Thy word is a lamp unto my feet, and a light unto my path.
Psalm 119:105

Presented

To

By

Date

This Certifies

That

And

Were United In

Holy Matrimony

Date

At

By

Witness

Witness

Births

Name

Date

Name

Date

Name

Date

Name

Date

Name

Date

Marriages

Deaths

Women of Color

STUDY BIBLE

Created by and for Contemporary Women
of African Descent

WORLD PUBLISHING
Iowa Falls, IA

NIA PUBLISHING
Atlanta, GA

Women of Color Study Bible

NIA PUBLISHING is an African-American owned company based in Atlanta, GA. Started in 1993 by Mel Banks, Jr., former marketing director for Urban Ministires, Inc., its first product was *The Children of Color Bible, King James Version* which has sold over 250,000 copies to date. The ownership, employees, and products of Nia Publishing are dedicated and committed to the cultural and spiritual growth of people of color, as individuals in the community and in the church.

The abbreviation *WBC* stands for *The Women's Bible Commentary,* eds. Carol Newsom and Sharon Ringe (Louisville, KY: Westminster/John Knox Press, 1992).

Published by: World Publishing, Inc.
Iowa Falls, IA 50126
U.S.A.

World Bibles are unconditionally guaranteed. If you are displeased with the manufacturing quality of this Bible, return it for a replacement.

1 2 3 4 5 6 7 8 06 05 04 03 02 01 00
RRD-C

Table of Contents

Acknowledgments 0-4
Why Affirm the Black Presence........0-6
Contributors 0-7
Focus on Genesis 22-1
Focus on Exodus............................54-1
Focus on Leviticus 54-6
Focus on Numbers 54-10
Focus on Deuteronomy 150-1
Focus on Joshua 150-5
Focus on Judges 150-8
Focus on Ruth............................150-14
Focus on 1 and 2 Samuel 246-1
Focus on 1 and 2 Kings................278-1
Focus on 1 and 2 Chronicles........278-7
Focus on Ezra and Nehemiah 374-1
Focus on Esther 374-4
Focus on Job...............................406-1
Focus on the Psalms....................406-4
Focus on Proverbs 470-1
Focus on Ecclesiastes..................470-4
Focus on the Song of Solomon 470-6
Focus on Isaiah............................470-8
Focus on Jeremiah 470-12
Focus on Lamentations..............470-14
Focus on Ezekiel..........................598-1
Focus on Daniel 598-5
Focus on Hosea 598-8
Focus on Joel 598-11
Focus on Amos 598-13
Focus on Obadiah 598-16
Focus on Jonah..........................598-18
Focus on Micah..........................598-20
Focus on Nahum 662-1
Focus on Habakkuk......................662-3
Focus on Zephaniah 662-6
Focus on Haggai 662-8
Focus on Zechariah....................662-11
Focus on Malachi 662-14
Focus on Matthew........................694-1
Focus on Mark 694-3
Focus on Luke..............................726-1
Focus on John..............................758-1
Focus on Acts 790-1
Focus on Romans 790-6
Focus on 1 Corinthians................822-1
Focus on 2 Corinthians................822-3
Focus on Galatians 822-5
Focus on Ephesians 822-8
Focus on Philippians..................822-10
Focus on Colossians 822-13
Focus on 1 Thessalonians..........822-16
Focus on 2 Thessalonians..........822-18
Focus on 1 Timothy......................854-1
Focus on 2 Timothy......................854-3
Focus on Titus..............................854-5
Focus on Philemon 854-7
Focus on Hebrews......................854-10
Focus on James 854-13
Focus on 1 Peter........................854-16
Focus on 2 Peter........................854-19
Focus on 1, 2, and 3 John..........854-21
Focus on Jude............................854-25
Focus on Revelation 886-1
Concluding Notes 918-1
God's Plan for Saving People........918-3
Breaking the Silence 918-4
Biographies of Contributors 918-6
Features Index 918-28
Women in the Bible....................918-30

Acknowledgments

NOTE FROM THE PUBLISHER

This Bible is dedicated to my mother, Olive Perkins Banks, whose love for the Lord, wit and wisdom, tender love, gentle prodding, and humble guidance has motivated and inspired me to attempt mighty feats. And to my sister Patrice Banks-Lee, whose unending dedication to education has inspired this project. I want you both to know that even though I don't say it enough—I love you!

—Mel Banks II
Publisher

General Editor: Marjorie Lawson
Bible Commentator, Notes, and Prayers: Dr. Linda H. Hollies, Ph.D.
Editorial Oversight: Dr. Melvin Banks Sr., Ph.D
Copy Editors: Alfreda Vaughn, Dr. Monifa A. Jumanne, Ph.D., Dr. Colleen Birchett, Ph.D., James Anyike
Typesetting: Cheryl Wilson
Concept, Cover, and Layout Design: Mel Banks II
Executive Consultant and Concept Development: Michele Clark Jenkins
Editorial Assistant: Candace Taylor
Cover Art: Larry Smith and Associates

Special thanks to: Nieta Wigginton, Jamie Ingram, LaKeisha Walker, Raquel Gray, Shanta Smith, Shekeva Phillips, Steven Stafford, Lois Bonner, Ellis Manns, Michael "Airplay"Austin, Reginald Banks, Arnold Hennings, Katrina Williams, Daya Parham, Bridgette Tate, Shana Jarrett and the many friends, family and supporters too numerous to name.

NOTE FROM J. ALFRED SMITH

Ms. Marjorie H. Lawson has the excellence required for serving as editor of the *Women of Color Study Bible.* My judgment is based on her editorial and executive assistance given to me during my term as President of The Progressive National Baptist Convention and her editorial assistance given to me in the publication of several of my published books and manuscripts which I published for academic settings.

Her choice of highly educated and well-disciplined women scholars who had to have far better credentials than the majority of male clergy is evidence of the quality you will find in the notes of the *Women of Color Study Bible.* I am convinced that God will use this Study Bible far above our greatest imagination for the lofty purpose of bringing all who read it closer to God and for the needed reconciling action to heal the wounds

that have contributed to the painful alienation between men and women.

May God be praised!

—J. Alfred Smith, Senior
Senior Pastor, Allen Temple Baptist Church
Oakland, California
Professor of Preaching and Church Ministries
American Baptist Seminary of the West
Berkeley, California

NOTE FROM THE GENERAL EDITOR

Throughout this project, I asked God so many times to give me strength and to help me get through just one more day. Therefore, I must give Him all the praise and glory! I must thank Him first. Thank you Lord for bringing me through. Thank you for the guardian angels, seen and unseen, that You sent to assist me, encourage me, support me, and pray with me. With sincere appreciation, gratefulness, and gratitude, I would like to acknowledge:

The African-American women contributors, who have labored in many different vineyards and in many different roles, towards essentially the same goal—to inspire, edify, encourage, emancipate women of color, and to see African-American women triumph! Thank you; without you, this Study Bible would not be possible.

Thank you to Cheryl Wilson, typesetter, and Alfreda Vaughn, copyeditor, for their assistance. They typed and retyped, read and reread the many profiles and essays over and over again, so that we could present professionally prepared essays. Linda Hollies for the countless hours required to provide the Life Lessons. Jerri Mayfield, Shekeva Phillips, Shanta Phillips, and Kishawn Wise, who worked closely with me and the contributors so that all deadlines could be met. Arthur S. Scott, my brother friend, who has encouraged and supported me through the years, who is always willing and available to provide theological help. Jacqueline Thompson, who assisted me in securing contributors for this project and provided a young, single, Christian, African-American woman's perspective to the essays included, and Sandra Varner who responded to my every call, understood, assisted, encouraged me during my low points, and was honest in her responses. She is a sister extraordinaire and an invaluable friend! Thank you also to my family and many friends who have always provided their assistance, whenever asked regardless of the need, encouragement, support, and prayers!

I would be remiss if I did not thank the members of the advisory/editorial board for all of their assistance. Last, but not least my thanks go to Melvin Banks, Jr. at Nia Publishing, Inc., who provided me with this incredible opportunity. It has been rewarding beyond belief!

—Marjorie H. Lawson, Editor

Foreword

WHY AFFIRM THE BLACK PRESENCE

Affirming the presence of Africans in the Bible is not an attempt to elevate Africans above other people. Rather, the purpose is to help correct the distortions, which have occurred over the last three to four hundred years. During biblical times, the color of a person's skin was irrelevant—a nonissue. If anything, people of African descent were revered—not because of their color, but because of their abilities. Only during the last three or four centuries have concerted attempts been made to eliminate the presence of people of color from the biblical record. The result of that distortion has been to leave people of African descent without their history, their culture, their values, and their sense of significance.

When people are deprived of their history and sense of importance they can more easily be dehumanized and demonized. In this way, subjugating, and controlling can more easily be justified. Examples are not hard to find. By dehumanizing and demonizing Jews, Hitler could justify eliminating them. By dehumanizing and demonizing Native Americans and Black people, pioneers of this country could eliminate the one and enslave the other. By demonizing other gang members, young people can justify killing their counterparts. Politicians demonize each other for their own advantage. It seems that humankind has a knack for demonizing each other for their own advantage!

The distortion of African history has occurred in a number of ways: through deliberate omissions and twisting of history by those who would take credit for everything good in the world; through the pictorial portrayal of biblical people as ethnically different from what they were—that is, African-Asian, through the failure of "scholars" and writers to acknowledge the distortions when confronted with the facts.

Of course, not all distortions have been deliberate. Some of it simply comes from the ignorant perpetuation of what has been received from others. Some of it stems from the desire, on the part of non-African-Asians to more closely identify themselves with biblical people. Whatever the motivation or method, the truth is that an accurate representation of history has not occurred. The notes of this Bible attempt to set the record straight. Interestingly enough, confirmation of the presence and role of Africans in the biblical record comes from both Black and non-Black scholars. The tragedy is that those, whose role it is to pass along the results of research to the general population, have done a poor job.

The Women of Color

STUDY BIBLE

Ms. Marjorie H. Lawson
General Editor

Reverend Jacqueline Thompson
Editorial Assistant

EDITORIAL/ADVISORY BOARD

Dr. P. June Anderson
Dr. Iva Carruthers
Dr. Faye S. Gunn
Reverend Barbara Heard
Dr. Linda Hollies
Reverend Mary Ann Allen Bellinger
Dr. Leah Gaskin Fitchue
Dr. Cynthia Hale
Reverend Jini Kilgore Ross

CONTRIBUTORS IN ALPHABETICAL ORDER

Reverend Estrelda Alexander
Mrs. Maude A. Alexander
Professor Linda L. Ammons
Dr. Pamela June Anderson
Reverend Chestina M. Archibald
Mrs. Marcia B. Armstead
Dr. Rhoenna P. Armster
Reverend Angela D. Aubry
Reverend Karen E. Mosby-Avery
Reverend Mary Anne Allen Bellinger
Reverend Cynthia B. Belt
Ms. Keya Belt
Reverend Bridgette Annette Black
Reverend Winfred Blagmond
Ms. Jetola Anderson-Blair
Reverend Michele Cotton Bohanon
Reverend Toni R. Booker
Reverend Linda E. Boston
Dr. Ann Bouie
Reverend Cookie Frances Lee Bracey
Reverend Nina Bryant
Reverend Marion Wyvetta Bullock
Attorney Candace Lorelle Byrd
Minister Terri L. Byrd
Reverend LaJuna D. Caldwell
Dr. Iva E. Carruthers
Reverend Jacquetta Chambers
Reverend DeeDee M. Coleman
Reverend Monica Anita Coleman
Dr. Suzan D. Johnson Cook
Reverend Charmayne Cooke
Reverend Maria-Alma Rainey Copeland
Dr. A. Elaine Crawford
Reverend Alice J. Burnette Davis
Reverend Katherine J. Davis
Reverend Sandra Demby
Reverend Alice Dise
Reverend Troy Janel Harrison-Dixon
Reverend LaSandra Melton-Dolberry
Reverend Marcia L. Dyson
Dr. Violet Lucinda Fisher
Dr. Leah Gaskin Fitchue
Dr. Margaret Elaine McCollins Flake
Reverend Andrea Beaden Foster
Dr. Abena Safiyah Fosua
Reverend Beverly Jackson Garvin
Ms. Portia George
Reverend Bridget Goines
Reverend Yar D. G. Bratcher Gono
Dr. Arlene W. Gordon
Dr. Deborah Denise Graham
Mrs. Easter M. Green
Dr. Faye S. Gunn
Dr. Cynthia L. Hale
Reverend Laverne C. Hall
Reverend Cecilia Swafford Harris

Reverend Gloria Harris
Mrs. Hattie G. Harris
Ms. Vanessa Hartsfield
Reverend Kellie V. Hayes
Reverend Raye Evelyn Haynes
Reverend Barbara Ann Heard
Reverend Vanessa Henderson
Dr. Avaneda D. Hobbs
Dr. Linda H. Hollies
Dr. Lottie Jones Hood
Dr. Janet Hopkins
Mrs. Joan E. Jackson
Reverend Darlene Moore-James
Reverend Deborah L. Shumake JaPhia
Dr. Diane H. Johnson
Reverend Frankye Anthea Sourie Johnson
Reverend Katurah Worrill Johnson
Reverend Wilma R. Johnson
Reverend Jolene Josey
Mrs.Marjorie L. Kimbrough
Dr. Barbara Lewis King
Reverend Bonita A. Kitt
Dr. Janette Chandler Koety
Dr. Linda Lee
Reverend Vanessa Stephens Lee
Reverend Ginger D. London
Dr. Carolyn B. Love
Mrs. Dinah Page Manns
Mrs. Ann Shenethia Manuel
Reverend Rosita Mathews
Ms. Loretta E. McBride
Dr. Dolores E. Lee McCabe
Chaplain Emma Louise McNair
Reverend Bernadine Grant McRipley
Reverend Andrea L. Middleton
Dr. Ella Pearson Mitchell
Dr. Sherry Davis Molock
Evangelist Alberiene Riene Adams-Morris
Dr. Camille Williams-Neal
Reverend Naomi E. Peete
Reverend Anita Adams Powell
Ms. Constance A. Richards
Ms. Shewanda Riley
Reverend Sheila Ford Robinson
Reverend Jini Kilgore Ross
Mrs. Cordelia Grace-Scott
Reverend Jannah Scott
Reverend Angela Stewart Sims
Reverend Claudette Elaine Sims
Dr. Kathryn Smallwood
Dr. Malvina V. Stephens
Reverend Dorothea J. Belt Stroman
Reverend Deborah Tinsley Taylor
Reverend Meriann Taylor
Reverend Jacqueline Thompson
Ms. Maxine Thompson
Dr. Lisa M. Smith-Vosper
Reverend Tanya S. Wade
Reverend N. S. "Robin" Walker
Reverend Elaine P. Walters
Reverend Cheryl D. Ward
Ms. Linda M. Washington
Dr. Elizabeth D. Watson
Reverend Vanessa Weatherspoon
Reverend Joan C. Webster
Dr. Joan L. Wharton
Reverend Barbara J. Whipple
Reverend Bessie Whitaker
Dr. Leah Elizabeth Mosley White
Dr. Bernadette Glover-Williams
Reverend Mary Newbern-Williams
Reverend Portia Turner Williamson
Reverend Jane E. Wood
Reverend Lois A. Wooden
Reverend Cynthia E. Woods
Mrs. Beverly Yates

THE
HOLY BIBLE

THE HOLY BIBLE

CONTAINING
THE OLD AND NEW TESTAMENTS

Translated out of the original tongues and with the
former translations diligently compared and
revised by His Majesty's special command.
Appointed to be read in churches.

AUTHORIZED KING JAMES VERSION

Classic Reference Bible
Red Letter Edition

WORLD
Bible Publishers, Inc.
Iowa Falls, IA 50126 U.S.A.

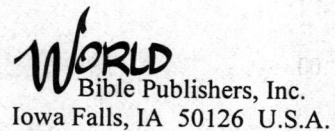

Classic Reference Bible, King James Version

Published by:
World Bible Publishers, Inc.
Iowa Falls, IA 50126 U.S.A.
All rights reserved.

KJV Concordance
Copyrighted 1988 by World Bible Publishers, Inc.
All rights reserved.

Color Maps
Copyright 1998 by World Bible Publishers, Inc.
All rights reserved.

2 3 4 5 6 7 8 02 01 00

CONTENTS

Books of the Old Testament

Book	Abbreviation	Page
Genesis	Gen.	1
Exodus	Ex.	43
Leviticus	Lev.	78
Numbers	Num.	104
Deuteronomy	Deut.	141
Joshua	Josh.	171
Judges	Judg.	192
Ruth	Ruth	212
1 Samuel	1 Sam.	215
2 Samuel	2 Sam.	242
1 Kings	1 Kings	264
2 Kings	2 Kings	290
1 Chronicles	1 Chron.	315
2 Chronicles	2 Chron.	339
Ezra	Ezra	367
Nehemiah	Neh.	376
Esther	Esther	388
Job	Job	394
Psalms	Ps.	416
Proverbs	Prov.	469
Ecclesiastes	Eccl.	487
Song of Solomon	SSol.	493
Isaiah	Isa.	497
Jeremiah	Jer.	537
Lamentations	Lam.	582
Ezekiel	Ezek.	586
Daniel	Dan.	628
Hosea	Hos.	641
Joel	Joel	647
Amos	Am.	650
Obadiah	Obad.	655
Jonah	Jonah	656
Micah	Mic.	658
Nahum	Nah.	662
Habakkuk	Hab.	664
Zephaniah	Zeph.	666
Haggai	Hag.	668
Zechariah	Zech.	669
Malachi	Mal.	677

Books of the New Testament

Book	Abbreviation	Page
Matthew	Matt.	683
Mark	Mark	710
Luke	Luke	727
John	John	756
Acts	Acts	777
Romans	Rom.	805
1 Corinthians	1 Cor.	816
2 Corinthians	2 Cor.	827
Galatians	Gal.	834
Ephesians	Eph.	838
Philippians	Phil.	842
Colossians	Col.	845
1 Thessalonians	1 Thess.	848
2 Thessalonians	2 Thess.	851
1 Timothy	1 Tim.	852
2 Timothy	2 Tim.	856
Titus	Tit.	858
Philemon	Philem.	860
Hebrews	Heb.	861
James	Jam.	869
1 Peter	1 Pet.	872
2 Peter	2 Pet.	875
1 John	1 John	878
2 John	2 John	881
3 John	3 John	882
Jude	Jude	883
Revelation	Rev.	884

Concordance 899

PREFACE

TO THE KING JAMES VERSION

TO THE MOST HIGH AND MIGHTY PRINCE

JAMES

BY THE GRACE OF GOD
KING OF GREAT BRITAIN, FRANCE, AND IRELAND
DEFENDER OF THE FAITH, &c.
The Translators of the Bible wish Grace, Mercy, and Peace
through JESUS CHRIST our Lord

Great and manifold were the blessings, most dread Sovereign, which Almighty God, the Father of all mercies, bestowed upon us the people of *England,* when first he sent Your Majesty's Royal Person to rule and reign over us. For whereas it was the expectation of many, who wished not well unto our *Sion,* that upon the setting of that bright *Occidental Star,* Queen *Elizabeth* of most happy memory, some thick and palpable clouds of darkness would so have overshadowed this Land, that men should have been in doubt which way they were to walk; and that it should hardly be known, who was to direct the unsettled State; the appearance of Your Majesty, as of the *Sun* in his strength, instantly dispelled those supposed and surmised mists, and gave unto all that were well affected exceeding cause of comfort; especially when we beheld the Government established in Your Highness, and Your hopeful Seed, by an undoubted Title, and this also accompanied with peace and tranquility at home and abroad.

But among all our joys, there was no one that more filled our hearts, than the blessed continuance of the preaching of God's sacred Word among us; which is that inestimable treasure, which excelleth all the riches of the earth; because the fruit thereof extendeth itself, not only to the time spent in this transitory world, but directeth and disposeth men unto that eternal happiness which is above in heaven.

Then not to suffer this to fall to the ground, but rather to take it up, and to continue it in that state, wherein the famous Predecessor of Your Highness did leave it: nay, to go forward with the confidence and resolution of a Man in maintaining the truth of Christ, and propagating it far and near, is that which hath so bound and firmly knit the hearts of all Your Majesty's loyal and religious people unto You, that Your very name is precious among them: their eye doth behold You with comfort, and they bless You in their hearts, as that sanctified Person who, under God, is the immediate Author of their true happiness. And this their contentment doth not diminish or decay, but every day increaseth and taketh strength, when they observe, that the zeal of Your Majesty toward the house of God doth not slack or go backward, but is more and more kindled, manifesting itself abroad in the farthest parts of *Christendom,* by writing in defence of the Truth, (which hath given such a blow unto that man of sin, as will not be healed,) and every day at home, by religious and learned discourse, by frequenting the house of God, by hearing the Word preached, by cherishing the Teachers thereof, by caring for the Church, as a most tender and loving nursing Father.

There are infinite arguments of this right Christian and religious affection in Your Majesty; but none is more forcible to declare it to others than the vehement and perpetuated desire of accomplishing and publishing of this work, which now with all humility we present unto Your Majesty. For when Your Highness had once out of deep judgment apprehended how convenient it was, that out of the Original Sacred Tongues, together with comparing of the labours, both in our own, and other foreign Languages, of many worthy men who went before us, there should be one more exact Translation

of the holy Scriptures into the *English Tongue;* Your Majesty did never desist to urge and to excite those to whom it was commended, that the work might be hastened, and that the business might be expedited in so decent a manner, as a matter of such importance might justly require.

And now at last, by the mercy of God, and the continuance of our labours, it being brought unto such a conclusion, as that we have great hopes that the Church of *England* shall reap good fruit thereby; we hold it our duty to offer it to Your Majesty, not only as to our King and Sovereign, but as to the principal Mover and Author of the work: humbly craving of Your most Sacred Majesty, that since things of this quality have ever been subject to the censures of illmeaning and discontented persons, it may receive approbation and patronage from so learned and judicious a Prince as Your Highness is, whose allowance and acceptance of our labours shall more honour and encourage us, than all the calumniations and hard interpretations of other men shall dismay us. So that if, on the one side, we shall be traduced by Popish Persons at home or abroad, who therefore will malign us, because we are poor instruments to make God's holy Truth to be yet more and more known unto the people, whom they desire still to keep in ignorance and darkness; or if, on the other side, we shall be maligned by self-conceited Brethren, who run their own ways, and give liking unto nothing, but what is framed by themselves, and hammered on their anvil; we may rest secure, supported within by the truth and innocency of a good conscience, having walked the ways of simplicity and integrity, as before the Lord; and sustained without by the powerful protection of Your Majesty's grace and favour, which will ever give countenance to honest and Christian endeavours against bitter censures and uncharitable imputations.

The Lord of heaven and earth bless Your Majesty with many and happy days, that, as his heavenly hand hath enriched Your Highness with many singular and extraordinary graces, so You may be the wonder of the world in this latter age for happiness and true felicity, to the honour of that great GOD, and the good of his Church, through Jesus Christ our Lord and only Saviour.

OLD TESTAMENT

GENESIS

Moses was the author of the first five books of the Bible, of which Genesis is the first. It was written between 1446 and 1406 B.C. Genesis takes its name from the Greek word meaning "origin" or "beginning." The book starts with the creation of the universe and the creation of man and woman. It describes the fall of man and woman into sin, and establishes God as the one true sovereign over all his creation. Genesis includes the accounts of Noah and the flood, the origin of the nations, the establishment of the Israelites as God's "chosen people," and the accounts of the lives of such people as Abraham, Isaac, Jacob, and Joseph.

I. Creation and the fall, 1:1–5:32
II. Noah and his descendants, 6:1–11:26
III. Abram (Abraham) and his descendants, 11:27–25:18
IV. Isaac, Jacob, and Esau, 25:19–36:43
V. The story of Joseph, 37:1–50:26

---

1 In the [a]beginning [b]God created the
heaven and the earth.
2 And the earth was without form, and
void; and darkness *was* upon the face of the
deep. [c]And the Spirit of God moved upon
the face of the waters.
3 [d]And God said, [e]Let there be light: and
there was light.
4 And God saw the light, that *it was* good:
and God divided the light from the darkness.
5 And God called the light [f]Day, and the
darkness he called Night. And the evening
and the morning were the first day.
6 ¶ And God said, [g]Let there be a firmament in the midst of the waters, and let it
divide the waters from the waters.
7 And God made the firmament, [h]and divided the waters which *were* under the firmament from the waters which *were*
[i]above the firmament: and it was so.
8 And God called the firmament Heaven.
And the evening and the morning were the
second day.
9 ¶ And God said, [j]Let the waters under
the heaven be gathered together unto one
place, and let the dry *land* appear: and it
was so.
10 And God called the dry *land* Earth; and
the gathering together of the waters called
he Seas: and God saw that *it was* good.
11 And God said, Let the earth [k]bring
forth grass, the herb yielding seed, *and* the
fruit tree yielding [l]fruit after his kind,
whose seed *is* in itself, upon the earth: and
it was so.
12 And the earth brought forth grass, *and*
herb yielding seed after his kind, and the
tree yielding fruit, whose seed *was* in itself,
after his kind: and God saw that *it was*
good.
13 And the evening and the morning were
the third day.
14 ¶ And God said, Let there be [m]lights in
the firmament of the heaven to divide the
day from the night; and let them be for

1:1 [a]John 1:1; Heb. 1:10 [b]Ps. 8:3; Isa. 44:24; Jer. 10:12; Zech. 12:1; Acts 14:15; Col. 1:16; Heb. 11:3; Rev. 4:11
1:2 [c]Ps. 33:6; Isa. 40:13
1:3 [d]Ps. 33:9 [e]2 Cor. 4:6
1:5 [f]Ps. 74:16
1:6 [g]Job 37:18; Ps. 136:5; Jer. 10:12
1:7 [h]Prov. 8:28 [i]Ps. 148:4
1:9 [j]Job 26:10; Ps. 33:7; Prov. 8:29; Jer. 5:22; 2 Pet. 3:5
1:11 [k]Heb. 6:7 [l]Luke 6:44
1:14 [m]Deut. 4:19; Ps. 74:16 [n]Ps. 74:17
1:16 [o]Ps. 136:7 [p]Ps. 8:3 [q]Job 38:7
1:18 [r]Jer. 31:35
1:21 [s]ch. 6:20; Ps. 104:26
1:22 [t]ch. 8:17
1:26 [u]ch. 5:1; Ps. 100:3; Eccl. 7:29; Acts 17:20; 1 Cor. 11:7; Eph. 4:24; Col. 3:10; Jam. 3:9 [v]ch. 9:2; Ps. 8:6

signs, and [n]for seasons, and for days, and
years:
15 And let them be for lights in the firmament of the heaven to give light upon the
earth: and it was so.
16 And God [o]made two great lights; the
greater light to rule the day, and [p]the lesser
light to rule the night: *he made* [q]the stars
also.
17 And God set them in the firmament of
the heaven to give light upon the earth,
18 And to [r]rule over the day and over the
night, and to divide the light from the darkness: and God saw that *it was* good.
19 And the evening and the morning were
the fourth day.
20 And God said, Let the waters bring
forth abundantly the moving creature that
hath life, and fowl *that* may fly above the
earth in the open firmament of heaven.
21 And [s]God created great whales, and
every living creature that moveth, which
the waters brought forth abundantly, after
their kind, and every winged fowl after his
kind: and God saw that *it was* good.
22 And God blessed them, saying, [t]Be
fruitful, and multiply, and fill the waters in
the seas, and let fowl multiply in the earth.
23 And the evening and the morning were
the fifth day.
24 ¶ And God said, Let the earth bring
forth the living creature after his kind, cattle, and creeping thing, and beast of the
earth after his kind: and it was so.
25 And God made the beast of the earth
after his kind, and cattle after their kind,
and every thing that creepeth upon the
earth after his kind: and God saw that *it was*
good.
26 ¶ And God said, [u]Let us make man in
our image, after our likeness: and [v]let them
have dominion over the fish of the sea, and
over the fowl of the air, and over the cattle,
and over all the earth, and over every creeping thing that creepeth upon the earth.
27 So God created man in his *own* image,

[w]in the image of God created he him; [x]male
and female created he them.
28 And God blessed them, and God said
unto them, [y]Be fruitful, and multiply, and
replenish the earth, and subdue it: and have
dominion over the fish of the sea, and over
the fowl of the air, and over every living
thing that moveth upon the earth.
29 ¶ And God said, Behold, I have given
you every herb bearing seed, which *is* upon
the face of all the earth, and every tree, in
the which *is* the fruit of a tree yielding seed;
[z]to you it shall be for meat.
30 And to [a]every beast of the earth, and
to every [b]fowl of the air, and to every thing
that creepeth upon the earth, wherein *there*
is life, *I have given* every green herb for
meat: and it was so.
31 [c]And God saw every thing that he had
made, and, behold, *it was* very good. And
the evening and the morning were the sixth
day.

2

Thus the heavens and the earth were
finished, and [d]all the host of them.
2 [e]And on the seventh day God ended his
work which he had made; and he rested on
the seventh day from all his work which he
had made.
3 And God [f]blessed the seventh day, and
sanctified it: because that in it he had rested
from all his work which God created and
made.
4 ¶ [g]These *are* the generations of the
heavens and of the earth when they were
created, in the day that the LORD God made
the earth and the heavens,
5 And every [h]plant of the field before it
was in the earth, and every herb of the field
before it grew: for the LORD God had not
[i]caused it to rain upon the earth, and *there*
was not a man [j]to till the ground.
6 But there went up a mist from the earth,
and watered the whole face of the ground.
7 And the LORD God formed man *of* the
[k]dust of the ground, and [l]breathed into his
[m]nostrils the breath of life; and [n]man became a living soul.
8 ¶ And the LORD God planted [o]a garden
[p]eastward in [q]Eden; and there [r]he put the
man whom he had formed.
9 And out of the ground made the LORD
God to grow [s]every tree that is pleasant to
the sight, and good for food; [t]the tree of life
also in the midst of the garden, [u]and the
tree of knowledge of good and evil.
10 And a river went out of Eden to water
the garden; and from thence it was parted,
and became into four heads.
11 The name of the first *is* Pison: that *is* it
which compasseth [v]the whole land of Havilah, where *there is* gold;
12 And the gold of that land *is* good:
[w]there *is* bdellium and the onyx stone.
13 And the name of the second river *is*
Gihon: the same *is* it that compasseth the
whole land of Ethiopia.
14 And the name of the third river *is*
[x]Hiddekel: that *is* it which goeth toward the
east of Assyria. And the fourth river *is* Euphrates.
15 And the LORD God took the man, and
[y]put him into the garden of Eden to dress it
and to keep it.
16 And the LORD God commanded the
man, saying, Of every tree of the garden
thou mayest freely eat:
17 [z]But of the tree of the knowledge of
good and evil, [a]thou shalt not eat of it: for
in the day that thou eatest thereof [b]thou
shalt surely die.
18 ¶ And the LORD God said, *It is* not good
that the man should be alone; [c]I will make
him an help meet for him.
19 [d]And out of the ground the LORD God
formed every beast of the field, and every
fowl of the air; and [e]brought *them* unto
Adam to see what he would call them: and
whatsoever Adam called every living creature, that *was* the name thereof.
20 And Adam gave names to all cattle,
and to the fowl of the air, and to every beast
of the field; but for Adam there was not
found an help meet for him.
21 And the LORD God caused a [f]deep
sleep to fall upon Adam, and he slept: and
he took one of his ribs, and closed up the
flesh instead thereof;
22 And the rib, which the LORD God had
taken from man, made he a woman, and
[g]brought her unto the man.
23 And Adam said, This *is* now [h]bone of
my bones, and flesh of my flesh: she shall be
called Woman, because she was [i]taken out
of Man.
24 [j]Therefore shall a man leave his father and his mother, and shall cleave unto
his wife: and they shall be one flesh.
25 [k]And they were both naked, the man
and his wife, and were not [l]ashamed.

3

Now [m]the serpent was [n]more subtil
than any beast of the field which the
LORD God had made. And he said unto the
woman, Yea, hath God said, Ye shall not eat
of every tree of the garden?
2 And the woman said unto the serpent,
We may eat of the fruit of the trees of the
garden:
3 [o]But of the fruit of the tree which *is* in
the midst of the garden, God hath said, Ye
shall not eat of it, neither shall ye touch it,
lest ye die.
4 [p]And the serpent said unto the woman,
Ye shall not surely die:
5 For God doth know that in the day ye
eat thereof, then [q]your eyes shall be
opened, and ye shall be as gods, knowing
good and evil.
6 And when the woman saw that the tree
was good for food, and that it *was* pleasant
to the eyes, and a tree to be desired to make
one wise, she took of the fruit thereof, [r]and
did eat, and gave also unto her husband
with her; [s]and he did eat.
7 And [t]the eyes of them both were
opened, [u]and they knew that they *were* na-

1:27 w1 Cor. 11:7 xch. 5:2; Mal. 2:15; Matt. 19:4; Mark 10:6
1:28 ych. 9:1; Lev. 26:9; Ps. 127:3
1:29 zch. 9:3; Job 36:31; Ps. 104:14; Acts 14:17
1:30 aPs. 145:15 bJob 38:41
1:31 cPs. 104:24; 1 Tim. 4:4
2:1 dPs. 33:6
2:2 eEx. 20:11; Deut. 5:14; Heb. 4:4
2:3 fNeh. 9:14; Isa. 58:13
2:4 gch. 1:1; Ps. 90:1
2:5 hch. 1:12; Ps. 104:14 iJob 38:26 jch. 3:23
2:7 kch. 3:19; Ps. 103:14; Eccl. 12:7; Isa. 64:8; 1 Cor. 15:47 lJob 33:4; Acts 17:25 mch. 7:22; Isa. 2:22 n1 Cor. 15:45
2:8 och. 13:10; Isa. 51:3; Ezek. 28:13; Joel 2:3 pch. 3:24 qch. 4:16; 2 Kings 19:12; Ezek. 27:23 rver. 15
2:9 sEzek. 31:8 tch. 3:22; Prov. 3:18; Rev. 2:7 uver. 17
2:11 vch. 25:18
2:12 wNum. 11:7
2:14 xDan. 10:4
2:15 yver. 8
2:17 zver. 9 ach. 3:1 bch. 3:3; Rom. 6:23; 1 Cor. 15:56; Jam. 1:15; 1 John 5:16
2:18 cch. 3:12; 1 Cor. 11:9; 1 Tim. 2:13
2:19 dch. 1:20 ech. 6:20; Ps. 8:6
2:21 fch. 15:12; 1 Sam. 26:12
2:22 gProv. 18:22; Heb. 13:4
2:23 hch. 29:14; Judg. 9:2; 2 Sam. 5:1; Eph. 5:30 i1 Cor. 11:8
2:24 jch. 31:15; Ps. 45:10; Matt. 19:5; Mark 10:7; 1 Cor. 6:16; Eph. 5:31
2:25 kch. 3:7 lEx. 32:25; Isa. 47:3
3:1 mRev. 12:9 nMatt. 10:16; 2 Cor. 11:3
3:3 och. 2:17
3:4 pver. 13; 2 Cor. 11:3; 1 Tim. 2:14
3:5 qver. 7; Acts 26:18
3:6 r1 Tim. 2:14 sver. 12
3:7 tver. 5 uch. 2:25

ked; and they sewed fig leaves together, and
made themselves aprons.
8 And they heard [v]the voice of the LORD
God walking in the garden in the cool of the
day: and Adam and his wife [w]hid themselves from the presence of the LORD God
amongst the trees of the garden.
9 And the LORD God called unto Adam,
and said unto him, Where *art* thou?
10 And he said, I heard thy voice in the
garden, [x]and I was afraid, because I *was*
naked; and I hid myself.
11 And he said, Who told thee that thou
wast naked? Hast thou eaten of the tree,
whereof I commanded thee that thou
shouldest not eat?
12 And the man said, [y]The woman whom
thou gavest *to be* with me, she gave me of
the tree, and I did eat.
13 And the LORD God said unto the
woman, What *is* this *that* thou hast done?
And the woman said, [z]The serpent beguiled me, and I did eat.
14 And the LORD God said [a]unto the serpent, Because thou hast done this, thou *art*
cursed above all cattle, and above every
beast of the field; upon thy belly shalt thou
go, and [b]dust shalt thou eat all the days of
thy life:
15 And I will put enmity between thee
and the woman, and between [c]thy seed and
[d]her seed; [e]it shall bruise thy head, and
thou shalt bruise his heel.
16 Unto the woman he said, I will greatly
multiply thy sorrow and thy conception; [f]in
sorrow thou shalt bring forth children;
[g]and thy desire *shall be* to thy husband, and
he shall [h]rule over thee.
17 And unto Adam he said, [i]Because
thou hast hearkened unto the voice of thy
wife, [j]and hast eaten of the tree, [k]of which
I commanded thee, saying, Thou shalt not
eat of it: [l]cursed *is* the ground for thy sake;
[m]in sorrow shalt thou eat *of* it all the days of
thy life;
18 [n]Thorns also and thistles shall it bring
forth to thee; and [o]thou shalt eat the herb of
the field;
19 [p]In the sweat of thy face shalt thou eat
bread, till thou return unto the ground; for
out of it wast thou taken: [q]for dust thou *art*,
and [r]unto dust shalt thou return.
20 And Adam called his wife's name Eve;
because she was the mother of all living.
21 Unto Adam also and to his wife did the
LORD God make coats of skins, and clothed
them.
22 ¶ And the LORD God said, [s]Behold, the
man is become as one of us, to know good
and evil: and now, lest he put forth his hand,
[t]and take also of the tree of life, and eat,
and live for ever:
23 Therefore the LORD God sent him forth
from the garden of Eden, [u]to till the ground
from whence he was taken.
24 So he drove out the man; and he placed
[v]at the east of the garden of Eden [w]Cheru-
bims, and a flaming sword which turned every way, to keep the way of the tree of life.

4 And Adam knew Eve his wife; and she
conceived, and bare Cain, and said, I
have gotten a man from the LORD.
2 And she again bare his brother Abel.
And Abel was a keeper of sheep, but Cain
was [x]a tiller of the ground.
3 And in process of time it came to pass,
that Cain brought [y]of the fruit of the
ground an offering unto the LORD.
4 And Abel, he also brought of [z]the firstlings of his flock and of the fat thereof. And
the LORD had [a]respect unto Abel and to his
offering:
5 But unto Cain and to his offering he had
not respect. And Cain was very wroth, [b]and
his countenance fell.
6 And the LORD said unto Cain, Why art
thou wroth? and why is thy countenance
fallen?
7 If thou doest well, shalt thou not be accepted? and if thou doest not well, sin lieth
at the door. And unto thee *shall be* his desire, and thou shalt rule over him.
8 And Cain talked with Abel his brother:
and it came to pass, when they were in the
field, that Cain rose up against Abel his
brother, and [c]slew him.
9 ¶ And the LORD said unto Cain, [d]Where
is Abel thy brother? And he said, [e]I know
not: *Am* I my brother's keeper?
10 And he said, What hast thou done? the
voice of thy brother's blood [f]crieth unto me
from the ground.
11 And now *art* thou cursed from the
earth, which hath opened her mouth to receive thy brother's blood from thy hand;
12 When thou tillest the ground, it shall
not henceforth yield unto thee her strength;
a fugitive and a vagabond shalt thou be in
the earth.
13 And Cain said unto the LORD, My punishment *is* greater than I can bear.
14 [g]Behold, thou hast driven me out this
day from the face of the earth; and [h]from
thy face shall I be hid; and I shall be a fugitive and a vagabond in the earth; and it shall
come to pass, [i]*that* every one that findeth
me shall slay me.
15 And the LORD said unto him, Therefore whosoever slayeth Cain, vengeance
shall be taken on him [j]sevenfold. And the
LORD [k]set a mark upon Cain, lest any finding him should kill him.
16 ¶ And Cain [l]went out from the presence of the LORD, and dwelt in the land of
Nod, on the east of Eden.
17 And Cain knew his wife; and she conceived, and bare Enoch: and he builded a
city, [m]and called the name of the city, after
the name of his son, Enoch.
18 And unto Enoch was born Irad: and
Irad begat Mehujael: and Mehujael begat
Methusael: and Methusael begat Lamech.
19 ¶ And Lamech took unto him two
wives: the name of the one *was* Adah, and
the name of the other Zillah.
20 And Adah bare Jabal: he was the fa-

3:8 [v]Job 38:1 [w]Job 31:33; Jer. 23:24; Am. 9:3
3:10 [x]ch. 2:25; Ex. 3:6; 1 John 3:20
3:12 [y]ch. 2:18; Job 31:33; Prov. 28:13
3:13 [z]ver. 4; 2 Cor. 11:3; 1 Tim. 2:14
3:14 [a]Ex. 21:29 [b]Isa. 65:25; Mic. 7:17
3:15 [c]Matt. 3:7; John 8:44; Acts 13:10; 1 John 3:8 [d]Ps. 132:11; Isa. 7:14; Mic. 5:3; Matt. 1:23; Luke 1:31; Gal. 4:4 [e]Rom. 16:20; Col. 2:15; Heb. 2:14; 1 John 5:5; Rev. 12:7
3:16 [f]Ps. 48:6; Isa. 13:8; John 16:21; 1 Tim. 2:15 [g]ch. 4:7 [h]1 Cor. 11:3; Eph. 5:22; 1 Tim. 2:11; Tit. 2:5; 1 Pet. 3:1
3:17 [i]1 Sam. 15:23 [j]ver. 6 [k]ch. 2:17 [l]Eccl. 1:2; Isa. 24:5; Rom. 8:20 [m]Job 5:7; Eccl. 2:23
3:18 [n]Job 31:40 [o]Ps. 104:14
3:19 [p]Eccl. 1:13; 2 Thess. 3:10 [q]ch. 2:7 [r]Job 21:26; Ps. 104:29; Eccl. 3:20; Rom. 5:12; Heb. 9:27
3:22 [s]ver. 5; Isa. 19:12; Jer. 22:23 [t]ch. 2:9
3:23 [u]ch. 4:2
3:24 [v]ch. 2:8 [w]Ps. 104:4; Heb. 1:7
4:2 [x]ch. 3:23
4:3 [y]Num. 18:12
4:4 [z]Num. 18:17; Prov. 3:9 [a]Heb. 11:4
4:5 [b]ch. 31:2
4:8 [c]Matt. 23:35; 1 John 3:12; Jude 11
4:9 [d]Ps. 9:12 [e]John 8:44
4:10 [f]Heb. 12:24; Rev. 6:10
4:14 [g]Job 15:20-24 [h]Ps. 51:11 [i]ch. 9:6; Num. 35:19
4:15 [j]Ps. 79:12 [k]Ezek. 9:4
4:16 [l]2 Kings 13:23; Jer. 23:29
4:17 [m]Ps. 49:11

ther of such as dwell in tents, and *of such as have* cattle.

21 And his brother's name *was* Jubal: he was the [n]father of all such as handle the harp and organ.

22 And Zillah, she also bare Tubal-cain, an instructer of every artificer in brass and iron: and the sister of Tubal-cain *was* Naamah.

23 And Lamech said unto his wives, Adah and Zillah, Hear my voice; ye wives of Lamech, hearken unto my speech: for I have slain a man to my wounding, and a young man to my hurt.

24 [o]If Cain shall be avenged sevenfold, truly Lamech seventy and sevenfold.

25 ¶ And Adam knew his wife again; and she bare a son, and [p]called his name Seth: For God, *said she,* hath appointed me another seed instead of Abel, whom Cain slew.

26 And to Seth, [q]to him also there was born a son; and he called his name Enos: then began men [r]to call upon the name of the LORD.

5 This *is* the [s]book of the generations of Adam. In the day that God created man, in [t]the likeness of God made he him;

2 [u]Male and female created he them; and blessed them, and called their name Adam, in the day when they were created.

3 ¶ And Adam lived an hundred and thirty years, and begat *a son* in his own likeness, after his image; and [v]called his name Seth:

4 [w]And the days of Adam after he had begotten Seth were eight hundred years: [x]and he begat sons and daughters:

5 And all the days that Adam lived were nine hundred and thirty years: [y]and he died.

6 And Seth lived an hundred and five years, and [z]begat Enos:

7 And Seth lived after he begat Enos eight hundred and seven years, and begat sons and daughters:

8 And all the days of Seth were nine hundred and twelve years: and he died.

9 ¶ And Enos lived ninety years, and begat Cainan:

10 And Enos lived after he begat Cainan eight hundred and fifteen years, and begat sons and daughters:

11 And all the days of Enos were nine hundred and five years: and he died.

12 ¶ And Cainan lived seventy years, and begat Mahalaleel:

13 And Cainan lived after he begat Mahalaleel eight hundred and forty years, and begat sons and daughters:

14 And all the days of Cainan were nine hundred and ten years: and he died.

15 ¶ And Mahalaleel lived sixty and five years, and begat Jared:

16 And Mahalaleel lived after he begat Jared eight hundred and thirty years, and begat sons and daughters:

17 And all the days of Mahalaleel were eight hundred ninety and five years: and he died.

18 ¶ And Jared lived an hundred sixty and two years, and he begat [a]Enoch:

19 And Jared lived after he begat Enoch eight hundred years, and begat sons and daughters:

20 And all the days of Jared were nine hundred sixty and two years: and he died.

21 ¶ And Enoch lived sixty and five years, and begat Methuselah:

22 And Enoch [b]walked with God after he begat Methuselah three hundred years, and begat sons and daughters:

23 And all the days of Enoch were three hundred sixty and five years:

24 And [c]Enoch walked with God: and he *was* not; for God took him.

25 And Methuselah lived an hundred eighty and seven years, and begat Lamech:

26 And Methuselah lived after he begat Lamech seven hundred eighty and two years, and begat sons and daughters:

27 And all the days of Methuselah were nine hundred sixty and nine years: and he died.

28 ¶ And Lamech lived an hundred eighty and two years, and begat a son:

29 And he called his name Noah, saying, This *same* shall comfort us concerning our work and toil of our hands, because of the ground [d]which the LORD hath cursed.

30 And Lamech lived after he begat Noah five hundred ninety and five years, and begat sons and daughters:

31 And all the days of Lamech were seven hundred seventy and seven years: and he died.

32 And Noah was five hundred years old: and Noah begat [e]Shem, Ham, [f]and Japheth.

6 And it came to pass, [g]when men began to multiply on the face of the earth, and daughters were born unto them,

2 That the sons of God saw the daughters of men that they *were* fair; and they [h]took them wives of all which they chose.

3 And the LORD said, [i]My spirit shall not always strive with man, [j]for that he also *is* flesh: yet his days shall be an hundred and twenty years.

4 There were giants in the earth in those days; and also after that, when the sons of God came in unto the daughters of men, and they bare *children* to them, the same *became* mighty men which *were* of old, men of renown.

5 ¶ And God saw that the wickedness of man *was* great in the earth, and *that* every [k]imagination of the thoughts of his heart *was* only evil continually.

6 And [l]it repented the LORD that he had made man on the earth, and it [m]grieved him at his heart.

7 And the LORD said, I will destroy man whom I have created from the face of the earth; both man, and beast, and the creep-

4:21 *n*Rom. 4:11
4:24 *o*ver. 15
4:25 *p*ch. 5:3
4:26 *q*ch. 5:6 *r*1 Kings 24; Ps. 116:17; Joel 2:32; Zeph. 3:9; 1 Cor. 1:2
5:1 *s*1 Chron. 1:1; Luke 3:36 *t*ch. 1:26; Eph. 4:24; Col. 3:10
5:2 *u*ch. 1:27
5:3 *v*ch. 4:25
5:4 *w*1 Chron. 1:1 *x*ch. 1:28
5:5 *y*ch. 3:19; Heb. 9:27
5:6 *z*ch. 4:26
5:18 *a*Jude 14
5:22 *b*ch. 6:9; 2 Kings 20:3; Ps. 16:8; Mic. 6:8; Mal. 2:6
5:24 *c*2 Kings 2:11; Heb. 11:5
5:29 *d*ch. 3:17
5:32 *e*ch. 6:10 *f*ch. 10:21
6:1 *g*ch. 1:28
6:2 *h*Deut. 7:3
6:3 *i*Gal. 5:16; 1 Pet. 3:19 *j*Ps. 78:39
6:5 *k*ch. 8:21; Deut. 29:19; Prov. 6:18; Matt. 15:19
6:6 *l*Num. 23:19; 1 Sam. 15:11; 2 Sam. 24:16; Mal. 3:6; Jam. 1:17 *m*Isa. 63:10; Eph. 4:30

ing thing, and the fowls of the air; for it
repenteth me that I have made them.
8 But Noah [n]found grace in the eyes of
the LORD.
9 ¶ These *are* the generations of Noah:
[o]Noah was a just man *and* perfect in his
generations, *and* Noah [p]walked with God.
10 And Noah begat three sons, [q]Shem,
Ham, and Japheth.
11 The earth also was corrupt [r]before
God, and the earth was [s]filled with violence.
12 And God [t]looked upon the earth, and,
behold, it was corrupt; for all flesh had corrupted his way upon the earth.
13 And God said unto Noah, [u]The end of
all flesh is come before me; for the earth is
filled with violence through them; [v]and, behold, I will destroy them with the earth.
14 ¶ Make thee an ark of gopher wood;
rooms shalt thou make in the ark, and shalt
pitch it within and without with pitch.
15 And this *is the fashion* which thou
shalt make it *of:* The length of the ark *shall
be* three hundred cubits, the breadth of it
fifty cubits, and the height of it thirty cubits.
16 A window shalt thou make to the ark,
and in a cubit shalt thou finish it above; and
the door of the ark shalt thou set in the side
thereof; *with* lower, second, and third *stories* shalt thou make it.
17 [w]And, behold, I, even I, do bring a
flood of waters upon the earth, to destroy all
flesh, wherein *is* the breath of life, from under heaven; *and* every thing that *is* in the
earth shall die.
18 But with thee will I establish my covenant; and [x]thou shalt come into the ark,
thou, and thy sons, and thy wife, and thy
sons' wives with thee.
19 And of every living thing of all flesh,
[y]two of every *sort* shalt thou bring into the
ark, to keep *them* alive with thee; they shall
be male and female.
20 Of fowls after their kind, and of cattle
after their kind, of every creeping thing of
the earth after his kind, two of every *sort*
[z]shall come unto thee, to keep *them* alive.
21 And take thou unto thee of all food that
is eaten, and thou shalt gather *it* to thee; and
it shall be for food for thee, and for them.
22 [a]Thus did Noah; [b]according to all that
God commanded him, so did he.

7

And the LORD said unto Noah, [c]Come
thou and all thy house into the ark; for
[d]thee have I seen righteous before me in
this generation.
2 Of every [e]clean beast thou shalt take to
thee by sevens, the male and his female:
[f]and of beasts that *are* not clean by two, the
male and his female.
3 Of fowls also of the air by sevens, the
male and the female; to keep seed alive
upon the face of all the earth.
4 For yet seven days, and I will cause it to
rain upon the earth [g]forty days and forty
nights; and every living substance that I
have made will I destroy from off the face of
the earth.
5 [h]And Noah did according unto all that
the LORD commanded him.
6 And Noah *was* six hundred years old
when the flood of waters was upon the
earth.
7 ¶ [i]And Noah went in, and his sons, and
his wife, and his sons' wives with him, into
the ark, because of the waters of the flood.
8 Of clean beasts, and of beasts that *are*
not clean, and of fowls, and of every thing
that creepeth upon the earth,
9 There went in two and two unto Noah
into the ark, the male and the female, as
God had commanded Noah.
10 And it came to pass after seven days,
that the waters of the flood were upon the
earth.
11 ¶ In the six hundredth year of Noah's
life, in the second month, the seventeenth
day of the month, the same day were all
[j]the fountains of the great deep broken up,
and [k]the windows of heaven were opened.
12 [l]And the rain was upon the earth forty
days and forty nights.
13 In the selfsame day [m]entered Noah,
and Shem, and Ham, and Japheth, the sons
of Noah, and Noah's wife, and the three
wives of his sons with them, into the ark;
14 [n]They, and every beast after his kind,
and all the cattle after their kind, and every
creeping thing that creepeth upon the earth
after his kind, and every fowl after his kind,
every bird of every sort.
15 And they [o]went in unto Noah into the
ark, two and two of all flesh, wherein *is* the
breath of life.
16 And they that went in, went in male
and female of all flesh, [p]as God had commanded him: and the LORD shut him in.
17 [q]And the flood was forty days upon
the earth; and the waters increased, and
bare up the ark, and it was lift up above the
earth.
18 And the waters prevailed, and were increased greatly upon the earth; [r]and the
ark went upon the face of the waters.
19 And the waters prevailed exceedingly
upon the earth; [s]and all the high hills, that
were under the whole heaven, were covered.
20 Fifteen cubits upward did the waters
prevail; and the mountains were covered.
21 [t]And all flesh died that moved upon
the earth, both of fowl, and of cattle, and
of beast, and of every creeping thing that
creepeth upon the earth, and every man:
22 All in [u]whose nostrils *was* the breath
of life, of all that *was* in the dry *land,* died.
23 And every living substance was destroyed which was upon the face of the
ground, both man, and cattle, and the creeping things, and the fowl of the heaven; and
they were destroyed from the earth: and
[v]Noah only remained *alive,* and they that
were with him in the ark.

6:8 [n]ch. 19:19; Ex. 33:12; Luke 1:30; Acts 7:46
6:9 [o]ch. 7:1; Ezek. 14:14; Rom. 1:17; Heb. 11:7; 2 Pet. 2:5 [p]ch. 5:22
6:10 [q]ch. 5:32
6:11 [r]ch. 7:1; 2 Chron. 34:27; Luke 1:6; Rom. 2:13 [s]Ezek. 8:17; Hab. 2:8
6:12 [t]ch. 18:21; Ps. 14:2
6:13 [u]Jer. 51:13; Ezek. 7:2; Am. 8:2; 1 Pet. 4:7 [v]ver. 17
6:17 [w]ver. 13; ch. 7:4; 2 Pet. 2:5
6:18 [x]ch. 7:1; 1 Pet. 3:20; 2 Pet. 2:5
6:19 [y]ch. 7:8
6:20 [z]ch. 2:19
6:22 [a]Ex. 40:16; Heb. 11:7 [b]ch. 7:5
7:1 [c]ver. 7; Matt. 24:38; Luke 17:26; Heb. 11:7; 1 Pet. 3:20; 2 Pet. 2:5 [d]ch. 6:9; Ps. 33:18; Prov. 10:9; 2 Pet. 2:9
7:2 [e]ver. 8; Lev. ch. 11 [f]Lev. 10:10; Ezek. 44:23
7:4 [g]ver. 12
7:5 [h]ch. 6:22
7:7 [i]ver. 1
7:11 [j]ch. 8:2; Prov. 8:28; Ezek. 26:19 [k]ch. 1:7; Ps. 78:23
7:12 [l]ver. 4:17
7:13 [m]ver. 1; ch. 6:18; Heb. 11:7; 1 Pet. 3:20; 2 Pet. 2:5
7:14 [n]ver. 2
7:15 [o]ch. 6:20
7:16 [p]ver. 2
7:17 [q]ver. 4
7:18 [r]Ps. 104:26
7:19 [s]Ps. 104:6; Jer. 3:23
7:21 [t]ch. 6:13; ver. 4; Job 22:16; Matt. 24:39; Luke 17:27; 2 Pet. 3:6
7:22 [u]ch. 2:7
7:23 [v]1 Pet. 3:20; 2 Pet. 2:5

24 [w]And the waters prevailed upon the earth an hundred and fifty days.

8 And God [x]remembered Noah, and every living thing, and all the cattle that *was* with him in the ark: [y]and God made a wind to pass over the earth, and the waters asswaged;

2 [z]The fountains also of the deep and the windows of heaven were stopped, and [a]the rain from heaven was restrained;

3 And the waters returned from off the earth continually: and after the end [b]of the hundred and fifty days the waters were abated.

4 And the ark rested in the seventh month, on the seventeenth day of the month, upon the mountains of Ararat.

5 And the waters decreased continually until the tenth month: in the tenth *month,* on the first *day* of the month, were the tops of the mountains seen.

6 ¶ And it came to pass at the end of forty days, that Noah opened [c]the window of the ark which he had made:

7 And he sent forth a raven, which went forth to and fro, until the waters were dried up from off the earth.

8 Also he sent forth a dove from him, to see if the waters were abated from off the face of the ground;

9 But the dove found no rest for the sole of her foot, and she returned unto him into the ark, for the waters *were* on the face of the whole earth: then he put forth his hand, and took her, and pulled her in unto him into the ark.

10 And he stayed yet other seven days; and again he sent forth the dove out of the ark;

11 And the dove came in to him in the evening; and, lo, in her mouth *was* an olive leaf pluckt off: so Noah knew that the waters were abated from off the earth.

12 And he stayed yet other seven days; and sent forth the dove; which returned not again unto him any more.

13 ¶ And it came to pass in the six hundredth and first year, in the first *month,* the first *day* of the month, the waters were dried up from off the earth: and Noah removed the covering of the ark, and looked, and, behold, the face of the ground was dry.

14 And in the second month, on the seven and twentieth day of the month, was the earth dried.

15 ¶ And God spake unto Noah, saying,

16 Go forth of the ark, [d]thou, and thy wife, and thy sons, and thy sons' wives with thee.

17 Bring forth with thee [e]every living thing that *is* with thee, of all flesh, *both* of fowl, and of cattle, and of every creeping thing that creepeth upon the earth; that they may breed abundantly in the earth, and [f]be fruitful, and multiply upon the earth.

18 And Noah went forth, and his sons, and his wife, and his sons' wives with him:

19 Every beast, every creeping thing, and every fowl, *and* whatsoever creepeth upon the earth, after their kinds, went forth out of the ark.

20 ¶ And Noah builded an altar unto the LORD; and took of [g]every clean beast, and of every clean fowl, and offered burnt offerings on the altar.

21 And the LORD smelled [h]a sweet savour; and the LORD said in his heart, I will not again [i]curse the ground any more for man's sake; for the [j]imagination of man's heart *is* evil from his youth; [k]neither will I again smite any more every thing living, as I have done.

22 [l]While the earth remaineth, seedtime and harvest, and cold and heat, and summer and winter, and [m]day and night shall not cease.

9 And God blessed Noah and his sons, and said unto them, [n]Be fruitful, and multiply, and replenish the earth.

2 [o]And the fear of you and the dread of you shall be upon every beast of the earth, and upon every fowl of the air, upon all that moveth *upon* the earth, and upon all the fishes of the sea; into your hand are they delivered.

3 [p]Every moving thing that liveth shall be meat for you; even as the [q]green herb have I given you [r]all things.

4 [s]But flesh with the life thereof, *which is* the blood thereof, shall ye not eat.

5 And surely your blood of your lives will I require; [t]at the hand of every beast will I require it, and [u]at the hand of man; at the hand of every [v]man's brother will I require the life of man.

6 [w]Whoso sheddeth man's blood, by man shall his blood be shed: [x]for in the image of God made he man.

7 And you, [y]be ye fruitful, and multiply; bring forth abundantly in the earth, and multiply therein.

8 ¶ And God spake unto Noah, and to his sons with him, saying,

9 And I, [z]behold, I establish [a]my covenant with you, and with your seed after you;

10 [b]And with every living creature that *is* with you, of the fowl, of the cattle, and of every beast of the earth with you; from all that go out of the ark, to every beast of the earth.

11 And [c]I will establish my covenant with you; neither shall all flesh be cut off any more by the waters of a flood; neither shall there any more be a flood to destroy the earth.

12 And God said, [d]This *is* the token of the covenant which I make between me and you and every living creature that *is* with you, for perpetual generations:

13 I do set [e]my bow in the cloud, and it shall be for a token of a covenant between me and the earth.

14 And it shall come to pass, when I bring a cloud over the earth, that the bow shall be seen in the cloud:

7:24 [w]ch. 7:11
8:1 [x]ch. 19:29; Ex. 2:24; 1 Sam. 1:19 [y]Ex. 14:21
8:2 [z]ch. 7:11 [a]Job 38:37
8:3 [b]ch. 7:24
8:6 [c]ch. 6:16
8:16 [d]ch. 7:13
8:17 [e]ch. 7:15 [f]ch. 1:22
8:20 [g]Lev. ch. 11
8:21 [h]Lev. 1:9; Ezek. 20:41; 2 Cor. 2:15; Eph. 5:2 [i]ch. 3:17 [j]ch. 6:5; Job 14:4; Ps. 51:5; Jer. 17:9; Matt. 15:19; Rom. 1:21 [k]ch. 9:11
8:22 [l]Isa. 54:8 [m]Jer. 33:20
9:1 [n]ch. 1:28; ver. 7; ch. 10:32
9:2 [o]ch. 1:28; Hos. 2:18
9:3 [p]Deut. 12:15; Acts 10:12 [q]ch. 1:29 [r]Rom. 14:14; 1 Cor. 10:23; Col. 2:16; 1 Tim. 4:3
9:4 [s]Lev. 17:10; Deut. 12:23; 1 Sam. 14:34; Acts 15:20
9:5 [t]Ex. 21:28 [u]ch. 4:9; Ps. 9:12 [v]Acts 17:26
9:6 [w]Ex. 21:12; Lev. 24:17; Matt. 26:52; Rev. 13:10 [x]ch. 1:27
9:7 [y]ver. 1
9:9 [z]ch. 6:18 [a]Isa. 54:9
9:10 [b]Ps. 145:9
9:11 [c]Isa. 54:9
9:12 [d]ch. 17:11
9:13 [e]Rev. 4:3

15 And [f]I will remember my covenant, which *is* between me and you and every living creature of all flesh; and the waters shall no more become a flood to destroy all flesh.

16 And the bow shall be in the cloud; and I will look upon it, that I may remember [g]the everlasting covenant between God and every living creature of all flesh that *is* upon the earth.

17 And God said unto Noah, This *is* the token of the covenant, which I have established between me and all flesh that *is* upon the earth.

18 ¶ And the sons of Noah, that went forth of the ark, were Shem, [h]and Ham, and Japheth: and Ham *is* the father of Canaan.

19 [i]These *are* the three sons of Noah: [j]and of them was the whole earth overspread.

20 And Noah began *to be* [k]an husbandman, and he planted a vineyard:

21 And he drank of the wine, [l]and was drunken; and he was uncovered within his tent.

22 And Ham, the father of Canaan, saw the nakedness of his father, and told his two brethren without.

23 [m]And Shem and Japheth took a garment, and laid *it* upon both their shoulders, and went backward, and covered the nakedness of their father; and their faces *were* backward, and they saw not their father's nakedness.

24 And Noah awoke from his wine, and knew what his younger son had done unto him.

25 And he said, [n]Cursed *be* Canaan; [o]a servant of servants shall he be unto his brethren.

26 And he said, [p]Blessed *be* the LORD God of Shem; and Canaan shall be his servant.

27 God shall enlarge Japheth, [q]and he shall dwell in the tents of Shem; and Canaan shall be his servant.

28 ¶ And Noah lived after the flood three hundred and fifty years.

29 And all the days of Noah were nine hundred and fifty years: and he died.

10 Now these *are* the generations of the sons of Noah, Shem, Ham, and Japheth: [r]and unto them were sons born after the flood.

2 [s]The sons of Japheth; Gomer, and Magog, and Madai, and Javan, and Tubal, and Meshech, and Tiras.

3 And the sons of Gomer; Ashkenaz, and Riphath, and Togarmah.

4 And the sons of Javan; Elishah, and Tarshish, Kittim, and Dodanim.

5 By these were [t]the isles of the Gentiles divided in their lands; every one after his tongue, after their families, in their nations.

6 ¶ [u]And the sons of Ham; Cush, and Mizraim, and Phut, and Canaan.

7 And the sons of Cush; Seba, and Havilah, and Sabtah, and Raamah, and Sabtecha: and the sons of Raamah; Sheba, and Dedan.

8 And Cush begat Nimrod: he began to be a mighty one in the earth.

9 He was a mighty [v]hunter [w]before the LORD: wherefore it is said, Even as Nimrod the mighty hunter before the LORD.

10 [x]And the beginning of his kingdom was Babel, and Erech, and Accad, and Calneh, in the land of Shinar.

11 Out of that land went forth Asshur, and builded Nineveh, and the city Rehoboth, and Calah,

12 And Resen between Nineveh and Calah: the same *is* a great city.

13 And Mizraim begat Ludim, and Anamim, and Lehabim, and Naphtuhim,

14 And Pathrusim, and Casluhim, ([y]out of whom came Philistim,) and Caphtorim.

15 ¶ And Canaan begat Sidon his firstborn, and Heth,

16 And the Jebusite, and the Amorite, and the Girgasite,

17 And the Hivite, and the Arkite, and the Sinite,

18 And the Arvadite, and the Zemarite, and the Hamathite: and afterward were the families of the Canaanites spread abroad.

19 [z]And the border of the Canaanites was from Sidon, as thou comest to Gerar, unto Gaza; as thou goest, unto Sodom, and Gomorrah, and Admah, and Zeboim, even unto Lasha.

20 These *are* the sons of Ham, after their families, after their tongues, in their countries, *and* in their nations.

21 ¶ Unto Shem also, the father of all the children of Eber, the brother of Japheth the elder, even to him were *children* born.

22 The [a]children of Shem; Elam, and Asshur, and Arphaxad, and Lud, and Aram.

23 And the children of Aram; Uz, and Hul, and Gether, and Mash.

24 And Arphaxad begat [b]Salah; and Salah begat Eber.

25 [c]And unto Eber were born two sons: the name of one *was* Peleg; for in his days was the earth divided; and his brother's name *was* Joktan.

26 And Joktan begat Almodad, and Sheleph, and Hazarmaveth, and Jerah,

27 And Hadoram, and Uzal, and Diklah,

28 And Obal, and Abimael, and Sheba,

29 And Ophir, and Havilah, and Jobab: all these *were* the sons of Joktan.

30 And their dwelling was from Mesha, as thou goest unto Sephar a mount of the east.

31 These *are* the sons of Shem, after their families, after their tongues, in their lands, after their nations.

32 [d]These *are* the families of the sons of Noah, after their generations, in their nations: [e]and by these were the nations divided in the earth after the flood.

11 And the whole earth was of one language, and of one speech.

2 And it came to pass, as they journeyed

9:15 [f]Ex. 28:12; Lev. 26:42; Ezek. 16:60
9:16 [g]ch. 17:13
9:18 [h]ch. 10:6
9:19 [i]ch. 5:32 [j]ch. 10:32; 1 Chron. 1:4
9:20 [k]ch. 3:19; Prov. 12:11
9:21 [l]Prov. 20:1; 1 Cor. 10:12
9:23 [m]Ex. 20:12; Gal. 6:1
9:25 [n]Deut. 27:16 [o]Josh. 9:23; 1 Kings 9:20
9:26 [p]Ps. 144:15; Heb. 11:16
9:27 [q]Eph. 2:13
10:1 [r]ch. 9:1
10:2 [s]1 Chron. 1:5
10:5 [t]Ps. 72:10; Jer. 2:10; Zeph. 2:11
10:6 [u]1 Chron. 1:8
10:9 [v]Jer. 16:16; Mic. 7:2 [w]ch. 6:11
10:10 [x]Mic. 5:6
10:14 [y]1 Chron. 1:12
10:19 [z]ch. 13:12; Num. 34:2-12; Josh. 12:7
10:22 [a]1 Chron. 1:17
10:24 [b]ch. 11:12
10:25 [c]1 Chron. 1:19
10:32 [d]ver. 1 [e]ch. 9:19

from the east, that they found a plain in the land of Shinar; and they dwelt there.

3 And they said one to another, Go to, let us make brick, and burn them throughly. And they had brick for stone, and slime had they for morter.

4 And they said, Go to, let us build us a city and a tower, [f]whose top *may reach* unto heaven; and let us make us a name, lest we be scattered abroad upon the face of the whole earth.

5 [g]And the LORD came down to see the city and the tower, which the children of men builded.

6 And the LORD said, Behold, [h]the people *is* one, and they have all [i]one language; and this they begin to do: and now nothing will be restrained from them, which they have [j]imagined to do.

7 Go to, [k]let us go down, and there confound their language, that they may [l]not understand one another's speech.

8 So [m]the LORD scattered them abroad from thence [n]upon the face of all the earth: and they left off to build the city.

9 Therefore is the name of it called Babel; [o]because the LORD did there confound the language of all the earth: and from thence did the LORD scatter them abroad upon the face of all the earth.

10 ¶ [p]These *are* the generations of Shem: Shem *was* an hundred years old, and begat Arphaxad two years after the flood:

11 And Shem lived after he begat Arphaxad five hundred years, and begat sons and daughters.

12 And Arphaxad lived five and thirty years, [q]and begat Salah:

13 And Arphaxad lived after he begat Salah four hundred and three years, and begat sons and daughters.

14 And Salah lived thirty years, and begat Eber:

15 And Salah lived after he begat Eber four hundred and three years, and begat sons and daughters.

16 [r]And Eber lived four and thirty years, and begat [s]Peleg:

17 And Eber lived after he begat Peleg four hundred and thirty years, and begat sons and daughters.

18 And Peleg lived thirty years, and begat Reu:

19 And Peleg lived after he begat Reu two hundred and nine years, and begat sons and daughters.

20 And Reu lived two and thirty years, and begat [t]Serug:

21 And Reu lived after he begat Serug two hundred and seven years, and begat sons and daughters.

22 And Serug lived thirty years, and begat Nahor:

23 And Serug lived after he begat Nahor two hundred years, and begat sons and daughters.

24 And Nahor lived nine and twenty years, and begat [u]Terah:

25 And Nahor lived after he begat Terah an hundred and nineteen years, and begat sons and daughters.

26 And Terah lived seventy years, and [v]begat Abram, Nahor, and Haran.

27 ¶ Now these *are* the generations of Terah: Terah begat Abram, Nahor, and Haran; and Haran begat Lot.

28 And Haran died before his father Terah in the land of his nativity, in Ur of the Chaldees.

29 And Abram and Nahor took them wives: the name of Abram's wife *was* [w]Sarai; and the name of Nahor's wife, [x]Milcah, the daughter of Haran, the father of Milcah, and the father of Iscah.

30 But [y]Sarai was barren; she *had* no child.

31 And Terah [z]took Abram his son, and Lot the son of Haran his son's son, and Sarai his daughter in law, his son Abram's wife; and they went forth with them from [a]Ur of the Chaldees, to go into [b]the land of Canaan; and they came unto Haran, and dwelt there.

32 And the days of Terah were two hundred and five years: and Terah died in Haran.

12 Now the [c]LORD had said unto Abram, Get thee out of thy country, and from thy kindred, and from thy father's house, unto a land that I will shew thee:

2 [d]And I will make of thee a great nation, [e]and I will bless thee, and make thy name great; [f]and thou shalt be a blessing:

3 [g]And I will bless them that bless thee, and curse him that curseth thee: [h]and in thee shall all families of the earth be blessed.

4 So Abram departed, as the LORD had spoken unto him; and Lot went with him: and Abram *was* seventy and five years old when he departed out of Haran.

5 And Abram took Sarai his wife, and Lot his brother's son, and all their substance that they had gathered, and [i]the souls that they had gotten [j]in Haran; and they went forth to go into the land of Canaan; and into the land of Canaan they came.

6 ¶ And Abram [k]passed through the land unto the place of Sichem, [l]unto the plain of Moreh. [m]And the Canaanite *was* then in the land.

7 [n]And the LORD appeared unto Abram, and said, [o]Unto thy seed will I give this land: and there builded he an [p]altar unto the LORD, who appeared unto him.

8 And he removed from thence unto a mountain on the east of Beth-el, and pitched his tent, *having* Beth-el on the west, and Hai on the east: and there he builded an altar unto the LORD, and [q]called upon the name of the LORD.

9 And Abram journeyed, [r]going on still toward the south.

10 ¶ And there was [s]a famine in the land: and [t]Abram went down into Egypt to so-

11:4 [f]Deut. 1:28
11:5 [g]ch. 18:21
11:6 [h]ch. 9:19; Acts 17:26 [i]ver. 1 [j]Ps. 2:1
11:7 [k]ch. 1:26; Ps. 2:4; Acts 2:4 [l]ch. 42:23; Deut. 28:49; Jer. 5:15; 1 Cor. 14:2
11:8 [m]Luke 1:51 [n]ch. 10:25
11:9 [o]1 Cor. 14:23
11:10 [p]ch. 10:22; 1 Chron. 1:17
11:12 [q]Luke 3:36
11:16 [r]1 Chron. 1:19 [s]Luke 3:35
11:20 [t]Luke 3:35
11:24 [u]Luke 3:34
11:26 [v]Josh. 24:2; 1 Chron. 1:26
11:29 [w]ch. 17:15 [x]ch. 22:20
11:30 [y]ch. 16:1
11:31 [z]ch. 12:1 [a]Neh. 9:7; Acts 7:4 [b]ch. 10:19
12:1 [c]ch. 15:7; Neh. 9:7; Isa. 41:2; Acts 7:3; Heb. 11:8
12:2 [d]ch. 17:6; Deut. 26:5; 1 Kings 3:8 [e]ch. 24:35 [f]ch. 28:4; Gal. 3:14
12:3 [g]ch. 27:29; Ex. 23:22; Num. 24:9 [h]ch. 18:18; Ps. 72:17; Acts 3:25; Gal. 3:8
12:5 [i]ch. 14:14 [j]ch. 11:31
12:6 [k]Heb. 11:9 [l]Deut. 11:30; Judg. 7:1 [m]ch. 10:18
12:7 [n]ch. 17:1 [o]ch. 13:15; Ps. 105:9 [p]ch. 13:4
12:8 [q]ch. 13:4
12:9 [r]ch. 13:3
12:10 [s]ch. 26:1 [t]Ps. 105:13

journ there; for the famine *was* [u]grievous in
the land.
11 And it came to pass, when he was
come near to enter into Egypt, that he said
unto Sarai his wife, Behold now, I know
that thou *art* [v]a fair woman to look upon:
12 Therefore it shall come to pass, when
the Egyptians shall see thee, that they shall
say, This *is* his wife: and they [w]will kill me,
but they will save thee alive.
13 [x]Say, I pray thee, thou *art* my sister:
that it may be well with me for thy sake; and
my soul shall live because of thee.
14 ¶ And it came to pass, that, when
Abram was come into Egypt, the Egyptians
[y]beheld the woman that she *was* very fair.
15 The princes also of Pharaoh saw her,
and commended her before Pharaoh: and
the woman was [z]taken into Pharaoh's
house.
16 And he [a]entreated Abram well for her
sake: and he had sheep, and oxen, and he
asses, and menservants, and maidservants,
and she asses, and camels.
17 And the LORD [b]plagued Pharaoh and
his house with great plagues because of Sarai Abram's wife.
18 And Pharaoh called Abram, and said,
[c]What *is* this *that* thou hast done unto me?
why didst thou not tell me that she *was* thy
wife?
19 Why saidst thou, She *is* my sister? so I
might have taken her to me to wife: now
therefore behold thy wife, take *her*, and go
thy way.
20 [d]And Pharaoh commanded *his* men
concerning him: and they sent him away,
and his wife, and all that he had.

13 And Abram went up out of Egypt, he,
and his wife, and all that he had, and
Lot with him, [e]into the south.
2 [f]And Abram *was* very rich in cattle, in
silver, and in gold.
3 And he went on his journeys [g]from the
south even to Beth-el, unto the place where
his tent had been at the beginning, between
Beth-el and Hai;
4 Unto the [h]place of the altar, which he
had made there at the first: and there
Abram [i]called on the name of the LORD.
5 ¶ And Lot also, which went with
Abram, had flocks, and herds, and tents.
6 And [j]the land was not able to bear
them, that they might dwell together: for
their substance was great, so that they
could not dwell together.
7 And there was [k]a strife between the
herdmen of Abram's cattle and the herdmen of Lot's cattle: [l]and the Canaanite and
the Perizzite dwelled then in the land.
8 And Abram said unto Lot, [m]Let there be
no strife, I pray thee, between me and thee,
and between my herdmen and thy herdmen; for we *be* brethren.
9 [n]*Is* not the whole land before thee? separate thyself, I pray thee, from me: [o]if *thou
wilt take* the left hand, then I will go to the
right; or if *thou depart* to the right hand,
then I will go to the left.
10 And Lot lifted up his eyes, and beheld
all [p]the plain of Jordan, that it *was* well
watered every where, before the LORD [q]de-
stroyed Sodom and Gomorrah, [r]*even* as the
garden of the LORD, like the land of Egypt,
as thou comest unto [s]Zoar.
11 Then Lot chose him all the plain of Jordan; and Lot journeyed east: and they separated themselves the one from the other.
12 Abram dwelled in the land of Canaan,
and Lot [t]dwelled in the cities of the plain,
and [u]pitched *his* tent toward Sodom.
13 But the men of Sodom [v]*were* wicked
and [w]sinners before the LORD exceedingly.
14 ¶ And the LORD said unto Abram, after
that Lot [x]was separated from him, Lift up
now thine eyes, and look from the place
where thou art [y]northward, and southward, and eastward, and westward:
15 For all the land which thou seest, [z]to
thee will I give it, and [a]to thy seed for ever.
16 And [b]I will make thy seed as the dust
of the earth: so that if a man can number the
dust of the earth, *then* shall thy seed also be
numbered.
17 Arise, walk through the land in the
length of it and in the breadth of it; for I will
give it unto thee.
18 Then Abram removed *his* tent, and
came and [c]dwelt in the plain of Mamre,
[d]which *is* in Hebron, and built there an altar unto the LORD.

14 And it came to pass in the days of
Amraphel king [e]of Shinar, Arioch
king of Ellasar, Chedorlaomer king of
[f]Elam, and Tidal king of nations;
2 *That these* made war with Bera king of
Sodom, and with Birsha king of Gomorrah,
Shinab king of [g]Admah, and Shemeber
king of Zeboiim, and the king of Bela,
which is [h]Zoar.
3 All these were joined together in the
vale of Siddim, [i]which is the salt sea.
4 Twelve years [j]they served Chedorlaomer, and in the thirteenth year they rebelled.
5 And in the fourteenth year came Chedorlaomer, and the kings that *were* with him,
and smote [k]the Rephaims [l]in Ashteroth
Karnaim, and the [m]Zuzims in Ham, [n]and
the Emims in Shaveh Kiriathaim,
6 [o]And the Horites in their mount Seir,
unto El-paran, which *is* by the wilderness.
7 And they returned, and came to En-
mishpat, which *is* Kadesh, and smote all the
country of the Amalekites, and also the Amorites, that dwelt [p]in Hazezon-tamar.
8 And there went out the king of Sodom,
and the king of Gomorrah, and the king of
Admah, and the king of Zeboiim, and the
king of Bela (the same *is* Zoar;) and they
joined battle with them in the vale of Siddim;
9 With Chedorlaomer the king of Elam,
and with Tidal king of nations, and Amra-

12:10 u ch. 43:1
12:11 v ver. 14; ch. 26:7
12:12 w ch. 20:11
12:13 x ch. 20:5
12:14 y ch. 39:7; Matt. 5:28
12:15 z ch. 20:2
12:16 a ch. 20:14
12:17 b ch. 20:18; 1 Chron. 16:21; Ps. 105:14; Heb. 13:4
12:18 c ch. 20:9
12:20 d Prov. 21:1
13:1 e ch. 12:9
13:2 f ch. 24:35; Ps. 112:3; Prov. 10:22
13:3 g ch. 12:8
13:4 h ch. 12:7 i Ps. 116:17
13:6 j ch. 36:7
13:7 k ch. 26:20 l ch. 12:6
13:8 m 1 Cor. 6:7
13:9 n ch. 20:15 o Rom. 12:18; Heb. 12:14; Jam. 3:17
13:10 p ch. 19:17; Deut. 34:3; Ps. 107:34 q ch. 19:24 r ch. 2:10; Isa. 51:3 s ch. 14:2
13:12 t ch. 19:29 u ch. 14:12; 2 Pet. 2:7
13:13 v ch. 18:20; Ezek. 16:49; 2 Pet. 2:7 w ch. 6:11
13:14 x ver. 11 y ch. 28:14
13:15 z ch. 12:7; Num. 34:12; Deut. 34:4; Acts 7:5 a 2 Chron. 20:7; Ps. 37:22
13:16 b ch. 15:5; Ex. 32:13; Num. 23:10; Deut. 1:10; 1 Kings 4:20; 1 Chron. 27:23; Isa. 48:19; Jer. 33:22; Rom. 4:16; Heb. 11:12
13:18 c ch. 14:13 d ch. 35:27
14:1 e ch. 10:10 f Isa. 11:11
14:2 g Deut. 29:23 h ch. 19:22
14:3 i Deut. 3:17; Num. 34:12; Josh. 3:16; Ps. 107:34
14:4 j ch. 9:26
14:5 k ch. 15:20; Deut. 3:11 l Josh. 12:4 m Deut. 2:20 n Deut. 2:10
14:6 o Deut. 2:12
14:7 p 2 Chron. 20:2

phel king of Shinar, and Arioch king of Ellasar; four kings with five.

10 And the vale of Siddim *was full of* [q]slimepits; and the kings of Sodom and Gomorrah fled, and fell there; and they that remained fled [r]to the mountain.

11 And they took [s]all the goods of Sodom and Gomorrah, and all their victuals, and went their way.

12 And they took Lot, Abram's [t]brother's son, [u]who dwelt in Sodom, and his goods, and departed.

13 ¶ And there came one that had escaped, and told Abram the Hebrew; for [v]he dwelt in the plain of Mamre the Amorite, brother of Eshcol, and brother of Aner: [w]and these *were* confederate with Abram.

14 And when Abram heard that [x]his brother was taken captive, he armed his trained *servants*, [y]born in his own house, three hundred and eighteen, and pursued *them* [z]unto Dan.

15 And he divided himself against them, he and his servants, by night, and [a]smote them, and pursued them unto Hobah, which *is* on the left hand of Damascus.

16 And he brought back [b]all the goods, and also brought again his brother Lot, and his goods, and the women also, and the people.

17 ¶ And the king of Sodom [c]went out to meet him [d]after his return from the slaughter of Chedorlaomer, and of the kings that *were* with him, at the valley of Shaveh, which *is* the [e]king's dale.

18 And [f]Melchizedek king of Salem brought forth bread and wine: and he *was* [g]the priest of [h]the most high God.

19 And he blessed him, and said, Blessed *be* Abram of the most high God, [i]possessor of heaven and earth:

20 And [j]blessed be the most high God, which hath delivered thine enemies into thy hand. And he gave him tithes [k]of all.

21 And the king of Sodom said unto Abram, Give me the persons, and take the goods to thyself.

22 And Abram said to the king of Sodom, I [l]have lift up mine hand unto the LORD, the most high God, [m]the possessor of heaven and earth,

23 That [n]I will not *take* from a thread even to a shoelatchet, and that I will not take any thing that *is* thine, lest thou shouldest say, I have made Abram rich:

24 Save only that which the young men have eaten, and the portion of the men [o]which went with me, Aner, Eshcol, and Mamre; let them take their portion.

15

After these things the word of the LORD came unto Abram [p]in a vision, saying, [q]Fear not, Abram: I *am* thy [r]shield, *and* thy exceeding [s]great reward.

2 And Abram said, Lord GOD, what wilt thou give me, [t]seeing I go childless, and the steward of my house *is* this Eliezer of Damascus?

3 And Abram said, Behold, to me thou hast given no seed: and, lo, [u]one born in my house is mine heir.

4 And, behold, the word of the LORD *came* unto him, saying, This shall not be thine heir; but he that [v]shall come forth out of thine own bowels shall be thine heir.

5 And he brought him forth abroad, and said, Look now toward heaven, and [w]tell the [x]stars, if thou be able to number them: and he said unto him, [y]So shall thy seed be.

6 And he [z]believed in the LORD; and he [a]counted it to him for righteousness.

7 And he said unto him, I *am* the LORD that [b]brought thee out of [c]Ur of the Chaldees, [d]to give thee this land to inherit it.

8 And he said, Lord GOD, [e]whereby shall I know that I shall inherit it?

9 And he said unto him, Take me an heifer of three years old, and a she goat of three years old, and a ram of three years old, and a turtledove, and a young pigeon.

10 And he took unto him all these, and [f]divided them in the midst, and laid each piece one against another: but [g]the birds divided he not.

11 And when the fowls came down upon the carcases, Abram drove them away.

12 And when the sun was going down, [h]a deep sleep fell upon Abram; and, lo, an horror of great darkness fell upon him.

13 And he said unto Abram, Know of a surety [i]that thy seed shall be a stranger in a land *that is* not theirs, and shall serve them; and [j]they shall afflict them four hundred years;

14 And also that nation, whom they shall serve, [k]will I judge: and afterward [l]shall they come out with great substance.

15 And [m]thou shalt go [n]to thy fathers in peace; [o]thou shalt be buried in a good old age.

16 But [p]in the fourth generation they shall come hither again: for the iniquity [q]of the Amorites [r]*is* not yet full.

17 And it came to pass, that, when the sun went down, and it was dark, behold a smoking furnace, and a burning lamp that [s]passed between those pieces.

18 In the same day the LORD [t]made a covenant with Abram, saying, [u]Unto thy seed have I given this land, from the river of Egypt unto the great river, the river Euphrates:

19 The Kenites, and the Kenizzites, and the Kadmonites,

20 And the Hittites, and the Perizzites, and the Rephaims,

21 And the Amorites, and the Canaanites, and the Girgashites, and the Jebusites.

16

Now Sarai Abram's wife [v]bare him no children: and she had an handmaid, [w]an Egyptian, whose name *was* [x]Hagar.

2 [y]And Sarai said unto Abram, Behold now, the LORD [z]hath restrained me from

14:10 [q]ch. 11:3 [r]ch. 19:17 **14:11** [s]ver. 16 **14:12** [t]ch. 12:5 [u]ch. 13:12 **14:13** [v]ch. 13:18 [w]ver. 24 **14:14** [x]ch. 13:8 [y]ch. 15:3; Eccl. 2:7 [z]Deut. 34:1; Judg. 18:29 **14:15** [a]Isa. 41:2 **14:16** [b]ver. 11 **14:17** [c]Judg. 11:34; 1 Sam. 18:6 [d]Heb. 7:1 [e]2 Sam. 18:18 **14:18** [f]Heb. 7:1 [g]Ps. 110:4; Heb. 5:6 [h]Mic. 6:6; Acts 16:17; Ruth 3:10; 2 Sam. 2:5 **14:19** [i]ver. 22; Matt. 11:25 **14:20** [j]ch. 24:27 [k]Heb. 7:4 **14:22** [l]Ex. 6:8; Dan. 12:7; Rev. 10:5 [m]ver. 19; ch. 21:33 **14:23** [n]Esther 9:15 **14:24** [o]ver. 13 **15:1** [p]Dan. 10:1; Acts 10:10 [q]ch. 26:24; Dan. 10:12; Luke 1:13 [r]Ps. 3:3 [s]Ps. 16:5; Prov. 11:18 **15:2** [t]Acts 7:5 **15:3** [u]ch. 14:14 **15:4** [v]2 Sam. 7:12; 2 Chron. 32:21 **15:5** [w]Ps. 147:4 [x]Jer. 33:22 [y]ch. 13:16; Ex. 32:13; Deut. 1:10; 1 Chron. 27:23; Rom. 4:18; Heb. 11:12 **15:6** [z]Rom. 4:3; Gal. 3:6; Jam. 2:23 [a]Ps. 106:31 **15:7** [b]ch. 12:1 [c]ch. 11:28 [d]Ps. 105:42; Rom. 4:13 **15:8** [e]ch. 24:13; Judg. 6:17; 1 Sam. 14:9; 2 Kings 20:8; Luke 1:18 **15:10** [f]Jer. 34:18 [g]Lev. 1:17 **15:12** [h]Gen. 2:21; Job 4:13 **15:13** [i]Ex. 12:40; Ps. 105:23; Acts 7:6 [j]Ex. 1:11; Ps. 105:25 **15:14** [k]Ex. 6:6; Deut. 6:22 [l]Ex. 12:36; Ps. 105:37 **15:15** [m]Job 5:26 [n]Acts 13:36 [o]ch. 25:8 **15:16** [p]Ex. 12:40 [q]1 Kings 21:26 [r]Dan. 8:23; Matt. 23:32; 1 Thess. 2:16 **15:17** [s]Jer. 34:18 **15:18** [t]ch. 24:7 [u]ch. 12:7; Ex. 23:31; Num. 34:3; Deut. 1:7; Josh. 1:4; 1 Kings 4:21; 2 Chron. 9:26; Neh. 9:8; Ps. 105:11; Isa. 27:12 **16:1** [v]ch. 15:2 [w]ch. 21:9 [x]Gal. 4:24 **16:2** [y]ch. 30:3 [z]ch. 20:18; 1 Sam. 1:5

bearing: I pray [a]thee, go in unto my maid;
it may be that I may obtain children by her.
And Abram [b]hearkened to the voice of Sarai.
3 And Sarai Abram's wife took Hagar her
maid the Egyptian, after Abram [c]had dwelt
ten years in the land of Canaan, and gave
her to her husband Abram to be his wife.
4 ¶ And he went in unto Hagar, and she
conceived: and when she saw that she had
conceived, her mistress was [d]despised in
her eyes.
5 And Sarai said unto Abram, My wrong
be upon thee: I have given my maid into thy
bosom; and when she saw that she had conceived, I was despised in her eyes: [e]the
LORD judge between me and thee.
6 [f]But Abram said unto Sarai, [g]Behold,
thy maid *is* in thy hand; do to her as it pleaseth thee. And when Sarai dealt hardly with
her, [h]she fled from her face.
7 ¶ And the angel of the LORD found her
by a fountain of water in the wilderness,
[i]by the fountain in the way to [j]Shur.
8 And he said, Hagar, Sarai's maid,
whence camest thou? and whither wilt thou
go? And she said, I flee from the face of my
mistress Sarai.
9 And the angel of the LORD said unto her,
Return to thy mistress, and [k]submit thyself
under her hands.
10 And the angel of the LORD said unto
her, [l]I will multiply thy seed exceedingly,
that it shall not be numbered for multitude.
11 And the angel of the LORD said unto
her, Behold, thou *art* with child, and shalt
bear a son, [m]and shalt call his name Ishmael; because the LORD hath heard thy affliction.
12 [n]And he will be a wild man; his hand
will be against every man, and every man's
hand against him; [o]and he shall dwell in the
presence of all his brethren.
13 And she called the name of the LORD
that spake unto her, Thou God seest me: for
she said, Have I also here looked after him
[p]that seeth me?
14 Wherefore the well was called [q]Beer-
lahai-roi; behold, *it is* [r]between Kadesh
and Bered.
15 ¶ And [s]Hagar bare Abram a son: and
Abram called his son's name, which Hagar
bare, [t]Ishmael.
16 And Abram *was* fourscore and six
years old, when Hagar bare Ishmael to
Abram.

17 And when Abram was ninety years
old and nine, the LORD [u]appeared to
Abram, and said unto him, [v]I *am* the Almighty God; [w]walk before me, and be thou
[x]perfect.
2 And I will make my covenant between
me and thee, and [y]will multiply thee exceedingly.
3 And Abram [z]fell on his face: and God
talked with him, saying,
4 As for me, behold, my covenant *is* with
thee, and thou shalt be [a]a father of many
nations.
5 Neither shall thy name any more be
called Abram, but [b]thy name shall be Abraham; [c]for a father of many nations have I
made thee.
6 And I will make thee exceeding fruitful,
and I will make [d]nations of thee, and
[e]kings shall come out of thee.
7 And I will [f]establish my covenant between me and thee and thy seed after thee
in their generations for an everlasting covenant, [g]to be a God unto thee, and to [h]thy
seed after thee.
8 And [i]I will give unto thee, and to thy
seed after thee, the land [j]wherein thou art
a stranger, all the land of Canaan, for an
everlasting possession; and [k]I will be their
God.
9 ¶ And God said unto Abraham, Thou
shalt keep my covenant therefore, thou, and
thy seed after thee in their generations.
10 This *is* my covenant, which ye shall
keep, between me and you and thy seed after thee; [l]Every man child among you shall
be circumcised.
11 And ye shall circumcise the flesh of
your foreskin; and it shall be [m]a token of the
covenant betwixt me and you.
12 And he that is eight days old [n]shall be
circumcised among you, every man child
in your generations, he that is born in the
house, or bought with money of any
stranger, which *is* not of thy seed.
13 He that is born in thy house, and he
that is bought with thy money, must needs
be circumcised: and my covenant shall be in
your flesh for an everlasting covenant.
14 And the uncircumcised man child
whose flesh of his foreskin is not circumcised, that soul [o]shall be cut off from his
people; he hath broken my covenant.
15 ¶ And God said unto Abraham, As for
Sarai thy wife, thou shalt not call her name
Sarai, but Sarah *shall* her name *be*.
16 And I will bless her, [p]and give thee a
son also of her: yea, I will bless her, and she
shall be *a mother* [q]of nations; kings of people shall be of her.
17 Then Abraham fell upon his face,
[r]and laughed, and said in his heart, Shall *a
child* be born unto him that is an hundred
years old? and shall Sarah, that is ninety
years old, bear?
18 And Abraham said unto God, O that
Ishmael might live before thee!
19 And God said, [s]Sarah thy wife shall
bear thee a son indeed; and thou shalt call
his name Isaac: and I will establish my covenant with him for an everlasting covenant,
and with his seed after him.
20 And as for Ishmael, I have heard thee:
Behold, I have blessed him, and will make
him fruitful, and [t]will multiply him exceedingly; [u]twelve princes shall he beget, [v]and
I will make him a great nation.
21 But my covenant will I establish with

16:2 [a]ch. 30:3 [b]ch. 3:17
16:3 [c]ch. 12:5
16:4 [d]2 Sam. 6:16; Prov. 30:21
16:5 [e]ch. 31:53; 1 Sam. 24:12
16:6 [f]Prov. 15:1; 1 Pet. 3:7 [g]Job 2:6; Ps. 106:41; Jer. 38:5 [h]Ex. 2:15
16:7 [i]ch. 25:18 [j]Ex. 15:22
16:9 [k]Tit. 2:9; 1 Pet. 2:18
16:10 [l]ch. 17:20
16:11 [m]ch. 17:19; Matt. 1:21; Luke 1:13
16:12 [n]ch. 21:20 [o]ch. 25:18
16:13 [p]ch. 31:42
16:14 [q]ch. 24:62 [r]Num. 13:26
16:15 [s]Gal. 4:22 [t]ver. 11
17:1 [u]ch. 12:1 [v]ch. 28:3; Ex. 6:3; Deut. 10:17 [w]ch. 5:22; 1 Kings 2:4; 2 Kings 20:3 [x]ch. 6:9; Deut. 18:13; Job 1:1; Matt. 5:48
17:2 [y]ch. 12:2
17:3 [z]ver. 17
17:4 [a]Rom. 4:11; Gal. 3:29
17:5 [b]Neh. 9:7 [c]Rom. 4:17
17:6 [d]ch. 35:11 [e]ver. 16; ch. 35:11; Matt. 1:6
17:7 [f]Gal. 3:17 [g]ch. 26:24; Heb. 11:16 [h]Rom. 9:8
17:8 [i]ch. 12:7; Ps. 105:9 [j]ch. 23:4 [k]Ex. 6:7; Lev. 26:12; Deut. 4:37
17:10 [l]Acts 7:8
17:11 [m]Acts 7:8; Rom. 4:11
17:12 [n]Lev. 12:3; Luke 2:21; John 7:22; Phil. 3:5
17:14 [o]Ex. 4:24
17:16 [p]ch. 18:10 [q]ch. 35:11; Gal. 4:31; 1 Pet. 3:6
17:17 [r]ch. 18:12
17:19 [s]ch. 18:10; Gal. 4:28
17:20 [t]ch. 16:10 [u]ch. 25:12 [v]ch. 21:18

Isaac, [w]which Sarah shall bear unto thee at
this set time in the next year.
22 And he left off talking with him, and
God went up from Abraham.
23 ¶ And Abraham took Ishmael his son,
and all that were born in his house, and all
that were bought with his money, every
male among the men of Abraham's house;
and circumcised the flesh of their foreskin
in the selfsame day, as God had said unto
him.
24 And Abraham *was* ninety years old
and nine, when he was circumcised in the
flesh of his foreskin.
25 And Ishmael his son *was* thirteen
years old, when he was circumcised in the
flesh of his foreskin.
26 In the selfsame day was Abraham circumcised, and Ishmael his son.
27 And [x]all the men of his house, born in
the house, and bought with money of the
stranger, were circumcised with him.

18 And the LORD appeared unto him in
the [y]plains of Mamre: and he sat in
the tent door in the heat of the day;
2 [z]And he lift up his eyes and looked,
and, lo, three men stood by him: [a]and when
he saw *them*, he ran to meet them from the
tent door, and bowed himself toward the
ground,
3 And said, My Lord, if now I have found
favour in thy sight, pass not away, I pray
thee, from thy servant:
4 Let [b]a little water, I pray you, be
fetched, and wash your feet, and rest yourselves under the tree:
5 And [c]I will fetch a morsel of bread, and
[d]comfort ye your hearts; after that ye shall
pass on: [e]for therefore are ye come to your
servant. And they said, So do, as thou hast
said.
6 And Abraham hastened into the tent
unto Sarah, and said, Make ready quickly
three measures of fine meal, knead *it*, and
make cakes upon the hearth.
7 And Abraham ran unto the herd, and
fetcht a calf tender and good, and gave *it*
unto a young man; and he hasted to dress it.
8 And [f]he took butter, and milk, and the
calf which he had dressed, and set *it* before
them; and he stood by them under the tree,
and they did eat.
9 ¶ And they said unto him, Where *is*
Sarah thy wife? And he said, Behold, [g]in
the tent.
10 And he said, I [h]will certainly return
unto thee [i]according to the time of life; and,
lo, [j]Sarah thy wife shall have a son. And
Sarah heard *it* in the tent door, which *was*
behind him.
11 Now [k]Abraham and Sarah *were* old
and well stricken in age; *and* it ceased to be
with Sarah [l]after the manner of women.
12 Therefore Sarah [m]laughed within herself, saying, [n]After I am waxed old shall I
have pleasure, my [o]lord being old also?
13 And the LORD said unto Abraham,
Wherefore did Sarah laugh, saying, Shall I
of a surety bear a child, which am old?
14 [p]Is any thing too hard for the LORD?
[q]At the time appointed I will return unto
thee, according to the time of life, and Sarah
shall have a son.
15 Then Sarah denied, saying, I laughed
not; for she was afraid. And he said, Nay;
but thou didst laugh.
16 ¶ And the men rose up from thence,
and looked toward Sodom: and Abraham
went with them [r]to bring them on the way.
17 And the LORD said, [s]Shall I hide from
Abraham that thing which I do;
18 Seeing that Abraham shall surely become a great and mighty nation, and all the
nations of the earth shall be [t]blessed in
him?
19 For I know him, [u]that he will command his children and his household after
him, and they shall keep the way of the
LORD, to do justice and judgment; that the
LORD may bring upon Abraham that which
he hath spoken of him.
20 And the LORD said, Because [v]the cry
of Sodom and Gomorrah is great, and because their sin is very grievous;
21 [w]I will go down now, and see whether
they have done altogether according to the
cry of it, which is come unto me; and if not,
[x]I will know.
22 And the men turned their faces from
thence, [y]and went toward Sodom: but
Abraham [z]stood yet before the LORD.
23 ¶ And Abraham [a]drew near, and said,
[b]Wilt thou also destroy the righteous with
the wicked?
24 [c]Peradventure there be fifty righteous
within the city: wilt thou also destroy and
not spare the place for the fifty righteous
that *are* therein?
25 That be far from thee to do after this
manner, to slay the righteous with the
wicked: and [d]that the righteous should be
as the wicked, that be far from thee: [e]Shall
not the Judge of all the earth do right?
26 And the LORD said, [f]If I find in Sodom
fifty righteous within the city, then I will
spare all the place for their sakes.
27 And Abraham answered and said,
[g]Behold now, I have taken upon me to
speak unto the Lord, which *am* [h]*but* dust
and ashes:
28 Peradventure there shall lack five of
the fifty righteous: wilt thou destroy all the
city for *lack of* five? And he said, If I find
there forty and five, I will not destroy *it*.
29 And he spake unto him yet again, and
said, Peradventure there shall be forty
found there. And he said, I will not do *it* for
forty's sake.
30 And he said *unto him*, Oh let not the
Lord be angry, and I will speak: Peradventure there shall thirty be found there. And
he said, I will not do *it*, if I find thirty there.
31 And he said, Behold now, I have taken
upon me to speak unto the Lord: Peradventure there shall be twenty found there. And

17:21 [w]ch. 21:2
17:27 [x]ch. 18:19
18:1 [y]ch. 13:18
18:2 [z]Heb. 13:2 [a]ch. 19:1; 1 Pet. 4:9
18:4 [b]ch. 19:2
18:5 [c]Judg. 6:18 [d]Judg. 19:5; Ps. 104:15 [e]ch. 19:8
18:8 [f]ch. 19:3
18:9 [g]ch. 24:67
18:10 [h]ver. 14 [i]2 Kings 4:16 [j]ch. 17:19; Rom. 9:9
18:11 [k]ch. 17:17; Rom. 4:19; Heb. 11:11 [l]ch. 31:35
18:12 [m]ch. 17:17 [n]Luke 1:18 [o]1 Pet. 3:6
18:14 [p]Jer. 32:17; Zech. 8:6; Matt. 3:9; Luke 1:37 [q]ch. 17:21; ver. 10; 2 Kings 4:16
18:16 [r]Rom. 15:24; 3 John 6
18:17 [s]Ps. 25:14; Am. 3:7; John 15:15
18:18 [t]ch. 12:3; Acts 3:25; Gal. 3:8
18:19 [u]Deut. 4:9; Josh. 24:15; Eph. 6:4
18:20 [v]ch. 4:10; Jam. 5:4
18:21 [w]ch. 11:5; Ex. 3:8 [x]Deut. 8:2; Josh. 22:22; Luke 16:15; 2 Cor. 11:11
18:22 [y]ch. 19:1 [z]ver. 1
18:23 [a]Heb. 10:22 [b]Num. 16:22; 2 Sam. 24:17
18:24 [c]Jer. 5:1
18:25 [d]Job 8:20; Isa. 3:10 [e]Job 8:3; Ps. 58:11; Rom. 3:6
18:26 [f]Jer. 5:1; Ezek. 22:30
18:27 [g]Luke 18:1 [h]ch. 3:19; Job 4:19; Eccl. 12:7; 1 Cor. 15:47; 2 Cor. 5:1

he said, I will not destroy *it* for twenty's
sake.
32 And he said, [i]Oh let not the Lord be
angry, and I will speak yet but this once:
Peradventure ten shall be found there.
[j]And he said, I will not destroy *it* for ten's
sake.
33 And the LORD went his way, as soon as
he had left communing with Abraham: and
Abraham returned unto his place.

19 And there [k]came two angels to
Sodom at even; and Lot sat in the
gate of Sodom: and [l]Lot seeing *them* rose
up to meet them; and he bowed himself with
his face toward the ground;
2 And he said, Behold now, my lords,
[m]turn in, I pray you, into your servant's
house, and tarry all night, and [n]wash your
feet, and ye shall rise up early, and go on
your ways. And they said, [o]Nay; but we will
abide in the street all night.
3 And he pressed upon them greatly; and
they turned in unto him, and entered into
his house; [p]and he made them a feast, and
did bake unleavened bread, and they did
eat.
4 ¶ But before they lay down, the men of
the city, *even* the men of Sodom, compassed
the house round, both old and young, all the
people from every quarter:
5 [q]And they called unto Lot, and said
unto him, Where *are* the men which came in
to thee this night? [r]bring them out unto us,
that we [s]may know them.
6 And [t]Lot went out at the door unto
them, and shut the door after him,
7 And said, I pray you, brethren, do not so
wickedly.
8 [u]Behold now, I have two daughters
which have not known man; let me, I pray
you, bring them out unto you, and do ye to
them as *is* good in your eyes: only unto
these men do nothing; [v]for therefore came
they under the shadow of my roof.
9 And they said, Stand back. And they
said *again,* This one *fellow* [w]came in to sojourn, [x]and he will needs be a judge: now
will we deal worse with thee, than with
them. And they pressed sore upon the man,
even Lot, and came near to break the door.
10 But the men put forth their hand, and
pulled Lot into the house to them, and shut
to the door.
11 And they smote the men [y]that *were* at
the door of the house with blindness, both
small and great: so that they wearied themselves to find the door.
12 ¶ And the men said unto Lot, Hast thou
here any besides? son in law, and thy sons,
and thy daughters, and whatsoever thou
hast in the city, [z]bring *them* out of this
place:
13 For we will destroy this place, because
the [a]cry of them is waxen great before the
face of the LORD; and [b]the LORD hath sent
us to destroy it.
14 And Lot went out, and spake unto his
sons in law, [c]which married his daughters,
and said, [d]Up, get you out of this place; for
the LORD will destroy this city. [e]But he
seemed as one that mocked unto his sons in
law.
15 ¶ And when the morning arose, then
the angels hastened Lot, saying, [f]Arise,
take thy wife, and thy two daughters, which
are here; lest thou be consumed in the iniquity of the city.
16 And while he lingered, the men laid
hold upon his hand, and upon the hand of
his wife, and upon the hand of his two
daughters; [g]the LORD being merciful unto
him: [h]and they brought him forth, and set
him without the city.
17 ¶ And it came to pass, when they had
brought them forth abroad, that he said,
[i]Escape for thy life; [j]look not behind thee,
neither stay thou in all the plain; escape to
the mountain, lest thou be consumed.
18 And Lot said unto them, Oh, [k]not so,
my Lord:
19 Behold now, thy servant hath found
grace in thy sight, and thou hast magnified
thy mercy, which thou hast shewed unto me
in saving my life; and I cannot escape to the
mountain, lest some evil take me, and I die:
20 Behold now, this city *is* near to flee
unto, and it *is* a little one: Oh, let me escape
thither, (*is* it not a little one?) and my soul
shall live.
21 And he said unto him, See, [l]I have
accepted thee concerning this thing also,
that I will not overthrow this city, for the
which thou hast spoken.
22 Haste thee, escape thither; for [m]I cannot do any thing till thou be come thither.
Therefore [n]the name of the city was called
Zoar.
23 ¶ The sun was risen upon the earth
when Lot entered into Zoar.
24 Then [o]the LORD rained upon Sodom
and upon Gomorrah brimstone and fire
from the LORD out of heaven;
25 And he overthrew those cities, and all
the plain, and all the inhabitants of the cities, and [p]that which grew upon the ground.
26 ¶ But his wife looked back from behind him, and she became [q]a pillar of salt.
27 ¶ And Abraham gat up early in the
morning to the place where [r]he stood before the LORD:
28 And he looked toward Sodom and Gomorrah, and toward all the land of the plain,
and beheld, and, lo, [s]the smoke of the country went up as the smoke of a furnace.
29 ¶ And it came to pass, when God destroyed the cities of the plain, that God [t]re-
membered Abraham, and sent Lot out of
the midst of the overthrow, when he overthrew the cities in the which Lot dwelt.
30 ¶ And Lot went up out of Zoar, and
[u]dwelt in the mountain, and his two daughters with him; for he feared to dwell in Zoar:
and he dwelt in a cave, he and his two
daughters.
31 And the firstborn said unto the younger, Our father *is* old, and *there is* not a man

18:32 [i]Judg. 6:39 [j]Jam. 5:16
19:1 [k]ch. 18:22 [l]ch. 18:1
19:2 [m]Heb. 13:2 [n]ch. 18:4 [o]Luke 24:28
19:3 [p]ch. 18:8
19:5 [q]Isa. 3:9 [r]Judg. 19:22 [s]ch. 4:1; Rom. 1:24; Jude 7
19:6 [t]Judg. 19:23
19:8 [u]Judg. 19:24 [v]ch. 18:5
19:9 [w]2 Pet. 2:7 [x]Ex. 2:14
19:11 [y]2 Kings 6:18; Acts 13:11
19:12 [z]ch. 7:1; 2 Pet. 2:7
19:13 [a]ch. 18:20 [b]1 Chron. 21:15
19:14 [c]Matt. 1:18 [d]Num. 16:21 [e]Ex. 9:21; Luke 17:28
19:15 [f]Num. 16:24; Rev. 18:4
19:16 [g]Luke 18:13; Rom. 9:15 [h]Ps. 34:22
19:17 [i]1 Kings 19:3 [j]ver. 26; Matt. 24:16; Luke 9:62; Phil. 3:13
19:18 [k]Acts 10:14
19:21 [l]Job 42:8; Ps. 145:19
19:22 [m]ch. 32:25; Ex. 32:10; Deut. 9:14; Mark 6:5 [n]ch. 13:10
19:24 [o]Deut. 29:23; Isa. 13:19; Jer. 20:16; Ezek. 16:49; Hos. 11:8; Am. 4:11; Zeph. 2:9; Luke 17:29; 2 Pet. 2:6; Jude 7
19:25 [p]ch. 14:3; Ps. 107:34
19:26 [q]Luke 17:32
19:27 [r]ch. 18:22
19:28 [s]Rev. 18:9
19:29 [t]ch. 8:1
19:30 [u]ver. 17

in the earth [v]to come in unto us after the
manner of all the earth:
32 Come, let us make our father drink
wine, and we will lie with him, that we
[w]may preserve seed of our father.
33 And they made their father drink wine
that night: and the firstborn went in, and lay
with her father; and he perceived not when
she lay down, nor when she arose.
34 And it came to pass on the morrow,
that the firstborn said unto the younger, Behold, I lay yesternight with my father: let us
make him drink wine this night also; and go
thou in, *and* lie with him, that we may preserve seed of our father.
35 And they made their father drink wine
that night also: and the younger arose, and
lay with him; and he perceived not when
she lay down, nor when she arose.
36 Thus were both the daughters of Lot
with child by their father.
37 And the firstborn bare a son, and
called his name Moab: [x]the same *is* the father of the Moabites unto this day.
38 And the younger, she also bare a son,
and called his name Ben-ammi: [y]the same
is the father of the children of Ammon unto
this day.

20 And Abraham journeyed from
[z]thence toward the south country,
and dwelled between [a]Kadesh and Shur,
and [b]sojourned in Gerar.
2 And Abraham said of Sarah his wife,
[c]She *is* my sister: and Abimelech king of
Gerar sent, and [d]took Sarah.
3 But [e]God came to Abimelech [f]in a
dream by night, and said to him, [g]Behold,
thou *art but* a dead man, for the woman
which thou hast taken; for she *is* a man's
wife.
4 But Abimelech had not come near her:
and he said, Lord, [h]wilt thou slay also a
righteous nation?
5 Said he not unto me, She *is* my sister?
and she, even she herself said, He *is* my
brother: [i]in the integrity of my heart and
innocency of my hands have I done this.
6 And God said unto him in a dream, Yea,
I know that thou didst this in the integrity of
thy heart; for [j]I also withheld thee from
sinning [k]against me: therefore suffered I
thee not to touch her.
7 Now therefore restore the man *his* wife;
[l]for he *is* a prophet, and he shall pray for
thee, and thou shalt live: and if thou restore
her not, [m]know thou that thou shalt surely
die, thou, [n]and all that *are* thine.
8 Therefore Abimelech rose early in the
morning, and called all his servants, and
told all these things in their ears: and the
men were sore afraid.
9 Then Abimelech called Abraham, and
said unto him, What hast thou done unto
us? and what have I offended thee, [o]that
thou hast brought on me and on my kingdom a great sin? thou hast done deeds unto
me [p]that ought not to be done.
10 And Abimelech said unto Abraham,
What sawest thou, that thou hast done this
thing?
11 And Abraham said, Because I thought,
Surely [q]the fear of God *is* not in this place;
and [r]they will slay me for my wife's sake.
12 And yet indeed [s]*she is* my sister; she
is the daughter of my father, but not the
daughter of my mother; and she became my
wife.
13 And it came to pass, when [t]God
caused me to wander from my father's
house, that I said unto her, This *is* thy kindness which thou shalt shew unto me; at every place whither we shall come, [u]say of
me, He *is* my brother.
14 And Abimelech [v]took sheep, and
oxen, and menservants, and womenservants, and gave *them* unto Abraham, and
restored him Sarah his wife.
15 And Abimelech said, Behold, [w]my
land *is* before thee: dwell where it pleaseth
thee.
16 And unto Sarah he said, Behold, I have
given [x]thy brother a thousand *pieces* of silver: [y]behold, he *is* to thee [z]a covering of
the eyes, unto all that *are* with thee, and
with all *other:* thus she was reproved.
17 ¶ So Abraham [a]prayed unto God: and
God healed Abimelech, and his wife, and
his maidservants; and they bare *children.*
18 For the LORD [b]had fast closed up all
the wombs of the house of Abimelech, because of Sarah Abraham's wife.

21 And the LORD [c]visited Sarah as he
had said, and the LORD did unto
Sarah [d]as he had spoken.
2 For Sarah [e]conceived, and bare Abraham a son in his old age, [f]at the set time of
which God had spoken to him.
3 And Abraham called the name of his
son that was born unto him, whom Sarah
bare to him, [g]Isaac.
4 And Abraham [h]circumcised his son
Isaac being eight days old, [i]as God had
commanded him.
5 And [j]Abraham was an hundred years
old, when his son Isaac was born unto him.
6 ¶ And Sarah said, [k]God hath made me
to laugh, *so that* all that hear [l]will laugh
with me.
7 And she said, Who would have said
unto Abraham, that Sarah should have
given children suck? [m]for I have born *him* a
son in his old age.
8 And the child grew, and was weaned:
and Abraham made a great feast the *same*
day that Isaac was weaned.
9 ¶ And Sarah saw the son of Hagar the
[n]Egyptian, [o]which she had born unto
Abraham, [p]mocking.
10 Wherefore she said unto Abraham,
[q]Cast out this bondwoman and her son: for
the son of this bondwoman shall not be heir
with my son, *even* with Isaac.
11 And the thing was very grievous in
Abraham's sight [r]because of his son.
12 ¶ And God said unto Abraham, Let it
not be grievous in thy sight because of the

19:31 [v]ch. 16:2; ch. 38:8; Deut. 25:5
19:32 [w]Mark 12:19
19:37 [x]Deut. 2:9
19:38 [y]Deut. 2:19
20:1 [z]ch. 18:1 [a]ch. 16:7 [b]ch. 26:6
20:2 [c]ch. 12:13 [d]ch. 12:15
20:3 [e]Ps. 105:14 [f]Job 33:15 [g]ver. 7
20:4 [h]ch. 18:23; ver. 18
20:5 [i]2 Kings 20:3; 2 Cor. 1:12
20:6 [j]ch. 31:7; Ex. 34:24; 1 Sam. 25:26 [k]ch. 39:9; Lev. 6:2; Ps. 51:4
20:7 [l]1 Sam. 7:5; 2 Kings 5:11; Job 42:8; Jam. 5:14; 1 John 5:16 [m]ch. 2:17 [n]Num. 16:32
20:9 [o]ch. 26:10; Ex. 32:21; Josh. 7:25 [p]ch. 34:7
20:11 [q]ch. 42:18; Ps. 36:1; Prov. 16:6 [r]ch. 12:12
20:12 [s]ch. 11:29
20:13 [t]ch. 12:1; Heb. 11:8 [u]ch. 12:13
20:14 [v]ch. 12:16
20:15 [w]ch. 13:9
20:16 [x]ver. 5 [y]ch. 26:11 [z]ch. 24:65
20:17 [a]Job 42:9
20:18 [b]ch. 12:17
21:1 [c]1 Sam. 2:21 [d]ch. 17:19; Gal. 4:23
21:2 [e]Acts 7:8; Gal. 4:22; Heb. 11:11 [f]ch. 17:21
21:3 [g]ch. 17:19
21:4 [h]Acts 7:8 [i]ch. 17:10
21:5 [j]ch. 17:1
21:6 [k]Ps. 126:2; Isa. 54:1; Gal. 4:27 [l]Luke 1:58
21:7 [m]ch. 18:11
21:9 [n]ch. 16:1 [o]ch. 16:15 [p]Gal. 4:22
21:10 [q]ch. 25:6; Gal. 4:30
21:11 [r]ch. 17:18

lad, and because of thy bondwoman; in all
that Sarah hath said unto thee, hearken
unto her voice; for [s]in Isaac shall thy seed
be called.
13 And also of the son of the bondwoman
will I make [t]a nation, because he *is* thy
seed.
14 And Abraham rose up early in the
morning, and took bread, and a bottle of
water, and gave *it* unto Hagar, putting *it* on
her shoulder, and the child, and [u]sent her
away: and she departed, and wandered in
the wilderness of Beer-sheba.
15 And the water was spent in the bottle,
and she cast the child under one of the
shrubs.
16 And she went, and sat her down over
against *him* a good way off, as it were a
bowshot: for she said, Let me not see the
death of the child. And she sat over against
him, and lift up her voice, and wept.
17 And [v]God heard the voice of the lad;
and the angel of God called to Hagar out of
heaven, and said unto her, What aileth thee,
Hagar? fear not; for God hath heard the
voice of the lad where he *is.*
18 Arise, lift up the lad, and hold him in
thine hand; for [w]I will make him a great
nation.
19 And [x]God opened her eyes, and she
saw a well of water; and she went, and filled
the bottle with water, and gave the lad
drink.
20 And God [y]was with the lad; and he
grew, and dwelt in the wilderness, [z]and became an archer.
21 And he dwelt in the wilderness of Paran: and his mother [a]took him a wife out of
the land of Egypt.
22 ¶ And it came to pass at that time, that
[b]Abimelech and Phichol the chief captain
of his host spake unto Abraham, saying,
[c]God *is* with thee in all that thou doest:
23 Now therefore [d]swear unto me here
by God that thou wilt not deal falsely with
me, nor with my son, nor with my son's son:
but according to the kindness that I have
done unto thee, thou shalt do unto me, and
to the land wherein thou hast sojourned.
24 And Abraham said, I will swear.
25 And Abraham reproved Abimelech
because of a well of water, which Abimelech's servants [e]had violently taken away.
26 And Abimelech said, I wot not who
hath done this thing: neither didst thou tell
me, neither yet heard I *of it,* but to day.
27 And Abraham took sheep and oxen,
and gave them unto Abimelech; and both of
them [f]made a covenant.
28 And Abraham set seven ewe lambs of
the flock by themselves.
29 And Abimelech said unto Abraham,
[g]What *mean* these seven ewe lambs which
thou hast set by themselves?
30 And he said, For *these* seven ewe
lambs shalt thou take of my hand, that
[h]they may be a witness unto me, that I have
digged this well.

21:12 [s]Rom. 9:7; Heb. 11:18
21:13 [t]ver. 18; ch. 16:10
21:14 [u]John 8:35
21:17 [v]Ex. 3:7
21:18 [w]ver. 13
21:19 [x]Num. 22:31; 2 Kings 6:17; Luke 24:16
21:20 [y]ch. 28:15 [z]ch. 16:12
21:21 [a]ch. 24:4
21:22 [b]ch. 20:2 [c]ch. 26:28
21:23 [d]Josh. 2:12; 1 Sam. 24:21
21:25 [e]ch. 26:15
21:27 [f]ch. 26:31
21:29 [g]ch. 33:8
21:30 [h]ch. 31:48
21:31 [i]ch. 26:33
21:33 [j]ch. 4:26 [k]Deut. 33:27; Isa. 40:28; Rom. 16:26; 1 Tim. 1:17
22:1 [l]1 Cor. 10:13; Heb. 11:17; Jam. 1:12; 1 Pet. 1:7
22:2 [m]Heb. 11:17 [n]2 Chron. 3:1
22:6 [o]John 19:17
22:9 [p]Heb. 11:17; Jam. 2:21
22:12 [q]1 Sam. 15:22; Mic. 6:7 [r]ch. 26:5; Jam. 2:22

31 Wherefore he [i]called that place Beer-
sheba; because there they sware both of
them.
32 Thus they made a covenant at Beer-
sheba: then Abimelech rose up, and Phichol
the chief captain of his host, and they returned into the land of the Philistines.
33 ¶ And *Abraham* planted a grove in
Beer-sheba, and [j]called there on the name
of the LORD, [k]the everlasting God.
34 And Abraham sojourned in the Philistines' land many days.
22 And it came to pass after these
things, that [l]God did tempt Abraham, and said unto him, Abraham: and he
said, Behold, *here* I *am.*
2 And he said, Take now thy son, [m]thine
only *son* Isaac, whom thou lovest, and get
thee [n]into the land of Moriah; and offer him
there for a burnt offering upon one of the
mountains which I will tell thee of.
3 ¶ And Abraham rose up early in the
morning, and saddled his ass, and took two
of his young men with him, and Isaac his
son, and clave the wood for the burnt offering, and rose up, and went unto the place of
which God had told him.
4 Then on the third day Abraham lifted
up his eyes, and saw the place afar off.
5 And Abraham said unto his young men,
Abide ye here with the ass; and I and the
lad will go yonder and worship, and come
again to you.
6 And Abraham took the wood of the
burnt offering, and [o]laid *it* upon Isaac his
son; and he took the fire in his hand, and a
knife; and they went both of them together.
7 And Isaac spake unto Abraham his father, and said, My father: and he said, Here
am I, my son. And he said, Behold the fire
and the wood: but where *is* the lamb for a
burnt offering?
8 And Abraham said, My son, God will
provide himself a lamb for a burnt offering:
so they went both of them together.
9 And they came to the place which God
had told him of; and Abraham built an altar
there, and [p]laid the wood in order, and
bound Isaac his son, and laid him on the
altar upon the wood.
10 And Abraham stretched forth his
hand, and took the knife to slay his son.
11 And the angel of the LORD called unto
him out of heaven, and said, Abraham,
Abraham: and he said, Here *am* I.
12 And he said, [q]Lay not thine hand upon
the lad, neither do thou any thing unto him:
for [r]now I know that thou fearest God, seeing thou hast not withheld thy son, thine
only *son* from me.
13 And Abraham lifted up his eyes, and
looked, and behold behind *him* a ram
caught in a thicket by his horns: and Abraham went and took the ram, and offered
him up for a burnt offering in the stead of
his son.
14 And Abraham called the name of that
place Jehovah-jireh: as it is said *to* this day,

In the mount of the LORD it shall be seen.
15 ¶ And the angel of the LORD called
unto Abraham out of heaven the second
time,
16 And said, [s]By myself have I sworn,
saith the LORD, for because thou hast done
this thing, and hast not withheld thy son,
thine only *son:*
17 That in blessing I will bless thee, and in
multiplying I will multiply thy seed [t]as the
stars of the heaven, [u]and as the sand which
is upon the sea shore; and [v]thy seed shall
possess [w]the gate of his enemies;
18 [x]And in thy seed shall all the nations
of the earth be blessed; [y]because thou hast
obeyed my voice.
19 So Abraham returned unto his young
men, and they rose up and went together to
[z]Beer-sheba; and Abraham dwelt at Beer-
sheba.
20 ¶ And it came to pass after these
things, that it was told Abraham, saying,
Behold, [a]Milcah, she hath also born children unto thy brother Nahor;
21 [b]Huz his firstborn, and Buz his
brother, and Kemuel the father [c]of Aram,
22 And Chesed, and Hazo, and Pildash,
and Jidlaph, and Bethuel.
23 And [d]Bethuel begat [e]Rebekah: these
eight Milcah did bear to Nahor, Abraham's
brother.
24 And his concubine, whose name *was*
Reumah, she bare also Tebah, and Gaham,
and Thahash, and Maachah.

23

And Sarah was an hundred and
seven and twenty years old: *these*
were the years of the life of Sarah.
2 And Sarah died in [f]Kirjath-arba; the
same *is* [g]Hebron in the land of Canaan: and
Abraham came to mourn for Sarah, and to
weep for her.
3 ¶ And Abraham stood up from before
his dead, and spake unto the sons of Heth,
saying,
4 [h]I *am* a stranger and a sojourner with
you: [i]give me a possession of a buryingplace with you, that I may bury my dead out
of my sight.
5 And the children of Heth answered
Abraham, saying unto him,
6 Hear us, my lord: thou *art* [j]a mighty
prince among us: in the choice of our sepulchres bury thy dead; none of us shall withhold from thee his sepulchre, but that thou
mayest bury thy dead.
7 And Abraham stood up, and bowed
himself to the people of the land, *even* to the
children of Heth.
8 And he communed with them, saying, If
it be your mind that I should bury my dead
out of my sight; hear me, and intreat for me
to Ephron the son of Zohar,
9 That he may give me the cave of Machpelah, which he hath, which *is* in the end of
his field; for as much money as it is worth he
shall give it me for a possession of a buryingplace amongst you.
10 And Ephron dwelt among the children

22:16 [s]Ps. 105:9; Luke 1:73; Heb. 6:13
22:17 [t]ch. 15:5; Jer. 33:22 [u]ch. 13:16 [v]ch. 24:60 [w]Mic. 1:9
22:18 [x]ch. 12:3; Acts 3:25; Gal. 3:8 [y]ver. 3; ch. 26:5
22:19 [z]ch. 21:31
22:20 [a]ch. 11:29
22:21 [b]Job 1:1 [c]Job 32:2
22:23 [d]ch. 24:15 [e]Rom. 9:10
23:2 [f]Josh. 14:15; Judg. 1:10 [g]ch. 13:18; ver. 19
23:4 [h]ch. 17:8; 1 Chron. 29:15; Ps. 105:12; Heb. 11:9 [i]Acts 7:5
23:6 [j]ch. 13:2
23:10 [k]ch. 34:20; Ruth 4:4
23:11 [l]2 Sam. 24:21-24
23:15 [m]Ex. 30:15; Ezek. 45:12
23:16 [n]Jer. 32:9
23:17 [o]ch. 25:9; Acts 7:16
23:20 [p]Ruth 4:7; Jer. 32:10
24:1 [q]ch. 18:11 [r]ch. 13:2; ver. 35; Ps. 112:3; Prov. 10:22
24:2 [s]ch. 15:2 [t]ver. 10; ch. 39:4 [u]ch. 47:29; 1 Chron. 29:24; Lam. 5:6
24:3 [v]ch. 14:22; Deut. 6:13; Josh. 2:12 [w]ch. 26:35; Ex. 34:16; Deut. 7:3
24:4 [x]ch. 28:2 [y]ch. 12:1

of Heth: and Ephron the Hittite answered
Abraham in the audience of the children of
Heth, *even* of all that [k]went in at the gate of
his city, saying,
11 [l]Nay, my lord, hear me: the field give
I thee, and the cave that *is* therein, I give it
thee; in the presence of the sons of my people give I it thee: bury thy dead.
12 And Abraham bowed down himself
before the people of the land.
13 And he spake unto Ephron in the audience of the people of the land, saying, But if
thou *wilt give it,* I pray thee, hear me: I will
give thee money for the field; take *it* of me,
and I will bury my dead there.
14 And Ephron answered Abraham, saying unto him,
15 My lord, hearken unto me: the land
is worth four hundred [m]shekels of silver;
what *is* that betwixt me and thee? bury
therefore thy dead.
16 And Abraham hearkened unto
Ephron; and Abraham [n]weighed to Ephron
the silver, which he had named in the audience of the sons of Heth, four hundred shekels of silver, current *money* with the
merchant.
17 ¶ And [o]the field of Ephron, which *was*
in Machpelah, which *was* before Mamre,
the field, and the cave which *was* therein,
and all the trees that *were* in the field, that
were in all the borders round about, were
made sure
18 Unto Abraham for a possession in the
presence of the children of Heth, before all
that went in at the gate of his city.
19 And after this, Abraham buried Sarah
his wife in the cave of the field of Machpelah before Mamre: the same *is* Hebron in
the land of Canaan.
20 And the field, and the cave that *is*
therein, [p]were made sure unto Abraham
for a possession of a buryingplace by the
sons of Heth.

24

And Abraham [q]was old, *and* well
stricken in age: and the LORD [r]had
blessed Abraham in all things.
2 And Abraham said [s]unto his eldest servant of his house, that [t]ruled over all that
he had, [u]Put, I pray thee, thy hand under
my thigh:
3 And I will make thee [v]swear by the
LORD, the God of heaven, and the God of the
earth, that [w]thou shalt not take a wife unto
my son of the daughters of the Canaanites,
among whom I dwell:
4 [x]But thou shalt go [y]unto my country,
and to my kindred, and take a wife unto my
son Isaac.
5 And the servant said unto him, Peradventure the woman will not be willing to
follow me unto this land: must I needs bring
thy son again unto the land from whence
thou camest?
6 And Abraham said unto him, Beware
thou that thou bring not my son thither
again.
7 ¶ The LORD God of heaven, which

[z]took me from my father's house, and from the land of my kindred, and which spake unto me, and that sware unto me, saying, [a]Unto thy seed will I give this land; [b]he shall send his angel before thee, and thou shalt take a wife unto my son from thence.

8 And if the woman will not be willing to follow thee, then [c]thou shalt be clear from this my oath: only bring not my son thither again.

9 And the servant put his hand under the thigh of Abraham his master, and sware to him concerning that matter.

10 ¶ And the servant took ten camels of the camels of his master, and departed; [d]for all the goods of his master *were* in his hand: and he arose, and went to Mesopotamia, unto [e]the city of Nahor.

11 And he made his camels to kneel down without the city by a well of water at the time of the evening, *even* the time [f]that women go out to draw *water.*

12 And he said, [g]O LORD God of my master Abraham, I pray thee, [h]send me good speed this day, and shew kindness unto my master Abraham.

13 Behold, [i]I stand *here* by the well of water; and [j]the daughters of the men of the city come out to draw water:

14 And let it come to pass, that the damsel to whom I shall say, Let down thy pitcher, I pray thee, that I may drink; and she shall say, Drink, and I will give thy camels drink also: *let the same be* she *that* thou hast appointed for thy servant Isaac; and [k]thereby shall I know that thou hast shewed kindness unto my master.

15 ¶ And it came to pass, before he had done speaking, that, behold, Rebekah came out, who was born to Bethuel, son of [l]Milcah, the wife of Nahor, Abraham's brother, with her pitcher upon her shoulder.

16 And the damsel [m]*was* very fair to look upon, a virgin, neither had any man known her: and she went down to the well, and filled her pitcher, and came up.

17 And the servant ran to meet her, and said, Let me, I pray thee, drink a little water of thy pitcher.

18 [n]And she said, Drink, my lord: and she hasted, and let down her pitcher upon her hand, and gave him drink.

19 And when she had done giving him drink, she said, I will draw *water* for thy camels also, until they have done drinking.

20 And she hasted, and emptied her pitcher into the trough, and ran again unto the well to draw *water,* and drew for all his camels.

21 And the man wondering at her held his peace, to wit whether [o]the LORD had made his journey prosperous or not.

22 And it came to pass, as the camels had done drinking, that the man took a golden [p]earring of half a shekel weight, and two bracelets for her hands of ten *shekels* weight of gold;

23 And said, Whose daughter *art* thou? tell me, I pray thee: is there room *in* thy father's house for us to lodge in?

24 And she said unto him, [q]I *am* the daughter of Bethuel the son of Milcah, which she bare unto Nahor.

25 She said moreover unto him, We have both straw and provender enough, and room to lodge in.

26 And the man [r]bowed down his head, and worshipped the LORD.

27 And he said, [s]Blessed *be* the LORD God of my master Abraham, who hath not left destitute my master of [t]his mercy and his truth: I *being* in the way, the LORD [u]led me to the house of my master's brethren.

28 And the damsel ran, and told *them of* her mother's house these things.

29 ¶ And Rebekah had a brother, and his name *was* [v]Laban: and Laban ran out unto the man, unto the well.

30 And it came to pass, when he saw the earring and bracelets upon his sister's hands, and when he heard the words of Rebekah his sister, saying, Thus spake the man unto me; that he came unto the man; and, behold, he stood by the camels at the well.

31 And he said, Come in, [w]thou blessed of the LORD; wherefore standest thou without? for I have prepared the house, and room for the camels.

32 ¶ And the man came into the house: and he ungirded his camels, and [x]gave straw and provender for the camels, and water to wash his feet, and the men's feet that *were* with him.

33 And there was set *meat* before him to eat: but he said, [y]I will not eat, until I have told mine errand. And he said, Speak on.

34 And he said, I *am* Abraham's servant.

35 And the LORD [z]hath blessed my master greatly; and he is become great: and he hath given him flocks, and herds, and silver, and gold, and menservants, and maidservants, and camels, and asses.

36 And Sarah my master's wife [a]bare a son to my master when she was old: and [b]unto him hath he given all that he hath.

37 And my master [c]made me swear, saying, Thou shalt not take a wife to my son of the daughters of the Canaanites, in whose land I dwell:

38 [d]But thou shalt go unto my father's house, and to my kindred, and take a wife unto my son.

39 [e]And I said unto my master, Peradventure the woman will not follow me.

40 [f]And he said unto me, The LORD, [g]before whom I walk, will send his angel with thee, and prosper thy way; and thou shalt take a wife for my son of my kindred, and of my father's house:

41 [h]Then shalt thou be clear from *this* my oath, when thou comest to my kindred; and if they give not thee *one,* thou shalt be clear from my oath.

42 And I came this day unto the well, and said, [i]O LORD God of my master Abraham,

24:7 [z]ch. 12:1 [a]ch. 12:7; Ex. 32:13; Deut. 1:8; Acts 7:5 [b]Ex. 23:20; Heb. 1:14
24:8 [c]Josh. 2:17
24:10 [d]ver. 2 [e]ch. 27:43
24:11 [f]Ex. 2:16; 1 Sam. 9:11
24:12 [g]ver. 27; ch. 26:24; Ex. 3:6 [h]Neh. 1:11; Ps. 37:5
24:13 [i]ver. 43 [j]ch. 29:9; Ex. 2:16
24:14 [k]Judg. 6:17; 1 Sam. 6:7
24:15 [l]ch. 11:29
24:16 [m]ch. 26:7
24:18 [n]1 Pet. 3:8
24:21 [o]ver. 12:56
24:22 [p]Ex. 32:2; Isa. 3:19; Ezek. 16:11; 1 Pet. 3:3
24:24 [q]ch. 22:23
24:26 [r]ver. 52; Ex. 4:31
24:27 [s]Ex. 18:10; Ruth 4:14; 1 Sam. 25:32; 2 Sam. 18:28; Luke 1:68 [t]ch. 32:10; Ps. 98:3 [u]ver. 48
24:29 [v]ch. 29:5
24:31 [w]ch. 26:29; Judg. 17:2; Ruth 3:10; Ps. 115:15
24:32 [x]ch. 43:24; Judg. 19:21
24:33 [y]Job 23:12; John 4:34; Eph. 6:5
24:35 [z]ver. 1; ch. 13:2
24:36 [a]ch. 21:2 [b]ch. 21:10
24:37 [c]ver. 3
24:38 [d]ver. 4
24:39 [e]ver. 5
24:40 [f]ver. 7 [g]ch. 17:1
24:41 [h]ver. 8
24:42 [i]ver. 12

if now thou do prosper my way which I go:

43 [j]Behold, I stand by the well of water; and it shall come to pass, that when the virgin cometh forth to draw *water,* and I say to her, Give me, I pray thee, a little water of thy pitcher to drink;

44 And she say to me, Both drink thou, and I will also draw for thy camels: *let* the same *be* the woman whom the LORD hath appointed out for my master's son.

45 [k]And before I had done [l]speaking in mine heart, behold, Rebekah came forth with her pitcher on her shoulder; and she went down unto the well, and drew *water:* and I said unto her, Let me drink, I pray thee.

46 And she made haste, and let down her pitcher from her *shoulder,* and said, Drink, and I will give thy camels drink also: so I drank, and she made the camels drink also.

47 And I asked her, and said, Whose daughter *art* thou? And she said, The daughter of Bethuel, Nahor's son, whom Milcah bare unto him: and I [m]put the earring upon her face, and the bracelets upon her hands.

48 [n]And I bowed down my head, and worshipped the LORD, and blessed the LORD God of my master Abraham, which had led me in the right way to take [o]my master's brother's daughter unto his son.

49 And now if ye will [p]deal kindly and truly with my master, tell me: and if not, tell me; that I may turn to the right hand, or to the left.

50 Then Laban and Bethuel answered and said, [q]The thing proceedeth from the LORD: we cannot [r]speak unto thee bad or good.

51 Behold, Rebekah [s]*is* before thee, take *her,* and go, and let her be thy master's son's wife, as the LORD hath spoken.

52 And it came to pass, that, when Abraham's servant heard their words, he [t]worshipped the LORD, *bowing himself* to the earth.

53 And the servant brought forth [u]jewels of silver, and jewels of gold, and raiment, and gave *them* to Rebekah: he gave also to her brother and to her mother [v]precious things.

54 And they did eat and drink, he and the men that *were* with him, and tarried all night; and they rose up in the morning, and he said, [w]Send me away unto my master.

55 And her brother and her mother said, Let the damsel abide with us *a few* days, at the least ten; after that she shall go.

56 And he said unto them, Hinder me not, seeing the LORD hath prospered my way; send me away that I may go to my master.

57 And they said, We will call the damsel, and enquire at her mouth.

58 And they called Rebekah, and said unto her, Wilt thou go with this man? And she said, I will go.

59 And they sent away Rebekah their sister, and [x]her nurse, and Abraham's servant, and his men.

60 And they blessed Rebekah, and said unto her, Thou *art* our sister, be thou [y]*the mother* of thousands of millions, and [z]let thy seed possess the gate of those which hate them.

61 ¶ And Rebekah arose, and her damsels, and they rode upon the camels, and followed the man: and the servant took Rebekah, and went his way.

62 And Isaac came from the way of the [a]well Lahai-roi; for he dwelt in the south country.

63 And Isaac went out [b]to meditate in the field at the eventide: and he lifted up his eyes, and saw, and, behold, the camels *were* coming.

64 And Rebekah lifted up her eyes, and when she saw Isaac, [c]she lighted off the camel.

65 For she *had* said unto the servant, What man *is* this that walketh in the field to meet us? And the servant *had* said, It *is* my master: therefore she took a vail, and covered herself.

66 And the servant told Isaac all things that he had done.

67 And Isaac brought her into his mother Sarah's tent, and took Rebekah, and she became his wife; and he loved her: and Isaac [d]was comforted after his mother's *death.*

25

Then again Abraham took a wife, and her name *was* Keturah.

2 And [e]she bare him Zimran, and Jokshan, and Medan, and Midian, and Ishbak, and Shuah.

3 And Jokshan begat Sheba, and Dedan. And the sons of Dedan were Asshurim, and Letushim, and Leummim.

4 And the sons of Midian; Ephah, and Epher, and Hanoch, and Abida, and Eldaah. All these *were* the children of Keturah.

5 ¶ And [f]Abraham gave all that he had unto Isaac.

6 But unto the sons of the concubines, which Abraham had, Abraham gave gifts, and [g]sent them away from Isaac his son, while he yet lived, eastward, unto [h]the east country.

7 And these *are* the days of the years of Abraham's life which he lived, an hundred threescore and fifteen years.

8 Then Abraham gave up the ghost, and [i]died in a good old age, an old man, and full *of years;* and [j]was gathered to his people.

9 And [k]his sons Isaac and Ishmael buried him in the cave of Machpelah, in the field of Ephron the son of Zohar the Hittite, which *is* before Mamre;

10 [l]The field which Abraham purchased of the sons of Heth: [m]there was Abraham buried, and Sarah his wife.

11 ¶ And it came to pass after the death of Abraham, that God blessed his son Isaac; and Isaac dwelt by the [n]well Lahai-roi.

12 ¶ Now these *are* the generations of Ishmael, Abraham's son, whom Hagar the

24:43 j ver. 13
24:45 k ver. 15 l 1 Sam. 1
24:47 m Ezek. 16:11
24:48 n ver. 26 o ch. 22:23
24:49 p ch. 47:29; Josh. 2:14
24:50 q Ps. 118:23; Matt. 21:42; Mark 12:11 r ch. 31:24
24:51 s ch. 20:15
24:52 t ver. 26
24:53 u Ex. 3:22 v 2 Chron. 21:3; Ezra 1:6
24:54 w ver. 56
24:59 x ch. 35:8
24:60 y ch. 17:16 z ch. 22:17
24:62 a ch. 16:14
24:63 b Josh. 1:8; Ps. 1:2
24:64 c Josh. 15:18
24:67 d ch. 38:12
25:2 e 1 Chron. 1:32
25:5 f ch. 24:36
25:6 g ch. 21:14 h Judg. 6:3
25:8 i ch. 15:15 j ch. 35:29
25:9 k ch. 35:29
25:10 l ch. 23:16 m ch. 49:31
25:11 n ch. 16:14

Egyptian, Sarah's handmaid, bare unto
Abraham:
13 And [o]these *are* the names of the sons
of Ishmael, by their names, according to
their generations: the firstborn of Ishmael,
Nebajoth; and Kedar, and Adbeel, and Mibsam,
14 And Mishma, and Dumah, and Massa,
15 Hadar, and Tema, Jetur, Naphish, and
Kedemah:
16 These *are* the sons of Ishmael, and
these *are* their names, by their towns, and
by their castles; [p]twelve princes according
to their nations.
17 And these *are* the years of the life of
Ishmael, an hundred and thirty and seven
years: and he [q]gave up the ghost and died;
and was gathered unto his people.
18 [r]And they dwelt from Havilah unto
Shur, that *is* before Egypt, as thou goest toward Assyria: *and* he died [s]in the presence
of all his brethren.
19 ¶ And these *are* the generations of
Isaac, Abraham's son: [t]Abraham begat
Isaac:
20 And Isaac was forty years old when he
took Rebekah to wife, [u]the daughter of Bethuel the Syrian of Padan-aram, the sister
to Laban the Syrian.
21 And Isaac intreated the LORD for his
wife, because she *was* barren: [v]and the
LORD was entreated of him, and [w]Rebekah
his wife conceived.
22 And the children struggled together
within her; and she said, If *it be* so, why *am*
I thus? [x]And she went to enquire of the
LORD.
23 And the LORD said unto her, [y]Two nations *are* in thy womb, and two manner of
people shall be separated from thy bowels;
and [z]*the one* people shall be stronger than
the other people; and [a]the elder shall serve
the younger.
24 ¶ And when her days to be delivered
were fulfilled, behold, *there were* twins in
her womb.
25 And the first came out red, [b]all over
like an hairy garment; and they called his
name Esau.
26 And after that came his brother out,
and [c]his hand took hold on Esau's heel; and
[d]his name was called Jacob: and Isaac *was*
threescore years old when she bare them.
27 And the boys grew: and Esau was a
[e]cunning hunter, a man of the field; and
Jacob *was* a [f]plain man, [g]dwelling in tents.
28 And Isaac loved Esau, because he did
[h]eat of *his* venison: [i]but Rebekah loved Jacob.
29 ¶ And Jacob sod pottage: and Esau
came from the field, and he *was* faint:
30 And Esau said to Jacob, Feed me, I
pray thee, with that same red *pottage;* for
I *am* faint: therefore was his name called
Edom.
31 And Jacob said, Sell me this day thy
birthright.
32 And Esau said, Behold, I *am* at the

25:13 [o]1 Chron. 1:29
25:16 [p]ch. 17:20
25:17 [q]ver. 8
25:18 [r]1 Sam. 15:7 [s]ch. 16:12
25:19 [t]Matt. 1:2
25:20 [u]ch. 22:23
25:21 [v]1 Chron. 5:20; 2 Chron. 33:13; Ezra 8:23 [w]Rom. 9:10
25:22 [x]1 Sam. 9:9
25:23 [y]ch. 17:16 [z]2 Sam. 8:14 [a]ch. 27:29; Mal. 1:3; Rom. 9:12
25:25 [b]ch. 27:11
25:26 [c]Hos. 12:3 [d]ch. 27:36
25:27 [e]ch. 27:3 [f]Job 1:1; Ps. 37:37 [g]Heb. 11:9
25:28 [h]ch. 27:19 [i]ch. 27:6
25:33 [j]Heb. 12:16
25:34 [k]Eccl. 8:15; Isa. 22:13; 1 Cor. 15:32
26:1 [l]ch. 12:10 [m]ch. 20:2
26:2 [n]ch. 12:1
26:3 [o]ch. 20:1; Ps. 39:12; Heb. 11:9 [p]ch. 28:15 [q]ch. 12:1 [r]ch. 13:15 [s]ch. 22:16; Ps. 105:9
26:4 [t]ch. 15:5 [u]ch. 12:3
26:5 [v]ch. 22:16
26:7 [w]ch. 12:13 [x]Prov. 29:25 [y]ch. 24:16
26:10 [z]ch. 20:9
26:11 [a]Ps. 105:15
26:12 [b]Matt. 13:8; Mark 4:8 [c]ver. 3; ch. 24:1; Job 42:12
26:13 [d]ch. 24:35; Ps. 112:3; Prov. 10:22
26:14 [e]ch. 37:11; Eccl. 4:4
26:15 [f]ch. 21:30
26:16 [g]Ex. 1:9

point to die: and what profit shall this birthright do to me?
33 And Jacob said, Swear to me this day;
and he sware unto him: and [j]he sold his
birthright unto Jacob.
34 Then Jacob gave Esau bread and pottage of lentiles; and [k]he did eat and drink,
and rose up, and went his way: thus Esau
despised *his* birthright.

26

And there was a famine in the land,
beside [l]the first famine that was in
the days of Abraham. And Isaac went unto
[m]Abimelech king of the Philistines unto Gerar.
2 And the LORD appeared unto him, and
said, Go not down into Egypt; dwell in [n]the
land which I shall tell thee of:
3 [o]Sojourn in this land, and [p]I will be
with thee, and [q]will bless thee; for unto
thee, and unto thy seed, [r]I will give all these
countries, and I will perform [s]the oath
which I sware unto Abraham thy father;
4 And [t]I will make thy seed to multiply as
the stars of heaven, and will give unto thy
seed all these countries; [u]and in thy seed
shall all the nations of the earth be blessed;
5 [v]Because that Abraham obeyed my
voice, and kept my charge, my commandments, my statutes, and my laws.
6 ¶ And Isaac dwelt in Gerar:
7 And the men of the place asked *him* of
his wife; and [w]he said, She *is* my sister: for
[x]he feared to say, *She is* my wife; lest, *said*
he, the men of the place should kill me for
Rebekah; because she [y]*was* fair to look
upon.
8 And it came to pass, when he had been
there a long time, that Abimelech king of
the Philistines looked out at a window, and
saw, and, behold, Isaac *was* sporting with
Rebekah his wife.
9 And Abimelech called Isaac, and said,
Behold, of a surety she *is* thy wife: and how
saidst thou, She *is* my sister? And Isaac said
unto him, Because I said, Lest I die for her.
10 And Abimelech said, What *is* this thou
hast done unto us? one of the people might
lightly have lien with thy wife, and [z]thou
shouldest have brought guiltiness upon us.
11 And Abimelech charged all *his* people,
saying, He that [a]toucheth this man or his
wife shall surely be put to death.
12 Then Isaac sowed in that land, and received in the same year [b]an hundredfold:
and the LORD [c]blessed him.
13 And the man [d]waxed great, and went
forward, and grew until he became very
great:
14 For he had possession of flocks, and
possession of herds, and great store of servants: and the Philistines [e]envied him.
15 For all the wells [f]which his father's
servants had digged in the days of Abraham
his father, the Philistines had stopped them,
and filled them with earth.
16 And Abimelech said unto Isaac, Go
from us; for [g]thou art much mightier
than we.

17 ¶ And Isaac departed thence, and pitched his tent in the valley of Gerar, and dwelt there.

18 And Isaac digged again the wells of water, which they had digged in the days of Abraham his father; for the Philistines had stopped them after the death of Abraham: [h]and he called their names after the names by which his father had called them.

19 And Isaac's servants digged in the valley, and found there a well of springing water.

20 And the herdmen of Gerar [i]did strive with Isaac's herdmen, saying, The water *is* ours: and he called the name of the well Esek; because they strove with him.

21 And they digged another well, and strove for that also: and he called the name of it Sitnah.

22 And he removed from thence, and digged another well; and for that they strove not: and he called the name of it Rehoboth; and he said, For now the LORD hath made room for us, and we shall [j]be fruitful in the land.

23 And he went up from thence to Beer-sheba.

24 And the LORD appeared unto him the same night, and said, [k]I *am* the God of Abraham thy father: [l]fear not, for [m]I *am* with thee, and will bless thee, and multiply thy seed for my servant Abraham's sake.

25 And he [n]builded an altar there, and [o]called upon the name of the LORD, and pitched his tent there: and there Isaac's servants digged a well.

26 ¶ Then Abimelech went to him from Gerar, and Ahuzzath one of his friends, [p]and Phichol the chief captain of his army.

27 And Isaac said unto them, Wherefore come ye to me, seeing [q]ye hate me, and have [r]sent me away from you?

28 And they said, We saw certainly that the LORD [s]was with thee: and we said, Let there be now an oath betwixt us, *even* betwixt us and thee, and let us make a covenant with thee;

29 That thou wilt do us no hurt, as we have not touched thee, and as we have done unto thee nothing but good, and have sent thee away in peace: [t]thou *art* now the blessed of the LORD.

30 [u]And he made them a feast, and they did eat and drink.

31 And they rose up betimes in the morning, and [v]sware one to another: and Isaac sent them away, and they departed from him in peace.

32 And it came to pass the same day, that Isaac's servants came, and told him concerning the well which they had digged, and said unto him, We have found water.

33 And he called it Shebah: [w]therefore the name of the city *is* Beer-sheba unto this day.

34 ¶ [x]And Esau was forty years old when he took to wife Judith the daughter of Beeri the Hittite, and Bashemath the daughter of Elon the Hittite:

35 Which [y]were a grief of mind unto Isaac and to Rebekah.

27 And it came to pass, that when Isaac was old, and [z]his eyes were dim, so that he could not see, he called Esau his eldest son, and said unto him, My son: and he said unto him, Behold, *here am* I.

2 And he said, Behold now, I am old, I [a]know not the day of my death:

3 [b]Now therefore take, I pray thee, thy weapons, thy quiver and thy bow, and go out to the field, and take me *some* venison;

4 And make me savoury meat, such as I love, and bring *it* to me, that I may eat; that my soul [c]may bless thee before I die.

5 And Rebekah heard when Isaac spake to Esau his son. And Esau went to the field to hunt *for* venison, *and* to bring *it*.

6 ¶ And Rebekah spake unto Jacob her son, saying, Behold, I heard thy father speak unto Esau thy brother, saying,

7 Bring me venison, and make me savoury meat, that I may eat, and bless thee before the LORD before my death.

8 Now therefore, my son, [d]obey my voice according to that which I command thee.

9 Go now to the flock, and fetch me from thence two good kids of the goats; and I will make them [e]savoury meat for thy father, such as he loveth:

10 And thou shalt bring *it* to thy father, that he may eat, and that he [f]may bless thee before his death.

11 And Jacob said to Rebekah his mother, Behold, [g]Esau my brother *is* a hairy man, and I *am* a smooth man:

12 My father peradventure will [h]feel me, and I shall seem to him as a deceiver; and I shall bring [i]a curse upon me, and not a blessing.

13 And his mother said unto him, [j]Upon me *be* thy curse, my son: only obey my voice, and go fetch me *them*.

14 And he went, and fetched, and brought *them* to his mother: and his mother [k]made savoury meat, such as his father loved.

15 And Rebekah took [l]goodly raiment of her eldest son Esau, which *were* with her in the house, and put them upon Jacob her younger son:

16 And she put the skins of the kids of the goats upon his hands, and upon the smooth of his neck:

17 And she gave the savoury meat and the bread, which she had prepared, into the hand of her son Jacob.

18 ¶ And he came unto his father, and said, My father: and he said, Here *am* I; who *art* thou, my son?

19 And Jacob said unto his father, I *am* Esau thy firstborn; I have done according as thou badest me: arise, I pray thee, sit and eat of my venison, [m]that thy soul may bless me.

20 And Isaac said unto his son, How *is it* that thou hast found *it* so quickly, my son?

26:18 [h]ch. 21:31
26:20 [i]ch. 21:25
26:22 [j]ch. 17:6; Ex. 1:7
26:24 [k]ch. 17:7; Ex. 3:6; Acts 7:32 [l]ch. 15:1 [m]ver. 3
26:25 [n]ch. 12:7 [o]Ps. 116:17
26:26 [p]ch. 21:22
26:27 [q]Judg. 11:7 [r]ver. 16
26:28 [s]ch. 21:22
26:29 [t]ch. 24:31; Ps. 115:15
26:30 [u]ch. 19:3
26:31 [v]ch. 21:31
26:33 [w]ch. 21:31
26:34 [x]ch. 36:2
26:35 [y]ch. 27:46
27:1 [z]ch. 48:10; 1 Sam. 3:2
27:2 [a]Prov. 27:1; Jam. 4:14
27:3 [b]ch. 25:27
27:4 [c]ver. 27; ch. 48:9; Deut. 33:1
27:8 [d]ver. 13
27:9 [e]ver. 4
27:10 [f]ver. 4
27:11 [g]ch. 25:25
27:12 [h]ver. 22 [i]ch. 9:25; Deut. 27:18
27:13 [j]ch. 43:9; 1 Sam. 25:24; 2 Sam. 14:9; Matt. 27:25
27:14 [k]ver. 4
27:15 [l]ver. 27
27:19 [m]ver. 4

And he said, Because the LORD thy God brought *it* to me.

21 And Isaac said unto Jacob, Come near, I pray thee, that I [n]may feel thee, my son, whether thou *be* my very son Esau or not.

22 And Jacob went near unto Isaac his father; and he felt him, and said, The voice *is* Jacob's voice, but the hands *are* the hands of Esau.

23 And he discerned him not, because [o]his hands were hairy, as his brother Esau's hands: so he blessed him.

24 And he said, *Art* thou my very son Esau? And he said, I *am*.

25 And he said, Bring *it* near to me, and I will eat of my son's venison, [p]that my soul may bless thee. And he brought *it* near to him, and he did eat: and he brought him wine, and he drank.

26 And his father Isaac said unto him, Come near now, and kiss me, my son.

27 And he came near, and kissed him: and he smelled the smell of his raiment, and blessed him, and said, See, [q]the smell of my son *is* as the smell of a field which the LORD hath blessed:

28 Therefore [r]God give thee of [s]the dew of heaven, and [t]the fatness of the earth, and [u]plenty of corn and wine:

29 [v]Let people serve thee, and nations bow down to thee: be lord over thy brethren, and [w]let thy mother's sons bow down to thee: [x]cursed *be* every one that curseth thee, and blessed *be* he that blesseth thee.

30 ¶ And it came to pass, as soon as Isaac had made an end of blessing Jacob, and Jacob was yet scarce gone out from the presence of Isaac his father, that Esau his brother came in from his hunting.

31 And he also had made savoury meat, and brought it unto his father, and said unto his father, Let my father arise, and [y]eat of his son's venison, that thy soul may bless me.

32 And Isaac his father said unto him, Who *art* thou? And he said, I *am* thy son, thy firstborn Esau.

33 And Isaac trembled very exceedingly, and said, Who? where *is* he that hath taken venison, and brought *it* me, and I have eaten of all before thou camest, and have blessed him? yea, [z]*and* he shall be blessed.

34 And when Esau heard the words of his father, [a]he cried with a great and exceeding bitter cry, and said unto his father, Bless me, *even* me also, O my father.

35 And he said, Thy brother came with subtilty, and hath taken away thy blessing.

36 And he said, [b]Is not he rightly named Jacob? for he hath supplanted me these two times: [c]he took away my birthright; and, behold, now he hath taken away my blessing. And he said, Hast thou not reserved a blessing for me?

37 And Isaac answered and said unto Esau, [d]Behold, I have made him thy lord, and all his brethren have I given to him for servants; and [e]with corn and wine have I sustained him: and what shall I do now unto thee, my son?

38 And Esau said unto his father, Hast thou but one blessing, my father? bless me, *even* me also, O my father. And Esau lifted up his voice, [f]and wept.

39 And Isaac his father answered and said unto him, Behold, [g]thy dwelling shall be the fatness of the earth, and of the dew of heaven from above;

40 And by thy sword shalt thou live, and [h]shalt serve thy brother; and [i]it shall come to pass when thou shalt have the dominion, that thou shalt break his yoke from off thy neck.

41 ¶ And Esau [j]hated Jacob because of the blessing wherewith his father blessed him: and Esau said in his heart, [k]The days of mourning for my father are at hand; [l]then will I slay my brother Jacob.

42 And these words of Esau her elder son were told to Rebekah: and she sent and called Jacob her younger son, and said unto him, Behold, thy brother Esau, as touching thee, doth [m]comfort himself, *purposing* to kill thee.

43 Now therefore, my son, obey my voice; and arise, flee thou to Laban my brother [n]to Haran;

44 And tarry with him a few days, until thy brother's fury turn away;

45 Until thy brother's anger turn away from thee, and he forget *that* which thou hast done to him: then I will send, and fetch thee from thence: why should I be deprived also of you both in one day?

46 And Rebekah said to Isaac, [o]I am weary of my life because of the daughters of Heth: [p]if Jacob take a wife of the daughters of Heth, such as these *which are* of the daughters of the land, what good shall my life do me?

28 And Isaac called Jacob, and [q]blessed him, and charged him, and said unto him, [r]Thou shalt not take a wife of the daughters of Canaan.

2 [s]Arise, go to [t]Padan-aram, to the house of [u]Bethuel thy mother's father; and take thee a wife from thence of the daughters of [v]Laban thy mother's brother.

3 [w]And God Almighty bless thee, and make thee fruitful, and multiply thee, that thou mayest be a multitude of people;

4 And give thee [x]the blessing of Abraham, to thee, and to thy seed with thee; that thou mayest inherit the land [y]wherein thou art a stranger, which God gave unto Abraham.

5 And Isaac sent away Jacob: and he went to Padan-aram unto Laban, son of Bethuel the Syrian, the brother of Rebekah, Jacob's and Esau's mother.

6 ¶ When Esau saw that Isaac had blessed Jacob, and sent him away to Padan-aram, to take him a wife from thence; and that as he blessed him he gave him a charge, saying, Thou shalt not take a wife of the daughters of Canaan;

27:21 [n]ver. 12
27:23 [o]ver. 16
27:25 [p]ver. 4
27:27 [q]Hos. 14:6
27:28 [r]Heb. 11:20 [s]Deut. 33:13; 2 Sam. 1:21 [t]ch. 45:18 [u]Deut. 33:28
27:29 [v]ch. 9:25 [w]ch. 49:8 [x]ch. 12:3; Num. 24:9
27:31 [y]ver. 4
27:33 [z]ch. 28:3; Rom. 11:29
27:34 [a]Heb. 12:17
27:36 [b]ch. 25:26 [c]ch. 25:33
27:37 [d]2 Sam. 8:14; ver. 29 [e]ver. 28
27:38 [f]Heb. 12:17
27:39 [g]ver. 28; Heb. 11:20
27:40 [h]ch. 25:23; Obad. 18; 2 Sam. 8:14 [i]2 Kings 8:20
27:41 [j]ch. 37:4 [k]ch. 50:3 [l]Obad. 10
27:42 [m]Ps. 64:5
27:43 [n]ch. 11:31
27:46 [o]ch. 26:35 [p]ch. 24:3
28:1 [q]ch. 27:33 [r]ch. 24:3
28:2 [s]Hos. 12:12 [t]ch. 25:20 [u]ch. 22:23 [v]ch. 24:29
28:3 [w]ch. 17:1
28:4 [x]ch. 12:2 [y]ch. 17:8

7 And that Jacob obeyed his father and
his mother, and was gone to Padan-aram;
8 And Esau seeing [z]that the daughters of
Canaan pleased not Isaac his father;
9 Then went Esau unto Ishmael, and took
unto the wives which he had [a]Mahalath the
daughter of Ishmael Abraham's son, the
[b]sister of Nebajoth, to be his wife.
10 ¶ And Jacob [c]went out from Beer-
sheba, and went toward [d]Haran.
11 And he lighted upon a certain place,
and tarried there all night, because the sun
was set; and he took of the stones of that
place, and put *them for* his pillows, and lay
down in that place to sleep.
12 And he [e]dreamed, and behold a ladder set up on the earth, and the top of it
reached to heaven: and behold [f]the angels
of God ascending and descending on it.
13 [g]And, behold, the LORD stood above it,
and said, [h]I *am* the LORD God of Abraham
thy father, and the God of Isaac: [i]the land
whereon thou liest, to thee will I give it, and
to thy seed;
14 And [j]thy seed shall be as the dust of
the earth, and thou shalt spread abroad [k]to
the west, and to the east, and to the north,
and to the south: and in thee and [l]in thy
seed shall all the families of the earth be
blessed.
15 And, behold, [m]I *am* with thee, and will
[n]keep thee in all *places* whither thou goest,
and will [o]bring thee again into this land; for
[p]I will not leave thee, [q]until I have done
that which I have spoken to thee of.
16 ¶ And Jacob awaked out of his sleep,
and he said, Surely the LORD is in [r]this
place; and I knew *it* not.
17 And he was afraid, and said, How
dreadful *is* this place! this *is* none other but
the house of God, and this *is* the gate of
heaven.
18 And Jacob rose up early in the morning, and took the stone that he had put *for*
his pillows, and [s]set it up *for* a pillar, [t]and
poured oil upon the top of it.
19 And he called the name of [u]that place
Beth-el: but the name of that city *was called*
Luz at the first.
20 [v]And Jacob vowed a vow, saying, If
[w]God will be with me, and will keep me in
this way that I go, and will give me [x]bread
to eat, and raiment to put on,
21 So that [y]I come again to my father's
house in peace; [z]then shall the LORD be my
God:
22 And this stone, which I have set *for* a
pillar, [a]shall be God's house: [b]and of all
that thou shalt give me I will surely give the
tenth unto thee.

29 Then Jacob went on his journey,
[c]and came into the land of the people of the east.
2 And he looked, and behold a well in the
field, and, lo, there *were* three flocks of
sheep lying by it; for out of that well they
watered the flocks: and a great stone *was*
upon the well's mouth.

28:8 [z]ch. 24:3
28:9 [a]ch. 36:3 [b]ch. 25:13
28:10 [c]Hos. 12:12 [d]Acts 7:2
28:12 [e]ch. 41:1; Job 33:15 [f]John 1:51; Heb. 1:14
28:13 [g]ch. 35:1 [h]ch. 26:24 [i]ch. 13:15
28:14 [j]ch. 13:16 [k]ch. 13:14; Deut. 12:20 [l]ch. 12:3
28:15 [m]ver. 20; ch. 26:24 [n]ch. 48:16; Ps. 121:5 [o]ch. 35:6 [p]Deut. 28:6; Josh. 1:5; 1 Kings 8:57; Heb. 13:5 [q]Num. 23:19
28:16 [r]Ex. 3:5; Josh. 5:15
28:18 [s]ch. 31:13 [t]Lev. 8:10; Num. 7:1
28:19 [u]Judg. 1:23; Hos. 4:15
28:20 [v]ch. 31:13; Judg. 11:30; 2 Sam. 15:8 [w]ver. 15 [x]1 Tim. 6:8
28:21 [y]Judg. 11:31; 2 Sam. 19:24 [z]Deut. 26:17; 2 Sam. 15:8; 2 Kings 5:17
28:22 [a]ch. 35:7 [b]Lev. 27:30
29:1 [c]Num. 23:7; Hos. 12:12
29:6 [d]ch. 43:27
29:9 [e]Ex. 2:16
29:10 [f]Ex. 2:17
29:11 [g]ch. 33:4
29:12 [h]ch. 13:8 [i]ch. 24:28
29:13 [j]ch. 24:29
29:14 [k]ch. 2:23; Judg. 9:2; 2 Sam. 5:1
29:18 [l]ch. 31:41; 2 Sam. 3:14
29:20 [m]ch. 30:26; Hos. 12:12
29:21 [n]Judg. 15:1

3 And thither were all the flocks gathered: and they rolled the stone from the
well's mouth, and watered the sheep, and
put the stone again upon the well's mouth in
his place.
4 And Jacob said unto them, My brethren,
whence *be* ye? And they said, Of Haran
are we.
5 And he said unto them, Know ye Laban
the son of Nahor? And they said, We know
him.
6 And he said unto them, [d]*Is* he well?
And they said, *He is* well: and, behold, Rachel his daughter cometh with the sheep.
7 And he said, Lo, *it is* yet high day, neither *is it* time that the cattle should be gathered together: water ye the sheep, and go
and feed *them*.
8 And they said, We cannot, until all the
flocks be gathered together, and *till* they
roll the stone from the well's mouth; then
we water the sheep.
9 ¶ And while he yet spake with them,
[e]Rachel came with her father's sheep: for
she kept them.
10 And it came to pass, when Jacob saw
Rachel the daughter of Laban his mother's
brother, and the sheep of Laban his
mother's brother, that Jacob went near, and
[f]rolled the stone from the well's mouth,
and watered the flock of Laban his mother's
brother.
11 And Jacob [g]kissed Rachel, and lifted
up his voice, and wept.
12 And Jacob told Rachel that he *was*
[h]her father's brother, and that he *was* Rebekah's son: [i]and she ran and told her father.
13 And it came to pass, when Laban
heard the tidings of Jacob his sister's son,
that [j]he ran to meet him, and embraced
him, and kissed him, and brought him to his
house. And he told Laban all these things.
14 And Laban said to him, [k]Surely thou
art my bone and my flesh. And he abode
with him the space of a month.
15 ¶ And Laban said unto Jacob, Because
thou *art* my brother, shouldest thou therefore serve me for nought? tell me, what *shall*
thy wages *be*?
16 And Laban had two daughters: the
name of the elder *was* Leah, and the name
of the younger *was* Rachel.
17 Leah *was* tender eyed; but Rachel *was*
beautiful and well favoured.
18 And Jacob loved Rachel; and said, [l]I
will serve thee seven years for Rachel thy
younger daughter.
19 And Laban said, *It is* better that I give
her to thee, than that I should give her to
another man: abide with me.
20 And Jacob [m]served seven years for
Rachel; and they seemed unto him *but* a few
days, for the love he had to her.
21 ¶ And Jacob said unto Laban, Give *me*
my wife, for my days are fulfilled, that I may
[n]go in unto her.

Focus on Genesis

The first book of the Bible, Genesis, introduces the reader to the Supreme Being, God, and provides a summary of God's revelation from Creation until the Israelites enter Egypt. It is a book with a significant number of "beginnings." It is the beginning of history and God's creation of a world populated with living, moving, and thinking beings. It also marks the beginning of God's promises, or covenants, with humankind.

HISTORICAL BACKGROUND TO GENESIS

Recent scholarship points toward the continent of Africa as the place where humanity began, and from there, people migrated to other parts of the earth. Thus the Garden of Eden would have been located there—perhaps the eastern shores along the Nile River. The Bible indicates that four rivers encompassed Eden—the Pison, the Gihon, the Hiddekel, and the Euphrates. The location of the latter two rivers is known. The first two are believed to be in Africa (See "The Place of Africa and Africans in the Old Testament and Its Environments," a Doctoral Dissertation, 1986 by David Tuesday Adamo, and others). Recent aerial photographs of the area indicate that ancient riverbeds are buried beneath the earth's surface. If so, the biblical indication of the Garden of Eden's location would be indisputable. Other anthropological and archaeological evidence also points to its African location.

Prior to the recent discoveries of humankind's origin in Africa, archaeological scholars suggested Mesopotamia as the most likely place for Eden. Even there, however, evidence points to the presence of Black people in early times. According to African scholar Cheikh Anta Diop and George Rawlinson, the Father of Assyriology, Mesopotamia was originally settled by Sumerians (about 5000 to 2500 B.C.), and these people migrated there from Africa. Rawlinson says that inscriptions, dialect, and tradition all point to these early inhabitants as African.

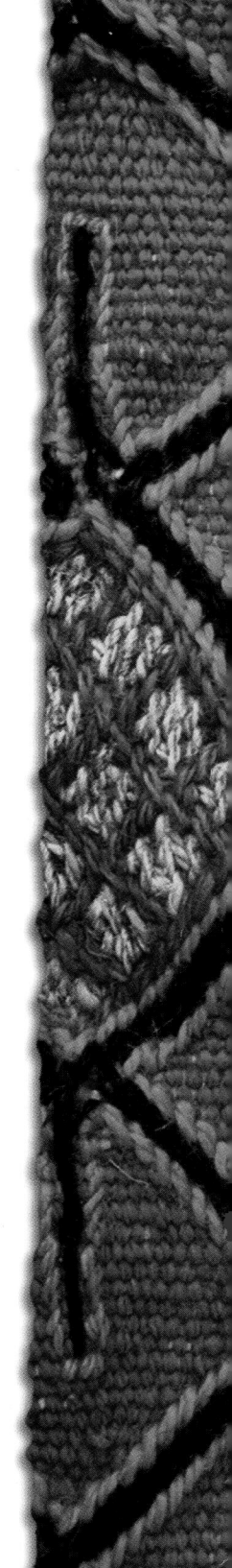

The picture that emerges from archaeology, anthropology, geography, and the biblical record is that humankind began in Africa. After the Noahic flood, the sons of Noah migrated in several directions: Japheth and his children went toward the north and west into Europe; Ham and his children lived in Mesopotamia/Asia as well as the continent of Africa (see Gen. 10:6–20); Shem and his children remained in Mesopotamia/ Asia. Historical records indicate that people of African descent can be identified all the way from the southern coasts of Africa into Asia and all around the Pacific Rim. Archaeological findings have been made of inscriptions and paintings on walls, pottery, and tombs in Mesopotamia and Egypt, which show these ancient people with African features. The term "Egypt" is a Greek term. Prior to the arrival of Greeks, the native people called their land "Kemet" which means, "land of the Blacks." While some scholars

have attempted to argue that the term refers to the black soil, other scholars including Diop have argued that it is indeed a reference to both the land and its people.

The Greek historian Herodotus, who lived in the fifth century B.C., visited Egypt and described the people as "black skinned with wooly hair."

Within the biblical record itself—besides the fact that the entire area was populated by people whose origins were in the continent of Africa—several geographical locations and people group names indicate the presence of Black people. Among them are these: Ham or Hamites (which means black or burnt face), Cush or Cushites (called Ethiopians in most translations), Mizraim or Mizraimites (the Hebrew word for Egypt), Phut, Canaan or Canaanites, Babel and Babylonians, Asshur or Assyrians. It is not necessary to assert that all these people were "coal" black to establish that they were of African heritage.

THE BLACK PRESENCE IN GENESIS

HAM/HAMITES are mentioned nine times in the Book of Genesis (chapters 5, 6, 7, 9, 10, 14). Hamites were the descendants of Noah through his son Ham. The name Ham means "black" or "burnt face." His descendants settled not only in Africa, but also in Mesopotamia and further east. They can today be found in all countries of the world. When it was discovered during the eighteenth century that Hamites were the source of much learning and discovery in Egypt, a new theory developed that Hamites must have been white; however, that theory is without merit.

MIZRAIM/EGYPT/EGYPTIANS are mentioned over 100 times in Genesis (chapters 10, 12, 13, 15, 21, 25, 26, 37, 39, 40, 41, 42, 43, 45, 46, 47, 48, 50). Mizraim is the Hebrew word designating the people otherwise called Egyptians. In fact, "Egypt" is a Greek term meaning "black." Prior to the conquering of that land by Alexander the Great in 332 B.C., the people along the Nile River called themselves "Kemites" and their land "Kemet," which means, "land of the blacks."

CANAAN/CANAANITES are mentioned over 40 times in Genesis (chapters 9, 10, 11, 12, 15, 16, 17, 23, 31, 33, 35, 36, 37, 42, 44, 45, 46, 47, 48, 50). According to Genesis 10:6, Canaanites were descendants of Ham, whose name means, "black." This son of Ham occupied the land where the Israelites eventually settled. Canaan gave birth to the Sidonites, Hittites, Jebusites, Amorites, Girgasites, Hivites, Arkites, Sinites, Arvadites, Zemarites, and Hamathites (Gen. 10:15–19).

Notable people of Hamitic Descent in Genesis include Melchizedek (Gen. 14:18–20); Hagar (Gen. 16:1ff.; 21:9ff.); Ephraim and Manasseh, sons of Joseph by Asenath, daughter of Poti-pherah, the Egyptian priest (Gen. 41:50–52).

Life Lessons

GENESIS 1–2

Chapters one and two record the creation of the universe, including the solar system, plants, fowl and other animals, and humankind. Fundamental to successful living in this world is the affirmation that the universe is not accidental, but the handiwork of an all-wise and all-powerful God. While we may not have all the details of how all things came into existence, we can confirm who created them.

Creating Wonder, I acknowledge and praise You for bringing all things into existence, including me. Help me to worship and appreciate You through the beauty of our world. Create in me a hunger to join You in the continuing creation left in our hands!

GENESIS 3

Chapter three relates the story of Adam and Eve's disobedience to God's Law, and their consequent expulsion from the Garden of Eden. It is because of Adam and Eve's alienation from God that each successive generation would be required to seek salvation through Jesus, who was God in human form, sent to earth as a man to redeem us.

Ancient of Days, I acknowledge that I, too, am a sinner, and fall short of Your glory. I thank You for knowing me and accepting me as I am. Help me to accept the grace of your forgiveness when I ask You for it because of the atoning sacrifice of Jesus, Your Son.

GENESIS 11—12

Chapters eleven and twelve tell us that in order to separate the children of Israel from other nations, God called upon Abram and Sarai (later renamed by God as Abraham and Sarah) to establish a nation, one that would ultimately produce the Savior. They were required to leave their homeland, Ur, and settle in Canaan. It was this journey of faith that symbolized the restoration of God's faith in man through the person of Abram (Abraham).

Dear God, help me, like Abram and Sarai, to obey Your clearly revealed will. When I am unsure of Your will, help me to trust You to clarify the path I should take.

GENESIS 15–17

In Genesis 15 and 17, God established two covenants with Abraham: The first was a promise to give Abraham and his descendants the land of Canaan; the second was the promise of a child born to Sarah that would signify the beginning of the Hebrew nation.

Covenant-Maker, help me to identify in Your Living Word those promises You have made for my benefit. Then, help me to trust You to fulfill them.

Women in GENESIS

EVE: THE FIRST AFRICAN WOMAN

When we create, we produce, bring into being, construct, discover, shape, and design. The "first" is a milestone for women of color. It is no secret that women of color have been the first in many areas. We have reigned throughout history as the first woman to do many things in God's creative world. The creation of Eve, the first woman of color, came forth on the sixth day of creation. Today, women of color have the authority to be creative any day of the week.

God made Eve as a helpmate to Adam. We find Eve in the first chapters of Genesis demonstrating the importance of men and women complementing one another, supporting one another, and empowering one another. When women of color first develop relationships, whether intimate, professional, familial, or social, we must first identify the importance of embracing and empowering one another. We should affirm the importance of being helpmates. I define helpmate not only in the sense of a husband and wife team, or a male and female relationship, but also inclusively from a biblical stance of women helping women, women helping men, women helping children, women helping others who may or may not be like them.

The womanist experience resonates with me when I think about Eve. Alice Walker coined the term "womanist." A womanist is one who values male and female relationships. The womanist is a free woman who loves to dance, sing, and watch the stars and moon. A womanist embraces and empowers all of God's creations.

The womanist Eve is constantly challenged to listen and hear God when God speaks to her. When we fail to hear God's voice, we move in the wrong direction and we commit sin. The late Dr. Howard Thurman, one of our great African-American theologians, said that anytime we go against God, we have committed a sin. The first sin of Eve was when she listened to the serpent instead of God (see Gen. 3:1–8). Here we see Eve going against the Word of God. There will be times when all of us listen to the wrong voice, but it's important to remember that we can always go to God and seek forgiveness. There is no need to hide from God. God wants us to confess our wrongs to Him.

In the Eve story God posed the question, "Where are you?" The question "Where are we in our relationship to God?" should be ever before us.

Women of color resonate with many colors. Some of us are black, some of us are brown, some of us are pecan, and some of us are chocolate or beige. Some of us are tall, short, skinny, fat, have long hair, braided hair, or no hair. Some of us are married, some single, some educated, and some uneducated. It does not matter where we are, we all know the story of Eve. We know that God has created us in His image.

Read Genesis 1:27; 2:18—4:25; Romans 5:18–19; 2 Corinthians 11:3; 1 Timothy 2:13–14.

—*P. Williamson*

HAGAR: BATTERED, BEATEN, AND REJECTED—BUT NOT ABANDONED

She was a young slave from Egypt who found herself in the midst of a foreign, nomad people. She was given a new name, Hagar, and a position as maidservant to Sarai, Abram's wife.

Sarai probably felt emotionally abandoned and socially scorned because she had not given birth to the son God had promised (Gen. 15:2–6). In accordance with the custom of that time, Sarai decided—and convinced Abram—to use Hagar as a surrogate concubine (Gen. 16:1–3).

It seems odd that Sarai would choose a woman who was not of her own cultural background and faith. Perhaps Hagar was special to Sarai or her slave status prevented refusal.

Hagar's temperament changed during pregnancy. She become insolent and arrogant toward Sarai. With Abram's permission, Sarai cruelly reprimanded Hagar. Because of Sarai's mistreatment, Hagar fled into the desert where she met an angel of God. He told her to return to Sarai and give birth to Abram's son, Ishmael, who would become the father of a nation. Hagar was amazed that the living God saw her. Filled with hope, Hagar returned and gave birth to her son (Gen. 16:4–15).

In God's time and by God's grace, the promised son, Isaac, was born to Sarah and Abraham (Gen. 21:1–8), whose names were changed by God before Isaac's birth. Now Sarah saw Hagar's child as a threat to Isaac's position as heir, so she implored Abraham to expel them (Gen. 21:9–14).

Hagar and Ishmael were sent into the desert with a meager supply of bread and water. When the water ran out, Hagar sat apart from her son, so as not to witness his death. Again, the angel of God appeared to reassure her of God's plan and to reveal to her a well of drinking water. Refreshed, renewed, and redirected, Hagar, now a free woman, set out to raise her son alone. Ishmael grew to be a strong, powerful man, an archer and a skilled hunter, and founder of the Arab nations. Ishmael married an Egyptian women (Gen. 21:14–21) and had 12 sons who became leaders of warrior tribes.

Disadvantaged and dispossessed women today can relate to Hagar. Many have experienced estrangement, prejudice, hardship, hopelessness, grief, and despair. Many have known the fear that accompanies being abandoned as an unwed, pregnant woman. Regardless of your circumstances, regardless of your social status, regardless of how many times you've been knocked down, battered and beaten by life, you cannot escape God's care. God provided for Hagar and her son, and He can and will provide for every woman. Just do as Hagar did and respond to God when He speaks to you.

Read Genesis 16; 21; 25:12–18.

See also the insight essays on Abandonment, Single Parenting, and Unwed Mothers.

—T. Wade

SARAH: IS ANYTHING TOO HARD FOR GOD?

Sarah is a woman after my heart. In some ways, I understand where she's coming from, being a woman of faith.

When God told Abraham to leave his father's household and go to the

country of God's choosing, Sarah was 65 years old and Abraham was 75.

The root meaning of the name "Sarah" is "to rule" and "princess." Sarah's name fits her personality. It was a name intended as a seal of the promise given to Abraham: "Kings of peoples shall be of her" (Gen. 17:16).

God spoke directly to Abraham and indirectly to Sarah. God said, "I will make of thee a great nation, and I will bless thee, and make thy name great; and thou shalt be a blessing: And I will bless them that bless thee, and curse him that curseth thee: and in thee shall all families of the earth be blessed" (Gen. 12:2–3). Abraham obeyed God, took Sarah, Lot (his nephew), and all of their possessions and headed for Canaan.

It is not said very often, but there are many African-American women who love their husbands, move when they say it's time to go, and happily submit to their leadership. Many of us are blessed to have strong men who listen to God and obey His Word. The Bible is our guide to a blessed marriage.

Hebrews 4:12–13 says, "What God has said isn't only alive and active, it's sharper than any double-edged sword. His word can cut through our spirits and souls and through our joints and marrow until it discovers the desires and thoughts of our hearts. Nothing is hidden from God" (paraphrased).

Armed with God's promises, Sarah began an awesome journey with her husband. She was a very beautiful woman. When they arrived in Egypt, the Pharaoh was impressed with her loveliness and desired to have her. Abraham, fearing that men would kill him, told Sarah to say she was his sister and deny being his wife. Abraham put Sarah in a compromising situation to save his own life. He surely forgot God's promises. Women of God, I encourage you to learn God's Word and know His promises for you. Develop closeness to God in prayer. If your beloved falters, you can help him stay in the will of God (Gen. 12).

God promised Abraham a second time that he would have descendants. Many years had passed and Sarah was past her childbearing years. She believed she would never have a child of her own for Abraham. Sarah then persuaded Abraham to take her Egyptian servant girl as a surrogate wife. Abraham, at 86 years old, could not resist this proposal. So, Ishmael was born to Hagar. Again, both Sarah and Abraham forgot God's ability to fulfill His promises. Sarah's attempt at assisting God had dire consequences for the descendants of Ishmael (Arabs) and Isaac (Israelites/Jews).

Sarah's bitter jealously and anger toward Hagar destroyed the family unit. "A woman's family is held together by her wisdom, but it can be destroyed by her foolishness" (Proverbs 14:1, paraphrased).

Sister Sarah did mess up, just as we sometimes mess up. But God keeps His promises! At age 90, Sarah became pregnant by Abraham when he was 100 years old. Is anything too hard for God?

Sarah gave birth to a son, Isaac, through whom all nations have been blessed in the person of the Messiah, our Lord and Savior, Jesus Christ.

Read Genesis 18:1–15.

See also the insight essays on Commitment, Infertility, and Submission.

—B. Yates

LOT'S WIFE: WHY LOOK BACK?

From Genesis 19, we know the story of Lot's wife, the spouse of a rich and influential man. Yet the Scripture does not record his wife's name or any information regarding her family. She disobeyed God. She looked back. She turned into a pillar of salt. Now, the rest of the story.

Although Lot, Abraham's nephew, chose to live in the midst of evil, God sent messengers to rescue Lot and his family from evil and its tragic consequences. When the angels came they found Lot sitting at the gate to the city. Lot was a man of substance. He had done well in this sinful city and was held in some respect. He was a power broker and apparently was willing to do whatever he had to in order to maintain his position in the community. Understand this: If Lot received power and respect, then his wife, Mrs. Lot, received some of the overflow "goodies" from what was given to him. She enjoyed the comforts afforded her because of him. As a couple they were determined to do whatever they needed to do to keep their place in "Sodom society."

Lot's wife is a perfect example of "Where your treasure is, there will your heart be also" (Matt. 6:21). She was destroyed because, although she started the right way, and even followed Lot outside the city, she looked back because she was not totally committed to giving up her old ways in obedience to God.

Think about all we as women/sisters have sometimes been willing to put up with when we have allowed ourselves to be belittled, put down, mistreated (verbally and physically) just to have a man. Lord, help us! We even sometimes allow our children to be mistreated because we want to maintain our position of "power partner," or girlfriend. Then when God releases us from that foolishness and makes a way out of no way, we dare to look back with some regret, some desire for what was—to a moment when things were good.

Those who put their hand to the gospel plow have no reason to look back now.

Read Genesis 19; Acts 7:39; Luke 17:31–32.

—M. Bellinger

LOT'S DAUGHTERS: A DECISION RESULTING IN DISASTER

In Genesis 19, we read that most of Lot's family was killed during the destruction of Sodom and Gomorrah. After God destroyed the cities, Lot and his two surviving daughters fled to the city of Zoar. But still afraid, he moved into a cave with them. Very little has been written about his two daughters except through their sons, Moab, and Ammon.

Lot's daughters, fearing that they would not be able to preserve their family following the destruction of Sodom and Gomorrah, chose incest with their father in order to continue their family's lineage. "Our father is old, and there is not a man in the earth to come in unto us after the manner of all the earth," the older daughter told her younger sister. "Come, let us make our father drink wine, and we will lie with him, that we may preserve seed of our father" (Gen. 19:31–32).

Both daughters conceived and gave birth to sons. The older daughter's son was called Moab, whose name in Hebrew means "of the same father."

The second daughter's son was named Ben-Ammi, called Ammon, which means "son of paternal kin." Moab and Ammon were the paternal ancestors of the Moabite and Ammonite tribes, trans-Jordan neighbors of Israel and people who have remained Israel's enemies throughout its history.

Nowhere in the Bible does the word incest appear, yet the Scriptures speak clearly on maintaining the purity of the family and they speak clearly against sexual relationships between family members (Lev. 18:6–18). Incest can lead to the destruction of the family, and God curses those who commit incest (Deut. 27:20–23). God's ministry is a holistic one, which means that He values the soul, mind, and body of every person.

Read Genesis 19:15–38.

—M. Copeland

REBEKAH: A WOMAN OF PASSION

Rebekah was the daughter of Bethuel, sister of Laban, (Gen. 24:29) wife of Isaac, and mother of Esau and Jacob. When Abraham desired to find a wife for his son Isaac, he sent a servant to the city of Nihor in Mesopotamia to choose a bride from his kinsmen who had remained in the region after he and Lot moved to Canaan. In that city, the servant met Rebekah and persuaded her to return with him to become Isaac's wife (Gen. 24).

Rebekah was barren for many years (about 20 years) of her marriage to Isaac. But Isaac interceded in prayer on his wife's behalf and, finally, Rebekah conceived twin boys—Jacob and Esau (Gen. 25:21–26).

Although Esau was the elder and entitled to his father's inheritance, Rebekah favored her younger son Jacob and desired that he gain his father's wealth. When the opportunity arose, Rebekah helped Jacob deceive his father. Isaac, who had become old, feeble, and blind, bestowed upon Jacob the family blessing and inheritance that was intended for Esau (Gen. 27:1–30).

Rebekah later protected Jacob from Esau's wrath by sending him to stay with her brother Laban in Haran. Unfortunately, Rebekah and Jacob were never reunited, and, upon her death, Rebekah was buried in the family burial ground at Machpelah.

It is instinctive and proper for a woman—a wife and mother—to love so passionately. But Rebekah's love for Jacob became a selfish, jealous love, which led to favoritism of one child over another. Her love for Jacob also led her to compromise her love and loyalty to her husband. She was determined to do what she thought would help Jacob gain the family inheritance.

How often have we heard of crimes of passion? Unlike Rebekah's case some have ultimately led to the death of innocent people. As mothers and spouses, we must take care that our love for our children and our spouses does not become an obsessive love—a love that would allow us to succumb to the temptation of Satan, to betray moral ethics, covenant relationships, and spiritual commitments. As women of God, our love should always be pure and subject to the Spirit of God.

God's love for us serves as the ultimate, true example of a pure love, a love that is unconditional, showing no bias or favoritism—a love that is not jealous or boastful. Finally, unselfish motives or desires define pure love: it bears all things, hopes all things, believes all things, and above all, never fails.

Read Genesis 24–27.
See also the insight essay on Infertility.

—T. Dixon

RACHEL: A WOMAN PASTOR

Born in a male-dominated society, Rachel would nonetheless be heard. While she possessed outstanding beauty and strength, and was the favored wife of Jacob, successive generations would distinguish Rachel most as a voice of leadership. Her voice would serve to epitomize caring and compassionate leadership that refuses to rest until the most defenseless and helpless of God's creatures are gathered in safety. Rachel is the first woman named among those who, in the early days of the patriarchs, held the chief occupation of keeping the sheep. She was a shepherdess, a woman pastor whose unrelenting voice defined the integrity of her work.

As the youngest of Laban's two daughters, Rachel gained her father's trust because of her ability to nurture and lead his sheep. The sheep knew her voice and had learned to obey it (Gen. 29:6).

Rachel's voice was not only recognized by the flock she tended, but was also recognized and respected by her fellow herdsmen. Hearing her shepherding call from afar, they refused to water their flocks until she and the rest of the flock arrived at the well (Gen. 29:8–9). Rachel had competently demonstrated that she, although female, was no less a shepherd than they were.

Daily she watched over the sheep, nursing the weak, healing the sick, binding up the injured, and searching for the lost. At night, she brought the flock home to the fold, counting them as they passed beneath the door rod, making certain that none were missing.

After marrying Jacob, Rachel set her heart towards shepherding the house of Israel. Finding, initially, that she was barren, she lifted her voice in jealous protest, insisting that Jacob sleep with her maid Bilhah, so, as she put it: "That I may also have children by her" (Gen. 30:3). Later, Rachel would give birth to two sons—Joseph and Benjamin. She would die while giving birth to Benjamin. But it is through her sons' offspring that Rachel would become known as the mother of the northern tribes of Israel.

A woman of courage, independence and determination, Rachel had a shepherd's heart. The prophet Jeremiah (Jer. 31:15) associated the sound of Rachel's voice with a loud cry—the cry of a mother shepherd whose young had fallen into the hands of their enemies; a voice that groaned with distress when even one sheep strayed or was at risk.

Read Genesis 29; 30:1–8, 22–26; 31:4, 14–19, 32–35; 33:2, 7; 35:16–20.

See also the essays on Favoritism, Infertility, Jealousy, and Suffering.

—D. Graham

LEAH GIRL: A STORY OF COURAGE, RESISTANCE, AND STRUGGLE

Leah's story is found in Genesis 29:31–35. She is a model for women longing to be loved, looking for validation, yearning to be affirmed. Leah is a model for women who recognize that the path they are on is a dead end,

yet desire to know which way to turn.

"Leah girl" came to my church last Sunday with her six children. She was tall and lanky built. Pretty eyes, but no other feature distinguishes her from most "sistas."

A member invited "Leah girl" because "Leah girl" had been drawn by her testimony. While on her post as a security guard, "Leah girl" overheard the lament of another young woman. This young woman had been "dis'd" by her man again. Their relationship was a series of unkept promises. "Leah girl" walked up and said, "Excuse me, it sounds like you're where I just left."

"Leah girl" had just found the courage to break free from the married man with whom she'd been involved. I bet the first five of her children are named, "This time he'll love me." I get the feeling, however, the youngest is named, "Now I will praise the Lord."

"Leah girl" came to my church last Sunday. She was hungry, thirsty, and looking for a relationship with the Lord. She had come to terms with the fact that validation, affirmation, and confirmation are gifts from the Lord and not empty promises from immoral brothers, "Leah girl" lifted her face to praise God.

"Leah girl" represents thousands of women looking for love in all the wrong places. The biblical Leah spent many years competing for Jacob's love, but one day she decided to look to the Lord instead. The story doesn't tell us what she did then, but it does tell us that she did not have any more children in an attempt to gain Jacob's affection. If your name is "Leah girl," take the first step today to develop a relationship with Christ. Let the Lord create in you that which will bring eternal satisfaction.

Read Genesis 29:16–17, 31–35; 35:23; Ruth 4:11.

—E. Walters

DINAH: THE STORY OF AN ABUSED WOMAN

Dinah is a forgotten woman of the Bible. Although she is a child of Jacob, there is no tribe named after her. There's no book in the Bible dedicated to her ministry or her prophetic words. In Genesis 34, we have an opportunity to read Dinah's story.

Very little is known about Dinah, the daughter of Jacob and Leah, outside of Genesis 34. Although Genesis 29:31—30:26 describes in detail the sons born to Jacob's wives, Leah and Rachel, and their concubines, as far as we know, Dinah is the only daughter of Jacob. Dinah's birth is mentioned in Genesis 30:21, almost as an afterthought.

In Genesis 34 we meet Dinah, the youngest of Jacob and Leah's children. Dinah left the Hebrew campsite to visit the women in the land. Scripture does not tell us why Dinah left the safety of her family.

While she was visiting with the women, Dinah was raped by Shechem. After raping her, Shechem declared his love for her. Unfortunately, this was not the first or last time a woman is abused in the name of love. When Jacob learned of his daughter's rape, he was silent. He didn't do anything, and then proceeded to bargain with Dinah's rapist in the interest of political harmony between the Hebrews and the Hivites. While Jacob tried to bargain, Dinah's brothers were plotting against the Hivites, and Dinah was noticeably absent from the proceedings. No one

noticed Dinah's absence. Instead, everyone ignored her tears. No one asked her whereabouts. And not until verse 26 does the reader learn that Dinah had been in Shechem's house all along.

As women of color, we may be able to relate to Dinah's story. We may know the experience of being devalued simply for being born female in a culture where male children are granted more prestige and promise. Sometimes we are abused in the name of love in so-called loving relationships, and those around us ignore our pain. Sometimes family members and friends are fully aware of the abuse, but choose to turn away in silence.

Is there any hope in this story? We can find hope in Simeon and Levi, Dinah's brothers. Although we cannot endorse their vengeful behavior, we can understand their anger after learning that their sister had been raped. It was these two brothers who declared that that "thing ought not to be done" (Gen. 34:7). They declared that a violation of one woman was an affront to the entire community. They were the ones who removed Dinah from her place of violation. Simeon and Levi took family seriously, truly acting as their sister's keeper. We can be Simeon and Levi to our abused sisters, declaring that physical and mental abuse are unacceptable and offend the entire community. We, too, can rescue our abused sisters from their place of violation.

Read Genesis 34.

See also the insight essay on Date Rape.

—M. Coleman

TAMAR: THE LINK BETWEEN JUDAH AND JESUS

Tamar's story is about the loss of two husbands, Er and Onan (Gen. 38:6–10), both sons of Judah. Childless, her future was questionable. She had two choices: 1) she could accept her lot in life; or 2) she could do something about it. Tamar made the second choice and became her own advocate.

Bound by law to marry another son of Judah or to be liberated by Judah to marry another man, she used her femininity and played on his manliness, dressing as a temple prostitute (Gen. 38:14–15). Her goal was security by any means necessary, even pregnancy out of wedlock. And, though she risked death if found guilty of adultery, she stole Judah's personal pledge by obtaining his seal, cord, and staff as proof of his participation in this sexually immoral act. Not only did Judah's personal items implicate him, they forced him to fulfill his responsibility to her as the father of her child.

When Judah realized that he had denied her justice under levirate law, he could only say, "She hath been more righteous than I" (Gen. 38:26). Tamar gave birth to twins, Pharez and Zarah (Gen. 38:29–30).

Critics will ask: "Why is this story found in the middle of Joseph's story?" One reason is that it prepares us for Genesis 49, in which Jacob blessed Judah, his fourth son, with his scepter, a symbol of birthright and kingship traditionally given to the firstborn. However, the immoral behavior of his three older brothers (Reuben, Simeon, and Levi) set the stage for this blessing to be passed to Judah. Thus, it is through the "Lion of

Judah" that the House of David is established. David's ancestry is traced back to Pharez, one of the twins fathered by Judah through his daughter-in-law, Tamar. Here we have the link between Judah and Jesus.

God works in amazing ways. Despite Tamar's deceitful act of harlotry, God sovereignly worked out His good plan. No human frailty could thwart His purposes.

Read Genesis 38; Deuteronomy 25:5; Matthew 1:3.

—K. Johnson

Insights

THE CREATION OF WOMAN

When God created man in His image and looked at what He had done, it was seen as very good (Gen. 1:26, 31). When God created the woman, He did something beyond the human's ability to grasp, do, or achieve. Initially, God created male and female together, both made in His image (Gen. 1:27). She was created equal to man, not inferior or superior, then separated to be uniquely different in her function. She was created for greatness!

How was the woman created? It began with God putting Adam into a deep sleep, taking out one of his ribs, and closing the place up with flesh (Gen. 2:21–24). The word flesh means "life itself" and "created life." God had to remove something "out of" Adam to create and make room for what He was bringing back to him—another life, woman.

God created the woman from the rib of man. In the Hebrew language, this word means "hidden support." She is his confidante, encourager, and inward strength. She is his "helper," the one most appropriate for his life. Helper does not imply inferiority. The word helper describes a "function" and not "worth." Women do not lose their worth when they assume the role of a helper. Adam expressed her purpose when he said, "This is now bone of my bones, and flesh of my flesh" (Gen. 2:23). He was literally saying that the woman was a part of him.

When God brought the woman to Adam, He brought into his life a trusted friend and a wife. She became something nothing else could be to him (Gen. 2:19–20). When Adam said "she shall be called Woman" (Gen. 2:23), he was declaring her into existence. Adam was also "praising" and "celebrating" her creation. Why? Because she was created out of a need he had (Gen. 2:18). The woman became his spiritual partner in the task of obedience to God, dominion over the earth, and extending the generations.

Man was made from the dust of the ground (Gen. 2:7), but the woman was made from man (Gen. 2:23). She received life from him. Her spirit and soul already existed when God created man's spirit (Gen. 1:27). Adam represents mankind, and the woman was named Eve because she was the mother of all living things (Gen. 3:20). As God's woman, created in His image, she is the door of life (Gen. 3:16). She was created with life, to bring life (Gen. 4:1), to nurture life (1 Sam. 1:9–28), and to be an example of life (Prov. 31:10–31). Every human life has received a woman's touch.

Woman was fearfully and wonderfully made (Ps. 139:14), purposefully saved (John 15:16), gifted for greatness (1 Cor. 12:4), empowered to accomplish God's will (Eph. 1:19), assigned to do great things (Matt. 28:1–10). She is a crown of glory (Prov. 12:4; Isa. 62:3), and a special treasure (Mal. 3:17). The woman was created for greatness!

Read Genesis 1:27–28; 2:22–24; 24:67.

Read the portrait on Eve..

—G. London

THE GIFT OF ALONENESS

You are single, but you aren't sure you want to be. You have read or heard the Word as recorded in Genesis 2:18, where God said, "It is not good that the man [or woman] should be alone." But the reality is, you are alone.

As singles, we struggle with being alone. Some of us hate being alone, going out, coming home, and eating alone. We can't stand being alone. But while we may be alone, we don't have to be lonely. Loneliness is an attitude; it is a state mind. We can be lonely even in a crowd. Loneliness is a decision; we can choose to be lonely or not.

When we are lonely, it may mean that we have not yet learned to enjoy our own company. We have not yet realized the gift of aloneness.

Everyone needs time to be alone. Aloneness is an investment. It is time to recharge one's emotional and spiritual batteries; a time to think and pray; a time to gain insight or find a solution to a pressing problem; rest after a battle or a long day; time to find grace to deal with life and all of its challenges; and time to hear from God.

Jesus took full advantage of His singleness and moments of aloneness or solitude.

Mark 1:35 says, "In the morning, rising up a great while before day, he went out, and departed into a solitary place, and there prayed."

It is when we are alone and still that God can speak to us most profoundly. Did He not tell the psalmist as recorded in Psalm 46:10, "Be still, and know that I am God"? We all need moments of aloneness to hear from God, reflect, meditate, and recreate.

Read Genesis 2:18; see also Mark 1:35; Psalm 46:10.

See also the insight essays on Loneliness, and Singleness.

—C. Hale

LET'S TALK ABOUT SEX

We live in a society that is saturated with sexual images. Every time we turn on the TV or go to the movies or listen to music, we hear and see sexual images. Products are sold using sex, ideas are promoted using sex, and standards are set using sex. Just think about the last movie you watched or the TV shows that you love. Think of your favorite toothpaste or your favorite car and remember how those items are advertised. With all the emphasis on sex from the world's perspective, it is difficult to hear what God has to say about sex.

God is not against sex. In fact, sexuality is God's gift to human beings. However, our sex-saturated society has distorted God's original intentions for sex. Most persons are looking for love and intimacy and settling for

sexual relationships. God's original intentions for sex are threefold:

Sex was intended for procreation. In Genesis 1:28, God gives human beings a command to be fruitful and multiply.

Sexual intercourse—along with a lifelong commitment of a man and woman to each other and before God—functioned as the seal of marriage. The marriage had been consummated. Genesis 2:18, 24–25 show us that the first man and the first woman were considered married after sexual intercourse. There are many Scriptures that affirm that sexual intercourse was the seal or the binding force of the marriage.

What often gets left out when we talk about the Bible's view of sex is God's gift of sex for marital pleasure. Hebrews 13:4 says that marriage is honorable and the bed undefiled. First Corinthians 7:2–5 expresses the understanding that the sexual act inside of marriage is important. The Song of Solomon is really a love song from the king to his bride and the bride to her husband. It expresses the beauty of the relationship between a man and a woman.

While God expresses His desire for us to fulfill our sexual desires only within the context of marriage, God does not say that our sexuality is sinful. What we are admonished to do is control those desires and bring them under the leadership of the Holy Spirit. Singleness and celibacy are gifts from God, and no less desirable or important to God than marriage. Since God created our bodies, our purpose is to honor God with our bodies. We do this by acknowledging the gift of sexuality, and using that gift in obedience to our Creator.

Read Genesis 2:18–25.

See also the essays on Adultery and Temptation.

—C. Belt

INFERTILITY

Infertility is one of the most hidden problems in the church. In biblical times, barrenness or infertility was viewed as a stigma and a curse. Thus, both Rachel in the Old Testament and Elizabeth in the New Testament exclaimed that their "reproach" has been removed when they each became pregnant (Gen. 30:23; Luke 1:24–25).

Although there are an equal number of male and female factors involved in infertility, women continue to feel stigmatized and cursed because of infertility. Infertility can represent a crisis of faith for many women. It violates our sense of femininity and infringes on our calling by God to "be fruitful, and multiply." We feel that we have failed our spouses and our ancestors. Sometimes we may even feel cursed by God: If children are a gift and we cannot have children, then we must be undeserving of the gift. Some women feel they are being punished for previous transgressions (e.g., abortions) or are accused of being selfish for delaying child rearing for educational or career goals.

Infertility also makes us question the nature of the God we serve. If God is the Provider and Divine Healer, then why doesn't God heal our barrenness? And if God will not bless us with a child, then why doesn't God at least take away our intense desire for a child? Sometimes well-meaning folks in church make it worse by asking if we have fasted and prayed like Hannah, as if we haven't taken our desires to the altar numerous times.

Church folk can sometimes be insensitive to the fact that certain holidays (e.g., Christmas, Mother's Day) are painful reminders of unwanted childlessness for women with infertility.

The good news is that God does hear the cries of those who suffer from infertility. God provides us with several models of how to keep our faith even when we don't receive the desires of our hearts (e.g., Job, Elijah). Women can also reframe what it means to "be fruitful, and multiply," by recognizing that we can help bring forth the next generation through other activities besides parenting (e.g., teaching, mentoring, and other helpful activities).

There are seven well-known cases of women in the Bible who were barren and who also received an announcement from God promising the end to the barrenness: Sarah (Gen. 18:9–15), Rebecca (Gen. 25:19–26), Rachel (Gen. 30:1–8, 22–24), the unnamed mother of Samson (Judg. 13:1–24), Hannah (1 Sam. 1:1–28), the Shunammite woman (2 Kin. 4:8–17), and Elizabeth (Luke 1:7–25; 39–80).

Read Genesis 16:1–2; Psalms 113:9; Luke 2:36.

Read the portraits on Hannah, Rebekah, Rachel, and Sarah. See also the insight essays on Anger, Motherhood, and Suffering.

—S. Molock

SUBMISSION

From the creation of Eve (Gen. 1:26–27; 2:18–21), women of color have been created to help meet the biblical requirements for God-glorifying fruitfulness. People are to submit to God first, and then mutually to one another. Otherwise, women of color—biblical and contemporary—may experience ethnic and gender-based impositions. Too often, submission implies a superior/inferior, master/slave, head/feet relationship, when, in fact, submission is measured by one's love for God. Submission does not mean subjecting yourself to abuse. Nor does it mean mindless acquiescence to the needs and desires of others. Women of color and women of God should embrace biblical submission. The success of biblical women is directly related to their submission—first to God—followed by the four other submissions the Bible requires: submit to one another, to leaders, to government, and to husbands.

Without exception, spiritually enabled women in the Bible were submissive to God. Esther provides a good example of submission. Even Hagar, a symbol of oppression, experienced a life-changing, liberating experience when she, as a refugee, submitted to God (Gen. 16:7–13). On the other hand, spiritually depraved women in the Bible eventually came to naught. Such is the case with Jezebel. Here is a woman who rebelled against submission to God, and her refusal cost her everything, including her kingdom and her life (1 Kin. 21:25; 2 Kin. 9:6–10, 30–37).

Those who submit their will to God will be empowered. On the other hand, those who rebel against God are continually disempowered. It can never be assumed that blind submission or obedience to a man—whether he is your husband, pastor, boss, or bishop—amounts to biblical submission. Indeed, those who are submitted to God's will begin submission where God's Word begins. When, in fact, this is the case, the specific submissions to government, leaders, and husbands, when applicable, will fol-

low as we begin where God's Word begins. Women submitted to God are elevated, blessed, enabled, and empowered.

Read Genesis 16:7–12.

—P.J. Anderson

UNWED MOTHERS

During biblical times, bearing a child out of wedlock brought severe consequences to the mother. In addition to shame and condemnation, the woman often experienced rejection by her family and ridicule by her social community. Many women were forced into a life of prostitution in an effort to support their children. In our society today, we still see a large number of unwed mothers. Many of these women, like women in biblical times, experience shame, ridicule, and rejection by friends and family. Due to circumstances, they find themselves in a cycle of poverty struggling to provide a decent life for themselves and their children. Although marriage is desirable and ordained by God, the Bible teaches us that regardless of the circumstances of a child's birth, God values the life of all children and has a divine plan for each child's life. In the story of Abraham and Sarah, God never stopped loving and caring for both Hagar and Ishmael. He provided water for her and her son in the wilderness. The name Ishmael in Hebrew means, "God hears" (Gen. 16; 21:8–20). Unwed mothers can find comfort in three biblical truths:

1. God loves and cares for them and their children (Mark 10:13–16).
2. God is willing and able to supply all of their needs according to His riches in glory (Phil. 4:19).
3. There is no condemnation for those who are in Christ Jesus (Rom. 8:1).

Read Genesis 16:6–16.

Read the portrait on Hagar. See also the insight essays on Date Rape and Motherhood.

—J. Thompson

22 And Laban gathered together all the men of the place, and [o]made a feast.

23 And it came to pass in the evening, that he took Leah his daughter, and brought her to him; and he went in unto her.

24 And Laban gave unto his daughter Leah Zilpah his maid *for* an handmaid.

25 And it came to pass, that in the morning, behold, it *was* Leah: and he said to Laban, What *is* this thou hast done unto me? did not I serve with thee for Rachel? wherefore then hast thou beguiled me?

26 And Laban said, It must not be so done in our country, to give the younger before the firstborn.

27 [p]Fulfil her week, and we will give thee this also for the service which thou shalt serve with me yet seven other years.

28 And Jacob did so, and fulfilled her week: and he gave him Rachel his daughter to wife also.

29 And Laban gave to Rachel his daughter Bilhah his handmaid to be her maid.

30 And he went in also unto Rachel, and he [q]loved also Rachel more than Leah, and served with him [r]yet seven other years.

31 ¶ And when the LORD [s]saw that Leah *was* hated, he [t]opened her womb: but Rachel *was* barren.

32 And Leah conceived, and bare a son, and she called his name Reuben: for she said, Surely the LORD hath [u]looked upon my affliction; now therefore my husband will love me.

33 And she conceived again, and bare a son; and said, Because the LORD hath heard that I *was* hated, he hath therefore given me this *son* also: and she called his name Simeon.

34 And she conceived again, and bare a son; and said, Now this time will my husband be joined unto me, because I have born him three sons: therefore was his name called Levi.

35 And she conceived again, and bare a son: and she said, Now will I praise the LORD: therefore she called his name [v]Judah; and left bearing.

30 And when Rachel saw that [w]she bare Jacob no children, Rachel [x]envied her sister; and said unto Jacob, Give me children, [y]or else I die.

2 And Jacob's anger was kindled against Rachel: and he said, [z]*Am* I in God's stead, who hath withheld from thee the fruit of the womb?

3 And she said, Behold [a]my maid Bilhah, go in unto her; [b]and she shall bear upon my knees, [c]that I may also have children by her.

4 And she gave him Bilhah her handmaid [d]to wife: and Jacob went in unto her.

5 And Bilhah conceived, and bare Jacob a son.

6 And Rachel said, God hath [e]judged me, and hath also heard my voice, and hath given me a son: therefore called she his name Dan.

29:22 [o]Judg. 14:10; John 2:1
29:27 [p]Judg. 14:12
29:30 [q]ver. 20; Deut. 21:15 [r]ch. 30:26; Hos. 12:12
29:31 [s]Ps. 127:3 [t]ch. 30:1
29:32 [u]Ex. 3:7; Deut. 26:7; Ps. 25:18
29:35 [v]Matt. 1:2
30:1 [w]ch. 29:31 [x]ch. 37:11 [y]Job 5:2
30:2 [z]ch. 16:2; 1 Sam. 1:5
30:3 [a]ch. 16:2 [b]ch. 50:23; Job 3:12 [c]ch. 16:2
30:4 [d]ch. 16:3
30:6 [e]Ps. 35:24; Lam. 3:59
30:8 [f]Matt. 4:13
30:9 [g]ver. 4
30:13 [h]Prov. 31:28; Luke 1:48
30:14 [i]ch. 25:30
30:15 [j]Num. 16:9
30:20 [k]Matt. 4:13
30:22 [l]ch. 8:1; 1 Sam. 1:19 [m]ch. 29:31
30:23 [n]1 Sam. 1:6; Isa. 4:1; Luke 1:25
30:24 [o]ch. 35:17
30:25 [p]ch. 24:54 [q]ch. 18:33
30:26 [r]ch. 29:20
30:27 [s]ch. 39:3 [t]ch. 25:24

7 And Bilhah Rachel's maid conceived again, and bare Jacob a second son.

8 And Rachel said, With great wrestlings have I wrestled with my sister, and I have prevailed: and she called his name [f]Naphtali.

9 When Leah saw that she had left bearing, she took Zilpah her maid, and [g]gave her Jacob to wife.

10 And Zilpah Leah's maid bare Jacob a son.

11 And Leah said, A troop cometh: and she called his name Gad.

12 And Zilpah Leah's maid bare Jacob a second son.

13 And Leah said, Happy am I, for the daughters [h]will call me blessed: and she called his name Asher.

14 ¶ And Reuben went in the days of wheat harvest, and found mandrakes in the field, and brought them unto his mother Leah. Then Rachel said to Leah, [i]Give me, I pray thee, of thy son's mandrakes.

15 And she said unto her, [j]*Is it* a small matter that thou hast taken my husband? and wouldest thou take away my son's mandrakes also? And Rachel said, Therefore he shall lie with thee to night for thy son's mandrakes.

16 And Jacob came out of the field in the evening, and Leah went out to meet him, and said, Thou must come in unto me; for surely I have hired thee with my son's mandrakes. And he lay with her that night.

17 And God hearkened unto Leah, and she conceived, and bare Jacob the fifth son.

18 And Leah said, God hath given me my hire, because I have given my maiden to my husband: and she called his name Issachar.

19 And Leah conceived again, and bare Jacob the sixth son.

20 And Leah said, God hath endued me *with* a good dowry; now will my husband dwell with me, because I have born him six sons: and she called his name [k]Zebulun.

21 And afterwards she bare a daughter, and called her name Dinah.

22 ¶ And God [l]remembered Rachel, and God hearkened to her, and [m]opened her womb.

23 And she conceived, and bare a son; and said, God hath taken away [n]my reproach:

24 And she called his name Joseph; and said, [o]The LORD shall add to me another son.

25 ¶ And it came to pass, when Rachel had born Joseph, that Jacob said unto Laban, [p]Send me away, that I may go unto [q]mine own place, and to my country.

26 Give *me* my wives and my children, [r]for whom I have served thee, and let me go: for thou knowest my service which I have done thee.

27 And Laban said unto him, I pray thee, if I have found favour in thine eyes, *tarry: for* [s]I have learned by experience that the LORD hath blessed me [t]for thy sake.

28 And he said, [u]Appoint me thy wages,
and I will give *it*.
29 And he said unto him, [v]Thou knowest
how I have served thee, and how thy cattle
was with me.
30 For *it was* little which thou hadst before I *came*, and it is *now* increased unto a
multitude; and the LORD hath blessed thee
since my coming: and now when shall I
[w]provide for mine own house also?
31 And he said, What shall I give thee?
And Jacob said, Thou shalt not give me any
thing: if thou wilt do this thing for me, I will
again feed *and* keep thy flock.
32 I will pass through all thy flock to day,
removing from thence all the speckled and
spotted cattle, and all the brown cattle
among the sheep, and the spotted and
speckled among the goats: and [x]*of such*
shall be my hire.
33 So shall my [y]righteousness answer for
me in time to come, when it shall come for
my hire before thy face: every one that *is*
not speckled and spotted among the goats,
and brown among the sheep, that shall be
counted stolen with me.
34 And Laban said, Behold, I would it
might be according to thy word.
35 And he removed that day the he goats
that were ringstraked and spotted, and all
the she goats that were speckled and spotted, *and* every one that had *some* white in it,
and all the brown among the sheep, and
gave *them* into the hand of his sons.
36 And he set three days' journey betwixt
himself and Jacob: and Jacob fed the rest of
Laban's flocks.
37 ¶ And [z]Jacob took him rods of green
poplar, and of the hazel and chestnut tree;
and pilled white strakes in them, and made
the white appear which *was* in the rods.
38 And he set the rods which he had
pilled before the flocks in the gutters in the
watering troughs when the flocks came to
drink, that they should conceive when they
came to drink.
39 And the flocks conceived before the
rods, and brought forth cattle ringstraked,
speckled, and spotted.
40 And Jacob did separate the lambs, and
set the faces of the flocks toward the ringstraked, and all the brown in the flock of
Laban; and he put his own flocks by themselves, and put them not unto Laban's cattle.
41 And it came to pass, whensoever the
stronger cattle did conceive, that Jacob laid
the rods before the eyes of the cattle in the
gutters, that they might conceive among the
rods.
42 But when the cattle were feeble, he put
them not in: so the feebler were Laban's,
and the stronger Jacob's.
43 And the man [a]increased exceedingly,
and [b]had much cattle, and maidservants,
and menservants, and camels, and asses.

31 And he heard the words of Laban's
sons, saying, Jacob hath taken away
all that *was* our father's; and of *that* which
was our father's hath he gotten all this
[c]glory.
2 And Jacob beheld [d]the countenance of
Laban, and, behold, it *was* not [e]toward him
as before.
3 And the LORD said unto Jacob, [f]Return
unto the land of thy fathers, and to thy kindred; and I will be with thee.
4 And Jacob sent and called Rachel and
Leah to the field unto his flock,
5 And said unto them, [g]I see your father's
countenance, that it *is* not toward me as before; but the God of my father [h]hath been
with me.
6 And [i]ye know that with all my power I
have served your father.
7 And your father hath deceived me, and
[j]changed my wages [k]ten times; but God
[l]suffered him not to hurt me.
8 If he said thus, [m]The speckled shall be
thy wages; then all the cattle bare speckled:
and if he said thus, The ringstraked shall be
thy hire; then bare all the cattle ringstraked.
9 Thus God hath [n]taken away the cattle
of your father, and given *them* to me.
10 And it came to pass at the time that the
cattle conceived, that I lifted up mine eyes,
and saw in a dream, and, behold, the rams
which leaped upon the cattle *were* ringstraked, speckled, and grisled.
11 And [o]the angel of God spake unto me
in a dream, *saying*, Jacob: and I said, Here
am I.
12 And he said, Lift up now thine eyes,
and see, all the rams which leap upon the
cattle *are* ringstraked, speckled, and
grisled: for [p]I have seen all that Laban doeth unto thee.
13 I *am* the God of Beth-el, [q]where thou
anointedst the pillar, *and* where thou vo-
wedst a vow unto me: now [r]arise, get thee
out from this land, and return unto the land
of thy kindred.
14 And Rachel and Leah answered and
said unto him, [s]*Is there* yet any portion or
inheritance for us in our father's house?
15 Are we not counted of him strangers?
for [t]he hath sold us, and hath quite devoured also our money.
16 For all the riches which God hath
taken from our father, that *is* our's, and our
children's: now then, whatsoever God hath
said unto thee, do.
17 ¶ Then Jacob rose up, and set his sons
and his wives upon camels;
18 And he carried away all his cattle, and
all his goods which he had gotten, the cattle
of his getting, which he had gotten in
Padan-aram, for to go to Isaac his father in
the land of Canaan.
19 And Laban went to shear his sheep:
and Rachel had stolen the [u]images that
were her father's.
20 And Jacob stole away unawares to Laban the Syrian, in that he told him not that
he fled.
21 So he fled with all that he had; and he

30:28 [u]ch. 29:15
30:29 [v]ch. 31:6; Matt. 24:45; Tit. 2:10
30:30 [w]1 Tim. 5:8
30:32 [x]ch. 31:8
30:33 [y]Ps. 37:6
30:37 [z]ch. 31:9-12
30:43 [a]ver. 30 [b]ch. 13:2
31:1 [c]Ps. 49:16
31:2 [d]ch. 4:5 [e]Deut. 28:54
31:3 [f]ch. 28:15
31:5 [g]ver. 2 [h]ver. 3
31:6 [i]ver. 38; ch. 30:29
31:7 [j]ver. 41 [k]Num. 14:22; Neh. 4:12; Job 19:3; Zech. 8:23 [l]ch. 20:6; Ps. 105:14
31:8 [m]ch. 30:32
31:9 [n]ver. 1
31:11 [o]ch. 48:16
31:12 [p]Ex. 3:7
31:13 [q]ch. 28:18 [r]ver. 3; ch. 32:9
31:14 [s]ch. 2:24
31:15 [t]ch. 29:15
31:19 [u]ch. 35:2

rose up, and passed over the river, and [v]set
his face *toward* the mount Gilead.
22 And it was told Laban on the third day
that Jacob was fled.
23 And he took [w]his brethren with him,
and pursued after him seven days' journey;
and they overtook him in the mount Gilead.
24 And God [x]came to Laban the Syrian
in a dream by night, and said unto him,
Take heed that thou [y]speak not to Jacob
either good or bad.
25 ¶ Then Laban overtook Jacob. Now
Jacob had pitched his tent in the mount: and
Laban with his brethren pitched in the
mount of Gilead.
26 And Laban said to Jacob, What hast
thou done, that thou hast stolen away unawares to me, and [z]carried away my daughters, as captives *taken* with the sword?
27 Wherefore didst thou flee away secretly, and steal away from me; and didst
not tell me, that I might have sent thee away
with mirth, and with songs, with tabret, and
with harp?
28 And hast not suffered me to [a]kiss my
sons and my daughters? [b]thou hast now
done foolishly in *so* doing.
29 It is in the power of my hand to do you
hurt: but the [c]God of your father spake
unto me [d]yesternight, saying, Take thou
heed that thou speak not to Jacob either
good or bad.
30 And now, *though* thou wouldest needs
be gone, because thou sore longedst after
thy father's house, *yet* wherefore hast thou
stolen my [e]gods?
31 And Jacob answered and said to Laban, Because I was afraid: for I said, Peradventure thou wouldest take by force thy
daughters from me.
32 With whomsoever thou findest thy
gods, [f]let him not live: before our brethren
discern thou what *is* thine with me, and take
it to thee. For Jacob knew not that Rachel
had stolen them.
33 And Laban went into Jacob's tent, and
into Leah's tent, and into the two maidservants' tents; but he found *them* not. Then
went he out of Leah's tent, and entered into
Rachel's tent.
34 Now Rachel had taken the images, and
put them in the camel's furniture, and sat
upon them. And Laban searched all the
tent, but found *them* not.
35 And she said to her father, Let it not
displease my lord that I cannot [g]rise up before thee; for the custom of women *is* upon
me. And he searched, but found not the images.
36 ¶ And Jacob was wroth, and chode
with Laban: and Jacob answered and said
to Laban, What *is* my trespass? what *is* my
sin, that thou hast so hotly pursued after me?
37 Whereas thou hast searched all my
stuff, what hast thou found of all thy household stuff? set *it* here before my brethren

31:21 [v]ch. 46:28; 2 Kings 12:17; Luke 9:51
31:23 [w]ch. 13:8
31:24 [x]ch. 20:3; Job 33:15; Matt. 1:20 [y]ch. 24:50
31:26 [z]1 Sam. 30:2
31:28 [a]ver. 55; Ruth 1:9; 1 Kings 19:20; Acts 20:37 [b]1 Sam. 13:13; 2 Chron. 16:9
31:29 [c]ver. 53; ch. 28:13 [d]ver. 24
31:30 [e]ver. 19; Judg. 18:24
31:32 [f]ch. 44:9
31:35 [g]Ex. 20:12; Lev. 19:32
31:39 [h]Ex. 22:10 [i]Ex. 22:12
31:41 [j]ch. 29:27 [k]ver. 7
31:42 [l]Ps. 124:1 [m]ver. 53; Isa. 8:13 [n]ch. 29:32; Ex. 3:7 [o]1 Chron. 12:17; Jude 9
31:44 [p]ch. 26:28 [q]Josh. 24:27
31:45 [r]ch. 28:18
31:48 [s]Josh. 24:27
31:49 [t]Judg. 11:29; 1 Sam. 7:5
31:53 [u]ch. 16:5 [v]ch. 21:23 [w]ver. 42

and thy brethren, that they may judge betwixt us both.
38 This twenty years *have* I *been* with
thee; thy ewes and thy she goats have not
cast their young, and the rams of thy flock
have I not eaten.
39 [h]That which was torn *of beasts* I
brought not unto thee; I bare the loss of it;
of [i]my hand didst thou require it, *whether*
stolen by day, or stolen by night.
40 *Thus* I was; in the day the drought consumed me, and the frost by night; and my
sleep departed from mine eyes.
41 Thus have I been twenty years in thy
house; I [j]served thee fourteen years for
thy two daughters, and six years for thy cattle: and [k]thou hast changed my wages ten
times.
42 [l]Except the God of my father, the God
of Abraham, and [m]the fear of Isaac, had
been with me, surely thou hadst sent me
away now empty. [n]God hath seen mine affliction and the labour of my hands, and
[o]rebuked *thee* yesternight.
43 ¶ And Laban answered and said unto
Jacob, *These* daughters *are* my daughters,
and *these* children *are* my children, and
these cattle *are* my cattle, and all that thou
seest *is* mine: and what can I do this day
unto these my daughters, or unto their children which they have born?
44 Now therefore come thou, [p]let us
make a covenant, I and thou; [q]and let it be
for a witness between me and thee.
45 And Jacob [r]took a stone, and set it up
for a pillar.
46 And Jacob said unto his brethren,
Gather stones; and they took stones, and
made an heap: and they did eat there upon
the heap.
47 And Laban called it Jegar-sahadutha:
but Jacob called it Galeed;
48 And Laban said, [s]This heap *is* a witness between me and thee this day. Therefore was the name of it called Galeed;
49 And [t]Mizpah; for he said, The LORD
watch between me and thee, when we are
absent one from another.
50 If thou shalt afflict my daughters, or
if thou shalt take *other* wives beside my
daughters, no man *is* with us; see, God *is*
witness betwixt me and thee.
51 And Laban said to Jacob, Behold this
heap, and behold *this* pillar, which I have
cast betwixt me and thee;
52 This heap *be* witness, and *this* pillar *be*
witness, that I will not pass over this heap to
thee, and that thou shalt not pass over this
heap and this pillar unto me, for harm.
53 The God of Abraham, and the God of
Nahor, the God of their father, [u]judge betwixt us. And Jacob [v]sware by [w]the fear of
his father Isaac.
54 Then Jacob offered sacrifice upon the
mount, and called his brethren to eat bread:
and they did eat bread, and tarried all night
in the mount.
55 And early in the morning Laban rose

up, and kissed his sons and his daughters,
and [x]blessed them: and Laban departed,
and [y]returned unto his place.
32 And Jacob went on his way, and
[z]the angels of God met him.
2 And when Jacob saw them, he said,
This *is* God's [a]host: and he called the name
of that place Mahanaim.
3 And Jacob sent messengers before him
to Esau his brother [b]unto the land of Seir,
[c]the country of Edom.
4 And he commanded them, saying,
[d]Thus shall ye speak unto my lord Esau;
Thy servant Jacob saith thus, I have sojourned with Laban, and stayed there until
now:
5 And [e]I have oxen, and asses, flocks,
and menservants, and womenservants: and
I have sent to tell my lord, that [f]I may find
grace in thy sight.
6 ¶ And the messengers returned to Jacob, saying, We came to thy brother Esau,
and also [g]he cometh to meet thee, and four
hundred men with him.
7 Then Jacob was greatly afraid and [h]dis-
tressed: and he divided the people that *was*
with him, and the flocks, and herds, and the
camels, into two bands;
8 And said, If Esau come to the one company, and smite it, then the other company
which is left shall escape.
9 ¶ [i]And Jacob said, [j]O God of my father Abraham, and God of my father Isaac,
the LORD [k]which saidst unto me, Return
unto thy country, and to thy kindred, and I
will deal well with thee:
10 I am not worthy of the least of all the
[l]mercies, and of all the truth, which thou
hast shewed unto thy servant; for with [m]my
staff I passed over this Jordan; and now I
am become two bands.
11 [n]Deliver me, I pray thee, from the
hand of my brother, from the hand of Esau:
for I fear him, lest he will come and smite
me, *and* [o]the mother with the children.
12 And [p]thou saidst, I will surely do thee
good, and make thy seed as the sand of the
sea, which cannot be numbered for multitude.
13 ¶ And he lodged there that same night;
and took of that which came to his hand [q]a
present for Esau his brother;
14 Two hundred she goats, and twenty he
goats, two hundred ewes, and twenty rams,
15 Thirty milch camels with their colts,
forty kine, and ten bulls, twenty she asses,
and ten foals.
16 And he delivered *them* into the hand of
his servants, every drove by themselves;
and said unto his servants, Pass over before
me, and put a space betwixt drove and
drove.
17 And he commanded the foremost, saying, When Esau my brother meeteth thee,
and asketh thee, saying, Whose *art* thou?
and whither goest thou? and whose *are*
these before thee?
18 Then thou shalt say, *They be* thy servant Jacob's; it *is* a present sent unto my
lord Esau: and, behold, also he *is* behind us.
19 And so commanded he the second, and
the third, and all that followed the droves,
saying, On this manner shall ye speak unto
Esau, when ye find him.
20 And say ye moreover, Behold, thy servant Jacob *is* behind us. For he said, I will
[r]appease him with the present that goeth
before me, and afterward I will see his face;
peradventure he will accept of me.
21 So went the present over before him:
and himself lodged that night in the company.
22 And he rose up that night, and took his
two wives, and his two womenservants, and
his eleven sons, [s]and passed over the ford
Jabbok.
23 And he took them, and sent them over
the brook, and sent over that he had.
24 ¶ And Jacob was left alone; and there
[t]wrestled a man with him until the breaking of the day.
25 And when he saw that he prevailed not
against him, he touched [u]the hollow of his
thigh; and the hollow of Jacob's thigh was
out of joint, as he wrestled with him.
26 And [v]he said, Let me go, for the day
breaketh. And he said, [w]I will not let thee
go, except thou bless me.
27 And he said unto him, What *is* thy
name? And he said, Jacob.
28 And he said, [x]Thy name shall be
called no more Jacob, but Israel: for as a
prince hast thou [y]power with God and
[z]with men, and hast prevailed.
29 And Jacob asked *him,* and said, Tell
me, I pray thee, thy name. And he said,
[a]Wherefore *is* it *that* thou dost ask after my
name? And he blessed him there.
30 And Jacob called the name of the place
Peniel: for [b]I have seen God face to face,
and my life is preserved.
31 And as he passed over Penuel the sun
rose upon him, and he halted upon his
thigh.
32 Therefore the children of Israel eat not
of the sinew which shrank, which *is* upon
the hollow of the thigh, unto this day: because he touched the hollow of Jacob's
thigh in the sinew that shrank.
33 And Jacob lifted up his eyes, and
looked, and, behold, [c]Esau came,
and with him four hundred men. And he
divided the children unto Leah, and unto
Rachel, and unto the two handmaids.
2 And he put the handmaids and their
children foremost, and Leah and her children after, and Rachel and Joseph hindermost.
3 And he passed over before them, and
[d]bowed himself to the ground seven times,
until he came near to his brother.
4 [e]And Esau ran to meet him, and embraced him, [f]and fell on his neck, and
kissed him: and they wept.
5 And he lifted up his eyes, and saw the
women and the children; and said, Who *are*

31:55 [x]ch. 28:1 [y]ch. 18:33
32:1 [z]Ps. 91:11; Heb. 1:14
32:2 [a]Josh. 5:14; Ps. 103:21; Luke 2:13
32:3 [b]ch. 33:14 [c]ch. 36:6; Deut. 2:5; Josh. 24:4
32:4 [d]Prov. 15:1
32:5 [e]ch. 30:43 [f]ch. 33:8
32:6 [g]ch. 33:1
32:7 [h]ch. 35:3
32:9 [i]Ps. 50:15 [j]ch. 28:13 [k]ch. 31:3
32:10 [l]ch. 24:27 [m]Job 8:7
32:11 [n]Ps. 59:1 [o]Hos. 10:14
32:12 [p]ch. 28:13
32:13 [q]ch. 43:11; Prov. 18:16
32:20 [r]Prov. 21:14
32:22 [s]Deut. 3:16
32:24 [t]Hos. 12:3; Eph. 6:12
32:25 [u]Matt. 26:41; 2 Cor. 12:7
32:26 [v]Luke 24:28 [w]Hos. 12:4
32:28 [x]ch. 35:10; 2 Kings 17:34 [y]Hos. 12:3 [z]ch. 25:31
32:29 [a]Judg. 13:18
32:30 [b]ch. 16:13; Ex. 24:11; Deut. 5:24; Judg. 6:22; Isa. 6:5
33:1 [c]ch. 32:6
33:3 [d]ch. 18:2
33:4 [e]ch. 32:28 [f]ch. 45:14

those with thee? And he said, The children [g]which God hath graciously given thy servant.

6 Then the handmaidens came near, they and their children, and they bowed themselves.

7 And Leah also with her children came near, and bowed themselves: and after came Joseph near and Rachel, and they bowed themselves.

8 And he said, What *meanest* thou by [h]all this drove which I met? And he said, *These are* [i]to find grace in the sight of my lord.

9 And Esau said, I have enough, my brother; keep that thou hast unto thyself.

10 And Jacob said, Nay, I pray thee, if now I have found grace in thy sight, then receive my present at my hand: for therefore I [j]have seen thy face, as though I had seen the face of God, and thou wast pleased with me.

11 Take, I pray thee, [k]my blessing that is brought to thee; because God hath dealt graciously with me, and because I have enough. [l]And he urged him, and he took *it*.

12 And he said, Let us take our journey, and let us go, and I will go before thee.

13 And he said unto him, My lord knoweth that the children *are* tender, and the flocks and herds with young *are* with me: and if men should overdrive them one day, all the flock will die.

14 Let my lord, I pray thee, pass over before his servant: and I will lead on softly, according as the cattle that goeth before me and the children be able to endure, until I come unto my lord [m]unto Seir.

15 And Esau said, Let me now leave with thee *some* of the folk that *are* with me. And he said, What needeth it? [n]let me find grace in the sight of my lord.

16 ¶ So Esau returned that day on his way unto Seir.

17 And Jacob journeyed to [o]Succoth, and built him an house, and made booths for his cattle: therefore the name of the place is called Succoth.

18 ¶ And Jacob came to [p]Shalem, a city of [q]Shechem, which *is* in the land of Canaan, when he came from Padan-aram; and pitched his tent before the city.

19 And [r]he bought a parcel of a field, where he had spread his tent, at the hand of the children of Hamor, Shechem's father, for an hundred pieces of money.

20 And he erected there an altar, and [s]called it El-elohe-Israel.

34 And [t]Dinah the daughter of Leah, which she bare unto Jacob, [u]went out to see the daughters of the land.

2 And when Shechem the son of Hamor the Hivite, prince of the country, [v]saw her, he [w]took her, and lay with her, and [x]defiled her.

3 And his soul clave unto Dinah the daughter of Jacob, and he loved the damsel, and spake kindly unto the damsel.

4 And Shechem [y]spake unto his father Hamor, saying, Get me this damsel to wife.

5 And Jacob heard that he had defiled Dinah his daughter: now his sons were with his cattle in the field: and Jacob [z]held his peace until they were come.

6 ¶ And Hamor the father of Shechem went out unto Jacob to commune with him.

7 And the sons of Jacob came out of the field when they heard *it:* and the men were grieved, and they [a]were very wroth, because he [b]had wrought folly in Israel in lying with Jacob's daughter; [c]which thing ought not to be done.

8 And Hamor communed with them, saying, The soul of my son Shechem longeth for your daughter: I pray you give her him to wife.

9 And make ye marriages with us, *and* give your daughters unto us, and take our daughters unto you.

10 And ye shall dwell with us: and [d]the land shall be before you; dwell and [e]trade ye therein, and [f]get you possessions therein.

11 And Shechem said unto her father and unto her brethren, Let me find grace in your eyes, and what ye shall say unto me I will give.

12 Ask me never so much [g]dowry and gift, and I will give according as ye shall say unto me: but give me the damsel to wife.

13 And the sons of Jacob answered Shechem and Hamor his father [h]deceitfully, and said, because he had defiled Dinah their sister:

14 And they said unto them, We cannot do this thing, to give our sister to one that is uncircumcised; for [i]that *were* a reproach unto us:

15 But in this will we consent unto you: If ye will be as we *be*, that every male of you be circumcised;

16 Then will we give our daughters unto you, and we will take your daughters to us, and we will dwell with you, and we will become one people.

17 But if ye will not hearken unto us, to be circumcised; then will we take our daughter, and we will be gone.

18 And their words pleased Hamor, and Shechem Hamor's son.

19 And the young man deferred not to do the thing, because he had delight in Jacob's daughter: and he *was* [j]more honourable than all the house of his father.

20 ¶ And Hamor and Shechem his son came unto the gate of their city, and communed with the men of their city, saying,

21 These men *are* peaceable with us; therefore let them dwell in the land, and trade therein; for the land, behold, *it is* large enough for them; let us take their daughters to us for wives, and let us give them our daughters.

22 Only herein will the men consent unto us for to dwell with us, to be one people, if every male among us be circumcised, as they *are* circumcised.

33:5 [g]ch. 48:9; Ps. 127:3; Isa. 8:18
33:8 [h]ch. 32:16 [i]ch. 32:5
33:10 [j]ch. 43:3; 2 Sam. 3:13; Matt. 18:10
33:11 [k]Judg. 1:15; 1 Sam. 25:27; 2 Kings 5:15 [l]2 Kings 5:23
33:14 [m]ch. 32:3
33:15 [n]ch. 34:11; Ruth 2:13
33:17 [o]Josh. 13:27; Judg. 8:5; Ps. 60:6
33:18 [p]John 3:23 [q]Josh. 24:1; Judg. 9:1
33:19 [r]Josh. 24:32; John 4:5
33:20 [s]ch. 35:7
34:1 [t]ch. 30:21 [u]Tit. 2:5
34:2 [v]ch. 6:2; Judg. 14:1 [w]ch. 20:2 [x]Deut. 22:29
34:4 [y]Judg. 14:2
34:5 [z]1 Sam. 10:27; 2 Sam. 13:20
34:7 [a]ch. 49:7; 2 Sam. 13:21 [b]Josh. 7:15; Judg. 20:6 [c]Deut. 23:17; 2 Sam. 13:12
34:10 [d]ch. 13:9 [e]ch. 42:34 [f]ch. 47:27
34:12 [g]Ex. 22:16; Deut. 22:29; 1 Sam. 18:25
34:13 [h]2 Sam. 13:24
34:14 [i]Josh. 5:9
34:19 [j]2 Chron. 4:9

23 *Shall* not their cattle and their substance and every beast of their's *be* ours? only let us consent unto them, and they will dwell with us.

24 And unto Hamor and unto Shechem his son hearkened all that [k]went out of the gate of his city; and every male was circumcised, all that went out of the gate of his city.

25 ¶ And it came to pass on the third day, when they were sore, that two of the sons of Jacob, [l]Simeon and Levi, Dinah's brethren, took each man his sword, and came upon the city boldly, and slew all the males.

26 And they slew Hamor and Shechem his son with the edge of the sword, and took Dinah out of Shechem's house, and went out.

27 The sons of Jacob came upon the slain, and spoiled the city, because they had defiled their sister.

28 They took their sheep, and their oxen, and their asses, and that which *was* in the city, and that which *was* in the field,

29 And all their wealth, and all their little ones, and their wives took they captive, and spoiled even all that *was* in the house.

30 And Jacob said to Simeon and Levi, [m]Ye have [n]troubled me [o]to make me to stink among the inhabitants of the land, among the Canaanites and the Perizzites: [p]and I *being* few in number, they shall gather themselves together against me, and slay me; and I shall be destroyed, I and my house.

31 And they said, Should he deal with our sister as with an harlot?

35 And God said unto Jacob, Arise, go up to [q]Beth-el, and dwell there: and make there an altar unto God, [r]that appeared unto thee [s]when thou fleddest from the face of Esau thy brother.

2 Then Jacob said unto his [t]household, and to all that *were* with him, Put away [u]the strange gods that *are* among you, and [v]be clean, and change your garments:

3 And let us arise, and go up to Beth-el; and I will make there an altar unto God, [w]who answered me in the day of my distress, [x]and was with me in the way which I went.

4 And they gave unto Jacob all the strange gods which *were* in their hand, and *all their* [y]earrings which *were* in their ears; and Jacob hid them under [z]the oak which *was* by Shechem.

5 And they journeyed: and [a]the terror of God was upon the cities that *were* round about them, and they did not pursue after the sons of Jacob.

6 ¶ So Jacob came to [b]Luz, which *is* in the land of Canaan, that *is*, Beth-el, he and all the people that *were* with him.

7 And he [c]built there an altar, and called the place El-beth-el: because [d]there God appeared unto him, when he fled from the face of his brother.

8 But [e]Deborah Rebekah's nurse died, and she was buried beneath Beth-el under an oak: and the name of it was called Allon-bachuth.

9 ¶ And [f]God appeared unto Jacob again, when he came out of Padan-aram, and blessed him.

10 And God said unto him, Thy name *is* Jacob: [g]thy name shall not be called any more Jacob, [h]but Israel shall be thy name: and he called his name Israel.

11 And God said unto him, [i]I *am* God Almighty: be fruitful and multiply; [j]a nation and a company of nations shall be of thee, and kings shall come out of thy loins;

12 And the land [k]which I gave Abraham and Isaac, to thee I will give it, and to thy seed after thee will I give the land.

13 And God [l]went up from him in the place where he talked with him.

14 And Jacob [m]set up a pillar in the place where he talked with him, *even* a pillar of stone: and he poured a drink offering thereon, and he poured oil thereon.

15 And Jacob called the name of the place where God spake with him, [n]Beth-el.

16 ¶ And they journeyed from Beth-el; and there was but a little way to come to Ephrath: and Rachel travailed, and she had hard labour.

17 And it came to pass, when she was in hard labour, that the midwife said unto her, Fear not; [o]thou shalt have this son also.

18 And it came to pass, as her soul was in departing, (for she died) that she called his name Ben-oni: but his father called him Benjamin.

19 And [p]Rachel died, and was buried in the way to [q]Ephrath, which *is* Beth-lehem.

20 And Jacob set a pillar upon her grave: that *is* the pillar of Rachel's grave [r]unto this day.

21 ¶ And Israel journeyed, and spread his tent beyond [s]the tower of Edar.

22 And it came to pass, when Israel dwelt in that land, that Reuben went and [t]lay with Bilhah his father's concubine: and Israel heard *it*. Now the sons of Jacob were twelve:

23 The sons of Leah; [u]Reuben, Jacob's firstborn, and Simeon, and Levi, and Judah, and Issachar, and Zebulun:

24 The sons of Rachel; Joseph, and Benjamin:

25 And the sons of Bilhah, Rachel's handmaid; Dan, and Naphtali:

26 And the sons of Zilpah, Leah's handmaid; Gad, and Asher: these *are* the sons of Jacob, which were born to him in Padan-aram.

27 ¶ And Jacob came unto Isaac his father unto [v]Mamre, unto the [w]city of Arbah, which *is* Hebron, where Abraham and Isaac sojourned.

28 And the days of Isaac were an hundred and fourscore years.

29 And Isaac gave up the ghost, and died, and [x]was gathered unto his people, *being* old and full of days: and [y]his sons Esau and Jacob buried him.

34:24 [k]ch. 23:10
34:25 [l]ch. 49:5
34:30 [m]ch. 49:6 [n]Josh. 7:25 [o]Ex. 5:21; 1 Sam. 13:4 [p]Deut. 4:27; Ps. 105:12
35:1 [q]ch. 28:19 [r]ch. 28:13 [s]ch. 27:43
35:2 [t]ch. 18:19; Josh. 24:15 [u]ch. 31:19; Josh. 24:2; 1 Sam. 7:3 [v]Ex. 19:10
35:3 [w]ch. 32:7; Ps. 107:6 [x]ch. 28:20
35:4 [y]Hos. 2:13 [z]Josh. 24:26; Judg. 9:6
35:5 [a]Ex. 15:16; Deut. 11:35; Josh. 2:9; 1 Sam. 14:15; 2 Chron. 14:14
35:6 [b]ch. 28:19
35:7 [c]Eccl. 5:4 [d]ch. 28:13
35:8 [e]ch. 24:59
35:9 [f]Hos. 12:4
35:10 [g]ch. 17:5 [h]ch. 32:28
35:11 [i]ch. 17:1; Ex. 6:3 [j]ch. 17:5
35:12 [k]ch. 12:7
35:13 [l]ch. 17:22
35:14 [m]ch. 28:18
35:15 [n]ch. 28:19
35:17 [o]ch. 30:24; 1 Sam. 4:20
35:19 [p]ch. 48:7 [q]Ruth 1:2; Mic. 5:2; Matt. 2:6
35:20 [r]1 Sam. 10:2; 2 Sam. 18:18
35:21 [s]Mic. 4:8
35:22 [t]ch. 49:4; 2 Sam. 16:22; 1 Chron. 5:1; 1 Cor. 5:1
35:23 [u]ch. 46:8; Ex. 1:2
35:27 [v]ch. 13:18 [w]Josh. 14:15
35:29 [x]ch. 15:15 [y]ch. 25:9

36

Now these *are* the generations of Esau, [z]who *is* Edom.

2 [a]Esau took his wives of the daughters of Canaan; Adah the daughter of Elon the Hittite, and [b]Aholibamah the daughter of Anah the daughter of Zibeon the Hivite;

3 And [c]Bashemath Ishmael's daughter, sister of Nebajoth.

4 And [d]Adah bare to Esau Eliphaz; and Bashemath bare Reuel;

5 And Aholibamah bare Jeush, and Jaalam, and Korah: these *are* the sons of Esau, which were born unto him in the land of Canaan.

6 And Esau took his wives, and his sons, and his daughters, and all the persons of his house, and his cattle, and all his beasts, and all his substance, which he had got in the land of Canaan; and went into the country from the face of his brother Jacob.

7 [e]For their riches were more than that they might dwell together; and [f]the land wherein they were strangers could not bear them because of their cattle.

8 Thus dwelt Esau in [g]mount Seir: [h]Esau *is* Edom.

9 ¶ And these *are* the generations of Esau the father of the Edomites in mount Seir:

10 These *are* the names of Esau's sons; [i]Eliphaz the son of Adah the wife of Esau, Reuel the son of Bashemath the wife of Esau.

11 And the sons of Eliphaz were Teman, Omar, Zepho, and Gatam, and Kenaz.

12 And Timna was concubine to Eliphaz Esau's son; and she bare to Eliphaz [j]Amalek: these *were* the sons of Adah Esau's wife.

13 And these *are* the sons of Reuel; Nahath, and Zerah, Shammah, and Mizzah: these were the sons of Bashemath Esau's wife.

14 ¶ And these were the sons of Aholibamah, the daughter of Anah the daughter of Zibeon, Esau's wife: and she bare to Esau Jeush, and Jaalam, and Korah.

15 ¶ These *were* dukes of the sons of Esau: the sons of Eliphaz the firstborn *son* of Esau; duke Teman, duke Omar, duke Zepho, duke Kenaz,

16 Duke Korah, duke Gatam, *and* duke Amalek: these *are* the dukes *that came* of Eliphaz in the land of Edom; these *were* the sons of Adah.

17 ¶ And these *are* the sons of Reuel Esau's son; duke Nahath, duke Zerah, duke Shammah, duke Mizzah: these *are* the dukes *that came* of Reuel in the land of Edom; these *are* the sons of Bashemath Esau's wife.

18 ¶ And these *are* the sons of Aholibamah Esau's wife; duke Jeush, duke Jaalam, duke Korah: these *were* the dukes *that came* of Aholibamah the daughter of Anah, Esau's wife.

19 These *are* the sons of Esau, who *is* Edom, and these *are* their dukes.

20 ¶ [k]These *are* the sons of Seir [l]the Horite, who inhabited the land; Lotan, and Shobal, and Zibeon, and Anah,

21 And Dishon, and Ezer, and Dishan: these *are* the dukes of the Horites, the children of Seir in the land of Edom.

22 And the children of Lotan were Hori and Hemam; and Lotan's sister *was* Timna.

23 And the children of Shobal *were* these; Alvan, and Manahath, and Ebal, Shepho, and Onam.

24 And these *are* the children of Zibeon; both Ajah, and Anah: this *was that* Anah that found [m]the mules in the wilderness, as he fed the asses of Zibeon his father.

25 And the children of Anah *were* these; Dishon, and Aholibamah the daughter of Anah.

26 And these *are* the children of Dishon; Hemdan, and Eshban, and Ithran, and Cheran.

27 The children of Ezer *are* these; Bilhan, and Zaavan, and Akan.

28 The children of Dishan *are* these; Uz, and Aran.

29 These *are* the dukes *that came* of the Horites; duke Lotan, duke Shobal, duke Zibeon, duke Anah,

30 Duke Dishon, duke Ezer, duke Dishan: these *are* the dukes *that came* of Hori, among their dukes in the land of Seir.

31 ¶ And [n]these *are* the kings that reigned in the land of Edom, before there reigned any king over the children of Israel.

32 And Bela the son of Beor reigned in Edom: and the name of his city *was* Dinhabah.

33 And Bela died, and Jobab the son of Zerah of Bozrah reigned in his stead.

34 And Jobab died, and Husham of the land of Temani reigned in his stead.

35 And Husham died, and Hadad the son of Bedad, who smote Midian in the field of Moab, reigned in his stead: and the name of his city *was* Avith.

36 And Hadad died, and Samlah of Masrekah reigned in his stead.

37 And Samlah died, and Saul of Rehoboth *by* the river reigned in his stead.

38 And Saul died, and Baal-hanan the son of Achbor reigned in his stead.

39 And Baal-hanan the son of Achbor died, and [o]Hadar reigned in his stead: and the name of his city *was* Pau; and his wife's name *was* Mehetabel, the daughter of Matred, the daughter of Mezahab.

40 And these *are* the names of [p]the dukes *that came* of Esau, according to their families, after their places, by their names; duke Timnah, duke Alvah, duke Jetheth,

41 Duke Aholibamah, duke Elah, duke Pinon,

42 Duke Kenaz, duke Teman, duke Mibzar,

43 Duke Magdiel, duke Iram: these *be* the dukes of Edom, according to their habitations in the land of their possession: he *is* Esau the father of the Edomites.

36:1 [z]ch. 25:30
36:2 [a]ch. 26:34 [b]ver. 25
36:3 [c]ch. 28:9
36:4 [d]1 Chron. 1:35
36:7 [e]ch. 13:6 [f]ch. 17:8
36:8 [g]ch. 32:3; Deut. 2:5; Josh. 24:4 [h]ver. 1
36:10 [i]1 Chron. 1:35
36:12 [j]Ex. 17:8; Num. 24:20; 1 Sam. 15:2
36:20 [k]1 Chron. 1:38 [l]ch. 14:6; Deut. 2:12
36:24 [m]Lev. 19:19
36:31 [n]1 Chron. 1:43
36:39 [o]Ex. 15:15; 1 Chron. 1:50
36:40 [p]1 Chron. 1:51

37 And Jacob dwelt in the land
[q]wherein his father was a stranger,
in the land of Canaan.
2 These *are* the generations of Jacob. Joseph, *being* seventeen years old, was feeding the flock with his brethren; and the lad
was with the sons of Bilhah, and with the
sons of Zilpah, his father's wives: and Joseph brought unto his father [r]their evil report.
3 Now Israel loved Joseph more than all
his children, because he *was* [s]the son of his
old age: and he made him a coat of *many*
colours.
4 And when his brethren saw that their
father loved him more than all his brethren,
they [t]hated him, and could not speak
peaceably unto him.
5 ¶ And Joseph dreamed a dream, and he
told *it* his brethren: and they hated him yet
the more.
6 And he said unto them, Hear, I pray
you, this dream which I have dreamed:
7 For, [u]behold, we *were* binding sheaves
in the field, and, lo, my sheaf arose, and also
stood upright; and, behold, your sheaves
stood round about, and made obeisance to
my sheaf.
8 And his brethren said to him, Shalt thou
indeed reign over us? or shalt thou indeed
have dominion over us? And they hated him
yet the more for his dreams, and for his
words.
9 ¶ And he dreamed yet another dream,
and told it his brethren, and said, Behold, I
have dreamed a dream more; and, behold,
[v]the sun and the moon and the eleven stars
made obeisance to me.
10 And he told *it* to his father, and to his
brethren: and his father rebuked him, and
said unto him, What *is* this dream that thou
hast dreamed? Shall I and thy mother and
[w]thy brethren indeed come to bow down
ourselves to thee to the earth?
11 And [x]his brethren envied him; but his
father [y]observed the saying.
12 ¶ And his brethren went to feed their
father's flock in Shechem.
13 And Israel said unto Joseph, Do not
thy brethren feed *the flock* in Shechem?
come, and I will send thee unto them. And
he said to him, Here *am I*.
14 And he said to him, Go, I pray thee, see
whether it be well with thy brethren, and
well with the flocks; and bring me word
again. So he sent him out of the vale of [z]He-
bron, and he came to Shechem.
15 ¶ And a certain man found him, and,
behold, *he was* wandering in the field: and
the man asked him, saying, What seekest
thou?
16 And he said, I seek my brethren: [a]tell
me, I pray thee, where they feed *their
flocks*.
17 And the man said, They are departed
hence; for I heard them say, Let us go to
[b]Dothan. And Joseph went after his brethren, and found them in Dothan.
18 And when they saw him afar off, even
before he came near unto them, [c]they conspired against him to slay him.
19 And they said one to another, Behold,
this dreamer cometh.
20 [d]Come now therefore, and let us slay
him, and cast him into some pit, and we will
say, Some evil beast hath devoured him:
and we shall see what will become of his
dreams.
21 And [e]Reuben heard *it*, and he delivered him out of their hands; and said, Let us
not kill him.
22 And Reuben said unto them, Shed no
blood, *but* cast him into this pit that *is* in the
wilderness, and lay no hand upon him; that
he might rid him out of their hands, to deliver him to his father again.
23 ¶ And it came to pass, when Joseph
was come unto his brethren, that they stript
Joseph out of his coat, *his* coat of *many* colours that *was* on him;
24 And they took him, and cast him into a
pit: and the pit *was* empty, *there was* no
water in it.
25 [f]And they sat down to eat bread: and
they lifted up their eyes and looked, and,
behold, a company of [g]Ishmeelites came
from Gilead, with their camels bearing spi-
cery and [h]balm and myrrh, going to carry
it down to Egypt.
26 And Judah said unto his brethren,
What profit *is it* if we slay our brother, and
[i]conceal his blood?
27 Come, and let us sell him to the Ishmeelites, and [j]let not our hand be upon
him; for he *is* [k]our brother *and* [l]our flesh.
And his brethren were content.
28 Then there passed by [m]Midianites
merchantmen; and they drew and lifted up
Joseph out of the pit, [n]and sold Joseph to
the Ishmeelites for [o]twenty *pieces* of silver:
and they brought Joseph into Egypt.
29 ¶ And Reuben returned unto the pit;
and, behold, Joseph *was* not in the pit; and
he [p]rent his clothes.
30 And he returned unto his brethren,
and said, The child [q]*is* not; and I, whither
shall I go?
31 And they took [r]Joseph's coat, and
killed a kid of the goats, and dipped the coat
in the blood;
32 And they sent the coat of *many* colours, and they brought *it* to their father;
and said, This have we found: know now
whether it *be* thy son's coat or no.
33 And he knew it, and said, *It is* my son's
coat; an [s]evil beast hath devoured him; Joseph is without doubt rent in pieces.
34 And Jacob [t]rent his clothes, and put
sackcloth upon his loins, and mourned for
his son many days.
35 And all his sons and all his daughters
[u]rose up to comfort him; but he refused to
be comforted; and he said, For [v]I will go
down into the grave unto my son mourning.
Thus his father wept for him.
36 And [w]the Midianites sold him into

37:1 *q*ch. 17:8; Heb. 11:9
37:2 *r*1 Sam. 2:22
37:3 *s*ch. 44:20
37:4 *t*ch. 27:41
37:7 *u*ch. 42:6
37:9 *v*ch. 46:29
37:10 *w*ch. 27:29
37:11 *x*Acts 7:9 *y*Dan. 7:28; Luke 2:19
37:14 *z*ch. 35:27
37:16 *a*SSol. 1:7
37:17 *b*2 Kings 6:13
37:18 *c*1 Sam. 19:1; Ps. 31:13; Matt. 27:1; Mark 14:1; John 11:53; Acts 23:12
37:20 *d*Prov. 1:11
37:21 *e*ch. 42:22
37:25 *f*Prov. 30:20; Am. 6:6 *g*ver. 28 *h*Jer. 8:22
37:26 *i*ch. 4:10; ver. 20; Job 16:18
37:27 *j*1 Sam. 18:17 *k*ch. 42:21 *l*ch. 29:14
37:28 *m*Judg. 6:3; ch. 45:4 *n*Ps. 105:17; Acts 7:9 *o*Matt. 27:9
37:29 *p*Job 1:20
37:30 *q*ch. 42:13; Jer. 31:15
37:31 *r*ver. 23
37:33 *s*ver. 20; ch. 44:28
37:34 *t*ver. 29; 2 Sam. 3:31
37:35 *u*2 Sam. 12:17 *v*ch. 42:38
37:36 *w*ch. 39:1

Egypt unto Potiphar, an officer of Pharaoh's, *and* captain of the guard.

38

And it came to pass at that time, that
Judah went down from his brethren,
and [x]turned in to a certain Adullamite,
whose name *was* Hirah.
2 And Judah [y]saw there a daughter of
a certain Canaanite, whose name *was*
[z]Shuah; and he took her, and went in unto
her.
3 And she conceived, and bare a son; and
he called his name [a]Er.
4 And she conceived again, and bare a
son; and she called his name [b]Onan.
5 And she yet again conceived, and bare
a son; and called his name [c]Shelah: and he
was at Chezib, when she bare him.
6 And Judah [d]took a wife for Er his firstborn, whose name *was* Tamar.
7 And [e]Er, Judah's firstborn, was wicked
in the sight of the LORD; [f]and the LORD slew
him.
8 And Judah said unto Onan, Go in unto
[g]thy brother's wife, and marry her, and
raise up seed to thy brother.
9 And Onan knew that the seed should
not be [h]his; and it came to pass, when he
went in unto his brother's wife, that he
spilled *it* on the ground, lest that he should
give seed to his brother.
10 And the thing which he did displeased
the LORD: wherefore he slew [i]him also.
11 Then said Judah to Tamar his daughter in law, [j]Remain a widow at thy father's
house, till Shelah my son be grown: for he
said, Lest peradventure he die also, as his
brethren *did.* And Tamar went and dwelt
[k]in her father's house.
12 ¶ And in process of time the daughter
of Shuah Judah's wife died; and Judah
[l]was comforted, and went up unto his
sheepshearers [m]to Timnath, he and his
friend Hirah the Adullamite.
13 And it was told Tamar, saying, Behold
thy father in law goeth up to Timnath to
shear his sheep.
14 And she put her widow's garments off
from her, and covered her with a vail, and
wrapped herself, and [n]sat in an open place,
which *is* by the way to Timnath; for she saw
[o]that Shelah was grown, and she was not
given unto him to wife.
15 When Judah saw her, he thought her
to be an harlot; because she had covered
her face.
16 And he turned unto her by the way,
and said, Go to, I pray thee, let me come in
unto thee; (for he knew not that she *was* his
daughter in law.) And she said, What wilt
thou give me, that thou mayest come in
unto me?
17 And he said, [p]I will send *thee* a kid
from the flock. And she said, [q]Wilt thou
give *me* a pledge, till thou send *it*?
18 And he said, What pledge shall I give
thee? And she said, [r]Thy signet, and thy
bracelets, and thy staff that *is* in thine hand.

38:1 [x]ch. 19:3; 2 Kings 4:8
38:2 [y]ch. 34:2 [z]1 Chron. 2:3
38:3 [a]ch. 46:12; Num. 26:19
38:4 [b]ch. 46:12; Num. 26:19
38:5 [c]ch. 46:12; Num. 26:20
38:6 [d]ch. 21:21
38:7 [e]ch. 46:12; Num. 26:19 [f]1 Chron. 2:3
38:8 [g]Deut. 25:5; Matt. 22:24
38:9 [h]Deut. 25:6
38:10 [i]ch. 46:12; Num. 26:19
38:11 [j]Ruth 1:13 [k]Lev. 22:13
38:12 [l]2 Sam. 13:39 [m]Josh. 15:10; Judg. 14:1
38:14 [n]Prov. 7:12 [o]ver. 11
38:17 [p]Ezek. 16:33 [q]ver. 20
38:18 [r]ver. 25
38:19 [s]ver. 14
38:24 [t]Judg. 19:2 [u]Lev. 21:9; Deut. 22:21
38:25 [v]ch. 37:32 [w]ver. 18
38:26 [x]ch. 37:33 [y]1 Sam. 24:17 [z]ver. 14 [a]Job 34:31
38:29 [b]ch. 46:12; Num. 26:20; 1 Chron. 2:4; Matt. 1:3
39:1 [c]ch. 37:36; Ps. 105:17 [d]ch. 37:28
39:2 [e]ver. 21; ch. 21:22; 1 Sam. 16:18; Acts 7:9
39:3 [f]Ps. 1:3
39:4 [g]ch. 18:3; ver. 21 [h]Gen. 24:2
39:5 [i]ch. 30:27

And he gave *it* her, and came in unto her,
and she conceived by him.
19 And she arose, and went away, and
[s]laid by her vail from her, and put on the
garments of her widowhood.
20 And Judah sent the kid by the hand
of his friend the Adullamite, to receive *his*
pledge from the woman's hand: but he
found her not.
21 Then he asked the men of that place,
saying, Where *is* the harlot, that *was* openly
by the way side? And they said, There was
no harlot in this *place.*
22 And he returned to Judah, and said, I
cannot find her; and also the men of the
place said, *that* there was no harlot in this
place.
23 And Judah said, Let her take *it* to her,
lest we be shamed: behold, I sent this kid,
and thou hast not found her.
24 ¶ And it came to pass about three
months after, that it was told Judah, saying,
Tamar thy daughter in law hath [t]played
the harlot; and also, behold, she *is* with
child by whoredom. And Judah said, Bring
her forth, [u]and let her be burnt.
25 When she *was* brought forth, she sent
to her father in law, saying, By the man,
whose these *are, am* I with child: and she
said, [v]Discern, I pray thee, whose *are* these,
[w]the signet, and bracelets, and staff.
26 And Judah [x]acknowledged *them,* and
said, [y]She hath been more righteous than I;
because that [z]I gave her not to Shelah my
son. And he knew her again [a]no more.
27 ¶ And it came to pass in the time of
her travail, that, behold, twins *were* in her
womb.
28 And it came to pass, when she travailed, that *the one* put out *his* hand: and the
midwife took and bound upon his hand a
scarlet thread, saying, This came out first.
29 And it came to pass, as he drew back
his hand, that, behold, his brother came out:
and she said, How hast thou broken forth?
this breach *be* upon thee: therefore his
name was called [b]Pharez.
30 And afterward came out his brother,
that had the scarlet thread upon his hand:
and his name was called Zarah.

39

And Joseph was brought down to
Egypt; and [c]Potiphar, an officer of
Pharaoh, captain of the guard, an Egyptian,
[d]bought him of the hands of the Ishmeelites, which had brought him down thither.
2 And [e]the LORD was with Joseph, and he
was a prosperous man; and he was in the
house of his master the Egyptian.
3 And his master saw that the LORD *was*
with him, and that the LORD [f]made all that
he did to prosper in his hand.
4 And Joseph [g]found grace in his sight,
and he served him: and he made him [h]over-
seer over his house, and all *that* he had he
put into his hand.
5 And it came to pass from the time *that*
he had made him overseer in his house, and
over all that he had, that [i]the LORD blessed

the Egyptian's house for Joseph's sake; and the blessing of the LORD was upon all that he had in the house, and in the field.

6 And he left all that he had in Joseph's hand; and he knew not ought he had, save the bread which he did eat. And Joseph [j]was *a* goodly *person,* and well favoured.

7 ¶ And it came to pass after these things, that his master's wife cast her eyes upon Joseph; and she said, [k]Lie with me.

8 But he refused, and said unto his master's wife, Behold, my master wotteth not what *is* with me in the house, and he hath committed all that he hath to my hand;

9 *There is* none greater in this house than I; neither hath he kept back any thing from me but thee, because thou *art* his wife: [l]how then can I do this great wickedness, and [m]sin against God?

10 And it came to pass, as she spake to Joseph day by day, that he hearkened not unto her, to lie by her, *or* to be with her.

11 And it came to pass about this time, that *Joseph* went into the house to do his business; and *there was* none of the men of the house there within.

12 And [n]she caught him by his garment, saying, Lie with me: and he left his garment in her hand, and fled, and got him out.

13 And it came to pass, when she saw that he had left his garment in her hand, and was fled forth,

14 That she called unto the men of her house, and spake unto them, saying, See, he hath brought in an Hebrew unto us to mock us; he came in unto me to lie with me, and I cried with a loud voice:

15 And it came to pass, when he heard that I lifted up my voice and cried, that he left his garment with me, and fled, and got him out.

16 And she laid up his garment by her, until his lord came home.

17 And she [o]spake unto him according to these words, saying, The Hebrew servant, which thou hast brought unto us, came in unto me to mock me:

18 And it came to pass, as I lifted up my voice and cried, that he left his garment with me, and fled out.

19 And it came to pass, when his master heard the words of his wife, which she spake unto him, saying, After this manner did thy servant to me; that his [p]wrath was kindled.

20 And Joseph's master took him, and [q]put him into the [r]prison, a place where the king's prisoners *were* bound: and he was there in the prison.

21 ¶ But the LORD was with Joseph, and shewed him mercy, and [s]gave him favour in the sight of the keeper of the prison.

22 And the keeper of the prison [t]committed to Joseph's hand all the prisoners that *were* in the prison; and whatsoever they did there, he was the doer *of it.*

23 The keeper of the prison looked not to any thing *that was* under his hand; because [u]the LORD was with him, and *that* which he did, the LORD made *it* to prosper.

40

And it came to pass after these things, *that* the [v]butler of the king of Egypt and *his* baker had offended their lord the king of Egypt.

2 And Pharaoh was [w]wroth against two *of* his officers, against the chief of the butlers, and against the chief of the bakers.

3 [x]And he put them in ward in the house of the captain of the guard, into the prison, the place where Joseph *was* bound.

4 And the captain of the guard charged Joseph with them, and he served them: and they continued a season in ward.

5 ¶ And they dreamed a dream both of them, each man his dream in one night, each man according to the interpretation of his dream, the butler and the baker of the king of Egypt, which *were* bound in the prison.

6 And Joseph came in unto them in the morning, and looked upon them, and, behold, they *were* sad.

7 And he asked Pharaoh's officers that *were* with him in the ward of his lord's house, saying, Wherefore look ye *so* sadly to day?

8 And they said unto him, [y]We have dreamed a dream, and *there is* no interpreter of it. And Joseph said unto them, [z]*Do* not interpretations *belong* to God? tell me *them,* I pray you.

9 And the chief butler told his dream to Joseph, and said to him, In my dream, behold, a vine *was* before me;

10 And in the vine *were* three branches: and it *was* as though it budded, *and* her blossoms shot forth; and the clusters thereof brought forth ripe grapes:

11 And Pharaoh's cup *was* in my hand: and I took the grapes, and pressed them into Pharaoh's cup, and I gave the cup into Pharaoh's hand.

12 And Joseph said unto him, [a]This *is* the interpretation of it: The three branches [b]*are* three days:

13 Yet within three days shall Pharaoh [c]lift up thine head, and restore thee unto thy place: and thou shalt deliver Pharaoh's cup into his hand, after the former manner when thou wast his butler.

14 But [d]think on me when it shall be well with thee, and [e]shew kindness, I pray thee, unto me, and make mention of me unto Pharaoh, and bring me out of this house:

15 For indeed I was stolen away out of the land of the Hebrews: [f]and here also have I done nothing that they should put me into the dungeon.

16 When the chief baker saw that the interpretation was good, he said unto Joseph, I also *was* in my dream, and, behold, *I had* three white baskets on my head:

17 And in the uppermost basket *there was* of all manner of bakemeats for Pharaoh; and the birds did eat them out of the basket upon my head.

39:6 [j]1 Sam. 16:12
39:7 [k]2 Sam. 13:11
39:9 [l]Prov. 6:29 [m]ch. 20:6; Lev. 6:2; 2 Sam. 12:13; Ps. 51:4
39:12 [n]Prov. 7:13
39:17 [o]Ex. 23:1; Ps. 120:3
39:19 [p]Prov. 6:34
39:20 [q]Ps. 105:18; 1 Pet. 2:19 [r]ch. 40:3
39:21 [s]Ex. 3:21; Ps. 106:46; Prov. 16:7; Dan. 1:9; Acts 7:9
39:22 [t]ch. 40:3
39:23 [u]ver. 2
40:1 [v]Neh. 1:11
40:2 [w]Prov. 16:14
40:3 [x]ch. 39:20
40:8 [y]ch. 41:15 [z]ch. 41:16; Dan. 2:11
40:12 [a]ver. 18; ch. 41:12; Judg. 7:14; Dan. 2:36 [b]ch. 41:26
40:13 [c]2 Kings 25:27; Ps. 3:3; Jer. 52:31
40:14 [d]Luke 23:42 [e]Josh. 2:12; 1 Sam. 20:14; 2 Sam. 9:1; 1 Kings 2:7
40:15 [f]ch. 39:20

18 And Joseph answered and said, [g]This *is* the interpretation thereof: The three baskets *are* three days:

19 [h]Yet within three days shall Pharaoh lift up thy head from off thee, and shall hang thee on a tree; and the birds shall eat thy flesh from off thee.

20 ¶ And it came to pass the third day, *which was* Pharaoh's [i]birthday, that he [j]made a feast unto all his servants: and he [k]lifted up the head of the chief butler and of the chief baker among his servants.

21 And he [l]restored the chief butler unto his butlership again; and [m]he gave the cup into Pharaoh's hand:

22 But he [n]hanged the chief baker: as Joseph had interpreted to them.

23 Yet did not the chief butler remember Joseph, but [o]forgat him.

41 And it came to pass at the end of two full years, that Pharaoh dreamed: and, behold, he stood by the river.

2 And, behold, there came up out of the river seven well favoured kine and fatfleshed; and they fed in a meadow.

3 And, behold, seven other kine came up after them out of the river, ill favoured and leanfleshed; and stood by the *other* kine upon the brink of the river.

4 And the ill favoured and leanfleshed kine did eat up the seven well favoured and fat kine. So Pharaoh awoke.

5 And he slept and dreamed the second time: and, behold, seven ears of corn came up upon one stalk, rank and good.

6 And, behold, seven thin ears and blasted with the east wind sprung up after them.

7 And the seven thin ears devoured the seven rank and full ears. And Pharaoh awoke, and, behold, *it was* a dream.

8 And it came to pass in the morning [p]that his spirit was troubled; and he sent and called for all the [q]magicians of Egypt, and all the [r]wise men thereof: and Pharaoh told them his dream; but *there was* none that could interpret them unto Pharaoh.

9 ¶ Then spake the chief butler unto Pharaoh, saying, I do remember my faults this day:

10 Pharaoh was [s]wroth with his servants, [t]and put me in ward in the captain of the guard's house, *both* me and the chief baker:

11 And [u]we dreamed a dream in one night, I and he; we dreamed each man according to the interpretation of his dream.

12 And *there was* there with us a young man, an Hebrew, [v]servant to the captain of the guard; and we told him, and he [w]interpreted to us our dreams; to each man according to his dream he did interpret.

13 And it came to pass, [x]as he interpreted to us, so it was; me he restored unto mine office, and him he hanged.

14 ¶ [y]Then Pharaoh sent and called Joseph, and they [z]brought him hastily [a]out of the dungeon: and he shaved *himself,* and changed his raiment, and came in unto Pharaoh.

15 And Pharaoh said unto Joseph, I have dreamed a dream, and *there is* none that can interpret it: [b]and I have heard say of thee, *that* thou canst understand a dream to interpret it.

16 And Joseph answered Pharaoh, saying, [c]*It is* not in me: [d]God shall give Pharaoh an answer of peace.

17 And Pharaoh said unto Joseph, [e]In my dream, behold, I stood upon the bank of the river:

18 And, behold, there came up out of the river seven kine, fatfleshed and well favoured; and they fed in a meadow:

19 And, behold, seven other kine came up after them, poor and very ill favoured and leanfleshed, such as I never saw in all the land of Egypt for badness:

20 And the lean and the ill favoured kine did eat up the first seven fat kine:

21 And when they had eaten them up, it could not be known that they had eaten them; but they *were* still ill favoured, as at the beginning. So I awoke.

22 And I saw in my dream, and, behold, seven ears came up in one stalk, full and good:

23 And, behold, seven ears, withered, thin, *and* blasted with the east wind, sprung up after them:

24 And the thin ears devoured the seven good ears: and [f]I told *this* unto the magicians; but *there was* none that could declare *it* to me.

25 ¶ And Joseph said unto Pharaoh, The dream of Pharaoh *is* one: [g]God hath shewed Pharaoh what he *is* about to do.

26 The seven good kine *are* seven years; and the seven good ears *are* seven years: the dream *is* one.

27 And the seven thin and ill favoured kine that came up after them *are* seven years; and the seven empty ears blasted with the east wind shall be [h]seven years of famine.

28 [i]This *is* the thing which I have spoken unto Pharaoh: What God *is* about to do he sheweth unto Pharaoh.

29 Behold, there come [j]seven years of great plenty throughout all the land of Egypt:

30 And there shall [k]arise after them seven years of famine; and all the plenty shall be forgotten in the land of Egypt; and the famine [l]shall consume the land;

31 And the plenty shall not be known in the land by reason of that famine following; for it *shall be* very grievous.

32 And for that the dream was doubled unto Pharaoh twice; *it is* because the [m]thing *is* established by God, and God will shortly bring it to pass.

33 Now therefore let Pharaoh look out a man discreet and wise, and set him over the land of Egypt.

34 Let Pharaoh do *this,* and let him ap-

40:18 [g]ver. 12
40:19 [h]ver. 13
40:20 [i]Matt. 14:6 [j]Mark 6:21 [k]ver. 13; Matt. 25:19
40:21 [l]ver. 13 [m]Neh. 2:1
40:22 [n]ver. 19
40:23 [o]Job 19:14; Ps. 31:12; Eccl. 9:15; Am. 6:6
41:8 [p]Dan. 2:1 [q]Ex. 7:11; Isa. 29:14; Dan. 1:20 [r]Matt. 2:1
41:10 [s]ch. 40:2 [t]ch. 39:20
41:11 [u]ch. 40:5
41:12 [v]ch. 37:36 [w]ch. 40:12
41:13 [x]ch. 40:22
41:14 [y]Ps. 105:20 [z]Dan. 2:25 [a]1 Sam. 2:8; Ps. 113:7
41:15 [b]ver. 12; Ps. 25:14; Dan. 5:16
41:16 [c]Dan. 2:30; Acts 3:12; 2 Cor. 3:5 [d]ch. 40:8; Dan. 2:22
41:17 [e]ver. 1
41:24 [f]ver. 8; Dan. 4:7
41:25 [g]Dan. 2:28; Rev. 4:1
41:27 [h]2 Kings 8:1
41:28 [i]ver. 25
41:29 [j]ver. 47
41:30 [k]ver. 54 [l]ch. 47:13
41:32 [m]Num. 23:19; Isa. 46:10

point officers over the land, and [n]take up
the fifth part of the land of Egypt in the
seven plenteous years.
35 And [o]let them gather all the food of
those good years that come, and lay up corn
under the hand of Pharaoh, and let them
keep food in the cities.
36 And that food shall be for store to the
land against the seven years of famine,
which shall be in the land of Egypt; that the
land [p]perish not through the famine.
37 ¶ And [q]the thing was good in the eyes
of Pharaoh, and in the eyes of all his servants.
38 And Pharaoh said unto his servants,
Can we find *such a one* as this *is*, a man [r]in
whom the Spirit of God *is*?
39 And Pharaoh said unto Joseph, Forasmuch as God hath shewed thee all this,
there is none so discreet and wise as thou
art:
40 [s]Thou shalt be over my house, and according unto thy word shall all my people
be ruled: only in the throne will I be greater
than thou.
41 And Pharaoh said unto Joseph, See, I
have [t]set thee over all the land of Egypt.
42 And Pharaoh [u]took off his ring from
his hand, and put it upon Joseph's hand,
and [v]arrayed him in vestures of fine linen,
[w]and put a gold chain about his neck;
43 And he made him to ride in the second
chariot which he had; [x]and they cried before him, Bow the knee: and he made him
ruler [y]over all the land of Egypt.
44 And Pharaoh said unto Joseph, I *am*
Pharaoh, and without thee shall no man lift
up his hand or foot in all the land of Egypt.
45 And Pharaoh called Joseph's name
Zaphnath-paaneah; and he gave him to
wife Asenath the daughter of Poti-pherah
priest of On. And Joseph went out over *all*
the land of Egypt.
46 And Joseph *was* thirty years old when
he [z]stood before Pharaoh king of Egypt.
And Joseph went out from the presence of
Pharaoh, and went throughout all the land
of Egypt.
47 And in the seven plenteous years the
earth brought forth by handfuls.
48 And he gathered up all the food of the
seven years, which were in the land of
Egypt, and laid up the food in the cities: the
food of the field, which *was* round about
every city, laid he up in the same.
49 And Joseph gathered corn [a]as the
sand of the sea, very much, until he left
numbering; for *it was* without number.
50 [b]And unto Joseph were born two sons
before the years of famine came, which Asenath the daughter of Poti-pherah priest of
On bare unto him.
51 And Joseph called the name of the
firstborn Manasseh: For God, *said he*, hath
made me forget all my toil, and all my father's house.
52 And the name of the second called he

41:34 [n]Prov. 6:6
41:35 [o]ver. 48
41:36 [p]ch. 47:15
41:37 [q]Ps. 105:19; Acts 7:10
41:38 [r]Num. 27:18; Job 32:8; Prov. 2:6; Dan. 4:8
41:40 [s]Ps. 105:21; Acts 7:10
41:41 [t]Dan. 6:3
41:42 [u]Esth. 3:10 [v]Esth. 8:15 [w]Dan. 5:7
41:43 [x]Esth. 6:9 [y]ch. 42:6; Acts 7:10
41:46 [z]1 Sam. 16:21; 1 Kings 12:6; Dan. 1:19
41:49 [a]ch. 22:17; Judg. 7:12; 1 Sam. 13:5; Ps. 78:27
41:50 [b]ch. 46:20
41:52 [c]ch. 49:22
41:54 [d]Ps. 105:16; Acts 7:11 [e]ver. 30
41:56 [f]ch. 42:6
41:57 [g]Deut. 9:28
42:1 [h]Acts 7:12
42:2 [i]ch. 43:8; Ps. 118:17; Isa. 38:1
42:4 [j]ver. 38
42:5 [k]Acts 7:11
42:6 [l]ch. 41:41 [m]ch. 37:7
42:9 [n]ch. 37:5
42:13 [o]ch. 37:30; Lam. 5:7
42:15 [p]1 Sam. 1:26

Ephraim: For God hath caused me to be
[c]fruitful in the land of my affliction.
53 ¶ And the seven years of plenteousness, that was in the land of Egypt, were
ended.
54 [d]And the seven years of dearth began
to come, [e]according as Joseph had said:
and the dearth was in all lands; but in all the
land of Egypt there was bread.
55 And when all the land of Egypt was
famished, the people cried to Pharaoh for
bread: and Pharaoh said unto all the Egyptians, Go unto Joseph; what he saith to
you, do.
56 And the famine was over all the face of
the earth: And Joseph opened all the storehouses, and [f]sold unto the Egyptians; and
the famine waxed sore in the land of Egypt.
57 [g]And all countries came into Egypt to
Joseph for to buy *corn*; because that the
famine was *so* sore in all lands.

42 Now when [h]Jacob saw that there
was corn in Egypt, Jacob said unto
his sons, Why do ye look one upon another?
2 And he said, Behold, I have heard that
there is corn in Egypt: get you down thither,
and buy for us from thence; that we may
[i]live, and not die.
3 ¶ And Joseph's ten brethren went down
to buy corn in Egypt.
4 But Benjamin, Joseph's brother, Jacob
sent not with his brethren; for he said, [j]Lest
peradventure mischief befall him.
5 And the sons of Israel came to buy *corn*
among those that came: for the famine was
[k]in the land of Canaan.
6 And Joseph *was* the governor [l]over the
land, *and* he *it was* that sold to all the people
of the land: and Joseph's brethren came,
and [m]bowed down themselves before him
with their faces to the earth.
7 And Joseph saw his brethren, and he
knew them, but made himself strange unto
them, and spake roughly unto them; and he
said unto them, Whence come ye? And they
said, From the land of Canaan to buy food.
8 And Joseph knew his brethren, but they
knew not him.
9 And Joseph [n]remembered the dreams
which he dreamed of them, and said unto
them, Ye *are* spies; to see the nakedness of
the land ye are come.
10 And they said unto him, Nay, my lord,
but to buy food are thy servants come.
11 We *are* all one man's sons; we *are* true
men, thy servants are no spies.
12 And he said unto them, Nay, but to see
the nakedness of the land ye are come.
13 And they said, Thy servants *are* twelve
brethren, the sons of one man in the land of
Canaan; and, behold, the youngest *is* this
day with our father, and one [o]*is* not.
14 And Joseph said unto them, That *is it*
that I spake unto you, saying, Ye *are* spies:
15 Hereby ye shall be proved: [p]By the life
of Pharaoh ye shall not go forth hence, except your youngest brother come hither.
16 Send one of you, and let him fetch your

brother, and ye shall be kept in prison, that your words may be proved, whether *there be any* truth in you: or else by the life of Pharaoh surely ye *are* spies.

17 And he put them all together into ward three days.

18 And Joseph said unto them the third day, This do, and live; [q]*for* I fear God:

19 If ye *be* true *men,* let one of your brethren be bound in the house of your prison: go ye, carry corn for the famine of your houses:

20 But [r]bring your youngest brother unto me, so shall your words be verified, and ye shall not die. And they did so.

21 ¶ And they said one to another, [s]We *are* verily guilty concerning our brother, in that we saw the anguish of his soul, when he besought us, and we would not hear; [t]therefore is this distress come upon us.

22 And Reuben answered them, saying, [u]Spake I not unto you, saying, Do not sin against the child; and ye would not hear? therefore, behold, also his blood is [v]required.

23 And they knew not that Joseph understood *them;* for he spake unto them by an interpreter.

24 And he turned himself about from them, and wept; and returned to them again, and communed with them, and took from them Simeon, and bound him before their eyes.

25 ¶ Then Joseph commanded to fill their sacks with corn, and to restore every man's money into his sack, and to give them provision for the way: and [w]thus did he unto them.

26 And they laded their asses with the corn, and departed thence.

27 And as [x]one of them opened his sack to give his ass provender in the inn, he espied his money; for, behold, it *was* in his sack's mouth.

28 And he said unto his brethren, My money is restored; and, lo, *it is* even in my sack: and their heart failed *them,* and they were afraid, saying one to another, What *is* this *that* God hath done unto us?

29 ¶ And they came unto Jacob their father unto the land of Canaan, and told him all that befell unto them; saying,

30 The man, *who is* the lord of the land, [y]spake roughly to us, and took us for spies of the country.

31 And we said unto him, We *are* true *men;* we are no spies:

32 We *be* twelve brethren, sons of our father; one *is* not, and the youngest *is* this day with our father in the land of Canaan.

33 And the man, the lord of the country, said unto us, [z]Hereby shall I know that ye *are* true *men;* leave one of your brethren *here* with me, and take *food for* the famine of your households, and be gone:

34 And bring your youngest brother unto me: then shall I know that ye *are* no spies, but *that* ye *are* true *men:* so will I deliver you your brother, and ye shall [a]traffick in the land.

35 ¶ And it came to pass as they emptied their sacks, that, behold, [b]every man's bundle of money *was* in his sack: and when *both* they and their father saw the bundles of money, they were afraid.

36 And Jacob their father said unto them, Me have ye [c]bereaved *of my children:* Joseph *is* not, and Simeon *is* not, and ye will take Benjamin *away:* all these things are against me.

37 And Reuben spake unto his father, saying, Slay my two sons, if I bring him not to thee: deliver him into my hand, and I will bring him to thee again.

38 And he said, My son shall not go down with you; for [d]his brother is dead, and he is left alone: [e]if mischief befall him by the way in the which ye go, then shall ye [f]bring down my gray hairs with sorrow to the grave.

43 And the famine *was* [g]sore in the land.

2 And it came to pass, when they had eaten up the corn which they had brought out of Egypt, their father said unto them, Go again, buy us a little food.

3 And Judah spake unto him, saying, The man did solemnly protest unto us, saying, Ye shall not see my face, except your [h]brother *be* with you.

4 If thou wilt send our brother with us, we will go down and buy thee food:

5 But if thou wilt not send *him,* we will not go down: for the man said unto us, Ye shall not see my face, except your brother *be* with you.

6 And Israel said, Wherefore dealt ye *so* ill with me, *as* to tell the man whether ye had yet a brother?

7 And they said, The man asked us straitly of our state, and of our kindred, saying, *Is* your father yet alive? have ye *another* brother? and we told him according to the tenor of these words: could we certainly know that he would say, Bring your brother down?

8 And Judah said unto Israel his father, Send the lad with me, and we will arise and go; that we may live, and not die, both we, and thou, *and* also our little ones.

9 I will be surety for him; of my hand shalt thou require him: [i]if I bring him not unto thee, and set him before thee, then let me bear the blame for ever:

10 For except we had lingered, surely now we had returned this second time.

11 And their father Israel said unto them, If *it must be* so now, do this; take of the best fruits in the land in your vessels, and [j]carry down the man a present, a little [k]balm, and a little honey, spices, and myrrh, nuts, and almonds:

12 And take double money in your hand; and the money [l]that was brought again in the mouth of your sacks, carry *it* again in

42:18 [q]Lev. 25:43; Neh. 5:15
42:20 [r]ver. 34; ch. 43:5
42:21 [s]Job 36:8; Hos. 5:15 [t]Prov. 21:13; Matt. 7:2
42:22 [u]ch. 37:21 [v]ch. 9:5; 1 Kings 2:32; 2 Chron. 24:22; Ps. 9:12; Luke 11:50
42:25 [w]Matt. 5:44; Rom. 12:17
42:27 [x]ch. 43:21
42:30 [y]ver. 7
42:33 [z]ver. 15
42:34 [a]ch. 34:10
42:35 [b]ch. 43:21
42:36 [c]ch. 43:14
42:38 [d]ver. 13 [e]ver. 4 [f]ch. 37:35
43:1 [g]ch. 41:54
43:3 [h]ch. 42:20
43:9 [i]ch. 44:32; Philem. 18
43:11 [j]ch. 32:20; Prov. 18:16 [k]ch. 37:25; Jer. 8:22
43:12 [l]ch. 42:25

your hand; peradventure it *was* an oversight:
13 Take also your brother, and arise, go
again unto the man:
14 And God Almighty give you mercy before the man, that he may send away your
other brother, and Benjamin. [m]If I be bereaved *of my children,* I am bereaved.
15 ¶ And the men took that present, and
they took double money in their hand, and
Benjamin; and rose up, and went down to
Egypt, and stood before Joseph.
16 And when Joseph saw Benjamin with
them, he said to the [n]ruler of his house,
Bring *these* men home, and slay, and make
ready; for *these* men shall dine with me at
noon.
17 And the man did as Joseph bade; and
the man brought the men into Joseph's
house.
18 And the men were afraid, because they
were brought into Joseph's house; and they
said, Because of the money that was returned in our sacks at the first time are
we brought in; that he may seek occasion
against us, and fall upon us, and take us for
bondmen, and our asses.
19 And they came near to the steward of
Joseph's house, and they communed with
him at the door of the house,
20 And said, O sir, [o]we came indeed
down at the first time to buy food:
21 And [p]it came to pass, when we came
to the inn, that we opened our sacks, and,
behold, *every* man's money *was* in the
mouth of his sack, our money in full weight:
and we have brought it again in our hand.
22 And other money have we brought
down in our hands to buy food: we cannot
tell who put our money in our sacks.
23 And he said, Peace *be* to you, fear not:
your God, and the God of your father, hath
given you treasure in your sacks: I had your
money. And he brought Simeon out unto
them.
24 And the man brought the men into Joseph's house, and [q]gave *them* water, and
they washed their feet; and he gave their
asses provender.
25 And they made ready the present
against Joseph came at noon: for they heard
that they should eat bread there.
26 ¶ And when Joseph came home, they
brought him the present which *was* in their
hand into the house, and [r]bowed themselves to him to the earth.
27 And he asked them of *their* welfare,
and said, *Is* your father well, the old man
[s]of whom ye spake? *Is* he yet alive?
28 And they answered, Thy servant our
father *is* in good health, he *is* yet alive.
[t]And they bowed down their heads, and
made obeisance.
29 And he lifted up his eyes, and saw his
brother Benjamin, [u]his mother's son, and
said, *Is* this your younger brother, [v]of
whom ye spake unto me? And he said, God
be gracious unto thee, my son.

43:14 [m]Esth. 4:16
43:16 [n]ch. 24:2
43:20 [o]ch. 42:3
43:21 [p]ch. 42:27
43:24 [q]ch. 18:4
43:26 [r]ch. 37:7
43:27 [s]ch. 42:11
43:28 [t]ch. 37:7
43:29 [u]ch. 35:17 [v]ch. 42:13
43:30 [w]1 Kings 3:26 [x]ch. 42:24
43:31 [y]ver. 25
43:32 [z]ch. 46:34; Ex. 8:26
43:34 [a]ch. 45:22
44:8 [b]ch. 43:21
44:9 [c]ch. 31:32
44:13 [d]ch. 37:29; Num. 14:6; 2 Sam. 1:11

30 And Joseph made haste; for [w]his bowels did yearn upon his brother: and he
sought *where* to weep; and he entered into
his chamber, and [x]wept there.
31 And he washed his face, and went out,
and refrained himself, and said, Set on
[y]bread.
32 And they set on for him by himself,
and for them by themselves, and for the
Egyptians, which did eat with him, by themselves: because the Egyptians might not eat
bread with the Hebrews; for that *is* [z]an
abomination unto the Egyptians.
33 And they sat before him, the firstborn
according to his birthright, and the youngest according to his youth: and the men
marvelled one at another.
34 And he took *and sent* messes unto
them from before him: but Benjamin's mess
was [a]five times so much as any of theirs.
And they drank, and were merry with him.
44 And he commanded the steward of
his house, saying, Fill the men's
sacks *with* food, as much as they can carry,
and put every man's money in his sack's
mouth.
2 And put my cup, the silver cup, in the
sack's mouth of the youngest, and his corn
money. And he did according to the word
that Joseph had spoken.
3 As soon as the morning was light, the
men were sent away, they and their asses.
4 *And* when they were gone out of the
city, *and* not *yet* far off, Joseph said unto
his steward, Up, follow after the men; and
when thou dost overtake them, say unto
them, Wherefore have ye rewarded evil for
good?
5 *Is* not this *it* in which my lord drinketh,
and whereby indeed he divineth? ye have
done evil in so doing.
6 ¶ And he overtook them, and he spake
unto them these same words.
7 And they said unto him, Wherefore
saith my lord these words? God forbid that
thy servants should do according to this
thing:
8 Behold, [b]the money, which we found in
our sacks' mouths, we brought again unto
thee out of the land of Canaan: how then
should we steal out of thy lord's house silver
or gold?
9 With whomsoever of thy servants it be
found, [c]both let him die, and we also will be
my lord's bondmen.
10 And he said, Now also *let* it *be* according unto your words: he with whom it is
found shall be my servant; and ye shall be
blameless.
11 Then they speedily took down every
man his sack to the ground, and opened every man his sack.
12 And he searched, *and* began at the eldest, and left at the youngest: and the cup
was found in Benjamin's sack.
13 Then they [d]rent their clothes, and
laded every man his ass, and returned to the
city.

14 And Judah and his brethren came to
Joseph's house; for he *was* yet there: and
they [e]fell before him on the ground.
15 And Joseph said unto them, What
deed *is* this that ye have done? wot ye not
that such a man as I can certainly divine?
16 And Judah said, What shall we say
unto my lord? what shall we speak? or how
shall we clear ourselves? God hath found
out the iniquity of thy servants: behold, [f]we
are my lord's servants, both we, and *he* also
with whom the cup is found.
17 And he said, [g]God forbid that I should
do so: *but* the man in whose hand the cup is
found, he shall be my servant; and as for
you, get you up in peace unto your father.
18 ¶ Then Judah came near unto him, and
said, Oh my lord, let thy servant, I pray thee,
speak a word in my lord's ears, and [h]let not
thine anger burn against thy servant: for
thou *art* even as Pharaoh.
19 My lord asked his servants, saying,
Have ye a father, or a brother?
20 And we said unto my lord, We have a
father, an old man, and [i]a child of his old
age, a little one; and his brother is dead, and
he alone is left of his mother, and his father
loveth him.
21 And thou saidst unto thy servants,
[j]Bring him down unto me, that I may set
mine eyes upon him.
22 And we said unto my lord, The lad cannot leave his father: for *if* he should leave
his father, *his father* would die.
23 And thou saidst unto thy servants,
[k]Except your youngest brother come down
with you, ye shall see my face no more.
24 And it came to pass when we came up
unto thy servant my father, we told him the
words of my lord.
25 And [l]our father said, Go again, *and*
buy us a little food.
26 And we said, We cannot go down: if
our youngest brother be with us, then will
we go down: for we may not see the man's
face, except our youngest brother *be*
with us.
27 And thy servant my father said unto
us, Ye know that [m]my wife bare me two
sons:
28 And the one went out from me, and I
said, [n]Surely he is torn in pieces; and I saw
him not since:
29 And if ye [o]take this also from me, and
mischief befall him, ye shall bring down my
gray hairs with sorrow to the grave.
30 Now therefore when I come to thy servant my father, and the lad *be* not with us;
seeing that [p]his life is bound up in the lad's
life;
31 It shall come to pass, when he seeth
that the lad *is* not *with us,* that he will die:
and thy servants shall bring down the gray
hairs of thy servant our father with sorrow
to the grave.
32 For thy servant became surety for the
lad unto my father, saying, [q]If I bring him
not unto thee, then I shall bear the blame to
my father for ever.
33 Now therefore, I pray thee, [r]let thy
servant abide instead of the lad a bondman
to my lord; and let the lad go up with his
brethren.
34 For how shall I go up to my father, and
the lad *be* not with me? lest peradventure I
see the evil that shall come on my father.

45 Then Joseph could not refrain himself before all them that stood by
him; and he cried, Cause every man to go
out from me. And there stood no man with
him, while Joseph made himself known
unto his brethren.
2 And he wept aloud: and the Egyptians
and the house of Pharaoh heard.
3 And Joseph said unto his brethren, [s]I
am Joseph; doth my father yet live? And his
brethren could not answer him; for they
were troubled at his presence.
4 And Joseph said unto his brethren,
Come near to me, I pray you. And they
came near. And he said I *am* Joseph your
brother, [t]whom ye sold into Egypt.
5 Now therefore [u]be not grieved, nor angry with yourselves, that ye sold me hither:
[v]for God did send me before you to preserve life.
6 For these two years *hath* the famine
been in the land: and yet *there are* five
years, in the which *there shall* neither *be*
earing nor harvest.
7 And God sent me before you to preserve
you a posterity in the earth, and to save
your lives by a great deliverance.
8 So now *it was* not you *that* sent me
hither, but God: and he hath made me [w]a
father to Pharaoh, and lord of all his house,
and a ruler throughout all the land of Egypt.
9 Haste ye, and go up to my father, and
say unto him, Thus saith thy son Joseph,
God hath made me lord of all Egypt: come
down unto me, tarry not:
10 And [x]thou shalt dwell in the land of
Goshen, and thou shalt be near unto me,
thou, and thy children, and thy children's
children, and thy flocks, and thy herds, and
all that thou hast:
11 And there will I nourish thee; for yet
there are five years of famine; lest thou, and
thy household, and all that thou hast, come
to poverty.
12 And, behold, your eyes see, and the
eyes of my brother Benjamin, that *it is* [y]my
mouth that speaketh unto you.
13 And ye shall tell my father of all my
glory in Egypt, and of all that ye have seen;
and ye shall haste and [z]bring down my father hither.
14 And he fell upon his brother Benjamin's neck, and wept; and Benjamin wept
upon his neck.
15 Moreover he kissed all his brethren,
and wept upon them: and after that his
brethren talked with him.
16 ¶ And the fame thereof was heard in
Pharaoh's house, saying, Joseph's brethren

44:14 [e]ch. 37:7
44:16 [f]ver. 9
44:17 [g]Prov. 17:15
44:18 [h]ch. 18:30; Ex. 32:22
44:20 [i]ch. 37:3
44:21 [j]ch. 42:15
44:23 [k]ch. 43:3
44:25 [l]ch. 43:2
44:27 [m]ch. 46:19
44:28 [n]ch. 37:33
44:29 [o]ch. 42:36
44:30 [p]1 Sam. 18:1
44:32 [q]ch. 43:9
44:33 [r]Ex. 32:32
45:3 [s]Acts 7:13
45:4 [t]ch. 37:28
45:5 [u]Isa. 40:2; 2 Cor. 2:7 [v]ch. 50:20; 2 Sam. 16:10; Ps. 105:16; Acts 4:24
45:8 [w]ch. 41:43; Judg. 17:10; Job 29:16
45:10 [x]ch. 47:1
45:12 [y]ch. 42:23
45:13 [z]Acts 7:14

are come: and it pleased Pharaoh well, and
his servants.
17 And Pharaoh said unto Joseph, Say
unto thy brethren, This do ye; lade your
beasts, and go, get you unto the land of Canaan;
18 And take your father and your households, and come unto me: and I will give you
the good of the land of Egypt, and ye shall
eat [a]the fat of the land.
19 Now thou art commanded, this do ye;
take you wagons out of the land of Egypt for
your little ones, and for your wives, and
bring your father, and come.
20 Also regard not your stuff; for the good
of all the land of Egypt *is* yours.
21 And the children of Israel did so: and
Joseph gave them wagons, according to the
commandment of Pharaoh, and gave them
provision for the way.
22 To all of them he gave each man
changes of raiment; but to Benjamin he
gave three hundred *pieces* of silver, and
[b]five changes of raiment.
23 And to his father he sent after this
manner; ten asses laden with the good
things of Egypt, and ten she asses laden
with corn and bread and meat for his father
by the way.
24 So he sent his brethren away, and they
departed: and he said unto them, See that ye
fall not out by the way.
25 ¶ And they went up out of Egypt, and
came into the land of Canaan unto Jacob
their father,
26 And told him, saying, Joseph *is* yet
alive, and he *is* governor over all the land of
Egypt. [c]And Jacob's heart fainted, for he
believed them not.
27 And they told him all the words of Joseph, which he had said unto them: and
when he saw the wagons which Joseph had
sent to carry him, the spirit of Jacob their
father revived:
28 And Israel said, *It is* enough; Joseph
my son *is* yet alive: I will go and see him
before I die.

46 And Israel took his journey with all
that he had, and came to [d]Beer-
sheba, and offered sacrifices [e]unto the God
of his father Isaac.
2 And God spake unto Israel [f]in the visions of the night, and said, Jacob, Jacob.
And he said, Here *am* I.
3 And he said, I *am* God, [g]the God of thy
father: fear not to go down into Egypt; for I
will there [h]make of thee a great nation:
4 [i]I will go down with thee into Egypt;
and I will also surely [j]bring thee up *again:*
and [k]Joseph shall put his hand upon thine
eyes.
5 And [l]Jacob rose up from Beer-sheba:
and the sons of Israel carried Jacob their
father, and their little ones, and their wives,
in the wagons [m]which Pharaoh had sent to
carry him.
6 And they took their cattle, and their
goods, which they had gotten in the land of
Canaan, and came into Egypt, [n]Jacob, and
all his seed with him:
7 His sons, and his sons' sons with him,
his daughters, and his sons' daughters, and
all his seed brought he with him into Egypt.
8 ¶ And [o]these *are* the names of the children of Israel, which came into Egypt, Jacob and his sons: [p]Reuben, Jacob's
firstborn.
9 And the sons of Reuben; Hanoch, and
Phallu, and Hezron, and Carmi.
10 ¶ And [q]the sons of Simeon; Jemuel,
and Jamin, and Ohad, and Jachin, and Zohar, and Shaul the son of a Canaanitish
woman.
11 ¶ And the sons of [r]Levi; Gershon, Kohath, and Merari.
12 ¶ And the sons of [s]Judah; Er, and
Onan, and Shelah, and Pharez, and Zarah:
but [t]Er and Onan died in the land of Canaan. And [u]the sons of Pharez were Hezron and Hamul.
13 ¶ [v]And the sons of Issachar; Tola, and
Phuvah, and Job, and Shimron.
14 ¶ And the sons of Zebulun; Sered, and
Elon, and Jahleel.
15 These *be* the sons of Leah, which she
bare unto Jacob in Padan-aram, with his
daughter Dinah: all the souls of his sons and
his daughters *were* thirty and three.
16 And the sons of Gad; [w]Ziphion, and
Haggi, Shuni, and Ezbon, Eri, and Arodi,
and Areli.
17 ¶ [x]And the sons of Asher; Jimnah, and
Ishuah, and Isui, and Beriah, and Serah
their sister: and the sons of Beriah; Heber,
and Malchiel.
18 [y]These *are* the sons of Zilpah, [z]whom
Laban gave to Leah his daughter, and these
she bare unto Jacob, *even* sixteen souls.
19 The sons of Rachel [a]Jacob's wife; Joseph, and Benjamin.
20 ¶ [b]And unto Joseph in the land of
Egypt were born Manasseh and Ephraim,
which Asenath the daughter of Poti-pherah
priest of On bare unto him.
21 [c]And the sons of Benjamin *were*
Belah, and Becher, and Ashbel, Gera, and
Naaman, [d]Ehi, and Rosh, [e]Muppim, and
Huppim, and Ard.
22 These *are* the sons of Rachel, which
were born to Jacob: all the souls *were* fourteen.
23 ¶ [f]And the sons of Dan; Hushim.
24 ¶ [g]And the sons of Naphtali; Jahzeel,
and Guni, and Jezer, and Shillem.
25 [h]These *are* the sons of Bilhah, [i]which
Laban gave unto Rachel his daughter, and
she bare these unto Jacob: all the souls *were*
seven.
26 [j]All the souls that came with Jacob
into Egypt, which came out of his loins,
besides Jacob's sons' wives, [k]all the souls
were threescore and six;
27 And the sons of Joseph, which were
born him in Egypt, *were* two souls: all the
souls of the house of Jacob, which came
into Egypt, *were* threescore and ten.

45:18 [a]ch. 27:28; Num. 18:12
45:22 [b]ch. 43:34
45:26 [c]Job 29:24; Ps. 126:1; Luke 24:11
46:1 [d]ch. 21:31 [e]ch. 26:24
46:2 [f]ch. 15:1; Job 33:14
46:3 [g]ch. 28:13 [h]ch. 12:2; Deut. 26:5
46:4 [i]ch. 28:15 [j]ch. 15:16; Ex. 3:8 [k]ch. 50:1
46:5 [l]Acts 7:15 [m]ch. 45:19
46:6 [n]Deut. 26:5; Josh. 24:4; Ps. 105:23; Isa. 52:4
46:8 [o]Ex. 1:1 [p]Num. 26:5; 1 Chron. 5:1
46:10 [q]Ex. 6:15; 1 Chron. 4:24
46:11 [r]1 Chron. 6:1
46:12 [s]1 Chron. 2:3 [t]ch. 38:3 [u]ch. 38:29; 1 Chron. 2:5
46:13 [v]1 Chron. 7:1
46:16 [w]Num. 26:15
46:17 [x]1 Chron. 7:30
46:18 [y]ch. 30:10 [z]ch. 29:24
46:19 [a]ch. 44:27
46:20 [b]ch. 41:50
46:21 [c]1 Chron. 7:6 [d]Num. 26:38 [e]Num. 26:39; 1 Chron. 7:12
46:23 [f]1 Chron. 7:12
46:24 [g]1 Chron. 7:13
46:25 [h]ch. 30:5 [i]ch. 29:29
46:26 [j]Ex. 1:5 [k]Deut. 10:22; Acts 7:14

28 ¶ And he sent Judah before him unto
Joseph, [l]to direct his face unto Goshen;
and they came [m]into the land of Goshen.
29 And Joseph made ready his chariot,
and went up to meet Israel his father, to
Goshen, and presented himself unto him;
and he [n]fell on his neck, and wept on his
neck a good while.
30 And Israel said unto Joseph, [o]Now let
me die, since I have seen thy face, because
thou *art* yet alive.
31 And Joseph said unto his brethren,
and unto his father's house, [p]I will go up,
and shew Pharaoh, and say unto him, My
brethren, and my father's house, which
were in the land of Canaan, are come
unto me;
32 And the men *are* shepherds, for their
trade hath been to feed cattle; and they have
brought their flocks, and their herds, and all
that they have.
33 And it shall come to pass, when Pharaoh shall call you, and shall say, [q]What *is*
your occupation?
34 That ye shall say, Thy servants' [r]trade
hath been about cattle [s]from our youth
even until now, both we, *and* also our fathers: that ye may dwell in the land of Goshen; for every shepherd *is* [t]an
abomination unto the Egyptians.

47

Then Joseph [u]came and told Pharaoh, and said, My father and my
brethren, and their flocks, and their herds,
and all that they have, are come out of the
land of Canaan; and, behold, they *are* in
[v]the land of Goshen.
2 And he took some of his brethren, *even*
five men, and [w]presented them unto Pharaoh.
3 And Pharaoh said unto his brethren,
[x]What *is* your occupation? And they said
unto Pharaoh, [y]Thy servants *are* shepherds, both we, *and* also our fathers.
4 They said moreover unto Pharaoh,
[z]For to sojourn in the land are we come;
for thy servants have no pasture for their
flocks; [a]for the famine *is* sore in the land of
Canaan: now therefore, we pray thee, let
thy servants [b]dwell in the land of Goshen.
5 And Pharaoh spake unto Joseph, saying, Thy father and thy brethren are come
unto thee:
6 [c]The land of Egypt *is* before thee; in the
best of the land make thy father and brethren to dwell; [d]in the land of Goshen let
them dwell: and if thou knowest *any* men of
activity among them, then make them rulers over my cattle.
7 And Joseph brought in Jacob his father,
and set him before Pharaoh: and Jacob
blessed Pharaoh.
8 And Pharaoh said unto Jacob, How old
art thou?
9 And Jacob said unto Pharaoh, [e]The
days of the years of my pilgrimage *are* an
hundred and thirty years: [f]few and evil
have the days of the years of my life been,
and [g]have not attained unto the days of the

46:28 [l]ch. 31:21 [m]ch. 47:1
46:29 [n]ch. 45:14
46:30 [o]Luke 2:29
46:31 [p]ch. 47:1
46:33 [q]ch. 47:2
46:34 [r]ver. 32 [s]ch. 30:35 [t]ch. 43:32; Ex. 8:26
47:1 [u]ch. 46:31 [v]ch. 45:10
47:2 [w]Acts 7:13
47:3 [x]ch. 46:33 [y]ch. 46:34
47:4 [z]ch. 15:13; Deut. 26:5 [a]ch. 43:1; Acts 7:11 [b]ch. 46:34
47:6 [c]ch. 20:15 [d]ver. 4
47:9 [e]Heb. 11:9; Ps. 39:12 [f]Job 14:1 [g]ch. 25:7
47:10 [h]ver. 7
47:11 [i]Ex. 1:11 [j]ver. 6
47:13 [k]ch. 41:30; Acts 7:11
47:14 [l]ch. 41:56
47:15 [m]ver. 19
47:22 [n]Ezra 7:24

years of the life of my fathers in the days of
their pilgrimage.
10 And Jacob [h]blessed Pharaoh, and
went out from before Pharaoh.
11 ¶ And Joseph placed his father and his
brethren, and gave them a possession in the
land of Egypt, in the best of the land, in the
land of [i]Rameses, [j]as Pharaoh had commanded.
12 And Joseph nourished his father, and
his brethren, and all his father's household,
with bread, according to *their* families.
13 ¶ And *there was* no bread in all the
land; for the famine *was* very sore, [k]so that
the land of Egypt and *all* the land of Canaan
fainted by reason of the famine.
14 [l]And Joseph gathered up all the
money that was found in the land of Egypt,
and in the land of Canaan, for the corn
which they bought: and Joseph brought the
money into Pharaoh's house.
15 And when money failed in the land of
Egypt, and in the land of Canaan, all the
Egyptians came unto Joseph, and said, Give
us bread: for [m]why should we die in thy
presence? for the money faileth.
16 And Joseph said, Give your cattle; and
I will give you for your cattle, if money fail.
17 And they brought their cattle unto Joseph: and Joseph gave them bread *in exchange* for horses, and for the flocks, and
for the cattle of the herds, and for the asses:
and he fed them with bread for all their cattle for that year.
18 When that year was ended, they came
unto him the second year, and said unto
him, We will not hide *it* from my lord, how
that our money is spent; my lord also hath
our herds of cattle; there is not ought left in
the sight of my lord, but our bodies, and our
lands:
19 Wherefore shall we die before thine
eyes, both we and our land? buy us and our
land for bread, and we and our land will be
servants unto Pharaoh: and give *us* seed,
that we may live, and not die, that the land
be not desolate.
20 And Joseph bought all the land of
Egypt for Pharaoh; for the Egyptians sold
every man his field, because the famine prevailed over them: so the land became Pharaoh's.
21 And as for the people, he removed
them to cities from *one* end of the borders of
Egypt even to the *other* end thereof.
22 [n]Only the land of the priests bought he
not; for the priests had a portion *assigned
them* of Pharaoh, and did eat their portion
which Pharaoh gave them: wherefore they
sold not their lands.
23 Then Joseph said unto the people, Behold, I have bought you this day and your
land for Pharaoh: lo, *here is* seed for you,
and ye shall sow the land.
24 And it shall come to pass in the increase, that ye shall give the fifth *part* unto
Pharaoh, and four parts shall be your own,
for seed of the field, and for your food, and

for them of your households, and for food
for your little ones.
25 And they said, Thou hast saved our
lives: [o]let us find grace in the sight of my
lord, and we will be Pharaoh's servants.
26 And Joseph made it a law over the
land of Egypt unto this day, *that* Pharaoh
should have the fifth *part;* [p]except the land
of the priests only, *which* became not Pharaoh's.
27 ¶ And Israel [q]dwelt in the land of
Egypt, in the country of Goshen; and they
had possessions therein, and [r]grew, and
multiplied exceedingly.
28 And Jacob lived in the land of Egypt
seventeen years: so the whole age of Jacob
was an hundred forty and seven years.
29 And the time [s]drew nigh that Israel
must die: and he called his son Joseph, and
said unto him, If now I have found grace in
thy sight, [t]put, I pray thee, thy hand under
my thigh, and [u]deal kindly and truly with
me; [v]bury me not, I pray thee, in Egypt:
30 But [w]I will lie with my fathers, and
thou shalt carry me out of Egypt, and [x]bury
me in their buryingplace. And he said, I will
do as thou hast said.
31 And he said, Swear unto me. And he
sware unto him. And [y]Israel bowed himself
upon the bed's head.

48

And it came to pass after these
things, that *one* told Joseph, Behold,
thy father *is* sick: and he took with him his
two sons, Manasseh and Ephraim.
2 And *one* told Jacob, and said, Behold,
thy son Joseph cometh unto thee: and Israel
strengthened himself, and sat upon the bed.
3 And Jacob said unto Joseph, God Almighty appeared unto me at [z]Luz in the
land of Canaan, and blessed me,
4 And said unto me, Behold, I will make
thee fruitful, and multiply thee, and I will
make of thee a multitude of people; and will
give this land to thy seed after thee [a]*for* an
everlasting possession.
5 ¶ And now thy [b]two sons, Ephraim and
Manasseh, which were born unto thee in
the land of Egypt before I came unto thee
into Egypt, *are* mine; as Reuben and Simeon, they shall be mine.
6 And thy issue, which thou begettest after them, shall be thine, *and* shall be called
after the name of their brethren in their inheritance.
7 And as for me, when I came from Pa-
dan, [c]Rachel died by me in the land of Canaan in the way, when yet *there was* but a
little way to come unto Ephrath: and I buried her there in the way of Ephrath; the
same *is* Beth-lehem.
8 And Israel beheld Joseph's sons, and
said, Who *are* these?
9 And Joseph said unto his father, [d]They
are my sons, whom God hath given me in
this *place.* And he said, Bring them, I pray
thee, unto me, and [e]I will bless them.
10 Now [f]the eyes of Israel were dim for
age, *so that* he could not see. And he

47:25 [o]ch. 33:15
47:26 [p]ver. 22
47:27 [q]ver. 11 [r]ch. 46:3
47:29 [s]Deut. 31:14; 1 Kings 2:1 [t]ch. 24:2 [u]ch. 24:49 [v]ch. 50:25
47:30 [w]2 Sam. 19:37 [x]ch. 49:29
47:31 [y]ch. 48:2; 1 Kings 1:47; Heb. 11:21
48:3 [z]ch. 28:13
48:4 [a]ch. 17:8
48:5 [b]ch. 41:50; Josh. 13:7
48:7 [c]ch. 35:9
48:9 [d]ch. 33:5 [e]ch. 27:4
48:10 [f]ch. 27:1 [g]ch. 27:27
48:11 [h]ch. 45:26
48:14 [i]ver. 19
48:15 [j]Heb. 11:21 [k]ch. 17:1
48:16 [l]ch. 28:15; Ps. 34:22 [m]Am. 9:12; Acts 15:17
48:17 [n]ver. 14
48:19 [o]ver. 14 [p]Num. 1:33; Deut. 33:17; Rev. 7:6
48:20 [q]Ruth 4:11
48:21 [r]ch. 46:4
48:22 [s]Josh. 24:32; John 4:5 [t]ch. 15:16; Josh. 17:14
49:1 [u]Deut. 33:1; Am. 3:7 [v]Deut. 4:30; Num. 24:14; Isa. 2:2; Jer. 23:20; Dan. 2:28; Acts 2:17; Heb. 1:2
49:2 [w]Ps. 34:11
49:3 [x]ch. 29:32 [y]Deut. 21:17; Ps. 78:51
49:4 [z]1 Chron. 5:1 [a]ch. 35:22; 1 Chron. 5:1; Deut. 27:20
49:5 [b]ch. 29:33 [c]Prov. 18:9 [d]ch. 34:25

brought them near unto him; and [g]he
kissed them, and embraced them.
11 And Israel said unto Joseph, [h]I had
not thought to see thy face: and, lo, God
hath shewed me also thy seed.
12 And Joseph brought them out from between his knees, and he bowed himself with
his face to the earth.
13 And Joseph took them both, Ephraim
in his right hand toward Israel's left hand,
and Manasseh in his left hand toward Israel's right hand, and brought *them* near
unto him.
14 And Israel stretched out his right
hand, and laid *it* upon Ephraim's head, who
was the younger, and his left hand upon
Manasseh's head, [i]guiding his hands wit-
tingly; for Manasseh *was* the firstborn.
15 ¶ And [j]he blessed Joseph, and said,
God, [k]before whom my fathers Abraham
and Isaac did walk, the God which fed me
all my life long unto this day,
16 The Angel [l]which redeemed me from
all evil, bless the lads; and let [m]my name be
named on them, and the name of my fathers
Abraham and Isaac; and let them grow into
a multitude in the midst of the earth.
17 And when Joseph saw that his father
[n]laid his right hand upon the head of
Ephraim, it displeased him: and he held up
his father's hand, to remove it from
Ephraim's head unto Manasseh's head.
18 And Joseph said unto his father, Not
so, my father: for this *is* the firstborn; put
thy right hand upon his head.
19 And his father refused, and said, [o]I
know *it,* my son, I know *it:* he also shall
become a people, and he also shall be great:
but truly [p]his younger brother shall be
greater than he, and his seed shall become
a multitude of nations.
20 And he blessed them that day, saying,
[q]In thee shall Israel bless, saying, God
make thee as Ephraim and as Manasseh:
and he set Ephraim before Manasseh.
21 And Israel said unto Joseph, Behold, I
die: but [r]God shall be with you, and bring
you again unto the land of your fathers.
22 Moreover [s]I have given to thee one
portion above thy brethren, which I took
out of the hand [t]of the Amorite with my
sword and with my bow.

49

And Jacob called unto his sons, and
said, Gather yourselves together,
that I may [u]tell you *that* which shall befall
you [v]in the last days.
2 Gather yourselves together, and hear,
ye sons of Jacob; and [w]hearken unto Israel
your father.
3 ¶ Reuben, thou *art* [x]my firstborn, my
might, [y]and the beginning of my strength,
the excellency of dignity, and the excellency of power:
4 Unstable as water, [z]thou shalt not excel; because thou [a]wentest up to thy father's bed; then defiledst thou *it:* he went up
to my couch.
5 ¶ [b]Simeon and Levi *are* [c]brethren; [d]in-

struments of cruelty *are in* their habitations.

6 O my soul, [e]come not thou into their secret; [f]unto their assembly, [g]mine honour, be not thou united: for [h]in their anger they slew a man, and in their selfwill they digged down a wall.

7 Cursed *be* their anger, for *it was* fierce; and their wrath, for it was cruel: [i]I will divide them in Jacob, and scatter them in Israel.

8 ¶ [j]Judah, thou *art he* whom thy brethren shall praise: [k]thy hand *shall be* in the neck of thine enemies; [l]thy father's children shall bow down before thee.

9 Judah *is* [m]a lion's whelp: from the prey, my son, thou art gone up: [n]he stooped down, he couched as a lion, and as an old lion; who shall rouse him up?

10 [o]The sceptre shall not depart from Judah, nor [p]a lawgiver [q]from between his feet, [r]until Shiloh come; [s]and unto him *shall* the gathering of the people *be.*

11 [t]Binding his foal unto the vine, and his ass's colt unto the choice vine; he washed his garments in wine, and his clothes in the blood of grapes:

12 His [u]eyes *shall be* red with wine, and his teeth white with milk.

13 ¶ [v]Zebulun shall dwell at the haven of the sea; and he *shall be* for an haven of ships; and his border *shall be* unto Zidon.

14 ¶ Issachar *is* a strong ass couching down between two burdens:

15 And he saw that rest *was* good, and the land that *it was* pleasant; and bowed [w]his shoulder to bear, and became a servant unto tribute.

16 ¶ [x]Dan shall judge his people, as one of the tribes of Israel.

17 [y]Dan shall be a serpent by the way, an adder in the path, that biteth the horse heels, so that his rider shall fall backward.

18 [z]I have waited for thy salvation, O LORD.

19 ¶ [a]Gad, a troop shall overcome him: but he shall overcome at the last.

20 ¶ Out of Asher his bread *shall be* fat, and he shall yield royal dainties.

21 ¶ [b]Naphtali *is* a hind let loose: he giveth goodly words.

22 ¶ Joseph *is* a fruitful bough, *even* a fruitful bough by a well; *whose* branches run over the wall:

23 The archers have [c]sorely grieved him, and shot *at him,* and hated him:

24 But his [d]bow abode in strength, and the arms of his hands were made strong by the hands of [e]the mighty *God* of Jacob; ([f]from thence [g]*is* the shepherd, [h]the stone of Israel:)

25 [i]*Even* by the God of thy father, who shall help thee; [j]and by the Almighty, [k]who shall bless thee with blessings of heaven above, blessings of the deep that lieth under, blessings of the breasts, and of the womb:

26 The blessings of thy father have prevailed above the blessings of my progenitors [l]unto the utmost bound of the everlasting hills: [m]they shall be on the head of Joseph, and on the crown of the head of him that was separate from his brethren.

27 ¶ Benjamin shall [n]ravin *as* a wolf: in the morning he shall devour the prey, [o]and at night he shall divide the spoil.

28 ¶ All these *are* the twelve tribes of Israel: and this *is it* that their father spake unto them, and blessed them; every one according to his blessing he blessed them.

29 And he charged them, and said unto them, I [p]am to be gathered unto my people: [q]bury me with my fathers [r]in the cave that *is* in the field of Ephron the Hittite,

30 In the cave that *is* in the field of Machpelah, which *is* before Mamre, in the land of Canaan, [s]which Abraham bought with the field of Ephron the Hittite for a possession of a buryingplace.

31 [t]There they buried Abraham and Sarah his wife; [u]there they buried Isaac and Rebekah his wife; and there I buried Leah.

32 The purchase of the field and of the cave that *is* therein *was* from the children of Heth.

33 And when Jacob had made an end of commanding his sons, he gathered up his feet into the bed, and yielded up the ghost, and [v]was gathered unto his people.

50 And Joseph [w]fell upon his father's face, and [x]wept upon him, and kissed him.

2 And Joseph commanded his servants the physicians to [y]embalm his father: and the physicians embalmed Israel.

3 And forty days were fulfilled for him; for so are fulfilled the days of those which are embalmed: and the Egyptians [z]mourned for him threescore and ten days.

4 And when the days of his mourning were past, Joseph spake unto [a]the house of Pharaoh, saying, If now I have found grace in your eyes, speak, I pray you, in the ears of Pharaoh, saying,

5 [b]My father made me swear, saying, Lo, I die: in my grave [c]which I have digged for me in the land of Canaan, there shalt thou bury me. Now therefore let me go up, I pray thee, and bury my father, and I will come again.

6 And Pharaoh said, Go up, and bury thy father, according as he made thee swear.

7 ¶ And Joseph went up to bury his father: and with him went up all the servants of Pharaoh, the elders of his house, and all the elders of the land of Egypt,

8 And all the house of Joseph, and his brethren, and his father's house: only their little ones, and their flocks, and their herds, they left in the land of Goshen.

9 And there went up with him both chariots and horsemen: and it was a very great company.

10 And they came to the threshingfloor of Atad, which *is* beyond Jordan, and there they [d]mourned with a great and very sore

49:6 [e]Prov. 1:15 [f]Ps. 26:9; Eph. 5:11 [g]Ps. 16:9 [h]ch. 34:26
49:7 [i]Josh. 19:1
49:8 [j]ch. 29:35; Deut. 33:7 [k]Ps. 18:40 [l]ch. 27:29; 1 Chron. 5:2
49:9 [m]Hos. 5:4; Rev. 5:5 [n]Num. 23:24
49:10 [o]Jer. 30:21 [p]Ps. 60:7 [q]Deut. 28:57 [r]Isa. 11:1; Ezek. 21:27; Matt. 21:9 [s]Isa. 2:2
49:11 [t]2 Kings 18:32
49:12 [u]Prov. 23:29
49:13 [v]Deut. 33:18
49:15 [w]1 Sam. 10:9
49:16 [x]Deut. 33:22; Judg. 18:1
49:17 [y]Judg. 18:27
49:18 [z]Ps. 25:6; Isa. 25:9
49:19 [a]Deut. 33:20; 1 Chron. 5:18
49:21 [b]Deut. 33:23
49:23 [c]ch. 37:4; Ps. 118:13
49:24 [d]Job 29:20; Ps. 37:15 [e]Ps. 132:2 [f]ch. 45:11 [g]Ps. 80:1 [h]Isa. 28:16
49:25 [i]ch. 28:13 [j]ch. 17:1 [k]Deut. 33:13
49:26 [l]Deut. 33:15; Hab. 3:6 [m]Deut. 33:16
49:27 [n]Judg. 20:21; Ezek. 22:25 [o]Num. 23:24; Esth. 8:11; Ezek. 39:10; Zech. 14:1
49:29 [p]ch. 15:15 [q]ch. 47:30; 2 Sam. 19:37 [r]ch. 50:13
49:30 [s]ch. 23:16
49:31 [t]ch. 23:19 [u]ch. 35:29
49:33 [v]ver. 29
50:1 [w]ch. 46:4 [x]2 Kings 13:14
50:2 [y]ver. 26; 2 Chron. 16:14; Matt. 26:12; Mark 14:8; Luke 24:1; John 12:7
50:3 [z]Num. 20:29; Deut. 34:8
50:4 [a]Esth. 4:2
50:5 [b]ch. 47:29 [c]2 Chron. 16:14; Isa. 22:16; Matt. 27:60
50:10 [d]2 Sam. 1:17; Acts 8:2

lamentation: [e]and he made a mourning for
his father seven days.
11 And when the inhabitants of the land,
the Canaanites, saw the mourning in the
floor of Atad, they said, This *is* a grievous
mourning to the Egyptians: wherefore the
name of it was called Abel-mizraim, which
is beyond Jordan.
12 And his sons did unto him according
as he commanded them:
13 For [f]his sons carried him into the land
of Canaan, and buried him in the cave of
the field of Machpelah, which Abraham
[g]bought with the field for a possession of a
buryingplace of Ephron the Hittite, before
Mamre.
14 ¶ And Joseph returned into Egypt, he,
and his brethren, and all that went up with
him to bury his father, after he had buried
his father.
15 ¶ And when Joseph's brethren saw
that their father was dead, [h]they said, Joseph will peradventure hate us, and will certainly requite us all the evil which we did
unto him.
16 And they sent a messenger unto Joseph, saying, Thy father did command before he died, saying,
17 So shall ye say unto Joseph, Forgive, I
pray thee now, the trespass of thy brethren,
and their sin; [i]for they did unto thee evil:
and now, we pray thee, forgive the trespass
of the servants of [j]the God of thy father.
And Joseph wept when they spake unto
him.
18 And his brethren also went and [k]fell
down before his face; and they said, Behold,
we *be* thy servants.
19 And Joseph said unto them, [l]Fear not:
[m]for *am* I in the place of God?
20 [n]But as for you, ye thought evil
against me; *but* [o]God meant it unto good, to
bring to pass, as *it is* this day, to save much
people alive.
21 Now therefore fear ye not: [p]I will
nourish you, and your little ones. And he
comforted them, and spake kindly unto
them.
22 ¶ And Joseph dwelt in Egypt, he, and
his father's house: and Joseph lived an hundred and ten years.
23 And Joseph saw Ephraim's children
[q]of the third *generation:* [r]the children also
of Machir the son of Manasseh [s]were
brought up upon Joseph's knees.
24 And Joseph said unto his brethren, I
die: and [t]God will surely visit you, and
bring you out of this land unto the land
[u]which he sware to Abraham, to Isaac, and
to Jacob.
25 And [v]Joseph took an oath of the children of Israel, saying, God will surely visit
you, and ye shall carry up my bones from
hence.
26 So Joseph died, *being* an hundred and
ten years old: and they [w]embalmed him,
and he was put in a coffin in Egypt.

50:10 e1 Sam. 31:13; Job 2:13
50:13 fch. 49:29; Acts 7:16 gch. 23:16
50:15 hJob 15:21
50:17 iProv. 28:13 jch. 49:25
50:18 kch. 37:7
50:19 lch. 45:5 mDeut. 32:35; Job 34:29; Rom. 12:19; Heb. 10:30; 2 Kings 5:7
50:20 nPs. 56:5; Isa. 10:7 och. 45:5; Acts 3:13
50:21 pch. 47:12; Matt. 5:44
50:23 qJob 42:16 rNum. 32:39 sch. 30:3
50:24 tch. 15:14; Ex. 3:16; Heb. 11:22 uch. 15:14
50:25 vEx. 13:19; Josh. 24:32; Acts 7:16
50:26 wver. 2

EXODUS

Exodus was written by Moses around 1446 B.C. The book of Exodus contains the story of the Israelites' bondage in Egypt, the raising of Moses as their leader, the confrontation between Moses and Pharaoh, the release of the people of Israel, their tortured journey toward the Promised Land, the giving of the law of God to his people, and the construction of the tabernacle. Familiar stories found in Exodus include the birth of Moses, his confrontation with God in the burning bush, the ten plagues against Egypt, the parting of the Red Sea, the giving of the Ten Commandments, and the construction of the Ark of the Covenant.

I. Israel's slavery in Egypt, 1:1–12:36
II. Moses leads the Israelites out of Egypt, 12:37–14:31
III. The Israelites in the Sinai, 15:1–40:38

1 Now [a]these *are* the names of the children of Israel, which came into Egypt;
every man and his household came with Jacob.
2 Reuben, Simeon, Levi, and Judah,
3 Issachar, Zebulun, and Benjamin,
4 Dan, and Naphtali, Gad, and Asher.
5 And all the souls that came out of the
loins of Jacob were [b]seventy souls: for Joseph was in Egypt *already*.
6 And [c]Joseph died, and all his brethren,
and all that generation.
7 ¶ [d]And the children of Israel were fruitful, and increased abundantly, and multiplied, and waxed exceeding mighty; and the
land was filled with them.
8 Now there [e]arose up a new king over
Egypt, which knew not Joseph.
9 And he said unto his people, Behold,
[f]the people of the children of Israel *are*
more and mightier than we:
10 [g]Come on, let us [h]deal wisely with
them; lest they multiply, and it come to
pass, that, when there falleth out any war,
they join also unto our enemies, and fight
against us, and *so* get them up out of the
land.
11 Therefore they did set over them taskmasters [i]to afflict them with their [j]bur-
dens. And they built for Pharaoh treasure
cities, Pithom [k]and Raamses.
12 But the more they afflicted them, the
more they multiplied and grew. And they
were grieved because of the children of Israel.
13 And the Egyptians made the children
of Israel to serve with rigour:
14 And they [l]made their lives bitter with
hard bondage, [m]in morter, and in brick, and
in all manner of service in the field: all their
service, wherein they made them serve, *was*
with rigour.
15 ¶ And the king of Egypt spake to the
Hebrew midwives, of which the name of the
one *was* Shiphrah, and the name of the
other Puah:
16 And he said, When ye do the office of
a midwife to the Hebrew women, and see
them upon the stools; if it *be* a son, then ye
shall kill him: but if it *be* a daughter, then
she shall live.
17 But the midwives [n]feared God, and
did not [o]as the king of Egypt commanded
them, but saved the men children alive.
18 And the king of Egypt called for the
midwives, and said unto them, Why have ye
done this thing, and have saved the men
children alive?
19 And [p]the midwives said unto Pharaoh, Because the Hebrew women *are* not as
the Egyptian women; for they *are* lively,
and are delivered ere the midwives come in
unto them.
20 [q]Therefore God dealt well with the
midwives: and the people multiplied, and
waxed very mighty.
21 And it came to pass, because the midwives feared God, [r]that he made them
houses.
22 And Pharaoh charged all his people,
saying, [s]Every son that is born ye shall cast
into the river, and every daughter ye shall
save alive.

2 And there went a [t]man of the house of
Levi, and took *to wife* a daughter of
Levi.
2 And the woman conceived, and bare a
son: and [u]when she saw him that he *was a*
goodly *child*, she hid him three months.
3 And when she could not longer hide
him, she took for him an ark of bulrushes,
and daubed it with slime and with pitch, and
put the child therein; and she laid *it* in the
flags by the river's brink.
4 [v]And his sister stood afar off, to wit
what would be done to him.
5 ¶ And the [w]daughter of Pharaoh came
down to wash *herself* at the river; and her
maidens walked along by the river's side;
and when she saw the ark among the flags,
she sent her maid to fetch it.
6 And when she had opened *it*, she saw
the child: and, behold, the babe wept. And
she had compassion on him, and said, This
is one of the Hebrews' children.
7 Then said his sister to Pharaoh's daugh-

1:1 [a]Gen. 46:8; ch. 6:14
1:5 [b]Gen. 46:26; ver. 20; Deut. 10:22
1:6 [c]Gen. 50:26; Acts 7:15
1:7 [d]Gen. 46:3; Deut. 26:5; Ps. 105:25; Acts 7:17
1:8 [e]Acts 7:18
1:9 [f]Ps. 105:24
1:10 [g]Ps. 10:2 [h]Job 5:13; Ps. 105:25; Prov. 16:25; Acts 7:19
1:11 [i]Gen. 15:13; ch. 3:7; Deut. 26:6 [j]ch. 2:11; Ps. 81:6 [k]Gen. 47:11
1:14 [l]ch. 2:23; Num. 20:15; Acts 7:19 [m]Ps. 81:6
1:17 [n]Prov. 16:6 [o]Dan. 3:16; Acts 5:29
1:19 [p]Josh. 2:4; 2 Sam. 17:19
1:20 [q]Prov. 11:18; Eccl. 8:12; Isa. 3:10; Heb. 6:10
1:21 [r]1 Sam. 2:35; 2 Sam. 7:11; 1 Kings 2:24; Ps. 127:1
1:22 [s]Acts 7:19
2:1 [t]ch. 6:20; Num. 26:59; 1 Chron. 23:14
2:2 [u]Acts 7:20; Heb. 11:23
2:4 [v]ch. 15:20; Num. 26:59
2:5 [w]Acts 7:21

ter, Shall I go and call to thee a nurse of the Hebrew women, that she may nurse the child for thee?

8 And Pharaoh's daughter said to her, Go. And the maid went and called the child's mother.

9 And Pharaoh's daughter said unto her, Take this child away, and nurse it for me, and I will give *thee* thy wages. And the woman took the child, and nursed it.

10 And the child grew, and she brought him unto Pharaoh's daughter, and he became [x]her son. And she called his name Moses: and she said, Because I drew him out of the water.

11 ¶ And it came to pass in those days, [y]when Moses was grown, that he went out unto his brethren, and looked on their [z]burdens: and he spied an Egyptian smiting an Hebrew, one of his brethren.

12 And he looked this way and that way, and when he saw that *there was* no man, he [a]slew the Egyptian, and hid him in the sand.

13 And [b]when he went out the second day, behold, two men of the Hebrews strove together: and he said to him that did the wrong, Wherefore smitest thou thy fellow?

14 And he said, [c]Who made thee a prince and a judge over us? intendest thou to kill me, as thou killedst the Egyptian? And Moses feared, and said, Surely this thing is known.

15 Now when Pharaoh heard this thing, he sought to slay Moses. But [d]Moses fled from the face of Pharaoh, and dwelt in the land of Midian: and he sat down by [e]a well.

16 [f]Now the priest of Midian had seven daughters: [g]and they came and drew *water*, and filled the troughs to water their father's flock.

17 And the shepherds came and drove them away: but Moses stood up and helped them, and [h]watered their flock.

18 And when they came to [i]Reuel their father, he said, How *is it that* ye are come so soon to day?

19 And they said, An Egyptian delivered us out of the hand of the shepherds, and also drew *water* enough for us, and watered the flock.

20 And he said unto his daughters, And where *is* he? why *is* it *that* ye have left the man? call him, that he may [j]eat bread.

21 And Moses was content to dwell with the man: and he gave Moses [k]Zipporah his daughter.

22 And she bare *him* a son, and he called his name [l]Gershom: for he said, I have been [m]a stranger in a strange land.

23 ¶ And it came to pass [n]in process of time, that the king of Egypt died: and the children of Israel [o]sighed by reason of the bondage, and they cried, and [p]their cry came up unto God by reason of the bondage.

24 And God [q]heard their groaning, and God [r]remembered his [s]covenant with Abraham, with Isaac, and with Jacob.

25 And God [t]looked upon the children of Israel, and God [u]had respect unto *them*.

3 Now Moses kept the flock of Jethro his father in law, [v]the priest of Midian: and he led the flock to the backside of the desert, and came to [w]the mountain of God, *even* to Horeb.

2 And [x]the angel of the LORD appeared unto him in a flame of fire out of the midst of a bush: and he looked, and, behold, the bush burned with fire, and the bush *was* not consumed.

3 And Moses said, I will now turn aside, and see this [y]great sight, why the bush is not burnt.

4 And when the LORD saw that he turned aside to see, God called [z]unto him out of the midst of the bush, and said, Moses, Moses. And he said, Here *am* I.

5 And he said, Draw not nigh hither: [a]put off thy shoes from off thy feet, for the place whereon thou standest *is* holy ground.

6 Moreover he said, [b]I *am* the God of thy father, the God of Abraham, the God of Isaac, and the God of Jacob. And Moses hid his face; for [c]he was afraid to look upon God.

7 ¶ And the LORD said, I have surely seen the affliction of my people which *are* in Egypt, and [d]have heard their cry [e]by reason of their taskmasters; for [f]I know their sorrows;

8 And [g]I am come down to [h]deliver them out of the hand of the Egyptians, and to bring them up out of that land [i]unto a good land and a large, unto a land [j]flowing with milk and honey; unto the place of [k]the Canaanites, and the Hittites, and the Amorites, and the Perizzites, and the Hivites, and the Jebusites.

9 Now therefore, behold, [l]the cry of the children of Israel is come unto me: and I have also seen the [m]oppression wherewith the Egyptians oppress them.

10 [n]Come now therefore, and I will send thee unto Pharaoh, that thou mayest bring forth my people the children of Israel out of Egypt.

11 ¶ And Moses said unto God, [o]Who *am* I, that I should go unto Pharaoh, and that I should bring forth the children of Israel out of Egypt?

12 And he said, [p]Certainly I will be with thee; and this *shall be* a token unto thee, that I have sent thee: When thou hast brought forth the people out of Egypt, ye shall serve God upon this mountain.

13 And Moses said unto God, Behold, *when* I come unto the children of Israel, and shall say unto them, The God of your fathers hath sent me unto you; and they shall say to me, What *is* his name? what shall I say unto them?

14 And God said unto Moses, I AM THAT I AM: and he said, Thus shalt thou say unto

2:10 [x]Acts 7:21
2:11 [y]Acts 7:23; Heb. 11:24 [z]ch. 1:11
2:12 [a]Acts 7:24
2:13 [b]Acts 7:26
2:14 [c]Acts 7:27
2:15 [d]Acts 7:29; Heb. 11:27 [e]Gen. 24:11
2:16 [f]ch. 3:1 [g]Gen. 24:11; 1 Sam. 9:11
2:17 [h]Gen. 20:10
2:18 [i]ch. 3:1; Num. 10:29
2:20 [j]Gen. 31:54
2:21 [k]ch. 4:25
2:22 [l]ch. 18:3 [m]Acts 7:29; Heb. 11:13
2:23 [n]ch. 7:7; Acts 7:30 [o]Num. 20:16; Deut. 26:7; Ps. 12:5 [p]Gen. 18:20; ch. 3:9; Deut. 24:15; Jam. 5:4
2:24 [q]ch. 6:5 [r]ch. 6:5; Ps. 105:8 [s]Gen. 15:14
2:25 [t]ch. 4:31; 1 Sam. 1:11; 2 Sam. 16:12; Luke 1:25 [u]ch. 3:7
3:1 [v]ch. 2:16 [w]ch. 18:5; 1 Kings 19:8
3:2 [x]Deut. 33:16; Isa. 63:9; Acts 7:30
3:3 [y]Ps. 111:2; Acts 7:31
3:4 [z]Deut. 33:16
3:5 [a]ch. 19:12; Josh. 5:15; Acts 7:33
3:6 [b]Gen. 28:13; ver. 15; ch. 4:5; Matt. 22:32; Mark 12:26; Luke 20:37; Acts 7:32 [c]1 Kings 19:13; Isa. 6:1; Neh. 9:9; Ps. 106:44; Acts 7:34
3:7 [d]ch. 2:23 [e]ch. 1:11 [f]Gen. 18:21; ch. 2:25
3:8 [g]Gen. 11:5 [h]ch. 6:6 [i]Deut. 1:25 [j]ver. 17; ch. 13:5; Num. 13:27; Deut. 26:9; Jer. 11:5; Ezek. 20:6 [k]Gen. 15:18
3:9 [l]ch. 2:23 [m]ch. 1:11
3:10 [n]Ps. 105:26; Mic. 6:4
3:11 [o]ch. 6:12; 1 Sam. 18:18; Isa. 6:5; Jer. 1:6
3:12 [p]Gen. 31:3; Deut. 31:23; Josh. 1:5; Rom. 8:31

the children of Israel, [q]I AM hath sent me unto you.

15 And God said moreover unto Moses, Thus shalt thou say unto the children of Israel, The LORD God of your fathers, the God of Abraham, the God of Isaac, and the God of Jacob, hath sent me unto you: this *is* [r]my name for ever, and this *is* my memorial unto all generations.

16 Go, and [s]gather the elders of Israel together, and say unto them, The LORD God of your fathers, the God of Abraham, of Isaac, and of Jacob, appeared unto me, saying, [t]I have surely visited you, and *seen* that which is done to you in Egypt:

17 And I have said, [u]I will bring you up out of the affliction of Egypt unto the land of the Canaanites, and the Hittites, and the Amorites, and the Perizzites, and the Hivites, and the Jebusites, unto a land flowing with milk and honey.

18 And [v]they shall hearken to thy voice: and [w]thou shalt come, thou and the elders of Israel, unto the king of Egypt, and ye shall say unto him, The LORD God of the Hebrews hath [x]met with us: and now let us go, we beseech thee, three days' journey into the wilderness, that we may sacrifice to the LORD our God.

19 ¶ And I am sure that the king of Egypt [y]will not let you go, no, not by a mighty hand.

20 And I will [z]stretch out my hand, and smite Egypt with [a]all my wonders which I will do in the midst thereof: and [b]after that he will let you go.

21 And [c]I will give this people favour in the sight of the Egyptians: and it shall come to pass, that, when ye go, ye shall not go empty:

22 [d]But every woman shall borrow of her neighbour, and of her that sojourneth in her house, jewels of silver, and jewels of gold, and raiment: and ye shall put *them* upon your sons, and upon your daughters; and [e]ye shall spoil the Egyptians.

4

And Moses answered and said, But, behold, they will not believe me, nor hearken unto my voice: for they will say, The LORD hath not appeared unto thee.

2 And the LORD said unto him, What *is* that in thine hand? And he said, [f]A rod.

3 And he said, Cast it on the ground. And he cast it on the ground, and it became a serpent; and Moses fled from before it.

4 And the LORD said unto Moses, Put forth thine hand, and take it by the tail. And he put forth his hand, and caught it, and it became a rod in his hand:

5 That they may [g]believe that [h]the LORD God of their fathers, the God of Abraham, the God of Isaac, and the God of Jacob, hath appeared unto thee.

6 ¶ And the LORD said furthermore unto him, Put now thine hand into thy bosom. And he put his hand into his bosom: and when he took it out, behold, his hand *was* leprous [i]as snow.

7 And he said, Put thine hand into thy bosom again. And he put his hand into his bosom again; and plucked it out of his bosom, and, behold, [j]it was turned again as his *other* flesh.

8 And it shall come to pass, if they will not believe thee, neither hearken to the voice of the first sign, that they will believe the voice of the latter sign.

9 And it shall come to pass, if they will not believe also these two signs, neither hearken unto thy voice, that thou shalt take of the water of the river, and pour *it* upon the dry *land:* and [k]the water which thou takest out of the river shall become blood upon the dry *land.*

10 ¶ And Moses said unto the LORD, O my Lord, I *am* not eloquent, neither heretofore, nor since thou hast spoken unto thy servant: but [l]I *am* slow of speech, and of a slow tongue.

11 And the LORD said unto him, [m]Who hath made man's mouth? or who maketh the dumb, or deaf, or the seeing, or the blind? have not I the LORD?

12 Now therefore go, and I will be [n]with thy mouth, and teach thee what thou shalt say.

13 And he said, O my Lord, [o]send, I pray thee, by the hand *of him whom* thou wilt send.

14 And the anger of the LORD was kindled against Moses, and he said, *Is* not Aaron the Levite thy brother? I know that he can speak well. And also, behold, [p]he cometh forth to meet thee: and when he seeth thee, he will be glad in his heart.

15 And [q]thou shalt speak unto him, and [r]put words in his mouth: and I will be with thy mouth, and with his mouth, and [s]will teach you what ye shall do.

16 And he shall be thy spokesman unto the people: and he shall be, *even* he shall be to thee instead of a mouth, and [t]thou shalt be to him instead of God.

17 And thou shalt take [u]this rod in thine hand, wherewith thou shalt do signs.

18 ¶ And Moses went and returned to Jethro his father in law, and said unto him, Let me go, I pray thee, and return unto my brethren which *are* in Egypt, and see whether they be yet alive. And Jethro said to Moses, Go in peace.

19 And the LORD said unto Moses in Midian, Go, return into Egypt: for [v]all the men are dead which sought thy life.

20 And Moses took his wife and his sons, and set them upon an ass, and he returned to the land of Egypt: and Moses took [w]the rod of God in his hand.

21 And the LORD said unto Moses, When thou goest to return into Egypt, see that thou do all those [x]wonders before Pharaoh, which I have put in thine hand: but [y]I will harden his heart, that he shall not let the people go.

22 And thou shalt say unto Pharaoh, Thus

3:14 [q]ch. 6:3; John 8:58; 2 Cor. 1:20; Heb. 13:8; Rev. 1:4
3:15 [r]Ps. 135:13; Hos. 12:5
3:16 [s]ch. 4:29 [t]Gen. 50:24; ch. 2:25; Luke 1:68
3:17 [u]Gen. 15:14; ver. 8
3:18 [v]ch. 4:31 [w]ch. 5:1 [x]Num. 23:3
3:19 [y]ch. 5:2
3:20 [z]ch. 6:6 [a]ch. 7 to ch. 13; Deut. 6:22; Neh. 9:10; Ps. 105:27; Jer. 32:20; Acts 7:36 [b]ch. 12:31
3:21 [c]ch. 11:3; Ps. 106:46; Prov. 16:7
3:22 [d]Gen. 15:14; ch. 11:2 [e]Job 27:17; Prov. 13:22; Ezek. 39:10
4:2 [f]ver. 17
4:5 [g]ch. 19:9 [h]ch. 3:15
4:6 [i]Num. 12:10; 2 Kings 5:27
4:7 [j]Deut. 32:39; Num. 12:13; 2 Kings 5:14; Matt. 8:3
4:9 [k]ch. 7:19
4:10 [l]ch. 6:12; Jer. 1:6
4:11 [m]Ps. 94:9
4:12 [n]Isa. 50:4; Jer. 1:9; Matt. 10:19; Mark 13:11; Luke 12:11
4:13 [o]Jonah 1:3
4:14 [p]ver. 27; 1 Sam. 10:2
4:15 [q]ch. 7:1 [r]Num. 22:38; Deut. 18:18; Isa. 51:16; Jer. 1:9 [s]Deut. 5:31
4:16 [t]ch. 7:1
4:17 [u]ver. 2
4:19 [v]ch. 2:15; Matt. 2:20
4:20 [w]ch. 17:9; Num. 20:8
4:21 [x]ch. 3:20 [y]ch. 7:3; Deut. 2:30; Josh. 11:20; Isa. 63:17; John 12:40; Rom. 9:18

saith the LORD, [z]Israel *is* my son, [a]*even* my firstborn:

23 And I say unto thee, Let my son go, that he may serve me: and if thou refuse to let him go, behold, [b]I will slay thy son, *even* thy firstborn.

24 ¶ And it came to pass by the way in the inn, that the LORD [c]met him, and sought to [d]kill him.

25 Then Zipporah took [e]a sharp stone, and cut off the foreskin of her son, and cast *it* at his feet, and said, Surely a bloody husband *art* thou to me.

26 So he let him go: then she said, A bloody husband *thou art,* because of the circumcision.

27 ¶ And the LORD said to Aaron, Go into the wilderness [f]to meet Moses. And he went, and met him in [g]the mount of God, and kissed him.

28 And Moses [h]told Aaron all the words of the LORD who had sent him, and all the [i]signs which he had commanded him.

29 ¶ And Moses and Aaron [j]went and gathered together all the elders of the children of Israel:

30 [k]And Aaron spake all the words which the LORD had spoken unto Moses, and did the signs in the sight of the people.

31 And the people [l]believed: and when they heard that the LORD had [m]visited the children of Israel, and that he [n]had looked upon their affliction, then [o]they bowed their heads and worshipped.

5 And afterward Moses and Aaron went in, and told Pharaoh, Thus saith the LORD God of Israel, Let my people go, that they may hold [p]a feast unto me in the wilderness.

2 And Pharaoh said, [q]Who *is* the LORD, that I should obey his voice to let Israel go? I know not the LORD, [r]neither will I let Israel go.

3 And they said, [s]The God of the Hebrews hath met with us: let us go, we pray thee, three days' journey into the desert, and sacrifice unto the LORD our God; lest he fall upon us with pestilence, or with the sword.

4 And the king of Egypt said unto them, Wherefore do ye, Moses and Aaron, let the people from their works? get you unto your [t]burdens.

5 And Pharaoh said, Behold, the people of the land now *are* [u]many, and ye make them rest from their burdens.

6 And Pharaoh commanded the same day the [v]taskmasters of the people, and their officers, saying,

7 Ye shall no more give the people straw to make brick, as heretofore: let them go and gather straw for themselves.

8 And the tale of the bricks, which they did make heretofore, ye shall lay upon them; ye shall not diminish *ought* thereof: for they *be* idle; therefore they cry, saying, Let us go *and* sacrifice to our God.

9 Let there more work be laid upon the men, that they may labour therein; and let them not regard vain words.

10 ¶ And the taskmasters of the people went out, and their officers, and they spake to the people, saying, Thus saith Pharaoh, I will not give you straw.

11 Go ye, get you straw where ye can find it: yet not ought of your work shall be diminished.

12 So the people were scattered abroad throughout all the land of Egypt to gather stubble instead of straw.

13 And the taskmasters hasted *them,* saying, Fulfil your works, *your* daily tasks, as when there was straw.

14 And the officers of the children of Israel, which Pharaoh's taskmasters had set over them, were beaten, *and* demanded, Wherefore have ye not fulfilled your task in making brick both yesterday and to day, as heretofore?

15 ¶ Then the officers of the children of Israel came and cried unto Pharaoh, saying, Wherefore dealest thou thus with thy servants?

16 There is no straw given unto thy servants, and they say to us, Make brick: and, behold, thy servants *are* beaten; but the fault *is* in thine own people.

17 But he said, Ye *are* idle, *ye are* idle: therefore ye say, Let us go *and* do sacrifice to the LORD.

18 Go therefore now, *and* work; for there shall no straw be given you, yet shall ye deliver the tale of bricks.

19 And the officers of the children of Israel did see *that* they *were* in evil *case,* after it was said, Ye shall not minish *ought* from your bricks of your daily task.

20 ¶ And they met Moses and Aaron, who stood in the way, as they came forth from Pharaoh:

21 [w]And they said unto them, The LORD look upon you, and judge; because ye have made our savour to be abhorred in the eyes of Pharaoh, and in the eyes of his servants, to put a sword in their hand to slay us.

22 And Moses returned unto the LORD, and said, Lord, wherefore hast thou *so* evil entreated this people? why *is* it *that* thou hast sent me?

23 For since I came to Pharaoh to speak in thy name, he hath done evil to this people; neither hast thou delivered thy people at all.

6 Then the LORD said unto Moses, Now shalt thou see what I will do to Pharaoh: for [x]with a strong hand shall he let them go, and with a strong hand [y]shall he drive them out of his land.

2 And God spake unto Moses, and said unto him, I *am* the LORD:

3 And I appeared unto Abraham, unto Isaac, and unto Jacob, by *the name of* [z]God Almighty, but by my name [a]JEHOVAH was I not known to them.

4 [b]And I have also established my covenant with them, [c]to give them the land

4:22 [z]Hos. 11:1; Rom. 9:4; 2 Cor. 6:18 [a]Jer. 31:9; Jam. 1:18
4:23 [b]ch. 11:5
4:24 [c]Num. 22:22 [d]Gen. 17:14
4:25 [e]Josh. 5:2
4:27 [f]ver. 14 [g]ch. 3:1
4:28 [h]ver. 15 [i]ver. 8
4:29 [j]ch. 3:16
4:30 [k]ver. 16
4:31 [l]ch. 3:18; ver. 8 [m]ch. 3:16 [n]ch. 2:25 [o]Gen. 24:26; ch. 12:27; 1 Chron. 29:20
5:1 [p]ch. 10:9
5:2 [q]2 Kings 18:35; Job 21:15 [r]ch. 3:19
5:3 [s]ch. 3:18
5:4 [t]ch. 1:11
5:5 [u]ch. 1:7
5:6 [v]ch. 1:11
5:21 [w]ch. 6:9
6:1 [x]ch. 3:19 [y]ch. 11:1
6:3 [z]Gen. 17:1 [a]ch. 3:14; Ps. 68:4; John 8:58; Rev. 1:4
6:4 [b]Gen. 15:18 [c]Gen. 17:8

of Canaan, the land of their pilgrimage, wherein they were strangers.

5 And [d]I have also heard the groaning of the children of Israel, whom the Egyptians keep in bondage; and I have remembered my covenant.

6 Wherefore say unto the children of Israel, [e]I *am* the LORD, and [f]I will bring you out from under the burdens of the Egyptians, and I will rid you out of their bondage, and I will [g]redeem you with a stretched out arm, and with great judgments:

7 And I will [h]take you to me for a people, and [i]I will be to you a God: and ye shall know that I *am* the LORD your God, which bringeth you out [j]from under the burdens of the Egyptians.

8 And I will bring you in unto the land, concerning the which I did [k]swear to give it to Abraham, to Isaac, and to Jacob; and I will give it you for an heritage: I *am* the LORD.

9 ¶ And Moses spake so unto the children of Israel: [l]but they hearkened not unto Moses for anguish of spirit, and for cruel bondage.

10 And the LORD spake unto Moses, saying,

11 Go in, speak unto Pharaoh king of Egypt, that he let the children of Israel go out of his land.

12 And Moses spake before the LORD, saying, Behold, the children of Israel have [m]not hearkened unto me; how then shall Pharaoh hear me, [n]who *am* of uncircumcised lips?

13 And the LORD spake unto Moses and unto Aaron, and gave them a charge unto the children of Israel, and unto Pharaoh king of Egypt, to bring the children of Israel out of the land of Egypt.

14 ¶ These *be* the heads of their fathers' houses: [o]The sons of Reuben the firstborn of Israel; Hanoch, and Pallu, Hezron, and Carmi: these *be* the families of Reuben.

15 [p]And the sons of Simeon; Jemuel, and Jamin, and Ohad, and Jachin, and Zohar, and Shaul the son of a Canaanitish woman: these *are* the families of Simeon.

16 ¶ And these *are* the names of [q]the sons of Levi according to their generations; Gershon, and Kohath, and Merari: and the years of the life of Levi *were* an hundred thirty and seven years.

17 [r]The sons of Gershon; Libni, and Shimi, according to their families.

18 And [s]the sons of Kohath; Amram, and Izhar, and Hebron, and Uzziel: and the years of the life of Kohath *were* an hundred thirty and three years.

19 And [t]the sons of Merari; Mahali and Mushi: these *are* the families of Levi according to their generations.

20 And [u]Amram took him Jochebed his father's sister to wife; and she bare him Aaron and Moses: and the years of the life of Amram *were* an hundred and thirty and seven years.

21 ¶ And [v]the sons of Izhar; Korah, and Nepheg, and Zichri.

22 And the [w]sons of Uzziel; Mishael, and Elzaphan, and Zithri.

23 And Aaron took him Elisheba, daughter of [x]Amminadab, sister of Naashon, to wife; and she bare him [y]Nadab, and Abihu, Eleazar, and Ithamar.

24 And the [z]sons of Korah; Assir, and Elkanah, and Abiasaph: these *are* the families of the Korhites.

25 And Eleazar Aaron's son took him *one* of the daughters of Putiel to wife; and [a]she bare him Phinehas: these *are* the heads of the fathers of the Levites according to their families.

26 These *are* that Aaron and Moses, [b]to whom the LORD said, Bring out the children of Israel from the land of Egypt according to their [c]armies.

27 These *are* they which [d]spake to Pharaoh king of Egypt, [e]to bring out the children of Israel from Egypt: these *are* that Moses and Aaron.

28 ¶ And it came to pass on the day *when* the LORD spake unto Moses in the land of Egypt,

29 That the LORD spake unto Moses, saying, [f]I *am* the LORD: [g]speak thou unto Pharaoh king of Egypt all that I say unto thee.

30 And Moses said before the LORD, Behold, [h]I *am* of uncircumcised lips, and how shall Pharaoh hearken unto me?

7 And the LORD said unto Moses, See, I have made thee [i]a god to Pharaoh: and Aaron thy brother shall be [j]thy prophet.

2 Thou [k]shalt speak all that I command thee: and Aaron thy brother shall speak unto Pharaoh, that he send the children of Israel out of his land.

3 And [l]I will harden Pharaoh's heart, and [m]multiply my [n]signs and my wonders in the land of Egypt.

4 But Pharaoh shall not hearken unto you, [o]that I may lay my hand upon Egypt, and bring forth mine armies, *and* my people the children of Israel, out of the land of Egypt [p]by great judgments.

5 And the Egyptians [q]shall know that I *am* the LORD, when I [r]stretch forth mine hand upon Egypt, and bring out the children of Israel from among them.

6 And Moses and Aaron [s]did as the LORD commanded them, so did they.

7 And Moses *was* [t]fourscore years old, and Aaron fourscore and three years old, when they spake unto Pharaoh.

8 ¶ And the LORD spake unto Moses and unto Aaron, saying,

9 When Pharaoh shall speak unto you, saying, [u]Shew a miracle for you: then thou shalt say unto Aaron, [v]Take thy rod, and cast *it* before Pharaoh, *and* it shall become a serpent.

10 ¶ And Moses and Aaron went in unto Pharaoh, and they did so [w]as the LORD had commanded: and Aaron cast down his rod

6:5 [d]ch. 2:24
6:6 [e]ver. 2 [f]ch. 3:17; Deut. 26:8; Ps. 81:6 [g]ch. 15:13; Deut. 7:8; 1 Chron. 17:21; Neh. 1:10
6:7 [h]Deut. 4:20; 2 Sam. 7:24 [i]Gen. 17:7; ch. 29:45; Deut. 29:13; Rev. 21:7 [j]ch. 5:4; Ps. 81:6
6:8 [k]Gen. 15:18
6:9 [l]ch. 5:21
6:12 [m]ver. 9 [n]ver. 30; ch. 4:10; Jer. 1:6
6:14 [o]Gen. 46:9; 1 Chron. 5:3
6:15 [p]1 Chron. 4:24; Gen. 46:10
6:16 [q]Gen. 46:11; Num. 3:17; 1 Chron. 6:1
6:17 [r]1 Chron. 6:17
6:18 [s]Num. 26:57; 1 Chron. 6:2
6:19 [t]1 Chron. 6:19
6:20 [u]ch. 2:1; Num. 26:59
6:21 [v]Num. 16:1; 1 Chron. 6:37
6:22 [w]Lev. 10:4; Num. 3:30
6:23 [x]Ruth 4:19; 1 Chron. 2:10; Matt. 1:4 [y]Lev. 10:1; Num. 3:2; 1 Chron. 6:3
6:24 [z]Num. 26:11
6:25 [a]Num. 25:7; Josh. 24:33
6:26 [b]ver. 13 [c]ch. 7:4; Num. 33:1
6:27 [d]ch. 5:1 [e]ver. 13; ch. 32:7; Ps. 77:20
6:29 [f]ver. 2 [g]ver. 11; ch. 7:2
6:30 [h]ver. 12; ch. 4:10
7:1 [i]ch. 4:16; Jer. 1:10 [j]ch. 4:16
7:2 [k]ch. 4:15
7:3 [l]ch. 4:21 [m]ch. 11:9 [n]ch. 4:7
7:4 [o]ch. 10:1 [p]ch. 6:6
7:5 [q]ver. 17; ch. 8:22; Ps. 9:16 [r]ch. 3:20
7:6 [s]ver. 2
7:7 [t]Deut. 29:5; Acts 7:23
7:9 [u]Isa. 7:11; John 2:18 [v]ch. 4:2
7:10 [w]ver. 9

before Pharaoh, and before his servants, and it [x]became a serpent.

11 Then Pharaoh also [y]called the wise men and [z]the sorcerers: now the magicians of Egypt, they also [a]did in like manner with their enchantments.

12 For they cast down every man his rod, and they became serpents: but Aaron's rod swallowed up their rods.

13 And he hardened Pharaoh's heart, that he hearkened not unto them; [b]as the LORD had said.

14 ¶ And the LORD said unto Moses, [c]Pharaoh's heart *is* hardened, he refuseth to let the people go.

15 Get thee unto Pharaoh in the morning; lo, he goeth out unto the water; and thou shalt stand by the river's brink against he come; and [d]the rod which was turned to a serpent shalt thou take in thine hand.

16 And thou shalt say unto him, [e]The LORD God of the Hebrews hath sent me unto thee, saying, Let my people go, [f]that they may serve me in the wilderness: and, behold, hitherto thou wouldest not hear.

17 Thus saith the LORD, In this [g]thou shalt know that I *am* the LORD: behold, I will smite with the rod that *is* in mine hand upon the waters which *are* in the river, and [h]they shall be turned [i]to blood.

18 And the fish that *is* in the river shall die, and the river shall stink; and the Egyptians shall [j]lothe to drink of the water of the river.

19 ¶ And the LORD spake unto Moses, Say unto Aaron, Take thy rod, and [k]stretch out thine hand upon the waters of Egypt, upon their streams, upon their rivers, and upon their ponds, and upon all their pools of water, that they may become blood; and *that* there may be blood throughout all the land of Egypt, both in *vessels of* wood, and in *vessels of* stone.

20 And Moses and Aaron did so, as the LORD commanded; and he [l]lifted up the rod, and smote the waters that *were* in the river, in the sight of Pharaoh, and in the sight of his servants; and all the [m]waters that *were* in the river were turned to blood.

21 And the fish that *was* in the river died; and the river stank, and the Egyptians [n]could not drink of the water of the river; and there was blood throughout all the land of Egypt.

22 [o]And the magicians of Egypt did so with their enchantments: and Pharaoh's heart was hardened, neither did he hearken unto them; [p]as the LORD had said.

23 And Pharaoh turned and went into his house, neither did he set his heart to this also.

24 And all the Egyptians digged round about the river for water to drink; for they could not drink of the water of the river.

25 And seven days were fulfilled, after that the LORD had smitten the river.

8 And the LORD spake unto Moses, Go unto Pharaoh, and say unto him, Thus saith the LORD, Let my people go, [q]that they may serve me.

2 And if thou [r]refuse to let *them* go, behold, I will smite all thy borders with [s]frogs:

3 And the river shall bring forth frogs abundantly, which shall go up and come into thine house, and into [t]thy bedchamber, and upon thy bed, and into the house of thy servants, and upon thy people, and into thine ovens, and into thy kneadingtroughs:

4 And the frogs shall come up both on thee, and upon thy people, and upon all thy servants.

5 ¶ And the LORD spake unto Moses, Say unto Aaron, [u]Stretch forth thine hand with thy rod over the streams, over the rivers, and over the ponds, and cause frogs to come up upon the land of Egypt.

6 And Aaron stretched out his hand over the waters of Egypt; and [v]the frogs came up, and covered the land of Egypt.

7 [w]And the magicians did so with their enchantments, and brought up frogs upon the land of Egypt.

8 ¶ Then Pharaoh called for Moses and Aaron, and said, [x]Intreat the LORD, that he may take away the frogs from me, and from my people; and I will let the people go, that they may do sacrifice unto the LORD.

9 And Moses said unto Pharaoh, Glory over me: when shall I intreat for thee, and for thy servants, and for thy people, to destroy the frogs from thee and thy houses, *that* they may remain in the river only?

10 And he said, To morrow. And he said, *Be it* according to thy word: that thou mayest know that [y]*there is* none like unto the LORD our God.

11 And the frogs shall depart from thee, and from thy houses, and from thy servants, and from thy people; they shall remain in the river only.

12 And Moses and Aaron went out from Pharaoh: and Moses [z]cried unto the LORD because of the frogs which he had brought against Pharaoh.

13 And the LORD did according to the word of Moses; and the frogs died out of the houses, out of the villages, and out of the fields.

14 And they gathered them together upon heaps: and the land stank.

15 But when Pharaoh saw that there was [a]respite, [b]he hardened his heart, and hearkened not unto them; as the LORD had said.

16 ¶ And the LORD said unto Moses, Say unto Aaron, Stretch out thy rod, and smite the dust of the land, that it may become lice throughout all the land of Egypt.

17 And they did so; for Aaron stretched out his hand with his rod, and smote the dust of the earth, and [c]it became lice in man, and in beast; all the dust of the land became lice throughout all the land of Egypt.

18 And [d]the magicians did so with their

7:10 [x]ch. 4:3
7:11 [y]Gen. 41:8 [z]2 Tim. 3:8 [a]ver. 22; ch. 8:7
7:13 [b]ch. 4:21; ver. 4
7:14 [c]ch. 8:15
7:15 [d]ch. 4:2
7:16 [e]ch. 3:18 [f]ch. 3:12
7:17 [g]ch. 5:2; ver. 5 [h]ch. 4:9 [i]Rev. 16:4
7:18 [j]ver. 24
7:19 [k]ch. 8:5
7:20 [l]ch. 17:5 [m]Ps. 78:44
7:21 [n]ver. 18
7:22 [o]ver. 11 [p]ver. 3
8:1 [q]ch. 3:12
8:2 [r]ch. 7:14 [s]Rev. 16:13
8:3 [t]Ps. 105:30
8:5 [u]ch. 7:19
8:6 [v]Ps. 78:45
8:7 [w]ch. 7:11
8:8 [x]ch. 9:28; Num. 21:7; 1 Kings 13:6; Acts 8:24
8:10 [y]ch. 9:14; Deut. 33:26; 2 Sam. 7:22; 1 Chron. 17:20; Ps. 86:8; Isa. 46:9; Jer. 10:6
8:12 [z]ver. 30; ch. 9:33; Jam. 5:16
8:15 [a]Eccl. 8:11 [b]ch. 7:14
8:17 [c]Ps. 105:31
8:18 [d]ch. 7:11

enchantments to bring forth lice, but they
[e]could not: so there were lice upon man,
and upon beast.
19 Then the magicians said unto Pharaoh, This *is* [f]the finger of God: and Pharaoh's [g]heart was hardened, and he
hearkened not unto them; as the LORD had
said.
20 ¶ And the LORD said unto Moses,
[h]Rise up early in the morning, and stand
before Pharaoh; lo, he cometh forth to the
water; and say unto him, Thus saith the
LORD, [i]Let my people go, that they may
serve me.
21 Else, if thou wilt not let my people go,
behold, I will send swarms *of flies* upon
thee, and upon thy servants, and upon thy
people, and into thy houses: and the houses
of the Egyptians shall be full of swarms *of
flies,* and also the ground whereon they *are.*
22 And [j]I will sever in that day the land
of Goshen, in which my people dwell, that
no swarms *of flies* shall be there; to the end
thou mayest know that I *am* the LORD in the
midst of the earth.
23 And I will put a division between my
people and thy people: to morrow shall this
sign be.
24 And the LORD did so; and [k]there came
a grievous swarm *of flies* into the house of
Pharaoh, and *into* his servants' houses, and
into all the land of Egypt: the land was corrupted by reason of the swarm *of flies.*
25 ¶ And Pharaoh called for Moses and
for Aaron, and said, Go ye, sacrifice to your
God in the land.
26 And Moses said, It is not meet so to do;
for we shall sacrifice [l]the abomination of
the Egyptians to the LORD our God: lo, shall
we sacrifice the abomination of the Egyptians before their eyes, and will they not
stone us?
27 We will go [m]three days' journey into
the wilderness, and sacrifice to the LORD
our God, as [n]he shall command us.
28 And Pharaoh said, I will let you go,
that ye may sacrifice to the LORD your God
in the wilderness; only ye shall not go very
far away: [o]intreat for me.
29 And Moses said, Behold, I go out from
thee, and I will intreat the LORD that the
swarms *of flies* may depart from Pharaoh,
from his servants, and from his people, to
morrow: but let not Pharaoh [p]deal deceitfully any more in not letting the people go to
sacrifice to the LORD.
30 And Moses went out from Pharaoh,
and [q]intreated the LORD.
31 And the LORD did according to the
word of Moses; and he removed the swarms
of flies from Pharaoh, from his servants,
and from his people; there remained not
one.
32 And Pharaoh [r]hardened his heart at
this time also, neither would he let the people go.
9 Then the LORD said unto Moses, [s]Go in
unto Pharaoh, and tell him, Thus saith
the LORD God of the Hebrews, Let my people go, that they may serve me.
2 For if thou [t]refuse to let *them* go, and
wilt hold them still,
3 Behold, the [u]hand of the LORD is upon
thy cattle which *is* in the field, upon the
horses, upon the asses, upon the camels,
upon the oxen, and upon the sheep: *there
shall be* a very grievous murrain.
4 And [v]the LORD shall sever between the
cattle of Israel and the cattle of Egypt: and
there shall nothing die of all *that is* the children's of Israel.
5 And the LORD appointed a set time, saying, To morrow the LORD shall do this thing
in the land.
6 And the LORD did that thing on the morrow, and [w]all the cattle of Egypt died: but of
the cattle of the children of Israel died not
one.
7 And Pharaoh sent, and, behold, there
was not one of the cattle of the Israelites
dead. And [x]the heart of Pharaoh was hardened, and he did not let the people go.
8 ¶ And the LORD said unto Moses and
unto Aaron, Take to you handfuls of ashes
of the furnace, and let Moses sprinkle it toward the heaven in the sight of Pharaoh.
9 And it shall become small dust in all the
land of Egypt, and shall be [y]a boil breaking
forth *with* blains upon man, and upon
beast, throughout all the land of Egypt.
10 And they took ashes of the furnace,
and stood before Pharaoh; and Moses sprinkled it up toward heaven; and it became [z]a
boil breaking forth *with* blains upon man,
and upon beast.
11 And the [a]magicians could not stand
before Moses because of the boils; for the
boil was upon the magicians, and upon all
the Egyptians.
12 And the LORD hardened the heart of
Pharaoh, and he hearkened not unto them;
[b]as the LORD had spoken unto Moses.
13 ¶ And the LORD said unto Moses,
[c]Rise up early in the morning, and stand
before Pharaoh, and say unto him, Thus
saith the LORD God of the Hebrews, Let my
people go, that they may serve me.
14 For I will at this time send all my
plagues upon thine heart, and upon thy servants, and upon thy people; [d]that thou
mayest know that *there is* none like me in
all the earth.
15 For now I will [e]stretch out my hand,
that I may smite thee and thy people with
pestilence; and thou shalt be cut off from
the earth.
16 And in very deed for [f]this *cause* have
I raised thee up, for to shew *in* thee my
power; and that my name may be declared
throughout all the earth.
17 As yet exaltest thou thyself against my
people, that thou wilt not let them go?
18 Behold, to morrow about this time I
will cause it to rain a very grievous hail,
such as hath not been in Egypt since the
foundation thereof even until now.

8:18 [e]Luke 10:18; 2 Tim. 3:8
8:19 [f]1 Sam. 6:3; Ps. 8:3; Matt. 12:28; Luke 11:20 [g]ver. 15
8:20 [h]ch. 7:15 [i]ver. 1
8:22 [j]ch. 9:4
8:24 [k]Ps. 78:45
8:26 [l]Gen. 43:32; Deut. 7:25
8:27 [m]ch. 3:18 [n]ch. 3:12
8:28 [o]ver. 8; ch. 9:28; 1 Kings 13:6
8:29 [p]ver. 15
8:30 [q]ver. 12
8:32 [r]ver. 15; ch. 4:21
9:1 [s]ch. 8:1
9:2 [t]ch. 8:2
9:3 [u]ch. 7:4
9:4 [v]ch. 8:22
9:6 [w]Ps. 78:50
9:7 [x]ch. 7:14
9:9 [y]Rev. 16:2
9:10 [z]Deut. 28:27
9:11 [a]ch. 8:18; 2 Tim. 3:9
9:12 [b]ch. 4:21
9:13 [c]ch. 8:20
9:14 [d]ch. 8:10
9:15 [e]ch. 3:20
9:16 [f]ch. 14:17; Prov. 16:4; Rom. 9:17; 1 Pet. 2:9

19 Send therefore now, *and* gather thy
cattle, and all that thou hast in the field; *for*
upon every man and beast which shall be
found in the field, and shall not be brought
home, the hail shall come down upon them,
and they shall die.
20 He that feared the word of the LORD
among the servants of Pharaoh made his
servants and his cattle flee into the houses:
21 And he that regarded not the word of
the LORD left his servants and his cattle in
the field.
22 ¶ And the LORD said unto Moses,
Stretch forth thine hand toward heaven,
that there may be [g]hail in all the land of
Egypt, upon man, and upon beast, and upon
every herb of the field, throughout the land
of Egypt.
23 And Moses stretched forth his rod toward heaven: and [h]the LORD sent thunder
and hail, and the fire ran along upon the
ground; and the LORD rained hail upon the
land of Egypt.
24 So there was hail, and fire mingled
with the hail, very grievous, such as there
was none like it in all the land of Egypt
since it became a nation.
25 And the hail smote throughout all the
land of Egypt all that *was* in the field, both
man and beast; and the hail [i]smote every
herb of the field, and brake every tree of the
field.
26 [j]Only in the land of Goshen, where
the children of Israel *were,* was there no
hail.
27 ¶ And Pharaoh sent, and called for
Moses and Aaron, and said unto them, [k]I
have sinned this time: [l]the LORD *is* righteous, and I and my people *are* wicked.
28 [m]Intreat the LORD (for *it is* enough)
that there be no *more* mighty thunderings
and hail; and I will let you go, and ye shall
stay no longer.
29 And Moses said unto him, As soon as
I am gone out of the city, I will [n]spread
abroad my hands unto the LORD; *and* the
thunder shall cease, neither shall there be
any more hail; that thou mayest know how
that the [o]earth *is* the LORD's.
30 But as for thee and thy servants, [p]I
know that ye will not yet fear the LORD God.
31 And the flax and the barley was smitten: [q]for the barley *was* in the ear, and the
flax *was* bolled.
32 But the wheat and the rie were not
smitten: for they *were* not grown up.
33 And Moses went out of the city from
Pharaoh, and [r]spread abroad his hands
unto the LORD: and the thunders and hail
ceased, and the rain was not poured upon
the earth.
34 And when Pharaoh saw that the rain
and the hail and the thunders were ceased,
he sinned yet more, and hardened his heart,
he and his servants.
35 And [s]the heart of Pharaoh was hardened, neither would he let the children of
Israel go; as the LORD had spoken by Moses.

9:22 *g*Rev. 16:21
9:23 *h*Josh. 10:11; Ps. 18:13; Isa. 30:30; Ezek. 38:22; Rev. 8:7
9:25 *i*Ps. 105:33
9:26 *j*ch. 8:22; Isa. 32:18
9:27 *k*ch. 10:16 *l*2 Chron. 12:6; Ps. 129:4; Lam. 1:18; Dan. 9:14
9:28 *m*ch. 8:8; Acts 8:24
9:29 *n*1 Kings 8:22; Ps. 143:6; Isa. 1:15 *o*Ps. 24:1; 1 Cor. 10:26
9:30 *p*Isa. 26:10
9:31 *q*Ruth 1:22
9:33 *r*ver. 29; ch. 8:12
9:35 *s*ch. 4:21
10:1 *t*ch. 4:21 *u*ch. 7:4
10:2 *v*Deut. 4:9; Ps. 44:1; Joel 1:3
10:3 *w*1 Kings 21:29; 2 Chron. 7:14; Job 42:6; Jer. 13:18; Jam. 4:10; 1 Pet. 5:6
10:4 *x*Prov. 30:27; Rev. 9:3
10:5 *y*ch. 9:32; Joel 1:4
10:6 *z*ch. 8:3
10:7 *a*ch. 23:33; Josh. 23:13; 1 Sam. 18:21; Eccl. 7:26; 1 Cor. 7:35
10:9 *b*ch. 5:1
10:12 *c*ch. 7:19 *d*ver. 4
10:14 *e*Ps. 78:46 *f*Joel 2:2

10 And the LORD said unto Moses, Go in
unto Pharaoh: [t]for I have hardened
his heart, and the heart of his servants,
[u]that I might shew these my signs before
him:
2 And that [v]thou mayest tell in the ears of
thy son, and of thy son's son, what things I
have wrought in Egypt, and my signs which
I have done among them; that ye may know
how that I *am* the LORD.
3 And Moses and Aaron came in unto
Pharaoh, and said unto him, Thus saith the
LORD God of the Hebrews, How long wilt
thou refuse to [w]humble thyself before me?
let my people go, that they may serve me.
4 Else, if thou refuse to let my people go,
behold, to morrow will I bring the [x]locusts
into thy coast:
5 And they shall cover the face of the
earth, that one cannot be able to see the
earth: and [y]they shall eat the residue of that
which is escaped, which remaineth unto
you from the hail, and shall eat every tree
which groweth for you out of the field:
6 And they [z]shall fill thy houses, and the
houses of all thy servants, and the houses of
all the Egyptians; which neither thy fathers,
nor thy fathers' fathers have seen, since the
day that they were upon the earth unto this
day. And he turned himself, and went out
from Pharaoh.
7 And Pharaoh's servants said unto him,
How long shall this man be [a]a snare unto
us? let the men go, that they may serve the
LORD their God: knowest thou not yet that
Egypt is destroyed?
8 And Moses and Aaron were brought
again unto Pharaoh: and he said unto them,
Go, serve the LORD your God: *but* who *are*
they that shall go?
9 And Moses said, We will go with our
young and with our old, with our sons and
with our daughters, with our flocks and
with our herds will we go; for [b]we *must*
hold a feast unto the LORD.
10 And he said unto them, Let the LORD
be so with you, as I will let you go, and your
little ones: look *to it;* for evil *is* before you.
11 Not so: go now ye *that are* men, and
serve the LORD; for that ye did desire. And
they were driven out from Pharaoh's presence.
12 ¶ And the LORD said unto Moses,
[c]Stretch out thine hand over the land of
Egypt for the locusts, that they may come
up upon the land of Egypt, and [d]eat every
herb of the land, *even* all that the hail hath
left.
13 And Moses stretched forth his rod over
the land of Egypt, and the LORD brought an
east wind upon the land all that day, and all
that night; *and* when it was morning, the
east wind brought the locusts.
14 And [e]the locusts went up over all the
land of Egypt, and rested in all the coasts of
Egypt: very grievous *were they;* [f]before
them there were no such locusts as they,
neither after them shall be such.

15 For they [g]covered the face of the whole earth, so that the land was darkened; and they [h]did eat every herb of the land, and all the fruit of the trees which the hail had left: and there remained not any green thing in the trees, or in the herbs of the field, through all the land of Egypt.

16 ¶ Then Pharaoh called for Moses and Aaron in haste; and he said, [i]I have sinned against the LORD your God, and against you.

17 Now therefore forgive, I pray thee, my sin only this once, and [j]intreat the LORD your God, that he may take away from me this death only.

18 And he [k]went out from Pharaoh, and intreated the LORD.

19 And the LORD turned a mighty strong west wind, which took away the locusts, and cast them [l]into the Red sea; there remained not one locust in all the coasts of Egypt.

20 But the LORD [m]hardened Pharaoh's heart, so that he would not let the children of Israel go.

21 ¶ And the LORD said unto Moses, [n]Stretch out thine hand toward heaven, that there may be darkness over the land of Egypt, even darkness *which* may be felt.

22 And Moses stretched forth his hand toward heaven; and there was a [o]thick darkness in all the land of Egypt three days:

23 They saw not one another, neither rose any from his place for three days: [p]but all the children of Israel had light in their dwellings.

24 ¶ And Pharaoh called unto Moses, and [q]said, Go ye, serve the LORD; only let your flocks and your herds be stayed: let your [r]little ones also go with you.

25 And Moses said, Thou must give us also sacrifices and burnt offerings, that we may sacrifice unto the LORD our God.

26 Our cattle also shall go with us; there shall not an hoof be left behind; for thereof must we take to serve the LORD our God; and we know not with what we must serve the LORD, until we come thither.

27 ¶ But the LORD [s]hardened Pharaoh's heart, and he would not let them go.

28 And Pharaoh said unto him, Get thee from me, take heed to thyself, see my face no more; for in *that* day thou seest my face thou shalt die.

29 And Moses said, Thou hast spoken well, [t]I will see thy face again no more.

11 And the LORD said unto Moses, Yet will I bring one plague *more* upon Pharaoh, and upon Egypt; afterwards he will let you go hence: [u]when he shall let *you* go, he shall surely thrust you out hence altogether.

2 Speak now in the ears of the people, and let every man borrow of his neighbour, and every woman of her neighbour, [v]jewels of silver, and jewels of gold.

3 [w]And the LORD gave the people favour in the sight of the Egyptians. Moreover, the man [x]Moses *was* very great in the land of Egypt, in the sight of Pharaoh's servants, and in the sight of the people.

4 And Moses said, Thus saith the LORD, [y]About midnight will I go out into the midst of Egypt:

5 And [z]all the firstborn in the land of Egypt shall die, from the firstborn of Pharaoh that sitteth upon his throne, even unto the firstborn of the maidservant that *is* behind the mill; and all the firstborn of beasts.

6 [a]And there shall be a great cry throughout all the land of Egypt, such as there was none like it, nor shall be like it any more.

7 [b]But against any of the children of Israel [c]shall not a dog move his tongue, against man or beast: that ye may know how that the LORD doth put a difference between the Egyptians and Israel.

8 And [d]all these thy servants shall come down unto me, and bow down themselves unto me, saying, Get thee out, and all the people that follow thee: and after that I will go out. And he went out from Pharaoh in a great anger.

9 And the LORD said unto Moses, [e]Pharaoh shall not hearken unto you; that [f]my wonders may be multiplied in the land of Egypt.

10 And Moses and Aaron did all these wonders before Pharaoh: [g]and the LORD hardened Pharaoh's heart, so that he would not let the children of Israel go out of his land.

12 And the LORD spake unto Moses and Aaron in the land of Egypt, saying,

2 [h]This month *shall be* unto you the beginning of months: it *shall be* the first month of the year to you.

3 ¶ Speak ye unto all the congregation of Israel, saying, In the tenth *day* of this month they shall take to them every man a lamb, according to the house of *their* fathers, a lamb for an house:

4 And if the household be too little for the lamb, let him and his neighbour next unto his house take *it* according to the number of the souls; every man according to his eating shall make your count for the lamb.

5 Your lamb shall be [i]without blemish, a male of the first year: ye shall take *it* out from the sheep, or from the goats:

6 And ye shall keep it up until the [j]fourteenth day of the same month: and the whole assembly of the congregation of Israel shall kill it in the evening.

7 And they shall take of the blood, and strike *it* on the two side posts and on the upper doorpost of the houses, wherein they shall eat it.

8 And they shall eat the flesh in that night, roast with fire, and [k]unleavened bread; *and* with bitter *herbs* they shall eat it.

9 Eat not of it raw, nor sodden at all with water, but [l]roast *with* fire; his head with his legs, and with the purtenance thereof.

10 [m]And ye shall let nothing of it remain

10:15 [g]ver. 5 [h]Ps. 105:35
10:16 [i]ch. 9:27
10:17 [j]ch. 9:28; 1 Kings 13:6
10:18 [k]ch. 8:30
10:19 [l]Joel 2:20
10:20 [m]ch. 4:21
10:21 [n]ch. 9:22
10:22 [o]Ps. 105:28
10:23 [p]ch. 8:22
10:24 [q]ver. 8 [r]ver. 10
10:27 [s]ver. 20; ch. 4:21
10:29 [t]Heb. 11:27
11:1 [u]ch. 12:31
11:2 [v]ch. 3:22
11:3 [w]ch. 3:21; Ps. 106:46 [x]2 Sam. 7:9; Esth. 9:4
11:4 [y]ch. 12:12; Am. 5:17
11:5 [z]ch. 12:12; Am. 4:10
11:6 [a]ch. 12:30; Am. 5:17
11:7 [b]ch. 8:22 [c]Josh. 10:21
11:8 [d]ch. 12:33
11:9 [e]ch. 3:19 [f]ch. 7:3
11:10 [g]ch. 10:20; Rom. 2:5
12:2 [h]ch. 13:4; Deut. 16:1
12:5 [i]Lev. 22:19; Mal. 1:8; Heb. 9:14; 1 Pet. 1:19
12:6 [j]Lev. 23:5; Num. 9:3; Deut. 16:1
12:8 [k]ch. 34:25; Deut. 16:3; Num. 9:11; 1 Cor. 5:8
12:9 [l]Deut. 16:7
12:10 [m]ch. 23:18

until the morning; and that which remaineth of it until the morning ye shall burn with fire.

11 ¶ And thus shall ye eat it; *with* your loins girded, your shoes on your feet, and your staff in your hand; and ye shall eat it in haste: [n]it *is* the LORD's passover.

12 For I [o]will pass through the land of Egypt this night, and will smite all the firstborn in the land of Egypt, both man and beast; and [p]against all the gods of Egypt I will execute judgment: [q]I *am* the LORD.

13 And the blood shall be to you for a token upon the houses where ye *are:* and when I see the blood, I will pass over you, and the plague shall not be upon you to destroy *you,* when I smite the land of Egypt.

14 And this day shall be unto you [r]for a memorial; and ye shall keep it a [s]feast to the LORD throughout your generations; ye shall keep it a feast [t]by an ordinance for ever.

15 [u]Seven days shall ye eat unleavened bread; even the first day ye shall put away leaven out of your houses: for whosoever eateth leavened bread from the first day until the seventh day, [v]that soul shall be cut off from Israel.

16 And in the first day *there shall be* [w]an holy convocation, and in the seventh day there shall be an holy convocation to you; no manner of work shall be done in them, save *that* which every man must eat, that only may be done of you.

17 And ye shall observe *the feast of* unleavened bread; for [x]in this selfsame day have I brought your armies out of the land of Egypt: therefore shall ye observe this day in your generations by an ordinance for ever.

18 ¶ [y]In the first *month,* on the fourteenth day of the month at even, ye shall eat unleavened bread, until the one and twentieth day of the month at even.

19 [z]Seven days shall there be no leaven found in your houses: for whosoever eateth that which is leavened, [a]even that soul shall be cut off from the congregation of Israel, whether he be a stranger, or born in the land.

20 Ye shall eat nothing leavened; in all your habitations shall ye eat unleavened bread.

21 ¶ Then Moses called for all the elders of Israel, and said unto them, [b]Draw out and take you a lamb according to your families, and kill the passover.

22 [c]And ye shall take a bunch of hyssop, and dip *it* in the blood that *is* in the bason, and [d]strike the lintel and the two side posts with the blood that *is* in the bason; and none of you shall go out at the door of his house until the morning.

23 [e]For the LORD will pass through to smite the Egyptians; and when he seeth the blood upon the lintel, and on the two side posts, the LORD will pass over the door, and [f]will not suffer [g]the destroyer to come in unto your houses to smite *you.*

24 And ye shall observe this thing for an ordinance to thee and to thy sons for ever.

25 And it shall come to pass, when ye be come to the land which the LORD will give you, [h]according as he hath promised, that ye shall keep this service.

26 [i]And it shall come to pass, when your children shall say unto you, What mean ye by this service?

27 That ye shall say, [j]It *is* the sacrifice of the LORD's passover, who passed over the houses of the children of Israel in Egypt, when he smote the Egyptians, and delivered our houses. And the people [k]bowed the head and worshipped.

28 And the children of Israel went away, and [l]did as the LORD had commanded Moses and Aaron, so did they.

29 ¶ [m]And it came to pass, that at midnight [n]the LORD smote all the firstborn in the land of Egypt, [o]from the firstborn of Pharaoh that sat on his throne unto the firstborn of the captive that *was* in the dungeon; and all the firstborn of cattle.

30 And Pharaoh rose up in the night, he, and all his servants, and all the Egyptians; and there was a [p]great cry in Egypt; for *there was* not a house where *there was* not one dead.

31 ¶ And [q]he called for Moses and Aaron by night, and said, Rise up, *and* get you forth from among my people, [r]both ye and the children of Israel; and go, serve the LORD, as ye have said.

32 [s]Also take your flocks and your herds, as ye have said, and be gone; and [t]bless me also.

33 [u]And the Egyptians were urgent upon the people, that they might send them out of the land in haste; for they said, [v]We *be* all dead *men.*

34 And the people took their dough before it was leavened, their kneadingtroughs being bound up in their clothes upon their shoulders.

35 And the children of Israel did according to the word of Moses; and they borrowed of the Egyptians [w]jewels of silver, and jewels of gold, and raiment:

36 [x]And the LORD gave the people favour in the sight of the Egyptians, so that they lent unto them *such things as they required.* And [y]they spoiled the Egyptians.

37 ¶ And [z]the children of Israel journeyed from [a]Rameses to Succoth, about [b]six hundred thousand on foot *that were* men, beside children.

38 And a mixed multitude went up also with them; and flocks, and herds, *even* very much cattle.

39 And they baked unleavened cakes of the dough which they brought forth out of Egypt, for it was not leavened; because [c]they were thrust out of Egypt, and could not tarry, neither had they prepared for themselves any victual.

12:11 [n]Deut. 16:5
12:12 [o]ch. 11:4; Am. 5:17 [p]Num. 33:4 [q]ch. 6:2
12:14 [r]ch. 13:9 [s]Lev. 23:4; 2 Kings 23:21 [t]ver. 24
12:15 [u]ch. 13:6; Lev. 23:5; Num. 28:17; Deut. 16:3; 1 Cor. 5:7 [v]Gen. 17:14; Num. 9:13
12:16 [w]Lev. 23:7; Num. 28:18
12:17 [x]ch. 13:3
12:18 [y]Lev. 23:5; Num. 28:16
12:19 [z]Ex. 23:15; Deut. 16:3; 1 Cor. 5:7 [a]Num. 9:13
12:21 [b]ver. 3; Num. 9:4; Josh. 5:10; 2 Kings 23:21; Ezra 6:20; Matt. 26:18; Mark 14:12-16; Luke 22:7
12:22 [c]Heb. 11:28 [d]ver. 7
12:23 [e]ver. 12 [f]Ezek. 9:6; Rev. 7:3 [g]2 Sam. 24:16; 1 Cor. 10:10; Heb. 11:28
12:25 [h]ch. 3:8
12:26 [i]ch. 13:8; Deut. 32:7; Josh. 4:6; Ps. 78:6
12:27 [j]ver. 11 [k]ch. 4:31
12:28 [l]Heb. 11:28
12:29 [m]ch. 11:4 [n]Num. 8:17; Ps. 78:51 [o]ch. 4:23
12:30 [p]ch. 11:6; Prov. 21:13; Am. 5:17; Jam. 2:13
12:31 [q]ch. 11:1; Ps. 105:38 [r]ch. 10:9
12:32 [s]ch. 10:26 [t]Gen. 27:34
12:33 [u]ch. 11:8; Ps. 105:38 [v]Gen. 20:3
12:35 [w]ch. 3:22
12:36 [x]ch. 3:21 [y]Gen. 15:14; ch. 3:22; Ps. 105:37
12:37 [z]Num. 33:3 [a]Gen. 47:11 [b]Gen. 12:2; ch. 38:26; Num. 1:46
12:39 [c]ch. 6:1

40 ¶ Now the sojourning of the children of Israel, who dwelt in Egypt, *was* [d]four hundred and thirty years.

41 And it came to pass at the end of the four hundred and thirty years, even the selfsame day it came to pass, that all [e]the hosts of the LORD went out from the land of Egypt.

42 It *is* [f]a night to be much observed unto the LORD for bringing them out from the land of Egypt: this *is* that night of the LORD to be observed of all the children of Israel in their generations.

43 ¶ And the LORD said unto Moses and Aaron, This *is* [g]the ordinance of the passover: There shall no stranger eat thereof:

44 But every man's servant that is bought for money, when thou hast [h]circumcised him, then shall he eat thereof.

45 [i]A foreigner and an hired servant shall not eat thereof.

46 In one house shall it be eaten; thou shalt not carry forth ought of the flesh abroad out of the house; [j]neither shall ye break a bone thereof.

47 [k]All the congregation of Israel shall keep it.

48 And [l]when a stranger shall sojourn with thee, and will keep the passover to the LORD, let all his males be circumcised, and then let him come near and keep it; and he shall be as one that is born in the land: for no uncircumcised person shall eat thereof.

49 [m]One law shall be to him that is homeborn, and unto the stranger that sojourneth among you.

50 Thus did all the children of Israel; as the LORD commanded Moses and Aaron, so did they.

51 [n]And it came to pass the selfsame day, *that* the LORD did bring the children of Israel out of the land of Egypt [o]by their armies.

13 And the LORD spake unto Moses, saying,

2 [p]Sanctify unto me all the firstborn, whatsoever openeth the womb among the children of Israel, *both* of man and of beast: it *is* mine.

3 ¶ And Moses said unto the people, [q]Remember this day, in which ye came out from Egypt, out of the house of bondage; for [r]by strength of hand the LORD brought you out from this *place:* [s]there shall no leavened bread be eaten.

4 [t]This day came ye out in the month Abib.

5 ¶ And it shall be when the LORD shall [u]bring thee into the land of the Canaanites, and the Hittites, and the Amorites, and the Hivites, and the Jebusites, which he [v]sware unto thy fathers to give thee, a land flowing with milk and honey, [w]that thou shalt keep this service in this month.

6 [x]Seven days thou shalt eat unleavened bread, and in the seventh day *shall be* a feast to the LORD.

7 Unleavened bread shall be eaten seven days; and there shall [y]no leavened bread be seen with thee, neither shall there be leaven seen with thee in all thy quarters.

8 ¶ And thou shalt [z]shew thy son in that day, saying, *This is done* because of that *which* the LORD did unto me when I came forth out of Egypt.

9 And it shall be for [a]a sign unto thee upon thine hand, and for a memorial between thine eyes, that the LORD's law may be in thy mouth: for with a strong hand hath the LORD brought thee out of Egypt.

10 [b]Thou shalt therefore keep this ordinance in his season from year to year.

11 ¶ And it shall be when the LORD shall bring thee into the land of the Canaanites, as he sware unto thee and to thy fathers, and shall give it thee,

12 [c]That thou shalt set apart unto the LORD all that openeth the matrix, and every firstling that cometh of a beast which thou hast; the males *shall be* the LORD's.

13 And [d]every firstling of an ass thou shalt redeem with a lamb; and if thou wilt not redeem it, then thou shalt break his neck: and all the firstborn of man among thy children [e]shalt thou redeem.

14 ¶ [f]And it shall be when thy son asketh thee in time to come, saying, What *is* this? that thou shalt say unto him, [g]By strength of hand the LORD brought us out from Egypt, from the house of bondage:

15 And it came to pass, when Pharaoh would hardly let us go, that [h]the LORD slew all the firstborn in the land of Egypt, both the firstborn of man, and the firstborn of beast: therefore I sacrifice to the LORD all that openeth the matrix, being males; but all the firstborn of my children I redeem.

16 And it shall be for [i]a token upon thine hand, and for frontlets between thine eyes: for by strength of hand the LORD brought us forth out of Egypt.

17 ¶ And it came to pass, when Pharaoh had let the people go, that God led them not *through* the way of the land of the Philistines, although that *was* near; for God said, Lest peradventure the people [j]repent when they see war, and [k]they return to Egypt:

18 But God [l]led the people about, *through* the way of the wilderness of the Red sea: and the children of Israel went up harnessed out of the land of Egypt.

19 And Moses took the bones of Joseph with him: for he had straitly sworn the children of Israel, saying, [m]God will surely visit you; and ye shall carry up my bones away hence with you.

20 ¶ And [n]they took their journey from Succoth, and encamped in Etham, in the edge of the wilderness.

21 And [o]the LORD went before them by day in a pillar of a cloud, to lead them the way; and by night in a pillar of fire, to give them light; to go by day and night:

22 He took not away the pillar of the cloud by day, nor the pillar of fire by night, *from* before the people.

12:40 [d]Gen. 15:13; Acts 7:6; Gal. 3:17
12:41 [e]ch. 7:4
12:42 [f]Deut. 16:6
12:43 [g]Num. 9:14
12:44 [h]Gen. 17:12
12:45 [i]Lev. 22:10
12:46 [j]Num. 9:12; John 19:33
12:47 [k]ver. 6; Num. 9:13
12:48 [l]Num. 9:14
12:49 [m]Num. 9:14; Gal. 3:28
12:51 [n]ver. 41 [o]ch. 6:26
13:2 [p]ver. 12; ch. 22:29; Lev. 27:26; Num. 3:13; Deut. 15:19; Luke 2:23
13:3 [q]ch. 12:42; Deut. 16:3 [r]ch. 6:1 [s]ch. 12:8
13:4 [t]ch. 23:15; Deut. 16:1
13:5 [u]ch. 3:8 [v]ch. 6:8 [w]ch. 12:25
13:6 [x]ch. 12:15
13:7 [y]ch. 12:19
13:8 [z]ver. 14; ch. 12:26
13:9 [a]ver. 16; ch. 12:14; Num. 15:39; Deut. 6:8; Prov. 1:9; Isa. 49:16; Jer. 22:24; Matt. 23:5
13:10 [b]ch. 12:14
13:12 [c]ver. 2; ch. 22:29; Lev. 27:26; Num. 8:17; Deut. 15:19; Ezek. 44:30
13:13 [d]ch. 34:20; Num. 18:15 [e]Num. 3:46
13:14 [f]ch. 12:26; Deut. 6:20; Josh. 4:6 [g]ver. 3
13:15 [h]ch. 12:29
13:16 [i]ver. 9
13:17 [j]ch. 14:11; Num. 14:1-4 [k]Deut. 17:16
13:18 [l]ch. 14:2; Num. 33:6
13:19 [m]Gen. 50:25; Josh. 24:32; Acts 7:16
13:20 [n]Num. 33:6
13:21 [o]ch. 14:19; Num. 9:15; Deut. 1:33; Neh. 9:12; Ps. 78:14; Isa. 4:5; 1 Cor. 10:1

14 And the LORD spake unto Moses,
saying,
2 Speak unto the children of Israel, [p]that
they turn and encamp before [q]Pi-hahiroth,
between [r]Migdol and the sea, over against
Baal-zephon: before it shall ye encamp by
the sea.
3 For Pharaoh will say of the children of
Israel, [s]They *are* entangled in the land, the
wilderness hath shut them in.
4 And [t]I will harden Pharaoh's heart,
that he shall follow after them; and I [u]will
be honoured upon Pharaoh, and upon all
his host; [v]that the Egyptians may know
that I *am* the LORD. And they did so.
5 ¶ And it was told the king of Egypt that
the people fled: and [w]the heart of Pharaoh
and of his servants was turned against the
people, and they said, Why have we done
this, that we have let Israel go from serving us?
6 And he made ready his chariot, and
took his people with him:
7 And he took [x]six hundred chosen chariots, and all the chariots of Egypt, and captains over every one of them.
8 And the LORD [y]hardened the heart of
Pharaoh king of Egypt, and he pursued after the children of Israel: and [z]the children
of Israel went out with an high hand.
9 But the [a]Egyptians pursued after them,
all the horses *and* chariots of Pharaoh, and
his horsemen, and his army, and overtook
them encamping by the sea, beside Pi-
hahiroth, before Baal-zephon.
10 ¶ And when Pharaoh drew nigh, the
children of Israel lifted up their eyes, and,
behold, the Egyptians marched after them;
and they were sore afraid: and the children
of Israel [b]cried out unto the LORD.
11 [c]And they said unto Moses, Because
there were no graves in Egypt, hast thou
taken us away to die in the wilderness?
wherefore hast thou dealt thus with us, to
carry us forth out of Egypt?
12 [d]*Is* not this the word that we did tell
thee in Egypt, saying, Let us alone, that we
may serve the Egyptians? For *it had been*
better for us to serve the Egyptians, than
that we should die in the wilderness.
13 ¶ And Moses said unto the people,
[e]Fear ye not, stand still, and see the salvation of the LORD, which he will shew to you
to day: for the Egyptians whom ye have
seen to day, ye shall see them again no more
for ever.
14 [f]The LORD shall fight for you, and ye
shall [g]hold your peace.
15 ¶ And the LORD said unto Moses,
Wherefore criest thou unto me? speak unto
the children of Israel, that they go forward:
16 But [h]lift thou up thy rod, and stretch
out thine hand over the sea, and divide it:
and the children of Israel shall go on dry
ground through the midst of the sea.
17 And I, behold, I will [i]harden the
hearts of the Egyptians, and they shall follow them: and I will [j]get me honour upon
Pharaoh, and upon all his host, upon his
chariots, and upon his horsemen.
18 And the Egyptians [k]shall know that I
am the LORD, when I have gotten me honour upon Pharaoh, upon his chariots, and
upon his horsemen.
19 ¶ And the angel of God, [l]which went
before the camp of Israel, removed and
went behind them; and the pillar of the
cloud went from before their face, and stood
behind them:
20 And it came between the camp of the
Egyptians and the camp of Israel; and [m]it
was a cloud and darkness *to them*, but it
gave light by night *to these:* so that the one
came not near the other all the night.
21 And Moses [n]stretched out his hand
over the sea; and the LORD caused the sea to
go *back* by a strong east wind all that night,
and [o]made the sea dry *land*, and the waters
were [p]divided.
22 And [q]the children of Israel went into
the midst of the sea upon the dry *ground:*
and the waters *were* [r]a wall unto them on
their right hand, and on their left.
23 ¶ And the Egyptians pursued, and
went in after them to the midst of the sea,
even all Pharaoh's horses, his chariots, and
his horsemen.
24 And it came to pass, that in the morning watch [s]the LORD looked unto the host
of the Egyptians through the pillar of fire
and of the cloud, and troubled the host of
the Egyptians,
25 And took off their chariot wheels, that
they drave them heavily: so that the Egyptians said, Let us flee from the face of Israel;
for the LORD [t]fighteth for them against the
Egyptians.
26 ¶ And the LORD said unto Moses,
[u]Stretch out thine hand over the sea, that
the waters may come again upon the Egyptians, upon their chariots, and upon their
horsemen.
27 And Moses stretched forth his hand
over the sea, and the sea [v]returned to his
strength when the morning appeared; and
the Egyptians fled against it; and the LORD
[w]overthrew the Egyptians in the midst of
the sea.
28 And [x]the waters returned, and [y]cov-
ered the chariots, and the horsemen, *and* all
the host of Pharaoh that came into the sea
after them; there remained not so much as
one of them.
29 [z]But the children of Israel walked
upon dry *land* in the midst of the sea; and
the waters *were* a wall unto them on their
right hand, and on their left.
30 Thus the LORD [a]saved Israel that day
out of the hand of the Egyptians; and Israel
[b]saw the Egyptians dead upon the sea
shore.
31 And Israel saw that great work which
the LORD did upon the Egyptians: and the
people feared the LORD, and [c]believed the
LORD, and his servant Moses.

14:2 *p*ch. 13:18 *q*Num. 33:7 *r*Jer. 44:1
14:3 *s*Ps. 71:11
14:4 *t*ch. 4:21 *u*ch. 9:16; ver. 17:18; Rom. 9:17 *v*ch. 7:5
14:5 *w*Ps. 105:25
14:7 *x*ch. 15:4
14:8 *y*ver. 4 *z*ch. 6:1; Num. 33:3
14:9 *a*ch. 15:9; Josh. 24:6
14:10 *b*Josh. 24:7; Neh. 9:9; Ps. 34:17
14:11 *c*Ps. 106:7
14:12 *d*ch. 5:21
14:13 *e*2 Chron. 20:15; Isa. 41:10
14:14 *f*ver. 25; Deut. 1:30; Josh. 10:14; 2 Chron. 20:29; Neh. 4:20; Isa. 31:4 *g*Isa. 30:15
14:16 *h*ver. 21; ch. 7:19
14:17 *i*ver. 8; ch. 7:3 *j*ver. 4
14:18 *k*ver. 4
14:19 *l*ch. 13:21; Num. 20:16; Isa. 63:9
14:20 *m*Isa. 8:14; 2 Cor. 4:3
14:21 *n*ver. 16 *o*Ps. 66:6 *p*ch. 15:8; Josh. 3:16; Neh. 9:11; Ps. 74:13; Isa. 63:12
14:22 *q*ver. 29; ch. 15:19; Num. 33:8; Ps. 66:6; Isa. 63:13; 1 Cor. 10:1; Heb. 11:29 *r*Hab. 3:10
14:24 *s*Ps. 77:17
14:25 *t*ver. 14
14:26 *u*ver. 16
14:27 *v*Josh. 4:18 *w*ch. 15:1
14:28 *x*Hab. 3:8 *y*Ps. 106:11
14:29 *z*ver. 22; Ps. 77:20
14:30 *a*Ps. 106:8 *b*Ps. 58:10
14:31 *c*ch. 4:31; Ps. 106:12; John 2:11

FOCUS ON EXODUS

Deliverance from more than 400 years of slavery demands many changes, including an expanded vision of a people who had been oppressed and enslaved, new leadership, and the establishment of community. The years of bondage and harsh labor had not prepared this fragmented people to become God's great nation. As a result, it took many generations for the Hebrews to become a cohesive people possessing power and independence.

Exodus is the story of God, giving birth to a nation. It is God's labor to expel the emerging nation from enslavement into the birth of freedom and a Promised Land! Women played their roles as orchestrated by God.

HISTORICAL BACKGROUND TO EXODUS

The history of the land called Egypt can be traced back to about 12,000 B.C. By 6000–5000 B.C., the Nile Valley had become a population center. By 4000 B.C., the more advanced Badarian culture was known to have "Negroid features." By 2000 B.C. (about the time when Abraham would have entered Egypt), the northern inhabitants had conquered their southern Cushite neighbors. By the time Joseph rose to power in Egypt, about 1715 B.C., the "possible descendants of Ham" were ruling Egypt. Jacob moved to Egypt around 1706 B.C. This pushes the date of the Exodus to about 1300 B.C., if the Israelites were in Egypt 400 years, as the Bible seems to indicate. The date of 1300 B.C., however, conflicts with other indications (1 Kin. 6:1) that the Exodus could have been around 1440 B.C. While the exact date is unknown, the history of their sojourn into and departure from Egypt is undeniable. That the Egyptians were and are Black is well known among recognized scholars, though western biblical commentators and artists have portrayed and depicted them as European Caucasians.

THE BLACK PRESENCE IN EXODUS

Based on geography, archaeology, anthropology, historical evidence, and biblical references, one can say that the events recorded in the Book of Exodus occurred in an area occupied and influenced by people of African descent (see Introduction to Genesis).

Recorded Egyptian history can be traced back to nearly 12,000 B.C., even further in certain instances. Some scholars find evidence that much of what the Egyptians knew was learned from their southern neighbors, the Nubians. While Egypt, itself African, is noteworthy for its cultural and intellectual superiority, it is refreshing to discover that people who lived farther south were, in antiquity, very learned and skilled people also.

The name Egypt or Egyptian is the Greek word for the people of that

land (native people called their country "Kemet" before the Greeks arrived). The name occurs over 150 times in the Book of Exodus, indicating how pervasive people of color were in the events that transpired there. As descendants of Ham, Egyptians demonstrated outstanding intelligence and creativity.

Canaan and Canaanites, also descendants of Ham, are mentioned 11 times in Exodus (chapters 3, 6, 13, 15, 16, 23, 33, 34).

NOTABLE BLACK PERSONALITIES IN EXODUS

Zipporah, daughter of Jethro, the Midianite high priest, who married Moses (Ex. 2:21; 4:25–26). She is referred to as Ethiopian, or Cushite (Num. 12:1).

Jethro, father of Zipporah and father-in-law of Moses (Ex. 2:16–21; 18), advised Moses on how to handle the large numbers of people who were coming to Moses with complaints. Today's business gurus point to Jethro as the pioneer in effective organizational principles. Seldom, if ever, do they identify the man who gave Moses wise advice as of African-Asiatic descent.

Pharaoh's daughter (Ex. 2:5–10). Although her name is not mentioned, we are aware that it was God working in and through her to receive a male, Hebrew infant, despite her father's mandate that they should all be killed. In her courts, he was fed, educated, and raised to be fully prepared for his appointed role of deliverer of the people of God.

Life Lessons

EXODUS 1

Shiphrah and Puah, Hebrew midwives, feared God and did not kill Hebrew children, thereby disobeying the Egyptian pharaoh. With passive resistance and covert actions, these two women defied the wicked law of Pharaoh. With great risk to their own lives, these women contradicted man-made laws to work with the God of Israel. "We must obey God before humans" (see Acts 4:19). Like them, and the more recent examples of Ms. Rosa Parks and Dr. Martin Luther King, Jr., we must be prepared to suffer for our convictions.

Birthing God, You who give birth to thoughts, dreams, and visions, help me to be ready to participate with You in bringing forth renewed life.

EXODUS 2

Moses had a passionate desire to see his people liberated from Egyptian bondage—not unlike other leaders who see their people enslaved. Moses lashed out, killing one Egyptian at a time—a method that was doomed. As

events unfold in the Book of Exodus, we can see that God never chided Moses for desiring liberation. Rather, God directed him to use a more effective strategy—the divine strategy. The human desire for liberation is undeniable. Such efforts must be God-directed and God-empowered to be effective.

Liberator, give me a heart for freedom! Loose the shackles from my mind in order that I may be free to live fully for You.

EXODUS 3

"I have surely seen the afflictions of my people which are in Egypt, and have heard their cry by reason of their taskmasters; for I know their sorrows; And I am come down to deliver them out of the hand of the Egyptians" (Ex. 3:7–8) reveals God's perfect knowledge and passionate concern for Israel. Though God may not respond when we think He should and in the ways we think, God cares and will respond at the right time and in the best way. Until the Ancient of Days acts, we must trust, wait, and be of good courage (Ps. 27:14).

Seeing, Hearing, Knowing, and Coming One, I stand in awe of Your awareness of my every need.

EXODUS 3

"I AM THAT I AM" (Ex. 3:14). God revealed Himself to Moses as the "I AM." In doing so, God conveyed to Moses that the pre-existing, self-sustaining One needed no external help. God's words to Moses assured him that Yahweh was totally capable of being whatever Israelites—or anyone—would need!

Great I AM, thank You for being present with me even now. Help me to remember that You are not known as the Great used to be!

EXODUS 4

Moses offered several excuses to avoid accepting God's commission (Ex. 4:1, 13), but in the end he obeyed (Ex. 4:19–20). God never objects to our honesty in questioning the direction for our lives. Nevertheless, to disobey is not wise, as many servants of God have discovered.

Perfect Direction, thank You for providing perfect guidance in my life. Thank You for an example in the women who steadfastly held to their commissions. Enable me to follow them in faithfulness.

EXODUS 7–11

Ten plagues were inflicted upon Pharaoh and the Egyptians before the Israelites were finally released after 430 years of servitude. One cannot fathom God's timing in bringing deliverance. Those who insist that God must always answer their prayers at the time and in the manner they prescribe have a lot to learn about God. This chapter provides us with the laments of distraught mothers who arose, early in the morning, to discover their oldest sons were dead. There was no comfort for their grief.

Prayer-Answering God, thank You for our freedom and deliverance, regardless of the various attempts to keep us enslaved.

EXODUS 12

Applying blood to the doorposts and eating the Passover lamb were prerequisites for experiencing deliverance from the angel of death and

Egyptian bondage. The blood symbolized the people's trust in the provision God made to spare their firstborn—the slain lamb died that their children might live. Eating the meat symbolized the Israelites' acceptance of God's provision. That symbolism would eventually apply to the Lord Jesus who became God's Lamb to take away the sins of the world (John 1:29). Our trust in the atoning sacrificial death of Jesus Christ on the cross brings deliverance from the bondage of sin and birth into His eternal kingdom.

Passover Lamb, how amazing is Your self-giving blood sacrifice that allows me to bypass death and destruction and grants me eternal life!

EXODUS 12

"A mixed multitude went up also with them" (Ex. 12:38). This mixed group undoubtedly consisted of non-Hebrews who decided to cast their lot with the Israelites and their God. As such, the group, which eventually arrived in Canaan, was mixed—held together by the Sinaitic covenant under the leadership of Moses and, later, Joshua. God's true church today is a "mixed" group of people, all of whom declare Jesus Christ to be Lord.

Calling God, I'm grateful that You allow the mixed-up, messed-up, and confused to be included among those You call Your people.

EXODUS 13

"God led the people about through the way of the wilderness" (Ex. 13:18). The distance between Egypt and Canaan was less than 200 miles. The Israelites could have made the journey in a few days if they had taken the shortest route, but God had other plans. Because God knew what lay ahead—and the disobedient mindset of the people—the 40-year period of wandering was a learning experience. Similarly, sometimes we are led in roundabout ways because God knows things we do not. We can accept God's way for us as best even when we do not understand it (Ps. 32:8).

Leading God, Your way is always perfect, even when I'm feeling as if I'm in charge. Lead me, guide me, along life's way. With You in charge, I cannot stray.

EXODUS 14

"And Moses said unto the people, Fear ye not, stand still, and see the salvation of the LORD . . . The LORD shall fight for you, and ye shall hold your peace" (Ex. 14:13–14). At certain times in our Christian walk, we must "stand still, and see the salvation of the LORD." At other times we must—in faith—get moving! Knowing when to act is critical. Through faith and fellowship with God, and in a covenant relationship with other like-minded Christians, we discover the appropriate action at the right moment.

Direction Provider, make Your will for my life clear. Strengthen me to know the difference between Your will and mine, and then, to follow Your directions.

EXODUS 15

The dance of the prophet Miriam and all the women is recorded after the triumphal crossing over the Red Sea from slavery into freedom. "For the horse of Pharaoh went in with his chariots and with his horsemen into the sea, and the LORD brought again the waters of the sea upon them; but the children of Israel went on dry land in the midst of the sea. And Miriam the

prophet, the sister of Aaron, took a timbrel in her hand; and all the women went out after her with timbrels and with dances. And Miriam answered them, Sing ye to the LORD, for he hath triumphed gloriously; the horse and his rider hath he thrown into the sea" (Ex. 15:19–21). Miriam led in celebration with authority that called all the other women to follow. The song of praise she sang is recorded. She wrote liturgy and performed liturgical dance without question or censor. What happened later to end her leadership role is not clear. There is no further transmission of her title or function. However, we do know that she was used by God to lead in worship and praise.

Lord of the Dance, when the horse and riders in my life have been drowned by Your greatness, teach me, like Miriam, to dance and to sing for the victory!

EXODUS 17

"Is the LORD among us, or not?" (Ex. 17:7). The people were thirsty and complained to Moses. God instructed Moses to strike a rock with the shepherd's rod he had used to bring down calamity upon the Egyptians. The place was called Massah to memorialize the people's testing of God, and Meribah to memorialize their arguing with God. Despite all God had done in delivering the people and providing food and meat, they complained and questioned God's commitment to provide for them. Though we are invited to come boldly and lay our every petition before God, we grieve the compassionate heart of God when we, like the Israelites, question God's love for and commitment to us.

Omnipresent Wonder, forgive me for "forgetting" that You are committed to my highest good, trustworthy without a doubt, and faithful to Your every promise.

EXODUS 18

Moses' father-in-law visited him and noticed how he attempted to do all the work himself. Jethro counseled him to share the load with others. The principle of dividing and sharing authority and responsibilities is one that has enabled giant corporations and governments to accomplish much more than they would otherwise have. Still, some leaders try to do everything, only to burn themselves out.

Almighty Counselor, gift me with administrative insight, so that the ministry You have called me to fulfill might not become a burden.

EXODUS 19–24

The Israelites agreed to a covenant that Yahweh would be their God and they would obey Him willingly (Ex. 24:3). The covenant (Ex. 20) followed the pattern of ancient covenants: God identified Himself as the God who would deliver them and then established expectations for them. While the Sinaitic covenant was a specific agreement between God (Yahweh) and the Israelites, the Ten Commandments reflect His eternal moral foundation applicable at all times to all people. The New Testament makes clear we are not justified by keeping the Law (Gal. 3:11); however, the same New Testament makes clear we must not violate the principles of these commandments (Matt. 5:17–20; James 2:10–11).

Covenant-Making and Covenant-Keeping God, enable me to keep my word. Thank You for keeping covenant with me, even when I've failed.

EXODUS 25–30

The tabernacle, with all its furnishings, reflected the Egyptian influence in design. While God gave clear instructions on what these items of worship were to look like, this apparently did not rule out the use of furniture-building knowledge. More important is that God provided a means whereby the Israelites could approach a holy God. Similarly, God has provided Jesus Christ as our High Priest so we can approach the throne to find gracious help in our times of need (Heb. 4:14–16).

Divine Designer, build my life to be pleasing for dwelling in Your presence.

EXODUS 32

While Moses was upon Mount Sinai receiving the Ten Commandments, Israel turned to idolatry and revelry. God threatened to destroy them. Moses interceded on behalf of the people, and God retreated. How much divine anger has been turned away because some saintly father or mother poured out his or her heart to God on behalf of a wayward child? Praise God for intercessors!

Faithful God, thank You for the magnificent gift of Your amazing grace. I continue to turn to forms of idolatry and even revelry, despite my very best intentions. Yet, You continue to intercede on my behalf. Be glorified through my life.

FOCUS ON LEVITICUS

The Book of Leviticus deals with the many rules God mandated to establish a worshiping nation. The conduct of civil government is outlined. Women are included with reference to sexual relations, marriage, childbearing, menstruation, and home teaching. Personal conduct set the stage for community interactions. Both the priestly and holiness codes detailed how life should be lived in this new and emerging nation, whose headquarters would be the temple at Jerusalem.

The first dwelling place of God was a portable sanctuary, the tabernacle, built with precious gems and metals taken out of Egypt by the Israelites. Each person was required to contribute an offering from the very best articles he or she had. The women provided the brass mirrors, which were used to make the basin in the outer court where the blood from the sacrifices was mixed with water.

Childbirth is one of a woman's gifts from God, providing her with both life and death. In bringing forth new life, it is believed that this is the one time that women are closest to death; and when all other creatures are weakened during a loss of blood, a woman is considered at the height of health. Therefore, the issue of blood is a central focus of the Book of Leviticus.

Women can glean a better understanding of our self-worth by reading Leviticus.

THE BLACK PRESENCE IN LEVITICUS

The Book of Leviticus gives instructions for the building of the tabernacle and instructs Israel on how worship should be carried out. Scholars have pointed out that while God gave specific instructions on what the tabernacle was to look like, the construction was not unlike objects used for worship in Egyptian society (see the *NIV Study Bible*, p. 124, 126). God gave Bezaleel and Aholiab (Ex. 31) exceptional gifts to oversee and carry out the project. Although they had been given specific instructions on how offerings were to be made acceptable in their presentation, Nadab and Abihu, two of Aaron and Elisheba's (the name assigned to Aaron's wife by Hebrew scholars) sons, were burned alive for presenting "strange fire" before the altar (Lev. 10:1–2). The use of altars and offerings was a common practice among the peoples of Africa and northeast Africa (i.e., Palestine) prior to these instructions. All of the materials used in the construction of the first place of worship were brought from Egypt.

LEVITICUS 1–6

In order to draw near to God and remain in harmony with God, two major categories of sacrifice were employed—joyful and sorrowful—both of which consisted of purification and guilt sacrifices. Many complex details were involved with these demanding, bloody rituals. Many occasions, seasons, and festivals required the fulfilling of vows before the priest. The word sacrifice in Hebrew means "to draw near," and in English is more clearly rendered as "to make sacred." The offerings were to be a means of compensation for sins and protection from divine punishment. The underlying purpose of sacrifice was to keep the people in harmony with their God. A handbook, Leviticus, was required to ensure an orderly and decent method of being right with God.

Lord, prepare me to be a sacrifice acceptable in Your sight.

LEVITICUS 7–8

The trespass, peace, thanksgiving, free will, and vow offerings were outlined in this section of Leviticus. It was the responsibility of the women in Levite households to ensure the purity of their house through the keeping of a kosher kitchen and diet. Unmarried females were allowed to eat from the holy sacrifices. However, no woman was allowed to eat from the most holy sacrifices, which were the burnt guilt and sin offerings; these were restricted to the male priests. In the days of the temple, Levite women sang, played musical instruments, participated in choirs, and choreographed and performed sacred dances based on the dances led by the prophet Miriam. Home rituals were oftentimes left in the hands of capable and trusted women.

Holy One, purify me so that I might serve You in all I do.

LEVITICUS 9–11

At the consecration of the Tabernacle, a divine fire descended to consume the prepared sacrifices that lay upon the altar. When his sons were killed after offering "strange fire," Aaron was not even permitted to grieve.

The Torah signified that if a female Levite married a male Levite, when she died he could not grieve, for the male priests were only allowed to mourn their blood relatives. Since these were his sons, we would expect to hear Aaron's grief. However, he was silent.

Leviticus also provides several guidelines for the use of food, the type of food to be consumed, and its proper preparation. Maintaining the system of strict dietary, or kosher, laws fell upon women. A list of forbidden animals, purity laws, and rules about vessels for cooking and storing food are also included in this part of Leviticus. This entire process is a way of sensitizing the hearts of a nation toward a delivering God. All of the people had to understand the proper conduct of a holy life. These laws teach a respect for all life as well as for the Giver of all life!

Purifying One, take all of me and make me fit for use as Your dwelling place.

LEVITICUS 12–13

Childbirth and leprosy were placed in the context of ritual purity. "According to the days of the separation for her infirmity shall she be unclean" (Lev. 12:2). This law placed certain restrictions upon childbearing women. During a specified period (one week after bearing a son and two weeks after a daughter), a woman was declared ritually impure. She was restricted from her husband's bed and certain religious areas. This time of restriction was due to her "blood defilement," when it was believed that her presence and touch could contaminate others. After birthing and waiting the required time period, a woman had to take both a purification and burnt offering to the priest.

Birthing God, hear the pain of my heart and send Your healing power to comfort me.

LEVITICUS 14–15

Isolation, sacrificial atonement, and public ritual were required in order to participate in the religious life of the community. However, menstruation, an ongoing and predictable discharge, rendered the average woman impure about one quarter of her life!

Life-Giver, make my days apart from others more meaningful with You!

LEVITICUS 16–17

The ritual of atonement was set forth to allow the most holy man in the community to approach God on behalf of all others after sending the scapegoat into the wilderness (Lev. 16:8–22). A bull had to be sacrificed on behalf of the priest, and a goat was offered for the community. These two sin offerings made atonement for the sins of the people. The blood from both animals was used to cleanse the tabernacle and the altar. Once again, we face the paradox of blood both purifying and defiling: "For the life of the flesh is in the blood: and I have given it to you upon the altar to make an atonement for your souls: for it is the blood that maketh an atonement for the soul" (Lev. 17:11).

Redeemer, thank You for being my ultimate sin offering.

LEVITICUS 18

Chapter 18 detailed sexual boundaries, including incest, adultery, bestiality, homosexuality, and sexual contact with a menstruating woman. The pharaohs made a practice of marrying their own mothers and sisters. And some of the pagan cults practiced strange sexual couplings. God forbade these practices and regulated the boundaries of sexual contact. In the blending of complex family relationships, it was a safeguard to many women that the boundaries were specifically spelled out. The laws of conduct condemned all adultery, homosexuality, and bestiality.

Boundary-Maker, thank You for providing for my safety and the safety of my sisters.

LEVITICUS 19–20

Social, economic, sexual, and ritual conduct were clarified in order to protect weaker members of society: to ensure justice, respect for nature, and preserve the religious codes. The command was given, "Ye shall be holy: for I the LORD your God am holy" (Lev. 19:2). Proper behavior in the community was a mandate. Consequences for unholy behavior are detailed in Leviticus.

Additionally, the practice of body tattoo was addressed in this section: "Ye shall not make any cuttings in your flesh for the dead, nor print any marks upon you" (Lev. 19:28). Tattooing was viewed as a foreign custom, often in honor of a cultic god or goddess. Sorcery, magic readings, and communing with spirits were condemned and banned among God's people. Some contemporary female rabbis believe that this particular taboo, repeated three times in 34 verses, was most directly aimed at strong women who were practicing spiritual leadership and threatening the patriarchal authority that was in place. However, the Law states: "And ye shall not walk in the manners of the nation, which I cast out before you: for they committed all these things, and therefore I abhorred them" (Lev. 20:23). Israel was to be a light to the world, not a follower of other countries.

Sanctifying One, make me unique and distinct from the world.

LEVITICUS 21–24

The roles and duties of the priests were also detailed. Holy men were required to marry holy women. The observance of holy days and festivals, including the Sabbath, and observance of special seasons, were outlined. Women were responsible for the preparation of the home—meaning that they had to be familiar with the dietary laws. Specific instructions were outlined regarding the sacred anointing oil and showbread displayed upon the table in the sanctuary.

Bread of Heaven, feed me until I want no more.

LEVITICUS 25–26

"And the sabbath of the land shall be meat for you; for thee, and for thy servant, and for thy maid, and for thy hired servant, and for thy stranger that sojourneth with thee" (Lev. 25:6). The land and its people were to be rested every seven years (Lev. 25:3–4). In a social framework, this allowed all participants to have a fresh start and not to be overbur-

dened by debt (25:6ff.). When the laws were first compiled, women were not permitted to own land or property, or to become heirs, thereby making sabbaticals and jubilee irrelevant to women directly.

LEVITICUS 26–27

God concluded this book of the communal Holiness Codes with both a promise of blessing and shalom (peace) if the people would obey. The promise extended to the land, which was an important part of the covenant. Yet the threat of impending doom was stated firmly: If the people did not follow the laws of conduct as outlined, there would be famine, destruction, and exile.

Blessed Holy One, take my life and let it be, always and forever a praise unto Thee!

FOCUS ON NUMBERS

Numbered among the notable women in this historical record were some significant leaders, including Miriam, the prophet and sister of Moses and Aaron. Her aggressive nature helped lead to the creation of liturgical dance as a continuing worship form. We already know her (from the Books of Exodus and Leviticus) as a poet and composer. In this record, we find her arguing with Moses and stricken with leprosy (Num. 12). She was exiled to the outskirts of the camp for seven days. Later, her eulogy was briefly provided (Num. 20).

We also meet a Midianite woman named Cozbi, the daughter of a tribal chief (Num. 25). Yet she acted as if she was one of the temple prostitutes who led the men of Israel away from God. Her lover, Zimri, was the son of a clan chief. Their murderer, Phinehas, was the grandson of Aaron and heir to the position of high priest. Sexual excess was a known characteristic of Mediterranean cultic practices. For this reason, the Israelites were warned repeatedly to keep themselves separate from the world of idol worshipers. Sexual excess was the sin. Death was the result.

The story of five sisters and their fight for the family's inheritance is also related in Numbers. We find the daughters of Zelophehad—Mahlah, Noah, Hoglah, Milcah, and Tirzah—were left without an inheritance when their father died and left no son as his heir (women could not inherit). As faithful followers of God and Moses, the women demanded a meeting at the entrance of the tabernacle and stood before Moses, Eleazar, the priest, other leaders, and the whole assembly (Num. 27:1–3) and demanded justice! Without a support group, without civil rights amendments, and without a public platform upon which they could base their argument, these bodacious women made their case and the Lord allowed them to have what was rightfully theirs.

Israelite women believed that God loved them equally! Prophetic, creative, wise, strong, bold, and pious: these are the words that describe the women numbered among the people of God.

THE BLACK PRESENCE IN NUMBERS

Chapter one lists the 12 tribes of Israel and the number of descendants in each. All of these sons, except Benjamin, had been born to Jacob while he lived with his Semite relatives in Padan-aram, Mesopotamia (Gen. 27:41–31:21), a land occupied by Cushites and Semites.

The descendants of Joseph, Ephraim, and Manasseh are identified among the tribes listed (Num. 1:10). These were sons born to Joseph by his Egyptian wife, Asenath, the daughter of Poti-pherah, priest of On.

Chapter 12 records the confrontation of Miriam and Aaron with Moses because of his Ethiopian (or Cushite) wife, Zipporah. Some scholars suggest that they objected to her because of the difference in her culture or religion, since all people of the time were dark-complexioned.

Moses sent spies to scout out the land of Canaan (Num.13:17). The land promised to Abraham by God was occupied by Canaanites, descendants of one of the sons of Ham. Descendants of Canaan included the Sidonians, Hittites (Heth), Jebusites, Amorites, Girgasites, Hivites, Arkites, Sinites, Arvadites, Zemarites and Hamathites (Gen. 10:15–18). Many, if not all, of these nations lived in Canaan. When the land was promised to Abraham, God stipulated that it could not be claimed until 400 years after the death of Abraham because, "the iniquity of the Amorites is not yet full" (Gen. 15:16). Unfortunately, by the time of the Exodus, these nations had become very corrupt and God's strategy for judging them was to allow the Israelites to conquer and drive them out.

The Lord instructed Moses to declare war on the Midianites because they had enticed Israel to turn away from Him (Num. 25:6–18). Midianites were the descendants of Abraham and Keturah, the African woman Abraham married in Genesis 25:1. Since Moses' wife, Zipporah, was Ethiopian and lived in the land of Midian (Ex. 2:15–21; Num. 12:1), we can draw the conclusion that some Midianites were Ethiopian.

NUMBERS 1–4

The Book of Numbers begins with a census, which was a means of determining who was of arms-bearing age, or who could become a soldier to defend the land promised to God's people. The Levites were exempt due to their sacred roles of the priesthood. Of course, in biblical times, women were not counted in this census; but God counted them as His faithful followers. The first chapters are filled with family history, laws, and arrangements for tribal camps.

God who counts, thank You for counting me in the number, as a warrior for You!

NUMBERS 5–6

The purity of the camp, restitution for wrongs, the requirements for Nazirites, and the priestly blessing are outlined. Of note to women is the

section beginning with Numbers 5:11, where the test for an unfaithful wife is detailed. This is the only example in all of the Bible of a "trial by ordeal." It is a ritual for judging a woman's innocence or guilt by subjecting her to a physical test. During the ritual, the priest placed the husband's offering upon his wife's hands, so that she became the altar! A bitter potion of dirt and ink was mixed and the woman was to swear her innocence in being unfaithful to her husband. If she was guilty, her thighs and abdomen would rot after drinking the potion. "And if the woman be not defiled, but be clean; then she shall be free, and shall conceive seed" (Num. 5:28). Centuries later, Rabbi Yohanan ben Zakkai outlawed this ritual even while the temple was standing because he recognized how destructive marital jealousy could be to the stability of the family.

This section concludes with God's blessing, extended to the people through the priesthood. It was originally given to Moses, passed on to Aaron, and then on to Aaron's sons: "The LORD bless thee, and keep thee: The LORD make his face shine upon thee, and be gracious unto thee: The LORD lift up his countenance upon thee, and give thee peace. And they shall put my name upon the children of Israel; and I will bless them" (Num. 6:24–27).

One True Father, thank You for bestowing both Your punishments and Your blessings upon us, because only You know what is truly good for us.

NUMBERS 7–10

This section of Numbers covers the official set up and dedication of the tabernacle; the cloud covering the tabernacle, and the silver trumpets designed for calling the community together and for having the camps set out.

Hovering and Calling God, let me sense Your presence and know Your voice.

NUMBERS 12

Miriam and Aaron begin to talk against Moses because of his Cushite wife, Zipporah. It is interesting to note that we find Miriam's name—a woman's—mentioned first. They questioned his authority as the primary one through whom God spoke to the children of Israel. God demanded both of them to step forward at the entrance to the tent. Both were chastised and "the anger of the LORD was kindled against them" (Num. 12:9). However, when the cloud lifted and God was gone, there stood Miriam, white with leprosy! For seven days Miriam was put outside the camp for shame, disgrace, and humiliation. However, Aaron was not punished. One view holds that since Aaron had already lost two sons, the two who offered "strange fire," that this time his punishment was mental. In other words, he was forced to watch his sister suffer for the sin they both committed. Miriam was punished severely for challenging the authority of her brother, whom God had selected as representative and deliverer.

Seeing, Hearing Judge, forgive me when I question those in authority.

NUMBERS 13–14

Twelve spies were sent out to explore the Promised Land of Canaan. Joshua and Caleb were the only ones to come back with a favorable

report: "If the LORD delight in us, then he will bring us into this land, and give it us . . . rebel not ye against the LORD, neither fear ye the people of the land; . . . their defence is departed from them, and the LORD is with us: fear them not" (Num. 14:8–9). The people, however, chose to listen to the negative reports of the other ten spies and rebellion broke out. Talk of stoning their leaders erupted and God's anger was apparent. The men responsible for spreading the negative reports were struck down by God and died of a plague (Num. 14:37). All the people over 20 years of age were doomed never to see the Promised Land.

Lord, I believe. Help my unbelief! Don't ever let me sell You short!

NUMBERS 16

Korah, a Levite, and certain Reubenites became insolent and rose up against Moses. God threatened to kill the whole assembly except for Moses and Aaron (Num. 16:21). Moses and Aaron begged for the people's lives. God sent earthquakes and consuming fire to rid the camp of rebellion (16:31–35). Fourteen thousand seven hundred people lost their lives from a plague.

Holy One, rid my heart of rebellion!

NUMBERS 20

The death of Miriam is noted. She was buried in the desert of Zin at Kadesh. The record holds that she died on the tenth day of the month of Nisan, 40 years to the day after the Israelites killed the first Passover lamb, and one year before they crossed over into the Promised Land. A day of fasting for women was customary to honor her memory. At the time of her death, there was no water for the community. What a paradox, since she was the girl who stood watch over the waters where her brother was hidden. She was there when Pharaoh's daughter drew her brother from the water and named him. And she walked, along with her brothers, across the dry land of the Red Sea into liberation. Yet she died in a dry place.

O God, give me living water—water that can quench my soul's thirst for You.

NUMBERS 21

The children of Israel began to grumble about the lack of bread and water and their dislike for the food they were receiving from God while in the desert. Because of their complaining, the Lord sent venomous snakes among the people to bite them. Many people died as a result of this (Num. 21:6). The people cried out to Moses in repentance and asked him to pray to the Lord to stop the vicious snake attack. God responded by instructing Moses: "Make thee a fiery serpent, and set it upon a pole: and it shall come to pass, that every one that is bitten, when he looketh upon it, shall live" (Num. 21:8).

I will lift up mine eyes unto the hills, from whence cometh my help. My help cometh from the LORD, which made heaven and earth (Ps. 121:1–2).

NUMBERS 22–24

Here is Balak, Balaam, and the talking jackass. God used Balaam's donkey to get his attention. What must God use to get our attention?

Lord, thank You for all the special things You do to grab my attention—even dying on a cross.

NUMBERS 25

The men of Israel began to indulge in sexual immorality with Moabite women who invited them to the sacrificial ceremonies dedicated to their false gods (Num. 25:1–3). This occured just after Balaam announced the blessings of God upon the people. The people turned away from God to worship idols! One bold sinner (Zimri, a leader of the tribe of Simeon) had the audacity to engage in sexual relations with a Midianite woman (Cozbi, the daughter of the tribal chief Zur) in front of Moses and the entire assembly of Israel (Num. 25:6). Aaron's grandson, Phinehas, became so outraged that he killed them both. Twenty-four thousand Israelites were killed by a plague because of their sexual misconduct and whorish acts in seeking after false gods.

Jealous God, help me to worship You and not false gods like money, fame, or sexual depravity.

NUMBERS 27

The daughters of Zelophehad came before Moses with a request to inherit the property that would have been passed on to their father's sons. Because he had been a loyal follower, yet left no sons to inherit, the sisters reasoned that they were due to receive his share of the Promised Land. They petitioned the full assembly—something that had never before been done by women. Moses then brought their case before the Lord, and God agreed with their rationale. A new law was established allowing women to receive inheritances.

Gracious God, give me wisdom so that I may know the blessings in store for me!

NUMBERS 34–35

In these two chapters God established specific land boundaries for the Israelites when they entered the land of Canaan. Forty-eight towns were set aside specifically for the Levites, six of which were to be used as places of refuge (Num. 35:6).

Divine Refuge, let me hide under the shelter of Your wings.

NUMBERS 36

Numbers closes with Moses' instructions to the daughters of Zelophehad regarding the inheritance of their father's land: "This is the thing which the Lord doth command concerning the daughters of Zelophehad, saying, Let them marry to whom they think best; only to the family of the tribe of their father shall they marry" (Num. 36:6). The daughters chose to marry their paternal first cousins from the tribe of Manasseh, "And they were married into the families of the sons of Manasseh the son of Joseph, and their inheritance remained in the tribe of the family of their father" (Num. 36:12).

Provider and Protector of women, please continue to attend to us with gracious care.

Women in EXODUS, LEVITICUS, AND NUMBERS

ZIPPORAH: THE UNDISTINGUISHED WIFE

The African-American woman of today has the potential to carry out the purpose for which she was created. It is not necessary that she live in the shadow of another person in order to establish a spiritual legacy. Historically, many women merely faded into the background, unnamed and unnoticed. Tradition and culture were often the factors for limiting a woman's identity to being connected to someone else. Women were identified as the daughter of, the sister of, the wife of, or the mother of a particular man. In the Old Testament, of course, there are a few whose individual character comes into the forefront, including Sarah, Ruth, Hannah, Abigail, and Esther. But her father's distinction and husband's prominence shadowed Zipporah, like a number of others. As an undistinguished wife, we can only surmise about her character from the few times she is mentioned and the one time she is quoted (Ex. 2:21; 4:24–26; 18:1–5; Num. 12:1).

Zipporah's name means "little bird or sparrow indicative of its twittering," which leads one to imagine her appearance and voice. However, this does not diminish the fact of her courage, which is seen when she is first introduced. She came into view as one of seven daughters, possibly the oldest, of the Midianite priest, Jethro (also known as Reuel, Jether, and Hobab). The Midianites were a nomadic group of tribes who roamed about Sinai and were descended from Abraham and Keturah (they were sometimes referred to as Cushites). In Genesis, Midianites were seen as traders; in Exodus, as shepherds. Jethro's daughters were courageous to face daily harassment by other shepherds when watering their father's flocks. After Moses helped the daughters, their father repaid him with hospitality and, eventually, with permission to marry Zipporah.

As the wife of Moses and mother of Gershom and Eliezer, Zipporah did not share the same spiritual values as her husband. Therefore, the sacred traditions of Israel were neglected. For awhile, Moses compromised with his unbelieving wife. While returning to Egypt, Moses became ill and his life was spared only after one of the boys was circumcised. The issue was the rite of circumcision. A wife's resistance to God's will not only endangers God's divine purpose for the couple's life, but it also places her family in spiritual jeopardy.

Zipporah's action and words of reproach lead us to assume that the root of the problem was due to her prejudice and rebellion of a rite not practiced among her people. However, her actions saved her husband's life. Unlike the marriages of Abraham and Sarah, Isaac and Rebecca, or Ruth and Boaz, Zipporah and Moses' marriage appears to be mismatched because of their different personal views.

Read Exodus 4:20–26; 18:2–3.

Read the insight essay on the Value of Motherhood.

—*A. Aubry*

JOCHEBED: SHE KNEW IT WOULD TAKE A VILLAGE

Somehow Jochebed knew it would take a village not only to raise her child, but also to save his life. So she started calling on that village from the day of his birth.

The first two village members were midwives named Shiphrah and Puah, who were ordered to kill all male babies born to Hebrew women. But these midwives lied to the king that the "Hebrew women are not as the Egyptian women; for they are lively and are delivered ere the midwives come in unto them" (Ex. 1:19). This refusal to kill the male babies was the first step in saving Moses, Jochebed's son.

Jochebed herself performed the second step by managing to conceal her baby for three months, defying the order to throw him into the Nile River. During that time she carefully constructed a basket of bulrushes and pitch (to waterproof it) (Ex. 2:3); she observed the bathing patterns of Pharaoh's daughter, the princess; and she coached her daughter, Miriam, so that she would know what to say and do when the princess found the baby.

The third step involved the next village member, Miriam. Jochebed was confident that she had coached her daughter well and had placed her in just the right spot to observe the basket and Pharaoh's daughter. Jochebed could have hidden herself, but she might have been seen and her plan exposed. So she relied on Miriam, knowing that if anything went awry, Miriam would alert her. Jochebed also knew that Miriam had fully comprehended her coaching and knew how to suddenly appear and suggest the appropriate nurse for the discovered child.

The next step involved the unsuspecting village member, Pharaoh's daughter. She discovered the beautiful baby who had managed to cry on cue. Then, before she had a chance to make a decision, Miriam offered to summon a wet nurse who could feed and care for the baby.

The princess raised this Hebrew child in luxury as her own son, naming him Moses "Because I drew him out of the water" (Ex. 2:10b).

Yes, Jochebed knew that it would take a village to raise her child, and she used that village well. She was a loving, caring, concerned, resourceful, determined mother. And she was faithful. God heard her prayers and intervened on her behalf. He honored her steadfast purpose by using her children, Aaron and Miriam, to help Moses lead His people out of bondage.

Jochebed was a woman of courage who feared only God, not man. She had a strong faith in His promises. She teaches us that it doesn't matter who you are or what your circumstances are, but how you deal with the lumps and bumps—the challenges and responsibilities that come with being a woman and a mother.

Read Exodus 1:15–2:10; Numbers 26:59; Hebrews 11:23–29.
Read the insight essay on Motherhood.

—M. Kimbrough

MIRIAM: PLAGUED BY JEALOUSY

Miriam was the daughter of Amram and Jochebed, and sister of Aaron and Moses. She is believed to be the sibling who watched the basket that held Moses float through the bulrushes to the Pharaoh's palace. Miriam watched from afar as Pharoah's daughter retrieved the basket, and immedi-

ately claimed Moses as her son. Miriam offered to get a wet nurse—the child's own mother, unbeknownst to Pharoah's daughter (Ex. 2:7).

Years later, after Moses fled Egypt and settled in Midian, he met Zipporah, the eldest daughter of Jethro, a Midian priest, and took her as his wife (Ex. 2:15–21).

Some time later, Miriam, along with Aaron, criticized Moses for taking Zipporah, a Midianite woman, to be his wife. We are not certain, however, that Zipporah is to be identified as this wife that Miriam and Aaron spoke against (Num. 12:1). It is possible (though not necessarily so) that the Ethiopian wife mentioned was a second wife of Moses. In addition to their criticisms, both Miriam and Aaron questioned and challenged Moses' sole right to speak for God to the people. As a result of instigating a rebellion against Moses—which initially stemmed from jealousy—Miriam was stricken with leprosy (Num. 12:9–10).

After Moses and Aaron interceded with God on Miriam's behalf, she was healed of her leprosy seven days after being placed under "exclusion" (Num. 12:11–15). When Miriam died, she was buried in Kadesh (Num. 20:1).

The spirit of Miriam is alive and well in many women today. We suffer daily physical and spiritual calamities as a result of deeply rooted jealousies that we harbor. It is jealousy which creates criticism and envy of our friends, loved ones, and even strangers. Jealousy and the actions which result from it are not of God.

So then, how do we thwart or control jealousy? How do we prevent ourselves from suffering Miriam's plight? We must be reborn each day, seeking God in our every thought and action. Pray to Him for the strength that will enable you to be Spirit-minded, Christ-centered and God-directed in your home, your workplace, your community, and, most of all, your church.

Read Exodus 2:4–10; 15:20; Numbers 12:1–16; 20:1; 26:59; Deuteronomy 24:9; Micah 6:4.

—T. Dixon

ZELOPHEHAD'S DAUGHTERS: SEEKING AN INHERITANCE

"Then came the daughters of Zelophehad" (Num. 27:1). That opening is filled with symbolism. "Then" implies that we pick up the story in progress. There has been some action and actors—then, the daughters came forward. We get the feeling that they had been left out, but now they are coming forward. Now they have made an opening for themselves. They have begun the process of unraveling a tight-knit system that kept women out.

The biblical record speaks of daughters as well as sons—however, the daughters usually appear in the background. The genealogies go on listing sons, but what about the daughters? Even Adam and Eve had daughters (see Gen. 5:1–4). There are other biblical stories of daughters, usually unnamed. Mentioning someone's name had special meaning to the Israelites for the following reasons:

1) The power to name a person, place, or thing showed authority over whatever was being named;

2) When an Israelite male gave his full name, it included his house/family (in Hebrew, *bet-ab,* i.e., "father's house"), clan *(mispaha),* and tribe *(sebet/matteh).* Thus, while a man's identity was reflected in his

name, this was not true for women because they were identified with the house of their father or husband.

Daughters are a part of the biblical story, sometimes even crucial to particular stories, but often this is not obvious. For example, the story of the Exodus still inspires people with the desire to be liberated. In this legendary story, after giving the glory to God for delivering the people from bondage, Moses still took on a heroic role that was almost superhuman. It therefore becomes easy to overlook the women who played a role in preparing Moses to be an instrument of God's justice.

In spite of the significance of these women to the liberation of the Israelites, there seemed to be no prominent role for women who found themselves in the wilderness after leaving Egypt. While we think of the Book of Numbers as a census or numbering of the tribes and clans, the title in Hebrew is called "in the wilderness" *(bemidbar).* Women have often had a feeling of being in the wilderness. The daughters of Zelophehad found themselves in the wilderness both literally and figuratively. They were in the midst of a people who wanted to be freed from slavery in Egypt, yet complained about the precarious insecurity of freedom in the wilderness.

Nonetheless, when it came time to allot the inheritance that God promised, you can be sure that all the men, good and bad, were there to claim their share. Zelophehad was not one who rebelled against God, and undoubtedly had hopes for his share in inheriting the land. But he died and left no male heirs, only five daughters. It was tradition in Israel that a family inheritance remained in the family through a male relative, thus perpetuating the ancestral name. Zelophehad's daughters made a request that not only challenged tradition, but also changed the laws of the community. Their actions were personal, yet brought about change in the legal and cultural system by becoming case law.

The five daughters—Mahlah, Noah, Hoglah, Milcah, and Tirzah—were amazing women. They recognized they could no longer be passive. They were not trying to be aggressive and annihilate the values and norms of their culture, yet they were taking a risk. They were asserting their claim within the context of their religious, cultural, and legal system. Their speech took on the form of *nachalah,* which means "inheritance," but also implied a sense of occupation of land. They put themselves in a position of being damned or blessed. The portions given to Mahlah, Noah, Hoglah, Milcah, and Tirzah demonstrated that God does not give women secondary status. It reflected God's concern for women. The fact that they did receive a portion in the land reflected their faith in God and His sense of justice for their welfare and personal security. They asked and they received. Oftentimes we receive not, because we ask not!

The story of Zelophehad's daughters in Numbers 27:1–11 provides the following lesson for women today: Proclaim who you are and that you have God-given rights. Know how your culture constrains or supports you as you claim your rights, and know that asserting yourself can lead to changes in the society that will benefit future generations.

Read Numbers 27:1–11; 36:2–11.

See also the insight essay on Children. See also the portraits on Achsah and a Virtuous Woman of Proverbs.

—B. McRipley

Insights

THE VALUE OF MOTHERHOOD

A mother is the female parent, the one who bears the children. To be a mother is one of the most important tasks that God could have entrusted to women. In Genesis 3:16, God said to the woman, "I will greatly multiply thy sorrow and thy conception; in sorrow thou shalt bring forth children." What once was a curse, was turned by God into the greatest blessing God could have bestowed upon the woman. God chose women as the vessels through which He would reproduce His greatest creation: humankind. God chose a special woman named Mary as the vehicle through which He would bring salvation to a dying world (Matt. 1:18–23; Luke 1:27–33).

Motherhood is not a responsibility to be taken lightly. Mothers are charged with shaping, molding, teaching, and nurturing the lives that are placed in their care (2 Tim. 1:3–5). We must teach our children about God, His principles, and His plan for their lives. The Bible tells us in Proverbs 22:6 that we are to train our children in the way they should go and when they are old, they will not depart from it.

A mother is also charged with loving her children. There is a special bond that exists between loving mothers and their children. There is no earthly love like a mother's love. It can only be compared to the love God has for His people (Isa. 49:14–16). A mother's love is enduring.

For a mother, there is no price too high in order to protect her children—even if it means self-sacrifice. In order to keep her son Moses from being killed, Jochebed hid him for three months, after which she placed him in the river to be found and raised by the Pharoah's daughter (Ex. 2:1–8). The unnamed woman in 1 Kings 3:26 was willing to risk losing her son to another woman in order to protect his life. Hagar, wandering in the wilderness, wept for her son. God responded to her cry and revealed a well of water to quench their thirst (Gen. 21:14–19). Hannah loved her son, yet she willingly offered him to the Lord (1 Sam. 1:27–28).

"The hand that rocks the cradle is the hand that rules the world." This proverb speaks to the influence a mother has in the life of her children. Mothers are to use that influence to instill godly morals and values in their children. Many mothers have the tremendous task of balancing home, family, and career. Others struggle with raising children alone and some others are experiencing motherhood for the second time around. Even the best mothers get tired and weary. Pray and ask God for the grace and strength necessary to complete the job you have been given as women and you will receive your just reward. Your children shall arise and call you blessed (Prov. 31:28).

Read Exodus 2:1–10, 20:12; see also Genesis 4:1; 1 Samuel 1:27–28; John 3:16.

See also the insight essays on Children and Motherhood. Read the portraits on Hagar, Hannah, Athaliah, Herodias and Salome, Jochebed, Samson's Mother.

—*E. Green*

FRUIT OF THE SPIRIT: THE FAITHFULNESS OF GOD

Faithfulness is an attribute which, in the Bible, is applied to both God and humans. As it applies to God, it means that God is absolutely reliable. He is not fickle, but is steadfast and constant in His dealings with His creation which, of course, includes us. The word is used to convey to us how unchanging and loyal God is in His love for us. He does not love us one day and change His mind on another day. His love for us does not change when we fail Him. God may discipline us when we go astray, but His love does not change.

In the Book of Exodus, we see that God was faithful to His people time and again—even though they were continually whining they were better off back in Egypt. When they worship idols (Ex. 32), God wanted to destroy them all and start again with Moses. But Moses had faith in the love and faithfulness of God. "Remember Abraham, Isaac, and Israel, thy servants, to whom thou swarest by thine own self, and saidst unto them, I will multiply your seed as the stars of heaven, and all this land that I have spoken of will I give unto your seed, and they shall inherit it for ever" (Ex. 32:13). What faith and courage to talk to an angry Father and know that He will keep His promises—even when we truly deserve His wrath and not His favor.

The Old and New Testaments praise God for His faithfulness, and Scripture challenges us as His children to develop faithfulness in our lives. Unwavering trust and steadfast loyalty are two virtues that are essential for our personal and spiritual growth.

African-American women must abide truthfully to their positions of faithfulness as mothers, friends, and leaders. God's faithfulness toward man mirrors an example of how faithfulness leads to productivity, resulting in the fruit of diligence, security, and reliability. It also creates an atmosphere of stability—not only for self, but also for other lives as well. Our dependability and commitment to others will manifest itself in our faithfulness, love, and service to them.

In viewing the life of Jesus Christ, we note how confidence in the divine plans, will, and purposes of the Father provoked Him to actions of faithfulness that allowed Him to carry out the will, the purposes, and the plans of God. When African-American women begin to believe in the fulfilled plans of God, there will be a commitment to proclaim His faithfulness to all generations (Ps. 89:1), even in the midst of trials, tribulations, and suffering.

Always remind yourself that the faithfulness of God is not determined by the faithfulness of people. God does not waver in His position as God, and His position of faithfulness is not proven or affirmed by one person. God remains faithful, because He is the I AM (Ex. 3:14). Our unfailing faith will be rewarded for all eternity.

Read Exodus 3:14.

See also the insight essays on Commitment, Fruit of the Spirit, and Perseverance. Read the portrait on Ruth.

—*T. Byrd*

DANCE, SISTERS, DANCE

Dance is an art form used to express and stir our emotions and the emotions of others. In many other countries, dance is an important part of

the culture as well as an intricate part of all celebrations.

Our sister Miriam, the prophet, called the women together to dance and sing for the victory of crossing the Red Sea (Ex. 15:20). Miriam led the way for the women to engage in dancing. Yes! They danced because of the powerful intervention of the almighty and merciful God who had made a way out of no way. Because of this intervention, they lifted this song: "Sing ye to the LORD, for he hath triumphed gloriously: the horse and his rider hath he thrown into the sea" (Ex. 15:21).

The Old Testament Scriptures record how dance was used to express joy and praise to the Lord (2 Sam. 6:14; Ps. 149:3; 150:4; Jer. 31:4). Much of the dance was generally done by women (Ex. 15:20–21; Judg. 21:19–21). In this generation, we can sing our own victory song and dance before God, who has brought us through our personal "Red Sea" experience. He has brought us through sickness, pain, suffering, trials, tribulation, abuse, and unpleasant situations and circumstances. Sisters, stop right now and just rejoice in the Lord and dance before Him!

Read Exodus 15:20–21; Psalm 30:11–12; 1 Corinthians 10:31.
Read the portrait on Herodias and Salome.

—C. Bracey

ATTRIBUTES OF GOD: JEALOUSY

As an African-American woman, and an ordained minister, I have often contemplated the divine attributes of God. My Creator is Immutable, Omnipotent, Omnipresent, Omniscient, Perfect, Holy, and Infinite—the Divine Nature! Yet, this unequaled God allows this humble daughter to share in and experience God's attributes of love, goodness, justice, mercy, presence, suffering, wisdom, and jealousy.

Jealousy? Yes, sister-friend. God is jealous!

Understandably, jealousy is a different concept to attribute to a Holy God. In a secular sense of the word, jealousy is negatively defined in terms of human relationships. However, divine Jealousy with the capital "J" aligns with the character of God. God's jealousy does not covet something that belongs to another, but something that belongs to Him. The relationship between God and His children is to be an exclusive one (Ex. 34:27).

The jealousy with the lowercase "j" is indicative of the "lowercase" human condition. From a social, cultural, mental, emotional, and historical perspective, the term "jealousy" signals a condition of being possessive, resentful, insecure, distrusting, and uncontrollably angry. We see these characteristics displayed even among the Christian Sisters—Clergy Sisters included! Yet the key to understanding God's divine Jealousy is in God's covenant: "Thou shalt have no other gods before me. Thou shalt not make unto thee any graven image. . . . Thou shalt not bow down thyself to them, nor serve them: for I the LORD thy God am a jealous God" (Ex. 20:3,4a,5a). "Thou shalt worship no other god: for the LORD, whose name is Jealous, is a jealous God" (Ex. 34:14).

Yes, God is divinely jealous and madly in love with you!

Read Exodus 34:14, 27; see Deuteronomy 6:14–15; 29:20; 32:16–21; 1 Corinthians 10:21–22; James 4:4–5.

See also the insight essays on Attributes of God.

—W. Blagmond

ATTRIBUTES OF GOD: HE IS OMNIPRESENT

Human language cannot adequately describe the splendor of God because human beings in their mortal state cannot fully comprehend the magnitude of His majesty. Knowing God is an inexhaustible theme—a study that will take an eternity to explore.

The active presence of God in places and in relationships is shown throughout the Old and New Testaments. There is no place without God and no place beyond God, as King Solomon confesses (2 Chron. 6:18).

God is! He is "Alpha and Omega, the beginning and the end, the first and the last," (Rev. 22:13). He is "the same yesterday, and to day, and for ever" (Heb. 13:8). He is everywhere at the same time (Eph. 4:6). God is the Creator of the universe. He is omnipresent—ever present in the person of the Holy Spirit. All believers experience his presence. He is omniscient—all wise, all knowing. God knows a woman's secret thoughts. He desires to have a relationship with every woman (see John 1:1–18), and He will not come in and out of her life. He is omnipotent—all powerful—"strong and mighty, the LORD mighty in battle" (Ps. 24:8).

If Moses had been asked, he would have proclaimed: "The LORD God, merciful and gracious, longsuffering, and abundant in goodness and truth" (Ex. 34:6). David would say: "God is our refuge and strength, a very present help in trouble" (Ps. 46:1). Daniel, Shadrach, Meshach, and Abed-nego would declare: "He is a deliverer." John the Baptist would exclaim: He is "the Lamb of God, which taketh away the sin of the world" (John 1:29). Mary of Magdala would say: "He is a loving, forgiving Savior."

God's love—bountiful, immeasurable, and unconditional—demonstrates how much He wants each one of His children to be saved. He made the supreme sacrifice of sending His only Son into a sinful world, not only to live an exemplary life but also to die that we might have eternal life. "Christ was treated as we deserve, that we might be treated as He deserves. He suffered the death which was ours that we might live the life which was His" (*The Desire of Ages*, p. 7). Such love, such grace!

God wants us to know Him—up close and personal—through prayer and through a daily study of His Word. Get to know Him better. He is a Friend who sticks closer than a sister.

Read Exodus 34:6; 2 Chronicles 6; see also Psalms 16:11; 23; 33:18; 34:15; 104; 121; Jeremiah 23:23–24; Philippians 1:6.

Read the insight essays on the Attributes of God.

—*R. Armster*

ANGER: ACT OR REACT

Anger can be defined as a strong feeling of belligerence aroused by a real or supposed inequity. God's anger was kindled against Miriam and Aaron when they talked against Moses because of his Ethiopian wife. Miriam became leprous (Num. 12:9–10).

"The LORD is merciful and gracious, slow to anger, and plenteous in mercy" (Ps. 103:8). God's anger is accepted as a holy response to our rebellion and sin—the destruction of Sodom and Gomorrah is an example (Gen. 19:1–25; Deut. 29:23).

As Black women, we are often accused of wearing our hearts on our sleeves, meaning we are more likely to react to an inequity rather than

thinking it through. Too often we allow anger to consume us to the point of not being able to move. Because of God's steadfast love toward us, we can step back from the situation and wait for divine leading. We need to become students of the Word of God, for it is our sword and shield. "Be ye angry and sin not" (Eph. 4:26). "Not rendering evil for evil or railing [abuse] for railing: but contrariwise blessing; knowing that ye are thereunto called, that ye should inherit a blessing" (1 Pet. 3:9).

When confronted by circumstances or situations that you perceive as unjust, don't react too quickly even though you may feel hurt or threatened. Don't follow your first impulse to curse. This angry response is sinful. Wait on the Lord. Anger may boil within, but praise the Lord. We need to ask ourselves if we are willing to trust God enough to release our anger into His care. Can we focus on the energy our anger produces into positive action? We need to be constant in prayer so that, when we are bumped, what spills out is wisdom from on high. "The mouth of the just bringeth forth wisdom" (Prov. 10:31).

A woman who acts instead of reacts is a woman secure in who she is, what she believes, and how she is to respond (Col. 3:23–24). Her reactions are not determined by another's actions. She is guided by the wisdom of the Lord.

Our God is glorified when we act rather than react.

Read Numbers 12:9–10; see also Proverbs 16:1–3; Galatians 5:22–26; 6:6–10; Ephesians 4:30–32.

Read the insight essays on Attributes of God, Forgiveness, and Fruit of the Spirit,

—J. Wood

REBELLION

Rebellion is defined as open resistance to authority. A rebellious spirit is one that defies authority. This includes the human authority that God has set in place, such as parents, employers, the government and the church. God deals very harshly with those who are rebellious. The first generation of Israelites died in the wilderness because of rebellion. Moses never got to see the Promised Land because of his rebellion at Meribah (Num. 20:7). The sons of Korah and their company were consumed by fire because of their rebellion (Num. 16:35). Rebellion begins with the seeds of discontentment and generally involves envy of someone or something. Korah was envious of the authority God had given Moses and Aaron (Num. 16:1–3). The Israelites were dissatisfied with their position in the wilderness. They began to feel that God was not capable of fulfilling His promises. They lost faith in the Sovereign power of God, disregarded their God-given leaders, and began to follow after their own way.

The Bible speaks of several kinds of rebellion. In Hebrews 3:8, the Bible speaks of hard-heartedness as a form of rebellion. In Isaiah 65:2, the Bible says following after one's own thoughts and ways is a form of rebellion. In Psalm 78:17, the Bible says that provoking God is a form of rebellion. At the center of all rebellion is sin, falling short of God's standard. We must learn to think like Paul, who says in Philippians 4:11, "for I have learned, in whatsoever state I am, therewith to be content."

We must trust God with all of our hearts to bring about His expected

end, believing that all things work together for the good of them that love God and are called according to His purpose.

See also the insight essay on Submission.

—*J. Thompson*

15 Then sang [d]Moses and the children
of Israel this song unto the LORD, and
spake, saying, I will [e]sing unto the LORD,
for he hath triumphed gloriously: the horse
and his rider hath he thrown into the sea.
2 The LORD *is* my strength and [f]song,
and he is become my salvation: he *is* my
God, and I will prepare him [g]an habitation;
my [h]father's God, and I [i]will exalt him.
3 The LORD *is* a man of [j]war: the LORD *is*
his [k]name.
4 [l]Pharaoh's chariots and his host hath
he cast into the sea: [m]his chosen captains
also are drowned in the Red sea.
5 [n]The depths have covered them: [o]they
sank into the bottom as a stone.
6 [p]Thy right hand, O LORD, is become
glorious in power: thy right hand, O LORD,
hath dashed in pieces the enemy.
7 And in the greatness of thine [q]excel-
lency thou hast overthrown them that rose
up against thee: thou sentest forth thy
wrath, *which* [r]consumed them [s]as stubble.
8 And [t]with the blast of thy nostrils the
waters were gathered together, [u]the floods
stood upright as an heap, *and* the depths
were congealed in the heart of the sea.
9 [v]The enemy said, I will pursue, I will
overtake, I will [w]divide the spoil; my lust
shall be satisfied upon them; I will draw my
sword, my hand shall destroy them.
10 Thou didst [x]blow with thy wind, [y]the
sea covered them: they sank as lead in the
mighty waters.
11 [z]Who *is* like unto thee, O LORD,
among the gods? who *is* like thee, [a]glorious
in holiness, fearful *in* praises, [b]doing wonders?
12 Thou stretchedst out [c]thy right hand,
the earth swallowed them.
13 Thou in thy mercy hast [d]led forth the
people *which* thou hast redeemed: thou hast
guided *them* in thy strength unto [e]thy holy
habitation.
14 [f]The people shall hear, *and* be afraid:
[g]sorrow shall take hold on the inhabitants
of Palestina.
15 [h]Then [i]the dukes of Edom shall be
amazed; [j]the mighty men of Moab, trembling shall take hold upon them; [k]all the
inhabitants of Canaan shall melt away.
16 [l]Fear and dread shall fall upon them;
by the greatness of thine arm they shall be
as still [m]as a stone; till thy people pass over,
O LORD, till the people pass over, [n]*which*
thou hast purchased.
17 Thou shalt bring them in, and [o]plant
them in the mountain of thine inheritance,
in the place, O LORD, *which* thou hast made
for thee to dwell in, *in* the [p]Sanctuary,
O Lord, *which* thy hands have established.
18 [q]The LORD shall reign for ever and
ever.
19 For the [r]horse of Pharaoh went in
with his chariots and with his horsemen
into the sea, and [s]the LORD brought again
the waters of the sea upon them; but the
children of Israel went on dry *land* in the
midst of the sea.
20 ¶ And Miriam the [t]prophetess, [u]the
sister of Aaron, [v]took a timbrel in her hand;
and all the women went out after her [w]with
timbrels and with dances.
21 And Miriam [x]answered them, [y]Sing
ye to the LORD, for he hath triumphed gloriously; the horse and his rider hath he
thrown into the sea.
22 So Moses brought Israel from the Red
sea, and they went out into the wilderness
of [z]Shur; and they went three days in the
wilderness, and found no water.
23 ¶ And when they came to [a]Marah,
they could not drink of the waters of Marah,
for they *were* bitter: therefore the name of it
was called Marah.
24 And the people [b]murmured against
Moses, saying, What shall we drink?
25 And he [c]cried unto the LORD; and the
LORD shewed him a tree, [d]*which* when he
had cast into the waters, the waters were
made sweet: there he [e]made for them a
statute and an ordinance, and there [f]he
proved them,
26 And said, [g]If thou wilt diligently
hearken to the voice of the LORD thy God,
and wilt do that which is right in his sight,
and wilt give ear to his commandments, and
keep all his statutes, I will put none of these
[h]diseases upon thee, which I have brought
upon the Egyptians: for I *am* the LORD [i]that
healeth thee.
27 ¶ [j]And they came to Elim, where *were*
twelve wells of water, and threescore and
ten palm trees: and they encamped there by
the waters.

16 And they [k]took their journey from
Elim, and all the congregation of the
children of Israel came unto the wilderness
of [l]Sin, which *is* between Elim and Sinai,
on the fifteenth day of the second month
after their departing out of the land of
Egypt.
2 And the whole congregation of the children of Israel [m]murmured against Moses
and Aaron in the wilderness:
3 And the children of Israel said unto
them, [n]Would to God we had died by the
hand of the LORD in the land of Egypt,
[o]when we sat by the flesh pots, *and* when
we did eat bread to the full; for ye have
brought us forth into this wilderness, to kill
this whole assembly with hunger.
4 ¶ Then said the LORD unto Moses, Behold, I will rain [p]bread from heaven for
you; and the people shall go out and gather
a certain rate every day, that I may [q]prove
them, whether they will walk in my law,
or no.
5 And it shall come to pass, that on the
sixth day they shall prepare *that* which

15:1 [d]Judg. 5:1; 2 Sam. 22:1; Ps. 106:12 [e]ver. 21
15:2 [f]Deut. 10:21; Ps. 18:2; Isa. 12:2; Hab. 3:18 [g]Gen. 28:21; 2 Sam. 7:5; Ps. 132:5 [h]ch. 3:15 [i]2 Sam. 22:47; Ps. 99:5; Isa. 25:1
15:3 [j]Ps. 24:8; Rev. 19:11 [k]ch. 6:3; Ps. 83:18
15:4 [l]ch. 14:28 [m]ch. 14:7
15:5 [n]ch. 14:28 [o]Neh. 9:11
15:6 [p]Ps. 118:15
15:7 [q]Deut. 33:26 [r]Ps. 59:13 [s]Isa. 5:24
15:8 [t]ch. 14:21; 2 Sam. 22:16; Job 4:9; 2 Thess. 2:8 [u]Ps. 78:13; Hab. 3:10
15:9 [v]Judg. 5:30 [w]Gen. 49:27; Isa. 53:12; Luke 11:22
15:10 [x]ch. 14:21; Ps. 147:18 [y]ver. 5; ch. 14:28
15:11 [z]2 Sam. 7:22; 1 Kings 8:23; Ps. 71:19; Jer. 10:6 [a]Isa. 6:3 [b]Ps. 77:14
15:12 [c]ver. 6
15:13 [d]Ps. 77:15; Isa. 63:12; Jer. 2:6 [e]Ps. 78:54
15:14 [f]Num. 14:14; Deut. 2:25; Josh. 2:9 [g]Ps. 48:6
15:15 [h]Gen. 36:40 [i]Deut. 2:4 [j]Num. 22:3; Hab. 3:7 [k]Josh. 5:1
15:16 [l]Deut. 2:25; Josh. 2:9 [m]1 Sam. 25:37 [n]ch. 19:5; Deut. 32:9; 2 Sam. 7:23; Ps. 74:2; Isa. 43:1; Jer. 31:11; Tit. 2:14; 1 Pet. 2:9; 2 Pet. 2:1
15:17 [o]Ps. 44:2 [p]Ps. 78:54
15:18 [q]Ps. 10:16; Isa. 57:15
15:19 [r]ch. 14:23; Prov. 21:31 [s]ch. 14:28
15:20 [t]Judg. 4:4; 1 Sam. 10:5 [u]Num. 26:59 [v]1 Sam. 18:6 [w]Judg. 11:34; 2 Sam. 6:16; Ps. 68:11
15:21 [x]1 Sam. 18:7 [y]ver. 1
15:22 [z]Gen. 16:7
15:23 [a]Num. 33:8
15:24 [b]ch. 16:2
15:25 [c]ch. 14:10; Ps. 50:15 [d]2 Kings 2:21 [e]Josh. 24:25 [f]ch. 16:4; Deut. 8:2; Judg. 2:22; Ps. 66:10

15:26 [g]Deut. 7:12 [h]Deut. 28:27 [i]ch. 23:25; Ps. 41:3 **15:27** [j]Num. 33:9
16:1 [k]Num. 33:10 [l]Ezek. 30:15 **16:2** [m]ch. 15:24; Ps. 106:25; 1 Cor. 10:10 **16:3** [n]Lam. 4:9 [o]Num. 11:4 **16:4** [p]Ps. 78:24; John 6:31; 1 Cor. 10:3 [q]ch. 15:25; Deut. 8:2

they bring in; and [r]it shall be twice as much
as they gather daily.
6 And Moses and Aaron said unto all the
children of Israel, [s]At even, then ye shall
know that the LORD hath brought you out
from the land of Egypt:
7 And in the morning, then ye shall see
[t]the glory of the LORD; for that he heareth
your murmurings against the LORD: and
[u]what *are* we, that ye murmur against us?
8 And Moses said, *This shall be*, when the
LORD shall give you in the evening flesh to
eat, and in the morning bread to the full; for
that the LORD heareth your murmurings
which ye murmur against him: and what
are we? your murmurings *are* not against
us, but [v]against the LORD.
9 ¶ And Moses spake unto Aaron, Say
unto all the congregation of the children of
Israel, [w]Come near before the LORD: for he
hath heard your murmurings.
10 And it came to pass, as Aaron spake
unto the whole congregation of the children
of Israel, that they looked toward the wilderness, and, behold, the glory of the LORD
[x]appeared in the cloud.
11 ¶ And the LORD spake unto Moses,
saying,
12 [y]I have heard the murmurings of the
children of Israel: speak unto them, saying,
[z]At even ye shall eat flesh, and [a]in the
morning ye shall be filled with bread; and
ye shall know that I *am* the LORD your God.
13 And it came to pass, that at even [b]the
quails came up, and covered the camp: and
in the morning [c]the dew lay round about
the host.
14 And when the dew that lay was gone
up, behold, upon the face of the wilderness
there lay [d]a small round thing, *as* small as
the hoar frost on the ground.
15 And when the children of Israel saw *it*,
they said one to another, It *is* manna: for
they wist not what it *was*. And Moses said
unto them, [e]This *is* the bread which the
LORD hath given you to eat.
16 ¶ This *is* the thing which the LORD hath
commanded, Gather of it every man according to his eating, [f]an omer for every man,
according to the number of your persons;
take ye every man for *them* which *are* in his
tents.
17 And the children of Israel did so, and
gathered, some more, some less.
18 And when they did mete *it* with an
omer, [g]he that gathered much had nothing
over, and he that gathered little had no lack;
they gathered every man according to his
eating.
19 And Moses said, Let no man leave of it
till the morning.
20 Notwithstanding they hearkened not
unto Moses; but some of them left of it until
the morning, and it bred worms, and stank:
and Moses was wroth with them.
21 And they gathered it every morning,
every man according to his eating: and
when the sun waxed hot, it melted.

16:5 [r]ver. 22; Lev. 25:21
16:6 [s]ver. 12; Num. 16:28
16:7 [t]ver. 10; Isa. 35:2; John 11:4 [u]Num. 16:11
16:8 [v]1 Sam. 8:7; Luke 10:16; Rom. 13:2
16:9 [w]Num. 16:16
16:10 [x]ver. 7; ch. 13:21; Num. 16:19; 1 Kings 8:10
16:12 [y]ver. 8 [z]ver. 6 [a]ver. 7
16:13 [b]Num. 11:31; Ps. 78:27 [c]Num. 11:9
16:14 [d]Num. 11:7; Deut. 8:3; Neh. 9:15; Ps. 78:24
16:15 [e]John 6:31; 1 Cor. 10:3
16:16 [f]ver. 36
16:18 [g]2 Cor. 8:15
16:23 [h]Gen. 2:3; ch. 20:8; Lev. 23:3
16:24 [i]ver. 20
16:26 [j]ch. 20:9
16:28 [k]2 Kings 17:14; Ps. 78:10
16:31 [l]Num. 11:7
16:33 [m]Heb. 9:4
16:34 [n]ch. 25:16; Num. 17:10; Deut. 10:5; 1 Kings 8:9
16:35 [o]Num. 33:38; Deut. 8:2; Neh. 9:20; John 6:31 [p]Josh. 5:12; Neh. 9:15
17:1 [q]ch. 16:1; Num. 33:12
17:2 [r]Num. 20:3 [s]Deut. 6:16; Ps. 78:18; Isa. 7:12; Matt. 4:7; 1 Cor. 10:9

22 ¶ And it came to pass, *that* on the sixth
day they gathered twice as much bread, two
omers for one *man*: and all the rulers of the
congregation came and told Moses.
23 And he said unto them, This *is that*
which the LORD hath said, To morrow *is*
[h]the rest of the holy sabbath unto the LORD:
bake *that* which ye will bake *to day*, and
seethe that ye will seethe; and that which
remaineth over lay up for you to be kept
until the morning.
24 And they laid it up till the morning, as
Moses bade: and it did not [i]stink, neither
was there any worm therein.
25 And Moses said, Eat that to day; for to
day *is* a sabbath unto the LORD: to day ye
shall not find it in the field.
26 [j]Six days ye shall gather it; but on the
seventh day, *which is* the sabbath, in it there
shall be none.
27 ¶ And it came to pass, *that* there went
out *some* of the people on the seventh day
for to gather, and they found none.
28 And the LORD said unto Moses, How
long [k]refuse ye to keep my commandments
and my laws?
29 See, for that the LORD hath given you
the sabbath, therefore he giveth you on the
sixth day the bread of two days; abide ye
every man in his place, let no man go out of
his place on the seventh day.
30 So the people rested on the seventh
day.
31 And the house of Israel called the
name thereof Manna: and [l]it *was* like coriander seed, white; and the taste of it *was*
like wafers *made* with honey.
32 ¶ And Moses said, This *is* the thing
which the LORD commandeth, Fill an omer
of it to be kept for your generations; that
they may see the bread wherewith I have
fed you in the wilderness, when I brought
you forth from the land of Egypt.
33 And Moses said unto Aaron, [m]Take a
pot, and put an omer full of manna therein,
and lay it up before the LORD, to be kept for
your generations.
34 As the LORD commanded Moses, so
Aaron laid it up [n]before the Testimony, to
be kept.
35 And the children of Israel did eat
manna [o]forty years, [p]until they came to a
land inhabited; they did eat manna, until
they came unto the borders of the land of
Canaan.
36 Now an omer *is* the tenth *part* of an
ephah.

17 And [q]all the congregation of the
children of Israel journeyed from the
wilderness of Sin, after their journeys, according to the commandment of the LORD,
and pitched in Rephidim: and *there was* no
water for the people to drink.
2 [r]Wherefore the people did chide with
Moses, and said, Give us water that we may
drink. And Moses said unto them, Why
chide ye with me? wherefore do ye [s]tempt
the LORD?

3 And the people thirsted there for water; and the people [t]murmured against Moses, and said, Wherefore *is* this *that* thou hast brought us up out of Egypt, to kill us and our children and our cattle with thirst?

4 And Moses [u]cried unto the LORD, saying, What shall I do unto this people? they be almost ready to [v]stone me.

5 And the LORD said unto Moses, [w]Go on before the people, and take with thee of the elders of Israel; and thy rod, wherewith [x]thou smotest the river, take in thine hand, and go.

6 [y]Behold, I will stand before thee there upon the rock in Horeb; and thou shalt smite the rock, and there shall come water out of it, that the people may drink. And Moses did so in the sight of the elders of Israel.

7 And he called the name of the place [z]Massah, and Meribah, because of the chiding of the children of Israel, and because they tempted the LORD, saying, Is the LORD among us, or not?

8 ¶ [a]Then came Amalek, and fought with Israel in Rephidim.

9 And Moses said unto [b]Joshua, Choose us out men, and go out, fight with Amalek: to morrow I will stand on the top of the hill with [c]the rod of God in mine hand.

10 So Joshua did as Moses had said to him, and fought with Amalek: and Moses, Aaron, and Hur went up to the top of the hill.

11 And it came to pass, when Moses [d]held up his hand, that Israel prevailed: and when he let down his hand, Amalek prevailed.

12 But Moses' hands *were* heavy; and they took a stone, and put *it* under him, and he sat thereon; and Aaron and Hur stayed up his hands, the one on the one side, and the other on the other side; and his hands were steady until the going down of the sun.

13 And Joshua discomfited Amalek and his people with the edge of the sword.

14 And the LORD said unto Moses, [e]Write this *for* a memorial in a book, and rehearse *it* in the ears of Joshua: for [f]I will utterly put out the remembrance of Amalek from under heaven.

15 And Moses built an altar, and called the name of it Jehovah-nissi:

16 For he said, Because the LORD hath sworn *that* the LORD *will have* war with Amalek from generation to generation.

18 When [g]Jethro, the priest of Midian, Moses' father in law, heard of all that [h]God had done for Moses, and for Israel his people, *and* that the LORD had brought Israel out of Egypt;

2 Then Jethro, Moses' father in law, took Zipporah, Moses' wife, [i]after he had sent her back,

3 And her [j]two sons; of which the [k]name of the one *was* Gershom; for he said, I have been an alien in a strange land:

4 And the name of the other *was* Eliezer; for the God of my father, *said he, was* mine help, and delivered me from the sword of Pharaoh:

5 And Jethro, Moses' father in law, came with his sons and his wife unto Moses into the wilderness, where he encamped at [l]the mount of God:

6 And he said unto Moses, I thy father in law Jethro am come unto thee, and thy wife, and her two sons with her.

7 ¶ And Moses [m]went out to meet his father in law, and did obeisance, and [n]kissed him; and they asked each other of *their* welfare; and they came into the tent.

8 And Moses told his father in law all that the LORD had done unto Pharaoh and to the Egyptians for Israel's sake, *and* all the travail that had come upon them by the way, and *how* the LORD [o]delivered them.

9 And Jethro rejoiced for all the goodness which the LORD had done to Israel, whom he had delivered out of the hand of the Egyptians.

10 And Jethro said, [p]Blessed *be* the LORD, who hath delivered you out of the hand of the Egyptians, and out of the hand of Pharaoh, who hath delivered the people from under the hand of the Egyptians.

11 Now I know that the LORD *is* [q]greater than all gods: [r]for in the thing wherein they dealt [s]proudly *he was* above them.

12 And Jethro, Moses' father in law, took a burnt offering and sacrifices for God: and Aaron came, and all the elders of Israel, to eat bread with Moses' father in law [t]before God.

13 ¶ And it came to pass on the morrow, that Moses sat to judge the people: and the people stood by Moses from the morning unto the evening.

14 And when Moses' father in law saw all that he did to the people, he said, What *is* this thing that thou doest to the people? why sittest thou thyself alone, and all the people stand by thee from morning unto even?

15 And Moses said unto his father in law, Because [u]the people come unto me to enquire of God:

16 When they have [v]a matter, they come unto me; and I judge between one and another, and I do [w]make *them* know the statutes of God, and his laws.

17 And Moses' father in law said unto him, The thing that thou doest *is* not good.

18 Thou wilt surely wear away, both thou, and this people that *is* with thee: for this thing *is* too heavy for thee: [x]thou art not able to perform it thyself alone.

19 Hearken now unto my voice, I will give thee counsel, and [y]God shall be with thee: Be thou [z]for the people to God-ward, that thou mayest [a]bring the causes unto God:

20 And thou shalt [b]teach them ordinances and laws, and shalt shew them [c]the way wherein they must walk, and [d]the work that they must do.

21 Moreover thou shalt provide out of all the people [e]able men, such as [f]fear God,

17:3 [t]ch. 16:2
17:4 [u]ch. 14:15 [v]1 Sam. 30:6; John 8:59
17:5 [w]Ezek. 2:6 [x]ch. 7:20; Num. 20:8
17:6 [y]Num. 20:10; Ps. 78:15; 1 Cor. 10:4
17:7 [z]Num. 20:13; Ps. 81:7; Heb. 3:8
17:8 [a]Gen. 36:12; Num. 24:20; Deut. 25:17; 1 Sam. 15:2
17:9 [b]Acts 7:45; Heb. 4:8 [c]ch. 4:20
17:11 [d]Jam. 5:16
17:14 [e]ch. 34:27 [f]Num. 24:20; Deut. 25:19; 1 Sam. 15:3; 2 Sam. 8:12; Ezra 9:14
18:1 [g]ch. 2:16 [h]Ps. 44:1
18:2 [i]ch. 4:26
18:3 [j]Acts 7:29 [k]ch. 2:22
18:5 [l]ch. 3:1
18:7 [m]Gen. 14:17; 1 Kings 2:19 [n]Gen. 29:13
18:8 [o]Ps. 78:42
18:10 [p]Gen. 14:20; 2 Sam. 18:28; Luke 1:68
18:11 [q]2 Chron. 2:5; Ps. 95:3 [r]ch. 1:10 [s]1 Sam. 2:3; Neh. 9:10; Job 40:11; Ps. 31:23; Luke 1:51
18:12 [t]Deut. 12:7; 1 Chron. 29:22; 1 Cor. 10:18
18:15 [u]Lev. 24:12; Num. 15:34
18:16 [v]ch. 23:7; Deut. 17:8; 2 Sam. 15:3; Job 31:13; Acts 18:15; 1 Cor. 6:1 [w]Lev. 24:15; Num. 15:35
18:18 [x]Num. 11:14; Deut. 1:9
18:19 [y]ch. 3:12 [z]ch. 4:16; Deut. 5:5 [a]Num. 27:5
18:20 [b]Deut. 4:1 [c]Ps. 143:8 [d]Deut. 1:18
18:21 [e]ver. 25; Deut. 1:15; 2 Chron. 19:5-10; Acts 6:3 [f]Gen. 42:18; 2 Sam. 23:3; 2 Chron. 19:9

[g]men of truth, [h]hating covetousness; and
place *such* over them, *to be* rulers of thousands, *and* rulers of hundreds, rulers of fifties, and rulers of tens:
22 And let them judge the people [i]at all
seasons: [j]and it shall be, *that* every great
matter they shall bring unto thee, but every
small matter they shall judge: so shall it be
easier for thyself, and [k]they shall bear *the*
burden with thee.
23 If thou shalt do this thing, and God
command thee *so*, then thou shalt be [l]able
to endure, and all this people shall also go to
[m]their place in peace.
24 So Moses hearkened to the voice of his
father in law, and did all that he had said.
25 And [n]Moses chose able men out of all
Israel, and made them heads over the people, rulers of thousands, rulers of hundreds,
rulers of fifties, and rulers of tens.
26 And they [o]judged the people at all seasons: the [p]hard causes they brought unto
Moses, but every small matter they judged
themselves.
27 ¶ And Moses let his father in law depart; and [q]he went his way into his own
land.

19 In the third month, when the children of Israel were gone forth out of
the land of Egypt, the same day [r]came they
into the wilderness of Sinai.
2 For they were departed from [s]Rephi-
dim, and were come *to* the desert of Sinai,
and had pitched in the wilderness; and
there Israel camped before [t]the mount.
3 And [u]Moses went up unto God, and the
LORD [v]called unto him out of the mountain,
saying, Thus shalt thou say to the house of
Jacob, and tell the children of Israel;
4 [w]Ye have seen what I did unto the
Egyptians, and *how* [x]I bare you on eagles'
wings, and brought you unto myself.
5 Now [y]therefore, if ye will obey my
voice indeed, and keep my covenant, then
[z]ye shall be a peculiar treasure unto me
above [a]all people: for all the earth *is* mine:
6 And ye shall be unto me a [b]kingdom of
priests, and an [c]holy nation. These *are* the
words which thou shalt speak unto the children of Israel.
7 ¶ And Moses came and called for the
elders of the people, and laid before their
faces all these words which the LORD commanded him.
8 And [d]all the people answered together,
and said, All that the LORD hath spoken we
will do. And Moses returned the words of
the people unto the LORD.
9 And the LORD said unto Moses, Lo, I
come unto thee [e]in a thick cloud, [f]that the
people may hear when I speak with thee,
and [g]believe thee for ever. And Moses told
the words of the people unto the LORD.
10 ¶ And the LORD said unto Moses, Go
unto the people, and [h]sanctify them to day
and to morrow, and let them [i]wash their
clothes,
11 And be ready against the third day: for
the third day the LORD [j]will come down in
the sight of all the people upon mount Sinai.
12 And thou shalt set bounds unto the
people round about, saying, Take heed to
yourselves, *that ye* go *not* up into the
mount, or touch the border of it: [k]whoso-
ever toucheth the mount shall be surely put
to death:
13 There shall not an hand touch it, but
he shall surely be stoned, or shot through;
whether *it be* beast or man, it shall not live:
when the [l]trumpet soundeth long, they
shall come up to the mount.
14 ¶ And Moses went down from the
mount unto the people, and [m]sanctified the
people; and they washed their clothes.
15 And he said unto the people, [n]Be
ready against the third day: [o]come not at
your wives.
16 ¶ And it came to pass on the third day
in the morning, that there were [p]thunders
and lightnings, and a [q]thick cloud upon the
mount, and the [r]voice of the trumpet exceeding loud; so that all the people that *was*
in the camp [s]trembled.
17 And [t]Moses brought forth the people
out of the camp to meet with God; and they
stood at the nether part of the mount.
18 And [u]mount Sinai was altogether on a
smoke, because the LORD descended upon it
[v]in fire: [w]and the smoke thereof ascended
as the smoke of a furnace, and [x]the whole
mount quaked greatly.
19 And [y]when the voice of the trumpet
sounded long, and waxed louder and
louder, [z]Moses spake, and [a]God answered
him by a voice.
20 And the LORD came down upon mount
Sinai, on the top of the mount: and the LORD
called Moses *up* to the top of the mount; and
Moses went up.
21 And the LORD said unto Moses, Go
down, charge the people, lest they break
through unto the LORD [b]to gaze, and many
of them perish.
22 And let the priests also, which come
near to the LORD, [c]sanctify themselves, lest
the LORD [d]break forth upon them.
23 And Moses said unto the LORD, The
people cannot come up to mount Sinai: for
thou chargedst us, saying, [e]Set bounds
about the mount, and sanctify it.
24 And the LORD said unto him, Away,
get thee down, and thou shalt come up,
thou, and Aaron with thee: but let not the
priests and the people break through to
come up unto the LORD, lest he break forth
upon them.
25 So Moses went down unto the people,
and spake unto them.

20 And God spake [f]all these words,
saying,
2 [g]I *am* the LORD thy God, which have
brought thee out of the land of Egypt, [h]out
of the house of bondage.

18:21 [g]Ezek. 18:8 [h]Deut. 16:19
18:22 [i]ver. 26 [j]ver. 26; Lev. 24:11; Num. 15:33; Deut. 1:17 [k]Num. 11:17
18:23 [l]ver. 18 [m]Gen. 18:33; ch. 16:29; 2 Sam. 19:39
18:25 [n]Deut. 1:15; Acts 6:5
18:26 [o]ver. 22 [p]Job 29:16
18:27 [q]Num. 10:29
19:1 [r]Num. 33:15
19:2 [s]ch. 17:1 [t]ch. 3:1
19:3 [u]ch. 20:21; Acts 7:38 [v]ch. 3:4
19:4 [w]Deut. 29:2 [x]Deut. 32:11; Isa. 63:9; Rev. 12:14
19:5 [y]Deut. 5:2 [z]Deut. 4:20; 1 Kings 8:53; Ps. 135:4; SSol. 8:12; Isa. 41:8; Jer. 10:16; Mal. 3:17; Tit. 2:14 [a]ch. 9:29; Deut. 10:14; Job 41:11; Ps. 24:1; 1 Cor. 10:26
19:6 [b]Deut. 33:2; 1 Pet. 2:5; Rev. 1:6 [c]Lev. 20:24; Deut. 7:6; Isa. 62:12; 1 Cor. 3:17; 1 Thess. 5:27
19:8 [d]ch. 24:3; Deut. 5:27
19:9 [e]ver. 16; ch. 20:21; Deut. 4:11; Ps. 18:11; Matt. 17:5 [f]Deut. 4:12; John 12:29 [g]ch. 14:31
19:10 [h]Lev. 11:44; Heb. 10:22 [i]ver. 14; Gen. 35:2; Lev. 15:5
19:11 [j]ver. 16; ch. 34:5; Deut. 33:2
19:12 [k]Heb. 12:20
19:13 [l]ver. 16
19:14 [m]ver. 10
19:15 [n]ver. 11 [o]1 Sam. 21:4; Zech. 7:3; 1 Cor. 7:5
19:16 [p]Ps. 77:18; Heb. 12:18; Rev. 4:5 [q]ver. 9; ch. 40:34; 2 Chron. 5:14 [r]Rev. 1:10 [s]Heb. 12:21
19:17 [t]Deut. 4:10
19:18 [u]Deut. 4:11; Judg. 5:5; Ps. 68:7; Isa. 6:4; Hab. 3:3 [v]ch. 3:2; 2 Chron. 7:1 [w]Gen. 15:17; Ps. 144:5; Rev. 15:8 [x]Ps. 68:8; Jer. 4:24; Heb. 12:26
19:19 [y]ver. 13 [z]Heb. 12:21 [a]Neh. 9:13; Ps. 81:7
19:21 [b]ch. 3:5; 1 Sam. 6:19
19:22 [c]Lev. 10:3 [d]2 Sam. 6:7
19:23 [e]ver. 12; Josh. 3:4
20:1 [f]Deut. 5:22
20:2 [g]Lev. 26:1; Deut. 5:6; Ps. 81:10; Hos. 13:4 [h]ch. 13:3

3 [i]Thou shalt have no other gods before me.

4 [j]Thou shalt not make unto thee any graven image, or any likeness *of any thing* that *is* in heaven above, or that *is* in the earth beneath, or that *is* in the water under the earth:

5 [k]Thou shalt not bow down thyself to them, nor serve them: for I the LORD thy God *am* [l]a jealous God, [m]visiting the iniquity of the fathers upon the children unto the third and fourth *generation* of them that hate me;

6 And [n]shewing mercy unto thousands of them that love me, and keep my commandments.

7 [o]Thou shalt not take the name of the LORD thy God in vain; for the LORD [p]will not hold him guiltless that taketh his name in vain.

8 [q]Remember the sabbath day, to keep it holy.

9 [r]Six days shalt thou labour, and do all thy work:

10 But the [s]seventh day *is* the sabbath of the LORD thy God: *in it* thou shalt not do any work, thou, nor thy son, nor thy daughter, thy manservant, nor thy maidservant, nor thy cattle, [t]nor thy stranger that *is* within thy gates:

11 For [u]*in* six days the LORD made heaven and earth, the sea, and all that in them *is*, and rested the seventh day: wherefore the LORD blessed the sabbath day, and hallowed it.

12 ¶ [v]Honour thy father and thy mother: that thy days may be long upon the land which the LORD thy God giveth thee.

13 [w]Thou shalt not kill.

14 [x]Thou shalt not commit adultery.

15 [y]Thou shalt not steal.

16 [z]Thou shalt not bear false witness against thy neighbour.

17 [a]Thou shalt not covet thy neighbour's house, [b]thou shalt not covet thy neighbour's wife, nor his manservant, nor his maidservant, nor his ox, nor his ass, nor any thing that *is* thy neighbour's.

18 ¶ And [c]all the people [d]saw the thunderings, and the lightnings, and the noise of the trumpet, and the mountain [e]smoking: and when the people saw *it*, they removed, and stood afar off.

19 And they said unto Moses, [f]Speak thou with us, and we will hear: but [g]let not God speak with us, lest we die.

20 And Moses said unto the people, [h]Fear not: [i]for God is come to prove you, and [j]that his fear may be before your faces, that ye sin not.

21 And the people stood afar off, and Moses drew near unto the [k]thick darkness where God *was*.

22 ¶ And the LORD said unto Moses, Thus thou shalt say unto the children of Israel, Ye have seen that I have talked with you [l]from heaven.

23 Ye shall not make [m]with me gods of silver, neither shall ye make unto you gods of gold.

24 ¶ An altar of earth thou shalt make unto me, and shalt sacrifice thereon thy burnt offerings, and thy peace offerings, [n]thy sheep, and thine oxen: in all [o]places where I record my name I will come unto thee, and I will [p]bless thee.

25 And [q]if thou wilt make me an altar of stone, thou shalt not build it of hewn stone: for if thou lift up thy tool upon it, thou hast polluted it.

26 Neither shalt thou go up by steps unto mine altar, that thy nakedness be not discovered thereon.

21 Now these *are* the judgments which thou shalt [r]set before them.

2 [s]If thou buy an Hebrew servant, six years he shall serve: and in the seventh he shall go out free for nothing.

3 If he came in by himself, he shall go out by himself: if he were married, then his wife shall go out with him.

4 If his master have given him a wife, and she have born him sons or daughters; the wife and her children shall be her master's, and he shall go out by himself.

5 [t]And if the servant shall plainly say, I love my master, my wife, and my children; I will not go out free:

6 Then his master shall bring him unto the [u]judges; he shall also bring him to the door, or unto the door post; and his master shall [v]bore his ear through with an aul; and he shall serve him for ever.

7 ¶ And if a man [w]sell his daughter to be a maidservant, she shall not go out [x]as the menservants do.

8 If she please not her master, who hath betrothed her to himself, then shall he let her be redeemed: to sell her unto a strange nation he shall have no power, seeing he hath dealt deceitfully with her.

9 And if he have betrothed her unto his son, he shall deal with her after the manner of daughters.

10 If he take him another *wife;* her food, her raiment, [y]and her duty of marriage, shall he not diminish.

11 And if he do not these three unto her, then shall she go out free without money.

12 ¶ [z]He that smiteth a man, so that he die, shall be surely put to death.

13 And [a]if a man lie not in wait, but God [b]deliver *him* into his hand; then [c]I will appoint thee a place whither he shall flee.

14 But if a man come [d]presumptuously upon his neighbour, to slay him with guile; [e]thou shalt take him from mine altar, that he may die.

20:3 *i*Deut. 5:7; 2 Kings 17:35; Jer. 25:6
20:4 *j*Lev. 26:1; Deut. 4:16; Ps. 97:7
20:5 *k*ch. 23:24; Josh. 23:7; 2 Kings 17:35; Isa. 44:15 *l*ch. 34:14; Deut. 4:24; Josh. 24:19; Nah. 1:2 *m*ch. 34:7; Lev. 20:5; Num. 14:18; 1 Kings 21:29; Job 5:4; Ps. 79:8; Isa. 14:20; Jer. 2:9
20:6 *n*ch. 34:7; Deut. 7:9; Ps. 89:34; Rom. 11:28
20:7 *o*ch. 23:1; Lev. 19:12; Deut. 5:11; Ps. 15:4; Matt. 5:33 *p*Mic. 6:11
20:8 *q*ch. 31:13; Lev. 19:3; Deut. 5:12
20:9 *r*ch. 23:12; Lev. 23:3; Ezek. 20:12; Luke 13:14
20:10 *s*Gen. 2:2; ch. 16:26 *t*Neh. 13:16
20:11 *u*Gen. 2:2
20:12 *v*ch. 23:26; Lev. 19:3; Deut. 5:16; Jer. 35:7; Matt. 15:4; Mark 7:10; Luke 18:20; Eph. 6:2
20:13 *w*Deut. 5:17; Matt. 5:21; Rom. 13:9
20:14 *x*Deut. 5:18; Matt. 5:27
20:15 *y*Lev. 19:11; Deut. 5:19; Matt. 19:18; Rom. 13:9; 1 Thess. 4:6
20:16 *z*ch. 23:1; Deut. 5:20; Matt. 19:18
20:17 *a*Deut. 5:21; Mic. 2:2; Hab. 2:9; Luke 12:15; Acts 20:33; Rom. 7:7; Eph. 5:3; Heb. 13:5 *b*Job 31:9; Prov. 6:29; Jer. 5:8; Matt. 5:28
20:18 *c*Heb. 12:18 *d*Rev. 1:10 *e*ch. 19:18
20:19 *f*Deut. 5:27; Gal. 3:19; Heb. 12:19 *g*Deut. 5:25
20:20 *h*1 Sam. 12:20; Isa. 41:10 *i*Gen. 22:1; Deut. 13:3 *j*Deut. 4:10; Prov. 3:7; Isa. 8:13
20:21 *k*ch. 19:16; Deut. 5:5; 1 Kings 8:12
20:22 *l*Deut. 4:36; Neh. 9:13
20:23 *m*ch. 32:1
20:24 *n*Lev. 1:2 *o*Deut. 12:5 *p*Gen. 12:2; Deut. 7:13
20:25 *q*Deut. 27:5; Josh. 8:31
21:1 *r*ch. 24:3
21:2 *s*Lev. 25:39; Deut. 15:12; Jer. 34:14
21:5 *t*Deut. 15:16
21:6 *u*ch. 12:12 *v*Ps. 40:6
21:7 *w*Neh. 5:5 *x*ver. 2
21:10 *y*1 Cor. 7:5
21:12 *z*Gen. 9:6; Lev. 24:17; Num. 35:30; Matt. 26:52
21:13 *a*Num. 35:22; Deut. 19:4 *b*1 Sam. 24:4 *c*Num. 35:11; Deut. 19:3; Josh. 20:2
21:14 *d*Num. 15:30; Deut. 19:11; Heb. 10:26 *e*1 Kings 2:28-34; 2 Kings 11:15

15 ¶ And he that smiteth his father, or his mother, shall be surely put to death.

16 ¶ And [f]he that stealeth a man, and [g]selleth him, or if he be [h]found in his hand, he shall surely be put to death.

17 ¶ And [i]he that curseth his father, or his mother, shall surely be put to death.

18 ¶ And if men strive together, and one smite another with a stone, or with *his* fist, and he die not, but keepeth *his* bed:

19 If he rise again, and walk abroad [j]upon his staff, then shall he that smote *him* be quit: only he shall pay *for* the loss of his time, and shall cause *him* to be thoroughly healed.

20 ¶ And if a man smite his servant, or his maid, with a rod, and he die under his hand; he shall be surely punished.

21 Notwithstanding, if he continue a day or two, he shall not be punished: for [k]he *is* his money.

22 ¶ If men strive, and hurt a woman with child, so that her fruit depart *from her*, and yet no mischief follow: he shall be surely punished, according as the woman's husband will lay upon him; and he shall [l]pay as the judges *determine*.

23 And if *any* mischief follow, then thou shalt give life for life,

24 [m]Eye for eye, tooth for tooth, hand for hand, foot for foot,

25 Burning for burning, wound for wound, stripe for stripe.

26 ¶ And if a man smite the eye of his servant, or the eye of his maid, that it perish; he shall let him go free for his eye's sake.

27 And if he smite out his manservant's tooth, or his maidservant 's tooth, he shall let him go free for his tooth's sake.

28 ¶ If an ox gore a man or a woman, that they die: then [n]the ox shall be surely stoned, and his flesh shall not be eaten; but the owner of the ox *shall be* quit.

29 But if the ox were wont to push with his horn in time past, and it hath been testified to his owner, and he hath not kept him in, but that he hath killed a man or a woman; the ox shall be stoned, and his owner also shall be put to death.

30 If there be laid on him a sum of money, then he shall give for [o]the ransom of his life whatsoever is laid upon him.

31 Whether he have gored a son, or have gored a daughter, according to this judgment shall it be done unto him.

32 If the ox shall push a manservant or a maidservant; he shall give unto their master [p]thirty shekels of silver, and the [q]ox shall be stoned.

33 ¶ And if a man shall open a pit, or if a man shall dig a pit, and not cover it, and an ox or an ass fall therein;

34 The owner of the pit shall make *it* good, *and* give money unto the owner of them; and the dead *beast* shall be his.

35 ¶ And if one man's ox hurt another's, that he die; then they shall sell the live ox, and divide the money of it; and the dead *ox* also they shall divide.

36 Or if it be known that the ox hath used to push in time past, and his owner hath not kept him in; he shall surely pay ox for ox; and the dead shall be his own.

22 If a man shall steal an ox, or a sheep, and kill it, or sell it; he shall restore five oxen for an ox, and [r]four sheep for a sheep.

2 ¶ If a thief be found [s]breaking up, and be smitten that he die, *there shall* [t]no blood *be shed* for him.

3 If the sun be risen upon him, *there shall be* blood *shed* for him; *for* he should make full restitution: if he have nothing, then he shall be [u]sold for his theft.

4 If the theft be certainly [v]found in his hand alive, whether it be ox, or ass, or sheep; he shall [w]restore double.

5 ¶ If a man shall cause a field or vineyard to be eaten, and shall put in his beast, and shall feed in another man's field; of the best of his own field, and of the best of his own vineyard, shall he make restitution.

6 ¶ If fire break out, and catch in thorns, so that the stacks of corn, or the standing corn, or the field, be consumed *therewith;* he that kindled the fire shall surely make restitution.

7 ¶ If a man shall deliver unto his neighbour money or stuff to keep, and it be stolen out of the man's house; [x]if the thief be found, let him pay double.

8 If the thief be not found, then the master of the house shall be brought unto the [y]judges, *to see* whether he have put his hand unto his neighbour's goods.

9 For all manner of trespass, *whether it be* for ox, for ass, for sheep, for raiment, *or* for any manner of lost thing, which *another* challengeth to be his, the [z]cause of both parties shall come before the judges; *and* whom the judges shall condemn, he shall pay double unto his neighbour.

10 If a man deliver unto his neighbour an ass, or an ox, or a sheep, or any beast, to keep; and it die, or be hurt, or driven away, no man seeing *it:*

11 *Then* shall an [a]oath of the LORD be between them both, that he hath not put his hand unto his neighbour's goods; and the owner of it shall accept *thereof,* and he shall not make *it* good.

12 And [b]if it be stolen from him, he shall make restitution unto the owner thereof.

13 If it be torn in pieces, *then* let him bring it *for* witness, *and* he shall not make good that which was torn.

14 ¶ And if a man borrow *ought* of his neighbour, and it be hurt, or die, the owner thereof *being* not with it, he shall surely make *it* good.

15 *But* if the owner thereof *be* with it, he shall not make *it* good: if it *be* an hired *thing,* it came for his hire.

16 ¶ And [c]if a man entice a maid that

21:16 [f]Deut. 24:7 [g]Gen. 37:28 [h]ch. 22:4
21:17 [i]Lev. 20:9; Prov. 20:20; Matt. 15:4; Mark 7:10
21:19 [j]2 Sam. 3:29
21:21 [k]Lev. 25:45
21:22 [l]ver. 30; Deut. 22:18
21:24 [m]Lev. 24:20; Deut. 19:21; Matt. 5:38
21:28 [n]Gen. 9:5
21:30 [o]ver. 22; Num. 35:31
21:32 [p]Zech. 11:12; Matt. 26:15; Phil. 2:7 [q]ver. 28
22:1 [r]2 Sam. 12:6; Prov. 6:31; Luke 19:8
22:2 [s]Matt. 24:43 [t]Num. 35:27
22:3 [u]ch. 21:2
22:4 [v]ch. 21:16 [w]ver. 1; Prov. 6:31
22:7 [x]ver. 4
22:8 [y]ch. 21:6
22:9 [z]Deut. 25:1; 2 Chron. 19:10
22:11 [a]Heb. 6:16
22:12 [b]Gen. 31:39
22:16 [c]Deut. 22:28

is not betrothed, and lie with her, he shall
surely endow her to be his wife.
17 If her father utterly refuse to give her
unto him, he shall pay money according to
the [d]dowry of virgins.
18 ¶ [e]Thou shalt not suffer a witch to live.
19 ¶ [f]Whosoever lieth with a beast shall
surely be put to death.
20 ¶ [g]He that sacrificeth unto *any* god,
save unto the LORD only, he shall be utterly
destroyed.
21 ¶ [h]Thou shalt neither vex a stranger,
nor oppress him: for ye were strangers in
the land of Egypt.
22 [i]Ye shall not afflict any widow, or fatherless child.
23 If thou afflict them in any wise, and
they [j]cry at all unto me, I will surely [k]hear
their cry;
24 And my [l]wrath shall wax hot, and I
will kill you with the sword; and [m]your
wives shall be widows, and your children
fatherless.
25 ¶ [n]If thou lend money to *any of* my
people *that is* poor by thee, thou shalt not
be to him as an usurer, neither shalt thou
lay upon him usury.
26 [o]If thou at all take thy neighbour's raiment to pledge, thou shalt deliver it unto
him by that the sun goeth down:
27 For that *is* his covering only, it *is* his
raiment for his skin: wherein shall he sleep?
and it shall come to pass, when he [p]crieth
unto me, that I will hear; for I *am* [q]gracious.
28 ¶ [r]Thou shalt not revile the gods, nor
curse the ruler of thy people.
29 ¶ Thou shalt not delay *to offer* [s]the
first of thy ripe fruits, and of thy liquors:
[t]the firstborn of thy sons shalt thou give
unto me.
30 [u]Likewise shalt thou do with thine
oxen, *and* with thy sheep: [v]seven days it
shall be with his dam; on the eighth day
thou shalt give it me.
31 ¶ And ye shall be [w]holy men unto me:
[x]neither shall ye eat *any* flesh *that is* torn of
beasts in the field; ye shall cast it to the
dogs.

23 Thou [y]shalt not raise a false report:
put not thine hand with the wicked to
be an [z]unrighteous witness.
2 ¶ [a]Thou shalt not follow a multitude to
do evil; [b]neither shalt thou speak in a cause
to decline after many to wrest *judgment:*
3 ¶ Neither shalt thou countenance a poor
man in his cause.
4 ¶ [c]If thou meet thine enemy's ox or his
ass going astray, thou shalt surely bring it
back to him again.
5 [d]If thou see the ass of him that hateth
thee lying under his burden, and wouldest
forbear to help him, thou shalt surely help
with him.
6 ¶ [e]Thou shalt not wrest the judgment of
thy poor in his cause.
7 [f]Keep thee far from a false matter;
[g]and the innocent and righteous slay thou
not: for [h]I will not justify the wicked.
8 ¶ And [i]thou shalt take no gift: for the
gift blindeth the wise, and perverteth the
words of the righteous.
9 ¶ Also [j]thou shalt not oppress a
stranger: for ye know the heart of a
stranger, seeing ye were strangers in the
land of Egypt.
10 And [k]six years thou shalt sow thy
land, and shalt gather in the fruits thereof:
11 But the seventh *year* thou shalt let it
rest and lie still; that the poor of thy people
may eat: and what they leave the beasts of
the field shall eat. In like manner thou shalt
deal with thy vineyard, *and* with thy olive-
yard.
12 [l]Six days thou shalt do thy work, and
on the seventh day thou shalt rest: that
thine ox and thine ass may rest, and the son
of thy handmaid, and the stranger, may be
refreshed.
13 And in all *things* that I have said unto
you [m]be circumspect: and [n]make no mention of the name of other gods, neither let it
be heard out of thy mouth.
14 ¶ [o]Three times thou shalt keep a feast
unto me in the year.
15 [p]Thou shalt keep the feast of unleavened bread: (thou shalt eat unleavened
bread seven days, as I commanded thee, in
the time appointed of the month Abib; for in
it thou camest out from Egypt: [q]and none
shall appear before me empty:)
16 [r]And the feast of harvest, the firstfruits of thy labours, which thou hast sown
in the field: and [s]the feast of ingathering,
which is in the end of the year, when thou
hast gathered in thy labours out of the field.
17 [t]Three times in the year all thy males
shall appear before the Lord GOD.
18 [u]Thou shalt not offer the blood of my
sacrifice with leavened bread; neither shall
the fat of my sacrifice remain until the
morning.
19 [v]The first of the firstfruits of thy land
thou shalt bring into the house of the LORD
thy God. [w]Thou shalt not seethe a kid in his
mother's milk.
20 ¶ [x]Behold, I send an Angel before
thee, to keep thee in the way, and to bring
thee into the place which I have prepared.
21 Beware of him, and obey his voice,
[y]provoke him not; for he will [z]not pardon
your transgressions: for [a]my name *is* in
him.
22 But if thou shalt indeed obey his voice,
and do all that I speak; then [b]I will be an
enemy unto thine enemies, and an adversary unto thine adversaries.
23 [c]For mine Angel shall go before thee,
and [d]bring thee in unto the Amorites, and
the Hittites, and the Perizzites, and the Ca-

22:17 dGen. 34:12; 1 Sam. 18:25
22:18 eLev. 19:26; 1 Sam. 28:3
22:19 fLev. 18:23
22:20 gNum. 25:2
22:21 hch. 23:9; Jer. 7:6; Zech. 7:10; Mal. 3:5
22:22 iPs. 94:6; Isa. 1:17
22:23 jJob 35:9; Luke 18:7 kver. 23; Ps. 18:6; Jam. 5:4
22:24 lJob 31:23; Ps. 69:24 mPs. 109:9; Lam. 5:3
22:25 nNeh. 5:7; Ps. 15:5; Ezek. 18:8
22:26 oJob 22:6; Ezek. 18:7; Am. 2:8
22:27 pver. 23 qch. 34:6; Ps. 86:15
22:28 rEccl. 10:20; Acts 23:5
22:29 sch. 23:16; Prov. 3:9 tch. 13:2
22:30 uDeut. 15:19 vLev. 22:27
22:31 wch. 19:6 xLev. 22:8; Ezek. 4:14
23:1 yver. 7; ch. 16:3; 2 Sam. 19:27; Ps. 15:3 zch. 20:16; 1 Kings 21:10; Ps. 35:11; Matt. 26:59; Acts 6:11
23:2 aGen. 7:1; ch. 32:1; Josh. 24:15; 1 Sam. 15:9; Job 31:34; Matt. 27:24; Luke 23:23; Acts 24:27 bver. 6; Ps. 72:2
23:4 cJob 31:29; Matt. 5:44; Rom. 12:20
23:5 dDeut. 22:4
23:6 ever. 2; Job 31:13; Isa. 10:1; Jer. 5:28; Am. 5:12; Mal. 3:5
23:7 fver. 1; Luke 3:14; Eph. 4:25 gPs. 94:21; Jer. 7:6; Matt. 27:4 hch. 34:7; Rom. 1:18
23:8 i1 Sam. 8:3; Ps. 26:10; Prov. 15:27; Isa. 1:23; Ezek. 22:12; Am. 5:12; Acts 24:26
23:9 jch. 22:21; Ps. 94:6; Ezek. 22:7; Mal. 3:5
23:10 kLev. 25:3
23:12 lch. 20:8; Luke 13:14
23:13 mJosh. 22:5; Ps. 39:1; Eph. 5:15 nNum. 32:38; Josh. 23:7; Ps. 16:4; Hos. 2:17; Zech. 13:2
23:14 och. 34:23

23:15 pch. 12:15 qch. 34:20 **23:16** rch. 34:22 sDeut. 16:13
23:17 tch. 34:23 **23:18** uch. 12:8 **23:19** vch. 22:29; Neh. 10:35 wch. 34:26 **23:20** xch. 14:19; Josh. 5:13; Ps. 91:11; Isa. 63:9 **23:21** yPs. 78:40; Eph. 4:30; Heb. 3:10 zch. 32:34; Heb. 3:11; 1 John 5:16 aIsa. 9:6; John 10:30 **23:22** bGen. 12:3; Jer. 30:20
23:23 cver. 20 dJosh. 24:8

naanites, the Hivites, and the Jebusites: and I will cut them off.

24 Thou shalt not [e]bow down to their gods, nor serve them, [f]nor do after their works: [g]but thou shalt utterly overthrow them, and quite break down their images.

25 And ye shall [h]serve the LORD your God, and [i]he shall bless thy bread, and thy water; and [j]I will take sickness away from the midst of thee.

26 ¶ [k]There shall nothing cast their young, nor be barren, in thy land: the number of thy days I will [l]fulfil.

27 I will send [m]my fear before thee, and will [n]destroy all the people to whom thou shalt come, and I will make all thine enemies turn their backs unto thee.

28 And [o]I will send hornets before thee, which shall drive out the Hivite, the Canaanite, and the Hittite, from before thee.

29 [p]I will not drive them out from before thee in one year; lest the land become desolate, and the beast of the field multiply against thee.

30 By little and little I will drive them out from before thee, until thou be increased, and inherit the land.

31 And [q]I will set thy bounds from the Red sea even unto the sea of the Philistines, and from the desert unto the river: for I will [r]deliver the inhabitants of the land into your hand; and thou shalt drive them out before thee.

32 [s]Thou shalt make no covenant with them, nor with their gods.

33 They shall not dwell in thy land, lest they make thee sin against me: for if thou serve their gods, [t]it will surely be a snare unto thee.

24 And he said unto Moses, Come up unto the LORD, thou, and Aaron, [u]Nadab, and Abihu, [v]and seventy of the elders of Israel; and worship ye afar off.

2 And Moses [w]alone shall come near the LORD: but they shall not come nigh; neither shall the people go up with him.

3 ¶ And Moses came and told the people all the words of the LORD, and all the judgments: and all the people answered with one voice, and said, [x]All the words which the LORD hath said will we do.

4 And Moses [y]wrote all the words of the LORD, and rose up early in the morning, and builded an altar under the hill, and twelve [z]pillars, according to the twelve tribes of Israel.

5 And he sent young men of the children of Israel, which offered burnt offerings, and sacrificed peace offerings of oxen unto the LORD.

6 And Moses [a]took half of the blood, and put *it* in basons; and half of the blood he sprinkled on the altar.

7 And he [b]took the book of the covenant, and read in the audience of the people: and they said, [c]All that the LORD hath said will we do, and be obedient.

8 And Moses took the blood, and sprinkled *it* on the people, and said, Behold [d]the blood of the covenant, which the LORD hath made with you concerning all these words.

9 ¶ Then [e]went up Moses, and Aaron, Nadab, and Abihu, and seventy of the elders of Israel:

10 And they [f]saw the God of Israel: and *there was* under his feet as it were a paved work of a [g]sapphire stone, and as it were the [h]body of heaven in *his* clearness.

11 And upon the nobles of the children of Israel he [i]laid not his hand: also [j]they saw God, and did [k]eat and drink.

12 ¶ And the LORD said unto Moses, [l]Come up to me into the mount, and be there: and I will give thee [m]tables of stone, and a law, and commandments which I have written; that thou mayest teach them.

13 And Moses rose up, and [n]his minister Joshua: and Moses [o]went up into the mount of God.

14 And he said unto the elders, Tarry ye here for us, until we come again unto you: and behold, Aaron and Hur *are* with you: if any man have any matters to do, let him come unto them.

15 And Moses went up into the mount, and [p]a cloud covered the mount.

16 And [q]the glory of the LORD abode upon mount Sinai, and the cloud covered it six days: and the seventh day he called unto Moses out of the midst of the cloud.

17 And the sight of the glory of the LORD *was* like [r]devouring fire on the top of the mount in the eyes of the children of Israel.

18 And Moses went into the midst of the cloud, and gat him up into the mount: and [s]Moses was in the mount forty days and forty nights.

25 And the LORD spake unto Moses, saying,

2 Speak unto the children of Israel, that they bring me an offering: [t]of every man that giveth it willingly with his heart ye shall take my offering.

3 And this *is* the offering which ye shall take of them; gold, and silver, and brass,

4 And blue, and purple, and scarlet, and fine linen, and goats' *hair*,

5 And rams' skins dyed red, and badgers' skins, and shittim wood,

6 [u]Oil for the light, [v]spices for anointing oil, and for [w]sweet incense,

7 Onyx stones, and stones to be set in the [x]ephod, and in the [y]breastplate.

8 And let them make me a [z]sanctuary; that [a]I may dwell among them.

9 [b]According to all that I shew thee, *after* the pattern of the tabernacle, and the pattern of all the instruments thereof, even so shall ye make *it*.

10 ¶ [c]And they shall make an ark *of* shittim wood: two cubits and a half *shall be* the length thereof, and a cubit and a half the

23:24 [e]ch. 20:5 [f]Lev. 18:3 [g]ch. 34:13 **23:25** [h]Josh. 22:5; Matt. 4:10 [i]Deut. 7:13 [j]ch. 15:26 **23:26** [k]Deut. 7:14; Job 21:10 [l]Gen. 25:8; Ps. 55:23 **23:27** [m]Gen. 35:5; ch. 15:14; Josh. 2:9; 2 Chron. 14:14 [n]Deut. 7:23 **23:28** [o]Deut. 7:20 **23:29** [p]Deut. 7:22 **23:31** [q]Gen. 15:18; Ps. 72:8 [r]Josh. 21:44; Judg. 1:4 **23:32** [s]ch. 34:12; Deut. 7:2 **23:33** [t]ch. 34:12; Deut. 7:16; Josh. 23:13; Judg. 2:3; 1 Sam. 18:21; Ps. 106:36 **24:1** [u]ch. 28:1; Lev. 10:1 [v]ch. 1:5; Num. 11:16 **24:2** [w]ver. 13 **24:3** [x]ver. 7; ch. 19:8; Deut. 5:27; Gal. 3:19 **24:4** [y]Deut. 31:9 [z]Gen. 28:18 **24:6** [a]Heb. 9:18 **24:7** [b]Heb. 9:19 [c]ver. 3 **24:8** [d]Heb. 9:20; 1 Pet. 1:2 **24:9** [e]ver. 1 **24:10** [f]Gen. 32:30; ch. 3:6; ch. 33:20; Judg. 13:22; Isa. 6:1; John 1:18; 1 Tim. 6:16; 1 John 4:12 [g]Ezek. 1:26; Rev. 4:3 [h]Matt. 17:2 **24:11** [i]ch. 19:21 [j]ver. 10; ch. 33:20; Gen. 16:13; Deut. 4:33; Judg. 13:22 [k]Gen. 31:54; ch. 18:12; 1 Cor. 10:18 **24:12** [l]ver. 2 [m]ch. 31:18; Deut. 5:22 **24:13** [n]ch. 32:17 [o]ver. 2 **24:15** [p]ch. 19:9; Matt. 17:5 **24:16** [q]ch. 16:10; Num. 14:10 **24:17** [r]ch. 3:2; Deut. 4:36; Heb. 12:18 **24:18** [s]ch. 34:28; Deut. 9:9 **25:2** [t]ch. 35:5; 1 Chron. 29:3; Ezra 2:68; Neh. 11:2; 2 Cor. 8:12 **25:6** [u]ch. 27:20 [v]ch. 30:23 [w]ch. 30:34 **25:7** [x]ch. 28:4 [y]ch. 28:15 **25:8** [z]ch. 36:1; Lev. 4:6; Heb. 9:1 [a]ch. 29:45; 1 Kings 6:13; 2 Cor. 6:16; Heb. 3:6; Rev. 21:3 **25:9** [b]ver. 40 **25:10** [c]ch. 37:1; Deut. 10:3; Heb. 9:4

breadth thereof, and a cubit and a half the height thereof.

11 And thou shalt overlay it with pure gold, within and without shalt thou overlay it, and shalt make upon it a crown of gold round about.

12 And thou shalt cast four rings of gold for it, and put *them* in the four corners thereof; and two rings *shall be* in the one side of it, and two rings in the other side of it.

13 And thou shalt make staves *of* shittim wood, and overlay them with gold.

14 And thou shalt put the staves into the rings by the sides of the ark, that the ark may be borne with them.

15 [d]The staves shall be in the rings of the ark: they shall not be taken from it.

16 And thou shalt put into the ark [e]the testimony which I shall give thee.

17 And [f]thou shalt make a mercy seat *of* pure gold: two cubits and a half *shall be* the length thereof, and a cubit and a half the breadth thereof.

18 And thou shalt make two cherubims *of* gold, *of* beaten work shalt thou make them, in the two ends of the mercy seat.

19 And make one cherub on the one end, and the other cherub on the other end: *even* of the mercy seat shall ye make the cherubims on the two ends thereof.

20 And [g]the cherubims shall stretch forth *their* wings on high, covering the mercy seat with their wings, and their faces *shall look* one to another; toward the mercy seat shall the faces of the cherubims be.

21 [h]And thou shalt put the mercy seat above upon the ark; and [i]in the ark thou shalt put the testimony that I shall give thee.

22 And [j]there I will meet with thee, and I will commune with thee from above the mercy seat, from [k]between the two cherubims which *are* upon the ark of the testimony, of all *things* which I will give thee in commandment unto the children of Israel.

23 ¶ [l]Thou shalt also make a table *of* shittim wood: two cubits *shall be* the length thereof, and a cubit the breadth thereof, and a cubit and a half the height thereof.

24 And thou shalt overlay it with pure gold, and make thereto a crown of gold round about.

25 And thou shalt make unto it a border of an hand breadth round about, and thou shalt make a golden crown to the border thereof round about.

26 And thou shalt make for it four rings of gold, and put the rings in the four corners that *are* on the four feet thereof.

27 Over against the border shall the rings be for places of the staves to bear the table.

28 And thou shalt make the staves *of* shittim wood, and overlay them with gold, that the table may be borne with them.

29 And thou shalt make [m]the dishes thereof, and spoons thereof, and covers thereof, and bowls thereof, to cover withal: *of* pure gold shalt thou make them.

30 And thou shalt set upon the table [n]shewbread before me alway.

31 ¶ [o]And thou shalt make a candlestick *of* pure gold: *of* beaten work shall the candlestick be made: his shaft, and his branches, his bowls, his knops, and his flowers, shall be of the same.

32 And six branches shall come out of the sides of it; three branches of the candlestick out of the one side, and three branches of the candlestick out of the other side:

33 Three bowls made like unto almonds, *with* a knop and a flower in one branch; and three bowls made like almonds in the other branch, *with* a knop and a flower: so in the six branches that come out of the candlestick.

34 And in the candlestick *shall be* four bowls made like unto almonds, *with* their knops and their flowers.

35 And *there shall be* a knop under two branches of the same, and a knop under two branches of the same, and a knop under two branches of the same, according to the six branches that proceed out of the candlestick.

36 Their knops and their branches shall be of the same: all it *shall be* one beaten work *of* pure gold.

37 And thou shalt make the seven lamps thereof: and [p]they shall light the lamps thereof, that they may [q]give light over against it.

38 And the tongs thereof, and the snuffdishes thereof, *shall be of* pure gold.

39 *Of* a talent of pure gold shall he make it, with all these vessels.

40 And [r]look that thou make *them* after their pattern, which was shewed thee in the mount.

26 Moreover [s]thou shalt make the tabernacle *with* ten curtains *of* fine twined linen, and blue, and purple, and scarlet: *with* cherubims of cunning work shalt thou make them.

2 The length of one curtain *shall be* eight and twenty cubits, and the breadth of one curtain four cubits: and every one of the curtains shall have one measure.

3 The five curtains shall be coupled together one to another; and *other* five curtains *shall be* coupled one to another.

4 And thou shalt make loops of blue upon the edge of the one curtain from the selvedge in the coupling; and likewise shalt thou make in the uttermost edge of *another* curtain, in the coupling of the second.

5 Fifty loops shalt thou make in the one curtain, and fifty loops shalt thou make in the edge of the curtain that *is* in the coupling of the second; that the loops may take hold one of another.

6 And thou shalt make fifty taches of gold, and couple the curtains together with the taches: and it shall be one tabernacle.

7 ¶ And [t]thou shalt make curtains *of* goats' *hair* to be a covering upon the tabernacle: eleven curtains shalt thou make.

25:15 [d]1 Kings 8:8
25:16 [e]ch. 16:34; Deut. 10:2; 1 Kings 8:9; 2 Kings 11:12; Heb. 9:4
25:17 [f]ch. 37:6; Rom. 3:25; Heb. 9:5
25:20 [g]1 Kings 8:7; 1 Chron. 28:18; Heb. 9:5
25:21 [h]ch. 26:34 [i]ver. 16
25:22 [j]ch. 29:42; Lev. 16:2; Num. 17:4 [k]Num. 7:89; 1 Sam. 4:4; 2 Sam. 6:2; 2 Kings 19:15; Ps. 80:1; Isa. 37:16
25:23 [l]ch. 37:10; 1 Kings 7:48; 2 Chron. 4:8; Heb. 9:2
25:29 [m]ch. 37:16; Num. 4:7
25:30 [n]Lev. 24:5
25:31 [o]ch. 37:17; 1 Kings 7:49; Zech. 4:2; Heb. 9:2; Rev. 1:12
25:37 [p]ch. 27:21; Lev. 24:3; 2 Chron. 13:11 [q]Num. 8:2
25:40 [r]ch. 26:30; Num. 8:4; 1 Chron. 28:11; Acts 7:44; Heb. 8:5
26:1 [s]ch. 36:8
26:7 [t]ch. 36:14

8 The length of one curtain *shall be* thirty cubits, and the breadth of one curtain four cubits: and the eleven curtains *shall be all* of one measure.

9 And thou shalt couple five curtains by themselves, and six curtains by themselves, and shalt double the sixth curtain in the forefront of the tabernacle.

10 And thou shalt make fifty loops on the edge of the one curtain *that is* outmost in the coupling, and fifty loops in the edge of the curtain which coupleth the second.

11 And thou shalt make fifty taches of brass, and put the taches into the loops, and couple the tent together, that it may be one.

12 And the remnant that remaineth of the curtains of the tent, the half curtain that remaineth, shall hang over the backside of the tabernacle.

13 And a cubit on the one side, and a cubit on the other side of that which remaineth in the length of the curtains of the tent, it shall hang over the sides of the tabernacle on this side and on that side, to cover it.

14 And [u]thou shalt make a covering for the tent *of* rams' skins dyed red, and a covering above *of* badgers' skins.

15 ¶ And thou shalt make boards for the tabernacle *of* shittim wood standing up.

16 Ten cubits *shall be* the length of a board, and a cubit and a half *shall be* the breadth of one board.

17 Two tenons *shall there be* in one board, set in order one against another: thus shalt thou make for all the boards of the tabernacle.

18 And thou shalt make the boards for the tabernacle, twenty boards on the south side southward.

19 And thou shalt make forty sockets of silver under the twenty boards; two sockets under one board for his two tenons, and two sockets under another board for his two tenons.

20 And for the second side of the tabernacle on the north side *there shall be* twenty boards:

21 And their forty sockets *of* silver; two sockets under one board, and two sockets under another board.

22 And for the sides of the tabernacle westward thou shalt make six boards.

23 And two boards shalt thou make for the corners of the tabernacle in the two sides.

24 And they shall be coupled together beneath, and they shall be coupled together above the head of it unto one ring: thus shall it be for them both; they shall be for the two corners.

25 And they shall be eight boards, and their sockets *of* silver, sixteen sockets; two sockets under one board, and two sockets under another board.

26 ¶ And thou shalt make bars *of* shittim wood; five for the boards of the one side of the tabernacle,

27 And five bars for the boards of the other side of the tabernacle, and five bars for the boards of the side of the tabernacle, for the two sides westward.

28 And the middle bar in the midst of the boards shall reach from end to end.

29 And thou shalt overlay the boards with gold, and make their rings *of* gold *for* places for the bars: and thou shalt overlay the bars with gold.

30 And thou shalt rear up the tabernacle [v]according to the fashion thereof which was shewed thee in the mount.

31 ¶ And [w]thou shalt make a vail *of* blue, and purple, and scarlet, and fine twined linen of cunning work: with cherubims shall it be made:

32 And thou shalt hang it upon four pillars of shittim *wood* overlaid with gold: their hooks *shall be of* gold, upon the four sockets of silver.

33 ¶ And thou shalt hang up the vail under the taches, that thou mayest bring in thither within the vail [x]the ark of the testimony: and the vail shall divide unto you between [y]the holy *place* and the most holy.

34 And [z]thou shalt put the mercy seat upon the ark of the testimony in the most holy *place.*

35 And [a]thou shalt set the table without the vail, and [b]the candlestick over against the table on the side of the tabernacle toward the south: and thou shalt put the table on the north side.

36 And [c]thou shalt make an hanging for the door of the tent, *of* blue, and purple, and scarlet, and fine twined linen, wrought with needlework.

37 And thou shalt make for the hanging [d]five pillars *of* shittim *wood,* and overlay them with gold, *and* their hooks *shall be of* gold: and thou shalt cast five sockets of brass for them.

27 And thou shalt make [e]an altar *of* shittim wood, five cubits long, and five cubits broad; the altar shall be foursquare: and the height thereof *shall be* three cubits.

2 And thou shalt make the horns of it upon the four corners thereof: his horns shall be of the same: and [f]thou shalt overlay it with brass.

3 And thou shalt make his pans to receive his ashes, and his shovels, and his basons, and his fleshhooks, and his firepans: all the vessels thereof thou shalt make *of* brass.

4 And thou shalt make for it a grate of network *of* brass; and upon the net shalt thou make four brasen rings in the four corners thereof.

5 And thou shalt put it under the compass of the altar beneath, that the net may be even to the midst of the altar.

6 And thou shalt make staves for the altar, staves *of* shittim wood, and overlay them with brass.

7 And the staves shall be put into the rings, and the staves shall be upon the two sides of the altar, to bear it.

26:14 *u*ch. 36:19
26:30 *v*ch. 25:9; Acts 7:44; Heb. 8:5
26:31 *w*ch. 36:35; Lev. 16:2; 2 Chron. 3:14; Matt. 27:51; Heb. 9:3
26:33 *x*ch. 25:16 *y*Lev. 16:2; Heb. 9:2
26:34 *z*ch. 25:21; Heb. 9:5
26:35 *a*ch. 40:22; Heb. 9:2 *b*ch. 40:24
26:36 *c*ch. 36:37
26:37 *d*ch. 36:38
27:1 *e*ch. 38:1; Ezek. 43:13
27:2 *f*Num. 16:38

8 Hollow with boards shalt thou make it: [g]as it was shewed thee in the mount, so shall they make *it*.

9 ¶ And [h]thou shalt make the court of the tabernacle: for the south side southward *there shall be* hangings for the court *of* fine twined linen of an hundred cubits long for one side:

10 And the twenty pillars thereof and their twenty sockets *shall be of* brass; the hooks of the pillars and their fillets *shall be of* silver.

11 And likewise for the north side in length *there shall be* hangings of an hundred *cubits* long, and his twenty pillars and their twenty sockets *of* brass; the hooks of the pillars and their fillets *of* silver.

12 And *for* the breadth of the court on the west side *shall be* hangings of fifty cubits: their pillars ten, and their sockets ten.

13 And the breadth of the court on the east side eastward *shall be* fifty cubits.

14 The hangings of one side *of the gate shall be* fifteen cubits: their pillars three, and their sockets three.

15 And on the other side *shall be* hangings fifteen *cubits*: their pillars three, and their sockets three.

16 ¶ And for the gate of the court *shall be* an hanging of twenty cubits, *of* blue, and purple, and scarlet, and fine twined linen, wrought with needlework: *and* their pillars *shall be* four, and their sockets four.

17 All the pillars round about the court *shall be* filleted with silver; their hooks *shall be of* silver, and their sockets *of* brass.

18 The length of the court *shall be* an hundred cubits, and the breadth fifty every where, and the height five cubits *of* fine twined linen, and their sockets *of* brass.

19 All the vessels of the tabernacle in all the service thereof, and all the pins thereof, and all the pins of the court, *shall be of* brass.

20 ¶ And [i]thou shalt command the children of Israel, that they bring thee pure oil olive beaten for the light, to cause the lamp to burn always.

21 In the tabernacle of the congregation [j]without the vail, which *is* before the testimony, [k]Aaron and his sons shall order it from evening to morning before the LORD: [l]*it shall be* a statute for ever unto their generations on the behalf of the children of Israel.

28 And take thou unto thee [m]Aaron thy brother, and his sons with him, from among the children of Israel, that he may minister unto me in the priest's office, *even* Aaron, Nadab and Abihu, Eleazar and Ithamar, Aaron's sons.

2 And [n]thou shalt make holy garments for Aaron thy brother for glory and for beauty.

3 And [o]thou shalt speak unto all *that are* wise hearted, [p]whom I have filled with the spirit of wisdom, that they may make Aaron's garments to consecrate him, that he may minister unto me in the priest's office.

4 And these *are* the garments which they shall make; [q]a breastplate, and [r]an ephod, and [s]a robe, and [t]a broidered coat, a mitre, and a girdle: and they shall make holy garments for Aaron thy brother, and his sons, that he may minister unto me in the priest's office.

5 And they shall take gold, and blue, and purple, and scarlet, and fine linen.

6 ¶ [u]And they shall make the ephod *of* gold, *of* blue, and *of* purple, *of* scarlet, and fine twined linen, with cunning work.

7 It shall have the two shoulderpieces thereof joined at the two edges thereof; and *so* it shall be joined together.

8 And the curious girdle of the ephod, which *is* upon it, shall be of the same, according to the work thereof; *even of* gold, *of* blue, and purple, and scarlet, and fine twined linen.

9 And thou shalt take two onyx stones, and grave on them the names of the children of Israel:

10 Six of their names on one stone, and *the other* six names of the rest on the other stone, according to their birth.

11 With the work of an engraver in stone, *like* the engravings of a signet, shalt thou engrave the two stones with the names of the children of Israel: thou shalt make them to be set in ouches of gold.

12 And thou shalt put the two stones upon the shoulders of the ephod *for* stones of memorial unto the children of Israel: and [v]Aaron shall bear their names before the LORD upon his two shoulders [w]for a memorial.

13 And thou shalt make ouches *of* gold;

14 And two chains *of* pure gold at the ends; *of* wreathen work shalt thou make them, and fasten the wreathen chains to the ouches.

15 ¶ And [x]thou shalt make the breastplate of judgment with cunning work; after the work of the ephod thou shalt make it; *of* gold, *of* blue, and *of* purple, and *of* scarlet, and *of* fine twined linen, shalt thou make it.

16 Foursquare it shall be *being* doubled; a span *shall be* the length thereof, and a span *shall be* the breadth thereof.

17 [y]And thou shalt set in it settings of stones, *even* four rows of stones: *the first* row *shall be* a sardius, a topaz, and a carbuncle: *this shall be* the first row.

18 And the second row *shall be* an emerald, a sapphire, and a diamond.

19 And the third row a ligure, an agate, and an amethyst.

20 And the fourth row a beryl, and an onyx, and a jasper: they shall be set in gold in their inclosings.

21 And the stones shall be with the names of the children of Israel, twelve, according to their names, *like* the engravings of a signet; every one with his name shall they be according to the twelve tribes.

27:8 [g]ch. 25:40
27:9 [h]ch. 38:9
27:20 [i]Lev. 24:2
27:21 [j]ch. 26:31 [k]ch. 30:8; 1 Sam. 3:3; 2 Chron. 13:11 [l]ch. 28:43; Lev. 3:17; Num. 18:23; 1 Sam. 30:25
28:1 [m]Num. 18:7; Heb. 5:1
28:2 [n]ch. 29:5; Lev. 8:7; Num. 20:26
28:3 [o]ch. 31:6 [p]ch. 31:3
28:4 [q]ver. 15 [r]ver. 6 [s]ver. 31 [t]ver. 39
28:6 [u]ch. 39:2
28:12 [v]ver. 29; ch. 39:7 [w]Josh. 4:7; Zech. 6:14
28:15 [x]ch. 39:8
28:17 [y]ch. 39:10

22 ¶ And thou shalt make upon the breastplate chains at the ends *of* wreathen work *of* pure gold.

23 And thou shalt make upon the breastplate two rings of gold, and shalt put the two rings on the two ends of the breastplate.

24 And thou shalt put the two wreathen *chains* of gold in the two rings *which are* on the ends of the breastplate.

25 And *the other* two ends of the two wreathen *chains* thou shalt fasten in the two ouches, and put *them* on the shoulder pieces of the ephod before it.

26 ¶ And thou shalt make two rings of gold, and thou shalt put them upon the two ends of the breastplate in the border thereof, which *is* in the side of the ephod inward.

27 And two *other* rings of gold thou shalt make, and shalt put them on the two sides of the ephod underneath, toward the forepart thereof, over against the *other* coupling thereof, above the curious girdle of the ephod.

28 And they shall bind the breastplate by the rings thereof unto the rings of the ephod with a lace of blue, that *it* may be above the curious girdle of the ephod, and that the breastplate be not loosed from the ephod.

29 And Aaron shall bear the names of the children of Israel in the breastplate of judgment upon his heart, when he goeth in unto the holy *place,* [z]for a memorial before the LORD continually.

30 ¶ And [a]thou shalt put in the breastplate of judgment the Urim and the Thummim; and they shall be upon Aaron's heart, when he goeth in before the LORD: and Aaron shall bear the judgment of the children of Israel upon his heart before the LORD continually.

31 ¶ And [b]thou shalt make the robe of the ephod all *of* blue.

32 And there shall be an hole in the top of it, in the midst thereof: it shall have a binding of woven work round about the hole of it, as it were the hole of an habergeon, that it be not rent.

33 ¶ And *beneath* upon the hem of it thou shalt make pomegranates *of* blue, and *of* purple, and *of* scarlet, round about the hem thereof; and bells of gold between them round about:

34 A golden bell and a pomegranate, a golden bell and a pomegranate, upon the hem of the robe round about.

35 And it shall be upon Aaron to minister: and his sound shall be heard when he goeth in unto the holy *place* before the LORD, and when he cometh out, that he die not.

36 ¶ And [c]thou shalt make a plate *of* pure gold, and grave upon it, *like* the engravings of a signet, HOLINESS TO THE LORD.

37 And thou shalt put it on a blue lace, that it may be upon the mitre; upon the forefront of the mitre it shall be.

38 And it shall be upon Aaron's forehead, that Aaron may [d]bear the iniquity of the holy things, which the children of Israel shall hallow in all their holy gifts; and it shall be always upon his forehead, that they may be [e]accepted before the LORD.

39 ¶ And thou shalt embroider the coat of fine linen, and thou shalt make the mitre of fine linen, and thou shalt make the girdle *of* needlework.

40 ¶ [f]And for Aaron's sons thou shalt make coats, and thou shalt make for them girdles, and bonnets shalt thou make for them, for glory and for beauty.

41 And thou shalt put them upon Aaron thy brother, and his sons with him; and shalt [g]anoint them, and [h]consecrate them, and sanctify them, that they may minister unto me in the priest's office.

42 And thou shalt make them [i]linen breeches to cover their nakedness; from the loins even unto the thighs they shall reach:

43 And they shall be upon Aaron, and upon his sons, when they come in unto the tabernacle of the congregation, or when they come near [j]unto the altar to minister in the holy *place;* that they [k]bear not iniquity, and die: [l]*it shall be* a statute for ever unto him and his seed after him.

29 And this *is* the thing that thou shalt do unto them to hallow them, to minister unto me in the priest's office: [m]Take one young bullock, and two rams without blemish,

2 And [n]unleavened bread, and cakes unleavened tempered with oil, and wafers unleavened anointed with oil: *of* wheaten flour shalt thou make them.

3 And thou shalt put them into one basket, and bring them in the basket, with the bullock and the two rams.

4 And Aaron and his sons thou shalt bring unto the door of the tabernacle of the congregation, [o]and shalt wash them with water.

5 [p]And thou shalt take the garments, and put upon Aaron the coat, and the robe of the ephod, and the ephod, and the breastplate, and gird him with [q]the curious girdle of the ephod:

6 [r]And thou shalt put the mitre upon his head, and put the holy crown upon the mitre.

7 Then shalt thou take the anointing [s]oil, and pour *it* upon his head, and anoint him.

8 And [t]thou shalt bring his sons, and put coats upon them.

9 And thou shalt gird them with girdles, Aaron and his sons, and put the bonnets on them: and [u]the priest's office shall be theirs for a perpetual statute: and thou shalt [v]consecrate Aaron and his sons.

10 And thou shalt cause a bullock to be brought before the tabernacle of the congregation: and [w]Aaron and his sons shall put their hands upon the head of the bullock.

11 And thou shalt kill the bullock before the LORD, *by* the door of the tabernacle of the congregation.

28:29 [z]ver. 12
28:30 [a]Lev. 8:8; Num. 27:21; Deut. 33:8; 1 Sam. 28:6; Ezra 2:63; Neh. 7:65
28:31 [b]ch. 39:22
28:36 [c]ch. 39:30; Zech. 14:20
28:38 [d]ver. 43; Lev. 10:17; Num. 18:1; Isa. 53:11; Ezek. 4:4; John 1:29; Heb. 9:28; 1 Pet. 2:24 [e]Lev. 1:4; Isa. 56:7
28:40 [f]ver. 4; ch. 39:27; Ezek. 44:17
28:41 [g]ch. 29:7; Lev. 10:7 [h]ch. 29:9; Lev. ch. 8; Heb. 7:28
28:42 [i]ch. 39:28; Lev. 6:10; Ezek. 44:18
28:43 [j]ch. 20:26 [k]Lev. 5:1; Num. 9:13 [l]ch. 27:21; Lev. 17:7
29:1 [m]Lev. 8:2
29:2 [n]Lev. 2:4
29:4 [o]ch. 40:12; Lev. 8:6; Heb. 10:22
29:5 [p]ch. 28:2; Lev. 8:7 [q]ch. 28:8
29:6 [r]Lev. 8:9
29:7 [s]ch. 28:41; Lev. 8:12; Num. 35:25
29:8 [t]Lev. 8:13
29:9 [u]Num. 18:7 [v]ch. 28:41; Lev. 8:22; Heb. 7:28
29:10 [w]Lev. 1:4

12 And thou [x]shalt take of the blood of the bullock, and put *it* upon [y]the horns of the altar with thy finger, and pour all the blood beside the bottom of the altar.

13 And [z]thou shalt take all the fat that covereth the inwards, and the caul *that is* above the liver, and the two kidneys, and the fat that *is* upon them, and burn *them* upon the altar.

14 But [a]the flesh of the bullock, and his skin, and his dung, shalt thou burn with fire without the camp: it *is* a sin offering.

15 ¶ [b]Thou shalt also take one ram; and Aaron and his sons shall [c]put their hands upon the head of the ram.

16 And thou shalt slay the ram, and thou shalt take his blood, and sprinkle *it* around about upon the altar.

17 And thou shalt cut the ram in pieces, and wash the inwards of him, and his legs, and put *them* unto his pieces, and unto his head.

18 And thou shalt burn the whole ram upon the altar: it *is* a burnt offering unto the LORD: it *is* a [d]sweet savour, an offering made by fire unto the LORD.

19 ¶ [e]And thou shalt take the other ram; and Aaron and his sons shall put their hands upon the head of the ram.

20 Then shalt thou kill the ram, and take of his blood, and put *it* upon the tip of the right ear of Aaron, and upon the tip of the right ear of his sons, and upon the thumb of their right hand, and upon the great toe of their right foot, and sprinkle the blood upon the altar round about.

21 And thou shalt take of the blood that *is* upon the altar, and of [f]the anointing oil, and sprinkle *it* upon Aaron, and upon his garments, and upon his sons, and upon the garments of his sons with him: and [g]he shall be hallowed, and his garments, and his sons, and his sons' garments with him.

22 Also thou shalt take of the ram the fat and the rump, and the fat that covereth the inwards, and the caul *above* the liver, and the two kidneys, and the fat that *is* upon them, and the right shoulder; for it *is* a ram of consecration:

23 [h]And one loaf of bread, and one cake of oiled bread, and one wafer out of the basket of the unleavened bread that *is* before the LORD:

24 And thou shalt put all in the hands of Aaron, and in the hands of his sons; and shalt [i]wave them *for* a wave offering before the LORD.

25 [j]And thou shalt receive them of their hands, and burn *them* upon the altar for a burnt offering, for a sweet savour before the LORD: it *is* an offering made by fire unto the LORD.

26 And thou shalt take [k]the breast of the ram of Aaron's consecration, and wave it *for* a wave offering before the LORD: and [l]it shall be thy part.

27 And thou shalt sanctify [m]the breast of the wave offering, and the shoulder of the

29:12 [x]Lev. 8:15 [y]ch. 27:2
29:13 [z]Lev. 3:3
29:14 [a]Lev. 4:11; Heb. 13:11
29:15 [b]Lev. 8:18 [c]Lev. 1:4-9
29:18 [d]Gen. 8:21
29:19 [e]ver. 3; Lev. 8:22
29:21 [f]ch. 30:25; Lev. 8:30 [g]ver. 1; Heb. 9:22
29:23 [h]Lev. 8:26
29:24 [i]Lev. 7:30
29:25 [j]Lev. 8:28
29:26 [k]Lev. 8:29 [l]Ps. 99:6
29:27 [m]Lev. 7:31; Num. 18:11; Deut. 18:3
29:28 [n]Lev. 10:15 [o]Lev. 7:34
29:29 [p]Num. 20:26 [q]Num. 18:8
29:30 [r]Num. 20:28 [s]Lev. 8:35
29:31 [t]Lev. 8:31
29:32 [u]Matt. 12:4
29:33 [v]Lev. 10:14 [w]Lev. 22:10
29:34 [x]Lev. 8:32
29:35 [y]Ex. 40:12; Lev. 8:33
29:36 [z]Heb. 10:11 [a]ch. 30:26
29:37 [b]ch. 40:10 [c]ch. 30:29; Matt. 23:19
29:38 [d]Num. 28:3; 1 Chron. 16:40; 2 Chron. 2:4; Ezra 3:3 [e]Dan. 9:27
29:39 [f]2 Kings 16:15; Ezek. 46:13
29:41 [g]1 Kings 18:29; 2 Kings 16:15; Ezra 9:4; Ps. 141:2; Dan. 9:21
29:42 [h]ver. 38; ch. 30:8; Num. 28:6; Dan. 8:11

heave offering, which is waved, and which is heaved up, of the ram of the consecration, *even* of *that* which *is* for Aaron, and of *that* which is for his sons:

28 And it shall be Aaron's and his sons' [n]by a statute for ever from the children of Israel: for it *is* an heave offering: and [o]it shall be an heave offering from the children of Israel of the sacrifice of their peace offerings, *even* their heave offering unto the LORD.

29 ¶ And the holy garments of Aaron [p]shall be his sons' after him, [q]to be anointed therein, and to be consecrated in them.

30 *And* [r]that son that is priest in his stead shall put them on [s]seven days, when he cometh into the tabernacle of the congregation to minister in the holy *place*.

31 ¶ And thou shalt take the ram of the consecration, and [t]seethe his flesh in the holy place.

32 And Aaron and his sons shall eat the flesh of the ram, and the [u]bread that *is* in the basket, *by* the door of the tabernacle of the congregation.

33 And [v]they shall eat those things wherewith the atonement was made, to consecrate *and* to sanctify them: [w]but a stranger shall not eat *thereof*, because they *are* holy.

34 And if ought of the flesh of the consecrations, or of the bread, remain unto the morning, then [x]thou shalt burn the remainder with fire: it shall not be eaten, because it *is* holy.

35 And thus shalt thou do unto Aaron, and to his sons, according to all *things* which I have commanded thee: [y]seven days shalt thou consecrate them.

36 And thou shalt [z]offer every day a bullock *for* a sin offering for atonement: and thou shalt cleanse the altar, when thou hast made an atonement for it, [a]and thou shalt anoint it, to sanctify it.

37 Seven days thou shalt make an atonement for the altar, and sanctify it; [b]and it shall be an altar most holy: [c]whatsoever toucheth the altar shall be holy.

38 ¶ Now this *is that* which thou shalt offer upon the altar; [d]two lambs of the first year [e]day by day continually.

39 The one lamb thou shalt offer [f]in the morning; and the other lamb thou shalt offer at even:

40 And with the one lamb a tenth deal of flour mingled with the fourth part of an hin of beaten oil; and the fourth part of an hin of wine *for* a drink offering.

41 And the other lamb thou shalt [g]offer at even, and shalt do thereto according to the meat offering of the morning, and according to the drink offering thereof, for a sweet savour, an offering made by fire unto the LORD.

42 *This shall be* [h]a continual burnt offering throughout your generations *at* the door of the tabernacle of the congregation

before the LORD: [i]where I will meet you, to speak there unto thee.

43 And there I will meet with the children of Israel, and *the tabernacle* [j]shall be sanctified by my glory.

44 And I will sanctify the tabernacle of the congregation, and the altar: I will [k]sanctify also both Aaron and his sons, to minister to me in the priest's office.

45 And [l]I will dwell among the children of Israel, and will be their God.

46 And they shall know that [m]I *am* the LORD their God, that brought them forth out of the land of Egypt, that I may dwell among them: I *am* the LORD their God.

30

And thou shalt make [n]an altar [o]to burn incense upon: *of* shittim wood shalt thou make it.

2 A cubit *shall be* the length thereof, and a cubit the breadth thereof; foursquare shall it be: and two cubits *shall be* the height thereof: the horns thereof *shall be* of the same.

3 And thou shalt overlay it with pure gold, the top thereof, and the sides thereof round about, and the horns thereof; and thou shalt make unto it a crown of gold round about.

4 And two golden rings shalt thou make to it under the crown of it, by the two corners thereof, upon the two sides of it shalt thou make *it;* and they shall be for places for the staves to bear it withal.

5 And thou shalt make the staves *of* shittim wood, and overlay them with gold.

6 And thou shalt put it before the vail that *is* by the ark of the testimony, before the [p]mercy seat that *is* over the testimony, where I will meet with thee.

7 And Aaron shall burn thereon [q]sweet incense every morning: when [r]he dresseth the lamps, he shall burn incense upon it.

8 And when Aaron lighteth the lamps at even, he shall burn incense upon it, a perpetual incense before the LORD throughout your generations.

9 Ye shall offer no [s]strange incense thereon, nor burnt sacrifice, nor meat offering; neither shall ye pour drink offering thereon.

10 And [t]Aaron shall make an atonement upon the horns of it once in a year with the blood of the sin offering of atonements: once in the year shall he make atonement upon it throughout your generations: it *is* most holy unto the LORD.

11 ¶ And the LORD spake unto Moses, saying,

12 [u]When thou takest the sum of the children of Israel after their number, then shall they give every man [v]a ransom for his soul unto the LORD, when thou numberest them; that there be no [w]plague among them, when *thou* numberest them.

13 [x]This they shall give, every one that passeth among them that are numbered, half a shekel after the shekel of the sanctuary: ([y]a shekel *is* twenty gerahs:) [z]an half shekel *shall be* the offering of the LORD.

14 Every one that passeth among them that are numbered, from twenty years old and above, shall give an offering unto the LORD.

15 The [a]rich shall not give more, and the poor shall not give less than half a shekel, when *they* give an offering unto the LORD, to make an [b]atonement for your souls.

16 And thou shalt take the atonement money of the children of Israel, and [c]shalt appoint it for the service of the tabernacle of the congregation; that it may be [d]a memorial unto the children of Israel before the LORD, to make an atonement for your souls.

17 ¶ And the LORD spake unto Moses, saying,

18 [e]Thou shalt also make a laver *of* brass, and his foot *also of* brass, to wash *withal:* and thou shalt [f]put it between the tabernacle of the congregation and the altar, and thou shalt put water therein.

19 For Aaron and his sons [g]shall wash their hands and their feet thereat:

20 When they go into the tabernacle of the congregation, they shall wash with water, that they die not; or when they come near to the altar to minister, to burn offering made by fire unto the LORD:

21 So they shall wash their hands and their feet, that they die not: and [h]it shall be a statute for ever to them, *even* to him and to his seed throughout their generations.

22 ¶ Moreover the LORD spake unto Moses, saying,

23 Take thou also unto thee [i]principal spices, of pure [j]myrrh five hundred *shekels,* and of sweet cinnamon half so much, *even* two hundred and fifty *shekels,* and of sweet [k]calamus two hundred and fifty *shekels,*

24 And of [l]cassia five hundred *shekels,* after the shekel of the sanctuary, and of oil olive an [m]hin:

25 And thou shalt make it an oil of holy ointment, an ointment compound after the art of the apothecary: it shall be [n]an holy anointing oil.

26 [o]And thou shalt anoint the tabernacle of the congregation therewith, and the ark of the testimony,

27 And the table and all his vessels, and the candlestick and his vessels, and the altar of incense,

28 And the altar of burnt offering with all his vessels, and the laver and his foot.

29 And thou shalt sanctify them, that they may be most holy: [p]whatsoever toucheth them shall be holy.

30 [q]And thou shalt anoint Aaron and his sons, and consecrate them, that *they* may minister unto me in the priest's office.

31 And thou shalt speak unto the children of Israel, saying, This shall be an holy anointing oil unto me throughout your generations.

32 Upon man's flesh shall it not be

29:42 [i]ch. 25:22; Num. 17:4
29:43 [j]ch. 40:34; 1 Kings 8:11; 2 Chron. 5:14; Ezek. 43:5; Hag. 2:7; Mal. 3:1
29:44 [k]Lev. 21:15
29:45 [l]Ex. 25:8; Lev. 26:12; Zech. 2:10; John 14:17; 2 Cor. 6:16; Rev. 21:3
29:46 [m]ch. 20:2
30:1 [n]ch. 37:25 [o]ver. 7; Lev. 4:7-18; Rev. 8:3
30:6 [p]ch. 25:21
30:7 [q]ver. 34; 1 Sam. 2:28; 1 Chron. 23:13; Luke 1:9 [r]ch. 27:21
30:9 [s]Lev. 10:1
30:10 [t]Lev. 16:18
30:12 [u]ch. 38:25; Num. 1:2; 2 Sam. 24:2 [v]Job 33:24; Ps. 49:7; Matt. 20:28; Mark 10:45; 1 Tim. 2:6; 1 Pet. 1:18 [w]2 Sam. 24:15
30:13 [x]Matt. 17:24 [y]Lev. 27:25; Num. 3:47; Ezek. 45:12 [z]ch. 38:26
30:15 [a]Job 34:19; Prov. 22:2; Eph. 6:9; Col. 3:25 [b]ver. 12
30:16 [c]ch. 38:25 [d]Num. 16:40
30:18 [e]ch. 38:8; 1 Kings 7:38 [f]ch. 40:7
30:19 [g]ch. 40:31; Ps. 26:6; Isa. 52:11; John 13:10; Heb. 10:22
30:21 [h]ch. 28:43
30:23 [i]SSol. 4:14; Ezek. 27:22 [j]Ps. 45:8; Prov. 7:17 [k]SSol. 4:14; Jer. 6:20
30:24 [l]Ps. 45:8 [m]ch. 29:40
30:25 [n]ch. 37:29; Num. 35:25; Ps. 89:20
30:26 [o]ch. 40:9; Lev. 8:10; Num. 7:1
30:29 [p]ch. 29:37
30:30 [q]ch. 29:7; Lev. 8:12

poured, neither shall ye make *any other* like it, after the composition of it: [r]it *is* holy, *and* it shall be holy unto you.

33 [s]Whosoever compoundeth *any* like it, or whosoever putteth *any* of it upon a stranger, [t]shall even be cut off from his people.

34 ¶ And the LORD said unto Moses, [u]Take unto thee sweet spices, stacte, and onycha, and galbanum; *these* sweet spices with pure frankincense: of each shall there be a like *weight:*

35 And thou shalt make it a perfume, a confection [v]after the art of the apothecary, tempered together, pure *and* holy:

36 And thou shalt beat *some* of it very small, and put of it before the testimony in the tabernacle of the congregation, [w]where I will meet with thee: [x]it shall be unto you most holy.

37 And *as for* the perfume which thou shalt make, [y]ye shall not make to yourselves according to the composition thereof: it shall be unto thee holy for the LORD.

38 [z]Whosoever shall make like unto that, to smell thereto, shall even be cut off from his people.

31 And the LORD spake unto Moses, saying,

2 [a]See, I have called by name Bezaleel the [b]son of Uri, the son of Hur, of the tribe of Judah:

3 And I have [c]filled him with the spirit of God, in wisdom, and in understanding, and in knowledge, and in all manner of workmanship,

4 To devise cunning works, to work in gold, and in silver, and in brass,

5 And in cutting of stones, to set *them,* and in carving of timber, to work in all manner of workmanship.

6 And I, behold, I have given with him [d]Aholiab, the son of Ahisamach, of the tribe of Dan: and in the hearts of all that are [e]wise hearted I have put wisdom, that they may make all that I have commanded thee;

7 [f]The tabernacle of the congregation, and [g]the ark of the testimony, and [h]the mercy seat that *is* thereupon, and all the furniture of the tabernacle,

8 And [i]the table and his furniture, and [j]the pure candlestick with all his furniture, and the altar of incense,

9 And [k]the altar of burnt offering with all his furniture, and [l]the laver and his foot,

10 And [m]the cloths of service, and the holy garments for Aaron the priest, and the garments of his sons, to minister in the priest's office,

11 [n]And the anointing oil, and [o]sweet incense for the holy *place:* according to all that I have commanded thee shall they do.

12 ¶ And the LORD spake unto Moses, saying,

13 Speak thou also unto the children of Israel, saying, [p]Verily my sabbaths ye shall keep: for it *is* a sign between me and you throughout your generations; that *ye* may know that I *am* the LORD that doth sanctify you.

14 [q]Ye shall keep the sabbath therefore; for it *is* holy unto you: every one that defileth it shall surely be put to death: for [r]whosoever doeth *any* work therein, that soul shall be cut off from among his people.

15 [s]Six days may work be done; but in the [t]seventh *is* the sabbath of rest, holy to the LORD: whosoever doeth *any* work in the sabbath day, he shall surely be put to death.

16 Wherefore the children of Israel shall keep the sabbath, to observe the sabbath throughout their generations, *for* a perpetual covenant.

17 It *is* [u]a sign between me and the children of Israel for ever: for [v]*in* six days the LORD made heaven and earth, and on the seventh day he rested, and was refreshed.

18 ¶ And he gave unto Moses, when he had made an end of communing with him upon mount Sinai, [w]two tables of testimony, tables of stone, written with the finger of God.

32 And when the people saw that Moses [x]delayed to come down out of the mount, the people gathered themselves together unto Aaron, and said unto him, [y]Up, make us gods, which shall [z]go before us; for *as for* this Moses, the man that brought us up out of the land of Egypt, we wot not what is become of him.

2 And Aaron said unto them, Break off the [a]golden earrings, which *are* in the ears of your wives, of your sons, and of your daughters, and bring *them* unto me.

3 And all the people brake off the golden earrings which *were* in their ears, and brought *them* unto Aaron.

4 [b]And he received *them* at their hand, and fashioned it with a graving tool, after he had made it a molten calf: and they said, These *be* thy gods, O Israel, which brought thee up out of the land of Egypt.

5 And when Aaron saw *it,* he built an altar before it; and Aaron made [c]proclamation, and said, To morrow *is* a feast to the LORD.

6 And they rose up early on the morrow, and offered burnt offerings, and brought peace offerings; and the [d]people sat down to eat and to drink, and rose up to play.

7 ¶ And the LORD said unto Moses, [e]Go, get thee down; for thy people, which thou broughtest out of the land of Egypt, [f]have corrupted *themselves:*

8 They have turned aside quickly out of the way which [g]I commanded them: they have made them a molten calf, and have worshipped it, and have sacrificed thereunto, and said, [h]These *be* thy gods, O Israel, which have brought thee up out of the land of Egypt.

9 And the LORD said unto Moses, [i]I have seen this people, and, behold, it *is* a stiffnecked people:

10 Now therefore [j]let me alone, that [k]my wrath may wax hot against them, and that

30:32 [r]ver. 25
30:33 [s]ver. 38 [t]Gen. 17:14; ch. 12:15; Lev. 7:20
30:34 [u]ch. 25:6
30:35 [v]ver. 25
30:36 [w]ch. 29:42; Lev. 16:2 [x]ver. 32; ch. 29:37; Lev. 2:3
30:37 [y]ver. 32
30:38 [z]ver. 33
31:2 [a]ch. 35:30 [b]1 Chron. 2:20
31:3 [c]ch. 35:31; 1 Kings 7:14
31:6 [d]ch. 35:34 [e]ch. 28:3
31:7 [f]ch. 36:8 [g]ch. 37:1 [h]ch. 37:6
31:8 [i]ch. 37:10 [j]ch. 37:17
31:9 [k]ch. 38:1 [l]ch. 38:8
31:10 [m]ch. 39:1; Num. 4:5
31:11 [n]ch. 30:25 [o]ch. 30:34
31:13 [p]Lev. 19:3; Ezek. 20:12
31:14 [q]ch. 20:8; Deut. 5:12; Ezek. 20:12 [r]ch. 35:2; Num. 15:35
31:15 [s]ch. 20:9 [t]Gen. 2:2; ch. 16:23
31:17 [u]ver. 13; Ezek. 20:12 [v]Gen. 1:31
31:18 [w]ch. 24:12; Deut. 4:13; 2 Cor. 3:3
32:1 [x]ch. 24:18; Deut. 9:9 [y]Acts 7:40 [z]ch. 13:21
32:2 [a]Judg. 8:24
32:4 [b]ch. 20:23; Deut. 9:16; Judg. 17:3; 1 Kings 12:28; Neh. 9:18; Ps. 106:19; Isa. 46:6; Acts 7:41; Rom. 1:23
32:5 [c]Lev. 23:2; 2 Kings 10:20; 2 Chron. 30:5
32:6 [d]1 Cor. 10:7
32:7 [e]Deut. 9:12; ver. 1; ch. 33:1; Dan. 9:24 [f]Gen. 6:11; Deut. 4:16; Judg. 2:19; Hos. 9:9
32:8 [g]ch. 20:3; Deut. 9:16 [h]1 Kings 12:28
32:9 [i]ch. 33:3; Deut. 9:6; 2 Chron. 30:8; Isa. 48:4; Acts 7:51
32:10 [j]Deut. 9:14 [k]ch. 22:24

I may consume them: and [l]I will make of thee a great nation.

11 [m]And Moses besought the LORD his God, and said, LORD, why doth thy wrath wax hot against thy people, which thou hast brought forth out of the land of Egypt with great power, and with a mighty hand?

12 [n]Wherefore should the Egyptians speak, and say, For mischief did he bring them out, to slay them in the mountains, and to consume them from the face of the earth? Turn from thy fierce wrath, and [o]repent of this evil against thy people.

13 Remember Abraham, Isaac, and Israel, thy servants, to whom thou [p]swarest by thine own self, and saidst unto them, [q]I will multiply your seed as the stars of heaven, and all this land that I have spoken of will I give unto your seed, and they shall inherit *it* for ever.

14 And the LORD [r]repented of the evil which he thought to do unto his people.

15 ¶ And [s]Moses turned, and went down from the mount, and the two tables of the testimony *were* in his hand: the tables *were* written on both their sides; on the one side and on the other *were* they written.

16 And the [t]tables *were* the work of God, and the writing *was* the writing of God, graven upon the tables.

17 And when Joshua heard the noise of the people as they shouted, he said unto Moses, *There is* a noise of war in the camp.

18 And he said, *It is* not the voice of *them that* shout for mastery, neither *is it* the voice of *them that* cry for being overcome: *but* the noise of *them that* sing do I hear.

19 ¶ And it came to pass, as soon as he came nigh unto the camp, that [u]he saw the calf, and the dancing: and Moses' anger waxed hot, and he cast the tables out of his hands, and brake them beneath the mount.

20 [v]And he took the calf which they had made, and burnt *it* in the fire, and ground *it* to powder, and strawed *it* upon the water, and made the children of Israel drink *of it*.

21 And Moses said unto Aaron, [w]What did this people unto thee, that thou hast brought so great a sin upon them?

22 And Aaron said, Let not the anger of my lord wax hot: [x]thou knowest the people, that they *are set* on mischief.

23 For they said unto me, [y]Make us gods, which shall go before us: for *as for* this Moses, the man that brought us up out of the land of Egypt, we wot not what is become of him.

24 And I said unto them, Whosoever hath any gold, let them break *it* off. So they gave *it* me: then I cast it into the fire, and there [z]came out this calf.

25 ¶ And when Moses saw that the people *were* [a]naked; (for Aaron [b]had made them naked unto *their* shame among their enemies:)

26 Then Moses stood in the gate of the camp, and said, Who *is* on the LORD's side? *let him come* unto me. And all the sons of Levi gathered themselves together unto him.

27 And he said unto them, Thus saith the LORD God of Israel, Put every man his sword by his side, *and* go in and out from gate to gate throughout the camp, and [c]slay every man his brother, and every man his companion, and every man his neighbour.

28 And the children of Levi did according to the word of Moses: and there fell of the people that day about three thousand men.

29 [d]For Moses had said, Consecrate yourselves to day to the LORD, even every man upon his son, and upon his brother; that he may bestow upon you a blessing this day.

30 ¶ And it came to pass on the morrow, that Moses said unto the people, [e]Ye have sinned a great sin: and now I will go up unto the LORD; [f]peradventure I shall [g]make an atonement for your sin.

31 And Moses [h]returned unto the LORD, and said, Oh, this people have sinned a great sin, and have [i]made them gods of gold.

32 Yet now, if thou wilt forgive their sin—; and if not, [j]blot me, I pray thee, [k]out of thy book which thou hast written.

33 And the LORD said unto Moses, [l]Whosoever hath sinned against me, him will I blot out of my book.

34 Therefore now go, lead the people unto *the place* of which I have spoken unto thee: [m]behold, mine Angel shall go before thee: nevertheless [n]in the day when I visit I will visit their sin upon them.

35 And the LORD plagued the people, because [o]they made the calf, which Aaron made.

33

And the LORD said unto Moses, Depart, *and* go up hence, thou [p]and the people which thou hast brought up out of the land of Egypt, unto the land which I sware unto Abraham, to Isaac, and to Jacob, saying, [q]Unto thy seed will I give it:

2 [r]And I will send an angel before thee; [s]and I will drive out the Canaanite, the Amorite, and the Hittite, and the Perizzite, the Hivite, and the Jebusite:

3 [t]Unto a land flowing with milk and honey: [u]for I will not go up in the midst of thee; for thou *art* a [v]stiffnecked people: lest [w]I consume thee in the way.

4 ¶ And when the people heard these evil tidings, [x]they mourned: [y]and no man did put on him his ornaments.

5 For the LORD had said unto Moses, Say unto the children of Israel, [z]Ye *are* a stiffnecked people: I will come up [a]into the midst of thee in a moment, and consume thee: therefore now put off thy ornaments from thee, that I may [b]know what to do unto thee.

6 And the children of Israel stripped themselves of their ornaments by the mount Horeb.

7 And Moses took the tabernacle, and pitched it without the camp, afar off from

32:10 [l]Num. 14:12
32:11 [m]Deut. 9:18; Ps. 74:1
32:12 [n]Num. 14:13; Deut. 9:28 [o]ver. 14
32:13 [p]Gen. 22:16; Heb. 6:13 [q]Gen. 12:7
32:14 [r]Deut. 32:26; 2 Sam. 24:16; 1 Chron. 21:15; Ps. 106:45; Jer. 18:8; Joel 2:13; Jonah 3:10
32:15 [s]Deut. 9:15
32:16 [t]ch. 31:18
32:19 [u]Deut. 9:16
32:20 [v]Deut. 9:21
32:21 [w]Gen. 20:9
32:22 [x]ch. 14:11
32:23 [y]ver. 1
32:24 [z]ver. 4
32:25 [a]ch. 33:4 [b]2 Chron. 28:19
32:27 [c]Num. 25:5; Deut. 33:9
32:29 [d]Num. 25:11; Deut. 13:6-11; 1 Sam. 15:18; Prov. 21:3; Zech. 13:3; Matt. 10:37
32:30 [e]1 Sam. 12:20; Luke 15:18 [f]2 Sam. 16:12; Am. 5:15 [g]Num. 25:13
32:31 [h]Deut. 9:18 [i]ch. 20:23
32:32 [j]Ps. 69:28; Rom. 9:3 [k]Ps. 56:8; Dan. 12:1; Phil. 4:3; Rev. 3:5
32:33 [l]Lev. 23:30; Ezek. 18:4
32:34 [m]ch. 33:2; Num. 20:16 [n]Deut. 32:35; Am. 3:14; Rom. 2:5
32:35 [o]2 Sam. 12:9; Acts 7:41
33:1 [p]ch. 32:7 [q]Gen. 12:7; ch. 32:13
33:2 [r]ch. 32:34 [s]Deut. 7:22; Josh. 24:11
33:3 [t]ch. 3:8 [u]ver. 15 [v]ch. 32:9; Deut. 9:6 [w]ch. 23:21; Num. 16:21
33:4 [x]Num. 14:1 [y]Lev. 10:6; 2 Sam. 19:24; 1 Kings 21:27; 2 Kings 19:1; Esth. 4:1; Ezra 9:3; Job 1:20; Isa. 32:11; Ezek. 24:17
33:5 [z]ver. 3 [a]Num. 16:45 [b]Deut. 8:2; Ps. 139:23

the camp, [c]and called it the Tabernacle of
the congregation. And it came to pass, *that*
every one which [d]sought the LORD went out
unto the tabernacle of the congregation,
which *was* without the camp.
8 And it came to pass, when Moses went
out unto the tabernacle, *that* all the people
rose up, and stood every man [e]*at* his tent
door, and looked after Moses, until he was
gone into the tabernacle.
9 And it came to pass, as Moses entered
into the tabernacle, the cloudy pillar descended, and stood *at* the door of the tabernacle, and *the LORD* [f]talked with Moses.
10 And all the people saw the cloudy pillar stand *at* the tabernacle door: and all the
people rose up and [g]worshipped, every
man *in* his tent door.
11 And [h]the LORD spake unto Moses face
to face, as a man speaketh unto his friend.
And he turned again into the camp: but [i]his
servant Joshua, the son of Nun, a young
man, departed not out of the tabernacle.
12 ¶ And Moses said unto the LORD, [j]See,
thou sayest unto me, Bring up this people:
and thou hast not let me know whom thou
wilt send with me. Yet thou hast said, [k]I
know thee by name, and thou hast also
found grace in my sight.
13 Now therefore, I pray thee, [l]if I have
found grace in thy sight, [m]shew me now thy
way, that I may know thee, that I may find
grace in thy sight: and consider that this
nation *is* [n]thy people.
14 And he said, [o]My presence shall go
with thee, and I will give thee [p]rest.
15 And he said unto him, [q]If thy presence
go not *with me,* carry us not up hence.
16 For wherein shall it be known here
that I and thy people have found grace in
thy sight? [r]*is it* not in that thou goest with
us? so [s]shall we be separated, I and thy
people, from all the people that *are* upon the
face of the earth.
17 And the LORD said unto Moses, [t]I will
do this thing also that thou hast spoken: for
[u]thou hast found grace in my sight, and I
know thee by name.
18 And he said, I beseech thee, shew me
[v]thy glory.
19 And he said, [w]I will make all my goodness pass before thee, and I will proclaim
the name of the LORD before thee; [x]and will
be [y]gracious to whom I will be gracious,
and will shew mercy on whom I will shew
mercy.
20 And he said, Thou canst not see my
face: for [z]there shall no man see me, and
live.
21 And the LORD said, Behold, *there is* a
place by me, and thou shalt stand upon a
rock:
22 And it shall come to pass, while my
glory passeth by, that I will put thee [a]in a
clift of the rock, and will [b]cover thee with
my hand while I pass by:
23 And I will take away mine hand, and
thou shalt see my back parts: but my face
shall [c]not be seen.
34 And the LORD said unto Moses,
[d]Hew thee two tables of stone like
unto the first: [e]and I will write upon *these*
tables the words that were in the first tables,
which thou brakest.
2 And be ready in the morning, and come
up in the morning unto mount Sinai, and
present thyself there to me [f]in the top of the
mount.
3 And no man shall [g]come up with thee,
neither let any man be seen throughout all
the mount; neither let the flocks nor herds
feed before that mount.
4 ¶ And he hewed two tables of stone like
unto the first; and Moses rose up early in the
morning, and went up unto mount Sinai, as
the LORD had commanded him, and took in
his hand the two tables of stone.
5 And the LORD descended in the cloud,
and stood with him there, and [h]proclaimed
the name of the LORD.
6 And the LORD passed by before him,
and proclaimed, The LORD, The LORD
[i]God, merciful and gracious, longsuffering,
and abundant in [j]goodness and [k]truth,
7 [l]Keeping mercy for thousands, [m]for-
giving iniquity and transgression and sin,
and [n]that will by no means clear *the guilty;*
visiting the iniquity of the fathers upon the
children, and upon the children's children,
unto the third and to the fourth *generation.*
8 And Moses made haste, and [o]bowed his
head toward the earth, and worshipped.
9 And he said, If now I have found grace
in thy sight, O Lord, [p]let my Lord, I pray
thee, go among us; for [q]it *is* a stiffnecked
people; and pardon our iniquity and our sin,
and take us for [r]thine inheritance.
10 ¶ And he said, Behold, [s]I make a covenant: before all thy people I will [t]do mar-
vels, such as have not been done in all the
earth, nor in any nation: and all the people
among which thou *art* shall see the work of
the LORD: for it *is* [u]a terrible thing that I will
do with thee.
11 [v]Observe thou that which I command
thee this day: behold, [w]I drive out before
thee the Amorite, and the Canaanite, and
the Hittite, and the Perizzite, and the Hivite,
and the Jebusite.
12 [x]Take heed to thyself, lest thou make
a covenant with the inhabitants of the land
whither thou goest, lest it be for [y]a snare in
the midst of thee:
13 But ye shall [z]destroy their altars,
break their images, and [a]cut down their
groves:
14 For thou shalt worship [b]no other god:
for the LORD, whose [c]name *is* Jealous, *is* a
[d]jealous God:
15 [e]Lest thou make a covenant with the

33:7 [c]ch. 29:42 [d]Deut. 4:29; 2 Sam. 21:1 **33:8** [e]Num. 16:27 **33:9** [f]ch. 25:22; Ps. 99:7 **33:10** [g]ch. 4:31 **33:11** [h]Gen. 32:30; Num. 12:8; Deut. 34:10 [i]ch. 24:13 **33:12** [j]ch. 32:34 [k]ver. 17; Gen. 18:19; Ps. 1:6; Jer. 1:5; John 10:14; 2 Tim. 2:19 **33:13** [l]ch. 34:9 [m]Ps. 25:4 [n]Deut. 9:26; Joel 2:17 **33:14** [o]ch. 13:21; Isa. 63:9 [p]Deut. 3:20; Josh. 21:44; Ps. 95:11 **33:15** [q]ver. 3; ch. 34:9 **33:16** [r]Num. 14:14 [s]ch. 34:10; Deut. 4:7; 2 Sam. 7:23; 1 Kings 8:53; Ps. 147:20 **33:17** [t]Gen. 19:21; Jam. 5:16 [u]ver. 12 **33:18** [v]ver. 20; 1 Tim. 6:16 **33:19** [w]ch. 34:5; Jer. 31:14 [x]Rom. 9:15 [y]Rom. 4:4 **33:20** [z]Gen. 32:30; ch. 24:10; Deut. 5:24; Judg. 6:22; Isa. 6:5; Rev. 1:16 **33:22** [a]Isa. 2:21 [b]Ps. 91:1 **33:23** [c]ver. 20; John 1:18 **34:1** [d]ch. 32:16; Deut. 10:1 [e]ver. 28; Deut. 10:2 **34:2** [f]ch. 19:20 **34:3** [g]ch. 19:12 **34:5** [h]ch. 33:19; Num. 14:17 **34:6** [i]Num. 14:18; 2 Chron. 30:9; Neh. 9:17; Ps. 86:15; Joel 2:13 [j]Ps. 31:19; Rom. 2:4 [k]Ps. 57:10 **34:7** [l]ch. 20:6; Deut. 5:10; Ps. 86:15; Jer. 32:18; Dan. 9:4 [m]Ps. 103:3; Dan. 9:9; Eph. 4:32; 1 John 1:9 [n]ch. 23:7; Josh. 24:19; Job 10:14; Mic. 6:11; Nah. 1:3 **34:8** [o]ch. 4:31 **34:9** [p]ch. 33:15 [q]ch. 33:3 [r]Deut. 32:9; Ps. 28:9; Jer. 10:16; Zech. 2:12 **34:10** [s]Deut. 5:2 [t]Deut. 4:32; 2 Sam. 7:23; Ps. 77:14 [u]Deut. 10:21; Ps. 145:6; Isa. 64:3 **34:11** [v]Deut. 5:32 [w]ch. 33:2
34:12 [x]ch. 23:32; Deut. 7:2; Judg. 2:2 [y]ch. 23:33 **34:13** [z]ch. 23:24; Deut. 12:3; Judg. 2:2 [a]Deut. 7:5; Judg. 6:25; 2 Kings 18:4; 2 Chron. 31:1
34:14 [b]ch. 20:3 [c]Isa. 9:6 [d]ch. 20:5 **34:15** [e]ver. 12

inhabitants of the land, and they [f]go a whoring after their gods, and do sacrifice unto their gods, and *one* [g]call thee, and thou [h]eat of his sacrifice;

16 And thou take of [i]their daughters unto thy sons, and their daughters [j]go a whoring after their gods, and make thy sons go a whoring after their gods.

17 [k]Thou shalt make thee no molten gods.

18 ¶ The feast of [l]unleavened bread shalt thou keep. Seven days thou shalt eat unleavened bread, as I commanded thee, in the time of the month Abib: for in the [m]month Abib thou camest out from Egypt.

19 [n]All that openeth the matrix *is* mine; and every firstling among thy cattle, *whether* ox or sheep, *that is male*.

20 But [o]the firstling of an ass thou shalt redeem with a lamb: and if thou redeem *him* not, then shalt thou break his neck. All the firstborn of thy sons thou shalt redeem. And none shall appear before me [p]empty.

21 ¶ [q]Six days thou shalt work, but on the seventh day thou shalt rest: in earing time and in harvest thou shalt rest.

22 ¶ [r]And thou shalt observe the feast of weeks, of the firstfruits of wheat harvest, and the feast of ingathering at the year's end.

23 ¶ [s]Thrice in the year shall all your men children appear before the Lord GOD, the God of Israel.

24 For I will [t]cast out the nations before thee, and [u]enlarge thy borders: [v]neither shall any man desire thy land, when thou shalt go up to appear before the LORD thy God thrice in the year.

25 [w]Thou shalt not offer the blood of my sacrifice with leaven; [x]neither shall the sacrifice of the feast of the passover be left unto the morning.

26 [y]The first of the firstfruits of thy land thou shalt bring unto the house of the LORD thy God. [z]Thou shalt not seethe a kid in his mother's milk.

27 And the LORD said unto Moses, Write thou [a]these words: for after the tenor of these words I have made a covenant with thee and with Israel.

28 [b]And he was there with the LORD forty days and forty nights; he did neither eat bread, nor drink water. And [c]he wrote upon the tables the words of the covenant, the ten commandments.

29 ¶ And it came to pass, when Moses came down from mount Sinai with the [d]two tables of testimony in Moses' hand, when he came down from the mount, that Moses wist not that [e]the skin of his face shone while he talked with him.

30 And when Aaron and all the children of Israel saw Moses, behold, the skin of his face shone; and they were afraid to come nigh him.

31 And Moses called unto them; and Aaron and all the rulers of the congregation returned unto him: and Moses talked with them.

32 And afterward all the children of Israel came nigh: [f]and he gave them in commandment all that the LORD had spoken with him in mount Sinai.

33 And *till* Moses had done speaking with them, he put [g]a vail on his face.

34 But [h]when Moses went in before the LORD to speak with him, he took the vail off, until he came out. And he came out, and spake unto the children of Israel *that* which he was commanded.

35 And the children of Israel saw the face of Moses, that the skin of Moses' face shone: and Moses put the vail upon his face again, until he went in to speak with him.

35

And Moses gathered all the congregation of the children of Israel together, and said unto them, [i]These *are* the words which the LORD hath commanded, that *ye* should do them.

2 [j]Six days shall work be done, but on the seventh day there shall be to you an holy day, a sabbath of rest to the LORD: whosoever doeth work therein shall be put to death.

3 [k]Ye shall kindle no fire throughout your habitations upon the sabbath day.

4 ¶ And Moses spake unto all the congregation of the children of Israel, saying, [l]This *is* the thing which the LORD commanded, saying,

5 Take ye from among you an offering unto the LORD: [m]whosoever *is* of a willing heart, let him bring it, an offering of the LORD; gold, and silver, and brass,

6 And blue, and purple, and scarlet, and fine linen, and goats' *hair*,

7 And rams' skins dyed red, and badgers' skins, and shittim wood,

8 And oil for the light, [n]and spices for anointing oil, and for the sweet incense,

9 And onyx stones, and stones to be set for the ephod, and for the breastplate.

10 And [o]every wise hearted among you shall come, and make all that the LORD hath commanded;

11 [p]The tabernacle, his tent, and his covering, his taches, and his boards, his bars, his pillars, and his sockets,

12 [q]The ark, and the staves thereof, *with* the mercy seat, and the vail of the covering,

13 The [r]table, and his staves, and all his vessels, [s]and the shewbread,

14 [t]The candlestick also for the light, and his furniture, and his lamps, with the oil for the light,

15 [u]And the incense altar, and his staves, [v]and the anointing oil, and [w]the sweet incense, and the hanging for the door at the entering in of the tabernacle,

16 [x]The altar of burnt offering, with his brasen grate, his staves, and all his vessels, the laver and his foot,

17 [y]The hangings of the court, his pillars, and their sockets, and the hanging for the door of the court,

34:15 *f*Deut. 31:16; Judg. 2:17; Jer. 3:9; Ezek. 6:9 *g*Num. 25:2; 1 Cor. 10:27 *h*Ps. 106:28; 1 Cor. 8:4
34:16 *i*Deut. 7:3; 1 Kings 11:2; Ezra 9:2; Neh. 13:25 *j*Num. 25:1; 1 Kings 11:4
34:17 *k*ch. 32:8; Lev. 19:4
34:18 *l*ch. 12:15 *m*ch. 13:4
34:19 *n*ch. 13:2; Ezek. 44:30; Luke 2:23
34:20 *o*ch. 13:13; Num. 18:15 *p*ch. 23:15; Deut. 16:16; 1 Sam. 9:7; 2 Sam. 24:24
34:21 *q*ch. 20:9; Deut. 5:12; Luke 13:14
34:22 *r*ch. 23:16; Deut. 16:10
34:23 *s*ch. 23:14; Deut. 16:16
34:24 *t*ch. 33:2; Lev. 18:24; Deut. 7:1; Ps. 78:55 *u*Deut. 12:20 *v*Gen. 35:5; 2 Chron. 17:10; Prov. 16:7; Acts 18:10
34:25 *w*ch. 23:18 *x*ch. 12:10
34:26 *y*ch. 23:19; Deut. 26:2 *z*ch. 23:19; Deut. 14:21
34:27 *a*ver. 10; Deut. 4:13
34:28 *b*ch. 24:18; Deut. 9:9 *c*ver. 1; ch. 31:18; Deut. 4:13
34:29 *d*ch. 32:15 *e*Matt. 17:2; 2 Cor. 3:7
34:32 *f*ch. 24:3
34:33 *g*2 Cor. 3:13
34:34 *h*2 Cor. 3:16
35:1 *i*ch. 34:32
35:2 *j*ch. 20:9; Lev. 23:3; Num. 15:32; Deut. 5:12; Luke 13:14
35:3 *k*ch. 16:23
35:4 *l*ch. 25:1
35:5 *m*ch. 25:2
35:8 *n*ch. 25:6
35:10 *o*ch. 31:6
35:11 *p*ch. 26:1
35:12 *q*ch. 25:10
35:13 *r*ch. 25:23 *s*ch. 25:30; Lev. 24:5
35:14 *t*ch. 25:31
35:15 *u*ch. 30:1 *v*ch. 30:23 *w*ch. 30:34
35:16 *x*ch. 27:1
35:17 *y*ch. 27:9

18 The pins of the tabernacle, and the pins of the court, and their cords,

19 [z]The cloths of service, to do service in the holy *place*, the holy garments for Aaron the priest, and the garments of his sons, to minister in the priest's office.

20 ¶ And all the congregation of the children of Israel departed from the presence of Moses.

21 And they came, every one [a]whose heart stirred him up, and every one whom his spirit made willing, *and* they brought the LORD's offering to the work of the tabernacle of the congregation, and for all his service, and for the holy garments.

22 And they came, both men and women, as many as were willing hearted, *and* brought bracelets, and earrings, and rings, and tablets, all jewels of gold: and every man that offered *offered* an offering of gold unto the LORD.

23 And [b]every man, with whom was found blue, and purple, and scarlet, and fine linen, and goats' *hair*, and red skins of rams, and badgers' skins, brought *them*.

24 Every one that did offer an offering of silver and brass brought the LORD's offering: and every man, with whom was found shittim wood for any work of the service, brought *it*.

25 And all the women that were [c]wise hearted did spin with their hands, and brought that which they had spun, *both* of blue, and of purple, *and* of scarlet, and of fine linen.

26 And all the women whose heart stirred them up in wisdom spun goats' *hair*.

27 And [d]the rulers brought onyx stones, and stones to be set, for the ephod, and for the breastplate;

28 And [e]spice, and oil for the light, and for the anointing oil, and for the sweet incense.

29 The children of Israel brought a [f]willing offering unto the LORD, every man and woman, whose heart made them willing to bring for all manner of work, which the LORD had commanded to be made by the hand of Moses.

30 ¶ And Moses said unto the children of Israel, See, [g]the LORD hath called by name Bezaleel the son of Uri, the son of Hur, of the tribe of Judah;

31 And he hath filled him with the spirit of God, in wisdom, in understanding, and in knowledge, and in all manner of workmanship;

32 And to devise curious works, to work in gold, and in silver, and in brass,

33 And in the cutting of stones, to set *them*, and in carving of wood, to make any manner of cunning work.

34 And he hath put in his heart that he may teach, *both* he, and [h]Aholiab, the son of Ahisamach, of the tribe of Dan.

35 Them hath he [i]filled with wisdom of heart, to work all manner of work, of the engraver, and of the cunning workman, and of the embroiderer, in blue, and in purple, in scarlet, and in fine linen, and of the weaver, *even* of them that do any work, and of those that devise cunning work.

35:19 [z]ch. 31:10; Num. 4:5
35:21 [a]ver. 5; ch. 25:2; 1 Chron. 28:2; Ezra 7:27; 2 Cor. 8:12
35:23 [b]1 Chron. 29:8
35:25 [c]ch. 28:3; 2 Kings 23:7; Prov. 31:19
35:27 [d]1 Chron. 29:6; Ezra 2:68
35:28 [e]ch. 30:23
35:29 [f]ver. 21; 1 Chron. 29:9
35:30 [g]ch. 31:2
35:34 [h]ch. 31:6
35:35 [i]ver. 31; ch. 31:3; 1 Kings 7:14; 2 Chron. 2:14; Isa. 28:26
36:1 [j]ch. 28:3 [k]ch. 25:8
36:2 [l]ch. 35:2; 1 Chron. 29:5
36:3 [m]ch. 35:27
36:5 [n]2 Cor. 8:2
36:8 [o]ch. 26:1
36:12 [p]ch. 26:5
36:14 [q]ch. 26:7

36

Then wrought Bezaleel and Aholiab, and every [j]wise hearted man, in whom the LORD put wisdom and understanding to know how to work all manner of work for the service of the [k]sanctuary, according to all that the LORD had commanded.

2 And Moses called Bezaleel and Aholiab, and every wise hearted man, in whose heart the LORD had put wisdom, *even* every one [l]whose heart stirred him up to come unto the work to do it:

3 And they received of Moses all the offering, which the children of Israel [m]had brought for the work of the service of the sanctuary, to make it *withal*. And they brought yet unto him free offerings every morning.

4 And all the wise men, that wrought all the work of the sanctuary, came every man from his work which they made;

5 ¶ And they spake unto Moses, saying, [n]The people bring much more than enough for the service of the work, which the LORD commanded to make.

6 And Moses gave commandment, and they caused it to be proclaimed throughout the camp, saying, Let neither man nor woman make any more work for the offering of the sanctuary. So the people were restrained from bringing.

7 For the stuff they had was sufficient for all the work to make it, and too much.

8 ¶ [o]And every wise hearted man among them that wrought the work of the tabernacle made ten curtains *of* fine twined linen, and blue, and purple, and scarlet: *with* cherubims of cunning work made he them.

9 The length of one curtain *was* twenty and eight cubits, and the breadth of one curtain four cubits: the curtains *were* all of one size.

10 And he coupled the five curtains one unto another: and *the other* five curtains he coupled one unto another.

11 And he made loops of blue on the edge of one curtain from the selvedge in the coupling: likewise he made in the uttermost side of *another* curtain, in the coupling of the second.

12 [p]Fifty loops made he in one curtain, and fifty loops made he in the edge of the curtain which *was* in the coupling of the second: the loops held one *curtain* to another.

13 And he made fifty taches of gold, and coupled the curtains one unto another with the taches: so it became one tabernacle.

14 ¶ [q]And he made curtains *of* goats' *hair* for the tent over the tabernacle: eleven curtains he made them.

15 The length of one curtain *was* thirty cubits, and four cubits *was* the breadth of

one curtain: the eleven curtains *were* of one size.

16 And he coupled five curtains by themselves, and six curtains by themselves.

17 And he made fifty loops upon the uttermost edge of the curtain in the coupling, and fifty loops made he upon the edge of the curtain which coupleth the second.

18 And he made fifty taches *of* brass to couple the tent together, that it might be one.

19 [r]And he made a covering for the tent *of* rams' skins dyed red, and a covering *of* badgers' skins above *that*.

20 ¶ [s]And he made boards for the tabernacle *of* shittim wood, standing up.

21 The length of a board *was* ten cubits, and the breadth of a board one cubit and a half.

22 One board had two tenons, equally distant one from another: thus did he make for all the boards of the tabernacle.

23 And he made boards for the tabernacle; twenty boards for the south side southward:

24 And forty sockets of silver he made under the twenty boards; two sockets under one board for his two tenons, and two sockets under another board for his two tenons.

25 And for the other side of the tabernacle, *which is* toward the north corner, he made twenty boards,

26 And their forty sockets of silver; two sockets under one board, and two sockets under another board.

27 And for the sides of the tabernacle westward he made six boards.

28 And two boards made he for the corners of the tabernacle in the two sides.

29 And they were coupled beneath, and coupled together at the head thereof, to one ring: thus he did to both of them in both the corners.

30 And there were eight boards; and their sockets *were* sixteen sockets of silver, under every board two sockets.

31 ¶ And he made [t]bars of shittim wood; five for the boards of the one side of the tabernacle,

32 And five bars for the boards of the other side of the tabernacle, and five bars for the boards of the tabernacle for the sides westward.

33 And he made the middle bar to shoot through the boards from the one end to the other.

34 And he overlaid the boards with gold, and made their rings *of* gold *to be* places for the bars, and overlaid the bars with gold.

35 ¶ And he made [u]a vail *of* blue, and purple, and scarlet, and fine twined linen: *with* cherubims made he it of cunning work.

36 And he made thereunto four pillars *of* shittim *wood*, and overlaid them with gold: their hooks *were of* gold; and he cast for them four sockets of silver.

37 ¶ And he made an [v]hanging for the tabernacle door *of* blue, and purple, and scarlet, and fine twined linen, of needlework;

38 And the five pillars of it with their hooks: and he overlaid their chapiters and their fillets with gold: but their five sockets *were of* brass.

36:19 [r]ch. 26:14
36:20 [s]ch. 26:15
36:31 [t]ch. 26:26
36:35 [u]ch. 26:31
36:37 [v]ch. 26:36
37:1 [w]ch. 25:10
37:6 [x]ch. 25:17
37:10 [y]ch. 25:23
37:16 [z]ch. 25:29
37:17 [a]ch. 25:31

37 And Bezaleel made [w]the ark *of* shittim wood: two cubits and a half *was* the length of it, and a cubit and a half the breadth of it, and a cubit and a half the height of it:

2 And he overlaid it with pure gold within and without, and made a crown of gold to it round about.

3 And he cast for it four rings of gold, *to be set* by the four corners of it; even two rings upon the one side of it, and two rings upon the other side of it.

4 And he made staves *of* shittim wood, and overlaid them with gold.

5 And he put the staves into the rings by the sides of the ark, to bear the ark.

6 ¶ And he made the [x]mercy seat *of* pure gold: two cubits and a half *was* the length thereof, and one cubit and a half the breadth thereof.

7 And he made two cherubims *of* gold, beaten out of one piece made he them, on the two ends of the mercy seat;

8 One cherub on the end on this side, and another cherub on the *other* end on that side: out of the mercy seat made he the cherubims on the two ends thereof.

9 And the cherubims spread out *their* wings on high, *and* covered with their wings over the mercy seat, with their faces one to another; *even* to the mercy seatward were the faces of the cherubims.

10 ¶ And he made [y]the table *of* shittim wood: two cubits *was* the length thereof, and a cubit the breadth thereof, and a cubit and a half the height thereof:

11 And he overlaid it with pure gold, and made thereunto a crown of gold round about.

12 Also he made thereunto a border of an hand breadth round about; and made a crown of gold for the border thereof round about.

13 And he cast for it four rings of gold, and put the rings upon the four corners that *were* in the four feet thereof.

14 Over against the border were the rings, the places for the staves to bear the table.

15 And he made the staves *of* shittim wood, and overlaid them with gold, to bear the table.

16 And he made the vessels which *were* upon the table, his [z]dishes, and his spoons, and his bowls, and his covers to cover withal, *of* pure gold.

17 ¶ And he made the [a]candlestick *of* pure gold: *of* beaten work made he the candlestick; his shaft, and his branch, his bowls, his knops, and his flowers, were of the same:

18 And six branches going out of the

sides thereof; three branches of the candlestick out of the one side thereof, and three branches of the candlestick out of the other side thereof:

19 Three bowls made after the fashion of almonds in one branch, a knop and a flower; and three bowls made like almonds in another branch, a knop and a flower: so throughout the six branches going out of the candlestick.

20 And in the candlestick *were* four bowls made like almonds, his knops, and his flowers:

21 And a knop under two branches of the same, and a knop under two branches of the same, and a knop under two branches of the same, according to the six branches going out of it.

22 Their knops and their branches were of the same: all of it *was* one beaten work *of* pure gold.

23 And he made his seven lamps, and his snuffers, and his snuffdishes, *of* pure gold.

24 *Of* a talent of pure gold made he it, and all the vessels thereof.

25 ¶ [b]And he made the incense altar *of* shittim wood: the length of it *was* a cubit, and the breadth of it a cubit; *it was* foursquare; and two cubits *was* the height of it; the horns thereof were of the same.

26 And he overlaid it with pure gold, *both* the top of it, and the sides thereof round about, and the horns of it: also he made unto it a crown of gold round about.

27 And he made two rings of gold for it under the crown thereof, by the two corners of it, upon the two sides thereof, to be places for the staves to bear it withal.

28 And he made the staves *of* shittim wood, and overlaid them with gold.

29 ¶ And he made [c]the holy anointing oil, and the pure incense of sweet spices, according to the work of the apothecary.

38 And [d]he made the altar of burnt offering *of* shittim wood: five cubits *was* the length thereof, and five cubits the breadth thereof; *it was* foursquare; and three cubits the height thereof.

2 And he made the horns thereof on the four corners of it; the horns thereof were of the same: and he overlaid it with brass.

3 And he made all the vessels of the altar, the pots, and the shovels, and the basons, *and* the fleshhooks, and the firepans: all the vessels thereof made he *of* brass.

4 And he made for the altar a brasen grate of network under the compass thereof beneath unto the midst of it.

5 And he cast four rings for the four ends of the grate of brass, *to be* places for the staves.

6 And he made the staves *of* shittim wood, and overlaid them with brass.

7 And he put the staves into the rings on the sides of the altar, to bear it withal; he made the altar hollow with boards.

8 ¶ And he made [e]the laver *of* brass, and the foot of it *of* brass, of the lookingglasses of *the women* assembling, which assembled *at* the door of the tabernacle of the congregation.

9 ¶ And he made [f]the court: on the south side southward the hangings of the court *were of* fine twined linen, an hundred cubits:

10 Their pillars *were* twenty, and their brasen sockets twenty; the hooks of the pillars and their fillets *were of* silver.

11 And for the north side *the hangings were* an hundred cubits, their pillars *were* twenty, and their sockets of brass twenty; the hooks of the pillars and their fillets *of* silver.

12 And for the west side *were* hangings of fifty cubits, their pillars ten, and their sockets ten; the hooks of the pillars and their fillets *of* silver.

13 And for the east side eastward fifty cubits.

14 The hangings of the one side *of the gate were* fifteen cubits; their pillars three, and their sockets three.

15 And for the other side of the court gate, on this hand and that hand, *were* hangings of fifteen cubits; their pillars three, and their sockets three.

16 All the hangings of the court round about *were* of fine twined linen.

17 And the sockets for the pillars *were of* brass; the hooks of the pillars and their fillets *of* silver; and the overlaying of their chapiters *of* silver; and all the pillars of the court *were* filleted with silver.

18 And the hanging for the gate of the court *was* needlework, *of* blue, and purple, and scarlet, and fine twined linen: and twenty cubits *was* the length, and the height in the breadth *was* five cubits, answerable to the hangings of the court.

19 And their pillars *were* four, and their sockets *of* brass four; their hooks *of* silver, and the overlaying of their chapiters and their fillets *of* silver.

20 And all the [g]pins of the tabernacle, and of the court round about, *were of* brass.

21 ¶ This is the sum of the tabernacle, *even* of [h]the tabernacle of testimony, as it was counted, according to the commandment of Moses, *for* the service of the Levites, [i]by the hand of Ithamar, son to Aaron the priest.

22 And [j]Bezaleel the son of Uri, the son of Hur, of the tribe of Judah, made all that the LORD commanded Moses.

23 And with him *was* Aholiab, son of Ahisamach, of the tribe of Dan, an engraver, and a cunning workman, and an embroiderer in blue, and in purple, and in scarlet, and fine linen.

24 All the gold that was occupied for the work in all the work of the holy *place*, even the gold of the offering, was twenty and nine talents, and seven hundred and thirty shekels, after [k]the shekel of the sanctuary.

25 And the silver of them that were numbered of the congregation *was* an hundred

37:25 [b]ch. 30:1
37:29 [c]ch. 30:23
38:1 [d]ch. 27:1
38:8 [e]ch. 30:18
38:9 [f]ch. 27:9
38:20 [g]ch. 27:19
38:21 [h]Num. 1:50; 2 Chron. 24:6; Acts 7:44 [i]Num. 4:28
38:22 [j]ch. 31:2
38:24 [k]ch. 30:13; Lev. 5:15; Num. 3:47

talents, and a thousand seven hundred and threescore and fifteen shekels, after the shekel of the sanctuary:

26 [l]A bekah for every man, *that is,* half a shekel, after the shekel of the sanctuary, for every one that went to be numbered, from twenty years old and upward, for [m]six hundred thousand and three thousand and five hundred and fifty *men.*

27 And of the hundred talents of silver were cast [n]the sockets of the sanctuary, and the sockets of the vail; an hundred sockets of the hundred talents, a talent for a socket.

28 And of the thousand seven hundred seventy and five *shekels* he made hooks for the pillars, and overlaid their chapiters, and filleted them.

29 And the brass of the offering *was* seventy talents, and two thousand and four hundred shekels.

30 And therewith he made the sockets to the door of the tabernacle of the congregation, and the brasen altar, and the brasen grate for it, and all the vessels of the altar,

31 And the sockets of the court round about, and the sockets of the court gate, and all the pins of the tabernacle, and all the pins of the court round about.

39 And of [o]the blue, and purple, and scarlet, they made [p]cloths of service, to do service in the holy *place,* and made the holy garments for Aaron; [q]as the LORD commanded Moses.

2 [r]And he made the ephod *of* gold, blue, and purple, and scarlet, and fine twined linen.

3 And they did beat the gold into thin plates, and cut *it into* wires, to work *it* in the blue, and in the purple, and in the scarlet, and in the fine linen, *with* cunning work.

4 They made shoulderpieces for it, to couple *it* together: by the two edges was it coupled together.

5 And the curious girdle of his ephod, that *was* upon it, *was* of the same, according to the work thereof; *of* gold, blue, and purple, and scarlet, and fine twined linen; as the LORD commanded Moses.

6 ¶ [s]And they wrought onyx stones inclosed in ouches of gold, graven, as signets are graven, with the names of the children of Israel.

7 And he put them on the shoulders of the ephod, *that they should be* stones for a [t]memorial to the children of Israel; as the LORD commanded Moses.

8 ¶ [u]And he made the breastplate *of* cunning work, like the work of the ephod; *of* gold, blue, and purple, and scarlet, and fine twined linen.

9 It was foursquare; they made the breastplate double: a span *was* the length thereof, and a span the breadth thereof, *being* doubled.

10 [v]And they set in it four rows of stones: *the first* row *was* a sardius, a topaz, and a carbuncle: this *was* the first row.

11 And the second row, an emerald, a sapphire, and a diamond.

12 And the third row, a ligure, an agate, and an amethyst.

13 And the fourth row, a beryl, an onyx, and a jasper: *they were* inclosed in ouches of gold in their inclosings.

14 And the stones *were* according to the names of the children of Israel, twelve, according to their names, *like* the engravings of a signet, every one with his name, according to the twelve tribes.

15 And they made upon the breastplate chains at the ends, *of* wreathed work *of* pure gold.

16 And they made two ouches *of* gold, and two gold rings; and put the two rings in the two ends of the breastplate.

17 And they put the two wreathed chains of gold in the two rings on the ends of the breastplate.

18 And the two ends of the two wreathed chains they fastened in the two ouches, and put them on the shoulderpieces of the ephod, before it.

19 And they made two rings of gold, and put *them* on the two ends of the breastplate, upon the border of it, which *was* on the side of the ephod inward.

20 And they made two *other* golden rings, and put them on the two sides of the ephod underneath, toward the forepart of it, over against the *other* coupling thereof, above the curious girdle of the ephod.

21 And they did bind the breastplate by his rings unto the rings of the ephod with a lace of blue, that it might be above the curious girdle of the ephod, and that the breastplate might not be loosed from the ephod; as the LORD commanded Moses.

22 ¶ [w]And he made the robe of the ephod *of* woven work, all *of* blue.

23 And *there was* an hole in the midst of the robe, as the hole of an habergeon, *with* a band round about the hole, that it should not rend.

24 And they made upon the hems of the robe pomegranates *of* blue, and purple, and scarlet, *and* twined *linen.*

25 And they made [x]bells *of* pure gold, and put the bells between the pomegranates upon the hem of the robe, round about between the pomegranates;

26 A bell and a pomegranate, a bell and a pomegranate, round about the hem of the robe to minister *in;* as the LORD commanded Moses.

27 ¶ [y]And they made coats *of* fine linen *of* woven work for Aaron, and for his sons,

28 [z]And a mitre *of* fine linen, and goodly bonnets *of* fine linen, and [a]linen breeches *of* fine twined linen,

29 [b]And a girdle *of* fine twined linen, and blue, and purple, and scarlet, *of* needlework; as the LORD commanded Moses.

30 ¶ [c]And they made the plate of the holy crown *of* pure gold, and wrote upon it a

38:26 [l]ch. 30:13 [m]Num. 1:46
38:27 [n]ch. 26:19
39:1 [o]ch. 35:23 [p]ch. 31:10 [q]ch. 28:4
39:2 [r]ch. 28:6
39:6 [s]ch. 28:9
39:7 [t]ch. 28:12
39:8 [u]ch. 28:15
39:10 [v]ch. 28:17
39:22 [w]ch. 28:31
39:25 [x]ch. 28:33
39:27 [y]ch. 28:39
39:28 [z]ch. 28:4; Ezek. 44:18 [a]ch. 28:42
39:29 [b]ch. 28:39
39:30 [c]ch. 28:36

writing, *like to* the engravings of a signet, HOLINESS TO THE LORD.

31 And they tied unto it a lace of blue, to fasten *it* on high upon the mitre; as the LORD commanded Moses.

32 ¶ Thus was all the work of the tabernacle of the tent of the congregation finished: and the children of Israel did [d]according to all that the LORD commanded Moses, so did they.

33 ¶ And they brought the tabernacle unto Moses, the tent, and all his furniture, his taches, his boards, his bars, and his pillars, and his sockets,

34 And the covering of rams' skins dyed red, and the covering of badgers' skins, and the vail of the covering,

35 The ark of the testimony, and the staves thereof, and the mercy seat,

36 The table, *and* all the vessels thereof, and the shewbread,

37 The pure candlestick, *with* the lamps thereof, *even with* the lamps to be set in order, and all the vessels thereof, and the oil for light,

38 And the golden altar, and the anointing oil, and the sweet incense, and the hanging for the tabernacle door,

39 The brasen altar, and his grate of brass, his staves, and all his vessels, the laver and his foot,

40 The hangings of the court, his pillars, and his sockets, and the hanging for the court gate, his cords, and his pins, and all the vessels of the service of the tabernacle, for the tent of the congregation,

41 The cloths of service to do service in the holy *place*, and the holy garments for Aaron the priest, and his sons' garments, to minister in the priest's office.

42 According to all that the LORD commanded Moses, so the children of Israel [e]made all the work.

43 And Moses did look upon all the work, and, behold, they had done it as the LORD had commanded, even so had they done it: and Moses [f]blessed them.

40 And the LORD spake unto Moses, saying,

2 On the first day of the [g]first month shalt thou set up [h]the tabernacle of the tent of the congregation.

3 And [i]thou shalt put therein the ark of the testimony, and cover the ark with the vail.

4 And [j]thou shalt bring in the table, and [k]set in order the things that are to be set in order upon it; [l]and thou shalt bring in the candlestick, and light the lamps thereof.

5 [m]And thou shalt set the altar of gold for the incense before the ark of the testimony, and put the hanging of the door to the tabernacle.

6 And thou shalt set the altar of the burnt offering before the door of the tabernacle of the tent of the congregation.

7 And [n]thou shalt set the laver between the tent of the congregation and the altar, and shalt put water therein.

8 And thou shalt set up the court round about, and hang up the hanging at the court gate.

9 And thou shalt take the anointing oil, and [o]anoint the tabernacle, and all that *is* therein, and shalt hallow it, and all the vessels thereof: and it shall be holy.

10 And thou shalt anoint the altar of the burnt offering, and all his vessels, and sanctify the altar: and [p]it shall be an altar most holy.

11 And thou shalt anoint the laver and his foot, and sanctify it.

12 [q]And thou shalt bring Aaron and his sons unto the door of the tabernacle of the congregation, and wash them with water.

13 And thou shalt put upon Aaron the holy garments, [r]and anoint him, and sanctify him; that he may minister unto me in the priest's office.

14 And thou shalt bring his sons, and clothe them with coats:

15 And thou shalt anoint them, as thou didst anoint their father, that they may minister unto me in the priest's office: for their anointing shall surely [s]be an everlasting priesthood throughout their generations.

16 Thus did Moses: according to all that the LORD commanded him, so did he.

17 ¶ And it came to pass in the first month in the second year, on the first *day* of the month, *that* the [t]tabernacle was reared up.

18 And Moses reared up the tabernacle, and fastened his sockets, and set up the boards thereof, and put in the bars thereof, and reared up his pillars.

19 And he spread abroad the tent over the tabernacle, and put the covering of the tent above upon it; as the LORD commanded Moses.

20 ¶ And he took and put [u]the testimony into the ark, and set the staves on the ark, and put the mercy seat above upon the ark:

21 And he brought the ark into the tabernacle, and [v]set up the vail of the covering, and covered the ark of the testimony; as the LORD commanded Moses.

22 ¶ [w]And he put the table in the tent of the congregation, upon the side of the tabernacle northward, without the vail.

23 [x]And he set the bread in order upon it before the LORD; as the LORD had commanded Moses.

24 ¶ [y]And he put the candlestick in the tent of the congregation, over against the table, on the side of the tabernacle southward.

25 And [z]he lighted the lamps before the LORD; as the LORD commanded Moses.

26 ¶ [a]And he put the golden altar in the tent of the congregation before the vail:

27 [b]And he burnt sweet incense thereon; as the LORD commanded Moses.

28 ¶ [c]And he set up the hanging *at* the door of the tabernacle.

29 [d]And he put the altar of burnt offering

39:32 [d]ver. 42; ch. 25:40
39:42 [e]ch. 35:10
39:43 [f]Lev. 9:22; Num. 6:23; Josh. 22:6; 2 Sam. 6:18; 1 Kings 8:14; 2 Chron. 30:27
40:2 [g]ch. 12:2 [h]ver. 17
40:3 [i]ver. 21; ch. 26:33; Num. 4:5
40:4 [j]ver. 22; ch. 26:35 [k]ver. 23; ch. 25:30; Lev. 24:5 [l]ver. 24
40:5 [m]ver. 26
40:7 [n]ver. 30; ch. 30:18
40:9 [o]ch. 30:26
40:10 [p]ch. 29:36
40:12 [q]Lev. 8:1-13
40:13 [r]ch. 28:41
40:15 [s]Num. 25:13
40:17 [t]ver. 1; Num. 7:1
40:20 [u]ch. 25:16
40:21 [v]ch. 26:33
40:22 [w]ch. 26:35
40:23 [x]ver. 4
40:24 [y]ch. 26:35
40:25 [z]ver. 4; ch. 25:37
40:26 [a]ver. 5; ch. 30:6
40:27 [b]ch. 30:7
40:28 [c]ver. 5; ch. 26:36
40:29 [d]ver. 6

by the door of the tabernacle of the tent of
the congregation, and [e]offered upon it the
burnt offering and the meat offering; as the
LORD commanded Moses.
30 ¶ [f]And he set the laver between the
tent of the congregation and the altar, and
put water there, to wash *withal.*
31 And Moses and Aaron and his sons
washed their hands and their feet thereat:
32 When they went into the tent of the
congregation, and when they came near
unto the altar, they washed; [g]as the LORD
commanded Moses.
33 [h]And he reared up the court round
about the tabernacle and the altar, and set
up the hanging of the court gate. So Moses
finished the work.

40:29 [e]ch. 29:38
40:30 [f]ver. 7; ch. 30:18
40:32 [g]ch. 30:19
40:33 [h]ver. 8; ch. 27:9
40:34 [i]ch. 29:43; Lev. 16:2; Num. 9:15; 1 Kings 8:10; 2 Chron. 5:13; Isa. 6:4; Hag. 2:7; Rev. 15:8
40:35 [j]Lev. 16:2; 1 Kings 8:11; 2 Chron. 5:14
40:36 [k]Num. 9:17; Neh. 9:19
40:37 [l]Num. 9:19-22
40:38 [m]ch. 13:21; Num. 9:15

34 ¶ [i]Then a cloud covered the tent of the
congregation, and the glory of the LORD
filled the tabernacle.
35 And Moses [j]was not able to enter into
the tent of the congregation, because the
cloud abode thereon, and the glory of the
LORD filled the tabernacle.
36 [k]And when the cloud was taken up
from over the tabernacle, the children of Israel went onward in all their journeys:
37 But [l]if the cloud were not taken up,
then they journeyed not till the day that it
was taken up.
38 For [m]the cloud of the LORD *was* upon
the tabernacle by day, and fire was on it by
night, in the sight of all the house of Israel,
throughout all their journeys.

LEVITICUS

Leviticus was written by Moses between 1450 B.C. and 1410 B.C. The book of Leviticus takes its name from one of the twelve tribes of Israel, the Levites, from whose ranks came the priests that served in the tabernacle. Leviticus gives the details of the sacrificial system established by God, the various offerings and their significance, and the duties of the priests. Leviticus also contains laws dealing with the daily activities of the people including cleanliness, sexual morality, disease control, and criminal activities.

I. The sacrificial system defined, 1:1–10:20
II. The laws of God for the people, 11:1–15:33
III. The Day of Atonement, 16:1–17:16
IV. Other laws of God for the people, 18:1–27:34

---

1 And the LORD [a]called unto Moses, and
spake unto him [b]out of the tabernacle
of the congregation, saying,
2 Speak unto the children of Israel, and
say unto them, [c]If any man of you bring an
offering unto the LORD, ye shall bring your
offering of the cattle, *even* of the herd, and
of the flock.
3 If his offering *be* a burnt sacrifice of the
herd, let him offer a male [d]without blemish:
he shall offer it of his own voluntary will at
the door of the tabernacle of the congregation before the LORD.
4 [e]And he shall put his hand upon the
head of the burnt offering; and it shall be
[f]accepted for him [g]to make atonement for
him.
5 And he shall kill the [h]bullock before the
LORD: [i]and the priests, Aaron's sons, shall
bring the blood, [j]and sprinkle the blood
round about upon the altar that *is by* the
door of the tabernacle of the congregation.
6 And he shall flay the burnt offering, and
cut it into his pieces.
7 And the sons of Aaron the priest shall
put fire upon the altar, and [k]lay the wood in
order upon the fire:

1:1 [a]Ex. 19:3 [b]Ex. 40:34; Num. 12:4
1:2 [c]ch. 22:18
1:3 [d]Ex. 12:5; ch. 3:1; Deut. 15:21; Mal. 1:14; Eph. 5:27; Heb. 9:14; 1 Pet. 1:19
1:4 [e]ch. 4:15; Ex. 29:10 [f]ch. 22:21; Isa. 56:7; Rom. 12:1; Phil. 4:18 [g]ch. 4:20; Num. 15:25; 2 Chron. 29:23; Rom. 5:11
1:5 [h]Mic. 6:6 [i]2 Chron. 35:11; Heb. 10:11 [j]ch. 3:8; Heb. 12:24; 1 Pet. 1:2
1:7 [k]Gen. 22:9
1:9 [l]Gen. 8:21; Ezek. 20:28; 2 Cor. 2:15; Eph. 5:2; Phil. 4:18
1:10 [m]ver. 3
1:11 [n]ver. 5

8 And the priests, Aaron's sons, shall lay
the parts, the head, and the fat, in order
upon the wood that *is* on the fire which *is*
upon the altar:
9 But his inwards and his legs shall he
wash in water: and the priest shall burn all
on the altar, *to be* a burnt sacrifice, an offering made by fire, of a [l]sweet savour unto
the LORD.
10 ¶ And if his offering *be* of the flocks,
namely, of the sheep, or of the goats, for
a burnt sacrifice; he shall bring it a male
[m]without blemish.
11 [n]And he shall kill it on the side of the
altar northward before the LORD: and the
priests, Aaron's sons, shall sprinkle his
blood round about upon the altar.
12 And he shall cut it into his pieces, with
his head and his fat: and the priest shall lay
them in order on the wood that *is* on the fire
which *is* upon the altar:
13 But he shall wash the inwards and the
legs with water: and the priest shall bring *it*
all, and burn *it* upon the altar: it *is* a burnt
sacrifice, an offering made by fire, of a
sweet savour unto the LORD.
14 ¶ And if the burnt sacrifice for his of-

fering to the LORD be of fowls, then he shall bring his offering of [o]turtledoves, or of young pigeons.

15 And the priest shall bring it unto the altar, and wring off his head, and burn *it* on the altar; and the blood thereof shall be wrung out at the side of the altar:

16 And he shall pluck away his crop with his feathers, and cast it [p]beside the altar on the east part, by the place of the ashes:

17 And he shall cleave it with the wings thereof, *but* [q]shall not divide *it* asunder: and the priest shall burn it upon the altar, upon the wood that *is* upon the fire: [r]it *is* a burnt sacrifice, an offering made by fire, of a sweet savour unto the LORD.

2 And when any will offer [s]a meat offering unto the LORD, his offering shall be *of* fine flour; and he shall pour oil upon it, and put frankincense thereon:

2 And he shall bring it to Aaron's sons the priests: and he shall take thereout his handful of the flour thereof, and of the oil thereof, with all the frankincense thereof; and the priest shall burn [t]the memorial of it upon the altar, *to be* an offering made by fire, of a sweet savour unto the LORD:

3 And [u]the remnant of the meat offering *shall be* Aaron's and his sons': [v]*it is* a thing most holy of the offerings of the LORD made by fire.

4 ¶ And if thou bring an oblation of a meat offering baken in the oven, *it shall be* unleavened cakes of fine flour mingled with oil, or unleavened wafers [w]anointed with oil.

5 ¶ And if thy oblation *be* a meat offering *baken* in a pan, it shall be *of* fine flour unleavened, mingled with oil.

6 Thou shalt part it in pieces, and pour oil thereon: it *is* a meat offering.

7 ¶ And if thy oblation *be* a meat offering *baken* in the fryingpan, it shall be made *of* fine flour with oil.

8 And thou shalt bring the meat offering that is made of these things unto the LORD: and when it is presented unto the priest, he shall bring it unto the altar.

9 And the priest shall take from the meat offering a memorial [x]thereof, and shall burn *it* upon the altar: *it is* an [y]offering made by fire, of a sweet savour unto the LORD.

10 And [z]that which is left of the meat offering *shall be* Aaron's and his sons': *it is* a thing most holy of the offerings of the LORD made by fire.

11 No meat offering, which ye shall bring unto the LORD, shall be made with leaven: for ye shall burn no [a]leaven, nor any honey, in any offering of the LORD made by fire.

12 ¶ [b]As for the oblation of the firstfruits, ye shall offer them unto the LORD: but they shall not be burnt on the altar for a sweet savour.

13 And every oblation of thy meat offering [c]shalt thou season with salt; neither shalt thou suffer [d]the salt of the covenant of thy God to be lacking from thy meat offering: [e]with all thine offerings thou shalt offer salt.

14 And if thou offer a meat offering of thy firstfruits unto the LORD, [f]thou shalt offer for the meat offering of thy firstfruits green ears of corn dried by the fire, *even* corn beaten out of [g]full ears.

15 And [h]thou shalt put oil upon it, and lay frankincense thereon: it *is* a meat offering.

16 And the priest shall burn [i]the memorial of it, *part* of the beaten corn thereof, and *part* of the oil thereof, with all the frankincense thereof: *it is* an offering made by fire unto the LORD.

3 And if his oblation *be* a [j]sacrifice of peace offering, if he offer *it* of the herd; whether *it be* a male or female, he shall offer it [k]without blemish before the LORD.

2 And [l]he shall lay his hand upon the head of his offering, and kill it *at* the door of the tabernacle of the congregation: and Aaron's sons the priests shall sprinkle the blood upon the altar round about.

3 And he shall offer of the sacrifice of the peace offering an offering made by fire unto the LORD; [m]the fat that covereth the inwards, and all the fat that *is* upon the inwards,

4 And the two kidneys, and the fat that *is* on them, which *is* by the flanks, and the caul above the liver, with the kidneys, it shall he take away.

5 And Aaron's sons [n]shall burn it on the altar upon the burnt sacrifice, which *is* upon the wood that *is* on the fire: *it is* an offering made by fire, of a sweet savour unto the LORD.

6 ¶ And if his offering for a sacrifice of peace offering unto the LORD *be* of the flock; male or female, [o]he shall offer it without blemish.

7 If he offer a lamb for his offering, then shall he offer it before the LORD.

8 And he shall lay his hand upon the head of his offering, and kill it before the tabernacle of the congregation: and Aaron's sons shall sprinkle the blood thereof round about upon the altar.

9 And he shall offer of the sacrifice of the peace offering an offering made by fire unto the LORD; the fat thereof, *and* the whole rump, it shall he take off hard by the backbone; and the fat that covereth the inwards, and all the fat that *is* upon the inwards,

10 And the two kidneys, and the fat that *is* upon them, which *is* by the flanks, and the caul above the liver, with the kidneys, it shall he take away.

11 And the priest shall burn it upon the altar: *it is* [p]the food of the offering made by fire unto the LORD.

12 ¶ And if his offering *be* a goat, then [q]he shall offer it before the LORD.

13 And he shall lay his hand upon the head of it, and kill it before the tabernacle of the congregation: and the sons of Aaron

1:14 *o*ch. 5:7; Luke 2:24
1:16 *p*ch. 6:10
1:17 *q*Gen. 15:10 *r*ver. 9
2:1 *s*ch. 6:14; Num. 15:4
2:2 *t*ver. 9; Isa. 66:3; Acts 10:4
2:3 *u*ch. 7:9 *v*Ex. 29:37; Num. 18:9
2:4 *w*Ex. 29:2
2:9 *x*ver. 2 *y*Ex. 29:18
2:10 *z*ver. 3
2:11 *a*ch. 6:17; Matt. 16:12; Mark 8:15; Luke 12:1; 1 Cor. 5:8; Gal. 5:9
2:12 *b*Ex. 22:29; ch. 23:10
2:13 *c*Mark 9:49; Col. 4:6 *d*Num. 18:19 *e*Ezek. 43:24
2:14 *f*ch. 23:10 *g*2 Kings 4:42
2:15 *h*ver. 1
2:16 *i*ver. 2
3:1 *j*ch. 7:11 *k*ch. 1:3
3:2 *l*ch. 1:4; Ex. 29:10
3:3 *m*Ex. 29:13; ch. 4:8
3:5 *n*ch. 6:12; Ex. 29:13
3:6 *o*ver. 1
3:11 *p*ch. 21:6; Ezek. 44:7; Mal. 1:7
3:12 *q*ver. 1

shall sprinkle the blood thereof upon the
altar round about.
14 And he shall offer thereof his offering,
even an offering made by fire unto the
LORD; the fat that covereth the inwards, and
all the fat that *is* upon the inwards,
15 And the two kidneys, and the fat that *is*
upon them, which *is* by the flanks, and the
caul above the liver, with the kidneys, it
shall he take away.
16 And the priest shall burn them upon
the altar: *it is* the food of the offering made
by fire for a sweet savour: [r]all the fat *is* the
LORD'S.
17 *It shall be* a [s]perpetual statute for your
generations throughout all your dwellings,
that ye eat neither [t]fat nor [u]blood.

4 And the LORD spake unto Moses, saying,
2 Speak unto the children of Israel, saying, [v]If a soul shall sin through ignorance
against any of the commandments of the
LORD *concerning things* which ought not to
be done, and shall do against any of them:
3 [w]If the priest that is anointed do sin according to the sin of the people; then let him
bring for his sin, which he hath sinned, [x]a
young bullock without blemish unto the
LORD for a sin offering.
4 And he shall bring the bullock [y]unto
the door of the tabernacle of the congregation before the LORD; and shall lay his hand
upon the bullock's head, and kill the bullock
before the LORD.
5 And the priest that is anointed [z]shall
take of the bullock's blood, and bring it to
the tabernacle of the congregation:
6 And the priest shall dip his finger in the
blood, and sprinkle of the blood seven times
before the LORD, before the vail of the sanctuary.
7 And the priest shall [a]put *some* of the
blood upon the horns of the altar of sweet
incense before the LORD, which *is* in the tabernacle of the congregation; and shall pour
[b]all the blood of the bullock at the bottom
of the altar of the burnt offering, which *is at*
the door of the tabernacle of the congregation.
8 And he shall take off from it all the fat
of the bullock for the sin offering; the fat
that covereth the inwards, and all the fat
that *is* upon the inwards,
9 And the two kidneys, and the fat that *is*
upon them, which *is* by the flanks, and the
caul above the liver, with the kidneys, it
shall he take away,
10 [c]As it was taken off from the bullock
of the sacrifice of peace offerings: and the
priest shall burn them upon the altar of the
burnt offering.
11 [d]And the skin of the bullock, and all
his flesh, with his head, and with his legs,
and his inwards, and his dung,
12 Even the whole bullock shall he carry
forth without the camp unto a clean place,
[e]where the ashes are poured out, and
[f]burn him on the wood with fire: where the
ashes are poured out shall he be burnt.
13 ¶ And [g]if the whole congregation of
Israel sin through ignorance, [h]and the
thing be hid from the eyes of the assembly,
and they have done *somewhat against* any
of the commandments of the LORD *concerning things* which should not be done, and
are guilty;
14 When the sin, which they have sinned
against it, is known, then the congregation
shall offer a young bullock for the sin, and
bring him before the tabernacle of the congregation.
15 And the elders of the congregation
[i]shall lay their hands upon the head of the
bullock before the LORD: and the bullock
shall be killed before the LORD.
16 [j]And the priest that is anointed shall
bring of the bullock's blood to the tabernacle of the congregation:
17 And the priest shall dip his finger *in
some* of the blood, and sprinkle *it* seven
times before the LORD, *even* before the vail.
18 And he shall put *some* of the blood
upon the horns of the altar which *is* before
the LORD, that *is* in the tabernacle of the
congregation, and shall pour out all the
blood at the bottom of the altar of the burnt
offering, which *is at* the door of the tabernacle of the congregation.
19 And he shall take all his fat from him,
and burn *it* upon the altar.
20 And he shall do with the bullock as he
did [k]with the bullock for a sin offering, so
shall he do with this: [l]and the priest shall
make an atonement for them, and it shall be
forgiven them.
21 And he shall carry forth the bullock
without the camp, and burn him as he
burned the first bullock: it *is* a sin offering
for the congregation.
22 ¶ When a ruler hath sinned, and [m]done
somewhat through ignorance *against* any
of the commandments of the LORD his God
concerning things which should not be
done, and is guilty;
23 Or [n]if his sin, wherein he hath sinned,
come to his knowledge; he shall bring his
offering, a kid of the goats, a male without
blemish:
24 And [o]he shall lay his hand upon the
head of the goat, and kill it in the place
where they kill the burnt offering before the
LORD: it *is* a sin offering.
25 [p]And the priest shall take of the blood
of the sin offering with his finger, and put *it*
upon the horns of the altar of burnt offering,
and shall pour out his blood at the bottom of
the altar of burnt offering.
26 And he shall burn all his fat upon the
altar, as [q]the fat of the sacrifice of peace
offerings: [r]and the priest shall make an
atonement for him as concerning his sin,
and it shall be forgiven him.
27 ¶ And [s]if any one of the common people sin through ignorance, while he doeth
somewhat against any of the command-

3:16 [r]ch. 7:23; 1 Sam. 2:15; 2 Chron. 7:7
3:17 [s]ch. 6:18 [t]ver. 16; Deut. 32:14; Neh. 8:10 [u]Gen. 9:4; ch. 7:23; Deut. 12:16; 1 Sam. 14:33; Ezek. 44:7
4:2 [v]ch. 5:15; Num. 15:22; 1 Sam. 14:27; Ps. 19:12
4:3 [w]ch. 8:12 [x]ch. 9:2
4:4 [y]ch. 1:3
4:5 [z]ch. 16:14; Num. 19:4
4:7 [a]ch. 8:15 [b]ch. 5
4:10 [c]ch. 3:3
4:11 [d]Ex. 29:14; Num. 19:5
4:12 [e]ch. 6:11 [f]Heb. 13:11
4:13 [g]Num. 15:24; Josh. 7:11 [h]ch. 5:2
4:15 [i]ch. 1:4
4:16 [j]ver. 5; Heb. 9:12
4:20 [k]ver. 3 [l]Num. 15:25; Dan. 9:24; Rom. 5:11; Heb. 2:17; 1 John 1:7
4:22 [m]ver. 2
4:23 [n]ver. 14
4:24 [o]ver. 4
4:25 [p]ver. 30
4:26 [q]ch. 3:5 [r]ver. 20; Num. 15:28
4:27 [s]ver. 2; Num. 15:28

ments of the LORD *concerning things* which ought not to be done, and be guilty;

28 Or [t]if his sin, which he hath sinned, come to his knowledge: then he shall bring his offering, a kid of the goats, a female without blemish, for his sin which he hath sinned.

29 [u]And he shall lay his hand upon the head of the sin offering, and slay the sin offering in the place of the burnt offering.

30 And the priest shall take of the blood thereof with his finger, and put *it* upon the horns of the altar of burnt offering, and shall pour out all the blood thereof at the bottom of the altar.

31 And [v]he shall take away all the fat thereof, [w]as the fat is taken away from off the sacrifice of peace offerings; and the priest shall burn *it* upon the altar for a [x]sweet savour unto the LORD; [y]and the priest shall make an atonement for him, and it shall be forgiven him.

32 And if he bring a lamb for a sin offering, [z]he shall bring it a female without blemish.

33 And he shall lay his hand upon the head of the sin offering, and slay it for a sin offering in the place where they kill the burnt offering.

34 And the priest shall take of the blood of the sin offering with his finger, and put *it* upon the horns of the altar of burnt offering, and shall pour out all the blood thereof at the bottom of the altar:

35 And he shall take away all the fat thereof, as the fat of the lamb is taken away from the sacrifice of the peace offerings; and the priest shall burn them upon the altar, [a]according to the offerings made by fire unto the LORD: [b]and the priest shall make an atonement for his sin that he hath committed, and it shall be forgiven him.

5

And if a soul sin, [c]and hear the voice of swearing, and *is* a witness, whether he hath seen or known *of it;* if he do not utter *it,* then he shall [d]bear his iniquity.

2 Or [e]if a soul touch any unclean thing, whether *it be* a carcase of an unclean beast, or a carcase of unclean cattle, or the carcase of unclean creeping things, and *if* it be hidden from him; he also shall be unclean, and [f]guilty.

3 Or if he touch [g]the uncleanness of man, whatsoever uncleanness *it be* that a man shall be defiled withal, and it be hid from him; when he knoweth *of it,* then he shall be guilty.

4 Or if a soul swear, pronouncing with *his* lips [h]to do evil, or [i]to do good, whatsoever *it be* that a man shall pronounce with an oath, and it be hid from him; when he knoweth *of it,* then he shall be guilty in one of these.

5 And it shall be, when he shall be guilty in one of these *things,* that he shall [j]confess that he hath sinned in that *thing:*

6 And he shall bring his trespass offering unto the LORD for his sin which he hath sinned, a female from the flock, a lamb or a kid of the goats, for a sin offering; and the priest shall make an atonement for him concerning his sin.

7 And [k]if he be not able to bring a lamb, then he shall bring for his trespass, which he hath committed, two [l]turtledoves, or two young pigeons, unto the LORD; one for a sin offering, and the other for a burnt offering.

8 And he shall bring them unto the priest, who shall offer *that* which *is* for the sin offering first, and [m]wring off his head from his neck, but shall not divide *it* asunder:

9 And he shall sprinkle of the blood of the sin offering upon the side of the altar; and [n]the rest of the blood shall be wrung out at the bottom of the altar: it *is* a sin offering.

10 And he shall offer the second *for* a burnt offering, according to the [o]manner: [p]and the priest shall make an atonement for him for his sin which he hath sinned, and it shall be forgiven him.

11 ¶ But if he be not able to bring two turtledoves, or two young pigeons, then he that sinned shall bring for his offering the tenth part of an ephah of fine flour for a sin offering; [q]he shall put no oil upon it, neither shall he put *any* frankincense thereon: for it *is* a sin offering.

12 Then shall he bring it to the priest, and the priest shall take his handful of it, [r]*even* a memorial thereof, and burn *it* on the altar, according to the offerings made by fire unto the LORD: it *is* a sin offering.

13 [s]And the priest shall make an atonement for him as touching his sin that he hath sinned in one of these, and it shall be forgiven him: and [t]*the remnant* shall be the priest's, as a meat offering.

14 ¶ And the LORD spake unto Moses, saying,

15 [u]If a soul commit a trespass, and sin through ignorance, in the holy things of the LORD; then [v]he shall bring for his trespass unto the LORD a ram without blemish out of the flocks, with thy estimation by shekels of silver, after [w]the shekel of the sanctuary, for a trespass offering:

16 And he shall make amends for the harm that he hath done in the holy thing, and [x]shall add the fifth part thereto, and give it unto the priest: [y]and the priest shall make an atonement for him with the ram of the trespass offering, and it shall be forgiven him.

17 ¶ And if a [z]soul sin, and commit any of these things which are forbidden to be done by the commandments of the LORD; [a]though he wist *it* not, yet is he [b]guilty, and shall bear his iniquity.

18 [c]And he shall bring a ram without blemish out of the flock, with thy estimation, for a trespass offering, unto the priest: [d]and the priest shall make an atonement for him concerning his ignorance wherein he erred and wist *it* not, and it shall be forgiven him.

4:28 [t]ver. 23
4:29 [u]ver. 4
4:31 [v]ch. 3:14 [w]ch. 3:3 [x]Ex. 29:18; ch. 1:9 [y]ver. 26
4:32 [z]ver. 28
4:35 [a]ch. 3:5 [b]ver. 26
5:1 [c]1 Kings 8:31; Matt. 26:63 [d]ver. 17; ch. 7:18; Num. 9:13
5:2 [e]ch. 11:24; Num. 19:11 [f]ver. 17
5:3 [g]ch. 12
5:4 [h]1 Sam. 25:22; Acts 23:12 [i]Mark 6:23
5:5 [j]ch. 16:21; Num. 5:7; Ezra 10:11
5:7 [k]ch. 12:8 [l]ch. 1:14
5:8 [m]ch. 1:15
5:9 [n]ch. 4:7
5:10 [o]ch. 1:14 [p]ch. 4:26
5:11 [q]Num. 5:15
5:12 [r]ch. 2:2
5:13 [s]ch. 4:26 [t]ch. 2:3
5:15 [u]ch. 22:14 [v]Ezra 10:19 [w]Ex. 30:13; ch. 27:25
5:16 [x]ch. 6:5; Num. 5:7 [y]ch. 4:26
5:17 [z]ch. 4:2 [a]ver. 15; ch. 4:2; Ps. 19:12; Luke 12:48 [b]ver. 1
5:18 [c]ver. 15 [d]ver. 16

19 It *is* a trespass offering: [e]he hath certainly trespassed against the LORD.

6 And the LORD spake unto Moses, saying,

2 If a soul sin, and [f]commit a trespass against the LORD, and [g]lie unto his neighbour in that [h]which was delivered him to keep, or in fellowship, or in a thing taken away by violence, or hath [i]deceived his neighbour;

3 Or [j]have found that which was lost, and lieth concerning it, and [k]sweareth falsely; in any of all these that a man doeth, sinning therein:

4 Then it shall be, because he hath sinned, and is guilty, that he shall restore that which he took violently away, or the thing which he hath deceitfully gotten, or that which was delivered him to keep, or the lost thing which he found,

5 Or all that about which he hath sworn falsely; he shall even [l]restore it in the principal, and shall add the fifth part more thereto, *and* give it unto him to whom it appertaineth, in the day of his trespass offering.

6 And he shall bring his trespass offering unto the LORD, [m]a ram without blemish out of the flock, with thy estimation, for a trespass offering, unto the priest:

7 [n]And the priest shall make an atonement for him before the LORD: and it shall be forgiven him for any thing of all that he hath done in trespassing therein.

8 ¶ And the LORD spake unto Moses, saying,

9 Command Aaron and his sons, saying, This *is* the law of the burnt offering: It *is* the burnt offering, because of the burning upon the altar all night unto the morning, and the fire of the altar shall be burning in it.

10 [o]And the priest shall put on his linen garment, and his linen breeches shall he put upon his flesh, and take up the ashes which the fire hath consumed with the burnt offering on the altar, and he shall put them [p]beside the altar.

11 And [q]he shall put off his garments, and put on other garments, and carry forth the ashes without the camp [r]unto a clean place.

12 And the fire upon the altar shall be burning in it; it shall not be put out: and the priest shall burn wood on it every morning, and lay the burnt offering in order upon it; and he shall burn thereon [s]the fat of the peace offerings.

13 The fire shall ever be burning upon the altar; it shall never go out.

14 ¶ [t]And this *is* the law of the meat offering: the sons of Aaron shall offer it before the LORD, before the altar.

15 And he shall take of it his handful, of the flour of the meat offering, and of the oil thereof, and all the frankincense which *is* upon the meat offering, and shall burn *it* upon the altar *for* a sweet savour, *even* the [u]memorial of it, unto the LORD.

16 And [v]the remainder thereof shall Aaron and his sons eat: [w]with unleavened bread shall it be eaten in the holy place; in the court of the tabernacle of the congregation they shall eat it.

17 [x]It shall not be baken with leaven. [y]I have given it *unto them for* their portion of my offerings made by fire; [z]it *is* most holy, as *is* the sin offering, and as the trespass offering.

18 [a]All the males among the children of Aaron shall eat of it. [b]*It shall be* a statute for ever in your generations concerning the offerings of the LORD made by fire: [c]every one that toucheth them shall be holy.

19 ¶ And the LORD spake unto Moses, saying,

20 [d]This *is* the offering of Aaron and of his sons, which they shall offer unto the LORD in the day when he is anointed; the tenth part of an [e]ephah of fine flour for a meat offering perpetual, half of it in the morning, and half thereof at night.

21 In a pan it shall be made with oil; *and when it is* baken, thou shalt bring it in: *and* the baken pieces of the meat offering shalt thou offer *for* a sweet savour unto the LORD.

22 And the priest of his sons [f]that is anointed in his stead shall offer it: *it is* a statute for ever unto the LORD; [g]it shall be wholly burnt.

23 For every meat offering for the priest shall be wholly burnt: it shall not be eaten.

24 ¶ And the LORD spake unto Moses, saying,

25 Speak unto Aaron and to his sons, saying, [h]This *is* the law of the sin offering: [i]In the place where the burnt offering is killed shall the sin offering be killed before the LORD: [j]it *is* most holy.

26 [k]The priest that offereth it for sin shall eat it: [l]in the holy place shall it be eaten, in the court of the tabernacle of the congregation.

27 [m]Whatsoever shall touch the flesh thereof shall be holy: and when there is sprinkled of the blood thereof upon any garment, thou shalt wash that whereon it was sprinkled in the holy place.

28 But the earthen vessel wherein it is sodden [n]shall be broken: and if it be sodden in a brasen pot, it shall be both scoured, and rinsed in water.

29 [o]All the males among the priests shall eat thereof: [p]it *is* most holy.

30 [q]And no sin offering, whereof *any* of the blood is brought into the tabernacle of the congregation to reconcile *withal* in the holy *place,* shall be eaten: it shall be burnt in the fire.

7 Likewise [r]this *is* the law of the trespass offering: [s]it *is* most holy.

2 [t]In the place where they kill the burnt offering shall they kill the trespass offering: and the blood thereof shall he sprinkle round about upon the altar.

3 And he shall offer of it [u]all the fat

5:19 [e]Ezra 10:2
6:2 [f]Num. 5:6 [g]ch. 19:11; Acts 5:4; Col. 3:9 [h]Ex. 22:7 [i]Prov. 24:28
6:3 [j]Deut. 22:1 [k]Ex. 22:11; ch. 19:12; Jer. 7:9; Zech. 5:4
6:5 [l]ch. 5:16; Num. 5:7; 2 Sam. 12:6; Luke 19:8
6:6 [m]ch. 5:15
6:7 [n]ch. 4:26
6:10 [o]ch. 16:4; Ex. 28:39; Ezek. 44:17 [p]ch. 1:16
6:11 [q]Ezek. 44:19 [r]ch. 4:12
6:12 [s]ch. 3:3
6:14 [t]ch. 2:1; Num. 15:4
6:15 [u]ch. 2:2
6:16 [v]ch. 2:3; Ezek. 44:29 [w]ver. 26; ch. 10:12; Num. 18:10
6:17 [x]ch. 2:11 [y]Num. 18:9 [z]ver. 25; ch. 2:3; Ex. 29:37
6:18 [a]ver. 29; Num. 18:10 [b]ch. 3:17 [c]ch. 22:3; Ex. 29:37
6:20 [d]Ex. 29:2 [e]Ex. 1:36
6:22 [f]ch. 4:3 [g]Ex. 29:25
6:25 [h]ch. 4:2 [i]ch. 1:3 [j]ver. 17; ch. 21:22
6:26 [k]ch. 10:17; Num. 18:9; Ezek. 44:28 [l]ver. 16
6:27 [m]Ex. 29:37
6:28 [n]ch. 11:33
6:29 [o]ver. 18; Num. 18:10 [p]ver. 25
6:30 [q]ch. 4:7; Heb. 13:11
7:1 [r]ch. 5 [s]ch. 6:17
7:2 [t]ch. 1:3
7:3 [u]ch. 3:4; Ex. 29:13

thereof; the rump, and the fat that covereth the inwards,

4 And the two kidneys, and the fat that *is* on them, which *is* by the flanks, and the caul *that is* above the liver, with the kidneys, it shall he take away:

5 And the priest shall burn them upon the altar *for* an offering made by fire unto the LORD: it *is* a trespass offering.

6 [v]Every male among the priests shall eat thereof: it shall be eaten in the holy place: [w]it *is* most holy.

7 As the sin offering *is,* so *is* [x]the trespass offering: *there is* one law for them: the priest that maketh atonement therewith shall have *it.*

8 And the priest that offereth any man's burnt offering, *even* the priest shall have to himself the skin of the burnt offering which he hath offered.

9 And [y]all the meat offering that is baken in the oven, and all that is dressed in the fryingpan, and in the pan, shall be the priest's that offereth it.

10 And every meat offering, mingled with oil, and dry, shall all the sons of Aaron have, one *as much* as another.

11 And [z]this *is* the law of the sacrifice of peace offerings, which he shall offer unto the LORD.

12 If he offer it for a thanksgiving, then he shall offer with the sacrifice of thanksgiving unleavened cakes mingled with oil, and unleavened wafers [a]anointed with oil, and cakes mingled with oil, of fine flour, fried.

13 Besides the cakes, he shall offer *for* his offering [b]leavened bread with the sacrifice of thanksgiving of his peace offerings.

14 And of it he shall offer one out of the whole oblation *for* an heave offering unto the LORD, [c]*and* it shall be the priest's that sprinkleth the blood of the peace offerings.

15 [d]And the flesh of the sacrifice of his peace offerings for thanksgiving shall be eaten the same day that it is offered; he shall not leave any of it until the morning.

16 But [e]if the sacrifice of his offering *be* a vow, or a voluntary offering, it shall be eaten the same day that he offereth his sacrifice: and on the morrow also the remainder of it shall be eaten:

17 But the remainder of the flesh of the sacrifice on the third day shall be burnt with fire.

18 And if *any* of the flesh of the sacrifice of his peace offerings be eaten at all on the third day, it shall not be accepted, neither shall it be [f]imputed unto him that offereth it: it shall be an [g]abomination, and the soul that eateth of it shall bear his iniquity.

19 And the flesh that toucheth any unclean *thing* shall not be eaten; it shall be burnt with fire: and as for the flesh, all that be clean shall eat thereof.

20 But the soul that eateth *of* the flesh of the sacrifice of peace offerings, that *pertain* unto the LORD, [h]having his uncleanness upon him, even that soul [i]shall be cut off from his people.

21 Moreover the soul that shall touch any unclean *thing, as* [j]the uncleanness of man, or *any* [k]unclean beast, or any [l]abominable unclean *thing,* and eat of the flesh of the sacrifice of peace offerings, which *pertain* unto the LORD, even that soul [m]shall be cut off from his people.

22 ¶ And the LORD spake unto Moses, saying,

23 Speak unto the children of Israel, saying, [n]Ye shall eat no manner of fat, of ox, or of sheep, or of goat.

24 And the fat of the beast that dieth of itself, and the fat of that which is torn with beasts, may be used in any other use: but ye shall in no wise eat of it.

25 For whosoever eateth the fat of the beast, of which men offer an offering made by fire unto the LORD, even the soul that eateth *it* shall be cut off from his people.

26 [o]Moreover ye shall eat no manner of blood, *whether it be* of fowl or of beast, in any of your dwellings.

27 Whatsoever soul *it be* that eateth any manner of blood, even that soul shall be cut off from his people.

28 ¶ And the LORD spake unto Moses, saying,

29 Speak unto the children of Israel, saying, [p]He that offereth the sacrifice of his peace offerings unto the LORD shall bring his oblation unto the LORD of the sacrifice of his peace offerings.

30 [q]His own hands shall bring the offerings of the LORD made by fire, the fat with the breast, it shall he bring, that [r]the breast may be waved *for* a wave offering before the LORD.

31 [s]And the priest shall burn the fat upon the altar: [t]but the breast shall be Aaron's and his sons'.

32 And [u]the right shoulder shall ye give unto the priest *for* an heave offering of the sacrifices of your peace offerings.

33 He among the sons of Aaron, that offereth the blood of the peace offerings, and the fat, shall have the right shoulder for *his* part.

34 For [v]the wave breast and the heave shoulder have I taken of the children of Israel from off the sacrifices of their peace offerings, and have given them unto Aaron the priest and unto his sons by a statute for ever from among the children of Israel.

35 ¶ This *is the portion* of the anointing of Aaron, and of the anointing of his sons, out of the offerings of the LORD made by fire, in the day *when* he presented them to minister unto the LORD in the priest's office;

36 Which the LORD commanded to be given them of the children of Israel, [w]in the day that he anointed them, *by* a statute for ever throughout their generations.

37 This *is* the law [x]of the burnt offering, [y]of the meat offering, [z]and of the sin offering, [a]and of the trespass offering, [b]and of

7:6 [v]ch. 6:16; Num. 18:9 [w]ch. 2:3
7:7 [x]ch. 6:25
7:9 [y]ch. 2:3; Num. 18:9; Ezek. 44:29
7:11 [z]ch. 3:1
7:12 [a]ch. 2:4; Num. 6:15
7:13 [b]Am. 4:5
7:14 [c]Num. 18:8
7:15 [d]ch. 22:30
7:16 [e]ch. 19:6
7:18 [f]Num. 18:27 [g]ch. 11:10
7:20 [h]ch. 15:3 [i]Gen. 17:14
7:21 [j]ch. 12 [k]ch. 11:24 [l]Ezek. 4:14 [m]ver. 20
7:23 [n]ch. 3:17
7:26 [o]Gen. 9:4; ch. 3:17
7:29 [p]ch. 3:1
7:30 [q]ch. 3:3 [r]Ex. 29:24; ch. 8:27; Num. 6:20
7:31 [s]ch. 3:5 [t]ver. 34
7:32 [u]ver. 34; ch. 9:21; Num. 6:20
7:34 [v]Ex. 29:28; ch. 10:14; Num. 18:18; Deut. 18:3
7:36 [w]ch. 8:12; Ex. 40:13
7:37 [x]ch. 6:9 [y]ch. 6:14 [z]ch. 6:25 [a]ver. 1 [b]ch. 6:20; Ex. 29:1

the consecrations, and [c]of the sacrifice of the peace offerings;

38 Which the LORD commanded Moses in mount Sinai, in the day that he commanded the children of Israel [d]to offer their oblations unto the LORD, in the wilderness of Sinai.

8 And the LORD spake unto Moses, saying,

2 [e]Take Aaron and his sons with him, and [f]the garments, and [g]the anointing oil, and a bullock for the sin offering, and two rams, and a basket of unleavened bread;

3 And gather thou all the congregation together unto the door of the tabernacle of the congregation.

4 And Moses did as the LORD commanded him; and the assembly was gathered together unto the door of the tabernacle of the congregation.

5 And Moses said unto the congregation, [h]This *is* the thing which the LORD commanded to be done.

6 And Moses brought Aaron and his sons, [i]and washed them with water.

7 [j]And he put upon him the [k]coat, and girded him with the girdle, and clothed him with the robe, and put the ephod upon him, and he girded him with the curious girdle of the ephod, and bound *it* unto him therewith.

8 And he put the breastplate upon him: also he [l]put in the breastplate the Urim and the Thummim.

9 [m]And he put the mitre upon his head; also upon the mitre, *even* upon his forefront, did he put the golden plate, the holy crown; as the LORD [n]commanded Moses.

10 [o]And Moses took the anointing oil, and anointed the tabernacle and all that *was* therein, and sanctified them.

11 And he sprinkled thereof upon the altar seven times, and anointed the altar and all his vessels, both the laver and his foot, to sanctify them.

12 And he [p]poured of the anointing oil upon Aaron's head, and anointed him, to sanctify him.

13 [q]And Moses brought Aaron's sons, and put coats upon them, and girded them with girdles, and put bonnets upon them; as the LORD commanded Moses.

14 [r]And he brought the bullock for the sin offering: and Aaron and his sons [s]laid their hands upon the head of the bullock for the sin offering.

15 And he slew *it;* [t]and Moses took the blood, and put *it* upon the horns of the altar round about with his finger, and purified the altar, and poured the blood at the bottom of the altar, and sanctified it, to make reconciliation upon it.

16 [u]And he took all the fat that *was* upon the inwards, and the caul *above* the liver, and the two kidneys, and their fat, and Moses burned *it* upon the altar.

17 But the bullock, and his hide, his flesh, and his dung, he burnt with fire without the camp; as the LORD [v]commanded Moses.

7:37 [c]ver. 11
7:38 [d]ch. 1:2
8:2 [e]Ex. 29:1 [f]Ex. 28:2 [g]Ex. 30:24
8:5 [h]Ex. 29:4
8:6 [i]Ex. 29:4
8:7 [j]Ex. 29:5 [k]Ex. 28:4
8:8 [l]Ex. 28:30
8:9 [m]Ex. 29:6 [n]Ex. 28:37
8:10 [o]Ex. 30:26
8:12 [p]ch. 21:10; Ex. 29:7; Ps. 133:2
8:13 [q]Ex. 29:8
8:14 [r]Ex. 29:10; Ezek. 43:19 [s]ch. 4:4
8:15 [t]Ex. 29:12; ch. 4:7; Ezek. 43:20; Heb. 9:22
8:16 [u]Ex. 29:13; ch. 4:8
8:17 [v]ch. 4:11; Ex. 29:14
8:18 [w]Ex. 29:15
8:21 [x]Ex. 29:18
8:22 [y]Ex. 29:19
8:25 [z]Ex. 29:22
8:26 [a]Ex. 29:23
8:27 [b]Ex. 29:24
8:28 [c]Ex. 29:25
8:29 [d]Ex. 29:26
8:30 [e]Ex. 29:21; Num. 3:3
8:31 [f]Ex. 29:31
8:32 [g]Ex. 29:34

18 ¶ [w]And he brought the ram for the burnt offering: and Aaron and his sons laid their hands upon the head of the ram.

19 And he killed *it;* and Moses sprinkled the blood upon the altar round about.

20 And he cut the ram into pieces; and Moses burnt the head, and the pieces, and the fat.

21 And he washed the inwards and the legs in water; and Moses burnt the whole ram upon the altar: it *was* a burnt sacrifice for a sweet savour, *and* an offering made by fire unto the LORD; [x]as the LORD commanded Moses.

22 ¶ And [y]he brought the other ram, the ram of consecration: and Aaron and his sons laid their hands upon the head of the ram.

23 And he slew *it;* and Moses took of the blood of it, and put *it* upon the tip of Aaron's right ear, and upon the thumb of his right hand, and upon the great toe of his right foot.

24 And he brought Aaron's sons, and Moses put of the blood upon the tip of their right ear, and upon the thumbs of their right hands, and upon the great toes of their right feet: and Moses sprinkled the blood upon the altar round about.

25 [z]And he took the fat, and the rump, and all the fat that *was* upon the inwards, and the caul *above* the liver, and the two kidneys, and their fat, and the right shoulder:

26 [a]And out of the basket of unleavened bread, that *was* before the LORD, he took one unleavened cake, and a cake of oiled bread, and one wafer, and put *them* on the fat, and upon the right shoulder:

27 And he put all [b]upon Aaron's hands, and upon his sons' hands, and waved them *for* a wave offering before the LORD.

28 [c]And Moses took them from off their hands, and burnt *them* on the altar upon the burnt offering: they *were* consecrations for a sweet savour: it *is* an offering made by fire unto the LORD.

29 And Moses took the breast, and waved it *for* a wave offering before the LORD: *for* of the ram of consecration it was Moses' [d]part; as the LORD commanded Moses.

30 And [e]Moses took of the anointing oil, and of the blood which *was* upon the altar, and sprinkled *it* upon Aaron, *and* upon his garments, and upon his sons, and upon his sons' garments with him; and sanctified Aaron, *and* his garments, and his sons, and his sons' garments with him.

31 ¶ And Moses said unto Aaron and to his sons, [f]Boil the flesh *at* the door of the tabernacle of the congregation: and there eat it with the bread that *is* in the basket of consecrations, as I commanded, saying, Aaron and his sons shall eat it.

32 [g]And that which remaineth of the flesh and of the bread shall ye burn with fire.

33 And ye shall not go out of the door of

the tabernacle of the congregation *in* seven days, until the days of your consecration be at an end: for [h]seven days shall he consecrate you.

34 [i]As he hath done this day, *so* the LORD hath commanded to do, to make an atonement for you.

35 Therefore shall ye abide *at* the door of the tabernacle of the congregation day and night seven days, and [j]keep the charge of the LORD, that ye die not: for so I am commanded.

36 So Aaron and his sons did all things which the LORD commanded by the hand of Moses.

9 And [k]it came to pass on the eighth day, *that* Moses called Aaron and his sons, and the elders of Israel;

2 And he said unto Aaron, [l]Take thee a young calf for a sin offering, [m]and a ram for a burnt offering, without blemish, and offer *them* before the LORD.

3 And unto the children of Israel thou shalt speak, saying, [n]Take ye a kid of the goats for a sin offering; and a calf and a lamb, *both* of the first year, without blemish, for a burnt offering;

4 Also a bullock and a ram for peace offerings, to sacrifice before the LORD; and [o]a meat offering mingled with oil: for [p]to day the LORD will appear unto you.

5 ¶ And they brought *that* which Moses commanded before the tabernacle of the congregation: and all the congregation drew near and stood before the LORD.

6 And Moses said, This *is* the thing which the LORD commanded that ye should do: and [q]the glory of the LORD shall appear unto you.

7 And Moses said unto Aaron, Go unto the altar, and [r]offer thy sin offering, and thy burnt offering, and make an atonement for thyself, and for the people: and [s]offer the offering of the people, and make an atonement for them; as the LORD commanded.

8 ¶ Aaron therefore went unto the altar, and slew the calf of the sin offering, which *was* for himself.

9 [t]And the sons of Aaron brought the blood unto him: and he dipped his finger in the blood, and [u]put *it* upon the horns of the altar, and poured out the blood at the bottom of the altar:

10 [v]But the fat, and the kidneys, and the caul above the liver of the sin offering, he burnt upon the altar; [w]as the LORD commanded Moses.

11 [x]And the flesh and the hide he burnt with fire without the camp.

12 And he slew the burnt offering; and Aaron's sons presented unto him the blood, [y]which he sprinkled round about upon the altar.

13 [z]And they presented the burnt offering unto him, with the pieces thereof, and the head: and he burnt *them* upon the altar.

14 [a]And he did wash the inwards and the legs, and burnt *them* upon the burnt offering on the altar.

15 ¶ [b]And he brought the people's offering, and took the goat, which *was* the sin offering for the people, and slew it, and offered it for sin, as the first.

16 And he brought the burnt offering, and offered it [c]according to the manner.

17 And he brought [d]the meat offering, and took an handful thereof, and burnt *it* upon the altar, [e]beside the burnt sacrifice of the morning.

18 He slew also the bullock and the ram *for* [f]a sacrifice of peace offerings, which *was* for the people: and Aaron's sons presented unto him the blood, which he sprinkled upon the altar round about,

19 And the fat of the bullock and of the ram, the rump, and that which covereth *the inwards*, and the kidneys, and the caul *above* the liver:

20 And they put the fat upon the breasts, [g]and he burnt the fat upon the altar:

21 And the breasts and the right shoulder Aaron waved [h]*for* a wave offering before the LORD; as Moses commanded.

22 And Aaron lifted up his hand toward the people, and [i]blessed them, and came down from offering of the sin offering, and the burnt offering, and peace offerings.

23 And Moses and Aaron went into the tabernacle of the congregation, and came out, and blessed the people: [j]and the glory of the LORD appeared unto all the people.

24 And [k]there came a fire out from before the LORD, and consumed upon the altar the burnt offering and the fat: *which* when all the people saw, [l]they shouted, and fell on their faces.

10 And [m]Nadab and Abihu, the sons of Aaron, [n]took either of them his censer, and put fire therein, and put incense thereon, and offered [o]strange fire before the LORD, which he commanded them not.

2 And there [p]went out fire from the LORD, and devoured them, and they died before the LORD.

3 Then Moses said unto Aaron, This *is it* that the LORD spake, saying, I will be sanctified in them [q]that come nigh me, and before all the people I will be [r]glorified. [s]And Aaron held his peace.

4 And Moses called Mishael and Elzaphan, the sons of [t]Uzziel the uncle of Aaron, and said unto them, Come near, [u]carry your brethren from before the sanctuary out of the camp.

5 So they went near, and carried them in their coats out of the camp; as Moses had said.

6 And Moses said unto Aaron, and unto Eleazar and unto Ithamar, his sons, [v]Uncover not your heads, neither rend your clothes; lest ye die, and lest [w]wrath come upon all the people: but let your brethren, the whole house of Israel, bewail the burning which the LORD hath kindled.

7 [x]And ye shall not go out from the door

8:33 [h]Ex. 29:30; Ezek. 43:25
8:34 [i]Heb. 7:16
8:35 [j]Num. 3:7; Deut. 11:1; 1 Kings 2:3
9:1 [k]Ezek. 43:27
9:2 [l]ch. 4:3; Ex. 29:1 [m]ch. 8:18
9:3 [n]ch. 4:23; Ezra 6:17
9:4 [o]ch. 2:4 [p]ver. 6; Ex. 29:43
9:6 [q]ver. 23; Ex. 24:16
9:7 [r]ch. 4:3; 1 Sam. 3:14; Heb. 5:3 [s]ch. 4:16; Heb. 5:1
9:9 [t]ch. 8:15 [u]ch. 4:17
9:10 [v]ch. 8:16 [w]ch. 4:8
9:11 [x]ch. 4:11
9:12 [y]ch. 1:5
9:13 [z]ch. 8:20
9:14 [a]ch. 8:21
9:15 [b]ver. 3; Isa. 53:10; Heb. 2:17
9:16 [c]ch. 1:3
9:17 [d]ver. 4; ch. 2:1 [e]Ex. 29:38
9:18 [f]ch. 3:1
9:20 [g]ch. 3:5
9:21 [h]Ex. 29:24; ch. 7:30
9:22 [i]Num. 6:23; Deut. 21:5; Luke 24:50
9:23 [j]ver. 6; Num. 14:10
9:24 [k]Gen. 4:4; Judg. 6:21; 1 Kings 18:38; 2 Chron. 7:1; Ps. 20:3 [l]1 Kings 18:39; 2 Chron. 7:3; Ezra 3:11
10:1 [m]ch. 11:6; Num. 3:3; 1 Chron. 24:2 [n]ch. 16:12; Num. 16:18 [o]Ex. 30:9
10:2 [p]ch. 9:24; Num. 16:35; 2 Sam. 6:7
10:3 [q]Ex. 19:22; ch. 21:6; Isa. 52:11; Ezek. 20:41 [r]Isa. 49:3; Ezek. 28:22; John 13:31; 2 Thess. 1:10 [s]Ps. 39:9
10:4 [t]Ex. 6:18; Num. 3:19 [u]Luke 7:12; Acts 5:6
10:6 [v]Ex. 33:5; ch. 13:45; Num. 6:6; Deut. 33:9; Ezek. 24:16 [w]Num. 16:22; Josh. 7:1; 2 Sam. 24:1
10:7 [x]ch. 21:12

of the tabernacle of the congregation, lest
ye die: [y]for the anointing oil of the LORD *is*
upon you. And they did according to the
word of Moses.
8 ¶ And the LORD spake unto Aaron, saying,
9 [z]Do not drink wine nor strong drink,
thou, nor thy sons with thee, when ye go
into the tabernacle of the congregation, lest
ye die: *it shall be* a statute for ever throughout your generations:
10 And that ye may [a]put difference between holy and unholy, and between unclean and clean;
11 [b]And that ye may teach the children of
Israel all the statutes which the LORD hath
spoken unto them by the hand of Moses.
12 ¶ And Moses spake unto Aaron, and
unto Eleazar and unto Ithamar, his sons
that were left, Take [c]the meat offering that
remaineth of the offerings of the LORD
made by fire, and eat it without leaven beside the altar: for [d]it *is* most holy:
13 And ye shall eat it in the holy place,
because it *is* thy due, and thy sons' due, of
the sacrifices of the LORD made by fire: for
[e]so I am commanded.
14 And [f]the wave breast and heave
shoulder shall ye eat in a clean place; thou,
and thy sons, and thy daughters with thee:
for *they be* thy due, and thy sons' due,
which are given out of the sacrifices of
peace offerings of the children of Israel.
15 [g]The heave shoulder and the wave
breast shall they bring with the offerings
made by fire of the fat, to wave *it for* a wave
offering before the LORD; and it shall be
thine, and thy sons' with thee, by a statute
for ever; as the LORD hath commanded.
16 ¶ And Moses diligently sought [h]the
goat of the sin offering, and, behold, it was
burnt: and he was angry with Eleazar and
Ithamar, the sons of Aaron *which were* left
alive, saying,
17 [i]Wherefore have ye not eaten the sin
offering in the holy place, seeing it *is* most
holy, and *God* hath given it you to bear the
iniquity of the congregation, to make atonement for them before the LORD?
18 Behold, [j]the blood of it was not
brought in within the holy *place:* ye should
indeed have eaten it in the holy *place,* [k]as
I commanded.
19 And Aaron said unto Moses, Behold,
[l]this day have they offered their sin offering and their burnt offering before the
LORD; and such things have befallen me:
and *if* I had eaten the sin offering to day,
[m]should it have been accepted in the sight
of the LORD?
20 And when Moses heard *that,* he was
content.
11 And the LORD spake unto Moses and
to Aaron, saying unto them,
2 Speak unto the children of Israel, saying, [n]These *are* the beasts which ye shall
eat among all the beasts that *are* on the
earth.

10:7 [y]Ex. 28:41; ch. 8:30
10:9 [z]Ezek. 44:21; Luke 1:15; 1 Tim. 3:3; Tit. 1:7
10:10 [a]ch. 11:47; Jer. 15:19; Ezek. 22:26
10:11 [b]Deut. 24:8; Neh. 8:2; Jer. 18:18; Mal. 2:7
10:12 [c]Ex. 29:2; ch. 6:16; Num. 18:9 [d]ch. 21:22
10:13 [e]ch. 2:3
10:14 [f]Ex. 29:24; ch. 7:31; Num. 18:11
10:15 [g]ch. 7:19
10:16 [h]ch. 9:3
10:17 [i]ch. 6:26
10:18 [j]ch. 6:30 [k]ch. 6:26
10:19 [l]ch. 9:8 [m]Jer. 6:20; Hos. 9:4; Mal. 1:10
11:2 [n]Deut. 14:4; Acts 10:12
11:7 [o]Isa. 65:4
11:8 [p]Isa. 52:11; Matt. 15:11; Mark 7:2; Acts 10:14; Rom. 14:14; 1 Cor. 8:8; Col. 2:16; Heb. 9:10
11:9 [q]Deut. 14:9
11:10 [r]ch. 7:18; Deut. 14:3
11:13 [s]Deut. 14:12
11:22 [t]Matt. 3:4; Mark 1:6

3 Whatsoever parteth the hoof, and is clovenfooted, *and* cheweth the cud, among the
beasts, that shall ye eat.
4 Nevertheless these shall ye not eat of
them that chew the cud, or of them that
divide the hoof: *as* the camel, because he
cheweth the cud, but divideth not the hoof;
he *is* unclean unto you.
5 And the coney, because he cheweth the
cud, but divideth not the hoof; he *is* unclean
unto you.
6 And the hare, because he cheweth the
cud, but divideth not the hoof; he *is* unclean
unto you.
7 And the swine, though he divide the
hoof, and be clovenfooted, yet he cheweth
not the cud; [o]he *is* unclean to you.
8 Of their flesh shall ye not eat, and their
carcase shall ye not touch; [p]they *are* unclean to you.
9 ¶ [q]These shall ye eat of all that *are* in
the waters: whatsoever hath fins and scales
in the waters, in the seas, and in the rivers,
them shall ye eat.
10 And all that have not fins and scales in
the seas, and in the rivers, of all that move
in the waters, and of any living thing which
is in the waters, they *shall be* an [r]abomina-
tion unto you:
11 They shall be even an abomination
unto you; ye shall not eat of their flesh, but
ye shall have their carcases in abomination.
12 Whatsoever hath no fins nor scales in
the waters, that *shall be* an abomination
unto you.
13 ¶ [s]And these *are they which* ye shall
have in abomination among the fowls; they
shall not be eaten, they *are* an abomination:
the eagle, and the ossifrage, and the ospray,
14 And the vulture, and the kite after his
kind;
15 Every raven after his kind;
16 And the owl, and the night hawk, and
the cuckow, and the hawk after his kind,
17 And the little owl, and the cormorant,
and the great owl,
18 And the swan, and the pelican, and the
gier eagle,
19 And the stork, the heron after her
kind, and the lapwing, and the bat.
20 All fowls that creep, going upon *all*
four, *shall be* an abomination unto you.
21 Yet these may ye eat of every flying
creeping thing that goeth upon *all* four,
which have legs above their feet, to leap
withal upon the earth;
22 *Even* these of them ye may eat; [t]the
locust after his kind, and the bald locust after his kind, and the beetle after his kind,
and the grasshopper after his kind.
23 But all *other* flying creeping things,
which have four feet, *shall be* an abomination unto you.
24 And for these ye shall be unclean:
whosoever toucheth the carcase of them
shall be unclean until the even.
25 And whosoever beareth *ought* of the

carcase of them [u]shall wash his clothes, and be unclean until the even.

26 *The carcases* of every beast which divideth the hoof, and *is* not clovenfooted, nor cheweth the cud, *are* unclean unto you: every one that toucheth them shall be unclean.

27 And whatsoever goeth upon his paws, among all manner of beasts that go on *all* four, those *are* unclean unto you: whoso toucheth their carcase shall be unclean until the even.

28 And he that beareth the carcase of them shall wash his clothes, and be unclean until the even: they *are* unclean unto you.

29 ¶ These also *shall be* unclean unto you among the creeping things that creep upon the earth; the weasel, and [v]the mouse, and the tortoise after his kind,

30 And the ferret, and the chameleon, and the lizard, and the snail, and the mole.

31 These *are* unclean to you among all that creep: whosoever doth touch them, when they be dead, shall be unclean until the even.

32 And upon whatsoever *any* of them, when they are dead, doth fall, it shall be unclean; whether *it be* any vessel of wood, or raiment, or skin, or sack, whatsoever vessel *it be*, wherein *any* work is done, [w]it must be put into water, and it shall be unclean until the even; so it shall be cleansed.

33 And every earthen vessel, whereinto *any* of them falleth, whatsoever *is* in it shall be unclean; and [x]ye shall break it.

34 Of all meat which may be eaten, *that* on which *such* water cometh shall be unclean: and all drink that may be drunk in every *such* vessel shall be unclean.

35 And every *thing* whereupon *any part* of their carcase falleth shall be unclean; *whether it be* oven, or ranges for pots, they shall be broken down: *for* they *are* unclean, and shall be unclean unto you.

36 Nevertheless a fountain or pit, *wherein there is* plenty of water, shall be clean: but that which toucheth their carcase shall be unclean.

37 And if *any part* of their carcase fall upon any sowing seed which is to be sown, it *shall be* clean.

38 But if *any* water be put upon the seed, and *any part* of their carcase fall thereon, it *shall be* unclean unto you.

39 And if any beast, of which ye may eat, die; he that toucheth the carcase thereof shall be unclean until the even.

40 And [y]he that eateth of the carcase of it shall wash his clothes, and be unclean until the even: he also that beareth the carcase of it shall wash his clothes, and be unclean until the even.

41 And every creeping thing that creepeth upon the earth *shall be* an abomination; it shall not be eaten.

42 Whatsoever goeth upon the belly, and whatsoever goeth upon *all* four, or whatsoever hath more feet among all creeping things that creep upon the earth, them ye shall not eat; for they are an abomination.

43 [z]Ye shall not make yourselves abominable with any creeping thing that creepeth, neither shall ye make yourselves unclean with them, that ye should be defiled thereby.

44 For I *am* the LORD your God: ye shall therefore sanctify yourselves, and [a]ye shall be holy; for I *am* holy: neither shall ye defile yourselves with any manner of creeping thing that creepeth upon the earth.

45 [b]For I *am* the LORD that bringeth you up out of the land of Egypt, to be your God: [c]ye shall therefore be holy, for I *am* holy.

46 This *is* the law of the beasts, and of the fowl, and of every living creature that moveth in the waters, and of every creature that creepeth upon the earth:

47 [d]To make a difference between the unclean and the clean, and between the beast that may be eaten and the beast that may not be eaten.

12 And the LORD spake unto Moses, saying,

2 Speak unto the children of Israel, saying, If a [e]woman have conceived seed, and born a man child, then [f]she shall be unclean seven days; [g]according to the days of the separation for her infirmity shall she be unclean.

3 And in the [h]eighth day the flesh of his foreskin shall be circumcised.

4 And she shall then continue in the blood of her purifying three and thirty days; she shall touch no hallowed thing, nor come into the sanctuary, until the days of her purifying be fulfilled.

5 But if she bear a maid child, then she shall be unclean two weeks, as in her separation: and she shall continue in the blood of her purifying threescore and six days.

6 And [i]when the days of her purifying are fulfilled, for a son, or for a daughter, she shall bring a lamb of the first year for a burnt offering, and a young pigeon, or a turtledove, for a sin offering, unto the door of the tabernacle of the congregation, unto the priest:

7 Who shall offer it before the LORD, and make an atonement for her; and she shall be cleansed from the issue of her blood. This *is* the law for her that hath born a male or a female.

8 [j]And if she be not able to bring a lamb, then she shall bring two turtles, or two young pigeons; the one for the burnt offering, and the other for a sin offering: [k]and the priest shall make an atonement for her, and she shall be clean.

13 And the LORD spake unto Moses and Aaron, saying,

2 When a man shall have in the skin of his flesh a rising, [l]a scab, or bright spot, and it be in the skin of his flesh *like* the plague of leprosy; [m]then he shall be brought unto Aaron the priest, or unto one of his sons the priests:

11:25 [u]ch. 14:8; Num. 19:10
11:29 [v]Isa. 66:17
11:32 [w]ch. 15:12
11:33 [x]ch. 6:28
11:40 [y]ch. 17:15; Deut. 14:21; Ezek. 4:14
11:43 [z]ch. 20:25
11:44 [a]Ex. 19:6; ch. 19:2; 1 Thess. 4:7; 1 Pet. 1:15
11:45 [b]Ex. 6:7 [c]ver. 44
11:47 [d]ch. 10:10
12:2 [e]ch. 15:19 [f]Luke 2:22 [g]ch. 15:19
12:3 [h]Gen. 17:12; Luke 1:59; John 7:22
12:6 [i]Luke 2:22
12:8 [j]ch. 5:7; Luke 2:24 [k]ch. 4:26
13:2 [l]Deut. 28:27; Isa. 3:17 [m]Deut. 17:8; Luke 17:14

3 And the priest shall look on the plague in the skin of the flesh: and *when* the hair in the plague is turned white, and the plague in sight *be* deeper than the skin of his flesh, it *is* a plague of leprosy: and the priest shall look on him, and pronounce him unclean.

4 If the bright spot *be* white in the skin of his flesh, and in sight *be* not deeper than the skin, and the hair thereof be not turned white; then the priest shall shut up *him that hath* the plague seven days:

5 And the priest shall look on him the seventh day: and, behold, *if* the plague in his sight be at a stay, *and* the plague spread not in the skin; then the priest shall shut him up seven days more:

6 And the priest shall look on him again the seventh day: and, behold, *if* the plague *be* somewhat dark, *and* the plague spread not in the skin, the priest shall pronounce him clean: it *is but* a scab: and he [n]shall wash his clothes, and be clean.

7 But if the scab spread much abroad in the skin, after that he hath been seen of the priest for his cleansing, he shall be seen of the priest again:

8 And *if* the priest see that, behold, the scab spreadeth in the skin, then the priest shall pronounce him unclean: it *is* a leprosy.

9 ¶ When the plague of leprosy is in a man, then he shall be brought unto the priest;

10 [o]And the priest shall see *him:* and, behold, *if* the rising *be* white in the skin, and it have turned the hair white, and *there be* quick raw flesh in the rising;

11 It *is* an old leprosy in the skin of his flesh, and the priest shall pronounce him unclean, and shall not shut him up: for he *is* unclean.

12 And if a leprosy break out abroad in the skin, and the leprosy cover all the skin of *him that hath* the plague from his head even to his foot, wheresoever the priest looketh;

13 Then the priest shall consider: and, behold, *if* the leprosy have covered all his flesh, he shall pronounce *him* clean *that hath* the plague: it is all turned white: he *is* clean.

14 But when raw flesh appeareth in him, he shall be unclean.

15 And the priest shall see the raw flesh, and pronounce him to be unclean: *for* the raw flesh *is* unclean: it *is* a leprosy.

16 Or if the raw flesh turn again, and be changed unto white, he shall come unto the priest;

17 And the priest shall see him: and, behold, *if* the plague be turned into white; then the priest shall pronounce *him* clean *that hath* the plague: he *is* clean.

18 ¶ The flesh also, in which, *even* in the skin thereof, was a [p]boil, and is healed,

19 And in the place of the boil there be a white rising, or a bright spot, white, and somewhat reddish, and it be shewed to the priest;

13:6 [n]ch. 11:25

13:10 [o]Num. 12:10; 2 Kings 5:27; 2 Chron. 26:20

13:18 [p]Ex. 9:9

20 And if, when the priest seeth it, behold, it *be* in sight lower than the skin, and the hair thereof be turned white; the priest shall pronounce him unclean: it *is* a plague of leprosy broken out of the boil.

21 But if the priest look on it, and, behold, *there be* no white hairs therein, and *if* it *be* not lower than the skin, but *be* somewhat dark; then the priest shall shut him up seven days:

22 And if it spread much abroad in the skin, then the priest shall pronounce him unclean: it *is* a plague.

23 But if the bright spot stay in his place, *and* spread not, it *is* a burning boil; and the priest shall pronounce him clean.

24 ¶ Or if there be *any* flesh, in the skin whereof *there is* a hot burning, and the quick *flesh* that burneth have a white bright spot, somewhat reddish, or white;

25 Then the priest shall look upon it: and, behold, *if* the hair in the bright spot be turned white, and it *be in* sight deeper than the skin; it *is* a leprosy broken out of the burning: wherefore the priest shall pronounce him unclean: it *is* the plague of leprosy.

26 But if the priest look on it, and, behold, *there be* no white hair in the bright spot, and it *be* no lower than the *other* skin, but *be* somewhat dark; then the priest shall shut him up seven days:

27 And the priest shall look upon him the seventh day: *and* if it be spread much abroad in the skin, then the priest shall pronounce him unclean: it *is* the plague of leprosy.

28 And if the bright spot stay in his place, *and* spread not in the skin, but it *be* somewhat dark; it *is* a rising of the burning, and the priest shall pronounce him clean: for it *is* an inflammation of the burning.

29 ¶ If a man or woman have a plague upon the head or the beard;

30 Then the priest shall see the plague: and, behold, if it *be* in sight deeper than the skin; *and there be* in it a yellow thin hair; then the priest shall pronounce him unclean: it *is* a dry scall, *even* a leprosy upon the head or beard.

31 And if the priest look on the plague of the scall, and, behold, it *be* not in sight deeper than the skin, and *that there is* no black hair in it; then the priest shall shut up *him that hath* the plague of the scall seven days:

32 And in the seventh day the priest shall look on the plague: and, behold, *if* the scall spread not, and there be in it no yellow hair, and the scall *be* not in sight deeper than the skin;

33 He shall be shaven, but the scall shall he not shave; and the priest shall shut up *him that hath* the scall seven days more:

34 And in the seventh day the priest shall look on the scall: and, behold, *if* the scall be not spread in the skin, nor *be* in sight deeper than the skin; then the priest shall pro-

nounce him clean: and he shall wash his
clothes, and be clean.
35 But if the scall spread much in the skin
after his cleansing;
36 Then the priest shall look on him: and,
behold, if the scall be spread in the skin, the
priest shall not seek for yellow hair; he *is*
unclean.
37 But if the scall be in his sight at a stay,
and *that* there is black hair grown up
therein; the scall is healed, he *is* clean: and
the priest shall pronounce him clean.
38 ¶ If a man also or a woman have in the
skin of their flesh bright spots, *even* white
bright spots;
39 Then the priest shall look: and, behold,
if the bright spots in the skin of their flesh
be darkish white; it *is* a freckled spot *that*
groweth in the skin; he *is* clean.
40 And the man whose hair is fallen off
his head, he *is* bald; *yet is* he clean.
41 And he that hath his hair fallen off
from the part of his head toward his face, he
is forehead bald: *yet is* he clean.
42 And if there be in the bald head, or
bald forehead, a white reddish sore; it *is* a
leprosy sprung up in his bald head, or his
bald forehead.
43 Then the priest shall look upon it: and,
behold, *if* the rising of the sore *be* white reddish in his bald head, or in his bald forehead, as the leprosy appeareth in the skin of
the flesh;
44 He is a leprous man, he *is* unclean: the
priest shall pronounce him utterly unclean;
his plague *is* in his head.
45 And the leper in whom the plague *is*,
his clothes shall be rent, and his head bare,
and he shall [q]put a covering upon his upper
lip, and shall cry, [r]Unclean, unclean.
46 All the days wherein the plague *shall*
be in him he shall be defiled; he *is* unclean:
he shall dwell alone; [s]without the camp
shall his habitation *be*.
47 ¶ The garment also that the plague of
leprosy is in, *whether it be* a woollen garment, or a linen garment;
48 Whether *it be* in the warp, or woof; of
linen, or of woollen; whether in a skin, or in
any thing made of skin;
49 And if the plague be greenish or reddish in the garment, or in the skin, either in
the warp, or in the woof, or in any thing of
skin; it *is* a plague of leprosy, and shall be
shewed unto the priest:
50 And the priest shall look upon the
plague, and shut up *it that hath* the plague
seven days:
51 And he shall look on the plague on the
seventh day: if the plague be spread in the
garment, either in the warp, or in the woof,
or in a skin, *or* in any work that is made of
skin; the plague *is* [t]a fretting leprosy; it *is*
unclean.
52 He shall therefore burn that garment,
whether warp or woof, in woollen or in
linen, or any thing of skin, wherein the
plague is: for it *is* a fretting leprosy; it shall
be burnt in the fire.
53 And if the priest shall look, and, behold, the plague be not spread in the garment, either in the warp, or in the woof, or
in any thing of skin;
54 Then the priest shall command that
they wash *the thing* wherein the plague *is*,
and he shall shut it up seven days more:
55 And the priest shall look on the plague,
after that it is washed: and, behold, *if* the
plague have not changed his colour, and the
plague be not spread; it *is* unclean; thou
shalt burn it in the fire; it *is* fret inward,
whether it *be* bare within or without.
56 And if the priest look, and, behold, the
plague *be* somewhat dark after the washing
of it; then he shall rend it out of the garment,
or out of the skin, or out of the warp, or out
of the woof:
57 And if it appear still in the garment,
either in the warp, or in the woof, or in any
thing of skin; it *is* a spreading *plague:* thou
shalt burn that wherein the plague *is* with
fire.
58 And the garment, either warp, or woof,
or whatsoever thing of skin *it be,* which
thou shalt wash, if the plague be departed
from them, then it shall be washed the second time, and shall be clean.
59 This *is* the law of the plague of leprosy
in a garment of woollen or linen, either in
the warp, or woof, or any thing of skins, to
pronounce it clean, or to pronounce it unclean.

14 And the LORD spake unto Moses,
saying,
2 This shall be the law of the leper in the
day of his cleansing: He [u]shall be brought
unto the priest:
3 And the priest shall go forth out of the
camp; and the priest shall look, and, behold,
if the plague of leprosy be healed in the
leper;
4 Then shall the priest command to take
for him that is to be cleansed two birds alive
and clean, and [v]cedar wood, and [w]scarlet,
and [x]hyssop:
5 And the priest shall command that one
of the birds be killed in an earthen vessel
over running water:
6 As for the living bird, he shall take it,
and the cedar wood, and the scarlet, and the
hyssop, and shall dip them and the living
bird in the blood of the bird *that was* killed
over the running water:
7 And he shall [y]sprinkle upon him that
is to be cleansed from the leprosy [z]seven
times, and shall pronounce him clean, and
shall let the living bird loose into the open
field.
8 And he that is to be cleansed [a]shall
wash his clothes, and shave off all his hair,
[b]and wash himself in water, that he may be
clean: and after that he shall come into the
camp, and [c]shall tarry abroad out of his
tent seven days.
9 But it shall be on the seventh day, that

13:45 [q]Ezek. 24:17; Mic. 3:7 [r]Lam. 4:15
13:46 [s]Num. 5:2; 2 Kings 7:3; 2 Chron. 26:21; Luke 17:12
13:51 [t]ch. 14:44
14:2 [u]Matt. 8:2; Mark 1:40; Luke 5:12
14:4 [v]Num. 19:6 [w]Heb. 9:19 [x]Ps. 51:7
14:7 [y]Heb. 9:13 [z]2 Kings 5:10
14:8 [a]ch. 13:6 [b]ch. 11:25 [c]Num. 12:15

he shall shave all his hair off his head and his beard and his eyebrows, even all his hair he shall shave off: and he shall wash his clothes, also he shall wash his flesh in water, and he shall be clean.

10 And on the eighth day [d]he shall take two he lambs without blemish, and one ewe lamb of the first year without blemish, and three tenth deals of fine flour *for* [e]a meat offering, mingled with oil, and one log of oil.

11 And the priest that maketh *him* clean shall present the man that is to be made clean, and those things, before the LORD, *at* the door of the tabernacle of the congregation:

12 And the priest shall take one he lamb, and [f]offer him for a trespass offering, and the log of oil, and wave them *for* a wave offering before the LORD:

13 And he shall slay the lamb [g]in the place where he shall kill the sin offering and the burnt offering, in the holy place: for [h]as the sin offering *is* the priest's, *so is* the trespass offering: [i]it *is* most holy:

14 And the priest shall take *some* of the blood of the trespass offering, and the priest shall put *it* [j]upon the tip of the right ear of him that is to be cleansed, and upon the thumb of his right hand, and upon the great toe of his right foot:

15 And the priest shall take *some* of the log of oil, and pour *it* into the palm of his own left hand:

16 And the priest shall dip his right finger in the oil that *is* in his left hand, and shall sprinkle of the oil with his finger seven times before the LORD:

17 And of the rest of the oil that *is* in his hand shall the priest put upon the tip of the right ear of him that is to be cleansed, and upon the thumb of his right hand, and upon the great toe of his right foot, upon the blood of the trespass offering:

18 And the remnant of the oil that *is* in the priest's hand he shall pour upon the head of him that is to be cleansed: [k]and the priest shall make an atonement for him before the LORD.

19 And the priest shall offer [l]the sin offering, and make an atonement for him that is to be cleansed from his uncleanness; and afterward he shall kill the burnt offering:

20 And the priest shall offer the burnt offering and the meat offering upon the altar: and the priest shall make an atonement for him, and he shall be clean.

21 And [m]if he *be* poor, and cannot get so much; then he shall take one lamb *for* a trespass offering to be waved, to make an atonement for him, and one tenth deal of fine flour mingled with oil for a meat offering, and a log of oil;

22 [n]And two turtledoves, or two young pigeons, such as he is able to get; and the one shall be a sin offering, and the other a burnt offering.

23 [o]And he shall bring them on the eighth day for his cleansing unto the priest, unto the door of the tabernacle of the congregation, before the LORD.

24 [p]And the priest shall take the lamb of the trespass offering, and the log of oil, and the priest shall wave them *for* a wave offering before the LORD:

25 And he shall kill the lamb of the trespass offering, [q]and the priest shall take *some* of the blood of the trespass offering, and put *it* upon the tip of the right ear of him that is to be cleansed, and upon the thumb of his right hand, and upon the great toe of his right foot:

26 And the priest shall pour of the oil into the palm of his own left hand:

27 And the priest shall sprinkle with his right finger *some* of the oil that *is* in his left hand seven times before the LORD:

28 And the priest shall put of the oil that *is* in his hand upon the tip of the right ear of him that is to be cleansed, and upon the thumb of his right hand, and upon the great toe of his right foot, upon the place of the blood of the trespass offering:

29 And the rest of the oil that *is* in the priest's hand he shall put upon the head of him that is to be cleansed, to make an atonement for him before the LORD.

30 And he shall offer the one of [r]the turtledoves, or of the young pigeons, such as he can get;

31 *Even* such as he is able to get, the one *for* a sin offering, and the other *for* a burnt offering, with the meat offering: and the priest shall make an atonement for him that is to be cleansed before the LORD.

32 This *is* the law *of him* in whom *is* the plague of leprosy, whose hand is not able to get [s]*that which pertaineth* to his cleansing.

33 ¶ And the LORD spake unto Moses and unto Aaron, saying,

34 [t]When ye be come into the land of Canaan, which I give to you for a possession, and I put the plague of leprosy in a house of the land of your possession;

35 And he that owneth the house shall come and tell the priest, saying, It seemeth to me *there is* as it were [u]a plague in the house:

36 Then the priest shall command that they empty the house, before the priest go *into it* to see the plague, that all that *is* in the house be not made unclean: and afterward the priest shall go in to see the house:

37 And he shall look on the plague, and, behold, *if* the plague *be* in the walls of the house with hollow strakes, greenish or reddish, which in sight *are* lower than the wall;

38 Then the priest shall go out of the house to the door of the house, and shut up the house seven days:

39 And the priest shall come again the seventh day, and shall look: and, behold, *if* the plague be spread in the walls of the house;

40 Then the priest shall command that they take away the stones in which the

14:10 [d]Matt. 8:4; Mark 1:44; Luke 5:14 [e]ch. 2:1; Num. 15:4
14:12 [f]ch. 5:2
14:13 [g]Ex. 29:11; ch. 1:5 [h]ch. 7:7 [i]ch. 2:3
14:14 [j]Ex. 29:20; ch. 8:23
14:18 [k]ch. 4:26
14:19 [l]ch. 5:1
14:21 [m]ch. 5:7
14:22 [n]ch. 12:8
14:23 [o]ver. 11
14:24 [p]ver. 12
14:25 [q]ver. 14
14:30 [r]ver. 22; ch. 15:15
14:32 [s]ver. 10
14:34 [t]Gen. 17:8; Num. 32:22; Deut. 7:1
14:35 [u]Ps. 91:10; Prov. 3:33; Zech. 5:4

plague *is*, and they shall cast them into an unclean place without the city:

41 And he shall cause the house to be scraped within round about, and they shall pour out the dust that they scrape off without the city into an unclean place:

42 And they shall take other stones, and put *them* in the place of those stones; and he shall take other morter, and shall plaister the house.

43 And if the plague come again, and break out in the house, after that he hath taken away the stones, and after he hath scraped the house, and after it is plaistered;

44 Then the priest shall come and look, and, behold, *if* the plague be spread in the house, it *is* [v]a fretting leprosy in the house: it *is* unclean.

45 And he shall break down the house, the stones of it, and the timber thereof, and all the morter of the house; and he shall carry *them* forth out of the city into an unclean place.

46 Moreover, he that goeth into the house all the while that it is shut up shall be unclean until the even.

47 And he that lieth in the house shall wash his clothes; and he that eateth in the house shall wash his clothes.

48 And if the priest shall come in, and look *upon it*, and, behold, the plague hath not spread in the house, after the house was plaistered: then the priest shall pronounce the house clean, because the plague is healed.

49 And [w]he shall take to cleanse the house two birds, and cedar wood, and scarlet, and hyssop:

50 And he shall kill the one of the birds in an earthen vessel over running water:

51 And he shall take the cedar wood, and the hyssop, and the scarlet, and the living bird, and dip them in the blood of the slain bird, and in the running water, and sprinkle the house seven times:

52 And he shall cleanse the house with the blood of the bird, and with the running water, and with the living bird, and with the cedar wood, and with the hyssop, and with the scarlet:

53 But he shall let go the living bird out of the city into the open fields, and [x]make an atonement for the house: and it shall be clean.

54 This *is* the law for all manner of plague of leprosy, and [y]scall,

55 And for the [z]leprosy of a garment, [a]and of a house,

56 And [b]for a rising, and for a scab, and for a bright spot:

57 To [c]teach when *it is* unclean, and when *it is* clean: this *is* the law of leprosy.

15 And the LORD spake unto Moses and to Aaron, saying,

2 Speak unto the children of Israel, and say unto them, [d]When any man hath a running issue out of his flesh, *because of* his issue he *is* unclean.

3 And this shall be his uncleanness in his issue: whether his flesh run with his issue, or his flesh be stopped from his issue, it *is* his uncleanness.

4 Every bed, whereon he lieth that hath the issue, is unclean: and every thing, whereon he sitteth, shall be unclean.

5 And whosoever toucheth his bed shall wash his clothes, [e]and bathe *himself* in water, and be unclean until the even.

6 And he that sitteth on *any* thing whereon he sat that hath the issue shall wash his clothes, and bathe *himself* in water, and be unclean until the even.

7 And he that toucheth the flesh of him that hath the issue shall wash his clothes, and bathe *himself* in water, and be unclean until the even.

8 And if he that hath the issue spit upon him that is clean; then he shall wash his clothes, and bathe *himself* in water, and be unclean until the even.

9 And what saddle soever he rideth upon that hath the issue shall be unclean.

10 And whosoever toucheth any thing that was under him shall be unclean until the even: and he that beareth *any of* those things shall wash his clothes, and bathe *himself* in water, and be unclean until the even.

11 And whomsoever he toucheth that hath the issue, and hath not rinsed his hands in water, he shall wash his clothes, and bathe *himself* in water, and be unclean until the even.

12 And the [f]vessel of earth, that he toucheth which hath the issue, shall be broken: and every vessel of wood shall be rinsed in water.

13 And when he that hath an issue is cleansed of his issue; then [g]he shall number to himself seven days for his cleansing, and wash his clothes, and bathe his flesh in running water, and shall be clean.

14 And on the eighth day he shall take to him [h]two turtledoves, or two young pigeons, and come before the LORD unto the door of the tabernacle of the congregation, and give them unto the priest:

15 And the priest shall offer them, [i]the one *for* a sin offering, and the other *for* a burnt offering; [j]and the priest shall make an atonement for him before the LORD for his issue.

16 And [k]if any man's seed of copulation go out from him, then he shall wash all his flesh in water, and be unclean until the even.

17 And every garment, and every skin, whereon is the seed of copulation, shall be washed with water, and be unclean until the even.

18 The woman also with whom man shall lie *with* seed of copulation, they shall *both* bathe *themselves* in water, and [l]be unclean until the even.

19 ¶ And [m]if a woman have an issue, *and* her issue in her flesh be blood, she shall be

14:44 [v]ch. 13:51; Zech. 5:4
14:49 [w]ver. 4
14:53 [x]ver. 20
14:54 [y]ch. 13:30
14:55 [z]ch. 13:47 [a]ver. 34
14:56 [b]ch. 13:2
14:57 [c]Deut. 24:8; Ezek. 44:23
15:2 [d]ch. 22:4; Num. 5:2; 2 Sam. 3:29; Matt. 9:20; Mark 5:25; Luke 8:43
15:5 [e]ch. 11:25
15:12 [f]ch. 6:28
15:13 [g]ver. 28; ch. 14:8
15:14 [h]ch. 14:22
15:15 [i]ch. 14:30 [j]ch. 14:19
15:16 [k]ch. 22:4; Deut. 23:10
15:18 [l]1 Sam. 21:4
15:19 [m]ch. 12:2

put apart seven days: and whosoever toucheth her shall be unclean until the even.

20 And every thing that she lieth upon in her separation shall be unclean: every thing also that she sitteth upon shall be unclean.

21 And whosoever toucheth her bed shall wash his clothes, and bathe *himself* in water, and be unclean until the even.

22 And whosoever toucheth any thing that she sat upon shall wash his clothes, and bathe *himself* in water, and be unclean until the even.

23 And if it *be* on *her* bed, or on any thing whereon she sitteth, when he toucheth it, he shall be unclean until the even.

24 And [n]if any man lie with her at all, and her flowers be upon him, he shall be unclean seven days; and all the bed whereon he lieth shall be unclean.

25 And if [o]a woman have an issue of her blood many days out of the time of her separation, or if it run beyond the time of her separation; all the days of the issue of her uncleanness shall be as the days of her separation: she *shall be* unclean.

26 Every bed whereon she lieth all the days of her issue shall be unto her as the bed of her separation: and whatsoever she sitteth upon shall be unclean, as the uncleanness of her separation.

27 And whosoever toucheth those things shall be unclean, and shall wash his clothes, and bathe *himself* in water, and be unclean until the even.

28 But [p]if she be cleansed of her issue, then she shall number to herself seven days, and after that she shall be clean.

29 And on the eighth day she shall take unto her two turtles, or two young pigeons, and bring them unto the priest, to the door of the tabernacle of the congregation.

30 And the priest shall offer the one *for* a sin offering, and the other *for* a burnt offering; and the priest shall make an atonement for her before the LORD for the issue of her uncleanness.

31 Thus shall ye [q]separate the children of Israel from their uncleanness; that they die not in their uncleanness, when they [r]defile my tabernacle that *is* among them.

32 [s]This *is* the law of him that hath an issue, [t]and *of him* whose seed goeth from him, and is defiled therewith;

33 [u]And of her that is sick of her flowers, and of him that hath an issue, of the man, [v]and of the woman, [w]and of him that lieth with her that is unclean.

16 And the LORD spake unto Moses after [x]the death of the two sons of Aaron, when they offered before the LORD, and died;

2 And the LORD said unto Moses, Speak unto Aaron thy brother, that he [y]come not at all times into the holy *place* within the vail before the mercy seat, which *is* upon the ark; that he die not: for [z]I will appear in the cloud upon the mercy seat.

3 Thus shall Aaron [a]come into the holy *place:* [b]with a young bullock for a sin offering, and a ram for a burnt offering.

4 He shall put on [c]the holy linen coat, and he shall have the linen breeches upon his flesh, and shall be girded with a linen girdle, and with the linen mitre shall he be attired: these are *holy* garments; therefore [d]shall he wash his flesh in water, and *so* put them on.

5 And he shall take of [e]the congregation of the children of Israel two kids of the goats for a sin offering, and one ram for a burnt offering.

6 And Aaron shall offer his bullock of the sin offering, which *is* for himself, and [f]make an atonement for himself, and for his house.

7 And he shall take the two goats, and present them before the LORD *at* the door of the tabernacle of the congregation.

8 And Aaron shall cast lots upon the two goats; one lot for the LORD, and the other lot for the scapegoat.

9 And Aaron shall bring the goat upon which the LORD's lot fell, and offer him *for* a sin offering.

10 But the goat, on which the lot fell to be the scapegoat, shall be presented alive before the LORD, to make [g]an atonement with him, *and* to let him go for a scapegoat into the wilderness.

11 And Aaron shall bring the bullock of the sin offering, which *is* for himself, and shall make an atonement for himself, and for his house, and shall kill the bullock of the sin offering which *is* for himself:

12 And he shall take [h]a censer full of burning coals of fire from off the altar before the LORD, and his hands full of [i]sweet incense beaten small, and bring *it* within the vail:

13 [j]And he shall put the incense upon the fire before the LORD, that the cloud of the incense may cover the [k]mercy seat that *is* upon the testimony, that he die not:

14 And [l]he shall take of the blood of the bullock, and [m]sprinkle *it* with his finger upon the mercy seat eastward; and before the mercy seat shall he sprinkle of the blood with his finger seven times.

15 ¶ [n]Then shall he kill the goat of the sin offering, that *is* for the people, and bring his blood [o]within the vail, and do with that blood as he did with the blood of the bullock, and sprinkle it upon the mercy seat, and before the mercy seat:

16 And he shall [p]make an atonement for the holy *place,* because of the uncleanness of the children of Israel, and because of their transgressions in all their sins: and so shall he do for the tabernacle of the congregation, that remaineth among them in the midst of their uncleanness.

17 [q]And there shall be no man in the tabernacle of the congregation when he goeth in to make an atonement in the holy *place,* until he come out, and have made an atone-

15:24 *n*ch. 20:18
15:25 *o*Matt. 9:20; Mark 5:25; Luke 8:43
15:28 *p*ver. 13
15:31 *q*ch. 11:47; Deut. 24:8; Ezek. 44:23 *r*Num. 5:3; Ezek. 5:11
15:32 *s*ver. 2 *t*ver. 16
15:33 *u*ver. 19 *v*ver. 25 *w*ver. 24
16:1 *x*ch. 10:1
16:2 *y*Ex. 30:10; ch. 23:27; Heb. 9:7 *z*Ex. 25:22; 1 Kings 8:10
16:3 *a*Heb. 9:7 *b*ch. 4:3
16:4 *c*Ex. 28:39; ch. 6:10; Ezek. 44:17 *d*Ex. 30:20; ch. 8:6
16:5 *e*ch. 4:14; Num. 29:11; 2 Chron. 29:21; Ezra 6:17; Ezek. 45:22
16:6 *f*ch. 9:7; Heb. 5:2
16:10 *g*1 John 2:2
16:12 *h*ch. 10:1; Num. 16:18; Rev. 8:5 *i*Ex. 30:34
16:13 *j*Ex. 30:1; Num. 16:7; Rev. 8:3 *k*Ex. 25:21
16:14 *l*ch. 4:5; Heb. 9:13 *m*ch. 4:6
16:15 *n*Heb. 2:17 *o*ver. 2; Heb. 6:19
16:16 *p*Ex. 29:36; Ezek. 45:18; Heb. 9:22
16:17 *q*Ex. 34:3; Luke 1:10

ment for himself, and for his household, and for all the congregation of Israel.

18 And he shall go out unto the altar that *is* before the LORD, and [r]make an atonement for it; and shall take of the blood of the bullock, and of the blood of the goat, and put *it* upon the horns of the altar round about.

19 And he shall sprinkle of the blood upon it with his finger seven times, and cleanse it, and [s]hallow it from the uncleanness of the children of Israel.

20 ¶ And when he hath made an end of [t]reconciling the holy *place*, and the tabernacle of the congregation, and the altar, he shall bring the live goat:

21 And Aaron shall lay both his hands upon the head of the live goat, and confess over him all the iniquities of the children of Israel, and all their transgressions in all their sins, [u]putting them upon the head of the goat, and shall send *him* away by the hand of a fit man into the wilderness:

22 And the goat shall [v]bear upon him all their iniquities unto a land not inhabited: and he shall let go the goat in the wilderness.

23 And Aaron shall come into the tabernacle of the congregation, [w]and shall put off the linen garments, which he put on when he went into the holy *place*, and shall leave them there:

24 And he shall wash his flesh with water in the holy place, and put on his garments, and come forth, [x]and offer his burnt offering, and the burnt offering of the people, and make an atonement for himself, and for the people.

25 And [y]the fat of the sin offering shall he burn upon the altar.

26 And he that let go the goat for the scapegoat shall wash his clothes, [z]and bathe his flesh in water, and afterward come into the camp.

27 [a]And the bullock *for* the sin offering, and the goat *for* the sin offering, whose blood was brought in to make atonement in the holy *place*, shall *one* carry forth without the camp; and they shall burn in the fire their skins, and their flesh, and their dung.

28 And he that burneth them shall wash his clothes, and bathe his flesh in water, and afterward he shall come into the camp.

29 ¶ And *this* shall be a statute for ever unto you: *that* [b]in the seventh month, on the tenth *day* of the month, ye shall afflict your souls, and do no work at all, *whether it be* one of your own country, or a stranger that sojourneth among you:

30 For on that day shall *the priest* make an atonement for you, to [c]cleanse you, *that* ye may be clean from all your sins before the LORD.

31 [d]It *shall be* a sabbath of rest unto you, and ye shall afflict your souls, by a statute for ever.

32 [e]And the priest, whom he shall anoint, and whom he shall [f]consecrate to minister in the priest's office in his father's stead, shall make the atonement, and [g]shall put on the linen clothes, *even* the holy garments:

33 And [h]he shall make an atonement for the holy sanctuary, and he shall make an atonement for the tabernacle of the congregation, and for the altar, and he shall make an atonement for the priests, and for all the people of the congregation.

34 [i]And this shall be an everlasting statute unto you, to make an atonement for the children of Israel for all their sins [j]once a year. And he did as the LORD commanded Moses.

17 And the LORD spake unto Moses, saying,

2 Speak unto Aaron, and unto his sons, and unto all the children of Israel, and say unto them; This *is* the thing which the LORD hath commanded, saying,

3 What man soever *there be* of the house of Israel, [k]that killeth an ox, or lamb, or goat, in the camp, or that killeth *it* out of the camp,

4 [l]And bringeth it not unto the door of the tabernacle of the congregation, to offer an offering unto the LORD before the tabernacle of the LORD; blood shall be [m]imputed unto that man; he hath shed blood; and that man [n]shall be cut off from among his people:

5 To the end that the children of Israel may bring their sacrifices, [o]which they offer in the open field, even that they may bring them unto the LORD, unto the door of the tabernacle of the congregation, unto the priest, and offer them *for* peace offerings unto the LORD.

6 And the priest [p]shall sprinkle the blood upon the altar of the LORD *at* the door of the tabernacle of the congregation, and [q]burn the fat for a sweet savour unto the LORD.

7 And they shall no more offer their sacrifices [r]unto devils, after whom they [s]have gone a whoring. This shall be a statute for ever unto them throughout their generations.

8 ¶ And thou shalt say unto them, Whatsoever man *there be* of the house of Israel, or of the strangers which sojourn among you, [t]that offereth a burnt offering or sacrifice,

9 And [u]bringeth it not unto the door of the tabernacle of the congregation, to offer it unto the LORD; even that man shall be cut off from among his people.

10 ¶ [v]And whatsoever man *there be* of the house of Israel, or of the strangers that sojourn among you, that eateth any manner of blood; [w]I will even set my face against that soul that eateth blood, and will cut him off from among his people.

11 [x]For the life of the flesh *is* in the blood: and I have given it to you upon the altar [y]to make an atonement for your souls: for [z]it *is* the blood *that* maketh an atonement for the soul.

16:18 [r]Ex. 30:10; ch. 4:7; Heb. 9:22
16:19 [s]Ezek. 43:20
16:20 [t]ver. 16; Ezek. 45:20
16:21 [u]Isa. 53:6
16:22 [v]Isa. 53:11; John 1:29; Heb. 9:28; 1 Pet. 2:24
16:23 [w]Ezek. 42:14
16:24 [x]ver. 3
16:25 [y]ch. 4:10
16:26 [z]ch. 15:5
16:27 [a]ch. 4:12; Heb. 13:11
16:29 [b]Ex. 30:10; ch. 23:27; Num. 29:7; Isa. 58:3; Dan. 10:3
16:30 [c]Ps. 51:2; Jer. 33:8; Eph. 5:26; Heb. 9:13; 1 John 1:7
16:31 [d]ch. 23:32
16:32 [e]ch. 4:3 [f]Ex. 29:29; Num. 20:26 [g]ver. 4
16:33 [h]ver. 6
16:34 [i]ch. 23:31; Num. 29:7 [j]Ex. 30:10; Heb. 9:7
17:3 [k]Deut. 12:5
17:4 [l]Deut. 12:5 [m]Rom. 5:13 [n]Gen. 17:14
17:5 [o]Gen. 21:33; Deut. 12:2; 1 Kings 14:23; 2 Kings 16:4; 2 Chron. 28:4; Ezek. 20:28
17:6 [p]ch. 3:2 [q]Ex. 29:18; ch. 3:5; Num. 18:17
17:7 [r]Deut. 32:17; 2 Chron. 11:15; Ps. 106:37; 1 Cor. 10:20; Rev. 9:20 [s]Ex. 34:15; ch. 20:5; Deut. 31:16; Ezek. 23:8
17:8 [t]ch. 1:2
17:9 [u]ver. 4
17:10 [v]Gen. 9:4; ch. 3:17; Deut. 12:16; 1 Sam. 14:33; Ezek. 44:7 [w]ch. 20:3; Jer. 44:11; Ezek. 14:8
17:11 [x]ver. 14 [y]Matt. 26:28; Mark 14:24; Rom. 3:25; Eph. 1:7; Col. 1:14; Heb. 13:12; 1 Pet. 1:2; 1 John 1:7; Rev. 1:5 [z]Heb. 9:22

12 Therefore I said unto the children of Israel, No soul of you shall eat blood, neither shall any stranger that sojourneth among you eat blood.

13 And whatsoever man *there be* of the children of Israel, or of the strangers that sojourn among you, which [a]hunteth and catcheth any beast or fowl that may be eaten; he shall even [b]pour out the blood thereof, and [c]cover it with dust.

14 [d]For *it is* the life of all flesh; the blood of it *is* for the life thereof: therefore I said unto the children of Israel, Ye shall eat the blood of no manner of flesh; for the life of all flesh *is* the blood thereof: whosoever eateth it shall be cut off.

15 [e]And every soul that eateth that which died *of itself,* or that which was torn *with beasts, whether it be* one of your own country, or a stranger, [f]he shall both wash his clothes, [g]and bathe *himself* in water, and be unclean until the even: then shall he be clean.

16 But if he wash *them* not, nor bathe his flesh; then [h]he shall bear his iniquity.

18 And the LORD spake unto Moses, saying,

2 Speak unto the children of Israel, and say unto them, [i]I am the LORD your God.

3 [j]After the doings of the land of Egypt, wherein ye dwelt, shall ye not do: and [k]after the doings of the land of Canaan, whither I bring you, shall ye not do: neither shall ye walk in their ordinances.

4 [l]Ye shall do my judgments, and keep mine ordinances, to walk therein: I *am* the LORD your God.

5 Ye shall therefore keep my statutes, and my judgments: [m]which if a man do, he shall live in them: [n]I *am* the LORD.

6 ¶ None of you shall approach to any that is near of kin to him, to uncover *their* nakedness: I *am* the LORD.

7 [o]The nakedness of thy father, or the nakedness of thy mother, shalt thou not uncover: she *is* thy mother; thou shalt not uncover her nakedness.

8 [p]The nakedness of thy father's wife shalt thou not uncover: it *is* thy father's nakedness.

9 [q]The nakedness of thy sister, the daughter of thy father, or daughter of thy mother, *whether she be* born at home, or born abroad, *even* their nakedness thou shalt not uncover.

10 The nakedness of thy son's daughter, or of thy daughter's daughter, *even* their nakedness thou shalt not uncover: for theirs *is* thine own nakedness.

11 The nakedness of thy father's wife's daughter, begotten of thy father, she *is* thy sister, thou shalt not uncover her nakedness.

12 [r]Thou shalt not uncover the nakedness of thy father's sister: she *is* thy father's near kinswoman.

13 Thou shalt not uncover the nakedness of thy mother's sister: for she *is* thy mother's near kinswoman.

14 [s]Thou shalt not uncover the nakedness of thy father's brother, thou shalt not approach to his wife: she *is* thine aunt.

15 [t]Thou shalt not uncover the nakedness of thy daughter in law: she *is* thy son's wife; thou shalt not uncover her nakedness.

16 [u]Thou shalt not uncover the nakedness of thy brother's wife: it *is* thy brother's nakedness.

17 [v]Thou shalt not uncover the nakedness of a woman and her daughter, neither shalt thou take her son's daughter, or her daughter's daughter, to uncover her nakedness; *for* they *are* her near kinswomen: it *is* wickedness.

18 Neither shalt thou take a wife to her sister, [w]to vex *her,* to uncover her nakedness, beside the other in her life *time.*

19 [x]Also thou shalt not approach unto a woman to uncover her nakedness, as long as she is put apart for her uncleanness.

20 Moreover [y]thou shalt not lie carnally with thy neighbour's wife, to defile thyself with her.

21 And thou shalt not let any of thy seed [z]pass through *the fire* to [a]Molech, neither shalt thou [b]profane the name of thy God: I *am* the LORD.

22 [c]Thou shalt not lie with mankind, as with womankind: it *is* abomination.

23 [d]Neither shalt thou lie with any beast to defile thyself therewith: neither shall any woman stand before a beast to lie down thereto: it *is* [e]confusion.

24 [f]Defile not ye yourselves in any of these things: [g]for in all these the nations are defiled which I cast out before you:

25 And [h]the land is defiled: therefore I do [i]visit the iniquity thereof upon it, and the land itself [j]vomiteth out her inhabitants.

26 [k]Ye shall therefore keep my statutes and my judgments, and shall not commit *any* of these abominations; *neither* any of your own nation, nor any stranger that sojourneth among you:

27 (For all these abominations have the men of the land done, which *were* before you, and the land is defiled;)

28 That [l]the land spue not you out also, when ye defile it, as it spued out the nations that *were* before you.

29 For whosoever shall commit any of these abominations, even the souls that commit *them* shall be cut off from among their people.

30 Therefore shall ye keep mine ordinance, [m]that *ye* commit not *any one* of these abominable customs, which were committed before you, and that ye [n]defile not yourselves therein: [o]I *am* the LORD your God.

19 And the LORD spake unto Moses, saying,

2 Speak unto all the congregation of the

17:13 [a]ch. 7:26 [b]Deut. 12:16 [c]Ezek. 24:7 **17:14** [d]ver. 11; Gen. 9:4; Deut. 12:23 **17:15** [e]Ex. 22:31; ch. 22:8; Deut. 14:21; Ezek. 4:14 [f]ch. 11:25 [g]ch. 15:5 **17:16** [h]ch. 5:1; Num. 19:20 **18:2** [i]ver. 4; Ex. 6:7; ch. 11:44; Ezek. 20:5 **18:3** [j]Ezek. 20:7 [k]Ex. 23:24; ch. 20:23; Deut. 12:4 **18:4** [l]Deut. 4:1; Ezek. 20:19 **18:5** [m]Ezek. 20:11; Luke 10:28; Rom. 10:5; Gal. 3:12 [n]Ex. 6:2; Mal. 3:6 **18:7** [o]ch. 20:11 **18:8** [p]Gen. 49:4; ch. 20:11; Deut. 22:30; Ezek. 22:10; Am. 2:7; 1 Cor. 5:1 **18:9** [q]ch. 20:17; 2 Sam. 13:12; Ezek. 22:11 **18:12** [r]ch. 20:19 **18:14** [s]ch. 20:20 **18:15** [t]Gen. 38:18; ch. 20:12; Ezek. 22:11 **18:16** [u]ch. 20:21; Deut. 25:5; Matt. 14:4; Mark 12:19 **18:17** [v]ch. 20:14 **18:18** [w]1 Sam. 1:6 **18:19** [x]ch. 20:18; Ezek. 18:6 **18:20** [y]ch. 20:10; Ex. 20:14; Deut. 5:18; Prov. 6:29; Mal. 3:5; Matt. 5:27; Rom. 2:22; 1 Cor. 6:9; Heb. 13:4 **18:21** [z]ch. 20:2; 2 Kings 16:3; Jer. 19:5; Ezek. 20:31 [a]1 Kings 11:7; Acts 7:43 [b]ch. 19:12; Ezek. 36:20; Mal. 1:12 **18:22** [c]ch. 20:13; Rom. 1:27; 1 Cor. 6:9; 1 Tim. 1:10 **18:23** [d]ch. 20:15; Ex. 22:19 [e]ch. 20:12 **18:24** [f]ver. 30; Matt. 15:18; Mark 7:21; 1 Cor. 3:17 [g]ch. 20:23; Deut. 18:12 **18:25** [h]Num. 35:34; Jer. 2:7; Ezek. 36:17 [i]Ps. 89:32; Isa. 26:21; Jer. 5:9; Hos. 2:13 [j]ver. 28 **18:26** [k]ver. 5:30; ch. 20:22 **18:28** [l]ch. 20:22; Jer. 9:19; Ezek. 36:13 **18:30** [m]ver. 3; ch. 20:23; Deut. 18:9 [n]ver. 24 [o]ver. 2

children of Israel, and say unto them, [p]Ye shall be holy: for I the LORD your God *am* holy.

3 ¶ [q]Ye shall fear every man his mother, and his father, and [r]keep my sabbaths: I *am* the LORD your God.

4 ¶ [s]Turn ye not unto idols, [t]nor make to yourselves molten gods: I *am* the LORD your God.

5 ¶ And [u]if ye offer a sacrifice of peace offerings unto the LORD, ye shall offer it at your own will.

6 It shall be eaten the same day ye offer it, and on the morrow: and if ought remain until the third day, it shall be burnt in the fire.

7 And if it be eaten at all on the third day, it *is* abominable; it shall not be accepted.

8 Therefore *every one* that eateth it shall bear his iniquity, because he hath profaned the hallowed thing of the LORD: and that soul shall be cut off from among his people.

9 ¶ And [v]when ye reap the harvest of your land, thou shalt not wholly reap the corners of thy field, neither shalt thou gather the gleanings of thy harvest.

10 And thou shalt not glean thy vineyard, neither shalt thou gather *every* grape of thy vineyard; thou shalt leave them for the poor and stranger: I *am* the LORD your God.

11 ¶ [w]Ye shall not steal, [x]neither deal falsely, neither lie one to another.

12 ¶ And ye shall not [y]swear by my name falsely, [z]neither shalt thou profane the name of thy God: I *am* the LORD.

13 ¶ [a]Thou shalt not defraud thy neighbour, neither rob *him:* [b]the wages of him that is hired shall not abide with thee all night until the morning.

14 ¶ Thou shalt not curse the deaf, [c]nor put a stumblingblock before the blind, but shalt [d]fear thy God: I *am* the LORD.

15 ¶ [e]Ye shall do no unrighteousness in judgment: thou shalt not respect the person of the poor, nor honour the person of the mighty: *but* in righteousness shalt thou judge thy neighbour.

16 ¶ [f]Thou shalt not go up and down *as* a talebearer among thy people: neither shalt thou [g]stand against the blood of thy neighbour: I *am* the LORD.

17 ¶ [h]Thou shalt not hate thy brother in thine heart: [i]thou shalt in any wise rebuke thy neighbour, and not suffer sin upon him.

18 ¶ [j]Thou shalt not avenge, nor bear any grudge against the children of thy people, [k]but thou shalt love thy neighbour as thyself: I *am* the LORD.

19 ¶ Ye shall keep my statutes. Thou shalt not let thy cattle gender with a diverse kind: [l]thou shalt not sow thy field with mingled seed: [m]neither shall a garment mingled of linen and woollen come upon thee.

20 ¶ And whosoever lieth carnally with a woman, that *is* a bondmaid, betrothed to an husband, and not at all redeemed, nor freedom given her; she shall be scourged; they shall not be put to death, because she was not free.

21 And [n]he shall bring his trespass offering unto the LORD, unto the door of the tabernacle of the congregation, *even* a ram for a trespass offering.

22 And the priest shall make an atonement for him with the ram of the trespass offering before the LORD for his sin which he hath done: and the sin which he hath done shall be forgiven him.

23 ¶ And when ye shall come into the land, and shall have planted all manner of trees for food, then ye shall count the fruit thereof as uncircumcised: three years shall it be as uncircumcised unto you: it shall not be eaten of.

24 But in the fourth year all the fruit thereof shall be holy [o]to praise the LORD *withal.*

25 And in the fifth year shall ye eat of the fruit thereof, that it may yield unto you the increase thereof: I *am* the LORD your God.

26 ¶ [p]Ye shall not eat *any thing* with the blood: [q]neither shall ye use enchantment, nor observe times.

27 [r]Ye shall not round the corners of your heads, neither shalt thou mar the corners of thy beard.

28 Ye shall not [s]make any cuttings in your flesh for the dead, nor print any marks upon you: I *am* the LORD.

29 ¶ [t]Do not prostitute thy daughter, to cause her to be a whore; lest the land fall to whoredom, and the land become full of wickedness.

30 ¶ [u]Ye shall keep my sabbaths, and [v]reverence my sanctuary: I *am* the LORD.

31 ¶ [w]Regard not them that have familiar spirits, neither seek after wizards, to be defiled by them: I *am* the LORD your God.

32 ¶ [x]Thou shalt rise up before the hoary head, and honour the face of the old man, and [y]fear thy God: I *am* the LORD.

33 ¶ And [z]if a stranger sojourn with thee in your land, ye shall not vex him.

34 [a]*But* the stranger that dwelleth with you shall be unto you as one born among you, and [b]thou shalt love him as thyself; for ye were strangers in the land of Egypt: I *am* the LORD your God.

35 ¶ [c]Ye shall do no unrighteousness in judgment, in meteyard, in weight, or in measure.

36 [d]Just balances, just weights, a just ephah, and a just hin, shall ye have: I *am* the LORD your God, which brought you out of the land of Egypt.

37 [e]Therefore shall ye observe all my statutes, and all my judgments, and do them: I *am* the LORD.

20 And the LORD spake unto Moses, saying,

2 [f]Again, thou shalt say to the children of

19:2 [p]ch. 11:44; 1 Pet. 1:16
19:3 [q]Ex. 20:12 [r]Ex. 20:8
19:4 [s]Ex. 20:4; ch. 26:1; 1 Cor. 10:14; 1 John 5:21 [t]Ex. 34:17; Deut. 27:15
19:5 [u]ch. 7:16
19:9 [v]ch. 23:22; Deut. 24:19; Ruth 2:15
19:11 [w]Ex. 20:15; Deut. 5:19 [x]ch. 6:2; Eph. 4:25; Col. 3:9
19:12 [y]Ex. 20:7; ch. 6:3; Deut. 5:11; Matt. 5:33; Jam. 5:12 [z]ch. 18:21
19:13 [a]Mark 10:19; 1 Thess. 4:6 [b]Deut. 24:14; Mal. 3:5; Jam. 5:4
19:14 [c]Deut. 27:18; Rom. 14:13 [d]ver. 32; ch. 25:17; Gen. 42:18; Eccl. 5:7; 1 Pet. 2:17
19:15 [e]Ex. 23:2; Deut. 1:17; Ps. 82:2; Prov. 24:23; Jam. 2:9
19:16 [f]Ex. 23:1; Ps. 15:3; Prov. 11:13; Ezek. 22:9 [g]Ex. 23:1; 1 Kings 21:13; Matt. 26:60
19:17 [h]1 John 2:9 [i]Matt. 18:15; Luke 17:3; Gal. 6:1; Eph. 5:11; 1 Tim. 5:20; 2 Tim. 4:2; Tit. 1:13
19:18 [j]2 Sam. 13:22; Prov. 20:22; Rom. 12:17; Gal. 5:20; Eph. 4:31; 1 Pet. 2:1; Jam. 5:9 [k]Matt. 5:43; Rom. 13:9; Gal. 5:14; Jam. 2:8
19:19 [l]Deut. 22:9 [m]Deut. 22:11
19:21 [n]ch. 5:15
19:24 [o]Deut. 12:17; Prov. 3:9
19:26 [p]ch. 17:10; Deut. 12:23 [q]Deut. 18:10; 1 Sam. 15:23; 2 Kings 17:17; 2 Chron. 33:6; Mal. 3:5
19:27 [r]ch. 21:5; Jer. 9:26; Isa. 15:2
19:28 [s]ch. 21:5; Deut. 14:1; Jer. 16:6
19:29 [t]Deut. 23:17
19:30 [u]ver. 3; ch. 26:2 [v]Eccl. 5:1
19:31 [w]Ex. 22:18; ch. 20:6; Deut. 18:10; 1 Sam. 28:7; 1 Chron. 10:13; Isa. 8:19; Acts 16:16
19:32 [x]Prov. 20:29; 1 Tim. 5:1 [y]ver. 14
19:33 [z]Ex. 22:21
19:34 [a]Ex. 12:48 [b]Deut. 10:19
19:35 [c]ver. 15
19:36 [d]Deut. 25:13; Prov. 11:1
19:37 [e]ch. 18:4; Deut. 4:5
20:2 [f]ch. 18:21

Israel, [g]Whosoever *he be* of the children of
Israel, or of the strangers that sojourn in
Israel, that giveth *any* of his seed unto Molech; he shall surely be put to death: the
people of the land shall stone him with
stones.
3 And [h]I will set my face against that
man, and will cut him off from among his
people; because he hath given of his seed
unto Molech, to [i]defile my sanctuary, and
[j]to profane my holy name.
4 And if the people of the land do any
ways hide their eyes from the man, when he
giveth of his seed unto Molech, and [k]kill
him not:
5 Then [l]I will set my face against that
man, and [m]against his family, and will cut
him off, and all that [n]go a whoring after
him, to commit whoredom with Molech,
from among their people.
6 ¶ And [o]the soul that turneth after such
as have familiar spirits, and after wizards,
to go a whoring after them, I will even set
my face against that soul, and will cut him
off from among his people.
7 ¶ [p]Sanctify yourselves therefore, and
be ye holy: for I *am* the LORD your God.
8 [q]And ye shall keep my statutes, and do
them: [r]I *am* the LORD which sanctify you.
9 ¶ [s]For every one that curseth his father
or his mother shall be surely put to death:
he hath cursed his father or his mother;
[t]his blood *shall be* upon him.
10 ¶ And [u]the man that committeth adultery with *another* man's wife, *even he* that
committeth adultery with his neighbour's
wife, the adulterer and the adulteress shall
surely be put to death.
11 [v]And the man that lieth with his father's wife hath uncovered his father's nakedness: both of them shall surely be put to
death; their blood *shall be* upon them.
12 [w]And if a man lie with his daughter in
law, both of them shall surely be put to
death: [x]they have wrought confusion; their
blood *shall be* upon them.
13 [y]If a man also lie with mankind, as he
lieth with a woman, both of them have committed an abomination: they shall surely be
put to death; their blood *shall be* upon them.
14 [z]And if a man take a wife and her
mother, it *is* wickedness: they shall be burnt
with fire, both he and they; that there be no
wickedness among you.
15 [a]And if a man lie with a beast, he shall
surely be put to death; and ye shall slay the
beast.
16 And if a woman approach unto any
beast, and lie down thereto, thou shalt kill
the woman, and the beast: they shall surely
be put to death; their blood *shall be* upon
them.
17 [b]And if a man shall take his sister, his
father's daughter, or his mother's daughter,
and see her nakedness, and she see his nakedness; it *is* a wicked thing; and they shall
be cut off in the sight of their people: he
hath uncovered his sister's nakedness; he
shall bear his iniquity.
18 [c]And if a man shall lie with a woman
having her sickness, and shall uncover her
nakedness; he hath discovered her fountain, and she hath uncovered the fountain of
her blood: and both of them shall be cut off
from among their people.
19 [d]And thou shalt not uncover the nakedness of thy mother's sister, nor of thy
father's sister: [e]for he uncovereth his near
kin: they shall bear their iniquity.
20 [f]And if a man shall lie with his uncle's
wife, he hath uncovered his uncle's nakedness: they shall bear their sin; they shall die
childless.
21 [g]And if a man shall take his brother's
wife, it *is* an unclean thing: he hath uncovered his brother's nakedness; they shall be
childless.
22 ¶ Ye shall therefore keep all my [h]stat-
utes, and all my judgments, and do them:
that the land, whither I bring you to dwell
therein, [i]spue you not out.
23 [j]And ye shall not walk in the manners
of the nation, which I cast out before you:
for they committed all these things, and
[k]therefore I abhorred them.
24 But [l]I have said unto you, Ye shall
inherit their land, and I will give it unto you
to possess it, a land that floweth with milk
and honey: I *am* the LORD your God,
[m]which have separated you from *other* people.
25 [n]Ye shall therefore put difference between clean beasts and unclean, and between unclean fowls and clean: [o]and ye
shall not make your souls abominable by
beast, or by fowl, or by any manner of living
thing that creepeth on the ground, which I
have separated from you as unclean.
26 And ye shall be holy unto me: [p]for I
the LORD *am* holy, and [q]have severed you
from *other* people, that ye should be mine.
27 ¶ [r]A man also or woman that hath a
familiar spirit, or that is a wizard, shall
surely be put to death: they shall stone them
with stones: [s]their blood *shall be* upon
them.

21 And the LORD said unto Moses,
Speak unto the priests the sons of
Aaron, and say unto them, [t]There shall
none be defiled for the dead among his people:
2 But for his kin, that is near unto him,
that is, for his mother, and for his father,
and for his son, and for his daughter, and
for his brother,
3 And for his sister a virgin, that is nigh
unto him, which hath had no husband; for
her may he be defiled.
4 *But* he shall not defile himself, *being*
a chief man among his people, to profane
himself.
5 [u]They shall not make baldness upon
their head, neither shall they shave off the
corner of their beard, nor make any cuttings
in their flesh.

20:2 [g]ch. 18:21; Deut. 12:31; 2 Kings 17:17; 2 Chron. 33:6; Jer. 7:31; Ezek. 20:26
20:3 [h]ch. 17:10 [i]Ezek. 5:11 [j]ch. 18:21
20:4 [k]Deut. 17:2
20:5 [l]ch. 17:10 [m]Ex. 20:5 [n]ch. 17:7
20:6 [o]ch. 19:31
20:7 [p]ch. 11:44; 1 Pet. 1:16
20:8 [q]ch. 19:37 [r]Ex. 31:13; ch. 21:8; Ezek. 37:28
20:9 [s]Ex. 21:17; Deut. 27:16; Prov. 20:20; Matt. 15:4 [t]ver. 11; 2 Sam. 1:16
20:10 [u]ch. 18:20; Deut. 22:22; John 8:4
20:11 [v]ch. 18:8; Deut. 27:23
20:12 [w]ch. 18:15 [x]ch. 18:23
20:13 [y]Gen. 19:5; ch. 18:22; Deut. 23:17; Judg. 19:22
20:14 [z]ch. 18:17; Deut. 27:23
20:15 [a]ch. 18:23; Deut. 27:21
20:17 [b]Gen. 20:12; ch. 18:9; Deut. 27:22
20:18 [c]ch. 15:24
20:19 [d]ch. 18:12 [e]ch. 18:6
20:20 [f]ch. 18:14
20:21 [g]ch. 18:16
20:22 [h]ch. 18:26 [i]ch. 18:25
20:23 [j]ch. 18:3 [k]ch. 18:27; Deut. 9:5
20:24 [l]Ex. 3:17 [m]ver. 26; Ex. 19:5; Deut. 7:6; 1 Kings 8:53
20:25 [n]ch. 11:47; Deut. 14:4 [o]ch. 11:43
20:26 [p]ver. 7; ch. 19:2; 1 Pet. 1:16 [q]ver. 24; Tit. 2:14
20:27 [r]ch. 19:31; Ex. 22:18; Deut. 18:10; 1 Sam. 28:7 [s]ver. 9
21:1 [t]Ezek. 44:25
21:5 [u]ch. 19:27; Deut. 14:1; Ezek. 44:20

6 They shall be holy unto their God, and [v]not profane the name of their God: for the offerings of the LORD made by fire, *and* [w]the bread of their God, they do offer: therefore they shall be holy.

7 [x]They shall not take a wife *that is* a whore, or profane; neither shall they take a woman [y]put away from her husband: for he *is* holy unto his God.

8 Thou shalt sanctify him therefore; for he offereth the bread of thy God: he shall be holy unto thee: [z]for I the LORD, which sanctify you, *am* holy.

9 ¶ [a]And the daughter of any priest, if she profane herself by playing the whore, she profaneth her father: she shall be burnt with fire.

10 [b]And *he that is* the high priest among his brethren, upon whose head the anointing oil was poured, and [c]that is consecrated to put on the garments, [d]shall not uncover his head, nor rend his clothes;

11 Neither shall he [e]go in to any dead body, nor defile himself for his father, or for his mother;

12 [f]Neither shall he go out of the sanctuary, nor profane the sanctuary of his God; for [g]the crown of the anointing oil of his God *is* upon him: I *am* the LORD.

13 And [h]he shall take a wife in her virginity.

14 A widow, or a divorced woman, or profane, *or* an harlot, these shall he not take: but he shall take a virgin of his own people to wife.

15 Neither shall he profane his seed among his people: for [i]I the LORD do sanctify him.

16 ¶ And the LORD spake unto Moses, saying,

17 Speak unto Aaron, saying, Whosoever *he be* of thy seed in their generations that hath *any* blemish, let him not [j]approach to offer the bread of his God.

18 For whatsoever man *he be* that hath a blemish, he shall not approach: a blind man, or a lame, or he that hath a flat nose, or any thing [k]superfluous,

19 Or a man that is brokenfooted, or brokenhanded,

20 Or crookbackt, or a dwarf, or that hath a blemish in his eye, or be scurvy, or scabbed, or [l]hath his stones broken;

21 No man that hath a blemish of the seed of Aaron the priest shall come nigh to [m]offer the offerings of the LORD made by fire: he hath a blemish; he shall not come nigh to offer the bread of his God.

22 He shall eat the bread of his God, *both* of the [n]most holy, and of the [o]holy.

23 Only he shall not go in unto the vail, nor come nigh unto the altar, because he hath a blemish; that [p]he profane not my sanctuaries: for I the LORD do sanctify them.

24 And Moses told *it* unto Aaron, and to his sons, and unto all the children of Israel.

22

And the LORD spake unto Moses, saying,

2 Speak unto Aaron and to his sons, that they [q]separate themselves from the holy things of the children of Israel, and that they [r]profane not my holy name *in those things* which they [s]hallow unto me: I *am* the LORD.

3 Say unto them, Whosoever *he be* of all your seed among your generations, that goeth unto the holy things, which the children of Israel hallow unto the LORD, [t]having his uncleanness upon him, that soul shall be cut off from my presence: I *am* the LORD.

4 What man soever of the seed of Aaron *is* a leper, or hath [u]a running issue; he shall not eat of the holy things, [v]until he be clean. And [w]whoso toucheth any thing *that is* unclean *by* the dead, or [x]a man whose seed goeth from him;

5 Or [y]whosoever toucheth any creeping thing, whereby he may be made unclean, or [z]a man of whom he may take uncleanness, whatsoever uncleanness he hath;

6 The soul which hath touched any such shall be unclean until even, and shall not eat of the holy things, unless he [a]wash his flesh with water.

7 And when the sun is down, he shall be clean, and shall afterward eat of the holy things; because [b]it *is* his food.

8 [c]That which dieth of itself, or is torn *with beasts*, he shall not eat to defile himself therewith: I *am* the LORD.

9 They shall therefore keep mine ordinance, [d]lest they bear sin for it, and die therefore, if they profane it: I the LORD do sanctify them.

10 [e]There shall no stranger eat *of* the holy thing: a sojourner of the priest, or an hired servant, shall not eat *of* the holy thing.

11 But if the priest buy *any* soul with his money, he shall eat of it, and he that is born in his house: [f]they shall eat of his meat.

12 If the priest's daughter also be *married* unto a stranger, she may not eat of an offering of the holy things.

13 But if the priest's daughter be a widow, or divorced, and have no child, and is [g]returned unto her father's house, [h]as in her youth, she shall eat of her father's meat: but there shall no stranger eat thereof.

14 ¶ [i]And if a man eat *of* the holy thing unwittingly, then he shall put the fifth *part* thereof unto it, and shall give *it* unto the priest with the holy thing.

15 And [j]they shall not profane the holy things of the children of Israel, which they offer unto the LORD;

16 Or suffer them [k]to bear the iniquity of trespass, when they eat their holy things: for I the LORD do sanctify them.

17 ¶ And the LORD spake unto Moses, saying,

18 Speak unto Aaron, and to his sons, and unto all the children of Israel, and say unto them, [l]Whatsoever *he be* of the house of Israel, or of the strangers in Israel, that will offer his oblation for all his vows, and for all

21:6 [v]ch. 18:21 [w]ch. 3:11
21:7 [x]Ezek. 44:22 [y]Deut. 24:1
21:8 [z]ch. 20:7
21:9 [a]Gen. 38:24
21:10 [b]Ex. 29:29; ch. 8:12; Num. 35:25 [c]Ex. 28:2; ch. 16:32 [d]ch. 10:6
21:11 [e]ver. 1; Num. 19:14
21:12 [f]ch. 10:7 [g]Ex. 28:36; ch. 8:9
21:13 [h]ver. 7; Ezek. 44:22
21:15 [i]ver. 8
21:17 [j]ch. 10:3; Num. 16:5; Ps. 64:4
21:18 [k]ch. 22:23
21:20 [l]Deut. 23:1
21:21 [m]ver. 6
21:22 [n]ch. 2:3; Num. 18:9 [o]ch. 22:10; Num. 18:19
21:23 [p]ver. 12
22:2 [q]Num. 6:3 [r]ch. 18:21 [s]Ex. 28:38; Num. 18:32; Deut. 15:19
22:3 [t]ch. 7:20
22:4 [u]ch. 15:2 [v]ch. 14:2 [w]Num. 19:11 [x]ch. 15:16
22:5 [y]ch. 11:24 [z]ch. 15:7
22:6 [a]ch. 15:5; Heb. 10:22
22:7 [b]ch. 21:22; Num. 18:11
22:8 [c]Ex. 22:31; ch. 17:15; Ezek. 44:31
22:9 [d]Ex. 28:43; Num. 18:22
22:10 [e]1 Sam. 21:6
22:11 [f]Num. 18:11
22:13 [g]Gen. 38:11 [h]ch. 10:14; Num. 18:11
22:14 [i]ch. 5:15
22:15 [j]Num. 18:32
22:16 [k]ver. 9
22:18 [l]ch. 1:2; Num. 15:14

his freewill offerings, which they will offer
unto the LORD for a burnt offering;
19 [m]*Ye shall offer* at your own will a male
without blemish, of the beeves, of the sheep,
or of the goats.
20 [n]*But* whatsoever hath a blemish, *that*
shall ye not offer: for it shall not be acceptable for you.
21 And [o]whosoever offereth a sacrifice
of peace offerings unto the LORD [p]to accomplish *his* vow, or a freewill offering in
beeves or sheep, it shall be perfect to be
accepted; there shall be no blemish therein.
22 [q]Blind, or broken, or maimed, or having a wen, or scurvy, or scabbed, ye shall
not offer these unto the LORD, nor make
[r]an offering by fire of them upon the altar
unto the LORD.
23 Either a bullock or a lamb that hath
any thing [s]superfluous or lacking in his
parts, that mayest thou offer *for* a freewill
offering; but for a vow it shall not be accepted.
24 Ye shall not offer unto the LORD that
which is bruised, or crushed, or broken, or
cut; neither shall ye make *any offering
thereof* in your land.
25 Neither [t]from a stranger's hand shall
ye offer [u]the bread of your God of any of
these; because their [v]corruption *is* in them,
and blemishes *be* in them: they shall not be
accepted for you.
26 ¶ And the LORD spake unto Moses,
saying,
27 [w]When a bullock, or a sheep, or a goat,
is brought forth, then it shall be seven days
under the dam; and from the eighth day and
thenceforth it shall be accepted for an offering made by fire unto the LORD.
28 And *whether it be* cow or ewe, ye shall
not kill it [x]and her young both in one day.
29 ¶ And when ye will [y]offer a sacrifice
of thanksgiving unto the LORD, offer *it* at
your own will.
30 On the same day it shall be eaten up;
ye shall leave [z]none of it until the morrow:
I *am* the LORD.
31 [a]Therefore shall ye keep my commandments, and do them: I *am* the LORD.
32 [b]Neither shall ye profane my holy
name; but [c]I will be hallowed among the
children of Israel: I *am* the LORD which
[d]hallow you,
33 [e]That brought you out of the land of
Egypt, to be your God: I *am* the LORD.
23 And the LORD spake unto Moses,
saying,
2 Speak unto the children of Israel, and
say unto them, *Concerning* [f]the feasts of
the LORD, which ye shall [g]proclaim *to be*
holy convocations, *even* these *are* my
feasts.
3 [h]Six days shall work be done: but the
seventh day *is* the sabbath of rest, an holy
convocation; ye shall do no work *therein:* it
is the sabbath of the LORD in all your dwellings.
4 ¶ [i]These *are* the feasts of the LORD,

22:19 [m]ch. 1:3
22:20 [n]Deut. 15:21; Mal. 1:8; Eph. 5:27; Heb. 9:14; 1 Pet. 1:19
22:21 [o]ch. 3:1 [p]ch. 7:16; Num. 15:3; Deut. 23:21; Ps. 61:8; Eccl. 5:4
22:22 [q]ver. 20; Mal. 1:8 [r]ch. 1:9
22:23 [s]ch. 21:18
22:25 [t]Num. 15:15 [u]ch. 21:6 [v]Mal. 1:14
22:27 [w]Ex. 22:30
22:28 [x]Deut. 22:6
22:29 [y]ch. 7:12; Ps. 107:22; Am. 4:5
22:30 [z]ch. 7:15
22:31 [a]ch. 19:37; Num. 15:40; Deut. 4:40
22:32 [b]ch. 18:21 [c]ch. 10:3; Matt. 6:9; Luke 11:2 [d]ch. 20:8
22:33 [e]Ex. 6:7; ch. 11:45; Num. 15:41
23:2 [f]ver. 4:37 [g]Ex. 32:5; 2 Kings 10:20; Ps. 81:3
23:3 [h]Ex. 20:9; ch. 19:3; Deut. 5:13; Luke 13:14
23:4 [i]ver. 2; Ex. 23:14
23:5 [j]Ex. 12:6; Num. 9:2; Deut. 16:1-8; Josh. 5:10
23:7 [k]Ex. 12:16; Num. 28:18
23:10 [l]Ex. 23:16; Num. 15:2; Deut. 16:9; Josh. 3:15 [m]Rom. 11:16; 1 Cor. 15:20; Jam. 1:18; Rev. 14:4
23:11 [n]Ex. 29:24
23:13 [o]ch. 2:14
23:15 [p]ch. 25:8; Ex. 34:22; Deut. 16:9
23:16 [q]Acts 2:1 [r]Num. 28:26
23:17 [s]Ex. 23:16; Num. 15:17; Deut. 26:1
23:19 [t]ch. 4:23; Num. 28:30 [u]ch. 3:1

even holy convocations, which ye shall proclaim in their seasons.
5 [j]In the fourteenth *day* of the first
month at even *is* the LORD's passover.
6 And on the fifteenth day of the same
month *is* the feast of unleavened bread unto
the LORD: seven days ye must eat unleavened bread.
7 [k]In the first day ye shall have an holy
convocation: ye shall do no servile work
therein.
8 But ye shall offer an offering made by
fire unto the LORD seven days: in the seventh day *is* an holy convocation: ye shall do
no servile work *therein.*
9 ¶ And the LORD spake unto Moses, saying,
10 Speak unto the children of Israel, and
say unto them, [l]When ye be come into the
land which I give unto you, and shall reap
the harvest thereof, then ye shall bring a
sheaf of [m]the firstfruits of your harvest unto
the priest:
11 And he shall [n]wave the sheaf before
the LORD, to be accepted for you: on the
morrow after the sabbath the priest shall
wave it.
12 And ye shall offer that day when ye
wave the sheaf an he lamb without blemish
of the first year for a burnt offering unto the
LORD.
13 [o]And the meat offering thereof *shall
be* two tenth deals of fine flour mingled with
oil, an offering made by fire unto the LORD
for a sweet savour: and the drink offering
thereof *shall be* of wine, the fourth *part* of
an hin.
14 And ye shall eat neither bread, nor
parched corn, nor green ears, until the selfsame day that ye have brought an offering
unto your God: *it shall be* a statute for ever
throughout your generations in all your
dwellings.
15 ¶ And [p]ye shall count unto you from
the morrow after the sabbath, from the day
that ye brought the sheaf of the wave offering; seven sabbaths shall be complete:
16 Even unto the morrow after the seventh sabbath shall ye number [q]fifty days;
and ye shall offer [r]a new meat offering
unto the LORD.
17 Ye shall bring out of your habitations
two wave loaves of two tenth deals: they
shall be of fine flour; they shall be baken
with leaven; *they are* [s]the firstfruits unto
the LORD.
18 And ye shall offer with the bread seven
lambs without blemish of the first year, and
one young bullock, and two rams: they shall
be *for* a burnt offering unto the LORD, with
their meat offering, and their drink offerings, *even* an offering made by fire, of sweet
savour unto the LORD.
19 Then ye shall sacrifice [t]one kid of the
goats for a sin offering, and two lambs of
the first year for a sacrifice of [u]peace offerings.
20 And the priest shall wave them with

the bread of the firstfruits *for* a wave offering before the LORD, with the two lambs:
[v]they shall be holy to the LORD for the
priest.
21 And ye shall proclaim on the selfsame
day, *that* it may be an holy convocation
unto you: ye shall do no servile work
therein: it shall be a statute for ever in all
your dwellings throughout your generations.
22 ¶ And [w]when ye reap the harvest of
your land, thou shalt not make clean riddance of the corners of thy field when thou
reapest, [x]neither shalt thou gather any
gleaning of thy harvest: thou shalt leave
them unto the poor, and to the stranger: I
am the LORD your God.
23 ¶ And the LORD spake unto Moses,
saying,
24 Speak unto the children of Israel, saying, In the [y]seventh month, in the first *day*
of the month, shall ye have a sabbath, [z]a
memorial of blowing of trumpets, an holy
convocation.
25 Ye shall do no servile work *therein:*
but ye shall offer an offering made by fire
unto the LORD.
26 ¶ And the LORD spake unto Moses,
saying,
27 [a]Also on the tenth *day* of this seventh
month *there shall be* a day of atonement: it
shall be an holy convocation unto you; and
ye shall afflict your souls, and offer an offering made by fire unto the LORD.
28 And ye shall do no work in that same
day: for it *is* a day of atonement, to make an
atonement for you before the LORD your
God.
29 For whatsoever soul *it be* that shall not
be afflicted in that same day, [b]he shall be
cut off from among his people.
30 And whatsoever soul *it be* that doeth
any work in that same day, [c]the same soul
will I destroy from among his people.
31 Ye shall do no manner of work: *it shall
be* a statute for ever throughout your generations in all your dwellings.
32 It *shall be* unto you a sabbath of rest,
and ye shall afflict your souls: in the ninth
day of the month at even, from even unto
even, shall ye celebrate your sabbath.
33 ¶ And the LORD spake unto Moses,
saying,
34 Speak unto the children of Israel, saying, [d]The fifteenth day of this seventh
month *shall be* the feast of tabernacles *for*
seven days unto the LORD.
35 On the first day *shall be* an holy convocation: ye shall do no servile work *therein.*
36 Seven days ye shall offer an offering
made by fire unto the LORD: [e]on the eighth
day shall be an holy convocation unto you;
and ye shall offer an offering made by fire
unto the LORD: it *is* a [f]solemn assembly;
and ye shall do no servile work *therein.*
37 [g]These *are* the feasts of the LORD,
which ye shall proclaim *to be* holy convocations, to offer an offering made by fire unto

23:20 [v]Num. 18:12; Deut. 18:4
23:22 [w]ch. 19:9 [x]Deut. 24:19
23:24 [y]Num. 29:1 [z]ch. 25:9
23:27 [a]ch. 16:30; Num. 29:7
23:29 [b]Gen. 17:14
23:30 [c]ch. 20:3
23:34 [d]Ex. 23:16; Num. 29:12; Deut. 16:13; Ezra 3:4; Neh. 8:14; Zech. 14:16; John 7:2
23:36 [e]Num. 29:35; Neh. 8:18; John 7:37 [f]Deut. 16:8; 2 Chron. 7:9; Neh. 8:18; Joel 1:14
23:37 [g]ver. 2
23:38 [h]Num. 29:39
23:39 [i]Ex. 23:16; Deut. 16:13
23:40 [j]Neh. 8:15 [k]Deut. 16:14
23:41 [l]Num. 29:12; Neh. 8:18
23:42 [m]Neh. 8:14
23:43 [n]Deut. 31:13; Ps. 78:5
23:44 [o]ver. 2
24:2 [p]Ex. 27:20
24:4 [q]Ex. 31:8
24:5 [r]Ex. 25:30
24:6 [s]1 Kings 7:48; 2 Chron. 4:19; Heb. 9:2
24:8 [t]Num. 4:7; 1 Chron. 9:32; 2 Chron. 2:4
24:9 [u]1 Sam. 21:6; Matt. 12:4; Mark 2:26; Luke 6:4 [v]Ex. 29:33; ch. 8:3

the LORD, a burnt offering, and a meat offering, a sacrifice, and drink offerings, every
thing upon his day:
38 [h]Beside the sabbaths of the LORD, and
beside your gifts, and beside all your vows,
and beside all your freewill offerings, which
ye give unto the LORD.
39 Also in the fifteenth day of the seventh
month, when ye have [i]gathered in the fruit
of the land, ye shall keep a feast unto the
LORD seven days: on the first day *shall be* a
sabbath, and on the eighth day *shall be* a
sabbath.
40 And [j]ye shall take you on the first day
the boughs of goodly trees, branches of
palm trees, and the boughs of thick trees,
and willows of the brook; [k]and ye shall rejoice before the LORD your God seven days.
41 [l]And ye shall keep it a feast unto the
LORD seven days in the year. *It shall be* a
statute for ever in your generations: ye shall
celebrate it in the seventh month.
42 [m]Ye shall dwell in booths seven days;
all that are Israelites born shall dwell in
booths:
43 [n]That your generations may know
that I made the children of Israel to dwell in
booths, when I brought them out of the land
of Egypt: I *am* the LORD your God.
44 And Moses [o]declared unto the children of Israel the feasts of the LORD.

24 And the LORD spake unto Moses,
saying,
2 [p]Command the children of Israel, that
they bring unto thee pure oil olive beaten
for the light, to cause the lamps to burn continually.
3 Without the vail of the testimony, in the
tabernacle of the congregation, shall Aaron
order it from the evening unto the morning
before the LORD continually: *it shall be* a
statute for ever in your generations.
4 He shall order the lamps upon [q]the
pure candlestick before the LORD continually.
5 ¶ And thou shalt take fine flour, and
bake twelve [r]cakes thereof: two tenth deals
shall be in one cake.
6 And thou shalt set them in two rows, six
on a row, [s]upon the pure table before the
LORD.
7 And thou shalt put pure frankincense
upon *each* row, that it may be on the bread
for a memorial, *even* an offering made by
fire unto the LORD.
8 [t]Every sabbath he shall set it in order
before the LORD continually, *being taken*
from the children of Israel by an everlasting
covenant.
9 And [u]it shall be Aaron's and his sons';
[v]and they shall eat it in the holy place: for
it *is* most holy unto him of the offerings of
the LORD made by fire by a perpetual statute.
10 ¶ And the son of an Israelitish woman,
whose father *was* an Egyptian, went out
among the children of Israel: and this son of

the Israelitish *woman* and a man of Israel
strove together in the camp;
11 And the Israelitish woman's son
[w]blasphemed the name of *the* LORD, and
[x]cursed. And they [y]brought him unto Moses:
(and his mother's name *was* Shelomith,
the daughter of Dibri, of the tribe of Dan:)
12 And they [z]put him in ward, [a]that the
mind of the LORD might be shewed them.
13 And the LORD spake unto Moses, saying,
14 Bring forth him that hath cursed without
the camp; and let all that heard *him* [b]lay
their hands upon his head, and let all the
congregation stone him.
15 And thou shalt speak unto the children
of Israel, saying, Whosoever curseth his
God [c]shall bear his sin.
16 And he that [d]blasphemeth the name of
the LORD, he shall surely be put to death,
and all the congregation shall certainly
stone him: as well the stranger, as he that is
born in the land, when he blasphemeth the
name *of the LORD*, shall be put to death.
17 ¶ [e]And he that killeth any man shall
surely be put to death.
18 [f]And he that killeth a beast shall
make it good; beast for beast.
19 And if a man cause a blemish in his
neighbour; as [g]he hath done, so shall it be
done to him;
20 Breach for breach, eye for eye, tooth
for tooth: as he hath caused a blemish in a
man, so shall it be done to him *again*.
21 [h]And he that killeth a beast, he shall
restore it: [i]and he that killeth a man, he
shall be put to death.
22 Ye shall have [j]one manner of law, as
well for the stranger, as for one of your own
country: for I *am* the LORD your God.
23 ¶ And Moses spake to the children of
Israel, [k]that they should bring forth him
that had cursed out of the camp, and stone
him with stones. And the children of Israel
did as the LORD commanded Moses.

25

And the LORD spake unto Moses in
mount Sinai, saying,
2 Speak unto the children of Israel, and
say unto them, When ye come into the land
which I give you, then shall the land keep
[l]a sabbath unto the LORD.
3 Six years thou shalt sow thy field, and
six years thou shalt prune thy vineyard, and
gather in the fruit thereof;
4 But in the seventh year shall be a sabbath
of rest unto the land, a sabbath for the
LORD: thou shalt neither sow thy field, nor
prune thy vineyard.
5 [m]That which groweth of its own accord
of thy harvest thou shalt not reap, neither
gather the grapes of thy vine undressed: *for*
it is a year of rest unto the land.
6 And the sabbath of the land shall be
meat for you; for thee, and for thy servant,
and for thy maid, and for thy hired servant,
and for thy stranger that sojourneth with
thee.
7 And for thy cattle, and for the beast that

24:11 [w]ver. 16 [x]Job 1:5; Isa. 8:21 [y]Ex. 18:22
24:12 [z]Num. 15:34 [a]Ex. 18:15; Num. 27:5
24:14 [b]Deut. 13:9
24:15 [c]ch. 5:1; Num. 9:13
24:16 [d]1 Kings 21:10; Ps. 74:10; Matt. 12:31; Mark 3:28; Jam. 2:7
24:17 [e]Ex. 21:12; Num. 35:31; Deut. 19:11
24:18 [f]ver. 21
24:19 [g]Ex. 21:24; Deut. 19:21; Matt. 5:38
24:21 [h]Ex. 21:33; ver. 18 [i]ver. 17
24:22 [j]Ex. 12:49; ch. 19:34; Num. 15:16
24:23 [k]ver. 14
25:2 [l]Ex. 23:10; ch. 26:34; 2 Chron. 36:21
25:5 [m]2 Kings 19:29
25:9 [n]ch. 23:24
25:10 [o]Isa. 61:2; Jer. 34:8; Luke 4:19 [p]ver. 13; Num. 36:4
25:11 [q]ver. 5
25:12 [r]ver. 6
25:13 [s]ver. 10; ch. 27:24; Num. 36:4
25:14 [t]ver. 17; ch. 19:13; 1 Sam. 12:3; Mic. 2:2; 1 Cor. 6:8
25:15 [u]ch. 27:18
25:17 [v]ver. 14 [w]ver. 43; ch. 19:14
25:18 [x]ch. 19:37 [y]ch. 26:5; Deut. 12:10; Ps. 4:8; Prov. 1:33; Jer. 23:6
25:19 [z]ch. 26:5; Ezek. 34:25
25:20 [a]Matt. 6:25 [b]ver. 4
25:21 [c]Ex. 16:29; Deut. 28:8
25:22 [d]2 Kings 19:29 [e]Josh. 5:11
25:23 [f]Deut. 32:43; 2 Chron. 7:20; Ps. 85:1; Joel 2:18 [g]1 Chron. 29:15; Ps. 39:12; 1 Pet. 2:11
25:25 [h]Ruth 2:20 [i]Ruth 3:2; Jer. 32:7

are in thy land, shall all the increase thereof
be meat.
8 ¶ And thou shalt number seven sabbaths
of years unto thee, seven times seven
years; and the space of the seven sabbaths
of years shall be unto thee forty and nine
years.
9 Then shalt thou cause the trumpet of the
jubile to sound on the tenth *day* of the seventh
month, [n]in the day of atonement shall
ye make the trumpet sound throughout all
your land.
10 And ye shall hallow the fiftieth year,
and [o]proclaim liberty throughout *all* the
land unto all the inhabitants thereof: it shall
be a jubile unto you; [p]and ye shall return
every man unto his possession, and ye shall
return every man unto his family.
11 A jubile shall that fiftieth year be unto
you: [q]ye shall not sow, neither reap that
which groweth of itself in it, nor gather *the
grapes* in it of thy vine undressed.
12 For it *is* the jubile; it shall be holy unto
you: [r]ye shall eat the increase thereof out of
the field.
13 [s]In the year of this jubile ye shall return
every man unto his possession.
14 And if thou sell ought unto thy neighbour,
or buyest *ought* of thy neighbour's
hand, [t]ye shall not oppress one another:
15 [u]According to the number of years after
the jubile thou shalt buy of thy neighbour,
and according unto the number of
years of the fruits he shall sell unto thee:
16 According to the multitude of years
thou shalt increase the price thereof, and
according to the fewness of years thou shalt
diminish the price of it: for *according* to the
number *of the years* of the fruits doth he sell
unto thee.
17 [v]Ye shall not therefore oppress one
another; [w]but thou shalt fear thy God: for I
am the LORD your God.
18 ¶ [x]Wherefore ye shall do my statutes,
and keep my judgments, and do them; [y]and
ye shall dwell in the land in safety.
19 And the land shall yield her fruit, and
[z]ye shall eat your fill, and dwell therein in
safety.
20 And if ye shall say, [a]What shall we eat
the seventh year? behold, [b]we shall not
sow, nor gather in our increase:
21 Then I will [c]command my blessing
upon you in the sixth year, and it shall bring
forth fruit for three years.
22 [d]And ye shall sow the eighth year, and
eat *yet* of [e]old fruit until the ninth year;
until her fruits come in ye shall eat *of* the old
store.
23 ¶ The land shall not be sold for ever:
for [f]the land *is* mine; for ye *are* [g]strangers
and sojourners with me.
24 And in all the land of your possession
ye shall grant a redemption for the land.
25 ¶ [h]If thy brother be waxen poor, and
hath sold away *some* of his possession, and
if [i]any of his kin come to redeem it, then
shall he redeem that which his brother sold.

26 And if the man have none to redeem it, and himself be able to redeem it;

27 Then [i]let him count the years of the sale thereof, and restore the overplus unto the man to whom he sold it; that he may return unto his possession.

28 But if he be not able to restore *it* to him, then that which is sold shall remain in the hand of him that hath bought it until the year of jubile: [k]and in the jubile it shall go out, and he shall return unto his possession.

29 And if a man sell a dwelling house in a walled city, then he may redeem it within a whole year after it is sold; *within* a full year may he redeem it.

30 And if it be not redeemed within the space of a full year, then the house that *is* in the walled city shall be established for ever to him that bought it throughout his generations: it shall not go out in the jubile.

31 But the houses of the villages which have no wall round about them shall be counted as the fields of the country: they may be redeemed, and they shall go out in the jubile.

32 Notwithstanding [l]the cities of the Levites, *and* the houses of the cities of their possession, may the Levites redeem at any time.

33 And if a man purchase of the Levites, then the house that was sold, and the city of his possession, [m]shall go out in *the year of* jubile: for the houses of the cities of the Levites *are* their possession among the children of Israel.

34 But [n]the field of the suburbs of their cities may not be sold; for it *is* their perpetual possession.

35 ¶ And if thy brother be waxen poor, and fallen in decay with thee; then thou shalt [o]relieve him: *yea, though he be* a stranger, or a sojourner; that he may live with thee.

36 [p]Take thou no usury of him, or increase: but [q]fear thy God; that thy brother may live with thee.

37 Thou shalt not give him thy money upon usury, nor lend him thy victuals for increase.

38 [r]I *am* the LORD your God, which brought you forth out of the land of Egypt, to give you the land of Canaan, *and* to be your God.

39 ¶ And [s]if thy brother *that dwelleth* by thee be waxen poor, and be sold unto thee; thou shalt not compel him to serve as a bondservant:

40 *But* as an hired servant, *and* as a sojourner, he shall be with thee, *and* shall serve thee unto the year of jubile:

41 And *then* shall he depart from thee, *both* he and his children [t]with him, and shall return unto his own family, and [u]unto the possession of his fathers shall he return.

42 For they *are* [v]my servants, which I brought forth out of the land of Egypt: they shall not be sold as bondmen.

43 [w]Thou shalt not rule over him [x]with rigour; but [y]shalt fear thy God.

44 Both thy bondmen, and thy bondmaids, which thou shalt have, *shall be* of the heathen that are round about you; of them shall ye buy bondmen and bondmaids.

45 Moreover of [z]the children of the strangers that do sojourn among you, o them shall ye buy, and of their families tha *are* with you, which they begat in your land: and they shall be your possession.

46 And [a]ye shall take them as an inheritance for your children after you, to inherit *them for* a possession; they shall be your bondmen for ever: but over your brethren the children of Israel, [b]ye shall not rule one over another with rigour.

47 ¶ And if a sojourner or stranger wax rich by thee, and [c]thy brother *that dwelleth* by him wax poor, and sell himself unto the stranger *or* sojourner by thee, or to the stock of the stranger's family:

48 After that he is sold he may be redeemed again; one of his brethren may [d]redeem him:

49 Either his uncle, or his uncle's son, may redeem him, or *any* that is nigh of kin unto him of his family may redeem him; or if [e]he be able, he may redeem himself.

50 And he shall reckon with him that bought him from the year that he was sold to him unto the year of jubile: and the price of his sale shall be according unto the number of years, [f]according to the time of an hired servant shall it be with him.

51 If *there be* yet many years *behind,* according unto them he shall give again the price of his redemption out of the money that he was bought for.

52 And if there remain but few years unto the year of jubile, then he shall count with him, *and* according unto his years shall he give him again the price of his redemption.

53 *And* as a yearly hired servant shall he be with him: *and the other* shall not rule with rigour over him in thy sight.

54 And if he be not redeemed in these *years,* then [g]he shall go out in the year of jubile, *both* he, and his children with him.

55 For [h]unto me the children of Israel *are* servants; they *are* my servants whom I brought forth out of the land of Egypt: I *am* the LORD your God.

26

Ye shall make you [i]no idols nor graven image, neither rear you up a standing image, neither shall ye set up *any* image of stone in your land, to bow down unto it: for I *am* the LORD your God.

2 ¶ [j]Ye shall keep my sabbaths, and reverence my sanctuary: I *am* the LORD.

3 ¶ [k]If ye walk in my statutes, and keep my commandments, and do them;

4 [l]Then I will give you rain in due season, [m]and the land shall yield her increase, and the trees of the field shall yield their fruit.

5 And [n]your threshing shall reach unto the vintage, and the vintage shall reach

25:27 [i]ver. 50
25:28 [k]ver. 13
25:32 [l]Num. 35:2; Josh. 21:2
25:33 [m]ver. 28
25:34 [n]Acts 4:36
25:35 [o]Deut. 15:7; Ps. 37:26; Prov. 14:31; Luke 6:35; Acts 11:29; Rom. 12:18; 1 John 3:17
25:36 [p]Ex. 22:25; Deut. 23:19; Neh. 5:7; Ps. 15:5; Prov. 28:8; Ezek. 18:8 [q]ver. 17; Neh. 5:9
25:38 [r]ch. 22:32
25:39 [s]Ex. 21:2; Deut. 15:12; 1 Kings 9:22; 2 Kings 4:1; Neh. 5:5; Jer. 34:14
25:41 [t]Ex. 21:3 [u]ver. 28
25:42 [v]ver. 55; Rom. 6:22; 1 Cor. 7:23
25:43 [w]Eph. 6:9; Col. 4:1 [x]ver. 46; Ex. 1:13 [y]ver. 17; Ex. 1:17; Deut. 25:18; Mal. 3:5
25:45 [z]Isa. 56:3
25:46 [a]Isa. 14:2 [b]ver. 43
25:47 [c]ver. 25:35
25:48 [d]Neh. 5:5
25:49 [e]ver. 26
25:50 [f]Job 7:1; Isa. 16:14
25:54 [g]ver. 41; Ex. 21:2
25:55 [h]ver. 42
26:1 [i]Ex. 20:4; Deut. 5:8; Ps. 97:7
26:2 [j]ch. 19:30
26:3 [k]Deut. 11:13
26:4 [l]Isa. 30:23; Ezek. 34:26; Joel 2:23 [m]Ps. 67:6; Ezek. 34:27; Zech. 8:12
26:5 [n]Am. 9:13

unto the sowing time: and [o]ye shall eat your bread to the full, and [p]dwell in your land safely.

6 And [q]I will give peace in the land, and [r]ye shall lie down, and none shall make *you* afraid: and I will rid [s]evil beasts out of the land, neither shall [t]the sword go through your land.

7 And ye shall chase your enemies, and they shall fall before you by the sword.

8 And [u]five of you shall chase an hundred, and an hundred of you shall put ten thousand to flight: and your enemies shall fall before you by the sword.

9 For I will [v]have respect unto you, and [w]make you fruitful, and multiply you, and establish my covenant with you.

10 And ye shall eat [x]old store, and bring forth the old because of the new.

11 [y]And I will set my tabernacle among you: and my soul shall not [z]abhor you.

12 [a]And I will walk among you, and [b]will be your God, and ye shall be my people.

13 [c]I *am* the LORD your God, which brought you forth out of the land of Egypt, that ye should not be their bondmen; [d]and I have broken the bands of your yoke, and made you go upright.

14 ¶ [e]But if ye will not hearken unto me, and will not do all these commandments;

15 And if ye shall [f]despise my statutes, or if your soul abhor my judgments, so that ye will not do all my commandments, *but* that ye break my covenant:

16 I also will do this unto you; I will even appoint over you [g]terror, [h]consumption, and the burning ague, that shall [i]consume the eyes, and cause sorrow of heart: and [j]ye shall sow your seed in vain, for your enemies shall eat it.

17 And [k]I will set my face against you, and [l]ye shall be slain before your enemies: [m]they that hate you shall reign over you; and [n]ye shall flee when none pursueth you.

18 And if ye will not yet for all this hearken unto me, then I will punish you [o]seven times more for your sins.

19 And I will [p]break the pride of your power; and I [q]will make your heaven as iron, and your earth as brass:

20 And your [r]strength shall be spent in vain: for [s]your land shall not yield her increase, neither shall the trees of the land yield their fruits.

21 ¶ And if ye walk contrary unto me, and will not hearken unto me; I will bring seven times more plagues upon you according to your sins.

22 [t]I will also send wild beasts among you, which shall rob you of your children, and destroy your cattle, and make you few in number; and [u]your *high* ways shall be desolate.

23 And if ye [v]will not be reformed by me by these things, but will walk contrary unto me;

24 [w]Then will I also walk contrary unto you, and will punish you yet seven times for your sins.

25 And [x]I will bring a sword upon you, that shall avenge the quarrel of *my* covenant: and when ye are gathered together within your cities, [y]I will send the pestilence among you; and ye shall be delivered into the hand of the enemy.

26 [z]*And* when I have broken the staff of your bread, ten women shall bake your bread in one oven, and they shall deliver *you* your bread again by weight: and [a]ye shall eat, and not be satisfied.

27 And [b]if ye will not for all this hearken unto me, but walk contrary unto me;

28 Then I will walk contrary unto you also [c]in fury; and I, even I, will chastise you seven times for your sins.

29 [d]And ye shall eat the flesh of your sons, and the flesh of your daughters shall ye eat.

30 And [e]I will destroy your high places, and cut down your images, and [f]cast your carcases upon the carcases of your idols, and my soul shall [g]abhor you.

31 [h]And I will make your cities waste, and [i]bring your sanctuaries unto desolation, and I will not smell the savour of your sweet odours.

32 [j]And I will bring the land into desolation: and your enemies which dwell therein shall be [k]astonished at it.

33 And [l]I will scatter you among the heathen, and will draw out a sword after you: and your land shall be desolate, and your cities waste.

34 [m]Then shall the land enjoy her sabbaths, as long as it lieth desolate, and ye *be* in your enemies' land; *even* then shall the land rest, and enjoy her sabbaths.

35 As long as it lieth desolate it shall rest; because it did not rest in your [n]sabbaths, when ye dwelt upon it.

36 And upon them that are left *alive* of you [o]I will send a faintness into their hearts in the lands of their enemies; and [p]the sound of a shaken leaf shall chase them; and they shall flee, as fleeing from a sword; and they shall fall when none pursueth.

37 And [q]they shall fall one upon another, as it were before a sword, when none pursueth: and [r]ye shall have no power to stand before your enemies.

38 And ye shall perish among the heathen, and the land of your enemies shall eat you up.

39 And they that are left of you [s]shall pine away in their iniquity in your enemies'

26:5 [o]ch. 25:19; Deut. 11:15; Joel 2:19 [p]ch. 25:18; Job 11:18; Ezek. 34:25
26:6 [q]1 Chron. 22:9; Ps. 29:11; Isa. 45:7; Hag. 2:9 [r]Job 11:19; Ps. 3:5; Isa. 35:9; Jer. 30:10; Ezek. 34:25; Hos. 2:18; Zeph. 3:13 [s]2 Kings 17:25; Ezek. 5:17 [t]Ezek. 14:17
26:8 [u]Deut. 32:30; Josh. 23:10
26:9 [v]Ex. 2:25; 2 Kings 13:23 [w]Gen. 17:6; Neh. 9:23; Ps. 107:38
26:10 [x]ch. 25:22
26:11 [y]Ex. 25:8; Josh. 22:19; Ps. 76:2; Ezek. 37:26; Rev. 21:3 [z]ch. 20:23; Deut. 32:19
26:12 [a]2 Cor. 6:16 [b]Ex. 6:7; Jer. 7:23; Ezek. 11:20
26:13 [c]ch. 25:38 [d]Jer. 2:20; Ezek. 34:27
26:14 [e]Deut. 28:15; Lam. 2:17; Mal. 2:2
26:15 [f]ver. 43; 2 Kings 17:15
26:16 [g]Deut. 28:65; Jer. 15:8 [h]Deut. 28:22 [i]1 Sam. 2:33 [j]Deut. 28:33; Job 31:8; Jer. 5:17; Mic. 6:15
26:17 [k]ch. 17:10 [l]Deut. 28:25; Judg. 2:14; Jer. 19:7 [m]Ps. 106:41 [n]ver. 36; Ps. 53:5; Prov. 28:1
26:18 [o]1 Sam. 2:5; Ps. 119:164; Prov. 24:16
26:19 [p]Isa. 25:11; Ezek. 7:24 [q]Deut. 28:23
26:20 [r]Ps. 127:1; Isa. 49:4 [s]Deut. 11:17; Hag. 1:10
26:22 [t]Deut. 32:24; 2 Kings 17:25; Ezek. 5:17 [u]Judg. 5:6; 2 Chron. 15:5; Isa. 33:8; Lam. 1:4; Zech. 7:14
26:23 [v]Jer. 2:30; Am. 4:6-12
26:24 [w]2 Sam. 22:27; Ps. 18:26
26:25 [x]Ezek. 5:17 [y]Num. 14:12; Deut. 28:21; Jer. 14:12; Am. 4:10
26:26 [z]Ps. 105:16; Isa. 3:1; Ezek. 4:16 [a]Isa. 9:20; Mic. 6:14; Hag. 1:6
26:27 [b]ver. 21
26:28 [c]Isa. 59:18; Jer. 21:5; Ezek. 5:13
26:29 [d]Deut. 28:53; 2 Kings 6:29; Ezek. 5:10; Lam. 4:10
26:30 [e]2 Chron. 34:3; Isa. 27:9; Ezek. 6:3 [f]2 Kings 23:20; 2 Chron. 34:5 [g]Lev. 20:23; Ps. 78:59; Jer. 14:19
26:31 [h]Neh. 2:3; Jer. 4:7; Ezek. 6:6 [i]Ps. 74:7; Lam. 1:10; Ezek. 9:6
26:32 [j]Jer. 9:11 [k]Deut. 28:37; 1 Kings 9:8; Jer. 18:16; Ezek. 5:15
26:33 [l]Deut. 4:27; Ps. 44:11; Jer. 9:16; Ezek. 12:15; Zech. 7:14
26:34 [m]2 Chron. 36:21
26:35 [n]ch. 25:2
26:36 [o]Ezek. 21:7 [p]ver. 17; Job 15:21; Prov. 28:1
26:37 [q]Judg. 7:22; 1 Sam. 14:15; Isa. 10:4 [r]Josh. 7:12; Judg. 2:14
26:39 [s]Deut. 4:27; Neh. 1:9; Jer. 3:25; Ezek. 4:17; Hos. 5:15; Zech. 10:9

lands; and also in the iniquities of their fathers shall they pine away with them.
40 [t]If they shall confess their iniquity,
and the iniquity of their fathers, with their
trespass which they trespassed against me,
and that also they have walked contrary
unto me;
41 And *that* I also have walked contrary
unto them, and have brought them into the
land of their enemies; if then their [u]uncir-
cumcised hearts be [v]humbled, and they
then accept of the punishment of their iniquity:
42 Then will I [w]remember my covenant
with Jacob, and also my covenant with
Isaac, and also my covenant with Abraham
will I remember; and I will [x]remember the
land.
43 [y]The land also shall be left of them,
and shall enjoy her sabbaths, while she lieth
desolate without them: and they shall accept of the punishment of their iniquity: because, even because they [z]despised my
judgments, and because their soul abhorred
my statutes.
44 And yet for all that, when they be in
the land of their enemies, [a]I will not cast
them away, neither will I abhor them, to
destroy them utterly, and to break my covenant with them: for I *am* the LORD their
God.
45 But I will [b]for their sakes remember
the covenant of their ancestors, [c]whom I
brought forth out of the land of Egypt [d]in
the sight of the heathen, that I might be
their God: I *am* the LORD.
46 [e]These *are* the statutes and judgments
and laws, which the LORD made between
him and the children of Israel [f]in mount
Sinai by the hand of Moses.

27 And the LORD spake unto Moses,
saying,
2 Speak unto the children of Israel, and
say unto them, [g]When a man shall make a
singular vow, the persons *shall be* for the
LORD by thy estimation.
3 And thy estimation shall be of the male
from twenty years old even unto sixty years
old, even thy estimation shall be fifty shekels of silver, [h]after the shekel of the sanctuary.
4 And if it *be* a female, then thy estimation shall be thirty shekels.
5 And if *it be* from five years old even
unto twenty years old, then thy estimation
shall be of the male twenty shekels, and for
the female ten shekels.
6 And if *it be* from a month old even unto
five years old, then thy estimation shall be
of the male five shekels of silver, and for the
female thy estimation *shall be* three shekels
of silver.
7 And if *it be* from sixty years old and
above; if *it be* a male, then thy estimation
shall be fifteen shekels, and for the female
ten shekels.
8 But if he be poorer than thy estimation,
then he shall present himself before the
priest, and the priest shall value him; according to his ability that vowed shall the
priest value him.
9 And if *it be* a beast, whereof men bring
an offering unto the LORD, all that *any man*
giveth of such unto the LORD shall be holy.
10 He shall not alter it, nor change it, a
good for a bad, or a bad for a good: and if he
shall at all change beast for beast, then it
and the exchange thereof shall be holy.
11 And if *it be* any unclean beast, of
which they do not offer a sacrifice unto the
LORD, then he shall present the beast before
the priest:
12 And the priest shall value it, whether it
be good or bad: as thou valuest it, *who art*
the priest, so shall it be.
13 [i]But if he will at all redeem it, then he
shall add a fifth *part* thereof unto thy estimation.
14 ¶ And when a man shall sanctify his
house *to be* holy unto the LORD, then the
priest shall estimate it, whether it be good
or bad: as the priest shall estimate it, so
shall it stand.
15 [j]And if he that sanctified it will redeem his house, then he shall add the fifth
part of the money of thy estimation unto it,
and it shall be his.
16 And if a man shall sanctify unto the
LORD *some part* of a field of his possession,
then thy estimation shall be according to
the seed thereof: an homer of barley seed
shall be valued at fifty shekels of silver.
17 If he sanctify his field from the year of
jubile, according to thy estimation it shall
stand.
18 But if he sanctify his field after the jubile, then the priest shall [k]reckon unto him
the money according to the years that remain, even unto the year of the jubile, and
it shall be abated from thy estimation.
19 [l]And if he that sanctified the field will
in any wise redeem it, then he shall add the
fifth *part* of the money of thy estimation
unto it, and it shall be assured to him.
20 And if he will not redeem the field, or
if he have sold the field to another man, it
shall not be redeemed any more.
21 But the field, [m]when it goeth out in the
jubile, shall be holy unto the LORD, as a field
[n]devoted; [o]the possession thereof shall be
the priest's.
22 And if *a man* sanctify unto the LORD a
field which he hath bought, which *is* not of
the fields of [p]his possession;
23 [q]Then the priest shall reckon unto him
the worth of thy estimation, even unto the
year of the jubile: and he shall give thine
estimation in that day, *as* a holy thing unto
the LORD.
24 [r]In the year of the jubile the field shall
return unto him of whom it was bought,
even to him to whom the possession of the
land *did belong*.
25 And all thy estimations shall be according to the shekel of the sanctuary:
[s]twenty gerahs shall be the shekel.

26:40 [t]Num. 5:7; 1 Kings 8:33; Neh. 9:2; Dan. 9:3; Prov. 28:13; Luke 15:18; 1 John 1:9
26:41 [u]Jer. 6:10; Ezek. 44:7; Acts 7:51; Rom. 2:29; Col. 2:11 [v]1 Kings 21:29; 2 Chron. 12:6
26:42 [w]Ex. 2:24; Ps. 106:45; Ezek. 16:60 [x]Ps. 136:23
26:43 [y]ver. 34 [z]ver. 15
26:44 [a]Deut. 4:31; 2 Kings 13:23; Rom. 11:2
26:45 [b]Rom. 11:28 [c]ch. 22:33 [d]Ps. 98:2; Ezek. 20:9
26:46 [e]ch. 27:34; Deut. 6:1; John 1:17 [f]ch. 25:1
27:2 [g]Num. 6:2; Judg. 11:30; 1 Sam. 1:11
27:3 [h]Ex. 30:13
27:13 [i]ver. 15
27:15 [j]ver. 13
27:18 [k]ch. 25:15
27:19 [l]ver. 13
27:21 [m]ch. 25:10 [n]ver. 28 [o]Num. 18:14; Ezek. 44:29
27:22 [p]ch. 25:10
27:23 [q]ver. 18
27:24 [r]ch. 25:28
27:25 [s]Ex. 30:13; Num. 3:47; Ezek. 45:12

26 ¶ Only the [t]firstling of the beasts, which should be the LORD's firstling, no man shall sanctify it; whether *it be* ox, or sheep: it *is* the LORD's.

27 And if *it be* of an unclean beast, then he shall redeem *it* according to thine estimation, [u]and shall add a fifth *part* of it thereto: or if it be not redeemed, then it shall be sold according to thy estimation.

28 [v]Notwithstanding no devoted thing, that a man shall devote unto the LORD of all that he hath, *both* of man and beast, and of the field of his possession, shall be sold or redeemed: every devoted thing *is* most holy unto the LORD.

29 [w]None devoted, which shall be devoted of men, shall be redeemed; *but* shall surely be put to death.

30 And [x]all the tithe of the land, *whether* of the seed of the land, *or* of the fruit of the tree, *is* the LORD's: *it is* holy unto the LORD.

31 [y]And if a man will at all redeem *ought* of his tithes, he shall add thereto the fifth *part* thereof.

32 And concerning the tithe of the herd, or of the flock, *even* of whatsoever [z]passeth under the rod, the tenth shall be holy unto the LORD.

33 He shall not search whether it be good or bad, [a]neither shall he change it: and if he change it at all, then both it and the change thereof shall be holy; it shall not be redeemed.

34 [b]These *are* the commandments, which the LORD commanded Moses for the children of Israel in mount Sinai.

27:26 [t]Ex. 13:2; Num. 18:17; Deut. 15:19
27:27 [u]ver. 11
27:28 [v]ver. 21; Josh. 6:17
27:29 [w]Num. 21:2
27:30 [x]Gen. 28:22; Num. 18:21; 2 Chron. 31:5; Neh. 13:12; Mal. 3:8
27:31 [y]ver. 13
27:32 [z]Jer. 33:13; Ezek. 20:37; Mic. 7:14
27:33 [a]ver. 10
27:34 [b]ch. 26:46

NUMBERS

The book of Numbers was written by Moses at approximately the same time as Leviticus—sometime between 1450 B.C. and 1410 B.C. Numbers takes its name from the census of the Israelites described in the first four chapters. The census, however, is not the focal point of the book. The Israelites have left Egypt and now face an uncertain future as they journey toward the Promised Land of Canaan. They face hardships in the deserts of Sinai, their faltering faith, and a host of enemies. Their only hope in obtaining the land of Canaan rests in their faith in God.

I. The Israelites in the Sinai, 1:1–4:49
II. More laws of God for the people, 5:1–10:10
III. Toward the plains of Israel, 10:11–33:49
IV. Entering the land of Canaan, 33:50–36:13

1 And the LORD spake unto Moses [a]in the wilderness of Sinai, [b]in the tabernacle of the congregation, on the first *day* of the second month, in the second year after they were come out of the land of Egypt, saying,

2 [c]Take ye the sum of all the congregation of the children of Israel, after their families, by the house of their fathers, with the number of *their* names, every male by their polls;

3 From twenty years old and upward, all that are able to go forth to war in Israel: thou and Aaron shall number them by their armies.

4 And with you there shall be a man of every tribe; every one head of the house of his fathers.

5 ¶ And these *are* the names of the men that shall stand with you: of *the tribe of* Reuben; Elizur the son of Shedeur.

6 Of Simeon; Shelumiel the son of Zurishaddai.

7 Of Judah; Nahshon the son of Amminadab.

8 Of Issachar; Nethaneel the son of Zuar.

9 Of Zebulun; Eliab the son of Helon.

10 Of the children of Joseph: of Ephraim; Elishama the son of Ammihud: of Manasseh; Gamaliel the son of Pedahzur.

11 Of Benjamin; Abidan the son of Gideoni.

12 Of Dan; Ahiezer the son of Ammishaddai.

13 Of Asher; Pagiel the son of Ocran.

14 Of Gad; Eliasaph the son of [d]Deuel.

15 Of Naphtali; Ahira the son of Enan.

16 [e]These *were* the renowned of the congregation, princes of the tribes of their fathers, [f]heads of thousands in Israel.

17 ¶ And Moses and Aaron took these men which are expressed by *their* names:

18 And they assembled all the congregation together on the first *day* of the second month, and they declared their pedigrees after their families, by the house of their fathers, according to the number of the names, from twenty years old and upward, by their polls.

19 As the LORD commanded Moses, so he numbered them in the wilderness of Sinai.

1:1 [a]Ex. 19:1; Num. 10:11 [b]Ex. 25:22
1:2 [c]Ex. 30:12; ch. 26:2; 2 Sam. 24:2; 1 Chron. 21:2
1:14 [d]ch. 2:14
1:16 [e]ch. 7:2; 1 Chron. 27:16 [f]Ex. 18:21

20 And the children of Reuben, Israel's eldest son, by their generations, after their families, by the house of their fathers, according to the number of the names, by their polls, every male from twenty years old and upward, all that were able to go forth to war;

21 Those that were numbered of them, *even* of the tribe of Reuben, *were* forty and six thousand and five hundred.

22 ¶ Of the children of Simeon, by their generations, after their families, by the house of their fathers, those that were numbered of them, according to the number of the names, by their polls, every male from twenty years old and upward, all that were able to go forth to war;

23 Those that were numbered of them, *even* of the tribe of Simeon, *were* fifty and nine thousand and three hundred.

24 ¶ Of the children of Gad, by their generations, after their families, by the house of their fathers, according to the number of the names, from twenty years old and upward, all that were able to go forth to war;

25 Those that were numbered of them, *even* of the tribe of Gad, *were* forty and five thousand six hundred and fifty.

26 ¶ Of the children of Judah, by their generations, after their families, by the house of their fathers, according to the number of the names, from twenty years old and upward, all that were able to go forth to war;

27 Those that were numbered of them, *even* of the tribe of Judah, *were* threescore and fourteen thousand and six hundred.

28 ¶ Of the children of Issachar, by their generations, after their families, by the house of their fathers, according to the number of the names, from twenty years old and upward, all that were able to go forth to war;

29 Those that were numbered of them, *even* of the tribe of Issachar, *were* fifty and four thousand and four hundred.

30 ¶ Of the children of Zebulun, by their generations, after their families, by the house of their fathers, according to the number of the names, from twenty years old and upward, all that were able to go forth to war;

31 Those that were numbered of them, *even* of the tribe of Zebulun, *were* fifty and seven thousand and four hundred.

32 ¶ Of the children of Joseph, *namely*, of the children of Ephraim, by their generations, after their families, by the house of their fathers, according to the number of the names, from twenty years old and upward, all that were able to go forth to war;

33 Those that were numbered of them, *even* of the tribe of Ephraim, *were* forty thousand and five hundred.

34 ¶ Of the children of Manasseh, by their generations, after their families, by the house of their fathers, according to the number of the names, from twenty years old and upward, all that were able to go forth to war;

35 Those that were numbered of them, *even* of the tribe of Manasseh, *were* thirty and two thousand and two hundred.

36 ¶ Of the children of Benjamin, by their generations, after their families, by the house of their fathers, according to the number of the names, from twenty years old and upward, all that were able to go forth to war;

37 Those that were numbered of them, *even* of the tribe of Benjamin, *were* thirty and five thousand and four hundred.

38 ¶ Of the children of Dan, by their generations, after their families, by the house of their fathers, according to the number of the names, from twenty years old and upward, all that were able to go forth to war;

39 Those that were numbered of them, *even* of the tribe of Dan, *were* threescore and two thousand and seven hundred.

40 ¶ Of the children of Asher, by their generations, after their families, by the house of their fathers, according to the number of the names, from twenty years old and upward, all that were able to go forth to war;

41 Those that were numbered of them, *even* of the tribe of Asher, *were* forty and one thousand and five hundred.

42 ¶ Of the children of Naphtali, throughout their generations, after their families, by the house of their fathers, according to the number of the names, from twenty years old and upward, all that were able to go forth to war;

43 Those that were numbered of them, *even* of the tribe of Naphtali, *were* fifty and three thousand and four hundred.

44 [g]These *are* those that were numbered, which Moses and Aaron numbered, and the princes of Israel, *being* twelve men: each one was for the house of his fathers.

45 So were all those that were numbered of the children of Israel, by the house of their fathers, from twenty years old and upward, all that were able to go forth to war in Israel;

46 Even all they that were numbered were [h]six hundred thousand and three thousand and five hundred and fifty.

47 ¶ But [i]the Levites after the tribe of their fathers were not numbered among them.

48 For the LORD had spoken unto Moses, saying,

49 [j]Only thou shalt not number the tribe of Levi, neither take the sum of them among the children of Israel:

50 [k]But thou shalt appoint the Levites over the tabernacle of testimony, and over all the vessels thereof, and over all things that *belong* to it: they shall bear the tabernacle, and all the vessels thereof; and they shall minister unto it, [l]and shall encamp round about the tabernacle.

51 [m]And when the tabernacle setteth for-

1:44 [g]ch. 26:64
1:46 [h]Ex. 12:37; ch. 2:32
1:47 [i]ch. 2:33; ch. 3; 1 Chron. 6
1:49 [j]ch. 2:33
1:50 [k]Ex. 38:21; ch. 3:7 [l]ch. 3:23
1:51 [m]ch. 10:17

ward, the Levites shall take it down: and when the tabernacle is to be pitched, the Levites shall set it up: [n]and the stranger that cometh nigh shall be put to death.

52 And the children of Israel shall pitch their tents, every man by his own camp, and [o]every man by his own standard, throughout their hosts.

53 [p]But the Levites shall pitch round about the tabernacle of testimony, that there be no [q]wrath upon the congregation of the children of Israel: [r]and the Levites shall keep the charge of the tabernacle of testimony.

54 And the children of Israel did according to all that the LORD commanded Moses, so did they.

2 And the LORD spake unto Moses and unto Aaron, saying,

2 [s]Every man of the children of Israel shall pitch by his own standard, with the ensign of their father's house: [t]far off about the tabernacle of the congregation shall they pitch.

3 And on the east side toward the rising of the sun shall they of the standard of the camp of Judah pitch throughout their armies: and [u]Nahshon the son of Amminadab *shall be* captain of the children of Judah.

4 And his host, and those that were numbered of them, *were* threescore and fourteen thousand and six hundred.

5 And those that do pitch next unto him *shall be* the tribe of Issachar: and Nethaneel the son of Zuar *shall be* captain of the children of Issachar.

6 And his host, and those that were numbered thereof, *were* fifty and four thousand and four hundred.

7 *Then* the tribe of Zebulun: and Eliab the son of Helon *shall be* captain of the children of Zebulun.

8 And his host, and those that were numbered thereof, *were* fifty and seven thousand and four hundred.

9 All that were numbered in the camp of Judah *were* an hundred thousand and fourscore thousand and six thousand and four hundred, throughout their armies. [v]These shall first set forth.

10 ¶ On the south side *shall be* the standard of the camp of Reuben according to their armies: and the captain of the children of Reuben *shall be* Elizur the son of Shedeur.

11 And his host, and those that were numbered thereof, *were* forty and six thousand and five hundred.

12 And those which pitch by him *shall be* the tribe of Simeon: and the captain of the children of Simeon *shall be* Shelumiel the son of Zurishaddai.

13 And his host, and those that were numbered of them, *were* fifty and nine thousand and three hundred.

14 Then the tribe of Gad: and the captain of the sons of Gad *shall be* Eliasaph the son of Reuel.

15 And his host, and those that were numbered of them, *were* forty and five thousand and six hundred and fifty.

16 All that were numbered in the camp of Reuben *were* an hundred thousand and fifty and one thousand and four hundred and fifty, throughout their armies. [w]And they shall set forth in the second rank.

17 ¶ [x]Then the tabernacle of the congregation shall set forward with the camp of the Levites in the midst of the camp: as they encamp, so shall they set forward, every man in his place by their standards.

18 ¶ On the west side *shall be* the standard of the camp of Ephraim according to their armies: and the captain of the sons of Ephraim *shall be* Elishama the son of Ammihud.

19 And his host, and those that were numbered of them, *were* forty thousand and five hundred.

20 And by him *shall be* the tribe of Manasseh: and the captain of the children of Manasseh *shall be* Gamaliel the son of Pedahzur.

21 And his host, and those that were numbered of them, *were* thirty and two thousand and two hundred.

22 Then the tribe of Benjamin: and the captain of the sons of Benjamin *shall be* Abidan the son of Gideoni.

23 And his host, and those that were numbered of them, *were* thirty and five thousand and four hundred.

24 All that were numbered of the camp of Ephraim *were* an hundred thousand and eight thousand and an hundred, throughout their armies. [y]And they shall go forward in the third rank.

25 ¶ The standard of the camp of Dan *shall be* on the north side by their armies: and the captain of the children of Dan *shall be* Ahiezer the son of Ammishaddai.

26 And his host, and those that were numbered of them, *were* threescore and two thousand and seven hundred.

27 And those that encamp by him *shall be* the tribe of Asher: and the captain of the children of Asher *shall be* Pagiel the son of Ocran.

28 And his host, and those that were numbered of them, *were* forty and one thousand and five hundred.

29 ¶ Then the tribe of Naphtali: and the captain of the children of Naphtali *shall be* Ahira the son of Enan.

30 And his host, and those that were numbered of them, *were* fifty and three thousand and four hundred.

31 All they that were numbered in the camp of Dan *were* an hundred thousand and fifty and seven thousand and six hundred. [z]They shall go hindmost with their standards.

32 ¶ These *are* those which were numbered of the children of Israel by the house of their fathers: [a]all those that were numbered of the camps throughout their hosts

1:51 [n]ch. 3:10
1:52 [o]ch. 2:2
1:53 [p]ver. 50 [q]Lev. 10:6; ch. 8:19; 1 Sam. 6:19 [r]ch. 3:7; 1 Chron. 23:32; 2 Chron. 13:10
2:2 [s]ch. 1:52 [t]Josh. 3:4
2:3 [u]ch. 10:14; Ruth 4:20; 1 Chron. 2:10; Matt. 1:4; Luke 3:32
2:9 [v]ch. 10:14
2:16 [w]ch. 10:18
2:17 [x]ch. 10:17
2:24 [y]ch. 10:22
2:31 [z]ch. 10:25
2:32 [a]Ex. 38:26; ch. 1:46

were six hundred thousand and three thousand and five hundred and fifty.

33 But [b]the Levites were not numbered among the children of Israel; as the LORD commanded Moses.

34 And the children of Israel did according to all that the LORD commanded Moses: [c]so they pitched by their standards, and so they set forward, every one after their families, according to the house of their fathers.

3

These also *are* the generations of Aaron and Moses in the day *that* the LORD spake with Moses in mount Sinai.

2 And these *are* the names of the sons of Aaron; Nadab the [d]firstborn, and Abihu, Eleazar, and Ithamar.

3 These *are* the names of the sons of Aaron, [e]the priests which were anointed, whom he consecrated to minister in the priest's office.

4 [f]And Nadab and Abihu died before the LORD, when they offered strange fire before the LORD, in the wilderness of Sinai, and they had no children: and Eleazar and Ithamar ministered in the priest's office in the sight of Aaron their father.

5 ¶ And the LORD spake unto Moses, saying,

6 [g]Bring the tribe of Levi near, and present them before Aaron the priest, that they may minister unto him.

7 And they shall keep his charge, and the charge of the whole congregation before the tabernacle of the congregation, to do [h]the service of the tabernacle.

8 And they shall keep all the instruments of the tabernacle of the congregation, and the charge of the children of Israel, to do the service of the tabernacle.

9 And [i]thou shalt give the Levites unto Aaron and to his sons: they *are* wholly given unto him out of the children of Israel.

10 And thou shalt appoint Aaron and his sons, [j]and they shall wait on their priest's office: [k]and the stranger that cometh nigh shall be put to death.

11 And the LORD spake unto Moses, saying,

12 And I, behold, [l]I have taken the Levites from among the children of Israel instead of all the firstborn that openeth the matrix among the children of Israel: therefore the Levites shall be mine;

13 Because [m]all the firstborn *are* mine; [n]*for* on the day that I smote all the firstborn in the land of Egypt I hallowed unto me all the firstborn in Israel, both man and beast: mine shall they be: I *am* the LORD.

14 ¶ And the LORD spake unto Moses in the wilderness of Sinai, saying,

15 Number the children of Levi after the house of their fathers, by their families: [o]every male from a month old and upward shalt thou number them.

16 And Moses numbered them according to the word of the LORD, as he was commanded.

17 [p]And these were the sons of Levi by their names; Gershon, and Kohath, and Merari.

18 And these *are* the names of the sons of Gershon by their families; [q]Libni, and Shimei.

19 And the sons of Kohath by their families; [r]Amram, and Izehar, Hebron, and Uzziel.

20 [s]And the sons of Merari by their families; Mahli, and Mushi. These *are* the families of the Levites according to the house of their fathers.

21 Of Gershon *was* the family of the Libnites, and the family of the Shimites: these *are* the families of the Gershonites.

22 Those that were numbered of them, according to the number of all the males, from a month old and upward, *even* those that were numbered of them *were* seven thousand and five hundred.

23 [t]The families of the Gershonites shall pitch behind the tabernacle westward.

24 And the chief of the house of the father of the Gershonites *shall be* Eliasaph the son of Lael.

25 And [u]the charge of the sons of Gershon in the tabernacle of the congregation *shall be* [v]the tabernacle, and [w]the tent, [x]the covering thereof, and [y]the hanging for the door of the tabernacle of the congregation,

26 And [z]the hangings of the court, and [a]the curtain for the door of the court, which *is* by the tabernacle, and by the altar round about, and [b]the cords of it for all the service thereof.

27 ¶ [c]And of Kohath *was* the family of the Amramites, and the family of the Izeharites, and the family of the Hebronites, and the family of the Uzzielites: these *are* the families of the Kohathites.

28 In the number of all the males, from a month old and upward, *were* eight thousand and six hundred, keeping the charge of the sanctuary.

29 [d]The families of the sons of Kohath shall pitch on the side of the tabernacle southward.

30 And the chief of the house of the father of the families of the Kohathites *shall be* Elizaphan the son of Uzziel.

31 And [e]their charge *shall be* [f]the ark, and [g]the table, and [h]the candlestick, and [i]the altars, and the vessels of the sanctuary wherewith they minister, and [j]the hanging, and all the service thereof.

32 And Eleazar the son of Aaron the priest *shall be* chief over the chief of the Levites, *and have* the oversight of them that keep the charge of the sanctuary.

33 ¶ Of Merari *was* the family of the Mahlites, and the family of the Mushites: these *are* the families of Merari.

34 And those that were numbered of them, according to the number of all the males, from a month old and upward, *were* six thousand and two hundred.

35 And the chief of the house of the father

2:33 [b]ch. 1:47
2:34 [c]ch. 24:2
3:2 [d]Ex. 6:23
3:3 [e]Ex. 28:41; Lev. 8
3:4 [f]Lev. 10:1; ch. 26:61; 1 Chron. 24:2
3:6 [g]ch. 8:6
3:7 [h]ch. 1:50
3:9 [i]ch. 8:19
3:10 [j]ch. 18:7 [k]ver. 38; ch. 1:51
3:12 [l]ver. 41; ch. 8:16
3:13 [m]Ex. 13:2; Lev. 27:26; ch. 8:16; Luke 2:23 [n]Ex. 13:12; ch. 8:17
3:15 [o]ver. 39; ch. 26:62
3:17 [p]Gen. 46:11; Ex. 6:16; ch. 26:57; 1 Chron. 6:1
3:18 [q]Ex. 6:17
3:19 [r]Ex. 6:18
3:20 [s]Ex. 6:19
3:23 [t]ch. 1:53
3:25 [u]ch. 4:24 [v]Ex. 25:9 [w]Ex. 26:1 [x]Ex. 26:7 [y]Ex. 26:36
3:26 [z]Ex. 27:9 [a]Ex. 27:16 [b]Ex. 35:18
3:27 [c]1 Chron. 26:23
3:29 [d]ch. 1:53
3:31 [e]ch. 4:15 [f]Ex. 25:10 [g]Ex. 25:23 [h]Ex. 25:31 [i]Ex. 27:1 [j]Ex. 26:32

of the families of Merari *was* Zuriel the son of Abihail: [k]*these* shall pitch on the side of the tabernacle northward.

36 And [l]*under* the custody and charge of the sons of Merari *shall be* the boards of the tabernacle, and the bars thereof, and the pillars thereof, and the sockets thereof, and all the vessels thereof, and all that serveth thereto,

37 And the pillars of the court round about, and their sockets, and their pins, and their cords.

38 ¶ [m]But those that encamp before the tabernacle toward the east, *even* before the tabernacle of the congregation eastward, *shall be* Moses, and Aaron and his sons, [n]keeping the charge of the sanctuary [o]for the charge of the children of Israel; and [p]the stranger that cometh nigh shall be put to death.

39 [q]All that were numbered of the Levites, which Moses and Aaron numbered at the commandment of the LORD, throughout their families, all the males from a month old and upward, *were* twenty and two thousand.

40 ¶ And the LORD said unto Moses, [r]Number all the firstborn of the males of the children of Israel from a month old and upward, and take the number of their names.

41 [s]And thou shalt take the Levites for me (I *am* the LORD) instead of all the firstborn among the children of Israel; and the cattle of the Levites instead of all the firstlings among the cattle of the children of Israel.

42 And Moses numbered, as the LORD commanded him, all the firstborn among the children of Israel.

43 And all the firstborn males by the number of names, from a month old and upward, of those that were numbered of them, were twenty and two thousand two hundred and threescore and thirteen.

44 ¶ And the LORD spake unto Moses, saying,

45 [t]Take the Levites instead of all the firstborn among the children of Israel, and the cattle of the Levites instead of their cattle; and the Levites shall be mine: I *am* the LORD.

46 And for those that are to be [u]redeemed of the two hundred and threescore and thirteen of the firstborn of the children of Israel, [v]which are more than the Levites;

47 Thou shalt even take [w]five shekels apiece by the poll, after the shekel of the sanctuary shalt thou take *them:* ([x]the shekel *is* twenty gerahs:)

48 And thou shalt give the money, wherewith the odd number of them is to be redeemed, unto Aaron and to his sons.

49 And Moses took the redemption money of them that were over and above them that were redeemed by the Levites:

50 Of the firstborn of the children of Israel took he the money; [y]a thousand three hundred and threescore and five *shekels,* after the shekel of the sanctuary:

51 And Moses [z]gave the money of them that were redeemed unto Aaron and to his sons, according to the word of the LORD, as the LORD commanded Moses.

4

And the LORD spake unto Moses and unto Aaron, saying,

2 Take the sum of the sons of Kohath from among the sons of Levi, after their families, by the house of their fathers,

3 [a]From thirty years old and upward even until fifty years old, all that enter into the host, to do the work in the tabernacle of the congregation.

4 [b]This *shall be* the service of the sons of Kohath in the tabernacle of the congregation, *about* [c]the most holy things:

5 ¶ And when the camp setteth forward, Aaron shall come, and his sons, and they shall take down [d]the covering vail, and cover [e]the ark of testimony with it:

6 And shall put thereon the covering of badgers' skins, and shall spread over *it* a cloth wholly of blue, and shall put in [f]the staves thereof.

7 And upon the [g]table of shewbread they shall spread a cloth of blue, and put thereon the dishes, and the spoons, and the bowls, and covers to cover withal: and the continual bread shall be thereon:

8 And they shall spread upon them a cloth of scarlet, and cover the same with a covering of badgers' skins, and shall put in the staves thereof.

9 And they shall take a cloth of blue, and cover the [h]candlestick of the light, [i]and his lamps, and his tongs, and his snuffdishes, and all the oil vessels thereof, wherewith they minister unto it:

10 And they shall put it and all the vessels thereof within a covering of badgers' skins, and shall put *it* upon a bar.

11 And upon [j]the golden altar they shall spread a cloth of blue, and cover it with a covering of badgers' skins, and shall put to the staves thereof:

12 And they shall take all the instruments of ministry, wherewith they minister in the sanctuary, and put *them* in a cloth of blue, and cover them with a covering of badgers' skins, and shall put *them* on a bar:

13 And they shall take away the ashes from the altar, and spread a purple cloth thereon:

14 And they shall put upon it all the vessels thereof, wherewith they minister about it, *even* the censers, the fleshhooks, and the shovels, and the basons, all the vessels of the altar; and they shall spread upon it a covering of badgers' skins, and put to the staves of it.

15 And when Aaron and his sons have made an end of covering the sanctuary, and all the vessels of the sanctuary, as the camp is to set forward; after that, [k]the sons of Kohath shall come to bear *it:* [l]but they shall not touch *any* holy thing, lest they die.

3:35 [k]ch. 1:53
3:36 [l]ch. 4:31
3:38 [m]ch. 1:53 [n]ch. 18:5 [o]ver. 7 [p]ver. 10
3:39 [q]ch. 26:62
3:40 [r]ver. 15
3:41 [s]ver. 12
3:45 [t]ver. 12
3:46 [u]Ex. 13:13; ch. 18:15 [v]ver. 39
3:47 [w]Lev. 27:6; ch. 18:16 [x]Ex. 30:13; Lev. 27:25; ch. 18:16; Ezek. 45:12
3:50 [y]ver. 46
3:51 [z]ver. 48
4:3 [a]ch. 8:24; 1 Chron. 23:3
4:4 [b]ver. 15 [c]ver. 19
4:5 [d]Ex. 26:31 [e]Ex. 25:10
4:6 [f]Ex. 25:13
4:7 [g]Ex. 25:23; Lev. 24:6
4:9 [h]Ex. 25:31 [i]Ex. 25:37
4:11 [j]Ex. 30:1
4:15 [k]ch. 7:9; Deut. 31:9; 2 Sam. 6:13; 1 Chron. 15:2 [l]2 Sam. 6:6; 1 Chron. 13:9

[m]These *things are* the burden of the sons of Kohath in the tabernacle of the congregation.

16 ¶ And to the office of Eleazar the son of Aaron the priest *pertaineth* [n]the oil for the light, and the [o]sweet incense, and [p]the daily meat offering, and the [q]anointing oil, *and* the oversight of all the tabernacle, and of all that therein *is*, in the sanctuary, and in the vessels thereof.

17 ¶ And the LORD spake unto Moses and unto Aaron, saying,

18 Cut ye not off the tribe of the families of the Kohathites from among the Levites:

19 But thus do unto them, that they may live, and not die, when they approach unto [r]the most holy things. Aaron and his sons shall go in, and appoint them every one to his service and to his burden:

20 [s]But they shall not go in to see when the holy things are covered, lest they die.

21 ¶ And the LORD spake unto Moses, saying,

22 Take also the sum of the sons of Gershon, throughout the houses of their fathers, by their families;

23 [t]From thirty years old and upward until fifty years old shalt thou number them; all that enter in to perform the service, to do the work in the tabernacle of the congregation.

24 This *is* the service of the families of the Gershonites, to serve, and for burdens:

25 And [u]they shall bear the curtains of the tabernacle, and the tabernacle of the congregation, his covering, and the covering of the badgers' skins that *is* above upon it, and the hanging for the door of the tabernacle of the congregation,

26 And the hangings of the court, and the hanging for the door of the gate of the court, which *is* by the tabernacle and by the altar round about, and their cords, and all the instruments of their service, and all that is made for them: so shall they serve.

27 At the appointment of Aaron and his sons shall be all the service of the sons of the Gershonites, in all their burdens, and in all their service: and ye shall appoint unto them in charge all their burdens.

28 This *is* the service of the families of the sons of Gershon in the tabernacle of the congregation: and their charge *shall be* under the hand of Ithamar the son of Aaron the priest.

29 ¶ As for the sons of Merari, thou shalt number them after their families, by the house of their fathers;

30 [v]From thirty years old and upward even unto fifty years old shalt thou number them, every one that entereth into the service, to do the work of the tabernacle of the congregation.

31 And [w]this *is* the charge of their burden, according to all their service in the tabernacle of the congregation; [x]the boards of the tabernacle, and the bars thereof, and the pillars thereof, and sockets thereof,

32 And the pillars of the court round about, and their sockets, and their pins, and their cords, with all their instruments, and with all their service: and by name ye shall [y]reckon the instruments of the charge of their burden.

33 This *is* the service of the families of the sons of Merari, according to all their service, in the tabernacle of the congregation, under the hand of Ithamar the son of Aaron the priest.

34 ¶ [z]And Moses and Aaron and the chief of the congregation numbered the sons of the Kohathites after their families, and after the house of their fathers,

35 From thirty years old and upward even unto fifty years old, every one that entereth into the service, for the work in the tabernacle of the congregation:

36 And those that were numbered of them by their families were two thousand seven hundred and fifty.

37 These *were* they that were numbered of the families of the Kohathites, all that might do service in the tabernacle of the congregation, which Moses and Aaron did number according to the commandment of the LORD by the hand of Moses.

38 And those that were numbered of the sons of Gershon, throughout their families, and by the house of their fathers,

39 From thirty years old and upward even unto fifty years old, every one that entereth into the service, for the work in the tabernacle of the congregation,

40 Even those that were numbered of them, throughout their families, by the house of their fathers, were two thousand and six hundred and thirty.

41 [a]These *are* they that were numbered of the families of the sons of Gershon, of all that might do service in the tabernacle of the congregation, whom Moses and Aaron did number according to the commandment of the LORD.

42 ¶ And those that were numbered of the families of the sons of Merari, throughout their families, by the house of their fathers,

43 From thirty years old and upward even unto fifty years old, every one that entereth into the service, for the work in the tabernacle of the congregation,

44 Even those that were numbered of them after their families, were three thousand and two hundred.

45 These *be* those that were numbered of the families of the sons of Merari, whom Moses and Aaron numbered [b]according to the word of the LORD by the hand of Moses.

46 All those that were numbered of the Levites, whom Moses and Aaron and the chief of Israel numbered, after their families, and after the house of their fathers,

47 [c]From thirty years old and upward even unto fifty years old, every one that came to do the service of the ministry, and the service of the burden in the tabernacle of the congregation,

4:15 [m]ch. 3:31
4:16 [n]Ex. 25:6; Lev. 24:2 [o]Ex. 30:34 [p]Ex. 29:40 [q]Ex. 30:23
4:19 [r]ver. 4
4:20 [s]Ex. 19:21; 1 Sam. 6:19
4:23 [t]ver. 3
4:25 [u]ch. 3:25
4:30 [v]ver. 3
4:31 [w]ch. 3:36 [x]Ex. 26:15
4:32 [y]Ex. 38:21
4:34 [z]ver. 2
4:41 [a]ver. 22
4:45 [b]ver. 29
4:47 [c]ver. 3

48 Even those that were numbered of them, were eight thousand and five hundred and fourscore.

49 According to the commandment of the LORD they were numbered by the hand of Moses, [d]every one according to his service, and according to his burden: thus were they numbered of him, [e]as the LORD commanded Moses.

5 And the LORD spake unto Moses, saying,

2 Command the children of Israel, that they put out of the camp every [f]leper, and every one that hath an [g]issue, and whosoever is defiled by the [h]dead:

3 Both male and female shall ye put out, without the camp shall ye put them; that they defile not their camps, [i]in the midst whereof I dwell.

4 And the children of Israel did so, and put them out without the camp: as the LORD spake unto Moses, so did the children of Israel.

5 ¶ And the LORD spake unto Moses, saying,

6 Speak unto the children of Israel, [j]When a man or woman shall commit any sin that men commit, to do a trespass against the LORD, and that person be guilty;

7 [k]Then they shall confess their sin which they have done: and he shall recompense his trespass [l]with the principal thereof, and add unto it the fifth *part* thereof, and give *it* unto *him* against whom he hath trespassed.

8 But if the man have no kinsman to recompense the trespass unto, let the trespass be recompensed unto the LORD, *even* to the priest; beside [m]the ram of the atonement, whereby an atonement shall be made for him.

9 And every [n]offering of all the holy things of the children of Israel, which they bring unto the priest, shall be his.

10 And every man's hallowed things shall be his: whatsoever any man giveth the priest, it shall be [o]his.

11 ¶ And the LORD spake unto Moses, saying,

12 Speak unto the children of Israel, and say unto them, If any man's wife go aside, and commit a trespass against him,

13 And a man [p]lie with her carnally, and it be hid from the eyes of her husband, and be kept close, and she be defiled, and *there be* no witness against her, neither she be taken *with the manner;*

14 And the spirit of jealousy come upon him, and he be jealous of his wife, and she be defiled: or if the spirit of jealousy come upon him, and he be jealous of his wife, and she be not defiled:

15 Then shall the man bring his wife unto the priest, and he shall bring her offering for her, the tenth *part* of an ephah of barley meal; he shall pour no oil upon it, nor put frankincense thereon; for it *is* an offering of jealousy, an offering of memorial, [q]bringing iniquity to remembrance.

16 And the priest shall bring her near, and set her before the LORD:

17 And the priest shall take holy water in an earthen vessel; and of the dust that is in the floor of the tabernacle the priest shall take, and put *it* into the water:

18 And the priest shall set the woman before the LORD, and uncover the woman's head, and put the offering of memorial in her hands, which *is* the jealousy offering: and the priest shall have in his hand the bitter water that causeth the curse:

19 And the priest shall charge her by an oath, and say unto the woman, If no man have lain with thee, and if thou hast not gone aside to uncleanness *with another* instead of thy husband, be thou free from this bitter water that causeth the curse:

20 But if thou hast gone aside *to another* instead of thy husband, and if thou be defiled, and some man have lain with thee beside thine husband:

21 Then the priest shall [r]charge the woman with an oath of cursing, and the priest shall say unto the woman, [s]The LORD make thee a curse and an oath among thy people, when the LORD doth make thy thigh to rot, and thy belly to swell;

22 And this water that causeth the curse [t]shall go into thy bowels, to make *thy* belly to swell, and *thy* thigh to rot: [u]And the woman shall say, Amen, amen.

23 And the priest shall write these curses in a book, and he shall blot *them* out with the bitter water:

24 And he shall cause the woman to drink the bitter water that causeth the curse: and the water that causeth the curse shall enter into her, *and become* bitter.

25 Then the priest shall take the jealousy offering out of the woman's hand, and shall [v]wave the offering before the LORD, and offer it upon the altar:

26 [w]And the priest shall take an handful of the offering, *even* the memorial thereof, and burn *it* upon the altar, and afterward shall cause the woman to drink the water.

27 And when he hath made her to drink the water, then it shall come to pass, *that,* if she be defiled, and have done trespass against her husband, that the water that causeth the curse shall enter into her, *and become* bitter, and her belly shall swell, and her thigh shall rot: and the woman [x]shall be a curse among her people.

28 And if the woman be not defiled, but be clean; then she shall be free, and shall conceive seed.

29 This *is* the law of jealousies, when a wife goeth aside *to another* [y]instead of her husband, and is defiled;

30 Or when the spirit of jealousy cometh upon him, and he be jealous over his wife, and shall set the woman before the LORD, and the priest shall execute upon her all this law.

4:49 [d]ver. 15 [e]ver. 1
5:2 [f]Lev. 13:3 [g]Lev. 15:2 [h]Lev. 21:1; ch. 9:6
5:3 [i]Lev. 26:11; 2 Cor. 6:16
5:6 [j]Lev. 6:2
5:7 [k]Lev. 5:5; Josh. 7:19 [l]Lev. 6:5
5:8 [m]Lev. 6:6
5:9 [n]Ex. 29:28; Lev. 6:17; ch. 18:8; Deut. 18:3; Ezek. 44:29
5:10 [o]Lev. 10:13
5:13 [p]Lev. 18:20
5:15 [q]1 Kings 17:18; Ezek. 29:16
5:21 [r]Josh. 6:26; 1 Sam. 14:24; Neh. 10:29 [s]Jer. 29:22
5:22 [t]Ps. 109:18 [u]Deut. 27:15
5:25 [v]Lev. 8:27
5:26 [w]Lev. 2:2
5:27 [x]Deut. 28:37; Ps. 83:9; Jer. 24:9; Zech. 8:13
5:29 [y]ver. 19

31 Then shall the man be guiltless from iniquity, and this woman [z]shall bear her iniquity.

6

And the LORD spake unto Moses, saying,

2 Speak unto the children of Israel, and say unto them, When either man or woman shall [a]separate *themselves* to vow a vow of a Nazarite, to separate *themselves* unto the LORD:

3 [b]He shall separate *himself* from wine and strong drink, and shall drink no vinegar of wine, or vinegar of strong drink, neither shall he drink any liquor of grapes, nor eat moist grapes, or dried.

4 All the days of his separation shall he eat nothing that is made of the vine tree, from the kernels even to the husk.

5 All the days of the vow of his separation there shall no [c]razor come upon his head: until the days be fulfilled, in the which he separateth *himself* unto the LORD, he shall be holy, *and* shall let the locks of the hair of his head grow.

6 All the days that he separateth *himself* unto the LORD [d]he shall come at no dead body.

7 [e]He shall not make himself unclean for his father, or for his mother, for his brother, or for his sister, when they die: because the consecration of his God *is* upon his head.

8 All the days of his separation he *is* holy unto the LORD.

9 And if any man die very suddenly by him, and he hath defiled the head of his consecration; then he shall [f]shave his head in the day of his cleansing, on the seventh day shall he shave it.

10 And [g]on the eighth day he shall bring two turtles, or two young pigeons, to the priest, to the door of the tabernacle of the congregation:

11 And the priest shall offer the one for a sin offering, and the other for a burnt offering, and make an atonement for him, for that he sinned by the dead, and shall hallow his head that same day.

12 And he shall consecrate unto the LORD the days of his separation, and shall bring a lamb of the first year [h]for a trespass offering: but the days that were before shall be lost, because his separation was defiled.

13 ¶ And this *is* the law of the Nazarite, [i]when the days of his separation are fulfilled: he shall be brought unto the door of the tabernacle of the congregation:

14 And he shall offer his offering unto the LORD, one he lamb of the first year without blemish for a burnt offering, and one ewe lamb of the first year without blemish [j]for a sin offering, and one ram without blemish [k]for peace offerings,

15 And a basket of unleavened bread, [l]cakes of fine flour mingled with oil, and wafers of unleavened bread [m]anointed with oil, and their meat offering, and their [n]drink offerings.

16 And the priest shall bring *them* before the LORD, and shall offer his sin offering, and his burnt offering:

17 And he shall offer the ram *for* a sacrifice of peace offerings unto the LORD, with the basket of unleavened bread: the priest shall offer also his meat offering, and his drink offering.

18 [o]And the Nazarite shall shave the head of his separation *at* the door of the tabernacle of the congregation, and shall take the hair of the head of his separation, and put *it* in the fire which *is* under the sacrifice of the peace offerings.

19 And the priest shall take the [p]sodden shoulder of the ram, and one unleavened cake out of the basket, and one unleavened wafer, and [q]shall put *them* upon the hands of the Nazarite, after *the hair of* his separation is shaven:

20 And the priest shall wave them *for* a wave offering before the LORD: [r]this *is* holy for the priest, with the wave breast and heave shoulder: and after that the Nazarite may drink wine.

21 This *is* the law of the Nazarite who hath vowed, *and of* his offering unto the LORD for his separation, beside *that* that his hand shall get: according to the vow which he vowed, so he must do after the law of his separation.

22 ¶ And the LORD spake unto Moses, saying,

23 Speak unto Aaron and unto his sons, saying, On this wise [s]ye shall bless the children of Israel, saying unto them,

24 The LORD bless thee, and [t]keep thee:

25 The LORD [u]make his face shine upon thee, and [v]be gracious unto thee:

26 [w]The LORD lift up his countenance upon thee, and [x]give thee peace.

27 [y]And they shall put my name upon the children of Israel; and [z]I will bless them.

7

And it came to pass on the day that Moses had fully [a]set up the tabernacle, and had anointed it, and sanctified it, and all the instruments thereof, both the altar and all the vessels thereof, and had anointed them, and sanctified them;

2 That [b]the princes of Israel, heads of the house of their fathers, who *were* the princes of the tribes, and were over them that were numbered, offered:

3 And they brought their offering before the LORD, six covered wagons, and twelve oxen; a wagon for two of the princes, and for each one an ox: and they brought them before the tabernacle.

4 And the LORD spake unto Moses, saying,

5 Take *it* of them, that they may be to do the service of the tabernacle of the congregation; and thou shalt give them unto the Levites, to every man according to his service.

6 And Moses took the wagons and the oxen, and gave them unto the Levites.

7 Two wagons and four oxen [c]he gave

5:31 [z]Lev. 20:17
6:2 [a]Lev. 27:2; Judg. 13:5; Acts 21:23; Rom. 1:1
6:3 [b]Am. 2:12; Luke 1:15
6:5 [c]Judg. 13:5; 1 Sam. 1:11
6:6 [d]Lev. 21:11; ch. 19:11
6:7 [e]Lev. 21:1; ch. 9:6
6:9 [f]Acts 18:18
6:10 [g]Lev. 5:7
6:12 [h]Lev. 5:6
6:13 [i]Acts 21:26
6:14 [j]Lev. 4:2 [k]Lev. 3:6
6:15 [l]Lev. 2:4 [m]Ex. 29:2 [n]ch. 15:5
6:18 [o]Acts 21:24
6:19 [p]1 Sam. 2:15 [q]Ex. 29:23
6:20 [r]Ex. 29:27
6:23 [s]Lev. 9:22; 1 Chron. 23:13
6:24 [t]Ps. 121:7; John 17:11
6:25 [u]Ps. 31:16; Dan. 9:17 [v]Gen. 43:29
6:26 [w]Ps. 4:6 [x]John 14:27; 2 Thess. 3:16
6:27 [y]Deut. 28:10; 2 Chron. 7:14; Isa. 43:7; Dan. 9:18 [z]Ps. 115:12
7:1 [a]Ex. 40:18; Lev. 8:10
7:2 [b]ch. 1:4
7:7 [c]ch. 4:25

unto the sons of Gershon, according to their service:

8 [d]And four wagons and eight oxen he gave unto the sons of Merari, according unto their service, [e]under the hand of Ithamar the son of Aaron the priest.

9 But unto the sons of Kohath he gave none: because [f]the service of the sanctuary belonging unto them [g]*was that* they should bear upon their shoulders.

10 ¶ And the princes offered for [h]dedicating of the altar in the day that it was anointed, even the princes offered their offering before the altar.

11 And the LORD said unto Moses, They shall offer their offering, each prince on his day, for the dedicating of the altar.

12 ¶ And he that offered his offering the first day was [i]Nahshon the son of Amminadab, of the tribe of Judah:

13 And his offering *was* one silver charger, the weight thereof *was* an hundred and thirty *shekels*, one silver bowl of seventy shekels, after [j]the shekel of the sanctuary; both of them *were* full of fine flour mingled with oil for a [k]meat offering:

14 One spoon of ten *shekels* of gold, full of [l]incense:

15 [m]One young bullock, one ram, one lamb of the first year, for a burnt offering:

16 One kid of the goats for a [n]sin offering:

17 And for [o]a sacrifice of peace offerings, two oxen, five rams, five he goats, five lambs of the first year: this *was* the offering of Nahshon the son of Amminadab.

18 ¶ On the second day Nethaneel the son of Zuar, prince of Issachar, did offer:

19 He offered *for* his offering one silver charger, the weight whereof *was* an hundred and thirty *shekels*, one silver bowl of seventy shekels, after the shekel of the sanctuary; both of them full of fine flour mingled with oil for a meat offering:

20 One spoon of gold of ten *shekels*, full of incense:

21 One young bullock, one ram, one lamb of the first year, for a burnt offering:

22 One kid of the goats for a sin offering:

23 And for a sacrifice of peace offerings, two oxen, five rams, five he goats, five lambs of the first year: this *was* the offering of Nethaneel the son of Zuar.

24 ¶ On the third day Eliab the son of Helon, prince of the children of Zebulun, *did offer:*

25 His offering *was* one silver charger, the weight whereof *was* an hundred and thirty *shekels*, one silver bowl of seventy shekels, after the shekel of the sanctuary; both of them full of fine flour mingled with oil for a meat offering:

26 One golden spoon of ten *shekels*, full of incense:

27 One young bullock, one ram, one lamb of the first year, for a burnt offering:

28 One kid of the goats for a sin offering:

29 And for a sacrifice of peace offerings, two oxen, five rams, five he goats, five lambs of the first year: this *was* the offering of Eliab the son of Helon.

30 ¶ On the fourth day Elizur the son of Shedeur, prince of the children of Reuben, *did offer:*

31 His offering *was* one silver charger of the weight of an hundred and thirty *shekels*, one silver bowl of seventy shekels, after the shekel of the sanctuary; both of them full of fine flour mingled with oil for a meat offering:

32 One golden spoon of ten *shekels*, full of incense:

33 One young bullock, one ram, one lamb of the first year, for a burnt offering:

34 One kid of the goats for a sin offering:

35 And for a sacrifice of peace offerings, two oxen, five rams, five he goats, five lambs of the first year: this *was* the offering of Elizur the son of Shedeur.

36 ¶ On the fifth day Shelumiel the son of Zurishaddai, prince of the children of Simeon, *did offer:*

37 His offering *was* one silver charger, the weight whereof *was* an hundred and thirty *shekels*, one silver bowl of seventy shekels, after the shekel of the sanctuary; both of them full of fine flour mingled with oil for a meat offering:

38 One golden spoon of ten *shekels*, full of incense:

39 One young bullock, one ram, one lamb of the first year, for a burnt offering:

40 One kid of the goats for a sin offering:

41 And for a sacrifice of peace offerings, two oxen, five rams, five he goats, five lambs of the first year: this *was* the offering of Shelumiel the son of Zurishaddai.

42 ¶ On the sixth day Eliasaph the son of Deuel, prince of the children of Gad, *offered:*

43 His offering *was* one silver charger of the weight of an hundred and thirty *shekels*, a silver bowl of seventy shekels, after the shekel of the sanctuary; both of them full of fine flour mingled with oil for a meat offering:

44 One golden spoon of ten *shekels*, full of incense:

45 One young bullock, one ram, one lamb of the first year, for a burnt offering:

46 One kid of the goats for a sin offering:

47 And for a sacrifice of peace offerings, two oxen, five rams, five he goats, five lambs of the first year: this *was* the offering of Eliasaph the son of Deuel.

48 ¶ On the seventh day Elishama the son of Ammihud, prince of the children of Ephraim, *offered:*

49 His offering *was* one silver charger, the weight whereof *was* an hundred and thirty *shekels*, one silver bowl of seventy shekels, after the shekel of the sanctuary; both of them full of fine flour mingled with oil for a meat offering:

50 One golden spoon of ten *shekels*, full of incense:

7:8 [d]ch. 4:31 [e]ch. 4:28
7:9 [f]ch. 4:15 [g]ch. 4:6; 2 Sam. 6:13
7:10 [h]Deut. 20:5; 1 Kings 8:63; 2 Chron. 7:5; Ezra 6:16; Neh. 12:27; Ps. 30, title
7:12 [i]ch. 2:3
7:13 [j]Ex. 30:13 [k]Lev. 2:1
7:14 [l]Ex. 30:34
7:15 [m]Lev. 1:2
7:16 [n]Lev. 4:23
7:17 [o]Lev. 3:1

51 One young bullock, one ram, one lamb of the first year, for a burnt offering:
52 One kid of the goats for a sin offering:
53 And for a sacrifice of peace offerings, two oxen, five rams, five he goats, five lambs of the first year: this *was* the offering of Elishama the son of Ammihud.
54 ¶ On the eighth day *offered* Gamaliel the son of Pedahzur, prince of the children of Manasseh:
55 His offering *was* one silver charger of the weight of an hundred and thirty *shekels,* one silver bowl of seventy shekels, after the shekel of the sanctuary; both of them full of fine flour mingled with oil for a meat offering:
56 One golden spoon of ten *shekels,* full of incense:
57 One young bullock, one ram, one lamb of the first year, for a burnt offering:
58 One kid of the goats for a sin offering:
59 And for a sacrifice of peace offerings, two oxen, five rams, five he goats, five lambs of the first year: this *was* the offering of Gamaliel the son of Pedahzur.
60 ¶ On the ninth day Abidan the son of Gideoni, prince of the children of Benjamin, *offered:*
61 His offering *was* one silver charger, the weight whereof *was* an hundred and thirty *shekels,* one silver bowl of seventy shekels, after the shekel of the sanctuary; both of them full of fine flour mingled with oil for a meat offering:
62 One golden spoon of ten *shekels,* full of incense:
63 One young bullock, one ram, one lamb of the first year, for a burnt offering:
64 One kid of the goats for a sin offering:
65 And for a sacrifice of peace offerings, two oxen, five rams, five he goats, five lambs of the first year: this *was* the offering of Abidan the son of Gideoni.
66 ¶ On the tenth day Ahiezer the son of Ammishaddai, prince of the children of Dan, *offered:*
67 His offering *was* one silver charger, the weight whereof *was* an hundred and thirty *shekels,* one silver bowl of seventy shekels, after the shekel of the sanctuary; both of them full of fine flour mingled with oil for a meat offering:
68 One golden spoon of ten *shekels,* full of incense:
69 One young bullock, one ram, one lamb of the first year, for a burnt offering:
70 One kid of the goats for a sin offering:
71 And for a sacrifice of peace offerings, two oxen, five rams, five he goats, five lambs of the first year: this *was* the offering of Ahiezer the son of Ammishaddai.
72 ¶ On the eleventh day Pagiel the son of Ocran, prince of the children of Asher, *offered:*
73 His offering *was* one silver charger, the weight whereof *was* an hundred and thirty *shekels,* one silver bowl of seventy shekels, after the shekel of the sanctuary; both of them full of fine flour mingled with oil for a meat offering:
74 One golden spoon of ten *shekels,* full of incense:
75 One young bullock, one ram, one lamb of the first year, for a burnt offering:
76 One kid of the goats for a sin offering:
77 And for a sacrifice of peace offerings, two oxen, five rams, five he goats, five lambs of the first year: this *was* the offering of Pagiel the son of Ocran.
78 ¶ On the twelfth day Ahira the son of Enan, prince of the children of Naphtali, *offered:*
79 His offering *was* one silver charger, the weight whereof *was* an hundred and thirty *shekels,* one silver bowl of seventy shekels, after the shekel of the sanctuary; both of them full of fine flour mingled with oil for a meat offering:
80 One golden spoon of ten *shekels,* full of incense:
81 One young bullock, one ram, one lamb of the first year, for a burnt offering:
82 One kid of the goats for a sin offering:
83 And for a sacrifice of peace offerings, two oxen, five rams, five he goats, five lambs of the first year: this *was* the offering of Ahira the son of Enan.
84 This *was* the dedication of the altar, in the day when it was anointed, by the princes of Israel: twelve chargers of silver, twelve silver bowls, twelve spoons of gold:
85 Each charger of silver *weighing* an hundred and thirty *shekels,* each bowl seventy: all the silver vessels *weighed* two thousand and four hundred *shekels,* after the shekel of the sanctuary:
86 The golden spoons *were* twelve, full of incense, *weighing* ten *shekels* apiece, after the shekel of the sanctuary: all the gold of the spoons *was* an hundred and twenty *shekels.*
87 All the oxen for the burnt offering *were* twelve bullocks, the rams twelve, the lambs of the first year twelve, with their meat offering: and the kids of the goats for sin offering twelve.
88 And all the oxen for the sacrifice of the peace offerings *were* twenty and four bullocks, the rams sixty, the he goats sixty, the lambs of the first year sixty. This *was* the dedication of the altar, after that it was [p]anointed.
89 And when Moses was gone into the tabernacle of the congregation [q]to speak with him, then he heard [r]the voice of one speaking unto him from off the mercy seat that *was* upon the ark of testimony, from between the two cherubims: and he spake unto him.

8 And the LORD spake unto Moses, saying,
2 Speak unto Aaron, and say unto him, When thou [s]lightest the lamps, the seven lamps shall give light over against the candlestick.
3 And Aaron did so; he lighted the lamps

7:88 [p]ver. 1
7:89 [q]ch. 12:8; Ex. 33:9 [r]Ex. 25:22
8:2 [s]Ex. 25:37

thereof over against the candlestick, as the LORD commanded Moses.

4 [t]And this work of the candlestick *was of* beaten gold, unto the shaft thereof, unto the flowers thereof, *was* [u]beaten work: [v]according unto the pattern which the LORD had shewed Moses, so he made the candlestick.

5 ¶ And the LORD spake unto Moses, saying,

6 Take the Levites from among the children of Israel, and cleanse them.

7 And thus shalt thou do unto them, to cleanse them: Sprinkle [w]water of purifying upon them, and [x]let them shave all their flesh, and let them wash their clothes, and *so* make themselves clean.

8 Then let them take a young bullock with [y]his meat offering, *even* fine flour mingled with oil, and another young bullock shalt thou take for a sin offering.

9 [z]And thou shalt bring the Levites before the tabernacle of the congregation: [a]and thou shalt gather the whole assembly of the children of Israel together:

10 And thou shalt bring the Levites before the LORD: and the children of Israel [b]shall put their hands upon the Levites:

11 And Aaron shall offer the Levites before the LORD *for* an offering of the children of Israel, that they may execute the service of the LORD.

12 [c]And the Levites shall lay their hands upon the heads of the bullocks: and thou shalt offer the one *for* a sin offering, and the other *for* a burnt offering, unto the LORD, to make an atonement for the Levites.

13 And thou shalt set the Levites before Aaron, and before his sons, and offer them *for* an offering unto the LORD.

14 Thus shalt thou separate the Levites from among the children of Israel: and the Levites shall be [d]mine.

15 And after that shall the Levites go in to do the service of the tabernacle of the congregation: and thou shalt cleanse them, and [e]offer them *for* an offering.

16 For they *are* wholly given unto me from among the children of Israel; [f]instead of such as open every womb, *even instead of* the firstborn of all the children of Israel, have I taken them unto me.

17 [g]For all the firstborn of the children of Israel *are* mine, *both* man and beast: on the day that I smote every firstborn in the land of Egypt I sanctified them for myself.

18 And I have taken the Levites for all the firstborn of the children of Israel.

19 And [h]I have given the Levites *as* a gift to Aaron and to his sons from among the children of Israel, to do the service of the children of Israel in the tabernacle of the congregation, and to make an atonement for the children of Israel: [i]that there be no plague among the children of Israel, when the children of Israel come nigh unto the sanctuary.

20 And Moses, and Aaron, and all the congregation of the children of Israel, did to the Levites according unto all that the LORD commanded Moses concerning the Levites, so did the children of Israel unto them.

21 [j]And the Levites were purified, and they washed their clothes; [k]and Aaron offered them *as* an offering before the LORD; and Aaron made an atonement for them to cleanse them.

22 [l]And after that went the Levites in to do their service in the tabernacle of the congregation before Aaron, and before his sons: [m]as the LORD had commanded Moses concerning the Levites, so did they unto them.

23 ¶ And the LORD spake unto Moses, saying,

24 This *is it* that *belongeth* unto the Levites: [n]from twenty and five years old and upward they shall go in to wait upon the service of the tabernacle of the congregation:

25 And from the age of fifty years they shall cease waiting upon the service *thereof,* and shall serve no more:

26 But shall minister with their brethren in the tabernacle of the congregation, [o]to keep the charge, and shall do no service. Thus shalt thou do unto the Levites touching their charge.

9 And the LORD spake unto Moses in the wilderness of Sinai, in the first month of the second year after they were come out of the land of Egypt, saying,

2 Let the children of Israel also keep [p]the passover at his appointed season.

3 In the fourteenth day of this month, at even, ye shall keep it in his appointed season: according to all the rites of it, and according to all the ceremonies thereof, shall ye keep it.

4 And Moses spake unto the children of Israel, that they should keep the passover.

5 And [q]they kept the passover on the fourteenth day of the first month at even in the wilderness of Sinai: according to all that the LORD commanded Moses, so did the children of Israel.

6 ¶ And there were certain men, who were [r]defiled by the dead body of a man, that they could not keep the passover on that day: [s]and they came before Moses and before Aaron on that day:

7 And those men said unto him, We *are* defiled by the dead body of a man: wherefore are we kept back, that we may not offer an offering of the LORD in his appointed season among the children of Israel?

8 And Moses said unto them, Stand still, and [t]I will hear what the LORD will command concerning you.

9 ¶ And the LORD spake unto Moses, saying,

10 Speak unto the children of Israel, saying, If any man of you or of your posterity shall be unclean by reason of a dead body, or *be* in a journey afar off, yet he shall keep the passover unto the LORD.

8:4 [t]Ex. 25:31 [u]Ex. 25:18 [v]Ex. 25:40
8:7 [w]ch. 19:9 [x]Lev. 14:8
8:8 [y]Lev. 2:1
8:9 [z]Ex. 29:4 [a]Lev. 8:3
8:10 [b]Lev. 1:4
8:12 [c]Ex. 29:10
8:14 [d]ch. 3:45
8:15 [e]ver. 11
8:16 [f]ch. 3:12
8:17 [g]Ex. 13:2; ch. 3:13; Luke 2:23
8:19 [h]ch. 3:9 [i]ch. 1:53; 2 Chron. 26:16
8:21 [j]ver. 7 [k]ver. 11
8:22 [l]ver. 15 [m]ver. 5
8:24 [n]ch. 4:3; 1 Chron. 23:3
8:26 [o]ch. 1:53
9:2 [p]Ex. 12:1; Lev. 23:5; ch. 28:16; Deut. 16:1
9:5 [q]Josh. 5:10
9:6 [r]ch. 5:2; John 18:28 [s]Ex. 18:15; ch. 27:2
9:8 [t]ch. 27:5

11 [u]The fourteenth day of the second month at even they shall keep it, *and* [v]eat it with unleavened bread and bitter *herbs.*

12 [w]They shall leave none of it unto the morning, [x]nor break any bone of it: [y]according to all the ordinances of the passover they shall keep it.

13 But the man that *is* clean, and is not in a journey, and forbeareth to keep the passover, even the same soul [z]shall be cut off from among his people: because he [a]brought not the offering of the LORD in his appointed season, that man shall [b]bear his sin.

14 And if a stranger shall sojourn among you, and will keep the passover unto the LORD; according to the ordinance of the passover, and according to the manner thereof, so shall he do: [c]ye shall have one ordinance, both for the stranger, and for him that was born in the land.

15 ¶ And [d]on the day that the tabernacle was reared up the cloud covered the tabernacle, *namely,* the tent of the testimony: and [e]at even there was upon the tabernacle as it were the appearance of fire, until the morning.

16 So it was alway: the cloud covered it *by day,* and the appearance of fire by night.

17 And when the cloud [f]was taken up from the tabernacle, then after that the children of Israel journeyed: and in the place where the cloud abode, there the children of Israel pitched their tents.

18 At the commandment of the LORD the children of Israel journeyed, and at the commandment of the LORD they pitched: [g]as long as the cloud abode upon the tabernacle they rested in their tents.

19 And when the cloud tarried long upon the tabernacle many days, then the children of Israel [h]kept the charge of the LORD, and journeyed not.

20 And *so* it was, when the cloud was a few days upon the tabernacle; according to the commandment of the LORD they abode in their tents, and according to the commandment of the LORD they journeyed.

21 And *so* it was, when the cloud abode from even unto the morning, and *that* the cloud was taken up in the morning, then they journeyed: whether *it was* by day or by night that the cloud was taken up, they journeyed.

22 Or *whether it were* two days, or a month, or a year, that the cloud tarried upon the tabernacle, remaining thereon, the children of Israel [i]abode in their tents, and journeyed not: but when it was taken up, they journeyed.

23 At the commandment of the LORD they rested in the tents, and at the commandment of the LORD they journeyed: they [j]kept the charge of the LORD, at the commandment of the LORD by the hand of Moses.

10 And the LORD spake unto Moses, saying,

2 Make thee two trumpets of silver; of a whole piece shalt thou make them: that thou mayest use them for the [k]calling of the assembly, and for the journeying of the camps.

3 And when [l]they shall blow with them, all the assembly shall assemble themselves to thee at the door of the tabernacle of the congregation.

4 And if they blow *but* with one *trumpet,* then the princes, *which are* [m]heads of the thousands of Israel, shall gather themselves unto thee.

5 When ye blow an alarm, then [n]the camps that lie on the east parts shall go forward.

6 When ye blow an alarm the second time, then the camps that lie [o]on the south side shall take their journey: they shall blow an alarm for their journeys.

7 But when the congregation is to be gathered together, [p]ye shall blow, but ye shall not [q]sound an alarm.

8 [r]And the sons of Aaron, the priests, shall blow with the trumpets; and they shall be to you for an ordinance for ever throughout your generations.

9 And [s]if ye go to war in your land against the enemy that [t]oppresseth you, then ye shall blow an alarm with the trumpets; and ye shall be [u]remembered before the LORD your God, and ye shall be saved from your enemies.

10 Also [v]in the day of your gladness, and in your solemn days, and in the beginnings of your months, ye shall blow with the trumpets over your burnt offerings, and over the sacrifices of your peace offerings; that they may be to you [w]for a memorial before your God: I *am* the LORD your God.

11 ¶ And it came to pass on the twentieth *day* of the second month, in the second year, that the cloud [x]was taken up from off the tabernacle of the testimony.

12 And the children of Israel took [y]their journeys out of the [z]wilderness of Sinai; and the cloud rested in the [a]wilderness of Paran.

13 And they first took their journey [b]according to the commandment of the LORD by the hand of Moses.

14 ¶ [c]In the first *place* went the standard of the camp of the children of Judah according to their armies: and over his host *was* [d]Nahshon the son of Amminadab.

15 And over the host of the tribe of the children of Issachar *was* Nethaneel the son of Zuar.

16 And over the host of the tribe of the children of Zebulun *was* Eliab the son of Helon.

17 And [e]the tabernacle was taken down; and the sons of Gershon and the sons of Merari set forward, [f]bearing the tabernacle.

18 ¶ And [g]the standard of the camp of Reuben set forward according to their ar-

9:11 [u]2 Chron. 30:2 [v]Ex. 12:8
9:12 [w]Ex. 12:10 [x]Ex. 12:46; John 19:36 [y]Ex. 12:43
9:13 [z]Gen. 17:14; Ex. 12:15 [a]ver. 7 [b]ch. 5:31
9:14 [c]Ex. 12:49
9:15 [d]Ex. 40:34; Neh. 9:12; Ps. 78:14 [e]Ex. 13:21
9:17 [f]Ex. 40:36; ch. 10:11; Ps. 80:1
9:18 [g]1 Cor. 10:1
9:19 [h]ch. 1:53
9:22 [i]Ex. 40:36
9:23 [j]ver. 19
10:2 [k]Isa. 1:13
10:3 [l]Jer. 4:5; Joel 2:15
10:4 [m]Ex. 18:21; ch. 1:16
10:5 [n]ch. 2:3
10:6 [o]ch. 2:10
10:7 [p]ver. 3 [q]Joel 2:1
10:8 [r]ch. 31:6; Josh. 6:4; 1 Chron. 15:24; 2 Chron. 13:12
10:9 [s]ch. 31:6; Josh. 6:5; 2 Chron. 13:14 [t]Judg. 2:18; 1 Sam. 10:18; Ps. 106:42 [u]Gen. 8:1; Ps. 106:4
10:10 [v]ch. 29:1; Lev. 23:24; 1 Chron. 15:24; 2 Chron. 5:12; Ezra 3:10; Neh. 12:35; Ps. 81:3 [w]ver. 9
10:11 [x]ch. 9:17
10:12 [y]Ex. 40:36; ch. 2:9 [z]Ex. 19:1; ch. 1:1 [a]Gen. 21:21; ch. 12:16; Deut. 1:1
10:13 [b]ver. 5; ch. 2:34
10:14 [c]ch. 2:3 [d]ch. 1:7
10:17 [e]ch. 1:51 [f]ch. 4:24
10:18 [g]ch. 2:10

mies: and over his host *was* Elizur the son of Shedeur.

19 And over the host of the tribe of the children of Simeon *was* Shelumiel the son of Zurishaddai.

20 And over the host of the tribe of the children of Gad *was* Eliasaph the son of Deuel.

21 And the Kohathites set forward, bearing the [h]sanctuary: and *the other* did set up the tabernacle against they came.

22 ¶ And [i]the standard of the camp of the children of Ephraim set forward according to their armies: and over his host *was* Elishama the son of Ammihud.

23 And over the host of the tribe of the children of Manasseh *was* Gamaliel the son of Pedahzur.

24 And over the host of the tribe of the children of Benjamin *was* Abidan the son of Gideoni.

25 ¶ And [j]the standard of the camp of the children of Dan set forward, *which was* the rereward of all the camps throughout their hosts: and over his host *was* Ahiezer the son of Ammishaddai.

26 And over the host of the tribe of the children of Asher *was* Pagiel the son of Ocran.

27 And over the host of the tribe of the children of Naphtali *was* Ahira the son of Enan.

28 [k]Thus *were* the journeyings of the children of Israel according to their armies, when they set forward.

29 ¶ And Moses said unto Hobab, the son of [l]Raguel the Midianite, Moses' father in law, We are journeying unto the place of which the LORD said, [m]I will give it you: come thou with us, and [n]we will do thee good: for [o]the LORD hath spoken good concerning Israel.

30 And he said unto him, I will not go; but I will depart to mine own land, and to my kindred.

31 And he said, Leave us not, I pray thee; forasmuch as thou knowest how we are to encamp in the wilderness, and thou mayest be to us [p]instead of eyes.

32 And it shall be, if thou go with us, yea, it shall be, that [q]what goodness the LORD shall do unto us, the same will we do unto thee.

33 ¶ And they departed from [r]the mount of the LORD three days' journey: and the ark of the covenant of the LORD [s]went before them in the three days' journey, to search out a resting place for them.

34 And [t]the cloud of the LORD *was* upon them by day, when they went out of the camp.

35 And it came to pass, when the ark set forward, that Moses said, [u]Rise up, LORD, and let thine enemies be scattered; and let them that hate thee flee before thee.

36 And when it rested, he said, Return, O LORD, unto the many thousands of Israel.

11

And [v]*when* the people complained, it displeased the LORD: and the LORD heard *it;* [w]and his anger was kindled; and the [x]fire of the LORD burnt among them, and consumed *them that were* in the uttermost parts of the camp.

2 And the people cried unto Moses; and when Moses [y]prayed unto the LORD, the fire was quenched.

3 And he called the name of the place Taberah: because the fire of the LORD burnt among them.

4 ¶ And the [z]mixt multitude that *was* among them fell a lusting: and the children of Israel also wept again, and said, [a]Who shall give us flesh to eat?

5 [b]We remember the fish, which we did eat in Egypt freely; the cucumbers, and the melons, and the leeks, and the onions, and the garlick:

6 But now [c]our soul *is* dried away: *there is* nothing at all, beside this manna, *before* our eyes.

7 And [d]the manna *was* as coriander seed, and the colour thereof as the colour of [e]bdellium.

8 *And* the people went about, and gathered *it,* and ground *it* in mills, or beat *it* in a mortar, and baked *it* in pans, and made cakes of it: and the taste of it was as [f]the taste of fresh oil.

9 And [g]when the dew fell upon the camp in the night, the manna fell upon it.

10 ¶ Then Moses heard the people weep throughout their families, every man in the door of his tent: and [h]the anger of the LORD was kindled greatly; Moses also was displeased.

11 [i]And Moses said unto the LORD, Wherefore hast thou afflicted thy servant? and wherefore have I not found favour in thy sight, that thou layest the burden of all this people upon me?

12 Have I conceived all this people? have I begotten them, that thou shouldest say unto me, [j]Carry them in thy bosom, as a [k]nursing father beareth the sucking child, unto the land which thou [l]swarest unto their fathers?

13 [m]Whence should I have flesh to give unto all this people? for they weep unto me, saying, Give us flesh, that we may eat.

14 [n]I am not able to bear all this people alone, because *it is* too heavy for me.

15 And if thou deal thus with me, [o]kill me, I pray thee, out of hand, if I have found favour in thy sight; and let me not [p]see my wretchedness.

16 ¶ And the LORD said unto Moses, Gather unto me [q]seventy men of the elders of Israel, whom thou knowest to be the elders of the people, and [r]officers over them; and bring them unto the tabernacle of the congregation, that they may stand there with thee.

17 And I will [s]come down and talk with thee there: and [t]I will take of the spirit which *is* upon thee, and will put *it* upon

10:21 [h]ch. 4:4
10:22 [i]ch. 2:18
10:25 [j]ch. 2:25; Josh. 6:9
10:28 [k]ch. 2:34
10:29 [l]Ex. 2:18 [m]Gen. 12:7 [n]Judg. 1:16 [o]Gen. 32:12; Ex. 3:8
10:31 [p]Job 29:15
10:32 [q]Judg. 1:16
10:33 [r]Ex. 3:1 [s]Deut. 1:33; Josh. 3:3; Ps. 132:8; Jer. 31:2; Ezek. 20:6
10:34 [t]Ex. 13:21; Neh. 9:12
10:35 [u]Ps. 68:1
11:1 [v]Deut. 9:22 [w]Ps. 78:21 [x]Lev. 10:2; ch. 16:35; 2 Kings 1:12; Ps. 106:18
11:2 [y]Jam. 5:16
11:4 [z]Ex. 12:38 [a]Ps. 78:18; 1 Cor. 10:6
11:5 [b]Ex. 16:3
11:6 [c]ch. 21:5
11:7 [d]Ex. 16:14 [e]Gen. 2:12
11:8 [f]Ex. 16:31
11:9 [g]Ex. 16:13
11:10 [h]Ps. 78:21
11:11 [i]Deut. 1:12
11:12 [j]Isa. 40:11 [k]Isa. 49:23; 1 Thess. 2:7 [l]Gen. 26:3; Ex. 13:5
11:13 [m]Matt. 15:33; Mark 8:4
11:14 [n]Ex. 18:18
11:15 [o]1 Kings 19:4; Jonah 4:3 [p]Zeph. 3:15
11:16 [q]Ex. 24:1 [r]Deut. 16:18
11:17 [s]ver. 25; Gen. 11:5; Ex. 19:20 [t]1 Sam. 10:6; 2 Kings 2:15; Neh. 9:20; Isa. 44:3; Joel 2:28

them; and they shall bear the burden of the people with thee, that thou bear *it* not thyself alone.

18 And say thou unto the people, [u]Sanctify yourselves against to morrow, and ye shall eat flesh: for ye have wept [v]in the ears of the LORD, saying, Who shall give us flesh to eat? [w]for *it was* well with us in Egypt: therefore the LORD will give you flesh, and ye shall eat.

19 Ye shall not eat one day, nor two days, nor five days, neither ten days, nor twenty days;

20 [x]*But* even a whole month, until it come out at your nostrils, and it be loathsome unto you: because that ye have despised the LORD which *is* among you, and have wept before him, saying, [y]Why came we forth out of Egypt?

21 And Moses said, [z]The people, among whom I *am, are* six hundred thousand footmen; and thou hast said, I will give them flesh, that they may eat a whole month.

22 [a]Shall the flocks and the herds be slain for them, to suffice them? or shall all the fish of the sea be gathered together for them, to suffice them?

23 And the LORD said unto Moses, [b]Is the LORD's hand waxed short? thou shalt see now whether [c]my word shall come to pass unto thee or not.

24 ¶ And Moses went out, and told the people the words of the LORD, and [d]gathered the seventy men of the elders of the people, and set them round about the tabernacle.

25 And the LORD [e]came down in a cloud, and spake unto him, and took of the spirit that *was* upon him, and gave *it* unto the seventy elders: and it came to pass, *that,* [f]when the spirit rested upon them, [g]they prophesied, and did not cease.

26 But there remained two *of the* men in the camp, the name of the one *was* Eldad, and the name of the other Medad: and the spirit rested upon them; and they *were* of them that were written, but [h]went not out unto the tabernacle: and they prophesied in the camp.

27 And there ran a young man, and told Moses, and said, Eldad and Medad do prophesy in the camp.

28 And Joshua the son of Nun, the servant of Moses, *one* of his young men, answered and said, My lord Moses, [i]forbid them.

29 And Moses said unto him, Enviest thou for my sake? [j]would God that all the LORD's people were prophets, *and* that the LORD would put his spirit upon them!

30 And Moses gat him into the camp, he and the elders of Israel.

31 ¶ And there went forth a [k]wind from the LORD, and brought quails from the sea, and let *them* fall by the camp, as it were a day's journey on this side, and as it were a day's journey on the other side, round about the camp, and as it were two cubits *high* upon the face of the earth.

32 And the people stood up all that day, and all *that* night, and all the next day, and they gathered the quails: he that gathered least gathered ten [l]homers: and they spread *them* all abroad for themselves round about the camp.

33 And while the [m]flesh *was* yet between their teeth, ere it was chewed, the wrath of the LORD was kindled against the people, and the LORD smote the people with a very great plague.

34 And he called the name of that place Kibroth-hattaavah: because there they buried the people that lusted.

35 [n]*And* the people journeyed from Kibroth-hattaavah unto Hazeroth; and abode at Hazeroth.

12 And Miriam and Aaron spake against Moses because of the Ethiopian woman whom [o]he had married: for he had married an Ethiopian woman.

2 And they said, Hath the LORD indeed spoken only by Moses? [p]hath he not spoken also by us? And the LORD [q]heard *it.*

3 (Now the man Moses *was* very meek, above all the men which *were* upon the face of the earth.)

4 [r]And the LORD spake suddenly unto Moses, and unto Aaron, and unto Miriam, Come out ye three unto the tabernacle of the congregation. And they three came out.

5 [s]And the LORD came down in the pillar of the cloud, and stood *in* the door of the tabernacle, and called Aaron and Miriam: and they both came forth.

6 And he said, Hear now my words: If there be a prophet among you, *I* the LORD will make myself known unto him [t]in a vision, *and* will speak unto him [u]in a dream.

7 [v]My servant Moses *is* not so, [w]who *is* faithful in all [x]mine house.

8 With him will I speak [y]mouth to mouth, even [z]apparently, and not in dark speeches; and [a]the similitude of the LORD shall he behold: wherefore then [b]were ye not afraid to speak against my servant Moses?

9 And the anger of the LORD was kindled against them; and he departed.

10 And the cloud departed from off the tabernacle; and, [c]behold, Miriam *became* [d]leprous, *white* as snow: and Aaron looked upon Miriam, and, behold, *she was* leprous.

11 And Aaron said unto Moses, Alas, my lord, I beseech thee, [e]lay not the sin upon us, wherein we have done foolishly, and wherein we have sinned.

12 Let her not be [f]as one dead, of whom the flesh is half consumed when he cometh out of his mother's womb.

13 And Moses cried unto the LORD, saying, Heal her now, O God, I beseech thee.

14 ¶ And the LORD said unto Moses, [g]If her father had but spit in her face, should she not be ashamed seven days? let her be

11:18 [u]Ex. 19:10 [v]Ex. 16:7 [w]ver. 5; Acts 7:39
11:20 [x]Ps. 78:29 [y]ch. 21:5
11:21 [z]Gen. 12:2; Ex. 12:37; ch. 1:46
11:22 [a]2 Kings 7:2; Matt. 15:33; Mark 8:4; John 6:7
11:23 [b]Isa. 50:2 [c]ch. 23:19; Ezek. 12:25
11:24 [d]ver. 16
11:25 [e]ver. 17; ch. 12:5 [f]2 Kings 2:15 [g]1 Sam. 10:5; Joel 2:29; Acts 2:17; 1 Cor. 14:1
11:26 [h]1 Sam. 20:26; Jer. 36:5
11:28 [i]Mark 9:38; Luke 9:49; John 3:26
11:29 [j]1 Cor. 14:5
11:31 [k]Ex. 16:13; Ps. 78:26
11:32 [l]Ex. 16:36; Ezek. 45:11
11:33 [m]Ps. 78:30
11:35 [n]ch. 33:17
12:1 [o]Ex. 2:21
12:2 [p]Ex. 15:20; Mic. 6:4 [q]Gen. 29:33; ch. 11:1; 2 Kings 19:4; Isa. 37:4; Ezek. 35:12
12:4 [r]Ps. 76:9
12:5 [s]ch. 11:25
12:6 [t]Gen. 15:1; Job 33:15; Ezek. 1:1; Dan. 8:2; Luke 1:11; Acts 10:11 [u]Gen. 31:10; 1 Kings 3:5; Matt. 1:20
12:7 [v]Ps. 105:26 [w]Heb. 3:2 [x]1 Tim. 3:15
12:8 [y]Ex. 33:11; Deut. 34:10 [z]1 Cor. 13:12 [a]Ex. 33:19 [b]2 Pet. 2:10; Jude 8
12:10 [c]Deut. 24:9 [d]2 Kings 5:27; 2 Chron. 26:19
12:11 [e]2 Sam. 19:19; Prov. 30:32
12:12 [f]Ps. 88:4
12:14 [g]Heb. 12:9

[h]shut out from the camp seven days, and after that let her be received in *again*.

15 [i]And Miriam was shut out from the camp seven days: and the people journeyed not till Miriam was brought in *again*.

16 And afterward the people removed from [j]Hazeroth, and pitched in the wilderness of Paran.

13 And the LORD spake unto Moses, saying,

2 [k]Send thou men, that they may search the land of Canaan, which I give unto the children of Israel: of every tribe of their fathers shall ye send a man, every one a ruler among them.

3 And Moses by the commandment of the LORD sent them [l]from the wilderness of Paran: all those men *were* heads of the children of Israel.

4 And these *were* their names: of the tribe of Reuben, Shammua the son of Zaccur.

5 Of the tribe of Simeon, Shaphat the son of Hori.

6 [m]Of the tribe of Judah, [n]Caleb the son of Jephunneh.

7 Of the tribe of Issachar, Igal the son of Joseph.

8 Of the tribe of Ephraim, [o]Oshea the son of Nun.

9 Of the tribe of Benjamin, Palti the son of Raphu.

10 Of the tribe of Zebulun, Gaddiel the son of Sodi.

11 Of the tribe of Joseph, *namely*, of the tribe of Manasseh, Gaddi the son of Susi.

12 Of the tribe of Dan, Ammiel the son of Gemalli.

13 Of the tribe of Asher, Sethur the son of Michael.

14 Of the tribe of Naphtali, Nahbi the son of Vophsi.

15 Of the tribe of Gad, Geuel the son of Machi.

16 These *are* the names of the men which Moses sent to spy out the land. And Moses called [p]Oshea the son of Nun Jehoshua.

17 ¶ And Moses sent them to spy out the land of Canaan, and said unto them, Get you up this *way* [q]southward, and go up into [r]the mountain:

18 And see the land, what it *is;* and the people that dwelleth therein, whether they *be* strong or weak, few or many;

19 And what the land *is* that they dwell in, whether it *be* good or bad; and what cities *they be* that they dwell in, whether in tents, or in strong holds;

20 And what the land *is,* whether it *be* [s]fat or lean, whether there be wood therein, or not. And [t]be ye of good courage, and bring of the fruit of the land. Now the time *was* the time of the firstripe grapes.

21 ¶ So they went up, and searched the land [u]from the wilderness of Zin unto [v]Rehob, as men come to Hamath.

22 And they ascended by the south, and came unto Hebron; where [w]Ahiman, Sheshai, and Talmai, [x]the children of Anak, *were.* (Now [y]Hebron was built seven years before [z]Zoan in Egypt.)

23 [a]And they came unto the brook of Eshcol, and cut down from thence a branch with one cluster of grapes, and they bare it between two upon a staff; and *they brought* of the pomegranates, and of the figs.

24 The place was called the brook Eshcol, because of the cluster of grapes which the children of Israel cut down from thence.

25 And they returned from searching of the land after forty days.

26 ¶ And they went and came to Moses, and to Aaron, and to all the congregation of the children of Israel, [b]unto the wilderness of Paran, to [c]Kadesh; and brought back word unto them, and unto all the congregation, and shewed them the fruit of the land.

27 And they told him, and said, We came unto the land whither thou sentest us, and surely it floweth with [d]milk and honey; [e]and this *is* the fruit of it.

28 Nevertheless [f]the people *be* strong that dwell in the land, and the cities *are* walled, *and* very great: and moreover we saw [g]the children of Anak there.

29 [h]The Amalekites dwell in the land of the south: and the Hittites, and the Jebusites, and the Amorites, dwell in the mountains: and the Canaanites dwell by the sea, and by the coast of Jordan.

30 And [i]Caleb stilled the people before Moses, and said, Let us go up at once, and possess it; for we are well able to overcome it.

31 [j]But the men that went up with him said, We be not able to go up against the people; for they *are* stronger than we.

32 And they [k]brought up an evil report of the land which they had searched unto the children of Israel, saying, The land, through which we have gone to search it, *is* a land that eateth up the inhabitants thereof; and [l]all the people that we saw in it *are* men of a great stature.

33 And there we saw the giants, [m]the sons of Anak, *which come* of the giants: and we were in our own sight as [n]grasshoppers, and so we were [o]in their sight.

14 And all the congregation lifted up their voice, and cried; and [p]the people wept that night.

2 [q]And all the children of Israel murmured against Moses and against Aaron: and the whole congregation said unto them, Would God that we had died in the land of Egypt! or [r]would God we had died in this wilderness!

3 And wherefore hath the LORD brought us unto this land, to fall by the sword, that our wives and our children should be a prey? were it not better for us to return into Egypt?

4 And they said one to another, [s]Let us make a captain, and [t]let us return into Egypt.

5 Then [u]Moses and Aaron fell on their

12:14 [h]Lev. 13:46; ch. 5:2
12:15 [i]Deut. 24:9; 2 Chron. 26:20
12:16 [j]ch. 11:35
13:2 [k]ch. 32:8; Deut. 1:22
13:3 [l]ch. 12:16; Deut. 1:19
13:6 [m]ch. 34:19; 1 Chron. 4:15 [n]ver. 30; ch. 14:6; Josh. 14:6; Judg. 1:12
13:8 [o]ver. 16
13:16 [p]ver. 8; Ex. 17:9; ch. 14:6
13:17 [q]ver. 21 [r]Gen. 14:10; Judg. 1:9
13:20 [s]Neh. 9:25; Ezek. 34:14 [t]Deut. 31:6
13:21 [u]ch. 34:3; Josh. 15:1 [v]Josh. 19:28
13:22 [w]Josh. 11:21; Judg. 1:10 [x]ver. 33 [y]Josh. 21:11 [z]Ps. 78:12; Isa. 19:11
13:23 [a]Deut. 1:24
13:26 [b]ver. 3 [c]ch. 20:1; Deut. 1:19; Josh. 14:6
13:27 [d]Ex. 3:8 [e]Deut. 1:25
13:28 [f]Deut. 1:28 [g]ver. 33
13:29 [h]Ex. 17:8; ch. 14:43; Judg. 6:3; 1 Sam. 14:48
13:30 [i]ch. 14:6; Josh. 14:7
13:31 [j]ch. 32:9; Deut. 1:28; Josh. 14:8
13:32 [k]ch. 14:36 [l]Am. 2:9
13:33 [m]Deut. 1:28 [n]Isa. 40:22 [o]1 Sam. 17:42
14:1 [p]ch. 11:4
14:2 [q]Ex. 16:2; ch. 16:41; Ps. 106:25 [r]ver. 28
14:4 [s]Neh. 9:17 [t]Deut. 17:16; Acts 7:39
14:5 [u]ch. 16:4

faces before all the assembly of the congregation of the children of Israel.
6 ¶ [v]And Joshua the son of Nun, and Caleb the son of Jephunneh, *which were* of
them that searched the land, rent their
clothes:
7 And they spake unto all the company of
the children of Israel, saying, [w]The land,
which we passed through to search it, *is* an
exceeding good land.
8 If the LORD [x]delight in us, then he will
bring us into this land, and give it us; [y]a
land which floweth with milk and honey.
9 Only [z]rebel not ye against the LORD,
[a]neither fear ye the people of the land; for
[b]they *are* bread for us: their defence is departed from them, [c]and the LORD *is* with us:
fear them not.
10 [d]But all the congregation bade stone
them with stones. And [e]the glory of the
LORD appeared in the tabernacle of the congregation before all the children of Israel.
11 ¶ And the LORD said unto Moses, How
long will this people [f]provoke me? and how
long will it be ere they [g]believe me, for
all the signs which I have shewed among
them?
12 I will smite them with the pestilence,
and disinherit them, and [h]will make of thee
a greater nation and mightier than they.
13 ¶ And [i]Moses said unto the LORD,
Then the Egyptians shall hear *it*, (for thou
broughtest up this people in thy might from
among them;)
14 And they will tell *it* to the inhabitants
of this land: [j]*for* they have heard that thou
LORD *art* among this people, that thou LORD
art seen face to face, and *that* [k]thy cloud
standeth over them, and *that* thou goest before them, by day time in a pillar of a cloud,
and in a pillar of fire by night.
15 ¶ Now *if* thou shalt kill *all* this people
as one man, then the nations which have
heard the fame of thee will speak, saying,
16 Because the LORD was not [l]able to
bring this people into the land which he
sware unto them, therefore he hath slain
them in the wilderness.
17 And now, I beseech thee, let the power
of my LORD be great, according as thou hast
spoken, saying,
18 The LORD *is* [m]longsuffering, and of
great mercy, forgiving iniquity and transgression, and by no means clearing *the
guilty*, [n]visiting the iniquity of the fathers
upon the children unto the third and fourth
generation.
19 [o]Pardon, I beseech thee, the iniquity
of this people [p]according unto the greatness of thy mercy, and [q]as thou hast forgiven this people, from Egypt even until
now.
20 And the LORD said, I have pardoned
[r]according to thy word:
21 But *as* truly *as* I live, [s]all the earth
shall be filled with the glory of the LORD.
22 [t]Because all those men which have
seen my glory, and my miracles, which I did
in Egypt and in the wilderness, and have
tempted me now [u]these ten times, and have
not hearkened to my voice;
23 [v]Surely they shall not see the land
which I sware unto their fathers, neither
shall any of them that provoked me see it:
24 But my servant [w]Caleb, because he
had another spirit with him, and [x]hath followed me fully, him will I bring into the land
whereinto he went; and his seed shall possess it.
25 (Now the Amalekites and the Canaanites dwelt in the valley.) To morrow turn
you, [y]and get you into the wilderness by the
way of the Red sea.
26 ¶ And the LORD spake unto Moses and
unto Aaron, saying,
27 [z]How long *shall I bear with* this evil
congregation, which murmur against me?
[a]I have heard the murmurings of the children of Israel, which they murmur
against me.
28 Say unto them, [b]*As truly as* I live,
saith the LORD, [c]as ye have spoken in mine
ears, so will I do to you:
29 Your carcases shall fall in this wilderness; and [d]all that were numbered of you,
according to your whole number, from
twenty years old and upward, which have
murmured against me,
30 Doubtless ye shall not come into the
land, *concerning* which I sware to make you
dwell therein, [e]save Caleb the son of Jephunneh, and Joshua the son of Nun.
31 [f]But your little ones, which ye said
should be a prey, them will I bring in, and
they shall know the land which [g]ye have
despised.
32 But *as for* you, [h]your carcases, they
shall fall in this wilderness.
33 And your children shall [i]wander in
the wilderness [j]forty years, and [k]bear your
whoredoms, until your carcases be wasted
in the wilderness.
34 [l]After the number of the days in
which ye searched the land, *even* [m]forty
days, each day for a year, shall ye bear your
iniquities, *even* forty years, [n]and ye shall
know my breach of promise.
35 [o]I the LORD have said, I will surely do
it unto all [p]this evil congregation, that are
gathered together against me: in this wilderness they shall be consumed, and there
they shall die.
36 [q]And the men which Moses sent to
search the land, who returned, and made all
the congregation to murmur against him,
by bringing up a slander upon the land,
37 Even those men that did bring up the
evil report upon the land, [r]died by the
plague before the LORD.
38 [s]But Joshua the son of Nun, and Caleb
the son of Jephunneh, *which were* of the
men that went to search the land, lived *still*.
39 And Moses told these sayings unto all

14:6 [v]ver. 24; ch. 13:6
14:7 [w]ch. 13:27; Deut. 1:25
14:8 [x]Deut. 10:15; 2 Sam. 15:25; 1 Kings 10:9; Ps. 22:8; Isa. 62:4 [y]ch. 13:27
14:9 [z]Deut. 9:7 [a]Deut. 7:18 [b]ch. 24:8 [c]Gen. 48:21; Ex. 33:16; Deut. 20:1; Josh. 1:5; Judg. 1:22; 2 Chron. 13:12; Ps. 46:7; Isa. 41:10; Am. 5:14; Zech. 8:23
14:10 [d]Ex. 17:4 [e]Ex. 16:10; Lev. 9:23; ch. 16:19
14:11 [f]ver. 23; Deut. 9:7; Ps. 95:8; Heb. 3:8 [g]Deut. 1:32; Ps. 78:22; John 12:37; Heb. 3:18
14:12 [h]Ex. 32:10
14:13 [i]Ex. 32:12; Ps. 106:23; Deut. 9:26; Ezek. 20:9
14:14 [j]Ex. 15:14; Josh. 2:9 [k]Ex. 13:21; ch. 10:34; Neh. 9:12; Ps. 78:14
14:16 [l]Deut. 9:28; Josh. 7:9
14:18 [m]Ex. 34:6; Ps. 103:8; Jonah 4:2 [n]Ex. 20:5
14:19 [o]Ex. 34:9 [p]Ps. 106:45 [q]Ps. 78:38
14:20 [r]Ps. 106:23; Jam. 5:16; 1 John 5:14
14:21 [s]Ps. 72:19
14:22 [t]Deut. 1:35; Ps. 95:11; Heb. 3:17 [u]Gen. 31:7
14:23 [v]ch. 32:11; Ezek. 20:15
14:24 [w]Deut. 1:36; Josh. 14:6 [x]ch. 32:12
14:25 [y]Deut. 1:40
14:27 [z]ver. 11; Ex. 16:28; Matt. 17:7 [a]Ex. 16:12
14:28 [b]ver. 23; ch. 26:65; Deut. 1:35; Heb. 3:17 [c]ver. 2
14:29 [d]ch. 1:45
14:30 [e]ver. 38; ch. 26:65; Deut. 1:36
14:31 [f]Deut. 1:39 [g]Ps. 106:24
14:32 [h]1 Cor. 10:5; Heb. 3:17
14:33 [i]ch. 32:13; Ps. 107:40 [j]Deut. 2:14 [k]Ezek. 23:35
14:34 [l]ch. 13:25 [m]Ps. 95:10; Ezek. 4:6 [n]1 Kings 8:56; Ps. 77:8; Heb. 4:1

14:35 [o]ch. 23:19 [p]ver. 27; ch. 26:65; 1 Cor. 10:5 **14:36** [q]ch. 13:31
14:37 [r]1 Cor. 10:10; Heb. 3:17; Jude 5 **14:38** [s]ch. 26:65; Josh. 14:6

the children of Israel: [t]and the people
mourned greatly.
40 ¶ And they rose up early in the morning, and gat them up into the top of the
mountain, saying, Lo, [u]we *be here,* and will
go up unto the place which the LORD hath
promised: for we have sinned.
41 And Moses said, Wherefore now do
ye transgress [v]the commandment of the
LORD? but it shall not prosper.
42 [w]Go not up, for the LORD *is* not among
you; that ye be not smitten before your enemies.
43 For the Amalekites and the Canaanites
are there before you, and ye shall fall by the
sword: [x]because ye are turned away from
the LORD, therefore the LORD will not be
with you.
44 [y]But they presumed to go up unto the
hill top: nevertheless the ark of the covenant of the LORD, and Moses, departed not
out of the camp.
45 [z]Then the Amalekites came down,
and the Canaanites which dwelt in that hill,
and smote them, and discomfited them,
even unto [a]Hormah.

15

And the LORD spake unto Moses,
saying,
2 [b]Speak unto the children of Israel, and
say unto them, When ye be come into the
land of your habitations, which I give unto
you,
3 And [c]will make an offering by fire unto
the LORD, a burnt offering, or a sacrifice [d]in
performing a vow, or in a freewill offering,
or [e]in your solemn feasts, to make a [f]sweet
savour unto the LORD, of the herd, or of the
flock:
4 Then [g]shall he that offereth his offering
unto the LORD bring [h]a meat offering of a
tenth deal of flour mingled [i]with the fourth
part of an hin of oil.
5 [j]And the fourth *part* of an hin of wine
for a drink offering shalt thou prepare with
the burnt offering or sacrifice, for one lamb.
6 [k]Or for a ram, thou shalt prepare *for* a
meat offering two tenth deals of flour mingled with the third *part* of an hin of oil.
7 And for a drink offering thou shalt offer
the third *part* of an hin of wine, *for* a sweet
savour unto the LORD.
8 And when thou preparest a bullock *for*
a burnt offering, or *for* a sacrifice in performing a vow, or [l]peace offerings unto the
LORD:
9 Then shall he bring [m]with a bullock a
meat offering of three tenth deals of flour,
mingled with half an hin of oil.
10 And thou shalt bring for a drink offering half an hin of wine, *for* an offering made
by fire, of a sweet savour unto the LORD.
11 [n]Thus shall it be done for one bullock,
or for one ram, or for a lamb, or a kid.
12 According to the number that ye shall
prepare, so shall ye do to every one according to their number.
13 All that are born of the country shall
do these things after this manner, in offering an offering made by fire, of a sweet savour unto the LORD.
14 And if a stranger sojourn with you, or
whosoever *be* among you in your generations, and will offer an offering made by
fire, of a sweet savour unto the LORD; as ye
do, so he shall do.
15 [o]One ordinance *shall be both* for you
of the congregation, and also for the
stranger that sojourneth *with you,* an ordinance for ever in your generations: as ye
are, so shall the stranger be before the
LORD.
16 One law and one manner shall be for
you, and for the stranger that sojourneth
with you.
17 ¶ And the LORD spake unto Moses,
saying,
18 [p]Speak unto the children of Israel, and
say unto them, When ye come into the land
whither I bring you,
19 Then it shall be, that, when ye eat of
[q]the bread of the land, ye shall offer up an
heave offering unto the LORD.
20 [r]Ye shall offer up a cake of the first of
your dough *for* an heave offering: as *ye do*
[s]the heave offering of the threshingfloor,
so shall ye heave it.
21 Of the first of your dough ye shall give
unto the LORD an heave offering in your
generations.
22 ¶ And [t]if ye have erred, and not observed all these commandments, which the
LORD hath spoken unto Moses,
23 *Even* all that the LORD hath commanded you by the hand of Moses, from the
day that the LORD commanded *Moses,* and
henceforward among your generations;
24 Then it shall be, [u]if *ought* be committed by ignorance without the knowledge of
the congregation, that all the congregation
shall offer one young bullock for a burnt
offering, for a sweet savour unto the LORD,
[v]with his meat offering, and his drink offering, according to the manner, and [w]one kid
of the goats for a sin offering.
25 [x]And the priest shall make an atonement for all the congregation of the children
of Israel, and it shall be forgiven them; for
it *is* ignorance: and they shall bring their
offering, a sacrifice made by fire unto the
LORD, and their sin offering before the
LORD, for their ignorance:
26 And it shall be forgiven all the congregation of the children of Israel, and the
stranger that sojourneth among them; seeing all the people *were* in ignorance.
27 ¶ And [y]if any soul sin through ignorance, then he shall bring a she goat of the
first year for a sin offering.
28 [z]And the priest shall make an atonement for the soul that sinneth ignorantly,
when he sinneth by ignorance before the
LORD, to make an atonement for him; and it
shall be forgiven him.
29 [a]Ye shall have one law for him that
sinneth through ignorance, *both for* him
that is born among the children of Israel,

14:39 [t]Ex. 33:4
14:40 [u]Deut. 1:41
14:41 [v]ver. 25; 2 Chron. 24:20
14:42 [w]Deut. 1:42
14:43 [x]2 Chron. 15:2
14:44 [y]Deut. 1:43
14:45 [z]ver. 43; Deut. 1:44 [a]ch. 21:3; Judg. 1:17
15:2 [b]ver. 18; Lev. 23:10; Deut. 7:1
15:3 [c]Lev. 1:2 [d]Lev. 7:16 [e]Lev. 23:8; ch. 28:19; Deut. 16:10 [f]Gen. 8:21; Ex. 29:18
15:4 [g]Lev. 2:1 [h]Ex. 29:40; Lev. 23:13 [i]Lev. 14:10; ch. 28:5
15:5 [j]ch. 28:7
15:6 [k]ch. 28:12
15:8 [l]Lev. 7:11
15:9 [m]ch. 28:12
15:11 [n]ch. 28
15:15 [o]ver. 29; Ex. 12:49; ch. 9:14
15:18 [p]ver. 2; Deut. 26:1
15:19 [q]Josh. 5:11
15:20 [r]Deut. 26:2; Prov. 3:9 [s]Lev. 2:14
15:22 [t]Lev. 4:2
15:24 [u]Lev. 4:13 [v]ver. 8 [w]Lev. 4:23; ch. 28:15; Ezra 6:17
15:25 [x]Lev. 4:20
15:27 [y]Lev. 4:27
15:28 [z]Lev. 4:35
15:29 [a]ver. 15

and for the stranger that sojourneth among them.

30 ¶ [b]But the soul that doeth *ought* presumptuously, *whether he be* born in the land, or a stranger, the same reproacheth the LORD; and that soul shall be cut off from among his people.

31 Because he hath [c]despised the word of the LORD, and hath broken his commandment, that soul shall utterly be cut off; [d]his iniquity *shall be* upon him.

32 ¶ And while the children of Israel were in the wilderness, [e]they found a man that gathered sticks upon the sabbath day.

33 And they that found him gathering sticks brought him unto Moses and Aaron, and unto all the congregation.

34 And they put him [f]in ward, because it was not declared what should be done to him.

35 And the LORD said unto Moses, [g]The man shall be surely put to death: all the congregation shall [h]stone him with stones without the camp.

36 And all the congregation brought him without the camp, and stoned him with stones, and he died; as the LORD commanded Moses.

37 ¶ And the LORD spake unto Moses, saying,

38 Speak unto the children of Israel, and bid [i]them that they make them fringes in the borders of their garments throughout their generations, and that they put upon the fringe of the borders a ribband of blue:

39 And it shall be unto you for a fringe, that ye may look upon it, and remember all the commandments of the LORD, and do them; and that ye [j]seek not after your own heart and your own eyes, after which ye use [k]to go a whoring:

40 That ye may remember, and do all my commandments, and be [l]holy unto your God.

41 I *am* the LORD your God, which brought you out of the land of Egypt, to be your God: I *am* the LORD your God.

16 Now [m]Korah, the son of Izhar, the son of Kohath, the son of Levi, and Dathan and Abiram, the sons of Eliab, and On, the son of Peleth, sons of Reuben, took *men:*

2 And they rose up before Moses, with certain of the children of Israel, two hundred and fifty princes of the assembly, [n]famous in the congregation, men of renown:

3 And [o]they gathered themselves together against Moses and against Aaron, and said unto them, *Ye take* too much upon you, seeing [p]all the congregation *are* holy, every one of them, [q]and the LORD *is* among them: wherefore then lift ye up yourselves above the congregation of the LORD?

4 And when Moses heard *it*, [r]he fell upon his face:

5 And he spake unto Korah and unto all his company, saying, Even to morrow the LORD will shew who *are* his, and *who is* [s]holy; and will cause *him* to come near unto him: even *him* whom he hath [t]chosen will he cause to [u]come near unto him.

6 This do; Take you censers, Korah, and all his company;

7 And put fire therein, and put incense in them before the LORD to morrow: and it shall be *that* the man whom the LORD doth choose, he *shall be* holy: *ye take* too much upon you, ye sons of Levi.

8 And Moses said unto Korah, Hear, I pray you, ye sons of Levi:

9 *Seemeth it but* [v]a small thing unto you, that the God of Israel hath [w]separated you from the congregation of Israel, to bring you near to himself to do the service of the tabernacle of the LORD, and to stand before the congregation to minister unto them?

10 And he hath brought thee near *to him*, and all thy brethren the sons of Levi with thee: and seek ye the priesthood also?

11 For which cause *both* thou and all thy company *are* gathered together against the LORD: [x]and what *is* Aaron, that ye murmur against him?

12 ¶ And Moses sent to call Dathan and Abiram, the sons of Eliab: which said, We will not come up:

13 [y]*Is it* a small thing that thou hast brought us up out of a land that floweth with milk and honey, to kill us in the wilderness, except thou [z]make thyself altogether a prince over us?

14 Moreover thou hast not brought us into [a]a land that floweth with milk and honey, or given us inheritance of fields and vineyards: wilt thou put out the eyes of these men? we will not come up.

15 And Moses was very wroth, and said unto the LORD, [b]Respect not thou their offering: [c]I have not taken one ass from them, neither have I hurt one of them.

16 And Moses said unto Korah, [d]Be thou and all thy company [e]before the LORD, thou, and they, and Aaron, to morrow:

17 And take every man his censer, and put incense in them, and bring ye before the LORD every man his censer, two hundred and fifty censers; thou also, and Aaron, each *of you* his censer.

18 And they took every man his censer, and put fire in them, and laid incense thereon, and stood in the door of the tabernacle of the congregation with Moses and Aaron.

19 And Korah gathered all the congregation against them unto the door of the tabernacle of the congregation: and [f]the glory of the LORD appeared unto all the congregation.

20 And the LORD spake unto Moses and unto Aaron, saying,

21 [g]Separate yourselves from among this congregation, that I may [h]consume them in a moment.

22 And they [i]fell upon their faces, and said, O God, [j]the God of the spirits of all

15:30 [b]Deut. 17:12; Ps. 19:13; Heb. 10:26; 1 Pet. 2:10
15:31 [c]2 Sam. 12:9; Prov. 13:13 [d]Lev. 5:1; Ezek. 18:20
15:32 [e]Ex. 31:14
15:34 [f]Lev. 24:12
15:35 [g]Ex. 31:14 [h]Lev. 24:14; 1 Kings 21:13; Acts 7:58
15:38 [i]Deut. 22:12; Matt. 23:5
15:39 [j]Deut. 29:19; Job 31:7; Jer. 9:14; Ezek. 6:9 [k]Ps. 73:27; Jam. 4:4
15:40 [l]Lev. 11:44; Rom. 12:1; Col. 1:22; 1 Pet. 1:15
16:1 [m]Ex. 6:21; ch. 26:9; Jude 11
16:2 [n]ch. 26:9
16:3 [o]Ps. 106:16 [p]Ex. 19:6 [q]Ex. 29:45; ch. 14:14
16:4 [r]ch. 14:5
16:5 [s]ver. 3; Lev. 21:6 [t]Ex. 28:1; ch. 17:5; 1 Sam. 2:28; Ps. 105:26 [u]ch. 3:10; Lev. 10:3; Ezek. 40:46
16:9 [v]1 Sam. 18:23; Isa. 7:13 [w]ch. 3:41; Deut. 10:8
16:11 [x]Ex. 16:8; 1 Cor. 3:5
16:13 [y]ver. 9 [z]Ex. 2:14; Acts 7:27
16:14 [a]Ex. 3:8; Lev. 20:24
16:15 [b]Gen. 4:4 [c]1 Sam. 12:3; Acts 20:33; 2 Cor. 7:2
16:16 [d]ver. 6 [e]1 Sam. 12:3
16:19 [f]ver. 42; Ex. 16:7; Lev. 9:6; ch. 14:10
16:21 [g]Gen. 19:17; ver. 45; Jer. 51:6; Acts 2:40; Rev. 18:4 [h]ver. 45; Ex. 32:10
16:22 [i]ver. 45; ch. 14:5 [j]ch. 27:16; Job 12:10; Eccl. 12:7; Isa. 57:16; Zech. 12:1; Heb. 12:9

flesh, shall one man sin, and wilt thou be wroth with all the congregation?

23 ¶ And the LORD spake unto Moses, saying,

24 Speak unto the congregation, saying, Get you up from about the tabernacle of Korah, Dathan, and Abiram.

25 And Moses rose up and went unto Dathan and Abiram; and the elders of Israel followed him.

26 And he spake unto the congregation, saying, [k]Depart, I pray you, from the tents of these wicked men, and touch nothing of theirs, lest ye be consumed in all their sins.

27 So they gat up from the tabernacle of Korah, Dathan, and Abiram, on every side: and Dathan and Abiram came out, and stood in the door of their tents, and their wives, and their sons, and their little children.

28 And Moses said, [l]Hereby ye shall know that the LORD hath sent me to do all these works; for *I have* not *done them* [m]of mine own mind.

29 If these men die the common death of all men, or if they be [n]visited after the visitation of all men; *then* the LORD hath not sent me.

30 But if the LORD make [o]a new thing, and the earth open her mouth, and swallow them up, with all that *appertain* unto them, and they [p]go down quick into the pit; then ye shall understand that these men have provoked the LORD.

31 ¶ [q]And it came to pass, as he had made an end of speaking all these words, that the ground clave asunder that *was* under them:

32 And the earth opened her mouth, and swallowed them up, and their houses, and [r]all the men that *appertained* unto Korah, and all *their* goods.

33 They, and all that *appertained* to them, went down alive into the pit, and the earth closed upon them: and they perished from among the congregation.

34 And all Israel that *were* round about them fled at the cry of them: for they said, Lest the earth swallow us up *also*.

35 And there [s]came out a fire from the LORD, and consumed [t]the two hundred and fifty men that offered incense.

36 ¶ And the LORD spake unto Moses, saying,

37 Speak unto Eleazar the son of Aaron the priest, that he take up the censers out of the burning, and scatter thou the fire yonder; for [u]they are hallowed.

38 The censers of these [v]sinners against their own souls, let them make them broad plates *for* a covering of the altar: for they offered them before the LORD, therefore they are hallowed: [w]and they shall be a sign unto the children of Israel.

39 And Eleazar the priest took the brasen censers, wherewith they that were burnt had offered; and they were made broad *plates for* a covering of the altar:

16:26 *k*Gen. 19:12; Isa. 52:11; 2 Cor. 6:17; Rev. 18:4
16:28 *l*Ex. 3:12; Deut. 18:22; Zech. 2:9; John 5:36 *m*ch. 24:13; Jer. 23:16; Ezek. 13:17; John 5:30
16:29 *n*Ex. 20:5; Job 35:15; Isa. 10:3; Jer. 5:9
16:30 *o*Job 31:3; Isa. 28:21 *p*ver. 33; Ps. 55:15
16:31 *q*ch. 26:10; Deut. 11:6; Ps. 106:17
16:32 *r*ver. 17; 1 Chron. 6:22
16:35 *s*Lev. 10:2; ch. 11:1; Ps. 106:18 *t*ver. 17
16:37 *u*Lev. 27:28
16:38 *v*Prov. 20:2; Hab. 2:10 *w*ch. 17:10; Ezek. 14:8
16:40 *x*ch. 3:10; 2 Chron. 26:18
16:41 *y*ch. 14:2; Ps. 106:25
16:42 *z*Ex. 40:34 *a*ver. 19; ch. 20:6
16:45 *b*ver. 21 *c*ver. 22; ch. 20:6
16:46 *d*Lev. 10:6; ch. 1:53; 1 Chron. 27:24; Ps. 106:29
17:4 *e*Ex. 25:22
17:5 *f*ch. 16:5 *g*ch. 16:11

40 *To be* a memorial unto the children of Israel, [x]that no stranger, which *is* not of the seed of Aaron, come near to offer incense before the LORD; that he be not as Korah, and as his company: as the LORD said to him by the hand of Moses.

41 ¶ But on the morrow [y]all the congregation of the children of Israel murmured against Moses and against Aaron, saying, Ye have killed the people of the LORD.

42 And it came to pass, when the congregation was gathered against Moses and against Aaron, that they looked toward the tabernacle of the congregation: and, behold, [z]the cloud covered it, and [a]the glory of the LORD appeared.

43 And Moses and Aaron came before the tabernacle of the congregation.

44 ¶ And the LORD spake unto Moses, saying,

45 [b]Get you up from among this congregation, that I may consume them as in a moment. And [c]they fell upon their faces.

46 ¶ And Moses said unto Aaron, Take a censer, and put fire therein from off the altar, and put on incense, and go quickly unto the congregation, and make an atonement for them: [d]for there is wrath gone out from the LORD; the plague is begun.

47 And Aaron took as Moses commanded, and ran into the midst of the congregation; and, behold, the plague was begun among the people: and he put on incense, and made an atonement for the people.

48 And he stood between the dead and the living; and the plague was stayed.

49 Now they that died in the plague were fourteen thousand and seven hundred, besides them that died about the matter of Korah.

50 And Aaron returned unto Moses unto the door of the tabernacle of the congregation: and the plague was stayed.

17 And the LORD spake unto Moses, saying,

2 Speak unto the children of Israel, and take of every one of them a rod according to the house of *their* fathers, of all their princes according to the house of their fathers twelve rods: write thou every man's name upon his rod.

3 And thou shalt write Aaron's name upon the rod of Levi: for one rod *shall be* for the head of the house of their fathers.

4 And thou shalt lay them up in the tabernacle of the congregation before the testimony, [e]where I will meet with you.

5 And it shall come to pass, *that* the man's rod, [f]whom I shall choose, shall blossom: and I will make to cease from me the murmurings of the children of Israel, [g]whereby they murmur against you.

6 ¶ And Moses spake unto the children of Israel, and every one of their princes gave him a rod apiece, for each prince one, according to their fathers' houses, *even* twelve

rods: and the rod of Aaron *was* among their rods.

7 And Moses laid up the rods before the LORD in [h]the tabernacle of witness.

8 And it came to pass, that on the morrow Moses went into the tabernacle of witness; and, behold, the rod of Aaron for the house of Levi was budded, and brought forth buds, and bloomed blossoms, and yielded almonds.

9 And Moses brought out all the rods from before the LORD unto all the children of Israel: and they looked, and took every man his rod.

10 ¶ And the LORD said unto Moses, Bring [i]Aaron's rod again before the testimony, to be kept [j]for a token against the rebels; [k]and thou shalt quite take away their murmurings from me, that they die not.

11 And Moses did *so:* as the LORD commanded him, so did he.

12 And the children of Israel spake unto Moses, saying, Behold, we die, we perish, we all perish.

13 [l]Whosoever cometh any thing near unto the tabernacle of the LORD shall die: shall we be consumed with dying?

18 And the LORD said unto Aaron, [m]Thou and thy sons and thy father's house with thee shall [n]bear the iniquity of the sanctuary: and thou and thy sons with thee shall bear the iniquity of your priesthood.

2 And thy brethren also of the tribe of Levi, the tribe of thy father, bring thou with thee, that they may be [o]joined unto thee, and [p]minister unto thee: but [q]thou and thy sons with thee *shall minister* before the tabernacle of witness.

3 And they shall keep thy charge, and [r]the charge of all the tabernacle: [s]only they shall not come nigh the vessels of the sanctuary and the altar, [t]that neither they, nor ye also, die.

4 And they shall be joined unto thee, and keep the charge of the tabernacle of the congregation, for all the service of the tabernacle: [u]and a stranger shall not come nigh unto you.

5 And ye shall keep [v]the charge of the sanctuary, and the charge of the altar: [w]that there be no wrath any more upon the children of Israel.

6 And I, behold, I have [x]taken your brethren the Levites from among the children of Israel: [y]to you *they are* given *as* a gift for the LORD, to do the service of the tabernacle of the congregation.

7 Therefore [z]thou and thy sons with thee shall keep your priest's office for every thing of the altar, and [a]within the vail; and ye shall serve: I have given your priest's office *unto you as* a service of gift: and the stranger that cometh nigh shall be put to death.

8 ¶ And the LORD spake unto Aaron, Behold, [b]I also have given thee the charge of mine heave offerings of all the hallowed things of the children of Israel; unto thee have I given them [c]by reason of the anointing, and to thy sons, by an ordinance for ever.

9 This shall be thine of the most holy things, *reserved* from the fire: every oblation of theirs, every [d]meat offering of theirs, and every [e]sin offering of theirs, and every [f]trespass offering of theirs, which they shall render unto me, *shall be* most holy for thee and for thy sons.

10 [g]In the most holy *place* shalt thou eat it; every male shall eat it: it shall be holy unto thee.

11 And this *is* thine; [h]the heave offering of their gift, with all the wave offerings of the children of Israel: I have given them unto [i]thee, and to thy sons and to thy daughters with thee, by a statute for ever: [j]every one that is clean in thy house shall eat of it.

12 [k]All the best of the oil, and all the best of the wine, and of the wheat, [l]the firstfruits of them which they shall offer unto the LORD, them have I given thee.

13 *And* whatsoever is first ripe in the land, [m]which they shall bring unto the LORD, shall be thine; [n]every one that is clean in thine house shall eat *of* it.

14 [o]Every thing devoted in Israel shall be thine.

15 Every thing that openeth [p]the matrix in all flesh, which they bring unto the LORD, *whether it be* of men or beasts, shall be thine: nevertheless [q]the firstborn of man shalt thou surely redeem, and the firstling of unclean beasts shalt thou redeem.

16 And those that are to be redeemed from a month old shalt thou redeem, [r]according to thine estimation, for the money of five shekels, after the shekel of the sanctuary, [s]which *is* twenty gerahs.

17 [t]But the firstling of a cow, or the firstling of a sheep, or the firstling of a goat, thou shalt not redeem; they *are* holy: [u]thou shalt sprinkle their blood upon the altar, and shalt burn their fat *for* an offering made by fire, for a sweet savour unto the LORD.

18 And the flesh of them shall be thine, as the [v]wave breast and as the right shoulder are thine.

19 [w]All the heave offerings of the holy things, which the children of Israel offer unto the LORD, have I given thee, and thy sons and thy daughters with thee, by a statute for ever: [x]it *is* a covenant of salt for ever before the LORD unto thee and to thy seed with thee.

20 ¶ And the LORD spake unto Aaron, Thou shalt have no inheritance in their land, neither shalt thou have any part among them: [y]I *am* thy part and thine inheritance among the children of Israel.

21 And, behold, [z]I have given the children of Levi all the tenth in Israel for an inheritance, for their service which they serve, *even* [a]the service of the tabernacle of the congregation.

17:7 [h]Ex. 38:21; Num. 18:2; Acts 7:44
17:10 [i]Heb. 9:4 [j]ch. 16:38 [k]ver. 5
17:13 [l]ch. 1:51
18:1 [m]ch. 17:13 [n]Ex. 28:38
18:2 [o]Gen. 29:34 [p]ch. 3:6 [q]ch. 3:10
18:3 [r]ch. 3:25 [s]ch. 16:40 [t]ch. 4:15
18:4 [u]ch. 3:10
18:5 [v]Ex. 27:21; Lev. 24:3; ch. 8:2 [w]ch. 16:46
18:6 [x]ch. 3:12 [y]ch. 3:9
18:7 [z]ver. 5; ch. 3:10 [a]Heb. 9:3
18:8 [b]Lev. 6:16; ch. 5:9 [c]Ex. 29:29
18:9 [d]Lev. 2:2 [e]Lev. 4:22 [f]Lev. 5:1
18:10 [g]Lev. 6:16
18:11 [h]Ex. 29:27; Lev. 7:30 [i]Lev. 10:14; Deut. 18:3 [j]Lev. 22:2
18:12 [k]Ex. 23:19; Deut. 18:4; Neh. 10:35 [l]Ex. 22:29
18:13 [m]Ex. 22:29; Lev. 2:14; ch. 15:19; Deut. 26:2 [n]ver. 11
18:14 [o]Lev. 27:28
18:15 [p]Ex. 13:2; Lev. 27:26; ch. 3:13 [q]Ex. 13:13
18:16 [r]Lev. 27:2; ch. 3:47 [s]Ex. 30:13; Lev. 27:25; ch. 3:47; Ezek. 45:12
18:17 [t]Deut. 15:19 [u]Lev. 3:2
18:18 [v]Ex. 29:26; Lev. 7:31
18:19 [w]ver. 11 [x]Lev. 2:13; 2 Chron. 13:5
18:20 [y]Deut. 10:9; Josh. 13:14; Ps. 16:5; Ezek. 44:28
18:21 [z]ver. 24; Lev. 27:30; Neh. 10:37; Heb. 7:5 [a]ch. 3:7

22 [b]Neither must the children of Israel henceforth come nigh the tabernacle of the congregation, [c]lest they bear sin, and die.

23 [d]But the Levites shall do the service of the tabernacle of the congregation, and they shall bear their iniquity: *it shall be* a statute for ever throughout your generations, that among the children of Israel they have no inheritance.

24 [e]But the tithes of the children of Israel, which they offer *as* an heave offering unto the LORD, I have given to the Levites to inherit: therefore I have said unto them, [f]Among the children of Israel they shall have no inheritance.

25 ¶ And the LORD spake unto Moses, saying,

26 Thus speak unto the Levites, and say unto them, When ye take of the children of Israel the tithes which I have given you from them for your inheritance, then ye shall offer up an heave offering of it for the LORD, *even* [g]a tenth *part* of the tithe.

27 [h]And *this* your heave offering shall be reckoned unto you, as though *it were* the corn of the threshingfloor, and as the fulness of the winepress.

28 Thus ye also shall offer an heave offering unto the LORD of all your tithes, which ye receive of the children of Israel; and ye shall give thereof the LORD's heave offering to Aaron the priest.

29 Out of all your gifts ye shall offer every heave offering of the LORD, of all the best thereof, *even* the hallowed part thereof out of it.

30 Therefore thou shalt say unto them, When ye have heaved the best thereof from it, [i]then it shall be counted unto the Levites as the increase of the threshingfloor, and as the increase of the winepress.

31 And ye shall eat it in every place, ye and your households: for it *is* [j]your reward for your service in the tabernacle of the congregation.

32 And ye shall [k]bear no sin by reason of it, when ye have heaved from it the best of it: neither shall ye [l]pollute the holy things of the children of Israel, lest ye die.

19 And the LORD spake unto Moses and unto Aaron, saying,

2 This *is* the ordinance of the law which the LORD hath commanded, saying, Speak unto the children of Israel, that they bring thee a red heifer without spot, wherein *is* no blemish, [m]*and* upon which never came yoke:

3 And ye shall give her unto Eleazar the priest, that he may bring her [n]forth without the camp, and *one* shall slay her before his face:

4 And Eleazar the priest shall take of her blood with his finger, and [o]sprinkle of her blood directly before the tabernacle of the congregation seven times:

5 And *one* shall burn the heifer in his sight; [p]her skin, and her flesh, and her blood, with her dung, shall he burn:

18:22 [b]ch. 1:51 [c]Lev. 22:9
18:23 [d]ch. 3:7
18:24 [e]ver. 21 [f]ver. 20; Deut. 10:9
18:26 [g]Neh. 10:38
18:27 [h]ver. 30
18:30 [i]ver. 27
18:31 [j]Matt. 10:10; Luke 10:7; 1 Cor. 9:13; 1 Tim. 5:18
18:32 [k]Lev. 19:8 [l]Lev. 22:2
19:2 [m]Deut. 21:3; 1 Sam. 6:7
19:3 [n]Lev. 4:12; Heb. 13:11
19:4 [o]Lev. 4:6; Heb. 9:13
19:5 [p]Ex. 29:14; Lev. 4:11
19:6 [q]Lev. 14:4
19:7 [r]Lev. 11:25
19:9 [s]Heb. 9:13 [t]ver. 13; ch. 31:23
19:11 [u]ver. 16; Lev. 21:1; ch. 5:2; Lam. 4:14; Hag. 2:13
19:12 [v]ch. 31:19
19:13 [w]Lev. 15:31 [x]ver. 9; ch. 8:7 [y]Lev. 7:20
19:15 [z]Lev. 11:32; ch. 31:20
19:16 [a]ver. 11
19:17 [b]ver. 9
19:18 [c]Ps. 51:7
19:19 [d]Lev. 14:9
19:20 ever. 13

6 And the priest shall take [q]cedar wood, and hyssop, and scarlet, and cast *it* into the midst of the burning of the heifer.

7 [r]Then the priest shall wash his clothes, and he shall bathe his flesh in water, and afterward he shall come into the camp, and the priest shall be unclean until the even.

8 And he that burneth her shall wash his clothes in water, and bathe his flesh in water, and shall be unclean until the even.

9 And a man *that is* clean shall gather up [s]the ashes of the heifer, and lay *them* up without the camp in a clean place, and it shall be kept for the congregation of the children of Israel [t]for a water of separation: it *is* a purification for sin.

10 And he that gathereth the ashes of the heifer shall wash his clothes, and be unclean until the even: and it shall be unto the children of Israel, and unto the stranger that sojourneth among them, for a statute for ever.

11 ¶ [u]He that toucheth the dead body of any man shall be unclean seven days.

12 [v]He shall purify himself with it on the third day, and on the seventh day he shall be clean: but if he purify not himself the third day, then the seventh day he shall not be clean.

13 Whosoever toucheth the dead body of any man that is dead, and purifieth not himself, [w]defileth the tabernacle of the LORD; and that soul shall be cut off from Israel: because [x]the water of separation was not sprinkled upon him, he shall be unclean; [y]his uncleanness *is* yet upon him.

14 This *is* the law, when a man dieth in a tent: all that come into the tent, and all that *is* in the tent, shall be unclean seven days.

15 And every [z]open vessel, which hath no covering bound upon it, *is* unclean.

16 And [a]whosoever toucheth one that is slain with a sword in the open fields, or a dead body, or a bone of a man, or a grave, shall be unclean seven days.

17 And for an unclean *person* they shall take of the [b]ashes of the burnt heifer of purification for sin, and running water shall be put thereto in a vessel:

18 And a clean person shall take [c]hyssop, and dip *it* in the water, and sprinkle *it* upon the tent, and upon all the vessels, and upon the persons that were there, and upon him that touched a bone, or one slain, or one dead, or a grave:

19 And the clean *person* shall sprinkle upon the unclean on the third day, and on the seventh day: [d]and on the seventh day he shall purify himself, and wash his clothes, and bathe himself in water, and shall be clean at even.

20 But the man that shall be unclean, and shall not purify himself, that soul shall be cut off from among the congregation, because he hath [e]defiled the sanctuary of the LORD: the water of separation hath not been sprinkled upon him; he *is* unclean.

21 And it shall be a perpetual statute unto

them, that he that sprinkleth the water of separation shall wash his clothes; and he that toucheth the water of separation shall be unclean until even.

22 And [f]whatsoever the unclean *person* toucheth shall be unclean; and [g]the soul that toucheth *it* shall be unclean until even.

20 Then [h]came the children of Israel, *even* the whole congregation, into the desert of Zin in the first month: and the people abode in Kadesh; and [i]Miriam died there, and was buried there.

2 [j]And there was no water for the congregation: [k]and they gathered themselves together against Moses and against Aaron.

3 And the people [l]chode with Moses, and spake, saying, Would God that we had died [m]when our brethren died before the LORD!

4 And [n]why have ye brought up the congregation of the LORD into this wilderness, that we and our cattle should die there?

5 And wherefore have ye made us to come up out of Egypt, to bring us in unto this evil place? it *is* no place of seed, or of figs, or of vines, or of pomegranates; neither *is* there any water to drink.

6 And Moses and Aaron went from the presence of the assembly unto the door of the tabernacle of the congregation, and [o]they fell upon their faces: and [p]the glory of the LORD appeared unto them.

7 ¶ And the LORD spake unto Moses, saying,

8 [q]Take the rod, and gather thou the assembly together, thou, and Aaron thy brother, and speak ye unto the rock before their eyes; and it shall give forth his water, and [r]thou shalt bring forth to them water out of the rock: so thou shalt give the congregation and their beasts drink.

9 And Moses took the rod [s]from before the LORD, as he commanded him.

10 And Moses and Aaron gathered the congregation together before the rock, and he said unto them, [t]Hear now, ye rebels; must we fetch you water out of this rock?

11 And Moses lifted up his hand, and with his rod he smote the rock twice: and [u]the water came out abundantly, and the congregation drank, and their beasts *also*.

12 ¶ And the LORD spake unto Moses and Aaron, Because [v]ye believed me not, to [w]sanctify me in the eyes of the children of Israel, therefore ye shall not bring this congregation into the land which I have given them.

13 [x]This *is* the water of Meribah; because the children of Israel strove with the LORD, and he was sanctified in them.

14 ¶ [y]And Moses sent messengers from Kadesh unto the king of Edom, [z]Thus saith thy brother Israel, Thou knowest all the travail that hath befallen us:

15 [a]How our fathers went down into Egypt, [b]and we have dwelt in Egypt a long time; [c]and the Egyptians vexed us, and our fathers:

16 And [d]when we cried unto the LORD, he heard our voice, and [e]sent an angel, and hath brought us forth out of Egypt: and, behold, we *are* in Kadesh, a city in the uttermost of thy border:

17 [f]Let us pass, I pray thee, through thy country: we will not pass through the fields, or through the vineyards, neither will we drink *of* the water of the wells: we will go by the king's *high* way, we will not turn to the right hand nor to the left, until we have passed thy borders.

18 And Edom said unto him, Thou shalt not pass by me, lest I come out against thee with the sword.

19 And the children of Israel said unto him, We will go by the high way: and if I and my cattle drink of thy water, [g]then I will pay for it: I will only, without *doing* any thing *else*, go through on my feet.

20 And he said, [h]Thou shalt not go through. And Edom came out against him with much people, and with a strong hand.

21 Thus Edom [i]refused to give Israel passage through his border: wherefore Israel [j]turned away from him.

22 ¶ And the children of Israel, *even* the whole congregation, journeyed from [k]Kadesh, [l]and came unto mount Hor.

23 And the LORD spake unto Moses and Aaron in mount Hor, by the coast of the land of Edom, saying,

24 Aaron shall be [m]gathered unto his people: for he shall not enter into the land which I have given unto the children of Israel, because [n]ye rebelled against my word at the water of Meribah.

25 [o]Take Aaron and Eleazar his son, and bring them up unto mount Hor:

26 And strip Aaron of his garments, and put them upon Eleazar his son: and Aaron shall be gathered *unto his people*, and shall die there.

27 And Moses did as the LORD commanded: and they went up into mount Hor in the sight of all the congregation.

28 [p]And Moses stripped Aaron of his garments, and put them upon Eleazar his son; and [q]Aaron died there in the top of the mount: and Moses and Eleazar came down from the mount.

29 And when all the congregation saw that Aaron was dead, they mourned for Aaron [r]thirty days, *even* all the house of Israel.

21 And *when* [s]king Arad the Canaanite, which dwelt in the south, heard tell that Israel came [t]by the way of the spies; then he fought against Israel, and took *some* of them prisoners.

2 [u]And Israel vowed a vow unto the LORD, and said, If thou wilt indeed deliver this people into my hand, then [v]I will utterly destroy their cities.

3 And the LORD hearkened to the voice of Israel, and delivered up the Canaanites; and they utterly destroyed them and their cities: and he called the name of the place Hormah.

19:22 [f]Hag. 2:13 [g]Lev. 15:5
20:1 [h]ch. 33:36 [i]Ex. 15:20; ch. 26:59
20:2 [j]Ex. 17:1 [k]ch. 16:19
20:3 [l]Ex. 17:2; ch. 14:2 [m]ch. 11:1
20:4 [n]Ex. 17:3
20:6 [o]ch. 14:5 [p]ch. 14:10
20:8 [q]Ex. 17:5 [r]Neh. 9:15; Ps. 78:15; Isa. 43:20
20:9 [s]ch. 17:10
20:10 [t]Ps. 106:33
20:11 [u]Ex. 17:6; Deut. 8:15; 1 Cor. 10:4
20:12 [v]ch. 27:14; Deut. 1:37 [w]Lev. 10:3; Ezek. 20:41; 1 Pet. 3:15
20:13 [x]Deut. 33:8; Ps. 95:8
20:14 [y]Judg. 11:16 [z]Deut. 2:4; Obad. 10:12
20:15 [a]Gen. 46:6; Acts 7:15 [b]Ex. 12:40 [c]Ex. 1:11; Deut. 26:6; Acts 7:19
20:16 [d]Ex. 2:23 [e]Ex. 3:2
20:17 [f]ch. 21:22; Deut. 2:27
20:19 [g]Deut. 2:6
20:20 [h]Judg. 11:17
20:21 [i]Deut. 2:27 [j]Deut. 2:4; Judg. 11:18
20:22 [k]ch. 33:37 [l]ch. 21:4
20:24 [m]Gen. 25:8; ch. 27:13; Deut. 32:50 [n]ver. 12
20:25 [o]ch. 33:38; Deut. 32:50
20:28 [p]Ex. 29:29 [q]ch. 33:38; Deut. 10:6
20:29 [r]Deut. 34:38
21:1 [s]ch. 33:40; Judg. 1:16 [t]ch. 13:21
21:2 [u]Gen. 28:20; Judg. 11:30 [v]Lev. 27:28

4 ¶ And [w]they journeyed from mount Hor by the way of the Red sea, to [x]compass the land of Edom: and the soul of the people was much discouraged because of the way.

5 And the people [y]spake against God, and against Moses, [z]Wherefore have ye brought us up out of Egypt to die in the wilderness? for *there is* no bread, neither *is there any* water; and [a]our soul loatheth this light bread.

6 And [b]the LORD sent [c]fiery serpents among the people, and they bit the people; and much people of Israel died.

7 ¶ [d]Therefore the people came to Moses, and said, We have sinned, for [e]we have spoken against the LORD, and against thee; [f]pray unto the LORD, that he take away the serpents from us. And Moses prayed for the people.

8 And the LORD said unto Moses, Make thee a fiery serpent, and set it upon a pole: and it shall come to pass, that every one that is bitten, when he looketh upon it, shall live.

9 And [g]Moses made a serpent of brass, and put it upon a pole, and it came to pass, that if a serpent had bitten any man, when he beheld the serpent of brass, he lived.

10 ¶ And the children of Israel set forward, and [h]pitched in Oboth.

11 And they journeyed from Oboth, and [i]pitched at Ije-abarim, in the wilderness which *is* before Moab, toward the sunrising.

12 ¶ [j]From thence they removed, and pitched in the valley of Zared.

13 From thence they removed, and pitched on the other side of Arnon, which *is* in the wilderness that cometh out of the coasts of the Amorites: for [k]Arnon *is* the border of Moab, between Moab and the Amorites.

14 Wherefore it is said in the book of the wars of the LORD, What he did in the Red sea, and in the brooks of Arnon,

15 And at the stream of the brooks that goeth down to the dwelling of Ar, [l]and lieth upon the border of Moab.

16 And from thence *they went* [m]to Beer: that *is* the well whereof the LORD spake unto Moses, Gather the people together, and I will give them water.

17 ¶ [n]Then Israel sang this song, Spring up, O well; sing ye unto it:

18 The princes digged the well, the nobles of the people digged it, by *the direction of* [o]the lawgiver, with their staves. And from the wilderness *they went* to Mattanah:

19 And from Mattanah to Nahaliel: and from Nahaliel to Bamoth:

20 And from Bamoth *in* the valley, that *is* in the country of Moab, to the top of Pisgah, which looketh [p]toward Jeshimon.

21 ¶ And [q]Israel sent messengers unto Sihon king of the Amorites, saying,

22 [r]Let me pass through thy land: we will not turn into the fields, or into the vineyards; we will not drink *of* the waters of the well: *but* we will go along by the king's *high* way, until we be past thy borders.

23 [s]And Sihon would not suffer Israel to pass through his border: but Sihon gathered all his people together, and went out against Israel into the wilderness: [t]and he came to Jahaz, and fought against Israel.

24 And [u]Israel smote him with the edge of the sword, and possessed his land from Arnon unto Jabbok, even unto the children of Ammon: for the border of the children of Ammon *was* strong.

25 And Israel took all these cities: and Israel dwelt in all the cities of the Amorites, in Heshbon, and in all the villages thereof.

26 For Heshbon *was* the city of Sihon the king of the Amorites, who had fought against the former king of Moab, and taken all his land out of his hand, even unto Arnon.

27 Wherefore they that speak in proverbs say, Come into Heshbon, let the city of Sihon be built and prepared:

28 For there is [v]a fire gone out of Heshbon, a flame from the city of Sihon: it hath consumed [w]Ar of Moab, *and* the lords of the high places of Arnon.

29 Woe to thee, Moab! thou art undone, O people of [x]Chemosh: he hath given his sons that escaped, and his daughters, into captivity unto Sihon king of the Amorites.

30 We have shot at them; Heshbon is perished even [y]unto Dibon, and we have laid them waste even unto Nophah, which *reacheth* unto [z]Medeba.

31 ¶ Thus Israel dwelt in the land of the Amorites.

32 And Moses sent to spy out [a]Jaazer, and they took the villages thereof, and drove out the Amorites that *were* there.

33 ¶ [b]And they turned and went up by the way of Bashan: and Og the king of Bashan went out against them, he, and all his people, to the battle [c]at Edrei.

34 And the LORD said unto Moses, [d]Fear him not: for I have delivered him into thy hand, and all his people, and his land; and [e]thou shalt do to him as thou didst unto Sihon king of the Amorites, which dwelt at Heshbon.

35 [f]So they smote him, and his sons, and all his people, until there was none left him alive: and they possessed his land.

22 And [g]the children of Israel set forward, and pitched in the plains of Moab on this side Jordan *by* Jericho.

2 ¶ And [h]Balak the son of Zippor saw all that Israel had done to the Amorites.

3 And [i]Moab was sore afraid of the people, because they *were* many: and Moab was distressed because of the children of Israel.

4 And Moab said unto [j]the elders of Midian, Now shall this company lick up all *that are* round about us, as the ox licketh up the grass of the field. And Balak the son of Zippor *was* king of the Moabites at that time.

5 [k]He sent messengers therefore unto Balaam the son of Beor to [l]Pethor, which *is* by the river of the land of the children of his

21:4 [w]ch. 20:22 [x]Judg. 11:18
21:5 [y]Ps. 78:19 [z]Ex. 16:3 [a]ch. 11:6
21:6 [b]1 Cor. 10:9 [c]Deut. 8:15
21:7 [d]Ps. 78:34 [e]ver. 5 [f]Ex. 8:8; 1 Sam. 12:19; 1 Kings 13:6; Acts 8:24
21:9 [g]2 Kings 18:4; John 3:14
21:10 [h]ch. 33:43
21:11 [i]ch. 33:44
21:12 [j]Deut. 2:13
21:13 [k]ch. 22:36; Judg. 11:18
21:15 [l]Deut. 2:18
21:16 [m]Judg. 9:21
21:17 [n]Ex. 15:1; Ps. 105:2
21:18 [o]Isa. 33:22
21:20 [p]ch. 23:28
21:21 [q]Deut. 2:26; Judg. 11:19
21:22 [r]ch. 20:17
21:23 [s]Deut. 29:7 [t]Deut. 2:32; Judg. 11:20
21:24 [u]Deut. 2:33; Josh. 12:1; Neh. 9:22; Ps. 135:10; Am. 2:9
21:28 [v]Jer. 48:45 [w]Deut. 2:9; Isa. 15:1
21:29 [x]Judg. 11:24; 1 Kings 11:7; 2 Kings 23:13; Jer. 48:7
21:30 [y]Jer. 48:18 [z]Isa. 15:2
21:32 [a]ch. 32:1; Jer. 48:32
21:33 [b]Deut. 3:1 [c]Josh. 13:12
21:34 [d]Deut. 3:2 [e]ver. 24; Ps. 135:10
21:35 [f]Deut. 3:3
22:1 [g]ch. 33:48
22:2 [h]Judg. 11:25
22:3 [i]Ex. 15:15
22:4 [j]ch. 31:8; Josh. 13:21
22:5 [k]Deut. 23:4; Josh. 13:22; Neh. 13:1; Mic. 6:5; 2 Pet. 2:15; Jude 11; Rev. 2:14 [l]ch. 23:7; Deut. 23:4

people, to call him, saying, Behold, there is a people come out from Egypt: behold, they cover the face of the earth, and they abide over against me:

6 Come now therefore, I pray thee, [m]curse me this people; for they *are* too mighty for me: peradventure I shall prevail, *that* we may smite them, and *that* I may drive them out of the land: for I wot that he whom thou blessest *is* blessed, and he whom thou cursest is cursed.

7 And the elders of Moab and the elders of Midian departed with [n]the rewards of divination in their hand; and they came unto Balaam, and spake unto him the words of Balak.

8 And he said unto them, [o]Lodge here this night, and I will bring you word again, as the LORD shall speak unto me: and the princes of Moab abode with Balaam.

9 [p]And God came unto Balaam, and said, What men *are* these with thee?

10 And Balaam said unto God, Balak the son of Zippor, king of Moab, hath sent unto me, *saying*,

11 Behold, *there is* a people come out of Egypt, which covereth the face of the earth: come now, curse me them; peradventure I shall be able to overcome them, and drive them out.

12 And God said unto Balaam, Thou shalt not go with them; thou shalt not curse the people: for [q]they *are* blessed.

13 And Balaam rose up in the morning, and said unto the princes of Balak, Get you into your land: for the LORD refuseth to give me leave to go with you.

14 And the princes of Moab rose up, and they went unto Balak, and said, Balaam refuseth to come with us.

15 ¶ And Balak sent yet again princes, more, and more honourable than they.

16 And they came to Balaam, and said to him, Thus saith Balak the son of Zippor, Let nothing, I pray thee, hinder thee from coming unto me:

17 For I will promote thee unto very great honour, and I will do whatsoever thou sayest unto me: [r]come therefore, I pray thee, curse me this people.

18 And Balaam answered and said unto the servants of Balak, [s]If Balak would give me his house full of silver and gold, [t]I cannot go beyond the word of the LORD my God, to do less or more.

19 Now therefore, I pray you, [u]tarry ye also here this night, that I may know what the LORD will say unto me more.

20 [v]And God came unto Balaam at night, and said unto him, If the men come to call thee, rise up, *and* go with them; but [w]yet the word which I shall say unto thee, that shalt thou do.

21 And Balaam rose up in the morning, and saddled his ass, and went with the princes of Moab.

22 ¶ And God's anger was kindled because he went: [x]and the angel of the LORD stood in the way for an adversary against him. Now he was riding upon his ass, and his two servants *were* with him.

23 And [y]the ass saw the angel of the LORD standing in the way, and his sword drawn in his hand: and the ass turned aside out of the way, and went into the field: and Balaam smote the ass, to turn her into the way.

24 But the angel of the LORD stood in a path of the vineyards, a wall *being* on this side, and a wall on that side.

25 And when the ass saw the angel of the LORD, she thrust herself unto the wall, and crushed Balaam's foot against the wall: and he smote her again.

26 And the angel of the LORD went further, and stood in a narrow place, where *was* no way to turn either to the right hand or to the left.

27 And when the ass saw the angel of the LORD, she fell down under Balaam: and Balaam's anger was kindled, and he smote the ass with a staff.

28 And the LORD [z]opened the mouth of the ass, and she said unto Balaam, What have I done unto thee, that thou hast smitten me these three times?

29 And Balaam said unto the ass, Because thou hast mocked me: I would there were a sword in mine hand, [a]for now would I kill thee.

30 [b]And the ass said unto Balaam, *Am* not I thine ass, upon which thou hast ridden ever since *I was* thine unto this day? was I ever wont to do so unto thee? And he said, Nay.

31 Then the LORD [c]opened the eyes of Balaam, and he saw the angel of the LORD standing in the way, and his sword drawn in his hand: and he [d]bowed down his head, and fell flat on his face.

32 And the angel of the LORD said unto him, Wherefore hast thou smitten thine ass these three times? behold, I went out to withstand thee, because *thy* way is [e]perverse before me:

33 And the ass saw me, and turned from me these three times: unless she had turned from me, surely now also I had slain thee, and saved her alive.

34 And Balaam said unto the angel of the LORD, [f]I have sinned; for I knew not that thou stoodest in the way against me: now therefore, if it displease thee, I will get me back again.

35 And the angel of the LORD said unto Balaam, Go with the men: [g]but only the word that I shall speak unto thee, that thou shalt speak. So Balaam went with the princes of Balak.

36 ¶ And when Balak heard that Balaam was come, [h]he went out to meet him unto a city of Moab, [i]which *is* in the border of Arnon, which *is* in the utmost coast.

37 And Balak said unto Balaam, Did I not earnestly send unto thee to call thee? wherefore camest thou not unto me? am I

22:6 [m]ch. 23:7
22:7 [n]1 Sam. 9:7
22:8 [o]ver. 19
22:9 [p]Gen. 20:3; ver. 20
22:12 [q]ch. 23:20; Rom. 11:29
22:17 [r]ver. 6
22:18 [s]ch. 24:13 [t]1 Kings 22:14; 2 Chron. 18:13
22:19 [u]ver. 8
22:20 [v]ver. 9 [w]ver. 35; ch. 23:12
22:22 [x]Ex. 4:24
22:23 [y]2 Kings 6:17; Dan. 10:7; Acts 22:9; 2 Pet. 2:16; Jude 11
22:28 [z]2 Pet. 2:16
22:29 [a]Prov. 12:10
22:30 [b]2 Pet. 2:16
22:31 [c]Gen. 21:19; 2 Kings 6:17; Luke 24:16 [d]Ex. 34:8
22:32 [e]2 Pet. 2:14
22:34 [f]1 Sam. 15:24; 2 Sam. 12:13; Job 34:31
22:35 [g]ver. 20
22:36 [h]Gen. 14:17 [i]ch. 21:13

not able indeed [j]to promote thee to honour?

38 And Balaam said unto Balak, Lo, I am come unto thee: have I now any power at all to say any thing? [k]the word that God putteth in my mouth, that shall I speak.

39 And Balaam went with Balak, and they came unto Kirjath-huzoth.

40 And Balak offered oxen and sheep, and sent to Balaam, and to the princes that *were* with him.

41 And it came to pass on the morrow, that Balak took Balaam, and brought him up into the [l]high places of Baal, that thence he might see the utmost *part* of the people.

23 And Balaam said unto Balak, [m]Build me here seven altars, and prepare me here seven oxen and seven rams.

2 And Balak did as Balaam had spoken; and Balak and Balaam [n]offered on *every* altar a bullock and a ram.

3 And Balaam said unto Balak, [o]Stand by thy burnt offering, and I will go: peradventure the LORD will come [p]to meet me: and whatsoever he sheweth me I will tell thee. And he went to an high place.

4 [q]And God met Balaam: and he said unto him, I have prepared seven altars, and I have offered upon *every* altar a bullock and a ram.

5 And the LORD [r]put a word in Balaam's mouth, and said, Return unto Balak, and thus thou shalt speak.

6 And he returned unto him, and, lo, he stood by his burnt sacrifice, he, and all the princes of Moab.

7 And he [s]took up his parable, and said, Balak the king of Moab hath brought me from Aram, out of the mountains of the east, *saying*, [t]Come, curse me Jacob, and come, [u]defy Israel.

8 [v]How shall I curse, whom God hath not cursed? or how shall I defy, *whom* the LORD hath not defied?

9 For from the top of the rocks I see him, and from the hills I behold him: lo, [w]the people shall dwell alone, and [x]shall not be reckoned among the nations.

10 [y]Who can count the dust of Jacob, and the number of the fourth *part* of Israel? Let me die [z]the death of the righteous, and let my last end be like his!

11 And Balak said unto Balaam, What hast thou done unto me? [a]I took thee to curse mine enemies, and, behold, thou hast blessed *them* altogether.

12 And he answered and said, [b]Must I not take heed to speak that which the LORD hath put in my mouth?

13 And Balak said unto him, Come, I pray thee, with me unto another place, from whence thou mayest see them: thou shalt see but the utmost part of them, and shalt not see them all: and curse me them from thence.

14 ¶ And he brought him into the field of Zophim, to the top of Pisgah, [c]and built seven altars, and offered a bullock and a ram on *every* altar.

15 And he said unto Balak, Stand here by thy burnt offering, while I meet *the* LORD yonder.

16 And the LORD met Balaam, and [d]put a word in his mouth, and said, Go again unto Balak, and say thus.

17 And when he came to him, behold, he stood by his burnt offering, and the princes of Moab with him. And Balak said unto him, What hath the LORD spoken?

18 And he took up his parable, and said, [e]Rise up, Balak, and hear; hearken unto me, thou son of Zippor:

19 [f]God *is* not a man, that he should lie; neither the son of man, that he should repent: hath he said, and shall he not do *it?* or hath he spoken, and shall he not make it good?

20 Behold, I have received *commandment* to bless: and [g]he hath blessed; and I cannot reverse it.

21 [h]He hath not beheld iniquity in Jacob, neither hath he seen perverseness in Israel: [i]the LORD his God *is* with him, [j]and the shout of a king *is* among them.

22 [k]God brought them out of Egypt; he hath as it were [l]the strength of an unicorn.

23 Surely *there is* no enchantment against Jacob, neither *is there* any divination against Israel: according to this time it shall be said of Jacob and of Israel, [m]What hath God wrought!

24 Behold, the people shall rise up [n]as a great lion, and lift up himself as a young lion: [o]he shall not lie down until he eat *of* the prey, and drink the blood of the slain.

25 ¶ And Balak said unto Balaam, Neither curse them at all, nor bless them at all.

26 But Balaam answered and said unto Balak, Told not I thee, saying, [p]All that the LORD speaketh, that I must do?

27 ¶ And Balak said unto Balaam, [q]Come, I pray thee, I will bring thee unto another place; peradventure it will please God that thou mayest curse me them from thence.

28 And Balak brought Balaam unto the top of Peor, that looketh [r]toward Jeshimon.

29 And Balaam said unto Balak, [s]Build me here seven altars, and prepare me here seven bullocks and seven rams.

30 And Balak did as Balaam had said, and offered a bullock and a ram on *every* altar.

24 And when Balaam saw that it pleased the LORD to bless Israel, he went not, as at [t]other times, to seek for enchantments, but he set his face toward the wilderness.

2 And Balaam lifted up his eyes, and he saw Israel [u]abiding *in his tents* according to their tribes; and [v]the spirit of God came upon him.

3 [w]And he took up his parable, and said, Balaam the son of Beor hath said, and the man whose eyes are open hath said:

4 He hath said, which heard the words of

22:37 [j]ver. 17; ch. 24:11
22:38 [k]ch. 23:26; 1 Kings 22:14; 2 Chron. 18:13
22:41 [l]Deut. 12:2
23:1 [m]ver. 29
23:2 [n]ver. 14:30
23:3 [o]ver. 15 [p]ch. 24:1
23:4 [q]ver. 16
23:5 [r]ver. 16; ch. 22:35; Deut. 18:18; Jer. 1:9
23:7 [s]ver. 18; ch. 24:3; Job 27:1; Ps. 78:2; Ezek. 17:2; Mic. 2:4; Hab. 2:6 [t]ch. 22:6 [u]1 Sam. 17:10
23:8 [v]Isa. 47:12
23:9 [w]Deut. 33:28 [x]Ex. 33:16; Ezra 9:2; Eph. 2:14
23:10 [y]Gen. 13:16 [z]Ps. 116:15
23:11 [a]ch. 22:11
23:12 [b]ch. 22:38
23:14 [c]ver. 1
23:16 [d]ver. 5; ch. 22:35
23:18 [e]Judg. 3:20
23:19 [f]1 Sam. 15:29; Mal. 3:6; Rom. 11:29; Jam. 1:17; Tit. 1:2
23:20 [g]Gen. 12:2; Num. 22:12
23:21 [h]Rom. 4:7 [i]Ex. 13:21 [j]Ps. 89:15
23:22 [k]ch. 24:8 [l]Deut. 33:17; Job 39:10
23:23 [m]Ps. 31:19
23:24 [n]Gen. 49:9 [o]Gen. 49:27
23:26 [p]ver. 12; ch. 22:38; 1 Kings 22:14
23:27 [q]ver. 13
23:28 [r]ch. 21:20
23:29 [s]ver. 1
24:1 [t]ch. 23:3
24:2 [u]ch. 2:2 [v]ch. 11:25; 1 Sam. 10:10; 2 Chron. 15:1
24:3 [w]ch. 23:7

God, which saw the vision of the Almighty, [x]falling *into a trance,* but having his eyes open:

5 How goodly are thy tents, O Jacob, *and* thy tabernacles, O Israel!

6 As the valleys are they spread forth, as gardens by the river's side, [y]as the trees of lign aloes [z]which the LORD hath planted, *and* as cedar trees beside the waters.

7 He shall pour the water out of his buckets, and his seed *shall be* [a]in many waters, and his king shall be higher than [b]Agag, and his [c]kingdom shall be exalted.

8 [d]God brought him forth out of Egypt; he hath as it were the strength of an unicorn: he shall [e]eat up the nations his enemies, and shall [f]break their bones, and [g]pierce *them* through with his arrows.

9 [h]He couched, he lay down as a lion, and as a great lion: who shall stir him up? [i]Blessed *is* he that blesseth thee, and cursed *is* he that curseth thee.

10 ¶ And Balak's anger was kindled against Balaam, and he [j]smote his hands together: and Balak said unto Balaam, [k]I called thee to curse mine enemies, and, behold, thou hast altogether blessed *them* these three times.

11 Therefore now flee thou to thy place: [l]I thought to promote thee unto great honour; but, lo, the LORD hath kept thee back from honour.

12 And Balaam said unto Balak, Spake I not also to thy messengers which thou sentest unto me, saying,

13 [m]If Balak would give me his house full of silver and gold, I cannot go beyond the commandment of the LORD, to do *either* good or bad of mine own mind; *but* what the LORD saith, that will I speak?

14 And now, behold, I go unto my people: come *therefore, and* [n]I will advertise thee what this people shall do to thy people [o]in the latter days.

15 ¶ [p]And he took up his parable, and said, Balaam the son of Beor hath said, and the man whose eyes are open hath said:

16 He hath said, which heard the words of God, and knew the knowledge of the most High, *which* saw the vision of the Almighty, falling *into a trance,* but having his eyes open:

17 [q]I shall see him, but not now: I shall behold him, but not nigh: there shall come [r]a Star out of Jacob, and [s]a Sceptre shall rise out of Israel, and shall smite the corners of Moab, and destroy all the children of Sheth.

18 And [t]Edom shall be a possession, Seir also shall be a possession for his enemies; and Israel shall do valiantly.

19 [u]Out of Jacob shall come he that shall have dominion, and shall destroy him that remaineth of the city.

20 ¶ And when he looked on Amalek, he took up his parable, and said, Amalek *was* the first of the nations; but his latter end *shall be* that he perish for ever.

21 And he looked on the Kenites, and took up his parable, and said, Strong is thy dwellingplace, and thou puttest thy nest in a rock.

22 Nevertheless the Kenite shall be wasted, until Asshur shall carry thee away captive.

23 And he took up his parable, and said, Alas, who shall live when God doeth this!

24 And ships *shall come* from the coast of [v]Chittim, and shall afflict Asshur, and shall afflict [w]Eber, and he also shall perish for ever.

25 And Balaam rose up, and went and [x]returned to his place: and Balak also went his way.

25 And Israel abode in [y]Shittim, and [z]the people began to commit whoredom with the daughters of Moab.

2 And [a]they called the people unto [b]the sacrifices of their gods: and the people did eat, and [c]bowed down to their gods.

3 And Israel joined himself unto Baal-peor: and [d]the anger of the LORD was kindled against Israel.

4 And the LORD said unto Moses, [e]Take all the heads of the people, and hang them up before the LORD against the sun, [f]that the fierce anger of the LORD may be turned away from Israel.

5 And Moses said unto [g]the judges of Israel, [h]Slay ye every one his men that were joined unto Baal-peor.

6 ¶ And, behold, one of the children of Israel came and brought unto his brethren a Midianitish woman in the sight of Moses, and in the sight of all the congregation of the children of Israel, [i]who *were* weeping *before* the door of the tabernacle of the congregation.

7 And [j]when Phinehas, [k]the son of Eleazar, the son of Aaron the priest, saw *it,* he rose up from among the congregation, and took a javelin in his hand;

8 And he went after the man of Israel into the tent, and thrust both of them through, the man of Israel, and the woman through her belly. So [l]the plague was stayed from the children of Israel.

9 And [m]those that died in the plague were twenty and four thousand.

10 ¶ And the LORD spake unto Moses, saying,

11 [n]Phinehas, the son of Eleazar, the son of Aaron the priest, hath turned my wrath away from the children of Israel, while he was zealous for my sake among them, that I consumed not the children of Israel in [o]my jealousy.

12 Wherefore say, [p]Behold, I give unto him my covenant of peace:

13 And he shall have it, and [q]his seed after him, *even* the covenant of [r]an everlasting priesthood; because he was [s]zealous for his God, and [t]made an atonement for the children of Israel.

14 Now the name of the Israelite that was slain, *even* that was slain with the Midiani-

24:4 [x]1 Sam. 19:24; Ezek. 1:28; Dan. 8:18; 2 Cor. 12:2; Rev. 1:10
24:6 [y]Ps. 1:3; Jer. 17:8 [z]Ps. 104:16
24:7 [a]Jer. 51:13; Rev. 17:1 [b]1 Sam. 15:9 [c]2 Sam. 5:12; 1 Chron. 14:2
24:8 [d]ch. 23:22 [e]ch. 14:9 [f]Ps. 2:9; Isa. 38:13; Jer. 50:17 [g]Ps. 45:5; Jer. 50:9
24:9 [h]Gen. 49:9 [i]Gen. 12:3
24:10 [j]Ezek. 21:14 [k]ch. 23:11; Deut. 23:4; Josh. 24:9; Neh. 13:2
24:11 [l]ch. 22:17
24:13 [m]ch. 22:18
24:14 [n]Mic. 6:5; Rev. 2:14 [o]Gen. 49:1; Dan. 2:28
24:15 [p]ver. 3
24:17 [q]Rev. 1:7 [r]Matt. 2:2; Rev. 22:16 [s]Gen. 49:10; Ps. 110:2
24:18 [t]2 Sam. 8:14; Ps. 60:8
24:19 [u]Gen. 49:10
24:24 [v]Gen. 10:4; Dan. 11:30 [w]Gen. 10:21
24:25 [x]ch. 31:8
25:1 [y]ch. 33:49; Josh. 2:1; Mic. 6:5 [z]ch. 31:16; 1 Cor. 10:8
25:2 [a]Josh. 22:17; Ps. 106:28; Hos. 9:10 [b]Ex. 34:15; 1 Cor. 10:20 [c]Ex. 20:5
25:3 [d]Ps. 106:29
25:4 [e]Deut. 4:3; Josh. 22:17 [f]ver. 11; Deut. 13:17
25:5 [g]Ex. 18:21 [h]Ex. 32:27; Deut. 13:6
25:6 [i]Joel 2:17
25:7 [j]Ps. 106:30 [k]Ex. 6:25
25:8 [l]Ps. 106:30
25:9 [m]Deut. 4:3; 1 Cor. 10:8
25:11 [n]Ps. 106:30 [o]Ex. 20:5; Deut. 32:16; 1 Kings 14:22; Ps. 78:58; Ezek. 16:38; Zeph. 1:18
25:12 [p]Mal. 2:4
25:13 [q]1 Chron. 6:4 [r]Ex. 40:15 [s]Acts 22:3; Rom. 10:2 [t]Heb. 2:17

tish woman, *was* Zimri, the son of Salu, a prince of a chief house among the Simeonites.

15 And the name of the Midianitish woman that was slain *was* Cozbi, the daughter of [u]Zur; he *was* head over a people, *and* of a chief house in Midian.

16 ¶ And the LORD spake unto Moses, saying,

17 [v]Vex the Midianites, and smite them:

18 For they vex you with their [w]wiles, wherewith they have beguiled you in the matter of Peor, and in the matter of Cozbi, the daughter of a prince of Midian, their sister, which was slain in the day of the plague for Peor's sake.

26

26 And it came to pass after the plague, that the LORD spake unto Moses and unto Eleazar the son of Aaron the priest, saying,

2 [x]Take the sum of all the congregation of the children of Israel, [y]from twenty years old and upward, throughout their fathers' house, all that are able to go to war in Israel.

3 And Moses and Eleazar the priest spake with them [z]in the plains of Moab by Jordan *near* Jericho, saying,

4 *Take the sum of the people,* from twenty years old and upward; as the LORD [a]commanded Moses and the children of Israel, which went forth out of the land of Egypt.

5 ¶ [b]Reuben, the eldest son of Israel: the children of Reuben; Hanoch, *of whom cometh* the family of the Hanochites: of Pallu, the family of the Palluites:

6 Of Hezron, the family of the Hezronites: of Carmi, the family of the Carmites.

7 These *are* the families of the Reubenites: and they that were numbered of them were forty and three thousand and seven hundred and thirty.

8 And the sons of Pallu; Eliab.

9 And the sons of Eliab; Nemuel, and Dathan, and Abiram. This *is that* Dathan and Abiram, *which were* [c]famous in the congregation, who strove against Moses and against Aaron in the company of Korah, when they strove against the LORD:

10 [d]And the earth opened her mouth, and swallowed them up together with Korah, when that company died, what time the fire devoured two hundred and fifty men: [e]and they became a sign.

11 Notwithstanding [f]the children of Korah died not.

12 ¶ The sons of Simeon after their families: of [g]Nemuel, the family of the Nemuelites: of Jamin, the family of the Jaminites: of [h]Jachin, the family of the Jachinites:

13 Of [i]Zerah, the family of the Zarhites: of Shaul, the family of the Shaulites.

14 These *are* the families of the Simeonites, twenty and two thousand and two hundred.

15 ¶ The children of Gad after their families: of [j]Zephon, the family of the Zephonites: of Haggi, the family of the Haggites: of Shuni, the family of the Shunites:

16 Of Ozni, the family of the Oznites: of Eri, the family of the Erites:

17 Of [k]Arod, the family of the Arodites: of Areli, the family of the Arelites.

18 These *are* the families of the children of Gad according to those that were numbered of them, forty thousand and five hundred.

19 ¶ [l]The sons of Judah *were* Er and Onan: and Er and Onan died in the land of Canaan.

20 And [m]the sons of Judah after their families were; of Shelah, the family of the Shelanites: of Pharez, the family of the Pharzites: of Zerah, the family of the Zarhites.

21 And the sons of Pharez were; of Hezron, the family of the Hezronites: of Hamul, the family of the Hamulites.

22 These *are* the families of Judah according to those that were numbered of them, threescore and sixteen thousand and five hundred.

23 ¶ [n]*Of* the sons of Issachar after their families: *of* Tola, the family of the Tolaites: of Pua, the family of the Punites:

24 Of Jashub, the family of the Jashubites: of Shimron, the family of the Shimronites.

25 These *are* the families of Issachar according to those that were numbered of them, threescore and four thousand and three hundred.

26 ¶ [o]*Of* the sons of Zebulun after their families: of Sered, the family of the Sardites: of Elon, the family of the Elonites: of Jahleel, the family of the Jahleelites.

27 These *are* the families of the Zebulunites according to those that were numbered of them, threescore thousand and five hundred.

28 ¶ [p]The sons of Joseph after their families *were* Manasseh and Ephraim.

29 Of the sons of Manasseh: of [q]Machir, the family of the Machirites: and Machir begat Gilead: of Gilead *come* the family of the Gileadites.

30 These *are* the sons of Gilead: *of* [r]Jeezer, the family of the Jeezerites: of Helek, the family of the Helekites:

31 And *of* Asriel, the family of the Asrielites: and *of* Shechem, the family of the Shechemites:

32 And *of* Shemida, the family of the Shemidaites: and *of* Hepher, the family of the Hepherites.

33 ¶ And [s]Zelophehad the son of Hepher had no sons, but daughters: and the names of the daughters of Zelophehad *were* Mahlah, and Noah, Hoglah, Milcah, and Tirzah.

34 These *are* the families of Manasseh, and those that were numbered of them, fifty and two thousand and seven hundred.

35 ¶ These *are* the sons of Ephraim after their families: of Shuthelah, the family of the Shuthalhites: of [t]Becher, the family of

25:15 *u*ch. 31:8; Josh. 13:21
25:17 *v*ch. 31:2
25:18 *w*ch. 31:16; Rev. 2:14
26:2 *x*Ex. 30:12; ch. 1:2 *y*ch. 1:3
26:3 *z*ver. 63; ch. 22:1
26:4 *a*ch. 1:1
26:5 *b*Gen. 46:8; Ex. 6:14; 1 Chron. 5:1
26:9 *c*ch. 16:1
26:10 *d*ch. 16:32 *e*ch. 16:38; 1 Cor. 10:6; 2 Pet. 2:6
26:11 *f*Ex. 6:24; 1 Chron. 6:22
26:12 *g*Gen. 46:10; Ex. 6:15 *h*1 Chron. 4:24
26:13 *i*Gen. 46:10
26:15 *j*Gen. 46:16
26:17 *k*Gen. 46:16
26:19 *l*Gen. 38:2
26:20 *m*1 Chron. 2:3
26:23 *n*Gen. 46:13; 1 Chron. 7:1
26:26 *o*Gen. 46:14
26:28 *p*Gen. 46:20
26:29 *q*Josh. 17:1; 1 Chron. 7:14
26:30 *r*Josh. 17:2; Judg. 6:11
26:33 *s*ch. 27:1
26:35 *t*1 Chron. 7:20

the Bachrites: of Tahan, the family of the Tahanites.

36 And these *are* the sons of Shuthelah: of Eran, the family of the Eranites.

37 These *are* the families of the sons of Ephraim according to those that were numbered of them, thirty and two thousand and five hundred. These *are* the sons of Joseph after their families.

38 ¶ [u]The sons of Benjamin after their families: of Bela, the family of the Belaites: of Ashbel, the family of the Ashbelites: of [v]Ahiram, the family of the Ahiramites:

39 Of [w]Shupham, the family of the Shuphamites: of Hupham, the family of the Huphamites.

40 And the sons of Bela were [x]Ard and Naaman: *of Ard,* the family of the Ardites: *and* of Naaman, the family of the Naamites.

41 These *are* the sons of Benjamin after their families: and they that were numbered of them *were* forty and five thousand and six hundred.

42 ¶ [y]These *are* the sons of Dan after their families: of Shuham, the family of the Shuhamites. These *are* the families of Dan after their families.

43 All the families of the Shuhamites, according to those that were numbered of them, *were* threescore and four thousand and four hundred.

44 ¶ [z]*Of* the children of Asher after their families: of Jimna, the family of the Jimnites: of Jesui, the family of the Jesuites: of Beriah, the family of the Beriites.

45 Of the sons of Beriah: of Heber, the family of the Heberites: of Malchiel, the family of the Malchielites.

46 And the name of the daughter of Asher *was* Sarah.

47 These *are* the families of the sons of Asher according to those that were numbered of them; *who were* fifty and three thousand and four hundred.

48 ¶ [a]*Of* the sons of Naphtali after their families: of Jahzeel, the family of the Jahzeelites: of Guni, the family of the Gunites:

49 Of Jezer, the family of the Jezerites: of [b]Shillem, the family of the Shillemites.

50 These *are* the families of Naphtali according to their families: and they that were numbered of them *were* forty and five thousand and four hundred.

51 [c]These *were* the numbered of the children of Israel, six hundred thousand and a thousand seven hundred and thirty.

52 ¶ And the LORD spake unto Moses, saying,

53 [d]Unto these the land shall be divided for an inheritance according to the number of names.

54 [e]To many thou shalt give the more inheritance, and to few thou shalt give the less inheritance: to every one shall his inheritance be given according to those that were numbered of him.

55 Notwithstanding the land shall be [f]divided by lot: according to the names of the tribes of their fathers they shall inherit.

56 According to the lot shall the possession thereof be divided between many and few.

57 ¶ [g]And these *are* they that were numbered of the Levites after their families: of Gershon, the family of the Gershonites: of Kohath, the family of the Kohathites: of Merari, the family of the Merarites.

58 These *are* the families of the Levites: the family of the Libnites, the family of the Hebronites, the family of the Mahlites, the family of the Mushites, the family of the Korathites. And Kohath begat Amram.

59 And the name of Amram's wife *was* [h]Jochebed, the daughter of Levi, whom *her mother* bare to Levi in Egypt: and she bare unto Amram Aaron and Moses, and Miriam their sister.

60 [i]And unto Aaron was born Nadab and Abihu, Eleazar and Ithamar.

61 And [j]Nadab and Abihu died, when they offered strange fire before the LORD.

62 [k]And those that were numbered of them were twenty and three thousand, all males from a month old and upward: [l]for they were not numbered among the children of Israel, because there was [m]no inheritance given them among the children of Israel.

63 ¶ These *are* they that were numbered by Moses and Eleazar the priest, who numbered the children of Israel [n]in the plains of Moab by Jordan *near* Jericho.

64 [o]But among these there was not a man of them whom Moses and Aaron the priest numbered, when they numbered the children of Israel in the wilderness of Sinai.

65 For the LORD had said of them, They [p]shall surely die in the wilderness. And there was not left a man of them, [q]save Caleb the son of Jephunneh, and Joshua the son of Nun.

27

Then came the daughters of [r]Zelophehad, the son of Hepher, the son of Gilead, the son of Machir, the son of Manasseh, of the families of Manasseh the son of Joseph: and these *are* the names of his daughters; Mahlah, Noah, and Hoglah, and Milcah, and Tirzah.

2 And they stood before Moses, and before Eleazar the priest, and before the princes and all the congregation, *by* the door of the tabernacle of the congregation, saying,

3 Our father [s]died in the wilderness, and he was not in the company of them that gathered themselves together against the LORD [t]in the company of Korah; but died in his own sin, and had no sons.

4 Why should the name of our father be done away from among his family, because he hath no son? [u]Give unto us *therefore* a possession among the brethren of our father.

5 And Moses [v]brought their cause before the LORD.

26:38 [u]Gen. 46:21; 1 Chron. 7:6 [v]Gen. 46:21; 1 Chron. 8:1
26:39 [w]Gen. 46:21
26:40 [x]1 Chron. 8:3
26:42 [y]Gen. 46:23
26:44 [z]Gen. 46:17; 1 Chron. 7:30
26:48 [a]Gen. 46:24; 1 Chron. 7:13
26:49 [b]1 Chron. 7:13
26:51 [c]ch. 1:46
26:53 [d]Josh. 11:23
26:54 [e]ch. 33:54
26:55 [f]ch. 33:54; Josh. 11:23
26:57 [g]Gen. 46:11; Ex. 6:16; 1 Chron. 6:1
26:59 [h]Ex. 2:1
26:60 [i]ch. 3:2
26:61 [j]Lev. 10:1; ch. 3:4; 1 Chron. 24:2
26:62 [k]ch. 3:39 [l]ch. 1:49 [m]ch. 18:20; Deut. 10:9; Josh. 13:14
26:63 [n]ver. 3
26:64 [o]ch. 1; Deut. 2:14
26:65 [p]ch. 14:28; 1 Cor. 10:5 [q]ch. 14:30
27:1 [r]ch. 26:33; Josh. 17:3
27:3 [s]ch. 14:35 [t]ch. 16:1
27:4 [u]Josh. 17:4
27:5 [v]Ex. 18:15

6 ¶ And the LORD spake unto Moses, saying,

7 The daughters of Zelophehad speak right: [w]thou shalt surely give them a possession of an inheritance among their father's brethren; and thou shalt cause the inheritance of their father to pass unto them.

8 And thou shalt speak unto the children of Israel, saying, If a man die, and have no son, then ye shall cause his inheritance to pass unto his daughter.

9 And if he have no daughter, then ye shall give his inheritance unto his brethren.

10 And if he have no brethren, then ye shall give his inheritance unto his father's brethren.

11 And if his father have no brethren, then ye shall give his inheritance unto his kinsman that is next to him of his family, and he shall possess it: and it shall be unto the children of Israel [x]a statute of judgment, as the LORD commanded Moses.

12 ¶ And the LORD said unto Moses, [y]Get thee up into this mount Abarim, and see the land which I have given unto the children of Israel.

13 And when thou hast seen it, thou also [z]shalt be gathered unto thy people, as Aaron thy brother was gathered.

14 For ye [a]rebelled against my commandment in the desert of Zin, in the strife of the congregation, to sanctify me at the water before their eyes: that *is* the [b]water of Meribah in Kadesh in the wilderness of Zin.

15 ¶ And Moses spake unto the LORD, saying,

16 Let the LORD, [c]the God of the spirits of all flesh, set a man over the congregation,

17 [d]Which may go out before them, and which may go in before them, and which may lead them out, and which may bring them in; that the congregation of the LORD be not [e]as sheep which have no shepherd.

18 ¶ And the LORD said unto Moses, Take thee Joshua the son of Nun, a man [f]in whom *is* the spirit, and [g]lay thine hand upon him;

19 And set him before Eleazar the priest, and before all the congregation; and [h]give him a charge in their sight.

20 And [i]thou shalt put *some* of thine honour upon him, that all the congregation of the children of Israel [j]may be obedient.

21 [k]And he shall stand before Eleazar the priest, who shall ask *counsel* for him [l]after the judgment of Urim before the LORD: [m]at his word shall they go out, and at his word they shall come in, *both* he, and all the children of Israel with him, even all the congregation.

22 And Moses did as the LORD commanded him: and he took Joshua, and set him before Eleazar the priest, and before all the congregation:

23 And he laid his hands upon him, [n]and gave him a charge, as the LORD commanded by the hand of Moses.

27:7 [w]ch. 36:2
27:11 [x]ch. 35:29
27:12 [y]ch. 33:47; Deut. 3:27
27:13 [z]ch. 20:24; Deut. 10:6
27:14 [a]ch. 20:12; Deut. 1:37; Ps. 106:32 [b]Ex. 17:7
27:16 [c]ch. 16:22; Heb. 12:9
27:17 [d]Deut. 31:2; 1 Sam. 8:20; 2 Chron. 1:10 [e]1 Kings 22:17; Zech. 10:2; Matt. 9:36; Mark 6:34
27:18 [f]Gen. 41:38; Judg. 3:10; 1 Sam. 16:13 [g]Deut. 34:9
27:19 [h]Deut. 31:7
27:20 [i]ch. 11:17; 1 Sam. 10:6; 2 Kings 2:15 [j]Josh. 1:16
27:21 [k]Josh. 9:14; Judg. 1:1; 1 Sam. 23:9 [l]Ex. 28:30 [m]Josh. 9:14; 1 Sam. 22:10
27:23 [n]Deut. 3:28
28:2 [o]Lev. 3:11; Mal. 1:7
28:3 [p]Ex. 29:38
28:5 [q]Ex. 16:36; ch. 15:4 [r]Lev. 2:1 [s]Ex. 29:40
28:6 [t]Ex. 29:42; Am. 5:25
28:7 [u]Ex. 29:42
28:10 [v]Ezek. 46:4
28:11 [w]ch. 10:10; 1 Sam. 20:5; 1 Chron. 23:31; 2 Chron. 2:4; Ezra 3:5; Neh. 10:33; Isa. 1:13; Ezek. 45:17; Hos. 2:11; Col. 2:16
28:12 [x]ch. 15:4-12
28:15 [y]ver. 22; ch. 15:24
28:16 [z]Ex. 12:6; Lev. 23:5; ch. 9:3; Deut. 16:1; Ezek. 45:21
28:17 [a]Lev. 23:6
28:18 [b]Ex. 12:16; Lev. 23:7

28

And the LORD spake unto Moses, saying,

2 Command the children of Israel, and say unto them, My offering, *and* [o]my bread for my sacrifices made by fire, *for* a sweet savour unto me, shall ye observe to offer unto me in their due season.

3 And thou shalt say unto them, [p]This *is* the offering made by fire which ye shall offer unto the LORD; two lambs of the first year without spot day by day, *for* a continual burnt offering.

4 The one lamb shalt thou offer in the morning, and the other lamb shalt thou offer at even;

5 And [q]a tenth *part* of an ephah of flour for a [r]meat offering, mingled with the fourth *part* of an [s]hin of beaten oil.

6 *It is* [t]a continual burnt offering, which was ordained in mount Sinai for a sweet savour, a sacrifice made by fire unto the LORD.

7 And the drink offering thereof *shall be* the fourth *part* of a hin for the one lamb: [u]in the holy *place* shalt thou cause the strong wine to be poured unto the LORD *for* a drink offering.

8 And the other lamb shalt thou offer at even: as the meat offering of the morning, and as the drink offering thereof, thou shalt offer *it*, a sacrifice made by fire, of a sweet savour unto the LORD.

9 ¶ And on the sabbath day two lambs of the first year without spot, and two tenth deals of flour *for* a meat offering, mingled with oil, and the drink offering thereof:

10 *This is* [v]the burnt offering of every sabbath, beside the continual burnt offering, and his drink offering.

11 ¶ And [w]in the beginnings of your months ye shall offer a burnt offering unto the LORD; two young bullocks, and one ram, seven lambs of the first year without spot;

12 And [x]three tenth deals of flour *for* a meat offering, mingled with oil, for one bullock; and two tenth deals of flour *for* a meat offering, mingled with oil, for one ram;

13 And a several tenth deal of flour mingled with oil *for* a meat offering unto one lamb; *for* a burnt offering of a sweet savour, a sacrifice made by fire unto the LORD.

14 And their drink offerings shall be half an hin of wine unto a bullock, and the third *part* of an hin unto a ram, and a fourth *part* of an hin unto a lamb: this *is* the burnt offering of every month throughout the months of the year.

15 And [y]one kid of the goats for a sin offering unto the LORD shall be offered, beside the continual burnt offering, and his drink offering.

16 [z]And in the fourteenth day of the first month *is* the passover of the LORD.

17 [a]And in the fifteenth day of this month *is* the feast: seven days shall unleavened bread be eaten.

18 In the [b]first day *shall be* an holy con-

vocation; ye shall do no manner of servile work *therein:*

19 But ye shall offer a sacrifice made by fire *for* a burnt offering unto the LORD; two young bullocks, and one ram, and seven lambs of the first year: [c]they shall be unto you without blemish:

20 And their meat offering *shall be of* flour mingled with oil: three tenth deals shall ye offer for a bullock, and two tenth deals for a ram;

21 A several tenth deal shalt thou offer for every lamb, throughout the seven lambs:

22 And [d]one goat *for* a sin offering, to make an atonement for you.

23 Ye shall offer these beside the burnt offering in the morning, which *is* for a continual burnt offering.

24 After this manner ye shall offer daily, throughout the seven days, the meat of the sacrifice made by fire, of a sweet savour unto the LORD: it shall be offered beside the continual burnt offering, and his drink offering.

25 And [e]on the seventh day ye shall have an holy convocation; ye shall do no servile work.

26 ¶ Also [f]in the day of the firstfruits, when ye bring a new meat offering unto the LORD, after your weeks *be out,* ye shall have an holy convocation; ye shall do no servile work:

27 But ye shall offer the burnt offering for a sweet savour unto the LORD; [g]two young bullocks, one ram, seven lambs of the first year;

28 And their meat offering of flour mingled with oil, three tenth deals unto one bullock, two tenth deals unto one ram,

29 A several tenth deal unto one lamb, throughout the seven lambs;

30 *And* one kid of the goats, to make an atonement for you.

31 Ye shall offer *them* beside the continual burnt offering, and his meat offering, ([h]they shall be unto you without blemish) and their drink offerings.

29 And in the seventh month, on the first *day* of the month, ye shall have an holy convocation; ye shall do no servile work: [i]it is a day of blowing the trumpets unto you.

2 And ye shall offer a burnt offering for a sweet savour unto the LORD; one young bullock, one ram, *and* seven lambs of the first year without blemish:

3 And their meat offering *shall be of* flour mingled with oil, three tenth deals for a bullock, *and* two tenth deals for a ram,

4 And one tenth deal for one lamb, throughout the seven lambs:

5 And one kid of the goats *for* a sin offering, to make an atonement for you:

6 Beside [j]the burnt offering of the month, and his meat offering, and [k]the daily burnt offering, and his meat offering, and their drink offerings, [l]according unto their manner, for a sweet savour, a sacrifice made by fire unto the LORD.

7 ¶ And [m]ye shall have on the tenth *day* of this seventh month an holy convocation; and ye shall [n]afflict your souls: ye shall not do any work *therein:*

8 But ye shall offer a burnt offering unto the LORD *for* a sweet savour; one young bullock, one ram, *and* seven lambs of the first year; [o]they shall be unto you without blemish:

9 And their meat offering *shall be of* flour mingled with oil, three tenth deals to a bullock, *and* two tenth deals to one ram,

10 A several tenth deal for one lamb, throughout the seven lambs:

11 One kid of the goats *for* a sin offering; beside [p]the sin offering of atonement, and the continual burnt offering, and the meat offering of it, and their drink offerings.

12 ¶ And [q]on the fifteenth day of the seventh month ye shall have an holy convocation; ye shall do no servile work, and ye shall keep a feast unto the LORD seven days:

13 And [r]ye shall offer a burnt offering, a sacrifice made by fire, of a sweet savour unto the LORD; thirteen young bullocks, two rams, *and* fourteen lambs of the first year; they shall be without blemish:

14 And their meat offering *shall be of* flour mingled with oil, three tenth deals unto every bullock of the thirteen bullocks, two tenth deals to each ram of the two rams,

15 And a several tenth deal to each lamb of the fourteen lambs:

16 And one kid of the goats *for* a sin offering; beside the continual burnt offering, his meat offering, and his drink offering.

17 ¶ And on the second day *ye shall offer* twelve young bullocks, two rams, fourteen lambs of the first year without spot:

18 And their meat offering and their drink offerings for the bullocks, for the rams, and for the lambs, *shall be* according to their number, [s]after the manner:

19 And one kid of the goats *for* a sin offering; beside the continual burnt offering, and the meat offering thereof, and their drink offerings.

20 ¶ And on the third day eleven bullocks, two rams, fourteen lambs of the first year without blemish;

21 And their meat offering and their drink offerings for the bullocks, for the rams, and for the lambs, *shall be* according to their number, [t]after the manner:

22 And one goat *for* a sin offering; beside the continual burnt offering, and his meat offering, and his drink offering.

23 ¶ And on the fourth day ten bullocks, two rams, *and* fourteen lambs of the first year without blemish:

24 Their meat offering and their drink offerings for the bullocks, for the rams, and for the lambs, *shall be* according to their number, after the manner:

25 And one kid of the goats *for* a sin offer-

28:19 [c]ver. 31; Lev. 22:20; ch. 29:8; Deut. 15:21
28:22 [d]ver. 15
28:25 [e]Ex. 12:16; Lev. 23:8
28:26 [f]Ex. 23:16; Lev. 23:10; Deut. 16:10; Acts 2:1
28:27 [g]Lev. 23:18
28:31 [h]ver. 19
29:1 [i]Lev. 23:24
29:6 [j]ch. 28:11 [k]ch. 28:3 [l]ch. 15:11
29:7 [m]Lev. 16:29 [n]Ps. 35:13; Isa. 58:5
29:8 [o]ch. 28:19
29:11 [p]Lev. 16:3
29:12 [q]Lev. 23:33; Deut. 16:13; Ezek. 45:25
29:13 [r]Ezra 3:4
29:18 [s]ver. 3; ch. 15:12
29:21 [t]ver. 18

ing; beside the continual burnt offering, his
meat offering, and his drink offering.
26 ¶ And on the fifth day nine bullocks,
two rams, *and* fourteen lambs of the first
year without spot:
27 And their meat offering and their
drink offerings for the bullocks, for the
rams, and for the lambs, *shall be* according
to their number, after the manner:
28 And one goat *for* a sin offering; beside
the continual burnt offering, and his meat
offering, and his drink offering.
29 ¶ And on the sixth day eight bullocks,
two rams, *and* fourteen lambs of the first
year without blemish:
30 And their meat offering and their
drink offerings for the bullocks, for the
rams, and for the lambs, *shall be* according
to their number, after the manner:
31 And one goat *for* a sin offering; beside
the continual burnt offering, his meat offering, and his drink offering.
32 ¶ And on the seventh day seven bullocks, two rams, *and* fourteen lambs of the
first year without blemish:
33 And their meat offering and their
drink offerings for the bullocks, for the
rams, and for the lambs, *shall be* according
to their number, after the manner:
34 And one goat *for* a sin offering; beside
the continual burnt offering, his meat offering, and his drink offering.
35 ¶ On the eighth day ye shall have a
[u]solemn assembly: ye shall do no servile
work *therein:*
36 But ye shall offer a burnt offering, a
sacrifice made by fire, of a sweet savour
unto the LORD: one bullock, one ram, seven
lambs of the first year without blemish:
37 Their meat offering and their drink offerings for the bullock, for the ram, and for
the lambs, *shall be* according to their number, after the manner:
38 And one goat *for* a sin offering; beside
the continual burnt offering, and his meat
offering, and his drink offering.
39 These *things* ye shall do unto the LORD
in your [v]set feasts, beside your [w]vows, and
your freewill offerings, for your burnt offerings, and for your meat offerings, and for
your drink offerings, and for your peace offerings.
40 And Moses told the children of Israel
according to all that the LORD commanded
Moses.

30 And Moses spake unto [x]the heads of
the tribes concerning the children of
Israel, saying, This *is* the thing which the
LORD hath commanded.
2 [y]If a man vow a vow unto the LORD, or
[z]swear an oath to bind his soul with a bond;
he shall not break his word, he shall [a]do
according to all that proceedeth out of his
mouth.
3 If a woman also vow a vow unto the
LORD, and bind *herself* by a bond, *being* in
her father's house in her youth;
4 And her father hear her vow, and her
bond wherewith she hath bound her soul,
and her father shall hold his peace at her:
then all her vows shall stand, and every
bond wherewith she hath bound her soul
shall stand.
5 But if her father disallow her in the day
that he heareth; not any of her vows, or of
her bonds wherewith she hath bound her
soul, shall stand: and the LORD shall forgive
her, because her father disallowed her.
6 And if she had at all an husband, when
she vowed, or uttered ought out of her lips,
wherewith she bound her soul;
7 And her husband heard *it*, and held his
peace at her in the day that he heard *it:* then
her vows shall stand, and her bonds wherewith she bound her soul shall stand.
8 But if her husband [b]disallowed her on
the day that he heard *it;* then he shall make
her vow which she vowed, and that which
she uttered with her lips, wherewith she
bound her soul, of none effect: and the LORD
shall forgive her.
9 But every vow of a widow, and of her
that is divorced, wherewith they have
bound their souls, shall stand against her.
10 And if she vowed in her husband's
house, or bound her soul by a bond with an
oath;
11 And her husband heard *it*, and held his
peace at her, *and* disallowed her not: then
all her vows shall stand, and every bond
wherewith she bound her soul shall stand.
12 But if her husband hath utterly made
them void on the day he heard *them; then*
whatsoever proceeded out of her lips concerning her vows, or concerning the bond of
her soul, shall not stand: her husband hath
made them void; and the LORD shall forgive
her.
13 Every vow, and every binding oath to
afflict the soul, her husband may establish
it, or her husband may make it void.
14 But if her husband altogether hold his
peace at her from day to day; then he establisheth all her vows, or all her bonds, which
are upon her: he confirmeth them, because
he held his peace at her in the day that he
heard *them*.
15 But if he shall any ways make them
void after that he hath heard *them;* then he
shall bear her iniquity.
16 These *are* the statutes, which the LORD
commanded Moses, between a man and his
wife, between the father and his daughter,
being yet in her youth in her father's house.

31 And the LORD spake unto Moses,
saying,
2 [c]Avenge the children of Israel of the
Midianites: afterward shalt thou [d]be gathered unto thy people.
3 And Moses spake unto the people, saying, Arm some of yourselves unto the war,
and let them go against the Midianites, and
avenge the LORD of Midian.
4 Of every tribe a thousand, throughout
all the tribes of Israel, shall ye send to the
war.

29:35 [u]Lev. 23:36
29:39 [v]Lev. 23:2; 1 Chron. 23:31; 2 Chron. 31:3; Ezra 3:5; Neh. 10:33; Isa. 1:14 [w]Lev. 7:11
30:1 [x]ch. 1:4
30:2 [y]Lev. 27:2; Deut. 23:21; Judg. 11:30; Eccl. 5:4 [z]Lev. 5:4; Matt. 14:9; Acts 23:14 [a]Job 22:27; Ps. 22:25; Nah. 1:15
30:8 [b]Gen. 3:16
31:2 [c]ch. 25:17 [d]ch. 27:13

5 So there were delivered out of the thousands of Israel, a thousand of *every* tribe, twelve thousand armed for war.

6 And Moses sent them to the war, a thousand of *every* tribe, them and Phinehas the son of Eleazar the priest, to the war, with the holy instruments, and [e]the trumpets to blow in his hand.

7 And they warred against the Midianites, as the LORD commanded Moses; and [f]they slew all the [g]males.

8 And they slew the kings of Midian, beside the rest of them that were slain; *namely*, [h]Evi, and Rekem, and Zur, and Hur, and Reba, five kings of Midian: [i]Balaam also the son of Beor they slew with the sword.

9 And the children of Israel took *all* the women of Midian captives, and their little ones, and took the spoil of all their cattle, and all their flocks, and all their goods.

10 And they burnt all their cities wherein they dwelt, and all their goodly castles, with fire.

11 And [j]they took all the spoil, and all the prey, *both* of men and of beasts.

12 And they brought the captives, and the prey, and the spoil, unto Moses, and Eleazar the priest, and unto the congregation of the children of Israel, unto the camp at the plains of Moab, which *are* by Jordan *near* Jericho.

13 ¶ And Moses, and Eleazar the priest, and all the princes of the congregation, went forth to meet them without the camp.

14 And Moses was wroth with the officers of the host, *with* the captains over thousands, and captains over hundreds, which came from the battle.

15 And Moses said unto them, Have ye saved [k]all the women alive?

16 Behold, [l]these caused the children of Israel, through the [m]counsel of Balaam, to commit trespass against the LORD in the matter of Peor, and [n]there was a plague among the congregation of the LORD.

17 Now therefore [o]kill every male among the little ones, and kill every woman that hath known man by lying with him.

18 But all the women children, that have not known a man by lying with him, keep alive for yourselves.

19 And [p]do ye abide without the camp seven days: [q]whosoever hath killed any person, and whosoever hath touched any slain, purify *both* yourselves and your captives on the third day, and on the seventh day.

20 And purify all *your* raiment, and all that is made of skins, and all work of goats' *hair,* and all things made of wood.

21 ¶ And Eleazar the priest said unto the men of war which went to the battle, This *is* the ordinance of the law which the LORD commanded Moses;

22 Only the gold, and the silver, the brass, the iron, the tin, and the lead,

23 Every thing that may abide the fire, ye shall make *it* go through the fire, and it shall be clean: nevertheless it shall be purified [r]with the water of separation: and all that abideth not the fire ye shall make go through the water.

24 [s]And ye shall wash your clothes on the seventh day, and ye shall be clean, and afterward ye shall come into the camp.

25 ¶ And the LORD spake unto Moses, saying,

26 Take the sum of the prey that was taken, *both* of man and of beast, thou, and Eleazar the priest, and the chief fathers of the congregation:

27 And [t]divide the prey into two parts; between them that took the war upon them, who went out to battle, and between all the congregation:

28 And levy a tribute unto the LORD of the men of war which went out to battle: [u]one soul of five hundred, *both* of the persons, and of the beeves, and of the asses, and of the sheep:

29 Take *it* of their half, and give *it* unto Eleazar the priest, *for* an heave offering of the LORD.

30 And of the children of Israel's half, thou shalt take [v]one portion of fifty, of the persons, of the beeves, of the asses, and of the flocks, of all manner of beasts, and give them unto the Levites, [w]which keep the charge of the tabernacle of the LORD.

31 And Moses and Eleazar the priest did as the LORD commanded Moses.

32 And the booty, *being* the rest of the prey which the men of war had caught, was six hundred thousand and seventy thousand and five thousand sheep,

33 And threescore and twelve thousand beeves,

34 And threescore and one thousand asses,

35 And thirty and two thousand persons in all, of women that had not known man by lying with him.

36 And the half, *which was* the portion of them that went out to war, was in number three hundred thousand and seven and thirty thousand and five hundred sheep:

37 And the LORD's tribute of the sheep was six hundred and threescore and fifteen.

38 And the beeves *were* thirty and six thousand; of which the LORD's tribute *was* threescore and twelve.

39 And the asses *were* thirty thousand and five hundred; of which the LORD's tribute *was* threescore and one.

40 And the persons *were* sixteen thousand; of which the LORD's tribute *was* thirty and two persons.

41 And Moses gave the tribute, *which was* the LORD's heave offering, unto Eleazar the priest, [x]as the LORD commanded Moses.

42 And of the children of Israel's half, which Moses divided from the men that warred,

43 (Now the half *that pertained unto* the

31:6 [e]ch. 10:9
31:7 [f]Deut. 20:13; Judg. 21:11; 1 Sam. 27:9; 1 Kings 11:15 [g]Judg. 6:1
31:8 [h]Josh. 13:21 [i]Josh. 13:22
31:11 [j]Deut. 20:14
31:15 [k]Deut. 20:13; 1 Sam. 15:3
31:16 [l]ch. 25:2 [m]ch. 24:14; 2 Pet. 2:15; Rev. 2:14 [n]ch. 25:9
31:17 [o]Judg. 21:11
31:19 [p]ch. 5:2 [q]ch. 19:11
31:23 [r]ch. 19:9
31:24 [s]Lev. 11:25
31:27 [t]Josh. 22:8; 1 Sam. 30:4
31:28 [u]ver. 30
31:30 [v]ver. 42-47 [w]ch. 3:7
31:41 [x]ch. 18:8

congregation was three hundred thousand and thirty thousand *and* seven thousand and five hundred sheep,

44 And thirty and six thousand beeves,

45 And thirty thousand asses and five hundred,

46 And sixteen thousand persons;)

47 Even [y]of the children of Israel's half, Moses took one portion of fifty, *both* of man and of beast, and gave them unto the Levites, which kept the charge of the tabernacle of the LORD; as the LORD commanded Moses.

48 ¶ And the officers which *were* over thousands of the host, the captains of thousands, and captains of hundreds, came near unto Moses:

49 And they said unto Moses, Thy servants have taken the sum of the men of war which *are* under our charge, and there lacketh not one man of us.

50 We have therefore brought an oblation for the LORD, what every man hath gotten, of jewels of gold, chains, and bracelets, rings, earrings, and tablets, [z]to make an atonement for our souls before the LORD.

51 And Moses and Eleazar the priest took the gold of them, *even* all wrought jewels.

52 And all the gold of the offering that they offered up to the LORD, of the captains of thousands, and of the captains of hundreds, was sixteen thousand seven hundred and fifty shekels.

53 (*For* [a]the men of war had taken spoil, every man for himself.)

54 And Moses and Eleazar the priest took the gold of the captains of thousands and of hundreds, and brought it into the tabernacle of the congregation, [b]*for* a memorial for the children of Israel before the LORD.

32 Now the children of Reuben and the children of Gad had a very great multitude of cattle: and when they saw the land of [c]Jazer, and the land of Gilead, that, behold, the place *was* a place for cattle;

2 The children of Gad and the children of Reuben came and spake unto Moses, and to Eleazar the priest, and unto the princes of the congregation, saying,

3 Ataroth, and Dibon, and Jazer, and [d]Nimrah, and Heshbon, and Elealeh, and [e]Shebam, and Nebo, and [f]Beon,

4 *Even* the country [g]which the LORD smote before the congregation of Israel, *is* a land for cattle, and thy servants have cattle:

5 Wherefore, said they, if we have found grace in thy sight, let this land be given unto thy servants for a possession, *and* bring us not over Jordan.

6 ¶ And Moses said unto the children of Gad and to the children of Reuben, Shall your brethren go to war, and shall ye sit here?

7 And wherefore discourage ye the heart of the children of Israel from going over into the land which the LORD hath given them?

8 Thus did your fathers, [h]when I sent them from Kadesh-barnea [i]to see the land.

9 For [j]when they went up unto the valley of Eshcol, and saw the land, they discouraged the heart of the children of Israel, that they should not go into the land which the LORD had given them.

10 [k]And the LORD's anger was kindled the same time, and he sware, saying,

11 Surely none of the men that came up out of Egypt, [l]from twenty years old and upward, shall see the land which I sware unto Abraham, unto Isaac, and unto Jacob; because [m]they have not wholly followed me:

12 Save Caleb the son of Jephunneh the Kenezite, and Joshua the son of Nun: [n]for they have wholly followed the LORD.

13 And the LORD's anger was kindled against Israel, and he made them [o]wander in the wilderness forty years, until [p]all the generation, that had done evil in the sight of the LORD, was consumed.

14 And, behold, ye are risen up in your fathers' stead, an increase of sinful men, to augment yet the [q]fierce anger of the LORD toward Israel.

15 For if ye [r]turn away from after him, he will yet again leave them in the wilderness; and ye shall destroy all this people.

16 ¶ And they came near unto him, and said, We will build sheepfolds here for our cattle, and cities for our little ones:

17 But [s]we ourselves will go ready armed before the children of Israel, until we have brought them unto their place: and our little ones shall dwell in the fenced cities because of the inhabitants of the land.

18 [t]We will not return unto our houses, until the children of Israel have inherited every man his inheritance.

19 For we will not inherit with them on yonder side Jordan, or forward; [u]because our inheritance is fallen to us on this side Jordan eastward.

20 ¶ And [v]Moses said unto them, If ye will do this thing, if ye will go armed before the LORD to war,

21 And will go all of you armed over Jordan before the LORD, until he hath driven out his enemies from before him,

22 And [w]the land be subdued before the LORD: then afterward [x]ye shall return, and be guiltless before the LORD, and before Israel; and [y]this land shall be your possession before the LORD.

23 But if ye will not do so, behold, ye have sinned against the LORD: and be sure [z]your sin will find you out.

24 [a]Build you cities for your little ones, and folds for your sheep; and do that which hath proceeded out of your mouth.

25 And the children of Gad and the children of Reuben spake unto Moses, saying, Thy servants will do as my lord commandeth.

26 [b]Our little ones, our wives, our flocks, and all our cattle, shall be there in the cities of Gilead:

31:47 [y]ver. 30
31:50 [z]Ex. 30:12
31:53 [a]Deut. 20:14
31:54 [b]Ex. 30:16
32:1 [c]ch. 21:32; Josh. 13:25; 2 Sam. 24:5
32:3 [d]ver. 36 [e]ver. 38 [f]ver. 38
32:4 [g]ch. 21:24
32:8 [h]ch. 13:3 [i]Deut. 1:22
32:9 [j]ch. 13:24; Deut. 1:24
32:10 [k]ch. 14:11; Deut. 1:34
32:11 [l]ch. 14:28; Deut. 1:35 [m]ch. 14:24
32:12 [n]ch. 14:24; Deut. 1:36; Josh. 14:8
32:13 [o]ch. 14:33 [p]ch. 26:64
32:14 [q]Deut. 1:34
32:15 [r]Deut. 30:17; Josh. 22:16; 2 Chron. 7:19
32:17 [s]Josh. 4:12
32:18 [t]Josh. 22:4
32:19 [u]ver. 33; Josh. 12:1
32:20 [v]Deut. 3:18; Josh. 1:14
32:22 [w]Deut. 3:20; Josh. 11:23 [x]Josh. 22:4 [y]Deut. 3:12; Josh. 1:15
32:23 [z]Gen. 4:7; Isa. 59:12
32:24 [a]ver. 16
32:26 [b]Josh. 1:14

27 [c]But thy servants will pass over, every man armed for war, before the LORD to battle, as my lord saith.

28 So [d]concerning them Moses commanded Eleazar the priest, and Joshua the son of Nun, and the chief fathers of the tribes of the children of Israel:

29 And Moses said unto them, If the children of Gad and the children of Reuben will pass with you over Jordan, every man armed to battle, before the LORD, and the land shall be subdued before you; then ye shall give them the land of Gilead for a possession:

30 But if they will not pass over with you armed, they shall have possessions among you in the land of Canaan.

31 And the children of Gad and the children of Reuben answered, saying, As the LORD hath said unto thy servants, so will we do.

32 We will pass over armed before the LORD into the land of Canaan, that the possession of our inheritance on this side Jordan *may be* ours.

33 And [e]Moses gave unto them, *even* to the children of Gad, and to the children of Reuben, and unto half the tribe of Manasseh the son of Joseph, [f]the kingdom of Sihon king of the Amorites, and the kingdom of Og king of Bashan, the land, with the cities thereof in the coasts, *even* the cities of the country round about.

34 ¶ And the children of Gad built [g]Dibon, and Ataroth, and [h]Aroer,

35 And Atroth, Shophan, and Jaazer, and Jogbehah,

36 And [i]Beth-nimrah, and Beth-haran, [j]fenced cities: and folds for sheep.

37 And the children of Reuben [k]built Heshbon, and Elealeh, and Kirjathaim,

38 And [l]Nebo, and [m]Baal-meon, ([n]their names being changed,) and Shibmah: and gave other names unto the cities which they builded.

39 And the children of [o]Machir the son of Manasseh went to Gilead, and took it, and dispossessed the Amorite which *was* in it.

40 And Moses [p]gave Gilead unto Machir the son of Manasseh; and he dwelt therein.

41 And [q]Jair the son of Manasseh went and took the small towns thereof, and called them [r]Havoth-jair.

42 And Nobah went and took Kenath, and the villages thereof, and called it Nobah, after his own name.

33 These *are* the journeys of the children of Israel, which went forth out of the land of Egypt with their armies under the hand of Moses and Aaron.

2 And Moses wrote their goings out according to their journeys by the commandment of the LORD: and these *are* their journeys according to their goings out.

3 And they [s]departed from Rameses in [t]the first month, on the fifteenth day of the first month; on the morrow after the passover the children of Israel went out [u]with an high hand in the sight of all the Egyptians.

4 For the Egyptians buried all *their* firstborn, [v]which the LORD had smitten among them: [w]upon their gods also the LORD executed judgments.

5 [x]And the children of Israel removed from Rameses, and pitched in Succoth.

6 And they departed from [y]Succoth, and pitched in Etham, which *is* in the edge of the wilderness.

7 And [z]they removed from Etham, and turned again unto Pi-hahiroth, which *is* before Baal-zephon: and they pitched before Migdol.

8 And they departed from before Pi-hahiroth, and [a]passed through the midst of the sea into the wilderness, and went three days' journey in the wilderness of Etham, and pitched in Marah.

9 And they removed from Marah, and [b]came unto Elim: and in Elim *were* twelve fountains of water, and threescore and ten palm trees; and they pitched there.

10 And they removed from Elim, and encamped by the Red sea.

11 And they removed from the Red sea, and encamped in the [c]wilderness of Sin.

12 And they took their journey out of the wilderness of Sin, and encamped in Dophkah.

13 And they departed from Dophkah, and encamped in Alush.

14 And they removed from Alush, and encamped at [d]Rephidim, where was no water for the people to drink.

15 And they departed from Rephidim, and pitched in the [e]wilderness of Sinai.

16 And they removed from the desert of Sinai, and pitched [f]at Kibroth-hattaavah.

17 And they departed from Kibroth-hattaavah, and [g]encamped at Hazeroth.

18 And they departed from Hazeroth, and pitched in [h]Rithmah.

19 And they departed from Rithmah, and pitched at Rimmon-parez.

20 And they departed from Rimmon-parez, and pitched in Libnah.

21 And they removed from Libnah, and pitched at Rissah.

22 And they journeyed from Rissah, and pitched in Kehelathah.

23 And they went from Kehelathah, and pitched in mount Shapher.

24 And they removed from mount Shapher, and encamped in Haradah.

25 And they removed from Haradah, and pitched in Makheloth.

26 And they removed from Makheloth, and encamped at Tahath.

27 And they departed from Tahath, and pitched at Tarah.

28 And they removed from Tarah, and pitched in Mithcah.

29 And they went from Mithcah, and pitched in Hashmonah.

30 And they departed from Hashmonah, and [i]encamped at Moseroth.

32:27 [c]Josh. 4:12
32:28 [d]Josh. 1:13
32:33 [e]Deut. 3:12-17; Josh. 12:6 [f]ch. 21:24
32:34 [g]ch. 33:45 [h]Deut. 2:36
32:36 [i]ver. 3 [j]ver. 24
32:37 [k]ch. 21:27
32:38 [l]Isa. 46:1 [m]ch. 22:41 [n]ver. 3; Ex. 23:13; Josh. 23:7
32:39 [o]Gen. 50:23
32:40 [p]Deut. 3:12; Josh. 13:31
32:41 [q]Deut. 3:14; Josh. 13:30; 1 Chron. 2:21 [r]Judg. 10:4; 1 Kings 4:13
33:3 [s]Ex. 12:37 [t]Ex. 12:2 [u]Ex. 14:8
33:4 [v]Ex. 12:29 [w]Ex. 12:12; Isa. 19:1; Rev. 12:8
33:5 [x]Ex. 12:37
33:6 [y]Ex. 13:20
33:7 [z]Ex. 14:2
33:8 [a]Ex. 14:22
33:9 [b]Ex. 15:27
33:11 [c]Ex. 16:1
33:14 [d]Ex. 17:1
33:15 [e]Ex. 16:1
33:16 [f]ch. 11:34
33:17 [g]ch. 11:35
33:18 [h]ch. 12:16
33:30 [i]Deut. 10:6

31 And they departed from Moseroth,
and pitched in Bene-jaakan.
32 And they removed from [j]Bene-jaakan, and [k]encamped at Hor-hagidgad.
33 And they went from Hor-hagidgad,
and pitched in Jotbathah.
34 And they removed from Jotbathah,
and encamped at Ebronah.
35 And they departed from Ebronah,
[l]and encamped at Ezion-gaber.
36 And they removed from Ezion-gaber,
and pitched in the [m]wilderness of Zin,
which *is* Kadesh.
37 And they removed from [n]Kadesh, and
pitched in mount Hor, in the edge of the
land of Edom.
38 And [o]Aaron the priest went up into
mount Hor at the commandment of the
LORD, and died there, in the fortieth year
after the children of Israel were come out of
the land of Egypt, in the first *day* of the fifth
month.
39 And Aaron *was* an hundred and
twenty and three years old when he died in
mount Hor.
40 And [p]king Arad the Canaanite, which
dwelt in the south in the land of Canaan,
heard of the coming of the children of Israel.
41 And they departed from mount [q]Hor,
and pitched in Zalmonah.
42 And they departed from Zalmonah,
and pitched in Punon.
43 And they departed from Punon, and
[r]pitched in Oboth.
44 And [s]they departed from Oboth, and
pitched in [t]Ije-abarim, in the border of
Moab.
45 And they departed from Iim, and
pitched in [u]Dibon-gad.
46 And they removed from Dibon-gad,
and encamped in Almon-[v]diblathaim.
47 And they removed from Almon-diblathaim, [w]and pitched in the mountains
of Abarim, before Nebo.
48 And they departed from the mountains
of Abarim, and [x]pitched in the plains of
Moab by Jordan *near* Jericho.
49 And they pitched by Jordan, from
Beth-jesimoth *even* unto [y]Abel-shittim in
the plains of Moab.
50 ¶ And the LORD spake unto Moses in
the plains of Moab by Jordan *near* Jericho,
saying,
51 Speak unto the children of Israel, and
say unto them, [z]When ye are passed over
Jordan into the land of Canaan;
52 [a]Then ye shall drive out all the inhabitants of the land from before you, and destroy all their pictures, and destroy all their
molten images, and quite pluck down all
their high places:
53 And [b]ye shall dispossess *the inhabitants of* the land, and dwell therein: for I
have given you the land to possess it.
54 And ye shall divide the land by lot for
an inheritance among your families: *and* to
the more ye shall give the more inheritance,

33:32 [j]Gen. 36:27; Deut. 10:6; 1 Chron. 1:42 [k]Deut. 10:7
33:35 [l]Deut. 2:8; 1 Kings 9:26
33:36 [m]ch. 20:1
33:37 [n]ch. 20:22
33:38 [o]ch. 20:25; Deut. 10:6
33:40 [p]ch. 21:1
33:41 [q]ch. 21:4
33:43 [r]ch. 21:10
33:44 [s]ch. 21:11 [t]ch. 21:11
33:45 [u]ch. 32:34
33:46 [v]Jer. 48:22; Ezek. 6:14
33:47 [w]ch. 21:20; Deut. 32:49
33:48 [x]ch. 22:1
33:49 [y]ch. 25:1; Josh. 2:1
33:51 [z]Deut. 7:1; Josh. 3:17
33:52 [a]Ex. 23:24; Deut. 7:2; Josh. 11:12; Judg. 2:2
33:53 [b]ch. 26:53
33:55 [c]Ex. 23:33; Josh. 23:13; Judg. 2:3; Ps. 106:34; Ezek. 28:24
34:2 [d]Gen. 17:8; Deut. 1:7; Ps. 78:55; Ezek. 47:14
34:3 [e]Josh. 15:1; Ezek. 47:13 [f]Gen. 14:3; Josh. 15:2
34:4 [g]Josh. 15:3 [h]ch. 13:26 [i]Josh. 15:3
34:5 [j]Gen. 15:18; Josh. 15:4; 1 Kings 8:65; Isa. 27:12
34:7 [k]ch. 33:37
34:8 [l]ch. 13:21; 2 Kings 14:25 [m]Ezek. 47:15
34:9 [n]Ezek. 47:17
34:11 [o]2 Kings 23:33; Jer. 39:5 [p]Deut. 3:17; Josh. 11:2; Matt. 14:34; Luke 5:1
34:12 [q]ver. 3
34:13 [r]ver. 1; Josh. 14:1
34:14 [s]ch. 32:33; Josh. 14:2

and to the fewer ye shall give the less inheritance: every man's *inheritance* shall be in
the place where his lot falleth; according to
the tribes of your fathers ye shall inherit.
55 But if ye will not drive out the inhabitants of the land from before you; then it
shall come to pass, that those which ye let
remain of them *shall be* [c]pricks in your
eyes, and thorns in your sides, and shall vex
you in the land wherein ye dwell.
56 Moreover it shall come to pass, *that* I
shall do unto you, as I thought to do unto
them.

34

And the LORD spake unto Moses,
saying,
2 Command the children of Israel, and
say unto them, When ye come into [d]the
land of Canaan; (this *is* the land that shall
fall unto you for an inheritance, *even* the
land of Canaan with the coasts thereof:)
3 Then [e]your south quarter shall be from
the wilderness of Zin along by the coast of
Edom, and your south border shall be the
outmost coast of [f]the salt sea eastward:
4 And your border shall turn from the
south [g]to the ascent of Akrabbim, and pass
on to Zin: and the going forth thereof shall
be from the south [h]to Kadesh-barnea, and
shall go on to [i]Hazar-addar, and pass on to
Azmon:
5 And the border shall fetch a compass
from Azmon [j]unto the river of Egypt, and
the goings out of it shall be at the sea.
6 And *as for* the western border, ye shall
even have the great sea for a border: this
shall be your west border.
7 And this shall be your north border:
from the great sea ye shall point out for you
[k]mount Hor:
8 From mount Hor ye shall point out *your
border* [l]unto the entrance of Hamath; and
the goings forth of the border shall be to
[m]Zedad:
9 ¶ And the border shall go on to Ziphron,
and the goings out of it shall be at [n]Hazar-enan: this shall be your north border.
10 And ye shall point out your east border
from Hazar-enan to Shepham:
11 And the coast shall go down from Shepham [o]to Riblah, on the east side of Ain;
and the border shall descend, and shall
reach unto the side of the sea [p]of Chinnereth eastward:
12 And the border shall go down to Jordan, and the goings out of it shall be at [q]the
salt sea: this shall be your land with the
coasts thereof round about.
13 And Moses commanded the children
of Israel, saying, [r]This *is* the land which ye
shall inherit by lot, which the LORD commanded to give unto the nine tribes, and to
the half tribe:
14 [s]For the tribe of the children of Reuben according to the house of their fathers,
and the tribe of the children of Gad according to the house of their fathers, have received *their inheritance;* and half the tribe

of Manasseh have received their inheritance:
15 The two tribes and the half tribe have
received their inheritance on this side Jordan *near* Jericho eastward, toward the sunrising.
16 And the LORD spake unto Moses, saying,
17 These *are* the names of the men which
shall divide the land unto you: [t]Eleazar the
priest, and Joshua the son of Nun.
18 And ye shall take one [u]prince of every
tribe, to divide the land by inheritance.
19 And the names of the men *are* these:
Of the tribe of Judah, Caleb the son of Jephunneh.
20 And of the tribe of the children of Simeon, Shemuel the son of Ammihud.
21 Of the tribe of Benjamin, Elidad the
son of Chislon.
22 And the prince of the tribe of the children of Dan, Bukki the son of Jogli.
23 The prince of the children of Joseph,
for the tribe of the children of Manasseh,
Hanniel the son of Ephod.
24 And the prince of the tribe of the children of Ephraim, Kemuel the son of Shiph-
tan.
25 And the prince of the tribe of the children of Zebulun, Elizaphan the son of Par-
nach.
26 And the prince of the tribe of the children of Issachar, Paltiel the son of Azzan.
27 And the prince of the tribe of the children of Asher, Ahihud the son of Shelomi.
28 And the prince of the tribe of the children of Naphtali, Pedahel the son of Ammihud.
29 These *are they* whom the LORD commanded to divide the inheritance unto the
children of Israel in the land of Canaan.

35 And the LORD spake unto Moses in
the plains of Moab by Jordan *near*
Jericho, saying,
2 [v]Command the children of Israel, that
they give unto the Levites of the inheritance
of their possession, cities to dwell in; and ye
shall give *also* unto the Levites suburbs for
the cities round about them.
3 And the cities shall they have to dwell
in; and the suburbs of them shall be for their
cattle, and for their goods, and for all their
beasts.
4 And the suburbs of the cities, which ye
shall give unto the Levites, *shall reach* from
the wall of the city and outward a thousand
cubits round about.
5 And ye shall measure from without the
city on the east side two thousand cubits,
and on the south side two thousand cubits,
and on the west side two thousand
cubits, and on the north side two thousand
cubits; and the city *shall be* in the midst: this
shall be to them the suburbs of the cities.
6 And among the cities which ye shall
give unto the Levites *there shall be* [w]six cities for refuge, which ye shall appoint for the
manslayer, that he may flee thither: and to
them ye shall add forty and two cities.
7 *So* all the cities which ye shall give to
the Levites *shall be* [x]forty and eight cities:
them *shall ye give* with their suburbs.
8 And the cities which ye shall give *shall
be* [y]of the possession of the children of Israel: [z]from *them that have* many ye shall
give many; but from *them that have* few ye
shall give few: every one shall give of his
cities unto the Levites according to his inheritance which he inheriteth.
9 ¶ And the LORD spake unto Moses, saying,
10 Speak unto the children of Israel, and
say unto them, [a]When ye be come over Jordan into the land of Canaan;
11 Then [b]ye shall appoint you cities to be
cities of refuge for you; that the slayer may
flee thither, which killeth any person at unawares.
12 [c]And they shall be unto you cities for
refuge from the avenger; that the manslayer
die not, until he stand before the congregation in judgment.
13 And of these cities which ye shall give
[d]six cities shall ye have for refuge.
14 [e]Ye shall give three cities on this side
Jordan, and three cities shall ye give in the
land of Canaan, *which* shall be cities of refuge.
15 These six cities shall be a refuge, *both*
for the children of Israel, and [f]for the
stranger, and for the sojourner among
them: that every one that killeth any person
unawares may flee thither.
16 [g]And if he smite him with an instrument of iron, so that he die, he *is* a murderer: the murderer shall surely be put to
death.
17 And if he smite him with throwing a
stone, wherewith he may die, and he die, he
is a murderer: the murderer shall surely be
put to death.
18 Or *if* he smite him with an hand
weapon of wood, wherewith he may die,
and he die, he *is* a murderer: the murderer
shall surely be put to death.
19 [h]The revenger of blood himself shall
slay the murderer: when he meeteth him, he
shall slay him.
20 But [i]if he thrust him of hatred, or hurl
at him [j]by laying of wait, that he die;
21 Or in enmity smite him with his hand,
that he die: he that smote *him* shall surely
be put to death; *for* he *is* a murderer: the
revenger of blood shall slay the murderer,
when he meeteth him.
22 But if he thrust him suddenly [k]without
enmity, or have cast upon him any thing
without laying of wait,
23 Or with any stone, wherewith a man
may die, seeing *him* not, and cast *it* upon
him, that he die, and *was* not his enemy,
neither sought his harm:
24 Then [l]the congregation shall judge
between the slayer and the revenger of
blood according to these judgments:

34:17 [t]Josh. 14:1
34:18 [u]ch. 1:4
35:2 [v]Josh. 14:3; Ezek. 45:1
35:6 [w]ver. 13; Deut. 4:41; Josh. 20:2
35:7 [x]Josh. 21:41
35:8 [y]Josh. 21:3 [z]ch. 26:54
35:10 [a]Deut. 19:2; Josh. 20:2
35:11 [b]Ex. 21:13
35:12 [c]Deut. 19:6; Josh. 20:3
35:13 [d]ver. 6
35:14 [e]Deut. 4:41; Josh. 20:8
35:15 [f]ch. 15:16
35:16 [g]Ex. 21:12; Lev. 24:17; Deut. 19:11
35:19 [h]ver. 21; Deut. 19:6; Josh. 20:3
35:20 [i]Gen. 4:8; 2 Sam. 3:27; 1 Kings 2:31 [j]Ex. 21:14; Deut. 19:11
35:22 [k]Ex. 21:13
35:24 [l]ver. 12; Josh. 20:6

25 And the congregation shall deliver the slayer out of the hand of the revenger of blood, and the congregation shall restore him to the city of his refuge, whither he was fled: and [m]he shall abide in it unto the death of the high priest, [n]which was anointed with the holy oil.

26 But if the slayer shall at any time come without the border of the city of his refuge, whither he was fled;

27 And the revenger of blood find him without the borders of the city of his refuge, and the revenger of blood kill the slayer; he shall not be guilty of blood:

28 Because he should have remained in the city of his refuge until the death of the high priest: but after the death of the high priest the slayer shall return into the land of his possession.

29 So these *things* shall be for [o]a statute of judgment unto you throughout your generations in all your dwellings.

30 Whoso killeth any person, the murderer shall be put to death by the [p]mouth of witnesses: but one witness shall not testify against any person *to cause him* to die.

31 Moreover ye shall take no satisfaction for the life of a murderer, which *is* guilty of death: but he shall be surely put to death.

32 And ye shall take no satisfaction for him that is fled to the city of his refuge, that he should come again to dwell in the land, until the death of the priest.

33 So ye shall not pollute the land wherein ye *are:* for blood [q]it defileth the land: and the land cannot be cleansed of the blood that is shed therein, but [r]by the blood of him that shed it.

34 [s]Defile not therefore the land which ye shall inhabit, wherein I dwell: for [t]I the LORD dwell among the children of Israel.

36 And the chief fathers of the families of the [u]children of Gilead, the son of Machir, the son of Manasseh, of the families of the sons of Joseph, came near, and spake before Moses, and before the princes, the chief fathers of the children of Israel:

2 And they said, [v]The LORD commanded my lord to give the land for an inheritance by lot to the children of Israel: and [w]my lord was commanded by the LORD to give the inheritance of Zelophehad our brother unto his daughters.

3 And if they be married to any of the sons of the *other* tribes of the children of Israel, then shall their inheritance be taken from the inheritance of our fathers, and shall be put to the inheritance of the tribe whereunto they are received: so shall it be taken from the lot of our inheritance.

4 And when [x]the jubile of the children of Israel shall be, then shall their inheritance be put unto the inheritance of the tribe whereunto they are received: so shall their inheritance be taken away from the inheritance of the tribe of our fathers.

5 And Moses commanded the children of Israel according to the word of the LORD, saying, The tribe of the sons of Joseph [y]hath said well.

6 This *is* the thing which the LORD doth command concerning the daughters of Zelophehad, saying, Let them marry to whom they think best; [z]only to the family of the tribe of their father shall they marry.

7 So shall not the inheritance of the children of Israel remove from tribe to tribe: for every one of the children of Israel shall [a]keep himself to the inheritance of the tribe of his fathers.

8 And [b]every daughter, that possesseth an inheritance in any tribe of the children of Israel, shall be wife unto one of the family of the tribe of her father, that the children of Israel may enjoy every man the inheritance of his fathers.

9 Neither shall the inheritance remove from *one* tribe to another tribe; but every one of the tribes of the children of Israel shall keep himself to his own inheritance.

10 Even as the LORD commanded Moses, so did the daughters of Zelophehad:

11 [c]For Mahlah, Tirzah, and Hoglah, and Milcah, and Noah, the daughters of Zelophehad, were married unto their father's brothers' sons:

12 *And* they were married into the families of the sons of Manasseh the son of Joseph, and their inheritance remained in the tribe of the family of their father.

13 These *are* the commandments and the judgments, which the LORD commanded by the hand of Moses unto the children of Israel [d]in the plains of Moab by Jordan *near* Jericho.

35:25 [m]Josh. 20:6 [n]Ex. 29:7; Lev. 4:3
35:29 [o]ch. 27:11
35:30 [p]Deut. 17:6; Matt. 18:16; 2 Cor. 13:1; Heb. 10:28
35:33 [q]Ps. 106:38; Mic. 4:11 [r]Gen. 9:6
35:34 [s]Lev. 18:25; Deut. 21:23 [t]Ex. 29:45
36:1 [u]ch. 26:29
36:2 [v]ch. 26:55; Josh. 17:3 [w]ch. 27:1; Josh. 17:3
36:4 [x]Lev. 25:10
36:5 [y]ch. 27:7
36:6 [z]ver. 12
36:7 [a]1 Kings 21:3
36:8 [b]1 Chron. 23:22
36:11 [c]ch. 27:1
36:13 [d]ch. 26:3

DEUTERONOMY

Moses wrote this book between 1410 B.C. and 1406 B.C., although the description of Moses' death in chapter 34 could not have been written by him. In Deuteronomy the Israelites prepare to enter Canaan and Moses is near death. It describes the wanderings of the people in the Sinai, their trials and tribulations, their victories, and their heritage. The Ten Commandments are repeated in chapters 4 and 5 followed by other commands and laws to the people.

Joshua is selected as the successor to Moses and is the one to lead the people into Canaan. In chapters 32 and 33, Moses speaks to the people for the last time, recounts their journey, and offers his final blessing to the multitude.

I. Review of the Israelites' journey from Egypt, 1:1–4:43
II. The laws of God reviewed, 4:44–26:19
III. The covenant of God ratified, 27:1–30:20
IV. Moses and his final days, 31:1–34:12

---

1 These *be* the words which Moses spake unto all Israel [a]on this side Jordan in the wilderness, in the plain over against the Red *sea*, between Paran, and Tophel, and Laban, and Hazeroth, and Dizahab.

2 (*There are* eleven days' *journey* from Horeb by the way of mount Seir [b]unto Kadesh-barnea.)

3 And it came to pass [c]in the fortieth year, in the eleventh month, on the first *day* of the month, *that* Moses spake unto the children of Israel, according unto all that the LORD had given him in commandment unto them;

4 [d]After he had slain Sihon the king of the Amorites, which dwelt in Heshbon, and Og the king of Bashan, which dwelt at Astaroth [e]in Edrei:

5 On this side Jordan, in the land of Moab, began Moses to declare this law, saying,

6 The LORD our God spake unto us [f]in Horeb, saying, Ye have dwelt long [g]enough in this mount:

7 Turn you, and take your journey, and go to the mount of the Amorites, and unto all *the places* nigh thereunto, in the plain, in the hills, and in the vale, and in the south, and by the sea side, to the land of the Canaanites, and unto Lebanon, unto the great river, the river Euphrates.

8 Behold, I have set the land before you: go in and possess the land which the LORD sware unto your fathers, [h]Abraham, Isaac, and Jacob, to give unto them and to their seed after them.

9 ¶ And [i]I spake unto you at that time, saying, I am not able to bear you myself alone:

10 The LORD your God hath multiplied you, and, behold, [j]ye *are* this day as the stars of heaven for multitude.

11 ([k]The LORD God of your fathers make you a thousand times so many more as ye *are*, and bless you, [l]as he hath promised you!)

12 [m]How can I myself alone bear your cumbrance, and your burden, and your strife?

13 [n]Take you wise men, and understanding, and known among your tribes, and I will make them rulers over you.

14 And ye answered me, and said, The thing which thou hast spoken *is* good *for us* to do.

15 So I took the chief of your tribes, wise men, and known, [o]and made them heads over you, captains over thousands, and captains over hundreds, and captains over fifties, and captains over tens, and officers among your tribes.

16 And I charged your judges at that time, saying, Hear *the causes* between your brethren, and [p]judge righteously between *every* man and his [q]brother, and the stranger *that is* with him.

17 [r]Ye shall not respect persons in judgment; *but* ye shall hear the small as well as the great; ye shall not be afraid of the face of man; for [s]the judgment *is* God's: and the cause that is too hard for you, [t]bring *it* unto me, and I will hear it.

18 And I commanded you at that time all the things which ye should do.

19 ¶ And when we departed from Horeb, [u]we went through all that great and terrible wilderness, which ye saw by the way of the mountain of the Amorites, as the LORD our God commanded us; and [v]we came to Kadesh-barnea.

20 And I said unto you, Ye are come unto the mountain of the Amorites, which the LORD our God doth give unto us.

21 Behold, the LORD thy God hath set the land before thee: go up *and* possess *it*, as the LORD God of thy fathers hath said unto thee; [w]fear not, neither be discouraged.

22 ¶ And ye came near unto me every one of you, and said, We will send men before

1:1 [a]Josh. 9:1
1:2 [b]Num. 13:26; ch. 9:23
1:3 [c]Num. 33:38
1:4 [d]Num. 21:24 [e]Num. 21:33; Josh. 13:12
1:6 [f]Ex. 3:1 [g]Ex. 19:1; Num. 10:11
1:8 [h]Gen. 12:7
1:9 [i]Ex. 18:18; Num. 11:14
1:10 [j]Gen. 15:5; ch. 10:22
1:11 [k]2 Sam. 24:3 [l]Gen. 15:5; Ex. 32:13
1:12 [m]1 Kings 3:8
1:13 [n]Ex. 18:21; Num. 11:16
1:15 [o]Ex. 18:25
1:16 [p]ch. 16:18; John 7:24 [q]Lev. 24:22
1:17 [r]Lev. 19:15; ch. 16:19; 1 Sam. 16:7; Prov. 24:23; Jam. 2:1 [s]2 Chron. 19:6 [t]Ex. 18:22
1:19 [u]Num. 10:12; ch. 8:15; Jer. 2:6 [v]Num. 13:26
1:21 [w]Josh. 1:9

us, and they shall search us out the land, and bring us word again by what way we must go up, and into what cities we shall come.

23 And the saying pleased me well: and [x]I took twelve men of you, one of a tribe:

24 And [y]they turned and went up into the mountain, and came unto the valley of Eshcol, and searched it out.

25 And they took of the fruit of the land in their hands, and brought *it* down unto us, and brought us word again, and said, [z]*It is* a good land which the LORD our God doth give us.

26 [a]Notwithstanding ye would not go up, but rebelled against the commandment of the LORD your God:

27 And ye murmured in your tents, and said, Because the LORD [b]hated us, he hath brought us forth out of the land of Egypt, to deliver us into the hand of the Amorites, to destroy us.

28 Whither shall we go up? our brethren have discouraged our heart, saying, [c]The people *is* greater and taller than we; the cities *are* great and walled up to heaven; and moreover we have seen the sons of the [d]Anakims there.

29 Then I said unto you, Dread not, neither be afraid of them.

30 [e]The LORD your God which goeth before you, he shall fight for you, according to all that he did for you in Egypt before your eyes;

31 And in the wilderness, where thou hast seen how that the LORD thy God [f]bare thee, as a man doth bear his son, in all the way that ye went, until ye came into this place.

32 Yet in this thing [g]ye did not believe the LORD your God,

33 [h]Who went in the way before you, [i]to search you out a place to pitch your tents *in,* in fire by night, to shew you by what way ye should go, and in a cloud by day.

34 And the LORD heard the voice of your words, and was wroth, [j]and sware, saying,

35 [k]Surely there shall not one of these men of this evil generation see that good land, which I sware to give unto your fathers,

36 [l]Save Caleb the son of Jephunneh; he shall see it, and to him will I give the land that he hath trodden upon, and to his children, because [m]he hath wholly followed the LORD.

37 [n]Also the LORD was angry with me for your sakes, saying, Thou also shalt not go in thither.

38 [o]*But* Joshua the son of Nun, [p]which standeth before thee, he shall go in thither: [q]encourage him: for he shall cause Israel to inherit it.

39 [r]Moreover your little ones, which [s]ye said should be a prey, and your children, which in that day [t]had no knowledge between good and evil, they shall go in thither, and unto them will I give it, and they shall possess it.

40 [u]But *as for* you, turn you, and take your journey into the wilderness by the way of the Red sea.

41 Then ye answered and said unto me, [v]We have sinned against the LORD, we will go up and fight, according to all that the LORD our God commanded us. And when ye had girded on every man his weapons of war, ye were ready to go up into the hill.

42 And the LORD said unto me, Say unto them, [w]Go not up, neither fight; for I *am* not among you; lest ye be smitten before your enemies.

43 So I spake unto you; and ye would not hear, but rebelled against the commandment of the LORD, and [x]went presumptuously up into the hill.

44 And the Amorites, which dwelt in that mountain, came out against you, and chased you, [y]as bees do, and destroyed you in Seir, *even* unto Hormah.

45 And ye returned and wept before the LORD; but the LORD would not hearken to your voice, nor give ear unto you.

46 [z]So ye abode in Kadesh many days, according unto the days that ye abode *there.*

2 Then we turned, and took our journey into the wilderness by the way of the Red sea, [a]as the LORD spake unto me: and we compassed mount Seir many days.

2 And the LORD spake unto me, saying,

3 Ye have compassed this mountain [b]long enough: turn you northward.

4 And command thou the people, saying, [c]Ye *are* to pass through the coast of your brethren the children of Esau, which dwell in Seir; and they shall be afraid of you: take ye good heed unto yourselves therefore:

5 Meddle not with them; for I will not give you of their land, no, not so much as a foot breadth; [d]because I have given mount Seir unto Esau *for* a possession.

6 Ye shall buy meat of them for money, that ye may eat; and ye shall also buy water of them for money, that ye may drink.

7 For the LORD thy God hath blessed thee in all the works of thy hand: he knoweth thy walking through this great wilderness: [e]these forty years the LORD thy God *hath been* with thee; thou hast lacked nothing.

8 [f]And when we passed by from our brethren the children of Esau, which dwelt in Seir, through the way of the plain from [g]Elath, and from Ezion-gaber, we turned and passed by the way of the wilderness of Moab.

9 And the LORD said unto me, Distress not the Moabites, neither contend with them in battle: for I will not give thee of their land *for* a possession; because I have given [h]Ar unto [i]the children of Lot *for* a possession.

10 [j]The Emims dwelt therein in times past, a people great, and many, and tall, as [k]the Anakims;

11 Which also were accounted giants, as the Anakims; but the Moabites called them Emims.

1:23 [x]Num. 13:3
1:24 [y]Num. 13:22
1:25 [z]Num. 13:27
1:26 [a]Num. 14:1; Ps. 106:24
1:27 [b]ch. 9:28
1:28 [c]Num. 13:28; ch. 9:1 [d]Num. 13:28
1:30 [e]Ex. 14:14; Neh. 4:20
1:31 [f]Ex. 19:4; ch. 32:11; Isa. 46:3; Hos. 11:3; Acts 13:18
1:32 [g]Ps. 106:24; Jude 5
1:33 [h]Ex. 13:21; Ps. 78:14 [i]Num. 10:33; Ezek. 20:6
1:34 [j]ch. 2:14
1:35 [k]Num. 14:22; Ps. 95:11
1:36 [l]Num. 14:24; Josh. 14:9 [m]Num. 14:24
1:37 [n]Num. 20:12; ch. 3:26; Ps. 106:32
1:38 [o]Num. 14:30 [p]Ex. 24:13; 1 Sam. 16:22 [q]Num. 27:18; ch. 31:7
1:39 [r]Num. 14:31 [s]Num. 14:3 [t]Isa. 7:15; Rom. 9:11
1:40 [u]Num. 14:25
1:41 [v]Num. 14:40
1:42 [w]Num. 14:42
1:43 [x]Num. 14:44
1:44 [y]Ps. 118:12
1:46 [z]Num. 13:25; Judg. 11:17
2:1 [a]Num. 14:25; ch. 1:40
2:3 [b]ver. 7
2:4 [c]Num. 20:14
2:5 [d]Gen. 36:8; Josh. 24:4
2:7 [e]ch. 8:2
2:8 [f]Judg. 11:18 [g]1 Kings 9:26
2:9 [h]Num. 21:28 [i]Gen. 19:36
2:10 [j]Gen. 14:5 [k]Num. 13:22; ch. 9:2

12 [l]The Horims also dwelt in Seir beforetime; but the children of Esau succeeded them, when they had destroyed them from before them, and dwelt in their stead; as Israel did unto the land of his possession, which the LORD gave unto them.

13 Now rise up, *said I,* and get you over [m]the brook Zered. And we went over the brook Zered.

14 And the space in which we came [n]from Kadesh-barnea, until we were come over the brook Zered, *was* thirty and eight years; [o]until all the generation of the men of war were wasted out from among the host, [p]as the LORD sware unto them.

15 For indeed the [q]hand of the LORD was against them, to destroy them from among the host, until they were consumed.

16 ¶ So it came to pass, when all the men of war were consumed and dead from among the people,

17 That the LORD spake unto me, saying,

18 Thou art to pass over through Ar, the coast of Moab, this day:

19 And *when* thou comest nigh over against the children of Ammon, distress them not, nor meddle with them: for I will not give thee of the land of the children of Ammon *any* possession; because I have given it unto [r]the children of Lot *for* a possession.

20 (That also was accounted a land of giants: giants dwelt therein in old time; and the Ammonites call them [s]Zamzummims;

21 [t]A people great, and many, and tall, as the Anakims; but the LORD destroyed them before them; and they succeeded them, and dwelt in their stead:

22 As he did to the children of Esau, [u]which dwelt in Seir, when he destroyed [v]the Horims from before them; and they succeeded them, and dwelt in their stead even unto this day:

23 And [w]the Avims which dwelt in Hazerim, *even* unto [x]Azzah, [y]the Caphtorims, which came forth out of Caphtor, destroyed them, and dwelt in their stead.)

24 ¶ Rise ye up, take your journey, and [z]pass over the river Arnon: behold, I have given into thine hand Sihon the Amorite, king of Heshbon, and his land: begin to possess *it,* and contend with him in battle.

25 [a]This day will I begin to put the dread of thee and the fear of thee upon the nations *that are* under the whole heaven, who shall hear report of thee, and shall tremble, and be in anguish because of thee.

26 ¶ And I sent messengers out of the wilderness of Kedemoth unto Sihon king of Heshbon [b]with words of peace, saying,

27 [c]Let me pass through thy land: I will go along by the high way, I will neither turn unto the right hand nor to the left.

28 Thou shalt sell me meat for money, that I may eat; and give me water for money, that I may drink: [d]only I will pass through on my feet;

29 ([e]As the children of Esau which dwell in Seir, and the Moabites which dwell in Ar, did unto me;) until I shall pass over Jordan into the land which the LORD our God giveth us.

30 [f]But Sihon king of Heshbon would not let us pass by him: for [g]the LORD thy God [h]hardened his spirit, and made his heart obstinate, that he might deliver him into thy hand, as *appeareth* this day.

31 And the LORD said unto me, Behold, I have begun to [i]give Sihon and his land before thee: begin to possess, that thou mayest inherit his land.

32 [j]Then Sihon came out against us, he and all his people, to fight at Jahaz.

33 And [k]the LORD our God delivered him before us; and [l]we smote him, and his sons, and all his people.

34 And we took all his cities at that time, and [m]utterly destroyed the men, and the women, and the little ones, of every city, we left none to remain:

35 Only the cattle we took for a prey unto ourselves, and the spoil of the cities which we took.

36 [n]From Aroer, which *is* by the brink of the river of Arnon, and *from* the city that *is* by the river, even unto Gilead, there was not one city too strong for us: [o]the LORD our God delivered all unto us:

37 Only unto the land of the children of Ammon thou camest not, *nor* unto any place of the river [p]Jabbok, nor unto the cities in the mountains, nor unto [q]whatsoever the LORD our God forbad us.

3 Then we turned, and went up the way to Bashan: and [r]Og the king of Bashan came out against us, he and all his people, to battle [s]at Edrei.

2 And the LORD said unto me, Fear him not: for I will deliver him, and all his people, and his land, into thy hand; and thou shalt do unto him as thou didst unto [t]Sihon king of the Amorites, which dwelt at Heshbon.

3 So the LORD our God delivered into our hands Og also, the king of Bashan, and all his people: [u]and we smote him until none was left to him remaining.

4 And we took all his cities at that time, there was not a city which we took not from them, threescore cities, [v]all the region of Argob, the kingdom of Og in Bashan.

5 All these cities *were* fenced with high walls, gates, and bars; beside unwalled towns a great many.

6 And we utterly destroyed them, as we did unto Sihon king [w]of Heshbon, utterly destroying the men, women, and children, of every city.

7 But all the cattle, and the spoil of the cities, we took for a prey to ourselves.

8 And we took at that time out of the hand of the two kings of the Amorites the land that *was* on this side Jordan, from the river of Arnon unto mount Hermon;

9 (*Which* [x]Hermon the Sidonians call Sirion; and the Amorites call it [y]Shenir;)

10 [z]All the cities of the plain, and all Gil-

2:12 [l]ver. 22; Gen. 14:6
2:13 [m]Num. 21:12
2:14 [n]Num. 13:26 [o]Num. 14:33 [p]Num. 14:35; ch. 1:34; Ezek. 20:15
2:15 [q]Ps. 78:33
2:19 [r]Gen. 19:38
2:20 [s]Gen. 14:5
2:21 [t]ver. 10
2:22 [u]Gen. 36:8 [v]Gen. 14:6; ver. 12
2:23 [w]Josh. 13:3 [x]Jer. 25:20 [y]Gen. 10:14; Am. 9:7
2:24 [z]Num. 21:13; Judg. 11:18
2:25 [a]Ex. 15:14; ch. 11:25; Josh. 2:9
2:26 [b]ch. 20:10
2:27 [c]Num. 21:21; Judg. 11:19
2:28 [d]Num. 20:19
2:29 [e]Num. 20:18; ch. 23:3; Judg. 11:17
2:30 [f]Num. 21:23 [g]Josh. 11:20 [h]Ex. 4:21
2:31 [i]ch. 1:8
2:32 [j]Num. 21:23
2:33 [k]ch. 7:2 [l]Num. 21:24; ch. 29:7
2:34 [m]Lev. 27:28; ch. 7:2
2:36 [n]ch. 3:12; Josh. 13:9 [o]Ps. 44:3
2:37 [p]Gen. 32:22; Num. 21:24; ch. 3:16 [q]ver. 5
3:1 [r]Num. 21:33; ch. 29:7 [s]ch. 1:4
3:2 [t]Num. 21:24
3:3 [u]Num. 21:35
3:4 [v]1 Kings 4:13
3:6 [w]ch. 2:24; Ps. 135:10
3:9 [x]ch. 4:48; Ps. 29:6 [y]1 Chron. 5:23
3:10 [z]ch. 4:49

ead, and [a]all Bashan, unto Salchah and Edrei, cities of the kingdom of Og in Bashan.
11 [b]For only Og king of Bashan remained
of the remnant of [c]giants; behold, his bedstead *was* a bedstead of iron; *is* it not in
[d]Rabbath of the children of Ammon? nine
cubits *was* the length thereof, and four cubits the breadth of it, after the cubit of a
man.
12 And this land, *which* we possessed at
that time, [e]from Aroer, which *is* by the river
Arnon, and half mount Gilead, and [f]the cities thereof, gave I unto the Reubenites and
to the Gadites.
13 [g]And the rest of Gilead, and all Bashan, *being* the kingdom of Og, gave I unto
the half tribe of Manasseh; all the region of
Argob, with all Bashan, which was called
the land of giants.
14 [h]Jair the son of Manasseh took all the
country of Argob [i]unto the coasts of Ge-
shuri and Maachathi; and [j]called them after his own name, Bashan-havoth-jair, unto
this day.
15 [k]And I gave Gilead unto Machir.
16 And unto the Reubenites [l]and unto
the Gadites I gave from Gilead even unto
the river Arnon half the valley, and the border even unto the river Jabbok, [m]*which is*
the border of the children of Ammon;
17 The plain also, and Jordan, and the
coast *thereof*, from [n]Chinnereth [o]even
unto the sea of the plain, [p]*even* the salt sea,
under Ashdoth-pisgah eastward.
18 ¶ And I commanded you at that time,
saying, The LORD your God hath given you
this land to possess it: [q]ye shall pass over
armed before your brethren the children of
Israel, all *that are* meet for the war.
19 But your wives, and your little ones,
and your cattle, (*for* I know that ye have
much cattle,) shall abide in your cities
which I have given you;
20 Until the LORD have given rest unto
your brethren, as well as unto you, and *until*
they also possess the land which the LORD
your God hath given them beyond Jordan:
and *then* shall ye [r]return every man unto
his possession, which I have given you.
21 ¶ And [s]I commanded Joshua at that
time, saying, Thine eyes have seen all that
the LORD your God hath done unto these
two kings: so shall the LORD do unto all the
kingdoms whither thou passest.
22 Ye shall not fear them: for [t]the LORD
your God he shall fight for you.
23 And [u]I besought the LORD at that time,
saying,
24 O Lord GOD, thou hast begun to shew
thy servant [v]thy greatness, and thy mighty
hand: for [w]what God *is there* in heaven or
in earth, that can do according to thy works,
and according to thy might?
25 I pray thee, let me go over, and see
[x]the good land that *is* beyond Jordan, that
goodly mountain, and Lebanon.
26 But the LORD [y]was wroth with me for
your sakes, and would not hear me: and the
LORD said unto me, Let it suffice thee; speak
no more unto me of this matter.
27 [z]Get thee up into the top of Pisgah,
and lift up thine eyes westward, and northward, and southward, and eastward, and
behold *it* with thine eyes: for thou shalt not
go over this Jordan.
28 But [a]charge Joshua, and encourage
him, and strengthen him: for he shall go
over before this people, and he shall cause
them to inherit the land which thou shalt
see.
29 So we abode in [b]the valley over
against Beth-peor.

4 Now therefore hearken, O Israel, unto
[c]the statutes and unto the judgments,
which I teach you, for to do *them*, that ye
may live, and go in and possess the land
which the LORD God of your fathers giveth
you.
2 [d]Ye shall not add unto the word which
I command you, neither shall ye diminish
ought from it, that ye may keep the commandments of the LORD your God which I
command you.
3 Your eyes have seen what the LORD did
because of [e]Baal-peor: for all the men that
followed Baal-peor, the LORD thy God hath
destroyed them from among you.
4 But ye that did cleave unto the LORD
your God *are* alive every one of you this
day.
5 Behold, I have taught you statutes and
judgments, even as the LORD my God commanded me, that ye should do so in the land
whither ye go to possess it.
6 Keep therefore and do *them*; for this *is*
[f]your wisdom and your understanding in
the sight of the nations, which shall hear all
these statutes, and say, Surely this great nation *is* a wise and understanding people.
7 For [g]what nation *is there so* great, who
hath [h]God *so* nigh unto them, as the LORD
our God *is* in all *things that* we call upon
him *for*?
8 And what nation *is there so* great, that
hath statutes and judgments *so* righteous as
all this law, which I set before you this day?
9 Only take heed to thyself, and [i]keep
thy soul diligently, [j]lest thou forget the
things which thine eyes have seen, and lest
they depart from thy heart all the days of
thy life: but [k]teach them thy sons, and thy
sons' sons;
10 *Specially* [l]the day that thou stoodest
before the LORD thy God in Horeb, when the
LORD said unto me, Gather me the people
together, and I will make them hear my
words, that they may learn to fear me all the
days that they shall live upon the earth, and
that they may teach their children.
11 And ye came near and stood under the
mountain; and the [m]mountain burned with
fire unto the midst of heaven, with darkness, clouds, and thick darkness.
12 [n]And the LORD spake unto you out of
the midst of the fire: [o]ye heard the voice of

3:10 [a]Josh. 12:5
3:11 [b]Am. 2:9 [c]Gen. 14:5 [d]2 Sam. 12:26; Jer. 49:2; Ezek. 21:20
3:12 [e]ch. 2:36; Josh. 12:2 [f]Num. 32:33; Josh. 12:6
3:13 [g]Josh. 13:29
3:14 [h]1 Chron. 2:22 [i]Josh. 13:13; 2 Sam. 3:3 [j]Num. 32:41
3:15 [k]Num. 32:39
3:16 [l]2 Sam. 24:5 [m]Num. 21:24; Josh. 12:2
3:17 [n]Num. 34:11 [o]ch. 4:49; Num. 34:11; Josh. 12:3 [p]Gen. 14:3
3:18 [q]Num. 32:20
3:20 [r]Josh. 22:4
3:21 [s]Num. 27:18
3:22 [t]Ex. 14:14; ch. 1:30
3:23 [u]2 Cor. 12:8
3:24 [v]ch. 11:2 [w]Ex. 15:11; 2 Sam. 7:22; Ps. 71:19
3:25 [x]Ex. 3:8; ch. 4:22
3:26 [y]Num. 20:12; ch. 1:37; Ps. 106:32
3:27 [z]Num. 27:12
3:28 [a]Num. 27:18; ch. 1:38
3:29 [b]ch. 4:46
4:1 [c]Lev. 19:37; ch. 5:1; Ezek. 20:11; Rom. 10:5
4:2 [d]ch. 12:32; Josh. 1:7; Prov. 30:6; Eccl. 12:13; Rev. 22:18
4:3 [e]Num. 25:4; Josh. 22:17; Ps. 106:28
4:6 [f]Job 28:28; Ps. 19:7; Prov. 1:7
4:7 [g]2 Sam. 7:23 [h]Ps. 46:1; Isa. 55:6
4:9 [i]Prov. 4:23 [j]Prov. 3:1 [k]Gen. 18:19; ch. 6:7; Ps. 78:5; Eph. 6:4
4:10 [l]Ex. 19:9; Heb. 12:18
4:11 [m]Ex. 19:18; ch. 5:23
4:12 [n]ch. 5:4 over. 33

the words, but saw no similitude; [p]only *ye heard* a voice.

13 [q]And he declared unto you his covenant, which he commanded you to perform, *even* [r]ten commandments; and [s]he wrote them upon two tables of stone.

14 ¶ And [t]the LORD commanded me at that time to teach you statutes and judgments, that ye might do them in the land whither ye go over to possess it.

15 [u]Take ye therefore good heed unto yourselves; for ye saw no manner of [v]similitude on the day *that* the LORD spake unto you in Horeb out of the midst of the fire:

16 Lest ye [w]corrupt *yourselves,* and [x]make you a graven image, the similitude of any figure, [y]the likeness of male or female,

17 The likeness of any beast that *is* on the earth, the likeness of any winged fowl that flieth in the air,

18 The likeness of any thing that creepeth on the ground, the likeness of any fish that *is* in the waters beneath the earth:

19 And lest thou [z]lift up thine eyes unto heaven, and when thou seest the sun, and the moon, and the stars, *even* [a]all the host of heaven, shouldest be driven to [b]worship them, and serve them, which the LORD thy God hath divided unto all nations under the whole heaven.

20 But the LORD hath taken you, and [c]brought you forth out of the iron furnace, *even* out of Egypt, [d]to be unto him a people of inheritance, as *ye are* this day.

21 Furthermore [e]the LORD was angry with me for your sakes, and sware that I should not go over Jordan, and that I should not go in unto that good land, which the LORD thy God giveth thee *for* an inheritance:

22 But [f]I must die in this land, [g]I must not go over Jordan: but ye shall go over, and possess [h]that good land.

23 Take heed unto yourselves, [i]lest ye forget the covenant of the LORD your God, which he made with you, [j]and make you a graven image, *or* the likeness of any *thing,* which the LORD thy God hath forbidden thee.

24 For [k]the LORD thy God *is* a consuming fire, *even* [l]a jealous God.

25 ¶ When thou shalt beget children, and children's children, and ye shall have remained long in the land, and [m]shall corrupt *yourselves,* and make a graven image, *or* the likeness of any *thing,* and [n]shall do evil in the sight of the LORD thy God, to provoke him to anger:

26 [o]I call heaven and earth to witness against you this day, that ye shall soon utterly perish from off the land whereunto ye go over Jordan to possess it; ye shall not prolong *your* days upon it, but shall utterly be destroyed.

27 And the LORD [p]shall scatter you among the nations, and ye shall be left few in number among the heathen, whither the LORD shall lead you.

28 And [q]there ye shall serve gods, the work of men's hands, wood and stone, [r]which neither see, nor hear, nor eat, nor smell.

29 [s]But if from thence thou shalt seek the LORD thy God, thou shalt find *him,* if thou seek him with all thy heart and with all thy soul.

30 When thou art in tribulation, and all these things are come upon thee, [t]*even* in the latter days, if thou [u]turn to the LORD thy God, and shalt be obedient unto his voice;

31 (For the LORD thy God *is* [v]a merciful God;) he will not forsake thee, neither destroy thee, nor forget the covenant of thy fathers which he sware unto them.

32 For [w]ask now of the days that are past, which were before thee, since the day that God created man upon the earth, and *ask* [x]from the one side of heaven unto the other, whether there hath been *any such thing* as this great thing *is,* or hath been heard like it?

33 [y]Did *ever* people hear the voice of God speaking out of the midst of the fire, as thou hast heard, and live?

34 Or hath God assayed to go *and* take him a nation from the midst of *another* nation, [z]by temptations, [a]by signs, and by wonders, and by war, and [b]by a mighty hand, and [c]by a stretched out arm, [d]and by great terrors, according to all that the LORD your God did for you in Egypt before your eyes?

35 Unto thee it was shewed, that thou mightest know that the LORD he *is* God; [e]*there is* none else beside him.

36 [f]Out of heaven he made thee to hear his voice, that he might instruct thee: and upon earth he shewed thee his great fire; and thou heardest his words out of the midst of the fire.

37 And because [g]he loved thy fathers, therefore he chose their seed after them, and [h]brought thee out in his sight with his mighty power out of Egypt;

38 [i]To drive out nations from before thee greater and mightier than thou *art,* to bring thee in, to give thee their land *for* an inheritance, as *it is* this day.

39 Know therefore this day, and consider *it* in thine heart, that [j]the LORD he *is* God in heaven above, and upon the earth beneath: *there is* none else.

40 [k]Thou shalt keep therefore his statutes, and his commandments, which I command thee this day, [l]that it may go well with thee, and with thy children after thee, and that thou mayest prolong *thy* days upon the earth, which the LORD thy God giveth thee, for ever.

41 ¶ Then Moses [m]severed three cities on this side Jordan toward the sunrising;

42 [n]That the slayer might flee thither, which should kill his neighbour unawares, and hated him not in times past; and that

4:12 [p]Ex. 20:22; 1 Kings 19:12
4:13 [q]ch. 9:9 [r]Ex. 34:28 [s]Ex. 24:12
4:14 [t]Ex. 21:1
4:15 [u]Josh. 23:11 [v]Isa. 40:18
4:16 [w]Ex. 32:7 [x]Ex. 20:4; ver. 23; ch. 5:8 [y]Rom. 1:23
4:19 [z]ch. 17:3; Job 31:26 [a]Gen. 2:1; 2 Kings 17:16 [b]Rom. 1:25
4:20 [c]1 Kings 8:51; Jer. 11:4 [d]Ex. 19:5; ch. 9:29
4:21 [e]Num. 20:12; ch. 1:37
4:22 [f]2 Pet. 1:13 [g]ch. 3:27 [h]ch. 3:25
4:23 [i]ver. 9 [j]ver. 16; Ex. 20:4
4:24 [k]Ex. 24:17; ch. 9:3; Isa. 33:14; Heb. 12:29 [l]Ex. 20:5; ch. 6:15; Isa. 42:8
4:25 [m]ver. 16 [n]2 Kings 17:17
4:26 [o]ch. 30:18; Isa. 1:2; Mic. 6:2
4:27 [p]Lev. 26:33; ch. 28:62; Neh. 1:8
4:28 [q]ch. 28:64; 1 Sam. 26:19; Jer. 16:13 [r]Ps. 115:4; Isa. 44:9
4:29 [s]Lev. 26:39; ch. 30:1; 2 Chron. 15:4; Neh. 1:9; Isa. 55:6; Jer. 29:12
4:30 [t]Gen. 49:1; ch. 31:29; Jer. 23:20; Hos. 3:5 [u]Joel 2:12
4:31 [v]2 Chron. 30:9; Neh. 9:31; Ps. 116:5; Jonah 4:2
4:32 [w]Job 8:8 [x]Matt. 24:31
4:33 [y]Ex. 24:11; ch. 5:24
4:34 [z]ch. 7:19 [a]Ex. 7:3 [b]Ex. 13:3 [c]Ex. 6:6 [d]ch. 26:8
4:35 [e]ch. 32:39; 1 Sam. 2:2; Isa. 45:5; Mark 12:29
4:36 [f]Ex. 19:9; Heb. 12:18
4:37 [g]ch. 10:15 [h]Ex. 13:3
4:38 [i]ch. 7:1
4:39 [j]ver. 35; Josh. 2:11
4:40 [k]Lev. 22:31 [l]ch. 5:16; Eph. 6:3
4:41 [m]Num. 35:6
4:42 [n]ch. 19:4

fleeing unto one of these cities he might
live:
43 *Namely,* [o]Bezer in the wilderness, in
the plain country, of the Reubenites; and
Ramoth in Gilead, of the Gadites; and Golan
in Bashan, of the Manassites.
44 ¶ And this *is* the law which Moses set
before the children of Israel:
45 These *are* the testimonies, and the statutes, and the judgments, which Moses
spake unto the children of Israel, after they
came forth out of Egypt,
46 On this side Jordan, [p]in the valley
over against Beth-peor, in the land of Sihon
king of the Amorites, who dwelt at Heshbon, whom Moses and the children of Israel
[q]smote, after they were come forth out of
Egypt:
47 And they possessed his land, and the
land [r]of Og king of Bashan, two kings of
the Amorites, which *were* on this side Jordan toward the sunrising;
48 [s]From Aroer, which *is* by the bank
of the river Arnon, even unto mount Sion,
which *is* [t]Hermon,
49 And all the plain on this side Jordan
eastward, even unto the sea of the plain,
under the [u]springs of Pisgah.
5 And Moses called all Israel, and said
unto them, Hear, O Israel, the statutes
and judgments which I speak in your ears
this day, that ye may learn them, and keep,
and do them.
2 [v]The LORD our God made a covenant
with us in Horeb.
3 The LORD [w]made not this covenant with
our fathers, but with us, *even* us, who *are* all
of us here alive this day.
4 [x]The LORD talked with you face to face
in the mount out of the midst of the fire,
5 ([y]I stood between the LORD and you at
that time, to shew you the word of the LORD:
for [z]ye were afraid by reason of the fire,
and went not up into the mount;) saying,
6 ¶ [a]I *am* the LORD thy God, which
brought thee out of the land of Egypt, from
the house of bondage.
7 [b]Thou shalt have none other gods before me.
8 [c]Thou shalt not make thee *any* graven
image, *or* any likeness *of any thing* that *is* in
heaven above, or that *is* in the earth beneath, or that *is* in the waters beneath the
earth:
9 Thou shalt not bow down thyself unto
them, nor serve them: for I the LORD thy
God *am* a jealous God, [d]visiting the iniquity
of the fathers upon the children unto the
third and fourth *generation* of them that
hate me,
10 [e]And shewing mercy unto thousands
of them that love me and keep my commandments.
11 [f]Thou shalt not take the name of the
LORD thy God in vain: for the LORD will not
hold *him* guiltless that taketh his name in
vain.
12 [g]Keep the sabbath day to sanctify it,
as the LORD thy God hath commanded thee.
13 [h]Six days thou shalt labour, and do all
thy work:
14 But the seventh day *is* the [i]sabbath of
the LORD thy God: *in it* thou shalt not do any
work, thou, nor thy son, nor thy daughter,
nor thy manservant, nor thy maidservant,
nor thine ox, nor thine ass, nor any of thy
cattle, nor thy stranger that *is* within thy
gates; that thy manservant and thy maidservant may rest as well as thou.
15 [j]And remember that thou wast a servant in the land of Egypt, and *that* the LORD
thy God brought thee out thence [k]through
a mighty hand and by a stretched out arm:
therefore the LORD thy God commanded
thee to keep the sabbath day.
16 ¶ [l]Honour thy father and thy mother,
as the LORD thy God hath commanded thee;
[m]that thy days may be prolonged, and that
it may go well with thee, in the land which
the LORD thy God giveth thee.
17 [n]Thou shalt not kill.
18 [o]Neither shalt thou commit adultery.
19 [p]Neither shalt thou steal.
20 [q]Neither shalt thou bear false witness
against thy neighbour.
21 [r]Neither shalt thou desire thy neighbour's wife, neither shalt thou covet thy
neighbour's house, his field, or his manservant, or his maidservant, his ox, or his ass,
or any *thing* that *is* thy neighbour's.
22 ¶ These words the LORD spake unto all
your assembly in the mount out of the midst
of the fire, of the cloud, and of the thick
darkness, with a great voice: and he added
no more. And [s]he wrote them in two tables
of stone, and delivered them unto me.
23 [t]And it came to pass, when ye heard
the voice out of the midst of the darkness,
(for the mountain did burn with fire,) that ye
came near unto me, *even* all the heads of
your tribes, and your elders;
24 And ye said, Behold, the LORD our God
hath shewed us his glory and his greatness,
and [u]we have heard his voice out of the
midst of the fire: we have seen this day that
God doth talk with man, and he [v]liveth.
25 Now therefore why should we die? for
this great fire will consume us: [w]if we hear
the voice of the LORD our God any more,
then we shall die.
26 [x]For who *is there of* all flesh, that hath
heard the voice of the living God speaking
out of the midst of the fire, as we *have,* and
lived?
27 Go thou near, and hear all that the
LORD our God shall say: and [y]speak thou
unto us all that the LORD our God shall
speak unto thee; and we will hear *it,* and
do *it.*
28 And the LORD heard the voice of your
words, when ye spake unto me; and the
LORD said unto me, I have heard the voice of
the words of this people, which they have
spoken unto thee: [z]they have well said all
that they have spoken.
29 [a]O that there were such an heart in

4:43 [o]Josh. 20:8
4:46 [p]ch. 3:29 [q]Num. 21:24; ch. 1:4
4:47 [r]Num. 21:35; ch. 3:3
4:48 [s]ch. 2:36 [t]ch. 3:9; Ps. 133:3
4:49 [u]ch. 3:17
5:2 [v]Ex. 19:5; ch. 4:23
5:3 [w]Matt. 13:17; Heb. 8:9
5:4 [x]Ex. 19:9; ch. 4:33
5:5 [y]Ex. 20:21; Gal. 3:19 [z]Ex. 19:16
5:6 [a]Ex. 20:2; Lev. 26:1; ch. 6:4; Ps. 81:10
5:7 [b]Ex. 20:3
5:8 [c]Ex. 20:4
5:9 [d]Ex. 34:7
5:10 [e]Jer. 32:18; Dan. 9:4
5:11 [f]Ex. 20:7; Lev. 19:12; Matt. 5:33
5:12 [g]Ex. 20:8
5:13 [h]Ex. 23:12; Ezek. 20:12
5:14 [i]Gen. 2:2; Ex. 16:29; Heb. 4:4
5:15 [j]ch. 15:15 [k]ch. 4:34
5:16 [l]Ex. 20:12; Lev. 19:3; ch. 27:16; Eph. 6:2; Col. 3:20 [m]ch. 4:40
5:17 [n]Ex. 20:13; Matt. 5:21
5:18 [o]Ex. 20:14; Luke 18:20; Jam. 2:11
5:19 [p]Ex. 20:15; Rom. 13:9
5:20 [q]Ex. 20:16
5:21 [r]Ex. 20:17; Mic. 2:2; Hab. 2:9; Luke 12:15; Rom. 7:7
5:22 [s]Ex. 24:12; ch. 4:13
5:23 [t]Ex. 20:18
5:24 [u]Ex. 19:19 [v]ch. 4:33; Judg. 13:22
5:25 [w]ch. 18:16
5:26 [x]ch. 4:33
5:27 [y]Ex. 20:19; Heb. 12:19
5:28 [z]ch. 18:17
5:29 [a]ch. 32:29; Ps. 81:13; Isa. 48:18; Matt. 23:37; Luke 19:42

them, that they would fear me, and [b]keep all my commandments always, [c]that it might be well with them, and with their children for ever!

30 Go say to them, Get you into your tents again.

31 But as for thee, stand thou here by me, [d]and I will speak unto thee all the commandments, and the statutes, and the judgments, which thou shalt teach them, that they may do *them* in the land which I give them to possess it.

32 Ye shall observe to do therefore as the LORD your God hath commanded you: [e]ye shall not turn aside to the right hand or to the left.

33 Ye shall walk in [f]all the ways which the LORD your God hath commanded you, that ye may live, [g]and *that it may be* well with you, and *that* ye may prolong *your* days in the land which ye shall possess.

6 Now these *are* [h]the commandments, the statutes, and the judgments, which the LORD your God commanded to teach you, that ye might do *them* in the land whither ye go to possess it:

2 [i]That thou mightest fear the LORD thy God, to keep all his statutes and his commandments, which I command thee, thou, and thy son, and thy son's son, all the days of thy life; [j]and that thy days may be prolonged.

3 ¶ Hear therefore, O Israel, and observe to do *it;* that it may be well with thee, and that ye may increase mightily, [k]as the LORD God of thy fathers hath promised thee, in [l]the land that floweth with milk and honey.

4 [m]Hear, O Israel: The LORD our God *is* one LORD:

5 And [n]thou shalt love the LORD thy God [o]with all thine heart, and with all thy soul, and with all thy might.

6 And [p]these words, which I command thee this day, shall be in thine heart:

7 And [q]thou shalt teach them diligently unto thy children, and shalt talk of them when thou sittest in thine house, and when thou walkest by the way, and when thou liest down, and when thou risest up.

8 [r]And thou shalt bind them for a sign upon thine hand, and they shall be as frontlets between thine eyes.

9 [s]And thou shalt write them upon the posts of thy house, and on thy gates.

10 And it shall be, when the LORD thy God shall have brought thee into the land which he sware unto thy fathers, to Abraham, to Isaac, and to Jacob, to give thee great and goodly cities, [t]which thou buildedst not,

11 And houses full of all good *things*, which thou filledst not, and wells digged, which thou diggedst not, vineyards and olive trees, which thou plantedst not; [u]when thou shalt have eaten and be full;

12 *Then* beware lest thou forget the LORD, which brought thee forth out of the land of Egypt, from the house of bondage.

13 Thou shalt [v]fear the LORD thy God, and serve him, and [w]shalt swear by his name.

14 Ye shall not [x]go after other gods, [y]of the gods of the people which *are* round about you;

15 (For [z]the LORD thy God *is* a jealous God among you) [a]lest the anger of the LORD thy God be kindled against thee, and destroy thee from off the face of the earth.

16 ¶ [b]Ye shall not tempt the LORD your God, [c]as ye tempted *him* in Massah.

17 Ye shall [d]diligently keep the commandments of the LORD your God, and his testimonies, and his statutes, which he hath commanded thee.

18 And thou [e]shalt do *that which is* right and good in the sight of the LORD: that it may be well with thee, and that thou mayest go in and possess the good land which the LORD sware unto thy fathers,

19 [f]To cast out all thine enemies from before thee, as the LORD hath spoken.

20 *And* [g]when thy son asketh thee in time to come, saying, What *mean* the testimonies, and the statutes, and the judgments, which the LORD our God hath commanded you?

21 Then thou shalt say unto thy son, We were Pharaoh's bondmen in Egypt; and the LORD brought us out of Egypt [h]with a mighty hand:

22 [i]And the LORD shewed signs and wonders, great and sore, upon Egypt, upon Pharaoh, and upon all his household, before our eyes:

23 And he brought us out from thence, that he might bring us in, to give us the land which he sware unto our fathers.

24 And the LORD commanded us to do all these statutes, [j]to fear the LORD our God, [k]for our good always, that [l]he might preserve us alive, as *it is* at this day.

25 And [m]it shall be our righteousness, if we observe to do all these commandments before the LORD our God, as he hath commanded us.

7 When the [n]LORD thy God shall bring thee into the land whither thou goest to possess it, and hath cast out many nations before thee, [o]the Hittites, and the Girgashites, and the Amorites, and the Canaanites, and the Perizzites, and the Hivites, and the Jebusites, seven nations [p]greater and mightier than thou;

2 And when the LORD thy God shall [q]deliver them before thee; thou shalt smite them, *and* [r]utterly destroy them; [s]thou shalt make no covenant with them, nor shew mercy unto them:

3 [t]Neither shalt thou make marriages with them; thy daughter thou shalt not give unto his son, nor his daughter shalt thou take unto thy son.

4 For they will turn away thy son from following me, that they may serve other gods: [u]so will the anger of the LORD be kindled against you, and destroy thee suddenly.

5:29 [b]ch. 11:1 [c]ch. 4:40
5:31 [d]Gal. 3:19
5:32 [e]ch. 17:20; Josh. 1:7; Prov. 4:27
5:33 [f]ch. 10:12; Ps. 119:6; Jer. 7:23; Luke 1:6 [g]ch. 4:40
6:1 [h]ch. 4:1
6:2 [i]Ex. 20:20; ch. 10:12; Ps. 111:10; Eccl. 12:13 [j]ch. 4:40; Prov. 3:1
6:3 [k]Gen. 15:5 [l]Ex. 3:8
6:4 [m]Isa. 42:8; Mark 12:29; John 17:3; 1 Cor. 8:4
6:5 [n]ch. 10:12; Matt. 22:37; Mark 12:30; Luke 10:27 [o]2 Kings 23:25
6:6 [p]ch. 11:18; Ps. 37:31; Prov. 3:3; Isa. 51:7
6:7 [q]ch. 4:9; Ps. 78:4; Eph. 6:4
6:8 [r]Ex. 13:9; ch. 11:18; Prov. 3:3
6:9 [s]ch. 11:20; Isa. 57:8
6:10 [t]Josh. 24:13; Ps. 105:44
6:11 [u]ch. 8:10
6:13 [v]ch. 10:12; Matt. 4:10; Luke 4:8 [w]Ps. 63:11; Isa. 45:23; Jer. 4:2
6:14 [x]ch. 8:19; Jer. 25:6 [y]ch. 13:7
6:15 [z]Ex. 20:5; ch. 4:24 [a]ch. 7:4
6:16 [b]Matt. 4:7; Luke 4:12 [c]Ex. 17:2; Num. 20:3; 1 Cor. 10:9
6:17 [d]ch. 11:13; Ps. 119:4
6:18 [e]Ex. 15:26; ch. 12:28
6:19 [f]Num. 33:52
6:20 [g]Ex. 13:14
6:21 [h]Ex. 3:19
6:22 [i]Ex. 7; Ps. 135:9
6:24 [j]ver. 2 [k]ch. 10:13; Job 35:7; Jer. 32:39 [l]ch. 4:1; Ps. 41:2; Luke 10:28
6:25 [m]Lev. 18:5; ch. 24:13; Rom. 10:3
7:1 [n]ch. 31:3; Ps. 44:2 [o]Gen. 15:19; Ex. 33:2 [p]ch. 4:38
7:2 [q]ver. 23; ch. 23:14 [r]Lev. 27:28; Num. 33:52; ch. 20:16; Josh. 6:17 [s]Ex. 23:32; ch. 20:10; Judg. 2:2; Josh. 2:14; Judg. 1:24
7:3 [t]Josh. 23:12; 1 Kings 11:2; Ezra 9:2
7:4 [u]ch. 6:15

5 But thus shall ye deal with them; ye
shall [v]destroy their altars, and break down
their images, and cut down their groves,
and burn their graven images with fire.
6 [w]For thou *art* an holy people unto the
LORD thy God: [x]the LORD thy God hath chosen thee to be a special people unto himself,
above all people that *are* upon the face of
the earth.
7 The LORD did not set his love upon you,
nor choose you, because ye were more in
number than any people; for ye *were* [y]the
fewest of all people:
8 But [z]because the LORD loved you, and
because he would keep [a]the oath which he
had sworn unto your fathers, [b]hath the
LORD brought you out with a mighty hand,
and redeemed you out of the house of bondmen, from the hand of Pharaoh king of
Egypt.
9 Know therefore that the LORD thy God,
he *is* God, [c]the faithful God, [d]which keepeth covenant and mercy with them that love
him and keep his commandments to a thousand generations;
10 And [e]repayeth them that hate him to
their face, to destroy them: [f]he will not be
slack to him that hateth him, he will repay
him to his face.
11 Thou shalt therefore keep the commandments, and the statutes, and the judgments, which I command thee this day, to
do them.
12 ¶ [g]Wherefore it shall come to pass, if
ye hearken to these judgments, and keep,
and do them, that the LORD thy God shall
keep unto thee [h]the covenant and the
mercy which he sware unto thy fathers:
13 And he will [i]love thee, and bless thee,
and multiply thee: [j]he will also bless the
fruit of thy womb, and the fruit of thy land,
thy corn, and thy wine, and thine oil, the
increase of thy kine, and the flocks of thy
sheep, in the land which he sware unto thy
fathers to give thee.
14 Thou shalt be blessed above all people:
[k]there shall not be male or female barren
among you, or among your cattle.
15 And the LORD will take away from
thee all sickness, and will put none of the
[l]evil diseases of Egypt, which thou knowest, upon thee; but will lay them upon all
them that hate thee.
16 And [m]thou shalt consume all the people which the LORD thy God shall deliver
thee; [n]thine eye shall have no pity upon
them: neither shalt thou serve their gods;
for that *will be* [o]a snare unto thee.
17 If thou shalt say in thine heart, These
nations *are* more than I; how can I [p]dispos-
sess them?
18 [q]Thou shalt not be afraid of them: *but*
shalt well [r]remember what the LORD thy
God did unto Pharaoh, and unto all Egypt;
19 [s]The great temptations which thine
eyes saw, and the signs, and the wonders,
and the mighty hand, and the stretched out
arm, whereby the LORD thy God brought
thee out: so shall the LORD thy God do unto
all the people of whom thou art afraid.
20 [t]Moreover the LORD thy God will send
the hornet among them, until they that are
left, and hide themselves from thee, be destroyed.
21 Thou shalt not be affrighted at them:
for the LORD thy God *is* [u]among you, [v]a
mighty God and terrible.
22 [w]And the LORD thy God will put out
those nations before thee by little and little:
thou mayest not consume them at once, lest
the beasts of the field increase upon thee.
23 But the LORD thy God shall deliver
them unto thee, and shall destroy them with
a mighty destruction, until they be destroyed.
24 And [x]he shall deliver their kings into
thine hand, and thou shalt destroy their
name [y]from under heaven: [z]there shall no
man be able to stand before thee, until thou
have destroyed them.
25 The graven images of their gods [a]shall
ye burn with fire: thou [b]shalt not desire the
silver or gold *that is* on them, nor take *it*
unto thee, lest thou be [c]snared therein: for
it *is* [d]an abomination to the LORD thy God.
26 Neither shalt thou bring an abomination into thine house, lest thou be a cursed
thing like it: *but* thou shalt utterly detest it,
and thou shalt utterly abhor it; [e]for it *is* a
cursed thing.

8 All the commandments which I command thee this day [f]shall ye observe to
do, that ye may live, and multiply, and go in
and possess the land which the LORD sware
unto your fathers.
2 And thou shalt remember all the way
which the LORD thy God [g]led thee these
forty years in the wilderness, to humble
thee, *and* [h]to prove thee, [i]to know what
was in thine heart, whether thou wouldest
keep his commandments, or no.
3 And he humbled thee, and [j]suffered
thee to hunger, and [k]fed thee with manna,
which thou knewest not, neither did thy fathers know; that he might make thee know
that man doth [l]not live by bread only, but
by every *word* that proceedeth out of the
mouth of the LORD doth man live.
4 [m]Thy raiment waxed not old upon thee,
neither did thy foot swell, these forty years.
5 [n]Thou shalt also consider in thine
heart, that, as a man chasteneth his son, *so*
the LORD thy God chasteneth thee.
6 Therefore thou shalt keep the commandments of the LORD thy God, [o]to walk
in his ways, and to fear him.
7 For the LORD thy God bringeth thee into
a good land, [p]a land of brooks of water, of
fountains and depths that spring out of valleys and hills;
8 A land of wheat, and barley, and vines,
and fig trees, and pomegranates; a land of
oil olive, and honey;
9 A land wherein thou shalt eat bread
without scarceness, thou shalt not lack any
thing in it; a land [q]whose stones *are* iron,

7:5 [v]Ex. 23:24; ch. 12:2
7:6 [w]Ex. 19:6; ch. 14:2; Ps. 50:5; Jer. 2:3 [x]Ex. 19:5; Am. 3:2; 1 Pet. 2:9
7:7 [y]ch. 10:22
7:8 [z]ch. 10:15 [a]Ex. 32:13; Ps. 105:8; Luke 1:55 [b]Ex. 13:3
7:9 [c]Isa. 49:7; 1 Cor. 1:9; 2 Cor. 1:18; 1 Thess. 5:24; 2 Thess. 3:3; 2 Tim. 2:13; Heb. 11:11; 1 John 1:9 [d]Ex. 20:6; ch. 5:10; Neh. 1:5; Dan. 9:4
7:10 [e]Isa. 59:18; Nah. 1:2 [f]ch. 32:35
7:12 [g]Lev. 26:3; ch. 28:1 [h]Ps. 105:8; Luke 1:55
7:13 [i]John 14:21 [j]ch. 28:4
7:14 [k]Ex. 23:26
7:15 [l]Ex. 9:14; ch. 28:27
7:16 [m]ver. 2 [n]ch. 13:8 [o]Ex. 23:33; ch. 12:30; Judg. 8:27; Ps. 106:36
7:17 [p]Num. 33:53
7:18 [q]ch. 31:6 [r]Ps. 105:5
7:19 [s]ch. 4:34
7:20 [t]Ex. 23:28; Josh. 24:12
7:21 [u]Num. 11:20; Josh. 3:10 [v]ch. 10:17; Neh. 1:5
7:22 [w]Ex. 23:29
7:24 [x]Josh. 10:24 [y]Ex. 17:14; ch. 9:14 [z]ch. 11:25; Josh. 1:5
7:25 [a]ver. 5; Ex. 32:20; ch. 12:3; 1 Chron. 14:12 [b]Josh. 7:1 [c]Judg. 8:27; Zeph. 1:3 [d]ch. 17:1
7:26 [e]Lev. 27:28; ch. 13:17; Josh. 6:17
8:1 [f]ch. 4:1
8:2 [g]ch. 1:3; Ps. 136:16; Am. 2:10 [h]Ex. 16:4; ch. 13:3 [i]2 Chron. 32:31; John 2:25
8:3 [j]Ex. 16:2 [k]Ex. 16:12 [l]Ps. 104:29; Matt. 4:4; Luke 4:4
8:4 [m]ch. 29:5; Neh. 9:21
8:5 [n]2 Sam. 7:14; Ps. 89:32; Prov. 3:12; Heb. 12:5; Rev. 3:19
8:6 [o]ch. 5:33
8:7 [p]ch. 11:10
8:9 [q]ch. 33:25

and out of whose hills thou mayest dig brass.

10 [r]When thou hast eaten and art full, then thou shalt bless the LORD thy God for the good land which he hath given thee.

11 Beware that thou forget not the LORD thy God, in not keeping his commandments, and his judgments, and his statutes, which I command thee this day:

12 [s]Lest *when* thou hast eaten and art full, and hast built goodly houses, and dwelt *therein;*

13 And *when* thy herds and thy flocks multiply, and thy silver and thy gold is multiplied, and all that thou hast is multiplied;

14 [t]Then thine heart be lifted up, and thou [u]forget the LORD thy God, which brought thee forth out of the land of Egypt, from the house of bondage;

15 Who [v]led thee through that great and terrible wilderness, [w]*wherein were* fiery serpents, and scorpions, and drought, where *there was* no water; [x]who brought thee forth water out of the rock of flint;

16 Who fed thee in the wilderness with [y]manna, which thy fathers knew not, that he might humble thee, and that he might prove thee, [z]to do thee good at thy latter end;

17 [a]And thou say in thine heart, My power and the might of *mine* hand hath gotten me this wealth.

18 But thou shalt remember the LORD thy God: [b]for *it is* he that giveth thee power to get wealth, [c]that he may establish his covenant which he sware unto thy fathers, as *it is* this day.

19 And it shall be, if thou do at all forget the LORD thy God, and walk after other gods, and serve them, and worship them, [d]I testify against you this day that ye shall surely perish.

20 As the nations which the LORD destroyeth before your face, [e]so shall ye perish; because ye would not be obedient unto the voice of the LORD your God.

9 Hear, O Israel: Thou *art* to [f]pass over Jordan this day, to go in to possess nations [g]greater and mightier than thyself, cities great and [h]fenced up to heaven,

2 A people great and tall, [i]the children of the Anakims, whom thou knowest, and *of whom* thou hast heard *say,* Who can stand before the children of Anak!

3 Understand therefore this day, that the LORD thy God *is* he which [j]goeth over before thee; *as* a [k]consuming fire [l]he shall destroy them, and he shall bring them down before thy face: [m]so shalt thou drive them out, and destroy them quickly, as the LORD hath said unto thee.

4 [n]Speak not thou in thine heart, after that the LORD thy God hath cast them out from before thee, saying, For my righteousness the LORD hath brought me in to possess this land: but [o]for the wickedness of these nations the LORD doth drive them out from before thee.

8:10 [r]ch. 6:11
8:12 [s]ch. 28:47; Prov. 30:9; Hos. 13:6
8:14 [t]1 Cor. 4:7 [u]Ps. 106:21
8:15 [v]Isa. 63:12; Jer. 2:6 [w]Num. 21:6; Hos. 13:5 [x]Num. 20:11; Ps. 78:15
8:16 [y]ver. 3; Ex. 16:15 [z]Jer. 24:5; Heb. 12:11
8:17 [a]ch. 9:4; 1 Cor. 4:7
8:18 [b]Prov. 10:22; Hos. 2:8 [c]ch. 7:8
8:19 [d]ch. 4:26
8:20 [e]Dan. 9:11
9:1 [f]ch. 11:31; Josh. 3:16 [g]ch. 4:38 [h]ch. 1:28
9:2 [i]Num. 13:22
9:3 [j]ch. 31:3; Josh. 3:11 [k]ch. 4:24; Heb. 12:29 [l]ch. 7:23 [m]Ex. 23:31; ch. 7:24
9:4 [n]ch. 8:17; Rom. 11:6; 1 Cor. 4:4 [o]Gen. 15:16; Lev. 18:24; ch. 18:12
9:5 [p]Tit. 3:5 [q]Gen. 12:7
9:6 [r]ver. 13; Ex. 32:9
9:7 [s]Ex. 14:11; Num. 11:4; ch. 31:27
9:8 [t]Ex. 32:4; Ps. 106:19
9:9 [u]Ex. 24:12 [v]Ex. 24:18
9:10 [w]Ex. 31:18 [x]Ex. 19:17; ch. 4:10
9:12 [y]Ex. 32:7 [z]ch. 31:29; Judg. 2:17
9:13 [a]Ex. 32:9 [b]ver. 6; ch. 10:16; 2 Kings 17:14
9:14 [c]Ex. 32:10 [d]ch. 29:20; Ps. 9:5 [e]Num. 14:12
9:15 [f]Ex. 32:15 [g]Ex. 19:18; ch. 4:11
9:16 [h]Ex. 32:19
9:18 [i]Ex. 34:28; Ps. 106:23

5 [p]Not for thy righteousness, or for the uprightness of thine heart, dost thou go to possess their land: but for the wickedness of these nations the LORD thy God doth drive them out from before thee, and that he may perform [q]the word which the LORD sware unto thy fathers, Abraham, Isaac, and Jacob.

6 Understand therefore, that the LORD thy God giveth thee not this good land to possess it for thy righteousness; for thou *art* [r]a stiffnecked people.

7 ¶ Remember, *and* forget not, how thou provokedst the LORD thy God to wrath in the wilderness: [s]from the day that thou didst depart out of the land of Egypt, until ye came unto this place, ye have been rebellious against the LORD.

8 Also [t]in Horeb ye provoked the LORD to wrath, so that the LORD was angry with you to have destroyed you.

9 [u]When I was gone up into the mount to receive the tables of stone, *even* the tables of the covenant which the LORD made with you, then [v]I abode in the mount forty days and forty nights, I neither did eat bread nor drink water:

10 [w]And the LORD delivered unto me two tables of stone written with the finger of God; and on them *was written* according to all the words, which the LORD spake with you in the mount out of the midst of the fire, [x]in the day of the assembly.

11 And it came to pass at the end of forty days and forty nights, *that* the LORD gave me the two tables of stone, *even* the tables of the covenant.

12 And the LORD said unto me, [y]Arise, get thee down quickly from hence; for thy people which thou hast brought forth out of Egypt have corrupted *themselves;* they are [z]quickly turned aside out of the way which I commanded them; they have made them a molten image.

13 Furthermore [a]the LORD spake unto me, saying, I have seen this people, and, behold, [b]it *is* a stiffnecked people:

14 [c]Let me alone, that I may destroy them, and [d]blot out their name from under heaven: [e]and I will make of thee a nation mightier and greater than they.

15 [f]So I turned and came down from the mount, and [g]the mount burned with fire: and the two tables of the covenant *were* in my two hands.

16 And [h]I looked, and, behold, ye had sinned against the LORD your God, *and* had made you a molten calf: ye had turned aside quickly out of the way which the LORD had commanded you.

17 And I took the two tables, and cast them out of my two hands, and brake them before your eyes.

18 And I [i]fell down before the LORD, as at the first, forty days and forty nights: I did neither eat bread, nor drink water, because of all your sins which ye sinned, in doing

wickedly in the sight of the LORD, to provoke him to anger.

19 [j]For I was afraid of the anger and hot displeasure, wherewith the LORD was wroth against you to destroy you. [k]But the LORD hearkened unto me at that time also.

20 And the LORD was very angry with Aaron to have destroyed him: and I prayed for Aaron also the same time.

21 And [l]I took your sin, the calf which ye had made, and burnt it with fire, and stamped it, *and* ground *it* very small, *even* until it was as small as dust: and I cast the dust thereof into the brook that descended out of the mount.

22 And at [m]Taberah, and at [n]Massah, and at [o]Kibroth-hattaavah, ye provoked the LORD to wrath.

23 Likewise [p]when the LORD sent you from Kadesh-barnea, saying, Go up and possess the land which I have given you; then ye rebelled against the commandment of the LORD your God, and [q]ye believed him not, nor hearkened to his voice.

24 [r]Ye have been rebellious against the LORD from the day that I knew you.

25 [s]Thus I fell down before the LORD forty days and forty nights, as I fell down *at the first;* because the LORD had said he would destroy you.

26 [t]I prayed therefore unto the LORD, and said, O Lord GOD, destroy not thy people and thine inheritance, which thou hast redeemed through thy greatness, which thou hast brought forth out of Egypt with a mighty hand.

27 Remember thy servants, Abraham, Isaac, and Jacob; look not unto the stubbornness of this people, nor to their wickedness, nor to their sin:

28 Lest [u]the land whence thou broughtest us out say, [v]Because the LORD was not able to bring them into the land which he promised them, and because he hated them, he hath brought them out to slay them in the wilderness.

29 [w]Yet they *are* thy people and thine inheritance, which thou broughtest out by thy mighty power and by thy stretched out arm.

10 At that time the LORD said unto me, [x]Hew thee two tables of stone like unto the first, and come up unto me into the mount, and [y]make thee an ark of wood.

2 And I will write on the tables the words that were in the first tables which thou brakest, and [z]thou shalt put them in the ark.

3 And I made an ark *of* [a]shittim wood, and [b]hewed two tables of stone like unto the first, and went up into the mount, having the two tables in mine hand.

4 And [c]he wrote on the tables, according to the first writing, the ten commandments, [d]which the LORD spake unto you in the mount out of the midst of the fire [e]in the day of the assembly: and the LORD gave them unto me.

5 And I turned myself and [f]came down from the mount, and [g]put the tables in the ark which I had made; [h]and there they be, as the LORD commanded me.

6 ¶ And the children of Israel took their journey from Beeroth [i]of the children of Jaakan to [j]Mosera: [k]there Aaron died, and there he was buried; and Eleazar his son ministered in the priest's office in his stead.

7 [l]From thence they journeyed unto Gudgodah; and from Gudgodah to Jotbath, a land of rivers of waters.

8 ¶ At that time [m]the LORD separated the tribe of Levi, [n]to bear the ark of the covenant of the LORD, [o]to stand before the LORD to minister unto him, and [p]to bless in his name, unto this day.

9 [q]Wherefore Levi hath no part nor inheritance with his brethren; the LORD *is* his inheritance, according as the LORD thy God promised him.

10 And [r]I stayed in the mount, according to the first time, forty days and forty nights; and [s]the LORD hearkened unto me at that time also, *and* the LORD would not destroy thee.

11 [t]And the LORD said unto me, Arise, take *thy* journey before the people, that they may go in and possess the land, which I sware unto their fathers to give unto them.

12 ¶ And now, Israel, [u]what doth the LORD thy God require of thee, but [v]to fear the LORD thy God, [w]to walk in all his ways, and [x]to love him, and to serve the LORD thy God with all thy heart and with all thy soul,

13 To keep the commandments of the LORD, and his statutes, which I command thee this day [y]for thy good?

14 Behold, [z]the heaven and the heaven of heavens *is* the LORD's thy God, [a]the earth *also,* with all that therein *is.*

15 [b]Only the LORD had a delight in thy fathers to love them, and he chose their seed after them, *even* you above all people, as *it is* this day.

16 Circumcise therefore [c]the foreskin of your heart, and be no more [d]stiffnecked.

17 For the LORD your God *is* [e]God of gods, and [f]Lord of lords, a great God, [g]a mighty, and a terrible, which [h]regardeth not persons, nor taketh reward:

18 [i]He doth execute the judgment of the fatherless and widow, and loveth the stranger, in giving him food and raiment.

19 [j]Love ye therefore the stranger: for ye were strangers in the land of Egypt.

20 [k]Thou shalt fear the LORD thy God; him shalt thou serve, and to him shalt thou [l]cleave, [m]and swear by his name.

21 [n]He *is* thy praise, and he *is* thy God, [o]that hath done for thee these great and terrible things, which thine eyes have seen.

22 Thy fathers went down into Egypt [p]with threescore and ten persons; and now the LORD thy God hath made thee [q]as the stars of heaven for multitude.

9:19 [j]Ex. 32:10 [k]Ex. 32:14; ch. 10:10; Ps. 106:23
9:21 [l]Ex. 32:20; Isa. 31:7
9:22 [m]Num. 11:1 [n]Ex. 17:7 [o]Num. 11:4
9:23 [p]Num. 13:3 [q]Ps. 106:24
9:24 [r]ch. 31:27
9:25 [s]ver. 18
9:26 [t]Ex. 32:11
9:28 [u]Gen. 41:57; 1 Sam. 14:25 [v]Ex. 32:12; Num. 14:16
9:29 [w]ch. 4:20; 1 Kings 8:51; Neh. 1:10; Ps. 95:7
10:1 [x]Ex. 34:1 [y]Ex. 25:10
10:2 [z]Ex. 25:16
10:3 [a]Ex. 25:5 [b]Ex. 34:4
10:4 [c]Ex. 34:28 [d]Ex. 20:1 [e]Ex. 19:17; ch. 9:10
10:5 [f]Ex. 34:29 [g]Ex. 40:20 [h]1 Kings 8:9
10:6 [i]Num. 33:31 [j]Num. 33:30 [k]Num. 20:28
10:7 [l]Num. 33:32
10:8 [m]Num. 3:6 [n]Num. 4:15 [o]ch. 18:5 [p]Lev. 9:22; Num. 6:23; ch. 21:5
10:9 [q]Num. 18:20; ch. 18:1; Ezek. 44:28
10:10 [r]Ex. 34:28; ch. 9:18 [s]Ex. 32:14; ch. 9:19
10:11 [t]Ex. 32:34
10:12 [u]Mic. 6:8 [v]ch. 6:13 [w]ch. 5:33 [x]ch. 6:5; Matt. 22:37
10:13 [y]ch. 6:24
10:14 [z]1 Kings 8:27; Ps. 115:16 [a]Gen. 14:19; Ex. 19:5; Ps. 24:1
10:15 [b]ch. 4:37
10:16 [c]Lev. 26:41; ch. 30:6; Jer. 4:4; Rom. 2:28; Col. 2:11 [d]ch. 9:6
10:17 [e]Josh. 22:22; Ps. 136:2; Dan. 2:47 [f]Rev. 17:14 [g]ch. 7:21 [h]2 Chron. 19:7; Job 34:19; Acts 10:34; Rom. 2:11; Gal. 2:6; Eph. 6:9; Col. 3:25; 1 Pet. 1:17
10:18 [i]Ps. 68:5
10:19 [j]Lev. 19:33
10:20 [k]ch. 6:13; Matt. 4:10; Luke 4:8 [l]ch. 11:22 [m]Ps. 63:11
10:21 [n]Ex. 15:2; Ps. 22:3; Jer. 17:14 [o]1 Sam. 12:24; 2 Sam. 7:23; Ps. 106:21
10:22 [p]Gen. 46:27; Ex. 1:5; Acts 7:14 [q]Gen. 15:5; ch. 1:10

FOCUS ON DEUTERONOMY

The Book of Deuteronomy gives the final teachings of Moses to the children of Israel. As they prepare to enter the Promised Land without him, he stops to review all that God has taught them over the past 40 years. One is reminded, in this instance, of the repeated call of a mother to a child, or the love of a mother for a child she longs to see do well. This Book is the cry of a mother's heart aching with longing, filled with warnings, weary from repeating old information and rehashing known details. Moses reminds the people of their history with God and their moral obligation to Him as the people of the Covenant. Moses makes the central focus of this Book how God's children are to maintain a proper relationship with Him. The contractual agreement outlines the responsibilities of God and the community.

The Ten Commandments contain a historical prologue known as the Decalogue—guidelines set forth by God for daily living. "Love the LORD your God with all your heart and with all your soul" (Deut. 13:3). Here, the word *love* is significant when one recalls that God states "I, the LORD thy God am a jealous God" (Deut. 5:9). As we remember the bitter waters that the priest would make a wife drink when she was suspected of adultery by her jealous husband (Num. 5:11–31), we get a tiny hint of God's command for fidelity.

Moses has been told that he will not be allowed to enter the Promised Land because of his disobedience in striking the rock for water instead of speaking to it as God had commanded in Numbers 20:8–12. Moses addresses the people of God: women and men are instructed not to work on the Sabbath, a custom that continued even up to the days of our recent history. Our grandmothers would prepare Sunday dinner on Saturday. Sunday was the Lord's Day with no work and no play! Surely, women, as well as men, were not to use the Lord's name in vain, to steal, to commit adultery, or to murder.

"Happy art thou, O Israel: who is like unto thee, O people saved by the LORD, the shield of thy help, and who is the sword of thy excellency! And thine enemies shall be found liars unto thee; and thou shalt tread upon their high places" (Deut. 33:29). Moses dies, "And there arose not a prophet since in Israel like unto Moses, whom the LORD knew face to face" (Deut. 34:10).

Because of the original effort of a few women when he was a child, Moses the great deliverer is able to sleep in peace in Moab.

THE BLACK PRESENCE IN DEUTERONOMY

The structure of the Book of Deuteronomy follows the Hittite treaty format. Hittites were descendants of Ham through Canaan (Gen. 10:15). The existence of Hittites was once thought to be insignificant, but archaeological discoveries have shown that they were a very prominent and populous people. In the Hittite treaty format, a

king reviews what has been done for his vassal and then exhorts his people to remain loyal. In Deuteronomy, Moses reviews what God has done for Israel and exhorts the people to remain faithful to Yahweh (God).

Several times during his discourses, Moses makes reference to the land that the people are about to enter. He describes it as land occupied by Amorites (Deut. 1:4, 7, 20; 4:46–47). The Amorites were the descendants of Canaan, who was a son of Ham.

Life Lessons

DEUTERONOMY 1–4

Moses tells the people, "The Lord our God spake unto us in Horeb, saying Ye have dwelt long enough in this mount: Turn you, and take your journey" (Deut. 1:6). The journey from Horeb to Kadesh-barnea was only 11 days (Deut. 1:2). Yet, for over 40 years, 11 months, and 1 day, the Israelites had been stuck in the wilderness (Deut. 1:3). Our inability to trust God and follow God's instructions often puts us in a state of wandering. When we find ourselves in the same place, doing the same thing, and getting the same results while looking for *different* results, it is most likely God's way of saying, "Move it, girl!"

Moses appointed tribal leaders because he could not continue to govern the people alone. The people suggested that Moses send spies into the valley of Eshcol, and God agreed that this should be done before the people entered the Promised Land. Because the people did not believe that they could defeat the Amorites, they refused to enter. It was because of their disbelief that God allowed only Caleb, Joshua, and the next generation of Israelites to enter the Promised Land.

Director of Purpose, help me to move when You say move, so that I do not repeat the same mistakes! I know there is no other God but You, and I want to act on this knowledge.

DEUTERONOMY 5–6

The Ten Commandments are given to the people with the understanding that God is a jealous God: "I am the LORD your God . . . thou shalt have none other gods before me" (Deut. 5:6–7). Women today understand and long for a good, loving, and faithful husband. Within the context of marital fidelity, couples vow to have allegiance to just one spouse. The church is referred to as "the bride of Christ" and the marital context continues. The creed, which is drawn from these rules for proper worship and living, stems from God's decree, "I, the LORD your God, am a jealous God."

Thank You for being my Jealous Lord. Help me to stay faithful and true to You and to give You no cause to be jealous.

DEUTERONOMY 5

Although the Ten Commandments address the proper conduct of women (even slaves), it appears that women did not have equality under

ancient laws and customs. However, God does include women in the commandments to be faithful and true to God.

Holy One, help me to walk in all the ways You have commanded so that I may live and prosper for many days.

DEUTERONOMY 7

Driving out the established nations that were bigger and stronger than they was the next step for the Israelites in the new land. They were to "utterly destroy them; thou shalt make no covenant with them, nor show mercy unto them" (Deut. 7:2). The Hittites, Girgasites, Amorites, Canaanites, Perizzites, Hivites, and Jebusites were all descendants of Ham. The observation should be made that these nations were not being punished and disowned by God because they were black, but because they served idols and did not adhere to God's moral code. At any period in history, nations or individuals that reject the moral laws of God will reap the consequences of their behavior. God chooses the time and method: "For thou art an holy people unto the LORD thy God" (Deut. 7:6).

Divine Being, help me expel every idol from my life.

DEUTERONOMY 8–20

Moses cautions the people not to forget all that God has done for them (Deut. 8:1). Yet, he recalls for them how often they have forgotten God in the past. He reminds them of the golden calf they erected and how he had to receive new tablets containing the Ten Commandments because of their disobedience. He urges them to have reverence for God, to love and obey God, and to remember the place of true worship—the dwelling of God's name. "But unto the place which the LORD your God shall choose . . . thither thou shalt come, . . ." he said. "And thither ye shall bring your burnt offerings, and your sacrifices, and your tithes . . . and ye shall rejoice in all that ye put your hand unto . . . wherein the LORD thy God hath blessed thee" (Deut. 12:5–7). Levitical codes are studied, the jubilee years reinforced, and the occasions of seasons and festivals are detailed. Moses instructs the people to appoint judges who will judge fairly: "That which is altogether just shalt thou follow" (Deut. 16:18–20). The coronation of a king is prophesied (Deut. 17:4–20), and instructions for battle are laid before them: "When thou goest out to battle, be not afraid of them: for the LORD thy God is with thee" (Deut. 20:1).

Winning Warrior, fight my battles. Let my striving cease.

DEUTERONOMY 21

The role of women, particularly beautiful, captive women, is discussed (Deut. 21:11–14). It is agreed that women can be acquired during war, for they are part of the warriors' spoils or goods. When captured, a woman's head is shaven, her nails trimmed, and the clothes she wears discarded. Then, she is allowed a month of mourning for all that she lost when captured. It is the hope of the Torah that with a woman's beauty having been shorn and tossed away, the Israelite male would no longer find her attractive enough for marriage. But, if he desired her as a wife, the discarding of all "foreign" identity would make her eligible for marriage and religious conversion. Then, she could not be cast out, mistreated, or sold into slavery, even if the spouse is displeased. It would have been a dishonor to her womanhood.

Father, help me to know that I am always beautiful and worthy in Your eyes.

DEUTERONOMY 22

There was a steep price to be paid for not being a virgin when married. A bloodstained sheet was to be the evidence of virginity. Yet, here again we find much discussion about the issue of a woman's virginity being suspect. It was the father's role to keep his daughter pure. The tradition of rolling a white runner down the aisle before the father escorts the bride down the aisle was started because of this belief. If a man made a charge that his betrothed was not pure, but a bloodstained sheet was produced the next morning, the elders of the city would punish the male for bringing such disrespect upon the father of his bride!

When an accusation such as this was made against a woman, but proven false, three penalties could be levied against the husband: flogging, fines, and forfeiture of his right to ever divorce the woman.

O Protector, safeguard my innocence and defend me against false accusers.

DEUTERONOMY 24–28

Sex for procreation and pleasure is considered both sacred and necessary. The Law positively values sex within the confines of marriage. "When a man hath taken a new wife, he shall not go out to war, neither shall he be charged with any business: but he shall be free at home one year, and shall cheer up his wife which he hath taken" (Deut. 24:5).

The Bible also takes into account the needs of women who happen to be widows or slaves. "When thou cuttest down thine harvest in thy field, and hast forgot a sheaf in the field, thou shalt not go again to fetch it: it shall be for the stranger, for the fatherless, and for the widow: that the LORD thy God may bless thee in all the work of thine hands" (Deut. 24:19).

The Levirate marriage is instituted beginning with Deuteronomy 25:5. A woman who marries into a family must be passed on to the next brother in marriage if the one she marries dies or is killed before having any male heirs. The first male child would actually be the heir of the first husband. This provision made possible the care of the widowed woman and her children. Male sons were expected to care for their widowed mothers.

In his third and final address to the people, Moses lifts up the blessings of obedience to the sacred laws: "And it shall come to pass, if thou shalt hearken diligently unto the voice of the LORD thy God, to observe and to do all his commandments which I command thee this day, that the LORD thy God will set thee on high above all nations of the earth: And all these blessings shall come on thee, and overtake thee, if thou shalt hearken unto the voice of the LORD thy God" (Deut. 28:1–2). But the curse of disobedience is also laid before them: "But it shall come to pass, if thou wilt not hearken unto the voice of the LORD thy God, to observe to do all his commandments . . . that all these curses shall come upon thee, and overtake thee: Cursed shalt thou be in the city and . . . in the field. Cursed shall be thy basket and thy store. Cursed shall be the fruit of thy body, and the fruit of thy land . . . Cursed shalt thou be when thou comest in, and cursed shalt thou be when thou goest out" (Deut. 28:15–19).

God views the curse of barrenness and infertility as punishment for wrongdoing. Although this was a curse pronounced upon a nation, we can now understand why women throughout the ages have suffered great emotional suffering when unable to have children. It feels like an individual sin.

God who brings forth life, thank You for the opportunity to birth babies. To continue creation, You have gifted women with the ability to bring forth life. And, You allow us the privilege to birth ideas, visions, dreams, and plans that assist Your people on the journey to completeness. For every birth, we praise Your name.

DEUTERONOMY 31

This sums up Moses' narrative. The covenant is renewed. Prosperity is again detailed. The people are asked to choose life over death. Joshua is ordained as the new leader. Moses places the written law into the hands of the priests, who place it in the ark of the covenant. He instructs them to read it annually: "Gather the people together, men, and women, and children, and thy stranger that is within thy gates, that they may hear, and that they may learn, and fear the LORD your God, and observe to do all the words of this law" (Deut. 31:12). God tells Moses that the people of Israel will rebel after Moses' death—He foresees their hard hearts and stubborn ways (Deut. 31:14–18).

Dear Faithful One, help me to be faithful to You.

FOCUS ON JOSHUA

As the children of Israel prepare to enter and inhabit the Promised Land, we are introduced to the first woman we meet in the land of Canaan: Rahab. Canaan is a land of cunning, well-fortified enemies. It is interesting that this prostitute provides a hospitable and safe sanctuary for the agents of God's people. She is not a "churchgoer." She is not an upstanding citizen. However, she believes in the power of Israel's God, and decides to join the winning side and worship Israel's Almighty God.

Joshua, Israel's newly appointed leader, has been told to go in and possess the land. He who was once a spy himself and gave the "minority report" that Israel could "take" the land of giants (Num. 14:6) now sends spies for a new generation of Israelites. History is about to be made as Israel moves to take possession of the land and begins to establish itself as a sovereign nation with God as its leader.

Rahab is found to be a useful ally in this story of Israel's move forward from being wandering nomads to being settlers, vinedressers, and homeowners. With a divine mandate, the people of God struggle to push out those that God has ordained for destruction. Rahab, however, has another idea for her family.

Rahab risks her life by harboring Israelite spies. Her only request is recorded in Joshua 2:12–13: "Now therefore, I pray you, swear unto me by the LORD, since I have shewed you kindness, that ye will also shew

kindness unto my father's house, and give me a true token: and that ye will save alive my father, and my mother, and my brethren, and my sisters, and all that they have, and deliver our lives from death. And the men answered her, Our life for yours" (v. 14). Through her bold example, we discover that God can use the suspect and different.

Joshua was told by God: "Only be thou strong and very courageous . . . that thou mayest prosper withersoever thou goest" (Josh. 1:7). Rahab was strong and courageous. She negotiated her family's safety, saved the lives of spies, and ably assisted Israel in entering a new chapter of its existence. Joshua's closing statement that, "As for me and my house, we will serve the LORD" (Josh. 24:15), reflects the example set by Rahab at the very beginning of this book.

THE BLACK PRESENCE IN JOSHUA

The descendants of Ham and Canaan had occupied the Promised Land since the repopulating of the earth after the Flood. Perhaps the Canaanites were to be driven out of the land because of their "iniquities," according to Genesis 15:16. Israel's conquest was a "holy war" directed by God as judgment against a people whose corruption had reached the limits of His patience. While God's sentence was that the people should be completely destroyed, they were not. Subsequent events show that some Israelites intermarried with the Canaanites and also worshiped their gods.

Rahab, who hid the spies sent by Joshua (Joshua 2:1), was a Canaanite. Her faith is cited by New Testament writers as exemplary (see Hebrews 11:31; James 2:25). Rahab later became the ancestor of Boaz and King David. She is one of five women mentioned in Matthew's genealogy of Jesus (Matt. 1:5).

Life Lessons

JOSHUA 1–5

God assures Joshua of success if the words of Moses are adhered to. The spies are sent to "go view the land" (2:1). Upon arrival, they go first into Rahab's home. She risks her life by harboring them and by lying to the authorities about the spies' whereabouts. She requests safety only for herself and her family when the Israelites defeat the Canaanites. The Israelite spies tell her to mark her home by hanging a scarlet cord outside her window (v. 18). Upon the spies' return, the people of Israel cross the Jordan River and take 12 stones to mark the occasion of establishing their home (chaps. 3–4). Since the first generation of Israelites who left Egypt died in the wilderness due to their disobedience, Joshua requires that all males be circumcised again as a reminder of the covenant with God (5:1–8). God states at the conclusion of the ceremony, "This day, have I rolled away the reproach of Egypt from off of you" (Josh. 5:9). Thus begins a new period in their history.

Renewing Covenant Maker, circumcise my hard heart. Give me a heart ready and willing to do Your will.

JOSHUA 6–12

The walled city of Jericho is well fortified; yet God does not direct Joshua to arm the best-trained warriors for battle. Instead, seven priests carrying trumpets of ram's horns in front of the ark of the covenant are to march around the city once a day for six days (6:3–4a). The men of war follow them. On the seventh day, they are to march around the city seven times, with the priests blowing the trumpets. When the people hear the sound of a long blast on the trumpets, they are to give a loud shout. The wall of the city would collapse and the people able to enter (vv. 6:4b–5). All of the possessions of Jericho, with the exception of "silver, and gold, and vessels of brass and iron" are to be destroyed because the people are "accursed" (vv. 18–19). Yet one of the Israelite men, Achan, decided to be disobedient and to take a few keepsakes for himself (chap. 7). His sin caused God's anger to burn against Israel. When Israel began to lose battles, God demanded that Joshua search out the belongings of the entire congregation (vv. 10–24). Achan's disobedience brought death and destruction to all his family (v. 24): "And they raised over him a great heap of stones unto this day. So the LORD turned from the fierceness of his anger" (v. 26). The covenant with the Lord, "as Moses the servant of the LORD commanded" is renewed at Mount Ebal (8:30–34). Later, the sun stands still for a full day while the Israelite warriors battle successfully (10:13). The southern cities are conquered and the northern kings defeated—31 in all (12:24).

Conquering King, win the battles before me. Let Your Son "shine" upon me.

JOSHUA 13–21

The tribes of Israel divide the Promised Land. In the middle of the division we find women who receive property. One of these women is Achsah, the daughter of Caleb—one of the two spies who boldly proclaimed that Israel could take the land during the time of Moses (Num. 13:30; 14:6). "And Caleb said, He that smiteth Kirjath-sepher, and taketh it, to him will I give Achsah my daughter to wife" (15:16). Othniel, son of Kenaz, Caleb's brother, takes the city, and receives Achsah as his wife. One day Achsah makes a request of her father: "Give me a blessing; for thou hast given me a south land; give me also springs of water. And he gave her the upper springs, and the nether springs" (v. 19). Joshua 17:3–6 recounts the inheritance of Mahlah, Noah, Hoglah, Milcah, and Tirzah—the daughters of Zelophehad. The case of the daughters of Zelophehad was a precedent set during the time of Moses (Num. 27:1–11).

God of the marginalized and oppressed, thank You for looking out for the needs of women.

JOSHUA 21–24

God's people now inhabit the land of Canaan. Joshua bids farewell to the leaders (chaps. 23–24). The covenant is renewed at Shechem and the people present themselves to the Lord, declaring their faithfulness and allegiance to God after Joshua reminds them to make a choice about serving God: "If it seems evil unto you to serve the LORD, choose you this day

whom ye will serve; whether the gods which your fathers served that were on the other side of the flood, or the gods of the Amorites, in whose land ye dwell: but as for me and my house, we will serve the LORD" (24:15). And the people said to Joshua, "The LORD our God will we serve, and His voice will we obey" (v. 24). Joshua then dies and is buried in the Promised Land (v. 33).

My God, I will serve You.

FOCUS ON JUDGES

Sin, punishment, repentance, and salvation are the major themes in the Book of Judges. We meet a mighty woman warrior, Judge Deborah, a woman of fire. The stories depict the downward spiral that Israel seems bound to repeat. The settlement into a nation with leaders known as "judges" comes into focus. The stories play out like a recurring bad dream: Israel does wrong; God delivers them into the hands of their oppressors; Israel cries out to the Delivering God; Yahweh shows up and acts out on their behalf through a divinely appointed leader; deliverance comes; the people are faithful for a while; the land has rest and yields its increase; Israel forgets God; Israel does wrong; and the nightmare continues.

We find some unlikely leaders in this narrative: Gideon, who hides in a winepress trying to escape both attention and death; Deborah, sitting under a palm tree doing her daily work as wife of Lappidoth; and Jael, an outsider who helps set Israel free. We also are introduced to Delilah, who helped cause Samson's fall. Samson's penchant for choosing the wrong women and his own lack of discretion were the catalysts of his downfall.

Achsah, Caleb's daughter, makes another appearance as a woman who owns both land and water springs which keep it fertile. Although she shows up in the narrative like many women—as a "prize" for a military strategy—she makes her own move and ends up as a role model for the sisterhood. We see another picture of female victimization in the story of Jephthah's daughter. Jephthah longs to be a winning warrior so badly that he makes a vow that requires his daughter to be sacrificed (11:31–40). We are told of his genuine surprise and sorrow, but are also provided a glimpse of her courageous piety.

Oppression under the hands of mighty enemies seems to be Israel's chosen way of life. She is not content with Yahweh; she always seeks what she believes to be better gods. Yet God continues to come to the rescue. As always, the daughters of the Most High play significant roles.

THE BLACK PRESENCE IN JUDGES

People of Hamitic descent—the Canaanites, Amorites, Jebusites, Hivites, Hittites, and Perizzites—previously inhabited the Promised Land (3:5). As a judgment upon the people, God instructed the Israelites to carry out a holy war to annihilate them, but the Israelites never completely followed this command. As a result, God

used these Hamitic people and other surrounding nations to punish the Israelites for their disobedience.

One of the Israelites' repeated faults was the worship of the idol gods Baal and Ashtoreth (v. 7). Baal was the supreme male god and Ashtoreth the supreme female goddess.

King Jabin, a Canaanite king, oppressed Israel for 20 years (4:2). Jabin ruled from Hazor, a town in the northern section of the land. The Canaanites were a tough and stubborn people who were great warriors. But while they possessed many chariots and some of the best weaponry of the day, they were no match for Israel because of God's protection (1:19).

Midianites (6:2) were the descendants of Abraham and his Cushite wife, Keturah (Gen. 25:1). Keturah's Cushite identity can be deduced from the fact that Moses' wife, Zipporah, was from Midian. Numbers 12:1 specifically identifies Zipporah as an "Ethiopian woman."

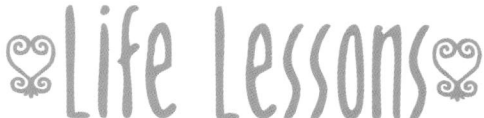

Life Lessons

JUDGES 2

Judges 2:1–3 states: "And an angel of the Lord came up from Gilgal to Bochim, and said, I made you to go up out of Egypt, and have brought you unto the land which I sware unto your fathers; and I said, I will never break my covenant with you. And ye shall make no league with the inhabitants of this land; ye shall throw down their altars: but ye have not obeyed my voice: why have ye done this? Wherefore I also said, I will not drive them out from before you; but they shall be as thorns in your sides, and their gods shall be a snare unto you." This proclamation sets the stage for Israel to be oppressed by its enemies in the Promised Land.

Covenant Maker, help me discover and then destroy every idol in my life so that You alone may rule.

JUDGES 2–3

"Nevertheless, the Lord raised up judges, which delivered them out of the hand of those that spoiled them. And yet they would not hearken unto their judges, but they went a whoring after other gods, and bowed themselves unto them: they turned quickly out of the way which their fathers walked in, obeying the commandments of the Lord; but they did not so. And when the Lord raised them up judges, then the Lord was with the judge, and delivered them out of the hand of their enemies all the days of the judge: for it repented the Lord because of their groanings by reason of them that oppressed them and vexed them. And it came to pass, when the judge was dead, that they returned, and corrupted themselves more than their fathers, in following other gods to serve them, and to bow down unto them; they ceased not from their own doings, nor from their stubborn ways. And the anger of the Lord was hot against Israel" (2:16–20).

The first judge is Othniel, son of Kenaz, Caleb's younger brother (3:9). Othniel also is the spouse of Achsah (1:11–15). Ehud becomes the second judge (3:15–30), and Shamgar the third (v. 31). When Israel continues to do evil, God acts: "And the LORD sold them into the hand of Jabin king of Canaan, that reigned in Hazor; . . . and the children of Israel cried unto the LORD . . . twenty years he mightily oppressed the children of Israel" (4:2–3).

Great Savior, deliver me from my repeated sinful cycles. Allow me to hear the voices of those who come with words of salvation. Turn Your anger from me that I may live an abundant life.

JUDGES 4–5

"Deborah, a prophetess, the wife of Lapidoth, she judged Israel at that time. And she dwelt under the palm tree of Deborah between Ramah and Beth-el in mount Ephraim: and the children of Israel came up to her for judgment. And she sent and called Barak" (4:4–6). It is interesting to note that Deborah is introduced as the wife of Lapidoth, whose name means "son of fire." So we might call her the "wife" or "woman of fire," although she stays close to home, doing what she has to do. Her husband's character, position, and deeds are not part of the record. We should not conclude that her role as wife is less important than her role as judge. As both prophet and judge, she has a relationship with Israel that is both religious and judicial. And, she is referred to as a "mother in Israel" (5:7). While we have not seen a primary female leader in Israel, Deborah could be perceived as "nursemaid to a politically incapacitated Israel" (*WBC*, 69). All that she learned as a girl to prepare her for womanhood, God now wants her to use in her role as judge.

When she summons a military commander, Barak comes. She gives him a word from the Lord—marching orders after twenty years of military oppression. But God's intention is to save Israel under the leadership of a judge, not military might. Barak is not opposed to going, but will only go if Deborah agrees to go with him. Deborah replies: "I will surely go with thee: notwithstanding the journey that thou takest shall not be for thine honour; for the LORD shall sell Sisera into the hand of a woman" (4:9). Deborah goes with Barak and 10,000 men to Kedesh (v. 10). Warrior Deborah goes into battle, and the hand of the saving and delivering God is with Israel.

Reliable Deliverer, I magnify Your great name for choosing me to do work worthy of You. Help me know that You can choose a woman to win the war for Your people. Thank You for being the God who never fails!

JUDGES 4–5

Sisera, commander of the Canaanite army, witnessed the destruction of his army at the hands of less skilled Israelites. He escapes on foot, seeking asylum in the tent of Hazor of the Heber clan. Because of their alliance, he feels secure entering Hazor's tent and making demands of Hazor's wife, Jael. Jael has more pressing matters to consider than an obsolete political alliance between her husband and this defeated commander. She is clearly a woman caught in the middle.

Jael welcomes Sisera and treats him with maternal care. When he falls asleep, assured of his safety, she drives a tent peg through his head,

leaving him to die. Jael not only wins her security; but in the song of Deborah and Barak, she wins Israel's praise as well (5:24–27). In their description of Jael's feat, her violent act becomes larger than life. Sisera had mistaken Jael's womanhood and kindness for weakness. He did not understand that God could use a woman. God had used Deborah to establish 40 years of peace in Israel (v. 31).

Equipping God, let me use the ways You have given me to bring down the unholy giants in my life.

JUDGES 6–8

"The LORD is with thee, thou mighty man of valour," says the angel of the Lord to Gideon, who hides from the Midianites in a winepress (6:12). God chooses Gideon, a man who is afraid to lead Israel, to be a judge. Gideon responds: "Oh my Lord, if the LORD be with us, why then is all this befallen us?" (v. 13). God does not answer this question, but summons Gideon to come out of hiding and "go in this thy might, and thou shalt save Israel from the hand of the Midianites: have not I sent thee?" (v. 14).

Gideon leads Israel in defeating the Midianites: "Thus was Midian subdued before the children of Israel, so that they lifted up their heads no more. And the country was in quietness forty years in the days of Gideon" (8:28).

Challenging God, if You can use a scared individual who is trying diligently to hide from the enemies of life, You can use me.

JUDGES 11

"Now Jephthah the Gileadite was a mighty man of valour, and he was the son of an harlot: and Gilead begat Jephthah" (11:1). Because of his mother's past, Jephthah is exiled from town, only to be sought in later years to command the army against the oppressive Ammonites: "Then Jephthah went with the elders of Gilead, and the people made him head and captain over them: and Jephthah uttered all his words before the LORD in Mizpeh" (v. 11). Wanting assurance of victory (and the town's continued acceptance), Jephthah makes a vow to God: "If thou shalt without fail deliver the children of Ammon into mine hands, then it shall be, that whatsoever cometh forth of the doors of my house to meet me . . . shall surely be the LORD's, and I will offer it up for a burnt offering" (vv. 30–31). His daughter pays the ultimate price for Israel's victory. Although we cannot be certain of the exact nature of the vow, the words of verse 31 are telling.

Jephthah does not specify what he expects to greet him on his arrival. Custom would have created the expectation that a slave or servant would greet the returning victor and master. So, the vow could have meant, more than likely, a servant would have been the sacrifice. Yet Jephthah does not anticipate that his daughter would greet him. Perhaps because of Yahweh, the daughter, whose name we never learn, responds, "Do to me according to that which hath proceeded out of thy mouth" (v. 36).

She then takes matters into her own hands and requests two months "that I may go up and down upon the mountains, and bewail my virginity, I and my fellows" (v. 37). She spends her remaining days with others like herself, who know what life is like in a violent society and who, in the end, will not forget her sacrifice. After she returns to be sacrificed, she becomes

a martyr in Israel. Whereas the song of Deborah recounts the deeds of a mighty God, the words of Jephthah's daughter describe the tragic end to the life of a girl, sacrificed needlessly because of her father's desire for a victory that God had already guaranteed by His presence (v. 29). From her short life comes the custom "that the daughters of Israel went yearly to lament the daughter of Jephthah the Gileadite four days in a year" (v. 40).

Lord, prepare me to be a living sacrifice!

JUDGES 13–16

The narrator relates the story of the birth of Samson to Manoah and his wife, who is not named. She is the one to whom the angel appears with the words of pronouncement and instructions for her infant to be set apart by God to begin the deliverance of Israel from the hands of the Philistines (13:3–5). Even when her husband demands an angelic reappearance due to both their long years of childlessness and his unbelief in a "woman's tale," the angel reappears to the wife (v. 9). Here, we see a foreshadowing of the story of Elisabeth, Zacharias, and the foretold coming of John the Baptist (see Luke 1). The child is born to begin the deliverance of the Israelites. They name him Samson (13:24).

Samson is a young man without boundaries. From the beginning we find him enchanted with the wrong women. He says to his parents, "I have seen a woman in Timnath of the daughters of the Philistines; now therefore get her for me to wife" (14:2).

"Loving a Philistine woman, spending his time in wine country, handling dead carcasses and eating unclean food hardly bode well for a Nazarite who is to be Israel's champion against the Philistines" (*WBC*, 72). Samson breaks all the rules. He does not become a military hero because Israel does not fight the Philistines. They have been oppressed for so long until it seems "their lot." At one point, when he has taken revenge upon the enemy, the men of Judah say to Samson, "Knowest thou not that the Philistines are rulers over us? what is this that thou hast done unto us?" (15:11). What is God to do with people who have no desire to be liberated from their oppressors?

It is only fair to recount that Samson's "rule-breaking" always seems to involve a type of woman not known as a "good Jewish girl"! His first wife is a Philistine, although his parents warn him of God's command against intermarriage, which leads to idol worship (14:1–3; see also Exodus 34:11–16; Numbers 25; Deuteronomy 7:3–4; Joshua 23:12; Judges 3:6; Ezra 9:1–2). Samson also frequents prostitutes (Judg. 16:1). In this we meet Delilah. We know her as the one responsible for Samson's ultimate downfall.

Mighty men in the community come and offer Delilah great wealth, for Samson has fallen in love with her, a fact that is no secret to the community (v. 4). "And the lords of the Philistines came up unto her, and said unto her, Entice him, and see wherein his great strength lieth, and by what means we may prevail against him . . . and we will give thee every one of us eleven hundred pieces of silver" (v. 5).

Samson loves Delilah, but Delilah abandons the love of a hunted man, for the security of wealth (vv. 6–20).

Jehovah-jireh, may my security come from You.

JUDGES 17

Micah steals 1,100 shekels from his mother and confesses that he has stolen them. She then blesses him (17:1–2). When he gives his mother the money, she declares, "I had wholly dedicated the silver unto the LORD from my hand for my son, to make a graven image and a molten image" (v. 3). The very things that God has forbidden—idols—are built and enshrined in the home of an Israelite. "And the man Micah had an house of gods, and made an ephod, and teraphim, and consecrated one of his sons, who became his priest" (v. 5). Private shrines to idols and priests not sanctioned by God show the great disdain that is now widespread in Israel. This mother-and-son story shows us how people of God, without close relationships with Him, will seek religious security in the same manner as their foreign neighbors.

Encountering One, let me always walk close with You.

JUDGES 19–21

The final Judges story also involves a woman and a Levite. "By focusing on Levites in the concluding episodes, the narrator communicates the extent of Israel's moral decline. The corruption that has infected the people and their deliverers has spread even to those who are entrusted with keeping Yahwistic tradition" (*WBC*, 75). This story is one of marital discord in which the Levite takes a concubine from Bethlehem in Judah who is unfaithful to him, and returns her to her father's house. After four months, the Levite goes to bring her back. On the way home, unwilling to stay another night, the man leaves and goes toward Jerusalem with his two saddled donkeys and his concubine (19:1–2, 10). It is here that trouble begins. An older man from the hill country of Ephraim, living in the area of the Benjamites, invites the group to spend the night at his home. While they are enjoying themselves, some of the wicked men of the city surround the house. Pounding on the door, they shout to the Levite's host, "Bring forth the man that came unto thine house, that we may know him" (v. 22). In other words, the men proposed to have sex with him. The older man counters with another proposition: "Behold, here is my daughter, a maiden, and his concubine; them I will bring out now, and humble ye them, and do with them what seemeth good unto you; but unto this man do not so vile a thing" (v. 24). The men refuse this offer. Nevertheless, the Levite sends out his concubine (v. 25).

The following morning, after the men have violated the concubine, she crawls back to the house from whence she came. There she dies. The Levite picks her up, places her on his donkey, and heads for home. When he reaches home, he takes a knife and cuts the body of his concubine into twelve parts and sends them into all of the areas of Israel (vv. 27–29). The deed is described thusly: "There was no such deed done nor seen from the day that the children of Israel came up out of the land of Egypt unto this day" (v. 30).

Like a sacrificial animal, riding upon a donkey, and sent piece by piece to every tribe of Israel, this nameless woman speaks in profound ways she has not spoken throughout the narrative. Her abused body speaks to all of Israel about abandonment, rejection, and betrayal of those who should have been her protectors. Her sacrificed body is a signal sent

by the Levite that his rights have been violated by the Benjamites. "Judah goes up first, not against a foreign enemy, but against other Israelites. The dismemberment is not that of an enemy king, but of an innocent and unprotected Israelite woman. The woman on a donkey rides not erect and determined to secure life, but she is limp and immobile, a victim of violence, the embodiment of betrayal and death" (*WBC*, 76). The slaughter continues and entire villages are ravished, for violence always begets violence (Judg. 20–21).

The narrator is quick to remind us that "in those days there was no king in Israel, but every man did that which was right in his own eyes" (17:6). The book progresses, and the violence becomes increasingly personal. From the progress of the nation (1:1–26) to the defense of the nation (4:1–5:31) to personal vengeance (14:1–16:31) to the wounded honor of the dishonorable (19:1–20:7), violence is no longer used as a tool for the common good, but as a weapon of anarchy.

God of new beginnings, help me learn from the lessons of yesterday. Let me be better because of my yesterdays.

Focus On
RUTH

The covenant vows between Ruth and Naomi are used in many marriage ceremonies even today. Ruth, a foreigner, takes the oath to the Israelites, as an invitation to her Israelite mother-in-law, Naomi, to "lean on me"! These two women teach us how to lean on each other for support, for survival, for community, and for the future. When Naomi grows old and tired, Ruth says, "I'll lead now." When Naomi decides that her life is at an end, Ruth says, "I'll begin now." When Naomi says, "Call me Mara, for life is bitter," Ruth takes her by the hand and makes her vow that life will be better. And together they walk into an unknown tomorrow.

With courage and determination, Ruth journeys with Naomi into a land with people and customs that are foreign to her. The women are left alone and without financial means; yet they risk leaving Moab to journey to Bethlehem.

Naomi is tired. Tired of relocating, as she had moved to Moab from Bethlehem years before during a famine. At that time, she had arrived with her spouse, Elimelech, and with expectations that her two sons would provide her with a secure future. Both her sons had grown up and intermarried with Moabite women, Ruth and Orpah. Then, her husband and both of her sons died and Naomi was left with her two daughters-in-law. Israelite custom made her responsible for their welfare. She felt that her back was to the wall. Naomi decided to return to her home, Bethlehem, for a famine had come to Moab. Knowing that she had some male kinsmen at home, she determined to send her daughters-in-law back to their parents, so that she could go home to perhaps die alone. Her time of motherhood was over.

At the crossroads, with an uncertain future ahead, Naomi bid both the women farewell. Orpah heeded her words and walked off the stage of bib-

lical history. Ruth swore to never leave nor forsake Naomi. Ruth covenanted to be her support and her provider-protector. Ruth's loyalty and sistership make the older, wise women of the community in Bethlehem agreed that she is better to Naomi than seven sons. Ruth and Naomi walked into a bright tomorrow as they tied themselves into the royal lineage of King David and Jesus Christ.

THE BLACK PRESENCE IN RUTH

The setting for the Book of Ruth is Canaan/Moab. The land of Canaan was given to the Israelites by God, having been promised to Abraham, Sarah, and their descendants at the time the Abrahamic covenant was made (Gen. 15). The reason for this transfer of ownership was the failure of the Canaanites to faithfully live up to God's expectations (Gen. 15; Lev. 18:24–25). Both the Canaanites and the Israelites were of African or Asiatic descent, since research shows that humankind began in Africa and spread from there into Asia.

According to Matthew 1:5, Boaz was a descendant of Rahab, who was a Hamite through Boaz's son Canaan.

Life Lessons

RUTH 1

We enter the scene in Moab, where there is a complex social situation involving gender issues, marital relationships, travel, and a growing sense of hopelessness. Today, Naomi would be classified as "depressed." First of all, her husband dies; he is followed in death by both of her sons. She has no male kinsmen close by. She is head of a household in which there are three widowed, childless women. Bitter and discouraged, she pronounces, "Call me not Naomi, call me Mara: for the Almighty hath dealt very bitterly with me. I went out full, and the LORD hath brought me home again empty" (1:20–21). She is afraid, for she realizes that she is a woman without resources for survival. Naomi was at rock bottom. She felt that there was nowhere else to go, so she decided to return to her home, Bethlehem.

Hope of the Hopeless, life is bitter. But You alone can make it better.

RUTH 1

Naomi kisses Orpah and Ruth and wishes them well: "Go, return each to her mother's house: the LORD deal kindly with you, as ye have dealt with the dead, and with me. The LORD grant you that ye may find rest, each of you in the house of her husband"(1:8–9). Naomi, Ruth, and Orpah are at a crossroads. They each know the past, but they don't have a clue as to what lies ahead. Naomi wishes that each of her daughters-in-law will find new husbands and have children. These are the requirements for a woman's survival in ancient Palestine.

Ruth declares, "Intreat me not to leave thee, or to return from following after thee: for whither thou goest, I will go; and where thou lodgest, I

will lodge: thy people shall be my people, and thy God my God: Where thou diest, will I die . . . and more also, if ought but death part thee and me" (vv. 16–17). In marriage the covenant is sealed with binding words. Ruth, a Gentile, is ready to forsake her homeland, her customs, and her gods. She is willing to risk binding her life with Naomi's. She is committed to taking care of another woman who has cared for her in days past. Declaring her intent, the women set out for Bethlehem.

Covenant relationships are not about equality. Covenant relationships are not about "What's in it for me?" Covenant relationships are about serving and meeting the needs of others. These women do not have blood ties to hold them together. They are not even of the same ethnic group. Yet Naomi and Ruth share love and the common desire to survive.

Holy One, guide me along the way. With You beside me, I cannot stray.

RUTH 2–3

It is Ruth's turn to take the initiative, and take the initiative she does! "And Ruth the Moabite, said unto Naomi, Let me now go to the field, and glean ears of corn after him in whose sight I shall find grace. . . and her hap was to light on a part of the field belonging unto Boaz, who was of the kindred of Elimelech" (2:2–3). "Then said Boaz unto his servant that was set over the reapers, Whose damsel is this? . . . It is the Moabitish damsel that came back with Naomi out of the country of Moab" (vv. 5–6). It is important to note that unlike Naomi, the narrative refers to Ruth by speaking of her ethnicity and not her name.

Harvester God, thank You for including me, an outsider, in the sweep of Your vast field.

RUTH 2

Boaz arranges for Ruth to remain in his field (2:8–10). He readily becomes her protector, including her in his field crew. She is able to feed and care for both herself and Naomi as she had sworn. "Blessed be he that did take knowledge of thee" (v.19) cries Naomi upon Ruth's return. "Blessed be the of the LORD!" (v.20). Ruth tells Naomi that his name is Boaz. It takes Naomi only minutes to recall that Boaz is a distant relative of her dead husband. "The man is near of kin unto us, one of our next kinsmen" (v.20).

By definition, a redeemer is one who retains or reclaims a property through purchase, thereby relieving oneself or another from obligation, lien, or slavery. Accordingly, it also reflects God's activity as the Deity who saves from sin, slavery, exile, and death. For Naomi, men function as representatives of heaven on earth (*WBC*, 81–82). Naomi recognizes the potential role of Boaz as a divinely guided redeemer who, as a relative of her husband, can reclaim the property that she could not. "So she kept fast by the maidens of Boaz to glean unto the end of barley harvest and of wheat harvest; and dwelt with her mother-in-law" (2:23). The roles of women supporting each other and working together are depicted as essential for survival.

Friend of the Friendless, grant me supportive community among my sisters.

RUTH 4

Ruth and Boaz marry and live happily ever after. Ruth then gives birth to a son, Obed. The women in the community tell Naomi, "Blessed be the LORD, which hath not left thee this day without a kinsman, that his name may be famous in Israel. And he shall be unto thee a restorer of thy life, and a nourisher of thine old age: for thy daughter-in-law, which loveth thee, which is better to thee than seven sons, hath born him" (4:14–15). Obed later becomes the father of Jesse, who is later the father of David. So a Moabite woman becomes part of the genealogy of Jesus Christ because she kept her covenant. Ruth's story is a true love story.

It is interesting to note that although the book is called Ruth, it ends with Naomi. She who was "empty" cares for the child. The women who greet them upon their arrival in Bethlehem name the child (v. 17).

Dear God, give me the name and identity that You have for me, even in a foreign land.

Women in Joshua, Judges, and Ruth

Achsah: Commodity's Daughter

Throughout Old Testament history, the roles of women have fallen into various categories, including daughter, wife, mother, prophet, harlot, heroine, prostitute, commander, victim, unwed mother, widow, queen, commander, and seducer, among others.

The story of Achsah, whose name in Hebrew means "bangle," "anklet," or "trinket," is found in the Books of Joshua and Judges. This discourse falls under the category of "commodity to commander." Caleb, the father of this young woman, had achieved fame as one of the spies of Israel. When he was engaged in conquering the land that had been promised to him, Achsah was used as the bargaining chip for her father's military campaign.

After fleeing Egypt, Israel wandered in the wilderness for 40 years. Caleb and Joshua were sent by Moses with ten others to scope out the land of Canaan (see Numbers 13–14). Caleb and Joshua were the only two of the twelve to give a positive "faith" report regarding Israel's ability to conquer the land. Consequently, they were the only two of their generation to inherit the promise of God in the new land that God had promised to Abraham's descendants.

At the age of 85, Caleb reminded Joshua of the promise that had been given him by Moses. Caleb was successful in driving out some of the inhabitants of the land that he had acquired; however, he needed help to conquer the land of Debir (formerly known as Kirjath-sepher). In order to do this, his daughter Achsah became the commodity that he traded in order to obtain the help necessary to conquer Debir. He said, "He that smiteth Kirjath-sepher, and taketh it, to him will I give Achsah my daughter to wife" (Josh. 15:16)

History does not record that Caleb had any other daughters besides Achsah (he had sons by his wife and concubines). However, it implies that a close relationship between father and daughter existed. Although her marriage to her cousin Othniel was a reward from her father, implications are that she found favor with her husband. She was wise enough to get her husband's consent to ask her father to give her a dowry of commercial value: "she moved him to ask of her father a field" (v. 18). It was obvious that she knew something about the area where she would live; her husband agreed. This area was part of the hill country. It was not known what exchanged between Caleb and his nephew, Othniel; however, Caleb wanted to know his daughter's wish: "What wouldest thou?" She answered, "Give me a blessing; for thou hast given me a south land; give me also springs of water" (vv. 18–19). So Caleb gave her the upper springs and the lower springs. In the

Book of Judges these springs are called "Upper Gulloth and Lower Gulloth."

The Negeb, the southern part of Judah, is a hot, dry region with less than eight inches of rainfall annually. Water is a necessity and the springs would help make life easier in this harsh country. The wording of Achsah's request suggests that she had some knowledge of what life was like in this area. She leaves an account of an obedient daughter, not bemoaning her fate but utilizing wisdom. There is no other mention of this couple in biblical history except that Achsah's husband, Othniel, became the first judge of Israel after Joshua's death (see Judg. 3:9–11).

Achsah had a winning combination of beauty and brains. She expressed an interest in her inheritance and in her future, which ultimately paid off for her husband Othniel.

Read Joshua 15:13–19; Judges 1:11–15; 3:9–11.

See also the portraits on A Virtuous Woman in Proverbs and Zelophehad's Daughters.

—M. Copeland

RAHAB: WILLING TO BE USED BY GOD

Rahab was a prostitute living near the side of the Jericho wall. When Joshua sent spies into Jericho, the spies lodged in Rahab's house (Josh. 2:1). When the king of Jericho sent soldiers in search of the spies, Rahab courageously hid them on the rooftop and told the king's soldiers that the spies were not there (vv. 2–4). Because of her great courage and kindness, the spies promised Rahab that her family would not be harmed during the takeover of Jericho.

Just before she helped the spies escape safely through a window, they instructed her to hang a scarlet cord from her window so that Joshua and the others would be able to identify the family that should be spared (vv. 17–18). Rahab told the spies how she heard stories about God's miracles, and that she recognized their God as the one true God (vv. 9–11).

Rahab's story has taught women throughout time that God will use those that He deems fit to fulfill His mission. God doesn't always choose the most righteous, but rather those who are the most willing.

Rahab's belief in God gave her the courage to help the spies. The greater news, however, is that in spite of the fact that she was a prostitute, God chose her to assist Joshua in his mission to capture Jericho. Her faith earns her a place in the "Hebrews Hall of Faith" (Heb. 11:31) and a listing in the genealogy of Jesus (Matt. 1:5).

When God comes into our hearts, we can truly become *new* people. We, however, must remain faithful in reaching for the courage and boldness that allow us to take the first steps toward Him.

Read Joshua 1:2, 11, 13; 2; Matthew 1:5–6; Hebrews 11:31; James 2:25.

See also the insight essays on Courage and Faith.

—T. Dixon

DEBORAH: AN UNCOMMON LEADER

Deborah's story begins thusly: "And the children of Israel again did evil in the sight of the LORD" (Judg. 4:1), which tells us that she ruled at a time when there was much unrest in the nation. Deborah reigned during

Israel's bondage under Jabin, king of Canaan, who resided in Hazor. Sisera, the captain of Jabin's army, was renowned for having 900 iron chariots, and was also known for his oppression of the Israelites (vv. 2–3).

Deborah's name means "bee," which is very appropriate, since she has the characteristics of the bee: she gathered the people to her as honey, but her sting was most fatal to her enemies. She was a godly woman—a prophet, poet, encourager, warrior, and ruler.

God chose Deborah to minister justice and to lead His people out of bondage into peace. Deborah sat under a palm tree to minister judgment and was one of several women distinguished in Scripture by her ability to discern the purposes of God.

Being an encourager, Deborah appealed to Israel's sense of freedom. In a way she was their wake-up call that God would forgive them if they would turn from their evil ways and return to Him. Deborah's words of wisdom, given to her by God, and commitment to Him inspired the people to a certainty of deliverance.

Deborah sent for Barak, the son of Abinoam, and approached him concerning the instructions God had given him and the promise of victory if he obeyed Him. Barak replied that he would lead their army to war if Deborah would go with him, but if she would not go, he would not go. Deborah agreed to go, but informed Barak that his victory would now be given to a woman. Deborah and Barak were useful to each other.

God delivered Sisera into the hands of Jael, who killed him with "a nail of the tent" (v. 21). Upon returning to the camp, Deborah and Barak sang a song of praise to the Lord and lifted up Jael for her bravery.

Deborah's story offers much insight for the African-American woman of today.

Read Judges 4–5.

—J. Josey

JAEL: JUST ANOTHER WOMAN ON THE LORD'S SIDE

Jael, though a celebrated heroine among Israelites, is an enigma. She is shrouded in mystery and speculation. We don't know much about her. We don't know who her people are—who she is the daughter of. She is just the wife of Heber the Kenite.

Though the Kenites were longtime allies of Israel, Heber was on the side of the enemy. Some say Heber is probably the one who tipped General Sisera off to where Israel's army was camped. Yet we do know that Jael had her own thoughts about the matter.

Jael may also have known Israel's God. She was probably familiar with the Abrahamic covenant: "I will bless them that bless thee, and curse him that curseth thee: And in thee shall all the families of the earth be blessed" (Gen. 12:3). The sequence of events suggest that Jael knew enough to know that being on the Lord's side was the better choice.

When Israel's victory was certain, Sisera ran for his life to his friend's house. Jael, standing in the doorway, invited him in. She gave him milk and covered him with her mantle. When he fell asleep, Jael took a hammer and used it to drive a tent peg through his temple (head), killing him.

We don't know much else in terms of details, but that's enough to celebrate this woman of great courage. Jael used what was at her disposal to accomplish what she understood to be her fight. She was obviously a woman of deep conviction. She had the big picture in view. Israel's victory meant victory for her and for her people.

There are times in a woman's life when she must take a stand. It may mean risking a career, social status, or something else more precious. Life presents us with many battles, many decisions. So choose carefully. Never go into battle unless you are on the Lord's side. Never fight for the sake of personal glory. Be certain that your motivation is the liberation and redemption of God's people.

Womanhood is honored as Deborah and Jael are used by God to accomplish His purpose of delivering His people from their enemies. Although Jael's victory is the fulfillment of Deborah's prophecy, I'm not so sure that Jael realized this. All that she may have known was that Israel was on the Lord's side. That was enough.

Read Judges 4:14–24; 5:17–27.

—*E. Walters*

THE WOMAN OF THEBEZ: ABIMELECH'S KILLER

She is a nameless woman. She is known best as the unknown woman who slew Abimelech, one of the sons of Gideon (Judg. 9:1), by throwing a millstone from the tower of Thebez, killing him (v. 53–54). It appears that Thebez is her home. Scripture gives no clue concerning her parentage.

The traditional work of women during this period was grinding grain with millstones and setting up tents with pegs. A millstone was considered a precious commodity.

At this time, the people of Thebez were under siege by Abimelech and his men (vv. 50–51). They had fled to the tower for safety. The woman probably used what she had on hand—the millstone—to defeat the enemy.

What can we learn from this woman? Obviously she was a woman who could assess the situation at hand, make a decision, and act on that decision with haste. Her immediate response to that moment not only saved her life but also the lives of all those who sought refuge in the tower. It appears that the woman acted unselfishly, understanding that in her culture, it was unlikely that she would receive any credit for her heroism. God used this unnamed woman to perform a small yet significant act.

How willing are we to step forward when called upon without worrying about "what's in it for me?" Each of us should be willing at any given moment to respond when a situation arises where God is directing us through the Holy Spirit. God knows the motives of our hearts and will reward us for the acts that reflect His glory. God called and the woman responded. This is a reminder to each of us to always be ready when God calls us, no matter what the task. God equips us for every task we are sent to do. All we need to do is be a willing vessel.

Read Judges 9; 2 Samuel 11:21.

—*J. Hopkins*

JEPHTHAH'S DAUGHTER: A PROMISE KEPT

She was so excited—Dad was coming home from battle, a successful battle, too. The Ammonites had been defeated, and Dad would be home for awhile.

She was probably "Daddy's little girl"—a favorite since she was his only child. She was young and full of life, young enough to dance, but old enough to think about the importance of marriage. As her father, Jephthah, approached the house, she went to meet him, running and dancing with tambourines in her hands, out of the house and across the field. With hair flying, she laughed and shouted her "hellos."

She never had a chance to finish her happy greeting. Instead, her father cut her off: "What disaster you've brought me! I made a foolish promise to the LORD. Now I can't break it" (Judg. 11:35). Her mind was racing: What had he said? What did he mean? What promise had he made to God? But her voice came steady and clear, and out of confidence and faith she said, "Do to me according to that which hath proceeded out of thy mouth; forasmuch as the LORD hath taken vengeance for thee of thine enemies" (Judg. 11:36). Her father's promise to God was more important than the consequences it held for her.

The ultimate fate of Jephthah's daughter isn't known. Some scholars speculate that she was actually killed. Others argue that it was highly unlikely she was sacrificed, since no priest would administer the ceremony. Others say she was set apart for God and never allowed to marry—in those days, a terrible fate for a woman, as she would have no family to support her or care for her.

Jephthah's daughter's life in the society of Judah was ruined because of a hastily voiced vow to God. But she knew that a promise to God was sacred. She didn't ask her father to break it. In maturity and faith, her only request was to have time to grieve with her friends.

Read Judges 11:29–40.

SAMSON'S MOTHER: THE STRENGTH OF A WIFE AND MOTHER

God sent an angel to an unnamed woman (Judg. 13). She was Samson's mother and Manoah's wife. At first glance, her namelessness implies that she was insignificant. Yet the angel spoke to the woman and revealed that the Lord would use her to birth one who would begin to deliver Israel from the Philistines.

Manoah's wife did not address the angel. Instead she told her husband what the Lord revealed. The angel appeared to the woman a second time. Although Manoah prayed, God did not send the angel directly to him. Why? After all, he was the head of the household. We could make a couple assumptions here: (1) God speaks to women who will share with their husbands the plan of salvation; and (2) women are encouraged to carry the story of salvation to others. (In Matthew 28:10, Jesus told the women, to "go tell.")

Manoah's wife was not a woman who aggressively tried to be her own boss. She heard God. She believed God. She led her husband to the messenger of God (the angel). Willingly, she was quiet while her husband questioned the angel. The angel replied, "Of all that I said unto the woman let

her beware" (Judg. 13:13). The responsibility was placed on the woman to do as God said. This woman demonstrated submissiveness to her husband's leadership, even though she was the one to whom the angel spoke.

As the vessel to bring forth deliverance for Israel, she was to refrain from certain things while carrying Israel's liberator. She was not to have alcohol or any unclean food. She was told how to nurture the life of this consecrated child. No razor was to come upon her son's head. He was to be set apart, and raised to be used for God's purpose. The child, Samson, would bring destruction to those who hated Israel (vv. 4–7, 13–14).

One of the mysteries of people of color has been their ability to survive the hardships of life and still maintain strength of body and mind. The strength of our women has consistently been faith in God. Samson's mother reminds us to listen to God's instructions and obey Him. Children who know their purpose can be great weapons against the enemies of God.

Read Judges 13.

See also the insight essays on Infertility and Motherhood.

—D. S. JaPhia

SAMSON'S BRIDE: NOTHING BY CHANCE

It is not by chance that Samson's marriage was the first recorded event of his adult life. Samson's bride was first mentioned in Judges 14:1–3 and, interestingly, was not described in the usual patriarchal biblical tradition of being the "daughter of . . ."; instead she is called "a Philistine woman in Timnah" (v. 2). She was characterized by where she lived. As a Philistine woman, she was a poor choice for a wife. The marriage was doomed from the beginning. Her loyalty to her past and her selfishness ultimately affected her future. Ask yourself how many times you've allowed your past to affect how you perceive the next level of personal, professional, and spiritual achievement. The story of this woman from Timnah shows what results from not recognizing how God's hand guides our lives.

Samson's bride manipulated him into telling her the secret of a riddle told at their wedding banquet. At the demands of her countrymen and their threats of death, she betrayed Samson. Samson, out of vengeance, returned to his father's house, while his wife was given to another (vv. 19–20). Unfortunately, the sad saga did not end there. After Samson exacted his revenge against the Philistines, his wife and father were murdered by the Philistines (15:1–6). More deaths followed (v. 8).

The key to understanding this oft-criticized woman is to look at who brought her into Samson's life. The astonishing answer is that God allowed her relationship with Samson. Judges 14:4 clearly shows that even his parents "knew not that it was of the LORD." Thus, God was orchestrating the circumstances so that Samson could confront the Philistines and "deliver Israel out of the hand of the Philistines" (Judg. 3:5). How reassuring it is to know that even when we make mistakes and disappoint ourselves, God's sovereign hand still controls the action! Others may not be able to see God in the situation, but we can be assured that God can use even our mistakes for our good! The woman of Timnah's presence in Samson's life provided a turning point in his life.

We need to recognize when God has placed us in a position of influ-

ence as Christian mothers, daughters, wives, sisters and coworkers. As Christians, we must lead lives strengthened by prayer and enhanced by the Word of God. Even when we feel that we do not know how God is using us, we can have the spiritual sensitivity to know that wherever God has placed us, we can make a difference.

Read Judges 14–15:8.

Read the insight essay on Rebellion.

—S. Riley

DELILAH: STRENGTH THAT BUILDS OR DESTROYS

The story of Samson and Delilah often generates more feedback about the weakness of Samson. Many questions arise regarding how Samson could be so clueless about Delilah's agenda to assist the Philistines in his demise. But the story of Samson and Delilah is not necessarily that simple. Delilah has a message for all women to take to heart. Delilah, like many women in the Bible, reminds us of the unusual strength women have—a strength that either builds or destroys. While women are naturally the weaker physically, they possess an exceptional yet subtle strength spiritually and emotionally.

It is important for women to be conscious of this strength because of its potential to both build and destroy. Women have the power to build up individuals, homes, communities, and churches. Likewise, that same power can also destroy. Delilah chose to destroy a man for money. She could have chosen to help build character as Deborah attempted to do with Barak. At the same time that Samson was destroyed, so were Delilah's people.

We women must be aware of the strength that God has given us and that Satan desires to use this strength for evil. It is our choice how this God-given strength will be used—to build or to destroy.

Read Judges 16.

See also the insight essay on Temptation.

—B. Whitaker

MICAH'S MOTHER: THE CONSEQUENCES OF IGNORING GOD

Little is known of Micah's mother except what is written in Judges 17. Apparently, she lived with her son in Ephraim, a region of Israel located in northeast Africa.

From her story, mothers can learn three things that they *should not* do:

1. *Be dishonest.* When one is dishonest, circumstances will not determine your actions—being dishonest will! When Micah returned the eleven hundred shekels of silver that he had stolen from his mother, she pretended that the silver was wholly consecrated to the Lord; therefore, she gave it back to him (Micah) to make a carved image and a cast idol. She then gave him only two hundred shekels of silver—a small fraction of her initial promise for the project (v. 4).

2. *Disobey the commandments.* By encouraging and participating with her son in making idols, Micah's mother broke God's most important commandment: "Thou shalt not make unto thee any graven image, or any likeness of any thing that is in heaven above, or that is in the earth beneath,

or that is in the water under the earth" (Ex. 20:4).

3. *Ignore your family's sinfulness.* In addition to participating in the making of idols, there is no indication that she tried to stop her son from installing her grandson, and later a Levite who was not a member of the priestly line, as priests. There were rules by which priests were to be chosen (see Ex. 28:41). She chose to ignore God's law. Consequently, her son's actions contributed to his—and Israel's—confusion in their religious lives.

Read Judges 17.

See also the insight essay on Motherhood.

—*A. Dise*

THE LEVITE'S CONCUBINE: BROKEN PIECES

This nineteenth chapter of Judges relates a horrific account of a woman's life and death in such graphic detail that it would cause one not to believe she is reading the Bible. The graphic details seem befitting of a Stephen King novel or movie script, but certainly not the Word of God.

This anonymous woman was the concubine of a Levite. The writer of the text informs us that she had been unfaithful to the Levite and left him, returning to her father. Her husband set out on a journey to convince her to come back home.

The Levite arrived at the home of his concubine's father to meet with her. There he spent many days conversing with her father. This is a scene of male bonding at its best. Finally, the Levite prepared for the journey home, accompanied by his concubine. We do not know if she was coerced or convinced to go, but she left with the Levite.

When evening came, they stopped in a town to rest and were taken in by a hospitable stranger. The men of the town swarmed to the man's door seeking to have sex with the Levite. Instead, the man offered his daughter and the Levite's concubine. Violation and death resulted. The subsequent dismemberment and distribution of the concubine's body led Israel to war.

In our lives, there are countless women who are broken into many pieces. There are many broken women who seem spread so thin that they have nothing left to give to themselves. Many of these women darken the doors of our churches and ministries; they remain anonymous, unheard, and unspoken to. They literally are standing at the threshold crying out for help and we step over them and continue on our own journeys, just as the Levite tried to do (see Judges 19:27).

But even when people don't know our names, God knows who we are. When society continues to rob us of our dignity, God is able to take every broken piece of our lives and bring about wholeness.

Read Judges 19–21.

Read insight essays on, Sexual Abuse, and Suffering.

—*C. Ward*

NAOMI'S STORY: CALL ME BITTER

This is Naomi's story, told as if she were writing directly to us:

My family left our hometown, Bethlehem, with noble aspirations. My husband and I packed up our two sons and moved to Moab, because there was a famine in Bethlehem and we'd heard that there was food and other

opportunities in Moab. So, we set out to make a mark for ourselves. We were comfortable in Moab. Our sons grew up and married Moabite women. Their names were Ruth and Orpah. Although I was concerned about these foreign women becoming part of our family, I grew to love them as my daughters.

One day the unthinkable happened: my husband died. I was thrown into the depths of despair. I thought that surely nothing worse could happen to me. I know now how foolish I was. My sons died soon after, leaving Ruth, Orpah, and me alone in a world that was not kind. At the time I thought, It's funny. While my name means "pleasantness," my spirit counters such a lighthearted name. Instead, my spirit says, "Call me bitter." Call me bitter, for the Lord has dealt harshly with me! Call me bitter.

After months of struggling in Moab, I decided to return to Bethlehem. I thought that at least my people were there and I could wait my time out to die. My daughters-in-law begged to return to Bethlehem with me because they were determined not to leave me alone. But what could I offer them? I was too old to have more sons. And even if I could, would they have waited until my sons were old enough to marry them? No, the best thing for Ruth and Orpah was to return to their mothers' homes. I convinced Orpah to leave, and she did so, weeping and despairing. But Ruth refused to go. Instead, she insisted, "Intreat me not to leave thee, or to return from following after thee: for whither thou goest, I will go; and where thou lodgest, I will lodge: thy people shall be my people, and thy God my God: Where thou diest, will I die, and there will I be buried: the LORD do so to me, and more also, if ought but death part thee and me" (2:16–17). Upon hearing this, I knew that Ruth was determined to accompany me. I allowed her to do so.

When we arrived in Bethlehem, I had only a small place for us to live. There was no food, and I was too old to work. When my friends tried to comfort me, all I could say was, "Call me bitter." Now I realize just how God blessed me by giving me Ruth. She gleaned in the fields so that we could eat. And when she was fortunate enough to be working on the property of one of my relatives, Boaz, she followed my advice and eventually married this kind man. Ruth and Boaz then took me into their home and provided for me. But my story does not end there. When Ruth had a son she brought him to me to nurse! Call me bitter—no! God has taken my bitterness and given me a garment of praise! I praise Him for Ruth because I now know that she is more valuable to me than ten sons!

Read Ruth 1–4.

Read the portrait on Ruth.

—C. Belt

RUTH: BEGINNING A NEW LIFE TOGETHER

Ruth is lifted up as an ideal prototype for the single woman. She was faithful, loyal, and willing to wait on her "Boaz." Her obedience and perseverance were rewarded with a husband and child.

The Book of Ruth and the woman Ruth have provided the biblical canon with a captivating voice that reaches far beyond what the writer of Ruth may have intended. Ruth holds more than a sentimental scriptural reference for a wedding or a life design for single women. Her story

poignantly highlights many of the issues that African-American women struggle with today (e.g., family, security, loss, racism, sexism, and survival). Ruth is best known for giving birth to Obed, an ancestor of David and consequently Jesus. But before she claimed her place in history as "mother," she added a unique imprint as woman and "sista." In Ruth 1:14, we find a Moabite widow making an unprecedented choice to "cling" or "cleave" to her Israelite widowed mother-in-law.

The relationship between Ruth and Naomi binds two women who could have easily chosen to become estranged. After the death of her husband (Naomi's son), Ruth was left with an uncertain future. She could have returned to her home, but there was no guarantee that her family would embrace her, since she had married an Israelite. The Israelites were longtime antagonists of her people. She could follow her mother-in-law, but there was similar uncertainty about how she would be received as a foreigner with scorned ethnic roots. Using her courage and strength, Ruth remained with or "clung" to Naomi. As a result, they were able to move beyond their given identities as wives and widows and establish different identities as partners and sojourners.

The return of Naomi to Bethlehem was the beginning of a new life for her and Ruth. Ruth worked in the fields of Naomi's relative, Boaz. Following the advice of Naomi, Ruth eventually won the love of Boaz, who bought the estate of Naomi and married Ruth.

Ruth's gift to us is a message about the value of collaboration, cooperation, friendship, love, and trust between two women. At a turning point in her life, Ruth continued a relationship that would become a great blessing for both women. By taking risks and working together, Ruth and Naomi were able to move forward together.

Read Leviticus 25:25; Ruth 1:14–17.

See the portrait on Naomi.

—K. Mosby-Avery

Insights

A GREAT CHALLENGE: TEACHING OUR CHILDREN

Striving for academic excellence is one of the greatest challenges facing many African-American students today. Several factors may be responsible for this. Perhaps, the most paralyzing factor is negative peer pressure. For example, many students try to study and strive for success but are stifled in their efforts by students who are on their way to the big city of Nowhere. Those students who want to excel are ostracized and constantly reminded: "You are trying to act white!" I have never been able to understand the logic couched in their implication that African-Americans are supposed to be ignorant. Admittedly, everyone wants to be accepted, loved, and respected. But when human wants are compromised at the expense of "a get-by education," the result is limited potential development. This, from an economic perspective, translates into unemployment

or limited income—a major step toward poverty.

Parents should expose their children to positive role models. By role models, I do not mean entertainers or athletes. I mean parents, extended and augmented families, church leaders, and community members who have the opportunity to mold lives and change attitudes on a daily basis. These are people who can participate in lifelong learning activities, demand high expectations from students, enhance self-esteem, and volunteer in schools as well as visit schools to model the importance of education. These are people who can exemplify and instill moral and spiritual values. These are people who can promote faith development and racial pride, by sharing their faith and ancestral stories. These are people who can demonstrate the importance of setting goals and reaching them. Certainly, these are people who can lend credence to the "It takes a village" concept. These are the role models that our young people need to see in action.

Finally, the very survival of our race compels us as parents and "village communities" to accept the challenge to help our youth understand that African-Americans in the past suffered, bled, and died in order for us to enter the door to opportunity today via education. Because of this, they do not have the right to nullify sacrifices made on our behalf by previous generations of African-Americans. Moreover, we must fulfill the mandates reflected in Deuteronomy 6:5–6 and Psalm 78:1–4. These mandates, coupled with our empowerment efforts, will not only sustain our heritage, but they will also be one of the greatest legacies that we can bequeath.

Throughout the Scriptures, the family is the basic source for the moral and practical teaching of children (Deut. 6:6–7). Women are a vital link in teaching their own children and mentoring younger women (2 Tim. 1:5).

Parents are admonished to teach their children with love and responsibility (Eph. 6:4–7), and children are to learn with an attitude of respect (Ex. 20:12; Lev. 19:3).

In complete darkness, we are all the same. It is only our knowledge and wisdom that separate us. Don't let your eyes deceive you!

Read Deuteronomy 6:5–7; see also Matthew 18:3.

See also the insight essays on Children and Parenting.

—H. Harris

INFLUENCE

Studying the Scriptures will reveal women who had tremendous influence over their families, communities, and nations. The same kind of influence is present today among women. Today's women also use their influence to lead, protest, raise children, and serve as shepherds over God's flock.

However, the point is to both confess and to show that all of us have the ability to affect the actions of others. We must be very sure that we are first being Christ-led ourselves. For one who exercises control over the thoughts and actions of others will be held liable by God for how they use this influence.

Deuteronomy 13 gives us some warnings about who we allow to lead us. Though the gift of pleasing and flowing words might be from God, sometimes these words guide us in the wrong direction—away from God.

God is, and will always be, the Creator. Although the First Mover is intrinsically involved in the "new," not every novel idea is from God.

Examine the message of anyone you might think to follow. Are they speaking basic truths? Will following their lead be beneficial for all concerned? Above all, are they sent by Christ to help you on this journey back to Him and wholeness?

Read Deuteronomy 13.

Read insight essays on Motherhood and Women's Ministries. See also the portraits on Abigail, Deborah, Esther, Huldah, Ruth, a Virtuous Woman in Proverbs, and the Widow's Mite.

—A. Adams-Morris

GRACIOUSNESS

Often the words *gracious* and *graciousness* evoke pictures of modest, weak women blindly bowing to the whims and fancies of those around them. But the word *gracious* refers to one who is marked by kindness and courtesy. The word that is translated *grace* in the Old Testament comes from the Hebrew verb *chanan* which means "to bend or stoop in kindness." The noun form *chen* conveys "favor." Simply stated, graciousness refers to one who is willing to acknowledge the concerns of others before her own.

Deborah was gracious in her dealings with Barak, captain of the Israelite army. Rather than chastising him for his apprehension in going to battle, she agreed to go with him in order to bring him comfort and ease his fears (Judg. 4). Abigail was gracious to David, who had a serious bone to pick with her husband (1 Sam. 25). Martha was gracious to Jesus and His disciples by opening her home to them as a place of rest (Luke 10:38). But the ultimate example of graciousness is God. It is the Almighty God through Christ who bends down to take on human form and be the Divine Gift to the world (Phil. 2:5–11), a world which could never be worthy of so great a gift. It is Christ who calls and equips His followers to a life of graciousness, even in the midst of a troubled world where being gracious is often difficult.

Graciousness is not a forced action but one that is done with what may appear as effortless skill. A woman who is gracious has the capacity to respond in joy to the various situations of life.

Graciousness does not imply the absence of anger. Instead the anger is expressed in wise and skillful ways based on a firm acknowledgment of God's sovereignty. It is graciousness that responds to the anxious concerns of former oppressors, just as Joseph did: "You thought evil against me: but God meant it unto good" (Gen. 50:20). Graciousness allows women to sing "nobody knows the trouble I've seen" and "glory hallelujah."

Read Judges 4; 1 Samuel 25; Luke 10:38–42.

Read the insight essays on Aging, the Fruit of the Spirit, and Vanity. Read the portraits on Abigail and Deborah.

—C. Williams-Neal

COURAGE TO HEAL

> And the angel of the Lord appeared unto him and said unto him, The Lord is with you, thou mighty man of valour (Judg. 6:12).

It takes great courage to become whole. The story of Gideon speaks to

women and men about courage and overcoming great obstacles. African-American women are women of great courage and dedication.

Our valor in the face of apparently insurmountable obstacles gives us the ability to heal and be healed. In Jeremiah 30:12, God tells His people, "Thy bruise is incurable, and thy wound is grevious." Yet in verse 17 of the same chapter, God says, "For I will restore unto thee, and I will heal thee of thy wounds."

A woman needs courage to choose wholeness. Why else would Jesus ask a man so obviously in need of healing whether he wanted to be healed. (See John 5:6.) As if He didn't know! It wasn't for His sake that He asked, but for the sake of the person in need of healing.

It takes courage to say, "I want to be healed." Some of us have the courage to be healed. We are willing to go through the painful process of transformation. We are willing to go through the excruciating elimination of parts of ourselves in order to be fully who we were created to be. We are willing to have our wounds exposed and cleansed. We come out on the other side of pain and exposure transformed—renewed time and time again. We survive and thrive to show our daughters and sons the way through the underbrush of childhood trauma, addiction, domestic abuse, racism, sexism, oppression, neglect, and hurt.

We are mighty women of valor. We have a divine battle plan. We have our troops in place. We have our marching orders, and we are ready to move out for the sake of healing and wholeness—again!

Where there's a will, there's a way. If you provide the will, God will provide the way.—Beverly Bailey Harvard

Read Judges 6.

See also the insight essay on Forgiveness.

—L. Lee

FRIENDSHIP: INTIMACY WITH OTHERS

In Scripture, no greater example of intimate friendship is portrayed than the relationship between Naomi and Ruth. In the words of Scripture, Ruth clung to Naomi (Ruth 1:14) and her vow to Naomi stands as one of the most beautiful commitments of friendship in history (Ruth 1:16–17).

They were friends that loved at all times—in good and bad situations. Their actions freely demonstrated the self-sacrificing love that builds intimacy in any relationship. This type of love would "lay down his life for his friend" as Jesus spoke of (see John 15:13).

Intimacy bears with it the great possibility for great pain. Betrayal is so much more hurtful when it comes at the hand of a trusted, intimate friend (Ps. 55:12–14). Intimate friendship is disrupted by petty disputation, lack of trustworthiness (Prov. 11:13), withholding kindness (Job 6:14), and whispering or gossip (Prov. 16:28). All of these things are intimacy breakers.

Read Ruth 1.

See also the portraits on Naomi and Ruth. See the insight essays on Friendship and Intimacy.

—E. Alexander

WHAT IS INTIMACY?

Unfortunately, our culture provides us with false images of intimacy. We have no role models. The television, with its soap operas filled with shallow relationships, and the movies, inundated with sex, seldom show in-depth relationships that exhibit real caring and sharing; nor do they show the risk and vulnerability of disclosure that are primary requisites for intimate relationships. Sex, materialism, and the lack of honest communication are the modern-day calling cards. Those of us who are introspective enough to expect more in a relationship are often left feeling disappointed and in search of more meaningful relationships—such as Ruth and Naomi had (Ruth 1). Yet it is important to have the courage of one's convictions and expectations in relationships.

There are a few factors that promote intimacy in a relationship. First, where there is no real communication between individuals there can be no real intimacy. The ability to share all of who we are with another person, and to risk rejection and perhaps even ridicule, are the first steps in intimacy. Another important prerequisite to an intimate relationship with another person is self-knowledge and the freedom that such knowledge brings to a relationship. Many of us are uncomfortable, as well as fearful, of getting to know the person behind the face we see in the mirror every day. Until we come to know that person on a deeply personal level, we will never be really happy with ourselves or in our relationships with others. We must get in touch with who we really are, face ourselves with all of our flaws, while at the same time acknowledge our strengths and the God-given gifts that we bring to a relationship with another individual. When we look to another person for our identity, we set ourselves up for disappointment and disillusionment. We must realize that our identity comes from our identity in God's eyes and the Holy Spirit within us.

As we come to know more fully who we are as women of color, we will be better able to engage in relationships more intimately than ever before. There's a strength that comes from knowing who you are in God that removes the fear of relationships. It allows you to be authentically who you are and to be honest with those whom God allows into your life. For some of us to reach this level of intimacy, healing from past relationships must take place. For others, a rebuilding of self-confidence and a renewed sense of womanhood has to occur. But as our relationship with God becomes more intimate, the more willing we should be to risk revealing ourselves to others and to trust God for the outcome of those interactions. Our relationship with God will determine our relationship with others. Without the risk that intimacy involves, either with ourselves or with others, we can never be all that He would have us to be.

Read Ruth 1.

Read the insight essay on Commitment.

—B. Heard

WIDOWS—DEPENDENCE UPON GOD

The widows recorded in Scripture make up a divine honor roll of believing women whose piety, commitment, faithfulness, and generosity make them examples for us to this very day (1 Tim. 5:9–10). Without God, the widow is the most wretched of creatures. Scripture advises that if a

widow is still young, she should remarry (Rom. 7:3; 1 Cor. 7:39; 1 Tim. 5:14). However, when a widow places her trust in God He promises to provide everything she needs and to be her decision-maker, a father to her children (Deut. 10:18), her defender-contender (Ps. 68:5; Isa. 1:17, 23), her guardian (Ps. 146:9), and the keeper and provider of her possessions (Prov. 15:25; 29:25; Jer. 49:9–11). He also promises to supply her "exceeding abundantly above all that we ask or think" (Eph. 3:20).

The Scriptures contain accounts of faithful widows whose stories still stir our hearts today. The examples of their faith, commitment, and courage are some of the Bible's most well-known examples of faithfulness. These accounts, from the Old Testament to the New, contains lessons and models for our behavior today.

Old Testament Widows: Naomi and Ruth (Ruth 1–4); the wise widow of Tekoah (2 Sam. 14:4–5); the widow of Zarephath who sustained Elijah during a famine (1 Kin. 17); the prophet's widow whose sons Elisha saved from being sold for debt (2 Kin. 4:1–7).

New Testament Widows: Anna (Luke 2:36–37); the widow who gave two mites in the temple (Mark 12:41–44; Luke 21:2); the widow of Nain whose only son Jesus raised from the dead (Luke 7:11–15).

Read Ruth 2.

See also the insight essay on Brokenness. See also the portraits on the Prophet's Widow, the Widow of Nain.

—J. Jackson

11 Therefore thou shalt [r]love the LORD
thy God, and [s]keep his charge, and
his statutes, and his judgments, and his
commandments, alway.
2 And know ye this day: for *I speak* not
with your children which have not known,
and which have not seen [t]the chastisement
of the LORD your God, [u]his greatness, [v]his
mighty hand, and his stretched out arm,
3 [w]And his miracles, and his acts, which
he did in the midst of Egypt unto Pharaoh
the king of Egypt, and unto all his land;
4 And what he did unto the army of
Egypt, unto their horses, and to their chariots; [x]how he made the water of the Red sea
to overflow them as they pursued after you,
and *how* the LORD hath destroyed them
unto this day;
5 And what he did unto you in the wilderness, until ye came into this place;
6 And [y]what he did unto Dathan and Abiram, the sons of Eliab, the son of Reuben:
how the earth opened her mouth, and swallowed them up, and their households, and
their tents, and all the substance that *was* in
their possession, in the midst of all Israel:
7 But [z]your eyes have seen all the great
acts of the LORD which he did.
8 Therefore shall ye keep all the commandments which I command you this day,
that ye may [a]be strong, and go in and possess the land, whither ye go to possess it;
9 And [b]that ye may prolong *your* days in
the land, [c]which the LORD sware unto your
fathers to give unto them and to their seed,
[d]a land that floweth with milk and honey.
10 ¶ For the land, whither thou goest in to
possess it, *is* not as the land of Egypt, from
whence ye came out, [e]where thou sowedst
thy seed, and wateredst *it* with thy foot, as
a garden of herbs:
11 [f]But the land, whither ye go to possess
it, *is* a land of hills and valleys, *and* drinketh
water of the rain of heaven:
12 A land which the LORD thy God careth
for: [g]the eyes of the LORD thy God *are* always upon it, from the beginning of the year
even unto the end of the year.
13 ¶ And it shall come to pass, if ye shall
hearken [h]diligently unto my commandments which I command you this day, [i]to
love the LORD your God, and to serve him
with all your heart and with all your soul,
14 That [j]I will give *you* the rain of your
land in his due season, [k]the first rain and
the latter rain, that thou mayest gather in
thy corn, and thy wine, and thine oil.
15 [l]And I will send grass in thy fields for
thy cattle, that thou mayest [m]eat and be full.
16 Take heed to yourselves, [n]that your
heart be not deceived, and ye turn aside,
and [o]serve other gods, and worship them;
17 And *then* [p]the LORD's wrath be kindled against you, and he [q]shut up the
heaven, that there be no rain, and that the
land yield not her fruit; and *lest* [r]ye perish
quickly from off the good land which the
LORD giveth you.
18 ¶ Therefore [s]shall ye lay up these my
words in your heart and in your soul, and
[t]bind them for a sign upon your hand, that
they may be as frontlets between your eyes.
19 [u]And ye shall teach them your children, speaking of them when thou sittest in
thine house, and when thou walkest by the
way, when thou liest down, and when thou
risest up.
20 [v]And thou shalt write them upon the
door posts of thine house, and upon thy
gates:
21 That [w]your days may be multiplied,
and the days of your children, in the land
which the LORD sware unto your fathers to
give them, [x]as the days of heaven upon the
earth.
22 ¶ For if [y]ye shall diligently keep all
these commandments which I command
you, to do them, to love the LORD your God,
to walk in all his ways, and [z]to cleave unto
him;
23 Then will the LORD [a]drive out all these
nations from before you, and ye shall [b]pos-
sess greater nations and mightier than
yourselves.
24 [c]Every place whereon the soles of
your feet shall tread shall be yours: [d]from
the wilderness and Lebanon, from the river,
the river Euphrates, even unto the uttermost sea shall your coast be.
25 [e]There shall no man be able to stand
before you: *for* the LORD your God shall
[f]lay the fear of you and the dread of you
upon all the land that ye shall tread upon,
[g]as he hath said unto you.
26 ¶ [h]Behold, I set before you this day a
blessing and a curse;
27 [i]A blessing, if ye obey the commandments of the LORD your God, which I command you this day:
28 And a [j]curse, if ye will not obey the
commandments of the LORD your God, but
turn aside out of the way which I command
you this day, to go after other gods, which
ye have not known.
29 And it shall come to pass, when the
LORD thy God hath brought thee in unto the
land whither thou goest to possess it, that
thou shalt put [k]the blessing upon mount
Gerizim, and the curse upon mount Ebal.
30 *Are* they not on the other side Jordan,
by the way where the sun goeth down, in
the land of the Canaanites, which dwell in
the champaign over against Gilgal, [l]beside
the plains of Moreh?
31 [m]For ye shall pass over Jordan to go in
to possess the land which the LORD your
God giveth you, and ye shall possess it, and
dwell therein.
32 And ye shall observe [n]to do all the
statutes and judgments which I set before
you this day.

12 These [o]*are* the statutes and judgments, which ye shall observe to do
in the land, which the LORD God of thy fathers giveth thee to possess it, [p]all the days
that ye live upon the earth.

11:1 [r]ch. 10:12 [s]Zech. 3:7
11:2 [t]ch. 8:5 [u]ch. 5:24 [v]ch. 7:19
11:3 [w]Ps. 78:12
11:4 [x]Ex. 14:27; Ps. 101:11
11:6 [y]Num. 16:1; Ps. 106:17
11:7 [z]ch. 5:3
11:8 [a]Josh. 1:6
11:9 [b]ch. 4:40; Prov. 10:27 [c]ch. 9:5 [d]Ex. 3:8
11:10 [e]Zech. 14:18
11:11 [f]ch. 8:7
11:12 [g]1 Kings 9:3
11:13 [h]ver. 22; ch. 6:17 [i]ch. 10:12
11:14 [j]Lev. 26:4; ch. 28:12 [k]Joel 2:23; Jam. 5:7
11:15 [l]Ps. 104:14 [m]ch. 6:11; Joel 2:19
11:16 [n]ch. 29:18; Job 31:27 [o]ch. 8:19
11:17 [p]ch. 6:15 [q]1 Kings 8:35; 2 Chron. 6:26 [r]ch. 4:26; Josh. 23:13
11:18 [s]ch. 6:6 [t]ch. 6:8
11:19 [u]ch. 4:9
11:20 [v]ch. 6:9
11:21 [w]ch. 4:40; Prov. 3:2 [x]Ps. 72:5
11:22 [y]ver. 13; ch. 6:17 [z]ch. 10:20
11:23 [a]ch. 4:38 [b]ch. 9:1
11:24 [c]Josh. 1:3 [d]Gen. 15:18; Ex. 23:31; Num. 34:3
11:25 [e]ch. 7:24 [f]ch. 2:25 [g]Ex. 23:27
11:26 [h]ch. 30:1
11:27 [i]ch. 28:2
11:28 [j]ch. 28:15
11:29 [k]ch. 27:12; Josh. 8:33
11:30 [l]Gen. 12:6; Judg. 7:1
11:31 [m]ch. 9:1; Josh. 1:11
11:32 [n]ch. 5:32
12:1 [o]ch. 6:1 [p]ch. 4:10; 1 Kings 8:40

2 [q]Ye shall utterly destroy all the places, wherein the nations which ye shall possess served their gods, [r]upon the high mountains, and upon the hills, and under every green tree:

3 And [s]ye shall overthrow their altars, and break their pillars, and burn their groves with fire; and ye shall hew down the graven images of their gods, and destroy the names of them out of that place.

4 [t]Ye shall not do so unto the LORD your God.

5 But unto the place which the LORD your God shall [u]choose out of all your tribes to put his name there, *even* unto his habitation shall ye seek, and thither thou shalt come:

6 And [v]thither ye shall bring your burnt offerings, and your sacrifices, and your [w]tithes, and heave offerings of your hand, and your vows, and your freewill offerings, and the firstlings of your herds and of your flocks:

7 And [x]there ye shall eat before the LORD your God, and [y]ye shall rejoice in all that ye put your hand unto, ye and your households, wherein the LORD thy God hath blessed thee.

8 Ye shall not do after all *the things* that we do here this day, [z]every man whatsoever *is* right in his own eyes.

9 For ye are not as yet come to the rest and to the inheritance, which the LORD your God giveth you.

10 But *when* [a]ye go over Jordan, and dwell in the land which the LORD your God giveth you to inherit, and *when* he giveth you rest from all your enemies round about, so that ye dwell in safety;

11 Then there shall be [b]a place which the LORD your God shall choose to cause his name to dwell there; thither shall ye bring all that I command you; your burnt offerings, and your sacrifices, your tithes, and the heave offering of your hand, and all your choice vows which ye vow unto the LORD:

12 And [c]ye shall rejoice before the LORD your God, ye, and your sons, and your daughters, and your menservants, and your maidservants, and the Levite that *is* within your gates; forasmuch as [d]he hath no part nor inheritance with you.

13 [e]Take heed to thyself that thou offer not thy burnt offerings in every place that thou seest:

14 [f]But in the place which the LORD shall choose in one of thy tribes, there thou shalt offer thy burnt offerings, and there thou shalt do all that I command thee.

15 Notwithstanding [g]thou mayest kill and eat flesh in all thy gates, whatsoever thy soul lusteth after, according to the blessing of the LORD thy God which he hath given thee: [h]the unclean and the clean may eat thereof, [i]as of the roebuck, and as of the hart.

16 [j]Only ye shall not eat the blood; ye shall pour it upon the earth as water.

17 ¶ Thou mayest not eat within thy gates the tithe of thy corn, or of thy wine, or of thy oil, or the firstlings of thy herds or of thy flock, nor any of thy vows which thou vowest, nor thy freewill offerings, or heave offering of thine hand:

18 [k]But thou must eat them before the LORD thy God in the place which the LORD thy God shall choose, thou, and thy son, and thy daughter, and thy manservant, and thy maidservant, and the Levite that *is* within thy gates: and thou shalt rejoice before the LORD thy God in all that thou puttest thine hands unto.

19 [l]Take heed to thyself that thou forsake not the Levite as long as thou livest upon the earth.

20 ¶ When the LORD thy God shall enlarge thy border, [m]as he hath promised thee, and thou shalt say, I will eat flesh, because thy soul longeth to eat flesh; thou mayest eat flesh, whatsoever thy soul lusteth after.

21 If the place which the LORD thy God hath chosen to put his name there be too far from thee, then thou shalt kill of thy herd and of thy flock, which the LORD hath given thee, as I have commanded thee, and thou shalt eat in thy gates whatsoever thy soul lusteth after.

22 [n]Even as the roebuck and the hart is eaten, so thou shalt eat them: the unclean and the clean shall eat *of* them alike.

23 [o]Only be sure that thou eat not the blood: [p]for the blood *is* the life; and thou mayest not eat the life with the flesh.

24 Thou shalt not eat it; thou shalt pour it upon the earth as water.

25 Thou shalt not eat it; [q]that it may go well with thee, and with thy children after thee, [r]when thou shalt do *that which is* right in the sight of the LORD.

26 Only thy [s]holy things which thou hast, and [t]thy vows, thou shalt take, and go unto the place which the LORD shall choose:

27 And [u]thou shalt offer thy burnt offerings, the flesh and the blood, upon the altar of the LORD thy God: and the blood of thy sacrifices shall be poured out upon the altar of the LORD thy God, and thou shalt eat the flesh.

28 Observe and hear all these words which I command thee, [v]that it may go well with thee, and with thy children after thee for ever, when thou doest *that which is* good and right in the sight of the LORD thy God.

29 ¶ When [w]the LORD thy God shall cut off the nations from before thee, whither thou goest to possess them, and thou succeedest them, and dwellest in their land;

30 Take heed to thyself [x]that thou be not snared by following them, after that they be destroyed from before thee; and that thou enquire not after their gods, saying, How did these nations serve their gods? even so will I do likewise.

31 [y]Thou shalt not do so unto the LORD

12:2 [q]Ex. 34:13; ch. 7:5 [r]2 Kings 16:4; Jer. 3:6
12:3 [s]Num. 33:52; Judg. 2:2
12:4 [t]ver. 31
12:5 [u]ver. 11; ch. 26:2; Josh. 9:27; 1 Kings 8:29; 2 Chron. 7:12; Ps. 78:68
12:6 [v]Lev. 17:3 [w]ver. 17; ch. 14:22
12:7 [x]ch. 14:26 [y]ver. 12; Lev. 23:40; ch. 16:11
12:8 [z]Judg. 17:6
12:10 [a]ch. 11:31
12:11 [b]ver. 5; Josh. 18:1; 1 Kings 8:29; Ps. 78:68
12:12 [c]ver. 7 [d]ch. 10:9
12:13 [e]Lev. 17:4
12:14 [f]ver. 11
12:15 [g]ver. 21 [h]ver. 22 [i]ch. 14:5
12:16 [j]Gen. 9:4; Lev. 7:26; ch. 15:23
12:18 [k]ver. 11
12:19 [l]ch. 4:27
12:20 [m]Gen. 15:18; Ex. 34:24; ch. 11:24
12:22 [n]ver. 15
12:23 [o]ver. 16 [p]Gen. 9:4; Lev. 17:11
12:25 [q]ch. 4:40; Isa. 3:10 [r]Ex. 15:26; ch. 13:18; 1 Kings 11:38
12:26 [s]Num. 5:9 [t]1 Sam. 1:21
12:27 [u]Lev. 1:5
12:28 [v]ver. 25
12:29 [w]Ex. 23:23; ch. 19:1; Josh. 23:4
12:30 [x]ch. 7:16
12:31 [y]ver. 4; Lev. 18:3; 2 Kings 17:15

thy God: for every abomination to the LORD which he hateth, have they done unto their gods; for [z]even their sons and their daughters they have burnt in the fire to their gods.

32 What thing soever I command you, observe to do it: [a]thou shalt not add thereto, nor diminish from it.

13 If there arise among you a prophet, or a [b]dreamer of dreams, [c]and giveth thee a sign or a wonder,

2 And [d]the sign or the wonder come to pass, whereof he spake unto thee, saying, Let us go after other gods, which thou hast not known, and let us serve them;

3 Thou shalt not hearken unto the words of that prophet, or that dreamer of dreams: for the LORD your God [e]proveth you, to know whether ye love the LORD your God with all your heart and with all your soul.

4 Ye shall [f]walk after the LORD your God, and fear him, and keep his commandments, and obey his voice, and ye shall serve him, and [g]cleave unto him.

5 And [h]that prophet, or that dreamer of dreams, shall be put to death; because he hath spoken to turn *you* away from the LORD your God, which brought you out of the land of Egypt, and redeemed you out of the house of bondage, to thrust thee out of the way which the LORD thy God commanded thee to walk in. [i]So shalt thou put the evil away from the midst of thee.

6 ¶ [j]If thy brother, the son of thy mother, or thy son, or thy daughter, or [k]the wife of thy bosom, or thy friend, [l]which *is* as thine own soul, entice thee secretly, saying, Let us go and serve other gods, which thou hast not known, thou, nor thy fathers;

7 *Namely,* of the gods of the people which *are* round about you, nigh unto thee, or far off from thee, from the *one* end of the earth even unto the *other* end of the earth;

8 Thou shalt [m]not consent unto him, nor hearken unto him; neither shall thine eye pity him, neither shalt thou spare, neither shalt thou conceal him:

9 But [n]thou shalt surely kill him; [o]thine hand shall be first upon him to put him to death, and afterwards the hand of all the people.

10 And thou shalt stone him with stones, that he die; because he hath sought to thrust thee away from the LORD thy God, which brought thee out of the land of Egypt, from the house of bondage.

11 And [p]all Israel shall hear, and fear, and shall do no more any such wickedness as this is among you.

12 ¶ [q]If thou shalt hear *say* in one of thy cities, which the LORD thy God hath given thee to dwell there, saying,

13 *Certain* men, the children of Belial, [r]are gone out from among you, and have [s]withdrawn the inhabitants of their city, saying, [t]Let us go and serve other gods, which ye have not known;

14 Then shalt thou enquire, and make search, and ask diligently; and, behold, *if it* *be* truth, *and* the thing certain, *that* such abomination is wrought among you;

15 Thou shalt surely smite the inhabitants of that city with the edge of the sword, [u]destroying it utterly, and all that *is* therein, and the cattle thereof, with the edge of the sword.

16 And thou shalt gather all the spoil of it into the midst of the street thereof, and shalt [v]burn with fire the city, and all the spoil thereof every whit, for the LORD thy God: and it shall be [w]an heap for ever; it shall not be built again.

17 And [x]there shall cleave nought of the cursed thing to thine hand: that the LORD may [y]turn from the fierceness of his anger, and shew thee mercy, and have compassion upon thee, and multiply thee, [z]as he hath sworn unto thy fathers;

18 When thou shalt hearken to the voice of the LORD thy God, [a]to keep all his commandments which I command thee this day, to do *that which is* right in the eyes of the LORD thy God.

14 Ye *are* [b]the children of the LORD your God: [c]ye shall not cut yourselves, nor make any baldness between your eyes for the dead.

2 [d]For thou *art* an holy people unto the LORD thy God, and the LORD hath chosen thee to be a peculiar people unto himself, above all the nations that *are* upon the earth.

3 ¶ [e]Thou shalt not eat any abominable thing.

4 [f]These *are* the beasts which ye shall eat: the ox, the sheep, and the goat,

5 The hart, and the roebuck, and the fallow deer, and the wild goat, and the pygarg, and the wild ox, and the chamois.

6 And every beast that parteth the hoof, and cleaveth the cleft into two claws, *and* cheweth the cud among the beasts, that ye shall eat.

7 Nevertheless these ye shall not eat of them that chew the cud, or of them that divide the cloven hoof; *as* the camel, and the hare, and the coney: for they chew the cud, but divide not the hoof; *therefore* they *are* unclean unto you.

8 And the swine, because it divideth the hoof, yet cheweth not the cud, it *is* unclean unto you: ye shall not eat of their flesh, [g]nor touch their dead carcase.

9 ¶ [h]These ye shall eat of all that *are* in the waters: all that have fins and scales shall ye eat:

10 And whatsoever hath not fins and scales ye may not eat; it *is* unclean unto you.

11 ¶ *Of* all clean birds ye shall eat.

12 [i]But these *are they* of which ye shall not eat: the eagle, and the ossifrage, and the ospray,

13 And the glede, and the kite, and the vulture after his kind,

14 And every raven after his kind,

15 And the owl, and the night hawk, and the cuckow, and the hawk after his kind,

12:31 [z]Lev. 18:21; ch. 18:10; Jer. 32:35; Ezek. 23:37
12:32 [a]ch. 4:2; Josh. 1:7; Prov. 30:6; Rev. 22:18
13:1 [b]Zech. 10:2 [c]Matt. 24:24; 2 Thess. 2:9
13:2 [d]ch. 18:22; Jer. 28:9; Matt. 7:22
13:3 [e]ch. 8:2; Matt. 24:24; 1 Cor. 11:19; 2 Thess. 2:11; Rev. 13:14
13:4 [f]2 Kings 23:3; 2 Chron. 34:31 [g]ch. 10:20
13:5 [h]ch. 18:20; Jer. 14:15; Zech. 13:3 [i]ch. 17:7; 1 Cor. 5:13
13:6 [j]ch. 17:2 [k]Gen. 16:5; ch. 28:54; Prov. 5:20; Mic. 7:5 [l]1 Sam. 18:1
13:8 [m]Prov. 1:10
13:9 [n]ch. 17:5 [o]ch. 17:7; Acts 7:58
13:11 [p]ch. 17:13
13:12 [q]Josh. 22:11; Judg. 20:1
13:13 [r]1 John 2:19; Jude 19 [s]2 Kings 17:21 [t]ver. 2
13:15 [u]Ex. 22:20; Lev. 27:28; Josh. 6:17
13:16 [v]Josh. 6:24 [w]Josh. 8:28; Isa. 17:1; Jer. 49:2
13:17 [x]ch. 7:26; Josh. 6:18 [y]Josh. 6:26 [z]Gen. 22:17
13:18 [a]ch. 12:25
14:1 [b]Rom. 8:16; Gal. 3:26 [c]Lev. 19:28; Jer. 16:6; 1 Thess. 4:13
14:2 [d]Lev. 20:26; ch. 7:6
14:3 [e]Ezek. 4:14; Acts 10:13
14:4 [f]Lev. 11:2
14:8 [g]Lev. 11:26
14:9 [h]Lev. 11:9
14:12 [i]Lev. 11:13

16 The little owl, and the great owl, and the swan,

17 And the pelican, and the gier eagle, and the cormorant,

18 And the stork, and the heron after her kind, and the lapwing, and the bat.

19 And [j]every creeping thing that flieth *is* unclean unto you: [k]they shall not be eaten.

20 *But of* all clean fowls ye may eat.

21 ¶ [l]Ye shall not eat *of* any thing that dieth of itself: thou shalt give it unto the stranger that *is* in thy gates, that he may eat it; or thou mayest sell it unto an alien: [m]for thou *art* an holy people unto the LORD thy God. [n]Thou shalt not seethe a kid in his mother's milk.

22 [o]Thou shalt truly tithe all the increase of thy seed, that the field bringeth forth year by year.

23 [p]And thou shalt eat before the LORD thy God, in the place which he shall choose to place his name there, the tithe of thy corn, of thy wine, and of thine oil, and the [q]firstlings of thy herds and of thy flocks; that thou mayest learn to fear the LORD thy God always.

24 And if the way be too long for thee, so that thou art not able to carry it; *or* [r]if the place be too far from thee, which the LORD thy God shall choose to set his name there, when the LORD thy God hath blessed thee:

25 Then shalt thou turn *it* into money, and bind up the money in thine hand, and shalt go unto the place which the LORD thy God shall choose:

26 And thou shalt bestow that money for whatsoever thy soul lusteth after, for oxen, or for sheep, or for wine, or for strong drink, or for whatsoever thy soul desireth: [s]and thou shalt eat there before the LORD thy God, and thou shalt rejoice, thou, and thine household,

27 And [t]the Levite that *is* within thy gates; thou shalt not forsake him: for [u]he hath no part nor inheritance with thee.

28 ¶ [v]At the end of three years thou shalt bring forth all the tithe of thine increase the same year, and shalt lay *it* up within thy gates:

29 [w]And the Levite, (because [x]he hath no part nor inheritance with thee,) and the stranger, and the fatherless, and the widow, which *are* within thy gates, shall come, and shall eat and be satisfied; that [y]the LORD thy God may bless thee in all the work of thine hand which thou doest.

15 At the end of [z]*every* seven years thou shalt make a release.

2 And this *is* the manner of the release: Every creditor that lendeth *ought* unto his neighbour shall release *it;* he shall not exact *it* of his neighbour, or of his brother; because it is called the LORD's release.

3 [a]Of a foreigner thou mayest exact *it again:* but *that* which is thine with thy brother thine hand shall release;

4 Save when there shall be no poor among you; [b]for the LORD shall greatly bless thee in the land which the LORD thy God giveth thee *for* an inheritance to possess it:

5 Only [c]if thou carefully hearken unto the voice of the LORD thy God, to observe to do all these commandments which I command thee this day.

6 For the LORD thy God blesseth thee, as he promised thee: and [d]thou shalt lend unto many nations, but thou shalt not borrow; and [e]thou shalt reign over many nations, but they shall not reign over thee.

7 ¶ If there be among you a poor man of one of thy brethren within any of thy gates in thy land which the LORD thy God giveth thee, [f]thou shalt not harden thine heart, nor shut thine hand from thy poor brother:

8 [g]But thou shalt open thine hand wide unto him, and shalt surely lend him sufficient for his need, *in that* which he wanteth.

9 Beware that there be not a thought in thy wicked heart, saying, The seventh year, the year of release, is at hand; and thine [h]eye be evil against thy poor brother, and thou givest him nought; and [i]he cry unto the LORD against thee, and [j]it be sin unto thee.

10 Thou shalt surely give him, and [k]thine heart shall not be grieved when thou givest unto him: because that [l]for this thing the LORD thy God shall bless thee in all thy works, and in all that thou puttest thine hand unto.

11 For [m]the poor shall never cease out of the land: therefore I command thee, saying, Thou shalt open thine hand wide unto thy brother, to thy poor, and to thy needy, in thy land.

12 ¶ *And* [n]if thy brother, an Hebrew man, or an Hebrew woman, be sold unto thee, and serve thee six years; then in the seventh year thou shalt let him go free from thee.

13 And when thou sendest him out free from thee, thou shalt not let him go away empty:

14 Thou shalt furnish him liberally out of thy flock, and out of thy floor, and out of thy winepress: *of that* wherewith the LORD thy God hath [o]blessed thee thou shalt give unto him.

15 And [p]thou shalt remember that thou wast a bondman in the land of Egypt, and the LORD thy God redeemed thee: therefore I command thee this thing to day.

16 And it shall be, [q]if he say unto thee, I will not go away from thee; because he loveth thee and thine house, because he is well with thee;

17 Then thou shalt take an aul, and thrust *it* through his ear unto the door, and he shall be thy servant for ever. And also unto thy maidservant thou shalt do likewise.

18 It shall not seem hard unto thee, when thou sendest him away free from thee; for he hath been worth [r]a double hired servant *to thee,* in serving thee six years: and the

14:19 [j]Lev. 11:20 [k]Lev. 11:21
14:21 [l]Lev. 17:15; Ezek. 4:14 [m]ver. 2 [n]Ex. 23:19
14:22 [o]Lev. 27:30; ch. 12:6; Neh. 10:37
14:23 [p]ch. 12:5 [q]ch. 15:19
14:24 [r]ch. 12:21
14:26 [s]ch. 12:7
14:27 [t]ch. 12:12 [u]Num. 18:20; ch. 18:1
14:28 [v]ch. 26:12; Am. 4:4
14:29 [w]ch. 26:12 [x]ver. 27; ch. 12:12 [y]ch. 15:10; Prov. 3:9; Mal. 3:10
15:1 [z]Ex. 21:2; Lev. 25:2; ch. 31:10; Jer. 34:14
15:3 [a]ch. 23:20
15:4 [b]ch. 28:8
15:5 [c]ch. 28
15:6 [d]ch. 28:12 [e]ch. 28:13; Prov. 22:7
15:7 [f]1 John 3:17
15:8 [g]Lev. 25:35; Matt. 5:42; Luke 6:34
15:9 [h]ch. 28:54; Prov. 23:6; Matt. 20:15 [i]ch. 24:15 [j]Matt. 25:41
15:10 [k]2 Cor. 9:5 [l]ch. 14:29; Ps. 41:1; Prov. 22:9
15:11 [m]Matt. 26:11; Mark 14:7; John 12:8
15:12 [n]Ex. 21:2; Lev. 25:39; Jer. 34:14
15:14 [o]Prov. 10:22
15:15 [p]ch. 5:15
15:16 [q]Ex. 21:5
15:18 [r]Isa. 16:14

LORD thy God shall bless thee in all that thou doest.

19 ¶ [s]All the firstling males that come of thy herd and of thy flock thou shalt sanctify unto the LORD thy God: thou shalt do no work with the firstling of thy bullock, nor shear the firstling of thy sheep.

20 [t]Thou shalt eat *it* before the LORD thy God year by year in the place which the LORD shall choose, thou and thy household.

21 [u]And if there be *any* blemish therein, *as if it be* lame, or blind, *or have* any ill blemish, thou shalt not sacrifice it unto the LORD thy God.

22 Thou shalt eat it within thy gates: [v]the unclean and the clean *person shall eat it* alike, as the roebuck, and as the hart.

23 [w]Only thou shalt not eat the blood thereof; thou shalt pour it upon the ground as water.

16 Observe the [x]month of Abib, and keep the passover unto the LORD thy God: for [y]in the month of Abib the LORD thy God brought thee forth out of Egypt [z]by night.

2 Thou shalt therefore sacrifice the passover unto the LORD thy God, of the flock and [a]the herd, in the [b]place which the LORD shall choose to place his name there.

3 [c]Thou shalt eat no leavened bread with it; seven days shalt thou eat unleavened bread therewith, *even* the bread of affliction; for thou camest forth out of the land of Egypt in haste: that thou mayest remember the day when thou camest forth out of the land of Egypt all the days of thy life.

4 [d]And there shall be no leavened bread seen with thee in all thy coast seven days; [e]neither shall there *any thing* of the flesh, which thou sacrificedst the first day at even, remain all night until the morning.

5 Thou mayest not sacrifice the passover within any of thy gates, which the LORD thy God giveth thee:

6 But at the place which the LORD thy God shall choose to place his name in, there thou shalt sacrifice the passover [f]at even, at the going down of the sun, at the season that thou camest forth out of Egypt.

7 And thou shalt [g]roast and eat *it* [h]in the place which the LORD thy God shall choose: and thou shalt turn in the morning, and go unto thy tents.

8 Six days thou shalt eat unleavened bread: and [i]on the seventh day *shall be* a solemn assembly to the LORD thy God: thou shalt do no work *therein*.

9 ¶ [j]Seven weeks shalt thou number unto thee: begin to number the seven weeks from *such time as* thou beginnest *to put* the sickle to the corn.

10 And thou shalt keep the feast of weeks unto the LORD thy God with a tribute of a freewill offering of thine hand, which thou shalt give *unto the LORD thy God,* [k]according as the LORD thy God hath blessed thee:

11 And [l]thou shalt rejoice before the LORD thy God, thou, and thy son, and thy daughter, and thy manservant, and thy maidservant, and the Levite that *is* within thy gates, and the stranger, and the fatherless, and the widow, that *are* among you, in the place which the LORD thy God hath chosen to place his name there.

12 [m]And thou shalt remember that thou wast a bondman in Egypt: and thou shalt observe and do these statutes.

13 ¶ [n]Thou shalt observe the feast of tabernacles seven days, after that thou hast gathered in thy corn and thy wine:

14 And [o]thou shalt rejoice in thy feast, thou, and thy son, and thy daughter, and thy manservant, and thy maidservant, and the Levite, the stranger, and the fatherless, and the widow, that *are* within thy gates.

15 [p]Seven days shalt thou keep a solemn feast unto the LORD thy God in the place which the LORD shall choose: because the LORD thy God shall bless thee in all thine increase, and in all the works of thine hands, therefore thou shalt surely rejoice.

16 ¶ [q]Three times in a year shall all thy males appear before the LORD thy God in the place which he shall choose; in the feast of unleavened bread, and in the feast of weeks, and in the feast of tabernacles: and [r]they shall not appear before the LORD empty:

17 Every man *shall give* as he is able, [s]according to the blessing of the LORD thy God which he hath given thee.

18 ¶ [t]Judges and officers shalt thou make thee in all thy gates, which the LORD thy God giveth thee, throughout thy tribes: and they shall judge the people with just judgment.

19 [u]Thou shalt not wrest judgment; [v]thou shalt not respect persons, [w]neither take a gift: for a gift doth blind the eyes of the wise, and pervert the words of the righteous.

20 That which is altogether just shalt thou follow, that thou mayest [x]live, and inherit the land which the LORD thy God giveth thee.

21 ¶ [y]Thou shalt not plant thee a grove of any trees near unto the altar of the LORD thy God, which thou shalt make thee.

22 [z]Neither shalt thou set thee up *any* image; which the LORD thy God hateth.

17 Thou [a]shalt not sacrifice unto the LORD thy God *any* bullock, or sheep, wherein is blemish, *or* any evilfavouredness: for that *is* an abomination unto the LORD thy God.

2 ¶ [b]If there be found among you, within any of thy gates which the LORD thy God giveth thee, man or woman, that hath wrought wickedness in the sight of the LORD thy God, [c]in transgressing his covenant,

3 And hath gone and served other gods, and worshipped them, either [d]the sun, or moon, or any of the host of heaven, [e]which I have not commanded;

4 [f]And it be told thee, and thou hast

15:19 [s]Ex. 13:2; Lev. 27:26; Num. 3:13
15:20 [t]ch. 12:5
15:21 [u]Lev. 22:20; ch. 17:1
15:22 [v]ch. 12:15
15:23 [w]ch. 12:16
16:1 [x]Ex. 12:2 [y]Ex. 13:4 [z]Ex. 12:29
16:2 [a]Num. 28:19 [b]ch. 12:5
16:3 [c]Ex. 12:15
16:4 [d]Ex. 13:7 [e]Ex. 12:10
16:6 [f]Ex. 12:6
16:7 [g]Ex. 12:8; 2 Chron. 35:13 [h]2 Kings 23:23; John 2:13
16:8 [i]Ex. 12:16; Lev. 23:8
16:9 [j]Ex. 23:16; Lev. 23:15; Num. 28:26; Acts 2:1
16:10 [k]ver. 17; 1 Cor. 16:2
16:11 [l]ch. 12:7; ver. 14
16:12 [m]ch. 15:15
16:13 [n]Ex. 23:16; Lev. 23:34; Num. 29:12
16:14 [o]Neh. 8:9
16:15 [p]Lev. 23:39
16:16 [q]Ex. 23:14 [r]Ex. 23:15
16:17 [s]ver. 10
16:18 [t]ch. 1:16; 1 Chron. 23:4; 2 Chron. 19:5
16:19 [u]Ex. 23:2; Lev. 19:15 [v]ch. 1:17; Prov. 24:23 [w]Ex. 23:8; Prov. 17:23; Eccl. 7:7
16:20 [x]Ezek. 18:5
16:21 [y]Ex. 34:13; 1 Kings 14:15; 2 Kings 17:16; 2 Chron. 33:3
16:22 [z]Lev. 26:1
17:1 [a]ch. 15:21; Mal. 1:8
17:2 [b]ch. 13:6 [c]Josh. 7:11; Judg. 2:20; 2 Kings 18:12; Hos. 8:1
17:3 [d]ch. 4:19; Job 31:26 [e]Jer. 7:22
17:4 [f]ch. 13:12

heard *of it,* and enquired diligently, and, behold, *it be* true, *and* the thing certain, *that*
such abomination is wrought in Israel:
5 Then shalt thou bring forth that man or
that woman, which have committed that
wicked thing, unto thy gates, *even* that man
or that woman, and [g]shalt stone them with
stones, till they die.
6 [h]At the mouth of two witnesses, or
three witnesses, shall he that is worthy of
death be put to death; *but* at the mouth of
one witness he shall not be put to death.
7 [i]The hands of the witnesses shall be
first upon him to put him to death, and afterward the hands of all the people. So [j]thou
shalt put the evil away from among you.
8 ¶ [k]If there arise a matter too hard for
thee in judgment, [l]between blood and
blood, between plea and plea, and between
stroke and stroke, *being* matters of controversy within thy gates: then shalt thou arise,
[m]and get thee up into the place which the
LORD thy God shall choose;
9 And [n]thou shalt come unto the priests
the Levites, and [o]unto the judge that shall
be in those days, and enquire; [p]and they
shall shew thee the sentence of judgment:
10 And thou shalt do according to the
sentence, which they of that place which the
LORD shall choose shall shew thee; and thou
shalt observe to do according to all that they
inform thee;
11 According to the sentence of the law
which they shall teach thee, and according
to the judgment which they shall tell thee,
thou shalt do: thou shalt not decline from
the sentence which they shall shew thee, *to*
the right hand, nor *to* the left.
12 And [q]the man that will do presumptuously, and will not hearken unto the priest
[r]that standeth to minister there before the
LORD thy God, or unto the judge, even that
man shall die: and [s]thou shalt put away the
evil from Israel.
13 [t]And all the people shall hear, and
fear, and do no more presumptuously.
14 ¶ When thou art come unto the land
which the LORD thy God giveth thee, and
shalt possess it, and shalt dwell therein, and
shalt say, [u]I will set a king over me, like as
all the nations that *are* about me;
15 Thou shalt in any wise set *him* king
over thee, [v]whom the LORD thy God shall
choose: *one* [w]from among thy brethren
shalt thou set king over thee: thou mayest
not set a stranger over thee, which *is* not thy
brother.
16 But he shall not multiply [x]horses to
himself, nor cause the people [y]to return to
Egypt, to the end that he should multiply
horses: forasmuch as [z]the LORD hath said
unto you, [a]Ye shall henceforth return no
more that way.
17 Neither shall he multiply wives to himself, that [b]his heart turn not away: neither
shall he greatly multiply to himself silver
and gold.
18 [c]And it shall be, when he sitteth upon
the throne of his kingdom, that he shall
write him a copy of this law in a book out of
[d]*that which is* before the priests the Levites:
19 And [e]it shall be with him, and he shall
read therein all the days of his life: that he
may learn to fear the LORD his God, to keep
all the words of this law and these statutes,
to do them:
20 That his heart be not lifted up above
his brethren, and that he [f]turn not aside
from the commandment, *to* the right hand,
or *to* the left: to the end that he may prolong
his days in his kingdom, he, and his children, in the midst of Israel.
18 The priests the Levites, *and* all the
tribe of Levi, [g]shall have no part nor
inheritance with Israel: they [h]shall eat the
offerings of the LORD made by fire, and his
inheritance.
2 Therefore shall they have no inheritance among their brethren: the LORD *is*
their inheritance, as he hath said unto them.
3 ¶ And this shall be the priest's due from
the people, from them that offer a sacrifice,
whether *it be* ox or sheep; and [i]they shall
give unto the priest the shoulder, and the
two cheeks, and the maw.
4 [j]The firstfruit *also* of thy corn, of thy
wine, and of thine oil, and the first of the
fleece of thy sheep, shalt thou give him.
5 For [k]the LORD thy God hath chosen him
out of all thy tribes, [l]to stand to minister in
the name of the LORD, him and his sons for
ever.
6 ¶ And if a Levite come from any of thy
gates out of all Israel, where he [m]sojourned,
and come with all the desire of his mind
[n]unto the place which the LORD shall
choose;
7 Then he shall minister in the name of
the LORD his God, [o]as all his brethren the
Levites *do,* which stand there before the
LORD.
8 They shall have like [p]portions to eat,
beside that which cometh of the sale of his
patrimony.
9 ¶ When thou art come into the land
which the LORD thy God giveth thee, [q]thou
shalt not learn to do after the abominations
of those nations.
10 There shall not be found among you
any one that maketh his son or his daughter
[r]to pass through the fire, [s]*or* that useth
divination, *or* an observer of times, or an
enchanter, or a witch,
11 [t]Or a charmer, or a consulter with familiar spirits, or a wizard, or a [u]necroman-
cer.
12 For all that do these things *are* an
abomination unto the LORD: and [v]because
of these abominations the LORD thy God
doth drive them out from before thee.
13 Thou shalt be perfect with the LORD
thy God.
14 For these nations, which thou shalt
possess, hearkened unto observers of times,

17:5 [g]Lev. 24:14; ch. 13:10; Josh. 7:25
17:6 [h]Num. 35:30; ch. 19:15; Matt. 18:16; John 8:17; 2 Cor. 13:1; 1 Tim. 5:19; Heb. 10:28
17:7 [i]ch. 13:9; Acts 7:58 [j]ver. 12; ch. 13:5
17:8 [k]2 Chron. 19:10; Hag. 2:11; Mal. 2:7 [l]Ex. 21:13; Num. 35:11; ch. 19:4 [m]ch. 12:5; Ps. 122:5
17:9 [n]Jer. 18:18 [o]ch. 19:17 [p]Ezek. 44:24
17:12 [q]Num. 15:30; Ezra 10:8; Hos. 4:4 [r]ch. 18:5 [s]ch. 13:5
17:13 [t]ch. 13:11
17:14 [u]1 Sam. 8:5
17:15 [v]1 Sam. 9:15; 1 Chron. 22:10 [w]Jer. 30:21
17:16 [x]1 Kings 4:26; Ps. 20:7 [y]Isa. 31:1; Ezek. 17:15 [z]Ex. 13:17; Num. 14:3 [a]ch. 28:68; Jer. 42:15; Hos. 11:5
17:17 [b]1 Kings 11:3
17:18 [c]2 Kings 11:12 [d]ch. 31:9; 2 Kings 22:8
17:19 [e]Josh. 1:8; Ps. 119:97
17:20 [f]ch. 5:32; 1 Kings 15:5
18:1 [g]Num. 18:20; ch. 10:9 [h]Num. 18:8; 1 Cor. 9:13
18:3 [i]Lev. 7:30-34
18:4 [j]Ex. 22:29; Num. 18:12
18:5 [k]Ex. 28:1; Num. 3:10 [l]ch. 10:8
18:6 [m]Num. 35:2 [n]ch. 12:5
18:7 [o]2 Chron. 31:2
18:8 [p]2 Chron. 31:4; Neh. 12:44
18:9 [q]Lev. 18:26; ch. 12:29
18:10 [r]Lev. 18:21; ch. 12:31 [s]Lev. 19:26; Isa. 8:19
18:11 [t]Lev. 20:27 [u]1 Sam. 28:7
18:12 [v]Lev. 18:24; ch. 9:4

and unto diviners: but as for thee, the LORD thy God hath not suffered thee so *to do.*

15 ¶ [w]The LORD thy God will raise up unto thee a Prophet from the midst of thee, of thy brethren, like unto me; unto him ye shall hearken;

16 According to all that thou desiredst of the LORD thy God in Horeb [x]in the day of the assembly, saying, [y]Let me not hear again the voice of the LORD my God, neither let me see this great fire any more, that I die not.

17 And the LORD said unto me, [z]They have well *spoken that* which they have spoken.

18 [a]I will raise them up a Prophet from among their brethren, like unto thee, and [b]will put my words in his mouth; [c]and he shall speak unto them all that I shall command him.

19 [d]And it shall come to pass, *that* whosoever will not hearken unto my words which he shall speak in my name, I will require *it* of him.

20 But [e]the prophet, which shall presume to speak a word in my name, which I have not commanded him to speak, or [f]that shall speak in the name of other gods, even that prophet shall die.

21 And if thou say in thine heart, How shall we know the word which the LORD hath not spoken?

22 [g]When a prophet speaketh in the name of the LORD, [h]if the thing follow not, nor come to pass, that *is* the thing which the LORD hath not spoken, *but* the prophet hath spoken it [i]presumptuously: thou shalt not be afraid of him.

19 When the LORD thy God [j]hath cut off the nations, whose land the LORD thy God giveth thee, and thou succeedest them, and dwellest in their cities, and in their houses;

2 [k]Thou shalt separate three cities for thee in the midst of thy land, which the LORD thy God giveth thee to possess it.

3 Thou shalt prepare thee a way, and divide the coasts of thy land, which the LORD thy God giveth thee to inherit, into three parts, that every slayer may flee thither.

4 ¶ And [l]this *is* the case of the slayer, which shall flee thither, that he may live: Whoso killeth his neighbour ignorantly, whom he hated not in time past;

5 As when a man goeth into the wood with his neighbour to hew wood, and his hand fetcheth a stroke with the axe to cut down the tree, and the head slippeth from the helve, and lighteth upon his neighbour, that he die; he shall flee unto one of those cities, and live:

6 [m]Lest the avenger of the blood pursue the slayer, while his heart is hot, and overtake him, because the way is long, and slay him; whereas he *was* not worthy of death, inasmuch as he hated him not in time past.

7 Wherefore I command thee, saying, Thou shalt separate three cities for thee.

8 And if the LORD thy God [n]enlarge thy coast, as he hath sworn unto thy fathers, and give thee all the land which he promised to give unto thy fathers;

9 If thou shalt keep all these commandments to do them, which I command thee this day, to love the LORD thy God, and to walk ever in his ways; [o]then shalt thou add three cities more for thee, beside these three:

10 That innocent blood be not shed in thy land, which the LORD thy God giveth thee *for* an inheritance, and *so* blood be upon thee.

11 ¶ But [p]if any man hate his neighbour, and lie in wait for him, and rise up against him, and smite him mortally that he die, and fleeth into one of these cities:

12 Then the elders of his city shall send and fetch him thence, and deliver him into the hand of the avenger of blood, that he may die.

13 [q]Thine eye shall not pity him, [r]but thou shalt put away *the guilt of* innocent blood from Israel, that it may go well with thee.

14 ¶ [s]Thou shalt not remove thy neighbour's landmark, which they of old time have set in thine inheritance, which thou shalt inherit in the land that the LORD thy God giveth thee to possess it.

15 ¶ [t]One witness shall not rise up against a man for any iniquity, or for any sin, in any sin that he sinneth: at the mouth of two witnesses, or at the mouth of three witnesses, shall the matter be established.

16 ¶ If a false witness [u]rise up against any man to testify against him *that which is* wrong;

17 Then both the men, between whom the controversy *is,* shall stand before the LORD, [v]before the priests and the judges, which shall be in those days;

18 And the judges shall make diligent inquisition: and, behold, *if* the witness *be* a false witness, *and* hath testified falsely against his brother;

19 [w]Then shall ye do unto him, as he had thought to have done unto his brother: so [x]shalt thou put the evil away from among you.

20 [y]And those which remain shall hear, and fear, and shall henceforth commit no more any such evil among you.

21 [z]And thine eye shall not pity; *but* [a]life *shall go* for life, eye for eye, tooth for tooth, hand for hand, foot for foot.

20 When thou goest out to battle against thine enemies, and seest [b]horses, and chariots, *and* a people more than thou, be not afraid of them: for the LORD thy God *is* [c]with thee, which brought thee up out of the land of Egypt.

2 And it shall be, when ye are come nigh unto the battle, that the priest shall approach and speak unto the people,

3 And shall say unto them, Hear, O Israel, ye approach this day unto battle against

18:15 [w]ver. 18; John 1:45; Acts 3:22
18:16 [x]ch. 9:10 [y]Ex. 20:19; Heb. 12:19
18:17 [z]ch. 5:28
18:18 [a]ver. 15; John 1:45; Acts 3:22 [b]Isa. 51:16; John 17:8 [c]John 4:25
18:19 [d]Acts 3:23
18:20 [e]ch. 13:5; Jer. 14:14; Zech. 13:3 [f]ch. 13:1; Jer. 2:8
18:22 [g]Jer. 28:9 [h]ch. 13:2 [i]ver. 20
19:1 [j]ch. 12:29
19:2 [k]Ex. 21:13; Num. 35:10; Josh. 20:2
19:4 [l]Num. 35:15; ch. 4:42
19:6 [m]Num. 35:12
19:8 [n]Gen. 15:18; ch. 12:20
19:9 [o]Josh. 20:7
19:11 [p]Ex. 21:12; Num. 35:16; ch. 27:24; Prov. 28:17
19:13 [q]ch. 13:8 [r]Num. 35:33; ch. 21:9; 1 Kings 2:31
19:14 [s]ch. 27:17; Job 24:2; Prov. 22:28; Hos. 5:10
19:15 [t]Num. 35:30; ch. 17:6; Matt. 18:16; John 8:17; 2 Cor. 13:1; 1 Tim. 5:19; Heb. 10:28
19:16 [u]Ps. 27:12
19:17 [v]ch. 17:9
19:19 [w]Prov. 19:5; Dan. 6:24 [x]ch. 13:5
19:20 [y]ch. 17:13
19:21 [z]ver. 13 [a]Ex. 21:23; Lev. 24:20; Matt. 5:38
20:1 [b]Ps. 20:7; Isa. 31:1 [c]Num. 23:21; ch. 31:6; 2 Chron. 13:12

your enemies: let not your hearts faint, fear not, and do not tremble, neither be ye terrified because of them;

4 For the LORD your God *is* he that goeth with you, [d]to fight for you against your enemies, to save you.

5 ¶ And the officers shall speak unto the people, saying, What man *is there* that hath built a new house, and hath not [e]dedicated it? let him go and return to his house, lest he die in the battle, and another man dedicate it.

6 And what man *is he* that hath planted a vineyard, and hath not *yet* eaten of it? let him *also* go and return unto his house, lest he die in the battle, and another man eat of it.

7 [f]And what man *is there* that hath betrothed a wife, and hath not taken her? let him go and return unto his house, lest he die in the battle, and another man take her.

8 And the officers shall speak further unto the people, and they shall say, [g]What man *is there that is* fearful and fainthearted? let him go and return unto his house, lest his brethren's heart faint as well as his heart.

9 And it shall be, when the officers have made an end of speaking unto the people, that they shall make captains of the armies to lead the people.

10 ¶ When thou comest nigh unto a city to fight against it, [h]then proclaim peace unto it.

11 And it shall be, if it make thee answer of peace, and open unto thee, then it shall be, *that* all the people *that is* found therein shall be tributaries unto thee, and they shall serve thee.

12 And if it will make no peace with thee, but will make war against thee, then thou shalt besiege it:

13 And when the LORD thy God hath delivered it into thine hands, [i]thou shalt smite every male thereof with the edge of the sword:

14 But the women, and the little ones, and [j]the cattle, and all that is in the city, *even* all the spoil thereof, shalt thou take unto thyself; and [k]thou shalt eat the spoil of thine enemies, which the LORD thy God hath given thee.

15 Thus shalt thou do unto all the cities *which are* very far off from thee, which *are* not of the cities of these nations.

16 But [l]of the cities of these people, which the LORD thy God doth give thee *for* an inheritance, thou shalt save alive nothing that breatheth:

17 But thou shalt utterly destroy them; *namely,* the Hittites, and the Amorites, the Canaanites, and the Perizzites, the Hivites, and the Jebusites; as the LORD thy God hath commanded thee:

18 That [m]they teach you not to do after all their abominations, which they have done unto their gods; so should ye [n]sin against the LORD your God.

19 ¶ When thou shalt besiege a city a long time, in making war against it to take it, thou shalt not destroy the trees thereof by forcing an axe against them: for thou mayest eat of them, and thou shalt not cut them down (for the tree of the field *is* man's *life*) to employ *them* in the siege:

20 Only the trees which thou knowest that they *be* not trees for meat, thou shalt destroy and cut them down; and thou shalt build bulwarks against the city that maketh war with thee, until it be subdued.

21

If *one* be found slain in the land which the LORD thy God giveth thee to possess it, lying in the field, *and* it be not known who hath slain him:

2 Then thy elders and thy judges shall come forth, and they shall measure unto the cities which *are* round about him that is slain:

3 And it shall be, *that* the city *which is* next unto the slain man, even the elders of that city shall take an heifer, which hath not been wrought with, *and* which hath not drawn in the yoke;

4 And the elders of that city shall bring down the heifer unto a rough valley, which is neither eared nor sown, and shall strike off the heifer's neck there in the valley:

5 And the priests the sons of Levi shall come near; for [o]them the LORD thy God hath chosen to minister unto him, and to bless in the name of the LORD; and [p]by their word shall every controversy and every stroke be *tried:*

6 And all the elders of that city, *that are* next unto the slain *man,* [q]shall wash their hands over the heifer that is beheaded in the valley:

7 And they shall answer and say, Our hands have not shed this blood, neither have our eyes seen *it.*

8 Be merciful, O LORD, unto thy people Israel, whom thou hast redeemed, [r]and lay not innocent blood unto thy people of Israel's charge. And the blood shall be forgiven them.

9 So [s]shalt thou put away the *guilt of* innocent blood from among you, when thou shalt do *that which is* right in the sight of the LORD.

10 ¶ When thou goest forth to war against thine enemies, and the LORD thy God hath delivered them into thine hands, and thou hast taken them captive,

11 And seest among the captives a beautiful woman, and hast a desire unto her, that thou wouldest have her to thy wife;

12 Then thou shalt bring her home to thine house; and she shall shave her head, and pare her nails;

13 And she shall put the raiment of her captivity from off her, and shall remain in thine house, and [t]bewail her father and her mother a full month: and after that thou shalt go in unto her, and be her husband, and she shall be thy wife.

14 And it shall be, if thou have no delight

20:4 [d]ch. 1:30; Josh. 23:10
20:5 [e]Neh. 12:27; Ps. 30, title
20:7 [f]ch. 24:5
20:8 [g]Judg. 7:3
20:10 [h]2 Sam. 20:18
20:13 [i]Num. 31:7
20:14 [j]Josh. 8:2 [k]Josh. 22:8
20:16 [l]Num. 21:2; ch. 7:1; Josh. 11:14
20:18 [m]ch. 7:4 [n]Ex. 23:33
21:5 [o]ch. 10:8; 1 Chron. 23:13 [p]ch. 17:8
21:6 [q]Ps. 19:12; Matt. 27:24
21:8 [r]Jonah 1:14
21:9 [s]ch. 19:13
21:13 [t]Ps. 45:10

in her, then thou shalt let her go whither she
will; but thou shalt not sell her at all for
money, thou shalt not make merchandise of
her, because thou hast [u]humbled her.
15 ¶ If a man have two wives, one beloved, [v]and another hated, and they have
born him children, *both* the beloved and the
hated; and *if* the firstborn son be hers that
was hated:
16 Then it shall be, [w]when he maketh his
sons to inherit *that* which he hath, *that* he
may not make the son of the beloved firstborn before the son of the hated, *which is
indeed* the firstborn:
17 But he shall acknowledge the son of
the hated *for* the firstborn, [x]by giving him
a double portion of all that he hath: for he *is*
[y]the beginning of his strength; [z]the right of
the firstborn *is* his.
18 ¶ If a man have a stubborn and rebellious son, which will not obey the voice of
his father, or the voice of his mother, and
that, when they have chastened him, will
not hearken unto them:
19 Then shall his father and his mother
lay hold on him, and bring him out unto the
elders of his city, and unto the gate of his
place;
20 And they shall say unto the elders of
his city, This our son *is* stubborn and rebellious, he will not obey our voice; *he is* a
glutton, and a drunkard.
21 And all the men of his city shall stone
him with stones, that he die: [a]so shalt thou
put evil away from among you; [b]and all Israel shall hear, and fear.
22 ¶ And if a man have committed a sin
[c]worthy of death, and he be to be put to
death, and thou hang him on a tree:
23 [d]His body shall not remain all night
upon the tree, but thou shalt in any wise
bury him that day; (for [e]he that is hanged *is*
accursed of God;) that [f]thy land be not defiled, which the LORD thy God giveth thee
for an inheritance.

22 Thou [g]shalt not see thy brother's ox
or his sheep go astray, and hide thyself from them: thou shalt in any case bring
them again unto thy brother.
2 And if thy brother *be* not nigh unto thee,
or if thou know him not, then thou shalt
bring it unto thine own house, and it shall
be with thee until thy brother seek after it,
and thou shalt restore it to him again.
3 In like manner shalt thou do with his
ass; and so shalt thou do with his raiment;
and with all lost thing of thy brother's,
which he hath lost, and thou hast found,
shalt thou do likewise: thou mayest not hide
thyself.
4 ¶ [h]Thou shalt not see thy brother's ass
or his ox fall down by the way, and hide
thyself from them: thou shalt surely help
him to lift *them* up again.
5 ¶ The woman shall not wear that which
pertaineth unto a man, neither shall a man
put on a woman's garment: for all that do so
are abomination unto the LORD thy God.
6 ¶ If a bird's nest chance to be before
thee in the way in any tree, or on the
ground, *whether they be* young ones, or
eggs, and the dam sitting upon the young,
or upon the eggs, [i]thou shalt not take the
dam with the young:
7 *But* thou shalt in any wise let the dam
go, and take the young to thee; [j]that it may
be well with thee, and *that* thou mayest prolong *thy* days.
8 ¶ When thou buildest a new house, then
thou shalt make a battlement for thy roof,
that thou bring not blood upon thine house,
if any man fall from thence.
9 ¶ [k]Thou shalt not sow thy vineyard
with divers seeds: lest the fruit of thy seed
which thou hast sown, and the fruit of thy
vineyard, be defiled.
10 ¶ [l]Thou shalt not plow with an ox and
an ass together.
11 ¶ [m]Thou shalt not wear a garment of
divers sorts, *as* of woollen and linen together.
12 ¶ Thou shalt make thee [n]fringes upon
the four quarters of thy vesture, wherewith
thou coverest *thyself*.
13 ¶ If any man take a wife, and [o]go in
unto her, and hate her,
14 And give occasions of speech against
her, and bring up an evil name upon her,
and say, I took this woman, and when I
came to her, I found her not a maid:
15 Then shall the father of the damsel,
and her mother, take and bring forth *the
tokens of* the damsel's virginity unto the elders of the city in the gate:
16 And the damsel's father shall say unto
the elders, I gave my daughter unto this
man to wife, and he hateth her;
17 And, lo, he hath given occasions of
speech *against her*, saying, I found not thy
daughter a maid; and yet these *are the tokens of* my daughter's virginity. And they
shall spread the cloth before the elders of
the city.
18 And the elders of that city shall take
that man and chastise him;
19 And they shall amerce him in an hundred *shekels* of silver, and give *them* unto
the father of the damsel, because he hath
brought up an evil name upon a virgin of
Israel: and she shall be his wife; he may not
put her away all his days.
20 But if this thing be true, *and the tokens
of* virginity be not found for the damsel:
21 Then they shall bring out the damsel to
the door of her father's house, and the men
of her city shall stone her with stones that
she die: because she hath [p]wrought folly
in Israel, to play the whore in her father's
house: [q]so shalt thou put evil away from
among you.
22 ¶ [r]If a man be found lying with a
woman married to an husband, then they
shall both of them die, *both* the man that lay
with the woman, and the woman: so shalt
thou put away evil from Israel.
23 ¶ If a damsel *that is* a virgin be [s]be-

21:14 [u]Gen. 34:2; ch. 22:29; Judg. 19:24
21:15 [v]Gen. 29:33
21:16 [w]1 Chron. 5:2; 2 Chron. 11:19
21:17 [x]1 Chron. 5:1 [y]Gen. 49:3 [z]Gen. 25:31
21:21 [a]ch. 13:5 [b]ch. 13:11
21:22 [c]ch. 19:6; Acts 23:29
21:23 [d]Josh. 8:29; John 19:31 [e]Gal. 3:13 [f]Lev. 18:25; Num. 35:34
22:1 [g]Ex. 23:4
22:4 [h]Ex. 23:5
22:6 [i]Lev. 22:28
22:7 [j]ch. 4:40
22:9 [k]Lev. 19:19
22:10 [l]2 Cor. 6:14
22:11 [m]Lev. 19:19
22:12 [n]Num. 15:38; Matt. 23:5
22:13 [o]Gen. 29:21; Judg. 15:1
22:21 [p]Gen. 34:7; Judg. 20:6; 2 Sam. 13:12 [q]ch. 13:5
22:22 [r]Lev. 20:10; John 8:5
22:23 [s]Matt. 1:18

trothed unto an husband, and a man find
her in the city, and lie with her;
24 Then ye shall bring them both out unto
the gate of that city, and ye shall stone them
with stones that they die; the damsel, because she cried not, *being* in the city; and
the man, because he hath [t]humbled his
neighbour's wife: [u]so thou shalt put away
evil from among you.
25 ¶ But if a man find a betrothed damsel
in the field, and the man force her, and lie
with her: then the man only that lay with
her shall die:
26 But unto the damsel thou shalt do
nothing; *there is* in the damsel no sin *worthy* of death: for as when a man riseth
against his neighbour, and slayeth him,
even so *is* this matter:
27 For he found her in the field, *and* the
betrothed damsel cried, and *there was* none
to save her.
28 ¶ [v]If a man find a damsel *that is* a
virgin, which is not betrothed, and lay hold
on her, and lie with her, and they be found;
29 Then the man that lay with her shall
give unto the damsel's father fifty *shekels* of
silver, and she shall be his wife; [w]because
he hath humbled her, he may not put her
away all his days.
30 ¶ [x]A man shall not take his father's
wife, nor [y]discover his father's skirt.
23 He that is wounded in the stones, or
hath his privy member cut off, shall
not enter into the congregation of the LORD.
2 A bastard shall not enter into the congregation of the LORD; even to his tenth
generation shall he not enter into the
congregation of the LORD.
3 [z]An Ammonite or Moabite shall not enter into the congregation of the LORD; even
to their tenth generation shall they not enter
into the congregation of the LORD for ever:
4 [a]Because they met you not with bread
and with water in the way, when ye came
forth out of Egypt; and [b]because they hired
against thee Balaam the son of Beor of Pe-
thor of Mesopotamia, to curse thee.
5 Nevertheless the LORD thy God would
not hearken unto Balaam; but the LORD thy
God turned the curse into a blessing unto
thee, because the LORD thy God loved thee.
6 [c]Thou shalt not seek their peace nor
their prosperity all thy days for ever.
7 ¶ Thou shalt not abhor an Edomite; [d]for
he *is* thy brother: thou shalt not abhor an
Egyptian; because [e]thou wast a stranger in
his land.
8 The children that are begotten of them
shall enter into the congregation of the
LORD in their third generation.
9 ¶ When the host goeth forth against
thine enemies, then keep thee from every
wicked thing.
10 ¶ [f]If there be among you any man,
that is not clean by reason of uncleanness
that chanceth him by night, then shall he go
abroad out of the camp, he shall not come
within the camp:

22:24 [t]ch. 21:14 [u]ver. 21
22:28 [v]Ex. 22:16
22:29 [w]ver. 24
22:30 [x]Lev. 18:8; ch. 27:20; 1 Cor. 5:1 [y]Ruth 3:9; Ezek. 16:8
23:3 [z]Neh. 13:1
23:4 [a]ch. 2:29 [b]Num. 22:5
23:6 [c]Ezra 9:12
23:7 [d]Gen. 25:24; Obad. 10:12 [e]Ex. 22:21; Lev. 19:34; ch. 10:19
23:10 [f]Lev. 15:16
23:11 [g]Lev. 15:5
23:14 [h]Lev. 26:12
23:15 [i]1 Sam. 30:15
23:16 [j]Ex. 22:21
23:17 [k]Lev. 19:29; Prov. 2:16 [l]Gen. 19:5; 2 Kings 23:7
23:19 [m]Ex. 22:25; Lev. 25:36; Neh. 5:2; Ps. 15:5; Luke 6:34
23:20 [n]Lev. 19:34 [o]ch. 15:10
23:21 [p]Num. 30:2; Eccl. 5:4
23:23 [q]Num. 30:2; Ps. 66:13
23:25 [r]Matt. 12:1; Mark 2:23; Luke 6:1
24:1 [s]Matt. 5:31; Mark 10:4

11 But it shall be, when evening cometh
on, [g]he shall wash *himself* with water: and
when the sun is down, he shall come into
the camp *again*.
12 ¶ Thou shalt have a place also without
the camp, whither thou shalt go forth
abroad:
13 And thou shalt have a paddle upon thy
weapon; and it shall be, when thou wilt ease
thyself abroad, thou shalt dig therewith,
and shalt turn back and cover that which
cometh from thee:
14 For the LORD thy God [h]walketh in the
midst of thy camp, to deliver thee, and to
give up thine enemies before thee; therefore
shall thy camp be holy: that he see no unclean thing in thee, and turn away from
thee.
15 ¶ [i]Thou shalt not deliver unto his
master the servant which is escaped from
his master unto thee:
16 He shall dwell with thee, *even* among
you, in that place which he shall choose in
one of thy gates, where it liketh him best:
[j]thou shalt not oppress him.
17 ¶ There shall be no whore [k]of the
daughters of Israel, nor [l]a sodomite of the
sons of Israel.
18 Thou shalt not bring the hire of a
whore, or the price of a dog, into the house
of the LORD thy God for any vow: for even
both these *are* abomination unto the LORD
thy God.
19 ¶ [m]Thou shalt not lend upon usury to
thy brother; usury of money, usury of victuals, usury of any thing that is lent upon
usury:
20 [n]Unto a stranger thou mayest lend
upon usury; but unto thy brother thou shalt
not lend upon usury: [o]that the LORD thy
God may bless thee in all that thou settest
thine hand to in the land whither thou goest
to possess it.
21 ¶ [p]When thou shalt vow a vow unto
the LORD thy God, thou shalt not slack to
pay it: for the LORD thy God will surely require it of thee; and it would be sin in thee.
22 But if thou shalt forbear to vow, it shall
be no sin in thee.
23 [q]That which is gone out of thy lips
thou shalt keep and perform; *even* a freewill
offering, according as thou hast vowed unto
the LORD thy God, which thou hast promised with thy mouth.
24 ¶ When thou comest into thy neighbour's vineyard, then thou mayest eat
grapes thy fill at thine own pleasure; but
thou shalt not put *any* in thy vessel.
25 When thou comest into the standing
corn of thy neighbour, [r]then thou mayest
pluck the ears with thine hand; but thou
shalt not move a sickle unto thy neighbour's
standing corn.
24 When a [s]man hath taken a wife, and
married her, and it come to pass that
she find no favour in his eyes, because he
hath found some uncleanness in her: then
let him write her a bill of divorcement, and

give *it* in her hand, and send her out of his house.

2 And when she is departed out of his house, she may go and be another man's *wife*.

3 And *if* the latter husband hate her, and write her a bill of divorcement, and giveth *it* in her hand, and sendeth her out of his house; or if the latter husband die, which took her *to be* his wife;

4 [t]Her former husband, which sent her away, may not take her again to be his wife, after that she is defiled; for that *is* abomination before the LORD: and thou shalt not cause the land to sin, which the LORD thy God giveth thee *for* an inheritance.

5 ¶ [u]When a man hath taken a new wife, he shall not go out to war, neither shall he be charged with any business: *but* he shall be free at home one year, and shall [v]cheer up his wife which he hath taken.

6 ¶ No man shall take the nether or the upper millstone to pledge: for he taketh *a man's* life to pledge.

7 ¶ [w]If a man be found stealing any of his brethren of the children of Israel, and maketh merchandise of him, or selleth him; then that thief shall die; [x]and thou shalt put evil away from among you.

8 ¶ Take heed in [y]the plague of leprosy, that thou observe diligently, and do according to all that the priests the Levites shall teach you: as I commanded them, *so* ye shall observe to do.

9 [z]Remember what the LORD thy God did [a]unto Miriam by the way, after that ye were come forth out of Egypt.

10 ¶ When thou dost lend thy brother any thing, thou shalt not go into his house to fetch his pledge.

11 Thou shalt stand abroad, and the man to whom thou dost lend shall bring out the pledge abroad unto thee.

12 And if the man *be* poor, thou shalt not sleep with his pledge:

13 [b]In any case thou shalt deliver him the pledge again when the sun goeth down, that he may sleep in his own raiment, and [c]bless thee: and [d]it shall be righteousness unto thee before the LORD thy God.

14 ¶ Thou shalt not [e]oppress an hired servant *that is* poor and needy, *whether he be* of thy brethren, or of thy strangers that *are* in thy land within thy gates:

15 At his day [f]thou shalt give *him* his hire, neither shall the sun go down upon it; for he *is* poor, and setteth his heart upon it: [g]lest he cry against thee unto the LORD, and it be sin unto thee.

16 [h]The fathers shall not be put to death for the children, neither shall the children be put to death for the fathers: every man shall be put to death for his own sin.

17 ¶ [i]Thou shalt not pervert the judgment of the stranger, *nor* of the fatherless; [j]nor take a widow's raiment to pledge:

18 But [k]thou shalt remember that thou wast a bondman in Egypt, and the LORD thy God redeemed thee thence: therefore I command thee to do this thing.

19 ¶ [l]When thou cuttest down thine harvest in thy field, and hast forgot a sheaf in the field, thou shalt not go again to fetch it: it shall be for the stranger, for the fatherless, and for the widow: that the LORD thy God may [m]bless thee in all the work of thine hands.

20 When thou beatest thine olive tree, thou shalt not go over the boughs again: it shall be for the stranger, for the fatherless, and for the widow.

21 When thou gatherest the grapes of thy vineyard, thou shalt not glean *it* afterward: it shall be for the stranger, for the fatherless, and for the widow.

22 And [n]thou shalt remember that thou wast a bondman in the land of Egypt: therefore I command thee to do this thing.

25

If there be a [o]controversy between men, and they come unto judgment, that *the judges* may judge them; then they [p]shall justify the righteous, and condemn the wicked.

2 And it shall be, if the wicked man *be* [q]worthy to be beaten, that the judge shall cause him to lie down, [r]and to be beaten before his face, according to his fault, by a certain number.

3 [s]Forty stripes he may give him, *and* not exceed: lest, *if* he should exceed, and beat him above these with many stripes, then thy brother should [t]seem vile unto thee.

4 ¶ [u]Thou shalt not muzzle the ox when he treadeth out *the corn*.

5 ¶ [v]If brethren dwell together, and one of them die, and have no child, the wife of the dead shall not marry without unto a stranger: her husband's brother shall go in unto her, and take her to him to wife, and perform the duty of an husband's brother unto her.

6 And it shall be, *that* the firstborn which she beareth [w]shall succeed in the name of his brother *which is* dead, that [x]his name be not put out of Israel.

7 And if the man like not to take his brother's wife, then let his brother's wife go up to the [y]gate unto the elders, and say, My husband's brother refuseth to raise up unto his brother a name in Israel, he will not perform the duty of my husband's brother.

8 Then the elders of his city shall call him, and speak unto him: and *if* he stand *to it*, and say, [z]I like not to take her;

9 Then shall his brother's wife come unto him in the presence of the elders, and [a]loose his shoe from off his foot, and spit in his face, and shall answer and say, So shall it be done unto that man that will not [b]build up his brother's house.

10 And his name shall be called in Israel, The house of him that hath his shoe loosed.

11 ¶ When men strive together one with another, and the wife of the one draweth near for to deliver her husband out of the hand of him that smiteth him, and putteth

24:4 [t]Jer. 3:1
24:5 [u]ch. 20:7 [v]Prov. 5:18
24:7 [w]Ex. 21:16 [x]ch. 19:19
24:8 [y]Lev. 13:2
24:9 [z]Luke 17:32; 1 Cor. 10:6 [a]Num. 12:10
24:13 [b]Ex. 22:26 [c]Job 29:11; 2 Cor. 9:13; 2 Tim. 1:18 [d]ch. 6:25; Ps. 106:31; Dan. 4:27
24:14 [e]Mal. 3:5
24:15 [f]Lev. 19:13; Jer. 22:13; Jam. 5:4 [g]Jam. 5:4
24:16 [h]2 Kings 14:6; 2 Chron. 25:4; Jer. 31:29; Ezek. 18:20
24:17 [i]Ex. 22:21; Prov. 22:22; Isa. 1:23; Jer. 5:28; Ezek. 22:29; Zech. 7:10; Mal. 3:5 [j]Ex. 22:26
24:18 [k]ver. 22; ch. 16:12
24:19 [l]Lev. 19:9 [m]ch. 15:10; Ps. 41:1; Prov. 19:17
24:22 [n]ver. 18
25:1 [o]ch. 19:17; Ezek. 44:24 [p]Prov. 17:15
25:2 [q]Luke 12:48 [r]Matt. 10:17
25:3 [s]2 Cor. 11:24 [t]Job 18:3
25:4 [u]Prov. 12:10; 1 Cor. 9:9; 1 Tim. 5:18
25:5 [v]Matt. 22:24; Mark 12:19; Luke 20:28
25:6 [w]Gen. 38:9 [x]Ruth 4:10
25:7 [y]Ruth 4:1
25:8 [z]Ruth 4:6
25:9 [a]Ruth 4:7 [b]Ruth 4:11

forth her hand, and taketh him by the secrets:

12 Then thou shalt cut off her hand, [c]thine eye shall not pity *her*.

13 ¶ [d]Thou shalt not have in thy bag divers weights, a great and a small.

14 Thou shalt not have in thine house divers measures, a great and a small.

15 *But* thou shalt have a perfect and just weight, a perfect and just measure shalt thou have: [e]that thy days may be lengthened in the land which the LORD thy God giveth thee.

16 For [f]all that do such things, *and* all that do unrighteously, *are* an abomination unto the LORD thy God.

17 ¶ [g]Remember what Amalek did unto thee by the way, when ye were come forth out of Egypt;

18 How he met thee by the way, and smote the hindmost of thee, *even* all *that were* feeble behind thee, when thou *wast* faint and weary; and he [h]feared not God.

19 Therefore it shall be, [i]when the LORD thy God hath given thee rest from all thine enemies round about, in the land which the LORD thy God giveth thee *for* an inheritance to possess it, *that* thou shalt [j]blot out the remembrance of Amalek from under heaven; thou shalt not forget *it*.

26

And it shall be, when thou *art* come in unto the land which the LORD thy God giveth thee *for* an inheritance, and possessest it, and dwellest therein;

2 [k]That thou shalt take of the first of all the fruit of the earth, which thou shalt bring of thy land that the LORD thy God giveth thee, and shalt put *it* in a basket, and shalt [l]go unto the place which the LORD thy God shall choose to place his name there.

3 And thou shalt go unto the priest that shall be in those days, and say unto him, I profess this day unto the LORD thy God, that I am come unto the country which the LORD sware unto our fathers for to give us.

4 And the priest shall take the basket out of thine hand, and set it down before the altar of the LORD thy God.

5 And thou shalt speak and say before the LORD thy God, [m]A Syrian [n]ready to perish *was* my father, and [o]he went down into Egypt, and sojourned there with a [p]few, and became there a nation, great, mighty, and populous:

6 And [q]the Egyptians evil entreated us, and afflicted us, and laid upon us hard bondage:

7 And [r]when we cried unto the LORD God of our fathers, the LORD heard our voice, and looked on our affliction, and our labour, and our oppression:

8 And [s]the LORD brought us forth out of Egypt with a mighty hand, and with an outstretched arm, and [t]with great terribleness, and with signs, and with wonders:

9 And he hath brought us into this place, and hath given us this land, *even* [u]a land that floweth with milk and honey.

10 And now, behold, I have brought the firstfruits of the land, which thou, O LORD, hast given me. And thou shalt set it before the LORD thy God, and worship before the LORD thy God:

11 And [v]thou shalt rejoice in every good *thing* which the LORD thy God hath given unto thee, and unto thine house, thou, and the Levite, and the stranger that *is* among you.

12 ¶ When thou hast made an end of tithing all the [w]tithes of thine increase the third year, *which is* [x]the year of tithing, and hast given *it* unto the Levite, the stranger, the fatherless, and the widow, that they may eat within thy gates, and be filled;

13 Then thou shalt say before the LORD thy God, I have brought away the hallowed things out of *mine* house, and also have given them unto the Levite, and unto the stranger, to the fatherless, and to the widow, according to all thy commandments which thou hast commanded me: I have not transgressed thy commandments, [y]neither have I forgotten *them:*

14 [z]I have not eaten thereof in my mourning, neither have I taken away *ought* thereof for *any* unclean *use,* nor given *ought* thereof for the dead: *but* I have hearkened to the voice of the LORD my God, *and* have done according to all that thou hast commanded me.

15 [a]Look down from thy holy habitation, from heaven, and bless thy people Israel, and the land which thou hast given us, as thou swarest unto our fathers, a land that floweth with milk and honey.

16 ¶ This day the LORD thy God hath commanded thee to do these statutes and judgments: thou shalt therefore keep and do them with all thine heart, and with all thy soul.

17 Thou hast [b]avouched the LORD this day to be thy God, and to walk in his ways, and to keep his statutes, and his commandments, and his judgments, and to hearken unto his voice:

18 And [c]the LORD hath avouched thee this day to be his peculiar people, as he hath promised thee, and that *thou* shouldest keep all his commandments;

19 And to make thee [d]high above all nations which he hath made, in praise, and in name, and in honour; and that thou mayest be [e]an holy people unto the LORD thy God, as he hath spoken.

27

And Moses with the elders of Israel commanded the people, saying, Keep all the commandments which I command you this day.

2 And it shall be, on the day [f]when ye shall pass over Jordan unto the land which the LORD thy God giveth thee, that [g]thou shalt set thee up great stones, and plaister them with plaister:

3 And thou shalt write upon them all the words of this law, when thou art passed over, that thou mayest go in unto the land

25:12 [c]ch. 19:13
25:13 [d]Lev. 19:35; Prov. 11:1; Ezek. 45:10; Mic. 6:11
25:15 [e]Ex. 20:12
25:16 [f]Prov. 11:1; 1 Thess. 4:6
25:17 [g]Ex. 17:8
25:18 [h]Ps. 36:1; Prov. 16:6; Rom. 3:18
25:19 [i]1 Sam. 15:3 [j]Ex. 17:14
26:2 [k]Ex. 23:19; Num. 18:13; ch. 16:10; Prov. 3:9 [l]ch. 12:5
26:5 [m]Hos. 12:12 [n]Gen. 43:1 [o]Gen. 46:1; Acts 7:15 [p]Gen. 46:27; ch. 10:22
26:6 [q]Ex. 1:11
26:7 [r]Ex. 2:23
26:8 [s]Ex. 12:37; ch. 5:15 [t]ch. 4:34
26:9 [u]Ex. 3:8
26:11 [v]ch. 12:7
26:12 [w]Lev. 27:30; Num. 18:24 [x]ch. 14:28
26:13 [y]Ps. 119:141
26:14 [z]Lev. 7:20; Hos. 9:4
26:15 [a]Isa. 63:15; Zech. 2:13
26:17 [b]Ex. 20:19
26:18 [c]Ex. 6:7; ch. 7:6
26:19 [d]ch. 4:7; Ps. 148:14 [e]Ex. 19:6; ch. 7:6; 1 Pet. 2:9
27:2 [f]Josh. 4:1 [g]Josh. 8:32

which the LORD thy God giveth thee, a land that floweth with milk and honey; as the LORD God of thy fathers hath promised thee.

4 Therefore it shall be when ye be gone over Jordan, *that* ye shall set up these stones, which I command you this day, [h]in mount Ebal, and thou shalt plaister them with plaister.

5 And there shalt thou build an altar unto the LORD thy God, an altar of stones: [i]thou shalt not lift up *any* iron *tool* upon them.

6 Thou shalt build the altar of the LORD thy God of whole stones: and thou shalt offer burnt offerings thereon unto the LORD thy God:

7 And thou shalt offer peace offerings, and shalt eat there, and rejoice before the LORD thy God.

8 And thou shalt write upon the stones all the words of this law very plainly.

9 ¶ And Moses and the priests the Levites spake unto all Israel, saying, Take heed, and hearken, O Israel; [j]this day thou art become the people of the LORD thy God.

10 Thou shalt therefore obey the voice of the LORD thy God, and do his commandments and his statutes, which I command thee this day.

11 ¶ And Moses charged the people the same day, saying,

12 These shall stand [k]upon mount Gerizim to bless the people, when ye are come over Jordan; Simeon, and Levi, and Judah, and Issachar, and Joseph, and Benjamin:

13 And [l]these shall stand upon mount Ebal to curse; Reuben, Gad, and Asher, and Zebulun, Dan, and Naphtali.

14 ¶ And [m]the Levites shall speak, and say unto all the men of Israel with a loud voice,

15 [n]Cursed *be* the man that maketh *any* graven or molten image, an abomination unto the LORD, the work of the hands of the craftsman, and putteth *it* in *a* secret *place*. [o]And all the people shall answer and say, Amen.

16 [p]Cursed *be* he that setteth light by his father or his mother. And all the people shall say, Amen.

17 [q]Cursed *be* he that removeth his neighbour's landmark. And all the people shall say, Amen.

18 [r]Cursed *be* he that maketh the blind to wander out of the way. And all the people shall say, Amen.

19 [s]Cursed *be* he that perverteth the judgment of the stranger, fatherless, and widow. And all the people shall say, Amen.

20 [t]Cursed *be* he that lieth with his father's wife; because he uncovereth his father's skirt. And all the people shall say, Amen.

21 [u]Cursed *be* he that lieth with any manner of beast. And all the people shall say, Amen.

22 [v]Cursed *be* he that lieth with his sister, the daughter of his father, or the daughter of his mother. And all the people shall say, Amen.

23 [w]Cursed *be* he that lieth with his mother in law. And all the people shall say, Amen.

24 [x]Cursed *be* he that smiteth his neighbour secretly. And all the people shall say, Amen.

25 [y]Cursed *be* he that taketh reward to slay an innocent person. And all the people shall say, Amen.

26 [z]Cursed *be* he that confirmeth not *all* the words of this law to do them. And all the people shall say, Amen.

28 And it shall come to pass, [a]if thou shalt hearken diligently unto the voice of the LORD thy God, to observe *and* to do all his commandments which I command thee this day, that the LORD thy God [b]will set thee on high above all nations of the earth:

2 And all these blessings shall come on thee, and [c]overtake thee, if thou shalt hearken unto the voice of the LORD thy God.

3 [d]Blessed *shalt* thou *be* in the city, and blessed *shalt* thou *be* [e]in the field.

4 Blessed *shall be* [f]the fruit of thy body, and the fruit of thy ground, and the fruit of thy cattle, the increase of thy kine, and the flocks of thy sheep.

5 Blessed *shall be* thy basket and thy store.

6 [g]Blessed *shalt* thou *be* when thou comest in, and blessed *shalt* thou *be* when thou goest out.

7 The LORD [h]shall cause thine enemies that rise up against thee to be smitten before thy face: they shall come out against thee one way, and flee before thee seven ways.

8 The LORD shall [i]command the blessing upon thee in thy storehouses, and in all that thou [j]settest thine hand unto; and he shall bless thee in the land which the LORD thy God giveth thee.

9 [k]The LORD shall establish thee an holy people unto himself, as he hath sworn unto thee, if thou shalt keep the commandments of the LORD thy God, and walk in his ways.

10 And all people of the earth shall see that thou art [l]called by the name of the LORD; and they shall be [m]afraid of thee.

11 And [n]the LORD shall make thee plenteous in goods, in the fruit of thy body, and in the fruit of thy cattle, and in the fruit of thy ground, in the land which the LORD sware unto thy fathers to give thee.

12 The LORD shall open unto thee his good treasure, the heaven [o]to give the rain unto thy land in his season, and [p]to bless all the work of thine hand: and [q]thou shalt lend unto many nations, and thou shalt not borrow.

13 And the LORD shall make thee [r]the head, and not the tail; and thou shalt be above only, and thou shalt not be beneath; if that thou hearken unto the commandments of the LORD thy God, which I com-

27:4 [h]ch. 11:29; Josh. 8:30
27:5 [i]Ex. 20:25; Josh. 8:31
27:9 [j]ch. 26:18
27:12 [k]ch. 11:29; Josh. 8:33; Judg. 9:7
27:13 [l]ch. 11:29; Josh. 8:33
27:14 [m]ch. 33:10; Josh. 8:33; Dan. 9:11
27:15 [n]Ex. 20:4; Lev. 19:4; ch. 4:16; Isa. 44:9; Hos. 13:2 [o]Num. 5:22; Jer. 11:5; 1 Cor. 14:16
27:16 [p]Ex. 20:12; Lev. 19:3; ch. 21:18
27:17 [q]ch. 19:14; Prov. 22:28
27:18 [r]Lev. 19:14
27:19 [s]Ex. 22:21; ch. 10:18; Mal. 3:5
27:20 [t]Lev. 18:8; ch. 22:30
27:21 [u]Lev. 18:23
27:22 [v]Lev. 18:9
27:23 [w]Lev. 18:17
27:24 [x]Ex. 20:13; Lev. 24:17; Num. 35:31; ch. 19:11
27:25 [y]Ex. 23:7; ch. 10:17; Ezek. 22:12
27:26 [z]ch. 28:15; Ps. 119:21; Jer. 11:3; Gal. 3:10
28:1 [a]Ex. 15:26; Lev. 26:3; Isa. 55:2 [b]ch. 26:19
28:2 [c]ver. 15; Zech. 1:6
28:3 [d]Ps. 128:1 [e]Gen. 39:5
28:4 [f]ver. 11; Gen. 22:17; ch. 7:13; Ps. 107:38; Prov. 10:22; 1 Tim. 4:8
28:6 [g]Ps. 121:8
28:7 [h]ver. 25; Lev. 26:7; 2 Sam. 22:38; Ps. 89:23
28:8 [i]Lev. 25:21 [j]ch. 15:10
28:9 [k]Ex. 19:5; ch. 7:6
28:10 [l]Num. 6:27; 2 Chron. 7:14; Isa. 63:19; Dan. 9:18 [m]ch. 11:25
28:11 [n]ver. 4; ch. 30:9; Prov. 10:22
28:12 [o]Lev. 26:4; ch. 11:14 [p]ch. 14:29 [q]ch. 15:6
28:13 [r]Isa. 9:14

mand thee this day, to observe and to do
them:
14 [s]And thou shalt not go aside from any
of the words which I command thee this
day, *to* the right hand, or *to* the left, to go
after other gods to serve them.
15 ¶ But it shall come to pass, [t]if thou
wilt not hearken unto the voice of the LORD
thy God, to observe to do all his commandments and his statutes which I command
thee this day; that all these curses shall
come upon thee, and [u]overtake thee:
16 Cursed *shalt* thou *be* [v]in the city, and
cursed *shalt* thou *be* in the field.
17 Cursed *shall be* thy basket and thy
store.
18 Cursed *shall be* the fruit of thy body,
and the fruit of thy land, the increase of thy
kine, and the flocks of thy sheep.
19 Cursed *shalt* thou *be* when thou comest in, and cursed *shalt* thou *be* when thou
goest out.
20 The LORD shall send upon thee [w]curs-
ing, [x]vexation, and [y]rebuke, in all that thou
settest thine hand unto for to do, until thou
be destroyed, and until thou perish quickly;
because of the wickedness of thy doings,
whereby thou hast forsaken me.
21 The LORD shall make [z]the pestilence
cleave unto thee, until he have consumed
thee from off the land, whither thou goest to
possess it.
22 [a]The LORD shall smite thee with a consumption, and with a fever, and with an inflammation, and with an extreme burning,
and with the sword, and with [b]blasting, and
with mildew; and they shall pursue thee until thou perish.
23 And [c]thy heaven that *is* over thy head
shall be brass, and the earth that *is* under
thee *shall be* iron.
24 The LORD shall make the rain of thy
land powder and dust: from heaven shall it
come down upon thee, until thou be destroyed.
25 [d]The LORD shall cause thee to be smitten before thine enemies: thou shalt go out
one way against them, and flee seven ways
before them: and [e]shalt be removed into all
the kingdoms of the earth.
26 And [f]thy carcase shall be meat unto
all fowls of the air, and unto the beasts of
the earth, and no man shall fray *them* away.
27 The LORD will smite thee with [g]the
botch of Egypt, and with [h]the emerods, and
with the scab, and with the itch, whereof
thou canst not be healed.
28 The LORD shall smite thee with madness, and blindness, and [i]astonishment of
heart:
29 And thou shalt [j]grope at noonday, as
the blind gropeth in darkness, and thou
shalt not prosper in thy ways: and thou
shalt be only oppressed and spoiled evermore, and no man shall save *thee.*
30 [k]Thou shalt betroth a wife, and another man shall lie with her: [l]thou shalt
build an house, and thou shalt not dwell
therein: [m]thou shalt plant a vineyard, and
shalt not gather the grapes thereof.
31 Thine ox *shall be* slain before thine
eyes, and thou shalt not eat thereof: thine
ass *shall be* violently taken away from before thy face, and shall not be restored to
thee: thy sheep *shall be* given unto thine
enemies, and thou shalt have none to rescue
them.
32 Thy sons and thy daughters *shall be*
given unto another people, and thine eyes
shall look, and [n]fail *with longing* for them
all the day long: and *there shall be* no might
in thine hand.
33 [o]The fruit of thy land, and all thy labours, shall a nation which thou knowest
not eat up; and thou shalt be only oppressed
and crushed alway:
34 So that thou shalt be mad [p]for the
sight of thine eyes which thou shalt see.
35 The LORD shall [q]smite thee in the
knees, and in the legs, with a sore botch that
cannot be healed, from the sole of thy foot
unto the top of thy head.
36 The LORD shall [r]bring thee, and thy
king which thou shalt set over thee, unto a
nation which neither thou nor thy fathers
have known; and [s]there shalt thou serve
other gods, wood and stone.
37 And thou shalt become [t]an astonishment, a proverb, [u]and a byword, among all
nations whither the LORD shall lead thee.
38 [v]Thou shalt carry much seed out into
the field, and shalt gather *but* little in; for
[w]the locust shall consume it.
39 Thou shalt plant vineyards, and dress
them, but shalt neither drink *of* the wine,
nor gather *the grapes;* for the worms shall
eat them.
40 Thou shalt have olive trees throughout
all thy coasts, but thou shalt not anoint *thyself* with the oil; for thine olive shall cast *his*
fruit.
41 Thou shalt beget sons and daughters,
but thou shalt not enjoy them; for [x]they
shall go into captivity.
42 All thy trees and fruit of thy land shall
the locust consume.
43 The stranger that *is* within thee shall
get up above thee very high; and thou shalt
come down very low.
44 [y]He shall lend to thee, and thou shalt
not lend to him: [z]he shall be the head, and
thou shalt be the tail.
45 Moreover [a]all these curses shall come
upon thee, and shall pursue thee, and overtake thee, till thou be destroyed; because
thou hearkenedst not unto the voice of the
LORD thy God, to keep his commandments
and his statutes which he commanded thee:
46 And they shall be upon thee [b]for a
sign and for a wonder, and upon thy seed
for ever.
47 [c]Because thou servedst not the LORD
thy God with joyfulness, and with gladness
of heart, [d]for the abundance of all *things;*
48 Therefore shalt thou serve thine enemies which the LORD shall send against

28:14 [s]ch. 5:32
28:15 [t]Lev. 26:14; Lam. 2:17; Dan. 9:11; Mal. 2:2 [u]ver. 2
28:16 [v]ver. 3
28:20 [w]Mal. 2:2 [x]1 Sam. 14:20; Zech. 14:13 [y]Ps. 80:16; Isa. 30:17
28:21 [z]Lev. 26:25; Jer. 24:10
28:22 [a]Lev. 26:16 [b]Am. 4:9
28:23 [c]Lev. 26:19
28:25 [d]ver. 7; Lev. 26:17; ch. 32:30; Isa. 30:17 [e]Jer. 15:4; Ezek. 23:46
28:26 [f]1 Sam. 17:44; Ps. 79:2; Jer. 7:33
28:27 [g]ver. 35; Ex. 9:9 [h]1 Sam. 5:6; Ps. 78:66
28:28 [i]Jer. 4:9
28:29 [j]Job 5:14; Isa. 59:10
28:30 [k]Job 31:10; Jer. 8:10 [l]Job 31:8; Jer. 12:13; Am. 5:11; Mic. 6:15; Zeph. 1:13 [m]ch. 20:6
28:32 [n]Ps. 119:82
28:33 [o]ver. 51; Lev. 26:16; Jer. 5:17
28:34 [p]ver. 67
28:35 [q]ver. 27
28:36 [r]2 Kings 17:4; 2 Chron. 33:11 [s]ch. 4:28; Jer. 16:13
28:37 [t]1 Kings 9:7; Jer. 24:9; Zech. 8:13 [u]Ps. 44:14
28:38 [v]Mic. 6:15; Hag. 1:6 [w]Joel 1:4
28:41 [x]Lam. 1:5
28:44 [y]ver. 12 [z]ver. 13; Lam. 1:5
28:45 [a]ver. 15
28:46 [b]Isa. 8:18; Ezek. 14:8
28:47 [c]Neh. 9:35 [d]ch. 32:15

thee, in hunger, and in thirst, and in nakedness, and in want of all *things:* and he [e]shall put a yoke of iron upon thy neck, until he have destroyed thee.

49 [f]The LORD shall bring a nation against thee from far, from the end of the earth, [g]*as swift* as the eagle flieth; a nation whose tongue thou shalt not understand;

50 A nation of fierce countenance, [h]which shall not regard the person of the old, nor shew favour to the young:

51 And he shall [i]eat the fruit of thy cattle, and the fruit of thy land, until thou be destroyed: which *also* shall not leave thee *either* corn, wine, or oil, *or* the increase of thy kine, or flocks of thy sheep, until he have destroyed thee.

52 And he shall [j]besiege thee in all thy gates, until thy high and fenced walls come down, wherein thou trustedst, throughout all thy land: and he shall besiege thee in all thy gates throughout all thy land, which the LORD thy God hath given thee.

53 And [k]thou shalt eat the fruit of thine own body, the flesh of thy sons and of thy daughters, which the LORD thy God hath given thee, in the siege, and in the straitness, wherewith thine enemies shall distress thee:

54 *So that* the man *that is* tender among you, and very delicate, [l]his eye shall be evil toward his brother, and toward [m]the wife of his bosom, and toward the remnant of his children which he shall leave:

55 So that he will not give to any of them of the flesh of his children whom he shall eat: because he hath nothing left him in the siege, and in the straitness, wherewith thine enemies shall distress thee in all thy gates.

56 The tender and delicate woman among you, which would not adventure to set the sole of her foot upon the ground for delicateness and tenderness, [n]her eye shall be evil toward the husband of her bosom, and toward her son, and toward her daughter,

57 And toward her young one that cometh out [o]from between her feet, and toward her children which she shall bear: for she shall eat them for want of all *things* secretly in the siege and straitness, wherewith thine enemy shall distress thee in thy gates.

58 If thou wilt not observe to do all the words of this law that are written in this book, that thou mayest fear [p]this glorious and fearful name, THE LORD THY GOD;

59 Then the LORD will make thy plagues [q]wonderful, and the plagues of thy seed, *even* great plagues, and of long continuance, and sore sicknesses, and of long continuance.

60 Moreover he will bring upon thee all [r]the diseases of Egypt, which thou wast afraid of; and they shall cleave unto thee.

61 Also every sickness, and every plague, which *is* not written in the book of this law, them will the LORD bring upon thee, until thou be destroyed.

62 And ye [s]shall be left few in number, whereas ye were [t]as the stars of heaven for multitude; because thou wouldest not obey the voice of the LORD thy God.

63 And it shall come to pass, *that* as the LORD [u]rejoiced over you to do you good, and to multiply you; so the LORD [v]will rejoice over you to destroy you, and to bring you to nought; and ye shall be plucked from off the land whither thou goest to possess it.

64 And the LORD [w]shall scatter thee among all people, from the one end of the earth even unto the other; and [x]there thou shalt serve other gods, which neither thou nor thy fathers have known, *even* wood and stone.

65 And [y]among these nations shalt thou find no ease, neither shall the sole of thy foot have rest: [z]but the LORD shall give thee there a trembling heart, and failing of eyes, and [a]sorrow of mind:

66 And thy life shall hang in doubt before thee; and thou shalt fear day and night, and shalt have none assurance of thy life:

67 [b]In the morning thou shalt say, Would God it were even! and at even thou shalt say, Would God it were morning! for the fear of thine heart wherewith thou shalt fear, and [c]for the sight of thine eyes which thou shalt see.

68 And the LORD [d]shall bring thee into Egypt again with ships, by the way whereof I spake unto thee, [e]Thou shalt see it no more again: and there ye shall be sold unto your enemies for bondmen and bondwomen, and no man shall buy *you.*

29

These *are* the words of the covenant, which the LORD commanded Moses to make with the children of Israel in the land of Moab, beside [f]the covenant which he made with them in Horeb.

2 ¶ And Moses called unto all Israel, and said unto them, [g]Ye have seen all that the LORD did before your eyes in the land of Egypt unto Pharaoh, and unto all his servants, and unto all his land;

3 [h]The great temptations which thine eyes have seen, the signs, and those great miracles:

4 Yet [i]the LORD hath not given you an heart to perceive, and eyes to see, and ears to hear, unto this day.

5 [j]And I have led you forty years in the wilderness: [k]your clothes are not waxen old upon you, and thy shoe is not waxen old upon thy foot.

6 [l]Ye have not eaten bread, neither have ye drunk wine or strong drink: that ye might know that I *am* the LORD your God.

7 And when ye came unto this place, [m]Sihon the king of Heshbon, and Og the king of Bashan, came out against us unto battle, and we smote them:

8 And we took their land, and [n]gave it for an inheritance unto the Reubenites, and to the Gadites, and to the half tribe of Manasseh.

9 [o]Keep therefore the words of this cov-

28:48 [e]Jer. 28:14
28:49 [f]Jer. 5:15; Luke 19:43 [g]Jer. 48:40; Lam. 4:19; Ezek. 17:3; Hos. 8:1
28:50 [h]2 Chron. 36:17; Isa. 47:6
28:51 [i]ver. 33; Isa. 1:7
28:52 [j]2 Kings 25:1
28:53 [k]Lev. 26:29; 2 Kings 6:28; Jer. 19:9; Lam. 2:20
28:54 [l]ch. 15:9 [m]ch. 13:6
28:56 [n]ver. 54
28:57 [o]Gen. 49:10
28:58 [p]Ex. 6:3
28:59 [q]Dan. 9:12
28:60 [r]ch. 7:15
28:62 [s]ch. 4:27 [t]ch. 10:22; Neh. 9:23
28:63 [u]ch. 30:9; Jer. 32:41 [v]Prov. 1:26; Isa. 1:24
28:64 [w]Lev. 26:33; ch. 4:27; Neh. 1:8; Jer. 16:13 [x]ver. 36
28:65 [y]Am. 9:4 [z]Lev. 26:36 [a]Lev. 26:16
28:67 [b]Job 7:4 [c]ver. 34
28:68 [d]Jer. 44:7; Hos. 8:13 [e]ch. 17:16
29:1 [f]ch. 5:2
29:2 [g]Ex. 19:4
29:3 [h]ch. 4:34
29:4 [i]Isa. 6:9; John 8:43; Acts 28:26; Eph. 4:18; 2 Thess. 2:11
29:5 [j]ch. 1:3 [k]ch. 8:4
29:6 [l]Ex. 16:12; ch. 8:3; Ps. 78:24
29:7 [m]Num. 21:23; ch. 2:32
29:8 [n]Num. 32:33; ch. 3:12
29:9 [o]ch. 4:6; Josh. 1:7; 1 Kings 2:3

enant, and do them, that ye may [p]prosper
in all that ye do.
10 ¶ Ye stand this day all of you before
the LORD your God; your captains of your
tribes, your elders, and your officers, *with*
all the men of Israel,
11 Your little ones, your wives, and thy
stranger that *is* in thy camp, from [q]the
hewer of thy wood unto the drawer of thy
water:
12 That thou shouldest enter into covenant with the LORD thy God, and [r]into his
oath, which the LORD thy God maketh with
thee this day:
13 That he may [s]establish thee to day for
a people unto himself, and *that* he may be
unto thee a God, [t]as he hath said unto thee,
and [u]as he hath sworn unto thy fathers, to
Abraham, to Isaac, and to Jacob.
14 Neither with you only [v]do I make this
covenant and this oath;
15 But with *him* that standeth here with
us this day before the LORD our God, [w]and
also with *him* that *is* not here with us this
day:
16 (For ye know how we have dwelt in the
land of Egypt; and how we came through
the nations which ye passed by;
17 And ye have seen their abominations,
and their idols, wood and stone, silver and
gold, which *were* among them:)
18 Lest there should be among you man,
or woman, or family, or tribe, [x]whose heart
turneth away this day from the LORD our
God, to go *and* serve the gods of these nations; [y]lest there should be among you a
root that beareth gall and wormwood;
19 And it come to pass, when he heareth
the words of this curse, that he bless himself
in his heart, saying, I shall have peace,
though I walk [z]in the imagination of mine
heart, [a]to add drunkenness to thirst:
20 [b]The LORD will not spare him, but
then [c]the anger of the LORD and [d]his jealousy shall smoke against that man, and all
the curses that are written in this book shall
lie upon him, and the LORD [e]shall blot out
his name from under heaven.
21 And the LORD [f]shall separate him
unto evil out of all the tribes of Israel, according to all the curses of the covenant that
are written in this book of the law:
22 So that the generation to come of your
children that shall rise up after you, and the
stranger that shall come from a far land,
shall say, when they see the plagues of that
land, and the sicknesses which the LORD
hath laid upon it;
23 *And that* the whole land thereof *is*
brimstone, [g]and salt, *and* burning, *that* it is
not sown, nor beareth, nor any grass groweth therein, [h]like the overthrow of Sodom
and Gomorrah, Admah, and Zeboim, which
the LORD overthrew in his anger, and in his
wrath:
24 Even all nations shall say, [i]Wherefore
hath the LORD done thus unto this land?
what *meaneth* the heat of this great anger?

29:9 [p]Josh. 1:7
29:11 [q]Josh. 9:21
29:12 [r]Neh. 10:29
29:13 [s]ch. 28:9 [t]Ex. 6:7 [u]Gen. 17:7
29:14 [v]Jer. 31:31; Heb. 8:7
29:15 [w]Acts 2:39; 1 Cor. 7:14
29:18 [x]ch. 11:16 [y]Acts 8:23; Heb. 12:15
29:19 [z]Num. 15:39; Eccl. 11:9 [a]Isa. 30:1
29:20 [b]Ezek. 14:7 [c]Ps. 74:1 [d]Ps. 79:5; Ezek. 23:25 [e]ch. 9:14
29:21 [f]Matt. 24:51
29:23 [g]Ps. 107:34; Jer. 17:6; Zeph. 2:9 [h]Gen. 19:24; Jer. 20:16
29:24 [i]1 Kings 9:8; Jer. 22:8
29:27 [j]Dan. 9:11
29:28 [k]1 Kings 14:15; 2 Chron. 7:20; Ps. 52:5; Prov. 2:22
30:1 [l]Lev. 26:40 [m]ch. 28 [n]ch. 4:29; 1 Kings 8:47
30:2 [o]Neh. 1:9; Isa. 55:7; Lam. 3:40; Joel 2:12
30:3 [p]Ps. 106:45; Jer. 29:14; Lam. 3:22 [q]Ps. 147:2; Jer. 32:37; Ezek. 34:13
30:4 [r]ch. 28:64; Neh. 1:9
30:6 [s]ch. 10:16; Jer. 32:39; Ezek. 11:19
30:9 [t]ch. 28:11 [u]ch. 28:63; Jer. 32:41

25 Then men shall say, Because they have
forsaken the covenant of the LORD God of
their fathers, which he made with them
when he brought them forth out of the land
of Egypt:
26 For they went and served other gods,
and worshipped them, gods whom they
knew not, and *whom* he had not given unto
them:
27 And the anger of the LORD was kindled
against this land, [j]to bring upon it all the
curses that are written in this book:
28 And the LORD [k]rooted them out of
their land in anger, and in wrath, and in
great indignation, and cast them into another land, as *it is* this day.
29 The secret *things belong* unto the
LORD our God: but those *things which are*
revealed *belong* unto us and to our children
for ever, that *we* may do all the words of this
law.

30 And [l]it shall come to pass, when
[m]all these things are come upon thee,
the blessing and the curse, which I have set
before thee, and [n]thou shalt call *them* to
mind among all the nations, whither the
LORD thy God hath driven thee,
2 And shalt [o]return unto the LORD thy
God, and shalt obey his voice according to
all that I command thee this day, thou and
thy children, with all thine heart, and with
all thy soul;
3 [p]That then the LORD thy God will turn
thy captivity, and have compassion upon
thee, and will return and [q]gather thee from
all the nations, whither the LORD thy God
hath scattered thee.
4 [r]If *any* of thine be driven out unto the
outmost *parts* of heaven, from thence will
the LORD thy God gather thee, and from
thence will he fetch thee:
5 And the LORD thy God will bring thee
into the land which thy fathers possessed,
and thou shalt possess it; and he will do thee
good, and multiply thee above thy fathers.
6 And [s]the LORD thy God will circumcise
thine heart, and the heart of thy seed, to
love the LORD thy God with all thine heart,
and with all thy soul, that thou mayest live.
7 And the LORD thy God will put all these
curses upon thine enemies, and on them
that hate thee, which persecuted thee.
8 And thou shalt return and obey the
voice of the LORD, and do all his commandments which I command thee this day.
9 [t]And the LORD thy God will make thee
plenteous in every work of thine hand, in
the fruit of thy body, and in the fruit of thy
cattle, and in the fruit of thy land, for good:
for the LORD will again [u]rejoice over thee
for good, as he rejoiced over thy fathers:
10 If thou shalt hearken unto the voice of
the LORD thy God, to keep his commandments and his statutes which are written in
this book of the law, *and* if thou turn unto
the LORD thy God with all thine heart, and
with all thy soul.
11 ¶ For this commandment which I com-

mand thee this day, [v]it *is* not hidden from
thee, neither *is* it far off.
12 [w]It *is* not in heaven, that thou shouldest say, Who shall go up for us to heaven,
and bring it unto us, that we may hear it,
and do it?
13 Neither *is* it beyond the sea, that thou
shouldest say, Who shall go over the sea for
us, and bring it unto us, that we may hear it,
and do it?
14 But the word *is* very nigh unto thee, in
thy mouth, and in thy heart, that thou mayest do it.
15 ¶ See, [x]I have set before thee this day
life and good, and death and evil;
16 In that I command thee this day to love
the LORD thy God, to walk in his ways, and
to keep his commandments and his statutes,
and his judgments, that thou mayest live
and multiply: and the LORD thy God shall
bless thee in the land whither thou goest to
possess it.
17 But if thine heart turn away, so that
thou wilt not hear, but shalt be drawn away,
and worship other gods, and serve them;
18 [y]I denounce unto you this day, that ye
shall surely perish, *and that* ye shall not
prolong *your* days upon the land, whither
thou passest over Jordan to go to possess it.
19 [z]I call heaven and earth to record this
day against you, *that* [a]I have set before you
life and death, blessing and cursing: therefore choose life, that both thou and thy seed
may live:
20 That thou mayest love the LORD thy
God, *and* that thou mayest obey his voice,
and that thou mayest cleave unto him: for
he *is* thy [b]life, and the length of thy days:
that thou mayest dwell in the land which the
LORD sware unto thy fathers, to Abraham,
to Isaac, and to Jacob, to give them.

31 And Moses went and spake these
words unto all Israel.
2 And he said unto them, I [c]*am* an hundred and twenty years old this day; I can no
more [d]go out and come in: also the LORD
hath said unto me, [e]Thou shalt not go over
this Jordan.
3 The LORD thy God, [f]he will go over before thee, *and* he will destroy these nations
from before thee, and thou shalt possess
them: *and* Joshua, he shall go over before
thee, [g]as the LORD hath said.
4 [h]And the LORD shall do unto them [i]as
he did to Sihon and to Og, kings of the Amorites, and unto the land of them, whom he
destroyed.
5 [j]And the LORD shall give them up before your face, that ye may do unto them
according unto all the commandments
which I have commanded you.
6 [k]Be strong and of a good courage,
[l]fear not, nor be afraid of them: for the
LORD thy God, [m]he *it is* that doth go with
thee; [n]he will not fail thee, nor forsake thee.
7 ¶ And Moses called unto Joshua, and
said unto him in the sight of all Israel, [o]Be
strong and of a good courage: for thou must
go with this people unto the land which the
LORD hath sworn unto their fathers to give
them; and thou shalt cause them to inherit it.
8 And the LORD, [p]he *it is* that doth go
before thee; [q]he will be with thee, he will
not fail thee, neither forsake thee: fear not,
neither be dismayed.
9 ¶ And Moses wrote this law, [r]and delivered it unto the priests the sons of Levi,
[s]which bare the ark of the covenant of the
LORD, and unto all the elders of Israel.
10 And Moses commanded them, saying,
At the end of *every* seven years, in the solemnity of the [t]year of release, [u]in the feast
of tabernacles,
11 When all Israel is come to [v]appear before the LORD thy God in the place which he
shall choose, [w]thou shalt read this law before all Israel in their hearing.
12 [x]Gather the people together, men, and
women, and children, and thy stranger that
is within thy gates, that they may hear, and
that they may learn, and fear the LORD your
God, and observe to do all the words of this
law:
13 And *that* their children, [y]which have
not known *any thing*, [z]may hear, and learn
to fear the LORD your God, as long as ye live
in the land whither ye go over Jordan to
possess it.
14 ¶ And the LORD said unto Moses, [a]Be-
hold, thy days approach that thou must die:
call Joshua, and present yourselves in the
tabernacle of the congregation, that [b]I may
give him a charge. And Moses and Joshua
went, and presented themselves in the tabernacle of the congregation.
15 And [c]the LORD appeared in the tabernacle in a pillar of a cloud: and the pillar of
the cloud stood over the door of the tabernacle.
16 ¶ And the LORD said unto Moses, Behold, thou shalt sleep with thy fathers; and
this people will [d]rise up, and [e]go a whoring
after the gods of the strangers of the land,
whither they go *to be* among them, and will
[f]forsake me, and [g]break my covenant
which I have made with them.
17 Then my anger shall be kindled
against them in that day, and [h]I will forsake
them, and I will [i]hide my face from them,
and they shall be devoured, and many evils
and troubles shall befall them; so that they
will say in that day, [j]Are not these evils
come upon us, because our God *is* [k]not
among us?
18 And [l]I will surely hide my face in that
day for all the evils which they shall have
wrought, in that they are turned unto other
gods.
19 Now therefore write ye this song for
you, and teach it the children of Israel: put
it in their mouths, that this song may be [m]a
witness for me against the children of Israel.
20 For when I shall have brought them
into the land which I sware unto their fa-

30:11 [v]Isa. 45:19
30:12 [w]Rom. 10:6
30:15 [x]ver. 1; ch. 11:26
30:18 [y]ch. 4:26
30:19 [z]ch. 4:26 [a]ver. 15
30:20 [b]Ps. 27:1; John 11:25
31:2 [c]Ex. 7:7; ch. 34:7 [d]Num. 27:17; 1 Kings 3:7 [e]Num. 20:12; ch. 3:27
31:3 [f]ch. 9:3 [g]Num. 27:21; ch. 3:28
31:4 [h]ch. 3:21 [i]Num. 21:24
31:5 [j]ch. 7:2
31:6 [k]Josh. 10:25; 1 Chron. 22:13 [l]ch. 1:29 [m]ch. 20:4 [n]Josh. 1:5; Heb. 13:5
31:7 [o]ver. 23; ch. 1:38; Josh. 1:6
31:8 [p]Ex. 13:21; ch. 9:3 [q]Josh. 1:5; 1 Chron. 28:20
31:9 [r]ver. 25; ch. 17:18 [s]Num. 4:15; Josh. 3:3; 1 Chron. 15:12
31:10 [t]ch. 15:1 [u]Lev. 23:34
31:11 [v]ch. 16:16 [w]Josh. 8:34; 2 Kings 23:2; Neh. 8:1
31:12 [x]ch. 4:10
31:13 [y]ch. 11:2 [z]Ps. 78:6
31:14 [a]Num. 27:13; ch. 34:5 [b]ver. 23; Num. 27:19
31:15 [c]Ex. 33:9
31:16 [d]Ex. 32:6 [e]Ex. 34:15; Judg. 2:17 [f]ch. 32:15; Judg. 2:12 [g]Judg. 2:20
31:17 [h]2 Chron. 15:2 [i]ch. 32:20; Ps. 104:29; Isa. 8:17; Ezek. 39:23 [j]Judg. 6:13 [k]Num. 14:42
31:18 [l]ver. 17
31:19 [m]ver. 26

thers, that floweth with milk and honey;
and they shall have eaten and filled themselves, [n]and waxen fat; [o]then will they turn
unto other gods, and serve them, and provoke me, and break my covenant.
21 And it shall come to pass, [p]when
many evils and troubles are befallen them,
that this song shall testify against them as a
witness; for it shall not be forgotten out of
the mouths of their seed: for [q]I know their
imagination [r]which they go about, even
now, before I have brought them into the
land which I sware.
22 ¶ Moses therefore wrote this song the
same day, and taught it the children of Israel.
23 [s]And he gave Joshua the son of Nun a
charge, and said, [t]Be strong and of a good
courage: for thou shalt bring the children
of Israel into the land which I sware unto
them: and I will be with thee.
24 ¶ And it came to pass, when Moses had
made an end of [u]writing the words of this
law in a book, until they were finished,
25 That Moses commanded the Levites,
which bare the ark of the covenant of the
LORD, saying,
26 Take this book of the law, [v]and put it
in the side of the ark of the covenant of the
LORD your God, that it may be there [w]for a
witness against thee.
27 [x]For I know thy rebellion, and thy
[y]stiff neck: behold, while I am yet alive
with you this day, ye have been rebellious
against the LORD; and how much more after
my death?
28 ¶ Gather unto me all the elders of your
tribes, and your officers, that I may speak
these words in their ears, [z]and call heaven
and earth to record against them.
29 For I know that after my death ye will
utterly [a]corrupt *yourselves,* and turn aside
from the way which I have commanded
you; and [b]evil will befall you [c]in the latter
days; because ye will do evil in the sight of
the LORD, to provoke him to anger through
the work of your hands.
30 And Moses spake in the ears of all the
congregation of Israel the words of this
song, until they were ended.

32
Give [d]ear, O ye heavens, and I will
speak; and hear, O earth, the words
of my mouth.
2 [e]My doctrine shall drop as the rain, my
speech shall distil as the dew, [f]as the small
rain upon the tender herb, and as the showers upon the grass:
3 Because I will publish the name of the
LORD: [g]ascribe ye greatness unto our God.
4 *He is* [h]the Rock, [i]his work *is* perfect:
for [j]all his ways *are* judgment: [k]a God of
truth and [l]without iniquity, just and right
is he.
5 [m]They have corrupted themselves, their
spot *is* not *the spot* of his children: *they are*
a [n]perverse and crooked generation.
6 Do ye thus [o]requite the LORD, O foolish
people and unwise? *is* not he [p]thy father
that hath [q]bought thee? hath he not [r]made
thee, and established thee?
7 ¶ Remember the days of old, consider
the years of many generations: [s]ask thy father, and he will shew thee; thy elders, and
they will tell thee.
8 When the most High [t]divided to the nations their inheritance, when he [u]separated
the sons of Adam, he set the bounds of the
people according to the number of the children of Israel.
9 For [v]the LORD's portion *is* his people;
Jacob *is* the lot of his inheritance.
10 He found him [w]in a desert land, and in
the waste howling wilderness; he led him
about, he [x]instructed him, he [y]kept him as
the apple of his eye.
11 [z]As an eagle stirreth up her nest, flut-
tereth over her young, spreadeth abroad
her wings, taketh them, beareth them on
her wings:
12 *So* the LORD alone did lead him, and
there was no strange god with him.
13 [a]He made him ride on the high places
of the earth, that he might eat the increase
of the fields; and he made him to suck
[b]honey out of the rock, and oil out of the
flinty rock;
14 Butter of kine, and milk of sheep, with
fat of lambs, and rams of the breed of Bashan, and goats, [c]with the fat of kidneys of
wheat; and thou didst drink the pure [d]blood
of the grape.
15 ¶ But [e]Jeshurun waxed fat, and
[f]kicked: [g]thou art waxen fat, thou art
grown thick, thou art covered *with fatness;*
then he [h]forsook God *which* [i]made him,
and lightly esteemed the [j]Rock of his salvation.
16 [k]They provoked him to jealousy with
strange *gods,* with abominations provoked
they him to anger.
17 [l]They sacrificed unto devils, not to
God; to gods whom they knew not, to new
gods that came newly up, whom your fathers feared not.
18 [m]Of the Rock *that* begat thee thou art
unmindful, and hast [n]forgotten God that
formed thee.
19 [o]And when the LORD saw *it,* he abhorred *them,* [p]because of the provoking of
his sons, and of his daughters.
20 And he said, [q]I will hide my face from
them, I will see what their end *shall be:* for
they *are* a very froward generation, [r]chil-
dren in whom *is* no faith.
21 [s]They have moved me to jealousy
with *that which is* not God; they have provoked me to anger [t]with their vanities: and
[u]I will move them to jealousy with *those
which are* not a people; I will provoke them
to anger with a foolish nation.
22 For [v]a fire is kindled in mine anger,
and shall burn unto the lowest hell, and
shall consume the earth with her increase,

31:20 [n]ch. 32:15; Neh. 9:25; Hos. 13:6 [o]ver. 16
31:21 [p]ver. 17 [q]Hos. 5:3 [r]Am. 5:25
31:23 [s]ver. 14 [t]ver. 7; Josh. 1:6
31:24 [u]ver. 9
31:26 [v]2 Kings 22:8 [w]ver. 19
31:27 [x]ch. 9:24 [y]Ex. 32:9; ch. 9:6
31:28 [z]ch. 30:19
31:29 [a]ch. 32:5; Judg. 2:19; Hos. 9:9 [b]ch. 28:15 [c]Gen. 49:1; ch. 4:30
32:1 [d]ch. 4:26; Ps. 50:4; Isa. 1:2; Jer. 2:12
32:2 [e]Isa. 55:10; 1 Cor. 3:6 [f]Ps. 72:6; Mic. 5:7
32:3 [g]1 Chron. 29:11
32:4 [h]2 Sam. 22:3; Ps. 18:2; Hab. 1:12 [i]2 Sam. 22:31 [j]Dan. 4:37; Rev. 15:3 [k]Jer. 10:10 [l]Job 34:10; Ps. 92:15
32:5 [m]ch. 31:29 [n]Matt. 17:17; Luke 9:41; Phil. 2:15
32:6 [o]Ps. 116:12 [p]Isa. 63:16 [q]Ps. 74:2 [r]ver. 15; Isa. 27:11
32:7 [s]Ex. 13:14; Ps. 44:1
32:8 [t]Zech. 9:2; Acts 17:26 [u]Gen. 11:8
32:9 [v]Ex. 15:16; 1 Sam. 10:1; Ps. 78:71
32:10 [w]ch. 8:15; Jer. 2:6; Hos. 13:5 [x]Deut. 4:36 [y]Ps. 17:8; Prov. 7:2; Zech. 2:8
32:11 [z]Ex. 19:4; ch. 1:31; Isa. 31:5; Hos. 11:3
32:13 [a]ch. 33:29; Isa. 58:14 [b]Job 29:6; Ps. 81:16
32:14 [c]Ps. 81:16 [d]Gen. 49:11
32:15 [e]ch. 33:5; Isa. 44:2 [f]1 Sam. 2:29 [g]ch. 31:20; Ps. 17:10; Jer. 2:7 [h]ch. 31:16; Isa. 1:4 [i]ver. 6; Isa. 51:13 [j]2 Sam. 22:47; Ps. 89:26
32:16 [k]1 Kings 14:22; 1 Cor. 10:22
32:17 [l]Lev. 17:7; Ps. 106:37; 1 Cor. 10:20; Rev. 9:20
32:18 [m]Isa. 17:10 [n]Jer. 2:32
32:19 [o]Judg. 2:14 [p]Isa. 1:2
32:20 [q]ch. 31:17 [r]Isa. 30:9; Matt. 17:17
32:21 [s]ver. 16; Ps. 78:58 [t]1 Sam. 12:21; Ps. 31:6; Acts 14:15 [u]Hos. 1:10; Rom. 10:19
32:22 [v]Jer. 15:14; Lam. 4:11

and set on fire the foundations of the mountains.

23 I will [w]heap mischiefs upon them; [x]I will spend mine arrows upon them.

24 *They shall be* burnt with hunger, and devoured with burning heat, and with bitter destruction: I will also send [y]the teeth of beasts upon them, with the poison of serpents of the dust.

25 [z]The sword without, and terror within, shall destroy both the young man and the virgin, the suckling *also* with the man of gray hairs.

26 [a]I said, I would scatter them into corners, I would make the remembrance of them to cease from among men:

27 Were it not that I feared the wrath of the enemy, lest their adversaries [b]should behave themselves strangely, *and* lest they should [c]say, Our hand *is* high, and the LORD hath not done all this.

28 For they *are* a nation void of counsel, [d]neither *is there any* understanding in them.

29 [e]O that they were wise, *that* they understood this, [f]*that* they would consider their latter end!

30 How should [g]one chase a thousand, and two put ten thousand to flight, except their Rock [h]had sold them, and the LORD had shut them up?

31 For [i]their rock *is* not as our Rock, [j]even our enemies themselves *being* judges.

32 For [k]their vine *is* of the vine of Sodom, and of the fields of Gomorrah: their grapes *are* grapes of gall, their clusters *are* bitter:

33 Their wine *is* [l]the poison of dragons, and the cruel [m]venom of asps.

34 *Is* not this [n]laid up in store with me, *and* sealed up among my treasures?

35 [o]To me *belongeth* vengeance, and recompence; their foot shall slide in *due* time: for [p]the day of their calamity *is* at hand, and the things that shall come upon them make haste.

36 [q]For the LORD shall judge his people, [r]and repent himself for his servants, when he seeth that *their* power is gone, and [s]*there is* none shut up, or left.

37 And he shall say, [t]Where *are* their gods, *their* rock in whom they trusted,

38 Which did eat the fat of their sacrifices, *and* drank the wine of their drink offerings? let them rise up and help you, *and* be your protection.

39 See now that [u]I, *even* I, *am* he, and [v]*there is* no god with me: [w]I kill, and I make alive; I wound, and I heal: neither *is there any* that can deliver out of my hand.

40 [x]For I lift up my hand to heaven, and say, I live for ever.

41 [y]If I whet my glittering sword, and mine hand take hold on judgment; [z]I will render vengeance to mine enemies, and will reward them that hate me.

42 I will make mine arrows [a]drunk with blood, and my sword shall devour flesh; *and that* with the blood of the slain and of the captives, from the beginning of [b]revenges upon the enemy.

43 [c]Rejoice, O ye nations, *with* his people: for he will [d]avenge the blood of his servants, and [e]will render vengeance to his adversaries, and [f]will be merciful unto his land, *and* to his people.

44 ¶ And Moses came and spake all the words of this song in the ears of the people, he, and Hoshea the son of Nun.

45 And Moses made an end of speaking all these words to all Israel:

46 And he said unto them, [g]Set your hearts unto all the words which I testify among you this day, which ye shall command your children to observe to do, all the words of this law.

47 For it *is* not a vain thing for you; [h]because it *is* your life: and through this thing ye shall prolong *your* days in the land, whither ye go over Jordan to possess it.

48 [i]And the LORD spake unto Moses that selfsame day, saying,

49 Get thee up into this [j]mountain Abarim, *unto* mount Nebo, which *is* in the land of Moab, that *is* over against Jericho; and behold the land of Canaan, which I give unto the children of Israel for a possession:

50 And die in the mount whither thou goest up, and be gathered unto thy people; as [k]Aaron thy brother died in mount Hor, and was gathered unto his people:

51 Because [l]ye trespassed against me among the children of Israel at the waters of Meribah-Kadesh, in the wilderness of Zin; because ye [m]sanctified me not in the midst of the children of Israel.

52 [n]Yet thou shalt see the land before *thee;* but thou shalt not go thither unto the land which I give the children of Israel.

33 And this *is* [o]the blessing, wherewith Moses [p]the man of God blessed the children of Israel before his death.

2 And he said, [q]The LORD came from Sinai, and rose up from Seir unto them; he shined forth from mount Paran, and he came with [r]ten thousands of saints: from his right hand *went* a fiery law for them.

3 Yea, [s]he loved the people; [t]all his saints *are* in thy hand: and they [u]sat down at thy feet; *every one* shall [v]receive of thy words.

4 [w]Moses commanded us a law, [x]*even* the inheritance of the congregation of Jacob.

5 And he was [y]king in [z]Jeshurun, when the heads of the people *and* the tribes of Israel were gathered together.

6 ¶ Let Reuben live, and not die; and let *not* his men be few.

7 ¶ And this *is the blessing* of Judah: and he said, Hear, LORD, the voice of Judah, and bring him unto his people: [a]let his hands be

32:23 [w]Isa. 26:15 [x]Ps. 7:12
32:24 [y]Lev. 26:22
32:25 [z]Lam. 1:20; 2 Cor. 7:5
32:26 [a]Ezek. 20:13
32:27 [b]Jer. 19:4 [c]Ps. 140:8
32:28 [d]Isa. 27:11
32:29 [e]ch. 5:29; Luke 19:42 [f]Isa. 47:7; Lam. 1:9
32:30 [g]Josh. 23:10 [h]Ps. 44:12; Isa. 50:1
32:31 [i]1 Sam. 2:2 [j]1 Sam. 4:8
32:32 [k]Isa. 1:10
32:33 [l]Ps. 58:4 [m]Ps. 140:3; Rom. 3:13
32:34 [n]Job 14:17; Rom. 2:5
32:35 [o]Ps. 94:1; Rom. 12:19 [p]2 Pet. 2:3
32:36 [q]Ps. 135:14 [r]Judg. 2:18 [s]1 Kings 14:10; 2 Kings 9:8
32:37 [t]Judg. 10:14
32:39 [u]Ps. 102:27; Isa. 41:4 [v]Isa. 45:5 [w]1 Sam. 2:6; Ps. 68:20
32:40 [x]Gen. 14:22
32:41 [y]Isa. 27:1 [z]Isa. 1:24
32:42 [a]Jer. 46:10 [b]Job 13:24
32:43 [c]Rom. 15:10 [d]Rev. 6:10 [e]ver. 41 [f]Ps. 35:1
32:46 [g]ch. 6:6; Ezek. 40:4
32:47 [h]ch. 30:19; Lev. 18:5; Prov. 3:2; Rom. 10:5
32:48 [i]Num. 27:12
32:49 [j]Num. 33:47; ch. 34:1
32:50 [k]Num. 20:25
32:51 [l]Num. 20:11 [m]Lev. 10:3
32:52 [n]Num. 27:12; ch. 34:4
33:1 [o]Gen. 49:28 [p]Ps. 90, title
33:2 [q]Ex. 19:18; Judg. 5:4; Hab. 3:3 [r]Ps. 68:17; Dan. 7:10; Acts 7:53; Gal. 3:19; Heb. 2:2; Rev. 5:11
33:3 [s]Ex. 19:5; ch. 7:7; Ps. 47:4; Hos. 11:1; Mal. 1:2 [t]ch. 7:6; 1 Sam. 2:9; Ps. 50:5 [u]Luke 10:39; Acts 22:3 [v]Prov. 2:1
33:4 [w]John 1:17 [x]Ps. 119:111
33:5 [y]Gen. 36:31; Judg. 9:2 [z]ch. 32:15
33:7 [a]Gen. 49:8

sufficient for him; and be thou [b]an help *to him* from his enemies.

8 ¶ And of Levi he said, [c]*Let* thy Thummim and thy Urim *be* with thy holy one, [d]whom thou didst prove at Massah, *and with* whom thou didst strive at the waters of Meribah;

9 Who said unto his father and to his mother, I have not [e]seen him; [f]neither did he acknowledge his brethren, nor knew his own children: for [g]they have observed thy word, and kept thy covenant.

10 [h]They shall teach Jacob thy judgments, and Israel thy law: [i]they shall put incense before thee, [j]and whole burnt sacrifice upon thine altar.

11 Bless, LORD, his substance, and [k]accept the work of his hands: smite through the loins of them that rise against him, and of them that hate him, that they rise not again.

12 ¶ *And* of Benjamin he said, The beloved of the LORD shall dwell in safety by him; *and the LORD* shall cover him all the day long, and he shall dwell between his shoulders.

13 ¶ And of Joseph he said, [l]Blessed of the LORD *be* his land, for the precious things of heaven, for [m]the dew, and for the deep that coucheth beneath,

14 And for the precious fruits *brought forth* by the sun, and for the precious things put forth by the moon,

15 And for the chief things of [n]the ancient mountains, and for the precious things [o]of the lasting hills,

16 And for the precious things of the earth and fulness thereof, and *for* the good will of [p]him that dwelt in the bush: let *the blessing* [q]come upon the head of Joseph, and upon the top of the head of him *that was* separated from his brethren.

17 His glory *is like* the [r]firstling of his bullock, and his horns *are like* [s]the horns of unicorns: with them [t]he shall push the people together to the ends of the earth: and [u]they *are* the ten thousands of Ephraim, and they *are* the thousands of Manasseh.

18 ¶ And of Zebulun he said, [v]Rejoice, Zebulun, in thy going out; and, Issachar, in thy tents.

19 They shall [w]call the people unto the mountain; there [x]they shall offer sacrifices of righteousness: for they shall suck *of* the abundance of the seas, and *of* treasures hid in the sand.

20 ¶ And of Gad he said, Blessed *be* he that [y]enlargeth Gad: he dwelleth as a lion, and teareth the arm with the crown of the head.

21 And [z]he provided the first part for himself, because there, *in* a portion of the lawgiver, *was he* seated; and [a]he came with the heads of the people, he executed the justice of the LORD, and his judgments with Israel.

33:7 [b]Ps. 146:5
33:8 [c]Ex. 28:30
33:8 [d]Ex. 17:7; Num. 20:13; ch. 8:2; Ps. 81:7
33:9 [e]Gen. 29:32; 1 Chron. 17:17; Job 37:24 [f]Ex. 32:26 [g]Jer. 18:18; Mal. 2:5
33:10 [h]Lev. 10:11; ch. 17:9; Ezek. 44:23; Mal. 2:7 [i]Ex. 30:7; Num. 16:40; 1 Sam. 2:28 [j]Lev. 1:9; Ps. 51:19; Ezek. 43:27
33:11 [k]2 Sam. 24:23; Ps. 20:3; Ezek. 20:40
33:13 [l]Gen. 49:25 [m]Gen. 27:28
33:15 [n]Gen. 49:26 [o]Hab. 3:6
33:16 [p]Ex. 3:2; Acts 7:30 [q]Gen. 49:26
33:17 [r]1 Chron. 5:1 [s]Num. 23:22; Ps. 92:10 [t]1 Kings 22:11; Ps. 44:5 [u]Gen. 48:19
33:18 [v]Gen. 49:13
33:19 [w]Isa. 2:3 [x]Ps. 4:5
33:20 [y]Josh. 13:10; 1 Chron. 12:8
33:21 [z]Num. 32:16 [a]Josh. 4:12
33:22 [b]Josh. 19:47; Judg. 18:27
33:23 [c]Gen. 49:21 [d]Josh. 19:32
33:24 [e]Gen. 49:20 [f]Job 29:6
33:25 [g]ch. 8:9
33:26 [h]Ex. 15:11; Ps. 86:8; Jer. 10:6 [i]ch. 32:15 [j]Ps. 68:4; Hab. 3:8
33:27 [k]Ps. 90:1 [l]ch. 9:3
33:28 [m]Num. 23:9; Jer. 23:6 [n]ch. 8:7 [o]Gen. 27:28; ch. 11:11
33:29 [p]Ps. 144:15 [q]2 Sam. 7:23 [r]Ps. 115:9 [s]2 Sam. 22:45; Ps. 18:44 [t]ch. 32:13
34:1 [u]Num. 27:12; ch. 32:49 [v]ch. 3:27 [w]Gen. 14:14
34:2 [x]ch. 11:24
34:3 [y]Judg. 1:16; 2 Chron. 28:15
34:4 [z]Gen. 12:7 [a]ch. 3:27
34:5 [b]ch. 32:50; Josh. 1:1
34:6 [c]Jude 9
34:7 [d]ch. 31:2 [e]Gen. 27:1; Josh. 14:10
34:8 [f]Gen. 50:3; Num. 20:29
34:9 [g]Isa. 11:2; Dan. 6:3 [h]Num. 27:18

22 ¶ And of Dan he said, Dan *is* a lion's whelp: [b]he shall leap from Bashan.

23 ¶ And of Naphtali he said, O Naphtali, [c]satisfied with favour, and full with the blessing of the LORD: [d]possess thou the west and the south.

24 ¶ And of Asher he said, [e]*Let* Asher *be* blessed with children; let him be acceptable to his brethren, and let him [f]dip his foot in oil.

25 Thy shoes *shall be* [g]iron and brass; and as thy days, *so shall* thy strength *be.*

26 ¶ *There is* [h]none like unto the God of [i]Jeshurun, [j]*who* rideth upon the heaven in thy help, and in his excellency on the sky.

27 The eternal God *is thy* [k]refuge, and underneath *are* the everlasting arms: and [l]he shall thrust out the enemy from before thee; and shall say, Destroy *them.*

28 [m]Israel then shall dwell in safety alone: [n]the fountain of Jacob *shall be* upon a land of corn and wine; also his [o]heavens shall drop down dew.

29 [p]Happy *art* thou, O Israel: [q]who *is* like unto thee, O people saved by the LORD, [r]the shield of thy help, and who *is* the sword of thy excellency! And thine enemies [s]shall be found liars unto thee; and [t]thou shalt tread upon their high places.

34

And Moses went up from the plains of Moab [u]unto the mountain of Nebo, to the top of Pisgah, that *is* over against Jericho. And the LORD [v]shewed him all the land of Gilead, [w]unto Dan,

2 And all Naphtali, and the land of Ephraim, and Manasseh, and all the land of Judah, [x]unto the utmost sea,

3 And the south, and the plain of the valley of Jericho, [y]the city of palm trees, unto Zoar.

4 And the LORD said unto him, [z]This *is* the land which I sware unto Abraham, unto Isaac, and unto Jacob, saying, I will give it unto thy seed: [a]I have caused thee to see *it* with thine eyes, but thou shalt not go over thither.

5 ¶ [b]So Moses the servant of the LORD died there in the land of Moab, according to the word of the LORD.

6 And he buried him in a valley in the land of Moab, over against Beth-peor: but [c]no man knoweth of his sepulchre unto this day.

7 ¶ [d]And Moses *was* an hundred and twenty years old when he died: [e]his eye was not dim, nor his natural force abated.

8 ¶ And the children of Israel wept for Moses in the plains of Moab [f]thirty days: so the days of weeping *and* mourning for Moses were ended.

9 ¶ And Joshua the son of Nun was full of the [g]spirit of wisdom; for [h]Moses had laid his hands upon him: and the children of Israel hearkened unto him, and did as the LORD commanded Moses.

10 ¶ And there [i]arose not a prophet since
in Israel like unto Moses, [j]whom the LORD
knew face to face,
11 In all [k]the signs and the wonders,
which the LORD sent him to do in the land of
Egypt to Pharaoh, and to all his servants,
and to all his land,
12 And in all that mighty hand, and in all
the great terror which Moses shewed in the
sight of all Israel.

34:10 [i]ch. 18:15 [j]Ex. 33:11; Num. 12:6; ch. 5:4
34:11 [k]ch. 4:34

JOSHUA

The book of Joshua was written by him except the account of his death in chapter 24. The date of writing could be as early as 1400 B.C., or as late as 1200 B.C. In this book the Israelites cross the Jordan into the land of Canaan with Joshua now the heir to Moses' leadership. There are two distinct parts to the book, the first describes the conquest of Canaan, the second gives explicit details of the dividing of the land among the tribes.

Probably the most recognized scriptures in the book are those describing the story of Joshua and the Israelites' conquest of the city of Jericho (6:1–6:27).

- **I. Entering the land of Canaan and conquering it, 1:1–12:24**
- **II. Dividing the land, 13:1–21:45**
- **III. Joshua's farewell, 22:1–24:33**

---

1 Now after the death of Moses the servant of the LORD it came to pass, that
the LORD spake unto Joshua the son of Nun,
Moses' [a]minister, saying,
2 [b]Moses my servant is dead; now therefore arise, go over this Jordan, thou, and all
this people, unto the land which I do give to
them, *even* to the children of Israel.
3 [c]Every place that the sole of your foot
shall tread upon, that have I given unto you,
as I said unto Moses.
4 [d]From the wilderness and this Lebanon
even unto the great river, the river Euphrates, all the land of the Hittites, and unto the
great sea toward the going down of the sun,
shall be your coast.
5 [e]There shall not any man be able to
stand before thee all the days of thy life: [f]as
I was with Moses, *so* [g]I will be with thee: [h]I
will not fail thee, nor forsake thee.
6 [i]Be strong and of a good courage: for
unto this people shalt thou divide for an inheritance the land, which I sware unto their
fathers to give them.
7 Only be thou strong and very courageous, that thou mayest observe to do according to all the law, [j]which Moses my
servant commanded thee: [k]turn not from it
to the right hand or *to* the left, that thou
mayest prosper whithersoever thou goest.
8 [l]This book of the law shall not depart
out of thy mouth; but [m]thou shalt meditate
therein day and night, that thou mayest observe to do according to all that is written
therein: for then thou shalt make thy way
prosperous, and then thou shalt have good
success.
9 [n]Have not I commanded thee? Be
strong and of a good courage; [o]be not
afraid, neither be thou dismayed: for the
LORD thy God *is* with thee whithersoever
thou goest.
10 ¶ Then Joshua commanded the officers of the people, saying,
11 Pass through the host, and command
the people, saying, Prepare you victuals; for
[p]within three days ye shall pass over this
Jordan, to go in to possess the land, which
the LORD your God giveth you to possess it.
12 ¶ And to the Reubenites, and to the
Gadites, and to half the tribe of Manasseh,
spake Joshua, saying,
13 Remember [q]the word which Moses
the servant of the LORD commanded you,
saying, The LORD your God hath given you
rest, and hath given you this land.
14 Your wives, your little ones, and your
cattle, shall remain in the land which Moses
gave you on this side Jordan; but ye shall
pass before your brethren armed, all the
mighty men of valour, and help them;
15 Until the LORD have given your brethren rest, as *he hath given* you, and they also
have possessed the land which the LORD
your God giveth them: [r]then ye shall return
unto the land of your possession, and enjoy
it, which Moses the LORD's servant gave
you on this side Jordan toward the sunrising.
16 ¶ And they answered Joshua, saying,
All that thou commandest us we will do,
and whithersoever thou sendest us, we
will go.
17 According as we hearkened unto Moses in all things, so will we hearken unto
thee: only the LORD thy God [s]be with thee,
as he was with Moses.
18 Whosoever *he be* that doth rebel
against thy commandment, and will not
hearken unto thy words in all that thou

1:1 [a]Ex. 24:13; Deut. 1:38
1:2 [b]Deut. 34:5
1:3 [c]Deut. 11:24; ch. 14:9
1:4 [d]Gen. 15:18; Ex. 23:31; Num. 34:3-12
1:5 [e]Deut. 7:24 [f]Ex. 3:12 [g]Deut. 31:8; ver. 9:17; ch. 3:7; Isa. 43:2 [h]Deut. 31:6; Heb. 13:5
1:6 [i]Deut. 31:7
1:7 [j]Num. 27:23; Deut. 31:7; ch. 11:15 [k]Deut. 5:32
1:8 [l]Deut. 17:18 [m]Ps. 1:2
1:9 [n]Deut. 31:7 [o]Ps. 27:1; Jer. 1:8
1:11 [p]Deut. 9:1; ch. 3:2
1:13 [q]Num. 32:20-28; ch. 22:2
1:15 [r]ch. 22:4
1:17 [s]ver. 5; 1 Sam. 20:13; 1 Kings 1:37

commandest him, he shall be put to death: only be strong and of a good courage.

2 And Joshua the son of Nun sent [t]out of Shittim two men to spy secretly, saying, Go view the land, even Jericho. And they went, and [u]came into an harlot's house, named [v]Rahab, and lodged there.

2 And [w]it was told the king of Jericho, saying, Behold, there came men in hither to night of the children of Israel to search out the country.

3 And the king of Jericho sent unto Rahab, saying, Bring forth the men that are come to thee, which are entered into thine house: for they be come to search out all the country.

4 [x]And the woman took the two men, and hid them, and said thus, There came men unto me, but I wist not whence they *were:*

5 And it came to pass *about the time* of shutting of the gate, when it was dark, that the men went out: whither the men went I wot not: pursue after them quickly; for ye shall overtake them.

6 But [y]she had brought them up to the roof of the house, and hid them with the stalks of flax, which she had laid in order upon the roof.

7 And the men pursued after them the way to Jordan unto the fords: and as soon as they which pursued after them were gone out, they shut the gate.

8 ¶ And before they were laid down, she came up unto them upon the roof;

9 And she said unto the men, I know that the LORD hath given you the land, and that [z]your terror is fallen upon us, and that all the inhabitants of the land faint because of you.

10 For we have heard how the LORD [a]dried up the water of the Red sea for you, when ye came out of Egypt; and [b]what ye did unto the two kings of the Amorites, that *were* on the other side Jordan, Sihon and Og, whom ye utterly destroyed.

11 And as soon as we had [c]heard *these things,* [d]our hearts did melt, neither did there remain any more courage in any man, because of you: for [e]the LORD your God, he *is* God in heaven above, and in earth beneath.

12 Now therefore, I pray you, [f]swear unto me by the LORD, since I have shewed you kindness, that ye will also shew kindness unto [g]my father's house, and [h]give me a true token:

13 And *that* ye will save alive my father, and my mother, and my brethren, and my sisters, and all that they have, and deliver our lives from death.

14 And the men answered her, Our life for your's, if ye utter not this our business. And it shall be, when the LORD hath given us the land, that [i]we will deal kindly and truly with thee.

15 Then she [j]let them down by a cord through the window: for her house *was* upon the town wall, and she dwelt upon the wall.

16 And she said unto them, Get you to the mountain, lest the pursuers meet you; and hide yourselves there three days, until the pursuers be returned: and afterward may ye go your way.

17 And the men said unto her, We *will be* [k]blameless of this thine oath which thou hast made us swear.

18 [l]Behold, *when* we come into the land, thou shalt bind this line of scarlet thread in the window which thou didst let us down by: [m]and thou shalt bring thy father, and thy mother, and thy brethren, and all thy father's household, home unto thee.

19 And it shall be, *that* whosoever shall go out of the doors of thy house into the street, his blood *shall be* upon his head, and we *will be* guiltless: and whosoever shall be with thee in the house, [n]his blood *shall be* on our head, if *any* hand be upon him.

20 And if thou utter this our business, then we will be quit of thine oath which thou hast made us to swear.

21 And she said, According unto your words, so *be* it. And she sent them away, and they departed: and she bound the scarlet line in the window.

22 And they went, and came unto the mountain, and abode there three days, until the pursuers were returned: and the pursuers sought *them* throughout all the way, but found *them* not.

23 ¶ So the two men returned, and descended from the mountain, and passed over, and came to Joshua the son of Nun, and told him all *things* that befell them:

24 And they said unto Joshua, Truly [o]the LORD hath delivered into our hands all the land; for even all the inhabitants of the country do faint because of us.

3 And Joshua rose early in the morning; and they removed [p]from Shittim, and came to Jordan, he and all the children of Israel, and lodged there before they passed over.

2 And it came to pass [q]after three days, that the officers went through the host;

3 And they commanded the people, saying, [r]When ye see the ark of the covenant of the LORD your God, [s]and the priests the Levites bearing it, then ye shall remove from your place, and go after it.

4 [t]Yet there shall be a space between you and it, about two thousand cubits by measure: come not near unto it, that ye may know the way by which ye must go: for ye have not passed *this* way heretofore.

5 And Joshua said unto the people, [u]Sanctify yourselves: for to morrow the LORD will do wonders among you.

6 And Joshua spake unto the priests, saying, [v]Take up the ark of the covenant, and pass over before the people. And they took up the ark of the covenant, and went before the people.

7 ¶ And the LORD said unto Joshua, This

2:1 *t*Num. 25:1 *u*Heb. 11:31; Jam. 2:25 *v*Matt. 1:5
2:2 *w*Ps. 127:1; Prov. 21:30
2:4 *x*2 Sam. 17:19
2:6 *y*Ex. 1:17; 2 Sam. 17:19
2:9 *z*Gen. 35:5; Ex. 23:27; Deut. 2:25
2:10 *a*Ex. 14:21; ch. 4:23 *b*Num. 21:24
2:11 *c*Ex. 15:14 *d*ch. 5:1; Isa. 13:7 *e*Deut. 4:39
2:12 *f*1 Sam. 20:14 *g*1 Tim. 5:8 *h*ver. 18
2:14 *i*Judg. 1:24; Matt. 5:7
2:15 *j*Acts 9:25
2:17 *k*Ex. 20:7
2:18 *l*ver. 12 *m*ch. 6:23
2:19 *n*Matt. 27:25
2:24 *o*Ex. 23:31; ch. 6:2
3:1 *p*ch. 2:1
3:2 *q*ch. 1:10
3:3 *r*Num. 10:33 *s*Deut. 31:9
3:4 *t*Ex. 19:12
3:5 *u*Ex. 19:10; Lev. 20:7; Num. 11:18; ch. 7:13; 1 Sam. 16:5; Joel 2:16
3:6 *v*Num. 4:15

day will I begin to [w]magnify thee in the sight of all Israel, that they may know that, [x]as I was with Moses, *so* I will be with thee.

8 And thou shalt command [y]the priests that bear the ark of the covenant, saying, When ye are come to the brink of the water of Jordan, [z]ye shall stand still in Jordan.

9 ¶ And Joshua said unto the children of Israel, Come hither, and hear the words of the LORD your God.

10 And Joshua said, Hereby ye shall know that [a]the living God *is* among you, and *that* he will without fail [b]drive out from before you the Canaanites, and the Hittites, and the Hivites, and the Perizzites, and the Girgashites, and the Amorites, and the Jebusites.

11 Behold, the ark of the covenant of [c]the Lord of all the earth passeth over before you into Jordan.

12 Now therefore [d]take you twelve men out of the tribes of Israel, out of every tribe a man.

13 And it shall come to pass, [e]as soon as the soles of the feet of the priests that bear the ark of the LORD, [f]the Lord of all the earth, shall rest in the waters of Jordan, *that* the waters of Jordan shall be cut off *from* the waters that come down from above; and they [g]shall stand upon an heap.

14 ¶ And it came to pass, when the people removed from their tents, to pass over Jordan, and the priests bearing the [h]ark of the covenant before the people;

15 And as they that bare the ark were come unto Jordan, and [i]the feet of the priests that bare the ark were dipped in the brim of the water, (for [j]Jordan overfloweth all his banks [k]all the time of harvest,)

16 That the waters which came down from above stood *and* rose up upon an heap very far from the city Adam, that *is* beside [l]Zaretan: and those that came down [m]toward the sea of the plain, *even* [n]the salt sea, failed, *and* were cut off: and the people passed over right against Jericho.

17 And the priests that bare the ark of the covenant of the LORD stood firm on dry ground in the midst of Jordan, [o]and all the Israelites passed over on dry ground, until all the people were passed clean over Jordan.

4 And it came to pass, when all the people were clean passed [p]over Jordan, that the LORD spake unto Joshua, saying,

2 [q]Take you twelve men out of the people, out of every tribe a man,

3 And command ye them, saying, Take you hence out of the midst of Jordan, out of the place where [r]the priests' feet stood firm, twelve stones, and ye shall carry them over with you, and leave them in [s]the lodging place, where ye shall lodge this night.

4 Then Joshua called the twelve men, whom he had prepared of the children of Israel, out of every tribe a man:

5 And Joshua said unto them, Pass over before the ark of the LORD your God into the midst of Jordan, and take ye up every man of you a stone upon his shoulder, according unto the number of the tribes of the children of Israel:

6 That this may be a sign among you, *that* [t]when your children ask *their fathers* in time to come, saying, What *mean* ye by these stones?

7 Then ye shall answer them, That [u]the waters of Jordan were cut off before the ark of the covenant of the LORD; when it passed over Jordan, the waters of Jordan were cut off: and these stones shall be for [v]a memorial unto the children of Israel for ever.

8 And the children of Israel did so as Joshua commanded, and took up twelve stones out of the midst of Jordan, as the LORD spake unto Joshua, according to the number of the tribes of the children of Israel, and carried them over with them unto the place where they lodged, and laid them down there.

9 And Joshua set up twelve stones in the midst of Jordan, in the place where the feet of the priests which bare the ark of the covenant stood: and they are there unto this day.

10 ¶ For the priests which bare the ark stood in the midst of Jordan, until every thing was finished that the LORD commanded Joshua to speak unto the people, according to all that Moses commanded Joshua: and the people hasted and passed over.

11 And it came to pass, when all the people were clean passed over, that the ark of the LORD passed over, and the priests, in the presence of the people.

12 And [w]the children of Reuben, and the children of Gad, and half the tribe of Manasseh, passed over armed before the children of Israel, as Moses spake unto them:

13 About forty thousand prepared for war passed over before the LORD unto battle, to the plains of Jericho.

14 ¶ On that day the LORD [x]magnified Joshua in the sight of all Israel; and they feared him, as they feared Moses, all the days of his life.

15 And the LORD spake unto Joshua, saying,

16 Command the priests that bear [y]the ark of the testimony, that they come up out of Jordan.

17 Joshua therefore commanded the priests, saying, Come ye up out of Jordan.

18 And it came to pass, when the priests that bare the ark of the covenant of the LORD were come up out of the midst of Jordan, *and* the soles of the priests' feet were lifted up unto the dry land, that the waters of Jordan returned unto their place, [z]and flowed over all his banks, as *they did* before.

19 ¶ And the people came up out of Jordan on the tenth *day* of the first month, and encamped [a]in Gilgal, in the east border of Jericho.

3:7 [w]ch. 4:14; 1 Chron. 29:25; 2 Chron. 1:1 [x]ch. 1:5
3:8 [y]ver. 3 [z]ver. 17
3:10 [a]Deut. 5:26; 1 Sam. 17:26; 2 Kings 19:4; Hos. 1:10; Matt. 16:16; 1 Thess. 1:9 [b]Ex. 33:2; Deut. 7:1; Ps. 44:2
3:11 [c]ver. 13; Mic. 4:13; Zech. 4:14
3:12 [d]ch. 4:2
3:13 [e]ver. 15 [f]ver. 11 [g]Ps. 78:13
3:14 [h]Acts 7:45
3:15 [i]ver. 13 [j]1 Chron. 12:15; Jer. 12:5 [k]ch. 4:18
3:16 [l]1 Kings 4:12 [m]Deut. 3:17 [n]Gen. 14:3; Num. 34:3
3:17 [o]Ex. 14:29
4:1 [p]Deut. 27:2; ch. 3:17
4:2 [q]ch. 3:12
4:3 [r]ch. 3:13 [s]ver. 19
4:6 [t]ver. 21; Ex. 12:26; Deut. 6:20; Ps. 44:1
4:7 [u]ch. 3:13 [v]Ex. 12:14; Num. 16:40
4:12 [w]Num. 32:20
4:14 [x]ch. 3:7
4:16 [y]Ex. 25:16
4:18 [z]ch. 3:15
4:19 [a]ch. 5:9

20 And [b]those twelve stones, which they
took out of Jordan, did Joshua pitch in Gilgal.
21 And he spake unto the children of Israel, saying, [c]When your children shall ask
their fathers in time to come, saying, What
mean these stones?
22 Then ye shall let your children know,
saying, [d]Israel came over this Jordan on
dry land.
23 For the LORD your God dried up the
waters of Jordan from before you, until ye
were passed over, as the LORD your God did
to the Red sea, [e]which he dried up from
before us, until we were gone over:
24 [f]That all the people of the earth might
know the hand of the LORD, that it *is*
[g]mighty: that ye might [h]fear the LORD your
God for ever.

5 And it came to pass, when all the kings
of the Amorites, which *were* on the side
of Jordan westward, and all the kings of
the Canaanites, [i]which *were* by the sea,
[j]heard that the LORD had dried up the waters of Jordan from before the children of
Israel, until we were passed over, that their
heart melted, [k]neither was there spirit in
them any more, because of the children of
Israel.
2 ¶ At that time the LORD said unto
Joshua, Make thee [l]sharp knives, and circumcise again the children of Israel the second time.
3 And Joshua made him sharp knives,
and circumcised the children of Israel at the
hill of the foreskins.
4 And this *is* the cause why Joshua did
circumcise: [m]All the people that came out of
Egypt, *that were* males, *even* all the men of
war, died in the wilderness by the way, after
they came out of Egypt.
5 Now all the people that came out were
circumcised: but all the people *that were*
born in the wilderness by the way as they
came forth out of Egypt, *them* they had not
circumcised.
6 For the children of Israel walked [n]forty
years in the wilderness, till all the people
that were men of war, which came out
of Egypt, were consumed, because they
obeyed not the voice of the LORD: unto
whom the LORD sware that [o]he would not
shew them the land, which the LORD sware
unto their fathers that he would give us, [p]a
land that floweth with milk and honey.
7 And [q]their children, *whom* he raised up
in their stead, them Joshua circumcised: for
they were uncircumcised, because they had
not circumcised them by the way.
8 And it came to pass, when they had
done circumcising all the people, that they
abode in their places in the camp, [r]till they
were whole.
9 And the LORD said unto Joshua, This
day have I rolled away [s]the reproach of
Egypt from off you. Wherefore the name of
the place is called [t]Gilgal unto this day.
10 ¶ And the children of Israel encamped
in Gilgal, and kept the passover [u]on the
fourteenth day of the month at even in the
plains of Jericho.
11 And they did eat of the old corn of the
land on the morrow after the passover, unleavened cakes, and parched *corn* in the
selfsame day.
12 ¶ And [v]the manna ceased on the morrow after they had eaten of the old corn of
the land; neither had the children of Israel
manna any more; but they did eat of the
fruit of the land of Canaan that year.
13 ¶ And it came to pass, when Joshua
was by Jericho, that he lifted up his eyes
and looked, and, behold, there stood [w]a
man over against him [x]with his sword
drawn in his hand: and Joshua went unto
him, and said unto him, *Art* thou for us, or
for our adversaries?
14 And he said, Nay; but *as* captain of
the host of the LORD am I now come. And
Joshua [y]fell on his face to the earth, and did
worship, and said unto him, What saith my
lord unto his servant?
15 And the captain of the LORD's host said
unto Joshua, [z]Loose thy shoe from off thy
foot; for the place whereon thou standest *is*
holy. And Joshua did so.

6 Now Jericho was straitly shut up because of the children of Israel: none
went out, and none came in.
2 And the LORD said unto Joshua, See, [a]I
have given into thine hand Jericho, and the
[b]king thereof, *and* the mighty men of valour.
3 And ye shall compass the city, all *ye*
men of war, *and* go round about the city
once. Thus shalt thou do six days.
4 And seven priests shall bear before the
ark seven [c]trumpets of rams' horns: and
the seventh day ye shall compass the city
seven times, and [d]the priests shall blow
with the trumpets.
5 And it shall come to pass, that when
they make a long *blast* with the ram's horn,
and when ye hear the sound of the trumpet,
all the people shall shout with a great shout;
and the wall of the city shall fall down flat,
and the people shall ascend up every man
straight before him.
6 ¶ And Joshua the son of Nun called the
priests, and said unto them, Take up the ark
of the covenant, and let seven priests bear
seven trumpets of rams' horns before the
ark of the LORD.
7 And he said unto the people, Pass on,
and compass the city, and let him that is
armed pass on before the ark of the LORD.
8 ¶ And it came to pass, when Joshua had
spoken unto the people, that the seven
priests bearing the seven trumpets of rams'
horns passed on before the LORD, and blew
with the trumpets: and the ark of the covenant of the LORD followed them.
9 ¶ And the armed men went before the
priests that blew with the trumpets, [e]and
the rereward came after the ark, *the priests*
going on, and blowing with the trumpets.

4:20 [b]ver. 3
4:21 [c]ver. 6
4:22 [d]ch. 3:17
4:23 [e]Ex. 14:21
4:24 [f]1 Kings 8:42; 2 Kings 19:19; Ps. 106:8 [g]Ex. 15:16; 1 Chron. 29:12; Ps. 89:13 [h]Ex. 14:31; Deut. 6:2; Ps. 89:7; Jer. 10:7
5:1 [i]Num. 13:29 [j]Ex. 15:14; ch. 2:9; Ps. 48:6; Ezek. 21:7 [k]1 Kings 10:5
5:2 [l]Ex. 4:25
5:4 [m]Num. 14:29; Deut. 2:16
5:6 [n]Num. 14:33; Deut. 1:3; Ps. 95:10 [o]Num. 14:23; Ps. 95:11; Heb. 3:11 [p]Ex. 3:8
5:7 [q]Num. 14:31; Deut. 1:39
5:8 [r]Gen. 34:25
5:9 [s]Gen. 34:14; Lev. 18:3; ch. 24:14; 1 Sam. 14:6; Ezek. 20:7 [t]ch. 4:19
5:10 [u]Ex. 12:6; Num. 9:5
5:12 [v]Ex. 16:35
5:13 [w]Gen. 18:2; Ex. 23:23; Zech. 1:8; Acts 1:10 [x]Num. 22:23
5:14 [y]Gen. 17:3
5:15 [z]Ex. 3:5; Acts 7:33
6:2 [a]ch. 2:9 [b]Deut. 7:24
6:4 [c]Judg. 7:16 [d]Num. 10:8
6:9 [e]Num. 10:25

10 And Joshua had commanded the people, saying, Ye shall not shout, nor make any noise with your voice, neither shall *any* word proceed out of your mouth, until the day I bid you shout; then shall ye shout.

11 So the ark of the LORD compassed the city, going about *it* once: and they came into the camp, and lodged in the camp.

12 ¶ And Joshua rose early in the morning, [f]and the priests took up the ark of the LORD.

13 And seven priests bearing seven trumpets of rams' horns before the ark of the LORD went on continually, and blew with the trumpets: and the armed men went before them; but the rereward came after the ark of the LORD, *the priests* going on, and blowing with the trumpets.

14 And the second day they compassed the city once, and returned into the camp: so they did six days.

15 And it came to pass on the seventh day, that they rose early about the dawning of the day, and compassed the city after the same manner seven times: only on that day they compassed the city seven times.

16 And it came to pass at the seventh time, when the priests blew with the trumpets, Joshua said unto the people, Shout; for the LORD hath given you the city.

17 ¶ And the city shall be accursed, *even* it, and all that *are* therein, to the LORD: only Rahab the harlot shall live, she and all that *are* with her in the house, because [g]she hid the messengers that we sent.

18 And ye, [h]in any wise keep *yourselves* from the accursed thing, lest ye make *yourselves* accursed, when ye take of the accursed thing, and make the camp of Israel a curse, [i]and trouble it.

19 But all the silver, and gold, and vessels of brass and iron, *are* consecrated unto the LORD: they shall come into the treasury of the LORD.

20 So the people shouted when *the priests* blew with the trumpets: and it came to pass, when the people heard the sound of the trumpet, and the people shouted with a great shout, that [j]the wall fell down flat, so that the people went up into the city, every man straight before him, and they took the city.

21 And they [k]utterly destroyed all that *was* in the city, both man and woman, young and old, and ox, and sheep, and ass, with the edge of the sword.

22 But Joshua had said unto the two men that had spied out the country, Go into the harlot's house, and bring out thence the woman, and all that she hath, [l]as ye sware unto her.

23 And the young men that were spies went in, and brought out Rahab, [m]and her father, and her mother, and her brethren, and all that she had; and they brought out all her kindred, and left them without the camp of Israel.

24 And they burnt the city with fire, and all that *was* therein: [n]only the silver, and the gold, and the vessels of brass and of iron, they put into the treasury of the house of the LORD.

25 And Joshua saved Rahab the harlot alive, and her father's household, and all that she had; and [o]she dwelleth in Israel *even* unto this day; because she hid the messengers, which Joshua sent to spy out Jericho.

26 ¶ And Joshua adjured *them* at that time, saying, [p]Cursed *be* the man before the LORD, that riseth up and buildeth this city Jericho: he shall lay the foundation thereof in his firstborn, and in his youngest *son* shall he set up the gates of it.

27 [q]So the LORD was with Joshua; and [r]his fame was *noised* throughout all the country.

7 But the children of Israel committed a trespass in the accursed thing: for [s]Achan, the son of Carmi, the son of Zabdi, the son of Zerah, of the tribe of Judah, took of the accursed thing: and the anger of the LORD was kindled against the children of Israel.

2 And Joshua sent men from Jericho to Ai, which *is* beside Beth-aven, on the east side of Beth-el, and spake unto them, saying, Go up and view the country. And the men went up and viewed Ai.

3 And they returned to Joshua, and said unto him, Let not all the people go up; but let about two or three thousand men go up and smite Ai; *and* make not all the people to labour thither; for they *are but* few.

4 So there went up thither of the people about three thousand men: [t]and they fled before the men of Ai.

5 And the men of Ai smote of them about thirty and six men: for they chased them *from* before the gate *even* unto Shebarim, and smote them in the going down: wherefore [u]the hearts of the people melted, and became as water.

6 ¶ And Joshua [v]rent his clothes, and fell to the earth upon his face before the ark of the LORD until the eventide, he and the elders of Israel, and [w]put dust upon their heads.

7 And Joshua said, Alas, O Lord GOD, [x]wherefore hast thou at all brought this people over Jordan, to deliver us into the hand of the Amorites, to destroy us? would to God we had been content, and dwelt on the other side Jordan!

8 O Lord, what shall I say, when Israel turneth their backs before their enemies!

9 For the Canaanites and all the inhabitants of the land shall hear *of it*, and shall environ us round, and [y]cut off our name from the earth: and [z]what wilt thou do unto thy great name?

10 ¶ And the LORD said unto Joshua, Get thee up; wherefore liest thou thus upon thy face?

11 [a]Israel hath sinned, and they have also transgressed my covenant which I

6:12 *f*Deut. 31:25
6:17 *g*ch. 2:4
6:18 *h*Deut. 7:26; ch. 7:1 *i*ch. 7:25; 1 Kings 18:17; Jonah 1:12
6:20 *j*ver. 5; Heb. 11:30
6:21 *k*Deut. 7:2
6:22 *l*ch. 2:14; Heb. 11:31
6:23 *m*ch. 2:13
6:24 *n*ver. 19
6:25 *o*Matt. 1:5
6:26 *p*1 Kings 16:34
6:27 *q*ch. 1:5 *r*ch. 9:1
7:1 *s*ch. 22:20
7:4 *t*Lev. 26:17; Deut. 28:25
7:5 *u*ch. 2:9; Lev. 26:36; Ps. 22:14
7:6 *v*Gen. 37:29 *w*1 Sam. 4:12; 2 Sam. 1:2; Neh. 9:1; Job 2:12
7:7 *x*Ex. 5:22; 2 Kings 3:10
7:9 *y*Ps. 83:4 *z*Ex. 32:12; Num. 14:13
7:11 *a*ver. 1

commanded them: [b]for they have even
taken of the accursed thing, and have also
stolen, and [c]dissembled also, and they have
put *it* even among their own stuff.
12 [d]Therefore the children of Israel could
not stand before their enemies, *but* turned
their backs before their enemies, because
[e]they were accursed: neither will I be with
you any more, except ye destroy the accursed from among you.
13 Up, [f]sanctify the people, and say,
[g]Sanctify yourselves against to morrow:
for thus saith the LORD God of Israel, *There*
is an accursed thing in the midst of thee,
O Israel: thou canst not stand before thine
enemies, until ye take away the accursed
thing from among you.
14 In the morning therefore ye shall be
brought according to your tribes: and it
shall be, *that* the tribe which [h]the LORD
taketh shall come according to the families
thereof; and the family which the LORD
shall take shall come by households; and
the household which the LORD shall take
shall come man by man.
15 [i]And it shall be, *that* he that is taken
with the accursed thing shall be burnt with
fire, he and all that he hath: because he hath
[j]transgressed the covenant of the LORD,
and because he [k]hath wrought folly in Israel.
16 ¶ So Joshua rose up early in the morning, and brought Israel by their tribes; and
the tribe of Judah was taken:
17 And he brought the family of Judah;
and he took the family of the Zarhites: and
he brought the family of the Zarhites man
by man; and Zabdi was taken:
18 And he brought his household man by
man; and Achan, the son of Carmi, the son
of Zabdi, the son of Zerah, of the tribe of
Judah, [l]was taken.
19 And Joshua said unto Achan, My son,
[m]give, I pray thee, glory to the LORD God of
Israel, [n]and make confession unto him; and
[o]tell me now what thou hast done; hide *it*
not from me.
20 And Achan answered Joshua, and
said, Indeed I have sinned against the LORD
God of Israel, and thus and thus have I
done:
21 When I saw among the spoils a goodly
Babylonish garment, and two hundred
shekels of silver, and a wedge of gold of
fifty shekels weight, then I coveted them,
and took them; and, behold, they *are* hid in
the earth in the midst of my tent, and the
silver under it.
22 So Joshua sent messengers, and they
ran unto the tent; and, behold, *it was* hid in
his tent, and the silver under it.
23 And they took them out of the midst of
the tent, and brought them unto Joshua, and
unto all the children of Israel, and laid them
out before the LORD.
24 And Joshua, and all Israel with him,
took Achan the son of Zerah, and the silver,
and the garment, and the wedge of gold,
and his sons, and his daughters, and his
oxen, and his asses, and his sheep, and his
tent, and all that he had: and they brought
them unto [p]the valley of Achor.
25 And Joshua said, [q]Why hast thou
troubled us? the LORD shall trouble thee this
day. [r]And all Israel stoned him with stones,
and burned them with fire, after they had
stoned them with stones.
26 And they [s]raised over him a great
heap of stones unto this day. So [t]the LORD
turned from the fierceness of his anger.
Wherefore the name of that place was
called, [u]The valley of Achor, unto this day.
8 And the LORD said unto Joshua, [v]Fear
not, neither be thou dismayed: take all
the people of war with thee, and arise, go up
to Ai: see, [w]I have given into thy hand the
king of Ai, and his people, and his city, and
his land:
2 And thou shalt do to Ai and her king as
thou didst unto [x]Jericho and her king: only
[y]the spoil thereof, and the cattle thereof,
shall ye take for a prey unto yourselves: lay
thee an ambush for the city behind it.
3 ¶ So Joshua arose, and all the people of
war, to go up against Ai: and Joshua chose
out thirty thousand mighty men of valour,
and sent them away by night.
4 And he commanded them, saying, Behold, [z]ye shall lie in wait against the city,
even behind the city: go not very far from
the city, but be ye all ready:
5 And I, and all the people that *are* with
me, will approach unto the city: and it shall
come to pass, when they come out against
us, as at the first, that [a]we will flee before
them,
6 (For they will come out after us) till we
have drawn them from the city; for they will
say, They flee before us, as at the first:
therefore we will flee before them.
7 Then ye shall rise up from the ambush,
and seize upon the city: for the LORD your
God will deliver it into your hand.
8 And it shall be, when ye have taken the
city, *that* ye shall set the city on fire: according to the commandment of the LORD shall
ye do. [b]See, I have commanded you.
9 ¶ Joshua therefore sent them forth: and
they went to lie in ambush, and abode between Beth-el and Ai, on the west side of Ai:
but Joshua lodged that night among the
people.
10 And Joshua rose up early in the morning, and numbered the people, and went up,
he and the elders of Israel, before the people
to Ai.
11 [c]And all the people, *even the people* of
war that *were* with him, went up, and drew
nigh, and came before the city, and pitched
on the north side of Ai: now *there was* a
valley between them and Ai.
12 And he took about five thousand men,
and set them to lie in ambush between Beth-
el and Ai, on the west side of the city.
13 And when they had set the people,
even all the host that *was* on the north of the

7:11 [b]ch. 6:17 [c]Acts 5:1
7:12 [d]Num. 14:45; Judg. 2:14 [e]Deut. 7:26; ch. 6:18
7:13 [f]Ex. 19:10 [g]ch. 3:5
7:14 [h]Prov. 16:33
7:15 [i]1 Sam. 14:38 [j]ver. 11 [k]Gen. 34:7; Judg. 20:6
7:18 [l]1 Sam. 14:42
7:19 [m]1 Sam. 6:5; Jer. 13:16; John 9:24 [n]Num. 5:6; 2 Chron. 30:22; Ps. 51:3; Dan. 9:4 [o]1 Sam. 14:43
7:24 [p]ver. 26; ch. 15:7
7:25 [q]ch. 6:18; 1 Chron. 2:7; Gal. 5:12 [r]Deut. 17:5
7:26 [s]ch. 8:29; 2 Sam. 18:17; Lam. 3:53 [t]Deut. 13:17; 2 Sam. 21:14 [u]ver. 24; Isa. 65:10; Hos. 2:15
8:1 [v]Deut. 1:21; ch. 1:9 [w]ch. 6:2
8:2 [x]ch. 6:21 [y]Deut. 20:14
8:4 [z]Judg. 20:29
8:5 [a]Judg. 20:32
8:8 [b]2 Sam. 13:28
8:11 [c]ver. 5

city, and their liers in wait on the west of the
city, Joshua went that night into the midst
of the valley.
14 ¶ And it came to pass, when the king
of Ai saw *it,* that they hasted and rose up
early, and the men of the city went out
against Israel to battle, he and all his people, at a time appointed, before the plain;
but he [d]wist not that *there were* liers in
ambush against him behind the city.
15 And Joshua and all Israel [e]made as if
they were beaten before them, and fled by
the way of the wilderness.
16 And all the people that *were* in Ai were
called together to pursue after them: and
they pursued after Joshua, and were drawn
away from the city.
17 And there was not a man left in Ai or
Beth-el, that went not out after Israel: and
they left the city open, and pursued after
Israel.
18 And the LORD said unto Joshua,
Stretch out the spear that *is* in thy hand toward Ai; for I will give it into thine hand.
And Joshua stretched out the spear that *he*
had in his hand toward the city.
19 And the ambush arose quickly out of
their place, and they ran as soon as he had
stretched out his hand: and they entered
into the city, and took it, and hasted and set
the city on fire.
20 And when the men of Ai looked behind
them, they saw, and, behold, the smoke of
the city ascended up to heaven, and they
had no power to flee this way or that way:
and the people that fled to the wilderness
turned back upon the pursuers.
21 And when Joshua and all Israel saw
that the ambush had taken the city, and that
the smoke of the city ascended, then they
turned again, and slew the men of Ai.
22 And the other issued out of the city
against them; so they were in the midst of
Israel, some on this side, and some on that
side: and they smote them, so that they [f]let
none of them remain or escape.
23 And the king of Ai they took alive, and
brought him to Joshua.
24 And it came to pass, when Israel had
made an end of slaying all the inhabitants of
Ai in the field, in the wilderness wherein
they chased them, and when they were all
fallen on the edge of the sword, until they
were consumed, that all the Israelites returned unto Ai, and smote it with the edge
of the sword.
25 And *so* it was, *that* all that fell that
day, both of men and women, *were* twelve
thousand, *even* all the men of Ai.
26 For Joshua drew not his hand back,
wherewith he stretched out the spear, until
he had utterly destroyed all the inhabitants
of Ai.
27 [g]Only the cattle and the spoil of that
city Israel took for a prey unto themselves,
according unto the word of the LORD which
he [h]commanded Joshua.
28 And Joshua burnt Ai, and made it [i]an
heap for ever, *even* a desolation unto this
day.
29 [j]And the king of Ai he hanged on a
tree until eventide: [k]and as soon as the sun
was down, Joshua commanded that they
should take his carcase down from the tree,
and cast it at the entering of the gate of the
city, and [l]raise thereon a great heap of
stones, *that remaineth* unto this day.
30 ¶ Then Joshua built an altar unto the
LORD God of Israel [m]in mount Ebal,
31 As Moses the servant of the LORD commanded the children of Israel, as it is written in the [n]book of the law of Moses, an
altar of whole stones, over which no man
hath lift up *any* iron: and [o]they offered
thereon burnt offerings unto the LORD, and
sacrificed peace offerings.
32 ¶ And [p]he wrote there upon the stones
a copy of the law of Moses, which he wrote
in the presence of the children of Israel.
33 And all Israel, and their elders, and officers, and their judges, stood on this side
the ark and on that side before the priests
the Levites, [q]which bare the ark of the covenant of the LORD, as well [r]the stranger, as
he that was born among them; half of them
over against mount Gerizim, and half of
them over against mount Ebal; [s]as Moses
the servant of the LORD had commanded
before, that they should bless the people of
Israel.
34 And afterward [t]he read all the words
of the law, [u]the blessings and cursings, according to all that is written in the book of
the law.
35 There was not a word of all that Moses
commanded, which Joshua read not before
all the congregation of Israel, [v]with the
women, and the little ones, and [w]the strangers that were conversant among them.
9 And it came to pass, when all the kings
which *were* on this side Jordan, in the
hills, and in the valleys, and in all the coasts
of [x]the great sea over against Lebanon,
[y]the Hittite, and the Amorite, the Canaanite, the Perizzite, the Hivite, and the Jebusite, heard *thereof;*
2 That they [z]gathered themselves together, to fight with Joshua and with Israel,
with one accord.
3 ¶ And when the inhabitants of [a]Gibeon
[b]heard what Joshua had done unto Jericho
and to Ai,
4 They did work wilily, and went and
made as if they had been ambassadors, and
took old sacks upon their asses, and wine
bottles, old, and rent, and bound up;
5 And old shoes and clouted upon their
feet, and old garments upon them; and all
the bread of their provision was dry *and*
mouldy.
6 And they went to Joshua [c]unto the
camp at Gilgal, and said unto him, and to
the men of Israel, We be come from a far
country: now therefore make ye a league
with us.
7 And the men of Israel said unto the [d]Hi-

8:14 [d]Judg. 20:34; Eccl. 9:12
8:15 [e]Judg. 20:36
8:22 [f]Deut. 7:2
8:27 [g]Num. 31:22 [h]ver. 2
8:28 [i]Deut. 13:16
8:29 [j]ch. 10:26; Ps. 107:40 [k]Deut. 21:23; ch. 10:27 [l]ch. 7:26
8:30 [m]Deut. 27:4
8:31 [n]Ex. 20:25; Deut. 27:5 [o]Ex. 20:24
8:32 [p]Deut. 27:2
8:33 [q]Deut. 31:9 [r]Deut. 31:12 [s]Deut. 11:29
8:34 [t]Deut. 31:11; Neh. 8:3 [u]Deut. 28:2
8:35 [v]Deut. 31:12 [w]ver. 33
9:1 [x]Num. 34:6 [y]Ex. 3:17
9:2 [z]Ps. 83:3
9:3 [a]ch. 10:2; 2 Sam. 21:1 [b]ch. 6:27
9:6 [c]ch. 5:10
9:7 [d]ch. 11:19

vites, Peradventure ye dwell among us; and
[e]how shall we make a league with you?
8 And they said unto Joshua, [f]We *are* thy
servants. And Joshua said unto them, Who
are ye? and from whence come ye?
9 And they said unto him, [g]From a very
far country thy servants are come because
of the name of the LORD thy God: for we
have [h]heard the fame of him, and all that he
did in Egypt,
10 And [i]all that he did to the two kings of
the Amorites, that *were* beyond Jordan, to
Sihon king of Heshbon, and to Og king of
Bashan, which *was* at Ashtaroth.
11 Wherefore our elders and all the inhabitants of our country spake to us, saying, Take victuals with you for the journey,
and go to meet them, and say unto them, We
are your servants: therefore now make ye a
league with us.
12 This our bread we took hot *for* our provision out of our houses on the day we came
forth to go unto you; but now, behold, it is
dry, and it is mouldy:
13 And these bottles of wine, which we
filled, *were* new; and, behold, they be rent:
and these our garments and our shoes are
become old by reason of the very long journey.
14 And the men took of their victuals,
[j]and asked not *counsel* at the mouth of the
LORD.
15 And [k]Joshua made peace with them,
and made a league with them, to let them
live: and the princes of the congregation
sware unto them.
16 ¶ And it came to pass at the end of
three days after they had made a league
with them, that they heard that they *were*
their neighbours, and *that* they dwelt
among them.
17 And the children of Israel journeyed,
and came unto their cities on the third day.
Now their cities *were* [l]Gibeon, and Chephirah, and Beeroth, and Kirjath-jearim.
18 And the children of Israel smote them
not, [m]because the princes of the congregation had sworn unto them by the LORD God
of Israel. And all the congregation murmured against the princes.
19 But all the princes said unto all the
congregation, We have sworn unto them by
the LORD God of Israel: now therefore we
may not touch them.
20 This we will do to them; we will even
let them live, lest [n]wrath be upon us, because of the oath which we sware unto
them.
21 And the princes said unto them, Let
them live; but let them be [o]hewers of wood
and drawers of water unto all the congregation; as the princes had [p]promised them.
22 ¶ And Joshua called for them, and he
spake unto them, saying, Wherefore have
ye beguiled us, saying, [q]We *are* very far
from you; when [r]ye dwell among us?
23 Now therefore ye *are* [s]cursed, and
there shall none of you be freed from being

9:7 [e]Ex. 23:32; Deut. 7:2; Judg. 2:2
9:8 [f]Deut. 20:11; 2 Kings 10:5
9:9 [g]Deut. 20:15 [h]Ex. 15:14; Josh. 2:10
9:10 [i]Num. 21:24
9:14 [j]Num. 27:21; Judg. 1:1; 1 Sam. 22:10; 2 Sam. 2:1; Isa. 30:1
9:15 [k]ch. 11:19; 2 Sam. 21:2
9:17 [l]ch. 18:25; Ezra 2:25
9:18 [m]Eccl. 5:2; Ps. 15:4
9:20 [n]2 Sam. 21:1; Ezek. 17:13; Zech. 5:3; Mal. 3:5
9:21 [o]Deut. 29:11 [p]ver. 15
9:22 [q]ver. 6 [r]ver. 16
9:23 [s]Gen. 9:25 [t]ver. 21
9:24 [u]Ex. 23:32; Deut. 7:1 [v]Ex. 15:14
9:25 [w]Gen. 16:6
9:27 [x]ver. 21 [y]Deut. 12:5
10:1 [z]ch. 6:21 [a]ch. 8:22 [b]ch. 9:15
10:2 [c]Ex. 15:14; Deut. 11:25
10:4 [d]ver. 1; ch. 9:15
10:5 [e]ch. 9:2
10:6 [f]ch. 5:10
10:7 [g]ch. 8:1
10:8 [h]ch. 11:6; Judg. 4:14 [i]ch. 1:5
10:10 [j]Judg. 4:15; 1 Sam. 7:10; Ps. 18:14; Isa. 28:21 [k]ch. 16:3

bondmen, and [t]hewers of wood and drawers of water for the house of my God.
24 And they answered Joshua, and said,
Because it was certainly told thy servants,
how that the LORD thy God [u]commanded
his servant Moses to give you all the land,
and to destroy all the inhabitants of the land
from before you, therefore [v]we were sore
afraid of our lives because of you, and have
done this thing.
25 And now, behold, we *are* [w]in thine
hand: as it seemeth good and right unto thee
to do unto us, do.
26 And so did he unto them, and delivered
them out of the hand of the children of Israel, that they slew them not.
27 And Joshua made them that day
[x]hewers of wood and drawers of water for
the congregation, and for the altar of the
LORD, even unto this day, [y]in the place
which he should choose.

10 Now it came to pass, when Adoni-
zedek king of Jerusalem had heard
how Joshua had taken Ai, and had utterly
destroyed it; [z]as he had done to Jericho and
her king, so he had done to [a]Ai and her
king; and [b]how the inhabitants of Gibeon
had made peace with Israel, and were
among them;
2 That they [c]feared greatly, because Gibeon *was* a great city, as one of the royal
cities, and because it *was* greater than Ai,
and all the men thereof *were* mighty.
3 Wherefore Adoni-zedek king of Jerusalem sent unto Hoham king of Hebron, and
unto Piram king of Jarmuth, and unto Japhia king of Lachish, and unto Debir king of
Eglon, saying,
4 Come up unto me, and help me, that we
may smite Gibeon: [d]for it hath made peace
with Joshua and with the children of Israel.
5 Therefore the five kings of the Amorites, the king of Jerusalem, the king of Hebron, the king of Jarmuth, the king of
Lachish, the king of Eglon, [e]gathered
themselves together, and went up, they and
all their hosts, and encamped before Gibeon, and made war against it.
6 ¶ And the men of Gibeon sent unto
Joshua [f]to the camp to Gilgal, saying,
Slack not thy hand from thy servants; come
up to us quickly, and save us, and help us:
for all the kings of the Amorites that dwell
in the mountains are gathered together
against us.
7 So Joshua ascended from Gilgal, he,
and [g]all the people of war with him, and all
the mighty men of valour.
8 ¶ And the LORD said unto Joshua, [h]Fear
them not: for I have delivered them into
thine hand; [i]there shall not a man of them
stand before thee.
9 Joshua therefore came unto them suddenly, *and* went up from Gilgal all night.
10 And the LORD [j]discomfited them before Israel, and slew them with a great
slaughter at Gibeon, and chased them along
the way that goeth up [k]to Beth-horon, and

smote them to [l]Azekah, and unto Makkedah.

11 And it came to pass, as they fled from before Israel, *and* were in the going down to Beth-horon, [m]that the LORD cast down great stones from heaven upon them unto Azekah, and they died: *they were* more which died with hailstones than *they* whom the children of Israel slew with the sword.

12 ¶ Then spake Joshua to the LORD in the day when the LORD delivered up the Amorites before the children of Israel, and he said in the sight of Israel, [n]Sun, stand thou still upon Gibeon; and thou, Moon, in the valley of [o]Ajalon.

13 And the sun stood still, and the moon stayed, until the people had avenged themselves upon their enemies. [p]*Is* not this written in the book of Jasher? So the sun stood still in the midst of heaven, and hasted not to go down about a whole day.

14 And there was [q]no day like that before it or after it, that the LORD hearkened unto the voice of a man: for [r]the LORD fought for Israel.

15 ¶ [s]And Joshua returned, and all Israel with him, unto the camp to Gilgal.

16 But these five kings fled, and hid themselves in a cave at Makkedah.

17 And it was told Joshua, saying, The five kings are found hid in a cave at Makkedah.

18 And Joshua said, Roll great stones upon the mouth of the cave, and set men by it for to keep them:

19 And stay ye not, *but* pursue after your enemies, and smite the hindmost of them; suffer them not to enter into their cities: for the LORD your God hath delivered them into your hand.

20 And it came to pass, when Joshua and the children of Israel had made an end of slaying them with a very great slaughter, till they were consumed, that the rest *which* remained of them entered into fenced cities.

21 And all the people returned to the camp to Joshua at Makkedah in peace: [t]none moved his tongue against any of the children of Israel.

22 Then said Joshua, Open the mouth of the cave, and bring out those five kings unto me out of the cave.

23 And they did so, and brought forth those five kings unto him out of the cave, the king of Jerusalem, the king of Hebron, the king of Jarmuth, the king of Lachish, *and* the king of Eglon.

24 And it came to pass, when they brought out those kings unto Joshua, that Joshua called for all the men of Israel, and said unto the captains of the men of war which went with him, Come near, [u]put your feet upon the necks of these kings. And they came near, and put their feet upon the necks of them.

25 And Joshua said unto them, [v]Fear not, nor be dismayed, be strong and of good courage: for [w]thus shall the LORD do to all your enemies against whom ye fight.

26 And afterward Joshua smote them, and slew them, and hanged them on five trees: and they [x]were hanging upon the trees until the evening.

27 And it came to pass at the time of the going down of the sun, *that* Joshua commanded, and they [y]took them down off the trees, and cast them into the cave wherein they had been hid, and laid great stones in the cave's mouth, *which remain* until this very day.

28 ¶ And that day Joshua took Makkedah, and smote it with the edge of the sword, and the king thereof he utterly destroyed, them, and all the souls that *were* therein; he let none remain: and he did to the king of Makkedah [z]as he did unto the king of Jericho.

29 Then Joshua passed from Makkedah, and all Israel with him, unto Libnah, and fought against Libnah:

30 And the LORD delivered it also, and the king thereof, into the hand of Israel; and he smote it with the edge of the sword, and all the souls that *were* therein; he let none remain in it; but did unto the king thereof as he did unto the king of Jericho.

31 ¶ And Joshua passed from Libnah, and all Israel with him, unto Lachish, and encamped against it, and fought against it:

32 And the LORD delivered Lachish into the hand of Israel, which took it on the second day, and smote it with the edge of the sword, and all the souls that *were* therein, according to all that he had done to Libnah.

33 ¶ Then Horam king of Gezer came up to help Lachish; and Joshua smote him and his people, until he had left him none remaining.

34 ¶ And from Lachish Joshua passed unto Eglon, and all Israel with him; and they encamped against it, and fought against it:

35 And they took it on that day, and smote it with the edge of the sword, and all the souls that *were* therein he utterly destroyed that day, according to all that he had done to Lachish.

36 And Joshua went up from Eglon, and all Israel with him, unto [a]Hebron; and they fought against it:

37 And they took it, and smote it with the edge of the sword, and the king thereof, and all the cities thereof, and all the souls that *were* therein; he left none remaining, according to all that he had done to Eglon; but destroyed it utterly, and all the souls that *were* therein.

38 ¶ And Joshua returned, and all Israel with him, to [b]Debir; and fought against it:

39 And he took it, and the king thereof, and all the cities thereof; and they smote them with the edge of the sword, and utterly destroyed all the souls that *were* therein; he left none remaining: as he had done to Hebron, so he did to Debir, and to the king

10:10 [l]ch. 15:35
10:11 [m]Ps. 18:13; Isa. 30:30; Rev. 16:21
10:12 [n]Isa. 28:21; Hab. 3:11 [o]Judg. 12:12
10:13 [p]2 Sam. 1:18
10:14 [q]Isa. 38:8 [r]Deut. 1:30; ver. 42
10:15 [s]ver. 43
10:21 [t]Ex. 11:7
10:24 [u]Ps. 107:40; Isa. 26:5; Mal. 4:3
10:25 [v]Deut. 31:6; ch. 1:9 [w]Deut. 3:21
10:26 [x]ch. 8:29
10:27 [y]Deut. 21:23; ch. 8:29
10:28 [z]ch. 6:21
10:36 [a]ch. 14:13; Judg. 1:10
10:38 [b]ch. 15:15; Judg. 1:11

thereof; as he had done also to Libnah, and to her king.

40 ¶ So Joshua smote all the country of the hills, and of the south, and of the vale, and of the springs, and all their kings: he left none remaining, but utterly destroyed all that breathed, as the LORD God of Israel [c]commanded.

41 And Joshua smote them from Kadesh-barnea even unto [d]Gaza, [e]and all the country of Goshen, even unto Gibeon.

42 And all these kings and their land did Joshua take at one time, [f]because the LORD God of Israel fought for Israel.

43 And Joshua returned, and all Israel with him, unto the camp to Gilgal.

11 And it came to pass, when Jabin king of Hazor had heard *those things*, that he [g]sent to Jobab king of Madon, and to the king [h]of Shimron, and to the king of Achshaph,

2 And to the kings that *were* on the north of the mountains, and of the plains south of [i]Chinneroth, and in the valley, and in the borders [j]of Dor on the west,

3 *And to* the Canaanite on the east and on the west, and *to* the Amorite, and the Hittite, and the Perizzite, and the Jebusite in the mountains, [k]and *to* the Hivite under [l]Hermon [m]in the land of Mizpeh.

4 And they went out, they and all their hosts with them, much people, [n]even as the sand that *is* upon the sea shore in multitude, with horses and chariots very many.

5 And when all these kings were met together, they came and pitched together at the waters of Merom, to fight against Israel.

6 ¶ And the LORD said unto Joshua, [o]Be not afraid because of them: for to morrow about this time will I deliver them up all slain before Israel: thou shalt [p]hough their horses, and burn their chariots with fire.

7 So Joshua came, and all the people of war with him, against them by the waters of Merom suddenly; and they fell upon them.

8 And the LORD delivered them into the hand of Israel, who smote them, and chased them unto great Zidon, and unto [q]Misrephoth-maim, and unto the valley of Mizpeh eastward; and they smote them, until they left them none remaining.

9 And Joshua did unto them [r]as the LORD bade him: he houghed their horses, and burnt their chariots with fire.

10 ¶ And Joshua at that time turned back, and took Hazor, and smote the king thereof with the sword: for Hazor beforetime was the head of all those kingdoms.

11 And they smote all the souls that *were* therein with the edge of the sword, utterly destroying *them*: there was not any left to breathe: and he burnt Hazor with fire.

12 And all the cities of those kings, and all the kings of them, did Joshua take, and smote them with the edge of the sword, *and* he utterly destroyed them, [s]as Moses the servant of the LORD commanded.

13 But *as for* the cities that stood still in their strength, Israel burned none of them, save Hazor only; *that* did Joshua burn.

14 And all the spoil of these cities, and the cattle, the children of Israel took for a prey unto themselves; but every man they smote with the edge of the sword, until they had destroyed them, neither left they any to breathe.

15 ¶ [t]As the LORD commanded Moses his servant, so [u]did Moses command Joshua, and [v]so did Joshua; he left nothing undone of all that the LORD commanded Moses.

16 So Joshua took all that land, [w]the hills, and all the south country, [x]and all the land of Goshen, and the valley, and the plain, and the mountain of Israel, and the valley of the same;

17 [y]*Even* from the mount Halak, that goeth up to Seir, even unto Baal-gad in the valley of Lebanon under mount Hermon: and [z]all their kings he took, and smote them, and slew them.

18 Joshua made war a long time with all those kings.

19 There was not a city that made peace with the children of Israel, save [a]the Hivites the inhabitants of Gibeon: all *other* they took in battle.

20 For [b]it was of the LORD to harden their hearts, that they should come against Israel in battle, that he might destroy them utterly, *and* that they might have no favour, but that he might destroy them, [c]as the LORD commanded Moses.

21 ¶ And at that time came Joshua, and cut off [d]the Anakims from the mountains, from Hebron, from Debir, from Anab, and from all the mountains of Judah, and from all the mountains of Israel: Joshua destroyed them utterly with their cities.

22 There was none of the Anakims left in the land of the children of Israel: only in Gaza, in [e]Gath, [f]and in Ashdod, there remained.

23 So Joshua took the whole land, [g]according to all that the LORD said unto Moses; and Joshua gave it for an inheritance unto Israel [h]according to their divisions by their tribes. [i]And the land rested from war.

12 Now these *are* the kings of the land, which the children of Israel smote, and possessed their land on the other side Jordan toward the rising of the sun, [j]from the river Arnon [k]unto mount Hermon, and all the plain on the east:

2 [l]Sihon king of the Amorites, who dwelt in Heshbon, *and* ruled from Aroer, which *is* upon the bank of the river Arnon, and from the middle of the river, and from half Gilead, even unto the river Jabbok, *which is* the border of the children of Ammon;

3 And [m]from the plain to the sea of Chinneroth on the east, and unto the sea of the plain, *even* the salt sea on the east, [n]the way to Beth-jeshimoth; and from the south, under [o]Ashdoth-pisgah:

4 ¶ And [p]the coast of Og king of Bashan,

10:40 [c]Deut. 20:16
10:41 [d]Gen. 10:19 [e]ch. 11:16
10:42 [f]ver. 14
11:1 [g]ch. 10:3 [h]ch. 19:15
11:2 [i]Num. 34:11 [j]ch. 17:11; Judg. 1:27; 1 Kings 4:11
11:3 [k]Judg. 3:3 [l]ch. 13:11 [m]Gen. 31:49
11:4 [n]Gen. 22:17; Judg. 7:12; 1 Sam. 13:5
11:6 [o]ch. 10:8 [p]2 Sam. 8:4
11:8 [q]ch. 13:6
11:9 [r]ver. 6
11:12 [s]Num. 33:52; Deut. 7:2
11:15 [t]Ex. 34:11 [u]Deut. 7:2 [v]ch. 1:7
11:16 [w]ch. 12:8 [x]ch. 10:41
11:17 [y]ch. 12:7 [z]Deut. 7:24; ch. 12:7
11:19 [a]ch. 9:3
11:20 [b]Deut. 2:30; Judg. 14:4; 1 Sam. 2:25; 1 Kings 12:15; Rom. 9:18 [c]Deut. 20:16
11:21 [d]Num. 13:22; Deut. 1:28; ch. 15:13
11:22 [e]1 Sam. 17:4 [f]ch. 15:46
11:23 [g]Num. 34:2 [h]Num. 26:53; ch. 14 [i]ch. 14:15; ver. 18
12:1 [j]Num. 21:24 [k]Deut. 3:8
12:2 [l]Num. 21:24; Deut. 2:33
12:3 [m]Deut. 3:17 [n]ch. 13:20 [o]Deut. 3:17
12:4 [p]Num. 21:35; Deut. 3:4

which was of [q]the remnant of the giants,
[r]that dwelt at Ashtaroth and at Edrei,
5 And reigned in [s]mount Hermon, [t]and
in Salcah, and in all Bashan, [u]unto the border of the Geshurites and the Maachathites,
and half Gilead, the border of Sihon king of
Heshbon.
6 [v]Them did Moses the servant of the
LORD and the children of Israel smite: and
[w]Moses the servant of the LORD gave it *for*
a possession unto the Reubenites, and the
Gadites, and the half tribe of Manasseh.
7 ¶ And these *are* the kings of the country
[x]which Joshua and the children of Israel
smote on this side Jordan on the west, from
Baal-gad in the valley of Lebanon even unto
the mount Halak, that goeth up to [y]Seir;
which Joshua [z]gave unto the tribes of Israel *for* a possession according to their divisions;
8 [a]In the mountains, and in the valleys,
and in the plains, and in the springs, and in
the wilderness, and in the south country;
[b]the Hittites, the Amorites, and the Canaanites, the Perizzites, the Hivites, and the
Jebusites:
9 ¶ [c]The king of Jericho, one; [d]the king
of Ai, which *is* beside Beth-el, one;
10 [e]The king of Jerusalem, one; the king
of Hebron, one;
11 The king of Jarmuth, one; the king of
Lachish, one;
12 The king of Eglon, one; [f]the king of
Gezer, one;
13 [g]The king of Debir, one; the king of
Geder, one;
14 The king of Hormah, one; the king of
Arad, one;
15 [h]The king of Libnah, one; the king of
Adullam, one;
16 [i]The king of Makkedah, one; [j]the
king of Beth-el, one;
17 The king of Tappuah, one; [k]the king of
Hepher, one;
18 The king of Aphek, one; the king of
Lasharon, one;
19 The king of Madon, one; [l]the king of
Hazor, one;
20 The king of [m]Shimron-meron, one; the
king of Achshaph, one;
21 The king of Taanach, one; the king of
Megiddo, one;
22 [n]The king of Kedesh, one; the king of
Jokneam of Carmel, one;
23 The king of Dor in the [o]coast of Dor,
one; the king of [p]the nations of Gilgal, one;
24 The king of Tirzah, one: all the kings
thirty and one.

13 Now Joshua [q]was old *and* stricken
in years; and the LORD said unto him,
Thou art old *and* stricken in years, and
there remaineth yet very much land to be
possessed.
2 [r]This *is* the land that yet remaineth:
[s]all the borders of the Philistines, and all
[t]Geshuri,
3 [u]From Sihor, which *is* before Egypt,
even unto the borders of Ekron northward,

12:4 [q]Deut. 3:11; ch. 13:12 [r]Deut. 1:4
12:5 [s]Deut. 3:8 [t]Deut. 3:10; ch. 13:11 [u]Deut. 3:14
12:6 [v]Num. 21:24 [w]Num. 32:29; Deut. 3:11; ch. 13:8
12:7 [x]ch. 11:17 [y]Gen. 14:6; Deut. 2:1 [z]ch. 11:23
12:8 [a]ch. 10:40 [b]Ex. 3:8; ch. 9:1
12:9 [c]ch. 6:2 [d]ch. 8:29
12:10 [e]ch. 10:23
12:12 [f]ch. 10:33
12:13 [g]ch. 10:38
12:15 [h]ch. 10:29
12:16 [i]ch. 10:28 [j]ch. 8:17; Judg. 1:22
12:17 [k]1 Kings 4:10
12:19 [l]ch. 11:10
12:20 [m]ch. 11:1
12:22 [n]ch. 19:37
12:23 [o]ch. 11:2 [p]Gen. 14:1; Isa. 9:1
13:1 [q]ch. 14:10
13:2 [r]Judg. 3:1 [s]Joel 3:4 [t]ver. 13; 2 Sam. 3:3
13:3 [u]Jer. 2:18 [v]Judg. 3:3; 1 Sam. 6:4; Zeph. 2:5 [w]Deut. 2:23
13:4 [x]ch. 19:30 [y]Judg. 1:34
13:5 [z]1 Kings 5:18; Ps. 83:7; Ezek. 27:9 [a]ch. 12:7
13:6 [b]ch. 11:8 [c]ch. 23:13; Judg. 2:21 [d]ch. 14:1
13:8 [e]Num. 32:33; Deut. 3:12; ch. 22:4
13:9 [f]ver. 16; Num. 21:30
13:10 [g]Num. 21:24
13:11 [h]ch. 12:5
13:12 [i]Deut. 3:11; ch. 12:4 [j]Num. 21:24
13:13 [k]ver. 11
13:14 [l]Num. 18:20; ch. 14:3 [m]ver. 33
13:16 [n]ch. 12:2 [o]Num. 21:28 [p]Num. 21:30; ver. 9
13:18 [q]Num. 21:23
13:19 [r]Num. 32:37 [s]Num. 32:38
13:20 [t]Deut. 3:17; ch. 12:3
13:21 [u]Deut. 3:10

which is counted to the Canaanite: [v]five
lords of the Philistines; the Gazathites, and
the Ashdothites, the Eshkalonites, the Gittites, and the Ekronites; also [w]the Avites:
4 From the south, all the land of the Canaanites, and Mearah that *is* beside the Sidonians, [x]unto Aphek, to the borders of
[y]the Amorites:
5 And the land of [z]the Giblites, and all
Lebanon, toward the sunrising, [a]from
Baal-gad under mount Hermon unto the entering into Hamath.
6 All the inhabitants of the hill country
from Lebanon unto [b]Misrephoth-maim,
and all the Sidonians, them [c]will I drive out
from before the children of Israel: only [d]di-
vide thou it by lot unto the Israelites for an
inheritance, as I have commanded thee.
7 Now therefore divide this land for an
inheritance unto the nine tribes, and the
half tribe of Manasseh,
8 With whom the Reubenites and the
Gadites have received their inheritance,
[e]which Moses gave them, beyond Jordan
eastward, *even* as Moses the servant of the
LORD gave them;
9 From Aroer, that *is* upon the bank of the
river Arnon, and the city that *is* in the midst
of the river, [f]and all the plain of Medeba
unto Dibon;
10 And [g]all the cities of Sihon king of the
Amorites, which reigned in Heshbon, unto
the border of the children of Ammon;
11 [h]And Gilead, and the border of the
Geshurites and Maachathites, and all
mount Hermon, and all Bashan unto Salcah;
12 All the kingdom of Og in Bashan,
which reigned in Ashtaroth and in Edrei,
who remained of [i]the remnant of the
giants: [j]for these did Moses smite, and cast
them out.
13 Nevertheless the children of Israel expelled [k]not the Geshurites, nor the Maachathites: but the Geshurites and the
Maachathites dwell among the Israelites
until this day.
14 [l]Only unto the tribe of Levi he gave
none inheritance; the sacrifices of the LORD
God of Israel made by fire *are* their inheritance, [m]as he said unto them.
15 ¶ And Moses gave unto the tribe of the
children of Reuben *inheritance* according
to their families.
16 And their coast was [n]from Aroer, that
is on the bank of the river Arnon, [o]and the
city that *is* in the midst of the river, [p]and all
the plain by Medeba;
17 Heshbon, and all her cities that *are*
in the plain; Dibon, and Bamoth-baal, and
Beth-baal-meon,
18 [q]And Jahazah, and Kedemoth, and
Mephaath,
19 [r]And Kirjathaim, and [s]Sibmah, and
Zareth-shahar in the mount of the valley,
20 And Beth-peor, and [t]Ashdoth-pisgah,
and Beth-jeshimoth,
21 [u]And all the cities of the plain, and all

the kingdom of Sihon king of the Amorites, which reigned in Heshbon, [v]whom Moses smote [w]with the princes of Midian, Evi, and Rekem, and Zur, and Hur, and Reba, *which were* dukes of Sihon, dwelling in the country.

22 ¶ [x]Balaam also the son of Beor, the soothsayer, did the children of Israel slay with the sword among them that were slain by them.

23 And the border of the children of Reuben was Jordan, and the border *thereof.* This *was* the inheritance of the children of Reuben after their families, the cities and the villages thereof.

24 And Moses gave *inheritance* unto the tribe of Gad, *even* unto the children of Gad according to their families.

25 [y]And their coast was Jazer, and all the cities of Gilead, [z]and half the land of the children of Ammon, unto Aroer that *is* before [a]Rabbah;

26 And from Heshbon unto Ramath-mizpeh, and Betonim; and from Mahanaim unto the border of Debir;

27 And in the valley, [b]Beth-aram, and Beth-nimrah, [c]and Succoth, and Zaphon, the rest of the kingdom of Sihon king of Heshbon, Jordan and *his* border, *even* unto the edge [d]of the sea of Chinnereth on the other side Jordan eastward.

28 This *is* the inheritance of the children of Gad after their families, the cities, and their villages.

29 ¶ And Moses gave *inheritance* unto the half tribe of Manasseh: and *this* was *the possession* of the half tribe of the children of Manasseh by their families.

30 And their coast was from Mahanaim, all Bashan, all the kingdom of Og king of Bashan, and [e]all the towns of Jair, which *are* in Bashan, threescore cities:

31 And half Gilead, and [f]Ashtaroth, and Edrei, cities of the kingdom of Og in Bashan, *were pertaining* unto the children of Machir the son of Manasseh, *even* to the one half of the [g]children of Machir by their families.

32 These *are the countries* which Moses did distribute for inheritance in the plains of Moab, on the other side Jordan, by Jericho, eastward.

33 [h]But unto the tribe of Levi Moses gave not *any* inheritance: the LORD God of Israel *was* their inheritance, [i]as he said unto them.

14 And these *are the countries* which the children of Israel inherited in the land of Canaan, [j]which Eleazar the priest, and Joshua the son of Nun, and the heads of the fathers of the tribes of the children of Israel, distributed for inheritance to them.

2 [k]By lot *was* their inheritance, as the LORD commanded by the hand of Moses, for the nine tribes, and *for* the half tribe.

3 [l]For Moses had given the inheritance of two tribes and an half tribe on the other side Jordan: but unto the Levites he gave none inheritance among them.

4 For [m]the children of Joseph were two tribes, Manasseh and Ephraim: therefore they gave no part unto the Levites in the land, save cities to dwell *in,* with their suburbs for their cattle and for their substance.

5 [n]As the LORD commanded Moses, so the children of Israel did, and they divided the land.

6 ¶ Then the children of Judah came unto Joshua in Gilgal: and Caleb the son of Jephunneh the [o]Kenezite said unto him, Thou knowest [p]the thing that the LORD said unto Moses the man of God concerning me and thee [q]in Kadesh-barnea.

7 Forty years old *was* I when Moses the servant of the LORD [r]sent me from Kadesh-barnea to espy out the land; and I brought him word again as *it was* in mine heart.

8 Nevertheless [s]my brethren that went up with me made the heart of the people melt: but I wholly [t]followed the LORD my God.

9 And Moses sware on that day, saying, [u]Surely the land [v]whereon thy feet have trodden shall be thine inheritance, and thy children's for ever, because thou hast wholly followed the LORD my God.

10 And now, behold, the LORD hath kept me alive, [w]as he said, these forty and five years, even since the LORD spake this word unto Moses, while *the children of* Israel wandered in the wilderness: and now, lo, I *am* this day fourscore and five years old.

11 [x]As yet I *am as* strong this day as *I was* in the day that Moses sent me: as my strength *was* then, even so *is* my strength now, for war, both [y]to go out, and to come in.

12 Now therefore give me this mountain, whereof the LORD spake in that day; for thou heardest in that day how [z]the Anakims *were* there, and *that* the cities *were* great *and* fenced: [a]if so be the LORD *will be* with me, then [b]I shall be able to drive them out, as the LORD said.

13 And Joshua [c]blessed him, [d]and gave unto Caleb the son of Jephunneh Hebron for an inheritance.

14 [e]Hebron therefore became the inheritance of Caleb the son of Jephunneh the Kenezite unto this day, because that he [f]wholly followed the LORD God of Israel.

15 And [g]the name of Hebron before *was* Kirjath-arba; *which Arba was* a great man among the Anakims. [h]And the land had rest from war.

15 *This* then was the lot of the tribe of the children of Judah by their families; [i]*even* to the border of Edom the [j]wilderness of Zin southward *was* the uttermost part of the south coast.

2 And their south border was from the shore of the salt sea, from the bay that looketh southward:

3 And it went out to the south side [k]to Maaleh-acrabbim, and passed along to Zin,

13:21 [v]Num. 21:24 [w]Num. 31:8
13:22 [x]Num. 22:5
13:25 [y]Num. 32:35 [z]Num. 21:26; Deut. 2:19; Judg. 11:13 [a]2 Sam. 11:1
13:27 [b]Num. 32:36 [c]Gen. 33:17; 1 Kings 7:46 [d]Num. 34:11
13:30 [e]Num. 32:41; 1 Chron. 2:23
13:31 [f]ch. 12:4 [g]Num. 32:39
13:33 [h]ver. 14; ch. 18:7 [i]Num. 18:20; Deut. 10:9
14:1 [j]Num. 34:17
14:2 [k]Num. 26:55
14:3 [l]ch. 13:8
14:4 [m]Gen. 48:5; 1 Chron. 5:1
14:5 [n]Num. 35:2; ch. 21:2
14:6 [o]Num. 32:12 [p]Num. 14:24; Deut. 1:36 [q]Num. 13:26
14:7 [r]Num. 13:6
14:8 [s]Num. 13:31; Deut. 1:28 [t]Num. 14:24; Deut. 1:36
14:9 [u]Num. 14:23; Deut. 1:36; ch. 1:3 [v]Num. 13:22
14:10 [w]Num. 14:30
14:11 [x]Deut. 34:7 [y]Deut. 31:2
14:12 [z]Num. 13:28 [a]Ps. 18:32; Rom. 8:31 [b]ch. 15:14; Judg. 1:20
14:13 [c]ch. 22:6 [d]ch. 10:37; Judg. 1:20; 1 Chron. 6:55
14:14 [e]ch. 21:12 [f]ver. 8
14:15 [g]Gen. 23:2; ch. 15:13 [h]ch. 11:23
15:1 [i]Num. 34:3 [j]Num. 33:36
15:3 [k]Num. 34:4

and ascended up on the south side unto
Kadesh-barnea, and passed along to Hezron, and went up to Adar, and fetched a
compass to Karkaa:
4 *From thence* it passed [l]toward Azmon,
and went out unto the river of Egypt; and
the goings out of that coast were at the sea:
this shall be your south coast.
5 And the east border *was* the salt sea,
even unto the end of Jordan. And *their* border in the north quarter *was* from the bay of
the sea at the uttermost part of Jordan:
6 And the border went up to [m]Beth-hogla,
and passed along by the north of Beth-
arabah; and the border went up [n]to the
stone of Bohan the son of Reuben:
7 And the border went up toward Debir
from [o]the valley of Achor, and so northward, looking toward Gilgal, that *is* before
the going up to Adummim, which *is* on the
south side of the river: and the border
passed toward the waters of En-shemesh,
and the goings out thereof were at [p]En-
rogel:
8 And the border went up [q]by the valley
of the son of Hinnom unto the south side of
the [r]Jebusite; the same *is* Jerusalem: and
the border went up to the top of the mountain that *lieth* before the valley of Hinnom
westward, which *is* at the end [s]of the valley
of the giants northward:
9 And the border was drawn from the top
of the hill unto [t]the fountain of the water
of Nephtoah, and went out to the cities of
mount Ephron; and the border was drawn
[u]to Baalah, which *is* [v]Kirjath-jearim:
10 And the border compassed from Baalah westward unto mount Seir, and passed
along unto the side of mount Jearim, which
is Chesalon, on the north side, and went
down to Beth-shemesh, and passed on to
[w]Timnah:
11 And the border went out unto the side
of [x]Ekron northward: and the border was
drawn to Shicron, and passed along to
mount Baalah, and went out unto Jabneel;
and the goings out of the border were at the
sea.
12 And the west border *was* [y]to the great
sea, and the coast *thereof*. This *is* the coast
of the children of Judah round about according to their families.
13 ¶ [z]And unto Caleb the son of Jephunneh he gave a part among the children of
Judah, according to the commandment of
the LORD to Joshua, *even* [a]the city of Arba
the father of Anak, which *city is* Hebron.
14 And Caleb drove thence [b]the three
sons of Anak, [c]Sheshai, and Ahiman, and
Talmai, the children of Anak.
15 And [d]he went up thence to the inhabitants of Debir: and the name of Debir before
was Kirjath-sepher.
16 ¶ [e]And Caleb said, He that smiteth
Kirjath-sepher, and taketh it, to him will I
give Achsah my daughter to wife.
17 And [f]Othniel the [g]son of Kenaz, the
brother of Caleb, took it: and he gave him
Achsah his daughter to wife.
18 [h]And it came to pass, as she came
unto him, that she moved him to ask of her
father a field: and [i]she lighted off *her* ass;
and Caleb said unto her, What wouldest
thou?
19 Who answered, Give me a [j]blessing;
for thou hast given me a south land; give me
also springs of water. And he gave her the
upper springs, and the nether springs.
20 This *is* the inheritance of the tribe of
the children of Judah according to their
families.
21 And the uttermost cities of the tribe of
the children of Judah toward the coast of
Edom southward were Kabzeel, and Eder,
and Jagur,
22 And Kinah, and Dimonah, and Ada-
dah,
23 And Kedesh, and Hazor, and Ithnan,
24 Ziph, and Telem, and Bealoth,
25 And Hazor, Hadattah, and Kerioth,
and Hezron, which *is* Hazor,
26 Amam, and Shema, and Moladah,
27 And Hazar-gaddah, and Heshmon,
and Beth-palet,
28 And Hazar-shual, and Beer-sheba,
and Bizjothjah,
29 Baalah, and Iim, and Azem,
30 And Eltolad, and Chesil, and Hormah,
31 And [k]Ziklag, and Madmannah, and
Sansannah,
32 And Lebaoth, and Shilhim, and Ain,
and Rimmon: all the cities *are* twenty and
nine, with their villages:
33 *And* in the valley, [l]Eshtaol, and Zo-
reah, and Ashnah,
34 And Zanoah, and En-gannim, Tappuah, and Enam,
35 Jarmuth, and Adullam, Socoh, and
Azekah,
36 And Sharaim, and Adithaim, and Ge-
derah, and Gederothaim; fourteen cities
with their villages:
37 Zenan, and Hadashah, and Migdal-
gad,
38 And Dilean, and Mizpeh, [m]and Joktheel,
39 Lachish, and Bozkath, and Eglon,
40 And Cabbon, and Lahmam, and Kith-
lish,
41 And Gederoth, Beth-dagon, and Naamah, and Makkedah; sixteen cities with
their villages:
42 Libnah, and Ether, and Ashan,
43 And Jiphtah, and Ashnah, and Nezib,
44 And Keilah, and Achzib, and Mareshah; nine cities with their villages:
45 Ekron, with her towns and her villages:
46 From Ekron even unto the sea, all that
lay near Ashdod, with their villages:
47 Ashdod with her towns and her villages, Gaza with her towns and her villages,
unto [n]the river of Egypt, and [o]the great
sea, and the border *thereof*:

15:4 *l*Num. 34:5
15:6 *m*ch. 18:19 *n*ch. 18:17
15:7 *o*ch. 7:26 *p*2 Sam. 17:17; 1 Kings 1:9
15:8 *q*ch. 18:16; 2 Kings 23:10; Jer. 19:2 *r*ch. 18:28; Judg. 1:21 *s*ch. 18:16
15:9 *t*ch. 18:15 *u*1 Chron. 13:6 *v*Judg. 18:12
15:10 *w*Gen. 38:13; Judg. 14:1
15:11 *x*ch. 19:43
15:12 *y*ver. 47; Num. 34:6
15:13 *z*ch. 14:13 *a*ch. 14:15
15:14 *b*Judg. 1:10 *c*Num. 13:22
15:15 *d*ch. 10:38; Judg. 1:11
15:16 *e*Judg. 1:12
15:17 *f*Judg. 1:13 *g*Num. 32:12; ch. 14:6
15:18 *h*Judg. 1:14 *i*Gen. 24:64; 1 Sam. 25:23
15:19 *j*Gen. 33:11
15:31 *k*1 Sam. 27:6
15:33 *l*Num. 13:23
15:38 *m*2 Kings 14:7
15:47 *n*ver. 4 *o*Num. 34:6

48 ¶ And in the mountains, Shamir, and Jattir, and Socoh,

49 And Dannah, and Kirjath-sannah, which *is* Debir,

50 And Anab, and Eshtemoh, and Anim,

51 [p]And Goshen, and Holon, and Giloh; eleven cities with their villages:

52 Arab, and Dumah, and Eshean,

53 And Janum, and Beth-tappuah, and Aphekah,

54 And Humtah, and [q]Kirjath-arba, which *is* Hebron, and Zior; nine cities with their villages:

55 Maon, Carmel, and Ziph, and Juttah,

56 And Jezreel, and Jokdeam, and Zanoah,

57 Cain, Gibeah, and Timnah; ten cities with their villages:

58 Halhul, Beth-zur, and Gedor,

59 And Maarath, and Beth-anoth, and Eltekon; six cities with their villages:

60 [r]Kirjath-baal, which *is* Kirjath-jearim, and Rabbah; two cities with their villages:

61 In the wilderness, Beth-arabah, Middin, and Secacah,

62 And Nibshan, and the city of Salt, and En-gedi; six cities with their villages.

63 ¶ As for the Jebusites the inhabitants of Jerusalem, [s]the children of Judah could not drive them out: [t]but the Jebusites dwell with the children of Judah at Jerusalem unto this day.

16 And the lot of the children of Joseph fell from Jordan by Jericho, unto the water of Jericho on the east, to the wilderness that goeth up from Jericho throughout mount Beth-el,

2 And goeth out from Beth-el to [u]Luz, and passeth along unto the borders of Archi to Ataroth,

3 And goeth down westward to the coast of Japhleti, [v]unto the coast of Beth-horon the nether, and to [w]Gezer: and the goings out thereof are at the sea.

4 [x]So the children of Joseph, Manasseh and Ephraim, took their inheritance.

5 ¶ And the border of the children of Ephraim according to their families was *thus:* even the border of their inheritance on the east side was [y]Ataroth-addar, [z]unto Beth-horon the upper;

6 And the border went out toward the sea to [a]Michmethah on the north side; and the border went about eastward unto Taanath-shiloh, and passed by it on the east to Janohah;

7 And it went down from Janohah to Ataroth, [b]and to Naarath, and came to Jericho, and went out at Jordan.

8 The border went out from Tappuah westward unto the [c]river Kanah; and the goings out thereof were at the sea. This *is* the inheritance of the tribe of the children of Ephraim by their families.

9 And [d]the separate cities for the children of Ephraim *were* among the inheritance of the children of Manasseh, all the cities with their villages.

10 [e]And they drave not out the Canaanites that dwelt in Gezer: but the Canaanites dwell among the Ephraimites unto this day, and serve under tribute.

17 There was also a lot for the tribe of Manasseh; for he *was* the [f]firstborn of Joseph; *to wit,* for [g]Machir the firstborn of Manasseh, the father of Gilead: because he was a man of war, therefore he had [h]Gilead and Bashan.

2 There was also *a lot* for [i]the rest of the children of Manasseh by their families; [j]for the children of Abiezer, and for the children of Helek, [k]and for the children of Asriel, and for the children of Shechem, [l]and for the children of Hepher, and for the children of Shemida: these *were* the male children of Manasseh the son of Joseph by their families.

3 ¶ But [m]Zelophehad, the son of Hepher, the son of Gilead, the son of Machir, the son of Manasseh, had no sons, but daughters: and these *are* the names of his daughters, Mahlah, and Noah, Hoglah, Milcah, and Tirzah.

4 And they came near before [n]Eleazar the priest, and before Joshua the son of Nun, and before the princes, saying, [o]The LORD commanded Moses to give us an inheritance among our brethren. Therefore according to the commandment of the LORD he gave them an inheritance among the brethren of their father.

5 And there fell ten portions to Manasseh, beside the land of Gilead and Bashan, which *were* on the other side Jordan;

6 Because the daughters of Manasseh had an inheritance among his sons: and the rest of Manasseh's sons had the land of Gilead.

7 ¶ And the coast of Manasseh was from Asher to [p]Michmethah, that *lieth* before Shechem; and the border went along on the right hand unto the inhabitants of En-tappuah.

8 *Now* Manasseh had the land of Tappuah: but [q]Tappuah on the border of Manasseh *belonged* to the children of Ephraim;

9 And the coast descended [r]unto the river Kanah, southward of the river: [s]these cities of Ephraim *are* among the cities of Manasseh: the coast of Manasseh also *was* on the north side of the river, and the outgoings of it were at the sea:

10 Southward *it was* Ephraim's, and northward *it was* Manasseh's, and the sea is his border; and they met together in Asher on the north, and in Issachar on the east.

11 [t]And Manasseh had in Issachar and in Asher [u]Beth-shean and her towns, and Ibleam and her towns, and the inhabitants of Dor and her towns, and the inhabitants of En-dor and her towns, and the inhabitants of Taanach and her towns, and the inhabitants of Megiddo and her towns, *even* three countries.

12 Yet [v]the children of Manasseh could

15:51 [p]ch. 10:41
15:54 [q]ch. 14:15
15:60 [r]ch. 18:14
15:63 [s]Judg. 1:8; 2 Sam. 5:6 [t]Judg. 1:21
16:2 [u]ch. 18:13; Judg. 1:26
16:3 [v]ch. 18:13; 2 Chron. 8:5 [w]1 Chron. 7:28; 1 Kings 9:15
16:4 [x]ch. 17:14
16:5 [y]ch. 18:13 [z]2 Chron. 8:5
16:6 [a]ch. 17:7
16:7 [b]1 Chron. 7:28
16:8 [c]ch. 17:9
16:9 [d]ch. 17:9
16:10 [e]Judg. 1:29; 1 Kings 9:16
17:1 [f]Gen. 41:51 [g]Gen. 50:23; Num. 26:29; 1 Chron. 7:14 [h]Deut. 3:15
17:2 [i]Num. 26:29-32 [j]1 Chron. 7:18 [k]Num. 26:31 [l]Num. 26:32
17:3 [m]Num. 26:33
17:4 [n]ch. 14:1 [o]Num. 27:6
17:7 [p]ch. 16:6
17:8 [q]ch. 16:8
17:9 [r]ch. 16:8 [s]ch. 16:9
17:11 [t]1 Chron. 7:29 [u]1 Sam. 31:10; 1 Kings 4:12
17:12 [v]Judg. 1:27

not drive out *the inhabitants of* those cities; but the Canaanites would dwell in that land.

13 Yet it came to pass, when the children of Israel were waxen strong, that they put the Canaanites to [w]tribute; but did not utterly drive them out.

14 [x]And the children of Joseph spake unto Joshua, saying, Why hast thou given me *but* [y]one lot and one portion to inherit, seeing I *am* [z]a great people, forasmuch as the LORD hath blessed me hitherto?

15 And Joshua answered them, If thou *be* a great people, *then* get thee up to the wood *country,* and cut down for thyself there in the land of the Perizzites and of the giants, if mount Ephraim be too narrow for thee.

16 And the children of Joseph said, The hill is not enough for us: and all the Canaanites that dwell in the land of the valley have [a]chariots of iron, *both they* who *are* of Beth-shean and her towns, and *they* who *are* [b]of the valley of Jezreel.

17 And Joshua spake unto the house of Joseph, *even* to Ephraim and to Manasseh, saying, Thou *art* a great people, and hast great power: thou shalt not have one lot *only:*

18 But the mountain shall be thine; for it *is* a wood, and thou shalt cut it down: and the outgoings of it shall be thine: for thou shalt drive out the Canaanites, [c]though they have iron chariots, *and* though they *be* strong.

18

And the whole congregation of the children of Israel assembled together [d]at Shiloh, and [e]set up the tabernacle of the congregation there. And the land was subdued before them.

2 And there remained among the children of Israel seven tribes, which had not yet received their inheritance.

3 And Joshua said unto the children of Israel, [f]How long *are* ye slack to go to possess the land, which the LORD God of your fathers hath given you?

4 Give out from among you three men for *each* tribe: and I will send them, and they shall rise, and go through the land, and describe it according to the inheritance of them; and they shall come *again* to me.

5 And they shall divide it into seven parts: [g]Judah shall abide in their coast on the south, and [h]the house of Joseph shall abide in their coasts on the north.

6 Ye shall therefore describe the land *into* seven parts, and bring *the description* hither to me, [i]that I may cast lots for you here before the LORD our God.

7 [j]But the Levites have no part among you; for the priesthood of the LORD *is* their inheritance: [k]and Gad, and Reuben, and half the tribe of Manasseh, have received their inheritance beyond Jordan on the east, which Moses the servant of the LORD gave them.

8 ¶ And the men arose, and went away: and Joshua charged them that went to describe the land, saying, Go and walk through the land, and describe it, and come again to me, that I may here cast lots for you before the LORD in Shiloh.

9 And the men went and passed through the land, and described it by cities into seven parts in a book, and came *again* to Joshua to the host at Shiloh.

10 ¶ And Joshua cast lots for them in Shiloh before the LORD: and there Joshua divided the land unto the children of Israel according to their divisions.

11 ¶ And the lot of the tribe of the children of Benjamin came up according to their families: and the coast of their lot came forth between the children of Judah and the children of Joseph.

12 [l]And their border on the north side was from Jordan; and the border went up to the side of Jericho on the north side, and went up through the mountains westward; and the goings out thereof were at the wilderness of Beth-aven.

13 And the border went over from thence toward Luz, to the side of Luz, [m]which *is* Beth-el, southward; and the border descended to Ataroth-adar, near the hill that *lieth* on the south side of the nether Beth-horon.

14 And the border was drawn *thence,* and compassed the corner of the sea southward, from the hill that *lieth* before Beth-horon southward; and the goings out thereof were at [n]Kirjath-baal, which *is* Kirjath-jearim, a city of the children of Judah: this *was* the west quarter.

15 And the south quarter *was* from the end of Kirjath-jearim, and the border went out on the west, and went out to [o]the well of waters of Nephtoah:

16 And the border came down to the end of the mountain that *lieth* before [p]the valley of the son of Hinnom, *and* which *is* in the valley of the giants on the north, and descended to the valley of Hinnom, to the side of Jebusi on the south, and descended to [q]En-rogel,

17 And was drawn from the north, and went forth to En-shemesh, and went forth toward Geliloth, which *is* over against the going up of Adummim, and descended to [r]the stone of Bohan the son of Reuben,

18 And passed along toward the side over against [s]Arabah northward, and went down unto Arabah:

19 And the border passed along to the side of Beth-hoglah northward: and the outgoings of the border were at the north bay of the salt sea at the south end of Jordan: this *was* the south coast.

20 And Jordan was the border of it on the east side. This *was* the inheritance of the children of Benjamin, by the coasts thereof round about, according to their families.

21 Now the cities of the tribe of the children of Benjamin according to their families were Jericho, and Beth-hoglah, and the valley of Keziz,

17:13 [w]ch. 16:10
17:14 [x]ch. 16:4 [y]Gen. 48:22 [z]Gen. 48:19; Num. 26:34
17:16 [a]Judg. 1:19 [b]ch. 19:18; 1 Kings 4:12
17:18 [c]Deut. 20:1
18:1 [d]ch. 19:51; Jer. 7:12 [e]Judg. 18:31; 1 Sam. 1:3
18:3 [f]Judg. 18:9
18:5 [g]ch. 15:1 [h]ch. 16:1
18:6 [i]ch. 14:2
18:7 [j]ch. 13:33 [k]ch. 13:8
18:12 [l]ch. 16:1
18:13 [m]Gen. 28:19; Judg. 1:23
18:14 [n]ch. 15:9
18:15 [o]ch. 15:9
18:16 [p]ch. 15:8 [q]ch. 15:7
18:17 [r]ch. 15:6
18:18 [s]ch. 15:6

22 And Beth-arabah, and Zemaraim, and Beth-el,
23 And Avim, and Parah, and Ophrah,
24 And Chephar-haammonai, and Ophni, and Gaba; twelve cities with their villages:
25 Gibeon, and Ramah, and Beeroth,
26 And Mizpeh, and Chephirah, and Mozah,
27 And Rekem, and Irpeel, and Taralah,
28 And Zelah, Eleph, and [t]Jebusi, which *is* Jerusalem, Gibeath, *and* Kirjath; fourteen cities with their villages. This *is* the inheritance of the children of Benjamin according to their families.

19 And the second lot came forth to Simeon, *even* for the tribe of the children of Simeon according to their families: [u]and their inheritance was within the inheritance of the children of Judah.
2 And [v]they had in their inheritance Beer-sheba, or Sheba, and Moladah,
3 And Hazar-shual, and Balah, and Azem,
4 And Eltolad, and Bethul, and Hormah,
5 And Ziklag, and Beth-marcaboth, and Hazar-susah,
6 And Beth-lebaoth, and Sharuhen; thirteen cities and their villages:
7 Ain, Remmon, and Ether, and Ashan; four cities and their villages:
8 And all the villages that *were* round about these cities to Baalath-beer, Ramath of the south. This *is* the inheritance of the tribe of the children of Simeon according to their families.
9 Out of the portion of the children of Judah *was* the inheritance of the children of Simeon: for the part of the children of Judah was too much for them: [w]therefore the children of Simeon had their inheritance within the inheritance of them.
10 ¶ And the third lot came up for the children of Zebulun according to their families: and the border of their inheritance was unto Sarid:
11 [x]And their border went up toward the sea, and Maralah, and reached to Dabbasheth, and reached to the river that *is* [y]before Jokneam;
12 And turned from Sarid eastward toward the sunrising unto the border of Chisloth-tabor, and then goeth out to Daberath, and goeth up to Japhia,
13 And from thence passeth on along on the east to Gittah-hepher, to Ittah-kazin, and goeth out to Remmon-methoar to Neah;
14 And the border compasseth it on the north side to Hannathon: and the outgoings thereof are in the valley of Jiphthah-el:
15 And Kattath, and Nahallal, and Shimron, and Idalah, and Beth-lehem: twelve cities with their villages.
16 This *is* the inheritance of the children of Zebulun according to their families, these cities with their villages.
17 ¶ *And* the fourth lot came out to Issachar, for the children of Issachar according to their families.
18 And their border was toward Jezreel, and Chesulloth, and Shunem,
19 And Haphraim, and Shihon, and Anaharath,
20 And Rabbith, and Kishion, and Abez,
21 And Remeth, and En-gannim, and En-haddah, and Beth-pazzez;
22 And the coast reached to Tabor, and Shahazimah, and Beth-shemesh; and the outgoings of their border were at Jordan: sixteen cities with their villages.
23 This *is* the inheritance of the tribe of the children of Issachar according to their families, the cities and their villages.
24 ¶ And the fifth lot came out for the tribe of the children of Asher according to their families.
25 And their border was Helkath, and Hali, and Beten, and Achshaph,
26 And Alammelech, and Amad, and Misheal; and reacheth to Carmel westward, and to Shihor-libnath;
27 And turneth toward the sunrising to Beth-dagon, and reacheth to Zebulun, and to the valley of Jiphthah-el toward the north side of Beth-emek, and Neiel, and goeth out to Cabul on the left hand,
28 And Hebron, and Rehob, and Hammon, and Kanah, [z]*even* unto great Zidon;
29 And *then* the coast turneth to Ramah, and to the strong city Tyre; and the coast turneth to Hosah; and the outgoings thereof are at the sea from the coast to [a]Achzib:
30 Ummah also, and Aphek, and Rehob: twenty and two cities with their villages.
31 This *is* the inheritance of the tribe of the children of Asher according to their families, these cities with their villages.
32 ¶ The sixth lot came out to the children of Naphtali, *even* for the children of Naphtali according to their families.
33 And their coast was from Heleph, from Allon to Zaanannim, and Adami, Nekeb, and Jabneel, unto Lakum; and the outgoings thereof were at Jordan:
34 And *then* [b]the coast turneth westward to Aznoth-tabor, and goeth out from thence to Hukkok, and reacheth to Zebulun on the south side, and reacheth to Asher on the west side, and to Judah upon Jordan toward the sunrising.
35 And the fenced cities *are* Ziddim, Zer, and Hammath, Rakkath, and Chinnereth,
36 And Adamah, and Ramah, and Hazor,
37 And Kedesh, and Edrei, and En-hazor,
38 And Iron, and Migdal-el, Horem, and Beth-anath, and Beth-shemesh; nineteen cities with their villages.
39 This *is* the inheritance of the tribe of the children of Naphtali according to their families, the cities and their villages.
40 ¶ *And* the seventh lot came out for the tribe of the children of Dan according to their families.
41 And the coast of their inheritance was Zorah, and Eshtaol, and Ir-shemesh,
42 And [c]Shaalabbin, and Ajalon, and Jethlah,

18:28 [t]ch. 15:8
19:1 [u]ver. 9
19:2 [v]1 Chron. 4:28
19:9 [w]ver. 1
19:11 [x]Gen. 49:13 [y]ch. 12:22
19:28 [z]ch. 11:8; Judg. 1:31
19:29 [a]Gen. 38:5; Judg. 1:31; Mic. 1:14
19:34 [b]Deut. 33:23
19:42 [c]Judg. 1:35

43 And Elon, and Thimnathah, and Ekron,
44 And Eltekeh, and Gibbethon, and Baalath,
45 And Jehud, and Bene-berak, and
Gath-rimmon,
46 And Me-jarkon, and Rakkon, with the
border before Japho.
47 And [d]the coast of the children of Dan
went out *too little* for them: therefore the
children of Dan went up to fight against Leshem, and took it, and smote it with the
edge of the sword, and possessed it, and
dwelt therein, and called Leshem, [e]Dan, after the name of Dan their father.
48 This *is* the inheritance of the tribe of
the children of Dan according to their families, these cities with their villages.
49 ¶ When they had made an end of dividing the land for inheritance by their coasts,
the children of Israel gave an inheritance to
Joshua the son of Nun among them:
50 According to the word of the LORD
they gave him the city which he asked, *even*
[f]Timnath-[g]serah in mount Ephraim: and
he built the city, and dwelt therein.
51 [h]These *are* the inheritances, which Eleazar the priest, and Joshua the son of Nun,
and the heads of the fathers of the tribes of
the children of Israel, divided for an inheritance by lot [i]in Shiloh before the LORD, at
the door of the tabernacle of the congregation. So they made an end of dividing the
country.

20 The LORD also spake unto Joshua,
saying,
2 Speak to the children of Israel, saying,
[j]Appoint out for you cities of refuge,
whereof I spake unto you by the hand of
Moses:
3 That the slayer that killeth *any* person
unawares *and* unwittingly may flee thither:
and they shall be your refuge from the
avenger of blood.
4 And when he that doth flee unto one of
those cities shall stand at the entering of
[k]the gate of the city, and shall declare his
cause in the ears of the elders of that city,
they shall take him into the city unto them,
and give him a place, that he may dwell
among them.
5 [l]And if the avenger of blood pursue
after him, then they shall not deliver the
slayer up into his hand; because he smote
his neighbour unwittingly, and hated him
not beforetime.
6 And he shall dwell in that city, [m]until
he stand before the congregation for judgment, *and* until the death of the high priest
that shall be in those days: then shall the
slayer return, and come unto his own city,
and unto his own house, unto the city from
whence he fled.
7 ¶ And they appointed [n]Kedesh in Galilee in mount Naphtali, and [o]Shechem in
mount Ephraim, and [p]Kirjath-arba, which
is Hebron, in the [q]mountain of Judah.
8 And on the other side Jordan by Jericho
eastward, they assigned [r]Bezer in the wilderness upon the plain out of the tribe of
Reuben, and [s]Ramoth in Gilead out of the
tribe of Gad, and [t]Golan in Bashan out of
the tribe of Manasseh.
9 [u]These were the cities appointed for all
the children of Israel, and for the stranger
that sojourneth among them, that whosoever killeth *any* person at unawares might
flee thither, and not die by the hand of the
avenger of blood, [v]until he stood before the
congregation.

21 Then came near the heads of the fathers of the Levites unto [w]Eleazar
the priest, and unto Joshua the son of Nun,
and unto the heads of the fathers of the
tribes of the children of Israel;
2 And they spake unto them at [x]Shiloh
in the land of Canaan, saying, [y]The LORD
commanded by the hand of Moses to give us
cities to dwell in, with the suburbs thereof
for our cattle.
3 And the children of Israel gave unto the
Levites out of their inheritance, at the commandment of the LORD, these cities and
their suburbs.
4 And the lot came out for the families of
the Kohathites: and [z]the children of Aaron
the priest, *which were* of the Levites, [a]had
by lot out of the tribe of Judah, and out of
the tribe of Simeon, and out of the tribe of
Benjamin, thirteen cities.
5 And [b]the rest of the children of Kohath
had by lot out of the families of the tribe of
Ephraim, and out of the tribe of Dan, and
out of the half tribe of Manasseh, ten cities.
6 And [c]the children of Gershon *had* by
lot out of the families of the tribe of Issachar, and out of the tribe of Asher, and out
of the tribe of Naphtali, and out of the half
tribe of Manasseh in Bashan, thirteen cities.
7 [d]The children of Merari by their families *had* out of the tribe of Reuben, and out
of the tribe of Gad, and out of the tribe of
Zebulun, twelve cities.
8 [e]And the children of Israel gave by lot
unto the Levites these cities with their suburbs, [f]as the LORD commanded by the hand
of Moses.
9 ¶ And they gave out of the tribe of the
children of Judah, and out of the tribe of the
children of Simeon, these cities which are
here mentioned by name,
10 [g]Which the children of Aaron, *being*
of the families of the Kohathites, *who were*
of the children of Levi, had: for theirs was
the first lot.
11 [h]And they gave them the city of Arba
the father of [i]Anak, which *city is* Hebron,
[j]in the hill *country* of Judah, with the suburbs thereof round about it.
12 But [k]the fields of the city, and the villages thereof, gave they to Caleb the son of
Jephunneh for his possession.
13 ¶ Thus [l]they gave to the children of
Aaron the priest [m]Hebron with her suburbs,
to be a city of refuge for the slayer; [n]and
Libnah with her suburbs,

19:47 [d]Judg. 18 [e]Judg. 18:29
19:50 [f]ch. 24:30 [g]1 Chron. 7:24
19:51 [h]Num. 34:17; ch. 14:1 [i]ch. 18:1
20:2 [j]Ex. 21:13; Num. 35:6; Deut. 19:2
20:4 [k]Ruth 4:1
20:5 [l]Num. 35:12
20:6 [m]Num. 35:12
20:7 [n]ch. 21:32; 1 Chron. 6:76 [o]ch. 21:21; 2 Chron. 10:1 [p]ch. 14:15 [q]Luke 1:39
20:8 [r]Deut. 4:43; ch. 21:36; 1 Chron. 6:78 [s]ch. 21:38; 1 Kings 22:3 [t]ch. 21:27
20:9 [u]Num. 35:15 [v]ver. 6
21:1 [w]ch. 14:1
21:2 [x]ch. 18:1 [y]Num. 35:2
21:4 [z]ver. 8 [a]ch. 24:33
21:5 [b]ver. 20
21:6 [c]ver. 27
21:7 [d]ver. 34
21:8 [e]ver. 3 [f]Num. 35:2
21:10 [g]ver. 4
21:11 [h]1 Chron. 6:55 [i]ch. 15:13 [j]ch. 20:7; Luke 1:39
21:12 [k]ch. 14:14; 1 Chron. 6:56
21:13 [l]1 Chron. 6:57 [m]ch. 15:54 [n]ch. 15:42

14 And [o]Jattir with her suburbs, [p]and
Eshtemoa with her suburbs,
15 And [q]Holon with her suburbs, [r]and
Debir with her suburbs,
16 And [s]Ain with her suburbs, [t]and Juttah with her suburbs, *and* [u]Beth-shemesh
with her suburbs; nine cities out of those
two tribes.
17 And out of the tribe of Benjamin,
[v]Gibeon with her suburbs, [w]Geba with her
suburbs,
18 Anathoth with her suburbs, and [x]Al-
mon with her suburbs; four cities.
19 All the cities of the children of Aaron,
the priests, *were* thirteen cities with their
suburbs.
20 ¶ [y]And the families of the children of
Kohath, the Levites which remained of the
children of Kohath, even they had the cities
of their lot out of the tribe of Ephraim.
21 For they gave them [z]Shechem with
her suburbs in mount Ephraim, *to be* a city
of refuge for the slayer; and Gezer with her
suburbs,
22 And Kibzaim with her suburbs, and
Beth-horon with her suburbs; four cities.
23 And out of the tribe of Dan, Eltekeh
with her suburbs, Gibbethon with her suburbs,
24 Aijalon with her suburbs, Gath-
rimmon with her suburbs; four cities.
25 And out of the half tribe of Manasseh,
Tanach with her suburbs, and Gath-
rimmon with her suburbs; two cities.
26 All the cities *were* ten with their suburbs for the families of the children of Kohath that remained.
27 ¶ [a]And unto the children of Gershon,
of the families of the Levites, out of the
other half tribe of Manasseh *they gave*
[b]Golan in Bashan with her suburbs, *to be* a
city of refuge for the slayer; and Beesh-
terah with her suburbs; two cities.
28 And out of the tribe of Issachar, Kishon with her suburbs, Dabareh with her
suburbs,
29 Jarmuth with her suburbs, En-gannim
with her suburbs; four cities.
30 And out of the tribe of Asher, Mishal
with her suburbs, Abdon with her suburbs,
31 Helkath with her suburbs, and Rehob
with her suburbs; four cities.
32 And out of the tribe of Naphtali, [c]Ke-
desh in Galilee with her suburbs, *to be* a city
of refuge for the slayer; and Hammoth-dor
with her suburbs, and Kartan with her suburbs; three cities.
33 All the cities of the Gershonites according to their families *were* thirteen cities
with their suburbs.
34 ¶ [d]And unto the families of the children of Merari, the rest of the Levites, out of
the tribe of Zebulun, Jokneam with her suburbs, and Kartah with her suburbs,
35 Dimnah with her suburbs, Nahalal
with her suburbs; four cities.
36 And out of the tribe of Reuben, [e]Bezer

21:14 [o]ch. 15:48 [p]ch. 15:50
21:15 [q]ch. 15:51; 1 Chron. 6:58 [r]ch. 15:49
21:16 [s]ch. 15:42; 1 Chron. 6:59 [t]ch. 15:55 [u]ch. 15:10
21:17 [v]ch. 18:25 [w]ch. 18:24
21:18 [x]1 Chron. 6:60
21:20 [y]ver. 5; 1 Chron. 6:66
21:21 [z]ch. 20:7
21:27 [a]ver. 6; 1 Chron. 6:71 [b]ch. 20:8
21:32 [c]ch. 20:7
21:34 [d]ver. 7; 1 Chron. 6:77
21:36 [e]ch. 20:8
21:38 [f]ch. 20:8
21:41 [g]Num. 35:7
21:43 [h]Gen. 13:15
21:44 [i]ch. 11:23 [j]Deut. 7:24
21:45 [k]ch. 23:14
22:2 [l]Num. 32:20; Deut. 3:18 [m]ch. 1:16
22:4 [n]Num. 32:33; Deut. 29:8; ch. 13:8
22:5 [o]Deut. 6:6 [p]Deut. 10:12
22:6 [q]Gen. 47:7; Ex. 39:43; ch. 14:13; 2 Sam. 6:18; Luke 24:50
22:7 [r]ch. 17:5

with her suburbs, and Jahazah with her
suburbs,
37 Kedemoth with her suburbs, and
Mephaath with her suburbs; four cities.
38 And out of the tribe of Gad, [f]Ramoth
in Gilead with her suburbs, *to be* a city of
refuge for the slayer; and Mahanaim with
her suburbs,
39 Heshbon with her suburbs, Jazer with
her suburbs; four cities in all.
40 So all the cities for the children of Merari by their families, which were remaining
of the families of the Levites, were *by* their
lot twelve cities.
41 [g]All the cities of the Levites within the
possession of the children of Israel *were*
forty and eight cities with their suburbs.
42 These cities were every one with their
suburbs round about them: thus *were* all
these cities.
43 ¶ And the LORD gave unto Israel [h]all
the land which he sware to give unto their
fathers; and they possessed it, and dwelt
therein.
44 [i]And the LORD gave them rest round
about, according to all that he sware unto
their fathers: and [j]there stood not a man of
all their enemies before them; the LORD delivered all their enemies into their hand.
45 [k]There failed not ought of any good
thing which the LORD had spoken unto the
house of Israel; all came to pass.

22

Then Joshua called the Reubenites,
and the Gadites, and the half tribe of
Manasseh,
2 And said unto them, Ye have kept [l]all
that Moses the servant of the LORD commanded you, [m]and have obeyed my voice in
all that I commanded you:
3 Ye have not left your brethren these
many days unto this day, but have kept the
charge of the commandment of the LORD
your God.
4 And now the LORD your God hath given
rest unto your brethren, as he promised
them: therefore now return ye, and get you
unto your tents, *and* unto the land of your
possession, [n]which Moses the servant of
the LORD gave you on the other side Jordan.
5 But [o]take diligent heed to do the commandment and the law, which Moses the
servant of the LORD charged you, [p]to love
the LORD your God, and to walk in all his
ways, and to keep his commandments, and
to cleave unto him, and to serve him with all
your heart and with all your soul.
6 So Joshua [q]blessed them, and sent
them away: and they went unto their tents.
7 ¶ Now to the *one* half of the tribe of
Manasseh Moses had given *possession* in
Bashan: [r]but unto the *other* half thereof
gave Joshua among their brethren on this
side Jordan westward. And when Joshua
sent them away also unto their tents, then
he blessed them,
8 And he spake unto them, saying, Return
with much riches unto your tents, and with
very much cattle, with silver, and with gold,

and with brass, and with iron, and with very much raiment: [s]divide the spoil of your enemies with your brethren.

9 ¶ And the children of Reuben and the children of Gad and the half tribe of Manasseh returned, and departed from the children of Israel out of Shiloh, which *is* in the land of Canaan, to go unto [t]the country of Gilead, to the land of their possession, whereof they were possessed, according to the word of the LORD by the hand of Moses.

10 ¶ And when they came unto the borders of Jordan, that *are* in the land of Canaan, the children of Reuben and the children of Gad and the half tribe of Manasseh built there an altar by Jordan, a great altar to see to.

11 ¶ And the children of Israel [u]heard say, Behold, the children of Reuben and the children of Gad and the half tribe of Manasseh have built an altar over against the land of Canaan, in the borders of Jordan, at the passage of the children of Israel.

12 And when the children of Israel heard *of it,* [v]the whole congregation of the children of Israel gathered themselves together at Shiloh, to go up to war against them.

13 And the children of Israel [w]sent unto the children of Reuben, and to the children of Gad, and to the half tribe of Manasseh, into the land of Gilead, [x]Phinehas the son of Eleazar the priest,

14 And with him ten princes, of each chief house a prince throughout all the tribes of Israel; and [y]each one *was* an head of the house of their fathers among the thousands of Israel.

15 ¶ And they came unto the children of Reuben, and to the children of Gad, and to the half tribe of Manasseh, unto the land of Gilead, and they spake with them, saying,

16 Thus saith the whole congregation of the LORD, What trespass *is* this that ye have committed against the God of Israel, to turn away this day from following the LORD, in that ye have builded you an altar, [z]that ye might rebel this day against the LORD?

17 *Is* the iniquity [a]of Peor too little for us, from which we are not cleansed until this day, although there was a plague in the congregation of the LORD,

18 But that ye must turn away this day from following the LORD? and it will be, *seeing* ye rebel to day against the LORD, that to morrow [b]he will be wroth with the whole congregation of Israel.

19 Notwithstanding, if the land of your possession *be* unclean, *then* pass ye over unto the land of the possession of the LORD, [c]wherein the LORD's tabernacle dwelleth, and take possession among us: but rebel not against the LORD, nor rebel against us, in building you an altar beside the altar of the LORD our God.

20 [d]Did not Achan the son of Zerah commit a trespass in the accursed thing, and wrath fell on all the congregation of Israel? and that man perished not alone in his iniquity.

21 ¶ Then the children of Reuben and the children of Gad and the half tribe of Manasseh answered, and said unto the heads of the thousands of Israel,

22 The LORD [e]God of gods, the LORD God of gods, he [f]knoweth, and Israel he shall know; if *it be* in rebellion, or if in transgression against the LORD, (save us not this day,)

23 That we have built us an altar to turn from following the LORD, or if to offer thereon burnt offering or meat offering, or if to offer peace offerings thereon, let the LORD himself [g]require *it;*

24 And if we have not *rather* done it for fear of *this* thing, saying, In time to come your children might speak unto our children, saying, What have ye to do with the LORD God of Israel?

25 For the LORD hath made Jordan a border between us and you, ye children of Reuben and children of Gad; ye have no part in the LORD: so shall your children make our children cease from fearing the LORD.

26 Therefore we said, Let us now prepare to build us an altar, not for burnt offering, nor for sacrifice:

27 But *that* it *may be* [h]a witness between us, and you, and our generations after us, that we might [i]do the service of the LORD before him with our burnt offerings, and with our sacrifices, and with our peace offerings; that your children may not say to our children in time to come, Ye have no part in the LORD.

28 Therefore said we, that it shall be, when they should *so* say to us or to our generations in time to come, that we may say *again,* Behold the pattern of the altar of the LORD, which our fathers made, not for burnt offerings, nor for sacrifices; but it *is* a witness between us and you.

29 God forbid that we should rebel against the LORD, and turn this day from following the LORD, [j]to build an altar for burnt offerings, for meat offerings, or for sacrifices, beside the altar of the LORD our God that *is* before his tabernacle.

30 ¶ And when Phinehas the priest, and the princes of the congregation and heads of the thousands of Israel which *were* with him, heard the words that the children of Reuben and the children of Gad and the children of Manasseh spake, it pleased them.

31 And Phinehas the son of Eleazar the priest said unto the children of Reuben, and to the children of Gad, and to the children of Manasseh, This day we perceive that the LORD *is* [k]among us, because ye have not committed this trespass against the LORD: now ye have delivered the children of Israel out of the hand of the LORD.

32 ¶ And Phinehas the son of Eleazar the priest, and the princes, returned from the children of Reuben, and from the children

22:8 [s]Num. 31:27; 1 Sam. 30:14
22:9 [t]Num. 32:1
22:11 [u]Deut. 13:12; Judg. 20:12
22:12 [v]Judg. 20:1
22:13 [w]Deut. 13:14; Judg. 20:12 [x]Ex. 6:25; Num. 25:7
22:14 [y]Num. 1:4
22:16 [z]Lev. 17:8; Deut. 12:13
22:17 [a]Num. 25:3; Deut. 4:3
22:18 [b]Num. 16:22
22:19 [c]ch. 18:1
22:20 [d]ch. 7:1
22:22 [e]Deut. 10:17 [f]1 Kings 8:39; Job 10:7; Ps. 44:21; Jer. 12:3; 2 Cor. 11:11
22:23 [g]Deut. 18:19; 1 Sam. 20:16
22:27 [h]Gen. 31:48; ch. 24:27; ver. 34 [i]Deut. 12:5
22:29 [j]Deut. 12:13
22:31 [k]Lev. 26:11; 2 Chron. 15:2

of Gad, out of the land of Gilead, unto the land of Canaan, to the children of Israel, and brought them word again.

33 And the thing pleased the children of Israel; and the children of Israel [l]blessed God, and did not intend to go up against them in battle, to destroy the land wherein the children of Reuben and Gad dwelt.

34 And the children of Reuben and the children of Gad called the altar *Ed:* for it *shall be* a witness between us that the LORD *is* God.

23 And it came to pass a long time after that the LORD [m]had given rest unto Israel from all their enemies round about, that Joshua [n]waxed old *and* stricken in age.

2 And Joshua [o]called for all Israel, *and* for their elders, and for their heads, and for their judges, and for their officers, and said unto them, I am old *and* stricken in age:

3 And ye have seen all that the LORD your God hath done unto all these nations because of you; for the [p]LORD your God *is* he that hath fought for you.

4 Behold, [q]I have divided unto you by lot these nations that remain, to be an inheritance for your tribes, from Jordan, with all the nations that I have cut off, even unto the great sea westward.

5 And the LORD your God, [r]he shall expel them from before you, and drive them from out of your sight; and ye shall possess their land, [s]as the LORD your God hath promised unto you.

6 [t]Be ye therefore very courageous to keep and to do all that is written in the book of the law of Moses, [u]that ye turn not aside therefrom *to* the right hand or *to* the left;

7 That ye [v]come not among these nations, these that remain among you; neither [w]make mention of the name of their gods, nor cause to swear *by them,* neither serve them, nor bow yourselves unto them:

8 But [x]cleave unto the LORD your God, as ye have done unto this day.

9 [y]For the LORD hath driven out from before you great nations and strong: but *as for* you, [z]no man hath been able to stand before you unto this day.

10 [a]One man of you shall chase a thousand: for the LORD your God, he *it is* that fighteth for you, [b]as he hath promised you.

11 [c]Take good heed therefore unto yourselves, that ye love the LORD your God.

12 Else if ye do in any wise [d]go back, and cleave unto the remnant of these nations, *even* these that remain among you, and shall [e]make marriages with them, and go in unto them, and they to you:

13 Know for a certainty that [f]the LORD your God will no more drive out *any of* these nations from before you; [g]but they shall be snares and traps unto you, and scourges in your sides, and thorns in your eyes, until ye perish from off this good land which the LORD your God hath given you.

14 And, behold, this day [h]I *am* going the way of all the earth: and ye know in all your hearts and in all your souls, that [i]not one thing hath failed of all the good things which the LORD your God spake concerning you; all are come to pass unto you, *and* not one thing hath failed thereof.

15 [j]Therefore it shall come to pass, *that* as all good things are come upon you, which the LORD your God promised you; so shall the LORD bring upon you [k]all evil things, until he have destroyed you from off this good land which the LORD your God hath given you.

16 When ye have transgressed the covenant of the LORD your God, which he commanded you, and have gone and served other gods, and bowed yourselves to them; then shall the anger of the LORD be kindled against you, and ye shall perish quickly from off the good land which he hath given unto you.

24 And Joshua gathered all the tribes of Israel to [l]Shechem, and [m]called for the elders of Israel, and for their heads, and for their judges, and for their officers; and they [n]presented themselves before God.

2 And Joshua said unto all the people, Thus saith the LORD God of Israel, [o]Your fathers dwelt on the other side of the flood in old time, *even* Terah, the father of Abraham, and the father of Nachor: and [p]they served other gods.

3 And [q]I took your father Abraham from the other side of the flood, and led him throughout all the land of Canaan, and multiplied his seed, and [r]gave him Isaac.

4 And I gave unto Isaac [s]Jacob and Esau: and I gave unto [t]Esau mount Seir, to possess it; [u]but Jacob and his children went down into Egypt.

5 [v]I sent Moses also and Aaron, and [w]I plagued Egypt, according to that which I did among them: and afterward I brought you out.

6 And I [x]brought your fathers out of Egypt: and [y]ye came unto the sea; [z]and the Egyptians pursued after your fathers with chariots and horsemen unto the Red sea.

7 And when they [a]cried unto the LORD, [b]he put darkness between you and the Egyptians, [c]and brought the sea upon them, and covered them; and [d]your eyes have seen what I have done in Egypt: and ye dwelt in the wilderness [e]a long season.

8 And I brought you into the land of the Amorites, which dwelt on the other side Jordan; [f]and they fought with you: and I gave them into your hand, that ye might possess their land; and I destroyed them from before you.

9 Then [g]Balak the son of Zippor, king of Moab, arose and warred against Israel, and [h]sent and called Balaam the son of Beor to curse you:

10 [i]But I would not hearken unto Balaam; [j]therefore he blessed you still: so I delivered you out of his hand.

11 And [k]you went over Jordan, and came unto Jericho: and [l]the men of Jericho

22:33 [l]1 Chron. 29:20; Neh. 8:6; Dan. 2:19; Luke 2:28
23:1 [m]ch. 21:44 [n]ch. 13:1
23:2 [o]Deut. 31:28; ch. 24:1; 1 Chron. 28:1
23:3 [p]Ex. 14:14; ch. 10:14
23:4 [q]ch. 13:2
23:5 [r]Ex. 23:30; Deut. 11:23; ch. 13:6 [s]Num. 33:53
23:6 [t]ch. 1:7 [u]Deut. 5:32
23:7 [v]Ex. 23:33; Deut. 7:2; Prov. 4:14; Eph. 5:11 [w]Ex. 23:13; Num. 32:38; Ps. 16:4; Jer. 5:7; Zeph. 1:5
23:8 [x]Deut. 10:20; ch. 22:5
23:9 [y]Deut. 11:23 [z]ch. 1:5
23:10 [a]Lev. 26:8; Deut. 32:30; Judg. 3:31; 2 Sam. 23:8 [b]Ex. 14:14; Deut. 3:22
23:11 [c]ch. 22:5
23:12 [d]Heb. 10:38; 2 Pet. 2:20 [e]Deut. 7:3
23:13 [f]Judg. 2:3 [g]Ex. 23:33; Num. 33:55; Deut. 7:16; 1 Kings 11:4
23:14 [h]1 Kings 2:2; Heb. 9:27 [i]ch. 21:45; Luke 21:33
23:15 [j]Deut. 28:63 [k]Lev. 26:16; Deut. 28:15
24:1 [l]Gen. 35:4 [m]ch. 23:2 [n]1 Sam. 10:19
24:2 [o]Gen. 11:26 [p]Gen. 31:53
24:3 [q]Gen. 12:1; Acts 7:2 [r]Gen. 21:2; Ps. 127:3
24:4 [s]Gen. 25:24 [t]Gen. 36:8; Deut. 2:5 [u]Gen. 46:1; Acts 7:15
24:5 [v]Ex. 3:10 [w]Ex. 7
24:6 [x]Ex. 12:37 [y]Ex. 14:2 [z]Ex. 14:9
24:7 [a]Ex. 14:10 [b]Ex. 14:20 [c]Ex. 14:27 [d]Deut. 4:34 [e]ch. 5:6
24:8 [f]Num. 21:21; Deut. 2:32
24:9 [g]Judg. 11:25 [h]Num. 22:5; Deut. 23:4
24:10 [i]Deut. 23:5 [j]Num. 23:11
24:11 [k]ch. 3:14 [l]ch. 6:1

fought against you, the Amorites, and the
Perizzites, and the Canaanites, and the Hittites, and the Girgashites, the Hivites, and
the Jebusites; and I delivered them into
your hand.
12 And [m]I sent the hornet before you,
which drave them out from before you, *even*
the two kings of the Amorites; *but* [n]not
with thy sword, nor with thy bow.
13 And I have given you a land for which
ye did not labour, and [o]cities which ye built
not, and ye dwell in them; of the vineyards
and oliveyards which ye planted not do ye
eat.
14 ¶ [p]Now therefore fear the LORD, and
serve him in [q]sincerity and in truth: and
[r]put away the gods which your fathers
served on the other side of the flood, and
[s]in Egypt; and serve ye the LORD.
15 And if it seem evil unto you to serve
the LORD, [t]choose you this day whom ye
will serve; whether [u]the gods which your
fathers served that *were* on the other side of
the flood, or [v]the gods of the Amorites, in
whose land ye dwell: [w]but as for me and my
house, we will serve the LORD.
16 And the people answered and said,
God forbid that we should forsake the
LORD, to serve other gods;
17 For the LORD our God, he *it is* that
brought us up and our fathers out of the
land of Egypt, from the house of bondage,
and which did those great signs in our sight,
and preserved us in all the way wherein we
went, and among all the people through
whom we passed:
18 And the LORD drave out from before us
all the people, even the Amorites which
dwelt in the land: *therefore* will we also
serve the LORD; for he *is* our God.
19 And Joshua said unto the people, [x]Ye
cannot serve the LORD: for he *is* an [y]holy
God; he *is* [z]a jealous God; [a]he will not forgive your transgressions nor your sins.
20 [b]If ye forsake the LORD, and serve
strange gods, [c]then he will turn and do you
hurt, and consume you, after that he hath
done you good.
21 And the people said unto Joshua, Nay;
but we will serve the LORD.
22 And Joshua said unto the people, Ye
are witnesses against yourselves that [d]ye
have chosen you the LORD, to serve him.
And they said, *We are* witnesses.
23 Now therefore [e]put away, *said he,* the
strange gods which *are* among you, and incline your heart unto the LORD God of Israel.
24 And the people said unto Joshua, The
LORD our God will we serve, and his voice
will we obey.
25 So Joshua [f]made a covenant with the
people that day, and set them a statute and
an ordinance [g]in Shechem.
26 ¶ And Joshua [h]wrote these words in
the book of the law of God, and took [i]a
great stone, and [j]set it up there [k]under an
oak, that *was* by the sanctuary of the LORD.
27 And Joshua said unto all the people,
Behold, this stone shall be [l]a witness unto
us; for [m]it hath heard all the words of the
LORD which he spake unto us: it shall be
therefore a witness unto you, lest ye deny
your God.
28 So [n]Joshua let the people depart, every man unto his inheritance.
29 ¶ [o]And it came to pass after these
things, that Joshua the son of Nun, the servant of the LORD, died, *being* an hundred
and ten years old.
30 And they buried him in the border of
his inheritance in [p]Timnath-serah, which *is*
in mount Ephraim, on the north side of the
hill of Gaash.
31 And [q]Israel served the LORD all the
days of Joshua, and all the days of the elders that overlived Joshua, and which had
[r]known all the works of the LORD, that he
had done for Israel.
32 ¶ And [s]the bones of Joseph, which the
children of Israel brought up out of Egypt,
buried they in Shechem, in a parcel of
ground [t]which Jacob bought of the sons of
Hamor the father of Shechem for an hundred pieces of silver: and it became the inheritance of the children of Joseph.
33 ¶ And Eleazar the son of Aaron died;
and they buried him in a hill *that pertained*
to [u]Phinehas his son, which was given him
in mount Ephraim.

24:12 [m]Ex. 23:28; Deut. 7:20 [n]Ps. 44:3
24:13 [o]Deut. 6:10; ch. 11:13
24:14 [p]Deut. 10:12; 1 Sam. 12:24 [q]Gen. 17:1; Deut. 18:13; Ps. 119:1; 2 Cor. 1:12; Eph. 6:24 [r]ver. 2; Lev. 17:7; Ezek. 20:18 [s]Ezek. 20:7
24:15 [t]Ruth 1:15; 1 Kings 18:21; Ezek. 20:39; John 6:67 [u]ver. 14 [v]Ex. 23:24; Deut. 13:7; Judg. 6:10 [w]Gen. 18:19
24:19 [x]Matt. 6:24 [y]Lev. 19:2; 1 Sam. 6:20; Ps. 99:5; Isa. 5:16 [z]Ex. 20:5 [a]Ex. 23:21
24:20 [b]1 Chron. 28:9; 2 Chron. 15:2; Ezra 8:22; Isa. 1:28; Jer. 17:13 [c]ch. 23:15; Isa. 63:10; Acts 7:42
24:22 [d]Ps. 119:173
24:23 [e]ver. 14; Gen. 35:2; Judg. 10:16; 1 Sam. 7:3
24:25 [f]Ex. 15:25; 2 Kings 11:17 [g]ver. 26
24:26 [h]Deut. 31:24 [i]Judg. 9:6 [j]Gen. 28:18; ch. 4:3 [k]Gen. 35:4
24:27 [l]Gen. 31:48; Deut. 31:19; ch. 22:27 [m]Deut. 32:1
24:28 [n]Judg. 2:6
24:29 [o]Judg. 2:8
24:30 [p]ch. 19:50; Judg. 2:9
24:31 [q]Judg. 2:7 [r]Deut. 11:2
24:32 [s]Gen. 50:25; Ex. 13:19 [t]Gen. 33:19
24:33 [u]Ex. 6:25; Judg. 20:28

JUDGES

Samuel wrote the book of Judges around 1000 B.C. The book of Judges covers approximately 300 years from the death of Joshua until the rise of the monarchy in Israel. During this tumultuous time several leaders, judges, are raised up to govern the people. Some of these men and women are heroic in their efforts while others rule over a people straying far from God.

The two best known characters in the book are Gideon (6:1–8:35) and Samson. Samson and his affair with Delilah is the best known story (16:1–16:31).

I. Israel following the death of Joshua, 1:1–3:6
II. Israel under the judges, 3:7–16:31
III. The failings during the period of the judges, 17:1–21:25

---

1 Now after the death of Joshua it came to pass, that the children of Israel [a]asked the LORD, saying, Who shall go up for us against the Canaanites first, to fight against them?

2 And the LORD said, [b]Judah shall go up: behold, I have delivered the land into his hand.

3 And Judah said unto Simeon his brother, Come up with me into my lot, that we may fight against the Canaanites; and [c]I likewise will go with thee into thy lot. So Simeon went with him.

4 And Judah went up; and the LORD delivered the Canaanites and the Perizzites into their hand: and they slew of them in [d]Bezek ten thousand men.

5 And they found Adoni-bezek in Bezek: and they fought against him, and they slew the Canaanites and the Perizzites.

6 But Adoni-bezek fled; and they pursued after him, and caught him, and cut off his thumbs and his great toes.

7 And Adoni-bezek said, Threescore and ten kings, having their thumbs and their great toes cut off, gathered *their meat* under my table: [e]as I have done, so God hath requited me. And they brought him to Jerusalem, and there he died.

8 Now [f]the children of Judah had fought against Jerusalem, and had taken it, and smitten it with the edge of the sword, and set the city on fire.

9 ¶ [g]And afterward the children of Judah went down to fight against the Canaanites, that dwelt in the mountain, and in the south, and in the valley.

10 And Judah went against the Canaanites that dwelt in Hebron: (now the name of Hebron before *was* [h]Kirjath-arba:) and they slew Sheshai, and Ahiman, and Talmai.

11 [i]And from thence he went against the inhabitants of Debir: and the name of Debir before *was* Kirjath-sepher:

12 [j]And Caleb said, He that smiteth Kirjath-sepher, and taketh it, to him will I give Achsah my daughter to wife.

13 And Othniel the son of Kenaz, [k]Caleb's younger brother, took it: and he gave him Achsah his daughter to wife.

14 [l]And it came to pass, when she came *to him,* that she moved him to ask of her father a field: and she lighted from off *her* ass; and Caleb said unto her, What wilt thou?

15 And she said unto him, [m]Give me a blessing: for thou hast given me a south land; give me also springs of water. And Caleb gave her the upper springs and the nether springs.

16 ¶ [n]And the children of the Kenite, Moses' father in law, went up out [o]of the city of palm trees with the children of Judah into the wilderness of Judah, which *lieth* in the south of [p]Arad; [q]and they went and dwelt among the people.

17 [r]And Judah went with Simeon his brother, and they slew the Canaanites that inhabited Zephath, and utterly destroyed it. And the name of the city was called [s]Hormah.

18 Also Judah took [t]Gaza with the coast thereof, and Askelon with the coast thereof, and Ekron with the coast thereof.

19 And [u]the LORD was with Judah; and he drave out *the inhabitants of* the mountain; but could not drive out the inhabitants of the valley, because they had [v]chariots of iron.

20 [w]And they gave Hebron unto Caleb, as Moses said: and he expelled thence the three sons of Anak.

21 [x]And the children of Benjamin did not drive out the Jebusites that inhabited Jerusalem; but the Jebusites dwell with the children of Benjamin in Jerusalem unto this day.

22 ¶ And the house of Joseph, they also went up against Beth-el: [y]and the LORD *was* with them.

23 And the house of Joseph [z]sent to descry Beth-el. (Now the name of the city before *was* [a]Luz.)

24 And the spies saw a man come forth out of the city, and they said unto him, Shew us, we pray thee, the entrance into the city, and [b]we will shew thee mercy.

1:1 [a]Num. 27:21; ch. 20:18
1:2 [b]Gen. 49:8
1:3 [c]ver. 17
1:4 [d]1 Sam. 11:8
1:7 [e]Lev. 24:19; 1 Sam. 15:33; Jam. 2:13
1:8 [f]Josh. 15:63
1:9 [g]Josh. 10:36
1:10 [h]Josh. 14:15
1:11 [i]Josh. 15:15
1:12 [j]Josh. 15:16
1:13 [k]ch. 3:9
1:14 [l]Josh. 15:18
1:15 [m]Gen. 33:11
1:16 [n]ch. 4:11; 1 Sam. 15:6; 1 Chron. 2:55; Jer. 35:2 [o]Deut. 34:3 [p]Num. 21:1 [q]Num. 10:32
1:17 [r]ver. 3 [s]Num. 21:3; Josh. 19:4
1:18 [t]Josh. 11:22
1:19 [u]ver. 2; 2 Kings 18:7 [v]Josh. 17:16
1:20 [w]Num. 14:24; Deut. 1:36; Josh. 14:9
1:21 [x]Josh. 15:63
1:22 [y]ver. 19
1:23 [z]Josh. 2:1; ch. 18:2 [a]Gen. 28:19
1:24 [b]Josh. 2:12

25 And when he shewed them the entrance into the city, they smote the city with the edge of the sword; but they let go the man and all his family.

26 And the man went into the land of the Hittites, and built a city, and called the name thereof Luz: which *is* the name thereof unto this day.

27 ¶ [c]Neither did Manasseh drive out *the inhabitants of* Beth-shean and her towns, nor Taanach and her towns, nor the inhabitants of Dor and her towns, nor the inhabitants of Ibleam and her towns, nor the inhabitants of Megiddo and her towns: but the Canaanites would dwell in that land.

28 And it came to pass, when Israel was strong, that they put the Canaanites to tribute, and did not utterly drive them out.

29 ¶ [d]Neither did Ephraim drive out the Canaanites that dwelt in Gezer; but the Canaanites dwelt in Gezer among them.

30 ¶ Neither did Zebulun drive out the inhabitants of Kitron, nor the [e]inhabitants of Nahalol; but the Canaanites dwelt among them, and became tributaries.

31 ¶ [f]Neither did Asher drive out the inhabitants of Accho, nor the inhabitants of Zidon, nor of Ahlab, nor of Achzib, nor of Helbah, nor of Aphik, nor of Rehob:

32 But the Asherites [g]dwelt among the Canaanites, the inhabitants of the land: for they did not drive them out.

33 ¶ [h]Neither did Naphtali drive out the inhabitants of Beth-shemesh, nor the inhabitants of Beth-anath; but he [i]dwelt among the Canaanites, the inhabitants of the land: nevertheless the inhabitants of Beth-shemesh and of Beth-anath [j]became tributaries unto them.

34 And the Amorites forced the children of Dan into the mountain: for they would not suffer them to come down to the valley:

35 But the Amorites would dwell in mount Heres [k]in Aijalon, and in Shaalbim: yet the hand of the house of Joseph prevailed, so that they became tributaries.

36 And the coast of the Amorites *was* [l]from the going up to Akrabbim, from the rock, and upward.

2 And an angel of the LORD came up from Gilgal [m]to Bochim, and said, I made you to go up out of Egypt, and have brought you unto the land which I sware unto your fathers; and [n]I said, I will never break my covenant with you.

2 And [o]ye shall make no league with the inhabitants of this land; [p]ye shall throw down their altars: [q]but ye have not obeyed my voice: why have ye done this?

3 Wherefore I also said, I will not drive them out from before you; but they shall be [r]*as thorns* in your sides, and [s]their gods shall be a [t]snare unto you.

4 And it came to pass, when the angel of the LORD spake these words unto all the children of Israel, that the people lifted up their voice, and wept.

5 And they called the name of that place Bochim: and they sacrificed there unto the LORD.

6 ¶ And when [u]Joshua had let the people go, the children of Israel went every man unto his inheritance to possess the land.

7 [v]And the people served the LORD all the days of Joshua, and all the days of the elders that outlived Joshua, who had seen all the great works of the LORD, that he did for Israel.

8 And [w]Joshua the son of Nun, the servant of the LORD, died, *being* an hundred and ten years old.

9 [x]And they buried him in the border of his inheritance in [y]Timnath-heres, in the mount of Ephraim, on the north side of the hill Gaash.

10 And also all that generation were gathered unto their fathers: and there arose another generation after them, which [z]knew not the LORD, nor yet the works which he had done for Israel.

11 ¶ And the children of Israel did evil in the sight of the LORD, and served Baalim:

12 And they [a]forsook the LORD God of their fathers, which brought them out of the land of Egypt, and followed [b]other gods, of the gods of the people that *were* round about them, and [c]bowed themselves unto them, and provoked the LORD to anger.

13 And they forsook the LORD, [d]and served Baal and Ashtaroth.

14 ¶ [e]And the anger of the LORD was hot against Israel, and he [f]delivered them into the hands of spoilers that spoiled them, and [g]he sold them into the hands of their enemies round about, so that they [h]could not any longer stand before their enemies.

15 Whithersoever they went out, the hand of the LORD was against them for evil, as the LORD had said, and [i]as the LORD had sworn unto them: and they were greatly distressed.

16 ¶ Nevertheless [j]the LORD raised up judges, which delivered them out of the hand of those that spoiled them.

17 And yet they would not hearken unto their judges, but they [k]went a whoring after other gods, and bowed themselves unto them: they turned quickly out of the way which their fathers walked in, obeying the commandments of the LORD; *but* they did not so.

18 And when the LORD raised them up judges, then [l]the LORD was with the judge, and delivered them out of the hand of their enemies all the days of the judge: [m]for it repented the LORD because of their groanings by reason of them that oppressed them and vexed them.

19 And it came to pass, [n]when the judge was dead, *that* they returned, and corrupted *themselves* more than their fathers, in following other gods to serve them, and to bow down unto them; they ceased not from their own doings, nor from their stubborn way.

20 ¶ [o]And the anger of the LORD was hot

1:27 c Josh. 17:11
1:29 d Josh. 16:10; 1 Kings 9:16
1:30 e Josh. 19:15
1:31 f Josh. 19:24-30
1:32 g Ps. 106:34
1:33 h Josh. 19:38 i ver. 32 j ver. 30
1:35 k Josh. 19:42
1:36 l Num. 34:4; Josh. 15:3
2:1 m ver. 5 n Gen. 17:7
2:2 o Deut. 7:2 p Deut. 12:3 q ver. 20; Ps. 106:34
2:3 r Josh. 23:13 s ch. 3:6 t Ex. 23:33; Deut. 7:16; Ps. 106:36
2:6 u Josh. 22:6
2:7 v Josh. 24:31
2:8 w Josh. 24:29
2:9 x Josh. 24:30 y Josh. 19:50
2:10 z Ex. 5:2; 1 Sam. 2:12; 1 Chron. 28:9; Jer. 9:3; Gal. 4:8; 2 Thess. 1:8; Tit. 1:16
2:12 a Deut. 31:16 b Deut. 6:14 c Ex. 20:5
2:13 d ch. 3:7; Ps. 106:36
2:14 e ch. 3:8; Ps. 106:40 f 2 Kings 17:20 g ch. 3:8; Ps. 44:12; Isa. 50:1 h Lev. 26:37; Josh. 7:12
2:15 i Lev. 26; Deut. 28
2:16 j ch. 3:9; 1 Sam. 12:11; Acts 13:20
2:17 k Ex. 34:15; Lev. 17:7
2:18 l Josh. 1:5 m Gen. 6:6; Deut. 32:36; Ps. 106:44
2:19 n ch. 3:12
2:20 o ver. 14

against Israel; and he said, Because that this people hath [p]transgressed my covenant which I commanded their fathers, and have not hearkened unto my voice;

21 [q]I also will not henceforth drive out any from before them of the nations which Joshua left when he died:

22 [r]That through them I may [s]prove Israel, whether they will keep the way of the LORD to walk therein, as their fathers did keep *it*, or not.

23 Therefore the LORD left those nations, without driving them out hastily; neither delivered he them into the hand of Joshua.

3 Now these *are* [t]the nations which the LORD left, to prove Israel by them, *even* as many *of Israel* as had not known all the wars of Canaan;

2 Only that the generations of the children of Israel might know, to teach them war, at the least such as before knew nothing thereof;

3 *Namely*, [u]five lords of the Philistines, and all the Canaanites, and the Sidonians, and the Hivites that dwelt in mount Lebanon, from mount Baal-hermon unto the entering in of Hamath.

4 [v]And they were to prove Israel by them, to know whether they would hearken unto the commandments of the LORD, which he commanded their fathers by the hand of Moses.

5 ¶ [w]And the children of Israel dwelt among the Canaanites, Hittites, and Amorites, and Perizzites, and Hivites, and Jebusites:

6 And [x]they took their daughters to be their wives, and gave their daughters to their sons, and served their gods.

7 [y]And the children of Israel did evil in the sight of the LORD, and forgat the LORD their God, [z]and served Baalim and [a]the groves.

8 ¶ Therefore the anger of the LORD was hot against Israel, and he [b]sold them into the hand of [c]Chushan-rishathaim king of Mesopotamia: and the children of Israel served Chushan-rishathaim eight years.

9 And when the children of Israel [d]cried unto the LORD, the LORD [e]raised up a deliverer to the children of Israel, who delivered them, *even* [f]Othniel the son of Kenaz, Caleb's younger brother.

10 And [g]the Spirit of the LORD came upon him, and he judged Israel, and went out to war: and the LORD delivered Chushan-rishathaim king of Mesopotamia into his hand; and his hand prevailed against Chushan-rishathaim.

11 And the land had rest forty years. And Othniel the son of Kenaz died.

12 ¶ [h]And the children of Israel did evil again in the sight of the LORD: and the LORD strengthened [i]Eglon the king of Moab against Israel, because they had done evil in the sight of the LORD.

13 And he gathered unto him the children of Ammon and [j]Amalek, and went and smote Israel, and possessed [k]the city of palm trees.

14 So the children of Israel [l]served Eglon the king of Moab eighteen years.

15 But when the children of Israel [m]cried unto the LORD, the LORD raised them up a deliverer, Ehud the son of Gera, a Benjamite, a man lefthanded: and by him the children of Israel sent a present unto Eglon the king of Moab.

16 But Ehud made him a dagger which had two edges, of a cubit length; and he did gird it under his raiment upon his right thigh.

17 And he brought the present unto Eglon king of Moab: and Eglon *was* a very fat man.

18 And when he had made an end to offer the present, he sent away the people that bare the present.

19 But he himself turned again [n]from the quarries that *were* by Gilgal, and said, I have a secret errand unto thee, O king: who said, Keep silence. And all that stood by him went out from him.

20 And Ehud came unto him; and he was sitting in a summer parlour, which he had for himself alone. And Ehud said, I have a message from God unto thee. And he arose out of *his* seat.

21 And Ehud put forth his left hand, and took the dagger from his right thigh, and thrust it into his belly:

22 And the haft also went in after the blade; and the fat closed upon the blade, so that he could not draw the dagger out of his belly; and the dirt came out.

23 Then Ehud went forth through the porch, and shut the doors of the parlour upon him, and locked them.

24 When he was gone out, his servants came; and when they saw that, behold, the doors of the parlour *were* locked, they said, Surely he covereth his feet in his summer chamber.

25 And they tarried till they were ashamed: and, behold, he opened not the doors of the parlour; therefore they took a key, and opened *them:* and, behold, their lord *was* fallen down dead on the earth.

26 And Ehud escaped while they tarried, and passed beyond the quarries, and escaped unto Seirath.

27 And it came to pass, when he was come, that [o]he blew a trumpet in the [p]mountain of Ephraim, and the children of Israel went down with him from the mount, and he before them.

28 And he said unto them, Follow after me: for [q]the LORD hath delivered your enemies the Moabites into your hand. And they went down after him, and took [r]the fords of Jordan toward Moab, and suffered not a man to pass over.

29 And they slew of Moab at that time about ten thousand men, all lusty, and all men of valour; and there escaped not a man.

30 So Moab was subdued that day under

2:20 [p]Josh. 23:16
2:21 [q]Josh. 23:13
2:22 [r]ch. 3:1 [s]Deut. 8:2
3:1 [t]ch. 2:21
3:3 [u]Josh. 13:3
3:4 [v]ch. 2:22
3:5 [w]Ps. 106:35
3:6 [x]Ex. 34:16; Deut. 7:3
3:7 [y]ch. 2:11 [z]ch. 2:13 [a]Ex. 34:13; Deut. 16:21; ch. 6:25
3:8 [b]ch. 2:14 [c]Hab. 3:7
3:9 [d]ver. 15; 1 Sam. 12:10; Neh. 9:27; Ps. 22:5 [e]ch. 2:16 [f]ch. 1:13
3:10 [g]Num. 27:18; ch. 6:34; 1 Sam. 11:6; 2 Chron. 15:1
3:12 [h]ch. 2:19 [i]1 Sam. 12:9
3:13 [j]ch. 5:14 [k]ch. 1:16
3:14 [l]Deut. 28:40
3:15 [m]ver. 9; Ps. 78:34
3:19 [n]Josh. 4:20
3:27 [o]ch. 5:14; 1 Sam. 13:3 [p]Josh. 17:15; ch. 7:24
3:28 [q]ch. 7:9; 1 Sam. 17:47 [r]Josh. 2:7; ch. 12:5

the hand of Israel. And [s]the land had rest fourscore years.

31 ¶ And after him was [t]Shamgar the son of Anath, which slew of the Philistines six hundred men [u]with an ox goad: [v]and he also delivered [w]Israel.

4

And [x]the children of Israel again did evil in the sight of the LORD, when Ehud was dead.

2 And the LORD [y]sold them into the hand of Jabin king of Canaan, that reigned in [z]Hazor; the captain of whose host *was* [a]Sisera, which dwelt in [b]Harosheth of the Gentiles.

3 And the children of Israel cried unto the LORD: for he had nine hundred [c]chariots of iron; and twenty years [d]he mightily oppressed the children of Israel.

4 ¶ And Deborah, a prophetess, the wife of Lapidoth, she judged Israel at that time.

5 [e]And she dwelt under the palm tree of Deborah between Ramah and Beth-el in mount Ephraim: and the children of Israel came up to her for judgment.

6 And she sent and called [f]Barak the son of Abinoam out [g]of Kedesh-naphtali, and said unto him, Hath not the LORD God of Israel commanded, *saying*, Go and draw toward mount Tabor, and take with thee ten thousand men of the children of Naphtali and of the children of Zebulun?

7 And [h]I will draw unto thee to the [i]river Kishon Sisera, the captain of Jabin's army, with his chariots and his multitude; and I will deliver him into thine hand.

8 And Barak said unto her, If thou wilt go with me, then I will go: but if thou wilt not go with me, *then* I will not go.

9 And she said, I will surely go with thee: notwithstanding the journey that thou takest shall not be for thine honour; for the LORD shall [j]sell Sisera into the hand of a woman. And Deborah arose, and went with Barak to Kedesh.

10 ¶ And Barak called [k]Zebulun and Naphtali to Kedesh; and he went up with ten thousand men [l]at his feet: and Deborah went up with him.

11 Now Heber [m]the Kenite, *which was* of the children of [n]Hobab the father in law of Moses, had severed himself from the Kenites, and pitched his tent unto the plain of Zaanaim, [o]which *is* by Kedesh.

12 And they shewed Sisera that Barak the son of Abinoam was gone up to mount Tabor.

13 And Sisera gathered together all his chariots, *even* nine hundred chariots of iron, and all the people that *were* with him, from Harosheth of the Gentiles unto the river of Kishon.

14 And Deborah said unto Barak, Up; for this *is* the day in which the LORD hath delivered Sisera into thine hand: [p]is not the LORD gone out before thee? So Barak went down from mount Tabor, and ten thousand men after him.

15 And [q]the LORD discomfited Sisera, and all *his* chariots, and all *his* host, with the edge of the sword before Barak; so that Sisera lighted down off *his* chariot, and fled away on his feet.

16 But Barak pursued after the chariots, and after the host, unto Harosheth of the Gentiles: and all the host of Sisera fell upon the edge of the sword; *and* there was not a man left.

17 Howbeit Sisera fled away on his feet to the tent of Jael the wife of Heber the Kenite: for *there was* peace between Jabin the king of Hazor and the house of Heber the Kenite.

18 ¶ And Jael went out to meet Sisera, and said unto him, Turn in, my lord, turn in to me; fear not. And when he had turned in unto her into the tent, she covered him with a mantle.

19 And he said unto her, Give me, I pray thee, a little water to drink; for I am thirsty. And she opened [r]a bottle of milk, and gave him drink, and covered him.

20 Again he said unto her, Stand in the door of the tent, and it shall be, when any man doth come and enquire of thee, and say, Is there any man here? that thou shalt say, No.

21 Then Jael Heber's wife [s]took a nail of the tent, and took an hammer in her hand, and went softly unto him, and smote the nail into his temples, and fastened it into the ground: for he was fast asleep and weary. So he died.

22 And, behold, as Barak pursued Sisera, Jael came out to meet him, and said unto him, Come, and I will shew thee the man whom thou seekest. And when he came into her *tent*, behold, Sisera lay dead, and the nail *was* in his temples.

23 So [t]God subdued on that day Jabin the king of Canaan before the children of Israel.

24 And the hand of the children of Israel prospered, and prevailed against Jabin the king of Canaan, until they had destroyed Jabin king of Canaan.

5

Then [u]sang Deborah and Barak the son of Abinoam on that day, saying,

2 Praise ye the LORD for the [v]avenging of Israel, [w]when the people willingly offered themselves.

3 [x]Hear, O ye kings; give ear, O ye princes; I, *even* I, will sing unto the LORD; I will sing *praise* to the LORD God of Israel.

4 LORD, [y]when thou wentest out of Seir, when thou marchedst out of the field of Edom, [z]the earth trembled, and the heavens dropped, the clouds also dropped water.

5 [a]The mountains melted from before the LORD, *even* [b]that Sinai from before the LORD God of Israel.

6 In the days of [c]Shamgar the son of Anath, in the days of [d]Jael, [e]the highways were unoccupied, and the travellers walked through byways.

7 *The inhabitants of* the villages ceased, they ceased in Israel, until that I Deborah arose, that I arose [f]a mother in Israel.

3:30 [s]ver. 11
3:31 [t]ch. 5:6; 1 Sam. 13:19 [u]1 Sam. 17:47 [v]ch. 2:16 [w]ch. 4:1; 1 Sam. 4:1
4:1 [x]ch. 2:19
4:2 [y]ch. 2:14 [z]Josh. 11:1 [a]1 Sam. 12:9; Ps. 83:9 [b]ver. 13
4:3 [c]ch. 1:19 [d]ch. 5:8; Ps. 106:42
4:5 [e]Gen. 35:8
4:6 [f]Heb. 11:32 [g]Josh. 19:37
4:7 [h]Ex. 14:4 [i]ch. 5:21; 1 Kings 18:40; Ps. 83:9
4:9 [j]ch. 2:14
4:10 [k]ch. 5:18 [l]Ex. 11:8; 1 Kings 20:10
4:11 [m]ch. 1:16 [n]Num. 10:29 [o]ver. 6
4:14 [p]Deut. 9:3; 2 Sam. 5:24; Ps. 68:7; Isa. 52:12
4:15 [q]Josh. 10:10; Ps. 83:9
4:19 [r]ch. 5:25
4:21 [s]ch. 5:26
4:23 [t]Ps. 18:47
5:1 [u]Ex. 15:1; Ps. 18, title
5:2 [v]Ps. 18:47 [w]2 Chron. 17:16
5:3 [x]Deut. 32:1; Ps. 2:10
5:4 [y]Deut. 33:2; Ps. 68:7 [z]2 Sam. 22:8; Ps. 68:8; Isa. 64:3; Hab. 3:3
5:5 [a]Deut. 4:11; Ps. 97:5 [b]Ex. 19:18
5:6 [c]ch. 3:31 [d]ch. 4:17 [e]Lev. 26:22; 2 Chron. 15:5; Isa. 33:8; Lam. 1:4
5:7 [f]Isa. 49:23

8 They [g]chose new gods; then *was* war in the gates: [h]was there a shield or spear seen among forty thousand in Israel?

9 My heart *is* toward the governors of Israel, that [i]offered themselves willingly among the people. Bless ye the LORD.

10 [j]Speak, ye [k]that ride on white asses, [l]ye that sit in judgment, and walk by the way.

11 *They that are delivered* from the noise of archers in the places of drawing water, there shall they rehearse the [m]righteous acts of the LORD, *even* the righteous acts *toward the inhabitants* of his villages in Israel: then shall the people of the LORD go down to the gates.

12 [n]Awake, awake, Deborah: awake, awake, utter a song: arise, Barak, and [o]lead thy captivity captive, thou son of Abinoam.

13 Then he made him that remaineth [p]have dominion over the nobles among the people: the LORD made me have dominion over the mighty.

14 [q]Out of Ephraim *was there* a root of them [r]against Amalek; after thee, Benjamin, among thy people; out of [s]Machir came down governors, and out of Zebulun they that handle the pen of the writer.

15 And the princes of Issachar *were* with Deborah; even Issachar, and also [t]Barak: he was sent on foot into the valley. For the divisions of Reuben *there were* great thoughts of heart.

16 Why abodest thou [u]among the sheepfolds, to hear the bleatings of the flocks? For the divisions of Reuben *there were* great searchings of heart.

17 [v]Gilead abode beyond Jordan: and why did Dan remain in ships? [w]Asher continued on the sea shore, and abode in his breaches.

18 [x]Zebulun and Naphtali *were* a people *that* jeoparded their lives unto the death in the high places of the field.

19 The kings came *and* fought, then fought the kings of Canaan in Taanach by the waters of Megiddo; [y]they took no gain of money.

20 [z]They fought from heaven; [a]the stars in their courses fought against Sisera.

21 [b]The river of Kishon swept them away, that ancient river, the river Kishon. O my soul, thou hast trodden down strength.

22 Then were the horsehoofs broken by the means of the pransings, the pransings of their mighty ones.

23 Curse ye Meroz, said the angel of the LORD, curse ye bitterly the inhabitants thereof; [c]because they came not to the help [d]of the LORD, to the help of the LORD against the mighty.

24 Blessed above women shall [e]Jael the wife of Heber the Kenite be, [f]blessed shall she be above women in the tent.

25 [g]He asked water, *and* she gave *him* milk; she brought forth butter in a lordly dish.

5:8 [g]Deut. 32:16; ch. 2:12 [h]1 Sam. 13:19; ch. 4:3
5:9 [i]ver. 2
5:10 [j]Ps. 105:2 [k]ch. 10:4 [l]Ps. 107:32
5:11 [m]1 Sam. 12:7; Ps. 145:7
5:12 [n]Ps. 57:8 [o]Ps. 68:18
5:13 [p]Ps. 49:14
5:14 [q]ch. 3:27 [r]ch. 3:13 [s]Num. 32:39
5:15 [t]ch. 4:14
5:16 [u]Num. 32:1
5:17 [v]Josh. 13:25 [w]Josh. 19:29
5:18 [x]ch. 4:10
5:19 [y]ver. 30; ch. 4:16; Ps. 44:12
5:20 [z]Josh. 10:11; Ps. 77:17 [a]ch. 4:15
5:21 [b]ch. 4:7
5:23 [c]ch. 21:9; Neh. 3:5 [d]1 Sam. 17:47
5:24 [e]ch. 4:17 [f]Luke 1:28
5:25 [g]ch. 4:19
5:26 [h]ch. 4:21
5:30 [i]Ex. 15:9
5:31 [j]Ps. 83:9 [k]2 Sam. 23:4 [l]Ps. 19:5
6:1 [m]ch. 2:19 [n]Hab. 3:7
6:2 [o]1 Sam. 13:6; Heb. 11:38
6:3 [p]ch. 3:13 [q]Gen. 29:1; ch. 7:12; 1 Kings 4:30; Job 1:3
6:4 [r]Lev. 26:16; Deut. 28:30; Mic. 6:15
6:5 [s]ch. 7:12
6:6 [t]ch. 3:15; Hos. 5:15
6:9 [u]Ps. 44:2
6:10 [v]2 Kings 17:35; Jer. 10:2

26 [h]She put her hand to the nail, and her right hand to the workmen's hammer; and with the hammer she smote Sisera, she smote off his head, when she had pierced and stricken through his temples.

27 At her feet he bowed, he fell, he lay down: at her feet he bowed, he fell: where he bowed, there he fell down dead.

28 The mother of Sisera looked out at a window, and cried through the lattice, Why is his chariot *so* long in coming? why tarry the wheels of his chariots?

29 Her wise ladies answered her, yea, she returned answer to herself,

30 [i]Have they not sped? have they *not* divided the prey; to every man a damsel *or* two; to Sisera a prey of divers colours, a prey of divers colours of needlework, of divers colours of needlework on both sides, *meet* for the necks of *them that take* the spoil?

31 [j]So let all thine enemies perish, O LORD: but *let* them that love him *be* [k]as the sun [l]when he goeth forth in his might. And the land had rest forty years.

6 And [m]the children of Israel did evil in the sight of the LORD: and the LORD delivered them into the hand [n]of Midian seven years.

2 And the hand of Midian prevailed against Israel: *and* because of the Midianites the children of Israel made them [o]the dens which *are* in the mountains, and caves, and strong holds.

3 And *so* it was, when Israel had sown, that the Midianites came up, and [p]the Amalekites, [q]and the children of the east, even they came up against them;

4 And they encamped against them, and [r]destroyed the increase of the earth, till thou come unto Gaza, and left no sustenance for Israel, neither sheep, nor ox, nor ass.

5 For they came up with their cattle and their tents, and they came [s]as grasshoppers for multitude; *for* both they and their camels were without number: and they entered into the land to destroy it.

6 And Israel was greatly impoverished because of the Midianites; and the children of Israel [t]cried unto the LORD.

7 ¶ And it came to pass, when the children of Israel cried unto the LORD because of the Midianites,

8 That the LORD sent a prophet unto the children of Israel, which said unto them, Thus saith the LORD God of Israel, I brought you up from Egypt, and brought you forth out of the house of bondage;

9 And I delivered you out of the hand of the Egyptians, and out of the hand of all that oppressed you, and [u]drave them out from before you, and gave you their land;

10 And I said unto you, I *am* the LORD your God; [v]fear not the gods of the Amorites, in whose land ye dwell: but ye have not obeyed my voice.

11 ¶ And there came an angel of the

LORD, and sat under an oak which *was* in
Ophrah, that *pertained* unto Joash [w]the
Abi-ezrite: and his son [x]Gideon threshed
wheat by the winepress, to hide *it* from the
Midianites.
12 And the [y]angel of the LORD appeared
unto him, and said unto him, The LORD *is*
[z]with thee, thou mighty man of valour.
13 And Gideon said unto him, Oh my
Lord, if the LORD be with us, why then is all
this befallen us? and [a]where *be* all his miracles [b]which our fathers told us of, saying,
Did not the LORD bring us up from Egypt?
but now the LORD hath [c]forsaken us, and
delivered us into the hands of the Midianites.
14 And the LORD looked upon him, and
said, [d]Go in this thy might, and thou shalt
save Israel from the hand of the Midianites:
[e]have not I sent thee?
15 And he said unto him, Oh my Lord,
wherewith shall I save Israel? behold, [f]my
family *is* poor in Manasseh, and I *am* the
least in my father's house.
16 And the LORD said unto him, [g]Surely
I will be with thee, and thou shalt smite the
Midianites as one man.
17 And he said unto him, If now I have
found grace in thy sight, then [h]shew me a
sign that thou talkest with me.
18 [i]Depart not hence, I pray thee, until I
come unto thee, and bring forth my present,
and set *it* before thee. And he said, I will
tarry until thou come again.
19 ¶ [j]And Gideon went in, and made
ready a kid, and unleavened cakes of an
ephah of flour: the flesh he put in a basket,
and he put the broth in a pot, and brought
it out unto him under the oak, and presented *it*.
20 And the angel of God said unto him,
Take the flesh and the unleavened cakes,
and [k]lay *them* upon this rock, and [l]pour
out the broth. And he did so.
21 ¶ Then the angel of the LORD put forth
the end of the staff that *was* in his hand, and
touched the flesh and the unleavened cakes;
and [m]there rose up fire out of the rock, and
consumed the flesh and the unleavened
cakes. Then the angel of the LORD departed
out of his sight.
22 And when Gideon [n]perceived that he
was an angel of the LORD, Gideon said,
Alas, O Lord GOD! [o]for because I have seen
an angel of the LORD face to face.
23 And the LORD said unto him, [p]Peace
be unto thee; fear not: thou shalt not die.
24 Then Gideon built an altar there unto
the LORD, and called it Jehovah-shalom:
unto this day it *is* yet [q]in Ophrah of the
Abi-ezrites.
25 ¶ And it came to pass the same night,
that the LORD said unto him, Take thy father's young bullock, even the second bullock of seven years old, and throw down the
altar of Baal that thy father hath, and [r]cut
down the grove that *is* by it:
26 And build an altar unto the LORD thy
God upon the top of this rock, in the ordered
place, and take the second bullock, and offer a burnt sacrifice with the wood of the
grove which thou shalt cut down.
27 Then Gideon took ten men of his servants, and did as the LORD had said unto
him: and *so* it was, because he feared his
father's household, and the men of the city,
that he could not do *it* by day, that he did *it*
by night.
28 ¶ And when the men of the city arose
early in the morning, behold, the altar of
Baal was cast down, and the grove was cut
down that *was* by it, and the second bullock
was offered upon the altar *that was* built.
29 And they said one to another, Who
hath done this thing? And when they enquired and asked, they said, Gideon the son
of Joash hath done this thing.
30 Then the men of the city said unto Joash, Bring out thy son, that he may die: because he hath cast down the altar of Baal,
and because he hath cut down the grove
that *was* by it.
31 And Joash said unto all that stood
against him, Will ye plead for Baal? will ye
save him? he that will plead for him, let him
be put to death whilst *it is yet* morning: if he
be a god, let him plead for himself, because
one hath cast down his altar.
32 Therefore on that day he called him
[s]Jerubbaal, saying, Let Baal plead against
him, because he hath thrown down his altar.
33 ¶ Then all [t]the Midianites and the
Amalekites and the children of the east
were gathered together, and went over, and
pitched in [u]the valley of Jezreel.
34 But [v]the Spirit of the LORD came upon
Gideon, and he [w]blew a trumpet; and Abiezer was gathered after him.
35 And he sent messengers throughout
all Manasseh; who also was gathered after
him: and he sent messengers unto Asher,
and unto Zebulun, and unto Naphtali; and
they came up to meet them.
36 ¶ And Gideon said unto God, If thou
wilt save Israel by mine hand, as thou hast
said,
37 [x]Behold, I will put a fleece of wool in
the floor; *and* if the dew be on the fleece
only, and *it be* dry upon all the earth *beside*,
then shall I know that thou wilt save Israel
by mine hand, as thou hast said.
38 And it was so: for he rose up early on
the morrow, and thrust the fleece together,
and wringed the dew out of the fleece, a
bowl full of water.
39 And Gideon said unto God, [y]Let not
thine anger be hot against me, and I will
speak but this once: let me prove, I pray
thee, but this once with the fleece; let it now
be dry only upon the fleece, and upon all the
ground let there be dew.
40 And God did so that night: for it was
dry upon the fleece only, and there was dew
on all the ground.

6:11 [w]Josh. 17:2 [x]Heb. 11:32
6:12 [y]ch. 13:3; Luke 1:11 [z]Josh. 1:5
6:13 [a]Ps. 89:49; Isa. 59:1 [b]Ps. 44:1 [c]2 Chron. 15:2
6:14 [d]1 Sam. 12:11; Heb. 11:32 [e]Josh. 1:9; ch. 4:6
6:15 [f]1 Sam. 9:21
6:16 [g]Ex. 3:12; Josh. 1:5
6:17 [h]Ex. 4:1-8; ver. 36; 2 Kings 20:8; Ps. 86:17; Isa. 7:11
6:18 [i]Gen. 18:3; ch. 13:15
6:19 [j]Gen. 18:6
6:20 [k]ch. 13:19 [l]1 Kings 18:33
6:21 [m]Lev. 9:24; 1 Kings 18:38; 2 Chron. 7:1
6:22 [n]ch. 13:21 [o]Gen. 16:13; Ex. 33:20; ch. 13:22
6:23 [p]Dan. 10:19
6:24 [q]ch. 8:32
6:25 [r]Ex. 34:13; Deut. 7:5
6:32 [s]1 Sam. 12:11; 2 Sam. 11:21; Jer. 11:13; Hos. 9:10
6:33 [t]ver. 3 [u]Josh. 17:16
6:34 [v]ch. 3:10; 1 Chron. 12:18; 2 Chron. 24:20 [w]Num. 10:3; ch. 3:27
6:37 [x]Ex. 4:3
6:39 [y]Gen. 18:32

7 Then [z]Jerubbaal, who *is* Gideon, and all the people that *were* with him, rose up early, and pitched beside the well of Harod: so that the host of the Midianites were on the north side of them, by the hill of Moreh, in the valley.

2 And the LORD said unto Gideon, The people that *are* with thee *are* too many for me to give the Midianites into their hands, lest Israel [a]vaunt themselves against me, saying, Mine own hand hath saved me.

3 Now therefore go to, proclaim in the ears of the people, saying, [b]Whosoever *is* fearful and afraid, let him return and depart early from mount Gilead. And there returned of the people twenty and two thousand; and there remained ten thousand.

4 And the LORD said unto Gideon, The people *are* yet *too* many; bring them down unto the water, and I will try them for thee there: and it shall be, *that* of whom I say unto thee, This shall go with thee, the same shall go with thee; and of whomsoever I say unto thee, This shall not go with thee, the same shall not go.

5 So he brought down the people unto the water: and the LORD said unto Gideon, Every one that lappeth of the water with his tongue, as a dog lappeth, him shalt thou set by himself; likewise every one that boweth down upon his knees to drink.

6 And the number of them that lapped, *putting* their hand to their mouth, were three hundred men: but all the rest of the people bowed down upon their knees to drink water.

7 And the LORD said unto Gideon, [c]By the three hundred men that lapped will I save you, and deliver the Midianites into thine hand: and let all the *other* people go every man unto his place.

8 So the people took victuals in their hand, and their trumpets: and he sent all *the rest of* Israel every man unto his tent, and retained those three hundred men: and the host of Midian was beneath him in the valley.

9 ¶ And it came to pass the same [d]night, that the LORD said unto him, Arise, get thee down unto the host; for I have delivered it into thine hand.

10 But if thou fear to go down, go thou with Phurah thy servant down to the host:

11 And thou shalt [e]hear what they say; and afterward shall thine hands be strengthened to go down unto the host. Then went he down with Phurah his servant unto the outside of the armed men that *were* in the host.

12 And the Midianites and the Amalekites and [f]all the children of the east lay along in the valley like grasshoppers for multitude; and their camels *were* without number, as the sand by the sea side for multitude.

13 And when Gideon was come, behold, *there was* a man that told a dream unto his fellow, and said, Behold, I dreamed a dream, and, lo, a cake of barley bread tumbled into the host of Midian, and came unto a tent, and smote it that it fell, and overturned it, that the tent lay along.

14 And his fellow answered and said, This *is* nothing else save the sword of Gideon the son of Joash, a man of Israel: *for* into his hand hath God delivered Midian, and all the host.

15 ¶ And it was *so*, when Gideon heard the telling of the dream, and the interpretation thereof, that he worshipped, and returned into the host of Israel, and said, Arise; for the LORD hath delivered into your hand the host of Midian.

16 And he divided the three hundred men *into* three companies, and he put a trumpet in every man's hand, with empty pitchers, and lamps within the pitchers.

17 And he said unto them, Look on me, and do likewise: and, behold, when I come to the outside of the camp, it shall be *that*, as I do, so shall ye do.

18 When I blow with a trumpet, I and all that *are* with me, then blow ye the trumpets also on every side of all the camp, and say, *The sword* of the LORD, and of Gideon.

19 ¶ So Gideon, and the hundred men that *were* with him, came unto the outside of the camp in the beginning of the middle watch; and they had but newly set the watch: and they blew the trumpets, and brake the pitchers that *were* in their hands.

20 And the three companies blew the trumpets, and brake the pitchers, and held the lamps in their left hands, and the trumpets in their right hands to blow *withal:* and they cried, The sword of the LORD, and of Gideon.

21 And they [g]stood every man in his place round about the camp: [h]and all the host ran, and cried, and fled.

22 And the three hundred [i]blew the trumpets, and [j]the LORD set [k]every man's sword against his fellow, even throughout all the host: and the host fled to Beth-shittah in Zererath, *and* to the border of Abel-meholah, unto Tabbath.

23 And the men of Israel gathered themselves together out of Naphtali, and out of Asher, and out of all Manasseh, and pursued after the Midianites.

24 ¶ And Gideon sent messengers throughout all [l]mount Ephraim, saying, Come down against the Midianites, and take before them the waters unto Beth-barah and Jordan. Then all the men of Ephraim gathered themselves together, and [m]took the waters unto [n]Beth-barah and Jordan.

25 And they took [o]two princes of the Midianites, Oreb and Zeeb; and they slew Oreb upon [p]the rock Oreb, and Zeeb they slew at the winepress of Zeeb, and pursued Midian, and brought the heads of Oreb and Zeeb to Gideon on the [q]other side Jordan.

8 And [r]the men of Ephraim said unto him, Why hast thou served us thus, that

---

7:1 [z]ch. 6:32
7:2 [a]Deut. 8:17; Isa. 10:13; 1 Cor. 1:29; 2 Cor. 4:7
7:3 [b]Deut. 20:8
7:7 [c]1 Sam. 14:6
7:9 [d]Gen. 46:2
7:11 [e]Gen. 24:14; ver. 13; 1 Sam. 14:9
7:12 [f]ch. 6:5
7:21 [g]Ex. 14:13; 2 Chron. 20:17 [h]2 Kings 7:7
7:22 [i]Josh. 6:4; 2 Cor. 4:7 [j]Ps. 83:9; Isa. 9:4 [k]1 Sam. 14:20; 2 Chron. 20:23
7:24 [l]ch. 3:27 [m]ch. 3:28 [n]John 1:28
7:25 [o]ch. 8:3; Ps. 83:11 [p]Isa. 10:26 [q]ch. 8:4
8:1 [r]ch. 12:1; 2 Sam. 19:41

thou calledst us not, when thou wentest to fight with the Midianites? And they did chide with him sharply.

2 And he said unto them, What have I done now in comparison of you? *Is* not the gleaning of the grapes of Ephraim better than the vintage of Abi-ezer?

3 [s]God hath delivered into your hands the princes of Midian, Oreb and Zeeb: and what was I able to do in comparison of you? Then their [t]anger was abated toward him, when he had said that.

4 ¶ And Gideon came to Jordan, *and* passed over, he, and the three hundred men that *were* with him, faint, yet pursuing *them.*

5 And he said unto the men of [u]Succoth, Give, I pray you, loaves of bread unto the people that follow me; for they *be* faint, and I am pursuing after Zebah and Zalmunna, kings of Midian.

6 ¶ And the princes of Succoth said, [v]*Are* the hands of Zebah and Zalmunna now in thine hand, that [w]we should give bread unto thine army?

7 And Gideon said, Therefore when the LORD hath delivered Zebah and Zalmunna into mine hand, [x]then I will tear your flesh with the thorns of the wilderness and with briers.

8 ¶ And he went up thence [y]to Penuel, and spake unto them likewise: and the men of Penuel answered him as the men of Succoth had answered *him.*

9 And he spake also unto the men of Penuel, saying, When I [z]come again in peace, [a]I will break down this tower.

10 ¶ Now Zebah and Zalmunna *were* in Karkor, and their hosts with them, about fifteen thousand *men,* all that were left of [b]all the hosts of the children of the east: for there fell an hundred and twenty thousand men that drew sword.

11 ¶ And Gideon went up by the way of them that dwelt in tents on the east of [c]Nobah and Jogbehah, and smote the host: for the host was [d]secure.

12 And when Zebah and Zalmunna fled, he pursued after them, and [e]took the two kings of Midian, Zebah and Zalmunna, and discomfited all the host.

13 ¶ And Gideon the son of Joash returned from battle before the sun *was up,*

14 And caught a young man of the men of Succoth, and enquired of him: and he described unto him the princes of Succoth, and the elders thereof, *even* threescore and seventeen men.

15 And he came unto the men of Succoth, and said, Behold Zebah and Zalmunna, with whom ye did [f]upbraid me, saying, *Are* the hands of Zebah and Zalmunna now in thine hand, that we should give bread unto thy men *that are* weary?

16 [g]And he took the elders of the city, and thorns of the wilderness and briers, and with them he taught the men of Succoth.

17 [h]And he beat down the tower of [i]Penuel, and slew the men of the city.

18 ¶ Then said he unto Zebah and Zalmunna, What manner of men *were they* whom ye slew at [j]Tabor? And they answered, As thou *art,* so *were* they; each one resembled the children of a king.

19 And he said, They *were* my brethren, *even* the sons of my mother: *as* the LORD liveth, if ye had saved them alive, I would not slay you.

20 And he said unto Jether his firstborn, Up, *and* slay them. But the youth drew not his sword: for he feared, because he *was* yet a youth.

21 Then Zebah and Zalmunna said, Rise thou, and fall upon us: for as the man *is, so is* his strength. And Gideon arose, and [k]slew Zebah and Zalmunna, and took away the ornaments that *were* on their camels' necks.

22 ¶ Then the men of Israel said unto Gideon, Rule thou over us, both thou, and thy son, and thy son's son also: for thou hast delivered us from the hand of Midian.

23 And Gideon said unto them, I will not rule over you, neither shall my son rule over you: [l]the LORD shall rule over you.

24 ¶ And Gideon said unto them, I would desire a request of you, that ye would give me every man the earrings of his prey. (For they had golden earrings, [m]because they *were* Ishmaelites.)

25 And they answered, We will willingly give *them.* And they spread a garment, and did cast therein every man the earrings of his prey.

26 And the weight of the golden earrings that he requested was a thousand and seven hundred *shekels* of gold; beside ornaments, and collars, and purple raiment that *was* on the kings of Midian, and beside the chains that *were* about their camels' necks.

27 And Gideon [n]made an ephod thereof, and put it in his city, *even* [o]in Ophrah: and all Israel [p]went thither a whoring after it: which thing became [q]a snare unto Gideon, and to his house.

28 ¶ Thus was Midian subdued before the children of Israel, so that they lifted up their heads no more. [r]And the country was in quietness forty years in the days of Gideon.

29 ¶ And Jerubbaal the son of Joash went and dwelt in his own house.

30 And Gideon had [s]threescore and ten sons of his body begotten: for he had many wives.

31 [t]And his concubine that *was* in Shechem, she also bare him a son, whose name he called Abimelech.

32 ¶ And Gideon the son of Joash died [u]in a good old age, and was buried in the sepulchre of Joash his father, [v]in Ophrah of the Abi-ezrites.

33 And it came to pass, [w]as soon a
eon was dead, that the children c
turned again, and [x]went a who
Baalim, [y]and made Baal-berith

8:3 [s]ch. 7:24; Phil. 2:3 [t]Prov. 15:1
8:5 [u]Gen. 33:17; Ps. 60:6
8:6 [v]1 Kings 20:11 [w]1 Sam. 25:11
8:7 [x]ver. 16
8:8 [y]Gen. 32:30; 1 Kings 12:25
8:9 [z]1 Kings 22:27 [a]ver. 17
8:10 [b]ch. 7:12
8:11 [c]Num. 32:35 [d]ch. 18:27; 1 Thess. 5:3
8:12 [e]Ps. 83:11
8:15 [f]ver. 6
8:16 [g]ver. 7
8:17 [h]ver. 9 [i]1 Kings 12:25
8:18 [j]ch. 4:6; Ps. 89:12
8:21 [k]Ps. 83:11
8:23 [l]1 Sam. 8:7
8:24 [m]Gen. 25:13
8:27 [n]ch. 17:5 [o]ch. 6:24 [p]Ps. 106:39 [q]Deut. 7:16
8:28 [r]ch. 5:31
8:30 [s]ch. 9:2
8:31 [t]ch. 9:1
8:32 [u]Gen. 25:8; Job 5:26 [v]ver. 27; ch. 6:24
8:33 [w]ch. 2:19 [x]ch. 2:17 [y]ch. 9:4

34 And the children of Israel [z]remembered not the LORD their God, who had delivered them out of the hands of all their enemies on every side:

35 [a]Neither shewed they kindness to the house of Jerubbaal, *namely,* Gideon, according to all the goodness which he had shewed unto Israel.

9

9 And Abimelech the son of Jerubbaal went to Shechem unto [b]his mother's brethren, and communed with them, and with all the family of the house of his mother's father, saying,

2 Speak, I pray you, in the ears of all the men of Shechem, Whether *is* better for you, either that all the sons of Jerubbaal, *which are* [c]threescore and ten persons, reign over you, or that one reign over you? remember also that I *am* [d]your bone and your flesh.

3 And his mother's brethren spake of him in the ears of all the men of Shechem all these words: and their hearts inclined to follow Abimelech; for they said, He *is* our [e]brother.

4 And they gave him threescore and ten *pieces* of silver out of the house of [f]Baal-berith, wherewith Abimelech hired [g]vain and light persons, which followed him.

5 And he went unto his father's house [h]at Ophrah, and [i]slew his brethren the sons of Jerubbaal, *being* threescore and ten persons, upon one stone: notwithstanding yet Jotham the youngest son of Jerubbaal was left; for he hid himself.

6 And all the men of Shechem gathered together, and all the house of Millo, and went, and made Abimelech king, by the plain of the pillar that *was* in Shechem.

7 ¶ And when they told *it* to Jotham, he went and stood in the top of [j]mount Gerizim, and lifted up his voice, and cried, and said unto them, Hearken unto me, ye men of Shechem, that God may hearken unto you.

8 [k]The trees went forth *on a time* to anoint a king over them; and they said unto the olive tree, [l]Reign thou over us.

9 But the olive tree said unto them, Should I leave my fatness, [m]wherewith by me they honour God and man, and go to be promoted over the trees?

10 And the trees said to the fig tree, Come thou, *and* reign over us.

11 But the fig tree said unto them, Should I forsake my sweetness, and my good fruit, and go to be promoted over the trees?

12 Then said the trees unto the vine, Come thou, *and* reign over us.

13 And the vine said unto them, Should I leave my wine, [n]which cheereth God and man, and go to be promoted over the trees?

14 Then said all the trees unto the bramble, Come thou, *and* reign over us.

15 And the bramble said unto the trees, If in truth ye anoint me king over you, *then* come *and* put your trust in my [o]shadow: and if not, [p]let fire come out of the bramble, and devour the [q]cedars of Lebanon.

16 Now therefore, if ye have done truly and sincerely, in that ye have made Abimelech king, and if ye have dealt well with Jerubbaal and his house, and have done unto him [r]according to the deserving of his hands;

17 (For my father fought for you, and adventured his life far, and delivered you out of the hand of Midian:

18 [s]And ye are risen up against my father's house this day, and have slain his sons, threescore and ten persons, upon one stone, and have made Abimelech, the son of his maidservant, king over the men of Shechem, because he *is* your brother;)

19 If ye then have dealt truly and sincerely with Jerubbaal and with his house this day, *then* [t]rejoice ye in Abimelech, and let him also rejoice in you:

20 But if not, [u]let fire come out from Abimelech, and devour the men of Shechem, and the house of Millo; and let fire come out from the men of Shechem, and from the house of Millo, and devour Abimelech.

21 And Jotham ran away, and fled, and went to [v]Beer, and dwelt there, for fear of Abimelech his brother.

22 ¶ When Abimelech had reigned three years over Israel,

23 Then [w]God sent an evil spirit between Abimelech and the men of Shechem; and the men of Shechem [x]dealt treacherously with Abimelech:

24 [y]That the cruelty *done* to the threescore and ten sons of Jerubbaal might come, and their blood be laid upon Abimelech their brother, which slew them; and upon the men of Shechem, which aided him in the killing of his brethren.

25 And the men of Shechem set liers in wait for him in the top of the mountains, and they robbed all that came along that way by them: and it was told Abimelech.

26 And Gaal the son of Ebed came with his brethren, and went over to Shechem: and the men of Shechem put their confidence in him.

27 And they went out into the fields, and gathered their vineyards, and trode *the grapes,* and made merry, and went into [z]the house of their god, and did eat and drink, and cursed Abimelech.

28 And Gaal the son of Ebed said, [a]Who *is* Abimelech, and who *is* Shechem, that we should serve him? *is* not *he* the son of Jerubbaal? and Zebul his officer? serve the men of [b]Hamor the father of Shechem: for why should we serve him?

29 And [c]would to God this people were under my hand! then would I remove Abimelech. And he said to Abimelech, Increase thine army, and come out.

30 ¶ And when Zebul the ruler of the city heard the words of Gaal the son of Ebed, his anger was kindled.

31 And he sent messengers unto Abimelech privily, saying, Behold, Gaal the son of Ebed and his brethren be come to Shechem;

8:34 [z]Ps. 78:11
8:35 [a]ch. 9:16; Eccl. 9:14
9:1 [b]ch. 8:31
9:2 [c]ch. 8:30 [d]Gen. 29:14
9:3 [e]Gen. 29:15
9:4 [f]ch. 8:33 [g]ch. 11:3; 2 Chron. 13:7; Prov. 12:11; Acts 17:5
9:5 [h]ch. 6:24 [i]2 Kings 11:1
9:7 [j]Deut. 11:29; Josh. 8:33; John 4:20
9:8 [k]2 Kings 14:9 [l]ch. 8:22
9:9 [m]Ps. 104:15
9:13 [n]Ps. 104:15
9:15 [o]Isa. 30:2; Dan. 4:12; Hos. 14:7 [p]ver. 20; Num. 21:28; Ezek. 19:14 [q]2 Kings 14:9; Ps. 104:16; Isa. 2:13; Ezek. 31:3
9:16 [r]ch. 8:35
9:18 [s]ver. 5
9:19 [t]Isa. 8:6; Phil. 3:3
9:20 [u]ver. 15
9:21 [v]2 Sam. 20:14
9:23 [w]1 Sam. 16:14; 1 Kings 12:15; 2 Chron. 10:15; Isa. 19:2 [x]Isa. 33:1
9:24 [y]1 Kings 2:32; Esth. 9:25; Ps. 7:16; Matt. 23:35
9:27 [z]ver. 4
9:28 [a]1 Sam. 25:10; 1 Kings 12:16 [b]Gen. 34:2
9:29 [c]2 Sam. 15:4

and, behold, they fortify the city against thee.

32 Now therefore up by night, thou and the people that *is* with thee, and lie in wait in the field:

33 And it shall be, *that* in the morning, as soon as the sun is up, thou shalt rise early, and set upon the city: and, behold, *when* he and the people that *is* with him come out against thee, then mayest thou do to them as thou shalt find occasion.

34 ¶ And Abimelech rose up, and all the people that *were* with him, by night, and they laid wait against Shechem in four companies.

35 And Gaal the son of Ebed went out, and stood in the entering of the gate of the city: and Abimelech rose up, and the people that *were* with him, from lying in wait.

36 And when Gaal saw the people, he said to Zebul, Behold, there come people down from the top of the mountains. And Zebul said unto him, Thou seest the shadow of the mountains as *if they were* men.

37 And Gaal spake again and said, See there come people down by the middle of the land, and another company come along by the plain of Meonenim.

38 Then said Zebul unto him, Where *is* now thy mouth, wherewith thou [d]saidst, Who *is* Abimelech, that we should serve him? *is* not this the people that thou hast despised? go out, I pray now, and fight with them.

39 And Gaal went out before the men of Shechem, and fought with Abimelech.

40 And Abimelech chased him, and he fled before him, and many were overthrown *and* wounded, *even* unto the entering of the gate.

41 And Abimelech dwelt at Arumah: and Zebul thrust out Gaal and his brethren, that they should not dwell in Shechem.

42 And it came to pass on the morrow, that the people went out into the field; and they told Abimelech.

43 And he took the people, and divided them into three companies, and laid wait in the field, and looked, and, behold, the people *were* come forth out of the city; and he rose up against them, and smote them.

44 And Abimelech, and the company that *was* with him, rushed forward, and stood in the entering of the gate of the city: and the two *other* companies ran upon all *the people* that *were* in the fields, and slew them.

45 And Abimelech fought against the city all that day; and [e]he took the city, and slew the people that *was* therein, and [f]beat down the city, and sowed it with salt.

46 ¶ And when all the men of the tower of Shechem heard *that*, they entered into an hold of the house [g]of the god Berith.

47 And it was told Abimelech, that all the men of the tower of Shechem were gathered together.

48 And Abimelech gat him up to mount [h]Zalmon, he and all the people that *were* with him; and Abimelech took an axe in his hand, and cut down a bough from the trees, and took it, and laid *it* on his shoulder, and said unto the people that *were* with him, What ye have seen me do, make haste, *and* do as I *have done*.

49 And all the people likewise cut down every man his bough, and followed Abimelech, and put *them* to the hold, and set the hold on fire upon them; so that all the men of the tower of Shechem died also, about a thousand men and women.

50 ¶ Then went Abimelech to Thebez, and encamped against Thebez, and took it.

51 But there was a strong tower within the city, and thither fled all the men and women, and all they of the city, and shut *it* to them, and gat them up to the top of the tower.

52 And Abimelech came unto the tower, and fought against it, and went hard unto the door of the tower to burn it with fire.

53 And a certain woman [i]cast a piece of a millstone upon Abimelech's head, and all to brake his skull.

54 Then [j]he called hastily unto the young man his armourbearer, and said unto him, Draw thy sword, and slay me, that men say not of me, A woman slew him. And his young man thrust him through, and he died.

55 And when the men of Israel saw that Abimelech was dead, they departed every man unto his place.

56 ¶ [k]Thus God rendered the wickedness of Abimelech, which he did unto his father, in slaying his seventy brethren:

57 And all the evil of the men of Shechem did God render upon their heads: and upon them came [l]the curse of Jotham the son of Jerubbaal.

10 And after Abimelech there [m]arose to defend Israel Tola the son of Puah, the son of Dodo, a man of Issachar; and he dwelt in Shamir in mount Ephraim.

2 And he judged Israel twenty and three years, and died, and was buried in Shamir.

3 ¶ And after him arose Jair, a Gileadite, and judged Israel twenty and two years.

4 And he had thirty sons that [n]rode on thirty ass colts, and they had thirty cities, [o]which are called Havoth-jair unto this day, which *are* in the land of Gilead.

5 And Jair died, and was buried in Camon.

6 ¶ And [p]the children of Israel did evil again in the sight of the LORD, and [q]served Baalim, and Ashtaroth, and [r]the gods of Syria, and the gods of [s]Zidon, and the gods of Moab, and the gods of the children of Ammon, and the gods of the Philistines, and forsook the LORD, and served not him.

7 And the anger of the LORD was hot against Israel, and he [t]sold them into the hands of the Philistines, and into the hands of the children of Ammon.

8 And that year they vexed and oppressed the children of Israel: eighteen years, all the children of Israel that *were* on

9:38 [d]ver. 28
9:45 [e]ver. 20 [f]Deut. 29:23; 1 Kings 12:25; 2 Kings 3:25
9:46 [g]ch. 8:33
9:48 [h]Ps. 68:14
9:53 [i]2 Sam. 11:21
9:54 [j]1 Sam. 31:4
9:56 [k]ver. 24; Job 31:3; Ps. 94:23; Prov. 5:22
9:57 [l]ver. 20
10:1 [m]ch. 2:16
10:4 [n]ch. 5:10 [o]Deut. 3:14
10:6 [p]ch. 2:11 [q]ch. 2:13 [r]ch. 2:12 [s]1 Kings 11:33; Ps. 106:36
10:7 [t]ch. 2:14; 1 Sam. 12:9

the other side Jordan in the land of the Amorites, which *is* in Gilead.

9 Moreover the children of Ammon passed over Jordan to fight also against Judah, and against Benjamin, and against the house of Ephraim; so that Israel was sore distressed.

10 ¶ [u]And the children of Israel cried unto the LORD, saying, We have sinned against thee, both because we have forsaken our God, and also served Baalim.

11 And the LORD said unto the children of Israel, *Did* not *I deliver you* [v]from the Egyptians, and [w]from the Amorites, [x]from the children of Ammon, [y]and from the Philistines?

12 [z]The Zidonians also, [a]and the Amalekites, and the Maonites, [b]did oppress you; and ye cried to me, and I delivered you out of their hand.

13 [c]Yet ye have forsaken me, and served other gods: wherefore I will deliver you no more.

14 Go and [d]cry unto the gods which ye have chosen; let them deliver you in the time of your tribulation.

15 ¶ And the children of Israel said unto the LORD, We have sinned: [e]do thou unto us whatsoever seemeth good unto thee; deliver us only, we pray thee, this day.

16 [f]And they put away the strange gods from among them, and served the LORD: and [g]his soul was grieved for the misery of Israel.

17 Then the children of Ammon were gathered together, and encamped in Gilead. And the children of Israel assembled themselves together, and encamped in [h]Mizpeh.

18 And the people *and* princes of Gilead said one to another, What man *is he* that will begin to fight against the children of Ammon? he shall [i]be head over all the inhabitants of Gilead.

11 Now [j]Jephthah the Gileadite was [k]a mighty man of valour, and he *was* the son of an harlot: and Gilead begat Jephthah.

2 And Gilead's wife bare him sons; and his wife's sons grew up, and they thrust out Jephthah, and said unto him, Thou shalt not inherit in our father's house; for thou *art* the son of a strange woman.

3 Then Jephthah fled from his brethren, and dwelt in the land of Tob: and there were gathered [l]vain men to Jephthah, and went out with him.

4 ¶ And it came to pass in process of time, that the children of Ammon made war against Israel.

5 And it was so, that when the children of Ammon made war against Israel, the elders of Gilead went to fetch Jephthah out of the land of Tob:

6 And they said unto Jephthah, Come, and be our captain, that we may fight with the children of Ammon.

7 And Jephthah said unto the elders of Gilead, [m]Did not ye hate me, and expel me out of my father's house? and why are ye come unto me now when ye are in distress?

8 [n]And the elders of Gilead said unto Jephthah, Therefore we [o]turn again to thee now, that thou mayest go with us, and fight against the children of Ammon, and be [p]our head over all the inhabitants of Gilead.

9 And Jephthah said unto the elders of Gilead, If ye bring me home again to fight against the children of Ammon, and the LORD deliver them before me, shall I be your head?

10 And the elders of Gilead said unto Jephthah, [q]The LORD be witness between us, if we do not so according to thy words.

11 Then Jephthah went with the elders of Gilead, and the people made him [r]head and captain over them: and Jephthah uttered all his words [s]before the LORD in Mizpeh.

12 ¶ And Jephthah sent messengers unto the king of the children of Ammon, saying, What hast thou to do with me, that thou art come against me to fight in my land?

13 And the king of the children of Ammon answered unto the messengers of Jephthah, [t]Because Israel took away my land, when they came up out of Egypt, from Arnon even unto [u]Jabbok, and unto Jordan: now therefore restore those *lands* again peaceably.

14 And Jephthah sent messengers again unto the king of the children of Ammon:

15 And said unto him, Thus saith Jephthah, [v]Israel took not away the land of Moab, nor the land of the children of Ammon:

16 But when Israel came up from Egypt, and [w]walked through the wilderness unto the Red sea, and [x]came to Kadesh;

17 Then [y]Israel sent messengers unto the king of Edom, saying, Let me, I pray thee, pass through thy land: [z]but the king of Edom would not hearken *thereto*. And in like manner they sent unto the king of Moab: but he would not *consent:* and Israel [a]abode in Kadesh.

18 Then they went along through the wilderness, and [b]compassed the land of Edom, and the land of Moab, and [c]came by the east side of the land of Moab, [d]and pitched on the other side of Arnon, but came not within the border of Moab: for Arnon *was* the border of Moab.

19 And [e]Israel sent messengers unto Sihon king of the Amorites, the king of Heshbon; and Israel said unto him, [f]Let us pass, we pray thee, through thy land into my place.

20 [g]But Sihon trusted not Israel to pass through his coast: but Sihon gathered all his people together, and pitched in Jahaz, and fought against Israel.

21 And the LORD God of Israel delivered Sihon and all his people into the hand of Israel, and they [h]smote them: so Israel possessed all the land of the Amorites, the inhabitants of that country.

10:10 [u]1 Sam. 12:10
10:11 [v]Ex. 14:30 [w]Num. 21:21 [x]ch. 3:12 [y]ch. 3:31
10:12 [z]ch. 5:19 [a]ch. 6:3 [b]Ps. 106:42
10:13 [c]Deut. 32:15; Jer. 2:13
10:14 [d]Deut. 32:37; 2 Kings 3:13; Jer. 2:28
10:15 [e]1 Sam. 3:18; 2 Sam. 15:26
10:16 [f]2 Chron. 7:14; Jer. 18:7 [g]Ps. 106:44; Isa. 63:9
10:17 [h]ch. 11:11; Gen. 31:49
10:18 [i]ch. 11:8
11:1 [j]Heb. 11:32 [k]ch. 6:12; 2 Kings 5:1
11:3 [l]ch. 9:4; 1 Sam. 22:2
11:7 [m]Gen. 26:27
11:8 [n]ch. 10:18 [o]Luke 17:4 [p]ch. 10:18
11:10 [q]Jer. 42:5
11:11 [r]ver. 8 [s]ch. 10:17; 1 Sam. 10:17
11:13 [t]Num. 21:24 [u]Gen. 32:22
11:15 [v]Deut. 2:9
11:16 [w]Num. 14:25; Deut. 1:40; Josh. 5:6 [x]Num. 13:26; Deut. 1:46
11:17 [y]Num. 20:14 [z]Num. 20:18 [a]Num. 20:1
11:18 [b]Num. 21:4; Deut. 2:1-8 [c]Num. 21:11 [d]Num. 21:13
11:19 [e]Num. 21:21; Deut. 2:26 [f]Num. 21:22; Deut. 2:27
11:20 [g]Num. 21:23; Deut. 2:32
11:21 [h]Num. 21:24; Deut. 2:33

22 And they possessed [i]all the coasts of the Amorites, from Arnon even unto Jabbok, and from the wilderness even unto Jordan.

23 So now the LORD God of Israel hath dispossessed the Amorites from before his people Israel, and shouldest thou possess it?

24 Wilt not thou possess that which [j]Chemosh thy god giveth thee to possess? So whomsoever [k]the LORD our God shall drive out from before us, them will we possess.

25 And now *art* thou any thing better than [l]Balak the son of Zippor, king of Moab? did he ever strive against Israel, or did he ever fight against them,

26 While Israel dwelt in [m]Heshbon and her towns, and in [n]Aroer and her towns, and in all the cities that *be* along by the coasts of Arnon, three hundred years? why therefore did ye not recover *them* within that time?

27 Wherefore I have not sinned against thee, but thou doest me wrong to war against me: the LORD [o]the Judge [p]be judge this day between the children of Israel and the children of Ammon.

28 Howbeit the king of the children of Ammon hearkened not unto the words of Jephthah which he sent him.

29 ¶ Then [q]the Spirit of the LORD came upon Jephthah, and he passed over Gilead, and Manasseh, and passed over Mizpeh of Gilead, and from Mizpeh of Gilead he passed over *unto* the children of Ammon.

30 And Jephthah [r]vowed a vow unto the LORD, and said, If thou shalt without fail deliver the children of Ammon into mine hands,

31 Then it shall be, that whatsoever cometh forth of the doors of my house to meet me, when I return in peace from the children of Ammon, [s]shall surely be the LORD'S, [t]and I will offer it up for a burnt offering.

32 ¶ So Jephthah passed over unto the children of Ammon to fight against them; and the LORD delivered them into his hands.

33 And he smote them from Aroer, even till thou come to [u]Minnith, *even* twenty cities, and unto the plain of the vineyards, with a very great slaughter. Thus the children of Ammon were subdued before the children of Israel.

34 ¶ And Jephthah came to [v]Mizpeh unto his house, and, behold, [w]his daughter came out to meet him with timbrels and with dances: and she *was his* only child; beside her he had neither son nor daughter.

35 And it came to pass, when he saw her, that he [x]rent his clothes, and said, Alas, my daughter! thou hast brought me very low, and thou art one of them that trouble me: for I [y]have opened my mouth unto the LORD, and [z]I cannot go back.

36 And she said unto him, My father, *if* thou hast opened thy mouth unto the LORD, [a]do to me according to that which hath proceeded out of thy mouth; forasmuch as [b]the LORD hath taken vengeance for thee of thine enemies, *even* of the children of Ammon.

37 And she said unto her father, Let this thing be done for me: let me alone two months, that I may go up and down upon the mountains, and bewail my virginity, I and my fellows.

38 And he said, Go. And he sent her away *for* two months: and she went with her companions, and bewailed her virginity upon the mountains.

39 And it came to pass at the end of two months, that she returned unto her father, who [c]did with her *according* to his vow which he had vowed: and she knew no man. And it was a custom in Israel,

40 *That* the daughters of Israel went yearly to lament the daughter of Jephthah the Gileadite four days in a year.

12 And [d]the men of Ephraim gathered themselves together, and went northward, and said unto Jephthah, Wherefore passedst thou over to fight against the children of Ammon, and didst not call us to go with thee? we will burn thine house upon thee with fire.

2 And Jephthah said unto them, I and my people were at great strife with the children of Ammon; and when I called you, ye delivered me not out of their hands.

3 And when I saw that ye delivered *me* not, I [e]put my life in my hands, and passed over against the children of Ammon, and the LORD delivered them into my hand: wherefore then are ye come up unto me this day, to fight against me?

4 Then Jephthah gathered together all the men of Gilead, and fought with Ephraim: and the men of Gilead smote Ephraim, because they said, Ye Gileadites [f]*are* fugitives of Ephraim among the Ephraimites, *and* among the Manassites.

5 And the Gileadites took the [g]passages of Jordan before the Ephraimites: and it was *so*, that when those Ephraimites which were escaped said, Let me go over; that the men of Gilead said unto him, *Art* thou an Ephraimite? If he said, Nay;

6 Then said they unto him, Say now Shibboleth: and he said Sibboleth: for he could not frame to pronounce *it* right. Then they took him, and slew him at the passages of Jordan: and there fell at that time of the Ephraimites forty and two thousand.

7 And Jephthah judged Israel six years. Then died Jephthah the Gileadite, and was buried in *one of* the cities of Gilead.

8 ¶ And after him Ibzan of Beth-lehem judged Israel.

9 And he had thirty sons, and thirty daughters, *whom* he sent abroad, and took in thirty daughters from abroad for his sons. And he judged Israel seven years.

10 Then died Ibzan, and was buried at Beth-lehem.

11:22 [i]Deut. 2:36
11:24 [j]Num. 21:29; 1 Kings 11:7; Jer. 48:7 [k]Deut. 9:4; Josh. 3:10
11:25 [l]Num. 22:2; Josh. 24:9
11:26 [m]Num. 21:25 [n]Deut. 2:36
11:27 [o]Gen. 18:25 [p]Gen. 16:5; 1 Sam. 24:12
11:29 [q]ch. 3:10
11:30 [r]Gen. 28:20; 1 Sam. 1:11
11:31 [s]Lev. 27:2; 1 Sam. 1:11 [t]Lev. 27:11; Ps. 66:13
11:33 [u]Ezek. 27:17
11:34 [v]ch. 10:17 [w]Ex. 15:20; 1 Sam. 18:6; Ps. 68:25; Jer. 31:4
11:35 [x]Gen. 37:29 [y]Eccl. 5:2 [z]Num. 30:2; Ps. 15:4; Eccl. 5:4
11:36 [a]Num. 30:2 [b]2 Sam. 18:19
11:39 [c]ver. 31; 1 Sam. 1:22
12:1 [d]ch. 8:1
12:3 [e]1 Sam. 19:5; Job 13:14; Ps. 119:109
12:4 [f]1 Sam. 25:10; Ps. 78:9
12:5 [g]Josh. 22:11; ch. 3:28

11 ¶ And after him Elon, a Zebulonite,
judged Israel; and he judged Israel ten
years.
12 And Elon the Zebulonite died, and was
buried in Aijalon in the country of Zebulun.
13 ¶ And after him Abdon the son of Hillel, a Pirathonite, judged Israel.
14 And he had forty sons and thirty nephews, that [h]rode on threescore and ten ass
colts: and he judged Israel eight years.
15 And Abdon the son of Hillel the Pirathonite died, and was buried in Pirathon in
the land of Ephraim, [i]in the mount of the
Amalekites.

13

And the children of Israel [j]did evil
again in the sight of the LORD; and
the LORD delivered them [k]into the hand of
the Philistines forty years.
2 ¶ And there was a certain man of [l]Zo-
rah, of the family of the Danites, whose
name *was* Manoah; and his wife *was* barren, and bare not.
3 And the [m]angel of the LORD appeared
unto the woman, and said unto her, Behold
now, thou *art* barren, and bearest not: but
thou shalt conceive, and bear a son.
4 Now therefore beware, I pray thee, and
[n]drink not wine nor strong drink, and eat
not any unclean *thing*:
5 For, lo, thou shalt conceive, and bear a
son; and no [o]razor shall come on his head:
for the child shall be [p]a Nazarite unto God
from the womb: and he shall [q]begin to deliver Israel out of the hand of the Philistines.
6 ¶ Then the woman came and told her
husband, saying, [r]A man of God came unto
me, and his [s]countenance *was* like the
countenance of an angel of God, very terrible: but I [t]asked him not whence he *was*,
neither told he me his name:
7 But he said unto me, Behold, thou shalt
conceive, and bear a son; and now drink no
wine nor strong drink, neither eat any unclean *thing*: for the child shall be a Nazarite
to God from the womb to the day of his
death.
8 ¶ Then Manoah intreated the LORD, and
said, O my Lord, let the man of God which
thou didst send come again unto us, and
teach us what we shall do unto the child that
shall be born.
9 And God hearkened to the voice of Manoah; and the angel of God came again unto
the woman as she sat in the field: but Manoah her husband *was* not with her.
10 And the woman made haste, and ran,
and shewed her husband, and said unto
him, Behold, the man hath appeared unto
me, that came unto me the *other* day.
11 And Manoah arose, and went after his
wife, and came to the man, and said unto
him, *Art* thou the man that spakest unto the
woman? And he said, I *am*.
12 And Manoah said, Now let thy words
come to pass. How shall we order the child,
and *how* shall we do unto him?
13 And the angel of the LORD said unto
Manoah, Of all that I said unto the woman
let her beware.
14 She may not eat of any *thing* that cometh of the vine, [u]neither let her drink wine
or strong drink, nor eat any unclean *thing*:
all that I commanded her let her observe.
15 ¶ And Manoah said unto the angel of
the LORD, I pray thee, [v]let us detain thee,
until we shall have made ready a kid for
thee.
16 And the angel of the LORD said unto
Manoah, Though thou detain me, I will not
eat of thy bread: and if thou wilt offer a
burnt offering, thou must offer it unto the
LORD. For Manoah knew not that he *was* an
angel of the LORD.
17 And Manoah said unto the angel of the
LORD, What *is* thy name, that when thy sayings come to pass we may do thee honour?
18 And the angel of the LORD said unto
him, [w]Why askest thou thus after my name,
seeing it *is* secret?
19 So Manoah took a kid with a meat offering, [x]and offered *it* upon a rock unto the
LORD: and *the angel* did wondrously; and
Manoah and his wife looked on.
20 For it came to pass, when the flame
went up toward heaven from off the altar,
that the angel of the LORD ascended in the
flame of the altar. And Manoah and his wife
looked on *it*, and [y]fell on their faces to the
ground.
21 But the angel of the LORD did no more
appear to Manoah and to his wife. [z]Then
Manoah knew that he *was* an angel of the
LORD.
22 And Manoah said unto his wife, [a]We
shall surely die, because we have seen God.
23 But his wife said unto him, If the LORD
were pleased to kill us, he would not have
received a burnt offering and a meat offering at our hands, neither would he have
shewed us all these *things*, nor would as at
this time have told us *such things* as these.
24 ¶ And the woman bare a son, and
called his name [b]Samson: and [c]the child
grew, and the LORD blessed him.
25 [d]And the Spirit of the LORD began to
move him at times in the camp of Dan [e]be-
tween Zorah and Eshtaol.

14

And Samson went down [f]to Timnath, and [g]saw a woman in Timnath
of the daughters of the Philistines.
2 And he came up, and told his father and
his mother, and said, I have seen a woman
in Timnath of the daughters of the Philistines: now therefore [h]get her for me to wife.
3 Then his father and his mother said
unto him, *Is there* never a woman among
the daughters of [i]thy brethren, or among
all my people, that thou goest to take a wife
of the [j]uncircumcised Philistines? And
Samson said unto his father, Get her for me;
for she pleaseth me well.
4 But his father and his mother knew not
that it *was* [k]of the LORD, that he sought an
occasion against the Philistines: for at that

12:14 [h]ch. 5:10
12:15 [i]ch. 3:13
13:1 [j]ch. 2:11 [k]1 Sam. 12:9
13:2 [l]Josh. 19:41
13:3 [m]ch. 6:12; Luke 1:11
13:4 [n]ver. 14; Num. 6:2; Luke 1:15
13:5 [o]Num. 6:5; 1 Sam. 1:11 [p]Num. 6:2 [q]1 Sam. 7:13; 2 Sam. 8:1; 1 Chron. 18:1
13:6 [r]Deut. 33:1; 1 Sam. 2:27; 1 Kings 17:24 [s]Matt. 28:3; Luke 9:29; Acts 6:15 [t]ver. 17
13:14 [u]ver. 4
13:15 [v]Gen. 18:5; ch. 6:18
13:18 [w]Gen. 32:29
13:19 [x]ch. 6:19
13:20 [y]Lev. 9:24; 1 Chron. 21:16; Ezek. 1:28; Matt. 17:6
13:21 [z]ch. 6:22
13:22 [a]Gen. 32:30; Ex. 33:20; Deut. 5:26; ch. 6:22
13:24 [b]Heb. 11:32 [c]1 Sam. 3:19; Luke 1:80
13:25 [d]ch. 3:10; 1 Sam. 11:6; Matt. 4:1 [e]Josh. 15:33; ch. 18:11
14:1 [f]Gen. 38:13; Josh. 15:10 [g]Gen. 34:2
14:2 [h]Gen. 21:21
14:3 [i]Gen. 24:3 [j]Gen. 34:14; Ex. 34:16; Deut. 7:3
14:4 [k]Josh. 11:20; 1 Kings 12:15; 2 Kings 6:33; 2 Chron. 10:15

time [l]the Philistines had dominion over Israel.
5 ¶ Then went Samson down, and his father and his mother, to Timnath, and came
to the vineyards of Timnath: and, behold, a
young lion roared against him.
6 And [m]the Spirit of the LORD came
mightily upon him, and he rent him as he
would have rent a kid, and *he had* nothing
in his hand: but he told not his father or his
mother what he had done.
7 And he went down, and talked with the
woman; and she pleased Samson well.
8 ¶ And after a time he returned to take
her, and he turned aside to see the carcase
of the lion: and, behold, *there was* a swarm
of bees and honey in the carcase of the lion.
9 And he took thereof in his hands, and
went on eating, and came to his father and
mother, and he gave them, and they did eat:
but he told not them that he had taken the
honey out of the carcase of the lion.
10 ¶ So his father went down unto the
woman: and Samson made there a feast; for
so used the young men to do.
11 And it came to pass, when they saw
him, that they brought thirty companions to
be with him.
12 ¶ And Samson said unto them, I will
now [n]put forth a riddle unto you: if ye can
certainly declare it me [o]within the seven
days of the feast, and find *it* out, then I will
give you thirty sheets and thirty [p]change of
garments:
13 But if ye cannot declare *it* me, then
shall ye give me thirty sheets and thirty
change of garments. And they said unto
him, Put forth thy riddle, that we may
hear it.
14 And he said unto them, Out of the eater
came forth meat, and out of the strong came
forth sweetness. And they could not in three
days expound the riddle.
15 And it came to pass on the seventh
day, that they said unto Samson's wife,
[q]Entice thy husband, that he may declare
unto us the riddle, [r]lest we burn thee and
thy father's house with fire: have ye called
us to take that we have? *is it* not *so*?
16 And Samson's wife wept before him,
and said, [s]Thou dost but hate me, and lovest me not: thou hast put forth a riddle unto
the children of my people, and hast not told
it me. And he said unto her, Behold, I have
not told *it* my father nor my mother, and
shall I tell *it* thee?
17 And she wept before him the seven
days, while their feast lasted: and it came to
pass on the seventh day, that he told her,
because she lay sore upon him: and she told
the riddle to the children of her people.
18 And the men of the city said unto him
on the seventh day before the sun went
down, What *is* sweeter than honey? and
what *is* stronger than a lion? And he said
unto them, If ye had not plowed with my
heifer, ye had not found out my riddle.
19 ¶ And [t]the Spirit of the LORD came
upon him, and he went down to Ashkelon,
and slew thirty men of them, and took their
spoil, and gave change of garments unto
them which expounded the riddle. And his
anger was kindled, and he went up to his
father's house.
20 But Samson's wife [u]was *given* to his
companion, whom he had used as [v]his
friend.

15 But it came to pass within a while
after, in the time of wheat harvest,
that Samson visited his wife with a kid; and
he said, I will go in to my wife into the
chamber. But her father would not suffer
him to go in.
2 And her father said, I verily thought
that thou hadst utterly [w]hated her; therefore I gave her to thy companion: *is* not her
younger sister fairer than she? take her, I
pray thee, instead of her.
3 ¶ And Samson said concerning them,
Now shall I be more blameless than the Philistines, though I do them a displeasure.
4 And Samson went and caught three
hundred foxes, and took firebrands, and
turned tail to tail, and put a firebrand in the
midst between two tails.
5 And when he had set the brands on fire,
he let *them* go into the standing corn of the
Philistines, and burnt up both the shocks,
and also the standing corn, with the vineyards *and* olives.
6 ¶ Then the Philistines said, Who hath
done this? And they answered, Samson, the
son in law of the Timnite, because he had
taken his wife, and given her to his companion. [x]And the Philistines came up, and
burnt her and her father with fire.
7 ¶ And Samson said unto them, Though
ye have done this, yet will I be avenged of
you, and after that I will cease.
8 And he smote them hip and thigh with
a great slaughter: and he went down and
dwelt in the top of the rock Etam.
9 ¶ Then the Philistines went up, and
pitched in Judah, and spread themselves
[y]in Lehi.
10 And the men of Judah said, Why are ye
come up against us? And they answered, To
bind Samson are we come up, to do to him
as he hath done to us.
11 Then three thousand men of Judah
went to the top of the rock Etam, and said to
Samson, Knowest thou not that the Philistines *are* [z]rulers over us? what *is* this *that*
thou hast done unto us? And he said unto
them, As they did unto me, so have I done
unto them.
12 And they said unto him, We are come
down to bind thee, that we may deliver thee
into the hand of the Philistines. And Samson said unto them, Swear unto me, that ye
will not fall upon me yourselves.
13 And they spake unto him, saying, No;
but we will bind thee fast, and deliver thee
into their hand: but surely we will not kill
thee. And they bound him with two new
cords, and brought him up from the rock.

14:4 [l]ch. 13:1; Deut. 28:48
14:6 [m]ch. 3:10; 1 Sam. 11:6
14:12 [n]1 Kings 10:1; Ezek. 17:2; Luke 14:7 [o]Gen. 29:27 [p]Gen. 45:22; 2 Kings 5:22
14:15 [q]ch. 16:5 [r]ch. 15:6
14:16 [s]ch. 16:15
14:19 [t]ch. 3:10
14:20 [u]ch. 15:2 [v]John 3:29
15:2 [w]ch. 14:20
15:6 [x]ch. 14:15
15:9 [y]ver. 19
15:11 [z]ch. 14:4

14 ¶ *And* when he came unto Lehi, the
Philistines shouted against him: and [a]the
Spirit of the LORD came mightily upon him,
and the cords that *were* upon his arms became as flax that was burnt with fire, and
his bands loosed from off his hands.
15 And he found a new jawbone of an ass,
and put forth his hand, and took it, and
[b]slew a thousand men therewith.
16 And Samson said, With the jawbone of
an ass, heaps upon heaps, with the jaw of an
ass have I slain a thousand men.
17 And it came to pass, when he had
made an end of speaking, that he cast away
the jawbone out of his hand, and called that
place Ramath-lehi.
18 ¶ And he was sore athirst, and called
on the LORD, and said, [c]Thou hast given
this great deliverance into the hand of thy
servant: and now shall I die for thirst, and
fall into the hand of the uncircumcised?
19 But God clave an hollow place that
was in the jaw, and there came water thereout; and when he had drunk, [d]his spirit
came again, and he revived: wherefore he
called the name thereof En-hakkore, which
is in Lehi unto this day.
20 And he judged Israel [e]in the days of
the Philistines twenty years.

16 Then went Samson to Gaza, and saw
there an harlot, and went in unto her.
2 *And it was told* the Gazites, saying,
Samson is come hither. And they [f]com-
passed *him* in, and laid wait for him all
night in the gate of the city, and were quiet
all the night, saying, In the morning, when
it is day, we shall kill him.
3 And Samson lay till midnight, and arose
at midnight, and took the doors of the gate
of the city, and the two posts, and went
away with them, bar and all, and put *them*
upon his shoulders, and carried them up to
the top of an hill that *is* before Hebron.
4 ¶ And it came to pass afterward, that
he loved a woman in the valley of Sorek,
whose name *was* Delilah.
5 And the lords of the Philistines came up
unto her, and said unto her, [g]Entice him,
and see wherein his great strength *lieth*,
and by what *means* we may prevail against
him, that we may bind him to afflict him:
and we will give thee every one of us eleven
hundred *pieces* of silver.
6 ¶ And Delilah said to Samson, Tell me,
I pray thee, wherein thy great strength *lieth*,
and wherewith thou mightest be bound to
afflict thee.
7 And Samson said unto her, If they bind
me with seven green withs that were never
dried, then shall I be weak, and be as another man.
8 Then the lords of the Philistines brought
up to her seven green withs which had not
been dried, and she bound him with them.
9 Now *there were* men lying in wait, abiding with her in the chamber. And she said
unto him, The Philistines *be* upon thee,
Samson. And he brake the withs, as a
thread of tow is broken when it toucheth the
fire. So his strength was not known.
10 And Delilah said unto Samson, Behold, thou hast mocked me, and told me
lies: now tell me, I pray thee, wherewith
thou mightest be bound.
11 And he said unto her, If they bind me
fast with new ropes that never were occupied, then shall I be weak, and be as another
man.
12 Delilah therefore took new ropes, and
bound him therewith, and said unto him,
The Philistines *be* upon thee, Samson. And
there were liers in wait abiding in the chamber. And he brake them from off his arms
like a thread.
13 And Delilah said unto Samson, Hitherto thou hast mocked me, and told me lies:
tell me wherewith thou mightest be bound.
And he said unto her, If thou weavest the
seven locks of my head with the web.
14 And she fastened *it* with the pin, and
said unto him, The Philistines *be* upon thee,
Samson. And he awaked out of his sleep,
and went away with the pin of the beam,
and with the web.
15 ¶ And she said unto him, [h]How canst
thou say, I love thee, when thine heart *is* not
with me? thou hast mocked me these three
times, and hast not told me wherein thy
great strength *lieth*.
16 And it came to pass, when she pressed
him daily with her words, and urged him, *so*
that his soul was vexed unto death;
17 That he [i]told her all his heart, and
said unto her, [j]There hath not come a razor
upon mine head; for I *have been* a Nazarite
unto God from my mother's womb: if I be
shaven, then my strength will go from me,
and I shall become weak, and be like any
other man.
18 And when Delilah saw that he had told
her all his heart, she sent and called for the
lords of the Philistines, saying, Come up
this once, for he hath shewed me all his
heart. Then the lords of the Philistines came
up unto her, and brought money in their
hand.
19 [k]And she made him sleep upon her
knees; and she called for a man, and she
caused him to shave off the seven locks of
his head; and she began to afflict him, and
his strength went from him.
20 And she said, The Philistines *be* upon
thee, Samson. And he awoke out of his
sleep, and said, I will go out as at other
times before, and shake myself. And he wist
not that the LORD [l]was departed from him.
21 ¶ But the Philistines took him, and put
out his eyes, and brought him down to
Gaza, and bound him with fetters of brass;
and he did grind in the prison house.
22 Howbeit the hair of his head began to
grow again after he was shaven.
23 Then the lords of the Philistines gathered them together for to offer a great sacrifice unto Dagon their god, and to rejoice: for

15:14 [a]ch. 3:10
15:15 [b]ch. 3:31; Lev. 26:8; Josh. 23:10
15:18 [c]Ps. 3:7
15:19 [d]Gen. 45:27; Isa. 40:29
15:20 [e]ch. 13:1
16:2 [f]1 Sam. 23:26; Ps. 118:10; Acts 9:24
16:5 [g]ch. 14:15; Prov. 2:16-19
16:15 [h]ch. 14:16
16:17 [i]Mic. 7:5 [j]Num. 6:5; ch. 13:5
16:19 [k]Prov. 7:26
16:20 [l]Num. 14:9; Josh. 7:12; 1 Sam. 16:14; 2 Chron. 15:2

they said, Our god hath delivered Samson our enemy into our hand.

24 And when the people saw him, they [m]praised their god: for they said, Our god hath delivered into our hands our enemy, and the destroyer of our country, which slew many of us.

25 And it came to pass, when their hearts were [n]merry, that they said, Call for Samson, that he may make us sport. And they called for Samson out of the prison house; and he made them sport: and they set him between the pillars.

26 And Samson said unto the lad that held him by the hand, Suffer me that I may feel the pillars whereupon the house standeth, that I may lean upon them.

27 Now the house was full of men and women; and all the lords of the Philistines *were* there; and *there were* upon the [o]roof about three thousand men and women, that beheld while Samson made sport.

28 And Samson called unto the LORD, and said, O Lord GOD, [p]remember me, I pray thee, and strengthen me, I pray thee, only this once, O God, that I may be at once avenged of the Philistines for my two eyes.

29 And Samson took hold of the two middle pillars upon which the house stood, and on which it was borne up, of the one with his right hand, and of the other with his left.

30 And Samson said, Let me die with the Philistines. And he bowed himself with *all his* might; and the house fell upon the lords, and upon all the people that *were* therein. So the dead which he slew at his death were more than *they* which he slew in his life.

31 Then his brethren and all the house of his father came down, and took him, and brought *him* up, and [q]buried him between Zorah and Eshtaol in the buryingplace of Manoah his father. And he judged Israel twenty years.

17 And there was a man of mount Ephraim, whose name *was* Micah.

2 And he said unto his mother, The eleven hundred *shekels* of silver that were taken from thee, about which thou cursedst, and spakest of also in mine ears, behold, the silver *is* with me; I took it. And his mother said, [r]Blessed *be thou* of the LORD, my son.

3 And when he had restored the eleven hundred *shekels* of silver to his mother, his mother said, I had wholly dedicated the silver unto the LORD from my hand for my son, to [s]make a graven image and a molten image: now therefore I will restore it unto thee.

4 Yet he restored the money unto his mother; and his mother [t]took two hundred *shekels* of silver, and gave them to the founder, who made thereof a graven image and a molten image: and they were in the house of Micah.

5 And the man Micah had an house of gods, and made an [u]ephod, and [v]teraphim, and consecrated one of his sons, who became his priest.

6 [w]In those days *there was* no king in Israel, [x]*but* every man did *that which was* right in his own eyes.

7 ¶ And there was a young man out of [y]Beth-lehem-judah of the family of Judah, who *was* a Levite, and he sojourned there.

8 And the man departed out of the city from Beth-lehem-judah to sojourn where he could find *a place:* and he came to mount Ephraim to the house of Micah, as he journeyed.

9 And Micah said unto him, Whence comest thou? And he said unto him, I *am* a Levite of Beth-lehem-judah, and I go to sojourn where I may find *a place.*

10 And Micah said unto him, Dwell with me, [z]and be unto me a [a]father and a priest, and I will give thee ten *shekels* of silver by the year, and a suit of apparel, and thy victuals. So the Levite went in.

11 And the Levite was content to dwell with the man; and the young man was unto him as one of his sons.

12 And Micah [b]consecrated the Levite; and the young man [c]became his priest, and was in the house of Micah.

13 Then said Micah, Now know I that the LORD will do me good, seeing I have a Levite to *my* priest.

18 In [d]those days *there was* no king in Israel: and in those days [e]the tribe of the Danites sought them an inheritance to dwell in; for unto that day *all their* inheritance had not fallen unto them among the tribes of Israel.

2 And the children of Dan sent of their family five men from their coasts, men of valour, from [f]Zorah, and from Eshtaol, [g]to spy out the land, and to search it; and they said unto them, Go, search the land: who when they came to mount Ephraim, to the [h]house of Micah, they lodged there.

3 When they *were* by the house of Micah, they knew the voice of the young man the Levite: and they turned in thither, and said unto him, Who brought thee hither? and what makest thou in this *place?* and what hast thou here?

4 And he said unto them, Thus and thus dealeth Micah with me, and hath [i]hired me, and I am his priest.

5 And they said unto him, [j]Ask counsel, we pray thee, [k]of God, that we may know whether our way which we go shall be prosperous.

6 And the priest said unto them, [l]Go in peace: before the LORD *is* your way wherein ye go.

7 ¶ Then the five men departed, and came to [m]Laish, and saw the people that *were* therein, [n]how they dwelt careless, after the manner of the Zidonians, quiet and secure; and *there was* no magistrate in the land, that might put *them* to shame in *any* thing; and they *were* far from the Zidonians, and had no business with *any* man.

8 And they came unto their brethren to

16:24 [m]Dan. 5:4
16:25 [n]ch. 9:27
16:27 [o]Deut. 22:8
16:28 [p]Jer. 15:15
16:31 [q]ch. 13:25
17:2 [r]Gen. 14:19; Ruth 3:10
17:3 [s]Ex. 20:4; Lev. 19:4
17:4 [t]Isa. 46:6
17:5 [u]ch. 8:27 [v]Gen. 31:19; Hos. 3:4
17:6 [w]ch. 18:1; Deut. 33:5 [x]Deut. 12:8
17:7 [y]Josh. 19:15; ch. 19:1; Ruth 1:1; Mic. 5:2; Matt. 2:1
17:10 [z]ch. 18:19 [a]Gen. 45:8; Job 29:16
17:12 [b]ver. 5 [c]ch. 18:30
18:1 [d]ch. 17:6 [e]Josh. 19:47
18:2 [f]ch. 13:25 [g]Num. 13:17; Josh. 2:1 [h]ch. 17:1
18:4 [i]ch. 17:10
18:5 [j]1 Kings 22:5; Isa. 30:1; Hos. 4:12 [k]ch. 17:5
18:6 [l]1 Kings 22:6
18:7 [m]Josh. 19:47 [n]ver. 27

[o]Zorah and Eshtaol: and their brethren said unto them, What *say* ye?

9 And they said, [p]Arise, that we may go up against them: for we have seen the land, and, behold, it *is* very good: and *are* ye [q]still? be not slothful to go, *and* to enter to possess the land.

10 When ye go, ye shall come unto a people [r]secure, and to a large land: for God hath given it into your hands; [s]a place where *there is* no want of any thing that *is* in the earth.

11 ¶ And there went from thence of the family of the Danites, out of Zorah and out of Eshtaol, six hundred men appointed with weapons of war.

12 And they went up, and pitched in [t]Kirjath-jearim, in Judah: wherefore they called that place [u]Mahaneh-dan unto this day: behold, *it is* behind Kirjath-jearim.

13 And they passed thence unto mount Ephraim, and came unto [v]the house of Micah.

14 ¶ [w]Then answered the five men that went to spy out the country of Laish, and said unto their brethren, Do ye know that [x]there is in these houses an ephod, and teraphim, and a graven image, and a molten image? now therefore consider what ye have to do.

15 And they turned thitherward, and came to the house of the young man the Levite, *even* unto the house of Micah, and saluted him.

16 And the [y]six hundred men appointed with their weapons of war, which *were* of the children of Dan, stood by the entering of the gate.

17 And [z]the five men that went to spy out the land went up, *and* came in thither, *and* took [a]the graven image, and the ephod, and the teraphim, and the molten image: and the priest stood in the entering of the gate with the six hundred men *that were* appointed with weapons of war.

18 And these went into Micah's house, and fetched the carved image, the ephod, and the teraphim, and the molten image. Then said the priest unto them, What do ye?

19 And they said unto him, Hold thy peace, [b]lay thine hand upon thy mouth, and go with us, [c]and be to us a father and a priest: *is it* better for thee to be a priest unto the house of one man, or that thou be a priest unto a tribe and a family in Israel?

20 And the priest's heart was glad, and he took the ephod, and the teraphim, and the graven image, and went in the midst of the people.

21 So they turned and departed, and put the little ones and the cattle and the carriage before them.

22 ¶ *And* when they were a good way from the house of Micah, the men that *were* in the houses near to Micah's house were gathered together, and overtook the children of Dan.

23 And they cried unto the children of Dan. And they turned their faces, and said unto Micah, What aileth thee, that thou comest with such a company?

24 And he said, Ye have taken away my gods which I made, and the priest, and ye are gone away: and what have I more? and what *is* this *that* ye say unto me, What aileth thee?

25 And the children of Dan said unto him, Let not thy voice be heard among us, lest angry fellows run upon thee, and thou lose thy life, with the lives of thy household.

26 And the children of Dan went their way: and when Micah saw that they *were* too strong for him, he turned and went back unto his house.

27 And they took *the things* which Micah had made, and the priest which he had, and [d]came unto Laish, unto a people *that were* at quiet and secure: [e]and they smote them with the edge of the sword, and burnt the city with fire.

28 And *there was* no deliverer, because it *was* [f]far from Zidon, and they had no business with *any* man; and it was in the valley that *lieth* [g]by Beth-rehob. And they built a city, and dwelt therein.

29 And [h]they called the name of the city [i]Dan, after the name of Dan their father, who was born unto Israel: howbeit the name of the city *was* Laish at the first.

30 ¶ And the children of Dan set up the graven image: and Jonathan, the son of Gershom, the son of Manasseh, he and his sons were priests to the tribe of Dan [j]until the day of the captivity of the land.

31 And they set them up Micah's graven image, which he made, [k]all the time that the house of God was in Shiloh.

19 And it came to pass in those days, [l]when *there was* no king in Israel, that there was a certain Levite sojourning on the side of mount Ephraim, who took to him a concubine out of [m]Beth-lehem-judah.

2 And his concubine played the whore against him, and went away from him unto her father's house to Beth-lehem-judah, and was there four whole months.

3 And her husband arose, and went after her, to speak friendly unto her, *and* to bring her again, having his servant with him, and a couple of asses: and she brought him into her father's house: and when the father of the damsel saw him, he rejoiced to meet him.

4 And his father in law, the damsel's father, retained him; and he abode with him three days: so they did eat and drink, and lodged there.

5 ¶ And it came to pass on the fourth day, when they arose early in the morning, that he rose up to depart: and the damsel's father said unto his son in law, [n]Comfort thine heart with a morsel of bread, and afterward go your way.

6 And they sat down, and did eat and drink both of them together: for the damsel's father had said unto the man, Be con-

18:8 [o]ver. 2
18:9 [p]Num. 13:30; Josh. 2:23 [q]1 Kings 22:3
18:10 [r]ver. 7 [s]Deut. 8:9
18:12 [t]Josh. 15:60 [u]ch. 13:25
18:13 [v]ver. 2
18:14 [w]1 Sam. 14:28 [x]ch. 17:5
18:16 [y]ver. 11
18:17 [z]ver. 2 [a]ch. 17:4
18:19 [b]Job 21:5; Prov. 30:32; Mic. 7:16 [c]ch. 17:10
18:27 [d]ver. 7; Deut. 33:22 [e]Josh. 19:47
18:28 [f]ver. 7 [g]Num. 13:21; 2 Sam. 10:6
18:29 [h]Josh. 19:47 [i]Gen. 14:14; ch. 20:1; 1 Kings 12:29
18:30 [j]ch. 13:1; 1 Sam. 4:2; Ps. 78:60
18:31 [k]Josh. 18:1; ch. 19:18
19:1 [l]ch. 17:6 [m]ch. 17:7
19:5 [n]Gen. 18:5

tent, I pray thee, and tarry all night, and let thine heart be merry.

7 And when the man rose up to depart, his father in law urged him: therefore he lodged there again.

8 And he arose early in the morning on the fifth day to depart: and the damsel's father said, Comfort thine heart, I pray thee. And they tarried until afternoon, and they did eat both of them.

9 And when the man rose up to depart, he, and his concubine, and his servant, his father in law, the damsel's father, said unto him, Behold, now the day draweth toward evening, I pray you tarry all night: behold, the day groweth to an end, lodge here, that thine heart may be merry; and to morrow get you early on your way, that thou mayest go home.

10 But the man would not tarry that night, but he rose up and departed, and came over against [o]Jebus, which *is* Jerusalem; and *there were* with him two asses saddled, his concubine also *was* with him.

11 *And* when they *were* by Jebus, the day was far spent; and the servant said unto his master, Come, I pray thee, and let us turn in into this city [p]of the Jebusites, and lodge in it.

12 And his master said unto him, We will not turn aside hither into the city of a stranger, that *is* not of the children of Israel; we will pass over [q]to Gibeah.

13 And he said unto his servant, Come, and let us draw near to one of these places to lodge all night, in Gibeah, or in [r]Ramah.

14 And they passed on and went their way; and the sun went down upon them *when they were* by Gibeah, which *belongeth* to Benjamin.

15 And they turned aside thither, to go in *and* to lodge in Gibeah: and when he went in, he sat him down in a street of the city: for *there was* no man that [s]took them into his house to lodging.

16 ¶ And, behold, there came an old man from [t]his work out of the field at even, which *was* also of mount Ephraim; and he sojourned in Gibeah: but the men of the place *were* Benjamites.

17 And when he had lifted up his eyes, he saw a wayfaring man in the street of the city: and the old man said, Whither goest thou? and whence comest thou?

18 And he said unto him, We *are* passing from Beth-lehem-judah toward the side of mount Ephraim; from thence *am* I: and I went to Beth-lehem-judah, but I *am now* going to [u]the house of the LORD; and there *is* no man that receiveth me to house.

19 Yet there is both straw and provender for our asses; and there is bread and wine also for me, and for thy handmaid, and for the young man *which is* with thy servants: *there is* no want of any thing.

20 And the old man said, [v]Peace *be* with thee; howsoever *let* all thy wants *lie* upon me; [w]only lodge not in the street.

21 [x]So he brought him into his house, and gave provender unto the asses: [y]and they washed their feet, and did eat and drink.

22 ¶ *Now* as they were making their hearts merry, behold, [z]the men of the city, certain [a]sons of Belial, beset the house round about, *and* beat at the door, and spake to the master of the house, the old man, saying, [b]Bring forth the man that came into thine house, that we may know him.

23 And [c]the man, the master of the house, went out unto them, and said unto them, Nay, my brethren, *nay,* I pray you, do not *so* wickedly; seeing that this man is come into mine house, [d]do not this folly.

24 [e]Behold, *here is* my daughter a maiden, and his concubine; them I will bring out now, and [f]humble ye them, and do with them what seemeth good unto you: but unto this man do not so vile a thing.

25 But the men would not hearken to him: so the man took his concubine, and brought her forth unto them; and they [g]knew her, and abused her all the night until the morning: and when the day began to spring, they let her go.

26 Then came the woman in the dawning of the day, and fell down at the door of the man's house where her lord *was,* till it was light.

27 And her lord rose up in the morning, and opened the doors of the house, and went out to go his way: and, behold, the woman his concubine was fallen down *at* the door of the house, and her hands *were* upon the threshold.

28 And he said unto her, Up, and let us be going. But [h]none answered. Then the man took her *up* upon an ass, and the man rose up, and gat him unto his place.

29 ¶ And when he was come into his house, he took a knife, and laid hold on his concubine, and [i]divided her, *together* with her bones, into twelve pieces, and sent her into all the coasts of Israel.

30 And it was so, that all that saw it said, There was no such deed done nor seen from the day that the children of Israel came up out of the land of Egypt unto this day: consider of it, [j]take advice, and speak *your minds.*

20 Then [k]all the children of Israel went out, and the congregation was gathered together as one man, [l]from Dan even to Beer-sheba, with the land of Gilead, unto the LORD [m]in Mizpeh.

2 And the chief of all the people, *even* of all the tribes of Israel, presented themselves in the assembly of the people of God, four hundred thousand footmen [n]that drew sword.

3 (Now the children of Benjamin heard that the children of Israel were gone up to Mizpeh.) Then said the children of Israel, Tell *us,* how was this wickedness?

4 And the Levite, the husband of the

19:10 [o]Josh. 18:28
19:11 [p]Josh. 15:8; ch. 1:21; 2 Sam. 5:6
19:12 [q]Josh. 18:28
19:13 [r]Josh. 18:25
19:15 [s]Matt. 25:43; Heb. 13:2
19:16 [t]Ps. 104:23
19:18 [u]Josh. 18:1; ch. 18:31; 1 Sam. 1:3
19:20 [v]Gen. 43:23; ch. 6:23 [w]Gen. 19:2
19:21 [x]Gen. 24:32 [y]Gen. 18:4; John 13:5
19:22 [z]Gen. 19:4; ch. 20:5; Hos. 9:9 [a]Deut. 13:13 [b]Gen. 19:5; Rom. 1:26
19:23 [c]Gen. 19:6 [d]2 Sam. 13:12
19:24 [e]Gen. 19:8 [f]Gen. 34:2; Deut. 21:14
19:25 [g]Gen. 4:1
19:28 [h]ch. 20:5
19:29 [i]ch. 20:6; 1 Sam. 11:7
19:30 [j]ch. 20:7; Prov. 13:10
20:1 [k]Deut. 13:12; Josh. 22:12; ch. 21:5; 1 Sam. 11:7 [l]ch. 18:29; 1 Sam. 3:20; 2 Sam. 3:10 [m]Judg. 10:17; 1 Sam. 7:5
20:2 [n]ch. 8:10

woman that was slain, answered and said, [o]I came into Gibeah that *belongeth* to Benjamin, I and my concubine, to lodge.

5 [p]And the men of Gibeah rose against me, and beset the house round about upon me by night, *and* thought to have slain me: [q]and my concubine have they forced, that she is dead.

6 And [r]I took my concubine, and cut her in pieces, and sent her throughout all the country of the inheritance of Israel: for they [s]have committed lewdness and folly in Israel.

7 Behold, ye *are* all children of Israel; [t]give here your advice and counsel.

8 ¶ And all the people arose as one man, saying, We will not any *of us* go to his tent, neither will we any *of us* turn into his house.

9 But now this *shall be* the thing which we will do to Gibeah; *we will go up* by lot against it;

10 And we will take ten men of an hundred throughout all the tribes of Israel, and an hundred of a thousand, and a thousand out of ten thousand, to fetch victual for the people, that they may do, when they come to Gibeah of Benjamin, according to all the folly that they have wrought in Israel.

11 So all the men of Israel were gathered against the city, knit together as one man.

12 ¶ [u]And the tribes of Israel sent men through all the tribe of Benjamin, saying, What wickedness *is* this that is done among you?

13 Now therefore deliver *us* the men, [v]the children of Belial, which *are* in Gibeah, that we may put them to death, and [w]put away evil from Israel. But the children of Benjamin would not hearken to the voice of their brethren the children of Israel:

14 But the children of Benjamin gathered themselves together out of the cities unto Gibeah, to go out to battle against the children of Israel.

15 And the children of Benjamin were numbered at that time out of the cities twenty and six thousand men that drew sword, beside the inhabitants of Gibeah, which were numbered seven hundred chosen men.

16 Among all this people *there were* seven hundred chosen men [x]lefthanded; every one could sling stones at a hair *breadth*, and not miss.

17 And the men of Israel, beside Benjamin, were numbered four hundred thousand men that drew sword: all these *were* men of war.

18 ¶ And the children of Israel arose, and [y]went up to the house of God, and [z]asked counsel of God, and said, Which of us shall go up first to the battle against the children of Benjamin? And the LORD said, Judah *shall go up* first.

19 And the children of Israel rose up in the morning, and encamped against Gibeah.

20 And the men of Israel went out to battle against Benjamin; and the men of Israel put themselves in array to fight against them at Gibeah.

21 And [a]the children of Benjamin came forth out of Gibeah, and destroyed down to the ground of the Israelites that day twenty and two thousand men.

22 And the people the men of Israel, encouraged themselves, and set their battle again in array in the place where they put themselves in array the first day.

23 ([b]And the children of Israel went up and wept before the LORD until even, and asked counsel of the LORD, saying, Shall I go up again to battle against the children of Benjamin my brother? And the LORD said, Go up against him.)

24 And the children of Israel came near against the children of Benjamin the second day.

25 And [c]Benjamin went forth against them out of Gibeah the second day, and destroyed down to the ground of the children of Israel again eighteen thousand men; all these drew the sword.

26 ¶ Then all the children of Israel, and all the people, [d]went up, and came unto the house of God, and wept, and sat there before the LORD, and fasted that day until even, and offered burnt offerings and peace offerings before the LORD.

27 And the children of Israel enquired of the LORD, (for [e]the ark of the covenant of God *was* there in those days,

28 [f]And Phinehas, the son of Eleazar, the son of Aaron, [g]stood before it in those days,) saying, Shall I yet again go out to battle against the children of Benjamin my brother, or shall I cease? And the LORD said, Go up; for to morrow I will deliver them into thine hand.

29 And Israel [h]set liers in wait round about Gibeah.

30 And the children of Israel went up against the children of Benjamin on the third day, and put themselves in array against Gibeah, as at other times.

31 And the children of Benjamin went out against the people, *and* were drawn away from the city; and they began to smite of the people, *and* kill, as at other times, in the highways, of which one goeth up to the house of God, and the other to Gibeah in the field, about thirty men of Israel.

32 And the children of Benjamin said, They *are* smitten down before us, as at the first. But the children of Israel said, Let us flee, and draw them from the city unto the highways.

33 And all the men of Israel rose up out of their place, and put themselves in array at Baal-tamar: and the liers in wait of Israel came forth out of their places, *even* out of the meadows of Gibeah.

34 And there came against Gibeah ten thousand chosen men out of all Israel, and the battle was sore: [i]but they knew not that evil *was* near them.

20:4 [o]ch. 19:15
20:5 [p]ch. 19:22 [q]ch. 19:25
20:6 [r]ch. 19:29 [s]Josh. 7:15
20:7 [t]ch. 19:30
20:12 [u]Deut. 13:14; Josh. 22:13
20:13 [v]Deut. 13:13; ch. 19:22 [w]Deut. 17
20:16 [x]ch. 3:15; 1 Chron. 12:2
20:18 [y]ver. 23 [z]Num. 27:21; ch. 1:1
20:21 [a]Gen. 49:27
20:23 [b]ver. 26
20:25 [c]ver. 21
20:26 [d]ver. 18
20:27 [e]Josh. 18:1; 1 Sam. 4:3
20:28 [f]Josh. 24:33 [g]Deut. 10:8
20:29 [h]Josh. 8:4
20:34 [i]Josh. 8:14; Isa. 47:11

35 And the LORD smote Benjamin before Israel: and the children of Israel destroyed of the Benjamites that day twenty and five thousand and an hundred men: all these drew the sword.

36 So the children of Benjamin saw that they were smitten: [j]for the men of Israel gave place to the Benjamites, because they trusted unto the liers in wait which they had set beside Gibeah.

37 [k]And the liers in wait hasted, and rushed upon Gibeah; and the liers in wait drew *themselves* along, and smote all the city with the edge of the sword.

38 Now there was an appointed sign between the men of Israel and the liers in wait, that they should make a great flame with smoke rise up out of the city.

39 And when the men of Israel retired in the battle, Benjamin began to smite *and* kill of the men of Israel about thirty persons: for they said, Surely they are smitten down before us, as *in* the first battle.

40 But when the flame began to arise up out of the city with a pillar of smoke, the Benjamites [l]looked behind them, and, behold, the flame of the city ascended up to heaven.

41 And when the men of Israel turned again, the men of Benjamin were amazed: for they saw that evil was come upon them.

42 Therefore they turned *their backs* before the men of Israel unto the way of the wilderness; but the battle overtook them; and them which *came* out of the cities they destroyed in the midst of them.

43 *Thus* they inclosed the Benjamites round about, *and* chased them, *and* trode them down with ease over against Gibeah toward the sunrising.

44 And there fell of Benjamin eighteen thousand men; all these *were* men of valour.

45 And they turned and fled toward the wilderness unto the rock of [m]Rimmon: and they gleaned of them in the highways five thousand men; and pursued hard after them unto Gidom, and slew two thousand men of them.

46 So that all which fell that day of Benjamin were twenty and five thousand men that drew the sword; all these *were* men of valour.

47 [n]But six hundred men turned and fled to the wilderness unto the rock Rimmon, and abode in the rock Rimmon four months.

48 And the men of Israel turned again upon the children of Benjamin, and smote them with the edge of the sword, as well the men of *every* city, as the beast, and all that came to hand: also they set on fire all the cities that they came to.

21 Now [o]the men of Israel had sworn in Mizpeh, saying, There shall not any of us give his daughter unto Benjamin to wife.

2 And the people came [p]to the house of God, and abode there till even before God, and lifted up their voices, and wept sore;

3 And said, O LORD God of Israel, why is this come to pass in Israel, that there should be to day one tribe lacking in Israel?

4 And it came to pass on the morrow, that the people rose early, and [q]built there an altar, and offered burnt offerings and peace offerings.

5 And the children of Israel said, Who *is there* among all the tribes of Israel that came not up with the congregation unto the LORD? [r]For they had made a great oath concerning him that came not up to the LORD to Mizpeh, saying, He shall surely be put to death.

6 And the children of Israel repented them for Benjamin their brother, and said, There is one tribe cut off from Israel this day.

7 How shall we do for wives for them that remain, seeing we have sworn by the LORD that we will not give them of our daughters to wives?

8 ¶ And they said, What one *is there* of the tribes of Israel that came not up to Mizpeh to the LORD? And, behold, there came none to the camp from [s]Jabesh-gilead to the assembly.

9 For the people were numbered, and, behold, *there were* none of the inhabitants of Jabesh-gilead there.

10 And the congregation sent thither twelve thousand men of the valiantest, and commanded them, saying, [t]Go and smite the inhabitants of Jabesh-gilead with the edge of the sword, with the women and the children.

11 And this *is* the thing that ye shall do, [u]Ye shall utterly destroy every male, and every woman that hath lain by man.

12 And they found among the inhabitants of Jabesh-gilead four hundred young virgins, that had known no man by lying with any male: and they brought them unto the camp to [v]Shiloh, which *is* in the land of Canaan.

13 And the whole congregation sent *some* to speak to the children of Benjamin [w]that *were* in the rock Rimmon, and to call peaceably unto them.

14 And Benjamin came again at that time; and they gave them wives which they had saved alive of the women of Jabesh-gilead: and yet so they sufficed them not.

15 And the people [x]repented them for Benjamin, because that the LORD had made a breach in the tribes of Israel.

16 ¶ Then the elders of the congregation said, How shall we do for wives for them that remain, seeing the women are destroyed out of Benjamin?

17 And they said, *There must be* an inheritance for them that be escaped of Benjamin, that a tribe be not destroyed out of Israel.

18 Howbeit we may not give them wives of our daughters: [y]for the children of Israel have sworn, saying, Cursed *be* he that giveth a wife to Benjamin.

20:36 [j]Josh. 8:15
20:37 [k]Josh. 8:19
20:40 [l]Josh. 8:20
20:45 [m]Josh. 15:32
20:47 [n]ch. 21:13
21:1 [o]ch. 20:1
21:2 [p]ch. 20:18
21:4 [q]2 Sam. 24:25
21:5 [r]Judg. 5:23
21:8 [s]1 Sam. 11:1
21:10 [t]ver. 5; 1 Sam. 11:7
21:11 [u]Num. 31:17
21:12 [v]Josh. 18:1
21:13 [w]ch. 20:47
21:15 [x]ver. 6
21:18 [y]ver. 1; Judg. 11:35

19 Then they said, Behold, *there is* a feast of the LORD in Shiloh yearly *in a place* which *is* on the north side of Beth-el, on the east side of the highway that goeth up from Beth-el to Shechem, and on the south of Lebonah.

20 Therefore they commanded the children of Benjamin, saying, Go and lie in wait in the vineyards;

21 And see, and, behold, if the daughters of Shiloh come out [z]to dance in dances, then come ye out of the vineyards, and catch you every man his wife of the daughters of Shiloh, and go to the land of Benjamin.

22 And it shall be, when their fathers or their brethren come unto us to complain, that we will say unto them, Be favourable unto them for our sakes: because we reserved not to each man his wife in the war: for ye did not give unto them at this time, *that* ye should be guilty.

23 And the children of Benjamin did so, and took *them* wives, according to their number, of them that danced, whom they caught: and they went and returned unto their inheritance, and [a]repaired the cities, and dwelt in them.

24 And the children of Israel departed thence at that time, every man to his tribe and to his family, and they went out from thence every man to his inheritance.

25 [b]In those days *there was* no king in Israel: [c]every man did *that which was* right in his own eyes.

21:21 [z]Ex. 15:20; ch. 11:34; 1 Sam. 18:6; Jer. 31:13
21:23 [a]ch. 20:48
21:25 [b]ch. 17:6 [c]Deut. 12:8; ch. 17:6

RUTH

Samuel is traditionally viewed as the author of Ruth, which was written in or about 1000 B.C. This book is the tender story of an embittered woman, Naomi, a kind, loving daughter-in-law Ruth, and a man called Boaz. Despite Naomi's bitterness, Ruth, with the help of Boaz, is able to bring a sense of fullness into Naomi's life. This book is a prime example of Christian love in action, and its powerful effects on people.

I. The backgrounds of Naomi and Ruth, 1:1–1:22
II. Ruth and Boaz, 2:1–4:17
III. Partial lineage of Boaz and Ruth's son, 4:18–4:22

1 Now it came to pass in the days when [a]the judges ruled, that there was [b]a famine in the land. And a certain man of [c]Beth-lehem-judah went to sojourn in the country of Moab, he, and his wife, and his two sons.

2 And the name of the man *was* Elimelech, and the name of his wife Naomi, and the name of his two sons Mahlon and Chilion, [d]Ephrathites of Beth-lehem-judah. And they came [e]into the country of Moab, and continued there.

3 And Elimelech Naomi's husband died; and she was left, and her two sons.

4 And they took them wives of the women of Moab; the name of the one *was* Orpah, and the name of the other Ruth: and they dwelled there about ten years.

5 And Mahlon and Chilion died also both of them; and the woman was left of her two sons and her husband.

6 ¶ Then she arose with her daughters in law, that she might return from the country of Moab: for she had heard in the country of Moab how that the LORD had [f]visited his people in [g]giving them bread.

7 Wherefore she went forth out of the place where she was, and her two daughters in law with her; and they went on the way to return unto the land of Judah.

8 And Naomi said unto her two daughters in law, [h]Go, return each to her mother's house: [i]the LORD deal kindly with you, as ye have dealt with [j]the dead, and with me.

9 The LORD grant you that ye may find [k]rest, each *of you* in the house of her husband. Then she kissed them; and they lifted up their voice, and wept.

10 And they said unto her, Surely we will return with thee unto thy people.

11 And Naomi said, Turn again, my daughters: why will ye go with me? *are* there yet *any more* sons in my womb, [l]that they may be your husbands?

12 Turn again, my daughters, go *your way;* for I am too old to have an husband. If I should say, I have hope, *if* I should have an husband also to night, and should also bear sons;

13 Would ye tarry for them till they were grown? would ye stay for them from having husbands? nay, my daughters; for it grieveth me much for your sakes that [m]the hand of the LORD is gone out against me.

14 And they lifted up their voice, and

1:1 [a]Judg. 2:16 [b]Gen. 12:10; 2 Kings 8:1 [c]Judg. 17:8
1:2 [d]Gen. 35:19 [e]Judg. 5:30
1:6 [f]Ex. 4:31; Luke 1:68 [g]Ps. 132:15; Matt. 6:11
1:8 [h]Josh. 24:15 [i]2 Tim. 1:16 [j]ver. 5; ch. 2:20
1:9 [k]ch. 3:1
1:11 [l]Gen. 38:11; Deut. 25:5
1:13 [m]Judg. 2:15; Job 19:21; Ps. 32:4

wept again: and Orpah kissed her mother in
law; but Ruth [n]clave unto her.
15 And she said, Behold, thy sister in law
is gone back unto her people, and unto [o]her
gods: [p]return thou after thy sister in law.
16 And Ruth said, [q]Intreat me not to
leave thee, *or* to return from following after
thee: for whither thou goest, I will go; and
where thou lodgest, I will lodge: [r]thy people *shall be* my people, and thy God my
God:
17 Where thou diest, will I die, and there
will I be buried: [s]the LORD do so to me, and
more also, *if ought* but death part thee
and me.
18 [t]When she saw that she was stedfastly minded to go with her, then she left
speaking unto her.
19 ¶ So they two went until they came to
Beth-lehem. And it came to pass, when they
were come to Beth-lehem, that [u]all the city
was moved about them, and they said, [v]*Is*
this Naomi?
20 And she said unto them, Call me not
Naomi, call me Mara: for the Almighty hath
dealt very bitterly with me.
21 I went out full, [w]and the LORD hath
brought me home again empty: why *then*
call ye me Naomi, seeing the LORD hath testified against me, and the Almighty hath afflicted me?
22 So Naomi returned, and Ruth the Moabitess, her daughter in law, with her,
which returned out of the country of Moab:
and they came to Beth-lehem [x]in the beginning of barley harvest.

2

And Naomi had a [y]kinsman of her husband's, a mighty man of wealth, of the
family of Elimelech; and his name *was*
[z]Boaz.
2 And Ruth the Moabitess said unto Naomi, Let me now go to the field, and [a]glean
ears of corn after *him* in whose sight I shall
find grace. And she said unto her, Go, my
daughter.
3 And she went, and came, and gleaned in
the field after the reapers: and her hap was
to light on a part of the field *belonging* unto
Boaz, who *was* of the kindred of Elimelech.
4 ¶ And, behold, Boaz came from Beth-
lehem, and said unto the reapers, [b]The
LORD *be* with you. And they answered him,
The LORD bless thee.
5 Then said Boaz unto his servant that
was set over the reapers, Whose damsel *is*
this?
6 And the servant that was set over the
reapers answered and said, It *is* the Moabitish damsel [c]that came back with Naomi out
of the country of Moab:
7 And she said, I pray you, let me glean
and gather after the reapers among the
sheaves: so she came, and hath continued
even from the morning until now, that she
tarried a little in the house.
8 Then said Boaz unto Ruth, Hearest thou
not, my daughter? Go not to glean in another field, neither go from hence, but abide
here fast by my maidens:
9 *Let* thine eyes *be* on the field that they
do reap, and go thou after them: have I not
charged the young men that they shall not
touch thee? and when thou art athirst, go
unto the vessels, and drink of *that* which
the young men have drawn.
10 Then she [d]fell on her face, and bowed
herself to the ground, and said unto him,
Why have I found grace in thine eyes, that
thou shouldest take knowledge of me, seeing I *am* a stranger?
11 And Boaz answered and said unto her,
It hath fully been shewed me, [e]all that thou
hast done unto thy mother in law since the
death of thine husband: and *how* thou hast
left thy father and thy mother, and the land
of thy nativity, and art come unto a people
which thou knewest not heretofore.
12 [f]The LORD recompense thy work, and
a full reward be given thee of the LORD God
of Israel, [g]under whose wings thou art
come to trust.
13 Then she said, [h]Let me find favour in
thy sight, my lord; for that thou hast comforted me, and for that thou hast spoken
friendly unto thine handmaid, [i]though I be
not like unto one of thine handmaidens.
14 And Boaz said unto her, At mealtime
come thou hither, and eat of the bread, and
dip thy morsel in the vinegar. And she sat
beside the reapers: and he reached her
parched *corn,* and she did eat, and [j]was
sufficed, and left.
15 And when she was risen up to glean,
Boaz commanded his young men, saying,
Let her glean even among the sheaves, and
reproach her not:
16 And let fall also *some* of the handfuls
of purpose for her, and leave *them,* that she
may glean *them,* and rebuke her not.
17 So she gleaned in the field until even,
and beat out that she had gleaned: and it
was about an ephah of barley.
18 ¶ And she took *it* up, and went into the
city: and her mother in law saw what she
had gleaned: and she brought forth, and
gave to her [k]that she had reserved after she
was sufficed.
19 And her mother in law said unto her,
Where hast thou gleaned to day? and where
wroughtest thou? blessed be he that did
[l]take knowledge of thee. And she shewed
her mother in law with whom she had
wrought, and said, The man's name with
whom I wrought to day *is* Boaz.
20 And Naomi said unto her daughter in
law, [m]Blessed *be* he of the LORD, who [n]hath
not left off his kindness to the living and to
the dead. And Naomi said unto her, The
man *is* near of kin unto us, [o]one of our next
kinsmen.
21 And Ruth the Moabitess said, He said
unto me also, Thou shalt keep fast by my
young men, until they have ended all my
harvest.
22 And Naomi said unto Ruth her daugh-

1:14 [n]Prov. 17:17
1:15 [o]Judg. 11:24 [p]Josh. 24:15; 2 Kings 2:2; Luke 24:28
1:16 [q]2 Kings 2:2 [r]ch. 2:11
1:17 [s]1 Sam. 3:17; 2 Sam. 19:13; 2 Kings 6:31
1:18 [t]Acts 21:14
1:19 [u]Matt. 21:10 [v]Isa. 23:7; Lam. 2:15
1:21 [w]Job 1:21
1:22 [x]Ex. 9:31; ch. 2:23; 2 Sam. 21:9
2:1 [y]ch. 3:2 [z]ch. 4:21
2:2 [a]Lev. 19:9; Deut. 24:19
2:4 [b]Ps. 129:7; Luke 1:28; 2 Thess. 3:16
2:6 [c]ch. 1:22
2:10 [d]1 Sam. 25:23
2:11 [e]ch. 1:14
2:12 [f]1 Sam. 24:19 [g]ch. 1:16; Ps. 17:8
2:13 [h]Gen. 33:15; 1 Sam. 1:18 [i]1 Sam. 25:41
2:14 [j]ver. 18
2:18 [k]ver. 14
2:19 [l]ver. 10; Ps. 41:1
2:20 [m]ch. 3:10; 2 Sam. 2:5; Job 29:13 [n]Prov. 17:17 [o]ch. 3:9

ter in law, *It is* good, my daughter, that thou go out with his maidens, that they meet thee not in any other field.

23 So she kept fast by the maidens of Boaz to glean unto the end of barley harvest and of wheat harvest; and dwelt with her mother in law.

3 Then Naomi her mother in law said unto her, My daughter, [p]shall I not seek [q]rest for thee, that it may be well with thee?

2 And now *is* not Boaz of our kindred, [r]with whose maidens thou wast? Behold, he winnoweth barley to night in the threshingfloor.

3 Wash thyself therefore, [s]and anoint thee, and put thy raiment upon thee, and get thee down to the floor: *but* make not thyself known unto the man, until he shall have done eating and drinking.

4 And it shall be, when he lieth down, that thou shalt mark the place where he shall lie, and thou shalt go in, and uncover his feet, and lay thee down; and he will tell thee what thou shalt do.

5 And she said unto her, All that thou sayest unto me I will do.

6 ¶ And she went down unto the floor, and did according to all that her mother in law bade her.

7 And when Boaz had eaten and drunk, and [t]his heart was merry, he went to lie down at the end of the heap of corn: and she came softly, and uncovered his feet, and laid her down.

8 ¶ And it came to pass at midnight, that the man was afraid, and turned himself: and, behold, a woman lay at his feet.

9 And he said, Who *art* thou? And she answered, I *am* Ruth thine handmaid: [u]spread therefore thy skirt over thine handmaid; for thou *art* [v]a near kinsman.

10 And he said, [w]Blessed *be* thou of the LORD, my daughter: *for* thou hast shewed more kindness in the latter end than [x]at the beginning, inasmuch as thou followedst not young men, whether poor or rich.

11 And now, my daughter, fear not; I will do to thee all that thou requirest: for all the city of my people doth know that thou *art* [y]a virtuous woman.

12 And now it is true that I *am thy* [z]near kinsman: howbeit [a]there is a kinsman nearer than I.

13 Tarry this night, and it shall be in the morning, *that* if he will [b]perform unto thee the part of a kinsman, well; let him do the kinsman's part: but if he will not do the part of a kinsman to thee, then will I do the part of a kinsman to thee, [c]*as* the LORD liveth: lie down until the morning.

14 ¶ And she lay at his feet until the morning: and she rose up before one could know another. And he said, [d]Let it not be known that a woman came into the floor.

15 Also he said, Bring the vail that *thou hast* upon thee, and hold it. And when she held it, he measured six *measures* of barley, and laid *it* on her: and she went into the city.

3:1 [p]1 Cor. 7:36; 1 Tim. 5:8 [q]ch. 1:9
3:2 [r]ch. 2:8
3:3 [s]2 Sam. 14:2
3:7 [t]Judg. 19:6; 2 Sam. 13:28; Esth. 1:10
3:9 [u]Ezek. 16:8 [v]ch. 2:20
3:10 [w]ch. 2:20 [x]ch. 1:8
3:11 [y]Prov. 12:4
3:12 [z]ver. 10 [a]ch. 4:1
3:13 [b]Deut. 25:5; ch. 4:5; Matt. 22:24 [c]Judg. 8:19; Jer. 4:2
3:14 [d]Rom. 12:17; 1 Cor. 10:32; 2 Cor. 8:21; 1 Thess. 5:22
3:18 [e]Ps. 37:3
4:1 [f]ch. 3:12
4:2 [g]1 Kings 21:8; Prov. 31:23
4:4 [h]Jer. 32:7 [i]Gen. 23:18 [j]Lev. 25:25
4:5 [k]Gen. 38:8; Deut. 25:5; ch. 3:13; Matt. 22:24
4:6 [l]ch. 3:12
4:7 [m]Deut. 25:7
4:10 [n]Deut. 25:6
4:11 [o]Ps. 127:3 [p]Deut. 25:9 [q]Gen. 35:16

16 And when she came to her mother in law, she said, Who *art* thou, my daughter? And she told her all that the man had done to her.

17 And she said, These six *measures* of barley gave he me; for he said to me, Go not empty unto thy mother in law.

18 Then said she, [e]Sit still, my daughter, until thou know how the matter will fall: for the man will not be in rest, until he have finished the thing this day.

4 Then went Boaz up to the gate, and sat him down there: and, behold, [f]the kinsman of whom Boaz spake came by; unto whom he said, Ho, such a one! turn aside, sit down here. And he turned aside, and sat down.

2 And he took ten men of [g]the elders of the city, and said, Sit ye down here. And they sat down.

3 And he said unto the kinsman, Naomi, that is come again out of the country of Moab, selleth a parcel of land, which *was* our brother Elimelech's:

4 And I thought to advertise thee, saying, [h]Buy *it* [i]before the inhabitants, and before the elders of my people. If thou wilt redeem *it*, redeem *it:* but if thou wilt not redeem *it*, *then* tell me, that I may know: [j]for *there is* none to redeem *it* beside thee; and I *am* after thee. And he said, I will redeem *it*.

5 Then said Boaz, What day thou buyest the field of the hand of Naomi, thou must buy *it* also of Ruth the Moabitess, the wife of the dead, [k]to raise up the name of the dead upon his inheritance.

6 ¶ [l]And the kinsman said, I cannot redeem *it* for myself, lest I mar mine own inheritance: redeem thou my right to thyself; for I cannot redeem *it*.

7 [m]Now this *was the manner* in former time in Israel concerning redeeming and concerning changing, for to confirm all things; a man plucked off his shoe, and gave *it* to his neighbour: and this *was* a testimony in Israel.

8 Therefore the kinsman said unto Boaz, Buy *it* for thee. So he drew off his shoe.

9 ¶ And Boaz said unto the elders, and *unto* all the people, Ye *are* witnesses this day, that I have bought all that *was* Elimelech's, and all that *was* Chilion's and Mahlon's, of the hand of Naomi.

10 Moreover Ruth the Moabitess, the wife of Mahlon, have I purchased to be my wife, to raise up the name of the dead upon his inheritance, [n]that the name of the dead be not cut off from among his brethren, and from the gate of his place: ye *are* witnesses this day.

11 And all the people that *were* in the gate, and the elders, said, *We are* witnesses. [o]The LORD make the woman that is come into thine house like Rachel and like Leah, which two did [p]build the house of Israel: and do thou worthily in [q]Ephratah, and be famous in Beth-lehem:

12 And let thy house be like the house of

Pharez, [r]whom Tamar bare unto Judah, of [s]the seed which the LORD shall give thee of this young woman.

13 ¶ So Boaz [t]took Ruth, and she was his wife: and when he went in unto her, [u]the LORD gave her conception, and she bare a son.

14 And [v]the women said unto Naomi, Blessed *be* the LORD, which hath not left thee this day without a kinsman, that his name may be famous in Israel.

15 And he shall be unto thee a restorer of *thy* life, and a nourisher of thine old age: for thy daughter in law, which loveth thee, which is [w]better to thee than seven sons, hath born him.

16 And Naomi took the child, and laid it in her bosom, and became nurse unto it.

17 [x]And the women her neighbours gave it a name, saying, There is a son born to Naomi; and they called his name Obed: he *is* the father of Jesse, the father of David.

18 ¶ Now these *are* the generations of Pharez: [y]Pharez begat Hezron,

19 And Hezron begat Ram, and Ram begat Amminadab,

20 And Amminadab begat [z]Nahshon, and Nahshon begat [a]Salmon,

21 And Salmon begat Boaz, and Boaz begat Obed,

22 And Obed begat Jesse, and Jesse begat [b]David.

4:12 [r]Gen. 38:29; 1 Chron. 2:4; Matt. 1:3 [s]1 Sam. 2:20
4:13 [t]ch. 3:11 [u]Gen. 29:31
4:14 [v]Luke 1:58; Rom. 12:15
4:15 [w]1 Sam. 1:8
4:17 [x]Luke 1:58
4:18 [y]1 Chron. 2:4; Matt. 1:3
4:20 [z]Num. 1:7 [a]Matt. 1:4
4:22 [b]1 Chron. 2:15; Matt. 1:6

1 SAMUEL

Samuel wrote the majority of this book in or after 1120 B.C. Samuel is the last of the judges of Israel and is the bridge between the times of the judges and the monarchy of Israel. Samuel is a prophet of God who warns the Israelites about the dangers of a king, but is unable to persuade them of those dangers. He lives during the reign of the first king, Saul, and the rise of David as king of Israel.

The story of David and Goliath is found in chapter 17.

I. Samuel and his reign as judge, 1:1–8:22
II. Saul as king of Israel, 9:1–15:35
III. The rise of David, 16:1–17:58
IV. The battle for control between Saul and David, 18:1–31:13

1

Now there was a certain man of Ramathaim-zophim, of mount Ephraim, and his name *was* [a]Elkanah, the son of Jeroham, the son of Elihu, the son of Tohu, the son of Zuph, [b]an Ephrathite:

2 And he had two wives; the name of the one *was* Hannah, and the name of the other Peninnah: and Peninnah had children, but Hannah had no children.

3 And this man went up out of his city [c]yearly [d]to worship and to sacrifice unto the LORD of hosts in [e]Shiloh. And the two sons of Eli, Hophni and Phinehas, the priests of the LORD, *were* there.

4 ¶ And when the time was that Elkanah [f]offered, he gave to Peninnah his wife, and to all her sons and her daughters, portions:

5 But unto Hannah he gave a worthy portion; for he loved Hannah: [g]but the LORD had shut up her womb.

6 And her adversary also [h]provoked her sore, for to make her fret, because the LORD had shut up her womb.

7 And *as* he did so year by year, when she went up to the house of the LORD, so she provoked her; therefore she wept, and did not eat.

8 Then said Elkanah her husband to her, Hannah, why weepest thou? and why eatest thou not? and why is thy heart grieved? *am* not I [i]better to thee than ten sons?

9 ¶ So Hannah rose up after they had eaten in Shiloh, and after they had drunk. Now Eli the priest sat upon a seat by a post of [j]the temple of the LORD.

10 [k]And she *was* in bitterness of soul, and prayed unto the LORD, and wept sore.

11 And she [l]vowed a vow, and said, O LORD of hosts, if thou wilt indeed [m]look on the affliction of thine handmaid, and [n]remember me, and not forget thine handmaid, but wilt give unto thine handmaid a man child, then I will give him unto the LORD all the days of his life, and [o]there shall no razor come upon his head.

12 And it came to pass, as she continued praying before the LORD, that Eli marked her mouth.

13 Now Hannah, she spake in her heart; only her lips moved, but her voice was not heard: therefore Eli thought she had been drunken.

14 And Eli said unto her, How long wilt thou be drunken? put away thy wine from thee.

15 And Hannah answered and said, No,

1:1 [a]1 Chron. 6:27 [b]Ruth 1:2
1:3 [c]Ex. 23:14; Deut. 16:16; Luke 2:41 [d]Deut. 12:5 [e]Josh. 18:1
1:4 [f]Deut. 12:17
1:5 [g]Gen. 30:2
1:6 [h]Job 24:21
1:8 [i]Ruth 4:15
1:9 [j]ch. 3:3
1:10 [k]Job 7:11
1:11 [l]Gen. 28:20; Num. 30:3; Judg. 11:30 [m]Gen. 29:32; Ex. 4:31; 2 Sam. 16:12; Ps. 25:18 [n]Gen. 8:1 [o]Num. 6:5; Judg. 13:5

my lord, I *am* a woman of a sorrowful spirit:
I have drunk neither wine nor strong drink,
but have [p]poured out my soul before the
LORD.
16 Count not thine handmaid for a daughter of [q]Belial: for out of the abundance of
my complaint and grief have I spoken hitherto.
17 Then Eli answered and said, [r]Go in
peace: and [s]the God of Israel grant *thee* thy
petition that thou hast asked of him.
18 And she said, [t]Let thine handmaid
find grace in thy sight. So the woman [u]went
her way, and did eat, and her countenance
was no more *sad.*
19 ¶ And they rose up in the morning
early, and worshipped before the LORD, and
returned, and came to their house to Ramah: and Elkanah [v]knew Hannah his wife;
and [w]the LORD remembered her.
20 Wherefore it came to pass, when the
time was come about after Hannah had conceived, that she bare a son, and called his
name Samuel, *saying,* Because I have asked
him of the LORD.
21 And the man Elkanah, and all his
house, [x]went up to offer unto the LORD the
yearly sacrifice, and his vow.
22 But Hannah went not up; for she said
unto her husband, *I will not go up* until the
child be weaned, and *then* I will [y]bring him,
that he may appear before the LORD, and
there [z]abide [a]for ever.
23 And [b]Elkanah her husband said unto
her, Do what seemeth thee good; tarry until
thou have weaned him; [c]only the LORD establish his word. So the woman abode, and
gave her son suck until she weaned him.
24 ¶ And when she had weaned him, she
[d]took him up with her, with three bullocks,
and one ephah of flour, and a bottle of wine,
and brought him unto [e]the house of the
LORD in Shiloh: and the child *was* young.
25 And they slew a bullock, and [f]brought
the child to Eli.
26 And she said, O my lord, [g]*as* thy soul
liveth, my lord, I *am* the woman that stood
by thee here, praying unto the LORD.
27 [h]For this child I prayed; and the LORD
hath given me my petition which I asked of
him:
28 [i]Therefore also I have lent him to the
LORD; as long as he liveth he shall be lent to
the LORD. And he [j]worshipped the LORD
there.
2 And Hannah [k]prayed, and said, [l]My
heart rejoiceth in the LORD, [m]mine horn
is exalted in the LORD: my mouth is enlarged over mine enemies; because I [n]re-
joice in thy salvation.
2 [o]*There is* none holy as the LORD: for
there is [p]none beside thee: neither *is there*
any rock like our God.
3 Talk no more so exceeding proudly;
[q]let *not* arrogancy come out of your mouth:
for the LORD *is* a God of knowledge, and by
him actions are weighed.
4 [r]The bows of the mighty men *are* broken, and they that stumbled are girded with
strength.
5 [s]*They that were* full have hired out
themselves for bread; and *they that were*
hungry ceased: so that [t]the barren hath
born seven; and [u]she that hath many children is waxed feeble.
6 [v]The LORD killeth, and maketh alive:
he bringeth down to the grave, and bringeth up.
7 The LORD [w]maketh poor, and maketh
rich: [x]he bringeth low, and lifteth up.
8 [y]He raiseth up the poor out of the dust,
and lifteth up the beggar from the dunghill,
[z]to set *them* among princes, and to make
them inherit the throne of glory: for [a]the
pillars of the earth *are* the LORD's, and he
hath set the world upon them.
9 [b]He will keep the feet of his saints, and
the wicked shall be silent in darkness; for
by strength shall no man prevail.
10 The adversaries of the LORD shall be
[c]broken to pieces; [d]out of heaven shall he
thunder upon them: [e]the LORD shall judge
the ends of the earth; and he shall give
strength unto his king, and [f]exalt the horn
of his anointed.
11 And Elkanah went to Ramah to his
house. [g]And the child did minister unto the
LORD before Eli the priest.
12 ¶ Now the sons of Eli *were* [h]sons of
Belial; [i]they knew not the LORD.
13 And the priests' custom with the people *was, that,* when any man offered sacrifice, the priest's servant came, while the
flesh was in seething, with a fleshhook of
three teeth in his hand;
14 And he struck *it* into the pan, or kettle,
or caldron, or pot; all that the fleshhook
brought up the priest took for himself. So
they did in Shiloh unto all the Israelites that
came thither.
15 Also before they [j]burnt the fat, the
priest's servant came, and said to the man
that sacrificed, Give flesh to roast for the
priest; for he will not have sodden flesh of
thee, but raw.
16 And *if* any man said unto him, Let
them not fail to burn the fat presently, and
then take *as much* as thy soul desireth; then
he would answer him, *Nay;* but thou shalt
give *it me* now: and if not, I will take *it* by
force.
17 Wherefore the sin of the young men
was very great [k]before the LORD: for men
[l]abhorred the offering of the LORD.
18 ¶ [m]But Samuel ministered before the
LORD, *being* a child, [n]girded with a linen
ephod.
19 Moreover his mother made him a little
coat, and brought *it* to him from year to
year, when she [o]came up with her husband
to offer the yearly sacrifice.
20 ¶ And Eli [p]blessed Elkanah and his
wife, and said, The LORD give thee seed of
this woman for the loan which is [q]lent to
the LORD. And they went unto their own
home.

1:15 [p]Ps. 62:8
1:16 [q]Deut. 13:13
1:17 [r]Judg. 18:6; Mark 5:34; Luke 7:50 [s]Ps. 20:4
1:18 [t]Gen. 33:15; Ruth 2:13 [u]Eccl. 9:7
1:19 [v]Gen. 4:1 [w]Gen. 30:22
1:21 [x]ver. 3
1:22 [y]Luke 2:22 [z]ver. 11 [a]Ex. 21:6
1:23 [b]Num. 30:7 [c]2 Sam. 7:25
1:24 [d]Deut. 12:5 [e]Josh. 18:1
1:25 [f]Luke 2:22
1:26 [g]Gen. 42:15; 2 Kings 2:2
1:27 [h]Matt. 7:7
1:28 [i]ver. 11 [j]Gen. 24:26
2:1 [k]Phil. 4:6 [l]Luke 1:46 [m]Ps. 92:10 [n]Ps. 9:14
2:2 [o]Ex. 15:11; Deut. 3:24; Ps. 86:8 [p]Deut. 4:35; 2 Sam. 22:32
2:3 [q]Ps. 94:4; Mal. 3:13; Jude 15
2:4 [r]Ps. 37:15
2:5 [s]Ps. 34:10; Luke 1:53 [t]Ps. 113:9 [u]Isa. 54:1; Jer. 15:9
2:6 [v]Deut. 32:39; Job 5:18; Hos. 6:1
2:7 [w]Job 1:21 [x]Ps. 75:7
2:8 [y]Ps. 113:7; Dan. 4:17; Luke 1:52 [z]Job 36:7 [a]Job 38:4; Ps. 24:2; Heb. 1:3
2:9 [b]Ps. 91:11
2:10 [c]Ps. 2:9 [d]ch. 7:10; Ps. 18:13 [e]Ps. 96:13 [f]Ps. 89:24
2:11 [g]ver. 18; ch. 3:1
2:12 [h]Deut. 13:13 [i]Judg. 2:10; Jer. 22:16; Rom. 1:28
2:15 [j]Lev. 3:3
2:17 [k]Gen. 6:11 [l]Mal. 2:8
2:18 [m]ver. 11 [n]Ex. 28:4; 2 Sam. 6:14
2:19 [o]ch. 1:3
2:20 [p]Gen. 14:19 [q]ch. 1:28

21 And the LORD [r]visited Hannah, so that she conceived, and bare three sons and two daughters. And the child Samuel [s]grew before the LORD.

22 ¶ Now Eli was very old, and heard all that his sons did unto all Israel; and how they lay with [t]the women that assembled *at* the door of the tabernacle of the congregation.

23 And he said unto them, Why do ye such things? for I hear of your evil dealings by all this people.

24 Nay, my sons; for *it is* no good report that I hear: ye make the LORD's people to transgress.

25 If one man sin against another, the judge shall judge him: but if a man [u]sin against the LORD, who shall intreat for him? Notwithstanding they hearkened not unto the voice of their father, [v]because the LORD would slay them.

26 And the child Samuel [w]grew on, and was [x]in favour both with the LORD, and also with men.

27 ¶ [y]And there came a man of God unto Eli, and said unto him, Thus saith the LORD, [z]Did I plainly appear unto the house of thy father, when they were in Egypt in Pharaoh's house?

28 And did I [a]choose him out of all the tribes of Israel *to be* my priest, to offer upon mine altar, to burn incense, to wear an ephod before me? and [b]did I give unto the house of thy father all the offerings made by fire of the children of Israel?

29 Wherefore [c]kick ye at my sacrifice and at mine offering, which I have commanded *in my* [d]habitation; and honourest thy sons above me, to make yourselves fat with the chiefest of all the offerings of Israel my people?

30 Wherefore the LORD God of Israel saith, [e]I said indeed *that* thy house, and the house of thy father, should walk before me for ever: but now the LORD saith, [f]Be it far from me; for them that honour me [g]I will honour, and [h]they that despise me shall be lightly esteemed.

31 Behold, [i]the days come, that I will cut off thine arm, and the arm of thy father's house, that there shall not be an old man in thine house.

32 And thou shalt see an enemy *in my* habitation, in all *the wealth* which *God* shall give Israel: and there shall not be [j]an old man in thine house for ever.

33 And the man of thine, *whom* I shall not cut off from mine altar, *shall be* to consume thine eyes, and to grieve thine heart: and all the increase of thine house shall die in the flower of their age.

34 And this *shall be* [k]a sign unto thee, that shall come upon thy two sons, on Hophni and Phinehas; [l]in one day they shall die both of them.

35 And [m]I will raise me up a faithful priest, *that* shall do according to *that* which *is* in mine heart and in my mind: and [n]I will build him a sure house; and he shall walk before [o]mine anointed for ever.

36 [p]And it shall come to pass, *that* every one that is left in thine house shall come *and* crouch to him for a piece of silver and a morsel of bread, and shall say, Put me, I pray thee, into one of the priests' offices, that I may eat a piece of bread.

2:21 [r]Gen. 21:1 [s]ver. 26; ch. 3:19; Judg. 13:24; Luke 1:80
2:22 [t]Ex. 38:8
2:25 [u]Num. 15:30 [v]Josh. 11:20; Prov. 15:10
2:26 [w]ver. 21 [x]Prov. 3:4; Luke 2:52; Acts 2:47; Rom. 14:18
2:27 [y]1 Kings 13:1 [z]Ex. 4:14
2:28 [a]Ex. 28:1; Num. 16:5 [b]Lev. 2:3; Num. 5:9
2:29 [c]Deut. 32:15 [d]Deut. 12:5
2:30 [e]Ex. 29:9 [f]Jer. 18:9 [g]Ps. 18:20 [h]Mal. 2:9
2:31 [i]ch. 4:11; 1 Kings 2:27; Ezek. 44:10
2:32 [j]Zech. 8:4
2:34 [k]1 Kings 13:3 [l]ch. 4:11
2:35 [m]1 Kings 2:35; 1 Chron. 29:22; Ezek. 44:15 [n]2 Sam. 7:11; 1 Kings 11:38 [o]Ps. 2:2
2:36 [p]1 Kings 2:27
3:1 [q]ch. 2:11 [r]ver. 21; Ps. 74:9; Am. 8:11
3:2 [s]Gen. 27:1; ch. 2:22
3:3 [t]Ex. 27:21; Lev. 24:3; 2 Chron. 13:11 [u]ch. 1:9
3:7 [v]Acts 19:2
3:11 [w]2 Kings 21:12; Jer. 19:3
3:12 [x]ch. 2:30-36
3:13 [y]ch. 2:29 [z]Ezek. 7:3 [a]ch. 2:12 [b]ch. 2:23
3:14 [c]Num. 15:30; Isa. 22:14

3 And [q]the child Samuel ministered unto the LORD before Eli. And [r]the word of the LORD was precious in those days; *there was* no open vision.

2 And it came to pass at that time, when Eli *was* laid down in his place, [s]and his eyes began to wax dim, *that* he could not see;

3 And ere [t]the lamp of God went out [u]in the temple of the LORD, where the ark of God *was,* and Samuel was laid down *to sleep;*

4 That the LORD called Samuel: and he answered, Here *am* I.

5 And he ran unto Eli, and said, Here *am* I; for thou calledst me. And he said, I called not; lie down again. And he went and lay down.

6 And the LORD called yet again, Samuel. And Samuel arose and went to Eli, and said, Here *am* I; for thou didst call me. And he answered, I called not, my son; lie down again.

7 Now Samuel [v]did not yet know the LORD, neither was the word of the LORD yet revealed unto him.

8 And the LORD called Samuel again the third time. And he arose and went to Eli, and said, Here *am* I; for thou didst call me. And Eli perceived that the LORD had called the child.

9 Therefore Eli said unto Samuel, Go, lie down: and it shall be, if he call thee, that thou shalt say, Speak, LORD; for thy servant heareth. So Samuel went and lay down in his place.

10 And the LORD came, and stood, and called as at other times, Samuel, Samuel. Then Samuel answered, Speak; for thy servant heareth.

11 ¶ And the LORD said to Samuel, Behold, I will do a thing in Israel, [w]at which both the ears of every one that heareth it shall tingle.

12 In that day I will perform against Eli [x]all *things* which I have spoken concerning his house: when I begin, I will also make an end.

13 [y]For I have told him that I will [z]judge his house for ever for the iniquity which he knoweth; because [a]his sons made themselves vile, and he [b]restrained them not.

14 And therefore I have sworn unto the house of Eli, that the iniquity of Eli's house [c]shall not be purged with sacrifice nor offering for ever.

15 ¶ And Samuel lay until the morning, and opened the doors of the house of the LORD. And Samuel feared to shew Eli the vision.

16 Then Eli called Samuel, and said, Samuel, my son. And he answered, Here *am* I.

17 And he said, What *is* the thing that *the* LORD hath said unto thee? I pray thee hide *it* not from me: [d]God do so to thee, and more also, if thou hide *any* thing from me of all the things that he said unto thee.

18 And Samuel told him every whit, and hid nothing from him. And he said, [e]It *is* the LORD: let him do what seemeth him good.

19 ¶ And Samuel [f]grew, and [g]the LORD was with him, [h]and did let none of his words fall to the ground.

20 And all Israel [i]from Dan even to Beer-sheba knew that Samuel *was* established *to be* a prophet of the LORD.

21 And the LORD appeared again in Shiloh: for the LORD revealed himself to Samuel in Shiloh by [j]the word of the LORD.

4 And the word of Samuel came to all Israel. Now Israel went out against the Philistines to battle, and pitched beside [k]Eben-ezer: and the Philistines pitched in Aphek.

2 And the Philistines put themselves in array against Israel: and when they joined battle, Israel was smitten before the Philistines: and they slew of the army in the field about four thousand men.

3 ¶ And when the people were come into the camp, the elders of Israel said, Wherefore hath the LORD smitten us to day before the Philistines? Let us fetch the ark of the covenant of the LORD out of Shiloh unto us, that, when it cometh among us, it may save us out of the hand of our enemies.

4 So the people sent to Shiloh, that they might bring from thence the ark of the covenant of the LORD of hosts, [l]which dwelleth *between* [m]the cherubims: and the two sons of Eli, Hophni and Phinehas, *were* there with the ark of the covenant of God.

5 And when the ark of the covenant of the LORD came into the camp, all Israel shouted with a great shout, so that the earth rang again.

6 And when the Philistines heard the noise of the shout, they said, What *meaneth* the noise of this great shout in the camp of the Hebrews? And they understood that the ark of the LORD was come into the camp.

7 And the Philistines were afraid, for they said, God is come into the camp. And they said, Woe unto us! for there hath not been such a thing heretofore.

8 Woe unto us! who shall deliver us out of the hand of these mighty Gods? these *are* the Gods that smote the Egyptians with all the plagues in the wilderness.

9 [n]Be strong, and quit yourselves like men, O ye Philistines, that ye be not servants unto the Hebrews, [o]as they have been to you: quit yourselves like men, and fight.

10 ¶ And the Philistines fought, and [p]Israel was smitten, and they fled every man into his tent: and there was a very great slaughter; for there fell of Israel thirty thousand footmen.

11 And [q]the ark of God was taken; and [r]the two sons of Eli, Hophni and Phinehas, were slain.

12 ¶ And there ran a man of Benjamin out of the army, and [s]came to Shiloh the same day with his clothes rent, and [t]with earth upon his head.

13 And when he came, lo, Eli sat upon [u]a seat by the wayside watching: for his heart trembled for the ark of God. And when the man came into the city, and told *it*, all the city cried out.

14 And when Eli heard the noise of the crying, he said, What *meaneth* the noise of this tumult? And the man came in hastily, and told Eli.

15 Now Eli was ninety and eight years old; and [v]his eyes were dim, that he could not see.

16 And the man said unto Eli, I *am* he that came out of the army, and I fled to day out of the army. And he said, [w]What is there done, my son?

17 And the messenger answered and said, Israel is fled before the Philistines, and there hath been also a great slaughter among the people, and thy two sons also, Hophni and Phinehas, are dead, and the ark of God is taken.

18 And it came to pass, when he made mention of the ark of God, that he fell from off the seat backward by the side of the gate, and his neck brake, and he died: for he was an old man, and heavy. And he had judged Israel forty years.

19 ¶ And his daughter in law, Phinehas' wife, was with child, *near* to be delivered: and when she heard the tidings that the ark of God was taken, and that her father in law and her husband were dead, she bowed herself and travailed; for her pains came upon her.

20 And about the time of her death [x]the women that stood by her said unto her, Fear not; for thou hast born a son. But she answered not, neither did she regard *it*.

21 And she named the child [y]I-chabod, saying, [z]The glory is departed from Israel: because the ark of God was taken, and because of her father in law and her husband.

22 And she said, The glory is departed from Israel: for the ark of God is taken.

5 And the Philistines took the ark of God, and brought it [a]from Eben-ezer unto Ashdod.

2 When the Philistines took the ark of God, they brought it into the house of [b]Dagon, and set it by Dagon.

3 ¶ And when they of Ashdod arose early on the morrow, behold, Dagon *was* [c]fallen upon his face to the earth before the ark of the LORD. And they took Dagon, and [d]set him in his place again.

4 And when they arose early on the morrow morning, behold, Dagon *was* fallen upon his face to the ground before the ark of the LORD; and [e]the head of Dagon and both the palms of his hands *were* cut off

3:17 [d]Ruth 1:17
3:18 [e]Job 1:21; Ps. 39:9; Isa. 39:8
3:19 [f]ch. 2:21 [g]Gen. 39:2 [h]ch. 9:6
3:20 [i]Judg. 20:1
3:21 [j]ver. 1
4:1 [k]ch. 5:1
4:4 [l]2 Sam. 6:2; Ps. 80:1 [m]Ex. 25:18; Num. 7:89
4:9 [n]1 Cor. 16:13 [o]Judg. 13:1
4:10 [p]ver. 2; Lev. 26:17; Deut. 28:25; Ps. 78:9
4:11 [q]ch. 2:32; Ps. 78:61 [r]ch. 2:34; Ps. 78:64
4:12 [s]2 Sam. 1:2 [t]Josh. 7:6; 2 Sam. 13:19; Neh. 9:1; Job 2:12
4:13 [u]ch. 1:9
4:15 [v]ch. 3:2
4:16 [w]2 Sam. 1:4
4:20 [x]Gen. 35:17
4:21 [y]ch. 14:3 [z]Ps. 26:8
5:1 [a]ch. 4:1
5:2 [b]Judg. 16:23
5:3 [c]Isa. 19:1 [d]Isa. 46:7
5:4 [e]Jer. 50:2; Ezek. 6:4; Mic. 1:7

upon the threshold; only *the stump of* Dagon was left to him.

5 Therefore neither the priests of Dagon, nor any that come into Dagon's house, [f]tread on the threshold of Dagon in Ashdod unto this day.

6 But [g]the hand of the LORD was heavy upon them of Ashdod, and he [h]destroyed them, and smote them with [i]emerods, *even* Ashdod and the coasts thereof.

7 And when the men of Ashdod saw that *it was* so, they said, The ark of the God of Israel shall not abide with us: for his hand is sore upon us, and upon Dagon our god.

8 They sent therefore and gathered all the lords of the Philistines unto them, and said, What shall we do with the ark of the God of Israel? And they answered, Let the ark of the God of Israel be carried about unto Gath. And they carried the ark of the God of Israel about *thither*.

9 And it was *so*, that, after they had carried it about, [j]the hand of the LORD was against the city [k]with a very great destruction: and [l]he smote the men of the city, both small and great, and they had emerods in their secret parts.

10 ¶ Therefore they sent the ark of God to Ekron. And it came to pass, as the ark of God came to Ekron, that the Ekronites cried out, saying, They have brought about the ark of the God of Israel to us, to slay us and our people.

11 So they sent and gathered together all the lords of the Philistines, and said, Send away the ark of the God of Israel, and let it go again to his own place, that it slay us not, and our people: for there was a deadly destruction throughout all the city; [m]the hand of God was very heavy there.

12 And the men that died not were smitten with the emerods: and the cry of the city went up to heaven.

6 And the ark of the LORD was in the country of the Philistines seven months.

2 And the Philistines [n]called for the priests and the diviners, saying, What shall we do to the ark of the LORD? tell us wherewith we shall send it to his place.

3 And they said, If ye send away the ark of the God of Israel, send it not [o]empty; but in any wise return him [p]a trespass offering: then ye shall be healed, and it shall [q]be known to you why his hand is not removed from you.

4 Then said they, What *shall be* the trespass offering which we shall return to him? They answered, Five golden emerods, and five golden mice, [r]*according to* the number of the lords of the Philistines: for one plague *was* on you all, and on your lords.

5 Wherefore ye shall make images of your emerods, and images of your mice that [s]mar the land; and ye shall [t]give glory unto the God of Israel: peradventure he will [u]lighten his hand from off you, and from off [v]your gods, and from off your land.

6 Wherefore then do ye harden your hearts, [w]as the Egyptians and Pharaoh hardened their hearts? when he had wrought wonderfully among them, [x]did they not let the people go, and they departed?

7 Now therefore make [y]a new cart, and take two milch kine, [z]on which there hath come no yoke, and tie the kine to the cart, and bring their calves home from them:

8 And take the ark of the LORD, and lay it upon the cart; and put [a]the jewels of gold, which ye return him *for* a trespass offering, in a coffer by the side thereof; and send it away, that it may go.

9 And see, if it goeth up by the way of his own coast to [b]Beth-shemesh, *then* he hath done us this great evil: but if not, then [c]we shall know that *it is* not his hand *that* smote us; it *was* a chance *that* happened to us.

10 ¶ And the men did so; and took two milch kine, and tied them to the cart, and shut up their calves at home:

11 And they laid the ark of the LORD upon the cart, and the coffer with the mice of gold and the images of their emerods.

12 And the kine took the straight way to the way of Beth-shemesh, *and* went along the highway, lowing as they went, and turned not aside *to* the right hand or *to* the left; and the lords of the Philistines went after them unto the border of Beth-shemesh.

13 And *they of* Beth-shemesh *were* reaping their wheat harvest in the valley: and they lifted up their eyes, and saw the ark, and rejoiced to see *it*.

14 And the cart came into the field of Joshua, a Beth-shemite, and stood there, where *there was* a great stone: and they clave the wood of the cart, and offered the kine a burnt offering unto the LORD.

15 And the Levites took down the ark of the LORD, and the coffer that *was* with it, wherein the jewels of gold *were*, and put *them* on the great stone: and the men of Beth-shemesh offered burnt offerings and sacrificed sacrifices the same day unto the LORD.

16 And when [d]the five lords of the Philistines had seen *it*, they returned to Ekron the same day.

17 [e]And these *are* the golden emerods which the Philistines returned *for* a trespass offering unto the LORD; for Ashdod one, for Gaza one, for Askelon one, for Gath one, for Ekron one;

18 And the golden mice, *according to* the number of all the cities of the Philistines *belonging* to the five lords, *both* of fenced cities, and of country villages, even unto the great *stone of* Abel, whereon they set down the ark of the LORD: *which stone remaineth* unto this day in the field of Joshua, the Beth-shemite.

19 ¶ And [f]he smote the men of Beth-shemesh, because they had looked into the ark of the LORD, even he smote of the people fifty thousand and threescore and ten men:

5:5 *f*Zeph. 1:9
5:6 *g*ver. 7; Ex. 9:3; Ps. 32:4; Acts 13:11 *h*ch. 6:5 *i*Deut. 28:27; Ps. 78:66
5:9 *j*Deut. 2:15; ch. 7:13 *k*ver. 11 *l*ver. 6; Ps. 78:66
5:11 *m*ver. 6
6:2 *n*Gen. 41:8; Ex. 7:11; Dan. 2:2; Matt. 2:4
6:3 *o*Ex. 23:15; Deut. 16:16 *p*Lev. 5:15 *q*ver. 9
6:4 *r*ver. 17; Josh. 13:3; Judg. 3:3
6:5 *s*ch. 5:6 *t*Josh. 7:19; Isa. 42:12; Mal. 2:2; John 9:24 *u*ch. 5:6; Ps. 39:10 *v*ch. 5:3
6:6 *w*Ex. 7:13 *x*Ex. 12:31
6:7 *y*2 Sam. 6:3 *z*Num. 19:2
6:8 *a*ver. 4
6:9 *b*Josh. 15:10 *c*ver. 3
6:16 *d*Josh. 13:3
6:17 *e*ver. 4
6:19 *f*Ex. 19:21; Num. 4:5; 2 Sam. 6:7

and the people lamented, because the LORD had smitten *many* of the people with a great slaughter.

20 And the men of Beth-shemesh said, [g]Who is able to stand before this holy LORD God? and to whom shall he go up from us?

21 ¶ And they sent messengers to the inhabitants of [h]Kirjath-jearim, saying, The Philistines have brought again the ark of the LORD; come ye down, *and* fetch it up to you.

7 And the men of [i]Kirjath-jearim came, and fetched up the ark of the LORD, and brought it into the house of [j]Abinadab in the hill, and sanctified Eleazar his son to keep the ark of the LORD.

2 And it came to pass, while the ark abode in Kirjath-jearim, that the time was long; for it was twenty years: and all the house of Israel lamented after the LORD.

3 ¶ And Samuel spake unto all the house of Israel, saying, If ye do [k]return unto the LORD with all your hearts, *then* [l]put away the strange gods and [m]Ashtaroth from among you, and [n]prepare your hearts unto the LORD, and [o]serve him only: and he will deliver you out of the hand of the Philistines.

4 Then the children of Israel did put away [p]Baalim and Ashtaroth, and served the LORD only.

5 And Samuel said, [q]Gather all Israel to Mizpeh, and I will pray for you unto the LORD.

6 And they gathered together to Mizpeh, [r]and drew water, and poured *it* out before the LORD, and [s]fasted on that day, and said there, [t]We have sinned against the LORD. And Samuel judged the children of Israel in Mizpeh.

7 And when the Philistines heard that the children of Israel were gathered together to Mizpeh, the lords of the Philistines went up against Israel. And when the children of Israel heard *it*, they were afraid of the Philistines.

8 And the children of Israel said to Samuel, [u]Cease not to cry unto the LORD our God for us, that he will save us out of the hand of the Philistines.

9 ¶ And Samuel took a sucking lamb, and offered *it for* a burnt offering wholly unto the LORD: and [v]Samuel cried unto the LORD for Israel; and the LORD heard him.

10 And as Samuel was offering up the burnt offering, the Philistines drew near to battle against Israel: [w]but the LORD thundered with a great thunder on that day upon the Philistines, and discomfited them; and they were smitten before Israel.

11 And the men of Israel went out of Mizpeh, and pursued the Philistines, and smote them, until *they came* under Beth-car.

12 Then Samuel [x]took a stone, and set *it* between Mizpeh and Shen, and called the name of it Eben-ezer, saying, Hitherto hath the LORD helped us.

13 ¶ [y]So the Philistines were subdued, and they [z]came no more into the coast of Israel: and the hand of the LORD was against the Philistines all the days of Samuel.

14 And the cities which the Philistines had taken from Israel were restored to Israel, from Ekron even unto Gath; and the coasts thereof did Israel deliver out of the hands of the Philistines. And there was peace between Israel and the Amorites.

15 And Samuel [a]judged Israel all the days of his life.

16 And he went from year to year in circuit to Beth-el, and Gilgal, and Mizpeh, and judged Israel in all those places.

17 And [b]his return *was* to Ramah; for there *was* his house; and there he judged Israel; and there he [c]built an altar unto the LORD.

8 And it came to pass, when Samuel was old, that he [d]made his [e]sons judges over Israel.

2 Now the name of his firstborn was Joel; and the name of his second, Abiah: *they were* judges in Beer-sheba.

3 And his sons [f]walked not in his ways, but turned aside [g]after lucre, and [h]took bribes, and perverted judgment.

4 Then all the elders of Israel gathered themselves together, and came to Samuel unto Ramah,

5 And said unto him, Behold, thou art old, and thy sons walk not in thy ways: now [i]make us a king to judge us like all the nations.

6 ¶ But the thing displeased Samuel, when they said, Give us a king to judge us. And Samuel prayed unto the LORD.

7 And the LORD said unto Samuel, Hearken unto the voice of the people in all that they say unto thee: for [j]they have not rejected thee, but [k]they have rejected me, that I should not reign over them.

8 According to all the works which they have done since the day that I brought them up out of Egypt even unto this day, wherewith they have forsaken me, and served other gods, so do they also unto thee.

9 Now therefore hearken unto their voice: howbeit yet protest solemnly unto them, and [l]shew them the manner of the king that shall reign over them.

10 ¶ And Samuel told all the words of the LORD unto the people that asked of him a king.

11 And he said, [m]This will be the manner of the king that shall reign over you: [n]He will take your sons, and appoint *them* for himself, for his chariots, and *to be* his horsemen; and *some* shall run before his chariots.

12 And he will appoint him captains over thousands, and captains over fifties; and *will set them* to ear his ground, and to reap his harvest, and to make his instruments of war, and instruments of his chariots.

13 And he will take your daughters *to be*

6:20 [g]2 Sam. 6:9; Mal. 3:2
6:21 [h]Josh. 18:14; Judg. 18:12; 1 Chron. 13:5
7:1 [i]ch. 6:21; Ps. 132:6 [j]2 Sam. 6:4
7:3 [k]Deut. 30:2-10; 1 Kings 8:48; Isa. 55:7; Hos. 6:1; Joel 2:12 [l]Gen. 35:2; Josh. 24:14 [m]Judg. 2:13 [n]2 Chron. 30:19; Job 11:13 [o]Deut. 6:13; Matt. 4:10; Luke 4:8
7:4 [p]Judg. 2:11
7:5 [q]Judg. 20:1; 2 Kings 25:23
7:6 [r]2 Sam. 14:14 [s]Neh. 9:1; Dan. 9:3; Joel 2:12 [t]Judg. 10:10; 1 Kings 8:47; Ps. 106:6
7:8 [u]Isa. 37:4
7:9 [v]Ps. 99:6; Jer. 15:1
7:10 [w]Josh. 10:10; Judg. 4:15; ch. 2:10; 2 Sam. 22:14
7:12 [x]Gen. 28:18; Josh. 4:9
7:13 [y]Judg. 13:1 [z]ch. 13:5
7:15 [a]ver. 6; ch. 12:11; Judg. 2:16
7:17 [b]ch. 8:4 [c]Judg. 21:4
8:1 [d]Deut. 16:18; 2 Chron. 19:5 [e]Judg. 5:10
8:3 [f]Jer. 22:15 [g]Ex. 18:21; 1 Tim. 3:3 [h]Deut. 16:19; Ps. 15:5
8:5 [i]ver. 19; Deut. 17:14; Hos. 13:10; Acts 13:21
8:7 [j]Ex. 16:8 [k]ch. 10:19; Hos. 13:10
8:9 [l]ver. 11
8:11 [m]Deut. 17:16; ch. 10:25 [n]ch. 14:52

confectionaries, and *to be* cooks, and *to be* bakers.

14 And [o]he will take your fields, and your vineyards, and your oliveyards, *even* the best *of them,* and give *them* to his servants.

15 And he will take the tenth of your seed, and of your vineyards, and give to his officers, and to his servants.

16 And he will take your menservants, and your maidservants, and your goodliest young men, and your asses, and put *them* to his work.

17 He will take the tenth of your sheep: and ye shall be his servants.

18 And ye shall cry out in that day because of your king which ye shall have chosen you; and the LORD [p]will not hear you in that day.

19 ¶ Nevertheless the people [q]refused to obey the voice of Samuel; and they said, Nay; but we will have a king over us;

20 That we also may be [r]like all the nations; and that our king may judge us, and go out before us, and fight our battles.

21 And Samuel heard all the words of the people, and he rehearsed them in the ears of the LORD.

22 And the LORD said to Samuel, [s]Hearken unto their voice, and make them a king. And Samuel said unto the men of Israel, Go ye every man unto his city.

9 Now there was a man of Benjamin, whose name *was* [t]Kish, the son of Abiel, the son of Zeror, the son of Bechorath, the son of Aphiah, a Benjamite, a mighty man of power.

2 And he had a son, whose name *was* Saul, a choice young man, and a goodly: and *there was* not among the children of Israel a goodlier person than he: [u]from his shoulders and upward *he was* higher than any of the people.

3 And the asses of Kish Saul's father were lost. And Kish said to Saul his son, Take now one of the servants with thee, and arise, go seek the asses.

4 And he passed through mount Ephraim, and passed through the land of [v]Shalisha, but they found *them* not: then they passed through the land of Shalim, and *there they were* not: and he passed through the land of the Benjamites, but they found *them* not.

5 *And* when they were come to the land of Zuph, Saul said to his servant that *was* with him, Come, and let us return; lest my father leave *caring* for the asses, and take thought for us.

6 And he said unto him, Behold now, *there is* in this city [w]a man of God, and *he is* an honourable man; [x]all that he saith cometh surely to pass: now let us go thither; peradventure he can shew us our way that we should go.

7 Then said Saul to his servant, But, behold, *if* we go, [y]what shall we bring the man? for the bread is spent in our vessels, and *there is* not a present to bring to the man of God: what have we?

8 And the servant answered Saul again, and said, Behold, I have here at hand the fourth part of a shekel of silver: *that* will I give to the man of God, to tell us our way.

9 (Beforetime in Israel, when a man [z]went to enquire of God, thus he spake, Come, and let us go to the seer: for *he that is* now *called* a Prophet was beforetime called [a]a Seer.)

10 Then said Saul to his servant, Well said; come, let us go. So they went unto the city where the man of God *was.*

11 ¶ *And* as they went up the hill to the city, [b]they found young maidens going out to draw water, and said unto them, Is the seer here?

12 And they answered them, and said, He is; behold, *he is* before you: make haste now, for he came to day to the city; for [c]*there is* a sacrifice of the people to day [d]in the high place:

13 As soon as ye be come into the city, ye shall straightway find him, before he go up to the high place to eat: for the people will not eat until he come, because he doth bless the sacrifice; *and* afterwards they eat that be bidden. Now therefore get you up; for about this time ye shall find him.

14 And they went up into the city: *and* when they were come into the city, behold, Samuel came out against them, for to go up to the high place.

15 ¶ [e]Now the LORD had told Samuel in his ear a day before Saul came, saying,

16 To morrow about this time I will send thee a man out of the land of Benjamin, [f]and thou shalt anoint him *to be* captain over my people Israel, that he may save my people out of the hand of the Philistines: for I have [g]looked upon my people, because their cry is come unto me.

17 And when Samuel saw Saul, the LORD said unto him, [h]Behold the man whom I spake to thee of! this same shall reign over my people.

18 Then Saul drew near to Samuel in the gate, and said, Tell me, I pray thee, where the seer's house *is.*

19 And Samuel answered Saul, and said, I *am* the seer: go up before me unto the high place; for ye shall eat with me to day, and to morrow I will let thee go, and will tell thee all that *is* in thine heart.

20 And as for [i]thine asses that were lost three days ago, set not thy mind on them; for they are found. And on whom [j]*is* all the desire of Israel? *Is it* not on thee, and on all thy father's house?

21 And Saul answered and said, [k]*Am* not I a Benjamite, of the [l]smallest of the tribes of Israel? and [m]my family the least of all the families of the tribe of Benjamin? wherefore then speakest thou so to me?

22 And Samuel took Saul and his servant, and brought them into the parlour, and made them sit in the chiefest place among them that were bidden, which *were* about thirty persons.

8:14 *o*1 Kings 21:7; Ezek. 46:18
8:18 *p*Prov. 1:25; Isa. 1:15; Mic. 3:4
8:19 *q*Jer. 44:16
8:20 *r*ver. 5
8:22 *s*ver. 7; Hos. 13:11
9:1 *t*ch. 14:51; 1 Chron. 8:33
9:2 *u*ch. 10:23
9:4 *v*2 Kings 4:42
9:6 *w*Deut. 33:1; 1 Kings 13:1 *x*ch. 3:19
9:7 *y*Judg. 6:18; 1 Kings 14:3; 2 Kings 4:42
9:9 *z*Gen. 25:22 *a*2 Sam. 24:11; 2 Kings 17:13; 1 Chron. 26:28; 2 Chron. 16:7; Isa. 30:10; Am. 7:12
9:11 *b*Gen. 24:11
9:12 *c*Gen. 31:54; ch. 16:2 *d*1 Kings 3:2
9:15 *e*ch. 15:1; Acts 13:21
9:16 *f*ch. 10:1 *g*Ex. 2:25
9:17 *h*ch. 16:12; Hos. 13:11
9:20 *i*ver. 3 *j*ch. 8:5
9:21 *k*ch. 15:17 *l*Judg. 20:46; Ps. 68:27 *m*Judg. 6:15

23 And Samuel said unto the cook, Bring the portion which I gave thee, of which I said unto thee, Set it by thee.

24 And the cook took up [n]the shoulder, and *that* which *was* upon it, and set *it* before Saul. And *Samuel* said, Behold that which is left! set *it* before thee, *and* eat: for unto this time hath it been kept for thee since I said, I have invited the people. So Saul did eat with Samuel that day.

25 ¶ And when they were come down from the high place into the city, *Samuel* communed with Saul upon [o]the top of the house.

26 And they arose early: and it came to pass about the spring of the day, that Samuel called Saul to the top of the house, saying, Up, that I may send thee away. And Saul arose, and they went out both of them, he and Samuel, abroad.

27 *And* as they were going down to the end of the city, Samuel said to Saul, Bid the servant pass on before us, (and he passed on,) but stand thou still a while, that I may shew thee the word of God.

10 Then [p]Samuel took a vial of oil, and poured *it* upon his head, [q]and kissed him, and said, *Is it* not because [r]the LORD hath anointed thee *to be* captain over [s]his inheritance?

2 When thou art departed from me to day, then thou shalt find two men by [t]Rachel's sepulchre in the border of Benjamin [u]at Zelzah; and they will say unto thee, The asses which thou wentest to seek are found: and, lo, thy father hath left the care of the asses, and sorroweth for you, saying, What shall I do for my son?

3 Then shalt thou go on forward from thence, and thou shalt come to the plain of Tabor, and there shall meet thee three men going up [v]to God to Beth-el, one carrying three kids, and another carrying three loaves of bread, and another carrying a bottle of wine:

4 And they will salute thee, and give thee two *loaves* of bread; which thou shalt receive of their hands.

5 After that thou shalt come to [w]the hill of God, [x]where *is* the garrison of the Philistines: and it shall come to pass, when thou art come thither to the city, that thou shalt meet a company of prophets coming down [y]from the high place with a psaltery, and a tabret, and a pipe, and a harp, before them; [z]and they shall prophesy:

6 And [a]the Spirit of the LORD will come upon thee, and [b]thou shalt prophesy with them, and shalt be turned into another man.

7 And let it be, when these [c]signs are come unto thee, *that* thou do as occasion serve thee; for [d]God *is* with thee.

8 And thou shalt go down before me [e]to Gilgal; and, behold, I will come down unto thee, to offer burnt offerings, *and* to sacrifice sacrifices of peace offerings: [f]seven days shalt thou tarry, till I come to thee, and shew thee what thou shalt do.

9 ¶ And it was *so,* that when he had turned his back to go from Samuel, God gave him another heart: and all those signs came to pass that day.

10 And [g]when they came thither to the hill, behold, [h]a company of prophets met him; and [i]the Spirit of God came upon him, and he prophesied among them.

11 And it came to pass, when all that knew him beforetime saw that, behold, he prophesied among the prophets, then the people said one to another, What *is* this *that* is come unto the son of Kish? [j]*Is* Saul also among the prophets?

12 And one of the same place answered and said, But [k]who *is* their father? Therefore it became a proverb, *Is* Saul also among the prophets?

13 And when he had made an end of prophesying, he came to the high place.

14 ¶ And Saul's uncle said unto him and to his servant, Whither went ye? And he said, To seek the asses: and when we saw that *they were* no where, we came to Samuel.

15 And Saul's uncle said, Tell me, I pray thee, what Samuel said unto you.

16 And Saul said unto his uncle, He told us plainly that the asses were found. But of the matter of the kingdom, whereof Samuel spake, he told him not.

17 ¶ And Samuel called the people together [l]unto the LORD [m]to Mizpeh;

18 And said unto the children of Israel, [n]Thus saith the LORD God of Israel, I brought up Israel out of Egypt, and delivered you out of the hand of the Egyptians, and out of the hand of all kingdoms, *and* of them that oppressed you:

19 [o]And ye have this day rejected your God, who himself saved you out of all your adversities and your tribulations; and ye have said unto him, *Nay,* but set a king over us. Now therefore present yourselves before the LORD by your tribes, and by your thousands.

20 And when Samuel had [p]caused all the tribes of Israel to come near, the tribe of Benjamin was taken.

21 When he had caused the tribe of Benjamin to come near by their families, the family of Matri was taken, and Saul the son of Kish was taken: and when they sought him, he could not be found.

22 Therefore they [q]enquired of the LORD further, if the man should yet come thither. And the LORD answered, Behold, he hath hid himself among the stuff.

23 And they ran and fetched him thence: and when he stood among the people, [r]he was higher than any of the people from his shoulders and upward.

24 And Samuel said to all the people, See ye him [s]whom the LORD hath chosen, that *there is* none like him among all the people? And all the people shouted, and said, [t]God save the king.

25 Then Samuel told the people [u]the

9:24 [n]Lev. 7:32; Ezek. 24:4
9:25 [o]Deut. 22:8; 2 Sam. 11:2; Acts 10:9
10:1 [p]ch. 9:16; 2 Kings 9:3 [q]Ps. 2:12 [r]Acts 13:21 [s]Deut. 32:9; Ps. 78:71
10:2 [t]Gen. 35:19 [u]Josh. 18:28
10:3 [v]Gen. 28:22
10:5 [w]ver. 10 [x]ch. 13:3 [y]ch. 9:12 [z]Ex. 15:20; 2 Kings 3:15; 1 Cor. 14:1
10:6 [a]Num. 11:25; ch. 16:13 [b]ver. 10; ch. 19:23
10:7 [c]Ex. 4:8; Luke 2:12 [d]Judg. 6:12
10:8 [e]ch. 11:14 [f]ch. 13:8
10:10 [g]ver. 5 [h]ch. 19:20 [i]ver. 6
10:11 [j]ch. 19:24; Matt. 13:54; John 7:15; Acts 4:13
10:12 [k]Isa. 54:13; John 6:45
10:17 [l]Judg. 11:11; ch. 11:15 [m]ch. 7:5
10:18 [n]Judg. 6:8
10:19 [o]ch. 8:7
10:20 [p]Josh. 7:14; Acts 1:24
10:22 [q]ch. 23:2
10:23 [r]ch. 9:2
10:24 [s]2 Sam. 21:6 [t]1 Kings 1:25; 2 Kings 11:12
10:25 [u]Deut. 17:14; ch. 8:11

manner of the kingdom, and wrote *it* in a book, and laid *it* up before the LORD. And Samuel sent all the people away, every man to his house.

26 ¶ And Saul also went home [v]to Gibeah; and there went with him a band of men, whose hearts God had touched.

27 [w]But the [x]children of Belial said, How shall this man save us? And they despised him, [y]and brought him no presents. But he held his peace.

11 Then [z]Nahash the Ammonite came up, and encamped against [a]Jabesh-gilead: and all the men of Jabesh said unto Nahash, [b]Make a covenant with us, and we will serve thee.

2 And Nahash the Ammonite answered them, On this *condition* will I make *a covenant* with you, that I may thrust out all your right eyes, and lay it *for* [c]a reproach upon all Israel.

3 And the elders of Jabesh said unto him, Give us seven days' respite, that we may send messengers unto all the coasts of Israel: and then, if *there be* no man to save us, we will come out to thee.

4 ¶ Then came the messengers [d]to Gibeah of Saul, and told the tidings in the ears of the people: and [e]all the people lifted up their voices, and wept.

5 And, behold, Saul came after the herd out of the field; and Saul said, What *aileth* the people that they weep? And they told him the tidings of the men of Jabesh.

6 [f]And the Spirit of God came upon Saul when he heard those tidings, and his anger was kindled greatly.

7 And he took a yoke of oxen, and [g]hewed them in pieces, and sent *them* throughout all the coasts of Israel by the hands of messengers, saying, [h]Whosoever cometh not forth after Saul and after Samuel, so shall it be done unto his oxen. And the fear of the LORD fell on the people, and they came out with one consent.

8 And when he numbered them in [i]Bezek, the children [j]of Israel were three hundred thousand, and the men of Judah thirty thousand.

9 And they said unto the messengers that came, Thus shall ye say unto the men of Jabesh-gilead, To morrow, by *that time* the sun be hot, ye shall have help. And the messengers came and shewed *it* to the men of Jabesh; and they were glad.

10 Therefore the men of Jabesh said, To morrow [k]we will come out unto you, and ye shall do with us all that seemeth good unto you.

11 And it was *so* on the morrow, that [l]Saul put the people [m]in three companies; and they came into the midst of the host in the morning watch, and slew the Ammonites until the heat of the day: and it came to pass, that they which remained were scattered, so that two of them were not left together.

12 ¶ And the people said unto Samuel, [n]Who *is* he that said, Shall Saul reign over us? [o]bring the men, that we may put them to death.

13 And Saul said, [p]There shall not a man be put to death this day: for to day [q]the LORD hath wrought salvation in Israel.

14 Then said Samuel to the people, Come, and let us go [r]to Gilgal, and renew the kingdom there.

15 And all the people went to Gilgal; and there they made Saul king [s]before the LORD in Gilgal; and [t]there they sacrificed sacrifices of peace offerings before the LORD; and there Saul and all the men of Israel rejoiced greatly.

12 And Samuel said unto all Israel, Behold, I have hearkened unto [u]your voice in all that ye said unto me, and [v]have made a king over you.

2 And now, behold, the king [w]walketh before you: [x]and I am old and grayheaded; and, behold, my sons *are* with you: and I have walked before you from my childhood unto this day.

3 Behold, here I *am*: witness against me before the LORD, and before [y]his anointed: [z]whose ox have I taken? or whose ass have I taken? or whom have I defrauded? whom have I oppressed? or of whose hand have I received *any* bribe to [a]blind mine eyes therewith? and I will restore it you.

4 And they said, Thou hast not defrauded us, nor oppressed us, neither hast thou taken ought of any man's hand.

5 And he said unto them, The LORD *is* witness against you, and his anointed *is* witness this day, [b]that ye have not found ought [c]in my hand. And they answered, *He is* witness.

6 ¶ And Samuel said unto the people, [d]*It is* the LORD that advanced Moses and Aaron, and that brought your fathers up out of the land of Egypt.

7 Now therefore stand still, that I may [e]reason with you before the LORD of all the righteous acts of the LORD, which he did to you and to your fathers.

8 [f]When Jacob was come into Egypt, and your fathers [g]cried unto the LORD, then the LORD [h]sent Moses and Aaron, which brought forth your fathers out of Egypt, and made them dwell in this place.

9 And when they [i]forgat the LORD their God, [j]he sold them into the hand of Sisera, captain of the host of Hazor, and into the hand of [k]the Philistines, and into the hand of the king [l]of Moab, and they fought against them.

10 And they cried unto the LORD, and said, [m]We have sinned, because we have forsaken the LORD, [n]and have served Baalim and Ashtaroth: but now [o]deliver us out of the hand of our enemies, and we will serve thee.

11 And the LORD sent [p]Jerubbaal, and Bedan, and [q]Jephthah, and [r]Samuel, and delivered you out of the hand of your enemies on every side, and ye dwelled safe.

10:26 v Judg. 20:14; ch. 11:4
10:27 w ch. 11:12 x Deut. 13:13 y 2 Sam. 8:2; 1 Kings 4:21; 2 Chron. 17:5; Ps. 72:10; Matt. 2:11
11:1 z ch. 12:12 a Judg. 21:8 b Gen. 26:28; Ex. 23:32; 1 Kings 20:34; Job 41:4; Ezek. 17:13
11:2 c Gen. 34:14; ch. 17:26
11:4 d ch. 10:26; 2 Sam. 21:6 e Judg. 2:4
11:6 f Judg. 3:10; ch. 10:10
11:7 g Judg. 19:29 h Judg. 21:5
11:8 i Judg. 1:5 j 2 Sam. 24:9
11:10 k ver. 3
11:11 l ch. 31:11 m Judg. 7:16
11:12 n ch. 10:27 o Luke 19:27
11:13 p 2 Sam. 19:22 q Ex. 14:13; ch. 19:5
11:14 r ch. 10:8
11:15 s ch. 10:17 t ch. 10:8
12:1 u ch. 8:5 v ch. 10:24
12:2 w Num. 27:17; ch. 8:20 x ch. 8:1
12:3 y ver. 5; ch. 10:1; 2 Sam. 1:14 z Num. 16:15; Acts 20:33; 1 Thess. 2:5 a Deut. 16:19
12:5 b John 18:38; Acts 23:9 c Ex. 22:4
12:6 d Mic. 6:4
12:7 e Isa. 1:18; Mic. 6:2
12:8 f Gen. 46:5 g Ex. 2:23 h Ex. 3:10
12:9 i Judg. 3:7 j Judg. 4:2 k Judg. 10:7 l Judg. 3:12
12:10 m Judg. 10:10 n Judg. 2:13 o Judg. 10:15
12:11 p Judg. 6:14 q Judg. 11:1 r ch. 7:13

12 And when ye saw that [s]Nahash the king of the children of Ammon came against you, [t]ye said unto me, Nay; but a king shall reign over us: when [u]the LORD your God *was* your king.

13 Now therefore [v]behold the king [w]whom ye have chosen, *and* whom ye have desired! and, behold, [x]the LORD hath set a king over you.

14 If ye will [y]fear the LORD, and serve him, and obey his voice, and not rebel against the commandment of the LORD, then shall both ye and also the king that reigneth over you continue following the LORD your God:

15 But if ye will [z]not obey the voice of the LORD, but rebel against the commandment of the LORD, then shall the hand of the LORD be against you, [a]as *it was* against your fathers.

16 ¶ Now therefore [b]stand and see this great thing, which the LORD will do before your eyes.

17 *Is it* not [c]wheat harvest to day? [d]I will call unto the LORD, and he shall send thunder and rain; that ye may perceive and see that [e]your wickedness *is* great, which ye have done in the sight of the LORD, in asking you a king.

18 So Samuel called unto the LORD; and the LORD sent thunder and rain that day: and [f]all the people greatly feared the LORD and Samuel.

19 And all the people said unto Samuel, [g]Pray for thy servants unto the LORD thy God, that we die not: for we have added unto all our sins *this* evil, to ask us a king.

20 ¶ And Samuel said unto the people, Fear not: ye have done all this wickedness: yet turn not aside from following the LORD, but serve the LORD with all your heart;

21 And [h]turn ye not aside: [i]for *then should ye go* after vain *things*, which cannot profit nor deliver; for they *are* vain.

22 For [j]the LORD will not forsake his people [k]for his great name's sake: because [l]it hath pleased the LORD to make you his people.

23 Moreover as for me, God forbid that I should sin against the LORD [m]in ceasing to pray for you: but [n]I will teach you the [o]good and the right way:

24 [p]Only fear the LORD, and serve him in truth with all your heart: for [q]consider how [r]great *things* he hath done for you.

25 But if ye shall still do wickedly, [s]ye shall be consumed, [t]both ye and your king.

13 Saul reigned one year; and when he had reigned two years over Israel,

2 Saul chose him three thousand *men* of Israel; *whereof* two thousand were with Saul in Michmash and in mount Beth-el, and a thousand were with Jonathan in [u]Gibeah of Benjamin: and the rest of the people he sent every man to his tent.

3 And Jonathan smote [v]the garrison of the Philistines that *was* in Geba, and the Philistines heard *of it*. And Saul blew the trumpet throughout all the land, saying, Let the Hebrews hear.

4 And all Israel heard say *that* Saul had smitten a garrison of the Philistines, and *that* Israel also was had in abomination with the Philistines. And the people were called together after Saul to Gilgal.

5 ¶ And the Philistines gathered themselves together to fight with Israel, thirty thousand chariots, and six thousand horsemen, and people as the sand which *is* on the sea shore in multitude: and they came up, and pitched in Michmash, eastward from Beth-aven.

6 When the men of Israel saw that they were in a strait, (for the people were distressed,) then the people [w]did hide themselves in caves, and in thickets, and in rocks, and in high places, and in pits.

7 And *some of* the Hebrews went over Jordan to the land of Gad and Gilead. As for Saul, he *was* yet in Gilgal, and all the people followed him trembling.

8 ¶ [x]And he tarried seven days, according to the set time that Samuel *had appointed:* but Samuel came not to Gilgal; and the people were scattered from him.

9 And Saul said, Bring hither a burnt offering to me, and peace offerings. And he offered the burnt offering.

10 And it came to pass, that as soon as he had made an end of offering the burnt offering, behold, Samuel came; and Saul went out to meet him, that he might salute him.

11 ¶ And Samuel said, What hast thou done? And Saul said, Because I saw that the people were scattered from me, and *that* thou camest not within the days appointed, and *that* the Philistines gathered themselves together at Michmash;

12 Therefore said I, The Philistines will come down now upon me to Gilgal, and I have not made supplication unto the LORD: I forced myself therefore, and offered a burnt offering.

13 And Samuel said to Saul, [y]Thou hast done foolishly: [z]thou hast not kept the commandment of the LORD thy God, which he commanded thee: for now would the LORD have established thy kingdom upon Israel for ever.

14 [a]But now thy kingdom shall not continue: [b]the LORD hath sought him a man after his own heart, and the LORD hath commanded him *to be* captain over his people, because thou hast not kept *that* which the LORD commanded thee.

15 And Samuel arose, and gat him up from Gilgal unto Gibeah of Benjamin. And Saul numbered the people *that were* present with him, about [c]six hundred men.

16 And Saul, and Jonathan his son, and the people *that were* present with them, abode in Gibeah of Benjamin: but the Philistines encamped in Michmash.

17 ¶ And the spoilers came out of the camp of the Philistines in three companies: one company turned unto the way *that*

12:12 [s]ch. 11:1 [t]ch. 8:3 [u]Judg. 8:23; ch. 8:7
12:13 [v]ch. 10:24 [w]ch. 8:5 [x]Hos. 13:11
12:14 [y]Josh. 24:14; Ps. 81:13
12:15 [z]Lev. 26:14; Deut. 28:15; Josh. 24:20 [a]ver. 9
12:16 [b]Ex. 14:13
12:17 [c]Prov. 26:1 [d]Josh. 10:12; ch. 7:9; Jam. 5:16 [e]ch. 8:7
12:18 [f]Ex. 14:31; Ezra 10:9
12:19 [g]Ex. 9:28; Jam. 5:15; 1 John 5:16
12:21 [h]Deut. 11:16 [i]Jer. 16:19; Hab. 2:18; 1 Cor. 8:4
12:22 [j]1 Kings 6:13; Ps. 94:14 [k]Josh. 7:9; Ps. 106:8; Jer. 14:21; Ezek. 20:9 [l]Deut. 7:7; Mal. 1:2
12:23 [m]Acts 12:5; Rom. 1:9; Col. 1:9; 2 Tim. 1:3 [n]Ps. 34:11; Prov. 4:11 [o]1 Kings 8:36; 2 Chron. 6:27; Jer. 6:16
12:24 [p]Eccl. 12:13 [q]Isa. 5:12 [r]Deut. 10:21; Ps. 126:2
12:25 [s]Josh. 24:20 [t]Deut. 28:36
13:2 [u]ch. 10:26
13:3 [v]ch. 10:5
13:6 [w]Judg. 6:2
13:8 [x]ch. 10:8
13:13 [y]2 Chron. 16:9 [z]ch. 15:11
13:14 [a]ch. 15:28 [b]Ps. 89:20; Acts 13:22
13:15 [c]ch. 14:2

leadeth to [d]Ophrah, unto the land of Shual:

18 And another company turned the way *to* [e]Beth-horon: and another company turned *to* the way of the border that looketh to the valley of [f]Zeboim toward the wilderness.

19 ¶ Now [g]there was no smith found throughout all the land of Israel: for the Philistines said, Lest the Hebrews make *them* swords or spears:

20 But all the Israelites went down to the Philistines, to sharpen every man his share, and his coulter, and his axe, and his mattock.

21 Yet they had a file for the mattocks, and for the coulters, and for the forks, and for the axes, and to sharpen the goads.

22 So it came to pass in the day of battle, that [h]there was neither sword nor spear found in the hand of any of the people that *were* with Saul and Jonathan: but with Saul and with Jonathan his son was there found.

23 [i]And the garrison of the Philistines went out to the passage of Michmash.

14 Now it came to pass upon a day, that Jonathan the son of Saul said unto the young man that bare his armour, Come, and let us go over to the Philistines' garrison, that *is* on the other side. But he told not his father.

2 And Saul tarried in the uttermost part of Gibeah under a pomegranate tree which *is* in Migron: and the people that *were* with him *were* [j]about six hundred men;

3 And [k]Ahiah, the son of Ahitub, [l]Ichabod's brother, the son of Phinehas, the son of Eli, the LORD's priest in Shiloh, [m]wearing an ephod. And the people knew not that Jonathan was gone.

4 ¶ And between the passages, by which Jonathan sought to go over [n]unto the Philistines' garrison, *there was* a sharp rock on the one side, and a sharp rock on the other side: and the name of the one *was* Bozez, and the name of the other Seneh.

5 The forefront of the one *was* situate northward over against Michmash, and the other southward over against Gibeah.

6 And Jonathan said to the young man that bare his armour, Come, and let us go over unto the garrison of these uncircumcised: it may be that the LORD will work for us: for *there is* no restraint to the LORD [o]to save by many or by few.

7 And his armourbearer said unto him, Do all that *is* in thine heart: turn thee; behold, I *am* with thee according to thy heart.

8 Then said Jonathan, Behold, we will pass over unto *these* men, and we will discover ourselves unto them.

9 If they say thus unto us, Tarry until we come to you; then we will stand still in our place, and will not go up unto them.

10 But if they say thus, Come up unto us; then we will go up: for the LORD hath delivered them into our hand: and [p]this *shall be* a sign unto us.

11 And both of them discovered themselves unto the garrison of the Philistines: and the Philistines said, Behold, the Hebrews come forth out of the holes where they had hid themselves.

- **13:17** [d]Josh. 18:23
- **13:18** [e]Josh. 16:3 [f]Neh. 11:34
- **13:19** [g]2 Kings 24:14; Jer. 24:1
- **13:22** [h]Judg. 5:8
- **13:23** [i]ch. 14:1
- **14:2** [j]ch. 13:15
- **14:3** [k]ch. 22:9 [l]ch. 4:21 [m]ch. 2:28
- **14:4** [n]ch. 13:23
- **14:6** [o]Judg. 7:4; 2 Chron. 14:11
- **14:10** [p]Gen. 24:14; Judg. 7:11
- **14:15** [q]2 Kings 7:7; Job 18:11 [r]ch. 13:17 [s]Gen. 35:5
- **14:16** [t]ver. 20
- **14:19** [u]Num. 27:21
- **14:20** [v]Judg. 7:22; 2 Chron. 20:23
- **14:22** [w]ch. 13:6
- **14:23** [x]Ex. 14:30; Ps. 44:6; Hos. 1:7 [y]ch. 13:5
- **14:24** [z]Josh. 6:26
- **14:25** [a]Deut. 9:28; Matt. 3:5

12 And the men of the garrison answered Jonathan and his armourbearer, and said, Come up to us, and we will shew you a thing. And Jonathan said unto his armourbearer, Come up after me: for the LORD hath delivered them into the hand of Israel.

13 And Jonathan climbed up upon his hands and upon his feet, and his armourbearer after him: and they fell before Jonathan; and his armourbearer slew after him.

14 And that first slaughter, which Jonathan and his armourbearer made, was about twenty men, within as it were an half acre of land, *which* a yoke *of oxen might plow.*

15 And [q]there was trembling in the host, in the field, and among all the people: the garrison, and [r]the spoilers, they also trembled, and the earth quaked: so it was [s]a very great trembling.

16 And the watchmen of Saul in Gibeah of Benjamin looked; and, behold, the multitude melted away, and they [t]went on beating down *one another.*

17 Then said Saul unto the people that *were* with him, Number now, and see who is gone from us. And when they had numbered, behold, Jonathan and his armourbearer *were* not *there.*

18 And Saul said unto Ahiah, Bring hither the ark of God. For the ark of God was at that time with the children of Israel.

19 ¶ And it came to pass, while Saul [u]talked unto the priest, that the noise that *was* in the host of the Philistines went on and increased: and Saul said unto the priest, Withdraw thine hand.

20 And Saul and all the people that *were* with him assembled themselves, and they came to the battle: and, behold, [v]every man's sword was against his fellow, *and there was* a very great discomfiture.

21 Moreover the Hebrews *that* were with the Philistines before that time, which went up with them into the camp *from the country* round about, even they also *turned* to be with the Israelites that *were* with Saul and Jonathan.

22 Likewise all the men of Israel which [w]had hid themselves in Mount Ephraim, *when* they heard that the Philistines fled, even they also followed hard after them in the battle.

23 [x]So the LORD saved Israel that day: and the battle passed over [y]unto Bethaven.

24 ¶ And the men of Israel were distressed that day: for Saul had [z]adjured the people, saying, Cursed *be* the man that eateth *any* food until evening, that I may be avenged on mine enemies. So none of the people tasted *any* food.

25 [a]And all *they of* the land came to a

wood; and there was [b]honey upon the ground.

26 And when the people were come into the wood, behold, the honey dropped; but no man put his hand to his mouth: for the people feared the oath.

27 But Jonathan heard not when his father charged the people with the oath: wherefore he put forth the end of the rod that *was* in his hand, and dipped it in an honeycomb, and put his hand to his mouth; and his eyes were enlightened.

28 Then answered one of the people, and said, Thy father straitly charged the people with an oath, saying, Cursed *be* the man that eateth *any* food this day. And the people were faint.

29 Then said Jonathan, My father hath troubled the land: see, I pray you, how mine eyes have been enlightened, because I tasted a little of this honey.

30 How much more, if haply the people had eaten freely to day of the spoil of their enemies which they found? for had there not been now a much greater slaughter among the Philistines?

31 And they smote the Philistines that day from Michmash to Aijalon: and the people were very faint.

32 And the people flew upon the spoil, and took sheep, and oxen, and calves, and slew *them* on the ground: and the people did eat *them* [c]with the blood.

33 ¶ Then they told Saul, saying, Behold, the people sin against the LORD, in that they eat with the blood. And he said, Ye have transgressed: roll a great stone unto me this day.

34 And Saul said, Disperse yourselves among the people, and say unto them, Bring me hither every man his ox, and every man his sheep, and slay *them* here, and eat; and sin not against the LORD in eating with the blood. And all the people brought every man his ox with him that night, and slew *them* there.

35 And Saul [d]built an altar unto the LORD: the same was the first altar that he built unto the LORD.

36 ¶ And Saul said, Let us go down after the Philistines by night, and spoil them until the morning light, and let us not leave a man of them. And they said, Do whatsoever seemeth good unto thee. Then said the priest, Let us draw near hither unto God.

37 And Saul asked counsel of God, Shall I go down after the Philistines? wilt thou deliver them into the hand of Israel? But [e]he answered him not that day.

38 And Saul said, [f]Draw ye near hither, all the chief of the people: and know and see wherein this sin hath been this day.

39 For, [g]as the LORD liveth, which saveth Israel, though it be in Jonathan my son, he shall surely die. But *there was* not a man among all the people *that* answered him.

40 Then said he unto all Israel, Be ye on one side, and I and Jonathan my son will be on the other side. And the people said unto Saul, Do what seemeth good unto thee.

41 Therefore Saul said unto the LORD God of Israel, [h]Give a perfect *lot*. [i]And Saul and Jonathan were taken: but the people escaped.

42 And Saul said, Cast *lots* between me and Jonathan my son. And Jonathan was taken.

43 Then Saul said to Jonathan, [j]Tell me what thou hast done. And Jonathan told him, and said, [k]I did but taste a little honey with the end of the rod that *was* in mine hand, *and,* lo, I must die.

44 And Saul answered, [l]God do so and more also: [m]for thou shalt surely die, Jonathan.

45 And the people said unto Saul, Shall Jonathan die, who hath wrought this great salvation in Israel? God forbid: [n]as the LORD liveth, there shall not one hair of his head fall to the ground; for he hath wrought with God this day. So the people rescued Jonathan, that he died not.

46 Then Saul went up from following the Philistines: and the Philistines went to their own place.

47 ¶ So Saul took the kingdom over Israel, and fought against all his enemies on every side, against Moab, and against the children of [o]Ammon, and against Edom, and against the kings of [p]Zobah, and against the Philistines: and whithersoever he turned himself, he vexed *them.*

48 And he gathered an host, and [q]smote the Amalekites, and delivered Israel out of the hands of them that spoiled them.

49 Now [r]the sons of Saul were Jonathan, and Ishui, and Melchi-shua: and the names of his two daughters *were these;* the name of the firstborn Merab, and the name of the younger Michal:

50 And the name of Saul's wife *was* Ahinoam, the daughter of Ahimaaz: and the name of the captain of his host *was* Abner, the son of Ner, Saul's uncle.

51 [s]And Kish *was* the father of Saul; and Ner the father of Abner *was* the son of Abiel.

52 And there was sore war against the Philistines all the days of Saul: and when Saul saw any strong man, or any valiant man, [t]he took him unto him.

15 Samuel also said unto Saul, [u]The LORD sent me to anoint thee *to be* king over his people, over Israel: now therefore hearken thou unto the voice of the words of the LORD.

2 Thus saith the LORD of hosts, I remember *that* which Amalek did to Israel, [v]how he laid *wait* for him in the way, when he came up from Egypt.

3 Now go and smite Amalek, and [w]utterly destroy all that they have, and spare them not; but slay both man and woman, infant and suckling, ox and sheep, camel and ass.

4 And Saul gathered the people together, and numbered them in Telaim, two hundred

14:25 [b]Ex. 3:8; Num. 13:27; Matt. 3:4
14:32 [c]Lev. 3:17; Deut. 12:16
14:35 [d]ch. 7:17
14:37 [e]ch. 28:6
14:38 [f]Josh. 7:14; ch. 10:19
14:39 [g]2 Sam. 12:5
14:41 [h]Prov. 16:33; Acts 1:24 [i]Josh. 7:16; ch. 10:20
14:43 [j]Josh. 7:19 [k]ver. 27
14:44 [l]Ruth 1:17 [m]ver. 39
14:45 [n]2 Sam. 14:11; 1 Kings 1:52; Luke 21:18
14:47 [o]ch. 11:11 [p]2 Sam. 10:6
14:48 [q]ch. 15:3
14:49 [r]ch. 31:2; 1 Chron. 8:33
14:51 [s]ch. 9:1
14:52 [t]ch. 8:11
15:1 [u]ch. 9:16
15:2 [v]Ex. 17:8; Num. 24:20; Deut. 25:17
15:3 [w]Lev. 27:28; Josh. 6:17

thousand footmen, and ten thousand men of
Judah.
5 And Saul came to a city of Amalek, and
laid wait in the valley.
6 ¶ And Saul said unto [x]the Kenites, [y]Go,
depart, get you down from among the Amalekites, lest I destroy you with them: for [z]ye
shewed kindness to all the children of Israel, when they came up out of Egypt. So
the Kenites departed from among the Amalekites.
7 [a]And Saul smote the Amalekites from
[b]Havilah *until* thou comest to [c]Shur, that *is*
over against Egypt.
8 And [d]he took Agag the king of the Amalekites alive, and [e]utterly destroyed all the
people with the edge of the sword.
9 But Saul and the people [f]spared Agag,
and the best of the sheep, and of the oxen,
and of the fatlings, and the lambs, and all
that was good, and would not utterly destroy them: but every thing *that was* vile
and refuse, that they destroyed utterly.
10 ¶ Then came the word of the LORD
unto Samuel, saying,
11 [g]It repenteth me that I have set up
Saul *to be* king: for he is [h]turned back from
following me, [i]and hath not performed my
commandments. And it [j]grieved Samuel;
and he cried unto the LORD all night.
12 And when Samuel rose early to meet
Saul in the morning, it was told Samuel,
saying, Saul came to [k]Carmel, and, behold,
he set him up a place, and is gone about, and
passed on, and gone down to Gilgal.
13 And Samuel came to Saul: and Saul
said unto him, [l]Blessed *be* thou of the
LORD: I have performed the commandment
of the LORD.
14 And Samuel said, What *meaneth* then
this bleating of the sheep in mine ears, and
the lowing of the oxen which I hear?
15 And Saul said, They have brought
them from the Amalekites: [m]for the people
spared the best of the sheep and of the oxen,
to sacrifice unto the LORD thy God; and the
rest we have utterly destroyed.
16 Then Samuel said unto Saul, Stay, and
I will tell thee what the LORD hath said to
me this night. And he said unto him,
Say on.
17 And Samuel said, [n]When thou *wast*
little in thine own sight, *wast* thou not *made*
the head of the tribes of Israel, and the LORD
anointed thee king over Israel?
18 And the LORD sent thee on a journey,
and said, Go and utterly destroy the sinners
the Amalekites, and fight against them until
they be consumed.
19 Wherefore then didst thou not obey
the voice of the LORD, but didst fly upon the
spoil, and didst evil in the sight of the LORD?
20 And Saul said unto Samuel, Yea, [o]I
have obeyed the voice of the LORD, and
have gone the way which the LORD sent me,
and have brought Agag the king of Amalek,
and have utterly destroyed the Amalekites.
21 [p]But the people took of the spoil,
sheep and oxen, the chief of the things
which should have been utterly destroyed,
to sacrifice unto the LORD thy God in Gilgal.
22 And Samuel said, [q]Hath the LORD *as*
great delight in burnt offerings and sacrifices, as in obeying the voice of the LORD?
Behold, [r]to obey *is* better than sacrifice,
and to hearken than the fat of rams.
23 For rebellion *is as* the sin of witchcraft,
and stubbornness *is as* iniquity and idolatry. Because thou hast rejected the word of
the LORD, [s]he hath also rejected thee from
being king.
24 ¶ [t]And Saul said unto Samuel, I have
sinned: for I have transgressed the commandment of the LORD, and thy words: because I [u]feared the people, and obeyed
their voice.
25 Now therefore, I pray thee, pardon my
sin, and turn again with me, that I may worship the LORD.
26 And Samuel said unto Saul, I will not
return with thee: [v]for thou hast rejected the
word of the LORD, and the LORD hath rejected thee from being king over Israel.
27 And as Samuel turned about to go
away, [w]he laid hold upon the skirt of his
mantle, and it rent.
28 And Samuel said unto him, [x]The LORD
hath rent the kingdom of Israel from thee
this day, and hath given it to a neighbour of
thine, *that is* better than thou.
29 And also the Strength of Israel [y]will
not lie nor repent: for he *is* not a man, that
he should repent.
30 Then he said, I have sinned: *yet* [z]hon-
our me now, I pray thee, before the elders of
my people, and before Israel, and turn again
with me, that I may worship the LORD thy
God.
31 So Samuel turned again after Saul;
and Saul worshipped the LORD.
32 ¶ Then said Samuel, Bring ye hither to
me Agag the king of the Amalekites. And
Agag came unto him delicately. And Agag
said, Surely the bitterness of death is past.
33 And Samuel said, [a]As thy sword hath
made women childless, so shall thy mother
be childless among women. And Samuel
hewed Agag in pieces before the LORD in
Gilgal.
34 ¶ Then Samuel went to Ramah; and
Saul went up to his house to [b]Gibeah of
Saul.
35 And [c]Samuel came no more to see
Saul until the day of his death: nevertheless
Samuel [d]mourned for Saul: and the LORD
[e]repented that he had made Saul king over
Israel.

16 And the LORD said unto Samuel,
[f]How long wilt thou mourn for Saul,
seeing [g]I have rejected him from reigning
over Israel? [h]fill thine horn with oil, and go,
I will send thee to Jesse the Beth-lehemite:
for [i]I have provided me a king among his
sons.
2 And Samuel said, How can I go? if Saul
hear *it*, he will kill me. And the LORD said,

15:6 [x]Num. 24:21; Judg. 1:16 [y]Gen. 18:25; Rev. 18:4 [z]Ex. 18:10; Num. 10:29
15:7 [a]ch. 14:48 [b]Gen. 2:11 [c]Gen. 16:7
15:8 [d]1 Kings 20:34 [e]ch. 30:1
15:9 [f]ver. 3
15:11 [g]ver. 35; Gen. 6:6; 2 Sam. 24:16 [h]Josh. 22:16; 1 Kings 9:6 [i]ch. 13:13; ver. 3 [j]ver. 35; ch. 16:1
15:12 [k]Josh. 15:55
15:13 [l]Gen. 14:19; Judg. 17:2; Ruth 3:10
15:15 [m]ver. 9; Gen. 3:12; Prov. 28:13
15:17 [n]ch. 9:21
15:20 [o]ver. 13
15:21 [p]ver. 15
15:22 [q]Ps. 50:8; Prov. 21:3; Isa. 1:11; Jer. 7:22; Mic. 6:6; Heb. 10:6 [r]Eccl. 5:1; Hos. 6:6; Matt. 5:24; Mark 12:33
15:23 [s]ch. 13:14
15:24 [t]2 Sam. 12:13 [u]Ex. 23:2; Prov. 29:25; Isa. 51:12
15:26 [v]ch. 2:30
15:27 [w]1 Kings 11:30
15:28 [x]ch. 28:17; 1 Kings 11:31
15:29 [y]Num. 23:19; Ezek. 24:14; 2 Tim. 2:13; Tit. 1:2
15:30 [z]John 5:44
15:33 [a]Ex. 17:11; Num. 14:45; Judg. 1:7
15:34 [b]ch. 11:4
15:35 [c]ch. 19:24 [d]ver. 11; ch. 16:1 [e]ver. 11
16:1 [f]ch. 15:35 [g]ch. 15:23 [h]ch. 9:16; 2 Kings 9:1 [i]Ps. 78:70; Acts 13:22

Take an heifer with thee, and say, [j]I am
come to sacrifice to the LORD.
3 And call Jesse to the sacrifice, and [k]I
will shew thee what thou shalt do: and
[l]thou shalt anoint unto me *him* whom I
name unto thee.
4 And Samuel did that which the LORD
spake, and came to Beth-lehem. And the elders of the town [m]trembled at his coming,
and said, [n]Comest thou peaceably?
5 And he said, Peaceably: I am come to
sacrifice unto the LORD: [o]sanctify yourselves, and come with me to the sacrifice.
And he sanctified Jesse and his sons, and
called them to the sacrifice.
6 ¶ And it came to pass, when they were
come, that he looked on [p]Eliab, and [q]said,
Surely the LORD's anointed *is* before him.
7 But the LORD said unto Samuel, Look
not on [r]his countenance, or on the height
of his stature; because I have refused him:
[s]for *the LORD seeth* not as man seeth; for
man [t]looketh on the outward appearance,
but the LORD looketh on the [u]heart.
8 Then Jesse called [v]Abinadab, and
made him pass before Samuel. And he said,
Neither hath the LORD chosen this.
9 Then Jesse made [w]Shammah to pass
by. And he said, Neither hath the LORD chosen this.
10 Again, Jesse made seven of his sons to
pass before Samuel. And Samuel said unto
Jesse, The LORD hath not chosen these.
11 And Samuel said unto Jesse, Are here
all *thy* children? And he said, [x]There remaineth yet the youngest, and, behold, he
keepeth the sheep. And Samuel said unto
Jesse, [y]Send and fetch him: for we will not
sit down till he come hither.
12 And he sent, and brought him in. Now
he *was* [z]ruddy, *and* withal of a beautiful
countenance, and goodly to look to. [a]And
the LORD said, Arise, anoint him: for this
is he.
13 Then Samuel took the horn of oil, and
[b]anointed him in the midst of his brethren:
and [c]the Spirit of the LORD came upon David from that day forward. So Samuel rose
up, and went to Ramah.
14 ¶ [d]But the Spirit of the LORD departed
from Saul, and [e]an evil spirit from the LORD
troubled him.
15 And Saul's servants said unto him, Behold now, an evil spirit from God troubleth
thee.
16 Let our lord now command thy servants, *which are* [f]before thee, to seek out a
man, *who is* a cunning player on an harp:
and it shall come to pass, when the evil
spirit from God is upon thee, that he shall
[g]play with his hand, and thou shalt be well.
17 And Saul said unto his servants, Provide me now a man that can play well, and
bring *him* to me.
18 Then answered one of the servants,
and said, Behold, I have seen a son of Jesse
the Beth-lehemite, *that is* cunning in playing, and [h]a mighty valiant man, and a man
of war, and prudent in matters, and a
comely person, and [i]the LORD *is* with him.
19 ¶ Wherefore Saul sent messengers
unto Jesse, and said, Send me David thy
son, [j]which *is* with the sheep.
20 And Jesse [k]took an ass *laden* with
bread, and a bottle of wine, and a kid, and
sent *them* by David his son unto Saul.
21 And David came to Saul, and [l]stood
before him: and he loved him greatly; and
he became his armourbearer.
22 And Saul sent to Jesse, saying, Let David, I pray thee, stand before me; for he hath
found favour in my sight.
23 And it came to pass, when [m]the *evil*
spirit from God was upon Saul, that David
took an harp, and played with his hand: so
Saul was refreshed, and was well, and the
evil spirit departed from him.

17 Now the Philistines [n]gathered together their armies to battle, and
were gathered together at [o]Shochoh, which
belongeth to Judah, and pitched between
Shochoh and Azekah, in Ephes-dammim.
2 And Saul and the men of Israel were
gathered together, and pitched by the valley
of Elah, and set the battle in array against
the Philistines.
3 And the Philistines stood on a mountain
on the one side, and Israel stood on a mountain on the other side: and *there was* a valley between them.
4 ¶ And there went out a champion out of
the camp of the Philistines, named [p]Goli-
ath, of [q]Gath, whose height *was* six cubits
and a span.
5 And *he had* an helmet of brass upon his
head, and he *was* armed with a coat of mail;
and the weight of the coat *was* five thousand shekels of brass.
6 And *he had* greaves of brass upon his
legs, and a target of brass between his
shoulders.
7 And the [r]staff of his spear *was* like a
weaver's beam; and his spear's head
weighed six hundred shekels of iron: and
one bearing a shield went before him.
8 And he stood and cried unto the armies
of Israel, and said unto them, Why are ye
come out to set *your* battle in array? *am* not
I a Philistine, and ye [s]servants to Saul?
choose you a man for you, and let him come
down to me.
9 If he be able to fight with me, and to kill
me, then will we be your servants: but if I
prevail against him, and kill him, then shall
ye be our servants, and [t]serve us.
10 And the Philistine said, I [u]defy the armies of Israel this day; give me a man, that
we may fight together.
11 When Saul and all Israel heard those
words of the Philistine, they were dismayed, and greatly afraid.
12 ¶ Now David *was* [v]the son of that
[w]Ephrathite of Beth-lehem-judah, whose
name *was* Jesse; and he had [x]eight sons:
and the man went among men *for* an old
man in the days of Saul.

16:2 j ch. 9:12
16:3 k Ex. 4:15; l ch. 9:16
16:4 m ch. 21:1; n 1 Kings 2:13; 2 Kings 9:22
16:5 o Ex. 19:10
16:6 p ch. 17:13; 1 Chron. 27:18; q 1 Kings 12:26
16:7 r Ps. 147:10; s Isa. 55:8; t 2 Cor. 10:7; u 1 Kings 8:39; 1 Chron. 28:9; Ps. 7:9; Jer. 11:20; Acts 1:24
16:8 v ch. 17:13
16:9 w ch. 17:13
16:11 x ch. 17:12; y 2 Sam. 7:8; Ps. 78:70
16:12 z ch. 17:42; SSol. 5:10; a ch. 9:17
16:13 b ch. 10:1; Ps. 89:20; c Num. 27:18; Judg. 11:29; ch. 10:6
16:14 d ch. 11:6; Judg. 16:20; Ps. 51:11; e Judg. 9:23; ch. 18:10
16:16 f Gen. 41:46; ver. 21; 1 Kings 10:8; g ver. 23; 2 Kings 3:15
16:18 h ch. 17:32; i ch. 3:19
16:19 j ver. 11; ch. 17:15
16:20 k ch. 10:27; Gen. 43:11; Prov. 18:16
16:21 l Gen. 41:46; 1 Kings 10:8; Prov. 22:29
16:23 m ver. 14
17:1 n ch. 13:5; o Josh. 15:35; 2 Chron. 28:18
17:4 p 2 Sam. 21:19; q Josh. 11:22
17:7 r 2 Sam. 21:19
17:8 s ch. 8:17
17:9 t ch. 11:1
17:10 u ver. 26; 2 Sam. 21:21
17:12 v ver. 58; Ruth 4:22; ch. 16:1; w Gen. 35:19; x ch. 16:10; 1 Chron. 2:13

13 And the three eldest sons of Jesse went *and* followed Saul to the battle: and the [y]names of his three sons that went to the battle *were* Eliab the firstborn, and next unto him Abinadab, and the third Shammah.
14 And David *was* the youngest: and the three eldest followed Saul.
15 But David went and returned from Saul [z]to feed his father's sheep at Bethlehem.
16 And the Philistine drew near morning and evening, and presented himself forty days.
17 And Jesse said unto David his son, Take now for thy brethren an ephah of this parched *corn,* and these ten loaves, and run to the camp to thy brethren;
18 And carry these ten cheeses unto the captain of *their* thousand, and [a]look how thy brethren fare, and take their pledge.
19 Now Saul, and they, and all the men of Israel, *were* in the valley of Elah, fighting with the Philistines.
20 ¶ And David rose up early in the morning, and left the sheep with a keeper, and took, and went, as Jesse had commanded him; and he came to the trench, as the host was going forth to the fight, and shouted for the battle.
21 For Israel and the Philistines had put the battle in array, army against army.
22 And David left his carriage in the hand of the keeper of the carriage, and ran into the army, and came and saluted his brethren.
23 And as he talked with them, behold, there came up the champion, the Philistine of Gath, Goliath by name, out of the armies of the Philistines, and spake [b]according to the same words: and David heard *them.*
24 And all the men of Israel, when they saw the man, fled from him, and were sore afraid.
25 And the men of Israel said, Have ye seen this man that is come up? surely to defy Israel is he come up: and it shall be, *that* the man who killeth him, the king will enrich him with great riches, and [c]will give him his daughter, and make his father's house free in Israel.
26 And David spake to the men that stood by him, saying, What shall be done to the man that killeth this Philistine, and taketh away [d]the reproach from Israel? for who *is* this [e]uncircumcised Philistine, that he should [f]defy the armies of [g]the living God?
27 And the people answered him after this manner, saying, [h]So shall it be done to the man that killeth him.
28 ¶ And Eliab his eldest brother heard when he spake unto the men; and Eliab's [i]anger was kindled against David, and he said, Why camest thou down hither? and with whom hast thou left those few sheep in the wilderness? I know thy pride, and the naughtiness of thine heart; for thou art come down that thou mightest see the battle.
29 And David said, What have I now done? [j]*Is there* not a cause?
30 ¶ And he turned from him toward another, and [k]spake after the same manner: and the people answered him again after the former manner.
31 And when the words were heard which David spake, they rehearsed *them* before Saul: and he sent for him.
32 ¶ And David said to Saul, [l]Let no man's heart fail because of him; [m]thy servant will go and fight with this Philistine.
33 And Saul said to David, [n]Thou art not able to go against this Philistine to fight with him: for thou *art but* a youth, and he a man of war from his youth.
34 And David said unto Saul, Thy servant kept his father's sheep, and there came a lion, and a bear, and took a lamb out of the flock:
35 And I went out after him, and smote him, and delivered *it* out of his mouth: and when he arose against me, I caught *him* by his beard, and smote him, and slew him.
36 Thy servant slew both the lion and the bear: and this uncircumcised Philistine shall be as one of them, seeing he hath defied the armies of the living God.
37 David said moreover, [o]The LORD that delivered me out of the paw of the lion, and out of the paw of the bear, he will deliver me out of the hand of this Philistine. And Saul said unto David, Go, and [p]the LORD be with thee.
38 ¶ And Saul armed David with his armour, and he put an helmet of brass upon his head; also he armed him with a coat of mail.
39 And David girded his sword upon his armour, and he assayed to go; for he had not proved *it.* And David said unto Saul, I cannot go with these; for I have not proved *them.* And David put them off him.
40 And he took his staff in his hand, and chose him five smooth stones out of the brook, and put them in a shepherd's bag which he had, even in a scrip; and his sling *was* in his hand: and he drew near to the Philistine.
41 And the Philistine came on and drew near unto David; and the man that bare the shield *went* before him.
42 And when the Philistine looked about, and saw David, he [q]disdained him: for he was *but* a youth, and [r]ruddy, and of a fair countenance.
43 And the Philistine said unto David, [s]*Am* I a dog, that thou comest to me with staves? And the Philistine cursed David by his gods.
44 And the Philistine [t]said to David, Come to me, and I will give thy flesh unto the fowls of the air, and to the beasts of the field.
45 Then said David to the Philistine, Thou comest to me with a sword, and with a

17:13 [y]ch. 16:6; 1 Chron. 2:13
17:15 [z]ch. 16:19
17:18 [a]Gen. 37:14
17:23 [b]ver. 8
17:25 [c]Josh. 15:16
17:26 [d]ch. 11:2 [e]ch. 14:6 [f]ver. 10 [g]Deut. 5:26
17:27 [h]ver. 25
17:28 [i]Gen. 37:4; Matt. 10:36
17:29 [j]ver. 17
17:30 [k]ver. 26
17:32 [l]Deut. 20:1 [m]ch. 16:18
17:33 [n]Num. 13:31; Deut. 9:2
17:37 [o]Ps. 18:16; 2 Cor. 1:10; 2 Tim. 4:17 [p]ch. 20:13; 1 Chron. 22:11
17:42 [q]Ps. 123:4; 1 Cor. 1:27 [r]ch. 16:12
17:43 [s]ch. 24:14; 2 Sam. 3:8; 2 Kings 8:13
17:44 [t]1 Kings 20:10

spear, and with a shield: [u]but I come to thee in the name of the LORD of hosts, the God of the armies of Israel, whom thou hast [v]defied.

46 This day will the LORD deliver thee into mine hand; and I will smite thee, and take thine head from thee; and I will give [w]the carcases of the host of the Philistines this day unto the fowls of the air, and to the wild beasts of the earth; [x]that all the earth may know that there is a God in Israel.

47 And all this assembly shall know that the LORD [y]saveth not with sword and spear: for [z]the battle *is* the LORD's, and he will give you into our hands.

48 And it came to pass, when the Philistine arose, and came and drew nigh to meet David, that David hasted, and ran toward the army to meet the Philistine.

49 And David put his hand in his bag, and took thence a stone, and slang *it*, and smote the Philistine in his forehead, that the stone sunk into his forehead; and he fell upon his face to the earth.

50 So [a]David prevailed over the Philistine with a sling and with a stone, and smote the Philistine, and slew him; but *there was* no sword in the hand of David.

51 Therefore David ran, and stood upon the Philistine, and took his sword, and drew it out of the sheath thereof, and slew him, and cut off his head therewith. And when the Philistines saw their champion was dead, [b]they fled.

52 And the men of Israel and of Judah arose, and shouted, and pursued the Philistines, until thou come to the valley, and to the gates of Ekron. And the wounded of the Philistines fell down by the way to [c]Shaaraim, even unto Gath, and unto Ekron.

53 And the children of Israel returned from chasing after the Philistines, and they spoiled their tents.

54 And David took the head of the Philistine, and brought it to Jerusalem; but he put his armour in his tent.

55 ¶ And when Saul saw David go forth against the Philistine, he said unto Abner, the captain of the host, Abner, [d]whose son *is* this youth? And Abner said, *As* thy soul liveth, O king, I cannot tell.

56 And the king said, Enquire thou whose son the stripling *is*.

57 And as David returned from the slaughter of the Philistine, Abner took him, and brought him before Saul [e]with the head of the Philistine in his hand.

58 And Saul said to him, Whose son *art* thou, *thou* young man? And David answered, [f]*I am* the son of thy servant Jesse the Beth-lehemite.

18

And it came to pass, when he had made an end of speaking unto Saul, that [g]the soul of Jonathan was knit with the soul of David, [h]and Jonathan loved him as his own soul.

2 And Saul took him that day, [i]and would let him go no more home to his father's house.

3 Then Jonathan and David made a covenant, because he loved him as his own soul.

4 And Jonathan stripped himself of the robe that *was* upon him, and gave it to David, and his garments, even to his sword, and to his bow, and to his girdle.

5 ¶ And David went out whithersoever Saul sent him, *and* behaved himself wisely: and Saul set him over the men of war, and he was accepted in the sight of all the people, and also in the sight of Saul's servants.

6 And it came to pass as they came, when David was returned from the slaughter of the Philistine, that [j]the women came out of all cities of Israel, singing and dancing, to meet king Saul, with tabrets, with joy, and with instruments of musick.

7 And the women [k]answered *one another* as they played, and said, [l]Saul hath slain his thousands, and David his ten thousands.

8 And Saul was very wroth, and the saying [m]displeased him; and he said, They have ascribed unto David ten thousands, and to me they have ascribed *but* thousands: and *what* can he have more but [n]the kingdom?

9 And Saul eyed David from that day and forward.

10 ¶ And it came to pass on the morrow, that [o]the evil spirit from God came upon Saul, [p]and he prophesied in the midst of the house: and David played with his hand, as at other times: [q]and *there was* a javelin in Saul's hand.

11 And Saul [r]cast the javelin; for he said, I will smite David even to the wall *with it*. And David avoided out of his presence twice.

12 ¶ And Saul was [s]afraid of David, because [t]the LORD was with him, and was [u]departed from Saul.

13 Therefore Saul removed him from him, and made him his captain over a thousand; and [v]he went out and came in before the people.

14 And David behaved himself wisely in all his ways; and [w]the LORD *was* with him.

15 Wherefore when Saul saw that he behaved himself very wisely, he was afraid of him.

16 But [x]all Israel and Judah loved David, because he went out and came in before them.

17 ¶ And Saul said to David, Behold my elder daughter Merab, [y]her will I give thee to wife: only be thou valiant for me, and fight [z]the LORD's battles. For Saul said, [a]Let not mine hand be upon him, but let the hand of the Philistines be upon him.

18 And David said unto Saul, [b]Who *am* I? and what *is* my life, *or* my father's family in Israel, that I should be son in law to the king?

19 But it came to pass at the time when

17:45 [u]2 Sam. 22:33; Ps. 124:8; 2 Cor. 10:4; Heb. 11:33 [v]ver. 10
17:46 [w]Deut. 28:26 [x]Josh. 4:24; 1 Kings 8:43; 2 Kings 19:19; Isa. 52:10
17:47 [y]Ps. 44:6; Hos. 1:7; Zech. 4:6 [z]2 Chron. 20:15
17:50 [a]Judg. 3:31; ch. 21:9
17:51 [b]Heb. 11:34
17:52 [c]Josh. 15:36
17:55 [d]ch. 16:21
17:57 [e]ver. 54
17:58 [f]ver. 12
18:1 [g]Gen. 44:30 [h]ch. 19:2; 2 Sam. 1:26; Deut. 13:6
18:2 [i]ch. 17:15
18:6 [j]Ex. 15:20; Judg. 11:34
18:7 [k]Ex. 15:21 [l]ch. 21:11
18:8 [m]Eccl. 4:4 [n]ch. 15:28
18:10 [o]ch. 16:14 [p]ch. 19:24; 1 Kings 18:29; Acts 16:16 [q]ch. 19:9
18:11 [r]ch. 19:10; Prov. 27:4
18:12 [s]ver. 15:29 [t]ch. 16:13 [u]ch. 16:14
18:13 [v]ver. 16; Num. 27:17; 2 Sam. 5:2
18:14 [w]Gen. 39:2; Josh. 6:27
18:16 [x]ver. 5
18:17 [y]ch. 17:25 [z]Num. 32:20; ch. 25:28 [a]ver. 21; 2 Sam. 12:9
18:18 [b]ver. 23; ch. 9:21; 2 Sam. 7:18

Merab Saul's daughter should have been
given to David, that she was given unto
[c]Adriel the [d]Meholathite to wife.
20 [e]And Michal Saul's daughter loved
David: and they told Saul, and the thing
pleased him.
21 And Saul said, I will give him her, that
she may be [f]a snare to him, and that [g]the
hand of the Philistines may be against him.
Wherefore Saul said to David, Thou shalt
[h]this day be my son in law in *the one of* the
twain.
22 ¶ And Saul commanded his servants,
saying, Commune with David secretly, and
say, Behold, the king hath delight in thee,
and all his servants love thee: now therefore
be the king's son in law.
23 And Saul's servants spake those
words in the ears of David. And David said,
Seemeth it to you *a* light *thing* to be a king's
son in law, seeing that I *am* a poor man, and
lightly esteemed?
24 And the servants of Saul told him, saying, On this manner spake David.
25 And Saul said, Thus shall ye say to David, The king desireth not any [i]dowry, but
an hundred foreskins of the Philistines, to
be [j]avenged of the king's enemies. But Saul
[k]thought to make David fall by the hand of
the Philistines.
26 And when his servants told David
these words, it pleased David well to be the
king's son in law: and [l]the days were not
expired.
27 Wherefore David arose and went, he
and [m]his men, and slew of the Philistines
two hundred men; and [n]David brought
their foreskins, and they gave them in full
tale to the king, that he might be the king's
son in law. And Saul gave him Michal his
daughter to wife.
28 ¶ And Saul saw and knew that the
LORD *was* with David, and *that* Michal
Saul's daughter loved him.
29 And Saul was yet the more afraid of
David; and Saul became David's enemy
continually.
30 Then the princes of the Philistines
[o]went forth: and it came to pass, after they
went forth, *that* David [p]behaved himself
more wisely than all the servants of Saul; so
that his name was much set by.

19 And Saul spake to Jonathan his son,
and to all his servants, that they
should kill David.
2 But Jonathan Saul's son [q]delighted
much in David: and Jonathan told David,
saying, Saul my father seeketh to kill thee:
now therefore, I pray thee, take heed to thyself until the morning, and abide in a secret
place, and hide thyself:
3 And I will go out and stand beside my
father in the field where thou *art*, and I will
commune with my father of thee; and what
I see, that I will tell thee.
4 ¶ And Jonathan [r]spake good of David
unto Saul his father, and said unto him,
Let not the king [s]sin against his servant,
against David; because he hath not sinned
against thee, and because his works *have
been* to thee-ward very good:
5 For he did put his [t]life in his hand,
and [u]slew the Philistine, and [v]the LORD
wrought a great salvation for all Israel: thou
sawest *it*, and didst rejoice: [w]wherefore
then wilt thou [x]sin against innocent blood,
to slay David without a cause?
6 And Saul hearkened unto the voice of
Jonathan: and Saul sware, *As* the LORD liveth, he shall not be slain.
7 And Jonathan called David, and Jonathan shewed him all those things. And Jonathan brought David to Saul, and he was in
his presence, [y]as in times past.
8 ¶ And there was war again: and David
went out, and fought with the Philistines,
and slew them with a great slaughter; and
they fled from him.
9 And [z]the evil spirit from the LORD was
upon Saul, as he sat in his house with his
javelin in his hand: and David played with
his hand.
10 And Saul sought to smite David even
to the wall with the javelin; but he slipped
away out of Saul's presence, and he smote
the javelin into the wall: and David fled, and
escaped that night.
11 [a]Saul also sent messengers unto David's house, to watch him, and to slay him in
the morning: and Michal David's wife told
him, saying, If thou save not thy life to
night, to morrow thou shalt be slain.
12 ¶ So Michal [b]let David down through
a window: and he went, and fled, and escaped.
13 And Michal took an image, and laid *it*
in the bed, and put a pillow of goats' *hair* for
his bolster, and covered *it* with a cloth.
14 And when Saul sent messengers to
take David, she said, He *is* sick.
15 And Saul sent the messengers *again* to
see David, saying, Bring him up to me in the
bed, that I may slay him.
16 And when the messengers were come
in, behold, *there was* an image in the bed,
with a pillow of goats' *hair* for his bolster.
17 And Saul said unto Michal, Why hast
thou deceived me so, and sent away mine
enemy, that he is escaped? And Michal answered Saul, He said unto me, Let me go;
[c]why should I kill thee?
18 ¶ So David fled, and escaped, and
came to Samuel to Ramah, and told him all
that Saul had done to him. And he and Samuel went and dwelt in Naioth.
19 And it was told Saul, saying, Behold,
David *is* at Naioth in Ramah.
20 And [d]Saul sent messengers to take
David: [e]and when they saw the company
of the prophets prophesying, and Samuel
standing *as* appointed over them, the Spirit
of God was upon the messengers of Saul,
and they also [f]prophesied.
21 And when it was told Saul, he sent
other messengers, and they prophesied

18:19 [c]2 Sam. 21:8 [d]Judg. 7:22
18:20 [e]ver. 28
18:21 [f]Ex. 10:7 [g]ver. 17 [h]ver. 26
18:25 [i]Gen. 34:12; Ex. 22:17 [j]ch. 14:24 [k]ver. 17
18:26 [l]ver. 21
18:27 [m]ver. 13 [n]2 Sam. 3:14
18:30 [o]2 Sam. 11:1 [p]ver. 5
19:2 [q]ch. 18:1
19:4 [r]Prov. 31:8 [s]Gen. 42:22; Ps. 35:12; Prov. 17:13; Jer. 18:20
19:5 [t]Judg. 9:17; ch. 28:21; Ps. 119:109 [u]ch. 17:49 [v]1 Sam. 11:13; 1 Chron. 11:14 [w]ch. 20:32 [x]Matt. 27:4
19:7 [y]ch. 16:21
19:9 [z]ch. 16:14
19:11 [a]Ps. 59, title
19:12 [b]Josh. 2:15; Acts 9:24
19:17 [c]2 Sam. 2:22
19:20 [d]John 7:32 [e]1 Cor. 14:3; ch. 10:5 [f]Num. 11:25; Joel 2:28

likewise. And Saul sent messengers again the third time, and they prophesied also.

22 Then went he also to Ramah, and came to a great well that *is* in Sechu: and he asked and said, Where *are* Samuel and David? And *one* said, Behold, *they be* at Naioth in Ramah.

23 And he went thither to Naioth in Ramah: and [g]the Spirit of God was upon him also, and he went on, and prophesied, until he came to Naioth in Ramah.

24 [h]And he stripped off his clothes also, and prophesied before Samuel in like manner, and lay down [i]naked all that day and all that night. Wherefore they say, [j]*Is* Saul also among the prophets?

20

And David fled from Naioth in Ramah, and came and said before Jonathan, What have I done? what *is* mine iniquity? and what *is* my sin before thy father, that he seeketh my life?

2 And he said unto him, God forbid; thou shalt not die: behold, my father will do nothing either great or small, but that he will shew it me: and why should my father hide this thing from me? it *is* not *so*.

3 And David sware moreover, and said, Thy father certainly knoweth that I have found grace in thine eyes; and he saith, Let not Jonathan know this, lest he be grieved: but truly, *as* the LORD liveth, and *as* thy soul liveth, *there is* but a step between me and death.

4 Then said Jonathan unto David, Whatsoever thy soul desireth, I will even do *it* for thee.

5 And David said unto Jonathan, Behold, to morrow *is* the [k]new moon, and I should not fail to sit with the king at meat: but let me go, that I may [l]hide myself in the field unto the third *day* at even.

6 If thy father at all miss me, then say, David earnestly asked *leave* of me that he might run [m]to Beth-lehem his city: for *there is* a yearly sacrifice there for all the family.

7 [n]If he say thus, *It is* well; thy servant shall have peace: but if he be very wroth, *then* be sure that [o]evil is determined by him.

8 Therefore thou shalt [p]deal kindly with thy servant; for [q]thou hast brought thy servant into a covenant of the LORD with thee: notwithstanding, [r]if there be in me iniquity, slay me thyself; for why shouldest thou bring me to thy father?

9 And Jonathan said, Far be it from thee: for if I knew certainly that evil were determined by my father to come upon thee, then would not I tell it thee?

10 Then said David to Jonathan, Who shall tell me? or what *if* thy father answer thee roughly?

11 ¶ And Jonathan said unto David, Come, and let us go out into the field. And they went out both of them into the field.

12 And Jonathan said unto David, O LORD God of Israel, when I have sounded my father about to morrow any time, *or* the third *day*, and, behold, *if there be* good toward David, and I then send not unto thee, and shew it thee;

13 [s]The LORD do so and much more to Jonathan: but if it please my father *to do* thee evil, then I will shew it thee, and send thee away, that thou mayest go in peace: and [t]the LORD be with thee, as he hath been with my father.

14 And thou shalt not only while yet I live shew me the kindness of the LORD, that I die not:

15 But *also* [u]thou shalt not cut off thy kindness from my house for ever: no, not when the LORD hath cut off the enemies of David every one from the face of the earth.

16 So Jonathan made *a covenant* with the house of David, *saying,* [v]Let the LORD even require *it* at the hand of David's enemies.

17 And Jonathan caused David to swear again, because he loved him: [w]for he loved him as he loved his own soul.

18 Then Jonathan said to David, [x]To morrow *is* the new moon: and thou shalt be missed, because thy seat will be empty.

19 And *when* thou hast stayed three days, *then* thou shalt go down quickly, and come to [y]the place where thou didst hide thyself when the business was *in hand,* and shalt remain by the stone Ezel.

20 And I will shoot three arrows on the side *thereof,* as though I shot at a mark.

21 And, behold, I will send a lad, *saying,* Go, find out the arrows. If I expressly say unto the lad, Behold, the arrows *are* on this side of thee, take them; then come thou: for *there is* peace to thee, and no hurt; [z]*as* the LORD liveth.

22 But if I say thus unto the young man, Behold, the arrows *are* beyond thee; go thy way: for the LORD hath sent thee away.

23 And *as touching* [a]the matter which thou and I have spoken of, behold, the LORD *be* between thee and me for ever.

24 ¶ So David hid himself in the field: and when the new moon was come, the king sat him down to eat meat.

25 And the king sat upon his seat, as at other times, *even* upon a seat by the wall: and Jonathan arose, and Abner sat by Saul's side, and David's place was empty.

26 Nevertheless Saul spake not any thing that day: for he thought, something hath befallen him, he *is* not clean; surely he *is* [b]not clean.

27 And it came to pass on the morrow, *which was* the second *day* of the month, that David's place was empty: and Saul said unto Jonathan his son, Wherefore cometh not the son of Jesse to meat, neither yesterday, nor to day?

28 And Jonathan [c]answered Saul, David earnestly asked *leave* of me *to go* to Beth-lehem:

29 And he said, Let me go, I pray thee; for our family hath a sacrifice in the city; and my brother, he hath commanded me *to be there:* and now, if I have found favour in

19:23 [g]ch. 10:10
19:24 [h]Isa. 20:2 [i]2 Sam. 6:14; Mic. 1:8 [j]ch. 10:11
20:5 [k]Num. 10:10 [l]ch. 19:2
20:6 [m]ch. 16:4
20:7 [n]Deut. 1:23; 2 Sam. 17:4 [o]ch. 25:17; Esth. 7:7
20:8 [p]Josh. 2:14 [q]ver. 16; ch. 18:3 [r]2 Sam. 14:32
20:13 [s]Ruth 1:17 [t]Josh. 1:5; ch. 17:37; 1 Chron. 22:11
20:15 [u]2 Sam. 9:1
20:16 [v]ch. 25:22; 2 Sam. 4:7
20:17 [w]ch. 18:1
20:18 [x]ver. 5
20:19 [y]ch. 19:2
20:21 [z]Jer. 4:2
20:23 [a]ver. 14
20:26 [b]Lev. 7:21
20:28 [c]ver. 6

thine eyes, let me get away, I pray thee, and
see my brethren. Therefore he cometh not
unto the king's table.
30 Then Saul's anger was kindled against
Jonathan, and he said unto him, Thou son
of the perverse rebellious *woman*, do not I
know that thou hast chosen the son of Jesse
to thine own confusion, and unto the confusion of thy mother's nakedness?
31 For as long as the son of Jesse liveth
upon the ground, thou shalt not be established, nor thy kingdom. Wherefore now
send and fetch him unto me, for he shall
surely die.
32 And Jonathan answered Saul his father, and said unto him, [d]Wherefore shall
he be slain? what hath he done?
33 And Saul [e]cast a javelin at him to
smite him: [f]whereby Jonathan knew that it
was determined of his father to slay David.
34 So Jonathan arose from the table in
fierce anger, and did eat no meat the second
day of the month: for he was grieved for
David, because his father had done him
shame.
35 ¶ And it came to pass in the morning,
that Jonathan went out into the field at the
time appointed with David, and a little lad
with him.
36 And he said unto his lad, Run, find out
now the arrows which I shoot. *And* as the
lad ran, he shot an arrow beyond him.
37 And when the lad was come to the
place of the arrow which Jonathan had
shot, Jonathan cried after the lad, and said,
Is not the arrow beyond thee?
38 And Jonathan cried after the lad,
Make speed, haste, stay not. And Jonathan's lad gathered up the arrows, and
came to his master.
39 But the lad knew not any thing: only
Jonathan and David knew the matter.
40 And Jonathan gave his artillery unto
his lad, and said unto him, Go, carry *them*
to the city.
41 ¶ *And* as soon as the lad was gone,
David arose out of *a place* toward the south,
and fell on his face to the ground, and
bowed himself three times: and they kissed
one another, and wept one with another,
until David exceeded.
42 And Jonathan said to David, [g]Go in
peace, forasmuch as we have sworn both of
us in the name of the LORD, saying, The
LORD be between me and thee, and between
my seed and thy seed for ever. And he arose
and departed: and Jonathan went into the
city.

21 Then came David to Nob to [h]Ahime-
lech the priest: and Ahimelech was
[i]afraid at the meeting of David, and said
unto him, Why *art* thou alone, and no man
with thee?
2 And David said unto Ahimelech the
priest, The king hath commanded me a
business, and hath said unto me, Let no
man know any thing of the business where-
about I send thee, and what I have commanded thee: and I have appointed *my*
servants to such and such a place.
3 Now therefore what is under thine
hand? give *me* five *loaves of* bread in mine
hand, or what there is present.
4 And the priest answered David, and
said, *There is* no common bread under mine
hand, but there is [j]hallowed bread; [k]if the
young men have kept themselves at least
from women.
5 And David answered the priest, and
said unto him, Of a truth women *have been*
kept from us about these three days, since I
came out, and the [l]vessels of the young
men are holy, and *the bread is* in a manner
common, yea, though it were sanctified this
day [m]in the vessel.
6 So the priest [n]gave him hallowed
bread: for there was no bread there but the
shewbread, [o]that was taken from before
the LORD, to put hot bread in the day when
it was taken away.
7 Now a certain man of the servants of
Saul *was* there that day, detained before the
LORD; and his name *was* [p]Doeg, an Edomite, the chiefest of the herdmen that *belonged* to Saul.
8 ¶ And David said unto Ahimelech, And
is there not here under thine hand spear or
sword? for I have neither brought my sword
nor my weapons with me, because the
king's business required haste.
9 And the priest said, The sword of Goliath the Philistine, whom thou slewest in
[q]the valley of Elah, [r]behold, it *is here*
wrapped in a cloth behind the ephod: if thou
wilt take that, take *it:* for *there is* no other
save that here. And David said, *There is*
none like that; give it me.
10 ¶ And David arose, and fled that day
for fear of Saul, and went to Achish the king
of Gath.
11 And [s]the servants of Achish said unto
him, *Is* not this David the king of the land?
did they not sing one to another of him in
dances, saying, [t]Saul hath slain his thousands, and David his ten thousands?
12 And David [u]laid up these words in his
heart, and was sore afraid of Achish the
king of Gath.
13 And [v]he changed his behaviour before
them, and feigned himself mad in their
hands, and scrabbled on the doors of the
gate, and let his spittle fall down upon his
beard.
14 Then said Achish unto his servants,
Lo, ye see the man is mad: wherefore *then*
have ye brought him to me?
15 Have I need of mad men, that ye have
brought this *fellow* to play the mad man in
my presence? shall this *fellow* come into my
house?

22 David therefore departed thence,
and [w]escaped [x]to the cave Adullam:
and when his brethren and all his father's
house heard *it*, they went down thither to
him.
2 [y]And every one *that was* in distress,

20:32 [d]ch. 19:5; Matt. 27:23; Luke 23:22
20:33 [e]ch. 18:11 [f]ver. 7
20:42 [g]ch. 1:17
21:1 [h]ch. 14:3; Mark 2:26 [i]ch. 16:4
21:4 [j]Ex. 25:30; Lev. 24:5; Matt. 12:4 [k]Ex. 19:15; Zech. 7:3
21:5 [l]1 Thess. 4:4 [m]Lev. 8:26
21:6 [n]Matt. 12:3; Mark 2:25; Luke 6:3 [o]Lev. 24:8
21:7 [p]ch. 22:9; Ps. 52, title
21:9 [q]ch. 17:2 [r]ch. 31:10
21:11 [s]Ps. 56, title [t]ch. 18:7
21:12 [u]Luke 2:19
21:13 [v]Ps. 34, title
22:1 [w]Ps. 57, title [x]2 Sam. 23:13
22:2 [y]Judg. 11:3

and every one that *was* in debt, and every
one *that was* discontented, gathered themselves unto him; and he became a captain
over them: and there were with him about
four hundred men.
3 ¶ And David went thence to Mizpeh of
Moab: and he said unto the king of Moab,
Let my father and my mother, I pray thee,
come forth, *and be* with you, till I know
what God will do for me.
4 And he brought them before the king of
Moab: and they dwelt with him all the while
that David was in the hold.
5 ¶ And the prophet [z]Gad said unto David, Abide not in the hold; depart, and get
thee into the land of Judah. Then David departed, and came into the forest of Hareth.
6 ¶ When Saul heard that David was discovered, and the men that *were* with him,
(now Saul abode in Gibeah under a tree in
Ramah, having his spear in his hand, and all
his servants *were* standing about him;)
7 Then Saul said unto his servants that
stood about him, Hear now, ye Benjamites;
will the son of Jesse [a]give every one of you
fields and vineyards, *and* make you all captains of thousands, and captains of hundreds;
8 That all of you have conspired against
me, and *there is* none that sheweth me that
[b]my son hath made a league with the son of
Jesse, and *there is* none of you that is sorry
for me, or sheweth unto me that my son
hath stirred up my servant against me, to lie
in wait, as at this day?
9 ¶ Then answered [c]Doeg the Edomite,
which was set over the servants of Saul, and
said, I saw the son of Jesse coming to Nob,
to [d]Ahimelech the son of [e]Ahitub.
10 [f]And he enquired of the LORD for him,
and [g]gave him victuals, and gave him the
sword of Goliath the Philistine.
11 Then the king sent to call Ahimelech
the priest, the son of Ahitub, and all his father's house, the priests that *were* in Nob:
and they came all of them to the king.
12 And Saul said, Hear now, thou son of
Ahitub. And he answered, Here I *am*, my
lord.
13 And Saul said unto him, Why have ye
conspired against me, thou and the son of
Jesse, in that thou hast given him bread,
and a sword, and hast enquired of God for
him, that he should rise against me, to lie in
wait, as at this day?
14 Then Ahimelech answered the king,
and said, And who *is so* faithful among all
thy servants as David, which is the king's
son in law, and goeth at thy bidding, and is
honourable in thine house?
15 Did I then begin to enquire of God for
him? be it far from me: let not the king impute *any* thing unto his servant, *nor* to all
the house of my father: for thy servant
knew nothing of all this, less or more.
16 And the king said, Thou shalt surely
die, Ahimelech, thou, and all thy father's
house.

22:5 [z]2 Sam. 24:11; 1 Chron. 21:9; 2 Chron. 29:25
22:7 [a]ch. 8:14
22:8 [b]ch. 18:3
22:9 [c]ch. 21:7; Ps. 52, title [d]ch. 21:1 [e]ch. 14:3
22:10 [f]Num. 27:21 [g]ch. 21:6
22:17 [h]Ex. 1:17
22:18 [i]ch. 2:31
22:19 [j]ver. 9
22:20 [k]ch. 23:6 [l]ch. 2:33
22:23 [m]1 Kings 2:26
23:1 [n]Josh. 15:44
23:2 [o]ver. 4; ch. 30:8; 2 Sam. 5:19
23:6 [p]ch. 22:20
23:9 [q]Num. 27:21; ch. 30:7

17 ¶ And the king said unto the footmen
that stood about him, Turn, and slay the
priests of the LORD; because their hand also
is with David, and because they knew when
he fled, and did not shew it to me. But the
servants of the king [h]would not put forth
their hand to fall upon the priests of the
LORD.
18 And the king said to Doeg, Turn thou,
and fall upon the priests. And Doeg the
Edomite turned, and he fell upon the
priests, and [i]slew on that day fourscore
and five persons that did wear a linen
ephod.
19 [j]And Nob, the city of the priests,
smote he with the edge of the sword, both
men and women, children and sucklings,
and oxen, and asses, and sheep, with the
edge of the sword.
20 ¶ [k]And one of the sons of Ahimelech
the son of Ahitub, named Abiathar, [l]es-
caped, and fled after David.
21 And Abiathar shewed David that Saul
had slain the LORD's priests.
22 And David said unto Abiathar, I knew
it that day, when Doeg the Edomite *was*
there, that he would surely tell Saul: I have
occasioned *the death* of all the persons of
thy father's house.
23 Abide thou with me, fear not: [m]for he
that seeketh my life seeketh thy life: but
with me thou *shalt be* in safeguard.

23

Then they told David, saying, Behold, the Philistines fight against
[n]Keilah, and they rob the threshingfloors.
2 Therefore David [o]enquired of the
LORD, saying, Shall I go and smite these
Philistines? And the LORD said unto David,
Go, and smite the Philistines, and save Keilah.
3 And David's men said unto him, Behold, we be afraid here in Judah: how much
more then if we come to Keilah against the
armies of the Philistines?
4 Then David enquired of the LORD yet
again. And the LORD answered him and
said, Arise, go down to Keilah; for I will
deliver the Philistines into thine hand.
5 So David and his men went to Keilah,
and fought with the Philistines, and brought
away their cattle, and smote them with a
great slaughter. So David saved the inhabitants of Keilah.
6 And it came to pass, when Abiathar the
son of Ahimelech [p]fled to David to Keilah,
that he came down *with* an ephod in his
hand.
7 ¶ And it was told Saul that David was
come to Keilah. And Saul said, God hath
delivered him into mine hand; for he is shut
in, by entering into a town that hath gates
and bars.
8 And Saul called all the people together
to war, to go down to Keilah, to besiege David and his men.
9 ¶ And David knew that Saul secretly
practised mischief against him; and [q]he

said to Abiathar the priest, Bring hither the ephod.

10 Then said David, O LORD God of Israel, thy servant hath certainly heard that Saul seeketh to come to Keilah, [r]to destroy the city for my sake.

11 Will the men of Keilah deliver me up into his hand? will Saul come down, as thy servant hath heard? O LORD God of Israel, I beseech thee, tell thy servant. And the LORD said, He will come down.

12 Then said David, Will the men of Keilah deliver me and my men into the hand of Saul? And the LORD said, They will deliver *thee* up.

13 ¶ Then David and his men, [s]*which were* about six hundred, arose and departed out of Keilah, and went whithersoever they could go. And it was told Saul that David was escaped from Keilah; and he forbare to go forth.

14 And David abode in the wilderness in strong holds, and remained in [t]a mountain in the wilderness of [u]Ziph. And Saul [v]sought him every day, but God delivered him not into his hand.

15 And David saw that Saul was come out to seek his life: and David *was* in the wilderness of Ziph in a wood.

16 ¶ And Jonathan Saul's son arose, and went to David into the wood, and strengthened his hand in God.

17 And he said unto him, Fear not: for the hand of Saul my father shall not find thee; and thou shalt be king over Israel, and I shall be next unto thee; and [w]that also Saul my father knoweth.

18 And they two [x]made a covenant before the LORD: and David abode in the wood, and Jonathan went to his house.

19 ¶ Then [y]came up the Ziphites to Saul to Gibeah, saying, Doth not David hide himself with us in strong holds in the wood, in the hill of Hachilah, which *is* on the south of Jeshimon?

20 Now therefore, O king, come down according to all the desire of thy soul to come down; and [z]our part *shall be* to deliver him into the king's hand.

21 And Saul said, Blessed *be* ye of the LORD; for ye have compassion on me.

22 Go, I pray you, prepare yet, and know and see his place where his haunt is, *and* who hath seen him there: for it is told me *that* he dealeth very subtilly.

23 See therefore, and take knowledge of all the lurking places where he hideth himself, and come ye again to me with the certainty, and I will go with you: and it shall come to pass, if he be in the land, that I will search him out throughout all the thousands of Judah.

24 And they arose, and went to Ziph before Saul: but David and his men *were* in the wilderness [a]of Maon, in the plain on the south of Jeshimon.

25 Saul also and his men went to seek *him.* And they told David: wherefore he came down into a rock, and abode in the wilderness of Maon. And when Saul heard *that,* he pursued after David in the wilderness of Maon.

26 And Saul went on this side of the mountain, and David and his men on that side of the mountain: [b]and David made haste to get away for fear of Saul; for Saul and his men [c]compassed David and his men round about to take them.

27 ¶ [d]But there came a messenger unto Saul, saying, Haste thee, and come; for the Philistines have invaded the land.

28 Wherefore Saul returned from pursuing after David, and went against the Philistines: therefore they called that place Sela-hammahlekoth.

29 ¶ And David went up from thence, and dwelt in strong holds at [e]En-gedi.

24 And it came to pass, [f]when Saul was returned from following the Philistines, that it was told him, saying, Behold, David *is* in the wilderness of En-gedi.

2 Then Saul took three thousand chosen men out of all Israel, and [g]went to seek David and his men upon the rocks of the wild goats.

3 And he came to the sheepcotes by the way, where *was* a cave; and [h]Saul went in to [i]cover his feet: and [j]David and his men remained in the sides of the cave.

4 [k]And the men of David said unto him, Behold the day of which the LORD said unto thee, Behold, I will deliver thine enemy into thine hand, that thou mayest do to him as it shall seem good unto thee. Then David arose, and cut off the skirt of Saul's robe privily.

5 And it came to pass afterward, that [l]David's heart smote him, because he had cut off Saul's skirt.

6 And he said unto his men, [m]The LORD forbid that I should do this thing unto my master, the LORD's anointed, to stretch forth mine hand against him, seeing he *is* the anointed of the LORD.

7 So David [n]stayed his servants with these words and suffered them not to rise against Saul. But Saul rose up out of the cave, and went on *his* way.

8 David also arose afterward, and went out of the cave, and cried after Saul, saying, My lord the king. And when Saul looked behind him, David stooped with his face to the earth, and bowed himself.

9 ¶ And David said to Saul, [o]Wherefore hearest thou men's words, saying, Behold, David seeketh thy hurt?

10 Behold, this day thine eyes have seen how that the LORD had delivered thee to day into mine hand in the cave: and *some* bade *me* kill thee: but *mine eye* spared thee; and I said, I will not put forth mine hand against my lord; for he *is* the LORD's anointed.

11 Moreover, my father, see, yea, see the skirt of thy robe in my hand: for in that I cut off the skirt of thy robe, and killed thee not, know thou and see that *there is* [p]neither

23:10 [r]ch. 22:19
23:13 [s]ch. 22:2
23:14 [t]Ps. 11:1 [u]Josh. 15:55 [v]Ps. 54:3
23:17 [w]ch. 24:20
23:18 [x]ch. 18:3; 2 Sam. 21:7
23:19 [y]ch. 26:1; Ps. 54, title
23:20 [z]Ps. 54:3
23:24 [a]Josh. 15:55; ch. 25:2
23:26 [b]Ps. 31:22 [c]Ps. 17:9
23:27 [d]2 Kings 19:9
23:29 [e]2 Chron. 20:2
24:1 [f]ch. 23:28
24:2 [g]Ps. 38:12
24:3 [h]Ps. 141:6 [i]Judg. 3:24 [j]Ps. 57, title
24:4 [k]ch. 26:8
24:5 [l]2 Sam. 24:10
24:6 [m]ch. 26:11
24:7 [n]Ps. 7:4; Matt. 5:44; Rom. 12:17
24:9 [o]Ps. 141:6; Prov. 16:28
24:11 [p]Ps. 7:3

evil nor transgression in mine hand, and I have not sinned against thee; yet thou [q]huntest my soul to take it.

12 [r]The LORD judge between me and thee, and the LORD avenge me of thee: but mine hand shall not be upon thee.

13 As saith the proverb of the ancients, Wickedness proceedeth from the wicked: but mine hand shall not be upon thee.

14 After whom is the king of Israel come out? after whom dost thou pursue? [s]after a dead dog, after [t]a flea.

15 [u]The LORD therefore be judge, and judge between me and thee, and [v]see, and [w]plead my cause, and deliver me out of thine hand.

16 ¶ And it came to pass, when David had made an end of speaking these words unto Saul, that Saul said, [x]*Is* this thy voice, my son David? And Saul lifted up his voice, and wept.

17 [y]And he said to David, Thou *art* [z]more righteous than I: for [a]thou hast rewarded me good, whereas I have rewarded thee evil.

18 And thou hast shewed this day how that thou hast dealt well with me: forasmuch as when [b]the LORD had delivered me into thine hand, thou killedst me not.

19 For if a man find his enemy, will he let him go well away? wherefore the LORD reward thee good for that thou hast done unto me this day.

20 And now, behold, [c]I know well that thou shalt surely be king, and that the kingdom of Israel shall be established in thine hand.

21 [d]Swear now therefore unto me by the LORD, [e]that thou wilt not cut off my seed after me, and that thou wilt not destroy my name out of my father's house.

22 And David sware unto Saul. And Saul went home; but David and his men gat them up unto [f]the hold.

25

And [g]Samuel died; and all the Israelites were gathered together, and [h]lamented him, and buried him in his house at Ramah. And David arose, and went down [i]to the wilderness of Paran.

2 And *there was* a man [j]in Maon, whose possessions *were* in [k]Carmel; and the man *was* very great, and he had three thousand sheep, and a thousand goats: and he was shearing his sheep in Carmel.

3 Now the name of the man *was* Nabal; and the name of his wife Abigail: and *she was* a woman of good understanding, and of a beautiful countenance: but the man *was* churlish and evil in his doings; and he *was* of the house of Caleb.

4 ¶ And David heard in the wilderness that Nabal did [l]shear his sheep.

5 And David sent out ten young men, and David said unto the young men, Get you up to Carmel, and go to Nabal, and greet him in my name:

6 And thus shall ye say to him that liveth *in prosperity*, [m]Peace *be* both to thee, and peace *be* to thine house, and peace *be* unto all that thou hast.

7 And now I have heard that thou hast shearers: now thy shepherds which were with us, we hurt them not, [n]neither was there ought missing unto them, all the while they were in Carmel.

8 Ask thy young men, and they will shew thee. Wherefore let the young men find favour in thine eyes: for we come in [o]a good day: give, I pray thee, whatsoever cometh to thine hand unto thy servants, and to thy son David.

9 And when David's young men came, they spake to Nabal according to all those words in the name of David, and ceased.

10 ¶ And Nabal answered David's servants, and said, [p]Who *is* David? and who *is* the son of Jesse? there be many servants now a days that break away every man from his master.

11 [q]Shall I then take my bread, and my water, and my flesh that I have killed for my shearers, and give *it* unto men, whom I know not whence they *be*?

12 So David's young men turned their way, and went again, and came and told him all those sayings.

13 And David said unto his men, Gird ye on every man his sword. And they girded on every man his sword; and David also girded on his sword: and there went up after David about four hundred men; and two hundred [r]abode by the stuff.

14 ¶ But one of the young men told Abigail, Nabal's wife, saying, Behold, David sent messengers out of the wilderness to salute our master; and he railed on them.

15 But the men *were* very good unto us, and [s]we were not hurt, neither missed we any thing, as long as we were conversant with them, when we were in the fields:

16 They were [t]a wall unto us both by night and day, all the while we were with them keeping the sheep.

17 Now therefore know and consider what thou wilt do; for [u]evil is determined against our master, and against all his household: for he *is such* a son of [v]Belial, that *a man* cannot speak to him.

18 ¶ Then Abigail made haste, and [w]took two hundred loaves, and two bottles of wine, and five sheep ready dressed, and five measures of parched *corn,* and an hundred clusters of raisins, and two hundred cakes of figs, and laid *them* on asses.

19 And she said unto her servants, [x]Go on before me; behold, I come after you. But she told not her husband Nabal.

20 And it was *so, as* she rode on the ass, that she came down by the covert of the hill, and, behold, David and his men came down against her; and she met them.

21 Now David had said, Surely in vain have I kept all that this *fellow* hath in the wilderness, so that nothing was missed of all that *pertained* unto him: and he hath [y]requited me evil for good.

24:11 [q]ch. 26:20
24:12 [r]Gen. 16:5; Judg. 11:27; ch. 26:10; Job 5:8
24:14 [s]ch. 17:43; 2 Sam. 9:8 [t]ch. 26:20
24:15 [u]ver. 12 [v]2 Chron. 24:22 [w]Ps. 35:1; Mic. 7:9
24:16 [x]ch. 26:17
24:17 [y]ch. 26:21 [z]Gen. 38:26 [a]Matt. 5:44
24:18 [b]ch. 26:23
24:20 [c]ch. 23:17
24:21 [d]Gen. 21:23 [e]2 Sam. 21:6
24:22 [f]ch. 23:29
25:1 [g]ch. 28:3 [h]Num. 20:29; Deut. 34:8 [i]Gen. 21:21; Ps. 120:5
25:2 [j]ch. 23:24 [k]Josh. 15:55
25:4 [l]Gen. 38:13; 2 Sam. 13:23
25:6 [m]1 Chron. 12:18; Ps. 122:7; Luke 10:5
25:7 [n]ver. 15
25:8 [o]Neh. 8:10; Esth. 9:19
25:10 [p]Judg. 9:28; Ps. 73:7
25:11 [q]Judg. 8:6
25:13 [r]ch. 30:24
25:15 [s]ver. 7
25:16 [t]Ex. 14:22; Job 1:10
25:17 [u]ch. 20:7 [v]Deut. 13:13; Judg. 19:22
25:18 [w]Gen. 32:13; Prov. 18:16
25:19 [x]Gen. 32:16
25:21 [y]Ps. 109:5; Prov. 17:13

22 [z]So and more also do God unto the enemies of David, if I [a]leave of all that *pertain* to him by the morning light [b]any that pisseth against the wall.

23 And when Abigail saw David, she hasted, [c]and lighted off the ass, and fell before David on her face, and bowed herself to the ground,

24 And fell at his feet, and said, Upon me, my lord, *upon* me *let this* iniquity *be:* and let thine handmaid, I pray thee, speak in thine audience, and hear the words of thine handmaid.

25 Let not my lord, I pray thee, regard this man of Belial, *even* Nabal: for as his name *is,* so *is* he; Nabal *is* his name, and folly *is* with him: but I thine handmaid saw not the young men of my lord, whom thou didst send.

26 Now therefore, my lord, [d]*as* the LORD liveth, and *as* thy soul liveth, seeing the LORD hath [e]withholden thee from coming to *shed* blood, and from [f]avenging thyself with thine own hand, now [g]let thine enemies, and they that seek evil to my lord, be as Nabal.

27 And now [h]this blessing which thine handmaid hath brought unto my lord, let it even be given unto the young men that follow my lord.

28 I pray thee, forgive the trespass of thine handmaid: for [i]the LORD will certainly make my lord a sure house; because my lord [j]fighteth the battles of the LORD, and [k]evil hath not been found in thee *all* thy days.

29 Yet a man is risen to pursue thee, and to seek thy soul: but the soul of my lord shall be bound in the bundle of life with the LORD thy God; and the souls of thine enemies, them shall he [l]sling out, *as out* of the middle of a sling.

30 And it shall come to pass, when the LORD shall have done to my lord according to all the good that he hath spoken concerning thee, and shall have appointed thee ruler over Israel;

31 That this shall be no grief unto thee, nor offence of heart unto my lord, either that thou hast shed blood causeless, or that my lord hath avenged himself: but when the LORD shall have dealt well with my lord, then remember thine handmaid.

32 ¶ And David said to Abigail, [m]Blessed *be* the LORD God of Israel, which sent thee this day to meet me:

33 And blessed *be* thy advice, and blessed *be* thou, which hast [n]kept me this day from coming to *shed* blood, and from avenging myself with mine own hand.

34 For in very deed, *as* the LORD God of Israel liveth, which hath [o]kept me back from hurting thee, except thou hadst hasted and come to meet me, surely there had [p]not been left unto Nabal by the morning light any that pisseth against the wall.

35 So David received of her hand *that* which she had brought him, and said unto her, [q]Go up in peace to thine house; see, I have hearkened to thy voice, and have [r]accepted thy person.

36 ¶ And Abigail came to Nabal; and, behold, [s]he held a feast in his house, like the feast of a king; and Nabal's heart *was* merry within him, for he *was* very drunken: wherefore she told him nothing, less or more, until the morning light.

37 But it came to pass in the morning, when the wine was gone out of Nabal, and his wife had told him these things, that his heart died within him, and he became *as* a stone.

38 And it came to pass about ten days *after,* that the LORD smote Nabal, that he died.

39 ¶ And when David heard that Nabal was dead, he said, [t]Blessed *be* the LORD, that hath [u]pleaded the cause of my reproach from the hand of Nabal, and hath [v]kept his servant from evil: for the LORD hath [w]returned the wickedness of Nabal upon his own head. And David sent and communed with Abigail, to take her to him to wife.

40 And when the servants of David were come to Abigail to Carmel, they spake unto her, saying, David sent us unto thee, to take thee to him to wife.

41 And she arose, and bowed herself on *her* face to the earth, and said, Behold, *let* [x]thine handmaid *be* a servant to wash the feet of the servants of my lord.

42 And Abigail hasted, and arose, and rode upon an ass, with five damsels of hers that went after her; and she went after the messengers of David, and became his wife.

43 David also took Ahinoam [y]of Jezreel; [z]and they were also both of them his wives.

44 ¶ But Saul had given [a]Michal his daughter, David's wife, to Phalti the son of Laish, which *was* of [b]Gallim.

26 And the Ziphites came unto Saul to Gibeah, saying, [c]Doth not David hide himself in the hill of Hachilah, *which is* before Jeshimon?

2 Then Saul arose, and went down to the wilderness of Ziph, having three thousand chosen men of Israel with him, to seek David in the wilderness of Ziph.

3 And Saul pitched in the hill of Hachilah, which *is* before Jeshimon, by the way. But David abode in the wilderness, and he saw that Saul came after him into the wilderness.

4 David therefore sent out spies, and understood that Saul was come in very deed.

5 ¶ And David arose, and came to the place where Saul had pitched: and David beheld the place where Saul lay, and [d]Abner the son of Ner, the captain of his host: and Saul lay in the trench, and the people pitched round about him.

6 Then answered David and said to Ahimelech the Hittite, and to Abishai [e]the son of Zeruiah, brother to Joab, saying, Who will [f]go down with me to Saul to the

25:22 [z]Ruth 1:17; ch. 3:17 [a]ver. 34 [b]1 Kings 14:10; 2 Kings 9:8
25:23 [c]Josh. 15:18; Judg. 1:14
25:26 [d]2 Kings 2:2 [e]Gen. 20:6; ver. 33 [f]Rom. 12:19 [g]2 Sam. 18:32
25:27 [h]Gen. 33:11; ch. 30:26; 2 Kings 5:15
25:28 [i]2 Sam. 7:11; 1 Kings 9:5; 1 Chron. 17:10 [j]ch. 18:17 [k]ch. 24:11
25:29 [l]Jer. 10:18
25:32 [m]Gen. 24:27; Ex. 18:10; Ps. 41:13; Luke 1:68
25:33 [n]ver. 26
25:34 [o]ver. 26 [p]ver. 22
25:35 [q]ch. 20:42; 2 Sam. 15:9; 2 Kings 5:19; Luke 7:50 [r]Gen. 19:21
25:36 [s]2 Sam. 13:23
25:39 [t]ver. 32 [u]Prov. 22:23 [v]ver. 26:34 [w]1 Kings 2:44; Ps. 7:16
25:41 [x]Ruth 2:10; Prov. 15:33
25:43 [y]Josh. 15:56 [z]ch. 27:3
25:44 [a]2 Sam. 3:14 [b]Isa. 10:30
26:1 [c]ch. 23:19; Ps. 54, title
26:5 [d]ch. 14:50
26:6 [e]1 Chron. 2:16 [f]Judg. 7:10

camp? And Abishai said, I will go down
with thee.
7 So David and Abishai came to the people by night: and, behold, Saul lay sleeping
within the trench, and his spear stuck in the
ground at his bolster: but Abner and the
people lay round about him.
8 Then said Abishai to David, God hath
delivered thine enemy into thine hand this
day: now therefore let me smite him, I pray
thee, with the spear even to the earth at
once, and I will not *smite* him the second
time.
9 And David said to Abishai, Destroy him
not: [g]for who can stretch forth his hand
against the LORD's anointed, and be guiltless?
10 David said furthermore, *As* the LORD
liveth, [h]the LORD shall smite him; or [i]his
day shall come to die; or he shall [j]descend
into battle, and perish.
11 [k]The LORD forbid that I should stretch
forth mine hand against the LORD's
anointed: but, I pray thee, take thou now the
spear that *is* at his bolster, and the cruse of
water, and let us go.
12 So David took the spear and the cruse
of water from Saul's bolster; and they gat
them away, and no man saw *it*, nor knew *it*,
neither awaked: for they *were* all asleep;
because [l]a deep sleep from the LORD was
fallen upon them.
13 ¶ Then David went over to the other
side, and stood on the top of an hill afar off;
a great space *being* between them:
14 And David cried to the people, and to
Abner the son of Ner, saying, Answerest
thou not, Abner? Then Abner answered and
said, Who *art* thou *that* criest to the king?
15 And David said to Abner, *Art* not thou
a *valiant* man? and who *is* like to thee in
Israel? wherefore then hast thou not kept
thy lord the king? for there came one of the
people in to destroy the king thy lord.
16 This thing *is* not good that thou hast
done. *As* the LORD liveth, ye *are* worthy to
die, because ye have not kept your master,
the LORD's anointed. And now see where
the king's spear *is*, and the cruse of water
that *was* at his bolster.
17 And Saul knew David's voice, and
said, [m]*Is* this thy voice, my son David? And
David said, *It is* my voice, my lord, O king.
18 And he said, [n]Wherefore doth my lord
thus pursue after his servant? for what have
I done? or what evil *is* in mine hand?
19 Now therefore, I pray thee, let my lord
the king hear the words of his servant. If the
LORD have [o]stirred thee up against me, let
him accept an offering: but if *they be* the
children of men, cursed *be* they before the
LORD; [p]for they have driven me out this day
from abiding in the [q]inheritance of the
LORD, saying, Go, serve other gods.
20 Now therefore, let not my blood fall to
the earth before the face of the LORD: for the
king of Israel is come out to seek [r]a flea,
as when one doth hunt a partridge in the
mountains.
21 ¶ Then said Saul, [s]I have sinned: return, my son David: for I will no more do
thee harm, because my soul was [t]precious
in thine eyes this day: behold, I have played
the fool, and have erred exceedingly.
22 And David answered and said, Behold
the king's spear! and let one of the young
men come over and fetch it.
23 [u]The LORD render to every man his
righteousness and his faithfulness: for the
LORD delivered thee into *my* hand to day,
but I would not stretch forth mine hand
against the LORD's anointed.
24 And, behold, as thy life was much set
by this day in mine eyes, so let my life be
much set by in the eyes of the LORD, and let
him deliver me out of all tribulation.
25 Then Saul said to David, Blessed *be*
thou, my son David: thou shalt both do
great *things*, and also shalt still [v]prevail. So
David went on his way, and Saul returned
to his place.

27

And David said in his heart, I shall
now perish one day by the hand of
Saul: *there is* nothing better for me than
that I should speedily escape into the land
of the Philistines; and Saul shall despair of
me, to seek me any more in any coast of
Israel: so shall I escape out of his hand.
2 And David arose, [w]and he passed over
with the six hundred men that *were* with
him [x]unto Achish, the son of Maoch, king
of Gath.
3 And David dwelt with Achish at Gath,
he and his men, every man with his household, *even* David [y]with his two wives, Ahinoam the Jezreelitess, and Abigail the
Carmelitess, Nabal's wife.
4 And it was told Saul that David was fled
to Gath: and he sought no more again for
him.
5 ¶ And David said unto Achish, If I have
now found grace in thine eyes, let them give
me a place in some town in the country, that
I may dwell there: for why should thy servant dwell in the royal city with thee?
6 Then Achish gave him Ziklag that day:
wherefore [z]Ziklag pertaineth unto the
kings of Judah unto this day.
7 And the time that David dwelt in the
country of the Philistines was a full year
and four months.
8 ¶ And David and his men went up, and
invaded [a]the Geshurites, [b]and the Gez-
rites, and the [c]Amalekites: for those *nations were* of old the inhabitants of the land,
[d]as thou goest to Shur, even unto the land
of Egypt.
9 And David smote the land, and left neither man nor woman alive, and took away
the sheep, and the oxen, and the asses, and
the camels, and the apparel, and returned,
and came to Achish.
10 And Achish said, Whither have ye
made a road to day? And David said,
Against the south of Judah, and against the

26:9 [g]ch. 24:6; 2 Sam. 1:16
26:10 [h]ch. 25:38; Ps. 94:1; Luke 18:7; Rom. 12:19 [i]Gen. 47:29; Deut. 31:14; Job 7:1; Ps. 37:13 [j]ch. 31:6
26:11 [k]ch. 24:6
26:12 [l]Gen. 2:21
26:17 [m]ch. 24:16
26:18 [n]ch. 24:9
26:19 [o]2 Sam. 16:11 [p]Deut. 4:28; Ps. 120:5 [q]2 Sam. 14:16
26:20 [r]ch. 24:14
26:21 [s]ch. 15:24 [t]ch. 18:30
26:23 [u]Ps. 7:8
26:25 [v]Gen. 32:28
27:2 [w]ch. 25:13 [x]ch. 21:10
27:3 [y]ch. 25:43
27:6 [z]Josh. 15:31
27:8 [a]Josh. 13:2 [b]Josh. 16:10; Judg. 1:29 [c]Ex. 17:16; ch. 15:7 [d]Gen. 25:18

south of [e]the Jerahmeelites, and against the south of [f]the Kenites.

11 And David saved neither man nor woman alive, to bring *tidings* to Gath, saying, Lest they should tell on us, saying, So did David, and so *will be* his manner all the while he dwelleth in the country of the Philistines.

12 And Achish believed David, saying, He hath made his people Israel utterly to abhor him; therefore he shall be my servant for ever.

28 And [g]it came to pass in those days, that the Philistines gathered their armies together for warfare, to fight with Israel. And Achish said unto David, Know thou assuredly, that thou shalt go out with me to battle, thou and thy men.

2 And David said to Achish, Surely thou shalt know what thy servant can do. And Achish said to David, Therefore will I make thee keeper of mine head for ever.

3 ¶ Now [h]Samuel was dead, and all Israel had lamented him, and buried him in Ramah, even in his own city. And Saul had put away [i]those that had familiar spirits, and the wizards, out of the land.

4 And the Philistines gathered themselves together, and came and pitched in [j]Shunem: and Saul gathered all Israel together, and they pitched in [k]Gilboa.

5 And when Saul saw the host of the Philistines, he was [l]afraid, and his heart greatly trembled.

6 And when Saul enquired of the LORD, [m]the LORD answered him not, neither by [n]dreams, nor [o]by Urim, nor by prophets.

7 ¶ Then said Saul unto his servants, Seek me a woman that hath a familiar spirit, that I may go to her, and enquire of her. And his servants said to him, Behold, *there is* a woman that hath a familiar spirit at En-dor.

8 And Saul disguised himself, and put on other raiment, and he went, and two men with him, and they came to the woman by night: and [p]he said, I pray thee, divine unto me by the familiar spirit, and bring me *him* up, whom I shall name unto thee.

9 And the woman said unto him, Behold, thou knowest what Saul hath done, how he hath [q]cut off those that have familiar spirits, and the wizards, out of the land: wherefore then layest thou a snare for my life, to cause me to die?

10 And Saul sware to her by the LORD, saying, *As* the LORD liveth, there shall no punishment happen to thee for this thing.

11 Then said the woman, Whom shall I bring up unto thee? And he said, Bring me up Samuel.

12 And when the woman saw Samuel, she cried with a loud voice: and the woman spake to Saul, saying, Why hast thou deceived me? for thou *art* Saul.

13 And the king said unto her, Be not afraid: for what sawest thou? And the woman said unto Saul, I saw [r]gods ascending out of the earth.

14 And he said unto her, What form *is* he of? And she said, An old man cometh up; and he *is* covered with [s]a mantle. And Saul perceived that it *was* Samuel, and he stooped with *his* face to the ground, and bowed himself.

15 ¶ And Samuel said to Saul, Why hast thou disquieted me, to bring me up? And Saul answered, [t]I am sore distressed; for the Philistines make war against me, and [u]God is departed from me, and [v]answereth me no more, neither by prophets, nor by dreams: therefore I have called thee, that thou mayest make known unto me what I shall do.

16 Then said Samuel, Wherefore then dost thou ask of me, seeing the LORD is departed from thee, and is become thine enemy?

17 And the LORD hath done to him, [w]as he spake by me: for the LORD hath rent the kingdom out of thine hand, and given it to thy neighbour, *even* to David:

18 [x]Because thou obeyedst not the voice of the LORD, nor executedst his fierce wrath upon Amalek, therefore hath the LORD done this thing unto thee this day.

19 Moreover the LORD will also deliver Israel with thee into the hand of the Philistines: and to morrow *shalt* thou and thy sons *be* with me: the LORD also shall deliver the host of Israel into the hand of the Philistines.

20 Then Saul fell straightway all along on the earth, and was sore afraid, because of the words of Samuel: and there was no strength in him; for he had eaten no bread all the day, nor all the night.

21 ¶ And the woman came unto Saul, and saw that he was sore troubled, and said unto him, Behold, thine handmaid hath obeyed thy voice, and I have [y]put my life in my hand, and have hearkened unto thy words which thou spakest unto me.

22 Now therefore, I pray thee, hearken thou also unto the voice of thine handmaid, and let me set a morsel of bread before thee; and eat, that thou mayest have strength, when thou goest on thy way.

23 But he refused, and said, I will not eat. But his servants, together with the woman, compelled him; and he hearkened unto their voice. So he arose from the earth, and sat upon the bed.

24 And the woman had a fat calf in the house; and she hasted, and killed it, and took flour, and kneaded *it*, and did bake unleavened bread thereof:

25 And she brought *it* before Saul, and before his servants; and they did eat. Then they rose up, and went away that night.

29 Now [z]the Philistines gathered together all their armies [a]to Aphek: and the Israelites pitched by a fountain which *is* in Jezreel.

2 And the lords of the Philistines passed on by hundreds, and by thousands: but Da-

27:10 [e]1 Chron. 2:9 [f]Judg. 1:16
28:1 [g]ch. 29:1
28:3 [h]ch. 25:1 [i]ver. 9; Ex. 22:18; Lev. 19:31; Deut. 18:10
28:4 [j]Josh. 19:18; 2 Kings 4:8 [k]ch. 31:1
28:5 [l]Job 18:11
28:6 [m]ch. 14:37; Prov. 1:28; Lam. 2:9 [n]Num. 12:6 [o]Ex. 28:30; Num. 27:21; Deut. 33:8
28:8 [p]Deut. 18:11; 1 Chron. 10:13; Isa. 8:19
28:9 [q]ver. 3
28:13 [r]Ex. 22:28
28:14 [s]ch. 15:27; 2 Kings 2:8
28:15 [t]Prov. 5:11 [u]ch. 18:12 [v]ver. 6
28:17 [w]ch. 15:28
28:18 [x]ch. 15:9; 1 Kings 20:42; 1 Chron. 10:13; Jer. 48:10
28:21 [y]Judg. 12:3; ch. 19:5; Job 13:14
29:1 [z]ch. 28:1 [a]ch. 4:1

vid and his men passed on in the rereward [b]with Achish.

3 Then said the princes of the Philistines, What *do* these Hebrews *here?* And Achish said unto the princes of the Philistines, *Is* not this David, the servant of Saul the king of Israel, which hath been with me [c]these days, or these years, and I have [d]found no fault in him since he fell *unto me* unto this day?

4 And the princes of the Philistines were wroth with him; and the princes of the Philistines said unto him, [e]Make this fellow return, that he may go again to his place which thou hast appointed him, and let him not go down with us to battle, lest [f]in the battle he be an adversary to us: for wherewith should he reconcile himself unto his master? *should it* not *be* with the heads of these men?

5 *Is* not this David, of whom they sang one to another in dances, saying, [g]Saul slew his thousands, and David his ten thousands?

6 ¶ Then Achish called David, and said unto him, Surely, *as* the LORD liveth, thou hast been upright, and [h]thy going out and thy coming in with me in the host *is* good in my sight: for [i]I have not found evil in thee since the day of thy coming unto me unto this day: nevertheless the lords favour thee not.

7 Wherefore now return, and go in peace, that thou displease not the lords of the Philistines.

8 ¶ And David said unto Achish, But what have I done? and what hast thou found in thy servant so long as I have been with thee unto this day, that I may not go fight against the enemies of my lord the king?

9 And Achish answered and said to David, I know that thou *art* good in my sight, [j]as an angel of God: notwithstanding [k]the princes of the Philistines have said, He shall not go up with us to the battle.

10 Wherefore now rise up early in the morning with thy master's servants that are come with thee: and as soon as ye be up early in the morning, and have light, depart.

11 So David and his men rose up early to depart in the morning, to return into the land of the Philistines. [l]And the Philistines went up to Jezreel.

30

And it came to pass, when David and his men were come to Ziklag on the third day, that the [m]Amalekites had invaded the south, and Ziklag, and smitten Ziklag, and burned it with fire;

2 And had taken the women captives, that *were* therein: they slew not any, either great or small, but carried *them* away, and went on their way.

3 ¶ So David and his men came to the city, and, behold, *it was* burned with fire; and their wives, and their sons, and their daughters, were taken captives.

4 Then David and the people that *were* with him lifted up their voice and wept, until they had no more power to weep.

5 And David's [n]two wives were taken captives, Ahinoam the Jezreelitess, and Abigail the wife of Nabal the Carmelite.

6 And David was greatly distressed; [o]for the people spake of stoning him, because the soul of all the people was grieved, every man for his sons and for his daughters: [p]but David encouraged himself in the LORD his God.

7 [q]And David said to Abiathar the priest, Ahimelech's son, I pray thee, bring me hither the ephod. And Abiathar brought thither the ephod to David.

8 [r]And David enquired at the LORD, saying, Shall I pursue after this troop? shall I overtake them? And he answered him, Pursue: for thou shalt surely overtake *them,* and without fail recover *all.*

9 So David went, he and the six hundred men that *were* with him, and came to the brook Besor, where those that were left behind stayed.

10 But David pursued, he and four hundred men: [s]for two hundred abode behind, which were so faint that they could not go over the brook Besor.

11 ¶ And they found an Egyptian in the field, and brought him to David, and gave him bread, and he did eat; and they made him drink water;

12 And they gave him a piece of a cake of figs, and two clusters of raisins: and [t]when he had eaten, his spirit came again to him: for he had eaten no bread, nor drunk *any* water, three days and three nights.

13 And David said unto him, To whom *belongest* thou? and whence *art* thou? And he said, I *am* a young man of Egypt, servant to an Amalekite; and my master left me, because three days agone I fell sick.

14 We made an invasion *upon* the south of [u]the Cherethites, and upon *the coast* which *belongeth* to Judah, and upon the south of [v]Caleb; and we burned Ziklag with fire.

15 And David said to him, Canst thou bring me down to this company? And he said, Swear unto me by God, that thou wilt neither kill me, nor deliver me into the hands of my master, and I will bring thee down to this company.

16 ¶ And when he had brought him down, behold, *they were* spread abroad upon all the earth, [w]eating and drinking, and dancing, because of all the great spoil that they had taken out of the land of the Philistines, and out of the land of Judah.

17 And David smote them from the twilight even unto the evening of the next day: and there escaped not a man of them, save four hundred young men, which rode upon camels, and fled.

18 And David recovered all that the Amalekites had carried away: and David rescued his two wives.

19 And there was nothing lacking to

29:2 [b]ch. 28:1
29:3 [c]ch. 27:7 [d]Dan. 6:5
29:4 [e]1 Chron. 12:19 [f]ch. 14:21
29:5 [g]ch. 18:7
29:6 [h]2 Sam. 3:25; 2 Kings 19:27 [i]ver. 3
29:9 [j]2 Sam. 14:17 [k]ver. 4
29:11 [l]2 Sam. 4:4
30:1 [m]ch. 15:7
30:5 [n]ch. 25:42; 2 Sam. 2:2
30:6 [o]Ex. 17:4 [p]Ps. 42:5; Hab. 3:17
30:7 [q]ch. 23:6
30:8 [r]ch. 23:2
30:10 [s]ver. 21
30:12 [t]Judg. 15:19; ch. 14:2
30:14 [u]ver. 16; 2 Sam. 8:18; 1 Kings 1:38; Ezek. 25:16; Zeph. 2:5 [v]Josh. 14:13
30:16 [w]1 Thess. 5:3

them, neither small nor great, neither sons nor daughters, neither spoil, nor any *thing* that they had taken to them: [x]David recovered all.

20 And David took all the flocks and the herds, *which* they drave before those *other* cattle, and said, This *is* David's spoil.

21 ¶ And David came to the [y]two hundred men, which were so faint that they could not follow David, whom they had made also to abide at the brook Besor: and they went forth to meet David, and to meet the people that *were* with him: and when David came near to the people, he saluted them.

22 Then answered all the wicked men, and *men* [z]of Belial, of those that went with David, and said, Because they went not with us, we will not give them *ought* of the spoil that we have recovered, save to every man his wife and his children, that they may lead *them* away, and depart.

23 Then said David, Ye shall not do so, my brethren, with that which the LORD hath given us, who hath preserved us, and delivered the company that came against us into our hand.

24 For who will hearken unto you in this matter? but [a]as his part *is* that goeth down to the battle, so *shall* his part *be* that tarrieth by the stuff: they shall part alike.

25 And it was *so* from that day forward, that he made it a statute and an ordinance for Israel unto this day.

26 ¶ And when David came to Ziklag, he sent of the spoil unto the elders of Judah, *even* to his friends, saying, Behold a present for you of the spoil of the enemies of the LORD;

27 To *them* which *were* in Beth-el, and to *them* which *were* in [b]south Ramoth, and to *them* which *were* in [c]Jattir,

28 And to *them* which *were* in [d]Aroer, and to *them* which *were* in Siphmoth, and to *them* which *were* in [e]Eshtemoa,

29 And to *them* which *were* in Rachal, and to *them* which *were* in the cities of [f]the Jerahmeelites, and to *them* which *were* in the cities of the [g]Kenites,

30 And to *them* which *were* in [h]Hormah, and to *them* which *were* in Chor-ashan, and to *them* which *were* in Athach,

31 And to *them* which *were* in [i]Hebron, and to all the places where David himself and his men were wont to haunt.

30:19 [x]ver. 8
30:21 [y]ver. 10
30:22 [z]Deut. 13:13; Judg. 19:22
30:24 [a]Num. 31:27; Josh. 22:8
30:27 [b]Josh. 19:8 [c]Josh. 15:48
30:28 [d]Josh. 13:16 [e]Josh. 15:50
30:29 [f]ch. 27:10 [g]Judg. 1:16
30:30 [h]Judg. 1:17
30:31 [i]Josh. 14:13; 2 Sam. 2:1
31:1 [j]1 Chron. 10:1-12 [k]ch. 28:4
31:2 [l]ch. 14:49; 1 Chron. 8:33
31:3 [m]2 Sam. 1:6
31:4 [n]Judg. 9:54 [o]ch. 14:6 [p]2 Sam. 1:14 [q]2 Sam. 1:10
31:9 [r]2 Sam. 1:20
31:10 [s]ch. 21:9 [t]Judg. 2:13 [u]2 Sam. 21:12 [v]Josh. 17:11; Judg. 1:27
31:11 [w]ch. 11:3
31:12 [x]ch. 11:1-11 [y]Jer. 34:5; Am. 6:10
31:13 [z]2 Sam. 2:4 [a]Gen. 50:10

31 Now [j]the Philistines fought against Israel: and the men of Israel fled from before the Philistines, and fell down slain in mount [k]Gilboa.

2 And the Philistines followed hard upon Saul and upon his sons; and the Philistines slew [l]Jonathan, and Abinadab, and Melchi-shua, Saul's sons.

3 And [m]the battle went sore against Saul, and the archers hit him; and he was sore wounded of the archers.

4 [n]Then said Saul unto his armourbearer, Draw thy sword, and thrust me through therewith; lest [o]these uncircumcised come and thrust me through, and abuse me. But his armourbearer would not; [p]for he was sore afraid. Therefore Saul took a sword, and [q]fell upon it.

5 And when his armourbearer saw that Saul was dead, he fell likewise upon his sword, and died with him.

6 So Saul died, and his three sons, and his armourbearer, and all his men, that same day together.

7 ¶ And when the men of Israel that *were* on the other side of the valley, and *they* that *were* on the other side Jordan, saw that the men of Israel fled, and that Saul and his sons were dead, they forsook the cities, and fled; and the Philistines came and dwelt in them.

8 And it came to pass on the morrow, when the Philistines came to strip the slain, that they found Saul and his three sons fallen in mount Gilboa.

9 And they cut off his head, and stripped off his armour, and sent into the land of the Philistines round about, to [r]publish *it in* the house of their idols, and among the people.

10 [s]And they put his armour in the house of [t]Ashtaroth: and [u]they fastened his body to the wall of [v]Beth-shan.

11 ¶ [w]And when the inhabitants of Jabesh-gilead heard of that which the Philistines had done to Saul;

12 [x]All the valiant men arose, and went all night, and took the body of Saul and the bodies of his sons from the wall of Beth-shan, and came to Jabesh, and [y]burnt them there.

13 And they took their bones, and [z]buried *them* under a tree at Jabesh, and [a]fasted seven days.

2 SAMUEL

Samuel wrote this book in or after 1120 B.C. Second Samuel offers a partial historical account of the reign of David as king of Israel. The book opens as David is crowned king and ends just a few years before his death. The most significant events in 2 Samuel are the consolidation of Israel into a single nation, David's conquests over the enemies of Israel, his affair with Bathsheba, and the results of David's sins against God.

David's indiscretion with Bathsheba and his attempted cover-up (Chapter 11) is probably the most recognized scripture from 2 Samuel.

I. David made king over Israel, 1:1–6:23
II. David expands the kingdom, 7:1–10:19
III. David's sins and their consequences, 11:1–20:26
IV. The conclusion of the kingdom under David, 21:1–24:25

---

1 Now it came to pass after the death of
Saul, when David was returned from
[a]the slaughter of the Amalekites, and David had abode two days in Ziklag;
2 It came even to pass on the third day,
that, behold, [b]a man came out of the camp
from Saul [c]with his clothes rent, and earth
upon his head: and *so* it was, when he came
to David, that he fell to the earth, and did
obeisance.
3 And David said unto him, From whence
comest thou? And he said unto him, Out of
the camp of Israel am I escaped.
4 And David said unto him, How went the
matter? I pray thee, tell me. And he answered, That the people are fled from the
battle, and many of the people also are
fallen and dead; and Saul and Jonathan his
son are dead also.
5 And David said unto the young man
that told him, How knowest thou that Saul
and Jonathan his son be dead?
6 And the young man that told him said,
As I happened by chance upon [d]mount Gilboa, behold, [e]Saul leaned upon his spear;
and, lo, the chariots and horsemen followed
hard after him.
7 And when he looked behind him, he
saw me, and called unto me. And I answered, Here *am* I.
8 And he said unto me, Who *art* thou?
And I answered him, I *am* an Amalekite.
9 He said unto me again, Stand, I pray
thee, upon me, and slay me: for anguish is
come upon me, because my life *is* yet whole
in me.
10 So I stood upon him, and [f]slew him,
because I was sure that he could not live
after that he was fallen: and I took the
crown that *was* upon his head, and the
bracelet that *was* on his arm, and have
brought them hither unto my lord.
11 Then David took hold on his clothes,
and [g]rent them; and likewise all the men
that *were* with him:
12 And they mourned, and wept, and
fasted until even, for Saul, and for Jonathan
his son, and for the people of the LORD, and

1:1 [a]1 Sam. 30:17
1:2 [b]ch. 4:10 [c]1 Sam. 4:12
1:6 [d]1 Sam. 31:1 [e]1 Sam. 31:2
1:10 [f]Judg. 9:54
1:11 [g]ch. 3:31
1:14 [h]Num. 12:8 [i]1 Sam. 31:4 [j]1 Sam. 24:6; Ps. 105:15
1:15 [k]ch. 4:10
1:16 [l]1 Sam. 26:9; 1 Kings 2:32 [m]ver. 10; Luke 19:22
1:18 [n]1 Sam. 31:3 [o]Josh. 10:33
1:19 [p]ver. 27
1:20 [q]Judg. 16:23; 1 Sam. 31:9; Mic. 1:10 [r]Ex. 15:20; Judg. 11:34; 1 Sam. 18:6 [s]1 Sam. 31:4
1:21 [t]1 Sam. 31:1 [u]Judg. 25:23; Job 3:3; Jer. 20:14 [v]1 Sam. 10:1
1:22 [w]1 Sam. 18:4
1:23 [x]Judg. 14:18

for the house of Israel; because they were
fallen by the sword.
13 ¶ And David said unto the young man
that told him, Whence *art* thou? And he answered, I *am* the son of a stranger, an Amalekite.
14 And David said unto him, [h]How wast
thou not [i]afraid to [j]stretch forth thine
hand to destroy the LORD's anointed?
15 And [k]David called one of the young
men, and said, Go near, *and* fall upon him.
And he smote him that he died.
16 And David said unto him, [l]Thy blood
be upon thy head; for [m]thy mouth hath testified against thee, saying, I have slain the
LORD's anointed.
17 ¶ And David lamented with this lamentation over Saul and over Jonathan his
son:
18 ([n]Also he bade them teach the children of Judah *the use of* the bow: behold, *it*
is written [o]in the book of Jasher.)
19 The beauty of Israel is slain upon thy
high places: [p]how are the mighty fallen!
20 [q]Tell *it* not in Gath, publish *it* not in
the streets of Askelon; lest [r]the daughters
of [s]the Philistines rejoice, lest the daughters of the uncircumcised triumph.
21 Ye [t]mountains of Gilboa, [u]*let there*
be no dew, neither *let there be* rain, upon
you, nor fields of offerings: for there the
shield of the mighty is vilely cast away, the
shield of Saul, *as though he had* not *been*
[v]anointed with oil.
22 From the blood of the slain, from the
fat of the mighty, [w]the bow of Jonathan
turned not back, and the sword of Saul returned not empty.
23 Saul and Jonathan *were* lovely and
pleasant in their lives, and in their death
they were not divided: they were swifter
than eagles, they were [x]stronger than lions.
24 Ye daughters of Israel, weep over
Saul, who clothed you in scarlet, with *other*
delights, who put on ornaments of gold
upon your apparel.
25 How are the mighty fallen in the midst

of the battle! O Jonathan, *thou wast* slain in thine high places.

26 I am distressed for thee, my brother Jonathan: very pleasant hast thou been unto me: [y]thy love to me was wonderful, passing the love of women.

27 [z]How are the mighty fallen, and the weapons of war perished!

2 And it came to pass after this, that David [a]enquired of the LORD, saying, Shall I go up into any of the cities of Judah? And the LORD said unto him, Go up. And David said, Whither shall I go up? And he said, Unto [b]Hebron.

2 So David went up thither, and his [c]two wives also, Ahinoam the Jezreelitess, and Abigail Nabal's wife the Carmelite.

3 And [d]his men that *were* with him did David bring up, every man with his household: and they dwelt in the cities of Hebron.

4 [e]And the men of Judah came, and there they anointed David king over the house of Judah. And they told David, saying, *That* [f]the men of Jabesh-gilead *were they* that buried Saul.

5 ¶ And David sent messengers unto the men of Jabesh-gilead, and said unto them, [g]Blessed *be* ye of the LORD, that ye have shewed this kindness unto your lord, *even* unto Saul, and have buried him.

6 And now [h]the LORD shew kindness and truth unto you: and I also will requite you this kindness, because ye have done this thing.

7 Therefore now let your hands be strengthened, and be ye valiant: for your master Saul is dead, and also the house of Judah have anointed me king over them.

8 ¶ But [i]Abner the son of Ner, captain of Saul's host, took Ish-bosheth the son of Saul, and brought him over to Mahanaim;

9 And made him king over Gilead, and over the Ashurites, and over Jezreel, and over Ephraim, and over Benjamin, and over all Israel.

10 Ish-bosheth Saul's son *was* forty years old when he began to reign over Israel, and reigned two years. But the house of Judah followed David.

11 And [j]the time that David was king in Hebron over the house of Judah was seven years and six months.

12 ¶ And Abner the son of Ner, and the servants of Ish-bosheth the son of Saul, went out from Mahanaim to [k]Gibeon.

13 And Joab the son of Zeruiah, and the servants of David, went out, and met together by [l]the pool of Gibeon: and they sat down, the one on the one side of the pool, and the other on the other side of the pool.

14 And Abner said to Joab, Let the young men now arise, and play before us. And Joab said, Let them arise.

15 Then there arose and went over by number twelve of Benjamin, which *pertained* to Ish-bosheth the son of Saul, and twelve of the servants of David.

16 And they caught every one his fellow by the head, and *thrust* his sword in his fellow's side; so they fell down together: wherefore that place was called Helkath-hazzurim, which *is* in Gibeon.

17 And there was a very sore battle that day; and Abner was beaten, and the men of Israel, before the servants of David.

18 ¶ And there were [m]three sons of Zeruiah there, Joab, and Abishai, and Asahel: and Asahel *was* [n]as light of foot [o]as a wild roe.

19 And Asahel pursued after Abner; and in going he turned not to the right hand nor to the left from following Abner.

20 Then Abner looked behind him, and said, *Art* thou Asahel? And he answered, I *am*.

21 And Abner said to him, Turn thee aside to thy right hand or to thy left, and lay thee hold on one of the young men, and take thee his armour. But Asahel would not turn aside from following of him.

22 And Abner said again to Asahel, Turn thee aside from following me: wherefore should I smite thee to the ground? how then should I hold up my face to Joab thy brother?

23 Howbeit he refused to turn aside: wherefore Abner with the hinder end of the spear smote him [p]under the fifth *rib*, that the spear came out behind him; and he fell down there, and died in the same place: and it came to pass, *that* as many as came to the place where Asahel fell down and died stood still.

24 Joab also and Abishai pursued after Abner: and the sun went down when they were come to the hill of Ammah, that *lieth* before Giah by the way of the wilderness of Gibeon.

25 ¶ And the children of Benjamin gathered themselves together after Abner, and became one troop, and stood on the top of an hill.

26 Then Abner called to Joab, and said, Shall the sword devour for ever? knowest thou not that it will be bitterness in the latter end? how long shall it be then, ere thou bid the people return from following their brethren?

27 And Joab said, *As* God liveth, unless [q]thou hadst spoken, surely then in the morning the people had gone up every one from following his brother.

28 So Joab blew a trumpet, and all the people stood still, and pursued after Israel no more, neither fought they any more.

29 And Abner and his men walked all that night through the plain, and passed over Jordan, and went through all Bithron, and they came to Mahanaim.

30 And Joab returned from following Abner: and when he had gathered all the people together, there lacked of David's servants nineteen men and Asahel.

31 But the servants of David had smitten of Benjamin, and of Abner's men, *so that* three hundred and threescore men died.

1:26 [y]1 Sam. 18:1
1:27 [z]ver. 19
2:1 [a]Judg. 1:1; 1 Sam. 23:2 [b]1 Sam. 30:31; ver. 11; ch. 5:1; 1 Kings 2:11
2:2 [c]1 Sam. 30:5
2:3 [d]1 Sam. 27:2; 1 Chron. 12:1
2:4 [e]ver. 11; ch. 5:5 [f]1 Sam. 31:11
2:5 [g]Ruth 2:20; Ps. 115:15
2:6 [h]2 Tim. 1:16
2:8 [i]1 Sam. 14:50
2:11 [j]ch. 5:5; 1 Kings 2:11
2:12 [k]Josh. 18:25
2:13 [l]Jer. 41:12
2:18 [m]1 Chron. 2:16 [n]1 Chron. 12:8 [o]Ps. 18:33; SSol. 2:17
2:23 [p]ch. 3:27
2:27 [q]ver. 14; Prov. 17:14

32 ¶ And they took up Asahel, and buried
him in the sepulchre of his father, which
was in Beth-lehem. And Joab and his men
went all night, and they came to Hebron at
break of day.

3 Now there was long war between the
house of Saul and the house of David:
but David waxed stronger and stronger,
and the house of Saul waxed weaker and
weaker.
2 ¶ And [r]unto David were sons born in
Hebron: and his firstborn was Amnon, [s]of
Ahinoam the Jezreelitess;
3 And his second, Chileab, of Abigail the
wife of Nabal the Carmelite; and the third,
Absalom the son of Maacah the daughter of
Talmai king of [t]Geshur;
4 And the fourth, [u]Adonijah the son of
Haggith; and the fifth, Shephatiah the son
of Abital;
5 And the sixth, Ithream, by Eglah David's wife. These were born to David in Hebron.
6 ¶ And it came to pass, while there was
war between the house of Saul and the
house of David, that Abner made himself
strong for the house of Saul.
7 And Saul had a concubine, whose name
was [v]Rizpah, the daughter of Aiah: and
Ish-bosheth said to Abner, Wherefore hast
thou [w]gone in unto my father's concubine?
8 Then was Abner very wroth for the
words of Ish-bosheth, and said, *Am* I [x]a
dog's head, which against Judah do shew
kindness this day unto the house of Saul thy
father, to his brethren, and to his friends,
and have not delivered thee into the hand of
David, that thou chargest me to day with a
fault concerning this woman?
9 [y]So do God to Abner, and more also,
except, [z]as the LORD hath sworn to David,
even so I do to him;
10 To translate the kingdom from the
house of Saul, and to set up the throne of
David over Israel and over Judah, [a]from
Dan even to Beer-sheba.
11 And he could not answer Abner a
word again, because he feared him.
12 ¶ And Abner sent messengers to David
on his behalf, saying, Whose *is* the land?
saying *also,* Make thy league with me, and,
behold, my hand *shall be* with thee, to bring
about all Israel unto thee.
13 ¶ And he said, Well; I will make a
league with thee: but one thing I require of
thee, that is, [b]Thou shalt not see my face,
except thou first bring [c]Michal Saul's
daughter, when thou comest to see my face.
14 And David sent messengers to Ish-
bosheth Saul's son, saying, Deliver *me* my
wife Michal, which I espoused to me [d]for an
hundred foreskins of the Philistines.
15 And Ish-bosheth sent, and took her
from *her* husband, *even* from [e]Phaltiel the
son of Laish.
16 And her husband went with her along
weeping behind her to [f]Bahurim. Then said
Abner unto him, Go, return. And he returned.
17 ¶ And Abner had communication with
the elders of Israel, saying, Ye sought for
David in times past *to be* king over you:
18 Now then do *it:* [g]for the LORD hath
spoken of David, saying, By the hand of my
servant David I will save my people Israel
out of the hand of the Philistines, and out of
the hand of all their enemies.
19 And Abner also spake in the ears of
[h]Benjamin: and Abner went also to speak
in the ears of David in Hebron all that
seemed good to Israel, and that seemed
good to the whole house of Benjamin.
20 So Abner came to David to Hebron,
and twenty men with him. And David made
Abner and the men that *were* with him a
feast.
21 And Abner said unto David, I will arise
and go, and [i]will gather all Israel unto my
lord the king, that they may make a league
with thee, and that thou mayest [j]reign over
all that thine heart desireth. And David sent
Abner away; and he went in peace.
22 ¶ And, behold, the servants of David
and Joab came from *pursuing* a troop, and
brought in a great spoil with them: but Abner *was* not with David in Hebron; for he
had sent him away, and he was gone in
peace.
23 When Joab and all the host that *was*
with him were come, they told Joab, saying,
Abner the son of Ner came to the king, and
he hath sent him away, and he is gone in
peace.
24 Then Joab came to the king, and said,
What hast thou done? behold, Abner came
unto thee; why *is* it *that* thou hast sent him
away, and he is quite gone?
25 Thou knowest Abner the son of Ner,
that he came to deceive thee, and to know
[k]thy going out and thy coming in, and to
know all that thou doest.
26 And when Joab was come out from
David, he sent messengers after Abner,
which brought him again from the well of
Sirah: but David knew *it* not.
27 And when Abner was returned to Hebron, Joab [l]took him aside in the gate to
speak with him quietly, and smote him
there [m]under the fifth *rib,* that he died, for
the blood of [n]Asahel his brother.
28 ¶ And afterward when David heard *it,*
he said, [o]I and my kingdom *are* guiltless
before the LORD for ever from the blood of
Abner the son of Ner:
29 [p]Let it rest on the head of Joab, and on
all his father's house; and let there not fail
from the house of Joab one [q]that hath an
issue, or that is a leper, or that leaneth on a
staff, or that falleth on the sword, or that
lacketh bread.
30 So Joab, and Abishai his brother slew
Abner, because he had slain their brother
[r]Asahel at Gibeon in the battle.
31 ¶ And David said to Joab, and to all the
people that *were* with him, [s]Rend your

3:2 [r]1 Chron. 3:1-4 [s]1 Sam. 25:43
3:3 [t]1 Sam. 27:8; ch. 13:37
3:4 [u]1 Kings 1:5
3:7 [v]ch. 21:8 [w]ch. 16:21
3:8 [x]Deut. 23:18; 1 Sam. 24:15; ch. 9:8
3:9 [y]Ruth 1:17; 1 Kings 19:2 [z]1 Sam. 15:28; 1 Chron. 12:23
3:10 [a]Judg. 20:1; ch. 17:11; 1 Kings 4:25
3:13 [b]Gen. 43:3 [c]1 Sam. 18:20
3:14 [d]1 Sam. 18:25
3:15 [e]1 Sam. 25:44
3:16 [f]ch. 19:16
3:18 [g]ver. 9
3:19 [h]1 Chron. 12:29
3:21 [i]ver. 10 [j]1 Kings 11:37
3:25 [k]1 Sam. 29:6; Isa. 37:28
3:27 [l]ch. 20:9; 1 Kings 2:5 [m]ch. 4:6 [n]ch. 2:23
3:28 [o]Deut. 19:13; 1 Kings 2:31
3:29 [p]1 Kings 2:32 [q]Lev. 15:2
3:30 [r]ch. 2:23
3:31 [s]Josh. 7:6; ch. 1:2

clothes, and [t]gird you with sackcloth, and mourn before Abner. And king David *himself* followed the bier.

32 And they buried Abner in Hebron: and the king lifted up his voice, and wept at the grave of Abner; and all the people wept.

33 And the king lamented over Abner, and said, Died Abner as a [u]fool dieth?

34 Thy hands *were* not bound, nor thy feet put into fetters: as a man falleth before wicked men, *so* fellest thou. And all the people wept again over him.

35 And when all the people came [v]to cause David to eat meat while it was yet day, David sware, saying, [w]So do God to me, and more also, if I taste bread, or ought else, [x]till the sun be down.

36 And all the people took notice *of it,* and it pleased them: as whatsoever the king did pleased all the people.

37 For all the people and all Israel understood that day that it was not of the king to slay Abner the son of Ner.

38 And the king said unto his servants, Know ye not that there is a prince and a great man fallen this day in Israel?

39 And I *am* this day weak, though anointed king; and these men the sons of Zeruiah [y]*be* too hard for me: [z]the LORD shall reward the doer of evil according to his wickedness.

4 And when Saul's son heard that Abner was dead in Hebron, [a]his hands were feeble, and all the Israelites were [b]troubled.

2 And Saul's son had two men *that were* captains of bands: the name of the one *was* Baanah, and the name of the other Rechab, the sons of Rimmon a Beerothite, of the children of Benjamin: (for [c]Beeroth also was reckoned to Benjamin:

3 And the Beerothites fled to [d]Gittaim, and were sojourners there until this day.)

4 And [e]Jonathan, Saul's son, had a son *that was* lame of *his* feet. He was five years old when the tidings came of Saul and Jonathan [f]out of Jezreel, and his nurse took him up, and fled: and it came to pass, as she made haste to flee, that he fell, and became lame. And his name *was* Mephibosheth.

5 And the sons of Rimmon the Beerothite, Rechab and Baanah, went, and came about the heat of the day to the house of Ish-bosheth, who lay on a bed at noon,

6 And they came thither into the midst of the house, *as though* they would have fetched wheat; and they smote him [g]under the fifth *rib:* and Rechab and Baanah his brother escaped.

7 For when they came into the house, he lay on his bed in his bedchamber, and they smote him, and slew him, and beheaded him, and took his head, and gat them away through the plain all night.

8 And they brought the head of Ish-bosheth unto David to Hebron, and said to the king, Behold the head of Ish-bosheth the son of Saul thine enemy, [h]which sought thy life; and the LORD hath avenged my lord the king this day of Saul, and of his seed.

9 ¶ And David answered Rechab and Baanah his brother, the sons of Rimmon the Beerothite, and said unto them, *As* the LORD liveth, [i]who hath redeemed my soul out of all adversity,

10 When [j]one told me, saying, Behold, Saul is dead, thinking to have brought good tidings, I took hold of him, and slew him in Ziklag, who *thought* that I would have given him a reward for his tidings:

11 How much more, when wicked men have slain a righteous person in his own house upon his bed? shall I not therefore now [k]require his blood of your hand, and take you away from the earth?

12 And David [l]commanded his young men, and they slew them, and cut off their hands and their feet, and hanged *them* up over the pool in Hebron. But they took the head of Ish-bosheth, and buried *it* in the [m]sepulchre of Abner in Hebron.

5 Then [n]came all the tribes of Israel to David unto Hebron, and spake, saying, Behold, [o]we *are* thy bone and thy flesh.

2 Also in time past, when Saul was king over us, [p]thou wast he that leddest out and broughtest in Israel: and the LORD said to thee, [q]Thou shalt feed my people Israel, and thou shalt be a captain over Israel.

3 [r]So all the elders of Israel came to the king to Hebron; [s]and king David made a league with them in Hebron [t]before the LORD: and they anointed David king over Israel.

4 ¶ David *was* thirty years old when he began to reign, [u]*and* he reigned forty years.

5 In Hebron he reigned over Judah [v]seven years and six months: and in Jerusalem he reigned thirty and three years over all Israel and Judah.

6 ¶ And the king and his men went [w]to Jerusalem unto [x]the Jebusites, the inhabitants of the land: which spake unto David, saying, Except thou take away the blind and the lame, thou shalt not come in hither: thinking, David cannot come in hither.

7 Nevertheless, David took the strong hold of Zion: [y]the same *is* the city of David.

8 And David said on that day, Whosoever getteth up to the gutter, and smiteth the Jebusites, and the lame and the blind, *that are* hated of David's soul, [z]*he shall be chief and captain.* Wherefore they said, The blind and the lame shall not come into the house.

9 So David dwelt in the fort, and called it [a]the city of David. And David built round about from Millo and inward.

10 And David went on, and grew great, and the LORD God of hosts *was* with him.

11 ¶ And [b]Hiram king of Tyre sent messengers to David, and cedar trees, and carpenters, and masons: and they built David an house.

12 And David perceived that the LORD had established him king over Israel, and

3:31 [t]Gen. 37:34
3:33 [u]ch. 13:12
3:35 [v]ch. 12:17; Jer. 16:7 [w]Ruth 1:17 [x]ch. 1:12
3:39 [y]ch. 19:7 [z]ch. 19:13; 1 Kings 2:5; Ps. 28:4; 2 Tim. 4:14
4:1 [a]Ezra 4:4; Isa. 13:7 [b]Matt. 2:3
4:2 [c]Josh. 18:25
4:3 [d]Neh. 11:33
4:4 [e]ch. 9:3 [f]1 Sam. 29:1
4:6 [g]ch. 2:23
4:8 [h]1 Sam. 19:2
4:9 [i]Gen. 48:16; 1 Kings 1:29; Ps. 31:7
4:10 [j]ch. 1:2
4:11 [k]Gen. 9:5
4:12 [l]ch. 1:15 [m]ch. 3:32
5:1 [n]1 Chron. 11:1 [o]Gen. 29:14
5:2 [p]1 Sam. 18:13 [q]1 Sam. 16:1; ch. 7:7; Ps. 78:71
5:3 [r]1 Chron. 11:3 [s]2 Kings 11:17 [t]Judg. 11:11; 1 Sam. 23:18
5:4 [u]1 Chron. 26:31
5:5 [v]ch. 2:11; 1 Chron. 3:4
5:6 [w]Judg. 1:21 [x]Josh. 15:63; Judg. 1:8
5:7 [y]ver. 9; 1 Kings 2:10
5:8 [z]1 Chron. 11:6-9
5:9 [a]ver. 7
5:11 [b]1 Kings 5:2; 1 Chron. 14:1

that he had exalted his kingdom for his people Israel's sake.

13 ¶ And [c]David took *him* more concubines and wives out of Jerusalem, after he was come from Hebron: and there were yet sons and daughters born to David.

14 And [d]these *be* the names of those that were born unto him in Jerusalem; Shammua, and Shobab, and Nathan, and Solomon,

15 Ibhar also, and Elishua, and Nepheg, and Japhia,

16 And Elishama, and Eliada, and Eliphalet.

17 ¶ [e]But when the Philistines heard that they had anointed David king over Israel, all the Philistines came up to seek David; and David heard *of it,* [f]and went down to the hold.

18 The Philistines also came and spread themselves in [g]the valley of Rephaim.

19 And David [h]enquired of the LORD, saying, Shall I go up to the Philistines? wilt thou deliver them into mine hand? And the LORD said unto David, Go up: for I will doubtless deliver the Philistines into thine hand.

20 And David came to [i]Baal-perazim, and David smote them there, and said, The LORD hath broken forth upon mine enemies before me, as the breach of waters. Therefore he called the name of that place Baal-perazim.

21 And there they left their images, and David and his men [j]burned them.

22 ¶ [k]And the Philistines came up yet again, and spread themselves in the valley of Rephaim.

23 And when [l]David enquired of the LORD, he said, Thou shalt not go up; *but* fetch a compass behind them, and come upon them over against the mulberry trees.

24 And let it be, when thou [m]hearest the sound of a going in the tops of the mulberry trees, that then thou shalt bestir thyself: for then [n]shall the LORD go out before thee, to smite the host of the Philistines.

25 And David did so, as the LORD had commanded him; and smote the Philistines from [o]Geba until thou come to [p]Gazer.

6 Again, David gathered together all *the* chosen *men* of Israel, thirty thousand.

2 And [q]David arose, and went with all the people that *were* with him from Baale of Judah, to bring up from thence the ark of God, whose name is called by the name of the LORD of hosts [r]that dwelleth *between* the cherubims.

3 And they set the ark of God [s]upon a new cart, and brought it out of the house of Abinadab that *was* in Gibeah: and Uzzah and Ahio, the sons of Abinadab, drave the new cart.

4 And they brought it out of [t]the house of Abinadab which *was* at Gibeah, accompanying the ark of God: and Ahio went before the ark.

5 And David and all the house of Israel played before the LORD on all manner of *instruments made of* fir wood, even on harps, and on psalteries, and on timbrels, and on cornets, and on cymbals.

6 ¶ And when they came to [u]Nachon's threshingfloor, Uzzah [v]put forth *his hand* to the ark of God, and took hold of it; for the oxen shook *it.*

7 And the anger of the LORD was kindled against Uzzah; and [w]God smote him there for *his* error; and there he died by the ark of God.

8 And David was displeased, because the LORD had made a breach upon Uzzah: and he called the name of the place Perez-uzzah to this day.

9 And [x]David was afraid of the LORD that day, and said, How shall the ark of the LORD come to me?

10 So David would not remove the ark of the LORD unto him into the city of David: but David carried it aside into the house of Obed-edom [y]the Gittite.

11 [z]And the ark of the LORD continued in the house of Obed-edom the Gittite three months: and the LORD [a]blessed Obed-edom, and all his household.

12 ¶ And it was told king David, saying, The LORD hath blessed the house of Obed-edom, and all that *pertaineth* unto him, because of the ark of God. [b]So David went and brought up the ark of God from the house of Obed-edom into the city of David with gladness.

13 And it was *so,* that when [c]they that bare the ark of the LORD had gone six paces, he sacrificed [d]oxen and fatlings.

14 And David [e]danced before the LORD with all *his* might; and David *was* girded [f]with a linen ephod.

15 [g]So David and all the house of Israel brought up the ark of the LORD with shouting, and with the sound of the trumpet.

16 And [h]as the ark of the LORD came into the city of David, Michal Saul's daughter looked through a window, and saw king David leaping and dancing before the LORD; and she despised him in her heart.

17 ¶ [i]And they brought in the ark of the LORD, and set it in [j]his place, in the midst of the tabernacle that David had pitched for it: and David [k]offered burnt offerings and peace offerings before the LORD.

18 And as soon as David had made an end of offering burnt offerings and peace offerings, [l]he blessed the people in the name of the LORD of hosts.

19 [m]And he dealt among all the people, *even* among the whole multitude of Israel, as well to the women as men, to every one a cake of bread, and a good piece *of flesh,* and a flagon *of wine.* So all the people departed every one to his house.

20 ¶ [n]Then David returned to bless his household. And Michal the daughter of Saul came out to meet David, and said, How glorious was the king of Israel to day, who [o]uncovered himself to day in the eyes of the

---

5:13 [c]Deut. 17:17; 1 Chron. 3:9
5:14 [d]1 Chron. 3:5
5:17 [e]1 Chron. 11:16 [f]ch. 23:14
5:18 [g]Josh. 15:8; Isa. 17:5
5:19 [h]ch. 2:1; 1 Sam. 23:2
5:20 [i]Isa. 28:21
5:21 [j]Deut. 7:5; 1 Chron. 14:12
5:22 [k]1 Chron. 14:13
5:23 [l]ver. 19
5:24 [m]2 Kings 7:6 [n]Judg. 4:14
5:25 [o]1 Chron. 14:16 [p]Josh. 16:10
6:2 [q]1 Chron. 13:5 [r]1 Sam. 4:4; Ps. 80:1
6:3 [s]Num. 7:9; 1 Sam. 6:7
6:4 [t]1 Sam. 7:1
6:6 [u]1 Chron. 13:9 [v]Num. 4:15
6:7 [w]1 Sam. 6:19
6:9 [x]Ps. 119:120; Luke 5:8
6:10 [y]1 Chron. 13:13
6:11 [z]1 Chron. 13:14 [a]Gen. 30:27
6:12 [b]1 Chron. 15:25
6:13 [c]Num. 4:15; Josh. 3:3; 1 Chron. 15:2 [d]1 Kings 8:5; 1 Chron. 15:26
6:14 [e]Ex. 15:20; Ps. 30:11 [f]1 Sam. 2:18; 1 Chron. 15:27
6:15 [g]1 Chron. 15:28
6:16 [h]1 Chron. 15:29
6:17 [i]1 Chron. 16:1 [j]1 Chron. 15:1; Ps. 132:8 [k]1 Kings 8:5
6:18 [l]1 Kings 8:55; 1 Chron. 16:2
6:19 [m]1 Chron. 16:3
6:20 [n]Ps. 30, title [o]ver. 14; 1 Sam. 19:24

FOCUS ON FIRST AND SECOND SAMUEL

Prayer petitions. Jealousy. Competition. Barrenness. Marriage. Birth. Rape. Incest. Workers. Mourners. Nurses. Caregivers. Wives. Abandoned. Singers. Silent lamenters. Rejoicing and thankful. We meet women in all of these states in the Books of 1 and 2 Samuel. As the nation of Israel becomes more centralized and hierarchical, the roles of women are brought into perspective. In a progressively degenerating society in which the people have ears closed to God, and even the priesthood has forgotten the voice that calls, God answers a woman's prayer. Thus we have the birth and leadership of Samuel.

We find the recorded prayer of a woman, as Hannah pleads with God to open her womb and allow her to have a son: "O LORD of hosts, if thou wilt indeed look on the affliction of thine handmaid, and remember me, and not forget thine handmaid, but wilt give unto thine handmaid a man child, then I will give him unto the LORD all the days of his life, and there shall no razor come upon his head" (1 Sam. 1:11).

This account also illustrates how God includes children in His plan, even when adults have chosen disobedience and idolatry. "And she said, Let thine handmaid find grace in thy sight. So the woman went her way, and did eat, and her countenance was no more sad" (1:18). Hannah's misery over her inability to conceive, which led to constant discord between her and her husband's second and more fertile wife, was a prayer request awaiting the proper time. Her child came on the scene when even the high priest could not receive a word from God (due to the sin of his sons). "And the child Samuel ministered unto the LORD before Eli. And the word of the LORD was precious in those days; there was no open vision" (3:1).

Hannah envisioned herself as a mother and remained hopeful that she would have a child eventually. Bathsheba envisioned herself as a wife and mother. She faced the reality of her sin with David, becoming a widow at his command, and having her firstborn child die because of their sin. Her laments are not recorded. Yet God did not forsake her. She later gave birth to Solomon. In 2 Samuel, David's daughter, Tamar, has a vision of becoming a wife and mother. Yet, her half-brother Amnon rapes her and then rejects her (2 Sam. 13). Many women know her story and her pain. In 1 Samuel, we see wise women who can talk to kings when prophets cannot reach their listening ear (2 Sam. 20).

Although males dominate these pages, 1 and 2 Samuel provide examples of women who show us how to live fully and faithfully. You don't want to miss the story of Abigail, who is married to Nabal (1 Sam. 25). She teaches us how to survive and thrive. Women are notable in these books, which detail the rise of Israel's greatest king, David, as told by Samuel.

THE BLACK PRESENCE IN FIRST AND SECOND SAMUEL

The Philistines figure prominently in 1 and 2 Samuel. They were the offspring of Ham's son, Mizraim (Gen. 10:6, 13), and occupied the coastal land of Canaan.

David and the king of Tyre developed a good business relationship (2 Sam. 5:11). Tyre and Sidon were key cities in Phoenicia. Phoenicians were the descendants of Ham through Canaan and were famous for their alphabet, sea navigation, trading, and manufacturing. Ezekiel 27 describes their riches and extensive trading around the Mediterranean Sea and throughout the known world.

David's wife, Bathsheba, was first married to Uriah, the Hittite (2 Sam. 11:3). Hittites were also descendants of Ham through Canaan (Gen. 10:15; 23:10).

Life Lessons

1 SAMUEL 1

First Samuel begins with the pain of a barren woman, Hannah, who believes in the power of prayer. Hannah is married to Elkanah, who also has a second wife, Peninnah. Peninnah is a constant source of vexation to Hannah. The family annually made a journey to Shiloh for worship and sacrifice. The context is set with these words: "But unto Hannah he gave a worthy portion; for he loved Hannah: but the Lord had shut up her womb . . . her adversary also provoked her sore . . . because the Lord had shut up her womb. And . . . he did so year by year" (1 Sam. 1:5–7). Yet Hannah was persistent in prayer. She had taken a stand with God and was relentless in her desire for a son. Her vow, made at the tabernacle, was even misunderstood by the high priest, who thought she was a drunk. "And it came to pass, as she continued praying before the Lord, that Eli marked her mouth. Now Hannah, she spake in her heart; only her lips moved, but her voice was not heard: therefore Eli thought she had been drunken" (vv. 12–13). But she petitioned until God agreed that the time was right: "Elkanah knew Hannah his wife, and the Lord remembered her" (v. 19).

Petition Grantor, I lay my heart's desire before You.

1 SAMUEL 2–4

After the consecration of her son, Samuel, Hannah's prayer of thanksgiving is recorded in 1 Samuel 2. When she keeps her promise and takes him to the tabernacle, Eli's poor judgment over his own sons' sins is made known. Eli's sons are described as wicked men who had no regard for the Lord (2:12). For this cause, God ceases speaking to Eli. But Hannah takes Samuel to the Tabernacle where he is trained by Eli to be a priest. God speaks to Samuel regarding Eli's house: "And Samuel grew, and the Lord was with him, and did let none of his words fall to the ground. And all Israel from Dan even to Beersheba knew that Samuel was established to

be a prophet of the Lord . . . And the word of Samuel came to all Israel" (3:19–4:1).

Later the Philistines capture the ark of the covenant (4:11). Eli dies when he learns of his sons' deaths. His daughter-in-law, the wife of Phinehas, was pregnant at the time. Overcome with grief from the death of her husband and father-in-law, she goes into labor. As she is about to die she names the child Ichabod, meaning "the glory has departed from Israel" (vv. 21–22).

Hovering Presence, don't leave us. We long to hear from You.

1 SAMUEL 7–17

The ark remains at Kirjath-jearim a long time (20 years in all). All the people of Israel mourn and seek the Lord (1 Sam. 7:2). Samuel subdues the Philistines at Mizpah and builds a stone memorial, naming it Ebenezer, saying, "Hitherto hath the Lord helped us" (1 Sam. 7:12). Samuel continues as judge over Israel all the days of his life, and builds an altar to the Lord at Ramah (vv. 15–17).

The people ask Samuel to appoint a king to lead them. The Lord tells him, "Hearken unto the voice of the people in all that they say unto thee: for they have not rejected thee, but they have rejected me" (8:7). Saul is chosen as king in chapter 9, then anointed in chapter 10. In chapter 11, Saul crushes the Ammonites. Chapter 12 shows Samuel bidding farewell to the nation, and in chapter 13, Samuel rebukes Saul, who takes it upon himself to do the ministry of the priest. In chapter 13, Samuel warns Saul that his kingdom will be taken away because of his (Saul's) disobedience. Saul's son, Jonathan, attacks the Philistines in chapter 14. The Lord rejects Saul as king in chapter 15. Chapter 16 shows Samuel anointing David, who kills Goliath in chapter 17. Saul jealousy of David prevails and he tries to kill him, which keeps David on the run (see chapters 18–28).

Abiding God, please don't take Your Holy Spirit away from me!

1 SAMUEL 25–31

David encounters Nabal and his wife, Abigail. She prevents David from shedding innocent blood, and he takes her and Ahinoam of Jezreel to be his wives. Abigail shows us how to prevent the loss of lives. Saul has given his daughter, Michal (another of David's wives) to Phalti, a man from Gallim (25:43–44).

David spares Saul's life and hides from him among the Philistines (chap. 27). "Now Samuel was dead, and all Israel had lamented him, and buried him in Ramah, even in his own city. And Saul had put away those that had familiar spirits, and the wizards, out of the land" (28:3). Saul then further disobeys God by seeking out a medium in Endor who summons up the spirit of Samuel (28:3–25). David is triumphant against the Philistines and the Amalekites (chaps. 29–30). Saul kills himself (chap. 31).

Giver of Wisdom, give me the wisdom of Abigail as I wrestle with fools.

2 SAMUEL 1–6

Second Samuel continues the story of Israel's monarchy. Second Samuel 1 finds David lamenting the deaths of Saul and Jonathan. David is anointed king over Judah (chap. 2). Second Samuel 3 details the politics of

marriage, as David's sons are listed along with the names of their mothers' political lineage. "In addition to Michal, Abigail, Ahinoam, and Bathsheba, 2 Samuel 5:13 notes that David took more concubines and wives. The purpose of these marriages would have been largely political, in order to forge relationships with neighboring kingdoms as with Maacah, the daughter of the king of Gershur and mother of Absalom" (*WBC,* 92). David welcomes Mephibosheth, the son of Jonathan, into his home and family. Jonathan, son of Saul, had a son who was lame in both feet. He was five years old when news about Saul and Jonathan came from Jezreel. His nurse picked him up and fled, but as she hurried to leave, he fell and became crippled (2 Sam. 4:4). David becomes king over all Israel and conquers Jerusalem (chap. 5). The ark of the covenant is returned to Jerusalem and David dances joyfully. Michal, watching from a window, despises David in her heart (6:16).

Sovereign One, use me in Your service to bring forth good fruit.

2 SAMUEL 11–12

David's relations with Bathsheba are recounted in 2 Samuel 11–12. David sends messengers to get her, has sex with her, then sends her home. When David receives word that Bathsheba has conceived, he tries to cover up the sin by having her husband, Uriah, sleep with his wife. When Uriah refuses to cooperate with this deception (which he doesn't even know anything about), David has Uriah placed in the front line of battle, where he is killed. Now Bathsheba is pregnant and widowed at the hand of the king (11:2–17). "And when the mourning was past, David sent and fetched her to his house, and she became his wife, and bare him a son. But the thing that David had done displeased the Lord" (v. 27).

All Knowing and All Seeing God, see those who would harm me.
And, let me see those I have harmed.

2 SAMUEL 12

The prophet Nathan comes and rebukes David with the story of a rich man, a poor man, and one little pet lamb. David points the finger of blame at himself. However, God announces the judgment: "The Lord also hath put away thy sin; thou shalt not die. Howbeit, because by this deed thou hast given great occasion to the enemies of the Lord to blaspheme, the child also that is born unto thee shall surely die" (12:13–14).

Maestro of Voiceless Melodies, catch the perfect pitch of my broken heart.

2 SAMUEL 13–20

The sin of the father affects his household. In 2 Samuel 13, Amnon, son of David, falls in love with his sister Tamar, then rapes her. "Nay, my brother, do not force me; for no such thing ought to be done in Israel: do not thou this folly. And I, whither shall I cause my shame to go?" (13:12–13). Her pleas are to no avail. Her brother, Absalom, kills Amnon and flees. Sin always brings division. In chapter 14, a wise woman of Tekoa is approached to talk to David about restoring harmony in his house. Absalom is sent for, but conspires to take his father's throne. Second Samuel 15–19 tells of the murder of Absalom and David's regret and return to Jerusalem. All of the men of Israel deserted David to follow

Sheba, son of Beliel. But the men of Judah stayed by their king (20:2). Another wise woman speaks to the commander of the army in 2 Samuel 20:16, providing wise counsel.

Ancient of Days, speak Your words of wise counsel through me.

2 SAMUEL 21

A mother's faithfulness even after her son's death is recounted with the heartwretching story of Rizpah, Saul's wife. For a sin Saul had committed against the Gibeonites, her two sons—along with the five sons of Saul's oldest daughter Merab—were killed and exposed on a hill before the Lord. All seven of them fell together and were put to death during the first days of the harvest: "Rizpah, the daughter of Aiah, took sackcloth and spread it for her upon the rock, from the beginning of harvest until water dropped upon them out of heaven, and suffered neither the birds of the air to rest on them by day, nor the beasts of the field by night" (21:10). It is a love story at its best. As a committee of one, she stayed for six months, keeping vigil over decaying flesh. When the rains came, David gave the boys a decent burial.

Merciful God, send Your refreshing rains to fall down on me and my seeming decay. I wait for the latter rains.

2 SAMUEL 22–24

In these chapters, we see the days of David draw to an end.

Mighty God, You have raised up a mighty nation and a great king. Now raise me and allow me to serve Your sovereign name!

Women in FIRST AND SECOND SAMUEL

HANNAH: A WOMAN WHO REFUSED TO SETTLE FOR NO

We never get used to disappointment. To live the life of a barren woman is heartbreaking. Hannah had been a barren woman for many years. She had become the scorn of other women, because having children, especially male children, was a symbol of wholeness. She was made to feel incomplete and inadequate as a wife and a woman. Hannah teaches us what to do when what we desire does not materialize. She helps us to handle the "nos" or "not yets" from God. Hannah helps us not to settle for anything less than what God desires for our lives.

Hannah's example teaches us the value of accepting the "nos" in our lives. She is a model for us in handling life's disappointments. She could have become depressed and resigned herself to her plight. She could have become bitter as so many people become when the thing for which they have prayed has not been fulfilled within a satisfactory period of time. However, Hannah re-emphasizes for us the value of prayer. Hannah continued to go to the tabernacle with her husband, Elkanah, to pray. She continued to worship God even though what she was asking for had not come. In other words, she responded to God as if He had already heard her prayer and had answered it with a son. She had not just her history, but the history of her people to stand on.

Hannah remained faithful to God. She continued to believe that God would say "yes." She never stopped believing that the God she served was able to help her. She steadfastly believed that God not only could, but would, answer her prayer.

Hannah also teaches us the value of waiting and not fainting. Although there were no signs that she would become a mother anytime soon, she never gave up hope. She continued to pray. The Bible tells us "And let us not be weary in well doing: for in due season we shall reap, if we faint not" (Gal. 6:9). God has promised that if we delight ourselves in Him, He will give us the desires of our heart.

Finally, when God did say "yes," Hannah honored Him by offering her son back to Him. She realized that her son was a gift from God. We must honor the Giver of the gift, for He honors those who honor Him.

Just because God has said "no" at this time does not mean "no" eternally. Sometimes God has to put all things in order before He can say "yes." Perhaps there are people and situations that He must work on before our "yes" can come.

Read 1 Samuel 1:1–12.
Read insight essays on Faith, Infertility, Motherhood, Prayer, Spiritually Naming Our Children, and Suffering.

—L. White

ABIGAIL: A WISE WOMAN DEALS WITH A TOUGH SITUATION

For the eyes of the LORD run to and fro throughout the whole earth, to shew himself strong in the behalf of them whose heart is perfect toward him (2 Chron. 16:9).

Samuel died and was buried in Ramah (1 Sam. 25:1). David, upon returning to the wilderness, sent greetings to Nabal, the rich husband of Abigail (1 Sam. 25:4–5). David proceeded to ask for a customary gift for services rendered while his men were on Nabal's property. Nabal refused in a very insulting manner. This behavior is not very surprising, however. Nabal's name means "fool" and he lived up to it. David took offense immediately and rounds up four hundred men to attack Nabal and his household. In the meantime, a young man overhears Nabal's remarks and warns Abigail of David's intentions. Abigail, being the intuitive, wise, beautiful black woman that she was, took loaves, skins, sheep, and other gifts and loaded them on donkeys to forestall David's assault on her household.

When Abigail approached David, she quickly dismounted and fell on her face in submission, accepting the blame for her husband's foolish remarks. Her positioning and soft words showed great respect for this man of God. She depended not only on her reasoning, but God's grace. She began to remind David of who he was. She also reminded him that vengeance belonged to the Lord, and that his Lord was the captain of the battlefield.

David repented, thanking Abigail for being an instrument of God by reminding him not to take matters into his own hands. Upon returning home Abigail found her husband drunk after a feast. She was not able to tell him any of what transpired earlier that day. When he awoke the next morning, she shared with him the previous day's events. When she confronted him, his heart became as stone. Ten days later "the LORD smote Nabal, that he died" (1 Sam. 25:38).

When David heard that Nabal was dead, he rejoiced in the judgment of God. Because of his regard for Abigail, he sent for her to be his wife.

Abigail earned David's respect. She illustrates for wives today the determination to make the best of a bad situation.

Read 1 Samuel 25:1–44; 2 Samuel 3:3.

—P. George

MICHAL AND THE WIVES OF BENJAMIN: STOLEN LIVES

As I look at the wives of the tribe of Benjamin, the daughters of Shiloh (Judg. 21), I become very saddened in my spirit. I am sad because their stories are our stories. But what is it that we can learn about right relationships with God and humanity? Scripture does not tell us too much about the daughters of Shiloh other than that they danced in rituals at a certain time and would later be stolen while doing so.

In contrast to the daughters of Shiloh, Michal knew David and loved him (see 1 Sam. 18:20). It's evident that she did because she risked her own life to save his (1 Sam. 19:11–17). And David loved Michal. I don't believe it was just for political reasons that he decided to retrieve his first bride after 14 years of separation (2 Sam. 3:14). Yet Michal had another side to her, for she worshiped idols (1 Sam. 19:13; see also 2 Sam. 6:16, 20). All of us can become guilty of idol worship in many ways. We start our girls off early in idol worship: chasing after designer clothes, after popularity, and for certain schools—as if education is a cure-all. The list can go on and on. Our materials goods, the longing for degrees, for power and prestige, for more money, and for many other possessions become our idols.

Michal was like any other young woman who makes her desire for a man a top priority. Girls become a certain age, and they start longing for holy matrimony. But are they equipped? They, too, can bring their idols into the marital relationship and not really understand the true commitment to God in marriage.

Unlike Michal, who longed for David, the daughters of Shiloh, or the wives of Benjamin, were stolen (Judg. 21:21–23). No doubt they had dreams of marriage to their own tribesmen. But instead they were taken by force and given to strong warriors in the near extinct tribe of Benjamin. These young virgins had no say in the matter.

Today, I suggest that parents talk with their daughters and listen to their desires and aspirations. No, I am not saying give in to them, but listen and teach them the responsibilities of marriage. Mothers must learn to both talk and listen. My daughter, Michele, recently became engaged. She is excited—she rightly should be. But is Michele really aware of what is required in a marriage today? Can I give her all of the answers, being divorced from her dad after six years of marriage? I don't think so.

Girls need to know that God wants a relationship and marriage with them, too. It's good to pray, wait, and then trust God. When one enters into a relationship blindly, lives are stolen, just as the daughters of Shiloh were. Relationships that are thrown together without godly consent and direction are merely stolen relationships. Stealth is involved. There is anger, abuse, violence, infidelity, adultery, and wasted years of unhappiness.

Michal was happy to be with David. But because of her contempt for the worship of God, she had to settle for being an aunt, instead of a mother. She was barren for her whole life (see 2 Sam. 6:23). We don't know how the daughters of Shiloh, who were stolen for marriage, felt about their destiny.

Women and girls of African ancestry, what is our destiny? Will we ever be truly happy in our marriages? If we get married, will it be enough to have that much-wanted and needed security, material goods, and the opportunity to see our children become educated and live productive lives? What will truly fulfill our desires for our daughters and ourselves? Certainly, God has a good plan for us. All we need to do is trust Him.

Read Judges 21; 1 Samuel 18:20–21; 14:49; 18:17–28; 25:44; 2 Samuel 3:12–16; 6:16, 23.

—B. Garvin

RIZPAH: A GRIEVING MOTHER

Rizpah is a relatively unknown mother in the Scriptures; yet her actions speaker louder than words. In Rizpah we see a mother who demonstrated love and compassion in order to preserve the remains of not only her two sons, but also the sons of another woman. She took a sackcloth—a symbol of mourning and distress—and placed it on a rock for herself. For six months she stayed there to protect the remains of these executed individuals from the vultures and jackals. Seven sons were put to death for their father's sin. For six months, Rizpah dealt with their death, face to face.

When King David heard of Rizpah's vigil, he was moved to provide a proper burial for corpses. While Rizpah couldn't save her sons lives, her courageous protection of them in death was rewarded.

Mothers all over this nation, especially African-American mothers, have found themselves in Rizpah's position. They find themselves taking on the vultures by day and the jackals by night. Today's vultures and jackals include racism and the drug culture that destroys everything that gets in its way. The phenomenon of crack strikes at the central nervous system of our community. It can make African-American children turn on their own mothers and African-American women give up their children—something even slavery couldn't do.

Statistics continue to knock at the door with tragic news. Each day many of our mothers learn that their children have been harmed in some way—socially, economically, educationally, psychologically, spiritually, or physically. We must grieve. We must pick up our sackcloth and grieve over the situations that now confront us. God hears and answers our prayers.

Read 2 Samuel 3:10; 21:8–14.

Read insight essays on Children, Grief, and Motherhood.

—*R. Walker*

BATHSHEBA: DESIRE AND DOMINANCE

The story of Bathsheba elicits different kinds of responses. It is a story of sin, sorrow, redemption, and consequence. It is a story of a powerful man who went after what he wanted and a woman who had little power to resist being used by him. We learn of the humanity of King David, the faithfulness of Uriah, and the silence of Bathsheba.

Women of color have experienced ultimate powerlessness. With our history of slavery, we understand oppression and male dominance. We understand a culture where women, especially women of color, are treated like pawns in the larger scheme of political progress and ambition. In Bathsheba's time, women had no voice, no power, no place in decision making. Their voices were rarely heard. One of the few times Bathsheba spoke was to send word to King David that she was pregnant. Her voice is silent for the remainder of the story, like so many other biblical women. So we don't really know Bathsheba's real predicament in this story. She may have felt reluctant to be with King David; she may have felt that she could not refuse the king; or she may have been a willing partner. We are uncertain as to what really happened. We do know that King David went to

great lengths to be with Bathsheba, and that he plotted her husband's death after learning that Bathsheba was pregnant. In this story, we learn that there are consequences for our behavior, that God's prophet spoke the truth even to the king, that sinful behavior is not acceptable to God, and that God forgives us when we confess our sins. Read the story of David and Bathsheba with the knowledge that God loves creation, and that God restores us to wholeness even when we fall from grace.

Read 2 Samuel 11:1–27; 12:15–24.

See also the insight essays on Adultery and Forgiveness. See also the portraits on the Adulteress of Proverbs, and the Forgiven Adulteress.

—M. Newbern-Williams

Insights

MARRIAGE

The marriage relationship is a great picture of the type of intimacy that God intended for all of creation. The "two becoming one flesh" (Gen. 2:24, Matt. 19:5, Mark 10:8, Eph. 5:28–33) signifies a closeness of two persons, who previously have been unrelated. They become so intimately connected that all other human relationships pale in comparison.

The biblical narrative tells us that before the Fall, Adam and Eve enjoyed a level of intimacy that, perhaps, cannot be recreated, given all of the implications of our falleness. There was nothing that they could not share, there was no self-consciousness or face-saving barriers between them. Put simply it says, "they were both naked, the man and his wife, and they were not ashamed" (Gen. 2:25). But, this speaks not only of physical nakedness, but also of a spiritual openness to each other, because there were no sinful secrets to taint the relationship. Genesis portrays marriage as God intended it—a mutual love and respect between one man and one woman. Later, as the Old Testament men began taking several wives in marriage (see Gen. 29:30; 1 Sam. 1:2), jealousy and strife entered the relationship, because often the husband would love one wife over another (1 Sam. 1:5).

Of course, the greatest example of marital intimacy in Scripture is the beautiful Song of Solomon, a story of the love between a king and a young maiden. It paints a picture of mutual devotion and adoration. It portrays two who delight in each other to the exclusion of all others (Song 7:10). Though it exalts physical beauty and intimacy (Song 4:1–15; 6:4–7; 7:17), it also speaks of the spiritual dimension of genuine love as emanating from the soul, or very core of our being (3:4). Such love, it says, is better "than wine" (Song 4:10) and "strong as death" (Song 8:6).

Read 1 Samuel 1.

—E. Alexander

COMMITMENT TO COMMUNITY

God answered Hannah's fervent prayers for a child only when Hannah pledged to give the child back to God. God wanted her to dedicate the child to serve Him. By serving God, Samuel could be used by God to serve as one of God's greatest prophets and to save the community from the selfish excesses of Eli's sons in the Tabernacle. God used Hannah's faithful cry of pain to fulfill God's purpose for the community.

Women of color who believe in Christ are in a special place in this world. We are people of color in a world where the noncolored population has both political and economic advantages. We also are women in a society that continues to be dominated by men. We live under a double-edged oppression that is painful. In spite of our own pain, or because of it, we have the special ability to see and to feel the struggles of those around us in a way that those in power cannot.

As believers in Christ, we know that God works through people on the opposite side of the political and economic power structure to create change and to move the world to new levels of civility. When we fervently pray and humble ourselves to God's will for our lives as Hannah did, we open ourselves to what God would have us give back to our communities. We give back to God by helping others and by becoming engaged in the struggle to create a political and economic system that recognizes the worth of all of God's children. By faithfully offering our best to God, like Hannah, we become empowered by God to create communities that reflect His love.

Read 1 Samuel 1:1–2:21.

See the portrait on Hannah.

—A. Davis

ATTRIBUTES OF GOD—RIGHTEOUSNESS

The judge had been paid off! The criminal was given a light sentence. The victim, a young black woman, who pressed charges against her boss for sexual harassment, sat stunned in the courtroom. She could not believe what she had just heard. What ever happened to righteousness and justice? How could the judge, who was sworn to uphold the law, take such a stand? Oh how she longed for a righteous judge! Have you ever been in a situation where you felt that justice and righteousness were thrown out of the window?

The Bible says, "the judgments of the LORD are true and righteous altogether. More to be desired are they than gold, yea, than much fine gold: sweeter also than honey and the honeycomb" (Ps. 19:9–10). These are words of assurance in a world where justice is for sale to the highest bidder, and righteousness is a scarce commodity. God's righteousness is immovable (Ps. 36:5–6). As the prophet Samuel pointed out to the people, God has always acted in a righteous manner when He has dealt with His people (see 1 Sam. 12:6–7). God's standards are nonnegotiable. His righteous nature assures us that God will always do what is right. God is the standard for "right." His ways are right because He is right, (Ps. 145:17), and God always acts in conformity with God's law. In a wishy-washy world, we can take courage in the fact that God never acts against His own nature. In fact, Jesus Christ came, was crucified, was buried, and rose again to satisfy the demands of God's righteousness. God dropped the charges on us, because of Christ's sacrifice.

God's righteousness challenges those who call on God to do what is right. The Bible says that because of the shed blood of Jesus Christ, we have the righteousness of God. How is God's righteousness reflected in us? How often do we act contrary to our nature as Christians?

Read 1 Samuel 12:6–15; Psalm 11:7; 116:5.

—C. Belt

INTUITION

Women have been said to have a certain way of "knowing things." It's often referred to as "mother wit" or "women's intuition." Biblically speaking, this certain way of knowing is called discernment. The word discern refers to one's ability to distinguish between, recognize, and comprehend that which is obscured from vision and reasoning. The Bible speaks of dis-

cernment in two aspects: (1) discerning of spirits (1 John 4:10)—the ability to distinguish between that which is good and godly and that which is evil; (2) discerning of human will (Heb. 4:12).

The gift of discernment is best epitomized in the life of Jesus Christ. He was able to discern the thoughts and hearts of those whom He encountered (Matt. 12:25, John 6:6). The gift of discernment allows one to see beyond words and actions in order to uncover hidden motivations and intent (Prov. 16:9). Because discernment is a gift from God, it is always subject to the written revelation of God—the Word of God.

Abigail was one of those women who had a gift of discernment. She exercised wisdom, by intervening on behalf of her husband and family with the future King of Israel, David, and averted what could have been destruction for her and her family. (See especially 1 Sam. 25:32–33.)

Read 1 Samuel 25.

Read insight essay on Influence. Read the portrait on Abigail.

—J. Thompson

DATE RAPE

Rape is a horrible, devastating experience. Victims may even find themselves in a life-threatening situation. The feelings of humiliation, helplessness, fear, and anger permeate their being. With date rape, women are not only physically and emotionally violated, but the pain is inflicted by someone they trust and with whom they are socially involved.

The story of Tamar in 2 Samuel 13 offers some solace. Tamar was sexually assaulted by someone she knew, then cast aside like dirt. That is often how a woman who has experienced date rape feels—dirty. She often asks herself, *How could I have been so foolish to trust him?* She is left feeling very alone and ashamed to look at herself. She may feel as though she has no one to whom she can talk. She may feel too ashamed to tell anyone. There are days when she just wants to scream—scream until the anger disappears or until her voice is no longer audible.

Other Christian women may try to soothe her by reminding her that "God will never put on you more than you can bear" or by saying, "Take your burdens to the Lord and leave them there." At those times words are not enough. What is needed is a breakthrough: inner peace and an elevation of one's low-as-it-can-go self-esteem.

A term in the Christian church that one hears but rarely gives much thought to is *purge*. To purge means "to rid one of guilt and defilement, to be free from impurity." Only God can purge the woman who has experienced date rape.

As you read God's holy and healing Word you rediscover the sense of security that is often destroyed when one has been physically and emotionally violated. In Psalm 91 the psalmist encourages himself by recalling the great, awesome power of God to protect and deliver His own from the evil that may befall them. As you read this psalm, allow the words to become personal. Talk to God as the psalmist did, allowing the cleansing power of God's Word to wash over your heart and soul (Eph. 5:26). Let His promises of security and protection release the dam full of frustration, pain, guilt, fear, memory, and stolen innocence within you. As you cry, pray. As you pray, yield. This is purging (Ps. 51:7).

Are you tired of carrying the guilt? Are you tired of feeling undeserving of true love—not really knowing how to love yourself? Yield to God's empowering spirit! "That he might present it to himself a glorious [woman], not having spot or wrinkle, or any such thing; but that it should be holy and without blemish" (Eph. 5:27).

When you find yourself reflecting on the negative past, speak aloud the affirmation that God has made you a little lower than angels and crowned you with glory and honor (Ps. 8:5). Praise God each day for the healing of your spirit and for the renewing of your mind (Rom. 12:1–2). You cannot control the actions of others but with God's love dwelling inside of you, you will endure.

Read 2 Samuel 13; see also Psalm 51:10–13; Romans 8:28; 2 Corinthians 1:3–4; Galatians 5:19–21; 1 Thessalonians 5:15; Hebrew 12:15.

See also the insight essays on Dating, Depression, and Suffering. Read the portraits on Dinah and Tamar.

—M. Thompson

SEXUAL ABUSE

Sexual abuse is probably the most violent, brutal, and degrading form of suffering. Flashbacks and night terrors will rob you of sleep. Sounds, sights, smells, and touch will trigger old memories. Trying to defend your honor can result in yelling, screaming, and character assassinations. You might be constantly blamed, shamed, misunderstood, or even called demon-possessed. The emotional pain might become so intense it causes you to consider ending your life or the life of your abuser. The stories of sexual abuse in the Bible appear in 2 Samuel 13:1–22, when Tamar was raped by her half-brother, Ammon, and in Genesis 34:2, when Dinah was raped by the prince Shechem.

Healing from sexual abuse is not an easy process, and it will take time and understanding to stop feeling like a victim. Healing might take years of crying, praying, journal writing, yelling, screaming, and psychotherapy to improve your self-esteem, poor self-image, and distorted body image. During that time, you will suffer, by not eating or sleeping, isolating yourself from others, and feeling alone, angry, misunderstood, and betrayed. You must find a way to deal with your suffering and anger. You can find comfort and encouragement in knowing that God will never leave or forsake you (Isa. 41:10; Heb. 13:5–6).

What Jesus says about life in Matthew 10:34–39 may explain part of why you experienced what you did. Be assured God is in control of your life—you can let go of the memories of abuse, stop focusing on them, and instead focus on living one day at a time before your loving God. God will send trustworthy people to journey with you and assist in your healing. Love yourself. Trust yourself. Love and trust God. He is with you and will never leave you. God knows, cares, and understands. The Scriptures do not offer any easy solutions to suffering. However, we should look at the way Christ handled suffering. He should be our model. The suffering He experienced on this earth and the heavenly victory he celebrates today shows us that our suffering is not in vain. With God's help, we will win the victory!

Read 2 Samuel 13:1–22; see also Genesis 34:1–31; Judges 11:29–40; Psalm 31.

See the insight essays on Domestic Violence, Overcoming Abuse, and Suffering. See the portraits on Dinah, Hagar, and Tamar.

—M. Taylor

BROKENHEARTEDNESS

A broken heart may be the result of broken promises, broken friendships, broken relationships, broken families, broken marriages, or the death of a child. Regardless of the source of brokenness, you feel as if your life has been shattered—just as Bathsheba and David felt when their baby boy died (see 2 Sam. 12:15–24). In many instances, the void seems too great to fill, and many women wonder how they can go on living.

As we study the Scriptures, we find that Jesus came to heal the brokenhearted (Luke 4:18). Women can take comfort in knowing that God is aware of the condition of our hearts (Heb. 4:14). The Bible teaches us that wherever our treasures are, our hearts will be there also (Matt. 6:21). Our healing begins when we learn to shift the focus of our heart from the broken circumstances to the All-Sufficiency of God. This process of refocusing our hearts begins with the transforming of our minds (Rom. 12:1). As we seek the Lord with all our heart, we must believe that God is thinking about us and cares for us. We need to feel free to come to God with our pain and sorrow, just as David and Bathsheba did (2 Sam. 12:16). We must believe God has a plan to give us hope and a bright future, and that God will be with us always—even in the midst of our deepest pain and sorrow (Jer. 29:11:14; Matt. 28:20).

As women begin to refocus their hearts and minds on God, Jehovah Rapha, the Lord God that heals, they will become the recipient of God's promise to heal the brokenhearted and bind the wounds of the afflicted (Jer. 30:17).

Read 2 Samuel 12:15–24.

—J. Thompson

WHAT GOD SAYS ABOUT SUCCESS

We all love "success." But what does God's Word say about success:

- God's definition of success is radically different from the world's ideas about success (1 Sam. 16:7; Isa. 55:8–9; Luke 16:15).
- Any success we enjoy (whether earthly or spiritual) comes from the hand of God (Gen. 39:3; Neh. 2:20; Jam. 1:17).
- God promises to bless and grant success when we carefully obey His Word (Deut. 29:9;1 Chr. 22:13; Ps. 1:1–3).
- Seeking the Lord is a prerequisite to success (2 Chr. 26:5; 31:21).
- Christ's assessment of us, not the opinions of our peers or culture, is the true measure of our success (2 Cor. 5:10)
- Faithful service is what makes us successful in the eyes of God (Matt. 25:14–30).
- Preparation, diligence, and skill will bring success (Prov. 22:29; Eccl. 10:10).
- An overabundance of "worldly success" may tempt us to forget God (Deut. 32:15; Prov. 30:9; Rev. 3:17).
- Gathering wise counsel from mentors and trusted advisors leads to success (Prov. 15:22).
- A commitment to God (marked by humble trust and wholehearted obedience) is necessary for success (Prov. 16:3).
- If someone does not know God, that person is a failure, regardless of how wise, powerful, or wealthy that person may be (Jer. 9:23–24).
- A person's final destiny must be considered before judging whether that person is a success (Ps. 73, especially verses 16–19).

handmaids of his servants, as one of the
[p]vain fellows shamelessly uncovereth himself!
21 And David said unto Michal, *It was*
before the LORD, [q]which chose me before
thy father, and before all his house, to appoint me ruler over the people of the LORD,
over Israel: therefore will I play before the
LORD.
22 And I will yet be more vile than thus,
and will be base in mine own sight: and of
the maidservants which thou hast spoken
of, of them shall I be had in honour.
23 Therefore Michal the daughter of Saul
had no child [r]unto the day of her death.

7 And it came to pass, [s]when the king sat
in his house, and the LORD had given
him rest round about from all his enemies;
2 That the king said unto Nathan the
prophet, See now, I dwell in [t]an house of
cedar, [u]but the ark of God dwelleth within
[v]curtains.
3 And Nathan said to the king, Go, do all
that *is* [w]in thine heart; for the LORD *is* with
thee.
4 ¶ And it came to pass that night, that the
word of the LORD came unto Nathan, saying,
5 Go and tell my servant David, Thus
saith the LORD, [x]Shalt thou build me an
house for me to dwell in?
6 Whereas I have not dwelt in *any* house
[y]since the time that I brought up the children of Israel out of Egypt, even to this day,
but have walked in [z]a tent and in a tabernacle.
7 In all *the places* wherein I have
[a]walked with all the children of Israel
spake I a word with any of the tribes of
Israel, whom I commanded [b]to feed my
people Israel, saying, Why build ye not me
an house of cedar?
8 Now therefore so shalt thou say unto
my servant David, Thus saith the LORD of
hosts, [c]I took thee from the sheepcote, from
following the sheep, to be ruler over my
people, over Israel:
9 And [d]I was with thee whithersoever
thou wentest, [e]and have cut off all thine
enemies out of thy sight, and have made
thee [f]a great name, like unto the name of
the great *men* that *are* in the earth.
10 Moreover I will appoint a place for my
people Israel, and will [g]plant them, that
they may dwell in a place of their own, and
move no more; [h]neither shall the children
of wickedness afflict them any more, as
beforetime,
11 And as [i]since the time that I commanded judges *to be* over my people Israel,
and have [j]caused thee to rest from all thine
enemies. Also the LORD telleth thee [k]that
he will make thee an house.
12 ¶ And [l]when thy days be fulfilled, and
thou [m]shalt sleep with thy fathers, [n]I will
set up thy seed after thee, which shall proceed out of thy bowels, and I will establish
his kingdom.

6:20 [p]Judg. 9:4
6:21 [q]1 Sam. 13:14
6:23 [r]1 Sam. 15:35; Isa. 22:14; Matt. 1:25
7:1 [s]1 Chron. 17:1
7:2 [t]ch. 5:11 [u]Acts 7:46 [v]Ex. 26:1
7:3 [w]1 Kings 8:17; 1 Chron. 22:7
7:5 [x]1 Kings 5:3; 1 Chron. 22:8
7:6 [y]1 Kings 8:16 [z]Ex. 40:18
7:7 [a]Lev. 26:11; Deut. 23:14 [b]ch. 5:2; Ps. 78:71; Matt. 2:6; Acts 20:28
7:8 [c]1 Sam. 16:11; Ps. 78:70
7:9 [d]1 Sam. 18:14; ch. 5:10 [e]1 Sam. 31:6; Ps. 89:23 [f]Gen. 12:2
7:10 [g]Ps. 44:2; Jer. 24:6; Am. 9:15 [h]Ps. 89:22
7:11 [i]Judg. 2:14; 1 Sam. 12:9; Ps. 106:42 [j]ver. 1 [k]Ex. 1:21; ver. 27; 1 Kings 11:38
7:12 [l]1 Kings 2:1 [m]Deut. 31:16; 1 Kings 1:21; Acts 13:36 [n]1 Kings 8:20; Ps. 132:11
7:13 [o]1 Kings 5:5; 1 Chron. 22:10 [p]ver. 16; Ps. 89:4
7:14 [q]Ps. 89:26; Heb. 1:5 [r]Ps. 89:30
7:15 [s]1 Sam. 15:23; 1 Kings 11:13
7:16 [t]ver. 13; Ps. 89:36; John 12:34
7:18 [u]Gen. 32:10
7:19 [v]ver. 12 [w]Isa. 55:8
7:20 [x]Gen. 18:19; Ps. 139:1
7:22 [y]1 Chron. 16:25; 2 Chron. 2:5; Ps. 48:1; Jer. 10:6 [z]Deut. 3:24; 1 Sam. 2:2; Ps. 86:8; Isa. 45:5
7:23 [a]Deut. 4:7; Ps. 147:20 [b]Deut. 9:26; Neh. 1:10
7:24 [c]Deut. 26:18 [d]Ps. 48:14
7:28 [e]John 17:17

13 [o]He shall build an house for my name,
and I will [p]stablish the throne of his kingdom for ever.
14 [q]I will be his father, and he shall be my
son. [r]If he commit iniquity, I will chasten
him with the rod of men, and with the
stripes of the children of men:
15 But my mercy shall not depart away
from him, [s]as I took *it* from Saul, whom I
put away before thee.
16 And [t]thine house and thy kingdom
shall be established for ever before thee: thy
throne shall be established for ever.
17 According to all these words, and according to all this vision, so did Nathan
speak unto David.
18 ¶ Then went king David in, and sat
before the LORD, and he said, [u]Who *am* I,
O Lord GOD? and what *is* my house, that
thou hast brought me hitherto?
19 And this was yet a small thing in thy
sight, O Lord GOD; [v]but thou hast spoken
also of thy servant's house for a great while
to come. [w]And *is* this the manner of man,
O Lord GOD?
20 And what can David say more unto
thee? for thou, Lord GOD, [x]knowest thy servant.
21 For thy word's sake, and according to
thine own heart, hast thou done all these
great things, to make thy servant know
them.
22 Wherefore [y]thou art great, O LORD
God: for [z]*there is* none like thee, neither *is*
there any God beside thee, according to all
that we have heard with our ears.
23 And [a]what one nation in the earth *is*
like thy people, *even* like Israel, whom God
went to redeem for a people to himself, and
to make him a name, and to do for you great
things and terrible, for thy land, before [b]thy
people, which thou redeemedst to thee from
Egypt, *from* the nations and their gods?
24 For [c]thou hast confirmed to thyself
thy people Israel *to be* a people unto thee
for ever: [d]and thou, LORD, art become their
God.
25 And now, O LORD God, the word that
thou hast spoken concerning thy servant,
and concerning his house, establish *it* for
ever, and do as thou hast said.
26 And let thy name be magnified for
ever, saying, The LORD of hosts *is* the God
over Israel: and let the house of thy servant
David be established before thee.
27 For thou, O LORD of hosts, God of Israel, hast revealed to thy servant, saying, I
will build thee an house: therefore hath thy
servant found in his heart to pray this
prayer unto thee.
28 And now, O Lord GOD, thou *art* that
God, and [e]thy words be true, and thou hast
promised this goodness unto thy servant:
29 Therefore now let it please thee to
bless the house of thy servant, that it may
continue for ever before thee: for thou,
O Lord GOD, hast spoken *it:* and with thy

blessing let the house of thy servant be blessed [f]for ever.

8 And [g]after this it came to pass, that David smote the Philistines, and subdued them: and David took Metheg-ammah out of the hand of the Philistines.

2 And [h]he smote Moab, and measured them with a line, casting them down to the ground; even with two lines measured he to put to death, and with one full line to keep alive. And *so* the Moabites [i]became David's servants, *and* [j]brought gifts.

3 ¶ David smote also Hadadezer, the son of Rehob, king of [k]Zobah, as he went to recover [l]his border at the river Euphrates.

4 And David took from him a thousand *chariots*, and seven hundred horsemen, and twenty thousand footmen: and David [m]houghed all the chariot *horses*, but reserved of them *for* an hundred chariots.

5 [n]And when the Syrians of Damascus came to succour Hadadezer king of Zobah, David slew of the Syrians two and twenty thousand men.

6 Then David put garrisons in Syria of Damascus: and the Syrians [o]became servants to David, *and* brought gifts. [p]And the LORD preserved David whithersoever he went.

7 And David took [q]the shields of gold that were on the servants of Hadadezer, and brought them to Jerusalem.

8 And from Betah, and from Berothai, cities of Hadadezer, king David took exceeding much brass.

9 ¶ When Toi king of Hamath heard that David had smitten all the host of Hadadezer,

10 Then Toi sent [r]Joram his son unto king David, to salute him, and to bless him, because he had fought against Hadadezer, and smitten him: for Hadadezer had wars with Toi. And *Joram* brought with him vessels of silver, and vessels of gold, and vessels of brass:

11 Which also king David [s]did dedicate unto the LORD, with the silver and gold that he had dedicated of all nations which he subdued;

12 Of Syria, and of Moab, and of the children of Ammon, and of the Philistines, and of Amalek, and of the spoil of Hadadezer, son of Rehob, king of Zobah.

13 And David gat *him* a name when he returned from smiting of the Syrians in [t]the valley of salt, [u]*being* eighteen thousand *men*.

14 ¶ And he put garrisons in Edom; throughout all Edom put he garrisons, and [v]all they of Edom became David's servants. [w]And the LORD preserved David whithersoever he went.

15 And David reigned over all Israel; and David executed judgment and justice unto all his people.

16 [x]And Joab the son of Zeruiah *was* over the host; and [y]Jehoshaphat the son of Ahilud *was* recorder;

17 And [z]Zadok the son of Ahitub, and Ahimelech the son of Abiathar, *were* the priests; and Seraiah *was* the scribe;

18 [a]And Benaiah the son of Jehoiada *was over* both the [b]Cherethites and the Pelethites; and David's sons were chief rulers.

9 And David said, Is there yet any that is left of the house of Saul, that I may [c]shew him kindness for Jonathan's sake?

2 And *there was* of the house of Saul a servant whose name *was* [d]Ziba. And when they had called him unto David, the king said unto him, *Art* thou Ziba? And he said, Thy servant *is he.*

3 And the king said, *Is* there not yet any of the house of Saul, that I may shew [e]the kindness of God unto him? And Ziba said unto the king, Jonathan hath yet a son, *which is* [f]lame on *his* feet.

4 And the king said unto him, Where *is* he? And Ziba said unto the king, Behold, he *is* in the house of [g]Machir, the son of Ammiel, in Lo-debar.

5 ¶ Then king David sent, and fetched him out of the house of Machir, the son of Ammiel, from Lo-debar.

6 Now when Mephibosheth, the son of Jonathan, the son of Saul, was come unto David, he fell on his face, and did reverence. And David said, Mephibosheth. And he answered, Behold thy servant!

7 ¶ And David said unto him, Fear not: [h]for I will surely shew thee kindness for Jonathan thy father's sake, and will restore thee all the land of Saul thy father; and thou shalt eat bread at my table continually.

8 And he bowed himself, and said, What *is* thy servant, that thou shouldest look upon such [i]a dead dog as I *am*?

9 ¶ Then the king called to Ziba, Saul's servant, and said unto him, [j]I have given unto thy master's son all that pertained to Saul and to all his house.

10 Thou therefore, and thy sons, and thy servants, shall till the land for him, and thou shalt bring in *the fruits,* that thy master's son may have food to eat: but Mephibosheth thy master's son [k]shall eat bread alway at my table. Now Ziba had [l]fifteen sons and twenty servants.

11 Then said Ziba unto the king, According to all that my lord the king hath commanded his servant, so shall thy servant do. As for Mephibosheth, *said the king,* he shall eat at my table, as one of the king's sons.

12 And Mephibosheth had a young son, [m]whose name *was* Micha. And all that dwelt in the house of Ziba *were* servants unto Mephibosheth.

13 So Mephibosheth dwelt in Jerusalem: [n]for he did eat continually at the king's table; and [o]was lame on both his feet.

10 And it came to pass after this, that the [p]king of the children of Ammon died, and Hanun his son reigned in his stead.

2 Then said David, I will shew kindness unto Hanun the son of Nahash, as his father

7:29 [f]ch. 22:51
8:1 [g]1 Chron. 18:1
8:2 [h]Num. 24:17 [i]ver. 6 [j]Ps. 72:10; 1 Sam. 10:27
8:3 [k]ch. 10:6; Ps. 60, title [l]Gen. 15:18
8:4 [m]Josh. 11:6
8:5 [n]1 Kings 11:23
8:6 [o]ver. 2 [p]ver. 14; ch. 7:9
8:7 [q]1 Kings 10:16
8:10 [r]1 Chron. 18:10
8:11 [s]1 Kings 7:51; 1 Chron. 18:11
8:13 [t]2 Kings 14:7 [u]1 Chron. 18:12; Ps. 60, title
8:14 [v]Gen. 27:29; Num. 24:18 [w]ver. 6
8:16 [x]ch. 19:13; 1 Chron. 11:6 [y]1 Kings 4:3
8:17 [z]1 Chron. 24:3
8:18 [a]1 Chron. 18:17 [b]1 Sam. 30:14
9:1 [c]1 Sam. 18:3; Prov. 27:10
9:2 [d]ch. 16:1
9:3 [e]1 Sam. 20:14 [f]ch. 4:4
9:4 [g]ch. 17:27
9:7 [h]ver. 1
9:8 [i]1 Sam. 24:14; ch. 16:9
9:9 [j]ch. 16:4
9:10 [k]ver. 7; ch. 19:28 [l]ch. 19:17
9:12 [m]1 Chron. 8:34
9:13 [n]ver. 7 [o]ver. 3
10:1 [p]1 Chron. 19:1

shewed kindness unto me. And David sent to comfort him by the hand of his servants for his father. And David's servants came into the land of the children of Ammon.

3 And the princes of the children of Ammon said unto Hanun their lord, Thinkest thou that David doth honour thy father, that he hath sent comforters unto thee? hath not David *rather* sent his servants unto thee, to search the city, and to spy it out, and to overthrow it?

4 Wherefore Hanun took David's servants, and shaved off the one half of their beards, and cut off their garments in the middle, [q]*even* to their buttocks, and sent them away.

5 When they told *it* unto David, he sent to meet them, because the men were greatly ashamed: and the king said, Tarry at Jericho until your beards be grown, and *then* return.

6 ¶ And when the children of Ammon saw that they [r]stank before David, the children of Ammon sent and hired [s]the Syrians of Beth-rehob, and the Syrians of Zoba, twenty thousand footmen, and of king Maacah a thousand men, and of Ish-tob twelve thousand men.

7 And when David heard of *it*, he sent Joab, and all the host of [t]the mighty men.

8 And the children of Ammon came out, and put the battle in array at the entering in of the gate: and [u]the Syrians of Zoba, and of Rehob, and Ish-tob, and Maacah, *were* by themselves in the field.

9 When Joab saw that the front of the battle was against him before and behind, he chose of all the choice *men* of Israel, and put *them* in array against the Syrians:

10 And the rest of the people he delivered into the hand of Abishai his brother, that he might put *them* in array against the children of Ammon.

11 And he said, If the Syrians be too strong for me, then thou shalt help me: but if the children of Ammon be too strong for thee, then I will come and help thee.

12 [v]Be of good courage, and let us [w]play the men for our people, and for the cities of our God: and [x]the LORD do that which seemeth him good.

13 And Joab drew nigh, and the people that *were* with him, unto the battle against the Syrians: and they fled before him.

14 And when the children of Ammon saw that the Syrians were fled, then fled they also before Abishai, and entered into the city. So Joab returned from the children of Ammon, and came to Jerusalem.

15 ¶ And when the Syrians saw that they were smitten before Israel, they gathered themselves together.

16 And Hadarezer sent, and brought out the Syrians that *were* beyond the river: and they came to Helam; and Shobach the captain of the host of Hadarezer *went* before them.

17 And when it was told David, he gathered all Israel together, and passed over Jordan, and came to Helam. And the Syrians set themselves in array against David, and fought with him.

18 And the Syrians fled before Israel; and David slew *the men of* seven hundred chariots of the Syrians, and forty thousand [y]horsemen, and smote Shobach the captain of their host, who died there.

19 And when all the kings *that were* servants to Hadarezer saw that they were smitten before Israel, they made peace with Israel, and [z]served them. So the Syrians feared to help the children of Ammon any more.

11 And it came to pass, after the year was expired, at the time when kings go forth *to battle*, that [a]David sent Joab, and his servants with him, and all Israel; and they destroyed the children of Ammon, and besieged Rabbah. But David tarried still at Jerusalem.

2 ¶ And it came to pass in an eveningtide, that David arose from off his bed, [b]and walked upon the roof of the king's house: and from the roof he [c]saw a woman washing herself; and the woman *was* very beautiful to look upon.

3 And David sent and enquired after the woman. And *one* said, *Is* not this Bathsheba, the daughter of Eliam, the wife [d]of Uriah the Hittite?

4 And David sent messengers, and took her; and she came in unto him, and [e]he lay with her; for she was [f]purified from her uncleanness: and she returned unto her house.

5 And the woman conceived, and sent and told David, and said, I *am* with child.

6 ¶ And David sent to Joab, *saying*, Send me Uriah the Hittite. And Joab sent Uriah to David.

7 And when Uriah was come unto him, David demanded *of him* how Joab did, and how the people did, and how the war prospered.

8 And David said to Uriah, Go down to thy house, and [g]wash thy feet. And Uriah departed out of the king's house, and there followed him a mess *of meat* from the king.

9 But Uriah slept at the door of the king's house with all the servants of his lord, and went not down to his house.

10 And when they had told David, saying, Uriah went not down unto his house, David said unto Uriah, Camest thou not from *thy* journey? why *then* didst thou not go down unto thine house?

11 And Uriah said unto David, [h]The ark, and Israel, and Judah, abide in tents; and [i]my lord Joab, and the servants of my lord, are encamped in the open fields; shall I then go into mine house, to eat and to drink, and to lie with my wife? *as* thou livest, and *as* thy soul liveth, I will not do this thing.

12 And David said to Uriah, Tarry here to day also, and to morrow I will let thee de-

10:4 [q]Isa. 20:4
10:6 [r]Gen. 34:30; Ex. 5:21; 1 Sam. 13:4 [s]ch. 8:3
10:7 [t]ch. 23:8
10:8 [u]ver. 6
10:12 [v]Deut. 31:6 [w]1 Sam. 4:9; 1 Cor. 16:13 [x]1 Sam. 3:18
10:18 [y]1 Chron. 19:18
10:19 [z]ch. 8:6
11:1 [a]1 Chron. 20:1
11:2 [b]Deut. 22:8 [c]Gen. 34:2; Job 31:1; Matt. 5:28
11:3 [d]ch. 23:39
11:4 [e]Ps. 51, title; Jam. 1:14 [f]Lev. 15:19
11:8 [g]Gen. 18:4
11:11 [h]ch. 7:2 [i]ch. 20:6

part. So Uriah abode in Jerusalem that day, and the morrow.

13 And when David had called him, he did eat and drink before him; and he made him [i]drunk: and at even he went out to lie on his bed [k]with the servants of his lord, but went not down to his house.

14 ¶ And it came to pass in the morning, that David [l]wrote a letter to Joab, and sent *it* by the hand of Uriah.

15 And he wrote in the letter, saying, Set ye Uriah in the forefront of the hottest battle, and retire ye from him, that he may [m]be smitten, and die.

16 And it came to pass, when Joab observed the city, that he assigned Uriah unto a place where he knew that valiant men *were.*

17 And the men of the city went out, and fought with Joab: and there fell *some* of the people of the servants of David; and Uriah the Hittite died also.

18 ¶ Then Joab sent and told David all the things concerning the war;

19 And charged the messenger, saying, When thou hast made an end of telling the matters of the war unto the king,

20 And if so be that the king's wrath arise, and he say unto thee, Wherefore approached ye so nigh unto the city when ye did fight? knew ye not that they would shoot from the wall?

21 Who smote [n]Abimelech the son of [o]Jerubbesheth? did not a woman cast a piece of a millstone upon him from the wall, that he died in Thebez? why went ye nigh the wall? then say thou, Thy servant Uriah the Hittite is dead also.

22 ¶ So the messenger went, and came and shewed David all that Joab had sent him for.

23 And the messenger said unto David, Surely the men prevailed against us, and came out unto us into the field, and we were upon them even unto the entering of the gate.

24 And the shooters shot from off the wall upon thy servants; and *some* of the king's servants be dead, and thy servant Uriah the Hittite is dead also.

25 Then David said unto the messenger, Thus shalt thou say unto Joab, Let not this thing displease thee, for the sword devoureth one as well as another: make thy battle more strong against the city, and overthrow it: and encourage thou him.

26 ¶ And when the wife of Uriah heard that Uriah her husband was dead, she mourned for her husband.

27 And when the mourning was past, David sent and fetched her to his house, and she [p]became his wife, and bare him a son. But the thing that David had done displeased the LORD.

12 And the LORD sent Nathan unto David. And [q]he came unto him, and [r]said unto him, There were two men in one city; the one rich, and the other poor.

2 The rich *man* had exceeding many flocks and herds:

3 But the poor *man* had nothing, save one little ewe lamb, which he had bought and nourished up: and it grew up together with him, and with his children; it did eat of his own meat, and drank of his own cup, and lay in his bosom, and was unto him as a daughter.

4 And there came a traveller unto the rich man, and he spared to take of his own flock and of his own herd, to dress for the wayfaring man that was come unto him; but took the poor man's lamb, and dressed it for the man that was come to him.

5 And David's anger was greatly kindled against the man; and he said to Nathan, *As* the LORD liveth, the man that hath done this *thing* shall surely die:

6 And he shall restore the lamb [s]fourfold, because he did this thing, and because he had no pity.

7 ¶ And Nathan said to David, Thou *art* the man. Thus saith the LORD God of Israel, I [t]anointed thee king over Israel, and I delivered thee out of the hand of Saul;

8 And I gave thee thy master's house, and thy master's wives into thy bosom, and gave thee the house of Israel and of Judah; and if *that had been* too little, I would moreover have given unto thee such and such things.

9 [u]Wherefore hast thou [v]despised the commandment of the LORD, to do evil in his sight? [w]thou hast killed Uriah the Hittite with the sword, and hast taken his wife *to be* thy wife, and hast slain him with the sword of the children of Ammon.

10 Now therefore [x]the sword shall never depart from thine house; because thou hast despised me, and hast taken the wife of Uriah the Hittite to be thy wife.

11 Thus saith the LORD, Behold, I will raise up evil against thee out of thine own house, and I will [y]take thy wives before thine eyes, and give *them* unto thy neighbour, and he shall lie with thy wives in the sight of this sun.

12 For thou didst *it* secretly: [z]but I will do this thing before all Israel, and before the sun.

13 [a]And David said unto Nathan, [b]I have sinned against the LORD. And Nathan said unto David, The LORD also hath [c]put away thy sin; thou shalt not die.

14 Howbeit, because by this deed thou hast given great occasion to the enemies of the LORD [d]to blaspheme, the child also *that is* born unto thee shall surely die.

15 And Nathan departed unto his house. And the LORD struck the child that Uriah's wife bare unto David, and it was very sick.

16 David therefore besought God for the child; and David fasted, and went in, and [e]lay all night upon the earth.

17 And the elders of his house arose, *and went* to him, to raise him up from the earth: but he would not, neither did he eat bread with them.

11:13 [i]Gen. 19:33 [k]ver. 9
11:14 [l]1 Kings 21:8
11:15 [m]ch. 12:9
11:21 [n]Judg. 9:53 [o]Judg. 6:32
11:27 [p]ch. 12:9
12:1 [q]Ps. 51, title [r]ch. 14:5; 1 Kings 20:35-41; Isa. 5:3
12:6 [s]Ex. 22:1; Luke 19:8
12:7 [t]1 Sam. 16:13
12:9 [u]1 Sam. 15:19 [v]Num. 15:31 [w]ch. 11:15
12:10 [x]Am. 7:9
12:11 [y]Deut. 28:30; ch. 16:22
12:12 [z]ch. 16:22
12:13 [a]1 Sam. 15:24 [b]ch. 24:10; Job 7:20; Ps. 32:5; Prov. 28:13 [c]ch. 24:10; Ps. 32:1; Job 7:21; Mic. 7:18; Zech. 3:4
12:14 [d]Isa. 52:5; Ezek. 36:20; Rom. 2:24
12:16 [e]ch. 13:31

18 And it came to pass on the seventh
day, that the child died. And the servants of
David feared to tell him that the child was
dead: for they said, Behold, while the child
was yet alive, we spake unto him, and he
would not hearken unto our voice: how will
he then vex himself, if we tell him that the
child is dead?
19 But when David saw that his servants
whispered, David perceived that the child
was dead: therefore David said unto his servants, Is the child dead? And they said, He
is dead.
20 Then David arose from the earth,
and washed, and [f]anointed *himself,* and
changed his apparel, and came into the
house of the LORD, and [g]worshipped: then
he came to his own house; and when he
required, they set bread before him, and he
did eat.
21 Then said his servants unto him, What
thing *is* this that thou hast done? thou didst
fast and weep for the child, *while it was*
alive; but when the child was dead, thou
didst rise and eat bread.
22 And he said, While the child was yet
alive, I fasted and wept: [h]for I said, Who
can tell *whether* GOD will be gracious to me,
that the child may live?
23 But now he is dead, wherefore should
I fast? can I bring him back again? I shall go
to him, but [i]he shall not return to me.
24 ¶ And David comforted Bath-sheba
his wife, and went in unto her, and lay with
her: and [j]she bare a son, and [k]he called his
name Solomon: and the LORD loved him.
25 And he sent by the hand of Nathan the
prophet; and he called his name Jedidiah,
because of the LORD.
26 ¶ And [l]Joab fought against [m]Rabbah
of the children of Ammon, and took the
royal city.
27 And Joab sent messengers to David,
and said, I have fought against Rabbah, and
have taken the city of waters.
28 Now therefore gather the rest of the
people together, and encamp against the
city, and take it: lest I take the city, and it be
called after my name.
29 And David gathered all the people together, and went to Rabbah, and fought
against it, and took it.
30 [n]And he took their king's crown from
off his head, the weight whereof *was* a talent of gold with the precious stones: and it
was *set* on David's head. And he brought
forth the spoil of the city in great abundance.
31 And he brought forth the people that
were therein, and put *them* under saws, and
under harrows of iron, and under axes of
iron, and made them pass through the
brickkiln: and thus did he unto all the cities
of the children of Ammon. So David and all
the people returned unto Jerusalem.

13 And it came to pass after this, [o]that
Absalom the son of David had a fair
sister, whose name *was* [p]Tamar; and Amnon the son of David loved her.
2 And Amnon was so vexed, that he fell
sick for his sister Tamar; for she *was* a virgin; and Amnon thought it hard for him to
do any thing to her.
3 But Amnon had a friend, whose name
was Jonadab, [q]the son of Shimeah David's
brother: and Jonadab *was* a very subtil
man.
4 And he said unto him, Why *art* thou,
being the king's son, lean from day to day?
wilt thou not tell me? And Amnon said unto
him, I love Tamar, my brother Absalom's
sister.
5 And Jonadab said unto him, Lay thee
down on thy bed, and make thyself sick:
and when thy father cometh to see thee, say
unto him, I pray thee, let my sister Tamar
come, and give me meat, and dress the meat
in my sight, that I may see *it,* and eat *it* at
her hand.
6 ¶ So Amnon lay down, and made himself sick: and when the king was come to
see him, Amnon said unto the king, I pray
thee, let Tamar my sister come, and [r]mak
me a couple of cakes in my sight, that I may
eat at her hand.
7 Then David sent home to Tamar, saying, Go now to thy brother Amnon's house,
and dress him meat.
8 So Tamar went to her brother Amnon's
house; and he was laid down. And she took
flour, and kneaded *it,* and made cakes in his
sight, and did bake the cakes.
9 And she took a pan, and poured *them*
out before him; but he refused to eat. And
Amnon said, [s]Have out all men from me.
And they went out every man from him.
10 And Amnon said unto Tamar, Bring
the meat into the chamber, that I may eat
of thine hand. And Tamar took the cakes
which she had made, and brought *them* into
the chamber to Amnon her brother.
11 And when she had brought *them* unto
him to eat, he [t]took hold of her, and said
unto her, Come lie with me, my sister.
12 And she answered him, Nay, my
brother, do not force me; for [u]no such thing
ought to be done in Israel: do not thou this
[v]folly.
13 And I, whither shall I cause my shame
to go? and as for thee, thou shalt be as one
of the fools in Israel. Now therefore, I pray
thee, speak unto the king; [w]for he will not
withhold me from thee.
14 Howbeit he would not hearken unto
her voice: but, being stronger than she,
[x]forced her, and lay with her.
15 ¶ Then Amnon hated her exceedingly;
so that the hatred wherewith he hated her
was greater than the love wherewith he had
loved her. And Amnon said unto her, Arise,
be gone.
16 And she said unto him, *There is* no
cause: this evil in sending me away *is*
greater than the other that thou didst unto
me. But he would not hearken unto her.

12:20 [f]Ruth 3:3 [g]Job 1:20
12:22 [h]Isa. 38:1; Jonah 3:9
12:23 [i]Job 7:8
12:24 [j]Matt. 1:6 [k]1 Chron. 22:9
12:26 [l]1 Chron. 20:1 [m]Deut. 3:11
12:30 [n]1 Chron. 20:2
13:1 [o]ch. 3:2 [p]1 Chron. 3:9
13:3 [q]1 Sam. 16:9
13:6 [r]Gen. 18:6
13:9 [s]Gen. 45:1
13:11 [t]Gen. 39:12
13:12 [u]Lev. 18:9 [v]Gen. 34:7; Judg. 19:23
13:13 [w]Lev. 18:9
13:14 [x]Deut. 22:25; ch. 12:11

17 Then he called his servant that ministered unto him, and said, Put now this *woman* out from me, and bolt the door after her.

18 And *she had* [y]a garment of divers colours upon her: for with such robes were the king's daughters *that were* virgins apparelled. Then his servant brought her out, and bolted the door after her.

19 ¶ And Tamar put [z]ashes on her head, and rent her garment of divers colours that *was* on her, and [a]laid her hand on her head, and went on crying.

20 And Absalom her brother said unto her, Hath Amnon thy brother been with thee? but hold now thy peace, my sister: he *is* thy brother; regard not this thing. So Tamar remained desolate in her brother Absalom's house.

21 ¶ But when king David heard of all these things, he was very wroth.

22 And Absalom spake unto his brother Amnon [b]neither good nor bad: for Absalom [c]hated Amnon, because he had forced his sister Tamar.

23 ¶ And it came to pass after two full years, that Absalom [d]had sheepshearers in Baal-hazor, which *is* beside Ephraim: and Absalom invited all the king's sons.

24 And Absalom came to the king, and said, Behold now, thy servant hath sheepshearers; let the king, I beseech thee, and his servants go with thy servant.

25 And the king said to Absalom, Nay, my son, let us not all now go, lest we be chargeable unto thee. And he pressed him: howbeit he would not go, but blessed him.

26 Then said Absalom, If not, I pray thee, let my brother Amnon go with us. And the king said unto him, Why should he go with thee?

27 But Absalom pressed him, that he let Amnon and all the king's sons go with him.

28 ¶ Now Absalom had commanded his servants, saying, Mark ye now when Amnon's [e]heart is merry with wine, and when I say unto you, Smite Amnon; then kill him, fear not: have not I commanded you? be courageous, and be valiant.

29 And the servants of Absalom did unto Amnon as Absalom had commanded. Then all the king's sons arose, and every man gat him up upon his mule, and fled.

30 ¶ And it came to pass, while they were in the way, that tidings came to David, saying, Absalom hath slain all the king's sons, and there is not one of them left.

31 Then the king arose, and [f]tare his garments, and [g]lay on the earth; and all his servants stood by with their clothes rent.

32 And [h]Jonadab, the son of Shimeah David's brother, answered and said, Let not my lord suppose *that* they have slain all the young men the king's sons; for Amnon only is dead: for by the appointment of Absalom this hath been determined from the day that he forced his sister Tamar.

33 Now therefore [i]let not my lord the king take the thing to his heart, to think that all the king's sons are dead: for Amnon only is dead.

34 [j]But Absalom fled. And the young man that kept the watch lifted up his eyes, and looked, and, behold, there came much people by the way of the hill side behind him.

35 And Jonadab said unto the king, Behold, the king's sons come: as thy servant said, so it is.

36 And it came to pass, as soon as he had made an end of speaking, that, behold, the king's sons came, and lifted up their voice and wept: and the king also and all his servants wept very sore.

37 ¶ But Absalom fled, and went to [k]Talmai, the son of Ammihud, king of Geshur. And *David* mourned for his son every day.

38 So Absalom fled, and went to [l]Geshur, and was there three years.

39 And *the soul of* king David longed to go forth unto Absalom: for he was [m]comforted concerning Amnon, seeing he was dead.

14

Now Joab the son of Zeruiah perceived that the king's heart *was* [n]toward Absalom.

2 And Joab sent to [o]Tekoah, and fetched thence a wise woman, and said unto her, I pray thee, feign thyself to be a mourner, [p]and put on now mourning apparel, and anoint not thyself with oil, but be as a woman that had a long time mourned for the dead:

3 And come to the king, and speak on this manner unto him. So Joab [q]put the words in her mouth.

4 ¶ And when the woman of Tekoah spake to the king, she [r]fell on her face to the ground, and did obeisance, and said, [s]Help, O king.

5 And the king said unto her, What aileth thee? And she answered, [t]I *am* indeed a widow woman, and mine husband is dead.

6 And thy handmaid had two sons, and they two strove together in the field, and *there was* none to part them, but the one smote the other, and slew him.

7 And, behold, [u]the whole family is risen against thine handmaid, and they said, Deliver him that smote his brother, that we may kill him, for the life of his brother whom he slew; and we will destroy the heir also: and so they shall quench my coal which is left, and shall not leave to my husband *neither* name nor remainder upon the earth.

8 And the king said unto the woman, Go to thine house, and I will give charge concerning thee.

9 And the woman of Tekoah said unto the king, My lord, O king, [v]the iniquity *be* on me, and on my father's house: [w]and the king and his throne *be* guiltless.

10 And the king said, Whosoever saith *ought* unto thee, bring him to me, and he shall not touch thee any more.

13:18 [y]Gen. 37:3; Judg. 5:30; Ps. 45:14
13:19 [z]Josh. 7:6; ch. 1:2; Job 2:12 [a]Jer. 2:37
13:22 [b]Gen. 24:50 [c]Lev. 19:17
13:23 [d]Gen. 38:12; 1 Sam. 25:4
13:28 [e]Judg. 19:6; Ruth 3:7; 1 Sam. 25:36; Esth. 1:10; Ps. 104:15
13:31 [f]ch. 1:11 [g]ch. 12:16
13:32 [h]ver. 3
13:33 [i]ch. 19:19
13:34 [j]ver. 38
13:37 [k]ch. 3:3
13:38 [l]ch. 14:23
13:39 [m]Gen. 38:12
14:1 [n]ch. 13:39
14:2 [o]2 Chron. 11:6 [p]Ruth 3:3
14:3 [q]ver. 19; Ex. 4:15
14:4 [r]1 Sam. 20:41; ch. 1:2 [s]2 Kings 6:26
14:5 [t]ch. 12:1
14:7 [u]Num. 35:19; Deut. 19:12
14:9 [v]Gen. 27:13; 1 Sam. 25:24; Matt. 27:25 [w]ch. 3:28; 1 Kings 2:33

11 Then said she, I pray thee, let the king remember the LORD thy God, that thou wouldest not suffer [x]the revengers of blood to destroy any more, lest they destroy my son. And he said, [y]As the LORD liveth, there shall not one hair of thy son fall to the earth.

12 Then the woman said, Let thine handmaid, I pray thee, speak *one* word unto my lord the king. And he said, Say on.

13 And the woman said, Wherefore then hast thou thought such a thing against [z]the people of God? for the king doth speak this thing as one which is faulty, in that the king doth not fetch home again [a]his banished.

14 For we [b]must needs die, and *are* as water spilt on the ground, which cannot be gathered up again; neither doth God respect *any* person: yet doth he [c]devise means, that his banished be not expelled from him.

15 Now therefore that I am come to speak of this thing unto my lord the king, *it is* because the people have made me afraid: and thy handmaid said, I will now speak unto the king; it may be that the king will perform the request of his handmaid.

16 For the king will hear, to deliver his handmaid out of the hand of the man *that would* destroy me and my son together out of the inheritance of God.

17 Then thine handmaid said, The word of my lord the king shall now be comfortable: for [d]as an angel of God, so *is* my lord the king to discern good and bad: therefore the LORD thy God will be with thee.

18 Then the king answered and said unto the woman, Hide not from me, I pray thee, the thing that I shall ask thee. And the woman said, Let my lord the king now speak.

19 And the king said, *Is not* the hand of Joab with thee in all this? And the woman answered and said, *As* thy soul liveth, my lord the king, none can turn to the right hand or to the left from ought that my lord the king hath spoken: for thy servant Joab, he bade me, and [e]he put all these words in the mouth of thine handmaid:

20 To fetch about this form of speech hath thy servant Joab done this thing: and my lord *is* wise, [f]according to the wisdom of an angel of God, to know all *things* that *are* in the earth.

21 ¶ And the king said unto Joab, Behold now, I have done this thing: go therefore, bring the young man Absalom again.

22 And Joab fell to the ground on his face, and bowed himself, and thanked the king: and Joab said, To day thy servant knoweth that I have found grace in thy sight, my lord, O king, in that the king hath fulfilled the request of his servant.

23 So Joab arose [g]and went to Geshur, and brought Absalom to Jerusalem.

24 And the king said, Let him turn to his own house, and let him [h]not see my face. So Absalom returned to his own house, and saw not the king's face.

25 ¶ But in all Israel there was none to be so much praised as Absalom for his beauty: [i]from the sole of his foot even to the crown of his head there was no blemish in him.

26 And when he polled his head, (for it was at every year's end that he polled *it:* because *the hair* was heavy on him, therefore he polled it:) he weighed the hair of his head at two hundred shekels after the king's weight.

27 And [j]unto Absalom there were born three sons, and one daughter, whose name *was* Tamar: she was a woman of a fair countenance.

28 ¶ So Absalom dwelt two full years in Jerusalem, [k]and saw not the king's face.

29 Therefore Absalom sent for Joab, to have sent him to the king; but he would not come to him: and when he sent again the second time, he would not come.

30 Therefore he said unto his servants, See, Joab's field is near mine, and he hath barley there; go and set it on fire. And Absalom's servants set the field on fire.

31 Then Joab arose, and came to Absalom unto *his* house, and said unto him, Wherefore have thy servants set my field on fire?

32 And Absalom answered Joab, Behold, I sent unto thee, saying, Come hither, that I may send thee to the king, to say, Wherefore am I come from Geshur? *it had been* good for me *to have been* there still: now therefore let me see the king's face; and if there be *any* iniquity in me, let him kill me.

33 So Joab came to the king, and told him and when he had called for Absalom, he came to the king, and bowed himself on his face to the ground before the king: and the king [l]kissed Absalom.

15 And [m]it came to pass after this, that Absalom [n]prepared him chariots and horses, and fifty men to run before him.

2 And Absalom rose up early, and stood beside the way of the gate: and it was *so,* that when any man that had a controversy came to the king for judgment, then Absalom called unto him, and said, Of what city *art* thou? And he said, Thy servant *is* of one of the tribes of Israel.

3 And Absalom said unto him, See, thy matters *are* good and right; but *there is* no man *deputed* of the king to hear thee.

4 Absalom said moreover, [o]Oh that I were made judge in the land, that every man which hath any suit or cause might come unto me, and I would do him justice!

5 And it was *so,* that when any man came nigh *to him* to do him obeisance, he put forth his hand, and took him, and kissed him.

6 And on this manner did Absalom to all Israel that came to the king for judgment: [p]so Absalom stole the hearts of the men of Israel.

7 ¶ And it came to pass [q]after forty years, that Absalom said unto the king, I pray thee, let me go and pay my vow, which I have vowed unto the LORD, in Hebron.

14:11 [x]Num. 35:19 [y]1 Sam. 14:45; Acts 27:34
14:13 [z]Judg. 20:2 [a]ch. 13:37
14:14 [b]Job 34:15; Heb. 9:27 [c]Num. 35:15
14:17 [d]ver. 20; ch. 19:27
14:19 [e]ver. 3
14:20 [f]ver. 17; ch. 19:27
14:23 [g]ch. 13:37
14:24 [h]Gen. 43:3; ch. 3:13
14:25 [i]Isa. 1:6
14:27 [j]ch. 18:18
14:28 [k]ver. 24
14:33 [l]Gen. 33:4; Luke 15:20
15:1 [m]ch. 12:11 [n]1 Kings 1:5
15:4 [o]Judg. 9:29
15:6 [p]Rom. 16:18
15:7 [q]1 Sam. 16:1

8 [r]For thy servant [s]vowed a vow [t]while I abode at Geshur in Syria, saying, If the LORD shall bring me again indeed to Jerusalem, then I will serve the LORD.

9 And the king said unto him, Go in peace. So he arose, and went to Hebron.

10 ¶ But Absalom sent spies throughout all the tribes of Israel, saying, As soon as ye hear the sound of the trumpet, then ye shall say, Absalom reigneth in Hebron.

11 And with Absalom went two hundred men out of Jerusalem, *that were* [u]called; and they went [v]in their simplicity, and they knew not any thing.

12 And Absalom sent for Ahithophel the Gilonite, [w]David's counsellor, from his city, *even* from [x]Giloh, while he offered sacrifices. And the conspiracy was strong; for the people [y]increased continually with Absalom.

13 ¶ And there came a messenger to David, saying, [z]The hearts of the men of Israel are after Absalom.

14 And David said unto all his servants that *were* with him at Jerusalem, Arise, and let us [a]flee; for we shall not *else* escape from Absalom: make speed to depart, lest he overtake us suddenly, and bring evil upon us, and smite the city with the edge of the sword.

15 And the king's servants said unto the king, Behold, thy servants *are ready to do* whatsoever my lord the king shall appoint.

16 And [b]the king went forth, and all his household after him. And the king left [c]ten women, *which were* concubines, to keep the house.

17 And the king went forth, and all the people after him, and tarried in a place that was far off.

18 And all his servants passed on beside him; [d]and all the Cherethites, and all the Pelethites, and all the Gittites, six hundred men which came after him from Gath, passed on before the king.

19 ¶ Then said the king to [e]Ittai the Gittite, Wherefore goest thou also with us? return to thy place, and abide with the king: for thou *art* a stranger, and also an exile.

20 Whereas thou camest *but* yesterday, should I this day make thee go up and down with us? seeing I go [f]whither I may, return thou, and take back thy brethren: mercy and truth *be* with thee.

21 And Ittai answered the king, and said, [g]*As* the LORD liveth, and *as* my lord the king liveth, surely in what place my lord the king shall be, whether in death or life, even there also will thy servant be.

22 And David said to Ittai, Go and pass over. And Ittai the Gittite passed over, and all his men, and all the little ones that *were* with him.

23 And all the country wept with a loud voice, and all the people passed over: the king also himself passed over the brook Kidron, and all the people passed over, toward the way of the [h]wilderness.

24 ¶ And lo Zadok also, and all the Levites *were* with him, [i]bearing the ark of the covenant of God: and they set down the ark of God; and Abiathar went up, until all the people had done passing out of the city.

25 And the king said unto Zadok, Carry back the ark of God into the city: if I shall find favour in the eyes of the LORD, he [j]will bring me again, and shew me *both* it, and his habitation:

26 But if he thus say, I have no [k]delight in thee; behold, *here am* I, [l]let him do to me as seemeth good unto him.

27 The king said also unto Zadok the priest, *Art not* thou a [m]seer? return into the city in peace, and [n]your two sons with you, Ahimaaz thy son, and Jonathan the son of Abiathar.

28 See, [o]I will tarry in the plain of the wilderness, until there come word from you to certify me.

29 Zadok therefore and Abiathar carried the ark of God again to Jerusalem: and they tarried there.

30 ¶ And David went up by the ascent of *mount* Olivet, and wept as he went up, and [p]had his head covered, and he went [q]barefoot: and all the people that *was* with him [r]covered every man his head, and they went up, [s]weeping as they went up.

31 ¶ And *one* told David, saying, [t]Ahithophel *is* among the conspirators with Absalom. And David said, O LORD, I pray thee, [u]turn the counsel of Ahithophel into foolishness.

32 ¶ And it came to pass, that *when* David was come to the top *of the mount*, where he worshipped God, behold, Hushai the [v]Archite came to meet him [w]with his coat rent, and earth upon his head:

33 Unto whom David said, If thou passest on with me, then thou shalt be [x]a burden unto me:

34 But if thou return to the city, and say unto Absalom, [y]I will be thy servant, O king; *as* I *have been* thy father's servant hitherto, so *will* I now also *be* thy servant: then mayest thou for me defeat the counsel of Ahithophel.

35 And *hast thou* not there with thee Zadok and Abiathar the priests? therefore it shall be, *that* what thing soever thou shalt hear out of the king's house, [z]thou shalt tell *it* to Zadok and Abiathar the priests.

36 Behold, *they have* there [a]with them their two sons, Ahimaaz Zadok's *son,* and Jonathan Abiathar's *son;* and by them ye shall send unto me every thing that ye can hear.

37 So Hushai [b]David's friend came into the city, [c]and Absalom came into Jerusalem.

16 And [d]when David was a little past the top *of the hill,* behold, [e]Ziba the servant of Mephibosheth met him, with a couple of asses saddled, and upon them two hundred *loaves* of bread, and an hundred

15:8 [r]1 Sam. 16:2 [s]Gen. 28:20 [t]ch. 13:38
15:11 [u]1 Sam. 9:13 [v]Gen. 20:5
15:12 [w]Ps. 41:9 [x]Josh. 15:51 [y]Ps. 3:1
15:13 [z]ver. 6; Judg. 9:3
15:14 [a]ch. 19:9; Ps. 3, title
15:16 [b]Ps. 3, title [c]ch. 16:21
15:18 [d]ch. 8:18
15:19 [e]ch. 18:2
15:20 [f]1 Sam. 23:13
15:21 [g]Ruth 1:16; Prov. 17:17
15:23 [h]ch. 16:2
15:24 [i]Num. 4:15
15:25 [j]Ps. 43:3
15:26 [k]Num. 14:8; 2 Sam. 22:20; 1 Kings 10:9; 2 Chron. 9:8; Isa. 62:4 [l]1 Sam. 3:18
15:27 [m]1 Sam. 9:9 [n]ch. 17:17
15:28 [o]ch. 17:16
15:30 [p]ch. 19:4; Esth. 6:12 [q]Isa. 20:2 [r]Jer. 14:3 [s]Ps. 126:6
15:31 [t]Ps. 3:1 [u]ch. 16:23
15:32 [v]Josh. 16:2 [w]ch. 1:2
15:33 [x]ch. 19:35
15:34 [y]ch. 16:19
15:35 [z]ch. 17:15
15:36 [a]ver. 27
15:37 [b]ch. 16:16; 1 Chron. 27:33 [c]ch. 16:15
16:1 [d]ch. 15:30 [e]ch. 9:2

bunches of raisins, and an hundred of summer fruits, and a bottle of wine.
2 And the king said unto Ziba, What
meanest thou by these? And Ziba said, The
asses *be* for the king's household to ride on;
and the bread and summer fruit for the
young men to eat; and the wine, [f]that such
as be faint in the wilderness may drink.
3 And the king said, And where *is* thy
master's son? [g]And Ziba said unto the king,
Behold, he abideth at Jerusalem: for he
said, To day shall the house of Israel restore
me the kingdom of my father.
4 [h]Then said the king to Ziba, Behold,
thine *are* all that *pertained* unto Mephibosheth. And Ziba said, I humbly beseech thee
that I may find grace in thy sight, my lord,
O king.
5 ¶ And when king David came to Bahurim, behold, thence came out a man of the
family of the house of Saul, whose name
was [i]Shimei, the son of Gera: he came
forth, and cursed still as he came.
6 And he cast stones at David, and at all
the servants of king David: and all the people and all the mighty men *were* on his right
hand and on his left.
7 And thus said Shimei when he cursed,
Come out, come out, thou bloody man, and
thou [j]man of Belial:
8 The LORD hath [k]returned upon thee all
[l]the blood of the house of Saul, in whose
stead thou hast reigned; and the LORD hath
delivered the kingdom into the hand of Absalom thy son: and, behold, thou *art taken*
in thy mischief, because thou *art* a bloody
man.
9 ¶ Then said Abishai the son of Zeruiah
unto the king, Why should this [m]dead dog
[n]curse my lord the king? let me go over, I
pray thee, and take off his head.
10 And the king said, [o]What have I to do
with you, ye sons of Zeruiah? so let him
curse, because [p]the LORD hath said unto
him, Curse David. [q]Who shall then say,
Wherefore hast thou done so?
11 And David said to Abishai, and to all
his servants, Behold, [r]my son, which
[s]came forth of my bowels, seeketh my life:
how much more now *may this* Benjamite *do
it*? let him alone, and let him curse; for the
LORD hath bidden him.
12 It may be that the LORD will look on
mine affliction, and that the LORD will [t]re-
quite me good for his cursing this day.
13 And as David and his men went by the
way, Shimei went along on the hill's side
over against him, and cursed as he went,
and threw stones at him, and cast dust.
14 And the king, and all the people that
were with him, came weary, and refreshed
themselves there.
15 ¶ And [u]Absalom, and all the people
the men of Israel, came to Jerusalem, and
Ahithophel with him.
16 And it came to pass, when Hushai the
Archite, [v]David's friend, was come unto

16:2 [f]ch. 15:23
16:3 [g]ch. 19:27
16:4 [h]Prov. 18:13
16:5 [i]ch. 19:16; 1 Kings 2:8
16:7 [j]Deut. 13:13
16:8 [k]Judg. 9:24; 1 Kings 2:32 [l]ch. 1:16
16:9 [m]1 Sam. 24:14; ch. 9:8 [n]Ex. 22:28
16:10 [o]ch. 19:22; 1 Pet. 2:23 [p]2 Kings 18:25; Lam. 3:38 [q]Rom. 9:20
16:11 [r]ch. 12:11 [s]Gen. 15:4
16:12 [t]Rom. 8:28
16:15 [u]ch. 15:37
16:16 [v]ch. 15:37
16:17 [w]ch. 19:25; Prov. 17:17
16:19 [x]ch. 15:34
16:21 [y]ch. 15:16 [z]Gen. 34:30; 1 Sam. 13:4 [a]ch. 2:7; Zech. 8:13
16:22 [b]ch. 12:11
16:23 [c]ch. 15:12
17:2 [d]Deut. 25:18; ch. 16:14 [e]Zech. 13:7
17:8 [f]Hos. 13:8

Absalom, that Hushai said unto Absalom,
God save the king, God save the king.
17 And Absalom said to Hushai, *Is* this
thy kindness to thy friend? [w]why wentest
thou not with thy friend?
18 And Hushai said unto Absalom, Nay;
but whom the LORD, and this people, and all
the men of Israel, choose, his will I be, and
with him will I abide.
19 And again, [x]whom should I serve?
should I not *serve* in the presence of his son?
as I have served in thy father's presence, so
will I be in thy presence.
20 ¶ Then said Absalom to Ahithophel,
Give counsel among you what we shall do.
21 And Ahithophel said unto Absalom,
Go in unto thy father's [y]concubines, which
he hath left to keep the house; and all Israel
shall hear that thou [z]art abhorred of thy
father: then shall [a]the hands of all that *are*
with thee be strong.
22 So they spread Absalom a tent upon
the top of the house; and Absalom went in
unto his father's concubines [b]in the sight of
all Israel.
23 And the counsel of Ahithophel, which
he counselled in those days, *was* as if a man
had enquired at the oracle of God: so *was* all
the counsel of Ahithophel [c]both with David
and with Absalom.

17

Moreover Ahithophel said unto Absalom, Let me now choose out twelve
thousand men, and I will arise and pursue
after David this night:
2 And I will come upon him while he *is*
[d]weary and weak handed, and will make
him afraid: and all the people that *are* with
him shall flee; and I will [e]smite the king
only:
3 And I will bring back all the people unto
thee: the man whom thou seekest *is* as if all
returned: *so* all the people shall be in peace.
4 And the saying pleased Absalom well,
and all the elders of Israel.
5 Then said Absalom, Call now Hushai
the Archite also, and let us hear likewise
what he saith.
6 And when Hushai was come to Absalom, Absalom spake unto him, saying,
Ahithophel hath spoken after this manner:
shall we do *after* his saying? if not; speak
thou.
7 And Hushai said unto Absalom, The
counsel that Ahithophel hath given *is* not
good at this time.
8 For, said Hushai, thou knowest thy father and his men, that they *be* mighty men,
and they *be* chafed in their minds, as [f]a
bear robbed of her whelps in the field: and
thy father *is* a man of war, and will not
lodge with the people.
9 Behold, he is hid now in some pit, or in
some *other* place: and it will come to pass,
when some of them be overthrown at the
first, that whosoever heareth it will say,
There is a slaughter among the people that
follow Absalom.
10 And he also *that is* valiant, whose

heart *is* as the heart of a lion, shall utterly [g]melt: for all Israel knoweth that thy father *is* a mighty man, and *they* which *be* with him *are* valiant men.

11 Therefore I counsel that all Israel be generally gathered unto thee, [h]from Dan even to Beer-sheba, [i]as the sand that *is* by the sea for multitude; and that thou go to battle in thine own person.

12 So shall we come upon him in some place where he shall be found, and we will light upon him as the dew falleth on the ground: and of him and of all the men that *are* with him there shall not be left so much as one.

13 Moreover, if he be gotten into a city, then shall all Israel bring ropes to that city, and we will draw it into the river, until there be not one small stone found there.

14 And Absalom and all the men of Israel said, The counsel of Hushai the Archite *is* better than the counsel of Ahithophel. For [j]the LORD had appointed to defeat the good counsel of Ahithophel, to the intent that the LORD might bring evil upon Absalom.

15 ¶ [k]Then said Hushai unto Zadok and to Abiathar the priests, Thus and thus did Ahithophel counsel Absalom and the elders of Israel; and thus and thus have I counselled.

16 Now therefore send quickly, and tell David, saying, Lodge not this night [l]in the plains of the wilderness, but speedily pass over; lest the king be swallowed up, and all the people that *are* with him.

17 [m]Now Jonathan and Ahimaaz [n]stayed by [o]En-rogel; for they might not be seen to come into the city: and a wench went and told them; and they went and told king David.

18 Nevertheless a lad saw them, and told Absalom: but they went both of them away quickly, and came to a man's house [p]in Bahurim, which had a well in his court; whither they went down.

19 And [q]the woman took and spread a covering over the well's mouth, and spread ground corn thereon; and the thing was not known.

20 And when Absalom's servants came to the woman to the house, they said, Where *is* Ahimaaz and Jonathan? And [r]the woman said unto them, They be gone over the brook of water. And when they had sought and could not find *them,* they returned to Jerusalem.

21 And it came to pass, after they were departed, that they came up out of the well, and went and told king David, and said unto David, [s]Arise, and pass quickly over the water: for thus hath Ahithophel counselled against you.

22 Then David arose, and all the people that *were* with him, and they passed over Jordan: by the morning light there lacked not one of them that was not gone over Jordan.

23 ¶ And when Ahithophel saw that his counsel was not followed, he saddled *his* ass, and arose, and gat him home to his house, to [t]his city, and put his household in order, and [u]hanged himself, and died, and was buried in the sepulchre of his father.

24 Then David came to [v]Mahanaim. And Absalom passed over Jordan, he and all the men of Israel with him.

25 ¶ And Absalom made Amasa captain of the host instead of Joab: which Amasa *was* a man's son, whose name *was* Ithra an Israelite, that went in to [w]Abigail the daughter of Nahash, sister to Zeruiah Joab's mother.

26 So Israel and Absalom pitched in the land of Gilead.

27 ¶ And it came to pass, when David was come to Mahanaim, that [x]Shobi the son of Nahash of Rabbah of the children of Ammon, and [y]Machir the son of Ammiel of Lo-debar, and [z]Barzillai the Gileadite of Rogelim,

28 Brought beds, and basons, and earthen vessels, and wheat, and barley, and flour, and parched *corn,* and beans, and lentiles, and parched *pulse,*

29 And honey, and butter, and sheep, and cheese of kine, for David, and for the people that *were* with him, to eat: for they said, The people *is* hungry, and weary, and thirsty, [a]in the wilderness.

18

And David numbered the people that *were* with him, and set captains of thousands and captains of hundreds over them.

2 And David sent forth a third part of the people under the hand of Joab, [b]and a third part under the hand of Abishai the son of Zeruiah, Joab's brother, and a third part under the hand of Ittai the Gittite. And the king said unto the people, I will surely go forth with you myself also.

3 [c]But the people answered, Thou shalt not go forth: for if we flee away, they will not care for us; neither if half of us die, will they care for us: but now *thou art* worth ten thousand of us: therefore now *it is* better that thou succour us out of the city.

4 And the king said unto them, What seemeth you best I will do. And the king stood by the gate side, and all the people came out by hundreds and by thousands.

5 And the king commanded Joab and Abishai and Ittai, saying, *Deal* gently for my sake with the young man, *even* with Absalom. [d]And all the people heard when the king gave all the captains charge concerning Absalom.

6 ¶ So the people went out into the field against Israel: and the battle was in the [e]wood of Ephraim;

7 Where the people of Israel were slain before the servants of David, and there was there a great slaughter that day of twenty thousand *men.*

8 For the battle was there scattered over the face of all the country: and the wood

17:10 [g]Josh. 2:11
17:11 [h]Judg. 20:1 [i]Gen. 22:17
17:14 [j]ch. 15:31
17:15 [k]ch. 15:35
17:16 [l]ch. 15:28
17:17 [m]ch. 15:27 [n]Josh. 2:4 [o]Josh. 15:7
17:18 [p]ch. 16:5
17:19 [q]Josh. 2:6
17:20 [r]Ex. 1:19; Josh. 2:4
17:21 [s]ver. 15
17:23 [t]ch. 15:12 [u]Matt. 27:5
17:24 [v]Gen. 32:2; Josh. 13:26; ch. 2:8
17:25 [w]1 Chron. 2:16
17:27 [x]ch. 10:1 [y]ch. 9:4 [z]ch. 19:31; 1 Kings 2:7
17:29 [a]ch. 16:2
18:2 [b]ch. 15:19
18:3 [c]ch. 21:17
18:5 [d]ver. 12
18:6 [e]Josh. 17:15

devoured more people that day than the sword devoured.

9 ¶ And Absalom met the servants of David. And Absalom rode upon a mule, and the mule went under the thick boughs of a great oak, and his head caught hold of the oak, and he was taken up between the heaven and the earth; and the mule that *was* under him went away.

10 And a certain man saw *it*, and told Joab, and said, Behold, I saw Absalom hanged in an oak.

11 And Joab said unto the man that told him, And, behold, thou sawest *him*, and why didst thou not smite him there to the ground? and I would have given thee ten *shekels* of silver, and a girdle.

12 And the man said unto Joab, Though I should receive a thousand *shekels* of silver in mine hand, *yet* would I not put forth mine hand against the king's son: [f]for in our hearing the king charged thee and Abishai and Ittai, saying, Beware that none *touch* the young man Absalom.

13 Otherwise I should have wrought falsehood against mine own life: for there is no matter hid from the king, and thou thyself wouldest have set thyself against *me*.

14 Then said Joab, I may not tarry thus with thee. And he took three darts in his hand, and thrust them through the heart of Absalom, while he *was* yet alive in the midst of the oak.

15 And ten young men that bare Joab's armour compassed about and smote Absalom, and slew him.

16 And Joab blew the trumpet, and the people returned from pursuing after Israel: for Joab held back the people.

17 And they took Absalom, and cast him into a great pit in the wood, and [g]laid a very great heap of stones upon him: and all Israel fled every one to his tent.

18 ¶ Now Absalom in his lifetime had taken and reared up for himself a pillar, which *is* in [h]the king's dale: for he said, [i]I have no son to keep my name in remembrance: and he called the pillar after his own name: and it is called unto this day, Absalom's place.

19 ¶ Then said Ahimaaz the son of Zadok, Let me now run, and bear the king tidings, how that the LORD hath avenged him of his enemies.

20 And Joab said unto him, Thou shalt not bear tidings this day, but thou shalt bear tidings another day: but this day thou shalt bear no tidings, because the king's son is dead.

21 Then said Joab to Cushi, Go tell the king what thou hast seen. And Cushi bowed himself unto Joab, and ran.

22 Then said Ahimaaz the son of Zadok yet again to Joab, But howsoever, let me, I pray thee, also run after Cushi. And Joab said, Wherefore wilt thou run, my son, seeing that thou hast no tidings ready?

23 But howsoever, *said he*, let me run. And he said unto him, Run. Then Ahimaaz ran by the way of the plain, and overran Cushi.

24 And David sat between the two gates: and [j]the watchman went up to the roof over the gate unto the wall, and lifted up his eyes, and looked, and behold a man running alone.

25 And the watchman cried, and told the king. And the king said, If he *be* alone, *there is* tidings in his mouth. And he came apace, and drew near.

26 And the watchman saw another man running: and the watchman called unto the porter, and said, Behold *another* man running alone. And the king said, He also bringeth tidings.

27 And the watchman said, Me thinketh the running of the foremost is like the running of Ahimaaz the son of Zadok. And the king said, He *is* a good man, and cometh with good tidings.

28 And Ahimaaz called, and said unto the king, All is well. And he fell down to the earth upon his face before the king, and said, Blessed *be* the LORD thy God, which hath delivered up the men that lifted up their hand against my lord the king.

29 And the king said, Is the young man Absalom safe? And Ahimaaz answered, When Joab sent the king's servant, and *me* thy servant, I saw a great tumult, but I knew not what *it was*.

30 And the king said *unto him*, Turn aside, *and* stand here. And he turned aside, and stood still.

31 And, behold, Cushi came; and Cushi said, Tidings, my lord the king: for the LORD hath avenged thee this day of all them that rose up against thee.

32 And the king said unto Cushi, *Is* the young man Absalom safe? And Cushi answered, The enemies of my lord the king, and all that rise against thee to do *thee* hurt, be as *that* young man *is*.

33 ¶ And the king was much moved, and went up to the chamber over the gate, and wept: and as he went, thus he said, [k]O my son Absalom, my son, my son Absalom! would God I had died for thee, O Absalom, my son, my son!

19 And it was told Joab, Behold, the king weepeth and mourneth for Absalom.

2 And the victory that day was *turned* into mourning unto all the people: for the people heard say that day how the king was grieved for his son.

3 And the people gat them by stealth that day [l]into the city, as people being ashamed steal away when they flee in battle.

4 But the king [m]covered his face, and the king cried with a loud voice, [n]O my son Absalom, O Absalom, my son, my son!

5 And Joab came into the house to the king, and said, Thou hast shamed this day the faces of all thy servants, which this day have saved thy life, and the lives of thy sons

18:12 [f]ver. 5
18:17 [g]Josh. 7:26
18:18 [h]Gen. 14:17 [i]ch. 14:27
18:24 [j]2 Kings 9:17
18:33 [k]ch. 19:4
19:3 [l]ver. 32
19:4 [m]ch. 15:30 [n]ch. 18:33

and of thy daughters, and the lives of thy
wives, and the lives of thy concubines;
6 In that thou lovest thine enemies, and
hatest thy friends. For thou hast declared
this day, that thou regardest neither princes
nor servants: for this day I perceive, that if
Absalom had lived, and all we had died this
day, then it had pleased thee well.
7 Now therefore arise, go forth, and
speak comfortably unto thy servants: for I
swear by the LORD, if thou go not forth,
there will not tarry one with thee this night:
and that will be worse unto thee than all the
evil that befell thee from thy youth until
now.
8 Then the king arose, and sat in the gate.
And they told unto all the people, saying,
Behold, the king doth sit in the gate. And all
the people came before the king: for Israel
had fled every man to his tent.
9 ¶ And all the people were at strife
throughout all the tribes of Israel, saying,
The king saved us out of the hand of our
enemies, and he delivered us out of the
hand of the Philistines; and now he is [o]fled
out of the land for Absalom.
10 And Absalom, whom we anointed over
us, is dead in battle. Now therefore why
speak ye not a word of bringing the king
back?
11 ¶ And king David sent to Zadok and to
Abiathar the priests, saying, Speak unto the
elders of Judah, saying, Why are ye the last
to bring the king back to his house? seeing
the speech of all Israel is come to the king,
even to his house.
12 Ye *are* my brethren, ye *are* [p]my bones
and my flesh: wherefore then are ye the last
to bring back the king?
13 [q]And say ye to Amasa, *Art* thou not of
my bone, and of my flesh? [r]God do so to
me, and more also, if thou be not captain of
the host before me continually in the room
of Joab.
14 And he bowed the heart of all the men
of Judah, [s]even as *the heart of* one man; so
that they sent *this word* unto the king, Return thou, and all thy servants.
15 So the king returned, and came to Jordan. And Judah came to [t]Gilgal, to go to
meet the king, to conduct the king over Jordan.
16 ¶ And [u]Shimei the son of Gera, a Benjamite, which *was* of Bahurim, hasted and
came down with the men of Judah to meet
king David.
17 And *there were* a thousand men of
Benjamin with him, and [v]Ziba the servant
of the house of Saul, and his fifteen sons
and his twenty servants with him; and they
went over Jordan before the king.
18 And there went over a ferry boat to
carry over the king's household, and to do
what he thought good. And Shimei the son
of Gera fell down before the king, as he was
come over Jordan;
19 And said unto the king, [w]Let not my
lord impute iniquity unto me, neither do
thou remember [x]that which thy servant did
perversely the day that my lord the king
went out of Jerusalem, that the king should
[y]take it to his heart.
20 For thy servant doth know that I have
sinned: therefore, behold, I am come the
first this day of all [z]the house of Joseph to
go down to meet my lord the king.
21 But Abishai the son of Zeruiah answered and said, Shall not Shimei be put
to death for this, because he [a]cursed the
LORD's anointed?
22 And David said, [b]What have I to do
with you, ye sons of Zeruiah, that ye should
this day be adversaries unto me? [c]shall
there any man be put to death this day in
Israel? for do not I know that I *am* this day
king over Israel?
23 Therefore [d]the king said unto Shimei,
Thou shalt not die. And the king sware unto
him.
24 ¶ And [e]Mephibosheth the son of Saul
came down to meet the king, and had neither dressed his feet, nor trimmed his beard,
nor washed his clothes, from the day the
king departed until the day he came *again*
in peace.
25 And it came to pass, when he was
come to Jerusalem to meet the king, that the
king said unto him, [f]Wherefore wentest
not thou with me, Mephibosheth?
26 And he answered, My lord, O king, my
servant deceived me: for thy servant said,
I will saddle me an ass, that I may ride
thereon, and go to the king; because thy servant *is* lame.
27 And [g]he hath slandered thy servant
unto my lord the king; [h]but my lord the
king *is* as an angel of God: do therefore
what is good in thine eyes.
28 For all *of* my father's house were but
dead men before my lord the king: [i]yet
didst thou set thy servant among them that
did eat at thine own table. What right therefore have I yet to cry any more unto the
king?
29 And the king said unto him, Why
speakest thou any more of thy matters? I
have said, Thou and Ziba divide the land.
30 And Mephibosheth said unto the king,
Yea, let him take all, forasmuch as my lord
the king is come again in peace unto his
own house.
31 ¶ And [j]Barzillai the Gileadite came
down from Rogelim, and went over Jordan
with the king, to conduct him over Jordan.
32 Now Barzillai was a very aged man,
even fourscore years old: and [k]he had provided the king of sustenance while he lay at
Mahanaim; for he *was* a very great man.
33 And the king said unto Barzillai, Come
thou over with me, and I will feed thee with
me in Jerusalem.
34 And Barzillai said unto the king, How
long have I to live, that I should go up with
the king unto Jerusalem?
35 I *am* this day [l]fourscore years old: *and*
can I discern between good and evil? can

19:9 [o]ch. 15:14
19:12 [p]ch. 5:1
19:13 [q]ch. 17:25 [r]Ruth 1:17
19:14 [s]Judg. 20:1
19:15 [t]Josh. 5:9
19:16 [u]ch. 16:5; 1 Kings 2:8
19:17 [v]ch. 9:2
19:19 [w]1 Sam. 22:15 [x]ch. 16:5 [y]ch. 13:33
19:20 [z]ch. 16:5
19:21 [a]Ex. 22:28
19:22 [b]ch. 16:10 [c]1 Sam. 11:13
19:23 [d]1 Kings 2:8
19:24 [e]ch. 9:6
19:25 [f]ch. 16:17
19:27 [g]ch. 16:3 [h]ch. 14:17
19:28 [i]ch. 9:7
19:31 [j]1 Kings 2:7
19:32 [k]ch. 17:27
19:35 [l]Ps. 90:10

thy servant taste what I eat or what I drink? can I hear any more the voice of singing men and singing women? wherefore then should thy servant be yet a burden unto my lord the king?

36 Thy servant will go a little way over Jordan with the king: and why should the king recompense it me with such a reward?

37 Let thy servant, I pray thee, turn back again, that I may die in mine own city, *and be buried* by the grave of my father and of my mother. But behold thy servant [m]Chimham; let him go over with my lord the king; and do to him what shall seem good unto thee.

38 And the king answered, Chimham shall go over with me, and I will do to him that which shall seem good unto thee: and whatsoever thou shalt require of me, *that* will I do for thee.

39 And all the people went over Jordan. And when the king was come over, the king [n]kissed Barzillai, and blessed him; and he returned unto his own place.

40 Then the king went on to Gilgal, and Chimham went on with him: and all the people of Judah conducted the king, and also half the people of Israel.

41 ¶ And, behold, all the men of Israel came to the king, and said unto the king, Why have our brethren the men of Judah stolen thee away, and [o]have brought the king, and his household, and all David's men with him, over Jordan?

42 And all the men of Judah answered the men of Israel, Because the king *is* [p]near of kin to us: wherefore then be ye angry for this matter? have we eaten at all of the king's *cost?* or hath he given us any gift?

43 And the men of Israel answered the men of Judah, and said, We have ten parts in the king, and we have also more *right* in David than ye: why then did ye despise us, that our advice should not be first had in bringing back our king? And [q]the words of the men of Judah were fiercer than the words of the men of Israel.

20 And there happened to be there a man of Belial, whose name *was* Sheba, the son of Bichri, a Benjamite: and he blew a trumpet, and said, [r]We have no part in David, neither have we inheritance in the son of Jesse: [s]every man to his tents, O Israel.

2 So every man of Israel went up from after David, *and* followed Sheba the son of Bichri: but the men of Judah clave unto their king, from Jordan even to Jerusalem.

3 ¶ And David came to his house at Jerusalem; and the king took the ten women *his* [t]concubines, whom he had left to keep the house, and put them in ward, and fed them, but went not in unto them. So they were shut up unto the day of their death, living in widowhood.

4 ¶ Then said the king to Amasa, [u]Assemble me the men of Judah within three days, and be thou here present.

5 So Amasa went to assemble *the men of* Judah: but he tarried longer than the set time which he had appointed him.

6 And David said to Abishai, Now shall Sheba the son of Bichri do us more harm than *did* Absalom: take thou [v]thy lord's servants, and pursue after him, lest he get him fenced cities, and escape us.

7 And there went out after him Joab's men, and the [w]Cherethites, and the Pelethites, and all the mighty men: and they went out of Jerusalem, to pursue after Sheba the son of Bichri.

8 When they *were* at the great stone which *is* in Gibeon, Amasa went before them. And Joab's garment that he had put on was girded unto him, and upon it a girdle *with* a sword fastened upon his loins in the sheath thereof; and as he went forth it fell out.

9 And Joab said to Amasa, *Art* thou in health, my brother? [x]And Joab took Amasa by the beard with the right hand to kiss him.

10 But Amasa took no heed to the sword that *was* in Joab's hand: so [y]he smote him therewith [z]in the fifth *rib,* and shed out his bowels to the ground, and struck him not again; and he died. So Joab and Abishai his brother pursued after Sheba the son of Bichri.

11 And one of Joab's men stood by him, and said, He that favoureth Joab, and he that *is* for David, *let him go* after Joab.

12 And Amasa wallowed in blood in the midst of the highway. And when the man saw that all the people stood still, he removed Amasa out of the highway into the field, and cast a cloth upon him, when he saw that every one that came by him stood still.

13 When he was removed out of the highway, all the people went on after Joab, to pursue after Sheba the son of Bichri.

14 ¶ And he went through all the tribes of Israel unto [a]Abel, and to Beth-maachah, and all the Berites: and they were gathered together, and went also after him.

15 And they came and besieged him in Abel of Beth-maachah, and they [b]cast up a bank against the city, and it stood in the trench: and all the people that *were* with Joab battered the wall, to throw it down.

16 ¶ Then cried a wise woman out of the city, Hear, hear; say, I pray you, unto Joab, Come near hither, that I may speak with thee.

17 And when he was come near unto her, the woman said, *Art* thou Joab? And he answered, I *am he.* Then she said unto him, Hear the words of thine handmaid. And he answered, I do hear.

18 Then she spake, saying, They were wont to speak in old time, saying, They shall surely ask *counsel* at Abel: and so they ended *the matter.*

19 I *am one of them that are* peaceable *and* faithful in Israel: thou seekest to destroy a city and a mother in Israel: why wilt

19:37 *m*1 Kings 2:7; Jer. 41:17
19:39 *n*Gen. 31:55
19:41 *o*ver. 15
19:42 *p*ver. 12
19:43 *q*Judg. 8:1
20:1 *r*ch. 19:43 *s*1 Kings 12:16; 2 Chron. 10:16
20:3 *t*ch. 15:16
20:4 *u*ch. 19:13
20:6 *v*ch. 11:11; 1 Kings 1:33
20:7 *w*ch. 8:18; 1 Kings 1:38
20:9 *x*Matt. 26:49; Luke 22:47
20:10 *y*1 Kings 2:5 *z*ch. 2:23
20:14 *a*2 Kings 15:29; 2 Chron. 16:4
20:15 *b*2 Kings 19:32

thou swallow up [c]the inheritance of the LORD?

20 And Joab answered and said, Far be it, far be it from me, that I should swallow up or destroy.

21 The matter *is* not so: but a man of mount Ephraim, Sheba the son of Bichri by name, hath lifted up his hand against the king, *even* against David: deliver him only and I will depart from the city. And the woman said unto Joab, Behold, his head shall be thrown to thee over the wall.

22 Then the woman went unto all the people [d]in her wisdom. And they cut off the head of Sheba the son of Bichri, and cast *it* out to Joab. And he blew a trumpet, and they retired from the city, every man to his tent. And Joab returned to Jerusalem unto the king.

23 ¶ Now [e]Joab *was* over all the host of Israel: and Benaiah the son of Jehoiada *was* over the Cherethites and over the Pelethites:

24 And Adoram *was* [f]over the tribute: and [g]Jehoshaphat the son of Ahilud *was* recorder:

25 And Sheva *was* scribe: and [h]Zadok and Abiathar *were* the priests:

26 [i]And Ira also the Jairite was a chief ruler about David.

21

Then there was a famine in the days of David three years, year after year; and David enquired of the LORD. And the LORD answered, *It is* for Saul, and for *his* bloody house, because he slew the Gibeonites.

2 And the king called the Gibeonites, and said unto them; (now the Gibeonites *were* not of the children of Israel, but [j]of the remnant of the Amorites; and the children of Israel had sworn unto them: and Saul sought to slay them in his zeal to the children of Israel and Judah.)

3 Wherefore David said unto the Gibeonites, What shall I do for you? and wherewith shall I make the atonement, that ye may bless [k]the inheritance of the LORD?

4 And the Gibeonites said unto him, We will have no silver nor gold of Saul, nor of his house; neither for us shalt thou kill any man in Israel. And he said, What ye shall say, *that* will I do for you.

5 And they answered the king, The man that consumed us, and that devised against us *that* we should be destroyed from remaining in any of the coasts of Israel,

6 Let seven men of his sons be delivered unto us, and we will hang them up unto the LORD [l]in Gibeah of Saul, [m]*whom* the LORD did choose. And the king said, I will give *them.*

7 But the king spared Mephibosheth, the son of Jonathan the son of Saul, because of [n]the LORD's oath that *was* between them, between David and Jonathan the son of Saul.

8 But the king took the two sons of [o]Rizpah the daughter of Aiah, whom she bare unto Saul, Armoni and Mephibosheth; and the five sons of Michal the daughter of Saul, whom she brought up for Adriel the son of Barzillai the Meholathite:

9 And he delivered them into the hands of the Gibeonites, and they hanged them in the hill [p]before the LORD: and they fell *all* seven together, and were put to death in the days of harvest, in the first *days,* in the beginning of barley harvest.

10 ¶ And [q]Rizpah the daughter of Aiah took sackcloth, and spread it for her upon the rock, [r]from the beginning of harvest until water dropped upon them out of heaven, and suffered neither the birds of the air to rest on them by day, nor the beasts of the field by night.

11 And it was told David what Rizpah the daughter of Aiah, the concubine of Saul, had done.

12 ¶ And David went and took the bones of Saul and the bones of Jonathan his son from the men of [s]Jabesh-gilead, which had stolen them from the street of Beth-shan, where the [t]Philistines had hanged them, when the Philistines had slain Saul in Gilboa:

13 And he brought up from thence the bones of Saul and the bones of Jonathan his son; and they gathered the bones of them that were hanged.

14 And the bones of Saul and Jonathan his son buried they in the country of Benjamin in [u]Zelah, in the sepulchre of Kish his father: and they performed all that the king commanded. And after that [v]God was intreated for the land.

15 ¶ Moreover the Philistines had yet war again with Israel; and David went down, and his servants with him, and fought against the Philistines: and David waxed faint.

16 And Ishbi-benob, which *was* of the sons of the giant, the weight of whose spear *weighed* three hundred *shekels* of brass in weight, he being girded with a new *sword,* thought to have slain David.

17 But Abishai the son of Zeruiah succoured him, and smote the Philistine, and killed him. Then the men of David sware unto him, saying, [w]Thou shalt go no more out with us to battle, that thou quench not the [x]light of Israel.

18 [y]And it came to pass after this, that there was again a battle with the Philistines at Gob: then [z]Sibbechai the Hushathite slew Saph, which *was* of the sons of the giant.

19 And there was again a battle in Gob with the Philistines, where Elhanan the son of Jaare-oregim, a Beth-lehemite, slew [a]*the brother of* Goliath the Gittite, the staff of whose spear *was* like a weaver's beam.

20 And [b]there was yet a battle in Gath, where was a man of *great* stature, that had on every hand six fingers, and on every foot six toes, four and twenty in number; and he also was born to the giant.

20:19 [c]1 Sam. 26:19; ch. 21:3
20:22 [d]Eccl. 9:14
20:23 [e]ch. 8:16
20:24 [f]1 Kings 4:6 [g]ch. 8:16; 1 Kings 4:3
20:25 [h]ch. 8:17; 1 Kings 4:4
20:26 [i]ch. 23:38
21:2 [j]Josh. 9:3
21:3 [k]ch. 20:19
21:6 [l]1 Sam. 10:26 [m]1 Sam. 10:24
21:7 [n]1 Sam. 18:3
21:8 [o]ch. 3:7
21:9 [p]ch. 6:17
21:10 [q]ver. 8; ch. 3:7 [r]Deut. 21:23
21:12 [s]1 Sam. 31:11 [t]1 Sam. 31:10
21:14 [u]Josh. 18:28 [v]Josh. 7:26; ch. 24:25
21:17 [w]ch. 18:3 [x]1 Kings 11:36; Ps. 132:17
21:18 [y]1 Chron. 20:4 [z]1 Chron. 11:29
21:19 [a]1 Chron. 20:5
21:20 [b]1 Chron. 20:6

21 And when he defied Israel, Jonathan
the son of [c]Shimea the brother of David
slew him.
22 [d]These four were born to the giant in
Gath, and fell by the hand of David, and by
the hand of his servants.

22 And David [e]spake unto the LORD the
words of this song in the day *that* the
LORD had [f]delivered him out of the hand of
all his enemies, and out of the hand of Saul:
2 And he said, [g]The LORD *is* my rock, and
my fortress, and my deliverer;
3 The God of my rock; [h]in him will I trust:
he is my [i]shield, and the [j]horn of my salvation, my high [k]tower, and my [l]refuge, my
saviour; thou savest me from violence.
4 I will call on the LORD, *who is* worthy to
be praised: so shall I be saved from mine
enemies.
5 When the waves of death compassed
me, the floods of ungodly men made me
afraid;
6 The [m]sorrows of hell compassed me
about; the snares of death prevented me;
7 In my distress [n]I called upon the LORD,
and cried to my God: and he did [o]hear my
voice out of his temple, and my cry *did enter*
into his ears.
8 Then [p]the earth shook and trembled;
[q]the foundations of heaven moved and
shook, because he was wroth.
9 There went up a smoke out of his nostrils, and [r]fire out of his mouth devoured:
coals were kindled by it.
10 He [s]bowed the heavens also, and
came down; and [t]darkness *was* under his
feet.
11 And he rode upon a cherub, and did
fly: and he was seen [u]upon the wings of the
wind.
12 And he made [v]darkness pavilions
round about him, dark waters, *and* thick
clouds of the skies.
13 Through the brightness before him
were [w]coals of fire kindled.
14 The LORD [x]thundered from heaven,
and the most High uttered his voice.
15 And he sent out [y]arrows, and scattered them; lightning, and discomfited
them.
16 And the channels of the sea appeared,
the foundations of the world were discovered, at the [z]rebuking of the LORD, at the
blast of the breath of his nostrils.
17 [a]He sent from above, he took me; he
drew me out of many waters;
18 [b]He delivered me from my strong enemy, *and* from them that hated me: for they
were too strong for me.
19 They prevented me in the day of my
calamity: but the LORD was my stay.
20 [c]He brought me forth also into a large
place: he delivered me, because he [d]de-
lighted in me.
21 [e]The LORD rewarded me according to
my righteousness: according to the [f]clean-
ness of my hands hath he recompensed me.
22 For I have [g]kept the ways of the LORD,
and have not wickedly departed from my
God.
23 For all his [h]judgments *were* before
me: and *as for* his statutes, I did not depart
from them.
24 I was also [i]upright before him, and
have kept myself from mine iniquity.
25 Therefore [j]the LORD hath recompensed me according to my righteousness;
according to my cleanness in his eye sight.
26 With [k]the merciful thou wilt shew thyself merciful, *and* with the upright man thou
wilt shew thyself upright.
27 With the pure thou wilt shew thyself
pure; and [l]with the froward thou wilt shew
thyself unsavoury.
28 And the [m]afflicted people thou wilt
save: but thine eyes *are* upon [n]the haughty,
that thou mayest bring *them* down.
29 For thou *art* my lamp, O LORD: and the
LORD will lighten my darkness.
30 For by thee I have run through a troop:
by my God have I leaped over a wall.
31 *As for* God, [o]his way *is* perfect; [p]the
word of the LORD *is* tried: he *is* a buckler t
all them that trust in him.
32 For [q]who *is* God, save the LORD? an
who *is* a rock, save our God?
33 God *is* my [r]strength *and* power: and
he [s]maketh my way [t]perfect.
34 He maketh my feet [u]like hinds' *feet:*
and [v]setteth me upon my high places.
35 [w]He teacheth my hands to war; so that
a bow of steel is broken by mine arms.
36 Thou hast also given me the shield of
thy salvation: and thy gentleness hath made
me great.
37 Thou hast [x]enlarged my steps under
me; so that my feet did not slip.
38 I have pursued mine enemies, and destroyed them; and turned not again until I
had consumed them.
39 And I have consumed them, and
wounded them, that they could not arise:
yea, they are fallen [y]under my feet.
40 For thou hast [z]girded me with
strength to battle: [a]them that rose up
against me hast thou subdued under me.
41 Thou hast also given me the [b]necks of
mine enemies, that I might destroy them
that hate me.
42 They looked, but *there was* none to
save; *even* [c]unto the LORD, but he answered
them not.
43 Then did I beat them as small [d]as the
dust of the earth, I did stamp them [e]as the
mire of the street, *and* did spread them
abroad.
44 [f]Thou also hast delivered me from the
strivings of my people, thou hast kept me *to
be* [g]head of the heathen: [h]a people *which* I
knew not shall serve me.
45 Strangers shall submit themselves
unto me: as soon as they hear, they shall be
obedient unto me.

21:21 [c]1 Sam. 16:9
21:22 [d]1 Chron. 20:8
22:1 [e]Ex. 15:1; Judg. 5:1 [f]Ps. 18, title
22:2 [g]Deut. 32:4; Ps. 18:2
22:3 [h]Heb. 2:13 [i]Gen. 15:1 [j]Luke 1:69 [k]Prov. 18:10 [l]Ps. 9:9; Jer. 16:19
22:6 [m]Ps. 116:3
22:7 [n]Ps. 116:4; Jonah 2:2 [o]Ex. 3:7; Ps. 34:6
22:8 [p]Judg. 5:4; Ps. 77:18 [q]Job 26:11
22:9 [r]Ps. 97:3; Hab. 3:5; Heb. 12:29
22:10 [s]Ps. 144:5; Isa. 64:1 [t]Ex. 20:21; 1 Kings 8:12; Ps. 97:2
22:11 [u]Ps. 104:3
22:12 [v]ver. 10; Ps. 97:2
22:13 [w]ver. 9
22:14 [x]Judg. 5:20; Ps. 29:3; Isa. 30:30
22:15 [y]Deut. 32:23; Ps. 7:13; Hab. 3:11
22:16 [z]Ex. 15:8; Nah. 1:4; Matt. 8:26
22:17 [a]Ps. 144:7
22:18 [b]ver. 1
22:20 [c]Ps. 31:8 [d]ch. 15:26; Ps. 22:8
22:21 [e]ver. 25; 1 Sam. 26:23; 1 Kings 8:32; Ps. 7:8 [f]Ps. 24:4
22:22 [g]Gen. 18:19; Ps. 119:3
22:23 [h]Deut. 7:12; Ps. 119:30
22:24 [i]Gen. 6:9; Job 1:1
22:25 [j]ver. 21
22:26 [k]Matt. 5:7
22:27 [l]Lev. 26:23
22:28 [m]Ex. 3:7; Ps. 72:12 [n]Job 40:11; Isa. 2:11; Dan. 4:37
22:31 [o]Deut. 32:4; Dan. 4:37; Rev. 15:3 [p]Ps. 12:6
22:32 [q]1 Sam. 2:2; Isa. 45:5
22:33 [r]Ex. 15:2; Ps. 27:1; Isa. 12:2 [s]Heb. 13:21 [t]Deut. 18:13; Job 22:3; Ps. 101:2
22:34 [u]ch. 2:18; Hab. 3:19 [v]Deut. 32:13; Isa. 33:16
22:35 [w]Ps. 144:1
22:37 [x]Prov. 4:12
22:39 [y]Mal. 4:3
22:40 [z]Ps. 18:32 [a]Ps. 44:5
22:41 [b]Gen. 49:8; Ex. 23:27; Josh. 10:24
22:42 [c]Job 27:9; Prov. 1:28; Isa. 1:15; Mic. 3:4
22:43 [d]2 Kings 13:7; Ps. 35:5; Dan. 2:35 [e]Isa. 10:6; Mic. 7:10; Zech. 10:5
22:44 [f]ch. 3:1 [g]Deut. 28:13; ch. 8:1-14; Ps. 2:8 [h]Isa. 55:5

46 Strangers shall fade away, and they shall be afraid [i]out of their close places.

47 The LORD liveth; and blessed *be* my rock; and exalted be the God of the [j]rock of my salvation.

48 It *is* God that avengeth me, and that [k]bringeth down the people under me,

49 And that bringeth me forth from mine enemies: thou also hast lifted me up on high above them that rose up against me: thou hast delivered me from the [l]violent man.

50 Therefore I will give thanks unto thee, O LORD, among [m]the heathen, and I will sing praises unto thy name.

51 [n]*He is* the tower of salvation for his king: and sheweth mercy to his [o]anointed, unto David, and [p]to his seed for evermore.

23 Now these *be* the last words of David. David the son of Jesse said, [q]and the man *who was* raised up on high, [r]the anointed of the God of Jacob, and the sweet psalmist of Israel, said,

2 [s]The Spirit of the LORD spake by me, and his word *was* in my tongue.

3 The God of Israel said, [t]the Rock of Israel spake to me, He that ruleth over men *must be* just, ruling [u]in the fear of God.

4 And [v]*he shall be* as the light of the morning, *when* the sun riseth, *even* a morning without clouds; *as* the tender grass *springing* out of the earth by clear shining after rain.

5 Although my house *be* not so with God; [w]yet he hath made with me an everlasting covenant, ordered in all *things*, and sure: for *this is* all my salvation, and all *my* desire, although he make *it* not to grow.

6 ¶ But *the sons* of Belial *shall be* all of them as thorns thrust away, because they cannot be taken with hands:

7 But the man *that* shall touch them must be fenced with iron and the staff of a spear; and they shall be utterly burned with fire in the *same* place.

8 ¶ These *be* the names of the mighty men whom David had: The Tachmonite that sat in the seat, chief among the captains; the same *was* Adino the Eznite: *he lift up his spear* against eight hundred, whom he slew at one time.

9 And after him *was* [x]Eleazar the son of Dodo the Ahohite, *one* of the three mighty men with David, when they defied the Philistines *that* were there gathered together to battle, and the men of Israel were gone away:

10 He arose, and smote the Philistines until his hand was weary, and his hand clave unto the sword: and the LORD wrought a great victory that day; and the people returned after him only to spoil.

11 And after him *was* [y]Shammah the son of Agee the Hararite. [z]And the Philistines were gathered together into a troop, where was a piece of ground full of lentiles: and the people fled from the Philistines.

12 But he stood in the midst of the ground, and defended it, and slew the Philistines: and the LORD wrought a great victory.

13 And [a]three of the thirty chief went down, and came to David in the harvest time unto [b]the cave of Adullam: and the troop of the Philistines pitched in [c]the valley of Rephaim.

14 And David *was* then in an [d]hold, and the garrison of the Philistines *was* then *in* Beth-lehem.

15 And David longed, and said, Oh that one would give me drink of the water of the well of Beth-lehem, which *is* by the gate!

16 And the three mighty men brake through the host of the Philistines, and drew water out of the well of Beth-lehem, that *was* by the gate, and took *it*, and brought *it* to David: nevertheless he would not drink thereof, but poured it out unto the LORD.

17 And he said, Be it far from me, O LORD, that I should do this: *is not this* [e]the blood of the men that went in jeopardy of their lives? therefore he would not drink it. These things did these three mighty men.

18 And [f]Abishai, the brother of Joab, the son of Zeruiah, was chief among three. And he lifted up his spear against three hundred, *and* slew *them*, and had the name among three.

19 Was he not most honourable of three? therefore he was their captain: howbeit he attained not unto the *first* three.

20 And Benaiah the son of Jehoiada, the son of a valiant man, of [g]Kabzeel, who had done many acts, [h]he slew two lionlike men of Moab: he went down also and slew a lion in the midst of a pit in time of snow:

21 And he slew an Egyptian, a goodly man: and the Egyptian had a spear in his hand; but he went down to him with a staff, and plucked the spear out of the Egyptian's hand, and slew him with his own spear.

22 These *things* did Benaiah the son of Jehoiada, and had the name among three mighty men.

23 He was more honourable than the thirty, but he attained not to the *first* three. And David set him [i]over his guard.

24 [j]Asahel the brother of Joab *was* one of the thirty; Elhanan the son of Dodo of Beth-lehem,

25 [k]Shammah the Harodite, Elika the Harodite,

26 Helez the Paltite, Ira the son of Ikkesh the Tekoite,

27 Abiezer the Anethothite, Mebunnai the Hushathite,

28 Zalmon the Ahohite, Maharai the Netophathite,

29 Heleb the son of Baanah, a Netophathite, Ittai the son of Ribai out of Gibeah of the children of Benjamin,

30 Benaiah the Pirathonite, Hiddai of the brooks of [l]Gaash,

31 Abi-albon the Arbathite, Azmaveth the Barhumite,

22:46 [i]Mic. 7:17
22:47 [j]Ps. 89:26
22:48 [k]Ps. 144:2
22:49 [l]Ps. 140:1
22:50 [m]Rom. 15:9
22:51 [n]Ps. 144:10 [o]Ps. 89:20 [p]ch. 7:12; Ps. 89:29
23:1 [q]ch. 7; Ps. 78:70 [r]1 Sam. 16:12; Ps. 89:20
23:2 [s]2 Pet. 1:21
23:3 [t]Deut. 32:4; ch. 22:2 [u]Ex. 18:21; 2 Chron. 19:7
23:4 [v]Judg. 5:31; Ps. 89:36; Prov. 4:18; Hos. 6:5
23:5 [w]ch. 7:15; Ps. 89:29; Isa. 55:3
23:9 [x]1 Chron. 11:12
23:11 [y]1 Chron. 11:27 [z]1 Chron. 11:13
23:13 [a]1 Chron. 11:15 [b]1 Sam. 22:1 [c]ch. 5:18
23:14 [d]1 Sam. 22:4
23:17 [e]Lev. 17:10
23:18 [f]1 Chron. 11:20
23:20 [g]Josh. 15:21 [h]Ex. 15:15; 1 Chron. 11:22
23:23 [i]ch. 8:18
23:24 [j]ch. 2:18
23:25 [k]1 Chron. 11:27
23:30 [l]Judg. 2:9

32 Eliahba the Shaalbonite, of the sons of Jashen, Jonathan,

33 Shammah the Hararite, Ahiam the son of Sharar the Hararite,

34 Eliphelet the son of Ahasbai, the son of the Maachathite, Eliam the son of Ahithophel the Gilonite,

35 Hezrai the Carmelite, Paarai the Arbite,

36 Igal the son of Nathan of Zobah, Bani the Gadite,

37 Zelek the Ammonite, Naharai the Beerothite, armourbearer to Joab the son of Zeruiah,

38 [m]Ira an Ithrite, Gareb an Ithrite,

39 [n]Uriah the Hittite: thirty and seven in all.

24 And [o]again the anger of the LORD was kindled against Israel, and he moved David against them to say, [p]Go, number Israel and Judah.

2 For the king said to Joab the captain of the host, which *was* with him, Go now through all the tribes of Israel, [q]from Dan even to Beer-sheba, and number ye the people, that [r]I may know the number of the people.

3 And Joab said unto the king, Now the LORD thy God add unto the people, how many soever they be, an hundredfold, and that the eyes of my lord the king may see *it*: but why doth my lord the king delight in this thing?

4 Notwithstanding the king's word prevailed against Joab, and against the captains of the host. And Joab and the captains of the host went out from the presence of the king, to number the people of Israel.

5 ¶ And they passed over Jordan, and pitched in [s]Aroer, on the right side of the city that *lieth* in the midst of the river of Gad, and toward [t]Jazer:

6 Then they came to Gilead, and to the land of Tahtim-hodshi; and they came to [u]Dan-jaan, and about to [v]Zidon,

7 And came to the strong hold of Tyre, and to all the cities of the Hivites, and of the Canaanites: and they went out to the south of Judah, *even* to Beer-sheba.

8 So when they had gone through all the land, they came to Jerusalem at the end of nine months and twenty days.

9 And Joab gave up the sum of the number of the people unto the king: [w]and there were in Israel eight hundred thousand valiant men that drew the sword; and the men of Judah *were* five hundred thousand men.

10 ¶ And [x]David's heart smote him after that he had numbered the people. And David said unto the LORD, [y]I have sinned greatly in that I have done: and now, I beseech thee, O LORD, take away the iniquity of thy servant; for I have [z]done very foolishly.

11 For when David was up in the morning, the word of the LORD came unto the prophet [a]Gad, David's [b]seer, saying,

12 Go and say unto David, Thus saith the LORD, I offer thee three *things;* choose thee one of them, that I may *do it* unto thee.

13 So Gad came to David, and told him, and said unto him, Shall [c]seven years of famine come unto thee in thy land? or wilt thou flee three months before thine enemies, while they pursue thee? or that there be three days' pestilence in thy land? now advise, and see what answer I shall return to him that sent me.

14 And David said unto Gad, I am in a great strait: let us fall now into the hand of the LORD; [d]for his mercies *are* great: and [e]let me not fall into the hand of man.

15 ¶ So [f]the LORD sent a pestilence upon Israel from the morning even to the time appointed: and there died of the people from Dan even to Beer-sheba seventy thousand men.

16 [g]And when the angel stretched out his hand upon Jerusalem to destroy it, [h]the LORD repented him of the evil, and said to the angel that destroyed the people, It is enough: stay now thine hand. And the angel of the LORD was by the threshingplace of [i]Araunah the Jebusite.

17 And David spake unto the LORD when he saw the angel that smote the people, and said, Lo, [j]I have sinned, and I have done wickedly: but these sheep, what have they done? let thine hand, I pray thee, be against me, and against my father's house.

18 ¶ And Gad came that day to David, and said unto him, [k]Go up, rear an altar unto the LORD in the threshingfloor of Araunah the Jebusite.

19 And David, according to the saying of Gad, went up as the LORD commanded.

20 And Araunah looked, and saw the king and his servants coming on toward him: and Araunah went out, and bowed himself before the king on his face upon the ground.

21 And Araunah said, Wherefore is my lord the king come to his servant? [l]And David said, To buy the threshingfloor of thee, to build an altar unto the LORD, that [m]the plague may be stayed from the people.

22 And Araunah said unto David, Let my lord the king take and offer up what *seemeth* good unto him: [n]behold, *here be* oxen for burnt sacrifice, and threshing instruments and *other* instruments of the oxen for wood.

23 All these *things* did Araunah, *as* a king, give unto the king. And Araunah said unto the king, The LORD thy God [o]accept thee.

24 And the king said unto Araunah, Nay; but I will surely buy *it* of thee at a price: neither will I offer burnt offerings unto the LORD my God of that which doth cost me

23:38 [m]ch. 20:26
23:39 [n]ch. 11:3
24:1 [o]ch. 21:1 [p]1 Chron. 27:23
24:2 [q]Judg. 20:1 [r]Jer. 17:5
24:5 [s]Deut. 2:36; Josh. 13:9 [t]Num. 32:1
24:6 [u]Josh. 19:47; Judg. 18:29 [v]Josh. 19:28; Judg. 18:28
24:9 [w]1 Chron. 21:5
24:10 [x]1 Sam. 24:5 [y]ch. 12:13 [z]1 Sam. 13:13
24:11 [a]1 Sam. 22:5 [b]1 Sam. 9:9; 1 Chron. 29:29
24:13 [c]1 Chron. 21:12
24:14 [d]Ps. 103:8 [e]Isa. 47:6; Zech. 1:15
24:15 [f]1 Chron. 21:14
24:16 [g]Ex. 12:23; 1 Chron. 21:15 [h]Gen. 6:6; 1 Sam. 15:11; Joel 2:13 [i]ver. 18; 1 Chron. 21:15; 2 Chron. 3:1
24:17 [j]1 Chron. 21:17
24:18 [k]1 Chron. 21:18
24:21 [l]Gen. 23:8-16 [m]Num. 16:48
24:22 [n]1 Kings 19:21
24:23 [o]Ezek. 20:40

nothing. So [p]David bought the threshingfloor and the oxen for fifty shekels of
silver.
25 And David built there an altar unto
the LORD, and offered burnt offerings and
peace offerings. [q]So the LORD was intreated for the land, and [r]the plague was
stayed from Israel.

24:24 [p]1 Chron. 21:24
24:25 [q]ch. 21:14 [r]ver. 21

1 KINGS

Jeremiah wrote 1 Kings sometime after 550 B.C. First Kings continues the historical account which began in 1 and 2 Samuel. David is growing old as the book begins, and his son, Solomon, is preparing to take the throne of Israel. Many of Solomon's accomplishments are described in the first few chapters of the book, but none more important than the temple (Chapters 6 through 8). Solomon's reign ends tragically and the kingdom is divided. The rest of the book details relations between the separate kingdoms.

The most famous story from 1 Kings is found in chapter 3 where Solomon's wisdom is tested.

I. Solomon assumes the throne of Israel, 1:1–2:46
II. Solomon's reign as king, 3:1–11:43
III. Israel divided again, 12:1–22:53

---

1 Now king David was old *and* stricken
in years; and they covered him with
clothes, but he gat no heat.
2 Wherefore his servants said unto him,
Let there be sought for my lord the king a
young virgin: and let her stand before the
king, and let her cherish him, and let her lie
in thy bosom, that my lord the king may get
heat.
3 So they sought for a fair damsel
throughout all the coasts of Israel, and
found Abishag a [a]Shunammite, and
brought her to the king.
4 And the damsel *was* very fair, and cherished the king, and ministered to him: but
the king knew her not.
5 ¶ Then [b]Adonijah the son of Haggith
exalted himself, saying, I will be king: and
[c]he prepared him chariots and horsemen,
and fifty men to run before him.
6 And his father had not displeased him
at any time in saying, Why hast thou done
so? and he also *was* a very goodly *man;*
[d]and *his mother* bare him after Absalom.
7 And he conferred with Joab the son of
Zeruiah, and with [e]Abiathar the priest: and
[f]they following Adonijah helped *him.*
8 But Zadok the priest, and Benaiah the
son of Jehoiada, and Nathan the prophet,
and [g]Shimei, and Rei, and [h]the mighty
men which *belonged* to David, were not
with Adonijah.
9 And Adonijah slew sheep and oxen and
fat cattle by the stone of Zoheleth, which *is*
by En-rogel, and called all his brethren the
king's sons, and all the men of Judah the
king's servants:
10 But Nathan the prophet, and Benaiah,
and the mighty men, and Solomon his
brother, he called not.
11 ¶ Wherefore Nathan spake unto Bathsheba the mother of Solomon, saying, Hast
thou not heard that Adonijah the son of
[i]Haggith doth reign, and David our lord
knoweth *it* not?
12 Now therefore come, let me, I pray
thee, give thee counsel, that thou mayest
save thine own life, and the life of thy son
Solomon.
13 Go and get thee in unto king David,
and say unto him, Didst not thou, my lord,
O king, swear unto thine handmaid, saying,
[j]Assuredly Solomon thy son shall reign after me, and he shall sit upon my throne?
why then doth Adonijah reign?
14 Behold, while thou yet talkest there
with the king, I also will come in after thee,
and confirm thy words.
15 ¶ And Bath-sheba went in unto the
king into the chamber: and the king was
very old; and Abishag the Shunammite
ministered unto the king.
16 And Bath-sheba bowed, and did obeisance unto the king. And the king said,
What wouldest thou?
17 And she said unto him, My lord, [k]thou
swarest by the LORD thy God unto thine
handmaid, *saying,* Assuredly Solomon thy
son shall reign after me, and he shall sit
upon my throne.
18 And now, behold, Adonijah reigneth;
and now, my lord the king, thou knowest *it*
not:
19 [l]And he hath slain oxen and fat cattle
and sheep in abundance, and hath called
all the sons of the king, and Abiathar the
priest, and Joab the captain of the host: but
Solomon thy servant hath he not called.
20 And thou, my lord, O king, the eyes of
all Israel *are* upon thee, that thou shouldest
tell them who shall sit on the throne of my
lord the king after him.
21 Otherwise it shall come to pass, when
my lord the king shall [m]sleep with his fa-

1:3 [a]Josh. 19:18
1:5 [b]2 Sam. 3:4 [c]2 Sam. 15:1
1:6 [d]2 Sam. 3:3; 1 Chron. 3:2
1:7 [e]2 Sam. 20:25 [f]ch. 2:22
1:8 [g]ch. 4:18 [h]2 Sam. 23:8
1:11 [i]2 Sam. 3:4
1:13 [j]1 Chron. 22:9
1:17 [k]ver. 13
1:19 [l]ver. 7
1:21 [m]Deut. 31:16; ch. 2:10

thers, that I and my son Solomon shall be
counted offenders.
22 ¶ And, lo, while she yet talked with the
king, Nathan the prophet also came in.
23 And they told the king, saying, Behold
Nathan the prophet. And when he was
come in before the king, he bowed himself
before the king with his face to the ground.
24 And Nathan said, My lord, O king,
hast thou said, Adonijah shall reign after
me, and he shall sit upon my throne?
25 [n]For he is gone down this day, and
hath slain oxen and fat cattle and sheep in
abundance, and hath called all the king's
sons, and the captains of the host, and Abiathar the priest; and, behold, they eat and
drink before him, and say, [o]God save king
Adonijah.
26 But me, *even* me thy servant, and Zadok the priest, and Benaiah the son of Jehoiada, and thy servant Solomon, hath he
not called.
27 Is this thing done by my lord the king,
and thou hast not shewed *it* unto thy servant, who should sit on the throne of my
lord the king after him?
28 ¶ Then king David answered and said,
Call me Bath-sheba. And she came into the
king's presence, and stood before the king.
29 And the king sware, and said, [p]*As* the
LORD liveth, that hath redeemed my soul
out of all distress,
30 [q]Even as I sware unto thee by the
LORD God of Israel, saying, Assuredly Solomon thy son shall reign after me, and he
shall sit upon my throne in my stead; even
so will I certainly do this day.
31 Then Bath-sheba bowed with *her* face
to the earth, and did reverence to the king,
and said, [r]Let my lord king David live for
ever.
32 ¶ And king David said, Call me Zadok
the priest, and Nathan the prophet, and Benaiah the son of Jehoiada. And they came
before the king.
33 The king also said unto them, [s]Take
with you the servants of your lord, and
cause Solomon my son to ride upon mine
own mule, and bring him down to [t]Gihon:
34 And let Zadok the priest and Nathan
the prophet [u]anoint him there king over Israel: and [v]blow ye with the trumpet, and
say, God save king Solomon.
35 Then ye shall come up after him, that
he may come and sit upon my throne; for he
shall be king in my stead: and I have appointed him to be ruler over Israel and over
Judah.
36 And Benaiah the son of Jehoiada answered the king, and said, Amen: the LORD
God of my lord the king say so *too*.
37 [w]As the LORD hath been with my lord
the king, even so be he with Solomon, and
[x]make his throne greater than the throne of
my lord king David.
38 So Zadok the priest, and Nathan the
prophet, [y]and Benaiah the son of Jehoiada,
and the Cherethites, and the Pelethites,

1:25 [n]ver. 19 [o]1 Sam. 10:24
1:29 [p]2 Sam. 4:9
1:30 [q]ver. 17
1:31 [r]Neh. 2:3; Dan. 2:4
1:33 [s]2 Sam. 20:6 [t]2 Chron. 32:30
1:34 [u]1 Sam. 10:1; 2 Sam. 2:4; ch. 19:16; 2 Kings 9:3 [v]2 Sam. 15:10; 2 Kings 9:13
1:37 [w]Josh. 1:5; 1 Sam. 20:13 [x]ver. 47
1:38 [y]2 Sam. 8:18
1:39 [z]Ex. 30:23; Ps. 89:20 [a]1 Chron. 29:22 [b]1 Sam. 10:24
1:42 [c]2 Sam. 18:27
1:46 [d]1 Chron. 29:23
1:47 [e]ver. 37 [f]Gen. 47:31
1:48 [g]ch. 3:6; Ps. 132:11
1:50 [h]ch. 2:28
1:52 [i]1 Sam. 14:45; 2 Sam. 14:11; Acts 27:34

went down, and caused Solomon to ride
upon king David's mule, and brought him to
Gihon.
39 And Zadok the priest took an horn of
[z]oil out of the tabernacle, and [a]anointed
Solomon. And they blew the trumpet; [b]and
all the people said, God save king Solomon.
40 And all the people came up after him,
and the people piped with pipes, and rejoiced with great joy, so that the earth rent
with the sound of them.
41 ¶ And Adonijah and all the guests that
were with him heard *it* as they had made an
end of eating. And when Joab heard the
sound of the trumpet, he said, Wherefore *is*
this noise of the city being in an uproar?
42 And while he yet spake, behold, Jonathan the son of Abiathar the priest came:
and Adonijah said unto him, Come in; for
[c]thou *art* a valiant man, and bringest good
tidings.
43 And Jonathan answered and said to
Adonijah, Verily our lord king David hath
made Solomon king.
44 And the king hath sent with him Zadok the priest, and Nathan the prophet, and
Benaiah the son of Jehoiada, and the Cherethites, and the Pelethites, and they have
caused him to ride upon the king's mule:
45 And Zadok the priest and Nathan the
prophet have anointed him king in Gihon:
and they are come up from thence rejoicing,
so that the city rang again. This *is* the noise
that ye have heard.
46 And also Solomon [d]sitteth on the
throne of the kingdom.
47 And moreover the king's servants
came to bless our lord king David, saying,
[e]God make the name of Solomon better
than thy name, and make his throne greater
than thy throne. [f]And the king bowed himself upon the bed.
48 And also thus said the king, Blessed *be*
the LORD God of Israel, which hath [g]given
one to sit on my throne this day, mine eyes
even seeing *it*.
49 And all the guests that *were* with Adonijah were afraid, and rose up, and went
every man his way.
50 ¶ And Adonijah feared because of Solomon, and arose, and went, and [h]caught
hold on the horns of the altar.
51 And it was told Solomon, saying, Behold, Adonijah feareth king Solomon: for,
lo, he hath caught hold on the horns of the
altar, saying, Let king Solomon swear unto
me to day that he will not slay his servant
with the sword.
52 And Solomon said, If he will shew
himself a worthy man, [i]there shall not an
hair of him fall to the earth: but if wickedness shall be found in him, he shall die.
53 So king Solomon sent, and they
brought him down from the altar. And he
came and bowed himself to king Solomon:
and Solomon said unto him, Go to thine
house.

2 Now [j]the days of David drew nigh that he should die; and he charged Solomon his son, saying,

2 [k]I go the way of all the earth: [l]be thou strong therefore, and shew thyself a man;

3 And keep the charge of the LORD thy God, to walk in his ways, to keep his statutes, and his commandments, and his judgments, and his testimonies, as it is written in the law of Moses, that thou mayest [m]prosper in all that thou doest, and whithersoever thou turnest thyself:

4 That the LORD may [n]continue his word which he spake concerning me, saying, [o]If thy children take heed to their way, to [p]walk before me in truth with all their heart and with all their soul, [q]there shall not fail thee (said he) a man on the throne of Israel.

5 Moreover thou knowest also what Joab the son of Zeruiah [r]did to me, *and* what he did to the two captains of the hosts of Israel, unto [s]Abner the son of Ner, and unto [t]Amasa the son of Jether, whom he slew, and shed the blood of war in peace, and put the blood of war upon his girdle that *was* about his loins, and in his shoes that *were* on his feet.

6 Do therefore [u]according to thy wisdom, and let not his hoar head go down to the grave in peace.

7 But shew kindness unto the sons of [v]Barzillai the Gileadite, and let them be of those that [w]eat at thy table: for so [x]they came to me when I fled because of Absalom thy brother.

8 And, behold, *thou hast* with thee [y]Shimei the son of Gera, a Benjamite of Bahurim, which cursed me with a grievous curse in the day when I went to Mahanaim: but [z]he came down to meet me at Jordan, and [a]I sware to him by the LORD, saying, I will not put thee to death with the sword.

9 Now therefore [b]hold him not guiltless: for thou *art* a wise man, and knowest what thou oughtest to do unto him; but his hoar head [c]bring thou down to the grave with blood.

10 So [d]David slept with his fathers, and was buried in [e]the city of David.

11 And the days that David [f]reigned over Israel *were* forty years: seven years reigned he in Hebron, and thirty and three years reigned he in Jerusalem.

12 ¶ [g]Then sat Solomon upon the throne of David his father; and his kingdom was established greatly.

13 ¶ And Adonijah the son of Haggith came to Bath-sheba the mother of Solomon. And she said, [h]Comest thou peaceably? And he said, Peaceably.

14 He said moreover, I have somewhat to say unto thee. And she said, Say on.

15 And he said, Thou knowest that the kingdom was [i]mine, and *that* all Israel set their faces on me, that I should reign: howbeit the kingdom is turned about, and is become my brother's: for [j]it was his from the LORD.

16 And now I ask one petition of thee, deny me not. And she said unto him, Say on.

17 And he said, Speak, I pray thee, unto Solomon the king, (for he will not say thee nay,) that he give me [k]Abishag the Shunammite to wife.

18 And Bath-sheba said, Well; I will speak for thee unto the king.

19 ¶ Bath-sheba therefore went unto king Solomon, to speak unto him for Adonijah. And the king rose up to meet her, and [l]bowed himself unto her, and sat down on his throne, and caused a seat to be set for the king's mother; [m]and she sat on his right hand.

20 Then she said, I desire one small petition of thee; *I pray thee,* say me not nay. And the king said unto her, Ask on, my mother: for I will not say thee nay.

21 And she said, Let Abishag the Shunammite be given to Adonijah thy brother to wife.

22 And king Solomon answered and said unto his mother, And why dost thou ask Abishag the Shunammite for Adonijah? ask for him the kingdom also; for he *is* mine elder brother; even for him, and for [n]Abiathar the priest, and for Joab the son of Zeruiah.

23 Then king Solomon sware by the LORD, saying, [o]God do so to me, and more also, if Adonijah have not spoken this word against his own life.

24 Now therefore, *as* the LORD liveth, which hath established me, and set me on the throne of David my father, and who hath made me an house, as he [p]promised, Adonijah shall be put to death this day.

25 And king Solomon sent by the hand of Benaiah the son of Jehoiada; and he fell upon him that he died.

26 ¶ And unto Abiathar the priest said the king, Get thee to [q]Anathoth, unto thine own fields; for thou *art* worthy of death: but I will not at this time put thee to death, [r]because thou barest the ark of the Lord GOD before David my father, and because [s]thou hast been afflicted in all wherein my father was afflicted.

27 So Solomon thrust out Abiathar from being priest unto the LORD; that he might [t]fulfil the word of the LORD, which he spake concerning the house of Eli in Shiloh.

28 ¶ Then tidings came to Joab: for Joab [u]had turned after Adonijah, though he turned not after Absalom. And Joab fled unto the tabernacle of the LORD, and [v]caught hold on the horns of the altar.

29 And it was told king Solomon that Joab was fled unto the tabernacle of the LORD; and, behold, *he is* by the altar. Then Solomon sent Benaiah the son of Jehoiada, saying, Go, fall upon him.

30 And Benaiah came to the tabernacle of the LORD, and said unto him, Thus saith the king, Come forth. And he said, Nay; but I will die here. And Benaiah brought the king

2:1 [j]Gen. 47:29; Deut. 31:14
2:2 [k]Josh. 23:14 [l]Deut. 17:19
2:3 [m]Deut. 29:9; Josh. 1:7; 1 Chron. 22:12
2:4 [n]2 Sam. 7:25 [o]Ps. 132:12 [p]2 Kings 20:3 [q]2 Sam. 7:12; ch. 8:25
2:5 [r]2 Sam. 3:39 [s]2 Sam. 3:27 [t]2 Sam. 20:10
2:6 [u]ver. 9; Prov. 20:26
2:7 [v]2 Sam. 12:31 [w]2 Sam. 9:7 [x]2 Sam. 17:27
2:8 [y]2 Sam. 16:5 [z]2 Sam. 19:18 [a]2 Sam. 19:23
2:9 [b]Ex. 20:7; Job 9:28 [c]Gen. 42:38
2:10 [d]ch. 1:21; Acts 2:29 [e]2 Sam. 5:7
2:11 [f]2 Sam. 5:4; 1 Chron. 29:26
2:12 [g]1 Chron. 29:23; 2 Chron. 1:1
2:13 [h]1 Sam. 16:4
2:15 [i]ch. 1:5 [j]1 Chron. 22:9; Prov. 21:30; Dan. 2:21
2:17 [k]ch. 1:3
2:19 [l]Ex. 20:12 [m]Ps. 45:9
2:22 [n]ch. 1:7
2:23 [o]Ruth 1:17
2:24 [p]2 Sam. 7:11; 1 Chron. 22:10
2:26 [q]Josh. 21:18 [r]1 Sam. 23:6; 2 Sam. 15:24 [s]1 Sam. 22:20; 2 Sam. 15:24
2:27 [t]1 Sam. 2:31-35
2:28 [u]ch. 1:7 [v]ch. 1:50

word again, saying, Thus said Joab, and thus he answered me.

31 And the king said unto him, [w]Do as he hath said, and fall upon him, and bury him; [x]that thou mayest take away the innocent blood, which Joab shed, from me, and from the house of my father.

32 And the LORD [y]shall return his blood upon his own head, who fell upon two men more righteous [z]and better than he, and slew them with the sword, my father David not knowing *thereof, to wit,* [a]Abner the son of Ner, captain of the host of Israel, and [b]Amasa the son of Jether, captain of the host of Judah.

33 Their blood shall therefore return upon the head of Joab, and [c]upon the head of his seed for ever: [d]but upon David, and upon his seed, and upon his house, and upon his throne, shall there be peace for ever from the LORD.

34 So Benaiah the son of Jehoiada went up, and fell upon him, and slew him: and he was buried in his own house in the wilderness.

35 ¶ And the king put Benaiah the son of Jehoiada in his room over the host: and [e]Zadok the priest did the king put in the room of [f]Abiathar.

36 ¶ And the king sent and called for [g]Shimei, and said unto him, Build thee an house in Jerusalem, and dwell there, and go not forth thence any whither.

37 For it shall be, *that* on the day thou goest out, and passest over [h]the brook Kidron, thou shalt know for certain that thou shalt surely die: [i]thy blood shall be upon thine own head.

38 And Shimei said unto the king, The saying *is* good: as my lord the king hath said, so will thy servant do. And Shimei dwelt in Jerusalem many days.

39 And it came to pass at the end of three years, that two of the servants of Shimei ran away unto [j]Achish son of Maachah king of Gath. And they told Shimei, saying, Behold, thy servants *be* in Gath.

40 And Shimei arose, and saddled his ass, and went to Gath to Achish to seek his servants: and Shimei went, and brought his servants from Gath.

41 And it was told Solomon that Shimei had gone from Jerusalem to Gath, and was come again.

42 And the king sent and called for Shimei, and said unto him, Did I not make thee to swear by the LORD, and protested unto thee, saying, Know for a certain, on the day thou goest out, and walkest abroad any whither, that thou shalt surely die? and thou saidst unto me, The word *that* I have heard *is* good.

43 Why then hast thou not kept the oath of the LORD, and the commandment that I have charged thee with?

44 The king said moreover to Shimei, Thou knowest [k]all the wickedness which thine heart is privy to, that thou didst to David my father: therefore the LORD shall [l]return thy wickedness upon thine own head;

45 And king Solomon *shall be* blessed, and [m]the throne of David shall be established before the LORD for ever.

46 So the king commanded Benaiah the son of Jehoiada; which went out, and fell upon him, that he died. And the [n]kingdom was established in the hand of Solomon.

3 And [o]Solomon made affinity with Pharaoh king of Egypt, and took Pharaoh's daughter, and brought her into the [p]city of David, until he had made an end of building his [q]own house, and [r]the house of the LORD, and [s]the wall of Jerusalem round about.

2 [t]Only the people sacrificed in high places, because there was no house built unto the name of the LORD, until those days.

3 And Solomon [u]loved the LORD, [v]walking in the statutes of David his father: only he sacrificed and burnt incense in high places.

4 And [w]the king went to Gibeon to sacrifice there; [x]for that *was* the great high place: a thousand burnt offerings did Solomon offer upon that altar.

5 ¶ [y]In Gibeon the LORD appeared to Solomon [z]in a dream by night: and God said, Ask what I shall give thee.

6 [a]And Solomon said, Thou hast shewed unto thy servant David my father great mercy, according as he [b]walked before thee in truth, and in righteousness, and in uprightness of heart with thee; and thou hast kept for him this great kindness, that thou [c]hast given him a son to sit on his throne, as *it is* this day.

7 And now, O LORD my God, thou hast made thy servant king instead of David my father: [d]and I *am but* a little child: I know not *how* [e]to go out or come in.

8 And thy servant *is* in the midst of thy people which thou [f]hast chosen, a great people, [g]that cannot be numbered nor counted for multitude.

9 [h]Give therefore thy servant an understanding heart [i]to judge thy people, that I may [j]discern between good and bad: for who is able to judge this thy so great a people?

10 And the speech pleased the Lord, that Solomon had asked this thing.

11 And God said unto him, Because thou hast asked this thing, and hast [k]not asked for thyself long life; neither hast asked riches for thyself, nor hast asked the life of thine enemies; but hast asked for thyself understanding to discern judgment;

12 [l]Behold, I have done according to thy words: [m]lo, I have given thee a wise and an understanding heart; so that there was none like thee before thee, neither after thee shall any arise like unto thee.

13 And I have also [n]given thee that which thou hast not asked, both [o]riches, and hon-

2:31 [w]Ex. 21:14 [x]Num. 35:33; Deut. 19:13
2:32 [y]Judg. 9:24; Ps. 7:16 [z]2 Chron. 21:13 [a]2 Sam. 3:27 [b]2 Sam. 20:10
2:33 [c]2 Sam. 3:29 [d]Prov. 25:5
2:35 [e]Num. 25:11; 1 Sam. 2:35; 1 Chron. 6:53 [f]ver. 27
2:36 [g]2 Sam. 16:5; ver. 8
2:37 [h]2 Sam. 15:23 [i]Lev. 20:9; Josh. 2:29; 2 Sam. 1:16
2:39 [j]1 Sam. 27:2
2:44 [k]2 Sam. 16:5 [l]Ps. 7:16; Ezek. 17:19
2:45 [m]Prov. 25:5
2:46 [n]ver. 12; 2 Chron. 1:1
3:1 [o]ch. 7:8 [p]2 Sam. 5:7 [q]ch. 7:1 [r]ch. 6:1 [s]ch. 9:15
3:2 [t]Lev. 17:3; Deut. 12:2; ch. 22:43
3:3 [u]Deut. 6:5; Ps. 31:23; Rom. 8:28; 1 Cor. 8:3 [v]ver. 6
3:4 [w]2 Chron. 1:3 [x]1 Chron. 16:39; 2 Chron. 1:3
3:5 [y]ch. 9:2; 2 Chron. 1:7 [z]Num. 12:6; Matt. 1:20
3:6 [a]2 Chron. 1:8 [b]ch. 2:4; 2 Kings 20:3; Ps. 15:2 [c]ch. 1:48
3:7 [d]1 Chron. 29:1 [e]Num. 27:17
3:8 [f]Deut. 7:6 [g]Gen. 13:16
3:9 [h]2 Chron. 1:10; Prov. 2:3-9; Jam. 1:5 [i]Ps. 72:1 [j]Heb. 5:14
3:11 [k]Jam. 4:3
3:12 [l]1 John 5:14 [m]ch. 4:29; Eccl. 1:16
3:13 [n]Matt. 6:33; Eph. 3:20 [o]ch. 4:21; Prov. 3:16

our: so that there shall not be any among the kings like unto thee all thy days.

14 And if thou wilt walk in my ways, to keep my statutes and my commandments, [p]as thy father David did walk, then I will [q]lengthen thy days.

15 And Solomon [r]awoke; and, behold, *it was* a dream. And he came to Jerusalem, and stood before the ark of the covenant of the LORD, and offered up burnt offerings, and offered peace offerings, and [s]made a feast to all his servants.

16 ¶ Then came there two women, *that were* harlots, unto the king, and [t]stood before him.

17 And the one woman said, O my lord, I and this woman dwell in one house; and I was delivered of a child with her in the house.

18 And it came to pass the third day after that I was delivered, that this woman was delivered also: and we *were* together; *there was* no stranger with us in the house, save we two in the house.

19 And this woman's child died in the night; because she overlaid it.

20 And she arose at midnight, and took my son from beside me, while thine handmaid slept, and laid it in her bosom, and laid her dead child in my bosom.

21 And when I rose in the morning to give my child suck, behold, it was dead: but when I had considered it in the morning, behold, it was not my son, which I did bear.

22 And the other woman said, Nay; but the living *is* my son, and the dead *is* thy son. And this said, No; but the dead *is* thy son, and the living *is* my son. Thus they spake before the king.

23 Then said the king, The one saith, This *is* my son that liveth, and thy son *is* the dead: and the other saith, Nay; but thy son *is* the dead, and my son *is* the living.

24 And the king said, Bring me a sword. And they brought a sword before the king.

25 And the king said, Divide the living child in two, and give half to the one, and half to the other.

26 Then spake the woman whose the living child *was* unto the king, for [u]her bowels yearned upon her son, and she said, O my lord, give her the living child, and in no wise slay it. But the other said, Let it be neither mine nor thine, *but* divide *it*.

27 Then the king answered and said, Give her the living child, and in no wise slay it: she *is* the mother thereof.

28 And all Israel heard of the judgment which the king had judged; and they feared the king: for they saw that the [v]wisdom of God *was* in him, to do judgment.

4 So king Solomon was king over all Israel.

2 And these *were* the princes which he had; Azariah the son of Zadok the priest,

3 Elihoreph and Ahiah, the sons of Shisha, scribes; [w]Jehoshaphat the son of Ahilud, the recorder.

4 And [x]Benaiah the son of Jehoiada *was* over the host: and Zadok and [y]Abiathar *were* the priests:

5 And Azariah the son of Nathan *was* over [z]the officers: and Zabud the son of Nathan *was* [a]principal officer, *and* [b]the king's friend:

6 And Ahishar *was* over the household: and [c]Adoniram the son of Abda *was* over the tribute.

7 ¶ And Solomon had twelve officers over all Israel, which provided victuals for the king and his household: each man his month in a year made provision.

8 And these *are* their names: the son of Hur, in mount Ephraim:

9 The son of Dekar, in Makaz, and in Shaalbim, and Beth-shemesh, and Elon-bethhanan:

10 The son of Hesed, in Aruboth; to him *pertained* Sochoh, and all the land of Hepher:

11 The son of Abinadab, in all the region of Dor; which had Taphath the daughter of Solomon to wife:

12 Baana the son of Ahilud; *to him pertained* Taanach and Megiddo, and all Bethshean, which *is* by Zartanah beneath Jezreel, from Beth-shean to Abel-meholah, *even* unto *the place that is* beyond Jokneam:

13 The son of Geber, in Ramoth-gilead; to him *pertained* [d]the towns of Jair the son of Manasseh, which *are* in Gilead; to him *also pertained* [e]the region of Argob, which *is* in Bashan, threescore great cities with walls and brasen bars:

14 Ahinadab the son of Iddo *had* Mahanaim:

15 Ahimaaz *was* in Naphtali; he also took Basmath the daughter of Solomon to wife:

16 Baanah the son of Hushai *was* in Asher and in Aloth:

17 Jehoshaphat the son of Paruah, in Issachar:

18 Shimei the son of Elah, in Benjamin:

19 Geber the son of Uri *was* in [f]the country of Gilead, *in* the country of Sihon king of the Amorites, and of Og king of Bashan; and *he was* the only officer which *was* in the land.

20 ¶ Judah and Israel *were* many, [g]as the sand which *is* by the sea in multitude, [h]eating and drinking, and making merry.

21 And [i]Solomon reigned over all kingdoms from [j]the river unto the land of the Philistines, and unto the border of Egypt: [k]they brought presents, and served Solomon all the days of his life.

22 ¶ And Solomon's provision for one day was thirty measures of fine flour, and threescore measures of meal,

23 Ten fat oxen, and twenty oxen out of the pastures, and an hundred sheep, beside harts, and roebucks, and fallowdeer, and fatted fowl.

24 For he had dominion over all *the region* on this side the river, from Tiphsah

3:14 [p]ch. 15:5 [q]Ps. 91:16; Prov. 3:2
3:15 [r]Gen. 41:7 [s]Gen. 40:20; ch. 8:65; Esth. 1:3; Dan. 5:1; Mark 6:21
3:16 [t]Num. 27:2
3:26 [u]Gen. 43:30; Isa. 49:15; Jer. 31:20; Hos. 11:8
3:28 [v]ver. 9
4:3 [w]2 Sam. 8:16
4:4 [x]ch. 2:35 [y]ch. 2:27
4:5 [z]ver. 7 [a]2 Sam. 8:18 [b]2 Sam. 15:37; 1 Chron. 27:33
4:6 [c]ch. 5:14
4:13 [d]Num. 32:41 [e]Deut. 3:4
4:19 [f]Deut. 3:8
4:20 [g]Gen. 22:17; ch. 3:8; Prov. 14:28 [h]Ps. 72:3; Mic. 4:4
4:21 [i]2 Chron. 9:26; Ps. 72:8 [j]Gen. 15:18; Josh. 1:4 [k]Ps. 68:29

even to Azzah, over [l]all the kings on this
side the river: and [m]he had peace on all
sides round about him.
25 And Judah and Israel [n]dwelt safely,
[o]every man under his vine and under his fig
tree, [p]from Dan even to Beer-sheba, all the
days of Solomon.
26 ¶ And [q]Solomon had forty thousand
stalls of [r]horses for his chariots, and twelve
thousand horsemen.
27 And [s]those officers provided victual
for king Solomon, and for all that came unto
king Solomon's table, every man in his
month: they lacked nothing.
28 Barley also and straw for the horses
and dromedaries brought they unto the
place where *the officers* were, every man
according to his charge.
29 ¶ And [t]God gave Solomon wisdom
and understanding exceeding much, and
largeness of heart, even as the sand that *is*
on the sea shore.
30 And Solomon's wisdom excelled the
wisdom of all the children [u]of the east
country, and all [v]the wisdom of Egypt.
31 For he was [w]wiser than all men; [x]than
Ethan the Ezrahite, [y]and Heman, and Chal-
col, and Darda, the sons of Mahol: and his
fame was in all nations round about.
32 And [z]he spake three thousand proverbs: and his [a]songs were a thousand and
five.
33 And he spake of trees, from the cedar
tree that *is* in Lebanon even unto the hyssop
that springeth out of the wall: he spake also
of beasts, and of fowl, and of creeping
things, and of fishes.
34 And [b]there came of all people to hear
the wisdom of Solomon, from all kings of
the earth, which had heard of his wisdom.

5

And [c]Hiram king of Tyre sent his servants unto Solomon; for he had heard
that they had anointed him king in the room
of his father: [d]for Hiram was ever a lover of
David.
2 And [e]Solomon sent to Hiram, saying,
3 Thou knowest how that David my father could not build an house unto the name
of the LORD his God [f]for the wars which
were about him on every side, until the
LORD put them under the soles of his feet.
4 But now the LORD my God hath given
me [g]rest on every side, *so that there is* neither adversary nor evil occurrent.
5 [h]And, behold, I purpose to build an
house unto the name of the LORD my God,
[i]as the LORD spake unto David my father,
saying, Thy son, whom I will set upon thy
throne in thy room, he shall build an house
unto my name.
6 Now therefore command thou that they
hew me [j]cedar trees out of Lebanon; and
my servants shall be with thy servants: and
unto thee will I give hire for thy servants
according to all that thou shalt appoint: for
thou knowest that *there is* not among us
any that can skill to hew timber like unto
the Sidonians.

4:24 [l]Ps. 72:11 [m]1 Chron. 22:9
4:25 [n]Jer. 23:6 [o]Mic. 4:4; Zech. 3:10 [p]Judg. 20:1
4:26 [q]ch. 10:26; 2 Chron. 1:14 [r]Deut. 17:16
4:27 [s]ver. 7
4:29 [t]ch. 3:12
4:30 [u]Gen. 25:6 [v]Acts 7:22
4:31 [w]ch. 3:12 [x]1 Chron. 15:19; Ps. 89, title [y]1 Chron. 2:6; Ps. 88, title
4:32 [z]Prov. 1:1; Eccl. 12:9 [a]SSol. 1:1
4:34 [b]ch. 10:1; 2 Chron. 9:1
5:1 [c]ver. 10; 2 Chron. 2:3 [d]2 Sam. 5:11; 1 Chron. 14:1; Am. 1:9
5:2 [e]2 Chron. 2:3
5:3 [f]1 Chron. 22:8
5:4 [g]ch. 4:24; 2 Chron. 22:9
5:5 [h]2 Chron. 2:4 [i]2 Sam. 7:13; 1 Chron. 17:12
5:6 [j]2 Chron. 2:8
5:9 [k]2 Chron. 2:16 [l]Ezra 3:7; Ezek. 27:17; Acts 12:20
5:11 [m]2 Chron. 2:10
5:12 [n]ch. 3:12
5:14 [o]ch. 4:6
5:15 [p]ch. 9:21; 2 Chron. 2:17
5:17 [q]1 Chron. 22:2
6:1 [r]2 Chron. 3:1 [s]Acts 7:47
6:2 [t]Ezek. 41:1

7 ¶ And it came to pass, when Hiram
heard the words of Solomon, that he rejoiced greatly, and said, Blessed *be* the
LORD this day, which hath given unto David
a wise son over this great people.
8 And Hiram sent to Solomon, saying, I
have considered the things which thou sentest to me for: *and* I will do all thy desire
concerning timber of cedar, and concerning
timber of fir.
9 My servants shall bring *them* down
from Lebanon unto the sea: [k]and I will convey them by sea in floats unto the place that
thou shalt appoint me, and will cause them
to be discharged there, and thou shalt receive *them:* and thou shalt accomplish my
desire, [l]in giving food for my household.
10 So Hiram gave Solomon cedar trees
and fir trees *according to* all his desire.
11 [m]And Solomon gave Hiram twenty
thousand measures of wheat *for* food to his
household, and twenty measures of pure
oil: thus gave Solomon to Hiram year by
year.
12 And the LORD gave Solomon wisdom,
[n]as he promised him: and there was peace
between Hiram and Solomon; and they two
made a league together.
13 ¶ And king Solomon raised a levy out
of all Israel; and the levy was thirty thousand men.
14 And he sent them to Lebanon, ten
thousand a month by courses: a month they
were in Lebanon, *and* two months at home:
and [o]Adoniram *was* over the levy.
15 [p]And Solomon had threescore and ten
thousand that bare burdens, and fourscore
thousand hewers in the mountains;
16 Beside the chief of Solomon's officers
which *were* over the work, three thousand
and three hundred, which ruled over the
people that wrought in the work.
17 And the king commanded, and they
brought great stones, costly stones, *and*
[q]hewed stones, to lay the foundation of the
house.
18 And Solomon's builders and Hiram's
builders did hew *them,* and the stonesquar-
ers: so they prepared timber and stones to
build the house.

6

And [r]it came to pass in the four hundred and eightieth year after the children of Israel were come out of the land of
Egypt, in the fourth year of Solomon's reign
over Israel, in the month Zif, which *is* the
second month, that [s]he began to build the
house of the LORD.
2 And [t]the house which king Solomon
built for the LORD, the length thereof *was*
threescore cubits, and the breadth thereof
twenty *cubits,* and the height thereof thirty
cubits.
3 And the porch before the temple of the
house, twenty cubits *was* the length thereof,
according to the breadth of the house; *and*
ten cubits *was* the breadth thereof before
the house.

4 And for the house he made [u]windows of narrow lights.

5 ¶ And against the wall of the house he built [v]chambers round about, *against* the walls of the house round about, *both* of the temple [w]and of the oracle: and he made chambers round about:

6 The nethermost chamber *was* five cubits broad, and the middle *was* six cubits broad, and the third *was* seven cubits broad: for without *in the wall* of the house he made narrowed rests round about, that *the beams* should not be fastened in the walls of the house.

7 And [x]the house, when it was in building, was built of stone made ready before it was brought thither: so that there was neither hammer nor axe *nor* any tool of iron heard in the house, while it was in building.

8 The door for the middle chamber *was* in the right side of the house: and they went up with winding stairs into the middle *chamber,* and out of the middle into the third.

9 [y]So he built the house, and finished it; and covered the house with beams and boards of cedar.

10 And *then* he built chambers against all the house, five cubits high: and they rested on the house with timber of cedar.

11 ¶ And the word of the LORD came to Solomon, saying,

12 *Concerning* this house which thou art in building, [z]if thou wilt walk in my statutes, and execute my judgments, and keep all my commandments to walk in them; then will I perform my word with thee, [a]which I spake unto David thy father:

13 And [b]I will dwell among the children of Israel, and will not [c]forsake my people Israel.

14 [d]So Solomon built the house, and finished it.

15 And he built the walls of the house within with boards of cedar, both the floor of the house, and the walls of the cieling: *and* he covered *them* on the inside with wood, and covered the floor of the house with planks of fir.

16 And he built twenty cubits on the sides of the house, both the floor and the walls with boards of cedar: he even built *them* for it within, *even* for the oracle, *even* for the [e]most holy *place.*

17 And the house, that *is,* the temple before it, was forty cubits *long.*

18 And the cedar of the house within *was* carved with knops and open flowers: all *was* cedar; there was no stone seen.

19 And the oracle he prepared in the house within, to set there the ark of the covenant of the LORD.

20 And the oracle in the forepart *was* twenty cubits in length, and twenty cubits in breadth, and twenty cubits in the height thereof: and he overlaid it with pure gold; and *so* covered the altar *which was of* cedar.

21 So Solomon overlaid the house within with pure gold: and he made a partition by the chains of gold before the oracle; and he overlaid it with gold.

22 And the whole house he overlaid with gold, until he had finished all the house: also [f]the whole altar that *was* by the oracle he overlaid with gold.

23 ¶ And within the oracle [g]he made two cherubims *of* olive tree, *each* ten cubits high.

24 And five cubits *was* the one wing of the cherub, and five cubits the other wing of the cherub: from the uttermost part of the one wing unto the uttermost part of the other *were* ten cubits.

25 And the other cherub *was* ten cubits: both the cherubims *were* of one measure and one size.

26 The height of the one cherub *was* ten cubits, and so *was it* of the other cherub.

27 And he set the cherubims within the inner house: and [h]they stretched forth the wings of the cherubims, so that the wing of the one touched the *one* wall, and the wing of the other cherub touched the other wall; and their wings touched one another in the midst of the house.

28 And he overlaid the cherubims with gold.

29 And he carved all the walls of the house round about with carved figures of cherubims and palm trees and open flowers, within and without.

30 And the floor of the house he overlaid with gold, within and without.

31 ¶ And for the entering of the oracle he made doors *of* olive tree: the lintel *and* side posts *were* a fifth part *of the wall.*

32 The two doors also *were of* olive tree; and he carved upon them carvings of cherubims and palm trees and open flowers, and overlaid *them* with gold, and spread gold upon the cherubims, and upon the palm trees.

33 So also made he for the door of the temple posts *of* olive tree, a fourth part *of the wall.*

34 And the two doors *were of* fir tree: the [i]two leaves of the one door *were* folding, and the two leaves of the other door *were* folding.

35 And he carved *thereon* cherubims and palm trees and open flowers: and covered *them* with gold fitted upon the carved work.

36 ¶ And he built the inner court with three rows of hewed stone, and a row of cedar beams.

37 ¶ [j]In the fourth year was the foundation of the house of the LORD laid, in the month Zif:

38 And in the eleventh year, in the month Bul, which *is* the eighth month, was the house finished throughout all the parts thereof, and according to all the fashion of it. So was he [k]seven years in building it.

7 But Solomon was building his own house [l]thirteen years, and he finished all his house.

2 ¶ He built also the house of the forest of

6:4 [u]Ezek. 40:16
6:5 [v]Ezek. 41:6 [w]ver. 16
6:7 [x]Deut. 27:5; ch. 5:18
6:9 [y]ver. 14
6:12 [z]ch. 2:4 [a]2 Sam. 7:13; 1 Chron. 22:10
6:13 [b]Ex. 25:8; Lev. 26:11; 2 Cor. 6:16; Rev. 21:3 [c]Deut. 31:6
6:14 [d]ver. 38
6:16 [e]Ex. 26:33; Lev. 16:2; ch. 8:6; 2 Chron. 3:8; Ezek. 45:3; Heb. 9:3
6:22 [f]Ex. 30:1
6:23 [g]Ex. 37:7; 2 Chron. 3:10
6:27 [h]Ex. 25:20; 2 Chron. 5:8
6:34 [i]Ezek. 41:23
6:37 [j]ver. 1
6:38 [k]ver. 1
7:1 [l]ch. 9:10; 2 Chron. 8:1

Lebanon; the length thereof *was* an hundred cubits, and the breadth thereof fifty
cubits, and the height thereof thirty cubits,
upon four rows of cedar pillars, with cedar
beams upon the pillars.
3 And *it was* covered with cedar above
upon the beams, that *lay* on forty five pillars, fifteen *in* a row.
4 And *there were* windows *in* three rows,
and light *was* against light *in* three ranks.
5 And all the doors and posts *were*
square, with the windows: and light *was*
against light *in* three ranks.
6 ¶ And he made a porch of pillars; the
length thereof *was* fifty cubits, and the
breadth thereof thirty cubits: and the porch
was before them: and the *other* pillars and
the thick beam *were* before them.
7 ¶ Then he made a porch for the throne
where he might judge, *even* the porch of
judgment: and *it was* covered with cedar
from one side of the floor to the other.
8 ¶ And his house where he dwelt *had*
another court within the porch, *which* was
of the like work. Solomon made also an
house for Pharaoh's daughter, [m]whom he
had taken *to wife,* like unto this porch.
9 All these *were of* costly stones, according to the measures of hewed stones, sawed
with saws, within and without, even from
the foundation unto the coping, and *so* on
the outside toward the great court.
10 And the foundation *was of* costly
stones, even great stones, stones of ten cubits, and stones of eight cubits.
11 And above *were* costly stones, after
the measures of hewed stones, and cedars.
12 And the great court round about *was*
with three rows of hewed stones, and a row
of cedar beams, both for the inner court of
the house of the LORD, [n]and for the porch of
the house.
13 ¶ And king Solomon sent and fetched
[o]Hiram out of Tyre.
14 [p]He *was* a widow's son of the tribe
of Naphtali, and [q]his father *was* a man of
Tyre, a worker in brass: and [r]he was filled
with wisdom, and understanding, and cunning to work all works in brass. And he
came to king Solomon, and wrought all his
work.
15 For he cast [s]two pillars of brass, of
eighteen cubits high apiece: and a line of
twelve cubits did compass either of them
about.
16 And he made two chapiters *of* molten
brass, to set upon the tops of the pillars: the
height of the one chapiter *was* five cubits,
and the height of the other chapiter *was* five
cubits:
17 *And* nets of checker work, and
wreaths of chain work, for the chapiters
which *were* upon the top of the pillars;
seven for the one chapiter, and seven for the
other chapiter.
18 And he made the pillars, and two rows
round about upon the one network, to cover
the chapiters that *were* upon the top, with
pomegranates: and so did he for the other
chapiter.
19 And the chapiters that *were* upon the
top of the pillars *were* of lily work in the
porch, four cubits.
20 And the chapiters upon the two pillars
had pomegranates also above, over against
the belly which *was* by the network: and the
pomegranates *were* [t]two hundred in rows
round about upon the other chapiter.
21 [u]And he set up the pillars in [v]the
porch of the temple: and he set up the right
pillar, and called the name thereof Jachin:
and he set up the left pillar, and called the
name thereof Boaz.
22 And upon the top of the pillars *was* lily
work: so was the work of the pillars finished.
23 ¶ And he made [w]a molten sea, ten cubits from the one brim to the other: *it was*
round all about, and his height *was* five cubits: and a line of thirty cubits did compass
it round about.
24 And under the brim of it round about
there were knops compassing it, ten in a
cubit, [x]compassing the sea round about:
the knops *were* cast in two rows, when it
was cast.
25 It stood upon [y]twelve oxen, three
looking toward the north, and three looking
toward the west, and three looking toward
the south, and three looking toward the
east: and the sea *was set* above upon them,
and all their hinder parts *were* inward.
26 And it *was* an hand breadth thick, and
the brim thereof was wrought like the brim
of a cup, with flowers of lilies: it contained
[z]two thousand baths.
27 ¶ And he made ten bases of brass; four
cubits *was* the length of one base, and four
cubits the breadth thereof, and three cubits
the height of it.
28 And the work of the bases *was* on this
manner: they had borders, and the borders
were between the ledges:
29 And on the borders that *were* between
the ledges *were* lions, oxen, and cherubims:
and upon the ledges *there was* a base
above: and beneath the lions and oxen *were*
certain additions made of thin work.
30 And every base had four brasen
wheels, and plates of brass: and the four
corners thereof had undersetters: under the
laver *were* undersetters molten, at the side
of every addition.
31 And the mouth of it within the chapiter
and above *was* a cubit: but the mouth
thereof *was* round *after* the work of the
base, a cubit and an half: and also upon the
mouth of it *were* gravings with their borders, foursquare, not round.
32 And under the borders *were* four
wheels; and the axletrees of the wheels
were joined to the base: and the height of a
wheel *was* a cubit and half a cubit.
33 And the work of the wheels *was* like
the work of a chariot wheel: their axletrees,

7:8 [m]ch. 3:1; 2 Chron. 8:11
7:12 [n]John 10:23; Acts 3:11
7:13 [o]ver. 40; 2 Chron. 4:11
7:14 [p]2 Chron. 2:14 [q]2 Chron. 4:16 [r]Ex. 31:3
7:15 [s]2 Kings 25:17; 2 Chron. 3:15; Jer. 52:21
7:20 [t]2 Chron. 3:16; Jer. 52:23
7:21 [u]2 Chron. 3:17 [v]ch. 6:3
7:23 [w]2 Kings 25:13; 2 Chron. 4:2; Jer. 52:17
7:24 [x]2 Chron. 4:3
7:25 [y]2 Chron. 4:4; Jer. 52:20
7:26 [z]2 Chron. 4:5

and their naves, and their felloes, and their spokes, *were* all molten.

34 And *there were* four undersetters to the four corners of one base: *and* the undersetters *were* of the very base itself.

35 And in the top of the base *was there* a round compass of half a cubit high: and on the top of the base the ledges thereof and the borders thereof *were* of the same.

36 For on the plates of the ledges thereof, and on the borders thereof, he graved cherubims, lions, and palm trees, according to the proportion of every one, and additions round about.

37 After this *manner* he made the ten bases: all of them had one casting, one measure, *and* one size.

38 ¶ Then [a]made he ten lavers of brass: one laver contained forty baths: *and* every laver was four cubits: *and* upon every one of the ten bases one laver.

39 And he put five bases on the right side of the house, and five on the left side of the house: and he set the sea on the right side of the house eastward over against the south.

40 ¶ And Hiram made the lavers, and the shovels, and the basons. So Hiram made an end of doing all the work that he made king Solomon for the house of the LORD:

41 The two pillars, and the *two* bowls of the chapiters that *were* on the top of the two pillars; and the two [b]networks, to cover the two bowls of the chapiters which *were* upon the top of the pillars;

42 And four hundred pomegranates for the two networks, *even* two rows of pomegranates for one network, to cover the two bowls of the chapiters that *were* upon the pillars;

43 And the ten bases, and ten lavers on the bases;

44 And one sea, and twelve oxen under the sea;

45 [c]And the pots, and the shovels, and the basons: and all these vessels, which Hiram made to king Solomon for the house of the LORD, *were of* bright brass.

46 [d]In the plain of Jordan did the king cast them, in the clay ground between [e]Succoth and [f]Zarthan.

47 And Solomon left all the vessels *unweighed*, because they were exceeding many: neither was the weight of the brass found out.

48 And Solomon made all the vessels that *pertained* unto the house of the LORD: [g]the altar of gold, and [h]the table of gold, whereupon [i]the shewbread *was*,

49 And the candlesticks of pure gold, five on the right *side*, and five on the left, before the oracle, with the flowers, and the lamps, and the tongs *of* gold,

50 And the bowls, and the snuffers, and the basons, and the spoons, and the censers *of* pure gold; and the hinges *of* gold, *both* for the doors of the inner house, the most holy *place, and* for the doors of the house, *to wit*, of the temple.

7:38 [a]2 Chron. 4:6
7:41 [b]ver. 17
7:45 [c]Ex. 27:3; 2 Chron. 4:16
7:46 [d]2 Chron. 4:17 [e]Gen. 33:17 [f]Josh. 3:16
7:48 [g]Ex. 37:25 [h]Ex. 37:10 [i]Ex. 25:30; Lev. 24:5-8
7:51 [j]2 Sam. 8:11; 2 Chron. 5:1
8:1 [k]2 Chron. 5:2 [l]2 Sam. 6:17 [m]2 Sam. 5:7
8:2 [n]Lev. 23:34; 2 Chron. 7:8
8:3 [o]Num. 4:15; Deut. 31:9; Josh. 3:3; 1 Chron. 15:14
8:4 [p]ch. 3:4; 2 Chron. 1:3
8:5 [q]2 Sam. 6:13
8:6 [r]2 Sam. 6:17 [s]Ex. 26:33; ch. 6:19 [t]ch. 6:27
8:8 [u]Ex. 25:14
8:9 [v]Ex. 25:21; Deut. 10:2 [w]Deut. 10:5; Heb. 9:4 [x]Ex. 40:20 [y]Ex. 34:27; Deut. 4:13; ver. 21
8:10 [z]Ex. 40:34; 2 Chron. 5:13
8:12 [a]2 Chron. 6:1 [b]Lev. 16:2; Ps. 18:11
8:13 [c]2 Sam. 7:13 [d]Ps. 132:14
8:14 [e]2 Sam. 6:18
8:15 [f]Luke 1:68 [g]2 Sam. 7:5

51 So was ended all the work that king Solomon made for the house of the LORD. And Solomon brought in the things [j]which David his father had dedicated; *even* the silver, and the gold, and the vessels, did he put among the treasures of the house of the LORD.

8 Then [k]Solomon assembled the elders of Israel, and all the heads of the tribes, the chief of the fathers of the children of Israel, unto king Solomon in Jerusalem, [l]that they might bring up the ark of the covenant of the LORD [m]out of the city of David, which *is* Zion.

2 And all the men of Israel assembled themselves unto king Solomon at the [n]feast in the month Ethanim, which *is* the seventh month.

3 And all the elders of Israel came, [o]and the priests took up the ark.

4 And they brought up the ark of the LORD, [p]and the tabernacle of the congregation, and all the holy vessels that *were* in the tabernacle, even those did the priests and the Levites bring up.

5 And king Solomon, and all the congregation of Israel, that were assembled unto him, *were* with him before the ark, [q]sacrificing sheep and oxen, that could not be told nor numbered for multitude.

6 And the priests [r]brought in the ark of the covenant of the LORD unto [s]his place, into the oracle of the house, to the most holy *place, even* [t]under the wings of the cherubims.

7 For the cherubims spread forth *their* two wings over the place of the ark, and the cherubims covered the ark and the staves thereof above.

8 And they [u]drew out the staves, that the ends of the staves were seen out in the holy *place* before the oracle, and they were not seen without: and there they are unto this day.

9 [v]*There was* nothing in the ark [w]save the two tables of stone, which Moses [x]put there at Horeb, [y]when the LORD made *a covenant* with the children of Israel, when they came out of the land of Egypt.

10 And it came to pass, when the priests were come out of the holy *place*, that the cloud [z]filled the house of the LORD,

11 So that the priests could not stand to minister because of the cloud: for the glory of the LORD had filled the house of the LORD.

12 ¶ [a]Then spake Solomon, The LORD said that he would dwell [b]in the thick darkness.

13 [c]I have surely built thee an house to dwell in, [d]a settled place for thee to abide in for ever.

14 And the king turned his face about, and [e]blessed all the congregation of Israel: (and all the congregation of Israel stood;)

15 And he said, [f]Blessed *be* the LORD God of Israel, which [g]spake with his mouth

unto David my father, and hath with his
hand fulfilled *it*, saying,
16 [h]Since the day that I brought forth my
people Israel out of Egypt, I chose no city
out of all the tribes of Israel to build an
house, that [i]my name might be therein; but
I chose [j]David to be over my people Israel.
17 And [k]it was in the heart of David my
father to build an house for the name of the
LORD God of Israel.
18 [l]And the LORD said unto David my
father, Whereas it was in thine heart to
build an house unto my name, thou didst
well that it was in thine heart.
19 Nevertheless [m]thou shalt not build the
house; but thy son that shall come forth out
of thy loins, he shall build the house unto
my name.
20 And the LORD hath performed his
word that he spake, and I am risen up in the
room of David my father, and sit on the
throne of Israel, [n]as the LORD promised,
and have built an house for the name of the
LORD God of Israel.
21 And I have set there a place for the ark,
wherein *is* [o]the covenant of the LORD,
which he made with our fathers, when he
brought them out of the land of Egypt.
22 ¶ And Solomon stood before [p]the altar
of the LORD in the presence of all the congregation of Israel, and [q]spread forth his
hands toward heaven:
23 And he said, LORD God of Israel,
[r]*there is* no God like thee, in heaven above,
or on earth beneath, [s]who keepest covenant and mercy with thy servants that
[t]walk before thee with all their heart:
24 Who hast kept with thy servant David
my father that thou promisedst him: thou
spakest also with thy mouth, and hast fulfilled *it* with thine hand, as *it is* this day.
25 Therefore now, LORD God of Israel,
keep with thy servant David my father that
thou promisedst him, saying, [u]There shall
not fail thee a man in my sight to sit on the
throne of Israel; so that thy children take
heed to their way, that they walk before me
as thou hast walked before me.
26 [v]And now, O God of Israel, let thy
word, I pray thee, be verified, which thou
spakest unto thy servant David my father.
27 But [w]will God indeed dwell on the
earth? behold, the heaven and [x]heaven of
heavens cannot contain thee; how much
less this house that I have builded?
28 Yet have thou respect unto the prayer
of thy servant, and to his supplication,
O LORD my God, to hearken unto the cry
and to the prayer, which thy servant prayeth before thee to day:
29 That thine eyes may be open toward
this house night and day, *even* toward the
place of which thou hast said, [y]My name
shall be there: that thou mayest hearken
unto the prayer which thy servant shall
make [z]toward this place.
30 [a]And hearken thou to the supplication
of thy servant, and of thy people Israel,
when they shall pray toward this place: and
hear thou in heaven thy dwelling place: and
when thou hearest, forgive.
31 ¶ If any man trespass against his
neighbour, and [b]an oath be laid upon him
to cause him to swear, and the oath come
before thine altar in this house:
32 Then hear thou in heaven, and do, and
judge thy servants, [c]condemning the
wicked, to bring his way upon his head; and
justifying the righteous, to give him according to his righteousness.
33 ¶ [d]When thy people Israel be smitten
down before the enemy, because they have
sinned against thee, and [e]shall turn again
to thee, and confess thy name, and pray,
and make supplication unto thee in this
house:
34 Then hear thou in heaven, and forgive
the sin of thy people Israel, and bring them
again unto the land which thou gavest unto
their fathers.
35 ¶ [f]When heaven is shut up, and there
is no rain, because they have sinned against
thee; if they pray toward this place, and
confess thy name, and turn from their sin,
when thou afflictest them:
36 Then hear thou in heaven, and forgive
the sin of thy servants, and of thy people
Israel, that thou [g]teach them [h]the good
way wherein they should walk, and give
rain upon thy land, which thou hast given to
thy people for an inheritance.
37 ¶ [i]If there be in the land famine, if
there be pestilence, blasting, mildew, locust, *or* if there be caterpiller; if their enemy
besiege them in the land of their cities;
whatsoever plague, whatsoever sickness
there be;
38 What prayer and supplication soever
be *made* by any man, *or* by all thy people
Israel, which shall know every man the
plague of his own heart, and spread forth
his hands toward this house:
39 Then hear thou in heaven thy dwelling
place, and forgive, and do, and give to every
man according to his ways, whose heart
thou knowest; (for thou, *even* thou only,
[j]knowest the hearts of all the children of
men;)
40 [k]That they may fear thee all the days
that they live in the land which thou gavest
unto our fathers.
41 Moreover concerning a stranger, that
is not of thy people Israel, but cometh out of
a far country for thy name's sake;
42 (For they shall hear of thy great name,
and of thy [l]strong hand, and of thy
stretched out arm;) when he shall come and
pray toward this house;
43 Hear thou in heaven thy dwelling
place, and do according to all that the
stranger calleth to thee for: [m]that all people
of the earth may know thy name, to [n]fear
thee, as *do* thy people Israel; and that they
may know that this house, which I have
builded, is called by thy name.
44 ¶ If thy people go out to battle against

8:16 [h]2 Sam. 7:6; 2 Chron. 6:5 [i]ver. 29; Deut. 12:11 [j]1 Sam. 16:1; 2 Sam. 7:8; 1 Chron. 28:4
8:17 [k]2 Sam. 7:2; 1 Chron. 17:1
8:18 [l]2 Chron. 6:8
8:19 [m]2 Sam. 7:5; ch. 5:3
8:20 [n]1 Chron. 28:5
8:21 [o]ver. 9; Deut. 31:26
8:22 [p]2 Chron. 6:12 [q]Ex. 9:33; Ezra 9:5; Isa. 1:15
8:23 [r]Ex. 15:11; 2 Sam. 7:22 [s]Deut. 7:9; Neh. 1:5; Dan. 9:4 [t]Gen. 17:1; ch. 3:6; 2 Kings 20:3
8:25 [u]ch. 2:4; 2 Sam. 7:12
8:26 [v]2 Sam. 7:25
8:27 [w]2 Chron. 2:6; Isa. 66:1; Jer. 23:24; Acts 7:49 [x]2 Cor. 12:2
8:29 [y]Deut. 12:11 [z]Dan. 6:10
8:30 [a]2 Chron. 20:9; Neh. 1:6
8:31 [b]Ex. 22:11
8:32 [c]Deut. 25:1
8:33 [d]Lev. 26:17; Deut. 28:25 [e]Lev. 26:39; Neh. 1:9
8:35 [f]Lev. 26:19; Deut. 28:23
8:36 [g]Ps. 25:4 [h]1 Sam. 12:23
8:37 [i]Lev. 26:16; Deut. 28:21; 2 Chron. 20:9
8:39 [j]1 Sam. 16:7; 1 Chron. 28:9; Ps. 11:4; Jer. 17:10; Acts 1:24
8:40 [k]Ps. 130:4
8:42 [l]Deut. 3:24
8:43 [m]1 Sam. 17:46; 2 Kings 19:19; Ps. 67:2 [n]Ps. 102:15

their enemy, whithersoever thou shalt send
them, and shall pray unto the LORD toward
the city which thou hast chosen, and *toward*
the house that I have built for thy name:
45 Then hear thou in heaven their prayer
and their supplication, and maintain their
cause.
46 If they sin against thee, ([o]for *there is*
no man that sinneth not,) and thou be angry
with them, and deliver them to the enemy,
so that they carry them away captives
[p]unto the land of the enemy, far or near,
47 [q]*Yet* if they shall bethink themselves
in the land whither they were carried captives, and repent, and make supplication
unto thee in the land of them that carried
them captives, [r]saying, We have sinned,
and have done perversely, we have committed wickedness;
48 And *so* [s]return unto thee with all their
heart, and with all their soul, in the land of
their enemies, which led them away captive, and [t]pray unto thee toward their land,
which thou gavest unto their fathers, the
city which thou hast chosen, and the house
which I have built for thy name:
49 Then hear thou their prayer and their
supplication in heaven thy dwelling place,
and maintain their cause,
50 And forgive thy people that have
sinned against thee, and all their transgressions wherein they have transgressed
against thee, and [u]give them compassion
before them who carried them captive, that
they may have compassion on them:
51 For [v]they *be* thy people, and thine inheritance, which thou broughtest forth out
of Egypt, [w]from the midst of the furnace of
iron:
52 That thine eyes may be open unto the
supplication of thy servant, and unto the
supplication of thy people Israel, to hearken
unto them in all that they call for unto thee.
53 For thou didst separate them from
among all the people of the earth, *to be*
thine inheritance, [x]as thou spakest by the
hand of Moses thy servant, when thou
broughtest our fathers out of Egypt, O Lord
GOD.
54 And it was *so*, that when Solomon had
made an end of praying all this prayer and
supplication unto the LORD, he arose from
before the altar of the LORD, from kneeling
on his knees with his hands spread up to
heaven.
55 And he stood, [y]and blessed all the
congregation of Israel with a loud voice,
saying,
56 Blessed *be* the LORD, that hath given
rest unto his people Israel, according to all
that he promised: [z]there hath not failed one
word of all his good promise, which he
promised by the hand of Moses his servant.
57 The LORD our God be with us, as he
was with our fathers: [a]let him not leave us,
nor forsake us:
58 That he may [b]incline our hearts unto
him, to walk in all his ways, and to keep his
commandments, and his statutes, and his
judgments, which he commanded our fathers.
59 And let these my words, wherewith I
have made supplication before the LORD, be
nigh unto the LORD our God day and night,
that he maintain the cause of his servant,
and the cause of his people Israel at all
times, as the matter shall require:
60 [c]That all the people of the earth may
know that [d]the LORD *is* God, *and that there*
is none else.
61 Let your [e]heart therefore be perfect
with the LORD our God, to walk in his statutes, and to keep his commandments, as at
this day.
62 ¶ And [f]the king, and all Israel with
him, offered sacrifice before the LORD.
63 And Solomon offered a sacrifice of
peace offerings, which he offered unto the
LORD, two and twenty thousand oxen, and
an hundred and twenty thousand sheep. So
the king and all the children of Israel dedicated the house of the LORD.
64 [g]The same day did the king hallow the
middle of the court that *was* before the
house of the LORD: for there he offered
burnt offerings, and meat offerings, and the
fat of the peace offerings: because [h]the brasen altar that *was* before the LORD *was* too
little to receive the burnt offerings, and
meat offerings, and the fat of the peace offerings.
65 And at that time Solomon held [i]a
feast, and all Israel with him, a great congregation, from [j]the entering in of Hamath
unto [k]the river of Egypt, before the LORD
our God, [l]seven days and seven days, *even*
fourteen days.
66 [m]On the eighth day he sent the people
away: and they blessed the king, and went
unto their tents joyful and glad of heart for
all the goodness that the LORD had done for
David his servant, and for Israel his people.

9 And [n]it came to pass, when Solomon
had finished the building of the house of
the LORD, [o]and the king's house, and [p]all
Solomon's desire which he was pleased
to do,
2 That the LORD appeared to Solomon the
second time, [q]as he had appeared unto him
at Gibeon.
3 And the LORD said unto him, [r]I have
heard thy prayer and thy supplication, that
thou hast made before me: I have hallowed
this house, which thou hast built, [s]to put
my name there for ever; [t]and mine eyes
and mine heart shall be there perpetually.
4 And if thou wilt [u]walk before me, [v]as
David thy father walked, in integrity of
heart, and in uprightness, to do according to
all that I have commanded thee, *and* wilt
keep my statutes and my judgments:
5 Then I will establish the throne of thy
kingdom upon Israel for ever, [w]as I promised to David thy father, saying, There shall
not fail thee a man upon the throne of Israel.
6 [x]*But* if ye shall at all turn from follow-

8:46 [o]2 Chron. 6:36; Prov. 20:9; Eccl. 7:20; Jam. 3:2; 1 John 1:8 [p]Lev. 26:34; Deut. 28:36
8:47 [q]Lev. 26:40 [r]Neh. 1:6; Ps. 106:6; Dan. 9:5
8:48 [s]Jer. 29:12 [t]Dan. 6:10
8:50 [u]Ezra 7:6; Ps. 106:46
8:51 [v]Deut. 9:29; Neh. 1:10 [w]Deut. 4:20; Jer. 11:4
8:53 [x]Ex. 19:5; Deut. 9:26
8:55 [y]2 Sam. 6:18
8:56 [z]Deut. 12:10; Josh. 21:45
8:57 [a]Deut. 31:6; Josh. 1:5
8:58 [b]Ps. 119:36
8:60 [c]Josh. 4:24; 1 Sam. 17:46; 2 Kings 19:19 [d]Deut. 4:35
8:61 [e]ch. 11:4; 2 Kings 20:3
8:62 [f]2 Chron. 7:4
8:64 [g]2 Chron. 7:7 [h]2 Chron. 4:1
8:65 [i]ver. 2; Lev. 23:34 [j]Num. 34:8; Josh. 13:5; Judg. 3:3; 2 Kings 14:25 [k]Gen. 15:18; Num. 34:5 [l]2 Chron. 7:8
8:66 [m]2 Chron. 7:9
9:1 [n]2 Chron. 7:11 [o]ch. 7:1 [p]2 Chron. 8:6
9:2 [q]ch. 3:5
9:3 [r]2 Kings 20:5; Ps. 10:17 [s]ch. 8:29 [t]Deut. 11:12
9:4 [u]Gen. 17:1 [v]ch. 11:4
9:5 [w]2 Sam. 7:12; ch. 2:4; 1 Chron. 22:10; Ps. 132:12
9:6 [x]2 Sam. 7:14; 2 Chron. 7:19; Ps. 89:30

ing me, ye or your children, and will not
keep my commandments *and* my statutes
which I have set before you, but go and
serve other gods, and worship them:
7 [y]Then will I cut off Israel out of the land
which I have given them; and this house,
which I have hallowed [z]for my name, will
I cast out of my sight; [a]and Israel shall be a
proverb and a byword among all people:
8 And [b]at this house, *which* is high, every
one that passeth by it shall be astonished,
and shall hiss; and they shall say, [c]Why
hath the LORD done thus unto this land, and
to this house?
9 And they shall answer, Because they
forsook the LORD their God, who brought
forth their fathers out of the land of Egypt,
and have taken hold upon other gods, and
have worshipped them, and served them:
therefore hath the LORD brought upon them
all this evil.
10 ¶ And [d]it came to pass at the end of
twenty years, when Solomon had built the
two houses, the house of the LORD, and the
king's house,
11 ([e]*Now* Hiram the king of Tyre had furnished Solomon with cedar trees and fir
trees, and with gold, according to all his desire,) that then king Solomon gave Hiram
twenty cities in the land of Galilee.
12 And Hiram came out from Tyre to see
the cities which Solomon had given him;
and they pleased him not.
13 And he said, What cities *are* these
which thou hast given me, my brother?
[f]And he called them the land of Cabul unto
this day.
14 And Hiram sent to the king sixscore
talents of gold.
15 ¶ And this *is* the reason of [g]the levy
which king Solomon raised; for to build the
house of the LORD, and his own house, and
[h]Millo, and the wall of Jerusalem, and [i]Ha-
zor, and [j]Megiddo, and [k]Gezer.
16 *For* Pharaoh king of Egypt had gone
up, and taken Gezer, and burnt it with fire,
[l]and slain the Canaanites that dwelt in the
city, and given it *for* a present unto his
daughter, Solomon's wife.
17 And Solomon built Gezer, and [m]Beth-
horon the nether,
18 And [n]Baalath, and Tadmor in the wilderness, in the land,
19 And all the cities of store that Solomon
had, and cities for [o]his chariots, and cities
for his horsemen, and that which Solomon
[p]desired to build in Jerusalem, and in Lebanon, and in all the land of his dominion.
20 [q]*And* all the people *that were* left of
the Amorites, Hittites, Perizzites, Hivites,
and Jebusites, which *were* not of the children of Israel,
21 Their children [r]that were left after
them in the land, [s]whom the children of
Israel also were not able utterly to destroy,
[t]upon those did Solomon levy a tribute of
[u]bondservice unto this day.
22 But of the children of Israel did Solomon [v]make no bondmen: but they *were*
men of war, and his servants, and his
princes, and his captains, and rulers of his
chariots, and his horsemen.
23 These *were* the chief of the officers
that *were* over Solomon's work, [w]five hundred and fifty, which bare rule over the people that wrought in the work.
24 ¶ But [x]Pharaoh's daughter came up
out of the city of David unto [y]her house
which *Solomon* had built for her: [z]then did
he build Millo.
25 ¶ [a]And three times in a year did Solomon offer burnt offerings and peace offerings upon the altar which he built unto the
LORD, and he burnt incense upon the altar
that *was* before the LORD. So he finished the
house.
26 ¶ And [b]king Solomon made a navy
of ships in [c]Ezion-geber, which *is* beside
Eloth, on the shore of the Red sea, in the
land of Edom.
27 [d]And Hiram sent in the navy his servants, shipmen that had knowledge of the
sea, with the servants of Solomon.
28 And they came to [e]Ophir, and fetched
from thence gold, four hundred and twenty
talents, and brought *it* to king Solomon.

10 And when the [f]queen of Sheba
heard of the fame of Solomon concerning the name of the LORD, she came [g]to
prove him with hard questions.
2 And she came to Jerusalem with a very
great train, with camels that bare spices,
and very much gold, and precious stones:
and when she was come to Solomon, she
communed with him of all that was in her
heart.
3 And Solomon told her all her questions:
there was not *any* thing hid from the king,
which he told her not.
4 And when the queen of Sheba had seen
all Solomon's wisdom, and the house that
he had built,
5 And the meat of his table, and the sitting
of his servants, and the attendance of his
ministers, and their apparel, and his cupbearers, [h]and his ascent by which he went
up unto the house of the LORD; there was no
more spirit in her.
6 And she said to the king, It was a true
report that I heard in mine own land of thy
acts and of thy wisdom.
7 Howbeit I believed not the words, until
I came, and mine eyes had seen *it*: and, behold, the half was not told me: thy wisdom
and prosperity exceedeth the fame which I
heard.
8 [i]Happy *are* thy men, happy *are* these
thy servants, which stand continually before thee, *and* that hear thy wisdom.
9 [j]Blessed be the LORD thy God, which
delighted in thee, to set thee on the throne
of Israel: because the LORD loved Israel for
ever, therefore made he thee king, [k]to do
judgment and justice.
10 And she [l]gave the king an hundred
and twenty talents of gold, and of spices

9:7 [y]Deut. 4:26; 2 Kings 17:23 [z]Jer. 7:14 [a]Deut. 28:37; Ps. 44:14
9:8 [b]2 Chron. 7:21 [c]Deut. 29:24; Jer. 22:8
9:10 [d]ch. 6:37; 2 Chron. 8:1
9:11 [e]2 Chron. 8:2
9:13 [f]Josh. 19:27
9:15 [g]ch. 5:13 [h]ver. 24; 2 Sam. 5:9 [i]Josh. 19:36 [j]Josh. 17:11 [k]Josh. 16:10; Judg. 1:29
9:16 [l]Josh. 16:10
9:17 [m]Josh. 16:3; 2 Chron. 8:5
9:18 [n]Josh. 19:44; 2 Chron. 8:4
9:19 [o]ch. 4:26 [p]ver. 1
9:20 [q]2 Chron. 8:7
9:21 [r]Judg. 1:21 [s]Josh. 15:63 [t]Judg. 1:28 [u]Gen. 9:25; Ezra 2:55; Neh. 7:57
9:22 [v]Lev. 25:39
9:23 [w]2 Chron. 8:10
9:24 [x]ch. 3:1; 2 Chron. 8:11 [y]ch. 7:8 [z]2 Sam. 5:9; ch. 11:27; 2 Chron. 32:5
9:25 [a]2 Chron. 8:12
9:26 [b]2 Chron. 8:17 [c]Num. 33:35; Deut. 2:8; ch. 22:48
9:27 [d]ch. 10:11
9:28 [e]Job 22:24
10:1 [f]2 Chron. 9:1; Matt. 12:42; Luke 11:31 [g]Judg. 12:12; Prov. 1:6
10:5 [h]1 Chron. 26:16
10:8 [i]Prov. 8:34
10:9 [j]ch. 5:7 [k]2 Sam. 8:15; Ps. 72:2; Prov. 8:15
10:10 [l]Ps. 72:10

very great store, and precious stones: there came no more such abundance of spices as these which the queen of Sheba gave to king Solomon.

11 [m]And the navy also of Hiram, that brought gold from Ophir, brought in from Ophir great plenty of almug trees, and precious stones.

12 [n]And the king made of the almug trees pillars for the house of the LORD, and for the king's house, harps also and psalteries for singers: there came no such [o]almug trees, nor were seen unto this day.

13 And king Solomon gave unto the queen of Sheba all her desire, whatsoever she asked, beside *that* which Solomon gave her of his royal bounty. So she turned and went to her own country, she and her servants.

14 ¶ Now the weight of gold that came to Solomon in one year was six hundred threescore and six talents of gold,

15 Beside *that he had* of the merchantmen, and of the traffick of the spice merchants, and [p]of all the kings of Arabia, and of the governors of the country.

16 ¶ And king Solomon made two hundred targets *of* beaten gold: six hundred *shekels* of gold went to one target.

17 And *he made* [q]three hundred shields *of* beaten gold; three pound of gold went to one shield: and the king put them in the [r]house of the forest of Lebanon.

18 ¶ [s]Moreover the king made a great throne of ivory, and overlaid it with the best gold.

19 The throne had six steps, and the top of the throne *was* round behind: and *there were* stays on either side on the place of the seat, and two lions stood beside the stays.

20 And twelve lions stood there on the one side and on the other upon the six steps: there was not the like made in any kingdom.

21 ¶ [t]And all king Solomon's drinking vessels *were of* gold, and all the vessels of the house of the forest of Lebanon *were of* pure gold; none *were of* silver: it was nothing accounted of in the days of Solomon.

22 For the king had at sea a navy of [u]Tharshish with the navy of Hiram: once in three years came the navy of Tharshish, bringing gold, and silver, ivory, and apes, and peacocks.

23 So [v]king Solomon exceeded all the kings of the earth for riches and for wisdom.

24 ¶ And all the earth sought to Solomon, to hear his wisdom, which God had put in his heart.

25 And they brought every man his present, vessels of silver, and vessels of gold, and garments, and armour, and spices, horses, and mules, a rate year by year.

26 ¶ [w]And Solomon [x]gathered together chariots and horsemen: and he had a thousand and four hundred chariots, and twelve

10:11 [m]ch. 9:27
10:12 [n]2 Chron. 9:11 [o]2 Chron. 9:10
10:15 [p]2 Chron. 9:24; Ps. 72:10
10:17 [q]ch. 14:26 [r]ch. 7:2
10:18 [s]2 Chron. 9:17
10:21 [t]2 Chron. 9:20
10:22 [u]Gen. 10:4; 2 Chron. 20:36
10:23 [v]ch. 3:12
10:26 [w]ch. 4:26; 2 Chron. 1:14 [x]Deut. 17:16
10:27 [y]2 Chron. 1:15-17
10:28 [z]Deut. 17:16; 2 Chron. 1:16 [a]Ezek. 27:7
10:29 [b]Josh. 1:4; 2 Kings 7:6
11:1 [c]Neh. 13:26 [d]Deut. 17:17
11:2 [e]Ex. 34:16; Deut. 7:3
11:4 [f]Deut. 17:17; Neh. 13:26 [g]ch. 8:61 [h]ch. 9:4
11:5 [i]ver. 33; Judg. 2:13; 2 Kings 23:13
11:7 [j]Num. 33:52 [k]Num. 21:29; Judg. 11:24 [l]2 Kings 23:13
11:9 [m]ver. 2 [n]ch. 3:5
11:10 [o]ch. 6:12
11:11 [p]ver. 31; ch. 12:15
11:13 [q]2 Sam. 7:15; Ps. 89:33

thousand horsemen, whom he bestowed in the cities for chariots, and with the king at Jerusalem.

27 [y]And the king made silver *to be* in Jerusalem as stones, and cedars made he *to be* as the sycomore trees that *are* in the vale, for abundance.

28 ¶ [z]And Solomon had horses brought out of Egypt, and [a]linen yarn: the king's merchants received the linen yarn at a price.

29 And a chariot came up and went out of Egypt for six hundred *shekels* of silver, and an horse for an hundred and fifty: [b]and so for all the kings of the Hittites, and for the kings of Syria, did they bring *them* out by their means.

11 But [c]king Solomon loved [d]many strange women, together with the daughter of Pharaoh, women of the Moabites, Ammonites, Edomites, Zidonians, *and* Hittites;

2 Of the nations *concerning* which the LORD said unto the children of Israel, [e]Ye shall not go in to them, neither shall they come in unto you: *for* surely they will turn away your heart after their gods: Solomon clave unto these in love.

3 And he had seven hundred wives, princesses, and three hundred concubines: and his wives turned away his heart.

4 For it came to pass, when Solomon was old, [f]*that* his wives turned away his heart after other gods: and his [g]heart was not perfect with the LORD his God, [h]as *was* the heart of David his father.

5 For Solomon went after [i]Ashtoreth the goddess of the Zidonians, and after Milcom the abomination of the Ammonites.

6 And Solomon did evil in the sight of the LORD, and went not fully after the LORD, as *did* David his father.

7 [j]Then did Solomon build an high place for [k]Chemosh, the abomination of Moab, in [l]the hill that *is* before Jerusalem, and for Molech, the abomination of the children of Ammon.

8 And likewise did he for all his strange wives, which burnt incense and sacrificed unto their gods.

9 ¶ And the LORD was angry with Solomon, because [m]his heart was turned from the LORD God of Israel, [n]which had appeared unto him twice,

10 And [o]had commanded him concerning this thing, that he should not go after other gods: but he kept not that which the LORD commanded.

11 Wherefore the LORD said unto Solomon, Forasmuch as this is done of thee, and thou hast not kept my covenant and my statutes, which I have commanded thee, [p]I will surely rend the kingdom from thee, and will give it to thy servant.

12 Notwithstanding in thy days I will not do it for David thy father's sake: *but* I will rend it out of the hand of thy son.

13 [q]Howbeit I will not rend away all the

kingdom; *but* will give [r]one tribe to thy son for David my servant's sake, and for Jerusalem's sake [s]which I have chosen.

14 ¶ And the LORD [t]stirred up an adversary unto Solomon, Hadad the Edomite: he *was* of the king's seed in Edom.

15 [u]For it came to pass, when David was in Edom, and Joab the captain of the host was gone up to bury the slain, [v]after he had smitten every male in Edom;

16 (For six months did Joab remain there with all Israel, until he had cut off every male in Edom:)

17 That Hadad fled, he and certain Edomites of his father's servants with him, to go into Egypt; Hadad *being* yet a little child.

18 And they arose out of Midian, and came to Paran: and they took men with them out of Paran, and they came to Egypt, unto Pharaoh king of Egypt; which gave him an house, and appointed him victuals, and gave him land.

19 And Hadad found great favour in the sight of Pharaoh, so that he gave him to wife the sister of his own wife, the sister of Tahpenes the queen.

20 And the sister of Tahpenes bare him Genubath his son, whom Tahpenes weaned in Pharaoh's house: and Genubath was in Pharaoh's household among the sons of Pharaoh.

21 [w]And when Hadad heard in Egypt that David slept with his fathers, and that Joab the captain of the host was dead, Hadad said to Pharaoh, Let me depart, that I may go to mine own country.

22 Then Pharaoh said unto him, But what hast thou lacked with me, that, behold, thou seekest to go to thine own country? And he answered, Nothing: howbeit let me go in any wise.

23 ¶ And God stirred him up *another* adversary, Rezon the son of Eliadah, which fled from his lord [x]Hadadezer king of Zobah:

24 And he gathered men unto him, and became captain over a band, [y]when David slew them *of Zobah:* and they went to Damascus, and dwelt therein, and reigned in Damascus.

25 And he was an adversary to Israel all the days of Solomon, beside the mischief that Hadad *did:* and he abhorred Israel, and reigned over Syria.

26 ¶ And [z]Jeroboam the son of Nebat, an Ephrathite of Zereda, Solomon's servant, whose mother's name *was* Zeruah, a widow woman, even he [a]lifted up *his* hand against the king.

27 And this *was* the cause that he lifted up *his* hand against the king: [b]Solomon built Millo, *and* repaired the breaches of the city of David his father.

28 And the man Jeroboam *was* a mighty man of valour: and Solomon seeing the young man that he was industrious, he made him ruler over all the charge of the house of Joseph.

29 And it came to pass at that time when Jeroboam went out of Jerusalem, that the prophet [c]Ahijah the Shilonite found him in the way; and he had clad himself with a new garment; and they two *were* alone in the field:

30 And Ahijah caught the new garment that *was* on him, and [d]rent it *in* twelve pieces:

31 And he said to Jeroboam, Take thee ten pieces: for [e]thus saith the LORD, the God of Israel, Behold, I will rend the kingdom out of the hand of Solomon, and will give ten tribes to thee:

32 (But he shall have one tribe for my servant David's sake, and for Jerusalem's sake, the city which I have chosen out of all the tribes of Israel:)

33 [f]Because that they have forsaken me, and have worshipped Ashtoreth the goddess of the Zidonians, Chemosh the god of the Moabites, and Milcom the god of the children of Ammon, and have not walked in my ways, to do *that which is* right in mine eyes, and *to keep* my statutes and my judgments, as *did* David his father.

34 Howbeit I will not take the whole kingdom out of his hand: but I will make him prince all the days of his life for David my servant's sake, whom I chose, because he kept my commandments and my statutes:

35 But [g]I will take the kingdom out of his son's hand, and will give it unto thee, *even* ten tribes.

36 And unto his son will I give one tribe, that [h]David my servant may have a light alway before me in Jerusalem, the city which I have chosen me to put my name there.

37 And I will take thee, and thou shalt reign according to all that thy soul desireth, and shalt be king over Israel.

38 And it shall be, if thou wilt hearken unto all that I command thee, and wilt walk in my ways, and do *that is* right in my sight, to keep my statutes and my commandments, as David my servant did; that [i]I will be with thee, and [j]build thee a sure house, as I built for David, and will give Israel unto thee.

39 And I will for this afflict the seed of David, but not for ever.

40 Solomon sought therefore to kill Jeroboam. And Jeroboam arose, and fled into Egypt, unto Shishak king of Egypt, and was in Egypt until the death of Solomon.

41 ¶ And [k]the rest of the acts of Solomon, and all that he did, and his wisdom, *are* they not written in the book of the acts of Solomon?

42 [l]And the time that Solomon reigned in Jerusalem over all Israel *was* forty years.

43 [m]And Solomon slept with his fathers, and was buried in the city of David his father: and [n]Rehoboam his son reigned in his stead.

11:13 [r]ch. 12:20 [s]Deut. 12:11
11:14 [t]1 Chron. 5:26
11:15 [u]2 Sam. 8:14; 1 Chron. 18:12 [v]Num. 24:19; Deut. 20:13
11:21 [w]1 Kings 2:10
11:23 [x]2 Sam. 8:3
11:24 [y]2 Sam. 8:3
11:26 [z]ch. 12:2; 2 Chron. 13:6 [a]2 Sam. 20:21
11:27 [b]ch. 9:24
11:29 [c]ch. 14:2
11:30 [d]1 Sam. 15:27
11:31 [e]ver. 11
11:33 [f]ver. 5
11:35 [g]ch. 12:16
11:36 [h]1 Kings 15:4; 2 Kings 8:19; Ps. 132:17
11:38 [i]Josh. 1:5 [j]2 Sam. 7:11
11:41 [k]2 Chron. 9:29
11:42 [l]2 Chron. 9:30
11:43 [m]2 Chron. 9:31 [n]Matt. 1:7

12 And [o]Rehoboam went to Shechem: for all Israel were come to Shechem to make him king.

2 And it came to pass, when [p]Jeroboam the son of Nebat, who was yet in [q]Egypt, heard *of it,* (for he was fled from the presence of king Solomon, and Jeroboam dwelt in Egypt;)

3 That they sent and called him. And Jeroboam and all the congregation of Israel came, and spake unto Rehoboam, saying,

4 Thy father made our [r]yoke grievous: now therefore make thou the grievous service of thy father, and his heavy yoke which he put upon us, lighter, and we will serve thee.

5 And he said unto them, Depart yet *for* three days, then come again to me. And the people departed.

6 ¶ And king Rehoboam consulted with the old men, that stood before Solomon his father while he yet lived, and said, How do ye advise that I may answer this people?

7 And they spake unto him, saying, [s]If thou wilt be a servant unto this people this day, and wilt serve them, and answer them, and speak good words to them, then they will be thy servants for ever.

8 But he forsook the counsel of the old men, which they had given him, and consulted with the young men that were grown up with him, *and* which stood before him:

9 And he said unto them, What counsel give ye that we may answer this people, who have spoken to me, saying, Make the yoke which thy father did put upon us lighter?

10 And the young men that were grown up with him spake unto him, saying, Thus shalt thou speak unto this people that spake unto thee, saying, Thy father made our yoke heavy, but make thou *it* lighter unto us; thus shalt thou say unto them, My little *finger* shall be thicker than my father's loins.

11 And now whereas my father did lade you with a heavy yoke, I will add to your yoke: my father hath chastised you with whips, but I will chastise you with scorpions.

12 ¶ So Jeroboam and all the people came to Rehoboam the third day, as the king had appointed, saying, Come to me again the third day.

13 And the king answered the people roughly, and forsook the old men's counsel that they gave him;

14 And spake to them after the counsel of the young men, saying, My father made your yoke heavy, and I will add to your yoke: my father *also* chastised you with whips, but I will chastise you with scorpions.

15 Wherefore the king hearkened not unto the people; for [t]the cause was from the LORD, that he might perform his saying, which the LORD [u]spake by Ahijah the Shilonite unto Jeroboam the son of Nebat.

16 ¶ So when all Israel saw that the king hearkened not unto them, the people answered the king, saying, [v]What portion have we in David? neither *have we* inheritance in the son of Jesse: to your tents, O Israel: now see to thine own house, David. So Israel departed unto their tents.

17 But [w]*as for* the children of Israel which dwelt in the cities of Judah, Rehoboam reigned over them.

18 Then king Rehoboam [x]sent Adoram, who *was* over the tribute; and all Israel stoned him with stones, that he died. Therefore king Rehoboam made speed to get him up to his chariot, to flee to Jerusalem.

19 So [y]Israel rebelled against the house of David unto this day.

20 And it came to pass, when all Israel heard that Jeroboam was come again, that they sent and called him unto the congregation, and made him king over all Israel: there was none that followed the house of David, but the tribe of Judah [z]only.

21 ¶ And when [a]Rehoboam was come to Jerusalem, he assembled all the house of Judah, with the tribe of Benjamin, an hundred and fourscore thousand chosen men, which were warriors, to fight against the house of Israel, to bring the kingdom again to Rehoboam the son of Solomon.

22 But [b]the word of God came unto Shemaiah the man of God, saying,

23 Speak unto Rehoboam, the son of Solomon, king of Judah, and unto all the house of Judah and Benjamin, and to the remnant of the people, saying,

24 Thus saith the LORD, Ye shall not go up, nor fight against your brethren the children of Israel: return every man to his house; [c]for this thing is from me. They hearkened therefore to the word of the LORD, and returned to depart, according to the word of the LORD.

25 ¶ Then Jeroboam [d]built Shechem in mount Ephraim, and dwelt therein; and went out from thence, and built [e]Penuel.

26 And Jeroboam said in his heart, Now shall the kingdom return to the house of David:

27 If this people [f]go up to do sacrifice in the house of the LORD at Jerusalem, then shall the heart of this people turn again unto their lord, *even* unto Rehoboam king of Judah, and they shall kill me, and go again to Rehoboam king of Judah.

28 Whereupon the king took counsel, and [g]made two calves *of* gold, and said unto them, It is too much for you to go up to Jerusalem: [h]behold thy gods, O Israel, which brought thee up out of the land of Egypt.

29 And he set the one in [i]Beth-el, and the other put he in [j]Dan.

30 And this thing became [k]a sin: for the people went *to worship* before the one, *even* unto Dan.

31 And he made an [l]house of high places, [m]and made priests of the lowest of

12:1 o2 Chron. 10:1
12:2 pch. 11:26 qch. 11:40
12:4 r1 Sam. 8:11-18; ch. 4:7
12:7 s2 Chron. 10:7; Prov. 15:1
12:15 tver. 24; Judg. 14:4; 2 Chron. 10:15 uch. 11:11
12:16 v2 Sam. 20:1
12:17 wch. 11:13
12:18 xch. 4:6
12:19 y2 Kings 17:21
12:20 zch. 11:13
12:21 a2 Chron. 11:1
12:22 b2 Chron. 11:2
12:24 cver. 15
12:25 dJudg. 9:45 eJudg. 8:17
12:27 fDeut. 12:5
12:28 g2 Kings 10:29 hEx. 32:4
12:29 iGen. 28:19; Hos. 4:15 jJudg. 18:29
12:30 kch. 13:34; 2 Kings 17:21
12:31 lch. 13:32 mNum. 3:10; ch. 13:33; 2 Kings 17:32; 2 Chron. 11:14; Ezek. 44:7

FOCUS ON FIRST AND SECOND KINGS

Miracles never cease! In the two books outlining the continuing monarchy of Israel, we discover eight miracle narratives. Five of these concern women and their involvement with either Elijah or Elisha. The Sidonian widow feeds the man of God, thereby saving herself and her son during a famine. Her caretaking provides the reason for her son to be brought back to life by the prophet. Another widow is supplied with oil to save herself and her boys from being sold into slavery, thanks to the intervention of Elisha. A wealthy Shunammite woman is given a child in exchange for the hospitality she provides for the prophet. When her son dies suddenly, she declares, "It is well," and the prophet makes that a reality. These miracles open another window through which to view the lives of women.

As Israel continues to grow as an agricultural nation, women are viewed as necessary for their labors and their ability to provide additional laborers with each child born. Large families were a necessity for survival. "A woman was never just a mother. As manager of an extended family household, she was largely responsible for its economic viability. As the wife of an influential citizen and the mother of wisely trained children, she had at least an indirect voice in village affairs. As a wise woman or a prophet, her authority was openly acknowledged" (*WBC*, 97). Given the culture of the time, 1 and 2 Kings will provide startling insights into the women behind, and sometimes upon, the thrones.

THE BLACK PRESENCE IN FIRST KINGS

Solomon befriends King Hiram of Tyre, a city in Phoenicia (1 Kin. 5:1ff). The people of Phoenicia were descendants of Ham through his son Canaan (called Sidon in Gen. 10:15). The Phoenicians were able to supply Solomon with all the timber he needed to construct the temple. Ezekiel 27 describes the richness and resourcefulness of these people. All the inhabitants of Canaan and Mesopotamia were people with black or dark complexions.

Solomon taxed the Amorites, Hittites, Hivites, Perizzites, and Jebusites (1 Kin. 9:20–21) all of whom were descendants of Canaan.

The queen of Sheba came to visit Solomon to learn all she could from him and to challenge his wisdom (10:1–13). Sheba was in southern Arabia, an area situated across from what is now known as Ethiopia. The queen of Sheba is mentioned twice in the table of nations (Gen. 10) as a direct descendant of Ham and of Shem. Josephus refers to her as the queen of Ethiopia. According to the Coptic Church tradition, she gave birth to a son, Menelek, who was fathered by Solomon.

Solomon married many women of the nations surrounding the Israelites, including the Egyptians and Hittites, who were descendants of Ham (1 Kin. 11:1). Jeroboam took refuge in Egypt when Solomon sought to kill him (v. 40). Jezebel, the wife of King Ahab, was a daughter of Ethbaal, king of the Zidonians. The Zidonians (or Sidonians) were people of Phoenicia, descendants of Ham through Canaan.

THE BLACK PRESENCE IN SECOND KINGS

King Pul (2 Kin. 15:19) and King Shalmaneser (17:3), kings of Assyria, first subjugated Israel, then deported the Israelites to the land of Assyria. These eastern kings were from the region of Mesopotamia, an area originally settled by black Sumerians. Hamites and Shemites lived in this area following the Flood.

Tirhakah, king of Ethiopia (19:9), attempted to defend Egypt against Assyria, but was defeated.

Life Lessons

1 KINGS 1–3

First Kings 1 introduces us to a dying King David. As factions rise to take the kingdom, David calls Bathsheba and promises the kingdom to their son, Solomon (1:28–31). In 1 Kings 2, Solomon is made king. David's son Adonijah, by Haggith, decided that he should be king instead and went to seek Bathsheba's help in securing Abishag, a Shunammite who took care of David, for his wife. She discussed it with Solomon, who in turn decided that Adonijah should be put to death for being so forward. With the kingdom firmly established, Solomon asked for wisdom to guide the people of God (3:1–15).

Two prostitutes who come to Solomon seeking judgment put his wisdom to the test (vv. 16–28). "This story's primary purpose is to establish the wisdom of Solomon, yet it provides insight into the lives of prostitutes in Israelite culture and into the humanity of all people, even those despised by society. The opening scene is arresting in its simple statement that two prostitutes can approach the king. The ability of people of such low social standing to have an audience with the king demonstrates the narrator's belief that Solomon was a champion of all Israelites" (*The Storyteller's Companion*, 142).

Compassionate God, give me a discerning spirit to know how to do what is just.

1 KINGS 7–11

In 1 Kings 7–10, Solomon builds the temple. The queen of Sheba hears of his wisdom and travels a great distance to test him with hard questions (1 Kin. 10:3). The queen is presented as one empowered to accredit others as having wisdom. She confirms Solomon's wisdom and presents him with riches and honor.

King Solomon, however, takes many foreign women as wives. They are from nations about which the Lord had told the Israelites, "Ye shall not go in to them, neither shall they come in unto you: for surely they will turn away your heart after their gods: Solomon clave unto these in love" (11:2). God raised up adversaries against Solomon in Hadad the Edomite (v. 14) and Jeroboam, son of Nebat (v. 26).

God declares to Jeroboam, "I will not take the whole kingdom out of his hand: but I will make him prince all the days of his life for David my servant's sake . . . But I will take the kingdom out of his son's hand, and will give it unto thee, even ten tribes. And unto his son will I give one tribe, that David my servant may have a light alway before me in Jerusalem, the city which I have chosen me to put my name there" (vv. 34–36). Solomon tries to kill Jeroboam, but Jeroboam flees to Egypt and remains there until Solomon's death. Solomon's son Rehoboam succeeds him as king (vv. 41–43).

Loving and Enabling God, keep me from that which is foreign to You and Your ways.

1 KINGS 12–16

The kingdom is divided. Jeroboam does evil in God's sight by setting up idols and saying to Israel, "It is too much for you to go up to Jerusalem: behold thy gods, O Israel, which brought thee up out of the land of Egypt . . . And this thing became a sin: for the people went to worship before the one, even unto Dan" (12:25–33). Jeroboam's son becomes ill, which prompts him to have his unnamed wife disguise herself and go to Shiloh to see Ahijah, the prophet of God (14:1–18). God warns Ahijah that the woman is coming. Ahijah does not allow her to keep up the pretense with him at all. He declares to her that because of the wickedness of her husband, her son will die as soon as she sets foot in the city! "The LORD shall raise him up a king over Israel, who shall cut off the house of Jeroboam that day. For the LORD shall smite Israel, as a reed is shaken in the water . . . because of the sins of Jeroboam, who did sin, and who made Israel" (vv. 14–16). Harsh punishment is pronounced upon the house of Jeroboam (vv. 10–12). And after twenty-two years as king, Jeroboam dies (v. 20).

Rehoboam, son of Solomon and Naamah, his Ammonite wife, rules in Judah as king. There is continual warfare between Rehoboam and Jeroboam until Rehoboam dies and his son, Abijam, succeeds him (14:21–31). Abijam's heart is not fully devoted to the Lord (15:3). There is war between Abijam and Jeroboam until Abijam dies and his son Asa succeeds him (v. 8). Asa rules for forty-one years. Asa does what is right in the eyes of the Lord (vv. 9–11). He even deposes his mother, Maacah (daughter of Abishalom), from her position as Queen Mother because of her idolatry (v. 13). Asa dies and his son, Jehoshaphat, succeeds him (v. 24). Following Jehoshaphat's reign, Nadab, the son of Jeroboam, becomes king of Israel. He does evil in the sight of the Lord (vv. 25–26). Baasha kills Nadab in the third year and becomes king (v. 28). He also does evil in the sight of the Lord (v. 34). When Baasha dies, his son, Elah, succeeds him (1 King 16:6). Elah's servant Zimri strikes down Elah and succeeds him as king (v. 10). Zimri's reign lasts seven days. He then dies because of the sins he had committed (v. 19). The people of Israel are then split into

two factions: half support Tibni son of Ginath and the other half support Omri. Omri becomes king of Israel, but does evil in the sight of the Lord (vv. 21–25). When he dies, his son, Ahab, became king (v. 28).

Holy One, guard my heart. Keep me from doing evil in Your sight.

1 KINGS 17–22

Chapter 17 introduces us to Elijah the Tishbite, who is called by God to tell Ahab, "As the LORD God of Israel liveth, before whom I stand, there shall not be dew nor rain these few years but according to my word" (17:1). Elijah is instructed to go to the brook Cherith (v. 3), east of the Jordan, where a miracle occurs—ravens feed him until the brook dries up. God sends Elijah to a widow in Zarephath because she obeyed Elijah's word. "Fear not; go and do as thou hast said: but make me thereof a little cake first, and bring it unto me, and after make for thee and for they son. For thus saith the LORD God of Israel, The barrel of meal shall not waste, neither shall the cruse of oil fail, until the day that the LORD sendeth rain upon the earth" (vv. 13–14). When the widow's son suddenly dies, she calls out to Elijah. The Lord hears Elijah's cry, and the boy is revived (v. 22).

Chapter 18 finds the land in its third year of famine. We are introduced to Ahab's wife, Jezebel—a Phoenician princess: "Now Obadiah feared the LORD greatly: For it was so, when Jezebel cut off the prophets of the LORD, that Obadiah took an hundred prophets, and hid them by fifty in a cave" (v. 4). Jezebel is a worshiper of Baal, which sets her at odds with God's prophets, particularly Elijah. In Chapter 18, she sends a messenger to Elijah stating, "So let the gods do to me, and more also if I make not thy life as the life of one of them by to morrow about this time." Elijah escapes to avoid death, but first performs a feat displaying God's power on Mount Carmel.

Elijah flees to Horeb (chap. 19) where the Lord appears to him. Benhadad attacks Samaria but Ahab defeats him (chap. 20) and is condemned to death by a prophet. In chapter 21, Ahab longs for Naboth's vineyard and Jezebel asks, "Doest thou now govern the kingdom of Israel? arise, and eat bread, and let thine heart be merry: I will give thee the vineyard of Naboth the Jezreelite" (v. 7).

Jezebel's perverted leadership results in her death and that of Ahab. "Thus saith the LORD, In the place where dogs licked the blood of Naboth shall dogs lick thy blood, even this" (v. 19) And concerning Jezebel, the Lord says, 'Dogs will devour Jezebel by the wall of Jezreel' " (v. 23). Ahab dies and his son Ahaziah takes the throne (22:40).

2 KINGS 2–8

The divided kingdom continues. Elijah passes on the mantle of faith to Elisha when he is taken up to heaven in a whirlwind (2:1–12). Joram, son of Ahab, becomes king. The Scriptures describe him thusly: "He wrought evil in the sight of the LORD" (3:2). The wife of a prophet approaches Elisha with the news that her sons will be sold into slavery to repay a debt (4:1). The power of God in Elisha is verified as the miracle of oil flows to fill enough jars for the widow to pay her debts and make enough money to survive (vv. 2–7). Later we find a wealthy woman in Shunem who makes a place for the "holy man of God" (vv. 9–10). When Elisha

sends his servant Gahazi to ask what can be done to pay for the hospitality, the woman asks for nothing! So Elisha prophesies that a son would be born to her and her aged spouse. One day her son dies. She goes straight to the Elisha and demands, "Did I desire a son of my lord? did I not say, Do not deceive me?" (v. 28). Elisha goes home with the distraught mother and the son is restored to life (v. 36). In chapter eight, we find the miracle of this woman's land being restored by the king after her seven years of exile. "Give back everything that belonged to her, including all the income from her land from the day she left the country until now" (8:6). Her faith has made her whole.

Granting Lord, restore unto me all that the enemy has stolen.

2 KINGS 5

Chapter five tells of the miracle of forgiveness in a young woman who helps the same military leader who captured her from her homeland and made her his wife's servant. The chapter is a testament to love at work in a foreign land. The young woman remains nameless; however, the narrator does provide some insight into her station in life. Naaman has leprosy, which would entail his forfeiting his military rank and position and going to live in the leper's camp. When the young woman discovers his secret, she tells his wife of the prophet, Elisha. Naaman is sent by the king to visit Elisha, who heals him when he dips seven times in the Jordan. Thanks to the nameless woman, Naaman discovers the power of the Lord.

Namer of the Nameless, name me "Love."

2 KINGS 6–11

Jezebel, with temptation and idolatry in her heart, meets her foretold doom in chapter nine: "So they threw her down: and some of her blood was sprinkled on the wall, and on the horses: and he trode her underfoot" (v. 33). Jezebel's downfall does not come about because of the way she wears makeup, fixes her hair, or uses charcoal upon her eyes. She is cursed when she decides that Baal is more powerful than the Living God is! Worshiping an idol that has no power caused her death.

Chapter 10 outlines the destruction of the house of Ahab. Chapter 11 provides the story of Athaliah, the only female who reigned as a ruler in Judah. Joram's legacy is recorded in 2 Kings 8:18: "He walked in the way of the kings of Israel, as did the house of Ahab: for the daughter of Ahab was his wife: and he did evil in the sight of the LORD." At the death of her son Ahaziah, Athaliah proceeds to kill his sons—her rivals to the throne. But Jehosheba, the daughter of King Jehoram and sister of Ahaziah, rescues Joash, son of Ahaziah, and keeps him hidden in the temple for six years while Athaliah rules Judah (11:1–3). Athaliah's ruthlessness is not surprising when we recall that she is the daughter of Ahab and Jezebel and a worshiper of Baal. As is the case with many of the other rulers, Athaliah does evil in the eyes of the Lord. Like her mother before her, she is killed outside of the temple and not even provided a decent burial. "And they laid hands on her; and she went the way by the which the horses came into the king's house: and there was she slain" (v. 16). "And all the people of the land rejoiced, and the city was in quiet: and they slew Athaliah with the sword beside the king's house. Seven years old was

Jehoash when he began to reign" (vv. 20–21).

The divided kingdom, a backsliding people, kings who continue the practice of evil and women who demand justice and interpret God's written Word complete the chronicles of the monarchy. In a world that has gone completely mad, two women engage in cannibalism, eating the son of one of the women. "And as the king of Israel was passing upon the wall, there cried a woman unto him, saying, Help my lord, O king. And he said, If the LORD do not help thee, whence shall I help thee?" (6:26–27). Instead of the wisdom of King Solomon, sought by two mothers in need of justice, the king can offer no help. This incident shows the dire consequences of a series of kings who "did evil in the eyes of the Lord" and led the divided nation into further chaos.

2 KINGS 22

When Josiah turns eight years old, he becomes king over Judah. "His mother's name was Jedidah, the daughter of Adaiah of Boscath. And he did what was right in the sight of the LORD, and walked in all the ways of David his father" (22:1–2). In the eighteenth year of his reign the Book of the Law is found as the temple is prepared for reconstruction. Hilkiah, the high priest and Shaphan, the secretary to the king, makes the discovery. When they report their findings to the king, he reacts with repentance. "He rent his clothes. And the king commanded Hilkiah the priest, and Ahikam the son of Shaphan, and Achbor the son of Michaiah, and Shaphan the scribe, and Asahiah a servant of the king's, saying, Go ye, enquire of the LORD for me, and for the people, and for all Judah, concerning the words of this book that is found" (vv. 11–13).

This empowered and powerful entourage goes straight to Huldah, a keeper of the wardrobes and a woman obviously known as "of the LORD." "Though many of the Hebrews were given to idolatry and were ignorant of God, still the lamp of divine truth was kept burning in the heart of a woman named Huldah. She possessed two great qualities, righteousness and prophetic insight. . . . This prophetic power, never trusted to the undeserving, was given to her because she loved God with all her heart" (*All of the Women of the Bible*, 1955). To this entourage, Huldah foretells with boldness and accuracy the doom of a people who stand and hear the written Word of God, declare they will do God's will, and yet return to do evil in the eyes of the Lord! As with all the prophets of God, she begins her interpretation with the words, "Thus saith the LORD God of Israel" (2 Kin. 22:15).

God of prophets, priests, and kings, You have called me to carry Your Word with boldness and clarity to the world in which I live and serve. Give me a greater heart to love You, a greater mind to envision the future, and a greater spirit to declare Your truth to all people!

FOCUS ON
FIRST AND SECOND CHRONICLES

Without women there would be no history to be chronicled! The genealogies are recorded from Adam to Abraham and finally to the glorious rise of King David in the first book. Although we find no notable deeds written about the roles of women in these two books, women are listed. In the second book, which begins with King Solomon and includes King Josiah's reform period and the final days of the kingdom, little is added that we have not already been told. Within these pages we discover a total of forty-two female names in the genealogy. There seems to be a special emphasis on the names listed of the mothers of Judah's twenty kings. Eleven queen mothers are especially noted: Bathsheba, mother of Solomon; Naamah, mother of Rehoboam; Micaiah, mother of Abihah; Maacha, mother of Asa; Azubah, mother of Jehoshaphat; Athaliah, mother of Ahaziah; Zibiah, mother of Joash; Jehoaddan, mother of Amaziah; Jecoliah, mother of Uzziah; Jerushah, mother of Jotham; and Abijah, mother of Hezekiah.

The chronicler's emphasis is on that "glorious past" which brought about the reign of King David and the abundance of God's blessings. The greatest event for these books is the building of and worship at the temple. King David is in the foreground. King Solomon is uplifted. Yet Bathsheba and the other women who helped build Israel are not forgotten.

THE BLACK PRESENCE IN 1 AND 2 CHRONICLES

The genealogies listed in 1 Chronicles include references to Adam through Noah, and the sons of Noah: Japheth, Ham, and Shem. Since recent scholarship points to East Africa as the probable origin of humankind, the Garden of Eden is believed to have been located there. After the Flood, the descendants of Noah migrated from Mt. Ararat into three geographic areas: Japheth to the north and west of Mt. Ararat, where Noah's ark landed (modern Turkey); Ham's descendants remained in northeast Africa or migrated south into Africa; Shemites remained in the northeast (and perhaps east) portion of Africa.

The genealogy of 1 Chronicles includes Abraham's children: Ishmael and Isaac. Two of Abraham's wives were Hagar and Keturah, both of whom were African (see Genesis 16; 25:1–4; 1 Chronicles 1:32–33). Since it is known that Midian, one of Abraham's children by Keturah, was the progenitor of Moses' wife, Zipporah, who was Ethiopian (Num. 12), it can be deduced that Keturah was also Ethiopian.

Reference is made to the Jebusites (1 Chron. 11:4), Philistines (11:15, 16; 14:8–16; 18:1), Amorites, Perizzites, and Hivites (2 Chron. 8:7). All of these tribes were descendants of Ham (Gen. 10:6–19).

Noted scholars have confirmed that Ham means "black."

The queen of Sheba (Josephus, the ancient historian, calls her the queen of Ethiopia) visited Solomon (2 Chron. 9:1–12). Sheba was located in southern Arabia where black people lived. Tradition says Solomon impregnated the queen, who gave birth to a son.

Shishak, king of Egypt, attacked Jerusalem with Lubims (Libyans), Sukkims, and Ethopians (Cushites) (2 Chron. 12:1–9). All of these attackers were of African origin.

Zerah, a Cushite, marched out against King Asa of Judah (14:9–15). Asa called on the Lord and God gave him the victory over Zerah's army.

Life Lessons

1 CHRONICLES 1–9

Chapters 1–9 list the people of God beginning with Adam. The story of *Roots* has reinforced for us the importance of knowing where you descended from and who your people are! In 1 Chronicles, there is no separating out the good, the bad, the pious, and the unrighteous. Their deeds are told and recounted. There are no "ideal" families. The people of God are birthed forth in full humanness. Their roles and assignments are listed that we might know the contributions they made to the overall history. They continue to show us that God uses the great and the small.

Potential Giver, thanks for showing us the worth of each individual in Your overall plan.

1 CHRONICLES 10–29

Chapters 10–29 detail how Saul takes his own life and David becomes king over Israel. Stories that detail the rise of a mighty king who conquers enemies like the Philistines and the household David establishes with wives and concubines are included. His bringing the ark of the covenant back to Jerusalem, writing songs of thanksgiving, making vows before God, and praying in humbleness over God's choice of him as king allow us to see God at work in a life. David's many victories, his plans for constructing the house of the Lord and the people who served him are detailed. The book concludes with Solomon's being acknowledged as king. David "died in a good old age, full of days, riches, and honour" (29:26).

Prospering Sovereign, thank You for choosing one who didn't look like, act like, or think of himself as "king material." Despite his appearance You looked at his heart and found him worthy! There is hope for me!

2 CHRONICLES 1–9

Solomon asks for wisdom and prepares to build the temple. Its furnishings are detailed and the ark is brought and put in place. The dedication takes place. "When Solomon had made an end of praying, the fire came down from heaven, and consumed the burnt offering and the sacri-

fices; and the glory of the LORD filled the house. And the priests could not enter into the house of the LORD, because the glory of the LORD had filled the LORD's house" (7:1–3).

Amazing Presence, let Your glory fill this place!

2 CHRONICLES 10–36

The rise of the line of Judaic kings is detailed, including the reign of Athaliah, the queen mother who ruled for six years (22:12). Jerusalem falls in the last chapter of the book, and the people are carried into exile in Babylon. Cyrus, king of Persia, is moved by God to send the people back home for the rebuilding of the land seventy years later.

Covenant-Remembering God, Your grace and mercy are astonishing.

Women in FIRST KINGS, SECOND KINGS, AND SECOND CHRONICLES

THE QUEEN OF SHEBA: IN SEARCH OF TRUE WISDOM

The queen of Sheba, also known as the queen of the South (Matt. 12:42; Luke 11:31), was perhaps one of the most powerful women of her day. Scholars generally agree that the area over which she reigned included parts of Ethiopia. The name Sheba (or Seba) implies that this queen was a woman of color. Seba or Sheba is mentioned a number of times as a descendent of Cush, who was a son of Ham (Gen. 10:7; 1 Chron. 1:9). Sheba is also mentioned as a grandson of Keturah, Abraham's second wife (Gen. 25:1–4; 1 Chron. 1:32). (Keturah is known as the mother of the Midianites, who are also commonly regarded as people of color.)

As we look at the exchange of gifts between the queen of Sheba and Solomon (1 Kin. 10:10–13; 2 Chron. 9:9–12), several points deserve further consideration. First of all, she came bearing gifts. The area from which the queen of Sheba hails was known for both gold and spices. She gave the king 120 talents of gold and scores of spices and jewels. Jewish historians give her credit for introducing the cultivation of certain spices, like balsam, to Israel. (See Josephus, *Antiquities*, 8.6.6.) The kinds of gifts she gave and the quantities of those gifts had never been seen in Judah.

Second, notice the gifts that Solomon gave the queen of Sheba. Though Solomon was known for being generous with his many guests, he was reported to have been exceptionally generous with the queen of Sheba. He gave her anything her heart desired. The total of the gifts he gave her exceeded what she had given him. They appear to have made a profound impression upon one another. His wisdom and opulence awed

the queen. And even though she was a woman of enormous wealth and wisdom, Solomon's magnificent wealth and wisdom overwhelmed her. And out of respect for him she gave the highest praise to his God. God gave the queen of Sheba a great tribute, also. He used her to show the Pharisees how foolish they were (see Matthew 12:42).

Solomon, who was reported to have had 700 wives and 300 concubines, obviously had special regard for this powerful woman of color. Jewish tradition tells us that Solomon and the queen of Sheba parented a son, believed to be King Menelek.

Read 1 Kings 9:26–28; 1 Kings 10; Matthew 12:42.

—S. Fosua

THE PROPHET'S WIDOW: COMMITTING TO GOD WHAT SHE HAS

Thine handmaid hath not any thing in the house, save a pot of oil (2 Kin. 4:2).

The widow was the least of all people in ancient society. She had no rights to her husband's inheritance and, upon his death, she became part of the inheritance of the eldest son. If she had no children, she was returned to her father's household. Thus, her vulnerable state made her easy prey for a creditor or anyone else who wished to take advantage of an already bad situation. Second Kings 4:1–7 records the plight of a prophet's widow and the miracle of mercy that restored her.

This woman was in a rather unique and closed society in Israel—that of the prophets. Yet she was no less vulnerable than other widows were. Her back was against the wall and her creditors were about to take her only means of survival—her two sons. Her story describes a marvelous truth that God works with what we have to do miraculous things! When she appealed to the prophet Elisha, he asked her, "Tell me, what hast thou in the house?" (v. 2). It was out of a simple pot of oil which she possessed that God met her needs. As she poured out the oil she witnessed God's abundant love. God provided her with the means to pay her creditors and to support her family. How often do we overlook what is in our house that God wants to use? We might look for great things and great people to move on our behalf, and yet these things and these people are powerless without God's intervention.

It is interesting that the widow mentioned the oil as the one thing of value or usefulness in her house. Oil, particularly olive oil, was a valued product in those days. Olive trees were very common and grew wild throughout the ancient Mediterranean basin, so the people found many uses for olive oil. It was used as a condiment, as a moisturizer for the skin after a bath, for anointing wounds, as fuel for lamps, and as a base for all perfumes, including the holy anointing oil of the priests.

Oil is also very symbolic in the Bible. It is a common symbol of the indwelling presence of the Holy Spirit while the dove is a symbol of His manifested presence. In the parable of the ten virgins, recorded in Matthew 25, Jesus reminds us to keep the lamp of our hearts filled with oil—the Holy Spirit—to ensure that the Bridegroom knows that we are prepared and anxiously awaiting His return. Again, God will use what is in our "house" in that final miracle of mercy.

The prophet's widow exemplifies God's concern for women. Through her example, we can know our need to have faith and to obey God's will.

Read 2 Kings 4:1–37.

See also the insight essay on Motherhood.

—L. Caldwell

HULDAH: TOO FAMOUS TO BE POPULAR

One of the greatest women in the Bible is introduced in 2 Kings 22. Her name is Huldah. Not much is recorded of Huldah's life, but the story of one event in her life serves to create an unforgettable profile of a woman called by God.

She lived during the reign of Jerusalem's King Josiah. This ruler, unlike his father and grandfather, "did that which was right in the sight of the LORD" (v. 2). When Hilkiah, the high priest, discovered the Book of the Law in the house of the Lord, King Josiah inquired of the Lord concerning the words of this book. So he sent his cabinet (the top men in the kingdom) to inquire of the Lord's pending judgment on His people. They sought counsel from the prophet Huldah. God used Huldah to deliver messages to the high priest and to the king (vv. 14–20). Huldah, not Jeremiah or Zephaniah (who were also prophets), was consulted. The consultation with Huldah demonstrates that God doesn't assign women secondary status, nor does He only use women for ministry when there are no men available.

Huldah's brief biography mentions only that she was the wife "of Shallum the son of Tikvah" (v. 14), who dwelt in the college in Jerusalem. That's all! Yet the king's men communed with her. To commune means that those engaged in conversation have something in common. The common cord that linked Huldah with the leader of the country and members of his cabinet was that they wanted to do what was pleasing in God's sight.

Huldah's home address, activities, and achievements were well known among the people in her land. Noteworthy women such as Huldah are sometimes too busy being famous to be popular. Remember, when God is honored, we are elevated in His eyes.

Read 2 Kings 22:14–20; 2 Chronicles 34:22–28; Nehemiah 6:14.

See also the insight essay on Women's Ministries.

—M. Armstead

THE SHUNAMMITE WOMAN: OUR SISTER'S GRIEF IS OUR GRIEF

How do we share our loss or losses with others? What can this unnamed wealthy woman tell us about faith, humility, hospitality, and grace? God had the author of 2 Kings record her story to help us deal with our own losses.

A woman of means and political clout, she was kind to everyone regardless of class. Her reward for humility, hospitality, and grace would be found in her profound understanding of her faith: the prophecy of Elisha that she and her elderly husband would bear a son. In later years, the child would die in her arms, the very arms that held him when he cried; the very arms that comforted him when he was ill; the very arms that fed him when he could not feed himself; and the very arms that taught him to prepare for his Torah lessons. Yet, although filled with grief, she did as the prophet of God told her to do. Obedience comes with a

price. Could we lay our child down and walk away? Could we hold fast to the promises of God? The Shunammite woman's faith and confident determination in the midst of grief resulted in the restoration of her son's life.

Miracles happen to us daily. Our grievous losses are sometimes precursors to hidden miracles yet to be revealed. Our faith unlocks the key to our understanding. As we journey through this story, we can envision the many blessings that unfolded for this Shunammite wife and mother.

Read 2 Kings 4:8–37; 8:1–6.

Read essays on Children and Faith.

—*B. Kitt*

JEZEBEL: THE WICKED QUEEN

Evil, idolatrous, reckless, rebellious, ungodly, wicked, and abuser of power are just a few of the descriptions associated Queen Jezebel, who was also a Baal prophet. Jezebel was born in Tyre, which was on the northern coast just above Israel. Her father was Ethbaal, king of Tyre and Sidon. Ethbaal was formally a priest of Astarte, who violently removed his brother, Phelles, from the throne. Jezebel grew up in a home and community that did not worship Yahweh. Instead she worshiped Baal. This stark difference in her background with that of Israel proved to be a source of great conflict.

In spite of the differences, Jezebel and Ahab were married. The Scriptures say that Ahab had seventy sons (2 Kin. 10:2), but do not disclose how many of them were the sons of Jezebel. In any case, she was the mother and stepmother to seventy sons and at least one known daughter, Athaliah, queen of Judah. While they were in the early stages of the marriage, Ahab permitted Baal worship in the temple. That was offensive to Yahweh. The extent of its offensiveness is reflected by the statement "There was none like unto Ahab, which did sell himself to work wickedness in the sight of the LORD, whom Jezebel his wife stirred up" (1 Kin. 21:25). Jezebel is remembered in like fashion for her evil in the sight of the Lord—her Baal worship and her cruelty to others.

Elijah was one of the prophets during the reign of Ahab. Since Elijah was called to be a prophet of Yahweh, he naturally opposed the king and queen. After a long draught there was a showdown between the prophet of Yahweh and the prophets of Baal. Jezebel had 450 Baal prophets and 400 Astarte prophets. Elijah challenged the Baal and Astarte prophets to ask their gods to rain down fire. They were unsuccessful. Then Elijah poured water on his wood and prayed for God to send fire. Yahweh produced fire while the false prophets' gods produced nothing. After Elijah won the struggle he ordered the deaths of all of the Baal and Astarte prophets (1 Kin. 18:40; 19:1). When Jezebel heard what Elijah had done she sent a message, "So let the gods do to me, and more also, if I make not thy life as the life of one of them by to morrow about this time" (19:2).

It has been said that the test of a true prophet is that his or her prediction comes true. Jezebel's prediction about taking Elijah's life did not come true. Of course, Elijah ran, but more important than that, Yahweh protected, fed, and sheltered Elijah. Conversely, Elijah prophesied about Jezebel. Second Kings 9:37 says, "The carcase of Jezebel shall be as dung upon the face of the field in the portion of Jezreel; so that they shall not say, This is Jezebel." Jezebel dolled herself up with thick eye makeup,

fancy clothes, and an eye-catching hairstyle. Then she stood at the window and called to Jehu. Two or three officers appeared at the window where Jezebel stood, and at the command of Jehu they pushed Jezebel out of the window. When Jehu looked for the corpse to pay respect to the daughter of a king "they found no more of her than the skull, and the feet, and the palms of her hands" (9:35). The evil in the house of Ahab caused the deaths of the Baal prophets, the death of Jezebel, the death of Ahab, and the death of the seventy sons of Ahab. Athaliah herself did not escape execution (see 2 Kings 11:16).

What lessons can we learn for today from the story of a wicked king and queen? Sometimes it seems like the wicked prosper and the righteous suffer, but this story informs the reader that there is a day of judgment. In that day the righteous will be rescued by a righteous and holy God. The righteous, the poor, the oppressed, and the downtrodden will suffer no more. The oppressed will be delivered from the snare of oppression and injustice. Ahab and Jezebel killed their neighbor, Naboth, to steal his little plot of land, but God calls each human being "to love your enemy" and the stranger. Yahweh calls us to live righteous, holy, and faithful lives. In the end the righteous will receive shelter in the time of storm, as was true with Elijah. Evil has its reward, as was seen through the deaths of Ahab, Jezebel, and their children.

Read 1 Kings 16:31; 19:1–2; 21:5–16; 2 Kings 9:10, 22, 30–37.

Read insight essay on Influence.

—D. McCabe

ATHALIAH: AN ANGRY WOMAN

Athaliah, at a glance, appears to be nothing short of wicked—hardcore, low down, good for nothing, rotten to the bone. She is the granddaughter of the idolatrous King Omri and the daughter of none other than the notorious King Ahab and Jezebel. Talk about a generational curse! The compendium of Athaliah's life is nothing short of a counselor's nightmare.

Imagine coming from the family into which she was born. Though her family had power and money, they weren't the most popular people around. It must have been a lonely existence. It must have also been a life of paranoia, looking over her shoulder every minute of the day, trusting no one. We can understand why Athaliah was mad at the world.

Prisons, detention centers, and rehabs are full of angry Athaliahs—angry women who lash out violently at anybody and everybody, trusting no one. Athaliahs believe that is the way of life. After all, that's the way it was with her mama and her mama before her.

Athaliahs tend to deny that their own anger is the problem. They usually blame their problems on something else: "I'm black. I'm poor. I'm fat. I'm ugly. Everybody's always picking on me." Athaliahs tend to see themselves as victims. This thinking ultimately produces what it believes. But, the excuse of victimization becomes a prison, trapping them in their own anger. Letting go of their anger at the world and its God is often difficult to do. But, letting go is the only way to give their burdens to Jesus and let Him truly love them.

Read 2 Kings 8:2; 11:13–20; 2 Chronicles 21:6–20; 22:3–5, 10; 23:12; 24:7.

Read essays on Influence and Rebellion.

—E. Walters

JEHOSHABEATH: GOD'S DELIVERER

Jehoshabeath was the daughter of King Jehoram, son of Jehoshaphat, son of Omir, the sixth king of Israel. Jehoram's wife was Athaliah, one of the most detestable rulers of Judah.

Athaliah's desire to rule after the deaths of her husband, King Jehoram and his successor, her son King Ahaziah, led her to kill off all those of the house of David who were the rightful heirs to the throne. These heirs were also her grandsons. However, this did not deter her from her task.

Jehoshabeath, which means "Jehovah is her oath," was used by God to redeem Joash from among the bodies of his brothers. She then hid him and his nursemaid in a bedchamber for six years. The temple provided a safe place for Joash and an environment where he could be prepared for his future as king. During that time Queen Athaliah ruled with a vengeance, never knowing that the one she hated was under her nose all the time. By rescuing Joash, Jehoshabeath became an instrument of God in His divine plan to keep His promise that a son of David would always be king.

Today, there are many who hate the name of Jesus Christ and will behave as Queen Athaliah in an attempt to destroy God's people. But believers must stand and trust God in order to determine the outcome of our enemy's plans. Whatever God's plans are for us, no amount of adversity can thwart them.

As Christian women we are to encourage one another. God's Word states: "Be not deceived; God is not mocked: for whatsoever a man soweth, that shall he also reap" (Gal. 6:7).

Whatever trials beset us we can trust our Lord to hide us in the shadow of His wings, and cause our enemies to become our footstools (see Matt. 22:44).

Read 2 Chronicles 22:11–12.

Read insight essay on Attributes of God.

—J. Josey

Insights

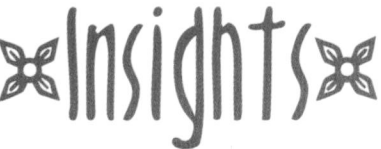

MOTHERHOOD

Motherhood is an expected, or sometimes unexpected, opportunity to introspectively look at the mirror image of oneself in the eyes of one's beloved. In the midst of this ministry called motherhood, the reflection can remind us of the unresolved issues that have been carefully tucked away and the revelation of the very remnant of good that God created in all of us.

To discover the good or perhaps not so good in oneself is to continue the lifelong journey of womanhood rather than motherhood. In order to fulfill the high calling of motherhood, self-discovery as a woman first, is paramount. When our children leave the nest (yes, they do leave) the image of you, the woman, will be in the mirror. Will you know her?

A wise mother builds her family up rather than tears them down with hurtful words. Our children will not remember so much what we said but how we said those words (see Prov. 14:1). Even while feeling a potpourri of emotions, motherhood is a 24-hour ministry of comfort (see Isa. 66:12–13).

Like a good roller-coaster ride, motherhood at times is a slow, fearful climb that suddenly drops only to disrupt the state of comfort and normalcy in our lives. When you realize that the ride has come to a halt, you can sometimes laugh and move on to the next adventure.

Motherhood is likened to a home study course in managing multiple projects, gathering school materials, providing economic stability, finding five-minute nutritional subsistence, and nurturing those entrusted in our care by physical, emotional, or spiritual birth. In this motherhood course, finding personal fulfillment becomes your goal during certain seasons of life (1 Kin. 3:26–27).

We may not be sure of the reasoning behind God's having chosen us to sacrifice so much, but it is a call we must answer. God's mothering representatives in our lives have sacrificed so much over the years. It is this sacrificial love toward us that drives us to pass this legacy on to our children. Take the example of the woman in 1 Kings 3:16–28. King Solomon knew that the natural mother loved her child so much that she would give her child over to another woman rather than to watch her child die. This is the hallmark of sacrificial love.

For women who consider motherhood a job because the valleys far outweigh the peaks, the valleys are necessary reminders. Sometimes the best way to understand God's will is to let go and let God have His way. We will learn more about the value in the valley as we allow God to work out the plan already predestined for our lives. We can't fulfill the call of motherhood without a daily consultation and guidance from our God (Acts 21:14). There is value in the valley because God is there with us.

In the forty-ninth chapter of Isaiah, the prophet uses an illustration of a newborn baby's mother to remind us that God's love for His people is unchanging. Isaiah reminds us that the love we have for those entrusted to our mothering care is like the sacrificial love God has for us. Because there is not a circumstance that can separate us from God's love, we ought not to allow anything to separate us from our love for our beloved. One that loves as God loves will correct and punish for the good of her beloved one's eternal destiny (Deut. 8:5).

A Spirit-led mother understands that in the midst of a disciplinary act, she must always show the kind of love that God shows when He disciplines us. Like our mothers would tell us, sometimes "it really does hurt me more than it does you!" Peace of mind will come through the foundational love God requires in the obedience to His Word.

As one songwriter says, "I'm so glad trouble don't last always." The song speaks of the child-maturing acts of mothering. In our maturation, we realize that sometimes putting regular deposits of love in early will return eternal dividends in the future. The eternal dividends may seem so far off. The returns are not measured by money, thank-you cards, or flowers. They are measured by a heavenly peace felt deep within, when your spirit whispers to your soul that you have fulfilled the mothering call on your life. Look again, mothers, in the eyes of your beloved!

Read 1 King 3:26–27.

Read the insight essays on Children, Motherhood, and Unwed Mothers. Read the portraits on Michah's Mother and Samson's Mother.

—A. Foster

RESPONSIBLE DECISIONS IN LEADERSHIP FOR WOMEN OF COLOR

Chapter twenty-two of 2 Kings provides a powerful backdrop for women of color in employing the principles of responsible decision making in leadership. God used Huldah, the prophet, as God's instrument to communicate the word of the Lord, and to warn the king of God's judgment for the nation's sinful, wayward acts. God's call transcends gender, race, cultural background, and human imperfection. God calls women and men to be His vehicles for truth, honesty, and justice in a world that has turned away from the Creator. When the appointed people came to Huldah, she heeded the word from the Lord, obeyed God's message, and interpreted it as she was led.

Throughout biblical history God has used women as agents of justice, agents of goodwill, and agents of the Gospel message. In this story, God used a prophet, Huldah, to speak and interpret God's word of coming disaster for the Hebrew people in the face of Israel's worship of other gods and ignorance of God's teachings. Deborah, Rahab, Phoebe, the woman Jesus talked to at the well, Mary (Jesus' mother), and countless others have shown courage and strength in their ability to make important decisions, to display exemplary leadership, and to speak the truth in love for God's people. God's appointed messenger was Huldah, who had the courage and insight to interpret the Book of the Law in a truthful and straightforward manner.

In our work in the world, God will place people in our lives from whom we can glean knowledge that will assure our success. We must call upon trusted leaders to assist us in the work for God's kingdom. The legacy Huldah left to us is one in which God leads us to discern carefully, to remain prayerful, and to speak the truth of God's justice and mercy.

Women of color face special challenges in the journey through life. Learning the important principles of responsible decision making, delegation, and teamwork require prayerful deliberation, strategic thinking, and dialogue with trusted mentors and friends. God has given us the gift of discernment in our decision making, creative thinking for our choices, and the ability to seek out allies and colleagues who will work with us in the professional arena. The gift of trusted friendship and mentoring was illustrated in the story of Huldah. Let us find a message in this story and apply it to our lives.

Read 2 Kings 22; see also Exodus 18:10-27; Joshua 24:15; Psalm 65:4; John 15:16.

Read portraits on Abigail, Deborah, Miriam, and Huldah. Read the insight essays on Leadership and Women's Ministries.

—M. Newbern-Williams

the people, which were not of the sons of
Levi.
32 And Jeroboam ordained a feast in the
eighth month, on the fifteenth day of the
month, like unto [n]the feast that *is* in Judah,
and he offered upon the altar. So did he in
Beth-el, sacrificing unto the calves that he
had made: [o]and he placed in Beth-el the
priests of the high places which he had
made.
33 So he offered upon the altar which he
had made in Beth-el the fifteenth day of the
eighth month, *even* in the month which he
had [p]devised of his own heart; and ordained a feast unto the children of Israel:
and he offered upon the altar, and [q]burnt
incense.

13 And, behold, there came [r]a man of
God out of Judah by the word of the
LORD unto Beth-el: [s]and Jeroboam stood
by the altar to burn incense.
2 And he cried against the altar in the
word of the LORD, and said, O altar, altar,
thus saith the LORD; Behold, a child shall be
born unto the house of David, [t]Josiah by
name; and upon thee shall he offer the
priests of the high places that burn incense
upon thee, and men's bones shall be burnt
upon thee.
3 And he gave [u]a sign the same day, saying, This *is* the sign which the LORD hath
spoken; Behold, the altar shall be rent, and
the ashes that *are* upon it shall be poured
out.
4 And it came to pass, when king Jeroboam heard the saying of the man of God,
which had cried against the altar in Beth-el,
that he put forth his hand from the altar,
saying, Lay hold on him. And his hand,
which he put forth against him, dried up, so
that he could not pull it in again to him.
5 The altar also was rent, and the ashes
poured out from the altar, according to the
sign which the man of God had given by the
word of the LORD.
6 And the king answered and said unto
the man of God, [v]Intreat now the face of the
LORD thy God, and pray for me, that my
hand may be restored me again. And the
man of God besought the LORD, and the
king's hand was restored him again, and
became as *it was* before.
7 And the king said unto the man of God,
Come home with me, and refresh thyself,
and [w]I will give thee a reward.
8 And the man of God said unto the king,
[x]If thou wilt give me half thine house, I will
not go in with thee, neither will I eat bread
nor drink water in this place:
9 For so was it charged me by the word of
the LORD, saying, [y]Eat no bread, nor drink
water, nor turn again by the same way that
thou camest.
10 So he went another way, and returned
not by the way that he came to Beth-el.
11 ¶ Now there dwelt an old prophet in
Beth-el; and his sons came and told him all
the works that the man of God had done

12:32 [n]Lev. 23:33; Num. 29:12; ch. 8:2 [o]Am. 7:13
12:33 [p]Num. 15:39 [q]ch. 13:1
13:1 [r]2 Kings 23:17 [s]ch. 12:32
13:2 [t]2 Kings 23:15
13:3 [u]Isa. 7:14; John 2:18; 1 Cor. 1:22
13:6 [v]Ex. 8:8; Num. 21:7; Acts 8:24; Jam. 5:16
13:7 [w]1 Sam. 9:7; 2 Kings 5:15
13:8 [x]Num. 22:18
13:9 [y]1 Cor. 5:11
13:16 [z]ver. 8
13:17 [a]ch. 20:35; 1 Thess. 4:15
13:22 [b]ver. 9
13:24 [c]ch. 20:36

that day in Beth-el: the words which he had
spoken unto the king, them they told also to
their father.
12 And their father said unto them, What
way went he? For his sons had seen what
way the man of God went, which came from
Judah.
13 And he said unto his sons, Saddle me
the ass. So they saddled him the ass: and he
rode thereon,
14 And went after the man of God, and
found him sitting under an oak: and he said
unto him, *Art* thou the man of God that
camest from Judah? And he said, I *am*.
15 Then he said unto him, Come home
with me, and eat bread.
16 And he said, [z]I may not return with
thee, nor go in with thee: neither will I eat
bread nor drink water with thee in this
place:
17 For it was said to me [a]by the word of
the LORD, Thou shalt eat no bread nor drink
water there, nor turn again to go by the way
that thou camest.
18 He said unto him, I *am* a prophet also
as thou *art;* and an angel spake unto me by
the word of the LORD, saying, Bring him
back with thee into thine house, that he may
eat bread and drink water. *But* he lied unto
him.
19 So he went back with him, and did eat
bread in his house, and drank water.
20 ¶ And it came to pass, as they sat at the
table, that the word of the LORD came unto
the prophet that brought him back:
21 And he cried unto the man of God that
came from Judah, saying, Thus saith the
LORD, Forasmuch as thou hast disobeyed
the mouth of the LORD, and hast not kept
the commandment which the LORD thy God
commanded thee,
22 But camest back, and hast eaten bread
and drunk water in the place, [b]of the which
the LORD did say to thee, Eat no bread, and
drink no water; thy carcase shall not come
unto the sepulchre of thy fathers.
23 ¶ And it came to pass, after he had
eaten bread, and after he had drunk, that
he saddled for him the ass, *to wit*, for the
prophet whom he had brought back.
24 And when he was gone, [c]a lion met
him by the way, and slew him: and his carcase was cast in the way, and the ass stood
by it, the lion also stood by the carcase.
25 And, behold, men passed by, and saw
the carcase cast in the way, and the lion
standing by the carcase: and they came and
told *it* in the city where the old prophet
dwelt.
26 And when the prophet that brought
him back from the way heard *thereof*, he
said, It *is* the man of God, who was disobedient unto the word of the LORD: therefore
the LORD hath delivered him unto the lion,
which hath torn him, and slain him, according to the word of the LORD, which he spake
unto him.

27 And he spake to his sons, saying, Saddle me the ass. And they saddled *him.*

28 And he went and found his carcase cast in the way, and the ass and the lion standing by the carcase: the lion had not eaten the carcase, nor torn the ass.

29 And the prophet took up the carcase of the man of God, and laid it upon the ass, and brought it back: and the old prophet came to the city, to mourn and to bury him.

30 And he laid his carcase in his own grave; and they mourned over him, *saying,* [d]Alas, my brother!

31 And it came to pass, after he had buried him, that he spake to his sons, saying, When I am dead, then bury me in the sepulchre wherein the man of God *is* buried; [e]lay my bones beside his bones:

32 [f]For the saying which he cried by the word of the LORD against the altar in Bethel, and against all the houses of the high places which *are* in the cities of [g]Samaria, shall surely come to pass.

33 ¶ [h]After this thing Jeroboam returned not from his evil way, but made again of the lowest of the people priests of the high places: whosoever would, he consecrated him, and he became *one* of the priests of the high places.

34 [i]And this thing became sin unto the house of Jeroboam, even [j]to cut *it* off, and to destroy *it* from off the face of the earth.

14 At that time Abijah the son of Jeroboam fell sick.

2 And Jeroboam said to his wife, Arise, I pray thee, and disguise thyself, that thou be not known to be the wife of Jeroboam; and get thee to Shiloh: behold, there *is* Ahijah the prophet, which told me that [k]*I should be* king over this people.

3 [l]And take with thee ten loaves, and cracknels, and a cruse of honey, and go to him: he shall tell thee what shall become of the child.

4 And Jeroboam's wife did so, and arose, [m]and went to Shiloh, and came to the house of Ahijah. But Ahijah could not see; for his eyes were set by reason of his age.

5 ¶ And the LORD said unto Ahijah, Behold, the wife of Jeroboam cometh to ask a thing of thee for her son; for he *is* sick: thus and thus shalt thou say unto her: for it shall be, when she cometh in, that she shall feign herself *to be* another *woman.*

6 And it was *so,* when Ahijah heard the sound of her feet, as she came in at the door, that he said, Come in, thou wife of Jeroboam; why feignest thou thyself *to be* another? for I *am* sent to thee *with* heavy *tidings.*

7 Go, tell Jeroboam, Thus saith the LORD God of Israel, [n]Forasmuch as I exalted thee from among the people, and made thee prince over my people Israel,

8 And [o]rent the kingdom away from the house of David, and gave it thee: and *yet* thou hast not been as my servant David, [p]who kept my commandments, and who followed me with all his heart, to do *that* only *which was* right in mine eyes;

9 But hast done evil above all that were before thee: [q]for thou hast gone and made thee other gods, and molten images, to provoke me to anger, and [r]hast cast me behind thy back:

10 Therefore, behold, [s]I will bring evil upon the house of Jeroboam, and [t]will cut off from Jeroboam him that pisseth against the wall, [u]*and* him that is shut up and left in Israel, and will take away the remnant of the house of Jeroboam, as a man taketh away dung, till it be all gone.

11 [v]Him that dieth of Jeroboam in the city shall the dogs eat; and him that dieth in the field shall the fowls of the air eat: for the LORD hath spoken *it.*

12 Arise thou therefore, get thee to thine own house: *and* [w]when thy feet enter into the city, the child shall die.

13 And all Israel shall mourn for him, and bury him: for he only of Jeroboam shall come to the grave, because in him [x]there is found *some* good thing toward the LORD God of Israel in the house of Jeroboam.

14 [y]Moreover the LORD shall raise him up a king over Israel, who shall cut off the house of Jeroboam that day: but what? even now.

15 For the LORD shall smite Israel, as a reed is shaken in the water, and he shall [z]root up Israel out of this [a]good land, which he gave to their fathers, and shall scatter them [b]beyond the river, [c]because they have made their groves, provoking the LORD to anger.

16 And he shall give Israel up because of the sins of Jeroboam, [d]who did sin, and who made Israel to sin.

17 ¶ And Jeroboam's wife arose, and departed, and came to [e]Tirzah: *and* [f]when she came to the threshold of the door, the child died;

18 And they buried him; and all Israel mourned for him, [g]according to the word of the LORD, which he spake by the hand of his servant Ahijah the prophet.

19 And the rest of the acts of Jeroboam, how he [h]warred, and how he reigned, behold, they *are* written in the book of the chronicles of the kings of Israel.

20 And the days which Jeroboam reigned *were* two and twenty years: and he slept with his fathers, and Nadab his son reigned in his stead.

21 ¶ And Rehoboam the son of Solomon reigned in Judah. [i]Rehoboam *was* forty and one years old when he began to reign, and he reigned seventeen years in Jerusalem, the city [j]which the LORD did choose out of all the tribes of Israel, to put his name there. [k]And his mother's name *was* Naamah an Ammonitess.

22 [l]And Judah did evil in the sight of the LORD, and they [m]provoked him to jealousy with their sins which they had committed, above all that their fathers had done.

13:30 [d]Jer. 22:18
13:31 [e]2 Kings 23:17
13:32 [f]ver. 2; 2 Kings 23:16 [g]ch. 16:24
13:33 [h]ch. 12:31; 2 Chron. 11:15
13:34 [i]ch. 12:30 [j]ch. 14:10
14:2 [k]ch. 11:31
14:3 [l]1 Sam. 9:7
14:4 [m]ch. 11:29
14:7 [n]2 Sam. 12:7; ch. 16:2
14:8 [o]ch. 11:31 [p]ch. 11:33
14:9 [q]ch. 12:28; 2 Chron. 11:15 [r]Neh. 9:26; Ps. 50:17; Ezek. 23:35
14:10 [s]ch. 15:29 [t]ch. 21:21; 2 Kings 9:8 [u]Deut. 32:36; 2 Kings 14:26
14:11 [v]ch. 16:4
14:12 [w]ver. 17
14:13 [x]2 Chron. 12:12
14:14 [y]ch. 15:27
14:15 [z]2 Kings 17:6; Ps. 52:5 [a]Josh. 23:15 [b]2 Kings 15:29 [c]Ex. 34:13; Deut. 12:3
14:16 [d]ch. 12:30
14:17 [e]ch. 16:6; SSol. 6:4 [f]ver. 12
14:18 [g]ver. 13
14:19 [h]2 Chron. 13:2
14:21 [i]2 Chron. 12:13 [j]ch. 11:36 [k]ver. 31
14:22 [l]2 Chron. 12:1 [m]Deut. 32:21; Ps. 78:58; 1 Cor. 10:22

23 For they also built them [n]high places,
and images, [o]and groves, on every high
hill, and [p]under every green tree.
24 [q]And there were also sodomites in the
land: *and* they did according to all the
abominations of the nations which the
LORD cast out before the children of Israel.
25 ¶ [r]And it came to pass in the fifth year
of king Rehoboam, *that* Shishak king of
Egypt came up against Jerusalem:
26 [s]And he took away the treasures of
the house of the LORD, and the treasures of
the king's house; he even took away all: and
he took away all the shields of gold [t]which
Solomon had made.
27 And king Rehoboam made in their
stead brasen shields, and committed *them*
unto the hands of the chief of the guard,
which kept the door of the king's house.
28 And it was *so*, when the king went into
the house of the LORD, that the guard bare
them, and brought them back into the guard
chamber.
29 ¶ [u]Now the rest of the acts of Rehoboam, and all that he did, *are* they not written in the book of the chronicles of the kings
of Judah?
30 And there was [v]war between Rehoboam and Jeroboam all *their* days.
31 [w]And Rehoboam slept with his fathers, and was buried with his fathers in the
city of David. [x]And his mother's name *was*
Naamah an Ammonitess. And [y]Abijam his
son reigned in his stead.

15

Now [z]in the eighteenth year of king
Jeroboam the son of Nebat reigned
Abijam over Judah.
2 Three years reigned he in Jerusalem.
[a]And his mother's name *was* [b]Maachah,
the daughter of [c]Abishalom.
3 And he walked in all the sins of his father, which he had done before him: and
[d]his heart was not perfect with the LORD his
God, as the heart of David his father.
4 Nevertheless [e]for David's sake did the
LORD his God give him a lamp in Jerusalem,
to set up his son after him, and to establish
Jerusalem:
5 Because David [f]did *that which was*
right in the eyes of the LORD, and turned not
aside from any *thing* that he commanded
him all the days of his life, [g]save only in the
matter of Uriah the Hittite.
6 [h]And there was war between Rehoboam and Jeroboam all the days of his life.
7 [i]Now the rest of the acts of Abijam, and
all that he did, *are* they not written in the
book of the chronicles of the kings of Judah? And there was war between Abijam
and Jeroboam.
8 [j]And Abijam slept with his fathers; and
they buried him in the city of David: and
Asa his son reigned in his stead.
9 ¶ And in the twentieth year of Jeroboam
king of Israel reigned Asa over Judah.
10 And forty and one years reigned he
in Jerusalem. And his mother's name *was*
Maachah, the daughter of Abishalom.

14:23 [n]Deut. 12:2; Ezek. 16:24 [o]2 Kings 17:9 [p]Isa. 57:5
14:24 [q]Deut. 23:17; ch. 15:12; 2 Kings 23:7
14:25 [r]ch. 11:40; 2 Chron. 12:2
14:26 [s]2 Chron. 12:9 [t]ch. 10:17
14:29 [u]2 Chron. 12:15
14:30 [v]ch. 12:24; 2 Chron. 12:15
14:31 [w]2 Chron. 12:16 [x]ver. 21 [y]2 Chron. 12:16; Matt. 1:7
15:1 [z]2 Chron. 13:1
15:2 [a]2 Chron. 11:20 [b]2 Chron. 13:2 [c]2 Chron. 11:21
15:3 [d]ch. 11:4; Ps. 119:80
15:4 [e]ch. 11:32; 2 Chron. 21:7
15:5 [f]ch. 14:8 [g]2 Sam. 11:4
15:6 [h]ch. 14:30
15:7 [i]2 Chron. 13:2
15:8 [j]2 Chron. 14:1
15:11 [k]2 Chron. 14:2
15:12 [l]ch. 14:24
15:13 [m]2 Chron. 15:16 [n]Ex. 32:20
15:14 [o]ch. 22:43; 2 Chron. 15:17 [p]ver. 3
15:17 [q]2 Chron. 16:1 [r]Josh. 18:25 [s]ch. 12:27
15:18 [t]2 Chron. 16:2 [u]ch. 11:23
15:20 [v]2 Kings 15:29 [w]Judg. 18:29 [x]2 Sam. 20:14
15:22 [y]2 Chron. 16:6 [z]Josh. 21:17 [a]Josh. 18:26
15:23 [b]2 Chron. 16:12
15:24 [c]2 Chron. 17:1 [d]Matt. 1:8

11 [k]And Asa did *that which was* right in
the eyes of the LORD, as *did* David his father.
12 [l]And he took away the sodomites out
of the land, and removed all the idols that
his fathers had made.
13 And also [m]Maachah his mother, even
her he removed from *being* queen, because
she had made an idol in a grove; and Asa
destroyed her idol, and [n]burnt *it* by the
brook Kidron.
14 [o]But the high places were not removed: nevertheless Asa's [p]heart was perfect with the LORD all his days.
15 And he brought in the things which his
father had dedicated, and the things which
himself had dedicated, into the house of the
LORD, silver, and gold, and vessels.
16 ¶ And there was war between Asa and
Baasha king of Israel all their days.
17 And [q]Baasha king of Israel went up
against Judah, and built [r]Ramah, [s]that he
might not suffer any to go out or come in to
Asa king of Judah.
18 Then Asa took all the silver and the
gold *that were* left in the treasures of the
house of the LORD, and the treasures of the
king's house, and delivered them into
the hand of his servants: and king Asa sent
them to [t]Ben-hadad, the son of Tabrimon,
the son of Hezion, king of Syria, that dwelt
at [u]Damascus, saying,
19 *There is* a league between me and thee,
and between my father and thy father: behold, I have sent unto thee a present of silver and gold; come and break thy league
with Baasha king of Israel, that he may depart from me.
20 So Ben-hadad hearkened unto king
Asa, and sent the captains of the hosts
which he had against the cities of Israel,
and smote [v]Ijon, and [w]Dan, and [x]Abel-
beth-maachah, and all Cinneroth, with all
the land of Naphtali.
21 And it came to pass, when Baasha
heard *thereof*, that he left off building of
Ramah, and dwelt in Tirzah.
22 [y]Then king Asa made a proclamation
throughout all Judah; none *was* exempted:
and they took away the stones of Ramah,
and the timber thereof, wherewith Baasha
had builded; and king Asa built with them
[z]Geba of Benjamin, and [a]Mizpah.
23 The rest of all the acts of Asa, and all
his might, and all that he did, and the cities
which he built, *are* they not written in the
book of the chronicles of the kings of Judah? Nevertheless [b]in the time of his old
age he was diseased in his feet.
24 And Asa slept with his fathers, and
was buried with his fathers in the city of
David his father: [c]and [d]Jehoshaphat his
son reigned in his stead.
25 ¶ And Nadab the son of Jeroboam began to reign over Israel in the second year
of Asa king of Judah, and reigned over Israel two years.
26 And he did evil in the sight of the

LORD, and walked in the way of his father, and in [e]his sin wherewith he made Israel to sin.

27 ¶ [f]And Baasha the son of Ahijah, of the house of Issachar, conspired against him; and Baasha smote him at [g]Gibbethon, which *belonged* to the Philistines; for Nadab and all Israel laid siege to Gibbethon.

28 Even in the third year of Asa king of Judah did Baasha slay him, and reigned in his stead.

29 And it came to pass, when he reigned, *that* he smote all the house of Jeroboam; he left not to Jeroboam any that breathed, until he had destroyed him, according unto [h]the saying of the LORD, which he spake by his servant Ahijah the Shilonite:

30 [i]Because of the sins of Jeroboam which he sinned, and which he made Israel sin, by his provocation wherewith he provoked the LORD God of Israel to anger.

31 ¶ Now the rest of the acts of Nadab, and all that he did, *are* they not written in the book of the chronicles of the kings of Israel?

32 [j]And there was war between Asa and Baasha king of Israel all their days.

33 In the third year of Asa king of Judah began Baasha the son of Ahijah to reign over all Israel in Tirzah, twenty and four years.

34 And he did evil in the sight of the LORD, and walked in [k]the way of Jeroboam, and in his sin wherewith he made Israel to sin.

16 Then the word of the LORD came to [l]Jehu the son of Hanani against Baasha, saying,

2 [m]Forasmuch as I exalted thee out of the dust, and made thee prince over my people Israel; and [n]thou hast walked in the way of Jeroboam, and hast made my people Israel to sin, to provoke me to anger with their sins;

3 Behold, I will [o]take away the posterity of Baasha, and the posterity of his house; and will make thy house like [p]the house of Jeroboam the son of Nebat.

4 [q]Him that dieth of Baasha in the city shall the dogs eat; and him that dieth of his in the fields shall the fowls of the air eat.

5 Now the rest of the acts of Baasha, and what he did, and his might, [r]*are* they not written in the book of the chronicles of the kings of Israel?

6 So Baasha slept with his fathers, and was buried in [s]Tirzah: and Elah his son reigned in his stead.

7 And also by the hand of the prophet [t]Jehu the son of Hanani came the word of the LORD against Baasha, and against his house, even for all the evil that he did in the sight of the LORD, in provoking him to anger with the work of his hands, in being like the house of Jeroboam; and because [u]he killed him.

8 ¶ In the twenty and sixth year of Asa king of Judah began Elah the son of Baasha to reign over Israel in Tirzah, two years.

9 [v]And his servant Zimri, captain of half *his* chariots, conspired against him, as he was in Tirzah, drinking himself drunk in the house of Arza steward of *his* house in Tirzah.

10 And Zimri went in and smote him, and killed him, in the twenty and seventh year of Asa king of Judah, and reigned in his stead.

11 ¶ And it came to pass, when he began to reign, as soon as he sat on his throne, *that* he slew all the house of Baasha: he left him [w]not one that pisseth against a wall, neither of his kinsfolks, nor of his friends.

12 Thus did Zimri destroy all the house of Baasha, [x]according to the word of the LORD, which he spake against Baasha [y]by Jehu the prophet,

13 For all the sins of Baasha, and the sins of Elah his son, by which they sinned, and by which they made Israel to sin, in provoking the LORD God of Israel to anger [z]with their vanities.

14 Now the rest of the acts of Elah, and all that he did, *are* they not written in the book of the chronicles of the kings of Israel?

15 ¶ In the twenty and seventh year of Asa king of Judah did Zimri reign seven days in Tirzah. And the people *were* encamped [a]against Gibbethon, which *belonged* to the Philistines.

16 And the people *that were* encamped heard say, Zimri hath conspired, and hath also slain the king: wherefore all Israel made Omri, the captain of the host, king over Israel that day in the camp.

17 And Omri went up from Gibbethon, and all Israel with him, and they besieged Tirzah.

18 And it came to pass, when Zimri saw that the city was taken, that he went into the palace of the king's house, and burnt the king's house over him with fire, and died.

19 For his sins which he sinned in doing evil in the sight of the LORD, [b]in walking in the way of Jeroboam, and in his sin which he did, to make Israel to sin.

20 Now the rest of the acts of Zimri, and his treason that he wrought, *are* they not written in the book of the chronicles of the kings of Israel?

21 ¶ Then were the people of Israel divided into two parts: half of the people followed Tibni the son of Ginath, to make him king; and half followed Omri.

22 But the people that followed Omri prevailed against the people that followed Tibni the son of Ginath: so Tibni died, and Omri reigned.

23 ¶ In the thirty and first year of Asa king of Judah began Omri to reign over Israel, twelve years: six years reigned he in Tirzah.

24 And he bought the hill Samaria of Shemer for two talents of silver, and built on the hill, and called the name of the city which

15:26 [e]ch. 12:30
15:27 [f]ch. 14:14 [g]Josh. 19:44; ch. 16:15
15:29 [h]ch. 14:10
15:30 [i]ch. 14:9
15:32 [j]ver. 16
15:34 [k]ch. 12:28
16:1 [l]ver. 7; 2 Chron. 19:2
16:2 [m]ch. 14:7 [n]ch. 15:34
16:3 [o]ver. 11 [p]ch. 14:10
16:4 [q]ch. 14:11
16:5 [r]2 Chron. 16:1
16:6 [s]ch. 14:17
16:7 [t]ver. 1 [u]ch. 15:27; Hos. 1:4
16:9 [v]2 Kings 9:31
16:11 [w]1 Sam. 25:22
16:12 [x]ver. 3 [y]ver. 1
16:13 [z]Deut. 32:21; 1 Sam. 12:21; Isa. 41:29; Jonah 2:8; 1 Cor. 8:4
16:15 [a]ch. 15:27
16:19 [b]ch. 12:28

he built, after the name of Shemer, owner of
the hill, [c]Samaria.
25 ¶ But [d]Omri wrought evil in the eyes
of the LORD, and did worse than all that
were before him.
26 For he [e]walked in all the way of Jeroboam the son of Nebat, and in his sin wherewith he made Israel to sin, to provoke the
LORD God of Israel to anger with their
[f]vanities.
27 Now the rest of the acts of Omri which
he did, and his might that he shewed, *are*
they not written in the book of the chronicles of the kings of Israel?
28 So Omri slept with his fathers, and was
buried in Samaria: and Ahab his son
reigned in his stead.
29 ¶ And in the thirty and eighth year of
Asa king of Judah began Ahab the son of
Omri to reign over Israel: and Ahab the
son of Omri reigned over Israel in Samaria
twenty and two years.
30 And Ahab the son of Omri did evil in
the sight of the LORD above all that *were*
before him.
31 And it came to pass, as if it had been a
light thing for him to walk in the sins of
Jeroboam the son of Nebat, [g]that he took to
wife Jezebel the daughter of Ethbaal king
of the [h]Zidonians, [i]and went and served
Baal, and worshipped him.
32 And he reared up an altar for Baal in
[j]the house of Baal, which he had built in
Samaria.
33 [k]And Ahab made a grove; and Ahab
[l]did more to provoke the LORD God of Israel to anger than all the kings of Israel that
were before him.
34 ¶ In his days did Hiel the Beth-elite
build Jericho: he laid the foundation thereof
in Abiram his firstborn, and set up the gates
thereof in his youngest *son* Segub, [m]accord-
ing to the word of the LORD, which he spake
by Joshua the son of Nun.

17

And Elijah the Tishbite, *who was* of
the inhabitants of Gilead, said unto
Ahab, [n]*As* the LORD God of Israel liveth,
[o]before whom I stand, [p]there shall not be
dew nor rain [q]these years, but according to
my word.
2 And the word of the LORD came unto
him, saying,
3 Get thee hence, and turn thee eastward,
and hide thyself by the brook Cherith, that
is before Jordan.
4 And it shall be, *that* thou shalt drink of
the brook; and I have commanded the ravens to feed thee there.
5 So he went and did according unto the
word of the LORD: for he went and dwelt by
the brook Cherith, that *is* before Jordan.
6 And the ravens brought him bread and
flesh in the morning, and bread and flesh in
the evening; and he drank of the brook.
7 And it came to pass after a while, that
the brook dried up, because there had been
no rain in the land.
8 ¶ And the word of the LORD came unto
him, saying,
9 Arise, get thee to [r]Zarephath, which
belongeth to Zidon, and dwell there: behold, I have commanded a widow woman
there to sustain thee.
10 So he arose and went to Zarephath.
And when he came to the gate of the city,
behold, the widow woman *was* there gathering of sticks: and he called to her, and
said, Fetch me, I pray thee, a little water in
a vessel, that I may drink.
11 And as she was going to fetch *it*, he
called to her, and said, Bring me, I pray
thee, a morsel of bread in thine hand.
12 And she said, *As* the LORD thy God
liveth, I have not a cake, but an handful of
meal in a barrel, and a little oil in a cruse:
and, behold, I *am* gathering two sticks, that
I may go in and dress it for me and my son,
that we may eat it, and die.
13 And Elijah said unto her, Fear not; go
and do as thou hast said: but make me
thereof a little cake first, and bring *it* unto
me, and after make for thee and for thy son.
14 For thus saith the LORD God of Israel,
The barrel of meal shall not waste, neither
shall the cruse of oil fail, until the day *that*
the LORD sendeth rain upon the earth.
15 And she went and did according to the
saying of Elijah: and she, and he, and her
house, did eat *many* days.
16 *And* the barrel of meal wasted not, neither did the cruse of oil fail, according to the
word of the LORD, which he spake by Elijah.
17 ¶ And it came to pass after these
things, *that* the son of the woman, the mistress of the house, fell sick; and his sickness
was so sore, that there was no breath left in
him.
18 And she said unto Elijah, [s]What have
I to do with thee, O thou man of God? art
thou come unto me to call my sin to remembrance, and to slay my son?
19 And he said unto her, Give me thy son.
And he took him out of her bosom, and carried him up into a loft, where he abode, and
laid him upon his own bed.
20 And he cried unto the LORD, and said,
O LORD my God, hast thou also brought evil
upon the widow with whom I sojourn, by
slaying her son?
21 [t]And he stretched himself upon the
child three times, and cried unto the LORD,
and said, O LORD my God, I pray thee, let
this child's soul come into him again.
22 And the LORD heard the voice of Elijah; and the soul of the child came into him
again, and he [u]revived.
23 And Elijah took the child, and brought
him down out of the chamber into the
house, and delivered him unto his mother:
and Elijah said, See, thy son liveth.
24 ¶ And the woman said to Elijah, Now
by this [v]I know that thou *art* a man of God,
and that the word of the LORD in thy mouth
is truth.

16:24 ch. 13:32; 2 Kings 17:24; John 4:4
16:25 [d]Mic. 6:16
16:26 [e]ver. 19 [f]ver. 13
16:31 [g]Deut. 7:3 [h]Judg. 18:7 [i]ch. 21:25; 2 Kings 10:18
16:32 [j]2 Kings 10:21
16:33 [k]2 Kings 13:6; Jer. 17:2 [l]ver. 30; ch. 21:25
16:34 [m]Josh. 6:26
17:1 [n]2 Kings 3:14 [o]Deut. 10:8 [p]Jam. 5:17 [q]Luke 4:25
17:9 [r]Obad. 20; Luke 4:26
17:18 [s]Luke 5:8
17:21 [t]2 Kings 4:34
17:22 [u]Heb. 11:35
17:24 [v]John 3:2

18 And it came to pass *after* [w]many days, that the word of the LORD came to Elijah in the third year, saying, Go, shew thyself unto Ahab; and [x]I will send rain upon the earth.

2 And Elijah went to shew himself unto Ahab. And *there was* a sore famine in Samaria.

3 And Ahab called Obadiah, which *was* the governor of *his* house. (Now Obadiah feared the LORD greatly:

4 For it was *so,* when Jezebel cut off the prophets of the LORD, that Obadiah took an hundred prophets, and hid them by fifty in a cave, and fed them with bread and water.)

5 And Ahab said unto Obadiah, Go into the land, unto all fountains of water, and unto all brooks: peradventure we may find grass to save the horses and mules alive, that we lose not all the beasts.

6 So they divided the land between them to pass throughout it: Ahab went one way by himself, and Obadiah went another way by himself.

7 ¶ And as Obadiah was in the way, behold, Elijah met him: and he knew him, and fell on his face, and said, *Art* thou that my lord Elijah?

8 And he answered him, I *am:* go, tell thy lord, Behold, Elijah *is here.*

9 And he said, What have I sinned, that thou wouldest deliver thy servant into the hand of Ahab, to slay me?

10 *As* the LORD thy God liveth, there is no nation or kingdom, whither my lord hath not sent to seek thee: and when they said, *He is* not *there;* he took an oath of the kingdom and nation, that they found thee not.

11 And now thou sayest, Go, tell thy lord, Behold, Elijah *is here.*

12 And it shall come to pass, *as soon as* I am gone from thee, that [y]the Spirit of the LORD shall carry thee whither I know not; and *so* when I come and tell Ahab, and he cannot find thee, he shall slay me: but I thy servant fear the LORD from my youth.

13 Was it not told my lord what I did when Jezebel slew the prophets of the LORD, how I hid an hundred men of the LORD's prophets by fifty in a cave, and fed them with bread and water?

14 And now thou sayest, Go, tell thy lord, Behold, Elijah *is here:* and he shall slay me.

15 And Elijah said, *As* the LORD of hosts liveth, before whom I stand, I will surely shew myself unto him to day.

16 So Obadiah went to meet Ahab, and told him: and Ahab went to meet Elijah.

17 ¶ And it came to pass, when Ahab saw Elijah, that Ahab said unto him, [z]*Art* thou he that [a]troubleth Israel?

18 And he answered, I have not troubled Israel; but thou, and thy father's house, [b]in that ye have forsaken the commandments of the LORD, and thou hast followed Baalim.

19 Now therefore send, *and* gather to me all Israel unto mount [c]Carmel, and the prophets of Baal four hundred and fifty, [d]and the prophets of the groves four hundred, which eat at Jezebel's table.

20 So Ahab sent unto all the children of Israel, and [e]gathered the prophets together unto mount Carmel.

21 And Elijah came unto all the people, and said, [f]How long halt ye between two opinions? if the LORD *be* God, follow him: but if [g]Baal, *then* follow him. And the people answered him not a word.

22 Then said Elijah unto the people, [h]I, *even* I only, remain a prophet of the LORD; [i]but Baal's prophets *are* four hundred and fifty men.

23 Let them therefore give us two bullocks; and let them choose one bullock for themselves, and cut it in pieces, and lay *it* on wood, and put no fire *under:* and I will dress the other bullock, and lay *it* on wood, and put no fire *under:*

24 And call ye on the name of your gods, and I will call on the name of the LORD: and the God that [j]answereth by fire, let him be God. And all the people answered and said, It is well spoken.

25 And Elijah said unto the prophets of Baal, Choose you one bullock for yourselves, and dress *it* first; for ye *are* many; and call on the name of your gods, but put no fire *under.*

26 And they took the bullock which was given them, and they dressed *it,* and called on the name of Baal from morning even until noon, saying, O Baal, hear us. But *there was* [k]no voice, nor any that answered. And they leaped upon the altar which was made.

27 And it came to pass at noon, that Elijah mocked them, and said, Cry aloud: for he *is* a god; either he is talking, or he is pursuing, or he is in a journey, *or* peradventure he sleepeth, and must be awaked.

28 And they cried aloud, and [l]cut themselves after their manner with knives and lancets, till the blood gushed out upon them.

29 And it came to pass, when midday was past, [m]and they prophesied until the *time* of the offering of the *evening* sacrifice, that *there was* [n]neither voice, nor any to answer, nor any that regarded.

30 And Elijah said unto all the people, Come near unto me. And all the people came near unto him. [o]And he repaired the altar of the LORD *that was* broken down.

31 And Elijah took twelve stones, according to the number of the tribes of the sons of Jacob, unto whom the word of the LORD came, saying, [p]Israel shall be thy name:

32 And with the stones he built an altar [q]in the name of the LORD: and he made a trench about the altar, as great as would contain two measures of seed.

33 And he [r]put the wood in order, and cut the bullock in pieces, and laid *him* on the wood, and said, Fill four barrels with water, and [s]pour *it* on the burnt sacrifice, and on the wood.

34 And he said, Do *it* the second time. And they did *it* the second time. And he

18:1 [w]Luke 4:25; Jam. 5:17 [x]Deut. 28:12
18:12 [y]2 Kings 2:16; Ezek. 3:12; Matt. 4:1; Acts 8:39
18:17 [z]ch. 21:20 [a]Josh. 7:25; Acts 16:20
18:18 [b]2 Chron. 15:2
18:19 [c]Josh. 19:26 [d]ch. 16:33
18:20 [e]ch. 22:6
18:21 [f]2 Kings 17:41; Matt. 6:24 [g]Josh. 24:15
18:22 [h]ch. 19:10 [i]ver. 19
18:24 [j]ver. 38; 1 Chron. 21:26
18:26 [k]Ps. 115:5; Jer. 10:5; 1 Cor. 8:4
18:28 [l]Lev. 19:28; Deut. 14:1
18:29 [m]1 Cor. 11:4 [n]ver. 26
18:30 [o]ch. 19:10
18:31 [p]Gen. 32:28; 2 Kings 17:34
18:32 [q]Col. 3:17
18:33 [r]Lev. 1:6 [s]Judg. 6:20

said, Do *it* the third time. And they did *it* the third time.

35 And the water ran round about the altar; and he filled [t]the trench also with water.

36 And it came to pass at *the time of* the offering of the *evening* sacrifice, that Elijah the prophet came near, and said, LORD [u]God of Abraham, Isaac, and of Israel, [v]let it be known this day that thou *art* God in Israel, and *that* I *am* thy servant, and *that* [w]I have done all these things at thy word.

37 Hear me, O LORD, hear me, that this people may know that thou *art* the LORD God, and *that* thou hast turned their heart back again.

38 Then [x]the fire of the LORD fell, and consumed the burnt sacrifice, and the wood, and the stones, and the dust, and licked up the water that *was* in the trench.

39 And when all the people saw *it*, they fell on their faces: and they said, [y]The LORD, he *is* the God; the LORD, he *is* the God.

40 And Elijah said unto them, [z]Take the prophets of Baal; let not one of them escape. And they took them: and Elijah brought them down to the brook Kishon, and [a]slew them there.

41 ¶ And Elijah said unto Ahab, Get thee up, eat and drink; for *there is* a sound of abundance of rain.

42 So Ahab went up to eat and to drink. And Elijah went up to the top of Carmel; [b]and he cast himself down upon the earth, and put his face between his knees,

43 And said to his servant, Go up now, look toward the sea. And he went up, and looked, and said, *There is* nothing. And he said, Go again seven times.

44 And it came to pass at the seventh time, that he said, Behold, there ariseth a little cloud out of the sea, like a man's hand. And he said, Go up, say unto Ahab, Prepare *thy chariot*, and get thee down, that the rain stop thee not.

45 And it came to pass in the mean while, that the heaven was black with clouds and wind, and there was a great rain. And Ahab rode, and went to Jezreel.

46 And the hand of the LORD was on Elijah; and he [c]girded up his loins, and ran before Ahab to the entrance of Jezreel.

19 And Ahab told Jezebel all that Elijah had done, and withal how he had [d]slain all the prophets with the sword.

2 Then Jezebel sent a messenger unto Elijah, saying, [e]So let the gods do *to me*, and more also, if I make not thy life as the life of one of them by to morrow about this time.

3 And when he saw *that*, he arose, and went for his life, and came to Beer-sheba, which *belongeth* to Judah, and left his servant there.

4 ¶ But he himself went a day's journey into the wilderness, and came and sat down under a juniper tree: and he [f]requested for himself that he might die; and said, It is enough; now, O LORD, take away my life; for I *am* not better than my fathers.

5 And as he lay and slept under a juniper tree, behold, then an angel touched him, and said unto him, Arise *and* eat.

6 And he looked, and, behold, *there was* a cake baken on the coals, and a cruse of water at his head. And he did eat and drink, and laid him down again.

7 And the angel of the LORD came again the second time, and touched him, and said, Arise *and* eat; because the journey *is* too great for thee.

8 And he arose, and did eat and drink, and went in the strength of that meat [g]forty days and forty nights unto [h]Horeb the mount of God.

9 ¶ And he came thither unto a cave, and lodged there; and, behold, the word of the LORD *came* to him, and he said unto him, What doest thou here, Elijah?

10 And he said, [i]I have been very [j]jealous for the LORD God of hosts: for the children of Israel have forsaken thy covenant, thrown down thine altars, and [k]slain thy prophets with the sword; and [l]I, *even* I only, am left; and they seek my life, to take it away.

11 And he said, Go forth, and stand [m]upon the mount before the LORD. And, behold, the LORD passed by, and [n]a great and strong wind rent the mountains, and brake in pieces the rocks before the LORD; *but* the LORD *was* not in the wind: and after the wind an earthquake; *but* the LORD *was* not in the earthquake:

12 And after the earthquake a fire; *but* the LORD *was* not in the fire: and after the fire a still small voice.

13 And it was *so*, when Elijah heard *it*, that [o]he wrapped his face in his mantle, and went out, and stood in the entering in of the cave. [p]And, behold, *there came* a voice unto him, and said, What doest thou here, Elijah?

14 [q]And he said, I have been very jealous for the LORD God of hosts: because the children of Israel have forsaken thy covenant, thrown down thine altars, and slain thy prophets with the sword; and I, *even* I only, am left; and they seek my life, to take it away.

15 And the LORD said unto him, Go, return on thy way to the wilderness of Damascus: [r]and when thou comest, anoint Hazael *to be* king over Syria:

16 And [s]Jehu the son of Nimshi shalt thou anoint *to be* king over Israel: and [t]Elisha the son of Shaphat of Abel-meholah shalt thou anoint *to be* prophet in thy room.

17 And [u]it shall come to pass, *that* him that escapeth the sword of Hazael shall Jehu slay: and him that escapeth from the sword of Jehu [v]shall Elisha slay.

18 [w]Yet I have left *me* seven thousand in Israel, all the knees which have not bowed unto Baal, [x]and every mouth which hath not kissed him.

18:35 [t]ver. 32
18:36 [u]Ex. 3:6 [v]ch. 8:43; 2 Kings 19:19; Ps. 83:18 [w]Num. 16:28
18:38 [x]Lev. 9:24; Judg. 6:21; 1 Chron. 21:26; 2 Chron. 7:1
18:39 [y]ver. 24
18:40 [z]2 Kings 10:25 [a]Deut. 13:5
18:42 [b]Jam. 5:17
18:46 [c]2 Kings 4:29
19:1 [d]ch. 18:40
19:2 [e]Ruth 1:17; ch. 20:10; 2 Kings 6:31
19:4 [f]Num. 11:15; Jonah 4:3
19:8 [g]Ex. 34:28; Deut. 9:9; Matt. 4:2 [h]Ex. 3:1
19:10 [i]Rom. 11:3 [j]Num. 25:11; Ps. 69:9 [k]ch. 18:4 [l]ch. 18:22; Rom. 11:3
19:11 [m]Ex. 24:12 [n]Ezek. 1:4
19:13 [o]Ex. 3:6; Isa. 6:2 [p]ver. 9
19:14 [q]ver. 10
19:15 [r]2 Kings 8:12
19:16 [s]2 Kings 9:1-3 [t]Luke 4:27
19:17 [u]2 Kings 8:12 [v]Hos. 6:5
19:18 [w]Rom. 11:4 [x]Hos. 13:2

19 ¶ So he departed thence, and found Elisha the son of Shaphat, who *was* plowing *with* twelve yoke *of oxen* before him, and he with the twelfth: and Elijah passed by him, and cast his mantle upon him.

20 And he left the oxen, and ran after Elijah, and said, [y]Let me, I pray thee, kiss my father and my mother, and *then* I will follow thee. And he said unto him, Go back again: for what have I done to thee?

21 And he returned back from him, and took a yoke of oxen, and slew them, and [z]boiled their flesh with the instruments of the oxen, and gave unto the people, and they did eat. Then he arose, and went after Elijah, and ministered unto him.

20 And Ben-hadad the king of Syria gathered all his host together: and *there were* thirty and two kings with him, and horses, and chariots: and he went up and besieged Samaria, and warred against it.

2 And he sent messengers to Ahab king of Israel into the city, and said unto him, Thus saith Ben-hadad,

3 Thy silver and thy gold *is* mine; thy wives also and thy children, *even* the goodliest, *are* mine.

4 And the king of Israel answered and said, My lord, O king, according to thy saying, I *am* thine, and all that I have.

5 And the messengers came again, and said, Thus speaketh Ben-hadad, saying, Although I have sent unto thee, saying, Thou shalt deliver me thy silver, and thy gold, and thy wives, and thy children;

6 Yet I will send my servants unto thee to morrow about this time, and they shall search thine house, and the houses of thy servants; and it shall be, *that* whatsoever is pleasant in thine eyes, they shall put *it* in their hand, and take *it* away.

7 Then the king of Israel called all the elders of the land, and said, Mark, I pray you, and see how this *man* seeketh mischief: for he sent unto me for my wives, and for my children, and for my silver, and for my gold; and I denied him not.

8 And all the elders and all the people said unto him, Hearken not *unto him*, nor consent.

9 Wherefore he said unto the messengers of Ben-hadad, Tell my lord the king, all that thou didst send for to thy servant at the first I will do: but this thing I may not do. And the messengers departed, and brought him word again.

10 And Ben-hadad sent unto him, and said, [a]The gods do so unto me, and more also, if the dust of Samaria shall suffice for handfuls for all the people that follow me.

11 And the king of Israel answered and said, Tell *him,* Let not him that girdeth on *his harness* boast himself as he that putteth it off.

12 And it came to pass, when *Ben-hadad* heard this message, as he *was* [b]drinking, he and the kings in the pavilions, that he said unto his servants, Set *yourselves in array.* And they set *themselves in array* against the city.

13 ¶ And, behold, there came a prophet unto Ahab king of Israel, saying, Thus saith the LORD, Hast thou seen all this great multitude? behold, [c]I will deliver it into thine hand this day; and thou shalt know that I *am* the LORD.

14 And Ahab said, By whom? And he said, Thus saith the LORD, *Even* by the young men of the princes of the provinces. Then he said, Who shall order the battle? And he answered, Thou.

15 Then he numbered the young men of the princes of the provinces, and they were two hundred and thirty two: and after them he numbered all the people, *even* all the children of Israel, *being* seven thousand.

16 And they went out at noon. But Ben-hadad *was* [d]drinking himself drunk in the pavilions, he and the kings, the thirty and two kings that helped him.

17 And the young men of the princes of the provinces went out first; and Ben-hadad sent out, and they told him, saying, There are men come out of Samaria.

18 And he said, Whether they be come out for peace, take them alive; or whether they be come out for war, take them alive.

19 So these young men of the princes of the provinces came out of the city, and the army which followed them.

20 And they slew every one his man: and the Syrians fled; and Israel pursued them: and Ben-hadad the king of Syria escaped on an horse with the horsemen.

21 And the king of Israel went out, and smote the horses and chariots, and slew the Syrians with a great slaughter.

22 ¶ And the prophet came to the king of Israel, and said unto him, Go, strengthen thyself, and mark, and see what thou doest: [e]for at the return of the year the king of Syria will come up against thee.

23 And the servants of the king of Syria said unto him, Their gods *are* gods of the hills; therefore they were stronger than we; but let us fight against them in the plain, and surely we shall be stronger than they.

24 And do this thing, Take the kings away, every man out of his place, and put captains in their rooms:

25 And number thee an army, like the army that thou hast lost, horse for horse, and chariot for chariot: and we will fight against them in the plain, *and* surely we shall be stronger than they. And he hearkened unto their voice, and did so.

26 And it came to pass at the return of the year, that Ben-hadad numbered the Syrians, and went up to [f]Aphek, to fight against Israel.

27 And the children of Israel were numbered, and were all present, and went against them: and the children of Israel pitched before them like two little flocks of kids; but the Syrians filled the country.

19:20 [y]Matt. 8:21; Luke 9:61
19:21 [z]2 Sam. 24:22
20:10 [a]ch. 19:2
20:12 [b]ver. 16
20:13 [c]ver. 28
20:16 [d]ver. 11; ch. 16:9
20:22 [e]2 Sam. 11:1
20:26 [f]Josh. 13:4

28 ¶ And there came a man of God, and
spake unto the king of Israel, and said, Thus
saith the LORD, Because the Syrians have
said, The LORD *is* God of the hills, but he *is*
not God of the valleys, therefore [g]will I deliver all this great multitude into thine hand,
and ye shall know that I *am* the LORD.
29 And they pitched one over against the
other seven days. And *so* it was, that in the
seventh day the battle was joined: and the
children of Israel slew of the Syrians an
hundred thousand footmen in one day.
30 But the rest fled to Aphek, into the city;
and *there* a wall fell upon twenty and seven
thousand of the men *that were* left. And
Ben-hadad fled, and came into the city, into
an inner chamber.
31 ¶ And his servants said unto him, Behold now, we have heard that the kings of
the house of Israel *are* merciful kings: let us,
I pray thee, [h]put sackcloth on our loins, and
ropes upon our heads, and go out to the
king of Israel: peradventure he will save thy
life.
32 So they girded sackcloth on their loins,
and *put* ropes on their heads, and came to
the king of Israel, and said, Thy servant
Ben-hadad saith, I pray thee, let me live.
And he said, *Is* he yet alive? he *is* my
brother.
33 Now the men did diligently observe
whether *any thing would come* from him,
and did hastily catch *it:* and they said, Thy
brother Ben-hadad. Then he said, Go ye,
bring him. Then Ben-hadad came forth to
him; and he caused him to come up into the
chariot.
34 And *Ben-hadad* said unto him, [i]The
cities, which my father took from thy father,
I will restore; and thou shalt make streets
for thee in Damascus, as my father made in
Samaria. Then *said Ahab,* I will send thee
away with this covenant. So he made a covenant with him, and sent him away.
35 ¶ And a certain man of [j]the sons of the
prophets said unto his neighbour [k]in the
word of the LORD, Smite me, I pray thee.
And the man refused to smite him.
36 Then said he unto him, Because thou
hast not obeyed the voice of the LORD, behold, as soon as thou art departed from me,
a lion shall slay thee. And as soon as he was
departed from him, [l]a lion found him, and
slew him.
37 Then he found another man, and said,
Smite me, I pray thee. And the man smote
him, so that in smiting he wounded *him.*
38 So the prophet departed, and waited
for the king by the way, and disguised himself with ashes upon his face.
39 And [m]as the king passed by, he cried
unto the king: and he said, Thy servant
went out into the midst of the battle; and,
behold, a man turned aside, and brought a
man unto me, and said, Keep this man: if by
any means he be missing, then [n]shall thy
life be for his life, or else thou shalt pay a
talent of silver.

20:28 [g]ver. 13
20:31 [h]Gen. 37:34
20:34 [i]ch. 15:20
20:35 [j]2 Kings 2:3 [k]ch. 13:17
20:36 [l]ch. 13:24
20:39 [m]2 Sam. 12:1 [n]2 Kings 10:24
20:42 [o]ch. 22:31-37
20:43 [p]ch. 21:4
21:2 [q]1 Sam. 8:14
21:3 [r]Lev. 25:23; Num. 36:7; Ezek. 46:18
21:10 [s]Ex. 22:28; Lev. 24:15; Acts 6:11 [t]Lev. 24:14
21:12 [u]Isa. 58:4

40 And as thy servant was busy here and
there, he was gone. And the king of Israel
said unto him, So *shall* thy judgment *be;*
thyself hast decided *it.*
41 And he hasted, and took the ashes
away from his face; and the king of Israel
discerned him that he *was* of the prophets.
42 And he said unto him, Thus saith the
LORD, [o]Because thou hast let go out of *thy*
hand a man whom I appointed to utter destruction, therefore thy life shall go for his
life, and thy people for his people.
43 And the king of Israel [p]went to his
house heavy and displeased, and came to
Samaria.

21 And it came to pass after these
things, *that* Naboth the Jezreelite
had a vineyard, which *was* in Jezreel, hard
by the palace of Ahab king of Samaria.
2 And Ahab spake unto Naboth, saying,
Give me thy [q]vineyard, that I may have it
for a garden of herbs, because it *is* near unto
my house: and I will give thee for it a better
vineyard than it; *or,* if it seem good to thee,
I will give thee the worth of it in money.
3 And Naboth said to Ahab, The LORD
forbid it me, [r]that I should give the inheritance of my fathers unto thee.
4 And Ahab came into his house heavy
and displeased because of the word which
Naboth the Jezreelite had spoken to him:
for he had said, I will not give thee the inheritance of my fathers. And he laid him
down upon his bed, and turned away his
face, and would eat no bread.
5 ¶ But Jezebel his wife came to him, and
said unto him, Why is thy spirit so sad, that
thou eatest no bread?
6 And he said unto her, Because I spake
unto Naboth the Jezreelite, and said unto
him, Give me thy vineyard for money; or
else, if it please thee, I will give thee *another*
vineyard for it: and he answered, I will not
give thee my vineyard.
7 And Jezebel his wife said unto him,
Dost thou now govern the kingdom of Israel? arise, *and* eat bread, and let thine
heart be merry: I will give thee the vineyard
of Naboth the Jezreelite.
8 So she wrote letters in Ahab's name,
and sealed *them* with his seal, and sent the
letters unto the elders and to the nobles that
were in his city, dwelling with Naboth.
9 And she wrote in the letters, saying,
Proclaim a fast, and set Naboth on high
among the people:
10 And set two men, sons of Belial, before
him, to bear witness against him, saying,
Thou didst [s]blaspheme God and the king.
And *then* carry him out, and [t]stone him,
that he may die.
11 And the men of his city, *even* the elders
and the nobles who were the inhabitants in
his city, did as Jezebel had sent unto them,
and as it *was* written in the letters which she
had sent unto them.
12 [u]They proclaimed a fast, and set Naboth on high among the people.

13 And there came in two men, children of Belial, and sat before him: and the men of Belial witnessed against him, *even* against Naboth, in the presence of the people, saying, Naboth did blaspheme God and the king. [v]Then they carried him forth out of the city, and stoned him with stones, that he died.

14 Then they sent to Jezebel, saying, Naboth is stoned, and is dead.

15 ¶ And it came to pass, when Jezebel heard that Naboth was stoned, and was dead, that Jezebel said to Ahab, Arise, take possession of the vineyard of Naboth the Jezreelite, which he refused to give thee for money: for Naboth is not alive, but dead.

16 And it came to pass, when Ahab heard that Naboth was dead, that Ahab rose up to go down to the vineyard of Naboth the Jezreelite, to take possession of it.

17 ¶ [w]And the word of the LORD came to Elijah the Tishbite, saying,

18 Arise, go down to meet Ahab king of Israel, [x]which *is* in Samaria: behold, *he is* in the vineyard of Naboth, whither he is gone down to possess it.

19 And thou shalt speak unto him, saying, Thus saith the LORD, Hast thou killed, and also taken possession? And thou shalt speak unto him, saying, Thus saith the LORD, [y]In the place where dogs licked the blood of Naboth shall dogs lick thy blood, even thine.

20 And Ahab said to Elijah, [z]Hast thou found me, O mine enemy? And he answered, I have found *thee:* because [a]thou hast sold thyself to work evil in the sight of the LORD.

21 Behold, [b]I will bring evil upon thee, and will take away thy posterity, and will cut off from Ahab [c]him that pisseth against the wall, and [d]him that is shut up and left in Israel,

22 And will make thine house like the house of [e]Jeroboam the son of Nebat, and like the house of [f]Baasha the son of Ahijah, for the provocation wherewith thou hast provoked *me* to anger, and made Israel to sin.

23 And [g]of Jezebel also spake the LORD, saying, The dogs shall eat Jezebel by the wall of Jezreel.

24 [h]Him that dieth of Ahab in the city the dogs shall eat; and him that dieth in the field shall the fowls of the air eat.

25 ¶ But [i]there was none like unto Ahab, which did sell himself to work wickedness in the sight of the LORD, [j]whom Jezebel his wife stirred up.

26 And he did very abominably in following idols, according to all *things* [k]as did the Amorites, whom the LORD cast out before the children of Israel.

27 And it came to pass, when Ahab heard those words, that he rent his clothes, and [l]put sackcloth upon his flesh, and fasted, and lay in sackcloth, and went softly.

28 And the word of the LORD came to Elijah the Tishbite, saying,

29 Seest thou how Ahab humbleth himself before me? because he humbleth himself before me, I will not bring the evil in his days: *but* [m]in his son's days will I bring the evil upon his house.

22 And they continued three years without war between Syria and Israel.

2 And it came to pass in the third year, that [n]Jehoshaphat the king of Judah came down to the king of Israel.

3 And the king of Israel said unto his servants, Know ye that [o]Ramoth in Gilead *is* ours, and we *be* still, *and* take it not out of the hand of the king of Syria?

4 And he said unto Jehoshaphat, Wilt thou go with me to battle to Ramoth-gilead? And Jehoshaphat said to the king of Israel, [p]I *am* as thou *art*, my people as thy people, my horses as thy horses.

5 And Jehoshaphat said unto the king of Israel, Enquire, I pray thee, at the word of the LORD to day.

6 Then the king of Israel [q]gathered the prophets together, about four hundred men, and said unto them, Shall I go against Ramoth-gilead to battle, or shall I forbear? And they said, Go up; for the Lord shall deliver *it* into the hand of the king.

7 And [r]Jehoshaphat said, *Is there* not here a prophet of the LORD besides, that we might enquire of him?

8 And the king of Israel said unto Jehoshaphat, *There is* yet one man, Micaiah the son of Imlah, by whom we may enquire of the LORD: but I hate him; for he doth not prophesy good concerning me, but evil. And Jehoshaphat said, Let not the king say so.

9 Then the king of Israel called an officer, and said, Hasten *hither* Micaiah the son of Imlah.

10 And the king of Israel and Jehoshaphat the king of Judah sat each on his throne, having put on their robes, in a void place in the entrance of the gate of Samaria; and all the prophets prophesied before them.

11 And Zedekiah the son of Chenaanah made him horns of iron: and he said, Thus saith the LORD, With these shalt thou push the Syrians, until thou have consumed them.

12 And all the prophets prophesied so, saying, Go up to Ramoth-gilead, and prosper: for the LORD shall deliver *it* into the king's hand.

13 And the messenger that was gone to call Micaiah spake unto him, saying, Behold now, the words of the prophets *declare* good unto the king with one mouth: let thy word, I pray thee, be like the word of one of them, and speak *that which is* good.

14 And Micaiah said, *As* the LORD liveth, [s]what the LORD saith unto me, that will I speak.

15 ¶ So he came to the king. And the king

21:13 [v]2 Kings 9:26
21:17 [w]Ps. 9:12
21:18 [x]ch. 13:32; 2 Chron. 22:9
21:19 [y]ch. 22:38
21:20 [z]ch. 18:17 [a]2 Kings 17:17; Rom. 7:14
21:21 [b]ch. 14:10; 2 Kings 9:8 [c]1 Sam. 25:22 [d]ch. 14:10
21:22 [e]ch. 15:29 [f]ch. 16:3
21:23 [g]2 Kings 9:36
21:24 [h]ch. 14:11
21:25 [i]ch. 16:30 [j]ch. 16:31
21:26 [k]Gen. 15:16; 2 Kings 21:11
21:27 [l]Gen. 37:34
21:29 [m]2 Kings 9:25
22:2 [n]2 Chron. 18:2
22:3 [o]Deut. 4:43
22:4 [p]2 Kings 3:7
22:6 [q]ch. 18:19
22:7 [r]2 Kings 3:11
22:14 [s]Num. 22:38

said unto him, Micaiah, shall we go against Ramoth-gilead to battle, or shall we forbear? And he answered him, Go, and prosper: for the LORD shall deliver *it* into the hand of the king.

16 And the king said unto him, How many times shall I adjure thee that thou tell me nothing but *that which is* true in the name of the LORD?

17 And he said, I saw all Israel [t]scattered upon the hills, as sheep that have not a shepherd: and the LORD said, These have no master: let them return every man to his house in peace.

18 And the king of Israel said unto Jehoshaphat, Did I not tell thee that he would prophesy no good concerning me, but evil?

19 And he said, Hear thou therefore the word of the LORD: [u]I saw the LORD sitting on his throne, [v]and all the host of heaven standing by him on his right hand and on his left.

20 And the LORD said, Who shall persuade Ahab, that he may go up and fall at Ramoth-gilead? And one said on this manner, and another said on that manner.

21 And there came forth a spirit, and stood before the LORD, and said, I will persuade him.

22 And the LORD said unto him, Wherewith? And he said, I will go forth, and I will be a lying spirit in the mouth of all his prophets. And he said, [w]Thou shalt persuade *him,* and prevail also: go forth, and do so.

23 [x]Now therefore, behold, the LORD hath put a lying spirit in the mouth of all these thy prophets, and the LORD hath spoken evil concerning thee.

24 But Zedekiah the son of Chenaanah went near, and smote Micaiah on the cheek, and said, [y]Which way went the Spirit of the LORD from me to speak unto thee?

25 And Micaiah said, Behold, thou shalt see in that day, when thou shalt go into an inner chamber to hide thyself.

26 And the king of Israel said, Take Micaiah, and carry him back unto Amon the governor of the city, and to Joash the king's son;

27 And say, Thus saith the king, Put this *fellow* in the prison, and feed him with bread of affliction and with water of affliction, until I come in peace.

28 And Micaiah said, If thou return at all in peace, [z]the LORD hath not spoken by me. And he said, Hearken, O people, every one of you.

29 So the king of Israel and Jehoshaphat the king of Judah went up to Ramoth-gilead.

30 And the king of Israel said unto Jehoshaphat, I will disguise myself, and enter into the battle; but put thou on thy robes. And the king of Israel [a]disguised himself, and went into the battle.

31 But the king of Syria commanded his thirty and two captains that had rule over his chariots, saying, Fight neither with small nor great, save only with the king of Israel.

32 And it came to pass, when the captains of the chariots saw Jehoshaphat, that they said, Surely it *is* the king of Israel. And they turned aside to fight against him: and Jehoshaphat [b]cried out.

33 And it came to pass, when the captains of the chariots perceived that it *was* not the king of Israel, that they turned back from pursuing him.

34 And a *certain* man drew a bow at a venture, and smote the king of Israel between the joints of the harness: wherefore he said unto the driver of his chariot, Turn thine hand, and carry me out of the host; for I am wounded.

35 And the battle increased that day: and the king was stayed up in his chariot against the Syrians, and died at even: and the blood ran out of the wound into the midst of the chariot.

36 And there went a proclamation throughout the host about the going down of the sun, saying, Every man to his city, and every man to his own country.

37 ¶ So the king died, and was brought to Samaria; and they buried the king in Samaria.

38 And *one* washed the chariot in the pool of Samaria; and the dogs licked up his blood; and they washed his armour; according [c]unto the word of the LORD which he spake.

39 Now the rest of the acts of Ahab, and all that he did, and [d]the ivory house which he made, and all the cities that he built, *are* they not written in the book of the chronicles of the kings of Israel?

40 So Ahab slept with his fathers; and Ahaziah his son reigned in his stead.

41 ¶ And [e]Jehoshaphat the son of Asa began to reign over Judah in the fourth year of Ahab king of Israel.

42 Jehoshaphat *was* thirty and five years old when he began to reign; and he reigned twenty and five years in Jerusalem. And his mother's name *was* Azubah the daughter of Shilhi.

43 And [f]he walked in all the ways of Asa his father; he turned not aside from it, doing *that which was* right in the eyes of the LORD: nevertheless [g]the high places were not taken away; *for* the people offered and burnt incense yet in the high places.

44 And [h]Jehoshaphat made peace with the king of Israel.

45 Now the rest of the acts of Jehoshaphat, and his might that he shewed, and how he warred, *are* they not written in the book of the chronicles of the kings of Judah?

46 [i]And the remnant of the sodomites, which remained in the days of his father Asa, he took out of the land.

47 [j]*There was* then no king in Edom: a deputy *was* king.

22:17 [t]Matt. 9:36
22:19 [u]Isa. 6:1; Dan. 7:9 [v]Job 1:6; Ps. 103:20; Dan. 7:10; Zech. 1:10; Matt. 18:10; Heb. 1:7
22:22 [w]Judg. 9:23; Job 12:16; Ezek. 14:9; 2 Thess. 2:11
22:23 [x]Ezek. 14:9
22:24 [y]2 Chron. 18:23
22:28 [z]Num. 16:29; Deut. 18:20
22:30 [a]2 Chron. 35:22
22:32 [b]2 Chron. 18:31; Prov. 13:20
22:38 [c]ch. 21:19
22:39 [d]Am. 3:15
22:41 [e]2 Chron. 20:31
22:43 [f]2 Chron. 17:3 [g]ch. 14:23; 2 Kings 12:3
22:44 [h]2 Chron. 19:2; 2 Cor. 6:14
22:46 [i]ch. 14:24
22:47 [j]Gen. 25:23; 2 Sam. 8:14; 2 Kings 3:9

48 [k]Jehoshaphat [l]made ships of Tharshish to go to Ophir for gold: [m]but they went
not; for the ships were broken at [n]Ezion-
geber.
49 Then said Ahaziah the son of Ahab
unto Jehoshaphat, Let my servants go with
thy servants in the ships. But Jehoshaphat
would not.
50 ¶ And [o]Jehoshaphat slept with his fathers, and was buried with his fathers in the
city of David his father: and Jehoram his
son reigned in his stead.
51 ¶ [p]Ahaziah the son of Ahab began to
reign over Israel in Samaria the seventeenth year of Jehoshaphat king of Judah,
and reigned two years over Israel.
52 And he did evil in the sight of the
LORD, and [q]walked in the way of his father,
and in the way of his mother, and in the way
of Jeroboam the son of Nebat, who made
Israel to sin:
53 For [r]he served Baal, and worshipped
him, and provoked to anger the LORD God
of Israel, according to all that his father had
done.

22:48 [k]2 Chron. 20:35 [l]ch. 10:22 [m]2 Chron. 20:37 [n]ch. 9:26
22:50 [o]2 Chron. 21:1
22:51 [p]ver. 40
22:52 [q]ch. 15:26
22:53 [r]Judg. 2:11; ch. 16:31

2 KINGS

Jeremiah wrote 2 Kings sometime after 550 B.C. Second Kings covers the history of Judah and Israel for approximately 250 years. Initially, there is relative peace and tranquility in both parts, but as the narrative continues, there is a succession of good and bad Kings in both. Before the book ends, both Israel and Judah lie in ruins, a result of disobeying God, and only God's unmerited love for his people save either.

Perhaps the most well known passage in 2 Kings would be the healing of Naaman, a Syrian leper (Chapter 5). Elisha is probably the most widely recognized person in 2 Kings.

I. The divided monarchy, 1:1–17:41
II. Kings in the remaining nation of Judah, 18:1–25:30

---

1 Then Moab [a]rebelled against Israel
[b]after the death of Ahab.
2 And Ahaziah fell down through a lattice
in his upper chamber that *was* in Samaria,
and was sick: and he sent messengers, and
said unto them, Go, enquire of Baal-zebub
the god of [c]Ekron whether I shall recover
of this disease.
3 But the angel of the LORD said to Elijah
the Tishbite, Arise, go up to meet the messengers of the king of Samaria, and say
unto them, *Is it* not because *there is* not a
God in Israel, *that* ye go to enquire of Baal-
zebub the god of Ekron?
4 Now therefore thus saith the LORD,
Thou shalt not come down from that bed on
which thou art gone up, but shalt surely die.
And Elijah departed.
5 ¶ And when the messengers turned
back unto him, he said unto them, Why are
ye now turned back?
6 And they said unto him, There came a
man up to meet us, and said unto us, Go,
turn again unto the king that sent you, and
say unto him, Thus saith the LORD, *Is it* not
because *there is* not a God in Israel, *that*
thou sendest to enquire of Baal-zebub the
god of Ekron? therefore thou shalt not come
down from that bed on which thou art gone
up, but shalt surely die.
7 And he said unto them, What manner of
man *was he* which came up to meet you,
and told you these words?
8 And they answered him, *He was* [d]an
hairy man, and girt with a girdle of leather
about his loins. And he said, It *is* Elijah the
Tishbite.
9 Then the king sent unto him a captain of
fifty with his fifty. And he went up to him:
and, behold, he sat on the top of an hill. And
he spake unto him, Thou man of God, the
king hath said, Come down.
10 And Elijah answered and said to the
captain of fifty, If I *be* a man of God, then
[e]let fire come down from heaven, and consume thee and thy fifty. And there came
down fire from heaven, and consumed him
and his fifty.
11 Again also he sent unto him another
captain of fifty with his fifty. And he answered and said unto him, O man of God,
thus hath the king said, Come down
quickly.
12 And Elijah answered and said unto
them, If I *be* a man of God, let fire come
down from heaven, and consume thee and
thy fifty. And the fire of God came down
from heaven, and consumed him and his
fifty.
13 ¶ And he sent again a captain of the
third fifty with his fifty. And the third captain of fifty went up, and came and fell on
his knees before Elijah, and besought him,

1:1 [a]2 Sam. 8:2 [b]ch. 3:5
1:2 [c]1 Sam. 5:10
1:8 [d]Zech. 13:4; Matt. 3:4
1:10 [e]Luke 9:54

and said unto him, O man of God, I pray
thee, let my life, and the life of these fifty thy
servants, [f]be precious in thy sight.
14 Behold, there came fire down from
heaven, and burnt up the two captains of
the former fifties with their fifties: therefore
let my life now be precious in thy sight.
15 And the angel of the LORD said unto
Elijah, Go down with him: be not afraid of
him. And he arose, and went down with him
unto the king.
16 And he said unto him, Thus saith the
LORD, Forasmuch as thou hast sent messengers to enquire of Baal-zebub the god of
Ekron, *is it* not because *there is* no God in
Israel to enquire of his word? therefore thou
shalt not come down off that bed on which
thou art gone up, but shalt surely die.
17 ¶ So he died according to the word of
the LORD which Elijah had spoken. And Jehoram reigned in his stead, in the second
year of Jehoram the son of Jehoshaphat
king of Judah; because he had no son.
18 Now the rest of the acts of Ahaziah
which he did, *are* they not written in the
book of the chronicles of the kings of Israel?
2 And it came to pass, when the LORD
would [g]take up Elijah into heaven by a
whirlwind, that Elijah went with [h]Elisha
from Gilgal.
2 And Elijah said unto Elisha, [i]Tarry
here, I pray thee; for the LORD hath sent me
to Beth-el. And Elisha said *unto him, As* the
LORD liveth, and [j]*as* thy soul liveth, I will
not leave thee. So they went down to Beth-
el.
3 And [k]the sons of the prophets that *were*
at Beth-el came forth to Elisha, and said
unto him, Knowest thou that the LORD will
take away thy master from thy head to day?
And he said, Yea, I know *it;* hold ye your
peace.
4 And Elijah said unto him, Elisha, tarry
here, I pray thee; for the LORD hath sent me
to Jericho. And he said, *As* the LORD liveth,
and *as* thy soul liveth, I will not leave thee.
So they came to Jericho.
5 And the sons of the prophets that *were*
at Jericho came to Elisha, and said unto
him, Knowest thou that the LORD will take
away thy master from thy head to day? And
he answered, Yea, I know *it;* hold ye your
peace.
6 And Elijah said unto him, Tarry, I pray
thee, here; for the LORD hath sent me to
Jordan. And he said, *As* the LORD liveth,
and *as* thy soul liveth, I will not leave thee.
And they two went on.
7 And fifty men of the sons of the prophets went, and stood to view afar off: and
they two stood by Jordan.
8 And Elijah took his mantle, and
wrapped *it* together, and smote the waters,
and [l]they were divided hither and thither,
so that they two went over on dry ground.
9 ¶ And it came to pass, when they were
gone over, that Elijah said unto Elisha, Ask
what I shall do for thee, before I be taken
away from thee. And Elisha said, I pray
thee, let a double portion of thy spirit be
upon me.
10 And he said, Thou hast asked a hard
thing: *nevertheless,* if thou see me *when I*
am taken from thee, it shall be so unto thee;
but if not, it shall not be *so.*
11 And it came to pass, as they still went
on, and talked, that, behold, *there appeared*
[m]a chariot of fire, and horses of fire, and
parted them both asunder; and Elijah went
up by a whirlwind into heaven.
12 ¶ And Elisha saw *it,* and he cried, [n]My
father, my father, the chariot of Israel, and
the horsemen thereof. And he saw him no
more: and he took hold of his own clothes,
and rent them in two pieces.
13 He took up also the mantle of Elijah
that fell from him, and went back, and stood
by the bank of Jordan;
14 And he took the mantle of Elijah that
fell from him, and smote the waters, and
said, Where *is* the LORD God of Elijah? and
when he also had smitten the waters, [o]they
parted hither and thither: and Elisha went
over.
15 And when the sons of the prophets
which *were* [p]to view at Jericho saw him,
they said, The spirit of Elijah doth rest on
Elisha. And they came to meet him, and
bowed themselves to the ground before
him.
16 ¶ And they said unto him, Behold now,
there be with thy servants fifty strong men;
let them go, we pray thee, and seek thy master: [q]lest peradventure the Spirit of the
LORD hath taken him up, and cast him upon
some mountain, or into some valley. And he
said, Ye shall not send.
17 And when they urged him till he was
ashamed, he said, Send. They sent therefore
fifty men; and they sought three days, but
found him not.
18 And when they came again to him, (for
he tarried at Jericho,) he said unto them,
Did I not say unto you, Go not?
19 ¶ And the men of the city said unto
Elisha, Behold, I pray thee, the situation of
this city *is* pleasant, as my lord seeth: but
the water *is* naught, and the ground barren.
20 And he said, Bring me a new cruse,
and put salt therein. And they brought *it* to
him.
21 And he went forth unto the spring of
the waters, and [r]cast the salt in there, and
said, Thus saith the LORD, I have healed
these waters; there shall not be from thence
any more death or barren *land.*
22 So the waters were healed unto this
day, according to the saying of Elisha which
he spake.
23 ¶ And he went up from thence unto
Beth-el: and as he was going up by the way,
there came forth little children out of the
city, and mocked him, and said unto him,
Go up, thou bald head; go up, thou bald
head.
24 And he turned back, and looked on

1:13 [f]1 Sam. 26:21; Ps. 72:14
2:1 [g]Gen. 5:24 [h]1 Kings 19:21
2:2 [i]Ruth 1:15 [j]1 Sam. 1:26; ver. 4; ch. 4:30
2:3 [k]1 Kings 20:35; ver. 5; ch. 4:1
2:8 [l]Ex. 14:21; Josh. 3:16; ver. 14
2:11 [m]ch. 6:17; Ps. 104:4
2:12 [n]ch. 13:14
2:14 [o]ver. 8
2:15 [p]ver. 7
2:16 [q]1 Kings 18:12; Ezek. 8:3; Acts 8:39
2:21 [r]Ex. 15:25; ch. 4:41; John 9:6

them, and cursed them in the name of the LORD. And there came forth two she bears out of the wood, and tare forty and two children of them.

25 And he went from thence to mount Carmel, and from thence he returned to Samaria.

3 Now [s]Jehoram the son of Ahab began to reign over Israel in Samaria in the eighteenth year of Jehoshaphat king of Judah, and reigned twelve years.

2 And he wrought evil in the sight of the LORD; but not like his father, and like his mother: for he put away the image of Baal [t]that his father had made.

3 Nevertheless he cleaved unto [u]the sins of Jeroboam the son of Nebat, which made Israel to sin; he departed not therefrom.

4 ¶ And Mesha king of Moab was a sheepmaster, and rendered unto the king of Israel an hundred thousand [v]lambs, and an hundred thousand rams, with the wool.

5 But it came to pass, when [w]Ahab was dead, that the king of Moab rebelled against the king of Israel.

6 ¶ And king Jehoram went out of Samaria the same time, and numbered all Israel.

7 And he went and sent to Jehoshaphat the king of Judah, saying, The king of Moab hath rebelled against me: wilt thou go with me against Moab to battle? And he said, I will go up: [x]I *am* as thou *art*, my people as thy people, *and* my horses as thy horses.

8 And he said, Which way shall we go up? And he answered, The way through the wilderness of Edom.

9 So the king of Israel went, and the king of Judah, and the king of Edom: and they fetched a compass of seven days' journey: and there was no water for the host, and for the cattle that followed them.

10 And the king of Israel said, Alas! that the LORD hath called these three kings together, to deliver them into the hand of Moab!

11 But [y]Jehoshaphat said, *Is there* not here a prophet of the LORD, that we may enquire of the LORD by him? And one of the king of Israel's servants answered and said, Here *is* Elisha the son of Shaphat, which poured water on the hands of Elijah.

12 And Jehoshaphat said, The word of the LORD is with him. So the king of Israel and Jehoshaphat and the king of Edom [z]went down to him.

13 And Elisha said unto the king of Israel, [a]What have I to do with thee? [b]get thee to the prophets of thy father, and to [c]the prophets of thy mother. And the king of Israel said unto him, Nay: for the LORD hath called these three kings together, to deliver them into the hand of Moab.

14 And Elisha said, [d]*As* the LORD of hosts liveth, before whom I stand, surely, were it not that I regard the presence of Jehoshaphat the king of Judah, I would not look toward thee, nor see thee.

15 But now bring me a [e]minstrel. And it came to pass, when the minstrel played, that [f]the hand of the LORD came upon him.

16 And he said, Thus saith the LORD, [g]Make this valley full of ditches.

17 For thus saith the LORD, Ye shall not see wind, neither shall ye see rain; yet that valley shall be filled with water, that ye may drink, both ye, and your cattle, and your beasts.

18 And this is *but* a light thing in the sight of the LORD: he will deliver the Moabites also into your hand.

19 And ye shall smite every fenced city, and every choice city, and shall fell every good tree, and stop all wells of water, and mar every good piece of land with stones.

20 And it came to pass in the morning, when [h]the meat offering was offered, that, behold, there came water by the way of Edom, and the country was filled with water.

21 ¶ And when all the Moabites heard that the kings were come up to fight against them, they gathered all that were able to put on armour, and upward, and stood in the border.

22 And they rose up early in the morning, and the sun shone upon the water, and the Moabites saw the water on the other side *as* red as blood:

23 And they said, This *is* blood: the kings are surely slain, and they have smitten one another: now therefore, Moab, to the spoil.

24 And when they came to the camp of Israel, the Israelites rose up and smote the Moabites, so that they fled before them: but they went forward smiting the Moabites, even in *their* country.

25 And they beat down the cities, and on every good piece of land cast every man his stone, and filled it; and they stopped all the wells of water, and felled all the good trees: only in [i]Kir-haraseth left they the stones thereof; howbeit the slingers went about *it*, and smote it.

26 ¶ And when the king of Moab saw that the battle was too sore for him, he took with him seven hundred men that drew swords, to break through *even* unto the king of Edom: but they could not.

27 Then [j]he took his eldest son that should have reigned in his stead, and offered him *for* a burnt offering upon the wall. And there was great indignation against Israel: [k]and they departed from him, and returned to *their own* land.

4 Now there cried a certain woman of the wives of [l]the sons of the prophets unto Elisha, saying, Thy servant my husband is dead; and thou knowest that thy servant did fear the LORD: and the creditor is come [m]to take unto him my two sons to be bondmen.

2 And Elisha said unto her, What shall I do for thee? tell me, what hast thou in the house? And she said, Thine handmaid hath not any thing in the house, save a pot of oil.

3 Then he said, Go, [n]borrow thee vessels

3:1 [s]ch. 1:17
3:2 [t]1 Kings 16:31
3:3 [u]1 Kings 12:28
3:4 [v]Isa. 16:1
3:5 [w]ch. 1:1
3:7 [x]1 Kings 22:4
3:11 [y]1 Kings 22:7
3:12 [z]ch. 2:25
3:13 [a]Ezek. 14:3 [b]Judg. 10:14; Ruth 1:15 [c]1 Kings 18:19
3:14 [d]1 Kings 17:1; ch. 5:16
3:15 [e]1 Sam. 10:5 [f]Ezek. 1:3
3:16 [g]ch. 4:3
3:20 [h]Ex. 29:39
3:25 [i]Isa. 16:7
3:27 [j]Am. 2:1 [k]ch. 8:20
4:1 [l]1 Kings 20:35 [m]Lev. 25:39; Matt. 18:25
4:3 [n]ch. 3:16

abroad of all thy neighbours, *even* empty vessels; borrow not a few.

4 And when thou art come in, thou shalt shut the door upon thee and upon thy sons, and shalt pour out into all those vessels, and thou shalt set aside that which is full.

5 So she went from him, and shut the door upon her and upon her sons, who brought *the vessels* to her; and she poured out.

6 And it came to pass, when the vessels were full, that she said unto her son, Bring me yet a vessel. And he said unto her, *There is* not a vessel more. And the oil stayed.

7 Then she came and told the man of God. And he said, Go, sell the oil, and pay thy debt, and live thou and thy children of the rest.

8 ¶ And it fell on a day, that Elisha passed to [o]Shunem, where *was* a great woman; and she constrained him to eat bread. And *so* it was, *that* as oft as he passed by, he turned in thither to eat bread.

9 And she said unto her husband, Behold now, I perceive that this *is* an holy man of God, which passeth by us continually.

10 Let us make a little chamber, I pray thee, on the wall; and let us set for him there a bed, and a table, and a stool, and a candlestick: and it shall be, when he cometh to us, that he shall turn in thither.

11 And it fell on a day, that he came thither, and he turned into the chamber, and lay there.

12 And he said to Gehazi his servant, Call this Shunammite. And when he had called her, she stood before him.

13 And he said unto him, Say now unto her, Behold, thou hast been careful for us with all this care; what *is* to be done for thee? wouldest thou be spoken for to the king, or to the captain of the host? And she answered, I dwell among mine own people.

14 And he said, What then *is* to be done for her? And Gehazi answered, Verily she hath no child, and her husband is old.

15 And he said, Call her. And when he had called her, she stood in the door.

16 And he said, [p]About this season, according to the time of life, thou shalt embrace a son. And she said, Nay, my lord, *thou* man of God, [q]do not lie unto thine handmaid.

17 And the woman conceived, and bare a son at that season that Elisha had said unto her, according to the time of life.

18 ¶ And when the child was grown, it fell on a day, that he went out to his father to the reapers.

19 And he said unto his father, My head, my head. And he said to a lad, Carry him to his mother.

20 And when he had taken him, and brought him to his mother, he sat on her knees till noon, and *then* died.

21 And she went up, and laid him on the bed of the man of God, and shut *the door* upon him, and went out.

22 And she called unto her husband, and said, Send me, I pray thee, one of the young men, and one of the asses, that I may run to the man of God, and come again.

23 And he said, Wherefore wilt thou go to him to day? *it is* neither new moon, nor sabbath. And she said, *It shall be* well.

24 Then she saddled an ass, and said to her servant, Drive, and go forward; slack not *thy* riding for me, except I bid thee.

25 So she went and came unto the man of God [r]to mount Carmel. And it came to pass, when the man of God saw her afar off, that he said to Gehazi his servant, Behold, *yonder is* that Shunammite:

26 Run now, I pray thee, to meet her, and say unto her, *Is it* well with thee? *is it* well with thy husband? *is it* well with the child? And she answered, *It is* well.

27 And when she came to the man of God to the hill, she caught him by the feet: but Gehazi came near to thrust her away. And the man of God said, Let her alone; for her soul *is* vexed within her: and the LORD hath hid *it* from me, and hath not told me.

28 Then she said, Did I desire a son of my lord? [s]did I not say, Do not deceive me?

29 Then he said to Gehazi, [t]Gird up thy loins, and take my staff in thine hand, and go thy way: if thou meet any man, [u]salute him not; and if any salute thee, answer him not again: and [v]lay my staff upon the face of the child.

30 And the mother of the child said, [w]*As* the LORD liveth, and *as* thy soul liveth, I will not leave thee. And he arose, and followed her.

31 And Gehazi passed on before them, and laid the staff upon the face of the child; but *there was* neither voice, nor hearing. Wherefore he went again to meet him, and told him, saying, The child is [x]not awaked.

32 And when Elisha was come into the house, behold, the child was dead, *and* laid upon his bed.

33 He [y]went in therefore, and shut the door upon them twain, [z]and prayed unto the LORD.

34 And he went up, and lay upon the child, and put his mouth upon his mouth, and his eyes upon his eyes, and his hands upon his hands: and [a]he stretched himself upon the child; and the flesh of the child waxed warm.

35 Then he returned, and walked in the house to and fro; and went up, [b]and stretched himself upon him: and [c]the child sneezed seven times, and the child opened his eyes.

36 And he called Gehazi, and said, Call this Shunammite. So he called her. And when she was come in unto him, he said, Take up thy son.

37 Then she went in, and fell at his feet, and bowed herself to the ground, and [d]took up her son, and went out.

38 ¶ And Elisha came again to [e]Gilgal: and *there was* a [f]dearth in the land; and the

4:8 [o]Josh. 19:18
4:16 [p]Gen. 18:10 [q]ver. 28
4:25 [r]ch. 2:25
4:28 [s]ver. 16
4:29 [t]1 Kings 18:46; ch. 9:1 [u]Luke 10:4 [v]Ex. 7:19; ch. 2:8; Acts 19:12
4:30 [w]ch. 2:2
4:31 [x]John 11:11
4:33 [y]ver. 4; Matt. 6:6 [z]1 Kings 17:20
4:34 [a]1 Kings 17:21; Acts 20:10
4:35 [b]1 Kings 17:21 [c]ch. 8:1
4:37 [d]1 Kings 17:23; Heb. 11:35
4:38 [e]ch. 2:1 [f]ch. 8:1

sons of the prophets *were* [g]sitting before
him: and he said unto his servant, Set on the
great pot, and seethe pottage for the sons of
the prophets.
39 And one went out into the field to
gather herbs, and found a wild vine, and
gathered thereof wild gourds his lap full,
and came and shred *them* into the pot of
pottage: for they knew *them* not.
40 So they poured out for the men to eat.
And it came to pass, as they were eating of
the pottage, that they cried out, and said,
O *thou* man of God, *there is* [h]death in the
pot. And they could not eat *thereof.*
41 But he said, Then bring meal. And [i]he
cast *it* into the pot; and he said, Pour out for
the people, that they may eat. And there
was no harm in the pot.
42 ¶ And there came a man from [j]Baal-
shalisha, [k]and brought the man of God
bread of the firstfruits, twenty loaves of barley, and full ears of corn in the husk thereof.
And he said, Give unto the people, that they
may eat.
43 And his servitor said, [l]What, should I
set this before an hundred men? He said
again, Give the people, that they may eat:
for thus saith the LORD, [m]They shall eat,
and shall leave *thereof.*
44 So he set *it* before them, and they did
eat, [n]and left *thereof,* according to the word
of the LORD.

5 Now [o]Naaman, captain of the host of
the king of Syria, was [p]a great man
with his master, and honourable, because
by him the LORD had given deliverance unto
Syria: he was also a mighty man in valour,
but he was a leper.
2 And the Syrians had gone out by companies, and had brought away captive out
of the land of Israel a little maid; and she
waited on Naaman's wife.
3 And she said unto her mistress, Would
God my lord *were* with the prophet that *is* in
Samaria! for he would recover him of his
leprosy.
4 And *one* went in, and told his lord, saying, Thus and thus said the maid that *is* of
the land of Israel.
5 And the king of Syria said, Go to, go,
and I will send a letter unto the king of Israel. And he departed, and [q]took with him
ten talents of silver, and six thousand *pieces*
of gold, and ten changes of raiment.
6 And he brought the letter to the king of
Israel, saying, Now when this letter is come
unto thee, behold, I have *therewith* sent Naaman my servant to thee, that thou mayest
recover him of his leprosy.
7 And it came to pass, when the king of
Israel had read the letter, that he rent his
clothes, and said, *Am* I [r]God, to kill and to
make alive, that this man doth send unto me
to recover a man of his leprosy? wherefore
consider, I pray you, and see how he seeketh a quarrel against me.
8 ¶ And it was *so,* when Elisha the man of
God had heard that the king of Israel had

4:38 [g]ch. 2:3; Luke 10:39; Acts 22:3
4:40 [h]Ex. 10:17
4:41 [i]Ex. 15:25; ch. 2:21; John 9:6
4:42 [j]1 Sam. 9:4 [k]1 Sam. 9:7; 1 Cor. 9:11; Gal. 6:6
4:43 [l]Luke 9:13; John 6:9 [m]Luke 9:17; John 6:11
4:44 [n]Matt. 14:20; John 6:13
5:1 [o]Luke 4:27 [p]Ex. 11:3
5:5 [q]1 Sam. 9:8; ch. 8:8
5:7 [r]Gen. 30:2; Deut. 32:39; 1 Sam. 2:6
5:10 [s]ch. 4:41; John 9:7
5:14 [t]Job 33:25 [u]Luke 4:27
5:15 [v]Dan. 2:47 [w]Gen. 33:11
5:16 [x]ch. 3:14 [y]Gen. 14:23; Matt. 10:8; Acts 8:18
5:18 [z]ch. 7:2

rent his clothes, that he sent to the king,
saying, Wherefore hast thou rent thy
clothes? let him come now to me, and he
shall know that there is a prophet in Israel.
9 So Naaman came with his horses and
with his chariot, and stood at the door of the
house of Elisha.
10 And Elisha sent a messenger unto him,
saying, Go and [s]wash in Jordan seven
times, and thy flesh shall come again to
thee, and thou shalt be clean.
11 But Naaman was wroth, and went
away, and said, Behold, I thought, He will
surely come out to me, and stand, and call
on the name of the LORD his God, and strike
his hand over the place, and recover the
leper.
12 *Are* not Abana and Pharpar, rivers of
Damascus, better than all the waters of Israel? may I not wash in them, and be clean?
So he turned and went away in a rage.
13 And his servants came near, and spake
unto him, and said, My father, *if* the prophet
had bid thee *do some* great thing, wouldest
thou not have done *it?* how much rather
then, when he saith to thee, Wash, and be
clean?
14 Then went he down, and dipped himself seven times in Jordan, according to the
saying of the man of God: and [t]his flesh
came again like unto the flesh of a little
child, and [u]he was clean.
15 ¶ And he returned to the man of God,
he and all his company, and came, and
stood before him: and he said, Behold, now
I know that *there is* [v]no God in all the earth,
but in Israel: now therefore, I pray thee,
take [w]a blessing of thy servant.
16 But he said, [x]*As* the LORD liveth, before whom I stand, [y]I will receive none.
And he urged him to take *it;* but he refused.
17 And Naaman said, Shall there not
then, I pray thee, be given to thy servant
two mules' burden of earth? for thy servant
will henceforth offer neither burnt offering
nor sacrifice unto other gods, but unto the
LORD.
18 In this thing the LORD pardon thy servant, *that* when my master goeth into the
house of Rimmon to worship there, and [z]he
leaneth on my hand, and I bow myself in the
house of Rimmon: when I bow down myself
in the house of Rimmon, the LORD pardon
thy servant in this thing.
19 And he said unto him, Go in peace. So
he departed from him a little way.
20 ¶ But Gehazi, the servant of Elisha the
man of God, said, Behold, my master hath
spared Naaman this Syrian, in not receiving
at his hands that which he brought: but, *as*
the LORD liveth, I will run after him, and
take somewhat of him.
21 So Gehazi followed after Naaman.
And when Naaman saw *him* running after
him, he lighted down from the chariot to
meet him, and said, *Is* all well?
22 And he said, All *is* well. My master
hath sent me, saying, Behold, even now

there be come to me from mount Ephraim
two young men of the sons of the prophets:
give them, I pray thee, a talent of silver, and
two changes of garments.
23 And Naaman said, Be content, take
two talents. And he urged him, and bound
two talents of silver in two bags, with two
changes of garments, and laid *them* upon
two of his servants; and they bare *them* before him.
24 And when he came to the tower, he
took *them* from their hand, and bestowed
them in the house: and he let the men go,
and they departed.
25 But he went in, and stood before his
master. And Elisha said unto him, Whence
comest thou, Gehazi? And he said, Thy servant went no whither.
26 And he said unto him, Went not mine
heart *with thee,* when the man turned again
from his chariot to meet thee? *Is it* a time to
receive money, and to receive garments,
and oliveyards, and vineyards, and sheep,
and oxen, and menservants, and maidservants?
27 The leprosy therefore of Naaman
[a]shall cleave unto thee, and unto thy seed
for ever. And he went out from his presence
[b]a leper *as white* as snow.
6 And [c]the sons of the prophets said unto
Elisha, Behold now, the place where we
dwell with thee is too strait for us.
2 Let us go, we pray thee, unto Jordan,
and take thence every man a beam, and let
us make us a place there, where we may
dwell. And he answered, Go ye.
3 And one said, Be content, I pray thee,
and go with thy servants. And he answered,
I will go.
4 So he went with them. And when they
came to Jordan, they cut down wood.
5 But as one was felling a beam, the axe
head fell into the water: and he cried, and
said, Alas, master! for it was borrowed.
6 And the man of God said, Where fell it?
And he shewed him the place. And [d]he cut
down a stick, and cast *it* in thither; and the
iron did swim.
7 Therefore said he, Take *it* up to thee.
And he put out his hand, and took it.
8 ¶ Then the king of Syria warred against
Israel, and took counsel with his servants,
saying, In such and such a place *shall be* my
camp.
9 And the man of God sent unto the king
of Israel, saying, Beware that thou pass not
such a place; for thither the Syrians are
come down.
10 And the king of Israel sent to the place
which the man of God told him and warned
him of, and saved himself there, not once
nor twice.
11 Therefore the heart of the king of Syria
was sore troubled for this thing; and he
called his servants, and said unto them, Will
ye not shew me which of us *is* for the king
of Israel?
12 And one of his servants said, None, my
lord, O king: but Elisha, the prophet that *is*
in Israel, telleth the king of Israel the words
that thou speakest in thy bedchamber.
13 ¶ And he said, Go and spy where he *is,*
that I may send and fetch him. And it was
told him, saying, Behold, *he is* in [e]Dothan.
14 Therefore sent he thither horses, and
chariots, and a great host: and they came by
night, and compassed the city about.
15 And when the servant of the man of
God was risen early, and gone forth, behold, an host compassed the city both with
horses and chariots. And his servant said
unto him, Alas, my master! how shall
we do?
16 And he answered, Fear not: for [f]they
that *be* with us *are* more than they that *be*
with them.
17 And Elisha prayed, and said, LORD, I
pray thee, open his eyes, that he may see.
And the LORD opened the eyes of the young
man; and he saw: and, behold, the mountain
was full of [g]horses and chariots of fire
round about Elisha.
18 And when they came down to him, Elisha prayed unto the LORD, and said, Smite
this people, I pray thee, with blindness. And
[h]he smote them with blindness according
to the word of Elisha.
19 ¶ And Elisha said unto them, This *is*
not the way, neither *is* this the city: follow
me, and I will bring you to the man whom ye
seek. But he led them to Samaria.
20 And it came to pass, when they were
come into Samaria, that Elisha said, LORD,
open the eyes of these *men,* that they may
see. And the LORD opened their eyes, and
they saw; and, behold, *they were* in the
midst of Samaria.
21 And the king of Israel said unto Elisha,
when he saw them, My father, shall I smite
them? shall I smite *them?*
22 And he answered, Thou shalt not smite
them: wouldest thou smite those whom
thou hast taken captive with thy sword and
with thy bow? [i]set bread and water before
them, that they may eat and drink, and go to
their master.
23 And he prepared great provision for
them: and when they had eaten and drunk,
he sent them away, and they went to their
master. So [j]the bands of Syria came no
more into the land of Israel.
24 ¶ And it came to pass after this, that
Ben-hadad king of Syria gathered all his
host, and went up, and besieged Samaria.
25 And there was a great famine in Samaria: and, behold, they besieged it, until
an ass's head was *sold* for fourscore *pieces*
of silver, and the fourth part of a cab of
dove's dung for five *pieces* of silver.
26 And as the king of Israel was passing
by upon the wall, there cried a woman unto
him, saying, Help, my lord, O king.
27 And he said, If the LORD do not help
thee, whence shall I help thee? out of the
barnfloor, or out of the winepress?
28 And the king said unto her, What ail-

5:27 [a]1 Tim. 6:10 [b]Ex. 4:6; Num. 12:10; ch. 15:5
6:1 [c]ch. 4:38
6:6 [d]ch. 2:21
6:13 [e]Gen. 37:17
6:16 [f]2 Chron. 32:7; Ps. 55:18; Rom. 8:31
6:17 [g]ch. 2:11; Ps. 34:7; Zech. 1:8
6:18 [h]Gen. 19:11
6:22 [i]Rom. 12:20
6:23 [j]ch. 5:2; ver. 8

eth thee? And she answered, This woman said unto me, Give thy son, that we may eat him to day, and we will eat my son to morrow.

29 So [k]we boiled my son, and did eat him: and I said unto her on the next day, Give thy son, that we may eat him: and she hath hid her son.

30 ¶ And it came to pass, when the king heard the words of the woman, that he [l]rent his clothes; and he passed by upon the wall, and the people looked, and, behold, *he had* sackcloth within upon his flesh.

31 Then he said, [m]God do so and more also to me, if the head of Elisha the son of Shaphat shall stand on him this day.

32 But Elisha sat in his house, and [n]the elders sat with him; and *the king* sent a man from before him: but ere the messenger came to him, he said to the elders, [o]See ye how this son of [p]a murderer hath sent to take away mine head? look, when the messenger cometh, shut the door, and hold him fast at the door: *is* not the sound of his master's feet behind him?

33 And while he yet talked with them, behold, the messenger came down unto him: and he said, Behold, this evil *is* of the LORD; [q]what should I wait for the LORD any longer?

7 Then Elisha said, Hear ye the word of the LORD; thus saith the LORD, [r]To morrow about this time *shall* a measure of fine flour *be sold* for a shekel, and two measures of barley for a shekel, in the gate of Samaria.

2 [s]Then a lord on whose hand the king leaned answered the man of God, and said, Behold, [t]*if* the LORD would make windows in heaven, might this thing be? And he said, Behold, thou shalt see *it* with thine eyes, but shalt not eat thereof.

3 ¶ And there were four leprous men [u]at the entering in of the gate: and they said one to another, Why sit we here until we die?

4 If we say, We will enter into the city, then the famine *is* in the city, and we shall die there: and if we sit still here, we die also. Now therefore come, and let us fall unto the host of the Syrians: if they save us alive, we shall live; and if they kill us, we shall but die.

5 And they rose up in the twilight, to go unto the camp of the Syrians: and when they were come to the uttermost part of the camp of Syria, behold, *there was* no man there.

6 For the Lord had made the host of the Syrians [v]to hear a noise of chariots, and a noise of horses, *even* the noise of a great host: and they said one to another, Lo, the king of Israel hath hired against us [w]the kings of the Hittites, and the kings of the Egyptians, to come upon us.

7 Wherefore they [x]arose and fled in the twilight, and left their tents, and their horses, and their asses, even the camp as it *was,* and fled for their life.

8 And when these lepers came to the uttermost part of the camp, they went into one tent, and did eat and drink, and carried thence silver, and gold, and raiment, and went and hid *it;* and came again, and entered into another tent, and carried thence *also,* and went and hid *it.*

9 Then they said one to another, We do not well: this day *is* a day of good tidings, and we hold our peace: if we tarry till the morning light, some mischief will come upon us: now therefore come, that we may go and tell the king's household.

10 So they came and called unto the porter of the city: and they told them, saying, We came to the camp of the Syrians, and, behold, *there was* no man there, neither voice of man, but horses tied, and asses tied, and the tents as they *were.*

11 And he called the porters; and they told *it* to the king's house within.

12 ¶ And the king arose in the night, and said unto his servants, I will now shew you what the Syrians have done to us. They know that we *be* hungry; therefore are they gone out of the camp to hide themselves in the field, saying, When they come out of the city, we shall catch them alive, and get into the city.

13 And one of his servants answered and said, Let *some* take, I pray thee, five of the horses that remain, which are left in the city, (behold, they *are* as all the multitude of Israel that are left in it: behold, *I say,* they *are* even as all the multitude of the Israelites that are consumed:) and let us send and see.

14 They took therefore two chariot horses; and the king sent after the host of the Syrians, saying, Go and see.

15 And they went after them unto Jordan: and, lo, all the way *was* full of garments and vessels, which the Syrians had cast away in their haste. And the messengers returned, and told the king.

16 And the people went out, and spoiled the tents of the Syrians. So a measure of fine flour was *sold* for a shekel, and two measures of barley for a shekel, [y]according to the word of the LORD.

17 ¶ And the king appointed the lord on whose hand he leaned to have the charge of the gate: and the people trode upon him in the gate, and he died, [z]as the man of God had said, who spake when the king came down to him.

18 And it came to pass as the man of God had spoken to the king, saying, [a]Two measures of barley for a shekel, and a measure of fine flour for a shekel, shall be to morrow about this time in the gate of Samaria:

19 And that lord answered the man of God, and said, Now, behold, *if* the LORD should make windows in heaven, might such a thing be? And he said, Behold, thou shalt see it with thine eyes, but shalt not eat thereof.

6:29 [k]Lev. 26:29; Deut. 28:53
6:30 [l]1 Kings 21:27
6:31 [m]Ruth 1:17; 1 Kings 19:2
6:32 [n]Ezek. 8:1 [o]Luke 13:32 [p]1 Kings 18:4
6:33 [q]Job 2:9
7:1 [r]ver. 18
7:2 [s]ver. 17 [t]Mal. 3:10
7:3 [u]Lev. 13:46
7:6 [v]2 Sam. 5:24; ch. 19:7; Job 15:21 [w]1 Kings 10:29
7:7 [x]Ps. 48:4; Prov. 28:1
7:16 [y]ver. 1
7:17 [z]ch. 6:32; ver. 2
7:18 [a]ver. 1

20 And so it fell out unto him: for the people trode upon him in the gate, and he died.

8 Then spake Elisha unto the woman, [b]whose son he had restored to life, saying, Arise, and go thou and thine household, and sojourn wheresoever thou canst sojourn: for the LORD [c]hath called for a famine; and it shall also come upon the land seven years.

2 And the woman arose, and did after the saying of the man of God: and she went with her household, and sojourned in the land of the Philistines seven years.

3 And it came to pass at the seven years' end, that the woman returned out of the land of the Philistines: and she went forth to cry unto the king for her house and for her land.

4 And the king talked with [d]Gehazi the servant of the man of God, saying, Tell me, I pray thee, all the great things that Elisha hath done.

5 And it came to pass, as he was telling the king how he had [e]restored a dead body to life, that, behold, the woman, whose son he had restored to life, cried to the king for her house and for her land. And Gehazi said, My lord, O king, this *is* the woman, and this *is* her son, whom Elisha restored to life.

6 And when the king asked the woman, she told him. So the king appointed unto her a certain officer, saying, Restore all that *was* hers, and all the fruits of the field since the day that she left the land, even until now.

7 ¶ And Elisha came to Damascus; and Ben-hadad the king of Syria was sick; and it was told him, saying, The man of God is come hither.

8 And the king said unto [f]Hazael, [g]Take a present in thine hand, and go, meet the man of God, and [h]enquire of the LORD by him, saying, Shall I recover of this disease?

9 So Hazael went to meet him, and took a present with him, even of every good thing of Damascus, forty camels' burden, and came and stood before him, and said, Thy son Ben-hadad king of Syria hath sent me to thee, saying, Shall I recover of this disease?

10 And Elisha said unto him, Go, say unto him, Thou mayest certainly recover: howbeit the LORD hath shewed me that [i]he shall surely die.

11 And he settled his countenance stedfastly, until he was ashamed: and the man of God [j]wept.

12 And Hazael said, Why weepeth my lord? And he answered, Because I know [k]the evil that thou wilt do unto the children of Israel: their strong holds wilt thou set on fire, and their young men wilt thou slay with the sword, and [l]wilt dash their children, and rip up their women with child.

13 And Hazael said, But what, [m]*is* thy servant a dog, that he should do this great thing? And Elisha answered, [n]The LORD hath shewed me that thou *shalt be* king over Syria.

14 So he departed from Elisha, and came to his master; who said to him, What said Elisha to thee? And he answered, He told me *that* thou shouldest surely recover.

15 And it came to pass on the morrow, that he took a thick cloth, and dipped *it* in water, and spread *it* on his face, so that he died: and Hazael reigned in his stead.

16 ¶ And in the fifth year of Joram the son of Ahab king of Israel, Jehoshaphat *being* then king of Judah, [o]Jehoram the son of Jehoshaphat king of Judah began to reign.

17 [p]Thirty and two years old was he when he began to reign; and he reigned eight years in Jerusalem.

18 And he walked in the way of the kings of Israel, as did the house of Ahab: for [q]the daughter of Ahab was his wife: and he did evil in the sight of the LORD.

19 Yet the LORD would not destroy Judah for David his servant's sake, [r]as he promised him to give him alway a light, *and* to his children.

20 ¶ In his days [s]Edom revolted from under the hand of Judah, [t]and made a king over themselves.

21 So Joram went over to Zair, and all the chariots with him: and he rose by night, and smote the Edomites which compassed him about, and the captains of the chariots: and the people fled into their tents.

22 Yet Edom revolted from under the hand of Judah unto this day. [u]Then Libnah revolted at the same time.

23 And the rest of the acts of Joram, and all that he did, *are* they not written in the book of the chronicles of the kings of Judah?

24 And Joram slept with his fathers, and was buried with his fathers in the city of David: and [v]Ahaziah his son reigned in his stead.

25 ¶ In the twelfth year of Joram the son of Ahab king of Israel did Ahaziah the son of Jehoram king of Judah begin to reign.

26 [w]Two and twenty years old *was* Ahaziah when he began to reign; and he reigned one year in Jerusalem. And his mother's name *was* Athaliah, the daughter of Omri king of Israel.

27 [x]And he walked in the way of the house of Ahab, and did evil in the sight of the LORD, as *did* the house of Ahab: for he *was* the son in law of the house of Ahab.

28 ¶ And he went [y]with Joram the son of Ahab to the war against Hazael king of Syria in Ramoth-gilead; and the Syrians wounded Joram.

29 And [z]king Joram went back to be healed in Jezreel of the wounds which the Syrians had given him at Ramah, when he fought against Hazael king of Syria. [a]And Ahaziah the son of Jehoram king of Judah went down to see Joram the son of Ahab in Jezreel, because he was sick.

8:1 *b*ch. 4:35 *c*Ps. 105:16; Hag. 1:11
8:4 *d*ch. 5:27
8:5 *e*ch. 4:35
8:8 *f*1 Kings 19:15 *g*1 Sam. 9:7; 1 Kings 14:3; ch. 5:5 *h*ch. 1:2
8:10 *i*ver. 15
8:11 *j*Luke 19:41
8:12 *k*ch. 10:32; Am. 1:3 *l*ch. 15:16; Hos. 13:16; Am. 1:13
8:13 *m*1 Sam. 17:43 *n*1 Kings 19:15
8:16 *o*2 Chron. 21:3
8:17 *p*2 Chron. 21:5
8:18 *q*ver. 26
8:19 *r*2 Sam. 7:13; 1 Kings 11:36; 2 Chron. 21:7
8:20 *s*Gen. 27:40; ch. 3:27; 2 Chron. 21:8 *t*1 Kings 22:47
8:22 *u*2 Chron. 21:10
8:24 *v*2 Chron. 22:1
8:26 *w*2 Chron. 22:2
8:27 *x*2 Chron. 22:3
8:28 *y*2 Chron. 22:5
8:29 *z*ch. 9:15 *a*ch. 9:16; 2 Chron. 22:6

9 And Elisha the prophet called one of
[b]the children of the prophets, and said
unto him, [c]Gird up thy loins, and take this
box of oil in thine hand, [d]and go to Ramoth-
gilead:
2 And when thou comest thither, look out
there Jehu the son of Jehoshaphat the son
of Nimshi, and go in, and make him arise up
from among [e]his brethren, and carry him
to an inner chamber;
3 Then [f]take the box of oil, and pour *it* on
his head, and say, Thus saith the LORD, I
have anointed thee king over Israel. Then
open the door, and flee, and tarry not.
4 ¶ So the young man, *even* the young
man the prophet, went to Ramoth-gilead.
5 And when he came, behold, the captains of the host *were* sitting; and he said, I
have an errand to thee, O captain. And Jehu
said, Unto which of all us? And he said, To
thee, O captain.
6 And he arose, and went into the house;
and he poured the oil on his head, and said
unto him, [g]Thus saith the LORD God of Israel, I have anointed thee king over the people of the LORD, *even* over Israel.
7 And thou shalt smite the house of Ahab
thy master, that I may avenge the blood of
my servants the prophets, and the blood of
all the servants of the LORD, [h]at the hand
of Jezebel.
8 For the whole house of Ahab shall perish: and [i]I will cut off from Ahab [j]him that
pisseth against the wall, and [k]him that is
shut up and left in Israel:
9 And I will make the house of Ahab like
the house of [l]Jeroboam the son of Nebat,
and like the house of [m]Baasha the son of
Ahijah:
10 [n]And the dogs shall eat Jezebel in the
portion of Jezreel, and *there shall be* none
to bury *her*. And he opened the door, and
fled.
11 ¶ Then Jehu came forth to the servants
of his lord: and *one* said unto him, *Is* all
well? wherefore came [o]this mad *fellow* to
thee? And he said unto them, Ye know the
man, and his communication.
12 And they said, *It is* false; tell us now.
And he said, Thus and thus spake he to
me, saying, Thus saith the LORD, I have
anointed thee king over Israel.
13 Then they hasted, and [p]took every
man his garment, and put *it* under him on
the top of the stairs, and blew with trumpets, saying, Jehu is king.
14 So Jehu the son of Jehoshaphat the
son of Nimshi conspired against Joram.
(Now Joram had kept Ramoth-gilead, he
and all Israel, because of Hazael king of
Syria.
15 But [q]king Joram was returned to be
healed in Jezreel of the wounds which the
Syrians had given him, when he fought with
Hazael king of Syria.) And Jehu said, If it be
your minds, *then* let none go forth *nor* escape out of the city to go to tell *it* in Jezreel.
16 So Jehu rode in a chariot, and went to
Jezreel; for Joram lay there. [r]And Ahaziah
king of Judah was come down to see Joram.
17 And there stood a watchman on the
tower in Jezreel, and he spied the company
of Jehu as he came, and said, I see a company. And Joram said, Take an horseman,
and send to meet them, and let him say, *Is
it* peace?
18 So there went one on horseback to
meet him, and said, Thus saith the king, *Is
it* peace? And Jehu said, What hast thou to
do with peace? turn thee behind me. And
the watchman told, saying, The messenger
came to them, but he cometh not again.
19 Then he sent out a second on horseback, which came to them, and said, Thus
saith the king, *Is it* peace? And Jehu answered, What hast thou to do with peace?
turn thee behind me.
20 And the watchman told, saying, He
came even unto them, and cometh not
again: and the driving *is* like the driving of
Jehu the son of Nimshi; for he driveth furiously.
21 And Joram said, Make ready. And his
chariot was made ready. And [s]Joram king
of Israel and Ahaziah king of Judah went
out, each in his chariot, and they went out
against Jehu, and met him in the portion of
Naboth the Jezreelite.
22 And it came to pass, when Joram saw
Jehu, that he said, *Is it* peace, Jehu? And
he answered, What peace, so long as the
whoredoms of thy mother Jezebel and her
witchcrafts *are so* many?
23 And Joram turned his hands, and fled,
and said to Ahaziah, *There is* treachery,
O Ahaziah.
24 And Jehu drew a bow with his full
strength, and smote Jehoram between his
arms, and the arrow went out at his heart,
and he sunk down in his chariot.
25 Then said *Jehu* to Bidkar his captain,
Take up, *and* cast him in the portion of the
field of Naboth the Jezreelite: for remember
how that, when I and thou rode together
after Ahab his father, [t]the LORD laid this
burden upon him;
26 Surely I have seen yesterday the blood
of Naboth, and the blood of his sons, saith
the LORD; and [u]I will requite thee in this
plat, saith the LORD. Now therefore take
and cast him into the plat *of ground*, according to the word of the LORD.
27 ¶ But when Ahaziah the king of Judah
saw *this*, he fled by the way of the garden
house. And Jehu followed after him, and
said, Smite him also in the chariot. *And they
did so* at the going up to Gur, which *is* by
Ibleam. And he fled to [v]Megiddo, and died
there.
28 And his servants carried him in a chariot to Jerusalem, and buried him in his sepulchre with his fathers in the city of David.
29 And in the eleventh year of Joram the
son of Ahab began Ahaziah to reign over
Judah.
30 ¶ And when Jehu was come to Jezreel,

9:1 [b]1 Kings 20:35 [c]ch. 4:29; Jer. 1:17 [d]ch. 8:28
9:2 [e]ver. 5
9:3 [f]1 Kings 19:16
9:6 [g]1 Kings 19:16; 2 Chron. 22:7
9:7 [h]1 Kings 18:4
9:8 [i]1 Kings 14:10 [j]1 Sam. 25:22 [k]Deut. 32:36
9:9 [l]1 Kings 14:10 [m]1 Kings 16:3
9:10 [n]1 Kings 21:23; ver. 35
9:11 [o]Jer. 29:26; John 10:20; Acts 26:24; 1 Cor. 4:10
9:13 [p]Matt. 21:7
9:15 [q]ch. 8:29
9:16 [r]ch. 8:29
9:21 [s]2 Chron. 22:7
9:25 [t]1 Kings 21:29
9:26 [u]1 Kings 21:19
9:27 [v]2 Chron. 22:9

Jezebel heard *of it;* [w]and she painted her face, and tired her head, and looked out at a window.

31 And as Jehu entered in at the gate, she said, [x]*Had* Zimri peace, who slew his master?

32 And he lifted up his face to the window, and said, Who *is* on my side? who? And there looked out to him two *or* three eunuchs.

33 And he said, Throw her down. So they threw her down: and *some* of her blood was sprinkled on the wall, and on the horses: and he trode her under foot.

34 And when he was come in, he did eat and drink, and said, Go, see now this cursed *woman,* and bury her: for [y]she *is* a king's daughter.

35 And they went to bury her: but they found no more of her than the skull, and the feet, and the palms of *her* hands.

36 Wherefore they came again, and told him. And he said, This *is* the word of the LORD, which he spake by his servant Elijah the Tishbite, saying, [z]In the portion of Jezreel shall dogs eat the flesh of Jezebel:

37 And the carcase of Jezebel shall be [a]as dung upon the face of the field in the portion of Jezreel; *so* that they shall not say, This *is* Jezebel.

10 And Ahab had seventy sons in Samaria. And Jehu wrote letters, and sent to Samaria, unto the rulers of Jezreel, to the elders, and to them that brought up Ahab's *children,* saying,

2 Now as soon as this letter cometh to you, seeing your master's sons *are* with you, and *there are* with you chariots and horses, a fenced city also, and armour;

3 Look even out the best and meetest of your master's sons, and set *him* on his father's throne, and fight for your master's house.

4 But they were exceedingly afraid, and said, Behold, two kings stood not before him: how then shall we stand?

5 And he that *was* over the house, and he that *was* over the city, the elders also, and the bringers up *of the children,* sent to Jehu, saying, We *are* thy servants, and will do all that thou shalt bid us; we will not make any king: do thou *that which is* good in thine eyes.

6 Then he wrote a letter the second time to them, saying, If ye *be* mine, and *if* ye will hearken unto my voice, take ye the heads of the men your master's sons, and come to me to Jezreel by to morrow this time. Now the king's sons, *being* seventy persons, *were* with the great men of the city, which brought them up.

7 And it came to pass, when the letter came to them, that they took the king's sons, and [b]slew seventy persons, and put their heads in baskets, and sent him *them* to Jezreel.

8 ¶ And there came a messenger, and told him, saying, They have brought the heads of the king's sons. And he said, Lay ye them in two heaps at the entering in of the gate until the morning.

9 And it came to pass in the morning, that he went out, and stood, and said to all the people, Ye *be* righteous: behold, [c]I conspired against my master, and slew him: but who slew all these?

10 Know now that there shall [d]fall unto the earth nothing of the word of the LORD, which the LORD spake concerning the house of Ahab: for the LORD hath done *that* which he spake [e]by his servant Elijah.

11 So Jehu slew all that remained of the house of Ahab in Jezreel, and all his great men, and his kinsfolks, and his priests, until he left him none remaining.

12 ¶ And he arose and departed, and came to Samaria. *And* as he *was* at the shearing house in the way,

13 [f]Jehu met with the brethren of Ahaziah king of Judah, and said, Who *are* ye? And they answered, We *are* the brethren of Ahaziah; and we go down to salute the children of the king and the children of the queen.

14 And he said, Take them alive. And they took them alive, and slew them at the pit of the shearing house, *even* two and forty men; neither left he any of them.

15 ¶ And when he was departed thence, he lighted on [g]Jehonadab the son of [h]Rechab *coming* to meet him: and he saluted him, and said to him, Is thine heart right, as my heart *is* with thy heart? And Jehonadab answered, It is. If it be, [i]give *me* thine hand. And he gave *him* his hand; and he took him up to him into the chariot.

16 And he said, Come with me, and see my [j]zeal for the LORD. So they made him ride in his chariot.

17 And when he came to Samaria, [k]he slew all that remained unto Ahab in Samaria, till he had destroyed him, according to the saying of the LORD, [l]which he spake to Elijah.

18 ¶ And Jehu gathered all the people together, and said unto them, [m]Ahab served Baal a little; *but* Jehu shall serve him much.

19 Now therefore call unto me all the [n]prophets of Baal, all his servants, and all his priests; let none be wanting: for I have a great sacrifice *to do* to Baal; whosoever shall be wanting, he shall not live. But Jehu did *it* in subtilty, to the intent that he might destroy the worshippers of Baal.

20 And Jehu said, Proclaim a solemn assembly for Baal. And they proclaimed *it.*

21 And Jehu sent through all Israel: and all the worshippers of Baal came, so that there was not a man left that came not. And they came into the [o]house of Baal; and the house of Baal was full from one end to another.

22 And he said unto him that *was* over the vestry, Bring forth vestments for all the worshippers of Baal. And he brought them forth vestments.

9:30 [w]Ezek. 23:40
9:31 [x]1 Kings 16:9-20
9:34 [y]1 Kings 16:31
9:36 [z]1 Kings 21:23
9:37 [a]Ps. 83:10
10:7 [b]1 Kings 21:21
10:9 [c]ch. 9:14
10:10 [d]1 Sam. 3:19 [e]1 Kings 21:19
10:13 [f]ch. 8:29; 2 Chron. 22:8
10:15 [g]Jer. 35:6 [h]1 Chron. 2:55 [i]Ezra 10:19
10:16 [j]1 Kings 19:10
10:17 [k]ch. 9:8; 2 Chron. 22:8 [l]1 Kings 21:21
10:18 [m]1 Kings 16:31
10:19 [n]1 Kings 22:6
10:21 [o]1 Kings 16:32

23 And Jehu went, and Jehonadab the son of Rechab, into the house of Baal, and said unto the worshippers of Baal, Search, and look that there be here with you none of the servants of the LORD, but the worshippers of Baal only.

24 And when they went in to offer sacrifices and burnt offerings, Jehu appointed fourscore men without, and said, *If* any of the men whom I have brought into your hands escape, *he that letteth him go,* [p]his life *shall be* for the life of him.

25 And it came to pass, as soon as he had made an end of offering the burnt offering, that Jehu said to the guard and to the captains, Go in, *and* slay them; let none come forth. And they smote them with the edge of the sword; and the guard and the captains cast *them* out, and went to the city of the house of Baal.

26 And they brought forth the [q]images out of the house of Baal, and burned them.

27 And they brake down the image of Baal, and brake down the house of Baal, [r]and made it a draught house unto this day.

28 Thus Jehu destroyed Baal out of Israel.

29 ¶ Howbeit, *from* the sins of Jeroboam the son of Nebat, who made Israel to sin, Jehu departed not from after them, *to wit,* [s]the golden calves that *were* in Beth-el, and that *were* in Dan.

30 And the LORD said unto Jehu, Because thou hast done well in executing *that which is* right in mine eyes, *and* hast done unto the house of Ahab according to all that *was* in mine heart, [t]thy children of the fourth *generation* shall sit on the throne of Israel.

31 But Jehu took no heed to walk in the law of the LORD God of Israel with all his heart: for he departed not from [u]the sins of Jeroboam, which made Israel to sin.

32 ¶ In those days the LORD began to cut Israel short: and [v]Hazael smote them in all the coasts of Israel;

33 From Jordan eastward, all the land of Gilead, the Gadites, and the Reubenites, and the Manassites, from Aroer, which *is* by the river Arnon, even [w]Gilead and Bashan.

34 Now the rest of the acts of Jehu, and all that he did, and all his might, *are* they not written in the book of the chronicles of the kings of Israel?

35 And Jehu slept with his fathers: and they buried him in Samaria. And Jehoahaz his son reigned in his stead.

36 And the time that Jehu reigned over Israel in Samaria *was* twenty and eight years.

11 And when [x]Athaliah [y]the mother of Ahaziah saw that her son was dead, she arose and destroyed all the seed royal.

2 But Jehosheba, the daughter of king Joram, sister of Ahaziah, took Joash the son of Ahaziah, and stole him from among the king's sons *which were* slain; and they hid him, *even* him and his nurse, in the bedchamber from Athaliah, so that he was not slain.

3 And he was with her hid in the house of the LORD six years. And Athaliah did reign over the land.

4 ¶ And [z]the seventh year Jehoiada sent and fetched the rulers over hundreds, with the captains and the guard, and brought them to him into the house of the LORD, and made a covenant with them, and took an oath of them in the house of the LORD, and shewed them the king's son.

5 And he commanded them, saying, This *is* the thing that ye shall do; A third part of you that enter in [a]on the sabbath shall even be keepers of the watch of the king's house;

6 And a third part *shall be* at the gate of Sur; and a third part at the gate behind the guard: so shall ye keep the watch of the house, that it be not broken down.

7 And two parts of all you that go forth on the sabbath, even they shall keep the watch of the house of the LORD about the king.

8 And ye shall compass the king round about, every man with his weapons in his hand: and he that cometh within the ranges, let him be slain: and be ye with the king as he goeth out and as he cometh in.

9 [b]And the captains over the hundreds did according to all *things* that Jehoiada the priest commanded: and they took every man his men that were to come in on the sabbath, with them that should go out on the sabbath, and came to Jehoiada the priest.

10 And to the captains over hundreds did the priest give king David's spears and shields, that *were* in the temple of the LORD.

11 And the guard stood, every man with his weapons in his hand, round about the king, from the right corner of the temple to the left corner of the temple, *along* by the altar and the temple.

12 And he brought forth the king's son, and put the crown upon him, and *gave him* the testimony; and they made him king, and anointed him; and they clapped their hands, and said, [c]God save the king.

13 ¶ [d]And when Athaliah heard the noise of the guard *and* of the people, she came to the people into the temple of the LORD.

14 And when she looked, behold, the king stood by [e]a pillar, as the manner *was,* and the princes and the trumpeters by the king, and all the people of the land rejoiced, and blew with trumpets: and Athaliah rent her clothes, and cried, Treason, Treason.

15 But Jehoiada the priest commanded the captains of the hundreds, the officers of the host, and said unto them, Have her forth without the ranges: and him that followeth her kill with the sword. For the priest had said, Let her not be slain in the house of the LORD.

16 And they laid hands on her; and she went by the way by the which the horses came into the king's house: and there was she slain.

17 ¶ [f]And Jehoiada made a covenant between the LORD and the king and the peo-

10:24 [p]1 Kings 20:39
10:26 [q]1 Kings 14:23
10:27 [r]Ezra 6:11; Dan. 2:5
10:29 [s]1 Kings 12:28
10:30 [t]ver. 35; ch. 13:1
10:31 [u]1 Kings 14:16
10:32 [v]ch. 8:12
10:33 [w]Am. 1:3
11:1 [x]2 Chron. 22:10 [y]ch. 8:26
11:4 [z]2 Chron. 23:1
11:5 [a]1 Chron. 9:25
11:9 [b]2 Chron. 23:8
11:12 [c]1 Sam. 10:24
11:13 [d]2 Chron. 23:12
11:14 [e]ch. 23:3; 2 Chron. 34:31
11:17 [f]2 Chron. 23:16

ple, that they should be the LORD's people;
[g]between the king also and the people.
18 And all the people of the land went
into the [h]house of Baal, and brake it down;
his altars and his images [i]brake they in
pieces thoroughly, and slew Mattan the
priest of Baal before the altars. And [j]the
priest appointed officers over the house of
the LORD.
19 And he took the rulers over hundreds,
and the captains, and the guard, and all the
people of the land; and they brought down
the king from the house of the LORD, and
came by the way of the gate of the guard to
the king's house. And he sat on the throne
of the kings.
20 And all the people of the land rejoiced,
and the city was in quiet: and they slew
Athaliah with the sword *beside* the king's
house.
21 [k]Seven years old *was* Jehoash when
he began to reign.

12 In the seventh year of Jehu [l]Jehoash
began to reign; and forty years
reigned he in Jerusalem. And his mother's
name *was* Zibiah of Beer-sheba.
2 And Jehoash did *that which was* right
in the sight of the LORD all his days wherein
Jehoiada the priest instructed him.
3 But [m]the high places were not taken
away: the people still sacrificed and burnt
incense in the high places.
4 ¶ And Jehoash said to the priests, [n]All
the money of the dedicated things that is
brought into the house of the LORD, *even*
[o]the money of every one that passeth *the
account*, the money that every man is set at,
and all the money that [p]cometh into any
man's heart to bring into the house of the
LORD,
5 Let the priests take *it* to them, every
man of his acquaintance: and let them repair the breaches of the house, wheresoever
any breach shall be found.
6 But it was *so, that* in the three and
twentieth year of king Jehoash [q]the priests
had not repaired the breaches of the house.
7 [r]Then king Jehoash called for Jehoiada
the priest, and the *other* priests, and said
unto them, Why repair ye not the breaches
of the house? now therefore receive no
more money of your acquaintance, but deliver it for the breaches of the house.
8 And the priests consented to receive no
more money of the people, neither to repair
the breaches of the house.
9 But Jehoiada the priest took [s]a chest,
and bored a hole in the lid of it, and set it
beside the altar, on the right side as one
cometh into the house of the LORD: and the
priests that kept the door put therein all the
money *that was* brought into the house of
the LORD.
10 And it was *so*, when they saw that
there was much money in the chest, that the
king's scribe and the high priest came up,
and they put up in bags, and told the money
that was found in the house of the LORD.

11 And they gave the money, being told,
into the hands of them that did the work,
that had the oversight of the house of the
LORD: and they laid it out to the carpenters
and builders, that wrought upon the house
of the LORD,
12 And to masons, and hewers of stone,
and to buy timber and hewed stone to repair
the breaches of the house of the LORD, and
for all that was laid out for the house to
repair *it*.
13 Howbeit [t]there were not made for the
house of the LORD bowls of silver, snuffers,
basons, trumpets, any vessels of gold, or
vessels of silver, of the money *that was*
brought into the house of the LORD:
14 But they gave that to the workmen,
and repaired therewith the house of the
LORD.
15 Moreover [u]they reckoned not with the
men, into whose hand they delivered the
money to be bestowed on workmen: for
they dealt faithfully.
16 [v]The trespass money and sin money
was not brought into the house of the LORD:
[w]it was the priests'.
17 ¶ Then [x]Hazael king of Syria went up,
and fought against Gath, and took it: and
[y]Hazael set his face to go up to Jerusalem.
18 And Jehoash king of Judah [z]took all
the hallowed things that Jehoshaphat, and
Jehoram, and Ahaziah, his fathers, kings
of Judah, had dedicated, and his own hallowed things, and all the gold *that was*
found in the treasures of the house of the
LORD, and in the king's house, and sent *it* to
Hazael king of Syria: and he went away
from Jerusalem.
19 ¶ And the rest of the acts of Joash, and
all that he did, *are* they not written in the
book of the chronicles of the kings of Judah?
20 And [a]his servants arose, and made a
conspiracy, and slew Joash in the house of
Millo, which goeth down to Silla.
21 For [b]Jozachar the son of Shimeath,
and Jehozabad the son of Shomer, his servants, smote him, and he died; and they buried him with his fathers in the city of David:
and [c]Amaziah his son reigned in his stead.

13 In the three and twentieth year of Joash the son of Ahaziah king of Judah
Jehoahaz the son of Jehu began to reign
over Israel in Samaria, *and reigned* seventeen years.
2 And he did *that which was* evil in the
sight of the LORD, and followed the sins of
Jeroboam the son of Nebat, which made Israel to sin; he departed not therefrom.
3 ¶ And [d]the anger of the LORD was kindled against Israel, and he delivered them
into the hand of [e]Hazael king of Syria, and
into the hand of Ben-hadad the son of Hazael, all *their* days.
4 And Jehoahaz [f]besought the LORD, and
the LORD hearkened unto him: for [g]he saw
the oppression of Israel, because the king of
Syria oppressed them.

11:17 [g]2 Sam. 5:3
11:18 [h]ch. 10:26 [i]Deut. 12:3; 2 Chron. 12:17 [j]2 Chron. 23:18
11:21 [k]2 Chron. 24:1
12:1 [l]2 Chron. 24:1
12:3 [m]1 Kings 15:14; ch. 14:4
12:4 [n]ch. 22:4 [o]Ex. 30:13 [p]Ex. 35:5; 1 Chron. 29:9
12:6 [q]2 Chron. 24:5
12:7 [r]2 Chron. 24:6
12:9 [s]2 Chron. 24:8
12:13 [t]2 Chron. 24:14
12:15 [u]ch. 22:7
12:16 [v]Lev. 5:15 [w]Lev. 7:7; Num. 18:9
12:17 [x]ch. 8:12 [y]2 Chron. 24:23
12:18 [z]1 Kings 15:18; ch. 18:15
12:20 [a]ch. 14:5; 2 Chron. 24:25
12:21 [b]2 Chron. 24:26 [c]2 Chron. 24:27
13:3 [d]Judg. 2:14 [e]ch. 8:12
13:4 [f]Ps. 78:34 [g]Ex. 3:7; ch. 14:26

5 ([h]And the LORD gave Israel a saviour, so that they went out from under the hand of the Syrians: and the children of Israel dwelt in their tents, as beforetime.

6 Nevertheless they departed not from the sins of the house of Jeroboam, who made Israel sin, *but* walked therein: [i]and there remained the grove also in Samaria.)

7 Neither did he leave of the people to Jehoahaz but fifty horsemen, and ten chariots, and ten thousand footmen; for the king of Syria had destroyed them, [j]and had made them like the dust by threshing.

8 ¶ Now the rest of the acts of Jehoahaz, and all that he did, and his might, *are* they not written in the book of the chronicles of the kings of Israel?

9 And Jehoahaz slept with his fathers; and they buried him in Samaria: and Joash his son reigned in his stead.

10 ¶ In the thirty and seventh year of Joash king of Judah began Jehoash the son of Jehoahaz to reign over Israel in Samaria, *and reigned* sixteen years.

11 And he did *that which was* evil in the sight of the LORD; he departed not from all the sins of Jeroboam the son of Nebat, who made Israel sin: *but* he walked therein.

12 [k]And the rest of the acts of Joash, and [l]all that he did, and [m]his might wherewith he fought against Amaziah king of Judah, *are* they not written in the book of the chronicles of the kings of Israel?

13 And Joash slept with his fathers; and Jeroboam sat upon his throne: and Joash was buried in Samaria with the kings of Israel.

14 ¶ Now Elisha was fallen sick of his sickness whereof he died. And Joash the king of Israel came down unto him, and wept over his face, and said, O my father, my father, [n]the chariot of Israel, and the horsemen thereof.

15 And Elisha said unto him, Take bow and arrows. And he took unto him bow and arrows.

16 And he said to the king of Israel, Put thine hand upon the bow. And he put his hand *upon it:* and Elisha put his hands upon the king's hands.

17 And he said, Open the window eastward. And he opened *it*. Then Elisha said, Shoot. And he shot. And he said, The arrow of the LORD's deliverance, and the arrow of deliverance from Syria: for thou shalt smite the Syrians in [o]Aphek, till thou have consumed *them.*

18 And he said, Take the arrows. And he took *them.* And he said unto the king of Israel, Smite upon the ground. And he smote thrice, and stayed.

19 And the man of God was wroth with him, and said, Thou shouldest have smitten five or six times; then hadst thou smitten Syria till thou hadst consumed *it:* [p]whereas now thou shalt smite Syria *but* thrice.

20 ¶ And Elisha died, and they buried him. And the bands of the Moabites invaded the land at the coming in of the year.

21 And it came to pass, as they were burying a man, that, behold, they spied a band *of men;* and they cast the man into the sepulchre of Elisha: and when the man was let down, and touched the bones of Elisha, he revived, and stood up on his feet.

22 ¶ But [q]Hazael king of Syria oppressed Israel all the days of Jehoahaz.

23 [r]And the LORD was gracious unto them, and had compassion on them, and [s]had respect unto them, [t]because of his covenant with Abraham, Isaac, and Jacob, and would not destroy them, neither cast he them from his presence as yet.

24 So Hazael king of Syria died; and Benhadad his son reigned in his stead.

25 And Jehoash the son of Jehoahaz took again out of the hand of Ben-hadad the son of Hazael the cities, which he had taken out of the hand of Jehoahaz his father by war. [u]Three times did Joash beat him, and recovered the cities of Israel.

14

In [v]the second year of Joash son of Jehoahaz king of Israel reigned [w]Amaziah the son of Joash king of Judah.

2 He was twenty and five years old when he began to reign, and reigned twenty and nine years in Jerusalem. And his mother's name *was* Jehoaddan of Jerusalem.

3 And he did *that which was* right in the sight of the LORD, yet not like David his father: he did according to all things as Joash his father did.

4 [x]Howbeit the high places were not taken away: as yet the people did sacrifice and burnt incense on the high places.

5 ¶ And it came to pass, as soon as the kingdom was confirmed in his hand, that he slew his servants [y]which had slain the king his father.

6 But the children of the murderers he slew not: according unto that which is written in the book of the law of Moses, wherein the LORD commanded, saying, [z]The fathers shall not be put to death for the children, nor the children be put to death for the fathers; but every man shall be put to death for his own sin.

7 [a]He slew of Edom in [b]the valley of salt ten thousand, and took Selah by war, [c]and called the name of it Joktheel unto this day.

8 ¶ [d]Then Amaziah sent messengers to Jehoash, the son of Jehoahaz son of Jehu, king of Israel, saying, Come, let us look one another in the face.

9 And Jehoash the king of Israel sent to Amaziah king of Judah, saying, [e]The thistle that *was* in Lebanon sent to the [f]cedar that *was* in Lebanon, saying, Give thy daughter to my son to wife: and there passed by a wild beast that *was* in Lebanon, and trode down the thistle.

10 Thou hast indeed smitten Edom, and [g]thine heart hath lifted thee up: glory *of this,* and tarry at home: for why shouldest

13:5 [h]ver. 25
13:6 [i]1 Kings 16:33
13:7 [j]Am. 1:3
13:12 [k]ch. 14:15 [l]ver. 14 [m]ch. 14:9; 2 Chron. 25:17
13:14 [n]ch. 2:12
13:17 [o]1 Kings 20:26
13:19 [p]ver. 25
13:22 [q]ch. 8:12
13:23 [r]ch. 14:27 [s]Ex. 2:24 [t]Ex. 32:13
13:25 [u]ver. 18
14:1 [v]ch. 13:10 [w]2 Chron. 25:1
14:4 [x]ch. 12:3
14:5 [y]ch. 12:20
14:6 [z]Deut. 24:16; Ezek. 18:4
14:7 [a]2 Chron. 25:11 [b]2 Sam. 8:13; Ps. 60, title [c]Josh. 15:38
14:8 [d]2 Chron. 25:17
14:9 [e]Judg. 9:8 [f]1 Kings 4:33
14:10 [g]Deut. 8:14; 2 Chron. 32:25; Ezek. 28:2; Hab. 2:4

thou meddle to *thy* hurt, that thou shouldest fall, *even* thou, and Judah with thee?

11 But Amaziah would not hear. Therefore Jehoash king of Israel went up; and he and Amaziah king of Judah looked one another in the face at [h]Beth-shemesh, which *belongeth* to Judah.

12 And Judah was put to the worse before Israel; and they fled every man to their tents.

13 And Jehoash king of Israel took Amaziah king of Judah, the son of Jehoash the son of Ahaziah, at Beth-shemesh, and came to Jerusalem, and brake down the wall of Jerusalem from [i]the gate of Ephraim unto [j]the corner gate, four hundred cubits.

14 And he took all [k]the gold and silver, and all the vessels that were found in the house of the LORD, and in the treasures of the king's house, and hostages, and returned to Samaria.

15 ¶ [l]Now the rest of the acts of Jehoash which he did, and his might, and how he fought with Amaziah king of Judah, *are* they not written in the book of the chronicles of the kings of Israel?

16 And Jehoash slept with his fathers, and was buried in Samaria with the kings of Israel; and Jeroboam his son reigned in his stead.

17 ¶ [m]And Amaziah the son of Joash king of Judah lived after the death of Jehoash son of Jehoahaz king of Israel fifteen years.

18 And the rest of the acts of Amaziah, *are* they not written in the book of the chronicles of the kings of Judah?

19 Now [n]they made a conspiracy against him in Jerusalem: and he fled to Lachish; but they sent after him to [o]Lachish, and slew him there.

20 And they brought him on horses: and he was buried at Jerusalem with his fathers in the city of David.

21 ¶ And all the people of Judah took [p]Azariah, which *was* sixteen years old, and made him king instead of his father Amaziah.

22 He built [q]Elath, and restored it to Judah, after that the king slept with his fathers.

23 ¶ In the fifteenth year of Amaziah the son of Joash king of Judah Jeroboam the son of Joash king of Israel began to reign in Samaria, *and reigned* forty and one years.

24 And he did *that which was* evil in the sight of the LORD: he departed not from all the sins of Jeroboam the son of Nebat, who made Israel to sin.

25 He restored the coast of Israel [r]from the entering of Hamath unto [s]the sea of the plain, according to the word of the LORD God of Israel, which he spake by the hand of his servant [t]Jonah, the son of Amittai, the prophet, which *was* of [u]Gath-hepher.

26 For the LORD [v]saw the affliction of Israel, *that it was* very bitter: for [w]*there was* not any shut up, nor any left, nor any helper for Israel.

27 [x]And the LORD said not that he would blot out the name of Israel from under heaven: but he saved them by the hand of Jeroboam the son of Joash.

28 ¶ Now the rest of the acts of Jeroboam, and all that he did, and his might, how he warred, and how he recovered Damascus, and Hamath, [y]*which belonged* to Judah, for Israel, *are* they not written in the book of the chronicles of the kings of Israel?

29 And Jeroboam slept with his fathers, *even* with the kings of Israel; and [z]Zachariah his son reigned in his stead.

15 In the twenty and seventh year of Jeroboam king of Israel [a]began [b]Azariah son of Amaziah king of Judah to reign.

2 Sixteen years old was he when he began to reign, and he reigned two and fifty years in Jerusalem. And his mother's name *was* Jecholiah of Jerusalem.

3 And he did *that which was* right in the sight of the LORD, according to all that his father Amaziah had done;

4 [c]Save that the high places were not removed: the people sacrificed and burnt incense still on the high places.

5 ¶ And the LORD [d]smote the king, so that he was a leper unto the day of his death, and [e]dwelt in a several house. And Jotham the king's son *was* over the house, judging the people of the land.

6 And the rest of the acts of Azariah, and all that he did, *are* they not written in the book of the chronicles of the kings of Judah?

7 So Azariah slept with his fathers; and [f]they buried him with his fathers in the city of David: and Jotham his son reigned in his stead.

8 ¶ In the thirty and eighth year of Azariah king of Judah did Zachariah the son of Jeroboam reign over Israel in Samaria six months.

9 And he did *that which was* evil in the sight of the LORD, as his fathers had done: he departed not from the sins of Jeroboam the son of Nebat, who made Israel to sin.

10 And Shallum the son of Jabesh conspired against him, and [g]smote him before the people, and slew him, and reigned in his stead.

11 And the rest of the acts of Zachariah, behold, they *are* written in the book of the chronicles of the kings of Israel.

12 This *was* [h]the word of the LORD which he spake unto Jehu, saying, Thy sons shall sit on the throne of Israel unto the fourth *generation*. And so it came to pass.

13 ¶ Shallum the son of Jabesh began to reign in the nine and thirtieth year of [i]Uzziah king of Judah; and he reigned a full month in Samaria.

14 For Menahem the son of Gadi went up from [j]Tirzah, and came to Samaria, and smote Shallum the son of Jabesh in Samaria, and slew him, and reigned in his stead.

14:11 [h]Josh. 19:38
14:13 [i]Neh. 8:16 [j]Jer. 31:38; Zech. 14:10
14:14 [k]1 Kings 7:51
14:15 [l]ch. 13:12
14:17 [m]2 Chron. 25:25
14:19 [n]2 Chron. 25:27 [o]Josh. 10:31
14:21 [p]ch. 15:13
14:22 [q]ch. 16:6; 2 Chron. 26:2
14:25 [r]Num. 13:21 [s]Deut. 3:17 [t]Jonah 1:1; Matt. 12:39 [u]Josh. 19:13
14:26 [v]ch. 13:4 [w]Deut. 32:36
14:27 [x]ch. 13:5
14:28 [y]2 Sam. 8:6; 1 Kings 11:24; 2 Chron. 8:3
14:29 [z]ch. 15:8
15:1 [a]ch. 14:21; 2 Chron. 26:1 [b]ver. 13
15:4 [c]ver. 35; ch. 12:3
15:5 [d]2 Chron. 26:19-21 [e]Lev. 13:46
15:7 [f]2 Chron. 26:23
15:10 [g]Am. 7:9
15:12 [h]ch. 10:30
15:13 [i]Matt. 1:8
15:14 [j]1 Kings 14:17

15 And the rest of the acts of Shallum, and his conspiracy which he made, behold, they *are* written in the book of the chronicles of the kings of Israel.

16 Then Menahem smote [k]Tiphsah, and all that *were* therein, and the coasts thereof from Tirzah: because they opened not *to him,* therefore he smote *it; and* all [l]the women therein that were with child he ripped up.

17 ¶ In the nine and thirtieth year of Azariah king of Judah began Menahem the son of Gadi to reign over Israel, *and reigned* ten years in Samaria.

18 And he did *that which was* evil in the sight of the LORD: he departed not all his days from the sins of Jeroboam the son of Nebat, who made Israel to sin.

19 *And* [m]Pul the king of Assyria came against the land: and Menahem gave Pul a thousand talents of silver, that his hand might be with him to [n]confirm the kingdom in his hand.

20 And Menahem exacted the money of Israel, *even* of all the mighty men of wealth, of each man fifty shekels of silver, to give to the king of Assyria. So the king of Assyria turned back, and stayed not there in the land.

21 ¶ And the rest of the acts of Menahem, and all that he did, *are* they not written in the book of the chronicles of the kings of Israel?

22 And Menahem slept with his fathers; and Pekahiah his son reigned in his stead.

23 ¶ In the fiftieth year of Azariah king of Judah Pekahiah the son of Menahem began to reign over Israel in Samaria, *and reigned* two years.

24 And he did *that which was* evil in the sight of the LORD: he departed not from the sins of Jeroboam the son of Nebat, who made Israel to sin.

25 But Pekah the son of Remaliah, a captain of his, conspired against him, and smote him in Samaria, in the palace of the king's house, with Argob and Arieh, and with him fifty men of the Gileadites: and he killed him, and reigned in his room.

26 And the rest of the acts of Pekahiah, and all that he did, behold, they *are* written in the book of the chronicles of the kings of Israel.

27 ¶ In the two and fiftieth year of Azariah king of Judah [o]Pekah the son of Remaliah began to reign over Israel in Samaria, *and reigned* twenty years.

28 And he did *that which was* evil in the sight of the LORD: he departed not from the sins of Jeroboam the son of Nebat, who made Israel to sin.

29 In the days of Pekah king of Israel [p]came Tiglath-pileser king of Assyria, and took [q]Ijon, and Abel-beth-maachah, and Janoah, and Kedesh, and Hazor, and Gilead, and Galilee, all the land of Naphtali, and carried them captive to Assyria.

30 And Hoshea the son of Elah made a conspiracy against Pekah the son of Remaliah, and smote him, and slew him, and [r]reigned in his stead, in the twentieth year of Jotham the son of Uzziah.

31 And the rest of the acts of Pekah, and all that he did, behold, they *are* written in the book of the chronicles of the kings of Israel.

32 ¶ In the second year of Pekah the son of Remaliah king of Israel began [s]Jotham the son of Uzziah king of Judah to reign.

33 Five and twenty years old was he when he began to reign, and he reigned sixteen years in Jerusalem. And his mother's name *was* Jerusha, the daughter of Zadok.

34 And he did *that which was* right in the sight of the LORD: he did [t]according to all that his father Uzziah had done.

35 ¶ [u]Howbeit the high places were not removed: the people sacrificed and burned incense still in the high places. [v]He built the higher gate of the house of the LORD.

36 ¶ Now the rest of the acts of Jotham, and all that he did, *are* they not written in the book of the chronicles of the kings of Judah?

37 In those days the LORD began to send against Judah [w]Rezin the king of Syria, and [x]Pekah the son of Remaliah.

38 And Jotham slept with his fathers, and was buried with his fathers in the city of David his father: and Ahaz his son reigned in his stead.

16 In the seventeenth year of Pekah the son of Remaliah [y]Ahaz the son of Jotham king of Judah began to reign.

2 Twenty years old *was* Ahaz when he began to reign, and reigned sixteen years in Jerusalem, and did not *that which was* right in the sight of the LORD his God, like David his father.

3 But he walked in the way of the kings of Israel, yea, [z]and made his son to pass through the fire, according to the [a]abominations of the heathen, whom the LORD cast out from before the children of Israel.

4 And he sacrificed and burnt incense in the high places, and [b]on the hills, and under every green tree.

5 ¶ [c]Then Rezin king of Syria and Pekah son of Remaliah king of Israel came up to Jerusalem to war: and they besieged Ahaz, but could not overcome *him.*

6 At that time Rezin king of Syria [d]recovered Elath to Syria, and drave the Jews from Elath: and the Syrians came to Elath, and dwelt there unto this day.

7 So Ahaz sent messengers [e]to Tiglath-pileser king of Assyria, saying, I *am* thy servant and thy son: come up, and save me out of the hand of the king of Syria, and out of the hand of the king of Israel, which rise up against me.

8 And Ahaz [f]took the silver and gold that was found in the house of the LORD, and in the treasures of the king's house, and sent *it for* a present to the king of Assyria.

9 And the king of Assyria hearkened unto

15:16 [k]1 Kings 4:24 [l]ch. 8:12
15:19 [m]1 Chron. 5:26; Isa. 9:1; Hos. 8:9 [n]ch. 14:5
15:27 [o]Isa. 7:1
15:29 [p]1 Chron. 5:26; Isa. 9:1 [q]1 Kings 15:20
15:30 [r]ch. 17:1; Hos. 10:3
15:32 [s]2 Chron. 27:1
15:34 [t]ver. 3
15:35 [u]ver. 4 [v]2 Chron. 27:3
15:37 [w]ch. 16:5; Isa. 7:1 [x]ver. 27
16:1 [y]2 Chron. 28:1
16:3 [z]Lev. 18:21; 2 Chron. 28:3; Ps. 106:37 [a]Deut. 12:31
16:4 [b]Deut. 12:2; 1 Kings 14:23
16:5 [c]Isa. 7:1
16:6 [d]ch. 14:22
16:7 [e]ch. 15:29
16:8 [f]ch. 12:18; 2 Chron. 28:21

him: for the king of Assyria went up against Damascus, and [g]took it, and carried *the people of* it captive to Kir, and slew Rezin.

10 ¶ And king Ahaz went to Damascus to meet Tiglath-pileser king of Assyria, and saw an altar that *was* at Damascus: and king Ahaz sent to Urijah the priest the fashion of the altar, and the pattern of it, according to all the workmanship thereof.

11 And Urijah the priest built an altar according to all that king Ahaz had sent from Damascus: so Urijah the priest made *it* against king Ahaz came from Damascus.

12 And when the king was come from Damascus, the king saw the altar: and [h]the king approached to the altar, and offered thereon.

13 And he burnt his burnt offering and his meat offering, and poured his drink offering, and sprinkled the blood of his peace offerings, upon the altar.

14 And he brought also the [i]brasen altar, which *was* before the LORD, from the forefront of the house, from between the altar and the house of the LORD, and put it on the north side of the altar.

15 And king Ahaz commanded Urijah the priest, saying, Upon the great altar burn [j]the morning burnt offering, and the evening meat offering, and the king's burnt sacrifice, and his meat offering, with the burnt offering of all the people of the land, and their meat offering, and their drink offerings; and sprinkle upon it all the blood of the burnt offering, and all the blood of the sacrifice: and the brasen altar shall be for me to enquire *by*.

16 Thus did Urijah the priest, according to all that king Ahaz commanded.

17 ¶ [k]And king Ahaz cut off [l]the borders of the bases, and removed the laver from off them; and took down [m]the sea from off the brasen oxen that *were* under it, and put it upon a pavement of stones.

18 And the covert for the sabbath that they had built in the house, and the king's entry without, turned he from the house of the LORD for the king of Assyria.

19 ¶ Now the rest of the acts of Ahaz which he did, *are* they not written in the book of the chronicles of the kings of Judah?

20 And Ahaz slept with his fathers, and [n]was buried with his fathers in the city of David: and Hezekiah his son reigned in his stead.

17 In the twelfth year of Ahaz king of Judah began [o]Hoshea the son of Elah to reign in Samaria over Israel nine years.

2 And he did *that which was* evil in the sight of the LORD, but not as the kings of Israel that were before him.

3 ¶ Against him came up [p]Shalmaneser king of Assyria; and Hoshea became his servant, and gave him presents.

4 And the king of Assyria found conspiracy in Hoshea: for he had sent messengers to So king of Egypt, and brought no present to the king of Assyria, as *he had done* year by year: therefore the king of Assyria shut him up, and bound him in prison.

5 ¶ Then [q]the king of Assyria came up throughout all the land, and went up to Samaria, and besieged it three years.

6 ¶ [r]In the ninth year of Hoshea the king of Assyria took Samaria, and [s]carried Israel away into Assyria, [t]and placed them in Halah and in Habor *by* the river of Gozan, and in the cities of the Medes.

7 For *so* it was, that the children of Israel had sinned against the LORD their God, which had brought them up out of the land of Egypt, from under the hand of Pharaoh king of Egypt, and had feared other gods,

8 And [u]walked in the statutes of the heathen, whom the LORD cast out from before the children of Israel, and of the kings of Israel, which they had made.

9 And the children of Israel did secretly *those* things that *were* not right against the LORD their God, and they built them high places in all their cities, [v]from the tower of the watchmen to the fenced city.

10 [w]And they set them up images and [x]groves [y]in every high hill, and under every green tree:

11 And there they burnt incense in all the high places, as *did* the heathen whom the LORD carried away before them; and wrought wicked things to provoke the LORD to anger:

12 For they served idols, [z]whereof the LORD had said unto them, [a]Ye shall not do this thing.

13 Yet the LORD testified against Israel, and against Judah, by all the prophets, *and by* all [b]the seers, saying, [c]Turn ye from your evil ways, and keep my commandments *and* my statutes, according to all the law which I commanded your fathers, and which I sent to you by my servants the prophets.

14 Notwithstanding they would not hear, but [d]hardened their necks, like to the neck of their fathers, that did not believe in the LORD their God.

15 And they rejected his statutes, [e]and his covenant that he made with their fathers, and his testimonies which he testified against them; and they followed [f]vanity, and [g]became vain, and went after the heathen that *were* round about them, *concerning* whom the LORD had charged them, that they should [h]not do like them.

16 And they left all the commandments of the LORD their God, and [i]made them molten images, *even* two calves, [j]and made a grove, and worshipped all the host of heaven, [k]and served Baal.

17 [l]And they caused their sons and their daughters to pass through the fire, and [m]used divination and enchantments, and [n]sold themselves to do evil in the sight of the LORD, to provoke him to anger.

18 Therefore the LORD was very angry

16:9 [g]Am. 1:5
16:12 [h]2 Chron. 26:16
16:14 [i]2 Chron. 4:1
16:15 [j]Ex. 29:39
16:17 [k]2 Chron. 28:24 [l]1 Kings 7:27 [m]1 Kings 7:23
16:20 [n]2 Chron. 28:27
17:1 [o]ch. 15:30
17:3 [p]ch. 18:9
17:5 [q]ch. 18:9
17:6 [r]ch. 18:10; Hos. 13:16 [s]Lev. 26:32; Deut. 28:36 [t]1 Chron. 5:26
17:8 [u]Lev. 18:3; Deut. 18:9; ch. 16:3
17:9 [v]ch. 18:8
17:10 [w]1 Kings 14:23; Isa. 57:5 [x]Ex. 34:13; Deut. 16:21; Mic. 5:14 [y]Deut. 12:2; ch. 16:4
17:12 [z]Ex. 20:3; Lev. 26:1; Deut. 5:7 [a]Deut. 4:19
17:13 [b]1 Sam. 9:9 [c]Jer. 18:11
17:14 [d]Deut. 31:27; Prov. 29:1
17:15 [e]Deut. 29:25 [f]Deut. 32:21; 1 Kings 16:13; 1 Cor. 8:4 [g]Ps. 115:8; Rom. 1:21 [h]Deut. 12:30
17:16 [i]Ex. 32:8; 1 Kings 12:28 [j]1 Kings 14:15 [k]1 Kings 16:31; ch. 11:18
17:17 [l]Lev. 18:21; ch. 16:3; Ezek. 23:37 [m]Deut. 18:10 [n]1 Kings 21:20

with Israel, and removed them out of his sight: there was none left [o]but the tribe of Judah only.

19 Also [p]Judah kept not the commandments of the LORD their God, but walked in the statutes of Israel which they made.

20 And the LORD rejected all the seed of Israel, and afflicted them, and [q]delivered them into the hand of spoilers, until he had cast them out of his sight.

21 For [r]he rent Israel from the house of David; and [s]they made Jeroboam the son of Nebat king: and Jeroboam drave Israel from following the LORD, and made them sin a great sin.

22 For the children of Israel walked in all the sins of Jeroboam which he did; they departed not from them;

23 Until the LORD removed Israel out of his sight, [t]as he had said by all his servants the prophets. [u]So was Israel carried away out of their own land to Assyria unto this day.

24 ¶ [v]And the king of Assyria brought *men* [w]from Babylon, and from Cuthah, and from [x]Ava, and from Hamath, and from Sepharvaim, and placed *them* in the cities of Samaria instead of the children of Israel: and they possessed Samaria, and dwelt in the cities thereof.

25 And so it was at the beginning of their dwelling there, *that* they feared not the LORD: therefore the LORD sent lions among them, which slew *some* of them.

26 Wherefore they spake to the king of Assyria, saying, The nations which thou hast removed, and placed in the cities of Samaria, know not the manner of the God of the land: therefore he hath sent lions among them, and, behold, they slay them, because they know not the manner of the God of the land.

27 Then the king of Assyria commanded, saying, Carry thither one of the priests whom ye brought from thence; and let them go and dwell there, and let him teach them the manner of the God of the land.

28 Then one of the priests whom they had carried away from Samaria came and dwelt in Beth-el, and taught them how they should fear the LORD.

29 Howbeit every nation made gods of their own, and put *them* in the houses of the high places which the Samaritans had made, every nation in their cities wherein they dwelt.

30 And the men of [y]Babylon made Succoth-benoth, and the men of Cuth made Nergal, and the men of Hamath made Ashima,

31 [z]And the Avites made Nibhaz and Tartak, and the Sepharvites [a]burnt their children in fire to Adrammelech and Anammelech, the gods of Sepharvaim.

32 So they feared the LORD, [b]and made unto themselves of the lowest of them priests of the high places, which sacrificed for them in the houses of the high places.

33 [c]They feared the LORD, and served their own gods, after the manner of the nations whom they carried away from thence.

34 Unto this day they do after the former manners: they fear not the LORD, neither do they after their statutes, or after their ordinances, or after the law and commandment which the LORD commanded the children of Jacob, [d]whom he named Israel;

35 With whom the LORD had made a covenant, and charged them, saying, [e]Ye shall not fear other gods, nor [f]bow yourselves to them, nor serve them, nor sacrifice to them:

36 But the LORD, who brought you up out of the land of Egypt with great power and [g]a stretched out arm, [h]him shall ye fear, and him shall ye worship, and to him shall ye do sacrifice.

37 And the statutes, and the ordinances, and the law, and the commandment, which he wrote for you, [i]ye shall observe to do for evermore; and ye shall not fear other gods.

38 And the covenant that I have made with you [j]ye shall not forget; neither shall ye fear other gods.

39 But the LORD your God ye shall fear; and he shall deliver you out of the hand of all your enemies.

40 Howbeit they did not hearken, but they did after their former manner.

41 [k]So these nations feared the LORD, and served their graven images, both their children, and their children's children: as did their fathers, so do they unto this day.

18 Now it came to pass in the third year of Hoshea son of Elah king of Israel, *that* [l]Hezekiah the son of Ahaz king of Judah began to reign.

2 Twenty and five years old was he when he began to reign; and he reigned twenty and nine years in Jerusalem. His mother's name also *was* [m]Abi, the daughter of Zachariah.

3 And he did *that which was* right in the sight of the LORD, according to all that David his father did.

4 ¶ [n]He removed the high places, and brake the images, and cut down the groves, and brake in pieces the [o]brasen serpent that Moses had made: for unto those days the children of Israel did burn incense to it: and he called it Nehushtan.

5 He [p]trusted in the LORD God of Israel; [q]so that after him was none like him among all the kings of Judah, nor *any* that were before him.

6 For he [r]clave to the LORD, *and* departed not from following him, but kept his commandments, which the LORD commanded Moses.

7 And the LORD [s]was with him; *and* he [t]prospered whithersoever he went forth: and he [u]rebelled against the king of Assyria, and served him not.

8 [v]He smote the Philistines, *even* unto Gaza, and the borders thereof, [w]from the tower of the watchmen to the fenced city.

9 ¶ And [x]it came to pass in the fourth

17:18 o1 Kings 11:13
17:19 pJer. 3:8
17:20 qch. 13:3
17:21 r1 Kings 11:11 s1 Kings 12:20
17:23 t1 Kings 14:16 uver. 6
17:24 vEzra 4:2 wver. 30 xch. 18:34
17:30 yver. 24
17:31 zEzra 4:9 aLev. 18:21; Deut. 12:31
17:32 b1 Kings 12:31
17:33 cZeph. 1:5
17:34 dGen. 32:28; 1 Kings 11:31
17:35 eJudg. 6:10 fEx. 20:5
17:36 gEx. 6:6 hDeut. 10:20
17:37 iDeut. 5:32
17:38 jDeut. 4:23
17:41 kver. 32
18:1 l2 Chron. 28:27; Matt. 1:9
18:2 m2 Chron. 29:1
18:4 n2 Chron. 31:1 oNum. 21:9
18:5 pch. 19:10; Job 13:15; Ps. 13:5 qch. 23:25
18:6 rDeut. 10:20; Josh. 23:8
18:7 s2 Chron. 15:2 t1 Sam. 18:5; Ps. 60:12 uch. 16:7
18:8 v1 Chron. 4:41; Isa. 14:29 wch. 17:9
18:9 xch. 17:3

year of king Hezekiah, which *was* the seventh year of Hoshea son of Elah king of Israel, *that* Shalmaneser king of Assyria came up against Samaria, and besieged it.

10 And at the end of three years they took it: *even* in the sixth year of Hezekiah, that *is* [y]the ninth year of Hoshea king of Israel, Samaria was taken.

11 [z]And the king of Assyria did carry away Israel unto Assyria, and put them [a]in Halah and in Habor *by* the river of Gozan, and in the cities of the Medes:

12 [b]Because they obeyed not the voice of the LORD their God, but transgressed his covenant, *and* all that Moses the servant of the LORD commanded, and would not hear *them,* nor do *them.*

13 ¶ Now [c]in the fourteenth year of king Hezekiah did Sennacherib king of Assyria come up against all the fenced cities of Judah, and took them.

14 And Hezekiah king of Judah sent to the king of Assyria to Lachish, saying, I have offended; return from me: that which thou puttest on me will I bear. And the king of Assyria appointed unto Hezekiah king of Judah three hundred talents of silver and thirty talents of gold.

15 And Hezekiah [d]gave *him* all the silver that was found in the house of the LORD, and in the treasures of the king's house.

16 At that time did Hezekiah cut off *the gold from* the doors of the temple of the LORD, and *from* the pillars which Hezekiah king of Judah had overlaid, and gave it to the king of Assyria.

17 ¶ And the king of Assyria sent Tartan and Rabsaris and Rab-shakeh from Lachish to king Hezekiah with a great host against Jerusalem. And they went up and came to Jerusalem. And when they were come up, they came and stood by the conduit of the upper pool, [e]which *is* in the highway of the fuller's field.

18 And when they had called to the king, there came out to them Eliakim the son of Hilkiah, which *was* over the household, and Shebna the scribe, and Joah the son of Asaph the recorder.

19 And Rab-shakeh said unto them, Speak ye now to Hezekiah, thus saith the great king, the king of Assyria, [f]What confidence *is* this wherein thou trustest?

20 Thou sayest, (but *they are but* vain words,) *I have* counsel and strength for the war. Now on whom dost thou trust, that thou rebellest against me?

21 [g]Now, behold, thou trustest upon the staff of this bruised reed, *even* upon Egypt, on which if a man lean, it will go into his hand, and pierce it: so *is* Pharaoh king of Egypt unto all that trust on him.

22 But if ye say unto me, We trust in the LORD our God: *is* not that he, [h]whose high places and whose altars Hezekiah hath taken away, and hath said to Judah and Jerusalem, Ye shall worship before this altar in Jerusalem?

23 Now therefore, I pray thee, give pledges to my lord the king of Assyria, and I will deliver thee two thousand horses, if thou be able on thy part to set riders upon them.

24 How then wilt thou turn away the face of one captain of the least of my master's servants, and put thy trust on Egypt for chariots and for horsemen?

25 Am I now come up without the LORD against this place to destroy it? The LORD said to me, Go up against this land, and destroy it.

26 Then said Eliakim the son of Hilkiah, and Shebna, and Joah, unto Rab-shakeh, Speak, I pray thee, to thy servants in the Syrian language; for we understand *it:* and talk not with us in the Jews' language in the ears of the people that *are* on the wall.

27 But Rab-shakeh said unto them, Hath my master sent me to thy master, and to thee, to speak these words? *hath he* not *sent me* to the men which sit on the wall, that they may eat their own dung, and drink their own piss with you?

28 Then Rab-shakeh stood and cried with a loud voice in the Jews' language, and spake, saying, Hear the word of the great king, the king of Assyria:

29 Thus saith the king, [i]Let not Hezekiah deceive you: for he shall not be able to deliver you out of his hand:

30 Neither let Hezekiah make you trust in the LORD, saying, The LORD will surely deliver us, and this city shall not be delivered into the hand of the king of Assyria.

31 Hearken not to Hezekiah: for thus saith the king of Assyria, Make *an agreement* with me by a present, and come out to me, and *then* eat ye every man of his own vine, and every one of his fig tree, and drink ye every one the waters of his cistern:

32 Until I come and take you away to a land like your own land, [j]a land of corn and wine, a land of bread and vineyards, a land of oil olive and of honey, that ye may live, and not die: and hearken not unto Hezekiah, when he persuadeth you, saying, The LORD will deliver us.

33 [k]Hath any of the gods of the nations delivered at all his land out of the hand of the king of Assyria?

34 [l]Where *are* the gods of Hamath, and of Arpad? where *are* the gods of Sepharvaim, Hena, and [m]Ivah? have they delivered Samaria out of mine hand?

35 Who *are* they among all the gods of the countries, that have delivered their country out of mine hand, [n]that the LORD should deliver Jerusalem out of mine hand?

36 But the people held their peace, and answered him not a word: for the king's commandment was, saying, Answer him not.

37 Then came Eliakim the son of Hilkiah, which *was* over the household, and Shebna the scribe, and Joah the son of Asaph the recorder, to Hezekiah [o]with *their* clothes

18:10 [y]ch. 17:6
18:11 [z]ch. 17:6 [a]1 Chron. 5:26
18:12 [b]ch. 17:7; Dan. 9:6
18:13 [c]2 Chron. 32:1; Isa. 36:1
18:15 [d]ch. 16:8
18:17 [e]Isa. 7:3
18:19 [f]2 Chron. 32:10
18:21 [g]Ezek. 29:6
18:22 [h]ver. 4; 2 Chron. 31:1
18:29 [i]2 Chron. 32:15
18:32 [j]Deut. 8:7
18:33 [k]ch. 19:12; 2 Chron. 32:14; Isa. 10:10
18:34 [l]ch. 19:13 [m]ch. 17:24
18:35 [n]Dan. 3:15
18:37 [o]Isa. 33:7

rent, and told him the words of Rab-shakeh.

19

And [p]it came to pass, when king Hezekiah heard *it,* that he rent his clothes, and covered himself with sackcloth, and went into the house of the LORD.

2 And he sent Eliakim, which *was* over the household, and Shebna the scribe, and the elders of the priests, covered with sackcloth, to [q]Isaiah the prophet the son of Amoz.

3 And they said unto him, Thus saith Hezekiah, This day *is* a day of trouble, and of rebuke, and blasphemy: for the children are come to the birth, and *there is* not strength to bring forth.

4 [r]It may be the LORD thy God will hear all the words of Rab-shakeh, [s]whom the king of Assyria his master hath sent to reproach the living God; and will [t]reprove the words which the LORD thy God hath heard: wherefore lift up *thy* prayer for the remnant that are left.

5 So the servants of king Hezekiah came to Isaiah.

6 ¶ [u]And Isaiah said unto them, Thus shall ye say to your master, Thus saith the LORD, Be not afraid of the words which thou hast heard, with which the [v]servants of the king of Assyria have blasphemed me.

7 Behold, I will send [w]a blast upon him, and he shall hear a rumour, and shall return to his own land; and I will cause him to fall by the sword in his own land.

8 ¶ So Rab-shakeh returned, and found the king of Assyria warring against Libnah: for he had heard that he was departed [x]from Lachish.

9 And [y]when he heard say of Tirhakah king of Ethiopia, Behold, he is come out to fight against thee: he sent messengers again unto Hezekiah, saying,

10 Thus shall ye speak to Hezekiah king of Judah, saying, Let not thy God [z]in whom thou trustest deceive thee, saying, Jerusalem shall not be delivered into the hand of the king of Assyria.

11 Behold, thou hast heard what the kings of Assyria have done to all lands, by destroying them utterly: and shalt thou be delivered?

12 [a]Have the gods of the nations delivered them which my fathers have destroyed; *as* Gozan, and Haran, and Rezeph, and the children of [b]Eden which *were* in Thelasar?

13 [c]Where *is* the king of Hamath, and the king of Arpad, and the king of the city of Sepharvaim, of Hena, and Ivah?

14 ¶ [d]And Hezekiah received the letter of the hand of the messengers, and read it: and Hezekiah went up into the house of the LORD, and spread it before the LORD.

15 And Hezekiah prayed before the LORD, and said, O LORD God of Israel, [e]which dwellest *between* the cherubims, [f]thou art the God, *even* thou alone, of all the kingdoms of the earth; thou hast made heaven and earth.

16 LORD, [g]bow down thine ear, and hear: [h]open, LORD, thine eyes, and see: and hear the words of Sennacherib, [i]which hath sent him to reproach the living God.

17 Of a truth, LORD, the kings of Assyria have destroyed the nations and their lands,

18 And have cast their gods into the fire: for they *were* no gods, but [j]the work of men's hands, wood and stone: therefore they have destroyed them.

19 Now therefore, O LORD our God, I beseech thee, save thou us out of his hand, [k]that all the kingdoms of the earth may know that thou *art* the LORD God, *even* thou only.

20 ¶ Then Isaiah the son of Amoz sent to Hezekiah, saying, Thus saith the LORD God of Israel, [l]*That* which thou hast prayed to me against Sennacherib king of Assyria [m]I have heard.

21 This *is* the word that the LORD hath spoken concerning him; The virgin [n]the daughter of Zion hath despised thee, *and* laughed thee to scorn; the daughter of Jerusalem [o]hath shaken her head at thee.

22 Whom hast thou reproached and blasphemed? and against whom hast thou exalted *thy* voice, and lifted up thine eyes on high? *even* against the [p]Holy *One* of Israel.

23 [q]By thy messengers thou hast reproached the Lord, and hast said, [r]With the multitude of my chariots I am come up to the height of the mountains, to the sides of Lebanon, and will cut down the tall cedar trees thereof, *and* the choice fir trees thereof: and I will enter into the lodgings of his borders, *and into* the forest of his Carmel.

24 I have digged and drunk strange waters, and with the sole of my feet have I dried up all the rivers of besieged places.

25 Hast thou not heard long ago *how* [s]I have done it, *and* of ancient times that I have formed it? now have I brought it to pass, that [t]thou shouldest be to lay waste fenced cities *into* ruinous heaps.

26 Therefore their inhabitants were of small power, they were dismayed and confounded; they were *as* the grass of the field, and *as* the green herb, *as* [u]the grass on the house tops, and *as corn* blasted before it be grown up.

27 But [v]I know thy abode, and thy going out, and thy coming in, and thy rage against me.

28 Because thy rage against me and thy tumult is come up into mine ears, therefore [w]I will put my hook in thy nose, and my bridle in thy lips, and I will turn thee back [x]by the way by which thou camest.

29 And this *shall be* [y]a sign unto thee, ye shall eat this year such things as grow of themselves, and in the second year that which springeth of the same; and in the third year sow ye, and reap, and plant vineyards, and eat the fruits thereof.

30 [z]And the remnant that is escaped of

19:1 [p]Isa. 37:1
19:2 [q]Luke 3:4
19:4 [r]2 Sam. 16:12 [s]ch. 18:35 [t]Ps. 50:21
19:6 [u]Isa. 37:6 [v]ch. 18:17
19:7 [w]ver. 35; Jer. 51:1
19:8 [x]ch. 18:14
19:9 [y]1 Sam. 23:27
19:10 [z]ch. 18:5
19:12 [a]ch. 18:33 [b]Ezek. 27:23
19:13 [c]ch. 18:34
19:14 [d]Isa. 37:14
19:15 [e]1 Sam. 4:4; Ps. 80:1 [f]1 Kings 18:39; Isa. 44:6; Jer. 10:10
19:16 [g]Ps. 31:2 [h]2 Chron. 6:40 [i]ver. 4
19:18 [j]Ps. 115:4; Jer. 10:3
19:19 [k]Ps. 83:18
19:20 [l]Isa. 37:21 [m]Ps. 65:2
19:21 [n]Lam. 2:13 [o]Job 16:4; Ps. 22:7; Lam. 2:15
19:22 [p]Ps. 71:22; Isa. 5:24; Jer. 51:5
19:23 [q]ch. 18:17 [r]Ps. 20:7
19:25 [s]Isa. 45:7 [t]Isa. 10:5
19:26 [u]Ps. 129:6
19:27 [v]Ps. 139:1
19:28 [w]Job 41:2; Ezek. 29:4; Am. 4:2 [x]ver. 33
19:29 [y]1 Sam. 2:34; ch. 20:8; Isa. 7:11; Luke 2:12
19:30 [z]2 Chron. 32:22

the house of Judah shall yet again take root
downward, and bear fruit upward.
31 For out of Jerusalem shall go forth a
remnant, and they that escape out of mount
Zion: [a]the zeal of the LORD *of hosts* shall do
this.
32 Therefore thus saith the LORD concerning the king of Assyria, He shall not
come into this city, nor shoot an arrow
there, nor come before it with shield, nor
cast a bank against it.
33 By the way that he came, by the same
shall he return, and shall not come into this
city, saith the LORD.
34 For [b]I will defend this city, to save it,
for mine own sake, and [c]for my servant
David's sake.
35 ¶ And [d]it came to pass that night, that
the angel of the LORD went out, and smote
in the camp of the Assyrians an hundred
fourscore and five thousand: and when they
arose early in the morning, behold, they
were all dead corpses.
36 So Sennacherib king of Assyria departed, and went and returned, and dwelt at
[e]Nineveh.
37 And it came to pass, as he was worshipping in the house of Nisroch his god,
that [f]Adrammelech and Sharezer his sons
[g]smote him with the sword: and they escaped into the land of Armenia. And [h]Esar-
haddon his son reigned in his stead.

20 In [i]those days was Hezekiah sick
unto death. And the prophet Isaiah
the son of Amoz came to him, and said unto
him, Thus saith the LORD, Set thine house in
order; for thou shalt die, and not live.
2 Then he turned his face to the wall, and
prayed unto the LORD, saying,
3 I beseech thee, O LORD, [j]remember
now how I have [k]walked before thee in
truth and with a perfect heart, and have
done *that which is* good in thy sight. And
Hezekiah wept sore.
4 And it came to pass, afore Isaiah was
gone out into the middle court, that the
word of the LORD came to him, saying,
5 Turn again, and tell Hezekiah [l]the captain of my people, Thus saith the LORD, the
God of David thy father, [m]I have heard thy
prayer, I have seen [n]thy tears: behold, I will
heal thee: on the third day thou shalt go up
unto the house of the LORD.
6 And I will add unto thy days fifteen
years; and I will deliver thee and this city
out of the hand of the king of Assyria; and
[o]I will defend this city for mine own sake,
and for my servant David's sake.
7 And [p]Isaiah said, Take a lump of figs.
And they took and laid *it* on the boil, and he
recovered.
8 ¶ And Hezekiah said unto Isaiah,
[q]What *shall* be the sign that the LORD will
heal me, and that I shall go up into the
house of the LORD the third day?
9 And Isaiah said, [r]This sign shalt thou
have of the LORD, that the LORD will do the
thing that he hath spoken: shall the shadow
go forward ten degrees, or go back ten degrees?
10 And Hezekiah answered, It is a light
thing for the shadow to go down ten degrees: nay, but let the shadow return backward ten degrees.
11 And Isaiah the prophet cried unto the
LORD: and [s]he brought the shadow ten degrees backward, by which it had gone down
in the dial of Ahaz.
12 ¶ [t]At that time Berodach-baladan, the
son of Baladan, king of Babylon, sent letters
and a present unto Hezekiah: for he had
heard that Hezekiah had been sick.
13 And [u]Hezekiah hearkened unto them,
and shewed them all the house of his precious things, the silver, and the gold, and
the spices, and the precious ointment, and
all the house of his armour, and all that was
found in his treasures: there was nothing in
his house, nor in all his dominion, that Hezekiah shewed them not.
14 ¶ Then came Isaiah the prophet unto
king Hezekiah, and said unto him, What
said these men? and from whence came
they unto thee? And Hezekiah said, They
are come from a far country, *even* from
Babylon.
15 And he said, What have they seen in
thine house? And Hezekiah answered, [v]All
the things that *are* in mine house have they
seen: there is nothing among my treasures
that I have not shewed them.
16 And Isaiah said unto Hezekiah, Hear
the word of the LORD.
17 Behold, the days come, that all that *is*
in thine house, and that which thy fathers
have laid up in store unto this day, [w]shall be
carried into Babylon: nothing shall be left,
saith the LORD.
18 And of thy sons that shall issue from
thee, which thou shalt beget, [x]shall they
take away; and they shall be eunuchs in the
palace of the king of Babylon.
19 Then said Hezekiah unto Isaiah,
[y]Good *is* the word of the LORD which thou
hast spoken. And he said, *Is it* not *good,* if
peace and truth be in my days?
20 ¶ [z]And the rest of the acts of Hezekiah, and all his might, and how he [a]made
a pool, and a conduit, and [b]brought water
into the city, *are* they not written in the
book of the chronicles of the kings of Judah?
21 And [c]Hezekiah slept with his fathers:
and Manasseh his son reigned in his stead.

21 Manasseh [d]*was* twelve years old
when he began to reign, and reigned
fifty and five years in Jerusalem. And his
mother's name *was* Hephzi-bah.
2 And he did *that which was* evil in the
sight of the LORD, [e]after the abominations
of the heathen, whom the LORD cast out before the children of Israel.
3 For he built up again the high places
[f]which Hezekiah his father had destroyed;
and he reared up altars for Baal, and made
a grove, [g]as did Ahab king of Israel; and

19:31 [a]Isa. 9:7
19:34 [b]ch. 20:6 [c]1 Kings 11:12
19:35 [d]2 Chron. 32:21; Isa. 37:36
19:36 [e]Gen. 10:11
19:37 [f]2 Chron. 32:21 [g]ver. 7 [h]Ezra 4:2
20:1 [i]2 Chron. 32:24; Isa. 38:1
20:3 [j]Neh. 13:22 [k]Gen. 17:1; 1 Kings 3:6
20:5 [l]1 Sam. 9:16 [m]ch. 19:20; Ps. 65:2 [n]Ps. 39:12
20:6 [o]ch. 19:34
20:7 [p]Isa. 38:21
20:8 [q]Judg. 6:17; Isa. 7:11
20:9 [r]Isa. 38:7
20:11 [s]Josh. 10:12; Isa. 38:8
20:12 [t]Isa. 39:1
20:13 [u]2 Chron. 32:27
20:15 [v]ver. 13
20:17 [w]ch. 24:13; Jer. 27:21
20:18 [x]ch. 24:12; 2 Chron. 33:11
20:19 [y]1 Sam. 3:18; Job 1:21; Ps. 39:9
20:20 [z]2 Chron. 32:32 [a]Neh. 3:16 [b]2 Chron. 32:30
20:21 [c]2 Chron. 32:33
21:1 [d]2 Chron. 33:1
21:2 [e]ch. 16:3
21:3 [f]ch. 18:4 [g]1 Kings 16:32

[h]worshipped all the host of heaven, and served them.

4 And [i]he built altars in the house of the LORD, of which the LORD said, [j]In Jerusalem will I put my name.

5 And he built altars for all the host of heaven in the two courts of the house of the LORD.

6 [k]And he made his son pass through the fire, and observed [l]times, and used enchantments, and dealt with familiar spirits and wizards: he wrought much wickedness in the sight of the LORD, to provoke *him* to anger.

7 And he set a graven image of the grove that he had made in the house, of which the LORD said to David, and to Solomon his son, [m]In this house, and in Jerusalem, which I have chosen out of all tribes of Israel, will I put my name for ever:

8 [n]Neither will I make the feet of Israel move any more out of the land which I gave their fathers; only if they will observe to do according to all that I have commanded them, and according to all the law that my servant Moses commanded them.

9 But they hearkened not: and Manasseh [o]seduced them to do more evil than did the nations whom the LORD destroyed before the children of Israel.

10 ¶ And the LORD spake by his servants the prophets, saying,

11 [p]Because Manasseh king of Judah hath done these abominations, [q]*and* hath done wickedly above all that the Amorites did, which *were* before him, and [r]hath made Judah also to sin with his idols:

12 Therefore thus saith the LORD God of Israel, Behold, I *am* bringing *such* evil upon Jerusalem and Judah, that whosoever heareth of it, both [s]his ears shall tingle.

13 And I will stretch over Jerusalem [t]the line of Samaria, and the plummet of the house of Ahab: and I will wipe Jerusalem as *a man* wipeth a dish, wiping *it*, and turning *it* upside down.

14 And I will forsake the remnant of mine inheritance, and deliver them into the hand of their enemies; and they shall become a prey and a spoil to all their enemies;

15 Because they have done *that which was* evil in my sight, and have provoked me to anger, since the day their fathers came forth out of Egypt, even unto this day.

16 [u]Moreover Manasseh shed innocent blood very much, till he had filled Jerusalem from one end to another; beside his sin wherewith he made Judah to sin, in doing *that which was* evil in the sight of the LORD.

17 ¶ Now [v]the rest of the acts of Manasseh, and all that he did, and his sin that he sinned, *are* they not written in the book of the chronicles of the kings of Judah?

18 And [w]Manasseh slept with his fathers, and was buried in the garden of his own house, in the garden of Uzza: and Amon his son reigned in his stead.

19 ¶ [x]Amon *was* twenty and two years old when he began to reign, and he reigned two years in Jerusalem. And his mother's name *was* Meshullemeth, the daughter of Haruz of Jotbah.

20 And he did *that which was* evil in the sight of the LORD, [y]as his father Manasseh did.

21 And he walked in all the way that his father walked in, and served the idols that his father served, and worshipped them:

22 And he [z]forsook the LORD God of his fathers, and walked not in the way of the LORD.

23 ¶ [a]And the servants of Amon conspired against him, and slew the king in his own house.

24 And the people of the land slew all them that had conspired against king Amon; and the people of the land made Josiah his son king in his stead.

25 Now the rest of the acts of Amon which he did, *are* they not written in the book of the chronicles of the kings of Judah?

26 And he was buried in his sepulchre in the garden of Uzza: and [b]Josiah his son reigned in his stead.

22

Josiah [c]*was* eight years old when he began to reign, and he reigned thirty and one years in Jerusalem. And his mother's name *was* Jedidah, the daughter of Adaiah of [d]Boscath.

2 And he did *that which was* right in the sight of the LORD, and walked in all the way of David his father, and [e]turned not aside to the right hand or to the left.

3 ¶ [f]And it came to pass in the eighteenth year of king Josiah, *that* the king sent Shaphan the son of Azaliah, the son of Meshullam, the scribe, to the house of the LORD, saying,

4 Go up to Hilkiah the high priest, that he may sum the silver which is [g]brought into the house of the LORD, which [h]the keepers of the door have gathered of the people.

5 And let them [i]deliver it into the hand of the doers of the work, that have the oversight of the house of the LORD: and let them give it to the doers of the work which *is* in the house of the LORD, to repair the breaches of the house,

6 Unto carpenters, and builders, and masons, and to buy timber and hewn stone to repair the house.

7 Howbeit [j]there was no reckoning made with them of the money that was delivered into their hand, because they dealt faithfully.

8 ¶ And Hilkiah the high priest said unto Shaphan the scribe, [k]I have found the book of the law in the house of the LORD. And Hilkiah gave the book to Shaphan, and he read it.

9 And Shaphan the scribe came to the king, and brought the king word again, and said, Thy servants have gathered the money that was found in the house, and have delivered it into the hand of them that do the

21:3 [h]Deut. 4:19; ch. 17:16
21:4 [i]Jer. 32:34 [j]2 Sam. 7:13; 1 Kings 8:29
21:6 [k]Lev. 18:21; ch. 16:3 [l]Lev. 19:26; ch. 17:17; Deut. 18:10
21:7 [m]2 Sam. 7:13; 1 Kings 8:29; ch. 23:27; Ps. 132:13; Jer. 32:34
21:8 [n]2 Sam. 7:10
21:9 [o]Prov. 29:12
21:11 [p]ch. 23:26; Jer. 15:4 [q]1 Kings 21:26 [r]ver. 9
21:12 [s]1 Sam. 3:11; Jer. 19:3
21:13 [t]Isa. 34:11; Lam. 2:8; Am. 7:7
21:16 [u]ch. 24:4
21:17 [v]2 Chron. 33:11-19
21:18 [w]2 Chron. 33:20
21:19 [x]2 Chron. 33:21-23
21:20 [y]ver. 2
21:22 [z]1 Kings 11:33
21:23 [a]2 Chron. 33:24
21:26 [b]Matt. 1:10
22:1 [c]2 Chron. 34:1 [d]Josh. 15:39
22:2 [e]Deut. 5:32
22:3 [f]2 Chron. 34:8
22:4 [g]ch. 12:4 [h]ch. 12:9; Ps. 84:10
22:5 [i]ch. 12:11
22:7 [j]ch. 12:15
22:8 [k]Deut. 31:24; 2 Chron. 34:14

work, that have the oversight of the house of the LORD.

10 And Shaphan the scribe shewed the king, saying, Hilkiah the priest hath delivered me a book. And Shaphan read it before the king.

11 And it came to pass, when the king had heard the words of the book of the law, that he rent his clothes.

12 And the king commanded Hilkiah the priest, and Ahikam the son of Shaphan, and [l]Achbor the son of Michaiah, and Shaphan the scribe, and Asahiah a servant of the king's, saying,

13 Go ye, enquire of the LORD for me, and for the people, and for all Judah, concerning the words of this book that is found: for great *is* [m]the wrath of the LORD that is kindled against us, because our fathers have not hearkened unto the words of this book, to do according unto all that which is written concerning us.

14 So Hilkiah the priest, and Ahikam, and Achbor, and Shaphan, and Asahiah, went unto Huldah the prophetess, the wife of Shallum the son of [n]Tikvah, the son of Harhas, keeper of the wardrobe; (now she dwelt in Jerusalem in the college;) and they communed with her.

15 ¶ And she said unto them, Thus saith the LORD God of Israel, Tell the man that sent you to me,

16 Thus saith the LORD, Behold, [o]I will bring evil upon this place, and upon the inhabitants thereof, *even* all the words of the book which the king of Judah hath read:

17 [p]Because they have forsaken me, and have burned incense unto other gods, that they might provoke me to anger with all the works of their hands; therefore my wrath shall be kindled against this place, and shall not be quenched.

18 But to [q]the king of Judah which sent you to enquire of the LORD, thus shall ye say to him, Thus saith the LORD God of Israel, *As touching* the words which thou hast heard;

19 Because thine [r]heart was tender, and thou hast [s]humbled thyself before the LORD, when thou heardest what I spake against this place, and against the inhabitants thereof, that they should become [t]a desolation and [u]a curse, and hast rent thy clothes, and wept before me; I also have heard *thee*, saith the LORD.

20 Behold therefore, I will gather thee unto thy fathers, and thou [v]shalt be gathered into thy grave in peace; and thine eyes shall not see all the evil which I will bring upon this place. And they brought the king word again.

23 And [w]the king sent, and they gathered unto him all the elders of Judah and of Jerusalem.

2 And the king went up into the house of the LORD, and all the men of Judah and all the inhabitants of Jerusalem with him, and the priests, and the prophets, and all the people, both small and great: and he read in their ears all the words of the book of the covenant [x]which was found in the house of the LORD.

3 ¶ And the king [y]stood by a pillar, and made a covenant before the LORD, to walk after the LORD, and to keep his commandments and his testimonies and his statutes with all *their* heart and all *their* soul, to perform the words of this covenant that were written in this book. And all the people stood to the covenant.

4 And the king commanded Hilkiah the high priest, and the priests of the second order, and the keepers of the door, to bring forth out of the temple of the LORD all the vessels that were made for Baal, and for [z]the grove, and for all the host of heaven: and he burned them without Jerusalem in the fields of Kidron, and carried the ashes of them unto Beth-el.

5 And he put down the idolatrous priests, whom the kings of Judah had ordained to burn incense in the high places in the cities of Judah, and in the places round about Jerusalem; them also that burned incense unto Baal, to the sun, and to the moon, and to the planets, and to [a]all the host of heaven.

6 And he brought out the [b]grove from the house of the LORD, without Jerusalem, unto the brook Kidron, and burned it at the brook Kidron, and stamped *it* small to powder, and cast the powder thereof upon [c]the graves of the children of the people.

7 And he brake down the houses [d]of the sodomites, that *were* by the house of the LORD, [e]where the women wove hangings for the grove.

8 And he brought all the priests out of the cities of Judah, and defiled the high places where the priests had burned incense, from [f]Geba to Beer-sheba, and brake down the high places of the gates that *were* in the entering in of the gate of Joshua the governor of the city, which *were* on a man's left hand at the gate of the city.

9 [g]Nevertheless the priests of the high places came not up to the altar of the LORD in Jerusalem, [h]but they did eat of the unleavened bread among their brethren.

10 And he defiled [i]Topheth, which *is* in [j]the valley of the children of Hinnom, [k]that no man might make his son or his daughter to pass through the fire to Molech.

11 And he took away the horses that the kings of Judah had given to the sun, at the entering in of the house of the LORD, by the chamber of Nathan-melech the chamberlain, which *was* in the suburbs, and burned the chariots of the sun with fire.

12 And the altars that *were* [l]on the top of the upper chamber of Ahaz, which the kings of Judah had made, and the altars which [m]Manasseh had made in the two courts of the house of the LORD, did the king beat down, and brake *them* down from

22:12 [l]2 Chron. 34:20
22:13 [m]Deut. 29:27
22:14 [n]2 Chron. 34:22
22:16 [o]Deut. 29:27; Dan. 9:11
22:17 [p]Deut. 29:25
22:18 [q]2 Chron. 34:26
22:19 [r]Ps. 51:17; Isa. 57:15 [s]1 Kings 21:29 [t]Lev. 26:31 [u]Jer. 26:6
22:20 [v]Ps. 37:37; Isa. 57:1
23:1 [w]2 Chron. 34:29
23:2 [x]ch. 22:8
23:3 [y]ch. 11:14
23:4 [z]ch. 21:3
23:5 [a]ch. 21:3
23:6 [b]ch. 21:7 [c]2 Chron. 34:4
23:7 [d]1 Kings 14:24 [e]Ezek. 16:16
23:8 [f]1 Kings 15:22
23:9 [g]Ezek. 44:10-14 [h]1 Sam. 2:36
23:10 [i]Isa. 30:33; Jer. 7:31 [j]Josh. 15:8 [k]Lev. 18:21; Deut. 18:10; Ezek. 23:37
23:12 [l]Jer. 19:13; Zeph. 1:5 [m]ch. 21:5

thence, and cast the dust of them into the brook Kidron.

13 And the high places that *were* before Jerusalem, which *were* on the right hand of the mount of corruption, which [n]Solomon the king of Israel had builded for Ashtoreth the abomination of the Zidonians, and for Chemosh the abomination of the Moabites, and for Milcom the abomination of the children of Ammon, did the king defile.

14 And he [o]brake in pieces the images, and cut down the groves, and filled their places with the bones of men.

15 ¶ Moreover the altar that *was* at Beth-el, *and* the high place [p]which Jeroboam the son of Nebat, who made Israel to sin, had made, both that altar and the high place he brake down, and burned the high place, *and* stamped *it* small to powder, and burned the grove.

16 And as Josiah turned himself, he spied the sepulchres that *were* there in the mount, and sent, and took the bones out of the sepulchres, and burned *them* upon the altar, and polluted it, according to the [q]word of the LORD which the man of God proclaimed, who proclaimed these words.

17 Then he said, What title *is* that that I see? And the men of the city told him, *It is* [r]the sepulchre of the man of God, which came from Judah, and proclaimed these things that thou hast done against the altar of Beth-el.

18 And he said, Let him alone; let no man move his bones. So they let his bones alone, with the bones of [s]the prophet that came out of Samaria.

19 And all the houses also of the high places that *were* [t]in the cities of Samaria, which the kings of Israel had made to provoke *the LORD* to anger, Josiah took away, and did to them according to all the acts that he had done in Beth-el.

20 And [u]he [v]slew all the priests of the high places that *were* there upon the altars, and [w]burned men's bones upon them, and returned to Jerusalem.

21 ¶ And the king commanded all the people, saying, [x]Keep the passover unto the LORD your God, [y]as *it is* written in the book of this covenant.

22 Surely [z]there was not holden such a passover from the days of the judges that judged Israel, nor in all the days of the kings of Israel, nor of the kings of Judah;

23 But in the eighteenth year of king Josiah, *wherein* this passover was holden to the LORD in Jerusalem.

24 ¶ Moreover [a]the *workers with* familiar spirits, and the wizards, and the images, and the idols, and all the abominations that were spied in the land of Judah and in Jerusalem, did Josiah put away, that he might perform the words of [b]the law, which were written in the book that Hilkiah the priest found in the house of the LORD.

25 [c]And like unto him was there no king before him, that turned to the LORD with all his heart, and with all his soul, and with all his might, according to all the law of Moses; neither after him arose there *any* like him.

26 ¶ Notwithstanding the LORD turned not from the fierceness of his great wrath, wherewith his anger was kindled against Judah, [d]because of all the provocations that Manasseh had provoked him withal.

27 And the LORD said, I will remove Judah also out of my sight, as [e]I have removed Israel, and will cast off this city Jerusalem which I have chosen, and the house of which I said, [f]My name shall be there.

28 Now the rest of the acts of Josiah, and all that he did, *are* they not written in the book of the chronicles of the kings of Judah?

29 ¶ [g]In his days Pharaoh-nechoh king of Egypt went up against the king of Assyria to the river Euphrates: and king Josiah went against him; and he slew him at [h]Megiddo, when he [i]had seen him.

30 [j]And his servants carried him in a chariot dead from Megiddo, and brought him to Jerusalem, and buried him in his own sepulchre. And [k]the people of the land took Jehoahaz the son of Josiah, and anointed him, and made him king in his father's stead.

31 ¶ Jehoahaz *was* twenty and three years old when he began to reign; and he reigned three months in Jerusalem. And his mother's name *was* [l]Hamutal, the daughter of Jeremiah of Libnah.

32 And he did *that which was* evil in the sight of the LORD, according to all that his fathers had done.

33 And Pharaoh-nechoh put him in bands [m]at Riblah in the land of Hamath, that he might not reign in Jerusalem; and put the land to a tribute of an hundred talents of silver, and a talent of gold.

34 And [n]Pharaoh-nechoh made Eliakim the son of Josiah king in the room of Josiah his father, and [o]turned his name to [p]Jehoiakim, and took Jehoahaz away: [q]and he came to Egypt, and died there.

35 And Jehoiakim gave [r]the silver and the gold to Pharaoh; but he taxed the land to give the money according to the commandment of Pharaoh: he exacted the silver and the gold of the people of the land, of every one according to his taxation, to give *it* unto Pharaoh-nechoh.

36 ¶ [s]Jehoiakim *was* twenty and five years old when he began to reign; and he reigned eleven years in Jerusalem. And his mother's name *was* Zebudah, the daughter of Pedaiah of Rumah.

37 And he did *that which was* evil in the sight of the LORD, according to all that his fathers had done.

24 In [t]his days Nebuchadnezzar king of Babylon came up, and Jehoiakim became his servant three years: then he turned and rebelled against him.

2 [u]And the LORD sent against him bands

23:13 [n]1 Kings 11:7
23:14 [o]Ex. 23:24; Deut. 7:5
23:15 [p]1 Kings 12:28
23:16 [q]1 Kings 13:2
23:17 [r]1 Kings 13:1
23:18 [s]1 Kings 13:31
23:19 [t]2 Chron. 34:6
23:20 [u]1 Kings 13:2 [v]Ex. 22:20; 1 Kings 18:40; ch. 11:18 [w]2 Chron. 34:5
23:21 [x]2 Chron. 35:1 [y]Ex. 12:3; Lev. 23:5; Num. 9:2; Deut. 16:2
23:22 [z]2 Chron. 35:18
23:24 [a]ch. 21:6 [b]Lev. 19:31; Deut. 18:11
23:25 [c]ch. 18:5
23:26 [d]ch. 21:11; Jer. 15:4
23:27 [e]ch. 17:18 [f]1 Kings 8:29; ch. 21:4
23:29 [g]2 Chron. 35:20 [h]Zech. 12:11 [i]ch. 14:8
23:30 [j]2 Chron. 35:24 [k]2 Chron. 36:1
23:31 [l]ch. 24:18
23:33 [m]ch. 25:6; Jer. 52:27
23:34 [n]2 Chron. 36:4 [o]ch. 24:17; Dan. 1:7 [p]Matt. 1:11 [q]Jer. 22:11; Ezek. 19:3
23:35 [r]ver. 33
23:36 [s]2 Chron. 36:5
24:1 [t]2 Chron. 36:6; Jer. 25:1; Dan. 1:1
24:2 [u]Ezek. 19:8; Jer. 25:9

of the Chaldees, and bands of the Syrians, and bands of the Moabites, and bands of the children of Ammon, and sent them against Judah to destroy it, [v]according to the word of the LORD, which he spake by his servants the prophets.

3 Surely at the commandment of the LORD came *this* upon Judah, to remove *them* out of his sight, [w]for the sins of Manasseh, according to all that he did;

4 [x]And also for the innocent blood that he shed: for he filled Jerusalem with innocent blood; which the LORD would not pardon.

5 ¶ Now the rest of the acts of Jehoiakim, and all that he did, *are* they not written in the book of the chronicles of the kings of Judah?

6 [y]So Jehoiakim slept with his fathers: and Jehoiachin his son reigned in his stead.

7 And [z]the king of Egypt came not again any more out of his land: for [a]the king of Babylon had taken from the river of Egypt unto the river Euphrates all that pertained to the king of Egypt.

8 ¶ [b]Jehoiachin *was* eighteen years old when he began to reign, and he reigned in Jerusalem three months. And his mother's name *was* Nehushta, the daughter of Elnathan of Jerusalem.

9 And he did *that which was* evil in the sight of the LORD, according to all that his father had done.

10 ¶ [c]At that time the servants of Nebuchadnezzar king of Babylon came up against Jerusalem, and the city was besieged.

11 And Nebuchadnezzar king of Babylon came against the city, and his servants did besiege it.

12 [d]And Jehoiachin the king of Judah went out to the king of Babylon, he, and his mother, and his servants, and his princes, and his officers: [e]and the king of Babylon [f]took him [g]in the eighth year of his reign.

13 [h]And he carried out thence all the treasures of the house of the LORD, and the treasures of the king's house, and [i]cut in pieces all the vessels of gold which Solomon king of Israel had made in the temple of the LORD, [j]as the LORD had said.

14 And [k]he carried away all Jerusalem, and all the princes, and all the mighty men of valour, [l]*even* ten thousand captives, and [m]all the craftsmen and smiths: none remained, save [n]the poorest sort of the people of the land.

15 And [o]he carried away Jehoiachin to Babylon, and the king's mother, and the king's wives, and his officers, and the mighty of the land, *those* carried he into captivity from Jerusalem to Babylon.

16 And [p]all the men of might, *even* seven thousand, and craftsmen and smiths a thousand, all *that were* strong *and* apt for war, even them the king of Babylon brought captive to Babylon.

17 ¶ And [q]the king of Babylon made Mattaniah [r]his father's brother king in his stead, and [s]changed his name to Zedekiah.

18 [t]Zedekiah *was* twenty and one years old when he began to reign, and he reigned eleven years in Jerusalem. And his mother's name *was* [u]Hamutal, the daughter of Jeremiah of Libnah.

19 [v]And he did *that which was* evil in the sight of the LORD, according to all that Jehoiakim had done.

20 For through the anger of the LORD it came to pass in Jerusalem and Judah, until he had cast them out from his presence, [w]that Zedekiah rebelled against the king of Babylon.

25 And it came to pass [x]in the ninth year of his reign, in the tenth month, in the tenth *day* of the month, *that* Nebuchadnezzar king of Babylon came, he, and all his host, against Jerusalem, and pitched against it; and they built forts against it round about.

2 And the city was besieged unto the eleventh year of king Zedekiah.

3 And on the ninth *day* of the [y]*fourth* month the famine prevailed in the city, and there was no bread for the people of the land.

4 ¶ And [z]the city was broken up, and all the men of war *fled* by night by the way of the gate between two walls, which *is* by the king's garden: (now the Chaldees *were* against the city round about:) and [a]*the king* went the way toward the plain.

5 And the army of the Chaldees pursued after the king, and overtook him in the plains of Jericho: and all his army were scattered from him.

6 So they took the king, and brought him up to the king of Babylon [b]to Riblah; and they gave judgment upon him.

7 And they slew the sons of Zedekiah before his eyes, and [c]put out the eyes of Zedekiah, and bound him with fetters of brass, and carried him to Babylon.

8 ¶ And in the fifth month, [d]on the seventh *day* of the month, which *is* [e]the nineteenth year of king Nebuchadnezzar king of Babylon, [f]came Nebuzar-adan, captain of the guard, a servant of the king of Babylon, unto Jerusalem:

9 [g]And he burnt the house of the LORD, [h]and the king's house, and all the houses of Jerusalem, and every great *man's* house burnt he with fire.

10 And all the army of the Chaldees, that *were with* the captain of the guard, [i]brake down the walls of Jerusalem round about.

11 [j]Now the rest of the people *that were* left in the city, and the fugitives that fell away to the king of Babylon, with the remnant of the multitude, did Nebuzar-adan the captain of the guard carry away.

12 But the captain of the guard [k]left of the poor of the land *to be* vinedressers and husbandmen.

13 And [l]the [m]pillars of brass that *were* in the house of the LORD, and [n]the bases, and

24:2 [v]ch. 20:17
24:3 [w]ch. 21:2
24:4 [x]ch. 21:16
24:6 [y]2 Chron. 36:6; Jer. 22:18
24:7 [z]Jer. 37:5 [a]Jer. 46:2
24:8 [b]2 Chron. 36:9
24:10 [c]Dan. 1:1
24:12 [d]Jer. 24:1; Ezek. 17:12 [e]Jer. 25:1 [f]ch. 25:27 [g]Jer. 52:28
24:13 [h]ch. 20:17; Isa. 39:6 [i]Dan. 5:2 [j]Jer. 20:5
24:14 [k]Jer. 24:1 [l]Jer. 52:28 [m]1 Sam. 13:19 [n]ch. 25:12; Jer. 40:7
24:15 [o]2 Chron. 36:10; Esth. 2:6; Jer. 22:24
24:16 [p]Jer. 52:28
24:17 [q]Jer. 37:1 [r]1 Chron. 3:15; 2 Chron. 36:10 [s]ch. 23:34; 2 Chron. 36:4
24:18 [t]2 Chron. 36:11; Jer. 37:1 [u]ch. 23:31
24:19 [v]2 Chron. 36:12
24:20 [w]2 Chron. 36:13; Ezek. 17:15
25:1 [x]2 Chron. 36:17; Jer. 34:2; Ezek. 24:1
25:3 [y]Jer. 39:2
25:4 [z]Jer. 39:2 [a]Jer. 39:4-7; Ezek. 12:12
25:6 [b]ch. 23:33; Jer. 52:9
25:7 [c]Jer. 39:7; Ezek. 12:13
25:8 [d]Jer. 52:12-14 [e]ch. 24:12 [f]Jer. 39:9
25:9 [g]2 Chron. 36:19; Ps. 79:1 [h]Jer. 39:8; Am. 2:5
25:10 [i]Neh. 1:3; Jer. 52:14
25:11 [j]Jer. 39:9
25:12 [k]ch. 24:14; Jer. 39:10
25:13 [l]ch. 20:17; Jer. 27:19 [m]1 Kings 7:15 [n]1 Kings 7:27

[o]the brasen sea that *was* in the house of the LORD, did the Chaldees break in pieces, and carried the brass of them to Babylon.

14 And [p]the pots, and the shovels, and the snuffers, and the spoons, and all the vessels of brass wherewith they ministered, took they away.

15 And the firepans, and the bowls, *and* such things as *were* of gold, *in* gold, and of silver, *in* silver, the captain of the guard took away.

16 The two pillars, one sea, and the bases which Solomon had made for the house of the LORD; [q]the brass of all these vessels was without weight.

17 [r]The height of the one pillar *was* eighteen cubits, and the chapiter upon it *was* brass: and the height of the chapiter three cubits; and the wreathen work, and pomegranates upon the chapiter round about, all of brass: and like unto these had the second pillar with wreathen work.

18 ¶ [s]And the captain of the guard took [t]Seraiah the chief priest, and [u]Zephaniah the second priest, and the three keepers of the door:

19 And out of the city he took an officer that was set over the men of war, and [v]five men of them that were in the king's presence, which were found in the city, and the principal scribe of the host, which mustered the people of the land, and threescore men of the people of the land *that were* found in the city:

20 And Nebuzar-adan captain of the guard took these, and brought them to the king of Babylon to Riblah:

21 And the king of Babylon smote them, and slew them at Riblah in the land of Hamath. [w]So Judah was carried away out of their land.

22 ¶ [x]And *as for* the people that remained in the land of Judah, whom Nebuchadnezzar king of Babylon had left, even over them he made Gedaliah the son of Ahikam, the son of Shaphan, ruler.

23 And when all the [y]captains of the armies, they and their men, heard that the king of Babylon had made Gedaliah governor, there came to Gedaliah to Mizpah, even Ishmael the son of Nethaniah, and Johanan the son of Careah, and Seraiah the son of Tanhumeth the Netophathite, and Jaazaniah the son of a Maachathite, they and their men.

24 And Gedaliah sware to them, and to their men, and said unto them, Fear not to be the servants of the Chaldees: dwell in the land, and serve the king of Babylon; and it shall be well with you.

25 But [z]it came to pass in the seventh month, that Ishmael the son of Nethaniah, the son of Elishama, of the seed royal, came, and ten men with him, and smote Gedaliah, that he died, and the Jews and the Chaldees that were with him at Mizpah.

26 And all the people, both small and great, and the captains of the armies, arose, [a]and came to Egypt: for they were afraid of the Chaldees.

27 ¶ [b]And it came to pass in the seven and thirtieth year of the captivity of Jehoiachin king of Judah, in the twelfth month, on the seven and twentieth *day* of the month, *that* Evil-merodach king of Babylon in the year that he began to reign [c]did lift up the head of Jehoiachin king of Judah out of prison;

28 And he spake kindly to him, and set his throne above the throne of the kings that *were* with him in Babylon;

29 And changed his prison garments: and he did [d]eat bread continually before him all the days of his life.

30 And his allowance *was* a continual allowance given him of the king, a daily rate for every day, all the days of his life.

25:13 [o]1 Kings 7:23
25:14 [p]Ex. 27:3; 1 Kings 7:45
25:16 [q]1 Kings 7:47
25:17 [r]1 Kings 7:15; Jer. 52:21
25:18 [s]Jer. 52:24 [t]1 Chron. 6:14; Ezra 7:1 [u]Jer. 21:1
25:19 [v]Jer. 52:25
25:21 [w]Lev. 26:33; Deut. 28:36; ch. 23:27
25:22 [x]Jer. 40:5
25:23 [y]Jer. 40:7
25:25 [z]Jer. 41:1
25:26 [a]Jer. 43:4
25:27 [b]Jer. 52:13 [c]Gen. 40:13
25:29 [d]2 Sam. 9:7

1 CHRONICLES

Tradition suggests that Ezra was the author of 1 Chronicles, written between 450 B.C. and 400 B.C. Much of the history found in the two books of Chronicles comes from Samuel and Kings. In 1 Chronicles, we are moved through history from Adam to the accession of Solomon to the throne of unified Israel.

I. The genealogies from Adam to David, 1:1–9:44
II. King David on the throne of Israel, 10:1–29:30
III. Solomon assumes the throne of Israel, 29:22–29:30

---

1 Adam, [a]Sheth, Enosh,
2 Kenan, Mahalaleel, Jered,
3 Henoch, Methuselah, Lamech,
4 Noah, Shem, Ham, and Japheth.
5 ¶ [b]The sons of Japheth; Gomer, and
Magog, and Madai, and Javan, and Tubal,
and Meshech, and Tiras.
6 And the sons of Gomer; Ashchenaz, and
Riphath, and Togarmah.
7 And the sons of Javan; Elishah, and
Tarshish, Kittim, and Dodanim.
8 ¶ [c]The sons of Ham; Cush, and Mizraim, Put, and Canaan.
9 And the sons of Cush; Seba, and Havilah, and Sabta, and Raamah, and Sabtecha.
And the sons of Raamah; Sheba, and Dedan.
10 And Cush [d]begat Nimrod: he began to
be mighty upon the earth.
11 And Mizraim begat Ludim, and Anamim, and Lehabim, and Naphtuhim,
12 And Pathrusim, and Casluhim, (of
whom came the Philistines,) and [e]Caph-
thorim.
13 And [f]Canaan begat Zidon his firstborn, and Heth,
14 The Jebusite also, and the Amorite,
and the Girgashite,
15 And the Hivite, and the Arkite, and the
Sinite,
16 And the Arvadite, and the Zemarite,
and the Hamathite.
17 ¶ The sons of [g]Shem; Elam, and Asshur, and Arphaxad, and Lud, and Aram,
and Uz, and Hul, and Gether, and Meshech.
18 And Arphaxad begat Shelah, and Shelah begat Eber.
19 And unto Eber were born two sons: the
name of the one *was* Peleg; because in his
days the earth was divided: and his
brother's name *was* Joktan.
20 And [h]Joktan begat Almodad, and
Sheleph, and Hazarmaveth, and Jerah,
21 Hadoram also, and Uzal, and Diklah,
22 And Ebal, and Abimael, and Sheba,
23 And Ophir, and Havilah, and Jobab.
All these *were* the sons of Joktan.
24 ¶ [i]Shem, Arphaxad, Shelah,
25 [j]Eber, Peleg, Reu,
26 Serug, Nahor, Terah,
27 [k]Abram; the same *is* Abraham.

1:1 [a]Gen. 4:25
1:5 [b]Gen. 10:2
1:8 [c]Gen. 10:6
1:10 [d]Gen. 10:8
1:12 [e]Deut. 2:23
1:13 [f]Gen. 10:15
1:17 [g]Gen. 10:22
1:20 [h]Gen. 10:26
1:24 [i]Gen. 11:10; Luke 3:34
1:25 [j]Gen. 11:15
1:27 [k]Gen. 17:5
1:28 [l]Gen. 21:2 [m]Gen. 16:11
1:29 [n]Gen. 25:13-16
1:32 [o]Gen. 25:1
1:34 [p]Gen. 21:2 [q]Gen. 25:25
1:35 [r]Gen. 36:9
1:38 [s]Gen. 36:20
1:41 [t]Gen. 36:25
1:43 [u]Gen. 36:31

28 The sons of Abraham; [l]Isaac, and
[m]Ishmael.
29 ¶ These *are* their generations: the
[n]firstborn of Ishmael, Nebaioth; then Kedar, and Adbeel, and Mibsam,
30 Mishma, and Dumah, Massa, Hadad,
and Tema,
31 Jetur, Naphish, and Kedemah. These
are the sons of Ishmael.
32 ¶ Now [o]the sons of Keturah, Abraham's concubine: she bare Zimran, and
Jokshan, and Medan, and Midian, and Ishbak, and Shuah. And the sons of Jokshan;
Sheba, and Dedan.
33 And the sons of Midian; Ephah, and
Epher, and Henoch, and Abida, and Eldaah.
All these *are* the sons of Keturah.
34 And [p]Abraham begat Isaac. [q]The
sons of Isaac; Esau and Israel.
35 ¶ The sons of [r]Esau; Eliphaz, Reuel,
and Jeush, and Jaalam, and Korah.
36 The sons of Eliphaz; Teman, and
Omar, Zephi, and Gatam, Kenaz, and
Timna, and Amalek.
37 The sons of Reuel; Nahath, Zerah,
Shammah, and Mizzah.
38 And [s]the sons of Seir; Lotan, and Shobal, and Zibeon, and Anah, and Dishon, and
Ezer, and Dishan.
39 And the sons of Lotan; Hori, and Ho-
mam: and Timna *was* Lotan's sister.
40 The sons of Shobal; Alian, and Manahath, and Ebal, Shephi, and Onam. And the
sons of Zibeon; Aiah, and Anah.
41 The sons of Anah; [t]Dishon. And the
sons of Dishon; Amram, and Eshban, and
Ithran, and Cheran.
42 The sons of Ezer; Bilhan, and Zavan,
and Jakan. The sons of Dishan; Uz, and
Aran.
43 ¶ Now these *are* the [u]kings that
reigned in the land of Edom before *any* king
reigned over the children of Israel; Bela the
son of Beor: and the name of his city *was*
Dinhabah.
44 And when Bela was dead, Jobab the
son of Zerah of Bozrah reigned in his stead.
45 And when Jobab was dead, Husham of
the land of the Temanites reigned in his
stead.
46 And when Husham was dead, Hadad
the son of Bedad, which smote Midian in the

field of Moab, reigned in his stead: and the name of his city *was* Avith.

47 And when Hadad was dead, Samlah of Masrekah reigned in his stead.

48 [v]And when Samlah was dead, Shaul of Rehoboth by the river reigned in his stead.

49 And when Shaul was dead, Baal-hanan the son of Achbor reigned in his stead.

50 And when Baal-hanan was dead, Hadad reigned in his stead: and the name of his city *was* Pai; and his wife's name *was* Mehetabel, the daughter of Matred, the daughter of Mezahab.

51 ¶ Hadad died also. And the [w]dukes of Edom were; duke Timnah, duke Aliah, duke Jetheth,

52 Duke Aholibamah, duke Elah, duke Pinon,

53 Duke Kenaz, duke Teman, duke Mibzar,

54 Duke Magdiel, duke Iram. These *are* the dukes of Edom.

2 These *are* the sons of Israel; [x]Reuben, Simeon, Levi, and Judah, Issachar, and Zebulun,

2 Dan, Joseph, and Benjamin, Naphtali, Gad, and Asher.

3 ¶ The sons of [y]Judah; Er, and Onan, and Shelah: *which* three were born unto him of the daughter of [z]Shua the Canaanitess. And [a]Er, the firstborn of Judah, was evil in the sight of the LORD; and he slew him.

4 And [b]Tamar his daughter in law bare him Pharez and Zerah. All the sons of Judah *were* five.

5 The sons of [c]Pharez; Hezron, and Hamul.

6 And the sons of Zerah; Zimri, [d]and Ethan, and Heman, and Calcol, and Dara: five of them in all.

7 And the sons of [e]Carmi; Achar, the troubler of Israel, who transgressed in the thing [f]accursed.

8 And the sons of Ethan; Azariah.

9 The sons also of Hezron, that were born unto him; Jerahmeel, and Ram, and Chelubai.

10 And Ram [g]begat Amminadab; and Amminadab begat Nahshon, [h]prince of the children of Judah;

11 And Nahshon begat Salma, and Salma begat Boaz,

12 And Boaz begat Obed, and Obed begat Jesse,

13 ¶ [i]And Jesse begat his firstborn Eliab, and Abinadab the second, and Shimma the third,

14 Nethaneel the fourth, Raddai the fifth,

15 Ozem the sixth, David the seventh:

16 Whose sisters *were* Zeruiah, and Abigail. [j]And the sons of Zeruiah; Abishai, and Joab, and Asahel, three.

17 And [k]Abigail bare Amasa: and the father of Amasa *was* Jether the Ishmeelite.

18 ¶ And Caleb the son of Hezron begat *children* of Azubah *his* wife, and of Jerioth: her sons *are* these; Jesher, and Shobab, and Ardon.

19 And when Azubah was dead, Caleb took unto him [l]Ephrath, which bare him Hur.

20 And Hur begat Uri, and Uri begat [m]Bezaleel.

21 ¶ And afterward Hezron went in to the daughter of [n]Machir the father of Gilead, whom he married when he *was* threescore years old; and she bare him Segub.

22 And Segub begat Jair, who had three and twenty cities in the land of Gilead.

23 [o]And he took Geshur, and Aram, with the towns of Jair, from them, with Kenath, and the towns thereof, *even* threescore cities. All these *belonged to* the sons of Machir the father of Gilead.

24 And after that Hezron was dead in Caleb-ephratah, then Abiah Hezron's wife bare him [p]Ashur the father of Tekoa.

25 ¶ And the sons of Jerahmeel the firstborn of Hezron were, Ram the firstborn, and Bunah, and Oren, and Ozem, *and* Ahijah.

26 Jerahmeel had also another wife, whose name *was* Atarah; she *was* the mother of Onam.

27 And the sons of Ram the firstborn of Jerahmeel were, Maaz, and Jamin, and Eker.

28 And the sons of Onam were, Shammai, and Jada. And the sons of Shammai; Nadab, and Abishur.

29 And the name of the wife of Abishur *was* Abihail, and she bare him Ahban, and Molid.

30 And the sons of Nadab; Seled, and Appaim: but Seled died without children.

31 And the sons of Appaim; Ishi. And the sons of Ishi; Sheshan. And [q]the children of Sheshan; Ahlai.

32 And the sons of Jada the brother of Shammai; Jether, and Jonathan: and Jether died without children.

33 And the sons of Jonathan; Peleth, and Zaza. These were the sons of Jerahmeel.

34 ¶ Now Sheshan had no sons, but daughters. And Sheshan had a servant, an Egyptian, whose name *was* Jarha.

35 And Sheshan gave his daughter to Jarha his servant to wife; and she bare him Attai.

36 And Attai begat Nathan, and Nathan begat [r]Zabad,

37 And Zabad begat Ephlal, and Ephlal begat Obed,

38 And Obed begat Jehu, and Jehu begat Azariah,

39 And Azariah begat Helez, and Helez begat Eleasah,

40 And Eleasah begat Sisamai, and Sisamai begat Shallum,

41 And Shallum begat Jekamiah, and Jekamiah begat Elishama.

42 ¶ Now the sons of Caleb the brother of Jerahmeel *were*, Mesha his firstborn, which

1:48 [v]Gen. 36:37
1:51 [w]Gen. 36:40
2:1 [x]Gen. 29:32
2:3 [y]Gen. 38:3; Num. 26:19 [z]Gen. 38:2 [a]Gen. 38:7
2:4 [b]Gen. 38:29; Matt. 1:3
2:5 [c]Gen. 46:12; Ruth 4:18
2:6 [d]1 Kings 4:31
2:7 [e]ch. 4:1 [f]Josh. 6:18
2:10 [g]Ruth 4:19; Matt. 1:4 [h]Num. 1:7
2:13 [i]2 Sam. 16:6
2:16 [j]2 Sam. 2:18
2:17 [k]2 Sam. 17:25
2:19 [l]ver. 50
2:20 [m]Ex. 31:2
2:21 [n]Num. 27:1
2:23 [o]Num. 32:41; Deut. 3:14; Josh. 13:30
2:24 [p]ch. 4:5
2:31 [q]ver. 34
2:36 [r]ch. 11:41

was the father of Ziph; and the sons of Mareshah the father of Hebron.
43 And the sons of Hebron; Korah, and
Tappuah, and Rekem, and Shema.
44 And Shema begat Raham, the father of
Jorkoam: and Rekem begat Shammai.
45 And the son of Shammai *was* Maon:
and Maon *was* the father of Beth-zur.
46 And Ephah, Caleb's concubine, bare
Haran, and Moza, and Gazez: and Haran
begat Gazez.
47 And the sons of Jahdai; Regem, and
Jotham, and Geshan, and Pelet, and Ephah,
and Shaaph.
48 Maachah, Caleb's concubine, bare
Sheber, and Tirhanah.
49 She bare also Shaaph the father of
Madmannah, Sheva the father of Mach-
benah, and the father of Gibea: and the
daughter of Caleb *was* [s]Achsah.
50 ¶ These were the sons of Caleb the son
of Hur, the firstborn of Ephratah; Shobal
the father of Kirjath-jearim,
51 Salma the father of Beth-lehem, Ha-
reph the father of Beth-gader.
52 And Shobal the father of Kirjath-
jearim had sons; Haroeh, *and* half of the
Manahethites.
53 And the families of Kirjath-jearim; the
Ithrites, and the Puhites, and the Shumath-
ites, and the Mishraites; of them came the
Zareathites, and the Eshtaulites.
54 The sons of Salma; Beth-lehem, and
the Netophathites, Ataroth, the house of
Joab, and half of the Manahethites, the Zo-
rites.
55 And the families of the scribes which
dwelt at Jabez; the Tirathites, the Shimeath-
ites, *and* Suchathites. These *are* the [t]Ke-
nites that came of Hemath, the father of the
house of [u]Rechab.

3 Now these were the sons of David,
which were born unto him in Hebron;
the firstborn [v]Amnon, of Ahinoam the
[w]Jezreelitess; the second Daniel, of Abigail
the Carmelitess:
2 The third, Absalom the son of Maachah
the daughter of Talmai king of Geshur: the
fourth, Adonijah the son of Haggith:
3 The fifth, Shephatiah of Abital: the
sixth, Ithream by [x]Eglah his wife.
4 *These* six were born unto him in Hebron; and [y]there he reigned seven years
and six months: and [z]in Jerusalem he
reigned thirty and three years.
5 [a]And these were born unto him in Jerusalem; Shimea, and Shobab, and Nathan,
and [b]Solomon, four, of Bath-shua the
daughter of Ammiel:
6 Ibhar also, and Elishama, and Eliphelet,
7 And Nogah, and Nepheg, and Japhia,
8 And Elishama, and Eliada, and Eliphelet, [c]nine.
9 *These were* all the sons of David, beside
the sons of the concubines, and [d]Tamar
their sister.
10 ¶ And Solomon's son *was* [e]Reho-
boam, Abia his son, Asa his son, Jehoshaphat his son,
11 Joram his son, Ahaziah his son, Joash
his son,
12 Amaziah his son, Azariah his son, Jotham his son,
13 Ahaz his son, Hezekiah his son, Manasseh his son,
14 Amon his son, Josiah his son.
15 And the sons of Josiah *were,* the firstborn Johanan, the second Jehoiakim, the
third Zedekiah, the fourth Shallum.
16 And the sons of [f]Jehoiakim: Jeconiah
his son, Zedekiah [g]his son.
17 ¶ And the sons of Jeconiah; Assir,
Salathiel [h]his son,
18 Malchiram also, and Pedaiah, and
Shenazar, Jecamiah, Hoshama, and Neda-
biah.
19 And the sons of Pedaiah *were,* Zerubbabel, and Shimei: and the sons of Zerubbabel; Meshullam, and Hananiah, and
Shelomith their sister:
20 And Hashubah, and Ohel, and Berechiah, and Hasadiah, Jushab-hesed, five.
21 And the sons of Hananiah; Pelatiah,
and Jesaiah: the sons of Rephaiah, the sons
of Arnan, the sons of Obadiah, the sons of
Shechaniah.
22 And the sons of Shechaniah; Shemaiah: and the sons of Shemaiah; [i]Hattush,
and Igeal, and Bariah, and Neariah, and
Shaphat, six.
23 And the sons of Neariah; Elioenai, and
Hezekiah, and Azrikam, three.
24 And the sons of Elioenai *were,* Ho-
daiah, and Eliashib, and Pelaiah, and Akkub, and Johanan, and Dalaiah, and Anani,
seven.

4 The sons of Judah; [j]Pharez, Hezron,
and Carmi, and Hur, and Shobal.
2 And Reaiah the son of Shobal begat Jahath; and Jahath begat Ahumai, and Lahad.
These *are* the families of the Zorathites.
3 And these *were of* the father of Etam;
Jezreel, and Ishma, and Idbash: and the
name of their sister *was* Hazelelponi:
4 And Penuel the father of Gedor, and
Ezer the father of Hushah. These *are* the
sons of [k]Hur, the firstborn of Ephratah, the
father of Beth-lehem.
5 ¶ And [l]Ashur the father of Tekoa had
two wives, Helah and Naarah.
6 And Naarah bare him Ahuzam, and Hepher, and Temeni, and Haahashtari. These
were the sons of Naarah.
7 And the sons of Helah *were,* Zereth, and
Jezoar, and Ethnan.
8 And Coz begat Anub, and Zobebah, and
the families of Aharhel the son of Harum.
9 ¶ And Jabez was [m]more honourable
than his brethren: and his mother called his
name Jabez, saying, Because I bare him
with sorrow.
10 And Jabez called on the God of Israel,
saying, Oh that thou wouldest bless me indeed, and enlarge my coast, and that thine
hand might be with me, and that thou

2:49 [s]Josh. 15:17
2:55 [t]Judg. 1:16 [u]Jer. 35:2
3:1 [v]2 Sam. 3:2 [w]Josh. 15:56
3:3 [x]2 Sam. 3:5
3:4 [y]2 Sam. 2:11 [z]2 Sam. 5:5
3:5 [a]2 Sam. 5:14; ch. 14:4 [b]2 Sam. 12:24
3:8 [c]2 Sam. 5:14
3:9 [d]2 Sam. 13:1
3:10 [e]1 Kings 11:43
3:16 [f]Matt. 1:11 [g]2 Kings 24:17
3:17 [h]Matt. 1:12
3:22 [i]Ezra 8:2
4:1 [j]Gen. 38:29
4:4 [k]ch. 2:50
4:5 [l]ch. 2:24
4:9 [m]Gen. 34:19

wouldest keep *me* from evil, that it may not grieve me! And God granted him that which he requested.

11 ¶ And Chelub the brother of Shuah begat Mehir, which *was* the father of Eshton.

12 And Eshton begat Beth-rapha, and Paseah, and Tehinnah the father of Ir-nahash. These *are* the men of Rechah.

13 And the sons of Kenaz; [n]Othniel, and Seraiah: and the sons of Othniel; Hathath.

14 And Meonothai begat Ophrah: and Seraiah begat Joab, the father of [o]the valley of Charashim; for they were craftsmen.

15 And the sons of Caleb the son of Jephunneh; Iru, Elah, and Naam: and the sons of Elah, even Kenaz.

16 And the sons of Jehaleleel; Ziph, and Ziphah, Tiria, and Asareel.

17 And the sons of Ezra *were*, Jether, and Mered, and Epher, and Jalon: and she bare Miriam, and Shammai, and Ishbah the father of Eshtemoa.

18 And his wife Jehudijah bare Jered the father of Gedor, and Heber the father of Socho, and Jekuthiel the father of Zanoah. And these *are* the sons of Bithiah the daughter of Pharaoh, which Mered took.

19 And the sons of *his* wife Hodiah the sister of Naham, the father of Keilah the Garmite, and Eshtemoa the Maachathite.

20 And the sons of Shimon *were*, Amnon, and Rinnah, Ben-hanan, and Tilon. And the sons of Ishi *were*, Zoheth, and Ben-zoheth.

21 ¶ The sons of Shelah [p]the son of Judah *were*, Er the father of Lecah, and Laadah the father of Mareshah, and the families of the house of them that wrought fine linen, of the house of Ashbea,

22 And Jokim, and the men of Chozeba, and Joash, and Saraph, who had the dominion in Moab, and Jashubi-lehem. And *these are* ancient things.

23 These *were* the potters, and those that dwelt among plants and hedges: there they dwelt with the king for his work.

24 ¶ The sons of Simeon *were*, Nemuel, and Jamin, Jarib, Zerah, *and* Shaul:

25 Shallum his son, Mibsam his son, Mishma his son.

26 And the sons of Mishma; Hamuel his son, Zacchur his son, Shimei his son.

27 And Shimei had sixteen sons and six daughters; but his brethren had not many children, neither did all their family multiply, like to the children of Judah.

28 And they dwelt at [q]Beer-sheba, and Moladah, and Hazar-shual,

29 And at Bilhah, and at Ezem, and at Tolad,

30 And at Bethuel, and at Hormah, and at Ziklag,

31 And at Beth-marcaboth, and Hazar-susim, and at Beth-birei, and at Shaaraim. These *were* their cities unto the reign of David.

32 And their villages *were*, Etam, and Ain, Rimmon, and Tochen, and Ashan, five cities:

33 And all their villages that *were* round about the same cities, unto Baal. These *were* their habitations, and their genealogy.

34 And Meshobab, and Jamlech, and Joshah the son of Amaziah,

35 And Joel, and Jehu the son of Josibiah, the son of Seraiah, the son of Asiel,

36 And Elioenai, and Jaakobah, and Jeshohaiah, and Asaiah, and Adiel, and Jesimiel, and Benaiah,

37 And Ziza the son of Shiphi, the son of Allon, the son of Jedaiah, the son of Shimri, the son of Shemaiah;

38 These mentioned by *their* names *were* princes in their families: and the house of their fathers increased greatly.

39 ¶ And they went to the entrance of Gedor, *even* unto the east side of the valley, to seek pasture for their flocks.

40 And they found fat pasture and good, and the land *was* wide, and quiet, and peaceable; for *they* of Ham had dwelt there of old.

41 And these written by name came in the days of Hezekiah king of Judah, and [r]smote their tents, and the habitations that were found there, and destroyed them utterly unto this day, and dwelt in their rooms: because *there was* pasture there for their flocks.

42 And *some* of them, *even* of the sons of Simeon, five hundred men, went to mount Seir, having for their captains Pelatiah, and Neariah, and Rephaiah, and Uzziel, the sons of Ishi.

43 And they smote [s]the rest of the Amalekites that were escaped, and dwelt there unto this day.

5 Now the sons of Reuben the firstborn of Israel, (for [t]he *was* the firstborn; but, forasmuch as he [u]defiled his father's bed, [v]his birthright was given unto the sons of Joseph the son of Israel: and the genealogy is not to be reckoned after the birthright.

2 For [w]Judah prevailed above his brethren, and of him *came* the [x]chief ruler; but the birthright *was* Joseph's:)

3 The sons, *I say*, of [y]Reuben the firstborn of Israel *were*, Hanoch, and Pallu, Hezron, and Carmi.

4 The sons of Joel; Shemaiah his son, Gog his son, Shimei his son,

5 Micah his son, Reaia his son, Baal his son,

6 Beerah his son, whom Tilgath-pilneser king of Assyria carried away *captive*: he *was* prince of the Reubenites.

7 And his brethren by their families, [z]when the genealogy of their generations was reckoned, *were* the chief, Jeiel, and Zechariah,

8 And Bela the son of Azaz, the son of Shema, the son of Joel, who dwelt in [a]Aroer, even unto Nebo and Baal-meon:

9 And eastward he inhabited unto the entering in of the wilderness from the river Euphrates: because their cattle were multiplied [b]in the land of Gilead.

4:13 [n]Josh. 15:17
4:14 [o]Neh. 11:35
4:21 [p]Gen. 38:1
4:28 [q]Josh. 19:2
4:41 [r]2 Kings 18:8
4:43 [s]1 Sam. 15:8
5:1 [t]Gen. 29:32 [u]Gen. 35:22 [v]Gen. 48:15
5:2 [w]Gen. 49:8; Ps. 60:7 [x]Mic. 5:2; Matt. 2:6
5:3 [y]Gen. 46:9; Ex. 6:14; Num. 26:5
5:7 [z]ver. 17
5:8 [a]Josh. 13:15
5:9 [b]Josh. 22:9

10 And in the days of Saul they made war [c]with the Hagarites, who fell by their hand: and they dwelt in their tents throughout all the east *land* of Gilead.

11 ¶ And the children of Gad dwelt over against them, in the land of [d]Bashan unto Salchah:

12 Joel the chief, and Shapham the next, and Jaanai, and Shaphat in Bashan.

13 And their brethren of the house of their fathers *were,* Michael, and Meshullam, and Sheba, and Jorai, and Jachan, and Zia, and Heber, seven.

14 These *are* the children of Abihail the son of Huri, the son of Jaroah, the son of Gilead, the son of Michael, the son of Jeshishai, the son of Jahdo, the son of Buz;

15 Ahi the son of Abdiel, the son of Guni, chief of the house of their fathers.

16 And they dwelt in Gilead in Bashan, and in her towns, and in all the suburbs of [e]Sharon, upon their borders.

17 All these were reckoned by genealogies in the days of [f]Jotham king of Judah, and in the days of [g]Jeroboam king of Israel.

18 ¶ The sons of Reuben, and the Gadites, and half the tribe of Manasseh, of valiant men, men able to bear buckler and sword, and to shoot with bow, and skilful in war, *were* four and forty thousand seven hundred and threescore, that went out to the war.

19 And they made war with the Hagarites, with [h]Jetur, and Nephish, and Nodab.

20 And [i]they were helped against them, and the Hagarites were delivered into their hand, and all that *were* with them: for they cried to God in the battle, and he was entreated of them; because they [j]put their trust in him.

21 And they took away their cattle; of their camels fifty thousand, and of sheep two hundred and fifty thousand, and of asses two thousand, and of men an hundred thousand.

22 For there fell down many slain, because the war *was* of God. And they dwelt in their steads until [k]the captivity.

23 ¶ And the children of the half tribe of Manasseh dwelt in the land: they increased from Bashan unto Baal-hermon and Senir, and unto mount Hermon.

24 And these *were* the heads of the house of their fathers, even Epher, and Ishi, and Eliel, and Azriel, and Jeremiah, and Hodaviah, and Jahdiel, mighty men of valour, famous men, *and* heads of the house of their fathers.

25 ¶ And they transgressed against the God of their fathers, and went a [l]whoring after the gods of the people of the land, whom God destroyed before them.

26 And the God of Israel stirred up the spirit of [m]Pul king of Assyria, and the spirit of [n]Tilgath-pilneser king of Assyria, and he carried them away, even the Reubenites, and the Gadites, and the half tribe of Manasseh, and brought them unto [o]Halah, and Habor, and Hara, and to the river Gozan, unto this day.

6 The sons of Levi; [p]Gershon, Kohath, and Merari.

2 And the sons of Kohath; Amram, [q]Izhar, and Hebron, and Uzziel.

3 And the children of Amram; Aaron, and Moses, and Miriam. The sons also of Aaron; [r]Nadab, and Abihu, Eleazar, and Ithamar.

4 ¶ Eleazar begat Phinehas, Phinehas begat Abishua,

5 And Abishua begat Bukki, and Bukki begat Uzzi,

6 And Uzzi begat Zerahiah, and Zerahiah begat Meraioth,

7 Meraioth begat Amariah, and Amariah begat Ahitub,

8 And [s]Ahitub begat Zadok, and [t]Zadok begat Ahimaaz,

9 And Ahimaaz begat Azariah, and Azariah begat Johanan,

10 And Johanan begat Azariah, (he *it is* [u]that executed the priest's office in the [v]temple that Solomon built in Jerusalem:)

11 And [w]Azariah begat Amariah, and Amariah begat Ahitub,

12 And Ahitub begat Zadok, and Zadok begat Shallum,

13 And Shallum begat Hilkiah, and Hilkiah begat Azariah,

14 And Azariah begat [x]Seraiah, and Seraiah begat Jehozadak,

15 And Jehozadak went *into captivity,* [y]when the LORD carried away Judah and Jerusalem by the hand of Nebuchadnezzar.

16 ¶ The sons of Levi; [z]Gershom, Kohath, and Merari.

17 And these *be* the names of the sons of Gershom; Libni, and Shimei.

18 And the sons of Kohath *were,* Amram, and Izhar, and Hebron, and Uzziel.

19 The sons of Merari; Mahli, and Mushi. And these *are* the families of the Levites according to their fathers.

20 Of Gershom; Libni his son, Jahath his son, [a]Zimmah his son,

21 Joah his son, Iddo his son, Zerah his son, Jeaterai his son.

22 The sons of Kohath; Amminadab his son, Korah his son, Assir his son,

23 Elkanah his son, and Ebiasaph his son, and Assir his son,

24 Tahath his son, Uriel his son, Uzziah his son, and Shaul his son.

25 And the sons of Elkanah; [b]Amasai, and Ahimoth.

26 *As for* Elkanah: the sons of Elkanah; Zophai his son, and [c]Nahath his son,

27 [d]Eliab his son, Jeroham his son, Elkanah his son.

28 And the sons of Samuel; the firstborn Vashni, and Abiah.

29 The sons of Merari; Mahli, Libni his son, Shimei his son, Uzza his son,

30 Shimea his son, Haggiah his son, Asaiah his son.

31 And these *are they* whom David set

5:10 [c]Gen. 25:12
5:11 [d]Josh. 13:11
5:16 [e]ch. 27:29
5:17 [f]2 Kings 15:5 [g]2 Kings 14:16
5:19 [h]Gen. 25:15; ch. 1:31
5:20 [i]ver. 22 [j]Ps. 22:4
5:22 [k]2 Kings 15:29
5:25 [l]2 Kings 17:7
5:26 [m]2 Kings 15:19 [n]2 Kings 15:29 [o]2 Kings 17:6
6:1 [p]Gen. 46:11; Ex. 6:16; Num. 26:57; ch. 23:6
6:2 [q]ver. 22
6:3 [r]Lev. 10:1
6:8 [s]2 Sam. 8:17 [t]2 Sam. 15:27
6:10 [u]2 Chron. 26:17 [v]1 Kings 6; 2 Chron. 3
6:11 [w]Ezra 7:3
6:14 [x]Neh. 11:11
6:15 [y]2 Kings 25:18
6:16 [z]Ex. 6:16
6:20 [a]ver. 42
6:25 [b]ver. 35
6:26 [c]ver. 34
6:27 [d]ver. 34

over the service of song in the house of the LORD, after that the [e]ark had rest.

32 And they ministered before the dwelling place of the tabernacle of the congregation with singing, until Solomon had built the house of the LORD in Jerusalem: and *then* they waited on their office according to their order.

33 And these *are* they that waited with their children. Of the sons of the Kohathites: Heman a singer, the son of Joel, the son of Shemuel,

34 The son of Elkanah, the son of Jeroham, the son of Eliel, the son of Toah,

35 The son of Zuph, the son of Elkanah, the son of Mahath, the son of Amasai,

36 The son of Elkanah, the son of Joel, the son of Azariah, the son of Zephaniah,

37 The son of Tahath, the son of Assir, the son of [f]Ebiasaph, the son of Korah,

38 The son of Izhar, the son of Kohath, the son of Levi, the son of Israel.

39 And his brother Asaph, who stood on his right hand, *even* Asaph the son of Berachiah, the son of Shimea,

40 The son of Michael, the son of Baaseiah, the son of Malchiah,

41 The son of [g]Ethni, the son of Zerah, the son of Adaiah,

42 The son of Ethan, the son of Zimmah, the son of Shimei,

43 The son of Jahath, the son of Gershom, the son of Levi.

44 And their brethren the sons of Merari *stood* on the left hand: Ethan the son of Kishi, the son of Abdi, the son of Malluch,

45 The son of Hashabiah, the son of Amaziah, the son of Hilkiah,

46 The son of Amzi, the son of Bani, the son of Shamer,

47 The son of Mahli, the son of Mushi, the son of Merari, the son of Levi.

48 Their brethren also the Levites *were* appointed unto all manner of service of the tabernacle of the house of God.

49 ¶ But Aaron and his sons offered [h]upon the altar of the burnt offering, and [i]on the altar of incense, *and were appointed* for all the work of the *place* most holy, and to make an atonement for Israel, according to all that Moses the servant of God had commanded.

50 And these *are* the sons of Aaron; Eleazar his son, Phinehas his son, Abishua his son,

51 Bukki his son, Uzzi his son, Zerahiah his son,

52 Meraioth his son, Amariah his son, Ahitub his son,

53 Zadok his son, Ahimaaz his son.

54 ¶ [j]Now these *are* their dwelling places throughout their castles in their coasts, of the sons of Aaron, of the families of the Kohathites: for theirs was the lot.

55 [k]And they gave them Hebron in the land of Judah, and the suburbs thereof round about it.

56 [l]But the fields of the city, and the villages thereof, they gave to Caleb the son of Jephunneh.

57 And [m]to the sons of Aaron they gave the cities of Judah, *namely*, Hebron, *the city* of refuge, and Libnah with her suburbs, and Jattir, and Eshtemoa, with their suburbs,

58 And Hilen with her suburbs, Debir with her suburbs,

59 And Ashan with her suburbs, and Beth-shemesh with her suburbs:

60 And out of the tribe of Benjamin; Geba with her suburbs, and Alemeth with her suburbs, and Anathoth with her suburbs. All their cities throughout their families *were* thirteen cities.

61 And unto the sons of Kohath, [n]*which were* left of the family of that tribe, *were cities given* out of the half tribe, *namely, out of* the half *tribe* of Manasseh, [o]by lot, ten cities.

62 And to the sons of Gershom throughout their families out of the tribe of Issachar, and out of the tribe of Asher, and out of the tribe of Naphtali, and out of the tribe of Manasseh in Bashan, thirteen cities.

63 Unto the sons of Merari *were given* by lot, throughout their families, out of the tribe of Reuben, and out of the tribe of Gad, and out of the tribe of Zebulun, [p]twelve cities.

64 And the children of Israel gave to the Levites *these* cities with their suburbs.

65 And they gave by lot out of the tribe of the children of Judah, and out of the tribe of the children of Simeon, and out of the tribe of the children of Benjamin, these cities, which are called by *their* names.

66 And [q]*the residue* of the families of the sons of Kohath had cities of their coasts out of the tribe of Ephraim.

67 [r]And they gave unto them, *of* the cities of refuge, Shechem in mount Ephraim with her suburbs; *they gave* also Gezer with her suburbs,

68 And [s]Jokmeam with her suburbs, and Beth-horon with her suburbs,

69 And Aijalon with her suburbs, and Gath-rimmon with her suburbs:

70 And out of the half tribe of Manasseh; Aner with her suburbs, and Bileam with her suburbs, for the family of the remnant of the sons of Kohath.

71 Unto the sons of Gershom *were given* out of the family of the half tribe of Manasseh, Golan in Bashan with her suburbs, and Ashtaroth with her suburbs:

72 And out of the tribe of Issachar; Kedesh with her suburbs, Daberath with her suburbs,

73 And Ramoth with her suburbs, and Anem with her suburbs:

74 And out of the tribe of Asher; Mashal with her suburbs, and Abdon with her suburbs,

75 And Hukok with her suburbs, and Rehob with her suburbs:

76 And out of the tribe of Naphtali; Kedesh in Galilee with her suburbs, and Ham-

6:31 [e]ch. 16:1
6:37 [f]Ex. 6:24
6:41 [g]ver. 21
6:49 [h]Lev. 1:9 [i]Ex. 30:7
6:54 [j]Josh. 21
6:55 [k]Josh. 21:11
6:56 [l]Josh. 14:13
6:57 [m]Josh. 21:13
6:61 [n]ver. 66 [o]Josh. 21:5
6:63 [p]Josh. 21:7
6:66 [q]ver. 61
6:67 [r]Josh. 21:21
6:68 [s]Josh. 21:22-35

mon with her suburbs, and Kirjathaim with her suburbs.

77 Unto the rest of the children of Merari *were given* out of the tribe of Zebulun, Rimmon with her suburbs, Tabor with her suburbs:

78 And on the other side Jordan by Jericho, on the east side of Jordan, *were given them* out of the tribe of Reuben, Bezer in the wilderness with her suburbs, and Jahzah with her suburbs,

79 Kedemoth also with her suburbs, and Mephaath with her suburbs:

80 And out of the tribe of Gad; Ramoth in Gilead with her suburbs, and Mahanaim with her suburbs,

81 And Heshbon with her suburbs, and Jazer with her suburbs.

7 Now the sons of Issachar *were*, [t]Tola, and Puah, Jashub, and Shimron, four.

2 And the sons of Tola; Uzzi, and Rephaiah, and Jeriel, and Jahmai, and Jibsam, and Shemuel, heads of their father's house, *to wit*, of Tola: *they were* valiant men of might in their generations; [u]whose number *was* in the days of David two and twenty thousand and six hundred.

3 And the sons of Uzzi; Izrahiah: and the sons of Izrahiah; Michael, and Obadiah, and Joel, Ishiah, five: all of them chief men.

4 And with them, by their generations, after the house of their fathers, *were* bands of soldiers for war, six and thirty thousand *men:* for they had many wives and sons.

5 And their brethren among all the families of Issachar *were* valiant men of might, reckoned in all by their genealogies fourscore and seven thousand.

6 ¶ *The sons* of [v]Benjamin; Bela, and Becher, and Jediael, three.

7 And the sons of Bela; Ezbon, and Uzzi, and Uzziel, and Jerimoth, and Iri, five; heads of the house of *their* fathers, mighty men of valour; and were reckoned by their genealogies twenty and two thousand and thirty and four.

8 And the sons of Becher; Zemira, and Joash, and Eliezer, and Elioenai, and Omri, and Jerimoth, and Abiah, and Anathoth, and Alameth. All these *are* the sons of Becher.

9 And the number of them, after their genealogy by their generations, heads of the house of their fathers, mighty men of valour, *was* twenty thousand and two hundred.

10 The sons also of Jediael; Bilhan: and the sons of Bilhan; Jeush, and Benjamin, and Ehud, and Chenaanah, and Zethan, and Tharshish, and Ahishahar.

11 All these the sons of Jediael, by the heads of their fathers, mighty men of valour, *were* seventeen thousand and two hundred *soldiers*, fit to go out for war *and* battle.

12 [w]Shuppim also, and Huppim, the children of Ir, *and* Hushim, the sons of Aher.

13 ¶ The sons of Naphtali; Jahziel, and Guni, and Jezer, and [x]Shallum, the sons of Bilhah.

7:1 *t*Gen. 46:13; Num. 26:23
7:2 *u*2 Sam. 24:1; ch. 27:1
7:6 *v*Gen. 46:21; Num. 26:38; ch. 8:1
7:12 *w*Num. 26:39
7:13 *x*Gen. 46:24
7:17 *y*1 Sam. 12:11
7:18 *z*Num. 26:30
7:20 *a*Num. 26:35
7:28 *b*Josh. 16:7
7:29 *c*Josh. 17:7 *d*Josh. 17:11
7:30 *e*Gen. 46:17; Num. 26:44
7:32 *f*ver. 34
7:34 *g*ver. 32

14 ¶ The sons of Manasseh; Ashriel, whom she bare: (*but* his concubine the Aramitess bare Machir the father of Gilead:

15 And Machir took to wife *the sister* of Huppim and Shuppim, whose sister's name *was* Maachah;) and the name of the second *was* Zelophehad: and Zelophehad had daughters.

16 And Maachah the wife of Machir bare a son, and she called his name Peresh; and the name of his brother *was* Sheresh; and his sons *were* Ulam and Rakem.

17 And the sons of Ulam; [y]Bedan. These *were* the sons of Gilead, the son of Machir, the son of Manasseh.

18 And his sister Hammoleketh bare Ishod, and [z]Abiezer, and Mahalah.

19 And the sons of Shemida were, Ahian, and Shechem, and Likhi, and Aniam.

20 ¶ And [a]the sons of Ephraim; Shuthelah, and Bered his son, and Tahath his son, and Eladah his son, and Tahath his son,

21 ¶ And Zabad his son, and Shuthelah his son, and Ezer, and Elead, whom the men of Gath *that were* born in *that* land slew, because they came down to take away their cattle.

22 And Ephraim their father mourned many days, and his brethren came to comfort him.

23 ¶ And when he went in to his wife, she conceived, and bare a son, and he called his name Beriah, because it went evil with his house.

24 (And his daughter *was* Sherah, who built Beth-horon the nether, and the upper, and Uzzen-sherah.)

25 And Rephah *was* his son, also Resheph, and Telah his son, and Tahan his son,

26 Laadan his son, Ammihud his son, Elishama his son,

27 Non his son, Jehoshua his son.

28 ¶ And their possessions and habitations *were*, Beth-el and the towns thereof, and eastward [b]Naaran, and westward Gezer, with the towns thereof; Shechem also and the towns thereof, unto Gaza and the towns thereof:

29 And by the borders of the children of [c]Manasseh, Beth-shean and her towns, Taanach and her towns, [d]Megiddo and her towns, Dor and her towns. In these dwelt the children of Joseph the son of Israel.

30 ¶ [e]The sons of Asher; Imnah, and Isuah, and Ishuai, and Beriah, and Serah their sister.

31 And the sons of Beriah; Heber, and Malchiel, who *is* the father of Birzavith.

32 And Heber begat Japhlet, and [f]Shomer, and Hotham, and Shua their sister.

33 And the sons of Japhlet; Pasach, and Bimhal, and Ashvath. These *are* the children of Japhlet.

34 And the sons of [g]Shamer; Ahi, and Rohgah, Jehubbah, and Aram.

35 And the sons of his brother Helem; Zophah, and Imna, and Shelesh, and Amal.

36 The sons of Zophah; Suah, and Harnepher, and Shual, and Beri, and Imrah,

37 Bezer, and Hod, and Shamma, and Shilshah, and Ithran, and Beera.

38 And the sons of Jether; Jephunneh, and Pispah, and Ara.

39 And the sons of Ulla; Arah, and Haniel, and Rezia.

40 All these *were* the children of Asher, heads of *their* father's house, choice *and* mighty men of valour, chief of the princes. And the number throughout the genealogy of them that were apt to the war *and* to battle *was* twenty and six thousand men.

8 Now Benjamin begat [h]Bela his firstborn, Ashbel the second, and Aharah the third,

2 Nohah the fourth, and Rapha the fifth.

3 And the sons of Bela were, Addar, and Gera, and Abihud,

4 And Abishua, and Naaman, and Ahoah,

5 And Gera, and Shephuphan, and Huram.

6 And these *are* the sons of Ehud: these are the heads of the fathers of the inhabitants of Geba, and they removed them to [i]Manahath:

7 And Naaman, and Ahiah, and Gera, he removed them, and begat Uzza, and Ahihud.

8 And Shaharaim begat *children* in the country of Moab, after he had sent them away; Hushim and Baara *were* his wives.

9 And he begat of Hodesh his wife, Jobab, and Zibia, and Mesha, and Malcham,

10 And Jeuz, and Shachia, and Mirma. These *were* his sons, heads of the fathers.

11 And of Hushim he begat Abitub, and Elpaal.

12 The sons of Elpaal; Eber, and Misham, and Shamed, who built Ono, and Lod, with the towns thereof:

13 Beriah also, and [j]Shema, who *were* heads of the fathers of the inhabitants of Aijalon, who drove away the inhabitants of Gath:

14 And Ahio, Shashak, and Jeremoth,

15 And Zebadiah, and Arad, and Ader,

16 And Michael, and Ispah, and Joha, the sons of Beriah;

17 And Zebadiah, and Meshullam, and Hezeki, and Heber,

18 Ishmerai also, and Jezliah, and Jobab, the sons of Elpaal;

19 And Jakim, and Zichri, and Zabdi,

20 And Elienai, and Zilthai, and Eliel,

21 And Adaiah, and Beraiah, and Shimrath, the sons of Shimhi;

22 And Ishpan, and Heber, and Eliel,

23 And Abdon, and Zichri, and Hanan,

24 And Hananiah, and Elam, and Antothijah,

25 And Iphedeiah, and Penuel, the sons of Shashak;

26 And Shamsherai, and Shehariah, and Athaliah,

27 And Jaresiah, and Eliah, and Zichri, the sons of Jeroham.

28 These *were* heads of the fathers, by their generations, chief *men*. These dwelt in Jerusalem.

29 And at Gibeon dwelt the father of Gibeon; whose [k]wife's name *was* Maachah:

30 And his firstborn son Abdon, and Zur, and Kish, and Baal, and Nadab,

31 And Gedor, and Ahio, and Zacher.

32 And Mikloth begat Shimeah. And these also dwelt with their brethren in Jerusalem, over against them.

33 ¶ And [l]Ner begat Kish, and Kish begat Saul, and Saul begat Jonathan, and Malchi-shua, and [m]Abinadab, and Eshbaal.

34 And the son of Jonathan *was* Merib-baal; and Merib-baal begat [n]Micah.

35 And the sons of Micah *were*, Pithon, and Melech, and Tarea, and Ahaz.

36 And Ahaz begat [o]Jehoadah; and Jehoadah begat Alemeth, and Azmaveth, and Zimri; and Zimri begat Moza,

37 And Moza begat Binea: [p]Rapha *was* his son, Eleasah his son, Azel his son:

38 And Azel had six sons, whose names *are* these, Azrikam, Bocheru, and Ishmael, and Sheariah, and Obadiah, and Hanan. All these *were* the sons of Azel.

39 And the sons of Eshek his brother *were*, Ulam his firstborn, Jehush the second, and Eliphelet the third.

40 And the sons of Ulam were mighty men of valour, archers, and had many sons, and sons' sons, an hundred and fifty. All these *are* of the sons of Benjamin.

9 So [q]all Israel were reckoned by genealogies; and, behold, they *were* written in the book of the kings of Israel and Judah, *who* were carried away to Babylon for their transgression.

2 ¶ [r]Now the first inhabitants that *dwelt* in their possessions in their cities *were*, the Israelites, the priests, Levites, and [s]the Nethinims.

3 And in [t]Jerusalem dwelt of the children of Judah, and of the children of Benjamin, and of the children of Ephraim, and Manasseh;

4 Uthai the son of Ammihud, the son of Omri, the son of Imri, the son of Bani, of the children of Pharez the son of Judah.

5 And of the Shilonites; Asaiah the firstborn, and his sons.

6 And of the sons of Zerah; Jeuel, and their brethren, six hundred and ninety.

7 And of the sons of Benjamin; Sallu the son of Meshullam, the son of Hodaviah, the son of Hasenuah,

8 And Ibneiah the son of Jeroham, and Elah the son of Uzzi, the son of Michri, and Meshullam the son of Shephathiah, the son of Reuel, the son of Ibnijah;

9 And their brethren, according to their generations, nine hundred and fifty and six. All these men *were* chief of the fathers in the house of their fathers.

10 ¶ [u]And of the priests; Jedaiah, and Jehoiarib, and Jachin,

8:1 [h]Gen. 46:21; Num. 26:38; ch. 7:6
8:6 [i]ch. 2:52
8:13 [j]ver. 21
8:29 [k]ch. 9:35
8:33 [l]1 Sam. 14:51 [m]1 Sam. 14:49
8:34 [n]2 Sam. 9:12
8:36 [o]ch. 9:42
8:37 [p]ch. 9:43
9:1 [q]Ezra 2:59
9:2 [r]Ezra 2:70; Neh. 7:73 [s]Josh. 9:27; Ezra 2:43
9:3 [t]Neh. 11:1
9:10 [u]Neh. 11:10

11 And Azariah the son of Hilkiah, the son of Meshullam, the son of Zadok, the son of Meraioth, the son of Ahitub, the ruler of the house of God;

12 And Adaiah the son of Jeroham, the son of Pashur, the son of Malchijah, and Maasiai the son of Adiel, the son of Jahzerah, the son of Meshullam, the son of Meshillemith, the son of Immer;

13 And their brethren, heads of the house of their fathers, a thousand and seven hundred and threescore; very able men for the work of the service of the house of God.

14 And of the Levites; Shemaiah the son of Hasshub, the son of Azrikam, the son of Hashabiah, of the sons of Merari;

15 And Bakbakkar, Heresh, and Galal, and Mattaniah the son of Micah, the son of Zichri, the son of Asaph;

16 And Obadiah the son of Shemaiah, the son of Galal, the son of Jeduthun, and Berechiah the son of Asa, the son of Elkanah, that dwelt in the villages of the Netophathites.

17 And the porters *were*, Shallum, and Akkub, and Talmon, and Ahiman, and their brethren: Shallum *was* the chief;

18 Who hitherto *waited* in the king's gate eastward: they *were* porters in the companies of the children of Levi.

19 And Shallum the son of Kore, the son of Ebiasaph, the son of Korah, and his brethren, of the house of his father, the Korahites, *were* over the work of the service, keepers of the gates of the tabernacle: and their fathers, *being* over the host of the LORD, *were* keepers of the entry.

20 And [v]Phinehas the son of Eleazar was the ruler over them in time past, *and* the LORD *was* with him.

21 *And* Zechariah the son of Meshelemiah *was* porter of the door of the tabernacle of the congregation.

22 All these *which were* chosen to be porters in the gates *were* two hundred and twelve. These were reckoned by their genealogy in their villages, whom [w]David and Samuel [x]the seer did ordain in their set office.

23 So they and their children *had* the oversight of the gates of the house of the LORD, *namely*, the house of the tabernacle, by wards.

24 In four quarters were the porters, toward the east, west, north, and south.

25 And their brethren, *which were* in their villages, *were* to come [y]after seven days from time to time with them.

26 For these Levites, the four chief porters, were in *their* set office, and were over the chambers and treasuries of the house of God.

27 ¶ And they lodged round about the house of God, because the charge *was* upon them, and the opening thereof every morning *pertained* to them.

28 And *certain* of them had the charge of the ministering vessels, that they should bring them in and out by tale.

29 *Some* of them also *were* appointed to oversee the vessels, and all the instruments of the sanctuary, and the fine flour, and the wine, and the oil, and the frankincense, and the spices.

30 And *some* of the sons of the priests made [z]the ointment of the spices.

31 And Mattithiah, *one* of the Levites, who *was* the firstborn of Shallum the Korahite, had the set office [a]over the things that were made in the pans.

32 And *other* of their brethren, of the sons of the Kohathites, [b]*were* over the shewbread, to prepare *it* every sabbath.

33 And these *are* [c]the singers, chief of the fathers of the Levites, *who remaining* in the chambers *were* free: for they were employed in *that* work day and night.

34 These chief fathers of the Levites *were* chief throughout their generations; these dwelt at Jerusalem.

35 ¶ And in Gibeon dwelt the father of Gibeon, Jehiel, whose wife's name *was* [d]Maachah:

36 And his firstborn son Abdon, then Zur, and Kish, and Baal, and Ner, and Nadab,

37 And Gedor, and Ahio, and Zechariah, and Mikloth.

38 And Mikloth begat Shimeam. And they also dwelt with their brethren at Jerusalem, over against their brethren.

39 [e]And Ner begat Kish; and Kish begat Saul; and Saul begat Jonathan, and Malchishua, and Abinadab, and Esh-baal.

40 And the son of Jonathan *was* Merib-baal: and Merib-baal begat Micah.

41 And the sons of Micah *were*, Pithon, and Melech, and Tahrea, [f]*and Ahaz*.

42 And Ahaz begat Jarah; and Jarah begat Alemeth, and Azmaveth, and Zimri; and Zimri begat Moza;

43 And Moza begat Binea; and Rephaiah his son, Eleasah his son, Azel his son.

44 And Azel had six sons, whose names *are* these, Azrikam, Bocheru, and Ishmael, and Sheariah, and Obadiah, and Hanan: these *were* the sons of Azel.

10 Now [g]the Philistines fought against Israel; and the men of Israel fled from before the Philistines, and fell down slain in mount Gilboa.

2 And the Philistines followed hard after Saul, and after his sons; and the Philistines slew Jonathan, and Abinadab, and Malchishua, the sons of Saul.

3 And the battle went sore against Saul, and the archers hit him, and he was wounded of the archers.

4 Then said Saul to his armourbearer, Draw thy sword, and thrust me through therewith; lest these uncircumcised come and abuse me. But his armourbearer would not; for he was sore afraid. So Saul took a sword, and fell upon it.

5 And when his armourbearer saw that

9:20 [v]Num. 31:6
9:22 [w]ch. 26:1 [x]1 Sam. 9:9
9:25 [y]2 Kings 11:5
9:30 [z]Ex. 30:23
9:31 [a]Lev. 2:5
9:32 [b]Lev. 24:8
9:33 [c]ch. 6:31
9:35 [d]ch. 8:29
9:39 [e]ch. 8:33
9:41 [f]ch. 8:35
10:1 [g]1 Sam. 31:1

Saul was dead, he fell likewise on the
sword, and died.
6 So Saul died, and his three sons, and all
his house died together.
7 And when all the men of Israel that
were in the valley saw that they fled, and
that Saul and his sons were dead, then they
forsook their cities, and fled: and the Philistines came and dwelt in them.
8 ¶ And it came to pass on the morrow,
when the Philistines came to strip the slain,
that they found Saul and his sons fallen in
mount Gilboa.
9 And when they had stripped him, they
took his head, and his armour, and sent into
the land of the Philistines round about, to
carry tidings unto their idols, and to the
people.
10 [h]And they put his armour in the house
of their gods, and fastened his head in the
temple of Dagon.
11 ¶ And when all Jabesh-gilead heard all
that the Philistines had done to Saul,
12 They arose, all the valiant men, and
took away the body of Saul, and the bodies
of his sons, and brought them to Jabesh,
and buried their bones under the oak in Jabesh, and fasted seven days.
13 ¶ So Saul died for his transgression
which he committed against the LORD,
[i]*even* against the word of the LORD, which
he kept not, and also for asking *counsel* of
one that had a familiar spirit, [j]to enquire
of it;
14 And enquired not of the LORD: therefore he slew him, and [k]turned the kingdom
unto David the son of Jesse.

11

Then [l]all Israel gathered themselves
to David unto Hebron, saying, Behold, we *are* thy bone and thy flesh.
2 And moreover in time past, even when
Saul was king, thou *wast* he that leddest out
and broughtest in Israel: and the LORD thy
God said unto thee, Thou shalt [m]feed my
people Israel, and thou shalt be ruler over
my people Israel.
3 Therefore came all the elders of Israel
to the king to Hebron; and David made a
covenant with them in Hebron before the
LORD; and [n]they anointed David king over
Israel, according to the word of the LORD by
[o]Samuel.
4 ¶ And David and all Israel [p]went to Jerusalem, which *is* Jebus; [q]where the Jebusites *were,* the inhabitants of the land.
5 And the inhabitants of Jebus said to David, Thou shalt not come hither. Nevertheless David took the castle of Zion, which *is*
the city of David.
6 And David said, Whosoever smiteth the
Jebusites first shall be chief and captain. So
Joab the son of Zeruiah went first up, and
was chief.
7 And David dwelt in the castle; therefore
they called it the city of David.
8 And he built the city round about, even
from Millo round about: and Joab repaired
the rest of the city.

10:10 [h]1 Sam. 31:10
10:13 [i]1 Sam. 13:13 [j]1 Sam. 28:7
10:14 [k]1 Sam. 15:28; 2 Sam. 3:9
11:1 [l]2 Sam. 5:1
11:2 [m]Ps. 78:71
11:3 [n]2 Sam. 5:3 [o]1 Sam. 16:1
11:4 [p]2 Sam. 5:6 [q]Judg. 1:21
11:10 [r]2 Sam. 23:8 [s]1 Sam. 16:1
11:15 [t]2 Sam. 23:13 [u]ch. 14:9
11:20 [v]2 Sam. 23:18
11:21 [w]2 Sam. 23:19
11:22 [x]2 Sam. 23:20

9 So David waxed greater and greater:
for the LORD of hosts *was* with him.
10 ¶ [r]These also *are* the chief of the
mighty men whom David had, who
strengthened themselves with him in his
kingdom, *and* with all Israel, to make him
king, according to [s]the word of the LORD
concerning Israel.
11 And this *is* the number of the mighty
men whom David had; Jashobeam, an
Hachmonite, the chief of the captains: he
lifted up his spear against three hundred
slain *by him* at one time.
12 And after him *was* Eleazar the son of
Dodo, the Ahohite, who *was one* of the
three mighties.
13 He was with David at Pas-dammim,
and there the Philistines were gathered together to battle, where was a parcel of
ground full of barley; and the people fled
from before the Philistines.
14 And they set themselves in the midst of
that parcel, and delivered it, and slew the
Philistines; and the LORD saved *them* by a
great deliverance.
15 ¶ Now three of the thirty captains
[t]went down to the rock to David, into the
cave of Adullam; and the host of the Philistines encamped [u]in the valley of Rephaim.
16 And David *was* then in the hold, and
the Philistines' garrison *was* then at Beth-
lehem.
17 And David longed, and said, Oh that
one would give me drink of the water of the
well of Beth-lehem, that *is* at the gate!
18 And the three brake through the host
of the Philistines, and drew water out of the
well of Beth-lehem, that *was* by the gate,
and took *it,* and brought *it* to David: but
David would not drink *of* it, but poured it
out to the LORD,
19 And said, My God forbid it me, that I
should do this thing: shall I drink the blood
of these men that have put their lives in
jeopardy? for with *the jeopardy of* their
lives they brought it. Therefore he would
not drink it. These things did these three
mightiest.
20 ¶ [v]And Abishai the brother of Joab, he
was chief of the three: for lifting up his
spear against three hundred, he slew *them,*
and had a name among the three.
21 [w]Of the three, he was more honourable than the two; for he was their captain:
howbeit he attained not to the *first* three.
22 Benaiah the son of Jehoiada, the son of
a valiant man of Kabzeel, who had done
many acts; [x]he slew two lionlike men of
Moab: also he went down and slew a lion in
a pit in a snowy day.
23 And he slew an Egyptian, a man of
great stature, five cubits high; and in the
Egyptian's hand *was* a spear like a weaver's
beam; and he went down to him with a staff,
and plucked the spear out of the Egyptian's
hand, and slew him with his own spear.
24 These *things* did Benaiah the son of

Jehoiada, and had the name among the three mighties.

25 Behold, he was honourable among the thirty, but attained not to the *first* three: and David set him over his guard.

26 ¶ Also the valiant men of the armies *were,* [y]Asahel the brother of Joab, Elhanan the son of Dodo of Beth-lehem,

27 Shammoth the Harorite, Helez the Pelonite,

28 Ira the son of Ikkesh the Tekoite, Abiezer the Antothite,

29 Sibbecai the Hushathite, Ilai the Ahohite,

30 Maharai the Netophathite, Heled the son of Baanah the Netophathite,

31 Ithai the son of Ribai of Gibeah, *that pertained* to the children of Benjamin, Benaiah the Pirathonite,

32 Hurai of the brooks of Gaash, Abiel the Arbathite,

33 Azmaveth the Baharumite, Eliahba the Shaalbonite,

34 The sons of Hashem the Gizonite, Jonathan the son of Shage the Hararite,

35 Ahiam the son of Sacar the Hararite, Eliphal the son of Ur,

36 Hepher the Mecherathite, Ahijah the Pelonite,

37 Hezro the Carmelite, Naarai the son of Ezbai,

38 Joel the brother of Nathan, Mibhar the son of Haggeri,

39 Zelek the Ammonite, Naharai the Berothite, the armourbearer of Joab the son of Zeruiah,

40 Ira the Ithrite, Gareb the Ithrite,

41 Uriah the Hittite, Zabad the son of Ahlai,

42 Adina the son of Shiza the Reubenite, a captain of the Reubenites, and thirty with him,

43 Hanan the son of Maachah, and Joshaphat the Mithnite,

44 Uzzia the Ashterathite, Shama and Jehiel the sons of Hothan the Aroerite,

45 Jediael the son of Shimri, and Joha his brother, the Tizite,

46 Eliel the Mahavite, and Jeribai, and Joshaviah, the sons of Elnaam, and Ithmah the Moabite,

47 Eliel, and Obed, and Jasiel the Mesobaite.

12 Now [z]these *are* they that came to David to [a]Ziklag, while he yet kept himself close because of Saul the son of Kish: and they *were* among the mighty men, helpers of the war.

2 *They were* armed with bows, and could use both the right hand and [b]the left in *hurling* stones and *shooting* arrows out of a bow, *even* of Saul's brethren of Benjamin.

3 The chief *was* Ahiezer, then Joash, the sons of Shemaah the Gibeathite; and Jeziel, and Pelet, the sons of Azmaveth; and Berachah, and Jehu the Antothite,

4 And Ismaiah the Gibeonite, a mighty man among the thirty, and over the thirty;

11:26 [y]2 Sam. 23:24
12:1 [z]1 Sam. 27:2 [a]1 Sam. 27:6
12:2 [b]Judg. 20:16
12:8 [c]2 Sam. 2:18
12:15 [d]Josh. 3:15
12:18 [e]2 Sam. 17:25
12:19 [f]1 Sam. 29:2 [g]1 Sam. 29:4
12:21 [h]1 Sam. 30:1

and Jeremiah, and Jahaziel, and Johanan, and Josabad the Gederathite,

5 Eluzai, and Jerimoth, and Bealiah, and Shemariah, and Shephatiah the Haruphite,

6 Elkanah, and Jesiah, and Azareel, and Joezer, and Jashobeam, the Korhites,

7 And Joelah, and Zebadiah, the sons of Jeroham of Gedor.

8 And of the Gadites there separated themselves unto David into the hold to the wilderness men of might, *and* men of war *fit* for the battle, that could handle shield and buckler, whose faces *were like* the faces of lions, and *were* [c]as swift as the roes upon the mountains;

9 Ezer the first, Obadiah the second, Eliab the third,

10 Mishmannah the fourth, Jeremiah the fifth,

11 Attai the sixth, Eliel the seventh,

12 Johanan the eighth, Elzabad the ninth,

13 Jeremiah the tenth, Machbanai the eleventh.

14 These *were* of the sons of Gad, captains of the host: one of the least *was* over an hundred, and the greatest over a thousand.

15 These *are* they that went over Jordan in the first month, when it had overflown all his [d]banks; and they put to flight all *them* of the valleys, *both* toward the east, and toward the west.

16 And there came of the children of Benjamin and Judah to the hold unto David.

17 And David went out to meet them, and answered and said unto them, If ye be come peaceably unto me to help me, mine heart shall be knit unto you: but if *ye be come* to betray me to mine enemies, seeing *there is* no wrong in mine hands, the God of our fathers look *thereon,* and rebuke *it.*

18 Then the spirit came upon [e]Amasai, *who was* chief of the captains, *and he said,* Thine *are we,* David, and on thy side, thou son of Jesse: peace, peace *be* unto thee, and peace *be* to thine helpers; for thy God helpeth thee. Then David received them, and made them captains of the band.

19 And there fell *some* of Manasseh to David, [f]when he came with the Philistines against Saul to battle: but they helped them not: for the lords of the Philistines upon advisement sent him away, saying, [g]He will fall to his master Saul to *the jeopardy of* our heads.

20 As he went to Ziklag, there fell to him of Manasseh, Adnah, and Jozabad, and Jediael, and Michael, and Jozabad, and Elihu, and Zilthai, captains of the thousands that *were* of Manasseh.

21 And they helped David against [h]the band *of the rovers:* for they *were* all mighty men of valour, and were captains in the host.

22 For at *that* time day by day there came to David to help him, until *it was* a great host, like the host of God.

23 ¶ And these *are* the numbers of the

bands *that were* ready armed to the war, *and* [i]came to David to Hebron, to [j]turn the kingdom of Saul to him, [k]according to the word of the LORD.

24 The children of Judah that bare shield and spear *were* six thousand and eight hundred, ready armed to the war.

25 Of the children of Simeon, mighty men of valour for the war, seven thousand and one hundred.

26 Of the children of Levi four thousand and six hundred.

27 And Jehoiada *was* the leader of the Aaronites, and with him *were* three thousand and seven hundred;

28 And [l]Zadok, a young man mighty of valour, and of his father's house twenty and two captains.

29 And of the children of Benjamin, the kindred of Saul, three thousand: for hitherto [m]the greatest part of them had kept the ward of the house of Saul.

30 And of the children of Ephraim twenty thousand and eight hundred, mighty men of valour, famous throughout the house of their fathers.

31 And of the half tribe of Manasseh eighteen thousand, which were expressed by name, to come and make David king.

32 And of the children of Issachar, [n]*which were men* that had understanding of the times, to know what Israel ought to do; the heads of them *were* two hundred; and all their brethren *were* at their commandment.

33 Of Zebulun, such as went forth to battle, expert in war, with all instruments of war, fifty thousand, which could keep rank: *they were* not of double heart.

34 And of Naphtali a thousand captains, and with them with shield and spear thirty and seven thousand.

35 And of the Danites expert in war twenty and eight thousand and six hundred.

36 And of Asher, such as went forth to battle, expert in war, forty thousand.

37 And on the other side of Jordan, of the Reubenites, and the Gadites, and of the half tribe of Manasseh, with all manner of instruments of war for the battle, an hundred and twenty thousand.

38 All these men of war, that could keep rank, came with a perfect heart to Hebron, to make David king over all Israel: and all the rest also of Israel *were* of one heart to make David king.

39 And there they were with David three days, eating and drinking: for their brethren had prepared for them.

40 Moreover they that were nigh them, *even* unto Issachar and Zebulun and Naphtali, brought bread on asses, and on camels, and on mules, and on oxen, *and* meat, meal, cakes of figs, and bunches of raisins, and wine, and oil, and oxen, and sheep abundantly: for *there was* joy in Israel.

13 And David consulted with the captains of thousands and hundreds, *and* with every leader.

2 And David said unto all the congregation of Israel, If *it seem* good unto you, and *that it be* of the LORD our God, let us send abroad unto our brethren every where, *that are* [o]left in all the land of Israel, and with them *also* to the priests and Levites *which are* in their cities *and* suburbs, that they may gather themselves unto us:

3 And let us bring again the ark of our God to us: [p]for we enquired not at it in the days of Saul.

4 And all the congregation said that they would do so: for the thing was right in the eyes of all the people.

5 So [q]David gathered all Israel together, from [r]Shihor of Egypt even unto the entering of Hemath, to bring the ark of God [s]from Kirjath-jearim.

6 And David went up, and all Israel, to [t]Baalah, *that is,* to Kirjath-jearim, which *belonged* to Judah, to bring up thence the ark of God the LORD, [u]that dwelleth *between* the cherubims, whose name is called *on it.*

7 And they carried the ark of God [v]in a new cart [w]out of the house of Abinadab: and [x]Uzza and Ahio drave the cart.

8 [y]And David and all Israel played before God with all *their* might, and with singing, and with harps, and with psalteries, and with timbrels, and with cymbals, and with trumpets.

9 ¶ And when they came unto the threshingfloor of Chidon, Uzza put forth his hand to hold the ark; for the oxen stumbled.

10 And the anger of the LORD was kindled against Uzza, and he smote him, [z]because he put his hand to the ark: and there he [a]died before God.

11 And David was displeased, because the LORD had made a breach upon Uzza: wherefore that place is called Perez-uzza to this day.

12 And David was afraid of God that day, saying, How shall I bring the ark of God *home* to me?

13 So David brought not the ark *home* to himself to the city of David, but carried it aside into the house of Obed-edom the Gittite.

14 [b]And the ark of God remained with the family of Obed-edom in his house three months. And the LORD blessed [c]the house of Obed-edom, and all that he had.

14 Now [d]Hiram king of Tyre sent messengers to David, and timber of cedars, with masons and carpenters, to build him an house.

2 And David perceived that the LORD had confirmed him king over Israel, for his kingdom was lifted up on high, because of his people Israel.

3 ¶ And David took more wives at Jerusalem: and David begat more sons and daughters.

12:23 [i]2 Sam. 2:3; ch. 11:1 [j]ch. 10:14 [k]1 Sam. 16:1
12:28 [l]2 Sam. 8:17
12:29 [m]2 Sam. 2:8
12:32 [n]Esth. 1:13
13:2 [o]1 Sam. 31:1; Isa. 37:4
13:3 [p]1 Sam. 7:1
13:5 [q]1 Sam. 7:1; 2 Sam. 6:1 [r]Josh. 13:3 [s]1 Sam. 6:21
13:6 [t]Josh. 15:9 [u]1 Sam. 4:4; 2 Sam. 6:2
13:7 [v]Num. 4:15; ch. 15:2 [w]1 Sam. 7:1 [x]2 Sam. 6:5
13:8 [y]2 Sam. 6:5
13:10 [z]Num. 4:15; ch. 15:13 [a]Lev. 10:2
13:14 [b]2 Sam. 6:11 [c]Gen. 30:27; ch. 26:5
14:1 [d]2 Sam. 5:11

4 Now [e]these *are* the names of *his* children which he had in Jerusalem; Shammua,
and Shobab, Nathan, and Solomon,
5 And Ibhar, and Elishua, and Elpalet,
6 And Nogah, and Nepheg, and Japhia,
7 And Elishama, and Beeliada, and Eliphalet.
8 ¶ And when the Philistines heard that
[f]David was anointed king over all Israel,
all the Philistines went up to seek David.
And David heard *of it,* and went out against
them.
9 And the Philistines came and spread
themselves [g]in the valley of Rephaim.
10 And David enquired of God, saying,
Shall I go up against the Philistines? and
wilt thou deliver them into mine hand? And
the LORD said unto him, Go up; for I will
deliver them into thine hand.
11 So they came up to Baal-perazim; and
David smote them there. Then David said,
God hath broken in upon mine enemies by
mine hand like the breaking forth of waters:
therefore they called the name of that place
Baal-perazim.
12 And when they had left their gods
there, David gave a commandment, and
they were burned with fire.
13 [h]And the Philistines yet again spread
themselves abroad in the valley.
14 Therefore David enquired again of
God; and God said unto him, Go not up after
them; turn away from them, [i]and come
upon them over against the mulberry trees.
15 And it shall be, when thou shalt hear a
sound of going in the tops of the mulberry
trees, *that* then thou shalt go out to battle:
for God is gone forth before thee to smite
the host of the Philistines.
16 David therefore did as God commanded him: and they smote the host of the
Philistines from [j]Gibeon even to Gazer.
17 And [k]the fame of David went out into
all lands; and the LORD [l]brought the fear of
him upon all nations.

15 And *David* made him houses in the
city of David, and prepared a place
for the ark of God, [m]and pitched for it a tent.
2 Then David said, None ought to carry
the [n]ark of God but the Levites: for them
hath the LORD chosen to carry the ark of
God, and to minister unto him for ever.
3 And David [o]gathered all Israel together
to Jerusalem, to bring up the ark of the
LORD unto his place, which he had prepared
for it.
4 And David assembled the children of
Aaron, and the Levites:
5 Of the sons of Kohath; Uriel the chief,
and his brethren an hundred and twenty:
6 Of the sons of Merari; Asaiah the chief,
and his brethren two hundred and twenty:
7 Of the sons of Gershom; Joel the chief,
and his brethren an hundred and thirty:
8 Of the sons of [p]Elizaphan; Shemaiah
the chief, and his brethren two hundred:
9 Of the sons of [q]Hebron; Eliel the chief,
and his brethren fourscore:
10 Of the sons of Uzziel; Amminadab the
chief, and his brethren an hundred and
twelve.
11 And David called for Zadok and Abiathar the priests, and for the Levites, for
Uriel, Asaiah, and Joel, Shemaiah, and
Eliel, and Amminadab,
12 And said unto them, Ye *are* the chief of
the fathers of the Levites: sanctify yourselves, *both* ye and your brethren, that ye
may bring up the ark of the LORD God of
Israel unto *the place that* I have prepared
for it.
13 For [r]because ye *did it* not at the first,
[s]the LORD our God made a breach upon us,
for that we sought him not after the due
order.
14 So the priests and the Levites sanctified themselves to bring up the ark of the
LORD God of Israel.
15 And the children of the Levites bare
the ark of God upon their shoulders with the
staves thereon, as [t]Moses commanded according to the word of the LORD.
16 And David spake to the chief of the
Levites to appoint their brethren *to be* the
singers with instruments of musick, psalteries and harps and cymbals, sounding, by
lifting up the voice with joy.
17 So the Levites appointed [u]Heman the
son of Joel; and of his brethren, [v]Asaph the
son of Berechiah; and of the sons of Merari
their brethren, [w]Ethan the son of Kushaiah;
18 And with them their brethren of the
second *degree,* Zechariah, Ben, and Jaaziel,
and Shemiramoth, and Jehiel, and Unni,
Eliab, and Benaiah, and Maaseiah, and
Mattithiah, and Elipheleh, and Mikneiah,
and Obed-edom, and Jeiel, the porters.
19 So the singers, Heman, Asaph, and
Ethan, *were appointed* to sound with cymbals of brass;
20 And Zechariah, and Aziel, and Shemiramoth, and Jehiel, and Unni, and Eliab,
and Maaseiah, and Benaiah, with psalteries
[x]on Alamoth;
21 And Mattithiah, and Elipheleh, and
Mikneiah, and Obed-edom, and Jeiel, and
Azaziah, with harps on the Sheminith to excel.
22 And Chenaniah, chief of the Levites,
was for song: he instructed about the song,
because he *was* skilful.
23 And Berechiah and Elkanah *were*
doorkeepers for the ark.
24 And Shebaniah, and Jehoshaphat, and
Nethaneel, and Amasai, and Zechariah, and
Benaiah, and Eliezer, the priests, [y]did blow
with the trumpets before the ark of God:
and Obed-edom and Jehiah *were* doorkeepers for the ark.
25 ¶ So [z]David, and the elders of Israel,
and the captains over thousands, went to
bring up the ark of the covenant of the LORD
out of the house of Obed-edom with joy.
26 And it came to pass, when God helped
the Levites that bare the ark of the covenant

14:4 [e]ch. 3:5
14:8 [f]2 Sam. 5:17
14:9 [g]ch. 11:15
14:13 [h]2 Sam. 5:22
14:14 [i]2 Sam. 5:23
14:16 [j]2 Sam. 5:25
14:17 [k]Josh. 6:27; 2 Chron. 26:8 [l]Deut. 2:25
15:1 [m]ch. 16:1
15:2 [n]Num. 4:2; Deut. 10:8
15:3 [o]1 Kings 8:1; ch. 13:5
15:8 [p]Ex. 6:22
15:9 [q]Ex. 6:18
15:13 [r]2 Sam. 6:3; ch. 13:7 [s]ch. 13:10
15:15 [t]Ex. 25:14; Num. 4:15
15:17 [u]ch. 6:33 [v]ch. 6:39 [w]ch. 6:44
15:20 [x]Ps. 46, title
15:24 [y]Num. 10:8; Ps. 81:3
15:25 [z]2 Sam. 6:12; 1 Kings 8:1

of the LORD, that they offered seven bullocks and seven rams.
27 And David *was* clothed with a robe of
fine linen, and all the Levites that bare the
ark, and the singers, and Chenaniah the
master of the song with the singers: David
also *had* upon him an ephod of linen.
28 [a]Thus all Israel brought up the ark of
the covenant of the LORD with shouting, and
with sound of the cornet, and with trumpets, and with cymbals, making a noise
with psalteries and harps.
29 ¶ And it came to pass, [b]*as* the ark of
the covenant of the LORD came to the city
of David, that Michal the daughter of Saul
looking out at a window saw king David
dancing and playing: and she despised him
in her heart.

16 So [c]they brought the ark of God, and
set it in the midst of the tent that
David had pitched for it: and they offered
burnt sacrifices and peace offerings before
God.
2 And when David had made an end of
offering the burnt offerings and the peace
offerings, he blessed the people in the name
of the LORD.
3 And he dealt to every one of Israel, both
man and woman, to every one a loaf of
bread, and a good piece of flesh, and a
flagon *of wine*.
4 ¶ And he appointed *certain* of the Levites to minister before the ark of the LORD,
and to [d]record, and to thank and praise the
LORD God of Israel:
5 Asaph the chief, and next to him Zechariah, Jeiel, and Shemiramoth, and Jehiel,
and Mattithiah, and Eliab, and Benaiah,
and Obed-edom: and Jeiel with psalteries
and with harps; but Asaph made a sound
with cymbals;
6 Benaiah also and Jahaziel the priests
with trumpets continually before the ark of
the covenant of God.
7 ¶ Then on that day David delivered
[e]first *this psalm* to thank the LORD into the
hand of Asaph and his brethren.
8 [f]Give thanks unto the LORD, call upon
his name, make known his deeds among the
people.
9 Sing unto him, sing psalms unto him,
talk ye of all his wondrous works.
10 Glory ye in his holy name: let the heart
of them rejoice that seek the LORD.
11 Seek the LORD and his strength, seek
his face continually.
12 Remember his marvellous works that
he hath done, his wonders, and the judgments of his mouth;
13 O ye seed of Israel his servant, ye children of Jacob, his chosen ones.
14 He *is* the LORD our God; his judgments
are in all the earth.
15 Be ye mindful always of his covenant;
the word *which* he commanded to a thousand generations;
16 *Even of the* [g]*covenant* which he made
with Abraham, and of his oath unto Isaac;
17 And hath confirmed the same to Jacob
for a law, *and* to Israel *for* an everlasting
covenant,
18 Saying, Unto thee will I give the land
of Canaan, the lot of your inheritance;
19 When ye were but few, [h]even a few,
and strangers in it.
20 And *when* they went from nation to
nation, and from *one* kingdom to another
people;
21 He suffered no man to do them wrong:
yea, he [i]reproved kings for their sakes,
22 *Saying*, [j]touch not mine anointed, and
do my prophets no harm.
23 [k]Sing unto the LORD, all the earth;
shew forth from day to day his salvation.
24 Declare his glory among the heathen;
his marvellous works among all nations.
25 For great *is* the LORD, and greatly to be
praised: he also *is* to be feared above all
gods.
26 For all the gods [l]of the people *are*
idols: but the LORD made the heavens.
27 Glory and honour *are* in his presence;
strength and gladness *are* in his place.
28 Give unto the LORD, ye kindreds of
the people, give unto the LORD glory and
strength.
29 Give unto the LORD the glory *due* unto
his name: bring an offering, and come before him: worship the LORD in the beauty of
holiness.
30 Fear before him, all the earth: the
world also shall be stable, that it be not
moved.
31 Let the heavens be glad, and let the
earth rejoice: and let *men* say among the
nations, The LORD reigneth.
32 Let the sea roar, and the fulness
thereof: let the fields rejoice, and all that *is*
therein.
33 Then shall the trees of the wood sing
out at the presence of the LORD, because he
cometh to judge the earth.
34 [m]O give thanks unto the LORD; for *he is*
good; for his mercy *endureth* for ever.
35 [n]And say ye, Save us, O God of our
salvation, and gather us together, and deliver us from the heathen, that we may give
thanks to thy holy name, *and* glory in thy
praise.
36 [o]Blessed *be* the LORD God of Israel for
ever and ever. And all [p]the people said,
Amen, and praised the LORD.
37 ¶ So he left there before the ark of the
covenant of the LORD Asaph and his brethren, to minister before the ark continually,
as every day's work required:
38 And Obed-edom with their brethren,
threescore and eight; Obed-edom also the
son of Jeduthun and Hosah *to be* porters:
39 And Zadok the priest, and his brethren
the priests, [q]before the tabernacle of the
LORD [r]in the high place that *was* at Gibeon,
40 To offer burnt offerings unto the LORD
upon the altar of the burnt offering continually [s]morning and evening, and *to do* ac-

15:28 [a]ch. 13:8
15:29 [b]2 Sam. 6:16
16:1 [c]2 Sam. 6:17-19
16:4 [d]Ps. 38
16:7 [e]2 Sam. 23:1
16:8 [f]Ps. 105:1-15
16:16 [g]Gen. 17:2
16:19 [h]Gen. 34:30
16:21 [i]Gen. 12:17; Ex. 7:15-18
16:22 [j]Ps. 105:15
16:23 [k]Ps. 96:1
16:26 [l]Lev. 19:4
16:34 [m]Ps. 106:1
16:35 [n]Ps. 106:47
16:36 [o]1 Kings 8:15 [p]Deut. 27:15
16:39 [q]ch. 21:29; 2 Chron. 1:3 [r]1 Kings 3:4
16:40 [s]Ex. 29:38; Num. 28:3

cording to all that is written in the law of the LORD, which he commanded Israel;

41 And with them Heman and Jeduthun, and the rest that were chosen, who were expressed by name, to give thanks to the LORD, [t]because his mercy *endureth* for ever;

42 And with them Heman and Jeduthun, with trumpets and cymbals for those that should make a sound, and with musical instruments of God. And the sons of Jeduthun *were* porters.

43 [u]And all the people departed every man to his house: and David returned to bless his house.

17 Now [v]it came to pass, as David sat in his house, that David said to Nathan the prophet, Lo, I dwell in an house of cedars, but the ark of the covenant of the LORD *remaineth* under curtains.

2 Then Nathan said unto David, Do all that *is* in thine heart; for God *is* with thee.

3 ¶ And it came to pass the same night, that the word of God came to Nathan, saying,

4 Go and tell David my servant, Thus saith the LORD, Thou shalt not build me an house to dwell in:

5 For I have not dwelt in an house since the day that I brought up Israel unto this day; but have gone from tent to tent, and from *one* tabernacle *to another*.

6 Wheresoever I have walked with all Israel, spake I a word to any of the judges of Israel, whom I commanded to feed my people, saying, Why have ye not built me an house of cedars?

7 Now therefore thus shalt thou say unto my servant David, Thus saith the LORD of hosts, I took thee from the sheepcote, *even* from following the sheep, that thou shouldest be ruler over my people Israel:

8 And I have been with thee whithersoever thou hast walked, and have cut off all thine enemies from before thee, and have made thee a name like the name of the great men that *are* in the earth.

9 Also I will ordain a place for my people Israel, and will plant them, and they shall dwell in their place, and shall be moved no more; neither shall the children of wickedness waste them any more, as at the beginning,

10 And since the time that I commanded judges *to be* over my people Israel. Moreover I will subdue all thine enemies. Furthermore I tell thee, that the LORD will build thee an house.

11 ¶ And it shall come to pass, when thy days be expired that thou must go *to be* with thy fathers, that I will raise up thy seed after thee, which shall be of thy sons; and I will establish his kingdom.

12 He shall build me an house, and I will stablish his throne for ever.

13 [w]I will be his father, and he shall be my son: and I will not take my mercy away from him, as I took *it* from *him* that was before thee:

14 But [x]I will settle him in mine house and in my kingdom for ever: and his throne shall be established for evermore.

15 According to all these words, and according to all this vision, so did Nathan speak unto David.

16 ¶ [y]And David the king came and sat before the LORD, and said, Who *am* I, O LORD God, and what *is* mine house, that thou hast brought me hitherto?

17 And *yet* this was a small thing in thine eyes, O God; for thou hast *also* spoken of thy servant's house for a great while to come, and hast regarded me according to the estate of a man of high degree, O LORD God.

18 What can David *speak* more to thee for the honour of thy servant? for thou knowest thy servant.

19 O LORD, for thy servant's sake, and according to thine own heart, hast thou done all this greatness, in making known all *these* great things.

20 O LORD, *there is* none like thee, neither *is there any* God beside thee, according to all that we have heard with our ears.

21 And what one nation in the earth *is* like thy people Israel, whom God went to redeem *to be* his own people, to make thee a name of greatness and terribleness, by driving out nations from before thy people, whom thou hast redeemed out of Egypt?

22 For thy people Israel didst thou make thine own people for ever; and thou, LORD, becamest their God.

23 Therefore now, LORD, let the thing that thou hast spoken concerning thy servant and concerning his house be established for ever, and do as thou hast said.

24 Let it even be established, that thy name may be magnified for ever, saying, The LORD of hosts *is* the God of Israel, *even* a God to Israel: and *let* the house of David thy servant *be* established before thee.

25 For thou, O my God, hast told thy servant that thou wilt build him an house: therefore thy servant hath found *in his heart* to pray before thee.

26 And now, LORD, thou art God, and hast promised this goodness unto thy servant:

27 Now therefore let it please thee to bless the house of thy servant, that it may be before thee for ever: for thou blessest, O LORD, and *it shall be* blessed for ever.

18 Now after this [z]it came to pass, that David smote the Philistines, and subdued them, and took Gath and her towns out of the hand of the Philistines.

2 And he smote Moab; and the Moabites became David's servants, *and* brought gifts.

3 ¶ And David smote Hadarezer king of Zobah unto Hamath, as he went to stablish his dominion by the river Euphrates.

4 And David took from him a thousand chariots, and [a]seven thousand horsemen, and twenty thousand footmen: David also

16:41 [t]ver. 34; 2 Chron. 5:13; Ezra 3:11; Jer. 33:11
16:43 [u]2 Sam. 6:19
17:1 [v]2 Sam. 7:1
17:13 [w]2 Sam. 7:14
17:14 [x]Luke 1:33
17:16 [y]2 Sam. 7:18
18:1 [z]2 Sam. 8:1
18:4 [a]2 Sam. 8:4

houghed all the chariot *horses,* but reserved of them an hundred chariots.

5 And when the Syrians of Damascus came to help Hadarezer king of Zobah, David slew of the Syrians two and twenty thousand men.

6 Then David put *garrisons* in Syria-damascus; and the Syrians became David's servants, *and* brought gifts. Thus the LORD preserved David whithersoever he went.

7 And David took the shields of gold that were on the servants of Hadarezer, and brought them to Jerusalem.

8 Likewise from Tibhath, and from Chun, cities of Hadarezer, brought David very much brass, wherewith [b]Solomon made the brasen sea, and the pillars, and the vessels of brass.

9 ¶ Now when Tou king of Hamath heard how David had smitten all the host of Hadarezer king of Zobah;

10 He sent Hadoram his son to king David, to enquire of his welfare, and to congratulate him, because he had fought against Hadarezer, and smitten him; (for Hadarezer had war with Tou;) and *with him* all manner of vessels of gold and silver and brass.

11 ¶ Them also king David dedicated unto the LORD, with the silver and the gold that he brought from all *these* nations; from Edom, and from Moab, and from the children of Ammon, and from the Philistines, and from Amalek.

12 Moreover Abishai the son of Zeruiah slew of the Edomites in the valley of salt [c]eighteen thousand.

13 ¶ [d]And he put garrisons in Edom; and all the Edomites became David's servants. Thus the LORD preserved David whithersoever he went.

14 ¶ So David reigned over all Israel, and executed judgment and justice among all his people.

15 And Joab the son of Zeruiah *was* over the host; and Jehoshaphat the son of Ahilud, recorder.

16 And Zadok the son of Ahitub, and Abimelech the son of Abiathar, *were* the priests; and Shavsha was scribe;

17 [e]And Benaiah the son of Jehoiada *was* over the Cherethites and the Pelethites; and the sons of David *were* chief about the king.

19 Now [f]it came to pass after this, that Nahash the king of the children of Ammon died, and his son reigned in his stead.

2 And David said, I will shew kindness unto Hanun the son of Nahash, because his father shewed kindness to me. And David sent messengers to comfort him concerning his father. So the servants of David came into the land of the children of Ammon to Hanun, to comfort him.

3 But the princes of the children of Ammon said to Hanun, Thinkest thou that David doth honour thy father, that he hath sent comforters unto thee? are not his servants come unto thee for to search, and to overthrow, and to spy out the land?

4 Wherefore Hanun took David's servants, and shaved them, and cut off their garments in the midst hard by their buttocks, and sent them away.

5 Then there went *certain,* and told David how the men were served. And he sent to meet them: for the men were greatly ashamed. And the king said, Tarry at Jericho until your beards be grown, and *then* return.

6 ¶ And when the children of Ammon saw that they had made themselves odious to David, Hanun and the children of Ammon sent a thousand talents of silver to hire them chariots and horsemen out of Mesopotamia, and out of Syria-maachah, [g]and out of Zobah.

7 So they hired thirty and two thousand chariots, and the king of Maachah and his people; who came and pitched before Medeba. And the children of Ammon gathered themselves together from their cities, and came to battle.

8 And when David heard *of it,* he sent Joab, and all the host of the mighty men.

9 And the children of Ammon came out, and put the battle in array before the gate of the city: and the kings that were come *were* by themselves in the field.

10 Now when Joab saw that the battle was set against him before and behind, he chose out of all the choice of Israel, and put *them* in array against the Syrians.

11 And the rest of the people he delivered unto the hand of Abishai his brother, and they set *themselves* in array against the children of Ammon.

12 And he said, If the Syrians be too strong for me, then thou shalt help me: but if the children of Ammon be too strong for thee, then I will help thee.

13 Be of good courage, and let us behave ourselves valiantly for our people, and for the cities of our God: and let the LORD do *that which is* good in his sight.

14 So Joab and the people that *were* with him drew nigh before the Syrians unto the battle; and they fled before him.

15 And when the children of Ammon saw that the Syrians were fled, they likewise fled before Abishai his brother, and entered into the city. Then Joab came to Jerusalem.

16 ¶ And when the Syrians saw that they were put to the worse before Israel, they sent messengers, and drew forth the Syrians that *were* beyond the river: and Shophach the captain of the host of Hadarezer *went* before them.

17 And it was told David; and he gathered all Israel, and passed over Jordan, and came upon them, and set *the battle* in array against them. So when David had put the battle in array against the Syrians, they fought with him.

18 But the Syrians fled before Israel; and David slew of the Syrians seven thousand

18:8 [b]1 Kings 7:15; 2 Chron. 4:12
18:12 [c]2 Sam. 8:13
18:13 [d]2 Sam. 8:14
18:17 [e]2 Sam. 8:18
19:1 [f]2 Sam. 10:1
19:6 [g]ch. 18:5

men which fought in chariots, and forty thousand footmen, and killed Shophach the captain of the host.

19 And when the servants of Hadarezer saw that they were put to the worse before Israel, they made peace with David, and became his servants: neither would the Syrians help the children of Ammon any more.

20 And [h]it came to pass, that after the year was expired, at the time that kings go out *to battle,* Joab led forth the power of the army, and wasted the country of the children of Ammon, and came and besieged Rabbah. But David tarried at Jerusalem. And [i]Joab smote Rabbah, and destroyed it.

2 And David [j]took the crown of their king from off his head, and found it to weigh a talent of gold, and *there were* precious stones in it; and it was set upon David's head: and he brought also exceeding much spoil out of the city.

3 And he brought out the people that *were* in it, and cut *them* with saws, and with harrows of iron, and with axes. Even so dealt David with all the cities of the children of Ammon. And David and all the people returned to Jerusalem.

4 ¶ And it came to pass after this, [k]that there arose war at Gezer with the Philistines; at which time [l]Sibbechai the Hushathite slew Sippai, *that was* of the children of the giant: and they were subdued.

5 And there was war again with the Philistines; and Elhanan the son of Jair slew Lahmi the brother of Goliath the Gittite, whose spear staff *was* like a weaver's beam.

6 And yet again [m]there was war at Gath, where was a man of *great* stature, whose fingers and toes *were* four and twenty, six *on each hand,* and six *on each foot:* and he also was the son of the giant.

7 But when he defied Israel, Jonathan the son of Shimea David's brother slew him.

8 These were born unto the giant in Gath; and they fell by the hand of David, and by the hand of his servants.

21 And [n]Satan stood up against Israel, and provoked David to number Israel.

2 And David said to Joab and to the rulers of the people, Go, number Israel from Beersheba even to Dan; [o]and bring the number of them to me, that I may know *it.*

3 And Joab answered, The LORD make his people an hundred times so many more as they *be:* but, my lord the king, *are* they not all my lord's servants? why then doth my lord require this thing? why will he be a cause of trespass to Israel?

4 Nevertheless the king's word prevailed against Joab. Wherefore Joab departed, and went throughout all Israel, and came to Jerusalem.

5 ¶ And Joab gave the sum of the number of the people unto David. And all *they of* Israel were a thousand thousand and an hundred thousand men that drew sword: and Judah *was* four hundred threescore and ten thousand men that drew sword.

6 [p]But Levi and Benjamin counted he not among them: for the king's word was abominable to Joab.

7 And God was displeased with this thing; therefore he smote Israel.

8 And David said unto God, [q]I have sinned greatly, because I have done this thing: [r]but now, I beseech thee, do away the iniquity of thy servant; for I have done very foolishly.

9 ¶ And the LORD spake unto Gad, David's [s]seer, saying,

10 Go and tell David, saying, Thus saith the LORD, I offer thee three *things:* choose thee one of them, that I may do *it* unto thee.

11 So Gad came to David, and said unto him, Thus saith the LORD, Choose thee

12 [t]Either three years' famine; or three months to be destroyed before thy foes, while that the sword of thine enemies overtaketh *thee;* or else three days the sword of the LORD, even the pestilence, in the land, and the angel of the LORD destroying throughout all the coasts of Israel. Now therefore advise thyself what word I shall bring again to him that sent me.

13 And David said unto Gad, I am in a great strait: let me fall now into the hand of the LORD; for very great *are* his mercies: but let me not fall into the hand of man.

14 ¶ So the LORD sent pestilence upon Israel: and there fell of Israel seventy thousand men.

15 And God sent an [u]angel unto Jerusalem to destroy it: and as he was destroying, the LORD beheld, and [v]he repented him of the evil, and said to the angel that destroyed, It is enough, stay now thine hand. And the angel of the LORD stood by the threshingfloor of Ornan the Jebusite.

16 And David lifted up his eyes, and [w]saw the angel of the LORD stand between the earth and the heaven, having a drawn sword in his hand stretched out over Jerusalem. Then David and the elders of *Israel, who were* clothed in sackcloth, fell upon their faces.

17 And David said unto God, *Is it* not I *that* commanded the people to be numbered? even I it is that have sinned and done evil indeed; but *as for* these sheep, what have they done? let thine hand, I pray thee, O LORD my God, be on me, and on my father's house; but not on thy people, that they should be plagued.

18 ¶ Then the [x]angel of the LORD commanded Gad to say to David, that David should go up, and set up an altar unto the LORD in the threshingfloor of Ornan the Jebusite.

19 And David went up at the saying of Gad, which he spake in the name of the LORD.

20 And Ornan turned back, and saw the

20:1 *h*2 Sam. 11:1 *i*2 Sam. 12:26
20:2 *j*2 Sam. 12:30
20:4 *k*2 Sam. 21:18 *l*ch. 11:29
20:6 *m*2 Sam. 21:20
21:1 *n*2 Sam. 24:1
21:2 *o*ch. 27:23
21:6 *p*ch. 27:24
21:8 *q*2 Sam. 24:10 *r*2 Sam. 12:13
21:9 *s*1 Sam. 9:9
21:12 *t*2 Sam. 24:13
21:15 *u*2 Sam. 24:16 *v*Gen. 6:6
21:16 *w*2 Chron. 3:1
21:18 *x*2 Chron. 3:1

angel; and his four sons with him hid themselves. Now Ornan was threshing wheat.
21 And as David came to Ornan, Ornan
looked and saw David, and went out of the
threshingfloor, and bowed himself to David
with *his* face to the ground.
22 Then David said to Ornan, Grant me
the place of *this* threshingfloor, that I may
build an altar therein unto the LORD: thou
shalt grant it me for the full price: that the
plague may be stayed from the people.
23 And Ornan said unto David, Take *it* to
thee, and let my lord the king do *that which*
is good in his eyes: lo, I give *thee* the oxen
also for burnt offerings, and the threshing
instruments for wood, and the wheat for the
meat offering; I give it all.
24 And king David said to Ornan, Nay;
but I will verily buy it for the full price: for
I will not take *that* which *is* thine for the
LORD, nor offer burnt offerings without
cost.
25 So [y]David gave to Ornan for the place
six hundred shekels of gold by weight.
26 And David built there an altar unto
the LORD, and offered burnt offerings and
peace offerings, and called upon the LORD;
and [z]he answered him from heaven by fire
upon the altar of burnt offering.
27 And the LORD commanded the angel;
and he put up his sword again into the
sheath thereof.
28 ¶ At that time when David saw that the
LORD had answered him in the threshingfloor of Ornan the Jebusite, then he sacrificed there.
29 [a]For the tabernacle of the LORD,
which Moses made in the wilderness, and
the altar of the burnt offering, *were* at that
season in the high place at [b]Gibeon.
30 But David could not go before it to enquire of God: for he was afraid because of
the sword of the angel of the LORD.

22 Then David said, [c]This *is* the house
of the LORD God, and this *is* the altar
of the burnt offering for Israel.
2 And David commanded to gather together [d]the strangers that *were* in the land
of Israel; and he set masons to hew wrought
stones to build the house of God.
3 And David prepared iron in abundance
for the nails for the doors of the gates, and
for the joinings; and brass in abundance
[e]without weight;
4 Also cedar trees in abundance: for the
[f]Zidonians and they of Tyre brought much
cedar wood to David.
5 And David said, [g]Solomon my son *is*
young and tender, and the house *that is* to
be builded for the LORD *must be* exceeding
magnifical, of fame and of glory throughout
all countries: I will *therefore* now make
preparation for it. So David prepared abundantly before his death.
6 ¶ Then he called for Solomon his son,
and charged him to build an house for the
LORD God of Israel.
7 And David said to Solomon, My son, as
for me, [h]it was in my mind to build an
house [i]unto the name of the LORD my God:
8 But the word of the LORD came to me,
saying, [j]Thou hast shed blood abundantly,
and hast made great wars: thou shalt not
build an house unto my name, because thou
hast shed much blood upon the earth in my
sight.
9 [k]Behold, a son shall be born to thee,
who shall be a man of rest; and I will give
him [l]rest from all his enemies round about:
for his name shall be Solomon, and I will
give peace and quietness unto Israel in his
days.
10 [m]He shall build an house for my name;
and [n]he shall be my son, and I *will be* his
father; and I will establish the throne of his
kingdom over Israel for ever.
11 Now, my son, [o]the LORD be with thee;
and prosper thou, and build the house of the
LORD thy God, as he hath said of thee.
12 Only the LORD [p]give thee wisdom and
understanding, and give thee charge concerning Israel, that thou mayest keep the
law of the LORD thy God.
13 [q]Then shalt thou prosper, if thou takest heed to fulfil the statutes and judgments
which the LORD charged Moses with concerning Israel: [r]be strong, and of good
courage; dread not, nor be dismayed.
14 Now, behold, in my trouble I have prepared for the house of the LORD an hundred
thousand talents of gold, and a thousand
thousand talents of silver; and of brass and
iron [s]without weight; for it is in abundance:
timber also and stone have I prepared; and
thou mayest add thereto.
15 Moreover *there are* workmen with
thee in abundance, hewers and workers of
stone and timber, and all manner of cunning men for every manner of work.
16 Of the gold, the silver, and the brass,
and the iron, *there is* no number. Arise
therefore, and be doing, and [t]the LORD be
with thee.
17 ¶ David also commanded all the
princes of Israel to help Solomon his son,
saying,
18 *Is* not the LORD your God with you?
[u]and hath he *not* given you rest on every
side? for he hath given the inhabitants of
the land into mine hand; and the land is
subdued before the LORD, and before his
people.
19 Now [v]set your heart and your soul to
seek the LORD your God; arise therefore,
and build ye the sanctuary of the LORD God,
to [w]bring the ark of the covenant of the
LORD, and the holy vessels of God, into the
house that is to be built [x]to the name of
the LORD.

23 So when David was old and full of
days, he made [y]Solomon his son
king over Israel.
2 ¶ And he gathered together all the
princes of Israel, with the priests and the
Levites.
3 Now the Levites were numbered from

21:25 [y]2 Sam. 24:24
21:26 [z]Lev. 9:24; 2 Chron. 3:1
21:29 [a]ch. 16:39 [b]1 Kings 3:4; ch. 16:39; 2 Chron. 1:3
22:1 [c]Deut. 12:5; 2 Sam. 24:18; ch. 21:18; 2 Chron. 3:1
22:2 [d]1 Kings 9:21
22:3 [e]ver. 14; 1 Kings 7:47
22:4 [f]1 Kings 5:6
22:5 [g]ch. 29:1
22:7 [h]2 Sam. 7:2; 1 Kings 8:17; ch. 17:1 [i]Deut. 12:5
22:8 [j]1 Kings 5:3; ch. 28:3
22:9 [k]ch. 28:5 [l]1 Kings 4:25
22:10 [m]2 Sam. 7:13; 1 Kings 5:5; ch. 17:12 [n]Heb. 1:5
22:11 [o]ver. 16
22:12 [p]1 Kings 3:9; Ps. 72:1
22:13 [q]Josh. 1:7; ch. 28:7 [r]Deut. 31:7; Josh. 1:6; ch. 28:20
22:14 [s]ver. 3
22:16 [t]ver. 11
22:18 [u]Deut. 12:10; Josh. 22:4; 2 Sam. 7:1; ch. 23:25
22:19 [v]2 Chron. 20:3 [w]1 Kings 8:6; 2 Chron. 5:7 [x]ver. 7; 1 Kings 5:3
23:1 [y]1 Kings 1:33-39; ch. 28:5

the age of [z]thirty years and upward: and
their number by their polls, man by man,
was thirty and eight thousand.
4 Of which, twenty and four thousand
were to set forward the work of the house of
the LORD; and six thousand *were* [a]officers
and judges:
5 Moreover four thousand *were* porters;
and four thousand praised the LORD with
the instruments [b]which I made, *said David,*
to praise *therewith.*
6 And [c]David divided them into courses
among the sons of Levi, *namely,* Gershon,
Kohath, and Merari.
7 ¶ Of the [d]Gershonites *were,* Laadan,
and Shimei.
8 The sons of Laadan; the chief *was* Jehiel, and Zetham, and Joel, three.
9 The sons of Shimei; Shelomith, and Ha-
ziel, and Haran, three. These *were* the chief
of the fathers of Laadan.
10 And the sons of Shimei *were,* Jahath,
Zina, and Jeush, and Beriah. These four
were the sons of Shimei.
11 And Jahath was the chief, and Zizah
the second: but Jeush and Beriah had not
many sons; therefore they were in one reckoning, according to *their* father's house.
12 ¶ [e]The sons of Kohath; Amram, Izhar,
Hebron, and Uzziel, four.
13 The sons of [f]Amram; Aaron and Moses: and [g]Aaron was separated, that he
should sanctify the most holy things, he and
his sons for ever, [h]to burn incense before
the LORD, [i]to minister unto him, and [j]to
bless in his name for ever.
14 Now *concerning* Moses the man of
God, [k]his sons were named of the tribe of
Levi.
15 [l]The sons of Moses *were,* Gershom,
and Eliezer.
16 Of the sons of Gershom, [m]Shebuel *was*
the chief.
17 And the sons of Eliezer *were,* [n]Reha-
biah the chief. And Eliezer had none other
sons; but the sons of Rehabiah were very
many.
18 Of the sons of Izhar; Shelomith the
chief.
19 [o]Of the sons of Hebron; Jeriah the
first, Amariah the second, Jahaziel the
third, and Jekameam the fourth.
20 Of the sons of Uzziel; Michah the first
and Jesiah the second.
21 ¶ [p]The sons of Merari; Mahli, and Mushi. The sons of Mahli; Eleazar, and [q]Kish.
22 And Eleazar died, and [r]had no sons,
but daughters: and their brethren the sons
of Kish [s]took them.
23 [t]The sons of Mushi; Mahli, and Eder,
and Jeremoth, three.
24 ¶ These *were* the sons of [u]Levi after
the house of their fathers; *even* the chief of
the fathers, as they were counted by number of names by their polls, that did the
work for the service of the house of the
LORD, from the age of [v]twenty years and
upward.
25 For David said, The LORD God of Israel
[w]hath given rest unto his people, that they
may dwell in Jerusalem for ever:
26 And also unto the Levites; they shall
no *more* [x]carry the tabernacle, nor any vessels of it for the service thereof.
27 For by the last words of David the Levites *were* numbered from twenty years old
and above:
28 Because their office *was* to wait on the
sons of Aaron for the service of the house of
the LORD, in the courts, and in the chambers, and in the purifying of all holy things,
and the work of the service of the house of
God;
29 Both for [y]the shewbread, and for [z]the
fine flour for meat offering, and for [a]the
unleavened cakes, and for [b]*that which is*
baked in the pan, and for that which is fried,
and for all manner of [c]measure and size;
30 And to stand every morning to thank
and praise the LORD, and likewise at even;
31 And to offer all burnt sacrifices unto
the LORD [d]in the sabbaths, in the new
moons, and on the [e]set feasts, by number,
according to the order commanded unto
them, continually before the LORD:
32 And that they should [f]keep the charge
of the tabernacle of the congregation, and
the charge of the holy *place,* and [g]the
charge of the sons of Aaron their brethren,
in the service of the house of the LORD.

24 Now *these are* the divisions of the
sons of Aaron. [h]The sons of Aaron;
Nadab, and Abihu, Eleazar, and Ithamar.
2 But [i]Nadab and Abihu died before
their father, and had no children: therefore
Eleazar and Ithamar executed the priest's
office.
3 And David distributed them, both Zadok of the sons of Eleazar, and Ahimelech
of the sons of Ithamar, according to their
offices in their service.
4 And there were more chief men found
of the sons of Eleazar than of the sons of
Ithamar; and *thus* were they divided.
Among the sons of Eleazar *there were* sixteen chief men of the house of *their* fathers,
and eight among the sons of Ithamar according to the house of their fathers.
5 Thus were they divided by lot, one sort
with another; for the governors of the sanctuary, and governors *of the house* of God,
were of the sons of Eleazar, and of the sons
of Ithamar.
6 And Shemaiah the son of Nethaneel the
scribe, *one* of the Levites, wrote them before the king, and the princes, and Zadok
the priest, and Ahimelech the son of Abiathar, and *before* the chief of the fathers of
the priests and Levites: one principal household being taken for Eleazar, and *one* taken
for Ithamar.
7 Now the first lot came forth to Jehoiarib, the second to Jedaiah,
8 The third to Harim, the fourth to Seo-
rim,

23:3 [z]Num. 4:3
23:4 [a]Deut. 16:18; ch. 26:29; 2 Chron. 19:8
23:5 [b]2 Chron. 29:25; Am. 6:5
23:6 [c]Ex. 6:16; Num. 26:57; ch. 6:1; 2 Chron. 8:14
23:7 [d]ch. 26:21
23:12 [e]Ex. 6:18
23:13 [f]Ex. 6:20 [g]Ex. 28:1; Heb. 5:4 [h]Ex. 30:7; Num. 16:40; 1 Sam. 2:28 [i]Deut. 21:5 [j]Num. 6:23
23:14 [k]ch. 26:23
23:15 [l]Ex. 2:22
23:16 [m]ch. 26:24
23:17 [n]ch. 26:25
23:19 [o]ch. 24:23
23:21 [p]ch. 24:26 [q]ch. 24:29
23:22 [r]ch. 24:28 [s]Num. 36:6
23:23 [t]ch. 24:30
23:24 [u]Num. 10:17 [v]Num. 1:3; ver. 27; Ezra 3:8
23:25 [w]ch. 22:18
23:26 [x]Num. 4:5
23:29 [y]Ex. 25:30 [z]Lev. 6:20; ch. 9:29 [a]Lev. 2:4 [b]Lev. 2:5 [c]Lev. 19:35
23:31 [d]Num. 10:10; Ps. 81:3 [e]Lev. 23:4
23:32 [f]Num. 1:53 [g]Num. 3:6-9
24:1 [h]Lev. 10:1; Num. 26:60
24:2 [i]Num. 3:4

9 The fifth to Malchijah, the sixth to Mijamin,

10 The seventh to Hakkoz, the eighth to [j]Abijah,

11 The ninth to Jeshua, the tenth to Shecaniah,

12 The eleventh to Eliashib, the twelfth to Jakim,

13 The thirteenth to Huppah, the fourteenth to Jeshebeab,

14 The fifteenth to Bilgah, the sixteenth to Immer,

15 The seventeenth to Hezir, the eighteenth to Aphses,

16 The nineteenth to Pethahiah, the twentieth to Jehezekel,

17 The one and twentieth to Jachin, the two and twentieth to Gamul,

18 The three and twentieth to Delaiah, the four and twentieth to Maaziah.

19 These *were* the orderings of them in their service [k]to come into the house of the LORD, according to their manner, under Aaron their father, as the LORD God of Israel had commanded him.

20 ¶ And the rest of the sons of Levi *were these:* Of the sons of Amram; [l]Shubael: of the sons of Shubael; Jehdeiah.

21 Concerning [m]Rehabiah: of the sons of Rehabiah, the first *was* Isshiah.

22 Of the Izharites; [n]Shelomoth: of the sons of Shelomoth; Jahath.

23 And the sons *of* [o]*Hebron;* Jeriah *the first,* Amariah the second, Jahaziel the third, Jekameam the fourth.

24 *Of* the sons of Uzziel; Michah: of the sons of Michah; Shamir.

25 The brother of Michah *was* Isshiah: of the sons of Isshiah; Zechariah.

26 [p]The sons of Merari *were* Mahli and Mushi: the sons of Jaaziah; Beno.

27 ¶ The sons of Merari by Jaaziah; Beno, and Shoham, and Zaccur, and Ibri.

28 Of Mahli *came* Eleazar, [q]who had no sons.

29 Concerning Kish: the son of Kish *was* Jerahmeel.

30 [r]The sons also of Mushi; Mahli, and Eder, and Jerimoth. These *were* the sons of the Levites after the house of their fathers.

31 These likewise cast lots over against their brethren the sons of Aaron in the presence of David the king, and Zadok, and Ahimelech, and the chief of the fathers of the priests and Levites, even the principal fathers over against their younger brethren.

25

Moreover David and the captains of the host separated to the service of the sons of [s]Asaph, and of Heman, and of Jeduthun, who should prophesy with harps, with psalteries, and with cymbals: and the number of the workmen according to their service was:

2 Of the sons of Asaph; Zaccur, and Joseph, and Nethaniah, and Asarelah, the sons of Asaph under the hands of Asaph, which prophesied according to the order of the king.

24:10 [j]Neh. 12:4; Luke 1:5
24:19 [k]ch. 9:25
24:20 [l]ch. 23:16
24:21 [m]ch. 23:17
24:22 [n]ch. 23:18
24:23 [o]ch. 23:19
24:26 [p]Ex. 6:19; ch. 23:21
24:28 [q]ch. 23:22
24:30 [r]ch. 23:23
25:1 [s]ch. 6:33
25:6 [t]ver. 2
25:8 [u]2 Chron. 23:13

3 Of Jeduthun: the sons of Jeduthun; Gedaliah, and Zeri, and Jeshaiah, Hashabiah, and Mattithiah, six, under the hands of their father Jeduthun, who prophesied with a harp, to give thanks and to praise the LORD.

4 Of Heman: the sons of Heman; Bukkiah, Mattaniah, Uzziel, Shebuel, and Jerimoth, Hananiah, Hanani, Eliathah, Giddalti, and Romamti-ezer, Joshbekashah, Mallothi, Hothir, *and* Mahazioth:

5 All these *were* the sons of Heman the king's seer in the words of God, to lift up the horn. And God gave to Heman fourteen sons and three daughters.

6 All these *were* under the hands of their father for song *in* the house of the LORD, with cymbals, psalteries, and harps, for the service of the house of God, [t]according to the king's order to Asaph, Jeduthun, and Heman.

7 So the number of them, with their brethren that were instructed in the songs of the LORD, *even* all that were cunning, was two hundred fourscore and eight.

8 ¶ And they cast lots, ward against *ward,* as well the small as the great, [u]the teacher as the scholar.

9 Now the first lot came forth for Asaph to Joseph: the second to Gedaliah, who with his brethren and sons *were* twelve:

10 The third to Zaccur, *he,* his sons, and his brethren, *were* twelve:

11 The fourth to Izri, *he,* his sons, and his brethren, *were* twelve:

12 The fifth to Nethaniah, *he,* his sons, and his brethren, *were* twelve:

13 The sixth to Bukkiah, *he,* his sons, and his brethren, *were* twelve:

14 The seventh to Jesharelah, *he,* his sons, and his brethren, *were* twelve:

15 The eighth to Jeshaiah, *he,* his sons, and his brethren, *were* twelve:

16 The ninth to Mattaniah, *he,* his sons, and his brethren, *were* twelve:

17 The tenth to Shimei, *he,* his sons, and his brethren, *were* twelve:

18 The eleventh to Azareel, *he,* his sons, and his brethren, *were* twelve:

19 The twelfth to Hashabiah, *he,* his sons, and his brethren, *were* twelve:

20 The thirteenth to Shubael, *he,* his sons, and his brethren, *were* twelve:

21 The fourteenth to Mattithiah, *he,* his sons, and his brethren, *were* twelve:

22 The fifteenth to Jeremoth, *he,* his sons, and his brethren, *were* twelve:

23 The sixteenth to Hananiah, *he,* his sons, and his brethren, *were* twelve:

24 The seventeenth to Joshbekashah, *he,* his sons, and his brethren, *were* twelve:

25 The eighteenth to Hanani, *he,* his sons, and his brethren, *were* twelve:

26 The nineteenth to Mallothi, *he,* his sons, and his brethren, *were* twelve:

27 The twentieth to Eliathah, *he,* his sons, and his brethren, *were* twelve:

28 The one and twentieth to Hothir, *he,* his sons, and his brethren, *were* twelve:

29 The two and twentieth to Giddalti, *he,* his sons, and his brethren, *were* twelve:

30 The three and twentieth to Mahazioth, *he,* his sons, and his brethren, *were* twelve:

31 The four and twentieth to Romamtiezer, *he,* his sons, and his brethren, *were* twelve.

26 Concerning the divisions of the porters: Of the Korhites *was* Meshelemiah the son of Kore, of the sons of Asaph.

2 And the sons of Meshelemiah *were,* Zechariah the firstborn, Jediael the second, Zebadiah the third, Jathniel the fourth,

3 Elam the fifth, Jehohanan the sixth, Elioenai the seventh.

4 Moreover the sons of Obed-edom *were,* Shemaiah the firstborn, Jehozabad the second, Joah the third, and Sacar the fourth, and Nethaneel the fifth,

5 Ammiel the sixth, Issachar the seventh, Peulthai the eighth: for God blessed him.

6 Also unto Shemaiah his son were sons born, that ruled throughout the house of their father: for they *were* mighty men of valour.

7 The sons of Shemaiah; Othni, and Rephael, and Obed, Elzabad, whose brethren *were* strong men, Elihu, and Semachiah.

8 All these of the sons of Obed-edom: they and their sons and their brethren, able men for strength for the service, *were* threescore and two of Obed-edom.

9 And Meshelemiah had sons and brethren, strong men, eighteen.

10 Also [v]Hosah, of the children of Merari, had sons; Simri the chief, (for *though* he was not the firstborn, yet his father made him the chief;)

11 Hilkiah the second, Tebaliah the third, Zechariah the fourth: all the sons and brethren of Hosah *were* thirteen.

12 Among these *were* the divisions of the porters, *even* among the chief men, *having* wards one against another, to minister in the house of the LORD.

13 ¶ And they cast lots, as well the small as the great, according to the house of their fathers, for every gate.

14 And the lot eastward fell to Shelemiah. Then for Zechariah his son, a wise counsellor, they cast lots; and his lot came out northward.

15 To Obed-edom southward; and to his sons the house of Asuppim.

16 To Shuppim and Hosah *the lot came forth* westward, with the gate Shallecheth, by the causeway of the going up, ward against ward.

17 Eastward *were* six Levites, northward four a day, southward four a day, and toward Asuppim two *and* two.

18 At Parbar westward, four at the causeway, *and* two at Parbar.

19 These *are* the divisions of the porters among the sons of Kore, and among the sons of Merari.

20 ¶ And of the Levites, Ahijah *was* [w]over the treasures of the house of God, and over the treasures of the dedicated things.

21 *As concerning* the sons of Laadan; the sons of the Gershonite Laadan, chief fathers, *even* of Laadan the Gershonite, *were* Jehieli.

22 The sons of Jehieli; Zetham, and Joel his brother, *which were* over the treasures of the house of the LORD.

23 Of the Amramites, *and* the Izharites, the Hebronites, *and* the Uzzielites:

24 And [x]Shebuel the son of Gershom, the son of Moses, *was* ruler of the treasures.

25 And his brethren by Eliezer; Rehabiah his son, and Jeshaiah his son, and Joram his son, and Zichri his son, and [y]Shelomith his son.

26 Which Shelomith and his brethren *were* over all the treasures of the dedicated things, which David the king, and the chief fathers, the captains over thousands and hundreds, and the captains of the host, had dedicated.

27 Out of the spoils won in battles did they dedicate to maintain the house of the LORD.

28 And all that Samuel [z]the seer, and Saul the son of Kish, and Abner the son of Ner, and Joab the son of Zeruiah, had dedicated; *and* whosoever had dedicated *any thing, it was* under the hand of Shelomith, and of his brethren.

29 ¶ Of the Izharites, Chenaniah and his sons *were* for the outward business over Israel, for [a]officers and judges.

30 *And* of the Hebronites, Hashabiah and his brethren, men of valour, a thousand and seven hundred, *were* officers among them of Israel on this side Jordan westward in all the business of the LORD, and in the service of the king.

31 Among the Hebronites *was* [b]Jerijah the chief, *even* among the Hebronites, according to the generations of his fathers. In the fortieth year of the reign of David they were sought for, and there were found among them mighty men of valour [c]at Jazer of Gilead.

32 And his brethren, men of valour, *were* two thousand and seven hundred chief fathers, whom king David made rulers over the Reubenites, the Gadites, and the half tribe of Manasseh, for every matter pertaining to God, and [d]affairs of the king.

27 Now the children of Israel after their number, *to wit,* the chief fathers and captains of thousands and hundreds, and their officers that served the king in any matter of the courses, which came in and went out month by month throughout all the months of the year, of every course *were* twenty and four thousand.

2 Over the first course for the first month *was* [e]Jashobeam the son of Zabdiel: and in his course *were* twenty and four thousand.

3 Of the children of Perez *was* the chief of all the captains of the host for the first month.

26:10 [v]ch. 16:38
26:20 [w]ch. 28:12; Mal. 3:10
26:24 [x]ch. 23:16
26:25 [y]ch. 23:18
26:28 [z]1 Sam. 9:9
26:29 [a]ch. 23:4
26:31 [b]ch. 23:19 [c]Josh. 21:39
26:32 [d]2 Chron. 19:11
27:2 [e]2 Sam. 23:8; ch. 11:11

4 And over the course of the second month *was* Dodai an Ahohite, and of his course *was* Mikloth also the ruler: in his course likewise *were* twenty and four thousand.

5 The third captain of the host for the third month *was* Benaiah the son of Jehoiada, a chief priest: and in his course *were* twenty and four thousand.

6 This *is that* Benaiah, *who was* [f]mighty *among* the thirty, and above the thirty: and in his course *was* Ammizabad his son.

7 The fourth *captain* for the fourth month *was* [g]Asahel the brother of Joab, and Zebadiah his son after him: and in his course *were* twenty and four thousand.

8 The fifth captain for the fifth month *was* Shamhuth the Izrahite: and in his course *were* twenty and four thousand.

9 The sixth *captain* for the sixth month *was* [h]Ira the son of Ikkesh the Tekoite: and in his course *were* twenty and four thousand.

10 The seventh *captain* for the seventh month *was* [i]Helez the Pelonite, of the children of Ephraim: and in his course *were* twenty and four thousand.

11 The eighth *captain* for the eighth month *was* [j]Sibbecai the Hushathite, of the Zarhites: and in his course *were* twenty and four thousand.

12 The ninth *captain* for the ninth month *was* [k]Abi-ezer the Anetothite, of the Benjamites: and in his course *were* twenty and four thousand.

13 The tenth *captain* for the tenth month *was* [l]Maharai the Netophathite, of the Zarhites: and in his course *were* twenty and four thousand.

14 The eleventh *captain* for the eleventh month *was* [m]Benaiah the Pirathonite, of the children of Ephraim: and in his course *were* twenty and four thousand.

15 The twelfth *captain* for the twelfth month *was* Heldai the Netophathite, of Othniel: and in his course *were* twenty and four thousand.

16 ¶ Furthermore over the tribes of Israel: the ruler of the Reubenites *was* Eliezer the son of Zichri: of the Simeonites, Shephatiah the son of Maachah:

17 Of the Levites, [n]Hashabiah the son of Kemuel: of the Aaronites, Zadok:

18 Of Judah, [o]Elihu, *one* of the brethren of David: of Issachar, Omri the son of Michael:

19 Of Zebulun, Ishmaiah the son of Obadiah: of Naphtali, Jerimoth the son of Azriel:

20 Of the children of Ephraim, Hoshea the son of Azaziah: of the half tribe of Manasseh, Joel the son of Pedaiah:

21 Of the half *tribe* of Manasseh in Gilead, Iddo the son of Zechariah: of Benjamin, Jaasiel the son of Abner:

22 Of Dan, Azareel the son of Jeroham. These *were* the princes of the tribes of Israel.

27:6 [f]2 Sam. 23:20; ch. 11:22
27:7 [g]2 Sam. 23:24; ch. 11:26
27:9 [h]ch. 11:28
27:10 [i]ch. 11:27
27:11 [j]2 Sam. 21:18; ch. 11:29
27:12 [k]ch. 11:28
27:13 [l]2 Sam. 23:28; ch. 11:30
27:14 [m]ch. 11:31
27:17 [n]ch. 26:30
27:18 [o]1 Sam. 16:6
27:23 [p]Gen. 15:5
27:24 [q]2 Sam. 24:15; ch. 21:7
27:33 [r]2 Sam. 15:12 [s]2 Sam. 15:37
27:34 [t]1 Kings 1:7 [u]ch. 11:6
28:1 [v]ch. 27:16 [w]ch. 27:1 [x]ch. 27:25 [y]ch. 11:10
28:2 [z]2 Sam. 7:2; Ps. 132:3 [a]Ps. 99:5
28:3 [b]2 Sam. 7:5; 1 Kings 5:3; ch. 17:4
28:4 [c]1 Sam. 16:7-13

23 ¶ But David took not the number of them from twenty years old and under: because [p]the LORD had said he would increase Israel like to the stars of the heavens.

24 Joab the son of Zeruiah began to number, but he finished not, because [q]there fell wrath for it against Israel; neither was the number put in the account of the chronicles of king David.

25 ¶ And over the king's treasures *was* Azmaveth the son of Adiel: and over the storehouses in the fields, in the cities, and in the villages, and in the castles, *was* Jehonathan the son of Uzziah:

26 And over them that did the work of the field for tillage of the ground *was* Ezri the son of Chelub:

27 And over the vineyards *was* Shimei the Ramathite: over the increase of the vineyards for the wine cellars *was* Zabdi the Shiphmite:

28 And over the olive trees and the sycomore trees that *were* in the low plains *was* Baal-hanan the Gederite: and over the cellars of oil *was* Joash:

29 And over the herds that fed in Sharon *was* Shitrai the Sharonite: and over the herds *that were* in the valleys *was* Shaphat the son of Adlai:

30 Over the camels also *was* Obil the Ishmaelite: and over the asses *was* Jehdeiah the Meronothite:

31 And over the flocks *was* Jaziz the Hagerite. All these *were* the rulers of the substance which *was* king David's.

32 Also Jonathan David's uncle was a counsellor, a wise man, and a scribe: and Jehiel the son of Hachmoni *was* with the king's sons:

33 And [r]Ahithophel *was* the king's counsellor: and [s]Hushai the Archite *was* the king's companion:

34 And after Ahithophel *was* Jehoiada the son of Benaiah, and [t]Abiathar: and the general of the king's army *was* [u]Joab.

28

And David assembled all the princes of Israel, [v]the princes of the tribes, and [w]the captains of the companies that ministered to the king by course, and the captains over the thousands, and captains over the hundreds, and [x]the stewards over all the substance and possession of the king, and of his sons, with the officers, and with [y]the mighty men, and with all the valiant men, unto Jerusalem.

2 Then David the king stood up upon his feet, and said, Hear me, my brethren, and my people: *As for me,* [z]I *had* in mine heart to build an house of rest for the ark of the covenant of the LORD, and for [a]the footstool of our God, and had made ready for the building:

3 But God said unto me, [b]Thou shalt not build an house for my name, because thou *hast been* a man of war, and hast shed blood.

4 Howbeit the LORD God of Israel [c]chose me before all the house of my father to be

king over Israel for ever: for he hath chosen
[d]Judah *to be* the ruler; and of the house
of Judah, [e]the house of my father; and
[f]among the sons of my father he liked me
to make *me* king over all Israel:
5 [g]And of all my sons, (for the LORD hath
given me many sons,) [h]he hath chosen Solomon my son to sit upon the throne of the
kingdom of the LORD over Israel.
6 And he said unto me, [i]Solomon thy
son, he shall build my house and my courts:
for I have chosen him *to be* my son, and I
will be his father.
7 Moreover I will establish his kingdom
for ever, [j]if he be constant to do my commandments and my judgments, as at this
day.
8 Now therefore in the sight of all Israel
the congregation of the LORD, and in the
audience of our God, keep and seek for all
the commandments of the LORD your God:
that ye may possess this good land, and
leave *it* for an inheritance for your children
after you for ever.
9 ¶ And thou, Solomon my son, [k]know
thou the God of thy father, and serve him
[l]with a perfect heart and with a willing
mind: for [m]the LORD searcheth all hearts,
and understandeth all the imaginations of
the thoughts: [n]if thou seek him, he will be
found of thee; but if thou forsake him, he
will cast thee off for ever.
10 Take heed now; [o]for the LORD hath
chosen thee to build an house for the sanctuary: be strong, and do *it*.
11 ¶ Then David gave to Solomon his son
[p]the pattern of the porch, and of the houses
thereof, and of the treasuries thereof, and of
the upper chambers thereof, and of the inner parlours thereof, and of the place of the
mercy seat,
12 And the pattern of all that he had by
the spirit, of the courts of the house of the
LORD, and of all the chambers round about,
[q]of the treasuries of the house of God, and
of the treasuries of the dedicated things:
13 Also for the courses of the priests and
the Levites, and for all the work of the service of the house of the LORD, and for all the
vessels of service in the house of the LORD.
14 *He gave* of gold by weight for *things* of
gold, for all instruments of all manner of
service; *silver also* for all instruments of silver by weight, for all instruments of every
kind of service:
15 Even the weight for the candlesticks of
gold, and for their lamps of gold, by weight
for every candlestick, and for the lamps
thereof: and for the candlesticks of silver by
weight, *both* for the candlestick, and *also*
for the lamps thereof, according to the use
of every candlestick.
16 And by weight *he gave* gold for the
tables of shewbread, for every table; and
likewise silver for the tables of silver:
17 Also pure gold for the fleshhooks, and
the bowls, and the cups: and for the golden
basons *he gave gold* by weight for every

28:4 [d]Gen. 49:8; ch. 5:2; Ps. 60:7 [e]1 Sam. 26:1 [f]1 Sam. 16:12
28:5 [g]ch. 3:1 [h]ch. 22:9
28:6 [i]2 Sam. 7:13; ch. 22:8; 2 Chron. 1:9
28:7 [j]ch. 22:13
28:9 [k]Jer. 9:24; Hos. 4:1; John 17:3 [l]2 Kings 20:3; Ps. 101:2 [m]1 Sam. 16:7; 1 Kings 8:39; ch. 29:17; Ps. 7:9; Prov. 17:3; Jer. 11:20; Rev. 2:23 [n]2 Chron. 15:2
28:10 [o]ver. 6
28:11 [p]Ex. 25:40; ver. 19
28:12 [q]ch. 26:20
28:18 [r]Ex. 25:18-22; 1 Sam. 4:4; 1 Kings 6:23
28:19 [s]Ex. 25:40; ver. 11
28:20 [t]Deut. 31:7; Josh. 1:6; ch. 22:13 [u]Josh. 1:5
28:21 [v]ch. 24 [w]Ex. 35:25
29:1 [x]1 Kings 3:7; ch. 22:5; Prov. 4:3
29:2 [y]Isa. 54:11; Rev. 21:18
29:4 [z]1 Kings 9:28
29:6 [a]ch. 27:1 [b]ch. 27:25

bason; and *likewise silver* by weight for every bason of silver:
18 And for the altar of incense refined
gold by weight; and gold for the pattern of
the chariot of the [r]cherubims, that spread
out *their wings*, and covered the ark of the
covenant of the LORD.
19 All *this, said David*, [s]the LORD made
me understand in writing by *his* hand upon
me, *even* all the works of this pattern.
20 And David said to Solomon his son,
[t]Be strong and of good courage, and do *it*:
fear not, nor be dismayed: for the LORD
God, *even* my God, *will be* with thee; [u]he
will not fail thee, nor forsake thee, until
thou hast finished all the work for the service of the house of the LORD.
21 And, behold, [v]the courses of the
priests and the Levites, *even they shall be
with thee* for all the service of the house of
God: and *there shall be* with thee for all
manner of workmanship [w]every willing
skilful man, for any manner of service: also
the princes and all the people *will be* wholly
at thy commandment.

29

Furthermore David the king said
unto all the congregation, Solomon
my son, whom alone God hath chosen, *is
yet* [x]young and tender, and the work *is*
great: for the palace *is* not for man, but for
the LORD God.
2 Now I have prepared with all my might
for the house of my God the gold for *things
to be made* of gold, and the silver for *things*
of silver, and the brass for *things* of brass,
the iron for *things* of iron, and wood for
things of wood; [y]onyx stones, and *stones* to
be set, glistering stones, and of divers colours, and all manner of precious stones, and
marble stones in abundance.
3 Moreover, because I have set my affection to the house of my God, I have of mine
own proper good, of gold and silver, *which*
I have given to the house of my God, over
and above all that I have prepared for the
holy house.
4 *Even* three thousand talents of gold, of
the gold of [z]Ophir, and seven thousand talents of refined silver, to overlay the walls of
the houses *withal*:
5 The gold for *things* of gold, and the silver for *things* of silver, and for all manner
of work *to be made* by the hands of artificers. And who *then* is willing to consecrate
his service this day unto the LORD?
6 ¶ Then [a]the chief of the fathers and
princes of the tribes of Israel, and the captains of thousands and of hundreds, with
[b]the rulers of the king's work, offered willingly,
7 And gave for the service of the house of
God of gold five thousand talents and ten
thousand drams, and of silver ten thousand
talents, and of brass eighteen thousand talents, and one hundred thousand talents of
iron.
8 And they with whom *precious* stones
were found gave *them* to the treasure of the

house of the LORD, by the hand of [c]Jehiel
the Gershonite.
9 Then the people rejoiced, for that they
offered willingly, because with perfect
heart they [d]offered willingly to the LORD:
and David the king also rejoiced with great
joy.
10 ¶ Wherefore David blessed the LORD
before all the congregation: and David said,
Blessed *be* thou, LORD God of Israel our father, for ever and ever.
11 [e]Thine, O LORD, *is* the greatness, and
the power, and the glory, and the victory,
and the majesty: for all *that is* in the heaven
and in the earth *is thine;* thine *is* the kingdom, O LORD, and thou art exalted as head
above all.
12 [f]Both riches and honour *come* of thee,
and thou reignest over all; and in thine hand
is power and might; and in thine hand *it is*
to make great, and to give strength unto all.
13 Now therefore, our God, we thank
thee, and praise thy glorious name.
14 But who *am* I, and what *is* my people,
that we should be able to offer so willingly
after this sort? for all things *come* of thee,
and of thine own have we given thee.
15 For [g]we *are* strangers before thee, and
sojourners, as *were* all our fathers: [h]our
days on the earth *are* as a shadow, and
there is none abiding.
16 O LORD our God, all this store that we
have prepared to build thee an house for
thine holy name *cometh* of thine hand, and
is all thine own.
17 I know also, my God, that thou [i]triest
the heart, and [j]hast pleasure in uprightness. As for me, in the uprightness of mine
heart I have willingly offered all these
things: and now have I seen with joy thy
people, which are present here, to offer willingly unto thee.
18 O LORD God of Abraham, Isaac, and of
Israel, our fathers, keep this for ever in the
imagination of the thoughts of the heart of
thy people, and prepare their heart unto
thee:
19 And [k]give unto Solomon my son a perfect heart, to keep thy commandments, thy

29:8 [c]ch. 26:21
29:9 [d]2 Cor. 9:7
29:11 [e]Matt. 6:13; 1 Tim. 1:17; Rev. 5:13
29:12 [f]Rom. 11:36
29:15 [g]ch. 39:12; Heb. 11:13; 1 Pet. 2:11 [h]Job 14:2; Ps. 90:9
29:17 [i]1 Sam. 16:7; ch. 28:9 [j]Prov. 11:20
29:19 [k]Ps. 72:1 [l]ver. 2; ch. 22:14
29:22 [m]1 Kings 1:35
29:24 [n]Eccl. 8:2
29:25 [o]1 Kings 3:13; 2 Chron. 1:12; Eccl. 2:9
29:27 [p]2 Sam. 5:4; 1 Kings 2:11 [q]2 Sam. 5:5
29:28 [r]Gen. 25:8 [s]ch. 23:1
29:30 [t]Dan. 2:21

testimonies, and thy statutes, and to do all
these things, and to build the palace, *for* the
which [l]I have made provision.
20 ¶ And David said to all the congregation, Now bless the LORD your God. And all
the congregation blessed the LORD God of
their fathers, and bowed down their heads,
and worshipped the LORD, and the king.
21 And they sacrificed sacrifices unto the
LORD, and offered burnt offerings unto the
LORD, on the morrow after that day, *even* a
thousand bullocks, a thousand rams, *and* a
thousand lambs, with their drink offerings,
and sacrifices in abundance for all Israel:
22 And did eat and drink before the LORD
on that day with great gladness. And they
made Solomon the son of David king the
second time, and [m]anointed *him* unto the
LORD *to be* the chief governor, and Zadok
to be priest.
23 Then Solomon sat on the throne of the
LORD as king instead of David his father,
and prospered; and all Israel obeyed him.
24 And all the princes, and the mighty
men, and all the sons likewise of king David, [n]submitted themselves unto Solomon
the king.
25 And the LORD magnified Solomon exceedingly in the sight of all Israel, and [o]be-
stowed upon him *such* royal majesty as had
not been on any king before him in Israel.
26 ¶ Thus David the son of Jesse reigned
over all Israel.
27 [p]And the time that he reigned over Israel *was* forty years; [q]seven years reigned
he in Hebron, and thirty and three *years*
reigned he in Jerusalem.
28 And he [r]died in a good old age, [s]full
of days, riches, and honour: and Solomon
his son reigned in his stead.
29 Now the acts of David the king, first
and last, behold, they *are* written in the
book of Samuel the seer, and in the book of
Nathan the prophet, and in the book of Gad
the seer,
30 With all his reign and his might, [t]and
the times that went over him, and over Israel, and over all the kingdoms of the countries.

2 CHRONICLES

Tradition suggests that Ezra was the author of 2 Chronicles, written between 450 B.C. and 400 B.C. 2 Chronicles continues the narrative of 1 Chronicles beginning with the reign of Solomon in Israel. A detailed explanation of the construction of the Temple is in the first seven chapters, then the historical narrative continues, following the succession of kings in Judah following Solomon's death.

I. Solomon and his reign, 1:1–9:31
II. The kings of Judah, 10:1–36:21
III. The decree of Cyrus, King of Persia, 36:22–36:23

---

1 And [a]Solomon the son of David was
strengthened in his kingdom, and [b]the
LORD his God *was* with him, and [c]magni-
fied him exceedingly.
2 Then Solomon spake unto all Israel, to
[d]the captains of thousands and of hundreds, and to the judges, and to every governor in all Israel, the chief of the fathers.
3 So Solomon, and all the congregation
with him, went to the high place that *was* at
[e]Gibeon; for there was the tabernacle of the
congregation of God, which Moses the servant of the LORD had made in the wilderness.
4 [f]But the ark of God had David brought
up from Kirjath-jearim to *the place which*
David had prepared for it: for he had
pitched a tent for it at Jerusalem.
5 Moreover [g]the brasen altar, that [h]Be-
zaleel the son of Uri, the son of Hur, had
made, he put before the tabernacle of the
LORD: and Solomon and the congregation
sought unto it.
6 And Solomon went up thither to the
brasen altar before the LORD, which *was* at
the tabernacle of the congregation, and [i]of-
fered a thousand burnt offerings upon it.
7 ¶ [j]In that night did God appear unto
Solomon, and said unto him, Ask what I
shall give thee.
8 And Solomon said unto God, Thou hast
shewed great mercy unto David my father,
and hast made me [k]to reign in his stead.
9 Now, O LORD God, let thy promise unto
David my father be established: [l]for thou
hast made me king over a people like the
dust of the earth in multitude.
10 [m]Give me now wisdom and knowledge, that I may [n]go out and come in before
this people: for who can judge this thy people, *that is so* great?
11 [o]And God said to Solomon, Because
this was in thine heart, and thou hast not
asked riches, wealth, or honour, nor the life
of thine enemies, neither yet hast asked
long life; but hast asked wisdom and knowledge for thyself, that thou mayest judge my
people, over whom I have made thee king:
12 Wisdom and knowledge *is* granted
unto thee; and I will give thee riches, and
wealth, and honour, such as [p]none of the

1:1 [a]1 Kings 2:46 [b]Gen. 39:2 [c]1 Chron. 29:25
1:2 [d]1 Chron. 27:1
1:3 [e]1 Kings 3:4; 1 Chron. 16:39
1:4 [f]1 Sam. 6:2; 1 Chron. 15:1
1:5 [g]Ex. 27:1 [h]Ex. 31:2
1:6 [i]1 Kings 3:4
1:7 [j]1 Kings 3:5
1:8 [k]1 Chron. 28:5
1:9 [l]1 Kings 3:7
1:10 [m]1 Kings 3:9 [n]Num. 27:17; Deut. 31:2
1:11 [o]1 Kings 3:11
1:12 [p]1 Chron. 29:25; ch. 9:22; Eccl. 2:9
1:14 [q]1 Kings 4:26; ch. 9:25
1:15 [r]1 Kings 10:27; ch. 9:27; Job 22:24
1:16 [s]1 Kings 10:28; ch. 9:28
2:1 [t]1 Kings 5:5
2:2 [u]1 Kings 5:15; ver. 18
2:3 [v]1 Chron. 14:1
2:4 [w]ver. 1 [x]Ex. 30:7 [y]Ex. 25:30; Lev. 24:8 [z]Num. 28:3
2:5 [a]Ps. 135:5
2:6 [b]1 Kings 8:27; ch. 6:18; Isa. 66:1

kings have had that *have been* before thee,
neither shall there any after thee have the
like.
13 ¶ Then Solomon came *from his jour-*
ney to the high place that *was* at Gibeon to
Jerusalem, from before the tabernacle of
the congregation, and reigned over Israel.
14 [q]And Solomon gathered chariots and
horsemen: and he had a thousand and four
hundred chariots, and twelve thousand
horsemen, which he placed in the chariot
cities, and with the king at Jerusalem.
15 [r]And the king made silver and gold at
Jerusalem *as plenteous* as stones, and cedar
trees made he as the sycomore trees that *are*
in the vale for abundance.
16 [s]And Solomon had horses brought
out of Egypt, and linen yarn: the king's merchants received the linen yarn at a price.
17 And they fetched up, and brought
forth out of Egypt a chariot for six hundred
shekels of silver, and an horse for an hundred and fifty: and so brought they out
horses for all the kings of the Hittites, and
for the kings of Syria, by their means.
2 And Solomon [t]determined to build an
house for the name of the LORD, and an
house for his kingdom.
2 And [u]Solomon told out threescore and
ten thousand men to bear burdens, and
fourscore thousand to hew in the mountain,
and three thousand and six hundred to
oversee them.
3 ¶ And Solomon sent to Huram the king
of Tyre, saying, [v]As thou didst deal with
David my father, and didst send him cedars
to build him an house to dwell therein, *even*
so deal with me.
4 Behold, [w]I build an house to the name of
the LORD my God, to dedicate *it* to him, *and*
[x]to burn before him sweet incense, and for
[y]the continual shewbread, and for [z]the
burnt offerings morning and evening, on
the sabbaths, and on the new moons, and on
the solemn feasts of the LORD our God. This
is an ordinance for ever to Israel.
5 And the house which I build *is* great: for
[a]great *is* our God above all gods.
6 [b]But who is able to build him an house,
seeing the heaven and heaven of heavens
cannot contain him? who *am* I then, that I

should build him an house, save only to
burn sacrifice before him?
7 Send me now therefore a man cunning
to work in gold, and in silver, and in brass,
and in iron, and in purple, and crimson, and
blue, and that can skill to grave with the
cunning men that *are* with me in Judah and
in Jerusalem, [c]whom David my father did
provide.
8 [d]Send me also cedar trees, fir trees, and
algum trees, out of Lebanon: for I know that
thy servants can skill to cut timber in Lebanon; and, behold, my servants *shall be* with
thy servants,
9 Even to prepare me timber in abundance: for the house which I am about to
build *shall be* wonderful great.
10 [e]And, behold, I will give to thy servants, the hewers that cut timber, twenty
thousand measures of beaten wheat, and
twenty thousand measures of barley, and
twenty thousand baths of wine, and twenty
thousand baths of oil.
11 ¶ Then Huram the king of Tyre answered in writing, which he sent to Solomon, [f]Because the LORD hath loved his
people, he hath made thee king over them.
12 Huram said moreover, [g]Blessed *be* the
LORD God of Israel, [h]that made heaven and
earth, who hath given to David the king a
wise son, endued with prudence and understanding, that might build an house for the
LORD, and an house for his kingdom.
13 And now I have sent a cunning man,
endued with understanding, of Huram my
father's,
14 [i]The son of a woman of the daughters
of Dan, and his father *was* a man of Tyre,
skilful to work in gold, and in silver, in
brass, in iron, in stone, and in timber, in
purple, in blue, and in fine linen, and
in crimson; also to grave any manner of
graving, and to find out every device which
shall be put to him, with thy cunning men,
and with the cunning men of my lord David
thy father.
15 Now therefore the wheat, and the barley, the oil, and the wine, which [j]my lord
hath spoken of, let him send unto his servants:
16 [k]And we will cut wood out of Lebanon, as much as thou shalt need: and we
will bring it to thee in floates by sea to
Joppa; and thou shalt carry it up to Jerusalem.
17 ¶ [l]And Solomon numbered all the
strangers that *were* in the land of Israel, after the numbering wherewith [m]David his father had numbered them; and they were
found an hundred and fifty thousand and
three thousand and six hundred.
18 And he set [n]threescore and ten thousand of them *to be* bearers of burdens, and
fourscore thousand *to be* hewers in the
mountain, and three thousand and six hundred overseers to set the people a work.
3 Then [o]Solomon began to build the
house of the LORD at [p]Jerusalem in
mount Moriah, where *the* LORD appeared
unto David his father, in the place that David had prepared in the threshingfloor of
[q]Ornan the Jebusite.
2 And he began to build in the second *day*
of the second month, in the fourth year of
his reign.
3 ¶ Now these *are the things* [r]*wherein*
Solomon was instructed for the building of
the house of God. The length by cubits after
the first measure *was* threescore cubits, and
the breadth twenty cubits.
4 And the [s]porch that *was* in the front *of
the house*, the length *of it was* according to
the breadth of the house, twenty cubits, and
the height *was* an hundred and twenty: and
he overlaid it within with pure gold.
5 And [t]the greater house he cieled with
fir tree, which he overlaid with fine gold,
and set thereon palm trees and chains.
6 And he garnished the house with precious stones for beauty: and the gold *was*
gold of Parvaim.
7 He overlaid also the house, the beams,
the posts, and the walls thereof, and the
doors thereof, with gold; and graved cherubims on the walls.
8 And he made the most holy house, the
length whereof *was* according to the
breadth of the house, twenty cubits, and the
breadth thereof twenty cubits: and he overlaid it with fine gold, *amounting* to six hundred talents.
9 And the weight of the nails *was* fifty
shekels of gold. And he overlaid the upper
chambers with gold.
10 [u]And in the most holy house he made
two cherubims of image work, and overlaid
them with gold.
11 ¶ And the wings of the cherubims *were*
twenty cubits long: one wing *of the one
cherub was* five cubits, reaching to the wall
of the house: and the other wing *was likewise* five cubits, reaching to the wing of the
other cherub.
12 And *one* wing of the other cherub *was*
five cubits, reaching to the wall of the
house: and the other wing *was* five cubits
also, joining to the wing of the other cherub.
13 The wings of these cherubims spread
themselves forth twenty cubits: and they
stood on their feet, and their faces *were* inward.
14 And he made the [v]vail *of* blue, and
purple, and crimson, and fine linen, and
wrought cherubims thereon.
15 Also he made before the house [w]two
pillars of thirty and five cubits high, and the
chapiter that *was* on the top of each of them
was five cubits.
16 And he made chains, *as* in the oracle,
and put *them* on the heads of the pillars;
and made [x]an hundred pomegranates, and
put *them* on the chains.
17 And he [y]reared up the pillars before
the temple, one on the right hand, and the
other on the left; and called the name of that

2:7 [c]1 Chron. 22:15
2:8 [d]1 Kings 5:6
2:10 [e]1 Kings 5:11
2:11 [f]1 Kings 10:9; ch. 9:8
2:12 [g]1 Kings 5:7 [h]Gen. 1; Ps. 33:6; Acts 4:24; Rev. 10:6
2:14 [i]1 Kings 7:13
2:15 [j]ver. 10
2:16 [k]1 Kings 5:8
2:17 [l]ver. 2; 1 Kings 5:13; ch. 8:7 [m]1 Chron. 22:2
2:18 [n]ver. 2
3:1 [o]1 Kings 6:1 [p]Gen. 22:2 [q]1 Chron. 21:18
3:3 [r]1 Kings 6:2
3:4 [s]1 Kings 6:3
3:5 [t]1 Kings 6:17
3:10 [u]1 Kings 6:23
3:14 [v]Ex. 26:31; Matt. 27:51; Heb. 9:3
3:15 [w]1 Kings 7:15-21; Jer. 52:21
3:16 [x]1 Kings 7:20
3:17 [y]1 Kings 7:21

on the right hand Jachin, and the name of that on the left Boaz.

4 Moreover he made [z]an altar of brass, twenty cubits the length thereof, and twenty cubits the breadth thereof, and ten cubits the height thereof.

2 ¶ [a]Also he made a molten sea of ten cubits from brim to brim, round in compass, and five cubits the height thereof; and a line of thirty cubits did compass it round about.

3 [b]And under it *was* the similitude of oxen, which did compass it round about: ten in a cubit, compassing the sea round about. Two rows of oxen *were* cast, when it was cast.

4 It stood upon twelve oxen, three looking toward the north, and three looking toward the west, and three looking toward the south, and three looking toward the east: and the sea *was set* above upon them, and all their hinder parts *were* inward.

5 And the thickness of it *was* an hand breadth, and the brim of it like the work of the brim of a cup, with flowers of lilies; *and* it received and held [c]three thousand baths.

6 ¶ He made also [d]ten lavers, and put five on the right hand, and five on the left, to wash in them: such things as they offered for the burnt offering they washed in them; but the sea *was* for the priests to wash in.

7 [e]And he made ten candlesticks of gold [f]according to their form, and set *them* in the temple, five on the right hand, and five on the left.

8 [g]He made also ten tables, and placed *them* in the temple, five on the right side, and five on the left. And he made an hundred basons of gold.

9 ¶ Furthermore [h]he made the court of the priests, and the great court, and doors for the court, and overlaid the doors of them with brass.

10 And [i]he set the sea on the right side of the east end, over against the south.

11 And [j]Huram made the pots, and the shovels, and the basons. And Huram finished the work that he was to make for king Solomon for the house of God;

12 *To wit,* the two pillars, and [k]the pommels, and the chapiters *which were* on the top of the two pillars, and the two wreaths to cover the two pommels of the chapiters which *were* on the top of the pillars;

13 And [l]four hundred pomegranates on the two wreaths; two rows of pomegranates on each wreath, to cover the two pommels of the chapiters which *were* upon the pillars.

14 He made also [m]bases, and lavers made he upon the bases;

15 One sea, and twelve oxen under it.

16 The pots also, and the shovels, and the fleshhooks, and all their instruments, did [n]Huram his father make to king Solomon for the house of the LORD of bright brass.

17 [o]In the plain of Jordan did the king cast them, in the clay ground between Succoth and Zeredathah.

18 [p]Thus Solomon made all these vessels in great abundance: for the weight of the brass could not be found out.

19 ¶ And [q]Solomon made all the vessels that *were for* the house of God, the golden altar also, and the tables whereon [r]the shewbread *was set;*

20 Moreover the candlesticks with their lamps, that they should burn [s]after the manner before the oracle, of pure gold;

21 And [t]the flowers, and the lamps, and the tongs, *made he of* gold, *and* that perfect gold;

22 And the snuffers, and the basons, and the spoons, and the censers, *of* pure gold: and the entry of the house, the inner doors thereof for the most holy *place,* and the doors of the house of the temple, *were of* gold.

5 Thus [u]all the work that Solomon made for the house of the LORD was finished: and Solomon brought in *all* the things that David his father had dedicated; and the silver, and the gold, and all the instruments, put he among the treasures of the house of God.

2 ¶ [v]Then Solomon assembled the elders of Israel, and all the heads of the tribes, the chief of the fathers of the children of Israel, unto Jerusalem, to bring up the ark of the covenant of the LORD [w]out of the city of David, which *is* Zion.

3 [x]Wherefore all the men of Israel assembled themselves unto the king [y]in the feast which *was* in the seventh month.

4 And all the elders of Israel came; and the Levites took up the ark.

5 And they brought up the ark, and the tabernacle of the congregation, and all the holy vessels that *were* in the tabernacle, these did the priests *and* the Levites bring up.

6 Also king Solomon, and all the congregation of Israel that were assembled unto him before the ark, sacrificed sheep and oxen, which could not be told nor numbered for multitude.

7 And the priests brought in the ark of the covenant of the LORD unto his place, to the oracle of the house, into the most holy *place, even* under the wings of the cherubims:

8 For the cherubims spread forth *their* wings over the place of the ark, and the cherubims covered the ark and the staves thereof above.

9 And they drew out the staves *of the ark,* that the ends of the staves were seen from the ark before the oracle; but they were not seen without. And there it is unto this day.

10 *There was* nothing in the ark save the two tables which Moses [z]put *therein* at Horeb, when the LORD made *a covenant* with the children of Israel, when they came out of Egypt.

11 ¶ And it came to pass, when the priests were come out of the holy *place:* (for all the

4:1 [z]Ex. 27:1; 2 Kings 16:14; Ezek. 43:13
4:2 [a]1 Kings 7:23
4:3 [b]1 Kings 7:24
4:5 [c]1 Kings 7:26
4:6 [d]1 Kings 7:38
4:7 [e]1 Kings 7:49 [f]Ex. 25:31; 1 Chron. 28:12
4:8 [g]1 Kings 7:48
4:9 [h]1 Kings 6:36
4:10 [i]1 Kings 7:39
4:11 [j]1 Kings 7:40
4:12 [k]1 Kings 7:41
4:13 [l]1 Kings 7:20
4:14 [m]1 Kings 7:27
4:16 [n]1 Kings 7:14
4:17 [o]1 Kings 7:46
4:18 [p]1 Kings 7:47
4:19 [q]1 Kings 7:48 [r]Ex. 25:30
4:20 [s]Ex. 27:20
4:21 [t]Ex. 25:31
5:1 [u]1 Kings 7:51
5:2 [v]1 Kings 8:1 [w]2 Sam. 6:12
5:3 [x]1 Kings 8:2 [y]ch. 7:8
5:10 [z]Deut. 10:2; ch. 6:11

priests *that were* present were sanctified, *and* did not *then* wait by course:

12 [a]Also the Levites *which were* the singers, all of them of Asaph, of Heman, of Jeduthun, with their sons and their brethren, *being* arrayed in white linen, having cymbals and psalteries and harps, stood at the east end of the altar, [b]and with them an hundred and twenty priests sounding with trumpets:)

13 It came even to pass, as the trumpeters and singers *were* as one, to make one sound to be heard in praising and thanking the LORD; and when they lifted up *their* voice with the trumpets and cymbals and instruments of musick, and praised the LORD, *saying*, [c]For *he is* good; for his mercy *endureth* for ever: that *then* the house was filled with a cloud, *even* the house of the LORD;

14 So that the priests could not stand to minister by reason of the cloud: [d]for the glory of the LORD had filled the house of God.

6 Then [e]said Solomon, The LORD hath said that he would dwell in the [f]thick darkness.

2 But I have built an house of habitation for thee, and a place for thy dwelling for ever.

3 And the king turned his face, and blessed the whole congregation of Israel: and all the congregation of Israel stood.

4 And he said, Blessed *be* the LORD God of Israel, who hath with his hands fulfilled *that* which he spake with his mouth to my father David, saying,

5 Since the day that I brought forth my people out of the land of Egypt I chose no city among all the tribes of Israel to build an house in, that my name might be there; neither chose I any man to be a ruler over my people Israel:

6 [g]But I have chosen Jerusalem, that my name might be there; and [h]have chosen David to be over my people Israel.

7 Now [i]it was in the heart of David my father to build an house for the name of the LORD God of Israel.

8 But the LORD said to David my father, Forasmuch as it was in thine heart to build an house for my name, thou didst well in that it was in thine heart:

9 Notwithstanding thou shalt not build the house; but thy son which shall come forth out of thy loins, he shall build the house for my name.

10 The LORD therefore hath performed his word that he hath spoken: for I am risen up in the room of David my father, and am set on the throne of Israel, as the LORD promised, and have built the house for the name of the LORD God of Israel.

11 And in it have I put the ark, [j]wherein *is* the covenant of the LORD, that he made with the children of Israel.

12 ¶ [k]And he stood before the altar of the LORD in the presence of all the congregation of Israel, and spread forth his hands:

13 For Solomon had made a brasen scaffold, of five cubits long, and five cubits broad, and three cubits high, and had set it in the midst of the court: and upon it he stood, and kneeled down upon his knees before all the congregation of Israel, and spread forth his hands toward heaven,

14 And said, O LORD God of Israel, [l]*there is* no God like thee in the heaven, nor in the earth; which keepest covenant, and *shewest* mercy unto thy servants, that walk before thee with all their hearts:

15 [m]Thou which hast kept with thy servant David my father that which thou hast promised him; and spakest with thy mouth, and hast fulfilled *it* with thine hand, as *it is* this day.

16 Now therefore, O LORD God of Israel, keep with thy servant David my father that which thou hast promised him, saying, [n]There shall not fail thee a man in my sight to sit upon the throne of Israel; [o]yet so that thy children take heed to their way to walk in my law, as thou hast walked before me.

17 Now then, O LORD God of Israel, let thy word be verified, which thou hast spoken unto thy servant David.

18 But will God in very deed dwell with men on the earth? [p]behold, heaven and the heaven of heavens cannot contain thee; how much less this house which I have built!

19 Have respect therefore to the prayer of thy servant, and to his supplication, O LORD my God, to hearken unto the cry and the prayer which thy servant prayeth before thee:

20 That thine eyes may be open upon this house day and night, upon the place whereof thou hast said that thou wouldest put thy name there; to hearken unto the prayer which thy servant prayeth toward this place.

21 Hearken therefore unto the supplications of thy servant, and of thy people Israel, which they shall make toward this place: hear thou from thy dwelling place, *even* from heaven; and when thou hearest, forgive.

22 ¶ If a man sin against his neighbour, and an oath be laid upon him to make him swear, and the oath come before thine altar in this house;

23 Then hear thou from heaven, and do, and judge thy servants, by requiting the wicked, by recompensing his way upon his own head; and by justifying the righteous, by giving him according to his righteousness.

24 ¶ And if thy people Israel be put to the worse before the enemy, because they have sinned against thee; and shall return and confess thy name, and pray and make supplication before thee in this house;

25 Then hear thou from the heavens, and forgive the sin of thy people Israel, and bring them again unto the land which thou gavest to them and to their fathers.

5:12 [a]1 Chron. 25:1 [b]1 Chron. 15:24
5:13 [c]1 Chron. 16:34; Ps. 136
5:14 [d]Ex. 40:35; ch. 7:2
6:1 [e]1 Kings 8:12 [f]Lev. 16:2
6:6 [g]ch. 12:13 [h]1 Chron. 28:4
6:7 [i]2 Sam. 7:2; 1 Chron. 17:1
6:11 [j]ch. 5:10
6:12 [k]1 Kings 8:22
6:14 [l]Ex. 15:11; Deut. 4:39
6:15 [m]1 Chron. 22:9
6:16 [n]2 Sam. 7:12; 1 Kings 2:4; ch. 7:18 [o]Ps. 132:12
6:18 [p]ch. 2:6; Isa. 66:1; Acts 7:49

26 ¶ When the [q]heaven is shut up, and
there is no rain, because they have sinned
against thee; *yet* if they pray toward this
place, and confess thy name, and turn from
their sin, when thou dost afflict them;
27 Then hear thou from heaven, and forgive the sin of thy servants, and of thy people Israel, when thou hast taught them the
good way, wherein they should walk; and
send rain upon thy land, which thou hast
given unto thy people for an inheritance.
28 ¶ If there [r]be dearth in the land, if
there be pestilence, if there be blasting, or
mildew, locusts, or caterpillers; if their enemies besiege them in the cities of their land;
whatsoever sore or whatsoever sickness
there be:
29 *Then* what prayer *or* what supplication
soever shall be made of any man, or of all
thy people Israel, when every one shall
know his own sore and his own grief, and
shall spread forth his hands in this house:
30 Then hear thou from heaven thy dwelling place, and forgive, and render unto every man according unto all his ways, whose
heart thou knowest; (for thou only [s]know-
est the hearts of the children of men:)
31 That they may fear thee, to walk in thy
ways, so long as they live in the land which
thou gavest unto our fathers.
32 ¶ Moreover concerning the stranger,
[t]which is not of thy people Israel, but is
come from a far country for thy great
name's sake, and thy mighty hand, and thy
stretched out arm; if they come and pray in
this house;
33 Then hear thou from the heavens, *even*
from thy dwelling place, and do according
to all that the stranger calleth to thee for;
that all people of the earth may know thy
name, and fear thee, as *doth* thy people Israel, and may know that this house which I
have built is called by thy name.
34 If thy people go out to war against
their enemies by the way that thou shalt
send them, and they pray unto thee toward
this city which thou hast chosen, and the
house which I have built for thy name;
35 Then hear thou from the heavens their
prayer and their supplication, and maintain
their cause.
36 If they sin against thee, (for *there is*
[u]no man which sinneth not,) and thou be
angry with them, and deliver them over before *their* enemies, and they carry them
away captives unto a land far off or near;
37 Yet *if* they bethink themselves in the
land whither they are carried captive, and
turn and pray unto thee in the land of their
captivity, saying, We have sinned, we have
done amiss, and have dealt wickedly;
38 If they return to thee with all their
heart and with all their soul in the land of
their captivity, whither they have carried
them captives, and pray toward their land,
which thou gavest unto their fathers, and
toward the city which thou hast chosen, and
toward the house which I have built for thy
name:
39 Then hear thou from the heavens, *even*
from thy dwelling place, their prayer and
their supplications, and maintain their
cause, and forgive thy people which have
sinned against thee.
40 Now, my God, let, I beseech thee, thine
eyes be open, and *let* thine ears *be* attent
unto the prayer *that is made* in this place.
41 Now [v]therefore arise, O LORD God,
into thy [w]resting place, thou, and the ark of
thy strength: let thy priests, O LORD God, be
clothed with salvation, and let thy saints
[x]rejoice in goodness.
42 O LORD God, turn not away the face of
thine anointed: [y]remember the mercies of
David thy servant.

7 Now [z]when Solomon had made an end
of praying, the [a]fire came down from
heaven, and consumed the burnt offering
and the sacrifices; and [b]the glory of the
LORD filled the house.
2 [c]And the priests could not enter into
the house of the LORD, because the glory of
the LORD had filled the LORD's house.
3 And when all the children of Israel saw
how the fire came down, and the glory of
the LORD upon the house, they bowed themselves with their faces to the ground upon
the pavement, and worshipped, and praised
the LORD, [d]*saying*, For *he is* good; [e]for his
mercy *endureth* for ever.
4 ¶ [f]Then the king and all the people offered sacrifices before the LORD.
5 And king Solomon offered a sacrifice of
twenty and two thousand oxen, and an hundred and twenty thousand sheep: so the
king and all the people dedicated the house
of God.
6 [g]And the priests waited on their offices:
the Levites also with instruments of musick
of the LORD, which David the king had
made to praise the LORD, because his mercy
endureth for ever, when David praised by
their ministry; and [h]the priests sounded
trumpets before them, and all Israel stood.
7 Moreover [i]Solomon hallowed the middle of the court that *was* before the house of
the LORD: for there he offered burnt offerings, and the fat of the peace offerings, because the brasen altar which Solomon had
made was not able to receive the burnt offerings, and the meat offerings, and the fat.
8 ¶ [j]Also at the same time Solomon kept
the feast seven days, and all Israel with him,
a very great congregation, from the entering in of Hamath unto [k]the river of Egypt.
9 And in the eighth day they made a solemn assembly: for they kept the dedicati
of the altar seven days, and the feast
days.
10 And [l]on the three and t
of the seventh month he
away into their tents, g
heart for the goodness t
shewed unto David, and t
Israel his people.

6:26 [q]1 Kings 17:1
6:28 [r]ch. 20:9
6:30 [s]1 Chron. 28:9
6:32 [t]John 12:20; Acts 8:27
6:36 [u]Prov. 20:9; Eccl. 7:20; Jam. 3:2; 1 John 1:8
6:41 [v]Ps. 132:8 [w]1 Chron. 28:2 [x]Neh. 9:25
6:42 [y]Ps. 132:1; Isa. 55:3
7:1 [z]1 Kings 8:54 [a]Lev. 9:24; Judg. 6:21; 1 Kings 18:38; 1 Chron. 21:26 [b]1 Kings 8:10; ch. 5:13; Ezek. 10:3
7:2 [c]ch. 5:14
7:3 [d]ch. 5:13; Ps. 136:1 [e]1 Chron. 16:41; ch. 20:21
7:4 [f]1 Kings 8:62
7:6 [g]1 Chron. 15:16 [h]ch. 5:12
7:7 [i]1 Kings 8:64
7:8 [j]1 Kings 8:65 [k]Josh. 13:3
7:10 [l]1 Kings 8:66

11 Thus [m]Solomon finished the house of the LORD, and the king's house: and all that came into Solomon's heart to make in the house of the LORD, and in his own house, he prosperously effected.

12 ¶ And the LORD appeared to Solomon by night, and said unto him, I have heard thy prayer, [n]and have chosen this place to myself for an house of sacrifice.

13 [o]If I shut up heaven that there be no rain, or if I command the locusts to devour the land, or if I send pestilence among my people;

14 If my people, which are called by my name, shall [p]humble themselves, and pray, and seek my face, and turn from their wicked ways; [q]then will I hear from heaven, and will forgive their sin, and will heal their land.

15 Now [r]mine eyes shall be open, and mine ears attent unto the prayer *that is made* in this place.

16 For now have [s]I chosen and sanctified this house, that my name may be there for ever: and mine eyes and mine heart shall be there perpetually.

17 [t]And as for thee, if thou wilt walk before me, as David thy father walked, and do according to all that I have commanded thee, and shalt observe my statutes and my judgments;

18 Then will I stablish the throne of thy kingdom, according as I have covenanted with David thy father, saying, [u]There shall not fail thee a man *to be* ruler in Israel.

19 [v]But if ye turn away, and forsake my statutes and my commandments, which I have set before you, and shall go and serve other gods, and worship them;

20 Then will I pluck them up by the roots out of my land which I have given them; and this house, which I have sanctified for my name, will I cast out of my sight, and will make it *to be* a proverb and a byword among all nations.

21 And this house, which is high, shall be an astonishment to every one that passeth by it; so that he shall say, [w]Why hath the LORD done thus unto this land, and unto this house?

22 And it shall be answered, Because they forsook the LORD God of their fathers, which brought them forth out of the land of Egypt, and laid hold on other gods, and worshipped them, and served them: therefore hath he brought all this evil upon them.

8 And [x]it came to pass at the end of twenty years, wherein Solomon had built the house of the LORD, and his own house,

2 That the cities which Huram had restored to Solomon, Solomon built them, and aused the children of Israel to dwell there.

3 And Solomon went to Hamath-zobah, prevailed against it.

And he built Tadmor in the wilder- and all the store cities, which he built ath.

5 Also he built Beth-horon the upper, and Beth-horon the nether, fenced cities, with walls, gates, and bars;

6 And Baalath, and all the store cities that Solomon had, and all the chariot cities, and the cities of the horsemen, and all that Solomon desired to build in Jerusalem, and in Lebanon, and throughout all the land of his dominion.

7 ¶ [z]*As for* all the people *that were* left of the Hittites, and the Amorites, and the Perizzites, and the Hivites, and the Jebusites, which *were* not of Israel,

8 *But* of their children, who were left after them in the land, whom the children of Israel consumed not, them did Solomon make to pay tribute until this day.

9 But of the children of Israel did Solomon make no servants for his work; but they *were* men of war, and chief of his captains, and captains of his chariots and horsemen.

10 And these *were* the chief of king Solomon's officers, *even* [a]two hundred and fifty, that bare rule over the people.

11 ¶ And Solomon [b]brought up the daughter of Pharaoh out of the city of David unto the house that he had built for her: for he said, My wife shall not dwell in the house of David king of Israel, because *the places are* holy, whereunto the ark of the LORD hath come.

12 ¶ Then Solomon offered burnt offerings unto the LORD on the altar of the LORD, which he had built before the porch,

13 Even after a certain rate [c]every day, offering according to the commandment of Moses, on the sabbaths, and on the new moons, and on the solemn feasts, [d]three times in the year, *even* in the feast of unleavened bread, and in the feast of weeks, and in the feast of tabernacles.

14 ¶ And he appointed, according to the order of David his father, the [e]courses of the priests to their service, and [f]the Levites to their charges, to praise and minister before the priests, as the duty of every day required: the [g]porters also by their courses at every gate: for so had David the man of God commanded.

15 And they departed not from the commandment of the king unto the priests and Levites concerning any matter, or concerning the treasures.

16 Now all the work of Solomon was prepared unto the day of the foundation of the house of the LORD, and until it was finished. *So* the house of the LORD was perfected.

17 ¶ Then went Solomon to [h]Ezion-geber, and to Eloth, at the sea side in the land of Edom.

18 [i]And Huram sent him by the hands of his servants ships, and servants that had knowledge of the sea; and they went with the servants of Solomon to Ophir, and took thence four hundred and fifty talents of gold, and brought *them* to king Solomon.

7:11 [m]1 Kings 9:1
7:12 [n]Deut. 12:5
7:13 [o]ch. 6:26
7:14 [p]Jam. 4:10 [q]ch. 6:27
7:15 [r]ch. 6:40
7:16 [s]1 Kings 9:3; ch. 6:6
7:17 [t]1 Kings 9:4
7:18 [u]ch. 6:16
7:19 [v]Lev. 26:14; Deut. 28:15
7:21 [w]Deut. 29:24; Jer. 22:8
8:1 [x]1 Kings 9:10
8:4 [y]1 Kings 9:17
8:7 [z]1 Kings 9:20
8:10 [a]1 Kings 9:23
8:11 [b]1 Kings 3:1
8:13 [c]Ex. 29:38; Num. 28:3 [d]Ex. 23:14; Deut. 16:16
8:14 [e]1 Chron. 24:1 [f]1 Chron. 25:1 [g]1 Chron. 9:17
8:17 [h]1 Kings 9:26
8:18 [i]1 Kings 9:27; ch. 9:10

9 And [j]when the queen of Sheba heard of
the fame of Solomon, she came to prove
Solomon with hard questions at Jerusalem,
with a very great company, and camels that
bare spices, and gold in abundance, and
precious stones: and when she was come to
Solomon, she communed with him of all
that was in her heart.
2 And Solomon told her all her questions:
and there was nothing hid from Solomon
which he told her not.
3 And when the queen of Sheba had seen
the wisdom of Solomon, and the house that
he had built,
4 And the meat of his table, and the sitting
of his servants, and the attendance of his
ministers, and their apparel; his cupbearers
also, and their apparel; and his ascent by
which he went up into the house of the
LORD; there was no more spirit in her.
5 And she said to the king, *It was* a true
report which I heard in mine own land of
thine acts, and of thy wisdom:
6 Howbeit I believed not their words, until I came, and mine eyes had seen *it*: and,
behold, the one half of the greatness of thy
wisdom was not told me: *for* thou exceedest
the fame that I heard.
7 Happy *are* thy men, and happy *are*
these thy servants, which stand continually
before thee, and hear thy wisdom.
8 Blessed be the LORD thy God, which delighted in thee to set thee on his throne, *to
be* king for the LORD thy God: because thy
God loved Israel, to establish them for ever,
therefore made he thee king over them, to
do judgment and justice.
9 And she gave the king an hundred and
twenty talents of gold, and of spices great
abundance, and precious stones: neither
was there any such spice as the queen of
Sheba gave king Solomon.
10 And the servants also of Huram, and
the servants of Solomon, [k]which brought
gold from Ophir, brought [l]algum trees and
precious stones.
11 And the king made *of* the algum trees
terraces to the house of the LORD, and to the
king's palace, and harps and psalteries for
singers: and there were none such seen before in the land of Judah.
12 And king Solomon gave to the queen
of Sheba all her desire, whatsoever she
asked, beside *that* which she had brought
unto the king. So she turned, and went
away to her own land, she and her servants.
13 ¶ Now the weight of gold that came to
Solomon in one year was six hundred and
threescore and six talents of gold;
14 Beside *that which* chapmen and merchants brought. And all the kings of Arabia
and governors of the country brought gold
and silver to Solomon.
15 ¶ And king Solomon made two hundred targets *of* beaten gold: six hundred
shekels of beaten gold went to one target.
16 And three hundred shields *made he of*
beaten gold: three hundred *shekels* of gold
went to one shield. And the king put them in
the house of the forest of Lebanon.
17 Moreover the king made a great
throne of ivory, and overlaid it with pure
gold.
18 And *there were* six steps to the throne,
with a footstool of gold, *which were* fastened to the throne, and stays on each side
of the sitting place, and two lions standing
by the stays:
19 And twelve lions stood there on the
one side and on the other upon the six steps.
There was not the like made in any kingdom.
20 ¶ And all the drinking vessels of king
Solomon *were of* gold, and all the vessels of
the house of the forest of Lebanon *were of*
pure gold: none *were of* silver; it was *not*
any thing accounted of in the days of Solomon.
21 For the king's ships went to Tarshish
with the servants of Huram: every three
years once came the ships of Tarshish
bringing gold, and silver, ivory, and apes,
and peacocks.
22 And king Solomon passed all the kings
of the earth in riches and wisdom.
23 ¶ And all the kings of the earth sought
the presence of Solomon, to hear his wisdom, that God had put in his heart.
24 And they brought every man his
present, vessels of silver, and vessels of
gold, and raiment, harness, and spices,
horses, and mules, a rate year by year.
25 ¶ And Solomon [m]had four thousand
stalls for horses and chariots, and twelve
thousand horsemen; whom he bestowed in
the chariot cities, and with the king at Jerusalem.
26 ¶ [n]And he reigned over all the kings
[o]from the river even unto the land of the
Philistines, and to the border of Egypt.
27 [p]And the king made silver in Jerusalem as stones, and cedar trees made he as
the sycomore trees that *are* in the low plains
in abundance.
28 [q]And they brought unto Solomon
horses out of Egypt, and out of all lands.
29 ¶ [r]Now the rest of the acts of Solomon, first and last, *are* they not written in
the book of Nathan the prophet, and in the
prophecy of [s]Ahijah the Shilonite, and in
the visions of [t]Iddo the seer against Jeroboam the son of Nebat?
30 [u]And Solomon reigned in Jerusalem
over all Israel forty years.
31 And Solomon slept with his fathers,
and he was buried in the city of David his
father: and Rehoboam his son reigned in his
stead.

10 And [v]Rehoboam went to Shechem:
for to Shechem were all Israel come
to make him king.
2 And it came to pass, when Jeroboam
the son of Nebat, who *was* in Egypt,
[w]whither he had fled from the presence of
Solomon the king, heard *it*, that Jeroboam
returned out of Egypt.

9:1 [j]1 Kings 10:1; Matt. 12:42; Luke 11:31
9:10 [k]ch. 8:18 [l]1 Kings 10:11
9:25 [m]1 Kings 4:26; ch. 1:14
9:26 [n]1 Kings 4:21 [o]Gen. 15:18; Ps. 72:8
9:27 [p]1 Kings 10:27; ch. 1:15
9:28 [q]1 Kings 10:28; ch. 1:16
9:29 [r]1 Kings 11:41 [s]1 Kings 11:29 [t]ch. 12:25
9:30 [u]1 Kings 11:42
10:1 [v]1 Kings 12:1
10:2 [w]1 Kings 11:40

3 And they sent and called him. So Jeroboam and all Israel came and spake to Rehoboam, saying,

4 Thy father made our yoke grievous: now therefore ease thou somewhat the grievous servitude of thy father, and his heavy yoke that he put upon us, and we will serve thee.

5 And he said unto them, Come again unto me after three days. And the people departed.

6 ¶ And king Rehoboam took counsel with the old men that had stood before Solomon his father while he yet lived, saying, What counsel give ye *me* to return answer to this people?

7 And they spake unto him, saying, If thou be kind to this people, and please them, and speak good words to them, they will be thy servants for ever.

8 But he forsook the counsel which the old men gave him, and took counsel with the young men that were brought up with him, that stood before him.

9 And he said unto them, What advice give ye that we may return answer to this people, which have spoken to me, saying, Ease somewhat the yoke that thy father did put upon us?

10 And the young men that were brought up with him spake unto him, saying, Thus shalt thou answer the people that spake unto thee, saying, Thy father made our yoke heavy, but make thou *it* somewhat lighter for us; thus shalt thou say unto them, My little *finger* shall be thicker than my father's loins.

11 For whereas my father put a heavy yoke upon you, I will put more to your yoke: my father chastised you with whips, but I *will chastise you* with scorpions.

12 So Jeroboam and all the people came to Rehoboam on the third day, as the king bade, saying, Come again to me on the third day.

13 And the king answered them roughly; and king Rehoboam forsook the counsel of the old men,

14 And answered them after the advice of the young men, saying, My father made your yoke heavy, but I will add thereto: my father chastised you with whips, but I *will chastise you* with scorpions.

15 So the king hearkened not unto the people: [x]for the cause was of God, that the LORD might perform his word, which he spake by the [y]hand of Ahijah the Shilonite to Jeroboam the son of Nebat.

16 ¶ And when all Israel *saw* that the king would not hearken unto them, the people answered the king, saying, What portion have we in David? and *we have* none inheritance in the son of Jesse: every man to your tents, O Israel: *and* now, David, see to thine own house. So all Israel went to their tents.

17 But *as for* the children of Israel that dwelt in the cities of Judah, Rehoboam reigned over them.

18 Then king Rehoboam sent Hadoram that *was* over the tribute; and the children of Israel stoned him with stones, that he died. But king Rehoboam made speed to get him up to *his* chariot, to flee to Jerusalem.

19 [z]And Israel rebelled against the house of David unto this day.

11 And [a]when Rehoboam was come to Jerusalem, he gathered of the house of Judah and Benjamin an hundred and fourscore thousand chosen *men,* which were warriors, to fight against Israel, that he might bring the kingdom again to Rehoboam.

2 But the word of the LORD came [b]to Shemaiah the man of God, saying,

3 Speak unto Rehoboam the son of Solomon, king of Judah, and to all Israel in Judah and Benjamin, saying,

4 Thus saith the LORD, Ye shall not go up, nor fight against your brethren: return every man to his house: for this thing is done of me. And they obeyed the words of the LORD, and returned from going against Jeroboam.

5 ¶ And Rehoboam dwelt in Jerusalem, and built cities for defence in Judah.

6 He built even Beth-lehem, and Etam, and Tekoa,

7 And Beth-zur, and Shoco, and Adullam,

8 And Gath, and Mareshah, and Ziph,

9 And Adoraim, and Lachish, and Azekah,

10 And Zorah, and Aijalon, and Hebron, which *are* in Judah and in Benjamin fenced cities.

11 And he fortified the strong holds, and put captains in them, and store of victual, and of oil and wine.

12 And in every several city *he put* shields and spears, and made them exceeding strong, having Judah and Benjamin on his side.

13 ¶ And the priests and the Levites that *were* in all Israel resorted to him out of all their coasts.

14 For the Levites left [c]their suburbs and their possession, and came to Judah and Jerusalem: for [d]Jeroboam and his sons had cast them off from executing the priest's office unto the LORD:

15 [e]And he ordained him priests for the high places, and for [f]the devils, and for [g]the calves which he had made.

16 [h]And after them out of all the tribes of Israel such as set their hearts to seek the LORD God of Israel came to Jerusalem, to sacrifice unto the LORD God of their fathers.

17 So they [i]strengthened the kingdom of Judah, and made Rehoboam the son of Solomon strong, three years: for three years they walked in the way of David and Solomon.

18 ¶ And Rehoboam took him Mahalath the daughter of Jerimoth the son of David to wife, *and* Abihail the daughter of Eliab the son of Jesse;

10:15 [x]1 Sam. 2:25; 1 Kings 12:15 [y]1 Kings 11:29
10:19 [z]1 Kings 12:19
11:1 [a]1 Kings 12:21
11:2 [b]ch. 12:15
11:14 [c]Num. 35:2 [d]ch. 13:9
11:15 [e]1 Kings 12:31; Hos. 13:2 [f]Lev. 17:7; 1 Cor. 10:20 [g]1 Kings 12:28
11:16 [h]ch. 15:9
11:17 [i]ch. 12:1

19 Which bare him children; Jeush, and
Shamariah, and Zaham.
20 And after her he took [j]Maachah the
daughter of Absalom; which bare him Abijah, and Attai, and Ziza, and Shelomith.
21 And Rehoboam loved Maachah the
daughter of Absalom above all his wives
and his concubines: (for he took eighteen
wives, and threescore concubines; and begat twenty and eight sons, and threescore
daughters.)
22 And Rehoboam [k]made Abijah the son
of Maachah the chief, *to be* ruler among his
brethren: for *he thought* to make him king.
23 And he dealt wisely, and dispersed of
all his children throughout all the countries
of Judah and Benjamin, unto every fenced
city: and he gave them victual in abundance. And he desired many wives.
12 And [l]it came to pass, when Rehoboam had established the kingdom,
and had strengthened himself, [m]he forsook
the law of the LORD, and all Israel with him.
2 [n]And it came to pass, *that* in the fifth
year of king Rehoboam Shishak king of
Egypt came up against Jerusalem, because
they had transgressed against the LORD,
3 With twelve hundred chariots, and
threescore thousand horsemen: and the
people *were* without number that came with
him out of Egypt; [o]the Lubims, the Suk-
kiims, and the Ethiopians.
4 And he took the fenced cities which *pertained* to Judah, and came to Jerusalem.
5 ¶ Then came [p]Shemaiah the prophet to
Rehoboam, and *to* the princes of Judah,
that were gathered together to Jerusalem
because of Shishak, and said unto them,
Thus saith the LORD, [q]Ye have forsaken
me, and therefore have I also left you in the
hand of Shishak.
6 Whereupon the princes of Israel and the
king [r]humbled themselves; and they said,
[s]The LORD *is* righteous.
7 And when the LORD saw that they humbled themselves, [t]the word of the LORD
came to Shemaiah, saying, They have humbled themselves; *therefore* I will not destroy
them, but I will grant them some deliverance; and my wrath shall not be poured out
upon Jerusalem by the hand of Shishak.
8 Nevertheless [u]they shall be his servants; that they may know [v]my service, and
the service of the kingdoms of the countries.
9 [w]So Shishak king of Egypt came up
against Jerusalem, and took away the treasures of the house of the LORD, and the treasures of the king's house; he took all: he
carried away also the shields of gold which
Solomon had [x]made.
10 Instead of which king Rehoboam
made shields of brass, and committed *them*
[y]to the hands of the chief of the guard, that
kept the entrance of the king's house.
11 And when the king entered into the
house of the LORD, the guard came and
fetched them, and brought them again into
the guard chamber.

11:20 [j]2 Kings 15:2; ch. 13:2
11:22 [k]Deut. 21:15
12:1 [l]ch. 11:17 [m]1 Kings 14:22
12:2 [n]1 Kings 14:24
12:3 [o]ch. 16:8
12:5 [p]ch. 11:2 [q]ch. 15:2
12:6 [r]Jam. 4:10 [s]Ex. 9:27
12:7 [t]1 Kings 21:28
12:8 [u]Isa. 26:13 [v]Deut. 28:47
12:9 [w]1 Kings 14:25 [x]1 Kings 10:16; ch. 9:15
12:10 [y]2 Sam. 8:18
12:13 [z]1 Kings 14:21 [a]ch. 6:6
12:15 [b]ch. 9:29 [c]1 Kings 14:30
12:16 [d]1 Kings 14:31
13:1 [e]1 Kings 15:1
13:2 [f]ch. 11:20
13:4 [g]Josh. 18:22
13:5 [h]2 Sam. 7:12 [i]Num. 18:19
13:6 [j]1 Kings 11:26
13:7 [k]Judg. 9:4
13:8 [l]1 Kings 12:28; Hos. 8:6
13:9 [m]ch. 11:14 [n]Ex. 29:35

12 And when he humbled himself, the
wrath of the LORD turned from him, that he
would not destroy *him* altogether: and also
in Judah things went well.
13 ¶ So king Rehoboam strengthened
himself in Jerusalem, and reigned: for [z]Re-
hoboam *was* one and forty years old when
he began to reign, and he reigned seventeen
years in Jerusalem, [a]the city which the
LORD had chosen out of all the tribes of
Israel, to put his name there. And his
mother's name *was* Naamah an Ammonitess.
14 And he did evil, because he prepared
not his heart to seek the LORD.
15 Now the acts of Rehoboam, first and
last, *are* they not written in the book of Shemaiah the prophet, [b]and of Iddo the seer
concerning genealogies? [c]And *there were*
wars between Rehoboam and Jeroboam
continually.
16 And Rehoboam slept with his fathers,
and was buried in the city of David: and
[d]Abijah his son reigned in his stead.
13 Now [e]in the eighteenth year of king
Jeroboam began Abijah to reign over
Judah.
2 He reigned three years in Jerusalem.
His mother's name also *was* [f]Michaiah the
daughter of Uriel of Gibeah. And there was
war between Abijah and Jeroboam.
3 And Abijah set the battle in array with
an army of valiant men of war, *even* four
hundred thousand chosen men: Jeroboam
also set the battle in array against him with
eight hundred thousand chosen men, *being*
mighty men of valour.
4 ¶ And Abijah stood up upon mount
[g]Zemaraim, which *is* in mount Ephraim,
and said, Hear me, thou Jeroboam, and all
Israel;
5 Ought ye not to know that the LORD
God of Israel [h]gave the kingdom over Israel
to David for ever, *even* to him and to his
sons [i]by a covenant of salt?
6 Yet Jeroboam the son of Nebat, the servant of Solomon the son of David, is risen
up, and hath [j]rebelled against his lord.
7 And there are gathered unto him [k]vain
men, the children of Belial, and have
strengthened themselves against Rehoboam the son of Solomon, when Rehoboam
was young and tenderhearted, and could
not withstand them.
8 And now ye think to withstand the kingdom of the LORD in the hand of the sons of
David; and ye *be* a great multitude, and
there are with you golden calves, which Jeroboam [l]made you for gods.
9 [m]Have ye not cast out the priests of the
LORD, the sons of Aaron, and the Levites,
and have made you priests after the manner
of the nations of *other* lands? [n]so that whosoever cometh to consecrate himself with a
young bullock and seven rams, *the same*
may be a priest of *them that are* no gods.
10 But as for us, the LORD *is* our God, and
we have not forsaken him; and the priests,

which minister unto the LORD, *are* the sons of Aaron, and the Levites *wait* upon *their* business:

11 [o]And they burn unto the LORD every morning and every evening burnt sacrifices and sweet incense: the [p]shewbread also *set they in order* upon the pure table; and the candlestick of gold with the lamps thereof, [q]to burn every evening: for we keep the charge of the LORD our God; but ye have forsaken him.

12 And, behold, God himself *is* with us for *our* captain, [r]and his priests with sounding trumpets to cry alarm against you. O children of Israel, [s]fight ye not against the LORD God of your fathers; for ye shall not prosper.

13 ¶ But Jeroboam caused an ambushment to come about behind them: so they were before Judah, and the ambushment *was* behind them.

14 And when Judah looked back, behold, the battle *was* before and behind: and they cried unto the LORD, and the priests sounded with the trumpets.

15 Then the men of Judah gave a shout: and as the men of Judah shouted, it came to pass, that God [t]smote Jeroboam and all Israel before Abijah and Judah.

16 And the children of Israel fled before Judah: and God delivered them into their hand.

17 And Abijah and his people slew them with a great slaughter: so there fell down slain of Israel five hundred thousand chosen men.

18 Thus the children of Israel were brought under at that time, and the children of Judah prevailed, [u]because they relied upon the LORD God of their fathers.

19 And Abijah pursued after Jeroboam, and took cities from him, Beth-el with the towns thereof, and Jeshanah with the towns thereof, and [v]Ephraim with the towns thereof.

20 Neither did Jeroboam recover strength again in the days of Abijah: and the LORD [w]struck him, and [x]he died.

21 ¶ But Abijah waxed mighty, and married fourteen wives, and begat twenty and two sons, and sixteen daughters.

22 And the rest of the acts of Abijah, and his ways, and his sayings, *are* written in the story of the prophet [y]Iddo.

14 So Abijah slept with his fathers, and they buried him in the city of David: and [z]Asa his son reigned in his stead. In his days the land was quiet ten years.

2 And Asa did *that which was* good and right in the eyes of the LORD his God:

3 For he took away the altars of the strange *gods,* and [a]the high places, and [b]brake down the images, [c]and cut down the groves:

4 And commanded Judah to seek the LORD God of their fathers, and to do the law and the commandment.

5 Also he took away out of all the cities of Judah the high places and the images: and the kingdom was quiet before him.

6 ¶ And he built fenced cities in Judah: for the land had rest, and he had no war in those years; because the LORD had given him rest.

7 Therefore he said unto Judah, Let us build these cities, and make about *them* walls and towers, gates, and bars, *while* the land *is* yet before us; because we have sought the LORD our God, we have sought *him,* and he hath given us rest on every side. So they built and prospered.

8 And Asa had an army *of men* that bare targets and spears, out of Judah three hundred thousand; and out of Benjamin, that bare shields and drew bows, two hundred and fourscore thousand: all these *were* mighty men of valour.

9 ¶ [d]And there came out against them Zerah the Ethiopian with an host of a thousand thousand, and three hundred chariots; and came unto [e]Mareshah.

10 Then Asa went out against him, and they set the battle in array in the valley of Zephathah at Mareshah.

11 And Asa [f]cried unto the LORD his God, and said, LORD, *it is* [g]nothing with thee to help, whether with many, or with them that have no power: help us, O LORD our God; for we rest on thee, and [h]in thy name we go against this multitude. O LORD, thou *art* our God; let not man prevail against thee.

12 So the LORD [i]smote the Ethiopians before Asa, and before Judah; and the Ethiopians fled.

13 And Asa and the people that *were* with him pursued them unto [j]Gerar: and the Ethiopians were overthrown, that they could not recover themselves; for they were destroyed before the LORD, and before his host; and they carried away very much spoil.

14 And they smote all the cities round about Gerar; for [k]the fear of the LORD came upon them: and they spoiled all the cities; for there was exceeding much spoil in them.

15 They smote also the tents of cattle, and carried away sheep and camels in abundance, and returned to Jerusalem.

15 And [l]the Spirit of God came upon Azariah the son of Oded:

2 And he went out to meet Asa, and said unto him, Hear ye me, Asa, and all Judah and Benjamin; [m]the LORD *is* with you, while ye be with him; and [n]if ye seek him, he will be found of you; but [o]if ye forsake him, he will forsake you.

3 Now [p]for a long season Israel *hath been* without the true God, and without [q]a teaching priest, and without law.

4 But [r]when they in their trouble did turn unto the LORD God of Israel, and sought him, he was found of them.

5 And [s]in those times *there was* no peace to him that went out, nor to him that came

13:11 [o]ch. 2:4 [p]Lev. 24:6 [q]Ex. 27:20; Lev. 24:2
13:12 [r]Num. 10:8 [s]Acts 5:39
13:15 [t]ch. 14:12
13:18 [u]1 Chron. 5:20; Ps. 22:5
13:19 [v]Josh. 15:9
13:20 [w]1 Sam. 25:38 [x]1 Kings 14:20
13:22 [y]ch. 12:15
14:1 [z]1 Kings 15:8
14:3 [a]1 Kings 15:14; ch. 15:17 [b]Ex. 34:13 [c]1 Kings 11:7
14:9 [d]ch. 16:8 [e]Josh. 15:44
14:11 [f]Ex. 14:10; ch. 13:14; Ps. 22:5 [g]1 Sam. 14:6 [h]1 Sam. 17:45; Prov. 18:10
14:12 [i]ch. 13:15
14:13 [j]Gen. 10:19
14:14 [k]Gen. 35:5; ch. 17:10
15:1 [l]Num. 24:2; Judg. 3:10; ch. 20:14
15:2 [m]Jam. 4:8 [n]ver. 4; 1 Chron. 28:9; ch. 33:12; Jer. 29:13; Matt. 7:7 [o]ch. 24:20
15:3 [p]Hos. 3:4 [q]Lev. 10:11
15:4 [r]Deut. 4:29
15:5 [s]Judg. 5:6

in, but great vexations *were* upon all the
inhabitants of the countries.
6 [t]And nation was destroyed of nation,
and city of city: for God did vex them with
all adversity.
7 Be ye strong therefore, and let not your
hands be weak: for your work shall be rewarded.
8 And when Asa heard these words, and
the prophecy of Oded the prophet, he took
courage, and put away the abominable idols
out of all the land of Judah and Benjamin,
and out of the cities [u]which he had taken
from mount Ephraim, and renewed the altar of the LORD, that *was* before the porch of
the LORD.
9 And he gathered all Judah and Benjamin, and [v]the strangers with them out of
Ephraim and Manasseh, and out of Simeon:
for they fell to him out of Israel in abundance, when they saw that the LORD his
God *was* with him.
10 So they gathered themselves together
at Jerusalem in the third month, in the fifteenth year of the reign of Asa.
11 [w]And they offered unto the LORD the
same time, of [x]the spoil *which* they had
brought, seven hundred oxen and seven
thousand sheep.
12 And they [y]entered into a covenant to
seek the LORD God of their fathers with all
their heart and with all their soul;
13 [z]That whosoever would not seek the
LORD God of Israel [a]should be put to death,
whether small or great, whether man or
woman.
14 And they sware unto the LORD with
a loud voice, and with shouting, and with
trumpets, and with cornets.
15 And all Judah rejoiced at the oath: for
they had sworn with all their heart, and
[b]sought him with their whole desire; and he
was found of them: and the LORD gave them
rest round about.
16 ¶ And also *concerning* [c]Maachah the
mother of Asa the king, he removed her
from *being* queen, because she had made an
idol in a grove: and Asa cut down her idol,
and stamped *it*, and burnt *it* at the brook
Kidron.
17 But [d]the high places were not taken
away out of Israel: nevertheless the heart of
Asa was perfect all his days.
18 ¶ And he brought into the house of
God the things that his father had dedicated, and that he himself had dedicated,
silver, and gold, and vessels.
19 And there was no *more* war unto the
five and thirtieth year of the reign of Asa.

16 In the six and thirtieth year of the
reign of Asa [e]Baasha king of Israel
came up against Judah, and built Ramah,
[f]to the intent that he might let none go out
or come in to Asa king of Judah.
2 Then Asa brought out silver and gold
out of the treasures of the house of the LORD
and of the king's house, and sent to Ben-
hadad king of Syria, that dwelt at Damascus, saying,
3 *There is* a league between me and thee,
as *there was* between my father and thy
father: behold, I have sent thee silver and
gold; go, break thy league with Baasha king
of Israel, that he may depart from me.
4 And Ben-hadad hearkened unto king
Asa, and sent the captains of his armies
against the cities of Israel; and they smote
Ijon, and Dan, and Abel-maim, and all the
store cities of Naphtali.
5 And it came to pass, when Baasha
heard *it*, that he left off building of Ramah,
and let his work cease.
6 Then Asa the king took all Judah; and
they carried away the stones of Ramah, and
the timber thereof, wherewith Baasha was
building; and he built therewith Geba and
Mizpah.
7 ¶ And at that time [g]Hanani the seer
came to Asa king of Judah, and said unto
him, [h]Because thou hast relied on the king
of Syria, and not relied on the LORD thy
God, therefore is the host of the king of
Syria escaped out of thine hand.
8 Were not [i]the Ethiopians and [j]the
Lubims a huge host, with very many chariots and horsemen? yet, because thou didst
rely on the LORD, he delivered them into
thine hand.
9 [k]For the eyes of the LORD run to and fro
throughout the whole earth, to shew himself strong in the behalf of *them* whose
heart *is* perfect toward him. Herein [l]thou
hast done foolishly: therefore from henceforth [m]thou shalt have wars.
10 Then Asa was wroth with the seer, and
[n]put him in a prison house; for *he was* in a
rage with him because of this *thing*. And
Asa oppressed *some* of the people the same
time.
11 ¶ [o]And, behold, the acts of Asa, first
and last, lo, they *are* written in the book of
the kings of Judah and Israel.
12 And Asa in the thirty and ninth year of
his reign was diseased in his feet, until his
disease *was* exceeding *great:* yet in his disease he [p]sought not to the LORD, but to the
physicians.
13 ¶ [q]And Asa slept with his fathers, and
died in the one and fortieth year of his reign.
14 And they buried him in his own sepulchres, which he had made for himself in the
city of David, and laid him in the bed which
was filled [r]with sweet odours and divers
kinds *of spices* prepared by the apothecaries' art: and they made [s]a very great burning for him.

17 And [t]Jehoshaphat his son reigned
in his stead, and strengthened himself against Israel.
2 And he placed forces in all the fenced
cities of Judah, and set garrisons in the land
of Judah, and in the cities of Ephraim,
[u]which Asa his father had taken.
3 And the LORD was with Jehoshaphat,
because he walked in the first ways of his

15:6 [t]Matt. 24:7
15:8 [u]ch. 13:19
15:9 [v]ch. 11:16
15:11 [w]ch. 14:15 [x]ch. 14:13
15:12 [y]2 Kings 23:3; ch. 34:31; Neh. 10:29
15:13 [z]Ex. 22:20 [a]Deut. 13:5
15:15 [b]ver. 2
15:16 [c]1 Kings 15:13
15:17 [d]ch. 14:3; 1 Kings 15:14
16:1 [e]1 Kings 15:17 [f]ch. 15:9
16:7 [g]1 Kings 16:1; ch. 19:2 [h]Isa. 31:1; Jer. 17:5
16:8 [i]ch. 14:9 [j]ch. 12:3
16:9 [k]Job 34:21; Prov. 5:21; Jer. 16:17; Zech. 4:10 [l]1 Sam. 13:13 [m]1 Kings 15:32
16:10 [n]ch. 18:26; Jer. 20:2; Matt. 14:3
16:11 [o]1 Kings 15:23
16:12 [p]Jer. 17:5
16:13 [q]1 Kings 15:24
16:14 [r]Gen. 50:2; Mark 16:1; John 19:39 [s]ch. 21:19; Jer. 34:5
17:1 [t]1 Kings 15:24
17:2 [u]ch. 15:8

father David, and sought not unto Baalim;

4 But sought to the LORD God of his father, and walked in his commandments, and not after [v]the doings of Israel.

5 Therefore the LORD stablished the kingdom in his hand; and all Judah [w]brought to Jehoshaphat presents; [x]and he had riches and honour in abundance.

6 And his heart was lifted up in the ways of the LORD: moreover [y]he took away the high places and groves out of Judah.

7 ¶ Also in the third year of his reign he sent to his princes, *even* to Ben-hail, and to Obadiah, and to Zechariah, and to Nethaneel, and to Michaiah, [z]to teach in the cities of Judah.

8 And with them *he sent* Levites, *even* Shemaiah, and Nethaniah, and Zebadiah, and Asahel, and Shemiramoth, and Jehonathan, and Adonijah, and Tobijah, and Tobadonijah, Levites; and with them Elishama and Jehoram, priests.

9 [a]And they taught in Judah, and *had* the book of the law of the LORD with them, and went about throughout all the cities of Judah, and taught the people.

10 ¶ And [b]the fear of the LORD fell upon all the kingdoms of the lands that *were* round about Judah, so that they made no war against Jehoshaphat.

11 Also *some* of the Philistines [c]brought Jehoshaphat presents, and tribute silver; and the Arabians brought him flocks, seven thousand and seven hundred rams, and seven thousand and seven hundred he goats.

12 ¶ And Jehoshaphat waxed great exceedingly; and he built in Judah castles, and cities of store.

13 And he had much business in the cities of Judah: and the men of war, mighty men of valour, *were* in Jerusalem.

14 And these *are* the numbers of them according to the house of their fathers: Of Judah, the captains of thousands; Adnah the chief, and with him mighty men of valour three hundred thousand.

15 And next to him *was* Jehohanan the captain, and with him two hundred and fourscore thousand.

16 And next him *was* Amasiah the son of Zichri, [d]who willingly offered himself unto the LORD; and with him two hundred thousand mighty men of valour.

17 And of Benjamin; Eliada a mighty man of valour, and with him armed men with bow and shield two hundred thousand.

18 And next him *was* Jehozabad, and with him an hundred and fourscore thousand ready prepared for the war.

19 These waited on the king, beside [e]*those* whom the king put in the fenced cities throughout all Judah.

18

Now Jehoshaphat [f]had riches and honour in abundance, and [g]joined affinity with Ahab.

2 [h]And after *certain* years he went down to Ahab to Samaria. And Ahab killed sheep and oxen for him in abundance, and for the people that *he had* with him, and persuaded him to go up *with him* to Ramoth-gilead.

3 And Ahab king of Israel said unto Jehoshaphat king of Judah, Wilt thou go with me to Ramoth-gilead? And he answered him, I *am* as thou *art*, and my people as thy people; and *we will be* with thee in the war.

4 ¶ And Jehoshaphat said unto the king of Israel, [i]Enquire, I pray thee, at the word of the LORD to day.

5 Therefore the king of Israel gathered together of prophets four hundred men, and said unto them, Shall we go to Ramoth-gilead to battle, or shall I forbear? And they said, Go up; for God will deliver *it* into the king's hand.

6 But Jehoshaphat said, *Is there* not here a prophet of the LORD besides, that we might enquire of him?

7 And the king of Israel said unto Jehoshaphat, *There is* yet one man, by whom we may enquire of the LORD: but I hate him; for he never prophesied good unto me, but always evil: the same *is* Micaiah the son of Imla. And Jehoshaphat said, Let not the king say so.

8 And the king of Israel called for one *of his* officers, and said, Fetch quickly Micaiah the son of Imla.

9 And the king of Israel and Jehoshaphat king of Judah sat either of them on his throne, clothed in *their* robes, and they sat in a void place at the entering in of the gate of Samaria; and all the prophets prophesied before them.

10 And Zedekiah the son of Chenaanah had made him horns of iron, and said, Thus saith the LORD, With these thou shalt push Syria until they be consumed.

11 And all the prophets prophesied so, saying, Go up to Ramoth-gilead, and prosper: for the LORD shall deliver *it* into the hand of the king.

12 And the messenger that went to call Micaiah spake to him, saying, Behold, the words of the prophets *declare* good to the king with one assent; let thy word therefore, I pray thee, be like one of theirs, and speak thou good.

13 And Micaiah said, *As* the LORD liveth, [j]even what my God saith, that will I speak.

14 And when he was come to the king, the king said unto him, Micaiah, shall we go to Ramoth-gilead to battle, or shall I forbear? And he said, Go ye up, and prosper, and they shall be delivered into your hand.

15 And the king said to him, How many times shall I adjure thee that thou say nothing but the truth to me in the name of the LORD?

16 Then he said, I did see all Israel scattered upon the mountains, as sheep that have no shepherd: and the LORD said, These have no master; let them return *therefore* every man to his house in peace.

17 And the king of Israel said to Jehosha-

17:4 [v]1 Kings 12:28
17:5 [w]1 Sam. 10:27; 1 Kings 10:25 [x]1 Kings 10:27; ch. 18:1
17:6 [y]1 Kings 22:43; ch. 15:17
17:7 [z]ch. 15:3
17:9 [a]ch. 35:3; Neh. 8:7
17:10 [b]Gen. 35:5
17:11 [c]2 Sam. 8:2
17:16 [d]Judg. 5:2
17:19 [e]ver. 2
18:1 [f]ch. 17:5 [g]2 Kings 8:18
18:2 [h]1 Kings 22:2
18:4 [i]1 Sam. 23:2; 2 Sam. 2:1
18:13 [j]Num. 22:18; 1 Kings 22:14

phat, Did I not tell thee *that* he would not prophesy good unto me, but evil?

18 Again he said, Therefore hear the word of the LORD; I saw the LORD sitting upon his throne, and all the host of heaven standing on his right hand and *on* his left.

19 And the LORD said, Who shall entice Ahab king of Israel, that he may go up and fall at Ramoth-gilead? And one spake saying after this manner, and another saying after that manner.

20 Then there came out a [k]spirit, and stood before the LORD, and said, I will entice him. And the LORD said unto him, Wherewith?

21 And he said, I will go out, and be a lying spirit in the mouth of all his prophets. And *the LORD* said, Thou shalt entice *him*, and thou shalt also prevail: go out, and do *even* so.

22 Now therefore, behold, [l]the LORD hath put a lying spirit in the mouth of these thy prophets, and the LORD hath spoken evil against thee.

23 Then Zedekiah the son of Chenaanah came near, and [m]smote Micaiah upon the cheek, and said, Which way went the Spirit of the LORD from me to speak unto thee?

24 And Micaiah said, Behold, thou shalt see on that day when thou shalt go into an inner chamber to hide thyself.

25 Then the king of Israel said, Take ye Micaiah, and carry him back to Amon the governor of the city, and to Joash the king's son;

26 And say, Thus saith the king, [n]Put this *fellow* in the prison, and feed him with bread of affliction and with water of affliction, until I return in peace.

27 And Micaiah said, If thou certainly return in peace, *then* hath not the LORD spoken by me. And he said, Hearken, all ye people.

28 So the king of Israel and Jehoshaphat the king of Judah went up to Ramoth-gilead.

29 And the king of Israel said unto Jehoshaphat, I will disguise myself, and will go to the battle; but put thou on thy robes. So the king of Israel disguised himself; and they went to the battle.

30 Now the king of Syria had commanded the captains of the chariots that *were* with him, saying, Fight ye not with small or great, save only with the king of Israel.

31 And it came to pass, when the captains of the chariots saw Jehoshaphat, that they said, It *is* the king of Israel. Therefore they compassed about him to fight: but Jehoshaphat cried out, and the LORD helped him; and God moved them *to depart* from him.

32 For it came to pass, that, when the captains of the chariots perceived that it was not the king of Israel, they turned back again from pursuing him.

33 And a *certain* man drew a bow at a venture, and smote the king of Israel between the joints of the harness: therefore he said to his chariot man, Turn thine hand, that thou mayest carry me out of the host; for I am wounded.

34 And the battle increased that day: howbeit the king of Israel stayed *himself* up in *his* chariot against the Syrians until the even: and about the time of the sun going down he died.

19

And Jehoshaphat the king of Judah returned to his house in peace to Jerusalem.

2 And Jehu the son of Hanani [o]the seer went out to meet him, and said to king Jehoshaphat, Shouldest thou help the ungodly, and [p]love them that hate the LORD? therefore *is* [q]wrath upon thee from before the LORD.

3 Nevertheless there are [r]good things found in thee, in that thou hast taken away the groves out of the land, and hast [s]prepared thine heart to seek God.

4 And Jehoshaphat dwelt at Jerusalem: and he went out again through the people from Beer-sheba to mount Ephraim, and brought them back unto the LORD God of their fathers.

5 ¶ And he set judges in the land throughout all the fenced cities of Judah, city by city,

6 And said to the judges, Take heed what ye do: for [t]ye judge not for man, but for the LORD, [u]who *is* with you in the judgment.

7 Wherefore now let the fear of the LORD be upon you; take heed and do *it*: for [v]*there is* no iniquity with the LORD our God, nor [w]respect of persons, nor taking of gifts.

8 ¶ Moreover in Jerusalem did Jehoshaphat [x]set of the Levites, and *of* the priests, and of the chief of the fathers of Israel, for the judgment of the LORD, and for controversies, when they returned to Jerusalem.

9 And he charged them, saying, Thus shall ye do [y]in the fear of the LORD, faithfully, and with a perfect heart.

10 [z]And what cause soever shall come to you of your brethren that dwell in their cities, between blood and blood, between law and commandment, statutes and judgments, ye shall even warn them that they trespass not against the LORD, and *so* [a]wrath come upon [b]you, and upon your brethren: this do, and ye shall not trespass.

11 And, behold, Amariah the chief priest *is* over you [c]in all matters of the LORD; and Zebadiah the son of Ishmael, the ruler of the house of Judah, for all the king's matters: also the Levites *shall be* officers before you. Deal courageously, and the LORD shall be [d]with the good.

20

It came to pass after this also, *that* the children of Moab, and the children of Ammon, and with them *other* beside the Ammonites, came against Jehoshaphat to battle.

2 Then there came some that told Jehoshaphat, saying, There cometh a great multitude against thee from beyond the sea on

18:20 [k]Job 1:6
18:22 [l]Job 12:16; Isa. 19:14; Ezek. 14:9
18:23 [m]Jer. 20:2; Mark 14:65; Acts 23:2
18:26 [n]ch. 16:10
19:2 [o]1 Sam. 9:9 [p]Ps. 139:21 [q]ch. 32:25
19:3 [r]ch. 12:12 [s]ch. 30:19; Ezra 7:10
19:6 [t]Deut. 1:17 [u]Ps. 82:1; Eccl. 5:8
19:7 [v]Deut. 32:4; Rom. 9:14 [w]Deut. 10:17; Job 34:19; Acts 10:34; Rom. 2:11; Gal. 2:6; Eph. 6:9; Col. 3:25; 1 Pet. 1:17
19:8 [x]Deut. 16:18; ch. 17:8
19:9 [y]2 Sam. 23:3
19:10 [z]Deut. 17:8 [a]Num. 16:46 [b]Ezek. 3:18
19:11 [c]1 Chron. 26:30 [d]ch. 15:2

this side Syria; and, behold, they *be* [e]in
Hazazon-tamar, which *is* [f]En-gedi.
3 And Jehoshaphat feared, and set himself to [g]seek the LORD, and [h]proclaimed a
fast throughout all Judah.
4 And Judah gathered themselves together, to ask *help* of the LORD: even out of
all the cities of Judah they came to seek the
LORD.
5 ¶ And Jehoshaphat stood in the congregation of Judah and Jerusalem, in the house
of the LORD, before the new court,
6 And said, O LORD God of our fathers,
art not thou [i]God in heaven? and [j]rulest
not thou over all the kingdoms of the heathen? and [k]in thine hand *is there not* power
and might, so that none is able to withstand
thee?
7 *Art* not thou [l]our God, *who* [m]didst
drive out the inhabitants of this land before
thy people Israel, and gavest it to the seed of
Abraham [n]thy friend for ever?
8 And they dwelt therein, and have built
thee a sanctuary therein for thy name, saying,
9 [o]If, *when* evil cometh upon us, *as* the
sword, judgment, or pestilence, or famine,
we stand before this house, and in thy presence, (for thy [p]name *is* in this house,) and
cry unto thee in our affliction, then thou wilt
hear and help.
10 And now, behold, the children of Ammon and Moab and mount Seir, whom thou
[q]wouldest not let Israel invade, when they
came out of the land of Egypt, but [r]they
turned from them, and destroyed them not;
11 Behold, *I say, how* they reward us, [s]to
come to cast us out of thy possession, which
thou hast given us to inherit.
12 O our God, wilt thou not [t]judge them?
for we have no might against this great
company that cometh against us; neither
know we what to do: but [u]our eyes *are* upon
thee.
13 And all Judah stood before the LORD,
with their little ones, their wives, and their
children.
14 ¶ Then upon Jahaziel the son of Zechariah, the son of Benaiah, the son of Jeiel,
the son of Mattaniah, a Levite of the sons of
Asaph, [v]came the Spirit of the LORD in the
midst of the congregation;
15 And he said, Hearken ye, all Judah,
and ye inhabitants of Jerusalem, and thou
king Jehoshaphat, Thus saith the LORD unto
you, [w]Be not afraid nor dismayed by reason
of this great multitude; for the battle *is* not
yours, but God's.
16 To morrow go ye down against them:
behold, they come up by the cliff of Ziz; and
ye shall find them at the end of the brook,
before the wilderness of Jeruel.
17 [x]Ye shall not *need* to fight in this *bat-*
tle: set yourselves, stand ye *still,* and see the
salvation of the LORD with you, O Judah
and Jerusalem: fear not, nor be dismayed;
to morrow go out against them: [y]for the
LORD *will be* with you.
18 And Jehoshaphat [z]bowed his head
with *his* face to the ground: and all Judah
and the inhabitants of Jerusalem fell before
the LORD, worshipping the LORD.
19 And the Levites, of the children of the
Kohathites, and of the children of the Korhites, stood up to praise the LORD God of
Israel with a loud voice on high.
20 ¶ And they rose early in the morning,
and went forth into the wilderness of Tekoa:
and as they went forth, Jehoshaphat stood
and said, Hear me, O Judah, and ye inhabitants of Jerusalem; [a]Believe in the LORD
your God, so shall ye be established; believe
his prophets, so shall ye prosper.
21 And when he had consulted with the
people, he appointed singers unto the LORD,
[b]and that should praise the beauty of holiness, as they went out before the army, and
to say, [c]Praise the LORD; [d]for his mercy
endureth for ever.
22 ¶ And when they began to sing and to
praise, [e]the LORD set ambushments against
the children of Ammon, Moab, and mount
Seir, which were come against Judah; and
they were smitten.
23 For the children of Ammon and Moab
stood up against the inhabitants of mount
Seir, utterly to slay and destroy *them:* and
when they had made an end of the inhabitants of Seir, every one helped to destroy
another.
24 And when Judah came toward the
watch tower in the wilderness, they looked
unto the multitude, and, behold, they *were*
dead bodies fallen to the earth, and none
escaped.
25 And when Jehoshaphat and his people
came to take away the spoil of them, they
found among them in abundance both
riches with the dead bodies, and precious
jewels, which they stripped off for themselves, more than they could carry away:
and they were three days in gathering of the
spoil, it was so much.
26 ¶ And on the fourth day they assembled themselves in the valley of Berachah;
for there they blessed the LORD: therefore
the name of the same place was called, The
valley of Berachah, unto this day.
27 Then they returned, every man of Judah and Jerusalem, and Jehoshaphat in the
forefront of them, to go again to Jerusalem
with joy; for the LORD had [f]made them to
rejoice over their enemies.
28 And they came to Jerusalem with psalteries and harps and trumpets unto the
house of the LORD.
29 And [g]the fear of God was on all the
kingdoms of *those* countries, when they
had heard that the LORD fought against the
enemies of Israel.
30 So the realm of Jehoshaphat was
quiet: for his [h]God gave him rest round
about.
31 ¶ [i]And Jehoshaphat reigned over Judah: *he was* thirty and five years old when
he began to reign, and he reigned twenty

20:2 [e]Gen. 14:7 [f]Josh. 15:62
20:3 [g]ch. 19:3 [h]Ezra 8:21; Jer. 36:9; Jonah 3:5
20:6 [i]Deut. 4:39; Josh. 2:11; 1 Kings 8:23; Matt. 6:9 [j]Ps. 47:2; Dan. 4:17 [k]1 Chron. 29:12; Ps. 62:11; Matt. 6:13
20:7 [l]Gen. 17:7; Ex. 6:7 [m]Ps. 44:2 [n]Isa. 41:8; Jam. 2:23
20:9 [o]1 Kings 8:33; ch. 6:28 [p]ch. 6:20
20:10 [q]Deut. 2:4 [r]Num. 20:21
20:11 [s]Ps. 83:12
20:12 [t]1 Sam. 3:13 [u]Ps. 25:15
20:14 [v]Num. 11:25; ch. 15:1
20:15 [w]Ex. 14:13; Deut. 1:29; ch. 32:7
20:17 [x]Ex. 14:13 [y]Num. 14:9; ch. 15:2
20:18 [z]Ex. 4:31
20:20 [a]Isa. 7:9
20:21 [b]1 Chron. 16:29 [c]1 Chron. 16:34; Ps. 136:1 [d]1 Chron. 16:41; ch. 5:13
20:22 [e]Judg. 7:22; 1 Sam. 14:20
20:27 [f]Neh. 12:43
20:29 [g]ch. 17:10
20:30 [h]ch. 15:15; Job 34:29
20:31 [i]1 Kings 22:41

and five years in Jerusalem. And his mother's name *was* Azubah the daughter of Shilhi.

32 And he walked in the way of Asa his father, and departed not from it, doing *that which was* right in the sight of the LORD.

33 Howbeit [j]the high places were not taken away: for as yet the people had not [k]prepared their hearts unto the God of their fathers.

34 Now the rest of the acts of Jehoshaphat, first and last, behold, they *are* written in the book of Jehu the son of Hanani, [l]who *is* mentioned in the book of the kings of Israel.

35 ¶ And after this [m]did Jehoshaphat king of Judah join himself with Ahaziah king of Israel, who did very wickedly:

36 And he joined himself with him to make ships to go to Tarshish: and they made the ships in Ezion-geber.

37 Then Eliezer the son of Dodavah of Mareshah prophesied against Jehoshaphat, saying, Because thou hast joined thyself with Ahaziah, the LORD hath broken thy works. [n]And the ships were broken, that they were not able to go to [o]Tarshish.

21

Now [p]Jehoshaphat slept with his fathers, and was buried with his fathers in the city of David. And Jehoram his son reigned in his stead.

2 And he had brethren the sons of Jehoshaphat, Azariah, and Jehiel, and Zechariah, and Azariah, and Michael, and Shephatiah: all these *were* the sons of Jehoshaphat king of Israel.

3 And their father gave them great gifts of silver, and of gold, and of precious things, with fenced cities in Judah: but the kingdom gave he to Jehoram; because he *was* the firstborn.

4 Now when Jehoram was risen up to the kingdom of his father, he strengthened himself, and slew all his brethren with the sword, and *divers* also of the princes of Israel.

5 ¶ [q]Jehoram *was* thirty and two years old when he began to reign, and he reigned eight years in Jerusalem.

6 And he walked in the way of the kings of Israel, like as did the house of Ahab: for he had the daughter of [r]Ahab to wife: and he wrought *that which was* evil in the eyes of the LORD.

7 Howbeit the LORD would not destroy the house of David, because of the covenant that he had made with David, and as he promised to give a light to him and to his [s]sons for ever.

8 ¶ [t]In his days the Edomites revolted from under the dominion of Judah, and made themselves a king.

9 Then Jehoram went forth with his princes, and all his chariots with him: and he rose up by night, and smote the Edomites which compassed him in, and the captains of the chariots.

10 So the Edomites revolted from under the hand of Judah unto this day. The same time *also* did Libnah revolt from under his hand; because he had forsaken the LORD God of his fathers.

11 Moreover he made high places in the mountains of Judah, and caused the inhabitants of Jerusalem to [u]commit fornication, and compelled Judah *thereto*.

12 ¶ And there came a writing to him from Elijah the prophet, saying, Thus saith the LORD God of David thy father, Because thou hast not walked in the ways of Jehoshaphat thy father, nor in the ways of Asa king of Judah,

13 But hast walked in the way of the kings of Israel, and hast [v]made Judah and the inhabitants of Jerusalem to [w]go a whoring, like to the [x]whoredoms of the house of Ahab, and also hast [y]slain thy brethren of thy father's house, *which were* better than thyself:

14 Behold, with a great plague will the LORD smite thy people, and thy children, and thy wives, and all thy goods:

15 And thou *shalt have* great sickness by [z]disease of thy bowels, until thy bowels fall out by reason of the sickness day by day.

16 ¶ Moreover the LORD [a]stirred up against Jehoram the spirit of the Philistines, and of the Arabians, that *were* near the Ethiopians:

17 And they came up into Judah, and brake into it, and carried away all the substance that was found in the king's house, and [b]his sons also, and his wives; so that there was never a son left him, save Jehoahaz, the youngest of his sons.

18 ¶ And after all this the LORD smote him [c]in his bowels with an incurable disease.

19 And it came to pass, that in process of time, after the end of two years, his bowels fell out by reason of his sickness: so he died of sore diseases. And his people made no burning for him, like [d]the burning of his fathers.

20 Thirty and two years old was he when he began to reign, and he reigned in Jerusalem eight years, and departed without being desired. Howbeit they buried him in the city of David, but not in the sepulchres of the kings.

22

And the inhabitants of Jerusalem made [e]Ahaziah his youngest son king in his stead: for the band of men that came with the Arabians to the camp had slain all the [f]eldest. So Ahaziah the son of Jehoram king of Judah reigned.

2 [g]Forty and two years old *was* Ahaziah when he began to reign, and he reigned one year in Jerusalem. His mother's name also *was* [h]Athaliah the daughter of Omri.

3 He also walked in the ways of the house of Ahab: for his mother was his counsellor to do wickedly.

4 Wherefore he did evil in the sight of the LORD like the house of Ahab: for they were his counsellors, after the death of his father to his destruction.

20:33 [j]ch. 17:6 [k]ch. 12:14
20:34 [l]1 Kings 16:1
20:35 [m]1 Kings 22:48
20:37 [n]1 Kings 22:48 [o]ch. 9:21
21:1 [p]1 Kings 22:50
21:5 [q]2 Kings 8:17
21:6 [r]ch. 22:2
21:7 [s]2 Sam. 7:12; 1 Kings 11:36; 2 Kings 8:19; Ps. 132:11
21:8 [t]2 Kings 8:20
21:11 [u]Lev. 17:7; ver. 13
21:13 [v]ver. 11 [w]Ex. 34:15; Deut. 31:16 [x]1 Kings 16:31-33; 2 Kings 9:22 [y]ver. 4
21:15 [z]ver. 18
21:16 [a]1 Kings 11:14
21:17 [b]ch. 24:7
21:18 [c]ver. 15
21:19 [d]ch. 16:14
22:1 [e]2 Kings 8:24; ch. 21:17; ver. 6 [f]ch. 21:17
22:2 [g]2 Kings 8:26 [h]ch. 21:6

5 ¶ He walked also after their counsel, and [i]went with Jehoram the son of Ahab king of Israel to war against Hazael king of Syria at Ramoth-gilead: and the Syrians smote Joram.

6 [j]And he returned to be healed in Jezreel because of the wounds which were given him at Ramah, when he fought with Hazael king of Syria. And Azariah the son of Jehoram king of Judah went down to see Jehoram the son of Ahab at Jezreel, because he was sick.

7 And the destruction of Ahaziah [k]was of God by coming to Joram: for when he was come, he [l]went out with Jehoram against Jehu the son of Nimshi, [m]whom the LORD had anointed to cut off the house of Ahab.

8 And it came to pass, that, when Jehu was [n]executing judgment upon the house of Ahab, and [o]found the princes of Judah, and the sons of the brethren of Ahaziah, that ministered to Ahaziah, he slew them.

9 [p]And he sought Ahaziah: and they caught him, (for he was hid in Samaria,) and brought him to Jehu: and when they had slain him, they buried him: because, said they, he *is* the son of Jehoshaphat, who [q]sought the LORD with all heart. So the house of Ahaziah had no power to keep still the kingdom.

10 ¶ [r]But when Athaliah the mother of Ahaziah saw that her son was dead, she arose and destroyed all the seed royal of the house of Judah.

11 But [s]Jehoshabeath, the daughter of the king, took Joash the son of Ahaziah, and stole him from among the king's sons that were slain, and put him and his nurse in a bedchamber. So Jehoshabeath, the daughter of king Jehoram, the wife of Jehoiada the priest, (for she was the sister of Ahaziah,) hid him from Athaliah, so that she slew him not.

12 And he was with them hid in the house of God six years: and Athaliah reigned over the land.

23 And [t]in the seventh year Jehoiada strengthened himself, and took the captains of hundreds, Azariah the son of Jeroham, and Ishmael the son of Jehohanan, and Azariah the son of Obed, and Maaseiah the son of Adaiah, and Elishaphat the son of Zichri, into covenant with him.

2 And they went about in Judah, and gathered the Levites out of all the cities of Judah, and the chief of the fathers of Israel, and they came to Jerusalem.

3 And all the congregation made a covenant with the king in the house of God. And he said unto them, Behold, the king's son shall reign, as the LORD hath [u]said of the sons of David.

4 This *is* the thing that ye shall do; A third part of you [v]entering on the sabbath, of the priests and of the Levites, *shall be* porters of the doors;

5 And a third part *shall be* at the king's house; and a third part at the gate of the foundation: and all the people *shall be* in the courts of the house of the LORD.

6 But let none come into the house of the LORD, save the priests, and [w]they that minister of the Levites; they shall go in, for they *are* holy: but all the people shall keep the watch of the LORD.

7 And the Levites shall compass the king round about, every man with his weapons in his hand; and whosoever *else* cometh into the house, he shall be put to death: but be ye with the king when he cometh in, and when he goeth out.

8 So the Levites and all Judah did according to all things that Jehoiada the priest had commanded, and took every man his men that were to come in on the sabbath, with them that were to go *out* on the sabbath: for Jehoiada the priest dismissed not [x]the courses.

9 Moreover Jehoiada the priest delivered to the captains of hundreds spears, and bucklers, and shields, that *had been* king David's, which *were* in the house of God.

10 And he set all the people, every man having his weapon in his hand, from the right side of the temple to the left side of the temple, along by the altar and the temple, by the king round about.

11 Then they brought out the king's son, and put upon him the crown, and [y]*gave him* the testimony, and made him king. And Jehoiada and his sons anointed him, and said, God save the king.

12 ¶ Now when Athaliah heard the noise of the people running and praising the king, she came to the people into the house of the LORD:

13 And she looked, and, behold, the king stood at his pillar at the entering in, and the princes and the trumpets by the king: and all the people of the land rejoiced, and sounded with trumpets, also the singers with instruments of musick, and [z]such as taught to sing praise. Then Athaliah rent her clothes, and said, Treason, Treason.

14 Then Jehoiada the priest brought out the captains of hundreds that were set over the host, and said unto them, Have her forth of the ranges: and whoso followeth her, let him be slain with the sword. For the priest said, Slay her not in the house of the LORD.

15 So they laid hands on her; and when she was come to the entering [a]of the horse gate by the king's house, they slew her there.

16 ¶ And Jehoiada made a covenant between him, and between all the people, and between the king, that they should be the LORD's people.

17 Then all the people went to the house of Baal, and brake it down, and brake his altars and his images in pieces, and [b]slew Mattan the priest of Baal before the altars.

18 Also Jehoiada appointed the offices of the house of the LORD by the hand of the priests the Levites, whom David had [c]distributed in the house of the LORD, to offer

22:5 [i]2 Kings 8:28
22:6 [j]2 Kings 9:15
22:7 [k]Judg. 14:4; 1 Kings 12:15; ch. 10:15 [l]2 Kings 9:21 [m]2 Kings 9:6
22:8 [n]2 Kings 10:10 [o]2 Kings 10:13
22:9 [p]2 Kings 9:27 [q]ch. 17:4
22:10 [r]2 Kings 11:1
22:11 [s]2 Kings 11:2
23:1 [t]2 Kings 11:4
23:3 [u]2 Sam. 7:12; 1 Kings 2:4; ch. 6:16
23:4 [v]1 Chron. 9:25
23:6 [w]1 Chron. 23:28
23:8 [x]1 Chron. 24
23:11 [y]Deut. 17:18
23:13 [z]1 Chron. 25:8
23:15 [a]Neh. 3:28
23:17 [b]Deut. 13:9
23:18 [c]1 Chron. 23:6

the burnt offerings of the LORD, as *it is* written in the [d]law of Moses, with rejoicing and
with singing, *as it was ordained* by David.
19 And he set the [e]porters at the gates of
the house of the LORD, that none *which was*
unclean in any thing should enter in.
20 [f]And he took the captains of hundreds, and the nobles, and the governors of
the people, and all the people of the land,
and brought down the king from the house
of the LORD: and they came through the
high gate into the king's house, and set the
king upon the throne of the kingdom.
21 And all the people of the land rejoiced:
and the city was quiet, after that they had
slain Athaliah with the sword.

24 Joash [g]*was* seven years old when he
began to reign, and he reigned forty
years in Jerusalem. His mother's name also
was Zibiah of Beer-sheba.
2 And Joash [h]did *that which was* right in
the sight of the LORD all the days of Jehoiada the priest.
3 And Jehoiada took for him two wives;
and he begat sons and daughters.
4 ¶ And it came to pass after this, *that*
Joash was minded to repair the house of the
LORD.
5 And he gathered together the priests
and the Levites, and said to them, Go out
unto the cities of Judah, and [i]gather of all
Israel money to repair the house of your
God from year to year, and see that ye hasten the matter. Howbeit the Levites hastened *it* not.
6 [j]And the king called for Jehoiada the
chief, and said unto him, Why hast thou not
required of the Levites to bring in out of
Judah and out of Jerusalem the collection,
according to the commandment of [k]Moses
the servant of the LORD, and of the congregation of Israel, for the [l]tabernacle of witness?
7 For [m]the sons of Athaliah, that wicked
woman, had broken up the house of God;
and also all the [n]dedicated things of the
house of the LORD did they bestow upon
Baalim.
8 And at the king's commandment [o]they
made a chest, and set it without at the gate
of the house of the LORD.
9 And they made a proclamation through
Judah and Jerusalem, to bring in to the
LORD [p]the collection *that* Moses the servant of God *laid* upon Israel in the wilderness.
10 And all the princes and all the people
rejoiced, and brought in, and cast into the
chest, until they had made an end.
11 Now it came to pass, that at what time
the chest was brought unto the king's office
by the hand of the Levites, and [q]when they
saw that *there was* much money, the king's
scribe and the high priest's officer came and
emptied the chest, and took it, and carried it
to his place again. Thus they did day by day,
and gathered money in abundance.
12 And the king and Jehoiada gave it to
such as did the work of the service of the
house of the LORD, and hired masons and
carpenters to repair the house of the LORD,
and also such as wrought iron and brass to
mend the house of the LORD.
13 So the workmen wrought, and the
work was perfected by them, and they set
the house of God in his state, and strengthened it.
14 And when they had finished *it,* they
brought the rest of the money before the
king and Jehoiada, [r]whereof were made
vessels for the house of the LORD, *even* vessels to minister, and to offer *withal,* and
spoons, and vessels of gold and silver. And
they offered burnt offerings in the house of
the LORD continually all the days of Jehoiada.
15 ¶ But Jehoiada waxed old, and was full
of days when he died; an hundred and thirty
years old *was he* when he died.
16 And they buried him in the city of David among the kings, because he had done
good in Israel, both toward God, and toward his house.
17 Now after the death of Jehoiada came
the princes of Judah, and made obeisance
to the king. Then the king hearkened unto
them.
18 And they left the house of the LORD
God of their fathers, and served [s]groves
and idols: and [t]wrath came upon Judah
and Jerusalem for this their trespass.
19 Yet he [u]sent prophets to them, to bring
them again unto the LORD; and they testified against them: but they would not give
ear.
20 And [v]the Spirit of God came upon
Zechariah the son of Jehoiada the priest,
which stood above the people, and said unto
them, Thus saith God, [w]Why transgress ye
the commandments of the LORD, that ye
cannot prosper? [x]because ye have forsaken
the LORD, he hath also forsaken you.
21 And they conspired against him, and
[y]stoned him with stones at the commandment of the king in the court of the house of
the LORD.
22 Thus Joash the king remembered not
the kindness which Jehoiada his father had
done to him, but slew his son. And when he
died, he said, The LORD look upon *it,* and
require *it.*
23 ¶ And it came to pass at the end of
the year, *that* [z]the host of Syria came up
against him: and they came to Judah and
Jerusalem, and destroyed all the princes of
the people from among the people, and sent
all the spoil of them unto the king of Damascus.
24 For the army of the Syrians [a]came
with a small company of men, and the LORD
[b]delivered a very great host into their hand,
because they had forsaken the LORD God of
their fathers. So they [c]executed judgment
against Joash.
25 And when they were departed from
him, (for they left him in great diseases,)

23:18 [d]Num. 28:2
23:19 [e]1 Chron. 26:1
23:20 [f]2 Kings 11:19
24:1 [g]2 Kings 11:21
24:2 [h]ch. 26:5
24:5 [i]2 Kings 12:4
24:6 [j]2 Kings 12:7 [k]Ex. 30:12 [l]Num. 1:50; Acts 7:44
24:7 [m]ch. 21:17 [n]2 Kings 12:4
24:8 [o]2 Kings 12:9
24:9 [p]ver. 16
24:11 [q]2 Kings 12:10
24:14 [r]2 Kings 12:13
24:18 [s]1 Kings 14:23 [t]Judg. 5:8; ch. 19:2
24:19 [u]ch. 36:15; Jer. 7:25
24:20 [v]ch. 15:1 [w]Num. 14:41 [x]ch. 15:2
24:21 [y]Matt. 23:35; Acts 7:58
24:23 [z]2 Kings 12:17
24:24 [a]Lev. 26:8; Deut. 32:30; Isa. 30:17 [b]Lev. 26:25; Deut. 28:25 [c]ch. 22:8; Isa. 10:5

[d]his own servants conspired against him for the blood of the [e]sons of Jehoiada the priest, and slew him on his bed, and he died: and they buried him in the city of David, but they buried him not in the sepulchres of the kings.

26 And these are they that conspired against him; Zabad the son of Shimeath an Ammonitess, and Jehozabad the son of Shimrith a Moabitess.

27 ¶ Now *concerning* his sons, and the greatness of [f]the burdens *laid* upon him, and the repairing of the house of God, behold, they *are* written in the story of the book of the kings. [g]And Amaziah his son reigned in his stead.

25 Amaziah [h]*was* twenty and five years old *when* he began to reign, and he reigned twenty and nine years in Jerusalem. And his mother's name *was* Jehoaddan of Jerusalem.

2 And he did *that which was* right in the sight of the LORD, [i]but not with a perfect heart.

3 ¶ [j]Now it came to pass, when the kingdom was established to him, that he slew his servants that had killed the king his father.

4 But he slew not their children, but *did* as *it is* written in the law in the book of Moses, where the LORD commanded, saying, [k]The fathers shall not die for the children, neither shall the children die for the fathers, but every man shall die for his own sin.

5 ¶ Moreover Amaziah gathered Judah together, and made them captains over thousands, and captains over hundreds, according to the houses of *their* fathers, throughout all Judah and Benjamin: and he numbered them [l]from twenty years old and above, and found them three hundred thousand choice *men, able* to go forth to war, that could handle spear and shield.

6 He hired also an hundred thousand mighty men of valour out of Israel for an hundred talents of silver.

7 But there came a man of God to him, saying, O king, let not the army of Israel go with thee; for the LORD *is* not with Israel, *to wit, with* all the children of Ephraim.

8 But if thou wilt go, do *it*, be strong for the battle: God shall make thee fall before the enemy: for God hath [m]power to help, and to cast down.

9 And Amaziah said to the man of God, But what shall we do for the hundred talents which I have given to the army of Israel? And the man of God answered, [n]The LORD is able to give thee much more than this.

10 Then Amaziah separated them, *to wit*, the army that was come to him out of Ephraim, to go home again: wherefore their anger was greatly kindled against Judah, and they returned home in great anger.

11 ¶ And Amaziah strengthened himself, and led forth his people, and went [o]to the valley of salt, and smote of the children of Seir ten thousand.

12 And *other* ten thousand *left* alive did the children of Judah carry away captive, and brought them unto the top of the rock, and cast them down from the top of the rock, that they all were broken in pieces.

13 ¶ But the soldiers of the army which Amaziah sent back, that they should not go with him to battle, fell upon the cities of Judah, from Samaria even unto Beth-horon, and smote three thousand of them, and took much spoil.

14 ¶ Now it came to pass, after that Amaziah was come from the slaughter of the Edomites, that [p]he brought the gods of the children of Seir, and set them up *to be* [q]his gods, and bowed down himself before them, and burned incense unto them.

15 Wherefore the anger of the LORD was kindled against Amaziah, and he sent unto him a prophet, which said unto him, Why hast thou sought after [r]the gods of the people, which [s]could not deliver their own people out of thine hand?

16 And it came to pass, as he talked with him, that *the king* said unto him, Art thou made of the king's counsel? forbear; why shouldest thou be smitten? Then the prophet forbare, and said, I know that God hath [t]determined to destroy thee, because thou hast done this, and hast not hearkened unto my counsel.

17 ¶ Then [u]Amaziah king of Judah took advice, and sent to Joash, the son of Jehoahaz, the son of Jehu, king of Israel, saying, Come, let us see one another in the face.

18 And Joash king of Israel sent to Amaziah king of Judah, saying, The thistle that *was* in Lebanon sent to the cedar that *was* in Lebanon, saying, Give thy daughter to my son to wife: and there passed by a wild beast that *was* in Lebanon, and trode down the thistle.

19 Thou sayest, Lo, thou hast smitten the Edomites; and thine heart lifteth thee up to boast: abide now at home; why shouldest thou meddle to *thine* hurt, that thou shouldest fall, *even* thou, and Judah with thee?

20 But Amaziah would not hear; for [v]it *came* of God, that he might deliver them into the hand *of their enemies*, because they [w]sought after the gods of Edom.

21 So Joash the king of Israel went up; and they saw one another in the face, *both* he and Amaziah king of Judah, at Beth-shemesh, which *belongeth* to Judah.

22 And Judah was put to the worse before Israel, and they fled every man to his tent.

23 And Joash the king of Israel took Amaziah king of Judah, the son of Joash, the son of [x]Jehoahaz, at Beth-shemesh, and brought him to Jerusalem, and brake down the wall of Jerusalem from the gate of Ephraim to the corner gate, four hundred cubits.

24 And *he took* all the gold and the silver, and all the vessels that were found in the house of God with Obed-edom, and the

24:25 [d]2 Kings 12:20 [e]ver. 21
24:27 [f]2 Kings 12:18 [g]2 Kings 12:21
25:1 [h]2 Kings 14:1
25:2 [i]2 Kings 14:4; ver. 14
25:3 [j]2 Kings 14:5
25:4 [k]Deut. 24:16; 2 Kings 14:6; Jer. 31:30; Ezek. 18:20
25:5 [l]Num. 1:3
25:8 [m]ch. 20:6
25:9 [n]Prov. 10:22
25:11 [o]2 Kings 14:7
25:14 [p]ch. 28:23 [q]Ex. 20:3
25:15 [r]Ps. 96:5 [s]ver. 11
25:16 [t]1 Sam. 2:25
25:17 [u]2 Kings 14:8
25:20 [v]1 Kings 12:15; ch. 22:7 [w]ver. 14
25:23 [x]ch. 21:17

treasures of the king's house, the hostages also, and returned to Samaria.

25 ¶ [y]And Amaziah the son of Joash king of Judah lived after the death of Joash son of Jehoahaz king of Israel fifteen years.

26 Now the rest of the acts of Amaziah, first and last, behold, *are* they not written in the book of the kings of Judah and Israel?

27 ¶ Now after the time that Amaziah did turn away from following the LORD they made a conspiracy against him in Jerusalem; and he fled to Lachish: but they sent to Lachish after him, and slew him there.

28 And they brought him upon horses, and buried him with his fathers in the city of Judah.

26 Then all the people of Judah took [z]Uzziah, who *was* sixteen years old, and made him king in the room of his father Amaziah.

2 He built Eloth, and restored it to Judah, after that the king slept with his fathers.

3 Sixteen years old *was* Uzziah when he began to reign, and he reigned fifty and two years in Jerusalem. His mother's name also *was* Jecoliah of Jerusalem.

4 And he did *that which was* right in the sight of the LORD, according to all that his father Amaziah did.

5 And [a]he sought God in the days of Zechariah, who [b]had understanding in the visions of God: and as long as he sought the LORD, God made him to prosper.

6 And he went forth and [c]warred against the Philistines, and brake down the wall of Gath, and the wall of Jabneh, and the wall of Ashdod, and built cities about Ashdod, and among the Philistines.

7 And God helped him against [d]the Philistines, and against the Arabians that dwelt in Gur-baal, and the Mehunims.

8 And the Ammonites [e]gave gifts to Uzziah: and his name spread abroad *even* to the entering in of Egypt; for he strengthened *himself* exceedingly.

9 Moreover Uzziah built towers in Jerusalem at the [f]corner gate, and at the valley gate, and at the turning *of the wall*, and fortified them.

10 Also he built towers in the desert, and digged many wells: for he had much cattle, both in the low country, and in the plains: husbandmen *also*, and vine dressers in the mountains, and in Carmel: for he loved husbandry.

11 Moreover Uzziah had an host of fighting men, that went out to war by bands, according to the number of their account by the hand of Jeiel the scribe and Maaseiah the ruler, under the hand of Hananiah, *one* of the king's captains.

12 The whole number of the chief of the fathers of the mighty men of valour *were* two thousand and six hundred.

13 And under their hand *was* an army, three hundred thousand and seven thousand and five hundred, that made war with mighty power, to help the king against the enemy.

14 And Uzziah prepared for them throughout all the host shields, and spears, and helmets, and habergeons, and bows, and slings *to cast* stones.

15 And he made in Jerusalem engines, invented by cunning men, to be on the towers and upon the bulwarks, to shoot arrows and great stones withal. And his name spread far abroad; for he was marvellously helped, till he was strong.

16 ¶ But [g]when he was strong, his heart was [h]lifted up to *his* destruction: for he transgressed against the LORD his God, and [i]went into the temple of the LORD to burn incense upon the altar of incense.

17 And [j]Azariah the priest went in after him, and with him fourscore priests of the LORD, *that were* valiant men:

18 And they withstood Uzziah the king, and said unto him, *It* [k]*appertaineth* not unto thee, Uzziah, to burn incense unto the LORD, but to the [l]priests the sons of Aaron, that are consecrated to burn incense: go out of the sanctuary; for thou hast trespassed; neither *shall it be* for thine honour from the LORD God.

19 Then Uzziah was wroth, and *had* a censer in his hand to burn incense: and while he was wroth with the priests, [m]the leprosy even rose up in his forehead before the priests in the house of the LORD, from beside the incense altar.

20 And Azariah the chief priest, and all the priests, looked upon him, and, behold, he *was* leprous in his forehead, and they thrust him out from thence; yea, himself [n]hasted also to go out, because the LORD had smitten him.

21 [o]And Uzziah the king was a leper unto the day of his death, and dwelt in a [p]several house, *being* a leper; for he was cut off from the house of the LORD: and Jotham his son *was* over the king's house, judging the people of the land.

22 ¶ Now the rest of the acts of Uzziah, first and last, did [q]Isaiah the prophet, the son of Amoz, write.

23 [r]So Uzziah slept with his fathers, and they buried him with his fathers in the field of the burial which *belonged* to the kings; for they said, He *is* a leper: and Jotham his son reigned in his stead.

27 Jotham [s]*was* twenty and five years old when he began to reign, and he reigned sixteen years in Jerusalem. His mother's name also *was* Jerushah, the daughter of Zadok.

2 And he did *that which was* right in the sight of the LORD, according to all that his father Uzziah did: howbeit he entered not into the temple of the LORD. And [t]the people did yet corruptly.

3 He built the high gate of the house of the LORD, and on the wall of Ophel he built much.

4 Moreover he built cities in the moun-

25:25 [y]2 Kings 14:17
26:1 [z]2 Kings 14:21
26:5 [a]ch. 24:2 [b]Gen. 41:15; Dan. 1:17
26:6 [c]Isa. 14:29
26:7 [d]ch. 21:16
26:8 [e]2 Sam. 8:2; ch. 17:11
26:9 [f]2 Kings 14:13; Neh. 3:13; Zech. 14:10
26:16 [g]Deut. 32:15 [h]Deut. 8:14; ch. 25:19 [i]2 Kings 16:12
26:17 [j]1 Chron. 6:10
26:18 [k]Num. 16:40 [l]Ex. 30:7
26:19 [m]Num. 12:10; 2 Kings 5:27
26:20 [n]Esth. 6:12
26:21 [o]2 Kings 15:5 [p]Lev. 13:46; Num. 5:2
26:22 [q]Isa. 1:1
26:23 [r]2 Kings 15:7; Isa. 6:1
27:1 [s]2 Kings 15:32
27:2 [t]2 Kings 15:35

tains of Judah, and in the forests he built castles and towers.

5 ¶ He fought also with the king of the Ammonites, and prevailed against them. And the children of Ammon gave him the same year an hundred talents of silver, and ten thousand measures of wheat, and ten thousand of barley. So much did the children of Ammon pay unto him, both the second year, and the third.

6 So Jotham became mighty, because he prepared his ways before the LORD his God.

7 ¶ Now the rest of the acts of Jotham, and all his wars, and his ways, lo, they *are* written in the book of the kings of Israel and Judah.

8 He was five and twenty years old when he began to reign, and reigned sixteen years in Jerusalem.

9 ¶ [u]And Jotham slept with his fathers, and they buried him in the city of David: and Ahaz his son reigned in his stead.

28 Ahaz [v]*was* twenty years old when he began to reign, and he reigned sixteen years in Jerusalem: but he did not *that which was* right in the sight of the LORD, like David his father:

2 For he walked in the ways of the kings of Israel, and made also [w]molten images for [x]Baalim.

3 Moreover he burnt incense in [y]the valley of the son of Hinnom, and burnt [z]his children in the fire, after the abominations of the heathen whom the LORD had cast out before the children of Israel.

4 He sacrificed also and burnt incense in the high places, and on the hills, and under every green tree.

5 Wherefore [a]the LORD his God delivered him into the hand of the king of Syria; and they [b]smote him, and carried away a great multitude of them captives, and brought *them* to Damascus. And he was also delivered into the hand of the king of Israel, who smote him with a great slaughter.

6 ¶ For [c]Pekah the son of Remaliah slew in Judah an hundred and twenty thousand in one day, *which were* all valiant men; because they had forsaken the LORD God of their fathers.

7 And Zichri, a mighty man of Ephraim, slew Maaseiah the king's son, and Azrikam the governor of the house, and Elkanah *that was* next to the king.

8 And the children of Israel carried away captive of their [d]brethren two hundred thousand, women, sons, and daughters, and took also away much spoil from them, and brought the spoil to Samaria.

9 But a prophet of the LORD was there, whose name *was* Oded: and he went out before the host that came to Samaria, and said unto them, Behold, [e]because the LORD God of your fathers was wroth with Judah, he hath delivered them into your hand, and ye have slain them in a rage *that* [f]reacheth up unto heaven.

10 And now ye purpose to keep under the children of Judah and Jerusalem for [g]bondmen and bondwomen unto you: *but are there* not with you, even with you, sins against the LORD your God?

11 Now hear me therefore, and deliver the captives again, which ye have taken captive of your brethren: [h]for the fierce wrath of the LORD *is* upon you.

12 Then certain of the heads of the children of Ephraim, Azariah the son of Johanan, Berechiah the son of Meshillemoth, and Jehizkiah the son of Shallum, and Amasa the son of Hadlai, stood up against them that came from the war,

13 And said unto them, Ye shall not bring in the captives hither: for whereas we have offended against the LORD *already*, ye intend to add *more* to our sins and to our trespass: for our trespass is great, and *there is* fierce wrath against Israel.

14 So the armed men left the captives and the spoil before the princes and all the congregation.

15 And the men [i]which were expressed by name rose up, and took the captives, and with the spoil clothed all that were naked among them, and arrayed them, and shod them, and [j]gave them to eat and to drink, and anointed them, and carried all the feeble of them upon asses, and brought them to Jericho, [k]the city of palm trees, to their brethren: then they returned to Samaria.

16 ¶ [l]At that time did king Ahaz send unto the kings of Assyria to help him.

17 For again the Edomites had come and smitten Judah, and carried away captives.

18 [m]The Philistines also had invaded the cities of the low country, and of the south of Judah, and had taken Beth-shemesh, and Ajalon, and Gederoth, and Shocho with the villages thereof, and Timnah with the villages thereof, Gimzo also and the villages thereof: and they dwelt there.

19 For the LORD brought Judah low because of Ahaz king of [n]Israel; for he [o]made Judah naked, and transgressed sore against the LORD.

20 And [p]Tilgath-pilneser king of Assyria came unto him, and distressed him, but strengthened him not.

21 For Ahaz took away a portion *out* of the house of the LORD, and *out* of the house of the king, and of the princes, and gave *it* unto the king of Assyria: but he helped him not.

22 ¶ And in the time of his distress did he trespass yet more against the LORD: this *is that* king Ahaz.

23 For [q]he sacrificed unto the gods of Damascus, which smote him: and he said, Because the gods of the kings of Syria help them, *therefore* will I sacrifice to them, that [r]they may help me. But they were the ruin of him, and of all Israel.

24 And Ahaz gathered together the vessels of the house of God, and cut in pieces the vessels of the house of God, [s]and shut up the doors of the house of the LORD, and

27:9 [u]2 Kings 15:38
28:1 [v]2 Kings 16:2
28:2 [w]Ex. 34:17; Lev. 19:4 [x]Judg. 2:11
28:3 [y]2 Kings 23:10 [z]Lev. 18:21; 2 Kings 16:3; ch. 33:6
28:5 [a]Isa. 7:1 [b]2 Kings 16:5
28:6 [c]2 Kings 15:27
28:8 [d]ch. 11:4
28:9 [e]Ps. 69:26; Isa. 10:5; Ezek. 25:12; Obad. 10; Zech. 1:15 [f]Ezra 9:6; Rev. 18:5
28:10 [g]Lev. 25:39
28:11 [h]Jam. 2:13
28:15 [i]ver. 12 [j]2 Kings 6:22; Prov. 25:21; Luke 6:27; Rom. 12:20 [k]Deut. 34:3; Judg. 1:16
28:16 [l]2 Kings 16:7
28:18 [m]Ezek. 16:27
28:19 [n]ch. 21:2 [o]Ex. 32:25
28:20 [p]2 Kings 15:29
28:23 [q]ch. 25:14 [r]Jer. 44:17
28:24 [s]ch. 29:3

he made him altars in every corner of Jerusalem.

25 And in every several city of Judah he made high places to burn incense unto other gods, and provoked to anger the LORD God of his fathers.

26 ¶ [t]Now the rest of his acts and of all his ways, first and last, behold, they *are* written in the book of the kings of Judah and Israel.

27 And Ahaz slept with his fathers, and they buried him in the city, *even* in Jerusalem: but they brought him not into the sepulchres of the kings of Israel: and Hezekiah his son reigned in his stead.

29 Hezekiah [u]began to reign *when he was* five and twenty years old, and he reigned nine and twenty years in Jerusalem. And his mother's name *was* Abijah, the daughter [v]of Zechariah.

2 And he did *that which was* right in the sight of the LORD, according to all that David his father had done.

3 ¶ He in the first year of his reign, in the first month, [w]opened the doors of the house of the LORD, and repaired them.

4 And he brought in the priests and the Levites, and gathered them together into the east street,

5 And said unto them, Hear me, ye Levites; [x]sanctify now yourselves, and sanctify the house of the LORD God of your fathers, and carry forth the filthiness out of the holy *place*.

6 For our fathers have trespassed, and done *that which was* evil in the eyes of the LORD our God, and have forsaken him, and have [y]turned away their faces from the habitation of the LORD, and turned *their* backs.

7 [z]Also they have shut up the doors of the porch, and put out the lamps, and have not burned incense nor offered burnt offerings in the holy *place* unto the God of Israel.

8 Wherefore the [a]wrath of the LORD was upon Judah and Jerusalem, and he hath delivered them to trouble, to astonishment, and to [b]hissing, as ye see with your eyes.

9 For, lo, [c]our fathers have fallen by the sword, and our sons and our daughters and our wives *are* in captivity for this.

10 Now *it is* in mine heart to make [d]a covenant with the LORD God of Israel, that his fierce wrath may turn away from us.

11 My sons, be not now negligent: for the LORD hath [e]chosen you to stand before him, to serve him, and that ye should minister unto him, and burn incense.

12 ¶ Then the Levites arose, Mahath the son of Amasai, and Joel the son of Azariah, of the sons of the Kohathites: and of the sons of Merari, Kish the son of Abdi, and Azariah the son of Jehalelel: and of the Gershonites; Joah the son of Zimmah, and Eden the son of Joah:

13 And of the sons of Elizaphan; Shimri, and Jeiel: and of the sons of Asaph; Zechariah, and Mattaniah:

28:26 [t]2 Kings 16:19
29:1 [u]2 Kings 18:1 [v]ch. 26:5
29:3 [w]ch. 28:24; ver. 7
29:5 [x]1 Chron. 15:12; ch. 35:6
29:6 [y]Jer. 2:27; Ezek. 8:16
29:7 [z]ch. 28:24
29:8 [a]ch. 24:18 [b]1 Kings 9:8; Jer. 18:16
29:9 [c]ch. 28:5
29:10 [d]ch. 15:12
29:11 [e]Num. 3:6
29:15 [f]ver. 5 [g]1 Chron. 23:28
29:19 [h]ch. 28:24
29:21 [i]Lev. 4:3
29:22 [j]Lev. 8:14; Heb. 9:21
29:23 [k]Lev. 4:15
29:24 [l]Lev. 14:20
29:25 [m]1 Chron. 16:4 [n]1 Chron. 23:5; ch. 8:14 [o]2 Sam. 24:11 [p]ch. 30:12
29:26 [q]1 Chron. 23:5; Am. 6:5 [r]Num. 10:8; 1 Chron. 15:24

14 And of the sons of Heman; Jehiel, and Shimei: and of the sons of Jeduthun; Shemaiah, and Uzziel.

15 And they gathered their brethren, and [f]sanctified themselves, and came, according to the commandment of the king, by the words of the LORD, [g]to cleanse the house of the LORD.

16 And the priests went into the inner part of the house of the LORD, to cleanse *it*, and brought out all the uncleanness that they found in the temple of the LORD into the court of the house of the LORD. And the Levites took *it*, to carry *it* out abroad into the brook Kidron.

17 Now they began on the first *day* of the first month to sanctify, and on the eighth day of the month came they to the porch of the LORD: so they sanctified the house of the LORD in eight days; and in the sixteenth day of the first month they made an end.

18 Then they went in to Hezekiah the king, and said, We have cleansed all the house of the LORD, and the altar of burnt offering, with all the vessels thereof, and the shewbread table, with all the vessels thereof.

19 Moreover all the vessels, which king Ahaz in his reign did [h]cast away in his transgression, have we prepared and sanctified, and, behold, they *are* before the altar of the LORD.

20 ¶ Then Hezekiah the king rose early, and gathered the rulers of the city, and went up to the house of the LORD.

21 And they brought seven bullocks, and seven rams, and seven lambs, and seven he goats, for a [i]sin offering for the kingdom, and for the sanctuary, and for Judah. And he commanded the priests the sons of Aaron to offer *them* on the altar of the LORD.

22 So they killed the bullocks, and the priests received the blood, and [j]sprinkled *it* on the altar: likewise, when they had killed the rams, they sprinkled the blood upon the altar: they killed also the lambs, and they sprinkled the blood upon the altar.

23 And they brought forth the he goats *for* the sin offering before the king and the congregation; and they laid their [k]hands upon them:

24 And the priests killed them, and they made reconciliation with their blood upon the altar, [l]to make an atonement for all Israel: for the king commanded *that* the burnt offering and the sin offering *should be made* for all Israel.

25 [m]And he set the Levites in the house of the LORD with cymbals, with psalteries, and with harps, [n]according to the commandment of David, and of [o]Gad the king's seer, and Nathan the prophet: [p]for *so was* the commandment of the LORD by his prophets.

26 And the Levites stood with the instruments [q]of David, and the priests with [r]the trumpets.

27 And Hezekiah commanded to offer the

burnt offering upon the altar. And when the burnt offering began, [s]the song of the LORD began *also* with the trumpets, and with the instruments *ordained* by David king of Israel.

28 And all the congregation worshipped, and the singers sang, and the trumpeters sounded: *and* all *this continued* until the burnt offering was finished.

29 And when they had made an end of offering, [t]the king and all that were present with him bowed themselves, and worshipped.

30 Moreover Hezekiah the king and the princes commanded the Levites to sing praise unto the LORD with the words of David, and of Asaph the seer. And they sang praises with gladness, and they bowed their heads and worshipped.

31 Then Hezekiah answered and said, Now ye have consecrated yourselves unto the LORD, come near and bring sacrifices and [u]thank offerings into the house of the LORD. And the congregation brought in sacrifices and thank offerings; and as many as were of a free heart, burnt offerings.

32 And the number of the burnt offerings, which the congregation brought, was threescore and ten bullocks, an hundred rams, *and* two hundred lambs: all these *were* for a burnt offering to the LORD.

33 And the consecrated things *were* six hundred oxen and three thousand sheep.

34 But the priests were too few, so that they could not flay all the burnt offerings: wherefore [v]their brethren the Levites did help them, till the work was ended, and until the *other* priests had sanctified themselves: [w]for the Levites *were* more [x]upright in heart to sanctify themselves than the priests.

35 And also the burnt offerings *were* in abundance, with [y]the fat of the peace offerings, and [z]the drink offerings for *every* burnt offering. So the service of the house of the LORD was set in order.

36 And Hezekiah rejoiced, and all the people, that God had prepared the people: for the thing was *done* suddenly.

30 And Hezekiah sent to all Israel and Judah, and wrote letters also to Ephraim and Manasseh, that they should come to the house of the LORD at Jerusalem, to keep the passover unto the LORD God of Israel.

2 For the king had taken counsel, and his princes, and all the congregation in Jerusalem, to keep the passover in the second [a]month.

3 For they could not keep it [b]at that time, [c]because the priests had not sanctified themselves sufficiently, neither had the people gathered themselves together to Jerusalem.

4 And the thing pleased the king and all the congregation.

5 So they established a decree to make proclamation throughout all Israel, from

29:27 [s]ch. 23:18
29:29 [t]ch. 20:18
29:31 [u]Lev. 7:12
29:34 [v]ch. 35:11 [w]ch. 30:3 [x]Ps. 7:10
29:35 [y]Lev. 3:16 [z]Num. 15:5
30:2 [a]Num. 9:10
30:3 [b]Ex. 12:6 [c]ch. 29:34
30:6 [d]Jer. 4:1; Joel 2:13 [e]2 Kings 15:19
30:7 [f]Ezek. 20:18 [g]ch. 29:8
30:8 [h]Deut. 10:16 [i]ch. 29:10
30:9 [j]Ps. 106:46 [k]Ex. 34:6 [l]Isa. 55:7
30:10 [m]ch. 36:16
30:11 [n]ch. 11:16; ver. 18
30:12 [o]Phil. 2:13 [p]ch. 29:25
30:14 [q]ch. 28:24
30:15 [r]ch. 29:34
30:17 [s]ch. 29:34
30:18 [t]ver. 11

Beer-sheba even to Dan, that they should come to keep the passover unto the LORD God of Israel at Jerusalem: for they had not done *it* of a long *time in such sort* as it was written.

6 So the posts went with the letters from the king and his princes throughout all Israel and Judah, and according to the commandment of the king, saying, Ye children of Israel, [d]turn again unto the LORD God of Abraham, Isaac, and Israel, and he will return to the remnant of you, that are escaped out of the hand of [e]the kings of Assyria.

7 And be not ye [f]like your fathers, and like your brethren, which trespassed against the LORD God of their fathers, *who* therefore [g]gave them up to desolation, as ye see.

8 Now be ye not [h]stiffnecked, as your fathers *were, but* yield yourselves unto the LORD, and enter into his sanctuary, which he hath sanctified for ever: and serve the LORD your God, [i]that the fierceness of his wrath may turn away from you.

9 For if ye turn again unto the LORD, your brethren and your children *shall find* [j]compassion before them that lead them captive, so that they shall come again into this land: for the LORD your God *is* [k]gracious and merciful, and will not turn away *his* face from you, if ye [l]return unto him.

10 So the posts passed from city to city through the country of Ephraim and Manasseh even unto Zebulun: but [m]they laughed them to scorn, and mocked them.

11 Nevertheless [n]divers of Asher and Manasseh and of Zebulun humbled themselves, and came to Jerusalem.

12 Also in Judah [o]the hand of God was to give them one heart to do the commandment of the king and of the princes, [p]by the word of the LORD.

13 ¶ And there assembled at Jerusalem much people to keep the feast of unleavened bread in the second month, a very great congregation.

14 And they arose and took away the [q]altars that *were* in Jerusalem, and all the altars for incense took they away, and cast *them* into the brook Kidron.

15 Then they killed the passover on the fourteenth *day* of the second month: and the priests and the Levites were [r]ashamed, and sanctified themselves, and brought in the burnt offerings into the house of the LORD.

16 And they stood in their place after their manner, according to the law of Moses the man of God: the priests sprinkled the blood, *which they received* of the hand of the Levites.

17 For *there were* many in the congregation that were not sanctified: [s]therefore the Levites had the charge of the killing of the passovers for every one *that was* not clean, to sanctify *them* unto the LORD.

18 For a multitude of the people, *even* [t]many of Ephraim, and Manasseh, Issachar, and Zebulun, had not cleansed them-

selves, [u]yet did they eat the passover otherwise than it was written. But Hezekiah prayed for them, saying, The good LORD pardon every one

19 *That* [v]prepareth his heart to seek God, the LORD God of his fathers, though *he be* not *cleansed* according to the purification of the sanctuary.

20 And the LORD hearkened to Hezekiah, and healed the people.

21 And the children of Israel that were present at Jerusalem kept [w]the feast of unleavened bread seven days with great gladness: and the Levites and the priests praised the LORD day by day, *singing* with loud instruments unto the LORD.

22 And Hezekiah spake comfortably unto all the Levites [x]that taught the good knowledge of the LORD: and they did eat throughout the feast seven days, offering peace offerings, and [y]making confession to the LORD God of their fathers.

23 And the whole assembly took counsel to keep [z]other seven days: and they kept *other* seven days with gladness.

24 For Hezekiah king of Judah [a]did give to the congregation a thousand bullocks and seven thousand sheep; and the princes gave to the congregation a thousand bullocks and ten thousand sheep: and a great number of priests [b]sanctified themselves.

25 And all the congregation of Judah, with the priests and the Levites, and all the congregation [c]that came out of Israel, and the strangers that came out of the land of Israel, and that dwelt in Judah, rejoiced.

26 So there was great joy in Jerusalem: for since the time of Solomon the son of David king of Israel *there was* not the like in Jerusalem.

27 ¶ Then the priests the Levites arose and [d]blessed the people: and their voice was heard, and their prayer came *up* to his holy dwelling place, *even* unto heaven.

31 Now when all this was finished, all Israel that were present went out to the cities of Judah, and [e]brake the images in pieces, and cut down the groves, and threw down the high places and the altars out of all Judah and Benjamin, in Ephraim also and Manasseh, until they had utterly destroyed them all. Then all the children of Israel returned, every man to his possession, into their own cities.

2 ¶ And Hezekiah appointed [f]the courses of the priests and the Levites after their courses, every man according to his service, the priests and Levites [g]for burnt offerings and for peace offerings, to minister, and to give thanks, and to praise in the gates of the tents of the LORD.

3 *He appointed* also the king's portion of his substance for the burnt offerings, *to wit*, for the morning and evening burnt offerings, and the burnt offerings for the sabbaths, and for the new moons, and for the set feasts, as *it is* written in the [h]law of the LORD.

4 Moreover he commanded the people that dwelt in Jerusalem to give the [i]portion of the priests and the Levites, that they might be encouraged in [j]the law of the LORD.

5 ¶ And as soon as the commandment came abroad, the children of Israel brought in abundance [k]the firstfruits of corn, wine, and oil, and honey, and of all the increase of the field; and the tithe of all *things* brought they in abundantly.

6 And *concerning* the children of Israel and Judah, that dwelt in the cities of Judah, they also brought in the tithe of oxen and sheep, and the [l]tithe of holy things which were consecrated unto the LORD their God, and laid *them* by heaps.

7 In the third month they began to lay the foundation of the heaps, and finished *them* in the seventh month.

8 And when Hezekiah and the princes came and saw the heaps, they blessed the LORD, and his people Israel.

9 Then Hezekiah questioned with the priests and the Levites concerning the heaps.

10 And Azariah the chief priest of the house of Zadok answered him, and said, [m]Since *the people* began to bring the offerings into the house of the LORD, we have had enough to eat, and have left plenty: for the LORD hath blessed his people; and that which is left *is* this great store.

11 ¶ Then Hezekiah commanded to prepare chambers in the house of the LORD; and they prepared *them*,

12 And brought in the offerings and the tithes and the dedicated *things* faithfully: [n]over which Cononiah the Levite *was* ruler, and Shimei his brother *was* the next.

13 And Jehiel, and Azaziah, and Nahath, and Asahel, and Jerimoth, and Jozabad, and Eliel, and Ismachiah, and Mahath, and Benaiah, *were* overseers under the hand of Cononiah and Shimei his brother, at the commandment of Hezekiah the king, and Azariah the ruler of the house of God.

14 And Kore the son of Imnah the Levite, the porter toward the east, *was* over the freewill offerings of God, to distribute the oblations of the LORD, and the most holy things.

15 And next him *were* Eden, and Miniamin, and Jeshua, and Shemaiah, Amariah, and Shecaniah, in the [o]cities of the priests, in *their* set office, to give to *their* brethren by courses, as well to the great as to the small:

16 Beside their genealogy of males, from three years old and upward, *even* unto every one that entereth into the house of the LORD, his daily portion for their service in their charges according to their courses;

17 Both to the genealogy of the priests by the house of their fathers, and the Levites [p]from twenty years old and upward, in their charges by their courses;

18 And to the genealogy of all their little

30:18 [u]Ex. 12:43
30:19 [v]ch. 19:3
30:21 [w]Ex. 12:15
30:22 [x]ch. 17:9; Deut. 33:10 [y]Ezra 10:11
30:23 [z]1 Kings 8:65
30:24 [a]ch. 35:7 [b]ch. 29:34
30:25 [c]ver. 11
30:27 [d]Num. 6:23
31:1 [e]2 Kings 18:4
31:2 [f]1 Chron. 23:6 [g]1 Chron. 23:30
31:3 [h]Num. 28
31:4 [i]Num. 18:8; Neh. 13:10 [j]Mal. 2:7
31:5 [k]Ex. 22:29; Neh. 13:12
31:6 [l]Lev. 27:30; Deut. 14:28
31:10 [m]Mal. 3:10
31:12 [n]Neh. 13:13
31:15 [o]Josh. 21:9
31:17 [p]1 Chron. 23

ones, their wives, and their sons, and their
daughters, through all the congregation: for
in their set office they sanctified themselves
in holiness:
19 Also of the sons of Aaron the priests,
which were in [q]the fields of the suburbs of
their cities, in every several city, the men
that were [r]expressed by name, to give portions to all the males among the priests, and
to all that were reckoned by genealogies
among the Levites.
20 ¶ And thus did Hezekiah throughout
all Judah, and [s]wrought *that which was*
good and right and truth before the LORD
his God.
21 And in every work that he began in the
service of the house of God, and in the law,
and in the commandments, to seek his God,
he did *it* with all his heart, and prospered.

32

32 After [t]these things, and the establishment thereof, Sennacherib king
of Assyria came, and entered into Judah,
and encamped against the fenced cities, and
thought to win them for himself.
2 And when Hezekiah saw that Sennacherib was come, and that he was purposed to
fight against Jerusalem,
3 He took counsel with his princes and his
mighty men to stop the waters of the fountains which *were* without the city: and they
did help him.
4 So there was gathered much people together, who stopped all the fountains, and
the brook that ran through the midst of the
land, saying, Why should the kings of Assyria come, and find much water?
5 Also [u]he strengthened himself, [v]and
built up all the wall that was broken, and
raised *it* up to the towers, and another wall
without, and repaired [w]Millo *in* the city of
David, and made darts and shields in abundance.
6 And he set captains of war over the people, and gathered them together to him in
the street of the gate of the city, and spake
comfortably to them, saying,
7 [x]Be strong and courageous, [y]be not
afraid nor dismayed for the king of Assyria,
nor for all the multitude that *is* with him: for
[z]*there be* more with us than with him:
8 With him *is* an [a]arm of flesh; but [b]with
us *is* the LORD our God to help us, and to
fight our battles. And the people rested
themselves upon the words of Hezekiah
king of Judah.
9 ¶ [c]After this did Sennacherib king of
Assyria send his servants to Jerusalem, (but
he *himself laid siege* against Lachish, and
all his power with him,) unto Hezekiah king
of Judah, and unto all Judah that *were* at
Jerusalem, saying,
10 [d]Thus saith Sennacherib king of Assyria, Whereon do ye trust, that ye abide in
the siege in Jerusalem?
11 Doth not Hezekiah persuade you to
give over yourselves to die by famine and
by thirst, saying, [e]The LORD our God shall
deliver us out of the hand of the king of
Assyria?
12 [f]Hath not the same Hezekiah taken
away his high places and his altars, and
commanded Judah and Jerusalem, saying,
Ye shall worship before one altar, and burn
incense upon it?
13 Know ye not what I and my fathers
have done unto all the people of *other*
lands? [g]were the gods of the nations of
those lands any ways able to deliver their
lands out of mine hand?
14 Who *was there* among all the gods of
those nations that my fathers utterly destroyed, that could deliver his people out of
mine hand, that your God should be able to
deliver you out of mine hand?
15 Now therefore [h]let not Hezekiah deceive you, nor persuade you on this manner,
neither yet believe him: for no god of any
nation or kingdom was able to deliver his
people out of mine hand, and out of the
hand of my fathers: how much less shall
your God deliver you out of mine hand?
16 And his servants spake yet *more*
against the LORD God, and against his servant Hezekiah.
17 [i]He wrote also letters to rail on the
LORD God of Israel, and to speak against
him, saying, [j]As the gods of the nations of
other lands have not delivered their people
out of mine hand, so shall not the God of
Hezekiah deliver his people out of mine
hand.
18 [k]Then they cried with a loud voice in
the Jews' speech, unto the people of Jerusalem [l]that *were* on the wall, to affright them,
and to trouble them; that they might take
the city.
19 And they spake against the God of Jerusalem, as against the gods of the people
of the earth, *which were* [m]the work of the
hands of man.
20 [n]And for this *cause* Hezekiah the
king, and [o]the prophet Isaiah the son of
Amoz, prayed and cried to heaven.
21 ¶ [p]And the LORD sent an angel, which
cut off all the mighty men of valour, and the
leaders and captains in the camp of the king
of Assyria. So he returned with shame of
face to his own land. And when he was
come into the house of his god, they that
came forth of his own bowels slew him
there with the sword.
22 Thus the LORD saved Hezekiah and the
inhabitants of Jerusalem from the hand of
Sennacherib the king of Assyria, and from
the hand of all *other*, and guided them on
every side.
23 And many brought gifts unto the LORD
to Jerusalem, and [q]presents to Hezekiah
king of Judah: so that he was [r]magnified in
the sight of all nations from thenceforth.
24 ¶ [s]In those days Hezekiah was sick to
the death, and prayed unto the LORD: and
he spake unto him, and he gave him a sign.
25 But Hezekiah [t]rendered not again according to the benefit *done* unto him; for

31:19 [q]Lev. 25:34; Num. 35:2 [r]ver. 12:13
31:20 [s]2 Kings 20:3
32:1 [t]2 Kings 18:13; Isa. 36:1
32:5 [u]Isa. 22:9 [v]ch. 25:23 [w]2 Sam. 5:9; 1 Kings 9:24
32:7 [x]Deut. 31:6 [y]ch. 20:15 [z]2 Kings 6:16
32:8 [a]Jer. 17:5; 1 John 4:4 [b]ch. 13:12; Rom. 8:31
32:9 [c]2 Kings 18:17
32:10 [d]2 Kings 18:19
32:11 [e]2 Kings 18:30
32:12 [f]2 Kings 18:22
32:13 [g]2 Kings 18:33
32:15 [h]2 Kings 18:29
32:17 [i]2 Kings 19:9 [j]2 Kings 19:12
32:18 [k]2 Kings 18:28 [l]2 Kings 18:26
32:19 [m]2 Kings 19:18
32:20 [n]2 Kings 19:15 [o]2 Kings 19:2
32:21 [p]2 Kings 19:35
32:23 [q]ch. 17:5 [r]ch. 1:1
32:24 [s]2 Kings 20:1; Isa. 38:1
32:25 [t]Ps. 116:12

[u]his heart was lifted up: [v]therefore there was wrath upon him, and upon Judah and Jerusalem.

26 [w]Notwithstanding Hezekiah humbled himself for the pride of his heart, *both* he and the inhabitants of Jerusalem, so that the wrath of the LORD came not upon them [x]in the days of Hezekiah.

27 ¶ And Hezekiah had exceeding much riches and honour: and he made himself treasuries for silver, and for gold, and for precious stones, and for spices, and for shields, and for all manner of pleasant jewels;

28 Storehouses also for the increase of corn, and wine, and oil; and stalls for all manner of beasts, and cotes for flocks.

29 Moreover he provided him cities, and possessions of flocks and herds in abundance: for [y]God had given him substance very much.

30 [z]This same Hezekiah also stopped the upper watercourse of Gihon, and brought it straight down to the west side of the city of David. And Hezekiah prospered in all his works.

31 ¶ Howbeit in *the business of* the ambassadors of the princes of Babylon, who [a]sent unto him to enquire of the wonder that was *done* in the land, God left him, to [b]try him, that he might know all *that was* in his heart.

32 ¶ Now the rest of the acts of Hezekiah, and his goodness, behold, they *are* written in [c]the vision of Isaiah the prophet, the son of Amoz, *and* in the [d]book of the kings of Judah and Israel.

33 [e]And Hezekiah slept with his fathers, and they buried him in the chiefest of the sepulchres of the sons of David: and all Judah and the inhabitants of Jerusalem did him [f]honour at his death. And Manasseh his son reigned in his stead.

33

Manasseh [g]*was* twelve years old when he began to reign, and he reigned fifty and five years in Jerusalem:

2 But did *that which was* evil in the sight of the LORD, like unto the [h]abominations of the heathen, whom the LORD had cast out before the children of Israel.

3 ¶ For he built again the high places which Hezekiah his father had [i]broken down, and he reared up altars for Baalim, and [j]made groves, and worshipped [k]all the host of heaven, and served them.

4 Also he built altars in the house of the LORD, whereof the LORD had said, [l]In Jerusalem shall my name be for ever.

5 And he built altars for all the host of heaven [m]in the two courts of the house of the LORD.

6 [n]And he caused his children to pass through the fire in the valley of the son of Hinnom: [o]also he observed times, and used enchantments, and used witchcraft, and [p]dealt with a familiar spirit, and with wizards: he wrought much evil in the sight of the LORD, to provoke him to anger.

7 And [q]he set a carved image, the idol which he had made, in the house of God, of which God had said to David and to Solomon his son, In [r]this house, and in Jerusalem, which I have chosen before all the tribes of Israel, will I put my name for ever:

8 [s]Neither will I any more remove the foot of Israel from out of the land which I have appointed for your fathers; so that they will take heed to do all that I have commanded them, according to the whole law and the statutes and the ordinances by the hand of Moses.

9 So Manasseh made Judah and the inhabitants of Jerusalem to err, *and* to do worse than the heathen, whom the LORD had destroyed before the children of Israel.

10 And the LORD spake to Manasseh, and to his people: but they would not hearken.

11 ¶ [t]Wherefore the LORD brought upon them the captains of the host of the king of Assyria, which took Manasseh among the thorns, and [u]bound him with fetters, and carried him to Babylon.

12 And when he was in affliction, he besought the LORD his God, and [v]humbled himself greatly before the God of his fathers,

13 And prayed unto him: and he was [w]intreated of him, and heard his supplication, and brought him again to Jerusalem into his kingdom. Then Manasseh [x]knew that the LORD he *was* God.

14 ¶ Now after this he built a wall without the city of David, on the west side of [y]Gihon, in the valley, even to the entering in at the fish gate, and compassed [z]about Ophel, and raised it up a very great height, and put captains of war in all the fenced cities of Judah.

15 And he took away the [a]strange gods, and the idol out of the house of the LORD, and all the altars that he had built in the mount of the house of the LORD, and in Jerusalem, and cast *them* out of the city.

16 And he repaired the altar of the LORD, and sacrificed thereon peace offerings and [b]thank offerings, and commanded Judah to serve the LORD God of Israel.

17 [c]Nevertheless the people did sacrifice still in the high places, *yet* unto the LORD their God only.

18 ¶ Now the rest of the acts of Manasseh, and his prayer unto his God, and the words of [d]the seers that spake to him in the name of the LORD God of Israel, behold, they *are written* in the book of the kings of Israel.

19 His prayer also, and *how God* was intreated of him, and all his sin, and his trespass, and the places wherein he built high places, and set up groves and graven images, before he was humbled: behold, they *are* written among the sayings of the seers.

20 ¶ [e]So Manasseh slept with his fathers, and they buried him in his own house: and Amon his son reigned in his stead.

21 ¶ [f]Amon *was* two and twenty years

32:25 [u]ch. 26:16; Hab. 2:4 [v]ch. 24:18
32:26 [w]Jer. 26:18 [x]2 Kings 20:19
32:29 [y]2 Chron. 29:12
32:30 [z]Isa. 22:9
32:31 [a]2 Kings 20:12; Isa. 39:1 [b]Deut. 8:2
32:32 [c]Isa. 36 [d]2 Kings 18
32:33 [e]2 Kings 20:21 [f]Prov. 10:7
33:1 [g]2 Kings 21:1
33:2 [h]Deut. 18:9; 2 Chron. 28:3
33:3 [i]2 Kings 18:4; ch. 30:14 [j]Deut. 16:21 [k]Deut. 17:3
33:4 [l]Deut. 12:11; 1 Kings 8:29; ch. 6:6
33:5 [m]ch. 4:9
33:6 [n]Lev. 18:21; Deut. 18:10; 2 Kings 23:10; ch. 28:3; Ezek. 23:37 [o]Deut. 18:10 [p]2 Kings 21:6
33:7 [q]2 Kings 21:7 [r]Ps. 132:14
33:8 [s]2 Sam. 7:10
33:11 [t]Deut. 28:36; Job 36:8 [u]Ps. 107:10
33:12 [v]1 Pet. 5:6
33:13 [w]1 Chron. 5:20; Ezra 8:23 [x]Ps. 9:16; Dan. 4:25
33:14 [y]1 Kings 1:33 [z]ch. 27:3
33:15 [a]ver. 3
33:16 [b]Lev. 7:12
33:17 [c]ch. 32:12
33:18 [d]1 Sam. 9:9
33:20 [e]2 Kings 21:18
33:21 [f]2 Kings 21:19

old when he began to reign, and reigned two years in Jerusalem.

22 But he did *that which was* evil in the sight of the LORD, as did Manasseh his father: for Amon sacrificed unto all the carved images which Manasseh his father had made, and served them;

23 And humbled not himself before the LORD, [g]as Manasseh his father had humbled himself; but Amon trespassed more and more.

24 [h]And his servants conspired against him, and slew him in his own house.

25 ¶ But the people of the land slew all them that had conspired against king Amon; and the people of the land made Josiah his son king in his stead.

34 Josiah [i]*was* eight years old when he began to reign, and he reigned in Jerusalem one and thirty years.

2 And he did *that which was* right in the sight of the LORD, and walked in the ways of David his father, and declined *neither* to the right hand, nor to the left.

3 ¶ For in the eighth year of his reign, while he was yet young, he began to [j]seek after the God of David his father: and in the twelfth year he began [k]to purge Judah and Jerusalem [l]from the high places, and the groves, and the carved images, and the molten images.

4 [m]And they brake down the altars of Baalim in his presence; and the images, that *were* on high above them, he cut down; and the groves, and the carved images, and the molten images, he brake in pieces, and made dust *of them*, [n]and strowed *it* upon the graves of them that had sacrificed unto them.

5 And he [o]burnt the bones of the priests upon their altars, and cleansed Judah and Jerusalem.

6 And *so did he* in the cities of Manasseh, and Ephraim, and Simeon, even unto Naphtali, with their mattocks round about.

7 And when he had broken down the altars and the groves, and had [p]beaten the graven images into powder, and cut down all the idols throughout all the land of Israel, he returned to Jerusalem.

8 ¶ Now [q]in the eighteenth year of his reign, when he had purged the land, and the house, he sent Shaphan the son of Azaliah, and Maaseiah the governor of the city, and Joah the son of Joahaz the recorder, to repair the house of the LORD his God.

9 And when they came to Hilkiah the high priest, they delivered [r]the money that was brought into the house of God, which the Levites that kept the doors had gathered of the hand of Manasseh and Ephraim, and of all the remnant of Israel, and of all Judah and Benjamin; and they returned to Jerusalem.

10 And they put *it* in the hand of the workmen that had the oversight of the house of the LORD, and they gave it to the workmen that wrought in the house of the LORD, to repair and amend the house:

11 Even to the artificers and builders gave they *it*, to buy hewn stone, and timber for couplings, and to floor the houses which the kings of Judah had destroyed.

12 And the men did the work faithfully: and the overseers of them *were* Jahath and Obadiah, the Levites, of the sons of Merari; and Zechariah and Meshullam, of the sons of the Kohathites, to set *it* forward; and *other of* the Levites, all that could skill of instruments of musick.

13 Also *they were* over the bearers of burdens, and *were* overseers of all that wrought the work in any manner of service: [s]and of the Levites *there were* scribes, and officers, and porters.

14 ¶ And when they brought out the money that was brought into the house of the LORD, Hilkiah the priest [t]found a book of the law of the LORD *given* by Moses.

15 And Hilkiah answered and said to Shaphan the scribe, I have found the book of the law in the house of the LORD. And Hilkiah delivered the book to Shaphan.

16 And Shaphan carried the book to the king, and brought the king word back again, saying, All that was committed to thy servants, they do *it*.

17 And they have gathered together the money that was found in the house of the LORD, and have delivered it into the hand of the overseers, and to the hand of the workmen.

18 Then Shaphan the scribe told the king, saying, Hilkiah the priest hath given me a book. And Shaphan read it before the king.

19 And it came to pass, when the king had heard the words of the law, that he rent his clothes.

20 And the king commanded Hilkiah, and Ahikam the son of Shaphan, and Abdon the son of Micah, and Shaphan the scribe, and Asaiah a servant of the king's, saying,

21 Go, enquire of the LORD for me, and for them that are left in Israel and in Judah, concerning the words of the book that is found: for great *is* the wrath of the LORD that is poured out upon us, because our fathers have not kept the word of the LORD, to do after all that is written in this book.

22 And Hilkiah, and *they* that the king *had appointed*, went to Huldah the prophetess, the wife of Shallum the son of [u]Tikvath, the son of Hasrah, keeper of the wardrobe; (now she dwelt in Jerusalem in the college:) and they spake to her to that *effect*.

23 ¶ And she answered them, Thus saith the LORD God of Israel, Tell ye the man that sent you to me,

24 Thus saith the LORD, Behold, I will bring evil upon this place, and upon the inhabitants thereof, *even* all the curses that are written in the book which they have read before the king of Judah:

25 Because they have forsaken me, and

33:23 *g*ver. 12
33:24 *h*2 Kings 21:23
34:1 *i*2 Kings 22:1
34:3 *j*ch. 15:2 *k*1 Kings 13:2 *l*ch. 33:17
34:4 *m*Lev. 26:30; 2 Kings 23:4 *n*2 Kings 23:4
34:5 *o*1 Kings 13:2
34:7 *p*Deut. 9:21
34:8 *q*2 Kings 22:3
34:9 *r*2 Kings 12:4
34:13 *s*1 Chron. 23:4
34:14 *t*2 Kings 22:8
34:22 *u*2 Kings 22:14

have burned incense unto other gods, that
they might provoke me to anger with all the
works of their hands; therefore my wrath
shall be poured out upon this place, and
shall not be quenched.
26 And as for the king of Judah, who sent
you to enquire of the LORD, so shall ye say
unto him, Thus saith the LORD God of Israel
concerning the words which thou hast
heard;
27 Because thine heart was tender, and
thou didst humble thyself before God, when
thou heardest his words against this place,
and against the inhabitants thereof, and
humbledst thyself before me, and didst rend
thy clothes, and weep before me; I have
even heard *thee* also, saith the LORD.
28 Behold, I will gather thee to thy fathers, and thou shalt be gathered to thy
grave in peace, neither shall thine eyes see
all the evil that I will bring upon this place,
and upon the inhabitants of the same. So
they brought the king word again.
29 ¶ [v]Then the king sent and gathered
together all the elders of Judah and Jerusalem.
30 And the king went up into the house of
the LORD, and all the men of Judah, and the
inhabitants of Jerusalem, and the priests,
and the Levites, and all the people, great
and small: and he read in their ears all the
words of the book of the covenant that was
found in the house of the LORD.
31 And the king stood in his [w]place, and
made a covenant before the LORD, to walk
after the LORD, and to keep his commandments, and his testimonies, and his statutes,
with all his heart, and with all his soul, to
perform the words of the covenant which
are written in this book.
32 And he caused all that were present in
Jerusalem and Benjamin to stand *to it*. And
the inhabitants of Jerusalem did according
to the covenant of God, the God of their
fathers.
33 And Josiah took away all the [x]abomi-
nations out of all the countries that *pertained* to the children of Israel, and made all
that were present in Israel to serve, *even* to
serve the LORD their God. [y]*And* all his days
they departed not from following the LORD,
the God of their fathers.

35

Moreover [z]Josiah kept a passover
unto the LORD in Jerusalem: and they
killed the passover on the [a]fourteenth *day*
of the first month.
2 And he set the priests in their [b]charges,
and [c]encouraged them to the service of the
house of the LORD,
3 And said unto the Levites [d]that taught
all Israel, which were holy unto the LORD,
[e]Put the holy ark [f]in the house which Solomon the son of David king of Israel did
build; [g]*it shall* not *be* a burden upon *your*
shoulders: serve now the LORD your God,
and his people Israel,
4 And prepare *yourselves* by the [h]houses
of your fathers, after your courses, accord-

34:29 [v]2 Kings 23:1
34:31 [w]2 Kings 11:14; ch. 6:13
34:33 [x]1 Kings 11:5 [y]Jer. 3:10
35:1 [z]2 Kings 23:21 [a]Ex. 12:6; Ezra 6:19
35:2 [b]ch. 23:18; Ezra 6:18 [c]ch. 29:5
35:3 [d]Deut. 23:10; ch. 30:22; Mal. 2:7 [e]ch. 84:14 [f]ch. 5:7 [g]1 Chron. 23:26
35:4 [h]1 Chron. 9:10 [i]1 Chron. 23 [j]ch. 8:14
35:5 [k]Ps. 134:1
35:6 [l]ch. 29:5; Ezra 6:20
35:7 [m]ch. 30:24
35:10 [n]Ezra 6:18
35:11 [o]ch. 29:22 [p]ch. 29:34
35:12 [q]Lev. 3:3
35:13 [r]Ex. 12:8; Deut. 16:7 [s]1 Sam. 2:13
35:15 [t]1 Chron. 25:1 [u]1 Chron. 9:17

ing to the [i]writing of David king of Israel,
and according to the [j]writing of Solomon
his son.
5 And [k]stand in the holy *place* according
to the divisions of the families of the fathers
of your brethren the people, and *after* the
division of the families of the Levites.
6 So kill the passover, and [l]sanctify
yourselves, and prepare your brethren, that
they may do according to the word of the
LORD by the hand of Moses.
7 And Josiah [m]gave to the people, of the
flock, lambs and kids, all for the passover
offerings, for all that were present, to the
number of thirty thousand, and three thousand bullocks: these *were* of the king's substance.
8 And his princes gave willingly unto the
people, to the priests, and to the Levites:
Hilkiah and Zechariah and Jehiel, rulers of
the house of God, gave unto the priests for
the passover offerings two thousand and six
hundred *small cattle* and three hundred
oxen.
9 Conaniah also, and Shemaiah and Nethaneel, his brethren, and Hashabiah and
Jeiel and Jozabad, chief of the Levites, gave
unto the Levites for passover offerings five
thousand *small cattle,* and five hundred
oxen.
10 So the service was prepared, and the
priests [n]stood in their place, and the Levites
in their courses, according to the king's
commandment.
11 And they killed the passover, and the
priests [o]sprinkled *the blood* from their
hands, and the Levites [p]flayed *them.*
12 And they removed the burnt offerings,
that they might give according to the divisions of the families of the people, to offer
unto the LORD, as *it is* written [q]in the book
of Moses. And so *did they* with the oxen.
13 And they [r]roasted the passover with
fire according to the ordinance: but the
other holy *offerings* [s]sod they in pots, and
in caldrons, and in pans, and divided *them*
speedily among all the people.
14 And afterward they made ready for
themselves, and for the priests: because the
priests the sons of Aaron *were busied* in offering of burnt offerings and the fat until
night; therefore the Levites prepared for
themselves, and for the priests the sons of
Aaron.
15 And the singers the sons of Asaph
were in their place, according to the [t]com-
mandment of David, and Asaph, and Heman, and Jeduthun the king's seer; and the
porters [u]*waited* at every gate; they might
not depart from their service; for their
brethren the Levites prepared for them.
16 So all the service of the LORD was prepared the same day, to keep the passover,
and to offer burnt offerings upon the altar of
the LORD, according to the commandment
of king Josiah.
17 And the children of Israel that were
present kept the passover at that time, and

the feast of [v]unleavened bread seven days.

18 And [w]there was no passover like to that kept in Israel from the days of Samuel the prophet; neither did all the kings of Israel keep such a passover as Josiah kept, and the priests, and the Levites, and all Judah and Israel that were present, and the inhabitants of Jerusalem.

19 In the eighteenth year of the reign of Josiah was this passover kept.

20 ¶ [x]After all this, when Josiah had prepared the temple, Necho king of Egypt came up to fight against Charchemish by Euphrates: and Josiah went out against him.

21 But he sent ambassadors to him, saying, What have I to do with thee, thou king of Judah? *I come* not against thee this day, but against the house wherewith I have war: for God commanded me to make haste: forbear thee from *meddling with* God, who *is* with me, that he destroy thee not.

22 Nevertheless Josiah would not turn his face from him, but [y]disguised himself, that he might fight with him, and hearkened not unto the words of Necho from the mouth of God, and came to fight in the valley of Megiddo.

23 And the archers shot at king Josiah; and the king said to his servants, Have me away; for I am sore wounded.

24 [z]His servants therefore took him out of that chariot, and put him in the second chariot that he had; and they brought him to Jerusalem, and he died, and was buried in *one of* the sepulchres of his fathers. And [a]all Judah and Jerusalem mourned for Josiah.

25 ¶ And Jeremiah [b]lamented for Josiah: and [c]all the singing men and the singing women spake of Josiah in their lamentations to this day, [d]and made them an ordinance in Israel: and, behold, they *are* written in the lamentations.

26 Now the rest of the acts of Josiah, and his goodness, according to *that which was* written in the law of the LORD,

27 And his deeds, first and last, behold, they *are* written in the book of the kings of Israel and Judah.

36 Then [e]the people of the land took Jehoahaz the son of Josiah, and made him king in his father's stead in Jerusalem.

2 Jehoahaz *was* twenty and three years old when he began to reign, and he reigned three months in Jerusalem.

3 And the king of Egypt put him down at Jerusalem, and condemned the land in an hundred talents of silver and a talent of gold.

4 And the king of Egypt made Eliakim his brother king over Judah and Jerusalem, and turned his name to Jehoiakim. And Necho took Jehoahaz his brother, and carried him to Egypt.

5 ¶ [f]Jehoiakim *was* twenty and five years old when he began to reign, and he reigned eleven years in Jerusalem: and he did *that which was* evil in the sight of the LORD his God.

6 [g]Against him came up Nebuchadnezzar king of Babylon, and bound him in fetters, to [h]carry him to Babylon.

7 [i]Nebuchadnezzar also carried of the vessels of the house of the LORD to Babylon, and put them in his temple at Babylon.

8 Now the rest of the acts of Jehoiakim, and his abominations which he did, and that which was found in him, behold, they *are* written in the book of the kings of Israel and Judah: and Jehoiachin his son reigned in his stead.

9 ¶ [j]Jehoiachin *was* eight years old when he began to reign, and he reigned three months and ten days in Jerusalem: and he did *that which was* evil in the sight of the LORD.

10 And when the year was expired, [k]king Nebuchadnezzar sent, and brought him to Babylon, [l]with the goodly vessels of the house of the LORD, and made [m]Zedekiah his brother king over Judah and Jerusalem.

11 ¶ [n]Zedekiah *was* one and twenty years old when he began to reign, and reigned eleven years in Jerusalem.

12 And he did *that which was* evil in the sight of the LORD his God, *and* humbled not himself before Jeremiah the prophet *speaking* from the mouth of the LORD.

13 And [o]he also rebelled against king Nebuchadnezzar, who had made him swear by God: but he [p]stiffened his neck, and hardened his heart from turning unto the LORD God of Israel.

14 ¶ Moreover all the chief of the priests, and the people, transgressed very much after all the abominations of the heathen; and polluted the house of the LORD which he had hallowed in Jerusalem.

15 [q]And the LORD God of their fathers sent to them by his messengers, rising up betimes, and sending; because he had compassion on his people, and on his dwelling place:

16 [r]But they mocked the messengers of God, and [s]despised his words, and [t]misused his prophets, until the [u]wrath of the LORD arose against his people, till *there was* no remedy.

17 [v]Therefore he brought upon them the king of the Chaldees, who [w]slew their young men with the sword in the house of their sanctuary, and had no compassion upon young man or maiden, old man, or him that stooped for age: he gave *them* all into his hand.

18 [x]And all the vessels of the house of God, great and small, and the treasures of the house of the LORD, and the treasures of the king, and of his princes; all *these* he brought to Babylon.

19 [y]And they burnt the house of God, and brake down the wall of Jerusalem, and burnt all the palaces thereof with fire, and destroyed all the goodly vessels thereof.

35:17 [v]Ex. 12:15; ch. 30:21
35:18 [w]2 Kings 23:22
35:20 [x]2 Kings 23:29; Jer. 46:2
35:22 [y]1 Kings 22:34
35:24 [z]2 Kings 23:30 [a]Zech. 12:11
35:25 [b]Lam. 4:20 [c]Matt. 9:23 [d]Jer. 22:20
36:1 [e]2 Kings 23:30
36:5 [f]2 Kings 23:36
36:6 [g]2 Kings 24:1 [h]2 Kings 24:6; Jer. 22:18
36:7 [i]2 Kings 24:13; Dan. 1:1
36:9 [j]2 Kings 24:8
36:10 [k]2 Kings 24:10-17 [l]Dan. 1:1 [m]Jer. 37:1
36:11 [n]2 Kings 24:18; Jer. 52:1
36:13 [o]Jer. 52:3; Ezek. 17:15 [p]2 Kings 17:14
36:15 [q]Jer. 25:3
36:16 [r]Jer. 5:12 [s]Prov. 1:25 [t]Jer. 32:3; Matt. 23:34 [u]Ps. 74:1
36:17 [v]Deut. 28:49; 2 Kings 25:1; Ezra 9:7 [w]Ps. 74:20
36:18 [x]2 Kings 25:13
36:19 [y]2 Kings 25:9; Ps. 74:6

20 And [z]them that had escaped from the sword carried he away to Babylon; [a]where they were servants to him and his sons until the reign of the kingdom of Persia:

21 To fulfil the word of the LORD by the mouth of [b]Jeremiah, until the land [c]had enjoyed her sabbaths: *for* as long as she lay desolate [d]she kept sabbath, to fulfil threescore and ten years.

22 ¶ [e]Now in the first year of Cyrus king of Persia, that the word of the LORD *spoken* by the mouth of [f]Jeremiah might be accomplished, the LORD stirred up the spirit of [g]Cyrus king of Persia, that he made a proclamation throughout all his kingdom, and *put it* also in writing, saying,

23 [h]Thus saith Cyrus king of Persia, All the kingdoms of the earth hath the LORD God of heaven given me; and he hath charged me to build him an house in Jerusalem, which *is* in Judah. Who *is there* among you of all his people? The LORD his God *be* with him, and let him go up.

36:20 [z]2 Kings 25:11 [a]Jer. 27:7
36:21 [b]Jer. 25:9 [c]Lev. 26:34; Dan. 9:2 [d]Lev. 25:4
36:22 [e]Ezra 1:1 [f]Jer. 25:12 [g]Isa. 44:28
36:23 [h]Ezra 1:2

EZRA

Ezra may be the writer of the majority of the text, written sometime between 456 B.C. and 440 B.C. Ezra begins where 2 Chronicles ends and covers a period of about 100 years. During this time the people of Israel return to their land and rebuild the Temple which was destroyed by Nebuchadnezzar. Following this Ezra brings about reform and spiritual revival in the land.

I. The return under Zerubbabel, 1:1–2:70
II. The Temple is rebuilt, 3:1–6:22
III. Ezra returns to Jerusalem, 7:1–10:44

---

1 Now in the first year of Cyrus king of Persia, that the word of the LORD [a]by the mouth of Jeremiah might be fulfilled, the LORD stirred up the spirit of Cyrus king of Persia, [b]that he made a proclamation throughout all his kingdom, and *put it* also in writing, saying,

2 Thus saith Cyrus king of Persia, The LORD God of heaven hath given me all the kingdoms of the earth; and he hath [c]charged me to build him an house at Jerusalem, which *is* in Judah.

3 Who *is there* among you of all his people? his God be with him, and let him go up to Jerusalem, which *is* in Judah, and build the house of the LORD God of Israel, ([d]he *is* the God,) which *is* in Jerusalem.

4 And whosoever remaineth in any place where he sojourneth, let the men of his place help him with silver, and with gold, and with goods, and with beasts, beside the freewill offering for the house of God that *is* in Jerusalem.

5 ¶ Then rose up the chief of the fathers of Judah and Benjamin, and the priests, and the Levites, with all *them* whose spirit [e]God had raised, to go up to build the house of the LORD which *is* in Jerusalem.

6 And all they that *were* about them strengthened their hands with vessels of silver, with gold, with goods, and with beasts, and with precious things, beside all *that* was willingly offered.

7 ¶ [f]Also Cyrus the king brought forth the vessels of the house of the LORD, [g]which Nebuchadnezzar had brought forth out of Jerusalem, and had put them in the house of his gods;

8 Even those did Cyrus king of Persia bring forth by the hand of Mithredath the treasurer, and numbered them unto [h]Sheshbazzar, the prince of Judah.

9 And this *is* the number of them: thirty chargers of gold, a thousand chargers of silver, nine and twenty knives,

10 Thirty basons of gold, silver basons of a second *sort* four hundred and ten, *and* other vessels a thousand.

11 All the vessels of gold and of silver *were* five thousand and four hundred. All *these* did Sheshbazzar bring up with *them* of the captivity that were brought up from Babylon unto Jerusalem.

2 Now [i]these *are* the children of the province that went up out of the captivity, of those which had been carried away, [j]whom Nebuchadnezzar the king of Babylon had carried away unto Babylon, and came again unto Jerusalem and Judah, every one unto his city;

2 Which came with Zerubbabel: Jeshua, Nehemiah, Seraiah, Reelaiah, Mordecai, Bilshan, Mispar, Bigvai, Rehum, Baanah. The number of the men of the people of Israel:

3 The children of Parosh, two thousand an hundred seventy and two.

1:1 [a]2 Chron. 36:22; Jer. 25:12 [b]ch. 5:13
1:2 [c]Isa. 44:28
1:3 [d]Dan. 6:26
1:5 [e]Phil. 2:13
1:7 [f]ch. 5:14 [g]2 Kings 24:13; 2 Chron. 36:7
1:8 [h]ch. 5:14
2:1 [i]Neh. 7:6 [j]2 Kings 24:14; 2 Chron. 36:20

4 The children of Shephatiah, three hundred seventy and two.

5 The children of Arah, [k]seven hundred seventy and five.

6 The children of [l]Pahath-moab, of the children of Jeshua *and* Joab, two thousand eight hundred and twelve.

7 The children of Elam, a thousand two hundred fifty and four.

8 The children of Zattu, nine hundred forty and five.

9 The children of Zaccai, seven hundred and threescore.

10 The children of Bani, six hundred forty and two.

11 The children of Bebai, six hundred twenty and three.

12 The children of Azgad, a thousand two hundred twenty and two.

13 The children of Adonikam, six hundred sixty and six.

14 The children of Bigvai, two thousand fifty and six.

15 The children of Adin, four hundred fifty and four.

16 The children of Ater of Hezekiah, ninety and eight.

17 The children of Bezai, three hundred twenty and three.

18 The children of Jorah, an hundred and twelve.

19 The children of Hashum, two hundred twenty and three.

20 The children of Gibbar, ninety and five.

21 The children of Beth-lehem, an hundred twenty and three.

22 The men of Netophah, fifty and six.

23 The men of Anathoth, an hundred twenty and eight.

24 The children of Azmaveth, forty and two.

25 The children of Kirjath-arim, Chephirah, and Beeroth, seven hundred and forty and three.

26 The children of Ramah and Gaba, six hundred twenty and one.

27 The men of Michmas, an hundred twenty and two.

28 The men of Beth-el and Ai, two hundred twenty and three.

29 The children of Nebo, fifty and two.

30 The children of Magbish, an hundred fifty and six.

31 The children of the other [m]Elam, a thousand two hundred fifty and four.

32 The children of Harim, three hundred and twenty.

33 The children of Lod, Hadid, and Ono, seven hundred twenty and five.

34 The children of Jericho, three hundred forty and five.

35 The children of Senaah, three thousand and six hundred and thirty.

36 ¶ The priests: the children of [n]Jedaiah, of the house of Jeshua, nine hundred seventy and three.

37 The children of [o]Immer, a thousand fifty and two.

38 The children of [p]Pashur, a thousand two hundred forty and seven.

39 The children of [q]Harim, a thousand and seventeen.

40 ¶ The Levites: the children of Jeshua and Kadmiel, of the children of Hodaviah, seventy and four.

41 ¶ The singers: the children of Asaph, an hundred twenty and eight.

42 ¶ The children of the porters: the children of Shallum, the children of Ater, the children of Talmon, the children of Akkub, the children of Hatita, the children of Shobai, *in* all an hundred thirty and nine.

43 ¶ [r]The Nethinims: the children of Ziha, the children of Hasupha, the children of Tabbaoth,

44 The children of Keros, the children of Siaha, the children of Padon,

45 The children of Lebanah, the children of Hagabah, the children of Akkub,

46 The children of Hagab, the children of Shalmai, the children of Hanan,

47 The children of Giddel, the children of Gahar, the children of Reaiah,

48 The children of Rezin, the children of Nekoda, the children of Gazzam,

49 The children of Uzza, the children of Paseah, the children of Besai,

50 The children of Asnah, the children of Mehunim, the children of Nephusim,

51 The children of Bakbuk, the children of Hakupha, the children of Harhur,

52 The children of Bazluth, the children of Mehida, the children of Harsha,

53 The children of Barkos, the children of Sisera, the children of Thamah,

54 The children of Neziah, the children of Hatipha.

55 ¶ The children of [s]Solomon's servants: the children of Sotai, the children of Sophereth, the children of Peruda,

56 The children of Jaalah, the children of Darkon, the children of Giddel,

57 The children of Shephatiah, the children of Hattil, the children of Pochereth of Zebaim, the children of Ami.

58 All the [t]Nethinims, and the children of [u]Solomon's servants, *were* three hundred ninety and two.

59 And these *were* they which went up from Tel-melah, Tel-harsa, Cherub, Addan, *and* Immer: but they could not shew their father's house, and their seed, whether they *were* of Israel:

60 The children of Delaiah, the children of Tobiah, the children of Nekoda, six hundred fifty and two.

61 ¶ And of the children of the priests: the children of Habaiah, the children of Koz, the children of Barzillai; which took a wife of the daughters of [v]Barzillai the Gileadite, and was called after their name:

62 These sought their register *among* those that were reckoned by genealogy, but

2:5 *k*Neh. 7:10
2:6 *l*Neh. 7:11
2:31 *m*ver. 7
2:36 *n*1 Chron. 24:7
2:37 *o*1 Chron. 24:14
2:38 *p*1 Chron. 9:12
2:39 *q*1 Chron. 24:8
2:43 *r*1 Chron. 9:2
2:55 *s*1 Kings 9:21
2:58 *t*Josh. 9:21; 1 Chron. 9:2 *u*1 Kings 9:21
2:61 *v*2 Sam. 17:27

they were not found: [w]therefore were they,
as polluted, put from the priesthood.
63 And the Tirshatha said unto them, that
they [x]should not eat of the most holy
things, till there stood up a priest with
[y]Urim and with Thummim.
64 ¶ [z]The whole congregation together
was forty and two thousand three hundred
and threescore,
65 Beside their servants and their maids,
of whom *there were* seven thousand three
hundred thirty and seven: and *there were*
among them two hundred singing men and
singing women.
66 Their horses *were* seven hundred
thirty and six; their mules, two hundred
forty and five;
67 Their camels, four hundred thirty and
five; *their* asses, six thousand seven hundred and twenty.
68 ¶ [a]And *some* of the chief of the fathers, when they came to the house of the
LORD which *is* at Jerusalem, offered freely
for the house of God to set it up in his place:
69 They gave after their ability unto the
[b]treasure of the work threescore and one
thousand drams of gold, and five thousand
pound of silver, and one hundred priests'
garments.
70 [c]So the priests, and the Levites, and
some of the people, and the singers, and the
porters, and the Nethinims, dwelt in their
cities, and all Israel in their cities.

3

And when the seventh month was
come, and the children of Israel *were* in
the cities, the people gathered themselves
together as one man to Jerusalem.
2 Then stood up Jeshua the son of Jozadak, and his brethren the priests, and Zerubbabel the son of [d]Shealtiel, and his
brethren, and builded the altar of the God of
Israel, to offer burnt offerings thereon, as *it
is* [e]written in the law of Moses the man of
God.
3 And they set the altar upon his bases;
for fear *was* upon them because of the people of those countries: and they offered
burnt offerings thereon unto the LORD, *even*
[f]burnt offerings morning and evening.
4 [g]They kept also the feast of tabernacles, [h]as *it is* written, and [i]*offered* the daily
burnt offerings by number, according to the
custom, as the duty of every day required;
5 And afterward *offered* the [j]continual
burnt offering, both of the new moons, and
of all the set feasts of the LORD that were
consecrated, and of every one that willingly
offered a freewill offering unto the LORD.
6 From the first day of the seventh month
began they to offer burnt offerings unto the
LORD. But the foundation of the temple of
the LORD was not *yet* laid.
7 They gave money also unto the masons,
and to the carpenters; and [k]meat, and
drink, and oil, unto them of Zidon, and to
them of Tyre, to bring cedar trees from Lebanon to the sea of [l]Joppa, [m]according to
the grant that they had of Cyrus king of
Persia.
8 ¶ Now in the second year of their coming unto the house of God at Jerusalem, in
the second month, began Zerubbabel the
son of Shealtiel, and Jeshua the son of Jozadak, and the remnant of their brethren the
priests and the Levites, and all they that
were come out of the captivity unto Jerusalem; [n]and appointed the Levites, from
twenty years old and upward, to set forward the work of the house of the LORD.
9 Then stood [o]Jeshua *with* his sons and
his brethren, Kadmiel and his sons, the sons
of Judah, together, to set forward the workmen in the house of God: the sons of Henadad, *with* their sons and their brethren the
Levites.
10 And when the builders laid the foundation of the temple of the LORD, [p]they set the
priests in their apparel with trumpets, and
the Levites the sons of Asaph with cymbals,
to praise the LORD, after the [q]ordinance of
David king of Israel.
11 [r]And they sang together by course in
praising and giving thanks unto the LORD;
[s]because *he is* good, [t]for his mercy *endureth* for ever toward Israel. And all the people shouted with a great shout, when they
praised the LORD, because the foundation of
the house of the LORD was laid.
12 [u]But many of the priests and Levites
and chief of the fathers, *who were* ancient
men, that had seen the first house, when the
foundation of this house was laid before
their eyes, wept with a loud voice; and
many shouted aloud for joy:
13 So that the people could not discern
the noise of the shout of joy from the noise
of the weeping of the people: for the people
shouted with a loud shout, and the noise
was heard afar off.

4

Now when [v]the adversaries of Judah
and Benjamin heard that the children of
the captivity builded the temple unto the
LORD God of Israel;
2 Then they came to Zerubbabel, and to
the chief of the fathers, and said unto them,
Let us build with you: for we seek your God,
as ye *do;* and we do sacrifice unto him
[w]since the days of Esar-haddon king of Assur, which brought us up hither.
3 But Zerubbabel, and Jeshua, and the
rest of the chief of the fathers of Israel, said
unto them, [x]Ye have nothing to do with us
to build an house unto our God; but we ourselves together will build unto the LORD
God of Israel, as [y]king Cyrus the king of
Persia hath commanded us.
4 Then [z]the people of the land weakened
the hands of the people of Judah, and troubled them in building,
5 And hired counsellors against them, to
frustrate their purpose, all the days of Cyrus
king of Persia, even until the reign of Darius
king of Persia.
6 And in the reign of Ahasuerus, in the
beginning of his reign, wrote they *unto him*

2:62 [w]Num. 3:10
2:63 [x]Lev. 22:2 [y]Ex. 28:30; Num. 27:21
2:64 [z]Neh. 7:67
2:68 [a]Neh. 7:70
2:69 [b]1 Chron. 26:20
2:70 [c]ch. 6:16; Neh. 7:73
3:2 [d]Matt. 1:12 [e]Deut. 12:5
3:3 [f]Num. 28:3
3:4 [g]Neh. 8:14; Zech. 14:16 [h]Ex. 23:16 [i]Num. 29:12
3:5 [j]Ex. 29:38; Num. 28:3
3:7 [k]1 Kings 5:6; 2 Chron. 2:10; Acts 12:20 [l]2 Chron. 2:16; Acts 9:36 [m]ch. 6:3
3:8 [n]1 Chron. 23:24
3:9 [o]ch. 2:40
3:10 [p]1 Chron. 16:5 [q]1 Chron. 6:31
3:11 [r]Ex. 15:21; 2 Chron. 7:3; Neh. 12:24 [s]1 Chron. 16:34; Ps. 136:1 [t]1 Chron. 16:41; Jer. 33:11
3:12 [u]Hag. 2:3
4:1 [v]ver. 7
4:2 [w]2 Kings 17:24; ver. 10
4:3 [x]Neh. 2:20 [y]ch. 1:1
4:4 [z]ch. 3:3

an accusation against the inhabitants of Judah and Jerusalem.

7 ¶ And in the days of Artaxerxes wrote Bishlam, Mithredath, Tabeel, and the rest of their companions, unto Artaxerxes king of Persia; and the writing of the letter *was* written in the Syrian tongue, and interpreted in the Syrian tongue.

8 Rehum the chancellor and Shimshai the scribe wrote a letter against Jerusalem to Artaxerxes the king in this sort:

9 Then *wrote* Rehum the chancellor, and Shimshai the scribe, and the rest of their companions; [a]the Dinaites, the Apharsathchites, the Tarpelites, the Apharsites, the Archevites, the Babylonians, the Susanchites, the Dehavites, *and* the Elamites,

10 [b]And the rest of the nations whom the great and noble Asnapper brought over, and set in the cities of Samaria, and the rest *that are* on this side the river, [c]and at such a time.

11 ¶ This *is* the copy of the letter that they sent unto him, *even* unto Artaxerxes the king; Thy servants the men on this side the river, and at such a time.

12 Be it known unto the king, that the Jews which came up from thee to us are come unto Jerusalem, building the rebellious and the bad city, and have set up the walls *thereof*, and joined the foundations.

13 Be it known now unto the king, that, if this city be builded, and the walls set up *again, then* will they not pay [d]toll, tribute, and custom, and *so* thou shalt endamage the revenue of the kings.

14 Now because we have maintenance from *the king's* palace, and it was not meet for us to see the king's dishonour, therefore have we sent and certified the king;

15 That search may be made in the book of the records of thy fathers: so shalt thou find in the book of the records, and know that this city *is* a rebellious city, and hurtful unto kings and provinces, and that they have moved sedition within the same of old time: for which cause was this city destroyed.

16 We certify the king that, if this city be builded *again*, and the walls thereof set up, by this means thou shalt have no portion on this side the river.

17 ¶ *Then* sent the king an answer unto Rehum the chancellor, and *to* Shimshai the scribe, and *to* the rest of their companions that dwell in Samaria, and *unto* the rest beyond the river, Peace, and at such a time.

18 The letter which ye sent unto us hath been plainly read before me.

19 And I commanded, and search hath been made, and it is found that this city of old time hath made insurrection against kings, and *that* rebellion and sedition have been made therein.

20 There have been mighty kings also over Jerusalem, which have [e]ruled over all *countries* [f]beyond the river; and toll, tribute, and custom, was paid unto them.

21 Give ye now commandment to cause these men to cease, and that this city be not builded, until *another* commandment shall be given from me.

22 Take heed now that ye fail not to do this: why should damage grow to the hurt of the kings?

23 ¶ Now when the copy of king Artaxerxes' letter *was* read before Rehum, and Shimshai the scribe, and their companions, they went up in haste to Jerusalem unto the Jews, and made them to cease by force and power.

24 Then ceased the work of the house of God which *is* at Jerusalem. So it ceased unto the second year of the reign of Darius king of Persia.

5 Then the prophets, [g]Haggai the prophet, and [h]Zechariah the son of Iddo, prophesied unto the Jews that *were* in Judah and Jerusalem in the name of the God of Israel, *even* unto them.

2 Then rose up [i]Zerubbabel the son of Shealtiel, and Jeshua the son of Jozadak, and began to build the house of God which *is* at Jerusalem: and with them *were* the prophets of God helping them.

3 ¶ At the same time came to them [j]Tatnai, governor on this side the river, and Shethar-boznai, and their companions, and said thus unto them, [k]Who hath commanded you to build this house, and to make up this wall?

4 [l]Then said we unto them after this manner, What are the names of the men that make this building?

5 But [m]the eye of their God was upon the elders of the Jews, that they could not cause them to cease, till the matter came to Darius: and then they returned [n]answer by letter concerning this *matter*.

6 ¶ The copy of the letter that Tatnai, governor on this side the river, and Shethar-boznai, [o]and his companions the Apharsachites, which *were* on this side the river, sent unto Darius the king:

7 They sent a letter unto him, wherein was written thus; Unto Darius the king, all peace.

8 Be it known unto the king, that we went into the province of Judea, to the house of the great God, which is builded with great stones, and timber is laid in the walls, and this work goeth fast on, and prospereth in their hands.

9 Then asked we those elders, *and* said unto them thus, [p]Who commanded you to build this house, and to make up these walls?

10 We asked their names also, to certify thee, that we might write the names of the men that *were* the chief of them.

11 And thus they returned us answer, saying, We are the servants of the God of heaven and earth, and build the house that was builded these many years ago, which a great king of Israel builded [q]and set up.

12 But [r]after that our fathers had pro-

4:9 [a]2 Kings 17:30
4:10 [b]ver. 1 [c]ver. 11:17
4:13 [d]ch. 7:24
4:20 [e]1 Kings 4:21; Ps. 72:8 [f]Gen. 15:18; Josh. 1:4
5:1 [g]Hag. 1:1 [h]Zech. 1:1
5:2 [i]ch. 3:2
5:3 [j]ver. 6; ch. 6:6 [k]ver. 9
5:4 [l]ver. 10
5:5 [m]ch. 7:6; Ps. 33:18 [n]ch. 6:6
5:6 [o]ch. 4:9
5:9 [p]ver. 3
5:11 [q]1 Kings 6:1
5:12 [r]2 Chron. 36:16

voked the God of heaven unto wrath, he gave them into the hand of [s]Nebuchadnezzar the king of Babylon, the Chaldean, who destroyed this house, and carried the people away into Babylon.

13 But in the first year of [t]Cyrus the king of Babylon *the same* king Cyrus made a decree to build this house of God.

14 And [u]the vessels also of gold and silver of the house of God, which Nebuchadnezzar took out of the temple that *was* in Jerusalem, and brought them into the temple of Babylon, those did Cyrus the king take out of the temple of Babylon, and they were delivered unto *one,* [v]whose name *was* Sheshbazzar, whom he had made governor;

15 And said unto him, Take these vessels, go, carry them into the temple that *is* in Jerusalem, and let the house of God be builded in his place.

16 Then came the same Sheshbazzar, *and* [w]laid the foundation of the house of God which *is* in Jerusalem: and since that time even until now hath it been in building, and [x]*yet* it is not finished.

17 Now therefore, if *it seem* good to the king, [y]let there be search made in the king's treasure house, which *is* there at Babylon, whether it be *so,* that a decree was made of Cyrus the king to build this house of God at Jerusalem, and let the king send his pleasure to us concerning this matter.

6 Then Darius the king made a decree, [z]and search was made in the house of the rolls, where the treasures were laid up in Babylon.

2 And there was found at Achmetha, in the palace that *is* in the province of the Medes, a roll, and therein *was* a record thus written:

3 In the first year of Cyrus the king *the same* Cyrus the king made a decree *concerning* the house of God at Jerusalem, Let the house be builded, the place where they offered sacrifices, and let the foundations thereof be strongly laid; the height thereof threescore cubits, *and* the breadth thereof threescore cubits;

4 [a]*With* three rows of great stones, and a row of new timber: and let the expenses be given out of the king's house:

5 And also let [b]the golden and silver vessels of the house of God, which Nebuchadnezzar took forth out of the temple which *is* at Jerusalem, and brought unto Babylon, be restored, and brought again unto the temple which *is* at Jerusalem, *every one* to his place, and place *them* in the house of God.

6 [c]Now *therefore,* Tatnai, governor beyond the river, Shethar-boznai, and your companions the Apharsachites, which *are* beyond the river, be ye far from thence:

7 Let the work of this house of God alone; let the governor of the Jews and the elders of the Jews build this house of God in his place.

8 Moreover I make a decree what ye shall do to the elders of these Jews for the building of this house of God: that of the king's goods, *even* of the tribute beyond the river, forthwith expenses be given unto these men, that they be not hindered.

9 And that which they have need of, both young bullocks, and rams, and lambs, for the burnt offerings of the God of heaven, wheat, salt, wine, and oil, according to the appointment of the priests which *are* at Jerusalem, let it be given them day by day without fail:

10 [d]That they may offer sacrifices of sweet savours unto the God of heaven, and [e]pray for the life of the king, and of his sons.

11 Also I have made a decree, that whosoever shall alter this word, let timber be pulled down from his house, and being set up, let him be hanged thereon; [f]and let his house be made a dunghill for this.

12 And the God that hath caused his [g]name to dwell there destroy all kings and people, that shall put to their hand to alter *and* to destroy this house of God which *is* at Jerusalem. I Darius have made a decree; let it be done with speed.

13 ¶ Then Tatnai, governor on this side the river, Shethar-boznai, and their companions, according to that which Darius the king had sent, so they did speedily.

14 [h]And the elders of the Jews builded, and they prospered through the prophesying of Haggai the prophet and Zechariah the son of Iddo. And they builded, and finished *it,* according to the commandment of the God of Israel, and according to the commandment of [i]Cyrus, and [j]Darius, and [k]Artaxerxes king of Persia.

15 And this house was finished on the third day of the month Adar, which was in the sixth year of the reign of Darius the king.

16 ¶ And the children of Israel, the priests, and the Levites, and the rest of the children of the captivity, kept [l]the dedication of this house of God with joy,

17 And [m]offered at the dedication of this house of God an hundred bullocks, two hundred rams, four hundred lambs; and for a sin offering for all Israel, twelve he goats, according to the number of the tribes of Israel.

18 And they set the priests in their [n]divisions, and the Levites in their [o]courses, for the service of God, which *is* at Jerusalem; [p]as it is written in the book of Moses.

19 And the children of the captivity kept the passover [q]upon the fourteenth *day* of the first month.

20 For the priests and the Levites were [r]purified together, all of them *were* pure, and [s]killed the passover for all the children of the captivity, and for their brethren the priests, and for themselves.

21 And the children of Israel, which were come again out of captivity, and all such as had separated themselves unto them from

5:12 *s*2 Kings 24:2
5:13 *t*ch. 1:1
5:14 *u*ch. 1:7 *v*Hag. 1:14
5:16 *w*ch. 3:8 *x*ch. 6:15
5:17 *y*ch. 6:1
6:1 *z*ch. 5:17
6:4 *a*1 Kings 6:36
6:5 *b*ch. 1:7
6:6 *c*ch. 5:3
6:10 *d*ch. 7:23; Jer. 29:7 *e*1 Tim. 2:1
6:11 *f*Dan. 2:5
6:12 *g*1 Kings 9:3
6:14 *h*ch. 5:1 *i*ch. 1:1; ver. 3 *j*ch. 4:24 *k*ch. 7:1
6:16 *l*1 Kings 8:63; 2 Chron. 7:5
6:17 *m*ch. 8:35
6:18 *n*1 Chron. 24:1 *o*1 Chron. 23:6 *p*Num. 3:6
6:19 *q*Ex. 12:6
6:20 *r*2 Chron. 30:15 *s*2 Chron. 35:11

the [t]filthiness of the heathen of the land, to seek the LORD God of Israel, did eat,

22 And kept the [u]feast of unleavened bread seven days with joy: for the LORD had made them joyful, and [v]turned the heart [w]of the king of Assyria unto them, to strengthen their hands in the work of the house of God, the God of Israel.

7 Now after these things, in the reign of [x]Artaxerxes king of Persia, Ezra the son of Seraiah, [y]the son of Azariah, the son of Hilkiah,

2 The son of Shallum, the son of Zadok, the son of Ahitub,

3 The son of Amariah, the son of Azariah, the son of Meraioth,

4 The son of Zerahiah, the son of Uzzi, the son of Bukki,

5 The son of Abishua, the son of Phinehas, the son of Eleazar, the son of Aaron the chief priest:

6 This Ezra went up from Babylon; and he *was* [z]a ready scribe in the law of Moses, which the LORD God of Israel had given: and the king granted him all his request, [a]according to the hand of the LORD his God upon him.

7 [b]And there went up *some* of the children of Israel, and of the priests, and [c]the Levites, and the singers, and the porters, and [d]the Nethinims, unto Jerusalem, in the seventh year of Artaxerxes the king.

8 And he came to Jerusalem in the fifth month, which *was* in the seventh year of the king.

9 For upon the first *day* of the first month began he to go up from Babylon, and on the first *day* of the fifth month came he to Jerusalem, [e]according to the good hand of his God upon him.

10 For Ezra had prepared his heart to [f]seek the law of the LORD, and to do *it,* and to [g]teach in Israel statutes and judgments.

11 ¶ Now this *is* the copy of the letter that the king Artaxerxes gave unto Ezra the priest, the scribe, *even* a scribe of the words of the commandments of the LORD, and of his statutes to Israel.

12 Artaxerxes, [h]king of kings, unto Ezra the priest, a scribe of the law of the God of heaven, perfect *peace,* [i]and at such a time.

13 I make a decree, that all they of the people of Israel, and *of* his priests and Levites, in my realm, which are minded of their own freewill to go up to Jerusalem, go with thee.

14 Forasmuch as thou art sent of the king, and of his [j]seven counsellors, to enquire concerning Judah and Jerusalem, according to the law of thy God which *is* in thine hand;

15 And to carry the silver and gold, which the king and his counsellors have freely offered unto the God of Israel, [k]whose habitation *is* in Jerusalem,

16 [l]And all the silver and gold that thou canst find in all the province of Babylon, with the freewill offering of the people, and of the priests, [m]offering willingly for the house of their God which *is* in Jerusalem:

17 That thou mayest buy speedily with this money bullocks, rams, lambs, with their [n]meat offerings and their drink offerings, and [o]offer them upon the altar of the house of your God which *is* in Jerusalem.

18 And whatsoever shall seem good to thee, and to thy brethren, to do with the rest of the silver and the gold, that do after the will of your God.

19 The vessels also that are given thee for the service of the house of thy God, *those* deliver thou before the God of Jerusalem.

20 And whatsoever more shall be needful for the house of thy God, which thou shalt have occasion to bestow, bestow *it* out of the king's treasure house.

21 And I, *even* I Artaxerxes the king, do make a decree to all the treasurers which *are* beyond the river, that whatsoever Ezra the priest, the scribe of the law of the God of heaven, shall require of you, it be done speedily,

22 Unto an hundred talents of silver, and to an hundred measures of wheat, and to an hundred baths of wine, and to an hundred baths of oil, and salt without prescribing *how much.*

23 Whatsoever is commanded by the God of heaven, let it be diligently done for the house of the God of heaven: for why should there be wrath against the realm of the king and his sons?

24 Also we certify you, that touching any of the priests and Levites, singers, porters, Nethinims, or ministers of this house of God, it shall not be lawful to impose toll, tribute, or custom, upon them.

25 And thou, Ezra, after the wisdom of thy God, that *is* in thine hand, [p]set magistrates and judges, which may judge all the people that *are* beyond the river, all such as know the laws of thy God; and [q]teach ye them that know *them* not.

26 And whosoever will not do the law of thy God, and the law of the king, let judgment be executed speedily upon him, whether *it be* unto death, or to banishment, or to confiscation of goods, or to imprisonment.

27 ¶ [r]Blessed *be* the LORD God of our fathers, [s]which hath put *such a thing* as this in the king's heart, to beautify the house of the LORD which *is* in Jerusalem:

28 And [t]hath extended mercy unto me before the king, and his counsellors, and before all the king's mighty princes. And I was strengthened as [u]the hand of the LORD my God *was* upon me, and I gathered together out of Israel chief men to go up with me.

8 These *are* now the chief of their fathers, and *this is* the genealogy of them that went up with me from Babylon, in the reign of Artaxerxes the king.

2 Of the sons of Phinehas; Gershom: of

6:21 [t]ch. 9:11
6:22 [u]Ex. 12:15; 2 Chron. 30:21 [v]Prov. 21:1 [w]2 Kings 23:29; 2 Chron. 33:11; ch. 1:1
7:1 [x]Neh. 2:1 [y]1 Chron. 6:14
7:6 [z]ver. 11 [a]ver. 9; ch. 8:22
7:7 [b]ch. 8:1 [c]ch. 8:15 [d]ch. 2:43
7:9 [e]ver. 6; Neh. 2:8
7:10 [f]Ps. 119:45 [g]ver. 6; Deut. 33:10; Neh. 8:1-8; Mal. 2:7
7:12 [h]Ezek. 26:7; Dan. 2:37 [i]ch. 4:10
7:14 [j]Esth. 1:14
7:15 [k]2 Chron. 6:2; Ps. 135:21
7:16 [l]ch. 8:25 [m]1 Chron. 29:6
7:17 [n]Num. 15:4-13 [o]Deut. 12:5
7:25 [p]Ex. 18:21; Deut. 16:18 [q]ver. 10; 2 Chron. 17:7; Mal. 2:7; Matt. 23:2
7:27 [r]1 Chron. 29:10 [s]ch. 6:22
7:28 [t]ch. 9:9 [u]ch. 5:5

the sons of Ithamar; Daniel: of the sons of David; [v]Hattush.

3 Of the sons of Shechaniah, of the sons of [w]Pharosh; Zechariah: and with him were reckoned by genealogy of the males an hundred and fifty.

4 Of the sons of Pahath-moab; Elihoenai the son of Zerahiah, and with him two hundred males.

5 Of the sons of Shechaniah; the son of Jahaziel, and with him three hundred males.

6 Of the sons also of Adin; Ebed the son of Jonathan, and with him fifty males.

7 And of the sons of Elam; Jeshaiah the son of Athaliah, and with him seventy males.

8 And of the sons of Shephatiah; Zebadiah the son of Michael, and with him fourscore males.

9 Of the sons of Joab; Obadiah the son of Jehiel, and with him two hundred and eighteen males.

10 And of the sons of Shelomith; the son of Josiphiah, and with him an hundred and threescore males.

11 And of the sons of Bebai; Zechariah the son of Bebai, and with him twenty and eight males.

12 And of the sons of Azgad; Johanan the son of Hakkatan, and with him an hundred and ten males.

13 And of the last sons of Adonikam, whose names *are* these, Eliphelet, Jeiel, and Shemaiah, and with them threescore males.

14 Of the sons also of Bigvai; Uthai, and Zabbud, and with them seventy males.

15 ¶ And I gathered them together to the river that runneth to Ahava; and there abode we in tents three days: and I viewed the people, and the priests, and found there none of the [x]sons of Levi.

16 Then sent I for Eliezer, for Ariel, for Shemaiah, and for Elnathan, and for Jarib, and for Elnathan, and for Nathan, and for Zechariah, and for Meshullam, chief men; also for Joiarib, and for Elnathan, men of understanding.

17 And I sent them with commandment unto Iddo the chief at the place Casiphia, and I told them what they should say unto Iddo, *and* to his brethren the Nethinims, at the place Casiphia, that they should bring unto us ministers for the house of our God.

18 And by the good hand of our God upon us they [y]brought us a man of understanding, of the sons of Mahli, the son of Levi, the son of Israel; and Sherebiah, with his sons and his brethren, eighteen;

19 And Hashabiah, and with him Jeshaiah of the sons of Merari, his brethren and their sons, twenty;

20 [z]Also of the Nethinims, whom David and the princes had appointed for the service of the Levites, two hundred and twenty Nethinims: all of them were expressed by name.

21 ¶ Then I [a]proclaimed a fast there, at the river of Ahava, that we might [b]afflict ourselves before our God, to seek of him a [c]right way for us, and for our little ones, and for all our substance.

22 For [d]I was ashamed to require of the king a band of soldiers and horsemen to help us against the enemy in the way: because we had spoken unto the king, saying, [e]The hand of our God *is* upon all them for [f]good that seek him; but his power and his wrath *is* [g]against all them that [h]forsake him.

23 So we fasted and besought our God for this: and he was [i]entreated of us.

24 ¶ Then I separated twelve of the chief of the priests, Sherebiah, Hashabiah, and ten of their brethren with them,

25 And weighed unto them [j]the silver, and the gold, and the vessels, *even* the offering of the house of our God, which the king, and his counsellors, and his lords, and all Israel *there* present, had offered:

26 I even weighed unto their hand six hundred and fifty talents of silver, and silver vessels an hundred talents, *and* of gold an hundred talents;

27 Also twenty basons of gold, of a thousand drams; and two vessels of fine copper, precious as gold.

28 And I said unto them, Ye *are* [k]holy unto the LORD; the vessels *are* [l]holy also; and the silver and the gold *are* a freewill offering unto the LORD God of your fathers.

29 Watch ye, and keep *them,* until ye weigh *them* before the chief of the priests and the Levites, and chief of the fathers of Israel, at Jerusalem, in the chambers of the house of the LORD.

30 So took the priests and the Levites the weight of the silver, and the gold, and the vessels, to bring *them* to Jerusalem unto the house of our God.

31 ¶ Then we departed from the river of Ahava on the twelfth *day* of the first month, to go unto Jerusalem: and [m]the hand of our God was upon us, and he delivered us from the hand of the enemy, and of such as lay in wait by the way.

32 And we [n]came to Jerusalem, and abode there three days.

33 ¶ Now on the fourth day was the silver and the gold and the vessels [o]weighed in the house of our God by the hand of Meremoth the son of Uriah the priest; and with him *was* Eleazar the son of Phinehas; and with them *was* Jozabad the son of Jeshua, and Noadiah the son of Binnui, Levites;

34 By number *and* by weight of every one: and all the weight was written at that time.

35 *Also* the children of those that had been carried away, which were come out of the captivity, [p]offered burnt offerings unto the God of Israel, twelve bullocks for all Israel, ninety and six rams, seventy and seven lambs, twelve he goats *for* a sin offering: all *this was* a burnt offering unto the LORD.

36 ¶ And they delivered the king's [q]commissions unto the king's lieutenants, and to

8:2 [v]1 Chron. 3:22
8:3 [w]ch. 2:3
8:15 [x]ch. 7:7
8:18 [y]Neh. 8:7
8:20 [z]ch. 2:43
8:21 [a]2 Chron. 20:3 [b]Lev. 16:29; Isa. 58:3 [c]Ps. 5:8
8:22 [d]1 Cor. 9:15 [e]ch. 7:6 [f]Ps. 33:18; Rom. 8:28 [g]Ps. 34:16 [h]2 Chron. 15:2
8:23 [i]1 Chron. 5:20; 2 Chron. 33:13; Isa. 19:22
8:25 [j]ch. 7:15
8:28 [k]Lev. 21:6; Deut. 33:8 [l]Lev. 22:2; Num. 4:4
8:31 [m]ch. 7:6
8:32 [n]Neh. 2:11
8:33 [o]ver. 26
8:35 [p]ch. 6:17
8:36 [q]ch. 7:21

the governors on this side the river: and
they furthered the people, and the house of
God.

9 Now when these things were done, the
princes came to me, saying, The people
of Israel, and the priests, and the Levites,
have not [r]separated themselves from the
people of the lands, [s]*doing* according to
their abominations, *even* of the Canaanites,
the Hittites, the Perizzites, the Jebusites, the
Ammonites, the Moabites, the Egyptians,
and the Amorites.
2 For they have [t]taken of their daughters
for themselves, and for their sons: so that
the [u]holy seed have [v]mingled themselves
with the people of *those* lands: yea, the
hand of the princes and rulers hath been
chief in this trespass.
3 And when I heard this thing, [w]I rent my
garment and my mantle, and plucked off
the hair of my head and of my beard, and
sat down [x]astonied.
4 Then were assembled unto me every
one that [y]trembled at the words of the God
of Israel, because of the transgression of
those that had been carried away; and I sat
astonied until the [z]evening sacrifice.
5 ¶ And at the evening sacrifice I arose up
from my heaviness; and having rent my
garment and my mantle, I fell upon my
knees, and [a]spread out my hands unto the
LORD my God,
6 And said, O my God, I am [b]ashamed
and blush to lift up my face to thee, my God:
for [c]our iniquities are increased over *our*
head, and our trespass is [d]grown up unto
the heavens.
7 Since the days of our fathers *have* [e]we
been in a great trespass unto this day; and
for our iniquities [f]have we, our kings, *and*
our priests, been delivered into the hand of
the kings of the lands, to the sword, to captivity, and to a spoil, and to [g]confusion of
face, as *it is* this day.
8 And now for a little space grace hath
been *shewed* from the LORD our God, to
leave us a remnant to escape, and to give us
a nail in his holy place, that our God may
[h]lighten our eyes, and give us a little reviving in our bondage.
9 [i]For we *were* bondmen; [j]yet our God
hath not forsaken us in our bondage, but
[k]hath extended mercy unto us in the sight
of the kings of Persia, to give us a reviving,
to set up the house of our God, and to repair
the desolations thereof, and to give us [l]a
wall in Judah and in Jerusalem.
10 And now, O our God, what shall we
say after this? for we have forsaken thy
commandments,
11 Which thou hast commanded by thy
servants the prophets, saying, The land,
unto which ye go to possess it, is an unclean
land with the [m]filthiness of the people of the
lands, with their abominations, which have
filled it from one end to another with their
uncleanness.
12 Now therefore [n]give not your daughters unto their sons, neither take their
daughters unto your sons, [o]nor seek their
peace or their wealth for ever: that ye may
be strong, and eat the good of the land, and
[p]leave *it* for an inheritance to your children
for ever.
13 And after all that is come upon us for
our evil deeds, and for our great trespass,
seeing that thou our God [q]hast punished us
less than our iniquities *deserve,* and hast
given us *such* deliverance as this;
14 Should we [r]again break thy commandments, and [s]join in affinity with the
people of these abominations? wouldest not
thou be [t]angry with us till thou hadst consumed *us,* so that *there should be* no remnant nor escaping?
15 O LORD God of Israel, [u]thou *art* righteous: for we remain yet escaped, as *it is*
this day: behold, we *are* [v]before thee [w]in
our trespasses: for we cannot [x]stand before
thee because of this.

10 Now [y]when Ezra had prayed, and
when he had confessed, weeping and
casting himself down [z]before the house of
God, there assembled unto him out of Israel
a very great congregation of men and
women and children: for the people wept
very sore.
2 And Shechaniah the son of Jehiel, *one*
of the sons of Elam, answered and said unto
Ezra, We have [a]trespassed against our
God, and have taken strange wives of the
people of the land: yet now there is hope in
Israel concerning this thing.
3 Now therefore let us make a [b]covenant
with our God to put away all the wives, and
such as are born of them, according to the
counsel of my lord, and of those that [c]trem-
ble at [d]the commandment of our God; and
let it be done according to the law.
4 Arise; for *this* matter *belongeth* unto
thee: we also *will be* with thee: [e]be of good
courage, and do *it.*
5 Then arose Ezra, and made the chief
priests, the Levites, and all Israel, [f]to swear
that they should do according to this word.
And they sware.
6 ¶ Then Ezra rose up from before the
house of God, and went into the chamber of
Johanan the son of Eliashib: and *when* he
came thither, he [g]did eat no bread, nor
drink water: for he mourned because of the
transgression of them that had been carried
away.
7 And they made proclamation throughout Judah and Jerusalem unto all the children of the captivity, that they should
gather themselves together unto Jerusalem;
8 And that whosoever would not come
within three days, according to the counsel
of the princes and the elders, all his substance should be forfeited, and himself separated from the congregation of those that
had been carried away.
9 ¶ Then all the men of Judah and Benjamin gathered themselves together unto Jerusalem within three days. It *was* the ninth

9:1 [r]ch. 6:21; Neh. 9:2 [s]Deut. 12:30
9:2 [t]Ex. 34:16; Deut. 7:3; Neh. 13:23 [u]Ex. 19:6; Deut. 7:6 [v]2 Cor. 6:14
9:3 [w]Job 1:20 [x]Ps. 143:4
9:4 [y]ch. 10:3; Isa. 66:2 [z]Ex. 29:39
9:5 [a]Ex. 9:29
9:6 [b]Dan. 9:7 [c]Ps. 38:4 [d]2 Chron. 28:9; Rev. 18:5
9:7 [e]Ps. 106:6; Dan. 9:5 [f]Deut. 28:36; Neh. 9:30 [g]Dan. 9:7
9:8 [h]Ps. 13:3
9:9 [i]Neh. 9:36 [j]Ps. 136:23 [k]ch. 7:28 [l]Isa. 5:2
9:11 [m]ch. 6:21
9:12 [n]Ex. 23:32; Deut. 7:3 [o]Deut. 23:6 [p]Prov. 13:22
9:13 [q]Ps. 103:10
9:14 [r]John 5:14; 2 Pet. 2:20 [s]ver. 2; Neh. 13:23 [t]Deut. 9:8
9:15 [u]Neh. 9:33; Dan. 9:14 [v]Rom. 3:19 [w]1 Cor. 15:17 [x]Ps. 130:3
10:1 [y]Dan. 9:20 [z]2 Chron. 20:9
10:2 [a]Neh. 13:27
10:3 [b]2 Chron. 34:31 [c]ch. 9:4 [d]Deut. 7:2
10:4 [e]1 Chron. 28:10
10:5 [f]Neh. 5:12
10:6 [g]Deut. 9:18

FOCUS ON EZRA AND NEHEMIAH

The Books of Ezra and Nehemiah look at the rebuilding of a nation after it has been in exile. King Cyrus, the king of Persia, decrees that the people are to go back to Jerusalem and rebuild the house of God. Fifty years have gone by since the Babylonians had destroyed the city of Jerusalem and sent its inhabitants off in shame. These acts of devastation altered the ways in which Israel had come to think of herself. Everything that had symbolized security was gone. There was no more monarchy. The land was taken and controlled by foreigners. The political, social, and religious climates were different. The dwelling place, which housed the name of God, was destroyed. Who were the returning exiles? How would the rebuilding take shape? Who were the women who once again were called upon to help repopulate the nation, replant the vineyards, and rebuild the family structures?

Jewish women take on a central character as Ezra calls the nation to repentance for its accepted practice of interethnic marriages. "Now therefore make confession unto the LORD God of your fathers, and do his pleasure: and separate yourselves from the people of the land, and from the strange wives" (Ezra 10:11). "Intermarriage endangered the physical as well as spiritual boundaries of the community. A non-Jewish partner who had legal control over property could rejoin the ethnic community of origin and remove land from Jewish jurisdiction. Children of such marriages could do likewise, reducing the actual land belonging to the Jewish community and hence the province of Judah" (*WBC*, 117).

As both "scribes" focus on the "new ways" of community reshaping in post-exilic times, a listing of the returnees is found in chapter two. Verse 55 lists the descendants of Sophereth, a name that is translated "the female scribe." Verse 61 of the listing recorded Barzillai—a man who had married a daughter of Barzillai, the Gileadite and was called by that name. Here we find that some males relinquished their family name for that of their wives, presumably for the wives' family inheritance!

If you read fast, it is possible to skip the lines in verses 64–67 that read: "The whole congregation together was forty and two thousand three hundred and threescore, Besides their servants and their maids of whom there were seven thousand three hundred thirty and seven: and there were among them two hundred singing men and singing women." Listed right after this the animals are numbered, which could cause a person to infer that the singers had very little value. However, they are numbered and named!

Women are given no voice in either of these books. However, it should be noted that their labors are listed in the record of Nehemiah 3:12: "Next unto him repaired Shallum the son of Halohesh, the ruler of the half part of Jerusalem, he and his daughters." And in Nehemiah 6:14, as the man of God labors on the wall and asks for God's intervention with those who try to intimidate him and stop his work, we find the name of "the prophetess

Noadiah." She is one of a handful of women named in Scripture as a prophet. (Miriam, Deborah, and Huldah come before the Exile. Anna is a New Testament prophet.) Why she contended against Nehemiah is not known.

In rebuilding the city, the infrastructures of governance, it is not surprising that the labor of women is noted. We see the hand of God bringing a covenanted people back to a right relationship with Himself throughout the books of Ezra and Nehemiah—from when the exiles began returning to their homeland to when they built an altar to the God of Israel, from when they resumed proper worship of God to when the rebuilt the walls of Jerusalem under Nehemiah's leadership.

THE BLACK PRESENCE IN EZRA AND NEHEMIAH

After the rebuilding of the temple, worship is reestablished. Furniture constructed and used in the tabernacle for worship was patterned after furniture found among other African-Egyptian countries. God certainly gave specific instructions to Moses on how to construct the tabernacle, but His instructions included furniture that resembled that in Egypt (see *NIV Study Bible*, 124, 126).

Leaders in the land came to Ezra complaining that the Israelites, including the Levites, had intermarried with the people of the land: the Canaanites, Hittites, Perizzites, Jebusites, Ammonites, Moabites, Egyptians, and Amorites (Ezra 9). All of these people, with the possible exception of the Ammonites and Moabites, were descendants of Ham, with Egypt being equivalent to Mizraim (Gen. 10:6–15). More than 100 men had married these foreign black women (Ezra 10).

Life Lessons

EZRA 1–2

Chapters one and two chronicle Cyrus, king of Persia, as a foreigner, Gentile, nonbeliever, outsider, and infidel! Yet it is recorded: "Now in the first year of Cyrus king of Persia, that the word of the LORD by the mouth of Jeremiah might be fulfilled, the LORD stirred up the spirit of Cyrus king of Persia, that he made a proclamation throughout all his kingdom, and put it also in writing, saying, Thus saith Cyrus king of Persia, The LORD God of heaven hath given me all the kingdoms of the earth; and he hath charged me to build him an house at Jerusalem, which is in Judah. . . . And whosoever remaineth in any place where he sojourneth, let the men of his place help him with silver, and with gold, and with goods, and with beasts, beside the freewill offering for the house of God that is in Jerusalem" (1:1–4).

Again, it is made perfectly clear that God will use anyone and anything to fulfill His purpose. When the people of God decide to worship idols, God raises up an "idol worshiper" with a mind to build a temple in Jerusalem! What Israel is unable to accomplish will be accomplish at the hand of a foreign king. The whole earth belongs to God! God gets the glory and the temple despite who "thinks" they own it. In the same manner that

the portable tabernacle in the wilderness was to be furnished by the "freewill offerings" that the Israelites collected from the Egyptians before the Exodus, once again the people are to bring the Lord an offering. God may not look like, act like, or be like what you expect. God will come disguised in "foreigners." Zerubbabel, a priest, began the work (3:8–9) and worship was restored. "So that the people could not discern the noise of the shout of joy from the noise of the weeping people: for the people shouted with a loud shout, and the noise was heard afar off" (v. 13).

Supplier of Every Need, help me to remember that my needs may be supplied by what is "foreign" to me. Any way You choose to bless me, let me receive it with gratitude.

EZRA 7–10

Despite opposition from diverse "ruling" factions and delays, the temple is rebuilt and dedicated. Ezra is "a ready scribe in the law of Moses, which the LORD God of Israel had given" (7:6). The king had granted him everything he asked, for the hand of the Lord was upon him. Ezra had devoted himself to the study and observance of the Law of the Lord, and to teaching its decrees and laws in Israel (vv. 1–10). And God speaks to Ezra about intermarriage: "The people of Israel, and the priests, and the Levites, have not separated themselves from the people of the lands, doing according to their abominations . . . they have taken of their daughters for themselves, and for their sons: so that the hold seed have mingled themselves with the people of those lands: yea, the hand of the princes and rulers hath chief in this trespass" (9:1–2). The people confess their sin: "We have trespassed against our God, and have taken strange wives of the people of the land: yet now there is hope in Israel concerning this thing" (10:2). "Then the congregation answered and said with a loud voice, As thou hast said, so must we do. . . . Let now our rulers of all the congregation stand, and let them which have taken strange wives in our cities come at appointed times . . . until the fierce wrath of our God for this matter be turned from us" (vv. 12–15). The Book of Ezra ends with a listing of all of the "guilty" parties.

Holy One, help me to remain alert and caring of those in the world around me. Keep me sensitive to those who have not yet come into the knowledge of You. And keep me separate from them in the ways I think and behave, so that I might influence them with my love for You.

NEHEMIAH 1–5

Chapters 1–2 outline the process of Nehemiah's preparation to rebuild the wall of Jerusalem. Chapters 3–5 show the building process and the opposition to that process. "They said unto me, The remnant that are left of the captivity there in the province are in great affliction and reproach: the wall of Jerusalem also is broken down, and the gates thereof are burned with fire. And it came to pass, when I heard these words, that I sat down and wept" (1:3–4). Nehemiah had a good job in the palace as the king's cupbearer. Yet he was distressed about the conditions of his homeland. His employer, King Artaxerxes, sent him to Jerusalem as the newly appointed governor to rebuild the city's walls. Faced with opposition and delay as he inspects the wall, Nehemiah declares to several of his critics: "The God of heaven, he will prosper us; therefore we his servants will arise and build:

but ye have not portion, nor right, nor memorial, in Jerusalem" (2:19–20).

Rebuilder of Torn and Burned Places, when others are working and I can't join in the labor, assist me with keeping my mouth shut so that I don't forfeit my share in Your generous rewards.

NEHEMIAH 6–13

The wall is completed (6:15). The doors to the gates are set in place. The gatekeepers, singers, and Levites are appointed. Guards are posted. "Now the city was large and great: but the people were few therein, and the houses were not builded. And my God put into mine heart to gather together the nobles, and the rulers, and the people, that they might be reckoned by genealogy of them which came up at the first, and found written therein" (7:4–5). "Upon the first day of the seventh month. And he read therein before the street that was before the water gate from the morning until midday, before the men and women, and those that could understand; and the ears of all the people were attentive unto the book of the law. . . . And all the people answered, Amen, Amen, with lifting up their hands: and they bowed their heads, and worshipped the LORD with their faces to the ground" (8:2–6). The people join in fasting, prayer and confession of their sin. In chapter nine, a signed agreement to keep the Law is enabled.

In chapter 10, the city of Jerusalem is repopulated. In chapter 11, the wall is dedicated. In chapters 12 and 13, new reforms by Ezra and Nehemiah are established.

Remember me, O my God, for good (Neh. 13:31).

FOCUS ON ESTHER

We know her as the queen who declared, "Will I go in unto the king, which is not according to the law: and if I perish, I perish" (4:16). Yet there is more to her than this often repeated declaration. This woman, a queen, is "passing" for the position she holds. It was Mordecai, her Jewish male relative, who told her to "pass." She was not to reveal her Jewish heritage, but to remain quiet during the national beauty contest. "Passing" is no new or recent tradition. Keeping quiet about one's identity has preserved many lives! Esther had no living parents.

We recognize that Esther was beautiful. We understand that she was no fool. And, we need to be aware that she was groomed for over a year in the art of pleasing the king. We don't know whether Esther went to the king's harem voluntarily. So in her actions, Esther teaches us how to make the best of bad situations. She instructs us in womanly wisdom, which was not taught in the courses that she was required to take. She helps us to realize that beauty is only skin deep. Wisdom comes from God!

Esther was in the right place at the right time. She did the right things for the right reasons. She saved her entire nation because she refused to "pass" on her relationship with God!

THE BLACK PRESENCE IN ESTHER

King Ahasuerus of Persia ruled from Ethiopia to India, from 486–465 B.C. (Esther 1:1). His sovereignty included north Africa, northeast Africa, Arabia, Asia, Mesopotamia, and India. Descendants of Ham and Shem, specifically Cushites, peopled all these lands.

Life Lessons

ESTHER 1

Vashti refuses to be viewed as an object for her husband, Xerxes. When she embarrasses him after he orders her to parade before his drunken associates, he has this reaction: "Therefore was the king very wroth, and his anger burned in him" (1:12). In consultation with his "wise men, which knew the times, (for so was the king's manner toward all that knew law and judgment" (v. 13). One spoke the truth: "Vashti the queen hath not done wrong to the king only, but also to all the princes, and to all the people that are in all the provinces of the king . . . Likewise shall the ladies of Persia and Media say this day unto all the king's princes, which have heard of the deed of the queen. Thus shall there arise too much contempt and wrath. If it please the king, let there go a royal commandment from him . . . that Vashti come no more before king Ahasuerus; and let the king give her royal estate unto another that is better than she" (vv. 16, 18–19).

Vashti's refusal sets the stage for a drunken group of "little boys" to become upset that their personal "kingdoms" may come tumbling down around their feet if their wives behave in this insulting and unseemly manner. Her name is to be stricken from the royal records as if she never existed! Yet, her refusal opens the way for God to move on behalf of the Israelites, who are living in exile without voice or land. Once again, God chooses to allow a foreigner—a woman—to be a vessel for bringing about deliverance as part of a greater plan.

Divine Planner, people come and go from the stage of life. Just allow me to play my role, with quiet strength and dignity.

ESTHER 2

"Let there be fair young virgins sought for the king: And let the king appoint officers in all the provinces of his kingdom, that they may gather together all the fair young virgins unto Shushan the palace, to the house of the women, unto the custody of Hege the king's chamberlain, keeper of women; and let their things for purification be given to them: And let the maiden which pleaseth the king be queen instead of Vashti. And the thing pleased the king; and he did so" (2:2–4). The search for a new queen begins. We meet Mordecai and his ward, Hadassah, both of whom are exiles from Jerusalem, and Mordecai has his own plans for Hadassah, whose Persian name is Esther. "He brought up Hadassah, that is, Esther, his uncle's daughter: for she had neither father nor mother, and the maid was fair and beautiful; whom Mordecai, when her father and mother were

dead, took for his own daughter" (v. 7). Esther is taken with other young women to the palace. She does not reveal her nationality, because Mordecai warns her not to do so." Mordecai walked every day before the court of the women's house, to know how Esther did, and what should become of her" (v. 11). A twelve-month beauty regimen is required for her training (v. 12). Then the young women are turned over to the eunuch in charge of the concubines (v. 14). Esther wins the favor of all (v. 15). Since she pleases the king, she becomes his queen (v. 17). Meanwhile, while Mordecai sits at the king's gates, he discovers a plot to kill the king. He reports the plot to Esther, who tells the king (vv. 21–23).

God who sees inward beauty, let me win favor in Your sight.

ESTHER 3–4

In chapter three, we meet Haman, a descendent of Agag, the king of the Amalekites, the most bitter enemy of the Jews. Haman is promoted higher than all the other nobles. Everyone kneels down to pay him homage with the exception of Mordecai. "When Haman saw that Mordecai bowed not, nor did him reverence, then was Haman full of wrath. And he thought scorn to lay hands on Mordecai alone; for they had shewed him the people of Mordecai: wherefore Haman sought to destroy all the Jews that were throughout the whole kingdom of Ahasuerus, even the people of Mordecai" (3:5). Haman reveals his plot to the king who gives it his stamp of approval. "Do with them as it seemeth good to thee" (v. 11). This is an attempt at ethnic cleansing at its ultimate. But, God provides a way of escape with Esther. In chapter four, Mordecai proceeds to remind Esther of her ethnic identity. "Think not with thyself that thou shalt escape in the king's house, more than all the Jews. For if thou altogether holdest thy peace at this time, then shall there enlargement and deliverance arise to the Jews from another place; but thou and thy father's house shall be destroyed: and who knoweth whether thou are come to the kingdom for such a time as this?" (4:13–14). Esther calls for a national fast among the Jews. She makes her declaration to go and see the king even though it may cause her to lose her life.

Bodacious God, the righteous are as bold as a lion. Let my roar be heard where needed today.

ESTHER 5

Knowing that Xerxes is an emotional man and not a rational thinker, Esther resorts to the old adage, "The way to a mans heart is through his stomach." She prepares a meal and invites both the king and Haman to attend. They come as she bids. While she's planning the meal, Haman is instructed by his wife, Zeresh, and all of his friends: "Let a gallows be made of fifty cubits high, and to morrow speak thou unto the king that Mordecai may be hanged thereon: then go thou in merrily with the king unto the banquet. And the thing pleased Haman; and he caused the gallows to be made" (5:14).

Great God, I hear You say, "When you dig a ditch, dig two. One for Your enemy; the other one for You!" Help me not to dig ditches!

ESTHER 6–9

A restless king gets up in the night and has the Book of Chronicles read to him. He decides to honor Mordecai. He asks Haman how to honor a worthy man. Haman thinks of himself as the worthy man and suggests a parade of pomp and circumstance. The king agrees. The God of irony has the king instruct Haman to parade Mordecai through the town! As Haman is lamenting this sad state of affairs, the eunuchs come to hurry him to Queen Esther's feast. At the feast, she tells the king of the plight of her people, the Jews. "Then Haman was afraid before the king and queen. And the king rising from the banquet of wine in his wrath went into the palace garden" (7:6–7). While the king is out, Haman throws himself on the mercy of Queen Esther, pleading for his life. The king reenters the room and accuses Haman of the attempted sexual assault of his queen. Haman later is hanged on the gallows he had prepared for Mordecai (vv. 8–10). The king makes this decree: "Behold, I have given Esther the house of Haman, and him they have hanged upon the gallows, because he laid his hand upon the Jews" (8:7). That decree is followed by another one: "The king granted the Jews which were in every city to gather themselves together, and to stand for their life, . . . And many of the people of the land became Jews; for the fear of the Jews fell upon them" (vv. 11, 17). The Jews are victorious. The holy day of Purim is instituted to signify this national day of rejoicing. It is an edict of the queen! (9:32).

Women in ESTHER

QUEEN VASHTI: A WOMAN OF STRENGTH

King Ahasuerus, the ruler of 127 provinces (from India to Ethiopia), celebrated his third year as ruler and gave a banquet for all his underlings. He and local leaders partied for 180 days—which is six months. This means six months of drinking, telling tall tales, and more drinking—plus whatever unmentionables they thought they were big enough to do. Their "after party" lasted seven days. Once everyone was good and drunk, as tradition says, they were then ready to make some decisions.

While the men became drunk at their own party, Queen Vashti gave a party for the women. On the seventh day of the after party, the king sent seven eunuchs to get Queen Vashti. She was told to come to the men's party wearing the royal crown. She was his trophy and he wanted to show her off.

The eunuchs came to the queen to deliver King Ahasuerus' message, but she would not come. She would not be made to look like a fool to these provincial women, to whom she was an example of all that a woman could be. She was not ignorant of the price she would have to pay, but she was willing to challenge the king's drunken foolishness in order to be true to herself. This woman was a strong sister—willing to take a chance for the good that she might be able to do for those who came behind her.

Sometimes we have to step out there and be an example so that those

who follow will know what can be done. Strength and wisdom are qualities which each of us needs to deal with one another wherever God has placed us.

We have but to remember our history: Hatshepsut, the queen of far antiquity; the beautiful warrior queen Makeda; Ann Zingha, the amazon queen of Matamba, West Africa; Sojourner Truth; Harriet Tubman; Mary McLeod Bethune; Marian Anderson; Barbara Jordan; Fannie Lou Hamer; and Rosa Parks, among others.

Read Esther 1–2.

Read the insight essays on Influence and Submission.

—M. Bellinger

Insights

LEADERSHIP: BRICK BY BRICK, TOGETHER

To see a model of leadership within the biblical text, read the Book of Nehemiah. Nehemiah exhibited organizational and administrative gifts. He was a man who knew how to conceptualize a job, organize the work and the workers, and—in spite of obstacles and naysayers—persist until the task was completed.

Someone once asked, "How do you eat an elephant?" The answer is one bite at a time. This brings to mind other questions: How do you rebuild a wall? Brick by brick. How do you restore a community? School by school, church by church, home by home, business by business. How do you restore a people? One child, one family, one soul at a time! People are more important than the task!

Nehemiah took a holistic approach to the restoration of Jerusalem. While rebuilding the wall was his initial project, he knew that the rebuilding process would not be complete until the people restored their relationship with God. We, the women of the African American community, must also take a holistic approach to restoring our communities. Restoring the institutions, our walls, is necessary to make our communities economically viable and financially stable. But restoring the institutions is not the only issue. Until the people have restored their relationship with God, the rebuilding process is incomplete—a patchwork solution at best.

As we seek to be equal partners in Nehemiah's "business plan," we must be willing to do our part to not only lay bricks, but also to lay a spiritual foundation for our children, our families and our neighbors. "Let us arise up and build. . . . [For] the God of heaven, he will prosper us" (Neh. 2:18, 20).

Leadership is an awesome responsibility. Leaders must seek godly counsel (Prov. 15:22), work willingly and energetically with others, and posses a servant's heart (Prov. 3:27). Let us work together, prayer by prayer, side by side, brick by brick. Nehemiah knew that it "would take a village," the whole village—men and women, sons and daughters—to get the work done. Let those of us with a mind to work get busy.

Read Nehemiah 2:17–20; Psalm 23; 122:6–9.

—D. Johnson

month, on the twentieth *day* of the month;
and [h]all the people sat in the street of the
house of God, trembling because of *this*
matter, and for the great rain.
10 And Ezra the priest stood up, and said
unto them, Ye have transgressed, and have
taken strange wives, to increase the trespass of Israel.
11 Now therefore [i]make confession unto
the LORD God of your fathers, and do his
pleasure: and [j]separate yourselves from
the people of the land, and from the strange
wives.
12 Then all the congregation answered
and said with a loud voice, As thou hast
said, so must we do.
13 But the people *are* many, and *it is* a
time of much rain, and we are not able to
stand without, neither *is this* a work of one
day or two: for we are many that have transgressed in this thing.
14 Let now our rulers of all the congregation stand, and let all them which have
taken strange wives in our cities come at
appointed times, and with them the elders
of every city, and the judges thereof, until
[k]the fierce wrath of our God for this matter
be turned from us.
15 ¶ Only Jonathan the son of Asahel and
Jahaziah the son of Tikvah were employed
about this *matter:* and Meshullam and
Shabbethai the Levite helped them.
16 And the children of the captivity did
so. And Ezra the priest, *with* certain chief of
the fathers, after the house of their fathers,
and all of them by *their* names, were separated, and sat down in the first day of the
tenth month to examine the matter.
17 And they made an end with all the men
that had taken strange wives by the first
day of the first month.
18 ¶ And among the sons of the priests
there were found that had taken strange
wives: *namely,* of the sons of Jeshua the son
of Jozadak, and his brethren; Maaseiah,
and Eliezer, and Jarib, and Gedaliah.
19 And they [l]gave their hands that they
would put away their wives; and *being*
[m]guilty, *they offered* a ram of the flock for
their trespass.
20 And of the sons of Immer; Hanani, and
Zebadiah.
21 And of the sons of Harim; Maaseiah,
and Elijah, and Shemaiah, and Jehiel, and
Uzziah.
22 And of the sons of Pashur; Elioenai,
Maaseiah, Ishmael, Nethaneel, Jozabad,
and Elasah.
23 Also of the Levites; Jozabad, and
Shimei, and Kelaiah, (the same *is* Kelita,)
Pethahiah, Judah, and Eliezer.
24 Of the singers also; Eliashib: and of the
porters; Shallum, and Telem, and Uri.
25 Moreover of Israel: of the sons of Parosh; Ramiah, and Jeziah, and Malchiah,
and Miamin, and Eleazar, and Malchijah,
and Benaiah.
26 And of the sons of Elam; Mattaniah,
Zechariah, and Jehiel, and Abdi, and Jeremoth, and Eliah.
27 And of the sons of Zattu; Elioenai, Eliashib, Mattaniah, and Jeremoth, and Zabad, and Aziza.
28 Of the sons also of Bebai; Jehohanan,
Hananiah, Zabbai, *and* Athlai.
29 And of the sons of Bani; Meshullam,
Malluch, and Adaiah, Jashub, and Sheal,
and Ramoth.
30 And of the sons of Pahath-moab;
Adna, and Chelal, Benaiah, Maaseiah, Mattaniah, Bezaleel, and Binnui, and Manasseh.
31 And *of* the sons of Harim; Eliezer, Ishi-
jah, Malchiah, Shemaiah, Shimeon,
32 Benjamin, Malluch, *and* Shemariah.
33 Of the sons of Hashum; Mattenai, Mat-
tathah, Zabad, Eliphelet, Jeremai, Manasseh, *and* Shimei.
34 Of the sons of Bani; Maadai, Amram,
and Uel,
35 Benaiah, Bedeiah, Chelluh,
36 Vaniah, Meremoth, Eliashib,
37 Mattaniah, Mattenai, and Jaasau,
38 And Bani, and Binnui, Shimei,
39 And Shelemiah, and Nathan, and Adaiah,
40 Machnadebai, Shashai, Sharai,
41 Azareel, and Shelemiah, Shemariah,
42 Shallum, Amariah, *and* Joseph.
43 Of the sons of Nebo; Jeiel, Mattithiah,
Zabad, Zebina, Jadau, and Joel, Benaiah.
44 All these had taken strange wives: and
some of them had wives by whom they had
children.

10:9 *h*1 Sam. 12:18
10:11 *i*Josh. 7:19; Prov. 28:13 *j*ver. 3
10:14 *k*2 Chron. 30:8
10:19 *l*2 Kings 10:15; 1 Chron. 29:24; 2 Chron. 30:8 *m*Lev. 6:4

NEHEMIAH

Nehemiah is probably the writer of the book of Nehemiah, written sometime between 445 B.C. and 425 B.C. Nehemiah contains information on the rebuilding of the walls around Jerusalem with additional information about the reforms and reformations made during Nehemiah's and Ezra's lifetime. Some of the records concerning the rebuilding of the walls are quite detailed, including a list of the builders (Chapter 3). The wall building project had many critics; Nehemiah gives an account of the opposition in chapters 4-6.

I. Nehemiah and the return to Jerusalem, 1:1–2:10
II. Rebuilding the walls of Jerusalem, 2:11–7:73
III. Ezra brings reforms to the people, 8:1–10:39
IV. The nation is rebuilt, 11:1–12:47
V. Revival spreads, 13:1–13:31

1 The words of [a]Nehemiah the son of Hachaliah. And it came to pass in the month Chisleu, in the twentieth year, as I was in Shushan the palace,

2 That Hanani, one of my brethren, came, he and *certain* men of Judah; and I asked them concerning the Jews that had escaped, which were left of the captivity, and concerning Jerusalem.

3 And they said unto me, The remnant that are left of the captivity there in the province *are* in great affliction and reproach: [b]the wall of Jerusalem also [c]*is* broken down, and the gates thereof are burned with fire.

4 ¶ And it came to pass, when I heard these words, that I sat down and wept, and mourned *certain* days, and fasted, and prayed before the God of heaven,

5 And said, I beseech thee, [d]O LORD God of heaven, the great and terrible God, [e]that keepeth covenant and mercy for them that love him and observe his commandments:

6 Let thine ear now be attentive, and [f]thine eyes open, that thou mayest hear the prayer of thy servant, which I pray before thee now, day and night, for the children of Israel thy servants, and [g]confess the sins of the children of Israel, which we have sinned against thee: both I and my father's house have sinned.

7 [h]We have dealt very corruptly against thee, and have [i]not kept the commandments, nor the statutes, nor the judgments, which thou commandedst thy servant Moses.

8 Remember, I beseech thee, the word that thou commandedst thy servant Moses, saying, [j]*If* ye transgress, I will scatter you abroad among the nations:

9 [k]But *if* ye turn unto me, and keep my commandments, and do them; [l]though there were of you cast out unto the uttermost part of the heaven, *yet* will I gather them from thence, and will bring them unto the place that I have chosen to set my name there.

10 [m]Now these *are* thy servants and thy people, whom thou hast redeemed by thy great power, and by thy strong hand.

11 O Lord, I beseech thee, [n]let now thine ear be attentive to the prayer of thy servant, and to the prayer of thy servants, who [o]desire to fear thy name: and prosper, I pray thee, thy servant this day, and grant him mercy in the sight of this man. For I was the king's [p]cupbearer.

2 And it came to pass in the month Nisan, in the twentieth year of [q]Artaxerxes the king, *that* wine *was* before him: and [r]I took up the wine, and gave *it* unto the king. Now I had not been *beforetime* sad in his presence.

2 Wherefore the king said unto me, Why *is* thy countenance sad, seeing thou *art* not sick? this *is* nothing *else* but [s]sorrow of heart. Then I was very sore afraid,

3 And said unto the king, [t]Let the king live for ever: why should not my countenance be sad, when [u]the city, the place of my fathers' sepulchres, *lieth* waste, and the gates thereof are consumed with fire?

4 Then the king said unto me, For what dost thou make request? So I prayed to the God of heaven.

5 And I said unto the king, If it please the king, and if thy servant have found favour in thy sight, that thou wouldest send me unto Judah, unto the city of my fathers' sepulchres, that I may build it.

6 And the king said unto me, (the queen also sitting by him,) For how long shall thy journey be? and when wilt thou return? So it pleased the king to send me; and I set him [v]a time.

7 Moreover I said unto the king, If it please the king, let letters be given me to the governors beyond the river, that they may convey me over till I come into Judah;

8 And a letter unto Asaph the keeper of the king's forest, that he may give me timber to make beams for the gates of the palace which *appertained* [w]to the house, and for the wall of the city, and for the house that I shall enter into. And the king granted

1:1 [a]ch. 10:1
1:3 [b]ch. 2:17 [c]2 Kings 25:10
1:5 [d]Dan. 9:4 [e]Ex. 20:6
1:6 [f]1 Kings 8:28; 2 Chron. 6:40; Dan. 9:17 [g]Dan. 9:20
1:7 [h]Ps. 106:6; Dan. 9:5 [i]Deut. 28:15
1:8 [j]Lev. 26:33; Deut. 4:25
1:9 [k]Lev. 26:39; Deut. 4:29 [l]Deut. 30:4
1:10 [m]Deut. 9:29; Dan. 9:15
1:11 [n]ver. 6 [o]Isa. 26:8; Heb. 13:18 [p]ch. 2:1
2:1 [q]Ezra 7:1 [r]ch. 1:11
2:2 [s]Prov. 15:13
2:3 [t]1 Kings 1:31; Dan. 2:4 [u]ch. 1:3
2:6 [v]ch. 5:14
2:8 [w]ch. 3:7

me, [x]according to the good hand of my God
upon me.
9 ¶ Then I came to the governors beyond
the river, and gave them the king's letters.
Now the king had sent captains of the army
and horsemen with me.
10 When Sanballat the Horonite, and Tobiah the servant, the Ammonite, heard *of it*,
it grieved them exceedingly that there was
come a man to seek the welfare of the children of Israel.
11 So I [y]came to Jerusalem, and was
there three days.
12 ¶ And I arose in the night, I and some
few men with me; neither told I *any* man
what my God had put in my heart to do at
Jerusalem: neither *was there any* beast with
me, save the beast that I rode upon.
13 And I went out by night [z]by the gate of
the valley, even before the dragon well, and
to the dung port, and viewed the walls of
Jerusalem, which were [a]broken down, and
the gates thereof were consumed with fire.
14 Then I went on to the gate of the fountain, and to the king's pool: but *there was* no
place for the beast *that was* under me to
pass.
15 Then went I up in the night by the
[b]brook, and viewed the wall, and turned
back, and entered by the gate of the valley,
and *so* returned.
16 And the rulers knew not whither I
went, or what I did; neither had I as yet told
it to the Jews, nor to the priests, nor to the
nobles, nor to the rulers, nor to the rest that
did the work.
17 ¶ Then said I unto them, Ye see the
distress that we *are* in, how Jerusalem *lieth*
waste, and the gates thereof are burned
with fire: come, and let us build up the wall
of Jerusalem, that we be no more [c]a reproach.
18 Then I told them of [d]the hand of my
God which was good upon me; as also the
king's words that he had spoken unto me.
And they said, Let us rise up and build. So
they [e]strengthened their hands for *this*
good *work*.
19 But when Sanballat the Horonite, and
Tobiah the servant, the Ammonite, and Geshem the Arabian, heard *it*, they [f]laughed
us to scorn, and despised us, and said, What
is this thing that ye do? [g]will ye rebel
against the king?
20 Then answered I them, and said unto
them, The God of heaven, he will prosper
us; therefore we his servants will arise and
build: [h]but ye have no portion, nor right,
nor memorial, in Jerusalem.

3 Then [i]Eliashib the high priest rose up
with his brethren the priests, [j]and they
builded the sheep gate; they sanctified it,
and set up the doors of it; [k]even unto the
tower of Meah they sanctified it, unto the
tower of [l]Hananeel.
2 And next unto him builded [m]the men of
Jericho. And next to them builded Zaccur
the son of Imri.

2:8 [x]Ezra 5:5; ver. 18
2:11 [y]Ezra 8:32
2:13 [z]2 Chron. 26:9; ch. 3:13 [a]ch. 1:3
2:15 [b]2 Sam. 15:23; Jer. 31:40
2:17 [c]ch. 1:3; Ps. 44:13; Jer. 24:9; Ezek. 5:14
2:18 [d]ver. 8 [e]2 Sam. 2:7
2:19 [f]Ps. 44:13 [g]ch. 6:6
2:20 [h]Ezra 4:3
3:1 [i]ch. 12:10 [j]John 5:2 [k]ch. 12:39 [l]Jer. 31:38; Zech. 14:10
3:2 [m]Ezra 2:34
3:3 [n]2 Chron. 33:14; ch. 12:39; Zeph. 1:10 [o]ch. 6:1
3:5 [p]Judg. 5:23
3:6 [q]ch. 12:39
3:7 [r]ch. 2:8
3:8 [s]ch. 12:38
3:11 [t]ch. 12:38
3:13 [u]ch. 2:13 [v]ch. 2:13
3:15 [w]ch. 2:14 [x]John 9:7
3:16 [y]2 Kings 20:20; Isa. 22:11

3 [n]But the fish gate did the sons of Hasse-
naah build, who *also* laid the beams thereof,
and [o]set up the doors thereof, the locks
thereof, and the bars thereof.
4 And next unto them repaired Meremoth
the son of Urijah, the son of Koz. And next
unto them repaired Meshullam the son of
Berechiah, the son of Meshezabeel. And
next unto them repaired Zadok the son of
Baana.
5 And next unto them the Tekoites repaired; but their nobles put not their necks
to [p]the work of their Lord.
6 Moreover [q]the old gate repaired Jehoiada the son of Paseah, and Meshullam the
son of Besodeiah; they laid the beams
thereof, and set up the doors thereof, and
the locks thereof, and the bars thereof.
7 And next unto them repaired Melatiah
the Gibeonite, and Jadon the Meronothite,
the men of Gibeon, and of Mizpah, unto the
[r]throne of the governor on this side the
river.
8 Next unto him repaired Uzziel the son
of Harhaiah, of the goldsmiths. Next unto
him also repaired Hananiah the son of *one*
of the apothecaries, and they fortified Jerusalem unto the [s]broad wall.
9 And next unto them repaired Rephaiah
the son of Hur, the ruler of the half part of
Jerusalem.
10 And next unto them repaired Jedaiah
the son of Harumaph, even over against his
house. And next unto him repaired Hattush
the son of Hashabniah.
11 Malchijah the son of Harim, and Hashub the son of Pahath-moab, repaired the
other piece, [t]and the tower of the furnaces.
12 And next unto him repaired Shallum
the son of Halohesh, the ruler of the half
part of Jerusalem, he and his daughters.
13 [u]The valley gate repaired Hanun, and
the inhabitants of Zanoah; they built it, and
set up the doors thereof, the locks thereof,
and the bars thereof, and a thousand cubits
on the wall unto [v]the dung gate.
14 But the dung gate repaired Malchiah
the son of Rechab, the ruler of part of Beth-
haccerem; he built it, and set up the doors
thereof, the locks thereof, and the bars
thereof.
15 But [w]the gate of the fountain repaired
Shallun the son of Col-hozeh, the ruler of
part of Mizpah; he built it, and covered it,
and set up the doors thereof, the locks
thereof, and the bars thereof, and the wall
of the pool of [x]Siloah by the king's garden,
and unto the stairs that go down from the
city of David.
16 After him repaired Nehemiah the son
of Azbuk, the ruler of the half part of Beth-
zur, unto *the place* over against the sepulchres of David, and to the [y]pool that was
made, and unto the house of the mighty.
17 After him repaired the Levites, Rehum
the son of Bani. Next unto him repaired
Hashabiah, the ruler of the half part of Keilah, in his part.

18 After him repaired their brethren, Bavai the son of Henadad, the ruler of the half part of Keilah.

19 And next to him repaired Ezer the son of Jeshua, the ruler of Mizpah, another piece over against the going up to the armoury at the [z]turning *of the wall.*

20 After him Baruch the son of Zabbai earnestly repaired the other piece, from the turning *of the wall* unto the door of the house of Eliashib the high priest.

21 After him repaired Meremoth the son of Urijah the son of Koz another piece, from the door of the house of Eliashib even to the end of the house of Eliashib.

22 And after him repaired the priests, the men of the plain.

23 After him repaired Benjamin and Hashub over against their house. After him repaired Azariah the son of Maaseiah the son of Ananiah by his house.

24 After him repaired Binnui the son of Henadad another piece, from the house of Azariah unto [a]the turning *of the wall,* even unto the corner.

25 Palal the son of Uzai, over against the turning *of the wall,* and the tower which lieth out from the king's high house, that *was* by the [b]court of the prison. After him Pedaiah the son of Parosh.

26 Moreover [c]the Nethinims dwelt in [d]Ophel, unto *the place* over against [e]the water gate toward the east, and the tower that lieth out.

27 After them the Tekoites repaired another piece, over against the great tower that lieth out, even unto the wall of Ophel.

28 From above the [f]horse gate repaired the priests, every one over against his house.

29 After them repaired Zadok the son of Immer over against his house. After him repaired also Shemaiah the son of Shechaniah, the keeper of the east gate.

30 After him repaired Hananiah the son of Shelemiah, and Hanun the sixth son of Zalaph, another piece. After him repaired Meshullam the son of Berechiah over against his chamber.

31 After him repaired Malchiah the goldsmith's son unto the place of the Nethinims, and of the merchants, over against the gate Miphkad, and to the going up of the corner.

32 And between the going up of the corner unto the sheep gate repaired the goldsmiths and the merchants.

4 But it came to pass, [g]that when Sanballat heard that we builded the wall, he was wroth, and took great indignation, and mocked the Jews.

2 And he spake before his brethren and the army of Samaria, and said, What do these feeble Jews? will they fortify themselves? will they sacrifice? will they make an end in a day? will they revive the stones out of the heaps of the rubbish which are burned?

3 Now [h]Tobiah the Ammonite *was* by him, and he said, Even that which they build, if a fox go up, he shall even break down their stone wall.

4 [i]Hear, O our God; for we are despised: and [j]turn their reproach upon their own head, and give them for a prey in the land of captivity:

5 And [k]cover not their iniquity, and let not their sin be blotted out from before thee: for they have provoked *thee* to anger before the builders.

6 So built we the wall; and all the wall was joined together unto the half thereof: for the people had a mind to work.

7 ¶ But it came to pass, *that* [l]when Sanballat, and Tobiah, and the Arabians, and the Ammonites, and the Ashdodites, heard that the walls of Jerusalem were made up, *and* that the breaches began to be stopped, then they were very wroth,

8 And [m]conspired all of them together to come *and* to fight against Jerusalem, and to hinder it.

9 Nevertheless [n]we made our prayer unto our God, and set a watch against them day and night, because of them.

10 And Judah said, The strength of the bearers of burdens is decayed, and *there is* much rubbish; so that we are not able to build the wall.

11 And our adversaries said, They shall not know, neither see, till we come in the midst among them, and slay them, and cause the work to cease.

12 ¶ And it came to pass, that when the Jews which dwelt by them came, they said unto us ten times, From all places whence ye shall return unto us *they will be upon you.*

13 ¶ Therefore set I in the lower places behind the wall, *and* on the higher places, I even set the people after their families with their swords, their spears, and their bows.

14 And I looked, and rose up, and said unto the nobles, and to the rulers, and to the rest of the people, [o]Be not ye afraid of them: remember the Lord, *which is* [p]great and terrible, and [q]fight for your brethren, your sons, and your daughters, your wives, and your houses.

15 And it came to pass, when our enemies heard that it was known unto us, [r]and God had brought their counsel to nought, that we returned all of us to the wall, every one unto his work.

16 And it came to pass from that time forth, *that* the half of my servants wrought in the work, and the other half of them held both the spears, the shields, and the bows, and the habergeons; and the rulers *were* behind all the house of Judah.

17 They which builded on the wall, and they that bare burdens, with those that laded, *every one* with one of his hands wrought in the work, and with the other *hand* held a weapon.

18 For the builders, every one had his sword girded by his side, and *so* builded.

3:19 [z]2 Chron. 26:9
3:24 [a]ver. 19
3:25 [b]Jer. 32:2
3:26 [c]Ezra 2:43; ch. 11:21 [d]2 Chron. 27:3 [e]ch. 8:1
3:28 [f]2 Kings 11:16; 2 Chron. 23:15; Jer. 31:40
4:1 [g]ch. 2:10
4:3 [h]ch. 2:10
4:4 [i]Ps. 123:3 [j]Ps. 79:12; Prov. 3:34
4:5 [k]Ps. 69:27; Jer. 18:23
4:7 [l]ver. 1
4:8 [m]Ps. 83:3
4:9 [n]Ps. 50:15
4:14 [o]Num. 14:9; Deut. 1:29 [p]Deut. 10:17 [q]2 Sam. 10:12
4:15 [r]Job 5:12

And he that sounded the trumpet *was* by me.

19 ¶ And I said unto the nobles, and to the rulers, and to the rest of the people, The work *is* great and large, and we are separated upon the wall, one far from another.

20 In what place *therefore* ye hear the sound of the trumpet, resort ye thither unto us: [s]our God shall fight for us.

21 So we laboured in the work: and half of them held the spears from the rising of the morning till the stars appeared.

22 Likewise at the same time said I unto the people, Let every one with his servant lodge within Jerusalem, that in the night they may be a guard to us, and labour on the day.

23 So neither I, nor my brethren, nor my servants, nor the men of the guard which followed me, none of us put off our clothes, *saving that* every one put them off for washing.

5 And there was a great [t]cry of the people and of their wives against their [u]brethren the Jews.

2 For there were that said, We, our sons, and our daughters, *are* many: therefore we take up corn *for them,* that we may eat, and live.

3 *Some* also there were that said, We have mortgaged our lands, vineyards, and houses, that we might buy corn, because of the dearth.

4 There were also that said, We have borrowed money for the king's tribute, *and that upon* our lands and vineyards.

5 Yet now [v]our flesh *is* as the flesh of our brethren, our children as their children: and, lo, we [w]bring into bondage our sons and our daughters to be servants, and *some* of our daughters are brought unto bondage *already:* neither *is it* in our power *to redeem them;* for other men have our lands and vineyards.

6 ¶ And I was very angry when I heard their cry and these words.

7 Then I consulted with myself, and I rebuked the nobles, and the rulers, and said unto them, [x]Ye exact usury, every one of his brother. And I set a great assembly against them.

8 And I said unto them, We after our ability have [y]redeemed our brethren the Jews, which were sold unto the heathen; and will ye even sell your brethren? or shall they be sold unto us? Then held they their peace, and found nothing *to answer.*

9 Also I said, It *is* not good that ye do: ought ye not to walk [z]in the fear of our God [a]because of the reproach of the heathen our enemies?

10 I likewise, *and* my brethren, and my servants, might exact of them money and corn: I pray you, let us leave off this usury.

11 Restore, I pray you, to them, even this day, their lands, their vineyards, their oliveyards, and their houses, also the hundredth *part* of the money, and of the corn, the wine, and the oil, that ye exact of them.

12 Then said they, We will restore *them,* and will require nothing of them; so will we do as thou sayest. Then I called the priests, [b]and took an oath of them, that they should do according to this promise.

13 Also [c]I shook my lap, and said, So God shake out every man from his house, and from his labour, that performeth not this promise, even thus be he shaken out, and emptied. And all the congregation said, Amen, and praised the LORD. [d]And the people did according to this promise.

14 ¶ Moreover from the time that I was appointed to be their governor in the land of Judah, from the twentieth year [e]even unto the two and thirtieth year of Artaxerxes the king, *that is,* twelve years, I and my brethren have not [f]eaten the bread of the governor.

15 But the former governors that *had been* before me were chargeable unto the people, and had taken of them bread and wine, beside forty shekels of silver; yea, even their servants bare rule over the people: but [g]so did not I, because of the [h]fear of God.

16 Yea, also I continued in the work of this wall, neither bought we any land: and all my servants *were* gathered thither unto the work.

17 Moreover *there were* [i]at my table an hundred and fifty of the Jews and rulers, beside those that came unto us from among the heathen that *are* about us.

18 Now *that* [j]which was prepared *for me* daily *was* one ox *and* six choice sheep; also fowls were prepared for me, and once in ten days store of all sorts of wine: yet for all this [k]required not I the bread of the governor, because the bondage was heavy upon this people.

19 [l]Think upon me, my God, for good, *according* to all that I have done for this people.

6 Now it came to pass, [m]when Sanballat, and Tobiah, and Geshem the Arabian, and the rest of our enemies, heard that I had builded the wall, and *that* there was no breach left therein; ([n]though at that time I had not set up the doors upon the gates;)

2 That Sanballat and Geshem [o]sent unto me, saying, Come, let us meet together in *some one of* the villages in the plain of [p]Ono. But they [q]thought to do me mischief.

3 And I sent messengers unto them, saying, I *am* doing a great work, so that I cannot come down: why should the work cease, whilst I leave it, and come down to you?

4 Yet they sent unto me four times after this sort; and I answered them after the same manner.

5 Then sent Sanballat his servant unto me in like manner the fifth time with an open letter in his hand;

6 Wherein *was* written, It is reported among the heathen, and Gashmu saith *it,*

4:20 [s]Ex. 14:14; Deut. 1:30; Josh. 23:10
5:1 [t]Isa. 5:7 [u]Lev. 25:35; Deut. 15:7
5:5 [v]Isa. 58:7 [w]Ex. 21:7; Lev. 25:39
5:7 [x]Ex. 22:25; Lev. 25:36; Ezek. 22:12
5:8 [y]Lev. 25:48
5:9 [z]Lev. 25:36 [a]2 Sam. 12:14; Rom. 2:24; 1 Pet. 2:12
5:12 [b]Ezra 10:5; Jer. 34:8
5:13 [c]Matt. 10:14; Acts 13:51 [d]2 Kings 23:3
5:14 [e]ch. 13:6 [f]1 Cor. 9:4
5:15 [g]2 Cor. 11:9 [h]ver. 9
5:17 [i]2 Sam. 9:7; 1 Kings 18:19
5:18 [j]1 Kings 4:22 [k]ver. 14
5:19 [l]ch. 13:22
6:1 [m]ch. 2:10 [n]ch. 3:1
6:2 [o]Prov. 26:24 [p]1 Chron. 8:12; ch. 11:35 [q]Ps. 37:12

[r]*that* thou and the Jews think to rebel: for which cause thou buildest the wall, that thou mayest be their king, according to these words.

7 And thou hast also appointed prophets to preach of thee at Jerusalem, saying, *There is* a king in Judah: and now shall it be reported to the king according to these words. Come now therefore, and let us take counsel together.

8 Then I sent unto him, saying, There are no such things done as thou sayest, but thou feignest them out of thine own heart.

9 For they all made us afraid, saying, Their hands shall be weakened from the work, that it be not done. Now therefore, *O God,* strengthen my hands.

10 Afterward I came unto the house of Shemaiah the son of Delaiah the son of Mehetabeel, who *was* shut up; and he said, Let us meet together in the house of God, within the temple, and let us shut the doors of the temple: for they will come to slay thee; yea, in the night will they come to slay thee.

11 And I said, Should such a man as I flee? and who *is there,* that, *being* as I *am,* would go into the temple to save his life? I will not go in.

12 And, lo, I perceived that God had not sent him; but that [s]he pronounced this prophecy against me: for Tobiah and Sanballat had hired him.

13 Therefore *was* he hired, that I should be afraid, and do so, and sin, and *that* they might have *matter* for an evil report, that they might reproach me.

14 [t]My God, think thou upon Tobiah and Sanballat according to these their works, and on the [u]prophetess Noadiah, and the rest of the prophets, that would have put me in fear.

15 ¶ So the wall was finished in the twenty and fifth *day* of *the month* Elul, in fifty and two days.

16 And it came to pass, that [v]when all our enemies heard *thereof,* and all the heathen that *were* about us saw *these things,* they were much cast down in their own eyes: for [w]they perceived that this work was wrought of our God.

17 ¶ Moreover in those days the nobles of Judah sent many letters unto Tobiah, and *the letters* of Tobiah came unto them.

18 For *there were* many in Judah sworn unto him, because he *was* the son in law of Shechaniah the son of Arah; and his son Johanan had taken the daughter of Meshullam the son of Berechiah.

19 Also they reported his good deeds before me, and uttered my words to him. *And* Tobiah sent letters to put me in fear.

7 Now it came to pass, when the wall was built, and I had [x]set up the doors, and the porters and the singers and the Levites were appointed,

2 That I gave my brother Hanani, and Hananiah the ruler [y]of the palace, charge over Jerusalem: for he *was* a faithful man, and [z]feared God above many.

3 And I said unto them, Let not the gates of Jerusalem be opened until the sun be hot; and while they stand by, let them shut the doors, and bar *them:* and appoint watches of the inhabitants of Jerusalem, every one in his watch, and every one *to be* over against his house.

4 Now the city *was* large and great: but the people *were* few therein, and the houses *were* not builded.

5 ¶ And my God put into mine heart to gather together the nobles, and the rulers, and the people, that they might be reckoned by genealogy. And I found a register of the genealogy of them which came up at the first, and found written therein,

6 [a]These *are* the children of the province, that went up out of the captivity, of those that had been carried away, whom Nebuchadnezzar the king of Babylon had carried away, and came again to Jerusalem and to Judah, every one unto his city;

7 Who came with Zerubbabel, Jeshua, Nehemiah, Azariah, Raamiah, Nahamani, Mordecai, Bilshan, Mispereth, Bigvai, Nehum, Baanah. The number, *I say,* of the men of the people of Israel *was this;*

8 The children of Parosh, two thousand an hundred seventy and two.

9 The children of Shephatiah, three hundred seventy and two.

10 The children of Arah, six hundred fifty and two.

11 The children of Pahath-moab, of the children of Jeshua and Joab, two thousand and eight hundred *and* eighteen.

12 The children of Elam, a thousand two hundred fifty and four.

13 The children of Zattu, eight hundred forty and five.

14 The children of Zaccai, seven hundred and threescore.

15 The children of Binnui, six hundred forty and eight.

16 The children of Bebai, six hundred twenty and eight.

17 The children of Azgad, two thousand three hundred twenty and two.

18 The children of Adonikam, six hundred threescore and seven.

19 The children of Bigvai, two thousand threescore and seven.

20 The children of Adin, six hundred fifty and five.

21 The children of Ater of Hezekiah, ninety and eight.

22 The children of Hashum, three hundred twenty and eight.

23 The children of Bezai, three hundred twenty and four.

24 The children of Hariph, an hundred and twelve.

25 The children of Gibeon, ninety and five.

26 The men of Beth-lehem and Netophah, an hundred fourscore and eight.

6:6 [r]ch. 2:19
6:12 [s]Ezek. 13:22
6:14 [t]ch. 13:29 [u]Ezek. 13:17
6:16 [v]ch. 2:10 [w]Ps. 126:2
7:1 [x]ch. 6:1
7:2 [y]ch. 2:8 [z]Ex. 18:21
7:6 [a]Ezra 2:1

27 The men of Anathoth, an hundred twenty and eight.

28 The men of Beth-azmaveth, forty and two.

29 The men of Kirjath-jearim, Chephirah, and Beeroth, seven hundred forty and three.

30 The men of Ramah and Geba, six hundred twenty and one.

31 The men of Michmas, an hundred and twenty and two.

32 The men of Beth-el and Ai, an hundred twenty and three.

33 The men of the other Nebo, fifty and two.

34 The children of the other [b]Elam, a thousand two hundred fifty and four.

35 The children of Harim, three hundred and twenty.

36 The children of Jericho, three hundred forty and five.

37 The children of Lod, Hadid, and Ono, seven hundred twenty and one.

38 The children of Senaah, three thousand nine hundred and thirty.

39 ¶ The priests: the children of [c]Jedaiah, of the house of Jeshua, nine hundred seventy and three.

40 The children of [d]Immer, a thousand fifty and two.

41 The children of [e]Pashur, a thousand two hundred forty and seven.

42 The children of [f]Harim, a thousand and seventeen.

43 ¶ The Levites: the children of Jeshua, of Kadmiel, *and* of the children of Hodevah, seventy and four.

44 ¶ The singers: the children of Asaph, an hundred forty and eight.

45 ¶ The porters: the children of Shallum, the children of Ater, the children of Talmon, the children of Akkub, the children of Hatita, the children of Shobai, an hundred thirty and eight.

46 ¶ The Nethinims: the children of Ziha, the children of Hashupha, the children of Tabbaoth,

47 The children of Keros, the children of Sia, the children of Padon,

48 The children of Lebana, the children of Hagaba, the children of Shalmai,

49 The children of Hanan, the children of Giddel, the children of Gahar,

50 The children of Reaiah, the children of Rezin, the children of Nekoda,

51 The children of Gazzam, the children of Uzza, the children of Phaseah,

52 The children of Besai, the children of Meunim, the children of Nephishesim,

53 The children of Bakbuk, the children of Hakupha, the children of Harhur,

54 The children of Bazlith, the children of Mehida, the children of Harsha,

55 The children of Barkos, the children of Sisera, the children of Tamah,

56 The children of Neziah, the children of Hatipha.

57 ¶ The children of Solomon's servants: the children of Sotai, the children of Sophereth, the children of Perida,

58 The children of Jaala, the children of Darkon, the children of Giddel,

59 The children of Shephatiah, the children of Hattil, the children of Pochereth of Zebaim, the children of Amon.

60 All the Nethinims, and the children of Solomon's servants, *were* three hundred ninety and two.

61 [g]And these *were* they which went up *also* from Tel-melah, Tel-haresha, Cherub, Addon, and Immer: but they could not shew their father's house, nor their seed, whether they *were* of Israel.

62 The children of Delaiah, the children of Tobiah, the children of Nekoda, six hundred forty and two.

63 ¶ And of the priests: the children of Habaiah, the children of Koz, the children of Barzillai, which took *one* of the daughters of Barzillai the Gileadite to wife, and was called after their name.

64 These sought their register *among* those that were reckoned by genealogy, but it was not found: therefore were they, as polluted, put from the priesthood.

65 And the Tirshatha said unto them, that they should not eat of the most holy things, till there stood *up* a priest with Urim and Thummim.

66 ¶ The whole congregation together *was* forty and two thousand three hundred and threescore,

67 Beside their manservants and their maidservants, of whom *there were* seven thousand three hundred thirty and seven: and they had two hundred forty and five singing men and singing women.

68 Their horses, seven hundred thirty and six: their mules, two hundred forty and five:

69 *Their* camels, four hundred thirty and five: six thousand seven hundred and twenty asses.

70 ¶ And some of the chief of the fathers gave unto the work. [h]The Tirshatha gave to the treasure a thousand drams of gold, fifty basons, five hundred and thirty priests' garments.

71 And *some* of the chief of the fathers gave to the treasure of the work [i]twenty thousand drams of gold, and two thousand and two hundred pounds of silver.

72 And *that* which the rest of the people gave *was* twenty thousand drams of gold, and two thousand pounds of silver, and threescore and seven priests' garments.

73 So the priests, and the Levites, and the porters, and the singers, and *some* of the people, and the Nethinims, and all Israel, dwelt in their cities; [j]and when the seventh month came, the children of Israel *were* in their cities.

8 And all [k]the people gathered themselves together as one man into the street that *was* [l]before the water gate; and they spake unto Ezra the [m]scribe to bring

7:34 [b]ver. 12
7:39 [c]1 Chron. 24:7
7:40 [d]1 Chron. 24:14
7:41 [e]1 Chron. 9:12
7:42 [f]1 Chron. 24:8
7:61 [g]Ezra 2:59
7:70 [h]ch. 8:9
7:71 [i]Ezra 2:69
7:73 [j]Ezra 3:1
8:1 [k]Ezra 3:1 [l]ch. 3:26 [m]Ezra 7:6

the book of the law of Moses, which the LORD had commanded to Israel.

2 And Ezra the priest brought [n]the law before the congregation both of men and women, and all that could hear with understanding, [o]upon the first day of the seventh month.

3 And he read therein before the street that *was* before the water gate from the morning until midday, before the men and the women, and those that could understand; and the ears of all the people *were attentive* unto the book of the law.

4 And Ezra the scribe stood upon a pulpit of wood, which they had made for the purpose; and beside him stood Mattithiah, and Shema, and Anaiah, and Urijah, and Hilkiah, and Maaseiah, on his right hand; and on his left hand, Pedaiah, and Mishael, and Malchiah, and Hashum, and Hashbadana, Zechariah, *and* Meshullam.

5 And Ezra opened the book in the sight of all the people; (for he was above all the people;) and when he opened it, all the people [p]stood up:

6 And Ezra blessed the LORD, the great God. And all the people [q]answered, Amen, Amen, with [r]lifting up their hands: and they [s]bowed their heads, and worshipped the LORD with *their* faces to the ground.

7 Also Jeshua, and Bani, and Sherebiah, Jamin, Akkub, Shabbethai, Hodijah, Maaseiah, Kelita, Azariah, Jozabad, Hanan, Pelaiah, and the Levites, [t]caused the people to understand the law: and the people *stood* in their place.

8 So they read in the book in the law of God distinctly, and gave the sense, and caused *them* to understand the reading.

9 ¶ [u]And Nehemiah, which *is* the Tirshatha, and Ezra the priest the scribe, [v]and the Levites that taught the people, said unto all the people, [w]This day *is* holy unto the LORD your God; [x]mourn not, nor weep. For all the people wept, when they heard the words of the law.

10 Then he said unto them, Go your way, eat the fat, and drink the sweet, [y]and send portions unto them for whom nothing is prepared: for *this* day *is* holy unto our Lord: neither be ye sorry; for the joy of the LORD is your strength.

11 So the Levites stilled all the people, saying, Hold your peace, for the day *is* holy; neither be ye grieved.

12 And all the people went their way to eat, and to drink, and to [z]send portions, and to make great mirth, because they had [a]understood the words that were declared unto them.

13 ¶ And on the second day were gathered together the chief of the fathers of all the people, the priests, and the Levites, unto Ezra the scribe, even to understand the words of the law.

14 And they found written in the law which the LORD had commanded by Moses, that the children of Israel should dwell in [b]booths in the feast of the seventh month:

15 And [c]that they should publish and proclaim in all their cities, and [d]in Jerusalem, saying, Go forth unto the mount, and [e]fetch olive branches, and pine branches, and myrtle branches, and palm branches, and branches of thick trees, to make booths, as *it is* written.

16 ¶ So the people went forth, and brought *them,* and made themselves booths, every one upon the [f]roof of his house, and in their courts, and in the courts of the house of God, and in the street of the [g]water gate, [h]and in the street of the gate of Ephraim.

17 And all the congregation of them that were come again out of the captivity made booths, and sat under the booths: for since the days of Jeshua the son of Nun unto that day had not the children of Israel done so. And there was very [i]great gladness.

18 Also [j]day by day, from the first day unto the last day, he read in the book of the law of God. And they kept the feast seven days; and on the eighth day *was* a solemn assembly, [k]according unto the manner.

9 Now in the twenty and fourth day of [l]this month the children of Israel were assembled with fasting, and with sackclothes, [m]and earth upon them.

2 And [n]the seed of Israel separated themselves from all strangers, and stood and confessed their sins, and the iniquities of their fathers.

3 And they stood up in their place, and [o]read in the book of the law of the LORD their God *one* fourth part of the day; and *another* fourth part they confessed, and worshipped the LORD their God.

4 ¶ Then stood up upon the stairs, of the Levites, Jeshua, and Bani, Kadmiel, Shebaniah, Bunni, Sherebiah, Bani, *and* Chenani, and cried with a loud voice unto the LORD their God.

5 Then the Levites, Jeshua, and Kadmiel, Bani, Hashabniah, Sherebiah, Hodijah, Shebaniah, *and* Pethahiah, said, Stand up *and* bless the LORD your God for ever and ever: and blessed be [p]thy glorious name, which is exalted above all blessing and praise.

6 [q]Thou, *even* thou, *art* LORD alone; [r]thou hast made heaven, [s]the heaven of heavens, with [t]all their host, the earth, and all *things* that *are* therein, the seas, and all that *is* therein, and thou [u]preservest them all; and the host of heaven worshippeth thee.

7 Thou *art* the LORD the God, who didst choose [v]Abram, and broughtest him forth out of Ur of the Chaldees, and gavest him the name of [w]Abraham;

8 And foundest his heart [x]faithful before thee, and madest a [y]covenant with him to give the land of the Canaanites, the Hittites, the Amorites, and the Perizzites, and the Jebusites, and the Girgashites, to give *it, I*

8:2 [n]Deut. 31:11 [o]Lev. 23:24
8:5 [p]Judg. 3:20
8:6 [q]1 Cor. 14:16 [r]Lam. 3:41; 1 Tim. 2:8 [s]Ex. 4:31; 2 Chron. 20:18
8:7 [t]Lev. 10:11; Deut. 33:10; 2 Chron. 17:7; Mal. 2:7
8:9 [u]Ezra 2:63; ch. 7:65 [v]2 Chron. 35:3; ver. 8 [w]Lev. 23:24; Num. 29:1 [x]Deut. 16:14; Eccl. 3:4
8:10 [y]Esth. 9:19; Rev. 11:10
8:12 [z]ver. 10 [a]ver. 7
8:14 [b]Lev. 23:34; Deut. 16:13
8:15 [c]Lev. 23:4 [d]Deut. 16:16 [e]Lev. 23:40
8:16 [f]Deut. 22:8 [g]ch. 12:37 [h]2 Kings 14:13; ch. 12:39
8:17 [i]2 Chron. 30:21
8:18 [j]Deut. 31:10 [k]Lev. 23:36; Num. 29:35
9:1 [l]ch. 8:2 [m]Josh. 7:6; 1 Sam. 4:12; 2 Sam. 1:2; Job 2:12
9:2 [n]Ezra 10:11; ch. 13:3
9:3 [o]ch. 8:7
9:5 [p]1 Chron. 29:13
9:6 [q]2 Kings 19:15; Ps. 86:10; Isa. 37:16 [r]Gen. 1:1; Ex. 20:11; Rev. 14:7 [s]Deut. 10:14; 1 Kings 8:27 [t]Gen. 2:1 [u]Ps. 36:6
9:7 [v]Gen. 11:31 [w]Gen. 17:5
9:8 [x]Gen. 15:6 [y]Gen. 12:7

say, to his seed, and [z]hast performed thy words; for thou *art* righteous:

9 [a]And didst see the affliction of our fathers in Egypt, and [b]heardest their cry by the Red sea;

10 And [c]shewedst signs and wonders upon Pharaoh, and on all his servants, and on all the people of his land: for thou knewest that they [d]dealt proudly against them. So didst thou [e]get thee a name, as *it is* this day.

11 [f]And thou didst divide the sea before them, so that they went through the midst of the sea on the dry land; and their persecutors thou threwest into the deeps, [g]as a stone into the mighty waters.

12 Moreover thou [h]leddest them in the day by a cloudy pillar; and in the night by a pillar of fire, to give them light in the way wherein they should go.

13 [i]Thou camest down also upon mount Sinai, and spakest with them from heaven, and gavest them [j]right judgments, and true laws, good statutes and commandments:

14 And madest known unto them thy [k]holy sabbath, and commandedst them precepts, statutes, and laws, by the hand of Moses thy servant:

15 And [l]gavest them bread from heaven for their hunger, and [m]broughtest forth water for them out of the rock for their thirst, and promisedst them that they should [n]go in to possess the land which thou hadst sworn to give them.

16 [o]But they and our fathers dealt proudly, and [p]hardened their necks, and hearkened not to thy commandments,

17 And refused to obey, [q]neither were mindful of thy wonders that thou didst among them; but hardened their necks, and in their rebellion appointed [r]a captain to return to their bondage; but thou *art* a God ready to pardon, [s]gracious and merciful, slow to anger, and of great kindness, and forsookest them not.

18 Yea, [t]when they had made them a molten calf, and said, This *is* thy God that brought thee up out of Egypt, and had wrought great provocations;

19 Yet thou in thy [u]manifold mercies forsookest them not in the wilderness: the [v]pillar of the cloud departed not from them by day, to lead them in the way; neither the pillar of fire by night, to shew them light, and the way wherein they should go.

20 Thou gavest also thy [w]good spirit to instruct them, and withheldest not thy [x]manna from their mouth, and gavest them [y]water for their thirst.

21 Yea, [z]forty years didst thou sustain them in the wilderness, *so that* they lacked nothing; their [a]clothes waxed not old, and their feet swelled not.

22 Moreover thou gavest them kingdoms and nations, and didst divide them into corners: so they possessed the land of [b]Sihon, and the land of the king of Heshbon, and the land of Og king of Bashan.

9:8 [z]Josh. 23:14
9:9 [a]Ex. 2:25
[b]Ex. 14:10
9:10 [c]Ex. 7
[d]Ex. 18:11
[e]Ex. 9:16; Isa. 63:12; Jer. 32:20; Dan. 9:15
9:11 [f]Ex. 14:21; Ps. 78:13
[g]Ex. 15:5
9:12 [h]Ex. 13:21
9:13 [i]Ex. 19:20
[j]Ps. 19:8; Rom. 7:12
9:14 [k]Gen. 2:3; Ex. 20:8
9:15 [l]Ex. 16:14; John 6:31
[m]Ex. 17:6; Num. 20:9
[n]Deut. 1:8
9:16 [o]ver. 29; Ps. 106:6
[p]Deut. 31:27; 2 Kings 17:14; 2 Chron. 30:8; Jer. 19:15
9:17 [q]Ps. 78:11
[r]Num. 14:4
[s]Ex. 34:6; Num. 14:18; Ps. 86:5; Joel 2:13
9:18 [t]Ex. 32:4
9:19 [u]ver. 27; Ps. 106:45
[v]Ex. 13:21; Num. 14:14; 1 Cor. 10:1
9:20 [w]Num. 11:17; Isa. 63:11
[x]Ex. 16:15; Josh. 5:12
[y]Ex. 17:6
9:21 [z]Deut. 2:7
[a]Deut. 8:4
9:22 [b]Num. 21:21
9:23 [c]Gen. 22:17
9:24 [d]Josh. 1:2
[e]Ps. 44:2
9:25 [f]ver. 35; Num. 13:27; Deut. 8:7; Ezek. 20:6
[g]Deut. 6:11
[h]Deut. 32:15
[i]Hos. 3:5
9:26 [j]Judg. 2:11; Ezek. 20:21
[k]1 Kings 14:9; Ps. 50:17
[l]1 Kings 18:4; 2 Chron. 24:20; Matt. 23:37; Acts 7:52
9:27 [m]Judg. 2:14; Ps. 106:41
[n]Ps. 106:44
[o]Judg. 2:18
9:28 [p]Judg. 3:11
[q]Ps. 106:43
9:29 [r]ver. 16
[s]Lev. 18:5; Ezek. 20:11; Rom. 10:5; Gal. 3:12
9:30 [t]2 Kings 17:13; 2 Chron. 36:15; Jer. 7:25
[u]Acts 7:51; 1 Pet. 1:11; 2 Pet. 1:21
[v]Isa. 5:5
9:31 [w]Jer. 4:27
[x]ver. 17
9:32 [y]Ex. 34:6; ch. 1:5
[z]2 Kings 17:3
9:33 [a]Dan. 9:14; Ps. 119:137
[b]Ps. 106:6; Dan. 9:5

23 [c]Their children also multipliedst thou as the stars of heaven, and broughtest them into the land, concerning which thou hadst promised to their fathers, that they should go in to possess *it.*

24 So [d]the children went in and possessed the land, and [e]thou subduedst before them the inhabitants of the land, the Canaanites, and gavest them into their hands, with their kings, and the people of the land, that they might do with them as they would.

25 And they took strong cities, and a [f]fat land, and possessed [g]houses full of all goods, wells digged, vineyards, and oliveyards, and fruit trees in abundance: so they did eat, and were filled, and [h]became fat, and delighted themselves in thy great [i]goodness.

26 Nevertheless they [j]were disobedient, and rebelled against thee, and [k]cast thy law behind their backs, and slew thy [l]prophets which testified against them to turn them to thee, and they wrought great provocations.

27 [m]Therefore thou deliveredst them into the hand of their enemies, who vexed them: and in the time of their trouble, when they cried unto thee, thou [n]heardest *them* from heaven; and according to thy manifold mercies [o]thou gavest them saviours, who saved them out of the hand of their enemies.

28 But after they had rest, [p]they did evil again before thee: therefore leftest thou them in the hand of their enemies, so that they had the dominion over them: yet when they returned, and cried unto thee, thou heardest *them* from heaven; and [q]many times didst thou deliver them according to thy mercies;

29 And testifiedst against them, that thou mightest bring them again unto thy law: yet they [r]dealt proudly, and hearkened not unto thy commandments, but sinned against thy judgments, ([s]which if a man do, he shall live in them;) and withdrew the shoulder, and hardened their neck, and would not hear.

30 Yet many years didst thou forbear them, and testifiedst [t]against them by thy spirit [u]in thy prophets: yet would they not give ear: [v]therefore gavest thou them into the hand of the people of the lands.

31 Nevertheless for thy great mercies' sake [w]thou didst not utterly consume them, nor forsake them; for thou *art* [x]a gracious and merciful God.

32 Now therefore, our God, the great, the [y]mighty, and the terrible God, who keepest covenant and mercy, let not all the trouble seem little before thee, that hath come upon us, on our kings, on our princes, and on our priests, and on our prophets, and on our fathers, and on all thy people, [z]since the time of the kings of Assyria unto this day.

33 Howbeit [a]thou *art* just in all that is brought upon us; for thou hast done right, but [b]we have done wickedly:

34 Neither have our kings, our princes,

our priests, nor our fathers, kept thy law,
nor hearkened unto thy commandments
and thy testimonies, wherewith thou didst
testify against them.
35 For they have [c]not served thee in their
kingdom, and in [d]thy great goodness that
thou gavest them, and in the large and [e]fat
land which thou gavest before them, neither
turned they from their wicked works.
36 Behold, [f]we *are* servants this day, and
for the land that thou gavest unto our fathers to eat the fruit thereof and the good
thereof, behold, we *are* servants in it:
37 And [g]it yieldeth much increase unto
the kings whom thou hast set over us because of our sins: also they have [h]dominion
over our bodies, and over our cattle, at their
pleasure, and we *are* in great distress.
38 And because of all this we [i]make a
sure *covenant,* and write *it;* and our princes,
Levites, *and* priests, [j]seal *unto it.*

10

Now those that sealed *were,* [k]Nehe-
miah, the Tirshatha, [l]the son of
Hachaliah, and Zidkijah,
2 [m]Seraiah, Azariah, Jeremiah,
3 Pashur, Amariah, Malchijah,
4 Hattush, Shebaniah, Malluch,
5 Harim, Meremoth, Obadiah,
6 Daniel, Ginnethon, Baruch,
7 Meshullam, Abijah, Mijamin,
8 Maaziah, Bilgai, Shemaiah: these *were*
the priests.
9 And the Levites: both Jeshua the son of
Azaniah, Binnui of the sons of Henadad,
Kadmiel;
10 And their brethren, Shebaniah, Hodijah, Kelita, Pelaiah, Hanan,
11 Micha, Rehob, Hashabiah,
12 Zaccur, Sherebiah, Shebaniah,
13 Hodijah, Bani, Beninu.
14 The chief of the people; [n]Parosh,
Pahath-moab, Elam, Zatthu, Bani,
15 Bunni, Azgad, Bebai,
16 Adonijah, Bigvai, Adin,
17 Ater, Hizkijah, Azzur,
18 Hodijah, Hashum, Bezai,
19 Hariph, Anathoth, Nebai,
20 Magpiash, Meshullam, Hezir,
21 Meshezabeel, Zadok, Jaddua,
22 Pelatiah, Hanan, Anaiah,
23 Hoshea, Hananiah, Hashub,
24 Hallohesh, Pileha, Shobek,
25 Rehum, Hashabnah, Maaseiah,
26 And Ahijah, Hanan, Anan,
27 Malluch, Harim, Baanah.
28 ¶ [o]And the rest of the people, the
priests, the Levites, the porters, the singers,
the Nethinims, [p]and all they that had separated themselves from the people of the
lands unto the law of God, their wives, their
sons, and their daughters, every one having
knowledge, and having understanding;
29 They clave to their brethren, their nobles, [q]and entered into a curse, and into an
oath, [r]to walk in God's law, which was
given by Moses the servant of God, and to
observe and do all the commandments of
the LORD our Lord, and his judgments and
his statutes;
30 And that we would not give [s]our
daughters unto the people of the land, nor
take their daughters for our sons:
31 [t]And *if* the people of the land bring
ware or any victuals on the sabbath day to
sell, *that* we would not buy it of them on the
sabbath, or on the holy day: and *that* we
would leave the [u]seventh year, and the
[v]exaction of every debt.
32 Also we made ordinances for us, to
charge ourselves yearly with the third part
of a shekel for the service of the house of
our God;
33 For [w]the shewbread, and for the [x]con-
tinual meat offering, and for the continual
burnt offering, of the sabbaths, of the new
moons, for the set feasts, and for the holy
things, and for the sin offerings to make an
atonement for Israel, and *for* all the work of
the house of our God.
34 And we cast the lots among the priests,
the Levites, and the people, [y]for the wood
offering, to bring *it* into the house of our
God, after the houses of our fathers, at times
appointed year by year, to burn upon the
altar of the LORD our God, [z]as *it is* written
in the law:
35 And [a]to bring the firstfruits of our
ground, and the firstfruits of all fruit of all
trees, year by year, unto the house of the
LORD:
36 Also the firstborn of our sons, and of
our cattle, as *it is* written [b]in the law, and
the firstlings of our herds and of our flocks,
to bring to the house of our God, unto the
priests that minister in the house of our
God:
37 [c]And *that* we should bring the firstfruits of our dough, and our offerings, and
the fruit of all manner of trees, of wine and
of oil, unto the priests, to the chambers of
the house of our God; and [d]the tithes of our
ground unto the Levites, that the same Levites might have the tithes in all the cities of
our tillage.
38 And the priest the son of Aaron shall
be with the Levites, [e]when the Levites take
tithes: and the Levites shall bring up the
tithe of the tithes unto the house of our God,
to [f]the chambers, into the treasure house.
39 For the children of Israel and the children of Levi [g]shall bring the offering of the
corn, of the new wine, and the oil, unto the
chambers, where *are* the vessels of
the sanctuary, and the priests that minister,
and the porters, and the singers: [h]and we
will not forsake the house of our God.

11

And the rulers of the people dwelt at
Jerusalem: the rest of the people also
cast lots, to bring one of ten to dwell in Jerusalem [i]the holy city, and nine parts *to
dwell* in *other* cities.
2 And the people blessed all the men, that
[j]willingly offered themselves to dwell at
Jerusalem.
3 ¶ [k]Now these *are* the chief of the prov-

9:35 [c]Deut. 28:47 [d]ver. 25 [e]ver. 25
9:36 [f]Deut. 28:48; Ezra 9:9
9:37 [g]Deut. 28:33 [h]Deut. 28:48
9:38 [i]2 Kings 23:3; 2 Chron. 29:10; ch. 10:29; Ezra 10:3 [j]ch. 10:1
10:1 [k]ch. 8:9 [l]ch. 1:1
10:2 [m]ch. 12:1-21
10:14 [n]Ezra 2:3; ch. 7:8
10:28 [o]Ezra 2:86-43 [p]Ezra 9:1; ch. 13:3
10:29 [q]Deut. 29:12; ch. 5:12; Ps. 119:106 [r]2 Kings 23:3; 2 Chron. 34:31
10:30 [s]Ex. 34:16; Deut. 7:3; Ezra 9:12
10:31 [t]Ex. 20:10; Lev. 23:3; Deut. 5:12; ch. 13:5 [u]Ex. 23:10; Lev. 25:4 [v]Deut. 15:1; ch. 5:12
10:33 [w]Lev. 24:5; 2 Chron. 2:4 [x]Num. 28
10:34 [y]ch. 13:31; Isa. 40:16 [z]Lev. 6:12
10:35 [a]Ex. 23:19; Lev. 19:23; Num. 18:12; Deut. 26:2
10:36 [b]Ex. 13:2; Lev. 27:26; Num. 18:15
10:37 [c]Lev. 23:17; Num. 15:19; Deut. 18:4 [d]Lev. 27:30; Num. 18:21
10:38 [e]Num. 18:26 [f]1 Chron. 9:26; 2 Chron. 31:11
10:39 [g]Deut. 12:6; 2 Chron. 31:12; ch. 13:12 [h]ch. 13:10
11:1 [i]ver. 18; Matt. 4:5
11:2 [j]Judg. 5:9
11:3 [k]1 Chron. 9:2

ince that dwelt in Jerusalem: but in the cities of Judah dwelt every one in his
possession in their cities, *to wit*, Israel, the
priests, and the Levites, and [l]the Nethinims, and [m]the children of Solomon's servants.
4 And [n]at Jerusalem dwelt *certain* of the
children of Judah, and of the children of
Benjamin. Of the children of Judah; Atha-
iah the son of Uzziah, the son of Zechariah,
the son of Amariah, the son of Shephatiah,
the son of Mahalaleel, of the children of
[o]Perez;
5 And Maaseiah the son of Baruch, the
son of Col-hozeh, the son of Hazaiah, the
son of Adaiah, the son of Joiarib, the son of
Zechariah, the son of Shiloni.
6 All the sons of Perez that dwelt at Jerusalem *were* four hundred threescore and
eight valiant men.
7 And these *are* the sons of Benjamin;
Sallu the son of Meshullam, the son of Joed,
the son of Pedaiah, the son of Kolaiah, the
son of Maaseiah, the son of Ithiel, the son of
Jesaiah.
8 And after him Gabbai, Sallai, nine hundred twenty and eight.
9 And Joel the son of Zichri *was* their
overseer: and Judah the son of Senuah *was*
second over the city.
10 [p]Of the priests: Jedaiah the son of Joiarib, Jachin.
11 Seraiah the son of Hilkiah, the son of
Meshullam, the son of Zadok, the son of
Meraioth, the son of Ahitub, *was* the ruler
of the house of God.
12 And their brethren that did the work of
the house *were* eight hundred twenty and
two: and Adaiah the son of Jeroham, the
son of Pelaliah, the son of Amzi, the son of
Zechariah, the son of Pashur, the son of
Malchiah.
13 And his brethren, chief of the fathers,
two hundred forty and two: and Amashai
the son of Azareel, the son of Ahasai, the
son of Meshillemoth, the son of Immer,
14 And their brethren, mighty men of valour, an hundred twenty and eight: and their
overseer *was* Zabdiel, the son of *one of* the
great men.
15 Also of the Levites: Shemaiah the son
of Hashub, the son of Azrikam, the son of
Hashabiah, the son of Bunni;
16 And Shabbethai and Jozabad, of the
chief of the Levites, *had* the oversight of
[q]the outward business of the house of God.
17 And Mattaniah the son of Micha, the
son of Zabdi, the son of Asaph, *was* the
principal to begin the thanksgiving in
prayer: and Bakbukiah the second among
his brethren, and Abda the son of Shammua, the son of Galal, the son of Jeduthun.
18 All the Levites in [r]the holy city *were*
two hundred fourscore and four.
19 Moreover the porters, Akkub, Talmon,
and their brethren that kept the gates, *were*
an hundred seventy and two.
20 ¶ And the residue of Israel, of the
priests, *and* the Levites, *were* in all the cities
of Judah, every one in his inheritance.
21 [s]But the Nethinims dwelt in Ophel:
and Ziha and Gispa *were* over the Nethinims.
22 The overseer also of the Levites at Jerusalem *was* Uzzi the son of Bani, the son of
Hashabiah, the son of Mattaniah, the son of
Micha. Of the sons of Asaph, the singers
were over the business of the house of God.
23 For [t]*it was* the king's commandment
concerning them, that a certain portion
should be for the singers, due for every day.
24 And Pethahiah the son of Meshezabeel, of the children of [u]Zerah the son
of Judah, *was* [v]at the king's hand in all matters concerning the people.
25 And for the villages, with their fields,
some of the children of Judah dwelt at
[w]Kirjath-arba, and *in* the villages thereof,
and at Dibon, and *in* the villages thereof,
and at Jekabzeel, and *in* the villages
thereof,
26 And at Jeshua, and at Moladah, and at
Beth-phelet,
27 And at Hazar-shual, and at Beer-
sheba, and *in* the villages thereof,
28 And at Ziklag, and at Mekonah, and in
the villages thereof,
29 And at En-rimmon, and at Zareah, and
at Jarmuth,
30 Zanoah, Adullam, and *in* their villages,
at Lachish, and the fields thereof, at Azekah, and *in* the villages thereof. And they
dwelt from Beer-sheba unto the valley of
Hinnom.
31 The children also of Benjamin from
Geba *dwelt* at Michmash, and Aija, and
Beth-el, and *in* their villages,
32 *And* at Anathoth, Nob, Ananiah,
33 Hazor, Ramah, Gittaim,
34 Hadid, Zeboim, Neballat,
35 Lod, and Ono, [x]the valley of craftsmen.
36 And of the Levites *were* divisions *in*
Judah, *and* in Benjamin.

12 Now these *are* the [y]priests and the
Levites that went up with Zerubba-
bel the son of Shealtiel, and Jeshua: [z]Sera-
iah, Jeremiah, Ezra,
2 Amariah, Malluch, Hattush,
3 Shechaniah, Rehum, Meremoth,
4 Iddo, Ginnetho, [a]Abijah,
5 Miamin, Maadiah, Bilgah,
6 Shemaiah, and Joiarib, Jedaiah,
7 Sallu, Amok, Hilkiah, Jedaiah. These
were the chief of the priests and of their
brethren in the days of [b]Jeshua.
8 Moreover the Levites: Jeshua, Binnui,
Kadmiel, Sherebiah, Judah, *and* Mattaniah,
[c]*which was* over the thanksgiving, he and
his brethren.
9 Also Bakbukiah and Unni, their brethren, *were* over against them in the watches.
10 ¶ And Jeshua begat Joiakim, Joiakim
also begat Eliashib, and Eliashib begat Joiada,

11:3 [l]Ezra 2:43 [m]Ezra 2:55
11:4 [n]1 Chron. 9:3 [o]Gen. 38:29
11:10 [p]1 Chron. 9:10
11:16 [q]1 Chron. 26:29
11:18 [r]ver. 1
11:21 [s]ch. 3:26
11:23 [t]Ezra 6:8
11:24 [u]Gen. 38:30 [v]1 Chron. 18:17
11:25 [w]Josh. 14:15
11:35 [x]1 Chron. 4:14
12:1 [y]Ezra 2:1 [z]ch. 10:2-8
12:4 [a]Luke 1:5
12:7 [b]Ezra 3:2; Hag. 1:1; Zech. 3:1
12:8 [c]ch. 11:17

11 And Joiada begat Jonathan, and Jonathan begat Jaddua.

12 And in the days of Joiakim were priests, the chief of the fathers: of Seraiah, Meraiah; of Jeremiah, Hananiah;

13 Of Ezra, Meshullam; of Amariah, Jehohanan;

14 Of Melicu, Jonathan; of Shebaniah, Joseph;

15 Of Harim, Adna; of Meraioth, Helkai;

16 Of Iddo, Zechariah; of Ginnethon, Meshullam;

17 Of Abijah, Zichri; of Miniamin, of Moadiah, Piltai;

18 Of Bilgah, Shammua; of Shemaiah, Jehonathan;

19 And of Joiarib, Mattenai; of Jedaiah, Uzzi;

20 Of Sallai, Kallai; of Amok, Eber;

21 Of Hilkiah, Hashabiah; of Jedaiah, Nethaneel.

22 ¶ The Levites in the days of Eliashib, Joiada, and Johanan, and Jaddua, *were* recorded chief of the fathers: also the priests, to the reign of Darius the Persian.

23 The sons of Levi, the chief of the fathers, *were* written in the book of the [d]chronicles, even until the days of Johanan the son of Eliashib.

24 And the chief of the Levites: Hashabiah, Sherebiah, and Jeshua the son of Kadmiel, with their brethren over against them, to praise *and* to give thanks, [e]according to the commandment of David the man of God, [f]ward over against ward.

25 Mattaniah, and Bakbukiah, Obadiah, Meshullam, Talmon, Akkub, *were* porters keeping the ward at the thresholds of the gates.

26 These *were* in the days of Joiakim the son of Jeshua, the son of Jozadak, and in the days of Nehemiah [g]the governor, and of Ezra the priest, [h]the scribe.

27 ¶ And at [i]the dedication of the wall of Jerusalem they sought the Levites out of all their places, to bring them to Jerusalem, to keep the dedication with gladness, [j]both with thanksgivings, and with singing, *with* cymbals, psalteries, and with harps.

28 And the sons of the singers gathered themselves together, both out of the plain country round about Jerusalem, and from the villages of Netophathi;

29 Also from the house of Gilgal, and out of the fields of Geba and Azmaveth: for the singers had builded them villages round about Jerusalem.

30 And the priests and the Levites purified themselves, and purified the people, and the gates, and the wall.

31 Then I brought up the princes of Judah upon the wall, and appointed two great *companies of them that gave* thanks, *whereof* [k]*one* went on the right hand upon the wall [l]toward the dung gate:

32 And after them went Hoshaiah, and half of the princes of Judah,

33 And Azariah, Ezra, and Meshullam,

34 Judah, and Benjamin, and Shemaiah, and Jeremiah,

35 And *certain* of the priests' sons [m]with trumpets; *namely*, Zechariah the son of Jonathan, the son of Shemaiah, the son of Mattaniah, the son of Michaiah, the son of Zaccur, the son of Asaph:

36 And his brethren, Shemaiah, and Azarael, Milalai, Gilalai, Maai, Nethaneel, and Judah, Hanani, with [n]the musical instruments of David the man of God, and Ezra the scribe before them.

37 [o]And at the fountain gate, which was over against them, they went up by [p]the stairs of the city of David, at the going up of the wall, above the house of David, even unto [q]the water gate eastward.

38 [r]And the other *company of them that gave* thanks went over against *them*, and I after them, and the half of the people upon the wall, from beyond [s]the tower of the furnaces even unto [t]the broad wall;

39 [u]And from above the gate of Ephraim, and above [v]the old gate, and above [w]the fish gate, [x]and the tower of Hananeel, and the tower of Meah, even unto [y]the sheep gate: and they stood still in [z]the prison gate.

40 So stood the two *companies of them that gave* thanks in the house of God, and I, and the half of the rulers with me:

41 And the priests; Eliakim, Maaseiah, Miniamin, Michaiah, Elioenai, Zechariah, *and* Hananiah, with trumpets;

42 And Maaseiah, and Shemaiah, and Eleazar, and Uzzi, and Jehohanan, and Malchijah, and Elam, and Ezer. And the singers sang loud, with Jezrahiah *their* overseer.

43 Also that day they offered great sacrifices, and rejoiced: for God had made them rejoice with great joy: the wives also and the children rejoiced: so that the joy of Jerusalem was heard even afar off.

44 ¶ [a]And at that time were some appointed over the chambers for the treasures, for the offerings, for the firstfruits, and for the tithes, to gather into them out of the fields of the cities the portions of the law for the priests and Levites: for Judah rejoiced for the priests and for the Levites that waited.

45 And both the singers and the porters kept the ward of their God, and the ward of the purification, [b]according to the commandment of David, *and* of Solomon his son.

46 For in the days of David [c]and Asaph of old *there were* chief of the singers, and songs of praise and thanksgiving unto God.

47 And all Israel in the days of Zerubbabel, and in the days of Nehemiah, gave the portions of the singers and the porters, every day his portion: [d]and they sanctified *holy things* unto the Levites; [e]and the Levites sanctified *them* unto the children of Aaron.

13 On that day [f]they read in the book of Moses in the audience of the people;

12:23 [d]1 Chron. 9:14
12:24 [e]1 Chron. 23 [f]Ezra 3:11
12:26 [g]ch. 8:9 [h]Ezra 7:6
12:27 [i]Deut. 20:5; Ps. 30, title [j]1 Chron. 25:6; 2 Chron. 5:13
12:31 [k]ver. 38 [l]ch. 2:13
12:35 [m]Num. 10:2
12:36 [n]1 Chron. 23:5
12:37 [o]ch. 2:14 [p]ch. 3:15 [q]ch. 3:26
12:38 [r]ver. 31 [s]ch. 3:11 [t]ch. 3:8
12:39 [u]2 Kings 14:13; ch. 8:16 [v]ch. 3:6 [w]ch. 3:3 [x]ch. 3:1 [y]ch. 3:32 [z]Jer. 32:2
12:44 [a]2 Chron. 13:11; ch. 13:5
12:45 [b]1 Chron. 25
12:46 [c]1 Chron. 25:1; 2 Chron. 29:30
12:47 [d]Num. 18:21 [e]Num. 18:26
13:1 [f]Deut. 31:11; 2 Kings 23:2; ch. 8:3; Isa. 34:16

and therein was found written, [g]that the Ammonite and the Moabite should not come into the congregation of God for ever;

2 Because they met not the children of Israel with bread and with water, but [h]hired Balaam against them, that he should curse them: [i]howbeit our God turned the curse into a blessing.

3 Now it came to pass, when they had heard the law, [j]that they separated from Israel all the mixed multitude.

4 ¶ And before this, Eliashib the priest, having the oversight of the chamber of the house of our God, *was* allied unto Tobiah:

5 And he had prepared for him a great chamber, [k]where aforetime they laid the meat offerings, the frankincense, and the vessels, and the tithes of the corn, the new wine, and the oil, [l]which was commanded *to be given* to the Levites, and the singers, and the porters; and the offerings of the priests.

6 But in all this *time* was not I at Jerusalem: [m]for in the two and thirtieth year of Artaxerxes king of Babylon came I unto the king, and after certain days obtained I leave of the king:

7 And I came to Jerusalem, and understood of the evil that Eliashib did for Tobiah, in [n]preparing him a chamber in the courts of the house of God.

8 And it grieved me sore: therefore I cast forth all the household stuff of Tobiah out of the chamber.

9 Then I commanded, and they [o]cleansed the chambers: and thither brought I again the vessels of the house of God, with the meat offering and the frankincense.

10 ¶ And I perceived that the portions of the Levites had [p]not been given *them:* for the Levites and the singers, that did the work, were fled every one to [q]his field.

11 Then [r]contended I with the rulers, and said, [s]Why is the house of God forsaken? And I gathered them together, and set them in their place.

12 [t]Then brought all Judah the tithe of the corn and the new wine and the oil unto the treasuries.

13 [u]And I made treasurers over the treasuries, Shelemiah the priest, and Zadok the scribe, and of the Levites, Pedaiah: and next to them *was* Hanan the son of Zaccur, the son of Mattaniah: for they were counted [v]faithful, and their office *was* to distribute unto their brethren.

14 [w]Remember me, O my God, concerning this, and wipe not out my good deeds that I have done for the house of my God, and for the offices thereof.

15 ¶ In those days saw I in Judah *some* treading wine presses [x]on the sabbath, and bringing in sheaves, and lading asses; as also wine, grapes, and figs, and all *manner of* burdens, [y]which they brought into Jerusalem on the sabbath day: and I testified *against them* in the day wherein they sold victuals.

13:1 [g]Deut. 23:3
13:2 [h]Num. 22:5; Josh. 24:9 [i]Num. 23:11; Deut. 23:5
13:3 [j]ch. 9:2
13:5 [k]ch. 12:44 [l]Num. 18:21
13:6 [m]ch. 5:14
13:7 [n]ver. 1
13:9 [o]2 Chron. 29:5
13:10 [p]Mal. 3:8 [q]Num. 35:2
13:11 [r]ver. 17; Prov. 28:4 [s]ch. 10:39
13:12 [t]ch. 10:38
13:13 [u]ch. 12:44; 2 Chron. 31:12 [v]ch. 7:2; 1 Cor. 4:2
13:14 [w]ver. 22; ch. 5:19
13:15 [x]Ex. 20:10 [y]Jer. 17:21; ch. 10:31
13:17 [z]ver. 11
13:18 [a]Jer. 17:21
13:19 [b]Lev. 23:32 [c]Jer. 17:21
13:22 [d]ch. 12:30 [e]ver. 14
13:23 [f]Ezra 9:2
13:25 [g]ver. 11; Prov. 28:4 [h]Ezra 10:5; ch. 10:29
13:26 [i]1 Kings 11:1 [j]1 Kings 3:13; 2 Chron. 1:12 [k]2 Sam. 12:24 [l]1 Kings 11:4
13:27 [m]Ezra 10:2
13:28 [n]ch. 12:10
13:29 [o]ch. 6:14 [p]Mal. 2:4

16 There dwelt men of Tyre also therein, which brought fish, and all manner of ware, and sold on the sabbath unto the children of Judah, and in Jerusalem.

17 [z]Then I contended with the nobles of Judah, and said unto them, What evil thing *is* this that ye do, and profane the sabbath day?

18 [a]Did not your fathers thus, and did not our God bring all this evil upon us, and upon this city? yet ye bring more wrath upon Israel by profaning the sabbath.

19 And it came to pass, that when the gates of Jerusalem [b]began to be dark before the sabbath, I commanded that the gates should be shut, and charged that they should not be opened till after the sabbath: [c]and *some* of my servants set I at the gates, *that* there should no burden be brought in on the sabbath day.

20 So the merchants and sellers of all kind of ware lodged without Jerusalem once or twice.

21 Then I testified against them, and said unto them, Why lodge ye about the wall? if ye do *so* again, I will lay hands on you. From that time forth came they no *more* on the sabbath.

22 And I commanded the Levites that [d]they should cleanse themselves, and *that* they should come *and* keep the gates, to sanctify the sabbath day. [e]Remember me, O my God, *concerning* this also, and spare me according to the greatness of thy mercy.

23 ¶ In those days also saw I Jews *that* [f]had married wives of Ashdod, of Ammon, *and* of Moab:

24 And their children spake half in the speech of Ashdod, and could not speak in the Jews' language, but according to the language of each people.

25 And I [g]contended with them, and cursed them, and smote certain of them, and plucked off their hair, and made them [h]swear by God, *saying,* Ye shall not give your daughters unto their sons, nor take their daughters unto your sons, or for yourselves.

26 [i]Did not Solomon king of Israel sin by these things? yet [j]among many nations was there no king like him, [k]who was beloved of his God, and God made him king over all Israel: [l]nevertheless even him did outlandish women cause to sin.

27 Shall we then hearken unto you to do all this great evil, to [m]transgress against our God in marrying strange wives?

28 And *one* of the sons [n]of Joiada, the son of Eliashib the high priest, *was* son in law to Sanballat the Horonite: therefore I chased him from me.

29 [o]Remember them, O my God, because they have defiled the priesthood, and [p]the covenant of the priesthood, and of the Levites.

30 [q]Thus cleansed I them from all strangers, and [r]appointed the wards of the priests and the Levites, every one in his business;

31 And for [s]the wood offering, at times appointed, and for the firstfruits. [t]Remember me, O my God, for good.

13:30 [q]ch. 10:30 [r]ch. 12:1
13:31 [s]ch. 10:34 [t]ver. 14

ESTHER

Some scholars have speculated that Ezra might have written the book in or close to 460 B.C. During the time of this book, God's people are still subject to anti-semitism that forced some of them to reject their heritage. The book of Esther tells a story of hope for the Jews of that day through the rise to power of a Jewish girl, Esther. Through Esther's influence with the king, an enemy of the Jews (Haman) is unmasked. This explains the origin of the Feast of Purim, a Jewish celebration marking Haman's death.

I. Esther becomes queen, 1:1–2:18
II. Haman's plot and Esther's intervention, 2:19–7:10
III. The Feasts of Purim, 8:1–10:3

---

1 Now it came to pass in the days of [a]Ahasuerus, (this *is* Ahasuerus which reigned, [b]from India even unto Ethiopia, [c]*over* an hundred and seven and twenty provinces:)

2 *That* in those days, when the king Ahasuerus [d]sat on the throne of his kingdom, which *was* in [e]Shushan the palace,

3 In the third year of his reign, he [f]made a feast unto all his princes and his servants; the power of Persia and Media, the nobles and princes of the provinces, *being* before him:

4 When he shewed the riches of his glorious kingdom and the honour of his excellent majesty many days, *even* an hundred and fourscore days.

5 And when these days were expired, the king made a feast unto all the people that were present in Shushan the palace, both unto great and small, seven days, in the court of the garden of the king's palace;

6 *Where were* white, green, and blue, *hangings*, fastened with cords of fine linen and purple to silver rings and pillars of marble: [g]the beds *were of* gold and silver, upon a pavement of red, and blue, and white, and black, marble.

7 And they gave *them* drink in vessels of gold, (the vessels being diverse one from another,) and royal wine in abundance, according to the state of the king.

8 And the drinking *was* according to the law; none did compel: for so the king had appointed to all the officers of his house, that they should do according to every man's pleasure.

9 Also Vashti the queen made a feast for the women *in* the royal house which *belonged* to king Ahasuerus.

10 ¶ On the seventh day, when [h]the heart of the king was merry with wine, he commanded Mehuman, Biztha, [i]Harbona, Bigtha, and Abagtha, Zethar, and Carcas, the seven chamberlains that served in the presence of Ahasuerus the king,

11 To bring Vashti the queen before the king with the crown royal, to shew the people and the princes her beauty: for she *was* fair to look on.

12 But the queen Vashti refused to come at the king's commandment by *his* chamberlains: therefore was the king very wroth, and his anger burned in him.

13 ¶ Then the king said to the [j]wise men, [k]which knew the times, (for so *was* the king's manner toward all that knew law and judgment:

14 And the next unto him *was* Carshena, Shethar, Admatha, Tarshish, Meres, Marsena, *and* Memucan, the [l]seven princes of Persia and Media, [m]which saw the king's face, *and* which sat the first in the kingdom;)

15 What shall we do unto the queen Vashti according to law, because she hath not performed the commandment of the king Ahasuerus by the chamberlains?

16 And Memucan answered before the king and the princes, Vashti the queen hath not done wrong to the king only, but also to all the princes, and to all the people that *are* in all the provinces of the king Ahasuerus.

17 For *this* deed of the queen shall come abroad unto all women, so that they shall [n]despise their husbands in their eyes, when it shall be reported, The king Ahasuerus commanded Vashti the queen to be brought in before him, but she came not.

18 *Likewise* shall the ladies of Persia and Media say this day unto all the king's princes, which have heard of the deed of the queen. Thus *shall there arise* too much contempt and wrath.

19 If it please the king, let there go a royal commandment from him, and let it be writ-

1:1 [a]Ezra 4:6; Dan. 9:1 [b]ch. 8:9 [c]Dan. 6:1
1:2 [d]1 Kings 1:46 [e]Neh. 1:1
1:3 [f]Gen. 40:20; ch. 2:18; Mark 6:21
1:6 [g]ch. 7:8; Ezek. 23:41; Am. 2:8
1:10 [h]2 Sam. 13:28 [i]ch. 7:9
1:13 [j]Jer. 10:7; Dan. 2:12; Matt. 2:1 [k]1 Chron. 12:32
1:14 [l]Ezra 7:14 [m]2 Kings 25:19
1:17 [n]Eph. 5:33

ten among the laws of the Persians and the Medes, that it be not altered, That Vashti come no more before king Ahasuerus; and let the king give her royal estate unto another that is better than she.

20 And when the king's decree which he shall make shall be published throughout all his empire, (for it is great,) all the wives shall [o]give to their husbands honour, both to great and small.

21 And the saying pleased the king and the princes; and the king did according to the word of Memucan:

22 For he sent letters into all the king's provinces, [p]into every province according to the writing thereof, and to every people after their language, that every man should [q]bear rule in his own house, and that *it* should be published according to the language of every people.

2 After these things, when the wrath of king Ahasuerus was appeased, he remembered Vashti, and what she had done, and [r]what was decreed against her.

2 Then said the king's servants that ministered unto him, Let there be fair young virgins sought for the king:

3 And let the king appoint officers in all the provinces of his kingdom, that they may gather together all the fair young virgins unto Shushan the palace, to the house of the women, unto the custody of Hege the king's chamberlain, keeper of the women; and let their things for purification be given *them:*

4 And let the maiden which pleaseth the king be queen instead of Vashti. And the thing pleased the king; and he did so.

5 ¶ *Now* in Shushan the palace there was a certain Jew, whose name *was* Mordecai, the son of Jair, the son of Shimei, the son of Kish, a Benjamite;

6 [s]Who had been carried away from Jerusalem with the captivity which had been carried away with Jeconiah king of Judah, whom Nebuchadnezzar the king of Babylon had carried away.

7 And he brought up Hadassah, that *is,* Esther, [t]his uncle's daughter: for she had neither father nor mother, and the maid *was* fair and beautiful; whom Mordecai, when her father and mother were dead, took for his own daughter.

8 ¶ So it came to pass, when the king's commandment and his decree was heard, and when many maidens were [u]gathered together unto Shushan the palace, to the custody of Hegai, that Esther was brought also unto the king's house, to the custody of Hegai, keeper of the women.

9 And the maiden pleased him, and she obtained kindness of him; and he speedily gave her her [v]things for purification, with such things as belonged to her, and seven maidens, *which were* meet to be given her, out of the king's house: and he preferred her and her maids unto the best *place* of the house of the women.

10 [w]Esther had not shewed her people nor her kindred: for Mordecai had charged her that she should not shew *it.*

11 And Mordecai walked every day before the court of the women's house, to know how Esther did, and what should become of her.

12 ¶ Now when every maid's turn was come to go in to king Ahasuerus, after that she had been twelve months, according to the manner of the women, (for so were the days of their purifications accomplished, *to wit,* six months with oil of myrrh, and six months with sweet odours, and with *other* things for the purifying of the women;)

13 Then thus came *every* maiden unto the king; whatsoever she desired was given her to go with her out of the house of the women unto the king's house.

14 In the evening she went, and on the morrow she returned into the second house of the women, to the custody of Shaashgaz, the king's chamberlain, which kept the concubines: she came in unto the king no more, except the king delighted in her, and that she were called by name.

15 ¶ Now when the turn of Esther, [x]the daughter of Abihail the uncle of Mordecai, who had taken her for his daughter, was come to go in unto the king, she required nothing but what Hegai the king's chamberlain, the keeper of the women, appointed. And Esther obtained favour in the sight of all them that looked upon her.

16 So Esther was taken unto king Ahasuerus into his house royal in the tenth month, which *is* the month Tebeth, in the seventh year of his reign.

17 And the king loved Esther above all the women, and she obtained grace and favour in his sight more than all the virgins; so that he set the royal crown upon her head, and made her queen instead of Vashti.

18 Then the king [y]made a great feast unto all his princes and his servants, *even* Esther's feast; and he made a release to the provinces, and gave gifts, according to the state of the king.

19 And when the virgins were gathered together the second time, then Mordecai sat [z]in the king's gate.

20 [a]Esther had not *yet* shewed her kindred nor her people; as Mordecai had charged her: for Esther did the commandment of Mordecai, like as when she was brought up with him.

21 ¶ In those days, while Mordecai sat in the king's gate, two of the king's chamberlains, Bigthan and Teresh, of those which kept the door, were wroth, and sought to lay hand on the king Ahasuerus.

22 And the thing was known to Mordecai, [b]who told *it* unto Esther the queen; and Esther certified the king *thereof* in Mordecai's name.

23 And when inquisition was made of the matter, it was found out; therefore they were both hanged on a tree: and it was writ-

1:20 [o]Eph. 5:33; Col. 3:18; 1 Pet. 3:1
1:22 [p]ch. 8:9 [q]Eph. 5:22; 1 Tim. 2:12
2:1 [r]ch. 1:19
2:6 [s]2 Kings 24:14; 2 Chron. 36:10; Jer. 24:1
2:7 [t]ver. 15
2:8 [u]ver. 3
2:9 [v]ver. 3
2:10 [w]ver. 20
2:15 [x]ver. 7
2:18 [y]ch. 1:3
2:19 [z]ver. 21; ch. 3:2
2:20 [a]ver. 10
2:22 [b]ch. 6:2

ten in [c]the book of the chronicles before the king.

3 After these things did king Ahasuerus promote Haman the son of Hammedatha the [d]Agagite, and advanced him, and set his seat above all the princes that *were* with him.

2 And all the king's servants, that *were* [e]in the king's gate, bowed, and reverenced Haman: for the king had so commanded concerning him. But Mordecai [f]bowed not, nor did *him* reverence.

3 Then the king's servants, which *were* in the king's gate, said unto Mordecai, Why transgressest thou the [g]king's commandment?

4 Now it came to pass, when they spake daily unto him, and he hearkened not unto them, that they told Haman, to see whether Mordecai's matters would stand: for he had told them that he *was* a Jew.

5 And when Haman saw that Mordecai [h]bowed not, nor did him reverence, then was Haman [i]full of wrath.

6 And he thought scorn to lay hands on Mordecai alone; for they had shewed him the people of Mordecai: wherefore Haman [j]sought to destroy all the Jews that *were* throughout the whole kingdom of Ahasuerus, *even* the people of Mordecai.

7 ¶ In the first month, that *is*, the month Nisan, in the twelfth year of king Ahasuerus, [k]they cast Pur, that *is*, the lot, before Haman from day to day, and from month to month, *to* the twelfth *month*, that *is*, the month Adar.

8 ¶ And Haman said unto king Ahasuerus, There is a certain people scattered abroad and dispersed among the people in all the provinces of thy kingdom; and [l]their laws *are* diverse from all people; neither keep they the king's laws: therefore it *is* not for the king's profit to suffer them.

9 If it please the king, let it be written that they may be destroyed: and I will pay ten thousand talents of silver to the hands of those that have the charge of the business, to bring *it* into the king's treasuries.

10 And the king [m]took [n]his ring from his hand, and gave it unto Haman the son of Hammedatha the Agagite, the Jews' enemy.

11 And the king said unto Haman, The silver *is* given to thee, the people also, to do with them as it seemeth good to thee.

12 [o]Then were the king's scribes called on the thirteenth day of the first month, and there was written according to all that Haman had commanded unto the king's lieutenants, and to the governors that *were* over every province, and to the rulers of every people of every province [p]according to the writing thereof, and *to* every people after their language; [q]in the name of king Ahasuerus was it written, and sealed with the king's ring.

13 And the letters were [r]sent by posts into all the king's provinces, to destroy, to kill, and to cause to perish, all Jews, both young and old, little children and women, [s]in one day, *even* upon the thirteenth *day* of the twelfth month, which *is* the month Adar, and [t]*to take* the spoil of them for a prey.

14 [u]The copy of the writing for a commandment to be given in every province was published unto all people, that they should be ready against that day.

15 The posts went out, being hastened by the king's commandment, and the decree was given in Shushan the palace. And the king and Haman sat down to drink; but [v]the city Shushan was perplexed.

4 When Mordecai perceived all that was done, Mordecai [w]rent his clothes, and put on sackcloth [x]with ashes, and went out into the midst of the city, and [y]cried with a loud and a bitter cry;

2 And came even before the king's gate: for none *might* enter into the king's gate clothed with sackcloth.

3 And in every province, whithersoever the king's commandment and his decree came, *there was* great mourning among the Jews, and fasting, and weeping, and wailing; and many lay in sackcloth and ashes.

4 ¶ So Esther's maids and her chamberlains came and told *it* her. Then was the queen exceedingly grieved; and she sent raiment to clothe Mordecai, and to take away his sackcloth from him: but he received *it* not.

5 Then called Esther for Hatach, *one* of the king's chamberlains, whom he had appointed to attend upon her, and gave him a commandment to Mordecai, to know what it *was*, and why it *was*.

6 So Hatach went forth to Mordecai unto the street of the city, which *was* before the king's gate.

7 And Mordecai told him of all that had happened unto him, and of [z]the sum of the money that Haman had promised to pay to the king's treasuries for the Jews, to destroy them.

8 Also he gave him [a]the copy of the writing of the decree that was given at Shushan to destroy them, to shew *it* unto Esther, and to declare *it* unto her, and to charge her that she should go in unto the king, to make supplication unto him, and to make request before him for her people.

9 And Hatach came and told Esther the words of Mordecai.

10 ¶ Again Esther spake unto Hatach, and gave him commandment unto Mordecai;

11 All the king's servants, and the people of the king's provinces, do know, that whosoever, whether man or woman, shall come unto the king into the [b]inner court, who is not called, [c]*there is* one law of his to put *him* to death, except such [d]to whom the king shall hold out the golden sceptre, that he may live: but I have not been called to come in unto the king these thirty days.

12 And they told to Mordecai Esther's words.

2:23 [c]ch. 6:1
3:1 [d]Num. 24:7; 1 Sam. 15:8
3:2 [e]ch. 2:19 [f]ver. 5; Ps. 15:4
3:3 [g]ver. 2
3:5 [h]ver. 2; ch. 5:9 [i]Dan. 3:19
3:6 [j]Ps. 83:4
3:7 [k]ch. 9:24
3:8 [l]Ezra 4:13; Acts 16:20
3:10 [m]Gen. 41:42 [n]ch. 8:2
3:12 [o]ch. 8:9 [p]ch. 1:22 [q]1 Kings 21:8; ch. 8:8
3:13 [r]ch. 8:10 [s]ch. 8:12 [t]ch. 8:11
3:14 [u]ch. 8:13
3:15 [v]ch. 8:15; Prov. 29:2
4:1 [w]2 Sam. 1:11 [x]Josh. 7:6; Ezek. 27:30 [y]Gen. 27:34
4:7 [z]ch. 3:9
4:8 [a]ch. 3:14
4:11 [b]ch. 5:1 [c]Dan. 2:9 [d]ch. 5:2

13 Then Mordecai commanded to answer Esther, Think not with thyself that thou shalt escape in the king's house, more than all the Jews.

14 For if thou altogether holdest thy peace at this time, *then* shall there enlargement and deliverance arise to the Jews from another place; but thou and thy father's house shall be destroyed: and who knoweth whether thou art come to the kingdom for *such* a time as this?

15 ¶ Then Esther bade *them* return Mordecai *this answer,*

16 Go, gather together all the Jews that are present in Shushan, and fast ye for me, and neither eat nor drink [e]three days, night or day: I also and my maidens will fast likewise; and so will I go in unto the king, which *is* not according to the law: [f]and if I perish, I perish.

17 So Mordecai went his way, and did according to all that Esther had commanded him.

5 Now it came to pass [g]on the third day, that Esther put on *her* royal *apparel,* and stood in [h]the inner court of the king's house, over against the king's house: and the king sat upon his royal throne in the royal house, over against the gate of the house.

2 And it was so, when the king saw Esther the queen standing in the court, *that* [i]she obtained favour in his sight: and [j]the king held out to Esther the golden sceptre that *was* in his hand. So Esther drew near, and touched the top of the sceptre.

3 Then said the king unto her, What wilt thou, queen Esther? and what *is* thy request? [k]it shall be even given thee to the half of the kingdom.

4 And Esther answered, If *it seem* good unto the king, let the king and Haman come this day unto the banquet that I have prepared for him.

5 Then the king said, Cause Haman to make haste, that he may do as Esther hath said. So the king and Haman came to the banquet that Esther had prepared.

6 ¶ [l]And the king said unto Esther at the banquet of wine, [m]What *is* thy petition? and it shall be granted thee: and what *is* thy request? even to the half of the kingdom it shall be performed.

7 Then answered Esther, and said, My petition and my request *is;*

8 If I have found favour in the sight of the king, and if it please the king to grant my petition, and to perform my request, let the king and Haman come to the banquet that I shall prepare for them, and I will do to morrow as the king hath said.

9 ¶ Then went Haman forth that day joyful and with a glad heart: but when Haman saw Mordecai in the king's gate, [n]that he stood not up, nor moved for him, he was full of indignation against Mordecai.

10 Nevertheless Haman [o]refrained himself: and when he came home, he sent and called for his friends, and Zeresh his wife.

11 And Haman told them of the glory of his riches, and [p]the multitude of his children, and all *the things* wherein the king had promoted him, and how he had [q]advanced him above the princes and servants of the king.

12 Haman said moreover, Yea, Esther the queen did let no man come in with the king unto the banquet that she had prepared but myself; and to morrow am I invited unto her also with the king.

13 Yet all this availeth me nothing, so long as I see Mordecai the Jew sitting at the king's gate.

14 ¶ Then said Zeresh his wife and all his friends unto him, Let a [r]gallows be made of fifty cubits high, and to morrow [s]speak thou unto the king that Mordecai may be hanged thereon: then go thou in merrily with the king unto the banquet. And the thing pleased Haman; and he caused [t]the gallows to be made.

6 On that night could not the king sleep, and he commanded to bring [u]the book of records of the chronicles; and they were read before the king.

2 And it was found written, that Mordecai had told of Bigthana and Teresh, two of the king's chamberlains, the keepers of the door, who sought to lay hand on the king Ahasuerus.

3 And the king said, What honour and dignity hath been done to Mordecai for this? Then said the king's servants that ministered unto him, There is nothing done for him.

4 And the king said, Who *is* in the court? Now Haman was come [v]into the outward court of the king's house, [w]to speak unto the king to hang Mordecai on the gallows that he had prepared for him.

5 And the king's servants said unto him, Behold, Haman standeth in the court. And the king said, Let him come in.

6 So Haman came in. And the king said unto him, What shall be done unto the man whom the king delighteth to honour? Now Haman thought in his heart, To whom would the king delight to do honour more than to myself?

7 And Haman answered the king, For the man whom the king delighteth to honour,

8 Let the royal apparel be brought which the king *useth* to wear, and [x]the horse that the king rideth upon, and the crown royal which is set upon his head:

9 And let this apparel and horse be delivered to the hand of one of the king's most noble princes, that they may array the man *withal* whom the king delighteth to honour, and bring him on horseback through the street of the city, [y]and proclaim before him, Thus shall it be done to the man whom the king delighteth to honour.

10 Then the king said to Haman, Make haste, *and* take the apparel and the horse, as thou hast said, and do even so to Morde-

4:16 [e]ch. 5:1 [f]Gen. 43:14
5:1 [g]ch. 4:16 [h]ch. 4:11
5:2 [i]Esth. 15:7; Prov. 21:1 [j]ch. 4:11
5:3 [k]Mark 6:23
5:6 [l]ch. 7:2 [m]ch. 9:12
5:9 [n]ch. 3:5
5:10 [o]2 Sam. 13:22
5:11 [p]ch. 9:7 [q]ch. 3:1
5:14 [r]ch. 7:9 [s]ch. 6:4 [t]ch. 7:10
6:1 [u]ch. 2:23
6:4 [v]ch. 5:1 [w]ch. 5:14
6:8 [x]1 Kings 1:33
6:9 [y]Gen. 41:43

cai the Jew, that sitteth at the king's gate: let nothing fail of all that thou hast spoken.

11 Then took Haman the apparel and the horse, and arrayed Mordecai, and brought him on horseback through the street of the city, and proclaimed before him, Thus shall it be done unto the man whom the king delighteth to honour.

12 ¶ And Mordecai came again to the king's gate. But Haman [z]hasted to his house mourning, [a]and having his head covered.

13 And Haman told Zeresh his wife and all his friends every *thing* that had befallen him. Then said his wise men and Zeresh his wife unto him, If Mordecai *be* of the seed of the Jews, before whom thou hast begun to fall, thou shalt not prevail against him, but shalt surely fall before him.

14 And while they *were* yet talking with him, came the king's chamberlains, and hasted to bring Haman unto [b]the banquet that Esther had prepared.

7 So the king and Haman came to banquet with Esther the queen.

2 And the king said again unto Esther on the second day [c]at the banquet of wine, What *is* thy petition, queen Esther? and it shall be granted thee: and what *is* thy request? and it shall be performed, *even* to the half of the kingdom.

3 Then Esther the queen answered and said, If I have found favour in thy sight, O king, and if it please the king, let my life be given me at my petition, and my people at my request:

4 For we are [d]sold, I and my people, to be destroyed, to be slain, and to perish. But if we had been sold for bondmen and bondwomen, I had held my tongue, although the enemy could not countervail the king's damage.

5 ¶ Then the king Ahasuerus answered and said unto Esther the queen, Who is he, and where is he, that durst presume in his heart to do so?

6 And Esther said, The adversary and enemy *is* this wicked Haman. Then Haman was afraid before the king and the queen.

7 ¶ And the king arising from the banquet of wine in his wrath *went* into the palace garden: and Haman stood up to make request for his life to Esther the queen; for he saw that there was evil determined against him by the king.

8 Then the king returned out of the palace garden into the place of the banquet of wine; and Haman was fallen upon [e]the bed whereon Esther *was*. Then said the king, Will he force the queen also before me in the house? As the word went out of king's mouth, they [f]covered Haman's face.

9 And [g]Harbonah, one of the chamberlains, said before the king, Behold also, [h]the gallows fifty cubits high, which Haman had made for Mordecai, who had spoken good for the king, standeth in the house of Haman. Then the king said, Hang him thereon.

10 So [i]they hanged Haman on the gallows that he had prepared for Mordecai. Then was the king's wrath pacified.

8 On that day did the king Ahasuerus give the house of Haman the Jews' enemy unto Esther the queen. And Mordecai came before the king; for Esther had told [j]what he *was* unto her.

2 And the king took off [k]his ring, which he had taken from Haman, and gave it unto Mordecai. And Esther set Mordecai over the house of Haman.

3 ¶ And Esther spake yet again before the king, and fell down at his feet, and besought him with tears to put away the mischief of Haman the Agagite, and his device that he had devised against the Jews.

4 Then [l]the king held out the golden sceptre toward Esther. So Esther arose, and stood before the king.

5 And said, If it please the king, and if I have found favour in his sight, and the thing *seem* right before the king, and I *be* pleasing in his eyes, let it be written to reverse the letters devised by Haman the son of Hammedatha the Agagite, which he wrote to destroy the Jews which *are* in all the king's provinces:

6 For how can I endure to see [m]the evil that shall come unto my people? or how can I endure to see the destruction of my kindred?

7 ¶ Then the king Ahasuerus said unto Esther the queen and to Mordecai the Jew, Behold, [n]I have given Esther the house of Haman, and him they have hanged upon the gallows, because he laid his hand upon the Jews.

8 Write ye also for the Jews, as it liketh you, in the king's name, and seal *it* with the king's ring: for the writing which is written in the king's name, and sealed with the king's ring, [o]may no man reverse.

9 [p]Then were the king's scribes called at that time in the third month, that *is*, the month Sivan, on the three and twentieth *day* thereof; and it was written according to all that Mordecai commanded unto the Jews, and to the lieutenants, and the deputies and rulers of the provinces which *are* [q]from India unto Ethiopia, an hundred twenty and seven provinces, unto every province [r]according to the writing thereof, and unto every people after their language, and to the Jews according to their writing, and according to their language.

10 [s]And he wrote in the king Ahasuerus' name, and sealed *it* with the king's ring, and sent letters by posts on horseback, *and* riders on mules, camels, *and* young dromedaries:

11 Wherein the king granted the Jews which *were* in every city to gather themselves together, and to stand for their life, to destroy, to slay, and to cause to perish, all the power of the people and province that

6:12 z2 Chron. 26:20 a2 Sam. 15:30; Jer. 14:3
6:14 bch. 5:8
7:2 cch. 5:6
7:4 dch. 3:9
7:8 ech. 1:6 fJob 9:24
7:9 gch. 1:10 hch. 5:14; Ps. 7:16; Prov. 11:5
7:10 iDan. 6:24; Ps. 37:35
8:1 jch. 2:7
8:2 kch. 3:10
8:4 lch. 4:11
8:6 mch. 7:4; Neh. 2:3
8:7 nver. 1; Prov. 13:22
8:8 och. 1:19; Dan. 6:8
8:9 pch. 3:12 qch. 1:1 rch. 1:22
8:10 s1 Kings 21:8; ch. 3:12

would assault them, *both* little ones and
women, and [t]*to take* the spoil of them for
a prey,
12 [u]Upon one day in all the provinces
of king Ahasuerus, *namely*, upon the thirteenth *day* of the twelfth month, which *is*
the month Adar.
13 [v]The copy of the writing for a commandment to be given in every province
was published unto all people, and that the
Jews should be ready against that day to
avenge themselves on their enemies.
14 *So* the posts that rode upon mules *and*
camels went out, being hastened and
pressed on by the king's commandment.
And the decree was given at Shushan the
palace.
15 ¶ And Mordecai went out from the
presence of the king in royal apparel of blue
and white, and with a great crown of gold,
and with a garment of fine linen and purple:
and [w]the city of Shushan rejoiced and was
glad.
16 The Jews had [x]light, and gladness,
and joy, and honour.
17 And in every province, and in every
city, whithersoever the king's commandment and his decree came, the Jews had joy
and gladness, a feast [y]and a good day. And
many of the people of the land [z]became
Jews; for [a]the fear of the Jews fell upon
them.
9 Now [b]in the twelfth month, that *is*, the
month Adar, on the thirteenth day of
the same, [c]when the king's commandment
and his decree drew near to be put in execution, in the day that the enemies of the Jews
hoped to have power over them, (though it
was turned to the contrary, that the Jews
[d]had rule over them that hated them;)
2 The Jews [e]gathered themselves together in their cities throughout all the
provinces of the king Ahasuerus, to [f]lay
hand on such as sought their hurt: and no
man could withstand them; for [g]the fear of
them fell upon all people.
3 And all the rulers of the provinces, and
the lieutenants, and the deputies, and officers of the king, helped the Jews; because
the fear of Mordecai fell upon them.
4 For Mordecai *was* great in the king's
house, and his fame went out throughout
all the provinces: for this man Mordecai
[h]waxed greater and greater.
5 Thus the Jews smote all their enemies
with the stroke of the sword, and slaughter,
and destruction, and did what they would
unto those that hated them.
6 And in Shushan the palace the Jews
slew and destroyed five hundred men.
7 And Parshandatha, and Dalphon, and
Aspatha,
8 And Poratha, and Adalia, and Aridatha,
9 And Parmashta, and Arisai, and Aridai,
and Vajezatha,
10 [i]The ten sons of Haman the son of
Hammedatha, the enemy of the Jews, slew

8:11 [t]ch. 9:10
8:12 [u]ch. 3:13
8:13 [v]ch. 3:14
8:15 [w]ch. 3:15; Prov. 29:2
8:16 [x]Ps. 97:11
8:17 [y]1 Sam. 25:8; ch. 9:19 [z]Ps. 18:43 [a]Gen. 35:5; Ex. 15:16; Deut. 2:25; ch. 9:2
9:1 [b]ch. 8:12 [c]ch. 3:13 [d]2 Sam. 22:41
9:2 [e]ch. 8:11 [f]Ps. 71:13 [g]ch. 8:17
9:4 [h]2 Sam. 3:1; 1 Chron. 11:9; Prov. 4:18
9:10 [i]ch. 5:11; Job 18:19; Ps. 21:10 [j]ch. 8:11
9:12 [k]ch. 5:6
9:13 [l]ch. 8:11 [m]2 Sam. 21:6
9:15 [n]ver. 2 [o]ver. 10
9:16 [p]ver. 2 [q]ch. 8:11
9:18 [r]ver. 11
9:19 [s]Deut. 16:11 [t]ch. 8:17 [u]ver. 22; Neh. 8:10
9:22 [v]Ps. 30:11 [w]ver. 19; Neh. 8:11
9:24 [x]ch. 3:6

they; [j]but on the spoil laid they not their
hand.
11 On that day the number of those that
were slain in Shushan the palace was
brought before the king.
12 And the king said unto Esther the
queen, The Jews have slain and destroyed
five hundred men in Shushan the palace,
and the ten sons of Haman; what have they
done in the rest of the king's provinces?
now [k]what *is* thy petition? and it shall be
granted thee: or what *is* thy request further?
and it shall be done.
13 Then said Esther, If it please the king,
let it be granted to the Jews which *are* in
Shushan to do to morrow also [l]according
unto this day's decree, and let Haman's ten
sons [m]be hanged upon the gallows.
14 And the king commanded it so to be
done: and the decree was given at Shushan;
and they hanged Haman's ten sons.
15 For the Jews that *were* in Shushan
[n]gathered themselves together on the fourteenth day also of the month Adar, and slew
three hundred men at Shushan; [o]but on the
prey they laid not their hand.
16 But the other Jews that *were* in the
king's provinces [p]gathered themselves together, and stood for their lives, and had
rest from their enemies, and slew of their
foes seventy and five thousand, [q]but they
laid not their hands on the prey,
17 On the thirteenth day of the month
Adar; and on the fourteenth day of the same
rested they, and made it a day of feasting
and gladness.
18 But the Jews that *were* at Shushan assembled together [r]on the thirteenth *day*
thereof, and on the fourteenth thereof; and
on the fifteenth *day* of the same they rested,
and made it a day of feasting and gladness.
19 Therefore the Jews of the villages, that
dwelt in the unwalled towns, made the fourteenth day of the month Adar [s]*a day of*
gladness and feasting, [t]and a good day,
and of [u]sending portions one to another.
20 ¶ And Mordecai wrote these things,
and sent letters unto all the Jews that *were*
in all the provinces of the king Ahasuerus,
both nigh and far,
21 To stablish *this* among them, that they
should keep the fourteenth day of the
month Adar, and the fifteenth day of the
same, yearly,
22 As the days wherein the Jews rested
from their enemies, and the month which
was [v]turned unto them from sorrow to joy,
and from mourning into a good day: that
they should make them days of feasting and
joy, and of [w]sending portions one to another, and gifts to the poor.
23 And the Jews undertook to do as they
had begun, and as Mordecai had written
unto them;
24 Because Haman the son of Hammedatha, the Agagite, the enemy of all the Jews,
[x]had devised against the Jews to destroy

them, and had cast Pur, that *is*, the lot, to consume them, and to destroy them;

25 But [y]when *Esther* came before the king, he commanded by letters that his wicked device, which he devised against the Jews, should [z]return upon his own head, and that he and his sons should be hanged on the gallows.

26 Wherefore they called these days Purim after the name of Pur. Therefore for all the words of [a]this letter, and *of that* which they had seen concerning this matter, and which had come unto them,

27 The Jews ordained, and took upon them, and upon their seed, and upon all such as [b]joined themselves unto them, so as it should not fail, that they would keep these two days according to their writing, and according to their *appointed* time every year;

28 And *that* these days *should be* remembered and kept throughout every generation, every family, every province, and every city; and *that* these days of Purim should not fail from among the Jews, nor the memorial of them perish from their seed.

29 Then Esther the queen, [c]the daughter of Abihail, and Mordecai the Jew, wrote with all authority, to confirm this [d]second letter of Purim.

30 And he sent the letters unto all the Jews, to [e]the hundred twenty and seven provinces of the kingdom of Ahasuerus, *with* words of peace and truth,

31 To confirm these days of Purim in their times *appointed*, according as Mordecai the Jew and Esther the queen had enjoined them, and as they had decreed for themselves and for their seed, the matters of [f]the fastings and their cry.

32 And the decree of Esther confirmed these matters of Purim; and it was written in the book.

10 And the king Ahasuerus laid a tribute upon the land, and *upon* [g]the isles of the sea.

2 And all the acts of his power and of his might, and the declaration of the greatness of Mordecai, [h]whereunto the king advanced him, *are* they not written in the book of the chronicles of the kings of Media and Persia?

3 For Mordecai the Jew *was* [i]next unto king Ahasuerus, and great among the Jews, and accepted of the multitude of his brethren, [j]seeking the wealth of his people, and speaking peace to all his seed.

9:25 [y]ver. 13; ch. 7:5 [z]ch. 7:10; Ps. 7:16
9:26 [a]ver. 20
9:27 [b]ch. 8:17; Isa. 56:3; Zech. 2:11
9:29 [c]ch. 2:15 [d]ch. 8:10
9:30 [e]ch. 1:1
9:31 [f]ch. 4:3
10:1 [g]Gen. 10:5; Ps. 72:10; Isa. 24:15
10:2 [h]ch. 8:15
10:3 [i]Gen. 41:40; 2 Chron. 28:7 [j]Neh. 2:10; Ps. 122:8

JOB

The authorship of Job is uncertain. Some say Job himself wrote the book while others have credited Solomon or Moses. The date of the writing of Job is unknown. This is the story of Job, a righteous man whom Satan believes can be corrupted and drawn away from God. God agrees to allow Satan to tempt and destroy much of what Job has. Satan hopes to prove Job will crumble under the assault. The remainder of the book records Job's search for answers to what is happening to him. Having resolved the issue, Job eventually recovers much of what he lost and learns a valuable lesson about God in the process.

I. Disaster strikes Job, 1:1–3:26
II. Job and his friends argue the cause, 4:1–31:40
III. Cause properly determined, 32:1–42:17

1 There was a man [a]in the land of Uz, whose name *was* [b]Job; and that man was [c]perfect and upright, and one that [d]feared God, and eschewed evil.

2 And there were born unto him seven sons and three daughters.

3 His substance also was seven thousand sheep, and three thousand camels, and five hundred yoke of oxen, and five hundred she asses, and a very great household; so that this man was the greatest of all the men of the east.

4 And his sons went and feasted *in their* houses, every one his day; and sent and called for their three sisters to eat and to drink with them.

5 And it was so, when the days of *their* feasting were gone about, that Job sent and sanctified them, and rose up early in the morning, [e]and offered burnt offerings *according* to the number of them all: for Job said, It may be that my sons have sinned, and [f]cursed God in their hearts. Thus did Job continually.

6 ¶ Now [g]there was a day [h]when the sons of God came to present themselves before the LORD, and Satan came also among them.

1:1 [a]Gen. 22:20 [b]Ezek. 14:14; Jam. 5:11 [c]Gen. 6:9; ch. 2:3 [d]Prov. 8:13
1:5 [e]Gen. 8:20; ch. 42:8 [f]1 Kings 21:10
1:6 [g]ch. 2:1 [h]1 Kings 22:19; ch. 38:7

7 And the LORD said unto Satan, Whence comest thou? Then Satan answered the LORD, and said, From [i]going to and fro in the earth, and from walking up and down in it.

8 And the LORD said unto Satan, [j]Hast thou considered my servant Job, that *there is* none like him in the earth, [k]a perfect and an upright man, one that feareth God, and escheweth evil?

9 Then Satan answered the LORD, and said, Doth Job fear God for nought?

10 [l]Hast not thou made an hedge about him, and about his house, and about all that he hath on every side? [m]thou hast blessed the work of his hands, and his substance is increased in the land.

11 [n]But put forth thine hand now, and touch all that he hath, and he will [o]curse thee to thy face.

12 And the LORD said unto Satan, Behold, all that he hath *is* in thy power; only upon himself put not forth thine hand. So Satan went forth from the presence of the LORD.

13 ¶ And there was a day [p]when his sons and his daughters *were* eating and drinking wine in their eldest brother's house:

14 And there came a messenger unto Job, and said, The oxen were plowing, and the asses feeding beside them:

15 And the Sabeans fell *upon them,* and took them away; yea, they have slain the servants with the edge of the sword; and I only am escaped alone to tell thee.

16 While he *was* yet speaking, there came also another, and said, The fire of God is fallen from heaven, and hath burned up the sheep, and the servants, and consumed them; and I only am escaped alone to tell thee.

17 While he *was* yet speaking, there came also another, and said, The Chaldeans made out three bands, and fell upon the camels, and have carried them away, yea, and slain the servants with the edge of the sword; and I only am escaped alone to tell thee.

18 While he *was* yet speaking, there came also another, and said, [q]Thy sons and thy daughters *were* eating and drinking wine in their eldest brother's house:

19 And, behold, there came a great wind from the wilderness, and smote the four corners of the house, and it fell upon the young men, and they are dead; and I only am escaped alone to tell thee.

20 Then Job arose, [r]and rent his mantle, and shaved his head, and [s]fell down upon the ground, and worshipped,

21 And said, [t]Naked came I out of my mother's womb, and naked shall I return thither: the LORD [u]gave, and the LORD hath [v]taken away; [w]blessed be the name of the LORD.

22 [x]In all this Job sinned not, nor charged God foolishly.

2 Again [y]there was a day when the sons of God came to present themselves before the LORD, and Satan came also among them to present himself before the LORD.

1:7 [i]ch. 2:2; Matt. 12:43; 1 Pet. 5:8
1:8 [j]ch. 2:3 [k]ver. 1
1:10 [l]Ps. 34:7; Isa. 5:2 [m]Ps. 128:1; Prov. 10:22
1:11 [n]ch. 2:5 [o]Isa. 8:21; Mal. 3:13
1:13 [p]Eccl. 9:12
1:18 [q]ver. 4
1:20 [r]Gen. 37:29; Ezra 9:3 [s]1 Pet. 5:6
1:21 [t]Ps. 49:17; Eccl. 5:15; 1 Tim. 6:7 [u]Eccl. 5:19; Jam. 1:17 [v]Matt. 20:15 [w]Eph. 5:20; 1 Thess. 5:18
1:22 [x]ch. 2:10
2:1 [y]ch. 1:6
2:2 [z]ch. 1:7
2:3 [a]ch. 1:1 [b]ch. 27:5 [c]ch. 9:17
2:5 [d]ch. 1:11 [e]ch. 19:20
2:6 [f]ch. 1:12
2:7 [g]Isa. 1:6
2:8 [h]2 Sam. 13:19; ch. 42:6; Ezek. 27:30; Matt. 11:21
2:9 [i]ch. 21:15 [j]ver. 3
2:10 [k]ch. 1:21; Rom. 12:12; Jam. 5:10 [l]ch. 1:22 [m]Ps. 39:1
2:11 [n]Prov. 17:17 [o]Gen. 36:11; Jer. 49:7 [p]Gen. 25:2 [q]ch. 42:11; Rom. 12:15
2:12 [r]Neh. 9:1; Lam. 2:10; Ezek. 27:30
2:13 [s]Gen. 50:10
3:3 [t]ch. 10:18; Jer. 15:10
3:5 [u]ch. 10:21; Ps. 23:4; Jer. 13:16; Am. 5:8

2 And the LORD said unto Satan, From whence comest thou? And [z]Satan answered the LORD, and said, From going to and fro in the earth, and from walking up and down in it.

3 And the LORD said unto Satan, Hast thou considered my servant Job, that *there is* none like him in the earth, [a]a perfect and an upright man, one that feareth God, and escheweth evil? and still he [b]holdeth fast his integrity, although thou movedst me against him, [c]to destroy him without cause.

4 And Satan answered the LORD, and said, Skin for skin, yea, all that a man hath will he give for his life.

5 [d]But put forth thine hand now, and touch his [e]bone and his flesh, and he will curse thee to thy face.

6 [f]And the LORD said unto Satan, Behold, he *is* in thine hand; but save his life.

7 ¶ So went Satan forth from the presence of the LORD, and smote Job with sore boils [g]from the sole of his foot unto his crown.

8 And he took him a potsherd to scrape himself withal; [h]and he sat down among the ashes.

9 ¶ Then said his wife unto him, [i]Dost thou still [j]retain thine integrity? curse God, and die.

10 But he said unto her, Thou speakest as one of the foolish women speaketh. What? [k]shall we receive good at the hand of God, and shall we not receive evil? [l]In all this did not Job [m]sin with his lips.

11 ¶ Now when Job's three [n]friends heard of all this evil that was come upon him, they came every one from his own place; Eliphaz the [o]Temanite, and Bildad the [p]Shuhite, and Zophar the Naamathite: for they had made an appointment together to come [q]to mourn with him and to comfort him.

12 And when they lifted up their eyes afar off, and knew him not, they lifted up their voice, and wept; and they rent every one his mantle, and [r]sprinkled dust upon their heads toward heaven.

13 So they sat down with him upon the ground [s]seven days and seven nights, and none spake a word unto him: for they saw that *his* grief was very great.

3 After this opened Job his mouth, and cursed his day.

2 And Job spake, and said,

3 [t]Let the day perish wherein I was born, and the night *in which* it was said, There is a man child conceived.

4 Let that day be darkness; let not God regard it from above, neither let the light shine upon it.

5 Let darkness and [u]the shadow of death stain it; let a cloud dwell upon it; let the blackness of the day terrify it.

6 *As for* that night, let darkness seize upon it; let it not be joined unto the days of

the year, let it not come into the number of
the months.

7 Lo, let that night be solitary, let no joyful voice come therein.

8 Let them curse it that curse the day,
[v]who are ready to raise up their mourning.

9 Let the stars of the twilight thereof be
dark; let it look for light, but *have* none;
neither let it see the dawning of the day:

10 Because it shut not up the doors of my
mother's womb, nor hid sorrow from mine
eyes.

11 [w]Why died I not from the womb? *why*
did I *not* give up the ghost when I came out
of the belly?

12 [x]Why did the knees prevent me? or
why the breasts that I should suck?

13 For now should I have lain still and
been quiet, I should have slept: then had I
been at rest,

14 With kings and counsellors of the
earth, which [y]built desolate places for
themselves;

15 Or with princes that had gold, who
filled their houses with silver:

16 Or [z]as an hidden untimely birth I had
not been; as infants *which* never saw light.

17 There the wicked cease *from* troubling; and there the weary be at rest.

18 *There* the prisoners rest together;
[a]they hear not the voice of the oppressor.

19 The small and great are there; and the
servant *is* free from his master.

20 [b]Wherefore is light given to him that
is in misery, and life unto the [c]bitter *in* soul;

21 Which [d]long for death, but it *cometh*
not; and dig for it more than [e]for hid treasures;

22 Which rejoice exceedingly, *and* are
glad, when they can find the grave?

23 *Why is light given* to a man whose way
is hid, [f]and whom God hath hedged in?

24 For my sighing cometh before I eat,
and my roarings are poured out like the waters.

25 For the thing which I greatly feared is
come upon me, and that which I was afraid
of is come unto me.

26 I was not in safety, neither had I rest,
neither was I quiet; yet trouble came.

4 Then Eliphaz the Temanite answered
and said,

2 *If* we assay to commune with thee, wilt
thou be grieved? but who can withhold himself from speaking?

3 Behold, thou hast instructed many, and
thou [g]hast strengthened the weak hands.

4 Thy words have upholden him that was
falling, and thou [h]hast strengthened the
feeble knees.

5 But now it is come upon thee, and thou
faintest; it toucheth thee, and thou art troubled.

6 *Is* not *this* [i]thy fear, [j]thy confidence,
thy hope, and the uprightness of thy ways?

7 Remember, I pray thee, [k]who *ever* perished, being innocent? or where were the
righteous cut off?

8 Even as I have seen, [l]they that plow
iniquity, and sow wickedness, reap the
same.

9 By the blast of God they perish, and
by the breath of his nostrils are they consumed.

10 The roaring of the lion, and the voice
of the fierce lion, and [m]the teeth of the
young lions, are broken.

11 [n]The old lion perisheth for lack of
prey, and the stout lion's whelps are scattered abroad.

12 Now a thing was secretly brought to
me, and mine ear received a little thereof.

13 [o]In thoughts from the visions of the
night, when deep sleep falleth on men,

14 Fear came upon me, and [p]trembling,
which made all my bones to shake.

15 Then a spirit passed before my face;
the hair of my flesh stood up:

16 It stood still, but I could not discern the
form thereof: an image *was* before mine
eyes, *there was* silence, and I heard a voice,
saying,

17 [q]Shall mortal man be more just than
God? shall a man be more pure than his
maker?

18 Behold, [r]he put no trust in his servants; and his angels he charged with folly:

19 [s]How much less *in* them that dwell in
[t]houses of clay, whose foundation *is* in the
dust, *which* are crushed before the moth?

20 [u]They are destroyed from morning to
evening: they perish for ever without any
regarding *it*.

21 [v]Doth not their excellency *which is* in
them go away? [w]they die, even without wisdom.

5 Call now, if there be any that will answer thee; and to which of the saints
wilt thou turn?

2 For wrath killeth the foolish man, and
envy slayeth the silly one.

3 [x]I have seen the foolish taking root: but
suddenly I cursed his habitation.

4 [y]His children are far from safety, and
they are crushed in the gate, [z]neither *is*
there any to deliver *them*.

5 Whose harvest the hungry eateth up,
and taketh it even out of the thorns, and
[a]the robber swalloweth up their substance.

6 Although affliction cometh not forth of
the dust, neither doth trouble spring out of
the ground;

7 Yet man is [b]born unto trouble, as the
sparks fly upward.

8 I would seek unto God, and unto God
would I commit my cause:

9 [c]Which doeth great things and unsearchable; marvellous things without
number:

10 [d]Who giveth rain upon the earth, and
sendeth waters upon the fields:

11 [e]To set up on high those that be low;
that those which mourn may be exalted to
safety.

12 [f]He disappointeth the devices of the

3:8 [v]Jer. 9:17
3:11 [w]ch. 10:18
3:12 [x]Gen. 30:3; Isa. 66:12
3:14 [y]ch. 15:28
3:16 [z]Ps. 58:8
3:18 [a]ch. 39:7
3:20 [b]Jer. 20:18 [c]1 Sam. 1:10; 2 Kings 4:27; Prov. 31:6
3:21 [d]Rev. 9:6 [e]Prov. 2:4
3:23 [f]ch. 19:8; Lam. 3:7
4:3 [g]Isa. 35:3
4:4 [h]Isa. 35:3
4:6 [i]ch. 1:1 [j]Prov. 3:26
4:7 [k]Ps. 37:25
4:8 [l]Ps. 7:14; Prov. 22:8; Hos. 10:13; Gal. 6:7
4:10 [m]Ps. 58:6
4:11 [n]Ps. 34:10
4:13 [o]ch. 33:15
4:14 [p]Hab. 3:16
4:17 [q]ch. 9:2
4:18 [r]ch. 15:15; 2 Pet. 2:4
4:19 [s]ch. 15:16 [t]2 Cor. 4:7
4:20 [u]Ps. 90:5
4:21 [v]Ps. 39:11 [w]ch. 36:12
5:3 [x]Ps. 37:35; Jer. 12:2
5:4 [y]Ps. 119:155 [z]Ps. 109:12
5:5 [a]ch. 18:9
5:7 [b]Gen. 3:17; 1 Cor. 10:13
5:9 [c]ch. 9:10; Ps. 40:5; Rom. 11:33
5:10 [d]ch. 28:26; Ps. 65:9; Jer. 5:24; Acts 14:17
5:11 [e]1 Sam. 2:7; Ps. 113:7
5:12 [f]Neh. 4:15; Ps. 33:10; Isa. 8:10

crafty, so that their hands cannot perform *their* enterprise.

13 [g]He taketh the wise in their own craftiness: and the counsel of the froward is carried headlong.

14 [h]They meet with darkness in the daytime, and grope in the noonday as in the night.

15 But [i]he saveth the poor from the sword, from their mouth, and from the hand of the mighty.

16 [j]So the poor hath hope, and iniquity stoppeth her mouth.

17 [k]Behold, happy *is* the man whom God correcteth: therefore despise not thou the chastening of the Almighty:

18 [l]For he maketh sore, and bindeth up: he woundeth, and his hands make whole.

19 [m]He shall deliver thee in six troubles: yea, in seven [n]there shall no evil touch thee.

20 [o]In famine he shall redeem thee from death: and in war from the power of the sword.

21 [p]Thou shalt be hid from the scourge of the tongue: neither shalt thou be afraid of destruction when it cometh.

22 At destruction and famine thou shalt laugh: [q]neither shalt thou be afraid of the beasts of the earth.

23 [r]For thou shalt be in league with the stones of the field: and the beasts of the field shall be at peace with thee.

24 And thou shalt know that thy tabernacle *shall be* in peace; and thou shalt visit thy habitation, and shalt not sin.

25 Thou shalt know also that [s]thy seed *shall be* great, and thine offspring [t]as the grass of the earth.

26 [u]Thou shalt come to *thy* grave in a full age, like as a shock of corn cometh in in his season.

27 Lo this, we have [v]searched it, so it *is;* hear it, and know thou *it* for thy good.

6 But Job answered and said,

2 Oh that my grief were throughly weighed, and my calamity laid in the balances together!

3 For now it would be heavier [w]than the sand of the sea: therefore my words are swallowed up.

4 [x]For the arrows of the Almighty *are* within me, the poison whereof drinketh up my spirit: [y]the terrors of God do set themselves in array against me.

5 Doth the wild ass bray when he hath grass? or loweth the ox over his fodder?

6 Can that which is unsavoury be eaten without salt? or is there *any* taste in the white of an egg?

7 The things *that* my soul refused to touch *are* as my sorrowful meat.

8 Oh that I might have my request; and that God would grant *me* the thing that I long for!

9 Even [z]that it would please God to destroy me; that he would let loose his hand, and cut me off!

10 Then should I yet have comfort; yea, I would harden myself in sorrow: let him not spare; for [a]I have not concealed the words of [b]the Holy One.

11 What *is* my strength, that I should hope? and what *is* mine end, that I should prolong my life?

12 *Is* my strength the strength of stones? or *is* my flesh of brass?

13 *Is* not my help in me? and is wisdom driven quite from me?

14 [c]To him that is afflicted pity *should be shewed* from his friend; but he forsaketh the fear of the Almighty.

15 [d]My brethren have dealt deceitfully as a brook, *and* [e]as the stream of brooks they pass away;

16 Which are blackish by reason of the ice, *and* wherein the snow is hid:

17 What time they wax warm, they vanish: when it is hot, they are consumed out of their place.

18 The paths of their way are turned aside; they go to nothing, and perish.

19 The troops of [f]Tema looked, the companies of [g]Sheba waited for them.

20 They were [h]confounded because they had hoped; they came thither, and were ashamed.

21 For now [i]ye are nothing; ye see *my* casting down, and [j]are afraid.

22 Did I say, Bring unto me? or, Give a reward for me of your substance?

23 Or, Deliver me from the enemy's hand? or, Redeem me from the hand of the mighty?

24 Teach me, and I will hold my tongue: and cause me to understand wherein I have erred.

25 How forcible are right words! but what doth your arguing reprove?

26 Do ye imagine to reprove words, and the speeches of one that is desperate, *which are* as wind?

27 Yea, ye overwhelm the fatherless, and ye [k]dig *a pit* for your friend.

28 Now therefore be content, look upon me; for *it is* evident unto you if I lie.

29 [l]Return, I pray you, let it not be iniquity; yea, return again, my righteousness *is* in it.

30 Is there iniquity in my tongue? cannot my taste discern perverse things?

7 *Is there* not [m]an appointed time to man upon earth? *are not* his days also like the days of an hireling?

2 As a servant earnestly desireth the shadow, and as an hireling looketh for *the reward of* his work:

3 So am I made to possess [n]months of vanity, and wearisome nights are appointed to me.

4 [o]When I lie down, I say, When shall I arise, and the night be gone? and I am full of tossings to and fro unto the dawning of the day.

5 My flesh is [p]clothed with worms and clods of dust; my skin is broken, and become loathsome.

5:13 [g]Ps. 9:15; 1 Cor. 3:19
5:14 [h]Deut. 28:29; Isa. 59:10; Am. 8:9
5:15 [i]Ps. 35:10
5:16 [j]1 Sam. 2:9; Ps. 107:42
5:17 [k]Ps. 94:12; Prov. 3:11; Heb. 12:5; Jam. 1:12; Rev. 3:19
5:18 [l]Deut. 32:39; 1 Sam. 2:6; Isa. 30:26; Hos. 6:1
5:19 [m]Ps. 34:19; Prov. 24:16; 1 Cor. 10:13 [n]Ps. 91:10
5:20 [o]Ps. 33:19
5:21 [p]Ps. 31:20
5:22 [q]Isa. 11:9; Ezek. 34:25
5:23 [r]Ps. 91:12; Hos. 2:18
5:25 [s]Ps. 112:2 [t]Ps. 72:16
5:26 [u]Prov. 9:11
5:27 [v]Ps. 111:2
6:3 [w]Prov. 27:3
6:4 [x]Ps. 38:2 [y]Ps. 88:15
6:9 [z]1 Kings 19:4
6:10 [a]Acts 20:20 [b]Lev. 19:2; Isa. 57:15; Hos. 11:9
6:14 [c]Prov. 17:17
6:15 [d]Ps. 38:11 [e]Jer. 15:18
6:19 [f]Gen. 25:15 [g]1 Kings 10:1; Ps. 72:10; Ezek. 27:22
6:20 [h]Jer. 14:3
6:21 [i]ch. 13:4 [j]Ps. 38:11
6:27 [k]Ps. 57:6
6:29 [l]ch. 17:10
7:1 [m]ch. 14:5; Ps. 39:4
7:3 [n]ch. 29:2
7:4 [o]Deut. 28:67; ch. 17:12
7:5 [p]Isa. 14:11

6 [q]My days are swifter than a weaver's shuttle, and are spent without hope.

7 O remember that [r]my life *is* wind: mine eye shall no more see good.

8 [s]The eye of him that hath seen me shall see me no *more:* thine eyes *are* upon me, and I *am* not.

9 *As* the cloud is consumed and vanisheth away: so [t]he that goeth down to the grave shall come up no *more.*

10 He shall return no more to his house, [u]neither shall his place know him any more.

11 Therefore I will [v]not refrain my mouth; I will speak in the anguish of my spirit; I will [w]complain in the bitterness of my soul.

12 *Am* I a sea, or a whale, that thou settest a watch over me?

13 [x]When I say, My bed shall comfort me, my couch shall ease my complaint;

14 Then thou scarest me with dreams, and terrifiest me through visions:

15 So that my soul chooseth strangling, *and* death rather than my life.

16 [y]I loathe *it;* I would not live alway: [z]let me alone; [a]for my days *are* vanity.

17 [b]What *is* man, that thou shouldest magnify him? and that thou shouldest set thine heart upon him?

18 And *that* thou shouldest visit him every morning, *and* try him every moment?

19 How long wilt thou not depart from me, nor let me alone till I swallow down my spittle?

20 I have sinned; what shall I do unto thee, [c]O thou preserver of men? why [d]hast thou set me as a mark against thee, so that I am a burden to myself?

21 And why dost thou not pardon my transgression, and take away mine iniquity? for now shall I sleep in the dust; and thou shalt seek me in the morning, but I *shall* not *be.*

8 Then answered Bildad the Shuhite, and said,

2 How long wilt thou speak these *things?* and *how long shall* the words of thy mouth *be like* a strong wind?

3 [e]Doth God pervert judgment? or doth the Almighty pervert justice?

4 If [f]thy children have sinned against him, and he have cast them away for their transgression;

5 [g]If thou wouldest seek unto God betimes, and make thy supplication to the Almighty;

6 If thou *wert* pure and upright; surely now he would awake for thee, and make the habitation of thy righteousness prosperous.

7 Though thy beginning was small, yet thy latter end should greatly increase.

8 [h]For enquire, I pray thee, of the former age, and prepare thyself to the search of their fathers:

9 (For [i]we *are but of* yesterday, and know nothing, because our days upon earth *are* a shadow:)

7:6 [q]ch. 9:25; Ps. 90:6; Isa. 38:12; Jam. 4:14
7:7 [r]Ps. 78:39
7:8 [s]ch. 20:9
7:9 [t]2 Sam. 12:23
7:10 [u]ch. 8:18; Ps. 103:16
7:11 [v]Ps. 39:1 [w]1 Sam. 1:10; ch. 10:1
7:13 [x]ch. 9:27
7:16 [y]ch. 10:1 [z]ch. 10:20; Ps. 39:13 [a]Ps. 62:9
7:17 [b]Ps. 8:4; Heb. 2:6
7:20 [c]Ps. 36:6 [d]ch. 16:12; Ps. 21:12; Lam. 3:12
8:3 [e]Gen. 18:25; Deut. 32:4; 2 Chron. 19:7; ch. 34:12; Dan. 9:14; Rom. 3:5
8:4 [f]ch. 1:5
8:5 [g]ch. 5:8
8:8 [h]Deut. 4:32; ch. 15:18
8:9 [i]Gen. 47:9; 1 Chron. 29:15; ch. 7:6; Ps. 39:5
8:12 [j]Ps. 129:6; Jer. 17:6
8:13 [k]ch. 11:20; Ps. 112:10; Prov. 10:28
8:15 [l]ch. 27:18
8:18 [m]ch. 7:10; Ps. 37:36
8:19 [n]Ps. 113:7
8:22 [o]Ps. 35:26
9:2 [p]Ps. 143:2; Rom. 3:20
9:4 [q]ch. 36:5
9:6 [r]Isa. 2:19; Hag. 2:6; Heb. 12:26 [s]ch. 26:11
9:8 [t]Gen. 1:6; Ps. 104:2
9:9 [u]Gen. 1:16; ch. 38:31; Am. 5:8
9:10 [v]ch. 5:9; Ps. 71:15
9:11 [w]ch. 23:8
9:12 [x]Isa. 45:9; Jer. 18:6; Rom. 9:20
9:13 [y]ch. 26:12; Isa. 30:7
9:15 [z]ch. 10:15
9:17 [a]ch. 2:3

10 Shall not they teach thee, *and* tell thee, and utter words out of their heart?

11 Can the rush grow up without mire? can the flag grow without water?

12 [j]Whilst it *is* yet in his greenness, *and* not cut down, it withereth before any *other* herb.

13 So *are* the paths of all that forget God; and the [k]hypocrite's hope shall perish:

14 Whose hope shall be cut off, and whose trust *shall be* a spider's web.

15 [l]He shall lean upon his house, but it shall not stand: he shall hold it fast, but it shall not endure.

16 He *is* green before the sun, and his branch shooteth forth in his garden.

17 His roots are wrapped about the heap, *and* seeth the place of stones.

18 [m]If he destroy him from his place, then *it* shall deny him, *saying,* I have not seen thee.

19 Behold, this *is* the joy of his way, and [n]out of the earth shall others grow.

20 Behold, God will not cast away a perfect *man,* neither will he help the evil doers:

21 Till he fill thy mouth with laughing, and thy lips with rejoicing.

22 They that hate thee shall be [o]clothed with shame; and the dwelling place of the wicked shall come to nought.

9 Then Job answered and said,

2 I know *it is* so of a truth: but how should [p]man be just with God?

3 If he will contend with him, he cannot answer him one of a thousand.

4 [q]*He is* wise in heart, and mighty in strength: who hath hardened *himself* against him, and hath prospered?

5 Which removeth the mountains, and they know not: which overturneth them in his anger.

6 Which [r]shaketh the earth out of her place, and [s]the pillars thereof tremble.

7 Which commandeth the sun, and it riseth not; and sealeth up the stars.

8 [t]Which alone spreadeth out the heavens, and treadeth upon the waves of the sea.

9 [u]Which maketh Arcturus, Orion, and Pleiades, and the chambers of the south.

10 [v]Which doeth great things past finding out; yea, and wonders without number.

11 [w]Lo, he goeth by me, and I see *him* not: he passeth on also, but I perceive him not.

12 [x]Behold, he taketh away, who can hinder him? who will say unto him, What doest thou?

13 *If* God will not withdraw his anger, [y]the proud helpers do stoop under him.

14 How much less shall I answer him, *and* choose out my words *to reason* with him?

15 [z]Whom, though I were righteous, *yet* would I not answer, *but* I would make supplication to my judge.

16 If I had called, and he had answered me; *yet* would I not believe that he had hearkened unto my voice.

17 For he breaketh me with a tempest, and multiplieth my wounds [a]without cause.

18 He will not suffer me to take my breath, but filleth me with bitterness.

19 If *I speak* of strength, lo, *he is* strong: and if of judgment, who shall set me a time *to plead?*

20 If I justify myself, mine own mouth shall condemn me: *if I say,* I *am* perfect, it shall also prove me perverse.

21 *Though* I *were* perfect, *yet* would I not know my soul: I would despise my life.

22 This *is* one *thing,* therefore I said *it,* [b]He destroyeth the perfect and the wicked.

23 If the scourge slay suddenly, he will laugh at the trial of the innocent.

24 The earth is given into the hand of the wicked: [c]he covereth the faces of the judges thereof; if not, where, *and* who *is* he?

25 Now [d]my days are swifter than a post: they flee away, they see no good.

26 They are passed away as the swift ships: [e]as the eagle *that* hasteth to the prey.

27 [f]If I say, I will forget my complaint, I will leave off my heaviness, and comfort *myself:*

28 [g]I am afraid of all my sorrows, I know that thou [h]wilt not hold me innocent.

29 *If* I be wicked, why then labour I in vain?

30 [i]If I wash myself with snow water, and make my hands never so clean;

31 Yet shalt thou plunge me in the ditch, and mine own clothes shall abhor me.

32 For [j]*he is* not a man, as I *am, that* I should answer him, *and* we should come together in judgment.

33 [k]Neither is there any daysman betwixt us, *that* might lay his hand upon us both.

34 [l]Let him take his rod away from me, and let not his fear terrify me:

35 *Then* would I speak, and not fear him; but *it is* not so with me.

10 My [m]soul is weary of my life; I will leave my complaint upon myself; [n]I will speak in the bitterness of my soul.

2 I will say unto God, Do not condemn me; shew me wherefore thou contendest with me.

3 *Is it* good unto thee that thou shouldest oppress, that thou shouldest despise the work of thine hands, and shine upon the counsel of the wicked?

4 Hast thou eyes of flesh? or [o]seest thou as man seeth?

5 *Are* thy days as the days of man? *are* thy years as man's days,

6 That thou inquirest after mine iniquity, and searchest after my sin?

7 [p]Thou knowest that I am not wicked; and *there is* none that can deliver out of thine hand.

8 [q]Thine hands have made me and fashioned me together round about; yet thou dost destroy me.

9 Remember, I beseech thee, that [r]thou hast made me as the clay; and wilt thou bring me into dust again?

9:22 [b]Eccl. 9:2; Ezek. 21:3
9:24 [c]2 Sam. 15:30; Jer. 14:4
9:25 [d]ch. 7:6
9:26 [e]Hab. 1:8
9:27 [f]ch. 7:13
9:28 [g]Ps. 119:120 [h]Ex. 20:7
9:30 [i]Jer. 2:22
9:32 [j]Eccl. 6:10; Isa. 45:9; Jer. 49:19; Rom. 9:20
9:33 [k]ver. 19; 1 Sam. 2:25
9:34 [l]ch. 13:20; Ps. 39:10
10:1 [m]1 Kings 19:4; ch. 7:16; Jonah 4:3 [n]ch. 7:11
10:4 [o]1 Sam. 16:7
10:7 [p]Ps. 139:1
10:8 [q]Ps. 119:73
10:9 [r]Gen. 2:7; Isa. 64:8
10:10 [s]Ps. 139:14
10:14 [t]Ps. 139:1
10:15 [u]Isa. 3:11 [v]ch. 9:12 [w]Ps. 25:18
10:16 [x]Isa. 38:13; Lam. 3:10
10:18 [y]ch. 3:11
10:20 [z]ch. 7:6; Ps. 39:5 [a]Ps. 39:13 [b]ch. 7:16
10:21 [c]Ps. 88:12 [d]Ps. 23:4
11:4 [e]ch. 6:10
11:6 [f]Ezra 9:13
11:7 [g]Eccl. 3:11; Rom. 11:33
11:10 [h]ch. 9:12; Rev. 3:7
11:11 [i]Ps. 10:11
11:12 [j]Ps. 73:22; Eccl. 3:18; Rom. 1:22

10 [s]Hast thou not poured me out as milk, and curdled me like cheese?

11 Thou hast clothed me with skin and flesh, and hast fenced me with bones and sinews.

12 Thou hast granted me life and favour, and thy visitation hath preserved my spirit.

13 And these *things* hast thou hid in thine heart: I know that this *is* with thee.

14 If I sin, then [t]thou markest me, and thou wilt not acquit me from mine iniquity.

15 If I be wicked, [u]woe unto me; [v]and *if* I be righteous, *yet* will I not lift up my head. *I am* full of confusion; therefore [w]see thou mine affliction;

16 For it increaseth. [x]Thou huntest me as a fierce lion: and again thou shewest thyself marvellous upon me.

17 Thou renewest thy witnesses against me, and increasest thine indignation upon me; changes and war *are* against me.

18 [y]Wherefore then hast thou brought me forth out of the womb? Oh that I had given up the ghost, and no eye had seen me!

19 I should have been as though I had not been; I should have been carried from the womb to the grave.

20 [z]*Are* not my days few? [a]cease *then, and* [b]let me alone, that I may take comfort a little,

21 Before I go *whence* I shall not return, [c]*even* to the land of darkness [d]and the shadow of death;

22 A land of darkness, as darkness *itself; and* of the shadow of death, without any order, and *where* the light *is* as darkness.

11 Then answered Zophar the Naamathite, and said,

2 Should not the multitude of words be answered? and should a man full of talk be justified?

3 Should thy lies make men hold their peace? and when thou mockest, shall no man make thee ashamed?

4 For [e]thou hast said, My doctrine *is* pure, and I am clean in thine eyes.

5 But oh that God would speak, and open his lips against thee;

6 And that he would shew thee the secrets of wisdom, that *they are* double to that which is! Know therefore that [f]God exacteth of thee *less* than thine iniquity *deserveth.*

7 [g]Canst thou by searching find out God? canst thou find out the Almighty unto perfection?

8 *It is* as high as heaven; what canst thou do? deeper than hell; what canst thou know?

9 The measure thereof *is* longer than the earth, and broader than the sea.

10 [h]If he cut off, and shut up, or gather together, then who can hinder him?

11 For [i]he knoweth vain men: he seeth wickedness also; will he not then consider *it?*

12 For [j]vain man would be wise, though man be born *like* a wild ass's colt.

13 [k]If thou [l]prepare thine heart, and [m]stretch out thine hands toward him;

14 If iniquity *be* in thine hand, put it far away, and [n]let not wickedness dwell in thy tabernacles.

15 [o]For then shalt thou lift up thy face without spot; yea, thou shalt be stedfast, and shalt not fear:

16 Because thou shalt [p]forget *thy* misery, *and* remember *it* as waters *that* pass away:

17 And *thine* age [q]shall be clearer than the noonday; thou shalt shine forth, thou shalt be as the morning.

18 And thou shalt be secure, because there is hope; yea, thou shalt dig *about thee, and* [r]thou shalt take thy rest in safety.

19 Also thou shalt lie down, and none shall make thee afraid; yea, many shall make suit unto thee.

20 But [s]the eyes of the wicked shall fail, and they shall not escape, and [t]their hope *shall be as* the giving up of the ghost.

12 And Job answered and said,

2 No doubt but ye *are* the people, and wisdom shall die with you.

3 But [u]I have understanding as well as you; I *am* not inferior to you: yea, who knoweth not such things as these?

4 [v]I am *as* one mocked of his neighbour, who [w]calleth upon God, and he answereth him: the just upright *man is* laughed to scorn.

5 [x]He that is ready to slip with *his* feet *is as* a lamp despised in the thought of him that is at ease.

6 [y]The tabernacles of robbers prosper, and they that provoke God are secure; into whose hand God bringeth *abundantly*.

7 But ask now the beasts, and they shall teach thee; and the fowls of the air, and they shall tell thee:

8 Or speak to the earth, and it shall teach thee: and the fishes of the sea shall declare unto thee.

9 Who knoweth not in all these that the hand of the LORD hath wrought this?

10 [z]In whose hand *is* the soul of every living thing, and the breath of all mankind.

11 [a]Doth not the ear try words? and the mouth taste his meat?

12 [b]With the ancient *is* wisdom; and in length of days understanding.

13 [c]With him *is* wisdom and strength, he hath counsel and understanding.

14 Behold, [d]he breaketh down, and it cannot be built again: he [e]shutteth up a man, and there can be no opening.

15 Behold, he [f]withholdeth the waters, and they dry up: also he [g]sendeth them out, and they overturn the earth.

16 [h]With him *is* strength and wisdom: the deceived and the deceiver *are* his.

17 He leadeth counsellors away spoiled, and [i]maketh the judges fools.

18 He looseth the bond of kings, and girdeth their loins with a girdle.

19 He leadeth princes away spoiled, and overthroweth the mighty.

20 [j]He removeth away the speech of the trusty, and taketh away the understanding of the aged.

21 [k]He poureth contempt upon princes, and weakeneth the strength of the mighty.

22 [l]He discovereth deep things out of darkness, and bringeth out to light the shadow of death.

23 [m]He increaseth the nations, and destroyeth them: he enlargeth the nations, and straiteneth them *again*.

24 He taketh away the heart of the chief of the people of the earth, and [n]causeth them to wander in a wilderness *where there is* no way.

25 [o]They grope in the dark without light, and he maketh them to [p]stagger like *a* drunken *man*.

13 Lo, mine eye hath seen all *this*, mine ear hath heard and understood it.

2 [q]What ye know, *the same* do I know also: I *am* not inferior unto you.

3 [r]Surely I would speak to the Almighty, and I desire to reason with God.

4 But ye *are* forgers of lies, [s]ye *are* all physicians of no value.

5 O that ye would altogether hold your peace! and [t]it should be your wisdom.

6 Hear now my reasoning, and hearken to the pleadings of my lips.

7 [u]Will ye speak wickedly for God? and talk deceitfully for him?

8 Will ye accept his person? will ye contend for God?

9 Is it good that he should search you out? or as one man mocketh another, do ye *so* mock him?

10 He will surely reprove you, if ye do secretly accept persons.

11 Shall not his excellency make you afraid? and his dread fall upon you?

12 Your remembrances *are* like unto ashes, your bodies to bodies of clay.

13 Hold your peace, let me alone, that I may speak, and let come on me what *will*.

14 Wherefore [v]do I take my flesh in my teeth, and [w]put my life in mine hand?

15 [x]Though he slay me, yet will I trust in him: [y]but I will maintain mine own ways before him.

16 He also *shall be* my salvation: for an hypocrite shall not come before him.

17 Hear diligently my speech, and my declaration with your ears.

18 Behold now, I have ordered *my* cause; I know that I shall be justified.

19 [z]Who *is* he *that* will plead with me? for now, if I hold my tongue, I shall give up the ghost.

20 [a]Only do not two *things* unto me: then will I not hide myself from thee.

21 [b]Withdraw thine hand far from me: and let not thy dread make me afraid.

22 Then call thou, and I will answer: or let me speak, and answer thou me.

23 How many *are* mine iniquities and sins? make me to know my transgression and my sin.

11:13 [k]ch. 5:8 [l]1 Sam. 7:3; Ps. 78:8 [m]Ps. 88:9
11:14 [n]Ps. 101:3
11:15 [o]Gen. 4:5; ch. 22:26; Ps. 119:6; 1 John 3:21
11:16 [p]Isa. 65:16
11:17 [q]Ps. 37:6; Isa. 58:8
11:18 [r]Lev. 26:5; Ps. 3:5; Prov. 3:24
11:20 [s]Lev. 26:16; Deut. 28:65 [t]ch. 8:14; Prov. 11:7
12:3 [u]ch. 13:2
12:4 [v]ch. 16:10 [w]Ps. 91:15
12:5 [x]Prov. 14:2
12:6 [y]ch. 21:7; Ps. 37:1; Jer. 12:1; Mal. 3:15
12:10 [z]Num. 16:22; Dan. 5:23; Acts 17:28
12:11 [a]ch. 34:3
12:12 [b]ch. 32:7
12:13 [c]ch. 9:4
12:14 [d]ch. 11:10 [e]Isa. 22:22; Rev. 3:7
12:15 [f]1 Kings 8:35 [g]Gen. 7:11
12:16 [h]ver. 13
12:17 [i]2 Sam. 15:31; Isa. 19:12; 1 Cor. 1:19
12:20 [j]ch. 32:9; Isa. 3:1
12:21 [k]Ps. 107:40; Dan. 2:21
12:22 [l]Dan. 2:22; Matt. 10:26; 1 Cor. 4:5
12:23 [m]Ps. 107:38; Isa. 9:3
12:24 [n]Ps. 107:4
12:25 [o]Deut. 28:29; ch. 5:14 [p]Ps. 107:27
13:2 [q]ch. 12:3
13:3 [r]ch. 23:3
13:4 [s]ch. 6:21
13:5 [t]Prov. 17:28
13:7 [u]ch. 17:5
13:14 [v]ch. 18:4 [w]1 Sam. 28:21; Ps. 119:109
13:15 [x]Ps. 23:4; Prov. 14:32 [y]ch. 27:5
13:19 [z]ch. 33:6; Isa. 50:8
13:20 [a]ch. 9:34
13:21 [b]Ps. 39:10

24 [c]Wherefore hidest thou thy face, and
[d]holdest me for thine enemy?
25 [e]Wilt thou break a leaf driven to and
fro? and wilt thou pursue the dry stubble?
26 For thou writest bitter things against
me, and [f]makest me to possess the iniquities of my youth.
27 [g]Thou puttest my feet also in the
stocks, and lookest narrowly unto all my
paths; thou settest a print upon the heels of
my feet.
28 And he, as a rotten thing, consumeth,
as a garment that is moth eaten.

14

Man *that is* born of a woman *is* of
few days, and [h]full of trouble.
2 [i]He cometh forth like a flower, and is
cut down: he fleeth also as a shadow, and
continueth not.
3 And [j]dost thou open thine eyes upon
such an one, and [k]bringest me into judgment with thee?
4 Who [l]can bring a clean *thing* out of an
unclean? not one.
5 [m]Seeing his days *are* determined, the
number of his months *are* with thee, thou
hast appointed his bounds that he cannot
pass;
6 [n]Turn from him, that he may rest, till he
shall accomplish, [o]as an hireling, his day.
7 For there is hope of a tree, if it be cut
down, [p]that it will sprout again, and that
the tender branch thereof will not cease.
8 Though the root thereof wax old in the
earth, and the stock thereof die in the
ground;
9 *Yet* through the scent of water it will
bud, and bring forth boughs like a plant.
10 But man dieth, and wasteth away: yea,
man giveth up the ghost, and where *is* he?
11 *As* the waters fail from the sea, and the
flood decayeth and drieth up:
12 So man lieth down, and riseth not: [q]till
the heavens *be* no more, they shall not
awake, nor be raised out of their sleep.
13 O that thou wouldest hide me in the
grave, that thou wouldest keep me secret,
until thy wrath be past, that thou wouldest
appoint me a set time, and remember me!
14 If a man die, shall he live *again?* all the
days of my appointed time [r]will I wait, [s]till
my change come.
15 [t]Thou shalt call, and I will answer
thee: thou wilt have a desire to the work of
thine hands.
16 [u]For now thou numberest my steps:
dost thou not watch over my sin?
17 [v]My transgression *is* sealed up in a
bag, and thou sewest up mine iniquity.
18 And surely the mountain falling cometh to nought, and the rock is removed out
of his place.
19 The waters wear the stones: thou
washest away the things which grow *out* of
the dust of the earth; and thou destroyest
the hope of man.
20 Thou prevailest for ever against him,
and he passeth: thou changest his countenance, and sendest him away.
21 His sons come to honour, and [w]he
knoweth *it* not; and they are brought low,
but he perceiveth *it* not of them.
22 But his flesh upon him shall have pain,
and his soul within him shall mourn.

15

Then answered Eliphaz the Temanite, and said,
2 Should a wise man utter vain knowledge, and fill his belly with the east wind?
3 Should he reason with unprofitable
talk? or with speeches wherewith he can do
no good?
4 Yea, thou castest off fear, and restrain-
est prayer before God.
5 For thy mouth uttereth thine iniquity,
and thou choosest the tongue of the crafty.
6 [x]Thine own mouth condemneth thee,
and not I: yea, thine own lips testify against
thee.
7 *Art* thou the first man *that* was born?
[y]or wast thou made before the hills?
8 [z]Hast thou heard the secret of God?
and dost thou restrain wisdom to thyself?
9 [a]What knowest thou, that we know
not? *what* understandest thou, which *is* not
in us?
10 [b]With us *are* both the grayheaded and
very aged men, much elder than thy father.
11 *Are* the consolations of God small with
thee? is there any secret thing with thee?
12 Why doth thine heart carry thee away?
and what do thy eyes wink at,
13 That thou turnest thy spirit against
God, and lettest *such* words go out of thy
mouth?
14 [c]What *is* man, that he should be
clean? and *he which is* born of a woman,
that he should be righteous?
15 [d]Behold, he putteth no trust in his
saints; yea, the heavens are not clean in his
sight.
16 [e]How much more abominable and
filthy *is* man, [f]which drinketh iniquity like
water?
17 I will shew thee, hear me; and that
which I have seen I will declare;
18 Which wise men have told [g]from their
fathers, and have not hid *it:*
19 Unto whom alone the earth was given,
and [h]no stranger passed among them.
20 The wicked man travaileth with pain
all *his* days, [i]and the number of years is
hidden to the oppressor.
21 A dreadful sound *is* in his ears: [j]in
prosperity the destroyer shall come upon
him.
22 He believeth not that he shall return
out of darkness, and he is waited for of the
sword.
23 He [k]wandereth abroad for bread, *saying,* Where *is it?* he knoweth that [l]the day
of darkness is ready at his hand.
24 Trouble and anguish shall make him
afraid; they shall prevail against him, as a
king ready to the battle.
25 For he stretcheth out his hand against
God, and strengtheneth himself against the
Almighty.

13:24 [c]Deut. 32:20; Ps. 13:1; Isa. 8:17 [d]Deut. 32:42; Ruth 1:21; ch. 16:9; Lam. 2:5
13:25 [e]Isa. 42:3
13:26 [f]ch. 20:11; Ps. 25:7
13:27 [g]ch. 33:11
14:1 [h]ch. 5:7; Eccl. 2:23
14:2 [i]ch. 8:9; Ps. 90:5; Isa. 40:6; Jam. 1:10; 1 Pet. 1:24
14:3 [j]Ps. 144:3 [k]Ps. 143:2
14:4 [l]Gen. 5:3; Ps. 51:5; John 3:6; Rom. 5:12; Eph. 2:3
14:5 [m]ch. 7:1
14:6 [n]ch. 7:16; Ps. 39:13 [o]ch. 7:1
14:7 [p]ver. 14
14:12 [q]Ps. 102:26; Isa. 51:6; Acts 3:21; Rom. 8:20; 2 Pet. 3:7; Rev. 20:11
14:14 [r]ch. 13:15 [s]ver. 7
14:15 [t]ch. 13:22
14:16 [u]ch. 10:6; Ps. 56:8; Prov. 5:21; Jer. 32:19
14:17 [v]Deut. 32:34; Hos. 13:12
14:21 [w]Eccl. 9:5; Isa. 63:16
15:6 [x]Luke 19:22
15:7 [y]Ps. 90:2; Prov. 8:25
15:8 [z]Rom. 11:34; 1 Cor. 2:11
15:9 [a]ch. 13:2
15:10 [b]ch. 32:6
15:14 [c]1 Kings 8:46; 2 Chron. 6:36; ch. 14:4; Ps. 14:3; Prov. 20:9; Eccl. 7:20; 1 John 1:8
15:15 [d]ch. 4:18
15:16 [e]ch. 4:19; Ps. 14:3 [f]ch. 34:7; Prov. 19:28
15:18 [g]ch. 8:8
15:19 [h]Joel 3:17
15:20 [i]Ps. 90:12
15:21 [j]1 Thess. 5:3
15:23 [k]Ps. 59:15 [l]ch. 18:12

26 He runneth upon him, *even* on *his* neck, upon the thick bosses of his bucklers:

27 [m]Because he covereth his face with his fatness, and maketh collops of fat on *his* flanks.

28 And he dwelleth in desolate cities, *and* in houses which no man inhabiteth, which are ready to become heaps.

29 He shall not be rich, neither shall his substance continue, neither shall he prolong the perfection thereof upon the earth.

30 He shall not depart out of darkness; the flame shall dry up his branches, and [n]by the breath of his mouth shall he go away.

31 Let not him that is deceived [o]trust in vanity: for vanity shall be his recompence.

32 It shall be accomplished [p]before his time, and his branch shall not be green.

33 He shall shake off his unripe grape as the vine, and shall cast off his flower as the olive.

34 For the congregation of hypocrites *shall be* desolate, and fire shall consume the tabernacles of bribery.

35 [q]They conceive mischief, and bring forth vanity, and their belly prepareth deceit.

16 Then Job answered and said,

2 I have heard many such things: [r]miserable comforters *are* ye all.

3 Shall vain words have an end? or what emboldeneth thee that thou answerest?

4 I also could speak as ye *do:* if your soul were in my soul's stead, I could heap up words against you, and [s]shake mine head at you.

5 *But* I would strengthen you with my mouth, and the moving of my lips should asswage *your grief.*

6 Though I speak, my grief is not asswaged: and *though* I forbear, what am I eased?

7 But now he hath made me weary: thou hast made desolate all my company.

8 And thou hast filled me with wrinkles, *which* is a witness *against me:* and my leanness rising up in me beareth witness to my face.

9 [t]He teareth *me* in his wrath, who hateth me: he gnasheth upon me with his teeth; [u]mine enemy sharpeneth his eyes upon me.

10 They have [v]gaped upon me with their mouth; they [w]have smitten me upon the cheek reproachfully; they have [x]gathered themselves together against me.

11 God [y]hath delivered me to the ungodly, and turned me over into the hands of the wicked.

12 I was at ease, but he hath broken me asunder: he hath also taken *me* by my neck, and shaken me to pieces, and [z]set me up for his mark.

13 His archers compass me round about, he cleaveth my reins asunder, and doth not spare; he poureth out my gall upon the ground.

14 He breaketh me with breach upon breach, he runneth upon me like a giant.

15 I have sewed sackcloth upon my skin, and [a]defiled my horn in the dust.

16 My face is foul with weeping, and on my eyelids *is* the shadow of death;

17 Not for *any* injustice in mine hands: also my prayer *is* pure.

18 O earth, cover not thou my blood, and [b]let my cry have no place.

19 Also now, behold, [c]my witness *is* in heaven, and my record *is* on high.

20 My friends scorn me: *but* mine eye poureth out *tears* unto God.

21 [d]O that one might plead for a man with God, as a man *pleadeth* for his neighbour!

22 When a few years are come, then I shall [e]go the way *whence* I shall not return.

17 My breath is corrupt, my days are extinct, [f]the graves *are ready* for me.

2 *Are there* not mockers with me? and doth not mine eye continue in their [g]provocation?

3 Lay down now, put me in a surety with thee; who *is* he *that* [h]will strike hands with me?

4 For thou hast hid their heart from understanding: therefore shalt thou not exalt *them.*

5 He that speaketh flattery to *his* friends, even the eyes of his children shall fail.

6 He hath made me also [i]a byword of the people; and aforetime I was as a tabret.

7 [j]Mine eye also is dim by reason of sorrow, and all my members *are* as a shadow.

8 Upright *men* shall be astonied at this, and the innocent shall stir up himself against the hypocrite.

9 The righteous also shall hold on his way, and he that hath [k]clean hands shall be stronger and stronger.

10 But as for you all, [l]do ye return, and come now: for I cannot find *one* wise *man* among you.

11 [m]My days are past, my purposes are broken off, *even* the thoughts of my heart.

12 They change the night into day: the light *is* short because of darkness.

13 If I wait, the grave *is* mine house: I have made my bed in the darkness.

14 I have said to corruption, Thou *art* my father: to the worm, *Thou art* my mother, and my sister.

15 And where *is* now my hope? as for my hope, who shall see it?

16 They shall go down [n]to the bars of the pit, when *our* [o]rest together *is* in the dust.

18 Then answered Bildad the Shuhite, and said,

2 How long *will it be ere* ye make an end of words? mark, and afterwards we will speak.

3 Wherefore are we [p]counted as beasts, *and* reputed vile in your sight?

4 [q]He teareth himself in his anger: shall

15:27 [m]ch. 17:10
15:30 [n]ch. 4:9
15:31 [o]Isa. 59:4
15:32 [p]ch. 22:16; Ps. 55:23
15:35 [q]Ps. 7:14; Isa. 59:4; Hos. 10:13
16:2 [r]ch. 13:4
16:4 [s]Ps. 22:7; Lam. 2:15
16:9 [t]ch. 10:16 [u]ch. 13:24
16:10 [v]Ps. 22:13 [w]Lam. 3:30; Mic. 5:1 [x]Ps. 35:15
16:11 [y]ch. 1:15
16:12 [z]ch. 7:20
16:15 [a]ch. 30:19; Ps. 7:5
16:18 [b]ch. 27:9; Ps. 66:18
16:19 [c]Rom. 1:9
16:21 [d]ch. 31:35; Eccl. 6:10; Isa. 45:9; Rom. 9:20
16:22 [e]Eccl. 12:5
17:1 [f]Ps. 88:3
17:2 [g]1 Sam. 1:6
17:3 [h]Prov. 6:1
17:6 [i]ch. 30:9
17:7 [j]Ps. 6:7
17:9 [k]Ps. 24:4
17:10 [l]ch. 6:29
17:11 [m]ch. 7:6
17:16 [n]ch. 18:13 [o]ch. 3:17
18:3 [p]Ps. 73:22
18:4 [q]ch. 13:14

the earth be forsaken for thee? and shall the rock be removed out of his place?

5 Yea, [r]the light of the wicked shall be put out, and the spark of his fire shall not shine.

6 The light shall be dark in his tabernacle, [s]and his candle shall be put out with him.

7 The steps of his strength shall be straitened, and [t]his own counsel shall cast him down.

8 For [u]he is cast into a net by his own feet, and he walketh upon a snare.

9 The gin shall take *him* by the heel, *and* [v]the robber shall prevail against him.

10 The snare *is* laid for him in the ground, and a trap for him in the way.

11 [w]Terrors shall make him afraid on every side, and shall drive him to his feet.

12 His strength shall be hungerbitten, and [x]destruction *shall be* ready at his side.

13 It shall devour the strength of his skin: *even* the firstborn of death shall devour his strength.

14 [y]His confidence shall be rooted out of his tabernacle, and it shall bring him to the king of terrors.

15 It shall dwell in his tabernacle, because *it is* none of his: brimstone shall be scattered upon his habitation.

16 [z]His roots shall be dried up beneath, and above shall his branch be cut off.

17 [a]His remembrance shall perish from the earth, and he shall have no name in the street.

18 He shall be driven from light into darkness, and chased out of the world.

19 [b]He shall neither have son nor nephew among his people, nor any remaining in his dwellings.

20 They that come after *him* shall be astonied at [c]his day, as they that went before were affrighted.

21 Surely such *are* the dwellings of the wicked, and this *is* the place *of him that* [d]knoweth not God.

19 Then Job answered and said,

2 How long will ye vex my soul, and break me in pieces with words?

3 These [e]ten times have ye reproached me: ye are not ashamed *that* ye make yourselves strange to me.

4 And be it indeed *that* I have erred, mine error remaineth with myself.

5 If indeed ye will [f]magnify *yourselves* against me, and plead against me my reproach:

6 Know now that God hath overthrown me, and hath compassed me with his net.

7 Behold, I cry out of wrong, but I am not heard: I cry aloud, but *there is* no judgment.

8 [g]He hath fenced up my way that I cannot pass, and he hath set darkness in my paths.

9 [h]He hath stripped me of my glory, and taken the crown *from* my head.

10 He hath destroyed me on every side, and I am gone: and mine hope hath he removed like a tree.

11 He hath also kindled his wrath against me, and [i]he counteth me unto him as *one of* his enemies.

12 His troops come together, and [j]raise up their way against me, and encamp round about my tabernacle.

13 [k]He hath put my brethren far from me, and mine acquaintance are verily estranged from me.

14 My kinsfolk have failed, and my familiar friends have forgotten me.

15 They that dwell in mine house, and my maids, count me for a stranger: I am an alien in their sight.

16 I called my servant, and he gave *me* no answer; I intreated him with my mouth.

17 My breath is strange to my wife, though I intreated for the children's *sake* of mine own body.

18 Yea, [l]young children despised me; I arose, and they spake against me.

19 [m]All my inward friends abhorred me: and they whom I loved are turned against me.

20 [n]My bone cleaveth to my skin and to my flesh, and I am escaped with the skin of my teeth.

21 Have pity upon me, have pity upon me, O ye my friends; [o]for the hand of God hath touched me.

22 Why do ye [p]persecute me as God, and are not satisfied with my flesh?

23 Oh that my words were now written! oh that they were printed in a book!

24 That they were graven with an iron pen and lead in the rock for ever!

25 For I know *that* my redeemer liveth, and *that* he shall stand at the latter *day* upon the earth:

26 And *though* after my skin *worms* destroy this *body,* yet [q]in my flesh shall I see God:

27 Whom I shall see for myself, and mine eyes shall behold, and not another; *though* my reins be consumed within me.

28 But ye should say, [r]Why persecute we him, seeing the root of the matter is found in me?

29 Be ye afraid of the sword: for wrath *bringeth* the punishments of the sword, [s]that ye may know *there is* a judgment.

20 Then answered Zophar the Naamathite, and said,

2 Therefore do my thoughts cause me to answer, and for *this* I make haste.

3 I have heard the check of my reproach, and the spirit of my understanding causeth me to answer.

4 Knowest thou *not* this of old, since man was placed upon earth,

5 [t]That the triumphing of the wicked *is* short, and the joy of the hypocrite *but* for a moment?

6 [u]Though his excellency mount up to the heavens, and his head reach unto the clouds;

7 *Yet* he shall perish for ever [v]like his

18:5 [r]Prov. 13:9
18:6 [s]ch. 21:17; Ps. 18:28
18:7 [t]ch. 5:13
18:8 [u]ch. 22:10; Ps. 9:15
18:9 [v]ch. 5:5
18:11 [w]ch. 15:21; Jer. 6:25
18:12 [x]ch. 15:23
18:14 [y]ch. 8:14; Ps. 112:10; Prov. 10:28
18:16 [z]ch. 29:19; Isa. 5:24; Am. 2:9; Mal. 4:1
18:17 [a]Ps. 34:16; Prov. 2:22
18:19 [b]Isa. 14:22; Jer. 22:30
18:20 [c]Ps. 37:13
18:21 [d]Jer. 9:3; 1 Thess. 4:5; 2 Thess. 1:8; Tit. 1:16
19:3 [e]Gen. 31:7; Lev. 26:26
19:5 [f]Ps. 38:16
19:8 [g]ch. 3:23; Ps. 88:8
19:9 [h]Ps. 89:44
19:11 [i]ch. 13:24; Lam. 2:5
19:12 [j]ch. 30:12
19:13 [k]Ps. 31:11
19:18 [l]2 Kings 2:23
19:19 [m]Ps. 41:9
19:20 [n]ch. 30:30; Ps. 102:5; Lam. 4:8
19:21 [o]ch. 1:11; Ps. 38:2
19:22 [p]Ps. 69:26
19:26 [q]Ps. 17:15; 1 Cor. 13:12; 1 John 3:2
19:28 [r]ver. 22
19:29 [s]Ps. 58:10
20:5 [t]Ps. 37:35
20:6 [u]Isa. 14:13; Obad. 3
20:7 [v]Ps. 83:10

own dung: they which have seen him shall
say, Where *is* he?
8 He shall fly away [w]as a dream, and
shall not be found: yea, he shall be chased
away as a vision of the night.
9 [x]The eye also *which* saw him shall *see*
him no more; neither shall his place any
more behold him.
10 His children shall seek to please the
poor, and his hands [y]shall restore their
goods.
11 His bones are full *of* [z]*the sin* of his
youth, [a]which shall lie down with him in
the dust.
12 Though wickedness be sweet in his
mouth, *though* he hide it under his tongue;
13 *Though* he spare it, and forsake it not;
but keep it still within his mouth:
14 *Yet* his meat in his bowels is turned, *it*
is the gall of asps within him.
15 He hath swallowed down riches, and
he shall vomit them up again: God shall cast
them out of his belly.
16 He shall suck the poison of asps: the
viper's tongue shall slay him.
17 He shall not see [b]the rivers, the floods,
the brooks of honey and butter.
18 That which he laboured for [c]shall he
restore, and shall not swallow *it* down: according to *his* substance *shall* the restitution
be, and he shall not rejoice *therein*.
19 Because he hath oppressed *and* hath
forsaken the poor; *because* he hath violently taken away an house which he
builded not;
20 [d]Surely he shall not feel quietness in
his belly, he shall not save of that which he
desired.
21 There shall none of his meat be left;
therefore shall no man look for his goods.
22 In the fulness of his sufficiency he
shall be in straits: every hand of the wicked
shall come upon him.
23 *When* he is about to fill his belly, *God*
shall cast the fury of his wrath upon him,
and shall rain *it* upon him [e]while he is eating.
24 [f]He shall flee from the iron weapon,
and the bow of steel shall strike him
through.
25 It is drawn, and cometh out of the
body; yea, [g]the glittering sword cometh out
of his gall: [h]terrors *are* upon him.
26 All darkness *shall be* hid in his secret
places: [i]a fire not blown shall consume
him; it shall go ill with him that is left in his
tabernacle.
27 The heaven shall reveal his iniquity;
and the earth shall rise up against him.
28 The increase of his house shall depart,
and his goods shall flow away in the day of
his wrath.
29 [j]This *is* the portion of a wicked man
from God, and the heritage appointed unto
him by God.

21 But Job answered and said,
2 Hear diligently my speech, and let
this be your consolations.
3 Suffer me that I may speak; and after
that I have spoken, [k]mock on.
4 As for me, *is* my complaint to man? and
if *it were so*, why should not my spirit be
troubled?
5 Mark me, and be astonished, [l]and lay
your hand upon *your* mouth.
6 Even when I remember I am afraid, and
trembling taketh hold on my flesh.
7 [m]Wherefore do the wicked live, become
old, yea, are mighty in power?
8 Their seed is established in their sight
with them, and their offspring before their
eyes.
9 Their houses *are* safe from fear, [n]nei-
ther *is* the rod of God upon them.
10 Their bull gendereth, and faileth not;
their cow calveth, and [o]casteth not her calf.
11 They send forth their little ones like a
flock, and their children dance.
12 They take the timbrel and harp, and
rejoice at the sound of the organ.
13 They [p]spend their days in wealth, and
in a moment go down to the grave.
14 [q]Therefore they say unto God, Depart
from us; for we desire not the knowledge of
thy ways.
15 [r]What *is* the Almighty, that we should
serve him? and [s]what profit should we
have, if we pray unto him?
16 Lo, their good *is* not in their hand: [t]the
counsel of the wicked is far from me.
17 [u]How oft is the candle of the wicked
put out! and *how oft* cometh their destruction upon them! *God* [v]distributeth sorrows
in his anger.
18 [w]They are as stubble before the wind,
and as chaff that the storm carrieth away.
19 God layeth up his iniquity [x]for his
children: he rewardeth him, and he shall
know *it*.
20 His eyes shall see his destruction, and
[y]he shall drink of the wrath of the Almighty.
21 For what pleasure *hath* he in his house
after him, when the number of his months is
cut off in the midst?
22 [z]Shall *any* teach God knowledge? seeing he judgeth those that are high.
23 One dieth in his full strength, being
wholly at ease and quiet.
24 His breasts are full of milk, and his
bones are moistened with marrow.
25 And another dieth in the bitterness of
his soul, and never eateth with pleasure.
26 They shall [a]lie down alike in the dust,
and the worms shall cover them.
27 Behold, I know your thoughts, and
the devices *which* ye wrongfully imagine
against me.
28 For ye say, [b]Where *is* the house of the
prince? and where *are* the dwelling places
of the wicked?
29 Have ye not asked them that go by the
way? and do ye not know their tokens,
30 [c]That the wicked is reserved to the
day of destruction? they shall be brought
forth to the day of wrath.

20:8 [w]Ps. 73:20
20:9 [x]ch. 7:8; Ps. 37:36
20:10 [y]ver. 18
20:11 [z]ch. 13:26; Ps. 25:7 [a]ch. 21:26
20:17 [b]Ps. 36:9; Jer. 17:6
20:18 [c]ver. 10
20:20 [d]Eccl. 5:13
20:23 [e]Num. 11:33; Ps. 78:30
20:24 [f]Isa. 24:18; Jer. 48:43; Am. 5:19
20:25 [g]ch. 16:13 [h]ch. 18:11
20:26 [i]Ps. 21:9
20:29 [j]ch. 27:13
21:3 [k]ch. 16:10
21:5 [l]Judg. 18:19; ch. 29:9; Ps. 39:9
21:7 [m]ch. 12:6; Ps. 17:10; Jer. 12:1; Hab. 1:16
21:9 [n]Ps. 73:5
21:10 [o]Ex. 23:26
21:13 [p]ch. 36:11
21:14 [q]ch. 22:17
21:15 [r]Ex. 5:2; ch. 34:9 [s]ch. 35:3; Mal. 3:14
21:16 [t]ch. 22:18; Ps. 1:1; Prov. 1:10
21:17 [u]ch. 18:6 [v]Luke 12:46
21:18 [w]Ps. 1:4; Isa. 17:13; Hos. 13:3
21:19 [x]Ex. 20:5
21:20 [y]Ps. 75:8; Isa. 51:17; Jer. 25:15; Rev. 14:10
21:22 [z]Isa. 40:13; Rom. 11:34; 1 Cor. 2:16
21:26 [a]ch. 20:11; Eccl. 9:2
21:28 [b]ch. 20:7
21:30 [c]Prov. 16:4; 2 Pet. 2:9

31 Who shall declare his way [d]to his face? and who shall repay him *what* he hath done?

32 Yet shall he be brought to the grave, and shall remain in the tomb.

33 The clods of the valley shall be sweet unto him, and [e]every man shall draw after him, as *there are* innumerable before him.

34 How then comfort ye me in vain, seeing in your answers there remaineth falsehood?

22

Then Eliphaz the Temanite answered and said,

2 [f]Can a man be profitable unto God, as he that is wise may be profitable unto himself?

3 *Is it* any pleasure to the Almighty, that thou art righteous? or *is it* gain *to him,* that thou makest thy ways perfect?

4 Will he reprove thee for fear of thee? will he enter with thee into judgment?

5 *Is* not thy wickedness great? and thine iniquities infinite?

6 For thou hast [g]taken a pledge from thy brother for nought, and stripped the naked of their clothing.

7 Thou hast not given water to the weary to drink, and thou [h]hast withholden bread from the hungry.

8 But *as for* the mighty man, he had the earth; and the honourable man dwelt in it.

9 Thou hast sent widows away empty, and the arms of [i]the fatherless have been broken.

10 Therefore [j]snares *are* round about thee, and sudden fear troubleth thee;

11 Or darkness, *that* thou canst not see; and abundance of [k]waters cover thee.

12 *Is* not God in the height of heaven? and behold the height of the stars, how high they are!

13 And thou sayest, [l]How doth God know? can he judge through the dark cloud?

14 [m]Thick clouds *are* a covering to him, that he seeth not; and he walketh in the circuit of heaven.

15 Hast thou marked the old way which wicked men have trodden?

16 Which [n]were cut down out of time, whose foundation was overflown with a flood:

17 [o]Which said unto God, Depart from us: and [p]what can the Almighty do for them?

18 Yet he filled their houses with good *things:* but [q]the counsel of the wicked is far from me.

19 [r]The righteous see *it,* and are glad: and the innocent laugh them to scorn.

20 Whereas our substance is not cut down, but the remnant of them the fire consumeth.

21 Acquaint now thyself with him, and [s]be at peace: thereby good shall come unto thee.

22 Receive, I pray thee, the law from his mouth, and [t]lay up his words in thine heart.

23 [u]If thou return to the Almighty, thou shalt be built up, thou shalt put away iniquity far from thy tabernacles.

24 Then shalt thou [v]lay up gold as dust, and the *gold* of Ophir as the stones of the brooks.

25 Yea, the Almighty shall be thy defence, and thou shalt have plenty of silver.

26 For then shalt thou have thy [w]delight in the Almighty, and [x]shalt lift up thy face unto God.

27 [y]Thou shalt make thy prayer unto him, and he shall hear thee, and thou shalt pay thy vows.

28 Thou shalt also decree a thing, and it shall be established unto thee: and the light shall shine upon thy ways.

29 When *men* are cast down, then thou shalt say, *There is* lifting up; and [z]he shall save the humble person.

30 He shall deliver the island of the innocent: and it is delivered by the pureness of thine hands.

23

Then Job answered and said,

2 Even to day *is* my complaint bitter: my stroke is heavier than my groaning.

3 [a]Oh that I knew where I might find him! *that* I might come *even* to his seat!

4 I would order *my* cause before him, and fill my mouth with arguments.

5 I would know the words *which* he would answer me, and understand what he would say unto me.

6 [b]Will he plead against me with *his* great power? No; but he would put *strength* in me.

7 There the righteous might dispute with him; so should I be delivered for ever from my judge.

8 [c]Behold, I go forward, but he *is* not *there;* and backward, but I cannot perceive him:

9 On the left hand, where he doth work, but I cannot behold *him:* he hideth himself on the right hand, that I cannot see *him:*

10 But he [d]knoweth the way that I take: *when* [e]he hath tried me, I shall come forth as gold.

11 [f]My foot hath held his steps, his way have I kept, and not declined.

12 Neither have I gone back from the commandment of his lips; [g]I have esteemed the words of his mouth more than my necessary *food.*

13 But he *is* in one *mind,* and [h]who can turn him? and *what* [i]his soul desireth, even *that* he doeth.

14 For he performeth *the thing that is* [j]appointed for me: and many such *things are* with him.

15 Therefore am I troubled at his presence: when I consider, I am afraid of him.

16 For God [k]maketh my heart soft, and the Almighty troubleth me:

17 Because I was not cut off before the

21:31 [d]Gal. 2:11
21:33 [e]Heb. 9:27
22:2 [f]ch. 35:7; Ps. 16:2; Luke 17:10
22:6 [g]Ex. 22:26; Deut. 24:10; ch. 24:3; Ezek. 18:12
22:7 [h]ch. 31:17; Deut. 15:7; Isa. 58:7; Ezek. 18:7; Matt. 25:42
22:9 [i]ch. 31:21; Isa. 10:2; Ezek. 22:7
22:10 [j]ch. 18:8
22:11 [k]Ps. 69:1; Lam. 3:54
22:13 [l]Ps. 10:11
22:14 [m]Ps. 139:11
22:16 [n]ch. 15:32; Ps. 55:23; Eccl. 7:17
22:17 [o]ch. 21:14 [p]Ps. 4:6
22:18 [q]ch. 21:16
22:19 [r]Ps. 58:10
22:21 [s]Isa. 27:5
22:22 [t]Ps. 119:11
22:23 [u]ch. 8:5
22:24 [v]2 Chron. 1:15
22:26 [w]ch. 27:10; Isa. 58:14 [x]ch. 11:15
22:27 [y]Ps. 50:14; Isa. 58:9
22:29 [z]Prov. 29:23; Jam. 4:6; 1 Pet. 5:5
23:3 [a]ch. 13:3
23:6 [b]Isa. 27:4
23:8 [c]ch. 9:11
23:10 [d]Ps. 139:1 [e]Ps. 17:3; Jam. 1:12
23:11 [f]Ps. 44:18
23:12 [g]John 4:32
23:13 [h]ch. 9:12; Rom. 9:19 [i]Ps. 115:3
23:14 [j]1 Thess. 3:3
23:16 [k]Ps. 22:14

darkness, *neither* hath he covered the darkness from my face.

24 Why, seeing [l]times are not hidden from the Almighty, do they that know him not see his days?

2 *Some* remove the [m]landmarks; they violently take away flocks, and feed *thereof.*

3 They drive away the ass of the fatherless, they [n]take the widow's ox for a pledge.

4 They turn the needy out of the way: [o]the poor of the earth hide themselves together.

5 Behold, *as* wild asses in the desert, go they forth to their work; rising betimes for a prey: the wilderness *yieldeth* food for them *and* for *their* children.

6 They reap *every one* his corn in the field: and they gather the vintage of the wicked.

7 They [p]cause the naked to lodge without clothing, that *they have* no covering in the cold.

8 They are wet with the showers of the mountains, and [q]embrace the rock for want of a shelter.

9 They pluck the fatherless from the breast, and take a pledge of the poor.

10 They cause *him* to go naked without clothing, and they take away the sheaf *from* the hungry;

11 *Which* make oil within their walls, *and* tread *their* winepresses, and suffer thirst.

12 Men groan from out of the city, and the soul of the wounded crieth out: yet God layeth not folly *to them.*

13 They are of those that rebel against the light; they know not the ways thereof, nor abide in the paths thereof.

14 [r]The murderer rising with the light killeth the poor and needy, and in the night is as a thief.

15 [s]The eye also of the adulterer waiteth for the twilight, [t]saying, No eye shall see me: and disguiseth *his* face.

16 In the dark they dig through houses, *which* they had marked for themselves in the daytime: they [u]know not the light.

17 For the morning *is* to them even as the shadow of death: if *one* know *them, they are in* the terrors of the shadow of death.

18 He *is* swift as the waters; their portion is cursed in the earth: he beholdeth not the way of the vineyards.

19 Drought and heat consume the snow waters: *so doth* the grave *those which* have sinned.

20 The womb shall forget him; the worm shall feed sweetly on him; [v]he shall be no more remembered; and wickedness shall be broken as a tree.

21 He evil entreateth the barren *that* beareth not: and doeth not good to the widow.

22 He draweth also the mighty with his power: he riseth up, and no *man* is sure of life.

23 *Though* it be given him *to be* in safety, whereon he resteth; yet [w]his eyes *are* upon their ways.

24 They are exalted for a little while, but are gone and brought low; they are taken out of the way as all *other,* and cut off as the tops of the ears of corn.

25 And if *it be* not *so* now, who will make me a liar, and make my speech nothing worth?

25 Then answered Bildad the Shuhite, and said,

2 Dominion and fear *are* with him, he maketh peace in his high places.

3 Is there any number of his armies? and upon whom doth not [x]his light arise?

4 [y]How then can man be justified with God? or how can he be clean *that is* born of a woman?

5 Behold even to the moon, and it shineth not; yea, the stars are not pure in his sight.

6 How much less man, *that is* [z]a worm? and the son of man, *which is* a worm?

26 But Job answered and said,

2 How hast thou helped *him that is* without power? *how* savest thou the arm *that hath* no strength?

3 How hast thou counselled *him that hath* no wisdom? and *how* hast thou plentifully declared the thing as it is?

4 To whom hast thou uttered words? and whose spirit came from thee?

5 Dead *things* are formed from under the waters, and the inhabitants thereof.

6 [a]Hell *is* naked before him, and destruction hath no covering.

7 [b]He stretcheth out the north over the empty place, *and* hangeth the earth upon nothing.

8 [c]He bindeth up the waters in his thick clouds; and the cloud is not rent under them.

9 He holdeth back the face of his throne, *and* spreadeth his cloud upon it.

10 [d]He hath compassed the waters with bounds, until the day and night come to an end.

11 The pillars of heaven tremble and are astonished at his reproof.

12 [e]He divideth the sea with his power, and by his understanding he smiteth through the proud.

13 [f]By his spirit he hath garnished the heavens; his hand hath formed [g]the crooked serpent.

14 Lo, these *are* parts of his ways: but how little a portion is heard of him? but the thunder of his power who can understand?

27 Moreover Job continued his parable, and said,

2 *As* God liveth, [h]*who* hath taken away my judgment; and the Almighty, *who* hath vexed my soul;

3 All the while my breath *is* in me, and the spirit of God *is* in my nostrils;

4 My lips shall not speak wickedness, nor my tongue utter deceit.

5 God forbid that I should justify you: till

24:1 [l]Acts 1:7
24:2 [m]Deut. 19:14; Prov. 22:28; Hos. 5:10
24:3 [n]ch. 22:6; Deut. 24:6
24:4 [o]Prov. 28:28
24:7 [p]Ex. 22:26; Deut. 24:12; ch. 22:6
24:8 [q]Lam. 4:5
24:14 [r]Ps. 10:8
24:15 [s]Prov. 7:9 [t]Ps. 10:11
24:16 [u]John 3:20
24:20 [v]Prov. 10:7
24:23 [w]Ps. 11:4; Prov. 15:3
25:3 [x]Jam. 1:17
25:4 [y]ch. 4:17; Ps. 130:3
25:6 [z]Ps. 22:6
26:6 [a]Ps. 139:8; Prov. 15:11; Heb. 4:13
26:7 [b]ch. 9:8; Ps. 24:2
26:8 [c]Prov. 30:4
26:10 [d]ch. 38:8; Ps. 33:7; Prov. 8:29; Jer. 5:22
26:12 [e]Ex. 14:21; Ps. 74:13; Isa. 51:15; Jer. 31:35
26:13 [f]Ps. 33:6 [g]Isa. 27:1
27:2 [h]ch. 34:5

FOCUS ON JOB

In the distant past, there was a man and a woman who seemed to have it all together. They had great wealth and spacious accommodations. They had a large family of seven good-looking, reverent sons and three beautiful daughters. In agricultural periods, having many children meant greater potential both for increasing the wealth and for having progeny to carry further the name and property. They had the respect of the community. You know the name of the man—Job. He was pious and enjoyed favor with God. What more could he and his wife ask of life?

Like most women of her time, our leading lady is unnamed. She worked the garden, cooked the food, grew the wheat, made bread, wove the clothes at the loom, supervised the household help, negotiated for what they did not grow, and of course, bore and raised the babies. She was simply the wife of Mr. Job. Mrs. Job or Mother Job was her entire identity. She has a small role in this book—the oldest book in Scripture. But, sometimes, players with small roles can provide much insight into the overall plot.

Job is the first book of wisdom literature. For women, it demands consideration. It looks into issues that are critical to our understanding of ourselves and the relationship of our "woman experience" and God. It brings to bear the ones we call "friends and sisters" when life has handed us some tragic matter to deal with. And we have to continue to wrestle with Rabbi Kushner's book and question, "Why do bad things happen to good people?" This book also makes us stop and consider why it is that we really do try to live a "righteous" life! Are we seeking some payoff when we try to do the right thing for the right reason? Do we truly feel that if we're "good," that bad things won't happen? Do we bet our lives on the fact that when things are going well, then God is smiling on us? Conversely, do we feel that when life turns upside down and even our right is taken for wrong that God has walked off and forgotten all about us? Job brings us face to face with just how small we are in the awesomeness of God's creation.

Mrs. Job is heard to only make one comment in the entire book. She gives her spouse what she feels is sound advice. Looking at her husband suffering the indignities of lost favor, dead children, lost wealth, and unfaithful friends, she asks him, "Dost thou still retain thine integrity? curse God, and die" (2:9). Job declares, "Thou speaketh as one of the foolish women speaketh. What? shall we receive good at the hand of God, and shall we not receive evil?" (v. 10).

In a time when children were considered a gift from God, we can assume that Job's wife was even more "gifted" at the end of the story. "The LORD blessed the latter end of Job more than his beginning. . . . He had also seven sons and three daughters. And he called the name of the first, Jemima; and the name of the second, Kezia; and the name of the

third, Keren-happuch. And in all the land were no women found so fair as the daughters of Job: and their father gave them inheritance among their brothers" (vv. 13–15). God understood and forgave Job's wife.

THE BLACK PRESENCE IN JOB

While no specific Scriptural reference can identify Job as black, the known environment of northeast Africa points to the likelihood that he was of Hamitic lineage. People groups mentioned in the Book of Job include the following: Sabeans (Job 1:15) were descendants of Cush (Gen. 10:7), who was a son of Ham. Eliphaz the Temanite (Job 2:11) was one of the 12 sons of Ishmael (Gen. 25:15), who was born to Abraham and Hagar, an Egyptian. Bildad the Shuhite (Job 2:11) was a descendant of Abraham and Keturah (Gen. 25:2). Sheba (Job 1:15; 6:19) was a descendant of Cush who was black (Gen. 10:7; 1 Chron. 1:9). Their people were called Sabeans, the queen of Sheba being well known among them (1 Kin. 10:1–13; Matt. 12:42). They traded in precious stones, incense (Isa. 60:6; Jer. 6:20), and slaves (Joel 3:8).

Life Lessons

JOB 1

Job exercised concern for his family. Experience demonstrates that once a parent, always a parent. Parents naturally provide for and nurture their children. Parents of adult children pray for and counsel as they have opportunity.

Parent of Parents, give me the wisdom to be the parent I need to be for my underage or grown children, as well as for those in my community.

JOB 1–2

Because of Job's great wealth and abundant blessing, Satan questions Job's motivations. God permits Job to be tested. God is keenly aware of our every human situation, and does permit testing. The tests are for our refinement as well as for the glory of God, who helps us to go through them and come out victoriously! When his wife comes to challenge his suffering, Job maintains that he has done no wrong.

Helper of the Helpless, when I am tested, please help me to draw close to You for strength and wisdom.

JOB 1

Job acknowledges the sovereignty of God when the bottom had fallen out of everything important to him. He says, "The LORD gave, and the LORD hath taken away; blessed be the name of the LORD" (1:21). Praising God when things are going well is commendable, but having the ability to offer praise when everything goes wrong is a sign of genuine maturity and trust.

Sovereign God, help me to praise You when things are going well and when they are not.

JOB 2–37

The friends and associates of Job come to "grieve" with him. They come with the common social understanding that Job has either sinned against God or has so contemplated sin until these tests are a warning. They urge Job to "fess up" and allow a contrite spirit to relieve him of this present distress. Job maintains his integrity. In the face of social pressure, Job lays his experience against community wisdom and norms. In the midst of painful suffering and the loss of all his relatives and friends, Job clings to his personal conviction that God would ultimately not disappoint him. He said, "I know that my redeemer liveth, and that he shall stand at the latter day upon the earth" (19:25–27).

Faithful Friend, when I am experiencing painful suffering and no one seems to understand, help me to know that You will never leave me, and that ultimately I will see Your hand in the midst of the most desperate situation and be filled with wisdom, which will lead me to unending joy.

JOB 23

Job, in the midst of his suffering, seeks God. He wants and needs answers as to why this situation is happening to him. He knows the hurt of feeling forsaken. Yet he also knows that faith need not falter in such desperate times. He testifies of having sought for God in every known direction. Despite the seeming fruitlessness of his search, Job remains confident that "[God] knoweth the way that I take: when he hath tried me, I shall come forth as gold" (23:10).

Testing God, in those times when I feel abandoned and alone, help me to know that You are still with me. Teach me not to doubt Your absence in times of testing.

JOB 38–41

God answers Job out of the whirlwind. Through His questions God reveals perfect knowledge, infinite wisdom, and vast immensity. God's questions help Job begin to understand His justice, love for creation, and absolute power. Job now knows that God is more than sufficient for all human needs. Faith in God's power and love are what sustains believers today through good times and bad.

Questioning God, help me to comprehend more about Your sufficiency. The story of Job helps me to better understand that You not only care for me, but that You care enough never to leave me nor forsake me.

JOB 42

Job repents. "I know that thou canst do every thing, . . . Wherefore I abhor myself, and repent in dust and ashes" (42:2–6). The end of the story is better than the beginning. "The LORD blessed the latter end of Job more than his beginning" (v. 12). The family fortune is restored. Mrs. Job births seven additional sons, but their names are not recorded. However, three beautiful daughters are born: Jemima, Kezia, and Keren-happuch. "In all the land were no women found so fair as the daughters of Job: and their father gave them inheritance among their brethren" (vv. 14–15). This is mighty good news!

Dear God, I repent, as Job did, of my sins. Let me enjoy Your blessing again.

FOCUS ON PSALMS

Singing. Adoration. Worship. Praise. Emoting. Feeling. Expressing. Exalting. Lamenting. Crying. Hating. Hurting. Begging. Pleading. Surviving. Thriving. Up. Down. Happy. Sad. The Psalms express these feelings and more! When our words are too inadequate and our prayers cannot quite grasp the fitting phrase, the psalms provide them. David is credited with writing most of these songs. He writes out of a wide range of emotions. His songs are filled with pathos and exuberance. He does not hesitate to reveal to God the deepest feelings known to men and women alike. For whatever state you find yourself in, there is a psalm to fit the occasion. Yet, no song is recorded for Bathsheba. Who heard and kept record of her laments to God? Only the Healer of Broken Hearts heard her melodic cries.

Every widowed, divorced, abandoned woman, every single sister who feels hopeless in her waiting, every married woman who longs for understanding and care—each left alone and unprotected from emotional scars—sings songs in the long sleepless watches of the night. When solitude is torture and the stars won't shine, women sing melodies. The angels catch their perfect pitch. Women who lose innocent children as sacrifices to violence, those who experience miscarriages, those who ache for a pregnancy that never comes, utter sounds of unbelievable range. The Maestro of Music receives every flawless note.

THE BLACK PRESENCE IN THE PSALMS

In addition to the general awareness that people reflected in Psalms are of African-Asiatic background, the following Psalms make specific reference to known black people:

Psalm 68:31: This Psalm includes a reference to Egypt and Cush (Ethiopia), people of black skin speaking of their submission and reverence for God.

Psalm 72:10: Psalm 72 is messianic in that it refers to the coming reign of the Messiah, God's anointed ruler. Far away kings shall bow before Him, including those of Sheba and Seba, both Hamitic countries in Arabia whose inhabitants were black.

Psalms 78:51; 105:23, 27; 106:22: These references are to Israel's sojourn in Egypt, further described as the land of Ham, people of African descent.

Psalm 110:4: This Psalm mentions Melchezidek, a priest/king in Jerusalem at the time that Abraham lived in the land. At that time, the descendants of Ham and Canaan occupied Jerusalem.

Psalm 137: This Psalm references Babylon, where the Israelites were taken after being deported from their land in 586 B.C. Babylonia was occupied by the descendants of Ham and Cush (Gen. 10:6–10).

Life Lessons

PSALM 1

Psalm 1 describes two types of people: the "blessed" person is one who orders his or her life according to the Word of God ("law of the LORD," v. 2). Such a person is stable, fruitful, enduring, and prosperous. In contrast, the "ungodly" person is unstable, unfruitful, and unprotected from certain judgment.

Blessing God, help me to find delight in Your word so that I will always choose the path that leads to the fulfilled, fruitful life in You. Help me to avoid the ungodly path that leads to a lack of fruitfulness, as well as judgment from You.

PSALM 8

Psalm 8 refers to the honor God has bestowed on us. We can know, feel, and act in ways similar to God's ways because we are made in that divine image, the *Imago Dei*. How marvelous is the God whose love, wisdom, and power were breathed into us "in the beginning!"

Creative Creator, I praise You for the honor You have bestowed on me in making me in Your image and likeness.

PSALM 16

Psalm 16 expresses the author's appreciation for the ability to enjoy a personal and intimate relationship with God. God is acknowledged as all sovereign and all sufficient (v. 5–6). The Psalm also expresses God's counsel (v. 7), God faithfulness (vv. 8–10), and ends with the affirmation of eternal joy at God's right hand—a never-ending relationship (vv. 9–11).

Inviting God, like the author, I also praise You for Your willingness to indwell those who believe in You, and for the blessings You provide both here and hereafter.

PSALM 18

In Psalm 18, David praises God for deliverance from Saul. His expressions, while reflective of his own unique culture and circumstances, reveal truths about God, which are applicable anytime: God is a secure place to stand in times of stress ("a rock," v. 2); God hears our calls for help (v. 6); God is faithful (v. 25); God turns our "gloom into light" (v. 28); and God's Word is flawless and therefore totally reliable (v. 30). David testifies that only God can enable us to maneuver through the most harrowing of circumstances (v. 33).

Delivering God, You have revealed such awesome truths in Your Living Word. Help me to appropriate these truths for my life so that I can function each day in ways that honor You, bless others, and satisfy me.

PSALM 23

In Psalm 23, David praises the Lord—who has been his shepherd—for sufficiency, rest, and refreshment (v. 2); restoration and guidance (v.

3); protection and discipline (v. 4); fellowship and honor (v. 5); and goodness and mercy both here on earth and in heaven forever.

Shepherding God, I thank You and praise You for Your sufficiency and comfort for me.

PSALM 27

Psalm 27 expresses the psalmist's confidence that the Lord will give him victory over those who desire to do him evil. Because the Lord (and no one else) is his "light" (v. 1) and the source of his well-being, whom should he fear? He has evaluated the essentials of life and has decided that "dwelling in the house of the LORD" (v. 4) and seeking God (v. 8) are at the top of his list! His delight in the Lord moves him to encourage others to do as he did: "Wait on the LORD" (v. 14), a concept which means to eagerly anticipate that God will do what is necessary.

God Who Comes, in light of Your provision for my well-being, help me to always give You all of my affection. Help me to trust You for the wisdom and strength to do the right thing, knowing that to "wait" does not always mean to be idle, but to be expectant, with total dependence on the wisdom and strength that You provide.

PSALM 37

In Psalm 37, David shares some lessons he has learned from walking with God: If you "trust in the LORD and do good" you will "dwell in the land" (v. 3). If you delight yourself in the Lord, the Lord will grant the desires of your heart (v. 4). If you commit your way unto God, your righteousness will shine (v. 6). If you don't run ahead of the Lord ("Be still and know"; Ps. 46:10), you will inherit the land (vv. 7–9). If the Lord delights in you, God will make your steps firm and will keep you from falling (v. 24).

Attentive God, You are teaching me some valuable lessons about Yourself. Help me to be responsive to Your teaching and to order my steps according to Your Word.

PSALM 42–43

The psalmist encourages others to "hope thou in God" (42:5, 11; 43:5). For Christian believers, hope is more than wishful anticipation that things will somehow get better. Because of our relationship with God who is all-sufficient for all our needs, our hope is certain because it is anchored in the One who cannot fail.

Hope of the World, I praise You for the hope You offer to those who place their trust in You. When I am tempted to be discouraged, please remind me that I need not be because You have promised victory for those whose confidence is in You. You are absolutely trustworthy.

PSALM 51

Psalm 51 is the prayer of repentance and confession which David prays after the man of God, Nathan, comes and points out that "you are the man" who has taken advantage of Uriah's "one little ewe lamb!" David prays for mercy because of God's unfailing love (v. 1). He asks for his sins to be blotted out, his soul cleansed (v. 2). Then David confesses to knowing his own sin. He understands God's right judgment against him (v. 4).

Then David helps us to comprehend that evil was implanted in us due to the original sin of our first parents, Adam and Eve (v. 5). And David begs of wisdom (v. 6). Restoration and joy are sought (v. 8). David asks for a pure heart and a steadfast spirit (v. 10). The appeal for God's Holy Spirit (the anointing) not to be taken from him is clear (v. 11). To be sustained by a spirit willing to do the right thing is voiced (v. 12). Then David promises to testify on God's behalf and to teach others to turn back to God after sin is committed (v. 13).

Restoring Redeemer, help me always to confess my sin and turn to You for healing, restoration, and forgiveness.

PSALM 87

Psalm 87:4 lists five nations that will be gathered to worship the Lord in Zion: Rahab, Babylon, Philistia, Tyre, and Cush. Each of these nations sprang from Ham (Gen. 10:6–10), and shows God's glorious plans for these people of color. These texts demonstrate that while people of African descent are often rejected or ignored in our day, such treatment does not represent the love and plan of God, who accepts people of every nation who love and obey Him (see Acts 10:34–35).

Inclusive God, thank You for Your love for all people. Thank You for Your wonderful and inclusive plan to include people of African descent among the diverse groups that You will gather in Zion.

PSALM 118

Psalm 118:8 is the exact center of the Bible! "It is better to trust in the LORD than to put confidence in man." "Who" you trust and "where" you seek refuge are the essential components of all religions. As women, it is good for us to be reminded that no human male can be our ultimate source. There is only one God! The Psalm's focus is on our having confidence in God's eternal, unchanging love. Regardless of the situations we face, this gives us both hope and confidence.

Trusting Refuge, "I shall not die, but live and declare the works of my LORD" (v. 17).

PSALM 139

In Psalm 139, David praises God for His omniscience, omnipresence, and omnipotence. God's knowledge is expressed in verses 1–6; God's omnipresence in verses 7–12; God's omnipotence, love, and providence in verses 13–18.

All-Seeing, All-Knowing, All-Powerful, and Everywhere-Present God, You are keenly aware of all that concerns me. When I am tempted to feel lonely, powerless, and abandoned, please remind me of who You are and what I mean to You.

PSALM 150

Psalm 150 is a closing hymn of praise. All of creation offers praise. Every musical instrument is tuned in praise to the Magnificent Creator. The worship of God resounds in every sphere of the universe. The anonymous writer of this hymn declares, "Let every thing that hath breath praise the LORD. Praise ye the LORD!" (150:6).

Praiseworthy God, all the universe exalts You. From the dry

sprouting desert to the bubbling singing waters; from the grand and lofty mountains to the small oak budding in the forest; from the aged planets to the newly "found" galaxy—all of creation praises only You. As they respond to Your voice thundering, even in the silence of the longest night, I add my tiny voice and offer You my humble praise!

Women in JOB

THE DAUGHTERS OF JOB: IDENTITY CHECK

The first chapter of Job contains a cursory mention of Job's daughters. The three nameless women are referenced in terms of their father's blameless character. Little information is given regarding the daughters. Their identity and place are juxtaposed to their relationship to their father and brothers. We are told of the strong familial bond between the brothers and sisters, and the faithful intercession made by a father who was full of integrity. Without warning Job's daughters, sons, and possessions are destroyed. Too many nameless African-American women have experienced a similar kind of death—the loss of relationships, identity, and place. When one's worth and identity are predicated upon others, death is imminent and can come at any moment—quickly and unexpectedly.

But then Job has another set of daughters. The daughters of Job in chapter 42 exemplify the restorative power of God. While the sons are not named in this chapter, the three daughters are. Naming the daughters instead of the sons was very unusual. So, too, was the fact that Job gave his daughters an inheritance along with his sons. Their names articulate their identity, place, and relations in life. Jemima means "dove." Perhaps this is a reference to the Spirit-filled life this woman would live. Kezia is a fragrant cinnamon or perfume. Her name foreshadows Mary's act of pouring perfume on the feet of Jesus and how the fragrance filled the entire room. (See John 12:3.) The word Keren-happuch means "horn of eye shadow or beautifier." This name has a note of personal care. Living for God involves first being filled with the Holy Spirit, sharing our love and gifts with others, and taking care of ourselves spiritually and physically. God's restorative power enables us to live in the fullness of life even when life's circumstances try to beat us down. Personal loss and death of identity are often a prelude to personal triumph and a holistic life.

Read Job 1:18; see also Numbers 27:1–11; 36:1–13.

Read the insight essay on the Attributes of God. Read the portrait on Zelophehad's Daughters.

—*A. E. Crawford*

JOB'S WIFE: THE MISUNDERSTOOD WOMAN

She is a woman buried in obscurity. Little thought is given to her plight, and in the eyes of most, she emerges as an evil temptress. Saint Augustine called her an "adjutant of the devil" *(diaboli adjutrix).* Calvin referred to her as "an organ of Satan" *(organum Satanae).*[1] For years, preachers have counted her among the female villains of the Bible. Few have viewed her as a co-sufferer with Job. Instead, she has been con-

demned to the pages of history as an insensitive woman.

However, we can see in the character of Job's wife a woman who experienced the same doubt and the same frustration that so many of us have experienced in our lifetime.[2] Exponentially and theoretically we can identify with this woman's losses and agony. Her moments of faithlessness were probably no greater than the moments of faithlessness and despair that we have experienced. We must not be so quick to condemn or judge her, for we cannot be sure that if we were in her shoes we would not have reacted in the same manner.

There was once a woman who lived in the land of Uz. She had a husband by the name of Job. The Bible says that he was a faithful man. Can we not believe that she was a faithful woman also?[3] They had seven sons and three daughters. They had numerous livestock and lived in a large house with a number of servants. Job was described as the greatest man in the kingdom, so we must believe that Job's wife was the greatest woman in the kingdom.

Then, at the hand of Satan, the test came. It is traditionally called "Job's Test," but it was "Mrs. Job's Test" as well. Their livestock and servants were destroyed, their money lost, and their children killed. The biblical camera then focuses on Job's grief, giving no attention to "Mrs. Job." Indeed, the heavenly wager that had been designated for her husband had destroyed her world too. The pain intensified when her husband was stricken with boils all over his body. We cannot be surprised that her faith faltered and she cried out to Job: "Dost thou still retain thine integrity? curse God, and die!" (See Job 2:9.) These are the words that have provoked commentators, past and present, to scorn Mrs. Job. However, anyone who has experienced great loss can understand her outburst. It is probable that she suggested death to Job because death is what she wished for herself. She felt that faith and courage were unattainable at that moment. Furthermore, we have all said things for which we have had to repent.

Verses 10–13 of the last chapter declares that the Lord blessed the latter part of Job's life with double the earthly possessions and ten more children. We can safely assume that the mother of the last ten children was the woman who was mother of the first ten. Restoration and reconciliation, then, were Mrs. Job's, just as they were Job's.

Read Job 2:9–10.

Read insight essay on Suffering.

—M. Flake

Notes

1 Marvin H. Pope, *Job: The Anchor Bible Series* (Garden City: Doubleday, 1965), 21.

2 This shift to first person in this section and the next one is intentional. The identified audience is Black Christian women, and when referring to them and their experiences the words *we* and *our* provide the platform for a stronger identification with Job's wife.

3 Marvin H. Pope records that Rabbinic exegesis of Job 2:10 suggests that the plural "Shall we" includes Job's wife, hence the implication that she, too, was righteous.iInsightsi

Insights

SUFFERING—PHYSICAL PAIN

Be patient therefore, brethren, unto the coming of the Lord. . . . Be ye also patient; stablish your hearts: for the coming of the Lord draweth nigh. (James 5:7–8)

The Bible does not give any easy answers to the question of suffering. Suffering, however, is assured. Job was a "perfect and an upright man" who feared God and shunned evil (Job 2:3). Yet, even he experienced severe pain and never uncovered the reason why God allowed him to suffer. Sometimes in our suffering, our human instinct leads us to ask the question, "Why, God?" The fifth chapter of James tells us to be patient until the Lord comes. (See verse 7.)

How does one remain patient in view of continuous, seemingly endless, suffering? Asking one to be patient in the midst of suffering is a difficult request. Remember that even in suffering, the sovereignty of God prevails. Job persevered and was finally able to see what the Lord had in His divine plan for him. We may not understand the reasons why, but rest assured that God is full of mercy and compassion. God is your help in every need. (See Psalm 46:10.) God feeds your every hunger. God walks beside you night and day through every moment of your way. Even in our suffering, God is with us.

The New Testament emphasizes the partnership between suffering and joy. Joy comes from knowing that God is truly our shepherd (see John 10:11) and suffers with us through our pain. God is full of mercy and compassion: helping us in our need; feeding us in our hunger, walking with us night and day. We can rest assured that even in our suffering, God is with us.

Read Job 1–2; see also Judges 11:29–48; 2 Samuel 13:1–22; 2 Kings 4:8–31.

Read the insight essays on Grief, Sacrificial Living, and Suffering. Read the portraits on Dinah, Rachel, the Shunammite Woman, and Tamar.

—A. Gordon

OVERCOMING ABUSE—THE PEOPLE COULD FLY

The People Could Fly is an African-American folktale written by Virginia Hamilton. This folktale speaks about struggles, insight, understanding, integration, and development of new ways of being. The folktale typifies our struggle. It tells of a people with tremendous mystical powers who were captured and taken into slavery, made miserable by slavery, and forgot their powers to fly. When they were taken from their homeland and the "sweet scent of Africa," they could no longer remember who they were. Though they kept their powers throughout slavery, they psychically internalized the negative messages of slavery. The intolerable state of slavery caused many slaves to fall dead in the hot sun, until an old man named Toby arose and spoke ancient words, long forgotten, to a fallen man. The words "went deep inside the man," revived him, and he "rolled

over on the air" and flew. Next was a pregnant woman who had been whipped with her baby on her back. Toby spoke the words to her. He went from one slave to the next saying the ancient words, and one by one they rose on the air, leaving behind them the burdens, shame, violence, and psyche of a victim. Toby reminded the people of who they were, and that ancient knowledge was the key to their freedom.

Women of color have lived in a world that has imposed its destructive actions of abuse and messages that bind, burden, and produce guilt and shame. Most have internalized these destructive messages and now find themselves laboring in arenas that God never created them to labor in. To internalize the violence is to become its victim. It is to forget that "every human life is a reflection of the divinity." We are created by God in His image (see Gen. 1:27). It is to forget that for us the divine testimony proclaimed, "It [is] very good" (Gen. 1:31). It is to forget that God cares enough to shape and make us in our mother's wombs (see Job 31:15; Ps. 22:9–10). It is to forget that as images of God we have the choice to reflect the true divine image or become a distorted image by "passing on as true what are false images of God." Internalizing the violence causes self blame rather than the ability to see ourselves as "in process" of becoming. "In process" means there is tremendous creative potential that mirrors the divine impulse to beget life. Not only in procreation, but within the human ability to develop new thought and grow spiritually, to let go of old destructive patterns that limit the Holy Spirit within us, and limit intellectual, psychological, and emotional development. Being a reflection of God shows vividly in our propensity to love, forgive, have patience with, and be in relationships.

Read Job 31:15; see also Genesis 1:27, 31; 9:6; Psalm 22:9–10.
Read the insight essay on Suffering.

—N. Bryant

FRUIT OF THE SPIRIT—JOY

The word *joy* is found more than 150 times in the Bible. Joy is a deep inner gladness that comes from a clear conscience. It is not the same as happiness, because happiness depends on what happens to you. That means that if you have a bad day, you are not happy. Joy comes from trusting God and believing in God's promises. "Let all those that put their trust in thee rejoice: let them ever shout for joy, because thou defendest them: let them also that love thy name be joyful in thee" (Ps. 5:11).

Joy is a result of our faith and obedience. (See John 15:10-11.) We can have joy, because our hope lies in God, and we know that God is faithful. Joy is not something that we can work for; joy is worked for us by the Holy Spirit. The Bible says the joy of the Lord is our strength (Neh. 8:10).

I have often wondered at the joy expressed in the hearts and of minds of our ancestors. These women and men experienced unimaginable suffering, dehumanizing conditions, and immobilizing fear—yet managed to be joyful. The lives of slaves held little happiness, but there were many times when the joyous cries of Africa's dark children could be heard. There were times when the slaves could momentarily set aside their bondage and freely dance and sing. The abundance of joy is in direct proportion to the intimacy and steadfastness of the believer's walk with God.

True joy is evident regardless of circumstances. Those who love God rejoice even in the midst of troubles (James 1:2-3). There were times when heaven itself looked down and wondered at the joy and adulation of God's children. This joy expressed itself most often when the slaves gathered in brush arbors, in fields, and in secret places for worship. That's the key to joy: giving honor to the most high God. Communion with God produces joy—joy like a river, joy unspeakable, joy flooding the soul!

The harshness of this world, especially as it relates to persons of color, mitigates against happiness. But God promises a joy that the world can't give, and the world can't take away. Spend time with God and receive your joy! "Be glad in the Lord, and rejoice, ye righteous: and shout for joy" (Ps. 32:11).

Read Ps. 5:11; 32:11; see also Nehemiah 8:10; James 1:2–3.
Read the insight essay on Fruit of the Spirit.

—C. Belt

GRACE AND MERCY

For many of us, grace and mercy don't seem to be very evident within the fabric of our lives. We see grace as something other than what we are and what we have, and mercy as the antidote to our suffering or that of another. We experience existence as loss, while living in the margins of life, outside the boundaries of God's kingdom. It seems beyond our ability to understand why or how we came to be this way in this place and time. For, if given the choice, perhaps we would have chosen something different for ourselves: a different face, different gender, different body, different race, different parents, different path, different gifts and talents.

At times, it is hard for us to see or feel the presence of God's grace and mercy in our lives because we perceive ourselves as unworthy and assume that what we cannot see or feel does not exist. Maybe we cannot see it because, as the writer of Psalm 23 says, it follows us. It is always there behind us, upholding us, supporting us, seeing us through life, death, and the darkest valleys. "Surely goodness and mercy shall follow me all the days of my life and I will dwell in the house of the LORD for ever" (v. 6).

God's mercy does not give us what we deserve. His grace gives us what we do not deserve! Blessed are those who remember God's grace and mercy are always with them and they are never alone. God's grace includes undeserved favor, unexpected acceptance, and unconditional love.

Read Psalm 23.

—D. Taylor

CONFIDENCE

Confidence, as defined, implies "a firm belief in oneself, without display of arrogance or conceit." Therefore, we must be careful that we are not consumed with self-will. For of all the possible sins against God, one of the most serious is that of self-will and pride.

True confidence begins with faith in God, in His Word, and in Jesus our Lord and Savior. God is the confidence of all the ends of the earth (Ps. 65:5). His grace is at work in you to produce the desire and power to do His will. Believing in Him, one can truly say, "I can do all things through Christ which strengtheneth me" (Phil. 4:13). "For the LORD shall be thy

confidence" (Prov. 3:26). "In all thy ways acknowledge him, and he shall direct thy path" (v. 5).

Seek the presence of God, for He calls us to do so. We can then identify with the words of the psalmist: "The LORD is my light and my salvation; whom shall I fear? The LORD is the strength of my life; of whom shall I be afraid. . . . Though an host should encamp against me, my heart shall not fear: though war shall rise against me, in this will I be confident" (Ps. 27:1, 3).

The ability to enjoy life and succeed in one's pursuits is a gift from God. When we are brought into a right relationship with Him and are submissive to Him, He then gives us joy and confidence in what we do.

One's confidence in oneself must be based on a solid foundation, which is God. He promises to do great things for those who wait for Him. Look to Him and persevere in hope, confidence, and patience (Isa. 64:4).

"[Be] confident of this very thing, that he which hath begun a good work [of confidence] in you will perform it until the day of Jesus Christ" (Phil. 1:6). "And this is the confidence that we have in him, that, if we ask anything according to his will, he heareth us" (1 John 5:14). If you believe in Him, "then shall thy light break forth as the morning" (Isa. 58:8).

Press on with confidence.

Read Psalm 27:1–3; see also Isaiah 30:1;, 32:17; Proverbs 14:16; 28:16; Romans 14:5.

Read the insight essay on Fruit of the Spirit.

—R. Haynes

FRUIT OF THE SPIRIT—KINDNESS

Kindness is treating others with love and respect. Kindness in the Old and New Testaments refers to love that is expressed in actions. Kindness is not a natural human trait. It must be developed in women to enable us to express that kindness to others in the name of God. Since God has been kind to us, we as God's children should show kindness to others even in the midst of conflict. Over and over again the Bible tells us that we must be kind to those who are poor and oppressed. Proverbs 14:31 says, "He that oppresseth the poor reproacheth his Maker: but he that honoureth him hath mercy on the poor." Often the kindness that we extend to others goes unnoticed. But we must always remember that God notices. My sisters, "be not weary in well doing" (2 Thess. 3:13). The kindness that God shows to His children is everlasting.

Read Psalm 31:21; 117:2; see also 2 Samuel 2:6; Nehemiah 9:17; 2 Peter 1:5–7.

Read the insight essays on the Attributes of God, Friendship, and the Fruit of the Spirit.

—C. Belt

FEAR

> I sought the LORD, and he heard me, and delivered me from all my fears. (Ps. 34:4)

"Why are you so afraid, Mommy?" my then six-year-old daughter, Maisha, asked, responding to my tightened grip on her hand and my hastened gait. "Don't you know that God made you half woman and half angel?" I stared into the serenity of her light-brown eyes twinkled in the

moonlight. Her calm became contagious. Although her assessment of my physical composition was wrong, her spiritual insight was correct: God had made me and God would protect me! My grasp on her small hand loosened as we continued down the long, dark walkway that led from the garage to our apartment's front entrance.

Despite our historic lineage of bravery, courage, and seemingly supernatural strength, we, African-American women, have often found ourselves alone and in the dark. Events flash at us from seemingly nowhere, and we are struck by fright. Shocked by the electrifying bolt of fear, we become paralyzed and forget that we are God's daughters. I understand the fears of women. Perhaps a sister fears that she will live alone or even die alone. Perhaps she fears that God is angry with her because she has not been given someone to be one with and to be fruitful and multiply with. If she is a single parent, she may be fearful that her paychecks won't meet all of her responsibilities. Or if she's married and her relationship is not going well, she fears it will end in divorce.

Whatever our current circumstances may be, we must refuse to, as theologian Howard Thurman writes, "allow the events of our life to make us a prisoner." Instead, we must remember that "our lives offer so much more than our immediate experience discloses to us." Harriet Tubman's work was done in the shadows of darkness and evil, but she ultimately prevailed. The apostle Paul urged the passengers on the doomed ship, sailing toward Rome, to "be of good cheer . . . for there stood by me this night the angel of God, whose I am, and whom I serve, saying, Fear not Paul . . . I believe God" (Acts 27:25). So should we.

Read Psalm 34.

—M. Dyson

BROKENNESS: A BIBLICAL PERSPECTIVE

In order to understand brokenness from a biblical perspective, it becomes important that we embrace and understand the idea of the covenant relationship between God and humanity. This idea is fundamental in understanding both the Old and New Testaments, or Old and New Covenants. First, the covenant with Israel came from the sovereign and gracious will of God; it was a divine perspective on Israel, and was the originating move that constitutes and identifies Israel as the people of God. For all time, God remained the faithful party in the covenant and never breaches the contract (Ex. 34:6).

The prophets continually encouraged the people to be faithful to God's covenant with them. They encouraged the Israelites not to break their covenant with God—and by extension, not to break their relationships with their fellow humanity. They exhorted the people to be faithful to God. We see illustrations of what a faithful relationship with God and others would look like throughout the prophets: a better marriage (Hos. 2:19–20); a more idealized and faithful servant model (Isa. 44:18ff); and a prophetic vision of an ultimately salvific future, wherein the New Covenant of God is written on the human heart (Jer. 31; Ezek. 36:7).

This hopeful and ultimate future is one to which we all look forward. Nevertheless, we humans continue to break our covenants with God and with other humans. The feeling of being brokenhearted, then, is most often a result of some manner of "breach of contract" or broken covenant. When

humans make a covenant with one another, promises are made; however, when one or more persons involved in the covenant relationship ceases to keep the promise, the result is what we call a "broken heart." This breach of covenant can take place in personal relationships, such as marriages, other love relationships, friendships, and so on.

When Christians experience brokenness due to their own breach of covenant or when someone breaks a covenant with them that results in brokenness for the child of God, there is a source of hope and remedy. It is at these times of helplessness and brokenness, when we are in the deepest valleys of hurt and despair, that God's salvation is closest to us, surrounding our heart. Our challenge is to risk opening our broken heart to the healing power of God's love. Our divine partnership is with God in Jesus Christ from everlasting to everlasting. This solemn promise of God is found in Psalm 34:18; 51:7–11; Isaiah 61:1. It is ratified and becomes the binding trust with Jesus Christ in 1 Corinthians 11:23–25. God does not want us to be brokenhearted. Wisdom teaches that when a covenant is broken, God offers forgiveness that can heal the wound and love that can mend the broken heart.

Read Psalm 34:18; see also Psalm 51:7–11; 147:3; Proverbs 15:13; Isaiah 61:1–3; Mark 5:36; Luke 4:18.

Read insight essays on Distress, Fear, Grief, and Loneliness.

—K. Smallwood

SINGLE PARENTING

Reproduction between male and female was, from the very beginning, a command from God (Gen. 1:27–28). "And God blessed them, and God said unto them, Be fruitful, and multiply, and replenish the earth, and subdue it" (Gen. 1:28). These passages in Genesis offers a definition of parenthood in its original state, and at the same time demonstrate God's command to procreate and bring forth offspring.

From the very beginning, it was established in the mind of God that adult men and women would be responsible for raising and caring for their young. It was not ordained that the young would be left to exist on their own and fend for themselves, without training and guidance. Rather, the young would be cared for, taught, fed, and nurtured by adults until the young ones could function in their environment, independently and without the immediate assistance of adults. Raising children is not an easy task, but God instructs us to raise them with kindness. Accordingly, the Scripture says in Eph. 6:4, "And ye fathers, provoke not your children to wrath, but bring them up in the nurture and admonition of the Lord."

While contemporary parenting styles differ considerably from Old Testament practices, the facts still remain that parenting is not an easy task. Even in two-parent households, issues surrounding child rearing often arise and become points of contention between parents. In single-parent families, the responsibilities of parenting are often overwhelming. And, with statistics projecting failure and painting dismal pictures of delinquency, drugs, and prison for children of single-parent families, there doesn't seem to be a hope for these children. The statistics and the evening news trumpet gloom and doom: the many stories of crime and destruction among children of single-parent households—especially African-American young

men. Yet, we must refuse to accept that kind of future for our children. Remember the Scripture that says, "For with God, nothing shall be impossible," (Luke 1:37). Pray and rely completely on God. Insist on a drug-free, smoke-free, violence-free, loving home for your children to grow up in. Keep your expectations high, without being unrealistic. Whenever choices about college are talked about, the discussion should be centered on which college to attend rather than whether or not to attend.

Life as a single parent will have its fair share of challenges. You might have to pinch pennies, sacrifice, and cry. You may not always be able to buy your children everything they want, and you may drive a used car. But, you will never be homeless. God will always provide for your needs. You will mature spiritually and develop an intimate relationship with the Lord. You will learn to trust Him in a most astounding way. Learn to take the Word of God from the pages of the Scriptures and apply it directly, literally and realistically into your life. Life lessons will be well learned, and you'll be grateful to God for teaching them to you.

Have great expectations for your children. Anticipate receiving the secret desires of your heart from the Lord. Take verses, like Ps. 37:4–5, to heart: "Delight thyself also in the Lord; and he shall give thee the desires of thine heart. Commit thy way unto the Lord; trust also in him; and he shall bring it to pass." Look for the needs in your life to be met. In fact, expect them. These blessings will come to you from your loving God who has your best interests at heart. "But my God shall supply all your needs according to his riches in glory by Christ Jesus," (Phil. 4:19).

Read Psalms 34:4, 37:4–5; see also Genesis 21:8–21; 2 Kings 4:1–7; Luke 7:11–17.

—S. Robinson

DATING

Many books, television shows, and experts endeavor to reveal the secrets of successful dating. Although the Bible does not specifically discuss dating, general biblical principles should govern our dating relationships. Whether you are considering dating someone or are currently in a dating relationship, the following questions should be considered:

1. Does your date have a growing relationship with Jesus Christ? The Bible teaches that we should not be unequally yoked with unbelievers (2 Cor. 6:14). Not only does this text speak to one's spirituality, but also to values, lifestyles, goals, and worldviews.

2. Are you placing God first in every area of your life? Oftentimes we allow ourselves to become preoccupied with our dating relationships, or lack thereof, due to our need for companionship. This preoccupation can take a toll on our commitment to Christ. We are exhorted to seek God first and in return we shall receive the desires of our heart. "Delight thyself also in the Lord; and he shall give thee the desires of thine heart. Commit thy way unto the Lord; trust also in him; and he shall bring it to pass" (Ps. 37:4–5).

Also remember that "all that glitters is not gold." We must look past outward appearances and other superficialities in dating relationships and allow God to reveal to us what's in the heart (Ps. 37:4–5; Prov. 27:19).

Read Psalm 37:4–5; Proverbs 27:19.

Read insight essays on Commitment and Love.

—J. Thompson

LONELINESS

The experience of "aloneness" is a reality at various times in a woman's life. It can be a frightening experience and leave us with a sense of abandonment and powerlessness. This very real and painful feeling is often a catalyst of loneliness. Even if it is not triggered by a single event, we sometimes become so tired of being tired that the thought of going on any longer is no longer appealing or meaningful. It is at times like this that we feel that no one can possibly understand.

The depth of despair that can accompany such feelings becomes fertile ground for thoughts of suicide and other forms of destructive release. Anything to ease the pain becomes a viable option. Out of the depths, our soul cries out for God in wordless prayers that emanate from holes so deeply hewn by our despair that rescue is incomprehensible. It is in these moments that we can lament with the psalmist, saying,

> As the hart panteth after the water brooks, so panteth my soul after thee, O God. My soul thirsteth for God, for the living God: when shall I come and appear before God? My tears have been my meat day and night, while they continually say unto me, Where is thy God? (Ps. 42:1–3).

The pain seems to take on a life of its own at such times. It engulfs us, taunts us, and can cause us to believe that God has indeed abandoned us.

It is at that very place that God is most present and most intimate. God, the "wholly other," is so immersed in the event and the moment that we may find it almost impossible to perceive His presence in the midst of our pain. God is as close as the very air we breathe. We cannot experience a human emotion that God is outside of. In ways that are often incomprehensible at the time, God is present at the point of our greatest sense of brokenness and abandonment. The theology of the profound love of God understands that God has entered the drama and trauma of our lives and even screams with us in despair. Jesus, who was in the beginning with God, and who is indeed God, promises never to leave or forsake us. The profound love of God moved Him to take on flesh and hang on a cross where He screamed in agony, "My God, my God, why . . ." (Matt. 27:46). This God, who is willing to be present in the thick of it all with each of us, spoke through the prophet Isaiah one day:

> Fear not: for I have redeemed thee, I have called thee by thy name; thou art mine. When thou passeth through the waters, I will be with thee; and through the rivers, they shall not overflow thee: when thou walkest through the fire, thou shalt not be burned; neither shall the flame kindle upon thee. For I am the LORD thy God, the Holy One of Israel, thy Savior, . . . thou wast precious in my sight, thou hast been honourable, and I have loved thee (Isa. 43:2–5a).

We might experience being alone. We might experience devastating events. Disappointments might feel like they are par for the course in our experiential reality. But our faith, which is the substance of things unseen (see Hebrews 11:1), invades the void, becomes our companion in the very midst of the loneliness, and whispers, "Fear thou not; for I am with thee" (Is. 41:10). Believe in God, for He is here.

Read Psalm 42.

Read the insight essays on Friendship and Singleness.

—C. Swafford Harris

FORGIVENESS: GOD'S EXTENDED MERCY

"Amazing grace, how sweet the sound that saved a wretch like me." Through God's grace we have forgiveness for our iniquities. As humans, we all have sinned and fallen short of the glory of God. As sinners, we are victims of the consequences of sin! (See Psalm 51:5; Romans 3:23;1 John 1:8–10.) All we must do to receive God's gracious gift is to confess our sin. He is faithful and just to forgive us (1 John 1:9). God's forgiveness is complete (Ps. 103), it is everlasting (Isa. 44:22), and it is always available (1 John 1:9). What joy it is to know that God willingly and gladly releases us from the debt of sin and restores our fellowship with Him. It is a debt we could never repay or eradicate. Although this gift was free for us, it cost Jesus His own precious blood (Rom. 5:19). But despite Jesus' great price for our forgiveness, He unconditionally bestowed it upon us (Eph. 4:32). As children of God we continually need pardoning. But to our benefit, there is always an ample supply of forgiveness flowing through the love of the Father. God's forgiveness is not automatically given. We must humble ourselves before Him, confess our sins, and cease from sinning. (See 1 Kings 21:27–29; Isaiah 1:16–17; Joel 2:12–13.)

In the world of business, a debt is defined as a financial obligation—something one is bound to pay. Some medium of exchange or currency is needed to erase the debt. That means we are liable for our sin. The payment is eternal punishment! However, Jesus provided the "currency" through His blood and paid our debt of sin, leaving those who trust Him debt free.

Because we are shaped in iniquity (Ps. 51:5), our greatest need is that of forgiveness. God forgives our sin (Mic. 7:18), removes it completely (Ps. 103:12), and forgets it forever (Ps. 25:7). Thanks be to God that Jesus Christ has met this need and has restored our fellowship with our heavenly Father!

Read Psalm 51.

Read the insight essays on Attributes of God and Forgiveness.

—D. Manns

FRUIT OF THE SPIRIT—PATIENCE

Women are familiar with waiting. Women of African descent especially know the attributes of waiting. We wait for the restoration of our homes and the revival of our communities. We wait for an end to racism and the elimination of sexism. We wait for our children to be recognized as young and gifted in a society that suppresses their beauty and talent. We wait for our men to overcome the burden of oppression and self-hatred. We wait for our relationships to be empowered and renewed; and we wait for ourselves to be made whole by the Word of God.

Yes, black women are familiar with waiting. We have waited with the strength, brilliance, and vision of Hagar, Ruth, and the queen of Sheba. Yet with our inheritance of faith, creativity, and power, we wait with patience. God desires that we reflect the image of the Holy Spirit that lives within us. The presence of the Holy Spirit should not be interpreted to mean that we wait with anxiety, irritation, confusion, or passive resignation. Waiting should not understood as being done with jealousy, envy, or with rage. It is an active response to opposition. Waiting with the patience God grants is not without movement.

Waiting with a God-given patience means moving with God; it means

allowing God to have His perfect way in our lives. This patience allows God to regenerate us. Our attitudes while waiting should reflect our anticipation that God will arrive and be victorious. God waits with us, moves for us, and has already worked matters out on our behalf!

Read Psalms 86:15; 130:5–6; Romans 5:3–5; 1 Corinthians 13:4–7; Galatians 5:22.

Read the insight essays on Attributes of God, Fruit of the Spirit, and Suffering. Read the portraits on Hagar, the Queen of Sheba, and Ruth.

—C. Cooke

COPING

My soul is full of troubles. (Ps. 88:3)

There hath no temptation taken you but such as is common to man: but God is faithful, who will not suffer you to be tempted above that ye are able; but will with the temptation also make a way to escape, that ye may be able to bear it (1 Cor. 10:13).

Caregiver, coach, cook, counselor, chaplain, chauffeur, confidant, craftsperson, conflict mediator, companion, consultant, special events coordinator, ever ready to inspire others toward excellence, wellness and faith—these are descriptions to which many women can relate. Trying to be all things to all people has left us high on intentions but low on energy. How do we juggle the roles, relationships, requests, and life requirements that vie continuously for our attention and response?

Covenant with God to be open to anxiety, frustration, and trouble. The situations are divinely orchestrated mentors to our souls. Give thanks for the conversion of obstacles into opportunities for growth, and receive the resilience inherent in God's grace.

Operate out of what's important instead of what's urgent. Beware of poor planning and personal or organizational needs hiding behind a mask of urgency. Immediacy plus availability plus ability doesn't equal obligation. Ask God to order your involvement and concentrate on what matters in the eternal scheme of things.

Purpose in your heart to recall previous victories and determine to display godly character toward yourself and others as you scale the currently "insurmountable." Avoid the cling of "legitimate" anger by showing courage, justice, and compassion.

Engage with whom and in what confirms your God-derived destiny. Every decision either advances or retards fulfillment.

Coping is the language of transition. When the tomorrow you long for today comes, may it find you strong in faith, wiser in life, and more sensitive to the voice of God than you are right now.

Psalm 88.

Read the insight essays on Stress Management and Temptation.

—B. Glover-Williams

BUMPING INTO OMNIPOTENCE

Have you ever been minding your own business, doing your own thing, then suddenly run smack-dab into the omnipotence of God? I know this may seem like a strange question, but I have. As a matter of fact, I've done it more than once. Every time I think I have my life figured out, every time I think I can read God's mind, every time I get the notion that *I*

am the omnipotent one who has the ability to fight my own battles—BAM! I run into the omnipotence of God.

The omnipotence of God? Wait a minute, you might say. I thought African-American women *were* omnipotent! You know—all powerful, almighty, ruling everything and everybody. Able to leap tall buildings of sexism, racism, and classism in a single bound. Able to raise small children to complete and healthy adulthood single-handedly. Able to handle all stressful situations with grace and poise, never letting the world see us sweat. Isn't that what it means to be a woman of color—to be able to take all of the trash the world dishes out and still come out smelling like a rose?

My sisters, let's face it—we are not omnipotent. To be omnipotent means to reign supreme with all (unlimited) authority. That is an attribute that belongs only to God. Our attempts to be so only lead to an emotional and physical breakdown. We must learn to let God be God. "Know ye that the LORD he is God: it is he that hath made us, and not we ourselves; we are his people, and the sheep of his pasture" (Ps. 100:3). We must learn that the Creator and Sustainer of the universe cares about us and hears our faintest cry. God never loses control, nor does He sleep (see Ps. 121:3). If you feel burdened, overwhelmed, or abandoned, and you can't take another unexpected turn in the road, remember God's words found in Jeremiah: "I know the thoughts that I think toward you, saith the LORD, thoughts of peace, and not of evil, to give you an unexpected end" (Jer. 29:11).

I have grown weary of bumping into the omnipotence of God and finding that God really does know best, that His ways are not my ways, and His thoughts are not my thoughts. I now live a surrendered life to God's will. There is nothing that I will encounter that God is not Lord over.

And so, my sister, just in case you are operating under the assumption that you are in control, prepare yourself to bump into the omnipotence of God.

"You are my witnesses, saith the LORD, and my servant whom I have chosen: that ye may know and believe me, and understand that I am he: before me there was no God formed, neither shall there be after me. I, even I, am the LORD; and besides me there is no savior" (Isa. 43:10–11).

Read Psalm 100:3; see also Psalm 19:1–4; 33:9; 86:8–10; 93:2–4; Titus 1:2; James 1:13.

Read the insight essay on Attributes of God.

—K. Hayes

GOD IS IMMUTABLE

How do you put a jigsaw puzzle together?

We know that if we find the pieces with the smooth edges, they will form our guide and we can build the framework or the perimeter of the puzzle. Once the working parameters have been established, we can proceed with certainty that all of the other jumbled parts of the puzzle will fit into place one piece at a time.

Through Jesus Christ, women have their framework for life. No matter how many pieces may seem to be mixed up, as long as we are guided by the smooth edges of God's Spirit, God's Word, and Christ's example, our hope is secure. God on the left, God on the right, God above, God beneath, God all around.

Our life in Christ gives us structure—not confinement but definition!

It is definite! It is unchangeable! The Bible shows us that the Immutable God has established the foundation and the framework for all creation from beginning to end.

> Of old hast thou laid the foundation of the earth: and the heavens are the work of thy hands. . . . they shall be changed: But thou art the same (Ps. 102:25–27).

As children of the Most High, we are a part of God's creation and God's plan. The puzzles in life serve to remind us that God has set the framework, and God does not change. God is sure.

When we cannot trust our jumbled circumstances, we can trust the promises of the God who is immutable: "I know the thoughts that I think toward you, saith the LORD, thoughts of peace, and not of evil, to give you an expected end" (Jer. 29:11). "The counsel of the LORD standeth for ever, the thoughts of his heart to all generations" (Ps. 33:11).

Read Psalm 102.

Read the insight essays on Attributes of God and Commitment.

—A. Middleton

DISTRESS

Psalm 107 covers all the forms of distress that most of us will see in our entire lifetime. This passage of Scripture addresses the distress of those who are lost and wandering; those who are imprisoned by someone or something; those who are sick in the mind or body; those who are being tossed about by some storm of life. The often repeated answer is: "Then they cried unto the LORD in their trouble, and he delivered them out of their distresses" (v. 6).

Because we are human, distresses will enter into our lives. But if we allow the Lord into our lives, we will have immediate access to the One who not only cares that we are troubled, but is also powerful enough to bring us out of our troubles. Sometimes we make the mistake of believing that when God brings us out of a situation, it will be resolved to our own satisfaction. We assume that God will agree with the way that we think the dilemma should be settled. Often God does not change the circumstances in order to relieve our problems. A change is made in us—in the way we view or react to what is going on around us and inside of us.

The peace of God is the answer to many of the things that cause sadness or needless worry. Once you allow God to control your life, you also learn to let problems be handled by Someone most capable of solving them. No matter how extreme your situation may appear to be in your own eyes, there is a God who is ready to deliver you. All you have to do is cry unto the Lord in your trouble, oftentimes with earnest prayers and fasting. You will be brought out of whatever your distress is. Guaranteed!

Read Psalm 107.

Read the insight essays on Depression and Suffering.

—A. Adams-Morris

GOD IS SOVEREIGN

We have an expectation of what we consider "fair." Sometimes we are bewildered when God does not meet our expectations. God's authority does not operate within the confines of who we think He should be,

because God is in control. God is accountable to no one and is supreme in authority, power, and rank (Ps. 115:3).

Many times we desire to serve a God whom we have created in our own respective images. As "modernized" women we tend to do away with those things that our foremothers taught us about fearing and submitting to God. Instead, some of us have elected to take a loftier road to spiritual enlightenment and self-satisfaction.

Yet the road that many of us have elected to travel is one that leads us away from the God of the Bible and takes us instead to the god of self-service. Although many of us consider ourselves women of God, the truth is that we are more often than not women with a god.

Some of us have metaphorical "full plates," where Christ is not the main course. We like our Jesus a la carte! To be women of God, we must foremost and perpetually recognize that God is not merely an important aspect of life. Rather, God *is* Life. Since all life comes from Him, He retains the ultimate authority over our lives (1 Tim. 6:15).

God is Sovereign. God is the Source and Authority of and over all that exists. God is not simply Sunday morning worship, Wednesday night prayer meeting, daily devotions, or Bible study class!

Jesus must be Lord of all if He is to be Lord at all. All things were made through Him, and without Him nothing was made that was made (John 1:3).

He is the great "I AM" (Exod. 3:14).

Read Psalm 115.

Read the insight essay on Attributes of God.

—*A. Middleton*

TEMPTATION

- Satan distorts the truth to tempt us.
  Genesis 3:1–7
- The second, lustful, look leads to sin.
  2 Samuel 11:1–27
- Building protective walls now keeps out temptation later.
  2 Chronicles 14:7
- When we give in to temptation and sin, we sin against God.
  Psalm 51:4
- Remembering God's Word will help us resist temptation.
  Proverbs 7:1–5
- Resolving to obey God will keep us from giving in.
  Daniel 1:8
- Jesus resisted Satan's temptation because he knew who he was and because he knew and obeyed God's Word.
  Matthew 4:1–11
- We should take temptation seriously.
  Matthew 18:7–9
- We can overcome temptation by watching and praying.
  Matthew 26:40–41
- God provides a way out of every temptation.
  1 Corinthians 10:13
- To avoid temptation, pursue righteousness.
  1 Timothy 6:11–12
- We should flee youthful desires, foolish arguments, and other temptations.
  2 Timothy 2:22–26
- Jesus was tempted in every way, just as we are, but he didn't give in. He knows what temptation feels like.
  Hebrews 4:15
- Temptations arise from our own sinful desires.
  James 1:12–16
- We shouldn't love the world—it will pass away.
  1 John 2:15–17

I die [i]I will not remove mine integrity from me.

6 My righteousness I [j]hold fast, and will not let it go: [k]my heart shall not reproach *me* so long as I live.

7 Let mine enemy be as the wicked, and he that riseth up against me as the unrighteous.

8 [l]For what *is* the hope of the hypocrite, though he hath gained, when God taketh away his soul?

9 [m]Will God hear his cry when trouble cometh upon him?

10 [n]Will he delight himself in the Almighty? will he always call upon God?

11 I will teach you by the hand of God: *that* which *is* with the Almighty will I not conceal.

12 Behold, all ye yourselves have seen *it;* why then are ye thus altogether vain?

13 [o]This *is* the portion of a wicked man with God, and the heritage of oppressors, *which* they shall receive of the Almighty.

14 [p]If his children be multiplied, *it is* for the sword: and [q]his offspring shall not be satisfied with bread.

15 Those that remain of him shall be buried in death: and his widows shall not weep.

16 Though he heap up silver as the dust, and prepare raiment as the clay;

17 He may prepare *it,* but [r]the just shall put *it* on, and the innocent shall divide the silver.

18 He buildeth his house as a moth, and [s]as a booth *that* the keeper maketh.

19 The rich man shall lie down, but he shall not be gathered: he openeth his eyes, and he *is* not.

20 [t]Terrors take hold on him as waters, a tempest stealeth him away in the night.

21 The east wind carrieth him away, and he departeth: and as a storm hurleth him out of his place.

22 For *God* shall cast upon him, and not spare: he would fain flee out of his hand.

23 *Men* shall clap their hands at him, and shall hiss him out of his place.

28

Surely there is a vein for the silver, and a place for gold *where* they fine *it.*

2 Iron is taken out of the earth, and brass *is* molten *out of* the stone.

3 He setteth an end to darkness, and searcheth out all perfection: the stones of darkness, and the shadow of death.

4 The flood breaketh out from the inhabitant; *even the waters* forgotten of the foot: they are dried up, they are gone away from men.

5 *As for* the earth, out of it cometh bread: and under it is turned up as it were fire.

6 The stones of it *are* the place of sapphires: and it hath dust of gold.

7 *There is* a path which no fowl knoweth, and which the vulture's eye hath not seen:

8 The lion's whelps have not trodden it, nor the fierce lion passed by it.

9 He putteth forth his hand upon the rock; he overturneth the mountains by the roots.

10 He cutteth out rivers among the rocks; and his eye seeth every precious thing.

11 He bindeth the floods from overflowing; and *the thing that is* hid bringeth he forth to light.

12 [u]But where shall wisdom be found? and where *is* the place of understanding?

13 Man knoweth not the [v]price thereof; neither is it found in the land of the living.

14 [w]The depth saith, It *is* not in me: and the sea saith, *It is* not with me.

15 It [x]cannot be gotten for gold, neither shall silver be weighed *for* the price thereof.

16 It cannot be valued with the gold of Ophir, with the precious onyx, or the sapphire.

17 The gold and the crystal cannot equal it: and the exchange of it *shall not be for* jewels of fine gold.

18 No mention shall be made of coral, or of pearls: for the price of wisdom *is* above rubies.

19 The topaz of Ethiopia shall not equal it, neither shall it be valued with pure gold.

20 [y]Whence then cometh wisdom? and where *is* the place of understanding?

21 Seeing it is hid from the eyes of all living, and kept close from the fowls of the air.

22 [z]Destruction and death say, We have heard the fame thereof with our ears.

23 God understandeth the way thereof, and he knoweth the place thereof.

24 For he looketh to the ends of the earth, *and* [a]seeth under the whole heaven;

25 [b]To make the weight for the winds; and he weigheth the waters by measure.

26 When he [c]made a decree for the rain, and a way for the lightning of the thunder:

27 Then did he see it, and declare it; he prepared it, yea, and searched it out.

28 And unto man he said, Behold, [d]the fear of the Lord, that *is* wisdom; and to depart from evil *is* understanding.

29

Moreover Job continued his parable, and said,

2 Oh that I were [e]as *in* months past, as *in* the days *when* God preserved me;

3 [f]When his candle shined upon my head, *and when* by his light I walked *through* darkness;

4 As I was in the days of my youth, when [g]the secret of God *was* upon my tabernacle;

5 When the Almighty *was* yet with me, *when* my children *were* about me;

6 When [h]I washed my steps with butter, and [i]the rock poured me out rivers of oil;

7 When I went out to the gate through the city, *when* I prepared my seat in the street!

8 The young men saw me, and hid themselves: and the aged arose, *and* stood up.

9 The princes refrained talking, and [j]laid *their* hand on their mouth.

10 The nobles held their peace, and their [k]tongue cleaved to the roof of their mouth.

11 When the ear heard *me,* then it blessed

27:5 [i]ch. 2:9
27:6 [j]ch. 2:3 [k]Acts 24:16
27:8 [l]Matt. 16:26; Luke 12:20
27:9 [m]ch. 35:12; Ps. 18:41; Prov. 1:28; Isa. 1:15; Jer. 14:12; Ezek. 8:18; Mic. 3:4; John 9:31; Jam. 4:3
27:10 [n]ch. 22:26
27:13 [o]ch. 20:29
27:14 [p]Deut. 28:41; Esth. 9:10; Hos. 9:13 [q]Ps. 78:64
27:17 [r]Prov. 28:8; Eccl. 2:26
27:18 [s]Isa. 1:8; Lam. 2:6
27:20 [t]ch. 18:11
28:12 [u]ver. 20; Eccl. 7:24
28:13 [v]Prov. 3:15
28:14 [w]ver. 22; Rom. 11:33
28:15 [x]Prov. 3:13
28:20 [y]ver. 12
28:22 [z]ver. 14
28:24 [a]Prov. 15:3
28:25 [b]Ps. 135:7
28:26 [c]ch. 38:25
28:28 [d]Deut. 4:6; Ps. 111:10; Prov. 1:7; Eccl. 12:13
29:2 [e]ch. 7:3
29:3 [f]ch. 18:6
29:4 [g]Ps. 25:14
29:6 [h]Gen. 49:11; Deut. 32:13; ch. 20:17 [i]Ps. 81:16
29:9 [j]ch. 21:5
29:10 [k]Ps. 137:6

me; and when the eye saw *me,* it gave witness to me:
12 Because [l]I delivered the poor that
cried, and the fatherless, and *him that had*
none to help him.
13 The blessing of him that was ready
to perish came upon me: and I caused the
widow's heart to sing for joy.
14 [m]I put on righteousness, and it clothed
me: my judgment *was* as a robe and a diadem.
15 I was [n]eyes to the blind, and feet *was*
I to the lame.
16 I *was* a father to the poor: and [o]the
cause *which* I knew not I searched out.
17 And I brake [p]the jaws of the wicked,
and plucked the spoil out of his teeth.
18 Then I said, [q]I shall die in my nest, and
I shall multiply *my* days as the sand.
19 [r]My root *was* spread out [s]by the waters, and the dew lay all night upon my
branch.
20 My glory *was* fresh in me, and [t]my
bow was renewed in my hand.
21 Unto me *men* gave ear, and waited,
and kept silence at my counsel.
22 After my words they spake not again;
and my speech dropped upon them.
23 And they waited for me as for the rain;
and they opened their mouth wide *as* for
[u]the latter rain.
24 *If* I laughed on them, they believed *it*
not; and the light of my countenance they
cast not down.
25 I chose out their way, and sat chief,
and dwelt as a king in the army, as one *that*
comforteth the mourners.

30 But now *they that are* younger than
I have me in derision, whose fathers
I would have disdained to have set with the
dogs of my flock.
2 Yea, whereto *might* the strength of their
hands *profit* me, in whom old age was perished?
3 For want and famine *they were* solitary;
fleeing into the wilderness in former time
desolate and waste.
4 Who cut up mallows by the bushes, and
juniper roots *for* their meat.
5 They were driven forth from among
men, (they cried after them as *after* a thief;)
6 To dwell in the cliffs of the valleys, *in*
caves of the earth, and *in* the rocks.
7 Among the bushes they brayed; under
the nettles they were gathered together.
8 *They were* children of fools, yea, children of base men: they were viler than the
earth.
9 [v]And now am I their song, yea, I am
their byword.
10 They abhor me, they flee far from me,
and spare not [w]to spit in my face.
11 Because he [x]hath loosed my cord, and
afflicted me, they have also let loose the bridle before me.
12 Upon *my* right *hand* rise the youth;
they push away my feet, and [y]they raise up
against me the ways of their destruction.
13 They mar my path, they set forward
my calamity, they have no helper.
14 They came *upon me* as a wide breaking in *of waters:* in the desolation they
rolled themselves *upon me.*
15 Terrors are turned upon me: they pursue my soul as the wind: and my welfare
passeth away as a cloud.
16 [z]And now my soul is poured out upon
me; the days of affliction have taken hold
upon me.
17 My bones are pierced in me in the
night season: and my sinews take no rest.
18 By the great force *of my disease* is my
garment changed: it bindeth me about as
the collar of my coat.
19 He hath cast me into the mire, and I am
become like dust and ashes.
20 I cry unto thee, and thou dost not hear
me: I stand up, and thou regardest me *not.*
21 Thou art become cruel to me: with
thy strong hand thou opposest thyself
against me.
22 Thou liftest me up to the wind; thou
causest me to ride *upon it,* and dissolvest
my substance.
23 For I know *that* thou wilt bring me *to*
death, and *to* the house [a]appointed for all
living.
24 Howbeit he will not stretch out *his*
hand to the grave, though they cry in his
destruction.
25 [b]Did not I weep for him that was in
trouble? was *not* my soul grieved for the
poor?
26 [c]When I looked for good, then evil
came *unto me:* and when I waited for light,
there came darkness.
27 My bowels boiled, and rested not: the
days of affliction prevented me.
28 [d]I went mourning without the sun: I
stood up, *and* I cried in the congregation.
29 [e]I am a brother to dragons, and a companion to owls.
30 [f]My skin is black upon me, and [g]my
bones are burned with heat.
31 My harp also is *turned* to mourning,
and my organ into the voice of them that
weep.

31 I made a covenant with mine [h]eyes;
why then should I think upon a
maid?
2 For what [i]portion of God *is there* from
above? and *what* inheritance of the Almighty from on high?
3 *Is* not destruction to the wicked? and a
strange *punishment* to the workers of iniquity?
4 [j]Doth not he see my ways, and count
all my steps?
5 If I have walked with vanity, or if my
foot hath hasted to deceit;
6 Let me be weighed in an even balance,
that God may know mine integrity.
7 If my step hath turned out of the way,
and [k]mine heart walked after mine eyes,
and if any blot hath cleaved to mine hands;

29:12 [l]Ps. 72:12; Prov. 21:13
29:14 [m]Deut. 24:13; Ps. 132:9; Isa. 59:17; Eph. 6:14; 1 Thess. 5:8
29:15 [n]Num. 10:31
29:16 [o]Prov. 29:7
29:17 [p]Ps. 58:6; Prov. 30:14
29:18 [q]Ps. 30:6
29:19 [r]ch. 18:16 [s]Ps. 1:3; Jer. 17:8
29:20 [t]Gen. 49:24
29:23 [u]Zech. 10:1
30:9 [v]ch. 17:6; Ps. 35:15; Lam. 3:14
30:10 [w]Num. 12:14; Deut. 25:9; Isa. 50:6; Matt. 26:67
30:11 [x]ch. 12:18
30:12 [y]ch. 19:12
30:16 [z]Ps. 42:4
30:23 [a]Heb. 9:27
30:25 [b]Ps. 35:13; Rom. 12:15
30:26 [c]Jer. 8:15
30:28 [d]Ps. 38:6
30:29 [e]Ps. 102:6; Mic. 1:8
30:30 [f]Ps. 119:83; Lam. 4:8 [g]Ps. 102:3
31:1 [h]Matt. 5:28
31:2 [i]ch. 20:29
31:4 [j]2 Chron. 16:9; ch. 34:21; Prov. 5:21; Jer. 32:19
31:7 [k]Num. 15:39; Eccl. 11:9; Ezek. 6:9; Matt. 5:29

8 *Then* [l]let me sow, and let another eat;
yea, let my offspring be rooted out.
9 If mine heart have been deceived by a
woman, or *if* I have laid wait at my neighbour's door;
10 *Then* let my wife grind unto [m]another,
and let others bow down upon her.
11 For this *is* an heinous crime; yea, [n]it *is*
an iniquity *to be punished by* the judges.
12 For it *is* a fire *that* consumeth to destruction, and would root out all mine increase.
13 If I did despise the cause of my manservant or of my maidservant, when they
contended with me;
14 What then shall I do when [o]God riseth
up? and when he visiteth, what shall I answer him?
15 [p]Did not he that made me in the womb
make him? and did not one fashion us in the
womb?
16 If I have withheld the poor from *their*
desire, or have caused the eyes of the
widow to fail;
17 Or have eaten my morsel myself alone,
and the fatherless hath not eaten thereof;
18 (For from my youth he was brought up
with me, as *with* a father, and I have guided
her from my mother's womb;)
19 If I have seen any perish for want of
clothing, or any poor without covering;
20 If his loins have not [q]blessed me, and
if he were *not* warmed with the fleece of my
sheep;
21 If I have lifted up my hand [r]against
the fatherless, when I saw my help in the
gate:
22 *Then* let mine arm fall from my shoulder blade, and mine arm be broken from the
bone.
23 For [s]destruction *from* God *was* a terror to me, and by reason of his highness I
could not endure.
24 [t]If I have made gold my hope, or have
said to the fine gold, *Thou art* my confidence;
25 [u]If I rejoice because my wealth *was*
great, and because mine hand had gotten
much;
26 [v]If I beheld the sun when it shined, or
the moon walking *in* brightness;
27 And my heart hath been secretly enticed, or my mouth hath kissed my hand:
28 This also *were* [w]an iniquity *to be punished by* the judge: for I should have denied
the God *that is* above.
29 [x]If I rejoiced at the destruction of him
that hated me, or lifted up myself when evil
found him:
30 [y]Neither have I suffered my mouth to
sin by wishing a curse to his soul.
31 If the men of my tabernacle said not,
Oh that we had of his flesh! we cannot be
satisfied.
32 [z]The stranger did not lodge in the
street: *but* I opened my doors to the traveller.
33 If I covered my transgressions [a]as
Adam, by hiding mine iniquity in my bosom:
34 Did I fear a great [b]multitude, or did
the contempt of families terrify me, that I
kept silence, *and* went not out of the door?
35 [c]Oh that one would hear me! behold,
my desire [d]*is, that* the Almighty would answer me, and *that* mine adversary had written a book.
36 Surely I would take it upon my shoulder, *and* bind it *as* a crown to me.
37 I would declare unto him the number
of my steps; as a prince would I go near unto
him.
38 If my land cry against me, or that the
furrows likewise thereof complain;
39 If [e]I have eaten the fruits thereof without money, or [f]have caused the owners
thereof to lose their life:
40 Let [g]thistles grow instead of wheat,
and cockle instead of barley. The words of
Job are ended.

32

So these three men ceased to answer
Job, because he *was* [h]righteous in
his own eyes.
2 Then was kindled the wrath of Elihu the
son of Barachel [i]the Buzite, of the kindred
of Ram: against Job was his wrath kindled,
because he justified himself rather than
God.
3 Also against his three friends was his
wrath kindled, because they had found no
answer, and *yet* had condemned Job.
4 Now Elihu had waited till Job had spoken, because they *were* elder than he.
5 When Elihu saw that *there was* no answer in the mouth of *these* three men, then
his wrath was kindled.
6 And Elihu the son of Barachel the Buzite answered and said, I *am* young, [j]and
ye *are* very old; wherefore I was afraid, and
durst not shew you mine opinion.
7 I said, Days should speak, and multitude of years should teach wisdom.
8 But *there is* a spirit in man: and [k]the
inspiration of the Almighty giveth them understanding.
9 [l]Great men are not *always* wise: neither do the aged understand judgment.
10 Therefore I said, Hearken to me; I also
will shew mine opinion.
11 Behold, I waited for your words; I gave
ear to your reasons, whilst ye searched out
what to say.
12 Yea, I attended unto you, and, behold,
there was none of you that convinced Job,
or that answered his words:
13 [m]Lest ye should say, We have found
out wisdom: God thrusteth him down, not
man.
14 Now he hath not directed *his* words
against me: neither will I answer him with
your speeches.
15 They were amazed, they answered no
more: they left off speaking.
16 When I had waited, (for they spake
not, but stood still, *and* answered no more;)

31:8 [l]Lev. 26:16; Deut. 28:30
31:10 [m]2 Sam. 12:11; Jer. 8:10
31:11 [n]Gen. 38:24; Lev. 20:10; Deut. 22:22; ver. 28
31:14 [o]Ps. 44:21
31:15 [p]ch. 34:19; Prov. 14:31; Mal. 2:10
31:20 [q]Deut. 24:13
31:21 [r]ch. 22:9
31:23 [s]Isa. 13:6; Joel 1:15
31:24 [t]Mark 10:24; 1 Tim. 6:17
31:25 [u]Ps. 62:10; Prov. 11:28
31:26 [v]Deut. 4:19; Ezek. 8:16
31:28 [w]ver. 11
31:29 [x]Prov. 17:5
31:30 [y]Matt. 5:44; Rom. 12:14
31:32 [z]Gen. 19:2; Judg. 19:20; Rom. 12:13; Heb. 13:2; 1 Pet. 4:9
31:33 [a]Gen. 3:8; Prov. 28:13; Hos. 6:7
31:34 [b]Ex. 23:2
31:35 [c]ch. 33:6 [d]ch. 13:22
31:39 [e]Jam. 5:4 [f]1 Kings 21:19
31:40 [g]Gen. 3:18
32:1 [h]ch. 33:9
32:2 [i]Gen. 22:21
32:6 [j]ch. 15:10
32:8 [k]1 Kings 3:12; ch. 35:11; Prov. 2:6; Eccl. 2:26; Dan. 1:17; Matt. 11:25; Jam. 1:5
32:9 [l]1 Cor. 1:26
32:13 [m]Jer. 9:23; 1 Cor. 1:29

17 *I said,* I will answer also my part, I also
will shew mine opinion.
18 For I am full of matter, the spirit within
me constraineth me.
19 Behold, my belly *is* as wine *which* hath
no vent; it is ready to burst like new bottles.
20 I will speak, that I may be refreshed: I
will open my lips and answer.
21 Let me not, I pray you, [n]accept any
man's person, neither let me give flattering
titles unto man.
22 For I know not to give flattering titles;
in so doing my maker would soon take me
away.

33 Wherefore, Job, I pray thee, hear my
speeches, and hearken to all my
words.
2 Behold, now I have opened my mouth,
my tongue hath spoken in my mouth.
3 My words *shall be of* the uprightness of
my heart: and my lips shall utter knowledge
clearly.
4 [o]The spirit of God hath made me, and
the breath of the Almighty hath given me
life.
5 If thou canst answer me, set *thy words*
in order before me, stand up.
6 [p]Behold, I *am* according to thy wish in
God's stead: I also am formed out of the
clay.
7 [q]Behold, my terror shall not make thee
afraid, neither shall my hand be heavy upon
thee.
8 Surely thou hast spoken in mine hearing, and I have heard the voice of *thy* words,
saying,
9 [r]I am clean without transgression, I *am*
innocent; neither *is there* iniquity in me.
10 Behold, he findeth occasions against
me, [s]he counteth me for his enemy,
11 [t]He putteth my feet in the stocks, he
marketh all my paths.
12 Behold, *in* this thou art not just: I will
answer thee, that God is greater than man.
13 Why dost thou [u]strive against him? for
he giveth not account of any of his matters.
14 [v]For God speaketh once, yea twice,
yet man perceiveth it not.
15 [w]In a dream, in a vision of the night,
when deep sleep falleth upon men, in slum-
berings upon the bed;
16 [x]Then he openeth the ears of men, and
sealeth their instruction,
17 That he may withdraw man *from his*
purpose, and hide pride from man.
18 He keepeth back his soul from the pit,
and his life from perishing by the sword.
19 He is chastened also with pain upon
his bed, and the multitude of his bones with
strong *pain:*
20 [y]So that his life abhorreth bread, and
his soul dainty meat.
21 His flesh is consumed away, that it
cannot be seen; and his bones *that* were not
seen stick out.
22 Yea, his soul draweth near unto the
grave, and his life to the destroyers.
23 If there be a messenger with him, an
interpreter, one among a thousand, to shew
unto man his uprightness:
24 Then he is gracious unto him, and
saith, Deliver him from going down to the
pit: I have found a ransom.
25 His flesh shall be fresher than a
child's: he shall return to the days of his
youth:
26 He shall pray unto God, and he will be
favourable unto him: and he shall see his
face with joy: for he will render unto man
his righteousness.
27 He looketh upon men, and *if any* [z]say,
I have sinned, and perverted *that which*
was right, and it [a]profited me not;
28 He will [b]deliver his soul from going
into the pit, and his life shall see the light.
29 Lo, all these *things* worketh God oftentimes with man,
30 [c]To bring back his soul from the pit, to
be enlightened with the light of the living.
31 Mark well, O Job, hearken unto me:
hold thy peace, and I will speak.
32 If thou hast anything to say, answer
me: speak, for I desire to justify thee.
33 If not, [d]hearken unto me: hold thy
peace, and I shall teach thee wisdom.

34 Furthermore Elihu answered and
said,
2 Hear my words, O ye wise *men;* and
give ear unto me, ye that have knowledge.
3 [e]For the ear trieth words, as the mouth
tasteth meat.
4 Let us choose to us judgment: let us
know among ourselves what *is* good.
5 For Job hath said, [f]I am righteous: and
[g]God hath taken away my judgment.
6 [h]Should I lie against my right? my
wound *is* incurable without transgression.
7 What man *is* like Job, [i]*who* drinketh up
scorning like water?
8 Which goeth in company with the
workers of iniquity, and walketh with
wicked men.
9 For [j]he hath said, It profiteth a man
nothing that he should delight himself with
God.
10 Therefore hearken unto me ye men of
understanding: [k]far be it from God, *that he*
should do wickedness; and *from* the Almighty, *that he should commit* iniquity.
11 [l]For the work of a man shall he render
unto him, and cause every man to find according to *his* ways.
12 Yea, surely God will not do wickedly,
neither will the Almighty [m]pervert judgment.
13 Who hath given him a charge over the
earth? or who hath disposed the whole
world?
14 If he set his heart upon man, *if* he
[n]gather unto himself his spirit and his
breath;
15 [o]All flesh shall perish together, and
man shall turn again unto dust.
16 If now *thou hast* understanding, hear
this: hearken to the voice of my words.
17 [p]Shall even he that hateth right gov-

32:21 [n]Lev. 19:15; Deut. 1:17; Prov. 24:23; Matt. 22:16
33:4 [o]Gen. 2:7
33:6 [p]ch. 9:34
33:7 [q]ch. 9:34
33:9 [r]ch. 9:17
33:10 [s]ch. 13:24
33:11 [t]ch. 13:27
33:13 [u]Isa. 45:9
33:14 [v]ch. 40:5; Ps. 62:11
33:15 [w]Num. 12:6; ch. 4:13
33:16 [x]ch. 36:10
33:20 [y]Ps. 107:18
33:27 [z]2 Sam. 12:13; Prov. 28:13; Luke 15:21; 1 John 1:9 [a]Rom. 6:21
33:28 [b]Isa. 38:17
33:30 [c]ver. 28; Ps. 56:13
33:33 [d]Ps. 34:11
34:3 [e]ch. 6:30
34:5 [f]ch. 33:9 [g]ch. 27:2
34:6 [h]ch. 9:17
34:7 [i]ch. 15:16
34:9 [j]ch. 9:22; Mal. 3:14
34:10 [k]Gen. 18:25; Deut. 32:4; 2 Chron. 19:7; ch. 8:3; Ps. 92:15; Rom. 9:14
34:11 [l]Ps. 62:12; Prov. 24:12; Jer. 32:19; Ezek. 33:20; Matt. 16:27; Rom. 2:6; 2 Cor. 5:10; 1 Pet. 1:17; Rev. 22:12
34:12 [m]ch. 8:3
34:14 [n]Ps. 104:29
34:15 [o]Gen. 3:19; Eccl. 12:7
34:17 [p]Gen. 18:25; 2 Sam. 23:3

ern? and wilt thou condemn him that is
most just?
18 [q]*Is it fit* to say to a king, *Thou art*
wicked? *and* to princes, *Ye are* ungodly?
19 *How much less to him* that [r]accepteth
not the persons of princes, nor regardeth
the rich more than the poor? for [s]they all
are the work of his hands.
20 In a moment shall they die, and the
people shall be troubled [t]at midnight, and
pass away: and the mighty shall be taken
away without hand.
21 [u]For his eyes *are* upon the ways of
man, and he seeth all his goings.
22 [v]*There is* no darkness, nor shadow of
death, where the workers of iniquity may
hide themselves.
23 For he will not lay upon man more
than right; that he should enter into judgment with God.
24 [w]He shall break in pieces mighty men
without number, and set others in their
stead.
25 Therefore he knoweth their works,
and he overturneth *them* in the night, so
that they are destroyed.
26 He striketh them as wicked men in the
open sight of others;
27 Because they [x]turned back from him,
and [y]would not consider any of his ways:
28 So that they [z]cause the cry of the poor
to come unto him, and he [a]heareth the cry
of the afflicted.
29 When he giveth quietness, who then
can make trouble? and when he hideth *his*
face, who then can behold him? whether *it*
be done against a nation, or against a man
only:
30 That the hypocrite reign not, lest [b]the
people be ensnared.
31 Surely it is meet to be said unto God, [c]I
have borne *chastisement,* I will not offend
any more:
32 *That which* I see not teach thou me: if
I have done iniquity, I will do no more.
33 *Should it be* according to thy mind? he
will recompense it, whether thou refuse, or
whether thou choose; and not I: therefore
speak what thou knowest.
34 Let men of understanding tell me, and
let a wise man hearken unto me.
35 [d]Job hath spoken without knowledge,
and his words *were* without wisdom.
36 My desire *is that* Job may be tried unto
the end because of *his* answers for wicked
men.
37 For he addeth rebellion unto his sin, he
clappeth *his hands* among us, and multiplieth his words against God.

35 Elihu spake moreover, and said,
2 Thinkest thou this to be right, *that*
thou saidst, My righteousness *is* more than
God's?
3 For [e]thou saidst, What advantage will it
be unto thee? *and,* What profit shall I have,
if I be cleansed from my sin?
4 I will answer thee, and [f]thy companions with thee.
5 [g]Look unto the heavens, and see; and
behold the clouds *which* are higher than
thou.
6 If thou sinnest, what doest thou
[h]against him? or *if* thy transgressions be
multiplied, what doest thou unto him?
7 [i]If thou be righteous, what givest thou
him? or what receiveth he of thine hand?
8 Thy wickedness *may hurt* a man as
thou *art;* and thy righteousness *may profit*
the son of man.
9 [j]By reason of the multitude of oppressions they make *the oppressed* to cry: they
cry out by reason of the arm of the mighty.
10 But none saith, [k]Where *is* God my
maker, [l]who giveth songs in the night;
11 Who [m]teacheth us more than the
beasts of the earth, and maketh us wiser
than the fowls of heaven?
12 [n]There they cry, but none giveth answer, because of the pride of evil men.
13 [o]Surely God will not hear vanity, neither will the Almighty regard it.
14 [p]Although thou sayest thou shalt not
see him, *yet* judgment *is* before him; therefore [q]trust thou in him.
15 But now, because *it is* not *so,* he hath
[r]visited in his anger; yet he knoweth *it* not
in great extremity:
16 [s]Therefore doth Job open his mouth
in vain; he multiplieth words without
knowledge.

36 Elihu also proceeded, and said,
2 Suffer me a little, and I will shew
thee that *I have* yet to speak on God's behalf.
3 I will fetch my knowledge from afar,
and will ascribe righteousness to my
Maker.
4 For truly my words *shall* not *be* false: he
that is perfect in knowledge *is* with thee.
5 Behold, God *is* mighty, and despiseth
not *any:* [t]*he is* mighty in strength *and* wisdom.
6 He preserveth not the life of the wicked:
but giveth right to the poor.
7 [u]He withdraweth not his eyes from the
righteous: but [v]with kings *are they* on the
throne; yea, he doth establish them for ever,
and they are exalted.
8 And [w]if *they be* bound in fetters, *and* be
holden in cords of affliction;
9 Then he sheweth them their work, and
their transgressions that they have exceeded.
10 [x]He openeth also their ear to discipline, and commandeth that they return
from iniquity.
11 If they obey and serve *him,* they shall
[y]spend their days in prosperity, and their
years in pleasures.
12 But if they obey not, they shall perish
by the sword, and they shall die without
knowledge.
13 But the hypocrites in heart [z]heap up
wrath: they cry not when he bindeth them.
14 [a]They die in youth, and their life *is*
among the unclean.

34:18 [q]Ex. 22:28
34:19 [r]Deut. 10:17; 2 Chron. 19:7; Acts 10:34; Rom. 2:11; Gal. 2:6; Eph. 6:9; Col. 3:25; 1 Pet. 1:17 [s]ch. 31:15
34:20 [t]Ex. 12:29
34:21 [u]2 Chron. 16:9; ch. 31:4; Ps. 34:15; Prov. 5:21; Jer. 16:17
34:22 [v]Ps. 139:12; Am. 9:2; Heb. 4:13
34:24 [w]Dan. 2:21
34:27 [x]1 Sam. 15:11 [y]Ps. 28:5; Isa. 5:12
34:28 [z]ch. 35:9; Jam. 5:4 [a]Ex. 22:23
34:30 [b]1 Kings 12:28; 2 Kings 21:9
34:31 [c]Dan. 9:7-14
34:35 [d]ch. 35:16
35:3 [e]ch. 21:15
35:4 [f]ch. 34:8
35:5 [g]ch. 22:12
35:6 [h]Prov. 8:36; Jer. 17:19
35:7 [i]ch. 22:2; Ps. 16:2; Prov. 9:12; Rom. 11:35
35:9 [j]Ex. 2:23; ch. 34:28
35:10 [k]Isa. 51:13 [l]Ps. 42:8; Acts 16:25
35:11 [m]Ps. 94:12
35:12 [n]Prov. 1:28
35:13 [o]ch. 27:9; Prov. 15:29; Isa. 1:15; Jer. 11:11
35:14 [p]ch. 9:11 [q]Ps. 37:5
35:15 [r]Ps. 89:32
35:16 [s]ch. 34:35
36:5 [t]ch. 9:4; Ps. 99:4
36:7 [u]Ps. 33:18 [v]Ps. 113:8
36:8 [w]Ps. 107:10
36:10 [x]ch. 33:16
36:11 [y]ch. 21:13; Isa. 1:19
36:13 [z]Rom. 2:5
36:14 [a]ch. 15:32; Ps. 55:23

15 He delivereth the poor in his affliction,
and openeth their ears in oppression.
16 Even so would he have removed thee
out of the strait [b]*into* a broad place, where
there is no straitness; and [c]that which
should be set on thy table *should be* full of
[d]fatness.
17 But thou hast fulfilled the judgment of
the wicked: judgment and justice take hold
on thee.
18 Because *there is* wrath, *beware* lest he
take thee away with *his* stroke: then [e]a
great ransom cannot deliver thee.
19 [f]Will he esteem thy riches? *no,* not
gold, nor all the forces of strength.
20 Desire not the night, when people are
cut off in their place.
21 Take heed, [g]regard not iniquity: for
[h]this hast thou chosen rather than affliction.
22 Behold, God exalteth by his power:
[i]who teacheth like him?
23 [j]Who hath enjoined him his way? or
[k]who can say, Thou hast wrought iniquity?
24 Remember that thou [l]magnify his
work, which men behold.
25 Every man may see it; man may behold *it* afar off.
26 Behold, God *is* great, and we [m]know
him not, [n]neither can the number of his
years be searched out.
27 For he [o]maketh small the drops of water: they pour down rain according to the
vapour thereof:
28 [p]Which the clouds do drop *and* distil
upon man abundantly.
29 Also can *any* understand the spread-
ings of the clouds, *or* the noise of his tabernacle?
30 Behold, he [q]spreadeth his light upon
it, and covereth the bottom of the sea.
31 For [r]by them judgeth he the people; he
[s]giveth meat in abundance.
32 [t]With clouds he covereth the light;
and commandeth it *not to shine* by *the
cloud* that cometh betwixt.
33 [u]The noise thereof sheweth concerning it, the cattle also concerning the vapour.
37 At this also my heart trembleth, and
is moved out of his place.
2 Hear attentively the noise of his voice,
and the sound *that* goeth out of his mouth.
3 He directeth it under the whole heaven,
and his lightning unto the ends of the earth.
4 After it [v]a voice roareth: he thundereth
with the voice of his excellency; and he will
not stay them when his voice is heard.
5 God thundereth marvellously with his
voice; [w]great things doeth he, which we
cannot comprehend.
6 For [x]he saith to the snow, Be thou *on*
the earth; likewise to the small rain, and to
the great rain of his strength.
7 He sealeth up the hand of every man;
[y]that all men may know his work.
8 Then the beasts [z]go into dens, and remain in their places.

36:16 [b]Ps. 18:19 [c]Ps. 23:5 [d]Ps. 36:8
36:18 [e]Ps. 49:7
36:19 [f]Prov. 11
36:21 [g]Ps. 66:18 [h]Heb. 11:25
36:22 [i]Isa. 40:13; Rom. 11:34; 1 Cor. 2:16
36:23 [j]ch. 34:13 [k]ch. 34:10
36:24 [l]Ps. 92:5; Rev. 15:3
36:26 [m]1 Cor. 13:12 [n]Ps. 90:2; Heb. 1:12
36:27 [o]Ps. 147:8
36:28 [p]Prov. 3:20
36:30 [q]ch. 37:3
36:31 [r]ch. 37:13 [s]Ps. 136:25; Acts 14:17
36:32 [t]Ps. 147:8
36:33 [u]1 Kings 18:41
37:4 [v]Ps. 29:3
37:5 [w]ch. 5:9; Rev. 15:3
37:6 [x]Ps. 147:16
37:7 [y]Ps. 109:27
37:8 [z]Ps. 104:22
37:10 [a]ch. 38:29; Ps. 147:17
37:12 [b]Ps. 148:8
37:13 [c]Ex. 9:18; 1 Sam. 12:18; Ezra 10:9; ch. 36:31 [d]ch. 38:26 [e]2 Sam. 21:10; 1 Kings 18:45
37:14 [f]Ps. 111:2
37:16 [g]ch. 36:29 [h]ch. 36:4
37:18 [i]Gen. 1:6; Isa. 44:24
37:23 [j]1 Tim. 6:16 [k]ch. 36:5
37:24 [l]Matt. 10:28 [m]Matt. 11:25; 1 Cor. 1:26
38:1 [n]Ex. 19:16; 1 Kings 19:11; Ezek. 1:4; Nah. 1:3
38:2 [o]ch. 34:35 [p]1 Tim. 1:7
38:3 [q]ch. 40:7
38:4 [r]Ps. 104:5; Prov. 8:29
38:7 [s]ch. 1:6
38:8 [t]Gen. 1:9; Ps. 33:7; Prov. 8:29; Jer. 5:22
38:10 [u]ch. 26:10

9 Out of the south cometh the whirlwind:
and cold out of the north.
10 [a]By the breath of God frost is given:
and the breadth of the waters is straitened.
11 Also by watering he wearieth the thick
cloud: he scattereth his bright cloud:
12 And it is turned round about by his
counsels: that they may [b]do whatsoever he
commandeth them upon the face of the
world in the earth.
13 [c]He causeth it to come, whether for
correction, or [d]for his land, or [e]for mercy.
14 Hearken unto this, O Job: stand still,
and [f]consider the wondrous works of God.
15 Dost thou know when God disposed
them, and caused the light of his cloud to
shine?
16 [g]Dost thou know the balancings of the
clouds, the wondrous works of [h]him which
is perfect in knowledge?
17 How thy garments *are* warm, when he
quieteth the earth by the south *wind?*
18 Hast thou with him [i]spread out the
sky, *which is* strong, *and* as a molten looking glass?
19 Teach us what we shall say unto him;
for we cannot order *our speech* by reason of
darkness.
20 Shall it be told him that I speak? if a
man speak, surely he shall be swallowed up.
21 And now *men* see not the bright light
which *is* in the clouds: but the wind passeth,
and cleanseth them.
22 Fair weather cometh out of the north:
with God *is* terrible majesty.
23 *Touching* the Almighty, [j]we cannot
find him out: [k]*he is* excellent in power, and
in judgment, and in plenty of justice: he will
not afflict.
24 Men do therefore [l]fear him: he re-
specteth not any *that are* [m]wise of heart.
38 Then the LORD answered Job [n]out of
the whirlwind, and said,
2 [o]Who *is* this that darkeneth counsel by
[p]words without knowledge?
3 [q]Gird up now thy loins like a man; for
I will demand of thee, and answer thou me.
4 [r]Where wast thou when I laid the foundations of the earth? declare, if thou hast
understanding.
5 Who hath laid the measures thereof, if
thou knowest? or who hath stretched the
line upon it?
6 Whereupon are the foundations thereof
fastened? or who laid the corner stone
thereof;
7 When the morning stars sang together,
and all [s]the sons of God shouted for joy?
8 [t]Or *who* shut up the sea with doors,
when it brake forth, *as if* it had issued out of
the womb?
9 When I made the cloud the garment
thereof, and thick darkness a swaddling-
band for it,
10 And [u]brake up for it my decreed *place,*
and set bars and doors,
11 And said, Hitherto shalt thou come,

but no further: and here shall thy proud
waves [v]be stayed?
12 Hast thou [w]commanded the morning
since thy days; *and* caused the dayspring to
know his place;
13 That it might take hold of the ends of
the earth, that [x]the wicked might be shaken
out of it?
14 It is turned as clay *to* the seal; and they
stand as a garment.
15 And from the wicked their [y]light is
withholden, and [z]the high arm shall be broken.
16 Hast thou [a]entered into the springs of
the sea? or hast thou walked in the search of
the depth?
17 Have [b]the gates of death been opened
unto thee? or hast thou seen the doors of the
shadow of death?
18 Hast thou perceived the breadth of the
earth? declare if thou knowest it all.
19 Where *is* the way *where* light dwelleth? and *as for* darkness, where *is* the place
thereof,
20 That thou shouldest take it to the
bound thereof, and that thou shouldest
know the paths *to* the house thereof?
21 Knowest thou *it*, because thou wast
then born? or *because* the number of thy
days *is* great?
22 Hast thou entered into [c]the treasures
of the snow? or hast thou seen the treasures
of the hail,
23 [d]Which I have reserved against the
time of trouble, against the day of battle and
war?
24 By what way is the light parted, *which*
scattereth the east wind upon the earth?
25 Who [e]hath divided a watercourse for
the overflowing of waters, or a way for the
lightning of thunder;
26 To cause it to rain on the earth, *where*
no man *is; on* the wilderness, wherein *there*
is no man;
27 [f]To satisfy the desolate and waste
ground; and to cause the bud of the tender
herb to spring forth?
28 [g]Hath the rain a father? or who hath
begotten the drops of dew?
29 Out of whose womb came the ice? and
the [h]hoary frost of heaven, who hath gen-
dered it?
30 The waters are hid as *with* a stone, and
the face of the deep is [i]frozen.
31 Canst thou bind the sweet influences
of [j]Pleiades, or loose the bands of Orion?
32 Canst thou bring forth Mazzaroth in
his season? or canst thou guide Arcturus
with his sons?
33 Knowest thou [k]the ordinances of
heaven? canst thou set the dominion
thereof in the earth?
34 Canst thou lift up thy voice to the
clouds, that abundance of waters may cover
thee?
35 Canst thou send lightnings, that they
may go, and say unto thee, Here we *are*?
36 [l]Who hath put wisdom in the inward
parts? or who hath given understanding to
the heart?
37 Who can number the clouds in wisdom? or who can stay the bottles of heaven,
38 When the dust groweth into hardness,
and the clods cleave fast together?
39 [m]Wilt thou hunt the prey for the lion?
or fill the appetite of the young lions,
40 When they couch in *their* dens, *and*
abide in the covert to lie in wait?
41 [n]Who provideth for the raven his
food? when his young ones cry unto God,
they wander for lack of meat.
39 Knowest thou the time when the wild
goats of the rock bring forth? *or*
canst thou mark when [o]the hinds do calve?
2 Canst thou number the months *that*
they fulfil? or knowest thou the time when
they bring forth?
3 They bow themselves, they bring forth
their young ones, they cast out their sorrows.
4 Their young ones are in good liking,
they grow up with corn; they go forth, and
return not unto them.
5 Who hath sent out the wild ass free? or
who hath loosed the bands of the wild ass?
6 [p]Whose house I have made the wilderness, and the barren land his dwellings.
7 He scorneth the multitude of the city,
neither regardeth he the crying of the
driver.
8 The range of the mountains *is* his pasture, and he searcheth after every green
thing.
9 Will the [q]unicorn be willing to serve
thee, or abide by thy crib?
10 Canst thou bind the unicorn with his
band in the furrow? or will he harrow the
valleys after thee?
11 Wilt thou trust him, because his
strength *is* great? or wilt thou leave thy labour to him?
12 Wilt thou believe him, that he will
bring home thy seed, and gather *it into* thy
barn?
13 *Gavest thou* the goodly wings unto the
peacocks? or wings and feathers unto the
ostrich?
14 Which leaveth her eggs in the earth,
and warmeth them in dust,
15 And forgetteth that the foot may crush
them, or that the wild beast may break
them.
16 She is [r]hardened against her young
ones, as though *they were* not her's: her labour is in vain without fear;
17 Because God hath deprived her of wisdom, neither hath he [s]imparted to her understanding.
18 What time she lifteth up herself on
high, she scorneth the horse and his rider.
19 Hast thou given the horse strength?
hast thou clothed his neck with thunder?
20 Canst thou make him afraid as a grasshopper? the glory of his nostrils *is* terrible.
21 He paweth in the valley, and rejoiceth

38:11 [v]Ps. 89:9
38:12 [w]Ps. 74:16
38:13 [x]Ps. 104:35
38:15 [y]ch. 18:5 [z]Ps. 10:15
38:16 [a]Ps. 77:19
38:17 [b]Ps. 9:13
38:22 [c]Ps. 135:7
38:23 [d]Ex. 9:18; Josh. 10:11; Isa. 30:30; Ezek. 13:11; Rev. 16:21
38:25 [e]ch. 28:26
38:27 [f]Ps. 107:35
38:28 [g]Jer. 14:22; Ps. 147:8
38:29 [h]Ps. 147:16
38:30 [i]ch. 37:10
38:31 [j]ch. 9:9; Am. 5:8
38:33 [k]Jer. 31:35
38:36 [l]ch. 32:8; Ps. 51:6; Eccl. 2:26
38:39 [m]Ps. 104:21
38:41 [n]Ps. 147:9; Matt. 6:26
39:1 [o]Ps. 29:9
39:6 [p]ch. 24:5; Jer. 2:24; Hos. 8:9
39:9 [q]Num. 23:22; Deut. 33:17
39:16 [r]Lam. 4:3
39:17 [s]ch. 35:11

in *his* strength: [t]he goeth on to meet the armed men.

22 He mocketh at fear, and is not affrighted; neither turneth he back from the sword.

23 The quiver rattleth against him, the glittering spear and the shield.

24 He swalloweth the ground with fierceness and rage: neither believeth he that *it is* the sound of the trumpet.

25 He saith among the trumpets, Ha, ha; and he smelleth the battle afar off, the thunder of the captains, and the shouting.

26 Doth the hawk fly by thy wisdom, *and* stretch her wings toward the south?

27 Doth the eagle mount up at thy command, and [u]make her nest on high?

28 She dwelleth and abideth on the rock, upon the crag of the rock, and the strong place.

29 From thence she seeketh the prey, *and* her eyes behold afar off.

30 Her young ones also suck up blood: and [v]where the slain *are,* there *is* she.

40 Moreover the LORD answered Job, and said,

2 Shall he that [w]contendeth with the Almighty instruct *him?* he that reproveth God, let him answer it.

3 ¶ Then Job answered the LORD, and said,

4 [x]Behold, I am vile; what shall I answer thee? [y]I will lay mine hand upon my mouth.

5 Once have I spoken; but I will not answer: yea, twice; but I will proceed no further.

6 ¶ [z]Then answered the LORD unto Job out of the whirlwind, and said,

7 [a]Gird up thy loins now like a man: [b]I will demand of thee, and declare thou unto me.

8 [c]Wilt thou also disannul my judgment? wilt thou condemn me, that thou mayest be righteous?

9 Hast thou an arm like God? or canst thou thunder with [d]a voice like him?

10 [e]Deck thyself now *with* majesty and excellency; and array thyself with glory and beauty.

11 Cast abroad the rage of thy wrath: and behold every one *that is* proud, and abase him.

12 Look on every one *that is* [f]proud, *and* bring him low; and tread down the wicked in their place.

13 Hide them in the dust together; *and* bind their faces in secret.

14 Then will I also confess unto thee that thine own right hand can save thee.

15 ¶ Behold now behemoth, which I made with thee; he eateth grass as an ox.

16 Lo now, his strength *is* in his loins, and his force *is* in the navel of his belly.

17 He moveth his tail like a cedar: the sinews of his stones are wrapped together.

18 His bones *are as* strong pieces of brass; his bones *are* like bars of iron.

19 He *is* the chief of the ways of God: he that made him can make his sword to approach *unto him.*

20 Surely the mountains [g]bring him forth food, where all the beasts of the field play.

21 He lieth under the shady trees, in the covert of the reed, and fens.

22 The shady trees cover him *with* their shadow; the willows of the brook compass him about.

23 Behold, he drinketh up a river, *and* hasteth not: he trusteth that he can draw up Jordan into his mouth.

24 He taketh it with his eyes: *his* nose pierceth through snares.

41 Canst thou draw out [h]leviathan with an hook? or his tongue with a cord *which* thou lettest down?

2 Canst thou [i]put an hook into his nose? or bore his jaw through with a thorn?

3 Will he make many supplications unto thee? will he speak soft *words* unto thee?

4 Will he make a covenant with thee? wilt thou take him for a servant for ever?

5 Wilt thou play with him as *with* a bird? or wilt thou bind him for thy maidens?

6 Shall the companions make a banquet of him? shall they part him among the merchants?

7 Canst thou fill his skin with barbed irons? or his head with fish spears?

8 Lay thine hand upon him, remember the battle, do no more.

9 Behold, the hope of him is in vain: shall not *one* be cast down even at the sight of him?

10 None *is so* fierce that dare stir him up: who then is able to stand before me?

11 [j]Who hath prevented me, that I should repay *him?* [k]*whatsoever is* under the whole heaven is mine.

12 I will not conceal his parts, nor his power, nor his comely proportion.

13 Who can discover the face of his garment? *or* who can come *to him* with his double bridle?

14 Who can open the doors of his face? his teeth *are* terrible round about.

15 *His* scales *are his* pride, shut up together *as with* a close seal.

16 One is so near to another, that no air can come between them.

17 They are joined one to another, they stick together, that they cannot be sundered.

18 By his neesings a light doth shine, and his eyes *are* like the eyelids of the morning.

19 Out of his mouth go burning lamps, *and* sparks of fire leap out.

20 Out of his nostrils goeth smoke, as *out* of a seething pot or caldron.

21 His breath kindleth coals, and a flame goeth out of his mouth.

22 In his neck remaineth strength, and sorrow is turned into joy before him.

23 The flakes of his flesh are joined together: they are firm in themselves; they cannot be moved.

39:21 [t]Jer. 8:6
39:27 [u]Jer. 49:16; Obad. 4
39:30 [v]Matt. 24:28; Luke 17:37
40:2 [w]ch. 33:13
40:4 [x]Ezra 9:6; ch. 42:6; Ps. 51:4 [y]ch. 29:9; Ps. 39:9
40:6 [z]ch. 38:1
40:7 [a]ch. 38:3 [b]ch. 42:4
40:8 [c]Ps. 51:4; Rom. 3:4
40:9 [d]ch. 37:4; Ps. 29:3
40:10 [e]Ps. 93:1
40:12 [f]Isa. 2:12; Dan. 4:37
40:20 [g]Ps. 104:14
41:1 [h]Ps. 104:26; Isa. 27:1
41:2 [i]Isa. 37:29
41:11 [j]Rom. 11:35 [k]Ex. 19:5; Deut. 10:14; Ps. 24:1; 1 Cor. 10:26

24 His heart is as firm as a stone; yea, as hard as a piece of the nether *millstone*.

25 When he raiseth up himself, the mighty are afraid: by reason of breakings they purify themselves.

26 The sword of him that layeth at him cannot hold: the spear, the dart, nor the habergeon.

27 He esteemeth iron as straw, *and* brass as rotten wood.

28 The arrow cannot make him flee: slingstones are turned with him into stubble.

29 Darts are counted as stubble: he laugheth at the shaking of a spear.

30 Sharp stones *are* under him: he spreadeth sharp pointed things upon the mire.

31 He maketh the deep to boil like a pot: he maketh the sea like a pot of ointment.

32 He maketh a path to shine after him; *one* would think the deep *to be* hoary.

33 Upon earth there is not his like, who is made without fear.

34 He beholdeth all high *things*: he *is* a king over all the children of pride.

42 Then Job answered the LORD, and said,

2 I know that thou [l]canst do every *thing*, and *that* no thought can be withholden from thee.

3 [m]Who *is* he that hideth counsel without knowledge? therefore have I uttered that I understood not; [n]things too wonderful for me, which I knew not.

4 Hear, I beseech thee, and I will speak: [o]I will demand of thee, and declare thou unto me.

5 I have heard of thee by the hearing of the ear: but now mine eye seeth thee.

6 Wherefore I [p]abhor *myself*, and repent in dust and ashes.

7 ¶ And it was *so*, that after the LORD had spoken these words unto Job, the LORD said to Eliphaz the Temanite, My wrath is kindled against thee, and against thy two friends: for ye have not spoken of me *the thing that is* right, as my servant Job *hath*.

8 Therefore take unto you now [q]seven bullocks and seven rams, and [r]go to my servant Job, and offer up for yourselves a burnt offering; and my servant Job shall [s]pray for you: for him will I accept: lest I deal with you *after your* folly, in that ye have not spoken of me *the thing which is* right, like my servant Job.

9 So Eliphaz the Temanite and Bildad the Shuhite *and* Zophar the Naamathite went, and did according as the LORD commanded them: the LORD also accepted Job.

10 [t]And the LORD turned the captivity of Job, when he prayed for his friends: also the LORD gave Job [u]twice as much as he had before.

11 Then came there unto him [v]all his brethren, and all his sisters, and all they that had been of his acquaintance before, and did eat bread with him in his house: and they bemoaned him, and comforted him over all the evil that the LORD had brought upon him: every man also gave him a piece of money, and every one an earring of gold.

12 So the LORD blessed [w]the latter end of Job more than his beginning: for he had [x]fourteen thousand sheep, and six thousand camels, and a thousand yoke of oxen, and a thousand she asses.

13 [y]He had also seven sons and three daughters.

14 And he called the name of the first, Jemima; and the name of the second, Kezia; and the name of the third, Keren-happuch.

15 And in all the land were no women found *so* fair as the daughters of Job: and their father gave them inheritance among their brethren.

16 After this [z]lived Job an hundred and forty years, and saw his sons, and his sons' sons, *even* four generations.

17 So Job died, *being* old and [a]full of days.

42:2 [l]Gen. 18:14; Matt. 19:26; Mark 10:27; Luke 18:27
42:3 [m]ch. 38:2 [n]Ps. 40:5
42:4 [o]ch. 38:3
42:6 [p]Ezra 9:6; ch. 40:4
42:8 [q]Num. 23:1 [r]Matt. 5:24 [s]Gen. 20:17; Jam. 5:15; 1 John 5:16
42:10 [t]Ps. 14:7 [u]Isa. 40:2
42:11 [v]ch. 19:13
42:12 [w]ch. 8:7; Jam. 5:11 [x]ch. 1:3
42:13 [y]ch. 1:2
42:16 [z]ch. 5:26; Prov. 3:16
42:17 [a]Gen. 25:8

PSALMS

The book of Psalms is written by various authors: David, Solomon, the sons of Korah, Asaph, Ethan, Moses, and Heman at different times. The book of Psalms is divided into five sections or books. The book of Psalms contains more familiar verses than any other book in the Bible; the most recognized is Psalm 23. The book also contains the longest chapter in the Bible, Psalm 119.

I. Book 1, 1:1–41:13
II. Book 2, 42:1–72:20
III. Book 3, 73:1–89:52
IV. Book 4, 90:1–106:48
V. Book 5, 107:1–150:6

BOOK I

1 Blessed [a]*is* the man that walketh not in the counsel of the ungodly, nor standeth in the way of sinners, [b]nor sitteth in the seat of the scornful.

2 But [c]his delight *is* in the law of the LORD; [d]and in his law doth he meditate day and night.

3 And he shall be like a tree [e]planted by the rivers of water, that bringeth forth his fruit in his season; his leaf also shall not wither; and whatsoever he doeth shall [f]prosper.

4 The ungodly *are* not so: but *are* [g]like the chaff which the wind driveth away.

5 Therefore the ungodly shall not stand in the judgment, nor sinners in the congregation of the righteous.

6 For [h]the LORD knoweth the way of the righteous: but the way of the ungodly shall perish.

2 Why [i]do the heathen rage, and the people imagine a vain thing?

2 The kings of the earth set themselves, and the rulers take counsel together, against the LORD, and against his [j]anointed, *saying,*

3 [k]Let us break their bands asunder, and cast away their cords from us.

4 [l]He that sitteth in the heavens [m]shall laugh: the Lord shall have them in derision.

5 Then shall he speak unto them in his wrath, and vex them in his sore displeasure.

6 Yet have I set my king [n]upon my holy hill of Zion.

7 I will declare the decree: the LORD hath said unto me, [o]Thou *art* my Son; this day have I begotten thee.

8 [p]Ask of me, and I shall give *thee* the heathen *for* thine inheritance, and the uttermost parts of the earth *for* thy possession.

9 [q]Thou shalt break them with a rod of iron; thou shalt dash them in pieces like a potter's vessel.

10 Be wise now therefore, O ye kings: be instructed, ye judges of the earth.

11 [r]Serve the LORD with fear, and rejoice [s]with trembling.

12 [t]Kiss the Son, lest he be angry, and ye perish *from* the way, when [u]his wrath is kindled but a little. [v]Blessed *are* all they that put their trust in him.

A Psalm of David, when he fled from Absalom his son.

3 LORD, [w]how are they increased that trouble me! many *are* they that rise up against me.

2 Many *there be* which say of my soul, [x]*There is* no help for him in God. Selah.

3 But thou, O LORD, *art* [y]a shield for me; my glory, and [z]the lifter up of mine head.

4 I cried unto the LORD with my voice, and [a]he heard me out of his [b]holy hill. Selah.

5 [c]I laid me down and slept; I awaked; for the LORD sustained me.

6 [d]I will not be afraid of ten thousands of people, that have set *themselves* against me round about.

7 Arise, O LORD; save me, O my God: [e]for thou hast smitten all mine enemies *upon* the cheek bone; thou hast broken the teeth of the ungodly.

8 [f]Salvation *belongeth* unto the LORD: thy blessing *is* upon thy people. Selah.

To the chief Musician on Neginoth, A Psalm of David.

4 Hear me when I call, O God of my righteousness: thou hast enlarged me *when I was* in distress; have mercy upon me, and hear my prayer.

2 O ye sons of men, how long *will ye turn* my glory into shame? *how long* will ye love vanity, *and* seek after leasing? Selah.

3 But know that the [g]LORD hath set apart him that is godly for himself: the LORD will hear when I call unto him.

4 [h]Stand in awe, and sin not: [i]commune with your own heart upon your bed, and be still. Selah.

5 Offer [j]the sacrifices of righteousness, and [k]put your trust in the LORD.

6 *There be* many that say, Who will shew

1:1 [a]Prov. 4:14 [b]Ps. 26:4; Jer. 15:17
1:2 [c]Ps. 119:35 [d]Josh. 1:8; Ps. 119:1
1:3 [e]Jer. 17:8; Ezek. 47:12 [f]Gen. 39:3; Ps. 128:2; Isa. 3:10
1:4 [g]Job 21:18; Ps. 35:5; Isa. 17:13; Hos. 13:3
1:6 [h]Ps. 37:18; Nah. 1:7; John 10:14; 2 Tim. 2:19
2:1 [i]Ps. 46:6; Acts 4:25
2:2 [j]Ps. 45:7; John 1:41
2:3 [k]Jer. 5:5; Luke 19:14
2:4 [l]Ps. 11:4 [m]Ps. 37:13; Prov. 1:26
2:6 [n]2 Sam. 5:7
2:7 [o]Acts 13:33; Heb. 1:5
2:8 [p]Ps. 22:27; Dan. 7:13; John 17:4
2:9 [q]Ps. 89:23; Rev. 2:27
2:11 [r]Heb. 12:28 [s]Phil. 2:12
2:12 [t]Gen. 41:40; 1 Sam. 10:1; John 5:23 [u]Rev. 6:16 [v]Ps. 34:8; Prov. 16:20; Isa. 30:18; Jer. 17:7; Rom. 9:33; 1 Pet. 2:6
3:1 [w]2 Sam. 15:12
3:2 [x]2 Sam. 16:8; Ps. 71:11
3:3 [y]Gen. 15:1; Ps. 28:7 [z]Ps. 27:6
3:4 [a]Ps. 34:4 [b]Ps. 2:6
3:5 [c]Lev. 26:6; Ps. 4:8; Prov. 3:24
3:6 [d]Ps. 27:3
3:7 [e]Job 16:10; Ps. 58:6; Lam. 3:30
3:8 [f]Prov. 21:31; Isa. 43:11; Jer. 3:23; Hos. 13:4; Jonah 2:9; Rev. 7:10
4:3 [g]2 Tim. 2:19; 2 Pet. 2:9
4:4 [h]Eph. 4:26 [i]Ps. 77:6; 2 Cor. 13:5
4:5 [j]Deut. 33:19; Ps. 50:14; 2 Sam. 15:12 [k]Ps. 37:3

us *any* good? [l]LORD, lift thou up the light of
thy countenance upon us.
7 Thou hast put [m]gladness in my heart,
more than in the time *that* their corn and
their wine increased.
8 [n]I will both lay me down in peace, and
sleep: [o]for thou, LORD, only makest me
dwell in safety.

To the chief Musician upon Nehiloth,
A Psalm of David.

5 Give ear to my words, O LORD, consider
my meditation.
2 Hearken unto the [p]voice of my cry, my
King, and my God: for [q]unto thee will I
pray.
3 [r]My voice shalt thou hear in the morning, O LORD; in the morning will I direct *my
prayer* unto thee, and will look up.
4 For thou *art* not a God that hath pleasure in wickedness: neither shall evil dwell
with thee.
5 [s]The foolish shall not stand in thy sight:
thou hatest all workers of iniquity.
6 [t]Thou shalt destroy them that speak
leasing: [u]the LORD will abhor the bloody
and deceitful man.
7 But as for me, I will come *into* thy house
in the multitude of thy mercy: *and* in thy
fear will I worship [v]toward thy holy temple.
8 [w]Lead me, O LORD, in thy righteousness because of mine enemies; [x]make thy
way straight before my face.
9 For *there is* no faithfulness in their
mouth; their inward part *is* very wickedness; [y]their throat *is* an open sepulchre;
[z]they flatter with their tongue.
10 Destroy thou them, O God; [a]let them
fall by their own counsels; cast them out in
the multitude of their transgressions, for
they have rebelled against thee.
11 But let all those that put their trust in
thee [b]rejoice: let them ever shout for joy,
because thou defendest them: let them also
that love thy name be joyful in thee.
12 For thou, LORD, [c]wilt bless the righteous; with favour wilt thou compass him as
with a shield.

To the chief Musician on Neginoth upon
Sheminith, A Psalm of David.

6 O [d]LORD, rebuke me not in thine anger,
neither chasten me in thy hot displeasure.
2 [e]Have mercy upon me, O LORD; for I
am weak: O LORD, [f]heal me; for my bones
are vexed.
3 My soul is also sore vexed: but thou,
O LORD, [g]how long?
4 Return, O LORD, deliver my soul: oh
save me for thy mercies' sake.
5 [h]For in death *there is* no remembrance
of thee: in the grave who shall give thee
thanks?
6 I am weary with my groaning; all the
night make I my bed to swim; I water my
couch with my tears.
7 [i]Mine eye is consumed because of
grief; it waxeth old because of all mine enemies.
8 [j]Depart from me, all ye workers of iniquity; for the LORD hath [k]heard the voice
of my weeping.
9 The LORD hath heard my supplication;
the LORD will receive my prayer.
10 Let all mine enemies be ashamed and
sore vexed: let them return *and* be ashamed
suddenly.

Shiggaion of David, which he sang unto the
LORD, concerning the words of Cush
the Benjamite.

7 O LORD my God, in thee do I put my
trust: [l]save me from all them that persecute me, and deliver me:
2 [m]Lest he tear my soul like a lion, [n]rend-
ing *it* in pieces, while *there is* none to deliver.
3 O LORD my God, [o]if I have done this; if
there be [p]iniquity in my hands;
4 If I have rewarded evil unto him that
was at peace with me; (yea, [q]I have delivered him that without cause is mine enemy:)
5 Let the enemy persecute my soul, and
take *it;* yea, let him tread down my life upon
the earth, and lay mine honour in the dust.
Selah.
6 Arise, O LORD, in thine anger, [r]lift up
thyself because of the rage of mine enemies:
and [s]awake for me *to* the judgment *that*
thou hast commanded.
7 So shall the congregation of the people
compass thee about: for their sakes therefore return thou on high.
8 The LORD shall judge the people: judge
me, O LORD, [t]according to my righteousness, and according to mine integrity *that is*
in me.
9 Oh let the wickedness of the wicked
come to an end; but establish the just: [u]for
the righteous God trieth the hearts and
reins.
10 My defence *is* of God, which saveth the
[v]upright in heart.
11 God judgeth the righteous, and God is
angry *with the wicked* every day.
12 If he turn not, he will [w]whet his sword;
he hath bent his bow, and made it ready.
13 He hath also prepared for him the instruments of death; [x]he ordaineth his arrows against the persecutors.
14 [y]Behold, he travaileth with iniquity,
and hath conceived mischief, and brought
forth falsehood.
15 He made a pit, and digged it, [z]and is
fallen into the ditch *which* he made.
16 [a]His mischief shall return upon his
own head, and his violent dealing shall
come down upon his own pate.
17 I will praise the LORD according to his
righteousness: and will sing praise to the
name of the LORD most high.

4:6 [l]Num. 6:26; Ps. 80:3
4:7 [m]Isa. 9:3
4:8 [n]Job 11:18; Ps. 3:5 [o]Lev. 25:18; Deut. 12:10
5:2 [p]Ps. 3:4 [q]Ps. 65:2
5:3 [r]Ps. 30:5
5:5 [s]Hab. 1:13
5:6 [t]Rev. 21:8 [u]Ps. 55:23
5:7 [v]1 Kings 8:29; Ps. 28:2
5:8 [w]Ps. 25:5 [x]Ps. 25:4
5:9 [y]Luke 11:44; Rom. 3:13 [z]Ps. 62:4
5:10 [a]2 Sam. 15:31
5:11 [b]Isa. 65:13
5:12 [c]Ps. 115:13
6:1 [d]Ps. 38:1; Jer. 10:24
6:2 [e]Ps. 41:4 [f]Hos. 6:1
6:3 [g]Ps. 90:13
6:5 [h]Ps. 30:9; Isa. 38:18
6:7 [i]Job 17:7; Ps. 31:9; Lam. 5:17
6:8 [j]Ps. 119:115; Matt. 7:23; Luke 13:27 [k]Ps. 3:4
7:1 [l]Ps. 31:15
7:2 [m]Isa. 38:13 [n]Ps. 50:22
7:3 [o]2 Sam. 16:7 [p]1 Sam. 24:11
7:4 [q]1 Sam. 24:7
7:6 [r]Ps. 94:2 [s]Ps. 44:23
7:8 [t]Ps. 18:20
7:9 [u]1 Sam. 16:7; 1 Chron. 28:9; Ps. 139:1; Jer. 11:20; Rev. 2:23
7:10 [v]Ps. 125:4
7:12 [w]Deut. 32:41
7:13 [x]Deut. 32:23; Ps. 64:7
7:14 [y]Job 15:35; Isa. 33:11; Jam. 1:15
7:15 [z]Esth. 7:10; Job 4:8; Ps. 9:15; Prov. 5:22; Eccl. 10:8
7:16 [a]1 Kings 2:32; Esth. 9:25

To the chief Musician upon Gittith,
A Psalm of David.

8 O LORD our Lord, how [b]excellent *is* thy
name in all the earth! who [c]hast set thy
glory above the heavens.
2 [d]Out of the mouth of babes and sucklings hast thou ordained strength because
of thine enemies, that thou mightest still
[e]the enemy and the avenger.
3 When I [f]consider thy heavens, the
work of thy fingers, the moon and the stars,
which thou hast ordained;
4 [g]What is man, that thou art mindful of
him? and the son of man, that thou visitest
him?
5 For thou hast made him a little lower
than the angels, and hast crowned him with
glory and honour.
6 [h]Thou madest him to have dominion
over the works of thy hands; [i]thou hast put
all *things* under his feet:
7 All sheep and oxen, yea, and the beasts
of the field;
8 The fowl of the air, and the fish of the
sea, *and whatsoever* passeth through the
paths of the seas.
9 [j]O LORD our Lord, how excellent *is* thy
name in all the earth!

To the chief Musician upon Muth-labben,
A Psalm of David.

9 I will praise *thee,* O LORD, with my
whole heart; I will shew forth all thy
marvellous works.
2 I will be glad and [k]rejoice in thee: I will
sing praise to thy name, O [l]thou most
High.
3 When mine enemies are turned back,
they shall fall and perish at thy presence.
4 For thou hast maintained my right and
my cause; thou satest in the throne judging
right.
5 Thou hast rebuked the heathen, thou
hast destroyed the wicked, thou hast [m]put
out their name for ever and ever.
6 O thou enemy, destructions are come to
a perpetual end: and thou hast destroyed
cities; their memorial is perished with them.
7 [n]But the LORD shall endure for ever: he
hath prepared his throne for judgment.
8 And [o]he shall judge the world in righteousness, he shall minister judgment to the
people in uprightness.
9 [p]The LORD also will be a refuge for the
oppressed, a refuge in times of trouble.
10 And they that [q]know thy name will
put their trust in thee: for thou, LORD, hast
not forsaken them that seek thee.
11 Sing praises to the LORD, which dwelleth in Zion: [r]declare among the people his
doings.
12 [s]When he maketh inquisition for
blood, he remembereth them: he forgetteth
not the cry of the humble.
13 Have mercy upon me, O LORD; consider my trouble *which I suffer* of them that
hate me, thou that liftest me up from the
gates of death:
14 That I may shew forth all thy praise in
the gates of the daughter of Zion: I will [t]re-
joice in thy salvation.
15 [u]The heathen are sunk down in the pit
that they made: in the net which they hid is
their own foot taken.
16 The LORD is [v]known *by* the judgment
which he executeth: the wicked is snared
in the work of his own hands. [w]Higgaion.
Selah.
17 The wicked shall be turned into hell,
and all the nations [x]that forget God.
18 [y]For the needy shall not alway be forgotten: [z]the expectation of the poor shall
not perish for ever.
19 Arise, O LORD; let not man prevail: let
the heathen be judged in thy sight.
20 Put them in fear, O LORD: *that* the nations may know themselves *to be but* men.
Selah.

10 Why standest thou afar off, O LORD?
why hidest thou *thyself* in times of
trouble?
2 The wicked in *his* pride doth persecute
the poor: [a]let them be taken in the devices
that they have imagined.
3 For the wicked [b]boasteth of his heart's
desire, and [c]blesseth the covetous, *whom*
the LORD abhorreth.
4 The wicked, through the pride of his
countenance, [d]will not seek *after God:* God
is not in all his [e]thoughts.
5 His ways are always grievous; [f]thy
judgments *are* far above out of his sight: *as
for* all his enemies, [g]he puffeth at them.
6 [h]He hath said in his heart, I shall not be
moved: [i]for *I shall* never *be* in adversity.
7 [j]His mouth is full of cursing and deceit
and fraud: [k]under his tongue *is* mischief
[l]and vanity.
8 He sitteth in the lurking places of the
villages: [m]in the secret places doth he murder the innocent: [n]his eyes are privily set
against the poor.
9 [o]He lieth in wait secretly as a lion in his
den: he lieth in wait to catch the poor: he
doth catch the poor, when he draweth him
into his net.
10 He croucheth, *and* humbleth himself,
that the poor may fall by his strong ones.
11 He hath said in his heart, God hath forgotten: [p]he hideth his face; he will never
see *it.*
12 Arise, O LORD; O God, [q]lift up thine
hand: forget not the humble.
13 Wherefore doth the wicked contemn
God? he hath said in his heart, Thou wilt not
require *it.*
14 Thou hast seen *it;* for thou beholdest
mischief and spite, to requite *it* with thy
hand: the poor [r]committeth himself unto
thee; [s]thou art the helper of the fatherless.
15 [t]Break thou the arm of the wicked and
the evil *man:* seek out his wickedness *till*
thou find none.
16 [u]The LORD *is* King for ever and ever:
the heathen are perished out of his land.
17 LORD, thou hast heard the desire of the

8:1 [b]Ps. 148:13 [c]Ps. 113:4
8:2 [d]Matt. 11:25; 1 Cor. 1:27 [e]Ps. 44:16
8:3 [f]Ps. 111:2
8:4 [g]Job 7:17; Ps. 144:3; Heb. 2:6
8:6 [h]Gen. 1:26 [i]1 Cor. 15:27; Heb. 2:8
8:9 [j]ver. 1
9:2 [k]Ps. 5:11 [l]Ps. 56:2
9:5 [m]Deut. 9:14; Prov. 10:7
9:7 [n]Ps. 102:12; Heb. 1:11
9:8 [o]Ps. 96:13
9:9 [p]Ps. 32:7
9:10 [q]Ps. 91:14
9:11 [r]Ps. 107:22
9:12 [s]Gen. 9:5
9:14 [t]Ps. 13:5
9:15 [u]Ps. 7:15; Prov. 5:22
9:16 [v]Ex. 7:5 [w]Ps. 19:14
9:17 [x]Job 8:13; Ps. 50:22
9:18 [y]ver. 12; Ps. 12:5 [z]Prov. 23:18
10:2 [a]Ps. 7:16; Prov. 5:22
10:3 [b]Ps. 94:4 [c]Prov. 28:4; Rom. 1:32
10:4 [d]Ps. 14:2 [e]Ps. 14:1
10:5 [f]Prov. 24:1; Isa. 26:11 [g]Ps. 12:5
10:6 [h]Ps. 30:6; Eccl. 8:11; Isa. 56:12 [i]Rev. 18:7
10:7 [j]Rom. 3:14 [k]Job 20:12 [l]Ps. 12:2
10:8 [m]Hab. 3:14 [n]Ps. 17:11
10:9 [o]Ps. 17:12; Mic. 7:2
10:11 [p]Job 22:13; Ps. 73:11; Ezek. 8:12
10:12 [q]Mic. 5:9
10:14 [r]2 Tim. 1:12; 1 Pet. 4:19 [s]Ps. 68:5; Hos. 14:3
10:15 [t]Ps. 37:17
10:16 [u]Ps. 29:10; Jer. 10:10; Lam. 5:19; Dan. 4:34; 1 Tim. 1:17

humble: thou wilt [v]prepare their heart,
thou wilt cause thine ear to hear:
18 To [w]judge the fatherless and the oppressed, that the man of the earth may no
more oppress.

To the chief Musician, *A Psalm* of David.

11 [x]In the LORD put I my trust: [y]how
say ye to my soul, Flee *as* a bird to
your mountain?
2 For, lo, [z]the wicked bend *their* bow,
[a]they make ready their arrow upon the
string, that they may privily shoot at the
upright in heart.
3 [b]If the foundations be destroyed, what
can the righteous do?
4 [c]The LORD *is* in his holy temple, the
LORD's [d]throne *is* in heaven: [e]his eyes behold, his eyelids try, the children of men.
5 The LORD [f]trieth the righteous: but the
wicked and him that loveth violence his
soul hateth.
6 [g]Upon the wicked he shall rain snares,
fire and brimstone, and an horrible tempest:
[h]*this shall be* the portion of their cup.
7 For the righteous LORD [i]loveth righteousness; [j]his countenance doth behold
the upright.

To the chief Musician upon Sheminith,
A Psalm of David.

12 Help, LORD; for [k]the godly man ceaseth; for the faithful fail from among
the children of men.
2 [l]They speak vanity every one with his
neighbour: [m]*with* flattering lips *and* with a
double heart do they speak.
3 The LORD shall cut off all flattering lips,
and the tongue that speaketh [n]proud
things:
4 Who have said, With our tongue will we
prevail; our lips *are* our own: who *is* lord
over us?
5 For the oppression of the poor, for the
sighing of the needy, [o]now will I arise, saith
the LORD; I will set *him* in safety *from him
that* [p]puffeth at him.
6 The words of the LORD *are* [q]pure
words: *as* silver tried in a furnace of earth,
purified seven times.
7 Thou shalt keep them, O LORD, thou
shalt preserve them from this generation
for ever.
8 The wicked walk on every side, when
the vilest men are exalted.

To the chief Musician, A Psalm of David.

13 How long wilt thou forget me,
O LORD? for ever? [r]how long wilt
thou hide thy face from me?
2 How long shall I take counsel in my
soul, *having* sorrow in my heart daily? how
long shall mine enemy be exalted over me?
3 Consider *and* hear me, O LORD my God:
[s]lighten mine eyes, [t]lest I sleep the *sleep of*
death;
4 [u]Lest mine enemy say, I have prevailed
against him; *and* those that trouble me rejoice when I am moved.
5 But I have [v]trusted in thy mercy; my
heart shall rejoice in thy salvation.
6 I will sing unto the LORD, because he
hath [w]dealt bountifully with me.

To the chief Musician, *A Psalm* of David.

14 The [x]fool hath said in his heart,
There is no God. [y]They are corrupt,
they have done abominable works, *there is*
none that doeth good.
2 [z]The LORD looked down from heaven
upon the children of men, to see if there
were any that did understand, *and* seek
God.
3 [a]They are all gone aside, they are *all*
together become filthy: *there is* none that
doeth good, no, not one.
4 Have all the workers of iniquity no
knowledge? who [b]eat up my people *as* they
eat bread, and [c]call not upon the LORD.
5 There were they in great fear: for God *is*
in the generation of the righteous.
6 Ye have shamed the counsel of the
poor, because the LORD *is* his [d]refuge.
7 [e]Oh that the salvation of Israel *were
come* out of Zion! [f]when the LORD bringeth
back the captivity of his people, Jacob shall
rejoice, *and* Israel shall be glad.

A Psalm of David.

15 LORD, [g]who shall abide in thy tabernacle? who shall dwell in [h]thy holy
hill?
2 [i]He that walketh uprightly, and worketh righteousness, and [j]speaketh the truth
in his heart.
3 [k]*He that* backbiteth not with his
tongue, nor doeth evil to his neighbour,
[l]nor taketh up a reproach against his
neighbour.
4 [m]In whose eyes a vile person is contemned; but he honoureth them that fear the
LORD. *He that* [n]sweareth to *his own* hurt,
and changeth not.
5 [o]*He that* putteth not out his money to
usury, [p]nor taketh reward against the innocent. He that doeth these *things* [q]shall
never be moved.

Michtam of David.

16 Preserve me, O God: [r]for in thee do
I put my trust.
2 *O my soul,* thou hast said unto the LORD,
Thou *art* my Lord: [s]my goodness *extendeth* not to thee;
3 *But* to the saints that *are* in the earth,
and *to* the excellent, in whom *is* all my delight.
4 Their sorrows shall be multiplied *that*
hasten *after* another *god:* their drink offerings of blood will I not offer, [t]nor take up
their names into my lips.
5 [u]The LORD *is* the portion of mine inheritance and [v]of my cup: thou maintainest my
lot.
6 The lines are fallen unto me in pleasant
places; yea, I have a goodly heritage.
7 I will bless the LORD, who hath given me

10:17 [v]1 Chron. 29:18
10:18 [w]Ps. 82:3; Isa. 11:4
11:1 [x]Ps. 56:11 [y]1 Sam. 26:19
11:2 [z]Ps. 64:3 [a]Ps. 21:12
11:3 [b]Ps. 82:5
11:4 [c]Hab. 2:20 [d]Ps. 2:4; Isa. 66:1; Matt. 5:34; Acts 7:49; Rev. 4:2 [e]Ps. 33:13
11:5 [f]Gen. 22:1; Jam. 1:12
11:6 [g]Gen. 19:24; Ezek. 38:22 [h]Gen. 43:34; 1 Sam. 1:4; Ps. 75:8
11:7 [i]Ps. 45:7 [j]Job 36:7; Ps. 33:18; 1 Pet. 3:12
12:1 [k]Isa. 57:1; Mic. 7:2
12:2 [l]Ps. 10:7 [m]Ps. 28:3; Jer. 9:8; Rom. 16:18
12:3 [n]1 Sam. 2:3; Ps. 17:10; Dan. 7:8
12:5 [o]Ex. 3:7; Isa. 33:10 [p]Ps. 10:5
12:6 [q]2 Sam. 22:31; Ps. 18:30; Prov. 30:5
13:1 [r]Deut. 31:17; Job 13:24; Ps. 44:24; Isa. 59:2
13:3 [s]Ezra 9:8 [t]Jer. 51:39
13:4 [u]Ps. 25:2
13:5 [v]Ps. 33:21
13:6 [w]Ps. 116:7
14:1 [x]Ps. 10:4 [y]Gen. 6:11; Rom. 3:10
14:2 [z]Ps. 33:13
14:3 [a]Rom. 3:10
14:4 [b]Jer. 10:25; Am. 8:4; Mic. 3:3 [c]Ps. 79:6; Isa. 64:7
14:6 [d]Ps. 9:9
14:7 [e]Ps. 53:6 [f]Job 42:10; Ps. 126:1
15:1 [g]Ps. 24:3 [h]Ps. 2:6
15:2 [i]Isa. 33:15 [j]Zech. 8:16; Eph. 4:25
15:3 [k]Lev. 19:16; Ps. 34:13 [l]Ex. 23:1
15:4 [m]Esth. 3:2 [n]Judg. 11:35
15:5 [o]Ex. 22:25; Lev. 25:36; Deut. 23:19; Ezek. 18:8 [p]Ex. 23:8; Deut. 16:19 [q]Ps. 16:8; 2 Pet. 1:10
16:1 [r]Ps. 25:20
16:2 [s]Job 22:2; Ps. 50:9; Rom. 11:35
16:4 [t]Ex. 23:13; Josh. 23:7; Hos. 2:16
16:5 [u]Deut. 32:9; Ps. 73:26; Jer. 10:16; Lam. 3:24 [v]Ps. 11:6

counsel: [w]my reins also instruct me in the night seasons.

8 [x]I have set the LORD always before me: because [y]*he is* at my right hand, [z]I shall not be moved.

9 Therefore my heart is glad, [a]and my glory rejoiceth: my flesh also shall rest in hope.

10 [b]For thou wilt not leave [c]my soul in hell; neither wilt thou suffer thine Holy One to see corruption.

11 Thou wilt shew me the [d]path of life: [e]in thy presence *is* fulness of joy; [f]at thy right hand *there are* pleasures for evermore.

A Prayer of David.

17 Hear the right, O LORD, attend unto my cry, give ear unto my prayer, *that goeth* not out of feigned lips.

2 Let my sentence come forth from thy presence; let thine eyes behold the things that are equal.

3 Thou hast proved mine heart; [g]thou hast visited *me* in the night; [h]thou hast tried me, *and* shalt find nothing; I am purposed *that* my mouth shall not transgress.

4 Concerning the works of men, by the word of thy lips I have kept *me from* the paths of the destroyer.

5 [i]Hold up my goings in thy paths, *that* my footsteps slip not.

6 [j]I have called upon thee, for thou wilt hear me, O God: incline thine ear unto me, *and hear* my speech.

7 [k]Shew thy marvellous lovingkindness, O thou that savest by thy right hand them which put their trust *in thee* from those that rise up *against them.*

8 [l]Keep me as the apple of the eye, [m]hide me under the shadow of thy wings,

9 From the wicked that oppress me, *from* my deadly enemies, *who* compass me about.

10 [n]They are inclosed in their own fat: with their mouth they [o]speak proudly.

11 They have now [p]compassed us in our steps: [q]they have set their eyes bowing down to the earth;

12 Like as a lion *that* is greedy of his prey, and as it were a young lion lurking in secret places.

13 Arise, O LORD, disappoint him, cast him down: deliver my soul from the wicked, [r]*which is* thy sword:

14 From men *which are* thy hand, O LORD, from men of the world, [s]*which have* their portion in *this* life, and whose belly thou fillest with thy hid *treasure*: they are full of children, and leave the rest of their *substance* to their babes.

15 As for me, [t]I will behold thy face in righteousness: [u]I shall be satisfied, when I awake, with thy likeness.

To the chief Musician, *A Psalm* of David, the servant of the LORD, who spake unto the LORD the words of this song in the day *that* the LORD delivered him from the hand of all his enemies, and from the hand of Saul: And he said,

18 I [v]will love thee, O LORD, my strength.

2 The LORD *is* my rock, and my fortress, and my deliverer; my God, my strength, [w]in whom I will trust; my buckler, and the horn of my salvation, *and* my high tower.

3 I will call upon the LORD, [x]*who is worthy* to be praised: so shall I be saved from mine enemies.

4 [y]The sorrows of death compassed me, and the floods of ungodly men made me afraid.

5 The sorrows of hell compassed me about: the snares of death prevented me.

6 In my distress I called upon the LORD, and cried unto my God: he heard my voice out of his temple, and my cry came before him, *even* into his ears.

7 [z]Then the earth shook and trembled; the foundations also of the hills moved and were shaken, because he was wroth.

8 There went up a smoke out of his nostrils, and fire out of his mouth devoured: coals were kindled by it.

9 [a]He bowed the heavens also, and came down: and darkness *was* under his feet.

10 [b]And he rode upon a cherub, and did fly: yea, [c]he did fly upon the wings of the wind.

11 He made darkness his secret place; [d]his pavilion round about him *were* dark waters *and* thick clouds of the skies.

12 [e]At the brightness *that was* before him his thick clouds passed, hail *stones* and coals of fire.

13 The LORD also thundered in the heavens, and the Highest [f]gave his voice; hail *stones* and coals of fire.

14 [g]Yea, he sent out his arrows, and scattered them; and he shot out lightnings, and discomfited them.

15 [h]Then the channels of waters were seen, and the foundations of the world were discovered at thy rebuke, O LORD, at the blast of the breath of thy nostrils.

16 [i]He sent from above, he took me, he drew me out of many waters.

17 He delivered me from my strong enemy, and from them which hated me: for they were too strong for me.

18 They prevented me in the day of my calamity: but the LORD was my stay.

19 [j]He brought me forth also into a large place; he delivered me, because he delighted in me.

20 [k]The LORD rewarded me according to my righteousness; according to the cleanness of my hands hath he recompensed me.

21 For I have kept the ways of the LORD, and have not wickedly departed from my God.

22 For all his judgments *were* before me,

16:7 [w]Ps. 17:3
16:8 [x]Acts 2:25 [y]Ps. 73:23 [z]Ps. 15:5
16:9 [a]Ps. 30:12
16:10 [b]Ps. 49:15; Acts 2:27 [c]Lev. 19:28; Num. 6:6
16:11 [d]Matt. 7:14 [e]Ps. 17:15; Matt. 5:8; 1 Cor. 13:12; 1 John 3:2 [f]Ps. 36:8
17:3 [g]Ps. 16:7 [h]Job 23:10; Ps. 26:2; Zech. 13:9; Mal. 3:2; 1 Pet. 1:7
17:5 [i]Ps. 119:133
17:6 [j]Ps. 116:2
17:7 [k]Ps. 31:21
17:8 [l]Deut. 32:10; Zech. 2:8 [m]Ruth 2:12; Ps. 36:7; Matt. 23:37
17:10 [n]Deut. 32:15; Job 15:27; Ps. 73:7 [o]1 Sam. 2:3; Ps. 31:18
17:11 [p]1 Sam. 23:26 [q]Ps. 10:8
17:13 [r]Isa. 10:5
17:14 [s]Ps. 73:12; Luke 16:25; Jam. 5:5
17:15 [t]1 John 3:2 [u]Ps. 4:6
18:1 [v]Ps. 144:1
18:2 [w]Heb. 2:13
18:3 [x]Ps. 76:4
18:4 [y]Ps. 116:3
18:7 [z]Acts 4:31
18:9 [a]Ps. 144:5
18:10 [b]Ps. 99:1 [c]Ps. 104:3
18:11 [d]Ps. 97:2
18:12 [e]Ps. 97:3
18:13 [f]Ps. 29:3
18:14 [g]Josh. 10:10; Ps. 144:6; Isa. 30:30
18:15 [h]Ex. 15:8; Ps. 106:9
18:16 [i]Ps. 144:7
18:19 [j]Ps. 31:8
18:20 [k]1 Sam. 24:20

and I did not put away his statutes from me.
23 I was also upright before him, and I kept myself from mine iniquity.
24 [l]Therefore hath the LORD recompensed me according to my righteousness, according to the cleanness of my hands in his eyesight.
25 [m]With the merciful thou wilt shew thyself merciful; with an upright man thou wilt shew thyself upright;
26 With the pure thou wilt shew thyself pure; and [n]with the froward thou wilt shew thyself froward.
27 For thou wilt save the afflicted people; but wilt bring down [o]high looks.
28 [p]For thou wilt light my candle: the LORD my God will enlighten my darkness.
29 For by thee I have run through a troop; and by my God have I leaped over a wall.
30 *As for* God, [q]his way *is* perfect: [r]the word of the LORD is tried: he *is* a buckler [s]to all those that trust in him.
31 [t]For who *is* God save the LORD? or who *is* a rock save our God?
32 *It is* God that [u]girdeth me with strength, and maketh my way perfect.
33 [v]He maketh my feet like hinds' *feet*, and [w]setteth me upon my high places.
34 [x]He teacheth my hands to war, so that a bow of steel is broken by mine arms.
35 Thou hast also given me the shield of thy salvation: and thy right hand hath holden me up, and thy gentleness hath made me great.
36 Thou hast enlarged my steps under me, [y]that my feet did not slip.
37 I have pursued mine enemies, and overtaken them: neither did I turn again till they were consumed.
38 I have wounded them that they were not able to rise: they are fallen under my feet.
39 For thou hast girded me with strength unto the battle: thou hast subdued under me those that rose up against me.
40 Thou hast also given me the necks of mine enemies; that I might destroy them that hate me.
41 They cried, but *there was* none to save *them:* [z]*even* unto the LORD, but he answered them not.
42 Then did I beat them small as the dust before the wind: I did [a]cast them out as the dirt in the streets.
43 [b]Thou hast delivered me from the strivings of the people; *and* [c]thou hast made me the head of the heathen: [d]a people *whom* I have not known shall serve me.
44 As soon as they hear of me, they shall obey me: the strangers [e]shall submit themselves unto me.
45 [f]The strangers shall fade away, and be afraid out of their close places.
46 The LORD liveth; and blessed *be* my rock; and let the God of my salvation be exalted.
47 *It is* God that avengeth me, [g]and subdueth the people under me.

18:24 [l]1 Sam. 26:23
18:25 [m]1 Kings 8:32
18:26 [n]Lev. 26:23; Prov. 3:34
18:27 [o]Ps. 101:5; Prov. 6:17
18:28 [p]Job 18:6
18:30 [q]Deut. 32:4; Dan. 4:37; Rev. 15:3 [r]Ps. 12:6; Prov. 30:5 [s]Ps. 17:7
18:31 [t]Deut. 32:31; 1 Sam. 2:2; Ps. 86:8; Isa. 45:5
18:32 [u]Ps. 91:2
18:33 [v]2 Sam. 2:18; Hab. 3:19 [w]Deut. 32:13
18:34 [x]Ps. 144:1
18:36 [y]Prov. 4:12
18:41 [z]Job 27:9; Prov. 1:28; Isa. 1:15; Jer. 11:11; Ezek. 8:18; Mic. 3:4; Zech. 7:13
18:42 [a]Zech. 10:5
18:43 [b]2 Sam. 2:9 [c]2 Sam. 8 [d]Isa. 52:15
18:44 [e]Deut. 33:29; Ps. 66:3
18:45 [f]Mic. 7:17
18:47 [g]Ps. 47:3
18:48 [h]Ps. 59:1
18:49 [i]Rom. 15:9
18:50 [j]Ps. 144:10 [k]2 Sam. 7:13
19:1 [l]Gen. 1:6; Isa. 40:22; Rom. 1:19
19:4 [m]Rom. 10:18
19:5 [n]Eccl. 1:5
19:7 [o]Ps. 111:7
19:8 [p]Ps. 12:6 [q]Ps. 13:3
19:10 [r]Ps. 119:72; Prov. 8:10 [s]Ps. 119:103
19:11 [t]Prov. 29:18
19:12 [u]Ps. 40:12 [v]Lev. 4:2 [w]Ps. 90:8
19:13 [x]Gen. 20:6; 1 Sam. 25:32 [y]Ps. 119:133; Rom. 6:12
19:14 [z]Ps. 51:15 [a]Isa. 43:14; 1 Thess. 1:10
20:1 [b]Prov. 18:10
20:2 [c]1 Kings 6:16; 2 Chron. 20:8; Ps. 73:17
20:4 [d]Ps. 21:2
20:5 [e]Ps. 19:4

48 He delivereth me from mine enemies: yea, [h]thou liftest me up above those that rise up against me: thou hast delivered me from the violent man.
49 [i]Therefore will I give thanks unto thee, O LORD, among the heathen, and sing praises unto thy name.
50 [j]Great deliverance giveth he to his king; and sheweth mercy to his anointed, to David, and to his seed [k]for evermore.

To the chief Musician, A Psalm of David.

19 The [l]heavens declare the glory of God; and the firmament sheweth his handiwork.
2 Day unto day uttereth speech, and night unto night sheweth knowledge.
3 *There is* no speech nor language, *where* their voice is not heard.
4 [m]Their line is gone out through all the earth, and their words to the end of the world. In them hath he set a tabernacle for the sun,
5 Which *is* as a bridegroom coming out of his chamber, [n]*and* rejoiceth as a strong man to run a race.
6 His going forth *is* from the end of the heaven, and his circuit unto the ends of it: and there is nothing hid from the heat thereof.
7 [o]The law of the LORD *is* perfect, converting the soul: the testimony of the LORD *is* sure, making wise the simple.
8 The statutes of the LORD *are* right, rejoicing the heart: [p]the commandment of the LORD *is* pure, [q]enlightening the eyes.
9 The fear of the LORD *is* clean, enduring for ever: the judgments of the LORD *are* true *and* righteous altogether.
10 More to be desired *are they* than gold, [r]yea, than much fine gold: [s]sweeter also than honey and the honeycomb.
11 Moreover by them is thy servant warned: *and* [t]in keeping of them *there is* great reward.
12 [u]Who can understand *his* errors? [v]cleanse thou me from [w]secret *faults.*
13 [x]Keep back thy servant also from presumptuous *sins;* [y]let them not have dominion over me: then shall I be upright, and I shall be innocent from the great transgression.
14 [z]Let the words of my mouth, and the meditation of my heart, be acceptable in thy sight, O LORD, my strength, and my [a]redeemer.

To the chief Musician, A Psalm of David.

20 The LORD hear thee in the day of trouble; [b]the name of the God of Jacob defend thee;
2 Send thee help from [c]the sanctuary, and strengthen thee out of Zion;
3 Remember all thy offerings, and accept thy burnt sacrifice; Selah.
4 [d]Grant thee according to thine own heart, and fulfil all thy counsel.
5 We will [e]rejoice in thy salvation, and

[f]in the name of our God we will set up *our* banners: the LORD fulfil all thy petitions.

6 Now know I that the LORD saveth [g]his anointed; he will hear him from his holy heaven with the saving strength of his right hand.

7 [h]Some *trust* in chariots, and some in horses: [i]but we will remember the name of the LORD our God.

8 They are brought down and fallen: but we are risen, and stand upright.

9 Save, LORD: let the king hear us when we call.

To the chief Musician, A Psalm of David.

21 The king shall joy in thy strength, O LORD; and [j]in thy salvation how greatly shall he rejoice!

2 [k]Thou hast given him his heart's desire, and hast not withholden the request of his lips. Selah.

3 For thou preventest him with the blessings of goodness: thou [l]settest a crown of pure gold on his head.

4 [m]He asked life of thee, *and* thou gavest *it* him, [n]*even* length of days for ever and ever.

5 His glory *is* great in thy salvation: honour and majesty hast thou laid upon him.

6 For thou hast made him most blessed for ever: [o]thou hast made him exceeding glad with thy countenance.

7 For the king trusteth in the LORD, and through the mercy of the most High he [p]shall not be moved.

8 Thine hand shall [q]find out all thine enemies: thy right hand shall find out those that hate thee.

9 [r]Thou shalt make them as a fiery oven in the time of thine anger: the LORD shall [s]swallow them up in his wrath, [t]and the fire shall devour them.

10 [u]Their fruit shalt thou destroy from the earth, and their seed from among the children of men.

11 For they intended evil against thee: they [v]imagined a mischievous device, *which* they are not able *to perform.*

12 Therefore shalt thou make them turn their back, *when* thou shalt make ready *thine arrows* upon thy strings against the face of them.

13 Be thou exalted, LORD, in thine own strength: *so* will we sing and praise thy power.

To the chief Musician upon Aijeleth Shahar, A Psalm of David.

22 My [w]God, my God, why hast thou forsaken me? *why art thou so* far from helping me, *and from* [x]the words of my roaring?

2 O my God, I cry in the daytime, but thou hearest not; and in the night season, and am not silent.

3 But thou *art* holy, *O thou* that inhabitest the [y]praises of Israel.

4 Our fathers trusted in thee: they trusted, and thou didst deliver them.

5 They cried unto thee, and were delivered: [z]they trusted in thee, and were not confounded.

6 But I *am* [a]a worm, and no man; [b]a reproach of men, and despised of the people.

7 [c]All they that see me laugh me to scorn: they shoot out the lip, [d]they shake the head, *saying,*

8 [e]He trusted on the LORD *that* he would deliver him: [f]let him deliver him, seeing he delighted in him.

9 [g]But thou *art* he that took me out of the womb: thou didst make me hope *when I was* upon my mother's breasts.

10 I was cast upon thee from the womb: [h]thou *art* my God from my mother's belly.

11 Be not far from me; for trouble *is* near; for *there is* none to help.

12 [i]Many bulls have compassed me: strong *bulls* of Bashan have beset me round.

13 [j]They gaped upon me *with* their mouths, *as* a ravening and a roaring lion.

14 I am poured out like water, [k]and all my bones are out of joint: [l]my heart is like wax; it is melted in the midst of my bowels.

15 [m]My strength is dried up like a potsherd; and [n]my tongue cleaveth to my jaws; and thou hast brought me into the dust of death.

16 For [o]dogs have compassed me: the assembly of the wicked have inclosed me: [p]they pierced my hands and my feet.

17 I may tell all my bones: [q]they look *and* stare upon me.

18 [r]They part my garments among them, and cast lots upon my vesture.

19 But be [s]not thou far from me, O LORD: O my strength, haste thee to help me.

20 Deliver my soul from the sword; [t]my darling from the power of the [u]dog.

21 [v]Save me from the lion's mouth: [w]for thou hast heard me from the horns of the unicorns.

22 [x]I will declare thy name unto [y]my brethren: in the midst of the congregation will I praise thee.

23 [z]Ye that fear the LORD, praise him; all ye the seed of Jacob, glorify him; and fear him, all ye the seed of Israel.

24 For he hath not despised nor abhorred the affliction of the afflicted; neither hath he hid his face from him; but [a]when he cried unto him, he heard.

25 [b]My praise *shall be* of thee in the great congregation: [c]I will pay my vows before them that fear him.

26 [d]The meek shall eat and be satisfied: they shall praise the LORD that seek him: your heart [e]shall live for ever.

27 [f]All the ends of the world shall remember and turn unto the LORD: [g]and all the kindreds of the nations shall worship before thee.

28 [h]For the kingdom *is* the LORD's: and he *is* the governor among the nations.

20:5 [f]Ex. 17:15; Ps. 60:4
20:6 [g]Ps. 2:2
20:7 [h]Ps. 33:16; Prov. 21:31; Isa. 31:1 [i]2 Chron. 32:8
21:1 [j]Ps. 20:5
21:2 [k]Ps. 20:4
21:3 [l]2 Sam. 12:30; 1 Chron. 20:2
21:4 [m]Ps. 61:5 [n]2 Sam. 7:19; Ps. 91:16
21:6 [o]Ps. 16:11; Acts 2:28
21:7 [p]Ps. 16:8
21:8 [q]1 Sam. 31:3
21:9 [r]Mal. 4:1 [s]Ps. 56:1 [t]Ps. 18:8; Isa. 26:11
21:10 [u]1 Kings 13:34; Job 18:16; Ps. 37:28; Isa. 14:20
21:11 [v]Ps. 2:1
22:1 [w]Matt. 27:46; Mark 15:34 [x]Heb. 5:7
22:3 [y]Deut. 10:21
22:5 [z]Ps. 25:2; Isa. 49:23; Rom. 9:33
22:6 [a]Job 25:6; Isa. 41:14 [b]Isa. 53:3
22:7 [c]Matt. 27:39; Mark 15:29; Luke 23:35 [d]Job 16:4; Ps. 109:25
22:8 [e]Matt. 27:43 [f]Ps. 91:14
22:9 [g]Ps. 71:6
22:10 [h]Isa. 46:3
22:12 [i]Deut. 32:14; Ps. 68:30; Ezek. 39:18; Am. 4:1
22:13 [j]Job 16:10; Ps. 35:21; Lam. 2:16
22:14 [k]Dan. 5:6 [l]Josh. 7:5; Job 23:16
22:15 [m]Prov. 17:22 [n]Job 29:10; Lam. 4:4; John 19:28
22:16 [o]Rev. 22:15 [p]Matt. 27:35; Mark 15:24; Luke 23:33; John 19:23
22:17 [q]Luke 23:27
22:18 [r]Luke 23:34; John 19:23
22:19 [s]ver. 11; Ps. 10:1
22:20 [t]Ps. 35:17 [u]ver. 16
22:21 [v]2 Tim. 4:17 [w]Isa. 34:7; Acts 4:27
22:22 [x]Heb. 2:12; Ps. 40:9 [y]John 20:17; Rom. 8:29
22:23 [z]Ps. 135:19
22:24 [a]Heb. 5:7
22:25 [b]Ps. 35:18 [c]Ps. 66:13; Eccl. 5:4
22:26 [d]Lev. 7:11; Ps. 69:32; Isa. 65:13 [e]John 6:51
22:27 [f]Ps. 2:8; Isa. 49:6 [g]Ps. 96:7
22:28 [h]Ps. 47:8; Obad. 21; Zech. 14:9; Matt. 6:13

29 [i]All *they that be* fat upon earth shall eat and worship: [j]all they that go down to the dust shall bow before him: and none can keep alive his own soul.

30 A seed shall serve him; [k]it shall be accounted to the Lord for a generation.

31 [l]They shall come, and shall declare his righteousness unto a people that shall be born, that he hath done *this*.

A Psalm of David.

23 The LORD *is* [m]my shepherd; [n]I shall not want.

2 [o]He maketh me to lie down in green pastures: [p]he leadeth me beside the still waters.

3 He restoreth my soul: [q]he leadeth me in the paths of righteousness for his name's sake.

4 Yea, though I walk through the valley of [r]the shadow of death, [s]I will fear no evil: [t]for thou *art* with me; thy rod and thy staff they comfort me.

5 [u]Thou preparest a table before me in the presence of mine enemies: thou [v]anointest my head with oil; my cup runneth over.

6 Surely goodness and mercy shall follow me all the days of my life: and I will dwell in the house of the LORD for ever.

A Psalm of David.

24 The [w]earth *is* the LORD'S, and the fulness thereof; the world, and they that dwell therein.

2 [x]For he hath founded it upon the seas, and established it upon the floods.

3 [y]Who shall ascend into the hill of the LORD? or who shall stand in his holy place?

4 [z]He that hath [a]clean hands, and [b]a pure heart; who hath not lifted up his soul unto vanity, nor [c]sworn deceitfully.

5 He shall receive the blessing from the LORD, and righteousness from the God of his salvation.

6 This *is* the generation of them that seek him, that [d]seek thy face, O Jacob. Selah.

7 [e]Lift up your heads, O ye gates; and be ye lift up, ye everlasting doors; [f]and the King of glory shall come in.

8 Who *is* this King of glory? The LORD strong and mighty, the LORD mighty in battle.

9 Lift up your heads, O ye gates; even lift *them* up, ye everlasting doors; and the King of glory shall come in.

10 Who is this King of glory? The LORD of hosts, he *is* the King of glory. Selah.

A Psalm of David.

25 Unto [g]thee, O LORD, do I lift up my soul.

2 O my God, I [h]trust in thee: let me not be ashamed, [i]let not mine enemies triumph over me.

3 Yea, let none that wait on thee be ashamed: let them be ashamed which transgress without cause.

4 [j]Shew me thy ways, O LORD; teach me thy paths.

5 Lead me in thy truth, and teach me: for thou *art* the God of my salvation; on thee do I wait all the day.

6 Remember, O LORD, [k]thy tender mercies and thy lovingkindnesses; for they *have been* ever of old.

7 Remember not [l]the sins of my youth, nor my transgressions: [m]according to thy mercy remember thou me for thy goodness' sake, O LORD.

8 Good and upright *is* the LORD: therefore will he teach sinners in the way.

9 The meek will he guide in judgment: and the meek will he teach his way.

10 All the paths of the LORD *are* mercy and truth unto such as keep his covenant and his testimonies.

11 [n]For thy name's sake, O LORD, pardon mine iniquity; [o]for it *is* great.

12 What man *is* he that feareth the LORD? [p]him shall he teach in the way *that* he shall choose.

13 [q]His soul shall dwell at ease; and [r]his seed shall inherit the earth.

14 [s]The secret of the LORD *is* with them that fear him; and he will shew them his covenant.

15 [t]Mine eyes *are* ever toward the LORD; for he shall pluck my feet out of the net.

16 [u]Turn thee unto me, and have mercy upon me; for I *am* desolate and afflicted.

17 The troubles of my heart are enlarged: *O* bring thou me out of my distresses.

18 [v]Look upon mine affliction and my pain; and forgive all my sins.

19 Consider mine enemies; for they are many; and they hate me with cruel hatred.

20 O keep my soul, and deliver me: [w]let me not be ashamed; for I put my trust in thee.

21 Let integrity and uprightness preserve me; for I wait on thee.

22 [x]Redeem Israel, O God, out of all his troubles.

A Psalm of David.

26 Judge [y]me, O LORD; for I have [z]walked in mine integrity: [a]I have trusted also in the LORD; *therefore* I shall not slide.

2 [b]Examine me, O LORD, and prove me; try my reins and my heart.

3 For thy lovingkindness *is* before mine eyes: and [c]I have walked in thy truth.

4 [d]I have not sat with vain persons, neither will I go in with dissemblers.

5 I have [e]hated the congregation of evildoers; [f]and will not sit with the wicked.

6 [g]I will wash mine hands in innocency: so will I compass thine altar, O LORD:

7 That I may publish with the voice of thanksgiving, and tell of all thy wondrous works.

8 LORD, [h]I have loved the habitation of thy house, and the place where thine honour dwelleth.

22:29 [i]Ps. 45:12 [j]Isa. 26:19; Phil. 2:10
22:30 [k]Ps. 87:6
22:31 [l]Ps. 78:6; Isa. 60:3; Rom. 3:21
23:1 [m]Isa. 40:11; Jer. 23:4; Ezek. 34:11; John 10:11; 1 Pet. 2:25; Rev. 7:17 [n]Phil. 4:19
23:2 [o]Ezek. 34:14 [p]Rev. 7:17
23:3 [q]Ps. 5:8; Prov. 8:20
23:4 [r]Job 3:5; Ps. 44:19 [s]Ps. 3:6 [t]Isa. 43:2
23:5 [u]Ps. 104:15 [v]Ps. 92:10
24:1 [w]Ex. 9:29; Deut. 10:14; Job 41:11; Ps. 50:12; 1 Cor. 10:26
24:2 [x]Gen. 1:9; Job 38:6; Ps. 104:5; 2 Pet. 3:5
24:3 [y]Ps. 15:1
24:4 [z]Isa. 33:15 [a]Job 17:9; 1 Tim. 2:8 [b]Matt. 5:8 [c]Ps. 15:4
24:6 [d]Ps. 27:8
24:7 [e]Isa. 26:2 [f]Ps. 97:6; Hag. 2:7; Mal. 3:1; 1 Cor. 2:8
25:1 [g]Ps. 86:4; Lam. 3:41
25:2 [h]Ps. 22:5; Isa. 28:16; Rom. 10:11 [i]Ps. 13:4
25:4 [j]Ex. 33:13; Ps. 5:1
25:6 [k]Ps. 103:17; Isa. 63:15; Jer. 33:11
25:7 [l]Job 13:26; Jer. 3:25 [m]Ps. 51:1
25:11 [n]Ps. 31:3 [o]Rom. 5:20
25:12 [p]Ps. 37:23
25:13 [q]Prov. 19:23 [r]Ps. 37:11
25:14 [s]Prov. 5:32; John 7:17
25:15 [t]Ps. 141:8
25:16 [u]Ps. 69:16
25:18 [v]2 Sam. 16:12
25:20 [w]ver. 2
25:22 [x]Ps. 130:8
26:1 [y]Ps. 7:8 [z]ver. 11; 2 Kings 20:3; Prov. 20:7 [a]Ps. 28:7; Prov. 29:25
26:2 [b]Ps. 7:9; Zech. 13:9
26:3 [c]2 Kings 20:3
26:4 [d]Ps. 1:1; Jer. 15:17
26:5 [e]Ps. 31:6 [f]Ps. 1:1
26:6 [g]Ex. 30:19; Ps. 73:13; 1 Tim. 2:8
26:8 [h]Ps. 27:4

9 [i]Gather not my soul with sinners, nor
my life with bloody men:
10 In whose hands *is* mischief, and their
right hand is full of [j]bribes.
11 But as for me, I will walk [k]in mine
integrity: redeem me, and be merciful
unto me.
12 [l]My foot standeth in an [m]even place:
[n]in the congregations will I bless the LORD.

A *Psalm* of David.

27 The LORD *is* [o]my light and [p]my salvation; whom shall I fear? [q]the LORD
is the strength of my life; of whom shall I be
afraid?
2 When the wicked, *even* mine enemies
and my foes, came upon me to [r]eat up my
flesh, they stumbled and fell.
3 [s]Though an host should encamp
against me, my heart shall not fear: though
war should rise against me, in this *will* I *be*
confident.
4 [t]One *thing* have I desired of the LORD,
that will I seek after; that I may [u]dwell in
the house of the LORD all the days of my life,
to behold [v]the beauty of the LORD, and to
enquire in his temple.
5 For [w]in the time of trouble he shall hide
me in his pavilion: in the secret of his tabernacle shall he hide me; he shall [x]set me up
upon a rock.
6 And now shall [y]mine head be lifted up
above mine enemies round about me: therefore will I offer in his tabernacle sacrifices
of joy; I will sing, yea, I will sing praises
unto the LORD.
7 Hear, O LORD, *when* I cry with my
voice: have mercy also upon me, and answer me.
8 *When thou saidst,* [z]Seek ye my face;
my heart said unto thee, Thy face, LORD,
will I seek.
9 [a]Hide not thy face *far* from me; put not
thy servant away in anger: thou hast been
my help; leave me not, neither forsake me,
O God of my salvation.
10 [b]When my father and my mother forsake me, then the LORD will take me up.
11 [c]Teach me thy way, O LORD, and lead
me in a plain path, because of mine enemies.
12 [d]Deliver me not over unto the will of
mine enemies: for [e]false witnesses are
risen up against me, and such as [f]breathe
out cruelty.
13 *I had fainted,* unless I had believed to
see the goodness of the LORD [g]in the land of
the living.
14 [h]Wait on the LORD: be of good courage, and he shall strengthen thine heart:
wait, I say, on the LORD.

A *Psalm* of David.

28 Unto thee will I cry, O LORD my rock;
[i]be not silent to me: [j]lest, *if* thou be
silent to me, I become like them that go
down into the pit.
2 Hear the voice of my supplications,
when I cry unto thee, [k]when I lift up my
hands [l]toward thy holy oracle.
3 [m]Draw me not away with the wicked,
and with the workers of iniquity, [n]which
speak peace to their neighbours, but mischief *is* in their hearts.
4 [o]Give them according to their deeds,
and according to the wickedness of their
endeavours: give them after the work of
their hands; render to them their desert.
5 Because [p]they regard not the works of
the LORD, nor the operation of his hands, he
shall destroy them, and not build them up.
6 Blessed *be* the LORD, because he hath
heard the voice of my supplications.
7 The LORD *is* [q]my strength and my
shield; my heart [r]trusted in him, and I am
helped: therefore my heart greatly rejoiceth; and with my song will I praise him.
8 The LORD *is* their strength, and he *is* the
[s]saving strength of his anointed.
9 Save thy people, and bless [t]thine inheritance: feed them also, [u]and lift them up for
ever.

A Psalm of David.

29 Give [v]unto the LORD, O ye mighty,
give unto the LORD glory and
strength.
2 Give unto the LORD the glory due unto
his name; worship the LORD in the [w]beauty
of holiness.
3 The voice of the LORD *is* upon the waters: [x]the God of glory thundereth: the
LORD *is* upon many waters.
4 The voice of the LORD *is* powerful; the
voice of the LORD *is* full of majesty.
5 The voice of the LORD breaketh the cedars; yea, the LORD breaketh [y]the cedars of
Lebanon.
6 [z]He maketh them also to skip like a
calf; Lebanon and [a]Sirion like a young unicorn.
7 The voice of the LORD divideth the
flames of fire.
8 The voice of the LORD shaketh the wilderness; the LORD shaketh the wilderness of
[b]Kadesh.
9 The voice of the LORD maketh [c]the
hinds to calve, and discovereth the forests:
and in his temple doth every one speak of
his glory.
10 The LORD [d]sitteth upon the flood; yea,
[e]the LORD sitteth King for ever.
11 [f]The LORD will give strength unto his
people; the LORD will bless his people with
peace.

A Psalm *and* Song *at* the dedication
of the house of David.

30 I will extol thee, O LORD; for thou
hast [g]lifted me up, and hast not
made my foes to [h]rejoice over me.
2 O LORD my God, I cried unto thee, and
thou hast [i]healed me.
3 O LORD, [j]thou hast brought up my soul
from the grave: thou hast kept me alive, that
I should not [k]go down to the pit.
4 [l]Sing unto the LORD, O ye saints of his,

26:9 [i]1 Sam. 25:29; Ps. 28:3
26:10 [j]Ex. 23:8; Deut. 16:19; 1 Sam. 8:3; Isa. 33:15
26:11 [k]ver. 1
26:12 [l]Ps. 40:2 [m]Ps. 27:11 [n]Ps. 22:22
27:1 [o]Ps. 84:11; Isa. 60:19; Mic. 7:8 [p]Ex. 15:2 [q]Ps. 62:2; Isa. 12:2
27:2 [r]Ps. 14:4
27:3 [s]Ps. 3:6
27:4 [t]Ps. 26:8 [u]Ps. 65:4; Luke 2:37 [v]Ps. 90:17
27:5 [w]Ps. 31:29; Isa. 4:6 [x]Ps. 40:2
27:6 [y]Ps. 3:3
27:8 [z]Ps. 24:6
27:9 [a]Ps. 69:17
27:10 [b]Isa. 49:15
27:11 [c]Ps. 25:4
27:12 [d]Ps. 35:25 [e]1 Sam. 22:9; 2 Sam. 16:7; Ps. 35:11 [f]Acts 9:1
27:13 [g]Ps. 56:13; Jer. 11:19; Ezek. 26:20
27:14 [h]Ps. 31:24; Isa. 25:9; Hab. 2:3
28:1 [i]Ps. 83:1 [j]Ps. 84:4
28:2 [k]1 Kings 6:22; Ps. 5:7 [l]Ps. 138:2
28:3 [m]Ps. 26:9 [n]Ps. 12:2; Jer. 9:8
28:4 [o]2 Tim. 4:14; Rev. 18:6
28:5 [p]Job 34:27; Isa. 5:12
28:7 [q]Ps. 18:2 [r]Ps. 13:5
28:8 [s]Ps. 20:6
28:9 [t]Deut. 9:29; 1 Kings 8:51 [u]Ezra 1:4
29:1 [v]1 Chron. 16:28; Ps. 96:7
29:2 [w]2 Chron. 20:21
29:3 [x]Job 37:4
29:5 [y]Isa. 2:13
29:6 [z]Ps. 114:4 [a]Deut. 3:9
29:8 [b]Num. 13:26
29:9 [c]Job 39:1
29:10 [d]Gen. 6:17; Job 38:8 [e]Ps. 10:16
29:11 [f]Ps. 28:8
30:1 [g]Ps. 28:9 [h]Ps. 25:2
30:2 [i]Ps. 6:2
30:3 [j]Ps. 86:13 [k]Ps. 28:1
30:4 [l]1 Chron. 16:4; Ps. 97:12

and give thanks at the remembrance of his holiness.

5 For [m]his anger *endureth but* a moment; [n]in his favour *is* life: weeping may endure for a night, [o]but joy *cometh* in the morning.

6 And [p]in my prosperity I said, I shall never be moved.

7 LORD, by thy favour thou hast made my mountain to stand strong: [q]thou didst hide thy face, *and* I was troubled.

8 I cried to thee, O LORD; and unto the LORD I made supplication.

9 What profit *is there* in my blood, when I go down to the pit? [r]Shall the dust praise thee? shall it declare thy truth?

10 Hear, O LORD, and have mercy upon me: LORD, be thou my helper.

11 [s]Thou hast turned for me my mourning into dancing: thou hast put off my sackcloth, and girded me with gladness;

12 To the end that *my* glory may sing praise to thee, and not be silent. O LORD my God, I will give thanks unto thee for ever.

To the chief Musician, A Psalm of David.

31 In [t]thee, O LORD, do I put my trust; let me never be ashamed: [u]deliver me in thy righteousness.

2 [v]Bow down thine ear to me; deliver me speedily: be thou my strong rock, for an house of defence to save me.

3 [w]For thou *art* my rock and my fortress; therefore [x]for thy name's sake lead me, and guide me.

4 Pull me out of the net that they have laid privily for me: for thou *art* my strength.

5 [y]Into thine hand I commit my spirit: thou hast redeemed me, O LORD God of truth.

6 I have hated them [z]that regard lying vanities: but I trust in the LORD.

7 I will be glad and rejoice in thy mercy: for thou hast considered my trouble; thou hast [a]known my soul in adversities;

8 And hast not [b]shut me up into the hand of the enemy: [c]thou hast set my feet in a large room.

9 Have mercy upon me, O LORD, for I am in trouble: [d]mine eye is consumed with grief, *yea,* my soul and my belly.

10 For my life is spent with grief, and my years with sighing: my strength faileth because of mine iniquity, and [e]my bones are consumed.

11 [f]I was a reproach among all mine enemies, but [g]especially among my neighbours, and a fear to mine acquaintance: [h]they that did see me without fled from me.

12 [i]I am forgotten as a dead man out of mind: I am like a broken vessel.

13 [j]For I have heard the slander of many: [k]fear *was* on every side: while they [l]took counsel together against me, they devised to take away my life.

14 But I trusted in thee, O LORD: I said, Thou *art* my God.

15 My times *are* in thy hand: deliver me from the hand of mine enemies, and from them that persecute me.

16 [m]Make thy face to shine upon thy servant: save me for thy mercies' sake.

17 [n]Let me not be ashamed, O LORD; for I have called upon thee: let the wicked be ashamed, *and* [o]let them be silent in the grave.

18 [p]Let the lying lips be put to silence; which [q]speak grievous things proudly and contemptuously against the righteous.

19 [r]*Oh* how great *is* thy goodness, which thou hast laid up for them that fear thee; *which* thou hast wrought for them that trust in thee before the sons of men!

20 [s]Thou shalt hide them in the secret of thy presence from the pride of man: [t]thou shalt keep them secretly in a pavilion from the strife of tongues.

21 Blessed *be* the LORD: for [u]he hath shewed me his marvellous kindness [v]in a strong city.

22 For [w]I said in my haste, [x]I am cut off from before thine eyes: nevertheless thou heardest the voice of my supplications when I cried unto thee.

23 [y]O love the LORD, all ye his saints: *for* the LORD preserveth the faithful, and plentifully rewardeth the proud doer.

24 [z]Be of good courage, and he shall strengthen your heart, all ye that hope in the LORD.

A Psalm of David, Maschil.

32 Blessed *is he whose* [a]transgression *is* forgiven, *whose* sin *is* covered.

2 Blessed *is* the man unto whom the LORD [b]imputeth not iniquity, and [c]in whose spirit *there is* no guile.

3 When I kept silence, my bones waxed old through my roaring all the day long.

4 For day and night thy [d]hand was heavy upon me: my moisture is turned into the drought of summer. Selah.

5 I acknowledged my sin unto thee, and mine iniquity have I not hid. [e]I said, I will confess my transgressions unto the LORD; and thou forgavest the iniquity of my sin. Selah.

6 [f]For this shall every one that is godly [g]pray unto thee in a time when thou mayest be found: surely in the floods of great waters they shall not come nigh unto him.

7 [h]Thou *art* my hiding place; thou shalt preserve me from trouble; thou shalt compass me about with [i]songs of deliverance. Selah.

8 I will instruct thee and teach thee in the way which thou shalt go: I will guide thee with mine eye.

9 [j]Be ye not as the horse, *or* as the mule, *which* have [k]no understanding: whose mouth must be held in with bit and bridle, lest they come near unto thee.

10 [l]Many sorrows *shall be* to the wicked: but [m]he that trusteth in the LORD, mercy shall compass him about.

11 [n]Be glad in the LORD, and rejoice, ye

30:5 [m]Ps. 103:9; Isa. 26:20; 2 Cor. 4:17 [n]Ps. 63:3 [o]Ps. 126:5
30:6 [p]Job 29:18
30:7 [q]Ps. 104:29
30:9 [r]Ps. 6:5; Isa. 38:18
30:11 [s]2 Sam. 6:14; Isa. 61:3; Jer. 31:4
31:1 [t]Ps. 22:5; Isa. 49:23 [u]Ps. 143:1
31:2 [v]Ps. 71:2
31:3 [w]Ps. 18:1 [x]Ps. 23:3
31:5 [y]Luke 23:46; Acts 7:59
31:6 [z]Jonah 2:8
31:7 [a]John 10:27
31:8 [b]Deut. 32:30; 1 Sam. 17:46 [c]Ps. 4:1
31:9 [d]Ps. 6:7
31:10 [e]Ps. 32:3
31:11 [f]Ps. 41:8; Isa. 53:4 [g]Job 19:13; Ps. 38:11 [h]Ps. 64:8
31:12 [i]Ps. 88:4
31:13 [j]Jer. 20:10 [k]Jer. 6:25; Lam. 2:22 [l]Matt. 27:1
31:16 [m]Num. 6:25; Ps. 4:6
31:17 [n]Ps. 25:2 [o]1 Sam. 2:9; Ps. 115:17
31:18 [p]Ps. 12:3 [q]1 Sam. 2:3; Ps. 94:4; Jude 15
31:19 [r]Isa. 64:4; 1 Cor. 2:9
31:20 [s]Ps. 27:5 [t]Job 5:21
31:21 [u]Ps. 17:7 [v]1 Sam. 23:7
31:22 [w]1 Sam. 23:26; Ps. 116:11 [x]Isa. 38:11; Lam. 3:54; Jonah 2:4
31:23 [y]Ps. 34:9
31:24 [z]Ps. 27:14
32:1 [a]Ps. 85:2; Rom. 4:6
32:2 [b]2 Cor. 5:19 [c]John 1:47
32:4 [d]1 Sam. 5:6; Job 33:7; Ps. 38:2
32:5 [e]Prov. 28:13; Isa. 65:24; Luke 15:18; 1 John 1:9
32:6 [f]1 Tim. 1:16 [g]Isa. 55:6; John 7:34
32:7 [h]Ps. 9:9 [i]Ex. 15:1; Judg. 5:1; 2 Sam. 22:1
32:9 [j]Prov. 26:3; Jam. 3:3 [k]Job 35:11
32:10 [l]Prov. 13:21; Rom. 2:9 [m]Ps. 34:8; Prov. 16:20; Jer. 17:7
32:11 [n]Ps. 64:10

righteous: and shout for joy, all *ye that are*
upright in heart.

33 Rejoice [o]in the LORD, O ye righteous: *for* [p]praise is comely for the
upright.
2 Praise the LORD with harp: sing unto
him with the psaltery [q]*and* an instrument of
ten strings.
3 [r]Sing unto him a new song; play skil-
fully with a loud noise.
4 For the word of the LORD *is* right; and all
his works *are done* in truth.
5 [s]He loveth righteousness and judgment: [t]the earth is full of the goodness of
the LORD.
6 [u]By the word of the LORD were the
heavens made; and [v]all the host of them
[w]by the breath of his mouth.
7 [x]He gathereth the waters of the sea together as an heap: he layeth up the depth in
storehouses.
8 Let all the earth fear the LORD: let all the
inhabitants of the world stand in awe of
him.
9 For [y]he spake, and it was *done;* he commanded, and it stood fast.
10 [z]The LORD bringeth the counsel of the
heathen to nought: he maketh the devices of
the people of none effect.
11 [a]The counsel of the LORD standeth for
ever, the thoughts of his heart to all generations.
12 [b]Blessed *is* the nation whose God *is*
the LORD; *and* the people *whom* he hath
[c]chosen for his own inheritance.
13 [d]The LORD looketh from heaven; he
beholdeth all the sons of men.
14 From the place of his habitation he
looketh upon all the inhabitants of the
earth.
15 He fashioneth their hearts alike; [e]he
considereth all their works.
16 [f]There is no king saved by the multitude of an host: a mighty man is not delivered by much strength.
17 [g]An horse *is* a vain thing for safety:
neither shall he deliver *any* by his great
strength.
18 [h]Behold, the eye of the LORD *is* [i]upon
them that fear him, upon them that hope in
his mercy;
19 To deliver their soul from death, and
[j]to keep them alive in famine.
20 [k]Our soul waiteth for the LORD: [l]he *is*
our help and our shield.
21 For our [m]heart shall rejoice in him, because we have trusted in his holy name.
22 Let thy mercy, O LORD, be upon us, according as we hope in thee.

A Psalm of David, when he changed his
behaviour before Abimelech; who drove him
away, and he departed.

34 I will [n]bless the LORD at all times: his
praise *shall* continually *be* in my
mouth.
2 My soul shall make her [o]boast in the
LORD: [p]the humble shall hear *thereof,* and
be glad.
3 O [q]magnify the LORD with me, and let
us exalt his name together.
4 I [r]sought the LORD, and he heard me,
and delivered me from all my fears.
5 They looked unto him, and were lightened: and their faces were not ashamed.
6 [s]This poor man cried, and the LORD
heard *him,* and [t]saved him out of all his
troubles.
7 [u]The angel of the LORD [v]encampeth
round about them that fear him, and delivereth them.
8 O [w]taste and see that the LORD *is* good:
[x]blessed *is* the man *that* trusteth in him.
9 [y]O fear the LORD, ye his saints: for
there is no want to them that fear him.
10 [z]The young lions do lack, and suffer
hunger: [a]but they that seek the LORD shall
not want any good *thing.*
11 Come, ye children, hearken unto me:
[b]I will teach you the fear of the LORD.
12 [c]What man *is he that* desireth life, *and*
loveth *many* days, that he may see good?
13 Keep thy tongue from evil, and thy lips
from [d]speaking guile.
14 [e]Depart from evil, and do good; [f]seek
peace, and pursue it.
15 [g]The eyes of the LORD *are* upon the
righteous, and his ears *are open* unto their
[h]cry.
16 [i]The face of the LORD *is* against them
that do evil, [j]to cut off the remembrance of
them from the earth.
17 *The righteous* cry, and [k]the LORD
heareth, and delivereth them out of all their
troubles.
18 [l]The LORD *is* nigh [m]unto them that are
of a broken heart; and saveth such as be of
a contrite spirit.
19 [n]Many *are* the afflictions of the righteous: [o]but the LORD delivereth him out of
them all.
20 He keepeth all his bones: [p]not one of
them is broken.
21 [q]Evil shall slay the wicked: and they
that hate the righteous shall be desolate.
22 The LORD [r]redeemeth the soul of his
servants: and none of them that trust in him
shall be desolate.

A Psalm of David.

35 Plead [s]*my cause,* O LORD, with them
that strive with me: [t]fight against
them that fight against me.
2 [u]Take hold of shield and buckler, and
stand up for mine help.
3 Draw out also the spear, and stop *the*
way against them that persecute me: say
unto my soul, I *am* thy salvation.
4 [v]Let them be confounded and put to
shame that seek after my soul: let them be
[w]turned back and brought to confusion that
devise my hurt.

33:1 [o]Ps. 32:11 [p]Ps. 147:1 **33:2** [q]Ps. 92:3 **33:3** [r]Ps. 96:1; Isa. 42:10; Rev. 5:9 **33:5** [s]Ps. 11:7 [t]Ps. 119:64 **33:6** [u]Gen. 1:6; Heb. 11:3; 2 Pet. 3:5 [v]Gen. 2:1 [w]Job 26:13 **33:7** [x]Gen. 1:9; Job 26:10 **33:9** [y]Gen. 1:3; Ps. 148:5 **33:10** [z]Isa. 8:10 **33:11** [a]Job 23:13; Prov. 19:21; Isa. 46:10 **33:12** [b]Ps. 65:4 [c]Ex. 19:5; Deut. 7:6 **33:13** [d]2 Chron. 16:9; Job 28:24; Ps. 11:4; Prov. 15:3 **33:15** [e]Job 34:21; Jer. 32:19 **33:16** [f]Ps. 44:6 **33:17** [g]Ps. 20:7; Prov. 21:31 **33:18** [h]Job 36:7; Ps. 34:15; 1 Pet. 3:12 [i]Ps. 147:11 **33:19** [j]Job 5:20; Ps. 37:19 **33:20** [k]Ps. 62:1 [l]Ps. 115:9 **33:21** [m]Ps. 13:5; Zech. 10:7; John 16:22 **34:1** [n]Eph. 5:20; 1 Thess. 5:18; 2 Thess. 1:3 **34:2** [o]Jer. 9:24; 1 Cor. 1:31; 2 Cor. 10:17 [p]Ps. 119:74 **34:3** [q]Ps. 69:30; Luke 1:46 **34:4** [r]Matt. 7:7; Luke 11:9 **34:6** [s]Ps. 3:4 [t]ver. 17; 2 Sam. 22:1 **34:7** [u]Dan. 6:22; Heb. 1:14 [v]Gen. 32:1; 2 Kings 6:17; Zech. 9:8 **34:8** [w]1 Pet. 2:3 [x]Ps. 2:12 **34:9** [y]Ps. 31:23 **34:10** [z]Job 4:10 [a]Ps. 84:11 **34:11** [b]Ps. 32:8 **34:12** [c]1 Pet. 3:10 **34:13** [d]1 Pet. 2:22 **34:14** [e]Ps. 37:27; Isa. 1:16 [f]Rom. 12:18; Heb. 12:14 **34:15** [g]Job 36:7; Ps. 33:18; 1 Pet. 3:12 [h]ver. 6 **34:16** [i]Lev. 17:10; Jer. 44:11; Am. 9:4 [j]Prov. 10:7 **34:17** [k]ver. 6; Ps. 145:19 **34:18** [l]Ps. 145:18 [m]Ps. 51:17; Isa. 57:15 **34:19** [n]Prov. 24:16; 2 Tim. 3:11 [o]ver. 6 **34:20** [p]John 19:36 **34:21** [q]Ps. 94:23 **34:22** [r]2 Sam. 4:9; 1 Kings 1:29; Ps. 71:23; Lam. 3:58 **35:1** [s]Ps. 43:1; Lam. 3:58 [t]Ex. 14:25 **35:2** [u]Isa. 42:13 **35:4** [v]ver. 26; Ps. 40:14 [w]Ps. 129:5

5 [x]Let them be as chaff before the wind: and let the angel of the LORD chase *them.*

6 Let their way be [y]dark and slippery: and let the angel of the LORD persecute them.

7 For without cause have they [z]hid for me their net *in* a pit, *which* without cause they have digged for my soul.

8 Let [a]destruction come upon him at unawares; and [b]let his net that he hath hid catch himself: into that very destruction let him fall.

9 And my soul shall be joyful in the LORD: [c]it shall rejoice in his salvation.

10 [d]All my bones shall say, LORD, [e]who *is* like unto thee, which deliverest the poor from him that is too strong for him, yea, the poor and the needy from him that spoileth him?

11 [f]False witnesses did rise up; they laid to my charge *things* that I knew not.

12 [g]They rewarded me evil for good *to* the spoiling of my soul.

13 But as for me, [h]when they were sick, my clothing *was* sackcloth: I humbled my soul with fasting; [i]and my prayer returned into mine own bosom.

14 I behaved myself as though *he had been* my friend *or* brother: I bowed down heavily, as one that mourneth *for his* mother.

15 But in mine adversity they rejoiced, and gathered themselves together: *yea,* [j]the abjects gathered themselves together against me, and I knew *it* not; they did [k]tear *me,* and ceased not:

16 With hypocritical mockers in feasts, [l]they gnashed upon me with their teeth.

17 Lord, how long wilt thou [m]look on? rescue my soul from their destructions, [n]my darling from the lions.

18 [o]I will give thee thanks in the great congregation: I will praise thee among much people.

19 [p]Let not them that are mine enemies wrongfully rejoice over me: *neither* [q]let them wink with the eye [r]that hate me without a cause.

20 For they speak not peace: but they devise deceitful matters against *them that are* quiet in the land.

21 Yea, they [s]opened their mouth wide against me, *and* said, [t]Aha, aha, our eye hath seen *it.*

22 *This* thou hast [u]seen, O LORD: [v]keep not silence: O Lord, be not [w]far from me.

23 [x]Stir up thyself, and awake to my judgment, *even* unto my cause, my God and my Lord.

24 [y]Judge me, O LORD my God, [z]according to thy righteousness; and [a]let them not rejoice over me.

25 [b]Let them not say in their hearts, Ah, so would we have it: let them not say, [c]We have swallowed him up.

26 [d]Let them be ashamed and brought to confusion together that rejoice at mine hurt: let them be [e]clothed with shame and dishonour that [f]magnify *themselves* against me.

27 [g]Let them shout for joy, and be glad, that favour my righteous cause: yea, let them [h]say continually, Let the LORD be magnified, [i]which hath pleasure in the prosperity of his servant.

28 [j]And my tongue shall speak of thy righteousness *and* of thy praise all the day long.

To the chief Musician, *A Psalm* of David the servant of the LORD.

36 The transgression of the wicked saith within my heart, *that* [k]*there is* no fear of God before his eyes.

2 For [l]he flattereth himself in his own eyes, until his iniquity be found to be hateful.

3 The words of his mouth *are* iniquity and [m]deceit: [n]he hath left off to be wise, *and* to do good.

4 [o]He deviseth mischief upon his bed; he setteth himself [p]in a way *that is* not good; he abhorreth not evil.

5 [q]Thy mercy, O LORD, *is* in the heavens; *and* thy faithfulness *reacheth* unto the clouds.

6 Thy righteousness *is* like the great mountains; [r]thy judgments *are* a great deep: O LORD, [s]thou preservest man and beast.

7 [t]How excellent *is* thy lovingkindness, O God! therefore the children of men [u]put their trust under the shadow of thy wings.

8 [v]They shall be abundantly satisfied with the fatness of thy house; and thou shalt make them drink of [w]the river [x]of thy pleasures.

9 [y]For with thee *is* the fountain of life: [z]in thy light shall we see light.

10 O continue thy lovingkindness [a]unto them that know thee; and thy righteousness to the [b]upright in heart.

11 Let not the foot of pride come against me, and let not the hand of the wicked remove me.

12 There are the workers of iniquity fallen: they are cast down, [c]and shall not be able to rise.

A Psalm of David.

37 Fret [d]not thyself because of evildoers, neither be thou envious against the workers of iniquity.

2 For they shall soon be cut down [e]like the grass, and wither as the green herb.

3 Trust in the LORD, and do good; *so* shalt thou dwell in the land, and verily thou shalt be fed.

4 [f]Delight thyself also in the LORD; and he shall give thee the desires of thine heart.

5 [g]Commit thy way unto the LORD; trust also in him; and he shall bring *it* to pass.

6 [h]And he shall bring forth thy righteousness as the light, and thy judgment as the noonday.

35:5 *x*Job 21:18; Ps. 1:4; Isa. 29:5; Hos. 13:3
35:6 *y*Ps. 73:18; Jer. 23:12
35:7 *z*Ps. 9:15
35:8 *a*1 Thess. 5:3 *b*Ps. 7:15; Prov. 5:22
35:9 *c*Ps. 13:5
35:10 *d*Ps. 51:8 *e*Ex. 15:11; Ps. 71:19
35:11 *f*Ps. 27:12
35:12 *g*Ps. 38:20; Jer. 18:20; John 10:32
35:13 *h*Job 30:25; Ps. 69:10 *i*Matt. 10:13; Luke 10:6
35:15 *j*Job 30:1 *k*Job 16:9
35:16 *l*Job 16:9; Ps. 37:12; Lam. 2:16
35:17 *m*Hab. 1:13 *n*Ps. 22:20
35:18 *o*Ps. 22:25
35:19 *p*Ps. 13:4 *q*Job 15:12; Prov. 6:13 *r*Ps. 69:4; Lam. 3:52; John 15:25
35:21 *s*Ps. 22:13 *t*Ps. 40:15
35:22 *u*Ex. 3:7; Acts 7:34 *v*Ps. 28:1 *w*Ps. 10:1
35:23 *x*Ps. 44:23
35:24 *y*Ps. 26:1 *z*2 Thess. 1:6 *a*ver. 19
35:25 *b*Ps. 27:12 *c*Lam. 2:16
35:26 *d*ver. 4; Ps. 40:14 *e*Ps. 109:29 *f*Ps. 38:16
35:27 *g*Rom. 12:15; 1 Cor. 12:26 *h*Ps. 70:4 *i*Ps. 149:4
35:28 *j*Ps. 50:15
36:1 *k*Rom. 3:18
36:2 *l*Deut. 29:19; Ps. 10:3
36:3 *m*Ps. 12:2 *n*Jer. 4:22
36:4 *o*Prov. 4:16; Mic. 2:1 *p*Isa. 65:2
36:5 *q*Ps. 57:10
36:6 *r*Job 11:8; Ps. 77:19; Rom. 11:33 *s*Job 7:20; Ps. 145:9; 1 Tim. 4:10
36:7 *t*Ps. 31:19 *u*Ruth 2:12; Ps. 17:8
36:8 *v*Ps. 65:4 *w*Job 20:17; Rev. 22:1 *x*Ps. 16:11
36:9 *y*Jer. 2:13; John 4:10 *z*1 Pet. 2:9
36:10 *a*Jer. 22:16 *b*Ps. 7:10
36:12 *c*Ps. 1:5
37:1 *d*ver. 7; Ps. 73:3; Prov. 23:17
37:2 *e*Ps. 90:5
37:4 *f*Isa. 58:14
37:5 *g*Ps. 55:22; Prov. 16:3; Matt. 6:25; Luke 12:22; 1 Pet. 5:7
37:6 *h*Job 11:17; Mic. 7:9

7 [i]Rest in the LORD, [j]and wait patiently for him: [k]fret not thyself because of him who prospereth in his way, because of the man who bringeth wicked devices to pass.

8 Cease from anger, and forsake wrath: [l]fret not thyself in any wise to do evil.

9 [m]For evildoers shall be cut off: but those that wait upon the LORD, they shall [n]inherit the earth.

10 For [o]yet a little while, and the wicked *shall* not *be:* yea, [p]thou shalt diligently consider his place, and it *shall* not *be.*

11 [q]But the meek shall inherit the earth; and shall delight themselves in the abundance of peace.

12 The wicked plotteth against the just, [r]and gnasheth upon him with his teeth.

13 [s]The Lord shall laugh at him: for he seeth that [t]his day is coming.

14 The wicked have drawn out the sword, and have bent their bow, to cast down the poor and needy, *and* to slay such as be of upright conversation.

15 [u]Their sword shall enter into their own heart, and their bows shall be broken.

16 [v]A little that a righteous man hath *is* better than the riches of many wicked.

17 For [w]the arms of the wicked shall be broken: but the LORD upholdeth the righteous.

18 The LORD [x]knoweth the days of the upright: and their inheritance shall be [y]for ever.

19 They shall not be ashamed in the evil time: and [z]in the days of famine they shall be satisfied.

20 But the wicked shall perish, and the enemies of the LORD *shall be* as the fat of lambs: they shall consume; [a]into smoke shall they consume away.

21 The wicked borroweth, and payeth not again: but [b]the righteous sheweth mercy, and giveth.

22 [c]For *such as be* blessed of him shall inherit the earth; and *they that be* cursed of him [d]shall be cut off.

23 [e]The steps of a *good* man are ordered by the LORD: and he delighteth in his way.

24 [f]Though he fall, he shall not be utterly cast down: for the LORD upholdeth *him with* his hand.

25 I have been young, and *now* am old; yet have I not seen the righteous forsaken, nor his seed [g]begging bread.

26 [h]*He is* ever merciful, and lendeth; and his seed *is* blessed.

27 [i]Depart from evil, and do good; and dwell for evermore.

28 For the LORD [j]loveth judgment, and forsaketh not his saints; they are preserved for ever: [k]but the seed of the wicked shall be cut off.

29 [l]The righteous shall inherit the land, and dwell therein for ever.

30 [m]The mouth of the righteous speaketh wisdom, and his tongue talketh of judgment.

37:7 [i]Ps. 62:1 [j]Isa. 30:15; Lam. 3:26 [k]ver. 1; Jer. 12:1
37:8 [l]Ps. 73:3; Eph. 4:26
37:9 [m]Job 27:13 [n]ver. 11; Isa. 57:13
37:10 [o]Heb. 10:36 [p]Job 7:10
37:11 [q]Matt. 5:5
37:12 [r]Ps. 35:16
37:13 [s]Ps. 2:4 [t]1 Sam. 26:10
37:15 [u]Mic. 5:6
37:16 [v]Prov. 15:16; 1 Tim. 6:6
37:17 [w]Job 38:15; Ps. 10:15; Ezek. 30:21
37:18 [x]Ps. 1:6 [y]Isa. 60:21
37:19 [z]Job 5:20; Ps. 33:19
37:20 [a]Ps. 102:3
37:21 [b]Ps. 112:5
37:22 [c]Prov. 3:33 [d]ver. 9
37:23 [e]1 Sam. 2:9; Prov. 16:9
37:24 [f]Ps. 34:19; Prov. 24:16; Mic. 7:8; 2 Cor. 4:9
37:25 [g]Job 15:23; Ps. 59:15
37:26 [h]Deut. 15:8; Ps. 112:5
37:27 [i]Ps. 34:14; Isa. 1:16
37:28 [j]Ps. 11:7 [k]Ps. 21:10; Prov. 2:22; Isa. 14:20
37:29 [l]Prov. 2:21
37:30 [m]Matt. 12:35
37:31 [n]Deut. 6:6; Ps. 40:8; Isa. 51:7
37:32 [o]Ps. 10:8
37:33 [p]2 Pet. 2:9 [q]Ps. 109:31
37:34 [r]ver. 9; Ps. 27:14; Prov. 20:22 [s]Ps. 52:5
37:35 [t]Job 5:3
37:36 [u]Job 20:5
37:37 [v]Isa. 32:17
37:38 [w]Ps. 1:4
37:39 [x]Ps. 3:8 [y]Ps. 9:9
37:40 [z]Isa. 31:5 [a]1 Chron. 5:20; Dan. 3:17
38:1 [b]Ps. 6:1
38:2 [c]Job 6:4 [d]Ps. 32:4
38:3 [e]Ps. 6:2
38:4 [f]Ezra 9:6; Ps. 40:12 [g]Matt. 11:28
38:6 [h]Ps. 35:14 [i]Job 30:28; Ps. 42:9
38:7 [j]Job 7:5 [k]ver. 3
38:8 [l]Job 3:24; Ps. 22:1; Isa. 59:11
38:10 [m]Ps. 6:7
38:11 [n]Ps. 31:11 [o]Luke 10:31 [p]Luke 23:49
38:12 [q]2 Sam. 17:1 [r]2 Sam. 16:7 [s]Ps. 35:20
38:13 [t]2 Sam. 16:10 [u]Ps. 39:2

31 [n]The law of his God *is* in his heart; none of his steps shall slide.

32 The wicked [o]watcheth the righteous, and seeketh to slay him.

33 The LORD [p]will not leave him in his hand, nor [q]condemn him when he is judged.

34 [r]Wait on the LORD, and keep his way, and he shall exalt thee to inherit the land: [s]when the wicked are cut off, thou shalt see *it.*

35 [t]I have seen the wicked in great power, and spreading himself like a green bay tree.

36 Yet he [u]passed away, and, lo, he *was* not: yea, I sought him, but he could not be found.

37 Mark the perfect *man,* and behold the upright: for [v]the end of *that* man *is* peace.

38 [w]But the transgressors shall be destroyed together: the end of the wicked shall be cut off.

39 But [x]the salvation of the righteous *is* of the LORD: *he is* their strength [y]in the time of trouble.

40 And [z]the LORD shall help them, and deliver them: he shall deliver them from the wicked, and save them, [a]because they trust in him.

A Psalm of David, to bring to remembrance.

38 O [b]LORD, rebuke me not in thy wrath: neither chasten me in thy hot displeasure.

2 For [c]thine arrows stick fast in me, and [d]thy hand presseth me sore.

3 *There is* no soundness in my flesh because of thine anger; [e]neither *is there any* rest in my bones because of my sin.

4 For [f]mine iniquities are gone over mine head: as an heavy burden they are too [g]heavy for me.

5 My wounds stink *and* are corrupt because of my foolishness.

6 I am troubled; [h]I am bowed down greatly; [i]I go mourning all the day long.

7 For my loins are filled with a [j]loathsome *disease:* and *there is* [k]no soundness in my flesh.

8 I am feeble and sore broken: [l]I have roared by reason of the disquietness of my heart.

9 Lord, all my desire *is* before thee; and my groaning is not hid from thee.

10 My heart panteth, my strength faileth me: as for [m]the light of mine eyes, it also is gone from me.

11 [n]My lovers and my friends [o]stand aloof from my sore; and my kinsmen [p]stand afar off.

12 They also that seek after my life [q]lay snares *for me:* and they that seek my hurt [r]speak mischievous things, and [s]imagine deceits all the day long.

13 But [t]I, as a deaf *man,* heard not; [u]and *I was* as a dumb man *that* openeth not his mouth.

14 Thus I was as a man that heareth not, and in whose mouth *are* no reproofs.

15 For in thee, O LORD, [v]do I hope: thou wilt hear, O Lord my God.

16 For I said, *Hear me,* [w]lest *otherwise* they should rejoice over me: when my [x]foot slippeth, they [y]magnify *themselves* against me.

17 For I *am* ready to halt, and my sorrow *is* continually before me.

18 For I will [z]declare mine iniquity; I will be [a]sorry for my sin.

19 But mine enemies *are* lively, *and* they are strong: and they that [b]hate me wrongfully are multiplied.

20 They also [c]that render evil for good are mine adversaries; [d]because I follow *the thing that* good *is.*

21 Forsake me not, O LORD: O my God, [e]be not far from me.

22 Make haste to help me, O Lord [f]my salvation.

To the chief Musician, *even* to Jeduthun, A Psalm of David.

39 I said, I will [g]take heed to my ways, that I sin not with my tongue: I will keep [h]my mouth with a bridle, [i]while the wicked is before me.

2 [j]I was dumb with silence, I held my peace, *even* from good; and my sorrow was stirred.

3 My heart was hot within me, while I was musing [k]the fire burned: *then* spake I with my tongue,

4 LORD, [l]make me to know mine end, and the measure of my days, what it *is; that* I may know how frail I *am.*

5 Behold, thou hast made my days *as* an hand breadth; and [m]mine age *is* as nothing before thee: [n]verily every man at his best state *is* altogether vanity. Selah.

6 Surely every man walketh in [o]a vain shew: surely they are disquieted in vain: [p]he heapeth up *riches,* and knoweth not who shall gather them.

7 And now, Lord, what wait I for? [q]my hope *is* in thee.

8 Deliver me from all my transgressions: make me not [r]the reproach of the foolish.

9 [s]I was dumb, I opened not my mouth; because [t]thou didst *it.*

10 [u]Remove thy stroke away from me: I am consumed by the blow of thine hand.

11 When thou with rebukes dost correct man for iniquity, thou makest his beauty [v]to consume away like a moth: [w]surely every man *is* vanity. Selah.

12 Hear my prayer, O LORD, and give ear unto my cry; hold not thy peace at my tears: [x]for I *am* a stranger with thee, *and* a sojourner, [y]as all my fathers *were.*

13 [z]O spare me, that I may recover strength, before I go hence, and [a]be no more.

38:15 [v]2 Sam. 16:12; Ps. 39:7
38:16 [w]Ps. 13:4 [x]Deut. 32:35 [y]Ps. 35:26
38:18 [z]Ps. 32:5; Prov. 28:13 [a]2 Cor. 7:9
38:19 [b]Ps. 35:39
38:20 [c]Ps. 35:12 [d]1 John 3:12
38:21 [e]Ps. 35:22
38:22 [f]Ps. 27:1; Isa. 12:2
39:1 [g]1 Kings 2:4; 2 Kings 10:31 [h]Ps. 141:3; Jam. 3:2 [i]Col. 4:5
39:2 [j]Ps. 38:13
39:3 [k]Jer. 20:9
39:4 [l]Ps. 90:12
39:5 [m]Ps. 90:4 [n]ver. 11; Ps. 62:9
39:6 [o]1 Cor. 7:31; Jam. 4:14 [p]Job 27:17; Eccl. 2:18; Luke 12:20
39:7 [q]Ps. 38:15
39:8 [r]Ps. 44:13
39:9 [s]Lev. 10:3; Job 40:4; Ps. 38:13 [t]2 Sam. 16:10; Job 2:10
39:10 [u]Job 9:34
39:11 [v]Job 4:19; Isa. 50:9; Hos. 5:12 [w]ver. 5
39:12 [x]Lev. 25:23; 1 Chron. 29:15; Ps. 119:19; 2 Cor. 5:6; Heb. 11:13; 1 Pet. 1:17 [y]Gen. 47:9
39:13 [z]Job 10:20 [a]Job 14:10
40:1 [b]Ps. 27:14
40:2 [c]Ps. 69:2 [d]Ps. 27:5 [e]Ps. 37:23
40:3 [f]Ps. 33:3 [g]Ps. 52:6
40:4 [h]Ps. 34:8; Jer. 17:7 [i]Ps. 101:3 [j]Ps. 125:5
40:5 [k]Ex. 11:15; Job 5:9; Ps. 71:15 [l]Isa. 55:8
40:6 [m]1 Sam. 15:22; Ps. 50:8; Isa. 1:11; Hos. 6:6; Matt. 9:13; Heb. 10:5
40:7 [n]Luke 24:44
40:8 [o]Ps. 119:16; John 4:34; Rom. 7:22 [p]Ps. 37:31; Jer. 31:33; 2 Cor. 3:3
40:9 [q]Ps. 22:22 [r]Ps. 119:13 [s]Ps. 139:2
40:10 [t]Acts 20:20
40:11 [u]Ps. 43:3
40:12 [v]Ps. 38:4 [w]Ps. 73:26
40:13 [x]Ps. 70:1
40:14 [y]Ps. 35:4
40:15 [z]Ps. 70:3 [a]Ps. 73:19
40:16 [b]Ps. 70:4 [c]Ps. 35:27
40:17 [d]Ps. 70:5 [e]1 Pet. 5:7
41:1 [f]Prov. 14:21

To the chief Musician, A Psalm of David.

40 I [b]waited patiently for the LORD; and he inclined unto me, and heard my cry.

2 He brought me up also out of an horrible pit, out of [c]the miry clay, and [d]set my feet upon a rock, *and* [e]established my goings.

3 [f]And he hath put a new song in my mouth, *even* praise unto our God: [g]many shall see *it,* and fear, and shall trust in the LORD.

4 [h]Blessed *is* that man that maketh the LORD his trust, and [i]respecteth not the proud, nor such as [j]turn aside to lies.

5 [k]Many, O LORD my God, *are* thy wonderful works *which* thou hast done, [l]and thy thoughts *which are* to us-ward: they cannot be reckoned up in order unto thee: *if* I would declare and speak *of them,* they are more than can be numbered.

6 [m]Sacrifice and offering thou didst not desire; mine ears hast thou opened: burnt offering and sin offering hast thou not required.

7 Then said I, Lo, I come: in the volume of the book *it is* [n]written of me,

8 [o]I delight to do thy will, O my God: yea, thy law *is* [p]within my heart.

9 [q]I have preached righteousness in the great congregation: lo, [r]I have not refrained my lips, O LORD, [s]thou knowest.

10 [t]I have not hid thy righteousness within my heart; I have declared thy faithfulness and thy salvation: I have not concealed thy lovingkindness and thy truth from the great congregation.

11 Withhold not thou thy tender mercies from me, O LORD: [u]let thy lovingkindness and thy truth continually preserve me.

12 For innumerable evils have compassed me about: [v]mine iniquities have taken hold upon me, so that I am not able to look up; they are more than the hairs of mine head: therefore [w]my heart faileth me.

13 [x]Be pleased, O LORD, to deliver me: O LORD, make haste to help me.

14 [y]Let them be ashamed and confounded together that seek after my soul to destroy it; let them be driven backward and put to shame that wish me evil.

15 [z]Let them be [a]desolate for a reward of their shame that say unto me, Aha, aha.

16 [b]Let all those that seek thee rejoice and be glad in thee: let such as love thy salvation [c]say continually, The LORD be magnified.

17 [d]But I *am* poor and needy; *yet* [e]the Lord thinketh upon me: thou *art* my help and my deliverer; make no tarrying, O my God.

To the chief Musician, A Psalm of David.

41 Blessed [f]*is* he that considereth the poor: the LORD will deliver him in time of trouble.

2 The LORD will preserve him, and keep him alive; *and* he shall be blessed upon the

earth: [g]and thou wilt not deliver him unto the will of his enemies.

3 The LORD will strengthen him upon the bed of languishing: thou wilt make all his bed in his sickness.

4 I said, LORD, be merciful unto me: [h]heal my soul; for I have sinned against thee.

5 Mine enemies speak evil of me, When shall he die, and his name perish?

6 And if he come to see *me,* he [i]speaketh vanity: his heart gathereth iniquity to itself; *when* he goeth abroad, he telleth *it.*

7 All that hate me whisper together against me: against me do they devise my hurt.

8 An evil disease, *say they,* cleaveth fast unto him: and *now* that he lieth he shall rise up no more.

9 [j]Yea, mine own familiar friend, in whom I trusted, [k]which did eat of my bread, hath lifted up *his* heel against me.

10 But thou, O LORD, be merciful unto me, and raise me up, that I may requite them.

11 By this I know that thou favourest me, because mine enemy doth not triumph over me.

12 And as for me, thou upholdest me in mine integrity, and [l]settest me before thy face for ever.

13 [m]Blessed *be* the LORD God of Israel from everlasting, and to everlasting. Amen, and Amen.

BOOK II

To the chief Musician, Maschil, for the sons of Korah.

42 As the hart panteth after the water brooks, so panteth my soul after thee, O God.

2 [n]My soul thirsteth for God, for [o]the living God: when shall I come and appear before God?

3 [p]My tears have been my meat day and night, while [q]they continually say unto me, Where *is* thy God?

4 When I remember these *things,* [r]I pour out my soul in me: for I had gone with the multitude, [s]I went with them to the house of God, with the voice of joy and praise, with a multitude that kept holyday.

5 [t]Why art thou cast down, O my soul? and *why* art thou disquieted in me? [u]hope thou in God: for I shall yet praise him *for* the help of his countenance.

6 O my God, my soul is cast down within me: therefore will I remember thee from the land of Jordan, and of the Hermonites, from the hill Mizar.

7 [v]Deep calleth unto deep at the noise of thy waterspouts: [w]all thy waves and thy billows are gone over me.

8 *Yet* the LORD will [x]command his lovingkindness in the daytime, and [y]in the night his song *shall be* with me, *and* my prayer unto the God of my life.

9 I will say unto God my rock, Why hast thou forgotten me? [z]why go I mourning because of the oppression of the enemy?

10 *As* with a sword in my bones, mine enemies reproach me; [a]while they say daily unto me, Where *is* thy God?

11 [b]Why art thou cast down, O my soul? and why art thou disquieted within me? hope thou in God: for I shall yet praise him, *who is* the health of my countenance, and my God.

43 [c]Judge me, O God, and [d]plead my cause against an ungodly nation: O deliver me from the deceitful and unjust man.

2 For thou *art* the God of [e]my strength: why dost thou cast me off? [f]why go I mourning because of the oppression of the enemy?

3 [g]O send out thy light and thy truth: let them lead me; let them bring me unto [h]thy holy hill, and to thy tabernacles.

4 Then will I go unto the altar of God, unto God my exceeding joy: yea, upon the harp will I praise thee, O God my God.

5 [i]Why art thou cast down, O my soul? and why art thou disquieted within me? hope in God: for I shall yet praise him, *who is* the health of my countenance, and my God.

To the chief Musician for the sons of Korah, Maschil.

44 We have heard with our ears, O God, [j]our fathers have told us, *what* work thou didst in their days, in the times of old.

2 *How* [k]thou didst drive out the heathen with thy hand, and plantedst them; *how* thou didst afflict the people, and cast them out.

3 For [l]they got not the land in possession by their own sword, neither did their own arm save them: but thy right hand, and thine arm, and the light of thy countenance, [m]because thou hadst a favour unto them.

4 [n]Thou art my King, O God: command deliverances for Jacob.

5 Through thee [o]will we push down our enemies: through thy name will we tread them under that rise up against us.

6 For [p]I will not trust in my bow, neither shall my sword save me.

7 But thou hast saved us from our enemies, and hast [q]put them to shame that hated us.

8 [r]In God we boast all the day long, and praise thy name for ever. Selah.

9 But [s]thou hast cast off, and put us to shame; and goest not forth with our armies.

10 Thou makest us to [t]turn back from the enemy: and they which hate us spoil for themselves.

11 [u]Thou hast given us like sheep *appointed* for meat; and hast [v]scattered us among the heathen.

12 [w]Thou sellest thy people for nought, and dost not increase *thy wealth* by their price.

13 [x]Thou makest us a reproach to our

41:2 g Ps. 27:12
41:4 h 2 Chron. 30:20; Ps. 6:2
41:6 i Ps. 12:2; Prov. 26:24
41:9 j 2 Sam. 15:12; Job 19:19; Ps. 55:12; Jer. 20:10 k Obad. 7; John 13:18
41:12 l Job 36:7; Ps. 34:15
41:13 m Ps. 106:48
42:2 n Ps. 63:1; John 7:37 o 1 Thess. 1:9
42:3 p Ps. 80:5 q ver. 10; Ps. 79:10
42:4 r Job 30:16; Ps. 62:8 s Isa. 30:29
42:5 t ver. 11 u Lam. 3:24
42:7 v Jer. 4:20; Ezek. 7:26 w Ps. 88:7; Jonah 2:3
42:8 x Lev. 25:21; Deut. 28:8; Ps. 133:3 y Job 35:10; Ps. 32:7
42:9 z Ps. 38:6
42:10 a ver. 3; Joel 2:17; Mic. 7:10
42:11 b ver. 5
43:1 c Ps. 26:1 d Ps. 35:1
43:2 e Ps. 28:7 f Ps. 42:9
43:3 g Ps. 40:11 h Ps. 3:4
43:5 i Ps. 42:5
44:1 j Ex. 12:26; Ps. 78:3
44:2 k Ex. 15:17; Deut. 7:1; Ps. 78:55
44:3 l Deut. 8:17; Josh. 24:12 m Deut. 4:37
44:4 n Ps. 74:12
44:5 o Dan. 8:4
44:6 p Ps. 33:16; Hos. 1:7
44:7 q Ps. 40:14
44:8 r Ps. 34:2; Jer. 9:24; Rom. 2:17
44:9 s Ps. 60:1
44:10 t Lev. 26:17; Deut. 28:25; Josh. 7:8
44:11 u Rom. 8:36 v Deut. 4:27; Ps. 60:1
44:12 w Isa. 52:3; Jer. 15:13
44:13 x Deut. 28:37; Ps. 79:4

neighbours, a scorn and a derision to them that are round about us.

14 [y]Thou makest us a byword among the heathen, [z]a shaking of the head among the people.

15 My confusion *is* continually before me, and the shame of my face hath covered me,

16 For the voice of him that reproacheth and blasphemeth; [a]by reason of the enemy and avenger.

17 [b]All this is come upon us; yet have we not forgotten thee, neither have we dealt falsely in thy covenant.

18 Our heart is not turned back, [c]neither have our steps declined from thy way;

19 Though thou hast sore broken us in [d]the place of dragons, and covered us [e]with the shadow of death.

20 If we have forgotten the name of our God, or [f]stretched out our hands to a strange god;

21 [g]Shall not God search this out? for he knoweth the secrets of the heart.

22 [h]Yea, for thy sake are we killed all the day long; we are counted as sheep for the slaughter.

23 [i]Awake, why sleepest thou, O Lord? arise, [j]cast *us* not off for ever.

24 [k]Wherefore hidest thou thy face, *and* forgettest our affliction and our oppression?

25 For [l]our soul is bowed down to the dust: our belly cleaveth unto the earth.

26 Arise for our help, and redeem us for thy mercies' sake.

To the chief Musician upon Shoshannim, for the sons of Korah, Maschil, A Song of loves.

45

My heart is inditing a good matter: I speak of the things which I have made touching the king: my tongue *is* the pen of a ready writer.

2 Thou art fairer than the children of men: [m]grace is poured into thy lips: therefore God hath blessed thee for ever.

3 Gird thy [n]sword upon *thy* thigh, [o]O *most* mighty, with thy glory and thy majesty.

4 [p]And in thy majesty ride prosperously because of truth and meekness *and* righteousness; and thy right hand shall teach thee terrible things.

5 Thine arrows *are* sharp in the heart of the king's enemies; *whereby* the people fall under thee.

6 [q]Thy throne, O God, *is* for ever and ever: the sceptre of thy kingdom *is* a right sceptre.

7 [r]Thou lovest righteousness, and hatest wickedness: therefore [s]God, thy God, [t]hath anointed thee with the oil [u]of gladness above thy fellows.

8 [v]All thy garments *smell* of myrrh, and aloes, *and* cassia, out of the ivory palaces, whereby they have made thee glad.

9 [w]Kings' daughters *were* among thy honourable women: [x]upon thy right hand did stand the queen in gold of Ophir.

10 Hearken, O daughter, and consider, and incline thine ear; [y]forget also thine own people, and thy father's house;

11 So shall the king greatly desire thy beauty: [z]for he *is* thy Lord; and worship thou him.

12 And the daughter of Tyre *shall be there* with a gift; *even* [a]the rich among the people shall intreat thy favour.

13 [b]The king's daughter *is* all glorious within: her clothing *is* of wrought gold.

14 [c]She shall be brought unto the king in raiment of needlework: the virgins her companions that follow her shall be brought unto thee.

15 With gladness and rejoicing shall they be brought: they shall enter into the king's palace.

16 Instead of thy fathers shall be thy children, [d]whom thou mayest make princes in all the earth.

17 [e]I will make thy name to be remembered in all generations: therefore shall the people praise thee for ever and ever.

To the chief Musician for the sons of Korah, A Song upon Alamoth.

46

God *is* our [f]refuge and strength, [g]a very present help in trouble.

2 Therefore will not we fear, though the earth be removed, and though the mountains be carried into the midst of the sea;

3 [h]*Though* the waters thereof roar *and* be troubled, *though* the mountains shake with the swelling thereof. Selah.

4 *There is* [i]a river, the streams whereof shall make glad [j]the city of God, the holy *place* of the tabernacles of the most High.

5 God *is* [k]in the midst of her; she shall not be moved: God shall help her, *and that* right early.

6 [l]The heathen raged, the kingdoms were moved: he uttered his voice, [m]the earth melted.

7 [n]The LORD of hosts *is* with us; the God of Jacob *is* our refuge. Selah.

8 [o]Come, behold the works of the LORD, what desolations he hath made in the earth.

9 [p]He maketh wars to cease unto the end of the earth; [q]he breaketh the bow, and cutteth the spear in sunder; [r]he burneth the chariot in the fire.

10 Be still, and know that I *am* God: [s]I will be exalted among the heathen, I will be exalted in the earth.

11 [t]The LORD of hosts *is* with us; the God of Jacob *is* our refuge. Selah.

To the chief Musician, A Psalm for the sons of Korah.

47

O [u]clap your hands, all ye people; shout unto God with the voice of triumph.

2 For the LORD most high *is* [v]terrible; [w]*he is* a great King over all the earth.

3 [x]He shall subdue the people under us, and the nations under our feet.

4 He shall choose our [y]inheritance for us, the excellency of Jacob whom he loved. Selah.

44:14 [y]Jer. 24:9 [z]2 Kings 19:21; Job 16:4; Ps. 22:7
44:16 [a]Ps. 8:2
44:17 [b]Dan. 9:13
44:18 [c]Job 23:11; Ps. 119:51
44:19 [d]Isa. 34:13 [e]Ps. 23:4
44:20 [f]Job 11:13; Ps. 68:31
44:21 [g]Job 31:14; Ps. 139:1; Jer. 17:10
44:22 [h]Rom. 8:36
44:23 [i]Ps. 7:6 [j]ver. 9
44:24 [k]Job 13:24; Ps. 13:1
44:25 [l]Ps. 119:25
45:2 [m]Luke 4:22
45:3 [n]Isa. 49:2; Heb. 4:12; Rev. 1:16 [o]Isa. 9:6
45:4 [p]Rev. 6:2
45:6 [q]Ps. 93:2; Heb. 1:8
45:7 [r]Ps. 33:5 [s]Isa. 61:1 [t]1 Kings 1:39 [u]Ps. 21:6
45:8 [v]SSol. 1:3
45:9 [w]SSol. 6:8 [x]1 Kings 2:9
45:10 [y]Deut. 21:13
45:11 [z]Ps. 95:6; Isa. 54:5
45:12 [a]Ps. 22:29; Isa. 49:23
45:13 [b]Rev. 19:7
45:14 [c]SSol. 1:4
45:16 [d]1 Pet. 2:9; Rev. 1:6
45:17 [e]Mal. 1:11
46:1 [f]Ps. 62:7 [g]Deut. 4:7; Ps. 145:18
46:3 [h]Ps. 93:3; Jer. 5:22; Matt. 7:25
46:4 [i]Isa. 8:7 [j]Ps. 48:1; Isa. 60:14
46:5 [k]Deut. 23:14; Isa. 12:6; Ezek. 43:7; Hos. 11:9; Joel 2:27; Zeph. 3:15; Zech. 2:5
46:6 [l]Ps. 2:1 [m]Josh. 2:9
46:7 [n]ver. 11; Num. 14:9; 2 Chron. 13:12
46:8 [o]Ps. 66:5
46:9 [p]Isa. 2:4 [q]Ps. 76:3 [r]Ezek. 39:9
46:10 [s]Isa. 2:11
46:11 [t]ver. 7
47:1 [u]Isa. 55:12
47:2 [v]Deut. 7:21; Neh. 1:5; Ps. 76:12 [w]Mal. 1:14
47:3 [x]Ps. 18:47
47:4 [y]1 Pet. 1:4

5 [z]God is gone up with a shout, the LORD
with the sound of a trumpet.
6 Sing praises to God, sing praises: sing
praises unto our King, sing praises.
7 [a]For God *is* the King of all the earth:
[b]sing ye praises with understanding.
8 [c]God reigneth over the heathen: God
sitteth upon the throne of his holiness.
9 The princes of the people are gathered
together, [d]*even* the people of the God of
Abraham: [e]for the shields of the earth *be-*
long unto God: he is greatly exalted.

A Song *and* Psalm for the sons of Korah.

48 Great *is* the LORD, and greatly to be
praised [f]in the city of our God, *in* the
[g]mountain of his holiness.
2 [h]Beautiful for situation, [i]the joy of the
whole earth, *is* mount Zion, [j]*on* the sides of
the north, [k]the city of the great King.
3 God is known in her palaces for a refuge.
4 For, lo, [l]the kings were assembled,
they passed by together.
5 They saw *it, and* so they marvelled; they
were troubled, *and* hasted away.
6 Fear [m]took hold upon them there, [n]*and*
pain, as of a woman in travail.
7 Thou [o]breakest the ships of Tarshish
[p]with an east wind.
8 As we have heard, so have we seen in
[q]the city of the LORD of hosts, in the city of
our God: God will [r]establish it for ever.
Selah.
9 We have thought of [s]thy lovingkindness, O God, in the midst of thy temple.
10 According to [t]thy name, O God, so *is*
thy praise unto the ends of the earth: thy
right hand is full of righteousness.
11 Let mount Zion rejoice, let the daughters of Judah be glad, because of thy judgments.
12 Walk about Zion, and go round about
her: tell the towers thereof.
13 Mark ye well her bulwarks, consider
her palaces; that ye may tell *it* to the generation following.
14 For this God *is* our God for ever and
ever: he will [u]be our guide *even* unto death.

To the chief Musician, A Psalm for the sons of Korah.

49 Hear this, all *ye* people; give ear, all
ye inhabitants of the world:
2 Both [v]low and high, rich and poor, together.
3 My mouth shall speak of wisdom; and
the meditation of my heart *shall be* of understanding.
4 [w]I will incline mine ear to a parable: I
will open my dark saying upon the harp.
5 Wherefore should I fear in the days of
evil, *when* [x]the iniquity of my heels shall
compass me about?
6 They that [y]trust in their wealth, and
boast themselves in the multitude of their
riches;
7 None *of them* can by any means redeem

47:5 [z]Ps. 68:24
47:7 [a]Zech. 14:9
[b]1 Cor. 14:15
47:8
[c]1 Chron. 16:31;
Ps. 93:1; Rev. 19:6
47:9 [d]Rom. 4:11
[e]Ps. 89:18
48:1 [f]Ps. 46:4
[g]Isa. 2:2; Mic. 4:1;
Zech. 8:3
48:2 [h]Ps. 50:2;
Jer. 3:19;
Lam. 2:15; Dan. 8:9
[i]Ezek. 20:6
[j]Isa. 14:13
[k]Matt. 5:35
48:4 [l]2 Sam. 10:6
48:6 [m]Ex. 15:15
[n]Hos. 13:13
48:7 [o]Ezek. 27:26
[p]Jer. 18:17
48:8 [q]ver. 1
[r]Isa. 2:2; Mic. 4:1
48:9 [s]Ps. 26:3
48:10
[t]Deut. 28:58;
Josh. 7:9;
Ps. 113:3;
Mal. 1:11
48:14 [u]Isa. 58:11
49:2 [v]Ps. 62:9
49:4 [w]Ps. 78:2;
Matt. 13:35
49:5 [x]Ps. 38:4
49:6 [y]Job 31:24;
Ps. 52:7;
Mark 10:24;
1 Tim. 6:17
49:7 [z]Matt. 16:26
49:8 [a]Job 36:18
49:9 [b]Ps. 89:48
49:10 [c]Eccl. 2:16
[d]Prov. 11:4;
Eccl. 2:18
49:11 [e]Gen. 4:17
49:12 [f]ver. 20;
Ps. 39:5
49:13 [g]Luke 12:20
49:14 [h]Ps. 47:3;
Dan. 7:22;
Mal. 4:3;
Luke 22:30;
1 Cor. 6:2;
Rev. 2:26
[i]Job 4:21;
Ps. 39:11
49:15 [j]Ps. 56:13;
Hos. 13:14
49:17 [k]Job 27:19
49:18
[l]Deut. 29:19;
Luke 12:19
49:19
[m]Gen. 15:15
[n]Job 33:30;
Ps. 56:13
49:20 [o]ver. 12
[p]Eccl. 3:19
50:1 [q]Neh. 9:32;
Isa. 9:6; Jer. 32:18
50:2 [r]Ps. 48:2
[s]Deut. 33:2;
Ps. 80:1
50:3 [t]Lev. 10:2;
Num. 16:35;
Ps. 97:3; Dan. 7:10
50:4 [u]Deut. 4:26;
Isa. 1:2; Mic. 6:1
50:5 [v]Deut. 33:3;
Isa. 13:3 [w]Ex. 24:7
50:6 [x]Ps. 97:6
[y]Ps. 75:7
50:7 [z]Ps. 81:8
[a]Ex. 20:2
50:8 [b]Isa. 1:11;
Jer. 7:22 [c]Hos. 6:6
50:9 [d]Mic. 6:6;
Acts 17:25

his brother, nor [z]give to God a ransom for
him:
8 (For [a]the redemption of their soul *is*
precious, and it ceaseth for ever:)
9 That he should still live for ever, *and*
[b]not see corruption.
10 For he seeth *that* [c]wise men die, likewise the fool and the brutish person perish,
[d]and leave their wealth to others.
11 Their inward thought *is, that* their
houses *shall continue* for ever, *and* their
dwelling places to all generations; they
[e]call *their* lands after their own names.
12 Nevertheless [f]man *being* in honour
abideth not: he is like the beasts *that* perish.
13 This their way *is* their [g]folly: yet their
posterity approve their sayings. Selah.
14 Like sheep they are laid in the grave;
death shall feed on them; and [h]the upright
shall have dominion over them in the morning; [i]and their beauty shall consume in the
grave from their dwelling.
15 But God [j]will redeem my soul from
the power of the grave: for he shall receive
me. Selah.
16 Be not thou afraid when one is made
rich, when the glory of his house is increased;
17 [k]For when he dieth he shall carry
nothing away: his glory shall not descend
after him.
18 Though while he lived [l]he blessed his
soul: and *men* will praise thee, when thou
doest well to thyself.
19 He shall [m]go to the generation of his
fathers; they shall never see [n]light.
20 [o]Man *that is* in honour, and understandeth not, [p]is like the beasts *that* perish.

A Psalm of Asaph.

50 The [q]mighty God, *even* the LORD,
hath spoken, and called the earth
from the rising of the sun unto the going
down thereof.
2 Out of Zion, [r]the perfection of beauty,
[s]God hath shined.
3 Our God shall come, and shall not keep
silence: [t]a fire shall devour before him, and
it shall be very tempestuous round about
him.
4 [u]He shall call to the heavens from
above, and to the earth, that he may judge
his people.
5 Gather [v]my saints together unto me;
[w]those that have made a covenant with me
by sacrifice.
6 And [x]the heavens shall declare his
righteousness: for [y]God *is* judge himself.
Selah.
7 [z]Hear, O my people, and I will speak;
O Israel, and I will testify against thee: [a]I
am God, *even* thy God.
8 [b]I will not reprove thee [c]for thy sacrifices or thy burnt offerings, *to have been*
continually before me.
9 [d]I will take no bullock out of thy house,
nor he goats out of thy folds.

10 For every beast of the forest *is* mine,
and the cattle upon a thousand hills.
11 I know all the fowls of the mountains:
and the wild beasts of the field *are* mine.
12 If I were hungry, I would not tell thee:
[e]for the world *is* mine, and the fulness
thereof.
13 Will I eat the flesh of bulls, or drink the
blood of goats?
14 [f]Offer unto God thanksgiving; and
[g]pay thy vows unto the most High:
15 And [h]call upon me in the day of trouble: I will deliver thee, and thou shalt [i]glo-
rify me.
16 But unto the wicked God saith, What
hast thou to do to declare my statutes, or
that thou shouldest take my covenant in thy
mouth?
17 [j]Seeing thou hatest instruction, and
[k]castest my words behind thee.
18 When thou sawest a thief, then thou
[l]consentedst with him, and hast been [m]par-
taker with adulterers.
19 Thou givest thy mouth to evil, and
[n]thy tongue frameth deceit.
20 Thou sittest *and* speakest against thy
brother; thou slanderest thine own mother's
son.
21 These *things* hast thou done, [o]and I
kept silence; [p]thou thoughtest that I was
altogether *such an one* as thyself: *but* [q]I
will reprove thee, and set *them* in order before thine eyes.
22 Now consider this, ye that [r]forget
God, lest I tear *you* in pieces, and *there be*
none to deliver.
23 [s]Whoso offereth praise glorifieth me:
and [t]to him that ordereth *his* conversation
aright will I shew the salvation of God.

To the chief Musician, A Psalm of David,
when Nathan the prophet came unto him,
after he had gone in to Bath-sheba.

51 Have mercy upon me, O God, according to thy lovingkindness: according unto the multitude of thy tender
mercies [u]blot out my transgressions.
2 [v]Wash me throughly from mine iniquity, and cleanse me from my sin.
3 For [w]I acknowledge my transgressions:
and my sin *is* ever before me.
4 [x]Against thee, thee only, have I sinned,
and done *this* evil [y]in thy sight: [z]that thou
mightest be justified when thou speakest,
and be clear when thou judgest.
5 [a]Behold, I was shapen in iniquity; [b]and
in sin did my mother conceive me.
6 Behold, thou desirest truth [c]in the inward parts: and in the hidden *part* thou
shalt make me to know wisdom.
7 [d]Purge me with hyssop, and I shall be
clean: wash me, and I shall be [e]whiter than
snow.
8 Make me to hear joy and gladness; *that*
the bones *which* thou hast broken [f]may rejoice.
9 [g]Hide thy face from my sins, and [h]blot
out all mine iniquities.

50:12 *e*Ex. 19:5; Deut. 10:14; Job 41:11; Ps. 24:1; 1 Cor. 10:26
50:14 *f*Hos. 14:2; Heb. 13:15 *g*Deut. 23:21; Job 22:27; Ps. 76:11; Eccl. 5:4
50:15 *h*Job 22:27; Ps. 91:15; Zech. 13:9 *i*ver. 23; Ps. 22:23
50:17 *j*Rom. 2:21 *k*Neh. 9:26
50:18 *l*Rom. 1:32 *m*1 Tim. 5:22
50:19 *n*Ps. 52:2
50:21 *o*Eccl. 8:11; Isa. 26:10 *p*Rom. 2:4 *q*Ps. 90:8
50:22 *r*Job 8:13; Ps. 9:17; Isa. 51:13
50:23 *s*Ps. 27:6; Rom. 12:1 *t*Gal. 6:16
51:1 *u*ver. 9; Isa. 43:25; Col. 2:14
51:2 *v*Heb. 9:14; 1 John 1:7; Rev. 1:5
51:3 *w*Ps. 32:5
51:4 *x*Gen. 20:6; Lev. 5:19; 2 Sam. 12:13 *y*Luke 15:21 *z*Rom. 3:4
51:5 *a*Job 14:4; Ps. 58:3; John 3:6; Rom. 5:12; Eph. 2:3 *b*Job 14:4
51:6 *c*Job 38:36
51:7 *d*Lev. 14:4; Num. 19:18; Heb. 9:19 *e*Isa. 1:18
51:8 *f*Matt. 5:4
51:9 *g*Jer. 16:17 *h*ver. 1
51:10 *i*Acts 15:9; Eph. 2:10
51:11 *j*Gen. 4:14; 2 Kings 13:23 *k*Rom. 8:9; Eph. 4:30
51:12 *l*2 Cor. 3:17
51:14 *m*2 Sam. 11:17 *n*Ps. 35:28
51:16 *o*Num. 15:27; Ps. 40:6; Isa. 1:11; Jer. 7:22; Hos. 6:6
51:17 *p*Ps. 34:18; Isa. 57:15
51:19 *q*Ps. 4:5; Mal. 3:3
52:1 *r*1 Sam. 21:7
52:2 *s*Ps. 50:19 *t*Ps. 57:4
52:3 *u*Jer. 9:4
52:5 *v*Prov. 2:22
52:6 *w*Job 22:19; Ps. 37:34; Mal. 1:5 *x*Ps. 58:10
52:7 *y*Ps. 49:6
52:8 *z*Jer. 11:16; Hos. 14:6
52:9 *a*Ps. 54:6
53:1 *b*Ps. 10:4 *c*Rom. 3:10
53:2 *d*Ps. 33:13 *e*2 Chron. 15:2

10 [i]Create in me a clean heart, O God;
and renew a right spirit within me.
11 Cast me not away [j]from thy presence;
and take not thy [k]holy spirit from me.
12 Restore unto me the joy of thy salvation; and uphold me *with thy* [l]free spirit.
13 *Then* will I teach transgressors thy
ways; and sinners shall be converted unto
thee.
14 Deliver me from [m]bloodguiltiness,
O God, thou God of my salvation: *and* [n]my
tongue shall sing aloud of thy righteousness.
15 O Lord, open thou my lips; and my
mouth shall shew forth thy praise.
16 For [o]thou desirest not sacrifice; else
would I give *it*: thou delightest not in burnt
offering.
17 [p]The sacrifices of God *are* a broken
spirit: a broken and a contrite heart, O God,
thou wilt not despise.
18 Do good in thy good pleasure unto
Zion: build thou the walls of Jerusalem.
19 Then shalt thou be pleased with [q]the
sacrifices of righteousness, with burnt offering and whole burnt offering: then shall
they offer bullocks upon thine altar.

To the chief Musician, Maschil, *A Psalm*
of David, when Doeg the Edomite came and
told Saul, and said unto him, David is come
to the house of Ahimelech.

52 Why boastest thou thyself in mischief, O [r]mighty man? the goodness
of God *endureth* continually.
2 [s]Thy tongue deviseth mischiefs; [t]like a
sharp razor, working deceitfully.
3 Thou lovest evil more than good; *and*
[u]lying rather than to speak righteousness.
Selah.
4 Thou lovest all devouring words, O
thou deceitful tongue.
5 God shall likewise destroy thee for ever,
he shall take thee away, and pluck thee out
of *thy* dwelling place, and [v]root thee out of
the land of the living. Selah.
6 [w]The righteous also shall see, and fear,
[x]and shall laugh at him:
7 Lo, *this is* the man *that* made not God
his strength; but [y]trusted in the abundance
of his riches, *and* strengthened himself in
his wickedness.
8 But I *am* [z]like a green olive tree in the
house of God: I trust in the mercy of God for
ever and ever.
9 I will praise thee for ever, because thou
hast done *it*: and I will wait on thy name;
[a]for *it is* good before thy saints.

To the chief Musician upon Mahalath,
Maschil, *A Psalm* of David.

53 The [b]fool hath said in his heart,
There is no God. Corrupt are they,
and have done abominable iniquity: [c]*there*
is none that doeth good.
2 God [d]looked down from heaven upon
the children of men, to see if there were *any*
that did understand, that did [e]seek God.
3 Every one of them is gone back: they

are altogether become filthy; *there is* none that doeth good, no, not one.

4 Have the workers of iniquity [f]no knowledge? who eat up my people *as* they eat bread: they have not called upon God.

5 [g]There were they in great fear, *where* no fear was: for God hath [h]scattered the bones of him that encampeth *against* thee: thou hast put *them* to shame, because God hath despised them.

6 [i]Oh that the salvation of Israel *were come* out of Zion! When God bringeth back the captivity of his people, Jacob shall rejoice, *and* Israel shall be glad.

To the chief Musician on Neginoth, Maschil, *A Psalm* of David, when the Ziphims came and said to Saul, Doth not David hide himself with us?

54 Save me, O God, by thy name, and judge me by thy strength.

2 Hear my prayer, O God; give ear to the words of my mouth.

3 For [j]strangers are risen up against me, and oppressors seek after my soul: they have not set God before them. Selah.

4 Behold, God *is* mine helper: [k]the Lord *is* with them that uphold my soul.

5 He shall reward evil unto mine enemies: cut them off [l]in thy truth.

6 I will freely sacrifice unto thee: I will praise thy name, O LORD; [m]for *it is* good.

7 For he hath delivered me out of all trouble: [n]and mine eye hath seen *his desire* upon mine enemies.

To the chief Musician on Neginoth, Maschil, *A Psalm* of David.

55 Give ear to my prayer, O God; and hide not thyself from my supplication.

2 Attend unto me, and hear me: I [o]mourn in my complaint, and make a noise;

3 Because of the voice of the enemy, because of the oppression of the wicked: [p]for they cast iniquity upon me, and in wrath they hate me.

4 [q]My heart is sore pained within me: and the terrors of death are fallen upon me.

5 Fearfulness and trembling are come upon me, and horror hath overwhelmed me.

6 And I said, Oh that I had wings like a dove! *for then* would I fly away, and be at rest.

7 Lo, *then* would I wander far off, *and* remain in the wilderness. Selah.

8 I would hasten my escape from the windy storm *and* tempest.

9 Destroy, O Lord, *and* divide their tongues: for I have seen [r]violence and strife in the city.

10 Day and night they go about it upon the walls thereof: mischief also and sorrow *are* in the midst of it.

11 Wickedness *is* in the midst thereof: deceit and guile depart not from her streets.

12 [s]For *it was* not an enemy *that* reproached me; then I could have borne *it:* neither *was it* he that hated me *that* did [t]magnify *himself* against me; then I would have hid myself from him:

13 But *it was* thou, a man mine equal, [u]my guide, and mine acquaintance.

14 We took sweet counsel together, *and* [v]walked unto the house of God in company.

15 Let death seize upon them, *and* let them [w]go down quick into hell: for wickedness *is* in their dwellings, *and* among them.

16 As for me, I will call upon God; and the LORD shall save me.

17 [x]Evening, and morning, and at noon, will I pray, and cry aloud: and he shall hear my voice.

18 He hath delivered my soul in peace from the battle *that was* against me: for [y]there were many with me.

19 God shall hear, and afflict them, [z]even he that abideth of old. Selah. Because they have no changes, therefore they fear not God.

20 He hath [a]put forth his hands against such as [b]be at peace with him: he hath broken his covenant.

21 [c]*The words* of his mouth were smoother than butter, but war *was* in his heart: his words were softer than oil, yet *were* they drawn swords.

22 [d]Cast thy burden upon the LORD, and he shall sustain thee: [e]he shall never suffer the righteous to be moved.

23 But thou, O God, shalt bring them down into the pit of destruction: [f]bloody and deceitful men [g]shall not live out half their days; but I will trust in thee.

To the chief Musician upon Jonath-elem-rechokim, Michtam of David, when the Philistines took him in Gath.

56 Be [h]merciful unto me, O God: for man would swallow me up; he fighting daily oppresseth me.

2 Mine enemies would daily [i]swallow *me* up: for *they be* many that fight against me, O thou most High.

3 What time I am afraid, I will trust in thee.

4 [j]In God I will praise his word, in God I have put my trust; [k]I will not fear what flesh can do unto me.

5 Every day they wrest my words: all their thoughts *are* against me for evil.

6 [l]They gather themselves together, they hide themselves, they mark my steps, [m]when they wait for my soul.

7 Shall they escape by iniquity? in *thine* anger cast down the people, O God.

8 Thou tellest my wanderings: put thou my tears into thy bottle: [n]*are they* not in thy book?

9 When I cry *unto thee,* then shall mine enemies turn back: this I know; for [o]God *is* for me.

10 [p]In God will I praise *his* word: in the LORD will I praise *his* word.

11 In God have I put my trust: I will not be afraid what man can do unto me.

53:4 [f]Jer. 4:22
53:5 [g]Lev. 26:17; Prov. 28:1 [h]Ezek. 6:5
53:6 [i]Ps. 14:7
54:3 [j]Ps. 86:14
54:4 [k]Ps. 118:7
54:5 [l]Ps. 89:49
54:6 [m]Ps. 52:9
54:7 [n]Ps. 59:10
55:2 [o]Isa. 38:14
55:3 [p]2 Sam. 16:7
55:4 [q]Ps. 116:3
55:9 [r]Jer. 6:7
55:12 [s]Ps. 41:9 [t]Ps. 35:26
55:13 [u]2 Sam. 15:12; Ps. 41:9; Jer. 9:4
55:14 [v]Ps. 42:4
55:15 [w]Num. 16:30
55:17 [x]Dan. 6:10; Luke 18:1; Acts 3:1; 1 Thess. 5:17
55:18 [y]2 Chron. 32:7
55:19 [z]Deut. 33:27
55:20 [a]Acts 12:1 [b]Ps. 7:4
55:21 [c]Ps. 28:3; Prov. 5:3
55:22 [d]Ps. 37:5; Matt. 6:25; Luke 12:22; 1 Pet. 5:7 [e]Ps. 37:24
55:23 [f]Ps. 5:6 [g]Job 15:32; Prov. 10:27; Eccl. 7:17
56:1 [h]Ps. 57:1
56:2 [i]Ps. 57:3
56:4 [j]ver. 10 [k]Ps. 118:6; Isa. 31:3; Heb. 13:6
56:6 [l]Ps. 59:3 [m]Ps. 71:10
56:8 [n]Mal. 3:16
56:9 [o]Rom. 8:31
56:10 [p]ver. 4

12 Thy vows *are* upon me, O God: I will render praises unto thee.

13 For [q]thou hast delivered my soul from death: *wilt* not *thou deliver* my feet from falling, that I may walk before God in [r]the light of the living?

To the chief Musician, Al-taschith, Michtam of David, when he fled from Saul in the cave.

57 Be [s]merciful unto me, O God, be merciful unto me: for my soul trusteth in thee: [t]yea, in the shadow of thy wings will I make my refuge, [u]until *these* calamities be overpast.

2 I will cry unto God most high; unto God [v]that performeth *all things* for me.

3 [w]He shall send from heaven, and save me *from* the reproach of him that would [x]swallow me up. Selah. God [y]shall send forth his mercy and his truth.

4 My soul *is* among lions: *and* I lie *even among* them that are set on fire, *even* the sons of men, [z]whose teeth *are* spears and arrows, and [a]their tongue a sharp sword.

5 [b]Be thou exalted, O God, above the heavens; *let* thy glory *be* above all the earth.

6 [c]They have prepared a net for my steps; my soul is bowed down: they have digged a pit before me, into the midst whereof they are fallen *themselves*. Selah.

7 [d]My heart is fixed, O God, my heart is fixed: I will sing and give praise.

8 Awake up, [e]my glory; awake, psaltery and harp: I *myself* will awake early.

9 [f]I will praise thee, O Lord, among the people: I will sing unto thee among the nations.

10 [g]For thy mercy *is* great unto the heavens, and thy truth unto the clouds.

11 [h]Be thou exalted, O God, above the heavens: *let* thy glory *be* above all the earth.

To the chief Musician, Al-taschith, Michtam of David.

58 Do ye indeed speak righteousness, O congregation? do ye judge uprightly, O ye sons of men?

2 Yea, in heart ye work wickedness; [i]ye weigh the violence of your hands in the earth.

3 [j]The wicked are estranged from the womb: they go astray as soon as they be born, speaking lies.

4 [k]Their poison *is* like the poison of a serpent: *they are* like [l]the deaf adder *that* stoppeth her ear;

5 Which will not hearken to the voice of charmers, charming never so wisely.

6 [m]Break their teeth, O God, in their mouth: break out the great teeth of the young lions, O LORD.

7 [n]Let them melt away as waters *which* run continually: *when* he bendeth *his bow to shoot* his arrows, let them be as cut in pieces.

8 As a snail *which* melteth, let *every one of them* pass away: [o]*like* the untimely birth of a woman, *that* they may not see the sun.

56:13 [q]Ps. 116:8 [r]Job 33:30
57:1 [s]Ps. 56:1 [t]Ps. 17:8 [u]Isa. 26:20
57:2 [v]Ps. 138:8
57:3 [w]Ps. 144:5 [x]Ps. 56:1 [y]Ps. 40:11
57:4 [z]Prov. 30:14 [a]Ps. 55:21
57:5 [b]ver. 11; Ps. 108:5
57:6 [c]Ps. 7:15
57:7 [d]Ps. 108:1
57:8 [e]Ps. 16:9
57:9 [f]Ps. 108:3
57:10 [g]Ps. 36:5
57:11 [h]ver. 5
58:2 [i]Ps. 94:20; Isa. 10:1
58:3 [j]Ps. 51:5; Isa. 48:8
58:4 [k]Ps. 140:3; Eccl. 10:11 [l]Jer. 8:17
58:6 [m]Job 4:10; Ps. 3:7
58:7 [n]Josh. 7:5; Ps. 112:10
58:8 [o]Job 3:16; Eccl. 6:3
58:9 [p]Prov. 10:25
58:10 [q]Ps. 52:6 [r]Ps. 68:23
58:11 [s]Ps. 92:15 [t]Ps. 67:4
59:1 [u]Ps. 18:48
59:3 [v]Ps. 56:6 [w]1 Sam. 24:11
59:4 [x]Ps. 35:23
59:6 [y]ver. 14
59:7 [z]Ps. 57:4; Prov. 12:18 [a]Ps. 10:11
59:8 [b]1 Sam. 19:16; Ps. 2:4
59:9 [c]ver. 17
59:10 [d]Ps. 21:3 [e]Ps. 54:7
59:11 [f]Gen. 4:12
59:12 [g]Prov. 12:13
59:13 [h]Ps. 7:9 [i]Ps. 83:18
59:14 [j]ver. 6
59:15 [k]Job 15:23; Ps. 109:10
59:17 [l]Ps. 18:1 [m]ver. 9

9 Before your pots can feel the thorns, he shall take them away [p]as with a whirlwind, both living, and in *his* wrath.

10 [q]The righteous shall rejoice when he seeth the vengeance: [r]he shall wash his feet in the blood of the wicked.

11 [s]So that a man shall say, Verily *there is* a reward for the righteous: verily he is a God that [t]judgeth in the earth.

To the chief Musician, Al-taschith, Michtam of David; when Saul sent, and they watched the house to kill him.

59 Deliver [u]me from mine enemies, O my God: defend me from them that rise up against me.

2 Deliver me from the workers of iniquity, and save me from bloody men.

3 For, lo, they lie in wait for my soul: [v]the mighty are gathered against me; [w]not *for* my transgression, nor *for* my sin, O LORD.

4 They run and prepare themselves without *my* fault: [x]awake to help me, and behold.

5 Thou therefore, O LORD God of hosts, the God of Israel, awake to visit all the heathen: be not merciful to any wicked transgressors. Selah.

6 [y]They return at evening: they make a noise like a dog, and go round about the city.

7 Behold, they belch out with their mouth: [z]swords *are* in their lips: for [a]who, *say they*, doth hear?

8 But [b]thou, O LORD, shalt laugh at them; thou shalt have all the heathen in derision.

9 *Because of* his strength will I wait upon thee: [c]for God *is* my defence.

10 The God of my mercy shall [d]prevent me: God shall let [e]me see *my desire* upon mine enemies.

11 [f]Slay them not, lest my people forget: scatter them by thy power; and bring them down, O Lord our shield.

12 [g]*For* the sin of their mouth *and* the words of their lips let them even be taken in their pride: and for cursing and lying *which* they speak.

13 [h]Consume *them* in wrath, consume *them*, that they *may* not *be*: and [i]let them know that God ruleth in Jacob unto the ends of the earth. Selah.

14 And [j]at evening let them return; *and* let them make a noise like a dog, and go round about the city.

15 Let them [k]wander up and down for meat, and grudge if they be not satisfied.

16 But I will sing of thy power; yea, I will sing aloud of thy mercy in the morning: for thou hast been my defence and refuge in the day of my trouble.

17 Unto thee, [l]O my strength, will I sing: [m]for God *is* my defence, *and* the God of my mercy.

To the chief Musician upon Shushan-eduth,
Michtam of David, to teach; when he strove
with Aram-naharaim and with Aram-zobah,
when Joab returned, and smote of Edom
in the valley of salt twelve thousand.

60 O God, [n]thou hast cast us off, thou
hast scattered us, thou hast been displeased; O turn thyself to us again.
2 Thou hast made the earth to tremble;
thou hast broken it: [o]heal the breaches
thereof; for it shaketh.
3 [p]Thou hast shewed thy people hard
things: [q]thou hast made us to drink the
wine of astonishment.
4 [r]Thou hast given a banner to them that
fear thee, that it may be displayed because
of the truth. Selah.
5 [s]That thy beloved may be delivered;
save *with* thy right hand, and hear me.
6 God hath [t]spoken in his holiness; I will
rejoice, I will [u]divide [v]Shechem, and mete
out [w]the valley of Succoth.
7 Gilead *is* mine, and Manasseh *is* mine;
[x]Ephraim also *is* the strength of mine head;
[y]Judah *is* my lawgiver;
8 [z]Moab *is* my washpot; [a]over Edom will
I cast out my shoe: [b]Philistia, triumph thou
because of me.
9 Who will bring me *into* the strong city?
who will lead me into Edom?
10 *Wilt* not thou, O God, *which* [c]hadst
cast us off? and *thou,* O God, *which* didst
[d]not go out with our armies?
11 Give us help from trouble: for [e]vain *is*
the help of man.
12 Through God [f]we shall do valiantly:
for he *it is that* shall [g]tread down our enemies.

To the chief Musician upon Neginah,
A Psalm of David.

61 Hear my cry, O God; attend unto my
prayer.
2 From the end of the earth will I cry unto
thee, when my heart is overwhelmed: lead
me to the rock *that* is higher than I.
3 For thou hast been a shelter for me, *and*
[h]a strong tower from the enemy.
4 [i]I will abide in thy tabernacle for ever:
[j]I will trust in the covert of thy wings.
Selah.
5 For thou, O God, hast heard my vows:
thou hast given *me* the heritage of those
that fear thy name.
6 [k]Thou wilt prolong the king's life: *and*
his years as many generations.
7 He shall abide before God for ever:
O prepare mercy [l]and truth, *which* may
preserve him.
8 So will I sing praise unto thy name for
ever, that I may daily perform my vows.

To the chief Musician, to Jeduthun,
A Psalm of David.

62 Truly [m]my soul waiteth upon God:
from him *cometh* my salvation.
2 [n]He only *is* my rock and my salvation;
he is my defence; [o]I shall not be greatly
moved.
3 How long will ye imagine mischief
against a man? ye shall be slain all of you:
[p]as a bowing wall *shall ye be, and as* a tot-
tering fence.
4 They only consult to cast *him* down
from his excellency: they delight in lies:
[q]they bless with their mouth, but they curse
inwardly. Selah.
5 [r]My soul, wait thou only upon God; for
my expectation *is* from him.
6 He only *is* my rock and my salvation: *he*
is my defence; I shall not be moved.
7 [s]In God *is* my salvation and my glory:
the rock of my strength, *and* my refuge, *is* in
God.
8 Trust in him at all times; ye people,
[t]pour out your heart before him: God *is* [u]a
refuge for us. Selah.
9 [v]Surely men of low degree *are* vanity,
and men of high degree *are* a lie: to be laid
in the balance, they *are* altogether *lighter*
than vanity.
10 Trust not in oppression, and become
not vain in robbery: [w]if riches increase, set
not your heart *upon them.*
11 God hath spoken [x]once; twice have I
heard this; that [y]power *belongeth* unto
God.
12 Also unto thee, O Lord, *belongeth*
[z]mercy: for [a]thou renderest to every man
according to his work.

A Psalm of David, when he was in the
wilderness of Judah.

63 O God, thou *art* my God; early will
I seek thee: [b]my soul thirsteth for
thee, my flesh longeth for thee in a dry and
thirsty land, where no water is;
2 To see [c]thy power and thy glory, so *as*
I have seen thee in the sanctuary.
3 [d]Because thy lovingkindness *is* better
than life, my lips shall praise thee.
4 Thus will I bless thee [e]while I live: I will
lift up my hands in thy name.
5 My soul shall be [f]satisfied as *with* marrow and fatness; and my mouth shall praise
thee with joyful lips:
6 When [g]I remember thee upon my bed,
and meditate on thee in the *night* watches.
7 Because thou hast been my help, therefore [h]in the shadow of thy wings will I rejoice.
8 My soul followeth hard after thee: thy
right hand upholdeth me.
9 But those *that* seek my soul, to destroy
it, shall go into the lower parts of the earth.
10 [i]They shall fall by the sword: they
shall be a portion for foxes.
11 But the king shall rejoice in God; [j]ev-
ery one that sweareth by him shall glory:
but the mouth of them that speak lies shall
be stopped.

To the chief Musician, A Psalm of David.

64 Hear my voice, O God, in my prayer:
preserve my life from fear of the enemy.
2 Hide me from the secret counsel of the

60:1 nPs. 44:9
60:2 o2 Chron. 7:14
60:3 pPs. 71:20 qIsa. 51:17; Jer. 25:15
60:4 rPs. 20:5
60:5 sPs. 108:6
60:6 tPs. 89:35 uJosh. 1:6 vGen. 12:6 wJosh. 13:27
60:7 xDeut. 33:17 yGen. 49:10
60:8 z2 Sam. 8:2 aPs. 108:9; 2 Sam. 8:14 b2 Sam. 8:1
60:10 cver. 1 dJosh. 7:12
60:11 ePs. 111:8
60:12 fNum. 24:18; 1 Chron. 19:13 gIsa. 63:3
61:3 hProv. 18:10
61:4 iPs. 27:4 jPs. 17:8
61:6 kPs. 21:4
61:7 lPs. 40:11; Prov. 20:28
62:1 mPs. 33:20
62:2 nver. 6 oPs. 37:24
62:3 pIsa. 30:13
62:4 qPs. 28:3
62:5 rver. 1
62:7 sJer. 3:23
62:8 t1 Sam. 1:15; Ps. 42:4; Lam. 2:19 uPs. 18:2
62:9 vPs. 39:5; Isa. 40:15; Rom. 3:4
62:10 wJob 31:25; Ps. 52:7; Luke 12:15; 1 Tim. 6:17
62:11 xJob 33:14 yRev. 19:1
62:12 zPs. 86:15; Dan. 9:9 aJob 34:11; Prov. 24:12; Jer. 32:19; Ezek. 7:27; Matt. 16:27; Rom. 2:6; 1 Cor. 3:8; 2 Cor. 5:10; Eph. 6:8; Col. 3:25; 1 Pet. 1:17; Rev. 22:12
63:1 bPs. 42:2
63:2 c1 Sam. 4:21; 1 Chron. 16:11; Ps. 27:4
63:3 dPs. 30:5
63:4 ePs. 104:33
63:5 fPs. 36:8
63:6 gPs. 42:8
63:7 hPs. 61:4
63:10 iEzek. 35:5
63:11 jDeut. 6:13; Isa. 45:23; Zeph. 1:5

wicked; from the insurrection of the workers of iniquity:
3 [k]Who whet their tongue like a sword,
[l]*and* bend *their bows to shoot* their arrows, *even* bitter words:
4 That they may shoot in secret at the perfect: suddenly do they shoot at him, and fear
not.
5 [m]They encourage themselves *in* an evil
matter: they commune of laying snares
privily; [n]they say, Who shall see them?
6 They search out iniquities; they accomplish a diligent search: both the inward
thought of every one *of them,* and the heart,
is deep.
7 [o]But God shall shoot at them *with* an
arrow; suddenly shall they be wounded.
8 So they shall make [p]their own tongue
to fall upon themselves: [q]all that see them
shall flee away.
9 [r]And all men shall fear, and shall [s]de-
clare the work of God; for they shall wisely
consider of his doing.
10 [t]The righteous shall be glad in the
LORD, and shall trust in him; and all the
upright in heart shall glory.

To the chief Musician, A Psalm *and* Song of David.

65 Praise waiteth for thee, O God, in
Sion: and unto thee shall the vow be
performed.
2 O thou that hearest prayer, [u]unto thee
shall all flesh come.
3 [v]Iniquities prevail against me: *as for*
our transgressions, thou shalt [w]purge them
away.
4 [x]Blessed *is the man whom* thou
[y]choosest, and causest to approach *unto*
thee, that he may dwell in thy courts: [z]we
shall be satisfied with the goodness of thy
house, *even* of thy holy temple.
5 *By* terrible things in righteousness wilt
thou answer us, O God of our salvation;
who art the confidence of [a]all the ends of
the earth, and of them that are afar off *upon*
the sea:
6 Which by his strength setteth fast the
mountains; [b]*being* girded with power:
7 [c]Which stilleth the noise of the seas,
the noise of their waves, [d]and the tumult of
the people.
8 They also that dwell in the uttermost
parts are afraid at thy tokens: thou makest
the outgoings of the morning and evening
to rejoice.
9 Thou [e]visitest the earth, and [f]waterest
it: thou greatly enrichest it [g]with the river
of God, *which* is full of water: thou preparest them corn, when thou hast so provided
for it.
10 Thou waterest the ridges thereof abundantly: thou settlest the furrows thereof:
thou makest it soft with showers: thou
blessest the springing thereof.
11 Thou crownest the year with thy goodness; and thy paths drop fatness.
12 They drop *upon* the pastures of the
wilderness: and the little hills rejoice on every side.
13 The pastures are clothed with flocks;
[h]the valleys also are covered over with
corn; they shout for joy, they also sing.

To the chief Musician, A Song *or* Psalm.

66 Make [i]a joyful noise unto God, all ye
lands:
2 Sing forth the honour of his name:
make his praise glorious.
3 Say unto God, How [j]terrible *art thou in*
thy works! [k]through the greatness of thy
power shall thine enemies submit themselves unto thee.
4 [l]All the earth shall worship thee, and
[m]shall sing unto thee; they shall sing *to* thy
name. Selah.
5 [n]Come and see the works of God: *he is*
terrible *in his* doing toward the children of
men.
6 [o]He turned the sea into dry *land:* [p]they
went through the flood on foot: there did we
rejoice in him.
7 He ruleth by his power for ever; [q]his
eyes behold the nations: let not the rebellious exalt themselves. Selah.
8 O bless our God, ye people, and make
the voice of his praise to be heard:
9 Which holdeth our soul in life, and
[r]suffereth not our feet to be moved.
10 For [s]thou, O God, hast proved us:
[t]thou hast tried us, as silver is tried.
11 [u]Thou broughtest us into the net; thou
laidst affliction upon our loins.
12 [v]Thou hast caused men to ride over
our heads; [w]we went through fire and
through water: but thou broughtest us out
into a wealthy *place.*
13 [x]I will go into thy house with burnt
offerings: [y]I will pay thee my vows,
14 Which my lips have uttered, and my
mouth hath spoken, when I was in trouble.
15 I will offer unto thee burnt sacrifices of
fatlings, with the incense of rams; I will offer bullocks with goats. Selah.
16 [z]Come *and* hear, all ye that fear God,
and I will declare what he hath done for my
soul.
17 I cried unto him with my mouth, and
he was extolled with my tongue.
18 [a]If I regard iniquity in my heart, the
Lord will not hear *me:*
19 *But* verily God [b]hath heard *me;* he
hath attended to the voice of my prayer.
20 Blessed *be* God, which hath not turned
away my prayer, nor his mercy from me.

To the chief Musician on Neginoth, A Psalm *or* Song.

67 God be merciful unto us, and bless
us; *and* [c]cause his face to shine upon
us; Selah.
2 That [d]thy way may be known upon
earth, [e]thy saving health among all nations.
3 [f]Let the people praise thee, O God; let
all the people praise thee.
4 O let the nations be glad and sing for

64:3 [k]Ps. 11:2 [l]Ps. 58:7; Jer. 9:3
64:5 [m]Prov. 1:11 [n]Ps. 10:11
64:7 [o]Ps. 7:12
64:8 [p]Prov. 12:13 [q]Ps. 31:11
64:9 [r]Ps. 40:3 [s]Jer. 50:28
64:10 [t]Ps. 32:11
65:2 [u]Isa. 66:23
65:3 [v]Ps. 38:4 [w]Ps. 51:2; Isa. 6:7; Heb. 9:14; 1 John 1:7
65:4 [x]Ps. 33:12 [y]Ps. 4:3 [z]Ps. 36:8
65:5 [a]Ps. 22:27
65:6 [b]Ps. 93:1
65:7 [c]Ps. 89:9; Matt. 8:26 [d]Ps. 76:10; Isa. 17:12
65:9 [e]Deut. 11:12 [f]Ps. 68:9; Jer. 5:24 [g]Ps. 46:4
65:13 [h]Isa. 55:12
66:1 [i]Ps. 100:1
66:3 [j]Ps. 65:5 [k]Ps. 18:44
66:4 [l]Ps. 22:27 [m]Ps. 96:1
66:5 [n]Ps. 46:8
66:6 [o]Ex. 14:21 [p]Josh. 3:14
66:7 [q]Ps. 11:4
66:9 [r]Ps. 121:3
66:10 [s]Ps. 17:3; Isa. 48:10 [t]Zech. 13:9; 1 Pet. 1:6
66:11 [u]Lam. 1:13
66:12 [v]Isa. 51:23 [w]Isa. 43:2
66:13 [x]Ps. 100:4 [y]Eccl. 5:4
66:16 [z]Ps. 34:11
66:18 [a]Job 27:9; Prov. 15:29; Isa. 1:15; John 9:31; Jam. 4:3
66:19 [b]Ps. 116:1
67:1 [c]Num. 6:25; Ps. 4:6
67:2 [d]Acts 18:25 [e]Luke 2:30; Tit. 2:11
67:3 [f]Ps. 66:4

joy: for [g]thou shalt judge the people righteously, and govern the nations upon earth. Selah.

5 Let the people praise thee, O God; let all the people praise thee.

6 [h]*Then* shall the earth yield her increase; *and* God, *even* our own God, shall bless us.

7 God shall bless us; and [i]all the ends of the earth shall fear him.

To the chief Musician, A Psalm *or* Song of David.

68 Let [j]God arise, let his enemies be scattered: let them also that hate him flee before him.

2 [k]As smoke is driven away, *so* drive *them* away: [l]as wax melteth before the fire, *so* let the wicked perish at the presence of God.

3 But [m]let the righteous be glad; let them rejoice before God: yea, let them exceedingly rejoice.

4 [n]Sing unto God, sing praises to his name: [o]extol him that rideth upon the heavens [p]by his name JAH, and rejoice before him.

5 [q]A father of the fatherless, and a judge of the widows, *is* God in his holy habitation.

6 [r]God setteth the solitary in families: [s]he bringeth out those which are bound with chains: but [t]the rebellious dwell in a dry *land*.

7 O God, [u]when thou wentest forth before thy people, when thou didst march through the wilderness; Selah:

8 [v]The earth shook, the heavens also dropped at the presence of God: *even* Sinai itself *was moved* at the presence of God, the God of Israel.

9 [w]Thou, O God, didst send a plentiful rain, whereby thou didst confirm thine inheritance, when it was weary.

10 Thy congregation hath dwelt therein: [x]thou, O God, hast prepared of thy goodness for the poor.

11 The Lord gave the word: great *was* the company of those that published *it*.

12 [y]Kings of armies did flee apace: and she that tarried at home divided the spoil.

13 [z]Though ye have lien among the pots, [a]*yet shall ye be as* the wings of a dove covered with silver, and her feathers with yellow gold.

14 [b]When the Almighty scattered kings in it, it was *white* as snow in Salmon.

15 The hill of God *is as* the hill of Bashan; an high hill *as* the hill of Bashan.

16 [c]Why leap ye, ye high hills? [d]*this is* the hill *which* God desireth to dwell in; yea, the LORD will dwell *in it* for ever.

17 [e]The chariots of God *are* twenty thousand, *even* thousands of angels: the Lord *is* among them, *as in* Sinai, in the holy *place*.

18 [f]Thou hast ascended on high, [g]thou hast led captivity captive: [h]thou hast received gifts for men; yea, *for* [i]the rebellious also, [j]that the LORD God might dwell *among them*.

19 Blessed *be* the Lord, *who* daily loadeth us *with benefits, even* the God of our salvation. Selah.

20 *He that is* our God *is* the God of salvation; and [k]unto GOD the Lord *belong* the issues from death.

21 But [l]God shall wound the head of his enemies, [m]*and* the hairy scalp of such an one as goeth on still in his trespasses.

22 The Lord said, I will bring [n]again from Bashan, I will bring *my people* again [o]from the depths of the sea:

23 [p]That thy foot may be dipped in the blood of *thine* enemies, [q]*and* the tongue of thy dogs in the same.

24 They have seen thy goings, O God; *even* the goings of my God, my King, in the sanctuary.

25 [r]The singers went before, the players on instruments *followed* after; among *them were* the damsels playing with timbrels.

26 Bless ye God in the congregations, *even* the Lord, from [s]the fountain of Israel.

27 There *is* [t]little Benjamin *with* their ruler, the princes of Judah *and* their council, the princes of Zebulun, *and* the princes of Naphtali.

28 Thy God hath [u]commanded thy strength: strengthen, O God, that which thou hast wrought for us.

29 Because of thy temple at Jerusalem [v]shall kings bring presents unto thee.

30 Rebuke the company of spearmen, [w]the multitude of the bulls, with the calves of the people, *till every one* [x]submit himself with pieces of silver: scatter thou the people *that* delight in war.

31 [y]Princes shall come out of Egypt; [z]Ethiopia shall soon [a]stretch out her hands unto God.

32 Sing unto God, ye kingdoms of the earth; O sing praises unto the Lord; Selah:

33 To him [b]that rideth upon the heavens of heavens, *which were* of old; lo, [c]he doth send out his voice, *and that* a mighty voice.

34 [d]Ascribe ye strength unto God: his excellency *is* over Israel, and his strength *is* in the clouds.

35 O God, [e]*thou art* terrible out of thy holy places: the God of Israel *is* he that giveth strength and power unto *his* people. Blessed *be* God.

To the chief Musician upon Shoshannim, *A Psalm* of David.

69 Save me, O God; for [f]the waters are come in unto *my* soul.

2 [g]I sink in deep mire, where *there is* no standing: I am come into deep waters, where the floods overflow me.

3 [h]I am weary of my crying: my throat is dried: [i]mine eyes fail while I wait for my God.

4 They that [j]hate me without a cause are more than the hairs of mine head: they that

67:4 gPs. 96:10 **67:6** hLev. 26:4; Ps. 85:12; Ezek. 34:27 **67:7** iPs. 22:27 **68:1** jNum. 10:35; Isa. 33:3 **68:2** kIsa. 9:18; Hos. 13:3 lPs. 97:5; Mic. 1:4 **68:3** mPs. 32:11 **68:4** nPs. 66:4 oDeut. 33:26; ver. 33 pEx. 6:3 **68:5** qPs. 10:14 **68:6** r1 Sam. 2:5; Ps. 113:9 sPs. 107:10; Acts 12:6 tPs. 107:34 **68:7** uEx. 13:21; Judg. 4:14; Hab. 3:13 **68:8** vEx. 19:16; Judg. 5:4; Isa. 64:1 **68:9** wDeut. 11:11; Ezek. 34:26 **68:10** xDeut. 26:5; Ps. 74:19 **68:12** yNum. 31:8; Josh. 10:16 **68:13** zPs. 81:6 aPs. 105:37 **68:14** bNum. 21:3; Josh. 10:10 **68:16** cPs. 114:4 dDeut. 12:5; 1 Kings 9:3; Ps. 87:1 **68:17** eDeut. 33:2; 2 Kings 6:16; Dan. 7:10; Heb. 12:22; Rev. 9:16 **68:18** fActs 1:9; Eph. 4:8 gJudg. 5:12 hActs 2:4 i1 Tim. 1:13 jPs. 78:60 **68:20** kDeut. 32:39; Prov. 4:23; Rev. 1:18 **68:21** lPs. 110:6; Hab. 3:13 mPs. 55:23 **68:22** nNum. 21:33 oEx. 14:22 **68:23** pPs. 58:10 q1 Kings 21:19 **68:25** r1 Chron. 13:8; Ps. 47:5 **68:26** sDeut. 33:28; Isa. 48:1 **68:27** t1 Sam. 9:21 **68:28** uPs. 42:8 **68:29** v1 Kings 10:10; 2 Chron. 32:23; Ps. 72:10; Isa. 60:16 **68:30** wPs. 22:12 x2 Sam. 8:2 **68:31** yIsa. 19:19 zPs. 72:9; Isa. 45:14; Zeph. 3:10; Acts 8:27 aPs. 44:20 **68:33** bPs. 18:10; ver. 4 cPs. 29:3 **68:34** dPs. 29:1 **68:35** ePs. 45:4 **69:1** fver. 2; Jonah 2:5 **69:2** gPs. 40:2 **69:3** hPs. 6:6 iPs. 119:82; Isa. 38:14 **69:4** jPs. 35:19; John 15:25

would destroy me, *being* mine enemies wrongfully, are mighty: then I restored *that* which I took not away.

5 O God, thou knowest my foolishness; and my sins are not hid from thee.

6 Let not them that wait on thee, O Lord GOD of hosts, be ashamed for my sake: let not those that seek thee be confounded for my sake, O God of Israel.

7 Because for thy sake I have borne reproach; shame hath covered my face.

8 [k]I am become a stranger unto my brethren, and an alien unto my mother's children.

9 [l]For the zeal of thine house hath eaten me up; [m]and the reproaches of them that reproached thee are fallen upon me.

10 [n]When I wept, *and chastened* my soul with fasting, that was to my reproach.

11 I made sackcloth also my garment; [o]and I became a proverb to them.

12 They that sit in the gate speak against me; and [p]I *was* the song of the drunkards.

13 But as for me, my prayer *is* unto thee, O LORD, [q]*in* an acceptable time: O God, in the multitude of thy mercy hear me, in the truth of thy salvation.

14 Deliver me out of the mire, and let me not sink: [r]let me be delivered from them that hate me, and out of [s]the deep waters.

15 Let not the waterflood overflow me, neither let the deep swallow me up, and let not the pit [t]shut her mouth upon me.

16 Hear me, O LORD; [u]for thy lovingkindness *is* good: [v]turn unto me according to the multitude of thy tender mercies.

17 And [w]hide not thy face from thy servant; for I am in trouble: hear me speedily.

18 Draw nigh unto my soul, *and* redeem it: deliver me because of mine enemies.

19 Thou hast known [x]my reproach, and my shame, and my dishonour: mine adversaries *are* all before thee.

20 Reproach hath broken my heart; and I am full of heaviness: and [y]I looked *for some* to take pity, but *there was* none; and for [z]comforters, but I found none.

21 They gave me also gall for my meat; [a]and in my thirst they gave me vinegar to drink.

22 [b]Let their table become a snare before them: and *that which should have been* for *their* welfare, *let it become* a trap.

23 [c]Let their eyes be darkened, that they see not; and make their loins continually to shake.

24 [d]Pour out thine indignation upon them, and let thy wrathful anger take hold of them.

25 [e]Let their habitation be desolate; *and* let none dwell in their tents.

26 For [f]they persecute [g]*him* whom thou hast smitten; and they talk to the grief of those whom thou hast wounded.

27 [h]Add iniquity unto their iniquity: [i]and let them not come into thy righteousness.

28 Let them [j]be blotted out of the book of the living, [k]and not be written with the righteous.

29 But I *am* poor and sorrowful: let thy salvation, O God, set me up on high.

30 [l]I will praise the name of God with a song, and will magnify him with thanksgiving.

31 [m]*This* also shall please the LORD better than an ox *or* bullock that hath horns and hoofs.

32 [n]The humble shall see *this, and* be glad: and [o]your heart shall live that seek God.

33 For the LORD heareth the poor, and despiseth not [p]his prisoners.

34 [q]Let the heaven and earth praise him, the seas, [r]and every thing that moveth therein.

35 [s]For God will save Zion, and will build the cities of Judah: that they may dwell there, and have it in possession.

36 [t]The seed also of his servants shall inherit it: and they that love his name shall dwell therein.

To the chief Musician, *A Psalm* of David, to bring to remembrance.

70 *Make haste,* [u]O God, to deliver me; make haste to help me, O LORD.

2 [v]Let them be ashamed and confounded that seek after my soul: let them be turned backward, and put to confusion, that desire my hurt.

3 [w]Let them be turned back for a reward of their shame that say, Aha, aha.

4 Let all those that seek thee rejoice and be glad in thee: and let such as love thy salvation say continually, Let God be magnified.

5 [x]But I *am* poor and needy: [y]make haste unto me, O God: thou *art* my help and my deliverer; O LORD, make no tarrying.

71 In [z]thee, O LORD, do I put my trust: let me never be put to confusion.

2 [a]Deliver me in thy righteousness, and cause me to escape: [b]incline thine ear unto me, and save me.

3 [c]Be thou my strong habitation, whereunto I may continually resort: thou hast given [d]commandment to save me; for thou *art* my rock and my fortress.

4 [e]Deliver me, O my God, out of the hand of the wicked, out of the hand of the unrighteous and cruel man.

5 For thou *art* [f]my hope, O Lord GOD: *thou art* my trust from my youth.

6 [g]By thee have I been holden up from the womb: thou art he that took me out of my mother's bowels: my praise *shall be* continually of thee.

7 [h]I am as a wonder unto many; but thou *art* my strong refuge.

8 Let [i]my mouth be filled *with* thy praise *and with* thy honour all the day.

9 [j]Cast me not off in the time of old age; forsake me not when my strength faileth.

10 For mine enemies speak against me;

69:8 kPs. 31:11; Isa. 53:3; John 1:11
69:9 lPs. 119:139; John 2:17 mPs. 89:50; Rom. 15:3
69:10 nPs. 35:13
69:11 o1 Kings 9:7; Jer. 24:9
69:12 pJob 30:9; Ps. 35:15
69:13 qIsa. 49:8; 2 Cor. 6:2
69:14 rPs. 144:7 sver. 1
69:15 tNum. 16:33
69:16 uPs. 63:3 vPs. 25:16
69:17 wPs. 27:9
69:19 xPs. 22:6; Isa. 53:3; Heb. 12:2
69:20 yPs. 142:4; Isa. 63:5 zJob 16:2
69:21 aMatt. 27:34; Mark 15:23; John 19:29
69:22 bRom. 11:9
69:23 cIsa. 6:9; John 12:39; Rom. 11:10; 2 Cor. 3:14
69:24 d1 Thess. 2:16
69:25 eMatt. 23:38; Acts 1:20
69:26 f2 Chron. 28:9; Zech. 1:15 gIsa. 53:4
69:27 hRom. 1:28 iIsa. 26:10; Rom. 9:31
69:28 jEx. 32:32; Phil. 4:3; Rev. 3:5 kEzek. 1:39; Luke 10:20; Heb. 12:23
69:30 lPs. 28:7
69:31 mPs. 50:13
69:32 nPs. 34:2 oPs. 22:26
69:33 pEph. 3:1
69:34 qPs. 96:11; Isa. 44:23 rIsa. 55:12
69:35 sPs. 51:18; Isa. 44:26
69:36 tPs. 102:28
70:1 uPs. 40:13
70:2 vPs. 35:4
70:3 wPs. 40:15
70:5 xPs. 40:17 yPs. 141:1
71:1 zPs. 25:2
71:2 aPs. 31:1 bPs. 17:6
71:3 cPs. 31:2 dPs. 44:4
71:4 ePs. 140:1
71:5 fJer. 17:7
71:6 gPs. 22:9; Isa. 46:3
71:7 hIsa. 8:18; Zech. 3:8; 1 Cor. 4:9
71:8 iPs. 35:28
71:9 jver. 18

and they that lay wait for my soul [k]take
counsel together,
11 Saying, God hath forsaken him: persecute and take him; for *there is* none to deliver *him*.
12 [l]O God, be not far from me: O my
God, [m]make haste for my help.
13 [n]Let them be confounded *and* consumed that are adversaries to my soul; let
them be covered *with* reproach and dishonour that seek my hurt.
14 But I will hope continually, and will yet
praise thee more and more.
15 [o]My mouth shall shew forth thy righteousness *and* thy salvation all the day; for
[p]I know not the numbers *thereof*.
16 I will go in the strength of the Lord
GOD: I will make mention of thy righteousness, *even* of thine only.
17 O God, thou hast taught me from my
youth: and hitherto have I declared thy
wondrous works.
18 [q]Now also when I am old and grayheaded, O God, forsake me not; until I have
shewed thy strength unto *this* generation,
and thy power to every one *that* is to come.
19 [r]Thy righteousness also, O God, *is*
very high, who hast done great things: [s]O
God, who *is* like unto thee!
20 [t]*Thou*, which hast shewed me great
and sore troubles, [u]shalt quicken me again,
and shalt bring me up again from the depths
of the earth.
21 Thou shalt increase my greatness, and
comfort me on every side.
22 I will also praise thee [v]with the psaltery, *even* thy truth, O my God: unto thee
will I sing with the harp, O thou [w]Holy One
of Israel.
23 My lips shall greatly rejoice when I
sing unto thee; and [x]my soul, which thou
hast redeemed.
24 [y]My tongue also shall talk of thy righteousness all the day long: for [z]they are
confounded, for they are brought unto
shame, that seek my hurt.

A Psalm for Solomon.

72 Give the king thy judgments, O God,
and thy righteousness unto the
king's son.
2 [a]He shall judge thy people with righteousness, and thy poor with judgment.
3 [b]The mountains shall bring peace to
the people, and the little hills, by righteousness.
4 [c]He shall judge the poor of the people,
he shall save the children of the needy, and
shall break in pieces the oppressor.
5 They shall fear thee [d]as long as the sun
and moon endure, throughout all generations.
6 [e]He shall come down like rain upon the
mown grass: as showers *that* water the
earth.
7 In his days shall the righteous flourish;
[f]and abundance of peace so long as the
moon endureth.

71:10 [k]2 Sam. 17:1; Matt. 27:1
71:12 [l]Ps. 22:11 [m]Ps. 70:1
71:13 [n]ver. 24; Ps. 35:4
71:15 [o]ver. 8; Ps. 35:28 [p]Ps. 40:5
71:18 [q]ver. 9
71:19 [r]Ps. 57:10 [s]Ps. 35:10
71:20 [t]Ps. 60:3 [u]Hos. 6:1
71:22 [v]Ps. 92:1 [w]2 Kings 19:22; Isa. 60:9
71:23 [x]Ps. 103:4
71:24 [y]ver. 8 [z]ver. 13
72:2 [a]Isa. 11:2
72:3 [b]Ps. 85:10; Isa. 32:17
72:4 [c]Isa. 11:4
72:5 [d]ver. 7; Ps. 89:36
72:6 [e]2 Sam. 23:4; Hos. 6:3
72:7 [f]Isa. 2:4; Dan. 2:44; Luke 1:33
72:8 [g]Ex. 23:31; 1 Kings 4:21; Ps. 2:8; Zech. 9:10
72:9 [h]Ps. 74:14 [i]Isa. 49:23; Mic. 7:17
72:10 [j]2 Chron. 9:21; Ps. 45:12; Isa. 49:7
72:11 [k]Isa. 49:22
72:12 [l]Job 29:12
72:14 [m]Ps. 116:15
72:16 [n]1 Kings 4:20
72:17 [o]Ps. 89:36 [p]Gen. 12:3; Jer. 4:2 [q]Luke 1:48
72:18 [r]1 Chron. 29:10; Ps. 41:13 [s]Ex. 15:11; Ps. 77:14
72:19 [t]Neh. 9:5 [u]Num. 14:21; Zech. 14:9
73:3 [v]Job 21:7; Ps. 37:1; Jer. 12:1
73:5 [w]Job 21:6
73:6 [x]Ps. 109:18
73:7 [y]Job 15:27; Ps. 17:10; Jer. 5:28
73:8 [z]Ps. 53:1 [a]Hos. 7:16 [b]2 Pet. 2:18; Jude 16
73:9 [c]Rev. 13:6
73:10 [d]Ps. 75:8
73:11 [e]Job 22:13; Ps. 10:11

8 [g]He shall have dominion also from sea
to sea, and from the river unto the ends of
the earth.
9 [h]They that dwell in the wilderness shall
bow before him; [i]and his enemies shall lick
the dust.
10 [j]The kings of Tarshish and of the isles
shall bring presents: the kings of Sheba and
Seba shall offer gifts.
11 [k]Yea, all kings shall fall down before
him: all nations shall serve him.
12 For he [l]shall deliver the needy when
he crieth; the poor also, and *him* that hath
no helper.
13 He shall spare the poor and needy, and
shall save the souls of the needy.
14 He shall redeem their soul from deceit
and violence: and [m]precious shall their
blood be in his sight.
15 And he shall live, and to him shall be
given of the gold of Sheba: prayer also shall
be made for him continually; *and* daily shall
he be praised.
16 There shall be an handful of corn in
the earth upon the top of the mountains; the
fruit thereof shall shake like Lebanon: [n]and
they of the city shall flourish like grass of
the earth.
17 [o]His name shall endure for ever: his
name shall be continued as long as the sun:
and [p]*men* shall be blessed in him: [q]all nations shall call him blessed.
18 [r]Blessed *be* the LORD God, the God of
Israel, [s]who only doeth wondrous things.
19 And [t]blessed *be* his glorious name for
ever: [u]and let the whole earth be filled *with*
his glory; Amen, and Amen.
20 The prayers of David the son of Jesse
are ended.

BOOK III

A Psalm of Asaph.

73 Truly God *is* good to Israel, *even* to
such as are of a clean heart.
2 But as for me, my feet were almost
gone; my steps had well nigh slipped.
3 [v]For I was envious at the foolish, *when*
I saw the prosperity of the wicked.
4 For *there are* no bands in their death:
but their strength *is* firm.
5 [w]They *are* not in trouble *as other* men;
neither are they plagued like *other* men.
6 Therefore pride compasseth them about
as a chain; violence covereth them [x]*as* a
garment.
7 [y]Their eyes stand out with fatness: they
have more than heart could wish.
8 [z]They are corrupt, and [a]speak wickedly *concerning* oppression: they [b]speak
loftily.
9 They set their mouth [c]against the heavens, and their tongue walketh through the
earth.
10 Therefore his people return hither:
[d]and waters of a full *cup* are wrung out to
them.
11 And they say, [e]How doth God know?
and is there knowledge in the most High?

12 Behold, these *are* the ungodly, who [f]prosper in the world; they increase *in* riches.

13 [g]Verily I have cleansed my heart *in* vain, and [h]washed my hands in innocency.

14 For all the day long have I been plagued, and chastened every morning.

15 If I say, I will speak thus; behold, I should offend *against* the generation of thy children.

16 [i]When I thought to know this, it *was* too painful for me;

17 Until [j]I went into the sanctuary of God; *then* understood I [k]their end.

18 Surely [l]thou didst set them in slippery places: thou castedst them down into destruction.

19 How are they *brought* into desolation, as in a moment! they are utterly consumed with terrors.

20 [m]As a dream when *one* awaketh; *so,* O Lord, [n]when thou awakest, thou shalt despise their image.

21 Thus my heart was [o]grieved, and I was pricked in my reins.

22 [p]So foolish *was* I, and ignorant: I was *as* a beast before thee.

23 Nevertheless I *am* continually with thee: thou hast holden *me* by my right hand.

24 [q]Thou shalt guide me with thy counsel, and afterward receive me *to* glory.

25 [r]Whom have I in heaven *but thee?* and *there is* none upon earth *that* I desire beside thee.

26 [s]My flesh and my heart faileth: *but* God *is* the strength of my heart, and [t]my portion for ever.

27 For, lo, [u]they that are far from thee shall perish: thou hast destroyed all them that [v]go a whoring from thee.

28 But *it is* good for me to [w]draw near to God: I have put my trust in the Lord GOD, that I may [x]declare all thy works.

Maschil of Asaph.

74 O God, why hast thou [y]cast *us* off for ever? *why* doth thine anger [z]smoke against [a]the sheep of thy pasture?

2 Remember thy congregation, [b]*which* thou hast purchased of old; the [c]rod of thine inheritance, *which* thou hast redeemed; this mount Zion, wherein thou hast dwelt.

3 Lift up thy feet unto the perpetual desolations; *even* all *that* the enemy hath done wickedly in the sanctuary.

4 [d]Thine enemies roar in the midst of thy congregations; [e]they set up their ensigns *for* signs.

5 *A man* was famous according as he had lifted up axes upon the thick trees.

6 But now they break down [f]the carved work thereof at once with axes and hammers.

7 [g]They have cast fire into thy sanctuary, they have defiled [h]*by casting down* the dwelling place of thy name to the ground.

8 [i]They said in their hearts, Let us destroy them together: they have burned up all the synagogues of God in the land.

9 We see not our signs: [j]*there is* no more any prophet: neither *is there* among us any that knoweth how long.

10 O God, how long shall the adversary reproach? shall the enemy blaspheme thy name for ever?

11 [k]Why withdrawest thou thy hand, even thy right hand? pluck *it* out of thy bosom.

12 For [l]God *is* my King of old, working salvation in the midst of the earth.

13 [m]Thou didst divide the sea by thy strength: [n]thou brakest the heads of the dragons in the waters.

14 Thou brakest the heads of leviathan in pieces, *and* gavest him [o]*to be* meat [p]to the people inhabiting the wilderness.

15 [q]Thou didst cleave the fountain and the flood: [r]thou driedst up mighty rivers.

16 The day *is* thine, the night also *is* thine: [s]thou hast prepared the light and the sun.

17 Thou hast [t]set all the borders of the earth: [u]thou hast made summer and winter.

18 [v]Remember this, *that* the enemy hath reproached, O LORD, and *that* [w]the foolish people have blasphemed thy name.

19 O deliver not the soul [x]of thy turtledove unto the multitude *of the wicked:* [y]forget not the congregation of thy poor for ever.

20 [z]Have respect unto the covenant: for the dark places of the earth are full of the habitations of cruelty.

21 O let not the oppressed return ashamed: let the poor and needy praise thy name.

22 Arise, O God, plead thine own cause: [a]remember how the foolish man reproacheth thee daily.

23 Forget not the voice of thine enemies: the tumult of those that rise up against thee increaseth continually.

To the chief Musician, Al-taschith, A Psalm *or* Song of Asaph.

75 Unto thee, O God, do we give thanks, *unto thee* do we give thanks: for *that* thy name is near thy wondrous works declare.

2 When I shall receive the congregation I will judge uprightly.

3 The earth and all the inhabitants thereof are dissolved: I bear up the pillars of it. Selah.

4 I said unto the fools, Deal not foolishly: and to the wicked, [b]Lift not up the horn:

5 Lift not up your horn on high: speak *not with* a stiff neck.

6 For promotion *cometh* neither from the east, nor from the west, nor from the south.

7 But [c]God *is* the judge: [d]he putteth down one, and setteth up another.

8 For [e]in the hand of the LORD *there is* a cup, and the wine is red; it is [f]full of mixture; and he poureth out of the same: [g]but

73:12 [f]ver. 3
73:13 [g]Job 21:15; Mal. 3:14 [h]Ps. 26:6
73:16 [i]Eccl. 8:17
73:17 [j]Ps. 77:13 [k]Ps. 37:38
73:18 [l]Ps. 35:6
73:20 [m]Job 20:8; Ps. 90:5; Isa. 29:7 [n]Ps. 78:65
73:21 [o]ver. 3
73:22 [p]Ps. 92:6; Prov. 30:2
73:24 [q]Ps. 32:8; Isa. 58:8
73:25 [r]Phil. 3:8
73:26 [s]Ps. 84:2 [t]Ps. 16:5
73:27 [u]Ps. 119:155 [v]Ex. 34:15; Num. 15:39; Jam. 4:4
73:28 [w]Heb. 10:22 [x]Ps. 107:22
74:1 [y]Ps. 44:9; Jer. 31:37 [z]Deut. 29:20 [a]Ps. 95:7
74:2 [b]Ex. 15:16; Deut. 9:29 [c]Deut. 32:9; Jer. 10:16
74:4 [d]Lam. 2:7 [e]Dan. 6:27
74:6 [f]1 Kings 6:18
74:7 [g]2 Kings 25:9 [h]Ps. 89:39
74:8 [i]Ps. 83:4
74:9 [j]1 Sam. 3:1; Am. 8:11
74:11 [k]Lam. 2:3
74:12 [l]Ps. 44:4
74:13 [m]Ex. 14:21 [n]Isa. 51:9; Ezek. 29:3
74:14 [o]Num. 14:9 [p]Ps. 72:9
74:15 [q]Ex. 17:5; Num. 20:11; Ps. 105:41; Isa. 48:21 [r]Josh. 3:13
74:16 [s]Gen. 1:14
74:17 [t]Acts 17:26 [u]Gen. 8:22
74:18 [v]ver. 22; Rev. 16:19 [w]Ps. 39:8
74:19 [x]SSol. 2:14 [y]Ps. 68:10
74:20 [z]Gen. 17:7; Lev. 26:44; Ps. 106:45; Jer. 33:21
74:22 [a]ver. 18; Ps. 89:51
75:4 [b]Zech. 1:21
75:7 [c]Ps. 50:6 [d]1 Sam. 2:7; Dan. 2:21
75:8 [e]Job 21:20; Ps. 60:3; Jer. 25:15; Rev. 14:10 [f]Prov. 23:30 [g]Ps. 73:10

the dregs thereof, all the wicked of the earth shall wring *them* out, *and* drink *them*.

9 But I will declare for ever; I will sing praises to the God of Jacob.

10 [h]All the horns of the wicked also will I cut off; *but* [i]the horns of the righteous shall be exalted.

To the chief Musician on Neginoth, A Psalm *or* Song of Asaph.

76 In [j]Judah *is* God known: his name *is* great in Israel.

2 In Salem also is his tabernacle, and his dwelling place in Zion.

3 [k]There brake he the arrows of the bow, the shield, and the sword, and the battle. Selah.

4 Thou *art* more glorious *and* excellent [l]than the mountains of prey.

5 [m]The stouthearted are spoiled, [n]they have slept their sleep: and none of the men of might have found their hands.

6 [o]At thy rebuke, O God of Jacob, both the chariot and horse are cast into a dead sleep.

7 Thou, *even* thou, *art* to be feared: and [p]who may stand in thy sight when once thou art angry?

8 [q]Thou didst cause judgment to be heard from heaven; [r]the earth feared, and was still,

9 When God [s]arose to judgment, to save all the meek of the earth. Selah.

10 [t]Surely the wrath of man shall praise thee: the remainder of wrath shalt thou restrain.

11 [u]Vow, and pay unto the LORD your God: [v]let all that be round about him bring presents unto him that ought to be feared.

12 He shall cut off the spirit of princes: [w]*he is* terrible to the kings of the earth.

To the chief Musician, to Jeduthun, A Psalm of Asaph.

77 I [x]cried unto God with my voice, *even* unto God with my voice; and he gave ear unto me.

2 [y]In the day of my trouble I [z]sought the Lord: my sore ran in the night, and ceased not: my soul refused to be comforted.

3 I remembered God, and was troubled: I complained, and [a]my spirit was overwhelmed. Selah.

4 Thou holdest mine eyes waking: I am so troubled that I cannot speak.

5 [b]I have considered the days of old, the years of ancient times.

6 I call to remembrance [c]my song in the night: [d]I commune with mine own heart: and my spirit made diligent search.

7 [e]Will the Lord cast off for ever? and will he [f]be favourable no more?

8 Is his mercy clean gone for ever? doth [g]*his* promise fail for evermore?

9 Hath God [h]forgotten to be gracious? hath he in anger shut up his tender mercies? Selah.

10 And I said, This *is* [i]my infirmity: *but* *I will remember* the years of the right hand of the most High.

11 [j]I will remember the works of the LORD: surely I will remember thy wonders of old.

12 I will meditate also of all thy work, and talk of thy doings.

13 [k]Thy way, O God, *is* in the sanctuary: [l]who *is so* great a God as *our* God?

14 Thou *art* the God that doest wonders: thou hast declared thy strength among the people.

15 [m]Thou hast with *thine* arm redeemed thy people, the sons of Jacob and Joseph. Selah.

16 [n]The waters saw thee, O God, the waters saw thee; they were afraid: the depths also were troubled.

17 The clouds poured out water: the skies sent out a sound: [o]thine arrows also went abroad.

18 The voice of thy thunder *was* in the heaven: [p]the lightnings lightened the world: [q]the earth trembled and shook.

19 [r]Thy way *is* in the sea, and thy path in the great waters, [s]and thy footsteps are not known.

20 [t]Thou leddest thy people like a flock by the hand of Moses and Aaron.

Maschil of Asaph.

78 Give [u]ear, O my people, *to* my law: incline your ears to the words of my mouth.

2 [v]I will open my mouth in a parable: I will utter dark sayings of old:

3 [w]Which we have heard and known, and our fathers have told us.

4 [x]We will not hide *them* from their children, [y]shewing to the generation to come the praises of the LORD, and his strength, and his wonderful works that he hath done.

5 For [z]he established a testimony in Jacob, and appointed a law in Israel, which he commanded our fathers, [a]that they should make them known to their children:

6 [b]That the generation to come might know *them, even* the children *which* should be born; *who* should arise and declare *them* to their children:

7 That they might set their hope in God, and not forget the works of God, but keep his commandments:

8 And [c]might not be as their fathers, [d]a stubborn and rebellious generation; a generation [e]*that* set not their heart aright, and whose spirit was not stedfast with God.

9 The children of Ephraim, *being* armed, *and* carrying bows, turned back in the day of battle.

10 [f]They kept not the covenant of God, and refused to walk in his law;

11 And [g]forgat his works, and his wonders that he had shewed them.

12 [h]Marvellous things did he in the sight of their fathers, in the land of Egypt, [i]*in* the field of Zoan.

13 [j]He divided the sea, and caused them

75:10 [h]Ps. 101:8; Jer. 48:25 [i]Ps. 89:17
76:1 [j]Ps. 48:1
76:3 [k]Ps. 46:9; Ezek. 39:9
76:4 [l]Ezek. 38:12
76:5 [m]Isa. 46:12 [n]Ps. 13:3; Jer. 51:39
76:6 [o]Ex. 15:1; Ezek. 39:20; Nah. 2:13; Zech. 12:4
76:7 [p]Nah. 1:6
76:8 [q]Ezek. 38:20 [r]2 Chron. 20:29
76:9 [s]Ps. 9:7
76:10 [t]Ex. 9:16; Ps. 65:7
76:11 [u]Eccl. 5:4 [v]2 Chron. 32:22; Ps. 68:29
76:12 [w]Ps. 68:35
77:1 [x]Ps. 3:4
77:2 [y]Ps. 50:15 [z]Isa. 26:9
77:3 [a]Ps. 142:3
77:5 [b]Deut. 32:7; Ps. 143:5; Isa. 51:9
77:6 [c]Ps. 42:8 [d]Ps. 4:4
77:7 [e]Ps. 74:1 [f]Ps. 85:1
77:8 [g]Rom. 9:6
77:9 [h]Isa. 49:15
77:10 [i]Ps. 31:22
77:11 [j]Ps. 143:5
77:13 [k]Ps. 73:17 [l]Ex. 15:11
77:15 [m]Ex. 6:6; Deut. 9:29
77:16 [n]Ex. 14:21; Josh. 3:15; Ps. 114:3; Hab. 3:8
77:17 [o]2 Sam. 22:15; Hab. 3:11
77:18 [p]Ps. 97:4 [q]2 Sam. 22:8
77:19 [r]Hab. 3:15 [s]Ex. 14:28
77:20 [t]Ex. 13:21; Ps. 78:52; Isa. 63:11; Hos. 12:13
78:1 [u]Isa. 51:4
78:2 [v]Ps. 49:4; Matt. 13:35
78:3 [w]Ps. 44:1
78:4 [x]Deut. 4:9; Joel 1:3 [y]Ex. 12:26; Josh. 4:6
78:5 [z]Ps. 147:19 [a]Deut. 4:9
78:6 [b]Ps. 102:18
78:8 [c]2 Kings 17:14; Ezek. 20:18 [d]Ex. 32:9; Deut. 9:6; Ps. 68:6 [e]ver. 37; 2 Chron. 20:33
78:10 [f]2 Kings 17:15
78:11 [g]Ps. 106:13
78:12 [h]Ex. 7 [i]Gen. 32:3; Num. 13:22; ver. 43; Isa. 19:11; Ezek. 30:14
78:13 [j]Ex. 14:21

to pass through; and [k]he made the waters to stand as an heap.

14 [l]In the daytime also he led them with a cloud, and all the night with a light of fire.

15 [m]He clave the rocks in the wilderness, and gave *them* drink as *out of* the great depths.

16 He brought [n]streams also out of the rock, and caused waters to run down like rivers.

17 And they sinned yet more against him by [o]provoking the most High in the wilderness.

18 And [p]they tempted God in their heart by asking meat for their lust.

19 [q]Yea, they spake against God; they said, Can God furnish a table in the wilderness?

20 [r]Behold, he smote the rock, that the waters gushed out, and the streams overflowed; can he give bread also? can he provide flesh for his people?

21 Therefore the LORD heard *this,* and [s]was wroth: so a fire was kindled against Jacob, and anger also came up against Israel;

22 Because they [t]believed not in God, and trusted not in his salvation:

23 Though he had commanded the clouds from above, [u]and opened the doors of heaven,

24 [v]And had rained down manna upon them to eat, and had given them of the corn of heaven.

25 Man did eat angels' food: he sent them meat to the full.

26 [w]He caused an east wind to blow in the heaven: and by his power he brought in the south wind.

27 He rained flesh also upon them as dust, and feathered fowls like as the sand of the sea:

28 And he let *it* fall in the midst of their camp, round about their habitations.

29 [x]So they did eat, and were well filled: for he gave them their own desire;

30 They were not estranged from their lust. But [y]while their meat *was* yet in their mouths,

31 The wrath of God came upon them, and slew the fattest of them, and smote down the chosen *men* of Israel.

32 For all this [z]they sinned still, and [a]believed not for his wondrous works.

33 [b]Therefore their days did he consume in vanity, and their years in trouble.

34 [c]When he slew them, then they sought him: and they returned and enquired early after God.

35 And they remembered that [d]God *was* their rock, and the high God [e]their redeemer.

36 Nevertheless they did [f]flatter him with their mouth, and they lied unto him with their tongues.

37 For [g]their heart was not right with him, neither were they stedfast in his covenant.

38 [h]But he, *being* full of compassion, forgave *their* iniquity, and destroyed *them* not: yea, many a time [i]turned he his anger away, [j]and did not stir up all his wrath.

39 For [k]he remembered [l]that they *were but* flesh; [m]a wind that passeth away, and cometh not again.

40 How oft did they [n]provoke him in the wilderness, *and* grieve him in the desert!

41 Yea, [o]they turned back and tempted God, and [p]limited the Holy One of Israel.

42 They remembered not his hand, *nor* the day when he delivered them from the enemy.

43 How [q]he had wrought his signs in Egypt, and his wonders in the field of Zoan:

44 [r]And had turned their rivers into blood; and their floods, that they could not drink.

45 [s]He sent divers sorts of flies among them, which devoured them; and [t]frogs, which destroyed them.

46 [u]He gave also their increase unto the caterpiller, and their labour unto the locust.

47 [v]He destroyed their vines with hail, and their sycomore trees with frost.

48 [w]He gave up their cattle also to the hail, and their flocks to hot thunderbolts.

49 He cast upon them the fierceness of his anger, wrath, and indignation, and trouble, by sending evil angels *among them.*

50 He made a way to his anger; he spared not their soul from death, but gave their life over to the pestilence;

51 [x]And smote all the firstborn in Egypt; the chief of *their* strength in [y]the tabernacles of Ham:

52 But [z]made his own people to go forth like sheep, and guided them in the wilderness like a flock.

53 And he [a]led them on safely, so that they feared not: but the sea [b]overwhelmed their enemies.

54 And he brought them to the border of his [c]sanctuary, *even to* this mountain, [d]*which* his right hand had purchased.

55 [e]He cast out the heathen also before them, and [f]divided them an inheritance by line, and made the tribes of Israel to dwell in their tents.

56 [g]Yet they tempted and provoked the most high God, and kept not his testimonies:

57 But [h]turned back, and dealt unfaithfully like their fathers: they were turned aside [i]like a deceitful bow.

58 [j]For they provoked him to anger with their [k]high places, and moved him to jealousy with their graven images.

59 When God heard *this,* he was wroth, and greatly abhorred Israel:

60 [l]So that he forsook the tabernacle of Shiloh, the tent *which* he placed among men;

61 [m]And delivered his strength into captivity, and his glory into the enemy's hand.

78:13 [k]Ex. 15:8; Ps. 33:7
78:14 [l]Ex. 13:21; Ps. 105:39
78:15 [m]Ex. 17:6; Num. 20:11; Ps. 105:41; 1 Cor. 10:4
78:16 [n]Deut. 9:21; Ps. 105:41
78:17 [o]Deut. 9:22; Ps. 95:8; Heb. 3:16
78:18 [p]Ex. 16:2
78:19 [q]Num. 11:4
78:20 [r]Ex. 17:6; Num. 20:11
78:21 [s]Num. 11:1
78:22 [t]Heb. 3:18; Jude 5
78:23 [u]Gen. 7:11; Mal. 3:10
78:24 [v]Ex. 16:4; Ps. 105:40; John 6:31; 1 Cor. 10:3
78:26 [w]Num. 11:31
78:29 [x]Num. 11:20
78:30 [y]Num. 11:33
78:32 [z]Num. 14 [a]ver. 22
78:33 [b]Num. 14:29
78:34 [c]Hos. 5:15
78:35 [d]Deut. 32:4 [e]Ex. 15:13; Deut. 7:8; Isa. 41:14
78:36 [f]Ezek. 33:31
78:37 [g]ver. 8
78:38 [h]Num. 14:18 [i]Isa. 48:9 [j]2 Kings 21:29
78:39 [k]Ps. 103:14 [l]Gen. 6:3; John 3:6 [m]Job 7:7; Jam. 4:14
78:40 [n]ver. 17; Ps. 95:9; Isa. 7:13; Eph. 4:30; Heb. 3:16
78:41 [o]Num. 14:22; Deut. 6:16 [p]ver. 20
78:43 [q]ver. 12; Ps. 105:27
78:44 [r]Ex. 7:20; Ps. 105:29
78:45 [s]Ex. 8:24; Ps. 105:31 [t]Ex. 8:6; Ps. 105:30
78:46 [u]Ex. 10:13; Ps. 105:34
78:47 [v]Ex. 9:23; Ps. 105:33
78:48 [w]Ex. 9:23; Ps. 105:32
78:51 [x]Ex. 12:29; Ps. 105:36 [y]Ps. 106:22
78:52 [z]Ps. 77:20
78:53 [a]Ex. 14:19 [b]Ex. 14:27
78:54 [c]Ex. 15:17 [d]Ps. 44:3
78:55 [e]Ps. 44:2 [f]Josh. 13:7; Ps. 136:21
78:56 [g]Judg. 2:11
78:57 [h]ver. 41; Ezek. 20:27 [i]Hos. 7:16
78:58 [j]Deut. 32:16; Judg. 2:12; Ezek. 20:28 [k]Deut. 12:2; 1 Kings 11:7

78:60 [l]1 Sam. 4:11; Jer. 7:12 **78:61** [m]Judg. 18:30

62 [n]He gave his people over also unto the
sword; and was wroth with his inheritance.
63 The fire consumed their young men;
and [o]their maidens were not given to marriage.
64 [p]Their priests fell by the sword; and
[q]their widows made no lamentation.
65 Then the Lord [r]awaked as one out of
sleep, *and* [s]like a mighty man that shouteth
by reason of wine.
66 And [t]he smote his enemies in the hinder parts: he put them to a perpetual reproach.
67 Moreover he refused the tabernacle of
Joseph, and chose not the tribe of Ephraim:
68 But chose the tribe of Judah, the mount
Zion [u]which he loved.
69 And he [v]built his sanctuary like high
palaces, like the earth which he hath established for ever.
70 [w]He chose David also his servant, and
took him from the sheepfolds:
71 From following the [x]ewes great with
young he brought him [y]to feed Jacob his
people, and Israel his inheritance.
72 So he fed them according to the [z]in-
tegrity of his heart; and guided them by the
skilfulness of his hands.

A Psalm of Asaph.

79 O God, the heathen are come into
[a]thine inheritance; [b]thy holy temple
have they defiled; [c]they have laid Jerusalem on heaps.
2 [d]The dead bodies of thy servants have
they given *to be* meat unto the fowls of the
heaven, the flesh of thy saints unto the
beasts of the earth.
3 Their blood have they shed like water
round about Jerusalem; [e]and *there was*
none to bury *them.*
4 [f]We are become a reproach to our
neighbours, a scorn and derision to them
that are round about us.
5 [g]How long, LORD? wilt thou be angry
for ever? shall thy [h]jealousy burn like fire?
6 [i]Pour out thy wrath upon the heathen
that have [j]not known thee, and upon the
kingdoms that have [k]not called upon thy
name.
7 For they have devoured Jacob, and laid
waste his dwelling place.
8 [l]O remember not against us former iniquities: let thy tender mercies speedily prevent us: for we are [m]brought very low.
9 [n]Help us, O God of our salvation, for
the glory of thy name: and deliver us, and
purge away our sins, [o]for thy name's sake.
10 [p]Wherefore should the heathen say,
Where *is* their God? let him be known
among the heathen in our sight *by* the re-
venging of the blood of thy servants *which*
is shed.
11 Let [q]the sighing of the prisoner come
before thee; according to the greatness of
thy power preserve thou those that are appointed to die;
12 And render unto our neighbours [r]sev-
enfold into their bosom [s]their reproach,
wherewith they have reproached thee,
O Lord.
13 So [t]we thy people and sheep of thy
pasture will give thee thanks for ever: [u]we
will shew forth thy praise to all generations.

To the chief Musician upon
Shoshannim-Eduth, A Psalm of Asaph.

80 Give ear, O Shepherd of Israel, thou
that leadest Joseph [v]like a flock;
[w]thou that dwellest *between* the cherubims,
[x]shine forth.
2 [y]Before Ephraim and Benjamin and
Manasseh stir up thy strength, and come
and save us.
3 [z]Turn us again, O God, [a]and cause thy
face to shine; and we shall be saved.
4 O LORD God of hosts, how long wilt
thou be angry against the prayer of thy people?
5 [b]Thou feedest them with the bread of
tears; and givest them tears to drink in great
measure.
6 [c]Thou makest us a strife unto our
neighbours: and our enemies laugh among
themselves.
7 [d]Turn us again, O God of hosts, and
cause thy face to shine; and we shall be
saved.
8 Thou hast brought [e]a vine out of Egypt:
[f]thou hast cast out the heathen, and
planted it.
9 Thou [g]preparedst *room* before it, and
didst cause it to take deep root, and it filled
the land.
10 The hills were covered with the
shadow of it, and the boughs thereof *were*
like the goodly cedars.
11 She sent out her boughs unto the sea,
and her branches [h]unto the river.
12 Why hast thou *then* [i]broken down her
hedges, so that all they which pass by the
way do pluck her?
13 The boar out of the wood doth waste
it, and the wild beast of the field doth devour it.
14 Return, we beseech thee, O God of
hosts: [j]look down from heaven, and behold, and visit this vine;
15 And the vineyard which thy right hand
hath planted, and the branch *that* thou
madest [k]strong for thyself.
16 *It is* burned with fire, *it is* cut down:
[l]they perish at the rebuke of thy countenance.
17 [m]Let thy hand be upon the man of thy
right hand, upon the son of man *whom* thou
madest strong for thyself.
18 So will not we go back from thee:
quicken us, and we will call upon thy name.
19 [n]Turn us again, O LORD God of hosts,
cause thy face to shine; and we shall be
saved.

78:62 [n]1 Sam. 4:10
78:63 [o]Jer. 7:34
78:64 [p]1 Sam. 4:11 [q]Job 27:15; Ezek. 24:23
78:65 [r]Ps. 44:23 [s]Isa. 42:13
78:66 [t]1 Sam. 5:6
78:68 [u]Ps. 87:2
78:69 [v]1 Kings 6
78:70 [w]1 Sam. 16:11; 2 Sam. 7:8
78:71 [x]Gen. 33:13; Isa. 40:11 [y]2 Sam. 5:2; 1 Chron. 11:2
78:72 [z]1 Kings 9:4
79:1 [a]Ex. 15:17; Ps. 74:2 [b]Ps. 74:7 [c]2 Kings 25:9; 2 Chron. 36:19; Mic. 3:12
79:2 [d]Jer. 7:33
79:3 [e]Ps. 141:7; Jer. 14:16; Rev. 11:9
79:4 [f]Ps. 44:13
79:5 [g]Ps. 74:1 [h]Zeph. 1:18
79:6 [i]Jer. 10:25; Rev. 16:1 [j]Isa. 45:4; 2 Thess. 1:8 [k]Ps. 53:4
79:8 [l]Isa. 64:9 [m]Deut. 28:43; Ps. 142:6
79:9 [n]2 Chron. 14:11 [o]Jer. 14:7
79:10 [p]Ps. 42:10
79:11 [q]Ps. 102:20
79:12 [r]Gen. 4:15; Isa. 65:6; Jer. 32:18; Luke 6:38 [s]Ps. 74:18
79:13 [t]Ps. 74:1 [u]Isa. 43:21
80:1 [v]Ps. 77:20 [w]Ex. 25:20; 1 Sam. 4:4; 2 Sam. 6:2; Ps. 99:1 [x]Deut. 33:2; Ps. 50:2
80:2 [y]Num. 2:18-23
80:3 [z]ver. 7; Lam. 5:21 [a]Num. 6:25; Ps. 4:6
80:5 [b]Ps. 42:3; Isa. 30:20
80:6 [c]Ps. 44:13
80:7 [d]ver. 3
80:8 [e]Isa. 5:1; Jer. 2:21; Ezek. 15:6 [f]Ps. 44:2
80:9 [g]Ex. 23:28; Josh. 24:12
80:11 [h]Ps. 72:8
80:12 [i]Ps. 89:40; Isa. 5:5; Nah. 2:2
80:14 [j]Isa. 63:15
80:15 [k]Isa. 49:5
80:16 [l]Ps. 39:11
80:17 [m]Ps. 89:21
80:19 [n]ver. 3

To the chief Musician upon Gittith, *A Psalm* of Asaph.

81 Sing aloud unto God our strength: make a joyful noise unto the God of Jacob.

2 Take a psalm, and bring hither the timbrel, the pleasant harp with the psaltery.

3 Blow up the trumpet in the new moon, in the time appointed, on our solemn feast day.

4 For [o]this *was* a statute for Israel, *and* a law of the God of Jacob.

5 This he ordained in Joseph *for* a testimony, when he went out through the land of Egypt: [p]*where* I heard a language *that* I understood not.

6 [q]I removed his shoulder from the burden: his hands were delivered [r]from the pots.

7 [s]Thou calledst in trouble, and I delivered thee; [t]I answered thee in the secret place of thunder: I [u]proved thee at the waters of Meribah. Selah.

8 [v]Hear, O my people, and I will testify unto thee: O Israel, if thou wilt hearken unto me;

9 [w]There shall no [x]strange god be in thee; neither shalt thou worship any strange god.

10 [y]I *am* the LORD thy God, which brought thee out of the land of Egypt: [z]open thy mouth wide, and I will fill it.

11 But my people would not hearken to my voice; and Israel would [a]none of me.

12 [b]So I gave them up unto their own hearts' lust: *and* they walked in their own counsels.

13 [c]Oh that my people had hearkened unto me, *and* Israel had walked in my ways!

14 I should soon have subdued their enemies, and turned my hand against their adversaries.

15 [d]The haters of the LORD should have submitted themselves unto him: but their time should have endured for ever.

16 He should [e]have fed them also with the finest of the wheat: and with honey [f]out of the rock should I have satisfied thee.

A Psalm of Asaph.

82 God [g]standeth in the congregation of the mighty; he judgeth among [h]the gods.

2 How long will ye judge unjustly, and [i]accept the persons of the wicked? Selah.

3 Defend the poor and fatherless: [j]do justice to the afflicted and needy.

4 [k]Deliver the poor and needy: rid *them* out of the hand of the wicked.

5 They [l]know not, neither will they understand; they walk on in darkness: [m]all the foundations of the earth are out of course.

6 [n]I have said, Ye *are* gods; and all of you *are* children of the most High.

7 But [o]ye shall die like men, and fall like one of the princes.

8 [p]Arise, O God, judge the earth: [q]for thou shalt inherit all nations.

81:4 oLev. 23:24; Num. 10:10
81:5 pPs. 114:1
81:6 qIsa. 9:4 rEx. 1:14
81:7 sEx. 2:23; Ps. 50:15 tEx. 19:19 uEx. 17:6; Num. 20:13
81:8 vPs. 50:7
81:9 wEx. 20:3 xDeut. 32:12; Isa. 43:12
81:10 yEx. 20:2 zPs. 37:3; John 15:7; Eph. 3:20
81:11 aEx. 32:1; Deut. 32:15
81:12 bActs 7:42; Rom. 1:24
81:13 cDeut. 5:29; Isa. 48:18
81:15 dPs. 18:45; Rom. 1:30
81:16 eDeut. 32:13; Ps. 147:14 fJob 29:6
82:1 g2 Chron. 19:6; Eccl. 5:8 hEx. 21:6
82:2 iDeut. 1:17; 2 Chron. 19:7; Prov. 18:5
82:3 jJer. 22:3
82:4 kJob 29:12; Prov. 24:11
82:5 lMic. 3:1 mPs. 11:3
82:6 nEx. 22:9; ver. 1; John 10:34
82:7 oJob 21:32; Ps. 49:12; Ezek. 31:14
82:8 pMic. 7:2 qPs. 2:8; Rev. 11:15
83:1 rPs. 28:1
83:2 sPs. 2:1; Acts 4:25 tPs. 81:15
83:3 uPs. 27:5
83:4 vEsth. 3:6; Jer. 11:19
83:6 w2 Chron. 20:1
83:9 xNum. 31:7; Judg. 7:22 yJudg. 4:15
83:10 z2 Kings 9:37; Zeph. 1:17
83:11 aJudg. 7:25 bJudg. 8:12
83:13 cIsa. 17:13 dPs. 35:5
83:14 eDeut. 33:22
83:15 fJob 9:17
83:16 gPs. 35:4
83:18 hPs. 59:13 iEx. 6:3 jPs. 92:8
84:1 kPs. 27:4
84:2 lPs. 42:1
84:4 mPs. 65:4
84:6 n2 Sam. 5:22
84:7 oProv. 4:18; 2 Cor. 3:18 pDeut. 16:16; Zech. 14:16

A Song *or* Psalm of Asaph.

83 Keep [r]not thou silence, O God: hold not thy peace, and be not still, O God.

2 For, lo, [s]thine enemies make a tumult: and they that [t]hate thee have lifted up the head.

3 They have taken crafty counsel against thy people, and consulted [u]against thy hidden ones.

4 They have said, Come, and [v]let us cut them off from *being* a nation; that the name of Israel may be no more in remembrance.

5 For they have consulted together with one consent: they are confederate against thee:

6 [w]The tabernacles of Edom, and the Ishmaelites; of Moab, and the Hagarenes;

7 Gebal, and Ammon, and Amalek; the Philistines with the inhabitants of Tyre;

8 Assur also is joined with them: they have holpen the children of Lot. Selah.

9 Do unto them as *unto* the [x]Midianites; as *to* [y]Sisera, as *to* Jabin, at the brook of Kison:

10 *Which* perished at En-dor: [z]they became *as* dung for the earth.

11 Make their nobles like [a]Oreb, and like Zeeb: yea, all their princes as [b]Zebah, and as Zalmunna:

12 Who said, Let us take to ourselves the houses of God in possession.

13 [c]O my God, make them like a wheel; [d]as the stubble before the wind.

14 As the fire burneth a wood, and as the flame [e]setteth the mountains on fire;

15 So persecute them [f]with thy tempest, and make them afraid with thy storm.

16 [g]Fill their faces with shame; that they may seek thy name, O LORD.

17 Let them be confounded and troubled for ever; yea, let them be put to shame, and perish:

18 [h]That *men* may know that thou, whose [i]name alone *is* JEHOVAH, *art* [j]the most high over all the earth.

To the chief Musician upon Gittith, A Psalm for the sons of Korah.

84 How [k]amiable *are* thy tabernacles, O LORD of hosts!

2 [l]My soul longeth, yea, even fainteth for the courts of the LORD: my heart and my flesh crieth out for the living God.

3 Yea, the sparrow hath found an house, and the swallow a nest for herself, where she may lay her young, *even* thine altars, O LORD of hosts, my King, and my God.

4 [m]Blessed *are* they that dwell in thy house: they will be still praising thee. Selah.

5 Blessed *is* the man whose strength *is* in thee; in whose heart *are* the ways *of them.*

6 *Who* passing through the valley [n]of Baca make it a well; the rain also filleth the pools.

7 They go [o]from strength to strength, *every one of them* in Zion [p]appeareth before God.

8 O LORD God of hosts, hear my prayer: give ear, O God of Jacob. Selah.

9 [q]Behold, O God our shield, and look upon the face of thine anointed.

10 For a day in thy courts *is* better than a thousand. I had rather be a doorkeeper in the house of my God, than to dwell in the tents of wickedness.

11 For the LORD God *is* a [r]sun and [s]shield: the LORD will give grace and glory: [t]no good *thing* will he withhold from them that walk uprightly.

12 O LORD of hosts, [u]blessed *is* the man that trusteth in thee.

To the chief Musician, A Psalm for the sons of Korah.

85 LORD, thou hast been favourable unto thy land: thou hast [v]brought back the captivity of Jacob.

2 [w]Thou hast forgiven the iniquity of thy people, thou hast covered all their sin. Selah.

3 Thou hast taken away all thy wrath: thou hast turned *thyself* from the fierceness of thine anger.

4 [x]Turn us, O God of our salvation, and cause thine anger toward us to cease.

5 [y]Wilt thou be angry with us for ever? wilt thou draw out thine anger to all generations?

6 Wilt thou not [z]revive us again: that thy people may rejoice in thee?

7 Shew us thy mercy, O LORD, and grant us thy salvation.

8 [a]I will hear what God the LORD will speak: for [b]he will speak peace unto his people, and to his saints: but let them not [c]turn again to folly.

9 Surely [d]his salvation *is* nigh them that fear him; [e]that glory may dwell in our land.

10 Mercy and truth are met together; [f]righteousness and peace have kissed *each other*.

11 [g]Truth shall spring out of the earth; and righteousness shall look down from heaven.

12 [h]Yea, the LORD shall give *that which is* good; and [i]our land shall yield her increase.

13 [j]Righteousness shall go before him; and shall set *us* in the way of his steps.

A Prayer of David.

86 Bow down thine ear, O LORD, hear me: for I *am* poor and needy.

2 Preserve my soul; for I *am* holy: O thou my God, save thy servant [k]that trusteth in thee.

3 [l]Be merciful unto me, O Lord: for I cry unto thee daily.

4 Rejoice the soul of thy servant: [m]for unto thee, O Lord, do I lift up my soul.

5 [n]For thou, Lord, *art* good, and ready to forgive; and plenteous in mercy unto all them that call upon thee.

6 Give ear, O LORD, unto my prayer; and attend to the voice of my supplications.

7 [o]In the day of my trouble I will call upon thee: for thou wilt answer me.

8 [p]Among the gods *there is* none like unto thee, O Lord; [q]neither *are there any works* like unto thy works.

9 [r]All nations whom thou hast made shall come and worship before thee, O Lord; and shall glorify thy name.

10 For thou *art* great, and [s]doest wondrous things: [t]thou *art* God alone.

11 [u]Teach me thy way, O LORD; I will walk in thy truth: unite my heart to fear thy name.

12 I will praise thee, O Lord my God, with all my heart: and I will glorify thy name for evermore.

13 For great *is* thy mercy toward me: and thou hast [v]delivered my soul from the lowest hell.

14 O God, [w]the proud are risen against me, and the assemblies of violent *men* have sought after my soul; and have not set thee before them.

15 [x]But thou, O Lord, *art* a God full of compassion, and gracious, longsuffering, and plenteous in mercy and truth.

16 O [y]turn unto me, and have mercy upon me; give thy strength unto thy servant, and save [z]the son of thine handmaid.

17 Shew me a token for good; that they which hate me may see *it*, and be ashamed: because thou, LORD, hast holpen me, and comforted me.

A Psalm *or* Song for the sons of Korah.

87 His foundation *is* [a]in the holy mountains.

2 [b]The LORD loveth the gates of Zion more than all the dwellings of Jacob.

3 [c]Glorious things are spoken of thee, O city of God. Selah.

4 I will make mention of [d]Rahab and Babylon to them that know me: behold Philistia, and Tyre, with Ethiopia; this *man* was born there.

5 And of Zion it shall be said, This and that man was born in her: and the highest himself shall establish her.

6 [e]The LORD shall count, when he [f]writeth up the people, *that* this *man* was born there. Selah.

7 As well the singers as the players on instruments *shall be there:* all my springs *are* in thee.

A Song *or* Psalm for the sons of Korah, to the chief Musician upon Mahalath Leannoth, Maschil of Heman the Ezrahite.

88 O LORD [g]God of my salvation, I have [h]cried day *and* night before thee:

2 Let my prayer come before thee: incline thine ear unto my cry;

3 For my soul is full of troubles: and my life [i]draweth nigh unto the grave.

4 [j]I am counted with them that go down into the pit: [k]I am as a man *that hath* no strength:

5 Free among the dead, like the slain that lie in the grave, whom thou rememberest no

84:9 [q]Gen. 15:1; ver. 11
84:11 [r]Isa. 60:19 [s]Gen. 15:1; ver. 9; Ps. 115:9; Prov. 2:7 [t]Ps. 34:9
84:12 [u]Ps. 2:12
85:1 [v]Ezra 1:11; Ps. 14:7; Jer. 30:18; Ezek. 39:25; Joel 3:1
85:2 [w]Ps. 32:1
85:4 [x]Ps. 80:7
85:5 [y]Ps. 74:1
85:6 [z]Hab. 3:2
85:8 [a]Hab. 2:1 [b]Zech. 9:10 [c]2 Pet. 2:20
85:9 [d]Isa. 46:13 [e]Zech. 2:5; John 1:14
85:10 [f]Ps. 72:3; Isa. 32:17; Luke 2:14
85:11 [g]Isa. 45:8
85:12 [h]Ps. 84:11; Jam. 1:17 [i]Ps. 67:6
85:13 [j]Ps. 89:14
86:2 [k]Isa. 26:3
86:3 [l]Ps. 56:1
86:4 [m]Ps. 25:1
86:5 [n]ver. 15; Ps. 130:7; Joel 2:13
86:7 [o]Ps. 50:15
86:8 [p]Ex. 15:11; Ps. 89:6 [q]Deut. 3:24
86:9 [r]Ps. 22:31; Isa. 43:7; Rev. 15:4
86:10 [s]Ex. 15:11; Ps. 72:18 [t]Deut. 6:3; Isa. 37:16; Mark 12:29; 1 Cor. 8:4; Eph. 4:6
86:11 [u]Ps. 25:4
86:13 [v]Ps. 56:13
86:14 [w]Ps. 54:3
86:15 [x]Ex. 34:6; Num. 14:18; Neh. 9:17; ver. 5; Ps. 103:8; Joel 2:13
86:16 [y]Ps. 25:16 [z]Ps. 116:16
87:1 [a]Ps. 48:1
87:2 [b]Ps. 78:67
87:3 [c]Isa. 60
87:4 [d]Ps. 89:10; Isa. 51:9
87:6 [e]Ps. 22:30 [f]Ezek. 13:9
88:1 [g]Ps. 27:9 [h]Luke 18:7
88:3 [i]Ps. 107:18
88:4 [j]Ps. 28:1 [k]Ps. 31:12

more: and they are [l]cut off from thy hand.
6 Thou hast laid me in the lowest pit, in
darkness, in the deeps.
7 Thy wrath lieth hard upon me, and
[m]thou hast afflicted *me* with all thy waves.
Selah.
8 [n]Thou hast put away mine acquaintance far from me; thou hast made me an
abomination unto them: [o]*I am* shut up, and
I cannot come forth.
9 [p]Mine eye mourneth by reason of affliction: LORD, [q]I have called daily upon
thee, [r]I have stretched out my hands unto
thee.
10 [s]Wilt thou shew wonders to the dead?
shall the dead arise *and* praise thee? Selah.
11 Shall thy lovingkindness be declared
in the grave? *or* thy faithfulness in destruction?
12 [t]Shall thy wonders be known in the
dark? [u]and thy righteousness in the land of
forgetfulness?
13 But unto thee have I cried, O LORD;
and [v]in the morning shall my prayer prevent thee.
14 LORD, [w]why castest thou off my soul?
why [x]hidest thou thy face from me?
15 I *am* afflicted and ready to die from *my*
youth up: *while* [y]I suffer thy terrors I am
distracted.
16 Thy fierce wrath goeth over me; thy
terrors have cut me off.
17 They came round about me daily like
water; they [z]compassed me about together.
18 [a]Lover and friend hast thou put far
from me, *and* mine acquaintance into darkness.

Maschil of Ethan the Ezrahite.

89 I [b]will sing of the mercies of the
LORD for ever: with my mouth will I
make known thy faithfulness to all generations.
2 For I have said, Mercy shall be built up
for ever: [c]thy faithfulness shalt thou establish in the very heavens.
3 [d]I have made a covenant with my chosen, I have [e]sworn unto David my servant,
4 [f]Thy seed will I establish for ever, and
build up thy throne [g]to all generations.
Selah.
5 And [h]the heavens shall praise thy wonders, O LORD: thy faithfulness also in the
congregation [i]of the saints.
6 For [j]who in the heaven can be compared unto the LORD? *who* among the sons
of the mighty can be likened unto the LORD?
7 [k]God is greatly to be feared in the assembly of the saints, and to be had in reverence of all *them that are* about him.
8 O LORD God of hosts, who *is* a strong
LORD [l]like unto thee? or to thy faithfulness
round about thee?
9 [m]Thou rulest the raging of the sea:
when the waves thereof arise, thou stillest
them.
10 [n]Thou hast broken Rahab in pieces, as

88:5 [l]Isa. 53:8
88:7 [m]Ps. 42:7
88:8 [n]Job 19:13; Ps. 31:11
[o]Lam. 3:7
88:9 [p]Ps. 38:10
[q]Ps. 86:3
[r]Job 11:13; Ps. 143:6
88:10 [s]Ps. 6:5; Isa. 38:18
88:12 [t]Job 10:21; Ps. 143:3
[u]Ps. 31:12; ver. 5; Eccl. 8:10
88:13 [v]Ps. 5:3
88:14 [w]Ps. 43:2
[x]Job 13:24; Ps. 13:1
88:15 [y]Job 6:4
88:17 [z]Ps. 22:16
88:18 [a]Job 19:13; Ps. 31:11
89:1 [b]Ps. 101:1
89:2 [c]Ps. 119:89
89:3
[d]1 Kings 8:16; Isa. 42:1
[e]2 Sam. 7:11; 1 Chron. 17:10; Jer. 30:9; Ezek. 34:23; Hos. 3:5
89:4 [f]ver. 29
[g]ver. 1; Luke 1:32
89:5 [h]Ps. 19:1; Rev. 7:10 [i]ver. 7
89:6 [j]Ps. 40:5
89:7 [k]Ps. 76:7
89:8 [l]Ex. 15:11; 1 Sam. 2:2; Ps. 35:10
89:9 [m]Ps. 65:7
89:10 [n]Ex. 14:26; Ps. 87:4; Isa. 30:7
89:11 [o]Gen. 1:1; 1 Chron. 29:11; Ps. 24:1
89:12 [p]Job 26:7
[q]Josh. 19:22
[r]Josh. 12:1
89:14 [s]Ps. 97:2
[t]Ps. 85:13
89:15
[u]Num. 10:10; Ps. 98:6 [v]Ps. 4:6
89:17 [w]ver. 24; Ps. 75:10
89:19 [x]ver. 3; 1 Kings 11:34
89:20
[y]1 Sam. 16:1
89:21 [z]Ps. 80:17
89:22
[a]2 Sam. 7:13
89:23 [b]2 Sam. 7:9
89:24 [c]Ps. 61:7
[d]ver. 17
89:25 [e]Ps. 72:8
89:26
[f]2 Sam. 7:14; 1 Chron. 22:10
[g]2 Sam. 22:47
89:27 [h]Ps. 2:7; Col. 1:15
[i]Num. 24:7
89:28 [j]Isa. 55:3
[k]ver. 34
89:29 [l]ver. 4
[m]ver. 4; Isa. 9:7; Jer. 33:17
[n]Deut. 11:21
89:30
[o]2 Sam. 7:14
[p]Ps. 119:53; Jer. 9:13
89:32
[q]2 Sam. 7:14; 1 Kings 11:31
89:33
[r]2 Sam. 7:13
89:35 [s]Am. 4:2

one that is slain; thou hast scattered thine
enemies with thy strong arm.
11 [o]The heavens *are* thine, the earth also
is thine: *as for* the world and the fulness
thereof, thou hast founded them.
12 [p]The north and the south thou hast
created them: [q]Tabor and [r]Hermon shall
rejoice in thy name.
13 Thou hast a mighty arm: strong is thy
hand, *and* high is thy right hand.
14 [s]Justice and judgment *are* the habitation of thy throne: [t]mercy and truth shall
go before thy face.
15 Blessed *is* the people that know the
[u]joyful sound: they shall walk, O LORD, in
the [v]light of thy countenance.
16 In thy name shall they rejoice all the
day: and in thy righteousness shall they be
exalted.
17 For thou *art* the glory of their strength:
[w]and in thy favour our horn shall be exalted.
18 For the LORD *is* our defence; and the
Holy One of Israel *is* our king.
19 Then thou spakest in vision to thy holy
one, and saidst, I have laid help upon *one*
that is mighty; I have exalted *one* [x]chosen
out of the people.
20 [y]I have found David my servant; with
my holy oil have I anointed him:
21 [z]With whom my hand shall be established: mine arm also shall strengthen him.
22 [a]The enemy shall not exact upon him;
nor the son of wickedness afflict him.
23 [b]And I will beat down his foes before
his face, and plague them that hate him.
24 But [c]my faithfulness and my mercy
shall be with him: and [d]in my name shall
his horn be exalted.
25 [e]I will set his hand also in the sea, and
his right hand in the rivers.
26 He shall cry unto me, Thou *art* [f]my
father, my God, and [g]the rock of my salvation.
27 Also I will make him [h]*my* firstborn,
[i]higher than the kings of the earth.
28 [j]My mercy will I keep for him for
evermore, and [k]my covenant shall stand
fast with him.
29 [l]His seed also will I make *to endure*
for ever, [m]and his throne [n]as the days of
heaven.
30 [o]If his children [p]forsake my law, and
walk not in my judgments;
31 If they break my statutes, and keep not
my commandments;
32 Then [q]will I visit their transgression
with the rod, and their iniquity with stripes.
33 [r]Nevertheless my lovingkindness will
I not utterly take from him, nor suffer my
faithfulness to fail.
34 My covenant will I not break, nor alter
the thing that is gone out of my lips.
35 Once have I sworn [s]by my holiness
that I will not lie unto David.

36 [t]His seed shall endure for ever, and
his throne [u]as the sun before me.
37 It shall be established for ever as the
moon, and *as* a faithful witness in heaven.
Selah.
38 But thou hast [v]cast off and [w]abhorred,
thou hast been wroth with thine anointed.
39 Thou hast made void the covenant of
thy servant: [x]thou hast profaned his crown
by casting it to the ground.
40 [y]Thou hast broken down all his
hedges; thou hast brought his strong holds
to ruin.
41 All that pass by the way spoil him: he
is [z]a reproach to his neighbours.
42 Thou hast set up the right hand of his
adversaries; thou hast made all his enemies
to rejoice.
43 Thou hast also turned the edge of his
sword, and hast not made him to stand in
the battle.
44 Thou hast made his glory to cease, and
[a]cast his throne down to the ground.
45 The days of his youth hast thou shortened: thou hast covered him with shame.
Selah.
46 [b]How long, LORD? wilt thou hide thyself for ever? [c]shall thy wrath burn like
fire?
47 [d]Remember how short my time is:
wherefore hast thou made all men in vain?
48 [e]What man *is he that* liveth, and shall
not [f]see death? shall he deliver his soul
from the hand of the grave? Selah.
49 Lord, where *are* thy former lovingkindnesses, *which* thou [g]swarest unto David [h]in thy truth?
50 Remember, Lord, the reproach of thy
servants; [i]*how* I do bear in my bosom *the
reproach of* all the mighty people;
51 [j]Wherewith thine enemies have reproached, O LORD; wherewith they have reproached the footsteps of thine anointed.
52 [k]Blessed *be* the LORD for evermore.
Amen, and Amen.

BOOK IV

A Prayer of Moses the man of God.

90 LORD, [l]thou hast been our dwelling
place in all generations.
2 [m]Before the mountains were brought
forth, or ever thou hadst formed the earth
and the world, even from everlasting to
everlasting, thou *art* God.
3 Thou turnest man to destruction; and
sayest, [n]Return, ye children of men.
4 [o]For a thousand years in thy sight *are
but* as yesterday when it is past, and *as* a
watch in the night.
5 Thou carriest them away as with a
flood; [p]they are *as* a sleep: in the morning
[q]*they are* like grass *which* groweth up.
6 [r]In the morning it flourisheth, and
groweth up; in the evening it is cut down,
and withereth.
7 For we are consumed by thine anger,
and by thy wrath are we troubled.
8 [s]Thou hast set our iniquities before
thee, our [t]secret *sins* in the light of thy
countenance.
9 For all our days are passed away in thy
wrath: we spend our years as a tale *that is
told*.
10 The days of our years *are* threescore
years and ten; and if by reason of strength
they be fourscore years, yet *is* their strength
labour and sorrow; for it is soon cut off, and
we fly away.
11 Who knoweth the power of thine anger? even according to thy fear, *so is* thy
wrath.
12 [u]So teach *us* to number our days, that
we may apply *our* hearts unto wisdom.
13 Return, O LORD, how long? and let it
[v]repent thee concerning thy servants.
14 O satisfy us early with thy mercy;
[w]that we may rejoice and be glad all our
days.
15 Make us glad according to the days
wherein thou hast afflicted us, *and* the years
wherein we have seen evil.
16 Let [x]thy work appear unto thy servants, and thy glory unto their children.
17 [y]And let the beauty of the LORD our
God be upon us: and [z]establish thou the
work of our hands upon us; yea, the work of
our hands establish thou it.
91 He [a]that dwelleth in the secret place
of the most High shall abide [b]under
the shadow of the Almighty.
2 [c]I will say of the LORD, *He is* my refuge
and my fortress: my God; in him will I trust.
3 Surely [d]he shall deliver thee from the
snare of the fowler, *and* from the noisome
pestilence.
4 [e]He shall cover thee with his feathers,
and under his wings shalt thou trust: his
truth *shall be thy* shield and buckler.
5 [f]Thou shalt not be afraid for the terror
by night; *nor* for the arrow *that* flieth by
day;
6 *Nor* for the pestilence *that* walketh in
darkness; *nor* for the destruction *that* wasteth at noonday.
7 A thousand shall fall at thy side, and ten
thousand at thy right hand; *but* it shall not
come nigh thee.
8 Only [g]with thine eyes shalt thou behold
and see the reward of the wicked.
9 Because thou hast made the LORD,
which is [h]my refuge, *even* the most High,
[i]thy habitation;
10 [j]There shall no evil befall thee, neither shall any plague come nigh thy dwelling.
11 [k]For he shall give his angels charge
over thee, to keep thee in all thy ways.
12 They shall bear thee up in *their* hands,
[l]lest thou dash thy foot against a stone.
13 Thou shalt tread upon the lion and adder: the young lion and the dragon shalt
thou trample under feet.
14 Because he hath set his love upon me,
therefore will I deliver him: I will set him on
high, because he hath [m]known my name.
15 [n]He shall call upon me, and I will an-

89:36 [t]2 Sam. 7:16; Luke 1:33; John 12:34; ver. 4:29 [u]Ps. 72:5; Jer. 33:20
89:38 [v]1 Chron. 28:9; Ps. 44:9 [w]Deut. 32:19; Ps. 78:59
89:39 [x]Ps. 74:7; Lam. 5:16
89:40 [y]Ps. 80:12
89:41 [z]Ps. 44:13
89:44 [a]ver. 39
89:46 [b]Ps. 79:5 [c]Ps. 78:63
89:47 [d]Job 7:7; Ps. 39:5
89:48 [e]Ps. 49:9 [f]Heb. 11:5
89:49 [g]2 Sam. 7:15; Isa. 55:3 [h]Ps. 54:5
89:50 [i]Ps. 69:9
89:51 [j]Ps. 74:22
89:52 [k]Ps. 41:13
90:1 [l]Deut. 33:27; Ezek. 11:16
90:2 [m]Prov. 8:25
90:3 [n]Gen. 3:19; Eccl. 12:7
90:4 [o]2 Pet. 3:8
90:5 [p]Ps. 73:20 [q]Ps. 103:15; Isa. 40:6
90:6 [r]Ps. 92:7; Job 14:2
90:8 [s]Ps. 50:21; Jer. 16:17 [t]Ps. 19:12
90:12 [u]Ps. 39:4
90:13 [v]Deut. 32:36; Ps. 135:14
90:14 [w]Ps. 85:6
90:16 [x]Hab. 3:2
90:17 [y]Ps. 27:4 [z]Isa. 26:12
91:1 [a]Ps. 27:5 [b]Ps. 17:8
91:2 [c]Ps. 142:5
91:3 [d]Ps. 124:7
91:4 [e]Ps. 17:8
91:5 [f]Job 5:19; Ps. 112:7; Prov. 3:23; Isa. 43:2
91:8 [g]Ps. 37:34; Mal. 1:5
91:9 [h]ver. 2 [i]Ps. 71:3
91:10 [j]Prov. 12:21
91:11 [k]Ps. 34:7; Matt. 4:6; Luke 4:10; Heb. 1:14
91:12 [l]Job 5:23; Ps. 37:24
91:14 [m]Ps. 9:10
91:15 [n]Ps. 50:15

swer him: [o]I *will be* with him in trouble; I will deliver him, and [p]honour him.

16 With long life will I satisfy him, and shew him my salvation.

A Psalm *or* Song for the sabbath day.

92 *It is* [q]*a* good *thing* to give thanks unto the LORD, and to sing praises unto thy name, O most High:

2 To [r]shew forth thy lovingkindness in the morning, and thy faithfulness every night,

3 [s]Upon an instrument of ten strings, and upon the psaltery; upon the harp with a solemn sound.

4 For thou, LORD, hast made me glad through thy work: I will triumph in the works of thy hands.

5 [t]O LORD, how great are thy works! *and* [u]thy thoughts are very deep.

6 [v]A brutish man knoweth not; neither doth a fool understand this.

7 When [w]the wicked spring as the grass, and when all the workers of iniquity do flourish; *it is* that they shall be destroyed for ever:

8 [x]But thou, LORD, *art most* high for evermore.

9 For, lo, thine enemies, O LORD, for, lo, thine enemies shall perish; all the workers of iniquity shall [y]be scattered.

10 But [z]my horn shalt thou exalt like *the horn of* an unicorn: I shall be [a]anointed with fresh oil.

11 [b]Mine eye also shall see *my desire* on mine enemies, *and* mine ears shall hear *my desire* of the wicked that rise up against me.

12 [c]The righteous shall flourish like the palm tree: he shall grow like a cedar in Lebanon.

13 Those that be planted in the house of the LORD shall [d]flourish in the courts of our God.

14 They shall still bring forth fruit in old age; they shall be fat and flourishing;

15 To shew that the LORD *is* upright: [e]*he is* my rock, and [f]*there is* no unrighteousness in him.

93 The [g]LORD reigneth, [h]he is clothed with majesty; the LORD is clothed with strength, [i]*wherewith* he hath girded himself: [j]the world also is stablished, that it cannot be moved.

2 [k]Thy throne *is* established of old: thou *art* from everlasting.

3 The floods have lifted up, O LORD, the floods have lifted up their voice; the floods lift up their waves.

4 [l]The LORD on high *is* mightier than the noise of many waters, *yea, than* the mighty waves of the sea.

5 Thy testimonies are very sure: holiness becometh thine house, O LORD, for ever.

94 O LORD God, [m]to whom vengeance belongeth; O God, to whom vengeance belongeth, shew thyself.

2 [n]Lift up thyself, thou [o]judge of the earth: render a reward to the proud.

91:15 [o]Isa. 43:2 [p]1 Sam. 2:30
92:1 [q]Ps. 147:1
92:2 [r]Ps. 89:1
92:3 [s]1 Chron. 23:5; Ps. 33:2
92:5 [t]Ps. 40:5 [u]Isa. 28:29; Rom. 11:33
92:6 [v]Ps. 73:22
92:7 [w]Job 12:6; Ps. 37:1; Jer. 12:1; Mal. 3:15
92:8 [x]Ps. 56:2
92:9 [y]Ps. 68:1
92:10 [z]Ps. 89:17 [a]Ps. 23:5
92:11 [b]Ps. 54:7
92:12 [c]Ps. 52:8; Isa. 65:22; Hos. 14:5
92:13 [d]Ps. 100:4
92:15 [e]Deut. 32:4 [f]Rom. 9:14
93:1 [g]Ps. 96:10; Isa. 52:7; Rev. 19:6 [h]Ps. 104:1 [i]Ps. 65:6 [j]Ps. 96:10
93:2 [k]Ps. 45:6; Prov. 8:22
93:4 [l]Ps. 65:7
94:1 [m]Deut. 32:35; Nah. 1:2
94:2 [n]Ps. 7:6 [o]Gen. 18:25
94:3 [p]Job 20:5
94:4 [q]Ps. 31:18; Jude 15
94:7 [r]Ps. 10:11
94:8 [s]Ps. 73:22
94:9 [t]Ex. 4:11; Prov. 20:12
94:10 [u]Job 35:11; Isa. 28:26
94:11 [v]1 Cor. 3:20
94:12 [w]Job 5:17; Prov. 3:11; 1 Cor. 11:32; Heb. 12:5
94:14 [x]1 Sam. 12:22; Rom. 11:1
94:17 [y]Ps. 124:1
94:18 [z]Ps. 38:16
94:20 [a]Am. 6:3 [b]Ps. 58:2; Isa. 10:1
94:21 [c]Matt. 27:1 [d]Ex. 23:7; Prov. 17:15
94:22 [e]Ps. 59:9
94:23 [f]Ps. 7:16; Prov. 2:22
95:1 [g]Ps. 100:1 [h]Deut. 32:15; 2 Sam. 22:47
95:3 [i]Ps. 96:4
95:5 [j]Gen. 1:9
95:6 [k]1 Cor. 6:20
95:7 [l]Ps. 79:13

3 LORD, [p]how long shall the wicked, how long shall the wicked triumph?

4 *How long* shall they [q]utter *and* speak hard things? *and* all the workers of iniquity boast themselves?

5 They break in pieces thy people, O LORD, and afflict thine heritage.

6 They slay the widow and the stranger, and murder the fatherless.

7 [r]Yet they say, The LORD shall not see, neither shall the God of Jacob regard *it*.

8 [s]Understand, ye brutish among the people: and *ye* fools, when will ye be wise?

9 [t]He that planted the ear, shall he not hear? he that formed the eye, shall he not see?

10 He that chastiseth the heathen, shall not he correct? he that [u]teacheth man knowledge, *shall not he know?*

11 [v]The LORD knoweth the thoughts of man, that they *are* vanity.

12 [w]Blessed *is* the man whom thou chastenest, O LORD, and teachest him out of thy law;

13 That thou mayest give him rest from the days of adversity, until the pit be digged for the wicked.

14 [x]For the LORD will not cast off his people, neither will he forsake his inheritance.

15 But judgment shall return unto righteousness: and all the upright in heart shall follow it.

16 Who will rise up for me against the evildoers? *or* who will stand up for me against the workers of iniquity?

17 [y]Unless the LORD *had been* my help, my soul had almost dwelt in silence.

18 When I said, [z]My foot slippeth; thy mercy, O LORD, held me up.

19 In the multitude of my thoughts within me thy comforts delight my soul.

20 Shall [a]the throne of iniquity have fellowship with thee, which [b]frameth mischief by a law?

21 [c]They gather themselves together against the soul of the righteous, and [d]condemn the innocent blood.

22 But the LORD is [e]my defence; and my God *is* the rock of my refuge.

23 And [f]he shall bring upon them their own iniquity, and shall cut them off in their own wickedness; *yea,* the LORD our God shall cut them off.

95 O come, let us sing unto the LORD: [g]let us make a joyful noise to [h]the rock of our salvation.

2 Let us come before his presence with thanksgiving, and make a joyful noise unto him with psalms.

3 For [i]the LORD *is* a great God, and a great King above all gods.

4 In his hand *are* the deep places of the earth: the strength of the hills *is* his also.

5 [j]The sea *is* his, and he made it: and his hands formed the dry *land*.

6 O come, let us worship and bow down: let [k]us kneel before the LORD our maker.

7 For he *is* our God; and [l]we *are* the peo-

ple of his pasture, and the sheep of his hand.
[m]To day if ye will hear his voice,
8 Harden not your heart, [n]as in the provocation, *and* as *in* the day of temptation in
the wilderness:
9 When [o]your fathers tempted me,
proved me, and [p]saw my work.
10 [q]Forty years long was I grieved with
this generation, and said, It *is* a people that
do err in their heart, and they have not
known my ways:
11 Unto whom [r]I sware in my wrath that
they should not enter into my rest.

96 O [s]sing unto the LORD a new song:
sing unto the LORD, all the earth.
2 Sing unto the LORD, bless his name;
shew forth his salvation from day to day.
3 Declare his glory among the heathen,
his wonders among all people.
4 For [t]the LORD *is* great, and [u]greatly to
be praised: [v]he *is* to be feared above all
gods.
5 For [w]all the gods of the nations *are*
idols: [x]but the LORD made the heavens.
6 Honor and majesty *are* before him:
strength and [y]beauty *are* in his sanctuary.
7 [z]Give unto the LORD, O ye kindreds of
the people, give unto the LORD glory and
strength.
8 Give unto the LORD the glory *due unto*
his name: bring an offering, and come into
his courts.
9 O worship the LORD [a]in the beauty of
holiness: fear before him, all the earth.
10 Say among the heathen *that* [b]the
LORD reigneth: the world also shall be established that it shall not be moved: [c]he
shall judge the people righteously.
11 [d]Let the heavens rejoice, and let the
earth be glad; [e]let the sea roar, and the fulness thereof.
12 Let the field be joyful, and all that *is*
therein: then shall all the trees of the wood
rejoice
13 Before the LORD: for he cometh, for he
cometh to judge the earth: [f]he shall judge
the world with righteousness, and the people with his truth.

97 The [g]LORD reigneth; let the earth rejoice; let the multitude of [h]isles be
glad *thereof.*
2 [i]Clouds and darkness *are* round about
him: [j]righteousness and judgment *are* the
habitation of his throne.
3 [k]A fire goeth before him, and burneth
up his enemies round about.
4 [l]His lightnings enlightened the world:
the earth saw, and trembled.
5 [m]The hills melted like wax at the presence of the LORD, at the presence of the
Lord of the whole earth.
6 [n]The heavens declare his righteousness, and all the people see his glory.
7 [o]Confounded be all they that serve
graven images, that boast themselves of
idols: [p]worship him, all *ye* gods.
8 Zion heard, and was glad; and the

95:7 [m]Heb. 3:7 **95:8** [n]Ex. 17:2; Num. 14:22; Deut. 6:16 **95:9** [o]Ps. 78:18; 1 Cor. 10:9 [p]Num. 14:22 **95:10** [q]Heb. 3:10 **95:11** [r]Num. 14:23; Heb. 3:11 **96:1** [s]1 Chron. 16:23-33; Ps. 33:3 **96:4** [t]Ps. 145:3 [u]Ps. 18:3 [v]Ps. 95:3 **96:5** [w]Jer. 10:11 [x]Ps. 115:15; Isa. 42:5 **96:6** [y]Ps. 29:2 **96:7** [z]Ps. 29:1 **96:9** [a]Ps. 29:2 **96:10** [b]Ps. 93:1; Rev. 11:15 [c]ver. 13; Ps. 67:4 **96:11** [d]Ps. 69:34 [e]Ps. 98:7 **96:13** [f]Ps. 67:4; Rev. 19:11 **97:1** [g]Ps. 96:10 [h]Isa. 60:9 **97:2** [i]1 Kings 8:12; Ps. 18:11 [j]Ps. 89:14 **97:3** [k]Ps. 18:8; Dan. 7:10; Hab. 3:5 **97:4** [l]Ex. 19:18; Ps. 77:18 **97:5** [m]Judg. 5:5; Mic. 1:4; Nah. 1:5 **97:6** [n]Ps. 19:1 **97:7** [o]Ex. 20:4; Lev. 26:1; Deut. 5:8 [p]Heb. 1:6 **97:9** [q]Ps. 83:18 [r]Ex. 18:11; Ps. 95:3 **97:10** [s]Ps. 34:14; Am. 5:15; Rom. 12:9 [t]Ps. 31:23; Prov. 2:8 [u]Ps. 37:39; Dan. 8:28 **97:11** [v]Job 22:28; Ps. 112:4; Prov. 4:18 **97:12** [w]Ps. 33:1 [x]Ps. 30:4 **98:1** [y]Ps. 33:3; Isa. 42:10 [z]Ex. 15:11; Ps. 77:14 [a]Ex. 15:6; Isa. 59:16 **98:2** [b]Isa. 52:10; Luke 2:30 [c]Isa. 62:2; Rom. 3:25 **98:3** [d]Luke 1:54 [e]Isa. 49:6; Luke 2:30; Acts 13:47 **98:4** [f]Ps. 95:1 **98:6** [g]Num. 10:10; 1 Chron. 15:28; 2 Chron. 29:27 **98:7** [h]Ps. 96:11 **98:8** [i]Isa. 55:12 **98:9** [j]Ps. 96:10 **99:1** [k]Ps. 93:1 [l]Ex. 25:22; Ps. 18:10 **99:2** [m]Ps. 97:9 **99:3** [n]Deut. 28:58; Rev. 15:4 **99:4** [o]Job 36:5 **99:5** [p]ver. 9 [q]1 Chron. 28:2; Ps. 132:7 [r]Lev. 19:2 **99:6** [s]Jer. 15:1 [t]Ex. 14:15; 1 Sam. 7:9

daughters of Judah rejoiced because of thy
judgments, O LORD.
9 For thou, LORD, *art* [q]high above all the
earth: [r]thou art exalted far above all gods.
10 Ye that love the LORD, [s]hate evil: [t]he
preserveth the souls of his saints; [u]he delivereth them out of the hand of the wicked.
11 [v]Light is sown for the righteous, and
gladness for the upright in heart.
12 [w]Rejoice in the LORD, ye righteous;
[x]and give thanks at the remembrance of his
holiness.

A Psalm.

98 O [y]sing unto the LORD a new song;
for [z]he hath done marvellous things:
[a]his right hand, and his holy arm, hath gotten him the victory.
2 [b]The LORD hath made known his salvation: [c]his righteousness hath he openly
shewed in the sight of the heathen.
3 He hath [d]remembered his mercy and
his truth toward the house of Israel: [e]all the
ends of the earth have seen the salvation of
our God.
4 [f]Make a joyful noise unto the LORD, all
the earth: make a loud noise, and rejoice,
and sing praise.
5 Sing unto the LORD with the harp; with
the harp, and the voice of a psalm.
6 [g]With trumpets and sound of cornet
make a joyful noise before the LORD, the
King.
7 [h]Let the sea roar, and the fulness
thereof; the world, and they that dwell
therein.
8 Let the floods [i]clap *their* hands: let the
hills be joyful together
9 Before the LORD; [j]for he cometh to
judge the earth: with righteousness shall he
judge the world, and the people with equity.

99 The [k]LORD reigneth; let the people
tremble: [l]he sitteth *between* the
cherubims; let the earth be moved.
2 The LORD *is* great in Zion; and he *is*
[m]high above all the people.
3 Let them praise [n]thy great and terrible
name; *for* it *is* holy.
4 [o]The king's strength also loveth judgment; thou dost establish equity, thou ex-
ecutest judgment and righteousness in
Jacob.
5 [p]Exalt ye the LORD our God, and worship at [q]his footstool; *for* [r]he *is* holy.
6 [s]Moses and Aaron among his priests,
and Samuel among them that call upon his
name; they [t]called upon the LORD, and he
answered them.
7 [u]He spake unto them in the cloudy pillar: they kept his testimonies, and the ordinance *that* he gave them.
8 Thou answeredst them, O LORD our
God: [v]thou wast a God that forgavest them,
though [w]thou tookest vengeance of their inventions.

99:7 [u]Ex. 33:9 **99:8** [v]Num. 14:20; Jer. 46:28; Zeph. 3:7 [w]Ex. 32:2; Num. 20:12; Deut. 9:20

9 [x]Exalt the LORD our God, and worship at his holy hill; for the LORD our God *is* holy.

A Psalm of praise.

100 Make [y]a joyful noise unto the LORD, all ye lands.

2 Serve the LORD with gladness: come before his presence with singing.

3 Know ye that the LORD he *is* God: [z]*it is* he *that* hath made us, and not we ourselves; [a]*we are* his people, and the sheep of his pasture.

4 [b]Enter into his gates with thanksgiving, *and* into his courts with praise: be thankful unto him, *and* bless his name.

5 For the LORD *is* good; [c]his mercy *is* everlasting; and his truth *endureth* to all generations.

A Psalm of David.

101 I [d]will sing of mercy and judgment: unto thee, O LORD, will I sing.

2 I will [e]behave myself wisely in a perfect way. O when wilt thou come unto me? I will [f]walk within my house with a perfect heart.

3 I will set no wicked thing before mine eyes: [g]I hate the work of them [h]that turn aside; *it* shall not cleave to me.

4 A froward heart shall depart from me: I will not [i]know a wicked *person*.

5 Whoso privily slandereth his neighbour, him will I cut off: [j]him that hath an high look and a proud heart will not I suffer.

6 Mine eyes *shall be* upon the faithful of the land, that they may dwell with me: he that walketh in a perfect way, he shall serve me.

7 He that worketh deceit shall not dwell within my house: he that telleth lies shall not tarry in my sight.

8 I will [k]early destroy all the wicked of the land; that I may cut off all wicked doers [l]from the city of the LORD.

A Prayer of the afflicted, when he is overwhelmed, and poureth out his complaint before the LORD.

102 Hear my prayer, O LORD, and let my cry [m]come unto thee.

2 [n]Hide not thy face from me in the day *when* I am in trouble; [o]incline thine ear unto me: in the day *when* I call answer me speedily.

3 [p]For my days are consumed like smoke, and [q]my bones are burned as an hearth.

4 My heart is smitten, and [r]withered like grass; so that I forget to eat my bread.

5 By reason of the voice of my groaning [s]my bones cleave to my skin.

6 [t]I am like [u]a pelican of the wilderness: I am like an owl of the desert.

7 I [v]watch, and am as a sparrow [w]alone upon the house top.

8 Mine enemies reproach me all the day; *and* they that are [x]mad against me are [y]sworn against me.

9 For I have eaten ashes like bread, and [z]mingled my drink with weeping,

10 Because of thine indignation and thy wrath: for [a]thou hast lifted me up, and cast me down.

11 [b]My days *are* like a shadow that declineth; and [c]I am withered like grass.

12 But [d]thou, O LORD, shalt endure for ever; and thy [e]remembrance unto all generations.

13 Thou shalt arise, *and* [f]have mercy upon Zion: for the time to favour her, yea, the [g]set time, is come.

14 For thy servants take pleasure in [h]her stones, and favour the dust thereof.

15 So the heathen shall [i]fear the name of the LORD, and all the kings of the earth thy glory.

16 When the LORD shall build up Zion, [j]he shall appear in his glory.

17 [k]He will regard the prayer of the destitute, and not despise their prayer.

18 This shall be [l]written for the generation to come: and [m]the people which shall be created shall praise the LORD.

19 For he hath [n]looked down from the height of his sanctuary; from heaven did the LORD behold the earth;

20 [o]To hear the groaning of the prisoner; to loose those that are appointed to death;

21 To [p]declare the name of the LORD in Zion, and his praise in Jerusalem;

22 When the people are gathered together, and the kingdoms, to serve the LORD.

23 He weakened my strength in the way; he [q]shortened my days.

24 [r]I said, O my God, take me not away in the midst of my days: [s]thy years *are* throughout all generations.

25 [t]Of old hast thou laid the foundation of the earth: and the heavens *are* the work of thy hands.

26 [u]They shall perish, but [v]thou shalt endure: yea, all of them shall wax old like a garment; as a vesture shalt thou change them, and they shall be changed:

27 But [w]thou *art* the same, and thy years shall have no end.

28 [x]The children of thy servants shall continue, and their seed shall be established before thee.

A Psalm of David.

103 Bless [y]the LORD, O my soul: and all that is within me, *bless* his holy name.

2 Bless the LORD, O my soul, and forget not all his benefits:

3 [z]Who forgiveth all thine iniquities; who [a]healeth all thy diseases;

4 Who [b]redeemeth thy life from destruction; [c]who crowneth thee with lovingkindness and tender mercies;

5 Who satisfieth thy mouth with good

99:9 [x]ver. 5; Ex. 15:2; Ps. 34:3
100:1 [y]Ps. 95:1
100:3 [z]Ps. 119:73; Eph. 2:10 [a]Ps. 95:7; Ezek. 34:30
100:4 [b]Ps. 66:13
100:5 [c]Ps. 136:1
101:1 [d]Ps. 89:1
101:2 [e]1 Sam. 18:14 [f]1 Kings 9:4
101:3 [g]Ps. 97:10 [h]Josh. 23:6; 1 Sam. 12:20; Ps. 40:4
101:4 [i]Matt. 7:23; 2 Tim. 2:19
101:5 [j]Ps. 18:27; Prov. 6:17
101:8 [k]Ps. 75:10; Jer. 21:12 [l]Ps. 48:2
102:1 [m]Ex. 2:23; 1 Sam. 9:16; Ps. 18:6
102:2 [n]Ps. 27:9 [o]Ps. 71:2
102:3 [p]Ps. 119:83; Jam. 4:14 [q]Job 30:30; Ps. 31:10; Lam. 1:13
102:4 [r]Ps. 37:2; ver. 11
102:5 [s]Job 19:20; Lam. 4:8
102:6 [t]Job 30:29 [u]Isa. 34:11; Zeph. 2:14
102:7 [v]Ps. 77:4 [w]Ps. 38:11
102:8 [x]Acts 26:11 [y]Acts 23:12
102:9 [z]Ps. 42:3
102:10 [a]Ps. 30:7
102:11 [b]Job 14:2; Ps. 109:23; Eccl. 6:12 [c]ver. 4; Isa. 40:6; Jam. 1:10
102:12 [d]ver. 26; Ps. 9:7; Lam. 5:19 [e]Ps. 135:13
102:13 [f]Isa. 60:10; Zech. 1:12 [g]Isa. 40:2
102:14 [h]Ps. 79:1
102:15 [i]1 Kings 8:43; Ps. 138:4; Isa. 60:3
102:16 [j]Isa. 60:1
102:17 [k]Neh. 1:6
102:18 [l]Rom. 15:4; 1 Cor. 10:11 [m]Ps. 22:31; Isa. 43:21
102:19 [n]Deut. 26:15; Ps. 14:2
102:20 [o]Ps. 79:11
102:21 [p]Ps. 22:22
102:23 [q]Job 21:21
102:24 [r]Isa. 38:10 [s]Ps. 90:2; Hab. 1:12
102:25 [t]Gen. 1:1; Heb. 1:10
102:26 [u]Isa. 34:4; Rom. 8:20; 2 Pet. 3:7 [v]ver. 12
102:27 [w]Mal. 3:6; Heb. 13:8; Jam. 1:17
102:28 [x]Ps. 69:36

103:1 [y]ver. 22; Ps. 104:1 **103:3** [z]Ps. 130:8; Isa. 33:24; Matt. 9:2; Mark 2:5; Luke 7:47 [a]Ex. 15:26; Ps. 147:3; Jer. 17:14 **103:4** [b]Ps. 34:22 [c]Ps. 5:12

things; so that [d]thy youth is renewed like the eagle's.

6 [e]The LORD executeth righteousness and judgment for all that are oppressed.

7 [f]He made known his ways unto Moses, his acts unto the children of Israel.

8 [g]The LORD *is* merciful and gracious, slow to anger, and plenteous in mercy.

9 [h]He will not always chide: neither will he keep *his anger* for ever.

10 [i]He hath not dealt with us after our sins; nor rewarded us according to our iniquities.

11 [j]For as the heaven is high above the earth, *so* great is his mercy toward them that fear him.

12 As far as the east is from the west, *so* far hath he [k]removed our transgressions from us.

13 [l]Like as a father pitieth *his* children, *so* the LORD pitieth them that fear him.

14 For he knoweth our frame; [m]he remembereth that we *are* [n]dust.

15 *As for* man, [o]his days *are* as grass: [p]as a flower of the field, so he flourisheth.

16 For the wind passeth over it, and it is gone; and [q]the place thereof shall know it no more.

17 But the mercy of the LORD *is* from everlasting to everlasting upon them that fear him, and his righteousness [r]unto children's children;

18 [s]To such as keep his covenant, and to those that remember his commandments to do them.

19 The LORD hath prepared his [t]throne in the heavens; and [u]his kingdom ruleth over all.

20 [v]Bless the LORD, ye his angels, that excel in strength, that [w]do his commandments, hearkening unto the voice of his word.

21 Bless ye the LORD, all *ye* [x]his hosts; [y]*ye* ministers of his, that do his pleasure.

22 [z]Bless the LORD, all his works in all places of his dominion: [a]bless the LORD, O my soul.

104 Bless [b]the LORD, O my soul. O LORD my God, thou art very great; [c]thou art clothed with honour and majesty.

2 [d]Who coverest *thyself* with light as *with* a garment: [e]who stretchest out the heavens like a curtain:

3 [f]Who layeth the beams of his chambers in the waters: [g]who maketh the clouds his chariot: [h]who walketh upon the wings of the wind:

4 [i]Who maketh his angels spirits; [j]his ministers a flaming fire:

5 [k]*Who* laid the foundations of the earth, *that* it should not be removed for ever.

6 [l]Thou coveredst it with the deep as *with* a garment: the waters stood above the mountains.

7 [m]At thy rebuke they fled; at the voice of thy thunder they hasted away.

8 [n]They go up by the mountains; they go down by the valleys unto [o]the place which thou hast founded for them.

9 [p]Thou hast set a bound that they may not pass over; [q]that they turn not again to cover the earth.

10 He sendeth the springs into the valleys, *which* run among the hills.

11 They give drink to every beast of the field: the wild asses quench their thirst.

12 By them shall the fowls of the heaven have their habitation, *which* sing among the branches.

13 [r]He watereth the hills from his chambers: [s]the earth is satisfied with [t]the fruit of thy works.

14 [u]He causeth the grass to grow for the cattle, and herb for the service of man: that he may bring forth [v]food out of the earth;

15 And [w]wine *that* maketh glad the heart of man, *and* oil to make *his* face to shine, and bread *which* strengtheneth man's heart.

16 The trees of the LORD are full *of sap;* the cedars of Lebanon, [x]which he hath planted;

17 Where the birds make their nests: *as for* the stork, the fir trees *are* her house.

18 The high hills *are* a refuge for the wild goats; *and* the rocks for [y]the conies.

19 [z]He appointed the moon for seasons: the sun [a]knoweth his going down.

20 [b]Thou makest darkness, and it is night: wherein all the beasts of the forest do creep *forth.*

21 [c]The young lions roar after their prey, and seek their meat from God.

22 The sun ariseth, they gather themselves together, and lay them down in their dens.

23 Man goeth forth unto [d]his work and to his labour until the evening.

24 [e]O LORD, how manifold are thy works! in wisdom hast thou made them all: the earth is full of thy riches.

25 *So is* this great and wide sea, wherein *are* things creeping innumerable, both small and great beasts.

26 There go the ships: *there is* that [f]leviathan, *whom* thou hast made to play therein.

27 [g]These wait all upon thee; that thou mayest give *them* their meat in due season.

28 *That* thou givest them they gather: thou openest thine hand, they are filled with good.

29 Thou hidest thy face, they are troubled: [h]thou takest away their breath, they die, and return to their dust.

30 [i]Thou sendest forth thy spirit, they are created: and thou renewest the face of the earth.

31 The glory of the LORD shall endure for ever: the LORD [j]shall rejoice in his works.

32 He looketh on the earth, and it [k]trembleth: [l]he toucheth the hills, and they smoke.

103:5 [d]Isa. 40:31
103:6 [e]Ps. 146:7
103:7 [f]Ps. 147:19
103:8 [g]Ex. 34:6; Num. 14:18; Deut. 5:10; Neh. 9:17; Ps. 86:15; Jer. 32:18
103:9 [h]Ps. 30:5; Isa. 57:16; Jer. 3:5; Mic. 7:18
103:10 [i]Ezra 9:13
103:11 [j]Ps. 57:10; Eph. 3:18
103:12 [k]Isa. 43:25; Mic. 7:18
103:13 [l]Mal. 3:17
103:14 [m]Ps. 78:39 [n]Gen. 3:19; Eccl. 12:7
103:15 [o]Ps. 90:5; 1 Pet. 1:24 [p]Job 14:1; Jam. 1:10
103:16 [q]Job 7:10
103:17 [r]Ex. 20:6
103:18 [s]Deut. 7:9
103:19 [t]Ps. 11:4 [u]Ps. 47:2; Dan. 4:25
103:20 [v]Ps. 148:2 [w]Matt. 6:10; Heb. 1:14
103:21 [x]Gen. 32:2; Josh. 5:14; Ps. 68:17 [y]Dan. 7:9; Heb. 1:14
103:22 [z]Ps. 145:10 [a]ver. 1
104:1 [b]Ps. 103:1; ver. 35 [c]Ps. 93:1
104:2 [d]Dan. 7:9 [e]Isa. 40:22
104:3 [f]Am. 9:6 [g]Isa. 19:1 [h]Ps. 18:10
104:4 [i]Heb. 1:7 [j]2 Kings 2:11
104:5 [k]Job 26:7; Ps. 24:2; Eccl. 1:4
104:6 [l]Gen. 7:19
104:7 [m]Gen. 8:1
104:8 [n]Gen. 8:5 [o]Job 38:10
104:9 [p]Job 26:10; Ps. 33:7; Jer. 5:22 [q]Gen. 9:11
104:13 [r]Ps. 147:8 [s]Ps. 65:9 [t]Jer. 10:13
104:14 [u]Gen. 1:29; Ps. 147:8 [v]Ps. 136:25; Job 28:5
104:15 [w]Judg. 9:13; Ps. 23:5; Prov. 31:6
104:16 [x]Num. 24:6
104:18 [y]Prov. 30:26
104:19 [z]Gen. 1:14 [a]Job 38:12
104:20 [b]Isa. 45:7
104:21 [c]Job 38:39; Joel 1:20
104:23 [d]Gen. 3:19
104:24 [e]Prov. 3:19
104:26 [f]Job 41:1
104:27 [g]Ps. 136:25
104:29 [h]Job 34:14; Ps. 146:4; Eccl. 12:7
104:30 [i]Isa. 32:15; Ezek. 37:9
104:31 [j]Gen. 1:31
104:32 [k]Hab. 3:10 [l]Ps. 144:5

33 [m]I will sing unto the LORD as long as I
live: I will sing praise to my God while I
have my being.
34 My meditation of him shall be sweet: I
will be glad in the LORD.
35 Let [n]the sinners be consumed out of
the earth, and let the wicked be no more.
[o]Bless thou the LORD, O my soul. Praise ye
the LORD.

105 O [p]give thanks unto the LORD;
call upon his name: [q]make
known his deeds among the people.
2 Sing unto him, sing psalms unto him:
[r]talk ye of all his wondrous works.
3 Glory ye in his holy name: let the heart
of them rejoice that seek the LORD.
4 Seek the LORD, and his strength: [s]seek
his face evermore.
5 [t]Remember his marvellous works that
he hath done; his wonders, and the judgments of his mouth;
6 O ye seed of Abraham his servant, ye
children of Jacob his chosen.
7 He *is* the LORD our God: [u]his judgments
are in all the earth.
8 He hath [v]remembered his covenant for
ever, the word *which* he commanded to a
thousand generations.
9 [w]Which *covenant* he made with Abraham, and his oath unto Isaac;
10 And confirmed the same unto Jacob
for a law, *and* to Israel *for* an everlasting
covenant:
11 Saying, [x]Unto thee will I give the land
of Canaan, the lot of your inheritance:
12 [y]When they were *but* a few men in
number; yea, very few, [z]and strangers in it.
13 When they went from one nation to
another, from *one* kingdom to another people;
14 [a]He suffered no man to do them
wrong: yea, [b]he reproved kings for their
sakes;
15 *Saying*, Touch not mine anointed, and
do my prophets no harm.
16 Moreover [c]he called for a famine upon
the land: he brake the whole [d]staff of bread.
17 [e]He sent a man before them, *even* Joseph, *who* [f]was sold for a servant:
18 [g]Whose feet they hurt with fetters: he
was laid in iron:
19 Until the time that his word came: [h]the
word of the LORD tried him.
20 [i]The king sent and loosed him; *even*
the ruler of the people, and let him go free.
21 [j]He made him lord of his house, and
ruler of all his substance:
22 To bind his princes at his pleasure; and
teach his senators wisdom.
23 [k]Israel also came into Egypt; and Jacob sojourned [l]in the land of Ham.
24 And [m]he increased his people greatly;
and made them stronger than their enemies.
25 [n]He turned their heart to hate his people, to deal subtilly with his servants.
26 [o]He sent Moses his servant; *and*
Aaron [p]whom he had chosen.
27 [q]They shewed his signs among them,
[r]and wonders in the land of Ham.
28 [s]He sent darkness, and made it dark;
and [t]they rebelled not against his word.
29 [u]He turned their waters into blood,
and slew their fish.
30 [v]Their land brought forth frogs in
abundance, in the chambers of their kings.
31 [w]He spake, and there came divers
sorts of flies, *and* lice in all their coasts.
32 [x]He gave them hail for rain, *and* flaming fire in their land.
33 [y]He smote their vines also and their
fig trees; and brake the trees of their coasts.
34 [z]He spake, and the locusts came, and
caterpillers, and that without number,
35 And did eat up all the herbs in their
land, and devoured the fruit of their ground.
36 [a]He smote also all the firstborn in
their land, [b]the chief of all their strength.
37 [c]He brought them forth also with silver and gold: and *there was* not one feeble
person among their tribes.
38 [d]Egypt was glad when they departed:
for the fear of them fell upon them.
39 [e]He spread a cloud for a covering; and
fire to give light in the night.
40 [f]*The people* asked, and he brought
quails, and [g]satisfied them with the bread
of heaven.
41 [h]He opened the rock, and the waters
gushed out; they ran in the dry places *like* a
river.
42 For he remembered [i]his holy promise,
and Abraham his servant.
43 And he brought forth his people with
joy, *and* his chosen with gladness:
44 [j]And gave them the lands of the heathen: and they inherited the labour of the
people;
45 [k]That they might observe his statutes,
and keep his laws. Praise ye the LORD.

106 Praise ye the LORD. [l]O [m]give
thanks unto the LORD; for *he is*
good: for his mercy *endureth* for ever.
2 [n]Who can utter the mighty acts of the
LORD? *who* can shew forth all his praise?
3 Blessed *are* they that keep judgment,
and he that [o]doeth righteousness at [p]all
times.
4 [q]Remember me, O LORD, with the favour *that thou bearest unto* thy people:
O visit me with thy salvation;
5 That I may see the good of thy chosen,
that I may rejoice in the gladness of thy nation, that I may glory with thine inheritance.
6 [r]We have sinned with our fathers, we
have committed iniquity, we have done
wickedly.
7 Our fathers understood not thy wonders in Egypt; they remembered not the
multitude of thy mercies; [s]but provoked
him at the sea, *even* at the Red sea.
8 Nevertheless he saved them [t]for his
name's sake, [u]that he might make his
mighty power to be known.

104:33 [m]Ps. 63:4
104:35 [n]Ps. 37:38; Prov. 2:22 [o]ver. 1
105:1 [p]1 Chron. 16:8-22; Isa. 12:4 [q]Ps. 145:4
105:2 [r]Ps. 77:12
105:4 [s]Ps. 27:8
105:5 [t]Ps. 77:11
105:7 [u]Isa. 26:9
105:8 [v]Luke 1:72
105:9 [w]Gen. 17:2; Luke 1:73; Heb. 6:17
105:11 [x]Gen. 13:15
105:12 [y]Gen. 34:30; Deut. 7:7 [z]Heb. 11:9
105:14 [a]Gen. 35:5 [b]Gen. 12:17
105:16 [c]Gen. 41:54 [d]Lev. 26:26; Isa. 3:1; Ezek. 4:16
105:17 [e]Gen. 45:5 [f]Gen. 37:28
105:18 [g]Gen. 39:20
105:19 [h]Gen. 41:25
105:20 [i]Gen. 41:14
105:21 [j]Gen. 41:40
105:23 [k]Gen. 46:6 [l]Ps. 78:51
105:24 [m]Ex. 1:7
105:25 [n]Ex. 1:8
105:26 [o]Ex. 3:10 [p]Num. 16:5
105:27 [q]Ex. 7; Ps. 78:43 [r]Ps. 106:22
105:28 [s]Ex. 10:22 [t]Ps. 99:7
105:29 [u]Ex. 7:20; Ps. 78:44
105:30 [v]Ex. 8:6; Ps. 78:45
105:31 [w]Ex. 8:17; Ps. 78:45
105:32 [x]Ex. 9:23; Ps. 78:48
105:33 [y]Ps. 78:47
105:34 [z]Ex. 10:4; Ps. 78:46
105:36 [a]Ex. 12:29; Ps. 78:51 [b]Gen. 49:3
105:37 [c]Ex. 12:35
105:38 [d]Ex. 12:33
105:39 [e]Ex. 13:21; Neh. 9:12
105:40 [f]Ex. 16:12; Ps. 78:18 [g]Ps. 78:24
105:41 [h]Ex. 17:6; Num. 20:11; Ps. 78:15; 1 Cor. 10:4
105:42 [i]Gen. 15:14
105:44 [j]Deut. 6:10; Josh. 13:7; Ps. 78:55
105:45 [k]Deut. 4:1
106:1 [l]1 Chron. 16:34 [m]Ps. 107:1
106:2 [n]Ps. 40:5
106:3 [o]Ps. 15:2 [p]Acts 24:16; Gal. 6:9
106:4 [q]Ps. 119:132
106:6 [r]Lev. 26:40; 1 Kings 8:47; Dan. 9:5
106:7 [s]Ex. 14:11
106:8 [t]Ezek. 20:14 [u]Ex. 9:16

9 [v]He rebuked the Red sea also, and it was dried up: so [w]he led them through the depths, as through the wilderness.

10 And he [x]saved them from the hand of him that hated *them,* and redeemed them from the hand of the enemy.

11 [y]And the waters covered their enemies: there was not one of them left.

12 [z]Then believed they his words; they sang his praise.

13 [a]They soon forgat his works; they waited not for his counsel:

14 [b]But lusted exceedingly in the wilderness, and tempted God in the desert.

15 [c]And he gave them their request; but [d]sent leanness into their soul.

16 [e]They envied Moses also in the camp, *and* Aaron the saint of the LORD.

17 [f]The earth opened and swallowed up Dathan, and covered the company of Abiram.

18 [g]And a fire was kindled in their company; the flame burned up the wicked.

19 [h]They made a calf in Horeb, and worshipped the molten image.

20 Thus [i]they changed their glory into the similitude of an ox that eateth grass.

21 They [j]forgat God their saviour, which had done great things in Egypt;

22 Wondrous works in [k]the land of Ham, *and* terrible things by the Red sea.

23 [l]Therefore he said that he would destroy them, had not Moses his chosen [m]stood before him in the breach, to turn away his wrath, lest he should destroy *them.*

24 Yea, they despised [n]the pleasant land, they [o]believed not his word:

25 [p]But murmured in their tents, *and* hearkened not unto the voice of the LORD.

26 [q]Therefore he [r]lifted up his hand against them, to overthrow them in the wilderness:

27 [s]To overthrow their seed also among the nations, and to scatter them in the lands.

28 [t]They joined themselves also unto Baal-peor, and ate the sacrifices of the dead.

29 Thus they provoked *him* to anger with their inventions: and the plague brake in upon them.

30 [u]Then stood up Phinehas, and executed judgment: and *so* the plague was stayed.

31 And that was counted unto him [v]for righteousness unto all generations for evermore.

32 [w]They angered *him* also at the waters of strife, [x]so that it went ill with Moses for their sakes:

33 [y]Because they provoked his spirit, so that he spake unadvisedly with his lips.

34 [z]They did not destroy the nations, [a]concerning whom the LORD commanded them:

35 [b]But were mingled among the heathen, and learned their works.

36 And [c]they served their idols: [d]which were a snare unto them.

37 Yea, [e]they sacrificed their sons and their daughters unto [f]devils,

38 And shed innocent blood, *even* the blood of their sons and of their daughters, whom they sacrificed unto the idols of Canaan: and [g]the land was polluted with blood.

39 Thus were they [h]defiled with their own works, and [i]went a whoring with their own inventions.

40 Therefore [j]was the wrath of the LORD kindled against his people, insomuch that he abhorred [k]his own inheritance.

41 And [l]he gave them into the hand of the heathen; and they that hated them ruled over them.

42 Their enemies also oppressed them, and they were brought into subjection under their hand.

43 [m]Many times did he deliver them; but they provoked *him* with their counsel, and were brought low for their iniquity.

44 Nevertheless he regarded their affliction, when [n]he heard their cry:

45 [o]And he remembered for them his covenant, and [p]repented [q]according to the multitude of his mercies.

46 [r]He made them also to be pitied of all those that carried them captives.

47 [s]Save us, O LORD our God, and gather us from among the heathen, to give thanks unto thy holy name, *and* to triumph in thy praise.

48 [t]Blessed *be* the LORD God of Israel from everlasting to everlasting: and let all the people say, Amen. Praise ye the LORD.

BOOK V

107 O [u]give thanks unto the LORD, for [v]*he is* good: for his mercy *endureth* for ever.

2 Let the redeemed of the LORD say *so,* [w]whom he hath redeemed from the hand of the enemy;

3 And [x]gathered them out of the lands, from the east, and from the west, from the north, and from the south.

4 They [y]wandered in [z]the wilderness in a solitary way; they found no city to dwell in.

5 Hungry and thirsty, their soul fainted in them.

6 [a]Then they cried unto the LORD in their trouble, *and* he delivered them out of their distresses.

7 And he led them forth by the [b]right way, that they might go to a city of habitation.

8 [c]Oh that *men* would praise the LORD *for*

106:9 [v]Ex. 14:21; Ps. 18:15; Nah. 1:4 [w]Isa. 63:11
106:10 [x]Ex. 14:30
106:11 [y]Ex. 14:27
106:12 [z]Ex. 14:31
106:13 [a]Ex. 15:24; Ps. 78:11
106:14 [b]Num. 11:4; Ps. 78:18; 1 Cor. 10:6
106:15 [c]Num. 11:31; Ps. 78:29 [d]Isa. 10:16
106:16 [e]Num. 16:1
106:17 [f]Num. 16:31; Deut. 11:6
106:18 [g]Num. 16:35
106:19 [h]Ex. 32:4
106:20 [i]Jer. 2:11; Rom. 1:23
106:21 [j]Ps. 78:11
106:22 [k]Ps. 78:51
106:23 [l]Ex. 32:10; Deut. 9:19; Ezek. 20:13 [m]Ezek. 13:5
106:24 [n]Deut. 8:7; Jer. 3:19; Ezek. 20:6 [o]Heb. 3:18
106:25 [p]Num. 14:2
106:26 [q]Num. 14:28; Ps. 95:11; Ezek. 20:15; Heb. 3:11 [r]Ex. 6:8; Deut. 32:40
106:27 [s]Lev. 26:33; Ps. 44:11; Ezek. 20:23
106:28 [t]Num. 25:2; Deut. 4:3; Hos. 9:10; Rev. 2:14
106:30 [u]Num. 25:7
106:31 [v]Num. 25:11
106:32 [w]Num. 20:3; Ps. 81:7 [x]Num. 20:12; Deut. 1:37
106:33 [y]Num. 20:10
106:34 [z]Judg. 1:21 [a]Deut. 7:2; Judg. 2:2
106:35 [b]Judg. 2:2; Isa. 2:6; 1 Cor. 5:6
106:36 [c]Judg. 2:12 [d]Ex. 23:33; Deut. 7:16; Judg. 2:3
106:37 [e]2 Kings 16:3; Isa. 57:5; Ezek. 16:20 [f]Lev. 17:7; Deut. 32:17; 2 Chron. 11:15; 1 Cor. 10:20
106:38 [g]Num. 35:33
106:39 [h]Ezek. 20:18 [i]Lev. 17:7; Num. 15:39; Ezek. 20:30
106:40 [j]Judg. 2:14; Ps. 78:59 [k]Deut. 9:29
106:41 [l]Judg. 2:14; Neh. 9:27
106:43 [m]Judg. 2:16; Neh. 9:27
106:44 [n]Judg. 3:9; Neh. 9:27
106:45 [o]Lev. 26:41 [p]Judg. 2:18 [q]Ps. 51:1; Isa. 63:7; Lam. 3:32
106:46 [r]Ezra 9:9; Jer. 42:12
106:47 [s]1 Chron. 16:35
106:48 [t]Ps. 41:13
107:1 [u]Ps. 106:1 [v]Ps. 119:68; Matt. 19:17
107:2 [w]Ps. 106:10
107:3 [x]Ps. 106:47; Isa. 43:5; Jer. 29:14; Ezek. 39:27
107:4 [y]ver. 40 [z]Deut. 32:10
107:6 [a]ver. 13; Ps. 50:15; Hos. 5:15
107:7 [b]Ezra 8:21
107:8 [c]ver. 15

his goodness, and *for* his wonderful works to the children of men!

9 For [d]he satisfieth the longing soul, and filleth the hungry soul with goodness.

10 Such as [e]sit in darkness and in the shadow of death, *being* [f]bound in affliction and iron;

11 Because they [g]rebelled against the words of God, and contemned [h]the counsel of the most High:

12 Therefore he brought down their heart with labour; they fell down, and *there was* [i]none to help.

13 [j]Then they cried unto the LORD in their trouble, *and* he saved them out of their distresses.

14 [k]He brought them out of darkness and the shadow of death, and brake their bands in sunder.

15 [l]Oh that *men* would praise the LORD *for* his goodness, and *for* his wonderful works to the children of men!

16 For he hath [m]broken the gates of brass, and cut the bars of iron in sunder.

17 Fools [n]because of their transgression, and because of their iniquities, are afflicted.

18 [o]Their soul abhorreth all manner of meat; and they [p]draw near unto the gates of death.

19 [q]Then they cry unto the LORD in their trouble, *and* he saveth them out of their distresses.

20 [r]He sent his word, and [s]healed them, and [t]delivered *them* from their destructions.

21 [u]Oh that *men* would praise the LORD *for* his goodness, and *for* his wonderful works to the children of men!

22 And [v]let them sacrifice the sacrifices of thanksgiving, and [w]declare his works with rejoicing.

23 They that go down to the sea in ships, that do business in great waters;

24 These see the works of the LORD, and his wonders in the deep.

25 For he commandeth, and [x]raiseth the stormy wind, which lifteth up the waves thereof.

26 They mount up to the heaven, they go down again to the depths: [y]their soul is melted because of trouble.

27 They reel to and fro, and stagger like a drunken man, and are at their wit's end.

28 [z]Then they cry unto the LORD in their trouble, and he bringeth them out of their distresses.

29 [a]He maketh the storm a calm, so that the waves thereof are still.

30 Then are they glad because they be quiet; so he bringeth them unto their desired haven.

31 [b]Oh that *men* would praise the LORD *for* his goodness, and *for* his wonderful works to the children of men!

32 Let them exalt him also [c]in the congregation of the people, and praise him in the assembly of the elders.

107:9 [d]Ps. 34:10; Luke 1:53
107:10 [e]Luke 1:79 [f]Job 36:8
107:11 [g]Lam. 3:42 [h]Ps. 73:24; Luke 7:30; Acts 20:27
107:12 [i]Ps. 22:11; Isa. 63:5
107:13 [j]ver. 6
107:14 [k]Ps. 68:6; Acts 12:7
107:15 [l]ver. 8
107:16 [m]Isa. 45:2
107:17 [n]Lam. 3:39
107:18 [o]Job 33:20 [p]Job 33:22; Ps. 9:13
107:19 [q]ver. 6
107:20 [r]2 Kings 20:4; Ps. 147:15; Matt. 8:8 [s]Ps. 30:2 [t]Job 33:28; Ps. 30:3
107:21 [u]ver. 8
107:22 [v]Lev. 7:12; Ps. 50:14; Heb. 13:15 [w]Ps. 9:11
107:25 [x]Jonah 1:4
107:26 [y]Ps. 22:14; Nah. 2:10
107:28 [z]ver. 6
107:29 [a]Ps. 89:9; Matt. 8:26
107:31 [b]ver. 8
107:32 [c]Ps. 22:22
107:33 [d]1 Kings 17:1
107:34 [e]Gen. 13:10
107:35 [f]Ps. 114:8; Isa. 41:18
107:38 [g]Gen. 12:2 [h]Ex. 1:7
107:39 [i]2 Kings 10:32
107:40 [j]Job 12:21
107:41 [k]1 Sam. 2:8; Ps. 113:7 [l]Ps. 78:52
107:42 [m]Job 22:19; Ps. 52:6 [n]Job 5:16; Ps. 63:11; Prov. 10:11; Rom. 3:19
107:43 [o]Ps. 64:9; Jer. 9:12; Hos. 14:9
108:1 [p]Ps. 57:7
108:2 [q]Ps. 57:8-11
108:5 [r]Ps. 57:5
108:6 [s]Ps. 60:5
108:8 [t]Gen. 49:10
108:10 [u]Ps. 60:9
108:13 [v]Ps. 60:12
109:1 [w]Ps. 83:1

33 He [d]turneth rivers into a wilderness, and the watersprings into dry ground;

34 A [e]fruitful land into barrenness, for the wickedness of them that dwell therein.

35 [f]He turneth the wilderness into a standing water, and dry ground into watersprings.

36 And there he maketh the hungry to dwell, that they may prepare a city for habitation;

37 And sow the fields, and plant vineyards, which may yield fruits of increase.

38 [g]He blesseth them also, so that they [h]are multiplied greatly; and suffereth not their cattle to decrease.

39 Again, they are [i]minished and brought low through oppression, affliction, and sorrow.

40 [j]He poureth contempt upon princes, and causeth them to wander in the wilderness, *where there is* no way.

41 [k]Yet setteth he the poor on high from affliction, and [l]maketh *him* families like a flock.

42 [m]The righteous shall see *it*, and rejoice: and all [n]iniquity shall stop her mouth.

43 [o]Whoso *is* wise, and will observe these *things*, even they shall understand the lovingkindness of the LORD.

A Song *or* Psalm of David.

108 O [p]God, my heart is fixed; I will sing and give praise, even with my glory.

2 [q]Awake, psaltery and harp: I *myself* will awake early.

3 I will praise thee, O LORD, among the people: and I will sing praises unto thee among the nations.

4 For thy mercy *is* great above the heavens: and thy truth *reacheth* unto the clouds.

5 [r]Be thou exalted, O God, above the heavens: and thy glory above all the earth;

6 [s]That thy beloved may be delivered: save *with* thy right hand, and answer me.

7 God hath spoken in his holiness; I will rejoice, I will divide Shechem, and mete out the valley of Succoth.

8 Gilead *is* mine; Manasseh *is* mine; Ephraim also *is* the strength of mine head; [t]Judah *is* my lawgiver;

9 Moab *is* my washpot; over Edom will I cast out my shoe; over Philistia will I triumph.

10 [u]Who will bring me into the strong city? who will lead me into Edom?

11 *Wilt* not *thou*, O God, *who* hast cast us off? and wilt not thou, O God, go forth with our hosts?

12 Give us help from trouble: for vain *is* the help of man.

13 [v]Through God we shall do valiantly: for he *it is that* shall tread down our enemies.

To the chief Musician, A Psalm of David.

109 Hold [w]not thy peace, O God of my praise;

2 For the mouth of the wicked and the mouth of the deceitful are opened against me: they have spoken against me with a lying tongue.

3 They compassed me about also with words of hatred; and fought against me [x]without a cause.

4 For my love they are my adversaries: but I *give myself unto* prayer.

5 And [y]they have rewarded me evil for good, and hatred for my love.

6 Set thou a wicked man over him: and let [z]Satan stand at his right hand.

7 When he shall be judged, let him be condemned: and [a]let his prayer become sin.

8 Let his days be few; *and* [b]let another take his office.

9 [c]Let his children be fatherless, and his wife a widow.

10 Let his children be continually vagabonds, and beg: let them seek *their bread* also out of their desolate places.

11 [d]Let the extortioner catch all that he hath; and let the strangers spoil his labour.

12 Let there be none to extend mercy unto him: neither let there be any to favour his fatherless children.

13 [e]Let his posterity be cut off; *and* in the generation following let their [f]name be blotted out.

14 [g]Let the iniquity of his fathers be remembered with the LORD; and let not the sin of his mother [h]be blotted out.

15 Let them be before the LORD continually, that he may [i]cut off the memory of them from the earth.

16 Because that he remembered not to shew mercy, but persecuted the poor and needy man, that he might even slay the [j]broken in heart.

17 [k]As he loved cursing, so let it come unto him: as he delighted not in blessing, so let it be far from him.

18 As he clothed himself with cursing like as with his garment, so let it [l]come into his bowels like water, and like oil into his bones.

19 Let it be unto him as the garment *which* covereth him, and for a girdle wherewith he is girded continually.

20 *Let* this *be* the reward of mine adversaries from the LORD, and of them that speak evil against my soul.

21 But do thou for me, O GOD the Lord, for thy name's sake: because thy mercy *is* good, deliver thou me.

22 For I *am* poor and needy, and my heart is wounded within me.

23 I am gone [m]like the shadow when it declineth: I am tossed up and down as the locust.

24 My [n]knees are weak through fasting; and my flesh faileth of fatness.

25 I became also a [o]reproach unto them: *when* they looked upon me [p]they shaked their heads.

26 Help me, O LORD my God: O save me according to thy mercy:

27 [q]That they may know that this *is* thy hand; *that* thou, LORD, hast done it.

28 [r]Let them curse, but bless thou: when they arise, let them be ashamed; but let [s]thy servant rejoice.

29 [t]Let mine adversaries be clothed with shame, and let them cover themselves with their own confusion, as with a mantle.

30 I will greatly praise the LORD with my mouth; yea, [u]I will praise him among the multitude.

31 For [v]he shall stand at the right hand of the poor, to save *him* from those that condemn his soul.

A Psalm of David.

110 The [w]LORD said unto my Lord, Sit thou at my right hand, until I make thine enemies thy footstool.

2 The LORD shall send the rod of thy strength out of Zion: rule thou in the midst of thine enemies.

3 [x]Thy people *shall be* willing in the day of thy power, [y]in the beauties of holiness from the womb of the morning: thou hast the dew of thy youth.

4 The LORD hath sworn, and [z]will not repent, [a]Thou *art* a priest for ever after the order of Melchizedek.

5 The Lord [b]at thy right hand shall strike through kings [c]in the day of his wrath.

6 He shall judge among the heathen, he shall fill *the places* with the dead bodies; [d]he shall wound the heads over many countries.

7 [e]He shall drink of the brook in the way: [f]therefore shall he lift up the head.

111 Praise ye the LORD. [g]I will praise the LORD with *my* whole heart, in the assembly of the upright, and *in* the congregation.

2 [h]The works of the LORD *are* great, [i]sought out of all them that have pleasure therein.

3 His work *is* [j]honourable and glorious: and his righteousness endureth for ever.

4 He hath made his wonderful works to be remembered: [k]the LORD *is* gracious and full of compassion.

5 He hath given [l]meat unto them that fear him: he will ever be mindful of his covenant.

6 He hath shewed his people the power of his works, that he may give them the heritage of the heathen.

7 The works of his hands *are* [m]verity and judgment; [n]all his commandments *are* sure.

8 [o]They stand fast for ever and ever, *and are* [p]done in truth and uprightness.

9 [q]He sent redemption unto his people: he hath commanded his covenant for ever: [r]holy and reverend *is* his name.

10 [s]The fear of the LORD *is* the beginning of wisdom: a good understanding have all they that do *his commandments:* his praise endureth for ever.

112 Praise ye the LORD. [t]Blessed *is* the man *that* feareth the LORD,

109:3 [x]Ps. 35:7; John 15:25
109:5 [y]Ps. 35:7
109:6 [z]Zech. 3:1
109:7 [a]Prov. 28:9
109:8 [b]Acts 1:20
109:9 [c]Ex. 22:24
109:11 [d]Job 5:5
109:13 [e]Job 18:19; Ps. 37:28 [f]Prov. 10:7
109:14 [g]Ex. 20:5 [h]Neh. 4:5; Jer. 18:23
109:15 [i]Job 18:17; Ps. 34:16
109:16 [j]Ps. 34:18
109:17 [k]Prov. 14:14; Ezek. 35:6
109:18 [l]Num. 5:22
109:23 [m]Ps. 102:11
109:24 [n]Heb. 12:12
109:25 [o]Ps. 22:6 [p]Matt. 27:39
109:27 [q]Job 37:7
109:28 [r]2 Sam. 16:11 [s]Isa. 65:14
109:29 [t]Ps. 35:26
109:30 [u]Ps. 35:18
109:31 [v]Ps. 16:8
110:1 [w]Ps. 45:6; Matt. 22:44; Mark 12:36; Luke 20:42; Acts 2:34; 1 Cor. 15:25; Heb. 1:13; 1 Pet. 3:22
110:3 [x]Judg. 5:2 [y]Ps. 96:9
110:4 [z]Num. 23:19 [a]Zech. 6:13; Heb. 5:6
110:5 [b]Ps. 16:8 [c]Ps. 2:5; Rom. 2:5; Rev. 11:18
110:6 [d]Ps. 68:21; Hab. 3:13
110:7 [e]Judg. 7:5 [f]Isa. 53:12
111:1 [g]Ps. 35:18
111:2 [h]Job 38; Ps. 92:5; Rev. 15:3 [i]Ps. 143:5
111:3 [j]Ps. 145:4
111:4 [k]Ps. 86:5
111:5 [l]Matt. 6:26
111:7 [m]Rev. 15:3 [n]Ps. 19:7
111:8 [o]Isa. 40:8; Matt. 5:18 [p]Ps. 19:9; Rev. 15:3
111:9 [q]Matt. 1:21; Luke 1:68 [r]Luke 1:49
111:10 [s]Deut. 4:6; Job 28:28; Prov. 1:7; Eccl. 12:13
112:1 [t]Ps. 128:1

that [u]delighteth greatly in his commandments.
2 [v]His seed shall be mighty upon earth:
the generation of the upright shall be
blessed.
3 [w]Wealth and riches *shall be* in his
house: and his righteousness endureth for
ever.
4 [x]Unto the upright there ariseth light in
the darkness: *he is* gracious, and full of
compassion, and righteous.
5 [y]A good man sheweth favour, and lendeth: he will guide his affairs [z]with discretion.
6 Surely [a]he shall not be moved for ever:
[b]the righteous shall be in everlasting remembrance.
7 [c]He shall not be afraid of evil tidings:
his [d]heart is fixed, [e]trusting in the LORD.
8 His heart *is* established, [f]he shall not be
afraid, until he [g]see *his desire* upon his enemies.
9 [h]He hath dispersed, he hath given to
the poor; [i]his righteousness endureth for
ever; [j]his horn shall be exalted with honour.
10 [k]The wicked shall see *it,* and be
grieved; [l]he shall gnash with his teeth, and
[m]melt away: [n]the desire of the wicked shall
perish.

113 Praise ye the LORD. [o]Praise, O ye
servants of the LORD, praise the
name of the LORD.
2 [p]Blessed be the name of the LORD from
this time forth and for evermore.
3 [q]From the rising of the sun unto the going down of the same the LORD's name *is* to
be praised.
4 The LORD *is* [r]high above all nations,
and [s]his glory above the heavens.
5 [t]Who *is* like unto the LORD our God,
who dwelleth on high,
6 [u]Who humbleth *himself* to behold *the
things that are* in heaven, and in the earth!
7 [v]He raiseth up the poor out of the dust,
and lifteth the needy out of the dunghill;
8 That he may [w]set *him* with princes,
even with the princes of his people.
9 [x]He maketh the barren woman to keep
house, *and to be* a joyful mother of children.
Praise ye the LORD.

114 When [y]Israel went out of Egypt,
the house of Jacob [z]from a people
of strange language;
2 [a]Judah was his sanctuary, *and* Israel
his dominion.
3 [b]The sea saw *it,* and fled: [c]Jordan was
driven back.
4 [d]The mountains skipped like rams, *and*
the little hills like lambs.
5 [e]What *ailed* thee, O thou sea, that thou
fleddest? thou Jordan, *that* thou wast
driven back?
6 Ye mountains, *that* ye skipped like
rams; *and* ye little hills, like lambs?
7 Tremble, thou earth, at the presence of
the Lord, at the presence of the God of Jacob;
8 [f]Which turned the rock *into* a standing
water, the flint into a fountain of waters.

115 Not [g]unto us, O LORD, not unto
us, but unto thy name give glory,
for thy mercy, *and* for thy truth's sake.
2 Wherefore should the heathen say,
[h]Where *is* now their God?
3 [i]But our God *is* in the heavens: he hath
done whatsoever he hath pleased.
4 [j]Their idols *are* silver and gold, the
work of men's hands.
5 They have mouths, but they speak not:
eyes have they, but they see not:
6 They have ears, but they hear not: noses
have they, but they smell not:
7 They have hands, but they handle not:
feet have they, but they walk not: neither
speak they through their throat.
8 [k]They that make them are like unto
them; *so is* every one that trusteth in them.
9 [l]O Israel, trust thou in the LORD: [m]he *is*
their help and their shield.
10 O house of Aaron, trust in the LORD: he
is their help and their shield.
11 Ye that fear the LORD, trust in the
LORD: he *is* their help and their shield.
12 The LORD hath been mindful of us: he
will bless *us;* he will bless the house of Israel; he will bless the house of Aaron.
13 [n]He will bless them that fear the LORD,
both small and great.
14 The LORD shall increase you more and
more, you and your children.
15 Ye *are* [o]blessed of the LORD [p]which
made heaven and earth.
16 The heaven, *even* the heavens, *are* the
LORD's: but the earth hath he given to the
children of men.
17 [q]The dead praise not the LORD, neither any that go down into silence.
18 [r]But we will bless the LORD from this
time forth and for evermore. Praise the
LORD.

116 I [s]love the LORD, because he hath
heard my voice *and* my supplications.
2 Because he hath inclined his ear unto
me, therefore will I call upon *him* as long as
I live.
3 [t]The sorrows of death compassed me,
and the pains of hell gat hold upon me: I
found trouble and sorrow.
4 Then called I upon the name of the
LORD; O LORD, I beseech thee, deliver my
soul.
5 [u]Gracious *is* the LORD, and [v]righteous;
yea, our God *is* merciful.
6 The LORD preserveth the simple: I was
brought low, and he helped me.
7 Return unto thy [w]rest, O my soul; for
[x]the LORD hath dealt bountifully with thee.
8 [y]For thou hast delivered my soul from
death, mine eyes from tears, *and* my feet
from falling.
9 I will walk before the LORD [z]in the land
of the living.

112:1 *u*Ps. 119:16 **112:2** *v*Ps. 25:13 **112:3** *w*Matt. 6:33 **112:4** *x*Job 11:17; Ps. 97:11 **112:5** *y*Ps. 37:26; Luke 6:35 *z*Eph. 5:15; Col. 4:5 **112:6** *a*Ps. 15:5 *b*Prov. 10:7 **112:7** *c*Prov. 1:33 *d*Ps. 57:7 *e*Ps. 64:10 **112:8** *f*Prov. 3:33 *g*Ps. 59:10 **112:9** *h*2 Cor. 9:9 *i*Deut. 24:13; ver. 3 *j*Ps. 75:10 **112:10** *k*Luke 13:28 *l*Ps. 37:12 *m*Ps. 58:7 *n*Prov. 10:28 **113:1** *o*Ps. 135:1 **113:2** *p*Dan. 2:20 **113:3** *q*Isa. 59:19; Mal. 1:11 **113:4** *r*Ps. 97:9 *s*Ps. 8:1 **113:5** *t*Ps. 89:6 **113:6** *u*Ps. 11:4; Isa. 57:15 **113:7** *v*1 Sam. 2:8; Ps. 107:41 **113:8** *w*Job 36:7 **113:9** *x*1 Sam. 2:5; Ps. 68:6; Isa. 54:1; Gal. 4:27 **114:1** *y*Ex. 13:3 *z*Ps. 81:5 **114:2** *a*Ex. 6:7; Deut. 27:9 **114:3** *b*Ex. 14:21; Ps. 77:16 *c*Josh. 3:13 **114:4** *d*Ps. 29:6; Hab. 3:6 **114:5** *e*Hab. 3:8 **114:8** *f*Ex. 17:6; Num. 20:11; Ps. 107:35 **115:1** *g*Isa. 48:11; Ezek. 36:32 **115:2** *h*Ps. 42:3; Joel 2:17 **115:3** *i*1 Chron. 16:26; Ps. 135:6; Dan. 4:35 **115:4** *j*Deut. 4:28; Ps. 135:15; Jer. 10:3 **115:8** *k*Ps. 135:18; Isa. 44:9; Jonah 2:8; Hab. 2:18 **115:9** *l*Ps. 118:2 *m*Ps. 38:20; Prov. 30:5 **115:13** *n*Ps. 128:1 **115:15** *o*Gen. 14:19 *p*Gen. 1:1; Ps. 96:5 **115:17** *q*Ps. 6:5; Isa. 38:18 **115:18** *r*Ps. 113:2; Dan. 2:20 **116:1** *s*Ps. 18:1 **116:3** *t*Ps. 18:4 **116:5** *u*Ps. 103:8 *v*Ezra 9:15; Neh. 9:8; Ps. 119:137 **116:7** *w*Jer. 6:16; Matt. 11:29 *x*Ps. 13:6 **116:8** *y*Ps. 56:13 **116:9** *z*Ps. 27:13

10 [a]I believed, therefore have I spoken: I was greatly afflicted:

11 [b]I said in my haste, [c]All men *are* liars.

12 What shall I render unto the LORD *for* all his benefits toward me?

13 I will take the cup of salvation, and call upon the name of the LORD.

14 [d]I will pay my vows unto the LORD now in the presence of all his people.

15 [e]Precious in the sight of the LORD *is* the death of his saints.

16 O LORD, truly [f]I *am* thy servant; I *am* thy servant, *and* [g]the son of thine handmaid: thou hast loosed my bonds.

17 I will offer to thee [h]the sacrifice of thanksgiving, and will call upon the name of the LORD.

18 [i]I will pay my vows unto the LORD now in the presence of all his people,

19 In the [j]courts of the LORD's house, in the midst of thee, O Jerusalem. Praise ye the LORD.

117 O [k]praise the LORD, all ye nations: praise him, all ye people.

2 For his merciful kindness is great toward us: and [l]the truth of the LORD *endureth* for ever. Praise ye the LORD.

118 O [m]give thanks unto the LORD; for *he is* good: because his mercy *endureth* for ever.

2 [n]Let Israel now say, that his mercy *endureth* for ever.

3 Let the house of Aaron now say, that his mercy *endureth* for ever.

4 Let them now that fear the LORD say, that his mercy *endureth* for ever.

5 [o]I called upon the LORD in distress: the LORD answered me, *and* [p]*set me* in a large place.

6 [q]The LORD *is* on my side; I will not fear: what can man do unto me?

7 [r]The LORD taketh my part with them that help me: therefore shall [s]I see *my desire* upon them that hate me.

8 [t]*It is* better to trust in the LORD than to put confidence in man.

9 [u]*It is* better to trust in the LORD than to put confidence in princes.

10 All nations compassed me about: but in the name of the LORD will I destroy them.

11 They [v]compassed me about; yea, they compassed me about: but in the name of the LORD I will destroy them.

12 They compassed me about [w]like bees; they are quenched [x]as the fire of thorns: for in the name of the LORD I will destroy them.

13 Thou hast thrust sore at me that I might fall: but the LORD helped me.

14 [y]The LORD *is* my strength and song, and is become my salvation.

15 The voice of rejoicing and salvation *is* in the tabernacles of the righteous: the right hand of the LORD doeth valiantly.

16 [z]The right hand of the LORD is exalted: the right hand of the LORD doeth valiantly.

17 [a]I shall not die, but live, and [b]declare the works of the LORD.

18 The LORD hath [c]chastened me sore: but he hath not given me over unto death.

19 [d]Open to me the gates of righteousness: I will go into them, *and* I will praise the LORD:

20 [e]This gate of the LORD, [f]into which the righteous shall enter.

21 I will praise thee: for thou hast [g]heard me, and [h]art become my salvation.

22 [i]The stone *which* the builders refused is become the head *stone* of the corner.

23 This is the LORD's doing; it *is* marvellous in our eyes.

24 This *is* the day *which* the LORD hath made; we will rejoice and be glad in it.

25 Save now, I beseech thee, O LORD: O LORD, I beseech thee, send now prosperity.

26 [j]Blessed *be* he that cometh in the name of the LORD: we have blessed you out of the house of the LORD.

27 God *is* the LORD, which hath shewed us [k]light: bind the sacrifice with cords, *even* unto the horns of the altar.

28 Thou *art* my God, and I will praise thee: [l]*thou art* my God, I will exalt thee.

29 [m]O give thanks unto the LORD; for *he is* good: for his mercy *endureth* for ever.

Aleph

119 Blessed *are* the undefiled in the way, [n]who walk in the law of the LORD.

2 Blessed *are* they that keep his testimonies, *and that* seek him with the whole heart.

3 [o]They also do no iniquity: they walk in his ways.

4 Thou hast commanded *us* to keep thy precepts diligently.

5 O that my ways were directed to keep thy statutes!

6 [p]Then shall I not be ashamed, when I have respect unto all thy commandments.

7 [q]I will praise thee with uprightness of heart, when I shall have learned thy righteous judgments.

8 I will keep thy statutes: O forsake me not utterly.

Beth

9 Wherewithal shall a young man cleanse his way? by taking heed *thereto* according to thy word.

10 With my whole heart have I [r]sought thee: O let me not [s]wander from thy commandments.

11 [t]Thy word have I hid in mine heart, that I might not sin against thee.

12 Blessed *art* thou, O LORD: [u]teach me thy statutes.

13 With my lips have I [v]declared all the judgments of thy mouth.

14 I have rejoiced in the way of thy testimonies, as *much as* in all riches.

15 I will [w]meditate in thy precepts, and have respect unto thy ways.

116:10 a2 Cor. 4:13
116:11 bPs. 31:22 cRom. 3:4
116:14 dver. 18; Ps. 22:25; Jonah 2:9
116:15 ePs. 72:14
116:16 fPs. 143:12 gPs. 86:16
116:17 hLev. 7:12; Ps. 50:14
116:18 iver. 14
116:19 jPs. 96:8
117:1 kRom. 15:11
117:2 lPs. 100:5
118:1 m1 Chron. 16:8; Ps. 106:1
118:2 nPs. 115:9
118:5 oPs. 120:1 pPs. 18:19
118:6 qPs. 27:1; Isa. 51:12; Heb. 13:6
118:7 rPs. 54:4 sPs. 59:10
118:8 tPs. 40:4; Jer. 17:5
118:9 uPs. 146:3
118:11 vPs. 88:17
118:12 wDeut. 1:44 xEccl. 7:6; Nah. 1:10
118:14 yEx. 15:2; Isa. 12:2
118:16 zEx. 15:6
118:17 aPs. 6:5; Hab. 1:12 bPs. 73:28
118:18 c2 Cor. 6:9
118:19 dIsa. 26:2
118:20 ePs. 24:7 fIsa. 35:8; Rev. 21:27
118:21 gPs. 116:1 hver. 14
118:22 iMatt. 21:42; Mark 12:10; Luke 20:17; Acts 4:11; Eph. 2:20; 1 Pet. 2:4
118:26 jZech. 4:7; Matt. 21:9; Mark 11:9; Luke 19:38
118:27 kEsth. 8:16; 1 Pet. 2:9
118:28 lEx. 15:2; Isa. 25:1
118:29 mver. 1
119:1 nPs. 128:1
119:3 o1 John 3:9
119:6 pJob 22:26; 1 John 2:28
119:7 qver. 171
119:10 r2 Chron. 15:15 sver. 21
119:11 tPs. 37:31; Luke 2:19
119:12 uver. 26; Ps. 25:4
119:13 vPs. 34:11
119:15 wPs. 1:2; ver. 23

16 I will [x]delight myself in thy statutes: I
will not forget thy word.

Gimel

17 [y]Deal bountifully with thy servant,
that I may live, and keep thy word.
18 Open thou mine eyes, that I may behold wondrous things out of thy law.
19 [z]I *am* a stranger in the earth: hide not
thy commandments from me.
20 [a]My soul breaketh for the longing
that it hath unto thy judgments at all times.
21 Thou hast rebuked the proud *that are*
cursed, which do [b]err from thy commandments.
22 [c]Remove from me reproach and contempt; for I have kept thy testimonies.
23 Princes also did sit *and* speak against
me: *but* thy servant did [d]meditate in thy
statutes.
24 [e]Thy testimonies also *are* my delight
and my counsellors.

Daleth

25 [f]My soul cleaveth unto the dust:
[g]quicken thou me according to thy word.
26 I have declared my ways, and thou
heardest me: [h]teach me thy statutes.
27 Make me to understand the way of thy
precepts: so [i]shall I talk of thy wondrous
works.
28 [j]My soul melteth for heaviness:
strengthen thou me according unto thy
word.
29 Remove from me the way of lying: and
grant me thy law graciously.
30 I have chosen the way of truth: thy
judgments have I laid *before me*.
31 I have stuck unto thy testimonies:
O LORD, put me not to shame.
32 I will run the way of thy commandments, when thou shalt [k]enlarge my heart.

He

33 [l]Teach me, O LORD, the way of thy
statutes; and I shall keep it [m]*unto* the end.
34 [n]Give me understanding, and I shall
keep thy law; yea, I shall observe it with *my*
whole heart.
35 Make me to go in the path of thy commandments; for therein do I [o]delight.
36 Incline my heart unto thy testimonies,
and not to [p]covetousness.
37 [q]Turn away mine eyes from [r]behold-
ing vanity; *and* [s]quicken thou me in thy
way.
38 [t]Stablish thy word unto thy servant,
who *is devoted* to thy fear.
39 Turn away my reproach which I fear:
for thy judgments *are* good.
40 Behold, I have [u]longed after thy precepts: [v]quicken me in thy righteousness.

Vau

41 [w]Let thy mercies come also unto me,
O LORD, *even* thy salvation, according to
thy word.
42 So shall I have wherewith to answer
him that reproacheth me: for I trust in thy
word.
43 And take not the word of truth utterly
out of my mouth; for I have hoped in thy
judgments.
44 So shall I keep thy law continually for
ever and ever.
45 And I will walk at liberty: for I seek thy
precepts.
46 [x]I will speak of thy testimonies also
before kings, and will not be ashamed.
47 And I will [y]delight myself in thy commandments, which I have loved.
48 My hands also will I lift up unto thy
commandments, which I have loved; and I
will [z]meditate in thy statutes.

Zain

49 Remember the word unto thy servant,
upon which thou hast caused me to [a]hope.
50 This *is* my [b]comfort in my affliction:
for thy word hath quickened me.
51 The proud have had me greatly [c]in derision: *yet* have I not [d]declined from thy
law.
52 I remembered thy judgments of old,
O LORD; and have comforted myself.
53 [e]Horror hath taken hold upon me because of the wicked that forsake thy law.
54 Thy statutes have been my songs in the
house of my pilgrimage.
55 [f]I have remembered thy name,
O LORD, in the night, and have kept thy law.
56 This I had, because I kept thy precepts.

Cheth

57 [g]*Thou art* my portion, O LORD: I have
said that I would keep thy words.
58 I intreated thy favour with *my* whole
heart: be merciful unto me [h]according to
thy word.
59 I [i]thought on my ways, and turned my
feet unto thy testimonies.
60 I made haste, and delayed not to keep
thy commandments.
61 The bands of the wicked have robbed
me: *but* I have not forgotten thy law.
62 [j]At midnight I will rise to give thanks
unto thee because of thy righteous judgments.
63 I *am* a companion of all *them* that fear
thee, and of them that keep thy precepts.
64 [k]The earth, O LORD, is full of thy
mercy; [l]teach me thy statutes.

Teth

65 Thou hast dealt well with thy servant,
O LORD, according unto thy word.
66 Teach me good judgment and knowledge: for I have believed thy commandments.
67 [m]Before I was afflicted I went astray:
but now have I kept thy word.
68 Thou *art* [n]good, and doest good;
[o]teach me thy statutes.
69 The proud have [p]forged a lie against
me: *but* I will keep thy precepts with *my*
whole heart.

119:16 [x]Ps. 1:2; ver. 35
119:17 [y]Ps. 116:7
119:19 [z]Gen. 47:9; 1 Chron. 29:15; Ps. 39:12; 2 Cor. 5:6; Heb. 11:13
119:20 [a]Ps. 42:1; ver. 40
119:21 [b]ver. 10
119:22 [c]Ps. 39:8
119:23 [d]ver. 15
119:24 [e]ver. 77
119:25 [f]Ps. 44:25 [g]ver. 40; Ps. 143:11
119:26 [h]ver. 12; Ps. 25:4
119:27 [i]Ps. 145:5
119:28 [j]Ps. 107:26
119:32 [k]1 Kings 4:29; Isa. 60:5; 2 Cor. 6:11
119:33 [l]ver. 12 [m]ver. 112; Matt. 10:22; Rev. 2:26
119:34 [n]ver. 73; Prov. 2:6; Jam. 1:5
119:35 [o]ver. 16
119:36 [p]Ezek. 33:31; Mark 7:21; Luke 12:15; 1 Tim. 6:10; Heb. 13:5
119:37 [q]Isa. 33:15 [r]Prov. 23:5 [s]ver. 40
119:38 [t]2 Sam. 7:25
119:40 [u]ver. 20 [v]ver. 25
119:41 [w]Ps. 106:4; ver. 77
119:46 [x]Ps. 138:1; Matt. 10:18; Acts 26:1
119:47 [y]ver. 16
119:48 [z]ver. 15
119:49 [a]ver. 74
119:50 [b]Rom. 15:4
119:51 [c]Jer. 20:7 [d]Job 23:11; Ps. 44:18; ver. 157
119:53 [e]Ezra 9:3
119:55 [f]Ps. 63:6
119:57 [g]Ps. 16:5; Jer. 10:16; Lam. 3:24
119:58 [h]ver. 41
119:59 [i]Luke 15:17
119:62 [j]Acts 16:25
119:64 [k]Ps. 33:5 [l]ver. 12
119:67 [m]ver. 71; Jer. 31:18; Heb. 12:11
119:68 [n]Ps. 106:1; Matt. 19:17 [o]ver. 12
119:69 [p]Job 13:4; Ps. 109:2

70 [q]Their heart is as fat as grease; *but* I
[r]delight in thy law.
71 [s]*It is* good for me that I have been
afflicted; that I might learn thy statutes.
72 [t]The law of thy mouth *is* better unto
me than thousands of gold and silver.

Jod

73 [u]Thy hands have made me and fashioned me: [v]give me understanding, that I
may learn thy commandments.
74 [w]They that fear thee will be glad when
they see me; because [x]I have hoped in thy
word.
75 I know, O LORD, that thy judgments
are right, and [y]*that* thou in faithfulness
hast afflicted me.
76 Let, I pray thee, thy merciful kindness
be for my comfort, according to thy word
unto thy servant.
77 [z]Let thy tender mercies come unto
me, that I may live: for [a]thy law *is* my delight.
78 Let the proud [b]be ashamed; [c]for they
dealt perversely with me without a cause:
but I will [d]meditate in thy precepts.
79 Let those that fear thee turn unto me,
and those that have known thy testimonies.
80 Let my heart be sound in thy statutes;
that I be not ashamed.

¼ Caph

81 [e]My soul fainteth for thy salvation:
but [f]I hope in thy word.
82 [g]Mine eyes fail for thy word, saying,
When wilt thou comfort me?
83 For [h]I am become like a bottle in the
smoke; *yet* do I not forget thy statutes.
84 [i]How many *are* the days of thy servant? [j]when wilt thou execute judgment on
them that persecute me?
85 [k]The proud have digged pits for me,
which *are* not after thy law.
86 All thy commandments *are* faithful:
[l]they persecute me [m]wrongfully; help
thou me.
87 They had almost consumed me upon
earth; but I forsook not thy precepts.
88 [n]Quicken me after thy lovingkindness; so shall I keep the testimony of thy
mouth.

Lamed

89 [o]For ever, O LORD, thy word is settled
in heaven.
90 Thy faithfulness *is* unto all generations: thou hast established the earth, and it
abideth.
91 They continue this day according to
[p]thine ordinances: for all *are* thy servants.
92 Unless [q]thy law *had been* my delights,
I should then have perished in mine affliction.
93 I will never forget thy precepts: for
with them thou hast quickened me.
94 I *am* thine, save me; for I have sought
thy precepts.
95 The wicked have waited for me to de-

119:70 [q]Ps. 17:10; Isa. 6:10; Acts 28:27 [r]ver. 35
119:71 [s]ver. 67; Heb. 12:10
119:72 [t]ver. 127; Ps. 19:10; Prov. 8:10
119:73 [u]Job 10:8; Ps. 100:3 [v]ver. 34
119:74 [w]Ps. 34:2 [x]ver. 49
119:75 [y]Heb. 12:10
119:77 [z]ver. 41 [a]ver. 24
119:78 [b]Ps. 25:3 [c]ver. 86 [d]ver. 23
119:81 [e]Ps. 73:26 [f]ver. 74
119:82 [g]ver. 123; Ps. 69:3
119:83 [h]Job 30:30
119:84 [i]Ps. 39:4 [j]Rev. 6:10
119:85 [k]Ps. 35:7; Prov. 16:27
119:86 [l]ver. 78 [m]Ps. 35:19
119:88 [n]ver. 40
119:89 [o]Ps. 89:2; Matt. 24:34; 1 Pet. 1:25
119:91 [p]Jer. 33:25
119:92 [q]ver. 24
119:96 [r]Matt. 5:18
119:97 [s]Ps. 1:2
119:98 [t]Deut. 4:6
119:99 [u]2 Tim. 3:15
119:100 [v]Job 32:7
119:101 [w]Prov. 1:15
119:103 [x]Ps. 19:10; Prov. 8:11
119:104 [y]ver. 128
119:105 [z]Prov. 6:23
119:106 [a]Neh. 10:29
119:107 [b]ver. 88
119:108 [c]Hos. 14:2; Heb. 13:15 [d]ver. 12
119:109 [e]Job 13:14
119:110 [f]Ps. 140:5 [g]ver. 10
119:111 [h]Deut. 33:4 [i]ver. 77
119:112 [j]ver. 33
119:114 [k]Ps. 32:7 [l]ver. 81
119:115 [m]Ps. 6:8; Matt. 7:23
119:116 [n]Ps. 25:2; Rom. 5:5
119:118 [o]ver. 21
119:119 [p]Ezek. 22:18
119:120 [q]Hab. 3:16

stroy me: *but* I will consider thy testimonies.
96 [r]I have seen an end of all perfection:
but thy commandment *is* exceeding broad.

Mem

97 O how love I thy law! [s]it *is* my meditation all the day.
98 Thou through thy commandments
hast made me [t]wiser than mine enemies:
for they *are* ever with me.
99 I have more understanding than all my
teachers: [u]for thy testimonies *are* my meditation.
100 [v]I understand more than the ancients, because I keep thy precepts.
101 I have [w]refrained my feet from every
evil way, that I might keep thy word.
102 I have not departed from thy judgments: for thou hast taught me.
103 [x]How sweet are thy words unto my
taste! *yea, sweeter* than honey to my
mouth!
104 Through thy precepts I get understanding: therefore [y]I hate every false way.

Nun

105 [z]Thy word *is* a lamp unto my feet,
and a light unto my path.
106 [a]I have sworn, and I will perform *it*,
that I will keep thy righteous judgments.
107 I am afflicted very much: [b]quicken
me, O LORD, according unto thy word.
108 Accept, I beseech thee, [c]the freewill
offerings of my mouth, O LORD, and [d]teach
me thy judgments.
109 [e]My soul *is* continually in my hand:
yet do I not forget thy law.
110 [f]The wicked have laid a snare for
me: yet I [g]erred not from thy precepts.
111 [h]Thy testimonies have I taken as an
heritage for ever: for [i]they *are* the rejoicing
of my heart.
112 I have inclined mine heart to perform
thy statutes alway, [j]*even unto* the end.

Samech

113 I hate *vain* thoughts: but thy law do I
love.
114 [k]Thou *art* my hiding place and my
shield: [l]I hope in thy word.
115 [m]Depart from me, ye evildoers: for I
will keep the commandments of my God.
116 Uphold me according unto thy word,
that I may live: and let me not [n]be ashamed
of my hope.
117 Hold thou me up, and I shall be safe:
and I will have respect unto thy statutes
continually.
118 Thou hast trodden down all them that
[o]err from thy statutes: for their deceit *is*
falsehood.
119 Thou puttest away all the wicked of
the earth [p]*like* dross: therefore I love thy
testimonies.
120 [q]My flesh trembleth for fear of thee;
and I am afraid of thy judgments.

Ain

121 I have done judgment and justice: leave me not to mine oppressors.

122 Be [r]surety for thy servant for good: let not the proud oppress me.

123 [s]Mine eyes fail for thy salvation, and for the word of thy righteousness.

124 Deal with thy servant according unto thy mercy, and [t]teach me thy statutes.

125 [u]I *am* thy servant; give me understanding, that I may know thy testimonies.

126 *It is* time for *thee,* LORD, to work: *for* they have made void thy law.

127 [v]Therefore I love thy commandments above gold; yea, above fine gold.

128 Therefore I esteem all *thy* precepts *concerning* all *things to be* right; *and* I [w]hate every false way.

Pe

129 Thy testimonies *are* wonderful: therefore doth my soul keep them.

130 The entrance of thy words giveth light; [x]it giveth understanding unto the simple.

131 I opened my mouth, and panted: for I [y]longed for thy commandments.

132 [z]Look thou upon me, and be merciful unto me, [a]as thou usest to do unto those that love thy name.

133 [b]Order my steps in thy word: and [c]let not any iniquity have dominion over me.

134 [d]Deliver me from the oppression of man: so will I keep thy precepts.

135 [e]Make thy face to shine upon thy servant; and [f]teach me thy statutes.

136 [g]Rivers of waters run down mine eyes, because they keep not thy law.

Tzaddi

137 [h]Righteous *art* thou, O LORD, and upright *are* thy judgments.

138 [i]Thy testimonies *that* thou hast commanded *are* righteous and very faithful.

139 [j]My zeal hath consumed me, because mine enemies have forgotten thy words.

140 [k]Thy word *is* very pure: therefore thy servant loveth it.

141 I *am* small and despised: *yet* do not I forget thy precepts.

142 Thy righteousness *is* an everlasting righteousness, and thy law *is* [l]the truth.

143 Trouble and anguish have taken hold on me: *yet* thy commandments *are* [m]my delights.

144 The righteousness of thy testimonies *is* everlasting: [n]give me understanding, and I shall live.

Koph

145 I cried with *my* whole heart; hear me, O LORD: I will keep thy statutes.

146 I cried unto thee; save me, and I shall keep thy testimonies.

147 [o]I prevented the dawning of the morning, and cried: [p]I hoped in thy word.

148 [q]Mine eyes prevent the *night* watches, that I might meditate in thy word.

149 Hear my voice according unto thy lovingkindness: O LORD, [r]quicken me according to thy judgment.

150 They draw nigh that follow after mischief: they are far from thy law.

151 Thou *art* [s]near, O LORD; [t]and all thy commandments *are* truth.

152 Concerning thy testimonies, I have known of old that thou hast founded them [u]for ever.

Resh

153 [v]Consider mine affliction, and deliver me: for I do not forget thy law.

154 [w]Plead my cause, and deliver me: [x]quicken me according to thy word.

155 [y]Salvation *is* far from the wicked: for they seek not thy statutes.

156 Great *are* thy tender mercies, O LORD: [z]quicken me according to thy judgments.

157 Many *are* my persecutors and mine enemies; *yet* do I not [a]decline from thy testimonies.

158 I beheld the transgressors, and [b]was grieved; because they kept not thy word.

159 Consider how I love thy precepts: [c]quicken me, O LORD, according to thy lovingkindness.

160 Thy word *is* true *from* the beginning: and every one of thy righteous judgments *endureth* for ever.

Schin

161 [d]Princes have persecuted me without a cause: but my heart standeth in awe of thy word.

162 I rejoice at thy word, as one that findeth great spoil.

163 I hate and abhor lying: *but* thy law do I love.

164 Seven times a day do I praise thee because of thy righteous judgments.

165 [e]Great peace have they which love thy law: and nothing shall offend them.

166 [f]LORD, I have hoped for thy salvation, and done thy commandments.

167 My soul hath kept thy testimonies; and I love them exceedingly.

168 I have kept thy precepts and thy testimonies: [g]for all my ways *are* before thee.

Tau

169 Let my cry come near before thee, O LORD: [h]give me understanding according to thy word.

170 Let my supplication come before thee: deliver me according to thy word.

171 [i]My lips shall utter praise, when thou hast taught me thy statutes.

172 My tongue shall speak of thy word: for all thy commandments *are* righteousness.

173 Let thine hand help me; for [j]I have chosen thy precepts.

119:122 [r]Heb. 7:22
119:123 [s]ver. 81
119:124 [t]ver. 12
119:125 [u]Ps. 116:16
119:127 [v]ver. 72; Ps. 19:10; Prov. 8:11
119:128 [w]ver. 104
119:130 [x]Ps. 19:7; Prov. 1:4
119:131 [y]ver. 20
119:132 [z]Ps. 106:4 [a]2 Thess. 1:6
119:133 [b]Ps. 17:5 [c]Ps. 19:13; Rom. 6:12
119:134 [d]Luke 1:74
119:135 [e]Ps. 4:6 [f]ver. 12
119:136 [g]Jer. 9:1; Ezek. 9:4
119:137 [h]Ezra 9:15; Neh. 9:33; Jer. 12:1; Dan. 9:7
119:138 [i]Ps. 19:7
119:139 [j]Ps. 69:9; John 2:17
119:140 [k]Ps. 12:6; Prov. 30:5
119:142 [l]ver. 151; Ps. 19:9; John 17:17
119:143 [m]ver. 77
119:144 [n]ver. 34
119:147 [o]Ps. 5:3 [p]ver. 74
119:148 [q]Ps. 63:1
119:149 [r]ver. 40
119:151 [s]Ps. 145:18 [t]ver. 142
119:152 [u]Luke 21:33
119:153 [v]Lam. 5:1
119:154 [w]1 Sam. 24:15; Ps. 35:1; Mic. 7:9 [x]ver. 40
119:155 [y]Job 5:4
119:156 [z]ver. 149
119:157 [a]Ps. 44:18; ver. 51
119:158 [b]ver. 136; Ezek. 9:4
119:159 [c]ver. 88
119:161 [d]1 Sam. 24:11; ver. 23
119:165 [e]Prov. 3:2; Isa. 32:17
119:166 [f]Gen. 49:18; ver. 174
119:168 [g]Prov. 5:21
119:169 [h]ver. 144
119:171 [i]ver. 7
119:173 [j]Josh. 24:22; Prov. 1:29; Luke 10:42

174 [k]I have longed for thy salvation, O LORD; and [l]thy law *is* my delight.

175 Let my soul live, and it shall praise thee; and let thy judgments help me.

176 [m]I have gone astray like a lost sheep; seek thy servant; for I do not forget thy commandments.

A Song of degrees.

120 In [n]my distress I cried unto the LORD, and he heard me.

2 Deliver my soul, O LORD, from lying lips, *and* from a deceitful tongue.

3 What shall be given unto thee? or what shall be done unto thee, thou false tongue?

4 Sharp arrows of the mighty, with coals of juniper.

5 Woe is me, that I sojourn in [o]Mesech, [p]*that* I dwell in the tents of Kedar!

6 My soul hath long dwelt with him that hateth peace.

7 I *am for* peace: but when I speak, they *are* for war.

A Song of degrees.

121 I will lift up mine eyes unto the hills, from whence cometh my help.

2 [q]My help *cometh* from the LORD, which made heaven and earth.

3 [r]He will not suffer thy foot to be moved: [s]he that keepeth thee will not slumber.

4 Behold, he that keepeth Israel shall neither slumber nor sleep.

5 The LORD *is* thy keeper: the LORD *is* [t]thy shade [u]upon thy right hand.

6 [v]The sun shall not smite thee by day, nor the moon by night.

7 The LORD shall preserve thee from all evil: he shall [w]preserve thy soul.

8 The LORD shall [x]preserve thy going out and thy coming in from this time forth, and even for evermore.

A Song of degrees of David.

122 I was glad when they said unto me, [y]Let us go into the house of the LORD.

2 Our feet shall stand within thy gates, O Jerusalem.

3 Jerusalem is builded as a city that is [z]compact together:

4 [a]Whither the tribes go up, the tribes of the LORD, unto [b]the testimony of Israel, to give thanks unto the name of the LORD.

5 [c]For there are set thrones of judgment, the thrones of the house of David.

6 [d]Pray for the peace of Jerusalem: they shall prosper that love thee.

7 Peace be within thy walls, *and* prosperity within thy palaces.

8 For my brethren and companions' sakes, I will now say, Peace *be* within thee.

9 Because of the house of the LORD our God I will [e]seek thy good.

119:174 [k]ver. 166 [l]ver. 16
119:176 [m]Isa. 53:6; Luke 15:4; 1 Pet. 2:25
120:1 [n]Ps. 118:5; Jonah 2:2
120:5 [o]Gen. 10:2; Ezek. 27:13 [p]Gen. 25:13; 1 Sam. 25:1; Jer. 49:28
121:2 [q]Ps. 124:8
121:3 [r]1 Sam. 2:9; Prov. 3:23 [s]Ps. 127:1; Isa. 27:3
121:5 [t]Isa. 25:4 [u]Ps. 16:8
121:6 [v]Ps. 91:5; Isa. 49:10; Rev. 7:16
121:7 [w]Ps. 41:2
121:8 [x]Deut. 28:6; Prov. 2:8
122:1 [y]Isa. 2:3; Zech. 8:21
122:3 [z]2 Sam. 5:9
122:4 [a]Ex. 23:17; Deut. 16:16 [b]Ex. 16:34
122:5 [c]Deut. 17:8; 2 Chron. 19:8
122:6 [d]Ps. 51:18
122:9 [e]Neh. 2:10
123:1 [f]Ps. 121:1 [g]Ps. 2:4
124:1 [h]Ps. 129:1
124:3 [i]Ps. 56:1; Prov. 1:12
124:7 [j]Ps. 91:3; Prov. 6:5
124:8 [k]Ps. 121:2 [l]Gen. 1:1; Ps. 134:3
125:3 [m]Prov. 22:8; Isa. 14:5
125:5 [n]Prov. 2:15 [o]Ps. 128:6; Gal. 6:16
126:1 [p]Acts 12:9
126:2 [q]Job 8:21
126:5 [r]Jer. 31:9

A Song of degrees.

123 Unto thee [f]lift I up mine eyes, O thou [g]that dwellest in the heavens.

2 Behold, as the eyes of servants *look* unto the hand of their masters, *and* as the eyes of a maiden unto the hand of her mistress; so our eyes *wait* upon the LORD our God, until that he have mercy upon us.

3 Have mercy upon us, O LORD, have mercy upon us: for we are exceedingly filled with contempt.

4 Our soul is exceedingly filled with the scorning of those that are at ease, *and* with the contempt of the proud.

A Song of degrees of David.

124 If *it had* not *been* the LORD who was on our side, [h]now may Israel say;

2 If *it had* not *been* the LORD who was on our side, when men rose up against us:

3 Then they had [i]swallowed us up quick, when their wrath was kindled against us:

4 Then the waters had overwhelmed us, the stream had gone over our soul:

5 Then the proud waters had gone over our soul.

6 Blessed *be* the LORD, who hath not given us *as* a prey to their teeth.

7 Our soul is escaped [j]as a bird out of the snare of the fowlers: the snare is broken, and we are escaped.

8 [k]Our help *is* in the name of the LORD, [l]who made heaven and earth.

A Song of degrees.

125 They that trust in the LORD *shall be* as mount Zion, *which* cannot be removed, *but* abideth for ever.

2 *As* the mountains *are* round about Jerusalem, so the LORD *is* round about his people from henceforth even for ever.

3 For [m]the rod of the wicked shall not rest upon the lot of the righteous; lest the righteous put forth their hands unto iniquity.

4 Do good, O LORD, unto *those that be* good, and to *them that are* upright in their hearts.

5 As for such as turn aside unto their [n]crooked ways, the LORD shall lead them forth with the workers of iniquity: *but* [o]peace *shall be* upon Israel.

A Song of degrees.

126 When the LORD turned again the captivity of Zion, [p]we were like them that dream.

2 Then [q]was our mouth filled with laughter, and our tongue with singing: then said they among the heathen, The LORD hath done great things for them.

3 The LORD hath done great things for us; *whereof* we are glad.

4 Turn again our captivity, O LORD, as the streams in the south.

5 [r]They that sow in tears shall reap in joy.

6 He that goeth forth and weepeth, bear-

ing precious seed, shall doubtless come
again with rejoicing, bringing his sheaves
with him.

A Song of degrees for Solomon.

127 Except the LORD build the house,
they labour in vain that build it:
except [s]the LORD keep the city, the watchman waketh *but* in vain.
2 *It is* vain for you to rise up early, to sit
up late, to [t]eat the bread of sorrows: *for* so
he giveth his beloved sleep.
3 Lo, [u]children *are* an heritage of the
LORD: *and* [v]the fruit of the womb *is his* reward.
4 As arrows *are* in the hand of a mighty
man; so *are* children of the youth.
5 Happy *is* the man that hath his quiver
full of them: [w]they shall not be ashamed,
but they shall speak with the enemies in the
gate.

A Song of degrees.

128 Blessed [x]*is* every one that feareth
the LORD; that walketh in his
ways.
2 [y]For thou shalt eat the labour of thine
hands: happy *shalt* thou *be,* and *it shall be*
well with thee.
3 Thy wife *shall be* [z]as a fruitful vine by
the sides of thine house: thy children [a]like
olive plants round about thy table.
4 Behold, that thus shall the man be
blessed that feareth the LORD.
5 [b]The LORD shall bless thee out of Zion:
and thou shalt see the good of Jerusalem all
the days of thy life.
6 Yea, thou shalt [c]see thy children's children, *and* [d]peace upon Israel.

A Song of degrees.

129 Many a time have they afflicted
me from [e]my youth, [f]may Israel
now say:
2 Many a time have they afflicted me
from my youth: yet they have not prevailed
against me.
3 The plowers plowed upon my back:
they made long their furrows.
4 The LORD *is* righteous: he hath cut asunder the cords of the wicked.
5 Let them all be confounded and turned
back that hate Zion.
6 Let them be as [g]the grass *upon* the
housetops, which withereth afore it groweth up:
7 Wherewith the mower filleth not his
hand; nor he that bindeth sheaves his bosom.
8 Neither do they which go by say, [h]The
blessing of the LORD *be* upon you: we bless
you in the name of the LORD.

A Song of degrees.

130 Out [i]of the depths have I cried
unto thee, O LORD.
2 Lord, hear my voice: let thine ears be
attentive to the voice of my supplications.
3 [j]If thou, LORD, shouldest mark iniquities, O Lord, who shall stand?
4 But *there is* [k]forgiveness with thee, that
[l]thou mayest be feared.
5 [m]I wait for the LORD, my soul doth wait,
and [n]in his word do I hope.
6 [o]My soul *waiteth* for the Lord more
than they that watch for the morning: *I say,*
more than they that watch for the morning.
7 [p]Let Israel hope in the LORD: for [q]with
the LORD *there is* mercy, and with him *is*
plenteous redemption.
8 And [r]he shall redeem Israel from all his
iniquities.

A Song of degrees of David.

131 LORD, my heart is not haughty,
nor mine eyes lofty: [s]neither do
I exercise myself in great matters, or in
things too high for me.
2 Surely I have behaved and quieted myself, [t]as a child that is weaned of his
mother: my soul *is* even as a weaned child.
3 [u]Let Israel hope in the LORD from
henceforth and for ever.

A Song of degrees.

132 LORD, remember David, *and* all
his afflictions:
2 How he sware unto the LORD, [v]*and*
vowed unto [w]the mighty *God* of Jacob;
3 Surely I will not come into the tabernacle of my house, nor go up into my bed;
4 I will [x]not give sleep to mine eyes, *or*
slumber to mine eyelids,
5 Until I [y]find out a place for the LORD, an
habitation for the mighty *God* of Jacob.
6 Lo, we heard of it [z]at Ephratah: [a]we
found it [b]in the fields of the wood.
7 We will go into his tabernacles: [c]we
will worship at his footstool.
8 [d]Arise, O LORD, into thy rest; thou, and
[e]the ark of thy strength.
9 Let thy priests [f]be clothed with righteousness; and let thy saints shout for joy.
10 For thy servant David's sake turn not
away the face of thine anointed.
11 [g]The LORD hath sworn *in* truth unto
David; he will not turn from it; [h]Of the fruit
of thy body will I set upon thy throne.
12 If thy children will keep my covenant
and my testimony that I shall teach them,
their children shall also sit upon thy throne
for evermore.
13 [i]For the LORD hath chosen Zion; he
hath desired *it* for his habitation.
14 [j]This *is* my rest for ever: here will I
dwell; for I have desired it.
15 [k]I will abundantly bless her provision:
I will satisfy her poor with bread.
16 [l]I will also clothe her priests with salvation: [m]and her saints shall shout aloud for
joy.
17 [n]There will I make the horn of David
to bud: [o]I have ordained a lamp for mine
anointed.
18 His enemies will I [p]clothe with shame:
but upon himself shall his crown flourish.

127:1 [s]Ps. 121:3
127:2 [t]Gen. 3:17
127:3 [u]Gen. 33:5; Josh. 24:3 [v]Deut. 28:4
127:5 [w]Job 5:4; Prov. 27:11
128:1 [x]Ps. 112:1
128:2 [y]Isa. 3:10
128:3 [z]Ezek. 19:10 [a]Ps. 52:8
128:5 [b]Ps. 134:3
128:6 [c]Gen. 50:23; Job 42:16 [d]Ps. 125:5
129:1 [e]Ezek. 23:3; Hos. 2:15 [f]Ps. 124:1
129:6 [g]Ps. 37:2
129:8 [h]Ruth 2:4; Ps. 118:26
130:1 [i]Lam. 3:55; Jonah 2:2
130:3 [j]Ps. 143:2; Rom. 3:20
130:4 [k]Ex. 34:7 [l]1 Kings 8:40; Ps. 2:11; Jer. 33:8
130:5 [m]Ps. 27:14; Isa. 8:17 [n]Ps. 119:81
130:6 [o]Ps. 63:6
130:7 [p]Ps. 131:3 [q]Ps. 86:5; Isa. 55:7
130:8 [r]Ps. 103:3; Matt. 1:21
131:1 [s]Rom. 12:16
131:2 [t]Matt. 18:3; 1 Cor. 14:20
131:3 [u]Ps. 130:7
132:2 [v]Ps. 65:1 [w]Gen. 49:24
132:4 [x]Prov. 6:4
132:5 [y]Acts 7:46
132:6 [z]1 Sam. 17:12 [a]1 Sam. 7:1 [b]1 Chron. 13:5
132:7 [c]Ps. 5:7
132:8 [d]Num. 10:35; 2 Chron. 6:41 [e]Ps. 78:61
132:9 [f]Job 29:14; ver. 16; Isa. 61:10
132:11 [g]Ps. 89:3 [h]2 Sam. 7:12; 1 Kings 8:25; 2 Chron. 6:16; Luke 1:69; Acts 2:30
132:13 [i]Ps. 48:1
132:14 [j]Ps. 68:16
132:15 [k]Ps. 147:14
132:16 [l]2 Chron. 6:41; ver. 9; Ps. 149:4 [m]Hos. 11:12
132:17 [n]Ezek. 29:21; Luke 1:69 [o]1 Kings 11:36; 2 Chron. 21:7
132:18 [p]Ps. 35:26

A Song of degrees of David.

133 Behold, how good and how pleasant *it is* for [q]brethren to dwell together in unity!

2 *It is* like [r]the precious ointment upon the head, that ran down upon the beard, *even* Aaron's beard: that went down to the skirts of his garments;

3 As the dew of [s]Hermon, *and as the dew* that descended upon the mountains of Zion: for [t]there the LORD commanded the blessing, *even* life for evermore.

A Song of degrees.

134 Behold, bless ye the LORD, [u]all *ye* servants of the LORD, [v]which by night stand in the house of the LORD.

2 [w]Lift up your hands *in* the sanctuary, and bless the LORD.

3 [x]The LORD that made heaven and earth [y]bless thee out of Zion.

135 Praise ye the LORD. Praise ye the name of the LORD; [z]praise *him*, O ye servants of the LORD.

2 [a]Ye that stand in the house of the LORD, in [b]the courts of the house of our God,

3 Praise the LORD; for [c]the LORD *is* good: sing praises unto his name; [d]for *it is* pleasant.

4 For [e]the LORD hath chosen Jacob unto himself, *and* Israel for his peculiar treasure.

5 For I know that [f]the LORD *is* great, and *that* our Lord *is* above all gods.

6 [g]Whatsoever the LORD pleased, *that* did he in heaven, and in earth, in the seas, and all deep places.

7 [h]He causeth the vapours to ascend from the ends of the earth; [i]he maketh lightnings for the rain; he bringeth the wind out of his [j]treasuries.

8 [k]Who smote the firstborn of Egypt, both of man and beast.

9 [l]*Who* sent tokens and wonders into the midst of thee, O Egypt, [m]upon Pharaoh, and upon all his servants.

10 [n]Who smote great nations, and slew mighty kings;

11 Sihon king of the Amorites, and Og king of Bashan, and [o]all the kingdoms of Canaan:

12 [p]And gave their land *for* an heritage, an heritage unto Israel his people.

13 [q]Thy name, O LORD, *endureth* for ever; *and* thy memorial, O LORD, throughout all generations.

14 [r]For the LORD will judge his people, and he will repent himself concerning his servants.

15 [s]The idols of the heathen *are* silver and gold, the work of men's hands.

16 They have mouths, but they speak not; eyes have they, but they see not;

17 They have ears, but they hear not; neither is there *any* breath in their mouths.

18 They that make them are like unto them: *so is* every one that trusteth in them.

19 [t]Bless the LORD, O house of Israel: bless the LORD, O house of Aaron:

133:1 [q]Gen. 13:8; Heb. 13:1
133:2 [r]Ex. 30:25
133:3 [s]Deut. 4:48 [t]Lev. 25:21; Deut. 28:8; Ps. 42:8
134:1 [u]Ps. 135:1 [v]1 Chron. 9:33
134:2 [w]1 Tim. 2:8
134:3 [x]Ps. 124:8 [y]Ps. 128:5
135:1 [z]Ps. 113:1
135:2 [a]Luke 2:37 [b]Ps. 92:13
135:3 [c]Ps. 119:68 [d]Ps. 147:1
135:4 [e]Ex. 19:5; Deut. 7:6
135:5 [f]Ps. 95:3
135:6 [g]Ps. 115:3
135:7 [h]Jer. 10:13 [i]Job 28:25; Zech. 10:1 [j]Job 38:22
135:8 [k]Ex. 12:12; Ps. 78:51
135:9 [l]Ex. 7 [m]Ps. 136:15
135:10 [n]Num. 21:24; Ps. 136:17
135:11 [o]Josh. 12:7
135:12 [p]Ps. 78:55
135:13 [q]Ex. 3:15; Ps. 102:12
135:14 [r]Deut. 32:36
135:15 [s]Ps. 115:4
135:19 [t]Ps. 115:9
135:21 [u]Ps. 134:3
136:1 [v]Ps. 106:1 [w]1 Chron. 16:34; 2 Chron. 20:21
136:2 [x]Deut. 10:17
136:4 [y]Ps. 72:18
136:5 [z]Gen. 1:1; Prov. 3:19; Jer. 51:15
136:6 [a]Gen. 1:9; Ps. 24:2; Jer. 10:12
136:7 [b]Gen. 1:14
136:8 [c]Gen. 1:16
136:10 [d]Ex. 12:29; Ps. 135:8
136:11 [e]Ex. 12:51
136:12 [f]Ex. 6:6
136:13 [g]Ex. 14:21; Ps. 78:13
136:15 [h]Ex. 14:27; Ps. 135:9
136:16 [i]Ex. 13:18; Deut. 8:15
136:17 [j]Ps. 135:10
136:18 [k]Deut. 29:7
136:19 [l]Num. 21:21
136:20 [m]Num. 21:33
136:21 [n]Josh. 12:1; Ps. 135:12
136:23 [o]Gen. 8:1; Deut. 32:36; Ps. 113:7
136:25 [p]Ps. 104:27

20 Bless the LORD, O house of Levi: ye that fear the LORD, bless the LORD.

21 Blessed be the LORD [u]out of Zion, which dwelleth at Jerusalem. Praise ye the LORD.

136 O [v]give thanks unto the LORD; for *he is* good: [w]for his mercy *endureth* for ever.

2 O give thanks unto [x]the God of gods: for his mercy *endureth* for ever.

3 O give thanks to the Lord of lords: for his mercy *endureth* for ever.

4 To him [y]who alone doeth great wonders: for his mercy *endureth* for ever.

5 [z]To him that by wisdom made the heavens: for his mercy *endureth* for ever.

6 [a]To him that stretched out the earth above the waters: for his mercy *endureth* for ever.

7 [b]To him that made great lights: for his mercy *endureth* for ever:

8 [c]The sun to rule by day: for his mercy *endureth* for ever:

9 The moon and stars to rule by night: for his mercy *endureth* for ever.

10 [d]To him that smote Egypt in their firstborn: for his mercy *endureth* for ever:

11 [e]And brought out Israel from among them: for his mercy *endureth* for ever:

12 [f]With a strong hand, and with a stretched out arm: for his mercy *endureth* for ever.

13 [g]To him which divided the Red sea into parts: for his mercy *endureth* for ever:

14 And made Israel to pass through the midst of it: for his mercy *endureth* for ever:

15 [h]But overthrew Pharaoh and his host in the Red sea: for his mercy *endureth* for ever.

16 [i]To him which led his people through the wilderness: for his mercy *endureth* for ever.

17 [j]To him which smote great kings: for his mercy *endureth* for ever:

18 [k]And slew famous kings: for his mercy *endureth* for ever:

19 [l]Sihon king of the Amorites: for his mercy *endureth* for ever:

20 [m]And Og the king of Bashan: for his mercy *endureth* for ever:

21 [n]And gave their land for an heritage: for his mercy *endureth* for ever:

22 *Even* an heritage unto Israel his servant: for his mercy *endureth* for ever.

23 Who [o]remembered us in our low estate: for his mercy *endureth* for ever:

24 And hath redeemed us from our enemies: for his mercy *endureth* for ever.

25 [p]Who giveth food to all flesh: for his mercy *endureth* for ever.

26 O give thanks unto the God of heaven: for his mercy *endureth* for ever.

137 By the rivers of Babylon, there we sat down, yea, we wept, when we remembered Zion.

2 We hanged our harps upon the willows in the midst thereof.

3 For there they that carried us away cap-

tive required of us a song; and they that [q]wasted us *required of us* mirth, *saying,* Sing us *one* of the songs of Zion.

4 How shall we sing the LORD's song in a strange land?

5 If I forget thee, O Jerusalem, let my right hand forget *her cunning.*

6 If I do not remember thee, let my [r]tongue cleave to the roof of my mouth; if I prefer not Jerusalem above my chief joy.

7 Remember, O LORD, [s]the children of Edom in the day of Jerusalem; who said, Rase *it,* rase *it, even* to the foundation thereof.

8 O daughter of Babylon, [t]who art to be destroyed; happy *shall he be,* [u]that rewardeth thee as thou hast served us.

9 Happy *shall he be,* that taketh and [v]dasheth thy little ones against the stones.

A Psalm of David.

138 I will praise thee with my whole heart: [w]before the gods will I sing praise unto thee.

2 [x]I will worship [y]toward thy holy temple, and praise thy name for thy lovingkindness and for thy truth: for thou hast [z]magnified thy word above all thy name.

3 In the day when I cried thou answeredst me, *and* strengthenedst me *with* strength in my soul.

4 [a]All the kings of the earth shall praise thee, O LORD, when they hear the words of thy mouth.

5 Yea, they shall sing in the ways of the LORD: for great *is* the glory of the LORD.

6 [b]Though the LORD *be* high, yet [c]hath he respect unto the lowly: but the proud he knoweth afar off.

7 [d]Though I walk in the midst of trouble, thou wilt revive me: thou shalt stretch forth thine hand against the wrath of mine enemies, and thy right hand shall save me.

8 [e]The LORD will perfect *that which* concerneth me: thy mercy, O LORD, *endureth* for ever: [f]forsake not the works of thine own hands.

To the chief Musician, A Psalm of David.

139 O LORD, [g]thou hast searched me, and known *me.*

2 [h]Thou knowest my downsitting and mine uprising, thou [i]understandest my thought afar off.

3 [j]Thou compassest my path and my lying down, and art acquainted *with* all my ways.

4 For *there is* not a word in my tongue, *but,* lo, O LORD, [k]thou knowest it altogether.

5 Thou hast beset me behind and before, and laid thine hand upon me.

6 [l]*Such* knowledge *is* too wonderful for me; it is high, I cannot *attain* unto it.

7 [m]Whither shall I go from thy spirit? or whither shall I flee from thy presence?

8 [n]If I ascend up into heaven, thou *art*

137:3 [q]Ps. 79:1
137:6 [r]Ezek. 3:26
137:7 [s]Jer. 49:7; Lam. 4:22; Ezek. 25:12; Obad. 10
137:8 [t]Isa. 13:1; Jer. 25:12 [u]Jer. 50:15; Rev. 18:6
137:9 [v]Isa. 13:16
138:1 [w]Ps. 119:46
138:2 [x]Ps. 28:2 [y]1 Kings 8:29; Ps. 5:7 [z]Isa. 42:21
138:4 [a]Ps. 102:15
138:6 [b]Ps. 113:5; Isa. 57:15 [c]Prov. 3:34; Jam. 4:6; 1 Pet. 5:5
138:7 [d]Ps. 23:3
138:8 [e]Ps. 57:2; Phil. 1:6 [f]Job 10:3
139:1 [g]Ps. 17:3; Jer. 12:3
139:2 [h]2 Kings 19:27 [i]Matt. 9:4; John 2:24
139:3 [j]Job 31:4
139:4 [k]Heb. 4:13
139:6 [l]Job 42:3; Ps. 40:5
139:7 [m]Jer. 23:24; Jonah 1:3
139:8 [n]Am. 9:2 [o]Job 26:6; Prov. 15:11
139:12 [p]Job 26:6; Dan. 2:22; Heb. 4:13
139:15 [q]Job 10:8; Eccl. 11:5
139:17 [r]Ps. 40:5
139:19 [s]Isa. 11:4 [t]Ps. 119:115
139:20 [u]Jude 15
139:21 [v]2 Chron. 19:2; Ps. 119:158
139:23 [w]Job 31:6; Ps. 26:2
139:24 [x]Ps. 5:8
140:1 [y]ver. 4
140:2 [z]Ps. 56:6
140:3 [a]Ps. 58:4; Rom. 3:13
140:4 [b]Ps. 74:1 [c]ver. 1
140:5 [d]Ps. 35:7; Jer. 18:22

there: [o]if I make my bed in hell, behold, thou *art there.*

9 *If* I take the wings of the morning, *and* dwell in the uttermost parts of the sea;

10 Even there shall thy hand lead me, and thy right hand shall hold me.

11 If I say, Surely the darkness shall cover me; even the night shall be light about me.

12 Yea, [p]the darkness hideth not from thee; but the night shineth as the day: the darkness and the light *are* both alike *to thee.*

13 For thou hast possessed my reins: thou hast covered me in my mother's womb.

14 I will praise thee; for I am fearfully *and* wonderfully made: marvellous *are* thy works; and *that* my soul knoweth right well.

15 [q]My substance was not hid from thee, when I was made in secret, *and* curiously wrought in the lowest parts of the earth.

16 Thine eyes did see my substance, yet being unperfect; and in thy book all *my members* were written, *which* in continuance were fashioned, when *as yet there was* none of them.

17 [r]How precious also are thy thoughts unto me, O God! how great is the sum of them!

18 *If* I should count them, they are more in number than the sand: when I awake, I am still with thee.

19 Surely thou wilt [s]slay the wicked, O God: [t]depart from me therefore, ye bloody men.

20 For they speak [u]against thee wickedly, *and* thine enemies take *thy name* in vain.

21 [v]Do not I hate them, O LORD, that hate thee? and am not I grieved with those that rise up against thee?

22 I hate them with perfect hatred: I count them mine enemies.

23 [w]Search me, O God, and know my heart: try me, and know my thoughts:

24 And see if *there be any* wicked way in me, and [x]lead me in the way everlasting.

To the chief Musician, A Psalm of David.

140 Deliver me, O LORD, from the evil man: [y]preserve me from the violent man;

2 Which imagine mischiefs in *their* heart; [z]continually are they gathered together *for* war.

3 They have sharpened their tongues like a serpent; [a]adders' poison *is* under their lips. Selah.

4 [b]Keep me, O LORD, from the hands of the wicked; [c]preserve me from the violent man; who have purposed to overthrow my goings.

5 [d]The proud have hid a snare for me, and cords; they have spread a net by the wayside; they have set gins for me. Selah.

6 I said unto the LORD, Thou *art* my God: hear the voice of my supplications, O LORD.

7 O GOD the Lord, the strength of my salvation, thou hast covered my head in the day of battle.

8 Grant not, O LORD, the desires of the wicked: further not his wicked device; [e]*lest* they exalt themselves. Selah.

9 *As for* the head of those that compass me about, [f]let the mischief of their own lips cover them.

10 [g]Let burning coals fall upon them: let them be cast into the fire; into deep pits, that they rise not up again.

11 Let not an evil speaker be established in the earth: evil shall hunt the violent man to overthrow *him.*

12 I know that the LORD will [h]maintain the cause of the afflicted, *and* the right of the poor.

13 Surely the righteous shall give thanks unto thy name: the upright shall dwell in thy presence.

A Psalm of David.

141 LORD, I cry unto thee: [i]make haste unto me; give ear unto my voice, when I cry unto thee.

2 Let [j]my prayer be set forth before thee [k]*as* incense; *and* [l]the lifting up of my hands *as* [m]the evening sacrifice.

3 Set a watch, O LORD, before my mouth; keep the door of my lips.

4 Incline not my heart to *any* evil thing, to practise wicked works with men that work iniquity: [n]and let me not eat of their dainties.

5 [o]Let the righteous smite me; *it shall be* a kindness: and let him reprove me; *it shall be* an excellent oil, *which* shall not break my head: for yet my prayer also *shall be* in their calamities.

6 When their judges are overthrown in stony places, they shall hear my words; for they are sweet.

7 Our bones are scattered [p]at the grave's mouth, as when one cutteth and cleaveth *wood* upon the earth.

8 But [q]mine eyes *are* unto thee, O GOD the Lord: in thee is my trust; leave not my soul destitute.

9 Keep me from [r]the snares *which* they have laid for me, and the gins of the workers of iniquity.

10 [s]Let the wicked fall into their own nets, whilst that I withal escape.

Maschil of David; A Prayer when he was in the cave.

142 I cried unto the LORD with my voice; with my voice unto the LORD did I make my supplication.

2 [t]I poured out my complaint before him; I shewed before him my trouble.

3 [u]When my spirit was overwhelmed within me, then thou knewest my path. [v]In the way wherein I walked have they privily laid a snare for me.

4 [w]I looked on *my* right hand, and beheld, but [x]*there was* no man that would know me: refuge failed me; no man cared for my soul.

5 I cried unto thee, O LORD: I said, [y]Thou *art* my refuge *and* [z]my portion [a]in the land of the living.

6 Attend unto my cry; for I am [b]brought very low: deliver me from my persecutors; for they are stronger than I.

7 Bring my soul out of prison, that I may praise thy name: [c]the righteous shall compass me about; [d]for thou shalt deal bountifully with me.

A Psalm of David.

143 Hear my prayer, O LORD, give ear to my supplications: [e]in thy faithfulness answer me, *and* in thy righteousness.

2 And [f]enter not into judgment with thy servant: for [g]in thy sight shall no man living be justified.

3 For the enemy hath persecuted my soul; he hath smitten my life down to the ground; he hath made me to dwell in darkness, as those that have been long dead.

4 [h]Therefore is my spirit overwhelmed within me; my heart within me is desolate.

5 [i]I remember the days of old; I meditate on all thy works; I muse on the work of thy hands.

6 [j]I stretch forth my hands unto thee: [k]my soul *thirsteth* after thee, as a thirsty land. Selah.

7 Hear me speedily, O LORD: my spirit faileth: hide not thy face from me, [l]lest I be like unto them that go down into the pit.

8 Cause me to hear thy lovingkindness [m]in the morning; for in thee do I trust: [n]cause me to know the way wherein I should walk; for [o]I lift up my soul unto thee.

9 Deliver me, O LORD, from mine enemies: I flee unto thee to hide me.

10 [p]Teach me to do thy will; for thou *art* my God: [q]thy spirit *is* good; lead me into [r]the land of uprightness.

11 [s]Quicken me, O LORD, for thy name's sake: for thy righteousness' sake bring my soul out of trouble.

12 And of thy mercy [t]cut off mine enemies, and destroy all them that afflict my soul: for [u]I *am* thy servant.

A Psalm of David.

144 Blessed *be* the LORD my strength, [v]which teacheth my hands to war, *and* my fingers to fight:

2 [w]My goodness, and my fortress; my high tower, and my deliverer; my shield, and *he* in whom I trust; who subdueth my people under me.

3 [x]LORD, what *is* man, that thou takest knowledge of him! *or* the son of man, that thou makest account of him!

4 [y]Man is like to vanity: [z]his days *are* as a shadow that passeth away.

5 [a]Bow thy heavens, O LORD, and come down: [b]touch the mountains, and they shall smoke.

140:8 [e]Deut. 32:27
140:9 [f]Ps. 7:16; Prov. 12:13
140:10 [g]Ps. 11:6
140:12 [h]1 Kings 8:45; Ps. 9:4
141:1 [i]Ps. 70:5
141:2 [j]Rev. 5:8 [k]Rev. 8:3 [l]Ps. 134:2; 1 Tim. 2:8 [m]Ex. 29:39
141:4 [n]Prov. 23:6
141:5 [o]Prov. 9:8; Gal. 6:1
141:7 [p]2 Cor. 1:9
141:8 [q]2 Chron. 20:12; Ps. 25:15
141:9 [r]Ps. 119:110
141:10 [s]Ps. 35:8
142:2 [t]Ps. 102, title; Isa. 26:16
142:3 [u]Ps. 143:4 [v]Ps. 140:5
142:4 [w]Ps. 69:20 [x]Ps. 31:11
142:5 [y]Ps. 46:1 [z]Ps. 16:5; Lam. 3:24 [a]Ps. 27:13
142:6 [b]Ps. 116:6
142:7 [c]Ps. 34:2 [d]Ps. 13:6
143:1 [e]Ps. 31:1
143:2 [f]Job 14:3 [g]Ex. 34:7; Job 4:17; Ps. 130:3; Eccl. 7:20; Rom. 3:20; Gal. 2:16
143:4 [h]Ps. 77:3
143:5 [i]Ps. 77:5
143:6 [j]Ps. 88:9 [k]Ps. 63:1
143:7 [l]Ps. 28:1
143:8 [m]Ps. 46:5 [n]Ps. 5:8 [o]Ps. 25:1
143:10 [p]Ps. 25:4 [q]Neh. 9:20 [r]Isa. 26:10
143:11 [s]Ps. 119:25
143:12 [t]Ps. 54:5 [u]Ps. 116:16
144:1 [v]2 Sam. 22:35; Ps. 18:34
144:2 [w]2 Sam. 22:2
144:3 [x]Job 7:17; Ps. 8:4; Heb. 2:6
144:4 [y]Job 4:19; Ps. 39:5 [z]Ps. 102:11
144:5 [a]Ps. 18:9; Isa. 64:1 [b]Ps. 104:32

6 [c]Cast forth lightning, and scatter them: shoot out thine arrows, and destroy them.

7 [d]Send thine hand from above; [e]rid me, and deliver me out of great waters, from the hand of [f]strange children;

8 Whose mouth [g]speaketh vanity, and their right hand *is* a right hand of falsehood.

9 I will [h]sing a new song unto thee, O God: upon a psaltery *and* an instrument of ten strings will I sing praises unto thee.

10 [i]*It is he* that giveth salvation unto kings: who delivereth David his servant from the hurtful sword.

11 [j]Rid me, and deliver me from the hand of strange children, whose mouth speaketh vanity, and their right hand *is* a right hand of falsehood:

12 That our sons *may be* [k]as plants grown up in their youth; *that* our daughters *may be* as corner stones, polished *after* the similitude of a palace:

13 *That* our garners *may be* full, affording all manner of store: *that* our sheep may bring forth thousands and ten thousands in our streets:

14 *That* our oxen *may be* strong to labour; *that there be* no breaking in, nor going out; that *there be* no complaining in our streets.

15 [l]Happy *is that* people, that is in such a case: *yea,* happy *is that* people, whose God *is* the LORD.

David's *Psalm* of praise.

145 I will extol thee, my God, O king; and I will bless thy name for ever and ever.

2 Every day will I bless thee; and I will praise thy name for ever and ever.

3 [m]Great *is* the LORD, and greatly to be praised; and [n]his greatness *is* unsearchable.

4 [o]One generation shall praise thy works to another, and shall declare thy mighty acts.

5 I will speak of the glorious honour of thy majesty, and of thy wondrous works.

6 And *men* shall speak of the might of thy terrible acts: and I will declare thy greatness.

7 They shall abundantly utter the memory of thy great goodness, and shall sing of thy righteousness.

8 [p]The LORD *is* gracious, and full of compassion; slow to anger, and of great mercy.

9 [q]The LORD *is* good to all: and his tender mercies *are* over all his works.

10 [r]All thy works shall praise thee, O LORD; and thy saints shall bless thee.

11 They shall speak of the glory of thy kingdom, and talk of thy power;

12 To make known to the sons of men his mighty acts, and the glorious majesty of his kingdom.

13 [s]Thy kingdom *is* an everlasting kingdom, and thy dominion *endureth* throughout all generations.

14 The LORD upholdeth all that fall, and [t]raiseth up all *those that be* bowed down.

15 [u]The eyes of all wait upon thee; and [v]thou givest them their meat in due season.

16 Thou openest thine hand, [w]and satisfiest the desire of every living thing.

17 The LORD *is* righteous in all his ways, and holy in all his works.

18 [x]The LORD *is* nigh unto all them that call upon him, to all that call upon him [y]in truth.

19 He will fulfil the desire of them that fear him: he also will hear their cry, and will save them.

20 [z]The LORD preserveth all them that love him: but all the wicked will he destroy.

21 My mouth shall speak the praise of the LORD: and let all flesh bless his holy name for ever and ever.

146 Praise ye the LORD. [a]Praise the LORD, O my soul.

2 [b]While I live will I praise the LORD: I will sing praises unto my God while I have any being.

3 [c]Put not your trust in princes, *nor* in the son of man, in whom *there is* no help.

4 [d]His breath goeth forth, he returneth to his earth; in that very day [e]his thoughts perish.

5 [f]Happy *is he* that *hath* the God of Jacob for his help, whose hope *is* in the LORD his God:

6 [g]Which made heaven, and earth, the sea, and all that therein *is:* which keepeth truth for ever:

7 [h]Which executeth judgment for the oppressed: [i]which giveth food to the hungry. [j]The LORD looseth the prisoners:

8 [k]The LORD openeth *the eyes of* the blind: [l]the LORD raiseth them that are bowed down: the LORD loveth the righteous:

9 [m]The LORD preserveth the strangers; he relieveth the fatherless and widow: [n]but the way of the wicked he turneth upside down.

10 [o]The LORD shall reign for ever, *even* thy God, O Zion, unto all generations. Praise ye the LORD.

147 Praise ye the LORD: for [p]*it is* good to sing praises unto our God; [q]for *it is* pleasant; *and* [r]praise is comely.

2 The LORD doth [s]build up Jerusalem: [t]he gathereth together the outcasts of Israel.

3 [u]He healeth the broken in heart, and bindeth up their wounds.

4 [v]He telleth the number of the stars; he calleth them all by *their* names.

5 [w]Great *is* our Lord, and of [x]great power: [y]his understanding *is* infinite.

6 [z]The LORD lifteth up the meek: he casteth the wicked down to the ground.

7 Sing unto the LORD with thanksgiving; sing praise upon the harp unto our God:

8 [a]Who covereth the heaven with clouds, who prepareth rain for the earth, who maketh grass to grow upon the mountains.

9 [b]He giveth to the beast his food, *and* [c]to the young ravens which cry.

10 [d]He delighteth not in the strength of

144:6 [c]Ps. 18:13
144:7 [d]Ps. 18:16 [e]ver. 11; Ps. 69:1 [f]Ps. 54:3; Mal. 2:11
144:8 [g]Ps. 12:2
144:9 [h]Ps. 33:2
144:10 [i]Ps. 18:50
144:11 [j]ver. 7
144:12 [k]Ps. 128:3
144:15 [l]Deut. 33:29; Ps. 33:12
145:3 [m]Ps. 96:4 [n]Job 5:9; Rom. 11:33
145:4 [o]Isa. 38:19
145:8 [p]Ex. 34:6; Num. 14:18; Ps. 86:5
145:9 [q]Ps. 100:5; Nah. 1:7
145:10 [r]Ps. 19:1
145:13 [s]Ps. 146:10; 1 Tim. 1:17
145:14 [t]Ps. 146:8
145:15 [u]Ps. 104:27 [v]Ps. 136:25
145:16 [w]Ps. 104:21
145:18 [x]Deut. 4:7 [y]John 4:24
145:20 [z]Ps. 31:23
146:1 [a]Ps. 103:1
146:2 [b]Ps. 104:33
146:3 [c]Ps. 118:8; Isa. 2:22
146:4 [d]Ps. 104:29; Eccl. 12:7; Isa. 2:22 [e]1 Cor. 2:6
146:5 [f]Ps. 144:15; Jer. 17:7
146:6 [g]Gen. 1:1; Rev. 14:7
146:7 [h]Ps. 103:6 [i]Ps. 107:9 [j]Ps. 68:6
146:8 [k]Matt. 9:30; John 9:7-32 [l]Ps. 145:14; Luke 13:13
146:9 [m]Deut. 10:18; Ps. 68:5 [n]Ps. 147:6
146:10 [o]Ex. 15:18; Ps. 10:16; Rev. 11:15
147:1 [p]Ps. 92:1 [q]Ps. 135:3 [r]Ps. 33:1
147:2 [s]Ps. 102:16 [t]Deut. 30:3
147:3 [u]Ps. 51:17; Isa. 57:15; Luke 4:18
147:4 [v]Gen. 15:5; Isa. 40:26
147:5 [w]1 Chron. 16:25; Ps. 48:1 [x]Neh. 1:3 [y]Isa. 40:28
147:6 [z]Ps. 146:8
147:8 [a]Job 38:26; Ps. 104:13
147:9 [b]Job 38:41; Ps. 104:27 [c]Job 38:41; Matt. 6:26
147:10 [d]Ps. 33:16; Hos. 1:7

the horse: he taketh not pleasure in the legs
of a man.
11 The LORD taketh pleasure in them that
fear him, in those that hope in his mercy.
12 Praise the LORD, O Jerusalem; praise
thy God, O Zion.
13 For he hath strengthened the bars of
thy gates; he hath blessed thy children
within thee.
14 [e]He maketh peace *in* thy borders, *and*
[f]filleth thee with the finest of the wheat.
15 [g]He sendeth forth his commandment
upon earth: his word runneth very swiftly.
16 [h]He giveth snow like wool: he scattereth the hoarfrost like ashes.
17 He casteth forth his ice like morsels:
who can stand before his cold?
18 [i]He sendeth out his word, and melteth
them: he causeth his wind to blow, *and* the
waters flow.
19 [j]He sheweth his word unto Jacob,
[k]his statutes and his judgments unto Israel.
20 [l]He hath not dealt so with any nation:
and *as for his* judgments, they have not
known them. Praise ye the LORD.

148

Praise ye the LORD. Praise ye the
LORD from the heavens: praise
him in the heights.
2 [m]Praise ye him, all his angels: praise ye
him, all his hosts.
3 Praise ye him, sun and moon: praise
him, all ye stars of light.
4 Praise him, [n]ye heavens of heavens,
and [o]ye waters that *be* above the heavens.
5 Let them praise the name of the LORD:
for [p]he commanded, and they were created.
6 [q]He hath also stablished them for ever
and ever: he hath made a decree which shall
not pass.
7 Praise the LORD from the earth, [r]ye
dragons, and all deeps:
8 Fire, and hail; snow, and vapour;
stormy wind [s]fulfilling his word:
9 [t]Mountains, and all hills; fruitful trees,
and all cedars:
10 Beasts, and all cattle; creeping things,
and flying fowl:
11 Kings of the earth, and all people;
princes, and all judges of the earth:
12 Both young men, and maidens; old
men, and children:
13 Let them praise the name of the LORD:
for [u]his name alone is excellent; [v]his glory
is above the earth and heaven.
14 [w]He also exalteth the horn of his people, [x]the praise of all his saints; *even* of the
children of Israel, [y]a people near unto him.
Praise ye the LORD.

149

Praise ye the LORD. [z]Sing unto
the LORD a new song, *and* his
praise in the congregation of saints.
2 Let Israel rejoice in [a]him that made
him: let the children of Zion be joyful in
their [b]King.
3 [c]Let them praise his name in the dance:
let them sing praises unto him with the timbrel and harp.
4 For [d]the LORD taketh pleasure in his
people: [e]he will beautify the meek with salvation.
5 Let the saints be joyful in glory: let them
[f]sing aloud upon their beds.
6 *Let* the high *praises* of God *be* in their
mouth, and [g]a twoedged sword in their
hand;
7 To execute vengeance upon the heathen, *and* punishments upon the people;
8 To bind their kings with chains, and
their nobles with fetters of iron;
9 [h]To execute upon them the judgment
written: [i]this honour have all his saints.
Praise ye the LORD.

150

Praise ye the LORD. Praise God in
his sanctuary: praise him in the
firmament of his power.
2 [j]Praise him for his mighty acts: praise
him according to his excellent [k]greatness.
3 Praise him with the sound of the trumpet: [l]praise him with the psaltery and harp.
4 Praise him [m]with the timbrel and dance:
praise him with [n]stringed instruments and
organs.
5 Praise him upon the loud [o]cymbals:
praise him upon the high sounding cymbals.
6 Let every thing that hath breath praise
the LORD. Praise ye the LORD.

147:14 [e]Isa. 60:17 [f]Ps. 132:15
147:15 [g]Ps. 107:20; Job 37:12
147:16 [h]Job 37:6
147:18 [i]Job 37:10; ver. 15
147:19 [j]Deut. 33:2; Ps. 76:1 [k]Mal. 4:4
147:20 [l]Deut. 4:32; Rom. 3:1
148:2 [m]Ps. 103:20
148:4 [n]1 Kings 8:27; 2 Cor. 12:2 [o]Gen. 1:7
148:5 [p]Gen. 1:1; Ps. 33:6
148:6 [q]Ps. 89:37; Jer. 31:35
148:7 [r]Isa. 43:20
148:8 [s]Ps. 147:15-18
148:9 [t]Isa. 44:23
148:13 [u]Ps. 8:1; Isa. 12:4 [v]Ps. 113:4
148:14 [w]Ps. 75:10 [x]Ps. 149:9 [y]Eph. 2:17
149:1 [z]Ps. 33:3; Isa. 42:10
149:2 [a]Job 35:10; Ps. 100:3; Isa. 54:5 [b]Zech. 9:9; Matt. 21:5
149:3 [c]Ps. 81:2
149:4 [d]Ps. 35:27 [e]Ps. 132:16
149:5 [f]Job 35:10
149:6 [g]Heb. 4:12; Rev. 1:16
149:9 [h]Deut. 7:1 [i]Ps. 148:14
150:2 [j]Ps. 145:5 [k]Deut. 3:24
150:3 [l]Ps. 81:2
150:4 [m]Ex. 15:20 [n]Ps. 33:2; Isa. 38:20
150:5 [o]1 Chron. 15:16

PROVERBS

Most of the book of Proverbs is attributed to Solomon, written around 950 B.C. Proverbs contains information and instructions for most aspects of life including sin, wealth, friends, idleness, poverty, the family, vengeance, humility, justice, and pride.

I. The purpose for the Proverbs, 1:1–1:7
II. The search for wisdom, 1:8–9:18
III. Specific Proverbs of Solomon, 10:1–24:34
IV. Proverbs of Solomon copied by Hezekiah's men, 25:1–29:27
V. The Words of Agur, 30:1–33
VI. The Words of Lemuel, 31:1–9
VII. The virtuous wife, 31:10–31:31

1 The [a]proverbs of Solomon the son of
David, king of Israel;
2 To know wisdom and instruction; to
perceive the words of understanding;
3 To [b]receive the instruction of wisdom,
justice, and judgment, and equity;
4 To give subtilty to the [c]simple, to the
young man knowledge and discretion.
5 [d]A wise *man* will hear, and will increase learning; and a man of understanding shall attain unto wise counsels:
6 To understand a proverb, and the interpretation; the words of the wise, and their
[e]dark sayings.
7 ¶ [f]The fear of the LORD *is* the beginning
of knowledge: *but* fools despise wisdom
and instruction.
8 [g]My son, hear the instruction of thy father, and forsake not the law of thy mother:
9 For [h]they *shall be* an ornament of grace
unto thy head, and chains about thy neck.
10 ¶ My son, if sinners entice thee, [i]con-
sent thou not.
11 If they say, Come with us, let us [j]lay
wait for blood, let us lurk privily for the
innocent without cause:
12 Let us swallow them up alive as the
grave; and whole, [k]as those that go down
into the pit:
13 We shall find all precious substance,
we shall fill our houses with spoil:
14 Cast in thy lot among us; let us all have
one purse:
15 My son, [l]walk not thou in the way
with them; [m]refrain thy foot from their path:
16 [n]For their feet run to evil, and make
haste to shed blood.
17 Surely in vain the net is spread in the
sight of any bird.
18 And they lay wait for their *own* blood;
they lurk privily for their *own* lives.
19 [o]So *are* the ways of every one that is
greedy of gain; *which* taketh away the life
of the owners thereof.
20 ¶ [p]Wisdom crieth without; she uttereth her voice in the streets:
21 She crieth in the chief place of concourse, in the openings of the gates: in the
city she uttereth her words, *saying*,
22 How long, ye simple ones, will ye love
simplicity? and the scorners delight in their
scorning, and fools hate knowledge?
23 Turn you at my reproof: behold, [q]I will
pour out my spirit unto you, I will make
known my words unto you.
24 ¶ [r]Because I have called, and ye refused; I have stretched out my hand, and no
man regarded;
25 But ye [s]have set at nought all my
counsel, and would none of my reproof:
26 [t]I also will laugh at your calamity; I
will mock when your fear cometh;
27 When [u]your fear cometh as desolation, and your destruction cometh as a
whirlwind; when distress and anguish cometh upon you.
28 [v]Then shall they call upon me, but I
will not answer; they shall seek me early,
but they shall not find me:
29 For that they [w]hated knowledge, and
did not [x]choose the fear of the LORD:
30 [y]They would none of my counsel: they
despised all my reproof.
31 Therefore [z]shall they eat of the fruit of
their own way, and be filled with their own
devices.
32 For the turning away of the simple
shall slay them, and the prosperity of fools
shall destroy them.
33 But [a]whoso hearkeneth unto me shall
dwell safely, and [b]shall be quiet from fear
of evil.

2 My son, if thou wilt receive my words,
and [c]hide my commandments with
thee;
2 So that thou incline thine ear unto wisdom, *and* apply thine heart to understanding;
3 Yea, if thou criest after knowledge, *and*
liftest up thy voice for understanding;
4 [d]If thou seekest her as silver, and
searchest for her as *for* hid treasures;
5 Then shalt thou understand the fear of
the LORD, and find the knowledge of God.
6 [e]For the LORD giveth wisdom: out of his
mouth *cometh* knowledge and understanding.
7 He layeth up sound wisdom for the righ-

1:1 [a]1 Kings 4:32; ch. 10:1; Eccl. 12:9
1:3 [b]ch. 2:1
1:4 [c]ch. 9:4
1:5 [d]ch. 9:9
1:6 [e]Ps. 78:2
1:7 [f]Job 28:28; Ps. 111:10; ch. 9:10; Eccl. 12:13
1:8 [g]ch. 4:1
1:9 [h]ch. 3:22
1:10 [i]Gen. 39:7; Ps. 1:1; Eph. 5:11
1:11 [j]Jer. 5:26
1:12 [k]Ps. 28:1
1:15 [l]Ps. 1:1; ch. 4:14 [m]Ps. 119:101
1:16 [n]Isa. 59:7; Rom. 3:15
1:19 [o]ch. 15:27; 1 Tim. 6:10
1:20 [p]ch. 8:1; John 7:37
1:23 [q]Joel 2:28
1:24 [r]Isa. 65:12; Jer. 7:13; Zech. 7:11
1:25 [s]Ps. 107:11; ver. 30; Luke 7:30
1:26 [t]Ps. 2:4
1:27 [u]ch. 10:24
1:28 [v]Job 27:9; Isa. 1:15; Jer. 11:11; Ezek. 8:18; Mic. 3:4; Zech. 7:13; Jam. 4:3
1:29 [w]Job 21:14; ver. 22 [x]Ps. 119:173
1:30 [y]ver. 25; Ps. 81:11
1:31 [z]Job 4:8; ch. 14:14; Isa. 3:11; Jer. 6:19
1:33 [a]Ps. 25:12 [b]Ps. 112:7
2:1 [c]ch. 4:21
2:4 [d]ch. 3:14; Matt. 13:44
2:6 [e]1 Kings 3:9; Jam. 1:5

teous: [f]*he is* a buckler to them that walk uprightly.

8 He keepeth the paths of judgment, and [g]preserveth the way of his saints.

9 Then shalt thou understand righteousness, and judgment, and equity; *yea,* every good path.

10 ¶ When wisdom entereth into thine heart, and knowledge is pleasant unto thy soul;

11 Discretion shall preserve thee, [h]understanding shall keep thee:

12 To deliver thee from the way of the evil *man,* from the man that speaketh froward things;

13 Who leave the paths of uprightness, to [i]walk in the ways of darkness;

14 Who [j]rejoice to do evil, *and* [k]delight in the frowardness of the wicked;

15 [l]Whose ways *are* crooked, and *they* froward in their paths:

16 To deliver thee from [m]the strange woman, [n]*even* from the stranger *which* flattereth with her words;

17 [o]Which forsaketh the guide of her youth, and forgetteth the covenant of her God.

18 For [p]her house inclineth unto death, and her paths unto the dead.

19 None that go unto her return again, neither take they hold of the paths of life.

20 That thou mayest walk in the way of good *men,* and keep the paths of the righteous.

21 [q]For the upright shall dwell in the land, and the perfect shall remain in it.

22 [r]But the wicked shall be cut off from the earth, and the transgressors shall be rooted out of it.

3 My son, forget not my law; [s]but let thine heart keep my commandments:

2 For length of days, and long life, and [t]peace, shall they add to thee.

3 Let not mercy and truth forsake thee: [u]bind them about thy neck; [v]write them upon the table of thine heart:

4 [w]So shalt thou find favour and good understanding in the sight of God and man.

5 ¶ [x]Trust in the LORD with all thine heart; [y]and lean not unto thine own understanding.

6 [z]In all thy ways acknowledge him, and he shall [a]direct thy paths.

7 ¶ [b]Be not wise in thine own eyes: [c]fear the LORD, and depart from evil.

8 It shall be health to thy navel, and [d]marrow to thy bones.

9 [e]Honour the LORD with thy substance, and with the firstfruits of all thine increase:

10 [f]So shall thy barns be filled with plenty, and thy presses shall burst out with new wine.

11 ¶ [g]My son, despise not the chastening of the LORD; neither be weary of his correction:

12 For whom the LORD loveth he correcteth; [h]even as a father the son *in whom* he delighteth.

13 ¶ [i]Happy *is* the man *that* findeth wisdom, and the man *that* getteth understanding.

14 [j]For the merchandise of it *is* better than the merchandise of silver, and the gain thereof than fine gold.

15 She *is* more precious than rubies: and [k]all the things thou canst desire are not to be compared unto her.

16 [l]Length of days *is* in her right hand; *and* in her left hand riches and honour.

17 [m]Her ways *are* ways of pleasantness, and all her paths *are* peace.

18 She *is* a [n]tree of life to them that lay hold upon her: and happy *is every one* that retaineth her.

19 [o]The LORD by wisdom hath founded the earth; by understanding hath he established the heavens.

20 [p]By his knowledge the depths are broken up, and [q]the clouds drop down the dew.

21 ¶ My son, let not them depart from thine eyes: keep sound wisdom and discretion:

22 So shall they be life unto thy soul, and [r]grace to thy neck.

23 [s]Then shalt thou walk in thy way safely, and thy foot shall not stumble.

24 [t]When thou liest down, thou shalt not be afraid: yea, thou shalt lie down, and thy sleep shall be sweet.

25 [u]Be not afraid of sudden fear, neither of the desolation of the wicked, when it cometh.

26 For the LORD shall be thy confidence, and shall keep thy foot from being taken.

27 ¶ [v]Withhold not good from them to whom it is due, when it is in the power of thine hand to do *it.*

28 [w]Say not unto thy neighbour, Go, and come again, and to morrow I will give; when thou hast it by thee.

29 Devise not evil against thy neighbour, seeing he dwelleth securely by thee.

30 ¶ [x]Strive not with a man without cause, if he have done thee no harm.

31 ¶ [y]Envy thou not the oppressor, and choose none of his ways.

32 For the froward *is* abomination to the LORD: [z]but his secret *is* with the righteous.

33 ¶ [a]The curse of the LORD *is* in the house of the wicked: but [b]he blesseth the habitation of the just.

34 [c]Surely he scorneth the scorners: but he giveth grace unto the lowly.

35 The wise shall inherit glory: but shame shall be the promotion of fools.

4 Hear, [d]ye children, the instruction of a father, and attend to know understanding.

2 For I give you good doctrine, forsake ye not my law.

3 For I was my father's son, [e]tender and only *beloved* in the sight of my mother.

4 [f]He taught me also, and said unto me, Let thine heart retain my words: [g]keep my commandments, and live.

5 [h]Get wisdom, get understanding: forget

2:7 *f*Ps. 84:11; ch. 30:5
2:8 *g*1 Sam. 2:9; Ps. 66:9
2:11 *h*ch. 6:22
2:13 *i*John 3:19
2:14 *j*ch. 10:23; Jer. 11:15 *k*Rom. 1:32
2:15 *l*Ps. 125:5
2:16 *m*ch. 5:20 *n*ch. 5:3
2:17 *o*Mal. 2:14
2:18 *p*ch. 7:27
2:21 *q*Ps. 37:29
2:22 *r*Job 18:17; Ps. 37:28
3:1 *s*Deut. 8:1
3:2 *t*Ps. 119:165
3:3 *u*Ex. 13:9; Deut. 6:8; ch. 6:21 *v*Jer. 17:1; 2 Cor. 3:3
3:4 *w*1 Sam. 2:26; Ps. 111:10; Luke 2:52; Acts 2:47; Rom. 14:18
3:5 *x*Ps. 37:3 *y*Jer. 9:23
3:6 *z*1 Chron. 28:9 *a*Jer. 10:23
3:7 *b*Rom. 12:16 *c*Job 1:1; ch. 16:6
3:8 *d*Job 21:24
3:9 *e*Ex. 22:29; Deut. 26:2; Mal. 3:10; Luke 14:13
3:10 *f*Deut. 28:8
3:11 *g*Job 5:17; Ps. 94:12; Heb. 12:5; Rev. 3:19
3:12 *h*Deut. 8:5
3:13 *i*ch. 8:34
3:14 *j*Job 28:13; Ps. 19:10; ch. 2:4
3:15 *k*Matt. 13:44
3:16 *l*ch. 8:18; 1 Tim. 4:8
3:17 *m*Matt. 11:29
3:18 *n*Gen. 2:9
3:19 *o*Ps. 104:24; ch. 8:27; Jer. 10:12
3:20 *p*Gen. 1:9 *q*Deut. 33:28; Job 36:28
3:22 *r*ch. 1:9
3:23 *s*Ps. 37:24; ch. 10:9
3:24 *t*Lev. 26:6; Ps. 3:5
3:25 *u*Ps. 91:5
3:27 *v*Rom. 13:7; Gal. 6:10
3:28 *w*Lev. 19:13; Deut. 24:15
3:30 *x*Rom. 12:18
3:31 *y*Ps. 37:1; ch. 24:1
3:32 *z*Ps. 25:14
3:33 *a*Lev. 26:14; Ps. 37:22; Zech. 5:4; Mal. 2:2 *b*Ps. 1:3
3:34 *c*Jam. 4:6; 1 Pet. 5:5
4:1 *d*Ps. 34:11; ch. 1:8
4:3 *e*1 Chron. 29:1
4:4 *f*1 Chron. 28:9; Eph. 6:4 *g*ch. 7:2
4:5 *h*ch. 2:2

Focus on PROVERBS

It is amazing to discover that hidden away among the wisdom of the varied collection of these instructional materials, we find a third version of the Creation Story! Wisdom speaks and details how she was "set up from everlasting, from the beginning, or ever the earth was" (8:23).

Proverbs is part of the wisdom literature segment of the Bible. The book received its final editing in the early postexilic period. The sages of the ages have contributed to this volume of short and often unrelated sayings, which cover a range of topics and subjects for making an emerging nation healthy, wealthy, and wise. Much of Proverbs is "borrowed" wisdom from the nations who influenced Israel's development. Solomon, who is credited as the main writer of Proverbs, often used contrasts to teach the difference between right and wrong—between moral and immoral behavior. In the wisdom tradition, God is viewed primarily as the Creator who has placed Wisdom among us to learn from and be led by. Wisdom is personified in chapter one as a woman. "Wisdom crieth without; she uttereth her voice in the streets: She crieth in the chief place of concourse, in the openings of the gates: in the city she uttereth her words, saying, How long, ye simple ones, will ye love simplicity? and the scorners delight in their scorning, and fools hate knowledge?" (1:20–22).

Wisdom does not belong to any one age, place, nation, or gender. Wisdom is a gift from God. "Whoso harkeneth unto me shall dwell safely, and shall be quiet from fear of evil" (v. 33). She is qualified to teach us because she watched the forming of the world: "I was by him, as one brought up with him" (v. 30). She clapped and danced in delight as the creatures of earth were being developed (8:30–31). She is filled with joy. She is expressive. She is a woman!

Most of us know "the Virtuous Woman" of chapter 31. She has been proclaimed as the ultimate vision of true Christian womanhood. What we have not been taught is that this chapter is a *massa,* or prophesy, from the mouth of a queen mother. "The words of king Lemuel, the prophecy [*massa]* that his mother taught him" (31:1). What we find is a woman telling her son, the king, "If you want a do-right woman, you need to be a do-right man!"

The queen mother knows that a "do-right" woman of great character is worth far more than rubies. She details that this sister is always on the ball: a good wife, eager worker, merchant, businesswoman, gardener, distributor, marketer, supervisor, real estate wheeler dealer, trader, craftsperson, missionary, seamstress, regal, royal, and a strong mother. Even without a network of support, civil rights amendments, college courses, and seminars in self-esteem building, this sister is called "blessed."

The entire collection of Wisdom literature is geared toward building strong leaders in families, communities, and in the nation. Women were

the primary instructors in early "home education." Our grandmothers passed many of these wise sayings down to us and described them as "just common sense." God named this "common sense" wisdom. "If any of you lack wisdom, let him ask of God that giveth to all men liberally" (James 1:5). We need wisdom in our lives. "Get wisdom, get understanding: forget it not; neither decline from the words of my mouth. Forsake her not, and she shall preserve thee: love her, and she shall keep thee. Wisdom is the principal thing; therefore get wisdom" (4:5–7).

THE BLACK PRESENCE IN PROVERBS

Section three (22:17–24:34) contains proverbs, which are very similar to proverbs contained in the African work, *The Instruction of Amen-em-Ope.* Although the relationship is debated (who copied whom), the similarities are striking and show the interrelatedness of the cultures and the respect each had for the other. The similarity of these proverbs is discussed in *The Bible Knowledge Commentary* (Wheaton, IL: Scripture Press, 1985, pp. 904–905, 954–960).

Life Lessons

PROVERBS 1

Proverbs 1:1–7 sets forth the purpose of the book which, among other objectives, is to impart wisdom, justice, judgment, and equity. These attributes should be the objectives of every person, especially those who claim identification with God. The author declares that in pursuit of these character traits the starting place is the "fear of the LORD" (v. 7). Since the Lord is wise, just, and impartial, our seeking to emulate these qualities will cause us to become "followers of God, as dear children" (Eph. 5:1).

Original One, help my striving to be more like You.

PROVERBS 3

Proverbs 3:5–6 has been referred to many times because it contains principles for discovering the will of God. Someone observed that 90 percent of ascertaining the will of God is having the desire to obey it once we know it. Someone else observed that these verses express action on the part of two parties: God and us. God's part is to direct our paths. Our part is to trust and not lean on our own understanding (v. 5). As long as we are doing our part we need not become stressed out wondering what God will do. God is a promise keeper!

Promise Keeper, deepen my will to follow where You lead.

PROVERBS 18

Proverbs 18:16 makes reference to the person who knows, develops, and operates in her or his spiritual gifts: "A man's gift maketh room for him, and bringeth him before great men." Neither people nor situations can block what God has in store for us if we are faithful in doing what God has given us to do. Spiritual gifts come from God alone. When we operate

within our area of giftedness, God opens the doors and takes us to places and people we could never imagine! The key is knowing your gift.

Gift Giver, stir within me the ability to walk in the area You have outlined through my spiritual gift.

PROVERBS 18

Proverbs 18:21 informs us that "death and life are in the power of the tongue." We get what we say! We create our worlds with our words. Since we are made in the *Imago Dei* (the divine image of God) who spoke the world into existence, we have the same creative powers. It is in our best interest to watch our words!

Wisdom of the Ages, guard my tongue and keep my life.

PROVERBS 22

Proverbs 22:1 indicates that a good name is preferable to great riches, and loving favor is preferred to silver and gold. One's character (what a person is when no one is looking) and reputation are of greater value than material treasures. That is because God is the ultimate Judge of our destiny and will look beyond our outward trappings to examine our hearts. Money has little value, especially when the owner has such low character as to be untrustworthy and uncaring.

Examiner of Hearts, grant me favor and a good name which honors You.

PROVERBS 22

Proverbs 22:6 exhorts parents to "train up a child in the way he should go: and when he is old, he will not depart from it." This proverb expresses results which are generally true, attested to by the many upright children who have been nurtured by godly parents. Experience demonstrates, however, that despite godly parents' efforts at "training . . . in the way they should go," a child may reject that training and go astray. In such cases, the Bible is not proved unreliable. The nature of proverbs is that they frequently express *general* truths—not absolute reality.

Ultimate Parent, I'm so glad that mothers and fathers I did not even know prayed for me to return to Your divine path.

PROVERBS 29

Proverbs 29:15 refutes the teachings of Dr. Spock! "The rod and reproof give wisdom: but a child left to himself bringeth his mother to shame." Here discipline is encouraged. Discipline is not abuse; it is love in action for the correction of wrong behavior. Because God loves us, we too are disciplined. Modern society has tried to steer us away from this course of action. All we have to do is look around us to see where this folly has brought us!

Strong Discipliner, both Your rod and Your staff comfort me.

PROVERBS 31

In Proverbs 31:10–31, a strong mother speaks to her son and describes the "virtuous" king and his selection of a "virtuous" woman. She is characterized by hard work, planning, and godly living—all for the benefit of her husband, children, and community. Her godly character is high-

lighted as the secret of her success (v. 30). The man who marries her knows that he has an invaluable prize!

Eternal God, help me to be the woman You would have me to be.

Focus on Ecclesiastes

"It's a man's world," sang James Brown. And in it, God is distant, untouchable, unknowable, and very much uninvolved—that is, if we listen to the author of Ecclesiastes! The author of Ecclesiastes examines life "under the sun" (Eccles. 1:3, 9, 14; 2:11, 17). According to that view, death seems to be "man's ultimate end"—and in light of death, all else is vanity and futility. A total of seven times we hear this writer exhort us to enjoy life because death is the inevitable end of us all. This, alone, is an unorthodox understanding of life and God. At the end of his book, the author comes to his conclusion and exhorts us to remember our Creator and fear Him, for He will judge everything we do (12:1, 13–14).

This book is attributed to King Solomon who has the wisdom, wealth, position, and strength to "do life his way." In this book, Solomon leads us to discover that all he received in life was not enough to satisfy his inner hunger. In this contemporary period, when women are struggling to come into their own and to be as "free" as men, this book offers us the wisdom that says achievements and accomplishments are not the ultimate rewards!

On a search to discover the "meaning" of life, this writer speaks of his tests of pleasure, status, and intellectual pursuits (2:1–11). None of these is found sufficient to give meaning to life. No matter how many slaves, concubines, singers, pleasure gardens, and fountains he acquired, he found no meaning in his possessions. His search for wisdom ended similarly, leading him to a hatred of his life (v. 17). "Significantly, the author never speaks of entertaining a meaningful relationship and so lives in a world where he is the only true subject. Nature, women, and other social inferiors remain objects for his use, so naturally he suffers the boredom of the elite who exist in a world populated only by themselves" (*WBC*, 154–155; see 2:18–19). But at the end of his work, the author teaches us the difficult lessons of his life. "Fear God, and keep his commandments: for this is the whole duty of man. For God shall bring every work into judgment, with every secret thing, whether it be good, or whether it be evil" (12:13–14).

For women, this book raises many questions. It allows us to envision with courage what a "different" world might look like where justice reigns and wisdom is supreme.

As we women wrestle with the "ladder of success," we might want to journal our climb. For if we truly take the wisdom of Solomon to heart, we will slow down, relax, and let God move us upward. "He hath made every thing beautiful in his time" (3:11).

THE BLACK PRESENCE IN ECCLESIASTES

Solomon's lineage can be traced back through David to Boaz. According to Matthew 1:5, the ancestor of Boaz was Rahab, who was a Canaanite and a descendant of Ham.

Life Lessons

ECCLESIASTES 1–2

The author describes his search for meaning in human affairs and concludes that all is "vanity and vexation of spirit" (2:11). He declares the monotony of nature and the impossibility of anything new: "The thing that hath been, it is that which shall be; and that which is done is that which shall be done: and there is no new thing under the sun" (1:9). He then admits to discovering what many people do not have, that "things" (status, wealth, possessions, and so on) cannot satisfy the deepest longings of the human heart. Though expressed differently, the African theologian, Augustine, came to the same conclusion: "Our souls are restless until we find our rest in God." Despite these knowledgeable observations, we continue the insatiable search for meaning in things. There is no question that physical needs are important; the error is in the imbalance of allowing materialism to outstrip the spiritual.

Satisfying Portion, help me to keep the proper balance between the material and the spiritual. Help me to know that it is my relationship with You that enables me to keep all things in proper perspective.

ECCLESIASTES 3

In chapter 3, the author expresses the belief that there is a time for everything and that these times are ordered by God who "hath made every thing beautiful in his time" (v. 11). The study in contrast is made simple by valuing the organization of our time. For there is time for everything and there are seasons for every purpose. Knowing how to discern the "time" and the "season" requires the wisdom of God. There is a "season" for nurturing others. There also is a time for nurturing oneself.

Unchanging God, teach me how to wisely manage my gift of time and seasons.

ECCLESIASTES 5

Ecclesiastes 5:18 declares that "it is good . . . to enjoy the good of all his labour that he taketh under the sun all the days of his life, which God giveth him." Making good choices is crucial to living a well-ordered and God-approved life. Therefore, it is essential that we gain a purpose for our lives. Living to our fullest potential is a requirement for a satisfying life. Just working to make money to survive does not bring satisfaction. To live fully requires that we discover our God-given purpose so that we can do what we love and allow the monetary benefits to follow!

Satisfier of the Longing Heart, let the very center of my being explode with my divine purpose breathed into me at my "beginning."

ECCLESIASTES 9–12

Ecclesiastes 12:13 gives the grand conclusion: "Fear God!" Life boils down to our personal relationship with the Creator of heaven and earth. What we amass in life will only grant temporary satisfaction. Regardless of how many "things" we acquire, how many people we supervise, how many mansions we build or how many obstacles we jump over in this life, there is only one chief requirement for eternal life and that is to keep the reverence of God as our first priority. We are to enjoy life such as it is, but focus on eternity. Since we cannot predict the future (9:1; 11:5–6) and only in this life can work be done, we are advised, "Whatsoever thy hand findeth to do, do it with thy might" (9:10). Wise people recognize the brevity of life (Ps. 90:10–12) and the critical nature of it. They establish worthwhile and God-approved goals and order their lives accordingly.

Heart's Desire, keep my eyes focused on You!

FOCUS ON SONG OF SOLOMON

Love is timeless. Love cuts across culture, social customs, and even religious tradition. Love is a free agent. No other book in the Christian canon is as straightforward about a woman's sexual feelings, thoughts, and desires.

The chief protagonist is a woman. And, she is a woman who declares frankly that she is black. "I am black, but comely, O ye daughters of Jerusalem, as the tents of Kedar, as the curtains of Solomon. Look not upon me, because I am black, because the sun hath looked upon me. My mother's children were angry with me; they made me the keeper of the vineyards; but mine own vineyard have I not kept" (Song 1:5–6). This book is a call for women of the dark earth to express their desires. In a sense, this is a mandate for sisters of the darker expression to take time to tend to themselves, to work their own garden. For in spite of her hue that is darker than that of the daughters of Jerusalem, she declares with boldness "My beloved is mine, and I am his" (2:16).

Renita Weems, Old Testament professor, says, this woman "feels good about herself and basks in her beloved's desire for her. In fact, her love and praise for her beloved (as well as his for her) are so forward, so uncompromising, so urgent, that it almost sounds argumentative" (*WBC*, 158).

Scholars continue to wrestle with what this book means to the church. Is it an allegory of the love of God for Israel? Is it the love of Christ for His bride, the church? There are many opinions and no positive conclusions. What we do know is that a black woman takes a significant portion of Scripture to express absolute love for her beloved. And, we find that her beloved responds in like manner.

THE BLACK PRESENCE IN THE SONG OF SOLOMON

1. Solomon's ancestry includes Rahab, the Canaanite son of Ham (see Matt. 1:5).

2. Some scholars believe the Shulamite woman refers to the Egyptian wife whom Solomon married (1 Kin. 3:1). Others believe she was from Lebanon (based on 4:8) where blacks also lived. She describes herself as "black" and "comely" (1:5) according to the Septuagint, (not "black, but comely" as the King James Version reads). Her blackness is compared to the "tents of Kedar" which were made of black goat's hair.

Life Lessons

SONG OF SOLOMON 1

The attraction between a male and female is natural and stated openly by a woman to her beloved (Song 1:1–4). There is a longing for sexual fulfillment. And, there is the warning that such attraction should not result in intimacy, until marriage has been consummated. In recent years, this clearly stated command by God that sexual activity should only occur within the bounds of marriage (Ex. 20:14) has been violated. The consequences have been disastrous: guilt, unwanted children, child abuse, and abortion, with its subsequent depression and guilt.

SONG OF SOLOMON 2

"I am sick with love" (2:5) reflects a deepening of the woman's affection for her lover. This growth of love points to the courtship that takes place between the two. Courtship should be a time when two lovers investigate their suitability for each other. Are they compatible for each other (which is not the same as sexual experimentation, which is clearly forbidden by the Bible)? Although accepted by contemporary social mores, exploited by movie and television themes, and virtually unheard of within the church, sex outside of marriage is expressly forbidden in Scripture (see Ex. 20:14). The scare of the sexually transmitted AIDS epidemic has caused media to take up the cry: "When you sleep with one, you sleep with all with whom that person has previously slept." It has been scientifically and medically documented, that there is no such thing as "safe sex." Any sex outside of marriage is sin.

God, giver of sexuality and self-control, keep me within your boundaries.

SONG OF SOLOMON 3–4

The wedding scene details how the lover, most likely Solomon, prepared for the wedding with an expensive chariot (3:9) in which to meet his bride (4:9). He describes her beauty and his deep love for her in anticipation of the ceremony (4:1–17). Changes in culture may result in different

formats for weddings, but the basic principle of lovers covenanting in the presence of witnesses to be loyal to each other need not change. For believers in Jesus Christ, that commitment ought to also be facilitated by a minister of the gospel. Additionally, our society requires the couple to obtain a marriage license in order to regulate the state's interest in married couples. The growing practice of persons simply living together without adhering to these fundamental principles violates biblical teaching.

O God, keep me like "a garden inclosed" until I covenant with a man in marriage (4:12).

SONG OF SOLOMON 5–6

The lovers are always making quick departures and hasty escapes. They continually want to get alone to deepen their relationship with each other. Weems suggests that this couple may have been in an interracial, interethnic marriage which would not have been sanctioned by the "town" (*WBC)*. Hence, the constant appeals to the "daughters of Jerusalem" as she seeks her beloved. As a married couple now (5:2–6:9), the wife describes the distance that has developed between herself and her husband either emotionally or literally (5:2–7). She senses the strained relationship and takes steps to strengthen it. In return, the husband reaffirms his love for his wife (6:3–9). Just as this relationship needed to be strengthened, so all marriage relationships need to be guarded. When distance develops between couples, steps need to be taken to renew it.

Dear God, strengthen my relationship with my husband. "I am my beloved's and my beloved is mine" (6:3).

SONG OF SOLOMON 6–8

The husband and wife celebrate each other's desirable traits (6:10–8:4). He celebrates her charm (7:1–9); she expresses her longing for him (8:1–4) as they become more intimate. Marriage permits ultimate intimacy between lovers. Such closeness points to and illustrates the abiding relationship believers can have with God through Jesus Christ. "I am my beloved's, and his desire is towards me" (7:10). This woman has come into her own. She has decided, "my vineyard, which is mine, is before me" to give (8:12). "The Song of Songs advocates balance in female and male relationships, urging mutuality, not domination; interdependence, not enmity" (*WBC*, 160).

Garden Giver, help me to plant, nurture, weed, grow, and harvest in my own yard.

FOCUS ON ISAIAH

Isaiah prophesied during a time of great political unrest, not only within Palestine, but in the surrounding nations as well. When Isaiah began his prophetic ministry about 742 B.C., the Assyrians were becoming the dominant power on the international scene. Eventually the Assyrians

conquered the northern kingdom of Israel in 722 B.C. and carried away thousands of the inhabitants to northern Mesopotamia.

When Isaiah saw what had happened to the northern kingdom, he urged the southern kingdom of Judah to repent of their sinful ways or experience the same fate.

Egypt, too, began to rise in power again after a period of decline. Sandwiched between two great superpowers, the kings of Judah vacillated in loyalty between Egypt and the eastern nations, depending on which they thought provided the best alliance. Isaiah counseled them to avoid relying on either, but to place their trust in Yahweh, their God.

Kings Jotham and Ahaz rejected the counsel of the prophet and aligned themselves with Assyria. Ahaz's son, Hezekiah, refused the alliance with this foreign nation. God rescued him from their hands. Following the death of Hezekiah, his son Manasseh became king of Judah. He is described as the worst the nation ever had, introducing Baal worship and the sacrifice of children. According to tradition, King Manasseh ordered Isaiah to be sawed in two.

Isaiah records God's disappointment with Israel's breaking of the covenant made with Him at Sinai and the punitive consequences that followed. In the midst of these pronouncements of judgment, the prophet calls on his people to repent in order to escape punishment (chaps. 1–5). After recording his vision of the throne of God (chap. 6), Isaiah writes about God's plan to judge not only Israel but the surrounding nations as well. Chapters 1–39 deal primarily with judgment, while chapters 40–66 focus on future restoration and blessings. These future blessings are said to not only benefit Israel but also the entire earth.

THE BLACK PRESENCE IN ISAIAH

Arabia: Mentioned in Isaiah 21:13. Located in northeast Africa, east of the Nile River, this area was occupied by the descendants of Shem and Ham. According to 2 Chronicles 21:16, the area is "near" Ethiopia. The peoples of this area are known to have been swarthy and black.

Assyria: Mentioned in Isaiah 7:17. In the Table of Nations (Gen. 10) Assyria (Asshur) is identified as a descendant of Shem. The people of this Mesopotamian area were Semitic, Hamitic, and Cushite—all of whom were black (see Introduction to Genesis).

Egypt: Mentioned in chapters 18–20. According to Genesis 10:6, Egyptians were the descendants of Ham, whose name means "black" or "burnt face." The history of Egypt can be traced back at least 10,000 years B.C. Prior to the arrival of Alexander the Great in 332 B.C., the people of that area called themselves *Kemet,* which means "black." Herodotus, a noted Greek historian who visited Egypt in the centuries prior to the birth of Christ, described the Egyptians as "black with wooly hair."

Ethiopia: Mentioned in chapters 18, 20, 37, 43, and 45. *Ethiopia* is the Greek word for *Cush* and describes the descendants of one of the sons of Ham. Cush means "black" and describes people who settled in Egypt and the Mesopotamian area. Some European schol-

ars, however, have sought to limit Ethiopians to the area just south of Egypt.

Midian: Mentioned in chapters 9–10 and 60. Midianites were the descendants of Abraham and Keturah (Gen. 25:2). With the knowledge that Moses' wife was from Midian, and therefore a Cushite, it can be deduced that Midianites were black.

Philistines: Mentioned in chapters 2, 9, and 11. Philistines were the descendants of Ham through Egypt. They migrated to Cyprus and from there to the southern coast of Palestine (see Genesis 10:14).

Life Lessons

ISAIAH 1–6

Isaiah 1:1–6:13 sets the stage for the work of the prophet. We are introduced to him and immediately hear the accusations of God against Israel. "Hear, O heavens, and give ear, O earth: for the LORD hath spoken, I have nourished and brought up children, and they have rebelled against me. The ox knoweth his owner, and the ass his master's crib: but Israel doth not know, my people doth not consider" (1:1–4). "How is the faithful city become an harlot! it was full of judgment; righteousness lodged in it; but now murderers" (v. 21). The great God of love, mercy, and justice has a severe complaint against these "children" who have walked away from the covenant.

It is easy to see how the imagery of a "woman gone bad" moves from a woman in particular to all of Israel as a whole. This is a forerunner of the common description of the church as "woman" and "bride of Christ." As the "spouse of the church," God is faithful to the covenant, providing and protecting as required by the vows of a covenantal relationship. However, the "wife," who is dependent, has "walked away," looking for another "lover." Judgment is pronounced upon Jerusalem and Judah.

We find several references to the roles of women in the rituals of the community. The roles of music making and lamenting are described in "The Song of the Vineyard" (chap. 5), and in the prophecy of 3:26, "Her gates shall lament and mourn; and she being desolate shall sit upon the ground." Even today, the role of "official" mourner belongs to the Jewish woman. Lamentations continue to be expressed through wailing and sitting on the ground, and an inability to dance or be lighthearted.

Tear Catcher, I am fulfilling my lamenting mission for Your people.

ISAIAH 7–9

Isaiah is clear about the time of his call to ministry: "In the year that King Uzziah died I saw also the Lord . . . also I heard the voice of the Lord saying, 'Whom shall I send, and who will go for us? Then I said, Here am I; send me' " (6:1, 8). One of his first assignments is to warn King Ahaz, as powerful enemies threaten: "If ye will not believe, surely ye shall not be established" (7: 9). Ahaz is encouraged to keep the faith, for the coming of Immanuel is foretold (v. 14).

Every enemy is told to "associate yourselves, O ye people, and ye shall be broken in pieces; . . . Take counsel together, and it shall come to nought; speak the word, and it shall not stand: for God is with us" (8:9–10). Yet Israel refuses to repent and return to God. Assyria will be raised up to get their attention. "And they shall look unto the earth; and behold trouble and darkness, dimness of anguish; and they shall be driven to darkness. Nevertheless the dimness shall not be such . . . For unto us a child is born, unto us a son is given: and the government shall be upon his shoulder: and his name shall be called Wonderful, Counselor, The mighty God, The everlasting Father, The Prince of Peace. Of the increase of his government and peace there shall be no end" (8:22–9:1, 6–7).

Wonderful Counselor, Mighty and Everlasting God, Prince of Peace, worthy is Your name!

ISAIAH 12–39

Jesus is called "a rod out of the stem of Jesse . . . a root of Jesse, which shall stand for an ensign of the people; to it shall the Gentiles seek: and his rest shall be glorious" (11:1, 10). Songs of praise for God's salvation are proclaimed in chapter 12. Then there is a series of woes against Israel's enemies intermingled with songs of praise for God's mercy throughout chapters 12–35.

When King Hezekiah reminds God of his walking in righteousness, deliverance is promised: "I have heard thy prayer, I have seen thy tears: behold, I will add unto thy days fifteen years. And I will deliver thee and this city out of the hand of the king of Assyria: and I will defend this city" (38:5–6). Thank God for a king who did "that which was right in the sight of the Lord" (2 Chron. 29:2) and stood as an intercessor for his people!

Watching Savior, let my life be a witness of Your deliverance.

ISAIAH 40

Chapter 40 has a change of tenor. "Comfort ye, comfort ye my people, saith your God. Speak ye comfortably to Jerusalem, and cry unto her, that her warfare is accomplished, that her iniquity is pardoned: for she hath received of the Lord's hand double for all her sins. The voice of him that crieth in the wilderness, Prepare ye the way of the Lord, make straight in the desert a highway for our God. Every valley shall be exalted, and every mountain and hill shall be made low: and the crooked shall be made straight, and the rough places plain: And the glory of the Lord shall be revealed, and all flesh shall see it together: for the mouth of the Lord hath spoken it" (vv. 1–6).

Helper of Israel, thank You for goodness and mercy at work on our behalf.

FOCUS ON JEREMIAH

The prophet Jeremiah wrote this book to warn Judah of impending judgment and to announce judgment upon the surrounding nations.

Jeremiah prophesied during the time when the new Babylonian empire was emerging. Assyria, which had been the dominant power, was defeated by Carchemish in 612 B.C. Egypt, observing the collapse of Assyria and fearful of a revived Babylonian Empire, entered the conflict on Assyria's side. Egypt and Babylon fought each other for a while, but eventually in 605 B.C. Babylon won. Nebuchadnezzar, the powerful general of Babylon, then chased the Egyptians to their border. On his way back home, he consolidated the vassal relationship with Judah and took some of the key people with him back to Babylon, including Daniel.

The prophet Jeremiah's call is described in Jeremiah 1. Jeremiah then details the judgment that awaits Judah (chaps. 2–45). In the midst of these prophecies a glimmer of hope is offered that Judah and Israel will one day be restored (chaps. 30–33). The prophet then turns to the surrounding nations to show that they will not escape judgment (chaps. 46–51). Chapter 52 concludes the book with a description of the fall of Jerusalem.

THE BLACK PRESENCE IN JEREMIAH

Babylon, Babylonians: Mentioned in chapters 20–52. The histories of Babylon and Assyria are intertwined with Assyria being located on the Tigris River and Babylon on the Euphrates River. Nimrod, son of Cush, whose name means "black," built both cities. Indications are that as early as 3000–2500 B.C., a group of black people known as Sumerians settled the area. According to Henry Rawlinson, the father of Assyriology, these Sumerians migrated there from Africa. In 747 B.C., Babylon achieved independence. However, in 699 B.C., Babylon became subject to Assyria and remained so until 625 when Nabopolassar asserted his independence from Assyria. His son Nebuchadnezzar became king in 605 B.C., and immediately began his conquest of the surrounding nations.

Chaldeans: Mentioned in chapters 21–52. *Chaldean* is one of the names given to the people who had Babylon as their capital. They lived in Ur, the area south of Babylon (Shinar) where Abraham lived prior to his departure to Haran and Canaan. Their language was very similar to Galla (Oromo), the scientific and religious Cushite language of Africa. They were likely a part of the migration that took place from Africa into the Mesopotamian area between 5000 and 2500 B.C.

Ethiopia: Mentioned in chapter 13, *Ethiopia* is the Greek word for Cush and describes the descendants of one of the sons of Ham. Ethiopians settled in Egypt and the Mesopotamian area, although some European scholars have sought to limit them to the area just

south of Egypt. Ebed-melech the Ethiopian performed an outstanding service when he rescued Jeremiah from a pit where the princes of Judah (chap. 38) had placed him. God promised him deliverance when the Babylonians invaded the land (39:16–18).

Kedar: Mentioned in 2:10. They are the descendants of Abraham and Hagar (Gen. 25:13).

Noph: Mentioned in 2:16.

Tahapanes: Mentioned in 2:16.

Life Lessons

JEREMIAH 1

In chapter one, Jeremiah begins with the introduction of his call and his resistance. God declares, "Before I formed thee in the belly I knew thee; and before thou camest forth out of the womb I sanctified thee, and I ordained thee a prophet unto the nations" (v. 5).

Then God gives this charge: "See, I have this day set thee over the nations and over the kingdoms, to root out, and to pull down, and to destroy, and to throw down, to build, and to plant" (v. 10). "Thou therefore gird up thy loins, and arise, and speak unto them all that I command thee: be not dismayed at their faces, lest I confound thee before them . . . [T]hey shall fight against thee; but they shall not prevail against thee; for I am with thee" (vv. 17–19).

Immanuel, You were with me in my forming and calling. Speak Your instructions to me again.

JEREMIAH 30–52

The remaining chapters up to chapter 45 concern themselves with failed leadership as prophets deceive the people with words of peace. A lying priest imprisons Jeremiah (20:1–6). Suffering and weeping occur as "Rachel [weeps] for her children" (31:15). We get a glimpse of hope threading its way through chapters 30–33. Healing and new life are promised and Jeremiah urges the people to believe that God will remove the yoke of bondage from their necks (30:8–9). Women will dance and laughter will be heard (31:13–14). Beginning with chapter 46, a message of destruction is proclaimed to the nations—a "day of the Lord's vengeance" for Israel's foes. The fall of Jerusalem is set as the last chapter—chapter 52–proclaims, "Thus Judah was carried away captive out of his own land" (v. 27).

Righteous Judge of Every Nation, help me remain true to You!

Focus on
LAMENTATIONS

Who knows better how to sit down and have a good cry than women? Who is better qualified to lift up her voice in lament over the loss of those she has borne in her womb and nurtured at her breast? Who has a better reason to cry than the wives, mothers, and daughters who are forced to survive, "by any means necessary?" when the male figures are carried off into exile or slain upon the bloody battlefields of war?

The sorrow of a broken heart is heard in the Book of Lamentations. In this "book of grief," we experience the anguish of "the daughter of Zion" (1:6). We watch and hear the wailing, mournful sounds after the walls have fallen and Nebuchadnezzar, king of Babylon, has taken the exiles into captivity.

Grief comes in various forms. It cannot accurately be described or articulated. It is a journey through a deep and lonesome valley, which changes you in many ways. Sometimes you can weep. Sometimes you can wail. Sometimes you can just moan. Sometimes you can only sit. Sometimes the sobs erupt like bombs. Sometimes the pain just grips. Sometimes you can see a particular object that makes the storm of sorrow suddenly descend upon you again. Sometimes you can sit in the dark and rock. Sometimes you cry as you work and walk. There is no one tried and true formula for grieving! Grief is heartbreaking. Grief can destroy. Grief also can heal.

We like to withdraw from others during our periods of grief. Some folks think we're crazy. Others feel that our tears and inability to stop crying indicate that we are in the process of losing our mind. However, this book teaches us that it's all right to grieve for however long the process requires.

> Laments are liturgical prayers or psalms in which the speakers complain to God about their circumstances and beg for release. Typical elements of the lament form appear in each of the five poems of Lamentations: a series of complaints, a statement of guilt, a request for God's favor, and a petition against enemies. Significantly absent from all five laments are the statements of praise . . . Nonetheless, the mere use of a lament is an act of fidelity, because the purpose of the lament is to address God in the midst of inexplicable suffering. (*WBC*, 178)

The grief contained within this body of laments is the collective grief of a nation. However, since it was the "official" role of women to be family mourners, we discover ourselves within these words of sorrow.

Jeremiah wrote Lamentations to record his grief over the devastation of Judah. After chasing the Egyptians into their land in 605 B.C., Nebuchadnezzar stopped in Judah to establish his control over that land. In 597 B.C., the Babylonian general returned to Jerusalem, removed Jehoiachin from the throne and placed Zedekiah in charge as a puppet king. Zedekiah rebelled in 596 B.C. and Nebuchadnezzar returned to completely wipe out the city. This time he put out Zedekiah's eyes and carried him off to Babylon

along with other people of Judah. This destruction of Jerusalem, which Jeremiah had warned his people would come and pleaded so passionately that they repent and avoid, is what the prophet now laments.

Lamentations 1 describes the condition of the devastated city. Chapter two explains why God determined to bring judgment on the city. Chapter three describes the prophet's grief over the condition of the city. Chapter four contrasts the former glory of the city with its present devastation. The remnant prays for restoration, as recorded in the last chapter.

THE BLACK PRESENCE IN LAMENTATIONS

Assyria is mentioned in Lamentations 5:6. According to Genesis 10, Nimrod, a son of Cush, built Asshur. Assyria retained a long, sometimes interrupted empire. Nineveh, the capital, was defeated during the battle of 612 B.C., when Babylon (also built by Nimrod) and Persia joined forces to defeat it. In 605 B.C., Babylon defeated Egypt, giving Babylon undisputed domination of the Fertile Crescent, a territory extending from Egypt to the Persian Gulf.

Life Lessons

LAMENTATIONS 2

Chapter two finds the voice of the daughter of Zion lifted in outrage as she shouts in outrage at God for killing the people of the city, lamenting, "The Lord hath swallowed up all the habitations of Jacob, and hath not pitied" (v. 1). How like the hearts of many inner city mothers who have lost children to what is termed "urban violence" does "she" sound! The daughter of Zion's prayer may help contemporary women in their prayer. "Her" voice evokes the pain of women who have lost their children, who know sexual abuse, or who are victims of war and famine. To pray with the daughter of Zion is to join with the struggles of women around the globe. It is to reject victimhood by embracing the anger that can provide energy to transform relationships. It is to pour out "thine heart like water before the face of the Lord" (v. 19).

God of My Heart, You know the pain of my soul, for You watched Your own child die.

LAMENTATIONS 3

Chapter three is spoken in the voice of a man. "I am the man that hath seen affliction" (v. 1). It is thought to be the wounded heart and spirit of Jeremiah. For 19 verses, he laments. Then there is a theological shift as he reflects on God's goodness in the past. "It is of the LORD's mercies that we are not consumed, because his compassions fail not. They are new every morning: great is thy faithfulness" (vv. 22–23). Hope is born!

Hope of the World, thank You for the tiny sparks of radiance that emerges in spite of the situations in which we find ourselves.

LAMENTATIONS 4

Chapter four contrasts the former Jerusalem to its present misery.

The plight of children seems to be a current concern: "The tongue of the sucking child cleaveth to the roof of his mouth for thirst: the young children ask bread, and no man breaketh it unto them. They that did feed delicately are desolate in the streets: they that were brought up in scarlet embrace dunghills" (vv. 4–5). Jeremiah leaves us with a vivid description of the fate of a people who have wandered far from their relationship with God. It was the sin of the people that had brought about their own destruction.

Bread of Heaven, feed me till I want no more.

LAMENTATIONS 5

Chapter five lifts up Jeremiah's prayer to God for mercy. The people join in a prayer for restoration and favor from God. "Remember, O LORD, what is come upon us: consider, and behold our reproach" (v. 1). The verses go on to describe the devastation (vv. 2–11). "By praying with her, women may be able to give voice to their pain and despair, and, by voicing it, by expressing their anger, they may be able to move beyond circumstances of impasse" (*WBC*, 181). May women be able to announce with the daughter of Zion "Turn thou us unto thee, O Lord, and we shall be turned; renew our days as of old" (5:21).

O Restorer, renew me and restore me, so that I may serve You.

Women in PROVERBS AND SONG OF SOLOMON

WISDOM PERSONIFIED: THE CRY OF WISDOM

Wisdom crieth without; she uttereth her voice in the streets (Prov. 1:20).

Woe is me! for I am undone; because I am a man of unclean lips, and I dwell in the midst of a people of unclean lips (Prov. 1:21).

Whatever else the text may be saying, it still reveals that there has been, and therefore there still can be, an image of femininity that includes sagacity. Indeed, we have long held an image of motherhood which did include great wisdom, although this image is confined to the narrow scope of home and childrearing. Ironically, that task of motherhood requires more intelligence than any other role, for there is no harder or more demanding task in the kingdom of God than that of rearing children. The world has long depended on this wisdom. The text would have us rebuild a symbol of wisdom which has a strong feminine alignment alongside whatever masculine connotations we give it. It would call us to establish a climate of the expectation that women will bring to the solution of the world's problems a precious perspective not available from any other source. It would call us to provide a fresh stimulus of challenge and a freeing of latent powers, because wisdom can be and is personified in the women of the world.

Wisdom is not portrayed in classical garments. She is not the cold, objective, dispassionate scholar. She cries her message all over town. She has a strange conviction that she cannot repress, and her "scholarship" is so centered on human concerns that she exceeds the bounds of dignity. She will hardly be caught out of touch with human realities and existential concerns, because she is in dialogue with people at the market, the courts, the highways, and the lofty walls of mass communication. Perhaps because she is a mother as well as a sage, she cannot view that which affects mothers' children with the detachment of a professor. She demands that her insights be implemented, and she is the personification of passionate practicality, as opposed to the almost helpless female. Her feelings are deeply involved in the use of her wisdom.

After the femininity of wisdom and the passionate character of her address of the issues, there is the clear fact that her understandings are constantly put to work in the marketplaces of the world. She cannot be content with smugness or arrogance in the mere fact that she *knows*. Her deep emotional involvement will not be satisfied with a mere love of truth. She demands application. She insists on being a doer of truth, rather than a hearer only. The fact that she must cry her message forth seems to suggest that she has not the power to apply her principles arbitrarily. But she does not hide behind her lack of dictatorial authority. She girds her loins and risks her image, choosing rather to have tried and lost than never to have tried at all. Wisdom in her early personification has not been permitted the luxury of truth for truth's sake. She has been in the cultural tradition of Africans and others who have quietly gone about the business of avoiding art for art's sake or music for music's sake, and persistently made all to be for the sake of all mankind. Wisdom is no distant dilettante—no pretty patron. She rolls up her sleeves and goes to work. She goes out into the marketplace.

The great question may well be, "Where in the world is there any such wisdom as the pretty picture that has been painted here?" I thank God that the answer is easy. The Bible is full of portrayals of this too often unrecognized wisdom in the feminine personification. Whether it be the stateswoman Abigail, or the businesswoman Lydia, or the humanitarian Dorcas, or the women of faith who went to the tomb to do something when everybody else was in shock and "out of it," the woman-wisdom of the Hebrew-Christian tradition has not been hidden. Nor could it be, even by a culture dominated by men.

Wisdom must never cease her cry, nor must the world ever cease to expect her to cry out and save us, lest we perish. Wisdom cries aloud in the street; in the markets she raises her voice; on top of the walls she cries out; at the entrance of the city gates she speaks.

Read Proverbs 1:20.

—E. Mitchell

THE ADULTERESS OF PROVERBS: THE PATH TO DEATH

Proverbs gives warning about the involvement with the adulteress or a "strange woman" (5:3) throughout chapters 5–9. She is an immoral woman and an unfaithful wife. She heads down a crooked path that leads to death. Her seductive speech is deceptive and cunning, resulting in an

unhealthy heart-crushing experience.

Her marriage vows are openly broken and disregarded. She has forgotten the covenant words of God. She uses words to describe the sex act to lure the man to her bed (7:16–18). Her trap is set during the night, beginning with a bold approach dressed like a harlot (vv. 10–13), inviting him over to her house assuring him of their privacy (vv. 19–20), and while flattering him, she then traps him (vv. 21–23).

She wants to possess the soul of her victim (6:26) and take his strength. She causes a wound and brings dishonor to his life (v. 33). His life is stricken in many ways: his body may become diseased, being publicly disgraced (5:11–14), and his soul destroyed (6:32).

"For the ways of man are before the eyes of the LORD" (5:21). Proverbs gives several ways a man can avoid the adulteress: pay attention to wisdom (v. 1); don't go near her door (v. 8); keep the law of God in his heart (7:3), and be ravished always with the sexual love of his wife (5:18–20).

The African-American woman is seen, at times, as the spiritual strength of the family. When the adulteress taints her life, it is devastating to her marriage and spirit. It poisons the husband-wife relationship, breaks trust, and eats away at the wife's ability to love. She can lose the ability to fulfill the marriage commitment, be afraid to trust, and become unwilling to be open with her spouse. Sadly to say, adultery can lead to divorce (Matt. 5:31–32), which divides her family and makes trusting another man difficult.

For the woman who is an adulteress, Jesus can forgive her sins (John 8:1–11) and create a clean heart within her (Ps. 51:10). She can become a woman devoted to Jesus and receiving eternal life, instead of being a woman who leads another life to death.

Read Proverbs 7–9.

Read the insight essays on Adultery and Temptation.

—G. London

A VIRTUOUS WOMAN IN PROVERBS: A STRONG WOMEN, DEPENDENT ON GOD

The virtuous woman in Proverbs 31 selects wool and flax, works with willing hands, brings her husband food, gets up while it is still dark, buys fields, plants vineyards, and so on. Virtuous means "strength," and this Proverb extols the dignity of women and emphasizes the importance of motherhood and home. A virtuous woman has strength and honor, and is able to bear up under many crosses and disappointments.

How many of us have held up under corporate America's glass ceilings, sexism, racism, unruly children, divorce, and single parenthood? A virtuous woman has words that are wise and kind. She knows how to temper her words and hold her peace if need be. She takes care of her household, meaning she can make a meal out of nothing, will stretch a week's worth of food into four weeks' worth; she can cook and clean with a baby on her hip while helping another child with homework. All of us can find ourselves in this virtuous woman. But how do we maintain our virtue? How are we able to be strong? It is through our reverence of God and our submitting to His will. We must put God above everything in our lives. We must seek Him; we must serve Him; we must witness to others about Him; we

must love Him with all our hearts, with all of our souls, and with all of our minds. Proverbs 30:30–31 says "Favour is deceitful, and beauty is vain: but a woman that feareth the LORD, she shall be praised. Give her of the fruit of her hands; and let her own works praise her in the gates." We strong women earn our reward by knowing God and seeking to please Him.

The Scriptures don't tell us *who* the woman in Proverbs 31 was—only *what* she was. A closer look at the virtuous woman can provide invaluable assistance to women today who are trying desperately to balance their lives.

Read Proverbs 31:10–31.

Read the insight essay on Influence. Read the portraits on Achsah and Zelophehad's Daughters.

—T. Booker

THE BRIDEGROOM AND HIS SHULAMITE BRIDE: SOULMATES IN LIFE

The Shulamite bride in Song of Solomon has been many things to many people. She has been classified as rich, poor, a commoner, and a princess. But she is first and foremost a woman in love. She is a woman who endured much to be with the one she loved. The bride speaks of their courtship, remembering how the groom looked and behaved towards her. She speaks of her engagement to him, of misunderstandings, and her dreams of being separated from him.

The length of their separation and her longing for him begins to trouble her sleep—not once, but twice. She longs for her best friend, her banner, her lover, and her lord. Even as she goes about her daily tasks, her mind is on the love of her life, the man who has swept her off her feet with kind words, gentle strength, and tender embraces.

When the bride and bridegroom finally reunite, it is with a joy reserved for people who have endured misunderstandings, temptations, and pain in order to be together. Alternately passionate and shy, the bride builds up her husband, loving him with the sweetness of her words and body. While she is jealous of him, she still loves him with all of her being. Her husband is both her brother and her friend—implying that they were soulmates before consummating their union.

The relationship between the Shulamite bride and her husband personifies love in its purest form—a monogamous relationship between a husband and wife who have an abiding respect and a replete and unassuming trust. This same desire is found in the spiritual relationship of knowing Jesus as Lord. We are to love Him with the same passion and all-consuming fire, the same jealousy and abiding love and respect with which we would love our spouse. With Jesus as the Bridegroom, we must come to Him with the same unabashed love that He demonstrates daily to Christians, those whom He considers His Shulamite bride.

Read Song of Solomon.

Read the insight essay on Commitment.

—M. Cotton Bohanon

Insights

RAISING CHILDREN: FINDING THE DISCIPLINARY BALANCE

Trust in the LORD with all thine heart; and lean not unto thine own understanding. In all thy ways acknowledge him, and he shall direct thy paths (Prov. 3:5–6).

Raising children is filled with challenges, victories, joys, and sorrows—learning experiences for you and hope for the children. Raising children includes introducing them to God at an early age. It includes a process of making disciples of them.

There are no perfect parents. Yet learning to listen both to God and our children will make the task a less stressful move from parent-controlled behavior to self-controlled, independent decision making. Ultimately, a God-controlled lifestyle, in which the child learns to make wise, God-honoring decisions, will be achieved.

The Bible teaches us that children are entitled to be respected for their childlike opinions. God teaches us when to use the rod and when to listen to correct unacceptable behavior. Correcting bad behavior promptly will prevent unacceptable patterns from being established. Discipline helps the child to understand that he or she not only disobeyed his/her parents, but God as well.

Listening to God and introducing children to Christ as babies, active listening, and guidance will enable children to make far better decisions throughout their lives. Consistent spiritual nurturing will ensure that your children will follow godly lives!

Read Proverbs 3:5–6; see also Exodus 20:12; Hebrews 12:10–11.

Read the insight essays on Parenting and Spiritual Discipline.

—*F. Johnson*

AGING—FOOTPRINTS ON THE SANDS OF TIME

A popular daytime soap opera introduced each episode with the image of an hourglass as a voice pronounces, "Like the sand through the hourglass, so are the days of our lives." The hourglass of life serves as a timer, an aging timepiece set in motion the moment we are born. Our "passing through," our aging, signifies movement from one realm to another.

As we age, as we "pass through the hourglass," the meaning and purpose of our lives unfold. Ecclesiastes 3:1 reminds us, "To every thing there is a season, and a time to every purpose under the heaven: A time to be born, and a time to die." Sands of time—seconds, minutes, hours, days, weeks, months, and years pass through the hourglass. Yet the passing sands do not merely count the days of our lives and settle into a meaningless heap at the bottom. They also carry footprints that mark the essence of our "passing through." Contained therein are imprints of all that we do to contribute to God's creative order, the impressions we make as we

touch people's lives and the trails we blaze for others to follow.

The footprints of other faithful pilgrims illuminate, inform, and enrich our lives, leaving a legacy of commitment to those things that are "true, whatsoever things are honest, whatsoever things are just, whatsoever things are pure" (Phil. 4:8). We are, therefore, challenged to do likewise. As we age, let us do so with grace, striving to use our gift of time to honor God and uplift others. Then one day our lives will be counted and remembered as testimonies of love and service, as we make our footprints on the sands of time.

A woman's looks, health, and her circumstances change with time. Many women attempt to cope with these changes by clinging to outward beauty, youthful behaviors, and past achievements. However, once we realize that we are made in accordance with God's plan, and that plan carries us through the change of time, we come to grips with aging. Women, as well as others who live each day for the Lord, will not only bear fruit while they are young, they will also bear fruit in their old age (Ps. 92:12–15).

Read Ecclesiastes 3.

Read insight essay on Widows.

—A. Powell

THE 3 M'S: MINISTRY, MARRIAGE, AND MOTHERHOOD—BALANCING HOME AND CAREER

Many sisters are now entering leadership roles in the ordained ministry, especially parish ministry. Some are accepting their "call" after a first or second career, when their children are grown and when their wedding anniversaries are in the double digits.

But what happens when one enters a pastorate as a single woman, one who has to date, marry, and then later bear children? This call is an increasingly new phenomenon, and I am one of those "3 M" women, who continuously has to strike a happy balance between the three (see Eccl. 3:1).

Ronald Cook came into my life when I was in my early thirties. I had never been married before but longed for a soul mate. One who is a senior pastor must be equally yoked spiritually. That means considering not how cute the brother is, but where he is in Christ. Can he be a prayer partner, a support to what God has chosen you to do? Can he be husband, a fun-loving partner in life? It is not easy to find such a man, but it is possible. Ron used Scriptures to "rap" to me. He prayed and fasted for me during some dark hours. Ron was the right, godly man. We were united in holy matrimony, and on our first anniversary, we had our first son, Samuel, whose name means gift from God. Three years later, we had our second son, Christopher.

I must tell you that my ministry, marriage, and motherhood are all thriving. There is very little "down" time, so I must stay healthy, stay focused, and be present and alone with my family whenever possible. Ron did not marry a "pastor," he married a *wife*. The children don't want a public figure; they want *Mommy*. The church also needs a leader. Can it all be done *well?* You'd better believe it! I am a blessed woman. The 3 Ms of marriage, ministry, and motherhood are working well for me.

Read Ecclesiastes 3:1; see also 1 Corinthians 4:2.

Read insight essay on Motherhood.

—S. Cook

ROMANCE: A BIBLICAL PERSPECTIVE

One would probably not think to look in the Bible for a definition of romance. But the deepest exposition of romance in its finest declaration can be found in the Song of Solomon. Solomon's devotional love poem sets the stage for a modern man and woman's ideal of courtship—an expression of love and promise. The words are so fervent and noble that centuries of Christian biblical scholars have identified the book as a divine allegory representing the love between Christ and His church.

It is not easy for the modern-day woman to embrace the noble words and sentiments of the long distant past. But African-American women, as well as women in general, are not so far removed from various servant roles. So often, even today, do these roles continue to describe the vocations of so many of us (nurse, teacher, waitress, cook, nanny, fast-food server, minister, and so on.) that it is still possible to understand the role of the *willing* servant. Our romantic relationships, however, do not always reflect our understanding.

In the Song of Solomon, the true depth of devotion possible for lovers is captured by the phrase "him [or her] whom my soul loveth" (1:7; 3:1). In other words, "the lover of my soul." This can easily be translated as "lover of my life." But there is an even deeper level of understanding possible in the translation. The Hebrew word *ahab* means, literally, "to have affection for." The Hebrew word *nephesh* means "soul, breathing, or breath." A more intriguing translation, then, for such a romantic lover could be "to have affection for the very breath of life in another person." This, then, is "true" romance. When such affection is felt during courtship, then one will find friendship, respect, and tenderness between the lovers (see 1:8–10; 2:3).

Read Song of Solomon 1:8–10; 2:3; see also Genesis 24:67; Proverbs 30:19; Ezekiel 16:4–14; Matthew 16:24–26; 2 Corinthians 11:2; Revelations 21:2.

Read the insight essays on Dating and Love.

—K. Smallwood

ATTRIBUTES OF GOD—HOLINESS

The word *holy* means "unique," "set apart," "unlike all others." The basic idea of holiness is that of distinctiveness. It is first applied to God and, by application, to people. God is separated from the universe. God is, by His very nature, holy. Sin does not exist in God; therefore, God does not deceive. This is an aspect of God that is very difficult to grasp. Our own understanding of holiness is limited by our attempts at being holy. We so often try to remake God in our own image, we cannot grasp the notion that God is distinct from His creation. God is the one and only (Isa. 40:25). In his great vision, Isaiah saw the Lord in His temple (see Isaiah 6). He saw God's glory and heard the angels declare, "Holy, holy, holy is the LORD of hosts: the whole earth is full of his glory" (v. 3).

Once Isaiah comprehended God's holiness, he understood his own sinfulness. He declared, "Woe is me! for I am undone; because I am a man of unclean lips, and I dwell in the midst of a people of unclean lips" (v. 5). True worship of God is possible only when we recognize His holiness. As we look at our communities, see the senseless violence by and against our children, and labor under the systematic racism of our society, it is important that we know who God is, and why we serve Him. Isaiah said to the people of Israel,

"Say ye not, A confederacy, to all them to whom this people shall say, A confederacy; neither fear ye their fear, not be afraid. Sanctify the LORD of hosts himself; and let him be your fear, and let him be your dread" (8:12-13).

Since the Lord alone is holy, we should not be surprised at the various scandals, sensationalistic news, and dire statistics. We also should not be sidetracked by them. Our response to a world gone haywire is to be still and know that God is God (Ps. 46:10).

Read Isaiah 8:40; see also Genesis 18:25; Exodus 33:17-23; Psalm 42:1-2; 100:3; Amos 4:2.

Read the insight essay on Attributes of God.

—*C. Belt*

SPIRITUAL DISCIPLINE

If you wander off the road to the right or the left, you will hear his voice behind you saying, "Here is the road. Follow it." (Isa. 30:21, paraphrased)

Life at its best sometimes demands so much of us. Often there are two things we don't have nor have enough of: spiritual energy (faith) and physical energy.

We are living in a fast-moving world. Our energies are absorbed and channeled in a complex society. Only a very few of us can deny this feeling of exhausting power from day to day—that feeling of I need to, I want to, but I can't.

We need to stop and ask ourselves, *What are we seeking? What are we running from?* We have lost control of ourselves by not seeking some basic foundations that will enable us to be our own person, by making ourselves responsible. Often we impose on ourselves high-risk expectations. Goals should be set before us. However, while we work toward them, we need to look to the right, left, and sometimes behind us as we move forward. Can you imagine getting into a car and driving without looking straight ahead? What about the sign that needs to be read that has been put there for our benefit? What about the risk of not stopping, not slowing down in a curve, not staying within the speed limits, not changing lanes without looking or ignoring "dead end" signs or "road washed out" signs?

Even though God blesses us, He anticipates our inability to live perfect lives. We are in motion not to *be*, but to *become*. This is why He tells us, "If you wander off the road to the right or the left, you will hear His voice behind you saying, 'Here is the road, follow it' " (Isa. 30:21, paraphrased).

We need to spend most of our time learning about ourselves as well as others. Take a tree, for example. If there is no new growth on the inside, there cannot be any on the outside. Likewise, unless we are deeply rooted in God, we will not grow. The very essence of growth lives within the infinite Creator who is the source of life.

Every woman should seek to become disciplined in order to grow spiritually. God helps us to make our way through the crevice of circumstances that we face daily.

Progress in the sense of acquisition has some value. Yet progress in the sense of *being* is a great deal more. We need to grow higher, deeper, and wider as time passes, to conquer difficulties and acquire more and more of God's power. Without spiritual discipline a woman cannot grow in faith or feel all of her facilities unfolding and truth descending into her

soul. With this discipline we feel more alive, more genuinely ourselves.

Remember, we are just passing through this wonderful and beautiful earth. God has given us every possible opportunity to live our lives to the utmost; to look upon every fresh impression; to develop every latent capacity; to grow as much as ever with His energy at work in us. Growth is within our grasp!

Read Isaiah 30:21.

Read the insight essays on Commitment and Fruit of the Spirit.

—E. McNair

STRESS MANAGEMENT: LEARNING TO SAY "NO"

One of the greatest combinations of blessings and burdens that black women carry around is the legacy of not being able to say "no." We are socialized to take care of our families, our friends, our communities, and everyone else but ourselves. A woman's natural desire for acceptance can create stress. Feeling that only you can meet the needs of your family and friends also will create stress. This anxiety can be compounded with the thought that our personal needs will not be met. This malady runs so deep that we are often consumed with guilt at the thought of putting our needs before someone else's. However, for the sake of sanity, sometimes that is just what we need to do.

Alleviating stress begins with learning to say "no" and recognizing your strengths and limitations. By taking time out to revive ourselves—spiritually, mentally, emotionally, and physically—we are actually doing our loved ones a favor because we are better equipped to attend to their needs. When we are tired, it is harder for our light to shine before others as the Bible commands us (see Matt. 5:16). The character Big Mama in the movie *Soul Food* serves as a good example of what happens when we take care of everybody else and reserve nothing for ourselves. Inevitably, we fall apart and the very people we feel compelled to take care of have to reverse roles with us.

The very idea of saying "no" drives many of us into hiding with the thought, "I shouldn't be so selfish," or "I can't put myself first. It's not right. They need me." True, putting oneself first is not always right, but rather than automatically saying "yes" to every request, we need to evaluate and determine when "no" is appropriate. Sometimes "no" is the right and healthy answer. Although it will not be easy, we must learn to say it. Self-deception, pride, and independence can prevent self-awareness and discernment (Jer. 17:9). God must give the self-awareness needed. He can show you where change is needed and lead you to bring about that change in your life (Ps. 139:23–24).

Having been programmed to say "yes" all our lives, saying "no" will feel uncomfortable at first. However, as you practice saying it and offering alternatives to the demands on your time and resources, saying "no" will become easier. Others will be taken aback at first, but you will feel better, and ultimately, serve them better. Once a woman acknowledges her dependence on God and submits to His will for her life, stress will disappear.

Read Jeremiah 17:9; see also Psalm 139:23–24.

Read insight essays on Depression and Distress.

—J. Anderson-Blair

it not; neither decline from the words of my
mouth.
6 Forsake her not, and she shall preserve
thee: [i]love her, and she shall keep thee.
7 [j]Wisdom *is* the principal thing; *there-*
fore get wisdom: and with all thy getting get
understanding.
8 [k]Exalt her, and she shall promote thee:
she shall bring thee to honour, when thou
dost embrace her.
9 She shall give to thine head [l]an ornament of grace: a crown of glory shall she
deliver to thee.
10 Hear, O my son, and receive my sayings; [m]and the years of thy life shall be
many.
11 I have taught thee in the way of wisdom; I have led thee in right paths.
12 When thou goest, [n]thy steps shall not
be straitened; [o]and when thou runnest,
thou shalt not stumble.
13 Take fast hold of instruction; let *her*
not go: keep her; for she *is* thy life.
14 ¶ [p]Enter not into the path of the
wicked, and go not in the way of evil *men*.
15 Avoid it, pass not by it, turn from it,
and pass away.
16 [q]For they sleep not, except they have
done mischief; and their sleep is taken
away, unless they cause *some* to fall.
17 For they eat the bread of wickedness,
and drink the wine of violence.
18 [r]But the path of the just [s]*is* as the
shining light, that shineth more and more
unto the perfect day.
19 [t]The way of the wicked *is* as darkness:
they know not at what they stumble.
20 ¶ My son, attend to my words; incline
thine ear unto my sayings.
21 [u]Let them not depart from thine eyes;
[v]keep them in the midst of thine heart.
22 For they *are* life unto those that find
them, and [w]health to all their flesh.
23 ¶ Keep thy heart with all diligence; for
out of it *are* the issues of life.
24 Put away from thee a froward mouth,
and perverse lips put far from thee.
25 Let thine eyes look right on, and let
thine eyelids look straight before thee.
26 Ponder the path of thy feet, and let all
thy ways be established.
27 [x]Turn not to the right hand nor to the
left: [y]remove thy foot from evil.

5 My son, attend unto my wisdom, *and*
bow thine ear to my understanding:
2 That thou mayest regard discretion, and
that thy lips may [z]keep knowledge.
3 ¶ [a]For the lips of a strange woman
drop *as* an honeycomb, and her mouth *is*
[b]smoother than oil:
4 But her end is [c]bitter as wormwood,
[d]sharp as a twoedged sword.
5 [e]Her feet go down to death; her steps
take hold on hell.
6 Lest thou shouldest ponder the path of
life, her ways are moveable, *that* thou canst
not know *them*.
7 Hear me now therefore, O ye children,

4:6 [i]2 Thess. 2:10
4:7 [j]Matt. 13:44; Luke 10:42
4:8 [k]1 Sam. 2:30
4:9 [l]ch. 1:9
4:10 [m]ch. 3:2
4:12 [n]Ps. 18:36 [o]Ps. 91:11
4:14 [p]Ps. 1:1; ch. 1:10
4:16 [q]Ps. 36:4; Isa. 57:20
4:18 [r]Matt. 5:14; Phil. 2:15 [s]2 Sam. 23:4
4:19 [t]1 Sam. 2:9; Job 18:5; Isa. 59:9; Jer. 23:12; John 12:35
4:21 [u]ch. 3:3 [v]ch. 2:1
4:22 [w]ch. 3:8
4:27 [x]Deut. 5:32; Josh. 1:7 [y]Isa. 1:16; Rom. 12:9
5:2 [z]Mal. 2:7
5:3 [a]ch. 2:16 [b]Ps. 55:21
5:4 [c]Eccl. 7:26 [d]Heb. 4:12
5:5 [e]ch. 7:27
5:12 [f]ch. 1:29 [g]ch. 1:25
5:18 [h]Mal. 2:14
5:19 [i]SSol. 2:9
5:20 [j]ch. 2:16
5:21 [k]2 Chron. 16:9; Job 31:4; ch. 15:3; Jer. 16:17; Hos. 7:2; Heb. 4:13
5:22 [l]Ps. 9:15
5:23 [m]Job 4:21
6:1 [n]ch. 11:15
6:4 [o]Ps. 132:4
6:6 [p]Job 12:7
6:9 [q]ch. 24:33
6:11 [r]ch. 10:4

and depart not from the words of my mouth.
8 Remove thy way far from her, and come
not nigh the door of her house:
9 Lest thou give thine honour unto others,
and thy years unto the cruel:
10 Lest strangers be filled with thy
wealth; and thy labours *be* in the house of a
stranger;
11 And thou mourn at the last, when thy
flesh and thy body are consumed,
12 And say, How have I [f]hated instruction, and my heart [g]despised reproof;
13 And have not obeyed the voice of my
teachers, nor inclined mine ear to them that
instructed me!
14 I was almost in all evil in the midst of
the congregation and assembly.
15 ¶ Drink waters out of thine own cistern, and running waters out of thine own
well.
16 Let thy fountains be dispersed abroad,
and rivers of waters in the streets.
17 Let them be only thine own, and not
strangers' with thee.
18 Let thy fountain be blessed: and rejoice with [h]the wife of thy youth.
19 [i]*Let her be as* the loving hind and
pleasant roe; let her breasts satisfy thee at
all times; and be thou ravished always with
her love.
20 And why wilt thou, my son, be ravished with [j]a strange woman, and embrace
the bosom of a stranger?
21 [k]For the ways of man *are* before the
eyes of the LORD, and he pondereth all his
goings.
22 ¶ [l]His own iniquities shall take the
wicked himself, and he shall be holden with
the cords of his sins.
23 [m]He shall die without instruction; and
in the greatness of his folly he shall go
astray.

6 My son, [n]if thou be surety for thy
friend, *if* thou hast stricken thy hand
with a stranger,
2 Thou art snared with the words of thy
mouth, thou art taken with the words of thy
mouth.
3 Do this now, my son, and deliver thyself, when thou art come into the hand of
thy friend; go, humble thyself, and make
sure thy friend.
4 [o]Give not sleep to thine eyes, nor slumber to thine eyelids.
5 Deliver thyself as a roe from the hand *of*
the hunter, and as a bird from the hand of
the fowler.
6 ¶ [p]Go to the ant, thou sluggard; consider her ways, and be wise:
7 Which having no guide, overseer, or
ruler,
8 Provideth her meat in the summer, *and*
gathereth her food in the harvest.
9 [q]How long wilt thou sleep, O sluggard?
when wilt thou arise out of thy sleep?
10 *Yet* a little sleep, a little slumber, a little folding of the hands to sleep:
11 [r]So shall thy poverty come as one that

travelleth, and thy want as an armed man.

12 ¶ A naughty person, a wicked man, walketh with a froward mouth.

13 [s]He winketh with his eyes, he speaketh with his feet, he teacheth with his fingers;

14 Frowardness *is* in his heart, [t]he deviseth mischief continually; [u]he soweth discord.

15 Therefore shall his calamity come suddenly; suddenly shall he [v]be broken [w]without remedy.

16 ¶ These six *things* doth the LORD hate: yea, seven *are* an abomination unto him:

17 [x]A proud look, [y]a lying tongue, and [z]hands that shed innocent blood,

18 [a]An heart that deviseth wicked imaginations, [b]feet that be swift in running to mischief,

19 [c]A false witness *that* speaketh lies, and he [d]that soweth discord among brethren.

20 ¶ [e]My son, keep thy father's commandment, and forsake not the law of thy mother:

21 [f]Bind them continually upon thine heart, *and* tie them about thy neck.

22 [g]When thou goest, it shall lead thee; when thou sleepest, [h]it shall keep thee; and *when* thou awakest, it shall talk with thee.

23 [i]For the commandment *is* a lamp; and the law *is* light; and reproofs of instruction *are* the way of life:

24 [j]To keep thee from the evil woman, from the flattery of the tongue of a strange woman.

25 [k]Lust not after her beauty in thine heart; neither let her take thee with her eyelids.

26 For [l]by means of a whorish woman *a man is brought* to a piece of bread: [m]and the adultress will [n]hunt for the precious life.

27 Can a man take fire in his bosom, and his clothes not be burned?

28 Can one go upon hot coals, and his feet not be burned?

29 So he that goeth in to his neighbour's wife; whosoever toucheth her shall not be innocent.

30 *Men* do not despise a thief, if he steal to satisfy his soul when he is hungry;

31 But *if* he be found, [o]he shall restore sevenfold; he shall give all the substance of his house.

32 *But* whoso committeth adultery with a woman [p]lacketh understanding: he *that* doeth it destroyeth his own soul.

33 A wound and dishonour shall he get; and his reproach shall not be wiped away.

34 For jealousy *is* the rage of a man: therefore he will not spare in the day of vengeance.

35 He will not regard any ransom; neither will he rest content, though thou givest many gifts.

7 My son, keep my words, and [q]lay up my commandments with thee.

2 [r]Keep my commandments, and live; [s]and my law as the apple of thine eye.

3 [t]Bind them upon thy fingers, write them upon the table of thine heart.

4 Say unto wisdom, Thou *art* my sister; and call understanding *thy* kinswoman:

5 [u]That they may keep thee from the strange woman, from the stranger *which* flattereth with her words.

6 ¶ For at the window of my house I looked through my casement,

7 And beheld among the simple ones, I discerned among the youths, a young man [v]void of understanding,

8 Passing through the street near her corner; and he went the way to her house,

9 [w]In the twilight, in the evening, in the black and dark night:

10 And, behold, there met him a woman *with* the attire of an harlot, and subtil of heart.

11 ([x]She *is* loud and stubborn; [y]her feet abide not in her house:

12 Now *is she* without, now in the streets, and lieth in wait at every corner.)

13 So she caught him, and kissed him, *and* with an impudent face said unto him,

14 *I have* peace offerings with me; this day have I payed my vows.

15 Therefore came I forth to meet thee, diligently to seek thy face, and I have found thee.

16 I have decked my bed with coverings of tapestry, with carved *works,* with [z]fine linen of Egypt.

17 I have perfumed my bed with myrrh, aloes, and cinnamon.

18 Come, let us take our fill of love until the morning: let us solace ourselves with loves.

19 For the goodman *is* not at home, he is gone a long journey:

20 He hath taken a bag of money with him, *and* will come home at the day appointed.

21 With [a]her much fair speech she caused him to yield, [b]with the flattering of her lips she forced him.

22 He goeth after her straightway, as an ox goeth to the slaughter, or as a fool to the correction of the stocks;

23 Till a dart strike through his liver; [c]as a bird hasteth to the snare, and knoweth not that it *is* for his life.

24 ¶ Hearken unto me now therefore, O ye children, and attend to the words of my mouth.

25 Let not thine heart decline to her ways, go not astray in her paths.

26 For she hath cast down many wounded: yea, [d]many strong *men* have been slain by her.

27 [e]Her house *is* the way to hell, going down to the chambers of death.

8 Doth not [f]wisdom cry? and understanding put forth her voice?

2 She standeth in the top of high places, by the way in the places of the paths.

6:13 [s]Job 15:12; Ps. 35:19; ch. 10:10
6:14 [t]Mic. 2:1 [u]ver. 19
6:15 [v]Jer. 19:11 [w]2 Chron. 36:16
6:17 [x]Ps. 18:27 [y]Ps. 120:2 [z]Isa. 1:15
6:18 [a]Gen. 6:5 [b]Isa. 59:7; Rom. 3:15
6:19 [c]Ps. 27:12; ch. 19:5 [d]ver. 14
6:20 [e]ch. 1:8; Eph. 6:1
6:21 [f]ch. 3:3
6:22 [g]ch. 3:23 [h]ch. 2:11
6:23 [i]Ps. 19:8
6:24 [j]ch. 2:16
6:25 [k]Matt. 5:28
6:26 [l]ch. 29:3 [m]Gen. 39:14 [n]Ezek. 13:18
6:31 [o]Ex. 22:1
6:32 [p]ch. 7:7
7:1 [q]ch. 2:1
7:2 [r]Lev. 18:5; ch. 4:4; Isa. 55:3 [s]Deut. 32:10
7:3 [t]Deut. 6:8; ch. 3:3
7:5 [u]ch. 2:16
7:7 [v]ch. 6:32
7:9 [w]Job 24:15
7:11 [x]ch. 9:13 [y]1 Tim. 5:13; Tit. 2:5
7:16 [z]Isa. 19:9
7:21 [a]ch. 5:3 [b]Ps. 12:2
7:23 [c]Eccl. 9:12
7:26 [d]Neh. 13:26
7:27 [e]ch. 2:18
8:1 [f]ch. 1:20

3 She crieth at the gates, at the entry of
the city, at the coming in at the doors.
4 Unto you, O men, I call; and my voice *is*
to the sons of man.
5 O ye simple, understand wisdom: and,
ye fools, be ye of an understanding heart.
6 Hear; for I will speak of [g]excellent
things; and the opening of my lips *shall be*
right things.
7 For my mouth shall speak truth; and
wickedness *is* an abomination to my lips.
8 All the words of my mouth *are* in righteousness; *there is* nothing froward or perverse in them.
9 They *are* all plain to him that understandeth, and right to them that find knowledge.
10 Receive my instruction, and not silver;
and knowledge rather than choice gold.
11 [h]For wisdom *is* better than rubies; and
all the things that may be desired are not to
be compared to it.
12 I wisdom dwell with prudence, and
find out knowledge of witty inventions.
13 [i]The fear of the LORD *is* to hate evil:
[j]pride, and arrogancy, and the evil way,
and [k]the froward mouth, do I hate.
14 Counsel *is* mine, and sound wisdom: I
am understanding; [l]I have strength.
15 [m]By me kings reign, and princes decree justice.
16 By me princes rule, and nobles, *even*
all the judges of the earth.
17 [n]I love them that love me; and [o]those
that seek me early shall find me.
18 [p]Riches and honour *are* with me; *yea,*
durable riches and righteousness.
19 [q]My fruit *is* better than gold, yea, than
fine gold; and my revenue than choice silver.
20 I lead in the way of righteousness, in
the midst of the paths of judgment:
21 That I may cause those that love me to
inherit substance; and I will fill their treasures.
22 [r]The LORD possessed me in the beginning of his way, before his works of old.
23 [s]I was set up from everlasting, from
the beginning, or ever the earth was.
24 When *there were* no depths, I was
brought forth; when *there were* no fountains abounding with water.
25 [t]Before the mountains were settled,
before the hills was I brought forth:
26 While as yet he had not made the
earth, nor the fields, nor the highest part of
the dust of the world.
27 When he prepared the heavens, I *was*
there: when he set a compass upon the face
of the depth:
28 When he established the clouds above:
when he strengthened the fountains of the
deep:
29 [u]When he gave to the sea his decree,
that the waters should not pass his commandment: when [v]he appointed the foundations of the earth:
30 [w]Then I was by him, *as* one brought up
with him: [x]and I was daily *his* delight, rejoicing always before him;
31 Rejoicing in the habitable part of his
earth; and [y]my delights *were* with the sons
of men.
32 Now therefore hearken unto me, O ye
children: for [z]blessed *are they that* keep
my ways.
33 Hear instruction, and be wise, and refuse it not.
34 [a]Blessed *is* the man that heareth me,
watching daily at my gates, waiting at the
posts of my doors.
35 For whoso findeth me findeth life, and
shall [b]obtain favour of the LORD.
36 But he that sinneth against me
[c]wrongeth his own soul: all they that hate
me love death.

9 Wisdom hath [d]builded her house, she
hath hewn out her seven pillars:
2 [e]She hath killed her beasts; [f]she hath
mingled her wine; she hath also furnished
her table.
3 She hath [g]sent forth her maidens: [h]she
crieth [i]upon the highest places of the city,
4 [j]Whoso *is* simple, let him turn in hither:
as for him that wanteth understanding, she
saith to him,
5 [k]Come, eat of my bread, and drink of
the wine *which* I have mingled.
6 Forsake the foolish, and live; and go in
the way of understanding.
7 He that reproveth a scorner getteth to
himself shame: and he that rebuketh a
wicked *man getteth* himself a blot.
8 [l]Reprove not a scorner, lest he hate
thee: [m]rebuke a wise man, and he will love
thee.
9 Give *instruction* to a wise *man,* and he
will be yet wiser: teach a just *man,* [n]and he
will increase in learning.
10 [o]The fear of the LORD *is* the beginning
of wisdom: and the knowledge of the holy *is*
understanding.
11 [p]For by me thy days shall be multiplied, and the years of thy life shall be increased.
12 [q]If thou be wise, thou shalt be wise for
thyself: but *if* thou scornest, thou alone shalt
bear *it.*
13 ¶ [r]A foolish woman *is* clamorous: *she*
is simple, and knoweth nothing.
14 For she sitteth at the door of her house,
on a seat [s]in the high places of the city,
15 To call passengers who go right on
their ways:
16 [t]Whoso *is* simple, let him turn in
hither: and *as for* him that wanteth understanding, she saith to him,
17 [u]Stolen waters are sweet, and bread
eaten in secret is pleasant.
18 But he knoweth not that [v]the dead *are*
there; *and that* her guests *are* in the depths
of hell.

10 The proverbs of Solomon. [w]A wise
son maketh a glad father: but a foolish son *is* the heaviness of his mother.
2 [x]Treasures of wickedness profit noth-

8:6 [g]ch. 22:20
8:11 [h]Job 28:15; Ps. 19:10; ch. 3:14
8:13 [i]ch. 16:6 [j]ch. 6:17 [k]ch. 4:24
8:14 [l]Eccl. 7:19
8:15 [m]Dan. 2:21; Rom. 13:1
8:17 [n]1 Sam. 2:30; Ps. 91:14; John 14:21 [o]Jam. 1:5
8:18 [p]ch. 3:16; Matt. 6:33
8:19 [q]ch. 3:14; ver. 10
8:22 [r]ch. 3:19; John 1:1
8:23 [s]Ps. 2:6
8:25 [t]Job 15:7
8:29 [u]Gen. 1:9; Job 38:10; Ps. 33:7; Jer. 5:22 [v]Job 38:4
8:30 [w]John 1:1 [x]Matt. 3:17; Col. 1:13
8:31 [y]Ps. 16:3
8:32 [z]Ps. 119:1; Luke 11:28
8:34 [a]ch. 3:13
8:35 [b]ch. 12:2
8:36 [c]ch. 20:2
9:1 [d]Matt. 16:18; Eph. 2:20; 1 Pet. 2:5
9:2 [e]Matt. 22:3 [f]ver. 5; ch. 23:30
9:3 [g]Rom. 10:15 [h]ch. 8:1 [i]ver. 14
9:4 [j]ver. 16; ch. 6:32; Matt. 11:25
9:5 [k]ver. 2; SSol. 5:1; Isa. 55:1; John 6:27
9:8 [l]Matt. 7:6 [m]Ps. 141:5
9:9 [n]Matt. 13:12
9:10 [o]Job 28:28; Ps. 111:10; ch. 1:7
9:11 [p]ch. 3:2
9:12 [q]Job 35:6; ch. 16:26
9:13 [r]ch. 7:11
9:14 [s]ver. 3
9:16 [t]ver. 4
9:17 [u]ch. 20:17
9:18 [v]ch. 2:18
10:1 [w]ch. 15:20
10:2 [x]Ps. 49:6; ch. 11:4; Luke 12:19

ing: [y]but righteousness delivereth from death.

3 [z]The LORD will not suffer the soul of the righteous to famish: but he casteth away the substance of the wicked.

4 [a]He becometh poor that dealeth *with* a slack hand: but [b]the hand of the diligent maketh rich.

5 He that gathereth in summer *is* a wise son: *but* he that sleepeth in harvest *is* [c]a son that causeth shame.

6 Blessings *are* upon the head of the just: but [d]violence covereth the mouth of the wicked.

7 [e]The memory of the just *is* blessed: but the name of the wicked shall rot.

8 The wise in heart will receive commandments: [f]but a prating fool shall fall.

9 [g]He that walketh uprightly walketh surely: but he that perverteth his ways shall be known.

10 [h]He that winketh with the eye causeth sorrow: [i]but a prating fool shall fall.

11 [j]The mouth of a righteous *man is* a well of life: but [k]violence covereth the mouth of the wicked.

12 Hatred stirreth up strifes: but [l]love covereth all sins.

13 In the lips of him that hath understanding wisdom is found: but [m]a rod *is* for the back of him that is void of understanding.

14 Wise *men* lay up knowledge: but [n]the mouth of the foolish *is* near destruction.

15 [o]The rich man's wealth *is* his strong city: the destruction of the poor *is* their poverty.

16 The labour of the righteous *tendeth* to life: the fruit of the wicked to sin.

17 He *is in* the way of life that keepeth instruction: but he that refuseth reproof erreth.

18 He that hideth hatred *with* lying lips, and [p]he that uttereth a slander, *is* a fool.

19 [q]In the multitude of words there wanteth not sin: but [r]he that refraineth his lips *is* wise.

20 The tongue of the just *is as* choice silver: the heart of the wicked *is* little worth.

21 The lips of the righteous feed many: but fools die for want of wisdom.

22 [s]The blessing of the LORD, it maketh rich, and he addeth no sorrow with it.

23 [t]*It is* as sport to a fool to do mischief: but a man of understanding hath wisdom.

24 [u]The fear of the wicked, it shall come upon him: but [v]the desire of the righteous shall be granted.

25 As the whirlwind passeth, [w]so *is* the wicked no *more:* but [x]the righteous *is* an everlasting foundation.

26 As vinegar to the teeth, and as smoke to the eyes, so *is* the sluggard to them that send him.

27 [y]The fear of the LORD prolongeth days: but [z]the years of the wicked shall be shortened.

28 The hope of the righteous *shall be* gladness: but the [a]expectation of the wicked shall perish.

29 The way of the LORD *is* strength to the upright: [b]but destruction *shall be* to the workers of iniquity.

30 [c]The righteous shall never be removed: but the wicked shall not inhabit the earth.

31 [d]The mouth of the just bringeth forth wisdom: but the froward tongue shall be cut out.

32 The lips of the righteous know what is acceptable: but the mouth of the wicked *speaketh* frowardness.

11

A [e]false balance *is* abomination to the LORD: but a just weight *is* his delight.

2 [f]*When* pride cometh, then cometh shame: but with the lowly *is* wisdom.

3 [g]The integrity of the upright shall guide them: but the perverseness of transgressors shall destroy them.

4 [h]Riches profit not in the day of wrath: but [i]righteousness delivereth from death.

5 The righteousness of the perfect shall direct his way: but the wicked shall fall by his own wickedness.

6 The righteousness of the upright shall deliver them: but [j]transgressors shall be taken in *their own* naughtiness.

7 [k]When a wicked man dieth, *his* expectation shall perish: and the hope of unjust *men* perisheth.

8 [l]The righteous is delivered out of trouble, and the wicked cometh in his stead.

9 An [m]hypocrite with *his* mouth destroyeth his neighbour: but through knowledge shall the just be delivered.

10 [n]When it goeth well with the righteous, the city rejoiceth: and when the wicked perish, *there is* shouting.

11 [o]By the blessing of the upright the city is exalted: but it is overthrown by the mouth of the wicked.

12 He that is void of wisdom despiseth his neighbour: but a man of understanding holdeth his peace.

13 [p]A talebearer revealeth secrets: but he that is of a faithful spirit concealeth the matter.

14 [q]Where no counsel *is*, the people fall: but in the multitude of counsellors *there is* safety.

15 [r]He that is surety for a stranger shall smart *for it:* and he that hateth suretiship is sure.

16 [s]A gracious woman retaineth honour: and strong *men* retain riches.

17 [t]The merciful man doeth good to his own soul: but *he that is* cruel troubleth his own flesh.

18 The wicked worketh a deceitful work: but [u]to him that soweth righteousness *shall be* a sure reward.

19 As righteousness *tendeth* to life: so he that pursueth evil *pursueth it* to his own death.

20 They that are of a froward heart *are*

10:2 [y]Dan. 4:27
10:3 [z]Ps. 10:14
10:4 [a]ch. 12:24 [b]ch. 13:4
10:5 [c]ch. 12:4
10:6 [d]ver. 11; Esth. 7:8
10:7 [e]Ps. 9:5; Eccl. 8:10
10:8 [f]ver. 10
10:9 [g]Ps. 23:4; ch. 28:18; Isa. 33:15
10:10 [h]ch. 6:13 [i]ver. 8
10:11 [j]Ps. 37:30; ch. 13:14 [k]Ps. 107:42; ver. 6
10:12 [l]ch. 17:9; 1 Cor. 13:4; 1 Pet. 4:8
10:13 [m]ch. 26:3
10:14 [n]ch. 18:7
10:15 [o]Job 31:24; Ps. 52:7; ch. 18:11; 1 Tim. 6:17
10:18 [p]Ps. 15:3
10:19 [q]Eccl. 5:3 [r]Jam. 3:2
10:22 [s]Gen. 24:35; Ps. 37:22
10:23 [t]ch. 14:9
10:24 [u]Job 15:21 [v]Ps. 145:19; Matt. 5:6; 1 John 5:14
10:25 [w]Ps. 37:9 [x]ver. 30; Ps. 15:5; Matt. 7:24
10:27 [y]ch. 9:11 [z]Job 15:32; Ps. 55:23; Eccl. 7:17
10:28 [a]Job 8:13; Ps. 112:10; ch. 11:7
10:29 [b]Ps. 1:6
10:30 [c]Ps. 37:22; ver. 25
10:31 [d]Ps. 37:30
11:1 [e]Lev. 19:35; Deut. 25:13-16; ch. 16:11
11:2 [f]ch. 15:33; Dan. 4:30
11:3 [g]ch. 13:6
11:4 [h]ch. 10:2; Ezek. 7:19; Zeph. 1:18 [i]Gen. 7:1
11:6 [j]ch. 5:22; Eccl. 10:8
11:7 [k]ch. 10:28
11:8 [l]ch. 21:18
11:9 [m]Job 8:13
11:10 [n]Esth. 8:15; ch. 28:12
11:11 [o]ch. 29:8
11:13 [p]Lev. 9:16; ch. 20:19
11:14 [q]1 Kings 12:1; ch. 15:22
11:15 [r]ch. 6:1
11:16 [s]ch. 31:30
11:17 [t]Matt. 5:7
11:18 [u]Hos. 10:12; Gal. 6:8; Jam. 3:18

abomination to the LORD: but *such as are*
upright in *their* way *are* his delight.
21 [v]*Though* hand *join* in hand, the
wicked shall not be unpunished: but [w]the
seed of the righteous shall be delivered.
22 *As* a jewel of gold in a swine's snout, *so*
is a fair woman which is without discretion.
23 The desire of the righteous *is* only
good: *but* the expectation of the wicked [x]*is*
wrath.
24 There is that [y]scattereth, and yet increaseth; and *there is* that withholdeth
more than is meet, but *it tendeth* to poverty.
25 [z]The liberal soul shall be made fat:
[a]and he that watereth shall be watered also
himself.
26 [b]He that withholdeth corn, the people
shall curse him: but [c]blessing *shall be* upon
the head of him that selleth *it*.
27 He that diligently seeketh good pro-
cureth favour: [d]but he that seeketh mischief, it shall come unto him.
28 [e]He that trusteth in his riches shall
fall: but [f]the righteous shall flourish as a
branch.
29 He that troubleth his own house [g]shall
inherit the wind: and the fool *shall be* servant to the wise of heart.
30 The fruit of the righteous *is* a tree of
life; and [h]he that winneth souls *is* wise.
31 [i]Behold, the righteous shall be recompensed in the earth: much more the wicked
and the sinner.
12 Whoso loveth instruction loveth
knowledge: but he that hateth reproof *is* brutish.
2 [j]A good *man* obtaineth favour of the
LORD: but a man of wicked devices will he
condemn.
3 A man shall not be established by wickedness: but the [k]root of the righteous shall
not be moved.
4 [l]A virtuous woman *is* a crown to her
husband: but she that maketh ashamed *is*
[m]as rottenness in his bones.
5 The thoughts of the righteous *are* right:
but the counsels of the wicked *are* deceit.
6 [n]The words of the wicked *are* to lie in
wait for blood: [o]but the mouth of the upright shall deliver them.
7 [p]The wicked are overthrown, and *are*
not: but the house of the righteous shall
stand.
8 A man shall be commended according
to his wisdom: [q]but he that is of a perverse
heart shall be despised.
9 [r]*He that is* despised, and hath a servant, *is* better than he that honoureth himself, and lacketh bread.
10 [s]A righteous *man* regardeth the life
of his beast: but the tender mercies of the
wicked *are* cruel.
11 [t]He that tilleth his land shall be satisfied with bread: but he that followeth vain
persons [u]*is* void of understanding.
12 The wicked desireth the net of evil
men: but the root of the righteous yieldeth
fruit.

11:21 [v]ch. 16:5 [w]Ps. 112:2
11:23 [x]Rom. 2:8
11:24 [y]Ps. 112:9
11:25 [z]2 Cor. 9:6 [a]Matt. 5:7
11:26 [b]Am. 8:5 [c]Job 29:13
11:27 [d]Esth. 7:10; Ps. 7:15
11:28 [e]Job 31:24; Ps. 52:7; Mark 10:24; Luke 12:21; 1 Tim. 6:17 [f]Ps. 1:3; Jer. 17:8
11:29 [g]Eccl. 5:16
11:30 [h]Dan. 12:3; 1 Cor. 9:19; Jam. 5:20
11:31 [i]Jer. 25:29; 1 Pet. 4:17
12:2 [j]ch. 8:35
12:3 [k]ch. 10:25
12:4 [l]ch. 31:23; 1 Cor. 11:7 [m]ch. 14:30
12:6 [n]ch. 1:11 [o]ch. 14:3
12:7 [p]Ps. 37:36; ch. 11:21; Matt. 7:24
12:8 [q]1 Sam. 25:17
12:9 [r]ch. 13:7
12:10 [s]Deut. 25:4
12:11 [t]Gen. 3:19; ch. 28:19 [u]ch. 6:32
12:13 [v]ch. 18:7 [w]2 Pet. 2:9
12:14 [x]ch. 13:2 [y]Isa. 3:10
12:15 [z]ch. 3:7; Luke 18:11
12:16 [a]ch. 29:11
12:17 [b]ch. 14:5
12:18 [c]Ps. 57:4
12:19 [d]Ps. 52:5; ch. 19:9
12:22 [e]ch. 6:17; Rev. 22:15
12:23 [f]ch. 13:16
12:24 [g]ch. 10:4
12:25 [h]ch. 15:13 [i]Isa. 50:4
13:1 [j]1 Sam. 2:25
13:2 [k]ch. 12:14
13:3 [l]Ps. 39:1; ch. 21:23; Jam. 3:2
13:4 [m]ch. 10:4
13:6 [n]ch. 11:3
13:7 [o]ch. 12:9

13 [v]The wicked is snared by the transgression of *his* lips: [w]but the just shall come
out of trouble.
14 [x]A man shall be satisfied with good by
the fruit of *his* mouth: [y]and the recompense
of a man's hands shall be rendered unto
him.
15 [z]The way of a fool *is* right in his own
eyes: but he that hearkeneth unto counsel *is*
wise.
16 [a]A fool's wrath is presently known:
but a prudent *man* covereth shame.
17 [b]*He that* speaketh truth sheweth forth
righteousness: but a false witness deceit.
18 [c]There is that speaketh like the pierc-
ings of a sword: but the tongue of the wise
is health.
19 The lip of truth shall be established for
ever: [d]but a lying tongue *is* but for a moment.
20 Deceit *is* in the heart of them that
imagine evil: but to the counsellors of peace
is joy.
21 There shall no evil happen to the just:
but the wicked shall be filled with mischief.
22 [e]Lying lips *are* abomination to the
LORD: but they that deal truly *are* his delight.
23 [f]A prudent man concealeth knowledge: but the heart of fools proclaimeth
foolishness.
24 [g]The hand of the diligent shall bear
rule: but the slothful shall be under tribute.
25 [h]Heaviness in the heart of man maketh it stoop: but [i]a good word maketh it
glad.
26 The righteous *is* more excellent than
his neighbour: but the way of the wicked
seduceth them.
27 The slothful *man* roasteth not that
which he took in hunting: but the substance
of a diligent man *is* precious.
28 In the way of righteousness *is* life; and
in the pathway *thereof there is* no death.
13 A wise son *heareth* his father's instruction: [j]but a scorner heareth not
rebuke.
2 [k]A man shall eat good by the fruit of *his*
mouth: but the soul of the transgressors
shall eat violence.
3 [l]He that keepeth his mouth keepeth his
life: *but* he that openeth wide his lips shall
have destruction.
4 [m]The soul of the sluggard desireth, and
hath nothing: but the soul of the diligent
shall be made fat.
5 A righteous *man* hateth lying: but a
wicked *man* is loathsome, and cometh to
shame.
6 [n]Righteousness keepeth *him that is* upright in the way: but wickedness overthroweth the sinner.
7 [o]There is that maketh himself rich, yet
hath nothing: *there is* that maketh himself
poor, yet *hath* great riches.
8 The ransom of a man's life *are* his
riches: but the poor heareth not rebuke.
9 The light of the righteous rejoiceth:

[p]but the lamp of the wicked shall be put out.

10 Only by pride cometh contention: but with the well advised *is* wisdom.

11 [q]Wealth *gotten* by vanity shall be diminished: but he that gathereth by labour shall increase.

12 Hope deferred maketh the heart sick: but [r]*when* the desire cometh, *it is* a tree of life.

13 Whoso [s]despiseth the word shall be destroyed: but he that feareth the commandment shall be rewarded.

14 [t]The law of the wise *is* a fountain of life, to depart from [u]the snares of death.

15 Good understanding giveth favour: but the way of transgressors *is* hard.

16 [v]Every prudent *man* dealeth with knowledge: but a fool layeth open *his* folly.

17 A wicked messenger falleth into mischief: but [w]a faithful ambassador *is* health.

18 Poverty and shame *shall be to* him that refuseth instruction: but [x]he that regardeth reproof shall be honoured.

19 [y]The desire accomplished is sweet to the soul: but *it is* abomination to fools to depart from evil.

20 He that walketh with wise *men* shall be wise: but a companion of fools shall be destroyed.

21 [z]Evil pursueth sinners: but to the righteous good shall be repaid.

22 A good *man* leaveth an inheritance to his children's children: and [a]the wealth of the sinner *is* laid up for the just.

23 [b]Much food *is in* the tillage of the poor: but there is *that is* destroyed for want of judgment.

24 [c]He that spareth his rod hateth his son: but he that loveth him chasteneth him betimes.

25 [d]The righteous eateth to the satisfying of his soul: but the belly of the wicked shall want.

14

Every [e]wise woman [f]buildeth her house: but the foolish plucketh it down with her hands.

2 He that walketh in his uprightness feareth the LORD: [g]but *he that is* perverse in his ways despiseth him.

3 In the mouth of the foolish *is* a rod of pride: [h]but the lips of the wise shall preserve them.

4 Where no oxen *are,* the crib *is* clean: but much increase *is* by the strength of the ox.

5 [i]A faithful witness will not lie: but a false witness will utter lies.

6 A scorner seeketh wisdom, and *findeth it* not: but [j]knowledge *is* easy unto him that understandeth.

7 Go from the presence of a foolish man, when thou perceivest not *in him* the lips of knowledge.

8 The wisdom of the prudent *is* to understand his way: but the folly of fools *is* deceit.

9 [k]Fools make a mock at sin: but among the righteous *there is* favour.

10 The heart knoweth his own bitterness; and a stranger doth not intermeddle with his joy.

11 [l]The house of the wicked shall be overthrown: but the tabernacle of the upright shall flourish.

12 [m]There is a way which seemeth right unto a man, but [n]the end thereof *are* the ways of death.

13 Even in laughter the heart is sorrowful; and [o]the end of that mirth *is* heaviness.

14 The backslider in heart shall be [p]filled with his own ways: and a good man *shall be satisfied* from himself.

15 The simple believeth every word: but the prudent *man* looketh well to his going.

16 [q]A wise *man* feareth, and departeth from evil: but the fool rageth, and is confident.

17 *He that is* soon angry dealeth foolishly: and a man of wicked devices is hated.

18 The simple inherit folly: but the prudent are crowned with knowledge.

19 The evil bow before the good; and the wicked at the gates of the righteous.

20 [r]The poor is hated even of his own neighbour: but the rich *hath* many friends.

21 He that despiseth his neighbour sinneth: [s]but he that hath mercy on the poor, happy *is* he.

22 Do they not err that devise evil? but mercy and truth *shall be* to them that devise good.

23 In all labour there is profit: but the talk of the lips *tendeth* only to penury.

24 The crown of the wise *is* their riches: *but* the foolishness of fools *is* folly.

25 [t]A true witness delivereth souls: but a deceitful *witness* speaketh lies.

26 In the fear of the LORD *is* strong confidence: and his children shall have a place of refuge.

27 [u]The fear of the LORD *is* a fountain of life, to depart from the snares of death.

28 In the multitude of people *is* the king's honour: but in the want of people *is* the destruction of the prince.

29 [v]*He that is* slow to wrath *is* of great understanding: but *he that is* hasty of spirit exalteth folly.

30 A sound heart *is* the life of the flesh: but [w]envy [x]the rottenness of the bones.

31 [y]He that oppresseth the poor reproacheth [z]his Maker: but he that honoureth him hath mercy on the poor.

32 The wicked is driven away in his wickedness: but [a]the righteous hath hope in his death.

33 Wisdom resteth in the heart of him that hath understanding: but [b]*that which is* in the midst of fools is made known.

34 Righteousness exalteth a nation: but sin *is* a reproach to any people.

35 [c]The king's favour *is* toward a wise servant: but his wrath is *against* him that causeth shame.

15

A [d]soft answer turneth away wrath: but [e]grievous words stir up anger.

2 The tongue of the wise useth knowledge

13:9 [p]Job 18:5; ch. 24:20
13:11 [q]ch. 10:2
13:12 [r]ver. 19
13:13 [s]2 Chron. 36:16
13:14 [t]ch. 10:11 [u]2 Sam. 22:6
13:16 [v]ch. 12:23
13:17 [w]ch. 25:23
13:18 [x]ch. 15:5
13:19 [y]ver. 12
13:21 [z]Ps. 32:10
13:22 [a]Job 27:16; ch. 28:8; Eccl. 2:26
13:23 [b]ch. 12:11
13:24 [c]ch. 19:18
13:25 [d]Ps. 34:10
14:1 [e]ch. 24:3 [f]Ruth 4:11
14:2 [g]Job 12:4
14:3 [h]ch. 12:6
14:5 [i]Ex. 20:16; ch. 6:19; ver. 25
14:6 [j]ch. 8:9
14:9 [k]ch. 10:23
14:11 [l]Job 8:15
14:12 [m]ch. 16:25 [n]Rom. 6:21
14:13 [o]ch. 5:4; Eccl. 2:2
14:14 [p]ch. 1:31
14:16 [q]ch. 22:3
14:20 [r]ch. 19:7
14:21 [s]Ps. 41:1
14:25 [t]ver. 5
14:27 [u]ch. 13:14
14:29 [v]ch. 16:32; Jam. 1:19
14:30 [w]Ps. 112:10 [x]ch. 12:4
14:31 [y]ch. 17:5; Matt. 25:40 [z]Job 31:15; ch. 22:2
14:32 [a]Job 13:15; Ps. 23:4; 2 Cor. 1:9; 2 Tim. 4:18
14:33 [b]ch. 12:16
14:35 [c]Matt. 24:45
15:1 [d]Judg. 8:1; ch. 25:15 [e]1 Sam. 25:10; 1 Kings 12:13

aright: [f]but the mouth of fools poureth out foolishness.

3 [g]The eyes of the LORD *are* in every place, beholding the evil and the good.

4 A wholesome tongue *is* a tree of life: but perverseness therein *is* a breach in the spirit.

5 [h]A fool despiseth his father's instruction: [i]but he that regardeth reproof is prudent.

6 In the house of the righteous *is* much treasure: but in the revenues of the wicked is trouble.

7 The lips of the wise disperse knowledge: but the heart of the foolish *doeth* not so.

8 [j]The sacrifice of the wicked *is* an abomination to the LORD: but the prayer of the upright *is* his delight.

9 The way of the wicked *is* an abomination unto the LORD: but he loveth him that [k]followeth after righteousness.

10 Correction *is* [l]grievous unto him that forsaketh the way: *and* [m]he that hateth reproof shall die.

11 [n]Hell and destruction *are* before the LORD: how much more then [o]the hearts of the children of men?

12 [p]A scorner loveth not one that reproveth him: neither will he go unto the wise.

13 [q]A merry heart maketh a cheerful countenance: but [r]by sorrow of the heart the spirit is broken.

14 The heart of him that hath understanding seeketh knowledge: but the mouth of fools feedeth on foolishness.

15 All the days of the afflicted *are* evil: [s]but he that is of a merry heart *hath* a continual feast.

16 [t]Better *is* little with the fear of the LORD than great treasure and trouble therewith.

17 [u]Better *is* a dinner of herbs where love is, than a stalled ox and hatred therewith.

18 [v]A wrathful man stirreth up strife: but *he that is* slow to anger appeaseth strife.

19 [w]The way of the slothful *man is* as an hedge of thorns: but the way of the righteous *is* made plain.

20 [x]A wise son maketh a glad father: but a foolish man despiseth his mother.

21 [y]Folly *is* joy to *him that is* destitute of wisdom: [z]but a man of understanding walketh uprightly.

22 [a]Without counsel purposes are disappointed: but in the multitude of counsellors they are established.

23 A man hath joy by the answer of his mouth: and [b]a word *spoken* in due season, how good *is it!*

24 [c]The way of life *is* above to the wise, that he may depart from hell beneath.

25 [d]The LORD will destroy the house of the proud: but [e]he will establish the border of the widow.

26 [f]The thoughts of the wicked *are* an abomination to the LORD: [g]but *the words* of the pure *are* pleasant words.

27 [h]He that is greedy of gain troubleth his own house; but he that hateth gifts shall live.

28 The heart of the righteous [i]studieth to answer: but the mouth of the wicked poureth out evil things.

29 [j]The LORD *is* far from the wicked: but [k]he heareth the prayer of the righteous.

30 The light of the eyes rejoiceth the heart: *and* a good report maketh the bones fat.

31 [l]The ear that heareth the reproof of life abideth among the wise.

32 He that refuseth instruction despiseth his own soul: but he that heareth reproof getteth understanding.

33 [m]The fear of the LORD *is* the instruction of wisdom; [n]and before honour *is* humility.

16

The [o]preparations of the heart in man, [p]and the answer of the tongue, *is* from the LORD.

2 [q]All the ways of a man *are* clean in his own eyes; but [r]the LORD weigheth the spirits.

3 [s]Commit thy works unto the LORD, and thy thoughts shall be established.

4 [t]The LORD hath made all *things* for himself: [u]yea, even the wicked for the day of evil.

5 [v]Every one *that is* proud in heart *is* an abomination to the LORD: [w]*though* hand *join* in hand, he shall not be unpunished.

6 [x]By mercy and truth iniquity is purged: and [y]by the fear of the LORD *men* depart from evil.

7 When a man's ways please the LORD, he maketh even his enemies to be at peace with him.

8 [z]Better *is* a little with righteousness than great revenues without right.

9 [a]A man's heart deviseth his way: [b]but the LORD directeth his steps.

10 A divine sentence *is* in the lips of the king: his mouth transgresseth not in judgment.

11 [c]A just weight and balance *are* the LORD's: all the weights of the bag *are* his work.

12 *It is* an abomination to kings to commit wickedness: for [d]the throne is established by righteousness.

13 [e]Righteous lips *are* the delight of kings; and they love him that speaketh right.

14 [f]The wrath of a king *is as* messengers of death: but a wise man will pacify it.

15 In the light of the king's countenance *is* life; and [g]his favour *is* [h]as a cloud of the latter rain.

16 [i]How much better *is it* to get wisdom than gold! and to get understanding rather to be chosen than silver!

17 The highway of the upright *is* to depart from evil: he that keepeth his way preserveth his soul.

18 [j]Pride *goeth* before destruction, and an haughty spirit before a fall.

15:2 [f]ver. 28; ch. 12:23
15:3 [g]Job 34:21; ch. 5:21; Jer. 16:17; Heb. 4:13
15:5 [h]ch. 10:1 [i]ch. 13:18; ver. 31
15:8 [j]ch. 21:27; Isa. 1:11; Jer. 6:20; Am. 5:22
15:9 [k]ch. 21:21; 1 Tim. 6:11
15:10 [l]1 Kings 22:8 [m]ch. 5:12
15:11 [n]Job 26:6; Ps. 139:8 [o]2 Chron. 6:30; Ps. 7:9; John 2:24; Acts 1:24
15:12 [p]Am. 5:10; 2 Tim. 4:3
15:13 [q]ch. 17:22 [r]ch. 12:25
15:15 [s]ch. 17:22
15:16 [t]Ps. 37:16; ch. 16:8; 1 Tim. 6:6
15:17 [u]ch. 17:1
15:18 [v]ch. 26:21
15:19 [w]ch. 22:5
15:20 [x]ch. 10:1
15:21 [y]ch. 10:23 [z]Eph. 5:15
15:22 [a]ch. 11:14
15:23 [b]ch. 25:11
15:24 [c]Phil. 3:20; Col. 3:1
15:25 [d]ch. 12:7 [e]Ps. 68:5
15:26 [f]ch. 6:16 [g]Ps. 37:30
15:27 [h]ch. 11:19; Isa. 5:8; Jer. 17:11
15:28 [i]1 Pet. 3:15
15:29 [j]Ps. 10:1 [k]Ps. 145:18
15:31 [l]ver. 5
15:33 [m]ch. 1:7 [n]ch. 18:12
16:1 [o]ver. 9; ch. 19:21; Jer. 10:23 [p]Matt. 10:19
16:2 [q]ch. 21:2 [r]1 Sam. 16:7
16:3 [s]Ps. 37:5; Matt. 6:25; Luke 12:22; Phil. 4:6; 1 Pet. 5:7
16:4 [t]Isa. 43:7; Rom. 11:36 [u]Job 21:30; Rom. 9:22
16:5 [v]ch. 6:17 [w]ch. 11:21
16:6 [x]Dan. 4:27; Luke 11:41 [y]ch. 14:16
16:8 [z]Ps. 37:16; ch. 15:16
16:9 [a]ver. 1; ch. 19:21 [b]Ps. 37:23; Prov. 20:24; Jer. 10:23
16:11 [c]Lev. 19:36; ch. 11:1
16:12 [d]ch. 25:5
16:13 [e]ch. 14:35
16:14 [f]ch. 19:12
16:15 [g]ch. 19:12 [h]Job 29:23; Zech. 10:1
16:16 [i]ch. 8:11
16:18 [j]ch. 11:2

19 Better *it is to be* of an humble spirit with the lowly, than to divide the spoil with the proud.

20 He that handleth a matter wisely shall find good: and whoso [k]trusteth in the LORD, happy *is* he.

21 The wise in heart shall be called prudent: and the sweetness of the lips increaseth learning.

22 [l]Understanding *is* a wellspring of life unto him that hath it: but the instruction of fools *is* folly.

23 [m]The heart of the wise teacheth his mouth, and addeth learning to his lips.

24 Pleasant words *are as* an honeycomb, sweet to the soul, and health to the bones.

25 [n]There is a way that seemeth right unto a man, but the end thereof *are* the ways of death.

26 [o]He that laboureth laboureth for himself; for his mouth craveth it of him.

27 An ungodly man diggeth up evil: and in his lips *there is* as a burning fire.

28 [p]A froward man soweth strife: and [q]a whisperer separateth chief friends.

29 A violent man [r]enticeth his neighbour, and leadeth him into the way *that is* not good.

30 He shutteth his eyes to devise froward things: moving his lips he bringeth evil to pass.

31 [s]The hoary head *is* a crown of glory, *if* it be found in the way of righteousness.

32 [t]*He that is* slow to anger *is* better than the mighty; and he that ruleth his spirit than he that taketh a city.

33 The lot is cast into the lap; but the whole disposing thereof *is* of the LORD.

17

Better *is* [u]a dry morsel, and quietness therewith, than an house full of sacrifices *with* strife.

2 A wise servant shall have rule over [v]a son that causeth shame, and shall have part of the inheritance among the brethren.

3 [w]The fining pot *is* for silver, and the furnace for gold: but the LORD trieth the hearts.

4 A wicked doer giveth heed to false lips; *and* a liar giveth ear to a naughty tongue.

5 [x]Whoso mocketh the poor reproacheth his Maker: *and* [y]he that is glad at calamities shall not be unpunished.

6 [z]Children's children *are* the crown of old men; and the glory of children *are* their fathers.

7 Excellent speech becometh not a fool: much less do lying lips a prince.

8 [a]A gift *is as* a precious stone in the eyes of him that hath it: whithersoever it turneth, it prospereth.

9 [b]He that covereth a transgression seeketh love; but [c]he that repeateth a matter separateth *very* friends.

10 A reproof entereth more into a wise man than an hundred stripes into a fool.

11 An evil *man* seeketh only rebellion: therefore a cruel messenger shall be sent against him.

16:20 [k]Ps. 2:12; Isa. 30:18; Jer. 17:7
16:22 [l]ch. 13:14
16:23 [m]Ps. 37:30; Matt. 12:34
16:25 [n]ch. 14:12
16:26 [o]ch. 9:12; Eccl. 6:7
16:28 [p]ch. 6:14 [q]ch. 17:9
16:29 [r]ch. 1:10
16:31 [s]ch. 20:29
16:32 [t]ch. 19:11
17:1 [u]ch. 15:17
17:2 [v]ch. 10:5
17:3 [w]Ps. 26:2; ch. 27:21; Jer. 17:10; Mal. 3:3
17:5 [x]ch. 14:31 [y]Job 31:29; Obad. 12
17:6 [z]Ps. 127:3
17:8 [a]ch. 18:16
17:9 [b]ch. 10:12 [c]ch. 16:28
17:12 [d]Hos. 13:8
17:13 [e]Ps. 109:4; Jer. 18:20; Rom. 12:17; 1 Thess. 5:15; 1 Pet. 3:9
17:14 [f]ch. 20:3; 1 Thess. 4:11
17:15 [g]Ex. 23:7; ch. 24:24; Isa. 5:23
17:16 [h]ch. 21:25
17:17 [i]Ruth 1:16; ch. 18:24
17:18 [j]ch. 6:1
17:19 [k]ch. 16:18
17:20 [l]Jam. 3:8
17:21 [m]ch. 10:1; ver. 25
17:22 [n]ch. 15:13 [o]Ps. 22:15
17:23 [p]Ex. 23:8
17:24 [q]ch. 14:6; Eccl. 2:14
17:25 [r]ch. 10:1; ver. 21
17:26 [s]ver. 15; ch. 18:5
17:27 [t]Jam. 1:19
17:28 [u]Job 13:5
18:4 [v]ch. 10:11 [w]Ps. 78:2
18:5 [x]Lev. 19:15; Deut. 1:17; ch. 24:23
18:7 [y]ch. 10:14; Eccl. 10:12
18:8 [z]ch. 12:18
18:9 [a]ch. 28:24
18:10 [b]2 Sam. 22:3; Ps. 18:2

12 Let [d]a bear robbed of her whelps meet a man, rather than a fool in his folly.

13 Whoso [e]rewardeth evil for good, evil shall not depart from his house.

14 The beginning of strife *is as* when one letteth out water: therefore [f]leave off contention, before it be meddled with.

15 [g]He that justifieth the wicked, and he that condemneth the just, even they both *are* abomination to the LORD.

16 Wherefore *is there* a price in the hand of a fool to get wisdom, [h]seeing *he hath* no heart *to it?*

17 [i]A friend loveth at all times, and a brother is born for adversity.

18 [j]A man void of understanding striketh hands, *and* becometh surety in the presence of his friend.

19 He loveth transgression that loveth strife: *and* [k]he that exalteth his gate seeketh destruction.

20 He that hath a froward heart findeth no good: and he that hath [l]a perverse tongue falleth into mischief.

21 [m]He that begetteth a fool *doeth it* to his sorrow: and the father of a fool hath no joy.

22 [n]A merry heart doeth good *like* a medicine: [o]but a broken spirit drieth the bones.

23 A wicked *man* taketh a gift out of the bosom [p]to pervert the ways of judgment.

24 [q]Wisdom *is* before him that hath understanding; but the eyes of a fool *are* in the ends of the earth.

25 [r]A foolish son *is* a grief to his father, and bitterness to her that bare him.

26 [s]Also to punish the just *is* not good, *nor* to strike princes for equity.

27 [t]He that hath knowledge spareth his words: *and* a man of understanding is of an excellent spirit.

28 [u]Even a fool, when he holdeth his peace, is counted wise: *and* he that shutteth his lips *is esteemed* a man of understanding.

18

Through desire a man, having separated himself, seeketh *and* intermeddleth with all wisdom.

2 A fool hath no delight in understanding, but that his heart may discover itself.

3 When the wicked cometh, *then* cometh also contempt, and with ignominy reproach.

4 [v]The words of a man's mouth *are as* deep waters, [w]*and* the wellspring of wisdom *as* a flowing brook.

5 [x]*It is* not good to accept the person of the wicked, to overthrow the righteous in judgment.

6 A fool's lips enter into contention, and his mouth calleth for strokes.

7 [y]A fool's mouth *is* his destruction, and his lips *are* the snare of his soul.

8 [z]The words of a talebearer *are* as wounds, and they go down into the innermost parts of the belly.

9 He also that is slothful in his work is [a]brother to him that is a great waster.

10 [b]The name of the LORD *is* a strong

tower: the righteous runneth into it, and is safe.

11 [c]The rich man's wealth *is* his strong city, and as an high wall in his own conceit.

12 [d]Before destruction the heart of man is haughty, and before honour *is* humility.

13 He that answereth a matter [e]before he heareth *it,* it *is* folly and shame unto him.

14 The spirit of a man will sustain his infirmity; but a wounded spirit who can bear?

15 The heart of the prudent getteth knowledge; and the ear of the wise seeketh knowledge.

16 [f]A man's gift maketh room for him, and bringeth him before great men.

17 *He that is* first in his own cause *seemeth* just; but his neighbour cometh and searcheth him.

18 The lot causeth contentions to cease, and parteth between the mighty.

19 A brother offended *is harder to be won* than a strong city: and *their* contentions *are* like the bars of a castle.

20 [g]A man's belly shall be satisfied with the fruit of his mouth; *and* with the increase of his lips shall he be filled.

21 [h]Death and life *are* in the power of the tongue: and they that love it shall eat the fruit thereof.

22 [i]*Whoso* findeth a wife findeth a good *thing,* and obtaineth favour of the LORD.

23 The poor useth intreaties; but the rich answereth [j]roughly.

24 A man *that hath* friends must shew himself friendly: [k]and there is a friend *that* sticketh closer than a brother.

19 Better [l]*is* the poor that walketh in his integrity, than *he that is* perverse in his lips, and is a fool.

2 Also, *that* the soul *be* without knowledge, *it is* not good; and he that hasteth with *his* feet sinneth.

3 The foolishness of man perverteth his way: [m]and his heart fretteth against the LORD.

4 [n]Wealth maketh many friends; but the poor is separated from his neighbour.

5 [o]A false witness shall not be unpunished, and *he that* speaketh lies shall not escape.

6 [p]Many will intreat the favour of the prince: and [q]every man *is* a friend to him that giveth gifts.

7 [r]All the brethren of the poor do hate him: how much more do his friends go [s]far from him? he pursueth *them with* words, *yet* they *are* wanting *to him.*

8 He that getteth wisdom loveth his own soul: he that keepeth understanding [t]shall find good.

9 [u]A false witness shall not be unpunished, and *he that* speaketh lies shall perish.

10 Delight is not seemly for a fool; much less [v]for a servant to have rule over princes.

11 [w]The discretion of a man deferreth his anger; [x]and *it is* his glory to pass over a transgression.

18:11 *c*ch. 10:15
18:12 *d*ch. 11:2
18:13 *e*John 7:51
18:16 *f*Gen. 32:20; 1 Sam. 25:27; ch. 17:8
18:20 *g*ch. 12:14
18:21 *h*Matt. 12:37
18:22 *i*ch. 19:14
18:23 *j*Jam. 2:3
18:24 *k*ch. 17:17
19:1 *l*ch. 28:6
19:3 *m*Ps. 37:7
19:4 *n*ch. 14:20
19:5 *o*ver. 9; Ex. 23:1; Deut. 19:16; ch. 6:19
19:6 *p*ch. 29:26 *q*ch. 17:8
19:7 *r*ch. 14:20 *s*Ps. 38:11
19:8 *t*ch. 16:20
19:9 *u*ver. 5
19:10 *v*ch. 30:22; Eccl. 10:6
19:11 *w*ch. 14:29; Jam. 1:19 *x*ch. 16:32
19:12 *y*ch. 16:14 *z*Hos. 14:5
19:13 *a*ch. 10:1 *b*ch. 21:9
19:14 *c*2 Cor. 12:14 *d*ch. 18:22
19:15 *e*ch. 6:9 *f*ch. 10:4
19:16 *g*Luke 10:28
19:17 *h*ch. 28:27; Eccl. 11:1; Matt. 10:42; 2 Cor. 9:6; Heb. 6:10
19:18 *i*ch. 13:24
19:21 *j*Job 23:13; Ps. 33:10; ch. 16:1; Isa. 14:26; Acts 5:39; Heb. 6:17
19:23 *k*1 Tim. 4:8
19:24 *l*ch. 15:19
19:25 *m*ch. 21:11 *n*Deut. 13:11 *o*ch. 9:8
19:26 *p*ch. 17:2
19:28 *q*Job 15:16
19:29 *r*ch. 10:13
20:1 *s*Gen. 9:21; ch. 23:29; Isa. 28:7; Hos. 4:11
20:2 *t*ch. 16:14 *u*ch. 8:36
20:3 *v*ch. 17:14
20:4 *w*ch. 10:4 *x*ch. 19:15
20:5 *y*ch. 18:4
20:6 *z*ch. 25:14; Matt. 6:2; Luke 18:11 *a*Ps. 12:1; Luke 18:8

12 [y]The king's wrath *is* as the roaring of a lion; but his favour *is* [z]as dew upon the grass.

13 [a]A foolish son *is* the calamity of his father: [b]and the contentions of a wife *are* a continual dropping.

14 [c]House and riches *are* the inheritance of fathers: and [d]a prudent wife *is* from the LORD.

15 [e]Slothfulness casteth into a deep sleep; and an idle soul shall [f]suffer hunger.

16 [g]He that keepeth the commandment keepeth his own soul; *but* he that despiseth his ways shall die.

17 [h]He that hath pity upon the poor lendeth unto the LORD; and that which he hath given will he pay him again.

18 [i]Chasten thy son while there is hope, and let not thy soul spare for his crying.

19 A man of great wrath shall suffer punishment: for if thou deliver *him,* yet thou must do it again.

20 Hear counsel, and receive instruction, that thou mayest be wise in thy latter end.

21 [j]*There are* many devices in a man's heart; nevertheless the counsel of the LORD, that shall stand.

22 The desire of a man *is* his kindness: and a poor man *is* better than a liar.

23 [k]The fear of the LORD *tendeth* to life: and *he that hath it* shall abide satisfied; he shall not be visited with evil.

24 [l]A slothful *man* hideth his hand in *his* bosom, and will not so much as bring it to his mouth again.

25 [m]Smite a scorner, and the simple [n]will beware: and [o]reprove one that hath understanding, *and* he will understand knowledge.

26 He that wasteth *his* father, *and* chaseth away *his* mother, *is* [p]a son that causeth shame, and bringeth reproach.

27 Cease, my son, to hear the instruction *that causeth* to err from the words of knowledge.

28 An ungodly witness scorneth judgment: and [q]the mouth of the wicked devoureth iniquity.

29 Judgments are prepared for scorners, [r]and stripes for the back of fools.

20 Wine [s]*is* a mocker, strong drink *is* raging: and whosoever is deceived thereby is not wise.

2 [t]The fear of a king *is* as the roaring of a lion: *whoso* provoketh him to anger [u]sinneth *against* his own soul.

3 [v]*It is* an honour for a man to cease from strife: but every fool will be meddling.

4 [w]The sluggard will not plow by reason of the cold; [x]*therefore* shall he beg in harvest, and *have* nothing.

5 [y]Counsel in the heart of man *is like* deep water; but a man of understanding will draw it out.

6 [z]Most men will proclaim every one his own goodness: but [a]a faithful man who can find?

7 [b]The just *man* walketh in his integrity: [c]his children *are* blessed after him.

8 [d]A king that sitteth in the throne of judgment scattereth away all evil with his eyes.

9 [e]Who can say, I have made my heart clean, I am pure from my sin?

10 [f]Divers weights, *and* divers measures, both of them *are* alike abomination to the LORD.

11 Even a child is [g]known by his doings, whether his work *be* pure, and whether *it be* right.

12 [h]The hearing ear, and the seeing eye, the LORD hath made even both of them.

13 [i]Love not sleep, lest thou come to poverty; open thine eyes, *and* thou shalt be satisfied with bread.

14 *It is* naught, *it is* naught, saith the buyer: but when he is gone his way, then he boasteth.

15 There is gold, and a multitude of rubies: but [j]the lips of knowledge *are* a precious jewel.

16 [k]Take his garment that is surety *for* a stranger: and take a pledge of him for a strange woman.

17 [l]Bread of deceit *is* sweet to a man; but afterwards his mouth shall be filled with gravel.

18 [m]*Every* purpose is established by counsel: [n]and with good advice make war.

19 [o]He that goeth about *as* a talebearer revealeth secrets: therefore meddle not with him [p]that flattereth with his lips.

20 [q]Whoso curseth his father or his mother, [r]his lamp shall be put out in obscure darkness.

21 [s]An inheritance *may be* gotten hastily at the beginning; [t]but the end thereof shall not be blessed.

22 [u]Say not thou, I will recompense evil; *but* [v]wait on the LORD, and he shall save thee.

23 [w]Divers weights *are* an abomination unto the LORD; and a false balance *is* not good.

24 [x]Man's goings *are* of the LORD; how can a man then understand his own way?

25 *It is* a snare to the man *who* devoureth *that which is* holy, and [y]after vows to make enquiry.

26 [z]A wise king scattereth the wicked, and bringeth the wheel over them.

27 [a]The spirit of man *is* the candle of the LORD, searching all the inward parts of the belly.

28 [b]Mercy and truth preserve the king: and his throne is upholden by mercy.

29 The glory of young men *is* their strength: and [c]the beauty of old men *is* the grey head.

30 The blueness of a wound cleanseth away evil: so *do* stripes the inward parts of the belly.

21 The king's heart *is* in the hand of the LORD, *as* the rivers of water: he turneth it whithersoever he will.

2 [d]Every way of a man *is* right in his own eyes: [e]but the LORD pondereth the hearts.

3 [f]To do justice and judgment *is* more acceptable to the LORD than sacrifice.

4 [g]An high look, and a proud heart, *and* the plowing of the wicked, *is* sin.

5 [h]The thoughts of the diligent *tend* only to plenteousness; but of every one *that is* hasty only to want.

6 [i]The getting of treasures by a lying tongue *is* a vanity tossed to and fro of them that seek death.

7 The robbery of the wicked shall destroy them; because they refuse to do judgment.

8 The way of man *is* froward and strange: but *as for* the pure, his work *is* right.

9 [j]*It is* better to dwell in a corner of the housetop, than with a brawling woman in a wide house.

10 [k]The soul of the wicked desireth evil: his neighbour findeth no favour in his eyes.

11 [l]When the scorner is punished, the simple is made wise: and when the wise is instructed, he receiveth knowledge.

12 The righteous *man* wisely considereth the house of the wicked: *but God* overthroweth the wicked for *their* wickedness.

13 [m]Whoso stoppeth his ears at the cry of the poor, he also shall cry himself, but shall not be heard.

14 [n]A gift in secret pacifieth anger: and a reward in the bosom strong wrath.

15 *It is* joy to the just to do judgment: [o]but destruction *shall be* to the workers of iniquity.

16 The man that wandereth out of the way of understanding shall remain in the congregation of the dead.

17 He that loveth pleasure *shall be* a poor man: he that loveth wine and oil shall not be rich.

18 [p]The wicked *shall be* a ransom for the righteous, and the transgressor for the upright.

19 [q]*It is* better to dwell in the wilderness, than with a contentious and an angry woman.

20 [r]*There is* treasure to be desired and oil in the dwelling of the wise; but a foolish man spendeth it up.

21 [s]He that followeth after righteousness and mercy findeth life, righteousness, and honour.

22 [t]A wise *man* scaleth the city of the mighty, and casteth down the strength of the confidence thereof.

23 [u]Whoso keepeth his mouth and his tongue keepeth his soul from troubles.

24 Proud *and* haughty scorner *is* his name, who dealeth in proud wrath.

25 [v]The desire of the slothful killeth him; for his hands refuse to labour.

26 He coveteth greedily all the day long: but the [w]righteous giveth and spareth not.

27 [x]The sacrifice of the wicked *is* abomination: how much more, *when* he bringeth it with a wicked mind?

20:7 [b]2 Cor. 1:12 [c]Ps. 37:26
20:8 [d]ver. 26
20:9 [e]1 Kings 8:46; 2 Chron. 6:36; Job 14:4; Ps. 51:5; Eccl. 7:20; 1 Cor. 4:4; 1 John 1:8
20:10 [f]Deut. 25:13; ver. 23; ch. 11:1; Mic. 6:10
20:11 [g]Matt. 7:16
20:12 [h]Ex. 4:11; Ps. 94:9
20:13 [i]ch. 6:9; Rom. 12:11
20:15 [j]Job 28:12; ch. 3:15
20:16 [k]ch. 22:26
20:17 [l]ch. 9:17
20:18 [m]ch. 15:22 [n]Luke 14:31
20:19 [o]ch. 11:13 [p]Rom. 16:18
20:20 [q]Ex. 21:17; Lev. 20:9; Matt. 15:4 [r]Job 18:5; ch. 24:20
20:21 [s]ch. 28:20 [t]Hab. 2:6
20:22 [u]Deut. 32:35; ch. 17:13; Rom. 12:17; 1 Thess. 5:15; 1 Pet. 3:9 [v]2 Sam. 16:12
20:23 [w]ver. 10
20:24 [x]Ps. 37:23; ch. 16:9; Jer. 10:23
20:25 [y]Eccl. 5:4
20:26 [z]Ps. 101:5; ver. 8
20:27 [a]1 Cor. 2:11
20:28 [b]Ps. 101:1; ch. 29:14
20:29 [c]ch. 16:31
21:2 [d]ch. 16:2 [e]ch. 24:12; Luke 16:15
21:3 [f]1 Sam. 15:22; Ps. 50:8; ch. 15:8; Isa. 1:11; Hos. 6:6; Mic. 6:7
21:4 [g]ch. 6:17
21:5 [h]ch. 10:4
21:6 [i]ch. 10:2; 2 Pet. 2:3
21:9 [j]ver. 19; ch. 19:13
21:10 [k]Jam. 4:5
21:11 [l]ch. 19:25
21:13 [m]Matt. 7:2; Jam. 2:13
21:14 [n]ch. 17:8
21:15 [o]ch. 10:29
21:18 [p]ch. 11:8; Isa. 43:3
21:19 [q]ver. 9
21:20 [r]Ps. 112:3; Matt. 25:3
21:21 [s]ch. 15:9; Matt. 5:6
21:22 [t]Eccl. 9:14
21:23 [u]ch. 12:13; Jam. 3:2
21:25 [v]ch. 13:4
21:26 [w]Ps. 37:26
21:27 [x]Ps. 50:9; ch. 15:8; Isa. 66:3; Jer. 6:20; Am. 5:22

28 [y]A false witness shall perish: but the man that heareth speaketh constantly.

29 A wicked man hardeneth his face: but *as for* the upright, he directeth his way.

30 [z]*There is* no wisdom nor understanding nor counsel against the LORD.

31 [a]The horse *is* prepared against the day of battle: but [b]safety *is* of the LORD.

22 A [c]*good* name *is* rather to be chosen than great riches, *and* loving favour rather than silver and gold.

2 [d]The rich and poor meet together: [e]the LORD *is* the maker of them all.

3 [f]A prudent *man* foreseeth the evil, and hideth himself: but the simple pass on, and are punished.

4 [g]By humility *and* the fear of the LORD *are* riches, and honour, and life.

5 [h]Thorns *and* snares *are* in the way of the froward: [i]he that doth keep his soul shall be far from them.

6 [j]Train up a child in the way he should go: and when he is old, he will not depart from it.

7 [k]The rich ruleth over the poor, and the borrower *is* servant to the lender.

8 [l]He that soweth iniquity shall reap vanity: and the rod of his anger shall fail.

9 [m]He that hath a bountiful eye shall be blessed; for he giveth of his bread to the poor.

10 [n]Cast out the scorner, and contention shall go out; yea, strife and reproach shall cease.

11 [o]He that loveth pureness of heart, *for* the grace of his lips the king *shall be* his friend.

12 The eyes of the LORD preserve knowledge, and he overthroweth the words of the transgressor.

13 [p]The slothful *man* saith, *There is* a lion without, I shall be slain in the streets.

14 [q]The mouth of strange women *is* a deep pit: [r]he that is abhorred of the LORD shall fall therein.

15 Foolishness *is* bound in the heart of a child; *but* [s]the rod of correction shall drive it far from him.

16 He that oppresseth the poor to increase his *riches, and* he that giveth to the rich, *shall* surely *come* to want.

17 Bow down thine ear, and hear the words of the wise, and apply thine heart unto my knowledge.

18 For *it is* a pleasant thing if thou keep them within thee; they shall withal be fitted in thy lips.

19 That thy trust may be in the LORD, I have made known to thee this day, even to thee.

20 Have not I written to thee [t]excellent things in counsels and knowledge,

21 [u]That I might make thee know the certainty of the words of truth; [v]that thou mightest answer the words of truth to them that send unto thee?

22 [w]Rob not the poor, because he *is* poor: [x]neither oppress the afflicted in the gate:

23 [y]For the LORD will plead their cause, and spoil the soul of those that spoiled them.

24 Make no friendship with an angry man; and with a furious man thou shalt not go:

25 Lest thou learn his ways, and get a snare to thy soul.

26 [z]Be not thou *one* of them that strike hands, *or* of them that are sureties for debts.

27 If thou hast nothing to pay, why should he [a]take away thy bed from under thee?

28 [b]Remove not the ancient landmark, which thy fathers have set.

29 Seest thou a man diligent in his business? he shall stand before kings; he shall not stand before mean *men*.

23 When thou sittest to eat with a ruler, consider diligently what *is* before thee:

2 And put a knife to thy throat, if thou *be* a man given to appetite.

3 Be not desirous of his dainties: for they *are* deceitful meat.

4 [c]Labour not to be rich: [d]cease from thine own wisdom.

5 Wilt thou set thine eyes upon that which is not? for *riches* certainly make themselves wings; they fly away as an eagle toward heaven.

6 [e]Eat thou not the bread of *him that hath* [f]an evil eye, neither desire thou his dainty meats:

7 For as he thinketh in his heart, so *is* he: Eat and drink, [g]saith he to thee; but his heart *is* not with thee.

8 The morsel *which* thou hast eaten shalt thou vomit up, and lose thy sweet words.

9 [h]Speak not in the ears of a fool: for he will despise the wisdom of thy words.

10 [i]Remove not the old landmark; and enter not into the fields of the fatherless:

11 [j]For their redeemer *is* mighty; he shall plead their cause with thee.

12 Apply thine heart unto instruction and thine ears to the words of knowledge.

13 [k]Withhold not correction from the child: for *if* thou beatest him with the rod, he shall not die.

14 Thou shalt beat him with the rod, and [l]shalt deliver his soul from hell.

15 My son, [m]if thine heart be wise, my heart shall rejoice, even mine.

16 Yea, my reins shall rejoice, when thy lips speak right things.

17 [n]Let not thine heart envy sinners: but [o]*be thou* in the fear of the LORD all the day long.

18 [p]For surely there is an end; and thine expectation shall not be cut off.

19 Hear thou, my son, and be wise, and [q]guide thine heart in the way.

20 [r]Be not among winebibbers; among riotous eaters of flesh:

21 For the drunkard and the glutton shall come to poverty: and [s]drowsiness shall clothe *a man* with rags.

22 [t]Hearken unto thy father that begat

21:28 y ch. 19:5
21:30 z Isa. 8:9; Jer. 9:23; Acts 5:39
21:31 a Ps. 20:7; Isa. 31:1 b Ps. 3:8
22:1 c Eccl. 7:1
22:2 d ch. 29:13; 1 Cor. 12:21 e Job 31:15; ch. 14:31
22:3 f ch. 14:16
22:4 g Ps. 112:3; Matt. 6:33
22:5 h ch. 15:19 i 1 John 5:18
22:6 j Eph. 6:4; 2 Tim. 3:15
22:7 k Jam. 2:6
22:8 l Job 4:8; Hos. 10:13
22:9 m 2 Cor. 9:6
22:10 n Gen. 21:9; Ps. 101:5
22:11 o Ps. 101:6; ch. 16:13
22:13 p ch. 26:13
22:14 q ch. 2:16 r Eccl. 7:26
22:15 s ch. 13:24
22:20 t ch. 8:6
22:21 u Luke 1:3 v 1 Pet. 3:15
22:22 w Ex. 23:6; Job 31:16 x Zech. 7:10; Mal. 3:5
22:23 y 1 Sam. 24:12; Ps. 12:5; ch. 23:11; Jer. 51:36
22:26 z ch. 6:1
22:27 a ch. 20:16
22:28 b Deut. 19:14; ch. 23:10
23:4 c ch. 28:20; 1 Tim. 6:9 d ch. 3:5; Rom. 12:16
23:6 e Ps. 141:4 f Deut. 15:9
23:7 g Ps. 12:2
23:9 h ch. 9:8; Matt. 7:6
23:10 i Deut. 19:14; ch. 22:28
23:11 j Job 31:21; ch. 22:23
23:13 k ch. 13:24
23:14 l 1 Cor. 5:5
23:15 m ver. 24; ch. 29:3
23:17 n Ps. 37:1; ch. 3:31 o ch. 28:14
23:18 p Ps. 37:37; ch. 24:14; Luke 16:25
23:19 q ch. 4:23
23:20 r Isa. 5:22; Matt. 24:49; Luke 21:34; Rom. 13:13; Eph. 5:18
23:21 s ch. 19:15
23:22 t ch. 1:8; Eph. 6:1

thee, and despise not thy mother when she is old.

23 [u]Buy the truth, and sell *it* not; *also* wisdom, and instruction, and understanding.

24 [v]The father of the righteous shall greatly rejoice: and he that begetteth a wise *child* shall have joy of him.

25 Thy father and thy mother shall be glad, and she that bare thee shall rejoice.

26 My son, give me thine heart, and let thine eyes observe my ways.

27 [w]For a whore *is* a deep ditch; and a strange woman *is* a narrow pit.

28 [x]She also lieth in wait as *for* a prey, and increaseth the transgressors among men.

29 [y]Who hath woe? who hath sorrow? who hath contentions? who hath babbling? who hath wounds without cause? who [z]hath redness of eyes?

30 [a]They that tarry long at the wine; they that go to seek [b]mixed wine.

31 Look not thou upon the wine when it is red, when it giveth his colour in the cup, *when* it moveth itself aright.

32 At the last it biteth like a serpent, and stingeth like an adder.

33 Thine eyes shall behold strange women, and thine heart shall utter perverse things.

34 Yea, thou shalt be as he that lieth down in the midst of the sea, or as he that lieth upon the top of a mast.

35 [c]They have stricken me, *shalt thou say, and* I was not sick; they have beaten me, *and* [d]I felt *it* not: [e]when shall I awake? I will seek it yet again.

24 Be not thou [f]envious against evil men, [g]neither desire to be with them.

2 [h]For their heart studieth destruction, and their lips talk of mischief.

3 Through wisdom is an house builded; and by understanding it is established:

4 And by knowledge shall the chambers be filled with all precious and pleasant riches.

5 [i]A wise man *is* strong; yea, a man of knowledge increaseth strength.

6 [j]For by wise counsel thou shalt make thy war: and in multitude of counsellors *there is* safety.

7 [k]Wisdom *is* too high for a fool: he openeth not his mouth in the gate.

8 He that [l]deviseth to do evil shall be called a mischievous person.

9 The thought of foolishness *is* sin: and the scorner *is* an abomination to men.

10 *If* thou faint in the day of adversity, thy strength *is* small.

11 [m]If thou forbear to deliver *them that are* drawn unto death, and *those that are* ready to be slain;

12 If thou sayest, Behold, we knew it not; doth not [n]he that pondereth the heart consider *it?* and he that keepeth thy soul, doth *not* he know *it?* and shall *not* he render to *every* man [o]according to his works?

13 My son, [p]eat thou honey, because *it is* good; and the honeycomb, *which is* sweet to thy taste:

14 [q]So *shall* the knowledge of wisdom *be* unto thy soul: when thou hast found *it,* [r]then there shall be a reward, and thy expectation shall not be cut off.

15 [s]Lay not wait, O wicked *man,* against the dwelling of the righteous; spoil not his resting place:

16 [t]For a just *man* falleth seven times, and riseth up again: [u]but the wicked shall fall into mischief.

17 [v]Rejoice not when thine enemy falleth, and let not thine heart be glad when he stumbleth:

18 Lest the LORD see *it,* and it displease him, and he turn away his wrath from him.

19 [w]Fret not thyself because of evil *men,* neither be thou envious at the wicked;

20 For [x]there shall be no reward to the evil *man;* [y]the candle of the wicked shall be put out.

21 My son, [z]fear thou the LORD and the king: *and* meddle not with them that are given to change:

22 For their calamity shall rise suddenly; and who knoweth the ruin of them both?

23 These *things* also *belong* to the wise. [a]*It is* not good to have respect of persons in judgment.

24 [b]He that saith unto the wicked, Thou *art* righteous; him shall the people curse, nations shall abhor him:

25 But to them that rebuke *him* shall be delight, and a good blessing shall come upon them.

26 *Every man* shall kiss *his* lips that giveth a right answer.

27 [c]Prepare thy work without, and make it fit for thyself in the field; and afterwards build thine house.

28 [d]Be not a witness against thy neighbour without cause; and deceive *not* with thy lips.

29 [e]Say not, I will do so to him as he hath done to me: I will render to the man according to his work.

30 I went by the field of the slothful, and by the vineyard of the man void of understanding;

31 And, lo, [f]it was all grown over with thorns, *and* nettles had covered the face thereof, and the stone wall thereof was broken down.

32 Then I saw, *and* considered *it* well: I looked upon *it, and* received instruction.

33 [g]*Yet* a little sleep, a little slumber, a little folding of the hands to sleep:

34 So shall thy poverty come *as* one that travelleth; and thy want as an armed man.

25 These [h]*are* also proverbs of Solomon, which the men of Hezekiah king of Judah copied out.

2 [i]*It is* the glory of God to conceal a

23:23 [u]ch. 4:5; Matt. 13:44
23:24 [v]ch. 10:1; ver. 15
23:27 [w]ch. 22:14
23:28 [x]ch. 7:12; Eccl. 7:26
23:29 [y]Isa. 5:11 [z]Gen. 49:12
23:30 [a]ch. 20:1; Eph. 5:18 [b]Ps. 75:8; ch. 9:2
23:35 [c]Jer. 5:3; ch. 27:22 [d]Eph. 4:19 [e]Deut. 29:19; Isa. 56:12
24:1 [f]Ps. 37:1; ch. 3:31; ver. 19 [g]Prov. 1:15
24:2 [h]Ps. 10:7
24:5 [i]ch. 21:22; Eccl. 9:16
24:6 [j]ch. 11:14; Luke 14:31
24:7 [k]Ps. 10:5; ch. 14:6
24:8 [l]Rom. 1:30
24:11 [m]Ps. 82:4; Isa. 58:6; 1 John 3:16
24:12 [n]ch. 21:2 [o]Job 34:11; Ps. 62:12; Jer. 32:19; Rom. 2:6; Rev. 2:23
24:13 [p]SSol. 5:1
24:14 [q]Ps. 19:10 [r]ch. 23:18
24:15 [s]Ps. 10:9
24:16 [t]Job 5:19; Ps. 34:19; Mic. 7:8 [u]Esth. 7:10; Am. 5:2; Rev. 18:21
24:17 [v]Job 31:29; Ps. 35:15; ch. 17:5; Obad. 12
24:19 [w]Ps. 37:1; ch. 23:17; ver. 1
24:20 [x]Ps. 11:6 [y]Job 18:5; ch. 13:9
24:21 [z]Rom. 13:7; 1 Pet. 2:17
24:23 [a]Lev. 19:15; Deut. 1:17; ch. 18:5; John 7:24
24:24 [b]ch. 17:15; Isa. 5:23
24:27 [c]1 Kings 5:17; Luke 14:28
24:28 [d]Eph. 4:25
24:29 [e]ch. 20:22; Matt. 5:39; Rom. 12:17
24:31 [f]Gen. 3:18
24:33 [g]ch. 6:9
25:1 [h]1 Kings 4:32
25:2 [i]Deut. 29:29; Rom. 11:33

thing: but the honour of kings *is* [i]to search out a matter.

3 The heaven for height, and the earth for depth, and the heart of kings *is* unsearchable.

4 [k]Take away the dross from the silver, and there shall come forth a vessel for the finer.

5 [l]Take away the wicked *from* before the king, and [m]his throne shall be established in righteousness.

6 Put not forth thyself in the presence of the king, and stand not in the place of great *men:*

7 [n]For better *it is* that it be said unto thee, Come up hither; than that thou shouldest be put lower in the presence of the prince whom thine eyes have seen.

8 [o]Go not forth hastily to strive, lest *thou know not* what to do in the end thereof, when thy neighbour hath put thee to shame.

9 [p]Debate thy cause with thy neighbour *himself;* and discover not a secret to another:

10 Lest he that heareth *it* put thee to shame, and thine infamy turn not away.

11 [q]A word fitly spoken *is like* apples of gold in pictures of silver.

12 *As* an earring of gold, and an ornament of fine gold, *so is* a wise reprover upon an obedient ear.

13 [r]As the cold of snow in the time of harvest, *so is* a faithful messenger to them that send him: for he refresheth the soul of his masters.

14 [s]Whoso boasteth himself of a false gift *is like* [t]clouds and wind without rain.

15 [u]By long forbearing is a prince persuaded, and a soft tongue breaketh the bone.

16 [v]Hast thou found honey? eat so much as is sufficient for thee, lest thou be filled therewith, and vomit it.

17 Withdraw thy foot from thy neighbour's house; lest he be weary of thee, and *so* hate thee.

18 [w]A man that beareth false witness against his neighbour *is* a maul, and a sword, and a sharp arrow.

19 Confidence in an unfaithful man in time of trouble *is like* a broken tooth, and a foot out of joint.

20 *As* he that taketh away a garment in cold weather, *and as* vinegar upon nitre, so *is* he that [x]singeth songs to an heavy heart.

21 [y]If thine enemy be hungry, give him bread to eat; and if he be thirsty, give him water to drink:

22 For thou shalt heap coals of fire upon his head, [z]and the LORD shall reward thee.

23 [a]The north wind driveth away rain: so *doth* an angry countenance [b]a backbiting tongue.

24 [c]*It is* better to dwell in the corner of the housetop, than with a brawling woman and in a wide house.

25 *As* cold waters to a thirsty soul, so *is* good news from a far country.

26 A righteous man falling down before the wicked *is as* a troubled fountain, and a corrupt spring.

27 [d]*It is* not good to eat much honey: so *for men* [e]to search their own glory *is not* glory.

28 [f]He that *hath* no rule over his own spirit *is like* a city *that is* broken down, *and* without walls.

26 As snow in summer, [g]and as rain in harvest, so honour is not seemly for a fool.

2 As the bird by wandering, as the swallow by flying, so [h]the curse causeless shall not come.

3 [i]A whip for the horse, a bridle for the ass, and a rod for the fool's back.

4 Answer not a fool according to his folly, lest thou also be like unto him.

5 [j]Answer a fool according to his folly, lest he be wise in his own conceit.

6 He that sendeth a message by the hand of a fool cutteth off the feet, *and* drinketh damage.

7 The legs of the lame are not equal: so *is* a parable in the mouth of fools.

8 As he that bindeth a stone in a sling, so *is* he that giveth honour to a fool.

9 *As* a thorn goeth up into the hand of a drunkard, so *is* a parable in the mouth of fools.

10 The great *God* that formed all *things* both rewardeth the fool, and rewardeth transgressors.

11 [k]As a dog returneth to his vomit, [l]*so* a fool returneth to his folly.

12 [m]Seest thou a man wise in his own conceit? *there is* more hope of a fool than of him.

13 [n]The slothful *man* saith, *There is* a lion in the way; a lion *is* in the streets.

14 *As* the door turneth upon his hinges, so *doth* the slothful upon his bed.

15 [o]The slothful hideth his hand in *his* bosom; it grieveth him to bring it again to his mouth.

16 The sluggard *is* wiser in his own conceit than seven men that can render a reason.

17 He that passeth by, *and* meddleth with strife *belonging* not to him, *is like* one that taketh a dog by the ears.

18 As a mad *man* who casteth firebrands, arrows, and death,

19 So *is* the man *that* deceiveth his neighbour, and saith, [p]Am not I in sport?

20 Where no wood is, *there* the fire goeth out: so [q]where *there is* no talebearer, the strife ceaseth.

21 [r]*As* coals *are* to burning coals, and wood to fire; so *is* a contentious man to kindle strife.

22 [s]The words of a talebearer *are* as wounds, and they go down into the innermost parts of the belly.

23 Burning lips and a wicked heart *are like* a potsherd covered with silver dross.

25:2 [i]Job 29:16
25:4 [k]2 Tim. 2:21
25:5 [l]ch. 20:8 [m]ch. 16:12
25:7 [n]Luke 14:8
25:8 [o]ch. 17:14; Matt. 5:25
25:9 [p]Matt. 5:25
25:11 [q]ch. 15:23; Isa. 50:4
25:13 [r]ch. 13:17
25:14 [s]ch. 20:6 [t]Jude 12
25:15 [u]Gen. 32:4; 1 Sam. 25:24; ch. 15:1
25:16 [v]ver. 27
25:18 [w]Ps. 57:4; ch. 12:18
25:20 [x]Dan. 6:18; Rom. 12:15
25:21 [y]Ex. 23:4; Matt. 5:44; Rom. 12:20
25:22 [z]2 Sam. 16:12
25:23 [a]Job 37:22 [b]Ps. 101:5
25:24 [c]ch. 19:13
25:27 [d]ver. 16 [e]ch. 27:2
25:28 [f]ch. 16:32
26:1 [g]1 Sam. 12:17
26:2 [h]Num. 23:8; Deut. 23:5
26:3 [i]Ps. 32:9; ch. 10:13
26:5 [j]Matt. 16:1-4
26:11 [k]2 Pet. 2:22 [l]Ex. 8:15
26:12 [m]ch. 29:20; Luke 18:11; Rom. 12:16; Rev. 3:17
26:13 [n]ch. 22:13
26:15 [o]ch. 19:24
26:19 [p]Eph. 5:4
26:20 [q]ch. 22:10
26:21 [r]ch. 15:18
26:22 [s]ch. 18:8

24 He that hateth dissembleth with his lips, and layeth up deceit within him;

25 [t]When he speaketh fair, believe him not: for *there are* seven abominations in his heart.

26 *Whose* hatred is covered by deceit, his wickedness shall be shewed before the *whole* congregation.

27 [u]Whoso diggeth a pit shall fall therein: and he that rolleth a stone, it will return upon him.

28 A lying tongue hateth *those that are* afflicted by it; and a flattering mouth worketh ruin.

27 Boast [v]not thyself of to morrow; for thou knowest not what a day may bring forth.

2 [w]Let another man praise thee, and not thine own mouth; a stranger, and not thine own lips.

3 A stone *is* heavy, and the sand weighty; but a fool's wrath *is* heavier than them both.

4 Wrath *is* cruel, and anger *is* outrageous; but [x]who *is* able to stand before envy?

5 [y]Open rebuke *is* better than secret love.

6 [z]Faithful *are* the wounds of a friend; but the kisses of an enemy *are* deceitful.

7 The full soul loatheth an honeycomb; but [a]to the hungry soul every bitter thing is sweet.

8 As a bird that wandereth from her nest, so *is* a man that wandereth from his place.

9 Ointment and perfume rejoice the heart: so *doth* the sweetness of a man's friend by hearty counsel.

10 Thine own friend, and thy father's friend, forsake not; neither go into thy brother's house in the day of thy calamity: *for* [b]better *is* a neighbour *that is* near than a brother far off.

11 [c]My son, be wise, and make my heart glad, [d]that I may answer him that reproacheth me.

12 [e]A prudent *man* foreseeth the evil, *and* hideth himself; *but* the simple pass on, *and* are punished.

13 [f]Take his garment that is surety for a stranger, and take a pledge of him for a strange woman.

14 He that blesseth his friend with a loud voice, rising early in the morning, it shall be counted a curse to him.

15 [g]A continual dropping in a very rainy day and a contentious woman are alike.

16 Whosoever hideth her hideth the wind, and the ointment of his right hand, *which* bewrayeth *itself*.

17 Iron sharpeneth iron; so a man sharpeneth the countenance of his friend.

18 [h]Whoso keepeth the fig tree shall eat the fruit thereof: so he that waiteth on his master shall be honoured.

19 As in water face *answereth* to face, so the heart of man to man.

20 [i]Hell and destruction are never full; so [j]the eyes of man are never satisfied.

21 [k]*As* the fining pot for silver, and the furnace for gold; so *is* a man to his praise.

22 [l]Though thou shouldest bray a fool in a mortar among wheat with a pestle, *yet* will not his foolishness depart from him.

23 Be thou diligent to know the state of thy flocks, *and* look well to thy herds.

24 For riches *are* not for ever: and doth the crown *endure* to every generation?

25 [m]The hay appeareth, and the tender grass sheweth itself, and herbs of the mountains are gathered.

26 The lambs *are* for thy clothing, and the goats *are* the price of the field.

27 And *thou shalt have* goats' milk enough for thy food, for the food of thy household, and *for* the maintenance for thy maidens.

28 The [n]wicked flee when no man pursueth: but the righteous are bold as a lion.

2 For the transgression of a land many *are* the princes thereof: but by a man of understanding *and* knowledge the state *thereof* shall be prolonged.

3 [o]A poor man that oppresseth the poor *is like* a sweeping rain which leaveth no food.

4 [p]They that forsake the law praise the wicked: [q]but such as keep the law contend with them.

5 [r]Evil men understand not judgment: but [s]they that seek the LORD understand all *things*.

6 [t]Better *is* the poor that walketh in his uprightness, than *he that is* perverse *in his* ways, though he *be* rich.

7 [u]Whoso keepeth the law *is* a wise son: but he that is a companion of riotous *men* shameth his father.

8 [v]He that by usury and unjust gain increaseth his substance, he shall gather it for him that will pity the poor.

9 [w]He that turneth away his ear from hearing the law, [x]even his prayer *shall be* abomination.

10 [y]Whoso causeth the righteous to go astray in an evil way, he shall fall himself into his own pit: [z]but the upright shall have good *things* in possession.

11 The rich man *is* wise in his own conceit; but the poor that hath understanding searcheth him out.

12 [a]When righteous *men* do rejoice, *there is* great glory: but when the wicked rise, a man is hidden.

13 [b]He that covereth his sins shall not prosper: but whoso confesseth and forsaketh *them* shall have mercy.

14 Happy *is* the man [c]that feareth alway: but [d]he that hardeneth his heart shall fall into mischief.

15 [e]*As* a roaring lion, and a ranging bear; [f]*so is* a wicked ruler over the poor people.

16 The prince that wanteth understanding *is* also a great oppressor: *but* he that hateth covetousness shall prolong *his* days.

17 [g]A man that doeth violence to the blood of *any* person shall flee to the pit; let no man stay him.

26:25 *t*Ps. 28:3; Jer. 9:8
26:27 *u*Ps. 7:15; ch. 28:10; Eccl. 10:8
27:1 *v*Luke 12:19; Jam. 4:13
27:2 *w*ch. 25:27
27:4 *x*1 John 3:12
27:5 *y*ch. 28:23; Gal. 2:14
27:6 *z*Ps. 141:5
27:7 *a*Job 6:7
27:10 *b*ch. 17:17
27:11 *c*ch. 10:1 *d*Ps. 127:5
27:12 *e*ch. 22:3
27:13 *f*Ex. 22:26; ch. 20:16
27:15 *g*ch. 19:13
27:18 *h*1 Cor. 9:7
27:20 *i*ch. 30:16; Hab. 2:5 *j*Eccl. 1:8
27:21 *k*ch. 17:3
27:22 *l*Isa. 1:5; Jer. 5:3; ch. 23:35
27:25 *m*Ps. 104:14
28:1 *n*Lev. 26:17; Ps. 53:5
28:3 *o*Matt. 18:28
28:4 *p*Ps. 10:3; Rom. 1:32 *q*1 Kings 18:18; Matt. 3:7; Eph. 5:11
28:5 *r*Ps. 92:6 *s*John 7:17; 1 Cor. 2:15; 1 John 2:20
28:6 *t*ch. 19:1; ver. 18
28:7 *u*ch. 29:3
28:8 *v*Job 27:16; ch. 13:22; Eccl. 2:26
28:9 *w*Zech. 7:11 *x*Ps. 66:18; ch. 15:8
28:10 *y*ch. 26:27 *z*Matt. 6:33
28:12 *a*ver. 28; ch. 11:10; Eccl. 10:6
28:13 *b*Ps. 32:3; 1 John 1:8
28:14 *c*Ps. 16:8; ch. 23:17 *d*Rom. 2:5
28:15 *e*1 Pet. 5:8 *f*Ex. 1:14; Matt. 2:16
28:17 *g*Gen. 9:6; Ex. 21:14

18 [h]Whoso walketh uprightly shall be saved: but [i]*he that is* perverse *in his* ways shall fall at once.

19 [j]He that tilleth his land shall have plenty of bread: but he that followeth after vain *persons* shall have poverty enough.

20 A faithful man shall abound with blessings: [k]but he that maketh haste to be rich shall not be innocent.

21 [l]To have respect of persons *is* not good: for [m]for a piece of bread *that* man will transgress.

22 [n]He that hasteth to be rich *hath* an evil eye, and considereth not that poverty shall come upon him.

23 [o]He that rebuketh a man afterwards shall find more favour than he that flattereth with the tongue.

24 Whoso robbeth his father or his mother, and saith, *It is* no transgression; the same [p]*is* the companion of a destroyer.

25 [q]He that is of a proud heart stirreth up strife: [r]but he that putteth his trust in the LORD shall be made fat.

26 He that trusteth in his own heart is a fool: but whoso walketh wisely, he shall be delivered.

27 [s]He that giveth unto the poor shall not lack: but he that hideth his eyes shall have many a curse.

28 [t]When the wicked rise, [u]men hide themselves: but when they perish, the righteous increase.

29 [v]He, that being often reproved hardeneth *his* neck, shall suddenly be destroyed, and that without remedy.

2 [w]When the righteous are in authority, the people rejoice: but when the wicked beareth rule, [x]the people mourn.

3 [y]Whoso loveth wisdom rejoiceth his father: [z]but he that keepeth company with harlots spendeth *his* substance.

4 The king by judgment establisheth the land: but he that receiveth gifts overthroweth it.

5 A man that flattereth his neighbour spreadeth a net for his feet.

6 In the transgression of an evil man *there is* a snare: but the righteous doth sing and rejoice.

7 [a]The righteous considereth the cause of the poor: *but* the wicked regardeth not to know *it*.

8 [b]Scornful men bring a city into a snare: but wise *men* [c]turn away wrath.

9 *If* a wise man contendeth with a foolish man, [d]whether he rage or laugh, *there is* no rest.

10 [e]The bloodthirsty hate the upright: but the just seek his soul.

11 A [f]fool uttereth all his mind: but a wise *man* keepeth it in till afterwards.

12 If a ruler hearken to lies, all his servants *are* wicked.

13 The poor and the deceitful man [g]meet together: [h]the LORD lighteneth both their eyes.

14 [i]The king that [j]faithfully judgeth the poor, his throne shall be established for ever.

15 [k]The rod and reproof give wisdom: but [l]a child left *to himself* bringeth his mother to shame.

16 When the wicked are multiplied, transgression increaseth: [m]but the righteous shall see their fall.

17 [n]Correct thy son, and he shall give thee rest; yea, he shall give delight unto thy soul.

18 [o]Where *there is* no vision, the people perish: but [p]he that keepeth the law, happy *is* he.

19 A servant will not be corrected by words: for though he understand he will not answer.

20 Seest thou a man *that is* hasty in his words? [q]*there is* more hope of a fool than of him.

21 He that delicately bringeth up his servant from a child shall have him become *his* son at the length.

22 [r]An angry man stirreth up strife, and a furious man aboundeth in transgression.

23 [s]A man's pride shall bring him low: but honour shall uphold the humble in spirit.

24 Whoso is partner with a thief hateth his own soul: [t]he heareth cursing, and bewrayeth *it* not.

25 [u]The fear of man bringeth a snare: but whoso putteth his trust in the LORD shall be safe.

26 [v]Many seek the ruler's favour; but *every* man's judgment *cometh* from the LORD.

27 An unjust man *is* an abomination to the just: and *he that is* upright in the way *is* abomination to the wicked.

30 The words of Agur the son of Jakeh, *even* [w]the prophecy: the man spake unto Ithiel, even unto Ithiel and Ucal,

2 [x]Surely I *am* more brutish than *any* man, and have not the understanding of a man.

3 I neither learned wisdom, nor have the knowledge of the holy.

4 [y]Who hath ascended up into heaven, or descended? [z]who hath gathered the wind in his fists? who hath bound the waters in a garment? who hath established all the ends of the earth? what *is* his name, and what *is* his son's name, if thou canst tell?

5 [a]Every word of God *is* pure: [b]he *is* a shield unto them that put their trust in him.

6 [c]Add thou not unto his words, lest he reprove thee, and thou be found a liar.

7 Two *things* have I required of thee; deny me *them* not before I die:

8 Remove far from me vanity and lies: give me neither poverty nor riches; [d]feed me with food convenient for me:

9 [e]Lest I be full, and deny *thee*, and say, Who *is* the LORD? or lest I be poor, and steal, and take the name of my God *in vain*.

10 Accuse not a servant unto his master, lest he curse thee, and thou be found guilty.

11 *There is* a generation *that* curseth

28:18 [h]ch. 10:9 [i]ver. 6
28:19 [j]ch. 12:11
28:20 [k]ch. 13:11; ver. 22; 1 Tim. 6:9
28:21 [l]ch. 18:5 [m]Ezek. 13:19
28:22 [n]ver. 20
28:23 [o]ch. 27:5
28:24 [p]ch. 18:9
28:25 [q]ch. 13:10 [r]1 Tim. 6:6
28:27 [s]Deut. 15:7; ch. 19:17
28:28 [t]ver. 12; ch. 29:2 [u]Job 24:4
29:1 [v]1 Sam. 2:25; 2 Chron. 36:16; ch. 1:24-27
29:2 [w]Esth. 8:15; ch. 11:10 [x]Esth. 3:15
29:3 [y]ch. 10:1 [z]ch. 5:9; Luke 15:13
29:7 [a]Job 29:16; Ps. 41:1
29:8 [b]ch. 11:11 [c]Ezek. 22:30
29:9 [d]Matt. 11:17
29:10 [e]Gen. 4:5; 1 John 3:12
29:11 [f]Judg. 16:17; ch. 12:16
29:13 [g]ch. 22:2 [h]Matt. 5:45
29:14 [i]ch. 20:28 [j]Ps. 72:2
29:15 [k]ver. 17 [l]ch. 10:1
29:16 [m]Ps. 37:36
29:17 [n]ch. 13:24; ver. 15
29:18 [o]1 Sam. 3:1; Am. 8:11 [p]John 13:17; Jam. 1:25
29:20 [q]ch. 26:12
29:22 [r]ch. 15:18
29:23 [s]Job 22:29; ch. 15:33; Isa. 66:2; Dan. 4:30; Matt. 23:12; Luke 14:11; Acts 12:23; Jam. 4:6; 1 Pet. 5:5
29:24 [t]Lev. 5:1
29:25 [u]Gen. 12:12
29:26 [v]Ps. 20:9; ch. 19:6
30:1 [w]ch. 31:1
30:2 [x]Ps. 73:22
30:4 [y]John 3:13 [z]Job 38:4; Ps. 104:3; Isa. 40:12
30:5 [a]Ps. 12:6 [b]Ps. 18:30
30:6 [c]Deut. 4:2; Rev. 22:18
30:8 [d]Matt. 6:11
30:9 [e]Deut. 8:12; Neh. 9:25; Job 31:24; Hos. 13:6

their father, and doth not bless their
mother.
12 *There is* a generation [f]*that are* pure in
their own eyes, and *yet* is not washed from
their filthiness.
13 *There is* a generation, O how [g]lofty
are their eyes! and their eyelids are
lifted up.
14 [h]*There is* a generation, whose teeth
are as swords, and their jaw teeth *as* knives,
[i]to devour the poor from off the earth, and
the needy from *among* men.
15 The horseleach hath two daughters,
crying, Give, give. There are three *things*
that are never satisfied, *yea*, four *things* say
not, *It is* enough:
16 [j]The grave; and the barren womb; the
earth *that* is not filled with water; and the
fire *that* saith not, *It is* enough.
17 [k]The eye *that* mocketh at *his* father,
and despiseth to obey *his* mother, the ravens of the valley shall pick it out, and the
young eagles shall eat it.
18 There be three *things which* are too
wonderful for me, yea, four which I know
not:
19 The way of an eagle in the air; the way
of a serpent upon a rock; the way of a ship
in the midst of the sea; and the way of a man
with a maid.
20 Such *is* the way of an adulterous
woman; she eateth, and wipeth her mouth,
and saith, I have done no wickedness.
21 For three *things* the earth is disquieted, and for four *which* it cannot bear:
22 [l]For a servant when he reigneth; and
a fool when he is filled with meat;
23 For an odious *woman* when she is married; and an handmaid that is heir to her
mistress.
24 There be four *things which are* little
upon the earth, but they *are* exceeding wise:
25 [m]The ants *are* a people not strong, yet
they prepare their meat in the summer;
26 [n]The conies *are but* a feeble folk, yet
make they their houses in the rocks;
27 The locusts have no king, yet go they
forth all of them by bands;
28 The spider taketh hold with her hands,
and is in kings' palaces.
29 There be three *things* which go well,
yea, four are comely in going:
30 A lion *which is* strongest among
beasts, and turneth not away for any;
31 A greyhound; an he goat also; and a
king, against whom *there is* no rising up.
32 If thou hast done foolishly in lifting up
thyself, or if thou hast thought evil, [o]*lay*
thine hand upon thy mouth.
33 Surely the churning of milk bringeth
forth butter, and the wringing of the nose
bringeth forth blood: so the forcing of wrath
bringeth forth strife.

31

The words of king Lemuel, [p]the
prophecy that his mother taught him.
2 What, my son? and what, [q]the son of
my womb? and what, the son of my vows?
3 [r]Give not thy strength unto women, nor
thy ways [s]to that which destroyeth kings.
4 [t]*It is* not for kings, O Lemuel, *it is* not
for kings to drink wine; nor for princes
strong drink:
5 [u]Lest they drink, and forget the law,
and pervert the judgment of any of the afflicted.
6 [v]Give strong drink unto him that is
ready to perish, and wine unto those that be
of heavy hearts.
7 Let him drink, and forget his poverty,
and remember his misery no more.
8 [w]Open thy mouth for the dumb [x]in the
cause of all such as are appointed to destruction.
9 Open thy mouth, [y]judge righteously,
and [z]plead the cause of the poor and
needy.
10 ¶ [a]Who can find a virtuous woman?
for her price *is* far above rubies.
11 The heart of her husband doth safely
trust in her, so that he shall have no need of
spoil.
12 She will do him good and not evil all
the days of her life.
13 She seeketh wool, and flax, and worketh willingly with her hands.
14 She is like the merchants' ships; she
bringeth her food from afar.
15 [b]She riseth also while it is yet night,
and [c]giveth meat to her household, and a
portion to her maidens.
16 She considereth a field, and buyeth it:
with the fruit of her hands she planteth a
vineyard.
17 She girdeth her loins with strength,
and strengtheneth her arms.
18 She perceiveth that her merchandise *is*
good: her candle goeth not out by night.
19 She layeth her hands to the spindle,
and her hands hold the distaff.
20 [d]She stretcheth out her hand to the
poor; yea, she reacheth forth her hands to
the needy.
21 She is not afraid of the snow for her
household: for all her household *are* clothed
with scarlet.
22 She maketh herself coverings of tapestry; her clothing *is* silk and purple.
23 [e]Her husband is known in the gates,
when he sitteth among the elders of the
land.
24 She maketh fine linen, and selleth *it*;
and delivereth girdles unto the merchant.
25 Strength and honour *are* her clothing;
and she shall rejoice in time to come.
26 She openeth her mouth with wisdom;
and in her tongue *is* the law of kindness.
27 She looketh well to the ways of her
household, and eateth not the bread of idleness.
28 Her children arise up, and call her
blessed; her husband *also*, and he praiseth
her.
29 Many daughters have done virtuously,
but thou excellest them all.

30:12 [f]Luke 18:11
30:13 [g]Ps. 131:1; ch. 6:17
30:14 [h]Job 29:17; Ps. 52:2; ch. 12:18 [i]Ps. 14:4; Am. 8:4
30:16 [j]ch. 27:20; Hab. 2:5
30:17 [k]Gen. 9:22; Lev. 20:9; ch. 20:20
30:22 [l]ch. 19:10; Eccl. 10:7
30:25 [m]ch. 6:6
30:26 [n]Ps. 104:18
30:32 [o]Job 21:5; Eccl. 8:3; Mic. 7:16
31:1 [p]ch. 30:1
31:2 [q]Isa. 49:15
31:3 [r]ch. 5:9 [s]Deut. 17:17; Neh. 13:26; ch. 7:26; Hos. 4:11
31:4 [t]Eccl. 10:17
31:5 [u]Hos. 4:11
31:6 [v]Ps. 104:15
31:8 [w]Job 29:15 [x]1 Sam. 19:4; Esth. 4:16
31:9 [y]Lev. 19:15; Deut. 1:16 [z]Job 29:12; Isa. 1:17; Jer. 22:16
31:10 [a]ch. 12:4
31:15 [b]Rom. 12:11 [c]Luke 12:42
31:20 [d]Eph. 4:28; Heb. 13:16
31:23 [e]ch. 12:4

30 Favour *is* deceitful, and beauty *is* vain: *but* a woman *that* feareth the LORD, she shall be praised.

31 Give her of the fruit of her hands; and let her own works praise her in the gates.

ECCLESIASTES

Solomon wrote Ecclesiastes sometime later than 970 B.C. Throughout the book of Ecclesiastes, the preacher (writer) tries to evaluate life in terms of various goals. The book becomes an essay of comparisons between the life of a person without God and one with a God-centered focus.

The phrase, "vanities of vanities, all is vanity" and "to everything there is a season" (Chapter 3) are probably the most recognized scripture from Ecclesiastes.

I. Introduction and theme, 1:1–1:2
II. The futility of human life, 1:3–2:23
III. Life as God intended, 2:24–3:22
IV. The problems of human life, 4:1–6:12
V. Coping in this life, 7:1–12:8
VI. Conclusion, 12:9–12:14

---

1 The words [a]of the Preacher, the son of David, king in Jerusalem.

2 [b]Vanity of vanities, saith the Preacher, vanity of vanities; [c]all *is* vanity.

3 [d]What profit hath a man of all his labour which he taketh under the sun?

4 *One* generation passeth away, and *another* generation cometh: [e]but the earth abideth for ever.

5 [f]The sun also ariseth, and the sun goeth down, and hasteth to his place where he arose.

6 [g]The wind goeth toward the south, and turneth about unto the north; it whirleth about continually, and the wind returneth again according to his circuits.

7 [h]All the rivers run into the sea; yet the sea *is* not full; unto the place from whence the rivers come, thither they return again.

8 All things *are* full of labour; man cannot utter *it:* [i]the eye is not satisfied with seeing, nor the ear filled with hearing.

9 [j]The thing that hath been, it *is that* which shall be; and that which is done *is* that which shall be done: and *there is* no new *thing* under the sun.

10 Is there *any* thing whereof it may be said, See, this *is* new? it hath been already of old time, which was before us.

11 *There is* no remembrance of former *things;* neither shall there be *any* remembrance of *things* that are to come with *those* that shall come after.

12 ¶ [k]I the Preacher was king over Israel in Jerusalem.

13 And I gave my heart to seek and search out by wisdom concerning all *things* that are done under heaven: [l]this sore travail hath God given to the sons of man to be exercised therewith.

14 I have seen all the works that are done under the sun; and, behold, all *is* vanity and vexation of spirit.

15 [m]*That which is* crooked cannot be made straight: and that which is wanting cannot be numbered.

16 I communed with mine own heart, saying, Lo, I am come to great estate, and have gotten [n]more wisdom than all *they* that have been before me in Jerusalem: yea, my heart had great experience of wisdom and knowledge.

17 [o]And I gave my heart to know wisdom, and to know madness and folly: I perceived that this also is vexation of spirit.

18 For [p]in much wisdom *is* much grief: and he that increaseth knowledge increaseth sorrow.

2 [q]I said in mine heart, Go to now, I will prove thee with mirth, therefore enjoy pleasure: and, behold, [r]this also *is* vanity.

2 [s]I said of laughter, *It is* mad: and of mirth, What doeth it?

3 [t]I sought in mine heart to give myself unto wine, yet acquainting mine heart with wisdom; and to lay hold on folly, till I might see what *was* that good for the sons of men, which they should do under the heaven all the days of their life.

4 I made me great works; I builded me houses; I planted me vineyards:

5 I made me gardens and orchards, and I planted trees in them of all *kind of* fruits:

6 I made me pools of water, to water therewith the wood that bringeth forth trees:

7 I got *me* servants and maidens, and had servants born in my house; also I had great possessions of great and small cattle above all that were in Jerusalem before me:

8 [u]I gathered me also silver and gold, and the peculiar treasure of kings and of the

1:1 [a]ver. 12; ch. 7:27
1:2 [b]Ps. 39:5; ch. 12:8 [c]Rom. 8:20
1:3 [d]ch. 2:22
1:4 [e]Ps. 104:5
1:5 [f]Ps. 19:5
1:6 [g]John 3:8
1:7 [h]Job 38:10; Ps. 104:8
1:8 [i]Prov. 27:20
1:9 [j]ch. 8:15
1:12 [k]ver. 1
1:13 [l]Gen. 3:19; ch. 3:10
1:15 [m]ch. 7:13
1:16 [n]1 Kings 3:12; ch. 2:9
1:17 [o]ch. 2:3; 1 Thess. 5:21
1:18 [p]ch. 12:12
2:1 [q]Luke 12:19 [r]Isa. 50:11
2:2 [s]Prov. 14:13; ch. 7:6
2:3 [t]ch. 1:17
2:8 [u]1 Kings 9:28

provinces: I gat me men singers and women
singers, and the delights of the sons of men,
as musical instruments, and that of all sorts.
9 So [v]I was great, and increased more
than all that were before me in Jerusalem:
also my wisdom remained with me.
10 And whatsoever mine eyes desired I
kept not from them, I withheld not my heart
from any joy; for my heart rejoiced in all my
labour: and [w]this was my portion of all my
labour.
11 Then I looked on all the works that my
hands had wrought, and on the labour that
I had laboured to do: and, behold, all *was*
[x]vanity and vexation of spirit, and *there*
was no profit under the sun.
12 ¶ And I turned myself to behold wisdom, [y]and madness, and folly: for what *can*
the man *do* that cometh after the king? *even*
that which hath been already done.
13 Then I saw that wisdom excelleth
folly, as far as light excelleth darkness.
14 [z]The wise man's eyes *are* in his head;
but the fool walketh in darkness: and I myself perceived also that [a]one event happeneth to them all.
15 Then said I in my heart, As it happeneth to the fool, so it happeneth even to me;
and why was I then more wise? Then I said
in my heart, that this also *is* vanity.
16 For *there is* no remembrance of the
wise more than of the fool for ever; seeing
that which now *is* in the days to come shall
all be forgotten. And how dieth the wise
man? as the fool.
17 Therefore I hated life; because the
work that is wrought under the sun *is* grievous unto me: for all *is* vanity and vexation of
spirit.
18 ¶ Yea, I hated all my labour which I
had taken under the sun: because [b]I should
leave it unto the man that shall be after me.
19 And who knoweth whether he shall be
a wise *man* or a fool? yet shall he have rule
over all my labour wherein I have laboured,
and wherein I have shewed myself wise under the sun. This *is* also vanity.
20 Therefore I went about to cause my
heart to despair of all the labour which I
took under the sun.
21 For there is a man whose labour *is* in
wisdom, and in knowledge, and in equity;
yet to a man that hath not laboured therein
shall he leave it *for* his portion. This also *is*
vanity and a great evil.
22 [c]For what hath man of all his labour,
and of the vexation of his heart, wherein he
hath laboured under the sun?
23 For all his days *are* [d]sorrows, and his
travail grief; yea, his heart taketh not rest in
the night. This is also vanity.
24 ¶ [e]*There is* nothing better for a man,
than that he should eat and drink, and *that*
he should make his soul enjoy good in his
labour. This also I saw, that it *was* from the
hand of God.
25 For who can eat, or who else can hasten *hereunto,* more than I?
26 For *God* giveth to a man that *is* good in
his sight wisdom, and knowledge, and joy:
but to the sinner he giveth travail, to gather
and to heap up, that [f]he may give to *him*
that is good before God. This also *is* vanity
and vexation of spirit.

3 To every *thing there is* a season, and
a [g]time to every purpose under the
heaven:
2 A time to be born, and [h]a time to die; a
time to plant, and a time to pluck up *that*
which is planted;
3 A time to kill, and a time to heal; a time
to break down, and a time to build up;
4 A time to weep, and a time to laugh; a
time to mourn, and a time to dance;
5 A time to cast away stones, and a time
to gather stones together; a time to embrace, and [i]a time to refrain from embracing;
6 A time to get, and a time to lose; a time
to keep, and a time to cast away;
7 A time to rend, and a time to sew; [j]a
time to keep silence, and a time to speak;
8 A time to love, and a time to [k]hate; a
time of war, and a time of peace.
9 [l]What profit hath he that worketh in
that wherein he laboureth?
10 [m]I have seen the travail, which God
hath given to the sons of men to be exercised in it.
11 He hath made every *thing* beautiful in
his time: also he hath set the world in their
heart, so that [n]no man can find out the
work that God maketh from the beginning
to the end.
12 [o]I know that *there is* no good in them,
but for *a man* to rejoice, and to do good in
his life.
13 And also [p]that every man should eat
and drink, and enjoy the good of all his labour, it *is* the gift of God.
14 I know that, whatsoever God doeth, it
shall be for ever: [q]nothing can be put to it,
nor any thing taken from it: and God doeth
it, that *men* should fear before him.
15 [r]That which hath been is now; and
that which is to be hath already been; and
God requireth that which is past.
16 ¶ And moreover [s]I saw under the sun
the place of judgment, *that* wickedness *was*
there; and the place of righteousness, *that*
iniquity *was* there.
17 I said in mine heart, [t]God shall judge
the righteous and the wicked: for *there is* [u]a
time there for every purpose and for every
work.
18 I said in mine heart concerning the estate of the sons of men, that God might
manifest them, and that they might see that
they themselves are beasts.
19 [v]For that which befalleth the sons of
men befalleth beasts; even one thing befalleth them: as the one dieth, so dieth the
other; yea, they have all one breath; so that
a man hath no preeminence above a beast:
for all *is* vanity.

2:9 [v]ch. 1:16
2:10 [w]ch. 3:22
2:11 [x]ch. 1:3
2:12 [y]ch. 1:17
2:14 [z]Prov. 17:24; ch. 8:1 [a]Ps. 49:10; ch. 9:2
2:18 [b]Ps. 49:10
2:22 [c]ch. 1:3
2:23 [d]Job 5:7
2:24 [e]ch. 3:12
2:26 [f]Job 27:16; Prov. 28:8
3:1 [g]ver. 17; ch. 8:6
3:2 [h]Heb. 9:27
3:5 [i]Joel 2:16; 1 Cor. 7:5
3:7 [j]Am. 5:13
3:8 [k]Luke 14:26
3:9 [l]ch. 1:3
3:10 [m]ch. 1:13
3:11 [n]ch. 8:17; Rom. 11:33
3:12 [o]ver. 22
3:13 [p]ch. 2:24
3:14 [q]Jam. 1:17
3:15 [r]ch. 1:9
3:16 [s]ch. 5:8
3:17 [t]Rom. 2:6; 2 Cor. 5:10; 2 Thess. 1:6 [u]ver. 1
3:19 [v]Ps. 49:12; ch. 2:16

20 All go unto one place; [w]all are of the dust, and all turn to dust again.

21 [x]Who knoweth the spirit of man that goeth upward, and the spirit of the beast that goeth downward to the earth?

22 [y]Wherefore I perceive that *there is* nothing better, than that a man should rejoice in his own works; for [z]that *is* his portion: [a]for who shall bring him to see what shall be after him?

4 So I returned, and considered all the [b]oppressions that are done under the sun: and behold the tears of *such as were* oppressed, and they had no comforter; and on the side of their oppressors *there was* power; but they had no comforter.

2 [c]Wherefore I praised the dead which are already dead more than the living which are yet alive.

3 [d]Yea, better *is he* than both they, which hath not yet been, who hath not seen the evil work that is done under the sun.

4 ¶ Again, I considered all travail, and every right work, that for this a man is envied of his neighbour. This *is* also vanity and vexation of spirit.

5 [e]The fool foldeth his hands together, and eateth his own flesh.

6 [f]Better *is* an handful *with* quietness, than both the hands full *with* travail and vexation of spirit.

7 ¶ Then I returned, and I saw vanity under the sun.

8 There is one *alone,* and *there is* not a second; yea, he hath neither child nor brother: yet *is there* no end of all his labour; neither is his [g]eye satisfied with riches; [h]neither *saith he,* For whom do I labour, and bereave my soul of good? This *is* also vanity, yea, it *is* a sore travail.

9 ¶ Two *are* better than one; because they have a good reward for their labour.

10 For if they fall, the one will lift up his fellow: but woe to him *that is* alone when he falleth; for *he hath* not another to help him up.

11 Again, if two lie together, then they have heat: but how can one be warm *alone?*

12 And if one prevail against him, two shall withstand him; and a threefold cord is not quickly broken.

13 ¶ Better *is* a poor and a wise child than an old and foolish king, who will no more be admonished.

14 For out of prison he cometh to reign; whereas also *he that is* born in his kingdom becometh poor.

15 I considered all the living which walk under the sun, with the second child that shall stand up in his stead.

16 *There is* no end of all the people, *even* of all that have been before them: they also that come after shall not rejoice in him. Surely this also *is* vanity and vexation of spirit.

5 Keep [i]thy foot when thou goest to the house of God, and be more ready to hear, [j]than to give the sacrifice of fools: for they consider not that they do evil.

2 Be not rash with thy mouth, and let not thine heart be hasty to utter *any* thing before God: for God *is* in heaven, and thou upon earth: therefore let thy words [k]be few.

3 For a dream cometh through the multitude of business; and [l]a fool's voice *is known* by multitude of words.

4 [m]When thou vowest a vow unto God, defer not to pay it; for *he hath* no pleasure in fools: [n]pay that which thou hast vowed.

5 [o]Better *is it* that thou shouldest not vow, than that thou shouldest vow and not pay.

6 Suffer not thy mouth to cause thy flesh to sin; [p]neither say thou before the angel, that it *was* an error: wherefore should God be angry at thy voice, and destroy the work of thine hands?

7 For in the multitude of dreams and many words *there are* also *divers* vanities: but [q]fear thou God.

8 ¶ If thou [r]seest the oppression of the poor, and violent perverting of judgment and justice in a province, marvel not at the matter: for [s]*he that is* higher than the highest regardeth; and *there be* higher than they.

9 ¶ Moreover the profit of the earth is for all: the king *himself* is served by the field.

10 He that loveth silver shall not be satisfied with silver; nor he that loveth abundance with increase: this *is* also vanity.

11 When goods increase, they are increased that eat them: and what good *is there* to the owners thereof, saving the beholding *of them* with their eyes?

12 The sleep of a labouring man *is* sweet, whether he eat little or much: but the abundance of the rich will not suffer him to sleep.

13 [t]There is a sore evil *which* I have seen under the sun, *namely,* riches kept for the owners thereof to their hurt.

14 But those riches perish by evil travai and he begetteth a son, and *there is* nothing in his hand.

15 [u]As he came forth of his mother's womb, naked shall he return to go as he came, and shall take nothing of his labour, which he may carry away in his hand.

16 And this also *is* a sore evil, *that* in all points as he came, so shall he go: and [v]what profit hath he [w]that hath laboured for the wind?

17 All his days also [x]he eateth in darkness, and *he hath* much sorrow and wrath with his sickness.

18 ¶ Behold *that* which I have seen: [y]*it is* good and comely *for one* to eat and to drink, and to enjoy the good of all his labour that he taketh under the sun all the days of his life, which God giveth him: [z]for it *is* his portion.

19 [a]Every man also to whom God hath given riches and wealth, and hath given him power to eat thereof, and to take his por-

3:20 [w]Gen. 3:19
3:21 [x]ch. 12:7
3:22 [y]ver. 12; ch. 2:24 [z]ch. 2:10 [a]ch. 6:12
4:1 [b]ch. 3:16
4:2 [c]Job 3:17
4:3 [d]Job 3:11; ch. 6:3
4:5 [e]Prov. 6:10
4:6 [f]Prov. 15:16
4:8 [g]Prov. 27:20; 1 John 2:16 [h]Ps. 39:6
5:1 [i]Ex. 3:5; Isa. 1:12 [j]1 Sam. 15:22; Ps. 50:8; Prov. 15:8; Hos. 6:6
5:2 [k]Prov. 10:19; Matt. 6:7
5:3 [l]Prov. 10:19
5:4 [m]Num. 30:2; Deut. 23:21; Ps. 50:14 [n]Ps. 66:13
5:5 [o]Prov. 20:25; Acts 5:4
5:6 [p]1 Cor. 11:10
5:7 [q]ch. 12:13
5:8 [r]ch. 3:16 [s]Ps. 12:5
5:13 [t]ch. 6:1
5:15 [u]Job 1:21; Ps. 49:17; 1 Tim. 6:7
5:16 [v]ch. 1:3 [w]Prov. 11:29
5:17 [x]Ps. 127:2
5:18 [y]ch. 2:24; 1 Tim. 6:17 [z]ch. 2:10
5:19 [a]ch. 2:24

tion, and to rejoice in his labour; this *is* the
gift of God.
20 For he shall not much remember the
days of his life; because God answereth *him*
in the joy of his heart.

6 There [b]is an evil which I have seen under the sun, and it *is* common among
men:
2 A man to whom God hath given riches,
wealth, and honour, [c]so that he wanteth
nothing for his soul of all that he desireth,
[d]yet God giveth him not power to eat
thereof, but a stranger eateth it: this *is*
vanity, and it *is* an evil disease.
3 ¶ If a man beget an hundred *children*,
and live many years, so that the days of his
years be many, and his soul be not filled
with good, and [e]also *that* he have no
burial; I say, *that* [f]an untimely birth *is* better than he.
4 For he cometh in with vanity, and departeth in darkness, and his name shall be
covered with darkness.
5 Moreover he hath not seen the sun, nor
known *any thing*: this hath more rest than
the other.
6 ¶ Yea, though he live a thousand years
twice *told*, yet hath he seen no good: do not
all go to one place?
7 [g]All the labour of man *is* for his mouth,
and yet the appetite is not filled.
8 For what hath the wise more than the
fool? what hath the poor, that knoweth to
walk before the living?
9 ¶ Better *is* the sight of the eyes than the
wandering of the desire: this *is* also vanity
and vexation of spirit.
10 That which hath been is named already, and it is known that it *is* man: [h]nei-
ther may he contend with him that is
mightier than he.
11 ¶ Seeing there be many things that increase vanity, what *is* man the better?
12 For who knoweth what *is* good for
man in *this* life, all the days of his vain life
which he spendeth as [i]a shadow? for [j]who
can tell a man what shall be after him under
the sun?

7 A [k]good name *is* better than precious
ointment; and the day of death than the
day of one's birth.
2 ¶ *It is* better to go to the house of mourning, than to go to the house of feasting: for
that *is* the end of all men; and the living will
lay *it* to his heart.
3 Sorrow *is* better than laughter: [l]for by
the sadness of the countenance the heart is
made better.
4 The heart of the wise *is* in the house of
mourning; but the heart of fools *is* in the
house of mirth.
5 [m]*It is* better to hear the rebuke of the
wise, than for a man to hear the song of
fools.
6 [n]For as the crackling of thorns under a
pot, so *is* the laughter of the fool: this also *is*
vanity.
7 ¶ Surely oppression maketh a wise man
mad; [o]and a gift destroyeth the heart.
8 Better *is* the end of a thing than the beginning thereof: *and* [p]the patient in spirit *is*
better than the proud in spirit.
9 [q]Be not hasty in thy spirit to be angry:
for anger resteth in the bosom of fools.
10 Say not thou, What is *the cause* that
the former days were better than these? for
thou dost not enquire wisely concerning
this.
11 ¶ Wisdom *is* good with an inheritance:
and *by it there is* profit [r]to them that see the
sun.
12 For wisdom *is* a defence, *and* money *is*
a defence: but the excellency of knowledge
is, that wisdom giveth life to them that
have it.
13 Consider the work of God: for [s]who
can make *that* straight, which he hath made
crooked?
14 [t]In the day of prosperity be joyful, but
in the day of adversity consider: God also
hath set the one over against the other, to
the end that man should find nothing after
him.
15 All *things* have I seen in the days of my
vanity: [u]there is a just *man* that perisheth in
his righteousness, and there is a wicked
man that prolongeth *his life* in his wickedness.
16 [v]Be not righteous over much; [w]neither
make thyself over wise: why shouldest thou
destroy thyself?
17 Be not over much wicked, neither be
thou foolish: [x]why shouldest thou die before thy time?
18 *It is* good that thou shouldest take hold
of this; yea, also from this withdraw not
thine hand: for he that feareth God shall
come forth of them all.
19 [y]Wisdom strengtheneth the wise more
than ten mighty *men* which are in the city.
20 [z]For *there is* not a just man upon
earth, that doeth good, and sinneth not.
21 Also take no heed unto all words that
are spoken; lest thou hear thy servant curse
thee:
22 For oftentimes also thine own heart
knoweth that thou thyself likewise hast
cursed others.
23 ¶ All this have I proved by wisdom: [a]I
said, I will be wise; but it *was* far from me.
24 [b]That which is far off, and [c]exceeding
deep, who can find it out?
25 [d]I applied mine heart to know, and to
search, and to seek out wisdom, and the
reason *of things*, and to know the wickedness of folly, even of foolishness *and* madness:
26 [e]And I find more bitter than death the
woman, whose heart *is* snares and nets, *and*
her hands *as* bands: whoso pleaseth God
shall escape from her; but the sinner shall
be taken by her.
27 Behold, this have I found, saith [f]the
preacher, *counting* one by one, to find out
the account:

6:1 b ch. 5:13
6:2 c Job 21:10; Ps. 17:14 d Luke 12:20
6:3 e 2 Kings 9:35; Isa. 14:19; Jer. 22:19 f Job 3:16; Ps. 58:8; ch. 4:3
6:7 g Prov. 16:26
6:10 h Job 9:32; Isa. 45:9; Jer. 49:19
6:12 i Ps. 102:11; Jam. 4:14 j Ps. 39:6; ch. 8:7
7:1 k Prov. 15:30
7:3 l 2 Cor. 7:10
7:5 m Ps. 141:5; Prov. 13:18
7:6 n Ps. 118:12; ch. 2:2
7:7 o Ex. 23:8; Deut. 16:19
7:8 p Prov. 14:29
7:9 q Prov. 14:17; Jam. 1:19
7:11 r ch. 11:7
7:13 s Job 12:14; ch. 1:15; Isa. 14:27
7:14 t ch. 3:4; Deut. 28:47
7:15 u ch. 8:14
7:16 v Prov. 25:16 w Rom. 12:3
7:17 x Job 15:32; Ps. 55:23; Prov. 10:27
7:19 y Prov. 21:22; ch. 9:16
7:20 z 1 Kings 8:46; 2 Chron. 6:36; Prov. 20:9; Rom. 3:23; 1 John 1:8
7:23 a Rom. 1:22
7:24 b Job 28:12; 1 Tim. 6:16 c Rom. 11:33
7:25 d ch. 1:17
7:26 e Prov. 5:3
7:27 f ch. 1:1

28 Which yet my soul seeketh, but I find
not: [g]one man among a thousand have I
found; but a woman among all those have I
not found.
29 Lo, this only have I found, [h]that God
hath made man upright; but [i]they have
sought out many inventions.

8 Who *is* as the wise *man?* and who knoweth the interpretation of a thing? [j]a
man's wisdom maketh his face to shine, and
[k]the boldness of his face shall be changed.
2 I *counsel thee* to keep the king's commandment, [l]and *that* in regard of the oath
of God.
3 [m]Be not hasty to go out of his sight:
stand not in an evil thing; for he doeth whatsoever pleaseth him.
4 Where the word of a king *is, there is*
power: and [n]who may say unto him, What
doest thou?
5 Whoso keepeth the commandment
shall feel no evil thing: and a wise man's
heart discerneth both time and judgment.
6 ¶ Because [o]to every purpose there is
time and judgment, therefore the misery of
man *is* great upon him.
7 [p]For he knoweth not that which shall
be: for who can tell him when it shall be?
8 [q]*There is* no man that hath power
[r]over the spirit to retain the spirit; neither
hath he power in the day of death: and *there*
is no discharge in *that* war; neither shall
wickedness deliver those that are given
to it.
9 All this have I seen, and applied my
heart unto every work that is done under
the sun: *there is* a time wherein one man
ruleth over another to his own hurt.
10 And so I saw the wicked buried, who
had come and gone from the place of the
holy, and they were forgotten in the city
where they had so done: this *is* also vanity.
11 [s]Because sentence against an evil
work is not executed speedily, therefore the
heart of the sons of men is fully set in them
to do evil.
12 ¶ [t]Though a sinner do evil an hundred
times, and his *days* be prolonged, yet surely
I know that [u]it shall be well with them that
fear God, which fear before him:
13 But it shall not be well with the wicked,
neither shall he prolong *his* days, *which are*
as a shadow; because he feareth not before
God.
14 There is a vanity which is done upon
the earth; that there be just *men,* unto whom
it [v]happeneth according to the work of the
wicked; again, there be wicked *men,* to
whom it happeneth according to the work
of the righteous: I said that this also *is*
vanity.
15 [w]Then I commended mirth, because a
man hath no better thing under the sun,
than to eat, and to drink, and to be merry:
for that shall abide with him of his labour
the days of his life, which God giveth him
under the sun.
16 ¶ When I applied mine heart to know
wisdom, and to see the business that is done
upon the earth: (for also *there is that* neither day nor night seeth sleep with his
eyes:)
17 Then I beheld all the work of God, that
[x]a man cannot find out the work that is
done under the sun: because though a man
labour to seek *it* out, yet he shall not find *it;*
yea farther; though a wise *man* think to
know *it,* [y]yet shall he not be able to find *it.*

9 For all this I considered in my heart
even to declare all this, [z]that the righteous, and the wise, and their works, *are* in
the hand of God: no man knoweth either
love or hatred *by* all *that is* before them.
2 [a]All *things come* alike to all: *there is*
one event to the righteous, and to the
wicked; to the good and to the clean, and to
the unclean; to him that sacrificeth, and to
him that sacrificeth not: as *is* the good, so *is*
the sinner; *and* he that sweareth, as *he* that
feareth an oath.
3 This *is* an evil among all *things* that are
done under the sun, that *there is* one event
unto all: yea, also the heart of the sons of
men is full of evil, and madness *is* in their
heart while they live, and after that *they go*
to the dead.
4 ¶ For to him that is joined to all the living there is hope: for a living dog is better
than a dead lion.
5 For the living know that they shall die:
but [b]the dead know not any thing, neither
have they any more a reward; for [c]the
memory of them is forgotten.
6 Also their love, and their hatred, and
their envy, is now perished; neither have
they any more a portion for ever in any
thing that is done under the sun.
7 ¶ Go thy way, [d]eat thy bread with joy,
and drink thy wine with a merry heart; for
God now accepteth thy works.
8 Let thy garments be always white; and
let thy head lack no ointment.
9 Live joyfully with the wife whom thou
lovest all the days of the life of thy vanity
which he hath given thee under the sun, all
the days of thy vanity: [e]for that *is* thy portion in *this* life, and in thy labour which
thou takest under the sun.
10 Whatsoever thy hand findeth to do, do
it with thy might; for *there is* no work, nor
device, nor knowledge, nor wisdom, in the
grave, whither thou goest.
11 ¶ I returned, [f]and saw under the sun,
that the race *is* not to the swift, nor the battle to the strong, neither yet bread to the
wise, nor yet riches to men of understanding, nor yet favour to men of skill; but time
and chance happeneth to them all.
12 For [g]man also knoweth not his time:
as the fishes that are taken in an evil net,
and as the birds that are caught in the snare;
so *are* the sons of men [h]snared in an evil
time, when it falleth suddenly upon them.
13 ¶ This wisdom have I seen also under
the sun, and it *seemed* great unto me:
14 [i]*There was* a little city, and few men

7:28 [g]Job 33:23; Ps. 12:1
7:29 [h]Gen. 1:27 [i]Gen. 3:6
8:1 [j]Prov. 4:8; Acts 6:15 [k]Deut. 28:50
8:2 [l]1 Chron. 29:24; Ezek. 17:18; Rom. 13:5
8:3 [m]ch. 10:4
8:4 [n]Job 34:18
8:6 [o]ch. 3:1
8:7 [p]Prov. 24:22; ch. 6:12
8:8 [q]Ps. 49:6 [r]Job 14:5
8:11 [s]Ps. 10:6; Isa. 26:10
8:12 [t]Isa. 65:20; Rom. 2:5 [u]Ps. 37:11; Prov. 1:32; Isa. 3:10; Matt. 25:34
8:14 [v]Ps. 73:14; ch. 2:14
8:15 [w]ch. 2:24
8:17 [x]Job 5:9; ch. 3:11; Rom. 11:33 [y]Ps. 73:16
9:1 [z]ch. 8:14
9:2 [a]Job 21:7; Ps. 73:3; Mal. 3:15
9:5 [b]Job 14:21; Isa. 63:16 [c]Job 7:8; Isa. 26:14
9:7 [d]ch. 8:15
9:9 [e]ch. 2:10
9:11 [f]Am. 2:14; Jer. 9:23
9:12 [g]ch. 8:7 [h]Prov. 29:6; Luke 12:20; 1 Thess. 5:3
9:14 [i]2 Sam. 20:16-22

within it; and there came a great king against it, and besieged it, and built great bulwarks against it:

15 Now there was found in it a poor wise man, and he by his wisdom delivered the city; yet no man remembered that same poor man.

16 [j]Then said I, Wisdom *is* better than strength: nevertheless [k]the poor man's wisdom *is* despised, and his words are not heard.

17 The words of wise *men are* heard in quiet more than the cry of him that ruleth among fools.

18 [l]Wisdom *is* better than weapons of war: but [m]one sinner destroyeth much good.

10 Dead flies cause the ointment of the apothecary to send forth a stinking savour: *so doth* a little folly him that is in reputation for wisdom *and* honour.

2 A wise man's heart *is* at his right hand; but a fool's heart at his left.

3 Yea also, when he that is a fool walketh by the way, his wisdom faileth *him*, [n]and he saith to every one *that* he *is* a fool.

4 If the spirit of the ruler rise up against thee, [o]leave not thy place; for [p]yielding pacifieth great offences.

5 There is an evil *which* I have seen under the sun, as an error *which* proceedeth from the ruler:

6 [q]Folly is set in great dignity, and the rich sit in low place.

7 I have seen servants [r]upon horses, and princes walking as servants upon the earth.

8 [s]He that diggeth a pit shall fall into it; and whoso breaketh an hedge, a serpent shall bite him.

9 Whoso removeth stones shall be hurt therewith; *and* he that cleaveth wood shall be endangered thereby.

10 If the iron be blunt, and he do not whet the edge, then must he put to more strength: but wisdom *is* profitable to direct.

11 Surely the serpent will bite [t]without enchantment; and a babbler is no better.

12 [u]The words of a wise man's mouth *are* gracious; but [v]the lips of a fool will swallow up himself.

13 The beginning of the words of his mouth *is* foolishness: and the end of his talk *is* mischievous madness.

14 [w]A fool also is full of words: a man cannot tell what shall be; and [x]what shall be after him, who can tell him?

15 The labour of the foolish wearieth every one of them, because he knoweth not how to go to the city.

16 ¶ [y]Woe to thee, O land, when thy king *is* a child, and thy princes eat in the morning!

17 Blessed *art* thou, O land, when thy king *is* the son of nobles, and [z]thy princes eat in due season, for strength, and not for drunkenness!

18 ¶ By much slothfulness the building decayeth; and through idleness of the hands the house droppeth through.

19 ¶ A feast is made for laughter, and [a]wine maketh merry: but money answereth all *things*.

20 ¶ [b]Curse not the king, no not in thy thought; and curse not the rich in thy bedchamber: for a bird of the air shall carry the voice, and that which hath wings shall tell the matter.

11 Cast thy bread [c]upon the waters: [d]for thou shalt find it after many days.

2 [e]Give a portion [f]to seven, and also to eight; [g]for thou knowest not what evil shall be upon the earth.

3 If the clouds be full of rain, they empty *themselves* upon the earth: and if the tree fall toward the south, or toward the north, in the place where the tree falleth, there it shall be.

4 He that observeth the wind shall not sow; and he that regardeth the clouds shall not reap.

5 As [h]thou knowest not what *is* the way of the spirit, [i]*nor* how the bones *do grow* in the womb of her that is with child: even so thou knowest not the works of God who maketh all.

6 In the morning sow thy seed, and in the evening withhold not thine hand: for thou knowest not whether shall prosper, either this or that, or whether they both *shall be* alike good.

7 ¶ Truly the light *is* sweet, and a pleasant *thing it is* for the eyes [j]to behold the sun:

8 But if a man live many years, *and* rejoice in them all; yet let him remember the days of darkness; for they shall be many. All that cometh *is* vanity.

9 ¶ Rejoice, O young man, in thy youth; and let thy heart cheer thee in the days of thy youth, [k]and walk in the ways of thine heart, and in the sight of thine eyes: but know thou, that for all these *things* [l]God will bring thee into judgment.

10 Therefore remove sorrow from thy heart, and [m]put away evil from thy flesh: [n]for childhood and youth *are* vanity.

12 Remember [o]now thy Creator in the days of thy youth, while the evil days come not, nor the years draw nigh, [p]when thou shalt say, I have no pleasure in them;

2 While the sun, or the light, or the moon, or the stars, be not darkened, nor the clouds return after the rain:

3 In the day when the keepers of the house shall tremble, and the strong men shall bow themselves, and the grinders cease because they are few, and those that look out of the windows be darkened,

4 And the doors shall be shut in the streets, when the sound of the grinding is low, and he shall rise up at the voice of the bird, and all [q]the daughters of musick shall be brought low;

5 Also *when* they shall be afraid of *that which is* high, and fears *shall be* in the way,

9:16 [j]Prov. 21:22; ch. 7:19; ver. 18 [k]Mark 6:2
9:18 [l]ver. 16 [m]Josh. 7:1
10:3 [n]Prov. 13:16
10:4 [o]ch. 8:3 [p]1 Sam. 25:24; Prov. 25:15
10:6 [q]Esth. 3:1
10:7 [r]Prov. 19:10
10:8 [s]Ps. 7:15; Prov. 26:27
10:11 [t]Ps. 58:4; Jer. 8:17
10:12 [u]Prov. 10:32 [v]Prov. 10:14
10:14 [w]Prov. 15:2 [x]ch. 3:22
10:16 [y]Isa. 3:4
10:17 [z]Prov. 31:4
10:19 [a]Ps. 104:15
10:20 [b]Ex. 22:28; Acts 23:5
11:1 [c]Isa. 32:20 [d]Deut. 15:10; Prov. 19:17; Matt. 10:42; 2 Cor. 9:8; Gal. 6:9; Heb. 6:10
11:2 [e]Ps. 112:9; Luke 6:30; 1 Tim. 6:18 [f]Mic. 5:5 [g]Eph. 5:16
11:5 [h]John 3:8 [i]Ps. 139:14
11:7 [j]ch. 7:11
11:9 [k]Num. 15:39 [l]ch. 12:14; Rom. 2:6-11
11:10 [m]2 Cor. 7:1; 2 Tim. 2:22 [n]Ps. 39:5
12:1 [o]Prov. 22:6; Lam. 3:27 [p]2 Sam. 19:35
12:4 [q]2 Sam. 19:35

and the almond tree shall flourish, and the
grasshopper shall be a burden, and desire
shall fail: because man goeth to [r]his long
home, and [s]the mourners go about the
streets:
6 Or ever the silver cord be loosed, or the
golden bowl be broken, or the pitcher be
broken at the fountain, or the wheel broken
at the cistern.
7 [t]Then shall the dust return to the earth
as it was: [u]and the spirit shall return unto
God [v]who gave it.
8 ¶ [w]Vanity of vanities, saith the
preacher; all *is* vanity.
9 And moreover, because the preacher
was wise, he still taught the people knowledge; yea, he gave good heed, and sought
out, *and* [x]set in order many proverbs.
10 The preacher sought to find out acceptable words: and *that which was* written
was upright, *even* words of truth.
11 The words of the wise *are* as goads,
and as nails fastened *by* the masters of assemblies, *which* are given from one shepherd.
12 And further, by these, my son, be admonished: of making many books *there is*
no end; and [y]much study *is* a weariness of
the flesh.
13 ¶ Let us hear the conclusion of the
whole matter: [z]Fear God, and keep his
commandments: for this *is* the whole *duty*
of man.
14 For [a]God shall bring every work into
judgment, with every secret thing, whether
it be good, or whether *it be* evil.

12:5 [r]Job 17:13 [s]Jer. 9:17
12:7 [t]Gen. 3:19; Job 34:15; Ps. 90:3 [u]ch. 3:21 [v]Num. 16:22; Job 34:14; Isa. 57:16; Zech. 12:1
12:8 [w]Ps. 62:9; ch. 1:2
12:9 [x]1 Kings 4:32
12:12 [y]ch. 1:18
12:13 [z]Deut. 6:2
12:14 [a]ch. 11:9; Matt. 12:36; Acts 17:30; Rom. 2:16; 1 Cor. 4:5; 2 Cor. 5:10

SONG OF SOLOMON

Solomon was the author of the Song of Solomon, written in 970 B.C. or later. This is the story of Solomon's love for a Shulamite woman, his efforts to court her, and his eventual marriage to her. The language is similar to a series of lyric poems written in dialogue form, each demonstrating a deepening love.

I. Solomon and the Shulamite woman meet, 1:1–2:7
II. The courtship begins, 2:8–3:5
III. The marriage, 3:6–3:11
IV. The marriage is consummated, 4:1–5:1
V. Problems beset the marriage, 5:2–6:13
VI. The marriage commitment continues, 7:1–8:14

---

1 The [a]song of songs, which *is* Solomon's.
2 Let him kiss me with the kisses of his
mouth: [b]for thy love *is* better than wine.
3 Because of the savour of thy good ointments thy name *is as* ointment poured forth,
therefore do the virgins love thee.
4 [c]Draw me, [d]we will run after thee: the
king [e]hath brought me into his chambers:
we will be glad and rejoice in thee, we will
remember thy love more than wine: the upright love thee.
5 I *am* black, but comely, O ye daughters
of Jerusalem, as the tents of Kedar, as the
curtains of Solomon.
6 Look not upon me, because I *am* black,
because the sun hath looked upon me: my
mother's children were angry with me; they
made me the keeper of the vineyards; *but*
mine own vineyard have I not kept.
7 Tell me, O thou whom my soul loveth,
where thou feedest, where thou makest *thy*
flock to rest at noon: for why should I be as
one that turneth aside by the flocks of thy
companions?
8 ¶ If thou know not, [f]O thou fairest
among women, go thy way forth by the
footsteps of the flock, and feed thy kids beside the shepherds' tents.
9 I have compared thee, [g]O my love, [h]to
a company of horses in Pharaoh's chariots.
10 [i]Thy cheeks are comely with rows *of*
jewels, thy neck with chains *of gold.*
11 We will make thee borders of gold
with studs of silver.
12 ¶ While the king *sitteth* at his table,
my spikenard sendeth forth the smell
thereof.
13 A bundle of myrrh *is* my wellbeloved
unto me; he shall lie all night betwixt my
breasts.
14 My beloved *is* unto me *as* a cluster of
camphire in the vineyards of En-gedi.
15 [j]Behold, thou *art* fair, my love; behold, thou *art* fair; thou *hast* doves' eyes.
16 Behold, thou *art* fair, my beloved, yea,
pleasant: also our bed *is* green.
17 The beams of our house *are* cedar, *and*
our rafters of fir.
2 I *am* the rose of Sharon, *and* the lily of
the valleys.

1:1 [a]1 Kings 4:32
1:2 [b]ch. 4:10
1:4 [c]Hos. 11:4; John 6:44 [d]Phil. 3:12 [e]Ps. 45:14; John 14:2; Eph. 2:6
1:8 [f]ch. 5:9
1:9 [g]ch. 2:2; John 15:14 [h]2 Chron. 1:16
1:10 [i]Ezek. 16:11
1:15 [j]ch. 4:1

2 As the lily among thorns, so *is* my love among the daughters.

3 As the apple tree among the trees of the wood, so *is* my beloved among the sons. I sat down under his shadow with great delight, [k]and his fruit *was* sweet to my taste.

4 He brought me to the banqueting house, and his banner over me *was* love.

5 Stay me with flagons, comfort me with apples: for I *am* sick of love.

6 [l]His left hand *is* under my head, and his right hand doth embrace me.

7 [m]I charge you, O ye daughters of Jerusalem, by the roes, and by the hinds of the field, that ye stir not up, nor awake *my* love, till he please.

8 ¶ The voice of my beloved! behold, he cometh leaping upon the mountains, skipping upon the hills.

9 [n]My beloved is like a roe or a young hart: behold, he standeth behind our wall, he looketh forth at the windows, shewing himself through the lattice.

10 My beloved spake, and said unto me, [o]Rise up, my love, my fair one, and come away.

11 For, lo, the winter is past, the rain is over *and* gone;

12 The flowers appear on the earth; the time of the singing *of birds* is come, and the voice of the turtle is heard in our land;

13 The fig tree putteth forth her green figs, and the vines *with* the tender grape give a *good* smell. [p]Arise, my love, my fair one, and come away.

14 ¶ O my dove, *that art* in the clefts of the rock, in the secret *places* of the stairs, let me see thy countenance, [q]let me hear thy voice; for sweet *is* thy voice, and thy countenance *is* comely.

15 Take us [r]the foxes, the little foxes, that spoil the vines: for our vines *have* tender grapes.

16 ¶ [s]My beloved *is* mine, and I *am* his: he feedeth among the lilies.

17 [t]Until the day break, and the shadows flee away, turn, my beloved, and be thou [u]like a roe or a young hart upon the mountains of Bether.

3 By [v]night on my bed I sought him whom my soul loveth: I sought him, but I found him not.

2 I will rise now, and go about the city in the streets, and in the broad ways I will seek him whom my soul loveth: I sought him, but I found him not.

3 [w]The watchmen that go about the city found me: *to whom I said,* Saw ye him whom my soul loveth?

4 *It was* but a little that I passed from them, but I found him whom my soul loveth: I held him, and would not let him go, until I had brought him into my mother's house, and into the chamber of her that conceived me.

5 [x]I charge you, O ye daughters of Jerusalem, by the roes, and by the hinds of the field, that ye stir not up, nor awake *my* love, till he please.

6 ¶ [y]Who *is* this that cometh out of the wilderness like pillars of smoke, perfumed with myrrh and frankincense, with all powders of the merchant?

7 Behold his bed, which *is* Solomon's; threescore valiant men *are* about it, of the valiant of Israel.

8 They all hold swords, *being* expert in war: every man *hath* his sword upon his thigh because of fear in the night.

9 King Solomon made himself a chariot of the wood of Lebanon.

10 He made the pillars thereof *of* silver, the bottom thereof *of* gold, the covering of it *of* purple, the midst thereof being paved *with* love, for the daughters of Jerusalem.

11 Go forth, O ye daughters of Zion, and behold king Solomon with the crown wherewith his mother crowned him in the day of his espousals, and in the day of the gladness of his heart.

4 Behold, [z]thou *art* fair, my love; behold, thou *art* fair; thou *hast* doves' eyes within thy locks: thy hair *is* as a [a]flock of goats, that appear from mount Gilead.

2 [b]Thy teeth *are* like a flock *of sheep that are even* shorn, which came up from the washing; whereof every one bear twins, and none *is* barren among them.

3 Thy lips *are* like a thread of scarlet, and thy speech *is* comely: [c]thy temples *are* like a piece of a pomegranate within thy locks.

4 [d]Thy neck *is* like the tower of David builded [e]for an armoury, whereon there hang a thousand bucklers, all shields of mighty men.

5 [f]Thy two breasts *are* like two young roes that are twins, which feed among the lilies.

6 [g]Until the day break, and the shadows flee away, I will get me to the mountain of myrrh, and to the hill of frankincense.

7 [h]Thou *art* all fair, my love; *there is* no spot in thee.

8 ¶ Come with me from Lebanon, *my* spouse, with me from Lebanon: look from the top of Amana, from the top of Shenir [i]and Hermon, from the lions' dens, from the mountains of the leopards.

9 Thou hast ravished my heart, my sister, *my* spouse; thou hast ravished my heart with one of thine eyes, with one chain of thy neck.

10 How fair is thy love, my sister, *my* spouse! [j]how much better is thy love than wine! and the smell of thine ointments than all spices!

11 Thy lips, O *my* spouse, drop *as* the honeycomb: [k]honey and milk *are* under thy tongue; and the smell of thy garments *is* [l]like the smell of Lebanon.

12 A garden inclosed *is* my sister, *my* spouse; a spring shut up, a fountain sealed.

13 Thy plants *are* an orchard of pomegranates, with pleasant fruits; camphire, with spikenard,

2:3 [k]Rev. 22:1
2:6 [l]ch. 8:3
2:7 [m]ch. 3:5
2:9 [n]ver. 17
2:10 [o]ver. 13
2:13 [p]ver. 10
2:14 [q]ch. 8:13
2:15 [r]Ps. 80:13; Ezek. 13:4; Luke 13:32
2:16 [s]ch. 6:3
2:17 [t]ch. 4:6 [u]ver. 9; ch. 8:14
3:1 [v]Isa. 26:9
3:3 [w]ch. 5:7
3:5 [x]ch. 2:7
3:6 [y]ch. 8:5
4:1 [z]ch. 1:15 [a]ch. 6:5
4:2 [b]ch. 6:6
4:3 [c]ch. 6:7
4:4 [d]ch. 7:4 [e]Neh. 3:19
4:5 [f]Prov. 5:19; ch. 7:3
4:6 [g]ch. 2:17
4:7 [h]Eph. 5:27
4:8 [i]Deut. 3:9
4:10 [j]ch. 1:2
4:11 [k]Prov. 24:13; ch. 5:1 [l]Gen. 27:27; Hos. 14:6

14 Spikenard and saffron; calamus and cinnamon, with all trees of frankincense; myrrh and aloes, with all the chief spices:

15 A fountain of gardens, a well of [m]living waters, and streams from Lebanon.

16 ¶ Awake, O north wind; and come, thou south; blow upon my garden, *that* the spices thereof may flow out. [n]Let my beloved come into his garden, and eat his pleasant fruits.

5 I [o]am come into my garden, my sister, *my* spouse: I have gathered my myrrh with my spice; [p]I have eaten my honeycomb with my honey; I have drunk my wine with my milk: eat, O [q]friends; drink, yea, drink abundantly, O beloved.

2 ¶ I sleep, but my heart waketh: *it is* the voice of my [r]beloved that knocketh, *saying,* Open to me, my sister, my love, my dove, my undefiled: for my head is filled with dew, *and* my locks with the drops of the night.

3 I have put off my coat; how shall I put it on? I have washed my feet; how shall I defile them?

4 My beloved put in his hand by the hole *of the door,* and my bowels were moved for him.

5 I rose up to open to my beloved; and my hands dropped *with* myrrh, and my fingers *with* sweet smelling myrrh, upon the handles of the lock.

6 I opened to my beloved; but my beloved had withdrawn himself, *and* was gone: my soul failed when he spake: [s]I sought him, but I could not find him; I called him, but he gave me no answer.

7 [t]The watchmen that went about the city found me, they smote me, they wounded me; the keepers of the walls took away my veil from me.

8 I charge you, O daughters of Jerusalem, if ye find my beloved, that ye tell him, that I *am* sick of love.

9 ¶ What *is* thy beloved more than *another* beloved, [u]O thou fairest among women? what *is* thy beloved more than *another* beloved, that thou dost so charge us?

10 My beloved *is* white and ruddy, the chiefest among ten thousand.

11 His head *is as* the most fine gold, his locks *are* bushy, *and* black as a raven.

12 [v]His eyes *are* as *the eyes* of doves by the rivers of waters, washed with milk, *and* fitly set.

13 His cheeks *are* as a bed of spices, *as* sweet flowers: his lips *like* lilies, dropping sweet smelling myrrh.

14 His hands *are as* gold rings set with the beryl: his belly *is as* bright ivory overlaid *with* sapphires.

15 His legs *are as* pillars of marble, set upon sockets of fine gold: his countenance *is* as Lebanon, excellent as the cedars.

16 His mouth *is* most sweet: yea, he *is* altogether lovely. This *is* my beloved, and this *is* my friend, O daughters of Jerusalem.

4:15 [m]John 4:10
4:16 [n]ch. 5:1
5:1 [o]ch. 4:16 [p]ch. 4:11 [q]Luke 15:7; John 3:29
5:2 [r]Rev. 3:20
5:6 [s]ch. 3:1
5:7 [t]ch. 3:3
5:9 [u]ch. 1:8
5:12 [v]ch. 1:15
6:1 [w]ch. 1:8
6:3 [x]ch. 2:16
6:4 [y]ver. 10
6:5 [z]ch. 4:1
6:6 [a]ch. 4:2
6:7 [b]ch. 4:3
6:10 [c]ver. 4
6:11 [d]ch. 7:12
7:1 [e]Ps. 45:13
7:3 [f]ch. 4:5
7:4 [g]ch. 4:4

6 Whither is thy beloved gone, [w]O thou fairest among women? whither is thy beloved turned aside? that we may seek him with thee.

2 My beloved is gone down into his garden, to the beds of spices, to feed in the gardens, and to gather lilies.

3 [x]I *am* my beloved's, and my beloved *is* mine: he feedeth among the lilies.

4 ¶ Thou *art* beautiful, O my love, as Tirzah, comely as Jerusalem, [y]terrible as *an army* with banners.

5 Turn away thine eyes from me, for they have overcome me: thy hair *is* [z]as a flock of goats that appear from Gilead.

6 [a]Thy teeth *are* as a flock of sheep which go up from the washing, whereof every one beareth twins, and *there is* not one barren among them.

7 [b]As a piece of a pomegranate *are* thy temples within thy locks.

8 There are threescore queens, and fourscore concubines, and virgins without number.

9 My dove, my undefiled is *but* one; she *is* the *only* one of her mother, she *is* the choice *one* of her that bare her. The daughters saw her, and blessed her; *yea,* the queens and the concubines, and they praised her.

10 ¶ Who *is* she *that* looketh forth as the morning, fair as the moon, clear as the sun, [c]*and* terrible as *an army* with banners?

11 I went down into the garden of nuts to see the fruits of the valley, *and* [d]to see whether the vine flourished, *and* the pomegranates budded.

12 Or ever I was aware, my soul made me *like* the chariots of Ammi-nadib.

13 Return, return, O Shulamite; return, return, that we may look upon thee. What will ye see in the Shulamite? As it were the company of two armies.

7 How beautiful are thy feet with shoes, [e]O prince's daughter! the joints of thy thighs *are* like jewels, the work of the hands of a cunning workman.

2 Thy navel *is like* a round goblet, *which* wanteth not liquor: thy belly *is like* an heap of wheat set about with lilies.

3 [f]Thy two breasts *are* like two young roes *that are* twins.

4 [g]Thy neck *is* as a tower of ivory; thine eyes *like* the fishpools in Heshbon, by the gate of Bath-rabbim: thy nose *is* as the tower of Lebanon which looketh toward Damascus.

5 Thine head upon thee *is* like Carmel, and the hair of thine head like purple; the king *is* held in the galleries.

6 How fair and how pleasant art thou, O love, for delights!

7 This thy stature is like to a palm tree, and thy breasts to clusters *of grapes.*

8 I said, I will go up to the palm tree, I will take hold of the boughs thereof: now also thy breasts shall be as clusters of the vine, and the smell of thy nose like apples;

9 And the roof of thy mouth like the best

wine for my beloved, that goeth *down*
sweetly, causing the lips of those that are
asleep to speak.
10 ¶ [h]I *am* my beloved's, and [i]his desire
is toward me.
11 Come, my beloved, let us go forth into
the field; let us lodge in the villages.
12 Let us get up early to the vineyards; let
us [j]see if the vine flourish, *whether* the tender grape appear, *and* the pomegranates
bud forth: there will I give thee my loves.
13 The [k]mandrakes give a smell, and at
our gates [l]*are* all manner of pleasant *fruits*,
new and old, *which* I have laid up for thee,
O my beloved.

8

O that thou *wert* as my brother, that
sucked the breasts of my mother! *when*
I should find thee without, I would kiss thee;
yea, I should not be despised.
2 I would lead thee, *and* bring thee into
my mother's house, *who* would instruct me:
I would cause thee to drink of [m]spiced wine
of the juice of my pomegranate.
3 [n]His left hand *should be* under my
head, and his right hand should embrace me.
4 [o]I charge you, O daughters of Jerusalem, that ye stir not up, nor awake *my* love,
until he please.
5 [p]Who *is* this that cometh up from the
wilderness, leaning upon her beloved? I
raised thee up under the apple tree: there
thy mother brought thee forth: there she
brought thee forth *that* bare thee.

7:10 [h]ch. 2:16 [i]Ps. 45:11
7:12 [j]ch. 6:11
7:13 [k]Gen. 30:14 [l]Matt. 13:52
8:2 [m]Prov. 9:2
8:3 [n]ch. 2:6
8:4 [o]ch. 2:7
8:5 [p]ch. 3:6
8:6 [q]Isa. 49:16; Jer. 22:24; Hag. 2:23
8:7 [r]Prov. 6:35
8:8 [s]Ezek. 23:33
8:11 [t]Matt. 21:33
8:13 [u]ch. 2:14
8:14 [v]Rev. 22:17 [w]ch. 2:17

6 ¶ [q]Set me as a seal upon thine heart, as
a seal upon thine arm: for love *is* strong as
death; jealousy *is* cruel as the grave: the
coals thereof *are* coals of fire, *which hath* a
most vehement flame.
7 Many waters cannot quench love, neither can the floods drown it: [r]if a man
would give all the substance of his house for
love, it would utterly be contemned.
8 ¶ [s]We have a little sister, and she hath
no breasts: what shall we do for our sister in
the day when she shall be spoken for?
9 If she *be* a wall, we will build upon her
a palace of silver: and if she *be* a door, we
will inclose her with boards of cedar.
10 I *am* a wall, and my breasts like towers: then was I in his eyes as one that found
favour.
11 Solomon had a vineyard at Baal-
hamon; [t]he let out the vineyard unto keepers; every one for the fruit thereof was to
bring a thousand *pieces* of silver.
12 My vineyard, which *is* mine, *is* before
me: thou, O Solomon, *must have* a thousand, and those that keep the fruit thereof
two hundred.
13 Thou that dwellest in the gardens, the
companions hearken to thy voice: [u]cause
me to hear *it*.
14 ¶ [v]Make haste, my beloved, and [w]be
thou like to a roe or to a young hart upon the
mountains of spices.

ISAIAH

Isaiah wrote this book prior to 680 B.C. Isaiah is a combination of prophecy concerning events that would affect Israel during and following Isaiah's lifetime, prophetical statements concerning the coming Messiah, and descriptions of Christ's coming kingdom. Throughout the middle of Isaiah, the theme of salvation and the place the Messiah would have in that redemptive plan is detailed. Isaiah 53 has long been a favorite chapter that describes Christ and his sufferings for the sinner.

I. Messages of denunciation and judgment, 1:1–23:18
II. Prophecies concerning God's final judgment and future blessings, 24:1–27:3
III. Further denunciation of Judah and Israel, 28:1–39:8
IV. God's greatness proclaimed, 40:1–48:22
V. Further prophecies concerning the Messiah, 49:1–57:21
VI. Further prophecies concerning Israel, 58:1–66:24

---

1 The [a]vision of Isaiah the son of Amoz, which he saw concerning Judah and Jerusalem in the days of Uzziah, Jotham, Ahaz, *and* Hezekiah, kings of Judah.

2 [b]Hear, O heavens, and give ear, O earth: for the LORD hath spoken, [c]I have nourished and brought up children, and they have rebelled against me.

3 [d]The ox knoweth his owner, and the ass his master's crib: *but* Israel [e]doth not know, my people [f]doth not consider.

4 Ah sinful nation, a people laden with iniquity, [g]a seed of evildoers, children that are corrupters: they have forsaken the LORD, they have provoked the Holy One of Israel unto anger, they are gone away backward.

5 ¶ [h]Why should ye be stricken any more? ye will revolt more and more: the whole head is sick, and the whole heart faint.

6 From the sole of the foot even unto the head *there is* no soundness in it; *but* wounds, and bruises, and putrifying sores: [i]they have not been closed, neither bound up, neither mollified with ointment.

7 [j]Your country *is* desolate, your cities *are* burned with fire: your land, strangers devour it in your presence, and *it is* desolate, as overthrown by strangers.

8 And the daughter of Zion is left [k]as a cottage in a vineyard, as a lodge in a garden of cucumbers, [l]as a besieged city.

9 [m]Except the LORD of hosts had left unto us a very small remnant, we should have been as [n]Sodom, *and* we should have been like unto Gomorrah.

10 ¶ Hear the word of the LORD, ye rulers [o]of Sodom; give ear unto the law of our God, ye people of Gomorrah.

11 To what purpose *is* the multitude of your [p]sacrifices unto me? saith the LORD: I am full of the burnt offerings of rams, and the fat of fed beasts; and I delight not in the blood of bullocks, or of lambs, or of he goats.

12 When ye come [q]to appear before me, who hath required this at your hand, to tread my courts?

13 Bring no more [r]vain oblations; incense is an abomination unto me; the new moons and sabbaths, [s]the calling of assemblies, I cannot away with; *it is* iniquity, even the solemn meeting.

14 Your [t]new moons and your [u]appointed feasts my soul hateth: they are a trouble unto me; [v]I am weary to bear *them.*

15 And [w]when ye spread forth your hands, I will hide mine eyes from you: [x]yea, when ye make many prayers, I will not hear: your hands are full of [y]blood.

16 ¶ [z]Wash you, make you clean; put away the evil of your doings from before mine eyes; [a]cease to do evil;

17 Learn to do well; [b]seek judgment, relieve the oppressed, judge the fatherless, plead for the widow.

18 Come now, and [c]let us reason together, saith the LORD: though your sins be as scarlet, [d]they shall be as white as snow; though they be red like crimson, they shall be as wool.

19 If ye be willing and obedient, ye shall eat the good of the land:

20 But if ye refuse and rebel, ye shall be devoured with the sword: [e]for the mouth of the LORD hath spoken *it.*

21 ¶ [f]How is the faithful city become an harlot! it was full of judgment; righteousness lodged in it; but now murderers.

22 [g]Thy silver is become dross, thy wine mixed with water:

23 [h]Thy princes *are* rebellious, and [i]companions of thieves: [j]every one loveth gifts, and followeth after rewards: they [k]judge not the fatherless, neither doth the cause of the widow come unto them.

24 Therefore saith the Lord, the LORD of hosts, the mighty One of Israel, Ah, [l]I will ease me of mine adversaries, and avenge me of mine enemies:

1:1 [a]Num. 12:6
1:2 [b]Deut. 32:1; Jer. 2:12; Ezek. 36:4; Mic. 1:2 [c]ch. 5:1
1:3 [d]Jer. 8:7 [e]Jer. 9:3 [f]ch. 5:12
1:4 [g]ch. 57:3; Matt. 3:7
1:5 [h]ch. 9:13; Jer. 2:30
1:6 [i]Jer. 8:22
1:7 [j]Deut. 28:51
1:8 [k]Job 27:18; Lam. 2:6 [l]Jer. 4:17
1:9 [m]Lam. 3:22; Rom. 9:29 [n]Gen. 19:24
1:10 [o]Deut. 32:32; Ezek. 16:46
1:11 [p]1 Sam. 15:22; Ps. 50:8; Prov. 15:8; ch. 66:3; Jer. 6:20; Am. 5:21; Mic. 6:7
1:12 [q]Ex. 23:17
1:13 [r]Matt. 15:9 [s]Joel 1:14
1:14 [t]Num. 28:11 [u]Lev. 23:2; Lam. 2:6 [v]ch. 43:24
1:15 [w]Job 27:29; Ps. 134:2; Prov. 1:28; ch. 59:2; Jer. 14:12; Mic. 3:4 [x]Ps. 66:18; 1 Tim. 2:8 [y]ch. 59:3
1:16 [z]Jer. 4:14 [a]Ps. 34:14; Am. 5:15; Rom. 12:9; 1 Pet. 3:11
1:17 [b]Jer. 22:3; Mic. 6:8; Zech. 7:9
1:18 [c]ch. 43:26; Mic. 6:2 [d]Ps. 51:7; Rev. 7:14
1:20 [e]Num. 23:19; Tit. 1:2
1:21 [f]Jer. 2:20
1:22 [g]Jer. 6:28; Ezek. 22:18
1:23 [h]Hos. 9:15 [i]Prov. 29:24 [j]Jer. 22:17; Ezek. 22:12; Hos. 4:18; Mic. 3:11 [k]Jer. 5:28; Zech. 7:10

1:24 [l]Deut. 28:63; Ezek. 5:13

25 ¶ And I will turn my hand upon thee, and [m]purely purge away thy dross, and take away all thy tin:

26 And I will restore thy judges [n]as at the first, and thy counsellors as at the beginning: afterward [o]thou shalt be called, The city of righteousness, the faithful city.

27 Zion shall be redeemed with judgment, and her converts with righteousness.

28 ¶ And the [p]destruction of the transgressors and of the sinners *shall be* together, and they that forsake the LORD shall be consumed.

29 For they shall be ashamed of [q]the oaks which ye have desired, [r]and ye shall be confounded for the gardens that ye have chosen.

30 For ye shall be as an oak whose leaf fadeth, and as a garden that hath no water.

31 [s]And the strong shall be [t]as tow, and the maker of it as a spark, and they shall both burn together, and none shall quench *them.*

2 The word that Isaiah the son of Amoz saw concerning Judah and Jerusalem.

2 And [u]it shall come to pass [v]in the last days, [w]*that* the mountain of the LORD's house shall be established in the top of the mountains, and shall be exalted above the hills; [x]and all nations shall flow unto it.

3 And many people shall go and say, [y]Come ye, and let us go up to the mountain of the LORD, to the house of the God of Jacob; and he will teach us of his ways, and we will walk in his paths: [z]for out of Zion shall go forth the law, and the word of the LORD from Jerusalem.

4 And he shall judge among the nations, and shall rebuke many people: and [a]they shall beat their swords into plowshares, and their spears into pruninghooks: nation shall not lift up sword against nation, [b]neither shall they learn war any more.

5 O house of Jacob, come ye, and let us [c]walk in the light of the LORD.

6 ¶ Therefore thou hast forsaken thy people the house of Jacob, because they be replenished [d]from the east, and [e]*are* soothsayers like the Philistines, [f]and they please themselves in the children of strangers.

7 [g]Their land also is full of silver and gold, neither *is there any* end of their treasures; their land is also full of horses, neither *is there any* end of their chariots:

8 [h]Their land also is full of idols; they worship the work of their own hands, that which their own fingers have made:

9 And the mean man boweth down, and the great man humbleth himself: therefore forgive them not.

10 ¶ [i]Enter into the rock, and hide thee in the dust, for fear of the LORD, and for the glory of his majesty.

11 The [j]lofty looks of man shall be humbled, and the haughtiness of men shall be bowed down, and the LORD alone shall be exalted [k]in that day.

12 For the day of the LORD of hosts *shall be* upon every *one that is* proud and lofty, and upon every *one that is* lifted up; and he shall be brought low:

13 And upon all [l]the cedars of Lebanon, *that are* high and lifted up, and upon all the oaks of Bashan,

14 And [m]upon all the high mountains, and upon all the hills *that are* lifted up,

15 And upon every high tower, and upon every fenced wall,

16 [n]And upon all the ships of Tarshish, and upon all pleasant pictures.

17 [o]And the loftiness of man shall be bowed down, and the haughtiness of men shall be made low: and the LORD alone shall be exalted [p]in that day.

18 And the idols he shall utterly abolish.

19 And they shall go into the [q]holes of the rocks, and into the caves of the earth, [r]for fear of the LORD, and for the glory of his majesty, when he ariseth [s]to shake terribly the earth.

20 [t]In that day a man shall cast his idols of silver, and his idols of gold, which they made *each one* for himself to worship, to the moles and to the bats;

21 [u]To go into the clefts of the rocks, and into the tops of the ragged rocks, [v]for fear of the LORD, and for the glory of his majesty, when he ariseth to shake terribly the earth.

22 [w]Cease ye from man, whose [x]breath *is* in his nostrils: for wherein is he to be accounted of?

3 For, behold, the Lord, the LORD of hosts, [y]doth take away from Jerusalem and from Judah [z]the stay and the staff, the whole stay of bread, and the whole stay of water,

2 [a]The mighty man, and the man of war, the judge, and the prophet, and the prudent, and the ancient,

3 The captain of fifty, and the honourable man, and the counsellor, and the cunning artificer, and the eloquent orator.

4 And I will give [b]children *to be* their princes, and babes shall rule over them.

5 And the people shall be oppressed, every one by another, and every one by his neighbour: the child shall behave himself proudly against the ancient, and the base against the honourable.

6 When a man shall take hold of his brother of the house of his father, *saying,* Thou hast clothing, be thou our ruler, and *let* this ruin *be* under thy hand:

7 In that day shall he swear, saying, I will not be an healer; for in my house *is* neither bread nor clothing: make me not a ruler of the people.

8 For [c]Jerusalem is ruined, and Judah is fallen: because their tongue and their doings *are* against the LORD, to provoke the eyes of his glory.

9 ¶ The shew of their countenance doth witness against them; and they declare their sin as [d]Sodom, they hide *it* not. Woe unto

1:25 *m*Jer. 6:29; Mal. 3:3
1:26 *n*Jer. 33:7 *o*Zech. 8:3
1:28 *p*Job 31:3; Ps. 1:6
1:29 *q*ch. 57:5 *r*ch. 65:3
1:31 *s*Ezek. 32:21 *t*ch. 43:17
2:2 *u*Mic. 4:1 *v*Gen. 49:1; Jer. 23:20 *w*Ps. 68:15 *x*Ps. 72:8; ch. 27:13
2:3 *y*Jer. 31:6; Zech. 8:21 *z*Luke 24:47
2:4 *a*Ps. 46:9; Hos. 2:18; Zech. 9:10 *b*Ps. 72:3
2:5 *c*Eph. 5:8
2:6 *d*Num. 23:7 *e*Deut. 18:14 *f*Ps. 106:35; Jer. 10:2
2:7 *g*Deut. 17:16
2:8 *h*Jer. 2:28
2:10 *i*ver. 19; Rev. 6:15
2:11 *j*ver. 17; ch. 5:15 *k*ch. 4:1; Jer. 30:7; Ezek. 38:14; Hos. 2:16; Joel 3:18; Am. 9:11; Obad. 8; Mic. 4:6; Zeph. 3:11; Zech. 9:16
2:13 *l*ch. 14:8; Ezek. 31:3; Zech. 11:1
2:14 *m*ch. 30:25
2:16 *n*1 Kings 10:22
2:17 *o*ver. 11 *p*ver. 11
2:19 *q*ver. 10; Hos. 10:8; Luke 23:30; Rev. 6:16 *r*2 Thess. 1:9 *s*ch. 30:32; Hag. 2:6; Heb. 12:26
2:20 *t*ch. 30:22
2:21 *u*ver. 19 *v*ver. 10
2:22 *w*Ps. 146:3; Jer. 17:5 *x*Job 27:3
3:1 *y*Jer. 37:21 *z*Lev. 26:26
3:2 *a*2 Kings 24:14
3:4 *b*Eccl. 10:16
3:8 *c*Mic. 3:12
3:9 *d*Gen. 13:13

their soul! for they have rewarded evil unto themselves.

10 Say ye to the righteous, [e]that *it shall be* well *with him:* [f]for they shall eat the fruit of their doings.

11 Woe unto the wicked! [g]*it shall be* ill *with him:* for the reward of his hands shall be given him.

12 ¶ *As for* my people, [h]children *are* their oppressors, and women rule over them. O my people, [i]they which lead thee cause *thee* to err, and destroy the way of thy paths.

13 The LORD standeth up [j]to plead, and standeth to judge the people.

14 The LORD will enter into judgment with the ancients of his people, and the princes thereof: for ye have eaten up [k]the vineyard; the spoil of the poor *is* in your houses.

15 What mean ye *that* ye [l]beat my people to pieces, and grind the faces of the poor? saith the Lord GOD of hosts.

16 ¶ Moreover the LORD saith, Because the daughters of Zion are haughty, and walk with stretched forth necks and wanton eyes, walking and mincing *as* they go, and making a tinkling with their feet:

17 Therefore the Lord will smite with [m]a scab the crown of the head of the daughters of Zion, and the LORD will [n]discover their secret parts.

18 In that day the Lord will take away the bravery of *their* tinkling ornaments *about their feet,* and *their* cauls, and *their* [o]round tires like the moon,

19 The chains, and the bracelets, and the mufflers,

20 The bonnets, and the ornaments of the legs, and the headbands, and the tablets, and the earrings,

21 The rings, and nose jewels,

22 The changeable suits of apparel, and the mantles, and the wimples, and the crisping pins,

23 The glasses, and the fine linen, and the hoods, and the vails.

24 And it shall come to pass, *that* instead of sweet smell there shall be stink; and instead of a girdle a rent; and instead of well set hair [p]baldness; and instead of a stomacher a girding of sackcloth; *and* burning instead of beauty.

25 Thy men shall fall by the sword, and thy mighty in the war.

26 [q]And her gates shall lament and mourn; and she *being* desolate [r]shall sit upon the ground.

4 And [s]in that day seven women shall take hold of one man, saying, We will [t]eat our own bread, and wear our own apparel: only let us be called by thy name, to take away [u]our reproach.

2 In that day shall [v]the branch of the LORD be beautiful and glorious, and the fruit of the earth *shall be* excellent and comely for them that are escaped of Israel.

3 And it shall come to pass, *that he that* is left in Zion, and *he that* remaineth in Jerusalem, [w]shall be called holy, *even* every one that is [x]written among the living in Jerusalem:

4 When [y]the Lord shall have washed away the filth of the daughters of Zion, and shall have purged the blood of Jerusalem from the midst thereof by the spirit of judgment, and by the spirit of burning.

5 And the LORD will create upon every dwelling place of mount Zion, and upon her assemblies, [z]a cloud and smoke by day, and [a]the shining of a flaming fire by night: for upon all the glory *shall be* a defence.

6 And there shall be a tabernacle for a shadow in the daytime from the heat, and [b]for a place of refuge, and for a covert from storm and from rain.

5 Now will I sing to my wellbeloved a song of my beloved touching [c]his vineyard. My wellbeloved hath a vineyard in a very fruitful hill:

2 And he fenced it, and gathered out the stones thereof, and planted it with the choicest vine, and built a tower in the midst of it, and also made a winepress therein: [d]and he looked that it should bring forth grapes, and it brought forth wild grapes.

3 And now, O inhabitants of Jerusalem, and men of Judah, [e]judge, I pray you, betwixt me and my vineyard.

4 What could have been done more to my vineyard, that I have not done in it? wherefore, when I looked that it should bring forth grapes, brought it forth wild grapes?

5 And now go to; I will tell you what I will do to my vineyard: [f]I will take away the hedge thereof, and it shall be eaten up; *and* break down the wall thereof, and it shall be trodden down:

6 And I will lay it waste: it shall not be pruned, nor digged; but there shall come up briers and thorns: I will also command the clouds that they rain no rain upon it.

7 For the vineyard of the LORD of hosts *is* the house of Israel, and the men of Judah his pleasant plant: and he looked for judgment, but behold oppression; for righteousness, but behold a cry.

8 ¶ Woe unto them that join [g]house to house, *that* lay field to field, till *there be* no place, that they may be placed alone in the midst of the earth!

9 [h]In mine ears *said* the LORD of hosts, Of a truth many houses shall be desolate, *even* great and fair, without inhabitant.

10 Yea, ten acres of vineyard shall yield one [i]bath, and the seed of an homer shall yield an ephah.

11 ¶ [j]Woe unto them that rise up early in the morning, *that* they may follow strong drink; that continue until night, *till* wine inflame them!

12 And the [k]harp, and the viol, the tabret, and pipe, and wine, are in their feasts: but [l]they regard not the work of the LORD, neither consider the operation of his hands.

13 ¶ [m]Therefore my people are gone into

3:10 [e]Eccl. 8:12 [f]Ps. 128:2
3:11 [g]Ps. 11:6; Eccl. 8:13
3:12 [h]ver. 4 [i]ch. 9:16
3:13 [j]Mic. 6:2
3:14 [k]ch. 5:7; Matt. 21:33
3:15 [l]ch. 58:4; Mic. 3:2
3:17 [m]Deut. 28:27 [n]ch. 47:2; Jer. 13:22; Nah. 3:5
3:18 [o]Judg. 8:21
3:24 [p]ch. 22:12; Mic. 1:16
3:26 [q]Jer. 14:2; Lam. 1:4 [r]Lam. 2:10
4:1 [s]ch. 2:11 [t]2 Thess. 3:12 [u]Luke 1:25
4:2 [v]Jer. 23:5; Zech. 3:8
4:3 [w]ch. 60:21 [x]Phil. 4:3; Rev. 3:5
4:4 [y]Mal. 3:2
4:5 [z]Ex. 13:21 [a]Zech. 2:5
4:6 [b]ch. 25:4
5:1 [c]Ps. 80:8; SSol. 8:12; ch. 27:2; Jer. 2:21; Matt. 21:33; Mark 12:1; Luke 20:9
5:2 [d]Deut. 32:6; ch. 1:2
5:3 [e]Rom. 3:4
5:5 [f]Ps. 80:12
5:8 [g]Mic. 2:2
5:9 [h]ch. 22:14
5:10 [i]Ezek. 45:11
5:11 [j]Prov. 23:29; Eccl. 10:16; ver. 22
5:12 [k]Am. 6:5 [l]Job 34:27; Ps. 28:5
5:13 [m]Hos. 4:6

captivity, [n]because *they have* no knowledge: and their honourable men *are* famished, and their multitude dried up with thirst.

14 Therefore hell hath enlarged herself, and opened her mouth without measure: and their glory, and their multitude, and their pomp, and he that rejoiceth, shall descend into it.

15 And [o]the mean man shall be brought down, and the mighty man shall be humbled, and the eyes of the lofty shall be humbled:

16 But the LORD of hosts shall be exalted in judgment, and God that is holy shall be sanctified in righteousness.

17 Then shall the lambs feed after their manner, and the waste places of [p]the fat ones shall strangers eat.

18 Woe unto them that draw iniquity with cords of vanity, and sin as it were with a cart rope:

19 [q]That say, Let him make speed, *and* hasten his work, that we may see *it:* and let the counsel of the Holy One of Israel draw nigh and come, that we may know *it!*

20 ¶ Woe unto them that call evil good, and good evil; that put darkness for light, and light for darkness; that put bitter for sweet, and sweet for bitter!

21 Woe unto *them that are* [r]wise in their own eyes, and prudent in their own sight!

22 [s]Woe unto *them that are* mighty to drink wine, and men of strength to mingle strong drink:

23 Which [t]justify the wicked for reward, and take away the righteousness of the righteous from him!

24 Therefore [u]as the fire devoureth the stubble, and the flame consumeth the chaff, *so* [v]their root shall be as rottenness, and their blossom shall go up as dust: because they have cast away the law of the LORD of hosts, and despised the word of the Holy One of Israel.

25 [w]Therefore is the anger of the LORD kindled against his people, and he hath stretched forth his hand against them, and hath smitten them: and [x]the hills did tremble, and their carcases *were* torn in the midst of the streets. [y]For all this his anger is not turned away, but his hand *is* stretched out still.

26 ¶ [z]And he will lift up an ensign to the nations from far, and will [a]hiss unto them from [b]the end of the earth: and, behold, [c]they shall come with speed swiftly:

27 None shall be weary nor stumble among them; none shall slumber nor sleep; neither [d]shall the girdle of their loins be loosed, nor the latchet of their shoes be broken:

28 [e]Whose arrows *are* sharp, and all their bows bent, their horses' hoofs shall be counted like flint, and their wheels like a whirlwind:

29 Their roaring *shall be* like a lion, they shall roar like young lions: yea, they shall roar, and lay hold of the prey, and shall carry *it* away safe, and none shall deliver *it*.

30 And in that day they shall roar against them like the roaring of the sea: and if *one* [f]look unto the land, behold darkness *and* sorrow, and the light is darkened in the heavens thereof.

6 In the year that [g]king Uzziah died I [h]saw also the Lord sitting upon a throne, high and lifted up, and his train filled the temple.

2 Above it stood the seraphims: each one had six wings; [i]with twain he covered his face, and with twain he covered his feet, and with twain he did fly.

3 And one cried unto another, and said, [j]Holy, holy, holy, *is* the LORD of hosts: [k]the whole earth *is* full of his glory.

4 And the posts of the door moved at the voice of him that cried, and [l]the house was filled with smoke.

5 ¶ [m]Then said I, Woe *is* me! for I am undone; because I *am* a man of unclean lips, and I dwell in the midst of a people of unclean lips: for mine eyes have seen the King, the LORD of hosts.

6 Then flew one of the seraphims unto me, having a live coal in his hand, *which* he had taken with the tongs from off [n]the altar:

7 And he [o]laid *it* upon my mouth, and said, Lo, this hath touched thy lips; and thine iniquity is taken away, and thy sin purged.

8 Also I heard the voice of the Lord, saying, Whom shall I send, and who will go for [p]us? Then said I, Here *am* I; send me.

9 ¶ And he said, Go, and tell this people, [q]Hear ye indeed, but understand not; and see ye indeed, but perceive not.

10 Make [r]the heart of this people fat, and make their ears heavy, and shut their eyes; [s]lest they see with their eyes, and hear with their ears, and understand with their heart, and convert, and be healed.

11 Then said I, Lord, how long? And he answered, [t]Until the cities be wasted without inhabitant, and the houses without man, and the land be utterly desolate,

12 [u]And the LORD have removed men far away, and *there be* a great forsaking in the midst of the land.

13 ¶ But yet in it *shall be* a tenth, and *it* shall return, and shall be eaten: as a teil tree, and as an oak, whose substance *is* in them, when they cast *their leaves: so* [v]the holy seed *shall be* the substance thereof.

7 And it came to pass in the days of [w]Ahaz the son of Jotham, the son of Uzziah, king of Judah, *that* Rezin the king of Syria, and Pekah the son of Remaliah, king of Israel, went up toward Jerusalem to war against it, but could not prevail against it.

2 And it was told the house of David, saying, Syria is confederate with Ephraim. And his heart was moved, and the heart of his people, as the trees of the wood are moved with the wind.

5:13 [n]ch. 1:3; Luke 19:44
5:15 [o]ch. 2:9
5:17 [p]ch. 10:16
5:19 [q]ch. 66:5; Jer. 17:15; Am. 5:18; 2 Pet. 3:3
5:21 [r]Prov. 3:7; Rom. 1:22
5:22 [s]ver. 11
5:23 [t]Prov. 17:15
5:24 [u]Ex. 15:7 [v]Job 18:16; Hos. 9:16; Am. 2:9
5:25 [w]2 Kings 22:13 [x]Jer. 4:24 [y]Lev. 26:14; ch. 9:12
5:26 [z]ch. 11:12 [a]ch. 7:18 [b]Deut. 28:49; Ps. 72:8; Mal. 1:11 [c]Joel 2:7
5:27 [d]Dan. 5:6
5:28 [e]Jer. 5:16
5:30 [f]ch. 8:22; Jer. 4:23; Lam. 3:2; Ezek. 32:7
6:1 [g]2 Kings 15:7 [h]1 Kings 22:19; John 12:41; Rev. 4:2
6:2 [i]Ezek. 1:11
6:3 [j]Rev. 4:8 [k]Ps. 72:19
6:4 [l]Ex. 40:34; 1 Kings 8:10
6:5 [m]Ex. 4:10; Judg. 6:22; Jer. 1:6
6:6 [n]Rev. 8:3
6:7 [o]Jer. 1:9; Dan. 10:16
6:8 [p]Gen. 1:26
6:9 [q]ch. 43:8; Matt. 13:14; Mark 4:12; Luke 8:10; John 12:40; Acts 28:26; Rom. 11:8
6:10 [r]Ps. 119:70; ch. 63:17 [s]Jer. 5:21
6:11 [t]Mic. 3:12
6:12 [u]2 Kings 25:21
6:13 [v]Ezra 9:2; Mal. 2:15; Rom. 11:5
7:1 [w]2 Kings 16:5; 2 Chron. 28:5

3 Then said the LORD unto Isaiah, Go forth now to meet Ahaz, thou, [x]and Shear-jashub thy son, at the end of the [y]conduit of the upper pool in the highway of the fuller's field;

4 And say unto him, Take heed, and be quiet; fear not, neither be fainthearted for the two tails of these smoking firebrands, for the fierce anger of Rezin with Syria, and of the son of Remaliah.

5 Because Syria, Ephraim, and the son of Remaliah, have taken evil counsel against thee, saying,

6 Let us go up against Judah, and vex it, and let us make a breach therein for us, and set a king in the midst of it, *even* the son of Tabeal:

7 Thus saith the Lord GOD, [z]It shall not stand, neither shall it come to pass.

8 [a]For the head of Syria *is* Damascus, and the head of Damascus *is* Rezin; and within threescore and five years shall Ephraim be broken, that it be not a people.

9 And the head of Ephraim *is* Samaria, and the head of Samaria *is* Remaliah's son. [b]If ye will not believe, surely ye shall not be established.

10 ¶ Moreover the LORD spake again unto Ahaz, saying,

11 [c]Ask thee a sign of the LORD thy God; ask it either in the depth, or in the height above.

12 But Ahaz said, I will not ask, neither will I tempt the LORD.

13 And he said, Hear ye now, O house of David; *Is it* a small thing for you to weary men, but will ye weary my God also?

14 Therefore the Lord himself shall give you a sign; [d]Behold, a virgin shall conceive, and bear [e]a son, and shall call his name [f]Immanuel.

15 Butter and honey shall he eat, that he may know to refuse the evil, and choose the good.

16 [g]For before the child shall know to refuse the evil, and choose the good, the land that thou abhorrest shall be forsaken of [h]both her kings.

17 ¶ [i]The LORD shall bring upon thee, and upon thy people, and upon thy father's house, days that have not come, from the day that [j]Ephraim departed from Judah; *even* the king of Assyria.

18 And it shall come to pass in that day, *that* the LORD [k]shall hiss for the fly that *is* in the uttermost part of the rivers of Egypt, and for the bee that *is* in the land of Assyria.

19 And they shall come, and shall rest all of them in the desolate valleys, and in [l]the holes of the rocks, and upon all thorns, and upon all bushes.

20 In the same day shall the Lord shave with a [m]razor that is hired, *namely,* by them beyond the river, by the king of Assyria, the head, and the hair of the feet: and it shall also consume the beard.

21 And it shall come to pass in that day, *that* a man shall nourish a young cow, and two sheep;

22 And it shall come to pass, for the abundance of milk *that* they shall give he shall eat butter: for butter and honey shall every one eat that is left in the land.

23 And it shall come to pass in that day, *that* every place shall be, where there were a thousand vines at a thousand silverlings, [n]it shall *even* be for briers and thorns.

24 With arrows and with bows shall *men* come thither; because all the land shall become briers and thorns.

25 And *on* all hills that shall be digged with the mattock, there shall not come thither the fear of briers and thorns: but it shall be for the sending forth of oxen, and for the treading of lesser cattle.

8 Moreover the LORD said unto me, Take thee a great roll, and [o]write in it with a man's pen concerning Maher-shalal-hash-baz.

2 And I took unto me faithful witnesses to record, [p]Uriah the priest, and Zechariah the son of Jeberechiah.

3 And I went unto the prophetess; and she conceived, and bare a son. Then said the LORD to me, Call his name Maher-shalal-hash-baz.

4 [q]For before the child shall have knowledge to cry, My father, and my mother, [r]the riches of Damascus and the spoil of Samaria shall be taken away before the king of Assyria.

5 ¶ The LORD spake also unto me again, saying,

6 Forasmuch as this people refuseth the waters of [s]Shiloah that go softly, and rejoice [t]in Rezin and Remaliah's son;

7 Now therefore, behold, the Lord bringeth up upon them the waters of the river, strong and many, *even* [u]the king of Assyria, and all his glory: and he shall come up over all his channels, and go over all his banks:

8 And he shall pass through Judah; he shall overflow and go over, [v]he shall reach *even* to the neck; and the stretching out of his wings shall fill the breadth of thy land, O [w]Immanuel.

9 ¶ [x]Associate yourselves, O ye people, and ye shall be broken in pieces; and give ear, all ye of far countries: gird yourselves, and ye shall be broken in pieces; gird yourselves, and ye shall be broken in pieces.

10 [y]Take counsel together, and it shall come to nought; speak the word, [z]and it shall not stand: [a]for God *is* with us.

11 ¶ For the LORD spake thus to me with a strong hand, and instructed me that I should not walk in the way of this people, saying,

12 Say ye not, A confederacy, to all *them to* whom [b]this people shall say, A confederacy; [c]neither fear ye their fear, nor be afraid.

13 [d]Sanctify the LORD of hosts himself;

7:3 [x]ch. 10:21 [y]2 Kings 18:17; ch. 36:2
7:7 [z]Prov. 21:30; ch. 8:10
7:8 [a]2 Sam. 8:6
7:9 [b]2 Chron. 20:20
7:11 [c]Judg. 6:36; Matt. 12:38
7:14 [d]Matt. 1:23; Luke 1:31 [e]ch. 9:6 [f]ch. 8:8
7:16 [g]ch. 8:4 [h]2 Kings 15:30
7:17 [i]2 Chron. 28:19 [j]1 Kings 12:16
7:18 [k]ch. 5:26
7:19 [l]ch. 2:19; Jer. 16:16
7:20 [m]2 Kings 16:7; 2 Chron. 28:20; Ezek. 5:1
7:23 [n]ch. 5:6
8:1 [o]ch. 30:8; Hab. 2:2
8:2 [p]2 Kings 16:10
8:4 [q]ch. 7:16 [r]2 Kings 15:29; ch. 17:3
8:6 [s]Neh. 3:15; John 9:7 [t]ch. 7:1
8:7 [u]ch. 10:12
8:8 [v]ch. 30:28 [w]ch. 7:14
8:9 [x]Joel 3:9
8:10 [y]Job 5:12 [z]ch. 7:7 [a]ch. 7:14; Acts 5:38; Rom. 8:13
8:12 [b]ch. 7:2 [c]1 Pet. 3:14
8:13 [d]Num. 20:12

and [e]*let* him *be* your fear, and *let* him *be* your dread.

14 And [f]he shall be for a sanctuary; but for [g]a stone of stumbling and for a rock of offence to both the houses of Israel, for a gin and for a snare to the inhabitants of Jerusalem.

15 And many among them shall [h]stumble, and fall, and be broken, and be snared, and be taken.

16 Bind up the testimony, seal the law among my disciples.

17 And I will wait upon the LORD, that [i]hideth his face from the house of Jacob, and I [j]will look for him.

18 [k]Behold, I and the children whom the LORD hath given me [l]*are* for signs and for wonders in Israel from the LORD of hosts, which dwelleth in mount Zion.

19 ¶ And when they shall say unto you, [m]Seek unto them that have familiar spirits, and unto wizards [n]that peep, and that mutter: should not a people seek unto their God? for the living [o]to the dead?

20 [p]To the law and to the testimony: if they speak not according to this word, *it is* because [q]*there is* no light in them.

21 And they shall pass through it, hardly bestead and hungry: and it shall come to pass, that when they shall be hungry, they shall fret themselves, and [r]curse their king and their God, and look upward.

22 And [s]they shall look unto the earth; and behold trouble and darkness, [t]dimness of anguish; and *they shall be* driven to darkness.

9 Nevertheless [u]the dimness *shall* not *be* such as *was* in her vexation, when at the [v]first he lightly afflicted the land of Zebulun and the land of Naphtali, and [w]afterward did more grievously afflict *her by* the way of the sea, beyond Jordan, in Galilee of the nations.

2 [x]The people that walked in darkness have seen a great light: they that dwell in the land of the shadow of death, upon them hath the light shined.

3 Thou hast multiplied the nation, *and* not increased the joy: they joy before thee according to the joy in harvest, *and* as *men* rejoice [y]when they divide the spoil.

4 For thou hast broken the yoke of his burden, and the [z]staff of his shoulder, the rod of his oppressor, as in the day of [a]Midian.

5 For every battle of the warrior *is* with confused noise, and garments rolled in blood; [b]but *this* shall be with burning *and* fuel of fire.

6 [c]For unto us a child is born, unto us a [d]son is given: and the [e]government shall be upon his shoulder: and his name shall be called [f]Wonderful, Counsellor, [g]The mighty God, The everlasting Father, [h]The Prince of Peace.

7 Of the increase of *his* government and peace [i]*there shall be* no end, upon the throne of David, and upon his kingdom, to order it, and to establish it with judgment and with justice from henceforth even for ever. The [j]zeal of the LORD of hosts will perform this.

8 ¶ The Lord sent a word into Jacob, and it hath lighted upon Israel.

9 And all the people shall know, *even* Ephraim and the inhabitant of Samaria, that say in the pride and stoutness of heart,

10 The bricks are fallen down, but we will build with hewn stones: the sycomores are cut down, but we will change *them into* cedars.

11 Therefore the LORD shall set up the adversaries of Rezin against him, and join his enemies together;

12 The Syrians before, and the Philistines behind; and they shall devour Israel with open mouth. [k]For all this his anger is not turned away, but his hand *is* stretched out still.

13 ¶ For [l]the people turneth not unto him that smiteth them, neither do they seek the LORD of hosts.

14 Therefore the LORD will cut off from Israel head and tail, branch and rush, [m]in one day.

15 The ancient and honourable, he *is* the head; and the prophet that teacheth lies, he *is* the tail.

16 For [n]the leaders of this people cause *them* to err; and *they that are* led of them *are* destroyed.

17 Therefore the Lord [o]shall have no joy in their young men, neither shall have mercy on their fatherless and widows: [p]for every one *is* an hypocrite and an evildoer, and every mouth speaketh folly. [q]For all this his anger is not turned away, but his hand *is* stretched out still.

18 ¶ For wickedness [r]burneth as the fire: it shall devour the briers and thorns, and shall kindle in the thickets of the forest, and they shall mount up *like* the lifting up of smoke.

19 Through the wrath of the LORD of hosts is [s]the land darkened, and the people shall be as the fuel of the fire: [t]no man shall spare his brother.

20 And he shall snatch on the right hand, and be hungry; and he shall eat on the left hand, [u]and they shall not be satisfied: [v]they shall eat every man the flesh of his own arm:

21 Manasseh, Ephraim; and Ephraim, Manasseh: *and* they together *shall be* against Judah. [w]For all this his anger is not turned away, but his hand *is* stretched out still.

10 Woe unto them that [x]decree unrighteous decrees, and that write grievousness *which* they have prescribed;

2 To turn aside the needy from judgment, and to take away the right from the poor of my people, that widows may be their prey, and *that* they may rob the fatherless!

3 And [y]what will ye do in [z]the day of visitation, and in the desolation *which* shall

8:13 [e]Ps. 76:7; Luke 12:5
8:14 [f]Ezek. 11:16 [g]ch. 28:16; Luke 2:34; Rom. 9:33; 1 Pet. 2:8
8:15 [h]Matt. 21:44; Luke 20:18; Rom. 9:32
8:17 [i]ch. 54:8 [j]Hab. 2:3; Luke 2:25
8:18 [k]Heb. 2:13 [l]Ps. 71:7; Zech. 3:8
8:19 [m]1 Sam. 28:8; ch. 19:3 [n]ch. 29:4 [o]Ps. 106:28
8:20 [p]Luke 16:29 [q]Mic. 3:6
8:21 [r]Rev. 16:11
8:22 [s]ch. 5:30 [t]ch. 9:1
9:1 [u]ch. 8:22 [v]2 Kings 15:29; 2 Chron. 16:4 [w]Lev. 26:24; 2 Kings 17:5; 1 Chron. 5:26
9:2 [x]Matt. 4:16; Eph. 5:8
9:3 [y]Judg. 5:30
9:4 [z]ch. 10:5 [a]Judg. 7:22; Ps. 83:9; ch. 10:26
9:5 [b]ch. 66:15
9:6 [c]ch. 7:14; Luke 2:11 [d]John 3:16 [e]Matt. 28:18; 1 Cor. 15:25 [f]Judg. 13:18 [g]Tit. 2:13 [h]Eph. 2:14
9:7 [i]Dan. 2:44; Luke 1:32 [j]2 Kings 19:31; ch. 37:32
9:12 [k]ch. 5:25; Jer. 4:8
9:13 [l]Jer. 5:3; Hos. 7:10
9:14 [m]ch. 10:17; Rev. 18:8
9:16 [n]ch. 3:12
9:17 [o]Ps. 147:10 [p]Mic. 7:2 [q]ver. 12; ch. 5:25
9:18 [r]ch. 10:17; Mal. 4:1
9:19 [s]ch. 8:22 [t]Mic. 7:2
9:20 [u]Lev. 26:26 [v]ch. 49:26; Jer. 19:9
9:21 [w]ver. 12; ch. 5:25
10:1 [x]Ps. 58:2
10:3 [y]Job 31:14 [z]Hos. 9:7; Luke 19:44

come from far? to whom will ye flee for
help? and where will ye leave your glory?
4 Without me they shall bow down under
the prisoners, and they shall fall under the
slain. [a]For all this his anger is not turned
away, but his hand *is* stretched out still.
5 ¶ O Assyrian, [b]the rod of mine anger,
and the staff in their hand is mine indignation.
6 I will send him against [c]an hypocritical
nation, and against the people of my wrath
will I [d]give him a charge, to take the spoil,
and to take the prey, and to tread them
down like the mire of the streets.
7 [e]Howbeit he meaneth not so, neither
doth his heart think so; but *it is* in his heart
to destroy and cut off nations not a few.
8 [f]For he saith, *Are* not my princes altogether kings?
9 *Is* not [g]Calno [h]as Carchemish? *is* not
Hamath as Arpad? *is* not Samaria [i]as Damascus?
10 As my hand hath found the kingdoms
of the idols, and whose graven images did
excel them of Jerusalem and of Samaria;
11 Shall I not, as I have done unto Samaria and her idols, so do to Jerusalem and
her idols?
12 Wherefore it shall come to pass, *that*
when the Lord hath performed his whole
work [j]upon mount Zion and on Jerusalem,
[k]I will punish the fruit of the stout heart of
the king of Assyria, and the glory of his
high looks.
13 [l]For he saith, By the strength of my
hand I have done *it,* and by my wisdom;
for I am prudent: and I have removed the
bounds of the people, and have robbed their
treasures, and I have put down the inhabitants like a valiant *man:*
14 And [m]my hand hath found as a nest
the riches of the people: and as one gathereth eggs *that are* left, have I gathered all the
earth; and there was none that moved the
wing, or opened the mouth, or peeped.
15 Shall [n]the axe boast itself against him
that heweth therewith? *or* shall the saw
magnify itself against him that shaketh it?
as if the rod should shake *itself* against
them that lift it up, *or* as if the staff should
lift up *itself, as if it were* no wood.
16 Therefore shall the Lord, the Lord of
hosts, send among his [o]fat ones leanness;
and under his glory he shall kindle a burning like the burning of a fire.
17 And the light of Israel shall be for a
fire, and his Holy One for a flame: [p]and it
shall burn and devour his thorns and his
briers in one day;
18 And shall consume the glory of his forest, and of [q]his fruitful field, both soul and
body: and they shall be as when a standard-
bearer fainteth.
19 And the rest of the trees of his forest
shall be few, that a child may write them.
20 ¶ And it shall come to pass in that day,
that the remnant of Israel, and such as are
escaped of the house of Jacob, [r]shall no
more again stay upon him that smote them;
but shall stay upon the LORD, the Holy One
of Israel, in truth.
21 [s]The remnant shall return, *even* the
remnant of Jacob, unto the mighty God.
22 [t]For though thy people Israel be as the
sand of the sea, [u]*yet* a remnant of them
shall return: [v]the consumption decreed
shall overflow with righteousness.
23 [w]For the Lord GOD of hosts shall make
a consumption, even determined, in the
midst of all the land.
24 ¶ Therefore thus saith the Lord GOD of
hosts, O my people that dwellest in Zion,
[x]be not afraid of the Assyrian: he shall
smite thee with a rod, and shall lift up his
staff against thee, after the manner of
[y]Egypt.
25 [z]For yet a very little while, [a]and the
indignation shall cease, and mine anger in
their destruction.
26 And the LORD of hosts shall stir up [b]a
scourge for him according to the slaughter
of [c]Midian at the rock of Oreb: and [d]*as* his
rod *was* upon the sea, so shall he lift it up
after the manner of Egypt.
27 And it shall come to pass in that day,
that [e]his burden shall be taken away from
off thy shoulder, and his yoke from off thy
neck, and the yoke shall be destroyed because of [f]the anointing.
28 He is come to Aiath, he is passed to
Migron; at Michmash he hath laid up his
carriages:
29 They are gone over the [g]passage: they
have taken up their lodging at Geba; Ramah
is afraid; [h]Gibeah of Saul is fled.
30 Lift up thy voice, O daughter [i]of Gallim: cause it to be heard unto [j]Laish, [k]O
poor Anathoth.
31 [l]Madmenah is removed; the inhabitants of Gebim gather themselves to flee.
32 As yet shall he remain [m]at Nob that
day: he shall [n]shake his hand *against* the
mount of [o]the daughter of Zion, the hill of
Jerusalem.
33 Behold, the Lord, the LORD of hosts,
shall lop the bough with terror: and [p]the
high ones of stature *shall be* hewn down,
and the haughty shall be humbled.
34 And he shall cut down the thickets of
the forest with iron, and Lebanon shall fall
by a mighty one.

11 And [q]there shall come forth a rod
out of the stem of [r]Jesse, and [s]a
Branch shall grow out of his roots:
2 [t]And the spirit of the LORD shall rest
upon him, the spirit of wisdom and understanding, the spirit of counsel and might,
the spirit of knowledge and of the fear of the
LORD;
3 And shall make him of quick understanding in the fear of the LORD: and he
shall not judge after the sight of his eyes,
neither reprove after the hearing of his ears:
4 But [u]with righteousness shall he judge
the poor, and reprove with equity for the
meek of the earth: and he shall [v]smite the

10:4 [a]ch. 5:25
10:5 [b]Jer. 51:20
10:6 [c]ch. 19:17 [d]Jer. 34:22
10:7 [e]Gen. 50:20; Mic. 4:12
10:8 [f]2 Kings 18:24
10:9 [g]Am. 6:2 [h]2 Chron. 35:20 [i]2 Kings 16:9
10:12 [j]2 Kings 19:31 [k]Jer. 50:18
10:13 [l]Isa. 37:24; Ezek. 28:4; Dan. 4:30
10:14 [m]Job 31:25
10:15 [n]Jer. 51:20
10:16 [o]ch. 5:17
10:17 [p]ch. 9:18
10:18 [q]2 Kings 19:23
10:20 [r]2 Kings 16:7; 2 Chron. 28:20
10:21 [s]ch. 7:3
10:22 [t]Rom. 9:27 [u]ch. 6:13 [v]ch. 28:22
10:23 [w]ch. 28:22; Dan. 9:27; Rom. 9:28
10:24 [x]ch. 37:6 [y]Ex. 14
10:25 [z]ch. 54:7 [a]Dan. 11:36
10:26 [b]2 Kings 19:35 [c]Judg. 7:25; ch. 9:4 [d]Ex. 14:26
10:27 [e]ch. 14:25 [f]Ps. 105:15; Dan. 9:24; 1 John 2:20
10:29 [g]1 Sam. 13:23 [h]1 Sam. 11:4
10:30 [i]1 Sam. 25:44 [j]Judg. 18:7 [k]Josh. 21:18
10:31 [l]Josh. 15:31
10:32 [m]1 Sam. 21:1; Neh. 11:32 [n]ch. 13:2 [o]ch. 37:22
10:33 [p]Am. 2:9
11:1 [q]ch. 53:2; Zech. 6:12; Rev. 5:5 [r]Acts 13:23; ver. 10 [s]ch. 4:2; Jer. 23:5
11:2 [t]ch. 61:1; Matt. 3:16; John 1:32
11:4 [u]Ps. 72:2; Rev. 19:11 [v]Job 4:9; Mal. 4:6; 2 Thess. 2:8; Rev. 1:16

earth with the rod of his mouth, and with
the breath of his lips shall he slay the
wicked.
5 And [w]righteousness shall be the girdle
of his loins, and faithfulness the girdle of his
reins.
6 [x]The wolf also shall dwell with the
lamb, and the leopard shall lie down with
the kid; and the calf and the young lion and
the fatling together; and a little child shall
lead them.
7 And the cow and the bear shall feed;
their young ones shall lie down together:
and the lion shall eat straw like the ox.
8 And the sucking child shall play on the
hole of the asp, and the weaned child shall
put his hand on the cockatrice' den.
9 [y]They shall not hurt nor destroy in all
my holy mountain: for [z]the earth shall be
full of the knowledge of the LORD, as the
waters cover the sea.
10 ¶ [a]And in that day [b]there shall be a
root of Jesse, which shall stand for an ensign of the people; to it shall the [c]Gentiles
seek: and [d]his rest shall be glorious.
11 And it shall come to pass [e]in that day,
that the Lord shall set his hand again the
second time to recover the remnant of his
people, which shall be left, [f]from Assyria,
and from Egypt, and from Pathros, and
from Cush, and from Elam, and from Shinar, and from Hamath, and from the islands
of the sea.
12 And he shall set up an ensign for the
nations, and shall assemble the outcasts of
Israel, and gather together [g]the dispersed
of Judah from the four corners of the earth.
13 [h]The envy also of Ephraim shall depart, and the adversaries of Judah shall be
cut off: Ephraim shall not envy Judah, and
Judah shall not vex Ephraim.
14 But they shall fly upon the shoulders of
the Philistines toward the west; they shall
spoil them of the east together: [i]they shall
lay their hand upon Edom and Moab; and
the children of Ammon [j]shall obey them.
15 And the LORD [k]shall utterly destroy
the tongue of the Egyptian sea; and with his
mighty wind shall he shake his hand over
the river, and shall smite it in the seven
streams, [l]and make *men* go over dryshod.
16 [m]And there shall be an highway for
the remnant of his people, which shall be
left, from Assyria; [n]like as it was to Israel in
the day that he came up out of the land of
Egypt.

12 And [o]in that day thou shalt say,
O LORD, I will praise thee: though
thou wast angry with me, thine anger is
turned away, and thou comfortedst me.
2 Behold, God *is* my salvation; I will trust,
and not be afraid: for the LORD [p]JEHOVAH
is my [q]strength and *my* song; he also is become my salvation.
3 Therefore with joy shall ye draw [r]wa-
ter out of the wells of salvation.
4 And in that day shall ye say, [s]Praise the
LORD, call upon his name, [t]declare his doings among the people, make mention that
his [u]name is exalted.
5 [v]Sing unto the LORD; for he hath done
excellent things: this *is* known in all the
earth.
6 [w]Cry out and shout, thou inhabitant of
Zion: for great *is* [x]the Holy One of Israel in
the midst of thee.

13 The [y]burden of Babylon, which Isaiah the son of Amoz did see.
2 [z]Lift ye up a banner [a]upon the high
mountain, exalt the voice unto them,
[b]shake the hand, that they may go into the
gates of the nobles.
3 I have commanded my sanctified ones,
I have also called [c]my mighty ones for mine
anger, *even* them that [d]rejoice in my highness.
4 The noise of a multitude in the mountains, like as of a great people; a tumultuous
noise of the kingdoms of nations gathered
together: the LORD of hosts mustereth the
host of the battle.
5 They come from a far country, from the
end of heaven, *even* the LORD, and the
weapons of his indignation, to destroy the
whole land.
6 ¶ Howl ye; [e]for the day of the LORD
is at hand; [f]it shall come as a destruction
from the Almighty.
7 Therefore shall all hands be faint, and
every man's heart shall melt:
8 And they shall be afraid: [g]pangs and
sorrows shall take hold of them; they shall
be in pain as a woman that travaileth: they
shall be amazed one at another; their faces
shall be as flames.
9 Behold, [h]the day of the LORD cometh,
cruel both with wrath and fierce anger, to
lay the land desolate: and he shall destroy
[i]the sinners thereof out of it.
10 For the stars of heaven and the con-
stellations thereof shall not give their light:
the sun shall be [j]darkened in his going
forth, and the moon shall not cause her light
to shine.
11 And I will punish the world for *their*
evil, and the wicked for their iniquity; [k]and
I will cause the arrogancy of the proud to
cease, and will lay low the haughtiness of
the terrible.
12 I will make a man more precious than
fine gold; even a man than the golden
wedge of Ophir.
13 [l]Therefore I will shake the heavens,
and the earth shall remove out of her place,
in the wrath of the LORD of hosts, and in
[m]the day of his fierce anger.
14 And it shall be as the chased roe, and
as a sheep that no man taketh up: [n]they
shall every man turn to his own people, and
flee every one into his own land.
15 Every one that is found shall be thrust
through; and every one that is joined *unto*
them shall fall by the sword.
16 Their children also shall be [o]dashed to
pieces before their eyes; their houses shall
be spoiled, and their wives ravished.

11:5 [w]Eph. 6:14
11:6 [x]ch. 65:25; Ezek. 34:25; Hos. 2:18
11:9 [y]Job 5:23; ch. 2:4 [z]Hab. 2:14
11:10 [a]ch. 2:11 [b]ver. 1; Rom. 15:12 [c]Rom. 15:10 [d]Heb. 4:1
11:11 [e]ch. 2:11 [f]Zech. 10:10
11:12 [g]John 7:35; Jam. 1:1
11:13 [h]Jer. 3:18; Ezek. 37:16; Hos. 1:11
11:14 [i]Dan. 11:41 [j]ch. 60:14
11:15 [k]Zech. 10:11 [l]Rev. 16:12
11:16 [m]ch. 19:23 [n]Ex. 14:29; ch. 51:10
12:1 [o]ch. 2:11
12:2 [p]Ps. 83:18 [q]Ex. 15:2; Ps. 118:14
12:3 [r]John 4:10
12:4 [s]1 Chron. 16:8; Ps. 105:1 [t]Ps. 145:4 [u]Ps. 34:3
12:5 [v]Ex. 15:1; Ps. 68:32
12:6 [w]ch. 54:1; Zeph. 3:14 [x]Ps. 71:22; ch. 41:14
13:1 [y]ch. 21:1; Jer. 50
13:2 [z]ch. 5:26; Jer. 50:2 [a]Jer. 51:25 [b]ch. 10:32
13:3 [c]Joel 3:11 [d]Ps. 149:2
13:6 [e]Zeph. 1:7; Rev. 6:17 [f]Job 31:23; Joel 1:15
13:8 [g]Ps. 48:6; ch. 21:3
13:9 [h]Mal. 4:1 [i]Ps. 104:35; Prov. 2:22
13:10 [j]ch. 24:21; Ezek. 32:7; Joel 2:31; Matt. 24:29; Mark 13:24; Luke 21:25
13:11 [k]ch. 2:17
13:13 [l]Hag. 2:6 [m]Ps. 110:5; Lam. 1:12
13:14 [n]Jer. 50:16
13:16 [o]Ps. 137:9; Nah. 3:10; Zech. 14:2

17 [p]Behold, I will stir up the Medes against them, which shall not regard silver; and *as for* gold, they shall not delight in it.

18 *Their* bows also shall dash the young men to pieces; and they shall have no pity on the fruit of the womb; their eye shall not spare children.

19 ¶ [q]And Babylon, the glory of kingdoms, the beauty of the Chaldees' excellency, shall be as when God overthrew [r]Sodom and Gomorrah.

20 [s]It shall never be inhabited, neither shall it be dwelt in from generation to generation: neither shall the Arabian pitch tent there; neither shall the shepherds make their fold there.

21 [t]But wild beasts of the desert shall lie there; and their houses shall be full of doleful creatures; and owls shall dwell there, and satyrs shall dance there.

22 And the wild beasts of the islands shall cry in their desolate houses, and dragons in *their* pleasant palaces: [u]and her time *is* near to come, and her days shall not be prolonged.

14 For the LORD [v]will have mercy on Jacob, and [w]will yet choose Israel, and set them in their own land: [x]and the strangers shall be joined with them, and they shall cleave to the house of Jacob.

2 And the people shall take them, [y]and bring them to their place: and the house of Israel shall possess them in the land of the LORD for servants and handmaids: and they shall take them captives, whose captives they were; [z]and they shall rule over their oppressors.

3 And it shall come to pass in the day that the LORD shall give thee rest from thy sorrow, and from thy fear, and from the hard bondage wherein thou wast made to serve,

4 ¶ That thou [a]shalt take up this proverb against the king of Babylon, and say, How hath the oppressor ceased! the [b]golden city ceased!

5 The LORD hath broken [c]the staff of the wicked, *and* the sceptre of the rulers.

6 He who smote the people in wrath with a continual stroke, he that ruled the nations in anger, is persecuted, *and* none hindereth.

7 The whole earth is at rest, *and* is quiet: they break forth into singing.

8 [d]Yea, the fir trees rejoice at thee, *and* the cedars of Lebanon, *saying,* Since thou art laid down, no feller is come up against us.

9 [e]Hell from beneath is moved for thee to meet *thee* at thy coming: it stirreth up the dead for thee, *even* all the chief ones of the earth; it hath raised up from their thrones all the kings of the nations.

10 All they shall speak and say unto thee, Art thou also become weak as we? art thou become like unto us?

11 Thy pomp is brought down to the grave, *and* the noise of thy viols: the worm is spread under thee, and the worms cover thee.

12 [f]How art thou fallen from heaven, O Lucifer, son of the morning! *how* art thou cut down to the ground, which didst weaken the nations!

13 For thou hast said in thine heart, [g]I will ascend into heaven, [h]I will exalt my throne above the stars of God: I will sit also upon the mount of the congregation, [i]in the sides of the north:

14 I will ascend above the heights of the clouds; [j]I will be like the most High.

15 Yet thou [k]shalt be brought down to hell, to the sides of the pit.

16 They that see thee shall narrowly look upon thee, *and* consider thee, *saying, Is* this the man that made the earth to tremble, that did shake kingdoms;

17 *That* made the world as a wilderness, and destroyed the cities thereof; *that* opened not the house of his prisoners?

18 All the kings of the nations, *even* all of them, lie in glory, every one in his own house.

19 But thou art cast out of thy grave like an abominable branch, *and as* the raiment of those that are slain, thrust through with a sword, that go down to the stones of the pit; as a carcase trodden under feet.

20 Thou shalt not be joined with them in burial, because thou hast destroyed thy land, *and* slain thy people: [l]the seed of evildoers shall never be renowned.

21 Prepare slaughter for his children [m]for the iniquity of their fathers; that they do not rise, nor possess the land, nor fill the face of the world with cities.

22 For I will rise up against them, saith the LORD of hosts, and cut off from Babylon [n]the name, and [o]remnant, [p]and son, and nephew, saith the LORD.

23 [q]I will also make it a possession for the bittern, and pools of water: and I will sweep it with the besom of destruction, saith the LORD of hosts.

24 ¶ The LORD of hosts hath sworn, saying, Surely as I have thought, so shall it come to pass; and as I have purposed, *so* shall it stand:

25 That I will break the Assyrian in my land, and upon my mountains tread him under foot: then shall [r]his yoke depart from off them, and his burden depart from off their shoulders.

26 This *is* the purpose that is purposed upon the whole earth: and this *is* the hand that is stretched out upon all the nations.

27 For the LORD of hosts hath [s]purposed, and who shall disannul *it?* and his hand *is* stretched out, and who shall turn it back?

28 In the year that [t]king Ahaz died was this burden.

29 ¶ Rejoice not thou, whole Palestina, [u]because the rod of him that smote thee is broken: for out of the serpent's root shall come forth a cockatrice, [v]and his fruit *shall be* a fiery flying serpent.

30 And the firstborn of the poor shall feed, and the needy shall lie down in safety:

13:17 [p]ch. 21:2; Jer. 51:11; Dan. 5:28
13:19 [q]ch. 14:4 [r]Gen. 19:24; Deut. 29:23; Jer. 49:18
13:20 [s]Jer. 50:3
13:21 [t]ch. 34:11; Rev. 18:2
13:22 [u]Jer. 51:33
14:1 [v]Ps. 102:13 [w]Zech. 1:17 [x]ch. 60:4; Eph. 2:12
14:2 [y]ch. 49:22 [z]ch. 60:14
14:4 [a]ch. 13:19; Hab. 2:6 [b]Rev. 18:16
14:5 [c]Ps. 125:3
14:8 [d]ch. 55:12; Ezek. 31:16
14:9 [e]Ezek. 32:21
14:12 [f]ch. 34:4
14:13 [g]Matt. 11:23 [h]Dan. 8:10 [i]Ps. 48:2
14:14 [j]ch. 47:8; 2 Thess. 2:4
14:15 [k]Matt. 11:23
14:20 [l]Job 18:19; Ps. 21:10
14:21 [m]Ex. 20:5; Matt. 23:35
14:22 [n]Prov. 10:7; Jer. 51:62 [o]1 Kings 14:10 [p]Job 18:19
14:23 [q]ch. 34:11; Zeph. 2:14
14:25 [r]ch. 10:27
14:27 [s]2 Chron. 20:6; Job 9:12; Ps. 33:11; Prov. 19:21; ch. 43:13; Dan. 4:31
14:28 [t]2 Kings 16:20
14:29 [u]2 Chron. 26:6 [v]2 Kings 18:8

and I will kill thy root with famine, and he shall slay thy remnant.

31 Howl, O gate; cry, O city; thou, whole Palestina, *art* dissolved: for there shall come from the north a smoke, and none *shall be* alone in his appointed times.

32 What shall *one* then answer the messengers of the nation? That [w]the LORD hath founded Zion, and [x]the poor of his people shall trust in it.

15 The [y]burden of Moab. Because in the night [z]Ar of Moab is laid waste, *and* brought to silence; because in the night Kir of Moab is laid waste, *and* brought to silence;

2 [a]He is gone up to Bajith, and to Dibon, the high places, to weep: Moab shall howl over Nebo, and over Medeba: [b]on all their heads *shall be* baldness, *and* every beard cut off.

3 In their streets they shall gird themselves with sackcloth: [c]on the tops of their houses, and in their streets, every one shall howl, weeping abundantly.

4 And Heshbon shall cry, [d]and Elealeh: their voice shall be heard *even* unto Jahaz: therefore the armed soldiers of Moab shall cry out; his life shall be grievous unto him.

5 [e]My heart shall cry out for Moab; his fugitives *shall flee* unto Zoar, an [f]heifer of three years old: for [g]by the mounting up of Luhith with weeping shall they go it up; for in the way of Horonaim they shall raise up a cry of destruction.

6 For the waters [h]of Nimrim shall be desolate: for the hay is withered away, the grass faileth, there is no green thing.

7 Therefore the abundance they have gotten, and that which they have laid up, shall they carry away to the brook of the willows.

8 For the cry is gone round about the borders of Moab; the howling thereof unto Eglaim, and the howling thereof unto Beerelim.

9 For the waters of Dimon shall be full of blood: for I will bring more upon Dimon, [i]lions upon him that escapeth of Moab, and upon the remnant of the land.

16 Send [j]ye the lamb to the ruler of the land [k]from Sela to the wilderness, unto the mount of the daughter of Zion.

2 For it shall be, *that*, as a wandering bird cast out of the nest, *so* the daughters of Moab shall be at the fords of [l]Arnon.

3 Take counsel, execute judgment; make thy shadow as the night in the midst of the noonday; hide the outcasts; bewray not him that wandereth.

4 Let mine outcasts dwell with thee, Moab; be thou a covert to them from the face of the spoiler: for the extortioner is at an end, the spoiler ceaseth, the oppressors are consumed out of the land.

5 And in mercy [m]shall the throne be established: and he shall sit upon it in truth in the tabernacle of David, [n]judging, and seeking judgment, and hasting righteousness.

14:32 [w]Ps. 87:1 [x]Zeph. 3:12; Zech. 11:11
15:1 [y]Jer. 48:1; Ezek. 25:8-11; Am. 2:1 [z]Num. 21:28
15:2 [a]ch. 16:12 [b]Lev. 21:5; ch. 3:24; Jer. 47:5; Ezek. 7:18
15:3 [c]Jer. 48:38
15:4 [d]ch. 16:9
15:5 [e]ch. 16:11; Jer. 48:31 [f]ch. 16:14; Jer. 48:34 [g]Jer. 48:5
15:6 [h]Num. 32:36
15:9 [i]2 Kings 17:25
16:1 [j]2 Kings 3:4 [k]2 Kings 14:7
16:2 [l]Num. 21:13
16:5 [m]Dan. 7:14; Mic. 4:7; Luke 1:33 [n]Ps. 72:2
16:6 [o]Jer. 48:29; Zeph. 2:10 [p]ch. 28:15
16:7 [q]Jer. 48:20 [r]2 Kings 3:25
16:8 [s]ch. 24:7 [t]ver. 9
16:9 [u]Jer. 48:32 [v]ch. 15:4
16:10 [w]ch. 24:8; Jer. 48:33
16:11 [x]ch. 15:5; Jer. 48:36
16:12 [y]ch. 15:2
16:14 [z]ch. 21:16
17:1 [a]2 Kings 16:9; Jer. 49:23; Am. 1:3; Zech. 9:1
17:2 [b]Jer. 7:33
17:3 [c]ch. 7:16
17:4 [d]ch. 10:16
17:5 [e]Jer. 51:33
17:6 [f]ch. 24:13
17:7 [g]Mic. 7:7

6 ¶ We have heard of the [o]pride of Moab; *he is* very proud: *even* of his haughtiness, and his pride, and his wrath: [p]*but* his lies *shall* not *be* so.

7 Therefore shall Moab [q]howl for Moab, every one shall howl: for the foundations [r]of Kir-hareseth shall ye mourn; surely *they are* stricken.

8 For [s]the fields of Heshbon languish, *and* [t]the vine of Sibmah: the lords of the heathen have broken down the principal plants thereof, they are come *even* unto Jazer, they wandered *through* the wilderness: her branches are stretched out, they are gone over the sea.

9 ¶ Therefore [u]I will bewail with the weeping of Jazer the vine of Sibmah: I will water thee with my tears, [v]O Heshbon, and Elealeh: for the shouting for thy summer fruits and for thy harvest is fallen.

10 And [w]gladness is taken away, and joy out of the plentiful field; and in the vineyards there shall be no singing, neither shall there be shouting: the treaders shall tread out no wine in *their* presses; I have made *their vintage* shouting to cease.

11 Wherefore [x]my bowels shall sound like an harp for Moab, and mine inward parts for Kir-haresh.

12 ¶ And it shall come to pass, when it is seen that Moab is weary on [y]the high place, that he shall come to his sanctuary to pray; but he shall not prevail.

13 This *is* the word that the LORD hath spoken concerning Moab since that time.

14 But now the LORD hath spoken, saying, Within three years, [z]as the years of an hireling, and the glory of Moab shall be contemned, with all that great multitude; and the remnant *shall be* very small *and* feeble.

17 The [a]burden of Damascus. Behold, Damascus is taken away from *being* a city, and it shall be a ruinous heap.

2 The cities of Aroer *are* forsaken: they shall be for flocks, which shall lie down, and [b]none shall make *them* afraid.

3 [c]The fortress also shall cease from Ephraim, and the kingdom from Damascus, and the remnant of Syria: they shall be as the glory of the children of Israel, saith the LORD of hosts.

4 And in that day it shall come to pass, *that* the glory of Jacob shall be made thin, and [d]the fatness of his flesh shall wax lean.

5 [e]And it shall be as when the harvestman gathereth the corn, and reapeth the ears with his arm; and it shall be as he that gathereth ears in the valley of Rephaim.

6 ¶ [f]Yet gleaning grapes shall be left in it, as the shaking of an olive tree, two *or* three berries in the top of the uppermost bough, four *or* five in the outmost fruitful branches thereof, saith the LORD God of Israel.

7 At that day shall a man [g]look to his Maker, and his eyes shall have respect to the Holy One of Israel.

8 And he shall not look to the altars, the work of his hands, neither shall respect *that*

which his fingers have made, either the
groves, or the images.
9 ¶ In that day shall his strong cities be
as a forsaken bough, and an uppermost
branch, which they left because of the children of Israel: and there shall be desolation.
10 Because thou hast forgotten [h]the God
of thy salvation, and hast not been mindful
of the rock of thy strength, therefore shalt
thou plant pleasant plants, and shalt set it
with strange slips:
11 In the day shalt thou make thy plant to
grow, and in the morning shalt thou make
thy seed to flourish: *but* the harvest *shall be*
a heap in the day of grief and of desperate
sorrow.
12 ¶ Woe to the multitude of many people, *which* make a noise [i]like the noise of
the seas; and to the rushing of nations, *that*
make a rushing like the rushing of mighty
waters!
13 The nations shall rush like the rushing
of many waters: but *God* shall [j]rebuke
them, and they shall flee far off, and [k]shall
be chased as the chaff of the mountains before the wind, and like a rolling thing before
the whirlwind.
14 And behold at eveningtide trouble; *and*
before the morning he *is* not. This *is* the
portion of them that spoil us, and the lot of
them that rob us.

18

Woe [l]to the land shadowing with
wings, which *is* beyond the rivers of
Ethiopia:
2 That sendeth ambassadors by the sea,
even in vessels of bulrushes upon the waters, *saying*, Go, ye swift messengers, to [m]a
nation scattered and peeled, to a people terrible from their beginning hitherto; a nation
meted out and trodden down, whose land
the rivers have spoiled!
3 All ye inhabitants of the world, and
dwellers on the earth, see ye, [n]when he lifteth up an ensign on the mountains; and
when he bloweth a trumpet, hear ye.
4 For so the LORD said unto me, I will take
my rest, and I will consider in my dwelling
place like a clear heat upon herbs, *and* like
a cloud of dew in the heat of harvest.
5 For afore the harvest, when the bud is
perfect, and the sour grape is ripening in the
flower, he shall both cut off the sprigs with
pruning hooks, and take away *and* cut
down the branches.
6 They shall be left together unto the
fowls of the mountains, and to the beasts of
the earth: and the fowls shall summer upon
them, and all the beasts of the earth shall
winter upon them.
7 ¶ In that time [o]shall the present be
brought unto the LORD of hosts of a people
scattered and peeled, and from a people terrible from their beginning hitherto; a nation
meted out and trodden under foot, whose
land the rivers have spoiled, to the place of
the name of the LORD of hosts, the mount
Zion.

17:10 [h]Ps. 68:19
17:12 [i]Jer. 6:23
17:13 [j]Ps. 9:5 [k]Ps. 83:13; Hos. 13:3
18:1 [l]ch. 20:4; Ezek. 30:4; Zeph. 2:12
18:2 [m]ver. 7
18:3 [n]ch. 5:26
18:7 [o]Ps. 68:31; ch. 16:1; Zeph. 3:10; Mal. 1:11
19:1 [p]Jer. 46:13; Ezek. 29 [q]Ps. 18:10 [r]Ex. 12:12; Jer. 43:12
19:2 [s]Judg. 7:22; 1 Sam. 14:16; 2 Chron. 20:23
19:3 [t]ch. 8:19
19:4 [u]ch. 20:4; Jer. 46:26; Ezek. 29:19
19:5 [v]Jer. 51:36; Ezek. 30:12
19:6 [w]2 Kings 19:24
19:9 [x]1 Kings 10:28; Prov. 7:16
19:11 [y]Num. 13:22
19:12 [z]1 Cor. 1:20
19:13 [a]Jer. 2:16
19:14 [b]1 Kings 22:22; ch. 29:10
19:15 [c]ch. 9:14
19:16 [d]Jer. 51:30; Nah. 3:13 [e]ch. 11:15

19

The [p]burden of Egypt. Behold, the
LORD [q]rideth upon a swift cloud, and
shall come into Egypt: and [r]the idols of
Egypt shall be moved at his presence, and
the heart of Egypt shall melt in the midst
of it.
2 And I will [s]set the Egyptians against
the Egyptians: and they shall fight every
one against his brother, and every one
against his neighbour; city against city, *and*
kingdom against kingdom.
3 And the spirit of Egypt shall fail in the
midst thereof; and I will destroy the counsel
thereof: and they shall [t]seek to the idols,
and to the charmers, and to them that have
familiar spirits, and to the wizards.
4 And the Egyptians will I give over [u]into
the hand of a cruel lord; and a fierce king
shall rule over them, saith the Lord, the
LORD of hosts.
5 [v]And the waters shall fail from the sea,
and the river shall be wasted and dried up.
6 And they shall turn the rivers far away;
and the brooks [w]of defence shall be emptied
and dried up: the reeds and flags shall
wither.
7 The paper reeds by the brooks, by the
mouth of the brooks, and every thing sown
by the brooks, shall wither, be driven away,
and be no *more*.
8 The fishers also shall mourn, and all
they that cast angle into the brooks shall
lament, and they that spread nets upon the
waters shall languish.
9 Moreover they that work in [x]fine flax,
and they that weave networks, shall be confounded.
10 And they shall be broken in the purposes thereof, all that make sluices *and*
ponds for fish.
11 ¶ Surely the princes of [y]Zoan *are*
fools, the counsel of the wise counsellors of
Pharaoh is become brutish: how say ye unto
Pharaoh, I *am* the son of the wise, the son of
ancient kings?
12 [z]Where *are* they? where *are* thy wise
men? and let them tell thee now, and let
them know what the LORD of hosts hath
purposed upon Egypt.
13 The princes of Zoan are become fools,
[a]the princes of Noph are deceived; they
have also seduced Egypt, *even they that are*
the stay of the tribes thereof.
14 The LORD hath mingled [b]a perverse
spirit in the midst thereof: and they have
caused Egypt to err in every work thereof,
as a drunken *man* staggereth in his vomit.
15 Neither shall there be *any* work for
Egypt, which [c]the head or tail, branch or
rush, may do.
16 In that day shall Egypt [d]be like unto
women: and it shall be afraid and fear because of the shaking of the hand of the
LORD of hosts, [e]which he shaketh over it.
17 And the land of Judah shall be a terror
unto Egypt, every one that maketh mention
thereof shall be afraid in himself, because of

the counsel of the LORD of hosts, which he
hath determined against it.
18 ¶ In that day shall five cities in the land
of Egypt [f]speak the language of Canaan,
and swear to the LORD of hosts; one shall be
called, The city of destruction.
19 In that day [g]shall there be an altar to
the LORD in the midst of the land of Egypt,
and a pillar at the border thereof to the
LORD.
20 And [h]it shall be for a sign and for a
witness unto the LORD of hosts in the land of
Egypt: for they shall cry unto the LORD because of the oppressors, and he shall send
them a saviour, and a great one, and he
shall deliver them.
21 And the LORD shall be known to
Egypt, and the Egyptians shall know the
LORD in that day, and [i]shall do sacrifice
and oblation; yea, they shall vow a vow
unto the LORD, and perform *it.*
22 And the LORD shall smite Egypt: he
shall smite and heal *it:* and they shall return
even to the LORD, and he shall be intreated
of them, and shall heal them.
23 ¶ In that day [j]shall there be a highway
out of Egypt to Assyria, and the Assyrian
shall come into Egypt, and the Egyptian
into Assyria, and the Egyptians shall serve
with the Assyrians.
24 In that day shall Israel be the third
with Egypt and with Assyria, *even* a blessing in the midst of the land:
25 Whom the LORD of hosts shall bless,
saying, Blessed *be* Egypt my people, and
Assyria [k]the work of my hands, and Israel
mine inheritance.
20 In the year that [l]Tartan came unto
Ashdod, (when Sargon the king of
Assyria sent him,) and fought against Ashdod, and took it;
2 At the same time spake the LORD by Isaiah the son of Amoz, saying, Go and loose
the [m]sackcloth from off thy loins, and put
off thy shoe from thy foot. And he did so,
[n]walking naked and barefoot.
3 And the LORD said, Like as my servant
Isaiah hath walked naked and barefoot
three years [o]*for* a sign and wonder upon
Egypt and upon Ethiopia;
4 So shall the king of Assyria lead away
the Egyptians prisoners, and the Ethiopians
captives, young and old, naked and barefoot, [p]even with *their* buttocks uncovered,
to the shame of Egypt.
5 [q]And they shall be afraid and ashamed
of Ethiopia their expectation, and of Egypt
their glory.
6 And the inhabitant of this isle shall say
in that day, Behold, such *is* our expectation,
whither we flee for help to be delivered
from the king of Assyria: and how shall we
escape?
21 The burden of the desert of the sea.
As [r]whirlwinds in the south pass
through; *so* it cometh from the desert, from
a terrible land.
2 A grievous vision is declared unto me;
[s]the treacherous dealer dealeth treacherously, and the spoiler spoileth. [t]Go up,
O Elam: besiege, O Media; all the sighing
thereof have I made to cease.
3 Therefore [u]are my loins filled with
pain: [v]pangs have taken hold upon me, as
the pangs of a woman that travaileth: I was
bowed down at the hearing *of it;* I was dismayed at the seeing *of it.*
4 My heart panted, fearfulness affrighted
me: [w]the night of my pleasure hath he
turned into fear unto me.
5 [x]Prepare the table, watch in the watch-
tower, eat, drink: arise, ye princes, *and*
anoint the shield.
6 For thus hath the Lord said unto me, Go,
set a watchman, let him declare what he
seeth.
7 [y]And he saw a chariot *with* a couple of
horsemen, a chariot of asses, *and* a chariot
of camels; and he hearkened diligently with
much heed:
8 And he cried, A lion: My lord, I stand
continually upon the [z]watchtower in the
daytime, and I am set in my ward whole
nights:
9 And, behold, here cometh a chariot of
men, *with* a couple of horsemen. And he
answered and said, [a]Babylon is fallen, is
fallen; and [b]all the graven images of her
gods he hath broken unto the ground.
10 [c]O my threshing, and the corn of my
floor: that which I have heard of the LORD of
hosts, the God of Israel, have I declared
unto you.
11 ¶ [d]The burden of Dumah. He calleth
to me out of Seir, Watchman, what of the
night? Watchman, what of the night?
12 The watchman said, The morning
cometh, and also the night: if ye will enquire, enquire ye: return, come.
13 ¶ [e]The burden upon Arabia. In the forest in Arabia shall ye lodge, O ye travelling
companies [f]of Dedanim.
14 The inhabitants of the land of Tema
brought water to him that was thirsty, they
prevented with their bread him that fled.
15 For they fled from the swords, from the
drawn sword, and from the bent bow, and
from the grievousness of war.
16 For thus hath the Lord said unto me,
Within a year, [g]according to the years of an
hireling, and all the glory of [h]Kedar shall
fail:
17 And the residue of the number of archers, the mighty men of the children of Kedar, shall be diminished: for the LORD God
of Israel hath spoken *it.*
22 The burden of the valley of vision.
What aileth thee now, that thou art
wholly gone up to the housetops?
2 Thou that art full of stirs, a tumultuous
city, [i]a joyous city: thy slain *men are* not
slain with the sword, nor dead in battle.
3 All thy rulers are fled together, they are
bound by the archers: all that are found in
thee are bound together, *which* have fled
from far.

19:18 [f]Zeph. 3:9
19:19 [g]Gen. 28:18; Ex. 24:4; Josh. 22:10
19:20 [h]Josh. 4:20
19:21 [i]Mal. 1:11
19:23 [j]ch. 11:16
19:25 [k]Ps. 100:3; ch. 29:23; Hos. 2:23; Eph. 2:10
20:1 [l]2 Kings 18:17
20:2 [m]Zech. 13:4 [n]1 Sam. 19:24; Mic. 1:8
20:3 [o]ch. 8:18
20:4 [p]2 Sam. 10:4; ch. 3:17; Jer. 13:22; Mic. 1:11
20:5 [q]2 Kings 18:21; ch. 30:3
21:1 [r]Zech. 9:14
21:2 [s]ch. 33:1 [t]ch. 13:17; Jer. 49:34
21:3 [u]ch. 15:5 [v]ch. 13:8
21:4 [w]Deut. 28:67
21:5 [x]Dan. 5:5
21:7 [y]ver. 9
21:8 [z]Hab. 2:1
21:9 [a]Jer. 51:8; Rev. 14:8 [b]ch. 46:1; Jer. 50:2
21:10 [c]Jer. 51:33
21:11 [d]1 Chron. 1:30; Jer. 49:7; Ezek. 35:2; Obad. 1
21:13 [e]Jer. 49:28 [f]1 Chron. 1:9
21:16 [g]ch. 16:14 [h]Ps. 120:5; ch. 60:7
22:2 [i]ch. 32:13

4 Therefore said I, Look away from me; [j]I will weep bitterly, labour not to comfort me, because of the spoiling of the daughter of my people.

5 [k]For *it is* a day of trouble, and of treading down, and of perplexity [l]by the Lord GOD of hosts in the valley of vision, breaking down the walls, and of crying to the mountains.

6 [m]And Elam bare the quiver with chariots of men *and* horsemen, and [n]Kir uncovered the shield.

7 And it shall come to pass, *that* thy choicest valleys shall be full of chariots, and the horsemen shall set themselves in array at the gate.

8 ¶ And he discovered the covering of Judah, and thou didst look in that day to the armour [o]of the house of the forest.

9 [p]Ye have seen also the breaches of the city of David, that they are many: and ye gathered together the waters of the lower pool.

10 And ye have numbered the houses of Jerusalem, and the houses have ye broken down to fortify the wall.

11 [q]Ye made also a ditch between the two walls for the water of the old pool: but ye have not looked unto [r]the maker thereof, neither had respect unto him that fashioned it long ago.

12 And in that day did the Lord GOD of hosts [s]call to weeping, and to mourning, and [t]to baldness, and to girding with sackcloth:

13 And behold joy and gladness, slaying oxen, and killing sheep, eating flesh, and drinking wine: [u]let us eat and drink; for to morrow we shall die.

14 [v]And it was revealed in mine ears by the LORD of hosts, Surely this iniquity [w]shall not be purged from you till ye die, saith the Lord GOD of hosts.

15 ¶ Thus saith the Lord GOD of hosts, Go, get thee unto this treasurer, *even* unto [x]Shebna, [y]which *is* over the house, *and say,*

16 What hast thou here? and whom hast thou here, that thou hast hewed thee out a sepulchre here, *as* he [z]that heweth him out a sepulchre on high, *and* that graveth an habitation for himself in a rock?

17 Behold, the LORD will carry thee away with a mighty captivity, [a]and will surely cover thee.

18 He will surely violently turn and toss thee *like* a ball into a large country: there shalt thou die, and there the chariots of thy glory *shall be* the shame of thy lord's house.

19 And I will drive thee from thy station, and from thy state shall he pull thee down.

20 ¶ And it shall come to pass in that day, that I will call my servant [b]Eliakim the son of Hilkiah:

21 And I will clothe him with thy robe, and strengthen him with thy girdle, and I will commit thy government into his hand: and he shall be a father to the inhabitants of Jerusalem, and to the house of Judah.

22 And the key of the house of David will I lay upon his shoulder; so he shall [c]open, and none shall shut; and he shall shut, and none shall open.

23 And I will fasten him *as* [d]a nail in a sure place; and he shall be for a glorious throne to his father's house.

24 And they shall hang upon him all the glory of his father's house, the offspring and the issue, all vessels of small quantity, from the vessels of cups, even to all the vessels of flagons.

25 In that day, saith the LORD of hosts, shall the nail that is fastened in the sure place be removed, and be cut down, and fall; and the burden that *was* upon it shall be cut off: for the LORD hath spoken *it.*

23 The [e]burden of Tyre. Howl, ye ships of Tarshish; for it is laid waste, so that there is no house, no entering in: [f]from the land of Chittim it is revealed to them.

2 Be still, ye inhabitants of the isle; thou whom the merchants of Zidon, that pass over the sea, have replenished.

3 And by great waters the seed of Sihor, the harvest of the river, *is* her revenue; and [g]she is a mart of nations.

4 Be thou ashamed, O Zidon: for the sea hath spoken, *even* the strength of the sea, saying, I travail not, nor bring forth children, neither do I nourish up young men, *nor* bring up virgins.

5 [h]As at the report concerning Egypt, *so* shall they be sorely pained at the report of Tyre.

6 Pass ye over to Tarshish; howl, ye inhabitants of the isle.

7 *Is* this your [i]joyous *city,* whose antiquity *is* of ancient days? her own feet shall carry her afar off to sojourn.

8 Who hath taken this counsel against Tyre, [j]the crowning *city,* whose merchants *are* princes, whose traffickers *are* the honourable of the earth?

9 The LORD of hosts hath purposed it, to stain the pride of all glory, *and* to bring into contempt all the honourable of the earth.

10 Pass through thy land as a river, O daughter of Tarshish: *there is* no more strength.

11 He stretched out his hand over the sea, he shook the kingdoms: the LORD hath given a commandment against the merchant *city,* to destroy the strong holds thereof.

12 And he said, [k]Thou shalt no more rejoice, O thou oppressed virgin, daughter of Zidon: arise, [l]pass over to Chittim; there also shalt thou have no rest.

13 Behold the land of the Chaldeans; this people was not, *till* the Assyrian founded it for them [m]that dwell in the wilderness: they set up the towers thereof, they raised up the palaces thereof; *and* he brought it to ruin.

14 [n]Howl, ye ships of Tarshish: for your strength is laid waste.

22:4 [j]Jer. 4:19
22:5 [k]ch. 37:3 [l]Lam. 1:5
22:6 [m]Jer. 49:35 [n]ch. 15:1
22:8 [o]1 Kings 7:2
22:9 [p]2 Kings 20:20; 2 Chron. 32:4
22:11 [q]Neh. 3:16 [r]ch. 37:26
22:12 [s]Joel 1:13 [t]Ezra 9:3; ch. 15:2; Mic. 1:16
22:13 [u]ch. 56:12; 1 Cor. 15:32
22:14 [v]ch. 5:9 [w]1 Sam. 3:14; Ezek. 24:13
22:15 [x]2 Kings 18:37; ch. 36:3 [y]1 Kings 4:6
22:16 [z]2 Sam. 18:18; Matt. 27:60
22:17 [a]Esth. 7:8
22:20 [b]2 Kings 18:18
22:22 [c]Job 12:14; Rev. 3:7
22:23 [d]Ezra 9:8
23:1 [e]Jer. 25:22; Ezek. 26; Am. 1:9; Zech. 9:2 [f]ver. 12
23:3 [g]Ezek. 27:3
23:5 [h]ch. 19:16
23:7 [i]ch. 22:2
23:8 [j]Ezek. 28:2
23:12 [k]Rev. 18:22 [l]ver. 1
23:13 [m]Ps. 72:9
23:14 [n]ver. 1; Ezek. 27:25

15 And it shall come to pass in that day,
that Tyre shall be forgotten seventy years,
according to the days of one king: after the
end of seventy years shall Tyre sing as an
harlot.
16 Take an harp, go about the city, thou
harlot that hast been forgotten; make sweet
melody, sing many songs, that thou mayest
be remembered.
17 ¶ And it shall come to pass after the
end of seventy years, that the LORD will visit
Tyre, and she shall turn to her hire, and
[o]shall commit fornication with all the kingdoms of the world upon the face of the
earth.
18 And her merchandise and her hire
[p]shall be holiness to the LORD: it shall not
be treasured nor laid up; for her merchandise shall be for them that dwell before the
LORD, to eat sufficiently, and for durable
clothing.

24 Behold, the LORD maketh the earth
empty, and maketh it waste, and
turneth it upside down, and scattereth
abroad the inhabitants thereof.
2 And it shall be, as with the people, so
with the [q]priest; as with the servant, so with
his master; as with the maid, so with her
mistress; [r]as with the buyer, so with the
seller; as with the lender, so with the borrower; as with the taker of usury, so with
the giver of usury to him.
3 The land shall be utterly emptied, and
utterly spoiled: for the LORD hath spoken
this word.
4 The earth mourneth *and* fadeth away,
the world languisheth *and* fadeth away, the
haughty people of the earth do languish.
5 [s]The earth also is defiled under the inhabitants thereof; because they have transgressed the laws, changed the ordinance,
broken the everlasting covenant.
6 Therefore hath [t]the curse devoured the
earth, and they that dwell therein are desolate: therefore the inhabitants of the earth
are burned, and few men left.
7 [u]The new wine mourneth, the vine languisheth, all the merryhearted do sigh.
8 The mirth [v]of tabrets ceaseth, the noise
of them that rejoice endeth, the joy of the
harp ceaseth.
9 They shall not drink wine with a song;
strong drink shall be bitter to them that
drink it.
10 The city of confusion is broken down:
every house is shut up, that no man may
come in.
11 *There is* a crying for wine in the
streets; all joy is darkened, the mirth of the
land is gone.
12 In the city is left desolation, and the
gate is smitten with destruction.
13 ¶ When thus it shall be in the midst of
the land among the people, [w]*there shall be*
as the shaking of an olive tree, *and* as the
gleaning grapes when the vintage is done.
14 They shall lift up their voice, they shall

23:17 [o]Rev. 17:2
23:18 [p]Zech. 14:20
24:2 [q]Hos. 4:9 [r]Ezek. 7:12
24:5 [s]Gen. 3:17; Num. 35:33
24:6 [t]Mal. 4:6
24:7 [u]ch. 16:8; Joel 1:10
24:8 [v]Jer. 7:34; Ezek. 26:13; Hos. 2:11; Rev. 18:22
24:13 [w]ch. 17:5
24:15 [x]Mal. 1:11
24:16 [y]Jer. 5:11
24:17 [z]1 Kings 19:17; Jer. 48:43; Am. 5:19
24:18 [a]Gen. 7:11 [b]Ps. 18:7
24:19 [c]Jer. 4:23
24:20 [d]ch. 19:14
24:21 [e]Ps. 76:12
24:23 [f]ch. 13:10; Ezek. 32:7; Joel 2:31 [g]Rev. 19:4 [h]Heb. 12:22
25:1 [i]Ex. 15:2; Ps. 118:28 [j]Ps. 98:1 [k]Num. 23:19
25:2 [l]ch. 21:9; Jer. 51:37
25:3 [m]Rev. 11:13
25:4 [n]ch. 4:6
25:6 [o]ch. 2:2 [p]Prov. 9:2; Matt. 22:4 [q]Dan. 7:14; Matt. 8:11
25:7 [r]2 Cor. 3:15; Eph. 4:18

sing for the majesty of the LORD, they shall
cry aloud from the sea.
15 Wherefore glorify ye the LORD in the
fires, *even* [x]the name of the LORD God of
Israel in the isles of the sea.
16 ¶ From the uttermost part of the earth
have we heard songs, *even* glory to the righteous. But I said, My leanness, my leanness,
woe unto me! [y]the treacherous dealers
have dealt treacherously; yea, the treacherous dealers have dealt very treacherously.
17 [z]Fear, and the pit, and the snare, *are*
upon thee, O inhabitant of the earth.
18 And it shall come to pass, *that* he who
fleeth from the noise of the fear shall fall
into the pit; and he that cometh up out of the
midst of the pit shall be taken in the snare:
for [a]the windows from on high are open,
and [b]the foundations of the earth do shake.
19 [c]The earth is utterly broken down, the
earth is clean dissolved, the earth is moved
exceedingly.
20 The earth shall [d]reel to and fro like a
drunkard, and shall be removed like a cottage; and the transgression thereof shall be
heavy upon it; and it shall fall, and not rise
again.
21 And it shall come to pass in that day,
that the LORD shall punish the host of the
high ones *that are* on high, [e]and the kings
of the earth upon the earth.
22 And they shall be gathered together,
as prisoners are gathered in the pit, and
shall be shut up in the prison, and after
many days shall they be visited.
23 Then the [f]moon shall be confounded,
and the sun ashamed, when the LORD of
hosts shall [g]reign in [h]mount Zion, and in
Jerusalem, and before his ancients gloriously.

25 O LORD, thou *art* my God; [i]I will exalt thee, I will praise thy name; [j]for
thou hast done wonderful *things;* [k]*thy*
counsels of old *are* faithfulness *and* truth.
2 For thou hast made [l]of a city an heap;
of a defenced city a ruin: a palace of strangers to be no city; it shall never be built.
3 Therefore shall the strong people [m]glo-
rify thee, the city of the terrible nations
shall fear thee.
4 For thou hast been a strength to the
poor, a strength to the needy in his distress,
[n]a refuge from the storm, a shadow from
the heat, when the blast of the terrible ones
is as a storm *against* the wall.
5 Thou shalt bring down the noise of
strangers, as the heat in a dry place; *even*
the heat with the shadow of a cloud: the
branch of the terrible ones shall be brought
low.
6 ¶ And in [o]this mountain shall [p]the
LORD of hosts make unto [q]all people a feast
of fat things, a feast of wines on the lees, of
fat things full of marrow, of wines on the
lees well refined.
7 And he will destroy in this mountain the
face of the covering cast over all people,
and [r]the vail that is spread over all nations.

8 He will [s]swallow up death in victory; and the Lord GOD will [t]wipe away tears from off all faces; and the rebuke of his people shall he take away from off all the earth: for the LORD hath spoken *it*.

9 ¶ And it shall be said in that day, Lo, this *is* our God; [u]we have waited for him, and he will save us: this *is* the LORD; we have waited for him, [v]we will be glad and rejoice in his salvation.

10 For in this mountain shall the hand of the LORD rest, and Moab shall be trodden down under him, even as straw is trodden down for the dunghill.

11 And he shall spread forth his hands in the midst of them, as he that swimmeth spreadeth forth *his hands* to swim: and he shall bring down their pride together with the spoils of their hands.

12 And the [w]fortress of the high fort of thy walls shall he bring down, lay low, *and* bring to the ground, *even* to the dust.

26 In [x]that day shall this song be sung in the land of Judah; We have a strong city; [y]salvation will *God* appoint *for* walls and bulwarks.

2 [z]Open ye the gates, that the righteous nation which keepeth the truth may enter in.

3 Thou wilt keep *him* in perfect peace, *whose* mind *is* stayed *on thee:* because he trusteth in thee.

4 Trust ye in the LORD for ever: [a]for in the LORD JEHOVAH *is* everlasting strength:

5 ¶ For he bringeth down them that dwell on high; [b]the lofty city, he layeth it low; he layeth it low, *even* to the ground; he bringeth it *even* to the dust.

6 The foot shall tread it down, *even* the feet of the poor, *and* the steps of the needy.

7 The way of the just *is* uprightness: [c]thou, most upright, dost weigh the path of the just.

8 Yea, [d]in the way of thy judgments, O LORD, have we waited for thee; the desire of *our* soul *is* to thy name, and to the remembrance of thee.

9 [e]With my soul have I desired thee in the night; yea, with my spirit within me will I seek thee early: for when thy judgments *are* in the earth, the inhabitants of the world will learn righteousness.

10 [f]Let favour be shewed to the wicked, *yet* will he not learn righteousness: in [g]the land of uprightness will he deal unjustly, and will not behold the majesty of the LORD.

11 LORD, *when* thy hand is lifted up, [h]they will not see: *but* they shall see, and be ashamed for *their* envy at the people; yea, the fire of thine enemies shall devour them.

12 ¶ LORD, thou wilt ordain peace for us: for thou also hast wrought all our works in us.

13 O LORD our God, [i]*other* lords beside thee have had dominion over us: *but* by thee only will we make mention of thy name.

14 *They are* dead, they shall not live; *they are* deceased, they shall not rise: therefore hast thou visited and destroyed them, and made all their memory to perish.

15 Thou hast increased the nation, O LORD, thou hast increased the nation: thou art glorified: thou hadst removed *it* far *unto* all the ends of the earth.

16 LORD, [j]in trouble have they visited thee, they poured out a prayer *when* thy chastening *was* upon them.

17 Like as [k]a woman with child, *that* draweth near the time of her delivery, is in pain, *and* crieth out in her pangs; so have we been in thy sight, O LORD.

18 We have been with child, we have been in pain, we have as it were brought forth wind; we have not wrought any deliverance in the earth; neither have [l]the inhabitants of the world fallen.

19 [m]Thy dead *men* shall live, *together with* my dead body shall they arise. [n]Awake and sing, ye that dwell in dust: for thy dew *is as* the dew of herbs, and the earth shall cast out the dead.

20 ¶ Come, my people, [o]enter thou into thy chambers, and shut thy doors about thee: hide thyself as it were [p]for a little moment, until the indignation be overpast.

21 For, behold, the LORD [q]cometh out of his place to punish the inhabitants of the earth for their iniquity: the earth also shall disclose her blood, and shall no more cover her slain.

27 In that day the LORD with his sore and great and strong sword shall punish leviathan the piercing serpent, [r]even leviathan that crooked serpent; and he shall slay [s]the dragon that *is* in the sea.

2 In that day [t]sing ye unto her, [u]A vineyard of red wine.

3 [v]I the LORD do keep it; I will water it every moment: lest *any* hurt it, I will keep it night and day.

4 Fury *is* not in me: who would set [w]the briers *and* thorns against me in battle? I would go through them, I would burn them together.

5 Or let him take hold [x]of my strength, *that* he may make peace with me; *and* he shall [y]make peace with me.

6 He shall cause them that come of Jacob [z]to take root: Israel shall blossom and bud, and fill the face of the world with fruit.

7 ¶ Hath he smitten him, as he smote those that smote him? *or* is he slain according to the slaughter of them that are slain by him?

8 [a]In measure, when it shooteth forth, thou wilt debate with it: [b]he stayeth his rough wind in the day of the east wind.

9 By this therefore shall the iniquity of Jacob be purged; and this *is* all the fruit to take away his sin; when he maketh all the stones of the altar as chalkstones that are beaten in sunder, the groves and images shall not stand up.

10 Yet the defenced city *shall be* desolate, *and* the habitation forsaken, and left like a wilderness: [c]there shall the calf feed, and

25:8 [s]Hos. 13:14; 1 Cor. 15:54; Rev. 20:14 [t]Rev. 7:17
25:9 [u]Gen. 49:18; Tit. 2:13 [v]Ps. 20:5
25:12 [w]ch. 26:5
26:1 [x]ch. 2:11 [y]ch. 60:18
26:2 [z]Ps. 118:19
26:4 [a]ch. 45:17
26:5 [b]ch. 25:12
26:7 [c]Ps. 37:23
26:8 [d]ch. 64:5
26:9 [e]Ps. 63:6; SSol. 3:1
26:10 [f]Eccl. 8:12; Rom. 2:4 [g]Ps. 143:10
26:11 [h]Job 34:27; Ps. 28:5; ch. 5:12
26:13 [i]2 Chron. 12:8
26:16 [j]Hos. 5:15
26:17 [k]ch. 13:8; John 16:21
26:18 [l]Ps. 17:14
26:19 [m]Ezek. 37:1 [n]Dan. 12:2
26:20 [o]Ex. 12:22 [p]Ps. 30:5; ch. 54:7; 2 Cor. 4:17
26:21 [q]Mic. 1:3; Jude 14
27:1 [r]Ps. 74:13 [s]ch. 51:9; Ezek. 29:3
27:2 [t]ch. 5:1 [u]Ps. 80:8; Jer. 2:21
27:3 [v]Ps. 121:4
27:4 [w]2 Sam. 23:6; ch. 9:18
27:5 [x]ch. 25:4 [y]Job 22:21
27:6 [z]ch. 37:31; Hos. 14:5
27:8 [a]Job 23:6; Ps. 6:1; Jer. 10:24; 1 Cor. 10:13 [b]Ps. 78:38
27:10 [c]ch. 17:2

there shall he lie down, and consume the branches thereof.

11 When the boughs thereof are withered, they shall be broken off: the women come, *and* set them on fire: for [d]it *is* a people of no understanding: therefore he that made them will not have mercy on them, and [e]he that formed them will shew them no favour.

12 ¶ And it shall come to pass in that day, *that* the LORD shall beat off from the channel of the river unto the stream of Egypt, and ye shall be gathered one by one, O ye children of Israel.

13 [f]And it shall come to pass in that day, [g]*that* the great trumpet shall be blown, and they shall come which were ready to perish in the land of Assyria, and the outcasts in the land of Egypt, and shall worship the LORD in the holy mount at Jerusalem.

28 Woe to [h]the crown of pride, to the drunkards of Ephraim, whose [i]glorious beauty *is* a fading flower, which *are* on the head of the fat valleys of them that are overcome with wine!

2 Behold, the Lord hath a mighty and strong one, [j]*which* as a tempest of hail *and* a destroying storm, as a flood of mighty waters overflowing, shall cast down to the earth with the hand.

3 [k]The crown of pride, the drunkards of Ephraim, shall be trodden under feet:

4 And [l]the glorious beauty, which *is* on the head of the fat valley, shall be a fading flower, *and* as the hasty fruit before the summer; which *when* he that looketh upon it seeth, while it is yet in his hand he eateth it up.

5 ¶ In that day shall the LORD of hosts be for a crown of glory, and for a diadem of beauty, unto the residue of his people,

6 And for a spirit of judgment to him that sitteth in judgment, and for strength to them that turn the battle to the gate.

7 ¶ But they also [m]have erred through wine, and through strong drink are out of the way; [n]the priest and the prophet have erred through strong drink, they are swallowed up of wine, they are out of the way through strong drink; they err in vision, they stumble *in* judgment.

8 For all tables are full of vomit *and* filthiness, *so that there is* no place *clean*.

9 ¶ [o]Whom shall he teach knowledge? and whom shall he make to understand doctrine? *them that are* weaned from the milk, *and* drawn from the breasts.

10 For precept *must be* upon precept, precept upon precept; line upon line, line upon line; here a little, *and* there a little:

11 For with [p]stammering lips and another tongue will he speak to this people.

12 To whom he said, This *is* the rest *wherewith* ye may cause the weary to rest; and this *is* the refreshing: yet they would not hear.

13 But the word of the LORD was unto them precept upon precept, precept upon precept; line upon line, line upon line; here a little, *and* there a little; that they might go, and fall backward, and be broken, and snared, and taken.

14 ¶ Wherefore hear the word of the LORD, ye scornful men, that rule this people which *is* in Jerusalem.

15 Because ye have said, We have made a covenant with death, and with hell are we at agreement; when the overflowing scourge shall pass through, it shall not come unto us: [q]for we have made lies our refuge, and under falsehood have we hid ourselves:

16 ¶ Therefore thus saith the Lord GOD, Behold, I lay in Zion for a foundation [r]a stone, a tried stone, a precious corner *stone*, a sure foundation: he that believeth shall not make haste.

17 Judgment also will I lay to the line, and righteousness to the plummet: and the hail shall sweep away [s]the refuge of lies, and the waters shall overflow the hiding place.

18 ¶ And your covenant with death shall be disannulled, and your agreement with hell shall not stand; when the overflowing scourge shall pass through, then ye shall be trodden down by it.

19 From the time that it goeth forth it shall take you: for morning by morning shall it pass over, by day and by night: and it shall be a vexation only *to* understand the report.

20 For the bed is shorter than that *a man* can stretch himself *on it:* and the covering narrower than that he can wrap himself *in it*.

21 For the LORD shall rise up as *in* mount [t]Perazim, he shall be wroth as *in* the valley of [u]Gibeon, that he may do his work, [v]his strange work; and bring to pass his act, his strange act.

22 Now therefore be ye not mockers, lest your bands be made strong: for I have heard from the Lord GOD of hosts [w]a consumption, even determined upon the whole earth.

23 ¶ Give ye ear, and hear my voice; hearken, and hear my speech.

24 Doth the plowman plow all day to sow? doth he open and break the clods of his ground?

25 When he hath made plain the face thereof, doth he not cast abroad the fitches, and scatter the cummin, and cast in the principal wheat and the appointed barley and the rie in their place?

26 For his God doth instruct him to discretion, *and* doth teach him.

27 For the fitches are not threshed with a threshing instrument, neither is a cart wheel turned about upon the cummin; but the fitches are beaten out with a staff, and the cummin with a rod.

28 Bread *corn* is bruised; because he will not ever be threshing it, nor break *it with* the wheel of his cart, nor bruise it *with* his horsemen.

29 This also cometh forth from the LORD

27:11 [d]Deut. 32:28; ch. 1:3; Jer. 8:7 [e]Deut. 32:18; ch. 43:1
27:13 [f]ch. 2:11 [g]Matt. 24:31; Rev. 11:15
28:1 [h]ver. 3 [i]ver. 4
28:2 [j]ch. 30:30; Ezek. 13:11
28:3 [k]ver. 1
28:4 [l]ver. 1
28:7 [m]Prov. 20:1; Hos. 4:11 [n]ch. 56:10
28:9 [o]Jer. 6:10
28:11 [p]1 Cor. 14:21
28:15 [q]Am. 2:4
28:16 [r]Gen. 49:24; Ps. 118:22; Matt. 21:42; Acts 4:11; Rom. 9:33; Eph. 2:20; 1 Pet. 2:6
28:17 [s]ver. 15
28:21 [t]2 Sam. 5:20; 1 Chron. 14:11 [u]Josh. 10:10; 2 Sam. 5:25; 1 Chron. 14:16 [v]Lam. 3:33
28:22 [w]ch. 10:22; Dan. 9:27

of hosts, [x]*which* *is* wonderful in counsel,
and excellent in working.

29

Woe [y]to Ariel, to Ariel, the city
[z]*where* David dwelt! add ye year to
year; let them kill sacrifices.
2 Yet I will distress Ariel, and there shall
be heaviness and sorrow: and it shall be
unto me as Ariel.
3 And I will camp against thee round
about, and will lay siege against thee with a
mount, and I will raise forts against thee.
4 And thou shalt be brought down, *and*
shalt speak out of the ground, and thy
speech shall be low out of the dust, and thy
voice shall be, as of one that hath a familiar
spirit, [a]out of the ground, and thy speech
shall whisper out of the dust.
5 Moreover the multitude of thy [b]strangers shall be like small dust, and the multitude of the terrible ones *shall be* [c]as chaff
that passeth away: yea, it shall be [d]at an
instant suddenly.
6 [e]Thou shalt be visited of the LORD of
hosts with thunder, and with earthquake,
and great noise, with storm and tempest,
and the flame of devouring fire.
7 ¶ [f]And the multitude of all the nations
that fight against Ariel, even all that fight
against her and her munition, and that distress her, shall be [g]as a dream of a night
vision.
8 [h]It shall even be as when an hungry
man dreameth, and, behold, he eateth; but
he awaketh, and his soul is empty: or as
when a thirsty man dreameth, and, behold,
he drinketh; but he awaketh, and, behold,
he is faint, and his soul hath appetite: so
shall the multitude of all the nations be, that
fight against mount Zion.
9 ¶ Stay yourselves, and wonder; cry ye
out, and cry: [i]they are drunken, [j]but not
with wine; they stagger, but not with strong
drink.
10 For [k]the LORD hath poured out upon
you the spirit of deep sleep, and hath
[l]closed your eyes: the prophets and your
rulers, [m]the seers hath he covered.
11 And the vision of all is become unto
you as the words of a book [n]that is sealed,
which *men* deliver to one that is learned,
saying, Read this, I pray thee: [o]and he
saith, I cannot; for it *is* sealed:
12 And the book is delivered to him that is
not learned, saying, Read this, I pray thee:
and he saith, I am not learned.
13 ¶ Wherefore the Lord said, [p]Forasmuch as this people draw near *me* with
their mouth, and with their lips do honour
me, but have removed their heart far from
me, and their fear toward me is taught by
[q]the precept of men:
14 [r]Therefore, behold, I will proceed to
do a marvellous work among this people,
even a marvellous work and a wonder: [s]for
the wisdom of their wise *men* shall perish,
and the understanding of their prudent *men*
shall be hid.
15 [t]Woe unto them that seek deep to hide

28:29 [x]Ps. 92:5; Jer. 32:19
29:1 [y]Ezek. 43:15 [z]2 Sam. 5:9
29:4 [a]ch. 8:19
29:5 [b]ch. 25:5 [c]Job 21:18; ch. 17:13 [d]ch. 30:13
29:6 [e]ch. 28:2
29:7 [f]ch. 37:36 [g]Job 20:8
29:8 [h]Ps. 73:20
29:9 [i]ch. 28:7 [j]ch. 51:21
29:10 [k]Rom. 11:8 [l]Ps. 69:23; ch. 6:10 [m]1 Sam. 9:9
29:11 [n]ch. 8:16 [o]Dan. 12:4; Rev. 5:1-5
29:13 [p]Ezek. 33:31; Matt. 15:8; Mark 7:6 [q]Col. 2:22
29:14 [r]Hab. 1:5 [s]Jer. 49:7; Obad. 8; 1 Cor. 1:19
29:15 [t]ch. 30:1 [u]Ps. 94:7
29:16 [v]ch. 45:9; Rom. 9:20
29:17 [w]ch. 32:15
29:18 [x]ch. 35:5
29:19 [y]ch. 61:1 [z]Jam. 2:5
29:20 [a]ch. 28:14 [b]Mic. 2:1
29:21 [c]Am. 5:10 [d]Prov. 28:21
29:22 [e]Josh. 24:3
29:23 [f]ch. 19:25; Eph. 2:10
29:24 [g]ch. 28:7
30:1 [h]ch. 29:15 [i]Deut. 29:19
30:2 [j]ch. 31:1 [k]Num. 27:21; Josh. 9:14; 1 Kings 22:7; Jer. 21:2
30:3 [l]ch. 20:5; Jer. 37:5
30:4 [m]ch. 19:11
30:5 [n]Jer. 2:36
30:6 [o]ch. 57:9; Hos. 8:9 [p]Deut. 8:15
30:7 [q]Jer. 37:7 [r]ver. 15; ch. 7:4

their counsel from the LORD, and their
works are in the dark, and [u]they say, Who
seeth us? and who knoweth us?
16 Surely your turning of things upside
down shall be esteemed as the potter's clay:
for shall the [v]work say of him that made it,
He made me not? or shall the thing framed
say of him that framed it, He had no understanding?
17 *Is* it not yet a very little while, and
[w]Lebanon shall be turned into a fruitful
field, and the fruitful field shall be esteemed
as a forest?
18 ¶ And [x]in that day shall the deaf hear
the words of the book, and the eyes of the
blind shall see out of obscurity, and out of
darkness.
19 [y]The meek also shall increase *their*
joy in the LORD, and [z]the poor among men
shall rejoice in the Holy One of Israel.
20 For the terrible one is brought to
nought, and [a]the scorner is consumed, and
all that [b]watch for iniquity are cut off:
21 That make a man an offender for a
word, and [c]lay a snare for him that reproveth in the gate, and turn aside the just [d]for
a thing of nought.
22 Therefore thus saith the LORD, [e]who
redeemed Abraham, concerning the house
of Jacob, Jacob shall not now be ashamed,
neither shall his face now wax pale.
23 But when he seeth his children, [f]the
work of mine hands, in the midst of him,
they shall sanctify my name, and sanctify
the Holy One of Jacob, and shall fear the
God of Israel.
24 They [g]also that erred in spirit shall
come to understanding, and they that murmured shall learn doctrine.

30

Woe to the rebellious children, saith
the LORD, [h]that take counsel, but not
of me; and that cover with a covering, but
not of my spirit, [i]that they may add sin to
sin:
2 [j]That walk to go down into Egypt, and
[k]have not asked at my mouth; to strengthen
themselves in the strength of Pharaoh, and
to trust in the shadow of Egypt!
3 [l]Therefore shall the strength of Pharaoh be your shame, and the trust in the
shadow of Egypt *your* confusion.
4 For his princes were at [m]Zoan, and his
ambassadors came to Hanes.
5 [n]They were all ashamed of a people
that could not profit them, nor be an help
nor profit, but a shame, and also a reproach.
6 [o]The burden of the beasts of the south:
into the land of trouble and anguish, from
whence *come* the young and old lion, [p]the
viper and fiery flying serpent, they will
carry their riches upon the shoulders of
young asses, and their treasures upon the
bunches of camels, to a people *that* shall
not profit *them.*
7 [q]For the Egyptians shall help in vain,
and to no purpose: therefore have I cried
concerning this, [r]Their strength *is* to sit
still.

8 ¶ Now go, [s]write it before them in a table, and note it in a book, that it may be for the time to come for ever and ever:

9 That [t]this *is* a rebellious people, lying children, children *that* will not hear the law of the LORD:

10 [u]Which say to the seers, See not; and to the prophets, Prophesy not unto us right things, [v]speak unto us smooth things, prophesy deceits:

11 Get you out of the way, turn aside out of the path, cause the Holy One of Israel to cease from before us.

12 Wherefore thus saith the Holy One of Israel, Because ye despise this word, and trust in oppression and perverseness, and stay thereon:

13 Therefore this iniquity shall be to you [w]as a breach ready to fall, swelling out in a high wall, whose breaking [x]cometh suddenly at an instant.

14 And [y]he shall break it as the breaking of the potters' vessel that is broken in pieces; he shall not spare: so that there shall not be found in the bursting of it a sherd to take fire from the hearth, or to take water *withal* out of the pit.

15 For thus saith the Lord GOD, the Holy One of Israel; [z]In returning and rest shall ye be saved; in quietness and in confidence shall be your strength: [a]and ye would not.

16 But ye said, No; for we will flee upon horses; therefore shall ye flee: and, We will ride upon the swift; therefore shall they that pursue you be swift.

17 [b]One thousand *shall flee* at the rebuke of one; at the rebuke of five shall ye flee: till ye be left as a beacon upon the top of a mountain, and as an ensign on an hill.

18 ¶ And therefore will the LORD wait, that he may be gracious unto you, and therefore will he be exalted, that he may have mercy upon you: for the LORD *is* a God of judgment: [c]blessed *are* all they that wait for him.

19 For the people [d]shall dwell in Zion at Jerusalem: thou shalt weep no more: he will be very gracious unto thee at the voice of thy cry; when he shall hear it, he will answer thee.

20 And *though* the Lord give you [e]the bread of adversity, and the water of affliction, yet shall not [f]thy teachers be removed into a corner any more, but thine eyes shall see thy teachers:

21 And thine ears shall hear a word behind thee, saying, This *is* the way, walk ye in it, when ye [g]turn to the right hand, and when ye turn to the left.

22 [h]Ye shall defile also the covering of thy graven images of silver, and the ornament of thy molten images of gold: thou shalt cast them away as a menstruous cloth; [i]thou shalt say unto it, Get thee hence.

23 [j]Then shall he give the rain of thy seed, that thou shalt sow the ground withal; and bread of the increase of the earth, and it shall be fat and plenteous: in that day shall thy cattle feed in large pastures.

24 The oxen likewise and the young asses that ear the ground shall eat clean provender, which hath been winnowed with the shovel and with the fan.

25 And there shall be [k]upon every high mountain, and upon every high hill, rivers *and* streams of waters in the day of the great slaughter, when the towers fall.

26 Moreover [l]the light of the moon shall be as the light of the sun, and the light of the sun shall be sevenfold, as the light of seven days, in the day that the LORD bindeth up the breach of his people, and healeth the stroke of their wound.

27 ¶ Behold, the name of the LORD cometh from far, burning *with* his anger, and the burden *thereof is* heavy: his lips are full of indignation, and his tongue as a devouring fire:

28 And [m]his breath, as an overflowing stream, [n]shall reach to the midst of the neck, to sift the nations with the sieve of vanity: and *there shall be* [o]a bridle in the jaws of the people, causing *them* to err.

29 Ye shall have a song, as in the night [p]*when* a holy solemnity is kept; and gladness of heart, as when one goeth with a pipe to come into the [q]mountain of the LORD, to the mighty One of Israel.

30 [r]And the LORD shall cause his glorious voice to be heard, and shall shew the lighting down of his arm, with the indignation of *his* anger, and *with* the flame of a devouring fire, *with* scattering, and tempest, [s]and hailstones.

31 For [t]through the voice of the LORD shall the Assyrian be beaten down, [u]*which* smote with a rod.

32 And *in* every place where the grounded staff shall pass, which the LORD shall lay upon him, *it* shall be with tabrets and harps: and in battles of [v]shaking will he fight with it.

33 [w]For Tophet *is* ordained of old; yea, for the king it is prepared; he hath made *it* deep and large: the pile thereof *is* fire and much wood; the breath of the LORD, like a stream of brimstone, doth kindle it.

31 Woe to them [x]that go down to Egypt for help; and [y]stay on horses, and trust in chariots, because *they are* many; and in horsemen, because they are very strong; but they look not unto the Holy One of Israel, [z]neither seek the LORD!

2 Yet he also *is* wise, and will bring evil, and [a]will not call back his words: but will arise against the house of the evildoers, and against the help of them that work iniquity.

3 Now the Egyptians *are* [b]men, and not God; and their horses flesh, and not spirit. When the LORD shall stretch out his hand, both he that helpeth shall fall, and he that is holpen shall fall down, and they all shall fail together.

4 For thus hath the LORD spoken unto me, [c]Like as the lion and the young lion roaring

30:8 [s]Hab. 2:2
30:9 [t]Deut. 32:20; ch. 1:4; ver. 1
30:10 [u]Jer. 11:21; Am. 2:12; Mic. 2:6 [v]1 Kings 22:13; Mic. 2:11
30:13 [w]Ps. 62:3 [x]ch. 29:5
30:14 [y]Ps. 2:9; Jer. 19:11
30:15 [z]ver. 7; ch. 7:4 [a]Matt. 23:37
30:17 [b]Rev. 26:8; Deut. 28:25; Josh. 23:10
30:18 [c]Ps. 2:12; Prov. 16:20; Jer. 17:7
30:19 [d]ch. 65:9
30:20 [e]1 Kings 22:27; Ps. 127:2 [f]Ps. 74:9; Am. 8:11
30:21 [g]Josh. 1:7
30:22 [h]2 Chron. 31:1; ch. 2:20 [i]Hos. 14:8
30:23 [j]Matt. 6:33; 1 Tim. 4:8
30:25 [k]ch. 2:14
30:26 [l]ch. 60:19
30:28 [m]ch. 11:4; 2 Thess. 2:8 [n]ch. 8:8 [o]ch. 37:29
30:29 [p]Ps. 42:4 [q]ch. 2:3
30:30 [r]ch. 29:6 [s]ch. 28:2
30:31 [t]ch. 37:26 [u]ch. 10:5
30:32 [v]ch. 11:15
30:33 [w]Jer. 7:31
31:1 [x]ch. 30:2; Ezek. 17:15 [y]Ps. 20:7; ch. 36:9 [z]Dan. 9:13; Hos. 7:7
31:2 [a]Num. 23:19
31:3 [b]Ps. 146:3
31:4 [c]Hos. 11:10; Am. 3:8

on his prey, when a multitude of shepherds is called forth against him, *he* will not be afraid of their voice, nor abase himself for the noise of them: [d]so shall the LORD of hosts come down to fight for mount Zion, and for the hill thereof.

5 [e]As birds flying, so will the LORD of hosts defend Jerusalem; [f]defending also he will deliver *it; and* passing over he will preserve *it*.

6 ¶ Turn ye unto *him from* whom the children of Israel have [g]deeply revolted.

7 For in that day every man shall [h]cast away his idols of silver, and his idols of gold, which your own hands have made unto you *for* [i]a sin.

8 ¶ Then shall the Assyrian [j]fall with the sword, not of a mighty man; and the sword, not of a mean man, shall devour him: but he shall flee from the sword, and his young men shall be discomfited.

9 And [k]he shall pass over to his strong hold for fear, and his princes shall be afraid of the ensign, saith the LORD, whose fire *is* in Zion, and his furnace in Jerusalem.

32

Behold, [l]a king shall reign in righteousness, and princes shall rule in judgment.

2 And a man shall be as an hiding place from the wind, and [m]a covert from the tempest; as rivers of water in a dry place, as the shadow of a great rock in a weary land.

3 And [n]the eyes of them that see shall not be dim, and the ears of them that hear shall hearken.

4 The heart also of the rash shall understand knowledge, and the tongue of the stammerers shall be ready to speak plainly.

5 The vile person shall be no more called liberal, nor the churl said *to be* bountiful.

6 For the vile person will speak villany, and his heart will work iniquity, to practise hypocrisy, and to utter error against the LORD, to make empty the soul of the hungry, and he will cause the drink of the thirsty to fail.

7 The instruments also of the churl *are* evil: he deviseth wicked devices to destroy the poor with lying words, even when the needy speaketh right.

8 But the liberal deviseth liberal things; and by liberal things shall he stand.

9 ¶ Rise up, ye women [o]that are at ease; hear my voice, ye careless daughters; give ear unto my speech.

10 Many days and years shall ye be troubled, ye careless women: for the vintage shall fail, the gathering shall not come.

11 Tremble, ye women that are at ease; be troubled, ye careless ones: strip you, and make you bare, and gird *sackcloth* upon *your* loins.

12 They shall lament for the teats, for the pleasant fields, for the fruitful vine.

13 [p]Upon the land of my people shall come up thorns *and* briers; yea, upon all the houses of joy *in* [q]the joyous city:

14 [r]Because the palaces shall be forsaken; the multitude of the city shall be left; the forts and towers shall be for dens for ever, a joy of wild asses, a pasture of flocks;

15 Until [s]the spirit be poured upon us from on high, and [t]the wilderness be a fruitful field, and the fruitful field be counted for a forest.

16 Then judgment shall dwell in the wilderness, and righteousness remain in the fruitful field.

17 [u]And the work of righteousness shall be peace; and the effect of righteousness quietness and assurance for ever.

18 And my people shall dwell in a peaceable habitation, and in sure dwellings, and in quiet resting places;

19 [v]When it shall hail, coming down [w]on the forest; and the city shall be low in a low place.

20 Blessed *are* ye that sow beside all waters, that send forth *thither* the feet of [x]the ox and the ass.

33

Woe to thee [y]that spoilest, and thou *wast* not spoiled; and dealest treacherously, and they dealt not treacherously with thee! [z]when thou shalt cease to spoil, thou shalt be spoiled; *and* when thou shalt make an end to deal treacherously, they shall deal treacherously with thee.

2 O LORD, be gracious unto us; [a]we have waited for thee: be thou their arm every morning, our salvation also in the time of trouble.

3 At the noise of the tumult the people fled; at the lifting up of thyself the nations were scattered.

4 And your spoil shall be gathered *like* the gathering of the caterpiller: as the running to and fro of locusts shall he run upon them.

5 [b]The LORD is exalted; for he dwelleth on high: he hath filled Zion with judgment and righteousness.

6 And wisdom and knowledge shall be the stability of thy times, *and* strength of salvation: the fear of the LORD *is* his treasure.

7 Behold, their valiant ones shall cry without: [c]the ambassadors of peace shall weep bitterly.

8 [d]The highways lie waste, the wayfaring man ceaseth: [e]he hath broken the covenant, he hath despised the cities, he regardeth no man.

9 [f]The earth mourneth *and* languisheth: Lebanon is ashamed *and* hewn down: Sharon is like a wilderness; and Bashan and Carmel shake off *their fruits*.

10 [g]Now will I rise, saith the LORD; now will I be exalted; now will I lift up myself.

11 [h]Ye shall conceive chaff, ye shall bring forth stubble: your breath, *as* fire, shall devour you.

12 And the people shall be *as* the burnings of lime: [i]*as* thorns cut up shall they be burned in the fire.

13 ¶ Hear, [j]ye *that are* far off, what I

31:4 *d*ch. 42:13
31:5 *e*Deut. 32:11; Ps. 91:4 *f*Ps. 37:40
31:6 *g*Hos. 9:9
31:7 *h*ch. 2:20 *i*1 Kings 12:30
31:8 *j*2 Kings 19:35; ch. 37:36
31:9 *k*ch. 37:37
32:1 *l*Ps. 45:1; Jer. 23:5; Hos. 3:5; Zech. 9:9
32:2 *m*ch. 4:6
32:3 *n*ch. 29:18
32:9 *o*Am. 6:1
32:13 *p*ch. 34:13; Hos. 9:6 *q*ch. 22:2
32:14 *r*ch. 27:10
32:15 *s*Ps. 104:30; Joel 2:28 *t*ch. 29:17
32:17 *u*Jam. 3:18
32:19 *v*ch. 30:30 *w*Zech. 11:2
32:20 *x*ch. 30:24
33:1 *y*ch. 21:2; Hab. 2:8 *z*Rev. 13:10
33:2 *a*ch. 25:9
33:5 *b*Ps. 97:9
33:7 *c*2 Kings 18:18
33:8 *d*Judg. 5:6 *e*2 Kings 18:14
33:9 *f*ch. 24:4
33:10 *g*Ps. 12:5
33:11 *h*Ps. 7:14; ch. 59:4
33:12 *i*ch. 9:18
33:13 *j*ch. 49:1

have done; and, ye *that are* near, acknowledge my might.

14 The sinners in Zion are afraid; fearfulness hath surprised the hypocrites. Who among us shall dwell with the devouring fire? who among us shall dwell with everlasting burnings?

15 He that [k]walketh righteously, and speaketh uprightly; he that despiseth the gain of oppressions, that shaketh his hands from holding of bribes, that stoppeth his ears from hearing of blood, and [l]shutteth his eyes from seeing evil;

16 He shall dwell on high: his place of defence *shall be* the munitions of rocks: bread shall be given him; his waters *shall be* sure.

17 Thine eyes shall see the king in his beauty: they shall behold the land that is very far off.

18 Thine heart shall meditate terror. [m]Where *is* the scribe? where *is* the receiver? where *is* he that counted the towers?

19 [n]Thou shalt not see a fierce people, [o]a people of a deeper speech than thou canst perceive; of a stammering tongue, *that thou canst* not understand.

20 [p]Look upon Zion, the city of our solemnities: thine eyes shall see [q]Jerusalem a quiet habitation, a tabernacle *that* shall not be taken down; [r]not one of [s]the stakes thereof shall ever be removed, neither shall any of the cords thereof be broken.

21 But there the glorious LORD *will be* unto us a place of broad rivers *and* streams; wherein shall go no galley with oars, neither shall gallant ship pass thereby.

22 For the LORD *is* our judge, the LORD *is* our [t]lawgiver, [u]the LORD *is* our king; he will save us.

23 Thy tacklings are loosed; they could not well strengthen their mast, they could not spread the sail: then is the prey of a great spoil divided; the lame take the prey.

24 And the inhabitant shall not say, I am sick: [v]the people that dwell therein *shall be* forgiven *their* iniquity.

34 [w]Come near, ye nations, to hear; and hearken, ye people: [x]let the earth hear, and all that is therein; the world, and all things that come forth of it.

2 For the indignation of the LORD *is* upon all nations, and *his* fury upon all their armies: he hath utterly destroyed them, he hath delivered them to the slaughter.

3 Their slain also shall be cast out, and [y]their stink shall come up out of their carcases, and the mountains shall be melted with their blood.

4 And [z]all the host of heaven shall be dissolved, and the heavens shall be [a]rolled together as a scroll: [b]and all their host shall fall down, as the leaf falleth off from the vine, and as a [c]falling *fig* from the fig tree.

5 For [d]my sword shall be bathed in heaven: behold, it [e]shall come down upon Idumea, and upon the people of my curse, to judgment.

6 The sword of the LORD is filled with blood, it is made fat with fatness, *and* with the blood of lambs and goats, with the fat of the kidneys of rams: for [f]the LORD hath a sacrifice in Bozrah, and a great slaughter in the land of Idumea.

7 And the unicorns shall come down with them, and the bullocks with the bulls; and their land shall be soaked with blood, and their dust made fat with fatness.

8 For *it is* the day of the LORD's [g]vengeance, *and* the year of recompences for the controversy of Zion.

9 [h]And the streams thereof shall be turned into pitch, and the dust thereof into brimstone, and the land thereof shall become burning pitch.

10 It shall not be quenched night nor day; [i]the smoke thereof shall go up for ever: [j]from generation to generation it shall lie waste; none shall pass through it for ever and ever.

11 ¶ [k]But the cormorant and the bittern shall possess it; the owl also and the raven shall dwell in it: and [l]he shall stretch out upon it the line of confusion, and the stones of emptiness.

12 They shall call the nobles thereof to the kingdom, but none *shall be* there, and all her princes shall be nothing.

13 And [m]thorns shall come up in her palaces, nettles and brambles in the fortresses thereof: and [n]it shall be an habitation of dragons, *and* a court for owls.

14 The wild beasts of the desert shall also meet with the wild beasts of the island, and the satyr shall cry to his fellow; the screech owl also shall rest there, and find for herself a place of rest.

15 There shall the great owl make her nest, and lay, and hatch, and gather under her shadow: there shall the vultures also be gathered, every one with her mate.

16 ¶ Seek ye out of the book of the LORD, and read: no one of these shall fail, none shall want her mate: for my mouth it hath commanded, and his spirit it hath gathered them.

17 And he hath cast the lot for them, and his hand hath divided it unto them by line: they shall possess it for ever, from generation to generation shall they dwell therein.

35 The [o]wilderness and the solitary place shall be glad for them; and the desert shall rejoice, and blossom as the rose.

2 [p]It shall blossom abundantly, and rejoice even with joy and singing: the glory of Lebanon shall be given unto it, the excellency of Carmel and Sharon, they shall see the glory of the LORD, *and* the excellency of our God.

3 ¶ [q]Strengthen ye the weak hands, and confirm the feeble knees.

4 Say to them *that are* of a fearful heart, Be strong, fear not: behold, your God will come *with* vengeance, *even* God *with* a recompence; he will come and save you.

33:15 [k]Ps. 15:2 [l]Ps. 119:37
33:18 [m]1 Cor. 1:20
33:19 [n]2 Kings 19:32 [o]Deut. 28:49; Jer. 5:15
33:20 [p]Ps. 48:12 [q]Ps. 46:5 [r]ch. 37:33 [s]ch. 54:2
33:22 [t]Jam. 4:12 [u]Ps. 89:18
33:24 [v]Jer. 50:20
34:1 [w]Ps. 49:1 [x]Deut. 32:1
34:3 [y]Joel 2:20
34:4 [z]Ps. 102:26; Ezek. 32:7; Joel 2:31; Matt. 24:29; 2 Pet. 3:10 [a]Rev. 6:14 [b]ch. 14:12 [c]Rev. 6:13
34:5 [d]Jer. 46:10 [e]Jer. 49:7; Mal. 1:4
34:6 [f]ch. 63:1; Jer. 49:13; Zeph. 1:7
34:8 [g]ch. 63:4
34:9 [h]Deut. 29:23
34:10 [i]Rev. 14:11 [j]Mal. 1:4
34:11 [k]ch. 14:23; Zeph. 2:14; Rev. 18:2 [l]2 Kings 21:13; Lam. 2:8
34:13 [m]ch. 32:13; Hos. 9:6 [n]ch. 13:21
35:1 [o]ch. 55:12
35:2 [p]ch. 32:15
35:3 [q]Job 4:3; Heb. 12:12

5 Then the [r]eyes of the blind shall be opened, and [s]the ears of the deaf shall be unstopped.

6 Then shall the [t]lame *man* leap as an hart, and the [u]tongue of the dumb sing: for in the wilderness shall [v]waters break out, and streams in the desert.

7 And the parched ground shall become a pool, and the thirsty land springs of water: in [w]the habitation of dragons, where each lay, *shall be* grass with reeds and rushes.

8 And an highway shall be there, and a way, and it shall be called The way of holiness; [x]the unclean shall not pass over it; but it *shall be* for those: the wayfaring men, though fools, shall not err *therein*.

9 [y]No lion shall be there, nor *any* ravenous beast shall go up thereon, it shall not be found there; but the redeemed shall walk *there*:

10 And the [z]ransomed of the LORD shall return, and come to Zion with songs and everlasting joy upon their heads: they shall obtain joy and gladness, and [a]sorrow and sighing shall flee away.

36 Now [b]it came to pass in the fourteenth year of king Hezekiah, *that* Sennacherib king of Assyria came up against all the defenced cities of Judah, and took them.

2 And the king of Assyria sent Rabshakeh from Lachish to Jerusalem unto king Hezekiah with a great army. And he stood by the conduit of the upper pool in the highway of the fuller's field.

3 Then came forth unto him Eliakim, Hilkiah's son, which was over the house, and Shebna the scribe, and Joah, Asaph's son, the recorder.

4 ¶ [c]And Rabshakeh said unto them, Say ye now to Hezekiah, Thus saith the great king, the king of Assyria, What confidence *is* this wherein thou trustest?

5 I say, *sayest thou*, (but *they are but* vain words) *I have* counsel and strength for war: now on whom dost thou trust, that thou rebellest against me?

6 Lo, thou trustest in the [d]staff of this broken reed, on Egypt; whereon if a man lean, it will go into his hand, and pierce it: so *is* Pharaoh king of Egypt to all that trust in him.

7 But if thou say to me, We trust in the LORD our God: *is it* not he, whose high places and whose altars Hezekiah hath taken away, and said to Judah and to Jerusalem, Ye shall worship before this altar?

8 Now therefore give pledges, I pray thee, to my master the king of Assyria, and I will give thee two thousand horses, if thou be able on thy part to set riders upon them.

9 How then wilt thou turn away the face of one captain of the least of my master's servants, and put thy trust on Egypt for chariots and for horsemen?

10 And am I now come up without the LORD against this land to destroy it? the LORD said unto me, Go up against this land, and destroy it.

11 ¶ Then said Eliakim and Shebna and Joah unto Rabshakeh, Speak, I pray thee, unto thy servants in the Syrian language; for we understand *it*: and speak not to us in the Jews' language, in the ears of the people that *are* on the wall.

12 ¶ But Rabshakeh said, Hath my master sent me to thy master and to thee to speak these words? *hath he* not *sent me* to the men that sit upon the wall, that they may eat their own dung, and drink their own piss with you?

13 Then Rabshakeh stood, and cried with a loud voice in the Jews' language, and said, Hear ye the words of the great king, the king of Assyria.

14 Thus saith the king, Let not Hezekiah deceive you: for he shall not be able to deliver you.

15 Neither let Hezekiah make you trust in the LORD, saying, The LORD will surely deliver us: this city shall not be delivered into the hand of the king of Assyria.

16 Hearken not to Hezekiah: for thus saith the king of Assyria, Make *an agreement* with me *by* a present, and come out to me: [e]and eat ye every one of his vine, and every one of his fig tree, and drink ye every one the waters of his own cistern;

17 Until I come and take you away to a land like your own land, a land of corn and wine, a land of bread and vineyards.

18 *Beware* lest Hezekiah persuade you, saying, The LORD will deliver us. Hath any of the gods of the nations delivered his land out of the hand of the king of Assyria?

19 Where *are* the gods of Hamath and Arphad? where *are* the gods of Sepharvaim? and have they delivered Samaria out of my hand?

20 Who *are they* among all the gods of these lands, that have delivered their land out of my hand, that the LORD should deliver Jerusalem out of my hand?

21 But they held their peace, and answered him not a word: for the king's commandment was, saying, Answer him not.

22 ¶ Then came Eliakim, the son of Hilkiah, that *was* over the household, and Shebna the scribe, and Joah, the son of Asaph, the recorder, to Hezekiah with *their* clothes rent, and told him the words of Rabshakeh.

37 And [f]it came to pass, when king Hezekiah heard *it*, that he rent his clothes, and covered himself with sackcloth, and went into the house of the LORD.

2 And he sent Eliakim, who *was* over the household, and Shebna the scribe, and the elders of the priests covered with sackcloth, unto Isaiah the prophet the son of Amoz.

3 And they said unto him, Thus saith Hezekiah, This day *is* a day of trouble, and of rebuke, and of blasphemy: for the children are come to the birth, and *there is* not strength to bring forth.

35:5 [r]ch. 29:18; Matt. 9:27; John 9:6 [s]Matt. 11:5; Mark 7:32
35:6 [t]Matt. 11:5; John 5:8; Acts 3:2 [u]ch. 32:4; Matt. 9:32 [v]ch. 41:18; John 7:38
35:7 [w]ch. 34:13
35:8 [x]ch. 52:1; Joel 3:17; Rev. 21:27
35:9 [y]Lev. 26:6; ch. 11:9; Ezek. 34:25
35:10 [z]ch. 51:11 [a]ch. 25:8; Rev. 7:17
36:1 [b]2 Kings 18:13; 2 Chron. 32:1
36:4 [c]2 Kings 18:19
36:6 [d]Ezek. 29:6
36:16 [e]Zech. 3:10
37:1 [f]2 Kings 19:1

4 It may be the LORD thy God will hear the words of Rabshakeh, whom the king of Assyria his master hath sent to reproach the living God, and will reprove the words which the LORD thy God hath heard: wherefore lift up *thy* prayer for the remnant that is left.

5 So the servants of king Hezekiah came to Isaiah.

6 ¶ And Isaiah said unto them, Thus shall ye say unto your master, Thus saith the LORD, Be not afraid of the words that thou hast heard, wherewith the servants of the king of Assyria have blasphemed me.

7 Behold, I will send a blast upon him, and he shall hear a rumour, and return to his own land; and I will cause him to fall by the sword in his own land.

8 ¶ So Rabshakeh returned, and found the king of Assyria warring against Libnah: for he had heard that he was departed from Lachish.

9 And he heard say concerning Tirhakah king of Ethiopia, He is come forth to make war with thee. And when he heard *it*, he sent messengers to Hezekiah, saying,

10 Thus shall ye speak to Hezekiah king of Judah, saying, Let not thy God, in whom thou trustest, deceive thee, saying, Jerusalem shall not be given into the hand of the king of Assyria.

11 Behold, thou hast heard what the kings of Assyria have done to all lands by destroying them utterly; and shalt thou be delivered?

12 Have the gods of the nations delivered them which my fathers have destroyed, *as* Gozan, and Haran, and Rezeph, and the children of Eden which *were* in Telassar?

13 Where *is* the king of [g]Hamath, and the king of Arphad, and the king of the city of Sepharvaim, Hena, and Ivah?

14 ¶ And Hezekiah received the letter from the hand of the messengers, and read it: and Hezekiah went up unto the house of the LORD, and spread it before the LORD.

15 And Hezekiah prayed unto the LORD, saying,

16 O LORD of hosts, God of Israel, that dwellest *between* the cherubims, thou *art* the God, *even* thou alone, of all the kingdoms of the earth: thou hast made heaven and earth.

17 [h]Incline thine ear, O LORD, and hear; open thine eyes, O LORD, and see: and hear all the words of Sennacherib, which hath sent to reproach the living God.

18 Of a truth, LORD, the kings of Assyria have laid waste all the nations, and their countries,

19 And have cast their gods into the fire: for they *were* no gods, but the work of men's hands, wood and stone: therefore they have destroyed them.

20 Now therefore, O LORD our God, save us from his hand, that all the kingdoms of the earth may know that thou *art* the LORD, *even* thou only.

21 ¶ Then Isaiah the son of Amoz sent unto Hezekiah, saying, Thus saith the LORD God of Israel, Whereas thou hast prayed to me against Sennacherib king of Assyria:

22 This *is* the word which the LORD hath spoken concerning him; The virgin, the daughter of Zion, hath despised thee, *and* laughed thee to scorn; the daughter of Jerusalem hath shaken her head at thee.

23 Whom hast thou reproached and blasphemed? and against whom hast thou exalted *thy* voice, and lifted up thine eyes on high? *even* against the Holy One of Israel.

24 By thy servants hast thou reproached the Lord, and hast said, By the multitude of my chariots am I come up to the height of the mountains, to the sides of Lebanon; and I will cut down the tall cedars thereof, *and* the choice fir trees thereof: and I will enter into the height of his border, *and* the forest of his Carmel.

25 I have digged, and drunk water; and with the sole of my feet have I dried up all the rivers of the besieged places.

26 Hast thou not heard long ago, *how* I have done it; *and* of ancient times, that I have formed it? now have I brought it to pass, that thou shouldest be to lay waste defenced cities *into* ruinous heaps.

27 Therefore their inhabitants *were* of small power, they were dismayed and confounded: they were *as* the grass of the field, and *as* the green herb, *as* the grass on the housetops, and *as corn* blasted before it be grown up.

28 But I know thy abode, and thy going out, and thy coming in, and thy rage against me.

29 Because thy rage against me, and thy tumult, is come up into mine ears, therefore [i]will I put my hook in thy nose, and my bridle in thy lips, and I will turn thee back by the way by which thou camest.

30 And this *shall be* a sign unto thee, Ye shall eat *this* year such as groweth of itself; and the second year that which springeth of the same: and in the third year sow ye, and reap, and plant vineyards, and eat the fruit thereof.

31 And the remnant that is escaped of the house of Judah shall again take root downward, and bear fruit upward:

32 For out of Jerusalem shall go forth a remnant, and they that escape out of mount Zion: the [j]zeal of the LORD of hosts shall do this.

33 Therefore thus saith the LORD concerning the king of Assyria, He shall not come into this city, nor shoot an arrow there, nor come before it with shields, nor cast a bank against it.

34 By the way that he came, by the same shall he return, and shall not come into this city, saith the LORD.

35 For I will [k]defend this city to save it for mine own sake, and for my servant David's sake.

36 Then the [l]angel of the LORD went

37:13 [g]Jer. 49:23
37:17 [h]Dan. 9:18
37:29 [i]ch. 30:28; Ezek. 38:4
37:32 [j]2 Kings 19:31; ch. 9:7
37:35 [k]2 Kings 20:6; ch. 38:6
37:36 [l]2 Kings 19:35

forth, and smote in the camp of the Assyrians a hundred and fourscore and five thousand: and when they arose early in the morning, behold, they *were* all dead corpses.

37 ¶ So Sennacherib king of Assyria departed, and went and returned, and dwelt at Nineveh.

38 And it came to pass, as he was worshipping in the house of Nisroch his god, that Adrammelech and Sharezer his sons smote him with the sword; and they escaped into the land of Armenia: and Esarhaddon his son reigned in his stead.

38 In [m]those days was Hezekiah sick unto death. And Isaiah the prophet the son of Amoz came unto him, and said unto him, Thus saith the LORD, [n]Set thine house in order: for thou shalt die, and not live.

2 Then Hezekiah turned his face toward the wall, and prayed unto the LORD,

3 And said, [o]Remember now, O LORD, I beseech thee, how I have walked before thee in truth and with a perfect heart, and have done *that which is* good in thy sight. And Hezekiah wept sore.

4 ¶ Then came the word of the LORD to Isaiah, saying,

5 Go, and say to Hezekiah, Thus saith the LORD, the God of David thy father, I have heard thy prayer, I have seen thy tears: behold, I will add unto thy days fifteen years.

6 And I will deliver thee and this city out of the hand of the king of Assyria: and [p]I will defend this city.

7 And this *shall be* [q]a sign unto thee from the LORD, that the LORD will do this thing that he hath spoken;

8 Behold, I will bring again the shadow of the degrees, which is gone down in the sun dial of Ahaz, ten degrees backward. So the sun returned ten degrees, by which degrees it was gone down.

9 ¶ The writing of Hezekiah king of Judah, when he had been sick, and was recovered of his sickness:

10 I said in the cutting off of my days, I shall go to the gates of the grave: I am deprived of the residue of my years.

11 I said, I shall not see the LORD, *even* the LORD, [r]in the land of the living: I shall behold man no more with the inhabitants of the world.

12 [s]Mine age is departed, and is removed from me as a shepherd's tent: I have cut off like a weaver my life: he will cut me off with pining sickness: from day *even* to night wilt thou make an end of me.

13 I reckoned till morning, *that*, as a lion, so will he break all my bones: from day *even* to night wilt thou make an end of me.

14 Like a crane *or* a swallow, so did I chatter: [t]I did mourn as a dove: mine eyes fail *with looking* upward: O LORD, I am oppressed; undertake for me.

15 What shall I say? he hath both spoken unto me, and himself hath done *it*: I shall go softly all my years [u]in the bitterness of my soul.

16 O Lord, by these *things men* live, and in all these *things is* the life of my spirit: so wilt thou recover me, and make me to live.

17 Behold, for peace I had great bitterness: but thou hast in love to my soul *delivered it* from the pit of corruption: for thou hast cast all my sins behind thy back.

18 For [v]the grave can *not* praise thee, death can *not* celebrate thee: they that go down into the pit cannot hope for thy truth.

19 The living, the living, he shall praise thee, as I *do* this day: [w]the father to the children shall make known thy truth.

20 The LORD *was ready* to save me: therefore we will sing my songs to the stringed instruments all the days of our life in the house of the LORD.

21 For [x]Isaiah had said, Let them take a lump of figs, and lay *it* for a plaister upon the boil, and he shall recover.

22 [y]Hezekiah also had said, What *is* the sign that I shall go up to the house of the LORD?

39 At [z]that time Merodach-baladan, the son of Baladan, king of Babylon, sent letters and a present to Hezekiah: for he had heard that he had been sick, and was recovered.

2 [a]And Hezekiah was glad of them, and shewed them the house of his precious things, the silver, and the gold, and the spices, and the precious ointment, and all the house of his armour, and all that was found in his treasures: there was nothing in his house, nor in all his dominion, that Hezekiah shewed them not.

3 ¶ Then came Isaiah the prophet unto king Hezekiah, and said unto him, What said these men? and from whence came they unto thee? And Hezekiah said, They are come from a far country unto me, *even* from Babylon.

4 Then said he, What have they seen in thine house? And Hezekiah answered, All that *is* in mine house have they seen: there is nothing among my treasures that I have not shewed them.

5 Then said Isaiah to Hezekiah, Hear the word of the LORD of hosts:

6 Behold, the days come, [b]that all that *is* in thine house, and *that* which thy fathers have laid up in store until this day, shall be carried to Babylon: nothing shall be left, saith the LORD.

7 And of thy sons that shall issue from thee, which thou shalt beget, shall they take away; and they shall be eunuchs in the palace of the king of Babylon.

8 Then said Hezekiah to Isaiah, [c]Good *is* the word of the LORD which thou hast spoken. He said moreover, For there shall be peace and truth in my days.

40 Comfort ye, comfort ye my people, saith your God.

2 Speak ye comfortably to Jerusalem, and cry unto her, that her warfare is accom-

38:1 [m]2 Kings 20:1; 2 Chron. 32:24 [n]2 Sam. 17:23
38:3 [o]Neh. 13:14
38:6 [p]ch. 37:35
38:7 [q]2 Kings 20:8; ch. 7:11
38:11 [r]Ps. 27:13
38:12 [s]Job 7:6
38:14 [t]ch. 59:11
38:15 [u]Job 7:11
38:18 [v]Ps. 6:5; Eccl. 9:10
38:19 [w]Deut. 4:9; Ps. 78:3
38:21 [x]2 Kings 20:7
38:22 [y]2 Kings 20:8
39:1 [z]2 Kings 20:12
39:2 [a]2 Chron. 32:31
39:6 [b]Jer. 20:5
39:8 [c]1 Sam. 3:18

plished, that her iniquity is pardoned: [d]for
she hath received of the LORD's hand double for all her sins.
3 ¶ [e]The voice of him that crieth in the
wilderness, [f]Prepare ye the way of the
LORD, [g]make straight in the desert a highway for our God.
4 Every valley shall be exalted, and every
mountain and hill shall be made low: [h]and
the crooked shall be made straight, and the
rough places plain:
5 And the glory of the LORD shall be revealed, and all flesh shall see *it* together: for
the mouth of the LORD hath spoken *it*.
6 The voice said, Cry. And he said, What
shall I cry? [i]All flesh *is* grass, and all the
goodliness thereof *is* as the flower of the
field:
7 The grass withereth, the flower fadeth:
because [j]the spirit of the LORD bloweth
upon it: surely the people *is* grass.
8 The grass withereth, the flower fadeth:
but [k]the word of our God shall stand for
ever.
9 ¶ O Zion, that bringest good tidings, get
thee up into the high mountain; O Jerusalem, that bringest good tidings, lift up thy
voice with strength; lift *it* up, be not afraid;
say unto the cities of Judah, Behold your
God!
10 Behold, the Lord GOD will come with
strong *hand*, and [l]his arm shall rule for
him: behold, [m]his reward *is* with him, and
his work before him.
11 He shall [n]feed his flock like a shepherd: he shall gather the lambs with his
arm, and carry *them* in his bosom, *and* shall
gently lead those that are with young.
12 ¶ [o]Who hath measured the waters in
the hollow of his hand, and meted out
heaven with the span, and comprehended
the dust of the earth in a measure, and
weighed the mountains in scales, and the
hills in a balance?
13 [p]Who hath directed the Spirit of the
LORD, or *being* his counsellor hath taught
him?
14 With whom took he counsel, and *who*
instructed him, and taught him in the path
of judgment, and taught him knowledge,
and shewed to him the way of understanding?
15 Behold, the nations *are* as a drop of a
bucket, and are counted as the small dust of
the balance: behold, he taketh up the isles
as a very little thing.
16 And Lebanon *is* not sufficient to burn,
nor the beasts thereof sufficient for a burnt
offering.
17 All nations before him *are* as [q]noth-
ing; and [r]they are counted to him less than
nothing, and vanity.
18 ¶ To whom then will ye [s]liken God? or
what likeness will ye compare unto him?
19 [t]The workman melteth a graven image, and the goldsmith spreadeth it over
with gold, and casteth silver chains.
20 He that *is* so impoverished that he hath
no oblation chooseth a tree *that* will not rot;
he seeketh unto him a cunning workman
[u]to prepare a graven image, *that* shall not
be moved.
21 [v]Have ye not known? have ye not
heard? hath it not been told you from the
beginning? have ye not understood from
the foundations of the earth?
22 *It is* he that sitteth upon the circle of
the earth, and the inhabitants thereof *are*
as grasshoppers; that [w]stretcheth out the
heavens as a curtain, and spreadeth them
out as a tent to dwell in:
23 That bringeth the [x]princes to nothing;
he maketh the judges of the earth as vanity.
24 Yea, they shall not be planted; yea,
they shall not be sown: yea, their stock shall
not take root in the earth: and he shall also
blow upon them, and they shall wither, and
the whirlwind shall take them away as stubble.
25 [y]To whom then will ye liken me, or
shall I be equal? saith the Holy One.
26 Lift up your eyes on high, and behold
who hath created these *things*, that bringeth out their host by number: [z]he calleth
them all by names by the greatness of his
might, for that *he is* strong in power; not one
faileth.
27 Why sayest thou, O Jacob, and speakest, O Israel, My way is hid from the LORD,
and my judgment is passed over from my
God?
28 ¶ Hast thou not known? hast thou not
heard, *that* the everlasting God, the LORD,
the Creator of the ends of the earth, fainteth
not, neither is weary? [a]*there is* no searching of his understanding.
29 He giveth power to the faint; and to
them that have no might he increaseth
strength.
30 Even the youths shall faint and be
weary, and the young men shall utterly fall:
31 But they that wait upon the LORD
[b]shall renew *their* strength; they shall
mount up with wings as eagles; they shall
run, and not be weary; *and* they shall walk,
and not faint.

41
Keep [c]silence before me, O islands;
and let the people renew *their*
strength: let them come near; then let them
speak: let us come near together to judgment.
2 Who raised up the righteous *man* [d]from
the east, called him to his foot, [e]gave the
nations before him, and made *him* rule over
kings? he gave *them* as the dust to his
sword, *and* as driven stubble to his bow.
3 He pursued them, *and* passed safely;
even by the way *that* he had not gone with
his feet.
4 [f]Who hath wrought and done *it*, calling
the generations from the beginning? I the
LORD, the [g]first, and with the last; I *am* he.
5 The isles saw *it*, and feared; the ends of
the earth were afraid, drew near, and came.
6 [h]They helped every one his neighbour;

40:2 [d]Job 42:10; ch. 61:7
40:3 [e]Matt. 3:3; Mark 1:3; Luke 3:4; John 1:23 [f]Mal. 3:1 [g]Ps. 68:4; ch. 49:11
40:4 [h]ch. 45:2
40:6 [i]Job 14:2; Ps. 90:5; Jam. 1:10; 1 Pet. 1:24
40:7 [j]Ps. 103:16
40:8 [k]John 12:34; 1 Pet. 1:25
40:10 [l]ch. 59:16 [m]ch. 62:11; Rev. 22:12
40:11 [n]ch. 49:10; Ezek. 34:23; John 10:11; Heb. 13:20; 1 Pet. 2:25; Rev. 7:17
40:12 [o]Prov. 30:4
40:13 [p]Job 21:22; Rom. 11:34; 1 Cor. 2:16
40:17 [q]Dan. 4:34 [r]Ps. 62:9
40:18 [s]ver. 25; ch. 46:5; Acts 17:29
40:19 [t]ch. 41:6; Jer. 10:3
40:20 [u]ch. 41:7; Jer. 10:4
40:21 [v]Ps. 19:1; Acts 14:17; Rom. 1:19
40:22 [w]Job 9:8; Ps. 104:2; ch. 42:5; Jer. 10:12
40:23 [x]Job 12:21; Ps. 107:40
40:25 [y]ver. 18; Deut. 4:15
40:26 [z]Ps. 147:4
40:28 [a]Ps. 147:5; Rom. 11:33
40:31 [b]Ps. 103:5
41:1 [c]Zech. 2:13
41:2 [d]ch. 46:11 [e]Gen. 14:14; ver. 25; ch. 45:1
41:4 [f]ver. 26; ch. 44:7 [g]ch. 43:10; Rev. 1:17
41:6 [h]ch. 40:19

and *every one* said to his brother, Be of good
courage.
7 [i]So the carpenter encouraged the goldsmith, *and* he that smootheth *with* the hammer him that smote the anvil, saying, It *is*
ready for the soldering: and he fastened it
with nails, [j]*that* it should not be moved.
8 But thou, Israel, *art* my servant, Jacob
whom I have [k]chosen, the seed of Abraham
my [l]friend.
9 *Thou* whom I have taken from the ends
of the earth, and called thee from the chief
men thereof, and said unto thee, Thou *art*
my servant; I have chosen thee, and not cast
thee away.
10 ¶ [m]Fear thou not; [n]for I *am* with thee:
be not dismayed; for I *am* thy God: I will
strengthen thee; yea, I will help thee; yea, I
will uphold thee with the right hand of my
righteousness.
11 Behold, all they that were incensed
against thee shall be [o]ashamed and confounded: they shall be as nothing; and they
that strive with thee shall perish.
12 Thou shalt seek them, and shalt not
find them, *even* them that contended with
thee: they that war against thee shall be as
nothing, and as a thing of nought.
13 For I the LORD thy God will hold thy
right hand, saying unto thee, [p]Fear not; I
will help thee.
14 Fear not, thou worm Jacob, *and* ye
men of Israel; I will help thee, saith the
LORD, and thy redeemer, the Holy One of
Israel.
15 Behold, [q]I will make thee a new sharp
threshing instrument having teeth: thou
shalt thresh the mountains, and beat *them*
small, and shalt make the hills as chaff.
16 Thou shalt [r]fan them, and the wind
shall carry them away, and the whirlwind
shall scatter them: and thou shalt rejoice in
the LORD, *and* [s]shalt glory in the Holy One
of Israel.
17 *When* the poor and needy seek water,
and *there is* none, *and* their tongue faileth
for thirst, I the LORD will hear them, *I* the
God of Israel will not forsake them.
18 I will open [t]rivers in high places, and
fountains in the midst of the valleys: I will
make the [u]wilderness a pool of water, and
the dry land springs of water.
19 I will plant in the wilderness the cedar,
the shittah tree, and the myrtle, and the oil
tree; I will set in the desert the fir tree, *and*
the pine, and the box tree together:
20 [v]That they may see, and know, and
consider, and understand together, that the
hand of the LORD hath done this, and the
Holy One of Israel hath created it.
21 Produce your cause, saith the LORD;
bring forth your strong *reasons,* saith the
King of Jacob.
22 [w]Let them bring *them* forth, and shew
us what shall happen: let them shew the former things, what they *be,* that we may consider them, and know the latter end of them;
or declare us things for to come.

41:7 [i]ch. 40:19 [j]ch. 40:20
41:8 [k]Deut. 7:6; Ps. 135:4; ch. 43:1 [l]2 Chron. 20:7; Jam. 2:23
41:10 [m]ver. 13; ch. 43:5 [n]Deut. 31:6
41:11 [o]Ex. 23:22; ch. 45:24; Zech. 12:3
41:13 [p]ver. 10
41:15 [q]Mic. 4:13; 2 Cor. 10:4
41:16 [r]Jer. 51:2 [s]ch. 45:25
41:18 [t]ch. 35:6 [u]Ps. 107:35
41:20 [v]Job 12:9
41:22 [w]ch. 45:21
41:23 [x]ch. 42:9; John 13:19 [y]Jer. 10:5
41:24 [z]Ps. 115:8; ch. 44:9; 1 Cor. 8:4
41:25 [a]Ezra 1:2 [b]ver. 2
41:26 [c]ch. 43:9
41:27 [d]ver. 4 [e]ch. 40:9
41:28 [f]ch. 63:5
41:29 [g]ver. 24
42:1 [h]ch. 43:10; Matt. 12:18; Phil. 2:7 [i]Matt. 3:17; Eph. 1:6 [j]ch. 11:2; John 3:34
42:4 [k]Gen. 40:10
42:5 [l]ch. 44:24; Zech. 12:1 [m]Ps. 136:6 [n]Acts 17:25
42:6 [o]ch. 43:1 [p]ch. 49:8 [q]ch. 49:6; Luke 2:32; Acts 13:47
42:7 [r]ch. 35:5 [s]ch. 61:1; Luke 4:18; 2 Tim. 2:26; Heb. 2:14 [t]ch. 9:2
42:8 [u]ch. 48:11
42:10 [v]Ps. 33:3 [w]Ps. 107:23

23 [x]Shew the things that are to come
hereafter, that we may know that ye *are*
gods: yea, [y]do good, or do evil, that we may
be dismayed, and behold *it* together.
24 Behold, [z]ye *are* of nothing, and your
work of nought: an abomination *is he that*
chooseth you.
25 I have raised up *one* from the north,
and he shall come: from the rising of the sun
[a]shall he call upon my name: [b]and he shall
come upon princes as *upon* morter, and as
the potter treadeth clay.
26 [c]Who hath declared from the beginning, that we may know? and beforetime,
that we may say, *He is* righteous? yea, *there
is* none that sheweth, yea, *there is* none that
declareth, yea, *there is* none that heareth
your words.
27 [d]The first [e]*shall say* to Zion, Behold,
behold them: and I will give to Jerusalem
one that bringeth good tidings.
28 [f]For I beheld, and *there was* no man;
even among them, and *there was* no counsellor, that, when I asked of them, could answer a word.
29 [g]Behold, they *are* all vanity; their
works *are* nothing: their molten images *are*
wind and confusion.
42 Behold [h]my servant, whom I uphold;
mine elect, *in whom* my soul [i]de-
lighteth; [j]I have put my spirit upon him: he
shall bring forth judgment to the Gentiles.
2 He shall not cry, nor lift up, nor cause
his voice to be heard in the street.
3 A bruised reed shall he not break, and
the smoking flax shall he not quench: he
shall bring forth judgment unto truth.
4 He shall not fail nor be discouraged, till
he have set judgment in the earth: [k]and the
isles shall wait for his law.
5 ¶ Thus saith God the LORD, [l]he that
created the heavens, and stretched them
out; [m]he that spread forth the earth, and
that which cometh out of it; [n]he that giveth
breath unto the people upon it, and spirit to
them that walk therein:
6 [o]I the LORD have called thee in righteousness, and will hold thine hand, and
will keep thee, [p]and give thee for a covenant of the people, for [q]a light of the Gentiles;
7 [r]To open the blind eyes, to [s]bring out
the prisoners from the prison, *and* them that
sit in [t]darkness out of the prison house.
8 I *am* the LORD: that *is* my name: and my
[u]glory will I not give to another, neither my
praise to graven images.
9 Behold, the former things are come to
pass, and new things do I declare: before
they spring forth I tell you of them.
10 [v]Sing unto the LORD a new song, *and*
his praise from the end of the earth, [w]ye
that go down to the sea, and all that is
therein; the isles, and the inhabitants
thereof.
11 Let the wilderness and the cities
thereof lift up *their voice,* the villages *that*
Kedar doth inhabit: let the inhabitants of

the rock sing, let them shout from the top of the mountains.

12 Let them give glory unto the LORD, and declare his praise in the islands.

13 The LORD shall go forth as a mighty man, he shall stir up jealousy like a man of war: he shall cry, [x]yea, roar; he shall prevail against his enemies.

14 I have long time holden my peace; I have been still, *and* refrained myself: *now* will I cry like a travailing woman; I will destroy and devour at once.

15 I will make waste mountains and hills, and dry up all their herbs; and I will make the rivers islands, and I will dry up the pools.

16 And I will bring the blind by a way *that* they knew not; I will lead them in paths *that* they have not known: I will make darkness light before them, and crooked things straight. These things will I do unto them, and not forsake them.

17 ¶ They shall be [y]turned back, they shall be greatly ashamed, that trust in graven images, that say to the molten images, Ye *are* our gods.

18 Hear, ye deaf; and look, ye blind, that ye may see.

19 [z]Who *is* blind, but my servant? or deaf, as my messenger *that* I sent? who *is* blind as *he that is* perfect, and blind as the LORD's servant?

20 Seeing many things, [a]but thou observest not; opening the ears, but he heareth not.

21 The LORD is well pleased for his righteousness' sake; he will magnify the law, and make *it* honourable.

22 But this *is* a people robbed and spoiled; *they are* all of them snared in holes, and they are hid in prison houses: they are for a prey, and none delivereth; for a spoil, and none saith, Restore.

23 Who among you will give ear to this? *who* will hearken and hear for the time to come?

24 Who gave Jacob for a spoil, and Israel to the robbers? did not the LORD, he against whom we have sinned? for they would not walk in his ways, neither were they obedient unto his law.

25 Therefore he hath poured upon him the fury of his anger, and the strength of battle: [b]and it hath set him on fire round about, [c]yet he knew not; and it burned him, yet he laid *it* not to heart.

43 But now thus saith the LORD [d]that created thee, O Jacob, [e]and he that formed thee, O Israel, Fear not: [f]for I have redeemed thee, [g]I have called *thee* by thy name; thou *art* mine.

2 [h]When thou passest through the waters, [i]I *will be* with thee; and through the rivers, they shall not overflow thee: when thou [j]walkest through the fire, thou shalt not be burned; neither shall the flame kindle upon thee.

3 For I *am* the LORD thy God, the Holy One of Israel, thy Saviour: [k]I gave Egypt *for* thy ransom, Ethiopia and Seba for thee.

4 Since thou wast precious in my sight, thou hast been honourable, and I have loved thee: therefore will I give men for thee, and people for thy life.

5 [l]Fear not: for I *am* with thee: I will bring thy seed from the east, and gather thee from the west;

6 I will say to the north, Give up; and to the south, Keep not back: bring my sons from far, and my daughters from the ends of the earth;

7 *Even* every one that is [m]called by my name: for [n]I have created him for my glory, [o]I have formed him; yea, I have made him.

8 ¶ [p]Bring forth the blind people that have eyes, and the deaf that have ears.

9 Let all the nations be gathered together, and let the people be assembled: [q]who among them can declare this, and shew us former things? let them bring forth their witnesses, that they may be justified: or let them hear, and say, *It is* truth.

10 [r]Ye *are* my witnesses, saith the LORD, [s]and my servant whom I have chosen: that ye may know and believe me, and understand that I *am* he: [t]before me there was no God formed, neither shall there be after me.

11 I, *even* I, [u]*am* the LORD; and beside me *there is* no saviour.

12 I have declared, and have saved, and I have shewed, when *there was* no [v]strange *god* among you: [w]therefore ye *are* my witnesses, saith the LORD, that I *am* God.

13 [x]Yea, before the day *was* I *am* he; and *there is* none that can deliver out of my hand: I will work, and who shall [y]let it?

14 ¶ Thus saith the LORD, your redeemer, the Holy One of Israel; For your sake I have sent to Babylon, and have brought down all their nobles, and the Chaldeans, whose cry *is* in the ships.

15 I *am* the LORD, your Holy One, the creator of Israel, your King.

16 Thus saith the LORD, which [z]maketh a way in the sea, and a [a]path in the mighty waters;

17 Which [b]bringeth forth the chariot and horse, the army and the power; they shall lie down together, they shall not rise: they are extinct, they are quenched as tow.

18 ¶ [c]Remember ye not the former things, neither consider the things of old.

19 Behold, I will do a [d]new thing; now it shall spring forth; shall ye not know it? [e]I will even make a way in the wilderness, *and* rivers in the desert.

20 The beast of the field shall honour me, the dragons and the owls: because [f]I give waters in the wilderness, *and* rivers in the desert, to give drink to my people, my chosen.

21 [g]This people have I formed for myself; they shall shew forth my praise.

22 ¶ But thou hast not called upon me, O Jacob; but thou [h]hast been weary of me, O Israel.

42:13 [x]ch. 31:4
42:17 [y]Ps. 97:7; ch. 1:29
42:19 [z]ch. 43:8; Ezek. 12:2; John 9:39
42:20 [a]Rom. 2:21
42:25 [b]2 Kings 25:9 [c]Hos. 7:9
43:1 [d]ver. 7 [e]ver. 21; ch. 44:2 [f]ch. 44:6 [g]ch. 42:6
43:2 [h]Ps. 66:12 [i]Deut. 31:6 [j]Dan. 3:25
43:3 [k]Prov. 11:8
43:5 [l]ch. 41:10; Jer. 30:10
43:7 [m]ch. 63:19; Jam. 2:7 [n]Ps. 100:3; ch. 29:23; John 3:3; 2 Cor. 5:17; Eph. 2:10 [o]ver. 1
43:8 [p]ch. 6:9; Ezek. 12:2
43:9 [q]ch. 41:21
43:10 [r]ch. 44:8 [s]ch. 42:1 [t]ch. 41:4
43:11 [u]ch. 45:21; Hos. 13:4
43:12 [v]Deut. 32:16; Ps. 81:9 [w]ch. 44:8; ver. 10
43:13 [x]Ps. 90:2; John 8:58 [y]Job 9:12; ch. 14:27
43:16 [z]Ex. 14:16; Ps. 77:19; ch. 51:10 [a]Josh. 3:13
43:17 [b]Ex. 14:4-9
43:18 [c]Jer. 16:14
43:19 [d]2 Cor. 5:17; Rev. 21:5 [e]Ex. 17:6; Num. 20:11; Deut. 8:15; Ps. 78:16; ch. 35:6
43:20 [f]ch. 48:21
43:21 [g]Ps. 102:18; ver. 1; Luke 1:74; Eph. 1:5
43:22 [h]Mal. 1:13

23 [i]Thou hast not brought me the small
cattle of thy burnt offerings; neither hast
thou honoured me with thy sacrifices. I
have not caused thee to serve with an offering, nor wearied thee with incense.
24 Thou hast bought me no sweet cane
with money, neither hast thou filled me with
the fat of thy sacrifices: but thou hast made
me to serve with thy sins, thou hast [j]wea-
ried me with thine iniquities.
25 I, *even* I, *am* he that [k]blotteth out thy
transgressions [l]for mine own sake, [m]and
will not remember thy sins.
26 Put me in remembrance: let us plead
together: declare thou, that thou mayest be
justified.
27 Thy first father hath sinned, and thy
teachers have transgressed against me.
28 Therefore [n]I have profaned the
princes of the sanctuary, [o]and have given
Jacob to the curse, and Israel to reproaches.

44 Yet now hear, [p]O Jacob my servant;
and Israel, whom I have chosen:
2 Thus saith the LORD that made thee,
[q]and formed thee from the womb, *which*
will help thee; Fear not, O Jacob, my servant; and thou, [r]Jesurun, whom I have chosen.
3 For I will [s]pour water upon him that is
thirsty, and floods upon the dry ground: I
will pour my spirit upon thy seed, and my
blessing upon thine offspring:
4 And they shall spring up *as* among the
grass, as willows by the water courses.
5 One shall say, I *am* the LORD's; and another shall call *himself* by the name of Jacob; and another shall subscribe *with* his
hand unto the LORD, and surname *himself*
by the name of Israel.
6 Thus saith the LORD the King of Israel,
[t]and his redeemer the LORD of hosts; [u]I *am*
the first, and I *am* the last; and beside me
there is no God.
7 And [v]who, as I, shall call, and shall declare it, and set it in order for me, since I
appointed the ancient people? and the
things that are coming, and shall come, let
them shew unto them.
8 Fear ye not, neither be afraid: [w]have not
I told thee from that time, and have declared
it? [x]ye *are* even my witnesses. Is there a
God beside me? yea, [y]*there is* no God; I
know not *any*.
9 ¶ [z]They that make a graven image *are*
all of them vanity; and their delectable
things shall not profit; and they *are* their
own witnesses; [a]they see not, nor know;
that they may be ashamed.
10 Who hath formed a god, or molten a
graven image [b]*that* is profitable for nothing?
11 Behold, all his fellows shall be
[c]ashamed: and the workmen, they *are* of
men: let them all be gathered together, let
them stand up; *yet* they shall fear, *and* they
shall be ashamed together.
12 [d]The smith with the tongs both worketh in the coals, and fashioneth it with hammers, and worketh it with the strength of
his arms: yea, he is hungry, and his strength
faileth: he drinketh no water, and is faint.
13 The carpenter stretcheth out *his* rule;
he marketh it out with a line; he fitteth it
with planes, and he marketh it out with the
compass, and maketh it after the figure of a
man, according to the beauty of a man; that
it may remain in the house.
14 He heweth him down cedars, and taketh the cypress and the oak, which he
strengtheneth for himself among the trees
of the forest: he planteth an ash, and the
rain doth nourish *it*.
15 Then shall it be for a man to burn: for
he will take thereof, and warm himself; yea,
he kindleth *it*, and baketh bread; yea, he
maketh a god, and worshippeth *it;* he maketh it a graven image, and falleth down
thereto.
16 He burneth part thereof in the fire;
with part thereof he eateth flesh; he roasteth roast, and is satisfied: yea, he warmeth
himself, and saith, Aha, I am warm, I have
seen the fire:
17 And the residue thereof he maketh a
god, *even* his graven image: he falleth down
unto it, and worshippeth *it*, and prayeth
unto it, and saith, Deliver me; for thou *art*
my god.
18 [e]They have not known nor understood: for [f]he hath shut their eyes, that they
cannot see; *and* their hearts, that they cannot understand.
19 And none [g]considereth in his heart,
neither *is there* knowledge nor understanding to say, I have burned part of it in the fire;
yea, also I have baked bread upon the coals
thereof; I have roasted flesh, and eaten *it:*
and shall I make the residue thereof an
abomination? shall I fall down to the stock
of a tree?
20 He feedeth on ashes: [h]a deceived heart
hath turned him aside, that he cannot deliver his soul, nor say, *Is there* not a lie in
my right hand?
21 ¶ Remember these, O Jacob and Israel; for [i]thou *art* my servant: I have
formed thee; thou *art* my servant: O Israel,
thou shalt not be forgotten of me.
22 [j]I have blotted out, as a thick cloud,
thy transgressions, and, as a cloud, thy sins:
return unto me; for [k]I have redeemed thee.
23 [l]Sing, O ye heavens; for the LORD
hath done *it:* shout, ye lower parts of the
earth: break forth into singing, ye mountains, O forest, and every tree therein: for
the LORD hath redeemed Jacob, and glorified himself in Israel.
24 Thus saith the LORD, [m]thy Redeemer,
and [n]he that formed thee from the womb, I
am the LORD that maketh all *things;* [o]that
stretcheth forth the heavens alone; that
spreadeth abroad the earth by myself;
25 That [p]frustrateth the tokens [q]of the
liars, and maketh diviners mad; that turneth
wise *men* backward, [r]and maketh their
knowledge foolish;

43:23 [i]Am. 5:25
43:24 [j]ch. 1:14; Mal. 2:17
43:25 [k]ch. 44:22; Jer. 50:20; Acts 3:19 [l]Ezek. 36:22 [m]ch. 1:18; Jer. 31:34
43:28 [n]ch. 47:6; Lam. 2:2 [o]Ps. 79:4; Jer. 24:9; Dan. 9:11; Zech. 8:13
44:1 [p]ver. 21; ch. 41:8; Jer. 30:10
44:2 [q]ch. 43:1 [r]Deut. 32:15
44:3 [s]ch. 35:7; Joel 2:28; John 7:38; Acts 2:18
44:6 [t]ver. 24; ch. 43:1 [u]ch. 41:4; Rev. 1:8
44:7 [v]ch. 41:4
44:8 [w]ch. 41:22 [x]ch. 43:10 [y]Deut. 4:35; 1 Sam. 2:2; 2 Sam. 22:32; ch. 45:5
44:9 [z]ch. 41:24 [a]Ps. 115:4
44:10 [b]Jer. 10:5; Hab. 2:18
44:11 [c]Ps. 97:7; ch. 1:29
44:12 [d]ch. 40:19; Jer. 10:3
44:18 [e]ch. 45:20 [f]2 Thess. 2:11
44:19 [g]ch. 46:8
44:20 [h]Hos. 4:12; Rom. 1:21; 2 Thess. 2:11
44:21 [i]ver. 1
44:22 [j]ch. 43:25 [k]ch. 43:1; 1 Cor. 6:20; 1 Pet. 1:18
44:23 [l]Ps. 69:34; ch. 42:10; Jer. 51:48; Rev. 18:20
44:24 [m]ch. 43:14; ver. 6 [n]ch. 43:1 [o]Job 9:8; Ps. 104:2; ch. 40:22
44:25 [p]ch. 47:13 [q]Jer. 50:36 [r]1 Cor. 1:20

26 [s]That confirmeth the word of his servant, and performeth the counsel of his
messengers; that saith to Jerusalem, Thou
shalt be inhabited; and to the cities of Judah, Ye shall be built, and I will raise up the
decayed places thereof:
27 [t]That saith to the deep, Be dry, and I
will dry up thy rivers:
28 That saith of Cyrus, *He is* my shepherd, and shall perform all my pleasure:
even saying to Jerusalem, [u]Thou shalt be
built; and to the temple, Thy foundation
shall be laid.

45 Thus saith the LORD to his anointed,
to Cyrus, whose [v]right hand I have
holden, [w]to subdue nations before him; and
I will loose the loins of kings, to open before
him the two leaved gates; and the gates
shall not be shut;
2 I will go before thee, [x]and make the
crooked places straight: [y]I will break in
pieces the gates of brass, and cut in sunder
the bars of iron:
3 And I will give thee the treasures of
darkness, and hidden riches of secret
places, [z]that thou mayest know that I, the
LORD, which [a]call *thee* by thy name, *am* the
God of Israel.
4 For [b]Jacob my servant's sake, and Israel mine elect, I have even called thee by
thy name: I have surnamed thee, though
thou hast [c]not known me.
5 ¶ I [d]*am* the LORD, and [e]*there is* none
else, *there is* no God beside me: [f]I girded
thee, though thou hast not known me:
6 [g]That they may know from the rising of
the sun, and from the west, that *there is*
none beside me. I *am* the LORD, and *there is*
none else.
7 I form the light, and create darkness: I
make peace, and [h]create evil: I the LORD do
all these *things*.
8 [i]Drop down, ye heavens, from above,
and let the skies pour down righteousness:
let the earth open, and let them bring forth
salvation, and let righteousness spring up
together; I the LORD have created it.
9 Woe unto him that striveth with [j]his
Maker! *Let* the potsherd *strive* with the pot-
sherds of the earth. [k]Shall the clay say to
him that fashioneth it, What makest thou?
or thy work, He hath no hands?
10 Woe unto him that saith unto *his* father, What begettest thou? or to the woman,
What hast thou brought forth?
11 Thus saith the LORD, the Holy One of
Israel, and his Maker, Ask me of things to
come concerning [l]my sons, and concerning [m]the work of my hands command
ye me.
12 [n]I have made the earth, and [o]created
man upon it: I, *even* my hands, have
stretched out the heavens, and [p]all their
host have I commanded.
13 [q]I have raised him up in righteousness, and I will direct all his ways: he shall
[r]build my city, and he shall let go my cap-

44:26 [s]Zech. 1:6
44:27 [t]Jer. 50:38
44:28 [u]2 Chron. 36:22; Ezra 1:1; ch. 45:13
45:1 [v]ch. 41:13 [w]ch. 41:2; Dan. 5:30
45:2 [x]ch. 40:4 [y]Ps. 107:16
45:3 [z]ch. 41:23 [a]Ex. 33:12; ch. 43:1
45:4 [b]ch. 44:1 [c]1 Thess. 4:5
45:5 [d]Deut. 4:35; ch. 44:8 [e]ver. 14:18 [f]Ps. 18:32
45:6 [g]Ps. 102:15; ch. 37:20; Mal. 1:11
45:7 [h]Am. 3:6
45:8 [i]Ps. 72:3
45:9 [j]ch. 64:8 [k]ch. 29:16; Jer. 18:6; Rom. 9:20
45:11 [l]Jer. 31:9 [m]Isa. 29:23
45:12 [n]ch. 42:5; Jer. 27:5 [o]Gen. 1:26 [p]Gen. 2:1
45:13 [q]ch. 41:2 [r]2 Chron. 36:22; Ezra 1:1; ch. 44:28 [s]ch. 52:3; Rom. 3:24
45:14 [t]Ps. 68:31; ch. 49:23; Zech. 8:22 [u]Ps. 149:8 [v]1 Cor. 14:25 [w]ver. 5
45:15 [x]Ps. 44:24; ch. 8:17
45:16 [y]ch. 44:11
45:17 [z]ch. 26:4; ver. 25; Rom. 11:26
45:18 [a]ch. 42:5 [b]ver. 5
45:19 [c]Deut. 30:11; ch. 48:16 [d]Ps. 19:8
45:20 [e]ch. 44:17; Rom. 1:22
45:21 [f]ch. 41:22 [g]ver. 5; ch. 44:8
45:22 [h]Ps. 22:27
45:23 [i]Gen. 22:16; Heb. 6:13 [j]Rom. 14:11; Phil. 2:10 [k]Gen. 31:53; Deut. 6:13; Ps. 63:11; ch. 65:16
45:24 [l]Jer. 23:5; 1 Cor. 1:30 [m]ch. 41:11
45:25 [n]ver. 17 [o]1 Cor. 1:31
46:1 [p]ch. 21:9; Jer. 50:2 [q]Jer. 10:5
46:2 [r]Jer. 48:7
46:3 [s]Ex. 19:4; Deut. 1:31; Ps. 71:6; ch. 63:9
46:4 [t]Ps. 102:27; Mal. 3:6

tives, [s]not for price nor reward, saith the
LORD of hosts.
14 Thus saith the LORD, [t]The labour of
Egypt, and merchandise of Ethiopia and of
the Sabeans, men of stature, shall come
over unto thee, and they shall be thine: they
shall come after thee; [u]in chains they shall
come over, and they shall fall down unto
thee, they shall make supplication unto
thee, *saying*, [v]Surely God *is* in thee; and
[w]*there is* none else, *there is* no God.
15 Verily thou *art* a God [x]that hidest thyself, O God of Israel, the Saviour.
16 They shall be ashamed, and also confounded, all of them: they shall go to confusion together *that are* [y]makers of idols.
17 [z]*But* Israel shall be saved in the LORD
with an everlasting salvation: ye shall not
be ashamed nor confounded world without
end.
18 For thus saith the LORD [a]that created
the heavens; God himself that formed the
earth and made it; he hath established it, he
created it not in vain, he formed it to be
inhabited: [b]I *am* the LORD; and *there is*
none else.
19 I have not spoken in [c]secret, in a dark
place of the earth: I said not unto the seed of
Jacob, Seek ye me in vain: [d]I the LORD
speak righteousness, I declare things that
are right.
20 ¶ Assemble yourselves and come;
draw near together, ye *that are* escaped of
the nations: [e]they have no knowledge that
set up the wood of their graven image, and
pray unto a god *that* cannot save.
21 Tell ye, and bring *them* near; yea, let
them take counsel together: [f]who hath declared this from ancient time? *who* hath told
it from that time? *have* not I the LORD? [g]and
there is no God else beside me; a just God
and a Saviour; *there is* none beside me.
22 [h]Look unto me, and be ye saved, all
the ends of the earth: for I *am* God, and
there is none else.
23 [i]I have sworn by myself, the word is
gone out of my mouth *in* righteousness, and
shall not return, That unto me every [j]knee
shall bow, [k]every tongue shall swear.
24 Surely, shall *one* say, in the LORD have
I [l]righteousness and strength: *even* to him
shall *men* come; and [m]all that are incensed
against him shall be ashamed.
25 [n]In the LORD shall all the seed of Israel
be justified, and [o]shall glory.

46 Bel [p]boweth down, Nebo stoopeth,
their idols were upon the beasts, and
upon the cattle: your carriages *were* heavy
loaden; [q]*they are* a burden to the weary
beast.
2 They stoop, they bow down together,
they could not deliver the burden, [r]but
themselves are gone into captivity.
3 ¶ Hearken unto me, O house of Jacob,
and all the remnant of the house of Israel,
[s]which are borne *by me* from the belly,
which are carried from the womb:
4 And *even* to *your* old age [t]I *am* he; and

even to hoar hairs [u]will I carry *you:* I have made, and I will bear; even I will carry, and will deliver *you.*
5 ¶ [v]To whom will ye liken me, and make *me* equal, and compare me, that we may be like?
6 [w]They lavish gold out of the bag, and weigh silver in the balance, *and* hire a goldsmith; and he maketh it a god: they fall down, yea, they worship.
7 [x]They bear him upon the shoulder, they carry him, and set him in his place, and he standeth; from his place shall he not remove: yea, [y]*one* shall cry unto him, yet can he not answer, nor save him out of his trouble.
8 Remember this, and shew yourselves men: [z]bring *it* again to mind, O ye transgressors.
9 [a]Remember the former things of old: for I *am* God, and [b]*there is* none else; *I am* God, and *there is* none like me,
10 [c]Declaring the end from the beginning, and from ancient times *the things* that are not *yet* done, saying, [d]My counsel shall stand, and I will do all my pleasure:
11 Calling a ravenous bird [e]from the east, the man [f]that executeth my counsel from a far country: yea, [g]I have spoken *it*, I will also bring it to pass; I have purposed *it*, I will also do it.
12 ¶ Hearken unto me, ye [h]stouthearted, [i]that *are* far from righteousness:
13 [j]I bring near my righteousness; it shall not be far off, and my salvation [k]shall not tarry: and I will place [l]salvation in Zion for Israel my glory.

47 Come [m]down, and [n]sit in the dust, O virgin daughter of Babylon, sit on the ground: *there is* no throne, O daughter of the Chaldeans: for thou shalt no more be called tender and delicate.
2 [o]Take the millstones, and grind meal: uncover thy locks, make bare the leg, uncover the thigh, pass over the rivers.
3 [p]Thy nakedness shall be uncovered, yea, thy shame shall be seen: [q]I will take vengeance, and I will not meet *thee as* a man.
4 *As for* [r]our redeemer, the LORD of hosts *is* his name, the Holy One of Israel.
5 Sit thou [s]silent, and get thee into darkness, O daughter of the Chaldeans: [t]for thou shalt no more be called, The lady of kingdoms.
6 ¶ [u]I was wroth with my people, [v]I have polluted mine inheritance, and given them into thine hand: thou didst shew them no mercy; [w]upon the ancient hast thou very heavily laid thy yoke.
7 ¶ And thou saidst, I shall be [x]a lady for ever: *so* that thou didst not [y]lay these *things* to thy heart, [z]neither didst remember the latter end of it.
8 Therefore hear now this, *thou that art* given to pleasures, that dwellest carelessly, that sayest in thine heart, [a]I *am*, and none else beside me; [b]I shall not sit *as* a widow, neither shall I know the loss of children:
9 But [c]these two *things* shall come to thee [d]in a moment in one day, the loss of children, and widowhood: they shall come upon thee in their perfection [e]for the multitude of thy sorceries, *and* for the great abundance of thine enchantments.
10 ¶ For thou [f]hast trusted in thy wickedness: [g]thou hast said, None seeth me. Thy wisdom and thy knowledge, it hath perverted thee; [h]and thou hast said in thine heart, I *am*, and none else beside me.
11 ¶ Therefore shall evil come upon thee; thou shalt not know from whence it riseth: and mischief shall fall upon thee; thou shalt not be able to put it off: and [i]desolation shall come upon thee suddenly, *which* thou shalt not know.
12 Stand now with thine enchantments, and with the multitude of thy sorceries, wherein thou hast laboured from thy youth; if so be thou shalt be able to profit, if so be thou mayest prevail.
13 [j]Thou art wearied in the multitude of thy counsels. Let now [k]the astrologers, the stargazers, the monthly prognosticators, stand up, and save thee from *these things* that shall come upon thee.
14 Behold, they shall be [l]as stubble; the fire shall burn them; they shall not deliver themselves from the power of the flame: *there shall* not *be* a coal to warm at, *nor* fire to sit before it.
15 Thus shall they be unto thee with whom thou hast laboured, *even* [m]thy merchants, from thy youth: they shall wander every one to his quarter; none shall save thee.

48 Hear ye this, O house of Jacob, which are called by the name of Israel, and [n]are come forth out of the waters of Judah, [o]which swear by the name of the LORD, and make mention of the God of Israel, [p]*but* not in truth, nor in righteousness.
2 For they call themselves [q]of the holy city, and [r]stay themselves upon the God of Israel; The LORD of hosts *is* his name.
3 [s]I have declared the former things from the beginning; and they went forth out of my mouth, and I shewed them; I did *them* suddenly, [t]and they came to pass.
4 Because I knew that thou *art* obstinate, and [u]thy neck *is* an iron sinew, and thy brow brass;
5 [v]I have even from the beginning declared *it* to thee; before it came to pass I shewed *it* thee: lest thou shouldest say, Mine idol hath done them; and my graven image, and my molten image, hath commanded them.
6 Thou hast heard, see all this; and will not ye declare *it?* I have shewed thee new things from this time, even hidden things, and thou didst not know them.
7 They are created now, and not from the beginning; even before the day when thou

46:4 *u*Ps. 48:14
46:5 *v*ch. 40:18
46:6 *w*ch. 40:19; Jer. 10:3
46:7 *x*Jer. 10:5 *y*ch. 45:20
46:8 *z*ch. 44:19
46:9 *a*Deut. 32:7 *b*ch. 45:5
46:10 *c*ch. 45:21 *d*Ps. 33:11; Prov. 19:21; Acts 5:39; Heb. 6:17
46:11 *e*ch. 41:2 *f*ch. 44:28 *g*Num. 23:19
46:12 *h*Ps. 76:5 *i*Rom. 10:3
46:13 *j*ch. 51:5; Rom. 1:17 *k*Hab. 2:3 *l*ch. 62:11
47:1 *m*Jer. 48:18 *n*ch. 3:26
47:2 *o*Ex. 11:5; Judg. 16:21; Matt. 24:41
47:3 *p*ch. 3:17; Jer. 13:22; Nah. 3:5 *q*Rom. 12:19
47:4 *r*ch. 43:3; Jer. 50:34
47:5 *s*1 Sam. 2:9 *t*ver. 7; ch. 13:19; Dan. 2:37
47:6 *u*2 Sam. 24:14; 2 Chron. 28:9; Zech. 1:15 *v*ch. 43:28 *w*Deut. 28:50
47:7 *x*ver. 5; Rev. 18:7 *y*ch. 46:8 *z*Deut. 32:29
47:8 *a*ver. 10; Zeph. 2:15 *b*Rev. 18:7
47:9 *c*ch. 51:19 *d*1 Thess. 5:3 *e*Nah. 3:4
47:10 *f*Ps. 52:7 *g*ch. 29:15; Ezek. 8:12 *h*ver. 8
47:11 *i*1 Thess. 5:3
47:13 *j*ch. 57:10 *k*ch. 44:25; Dan. 2:2
47:14 *l*Nah. 1:10; Mal. 4:1
47:15 *m*Rev. 18:11
48:1 *n*Ps. 68:26 *o*Deut. 6:13; ch. 65:16; Zeph. 1:5 *p*Jer. 4:2
48:2 *q*ch. 52:1 *r*Mic. 3:11; Rom. 2:17
48:3 *s*ch. 41:22 *t*Josh. 21:45
48:4 *u*Ex. 32:9; Deut. 31:27
48:5 *v*ver. 3

heardest them not; lest thou shouldest say,
Behold, I knew them.
8 Yea, thou heardest not; yea, thou knewest not; yea, from that time *that* thine ear
was not opened: for I knew that thou wouldest deal very treacherously, and wast called
[w]a transgressor from the womb.
9 ¶ [x]For my name's sake [y]will I defer
mine anger, and for my praise will I refrain
for thee, that I cut thee not off.
10 Behold, [z]I have refined thee, but not
with silver; I have chosen thee in the furnace of affliction.
11 [a]For mine own sake, *even* for mine
own sake, will I do *it:* for [b]how should *my*
name be polluted? and [c]I will not give my
glory unto another.
12 ¶ Hearken unto me, O Jacob and Is-
rael, my called; [d]I *am* he; I *am* the [e]first, I
also *am* the last.
13 [f]Mine hand also hath laid the foundation of the earth, and my right hand hath
spanned the heavens: *when* [g]I call unto
them, they stand up together.
14 [h]All ye, assemble yourselves, and
hear; which among them hath declared
these *things?* [i]The LORD hath loved him:
[j]he will do his pleasure on Babylon, and his
arm *shall be on* the Chaldeans.
15 I, *even* I, have spoken; yea, [k]I have
called him: I have brought him, and he shall
make his way prosperous.
16 ¶ Come ye near unto me, hear ye this;
[l]I have not spoken in secret from the beginning; from the time that it was, there *am* I:
and now [m]the Lord GOD, and his Spirit,
hath sent me.
17 Thus saith [n]the LORD, thy Redeemer,
the Holy One of Israel; I *am* the LORD thy
God which teacheth thee to profit, [o]which
leadeth thee by the way *that* thou shouldest go.
18 [p]O that thou hadst hearkened to my
commandments! [q]then had thy peace been
as a river, and thy righteousness as the
waves of the sea:
19 [r]Thy seed also had been as the sand,
and the offspring of thy bowels like the
gravel thereof; his name should not have
been cut off nor destroyed from before me.
20 ¶ [s]Go ye forth of Babylon, flee ye from
the Chaldeans, with a voice of singing declare ye, tell this, utter it *even* to the end
of the earth; say ye, The LORD hath [t]re-
deemed his servant Jacob.
21 And they [u]thirsted not *when* he led
them through the deserts: he [v]caused the
waters to flow out of the rock for them: he
clave the rock also, and the waters gushed
out.
22 [w]*There is* no peace, saith the LORD,
unto the wicked.

49

Listen, [x]O isles, unto me; and
hearken, ye people, from far; [y]The
LORD hath called me from the womb; from
the bowels of my mother hath he made
mention of my name.
2 And he hath made [z]my mouth like a
sharp sword; [a]in the shadow of his hand
hath he hid me, and made me [b]a polished
shaft; in his quiver hath he hid me;
3 And said unto me, [c]Thou *art* my servant, O Israel, [d]in whom I will be glorified.
4 [e]Then I said, I have laboured in vain, I
have spent my strength for nought, and in
vain: *yet* surely my judgment *is* with the
LORD, and my work with my God.
5 ¶ And now, saith the LORD [f]that formed
me from the womb *to be* his servant, to
bring Jacob again to him, Though Israel
[g]be not gathered, yet shall I be glorious in
the eyes of the LORD, and my God shall be
my strength.
6 And he said, It is a light thing that thou
shouldest be my servant to raise up the
tribes of Jacob, and to restore the preserved
of Israel: I will also give thee for a [h]light to
the Gentiles, that thou mayest be my salvation unto the end of the earth.
7 Thus saith the LORD, the Redeemer of
Israel, *and* his Holy One, [i]to him whom
man despiseth, to him whom the nation abhorreth, to a servant of rulers, [j]Kings shall
see and arise, princes also shall worship,
because of the LORD that is faithful, *and* the
Holy One of Israel, and he shall choose
thee.
8 Thus saith the LORD, [k]In an acceptable
time have I heard thee, and in a day of salvation have I helped thee: and I will preserve thee, [l]and give thee for a covenant of
the people, to establish the earth, to cause to
inherit the desolate heritages;
9 That thou mayest say [m]to the prisoners,
Go forth; to them that *are* in darkness, Shew
yourselves. They shall feed in the ways, and
their pastures *shall be* in all high places.
10 They shall not [n]hunger nor thirst;
[o]neither shall the heat nor sun smite them:
for he that hath mercy on them [p]shall lead
them, even by the springs of water shall he
guide them.
11 [q]And I will make all my mountains a
way, and my highways shall be exalted.
12 Behold, [r]these shall come from far:
and, lo, these from the north and from the
west; and these from the land of Sinim.
13 ¶ [s]Sing, O heavens; and be joyful,
O earth; and break forth into singing,
O mountains: for the LORD hath comforted
his people, and will have mercy upon his
afflicted.
14 [t]But Zion said, The LORD hath forsaken me, and my Lord hath forgotten me.
15 [u]Can a woman forget her sucking
child, that she should not have compassion
on the son of her womb? yea, they may forget, [v]yet will I not forget thee.
16 Behold, [w]I have graven thee upon the
palms of *my* hands; thy walls *are* continually before me.
17 Thy children shall make haste; [x]thy
destroyers and they that made thee waste
shall go forth of thee.
18 ¶ [y]Lift up thine eyes round about, and
behold: all these gather themselves to-

48:8 [w]Ps. 58:3
48:9 [x]Ps. 79:9; ch. 43:25; ver. 11; Ezek. 20:9 [y]Ps. 78:38
48:10 [z]Ps. 66:10
48:11 [a]ver. 9 [b]Deut. 32:26; Ezek. 20:9 [c]ch. 42:8
48:12 [d]Deut. 32:39 [e]ch. 41:4; Rev. 1:17
48:13 [f]Ps. 102:25 [g]ch. 40:26
48:14 [h]ch. 41:22 [i]ch. 45:1 [j]ch. 44:28
48:15 [k]ch. 45:1
48:16 [l]ch. 45:19 [m]ch. 61:1; Zech. 2:8
48:17 [n]ch. 43:14; ver. 20 [o]Ps. 32:8
48:18 [p]Deut. 32:29; Ps. 81:13 [q]Ps. 119:165
48:19 [r]Gen. 22:17; Hos. 1:10
48:20 [s]ch. 52:11; Jer. 50:8; Zech. 2:6; Rev. 18:4 [t]Ex. 19:4; ch. 44:22
48:21 [u]ch. 41:17 [v]Ex. 17:6; Num. 20:11; Ps. 105:41
48:22 [w]ch. 57:21
49:1 [x]ch. 41:1 [y]ver. 5; Jer. 1:5; Matt. 1:20; Luke 1:15; John 10:36; Gal. 1:15
49:2 [z]ch. 11:4; Hos. 6:5; Heb. 4:12; Rev. 1:16 [a]ch. 51:16 [b]Ps. 45:5
49:3 [c]ch. 42:1; Zech. 3:8 [d]ch. 44:23; John 13:31; Eph. 1:6
49:4 [e]Ezek. 3:19
49:5 [f]ver. 1 [g]Matt. 23:37
49:6 [h]ch. 42:6; Luke 2:32; Acts 13:47
49:7 [i]ch. 53:3; Matt. 26:67 [j]Ps. 72:10; ver. 23
49:8 [k]Ps. 69:13; 2 Cor. 6:2 [l]ch. 42:6
49:9 [m]ch. 42:7; Zech. 9:12
49:10 [n]Rev. 7:16 [o]Ps. 121:6 [p]Ps. 23:2
49:11 [q]ch. 40:4
49:12 [r]ch. 43:5
49:13 [s]ch. 44:23
49:14 [t]ch. 40:27
49:15 [u]Ps. 103:13; Mal. 3:17; Matt. 7:11 [v]Rom. 11:29
49:16 [w]Ex. 13:9; SSol. 8:6
49:17 [x]ver. 19
49:18 [y]ch. 60:4

gether, *and* come to thee. *As* I live, saith the LORD, thou shalt surely clothe thee with them all, [z]as with an ornament, and bind them *on thee*, as a bride *doeth*.

19 For thy waste and thy desolate places, and the land of thy destruction, [a]shall even now be too narrow by reason of the inhabitants, and they that swallowed thee up shall be far away.

20 [b]The children which thou shalt have, after thou hast lost the other, [c]shall say again in thine ears, The place *is* too strait for me: give place to me that I may dwell.

21 Then shalt thou say in thine heart, Who hath begotten me these, seeing I have lost my children, and am desolate, a captive, and removing to and fro? and who hath brought up these? Behold, I was left alone; these, where *had* they *been*?

22 [d]Thus saith the Lord GOD, Behold, I will lift up mine hand to the Gentiles, and set up my standard to the people: and they shall bring thy sons in *their* arms, and thy daughters shall be carried upon *their* shoulders.

23 [e]And kings shall be thy nursing fathers, and their queens thy nursing mothers: they shall bow down to thee with *their* face toward the earth, and [f]lick up the dust of thy feet; and thou shalt know that I *am* the LORD: for [g]they shall not be ashamed that wait for me.

24 ¶ [h]Shall the prey be taken from the mighty, or the lawful captive delivered?

25 But thus saith the LORD, Even the captives of the mighty shall be taken away, and the prey of the terrible shall be delivered: for I will contend with him that contendeth with thee, and I will save thy children.

26 And I will [i]feed them that oppress thee with their own flesh; and they shall be drunken with their own [j]blood, as with sweet wine: and all flesh [k]shall know that I the LORD *am* thy Saviour and thy Redeemer, the mighty One of Jacob.

50 Thus saith the LORD, Where *is* [l]the bill of your mother's divorcement, whom I have put away? or which of my [m]creditors *is it* to whom I have sold you? Behold, for your iniquities [n]have ye sold yourselves, and for your transgressions is your mother put away.

2 Wherefore, when I came, *was there* no man? [o]when I called, *was there* none to answer? [p]Is my hand shortened at all, that it cannot redeem? or have I no power to deliver? behold, [q]at my rebuke I [r]dry up the sea, I make the [s]rivers a wilderness: [t]their fish stinketh, because *there is* no water, and dieth for thirst.

3 [u]I clothe the heavens with blackness, [v]and I make sackcloth their covering.

4 [w]The Lord GOD hath given me the tongue of the learned, that I should know how to speak a word in season to *him that is* [x]weary: he wakeneth morning by morning, he wakeneth mine ear to hear as the learned.

5 ¶ The Lord GOD [y]hath opened mine ear, and I was not [z]rebellious, neither turned away back.

6 [a]I gave my back to the smiters, and [b]my cheeks to them that plucked off the hair: I hid not my face from shame and spitting.

7 For the Lord GOD will help me; therefore shall I not be confounded: therefore have [c]I set my face like a flint, and I know that I shall not be ashamed.

8 [d]*He is* near that justifieth me; who will contend with me? let us stand together: who *is* mine adversary? let him come near to me.

9 Behold, the Lord GOD will help me; who *is* he *that* shall condemn me? [e]lo, they all shall wax old as a garment; [f]the moth shall eat them up.

10 ¶ Who *is* among you that feareth the LORD, that obeyeth the voice of his servant, that [g]walketh *in* darkness, and hath no light? [h]let him trust in the name of the LORD, and stay upon his God.

11 Behold, all ye that kindle a fire, that compass *yourselves* about with sparks: walk in the light of your fire, and in the sparks *that ye* have kindled. [i]This shall ye have of mine hand; ye shall lie down [j]in sorrow.

51 Hearken [k]to me, [l]ye that follow after righteousness, ye that seek the LORD: look unto the rock *whence* ye are hewn, and to the hole of the pit *whence* ye are digged.

2 [m]Look unto Abraham your father, and unto Sarah *that* bare you: [n]for I called him alone, and [o]blessed him, and increased him.

3 For the LORD [p]shall comfort Zion: he will comfort all her waste places; and he will make her wilderness like Eden, and her desert [q]like the garden of the LORD; joy and gladness shall be found therein, thanksgiving, and the voice of melody.

4 ¶ Hearken unto me, my people; and give ear unto me, O my nation: [r]for a law shall proceed from me, and I will make my judgment to rest [s]for a light of the people.

5 [t]My righteousness *is* near; my salvation is gone forth, [u]and mine arms shall judge the people; [v]the isles shall wait upon me, and [w]on mine arm shall they trust.

6 [x]Lift up your eyes to the heavens, and look upon the earth beneath: for [y]the heavens shall vanish away like smoke, [z]and the earth shall wax old like a garment, and they that dwell therein shall die in like manner: but my salvation shall be for ever, and my righteousness shall not be abolished.

7 ¶ [a]Hearken unto me, ye that know righteousness, the people [b]in whose heart *is* my law; [c]fear ye not the reproach of men, neither be ye afraid of their revilings.

8 For [d]the moth shall eat them up like a garment, and the worm shall eat them like wool: but my righteousness shall be for ever, and my salvation from generation to generation.

49:18 [z]Prov. 17:6
49:19 [a]ch. 54:1; Zech. 2:4
49:20 [b]ch. 60:4 [c]Matt. 3:9; Rom. 11:11
49:22 [d]ch. 60:4
49:23 [e]Ps. 72:11; ver. 7; ch. 52:15 [f]Ps. 72:9; Mic. 7:17 [g]Ps. 34:22; Rom. 5:5
49:24 [h]Matt. 12:29; Luke 11:21
49:26 [i]ch. 9:20 [j]Rev. 14:20 [k]Ps. 9:16; ch. 60:16
50:1 [l]Deut. 24:1; Jer. 3:8; Hos. 2:2 [m]2 Kings 4:1; Matt. 18:25 [n]ch. 52:3
50:2 [o]Prov. 1:24; ch. 65:12; Jer. 7:13 [p]Num. 11:23; ch. 59:1 [q]Ps. 106:9; Nah. 1:4 [r]Ex. 14:21 [s]Josh. 3:16 [t]Ex. 7:18
50:3 [u]Ex. 10:21 [v]Rev. 6:12
50:4 [w]Ex. 4:11 [x]Matt. 11:28
50:5 [y]Ps. 40:6 [z]Matt. 26:39; John 14:31; Phil. 2:8; Heb. 10:5
50:6 [a]Matt. 26:67; John 18:22 [b]Lam. 3:30
50:7 [c]Ezek. 3:8
50:8 [d]Rom. 8:32
50:9 [e]Job 13:28; Ps. 102:26; ch. 51:6 [f]ch. 51:8
50:10 [g]Ps. 23:4 [h]2 Chron. 20:20; Ps. 20:7
50:11 [i]John 9:19 [j]Ps. 16:4
51:1 [k]ver. 7 [l]Rom. 9:30
51:2 [m]Rom. 4:1; Heb. 11:11 [n]Gen. 12:1 [o]Gen. 24:1
51:3 [p]Ps. 102:13; ch. 40:1; ver. 12 [q]Gen. 13:10; Joel 2:3
51:4 [r]ch. 2:3 [s]ch. 42:6
51:5 [t]ch. 46:13; Rom. 1:16 [u]Ps. 67:4 [v]ch. 60:9 [w]Rom. 1:16
51:6 [x]ch. 40:26 [y]Ps. 102:26; Matt. 24:35; 2 Pet. 3:10 [z]ch. 50:9
51:7 [a]ver. 1 [b]Ps. 37:31 [c]Matt. 10:28; Acts 5:41
51:8 [d]ch. 50:9

9 ¶ [e]Awake, awake, [f]put on strength, O arm of the LORD; awake, [g]as in the ancient days, in the generations of old. [h]*Art* thou not it that hath cut [i]Rahab, *and* wounded the [j]dragon?

10 *Art* thou not it which hath [k]dried the sea, the waters of the great deep; that hath made the depths of the sea a way for the ransomed to pass over?

11 Therefore [l]the redeemed of the LORD shall return, and come with singing unto Zion; and everlasting joy *shall be* upon their head: they shall obtain gladness and joy; *and* sorrow and mourning shall flee away.

12 I, *even* I, *am* he [m]that comforteth you: who *art* thou, that thou shouldest be afraid [n]of a man *that* shall die, and of the son of man *which* shall be made [o]*as* grass;

13 And forgettest the LORD thy maker, [p]that hath stretched forth the heavens, and laid the foundations of the earth; and hast feared continually every day because of the fury of the oppressor, as if he were ready to destroy? [q]and where *is* the fury of the oppressor?

14 The captive exile hasteneth that he may be loosed, [r]and that he should not die in the pit, nor that his bread should fail.

15 But I *am* the LORD thy God, that [s]divided the sea, whose waves roared: The LORD of hosts *is* his name.

16 And [t]I have put my words in thy mouth, and I [u]have covered thee in the shadow of mine hand, [v]that I may plant the heavens, and lay the foundations of the earth, and say unto Zion, Thou *art* my people.

17 ¶ [w]Awake, awake, stand up, O Jerusalem, which hast [x]drunk at the hand of the LORD the cup of his fury; [y]thou hast drunken the dregs of the cup of trembling, *and* wrung *them* out.

18 *There is* none to guide her among all the sons *whom* she hath brought forth; neither *is there any* that taketh her by the hand of all the sons *that* she hath brought up.

19 [z]These two *things* are come unto thee; who shall be sorry for thee? desolation, and destruction, and the famine, and the sword: [a]by whom shall I comfort thee?

20 [b]Thy sons have fainted, they lie at the head of all the streets, as a wild bull in a net: they are full of the fury of the LORD, the rebuke of thy God.

21 ¶ Therefore hear now this, thou afflicted, and drunken, [c]but not with wine:

22 Thus saith thy Lord the LORD, and thy God [d]*that* pleadeth the cause of his people, Behold, I have taken out of thine hand the cup of trembling, *even* the dregs of the cup of my fury; thou shalt no more drink it again:

23 But [e]I will put it into the hand of them that afflict thee; [f]which have said to thy soul, Bow down, that we may go over: and thou hast laid thy body as the ground, and as the street, to them that went over.

52 Awake, [g]awake; put on thy strength, O Zion; put on thy beautiful garments, O Jerusalem, [h]the holy city: for [i]henceforth there shall no more come into thee the uncircumcised [j]and the unclean.

2 [k]Shake thyself from the dust; arise, *and* sit down, O Jerusalem: [l]loose thyself from the bands of thy neck, O captive daughter of Zion.

3 For thus saith the LORD, [m]Ye have sold yourselves for nought; and ye shall be redeemed without money.

4 For thus saith the Lord GOD, My people went down aforetime into [n]Egypt to sojourn there; and the Assyrian oppressed them without cause.

5 Now therefore, what have I here, saith the LORD, that my people is taken away for nought? they that rule over them make them to howl, saith the LORD; and my name continually every day *is* [o]blasphemed.

6 Therefore my people shall know my name: therefore *they shall know* in that day that I *am* he that doth speak: behold, *it is* I.

7 ¶ [p]How beautiful upon the mountains are the feet of him that bringeth good tidings, that publisheth peace; that bringeth good tidings of good, that publisheth salvation; that saith unto Zion, [q]Thy God reigneth!

8 Thy watchmen shall lift up the voice; with the voice together shall they sing: for they shall see eye to eye, when the LORD shall bring again Zion.

9 ¶ Break forth into joy, sing together, ye waste places of Jerusalem: [r]for the LORD hath comforted his people, [s]he hath redeemed Jerusalem.

10 [t]The LORD hath made bare his holy arm in the eyes of all the nations; and [u]all the ends of the earth shall see the salvation of our God.

11 ¶ [v]Depart ye, depart ye, go ye out from thence, touch no unclean *thing;* go ye out of the midst of her; [w]be ye clean, that bear the vessels of the LORD.

12 For [x]ye shall not go out with haste, nor go by flight: [y]for the LORD will go before you; [z]and the God of Israel *will be* your rereward.

13 ¶ Behold, [a]my servant shall deal prudently, [b]he shall be exalted and extolled, and be very high.

14 As many were astonied at thee; his [c]visage was so marred more than any man, and his form more than the sons of men:

15 [d]So shall he sprinkle many nations; [e]the kings shall shut their mouths at him: for *that* [f]which had not been told them shall they see; and *that* which they had not heard shall they consider.

53 Who [g]hath believed our report? and to whom [h]is the arm of the LORD revealed?

2 For [i]he shall grow up before him as a tender plant, and as a root out of a dry

51:9 *e*Ps. 44:23; ch. 52:1 *f*Ps. 93:1; Rev. 11:17 *g*Ps. 44:1 *h*Job 26:12 *i*Ps. 87:4 *j*Ps. 74:13; ch. 27:1; Ezek. 29:3 **51:10** *k*Ex. 14:21; ch. 43:16 **51:11** *l*ch. 35:10 **51:12** *m*ver. 3; 2 Cor. 1:3 *n*Ps. 118:6 *o*ch. 40:6; 1 Pet. 1:24 **51:13** *p*Job 9:8; Ps. 104:2; ch. 40:22 *q*Job 20:7 **51:14** *r*Zech. 9:11 **51:15** *s*Ps. 74:13; Job 26:12; Jer. 31:35 **51:16** *t*Deut. 18:18; ch. 59:21; John 3:34 *u*ch. 49:2 *v*ch. 65:17 **51:17** *w*ch. 52:1 *x*Job 21:20; Jer. 25:15 *y*Deut. 28:28; Ps. 60:3; Ezek. 23:32; Zech. 12:2; Rev. 14:10 **51:19** *z*ch. 47:9 *a*Am. 7:2 **51:20** *b*Lam. 2:11 **51:21** *c*ver. 17; Lam. 3:15 **51:22** *d*Jer. 50:34 **51:23** *e*Jer. 25:17; Zech. 12:2 *f*Ps. 66:11 **52:1** *g*ch. 51:9 *h*Neh. 11:1; ch. 48:2; Matt. 4:5; Rev. 21:2 *i*ch. 35:8; Nah. 1:15 *j*Rev. 21:27 **52:2** *k*ch. 3:26 *l*Zech. 2:7 **52:3** *m*Ps. 44:12; ch. 45:13; Jer. 15:13 **52:4** *n*Gen. 46:6; Acts 7:14 **52:5** *o*Ezek. 36:20; Rom. 2:24 **52:7** *p*Nah. 1:15; Rom. 10:15 *q*Ps. 93:1 **52:9** *r*ch. 51:3 *s*ch. 48:20 **52:10** *t*Ps. 98:2 *u*Luke 3:6 **52:11** *v*ch. 48:20; Jer. 50:8; Zech. 2:6; 2 Cor. 6:17; Rev. 18:4 *w*Lev. 22:2 **52:12** *x*Ex. 12:33 *y*Mic. 2:13 *z*Ex. 14:19; Num. 10:25; ch. 58:8 **52:13** *a*ch. 42:1 *b*Phil. 2:9 **52:14** *c*Ps. 22:6; ch. 53:2 **52:15** *d*Ezek. 36:25; Acts 2:33; Heb. 9:13 *e*ch. 49:7 *f*ch. 55:5; Rom. 15:21; Eph. 3:5 **53:1** *g*John 12:38; Rom. 10:16 *h*ch. 51:9; Rom. 1:16; 1 Cor. 1:18 **53:2** *i*ch. 11:1

ground: [j]he hath no form nor comeliness;
and when we shall see him, *there is* no
beauty that we should desire him.
3 [k]He is despised and rejected of men;
a man of sorrows, and [l]acquainted with
grief: and we hid as it were *our* faces from
him; he was despised, and [m]we esteemed
him not.
4 ¶ Surely [n]he hath borne our griefs, and
carried our sorrows: yet we did esteem him
stricken, smitten of God, and afflicted.
5 But he *was* [o]wounded for our transgressions, *he was* bruised for our iniquities:
the chastisement of our peace *was* upon
him; and with his [p]stripes we are healed.
6 [q]All we like sheep have gone astray; we
have turned every one to his own way; and
the LORD hath laid on him the iniquity of us
all.
7 He was oppressed, and he was afflicted,
yet [r]he opened not his mouth: [s]he is
brought as a lamb to the slaughter, and as a
sheep before her shearers is dumb, so he
openeth not his mouth.
8 He was taken from prison and from
judgment: and who shall declare his generation? for [t]he was cut off out of the land of
the living: for the transgression of my people was he stricken.
9 [u]And he made his grave with the
wicked, and with the rich in his death; because he had done no violence, neither *was*
any [v]deceit in his mouth.
10 ¶ Yet it pleased the LORD to bruise him;
he hath put *him* to grief: when thou shalt
make his soul [w]an offering for sin, he shall
see *his* seed, [x]he shall prolong *his* days, and
[y]the pleasure of the LORD shall prosper in
his hand.
11 He shall see of the travail of his soul,
and shall be satisfied: [z]by his knowledge
shall [a]my righteous [b]servant [c]justify
many; [d]for he shall bear their iniquities.
12 [e]Therefore will I divide him *a portion*
with the great, [f]and he shall divide the
spoil with the strong; because he hath
poured out his soul unto death: and he was
[g]numbered with the transgressors; and he
bare the sin of many, and [h]made intercession for the transgressors.

54 [i]Sing, O barren, thou *that* didst not
bear; break forth into singing, and
cry aloud, thou *that* didst not travail with
child: for [j]more *are* the children of the desolate than the children of the married wife,
saith the LORD.
2 [k]Enlarge the place of thy tent, and let
them stretch forth the curtains of thine
habitations: spare not, lengthen thy cords,
and strengthen thy stakes;
3 For thou shalt break forth on the right
hand and on the left; [l]and thy seed shall
inherit the Gentiles, and make the desolate
cities to be inhabited.
4 Fear not; for thou shalt not be ashamed:
neither be thou confounded; for thou shalt
not be put to shame: for thou shalt forget the
shame of thy youth, and shalt not remember
the reproach of thy widowhood any more.
5 [m]For thy Maker *is* thine husband; the
[n]LORD of hosts *is* his name; and thy Redeemer the Holy One of Israel; [o]The God of
the whole earth shall he be called.
6 For the LORD [p]hath called thee as a
woman forsaken and grieved in spirit, and
a wife of youth, when thou wast refused,
saith thy God.
7 [q]For a small moment have I forsaken
thee; but with great mercies will I gather
thee.
8 In a little wrath I hid my face from thee
for a moment; [r]but with everlasting kindness will I have mercy on thee, saith the
LORD thy Redeemer.
9 For this *is as* the waters of [s]Noah unto
me: for *as* I have sworn that the waters of
Noah should no more go over the earth; so
have I sworn that I would not be wroth with
thee, nor rebuke thee.
10 For [t]the mountains shall depart, and
the hills be removed; [u]but my kindness
shall not depart from thee, neither shall the
covenant of my peace be removed, saith the
LORD that hath mercy on thee.
11 ¶ O thou afflicted, tossed with tempest, *and* not comforted, behold, I will lay
thy stones with [v]fair colours, and lay thy
foundations with sapphires.
12 And I will make thy windows of
agates, and thy gates of carbuncles, and all
thy borders of pleasant stones.
13 And all thy children *shall be* [w]taught
of the LORD; and [x]great *shall be* the peace
of thy children.
14 In righteousness shalt thou be established: thou shalt be far from oppression;
for thou shalt not fear: and from terror; for
it shall not come near thee.
15 Behold, they shall surely gather together, *but* not by me: whosoever shall
gather together against thee shall fall for
thy sake.
16 Behold, I have created the smith that
bloweth the coals in the fire, and that bringeth forth an instrument for his work; and I
have created the waster to destroy.
17 ¶ No weapon that is formed against
thee shall prosper; and every tongue *that*
shall rise against thee in judgment thou
shalt condemn. This *is* the heritage of the
servants of the LORD, [y]and their righteousness *is* of me, saith the LORD.

55 Ho, [z]every one that thirsteth, come
ye to the waters, and he that hath no
money; [a]come ye, buy, and eat; yea, come,
buy wine and milk without money and without price.
2 Wherefore do ye spend money for *that*
which is not bread? and your labour for *that*
which satisfieth not? hearken diligently
unto me, and eat ye *that which is* good, and
let your soul delight itself in fatness.
3 Incline your ear, and [b]come unto me:
hear, and your soul shall live; [c]and I will
make an everlasting covenant with you,
even the [d]sure mercies of David.

53:2 [j]ch. 52:14; Mark 9:12
53:3 [k]Ps. 22:6; ch. 49:7 [l]Heb. 4:15 [m]John 1:10
53:4 [n]Matt. 8:17; Heb. 9:28; 1 Pet. 2:24
53:5 [o]Rom. 4:25; 1 Cor. 15:3; 1 Pet. 3:18 [p]1 Pet. 2:24
53:6 [q]Ps. 119:176; 1 Pet. 2:25
53:7 [r]Matt. 26:63; Mark 14:61; 1 Pet. 2:23 [s]Acts 8:32
53:8 [t]Dan. 9:26
53:9 [u]Matt. 27:57 [v]1 Pet. 2:22; 1 John 3:5
53:10 [w]2 Cor. 5:21; 1 Pet. 2:24 [x]Rom. 6:9 [y]Eph. 1:5; 2 Thess. 1:11
53:11 [z]John 17:3; 2 Pet. 1:3 [a]1 John 2:1 [b]ch. 42:1 [c]Rom. 5:18 [d]ver. 4
53:12 [e]Ps. 2:8; Phil. 2:9 [f]Col. 2:15 [g]Mark 15:28; Luke 22:37 [h]Luke 23:34; Rom. 8:34; Heb. 7:25; 1 John 2:1
54:1 [i]Zeph. 3:14; Gal. 4:27 [j]1 Sam. 2:5
54:2 [k]ch. 49:19
54:3 [l]ch. 55:5
54:5 [m]Jer. 3:14 [n]Luke 1:32 [o]Zech. 14:9; Rom. 3:29
54:6 [p]ch. 62:4
54:7 [q]Ps. 30:5; ch. 26:20; 2 Cor. 4:17
54:8 [r]ch. 55:3; Jer. 31:3
54:9 [s]Gen. 8:21; ch. 55:11; Jer. 31:35
54:10 [t]Ps. 46:2; ch. 51:6; Matt. 5:18 [u]Ps. 89:33
54:11 [v]1 Chron. 29:2; Rev. 21:18
54:13 [w]ch. 11:9; Jer. 31:34; John 6:45; 1 Cor. 2:10; 1 Thess. 4:9; 1 John 2:20 [x]Ps. 119:165
54:17 [y]ch. 45:24
55:1 [z]John 4:14; Rev. 21:6 [a]Matt. 13:44; Rev. 3:18
55:3 [b]Matt. 11:28 [c]ch. 54:8; Jer. 32:40 [d]2 Sam. 7:8; Ps. 89:28; Acts 13:34

4 Behold, I have given him *for* [e]a witness to the people, [f]a leader and commander to the people.

5 [g]Behold, thou shalt call a nation *that* thou knowest not, [h]and nations *that* knew not thee shall run unto thee because of the LORD thy God, and for the Holy One of Israel; [i]for he hath glorified thee.

6 ¶ [j]Seek ye the LORD while he may be found, call ye upon him while he is near:

7 [k]Let the wicked forsake his way, and the unrighteous man [l]his thoughts: and let him return unto the LORD, [m]and he will have mercy upon him; and to our God, for he will abundantly pardon.

8 ¶ [n]For my thoughts *are* not your thoughts, neither *are* your ways my ways, saith the LORD.

9 [o]For *as* the heavens are higher than the earth, so are my ways higher than your ways, and my thoughts than your thoughts.

10 For [p]as the rain cometh down, and the snow from heaven, and returneth not thither, but watereth the earth, and maketh it bring forth and bud, that it may give seed to the sower, and bread to the eater:

11 [q]So shall my word be that goeth forth out of my mouth: it shall not return unto me void, but it shall accomplish that which I please, and it shall prosper *in the thing* whereto I sent it.

12 [r]For ye shall go out with joy, and be led forth with peace: the mountains and the hills shall [s]break forth before you into singing, and [t]all the trees of the field shall clap *their* hands.

13 [u]Instead of [v]the thorn shall come up the fir tree, and instead of the briar shall come up the myrtle tree: and it shall be to the LORD [w]for a name, for an everlasting sign *that* shall not be cut off.

56 Thus saith the LORD, Keep ye judgment, and do justice: [x]for my salvation *is* near to come, and my righteousness to be revealed.

2 Blessed *is* the man *that* doeth this, and the son of man *that* layeth hold on it; [y]that keepeth the sabbath from polluting it, and keepeth his hand from doing any evil.

3 ¶ Neither let [z]the son of the stranger, that hath joined himself to the LORD, speak, saying, The LORD hath utterly separated me from his people: neither let the eunuch say, Behold, I *am* a dry tree.

4 For thus saith the LORD unto the eunuchs that keep my sabbaths, and choose *the things* that please me, and take hold of my covenant;

5 Even unto them will I give in [a]mine house and within my walls a place [b]and a name better than of sons and of daughters: I will give them an everlasting name, that shall not be cut off.

6 Also the sons of the stranger, that join themselves to the LORD, to serve him, and to love the name of the LORD, to be his servants, every one that keepeth the sabbath from polluting it, and taketh hold of my covenant;

7 Even them will I [c]bring to my holy mountain, and make them joyful in my house of prayer: [d]their burnt offerings and their sacrifices *shall be* accepted upon mine altar; for [e]mine house shall be called an house of prayer [f]for all people.

8 The Lord GOD, [g]which gathereth the outcasts of Israel saith, [h]Yet will I gather *others* to him, beside those that are gathered unto him.

9 ¶ [i]All ye beasts of the field, come to devour, *yea*, all ye beasts in the forest.

10 His watchmen *are* [j]blind: they are all ignorant, [k]they *are* all dumb dogs, they cannot bark; sleeping, lying down, loving to slumber.

11 Yea, *they are* [l]greedy dogs *which* [m]can never have enough, and they *are* shepherds *that* cannot understand: they all look to their own way, every one for his gain, from his quarter.

12 Come ye, *say they*, I will fetch wine, and we will fill ourselves with strong drink; [n]and to morrow shall be as this day, *and* much more abundant.

57 The righteous perisheth, and no man layeth *it* to heart: and [o]merciful men *are* taken away, [p]none considering that the righteous is taken away from the evil *to come*.

2 He shall enter into peace: they shall rest in [q]their beds, *each one* walking *in* his uprightness.

3 ¶ But draw near hither, [r]ye sons of the sorceress, the seed of the adulterer and the whore.

4 Against whom do ye sport yourselves? against whom make ye a wide mouth, *and* draw out the tongue? *are* ye not children of transgression, a seed of falsehood,

5 Enflaming yourselves with idols [s]under every green tree, [t]slaying the children in the valleys under the clifts of the rocks?

6 Among the smooth *stones* of the stream *is* thy portion; they, they *are* thy lot: even to them hast thou poured a drink offering, thou hast offered a meat offering. Should I receive comfort in these?

7 [u]Upon a lofty and high mountain hast thou set [v]thy bed: even thither wentest thou up to offer sacrifice.

8 Behind the doors also and the posts hast thou set up thy remembrance: for thou hast discovered *thyself to another* than me, and art gone up; thou hast enlarged thy bed, and made thee *a covenant* with them; [w]thou lovedst their bed where thou sawest *it*.

9 And [x]thou wentest to the king with ointment, and didst increase thy perfumes, and didst send thy messengers far off, and didst debase *thyself even* unto hell.

10 Thou art wearied in the greatness of thy way; [y]*yet* saidst thou not, There is no hope: thou hast found the life of thine hand; therefore thou wast not grieved.

11 And [z]of whom hast thou been afraid

55:4 [e]John 18:37; Rev. 1:5 [f]Jer. 30:9; Ezek. 34:23; Hos. 3:5; Dan. 9:25
55:5 [g]ch. 52:15; Eph. 2:11 [h]ch. 60:5 [i]ch. 60:9; Acts 3:13
55:6 [j]Ps. 32:6; Matt. 5:25; John 7:34; 2 Cor. 6:1; Heb. 3:13
55:7 [k]ch. 1:16 [l]Zech. 8:17 [m]Ps. 130:7; Jer. 3:12
55:8 [n]2 Sam. 7:19
55:9 [o]Ps. 103:11
55:10 [p]Deut. 32:2
55:11 [q]ch. 54:9
55:12 [r]ch. 35:10 [s]Ps. 96:12; ch. 14:8 [t]1 Chron. 16:33
55:13 [u]ch. 41:19 [v]Mic. 7:4 [w]Jer. 13:11
56:1 [x]ch. 46:13; Matt. 3:2; Rom. 13:11
56:2 [y]ch. 58:13
56:3 [z]Deut. 23:1; Acts 8:27; 1 Pet. 1:1
56:5 [a]1 Tim. 3:15 [b]John 1:12; 1 John 3:1
56:7 [c]ch. 2:2; 1 Pet. 1:1 [d]Rom. 12:1; Heb. 13:15; 1 Pet. 2:5 [e]Matt. 21:13; Mark 11:17; Luke 19:46 [f]Mal. 1:11
56:8 [g]Ps. 147:2; ch. 11:12 [h]John 10:16; Eph. 1:10
56:9 [i]Jer. 12:9
56:10 [j]Matt. 15:14 [k]Phil. 3:2
56:11 [l]Mic. 3:11 [m]Ezek. 34:2
56:12 [n]Ps. 10:6; Prov. 23:35; ch. 22:13; Luke 12:19; 1 Cor. 15:32
57:1 [o]Ps. 12:1; Mic. 7:2 [p]1 Kings 14:13; 2 Kings 22:20
57:2 [q]2 Chron. 16:14
57:3 [r]Matt. 16:4
57:5 [s]2 Kings 16:4; Jer. 2:20 [t]Lev. 18:21; 2 Kings 16:3; Jer. 7:31; Ezek. 16:20
57:7 [u]Ezek. 16:16 [v]Ezek. 23:41
57:8 [w]Ezek. 16:26
57:9 [x]ch. 30:6; Ezek. 16:33; Hos. 7:11
57:10 [y]Jer. 2:25
57:11 [z]ch. 51:12

or feared, that thou hast lied, and hast not
remembered me, nor laid *it* to thy heart?
[a]have not I held my peace even of old, and
thou fearest me not?
12 I will declare thy righteousness, and
thy works; for they shall not profit thee.
13 ¶ When thou criest, let thy companies
deliver thee; but the wind shall carry them
all away; vanity shall take *them:* but he that
putteth his trust in me shall possess the
land, and shall inherit my holy mountain;
14 And shall say, [b]Cast ye up, cast ye up,
prepare the way, take up the stumblingblock out of the way of my people.
15 For thus saith the high and lofty One
that inhabiteth eternity, [c]whose name *is*
Holy; [d]I dwell in the high and holy *place,*
[e]with him also *that is* of a contrite and
humble spirit, [f]to revive the spirit of the
humble, and to revive the heart of the contrite ones.
16 [g]For I will not contend for ever, neither will I be always wroth: for the spirit
should fail before me, and the souls [h]*which*
I have made.
17 For the iniquity of [i]his covetousness
was I wroth, and smote him: [j]I hid me, and
was wroth, [k]and he went on frowardly in
the way of his heart.
18 I have seen his ways, and [l]will heal
him: I will lead him also, and restore comforts unto him and to [m]his mourners.
19 I create [n]the fruit of the lips; Peace,
peace [o]to *him that is* far off, and to *him that*
is near, saith the LORD; and I will heal him.
20 [p]But the wicked *are* like the troubled
sea, when it cannot rest, whose waters cast
up mire and dirt.
21 [q]*There is* no peace, saith my God, to
the wicked.

58 Cry aloud, spare not, lift up thy voice
like a trumpet, and shew my people
their transgression, and the house of Jacob
their sins.
2 Yet they seek me daily, and delight to
know my ways, as a nation that did righteousness, and forsook not the ordinance of
their God: they ask of me the ordinances of
justice; they take delight in approaching to
God.
3 ¶ [r]Wherefore have we fasted, *say they,*
and thou seest not? *wherefore* have we [s]af-
flicted our soul, and thou takest no knowledge? Behold, in the day of your fast ye find
pleasure, and exact all your labours.
4 [t]Behold, ye fast for strife and debate,
and to smite with the fist of wickedness: ye
shall not fast as *ye do this* day, to make your
voice to be heard on high.
5 Is it [u]such a fast that I have chosen? [v]a
day for a man to afflict his soul? *is it* to bow
down his head as a bulrush, and [w]to spread
sackcloth and ashes *under him?* wilt thou
call this a fast, and an acceptable day to the
LORD?
6 *Is* not this the fast that I have chosen? to
loose the bands of wickedness, [x]to undo the

57:11 [a]Ps. 50:21
57:14 [b]ch. 40:3
57:15 [c]Job 6:10; Luke 1:49 [d]Ps. 68:4; Zech. 2:13 [e]Ps. 34:18; ch. 66:2 [f]Ps. 147:3; ch. 61:1
57:16 [g]Ps. 85:5; Mic. 7:18 [h]Num. 16:22; Job 34:14; Heb. 12:9
57:17 [i]Jer. 6:13 [j]ch. 8:17 [k]ch. 9:13
57:18 [l]Jer. 3:22 [m]ch. 61:2
57:19 [n]Heb. 13:15 [o]Acts 2:39; Eph. 2:17
57:20 [p]Job 15:20; Prov. 4:16
57:21 [q]ch. 48:22
58:3 [r]Mal. 3:14 [s]Lev. 16:29
58:4 [t]1 Kings 21:9
58:5 [u]Zech. 7:5 [v]Lev. 16:29 [w]Esth. 4:3; Job 2:8; Dan. 9:3; Jonah 3:6
58:6 [x]Neh. 5:10 [y]Jer. 34:9
58:7 [z]Ezek. 18:7; Matt. 25:35 [a]Job 31:19 [b]Gen. 29:14; Neh. 5:5
58:8 [c]Job 11:17 [d]Ex. 14:19; ch. 52:12
58:9 [e]Ps. 12:2
58:12 [f]ch. 61:4
58:13 [g]ch. 56:2
58:14 [h]Job 22:26 [i]Deut. 32:13 [j]ch. 1:20; Mic. 4:4
59:1 [k]Num. 11:23; ch. 50:2
59:3 [l]ch. 1:15
59:4 [m]Job 15:35; Ps. 7:14
59:6 [n]Job 8:14
59:7 [o]Prov. 1:16; Rom. 3:15

heavy burdens, and [y]to let the oppressed go
free, and that ye break every yoke?
7 *Is it* not [z]to deal thy bread to the hungry, and that thou bring the poor that are
cast out to thy house? [a]when thou seest the
naked, that thou cover him; and that thou
hide not thyself from [b]thine own flesh?
8 ¶ [c]Then shall thy light break forth as
the morning, and thine health shall spring
forth speedily: and thy righteousness shall
go before thee; [d]the glory of the LORD shall
be thy rereward.
9 Then shalt thou call, and the LORD shall
answer; thou shalt cry, and he shall say,
Here I *am.* If thou take away from the midst
of thee the yoke, the putting forth of the
finger, and [e]speaking vanity;
10 And *if* thou draw out thy soul to the
hungry, and satisfy the afflicted soul; then
shall thy light rise in obscurity, and thy
darkness *be* as the noonday:
11 And the LORD shall guide thee continually, and satisfy thy soul in drought, and
make fat thy bones: and thou shalt be like a
watered garden, and like a spring of water,
whose waters fail not.
12 And *they that shall be* of thee [f]shall
build the old waste places: thou shalt raise
up the foundations of many generations;
and thou shalt be called, The repairer of the
breach, The restorer of paths to dwell in.
13 ¶ If [g]thou turn away thy foot from the
sabbath, *from* doing thy pleasure on my
holy day; and call the sabbath a delight, the
holy of the LORD, honourable; and shalt
honour him, not doing thine own ways, nor
finding thine own pleasure, nor speaking
thine own words:
14 [h]Then shalt thou delight thyself in the
LORD; and I will cause thee to [i]ride upon
the high places of the earth, and feed thee
with the heritage of Jacob thy father: [j]for
the mouth of the LORD hath spoken *it.*

59 Behold, the LORD's hand is not
[k]shortened, that it cannot save; neither his ear heavy, that it cannot hear:
2 But your iniquities have separated between you and your God, and your sins
have hid *his* face from you, that he will not
hear.
3 For [l]your hands are defiled with blood,
and your fingers with iniquity; your lips
have spoken lies, your tongue hath mut-
tered perverseness.
4 None calleth for justice, nor *any* pleadeth for truth: they trust in vanity, and speak
lies; [m]they conceive mischief, and bring
forth iniquity.
5 They hatch cockatrice' eggs, and weave
the spider's web: he that eateth of their eggs
dieth, and that which is crushed breaketh
out into a viper.
6 [n]Their webs shall not become garments, neither shall they cover themselves
with their works: their works *are* works of
iniquity, and the act of violence *is* in their
hands.
7 [o]Their feet run to evil, and they make

haste to shed innocent blood: their thoughts
are thoughts of iniquity; wasting and destruction *are* in their paths.
8 The way of peace they know not; and
there is no judgment in their goings: [p]they
have made them crooked paths: whosoever
goeth therein shall not know peace.
9 ¶ Therefore is judgment far from us,
neither doth justice overtake us: [q]we wait
for light, but behold obscurity; for brightness, *but* we walk in darkness.
10 [r]We grope for the wall like the blind,
and we grope as if *we had* no eyes: we stumble at noonday as in the night; *we are* in
desolate places as dead *men*.
11 We roar all like bears, and [s]mourn
sore like doves: we look for judgment, but
there is none; for salvation, *but* it is far off
from us.
12 For our transgressions are multiplied
before thee, and our sins testify against us:
for our transgressions *are* with us; and *as
for* our iniquities, we know them;
13 In transgressing and lying against the
LORD, and departing away from our God,
speaking oppression and revolt, conceiving
and uttering [t]from the heart words of falsehood.
14 And judgment is turned away backward, and justice standeth afar off: for truth
is fallen in the street, and equity cannot enter.
15 Yea, truth faileth; and he *that* departeth from evil maketh himself a prey. And
the LORD saw *it*, and it displeased him that
there was no judgment.
16 ¶ [u]And he saw that *there was* no man,
and [v]wondered that *there was* no intercessor: [w]therefore his arm brought salvation
unto him; and his righteousness, it sustained him.
17 [x]For he put on righteousness as a
breastplate, and an helmet of salvation
upon his head; and he put on the garments
of vengeance *for* clothing, and was clad
with zeal as a cloak.
18 [y]According to *their* deeds, accordingly he will repay, fury to his adversaries,
recompence to his enemies; to the islands
he will repay recompence.
19 [z]So shall they fear the name of the
LORD from the west, and his glory from the
rising of the sun. When the enemy shall
come in [a]like a flood, the Spirit of the LORD
shall lift up a standard against him.
20 ¶ And [b]the Redeemer shall come to
Zion, and unto them that turn from transgression in Jacob, saith the LORD.
21 [c]As for me, this *is* my covenant with
them, saith the LORD; My spirit that *is* upon
thee, and my words which I have put in thy
mouth, shall not depart out of thy mouth,
nor out of the mouth of thy seed, nor out
of the mouth of thy seed's seed, saith the
LORD, from henceforth and for ever.
60 Arise, [d]shine; for thy light is come,
and [e]the glory of the LORD is risen
upon thee.
2 For, behold, the darkness shall cover
the earth, and gross darkness the people:
but the LORD shall arise upon thee, and his
glory shall be seen upon thee.
3 And the [f]Gentiles shall come to thy
light, and kings to the brightness of thy rising.
4 [g]Lift up thine eyes round about, and
see: all they gather themselves together,
[h]they come to thee: thy sons shall come
from far, and thy daughters shall be nursed
at *thy* side.
5 Then thou shalt see, and flow together,
and thine heart shall fear, and be enlarged;
because [i]the abundance of the sea shall be
converted unto thee, the forces of the Gentiles shall come unto thee.
6 The multitude of camels shall cover
thee, the dromedaries of Midian and
[j]Ephah; all they from [k]Sheba shall come:
they shall bring [l]gold and incense; and
they shall shew forth the praises of the
LORD.
7 All the flocks of [m]Kedar shall be gathered together unto thee, the rams of Nebaioth shall minister unto thee: they shall
come up with acceptance on mine altar, and
[n]I will glorify the house of my glory.
8 Who *are* these *that* fly as a cloud, and
as the doves to their windows?
9 [o]Surely the isles shall wait for me, and
the ships of Tarshish first, [p]to bring thy
sons from far, [q]their silver and their gold
with them, [r]unto the name of the LORD thy
God, and to the Holy One of Israel, [s]be-
cause he hath glorified thee.
10 And [t]the sons of strangers shall build
up thy walls, [u]and their kings shall minister
unto thee: for [v]in my wrath I smote thee,
[w]but in my favour have I had mercy on thee.
11 Therefore thy gates [x]shall be open
continually; they shall not be shut day nor
night; that *men* may bring unto thee the
forces of the Gentiles, and *that* their kings
may be brought.
12 [y]For the nation and kingdom that will
not serve thee shall perish; yea, *those* nations shall be utterly wasted.
13 [z]The glory of Lebanon shall come
unto thee, the fir tree, the pine tree, and the
box together, to beautify the place of my
sanctuary; and I will make [a]the place of my
feet glorious.
14 The sons also of them that afflicted
thee shall come bending unto thee; and all
they that despised thee shall [b]bow themselves down at the soles of thy feet; and they
shall call thee, The city of the LORD, [c]The
Zion of the Holy One of Israel.
15 Whereas thou has been forsaken and
hated, so that no man went through *thee*, I
will make thee an eternal excellency, a joy
of many generations.
16 Thou shalt also suck the milk of the
Gentiles, [d]and shalt suck the breast of
kings: and thou shalt know that [e]I the LORD
am thy Saviour and thy Redeemer, the
mighty One of Jacob.

59:8 [p]Ps. 125:5; Prov. 2:15
59:9 [q]Jer. 8:15
59:10 [r]Deut. 28:29; Job 5:14; Am. 8:9
59:11 [s]ch. 38:14; Ezek. 7:16
59:13 [t]Matt. 12:34
59:16 [u]Ezek. 22:30 [v]Mark 6:6 [w]Ps. 98:1; ch. 63:5
59:17 [x]Eph. 6:14; 1 Thess. 5:8
59:18 [y]ch. 63:6
59:19 [z]Ps. 113:3; Mal. 1:11 [a]Rev. 12:15
59:20 [b]Rom. 11:26
59:21 [c]Heb. 8:10
60:1 [d]Eph. 5:14 [e]Mal. 4:2
60:3 [f]ch. 49:6; Rev. 21:24
60:4 [g]ch. 49:18 [h]ch. 49:20
60:5 [i]Rom. 11:25
60:6 [j]Gen. 25:4 [k]Ps. 72:10 [l]ch. 61:6; Matt. 2:11
60:7 [m]Gen. 25:13 [n]Hag. 2:7
60:9 [o]Ps. 72:10; ch. 42:4 [p]Gal. 4:26 [q]Ps. 68:30; Zech. 14:14 [r]Jer. 3:17 [s]ch. 55:5
60:10 [t]Zech. 6:15 [u]ch. 49:23; Rev. 21:24 [v]ch. 57:17 [w]ch. 54:7
60:11 [x]Rev. 21:25
60:12 [y]Zech. 14:17; Matt. 21:44
60:13 [z]ch. 35:2 [a]1 Chron. 28:2; Ps. 132:7
60:14 [b]ch. 49:23; Rev. 3:9 [c]Heb. 12:22; Rev. 14:1
60:16 [d]ch. 49:23 [e]ch. 43:3

17 For brass I will bring gold, and for iron
I will bring silver, and for wood brass, and
for stones iron: I will also make thy officers
peace, and thine exactors righteousness.
18 Violence shall no more be heard in thy
land, wasting nor destruction within thy
borders; but thou shalt call [f]thy walls Salvation, and thy gates Praise.
19 The [g]sun shall be no more thy light by
day; neither for brightness shall the moon
give light unto thee: but the LORD shall be
unto thee an everlasting light, and [h]thy God
thy glory.
20 [i]Thy sun shall no more go down; neither shall thy moon withdraw itself: for the
LORD shall be thine everlasting light, and
the days of thy mourning shall be ended.
21 [j]Thy people also *shall be* all righteous: [k]they shall inherit the land for ever,
[l]the branch of my planting, [m]the work of
my hands, that I may be glorified.
22 [n]A little one shall become a thousand,
and a small one a strong nation: I the LORD
will hasten it in his time.

61 The [o]Spirit of the Lord GOD *is*
upon me; because the LORD [p]hath
anointed me to preach good tidings unto the
meek; he hath sent me [q]to bind up the brokenhearted, to proclaim [r]liberty to the captives, and the opening of the prison to *them
that are* bound;
2 [s]To proclaim the acceptable year of the
LORD, and [t]the day of vengeance of our
God; [u]to comfort all that mourn;
3 To appoint unto them that mourn in
Zion, [v]to give unto them beauty for ashes,
the oil of joy for mourning, the garment of
praise for the spirit of heaviness; that they
might be called trees of righteousness, [w]the
planting of the LORD, [x]that he might be glorified.
4 ¶ And they shall [y]build the old wastes,
they shall raise up the former desolations,
and they shall repair the waste cities, the
desolations of many generations.
5 And [z]strangers shall stand and feed
your flocks, and the sons of the alien *shall
be* your plowmen and your vinedressers.
6 [a]But ye shall be named the Priests of
the LORD: *men* shall call you the Ministers
of our God: [b]ye shall eat the riches of the
Gentiles, and in their glory shall ye boast
yourselves.
7 ¶ [c]For your shame *ye shall have* double;
and *for* confusion they shall rejoice in their
portion: therefore in their land they shall
possess the double: everlasting joy shall be
unto them.
8 For [d]I the LORD love judgment, [e]I hate
robbery for burnt offering; and I will direct
their work in truth, [f]and I will make an
everlasting covenant with them.
9 And their seed shall be known among
the Gentiles, and their offspring among the
people: all that see them shall acknowledge
them, [g]that they *are* the seed *which* the
LORD hath blessed.
10 [h]I will greatly rejoice in the LORD, my
soul shall be joyful in my God; for [i]he hath
clothed me with the garments of salvation,
he hath covered me with the robe of righteousness, [j]as a bridegroom decketh *himself* with ornaments, and as a bride
adorneth *herself* with her jewels.
11 For as the earth bringeth forth her bud,
and as the garden causeth the things that
are sown in it to spring forth; so the Lord
GOD will cause [k]righteousness and [l]praise
to spring forth before all the nations.

62 For Zion's sake will I not hold my
peace, and for Jerusalem's sake I will
not rest, until the righteousness thereof go
forth as brightness, and the salvation
thereof as a lamp *that* burneth.
2 [m]And the Gentiles shall see thy righteousness, and all kings thy glory: [n]and
thou shalt be called by a new name, which
the mouth of the LORD shall name.
3 Thou shalt also be [o]a crown of glory in
the hand of the LORD, and a royal diadem in
the hand of thy God.
4 [p]Thou shalt no more be termed [q]For-
saken; neither shall thy land any more be
termed [r]Desolate: but thou shalt be called
Hephzi-bah, and thy land Beulah: for the
LORD delighteth in thee, and thy land shall
be married.
5 ¶ For *as* a young man marrieth a virgin,
so shall thy sons marry thee: and *as* the
bridegroom rejoiceth over the bride, *so*
[s]shall thy God rejoice over thee.
6 [t]I have set watchmen upon thy walls,
O Jerusalem, *which* shall never hold their
peace day nor night: ye that make mention
of the LORD, keep not silence,
7 And give him no rest, till he establish,
and till he make Jerusalem [u]a praise in the
earth.
8 The LORD hath sworn by his right hand,
and by the arm of his strength, Surely I will
no more [v]give thy corn *to be* meat for thine
enemies; and the sons of the stranger shall
not drink thy wine, for the which thou hast
laboured:
9 But they that have gathered it shall eat
it, and praise the LORD; and they that have
brought it together shall drink it [w]in the
courts of my holiness.
10 ¶ Go through, go through the gates;
[x]prepare ye the way of the people; cast up,
cast up the highway; gather out the stones;
[y]lift up a standard for the people.
11 Behold, the LORD hath proclaimed
unto the end of the world, [z]Say ye to the
daughter of Zion, Behold, thy salvation
cometh; behold, his [a]reward *is* with him,
and his work before him.
12 And they shall call them, The holy people, The redeemed of the LORD: and thou
shalt be called, Sought out, A city [b]not forsaken.

63 Who *is* this that cometh from Edom,
with dyed garments from Bozrah?
this *that is* glorious in his apparel, travelling in the greatness of his strength? I that
speak in righteousness, mighty to save.

60:18 [f]ch. 26:1
60:19 [g]Rev. 21:23 [h]Zech. 2:5
60:20 [i]Am. 8:9
60:21 [j]ch. 52:1; Rev. 21:27 [k]Ps. 37:11; Matt. 5:5 [l]ch. 61:3; Matt. 15:13; John 15:2 [m]ch. 29:23; Eph. 2:10
60:22 [n]Matt. 13:31
61:1 [o]ch. 11:2; Luke 4:18; John 1:32 [p]Ps. 45:7 [q]Ps. 147:3; ch. 57:15 [r]ch. 42:7; Jer. 34:8
61:2 [s]Lev. 25:9 [t]ch. 34:8; Mal. 4:1; 2 Thess. 1:7 [u]ch. 57:18; Matt. 5:4
61:3 [v]Ps. 30:11 [w]ch. 60:21 [x]John 15:8
61:4 [y]ch. 49:8; Ezek. 36:33-36
61:5 [z]Eph. 2:12
61:6 [a]Ex. 19:6; ch. 60:17; 1 Pet. 2:5; Rev. 1:6 [b]ch. 60:5
61:7 [c]ch. 40:2; Zech. 9:12
61:8 [d]Ps. 11:7 [e]ch. 1:11 [f]ch. 55:3
61:9 [g]ch. 65:23
61:10 [h]Hab. 3:18 [i]Ps. 132:9 [j]ch. 49:18; Rev. 21:2
61:11 [k]Ps. 72:3 [l]ch. 60:18
62:2 [m]ch. 60:3 [n]ver. 4; ch. 65:15
62:3 [o]Zech. 9:16
62:4 [p]Hos. 1:10; 1 Pet. 2:10 [q]ch. 49:14 [r]ch. 54:1
62:5 [s]ch. 65:19
62:6 [t]Ezek. 3:17
62:7 [u]ch. 61:11; Zeph. 3:20
62:8 [v]Deut. 28:31; Jer. 5:17
62:9 [w]Deut. 12:12
62:10 [x]ch. 40:3 [y]ch. 11:12
62:11 [z]Zech. 9:9; Matt. 21:5; John 12:15 [a]ch. 40:10; Rev. 22:12
62:12 [b]ver. 4

2 Wherefore [c]*art thou* red in thine apparel, and thy garments like him that treadeth in the winefat?

3 I have [d]trodden the winepress alone; and of the people *there was* none with me: for I will tread them in mine anger, and trample them in my fury; and their blood shall be sprinkled upon my garments, and I will stain all my raiment.

4 For the [e]day of vengeance *is* in mine heart, and the year of my redeemed is come.

5 [f]And I looked, and [g]*there was* none to help; and I wondered that *there was* none to uphold: therefore mine own [h]arm brought salvation unto me; and my fury, it upheld me.

6 And I will tread down the people in mine anger, and [i]make them drunk in my fury, and I will bring down their strength to the earth.

7 ¶ I will mention the lovingkindnesses of the LORD, *and* the praises of the LORD, according to all that the LORD hath bestowed on us, and the great goodness toward the house of Israel, which he hath bestowed on them according to his mercies, and according to the multitude of his lovingkindnesses.

8 For he said, Surely they *are* my people, children *that* will not lie: so he was their Saviour.

9 [j]In all their affliction he was afflicted, [k]and the angel of his presence saved them: [l]in his love and in his pity he redeemed them; and [m]he bare them, and carried them all the days of old.

10 ¶ But they [n]rebelled, and [o]vexed his holy Spirit: [p]therefore he was turned to be their enemy, *and* he fought against them.

11 Then he remembered the days of old, Moses, *and* his people, *saying,* Where *is* he that [q]brought them up out of the sea with the shepherd of his flock? [r]where *is* he that put his holy Spirit within him?

12 That led *them* by the right hand of Moses [s]with his glorious arm, [t]dividing the water before them, to make himself an everlasting name?

13 [u]That led them through the deep, as an horse in the wilderness, *that* they should not stumble?

14 As a beast goeth down into the valley, the Spirit of the LORD caused him to rest; so didst thou lead thy people, [v]to make thyself a glorious name.

15 ¶ [w]Look down from heaven, and behold [x]from the habitation of thy holiness and of thy glory: where *is* thy zeal and thy strength, the sounding [y]of thy bowels and of thy mercies toward me? are they restrained?

16 [z]Doubtless thou *art* our father, though Abraham be [a]ignorant of us, and Israel acknowledge us not: thou, O LORD, *art* our father, our redeemer; thy name *is* from everlasting.

17 ¶ O LORD, why hast thou [b]made us to err from thy ways, *and* [c]hardened our heart from thy fear? [d]Return for thy servants' sake, the tribes of thine inheritance.

18 [e]The people of thy holiness have possessed *it* but a little while: [f]our adversaries have trodden down thy sanctuary.

19 We are *thine:* thou never barest rule over them; they were not called by thy name.

64 Oh that thou wouldest [g]rend the heavens, that thou wouldest come down, that [h]the mountains might flow down at thy presence,

2 As *when* the melting fire burneth, the fire causeth the waters to boil, to make thy name known to thine adversaries, *that* the nations may tremble at thy presence!

3 When [i]thou didst terrible things *which* we looked not for, thou camest down, the mountains flowed down at thy presence.

4 For since the beginning of the world [j]*men* have not heard, nor perceived by the ear, neither hath the eye seen, O God, beside thee, *what* he hath prepared for him that waiteth for him.

5 Thou meetest him that rejoiceth [k]and worketh righteousness, [l]*those that* remember thee in thy ways: behold, thou art wroth; for we have sinned: [m]in those is continuance, and we shall be saved.

6 But we are all as an unclean *thing*, and all [n]our righteousnesses *are* as filthy rags; and we all do [o]fade as a leaf; and our iniquities, like the wind, have taken us away.

7 And [p]*there is* none that calleth upon thy name, that stirreth up himself to take hold of thee: for thou hast hid thy face from us, and hast consumed us, because of our iniquities.

8 [q]But now, O LORD, thou *art* our father; we *are* the clay, [r]and thou our potter; and we all *are* [s]the work of thy hand.

9 ¶ Be not [t]wroth very sore, O LORD, neither remember iniquity for ever: behold, see, we beseech thee, [u]we *are* all thy people.

10 Thy holy cities are a wilderness, Zion is a wilderness, [v]Jerusalem a desolation.

11 [w]Our holy and our beautiful house, where our fathers praised thee, is burned up with fire: and all [x]our pleasant things are laid waste.

12 [y]Wilt thou refrain thyself for these *things,* O LORD? [z]wilt thou hold thy peace, and afflict us very sore?

65 I [a]am sought of *them that* asked not *for me;* I am found of *them that* sought me not: I said, Behold me, behold me, unto a nation *that* [b]was not called by my name.

2 [c]I have spread out my hands all the day unto a rebellious people, which walketh in a way *that was* not good, after their own thoughts;

3 A people [d]that provoketh me to anger continually to my face; [e]that sacrificeth in gardens, and burneth incense upon altars of brick;

4 [f]Which remain among the graves, and

63:2 [c]Rev. 19:13
63:3 [d]Lam. 1:15; Rev. 14:19
63:4 [e]ch. 34:8
63:5 [f]ch. 41:28 [g]John 16:32 [h]Ps. 98:1; ch. 59:16
63:6 [i]Rev. 16:6
63:9 [j]Judg. 10:16; Zech. 2:8; Acts 9:4 [k]Ex. 14:19; Mal. 3:1; Acts 12:11 [l]Deut. 7:7 [m]Ex. 19:4; Deut. 1:31; ch. 46:3
63:10 [n]Ex. 15:24; Num. 14:11; Ps. 78:56 [o]Ps. 78:40; Acts 7:51; Eph. 4:30 [p]Ex. 23:21
63:11 [q]Ex. 14:30; Num. 14:13; Jer. 2:6 [r]Num. 11:17; Neh. 9:20; Dan. 4:8; Hag. 2:5
63:12 [s]Ex. 15:6 [t]Ex. 14:21; Josh. 3:16
63:13 [u]Ps. 106:9
63:14 [v]2 Sam. 7:23
63:15 [w]Deut. 26:15; Ps. 80:14 [x]Ps. 33:14 [y]Jer. 31:20; Hos. 11:8
63:16 [z]Deut. 32:6; 1 Chron. 29:10; ch. 64:8 [a]Job 14:21; Eccl. 9:5
63:17 [b]Ps. 119:10 [c]ch. 6:10; John 12:40; Rom. 9:18 [d]Num. 10:36; Ps. 90:13
63:18 [e]Deut. 7:6; ch. 62:12; Dan. 8:24 [f]Ps. 74:7
64:1 [g]Ps. 144:5 [h]Judg. 5:5; Mic. 1:4
64:3 [i]Ex. 34:10; Judg. 5:4; Ps. 68:8; Hab. 3:3
64:4 [j]Ps. 31:19; 1 Cor. 2:9
64:5 [k]Acts 10:35 [l]ch. 26:8 [m]Mal. 3:6
64:6 [n]Phil. 3:9 [o]Ps. 90:5
64:7 [p]Hos. 7:7
64:8 [q]ch. 63:16 [r]ch. 29:16; Jer. 18:6; Rom. 9:20 [s]Eph. 2:10
64:9 [t]Ps. 74:1 [u]Ps. 79:13
64:10 [v]Ps. 79:1
64:11 [w]2 Kings 25:9; Ps. 74:7; 2 Chron. 36:19 [x]Ezek. 24:21
64:12 [y]ch. 42:14 [z]Ps. 83:1
65:1 [a]Rom. 9:24; Eph. 2:12 [b]ch. 63:19
65:2 [c]Rom. 10:21
65:3 [d]Deut. 32:21 [e]Lev. 17:5; ch. 1:29
65:4 [f]Deut. 18:11

lodge in the monuments, [g]which eat
swine's flesh, and broth of abominable
things is in their vessels;
5 [h]Which say, Stand by thyself, come not
near to me; for I am holier than thou. These
are a smoke in my nose, a fire that burneth
all the day.
6 Behold, [i]*it is* written before me: [j]I will
not keep silence, [k]but will recompense,
even recompense into their bosom,
7 Your iniquities, and [l]the iniquities of
your fathers together, saith the LORD,
[m]which have burned incense upon the
mountains, [n]and blasphemed me upon the
hills: therefore will I measure their former
work into their bosom.
8 ¶ Thus saith the LORD, As the new wine
is found in the cluster, and *one* saith, Destroy it not; for [o]a blessing *is* in it: so will I
do for my servants' sakes, that I may not
destroy them all.
9 And I will bring forth a seed out of Jacob, and out of Judah an inheritor of my
mountains: and mine [p]elect shall inherit it,
and my servants shall dwell there.
10 And [q]Sharon shall be a fold of flocks,
and [r]the valley of Achor a place for the
herds to lie down in, for my people that
have sought me.
11 ¶ But ye *are* they that forsake the
LORD, that forget [s]my holy mountain, that
prepare [t]a table for that troop, and that furnish the drink offering unto that number.
12 Therefore will I number you to the
sword, and ye shall all bow down to the
slaughter: [u]because when I called, ye did
not answer; when I spake, ye did not hear;
but did evil before mine eyes, and did
choose *that* wherein I delighted not.
13 Therefore thus saith the Lord GOD, Behold, my servants shall eat, but ye shall be
hungry: behold, my servants shall drink,
but ye shall be thirsty: behold, my servants
shall rejoice, but ye shall be ashamed:
14 Behold, my servants shall sing for joy
of heart, but ye shall cry for sorrow of heart,
and [v]shall howl for vexation of spirit.
15 And ye shall leave your name [w]for a
curse unto [x]my chosen: for the Lord GOD
shall slay thee, and [y]call his servants by
another name:
16 [z]That he who blesseth himself in the
earth shall bless himself in the God of truth;
and [a]he that sweareth in the earth shall
swear by the God of truth; because the former troubles are forgotten, and because
they are hid from mine eyes.
17 ¶ For, behold, I create [b]new heavens
and a new earth: and the former shall not be
remembered, nor come into mind.
18 But be ye glad and rejoice for ever *in
that* which I create: for, behold, I create Jerusalem a rejoicing, and her people a joy.
19 And [c]I will rejoice in Jerusalem, and
joy in my people: and the [d]voice of weeping
shall be no more heard in her, nor the voice
of crying.
20 There shall be no more thence an infant of days, nor an old man that hath not
filled his days: for the child shall die an hundred years old; [e]but the sinner *being* an
hundred years old shall be accursed.
21 And [f]they shall build houses, and inhabit *them;* and they shall plant vineyards,
and eat the fruit of them.
22 They shall not build, and another inhabit; they shall not plant, and another eat:
for [g]as the days of a tree *are* the days of my
people, and [h]mine elect shall long enjoy the
work of their hands.
23 They shall not labour in vain, [i]nor
bring forth for trouble; for [j]they *are* the
seed of the blessed of the LORD, and their
offspring with them.
24 And it shall come to pass, that [k]before
they call, I will answer; and while they are
yet speaking, I will hear.
25 The [l]wolf and the lamb shall feed together, and the lion shall eat straw like the
bullock: [m]and dust *shall be* the serpent's
meat. They shall not hurt nor destroy in all
my holy mountain, saith the LORD.

66

Thus saith the LORD, [n]The heaven *is*
my throne, and the earth *is* my footstool: where *is* the house that ye build unto
me? and where *is* the place of my rest?
2 For all those *things* hath mine hand
made, and all those *things* have been, saith
the LORD: [o]but to this *man* will I look,
[p]*even to him that is* poor and of a contrite
spirit, and [q]trembleth at my word.
3 [r]He that killeth an ox *is as if* he slew a
man; he that sacrificeth a lamb, *as if* he [s]cut
off a dog's neck; he that offereth an oblation, *as if he offered* swine's blood; he that
burneth incense, *as if* he blessed an idol.
Yea, they have chosen their own ways, and
their soul delighteth in their abominations.
4 I also will choose their delusions, and
will bring their fears upon them; [t]because
when I called, none did answer; when I
spake, they did not hear: but they did evil
before mine eyes, and chose *that* in which
I delighted not.
5 ¶ Hear the word of the LORD, [u]ye that
tremble at his word; Your brethren that
hated you, that cast you out for my name's
sake, said, [v]Let the LORD be glorified: but
[w]he shall appear to your joy, and they shall
be ashamed.
6 A voice of noise from the city, a voice
from the temple, a voice of the LORD that
rendereth recompence to his enemies.
7 Before she travailed, she brought forth;
before her pain came, she was delivered of
a man child.
8 Who hath heard such a thing? who hath
seen such things? Shall the earth be made to
bring forth in one day? *or* shall a nation be
born at once? for as soon as Zion travailed,
she brought forth her children.
9 Shall I bring to the birth, and not cause
to bring forth? saith the LORD: shall I cause
to bring forth, and shut *the womb?* saith thy
God.
10 Rejoice ye with Jerusalem, and be glad

65:4 [g]Lev. 11:7; ch. 66:17
65:5 [h]Matt. 9:11; Luke 5:30; Jude 19
65:6 [i]Deut. 32:34; Mal. 3:16 [j]Ps. 50:3 [k]Ps. 79:12; Jer. 16:18; Ezek. 11:21
65:7 [l]Ex. 20:5 [m]Ezek. 18:6 [n]Ezek. 20:27
65:8 [o]Joel 2:14
65:9 [p]ver. 15; Matt. 24:22; Rom. 11:5
65:10 [q]ch. 33:9 [r]Josh. 7:24; Hos. 2:15
65:11 [s]ch. 56:7; ver. 25 [t]Ezek. 23:41; 1 Cor. 10:21
65:12 [u]2 Chron. 36:15; Prov. 1:24; ch. 66:4; Jer. 7:13; Zech. 7:7; Matt. 21:34-43
65:14 [v]Matt. 8:12; Luke 13:28
65:15 [w]Jer. 29:22; Zech. 8:13 [x]ver. 9 [y]ch. 62:2; Acts 11:26
65:16 [z]Ps. 72:17; Jer. 4:2 [a]Deut. 6:13; Ps. 63:11; ch. 19:18; Zeph. 1:5
65:17 [b]ch. 51:16; 2 Pet. 3:13; Rev. 21:1
65:19 [c]ch. 62:5 [d]ch. 35:10; Rev. 7:17
65:20 [e]Eccl. 8:12
65:21 [f]Lev. 26:16; Deut. 28:30; ch. 62:8; Am. 9:14
65:22 [g]Ps. 92:12 [h]ver. 9
65:23 [i]Deut. 28:41; Hos. 9:12 [j]ch. 61:9
65:24 [k]Ps. 32:5; Dan. 9:21
65:25 [l]ch. 11:6 [m]Gen. 3:14
66:1 [n]1 Kings 8:27; 2 Chron. 6:18; Matt. 5:34; Acts 7:48
66:2 [o]ch. 57:15 [p]Ps. 34:18 [q]Ezra 9:4; Prov. 28:14; ver. 5
66:3 [r]ch. 1:11 [s]Deut. 23:18
66:4 [t]Prov. 1:24; ch. 65:12; Jer. 7:13
66:5 [u]ver. 2 [v]ch. 5:19 [w]2 Thess. 1:10; Tit. 2:13

with her, all ye that love her: rejoice for joy
with her, all ye that mourn for her:
11 That ye may suck, and be satisfied
with the breasts of her consolations; that ye
may milk out, and be delighted with the
abundance of her glory.
12 For thus saith the LORD, Behold, [x]I
will extend peace to her like a river, and the
glory of the Gentiles like a flowing stream:
then shall ye [y]suck, ye shall be [z]borne
upon *her* sides, and be dandled upon *her*
knees.
13 As one whom his mother comforteth,
so will I comfort you; and ye shall be comforted in Jerusalem.
14 And when ye see *this,* your heart shall
rejoice, and [a]your bones shall flourish like
an herb: and the hand of the LORD shall be
known toward his servants, and *his* indignation toward his enemies.
15 [b]For, behold, the LORD will come with
fire, and with his chariots like a whirlwind,
to render his anger with fury, and his rebuke with flames of fire.
16 For by fire and by [c]his sword will the
LORD plead with all flesh: and the slain of
the LORD shall be many.
17 [d]They that sanctify themselves, and
purify themselves in the gardens behind
one *tree* in the midst, eating swine's flesh,
and the abomination, and the mouse, shall
be consumed together, saith the LORD.
18 For I *know* their works and their
thoughts: it shall come, that I will gather all
nations and tongues; and they shall come,
and see my glory.
19 [e]And I will set a sign among them, and
I will send those that escape of them unto
the nations, *to* Tarshish, Pul, and Lud, that
draw the bow, *to* Tubal and Javan, *to* the
isles afar off, that have not heard my fame,
neither have seen my glory; [f]and they shall
declare my glory among the Gentiles.
20 And they shall bring all your brethren
[g]*for* an offering unto the LORD out of all
nations upon horses, and in chariots, and
in litters, and upon mules, and upon swift
beasts, to my holy mountain Jerusalem,
saith the LORD, as the children of Israel
bring an offering in a clean vessel into the
house of the LORD.
21 And I will also take of them for
[h]priests *and* for Levites, saith the LORD.
22 For as [i]the new heavens and the new
earth, which I will make, shall remain before me, saith the LORD, so shall your seed
and your name remain.
23 And [j]it shall come to pass, *that* from
one new moon to another, and from one
sabbath to another, [k]shall all flesh come to
worship before me, saith the LORD.
24 And they shall go forth, and look upon
[l]the carcases of the men that have transgressed against me: for their [m]worm shall
not die, neither shall their fire be quenched;
and they shall be an abhorring unto all
flesh.

66:12 [x]ch. 48:18 [y]ch. 60:16 [z]ch. 49:22
66:14 [a]Ezek. 37:1
66:15 [b]ch. 9:5; 2 Thess. 1:8
66:16 [c]ch. 27:1
66:17 [d]ch. 65:3
66:19 [e]Luke 2:34 [f]Mal. 1:11
66:20 [g]Rom. 15:16
66:21 [h]Ex. 19:6; ch. 61:6; 1 Pet. 2:9; Rev. 1:6
66:22 [i]ch. 65:17; 2 Pet. 3:13; Rev. 21:1
66:23 [j]Zech. 14:16 [k]Ps. 65:2
66:24 [l]ver. 16 [m]Mark 9:44

JEREMIAH

Jeremiah wrote this book about 626 B.C. The majority of the book is about the period from 627 B.C. to 586 B.C. during which Judah and Israel drifted far from God and foreign powers controlled their land, even to the point of destroying Jerusalem. Despite this desolation, there is hope that restoration of the nation will come if the people return to and trust in God.

I. Jeremiah is called to minister, 1:1–1:19
II. Judah's sins and Jeremiah's warnings, 2:1–20:18
III. Denouncement of the kings, prophets, and people, 21:1–26:24
IV. Jeremiah's counsel and argument, 26:25–29:32
V. The promise of Judah's restoration, 30:1–33:26
VI. The fall of Jerusalem, 34:1–45:5
VII. Prophecies concerning other nations, 46:1–52:34

1 The words of Jeremiah the son of Hilkiah, of the priests that *were* [a]in Anathoth in the land of Benjamin:

2 To whom the word of the LORD came in the days of Josiah the son of Amon king of Judah, [b]in the thirteenth year of his reign.

3 It came also in the days of Jehoiakim the son of Josiah king of Judah, [c]unto the end of the eleventh year of Zedekiah the son of Josiah king of Judah, [d]unto the carrying away of Jerusalem captive [e]in the fifth month.

4 Then the word of the LORD came unto me, saying,

5 Before I [f]formed thee in the belly [g]I knew thee; and before thou camest forth out of the womb I [h]sanctified thee, *and* I ordained thee a prophet unto the nations.

6 Then said I, [i]Ah, Lord GOD! behold, I cannot speak: for I *am* a child.

7 ¶ But the LORD said unto me, Say not, I *am* a child: for thou shalt go to all that I shall send thee, and [j]whatsoever I command thee thou shalt speak.

8 [k]Be not afraid of their faces: for [l]I *am* with thee to deliver thee, saith the LORD.

9 Then the LORD put forth his hand, and [m]touched my mouth. And the LORD said unto me, Behold, I have [n]put my words in thy mouth.

10 [o]See, I have this day set thee over the nations and over the kingdoms, to [p]root out, and to pull down, and to destroy, and to throw down, to build, and to plant.

11 ¶ Moreover the word of the LORD came unto me, saying, Jeremiah, what seest thou? And I said, I see a rod of an almond tree.

12 Then said the LORD unto me, Thou hast well seen: for I will hasten my word to perform it.

13 And the word of the LORD came unto me the second time, saying, What seest thou? And I said, I see [q]a seething pot; and the face thereof *is* toward the north.

14 Then the LORD said unto me, Out of the [r]north an evil shall break forth upon all the inhabitants of the land.

15 For, lo, I will [s]call all the families of the kingdoms of the north, saith the LORD; and they shall come, and they shall [t]set every one his throne at the entering of the gates of Jerusalem, and against all the walls thereof round about, and against all the cities of Judah.

16 And I will utter my judgments against them touching all their wickedness, [u]who have forsaken me, and have burned incense unto other gods, and worshipped the works of their own hands.

17 ¶ Thou therefore [v]gird up thy loins, and arise, and speak unto them all that I command thee: [w]be not dismayed at their faces, lest I confound thee before them.

18 For, behold, I have made thee this day [x]a defenced city, and an iron pillar, and brasen walls against the whole land, against the kings of Judah, against the princes thereof, against the priests thereof, and against the people of the land.

19 And they shall fight against thee; but they shall not prevail against thee; [y]for I *am* with thee, saith the LORD, to deliver thee.

2 Moreover the word of the LORD came to me, saying,

2 Go and cry in the ears of Jerusalem, saying, Thus saith the LORD; I remember thee, the kindness of thy [z]youth, the love of thine espousals, [a]when thou wentest after me in the wilderness, in a land *that was* not sown.

3 [b]Israel *was* holiness unto the LORD, *and* [c]the firstfruits of his increase: [d]all that devour him shall offend; evil shall come upon them, saith the LORD.

4 Hear ye the word of the LORD, O house of Jacob, and all the families of the house of Israel:

5 ¶ Thus saith the LORD, [e]What iniquity have your fathers found in me, that they are gone far from me, [f]and have walked after vanity, and are become vain?

1:1 [a]Josh. 21:18; 1 Chron. 6:60; ch. 32:7
1:2 [b]ch. 25:3
1:3 [c]ch. 39:2 [d]ch. 52:12 [e]2 Kings 25:8
1:5 [f]Isa. 49:1 [g]Ex. 33:12 [h]Luke 1:15; Gal. 1:15
1:6 [i]Ex. 4:10; Isa. 6:5
1:7 [j]Num. 22:20; Matt. 28:20
1:8 [k]Ezek. 2:6; ver. 17 [l]Ex. 3:12; Deut. 31:6; Josh. 1:5; ch. 15:20; Acts 26:17; Heb. 13:6
1:9 [m]Isa. 6:7 [n]Isa. 51:16; ch. 5:14
1:10 [o]1 Kings 19:17 [p]ch. 18:7; 2 Cor. 10:4
1:13 [q]Ezek. 11:3
1:14 [r]ch. 4:6
1:15 [s]ch. 5:15 [t]ch. 39:3
1:16 [u]Deut. 28:20; ch. 17:13
1:17 [v]1 Kings 18:46; 2 Kings 4:29; Job 38:3; Luke 12:35; 1 Pet. 1:13 [w]Ex. 3:12; ver. 8; Ezek. 2:6
1:18 [x]Isa. 50:7; ch. 6:27
1:19 [y]ver. 8
2:2 [z]Ezek. 16:8; Hos. 2:15 [a]Deut. 2:7
2:3 [b]Ex. 19:5 [c]Jam. 1:18; Rev. 14:4 [d]ch. 12:14
2:5 [e]Isa. 5:4; Mic. 6:3 [f]2 Kings 17:15; Jonah 2:8

6 Neither said they, Where *is* the LORD
that [g]brought us up out of the land of Egypt,
that led us through [h]the wilderness,
through a land of deserts and of pits,
through a land of drought, and of the
shadow of death, through a land that no
man passed through, and where no man
dwelt?
7 And I brought you into [i]a plentiful
country, to eat the fruit thereof and the
goodness thereof; but when ye entered, ye
[j]defiled my land, and made mine heritage
an abomination.
8 The priests said not, Where *is* the LORD?
and they that handle the [k]law knew me not:
the pastors also transgressed against me,
[l]and the prophets prophesied by Baal, and
walked after *things that* [m]do not profit.
9 ¶ Wherefore [n]I will yet plead with you,
saith the LORD, and [o]with your children's
children will I plead.
10 For pass over the isles of Chittim, and
see; and send unto Kedar, and consider diligently, and see if there be such a thing.
11 [p]Hath a nation changed *their* gods,
which *are* [q]yet no gods? [r]but my people
have changed their glory for [s]*that which*
doth not profit.
12 [t]Be astonished, O ye heavens, at this,
and be horribly afraid, be ye very desolate,
saith the LORD.
13 For my people have committed two
evils; they have forsaken me the [u]fountain
of living waters, *and* hewed them out cisterns, broken cisterns, that can hold no water.
14 ¶ *Is* Israel [v]a servant? *is* he a homeborn *slave* ? why is he spoiled?
15 [w]The young lions roared upon him,
and yelled, and they made his land waste:
his cities are burned without inhabitant.
16 Also the children of Noph and
[x]Tahapanes have broken the crown of thy
head.
17 [y]Hast thou not procured this unto thyself, in that thou hast forsaken the LORD thy
God, when [z]he led thee by the way?
18 And now what hast thou to do [a]in the
way of Egypt, to drink the waters of [b]Si-
hor? or what hast thou to do in the way of
Assyria, to drink the waters of the river?
19 Thine own [c]wickedness shall correct
thee, and thy backslidings shall reprove
thee: know therefore and see that *it is* an
evil *thing* and bitter, that thou hast forsaken
the LORD thy God, and that my fear *is* not in
thee, saith the Lord GOD of hosts.
20 ¶ For of old time I have broken thy
yoke, *and* burst thy bands; and [d]thou
saidst, I will not transgress; when [e]upon
every high hill and under every green tree
thou wanderest, [f]playing the harlot.
21 Yet I had [g]planted thee a noble vine,
wholly a right seed: how then art thou
turned into [h]the degenerate plant of a
strange vine unto me?
22 For though thou [i]wash thee with
nitre, and take thee much soap, *yet* [j]thine
iniquity is marked before me, saith the Lord
GOD.
23 [k]How canst thou say, I am not polluted, I have not gone after Baalim? see thy
way [l]in the valley, know what thou hast
done: *thou art* a swift dromedary traversing
her ways;
24 [m]A wild ass used to the wilderness,
that snuffeth up the wind at her pleasure; in
her occasion who can turn her away? all
they that seek her will not weary themselves; in her month they shall find her.
25 Withhold thy foot from being unshod,
and thy throat from thirst: but [n]thou saidst,
There is no hope: no; for I have loved
[o]strangers, and after them will I go.
26 As the thief is ashamed when he is
found, so is the house of Israel ashamed;
they, their kings, their princes, and their
priests, and their prophets,
27 Saying to a stock, Thou *art* my father;
and to a stone, Thou hast brought me forth:
for they have turned *their* back unto me,
and not *their* face: but in the time of their
[p]trouble they will say, Arise, and save us.
28 But [q]where *are* thy gods that thou hast
made thee? let them arise, if they [r]can save
thee in the time of thy trouble: for [s]*according to* the number of thy cities are thy gods,
O Judah.
29 [t]Wherefore will ye plead with me? ye
all have transgressed against me, saith the
LORD.
30 In vain have I [u]smitten your children;
they received no correction: your own
sword hath [v]devoured your prophets, like a
destroying lion.
31 ¶ O generation, see ye the word of the
LORD. [w]Have I been a wilderness unto Israel? a land of darkness? wherefore say my
people, [x]We are lords; [y]we will come no
more unto thee?
32 Can a maid forget her ornaments, *or* a
bride her attire? yet my people [z]have forgotten me days without number.
33 Why trimmest thou thy way to seek
love? therefore hast thou also taught the
wicked ones thy ways.
34 Also in thy skirts is found [a]the blood
of the souls of the poor innocents: I have not
found it by secret search, but upon all these.
35 [b]Yet thou sayest, Because I am innocent, surely his anger shall turn from me.
Behold, [c]I will plead with thee, [d]because
thou sayest, I have not sinned.
36 [e]Why gaddest thou about so much to
change thy way? [f]thou also shalt be
ashamed of Egypt, [g]as thou wast ashamed
of Assyria.
37 Yea, thou shalt go forth from him, and
[h]thine hands upon thine head: for the LORD
hath rejected thy confidences, and thou
shalt not prosper in them.

3 They say, If a man put away his wife,
and she go from him, and become another man's, [i]shall he return unto her

2:6 [g]Isa. 63:9; Hos. 13:4 [h]Deut. 8:15
2:7 [i]Num. 13:27; Deut. 8:7 [j]Lev. 18:25; Num. 35:33; Ps. 78:58; ch. 3:1
2:8 [k]Mal. 2:6; Rom. 2:20 [l]ch. 23:13 [m]ver. 11; Hab. 2:18
2:9 [n]Ezek. 20:35; Mic. 6:2 [o]Ex. 20:5; Lev. 20:5
2:11 [p]Mic. 4:5 [q]Ps. 115:4; Isa. 37:19; ch. 16:20 [r]Ps. 106:20; Rom. 1:23 [s]ver. 8
2:12 [t]Isa. 1:2; ch. 6:19
2:13 [u]Ps. 36:9; ch. 17:13; John 4:14
2:14 [v]Ex. 4:22
2:15 [w]Isa. 1:7; ch. 4:7
2:16 [x]ch. 43:7
2:17 [y]ch. 4:18 [z]Deut. 32:10
2:18 [a]Isa. 30:1 [b]Josh. 13:3
2:19 [c]Isa. 3:9; Hos. 5:5
2:20 [d]Ex. 19:8; Josh. 24:18; Judg. 10:16; 1 Sam. 12:10 [e]Deut. 12:2; Isa. 57:5; ch. 3:6 [f]Ex. 34:15
2:21 [g]Ex. 15:17; Ps. 44:2; Isa. 5:1; Matt. 21:33; Mark 12:1; Luke 20:9 [h]Deut. 32:32; Isa. 1:21
2:22 [i]Job 9:30 [j]Deut. 32:34; Job 14:17; Hos. 13:12
2:23 [k]Prov. 30:12 [l]ch. 7:31
2:24 [m]Job 39:5; ch. 14:6
2:25 [n]ch. 18:12 [o]Deut. 32:16; ch. 3:13
2:27 [p]Judg. 10:10; Ps. 78:34; Isa. 26:16
2:28 [q]Deut. 32:37; Judg. 10:14 [r]Isa. 45:20 [s]ch. 11:13
2:29 [t]ver. 23
2:30 [u]Isa. 1:5; ch. 5:3 [v]2 Chron. 36:16; Neh. 9:26; Matt. 23:29; Acts 7:52; 1 Thess. 2:15
2:31 [w]ver. 5 [x]Ps. 12:4 [y]Deut. 32:15
2:32 [z]Ps. 106:21; ch. 13:25; Hos. 8:14
2:34 [a]Ps. 106:38; ch. 19:4
2:35 [b]ver. 23 [c]ver. 9 [d]Prov. 28:13; 1 John 1:8
2:36 [e]ver. 18; ch. 31:22; Hos. 5:13 [f]Isa. 30:3; ch. 37:7 [g]2 Chron. 28:16

2:37 [h]2 Sam. 13:19 **3:1** [i]Deut. 24:4

again? shall not that [j]land be greatly polluted? but thou hast [k]played the harlot with many lovers; [l]yet return again to me, saith the LORD.

2 Lift up thine eyes unto [m]the high places, and see where thou hast not been lien with. [n]In the ways hast thou sat for them, as the Arabian in the wilderness; [o]and thou hast polluted the land with thy whoredoms and with thy wickedness.

3 Therefore the [p]showers have been withholden, and there hath been no latter rain; and thou hadst a [q]whore's forehead, thou refusedst to be ashamed.

4 Wilt thou not from this time cry unto me, My father, thou *art* [r]the guide of [s]my youth?

5 [t]Will he reserve *his anger* for ever? will he keep *it* to the end? Behold, thou hast spoken and done evil things as thou couldest.

6 ¶ The LORD said also unto me in the days of Josiah the king, Hast thou seen *that* which [u]backsliding Israel hath done? she is [v]gone up upon every high mountain and under every green tree, and there hath played the harlot.

7 [w]And I said after she had done all these *things,* Turn thou unto me. But she returned not. And her treacherous [x]sister Judah saw *it.*

8 And I saw, when [y]for all the causes whereby backsliding Israel committed adultery I had [z]put her away, and given her a bill of divorce; [a]yet her treacherous sister Judah feared not, but went and played the harlot also.

9 And it came to pass through the lightness of her whoredom, that she [b]defiled the land, and committed adultery with [c]stones and with stocks.

10 And yet for all this her treacherous sister Judah hath not turned unto me [d]with her whole heart, but feignedly, saith the LORD.

11 And the LORD said unto me, [e]The backsliding Israel hath justified herself more than treacherous Judah.

12 ¶ Go and proclaim these words toward [f]the north, and say, Return, thou backsliding Israel, saith the LORD; *and* I will not cause mine anger to fall upon you: for I *am* [g]merciful, saith the LORD, *and* I will not keep *anger* for ever.

13 [h]Only acknowledge thine iniquity, that thou hast transgressed against the LORD thy God, and hast [i]scattered thy ways to the [j]strangers [k]under every green tree, and ye have not obeyed my voice, saith the LORD.

14 Turn, O backsliding children, saith the LORD; [l]for I am married unto you: and I will take you [m]one of a city, and two of a family, and I will bring you to Zion:

15 And I will give you [n]pastors according to mine heart, which shall [o]feed you with knowledge and understanding.

16 And it shall come to pass, when ye be multiplied and increased in the land, in those days, saith the LORD, they shall say no more, The ark of the covenant of the LORD: [p]neither shall it come to mind: neither shall they remember it; neither shall they visit *it;* neither shall *that* be done any more.

17 At that time they shall call Jerusalem the throne of the LORD; and all the nations shall be gathered unto it, [q]to the name of the LORD, to Jerusalem: neither shall they [r]walk any more after the imagination of their evil heart.

18 In those days [s]the house of Judah shall walk with the house of Israel, and they shall come together out of the land of [t]the north to [u]the land that I have given for an inheritance unto your fathers.

19 But I said, How shall I put thee among the children, and give thee [v]a pleasant land, a goodly heritage of the hosts of nations? and I said, Thou shalt call me, [w]My father; and shalt not turn away from me.

20 ¶ Surely *as* a wife treacherously departeth from her husband, so [x]have ye dealt treacherously with me, O house of Israel, saith the LORD.

21 A voice was heard upon [y]the high places, weeping *and* supplications of the children of Israel: for they have perverted their way, *and* they have forgotten the LORD their God.

22 [z]Return, ye backsliding children, *and* [a]I will heal your backslidings. Behold, we come unto thee; for thou *art* the LORD our God.

23 [b]Truly in vain *is salvation hoped for* from the hills, *and from* the multitude of mountains: [c]truly in the LORD our God *is* the salvation of Israel.

24 [d]For shame hath devoured the labour of our fathers from our youth; their flocks and their herds, their sons and their daughters.

25 We lie down in our shame, and our confusion covereth us: [e]for we have sinned against the LORD our God, we and our fathers, from our youth even unto this day, and [f]have not obeyed the voice of the LORD our God.

4 If thou wilt return, O Israel, saith the LORD, [g]return unto me: and if thou wilt put away thine abominations out of my sight, then shalt thou not remove.

2 [h]And thou shalt swear, The LORD liveth, [i]in truth, in judgment, and in righteousness; [j]and the nations shall bless themselves in him, and in him shall they [k]glory.

3 ¶ For thus saith the LORD to the men of Judah and Jerusalem, [l]Break up your fallow ground, and [m]sow not among thorns.

4 [n]Circumcise yourselves to the LORD, and take away the foreskins of your heart, ye men of Judah and inhabitants of Jerusalem: lest my fury come forth like fire, and burn that none can quench *it,* because of the evil of your doings.

5 Declare ye in Judah, and publish in Jerusalem; and say, Blow ye the trumpet in

3:1 [j]ch. 2:7 [k]ch. 2:20; Ezek. 16:26 [l]ch. 4:1; Zech. 1:3
3:2 [m]Deut. 12:2; ch. 2:20 [n]Gen. 38:14; Prov. 23:28; Ezek. 16:24 [o]ch. 2:7; ver. 9
3:3 [p]Lev. 26:19; Deut. 28:23; ch. 9:12 [q]ch. 5:3; Ezek. 3:7; Zeph. 3:5
3:4 [r]Prov. 2:17 [s]ch. 2:2; Hos. 2:15
3:5 [t]Ps. 77:7; Isa. 57:16; ver. 12
3:6 [u]ver. 11; ch. 7:24 [v]ch. 2:20
3:7 [w]2 Kings 17:13 [x]Ezek. 16:46
3:8 [y]Ezek. 23:9 [z]2 Kings 17:6 [a]Ezek. 23:11
3:9 [b]ch. 2:7; ver. 2 [c]ch. 2:27
3:10 [d]2 Chron. 34:33; Hos. 7:14
3:11 [e]Ezek. 16:51
3:12 [f]2 Kings 17:6 [g]Ps. 86:15; ver. 5
3:13 [h]Lev. 26:40; Deut. 30:1; Prov. 28:13 [i]ver. 2; Ezek. 16:15 [j]ch. 2:25 [k]Deut. 12:2
3:14 [l]ch. 31:32; Hos. 2:19 [m]Rom. 11:5
3:15 [n]ch. 23:4; Ezek. 34:23; Eph. 4:11 [o]Acts 20:28
3:16 [p]Isa. 65:17
3:17 [q]Isa. 60:9 [r]ch. 11:8
3:18 [s]Isa. 11:13; Ezek. 37:16-22; Hos. 1:11 [t]ver. 12; ch. 31:8 [u]Am. 9:15
3:19 [v]Ps. 106:24; Ezek. 20:6; Dan. 8:9 [w]Isa. 63:16
3:20 [x]Isa. 48:8; ch. 5:11
3:21 [y]Isa. 15:2
3:22 [z]ver. 14; Hos. 14:1 [a]Hos. 6:1
3:23 [b]Ps. 121:1 [c]Ps. 3:8
3:24 [d]ch. 11:13; Hos. 9:10
3:25 [e]Ezra 9:7 [f]ch. 22:21
4:1 [g]ch. 3:1; Joel 2:12
4:2 [h]Deut. 10:20; Isa. 45:23; ch. 5:2; Zech. 8:8 [i]Isa. 48:1 [j]Gen. 22:18; Ps. 72:17; Gal. 3:8 [k]Isa. 45:25; 1 Cor. 1:31
4:3 [l]Hos. 10:12 [m]Matt. 13:7
4:4 [n]Deut. 10:16; ch. 9:26; Col. 2:11; Rom. 2:28

the land: cry, gather together, and say, [o]As-
semble yourselves, and let us go into the
defenced cities.
6 Set up the standard toward Zion: retire,
stay not: for I will bring evil from the
[p]north, and a great destruction.
7 [q]The lion is come up from his thicket,
and [r]the destroyer of the Gentiles is on his
way; he is gone forth from his place [s]to
make thy land desolate; *and* thy cities shall
be laid waste, without an inhabitant.
8 For this [t]gird you with sackcloth, lament and howl: for the fierce anger of the
LORD is not turned back from us.
9 And it shall come to pass at that day,
saith the LORD, *that* the heart of the king
shall perish, and the heart of the princes;
and the priests shall be astonished, and the
prophets shall wonder.
10 Then said I, Ah, Lord GOD! [u]surely
thou hast greatly deceived this people and
Jerusalem, [v]saying, Ye shall have peace;
whereas the sword reacheth unto the soul.
11 At that time shall it be said to this people and to Jerusalem, [w]A dry wind of the
high places in the wilderness toward the
daughter of my people, not to fan, nor to
cleanse,
12 *Even* a full wind from those *places*
shall come unto me: now also [x]will I give
sentence against them.
13 Behold, he shall come up as clouds,
and [y]his chariots *shall be* as a whirlwind:
[z]his horses are swifter than eagles. Woe
unto us! for we are spoiled.
14 O Jerusalem, [a]wash thine heart from
wickedness, that thou mayest be saved.
How long shall thy vain thoughts lodge
within thee?
15 For a voice declareth [b]from Dan, and
publisheth affliction from mount Ephraim.
16 Make ye mention to the nations; behold, publish against Jerusalem, *that*
watchers come [c]from a far country, and
give out their voice against the cities of Judah.
17 [d]As keepers of a field, are they against
her round about; because she hath been rebellious against me, saith the LORD.
18 [e]Thy way and thy doings have procured these *things* unto thee; this *is* thy
wickedness, because it is bitter, because it
reacheth unto thine heart.
19 ¶ My [f]bowels, my bowels! I am pained
at my very heart; my heart maketh a noise
in me; I cannot hold my peace, because thou
hast heard, O my soul, the sound of the
trumpet, the alarm of war.
20 [g]Destruction upon destruction is
cried; for the whole land is spoiled: suddenly are [h]my tents spoiled, *and* my curtains in a moment.
21 How long shall I see the standard, *and*
hear the sound of the trumpet?
22 For my people *is* foolish, they have not
known me; they *are* sottish children, and
they have none understanding: [i]they *are*
wise to do evil, but to do good they have no
knowledge.
23 [j]I beheld the earth, and, lo, *it was*
[k]without form, and void; and the heavens,
and they *had* no light.
24 [l]I beheld the mountains, and, lo, they
trembled, and all the hills moved lightly.
25 I beheld, and, lo, *there was* no man,
and [m]all the birds of the heavens were fled.
26 I beheld, and, lo, the fruitful place *was*
a wilderness, and all the cities thereof were
broken down at the presence of the LORD,
and by his fierce anger.
27 For thus hath the LORD said, The
whole land shall be desolate; [n]yet will I not
make a full end.
28 For this [o]shall the earth mourn, and
[p]the heavens above be black: because I
have spoken *it,* I have purposed *it,* and
[q]will not repent, neither will I turn back
from it.
29 The whole city shall flee for the noise
of the horsemen and bowmen; they shall go
into thickets, and climb up upon the rocks:
every city *shall be* forsaken, and not a man
dwell therein.
30 And *when* thou *art* spoiled, what wilt
thou do? Though thou clothest thyself with
crimson, though thou deckest thee with ornaments of gold, [r]though thou rentest thy
face with painting, in vain shalt thou make
thyself fair; [s]*thy* lovers will despise thee,
they will seek thy life.
31 For I have heard a voice as of a woman
in travail, *and* the anguish as of her that
bringeth forth her first child, the voice of
the daughter of Zion, *that* bewaileth herself, *that* [t]spreadeth her hands, *saying,*
Woe *is* me now! for my soul is wearied because of murderers.

5

Run ye to and fro through the streets of
Jerusalem, and see now, and know, and
seek in the broad places thereof, [u]if ye can
find a man, [v]if there be *any* that executeth
judgment, that seeketh the truth; [w]and I will
pardon it.
2 And [x]though they say, [y]The LORD liveth; surely they [z]swear falsely.
3 O LORD, *are* not [a]thine eyes upon the
truth? thou hast [b]stricken them, but they
have not grieved; thou hast consumed them,
but [c]they have refused to receive correction: they have made their faces harder than
a rock; they have refused to return.
4 Therefore I said, Surely these *are* poor;
they are foolish: for [d]they know not the
way of the LORD, *nor* the judgment of their
God.
5 I will get me unto the great men, and
will speak unto them; for [e]they have known
the way of the LORD, *and* the judgment of
their God: but these have altogether [f]bro-
ken the yoke, *and* burst the bonds.
6 Wherefore [g]a lion out of the forest shall
slay them, [h]*and* a wolf of the evenings shall
spoil them, [i]a leopard shall watch over
their cities: every one that goeth out thence
shall be torn in pieces: because their trans-

4:5 [o]ch. 8:14
4:6 [p]ch. 1:13
4:7 [q]2 Kings 24:1; ch. 5:6; Dan. 7:4 [r]ch. 25:9 [s]Isa. 1:7; ch. 2:15
4:8 [t]Isa. 22:12; ch. 6:26
4:10 [u]Ezek. 14:9; 2 Thess. 2:11 [v]ch. 5:12
4:11 [w]ch. 51:1; Ezek. 17:10; Hos. 13:15
4:12 [x]ch. 1:16
4:13 [y]Isa. 5:28 [z]Deut. 28:49; Lam. 4:19; Hos. 8:1; Hab. 1:8
4:14 [a]Isa. 1:16; Jam. 4:8
4:15 [b]ch. 8:16
4:16 [c]ch. 5:15
4:17 [d]2 Kings 25:1
4:18 [e]Ps. 107:17; Isa. 50:1; ch. 2:17
4:19 [f]Isa. 15:5; ch. 9:1; Luke 19:42
4:20 [g]Ps. 42:7; Ezek. 7:26 [h]ch. 10:20
4:22 [i]Rom. 16:19
4:23 [j]Isa. 24:19 [k]Gen. 1:2
4:24 [l]Isa. 5:25; Ezek. 38:20
4:25 [m]Zeph. 1:3
4:27 [n]ch. 5:10
4:28 [o]Hos. 4:3 [p]Isa. 5:30 [q]Num. 23:19; ch. 7:16
4:30 [r]2 Kings 9:30; Ezek. 23:40 [s]ch. 22:20; Lam. 1:2
4:31 [t]Isa. 1:15; Lam. 1:17
5:1 [u]Ezek. 22:30 [v]Gen. 18:23; Ps. 12:1 [w]Gen. 18:26
5:2 [x]Tit. 1:16 [y]ch. 4:2 [z]ch. 7:9
5:3 [a]2 Chron. 16:9 [b]Isa. 1:5; ch. 2:30 [c]ch. 7:28; Zeph. 3:2
5:4 [d]ch. 7:8
5:5 [e]Mic. 3:1 [f]Ps. 2:3
5:6 [g]ch. 4:7 [h]Ps. 104:20; Hab. 1:8; Zeph. 3:3 [i]Hos. 13:7

gressions are many, *and* their backslidings
are increased.
7 ¶ How shall I pardon thee for this? thy
children have forsaken me, and [j]sworn by
them [k]*that are* no gods: [l]when I had fed
them to the full, they then committed adultery, and assembled themselves by troops
in the harlots' houses.
8 [m]They were *as* fed horses in the morning: every one [n]neighed after his neighbour's wife.
9 [o]Shall I not visit for these *things*? saith
the LORD: [p]and shall not my soul be
avenged on such a nation as this?
10 ¶ [q]Go ye up upon her walls, and destroy; [r]but make not a full end: take away
her battlements; for they *are* not the LORD'S.
11 For [s]the house of Israel and the house
of Judah have dealt very treacherously
against me, saith the LORD.
12 [t]They have belied the LORD, and said,
[u]*It is* not he; neither shall evil come upon
us; [v]neither shall we see sword nor famine:
13 And the prophets shall become wind,
and the word *is* not in them: thus shall it be
done unto them.
14 Wherefore thus saith the LORD God of
hosts, Because ye speak this word, [w]behold,
I will make my words in thy mouth fire, and
this people wood, and it shall devour them.
15 Lo, I will bring a [x]nation upon you
[y]from far, O house of Israel, saith the
LORD: it *is* a mighty nation, it *is* an ancient
nation, a nation whose language thou
knowest not, neither understandest what
they say.
16 Their quiver *is* as an open sepulchre,
they *are* all mighty men.
17 And they shall eat up thine [z]harvest,
and thy bread, *which* thy sons and thy
daughters should eat: they shall eat up thy
flocks and thine herds: they shall eat up
thy vines and thy fig trees: they shall impov-
erish thy fenced cities, wherein thou trustedst, with the sword.
18 Nevertheless in those days, saith the
LORD, I [a]will not make a full end with you.
19 ¶ And it shall come to pass, when ye
shall say, [b]Wherefore doeth the LORD our
God all these *things* unto us? then shalt thou
answer them, Like as ye have [c]forsaken
me, and served strange gods in your land,
so [d]shall ye serve strangers in a land *that*
is not yours.
20 Declare this in the house of Jacob, and
publish it in Judah, saying,
21 Hear now this, O [e]foolish people, and
without understanding; which have eyes,
and see not; which have ears, and hear not:
22 [f]Fear ye not me? saith the LORD: will
ye not tremble at my presence, which have
placed the sand *for* the [g]bound of the sea by
a perpetual decree, that it cannot pass it:
and though the waves thereof toss themselves, yet can they not prevail; though they
roar, yet can they not pass over it?
23 But this people hath a revolting and a
rebellious heart; they are revolted and gone.

5:7 [j]Josh. 23:7; Zeph. 1:5 [k]Deut. 32:21; Gal. 4:8 [l]Deut. 32:15
5:8 [m]Ezek. 22:11 [n]ch. 13:27
5:9 [o]ver. 29; ch. 9:9 [p]ch. 44:22
5:10 [q]ch. 39:8 [r]ch. 4:27; ver. 18
5:11 [s]ch. 3:20
5:12 [t]2 Chron. 36:16; ch. 4:10 [u]Isa. 28:15 [v]ch. 14:13
5:14 [w]ch. 1:9
5:15 [x]Deut. 28:49; Isa. 5:26; ch. 1:15 [y]Isa. 39:3; ch. 4:16
5:17 [z]Lev. 26:16; Deut. 28:31
5:18 [a]ch. 4:27
5:19 [b]Deut. 29:24; 1 Kings 9:8; ch. 13:22 [c]ch. 2:13 [d]Deut. 28:48
5:21 [e]Isa. 6:9; Ezek. 12:2; Matt. 13:14; John 12:40; Acts 28:26; Rom. 11:8
5:22 [f]Rev. 15:4 [g]Job 26:10; Ps. 104:9; Prov. 8:29
5:24 [h]Ps. 147:8; ch. 14:22; Matt. 5:45; Acts 14:17 [i]Deut. 11:14; Joel 2:23 [j]Gen. 8:22
5:25 [k]ch. 3:3
5:26 [l]Prov. 1:11; Hab. 1:15
5:28 [m]Deut. 32:15 [n]Isa. 1:23; Zech. 7:10 [o]Job 12:6; Ps. 73:12; ch. 12:1
5:29 [p]ver. 9; Mal. 3:5
5:30 [q]ch. 23:14; Hos. 6:10
5:31 [r]ch. 14:14; Ezek. 13:6 [s]Mic. 2:11
6:1 [t]Neh. 3:14 [u]ch. 1:14
6:3 [v]1 Kings 25:1; ch. 4:17
6:4 [w]ch. 51:27; Joel 3:9 [x]ch. 15:8
6:7 [y]Isa. 57:20 [z]Ps. 55:9; ch. 20:8; Ezek. 7:11
6:8 [a]Ezek. 23:18; Hos. 9:12
6:10 [b]Ex. 6:12; ch. 7:26; Acts 7:61 [c]ch. 20:8

24 Neither say they in their heart, Let us
now fear the LORD our God, [h]that giveth
rain, both the [i]former and the latter, in his
season: [j]he reserveth unto us the appointed
weeks of the harvest.
25 ¶ [k]Your iniquities have turned away
these *things*, and your sins have withholden
good *things* from you.
26 For among my people are found
wicked *men:* they [l]lay wait, as he that setteth snares; they set a trap, they catch men.
27 As a cage is full of birds, so *are* their
houses full of deceit: therefore they are become great, and waxen rich.
28 They are waxen [m]fat, they shine: yea,
they overpass the deeds of the wicked: they
judge not [n]the cause, the cause of the fatherless, [o]yet they prosper; and the right of
the needy do they not judge.
29 [p]Shall I not visit for these *things?* saith
the LORD: shall not my soul be avenged on
such a nation as this?
30 ¶ A wonderful and [q]horrible thing is
committed in the land;
31 The prophets prophesy [r]falsely, and
the priests bear rule by their means; and my
people [s]love *to have it* so: and what will ye
do in the end thereof?

6 O ye children of Benjamin, gather yourselves to flee out of the midst of Jerusalem, and blow the trumpet in Tekoa, and set
up a sign of fire in [t]Beth-haccerem: [u]for
evil appeareth out of the north, and great
destruction.
2 I have likened the daughter of Zion to a
comely and delicate *woman.*
3 The shepherds with their flocks shall
come unto her; [v]they shall pitch *their* tents
against her round about; they shall feed every one in his place.
4 [w]Prepare ye war against her; arise, and
let us go up [x]at noon. Woe unto us! for the
day goeth away, for the shadows of the evening are stretched out.
5 Arise, and let us go by night, and let us
destroy her palaces.
6 ¶ For thus hath the LORD of hosts said,
Hew ye down trees, and cast a mount
against Jerusalem: this *is* the city to be visited; she *is* wholly oppression in the midst of
her.
7 [y]As a fountain casteth out her waters,
so she casteth out her wickedness: [z]vio-
lence and spoil is heard in her; before me
continually *is* grief and wounds.
8 Be thou instructed, O Jerusalem, lest
[a]my soul depart from thee; lest I make thee
desolate, a land not inhabited.
9 ¶ Thus saith the LORD of hosts, They
shall throughly glean the remnant of Israel
as a vine: turn back thine hand as a
grapegatherer into the baskets.
10 To whom shall I speak, and give warning, that they may hear? behold, their [b]ear
is uncircumcised, and they cannot hearken:
behold, [c]the word of the LORD is unto them
a reproach; they have no delight in it.
11 Therefore I am full of the fury of the

LORD; [d]I am weary with holding in: I will
pour it out [e]upon the children abroad, and
upon the assembly of young men together:
for even the husband with the wife shall be
taken, the aged with *him that is* full of days.
12 And [f]their houses shall be turned unto
others, *with their* fields and wives together:
for I will stretch out my hand upon the inhabitants of the land, saith the LORD.
13 For from the least of them even unto
the greatest of them every one *is* given to
[g]covetousness; and from the prophet even
unto the priest every one dealeth falsely.
14 They have [h]healed also the hurt *of the
daughter* of my people slightly, [i]saying,
Peace, peace; when *there is* no peace.
15 Were they [j]ashamed when they had
committed abomination? nay, they were not
at all ashamed, neither could they blush:
therefore they shall fall among them that
fall: at the time *that* I visit them they shall
be cast down, saith the LORD.
16 Thus saith the LORD, Stand ye in the
ways, and see, and ask for the [k]old paths,
where *is* the good way, and walk therein,
and ye shall find [l]rest for your souls. But
they said, We will not walk *therein.*
17 Also I set [m]watchmen over you, *saying,* Hearken to the sound of the trumpet.
But they said, We will not hearken.
18 ¶ Therefore hear, ye nations, and
know, O congregation, what *is* among
them.
19 [n]Hear, O earth: behold, I will bring
evil upon this people, *even* [o]the fruit of
their thoughts, because they have not
hearkened unto my words, nor to my law,
but rejected it.
20 [p]To what purpose cometh there to me
incense [q]from Sheba, and the sweet cane
from a far country? [r]your burnt offerings
are not acceptable, nor your sacrifices
sweet unto me.
21 Therefore thus saith the LORD, Behold,
I will lay stumblingblocks before this people, and the fathers and the sons together
shall fall upon them; the neighbour and his
friend shall perish.
22 Thus saith the LORD, Behold, a people
cometh from the [s]north country, and a
great nation shall be raised from the sides
of the earth.
23 They shall lay hold on bow and spear;
they *are* cruel, and have no mercy; their
voice [t]roareth like the sea; and they ride
upon horses, set in array as men for war
against thee, O daughter of Zion.
24 We have heard the fame thereof: our
hands wax feeble: [u]anguish hath taken
hold of us, *and* pain, as of a woman in travail.
25 Go not forth into the field, nor walk by
the way; for the sword of the enemy *and*
fear *is* on every side.
26 ¶ O daughter of my people, [v]gird *thee*
with sackcloth, [w]and wallow thyself in
ashes: [x]make thee mourning, *as for* an only
son, most bitter lamentation: for the spoiler
shall suddenly come upon us.
27 I have set thee *for* a tower *and* [y]a fortress among my people, that thou mayest
know and try their way.
28 [z]They *are* all grievous revolters,
[a]walking with slanders: *they are* [b]brass
and iron; they *are* all corrupters.
29 The bellows are burned, the lead is
consumed of the fire; the founder melteth in
vain: for the wicked are not plucked away.
30 [c]Reprobate silver shall *men* call them,
because the LORD hath rejected them.

7 The word that came to Jeremiah from
the LORD, saying,
2 [d]Stand in the gate of the LORD's house,
and proclaim there this word, and say, Hear
the word of the LORD, all *ye of* Judah, that
enter in at these gates to worship the LORD.
3 Thus saith the LORD of hosts, the God of
Israel, [e]Amend your ways and your doings,
and I will cause you to dwell in this place.
4 [f]Trust ye not in lying words, saying,
The temple of the LORD, The temple of the
LORD, The temple of the LORD, *are* these.
5 For if ye throughly amend your ways
and your doings; if ye throughly [g]execute
judgment between a man and his neighbour;
6 *If* ye oppress not the stranger, the fatherless, and the widow, and shed not innocent blood in this place, [h]neither walk after
other gods to your hurt:
7 [i]Then will I cause you to dwell in this
place, in [j]the land that I gave to your fathers, for ever and ever.
8 ¶ Behold, [k]ye trust in [l]lying words,
that cannot profit.
9 [m]Will ye steal, murder, and commit
adultery, and swear falsely, and burn incense unto Baal, and [n]walk after other gods
whom ye know not;
10 [o]And come and stand before me in
this house, [p]which is called by my name,
and say, We are delivered to do all these
abominations?
11 Is [q]this house, which is called by my
name, become a [r]den of robbers in your
eyes? Behold, even I have seen *it,* saith the
LORD.
12 But go ye now unto [s]my place which
was in Shiloh, [t]where I set my name at the
first, and see [u]what I did to it for the wickedness of my people Israel.
13 And now, because ye have done all
these works, saith the LORD, and I spake
unto you, [v]rising up early and speaking,
but ye heard not; and I [w]called you, but ye
answered not;
14 Therefore will I do unto *this* house,
which is called by my name, wherein ye
trust, and unto the place which I gave to you
and to your fathers, as I have done to [x]Shi-
loh.
15 And I will cast you out of my sight, [y]as
I have cast out all your brethren, [z]*even* the
whole seed of Ephraim.
16 Therefore [a]pray not thou for this peo-

6:11 [d]ch. 20:9 [e]ch. 9:21
6:12 [f]Deut. 28:30; ch. 8:10
6:13 [g]Isa. 56:11; ch. 8:10; Mic. 3:5
6:14 [h]ch. 8:11; Ezek. 13:10 [i]ch. 4:10
6:15 [j]ch. 3:3
6:16 [k]Isa. 8:20; ch. 18:15; Mal. 4:4; Luke 16:29 [l]Matt. 11:29
6:17 [m]Isa. 21:11; ch. 25:4; Ezek. 3:17; Hab. 2:1
6:19 [n]Isa. 1:2 [o]Prov. 1:31
6:20 [p]Ps. 40:6; Isa. 1:11; Am. 5:21; Mic. 6:6 [q]Isa. 60:6 [r]ch. 7:21
6:22 [s]ch. 1:15
6:23 [t]Isa. 5:30
6:24 [u]ch. 4:31
6:26 [v]ch. 4:8 [w]ch. 25:34; Mic. 1:10 [x]Zech. 12:10
6:27 [y]ch. 1:18
6:28 [z]ch. 5:23 [a]ch. 9:4 [b]Ezek. 22:18
6:30 [c]Isa. 1:22
7:2 [d]ch. 26:2
7:3 [e]ch. 18:11
7:4 [f]Mic. 3:11
7:5 [g]ch. 22:3
7:6 [h]Deut. 6:14; ch. 13:10
7:7 [i]Deut. 4:40 [j]ch. 3:18
7:8 [k]ver. 4 [l]ch. 5:31
7:9 [m]1 Kings 18:21; Hos. 4:1; Zeph. 1:5 [n]Ex. 20:3; ver. 6
7:10 [o]Ezek. 23:39 [p]ver. 11; ch. 32:34
7:11 [q]Isa. 56:7 [r]Matt. 21:13; Mark 11:17; Luke 19:46
7:12 [s]Josh. 18:1; Judg. 18:31 [t]Deut. 12:11 [u]1 Sam. 4:10; Ps. 78:60; ch. 26:6
7:13 [v]2 Chron. 36:15; ver. 25; ch. 11:7 [w]Prov. 1:24; Isa. 65:12
7:14 [x]1 Sam. 4:10; Ps. 78:60; ch. 26:6
7:15 [y]2 Kings 17:23 [z]Ps. 78:67
7:16 [a]Ex. 32:10; ch. 11:14

ple, neither lift up cry nor prayer for them,
neither make intercession to me: [b]for I will
not hear thee.
17 ¶ Seest thou not what they do in the
cities of Judah and in the streets of Jerusalem?
18 [c]The children gather wood, and the
fathers kindle the fire, and the women
knead *their* dough, to make cakes to the
queen of heaven, and to [d]pour out drink
offerings unto other gods, that they may
provoke me to anger.
19 [e]Do they provoke me to anger? saith
the LORD: *do they* not *provoke* themselves
to the confusion of their own faces?
20 Therefore thus saith the Lord GOD; Behold, mine anger and my fury shall be
poured out upon this place, upon man, and
upon beast, and upon the trees of the field,
and upon the fruit of the ground; and it shall
burn, and shall not be quenched.
21 ¶ Thus saith the LORD of hosts, the God
of Israel; [f]Put your burnt offerings unto
your sacrifices, and eat flesh.
22 [g]For I spake not unto your fathers, nor
commanded them in the day that I brought
them out of the land of Egypt, concerning
burnt offerings or sacrifices:
23 But this thing commanded I them, saying, [h]Obey my voice, and [i]I will be your
God, and ye shall be my people: and walk ye
in all the ways that I have commanded you,
that it may be well unto you.
24 [j]But they hearkened not, nor inclined
their ear, but [k]walked in the counsels *and*
in the imagination of their evil heart, and
[l]went backward, and not forward.
25 Since the day that your fathers came
forth out of the land of Egypt unto this day
I have even [m]sent unto you all my servants
the prophets, [n]daily rising up early and
sending *them:*
26 [o]Yet they hearkened not unto me, nor
inclined their ear, but [p]hardened their
neck: [q]they did worse than their fathers.
27 Therefore [r]thou shalt speak all these
words unto them; but they will not hearken
to thee: thou shalt also call unto them; but
they will not answer thee.
28 But thou shalt say unto them, This *is*
a nation that obeyeth not the voice of the
LORD their God, [s]nor receiveth correction:
[t]truth is perished, and is cut off from their
mouth.
29 ¶ [u]Cut off thine hair, *O Jerusalem,* and
cast *it* away, and take up a lamentation on
high places; for the LORD hath rejected and
forsaken the generation of his wrath.
30 For the children of Judah have done
evil in my sight, saith the LORD: [v]they have
set their abominations in the house which is
called by my name, to pollute it.
31 And they have built the [w]high places
of Tophet, which *is* in the valley of the son
of Hinnom, to [x]burn their sons and their
daughters in the fire; [y]which I commanded
them not, neither came it into my heart.
32 ¶ Therefore, behold, [z]the days come,

7:16 [b]ch. 15:1
7:18 [c]ch. 44:17 [d]ch. 19:13
7:19 [e]Deut. 32:16
7:21 [f]Isa. 1:11; ch. 6:20; Hos. 8:13; Am. 5:21
7:22 [g]1 Sam. 15:22; Ps. 51:16; Hos. 6:6
7:23 [h]Ex. 15:26; Deut. 6:3; ch. 11:4 [i]Ex. 19:5; Lev. 26:12
7:24 [j]Ps. 81:11; ch. 11:8 [k]Deut. 29:19; Ps. 81:12 [l]ch. 2:27; Hos. 4:16
7:25 [m]2 Chron. 36:15; ch. 25:4 [n]ver. 13
7:26 [o]ver. 24; ch. 11:8 [p]Neh. 9:17; ch. 19:15 [q]ch. 16:12
7:27 [r]Ezek. 2:7
7:28 [s]ch. 5:3 [t]ch. 9:3
7:29 [u]Job 1:20; Isa. 15:2; ch. 16:6; Mic. 1:16
7:30 [v]2 Kings 21:4; 2 Chron. 33:4; ch. 23:11; Ezek. 7:20; Dan. 9:27
7:31 [w]2 Kings 23:10; ch. 19:5 [x]Ps. 106:38 [y]Deut. 17:3
7:32 [z]ch. 19:6 [a]2 Kings 23:10; ch. 19:11; Ezek. 6:5
7:33 [b]Deut. 28:26; Ps. 79:2; ch. 12:9
7:34 [c]Isa. 24:7; ch. 16:9; Ezek. 26:13; Hos. 2:11; Rev. 18:23 [d]Lev. 26:33; Isa. 1:7
8:2 [e]2 Kings 23:5; Ezek. 8:16 [f]ch. 22:19 [g]2 Kings 9:36; Ps. 83:10; ch. 9:22
8:3 [h]Job 3:21; Rev. 9:6
8:5 [i]ch. 7:24 [j]ch. 9:6 [k]ch. 5:3
8:6 [l]2 Pet. 3:9
8:7 [m]Isa. 1:3 [n]SSol. 2:12 [o]ch. 5:4
8:8 [p]Rom. 2:17
8:9 [q]ch. 6:15
8:10 [r]Deut. 28:30; ch. 6:12; Am. 5:11; Zeph. 1:13 [s]Isa. 56:11; ch. 6:13
8:11 [t]ch. 6:14 [u]Ezek. 13:10

saith the LORD, that it shall no more be
called Tophet, nor the valley of the son of
Hinnom, but the valley of slaughter: [a]for
they shall bury in Tophet, till there be no
place.
33 And the [b]carcases of this people shall
be meat for the fowls of the heaven, and for
the beasts of the earth; and none shall fray
them away.
34 Then will I cause to [c]cease from the
cities of Judah, and from the streets of Jerusalem, the voice of mirth, and the voice of
gladness, the voice of the bridegroom, and
the voice of the bride: for [d]the land shall be
desolate.
8 At that time, saith the LORD, they shall
bring out the bones of the kings of Judah, and the bones of his princes, and the
bones of the priests, and the bones of the
prophets, and the bones of the inhabitants
of Jerusalem, out of their graves:
2 And they shall spread them before the
sun, and the moon, and all the host of
heaven, whom they have loved, and whom
they have served, and after whom they have
walked, and whom they have sought, and
[e]whom they have worshipped: they shall
not be gathered, [f]nor be buried; they shall
be for [g]dung upon the face of the earth.
3 And [h]death shall be chosen rather than
life by all the residue of them that remain
of this evil family, which remain in all the
places whither I have driven them, saith the
LORD of hosts.
4 ¶ Moreover thou shalt say unto them,
Thus saith the LORD; Shall they fall, and not
arise? shall he turn away, and not return?
5 Why *then* is this people of Jerusalem
[i]slidden back by a perpetual backsliding?
[j]they hold fast deceit, [k]they refuse to return.
6 [l]I hearkened and heard, *but* they spake
not aright: no man repented him of his
wickedness, saying, What have I done? every one turned to his course, as the horse
rusheth into the battle.
7 Yea, [m]the stork in the heaven knoweth
her appointed times; and [n]the turtle and the
crane and the swallow observe the time of
their coming; but [o]my people know not the
judgment of the LORD.
8 How do ye say, We *are* wise, [p]and the
law of the LORD *is* with us? Lo, certainly in
vain made he *it;* the pen of the scribes *is* in
vain.
9 [q]The wise *men* are ashamed, they are
dismayed and taken: lo, they have rejected
the word of the LORD; and what wisdom *is*
in them?
10 Therefore [r]will I give their wives unto
others, *and* their fields to them that shall
inherit *them:* for every one from the least
even unto the greatest is given to [s]covet-
ousness, from the prophet even unto the
priest every one dealeth falsely.
11 For they have [t]healed the hurt of the
daughter of my people slightly, saying,
[u]Peace, peace; when *there is* no peace.

12 Were they [v]ashamed when they had committed abomination? nay, they were not at all ashamed, neither could they blush: therefore shall they fall among them that fall: in the time of their visitation they shall be cast down, saith the LORD.

13 ¶ I will surely consume them, saith the LORD: *there shall be* no grapes [w]on the vine, nor figs on the [x]fig tree, and the leaf shall fade; and *the things that* I have given them shall pass away from them.

14 Why do we sit still? [y]assemble yourselves, and let us enter into the defenced cities, and let us be silent there: for the LORD our God hath put us to silence, and given us [z]water of gall to drink, because we have sinned against the LORD.

15 We [a]looked for peace, but no good *came; and* for a time of health, and behold trouble!

16 The snorting of his horses was heard from [b]Dan: the whole land trembled at the sound of the neighing of his [c]strong ones; for they are come, and have devoured the land, and all that is in it; the city, and those that dwell therein.

17 For, behold, I will send serpents, cockatrices, among you, which *will* not *be* [d]charmed, and they shall bite you, saith the LORD.

18 ¶ *When* I would comfort myself against sorrow, my heart *is* faint in me.

19 Behold the voice of the cry of the daughter of my people because of them that dwell in [e]a far country: *Is* not the LORD in Zion? *is* not her king in her? Why have they [f]provoked me to anger with their graven images, *and* with strange vanities?

20 The harvest is past, the summer is ended, and we are not saved.

21 [g]For the hurt of the daughter of my people am I hurt; I am [h]black; astonishment hath taken hold on me.

22 *Is there* no [i]balm in Gilead; *is there* no physician there? why then is not the health of the daughter of my people recovered?

9

Oh [j]that my head were waters, and mine eyes a fountain of tears, that I might weep day and night for the slain of the daughter of my people!

2 Oh that I had in the wilderness a lodging place of wayfaring men; that I might leave my people, and go from them! for [k]they *be* all adulterers, an assembly of treacherous men.

3 And [l]they bend their tongues *like* their bow *for* lies: but they are not valiant for the truth upon the earth; for they proceed from evil to evil, and they [m]know not me, saith the LORD.

4 [n]Take ye heed every one of his neighbour, and trust ye not in any brother: for every brother will utterly supplant, and every neighbour will [o]walk with slanders.

5 And they will deceive every one his neighbour, and will not speak the truth: they have taught their tongue to speak lies, *and* weary themselves to commit iniquity.

6 Thine habitation *is* in the midst of deceit; through deceit they refuse to know me, saith the LORD.

7 Therefore thus saith the LORD of hosts, Behold, [p]I will melt them, and try them; [q]for how shall I do for the daughter of my people?

8 Their tongue *is as* an arrow shot out; it speaketh [r]deceit: *one* speaketh [s]peaceably to his neighbour with his mouth, but in heart he layeth his wait.

9 ¶ [t]Shall I not visit them for these *things?* saith the LORD: shall not my soul be avenged on such a nation as this?

10 For the mountains will I take up a weeping and wailing, and [u]for the habitations of the wilderness a lamentation, because they are burned up, so that none can pass through *them;* neither can *men* hear the voice of the cattle; [v]both the fowl of the heavens and the beast are fled; they are gone.

11 And I will make Jerusalem [w]heaps, *and* [x]a den of dragons; and I will make the cities of Judah desolate, without an inhabitant.

12 ¶ [y]Who *is* the wise man, that may understand this? and *who is he* to whom the mouth of the LORD hath spoken, that he may declare it, for what the land perisheth *and* is burned up like a wilderness, that none passeth through?

13 And the LORD saith, Because they have forsaken my law which I set before them, and have not obeyed my voice, neither walked therein;

14 But have [z]walked after the imagination of their own heart, and after Baalim, [a]which their fathers taught them:

15 Therefore thus saith the LORD of hosts, the God of Israel; Behold, I will [b]feed them, *even* this people, [c]with wormwood, and give them water of gall to drink.

16 I will [d]scatter them also among the heathen, whom neither they nor their fathers have known: [e]and I will send a sword after them, till I have consumed them.

17 ¶ Thus saith the LORD of hosts, Consider ye, and call for [f]the mourning women, that they may come; and send for cunning *women,* that they may come:

18 And let them make haste, and take up a wailing for us, that [g]our eyes may run down with tears, and our eyelids gush out with waters.

19 For a voice of wailing is heard out of Zion, How are we spoiled! we are greatly confounded, because we have forsaken the land, because [h]our dwellings have cast *us* out.

20 Yet hear the word of the LORD, O ye women, and let your ear receive the word of his mouth, and teach your daughters wailing, and every one her neighbour lamentation.

21 For death is come up into our windows, *and* is entered into our palaces, to cut

8:12 [v]ch. 3:3
8:13 [w]Isa. 5:1; Joel 1:7 [x]Matt. 21:19; Luke 13:6
8:14 [y]ch. 4:5 [z]ch. 9:15
8:15 [a]ch. 14:19
8:16 [b]ch. 4:15 [c]Judg. 5:22; ch. 47:3
8:17 [d]Ps. 58:4; Eccl. 10:11
8:19 [e]Isa. 39:3 [f]Deut. 32:21; Isa. 1:4
8:21 [g]ch. 4:19 [h]Joel 2:6; Nah. 2:10
8:22 [i]Gen. 37:25; ch. 46:11
9:1 [j]Isa. 22:4; ch. 4:19; Lam. 2:11
9:2 [k]ch. 5:7
9:3 [l]Ps. 64:3; Isa. 59:4 [m]1 Sam. 2:12; Hos. 4:1
9:4 [n]ch. 12:6; Mic. 7:5 [o]ch. 6:28
9:7 [p]Isa. 1:25; Mal. 3:3 [q]Hos. 11:8
9:8 [r]Ps. 12:2; ver. 3 [s]Ps. 28:3
9:9 [t]ch. 5:9
9:10 [u]ch. 12:4; Hos. 4:3 [v]ch. 4:25
9:11 [w]Isa. 25:2 [x]Isa. 13:22; ch. 10:22
9:12 [y]Ps. 107:43; Hos. 14:9
9:14 [z]ch. 3:17 [a]Gal. 1:14
9:15 [b]Ps. 80:5 [c]ch. 8:14; Lam. 3:15
9:16 [d]Lev. 26:33; Deut. 28:64 [e]Lev. 26:33; ch. 44:27; Ezek. 5:2
9:17 [f]2 Chron. 35:25; Job 3:8; Eccl. 12:5; Am. 5:16; Matt. 9:23
9:18 [g]ch. 14:17
9:19 [h]Lev. 18:28

off [i]the children from without, *and* the young men from the streets.

22 Speak, Thus saith the LORD, Even the carcases of men shall fall [j]as dung upon the open field, and as the handful after the harvestman, and none shall gather *them.*

23 ¶ Thus saith the LORD, [k]Let not the wise *man* glory in his wisdom, neither let the mighty *man* glory in his might, let not the rich *man* glory in his riches:

24 But [l]let him that glorieth glory in this, that he understandeth and knoweth me, that I *am* the LORD which exercise lovingkindness, judgment, and righteousness, in the earth: [m]for in these *things* I delight, saith the LORD.

25 ¶ Behold, the days come, saith the LORD, that [n]I will punish all *them which are* circumcised with the uncircumcised;

26 Egypt, and Judah, and Edom, and the children of Ammon, and Moab, and all *that are* in the [o]utmost corners, that dwell in the wilderness: for all *these* nations *are* uncircumcised, and all the house of Israel *are* [p]uncircumcised in the heart.

10 Hear ye the word which the LORD speaketh unto you, O house of Israel:

2 Thus saith the LORD, [q]Learn not the way of the heathen, and be not dismayed at the signs of heaven; for the heathen are dismayed at them.

3 For the customs of the people *are* vain: for [r]*one* cutteth a tree out of the forest, the work of the hands of the workman, with the axe.

4 They deck it with silver and with gold; they [s]fasten it with nails and with hammers, that it move not.

5 They *are* upright as the palm tree, [t]but speak not: they must needs be [u]borne, because they cannot go. Be not afraid of them; for [v]they cannot do evil, neither also *is it* in them to do good.

6 Forasmuch as *there is* none [w]like unto thee, O LORD; thou *art* great, and thy name *is* great in might.

7 [x]Who would not fear thee, O King of nations? for to thee doth it appertain: forasmuch as [y]among all the wise *men* of the nations, and in all their kingdoms, *there is* none like unto thee.

8 But they are altogether [z]brutish and foolish: the stock *is* a doctrine of vanities.

9 Silver spread into plates is brought from Tarshish, and [a]gold from Uphaz, the work of the workman, and of the hands of the founder: blue and purple *is* their clothing: they *are* all [b]the work of cunning *men.*

10 But the LORD *is* the true God, he *is* [c]the living God, and an [d]everlasting king: at his wrath the earth shall tremble, and the nations shall not be able to abide his indignation.

11 Thus shall ye say unto them, [e]The gods that have not made the heavens and the earth, *even* [f]they shall perish from the earth, and from under these heavens.

12 He [g]hath made the earth by his power, he hath [h]established the world by his wisdom, and [i]hath stretched out the heavens by his discretion.

13 [j]When he uttereth his voice, *there is* a multitude of waters in the heavens, and [k]he causeth the vapours to ascend from the ends of the earth; he maketh lightnings with rain, and bringeth forth the wind out of his treasures.

14 [l]Every man is [m]brutish in *his* knowledge: [n]every founder is confounded by the graven image: [o]for his molten image *is* falsehood, and *there is* no breath in them.

15 They *are* vanity, *and* the work of errors: in the time of their visitation [p]they shall perish.

16 [q]The portion of Jacob *is* not like them: for he *is* the former of all *things;* and [r]Israel *is* the rod of his inheritance: [s]The LORD of hosts *is* his name.

17 ¶ [t]Gather up thy wares out of the land, O inhabitant of the fortress.

18 For thus saith the LORD, Behold, I will [u]sling out the inhabitants of the land at this once, and will distress them, [v]that they may find *it so.*

19 ¶ [w]Woe is me for my hurt! my wound is grievous; but I said, [x]Truly this *is* a grief, and [y]I must bear it.

20 [z]My tabernacle is spoiled, and all my cords are broken: my children are gone forth of me, and they *are* not: *there is* none to stretch forth my tent any more, and to set up my curtains.

21 For the pastors are become brutish, and have not sought the LORD: therefore they shall not prosper, and all their flocks shall be scattered.

22 Behold, the noise of the bruit is come, and a great commotion out of the [a]north country, to make the cities of Judah desolate, *and* a [b]den of dragons.

23 ¶ O LORD, I know that the [c]way of man *is* not in himself: *it is* not in man that walketh to direct his steps.

24 O LORD, [d]correct me, but with judgment; not in thine anger, lest thou bring me to nothing.

25 [e]Pour out thy fury upon the heathen that [f]know thee not, and upon the families that call not on thy name: for they have eaten up Jacob, and [g]devoured him, and consumed him, and have made his habitation desolate.

11 The word that came to Jeremiah from the LORD, saying,

2 Hear ye the words of this covenant, and speak unto the men of Judah, and to the inhabitants of Jerusalem;

3 And say thou unto them, Thus saith the LORD God of Israel; [h]Cursed *be* the man that obeyeth not the words of this covenant,

4 Which I commanded your fathers in the day *that* I brought them forth out of the land of Egypt, [i]from the iron furnace, saying, [j]Obey my voice, and do them, according to all which I command you: so shall ye be my people, and I will be your God:

9:21 [i]ch. 6:11
9:22 [j]ch. 8:2
9:23 [k]Eccl. 9:11
9:24 [l]1 Cor. 1:31; 2 Cor. 10:17 [m]Mic. 6:8
9:25 [n]Rom. 2:8
9:26 [o]ch. 25:23 [p]Lev. 26:41; Ezek. 44:7; Rom. 2:28
10:2 [q]Lev. 18:3
10:3 [r]Isa. 40:19
10:4 [s]Isa. 41:7
10:5 [t]Ps. 115:5; Hab. 2:19; 1 Cor. 12:2 [u]Ps. 115:7; Isa. 46:1 [v]Isa. 41:23
10:6 [w]Ex. 15:11; Ps. 86:8
10:7 [x]Rev. 15:4 [y]Ps. 89:6
10:8 [z]Ps. 115:8; Isa. 41:29; Hab. 2:18; Zech. 10:2; Rom. 1:21
10:9 [a]Dan. 10:5 [b]Ps. 115:4
10:10 [c]1 Tim. 6:17 [d]Ps. 10:16
10:11 [e]Ps. 96:5 [f]ver. 15; Isa. 2:18; Zech. 13:2
10:12 [g]Gen. 1:1; Ps. 136:5; ch. 51:15 [h]Ps. 93:1 [i]Job 9:8; Ps. 104:2; Isa. 40:22
10:13 [j]Job 38:34 [k]Ps. 135:7
10:14 [l]ch. 51:17 [m]Prov. 30:2 [n]Isa. 42:17 [o]Hab. 2:18
10:15 [p]ver. 11
10:16 [q]Ps. 16:5; ch. 51:19; Lam. 3:24 [r]Deut. 32:9; Ps. 74:2 [s]Isa. 47:4; ch. 31:35
10:17 [t]ch. 6:1; Ezek. 12:3
10:18 [u]1 Sam. 25:29; ch. 16:13 [v]Ezek. 6:10
10:19 [w]ch. 4:19 [x]Ps. 77:10 [y]Mic. 7:9
10:20 [z]ch. 4:20
10:22 [a]ch. 1:15 [b]ch. 9:11
10:23 [c]Prov. 16:1
10:24 [d]Ps. 6:1; ch. 30:11
10:25 [e]Ps. 79:6 [f]Job 18:21; 1 Thess. 4:5; 2 Thess. 1:8 [g]ch. 8:16
11:3 [h]Deut. 27:26; Gal. 3:10
11:4 [i]Deut. 4:20; 1 Kings 8:51 [j]Lev. 26:3; ch. 7:23

5 That I may perform the [k]oath which I have sworn unto your fathers, to give them a land flowing with milk and honey, as *it is* this day. Then answered I, and said, So be it, O LORD.

6 Then the LORD said unto me, Proclaim all these words in the cities of Judah, and in the streets of Jerusalem, saying, Hear ye the words of this covenant, [l]and do them.

7 For I earnestly protested unto your fathers in the day *that* I brought them up out of the land of Egypt, *even* unto this day, [m]rising early and protesting, saying, Obey my voice.

8 [n]Yet they obeyed not, nor inclined their ear, but [o]walked every one in the imagination of their evil heart: therefore I will bring upon them all the words of this covenant, which I commanded *them* to do; but they did *them* not.

9 And the LORD said unto me, [p]A conspiracy is found among the men of Judah, and among the inhabitants of Jerusalem.

10 They are turned back to [q]the iniquities of their forefathers, which refused to hear my words; and they went after other gods to serve them: the house of Israel and the house of Judah have broken my covenant which I made with their fathers.

11 ¶ Therefore thus saith the LORD, Behold, I will bring evil upon them, which they shall not be able to escape; and [r]though they shall cry unto me, I will not hearken unto them.

12 Then shall the cities of Judah and inhabitants of Jerusalem go, and [s]cry unto the gods unto whom they offer incense: but they shall not save them at all in the time of their trouble.

13 For *according to* the number of thy [t]cities were thy gods, O Judah; and *according to* the number of the streets of Jerusalem have ye set up altars to *that* shameful thing, *even* altars to burn incense unto Baal.

14 Therefore [u]pray not thou for this people, neither lift up a cry or prayer for them: for I will not hear *them* in the time that they cry unto me for their trouble.

15 [v]What hath my beloved to do in mine house, *seeing* she hath [w]wrought lewdness with many, and [x]the holy flesh is passed from thee? when thou doest evil, then thou [y]rejoicest.

16 The LORD called thy name, [z]A green olive tree, fair, *and* of goodly fruit: with the noise of a great tumult he hath kindled fire upon it, and the branches of it are broken.

17 For the LORD of hosts, [a]that planted thee, hath pronounced evil against thee, for the evil of the house of Israel and of the house of Judah, which they have done against themselves to provoke me to anger in offering incense unto Baal.

18 ¶ And the LORD hath given me knowledge *of it,* and I know *it:* then thou shewedst me their doings.

19 But I *was* like a lamb *or* an ox *that* is brought to the slaughter; and I knew not that [b]they had devised devices against me, *saying,* Let us destroy the tree with the fruit thereof, [c]and let us cut him off from [d]the land of the living, that his name may be no more remembered.

20 But, O LORD of hosts, that judgest righteously, that [e]triest the reins and the heart, let me see thy vengeance on them: for unto thee have I revealed my cause.

21 Therefore thus saith the LORD of the men of Anathoth, [f]that seek thy life, saying, [g]Prophesy not in the name of the LORD, that thou die not by our hand:

22 Therefore thus saith the LORD of hosts, Behold, I will punish them: the young men shall die by the sword; their sons and their daughters shall die by famine:

23 And there shall be no remnant of them: for I will bring evil upon the men of Anathoth, *even* [h]the year of their visitation.

12 Righteous [i]*art* thou, O LORD, when I plead with thee: yet let me talk with thee of *thy* judgments: [j]Wherefore doth the way of the wicked prosper? *wherefore* are all they happy that deal very treacherously?

2 Thou hast planted them, yea, they have taken root: they grow, yea, they bring forth fruit: [k]thou *art* near in their mouth, and far from their reins.

3 But thou, O LORD, [l]knowest me: thou hast seen me, and [m]tried mine heart toward thee: pull them out like sheep for the slaughter, and prepare them for [n]the day of slaughter.

4 How long shall [o]the land mourn, and the herbs of every field wither, [p]for the wickedness of them that dwell therein? [q]the beasts are consumed, and the birds; because they said, He shall not see our last end.

5 ¶ If thou hast run with the footmen, and they have wearied thee, then how canst thou contend with horses? and *if* in the land of peace, *wherein* thou trustedst, *they wearied thee,* then how wilt thou do in [r]the swelling of Jordan?

6 For even [s]thy brethren, and the house of thy father, even they have dealt treacherously with thee; yea, they have called a multitude after thee: [t]believe them not, though they speak fair words unto thee.

7 ¶ I have forsaken mine house, I have left mine heritage; I have given the dearly beloved of my soul into the hand of her enemies.

8 Mine heritage is unto me as a lion in the forest; it crieth out against me: therefore have I hated it.

9 Mine heritage *is* unto me *as* a speckled bird, the birds round about *are* against her; come ye, assemble all the beasts of the field, [u]come to devour.

10 Many [v]pastors have destroyed [w]my vineyard, they have [x]trodden my portion under foot, they have made my pleasant portion a desolate wilderness.

11 They have made it desolate, *and being* desolate [y]it mourneth unto me; the whole

11:5 [k]Deut. 7:12; Ps. 105:9
11:6 [l]Rom. 2:13; Jam. 1:22
11:7 [m]ch. 7:13
11:8 [n]ch. 7:26 [o]ch. 3:17
11:9 [p]Ezek. 22:25; Hos. 6:9
11:10 [q]Ezek. 20:18
11:11 [r]Ps. 18:41; Prov. 1:28; Isa. 1:15; ch. 14:12; Ezek. 8:18; Mic. 3:4; Zech. 7:13
11:12 [s]Deut. 32:37
11:13 [t]ch. 2:28
11:14 [u]Ex. 32:10; ch. 7:16; 1 John 5:16
11:15 [v]Ps. 50:16; Isa. 1:11 [w]Ezek. 16:25 [x]Hag. 2:12; Tit. 1:15 [y]Prov. 2:14
11:16 [z]Ps. 52:8; Rom. 11:17
11:17 [a]Isa. 5:2; ch. 2:21
11:19 [b]ch. 18:18 [c]Ps. 83:4 [d]Ps. 27:13
11:20 [e]1 Sam. 16:7; 1 Chron. 28:9; Ps. 7:9; ch. 17:10; Rev. 2:23
11:21 [f]ch. 12:5 [g]Isa. 30:10; Am. 2:12; Mic. 2:6
11:23 [h]ch. 23:12; Luke 19:44
12:1 [i]Ps. 51:4 [j]Job 12:6; Ps. 37:1; ch. 5:28; Hab. 1:4; Mal. 3:15
12:2 [k]Isa. 29:13; Matt. 15:8; Mark 7:6
12:3 [l]Ps. 17:3 [m]ch. 11:20 [n]Jam. 5:5
12:4 [o]ch. 23:10; Hos. 4:3 [p]Ps. 107:34 [q]ch. 4:25; Hos. 4:3
12:5 [r]Josh. 3:15; 1 Chron. 12:15; ch. 49:19
12:6 [s]ch. 9:4 [t]Prov. 26:25
12:9 [u]Isa. 56:9; ch. 7:33
12:10 [v]ch. 6:3 [w]Isa. 5:1 [x]Isa. 63:18
12:11 [y]ver. 4

land is made desolate, because [z]no man
layeth *it* to heart.
12 The spoilers are come upon all high
places through the wilderness: for the
sword of the LORD shall devour from the
one end of the land even to the *other* end of
the land: no flesh shall have peace.
13 [a]They have sown wheat, but shall
reap thorns: they have put themselves to
pain, *but* shall not profit: and they shall be
ashamed of your revenues because of the
fierce anger of the LORD.
14 ¶ Thus saith the LORD against all mine
evil neighbours, that [b]touch the inheritance
which I have caused my people Israel to inherit; Behold, I will [c]pluck them out of their
land, and pluck out the house of Judah from
among them.
15 [d]And it shall come to pass, after that I
have plucked them out I will return, and
have compassion on them, [e]and will bring
them again, every man to his heritage, and
every man to his land.
16 And it shall come to pass, if they will
diligently learn the ways of my people, [f]to
swear by my name, The LORD liveth; as they
taught my people to swear by Baal; then
shall they be [g]built in the midst of my people.
17 But if they will not [h]obey, I will utterly
pluck up and destroy that nation, saith the
LORD.

13 Thus saith the LORD unto me, Go and
get thee a linen girdle, and put it
upon thy loins, and put it not in water.
2 So I got a girdle according to the word
of the LORD, and put *it* on my loins.
3 And the word of the LORD came unto me
the second time, saying,
4 Take the girdle that thou hast got,
which *is* upon thy loins, and arise, go to
Euphrates, and hide it there in a hole of the
rock.
5 So I went, and hid it by Euphrates, as
the LORD commanded me.
6 And it came to pass after many days,
that the LORD said unto me, Arise, go to
Euphrates, and take the girdle from thence,
which I commanded thee to hide there.
7 Then I went to Euphrates, and digged,
and took the girdle from the place where
I had hid it: and, behold, the girdle was
marred, it was profitable for nothing.
8 Then the word of the LORD came unto
me, saying,
9 Thus saith the LORD, After this manner
[i]will I mar the pride of Judah, and the great
pride of Jerusalem.
10 This evil people, which refuse to hear
my words, which [j]walk in the imagination
of their heart, and walk after other gods, to
serve them, and to worship them, shall even
be as this girdle, which is good for nothing.
11 For as the girdle cleaveth to the loins of
a man, so have I caused to cleave unto me
the whole house of Israel and the whole
house of Judah, saith the LORD; that [k]they
might be unto me for a people, and [l]for a
name, and for a praise, and for a glory: but
they would not hear.
12 ¶ Therefore thou shalt speak unto
them this word; Thus saith the LORD God of
Israel, Every bottle shall be filled with wine:
and they shall say unto thee, Do we not certainly know that every bottle shall be filled
with wine?
13 Then shalt thou say unto them, Thus
saith the LORD, Behold, I will fill all the inhabitants of this land, even the kings that sit
upon David's throne, and the priests, and
the prophets, and all the inhabitants of Jerusalem, [m]with drunkenness.
14 And [n]I will dash them one against another, even the fathers and the sons together, saith the LORD: I will not pity, nor
spare, nor have mercy, but destroy them.
15 ¶ Hear ye, and give ear; be not proud:
for the LORD hath spoken.
16 [o]Give glory to the LORD your God, before he cause [p]darkness, and before your
feet stumble upon the dark mountains, and,
while ye [q]look for light, he turn it into [r]the
shadow of death, *and* make *it* gross darkness.
17 But if ye will not hear it, my soul shall
weep in secret places for *your* pride; and
[s]mine eye shall weep sore, and run down
with tears, because the LORD's flock is carried away captive.
18 Say unto [t]the king and to the queen,
Humble yourselves, sit down: for your principalities shall come down, *even* the crown
of your glory.
19 The cities of the south shall be shut up,
and none shall open *them:* Judah shall be
carried away captive all of it, it shall be
wholly carried away captive.
20 Lift up your eyes, and behold them
[u]that come from the north: where *is* the
flock *that* was given thee, thy beautiful
flock?
21 What wilt thou say when he shall punish thee? for thou hast taught them *to be*
captains, *and* as chief over thee: shall not
[v]sorrows take thee, as a woman in travail?
22 ¶ And if thou say in thine heart,
[w]Wherefore come these things upon me?
For the greatness of thine iniquity are [x]thy
skirts discovered, *and* thy heels made bare.
23 Can the Ethiopian change his skin, or
the leopard his spots? *then* may ye also do
good, that are accustomed to do evil.
24 Therefore will I scatter them [y]as the
stubble that passeth away by the wind of
the wilderness.
25 [z]This *is* thy lot, the portion of thy measures from me, saith the LORD; because thou
hast forgotten me, and trusted in [a]false-
hood.
26 Therefore [b]will I discover thy skirts
upon thy face, that thy shame may appear.
27 I have seen thine adulteries, and thy
[c]neighings, the lewdness of thy whoredom,
and thine abominations [d]on the hills in the
fields. Woe unto thee, O Jerusalem! wilt

12:11 [z]Isa. 42:25
12:13 [a]Lev. 26:16; Deut. 28:38; Mic. 6:15; Hag. 1:6
12:14 [b]Zech. 2:8 [c]Deut. 30:3; ch. 32:37
12:15 [d]Ezek. 28:25 [e]Am. 9:14
12:16 [f]ch. 4:2 [g]Eph. 2:20; 1 Pet. 2:5
12:17 [h]Isa. 60:12
13:9 [i]Lev. 26:19
13:10 [j]ch. 9:14
13:11 [k]Ex. 19:5 [l]ch. 33:9
13:13 [m]Isa. 51:17; ch. 25:27
13:14 [n]Ps. 2:9
13:16 [o]Josh. 7:19 [p]Isa. 5:30; Am. 8:9 [q]Isa. 59:9 [r]Ps. 44:19
13:17 [s]ch. 9:1; Lam. 1:2
13:18 [t]2 Kings 24:12; ch. 22:26
13:20 [u]ch. 6:22
13:21 [v]ch. 6:24
13:22 [w]ch. 5:19 [x]Isa. 3:17; ver. 26; Ezek. 16:37; Nah. 3:5
13:24 [y]Ps. 1:4; Hos. 13:3
13:25 [z]Job 20:29; Ps. 11:6 [a]ch. 10:14
13:26 [b]ver. 22; Lam. 1:8; Ezek. 16:37; Hos. 2:10
13:27 [c]ch. 5:8 [d]Isa. 65:7; ch. 2:20; Ezek. 6:13

thou not be made clean? when *shall it* once *be*?

14 The word of the LORD that came to Jeremiah concerning the dearth.

2 Judah mourneth, and [e]the gates thereof languish; they are [f]black unto the ground; and [g]the cry of Jerusalem is gone up.

3 And their nobles have sent their little ones to the waters: they came to the pits, *and* found no water; they returned with their vessels empty; they were [h]ashamed and confounded, [i]and covered their heads.

4 Because the ground is chapt, for there was no rain in the earth, the plowmen were ashamed, they covered their heads.

5 Yea, the hind also calved in the field, and forsook *it*, because there was no grass.

6 And [j]the wild asses did stand in the high places, they snuffed up the wind like dragons; their eyes did fail, because *there was* no grass.

7 ¶ O LORD, though our iniquities testify against us, do thou *it* [k]for thy name's sake: for our backslidings are many; we have sinned against thee.

8 [l]O the hope of Israel, the saviour thereof in time of trouble, why shouldest thou be as a stranger in the land, and as a wayfaring man *that* turneth aside to tarry for a night?

9 Why shouldest thou be as a man astonied, as a mighty man [m]*that* cannot save? yet thou, O LORD, [n]*art* in the midst of us, and we are called by thy name; leave us not.

10 ¶ Thus saith the LORD unto this people, [o]Thus have they loved to wander, they have not refrained their feet, therefore the LORD doth not accept them; [p]he will now remember their iniquity, and visit their sins.

11 Then said the LORD unto me, [q]Pray not for this people for *their* good.

12 [r]When they fast, I will not hear their cry; and [s]when they offer burnt offering and an oblation, I will not accept them: but [t]I will consume them by the sword, and by the famine, and by the pestilence.

13 ¶ [u]Then said I, Ah, Lord GOD! behold, the prophets say unto them, Ye shall not see the sword, neither shall ye have famine; but I will give you assured peace in this place.

14 Then the LORD said unto me, [v]The prophets prophesy lies in my name: [w]I sent them not, neither have I commanded them, neither spake unto them: they prophesy unto you a false vision and divination, and a thing of nought, and the deceit of their heart.

15 Therefore thus saith the LORD concerning the prophets that prophesy in my name, and I sent them not, [x]yet they say, Sword and famine shall not be in this land; By sword and famine shall those prophets be consumed.

16 And the people to whom they prophesy shall be cast out in the streets of Jerusalem because of the famine and the sword; [y]and they shall have none to bury them, them, their wives, nor their sons, nor their daughters: for I will pour their wickedness upon them.

17 ¶ Therefore thou shalt say this word unto them; [z]Let mine eyes run down with tears night and day, and let them not cease: [a]for the virgin daughter of my people is broken with a great breach, with a very grievous blow.

18 If I go forth into [b]the field, then behold the slain with the sword! and if I enter into the city, then behold them that are sick with famine! yea, both the prophet and the priest go about into a land that they know not.

19 [c]Hast thou utterly rejected Judah? hath thy soul lothed Zion? why hast thou smitten us, and [d]*there is* no healing for us? [e]we looked for peace, and *there is* no good; and for the time of healing, and behold trouble!

20 We acknowledge, O LORD, our wickedness, *and* the iniquity of our fathers: for [f]we have sinned against thee.

21 Do not abhor *us*, for thy name's sake, do not disgrace the throne of thy glory: [g]remember, break not thy covenant with us.

22 [h]Are there *any* among [i]the vanities of the Gentiles that can cause rain? or can the heavens give showers? [j]*art* not thou he, O LORD our God? therefore we will wait upon thee: for thou hast made all these *things*.

15 Then said the LORD unto me, [k]Though [l]Moses and [m]Samuel stood before me, *yet* my mind *could* not *be* toward this people: cast *them* out of my sight, and let them go forth.

2 And it shall come to pass, if they say unto thee, Whither shall we go forth? then thou shalt tell them, Thus saith the LORD; [n]Such as *are* for death, to death; and such as *are* for the sword, to the sword; and such as *are* for the famine, to the famine; and such as *are* for the captivity, to the captivity.

3 And I will [o]appoint over them four kinds, saith the LORD: the sword to slay, and the dogs to tear, and [p]the fowls of the heaven, and the beasts of the earth, to devour and destroy.

4 And I will cause them to be [q]removed into all kingdoms of the earth, because of [r]Manasseh the son of Hezekiah king of Judah, for *that* which he did in Jerusalem.

5 For [s]who shall have pity upon thee, O Jerusalem? or who shall bemoan thee? or who shall go aside to ask how thou doest?

6 [t]Thou hast forsaken me, saith the LORD, thou art [u]gone backward: therefore will I stretch out my hand against thee, and destroy thee; [v]I am weary with repenting.

7 And I will fan them with a fan in the gates of the land; I will bereave *them* of children, I will destroy my people, *since* [w]they return not from their ways.

8 Their widows are increased to me above the sand of the seas: I have brought upon them against the mother of the young men a spoiler at noonday: I have caused *him*

14:2 [e]Isa. 3:26 [f]ch. 8:21 [g]1 Sam. 5:12
14:3 [h]Ps. 40:14 [i]2 Sam. 15:30
14:6 [j]ch. 2:24
14:7 [k]Ps. 25:11
14:8 [l]ch. 17:13
14:9 [m]Isa. 59:1 [n]Ex. 29:45; Lev. 26:11
14:10 [o]ch. 2:23 [p]Hos. 8:13
14:11 [q]Ex. 32:10; ch. 7:16
14:12 [r]Prov. 1:28; Isa. 1:15; ch. 11:11; Ezek. 8:18; Mic. 3:4; Zech. 7:13 [s]ch. 6:20 [t]ch. 9:16
14:13 [u]ch. 4:10
14:14 [v]ch. 27:10 [w]ch. 23:21
14:15 [x]ch. 5:12
14:16 [y]Ps. 79:3
14:17 [z]ch. 9:1; Lam. 1:16 [a]ch. 8:21
14:18 [b]Ezek. 7:15
14:19 [c]Lam. 5:22 [d]ch. 15:18 [e]ch. 8:15
14:20 [f]Ps. 106:6; Dan. 9:8
14:21 [g]Ps. 74:2
14:22 [h]Zech. 10:1 [i]Deut. 32:21 [j]Ps. 135:7; Isa. 30:23; ch. 5:24
15:1 [k]Ezek. 14:14 [l]Ex. 32:11; Ps. 99:6 [m]1 Sam. 7:9
15:2 [n]ch. 43:11; Ezek. 5:2; Zech. 11:9
15:3 [o]Lev. 26:16 [p]ch. 7:33; Deut. 28:26
15:4 [q]Deut. 28:25; ch. 24:9; Ezek. 23:46 [r]2 Kings 21:11
15:5 [s]Isa. 51:19
15:6 [t]ch. 2:13 [u]ch. 7:24 [v]Hos. 13:14
15:7 [w]Isa. 9:13; ch. 5:3; Am. 4:10

to fall upon it suddenly, and terrors upon the city.

9 [x]She that hath borne seven languisheth: she hath given up the ghost; [y]her sun is gone down while *it was* yet day: she hath been ashamed and confounded: and the residue of them will I deliver to the sword before their enemies, saith the LORD.

10 ¶ [z]Woe is me, my mother, that thou hast borne me a man of strife and a man of contention to the whole earth! I have neither lent on usury, nor men have lent to me on usury; *yet* every one of them doth curse me.

11 The LORD said, Verily it shall be well with thy remnant; verily I will cause [a]the enemy to entreat thee *well* in the time of evil and in the time of affliction.

12 Shall iron break the northern iron and the steel?

13 Thy substance and thy treasures will I give to the [b]spoil without price, and *that* for all thy sins, even in all thy borders.

14 And I will make *thee* to pass with thine enemies [c]into a land *which* thou knowest not: for a [d]fire is kindled in mine anger, *which* shall burn upon you.

15 ¶ O LORD, [e]thou knowest: remember me, and visit me, and [f]revenge me of my persecutors; take me not away in thy longsuffering: know that [g]for thy sake I have suffered rebuke.

16 Thy words were found, and I did [h]eat them; and [i]thy word was unto me the joy and rejoicing of mine heart: for I am called by thy name, O LORD God of hosts.

17 [j]I sat not in the assembly of the mockers, nor rejoiced; I sat alone because of thy hand: for thou hast filled me with indignation.

18 Why is my [k]pain perpetual, and my wound incurable, *which* refuseth to be healed? wilt thou be altogether unto me [l]as a liar, *and* [m]*as* waters *that* fail?

19 ¶ Therefore thus saith the LORD, [n]If thou return, then will I bring thee again, *and* thou shalt [o]stand before me: and if thou [p]take forth the precious from the vile, thou shalt be as my mouth: let them return unto thee; but return not thou unto them.

20 And I will make thee unto this people a fenced brasen [q]wall: and they shall fight against thee, but [r]they shall not prevail against thee: for I *am* with thee to save thee and to deliver thee, saith the LORD.

21 And I will deliver thee out of the hand of the wicked, and I will redeem thee out of the hand of the terrible.

16 The word of the LORD came also unto me, saying,

2 Thou shalt not take thee a wife, neither shalt thou have sons or daughters in this place.

3 For thus saith the LORD concerning the sons and concerning the daughters that are born in this place, and concerning their mothers that bare them, and concerning their fathers that begat them in this land;

4 They shall die of [s]grievous deaths; they shall not be [t]lamented; neither shall they be buried; *but* they shall be [u]as dung upon the face of the earth: and they shall be consumed by the sword, and by famine; and their [v]carcases shall be meat for the fowls of heaven, and for the beasts of the earth.

5 For thus saith the LORD, [w]Enter not into the house of mourning, neither go to lament nor bemoan them: for I have taken away my peace from this people, saith the LORD, *even* lovingkindness and mercies.

6 Both the great and the small shall die in this land: they shall not be buried, [x]neither shall *men* lament for them, nor [y]cut themselves, nor [z]make themselves bald for them:

7 Neither shall *men* tear *themselves* for them in mourning, to comfort them for the dead; neither shall *men* give them the cup of consolation to [a]drink for their father or for their mother.

8 Thou shalt not also go into the house of feasting, to sit with them to eat and to drink.

9 For thus saith the LORD of hosts, the God of Israel; Behold, [b]I will cause to cease out of this place in your eyes, and in your days, the voice of mirth, and the voice of gladness, the voice of the bridegroom, and the voice of the bride.

10 ¶ And it shall come to pass, when thou shalt shew this people all these words, and they shall say unto thee, [c]Wherefore hath the LORD pronounced all this great evil against us? or what *is* our iniquity? or what *is* our sin that we have committed against the LORD our God?

11 Then shalt thou say unto them, [d]Because your fathers have forsaken me, saith the LORD, and have walked after other gods, and have served them, and have worshipped them, and have forsaken me, and have not kept my law;

12 And ye have done [e]worse than your fathers; for, behold, [f]ye walk every one after the imagination of his evil heart, that they may not hearken unto me:

13 [g]Therefore will I cast you out of this land [h]into a land that ye know not, *neither* ye nor your fathers; and there shall ye serve other gods day and night; where I will not shew you favour.

14 ¶ Therefore, behold, the [i]days come, saith the LORD, that it shall no more be said, The LORD liveth, that brought up the children of Israel out of the land of Egypt;

15 But, The LORD liveth, that brought up the children of Israel from the land of the north, and from all the lands whither he had driven them: and [j]I will bring them again into their land that I gave unto their fathers.

16 ¶ Behold, I will send for many [k]fishers, saith the LORD, and they shall fish them; and after will I send for many hunters, and they shall hunt them from every mountain, and from every hill, and out of the holes of the rocks.

17 For mine [l]eyes *are* upon all their

15:9 [x]1 Sam. 2:5 [y]Am. 8:9
15:10 [z]Job 3:1; ch. 20:14
15:11 [a]ch. 39:11
15:13 [b]Ps. 44:12; ch. 17:3
15:14 [c]ch. 16:13 [d]Deut. 32:22
15:15 [e]ch. 12:3 [f]ch. 11:20 [g]Ps. 69:7
15:16 [h]Ezek. 3:1; Rev. 10:9 [i]Job 23:12; Ps. 119:72
15:17 [j]Ps. 1:1
15:18 [k]ch. 30:15 [l]ch. 1:18 [m]Job 6:15
15:19 [n]Zech. 3:7 over. 1 [p]Ezek. 22:26
15:20 [q]ch. 1:18 [r]ch. 20:11
16:4 [s]ch. 15:2 [t]ch. 22:18 [u]Ps. 83:10; ch. 8:2 [v]Ps. 79:2; ch. 7:33
16:5 [w]Ezek. 24:17
16:6 [x]ch. 22:18 [y]Lev. 19:28; Deut. 14:1; ch. 41:5 [z]Isa. 22:12; ch. 7:29
16:7 [a]Prov. 31:6
16:9 [b]Isa. 24:7; ch. 7:34; Ezek. 26:13; Hos. 2:11; Rev. 18:23
16:10 [c]Deut. 29:24; ch. 5:19
16:11 [d]Deut. 29:25; ch. 22:9
16:12 [e]ch. 7:26 [f]ch. 13:10
16:13 [g]Deut. 4:26 [h]ch. 15:14
16:14 [i]Isa. 43:18
16:15 [j]ch. 24:6
16:16 [k]Am. 4:2; Hab. 1:15
16:17 [l]Job 34:21; Prov. 5:21; ch. 32:19

ways: they are not hid from my face, neither is their iniquity hid from mine eyes.

18 And first I will recompense their iniquity and their sin [m]double; because [n]they have defiled my land, they have filled mine inheritance with the carcases of their detestable and abominable things.

19 O LORD, [o]my strength, and my fortress, and [p]my refuge in the day of affliction, the Gentiles shall come unto thee from the ends of the earth, and shall say, Surely our fathers have inherited lies, vanity, and *things* [q]wherein *there is* no profit.

20 Shall a man make gods unto himself, and [r]they *are* no gods?

21 Therefore, behold, I will this once cause them to know, I will cause them to know mine hand and my might; and they shall know that [s]my name *is* The LORD.

17 The sin of Judah *is* written with a [t]pen of iron, *and* with the point of a diamond: *it is* [u]graven upon the table of their heart, and upon the horns of your altars;

2 Whilst their children remember their altars and their [v]groves by the green trees upon the high hills.

3 O my mountain in the field, [w]I will give thy substance *and* all thy treasures to the spoil, *and* thy high places for sin, throughout all thy borders.

4 And thou, even thyself, shalt discontinue from thine heritage that I gave thee; and I will cause thee to serve thine enemies in [x]the land which thou knowest not: for [y]ye have kindled a fire in mine anger, *which* shall burn for ever.

5 ¶ Thus saith the LORD; [z]Cursed *be* the man that trusteth in man, and maketh [a]flesh his arm, and whose heart departeth from the LORD.

6 For he shall be [b]like the heath in the desert, and [c]shall not see when good cometh; but shall inhabit the parched places in the wilderness, [d]*in* a salt land and not inhabited.

7 [e]Blessed *is* the man that trusteth in the LORD, and whose hope the LORD is.

8 For he shall be [f]as a tree planted by the waters, and *that* spreadeth out her roots by the river, and shall not see when heat cometh, but her leaf shall be green; and shall not be careful in the year of drought, neither shall cease from yielding fruit.

9 ¶ The heart *is* deceitful above all *things*, and desperately wicked: who can know it?

10 I the LORD [g]search the heart, *I* try the reins, [h]even to give every man according to his ways, *and* according to the fruit of his doings.

11 *As* the partridge sitteth *on eggs*, and hatcheth *them* not; *so* he that getteth riches, and not by right, [i]shall leave them in the midst of his days, and at his end shall be [j]a fool.

12 ¶ A glorious high throne from the beginning *is* the place of our sanctuary.

13 O LORD, [k]the hope of Israel, [l]all that

16:18 [m]Isa. 40:2; ch. 17:18 [n]Ezek. 43:7
16:19 [o]Ps. 18:2 [p]ch. 17:17 [q]Isa. 44:10; ch. 2:11
16:20 [r]Isa. 37:19; ch. 2:11; Gal. 4:8
16:21 [s]Ex. 15:3; ch. 33:2; Am. 5:8
17:1 [t]Job 19:24 [u]Prov. 3:3; 2 Cor. 3:3
17:2 [v]Judg. 3:7; 2 Chron. 24:18; Isa. 1:29; ch. 2:20
17:3 [w]ch. 15:13
17:4 [x]ch. 16:13 [y]ch. 15:14
17:5 [z]Isa. 30:1 [a]Isa. 31:3
17:6 [b]ch. 48:6 [c]Job 20:17 [d]Deut. 29:23
17:7 [e]Ps. 2:12; Prov. 16:20; Isa. 30:18
17:8 [f]Job 8:16; Ps. 1:3
17:10 [g]1 Sam. 16:7; 1 Chron. 28:9; Ps. 7:9; Prov. 17:3; ch. 11:20; Rom. 8:27; Rev. 2:23 [h]Ps. 62:12; ch. 32:19; Rom. 2:6
17:11 [i]Ps. 55:23 [j]Luke 12:20
17:13 [k]ch. 14:8 [l]Ps. 73:27; Isa. 1:28 [m]Luke 10:20 [n]ch. 2:13
17:14 [o]Deut. 10:21; Ps. 109:1
17:15 [p]Isa. 5:19; Ezek. 12:22; Am. 5:18; 2 Pet. 3:4
17:16 [q]ch. 1:4
17:17 [r]ch. 16:19
17:18 [s]Ps. 35:4 [t]Ps. 25:2 [u]ch. 11:20
17:20 [v]ch. 19:3
17:21 [w]Num. 15:32; Neh. 13:19
17:22 [x]Ex. 20:8; Ezek. 20:12
17:23 [y]ch. 7:24
17:25 [z]ch. 22:4
17:26 [a]ch. 32:44 [b]Zech. 7:7 [c]Zech. 7:7 [d]Ps. 107:22
17:27 [e]ch. 21:14; Lam. 4:11; Am. 1:4 [f]2 Kings 25:9; ch. 52:13

forsake thee shall be ashamed, *and* they that depart from me shall be [m]written in the earth, because they have forsaken the LORD, the [n]fountain of living waters.

14 Heal me, O LORD, and I shall be healed; save me, and I shall be saved: for [o]thou *art* my praise.

15 ¶ Behold, they say unto me, [p]Where *is* the word of the LORD? let it come now.

16 As for me, [q]I have not hastened from *being* a pastor to follow thee: neither have I desired the woeful day; thou knowest: that which came out of my lips was *right* before thee.

17 Be not a terror unto me: [r]thou *art* my hope in the day of evil.

18 [s]Let them be confounded that persecute me, but [t]let not me be confounded: let them be dismayed, but let not me be dismayed: bring upon them the day of evil, and [u]destroy them with double destruction.

19 ¶ Thus said the LORD unto me; Go and stand in the gate of the children of the people, whereby the kings of Judah come in, and by the which they go out, and in all the gates of Jerusalem;

20 And say unto them, [v]Hear ye the word of the LORD, ye kings of Judah, and all Judah, and all the inhabitants of Jerusalem, that enter in by these gates:

21 Thus saith the LORD; [w]Take heed to yourselves, and bear no burden on the sabbath day, nor bring *it* in by the gates of Jerusalem;

22 Neither carry forth a burden out of your houses on the sabbath day, neither do ye any work, but hallow ye the sabbath day, as I [x]commanded your fathers.

23 [y]But they obeyed not, neither inclined their ear, but made their neck stiff, that they might not hear, nor receive instruction.

24 And it shall come to pass, if ye diligently hearken unto me, saith the LORD, to bring in no burden through the gates of this city on the sabbath day, but hallow the sabbath day, to do no work therein;

25 [z]Then shall there enter into the gates of this city kings and princes sitting upon the throne of David, riding in chariots and on horses, they, and their princes, the men of Judah, and the inhabitants of Jerusalem: and this city shall remain for ever.

26 And they shall come from the cities of Judah, and from [a]the places about Jerusalem, and from the land of Benjamin, and from [b]the plain, and from the mountains, and from [c]the south, bringing burnt offerings, and sacrifices, and meat offerings, and incense, and bringing [d]sacrifices of praise, unto the house of the LORD.

27 But if ye will not hearken unto me to hallow the sabbath day, and not to bear a burden, even entering in at the gates of Jerusalem on the sabbath day; then [e]will I kindle a fire in the gates thereof, [f]and it shall devour the palaces of Jerusalem, and it shall not be quenched.

18 The word which came to Jeremiah from the LORD, saying,

2 Arise, and go down to the potter's house, and there I will cause thee to hear my words.

3 Then I went down to the potter's house, and, behold, he wrought a work on the wheels.

4 And the vessel that he made of clay was marred in the hand of the potter: so he made it again another vessel, as seemed good to the potter to make *it*.

5 Then the word of the LORD came to me, saying,

6 O house of Israel, [g]cannot I do with you as this potter? saith the LORD. Behold, [h]as the clay *is* in the potter's hand, so *are* ye in mine hand, O house of Israel.

7 *At what* instant I shall speak concerning a nation, and concerning a kingdom, to [i]pluck up, and to pull down, and to destroy *it;*

8 [j]If that nation, against whom I have pronounced, turn from their evil, [k]I will repent of the evil that I thought to do unto them.

9 And *at what* instant I shall speak concerning a nation, and concerning a kingdom, to build and to plant *it;*

10 If it do evil in my sight, that it obey not my voice, then I will repent of the good, wherewith I said I would benefit them.

11 ¶ Now therefore go to, speak to the men of Judah, and to the inhabitants of Jerusalem, saying, Thus saith the LORD; Behold, I frame evil against you, and devise a device against you: [l]return ye now every one from his evil way, and make your ways and your doings good.

12 And they said, [m]There is no hope: but we will walk after our own devices, and we will every one do the imagination of his evil heart.

13 Therefore thus saith the LORD; [n]Ask ye now among the heathen, who hath heard such things: the virgin of Israel hath done [o]a very horrible thing.

14 Will *a man* leave the snow of Lebanon *which cometh* from the rock of the field? *or* shall the cold flowing waters that come from another place be forsaken?

15 Because my people hath forgotten [p]me, they have burned incense to [q]vanity, and they have caused them to stumble in their ways *from* the [r]ancient paths, to walk in paths, *in* a way not cast up;

16 To make their land [s]desolate, *and* a perpetual [t]hissing; every one that passeth thereby shall be astonished, and wag his head.

17 [u]I will scatter them [v]as with an east wind before the enemy: [w]I will shew them the back, and not the face, in the day of their calamity.

18 ¶ Then said they, [x]Come, and let us devise devices against Jeremiah; [y]for the law shall not perish from the priest, nor counsel from the wise, nor the word from the prophet. Come, and let us smite him with the tongue, and let us not give heed to any of his words.

19 Give heed to me, O LORD, and hearken to the voice of them that contend with me.

20 [z]Shall evil be recompensed for good? for [a]they have digged a pit for my soul. Remember that I stood before thee to speak good for them, *and* to turn away thy wrath from them.

21 Therefore [b]deliver up their children to the famine, and pour out their *blood* by the force of the sword; and let their wives be bereaved of their children, and *be* widows; and let their men be put to death; *let* their young men *be* slain by the sword in battle.

22 Let a cry be heard from their houses, when thou shalt bring a troop suddenly upon them: for [c]they have digged a pit to take me, and hid snares for my feet.

23 Yet, LORD, thou knowest all their counsel against me to slay *me:* [d]forgive not their iniquity, neither blot out their sin from thy sight, but let them be overthrown before thee; deal *thus* with them in the time of thine anger.

19 Thus saith the LORD, Go and get a potter's earthen bottle, and *take* of the ancients of the people, and of the ancients of the priests;

2 And go forth unto [e]the valley of the son of Hinnom, which *is* by the entry of the east gate, and proclaim there the words that I shall tell thee,

3 [f]And say, Hear ye the word of the LORD, O kings of Judah, and inhabitants of Jerusalem; Thus saith the LORD of hosts, the God of Israel; Behold, I will bring evil upon this place, the which whosoever heareth, his ears shall [g]tingle.

4 Because they [h]have forsaken me, and have estranged this place, and have burned incense in it unto other gods, whom neither they nor their fathers have known, nor the kings of Judah, and have filled this place with [i]the blood of innocents;

5 [j]They have built also the high places of Baal, to burn their sons with fire *for* burnt offerings unto Baal, [k]which I commanded not, nor spake *it*, neither came *it* into my mind:

6 Therefore, behold, the days come, saith the LORD, that this place shall no more be called Tophet, nor [l]The valley of the son of Hinnom, but The valley of slaughter.

7 And I will make void the counsel of Judah and Jerusalem in this place; [m]and I will cause them to fall by the sword before their enemies, and by the hands of them that seek their lives: and their [n]carcases will I give to be meat for the fowls of the heaven, and for the beasts of the earth.

8 And I will make this city [o]desolate, and an hissing; every one that passeth thereby shall be astonished and hiss because of all the plagues thereof.

9 And I will cause them to eat the [p]flesh of their sons and the flesh of their daugh-

18:6 [g]Isa. 45:9; Rom. 9:20 [h]Isa. 64:8
18:7 [i]ch. 1:10
18:8 [j]Ezek. 18:21 [k]ch. 26:3; Jonah 3:10
18:11 [l]2 Kings 27:13; ch. 7:3
18:12 [m]ch. 2:25
18:13 [n]ch. 2:10; 1 Cor. 5:1 [o]ch. 5:30
18:15 [p]ch. 2:13 [q]ch. 10:15 [r]ch. 6:16
18:16 [s]ch. 19:8 [t]1 Kings 9:8; Lam. 2:15; Mic. 6:16
18:17 [u]ch. 13:24 [v]Ps. 48:7 [w]ch. 2:27
18:18 [x]ch. 11:19 [y]Lev. 10:11; Mal. 2:7; John 7:48
18:20 [z]Ps. 109:4 [a]Ps. 35:7; ver. 22
18:21 [b]Ps. 109:9
18:22 [c]ver. 20
18:23 [d]Ps. 35:4; ch. 11:20
19:2 [e]Josh. 15:8; 2 Kings 23:10; ch. 7:31
19:3 [f]ch. 17:20 [g]1 Sam. 3:11; 2 Kings 21:12
19:4 [h]Deut. 28:20; Isa. 65:11; ch. 2:13 [i]2 Kings 21:16; ch. 2:34
19:5 [j]ch. 7:31 [k]Lev. 18:21
19:6 [l]Josh. 15:8
19:7 [m]Lev. 26:17; Deut. 28:25 [n]Ps. 79:2; ch. 7:33
19:8 [o]ch. 18:16
19:9 [p]Lev. 26:29; Deut. 28:53; Isa. 9:20; Lam. 4:10

ters, and they shall eat every one the flesh
of his friend in the siege and straitness,
wherewith their enemies, and they that
seek their lives, shall straiten them.
10 [q]Then shalt thou break the bottle in
the sight of the men that go with thee,
11 And shalt say unto them, Thus saith
the LORD of hosts; [r]Even so will I break this
people and this city, as *one* breaketh a potter's vessel, that cannot be made whole
again: and they shall [s]bury *them* in Tophet,
till *there be* no place to bury.
12 Thus will I do unto this place, saith the
LORD, and to the inhabitants thereof, and
even make this city as Tophet:
13 And the houses of Jerusalem, and the
houses of the kings of Judah, shall be defiled [t]as the place of Tophet, because of all
the houses upon whose [u]roofs they have
burned incense unto all the host of heaven,
and [v]have poured out drink offerings unto
other gods.
14 Then came Jeremiah from Tophet,
whither the LORD had sent him to prophesy;
and he stood in [w]the court of the LORD's
house, and said to all the people,
15 Thus saith the LORD of hosts, the God
of Israel; Behold, I will bring upon this city
and upon all her towns all the evil that I
have pronounced against it, because [x]they
have hardened their necks, that they might
not hear my words.

20 Now Pashur the son of [y]Immer the
priest, who *was* also chief governor
in the house of the LORD, heard that Jeremiah prophesied these things.
2 Then Pashur smote Jeremiah the
prophet, and put him in the stocks that *were*
in the high gate of Benjamin, which *was* by
the house of the LORD.
3 And it came to pass on the morrow, that
Pashur brought forth Jeremiah out of the
stocks. Then said Jeremiah unto him, The
LORD hath not called thy name Pashur, but
Magor-missabib.
4 For thus saith the LORD, Behold, I will
make thee a terror to thyself, and to all thy
friends: and they shall fall by the sword of
their enemies, and thine eyes shall behold
it: and I will give all Judah into the hand
of the king of Babylon, and he shall carry
them captive into Babylon, and shall slay
them with the sword.
5 Moreover I [z]will deliver all the strength
of this city, and all the labours thereof, and
all the precious things thereof, and all the
treasures of the kings of Judah will I give
into the hand of their enemies, which shall
spoil them, and take them, and carry them
to Babylon.
6 And thou, Pashur, and all that dwell in
thine house shall go into captivity: and thou
shalt come to Babylon, and there thou shalt
die, and shalt be buried there, thou, and all
thy friends, to whom thou hast [a]prophesied
lies.
7 ¶ O LORD, thou hast deceived me, and I
was deceived: [b]thou art stronger than I, and
hast prevailed: [c]I am in derision daily, every one mocketh me.
8 For since I spake, I cried out, [d]I cried
violence and spoil; because the word of the
LORD was made a reproach unto me, and a
derision, daily.
9 Then I said, I will not make mention of
him, nor speak any more in his name. But
his word was in mine heart as a [e]burning
fire shut up in my bones, and I was weary
with forbearing, and [f]I could not *stay.*
10 ¶ [g]For I heard the defaming of many,
fear on every side. Report, *say they,* and we
will report it. [h]All my familiars watched for
my halting, *saying,* Peradventure he will be
enticed, and we shall prevail against him,
and we shall take our revenge on him.
11 But [i]the LORD *is* with me as a mighty
terrible one: therefore my persecutors shall
stumble, and they shall not [j]prevail: they
shall be greatly ashamed; for they shall not
prosper: *their* [k]everlasting confusion shall
never be forgotten.
12 But, O LORD of hosts, that [l]triest the
righteous, *and* seest the reins and the heart,
[m]let me see thy vengeance on them: for unto
thee have I opened my cause.
13 Sing unto the LORD, praise ye the
LORD: for [n]he hath delivered the soul of the
poor from the hand of evildoers.
14 ¶ [o]Cursed *be* the day wherein I was
born: let not the day wherein my mother
bare me be blessed.
15 Cursed *be* the man who brought tidings to my father, saying, A man child is
born unto thee; making him very glad.
16 And let that man be as the cities which
the LORD [p]overthrew, and repented not:
and let him [q]hear the cry in the morning,
and the shouting at noontide;
17 [r]Because he slew me not from the
womb; or that my mother might have been
my grave, and her womb *to be* always great
with me.
18 [s]Wherefore came I forth out of the
womb to [t]see labour and sorrow, that my
days should be consumed with shame?

21 The word which came unto Jeremiah
from the LORD, when king Zedekiah
sent unto him [u]Pashur the son of Melchiah,
and [v]Zephaniah the son of Maaseiah the
priest, saying,
2 [w]Enquire, I pray thee, of the LORD for
us; for Nebuchadrezzar king of Babylon
maketh war against us; if so be that the
LORD will deal with us according to all his
wondrous works, that he may go up
from us.
3 ¶ Then said Jeremiah unto them, Thus
shall ye say to Zedekiah:
4 Thus saith the LORD God of Israel; Behold, I will turn back the weapons of war
that *are* in your hands, wherewith ye fight
against the king of Babylon, and *against* the
Chaldeans, which besiege you without the
walls, and [x]I will assemble them into
the midst of this city.
5 And I myself will fight against you with

19:10 [q]ch. 51:63
19:11 [r]Ps. 2:9; Isa. 30:14; Lam. 4:2 [s]ch. 7:32
19:13 [t]2 Kings 23:10 [u]2 Kings 23:12; ch. 32:29; Zeph. 1:5 [v]ch. 7:18
19:14 [w]2 Chron. 20:5
19:15 [x]ch. 7:26
20:1 [y]1 Chron. 24:14
20:5 [z]2 Kings 20:17; ch. 3:24
20:6 [a]ch. 14:13
20:7 [b]ch. 1:6 [c]Lam. 3:14
20:8 [d]ch. 6:7
20:9 [e]Job 32:18; Ps. 39:3 [f]Job 32:18; Acts 18:5
20:10 [g]Ps. 31:13 [h]Job 19:19; Ps. 41:9; Luke 11:53
20:11 [i]ch. 1:8 [j]ch. 15:20 [k]ch. 23:40
20:12 [l]ch. 11:20 [m]Ps. 54:7
20:13 [n]Ps. 35:9
20:14 [o]Job 3:3; ch. 15:10
20:16 [p]Gen. 19:25 [q]ch. 18:22
20:17 [r]Job 3:10
20:18 [s]Job 3:20 [t]Lam. 3:1
21:1 [u]ch. 38:1 [v]2 Kings 25:18; ch. 29:25
21:2 [w]ch. 37:3
21:4 [x]Isa. 13:4

an [y]outstretched hand and with a strong arm, even in anger, and in fury, and in great wrath.

6 And I will smite the inhabitants of this city, both man and beast: they shall die of a great pestilence.

7 And afterward, saith the LORD, [z]I will deliver Zedekiah king of Judah, and his servants, and the people, and such as are left in this city from the pestilence, from the sword, and from the famine, into the hand of Nebuchadrezzar king of Babylon, and into the hand of their enemies, and into the hand of those that seek their life: and he shall smite them with the edge of the sword; [a]he shall not spare them, neither have pity, nor have mercy.

8 ¶ And unto this people thou shalt say, Thus saith the LORD; Behold, [b]I set before you the way of life, and the way of death.

9 He that [c]abideth in this city shall die by the sword, and by the famine, and by the pestilence: but he that goeth out, and falleth to the Chaldeans that besiege you, he shall live, and [d]his life shall be unto him for a prey.

10 For I have [e]set my face against this city for evil, and not for good, saith the LORD: [f]it shall be given into the hand of the king of Babylon, and he shall [g]burn it with fire.

11 ¶ And touching the house of the king of Judah, *say*, Hear ye the word of the LORD;

12 O house of David, thus saith the LORD; [h]Execute judgment [i]in the morning, and deliver *him that is* spoiled out of the hand of the oppressor, lest my fury go out like fire, and burn that none can quench *it*, because of the evil of your doings.

13 Behold, [j]I *am* against thee, O inhabitant of the valley, *and* rock of the plain, saith the LORD; which say, [k]Who shall come down against us? or who shall enter into our habitations?

14 But I will punish you according to the [l]fruit of your doings, saith the LORD: and I will kindle a fire in the forest thereof, and [m]it shall devour all things round about it.

22 Thus saith the LORD; Go down to the house of the king of Judah, and speak there this word,

2 And say, [n]Hear the word of the LORD, O king of Judah, that sittest upon the throne of David, thou, and thy servants, and thy people that enter in by these gates:

3 Thus saith the LORD; [o]Execute ye judgment and righteousness, and deliver the spoiled out of the hand of the oppressor: and [p]do no wrong, do no violence to the stranger, the fatherless, nor the widow, neither shed innocent blood in this place.

4 For if ye do this thing indeed, [q]then shall there enter in by the gates of this house kings sitting upon the throne of David, riding in chariots and on horses, he, and his servants, and his people.

5 But if ye will not hear these words, [r]I swear by myself, saith the LORD, that this house shall become a desolation.

6 For thus saith the LORD unto the king's house of Judah; Thou *art* Gilead unto me, *and* the head of Lebanon: *yet* surely I will make thee a wilderness, *and* cities *which* are not inhabited.

7 And I will prepare destroyers against thee, every one with his weapons: and they shall cut down [s]thy choice cedars, [t]and cast *them* into the fire.

8 And many nations shall pass by this city, and they shall say every man to his neighbour, [u]Wherefore hath the LORD done thus unto this great city?

9 Then they shall answer, [v]Because they have forsaken the covenant of the LORD their God, and worshipped other gods, and served them.

10 ¶ Weep ye not for [w]the dead, neither bemoan him; *but* weep sore for him [x]that goeth away: for he shall return no more, nor see his native country.

11 For thus saith the LORD touching [y]Shallum the son of Josiah king of Judah, which reigned instead of Josiah his father, [z]which went forth out of this place; He shall not return thither any more:

12 But he shall die in the place whither they have led him captive, and shall see this land no more.

13 ¶ [a]Woe unto him that buildeth his house by unrighteousness, and his chambers by wrong; [b]*that* useth his neighbour's service without wages, and giveth him not for his work;

14 That saith, I will build me a wide house and large chambers, and cutteth him out windows; and *it is* cieled with cedar, and painted with vermilion.

15 Shalt thou reign, because thou closest *thyself* in cedar? [c]did not thy father eat and drink, and do judgment and justice, *and* then [d]*it was* well with him?

16 He judged the cause of the poor and needy; then *it was* well *with him: was* not this to know me? saith the LORD.

17 [e]But thine eyes and thine heart *are* not but for thy covetousness, and for to shed innocent blood, and for oppression, and for violence, to do *it*.

18 Therefore thus saith the LORD concerning Jehoiakim the son of Josiah king of Judah; [f]They shall not lament for him, *saying*, [g]Ah my brother! or, Ah sister! they shall not lament for him, *saying*, Ah lord! or, Ah his glory!

19 [h]He shall be buried with the burial of an ass, drawn and cast forth beyond the gates of Jerusalem.

20 ¶ Go up to Lebanon, and cry; and lift up thy voice in Bashan, and cry from the passages: for all thy lovers are destroyed.

21 I spake unto thee in thy prosperity; *but* thou saidst, I will not hear. [i]This *hath been* thy manner from thy youth, that thou obeyedst not my voice.

22 The wind shall eat up all [j]thy pastors,

21:5 [y]Ex. 6:6
21:7 [z]ch. 37:17 [a]Deut. 28:50; 2 Chron. 36:17
21:8 [b]Deut. 30:19
21:9 [c]ch. 38:2 [d]ch. 39:18
21:10 [e]Lev. 17:10; ch. 44:11; Am. 9:4 [f]ch. 38:3 [g]ch. 34:2
21:12 [h]ch. 22:3; Zech. 7:9 [i]Ps. 101:8
21:13 [j]Ezek. 13:8 [k]ch. 49:4
21:14 [l]Prov. 1:31; Isa. 3:10 [m]2 Chron. 36:19; ch. 52:13
22:2 [n]ch. 17:20
22:3 [o]ch. 21:12 [p]ver. 17
22:4 [q]ch. 17:25
22:5 [r]Heb. 6:13
22:7 [s]Isa. 37:24 [t]ch. 21:14
22:8 [u]Deut. 29:24; 1 Kings 9:8
22:9 [v]2 Kings 22:17; 2 Chron. 34:25
22:10 [w]2 Kings 22:20 [x]ver. 11
22:11 [y]1 Chron. 3:15; 2 Kings 23:30 [z]2 Kings 23:34
22:13 [a]2 Kings 23:35; ver. 18 [b]Lev. 19:13; Deut. 24:14; Mic. 3:10; Hab. 2:9; Jam. 5:4
22:15 [c]2 Kings 23:25 [d]Ps. 128:2; Isa. 3:10
22:17 [e]Ezek. 19:6
22:18 [f]ch. 16:4 [g]1 Kings 13:30
22:19 [h]2 Chron. 36:6; ch. 36:30
22:21 [i]ch. 3:25
22:22 [j]ch. 23:1

and [k]thy lovers shall go into captivity: surely then shalt thou be ashamed and confounded for all thy wickedness.

23 O inhabitant of Lebanon, that makest thy nest in the cedars, how gracious shalt thou be when pangs come upon thee, [l]the pain as of a woman in travail!

24 *As* I live, saith the LORD, [m]though Coniah the son of Jehoiakim king of Judah [n]were the signet upon my right hand, yet would I pluck thee thence;

25 [o]And I will give thee into the hand of them that seek thy life, and into the hand *of them* whose face thou fearest, even into the hand of Nebuchadrezzar king of Babylon, and into the hand of the Chaldeans.

26 [p]And I will cast thee out, and thy mother that bare thee, into another country, where ye were not born; and there shall ye die.

27 But to the land whereunto they desire to return, thither shall they not return.

28 *Is* this man Coniah a despised broken idol? *is he* [q]a vessel wherein *is* no pleasure? wherefore are they cast out, he and his seed, and are cast into a land which they know not?

29 [r]O earth, earth, earth, hear the word of the LORD.

30 Thus saith the LORD, Write ye this man [s]childless, a man *that* shall not prosper in his days: for no man of his seed shall prosper, [t]sitting upon the throne of David, and ruling any more in Judah.

23 Woe [u]be unto the pastors that destroy and scatter the sheep of my pasture! saith the LORD.

2 Therefore thus saith the LORD God of Israel against the pastors that feed my people; Ye have scattered my flock, and driven them away, and have not visited them: [v]behold, I will visit upon you the evil of your doings, saith the LORD.

3 And [w]I will gather the remnant of my flock out of all countries whither I have driven them, and will bring them again to their folds; and they shall be fruitful and increase.

4 And I will set up [x]shepherds over them which shall feed them: and they shall fear no more, nor be dismayed, neither shall they be lacking, saith the LORD.

5 ¶ Behold, [y]the days come, saith the LORD, that I will raise unto David a righteous Branch, and a King shall reign and prosper, [z]and shall execute judgment and justice in the earth.

6 [a]In his days Judah shall be saved, and Israel [b]shall dwell safely: and [c]this *is* his name whereby he shall be called, THE LORD OUR RIGHTEOUSNESS.

7 Therefore, behold, [d]the days come, saith the LORD, that they shall no more say, The LORD liveth, which brought up the children of Israel out of the land of Egypt;

8 But, The LORD liveth, which brought up and which led the seed of the house of Israel out of the north country, [e]and from all countries whither I had driven them; and they shall dwell in their own land.

9 ¶ Mine heart within me is broken because of the prophets; [f]all my bones shake; I am like a drunken man, and like a man whom wine hath overcome, because of the LORD, and because of the words of his holiness.

10 For [g]the land is full of adulterers; for [h]because of swearing the land mourneth; [i]the pleasant places of the wilderness are dried up, and their course is evil, and their force *is* not right.

11 For [j]both prophet and priest are profane; yea, [k]in my house have I found their wickedness, saith the LORD.

12 [l]Wherefore their way shall be unto them as slippery *ways* in the darkness: they shall be driven on, and fall therein: for I [m]will bring evil upon them, *even* the year of their visitation, saith the LORD.

13 And I have seen folly in the prophets of Samaria; [n]they prophesied in Baal, and [o]caused my people Israel to err.

14 I have seen also in the prophets of Jerusalem an horrible thing: [p]they commit adultery, and [q]walk in lies: they [r]strengthen also the hands of evildoers, that none doth return from his wickedness: they are all of them unto me as [s]Sodom, and the inhabitants thereof as Gomorrah.

15 Therefore thus saith the LORD of hosts concerning the prophets; Behold, I will feed them with [t]wormwood, and make them drink the water of gall: for from the prophets of Jerusalem is profaneness gone forth into all the land.

16 Thus saith the LORD of hosts, Hearken not unto the words of the prophets that prophesy unto you: they make you vain: [u]they speak a vision of their own heart, *and* not out of the mouth of the LORD.

17 They say still unto them that despise me, The LORD hath said, [v]Ye shall have peace; and they say unto every one that walketh after the imagination of his own heart, [w]No evil shall come upon you.

18 For [x]who hath stood in the counsel of the LORD, and hath perceived and heard his word? who hath marked his word, and heard *it?*

19 Behold, a [y]whirlwind of the LORD is gone forth in fury, even a grievous whirlwind: it shall fall grievously upon the head of the wicked.

20 The [z]anger of the LORD shall not return, until he have executed, and till he have performed the thoughts of his heart: [a]in the latter days ye shall consider it perfectly.

21 [b]I have not sent these prophets, yet they ran: I have not spoken to them, yet they prophesied.

22 But if they had [c]stood in my counsel, and had caused my people to hear my words, then they should have [d]turned them from their evil way, and from the evil of their doings.

22:22 [k]ver. 20
22:23 [l]ch. 6:24
22:24 [m]2 Kings 24:6; 1 Chron. 3:16; ch. 37:1 [n]SSol. 8:6; Hag. 2:23
22:25 [o]ch. 34:20
22:26 [p]2 Kings 24:15; 2 Chron. 36:10
22:28 [q]Ps. 31:12; ch. 48:38; Hos. 8:8
22:29 [r]Deut. 32:1; Isa. 1:2; Mic. 1:2
22:30 [s]1 Chron. 3:16; Matt. 1:12 [t]ch. 36:30
23:1 [u]ch. 10:21; Ezek. 34:2
23:2 [v]Ex. 32:34
23:3 [w]ch. 32:37; Ezek. 34:13
23:4 [x]ch. 3:15; Ezek. 34:23
23:5 [y]Isa. 4:2; ch. 33:14; Dan. 9:24; Zech. 3:8; John 1:45 [z]Ps. 72:2; Isa. 32:1
23:6 [a]Deut. 33:28; Zech. 14:11 [b]ch. 32:37 [c]ch. 33:16; 1 Cor. 1:30
23:7 [d]ch. 16:14
23:8 [e]Isa. 43:5; ver. 3
23:9 [f]Hab. 3:16
23:10 [g]ch. 5:7 [h]Hos. 4:2 [i]ch. 9:10
23:11 [j]ch. 6:13; Zeph. 3:4 [k]ch. 7:30; Ezek. 8:11
23:12 [l]Ps. 35:6; Prov. 4:19; ch. 13:16 [m]ch. 11:23
23:13 [n]ch. 2:8 [o]Isa. 9:16
23:14 [p]ch. 29:23 [q]ver. 26 [r]Ezek. 13:23 [s]Deut. 32:32; Isa. 1:9
23:15 [t]ch. 8:14
23:16 [u]ch. 14:14; ver. 21
23:17 [v]ch. 6:14; Ezek. 13:10; Zech. 10:2 [w]Mic. 3:11
23:18 [x]Job 15:8; 1 Cor. 2:16
23:19 [y]ch. 25:32
23:20 [z]ch. 30:24 [a]Gen. 49:1
23:21 [b]ch. 14:14
23:22 [c]ver. 18 [d]Jer. 25:5

23 *Am* I a God at hand, saith the LORD,
and not a God afar off?
24 Can any [e]hide himself in secret places
that I shall not see him? saith the LORD. [f]Do
not I fill heaven and earth? saith the LORD.
25 I have heard what the prophets said,
that prophesy lies in my name, saying, I
have dreamed, I have dreamed.
26 How long shall *this* be in the heart of
the prophets that prophesy lies? yea, *they*
are prophets of the deceit of their own
heart;
27 Which think to cause my people to forget my name by their dreams which they
tell every man to his neighbour, [g]as their
fathers have forgotten my name for Baal.
28 The prophet that hath a dream, let him
tell a dream; and he that hath my word, let
him speak my word faithfully. What *is* the
chaff to the wheat? saith the LORD.
29 *Is* not my word like as a fire? saith the
LORD; and like a hammer *that* breaketh the
rock in pieces?
30 Therefore, behold, [h]I *am* against the
prophets, saith the LORD, that steal my
words every one from his neighbour.
31 Behold, I *am* against the prophets,
saith the LORD, that use their tongues, and
say, He saith.
32 Behold, I *am* against them that prophesy false dreams, saith the LORD, and do tell
them, and cause my people to err by their
lies, and by [i]their lightness; yet I sent them
not, nor commanded them: therefore they
shall not profit this people at all, saith the
LORD.
33 ¶ And when this people, or the
prophet, or a priest, shall ask thee, saying,
What *is* [j]the burden of the LORD? thou shalt
then say unto them, What burden? [k]I will
even forsake you, saith the LORD.
34 And *as for* the prophet, and the priest,
and the people, that shall say, The burden of
the LORD, I will even punish that man and
his house.
35 Thus shall ye say every one to his
neighbour, and every one to his brother,
What hath the LORD answered? and, What
hath the LORD spoken?
36 And the burden of the LORD shall ye
mention no more; for every man's word
shall be his burden: for ye have perverted
the words of the living God, of the LORD of
hosts our God.
37 Thus shalt thou say to the prophet,
What hath the LORD answered thee? and,
What hath the LORD spoken?
38 But since ye say, The burden of the
LORD; therefore thus saith the LORD; Because ye say this word, The burden of the
LORD, and I have sent unto you, saying, Ye
shall not say, The burden of the LORD;
39 Therefore, behold, I, even I, [l]will utterly forget you, and [m]I will forsake you,
and the city that I gave you and your fathers, *and cast you* out of my presence:
40 And I will bring [n]an everlasting reproach upon you, and a perpetual shame,
which shall not be forgotten.

24 The [o]LORD shewed me, and, behold,
two baskets of figs *were* set before
the temple of the LORD, after that Nebuchadrezzar [p]king of Babylon had carried
away captive [q]Jeconiah the son of Jehoiakim king of Judah, and the princes of Judah, with the carpenters and smiths, from
Jerusalem, and had brought them to Babylon.
2 One basket *had* very good figs, *even* like
the figs *that are* first ripe: and the other
basket *had* very naughty figs, which could
not be eaten, they were so bad.
3 Then said the LORD unto me, What seest
thou, Jeremiah? And I said, Figs; the good
figs, very good; and the evil, very evil, that
cannot be eaten, they are so evil.
4 ¶ Again the word of the LORD came unto
me, saying,
5 Thus saith the LORD, the God of Israel;
Like these good figs, so will I acknowledge
them that are carried away captive of Judah, whom I have sent out of this place into
the land of the Chaldeans for *their* good.
6 For I will set mine eyes upon them for
good, and [r]I will bring them again to this
land: and [s]I will build them, and not pull
them down; and I will plant them, and not
pluck *them* up.
7 And I will give them [t]an heart to know
me, that I *am* the LORD: and they shall be
[u]my people, and I will be their God: for they
shall return unto me [v]with their whole
heart.
8 ¶ And as the evil [w]figs, which cannot be
eaten, they are so evil; surely thus saith the
LORD, So will I give Zedekiah the king of
Judah, and his princes, and the residue of
Jerusalem, that remain in this land, and
[x]them that dwell in the land of Egypt:
9 And I will deliver them to [y]be removed
into all the kingdoms of the earth for *their*
hurt, [z]*to be* a reproach and a proverb, a
taunt [a]and a curse, in all places whither I
shall drive them.
10 And I will send the sword, the famine,
and the pestilence, among them, till they be
consumed from off the land that I gave unto
them and to their fathers.

25 The word that came to Jeremiah concerning all the people of Judah [b]in
the fourth year of Jehoiakim the son of Josiah king of Judah, that *was* the first year of
Nebuchadrezzar king of Babylon;
2 The which Jeremiah the prophet spake
unto all the people of Judah, and to all the
inhabitants of Jerusalem, saying,
3 [c]From the thirteenth year of Josiah the
son of Amon king of Judah, even unto this
day, that *is* the three and twentieth year, the
word of the LORD hath come unto me, and
I have spoken unto you, rising early and
speaking; [d]but ye have not hearkened.
4 And the LORD hath sent unto you all his
servants the prophets, [e]rising early and

23:24 [e]Ps. 139:7; Am. 9:2 [f]1 Kings 8:27; Ps. 139:7
23:27 [g]Judg. 3:7
23:30 [h]Deut. 18:20; ch. 14:14
23:32 [i]Zeph. 3:4
23:33 [j]Mal. 1:1 [k]ver. 39
23:39 [l]Hos. 4:6 [m]ver. 33
23:40 [n]ch. 20:11
24:1 [o]Am. 7:1 [p]2 Kings 24:12; 2 Chron. 36:10 [q]ch. 22:24
24:6 [r]ch. 12:15 [s]ch. 32:41
24:7 [t]Deut. 30:6; ch. 32:39; Ezek. 11:19 [u]ch. 30:22 [v]ch. 29:13
24:8 [w]ch. 29:17 [x]ch. 43
24:9 [y]Deut. 28:25; 1 Kings 9:7; 2 Chron. 7:20; ch. 15:4 [z]Ps. 44:13 [a]ch. 29:18
25:1 [b]ch. 36:1
25:3 [c]ch. 1:2 [d]ch. 7:13
25:4 [e]ch. 7:13

sending *them;* but ye have not hearkened, nor inclined your ear to hear.

5 They said, [f]Turn ye again now every one from his evil way, and from the evil of your doings, and dwell in the land that the LORD hath given unto you and to your fathers for ever and ever:

6 And go not after other gods to serve them, and to worship them, and provoke me not to anger with the works of your hands; and I will do you no hurt.

7 Yet ye have not hearkened unto me, saith the LORD; that ye might [g]provoke me to anger with the works of your hands to your own hurt.

8 ¶ Therefore thus saith the LORD of hosts; Because ye have not heard my words,

9 Behold, I will send and take [h]all the families of the north, saith the LORD, and Nebuchadrezzar the king of Babylon, [i]my servant, and will bring them against this land, and against the inhabitants thereof, and against all these nations round about, and will utterly destroy them, and [j]make them an astonishment, and an hissing, and perpetual desolations.

10 Moreover I will take from them the [k]voice of mirth, and the voice of gladness, the voice of the bridegroom, and the voice of the bride, [l]the sound of the millstones, and the light of the candle.

11 And this whole land shall be a desolation, *and* an astonishment; and these nations shall serve the king of Babylon seventy years.

12 ¶ And it shall come to pass, [m]when seventy years are accomplished, *that* I will punish the king of Babylon, and that nation, saith the LORD, for their iniquity, and the land of the Chaldeans, [n]and will make it perpetual desolations.

13 And I will bring upon that land all my words which I have pronounced against it, *even* all that is written in this book, which Jeremiah hath prophesied against all the nations.

14 [o]For many nations [p]and great kings shall [q]serve themselves of them also: [r]and I will recompense them according to their deeds, and according to the works of their own hands.

15 ¶ For thus saith the LORD God of Israel unto me; Take the [s]wine cup of this fury at my hand, and cause all the nations, to whom I send thee, to drink it.

16 And [t]they shall drink, and be moved, and be mad, because of the sword that I will send among them.

17 Then took I the cup at the LORD's hand, and made all the nations to drink, unto whom the LORD had sent me:

18 *To wit,* Jerusalem, and the cities of Judah, and the kings thereof, and the princes thereof, to make them [u]a desolation, an astonishment, an hissing, and [v]a curse; as *it is* this day;

19 [w]Pharaoh king of Egypt, and his servants, and his princes, and all his people;

20 And all [x]the mingled people, and all the kings of [y]the land of Uz, [z]and all the kings of the land of the Philistines, and Ashkelon, and Azzah, and Ekron, and [a]the remnant of Ashdod,

21 [b]Edom, and [c]Moab, and the children of [d]Ammon,

22 And all the kings of [e]Tyrus, and all the kings of Zidon, and the kings of the isles which *are* beyond the [f]sea,

23 [g]Dedan, and Tema, and Buz, and all *that are* in the utmost corners,

24 And [h]all the kings of Arabia, and all the kings of the [i]mingled people that dwell in the desert,

25 And all the kings of Zimri, and all the kings of [j]Elam, and all the kings of the Medes,

26 [k]And all the kings of the north, far and near, one with another, and all the kingdoms of the world, which *are* upon the face of the earth: [l]and the king of Sheshach shall drink after them.

27 Therefore thou shalt say unto them, Thus saith the LORD of hosts, the God of Israel; [m]Drink ye, and [n]be drunken, and spue, and fall, and rise no more, because of the sword which I will send among you.

28 And it shall be, if they refuse to take the cup at thine hand to drink, then shalt thou say unto them, Thus saith the LORD of hosts; Ye shall certainly drink.

29 For, lo, [o]I begin to bring evil on the city [p]which is called by my name, and should ye be utterly unpunished? Ye shall not be unpunished: for [q]I will call for a sword upon all the inhabitants of the earth, saith the LORD of hosts.

30 Therefore prophesy thou against them all these words, and say unto them, The LORD shall [r]roar from on high, and utter his voice from [s]his holy habitation; he shall mightily roar upon [t]his habitation; he shall give [u]a shout, as they that tread *the grapes,* against all the inhabitants of the earth.

31 A noise shall come *even* to the ends of the earth; for the LORD hath [v]a controversy with the nations, [w]he will plead with all flesh; he will give them *that are* wicked to the sword, saith the LORD.

32 Thus saith the LORD of hosts, Behold, evil shall go forth from nation to nation, and [x]a great whirlwind shall be raised up from the coasts of the earth.

33 [y]And the slain of the LORD shall be at that day from *one* end of the earth even unto the *other* end of the earth: they shall not be [z]lamented, [a]neither gathered, nor buried; they shall be dung upon the ground.

34 ¶ [b]Howl, ye shepherds, and cry; and wallow yourselves *in the ashes,* ye principal of the flock: for the days of your slaughter and of your dispersions are accomplished; and ye shall fall like a pleasant vessel.

35 And the shepherds shall have no way to flee, nor the principal of the flock to escape.

36 A voice of the cry of the shepherds,

25:5 [f]2 Kings 17:13; ch. 18:11; Jonah 3:8
25:7 [g]Deut. 32:21; ch. 7:19
25:9 [h]ch. 1:15 [i]ch. 27:6; Isa. 44:28 [j]ch. 18:16
25:10 [k]Isa. 24:7; ch. 7:34; Ezek. 26:13; Hos. 2:11; Rev. 18:23 [l]Eccl. 12:4
25:12 [m]2 Chron. 36:21; Ezra 1:1; ch. 29:10; Dan. 9:2; 2 Kings 24:1; Ezra 1:1 [n]Isa. 13:19; ch. 50:3
25:14 [o]ch. 50:9 [p]ch. 50:41 [q]ch. 27:7 [r]ch. 50:29
25:15 [s]Job 21:20; Ps. 75:8; Isa. 51:17; Rev. 14:10
25:16 [t]ch. 51:7; Ezek. 23:34; Nah. 3:11
25:18 [u]ver. 9 [v]ch. 24:9
25:19 [w]ch. 46:2
25:20 [x]ver. 24 [y]Job 1:1 [z]ch. 47:1 [a]Isa. 20:1
25:21 [b]ch. 49:7 [c]ch. 48:1 [d]ch. 49:1
25:22 [e]ch. 47:4 [f]ch. 49:23
25:23 [g]ch. 49:8
25:24 [h]2 Chron. 9:14 [i]ver. 20; ch. 49:31; Ezek. 30:5
25:25 [j]ch. 49:34
25:26 [k]ch. 50:9 [l]ch. 51:41
25:27 [m]Hab. 2:16 [n]Isa. 51:21
25:29 [o]Prov. 11:31; ch. 49:12; Ezek. 9:6; Obad. 16; Luke 23:31; 1 Pet. 4:17 [p]Dan. 9:18 [q]Ezek. 38:21
25:30 [r]Isa. 42:13; Joel 3:16; Am. 1:2 [s]Ps. 11:4; ch. 17:12 [t]1 Kings 9:3; Ps. 132:14 [u]Isa. 16:9; ch. 48:33
25:31 [v]Hos. 4:1; Mic. 6:2 [w]Isa. 66:16; Joel 3:2
25:32 [x]ch. 23:19
25:33 [y]Isa. 66:16 [z]ch. 16:4 [a]Ps. 79:3; ch. 8:2; Rev. 11:9
25:34 [b]ch. 4:8

and an howling of the principal of the flock,
shall be heard: for the LORD hath spoiled
their pasture.
37 And the peaceable habitations are cut
down because of the fierce anger of the
LORD.
38 He hath forsaken [c]his covert, as the
lion: for their land is desolate because of the
fierceness of the oppressor, and because of
his fierce anger.

26 In the beginning of the reign of Jehoiakim the son of Josiah king of Judah came this word from the LORD, saying,
2 Thus saith the LORD; Stand in [d]the
court of the LORD's house, and speak unto
all the cities of Judah, which come to worship in the LORD's house, [e]all the words
that I command thee to speak unto them;
[f]diminish not a word:
3 [g]If so be they will hearken, and turn
every man from his evil way, that I may
[h]repent me of the evil, which I purpose to
do unto them because of the evil of their
doings.
4 And thou shalt say unto them, Thus
saith the LORD; [i]If ye will not hearken to
me, to walk in my law, which I have set
before you,
5 To hearken to the words of my servants
the prophets, [j]whom I sent unto you, both
rising up early, and sending *them,* but ye
have not hearkened;
6 Then will I make this house like [k]Shi-
loh, and will make this city [l]a curse to all
the nations of the earth.
7 So the priests and the prophets and all
the people heard Jeremiah speaking these
words in the house of the LORD.
8 ¶ Now it came to pass, when Jeremiah
had made an end of speaking all that the
LORD had commanded *him* to speak unto all
the people, that the priests and the prophets
and all the people took him, saying, Thou
shalt surely die.
9 Why hast thou prophesied in the name
of the LORD, saying, This house shall be like
Shiloh, and this city shall be desolate without an inhabitant? And all the people were
gathered against Jeremiah in the house of
the LORD.
10 ¶ When the princes of Judah heard
these things, then they came up from the
king's house unto the house of the LORD,
and sat down in the entry of the new gate of
the LORD's *house.*
11 Then spake the priests and the prophets unto the princes and to all the people,
saying, This man *is* worthy to die; [m]for he
hath prophesied against this city, as ye have
heard with your ears.
12 ¶ Then spake Jeremiah unto all the
princes and to all the people, saying, The
LORD sent me to prophesy against this
house and against this city all the words
that ye have heard.
13 Therefore now [n]amend your ways and
your doings, and obey the voice of the LORD
your God; and the LORD will [o]repent him of

25:38 [c]Ps. 76:2
26:2 [d]ch. 19:14 [e]Ezek. 3:10; Matt. 28:20 [f]Acts 20:27
26:3 [g]ch. 36:3 [h]ch. 18:8; Jonah 3:8
26:4 [i]Lev. 26:14; Deut. 28:15
26:5 [j]ch. 7:13
26:6 [k]1 Sam. 4:10; Ps. 78:60; ch. 7:12 [l]Isa. 65:15; ch. 24:9
26:11 [m]ch. 38:4
26:13 [n]ch. 7:3 [o]ver. 3
26:14 [p]ch. 38:5
26:17 [q]Acts 5:34
26:18 [r]Mic. 1:1 [s]Mic. 3:12
26:19 [t]2 Chron. 32:26 [u]Ex. 32:14; 2 Sam. 24:16 [v]Acts 5:39
26:24 [w]2 Kings 22:12; ch. 39:14
27:1 [x]ver. 3; ch. 28:1
27:2 [y]ch. 28:10; Ezek. 4:1

the evil that he hath pronounced against
you.
14 As for me, behold, [p]I *am* in your hand:
do with me as seemeth good and meet unto
you.
15 But know ye for certain, that if ye put
me to death, ye shall surely bring innocent
blood upon yourselves, and upon this city,
and upon the inhabitants thereof: for of a
truth the LORD hath sent me unto you to
speak all these words in your ears.
16 ¶ Then said the princes and all the people unto the priests and to the prophets;
This man *is* not worthy to die: for he hath
spoken to us in the name of the LORD our
God.
17 [q]Then rose up certain of the elders of
the land, and spake to all the assembly of
the people, saying,
18 [r]Micah the Morasthite prophesied in
the days of Hezekiah king of Judah, and
spake to all the people of Judah, saying,
Thus saith the LORD of hosts; [s]Zion shall be
plowed *like* a field, and Jerusalem shall become heaps, and the mountain of the house
as the high places of a forest.
19 Did Hezekiah king of Judah and all Judah put him at all to death? [t]did he not fear
the LORD, and besought the LORD, and the
LORD [u]repented him of the evil which he
had pronounced against them? [v]Thus
might we procure great evil against our
souls.
20 And there was also a man that prophesied in the name of the LORD, Urijah the son
of Shemaiah of Kirjath-jearim, who prophesied against this city and against this land
according to all the words of Jeremiah:
21 And when Jehoiakim the king, with all
his mighty men, and all the princes, heard
his words, the king sought to put him to
death: but when Urijah heard it, he was
afraid, and fled, and went into Egypt;
22 And Jehoiakim the king sent men into
Egypt, *namely,* Elnathan the son of Achbor,
and *certain* men with him into Egypt.
23 And they fetched forth Urijah out of
Egypt, and brought him unto Jehoiakim the
king; who slew him with the sword, and cast
his dead body into the graves of the common people.
24 Nevertheless [w]the hand of Ahikam the
son of Shaphan was with Jeremiah, that
they should not give him into the hand of
the people to put him to death.

27 In the beginning of the reign of Jehoiakim the son of Josiah [x]king of
Judah came this word unto Jeremiah from
the LORD, saying,
2 Thus saith the LORD to me; Make thee
bonds and yokes, [y]and put them upon thy
neck,
3 And send them to the king of Edom, and
to the king of Moab, and to the king of the
Ammonites, and to the king of Tyrus, and to
the king of Zidon, by the hand of the messengers which come to Jerusalem unto Zedekiah king of Judah;

4 And command them to say unto their masters, Thus saith the LORD of hosts, the God of Israel; Thus shall ye say unto your masters;

5 [z]I have made the earth, the man and the beast that *are* upon the ground, by my great power and by my outstretched arm, and [a]have given it unto whom it seemed meet unto me.

6 [b]And now have I given all these lands into the hand of Nebuchadnezzar the king of Babylon, [c]my servant; and [d]the beasts of the field have I given him also to serve him.

7 [e]And all nations shall serve him, and his son, and his son's son, [f]until the very time of his land come: [g]and then many nations and great kings shall serve themselves of him.

8 And it shall come to pass, *that* the nation and kingdom which will not serve the same Nebuchadnezzar the king of Babylon, and that will not put their neck under the yoke of the king of Babylon, that nation will I punish, saith the LORD, with the sword, and with the famine, and with the pestilence, until I have consumed them by his hand.

9 Therefore hearken not ye to your prophets, nor to your diviners, nor to your dreamers, nor to your enchanters, nor to your sorcerers, which speak unto you, saying, Ye shall not serve the king of Babylon:

10 [h]For they prophesy a lie unto you, to remove you far from your land; and that I should drive you out, and ye should perish.

11 But the nations that bring their neck under the yoke of the king of Babylon, and serve him, those will I let remain still in their own land, saith the LORD; and they shall till it, and dwell therein.

12 ¶ I spake also to [i]Zedekiah king of Judah according to all these words, saying, Bring your necks under the yoke of the king of Babylon, and serve him and his people, and live.

13 [j]Why will ye die, thou and thy people, by the sword, by the famine, and by the pestilence, as the LORD hath spoken against the nation that will not serve the king of Babylon?

14 Therefore hearken not unto the words of the prophets that speak unto you, saying, Ye shall not serve the king of Babylon: for they prophesy [k]a lie unto you.

15 For I have not sent them, saith the LORD, yet they prophesy a lie in my name; that I might drive you out, and that ye might perish, ye, and the prophets that prophesy unto you.

16 Also I spake to the priests and to all this people, saying, Thus saith the LORD; Hearken not to the words of your prophets that prophesy unto you, saying, Behold, [l]the vessels of the LORD's house shall now shortly be brought again from Babylon: for they prophesy a lie unto you.

17 Hearken not unto them; serve the king of Babylon, and live: wherefore should this city be laid waste?

18 But if they *be* prophets, and if the word of the LORD be with them, let them now make intercession to the LORD of hosts, that the vessels which are left in the house of the LORD, and *in* the house of the king of Judah, and at Jerusalem, go not to Babylon.

19 ¶ For thus saith the LORD of hosts [m]concerning the pillars, and concerning the sea, and concerning the bases, and concerning the residue of the vessels that remain in this city,

20 Which Nebuchadnezzar king of Babylon took not, when he carried away [n]captive Jeconiah the son of Jehoiakim king of Judah from Jerusalem to Babylon, and all the nobles of Judah and Jerusalem;

21 Yea, thus saith the LORD of hosts, the God of Israel, concerning the vessels that remain *in* the house of the LORD, and *in* the house of the king of Judah and of Jerusalem;

22 They shall be [o]carried to Babylon, and there shall they be until the day that I [p]visit them, saith the LORD; then [q]will I bring them up, and restore them to this place.

28

And [r]it came to pass the same year, in the beginning of the reign of Zedekiah king of Judah, in the fourth year, *and* in the fifth month, *that* Hananiah the son of Azur the prophet, which *was* of Gibeon, spake unto me in the house of the LORD, in the presence of the priests and of all the people, saying,

2 Thus speaketh the LORD of hosts, the God of Israel, saying, I have broken [s]the yoke of the king of Babylon.

3 [t]Within two full years will I bring again into this place all the vessels of the LORD's house, that Nebuchadnezzar king of Babylon took away from this place, and carried them to Babylon:

4 And I will bring again to this place Jeconiah the son of Jehoiakim king of Judah, with all the captives of Judah, that went into Babylon, saith the LORD: for I will break the yoke of the king of Babylon.

5 ¶ Then the prophet Jeremiah said unto the prophet Hananiah in the presence of the priests, and in the presence of all the people that stood in the house of the LORD,

6 Even the prophet Jeremiah said, [u]Amen: the LORD do so: the LORD perform thy words which thou hast prophesied, to bring again the vessels of the LORD's house, and all that is carried away captive, from Babylon into this place.

7 Nevertheless hear thou now this word that I speak in thine ears, and in the ears of all the people;

8 The prophets that have been before me and before thee of old prophesied both against many countries, and against great kingdoms, of war, and of evil, and of pestilence.

9 [v]The prophet which prophesieth of peace, when the word of the prophet shall

27:5 [z]Ps. 115:15; Isa. 45:12 [a]Ps. 115:16; Dan. 4:17
27:6 [b]ch. 28:14 [c]ch. 25:9; Ezek. 29:18 [d]ch. 28:14; Dan. 2:38
27:7 [e]2 Chron. 36:20 [f]ch. 25:12; Dan. 5:26 [g]ch. 25:14
27:10 [h]ver. 14
27:12 [i]ch. 28:1
27:13 [j]Ezek. 18:31
27:14 [k]ch. 14:14
27:16 [l]2 Chron. 36:7; ch. 28:3; Dan. 1:2
27:19 [m]2 Kings 25:13; ch. 52:17
27:20 [n]2 Kings 24:14; ch. 24:1
27:22 [o]2 Kings 25:13; 2 Chron. 36:18 [p]2 Chron. 36:21; ch. 29:10 [q]Ezra 1:7
28:1 [r]ch. 27:1
28:2 [s]ch. 27:12
28:3 [t]ch. 27:16
28:6 [u]1 Kings 1:36
28:9 [v]Deut. 18:22

come to pass, *then* shall the prophet be known, that the LORD hath truly sent him.

10 ¶ Then Hananiah the prophet took the [w]yoke from off the prophet Jeremiah's neck, and brake it.

11 And Hananiah spake in the presence of all the people, saying, Thus saith the LORD; Even so will I break the yoke of Nebuchadnezzar king of Babylon [x]from the neck of all nations within the space of two full years. And the prophet Jeremiah went his way.

12 ¶ Then the word of the LORD came unto Jeremiah *the prophet*, after that Hananiah the prophet had broken the yoke from off the neck of the prophet Jeremiah, saying,

13 Go and tell Hananiah, saying, Thus saith the LORD; Thou hast broken the yokes of wood; but thou shalt make for them yokes of iron.

14 For thus saith the LORD of hosts, the God of Israel; [y]I have put a yoke of iron upon the neck of all these nations, that they may serve Nebuchadnezzar king of Babylon; and they shall serve him: and [z]I have given him the beasts of the field also.

15 ¶ Then said the prophet Jeremiah unto Hananiah the prophet, Hear now, Hananiah; The LORD hath not sent thee; but [a]thou makest this people to trust in a lie.

16 Therefore thus saith the LORD; Behold, I will cast thee from off the face of the earth: this year thou shalt die, because thou hast taught [b]rebellion against the LORD.

17 So Hananiah the prophet died the same year in the seventh month.

29

Now these *are* the words of the letter that Jeremiah the prophet sent from Jerusalem unto the residue of the elders which were carried away captives, and to the priests, and to the prophets, and to all the people whom Nebuchadnezzar had carried away captive from Jerusalem to Babylon;

2 (After that [c]Jeconiah the king, and the queen, and the eunuchs, the princes of Judah and Jerusalem, and the carpenters, and the smiths, were departed from Jerusalem;)

3 By the hand of Elasah the son of Shaphan, and Gemariah the son of Hilkiah, (whom Zedekiah king of Judah sent unto Babylon to Nebuchadnezzar king of Babylon) saying,

4 Thus saith the LORD of hosts, the God of Israel, unto all that are carried away captives, whom I have caused to be carried away from Jerusalem unto Babylon;

5 [d]Build ye houses, and dwell *in them;* and plant gardens, and eat the fruit of them;

6 Take ye wives, and beget sons and daughters; and take wives for your sons, and give your daughters to husbands, that they may bear sons and daughters; that ye may be increased there, and not diminished.

7 And seek the peace of the city whither I have caused you to be carried away captives, [e]and pray unto the LORD for it: for in the peace thereof shall ye have peace.

8 ¶ For thus saith the LORD of hosts, the God of Israel; Let not your prophets and your diviners, that *be* in the midst of you, [f]deceive you, neither hearken to your dreams which ye cause to be dreamed.

9 [g]For they prophesy falsely unto you in my name: I have not sent them, saith the LORD.

10 ¶ For thus saith the LORD, That after [h]seventy years be accomplished at Babylon I will visit you, and perform my good word toward you, in causing you to return to this place.

11 For I know the thoughts that I think toward you, saith the LORD, thoughts of peace, and not of evil, to give you an expected end.

12 Then shall ye [i]call upon me, and ye shall go and pray unto me, and I will hearken unto you.

13 And [j]ye shall seek me, and find *me,* when ye shall search for me [k]with all your heart.

14 And [l]I will be found of you, saith the LORD: and I will turn away your captivity, and [m]I will gather you from all the nations, and from all the places whither I have driven you, saith the LORD; and I will bring you again into the place whence I caused you to be carried away captive.

15 ¶ Because ye have said, The LORD hath raised us up prophets in Babylon;

16 *Know* that thus saith the LORD of the king that sitteth upon the throne of David, and of all the people that dwelleth in this city, *and* of your brethren that are not gone forth with you into captivity;

17 Thus saith the LORD of hosts; Behold, I will send upon them the [n]sword, the famine, and the pestilence, and will make them like [o]vile figs, that cannot be eaten, they are so evil.

18 And I will persecute them with the sword, with the famine, and with the pestilence, and [p]will deliver them to be removed to all the kingdoms of the earth, to be [q]a curse, and an astonishment, and an hissing, and a reproach, among all the nations whither I have driven them:

19 Because they have not hearkened to my words, saith the LORD, which [r]I sent unto them by my servants the prophets, rising up early and sending *them;* but ye would not hear, saith the LORD.

20 ¶ Hear ye therefore the word of the LORD, all ye of the captivity, whom I have sent from Jerusalem to Babylon:

21 Thus saith the LORD of hosts, the God of Israel, of Ahab the son of Kolaiah, and of Zedekiah the son of Maaseiah, which prophesy a lie unto you in my name; Behold, I will deliver them into the hand of Nebuchadrezzar king of Babylon; and he shall slay them before your eyes;

22 [s]And of them shall be taken up a curse by all the captivity of Judah which *are* in

28:10 [w]ch. 27:2
28:11 [x]ch. 27:7
28:14 [y]Deut. 28:48; ch. 27:4 [z]ch. 27:6
28:15 [a]ch. 29:31; Ezek. 13:22
28:16 [b]Deut. 13:5; ch. 29:32
29:2 [c]2 Kings 24:12; ch. 22:26
29:5 [d]ver. 28
29:7 [e]Ezra 6:10; 1 Tim. 2:2
29:8 [f]ch. 14:14; Eph. 5:6
29:9 [g]ver. 31
29:10 [h]2 Chron. 36:21; Ezra 1:1; ch. 25:12; Dan. 9:2
29:12 [i]Dan. 9:3
29:13 [j]Lev. 26:39; Deut. 30:1 [k]ch. 24:7
29:14 [l]Deut. 4:7; Ps. 32:6; Isa. 55:6 [m]ch. 23:3
29:17 [n]ch. 24:10 [o]ch. 24:8
29:18 [p]Deut. 28:25; 2 Chron. 29:8; ch. 15:4 [q]ch. 20:6; ch. 42:18
29:19 [r]ch. 25:4
29:22 [s]Gen. 48:20; Isa. 65:15

Babylon, saying, The LORD make thee like Zedekiah and like Ahab, [t]whom the king of Babylon roasted in the fire;

23 Because [u]they have committed villany in Israel, and have committed adultery with their neighbours' wives, and have spoken lying words in my name, which I have not commanded them; even I know, and *am* a witness, saith the LORD.

24 ¶ *Thus* shalt thou also speak to Shemaiah the Nehelamite, saying,

25 Thus speaketh the LORD of hosts, the God of Israel, saying, Because thou hast sent letters in thy name unto all the people that *are* at Jerusalem, [v]and to Zephaniah the son of Maaseiah the priest, and to all the priests, saying,

26 The LORD hath made thee priest in the stead of Jehoiada the priest, that ye should be [w]officers in the house of the LORD, for every man *that is* [x]mad, and maketh himself a prophet, that thou shouldest [y]put him in prison, and in the stocks.

27 Now therefore why hast thou not reproved Jeremiah of Anathoth, which maketh himself a prophet to you?

28 For therefore he sent unto us *in* Babylon, saying, This *captivity is* long: [z]build ye houses, and dwell *in them;* and plant gardens, and eat the fruit of them.

29 And Zephaniah the priest read this letter in the ears of Jeremiah the prophet.

30 ¶ Then came the word of the LORD unto Jeremiah, saying,

31 Send to all them of the captivity, saying, Thus saith the LORD concerning Shemaiah the Nehelamite; Because that Shemaiah hath prophesied unto you, [a]and I sent him not, and he caused you to trust in a lie:

32 Therefore thus saith the LORD; Behold, I will punish Shemaiah the Nehelamite, and his seed: he shall not have a man to dwell among this people; neither shall he behold the good that I will do for my people, saith the LORD; [b]because he hath taught rebellion against the LORD.

30

The word that came to Jeremiah from the LORD, saying,

2 Thus speaketh the LORD God of Israel, saying, Write thee all the words that I have spoken unto thee in a book.

3 For, lo, the days come, saith the LORD, that [c]I will bring again the captivity of my people Israel and Judah, saith the LORD: [d]and I will cause them to return to the land that I gave to their fathers, and they shall possess it.

4 ¶ And these *are* the words that the LORD spake concerning Israel and concerning Judah.

5 For thus saith the LORD; We have heard a voice of trembling, of fear, and not of peace.

6 Ask ye now, and see whether a man doth travail with child? wherefore do I see every man with his hands on his loins, [e]as a woman in travail, and all faces are turned into paleness?

7 [f]Alas! for that day *is* great, [g]so that none *is* like it: it *is* even the time of Jacob's trouble; but he shall be saved out of it.

8 For it shall come to pass in that day, saith the LORD of hosts, *that* I will break his yoke from off thy neck, and will burst thy bonds, and strangers shall no more serve themselves of him:

9 But they shall serve the LORD their God, and [h]David their king, whom I will [i]raise up unto them.

10 ¶ Therefore [j]fear thou not, O my servant Jacob, saith the LORD; neither be dismayed, O Israel: for, lo, I will save thee from afar, and thy seed [k]from the land of their captivity; and Jacob shall return, and shall be in rest, and be quiet, and none shall make *him* afraid.

11 For I *am* with thee, saith the LORD, to save thee: [l]though I make a full end of all nations whither I have scattered thee, [m]yet will I not make a full end of thee: but I will correct thee [n]in measure, and will not leave thee altogether unpunished.

12 For thus saith the LORD, [o]Thy bruise *is* incurable, *and* thy wound *is* grievous.

13 *There is* none to plead thy cause, that thou mayest be bound up: [p]thou hast no healing medicines.

14 [q]All thy lovers have forgotten thee; they seek thee not; for I have wounded thee with the wound [r]of an enemy, with the chastisement [s]of a cruel one, for the multitude of thine iniquity; [t]*because* thy sins were increased.

15 Why [u]criest thou for thine affliction? thy sorrow *is* incurable for the multitude of thine iniquity: *because* thy sins were increased, I have done these things unto thee.

16 Therefore all they that devour thee [v]shall be devoured; and all thine adversaries, every one of them, shall go into captivity; and they that spoil thee shall be a spoil, and all that prey upon thee will I give for a prey.

17 [w]For I will restore health unto thee, and I will heal thee of thy wounds, saith the LORD; because they called thee an Outcast, *saying,* This *is* Zion, whom no man seeketh after.

18 ¶ Thus saith the LORD; Behold, [x]I will bring again the captivity of Jacob's tents, and [y]have mercy on his dwellingplaces; and the city shall be builded upon her own heap, and the palace shall remain after the manner thereof.

19 And [z]out of them shall proceed thanksgiving and the voice of them that make merry: [a]and I will multiply them, and they shall not be few; I will also glorify them, and they shall not be small.

20 Their children also shall be [b]as aforetime, and their congregation shall be established before me, and I will punish all that oppress them.

21 And their nobles shall be of them-

29:22 [t]Dan. 3:6
29:23 [u]ch. 23:14
29:25 [v]2 Kings 25:18; ch. 21:1
29:26 [w]ch. 20:1 [x]2 Kings 9:11; Acts 26:24 [y]ch. 20:2
29:28 [z]ver. 5
29:31 [a]ch. 28:15
29:32 [b]ch. 28:16
30:3 [c]ver. 18; ch. 32:44; Ezek. 39:25; Am. 9:14 [d]ch. 16:15
30:6 [e]ch. 4:31
30:7 [f]Joel 2:11; Am. 5:18; Zeph 1:14 [g]Dan. 12:1
30:9 [h]Isa. 55:3; Ezek. 34:23; Hos. 3:5 [i]Luke 1:69; Acts 2:30
30:10 [j]Isa. 41:13; ch. 46:27 [k]ch. 3:18
30:11 [l]Am. 9:8 [m]ch. 4:27 [n]Ps. 6:1; Isa. 27:8; ch. 10:24
30:12 [o]2 Chron. 36:16; ch. 15:18
30:13 [p]ch. 8:22
30:14 [q]Lam. 1:2 [r]Job 13:24 [s]Job 30:21 [t]ch. 5:6
30:15 [u]ch. 15:18
30:16 [v]Ex. 23:22; Isa. 33:1; ch. 10:25
30:17 [w]ch. 33:6
30:18 [x]ver. 3; ch. 33:7 [y]Ps. 102:13
30:19 [z]Isa. 35:10; ch. 31:4 [a]Zech. 10:8
30:20 [b]Isa. 1:26

selves, [c]and their governor shall proceed from the midst of them; and I will [d]cause him to draw near, and he shall approach unto me: for who *is* this that engaged his heart to approach unto me? saith the LORD.

22 And ye shall be [e]my people, and I will be your God.

23 Behold, the [f]whirlwind of the LORD goeth forth with fury, a continuing whirlwind: it shall fall with pain upon the head of the wicked.

24 The fierce anger of the LORD shall not return, until he hath done *it*, and until he have performed the intents of his heart: [g]in the latter days ye shall consider it.

31 At [h]the same time, saith the LORD, [i]will I be the God of all the families of Israel, and they shall be my people.

2 Thus saith the LORD, The people *which were* left of the sword found grace in the wilderness; *even* Israel, when [j]I went to cause him to rest.

3 The LORD hath appeared of old unto me, *saying*, Yea, [k]I have loved thee with [l]an everlasting love: therefore with lovingkindness have I [m]drawn thee.

4 Again [n]I will build thee, and thou shalt be built, O virgin of Israel: thou shalt again be adorned with thy [o]tabrets, and shalt go forth in the dances of them that make merry.

5 [p]Thou shalt yet plant vines upon the mountains of Samaria: the planters shall plant, and shall eat *them* as common things.

6 For there shall be a day, *that* the watchmen upon the mount Ephraim shall cry, [q]Arise ye, and let us go up to Zion unto the LORD our God.

7 For thus saith the LORD; [r]Sing with gladness for Jacob, and shout among the chief of the nations: publish ye, praise ye, and say, O LORD, save thy people, the remnant of Israel.

8 Behold, I will bring them [s]from the north country, and [t]gather them from the coasts of the earth, *and* with them the blind and the lame, the woman with child and her that travaileth with child together: a great company shall return thither.

9 [u]They shall come with weeping, and with supplications, will I lead them: I will cause them to walk [v]by the rivers of waters in a straight way, wherein they shall not stumble: for I am a father to Israel, and Ephraim *is* my [w]firstborn.

10 ¶ Hear the word of the LORD, O ye nations, and declare *it* in the isles afar off, and say, He that scattered Israel [x]will gather him, and keep him, as a shepherd *doth* his flock.

11 For [y]the LORD hath redeemed Jacob, and ransomed him [z]from the hand of *him that was* stronger than he.

12 Therefore they shall come and sing in [a]the height of Zion, and shall flow together to [b]the goodness of the LORD, for wheat, and for wine, and for oil, and for the young of the flock and of the herd: and their soul shall be as a [c]watered garden; [d]and they shall not sorrow any more at all.

13 Then shall the virgin rejoice in the dance, both young men and old together: for I will turn their mourning into joy, and will comfort them, and make them rejoice from their sorrow.

14 And I will satiate the soul of the priests with fatness, and my people shall be satisfied with my goodness, saith the LORD.

15 ¶ Thus saith the LORD; [e]A voice was heard in [f]Ramah, lamentation, *and* bitter weeping; Rahel weeping for her children refused to be comforted for her children, because [g]they *were* not.

16 Thus saith the LORD; Refrain thy voice from weeping, and thine eyes from tears: for thy work shall be rewarded, saith the LORD; and [h]they shall come again from the land of the enemy.

17 And there is hope in thine end, saith the LORD, that thy children shall come again to their own border.

18 ¶ I have surely heard Ephraim bemoaning himself *thus;* Thou hast chastised me, and I was chastised, as a bullock unaccustomed *to the yoke:* [i]turn thou me, and I shall be turned; for thou *art* the LORD my God.

19 Surely [j]after that I was turned, I repented; and after that I was instructed, I smote upon *my* thigh: I was ashamed, yea, even confounded, because I did bear the reproach of my youth.

20 *Is* Ephraim my dear son? *is he* a pleasant child? for since I spake against him, I do earnestly remember him still: [k]therefore my bowels are troubled for him; [l]I will surely have mercy upon him, saith the LORD.

21 Set thee up waymarks, make thee high heaps: [m]set thine heart toward the highway, *even* the way *which* thou wentest: turn again, O virgin of Israel, turn again to these thy cities.

22 ¶ How long wilt thou [n]go about, O thou [o]backsliding daughter? for the LORD hath created a new thing in the earth, A woman shall compass a man.

23 Thus saith the LORD of hosts, the God of Israel; As yet they shall use this speech in the land of Judah and in the cities thereof, when I shall bring again their captivity; [p]The LORD bless thee, O habitation of justice, *and* [q]mountain of holiness.

24 And there shall dwell in Judah itself, and [r]in all the cities thereof together, husbandmen, and they *that* go forth with flocks.

25 For I have satiated the weary soul, and I have replenished every sorrowful soul.

26 Upon this I awaked, and beheld; and my sleep was sweet unto me.

27 ¶ Behold, the days come, saith the LORD, that [s]I will sow the house of Israel and the house of Judah with the seed of man, and with the seed of beast.

28 And it shall come to pass, *that* like as

30:21 [c]Gen. 49:10 [d]Num. 16:5
30:22 [e]ch. 24:7; Ezek. 11:20
30:23 [f]ch. 23:19
30:24 [g]Gen. 49:1
31:1 [h]ch. 30:24 [i]ch. 30:22
31:2 [j]Num. 10:33; Deut. 1:33; Ps. 95:11; Isa. 63:14
31:3 [k]Mal. 1:2 [l]Rom. 11:28 [m]Hos. 11:4
31:4 [n]ch. 33:7 [o]Ex. 15:20; Judg. 11:34; Ps. 149:3
31:5 [p]Isa. 65:21; Am. 9:14
31:6 [q]Isa. 2:3; Mic. 4:2
31:7 [r]Isa. 12:5
31:8 [s]ch. 3:12 [t]Ezek. 20:34
31:9 [u]Ps. 126:5; ch. 50:4 [v]Isa. 35:8 [w]Ex. 4:22
31:10 [x]Isa. 40:11; Ezek. 34:12
31:11 [y]Isa. 44:23 [z]Isa. 49:24
31:12 [a]Ezek. 17:23 [b]Hos. 3:5 [c]Isa. 58:11 [d]Isa. 35:10; Rev. 21:4
31:15 [e]Matt. 2:17 [f]Josh. 18:25 [g]Gen. 42:13
31:16 [h]ver. 4; Ezra 1:5; Hos. 1:11
31:18 [i]Lam. 5:21
31:19 [j]Deut. 30:2
31:20 [k]Deut. 32:36; Isa. 63:15; Hos. 11:8 [l]Isa. 57:18; Hos. 14:4
31:21 [m]ch. 50:5
31:22 [n]ch. 2:18 [o]ch. 3:6
31:23 [p]Ps. 122:5; Isa. 1:26 [q]Zech. 8:3
31:24 [r]ch. 33:12
31:27 [s]Ezek. 36:9; Hos. 2:23; Zech. 10:9

I have [t]watched over them, [u]to pluck up,
and to break down, and to throw down, and
to destroy, and to afflict; so will I watch over
them, [v]to build, and to plant, saith the
LORD.
29 [w]In those days they shall say no more,
The fathers have eaten a sour grape, and
the children's teeth are set on edge.
30 [x]But every one shall die for his own
iniquity: every man that eateth the sour
grape, his teeth shall be set on edge.
31 ¶ Behold, the [y]days come, saith the
LORD, that I will make a new covenant with
the house of Israel, and with the house of
Judah:
32 Not according to the covenant that I
made with their fathers in the day *that* [z]I
took them by the hand to bring them out of
the land of Egypt; which my covenant they
brake, although I was an husband unto
them, saith the LORD:
33 [a]But this *shall be* the covenant that I
will make with the house of Israel; After
those days, saith the LORD, [b]I will put my
law in their inward parts, and write it in
their hearts; [c]and will be their God, and
they shall be my people.
34 And they shall teach no more every
man his neighbour, and every man his
brother, saying, Know the LORD: for [d]they
shall all know me, from the least of them
unto the greatest of them, saith the LORD:
for [e]I will forgive their iniquity, and I will
remember their sin no more.
35 ¶ Thus saith the LORD, [f]which giveth
the sun for a light by day, *and* the ordinances of the moon and of the stars for a
light by night, which divideth [g]the sea
when the waves thereof roar; [h]The LORD of
hosts *is* his name:
36 [i]If those ordinances depart from before me, saith the LORD, *then* the seed of
Israel also shall cease from being a nation
before me for ever.
37 Thus saith the LORD; [j]If heaven above
can be measured, and the foundations of the
earth searched out beneath, I will also cast
off all the seed of Israel for all that they
have done, saith the LORD.
38 ¶ Behold, the days come, saith the
LORD, that the city shall be built to the LORD
[k]from the tower of Hananeel unto the gate
of the corner.
39 And [l]the measuring line shall yet go
forth over against it upon the hill Gareb,
and shall compass about to Goath.
40 And the whole valley of the dead bodies, and of the ashes, and all the fields unto
the brook of Kidron, [m]unto the corner of the
horse gate toward the east, [n]*shall be* holy
unto the LORD; it shall not be plucked up,
nor thrown down any more for ever.

32

The word that came to Jeremiah
from the LORD [o]in the tenth year of
Zedekiah king of Judah, which *was* the
eighteenth year of Nebuchadrezzar.
2 For then the king of Babylon's army
besieged Jerusalem: and Jeremiah the
prophet was shut up [p]in the court of the
prison, which *was* in the king of Judah's
house.
3 For Zedekiah king of Judah had shut
him up, saying, Wherefore dost thou prophesy, and say, Thus saith the LORD, [q]Behold,
I will give this city into the hand of the king
of Babylon, and he shall take it;
4 And Zedekiah king of Judah [r]shall not
escape out of the hand of the Chaldeans, but
shall surely be delivered into the hand of
the king of Babylon, and shall speak with
him mouth to mouth, and his eyes shall behold his eyes;
5 And he shall lead Zedekiah to Babylon,
and there shall he be [s]until I visit him, saith
the LORD: [t]though ye fight with the Chaldeans, ye shall not prosper.
6 ¶ And Jeremiah said, The word of the
LORD came unto me, saying,
7 Behold, Hanameel the son of Shallum
thine uncle shall come unto thee, saying,
Buy thee my field that *is* in Anathoth: for
the [u]right of redemption *is* thine to buy *it*.
8 So Hanameel mine uncle's son came to
me in the court of the prison according to
the word of the LORD, and said unto me, Buy
my field, I pray thee, that *is* in Anathoth,
which *is* in the country of Benjamin: for the
right of inheritance *is* thine, and the redemption *is* thine; buy *it* for thyself. Then I
knew that this *was* the word of the LORD.
9 And I bought the field of Hanameel my
uncle's son, that *was* in Anathoth, and
[v]weighed him the money, *even* seventeen
shekels of silver.
10 And I subscribed the evidence, and
sealed *it*, and took witnesses, and weighed
him the money in the balances.
11 So I took the evidence of the purchase,
both that which was sealed *according* to the
law and custom, and that which was open:
12 And I gave the evidence of the purchase unto [w]Baruch the son of Neriah, the
son of Maaseiah, in the sight of Hanameel
mine uncle's *son*, and in the presence of the
[x]witnesses that subscribed the book of the
purchase, before all the Jews that sat in
the court of the prison.
13 ¶ And I charged Baruch before them,
saying,
14 Thus saith the LORD of hosts, the God
of Israel; Take these evidences, this evidence of the purchase, both which is sealed,
and this evidence which is open; and put
them in an earthen vessel, that they may
continue many days.
15 For thus saith the LORD of hosts, the
God of Israel; Houses and fields and vineyards [y]shall be possessed again in this
land.
16 ¶ Now when I had delivered the evidence of the purchase unto Baruch the son
of Neriah, I prayed unto the LORD, saying,
17 Ah Lord GOD! behold, [z]thou hast
made the heaven and the earth by thy great
power and stretched out arm, *and* [a]there is
nothing too hard for thee:

31:28 [t]ch. 44:27 [u]ch. 1:10 [v]ch. 24:6
31:29 [w]Ezek. 18:2
31:30 [x]Gal. 6:5
31:31 [y]ch. 32:40; Ezek. 37:26; Heb. 8:8-12
31:32 [z]Deut. 1:31
31:33 [a]ch. 32:40 [b]Ps. 40:8; Ezek. 11:19; 2 Cor. 3:3 [c]ch. 24:7
31:34 [d]Isa. 54:13; John 6:45; 1 Cor. 2:10; 1 John 2:20 [e]ch. 33:8; Mic. 7:18; Acts 10:43; Rom. 11:27
31:35 [f]Gen. 1:16; Ps. 72:5 [g]Isa. 51:15 [h]ch. 10:16
31:36 [i]Ps. 148:6; Isa. 54:9; ch. 33:20
31:37 [j]ch. 33:22
31:38 [k]Neh. 3:1; Zech. 14:10
31:39 [l]Ezek. 40:8; Zech. 2:1
31:40 [m]2 Chron. 23:15; Neh. 3:28 [n]Joel 3:17
32:1 [o]2 Kings 25:1; Jer. 39:1
32:2 [p]Neh. 3:25; ch. 33:1
32:3 [q]ch. 34:2
32:4 [r]ch. 34:3
32:5 [s]ch. 27:22 [t]ch. 21:4
32:7 [u]Lev. 25:24; Ruth 4:4
32:9 [v]Gen. 23:16; Zech. 11:12
32:12 [w]ch. 36:4 [x]Isa. 8:2
32:15 [y]ver. 37
32:17 [z]2 Kings 19:15 [a]Gen. 18:14; ver. 27; Luke 1:37

18 Thou shewest [b]lovingkindness unto
thousands, and recompensest the iniquity
of the fathers into the bosom of their children after them: the Great, [c]the Mighty
God, [d]the LORD of hosts, *is* his name;
19 [e]Great in counsel, and mighty in
work: for thine [f]eyes *are* open upon all the
ways of the sons of men: [g]to give every one
according to his ways, and according to the
fruit of his doings:
20 Which hast set signs and wonders in
the land of Egypt, *even* unto this day, and
in Israel, and among *other* men; and hast
made thee [h]a name, as at this day;
21 And [i]hast brought forth thy people Israel out of the land of Egypt with signs, and
with wonders, and with a strong hand, and
with a stretched out arm, and with great
terror;
22 And hast given them this land, which
thou didst swear to their fathers to give
them, [j]a land flowing with milk and honey;
23 And they came in, and possessed it;
but [k]they obeyed not thy voice, neither
walked in thy law; they have done nothing
of all that thou commandedst them to do:
therefore thou hast caused all this evil to
come upon them:
24 Behold the mounts, they are come unto
the city to take it; and the city [l]is given
into the hand of the Chaldeans, that fight
against it, because of [m]the sword, and of the
famine, and of the pestilence: and what thou
hast spoken is come to pass; and, behold,
thou seest *it*.
25 And thou hast said unto me, O Lord
GOD, Buy thee the field for money, and take
witnesses; for [n]the city is given into the
hand of the Chaldeans.
26 ¶ Then came the word of the LORD
unto Jeremiah, saying,
27 Behold, I *am* the LORD, the [o]God of all
flesh: [p]is there any thing too hard for me?
28 Therefore thus saith the LORD; Behold,
[q]I will give this city into the hand of the
Chaldeans, and into the hand of Nebuchadrezzar king of Babylon, and he shall
take it:
29 And the Chaldeans, that fight against
this city, shall come and [r]set fire on this
city, and burn it with the houses, [s]upon
whose roofs they have offered incense unto
Baal, and poured out drink offerings unto
other gods, to provoke me to anger.
30 For the children of Israel and the children of Judah [t]have only done evil before
me from their youth: for the children of Israel have only provoked me to anger with
the work of their hands, saith the LORD.
31 For this city hath been to me *as* a provocation of mine anger and of my fury from
the day that they built it even unto this day;
[u]that I should remove it from before my
face,
32 Because of all the evil of the children
of Israel and of the children of Judah, which
they have done to provoke me to anger,
[v]they, their kings, their princes, their
priests, and their prophets, and the men of
Judah, and the inhabitants of Jerusalem.
33 And they have turned unto me the
[w]back, and not the face: though I taught
them, [x]rising up early and teaching *them*,
yet they have not hearkened to receive instruction.
34 But they [y]set their abominations in the
house, which is called by my name, to defile it.
35 And they built the high places of Baal,
which *are* in the valley of the son of Hinnom, to [z]cause their sons and their daughters to pass through *the fire* unto [a]Molech;
[b]which I commanded them not, neither
came it into my mind, that they should do
this abomination, to cause Judah to sin.
36 ¶ And now therefore thus saith the
LORD, the God of Israel, concerning this
city, whereof ye say, [c]It shall be delivered
into the hand of the king of Babylon by the
sword, and by the famine, and by the pestilence;
37 Behold, I will [d]gather them out of all
countries, whither I have driven them in
mine anger, and in my fury, and in great
wrath; and I will bring them again unto this
place, and I will cause them [e]to dwell
safely:
38 And they shall be [f]my people, and I
will be their God:
39 And I will [g]give them one heart, and
one way, that they may fear me for ever, for
the good of them, and of their children after
them:
40 And [h]I will make an everlasting covenant with them, that I will not turn away
from them, to do them good; but [i]I will put
my fear in their hearts, that they shall not
depart from me.
41 Yea, [j]I will rejoice over them to do
them good, and [k]I will plant them in this
land assuredly with my whole heart and
with my whole soul.
42 For thus saith the LORD; [l]Like as I
have brought all this great evil upon this
people, so will I bring upon them all the
good that I have promised them.
43 And [m]fields shall be bought in this
land, [n]whereof ye say, *It is* desolate without
man or beast; it is given into the hand of the
Chaldeans.
44 Men shall buy fields for money, and
subscribe evidences, and seal *them*, and
take witnesses in [o]the land of Benjamin,
and in the places about Jerusalem, and in
the cities of Judah, and in the cities of the
mountains, and in the cities of the valley,
and in the cities of the south: for [p]I will
cause their captivity to return, saith the
LORD.

33

Moreover the word of the LORD came
unto Jeremiah the second time,
while he was yet [q]shut up in the court of the
prison, saying,
2 Thus saith the LORD the [r]maker
thereof, the LORD that formed it, to establish
it; [s]the LORD *is* his name;

32:18 [b]Ex. 20:6; Deut. 5:9 [c]Isa. 9:6 [d]ch. 10:16
32:19 [e]Isa. 28:29 [f]Job 34:21; Ps. 33:13; Prov. 5:21; ch. 16:17 [g]ch. 17:10
32:20 [h]Ex. 9:16; 1 Chron. 17:21; Isa. 63:12; Dan. 9:15
32:21 [i]Ex. 6:6; 2 Sam. 7:23; 1 Chron. 17:21; Ps. 136:11
32:22 [j]Ex. 3:8; ch. 11:5
32:23 [k]Neh. 9:26; ch. 11:8; Dan. 9:10-14
32:24 [l]ver. 25 [m]ch. 14:12
32:25 [n]ver. 24
32:27 [o]Num. 16:22 [p]ver. 17
32:28 [q]ver. 3
32:29 [r]ch. 21:10 [s]ch. 19:13
32:30 [t]ch. 2:7; Ezek. 20:28
32:31 [u]2 Kings 23:27
32:32 [v]Isa. 1:4; Dan. 9:8
32:33 [w]ch. 2:27 [x]ch. 7:13
32:34 [y]ch. 7:30; Ezek. 8:5
32:35 [z]ch. 7:31 [a]Lev. 18:21; 1 Kings 11:33 [b]ch. 7:31
32:36 [c]ver. 24
32:37 [d]Deut. 30:3; ch. 23:3; Ezek. 37:21 [e]ch. 23:6
32:38 [f]ch. 24:7
32:39 [g]ch. 24:7; Ezek. 11:19
32:40 [h]Isa. 55:3; ch. 31:31 [i]ch. 31:33
32:41 [j]Deut. 30:9; Zeph. 3:17 [k]ch. 24:6; Am. 9:15
32:42 [l]ch. 31:28
32:43 [m]ver. 15 [n]ch. 33:10
32:44 [o]ch. 17:26 [p]ch. 33:7
33:1 [q]ch. 32:2
33:2 [r]Isa. 37:26 [s]Ex. 15:3; Am. 5:8

3 [t]Call unto me, and I will answer thee, and shew thee great and mighty things, which thou knowest not.

4 For thus saith the LORD, the God of Israel, concerning the houses of this city, and concerning the houses of the kings of Judah, which are thrown down by [u]the mounts, and by the sword;

5 [v]They come to fight with the Chaldeans, but *it is* to fill them with the dead bodies of men, whom I have slain in mine anger and in my fury, and for all whose wickedness I have hid my face from this city.

6 Behold, [w]I will bring it health and cure, and I will cure them, and will reveal unto them the abundance of peace and truth.

7 And [x]I will cause the captivity of Judah and the captivity of Israel to return, and will build them, [y]as at the first.

8 And I will [z]cleanse them from all their iniquity, whereby they have sinned against me; and I will [a]pardon all their iniquities, whereby they have sinned, and whereby they have transgressed against me.

9 ¶ [b]And it shall be to me a name of joy, a praise and an honour before all the nations of the earth, which shall hear all the good that I do unto them: and they shall [c]fear and tremble for all the goodness and for all the prosperity that I procure unto it.

10 Thus saith the LORD; Again there shall be heard in this place, [d]which ye say *shall be* desolate without man and without beast, *even* in the cities of Judah, and in the streets of Jerusalem, that are desolate, without man, and without inhabitant, and without beast,

11 The [e]voice of joy, and the voice of gladness, the voice of the bridegroom, and the voice of the bride, the voice of them that shall say, [f]Praise the LORD of hosts: for the LORD *is* good; for his mercy *endureth* for ever: *and* of them that shall bring [g]the sacrifice of praise into the house of the LORD. For [h]I will cause to return the captivity of the land, as at the first, saith the LORD.

12 Thus saith the LORD of hosts; [i]Again in this place, which is desolate without man and without beast, and in all the cities thereof, shall be an habitation of shepherds causing *their* flocks to lie down.

13 [j]In the cities of the mountains, in the cities of the vale, and in the cities of the south, and in the land of Benjamin, and in the places about Jerusalem, and in the cities of Judah, shall the flocks [k]pass again under the hands of him that telleth *them*, saith the LORD.

14 [l]Behold, the days come, saith the LORD, that [m]I will perform that good thing which I have promised unto the house of Israel and to the house of Judah.

15 ¶ In those days, and at that time, will I cause the [n]Branch of righteousness to grow up unto David; and he shall execute judgment and righteousness in the land.

16 [o]In those days shall Judah be saved, and Jerusalem shall dwell safely: and this *is* *the name* wherewith she shall be called, The LORD our righteousness.

17 ¶ For thus saith the LORD; David shall never want a man to sit upon the throne of the house of Israel;

18 Neither shall the priests the Levites [p]want a man before me to [q]offer burnt offerings, and to kindle meat offerings, and to do sacrifice continually.

19 ¶ And the word of the LORD came unto Jeremiah, saying,

20 Thus saith the LORD; [r]If ye can break my covenant of the day, and my covenant of the night, and that there should not be day and night in their season;

21 *Then* may also [s]my covenant be broken with David my servant, that he should not have a son to reign upon his throne; and with the Levites the priests, my ministers.

22 As [t]the host of heaven cannot be numbered, neither the sand of the sea measured: so will I multiply the seed of David my servant, and the Levites that minister unto me.

23 Moreover the word of the LORD came to Jeremiah, saying,

24 Considerest thou not what this people have spoken, saying, [u]The two families which the LORD hath chosen, he hath even cast them off? thus they have despised my people, that they should be no more a nation before them.

25 Thus saith the LORD; If [v]my covenant *be* not with day and night, *and if* I have not [w]appointed the ordinances of heaven and earth;

26 [x]Then will I cast away the seed of Jacob, and David my servant, *so* that I will not take *any* of his seed *to be* rulers over the seed of Abraham, Isaac, and Jacob: for [y]I will cause their captivity to return, and have mercy on them.

34

The word which came unto Jeremiah from the LORD, [z]when Nebuchadnezzar king of Babylon, and all his army, and [a]all the kingdoms of the earth of his dominion, and all the people, fought against Jerusalem, and against all the cities thereof, saying,

2 Thus saith the LORD, the God of Israel; Go and speak to Zedekiah king of Judah, and tell him, Thus saith the LORD; Behold, [b]I will give this city into the hand of the king of Babylon, and [c]he shall burn it with fire:

3 And [d]thou shalt not escape out of his hand, but shalt surely be taken, and delivered into his hand; and thine eyes shall behold the eyes of the king of Babylon, and he shall speak with thee mouth to mouth, and thou shalt go to Babylon.

4 Yet hear the word of the LORD, O Zedekiah king of Judah; Thus saith the LORD of thee, Thou shalt not die by the sword:

5 *But* thou shalt die in peace: and with [e]the burnings of thy fathers, the former kings which were before thee, [f]so shall they burn *odours* for thee; and [g]they will

33:3 [t]Ps. 91:15; ch. 29:12
33:4 [u]ch. 32:24
33:5 [v]ch. 32:5
33:6 [w]ch. 30:17
33:7 [x]ch. 30:3; ver. 11 [y]Isa. 1:26; ch. 24:6
33:8 [z]Ezek. 36:25; Zech. 13:1; Heb. 9:13 [a]ch. 31:34; Mic. 7:18
33:9 [b]Isa. 62:7; ch. 13:11 [c]Isa. 60:5
33:10 [d]ch. 32:43
33:11 [e]ch. 7:34; Rev. 18:23 [f]1 Chron. 16:8; 2 Chron. 5:13; Ezra 3:11; Ps. 136:1; Isa. 12:4 [g]Lev. 7:12; Ps. 107:22 [h]ver. 7
33:12 [i]Isa. 65:10; ch. 31:24
33:13 [j]ch. 17:26 [k]Lev. 27:32
33:14 [l]ch. 23:5 [m]ch. 29:10
33:15 [n]Isa. 4:2; ch. 23:5
33:16 [o]ch. 23:6
33:18 [p]2 Sam. 7:16; 1 Kings 2:4; Ps. 89:29; Luke 1:32 [q]Rom. 12:1; 1 Pet. 2:5; Rev. 1:6
33:20 [r]Ps. 89:37; Isa. 54:9; ch. 31:36; ver. 25
33:21 [s]Ps. 89:34
33:22 [t]Gen. 13:16; ch. 31:37
33:24 [u]ver. 21
33:25 [v]ver. 20; Gen. 8:22 [w]Ps. 74:16; ch. 31:35
33:26 [x]ch. 31:37 [y]ver. 7; Ezra 2:1
34:1 [z]2 Kings 25:1; ch. 39:1 [a]ch. 1:15
34:2 [b]ch. 21:10 [c]ch. 32:29; ver. 22
34:3 [d]ch. 32:4
34:5 [e]2 Chron. 16:14 [f]Dan. 2:46 [g]ch. 22:18

lament thee, *saying,* Ah lord! for I have pronounced the word, saith the LORD.

6 Then Jeremiah the prophet spake all these words unto Zedekiah king of Judah in Jerusalem,

7 When the king of Babylon's army fought against Jerusalem, and against all the cities of Judah that were left, against Lachish, and against Azekah: for [h]these defenced cities remained of the cities of Judah.

8 ¶ *This is* the word that came unto Jeremiah from the LORD, after that the king Zedekiah had made a covenant with all the people which *were* at Jerusalem, to proclaim [i]liberty unto them;

9 [j]That every man should let his manservant, and every man his maidservant, *being* an Hebrew or an Hebrewess, go free; [k]that none should serve himself of them, *to wit,* of a Jew his brother.

10 Now when all the princes, and all the people, which had entered into the covenant, heard that every one should let his manservant, and every one his maidservant, go free, that none should serve themselves of them any more, then they obeyed, and let *them* go.

11 But [l]afterward they turned, and caused the servants and the handmaids, whom they had let go free, to return, and brought them into subjection for servants and for handmaids.

12 ¶ Therefore the word of the LORD came to Jeremiah from the LORD, saying,

13 Thus saith the LORD, the God of Israel; I made a covenant with your fathers in the day that I brought them forth out of the land of Egypt, out of the house of bondmen, saying,

14 At the end of [m]seven years let ye go every man his brother an Hebrew, which hath been sold unto thee; and when he hath served thee six years, thou shalt let him go free from thee: but your fathers hearkened not unto me, neither inclined their ear.

15 And ye were now turned, and had done right in my sight, in proclaiming liberty every man to his neighbour; and ye had [n]made a covenant before me [o]in the house which is called by my name:

16 But ye turned and [p]polluted my name, and caused every man his servant, and every man his handmaid, whom he had set at liberty at their pleasure, to return, and brought them into subjection, to be unto you for servants and for handmaids.

17 Therefore thus saith the LORD; Ye have not hearkened unto me, in proclaiming liberty, every one to his brother, and every man to his neighbour: [q]behold, I proclaim a liberty for you, saith the LORD, [r]to the sword, to the pestilence, and to the famine; and I will make you to be [s]removed into all the kingdoms of the earth.

18 And I will give the men that have transgressed my covenant, which have not performed the words of the covenant which they had made before me, when [t]they cut the calf in twain, and passed between the parts thereof,

19 The princes of Judah, and the princes of Jerusalem, the eunuchs, and the priests, and all the people of the land, which passed between the parts of the calf;

20 I will even give them into the hand of their enemies, and into the hand of them that seek their life: and their [u]dead bodies shall be for meat unto the fowls of the heaven, and to the beasts of the earth.

21 And Zedekiah king of Judah and his princes will I give into the hand of their enemies, and into the hand of them that seek their life, and into the hand of the king of Babylon's army, [v]which are gone up from you.

22 [w]Behold, I will command, saith the LORD, and cause them to return to this city; and they shall fight against it, [x]and take it, and burn it with fire: and [y]I will make the cities of Judah a desolation without an inhabitant.

35 The word which came unto Jeremiah from the LORD in the days of Jehoiakim the son of Josiah king of Judah, saying,

2 Go unto the house of the [z]Rechabites, and speak unto them, and bring them into the house of the LORD, into one of [a]the chambers, and give them wine to drink.

3 Then I took Jaazaniah the son of Jeremiah, the son of Habaziniah, and his brethren, and all his sons, and the whole house of the Rechabites;

4 And I brought them into the house of the LORD, into the chamber of the sons of Hanan, the son of Igdaliah, a man of God, which *was* by the chamber of the princes, which *was* above the chamber of Maaseiah the son of Shallum, [b]the keeper of the door:

5 And I set before the sons of the house of the Rechabites pots full of wine, and cups, and I said unto them, Drink ye wine.

6 But they said, We will drink no wine: for [c]Jonadab the son of Rechab our father commanded us, saying, Ye shall drink no wine, *neither* ye, nor your sons for ever:

7 Neither shall ye build house, nor sow seed, nor plant vineyard, nor have *any:* but all your days ye shall dwell in tents; [d]that ye may live many days in the land where ye *be* strangers.

8 Thus have we obeyed the voice of Jonadab the son of Rechab our father in all that he hath charged us, to drink no wine all our days, we, our wives, our sons, nor our daughters;

9 Nor to build houses for us to dwell in: neither have we vineyard, nor field, nor seed:

10 But we have dwelt in tents, and have obeyed, and done according to all that Jonadab our father commanded us.

11 But it came to pass, when Nebuchadrezzar king of Babylon came up into the land, that we said, Come, and let us go to Jerusalem for fear of the army of the

34:7 [h]2 Kings 18:13; 2 Chron. 11:5
34:8 [i]Ex. 21:2; Lev. 25:10; ver. 14
34:9 [j]Neh. 5:11 [k]Lev. 25:39-46
34:11 [l]ver. 21; ch. 37:5
34:14 [m]Ex. 21:2; Deut. 15:12
34:15 [n]2 Kings 23:3; Neh. 10:29 [o]ch. 7:10
34:16 [p]Ex. 20:7; Lev. 19:12
34:17 [q]Matt. 7:2; Gal. 6:7; Jam. 2:13 [r]ch. 32:24 [s]Deut. 28:25; ch. 29:18
34:18 [t]Gen. 15:10
34:20 [u]ch. 7:33
34:21 [v]ch. 37:5
34:22 [w]ch. 37:8 [x]ch. 38:3 [y]ch. 9:11
35:2 [z]2 Kings 10:15; 1 Chron. 2:55 [a]1 Kings 6:5
35:4 [b]2 Kings 12:9; 1 Chron. 9:18
35:6 [c]2 Kings 10:15
35:7 [d]Ex. 20:12; Eph. 6:2

Chaldeans, and for fear of the army of the Syrians: so we dwell at Jerusalem.

12 ¶ Then came the word of the LORD unto Jeremiah, saying,

13 Thus saith the LORD of hosts, the God of Israel; Go and tell the men of Judah and the inhabitants of Jerusalem, Will ye not [e]receive instruction to hearken to my words? saith the LORD.

14 The words of Jonadab the son of Rechab, that he commanded his sons not to drink wine, are performed; for unto this day they drink none, but obey their father's commandment: [f]notwithstanding I have spoken unto you, [g]rising early and speaking; but ye hearkened not unto me.

15 [h]I have sent also unto you all my servants the prophets, rising up early and sending *them*, saying, [i]Return ye now every man from his evil way, and amend your doings, and go not after other gods to serve them, and ye shall dwell in the land which I have given to you and to your fathers: but ye have not inclined your ear, nor hearkened unto me.

16 Because the sons of Jonadab the son of Rechab have performed the commandment of their father, which he commanded them; but this people hath not hearkened unto me:

17 Therefore thus saith the LORD God of hosts, the God of Israel; Behold, I will bring upon Judah and upon all the inhabitants of Jerusalem all the evil that I have pronounced against them: [j]because I have spoken unto them, but they have not heard; and I have called unto them, but they have not answered.

18 ¶ And Jeremiah said unto the house of the Rechabites, Thus saith the LORD of hosts, the God of Israel; Because ye have obeyed the commandment of Jonadab your father, and kept all his precepts, and done according unto all that he hath commanded you:

19 Therefore thus saith the LORD of hosts, the God of Israel; Jonadab the son of Rechab shall not want a man to [k]stand before me for ever.

36 And it came to pass in the fourth year of Jehoiakim the son of Josiah king of Judah, *that* this word came unto Jeremiah from the LORD, saying,

2 Take thee a [l]roll of a book, and [m]write therein all the words that I have spoken unto thee against Israel, and against Judah, and against [n]all the nations, from the day I spake unto thee, from the days of [o]Josiah, even unto this day.

3 [p]It may be that the house of Judah will hear all the evil which I purpose to do unto them; that they may [q]return every man from his evil way; that I may forgive their iniquity and their sin.

4 Then Jeremiah [r]called Baruch the son of Neriah: and [s]Baruch wrote from the mouth of Jeremiah all the words of the LORD, which he had spoken unto him, upon a roll of a book.

5 And Jeremiah commanded Baruch, saying, I *am* shut up; I cannot go into the house of the LORD:

6 Therefore go thou, and read in the roll, which thou hast written from my mouth, the words of the LORD in the ears of the people in the LORD's house upon [t]the fasting day: and also thou shalt read them in the ears of all Judah that come out of their cities.

7 [u]It may be they will present their supplication before the LORD, and will return every one from his evil way: for great *is* the anger and the fury that the LORD hath pronounced against this people.

8 And Baruch the son of Neriah did according to all that Jeremiah the prophet commanded him, reading in the book the words of the LORD in the LORD's house.

9 And it came to pass in the fifth year of Jehoiakim the son of Josiah king of Judah, in the ninth month, *that* they proclaimed a fast before the LORD to all the people in Jerusalem, and to all the people that came from the cities of Judah unto Jerusalem.

10 Then read Baruch in the book the words of Jeremiah in the house of the LORD, in the chamber of Gemariah the son of Shaphan the scribe, in the higher court, at the [v]entry of the new gate of the LORD's house, in the ears of all the people.

11 ¶ When Michaiah the son of Gemariah, the son of Shaphan, had heard out of the book all the words of the LORD,

12 Then he went down into the king's house, into the scribe's chamber: and, lo, all the princes sat there, *even* Elishama the scribe, and Delaiah the son of Shemaiah, and Elnathan the son of Achbor, and Gemariah the son of Shaphan, and Zedekiah the son of Hananiah, and all the princes.

13 Then Michaiah declared unto them all the words that he had heard, when Baruch read the book in the ears of the people.

14 Therefore all the princes sent Jehudi the son of Nethaniah, the son of Shelemiah, the son of Cushi, unto Baruch, saying, Take in thine hand the roll wherein thou hast read in the ears of the people, and come. So Baruch the son of Neriah took the roll in his hand, and came unto them.

15 And they said unto him, Sit down now, and read it in our ears. So Baruch read *it* in their ears.

16 Now it came to pass, when they had heard all the words, they were afraid both one and other, and said unto Baruch, We will surely tell the king of all these words.

17 And they asked Baruch, saying, Tell us now, how didst thou write all these words at his mouth?

18 Then Baruch answered them, He pronounced all these words unto me with his mouth, and I wrote *them* with ink in the book.

19 Then said the princes unto Baruch, Go,

35:13 [e]ch. 32:33
35:14 [f]2 Chron. 36:15 [g]ch. 7:13
35:15 [h]ch. 7:25 [i]ch. 18:11
35:17 [j]Prov. 1:24; Isa. 65:12; ch. 7:13
35:19 [k]ch. 15:19
36:2 [l]Isa. 8:1; Ezek. 2:9; Zech. 5:1 [m]ch. 30:2 [n]ch. 25:15 [o]ch. 25:3
36:3 [p]ver. 7; ch. 26:3 [q]ch. 18:8; Jonah 3:8
36:4 [r]ch. 32:12 [s]ch. 45:1
36:6 [t]Lev. 16:29; Acts 27:9
36:7 [u]ver. 3
36:10 [v]ch. 26:10

hide thee, thou and Jeremiah; and let no man know where ye be.

20 ¶ And they went in to the king into the court, but they laid up the roll in the chamber of Elishama the scribe, and told all the words in the ears of the king.

21 So the king sent Jehudi to fetch the roll: and he took it out of Elishama the scribe's chamber. And Jehudi read it in the ears of the king, and in the ears of all the princes which stood beside the king.

22 Now the king sat in [w]the winterhouse in the ninth month: and *there was a fire* on the hearth burning before him.

23 And it came to pass, *that* when Jehudi had read three or four leaves, he cut it with the penknife, and cast *it* into the fire that *was* on the hearth, until all the roll was consumed in the fire that *was* on the hearth.

24 Yet they were not afraid, nor [x]rent their garments, *neither* the king, nor any of his servants that heard all these words.

25 Nevertheless Elnathan and Delaiah and Gemariah had made intercession to the king that he would not burn the roll: but he would not hear them.

26 But the king commanded Jerahmeel the son of Hammelech, and Seraiah the son of Azriel, and Shelemiah the son of Abdeel, to take Baruch the scribe and Jeremiah the prophet: but the LORD hid them.

27 ¶ Then the word of the LORD came to Jeremiah, after that the king had burned the roll, and the words which Baruch wrote at the mouth of Jeremiah, saying,

28 Take thee again another roll, and write in it all the former words that were in the first roll, which Jehoiakim the king of Judah hath burned.

29 And thou shalt say to Jehoiakim king of Judah, Thus saith the LORD; Thou hast burned this roll, saying, Why hast thou written therein, saying, The king of Babylon shall certainly come and destroy this land, and shall cause to cease from thence man and beast?

30 Therefore thus saith the LORD of Jehoiakim king of Judah; [y]He shall have none to sit upon the throne of David: and his dead body shall be [z]cast out in the day to the heat, and in the night to the frost.

31 And I will punish him and his seed and his servants for their iniquity; and I will bring upon them, and upon the inhabitants of Jerusalem, and upon the men of Judah, all the evil that I have pronounced against them; but they hearkened not.

32 ¶ Then took Jeremiah another roll, and gave it to Baruch the scribe, the son of Neriah; who wrote therein from the mouth of Jeremiah all the words of the book which Jehoiakim king of Judah had burned in the fire: and there were added besides unto them many like words.

37 And king [a]Zedekiah the son of Josiah reigned instead of Coniah the son of Jehoiakim, whom Nebuchadrezzar king of Babylon made king in the land of Judah.

2 [b]But neither he, nor his servants, nor the people of the land, did hearken unto the words of the LORD, which he spake by the prophet Jeremiah.

3 And Zedekiah the king sent Jehucal the son of Shelemiah and [c]Zephaniah the son of Maaseiah the priest to the prophet Jeremiah, saying, Pray now unto the LORD our God for us.

4 Now Jeremiah came in and went out among the people: for they had not put him into prison.

5 Then [d]Pharaoh's army was come forth out of Egypt: [e]and when the Chaldeans that besieged Jerusalem heard tidings of them, they departed from Jerusalem.

6 ¶ Then came the word of the LORD unto the prophet Jeremiah, saying,

7 Thus saith the LORD, the God of Israel; Thus shall ye say to the king of Judah, [f]that sent you unto me to enquire of me; Behold, Pharaoh's army, which is come forth to help you, shall return to Egypt into their own land.

8 [g]And the Chaldeans shall come again, and fight against this city, and take it, and burn it with fire.

9 Thus saith the LORD; Deceive not yourselves, saying, The Chaldeans shall surely depart from us: for they shall not depart.

10 [h]For though ye had smitten the whole army of the Chaldeans that fight against you, and there remained *but* wounded men among them, *yet* should they rise up every man in his tent, and burn this city with fire.

11 ¶ [i]And it came to pass, that when the army of the Chaldeans was broken up from Jerusalem for fear of Pharaoh's army,

12 Then Jeremiah went forth out of Jerusalem to go into the land of Benjamin, to separate himself thence in the midst of the people.

13 And when he was in the gate of Benjamin, a captain of the ward *was* there, whose name *was* Irijah, the son of Shelemiah, the son of Hananiah; and he took Jeremiah the prophet, saying, Thou fallest away to the Chaldeans.

14 Then said Jeremiah, *It is* false; I fall not away to the Chaldeans. But he hearkened not to him: so Irijah took Jeremiah, and brought him to the princes.

15 Wherefore the princes were wroth with Jeremiah, and smote him, [j]and put him in prison in the house of Jonathan the scribe: for they had made that the prison.

16 ¶ When Jeremiah was entered into [k]the dungeon, and into the cabins, and Jeremiah had remained there many days;

17 Then Zedekiah the king sent, and took him out: and the king asked him secretly in his house, and said, Is there *any* word from the LORD? And Jeremiah said, There is: for, said he, thou shalt be delivered into the hand of the king of Babylon.

18 Moreover Jeremiah said unto king

36:22 [w]Am. 3:15
36:24 [x]2 Kings 22:11; Isa. 36:22
36:30 [y]ch. 22:30 [z]ch. 22:19
37:1 [a]2 Kings 24:17; 2 Chron. 36:10; ch. 22:24
37:2 [b]2 Chron. 36:12
37:3 [c]ch. 21:1
37:5 [d]2 Kings 24:7; Ezek. 17:15 [e]ver. 11; ch. 34:21
37:7 [f]ch. 21:2
37:8 [g]ch. 34:22
37:10 [h]ch. 21:4
37:11 [i]ver. 5
37:15 [j]ch. 38:26
37:16 [k]ch. 38:6

Zedekiah, What have I offended against thee, or against thy servants, or against this people, that ye have put me in prison?

19 Where *are* now your prophets which prophesied unto you, saying, The king of Babylon shall not come against you, nor against this land?

20 Therefore hear now, I pray thee, O my lord the king: let my supplication, I pray thee, be accepted before thee; that thou cause me not to return to the house of Jonathan the scribe, lest I die there.

21 Then Zedekiah the king commanded that they should commit Jeremiah [l]into the court of the prison, and that they should give him daily a piece of bread out of the bakers' street, [m]until all the bread in the city were spent. Thus Jeremiah remained in the court of the prison.

38

38 Then Shephatiah the son of Mattan, and Gedaliah the son of Pashur, and [n]Jucal the son of Shelemiah, and [o]Pashur the son of Malchiah, [p]heard the words that Jeremiah had spoken unto all the people, saying,

2 Thus saith the LORD, [q]He that remaineth in this city shall die by the sword, by the famine, and by the pestilence: but he that goeth forth to the Chaldeans shall live; for he shall have his life for a prey, and shall live.

3 Thus saith the LORD, [r]This city shall surely be given into the hand of the king of Babylon's army, which shall take it.

4 Therefore the princes said unto the king, We beseech thee, [s]let this man be put to death: for thus he weakeneth the hands of the men of war that remain in this city, and the hands of all the people, in speaking such words unto them: for this man seeketh not the welfare of this people, but the hurt.

5 Then Zedekiah the king said, Behold, he *is* in your hand: for the king *is* not *he that* can do *any* thing against you.

6 [t]Then took they Jeremiah, and cast him into the dungeon of Malchiah the son of Hammelech, that *was* in the court of the prison: and they let down Jeremiah with cords. And in the dungeon *there was* no water, but mire: so Jeremiah sunk in the mire.

7 ¶ [u]Now when Ebed-melech the Ethiopian, one of the eunuchs which was in the king's house, heard that they had put Jeremiah in the dungeon; the king then sitting in the gate of Benjamin;

8 Ebed-melech went forth out of the king's house, and spake to the king, saying,

9 My lord the king, these men have done evil in all that they have done to Jeremiah the prophet, whom they have cast into the dungeon; and he is like to die for hunger in the place where he is: for *there is* no more bread in the city.

10 Then the king commanded Ebed-melech the Ethiopian, saying, Take from hence thirty men with thee, and take up Jeremiah the prophet out of the dungeon, before he die.

11 So Ebed-melech took the men with him, and went into the house of the king under the treasury, and took thence old cast clouts and old rotten rags, and let them down by cords into the dungeon to Jeremiah.

12 And Ebed-melech the Ethiopian said unto Jeremiah, Put now *these* old cast clouts and rotten rags under thine armholes under the cords. And Jeremiah did so.

13 [v]So they drew up Jeremiah with cords, and took him up out of the dungeon: and Jeremiah remained [w]in the court of the prison.

14 ¶ Then Zedekiah the king sent, and took Jeremiah the prophet unto him into the third entry that *is* in the house of the LORD: and the king said unto Jeremiah, I will ask thee a thing; hide nothing from me.

15 Then Jeremiah said unto Zedekiah, If I declare *it* unto thee, wilt thou not surely put me to death? and if I give thee counsel, wilt thou not hearken unto me?

16 So Zedekiah the king sware secretly unto Jeremiah, saying, *As* the LORD liveth, [x]that made us this soul, I will not put thee to death, neither will I give thee into the hand of these men that seek thy life.

17 Then said Jeremiah unto Zedekiah, Thus saith the LORD, the God of hosts, the God of Israel; If thou wilt assuredly [y]go forth [z]unto the king of Babylon's princes, then thy soul shall live, and this city shall not be burned with fire; and thou shalt live, and thine house:

18 But if thou wilt not go forth to the king of Babylon's princes, then shall this city be given into the hand of the Chaldeans, and they shall burn it with fire, and [a]thou shalt not escape out of their hand.

19 And Zedekiah the king said unto Jeremiah, I am afraid of the Jews that are fallen to the Chaldeans, lest they deliver me into their hand, and they [b]mock me.

20 But Jeremiah said, They shall not deliver *thee*. Obey, I beseech thee, the voice of the LORD, which I speak unto thee: so it shall be well unto thee, and thy soul shall live.

21 But if thou refuse to go forth, this *is* the word that the LORD hath shewed me:

22 And, behold, all the women that are left in the king of Judah's house *shall be* brought forth to the king of Babylon's princes, and those *women* shall say, Thy friends have set thee on, and have prevailed against thee: thy feet are sunk in the mire, *and* they are turned away back.

23 So they shall bring out all thy wives and [c]thy children to the Chaldeans: and [d]thou shalt not escape out of their hand, but shalt be taken by the hand of the king of Babylon: and thou shalt cause this city to be burned with fire.

24 ¶ Then said Zedekiah unto Jeremiah, Let no man know of these words, and thou shalt not die.

25 But if the princes hear that I have

37:21 [l]ch. 32:2 [m]ch. 38:9
38:1 [n]ch. 37:3 [o]ch. 21:1 [p]ch. 21:8
38:2 [q]ch. 21:9
38:3 [r]ch. 21:10
38:4 [s]ch. 26:11
38:6 [t]ch. 37:21
38:7 [u]ch. 39:16
38:13 [v]ver. 6 [w]ch. 37:21
38:16 [x]Isa. 57:16
38:17 [y]2 Kings 24:12 [z]ch. 39:3
38:18 [a]ch. 32:4; ver. 23
38:19 [b]1 Sam. 31:4
38:23 [c]ch. 39:6 [d]ver. 18

talked with thee, and they come unto thee, and say unto thee, Declare unto us now what thou hast said unto the king, hide it not from us, and we will not put thee to death; also what the king said unto thee:

26 Then thou shalt say unto them, [e]I presented my supplication before the king, that he would not cause me to return [f]to Jonathan's house, to die there.

27 Then came all the princes unto Jeremiah, and asked him: and he told them according to all these words that the king had commanded. So they left off speaking with him; for the matter was not perceived.

28 So [g]Jeremiah abode in the court of the prison until the day that Jerusalem was taken: and he was *there* when Jerusalem was taken.

39 In the [h]ninth year of Zedekiah king of Judah, in the tenth month, came Nebuchadrezzar king of Babylon and all his army against Jerusalem, and they besieged it.

2 *And* in the eleventh year of Zedekiah, in the fourth month, the ninth *day* of the month, the city was broken up.

3 [i]And all the princes of the king of Babylon came in, and sat in the middle gate, *even* Nergal-sharezer, Samgar-nebo, Sarsechim, Rabsaris, Nergal-sharezer, Rabmag, with all the residue of the princes of the king of Babylon.

4 ¶ [j]And it came to pass, *that* when Zedekiah the king of Judah saw them, and all the men of war, then they fled, and went forth out of the city by night, by the way of the king's garden, by the gate betwixt the two walls: and he went out the way of the plain.

5 But the Chaldeans' army pursued after them, and [k]overtook Zedekiah in the plains of Jericho: and when they had taken him, they brought him up to Nebuchadnezzar king of Babylon to [l]Riblah in the land of Hamath, where he gave judgment upon him.

6 Then the king of Babylon slew the sons of Zedekiah in Riblah before his eyes: also the king of Babylon slew all the nobles of Judah.

7 Moreover [m]he put out Zedekiah's eyes, and bound him with chains, to carry him to Babylon.

8 ¶ [n]And the Chaldeans burned the king's house, and the houses of the people, with fire, and brake down the walls of Jerusalem.

9 [o]Then Nebuzar-adan the captain of the guard carried away captive into Babylon the remnant of the people that remained in the city, and those that fell away, that fell to him, with the rest of the people that remained.

10 But Nebuzar-adan the captain of the guard left of the poor of the people, which had nothing, in the land of Judah, and gave them vineyards and fields at the same time.

11 ¶ Now Nebuchadrezzar king of Babylon gave charge concerning Jeremiah to Nebuzar-adan the captain of the guard, saying,

12 Take him, and look well to him, and do him no harm; but do unto him even as he shall say unto thee.

13 So Nebuzar-adan the captain of the guard sent, and Nebushasban, Rabsaris, and Nergal-sharezer, Rab-mag, and all the king of Babylon's princes;

14 Even they sent, [p]and took Jeremiah out of the court of the prison, and committed him [q]unto Gedaliah the son of [r]Ahikam the son of Shaphan, that he should carry him home: so he dwelt among the people.

15 ¶ Now the word of the LORD came unto Jeremiah, while he was shut up in the court of the prison, saying,

16 Go and speak to [s]Ebed-melech the Ethiopian, saying, Thus saith the LORD of hosts, the God of Israel; Behold, [t]I will bring my words upon this city for evil, and not for good; and they shall be *accomplished* in that day before thee.

17 But I will deliver thee in that day, saith the LORD: and thou shalt not be given into the hand of the men of whom thou *art* afraid.

18 For I will surely deliver thee, and thou shalt not fall by the sword, but [u]thy life shall be for a prey unto thee: [v]because thou hast put thy trust in me, saith the LORD.

40 The word that came to Jeremiah from the LORD, [w]after that Nebuzar-adan the captain of the guard had let him go from Ramah, when he had taken him being bound in chains among all that were carried away captive of Jerusalem and Judah, which were carried away captive unto Babylon.

2 And the captain of the guard took Jeremiah, and [x]said unto him, The LORD thy God hath pronounced this evil upon this place.

3 Now the LORD hath brought *it*, and done according as he hath said: [y]because ye have sinned against the LORD, and have not obeyed his voice, therefore this thing is come upon you.

4 And now, behold, I loose thee this day from the chains which *were* upon thine hand. [z]If it seem good unto thee to come with me into Babylon, come; and I will look well unto thee: but if it seem ill unto thee to come with me into Babylon, forbear: behold, [a]all the land *is* before thee: whither it seemeth good and convenient for thee to go, thither go.

5 Now while he was not yet gone back, *he said,* Go back also to Gedaliah the son of Ahikam the son of Shaphan, [b]whom the king of Babylon hath made governor over the cities of Judah, and dwell with him among the people: or go wheresoever it seemeth convenient unto thee to go. So the captain of the guard gave him victuals and a reward, and let him go.

6 [c]Then went Jeremiah unto Gedaliah

38:26 [e]ch. 37:20 [f]ch. 37:15
38:28 [g]ch. 37:21
39:1 [h]2 Kings 15:1-4; ch. 52:4-7
39:3 [i]ch. 38:17
39:4 [j]2 Kings 25:4; ch. 52:7
39:5 [k]ch. 32:4 [l]2 Kings 23:33
39:7 [m]ch. 32:4; Ezek. 12:13
39:8 [n]2 Kings 25:9; ch. 38:18
39:9 [o]2 Kings 25:11; ch. 52:15
39:14 [p]ch. 38:28 [q]ch. 40:5 [r]ch. 26:24
39:16 [s]ch. 38:7 [t]Dan. 9:12
39:18 [u]ch. 21:9 [v]1 Chron. 5:20; Ps. 37:40
40:1 [w]ch. 39:14
40:2 [x]ch. 50:7
40:3 [y]Deut. 29:24; Dan. 9:11
40:4 [z]ch. 39:12 [a]Gen. 20:15
40:5 [b]2 Kings 25:22
40:6 [c]ch. 39:14

the son of Ahikam to [d]Mizpah; and dwelt with him among the people that were left in the land.

7 ¶ [e]Now when all the captains of the forces which *were* in the fields, *even* they and their men, heard that the king of Babylon had made Gedaliah the son of Ahikam governor in the land, and had committed unto him men, and women, and children, and of [f]the poor of the land, of them that were not carried away captive to Babylon;

8 Then they came to Gedaliah to Mizpah, [g]even Ishmael the son of Nethaniah, and Johanan and Jonathan the sons of Kareah, and Seraiah the son of Tanhumeth, and the sons of Ephai the Netophathite, and Jezaniah the son of a Maachathite, they and their men.

9 And Gedaliah the son of Ahikam the son of Shaphan sware unto them and to their men, saying, Fear not to serve the Chaldeans: dwell in the land, and serve the king of Babylon, and it shall be well with you.

10 As for me, behold, I will dwell at Mizpah to serve the Chaldeans, which will come unto us: but ye, gather ye wine, and summer fruits, and oil, and put *them* in your vessels, and dwell in your cities that ye have taken.

11 Likewise when all the Jews that *were* in Moab, and among the Ammonites, and in Edom, and that *were* in all the countries, heard that the king of Babylon had left a remnant of Judah, and that he had set over them Gedaliah the son of Ahikam the son of Shaphan;

12 Even all the Jews returned out of all places whither they were driven, and came to the land of Judah, to Gedaliah, unto Mizpah, and gathered wine and summer fruits very much.

13 ¶ Moreover Johanan the son of Kareah, and all the captains of the forces that *were* in the fields, came to Gedaliah to Mizpah,

14 And said unto him, Dost thou certainly know that [h]Baalis the king of the Ammonites hath sent Ishmael the son of Nethaniah to slay thee? But Gedaliah the son of Ahikam believed them not.

15 Then Johanan the son of Kareah spake to Gedaliah in Mizpah secretly, saying, Let me go, I pray thee, and I will slay Ishmael the son of Nethaniah, and no man shall know *it:* wherefore should he slay thee, that all the Jews which are gathered unto thee should be scattered, and the remnant in Judah perish?

16 But Gedaliah the son of Ahikam said unto Johanan the son of Kareah, Thou shalt not do this thing: for thou speakest falsely of Ishmael.

41 Now it came to pass in the seventh month, [i]*that* Ishmael the son of Nethaniah the son of Elishama, of the seed royal, and the princes of the king, even ten men with him, came unto Gedaliah the son of Ahikam to Mizpah; and there they did eat bread together in Mizpah.

2 Then arose Ishmael the son of Nethaniah, and the ten men that were with him, and [j]smote Gedaliah the son of Ahikam the son of Shaphan with the sword, and slew him, whom the king of Babylon had made governor over the land.

3 Ishmael also slew all the Jews that were with him, *even* with Gedaliah, at Mizpah, and the Chaldeans that were found there, *and* the men of war.

4 And it came to pass the second day after he had slain Gedaliah, and no man knew *it,*

5 That there came certain from Shechem, from Shiloh, and from Samaria, *even* fourscore men, [k]having their beards shaven, and their clothes rent, and having cut themselves, with offerings and incense in their hand, to bring *them* to [l]the house of the LORD.

6 And Ishmael the son of Nethaniah went forth from Mizpah to meet them, weeping all along as he went: and it came to pass, as he met them, he said unto them, Come to Gedaliah the son of Ahikam.

7 And it was *so,* when they came into the midst of the city, that Ishmael the son of Nethaniah slew them, *and cast them* into the midst of the pit, he, and the men that *were* with him.

8 But ten men were found among them that said unto Ishmael, Slay us not: for we have treasures in the field, of wheat, and of barley, and of oil, and of honey. So he forbare, and slew them not among their brethren.

9 Now the pit wherein Ishmael had cast all the dead bodies of the men, whom he had slain because of Gedaliah, *was* it [m]which Asa the king had made for fear of Baasha king of Israel: *and* Ishmael the son of Nethaniah filled it with *them that were* slain.

10 Then Ishmael carried away captive all the residue of the people that *were* in Mizpah, [n]*even* the king's daughters, and all the people that remained in Mizpah, [o]whom Nebuzar-adan the captain of the guard had committed to Gedaliah the son of Ahikam: and Ishmael the son of Nethaniah carried them away captive, and departed to go over to [p]the Ammonites.

11 ¶ But when Johanan the son of Kareah, and all [q]the captains of the forces that *were* with him, heard of all the evil that Ishmael the son of Nethaniah had done,

12 Then they took all the men, and went to fight with Ishmael the son of Nethaniah, and found him by [r]the great waters that *are* in Gibeon.

13 Now it came to pass, *that* when all the people which *were* with Ishmael saw Johanan the son of Kareah, and all the captains of the forces that *were* with him, then they were glad.

14 So all the people that Ishmael had carried away captive from Mizpah cast about

40:6 [d]Judg. 20:1
40:7 [e]2 Kings 25:23 [f]ch. 39:10
40:8 [g]ch. 41:1
40:14 [h]ch. 41:10
41:1 [i]2 Kings 25:25; ch. 40:6
41:2 [j]2 Kings 25:25
41:5 [k]Lev. 19:27; Deut. 14:1; Isa. 15:2 [l]2 Kings 25:9; 1 Sam. 1:7
41:9 [m]1 Kings 15:22; 2 Chron. 16:6
41:10 [n]ch. 43:6 [o]ch. 40:7 [p]ch. 40:14
41:11 [q]ch. 40:7
41:12 [r]2 Sam. 2:13

and returned, and went unto Johanan the son of Kareah.

15 But Ishmael the son of Nethaniah escaped from Johanan with eight men, and went to the Ammonites.

16 Then took Johanan the son of Kareah, and all the captains of the forces that *were* with him, all the remnant of the people whom he had recovered from Ishmael the son of Nethaniah, from Mizpah, after *that* he had slain Gedaliah the son of Ahikam, *even* mighty men of war, and the women, and the children, and the eunuchs, whom he had brought again from Gibeon:

17 And they departed, and dwelt in the habitation of [s]Chimham, which is by Bethlehem, to go to enter into Egypt,

18 Because of the Chaldeans: for they were afraid of them, because Ishmael the son of Nethaniah had slain Gedaliah the son of Ahikam, [t]whom the king of Babylon made governor in the land.

42 Then all the captains of the forces, [u]and Johanan the son of Kareah, and Jezaniah the son of Hoshaiah, and all the people from the least even unto the greatest, came near,

2 And said unto Jeremiah the prophet, Let, we beseech thee, our supplication be accepted before thee, and [v]pray for us unto the LORD thy God, *even* for all this remnant; (for we are left *but* [w]a few of many, as thine eyes do behold us:)

3 That the LORD thy God may shew us [x]the way wherein we may walk, and the thing that we may do.

4 Then Jeremiah the prophet said unto them, I have heard *you;* behold, I will pray unto the LORD your God according to your words; and it shall come to pass, *that* [y]whatsoever thing the LORD shall answer you, I will declare *it* unto you; I will [z]keep nothing back from you.

5 Then they said to Jeremiah, [a]The LORD be a true and faithful witness between us, if we do not even according to all things for the which the LORD thy God shall send thee to us.

6 Whether *it be* good, or whether *it be* evil, we will obey the voice of the LORD our God, to whom we send thee; [b]that it may be well with us, when we obey the voice of the LORD our God.

7 ¶ And it came to pass after ten days, that the word of the LORD came unto Jeremiah.

8 Then called he Johanan the son of Kareah, and all the captains of the forces which *were* with him, and all the people from the least even to the greatest,

9 And said unto them, Thus saith the LORD, the God of Israel, unto whom ye sent me to present your supplication before him;

10 If ye will still abide in this land, then [c]will I build you, and not pull *you* down, and I will plant you, and not pluck *you* up: for I [d]repent me of the evil that I have done unto you.

11 Be not afraid of the king of Babylon, of whom ye are afraid; be not afraid of him, saith the LORD: [e]for I *am* with you to save you, and to deliver you from his hand.

12 And [f]I will shew mercies unto you, that he may have mercy upon you, and cause you to return to your own land.

13 ¶ But if [g]ye say, We will not dwell in this land, neither obey the voice of the LORD your God,

14 Saying, No; but we will go into the land of Egypt, where we shall see no war, nor hear the sound of the trumpet, nor have hunger of bread; and there will we dwell:

15 And now therefore hear the word of the LORD, ye remnant of Judah; Thus saith the LORD of hosts, the God of Israel; If ye [h]wholly set [i]your faces to enter into Egypt, and go to sojourn there;

16 Then it shall come to pass, *that* the sword, [j]which ye feared, shall overtake you there in the land of Egypt, and the famine, whereof ye were afraid, shall follow close after you there in Egypt; and there ye shall die.

17 So shall it be with all the men that set their faces to go into Egypt to sojourn there; they shall die [k]by the sword, by the famine, and by the pestilence: and [l]none of them shall remain or escape from the evil that I will bring upon them.

18 For thus saith the LORD of hosts, the God of Israel; As mine anger and my fury hath been [m]poured forth upon the inhabitants of Jerusalem; so shall my fury be poured forth upon you, when ye shall enter into Egypt: and [n]ye shall be an execration, and an astonishment, and a curse, and a reproach; and ye shall see this place no more.

19 ¶ The LORD hath said concerning you, O ye remnant of Judah; [o]Go ye not into Egypt: know certainly that I have admonished you this day.

20 For ye dissembled in your hearts, when ye sent me unto the LORD your God, saying, [p]Pray for us unto the LORD our God; and according unto all that the LORD our God shall say, so declare unto us, and we will do *it.*

21 And *now* I have this day declared *it* to you; but ye have not obeyed the voice of the LORD your God, nor any *thing* for the which he hath sent me unto you.

22 Now therefore know certainly that [q]ye shall die by the sword, by the famine, and by the pestilence, in the place whither ye desire to go *and* to sojourn.

43 And it came to pass, *that* when Jeremiah had made an end of speaking unto all the people all the words of the LORD their God, for which the LORD their God had sent him to them, *even* all these words,

2 [r]Then spake Azariah the son of Hoshaiah, and Johanan the son of Kareah, and all the proud men, saying unto Jeremiah, Thou speakest falsely: the LORD our God hath not

41:17 [s]2 Sam. 19:37
41:18 [t]ch. 40:5
42:1 [u]ch. 40:8
42:2 [v]1 Sam. 7:8; Isa. 37:4; Jam. 5:16 [w]Lev. 26:22
42:3 [x]Ezra 8:21
42:4 [y]1 Kings 22:14 [z]1 Sam. 3:18; Acts 20:20
42:5 [a]Gen. 31:50
42:6 [b]Deut. 6:3; ch. 7:23
42:10 [c]ch. 24:6 [d]Deut. 32:36; ch. 18:8
42:11 [e]Isa. 43:5; Rom. 8:31
42:12 [f]Ps. 106:45
42:13 [g]ch. 44:16
42:15 [h]Deut. 17:16; ch. 44:12 [i]Luke 9:51
42:16 [j]Ezek. 11:8
42:17 [k]ch. 24:10; ver. 22 [l]ch. 44:14
42:18 [m]ch. 7:20 [n]ch. 18:16; Zech. 8:13
42:19 [o]Deut. 17:16
42:20 [p]ver. 2
42:22 [q]ver. 17; Ezek. 6:11
43:2 [r]ch. 42:1

sent thee to say, Go not into Egypt to sojourn there:

3 But Baruch the son of Neriah setteth thee on against us, for to deliver us into the hand of the Chaldeans, that they might put us to death, and carry us away captives into Babylon.

4 So Johanan the son of Kareah, and all the captains of the forces, and all the people, obeyed not the voice of the LORD, to dwell in the land of Judah.

5 But Johanan the son of Kareah, and all the captains of the forces, took [s]all the remnant of Judah, that were returned from all nations, whither they had been driven, to dwell in the land of Judah;

6 *Even* men, and women, and children, [t]and the king's daughters, [u]and every person that Nebuzar-adan the captain of the guard had left with Gedaliah the son of Ahikam the son of Shaphan, and Jeremiah the prophet, and Baruch the son of Neriah.

7 So they came into the land of Egypt: for they obeyed not the voice of the LORD: thus came they *even* to [v]Tahpanhes.

8 ¶ Then came the word of the LORD unto Jeremiah in Tahpanhes, saying,

9 Take great stones in thine hand, and hide them in the clay in the brickkiln, which *is* at the entry of Pharaoh's house in Tahpanhes, in the sight of the men of Judah;

10 And say unto them, Thus saith the LORD of hosts, the God of Israel; Behold, I will send and take Nebuchadrezzar the king of Babylon, [w]my servant, and will set his throne upon these stones that I have hid; and he shall spread his royal pavilion over them.

11 [x]And when he cometh, he shall smite the land of Egypt, *and deliver* such *as are* for death to death; and such *as are* for captivity to captivity; and [y]such *as are* for the sword to the sword.

12 And I will kindle a fire in the houses of [z]the gods of Egypt; and he shall burn them, and carry them away captives: and he shall array himself with the land of Egypt, as a shepherd putteth on his garment; and he shall go forth from thence in peace.

13 He shall break also the images of Bethshemesh, that *is* in the land of Egypt; and the houses of the gods of the Egyptians shall he burn with fire.

44 The word that came to Jeremiah concerning all the Jews which dwell in the land of Egypt, which dwell at [a]Migdol, and at [b]Tahpanhes, and at [c]Noph, and in the country of Pathros, saying,

2 Thus saith the LORD of hosts, the God of Israel; Ye have seen all the evil that I have brought upon Jerusalem, and upon all the cities of Judah; and, behold, this day they *are* [d]a desolation, and no man dwelleth therein,

3 Because of their wickedness which they have committed to provoke me to anger, in that they went [e]to burn incense, *and* to [f]serve other gods, whom they knew not, *neither* they, ye, nor your fathers.

4 Howbeit [g]I sent unto you all my servants the prophets, rising early and sending *them*, saying, Oh, do not this abominable thing that I hate.

5 But they hearkened not, nor inclined their ear to turn from their wickedness, to burn no incense unto other gods.

6 Wherefore [h]my fury and mine anger was poured forth, and was kindled in the cities of Judah and in the streets of Jerusalem; and they are wasted *and* desolate, as at this day.

7 Therefore now thus saith the LORD, the God of hosts, the God of Israel; Wherefore commit ye *this* great evil [i]against your souls, to cut off from you man and woman, child and suckling, out of Judah, to leave you none to remain;

8 In that ye [j]provoke me unto wrath with the works of your hands, burning incense unto other gods in the land of Egypt, whither ye be gone to dwell, that ye might cut yourselves off, and that ye might be [k]a curse and a reproach among all the nations of the earth?

9 Have ye forgotten the wickedness of your fathers, and the wickedness of the kings of Judah, and the wickedness of their wives, and your own wickedness, and the wickedness of your wives, which they have committed in the land of Judah, and in the streets of Jerusalem?

10 They are not humbled *even* unto this day, neither have they [l]feared, nor walked in my law, nor in my statutes, that I set before you and before your fathers.

11 ¶ Therefore thus saith the LORD of hosts, the God of Israel; Behold, [m]I will set my face against you for evil, and to cut off all Judah.

12 And I will take the remnant of Judah, that have set their faces to go into the land of Egypt to sojourn there, and [n]they shall all be consumed, *and* fall in the land of Egypt; they shall *even* be consumed by the sword *and* by the famine: they shall die, from the least even unto the greatest, by the sword and by the famine: and [o]they shall be an execration, *and* an astonishment, and a curse, and a reproach.

13 [p]For I will punish them that dwell in the land of Egypt, as I have punished Jerusalem, by the sword, by the famine, and by the pestilence:

14 So that none of the remnant of Judah, which are gone into the land of Egypt to sojourn there, shall escape or remain, that they should return into the land of Judah, to the which they have a desire to return to dwell there: for [q]none shall return but such as shall escape.

15 ¶ Then all the men which knew that their wives had burned incense unto other gods, and all the women that stood by, a great multitude, even all the people that

43:5 [s]ch. 40:11
43:6 [t]ch. 41:10 [u]ch. 39:10
43:7 [v]Isa. 30:4; ch. 2:16
43:10 [w]ch. 25:9; Ezek. 29:18
43:11 [x]ch. 44:13 [y]ch. 15:2; Zech. 11:9
43:12 [z]ch. 46:25
44:1 [a]Ex. 14:2; ch. 46:14 [b]ch. 43:7 [c]Isa. 19:13
44:2 [d]ch. 9:11
44:3 [e]ch. 19:4 [f]Deut. 13:6
44:4 [g]2 Chron. 36:15; ch. 7:25
44:6 [h]ch. 42:18
44:7 [i]Num. 16:38; ch. 7:19
44:8 [j]ch. 25:6 [k]ch. 42:18; ver. 12
44:10 [l]Prov. 28:14
44:11 [m]Lev. 17:10; ch. 21:10; Am. 9:4
44:12 [n]ch. 42:15 [o]ch. 42:18
44:13 [p]ch. 43:11
44:14 [q]ver. 28

dwelt in the land of Egypt, in Pathros, answered Jeremiah, saying,
16 *As for* the word that thou hast spoken
unto us in the name of the LORD, [r]we will
not hearken unto thee.
17 But we will certainly do [s]whatsoever
thing goeth forth out of our own mouth, to
burn incense unto the [t]queen of heaven,
and to pour out drink offerings unto her,
as we have done, we, and our fathers, our
kings, and our princes, in the cities of Judah, and in the streets of Jerusalem: for
then had we plenty of victuals, and were
well, and saw no evil.
18 But since we left off to burn incense to
the queen of heaven, and to pour out drink
offerings unto her, we have wanted all
things, and have been consumed by the
sword and by the famine.
19 [u]And when we burned incense to the
queen of heaven, and poured out drink offerings unto her, did we make her cakes to
worship her, and pour out drink offerings
unto her, without our men?
20 ¶ Then Jeremiah said unto all the people, to the men, and to the women, and to all
the people which had given him *that* answer, saying,
21 The incense that ye burned in the cities
of Judah, and in the streets of Jerusalem,
ye and your fathers, your kings, and your
princes, and the people of the land, did not
the LORD remember them, and came it *not*
into his mind?
22 So that the LORD could no longer bear,
because of the evil of your doings, *and* because of the abominations which ye have
committed; therefore is your land [v]a desolation, and an astonishment, and a curse,
without an inhabitant, [w]as at this day.
23 Because ye have burned incense, and
because ye have sinned against the LORD,
and have not obeyed the voice of the LORD,
nor walked in his law, nor in his statutes,
nor in his testimonies; [x]therefore this evil is
happened unto you, as at this day.
24 Moreover Jeremiah said unto all the
people, and to all the women, Hear the word
of the LORD, all Judah [y]that *are* in the land
of Egypt:
25 Thus saith the LORD of hosts, the God
of Israel, saying; [z]Ye and your wives have
both spoken with your mouths, and fulfilled
with your hand, saying, We will surely perform our vows that we have vowed, to burn
incense to the queen of heaven, and to pour
out drink offerings unto her: ye will surely
accomplish your vows, and surely perform
your vows.
26 Therefore hear ye the word of the
LORD, all Judah that dwell in the land of
Egypt; Behold, [a]I have sworn by my great
name, saith the LORD, that [b]my name shall
no more be named in the mouth of any man
of Judah in all the land of Egypt, saying,
The Lord GOD liveth.
27 [c]Behold, I will watch over them for
evil, and not for good: and all the men of
Judah that *are* in the land of Egypt [d]shall be
consumed by the sword and by the famine,
until there be an end of them.
28 Yet [e]a small number that escape the
sword shall return out of the land of Egypt
into the land of Judah, and all the remnant
of Judah, that are gone into the land of
Egypt to sojourn there, shall know whose
[f]words shall stand, mine, or theirs.
29 ¶ And this *shall be* a sign unto you,
saith the LORD, that I will punish you in this
place, that ye may know that my words
shall [g]surely stand against you for evil:
30 Thus saith the LORD; Behold, [h]I will
give Pharaoh-hophra king of Egypt into the
hand of his enemies, and into the hand of
them that seek his life; as I gave [i]Zedekiah
king of Judah into the hand of Nebuchadrezzar king of Babylon, his enemy, and
that sought his life.

45

The [j]word that Jeremiah the
prophet spake unto Baruch the son
of Neriah, when he had written these words
in a book at the mouth of Jeremiah, in the
fourth year of Jehoiakim the son of Josiah
king of Judah, saying,
2 Thus saith the LORD, the God of Israel,
unto thee, O Baruch;
3 Thou didst say, Woe is me now! for the
LORD hath added grief to my sorrow; I
fainted in my sighing, and I find no rest.
4 ¶ Thus shalt thou say unto him, The
LORD saith thus; Behold, [k]*that* which I have
built will I break down, and that which I
have planted I will pluck up, even this
whole land.
5 And seekest thou great things for thyself? seek *them* not: for, behold, [l]I will
bring evil upon all flesh, saith the LORD: but
thy life will I give unto thee [m]for a prey in
all places whither thou goest.

46

The word of the LORD which came to
Jeremiah the prophet against [n]the
Gentiles;
2 Against Egypt, [o]against the army of
Pharaoh-necho king of Egypt, which was
by the river Euphrates in Carchemish,
which Nebuchadrezzar king of Babylon
smote in the fourth year of Jehoiakim the
son of Josiah king of Judah.
3 [p]Order ye the buckler and shield, and
draw near to battle.
4 Harness the horses; and get up, ye
horsemen, and stand forth with *your* helmets; furbish the spears, *and* put on the
brigandines.
5 Wherefore have I seen them dismayed
and turned away back? and their mighty
ones are beaten down, and are fled apace,
and look not back: *for* [q]fear *was* round
about, saith the LORD.
6 Let not the swift flee away, nor the
mighty man escape; they shall [r]stumble,
and fall toward the north by the river Euphrates.
7 Who *is* this *that* cometh up [s]as a flood,
whose waters are moved as the rivers?
8 Egypt riseth up like a flood, and *his* wa-

44:16 [r]ch. 6:16
44:17 [s]Num. 30:12; Deut. 23:23; Judg. 11:36; ver. 25 [t]ch. 7:18
44:19 [u]ch. 7:18
44:22 [v]ch. 25:11 [w]ver. 6
44:23 [x]Dan. 9:11
44:24 [y]ch. 43:7; ver. 15
44:25 [z]ver. 15
44:26 [a]Gen. 22:16 [b]Ezek. 20:39
44:27 [c]ch. 1:10; Ezek. 7:6 [d]ver. 12
44:28 [e]ver. 14; Isa. 27:13 [f]ver. 17
44:29 [g]Ps. 33:11
44:30 [h]ch. 46:25; Ezek. 29:3 [i]ch. 39:5
45:1 [j]ch. 36:1
45:4 [k]Isa. 5:5
45:5 [l]ch. 25:26 [m]ch. 21:9
46:1 [n]ch. 25:15
46:2 [o]2 Kings 23:29; 2 Chron. 35:29
46:3 [p]ch. 51:11; Nah. 2:1
46:5 [q]ch. 6:25
46:6 [r]Dan. 11:19
46:7 [s]Isa. 8:7; ch. 47:2; Dan. 11:22

ters are moved like the rivers; and he saith,
I will go up, *and* will cover the earth; I will
destroy the city and the inhabitants thereof.
9 Come up, ye horses; and rage, ye chariots; and let the mighty men come forth; the
Ethiopians and the Libyans, [t]that handle
the shield; and the Lydians, that handle *and*
bend the bow.
10 For this *is* [u]the day of the Lord GOD
of hosts, a day of vengeance, that he may
avenge him of his adversaries: and [v]the
sword shall devour, and it shall be satiate
and made drunk with their blood: for the
Lord GOD of hosts [w]hath a sacrifice in the
north country by the river Euphrates.
11 [x]Go up into Gilead, and take balm, [y]O
virgin, the daughter of Egypt: in vain shalt
thou use many medicines; *for* [z]thou shalt
not be cured.
12 The nations have heard of thy shame,
and thy cry hath filled the land: for the
mighty man hath stumbled against the
mighty, *and* they are fallen both together.
13 ¶ The word that the LORD spake to Jeremiah the prophet, how Nebuchadrezzar
king of Babylon should come *and* [a]smite
the land of Egypt.
14 Declare ye in Egypt, and publish in
Migdol, and publish in Noph and in Tahpanhes: say ye, [b]Stand fast, and prepare
thee; for [c]the sword shall devour round
about thee.
15 Why are thy valiant *men* swept away?
they stood not, because the LORD did drive
them.
16 He made many to fall, yea, [d]one fell
upon another: and they said, Arise, and let
us go again to our own people, and to the
land of our nativity, from the oppressing
sword.
17 They did cry there, Pharaoh king of
Egypt *is but* a noise; he hath passed the time
appointed.
18 *As* I live, saith the King, [e]whose name
is the LORD of hosts, Surely as Tabor *is*
among the mountains, and as Carmel by the
sea, *so* shall he come.
19 O [f]thou daughter dwelling in Egypt,
furnish thyself [g]to go into captivity: for
Noph shall be waste and desolate without
an inhabitant.
20 Egypt *is like* a very fair [h]heifer, *but*
destruction cometh; it cometh [i]out of the
north.
21 Also her hired men *are* in the midst of
her like fatted bullocks; for they also are
turned back, *and* are fled away together:
they did not stand, because [j]the day of
their calamity was come upon them, *and* the
time of their visitation.
22 [k]The voice thereof shall go like a serpent; for they shall march with an army,
and come against her with axes, as hewers
of wood.
23 They shall [l]cut down her forest, saith
the LORD, though it cannot be searched; because they are more than [m]the grasshoppers, and *are* innumerable.
24 The daughter of Egypt shall be confounded; she shall be delivered into the
hand of [n]the people of the north.
25 The LORD of hosts, the God of Israel,
saith; Behold, I will punish the multitude of
[o]No, and Pharaoh, and Egypt, [p]with their
gods, and their kings; even Pharaoh, and *all*
them that trust in him:
26 [q]And I will deliver them into the hand
of those that seek their lives, and into the
hand of Nebuchadrezzar king of Babylon,
and into the hand of his servants: and [r]af-
terward it shall be inhabited, as in the days
of old, saith the LORD.
27 ¶ [s]But fear not thou, O my servant Jacob, and be not dismayed, O Israel: for, behold, I will save thee from afar off, and thy
seed from the land of their captivity; and
Jacob shall return, and be in rest and at
ease, and none shall make *him* afraid.
28 Fear thou not, O Jacob my servant,
saith the LORD: for I *am* with thee; for I will
make [t]a full end of all the nations whither
I have driven thee: but I will not make a full
end of thee, but correct thee in measure; yet
will I not leave thee wholly unpunished.

47

The word of the LORD that came to
Jeremiah the prophet [u]against the
Philistines, [v]before that Pharaoh smote
Gaza.
2 Thus saith the LORD; Behold, [w]waters
rise up [x]out of the north, and shall be an
overflowing flood, and shall overflow the
land, and all that is therein; the city, and
them that dwell therein: then the men shall
cry, and all the inhabitants of the land shall
howl.
3 At the [y]noise of the stamping of the
hoofs of his strong *horses,* at the rushing
of his chariots, *and at* the rumbling of his
wheels, the fathers shall not look back to
their children for feebleness of hands;
4 Because of the day that cometh to spoil
all the Philistines, *and* to cut off from
[z]Tyrus and Zidon every helper that remaineth: for the LORD will spoil the Philistines, [a]the remnant of the country of
[b]Caphtor.
5 [c]Baldness is come upon Gaza; [d]Ashke-
lon is cut off *with* the remnant of their valley: how long wilt thou [e]cut thyself?
6 O thou [f]sword of the LORD, how long
will it be ere thou be quiet? put up thyself
into thy scabbard, rest, and be still.
7 How can it be quiet, seeing the LORD
hath [g]given it a charge against Ashkelon,
and against the sea shore? there hath he
[h]appointed it.

48

Against [i]Moab thus saith the LORD
of hosts, the God of Israel; Woe unto
[j]Nebo! for it is spoiled: [k]Kiriathaim is confounded *and* taken: Misgab is confounded
and dismayed.
2 [l]*There shall be* no more praise of
Moab: in [m]Heshbon they have devised evil
against it; come, and let us cut it off from
being a nation. Also thou shalt be cut down,
O Madmen; the sword shall pursue thee.

46:9 [t]Isa. 66:19
46:10 [u]Isa. 13:6; Joel 1:15 [v]Deut. 32:42; Isa. 34:6 [w]Isa. 34:6; Ezek. 39:17; Zeph. 1:7
46:11 [x]ch. 8:22 [y]Isa. 47:1 [z]Ezek. 30:21
46:13 [a]Isa. 19:1; ch. 43:10; Ezek. 29
46:14 [b]ver. 3 [c]ver. 10
46:16 [d]Lev. 26:37
46:18 [e]Isa. 47:4; ch. 48:15
46:19 [f]ch. 48:18 [g]Isa. 20:4
46:20 [h]Hos. 10:11 [i]ch. 1:14; ver. 6
46:21 [j]Ps. 37:13; ch. 50:27
46:22 [k]Isa. 29:4
46:23 [l]Isa. 10:34 [m]Judg. 6:5
46:24 [n]ch. 1:15
46:25 [o]Ezek. 30:14; Nah. 3:8 [p]ch. 43:12; Ezek. 30:13
46:26 [q]ch. 44:30; Ezek. 32:11 [r]Ezek. 29:11
46:27 [s]Isa. 41:13; ch. 30:10
46:28 [t]ch. 10:24
47:1 [u]ch. 25:20; Ezek. 25:15; Zeph. 2:4 [v]Am. 1:6
47:2 [w]Isa. 8:7; ch. 46:7 [x]ch. 1:14
47:3 [y]ch. 8:16; Nah. 3:2
47:4 [z]ch. 25:22 [a]Ezek. 25:16; Am. 1:8 [b]Gen. 10:14
47:5 [c]Am. 1:7; Mic. 1:16; Zeph. 2:4; Zech. 9:5 [d]ch. 25:20 [e]ch. 16:6
47:6 [f]Deut. 32:41; Ezek. 21:3
47:7 [g]Ezek. 14:17 [h]Mic. 6:9
48:1 [i]Isa. 15; ch. 25:21; Ezek. 25:9; Am. 2:1 [j]Num. 32:38; Isa. 15:2 [k]Num. 32:37
48:2 [l]Isa. 16:14 [m]Isa. 15:4

3 [n]A voice of crying *shall be* from Horonaim, spoiling and great destruction.
4 Moab is destroyed; her little ones have
caused a cry to be heard.
5 [o]For in the going up of Luhith continual
weeping shall go up; for in the going down
of Horonaim the enemies have heard a cry
of destruction.
6 [p]Flee, save your lives, and be like the
[q]heath in the wilderness.
7 ¶ For because thou hast trusted in thy
works and in thy treasures, thou shalt also
be taken: and [r]Chemosh shall go forth into
captivity *with* his [s]priests and his princes
together.
8 And [t]the spoiler shall come upon every
city, and no city shall escape: the valley also
shall perish, and the plain shall be destroyed, as the LORD hath spoken.
9 [u]Give wings unto Moab, that it may flee
and get away: for the cities thereof shall be
desolate, without any to dwell therein.
10 [v]Cursed *be* he that doeth the work of
the LORD deceitfully, and cursed *be* he that
keepeth back his sword from blood.
11 ¶ Moab hath been at ease from his
youth, and he [w]hath settled on his lees, and
hath not been emptied from vessel to vessel,
neither hath he gone into captivity: therefore his taste remained in him, and his scent
is not changed.
12 Therefore, behold, the days come,
saith the LORD, that I will send unto him
wanderers, that shall cause him to wander,
and shall empty his vessels, and break their
bottles.
13 And Moab shall be ashamed of [x]Che-
mosh, as the house of Israel [y]was ashamed
of [z]Beth-el their confidence.
14 ¶ How say ye, [a]We *are* mighty and
strong men for the war?
15 [b]Moab is spoiled, and gone up *out of*
her cities, and his chosen young men are
[c]gone down to the slaughter, saith [d]the
King, whose name *is* The LORD of hosts.
16 The calamity of Moab *is* near to come,
and his affliction hasteth fast.
17 All ye that are about him, bemoan him;
and all ye that know his name, say, [e]How is
the strong staff broken, *and* the beautiful
rod!
18 [f]Thou daughter that dost inhabit [g]Di-
bon, come down from *thy* glory, and sit in
thirst; for [h]the spoiler of Moab shall come
upon thee, *and* he shall destroy thy strong
holds.
19 O inhabitant of [i]Aroer, [j]stand by the
way, and espy; ask him that fleeth, and her
that escapeth, *and* say, What is done?
20 Moab is confounded; for it is broken
down: [k]howl and cry; tell ye it in [l]Arnon,
that Moab is spoiled,
21 And judgment is come upon [m]the plain
country; upon Holon, and upon Jahazah,
and upon Mephaath,
22 And upon Dibon, and upon Nebo, and
upon Beth-diblathaim,
23 And upon Kiriathaim, and upon Beth-
gamul, and upon Beth-meon,
24 And upon [n]Kerioth, and upon Bozrah,
and upon all the cities of the land of Moab,
far or near.
25 [o]The horn of Moab is cut off, and his
[p]arm is broken, saith the LORD.
26 ¶ [q]Make ye him drunken: for he magnified *himself* against the LORD: Moab also
shall wallow in his vomit, and he also shall
be in derision.
27 For [r]was not Israel a derision unto
thee? [s]was he found among thieves? for
since thou spakest of him, thou skippedst
for joy.
28 O ye that dwell in Moab, leave the cities, and [t]dwell in the rock, and be like [u]the
dove *that* maketh her nest in the sides of the
hole's mouth.
29 We have heard the [v]pride of Moab, (he
is exceeding proud) his loftiness, and his
arrogancy, and his pride, and the haughtiness of his heart.
30 I know his wrath, saith the LORD; but *it
shall* not *be* so; [w]his lies shall not so effect *it*.
31 Therefore [x]will I howl for Moab, and I
will cry out for all Moab; *mine heart* shall
mourn for the men of Kir-heres.
32 [y]O vine of Sibmah, I will weep for thee
with the weeping of Jazer: thy plants are
gone over the sea, they reach *even* to the sea
of Jazer: the spoiler is fallen upon thy summer fruits and upon thy vintage.
33 And [z]joy and gladness is taken from
the plentiful field, and from the land of
Moab; and I have caused wine to fail from
the winepresses: none shall tread with
shouting; *their* shouting *shall be* no shouting.
34 [a]From the cry of Heshbon *even* unto
Elealeh, *and even* unto Jahaz, have they
uttered their voice, [b]from Zoar *even* unto
Horonaim, *as* an heifer of three years old:
for the waters also of Nimrim shall be desolate.
35 Moreover I will cause to cease in
Moab, saith the LORD, [c]him that offereth in
the high places, and him that burneth incense to his gods.
36 Therefore [d]mine heart shall sound for
Moab like pipes, and mine heart shall sound
like pipes for the men of Kir-heres: because
[e]the riches *that* he hath gotten are perished.
37 For [f]every head *shall be* bald, and every beard clipped: upon all the hands *shall
be* cuttings, and [g]upon the loins sackcloth.
38 *There shall be* lamentation generally
upon all the housetops of Moab, and in the
streets thereof: for I have broken Moab like
[h]a vessel wherein *is* no pleasure, saith the
LORD.
39 They shall howl, *saying,* How is it broken down! how hath Moab turned the back
with shame! so shall Moab be a derision and
a dismaying to all them about him.
40 For thus saith the LORD; Behold, [i]he

48:3 [n]ver. 5
48:5 [o]Isa. 15:5
48:6 [p]ch. 51:6 [q]ch. 17:6
48:7 [r]Num. 21:29; Judg. 11:24; Isa. 46:1; ch. 43:12 [s]ch. 49:3
48:8 [t]ch. 6:26; ver. 18
48:9 [u]Ps. 55:6; ver. 28
48:10 [v]Judg. 5:23; 1 Sam. 15:3; 1 Kings 20:42
48:11 [w]Zeph. 1:12
48:13 [x]Judg. 11:24; 1 Kings 11:7 [y]Hos. 10:6 [z]1 Kings 12:29
48:14 [a]Isa. 16:6
48:15 [b]ver. 8 [c]ch. 50:27 [d]ch. 46:18
48:17 [e]Isa. 9:4
48:18 [f]Isa. 47:1; ch. 46:19 [g]Num. 21:30; Isa. 15:2 [h]ver. 8
48:19 [i]Deut. 2:36 [j]1 Sam. 4:13
48:20 [k]Isa. 16:7 [l]Num. 21:13
48:21 [m]ver. 8
48:24 [n]ver. 41; Am. 2:2
48:25 [o]Ps. 75:10 [p]Ezek. 30:21
48:26 [q]ch. 25:15
48:27 [r]Zeph. 2:8 [s]ch. 2:26
48:28 [t]Ps. 55:6; ver. 9 [u]SSol. 2:14
48:29 [v]Isa. 16:6
48:30 [w]Isa. 16:6; ch. 50:36
48:31 [x]Isa. 15:5
48:32 [y]Isa. 16:8
48:33 [z]Isa. 16:10; Joel 1:12
48:34 [a]Isa. 15:4 [b]Isa. 15:5; ver. 5
48:35 [c]Isa. 15:2
48:36 [d]Isa. 15:5 [e]Isa. 15:7
48:37 [f]Isa. 15:2; ch. 47:5 [g]Gen. 37:34
48:38 [h]ch. 22:28
48:40 [i]Deut. 28:49; ch. 49:22; Dan. 7:4; Hos. 8:1; Hab. 1:8

shall fly as an eagle, and shall [j]spread his
wings over Moab.
41 [k]Kerioth is taken, and the strong holds
are surprised, and [l]the mighty men's
hearts in Moab at that day shall be as the
heart of a woman in her pangs.
42 And Moab shall be destroyed [m]from
being a people, because he hath magnified
himself against the LORD.
43 [n]Fear, and the pit, and the snare, *shall
be* upon thee, O inhabitant of Moab, saith
the LORD.
44 He that fleeth from the fear shall fall
into the pit; and he that getteth up out of the
pit shall be taken in the snare: for [o]I will
bring upon it, *even* upon Moab, the year of
their visitation, saith the LORD.
45 They that fled stood under the shadow
of Heshbon because of the force: but [p]a fire
shall come forth out of Heshbon, and a
flame from the midst of Sihon, and [q]shall
devour the corner of Moab, and the crown
of the head of the tumultuous ones.
46 [r]Woe be unto thee, O Moab! the people of Chemosh perisheth: for thy sons are
taken captives, and thy daughters captives.
47 ¶ Yet will I bring again the captivity of
Moab [s]in the latter days, saith the LORD.
Thus far *is* the judgment of Moab.

49 Concerning [t]the Ammonites, thus
saith the LORD; Hath Israel no sons?
hath he no heir? why *then* doth their king
inherit [u]Gad, and his people dwell in his
cities?
2 Therefore, behold, the days come, saith
the LORD, that I will cause an alarm of war
to be heard in [v]Rabbah of the Ammonites;
and it shall be a desolate heap, and her
daughters shall be burned with fire: then
shall Israel be heir unto them that were his
heirs, saith the LORD.
3 Howl, O Heshbon, for Ai is spoiled: cry,
ye daughters of Rabbah, [w]gird you with
sackcloth; lament, and run to and fro by the
hedges; for their king shall go into captivity,
and his [x]priests and his princes together.
4 Wherefore gloriest thou in the valleys,
thy flowing valley, O [y]backsliding daughter? that trusted in her treasures, [z]*saying,*
Who shall come unto me?
5 Behold, I will bring a fear upon thee,
saith the Lord GOD of hosts, from all those
that be about thee; and ye shall be driven
out every man right forth; and none shall
gather up him that wandereth.
6 And [a]afterward I will bring again the
captivity of the children of Ammon, saith
the LORD.
7 ¶ [b]Concerning Edom, thus saith the
LORD of hosts; [c]*Is* wisdom no more in Teman? [d]is counsel perished from the prudent? is their wisdom vanished?
8 [e]Flee ye, turn back, dwell deep,
O inhabitants of [f]Dedan; for I will bring
the calamity of Esau upon him, the time
that I will visit him.
9 If [g]grapegatherers come to thee, would
they not leave *some* gleaning grapes? if

48:40 [j]Isa. 8:8
48:41 [k]ver. 24 [l]Isa. 13:8; ch. 30:6; Mic. 4:9
48:42 [m]Ps. 83:4; Isa. 7:8
48:43 [n]Isa. 24:17
48:44 [o]ch. 11:23
48:45 [p]Num. 21:28 [q]Num. 24:17
48:46 [r]Num. 21:29
48:47 [s]ch. 49:6
49:1 [t]Ezek. 21:28; Am. 1:13; Zeph. 2:8 [u]Am. 1:13
49:2 [v]Ezek. 25:5; Am. 1:14
49:3 [w]Isa. 32:11; ch. 4:8 [x]ch. 48:7; Am. 1:15
49:4 [y]ch. 3:14 [z]ch. 21:13
49:6 [a]ver. 39
49:7 [b]Ezek. 25:12; Am. 1:11 [c]Obad. 8 [d]Isa. 19:11
49:8 [e]ver. 30 [f]ch. 25:23
49:9 [g]Obad. 5
49:10 [h]Mal. 1:3 [i]Isa. 17:14
49:12 [j]ch. 25:29; Obad. 16
49:13 [k]Gen. 22:16; Isa. 45:23; Am. 6:8 [l]Isa. 34:6
49:14 [m]Obad. 1:2
49:16 [n]Obad. 4 [o]Job 39:27 [p]Am. 9:2
49:17 [q]ch. 18:16
49:18 [r]Gen. 19:25; Deut. 29:23; ch. 50:40; Am. 4:11
49:19 [s]ch. 50:44 [t]ch. 12:5 [u]Ex. 15:11 [v]Job 41:10
49:20 [w]ch. 50:45
49:21 [x]ch. 50:46
49:22 [y]ch. 4:13
49:23 [z]Isa. 17:1; Am. 1:3; Zech. 9:1

thieves by night, they will destroy till they
have enough.
10 [h]But I have made Esau bare, I have
uncovered his secret places, and he shall
not be able to hide himself: his seed is
spoiled, and his brethren, and his neighbours, and [i]he *is* not.
11 Leave thy fatherless children, I will
preserve *them* alive; and let thy widows
trust in me.
12 For thus saith the LORD; Behold, [j]they
whose judgment *was* not to drink of the cup
have assuredly drunken; and *art* thou he
that shall altogether go unpunished? thou
shalt not go unpunished, but thou shalt
surely drink *of it.*
13 For [k]I have sworn by myself, saith the
LORD, that [l]Bozrah shall become a desolation, a reproach, a waste, and a curse; and
all the cities thereof shall be perpetual
wastes;
14 I have heard a [m]rumour from the
LORD, and an ambassador is sent unto the
heathen, *saying,* Gather ye together, and
come against her, and rise up to the battle.
15 For, lo, I will make thee small among
the heathen, *and* despised among men.
16 Thy terribleness hath deceived thee,
and the pride of thine heart, O thou that
dwellest in the clefts of the rock, that holdest the height of the hill: [n]though thou
shouldest make thy [o]nest as high as the eagle, [p]I will bring thee down from thence,
saith the LORD.
17 Also Edom shall be a desolation: [q]every one that goeth by it shall be astonished,
and shall hiss at all the plagues thereof.
18 [r]As in the overthrow of Sodom and
Gomorrah and the neighbour *cities* thereof,
saith the LORD, no man shall abide there,
neither shall a son of man dwell in it.
19 [s]Behold, he shall come up like a lion
from [t]the swelling of Jordan against the
habitation of the strong: but I will suddenly
make him run away from her: and who *is* a
chosen *man, that* I may appoint over her?
for [u]who *is* like me? and who will appoint
me the time? and [v]who *is* that shepherd
that will stand before me?
20 [w]Therefore hear the counsel of the
LORD, that he hath taken against Edom; and
his purposes, that he hath purposed against
the inhabitants of Teman: Surely the least
of the flock shall draw them out: surely he
shall make their habitations desolate with
them.
21 [x]The earth is moved at the noise of
their fall, at the cry the noise thereof was
heard in the Red sea.
22 Behold, [y]he shall come up and fly as
the eagle, and spread his wings over Bozrah: and at that day shall the heart of the
mighty men of Edom be as the heart of a
woman in her pangs.
23 ¶ [z]Concerning Damascus. Hamath is
confounded, and Arpad: for they have
heard evil tidings: they are fainthearted;

[a]*there is* sorrow on the sea; it cannot be quiet.

24 Damascus is waxed feeble, *and* turneth herself to flee, and fear hath seized on *her:* [b]anguish and sorrows have taken her, as a woman in travail.

25 How is [c]the city of praise not left, the city of my joy!

26 [d]Therefore her young men shall fall in her streets, and all the men of war shall be cut off in that day, saith the LORD of hosts.

27 And I will kindle a [e]fire in the wall of Damascus, and it shall consume the palaces of Ben-hadad.

28 ¶ [f]Concerning Kedar, and concerning the kingdoms of Hazor, which Nebuchadrezzar king of Babylon shall smite, thus saith the LORD; Arise ye, go up to Kedar, and spoil [g]the men of the east.

29 Their [h]tents and their flocks shall they take away: they shall take to themselves their curtains, and all their vessels, and their camels; and they shall cry unto them, [i]Fear *is* on every side.

30 ¶ [j]Flee, get you far off, dwell deep, O ye inhabitants of Hazor, saith the LORD; for Nebuchadrezzar king of Babylon hath taken counsel against you, and hath conceived a purpose against you.

31 Arise, get you up unto [k]the wealthy nation, that dwelleth without care, saith the LORD, which have neither gates nor bars, *which* [l]dwell alone.

32 And their camels shall be a booty, and the multitude of their cattle a spoil: and I will [m]scatter into all winds [n]them *that are* in the utmost corners; and I will bring their calamity from all sides thereof, saith the LORD.

33 And Hazor [o]shall be a dwelling for dragons, *and* a desolation for ever: [p]there shall no man abide there, nor *any* son of man dwell in it.

34 ¶ The word of the LORD that came to Jeremiah the prophet against [q]Elam in the beginning of the reign of Zedekiah king of Judah, saying,

35 Thus saith the LORD of hosts; Behold, I will break [r]the bow of Elam, the chief of their might.

36 And upon Elam will I bring the four winds from the four quarters of heaven, and [s]will scatter them toward all those winds; and there shall be no nation whither the outcasts of Elam shall not come.

37 For I will cause Elam to be dismayed before their enemies, and before them that seek their life: and I will bring evil upon them, *even* my fierce anger, saith the LORD; [t]and I will send the sword after them, till I have consumed them:

38 And I will [u]set my throne in Elam, and will destroy from thence the king and the princes, saith the LORD.

39 ¶ But it shall come to pass [v]in the latter days, *that* I will bring again the captivity of Elam, saith the LORD.

49:23 [a]Isa. 57:20
49:24 [b]Isa. 13:8; ch. 4:31; ver. 22
49:25 [c]ch. 33:9
49:26 [d]ch. 50:30
49:27 [e]Am. 1:4
49:28 [f]Isa. 21:13 [g]Judg. 6:3; Job 1:3
49:29 [h]Ps. 120:5 [i]ch. 6:25
49:30 [j]ver. 8
49:31 [k]Ezek. 38:11 [l]Num. 23:9; Deut. 33:28; Mic. 7:14
49:32 [m]Ezek. 5:10; ver. 36 [n]ch. 9:26
49:33 [o]ch. 9:11; Mal. 1:3 [p]ver. 18
49:34 [q]ch. 25:25
49:35 [r]Isa. 22:6
49:36 [s]ver. 32
49:37 [t]ch. 9:16
49:38 [u]ch. 43:10
49:39 [v]ch. 48:47; ver. 6
50:1 [w]Isa. 13:1
50:2 [x]Isa. 46:1; ch. 51:44 [y]ch. 43:12
50:3 [z]ch. 51:48 [a]Isa. 13:17; ver. 39
50:4 [b]Hos. 1:11 [c]Ezra 3:12; Ps. 126:5; ch. 31:9; Zech. 12:10 [d]Hos. 3:5
50:5 [e]ch. 31:31
50:6 [f]Isa. 53:6; ver. 17; 1 Pet. 2:25 [g]ch. 2:20
50:7 [h]Ps. 79:7 [i]ch. 40:2; Zech. 11:5 [j]ch. 2:3; Dan. 9:16 [k]Ps. 90:1 [l]Ps. 22:4
50:8 [m]Isa. 48:20; ch. 51:6; Zech. 2:6; Rev. 18:4
50:9 [n]ch. 15:14; ver. 3 [o]ver. 14 [p]2 Sam. 1:22
50:10 [q]Rev. 17:16
50:11 [r]Isa. 47:6 [s]Hos. 10:11
50:13 [t]ch. 25:12 [u]ch. 49:17
50:14 [v]ver. 9; ch. 51:2 [w]ch. 49:35; ver. 29
50:15 [x]1 Chron. 29:24; 2 Chron. 30:8; Lam. 5:6; Ezek. 17:18 [y]ch. 51:58 [z]ch. 51:6

50 The word that the LORD spake [w]against Babylon *and* against the land of the Chaldeans by Jeremiah the prophet.

2 Declare ye among the nations, and publish, and set up a standard; publish, *and* conceal not: say, Babylon is taken, [x]Bel is confounded, Merodach is broken in pieces; [y]her idols are confounded, her images are broken in pieces.

3 [z]For out of the north there cometh up [a]a nation against her, which shall make her land desolate, and none shall dwell therein: they shall remove, they shall depart, both man and beast.

4 ¶ In those days, and in that time, saith the LORD, the children of Israel shall come, [b]they and the children of Judah together, [c]going and weeping: they shall go, [d]and seek the LORD their God.

5 They shall ask the way to Zion with their faces thitherward, *saying*, Come, and let us join ourselves to the LORD in [e]a perpetual covenant *that* shall not be forgotten.

6 My people hath been [f]lost sheep: their shepherds have caused them to go astray, they have turned them away *on* [g]the mountains: they have gone from mountain to hill, they have forgotten their restingplace.

7 All that found them have [h]devoured them: and [i]their adversaries said, [j]We offend not, because they have sinned against the LORD, [k]the habitation of justice, even the LORD, [l]the hope of their fathers.

8 [m]Remove out of the midst of Babylon, and go forth out of the land of the Chaldeans, and be as the he goats before the flocks.

9 ¶ [n]For, lo, I will raise and cause to come up against Babylon an assembly of great nations from the north country: and they shall [o]set themselves in array against her; from thence she shall be taken: their arrows *shall be* as of a mighty expert man; [p]none shall return in vain.

10 And Chaldea shall be a spoil: [q]all that spoil her shall be satisfied, saith the LORD.

11 [r]Because ye were glad, because ye rejoiced, O ye destroyers of mine heritage, because ye are grown fat [s]as the heifer at grass, and bellow as bulls;

12 Your mother shall be sore confounded; she that bare you shall be ashamed: behold, the hindermost of the nations *shall be* a wilderness, a dry land, and a desert.

13 Because of the wrath of the LORD it shall not be inhabited, [t]but it shall be wholly desolate: [u]every one that goeth by Babylon shall be astonished, and hiss at all her plagues.

14 [v]Put yourselves in array against Babylon round about: all ye [w]that bend the bow, shoot at her, spare no arrows: for she hath sinned against the LORD.

15 Shout against her round about: she hath [x]given her hand: her foundations are fallen, [y]her walls are thrown down: for [z]it *is* the vengeance of the LORD: take ven-

geance upon her; [a]as she hath done, do
unto her.
16 Cut off the sower from Babylon, and
him that handleth the sickle in the time of
harvest: for fear of the oppressing sword
[b]they shall turn every one to his people,
and they shall flee every one to his own
land.
17 ¶ Israel *is* [c]a scattered sheep; [d]the lions have driven *him* away: first [e]the king of
Assyria hath devoured him; and last this
[f]Nebuchadrezzar king of Babylon hath
broken his bones.
18 Therefore thus saith the LORD of hosts,
the God of Israel; Behold, I will punish the
king of Babylon and his land, as I have punished the king of Assyria.
19 [g]And I will bring Israel again to his
habitation, and he shall feed on Carmel and
Bashan, and his soul shall be satisfied upon
mount Ephraim and Gilead.
20 In those days, and in that time, saith
the LORD, [h]the iniquity of Israel shall be
sought for, and *there shall be* none; and the
sins of Judah, and they shall not be found:
for I will pardon them [i]whom I reserve.
21 ¶ Go up against the land of Merathaim,
even against it, and against the inhabitants
of [j]Pekod: waste and utterly destroy after
them, saith the LORD, and do [k]according to
all that I have commanded thee.
22 [l]A sound of battle *is* in the land, and of
great destruction.
23 How is [m]the hammer of the whole
earth cut asunder and broken! how is Babylon become a desolation among the nations!
24 I have laid a snare for thee, and thou
art also taken, O Babylon, [n]and thou wast
not aware: thou art found, and also caught,
because thou hast striven against the LORD.
25 The LORD hath opened his armoury,
and hath brought forth [o]the weapons of his
indignation: for this *is* the work of the Lord
GOD of hosts in the land of the Chaldeans.
26 Come against her from the utmost border, open her storehouses: cast her up as
heaps, and destroy her utterly: let nothing
of her be left.
27 Slay all her [p]bullocks; let them go
down to the slaughter: woe unto them! for
their day is come, the time of their [q]visita-
tion.
28 The voice of them that flee and escape
out of the land of Babylon, [r]to declare in
Zion the vengeance of the LORD our God,
the vengeance of his temple.
29 Call together the archers against Babylon: [s]all ye that bend the bow, camp
against it round about; let none thereof escape: [t]recompense her according to her
work; according to all that she hath done,
do unto her: [u]for she hath been proud
against the LORD, against the Holy One of
Israel.
30 [v]Therefore shall her young men fall in
the streets, and all her men of war shall be
cut off in that day, saith the LORD.

31 Behold, I *am* against thee, *O thou* most
proud, saith the Lord GOD of hosts: for [w]thy
day is come, the time *that* I will visit thee.
32 And the most proud shall stumble and
fall, and none shall raise him up: and [x]I will
kindle a fire in his cities, and it shall devour
all round about him.
33 ¶ Thus saith the LORD of hosts; The
children of Israel and the children of Judah
were oppressed together: and all that took
them captives held them fast; they refused
to let them go.
34 [y]Their Redeemer *is* strong; [z]the LORD
of hosts *is* his name: he shall throughly
plead their cause, that he may give rest to
the land, and disquiet the inhabitants of
Babylon.
35 ¶ A sword *is* upon the Chaldeans, saith
the LORD, and upon the inhabitants of Babylon, and [a]upon her princes, and upon [b]her
wise *men*.
36 A sword *is* [c]upon the liars; and they
shall dote: a sword *is* upon her mighty men;
and they shall be dismayed.
37 A sword *is* upon their horses, and upon
their chariots, and upon all [d]the mingled
people that *are* in the midst of her; and
[e]they shall become as women: a sword *is*
upon her treasures; and they shall be
robbed.
38 [f]A drought *is* upon her waters; and
they shall be dried up: for it *is* the land of
[g]graven images, and they are mad upon
their idols.
39 [h]Therefore the wild beasts of the
desert with the wild beasts of the islands
shall dwell *there,* and the owls shall dwell
therein: [i]and it shall be no more inhabited
for ever; neither shall it be dwelt in from
generation to generation.
40 [j]As God overthrew Sodom and Gomorrah and the neighbour *cities* thereof,
saith the LORD; *so* shall no man abide there,
neither shall any son of man dwell therein.
41 [k]Behold, a people shall come from the
north, and a great nation, and many kings
shall be raised up from the coasts of the
earth.
42 [l]They shall hold the bow and the
lance: [m]they *are* cruel, and will not shew
mercy: [n]their voice shall roar like the sea,
and they shall ride upon horses, *every one*
put in array, like a man to the battle, against
thee, O daughter of Babylon.
43 The king of Babylon hath heard the
report of them, and his hands waxed feeble:
[o]anguish took hold of him, *and* pangs as of
a woman in travail.
44 [p]Behold, he shall come up like a lion
from the swelling of Jordan unto the habitation of the strong: but I will make them suddenly run away from her: and who *is* a
chosen *man, that* I may appoint over her?
for who *is* like me? and who will appoint me
the time? and [q]who *is* that shepherd that
will stand before me?
45 Therefore hear ye [r]the counsel of the
LORD, that he hath taken against Babylon;

50:15 [a]Ps. 137:8; ver. 29; Rev. 18:6
50:16 [b]Isa. 13:14; ch. 51:9
50:17 [c]ver. 6 [d]ch. 2:15 [e]2 Kings 17:6 [f]2 Kings 24:10
50:19 [g]Isa. 65:10; ch. 33:12; Ezek. 34:13
50:20 [h]ch. 31:34 [i]Isa. 1:9
50:21 [j]Ezek. 23:23 [k]2 Sam. 16:11; 2 Kings 18:25; 2 Chron. 36:23; Isa. 10:6; ch. 34:22
50:22 [l]ch. 51:54
50:23 [m]Isa. 14:6; ch. 51:20
50:24 [n]ch. 51:8; Dan. 5:30
50:25 [o]Isa. 13:5
50:27 [p]Ps. 22:12; Isa. 34:7; ch. 46:21 [q]ch. 48:44; ver. 31
50:28 [r]ch. 51:10
50:29 [s]ver. 14 [t]ver. 15; ch. 51:56; Rev. 18:6 [u]Isa. 47:10
50:30 [v]ch. 49:26
50:31 [w]ver. 27
50:32 [x]ch. 21:14
50:34 [y]Rev. 18:8 [z]Isa. 47:4
50:35 [a]Dan. 5:30 [b]Isa. 47:13
50:36 [c]Isa. 44:25; ch. 48:30
50:37 [d]ch. 25:20; Ezek. 30:5 [e]ch. 51:30; Nah. 3:13
50:38 [f]Isa. 44:27; ch. 51:32; Rev. 16:12 [g]ver. 2; ch. 51:44
50:39 [h]Isa. 13:21; ch. 51:37; Rev. 18:2 [i]Isa. 13:20; ch. 25:12
50:40 [j]Gen. 19:25; Isa. 13:19; ch. 49:18
50:41 [k]ver. 9; ch. 6:22; Rev. 17:16
50:42 [l]ch. 6:22 [m]Isa. 13:18 [n]Isa. 5:30
50:43 [o]ch. 49:24
50:44 [p]ch. 49:19 [q]Job 41:10; ch. 49:19
50:45 [r]Isa. 14:24; ch. 51:11

and his purposes, that he hath purposed
against the land of the Chaldeans: Surely
the least of the flock shall draw them out:
surely he shall make *their* habitation desolate with them.
46 [s]At the noise of the taking of Babylon
the earth is moved, and the cry is heard
among the nations.

51

Thus saith the LORD; Behold, I
will raise up against Babylon, and
against them that dwell in the midst of them
that rise up against me, [t]a destroying wind;
2 And will send unto Babylon [u]fanners,
that shall fan her, and shall empty her land:
[v]for in the day of trouble they shall be
against her round about.
3 Against *him that* bendeth [w]let the archer bend his bow, and against *him that*
lifteth himself up in his brigandine: and
spare ye not her young men; [x]destroy ye
utterly all her host.
4 Thus the slain shall fall in the land of
the Chaldeans, [y]and *they that are* thrust
through in her streets.
5 For Israel *hath* not *been* forsaken, nor
Judah of his God, of the LORD of hosts;
though their land was filled with sin against
the Holy One of Israel.
6 [z]Flee out of the midst of Babylon, and
deliver every man his soul: be not cut off
in her iniquity; for [a]this *is* the time of the
LORD's vengeance; [b]he will render unto her
a recompence.
7 [c]Babylon *hath been* a golden cup in
the LORD's hand, that made all the earth
drunken: [d]the nations have drunken of her
wine; therefore the nations [e]are mad.
8 Babylon is suddenly [f]fallen and destroyed: [g]howl for her; [h]take balm for her
pain, if so be she may be healed.
9 We would have healed Babylon, but she
is not healed: forsake her, and [i]let us go
every one into his own country: [j]for her
judgment reacheth unto heaven, and is
lifted up *even* to the skies.
10 The LORD hath [k]brought forth our
righteousness: come, and let us [l]declare in
Zion the work of the LORD our God.
11 [m]Make bright the arrows; gather the
shields: [n]the LORD hath raised up the spirit
of the kings of the Medes: [o]for his device *is*
against Babylon, to destroy it; because it *is*
[p]the vengeance of the LORD, the vengeance
of his temple.
12 [q]Set up the standard upon the walls of
Babylon, make the watch strong, set up the
watchmen, prepare the ambushes: for the
LORD hath both devised and done that
which he spake against the inhabitants of
Babylon.
13 [r]O thou that dwellest upon many waters, abundant in treasures, thine end is
come, *and* the measure of thy covetousness.
14 [s]The LORD of hosts hath sworn by
himself, *saying*, Surely I will fill thee with
men, [t]as with caterpillers; and they shall
lift [u]up a shout against thee.
15 [v]He hath made the earth by his power,

50:46 [s]Rev. 18:9
51:1 [t]2 Kings 19:7; ch. 4:11
51:2 [u]ch. 15:7 [v]ch. 50:14
51:3 [w]ch. 50:14 [x]ch. 50:21
51:4 [y]ch. 49:26
51:6 [z]ch. 50:8; Rev. 18:4 [a]ch. 50:15 [b]ch. 25:14
51:7 [c]Rev. 17:4 [d]Rev. 14:8 [e]ch. 25:16
51:8 [f]Isa. 21:9; Rev. 14:8 [g]ch. 48:20; Rev. 18:9 [h]ch. 46:11
51:9 [i]Isa. 13:4; ch. 50:16 [j]Rev. 18:5
51:10 [k]Ps. 37:6 [l]ch. 50:28
51:11 [m]ch. 46:4 [n]Isa. 13:17; ver. 28 [o]ch. 50:45 [p]ch. 50:28
51:12 [q]Nah. 2:1
51:13 [r]Rev. 17:1
51:14 [s]ch. 49:13; Am. 6:8 [t]Nah. 3:15 [u]ch. 50:15
51:15 [v]Gen. 1:1; ch. 10:12 [w]Job 9:8; Ps. 104:2; Isa. 40:22
51:16 [x]ch. 10:13 [y]Ps. 135:7
51:17 [z]ch. 10:14 [a]ch. 50:2
51:18 [b]ch. 10:15
51:19 [c]ch. 10:16
51:20 [d]Isa. 10:5; ch. 50:23
51:22 [e]2 Chron. 36:17
51:24 [f]ch. 50:15
51:25 [g]Isa. 13:2; Zech. 4:7 [h]Rev. 8:8
51:26 [i]ch. 50:40
51:27 [j]Isa. 13:2 [k]ch. 25:14 [l]ch. 50:41
51:28 [m]ver. 11
51:29 [n]ch. 50:13; ver. 43

he hath established the world by his wisdom, and [w]hath stretched out the heaven by
his understanding.
16 [x]When he uttereth *his* voice, *there is* a
multitude of waters in the heavens; and [y]he
causeth the vapours to ascend from the
ends of the earth: he maketh lightnings with
rain, and bringeth forth the wind out of his
treasures.
17 [z]Every man is brutish by *his* knowledge; every founder is confounded by the
graven image: [a]for his molten image *is*
falsehood, and *there is* no breath in them.
18 [b]They *are* vanity, the work of errors:
in the time of their visitation they shall perish.
19 [c]The portion of Jacob *is* not like them;
for he *is* the former of all things: and *Israel*
is the rod of his inheritance: the LORD of
hosts *is* his name.
20 [d]Thou *art* my battle axe *and* weapons
of war: for with thee will I break in pieces
the nations, and with thee will I destroy
kingdoms;
21 And with thee will I break in pieces the
horse and his rider; and with thee will I
break in pieces the chariot and his rider;
22 With thee also will I break in pieces
man and woman; and with thee will I break
in pieces [e]old and young; and with thee will
I break in pieces the young man and the
maid;
23 I will also break in pieces with thee the
shepherd and his flock; and with thee will I
break in pieces the husbandman and his
yoke of oxen; and with thee will I break in
pieces captains and rulers.
24 [f]And I will render unto Babylon and
to all the inhabitants of Chaldea all their
evil that they have done in Zion in your
sight, saith the LORD.
25 Behold, I *am* against thee, [g]O destroying mountain, saith the LORD, which destroyest all the earth: and I will stretch out
mine hand upon thee, and roll thee down
from the rocks, [h]and will make thee a burnt
mountain.
26 And they shall not take of thee a stone
for a corner, nor a stone for foundations;
[i]but thou shalt be desolate for ever, saith
the LORD.
27 [j]Set ye up a standard in the land, blow
the trumpet among the nations, [k]prepare
the nations against her, call together
against her [l]the kingdoms of Ararat,
Minni, and Ashchenaz; appoint a captain
against her; cause the horses to come up as
the rough caterpillers.
28 Prepare against her the nations with
[m]the kings of the Medes, the captains
thereof, and all the rulers thereof, and all
the land of his dominion.
29 And the land shall tremble and sorrow:
for every purpose of the LORD shall be performed against Babylon, [n]to make the land
of Babylon a desolation without an inhabitant.
30 The mighty men of Babylon have for-

born to fight, they have remained in *their*
holds: their might hath failed; [o]they became as women: they have burned her
dwellingplaces; [p]her bars are broken.
31 [q]One post shall run to meet another,
and one messenger to meet another, to
shew the king of Babylon that his city is
taken at *one* end,
32 And that [r]the passages are stopped,
and the reeds they have burned with fire,
and the men of war are affrighted.
33 For thus saith the LORD of hosts, the
God of Israel; The daughter of Babylon *is*
[s]like a threshingfloor, [t]*it is* time to thresh
her: yet a little while, [u]and the time of her
harvest shall come.
34 Nebuchadrezzar the king of Babylon
hath [v]devoured me, he hath crushed me, he
hath made me an empty vessel, he hath
swallowed me up like a dragon, he hath
filled his belly with my delicates, he
hath cast me out.
35 The violence done to me and to my
flesh *be* upon Babylon, shall the inhabitant
of Zion say; and my blood upon the inhabitants of Chaldea, shall Jerusalem say.
36 Therefore thus saith the LORD; Behold,
[w]I will plead thy cause, and take vengeance
for thee; [x]and I will dry up her sea, and
make her springs dry.
37 [y]And Babylon shall become heaps, a
dwellingplace for dragons, [z]an astonishment, and an hissing, without an inhabitant.
38 They shall roar together like lions:
they shall yell as lions' whelps.
39 In their heat I will make their feasts,
and [a]I will make them drunken, that they
may rejoice, and sleep a perpetual sleep,
and not wake, saith the LORD.
40 I will bring them down like lambs to
the slaughter, like rams with he goats.
41 How is [b]Sheshach taken! and how is
[c]the praise of the whole earth surprised!
how is Babylon become an astonishment
among the nations!
42 [d]The sea is come up upon Babylon:
she is covered with the multitude of the
waves thereof.
43 [e]Her cities are a desolation, a dry
land, and a wilderness, a land wherein no
man dwelleth, neither doth *any* son of man
pass thereby.
44 [f]And I will punish Bel in Babylon, and
I will bring forth out of his mouth that
which he hath swallowed up: and the nations shall not flow together any more unto
him: yea, [g]the wall of Babylon shall fall.
45 [h]My people, go ye out of the midst of
her, and deliver ye every man his soul from
the fierce anger of the LORD.
46 And lest your heart faint, and ye fear
[i]for the rumour that shall be heard in the
land; a rumour shall both come *one* year,
and after that in *another* year *shall come*
a rumour, and violence in the land, ruler
against ruler.
47 Therefore, behold, the days come, that
[j]I will do judgment upon the graven images
of Babylon: and her whole land shall be
confounded, and all her slain shall fall in
the midst of her.
48 Then [k]the heaven and the earth, and
all that *is* therein, shall sing for Babylon:
[l]for the spoilers shall come unto her from
the north, saith the LORD.
49 As Babylon *hath caused* the slain of
Israel to fall, so at Babylon shall fall the
slain of all the earth.
50 [m]Ye that have escaped the sword, go
away, stand not still: remember the LORD
afar off, and let Jerusalem come into your
mind.
51 [n]We are confounded, because we
have heard reproach: shame hath covered
our faces: for strangers are come into the
sanctuaries of the LORD's house.
52 Wherefore, behold, the days come,
saith the LORD, [o]that I will do judgment
upon her graven images: and through all
her land the wounded shall groan.
53 [p]Though Babylon should mount up to
heaven, and though she should fortify the
height of her strength, *yet* from me shall
spoilers come unto her, saith the LORD.
54 [q]A sound of a cry *cometh* from Babylon, and great destruction from the land of
the Chaldeans:
55 Because the LORD hath spoiled Babylon, and destroyed out of her the great
voice; when her waves do roar like great
waters, a noise of their voice is uttered:
56 Because the spoiler is come upon her,
even upon Babylon, and her mighty men
are taken, every one of their bows is broken: [r]for the LORD God of recompences
shall surely requite.
57 [s]And I will make drunk her princes,
and her wise *men*, her captains, and her rulers, and her mighty men: and they shall
sleep a perpetual sleep, and not wake, saith
[t]the King, whose name *is* the LORD of
hosts.
58 Thus saith the LORD of hosts; [u]The
broad walls of Babylon shall be utterly broken, and her high gates shall be burned
with fire; and [v]the people shall labour in
vain, and the folk in the fire, and they shall
be weary.
59 ¶ The word which Jeremiah the
prophet commanded Seraiah the son of Neriah, the son of Maaseiah, when he went
with Zedekiah the king of Judah into Babylon in the fourth year of his reign. And *this*
Seraiah *was* a quiet prince.
60 So Jeremiah wrote in a book all the
evil that should come upon Babylon, *even*
all these words that are written against Babylon.
61 And Jeremiah said to Seraiah, When
thou comest to Babylon, and shalt see, and
shalt read all these words;
62 Then shalt thou say, O LORD, thou hast
spoken against this place, to cut it off, that
[w]none shall remain in it, neither man nor
beast, but that it shall be desolate for ever.
63 And it shall be, when thou hast made

51:30 [o]Isa. 19:16; ch. 48:41 [p]Lam. 2:9; Am. 1:5; Nah. 3:13
51:31 [q]ch. 50:24
51:32 [r]ch. 50:38
51:33 [s]Isa. 21:10; Mic. 4:13; Am. 1:3 [t]Isa. 41:15; Hab. 3:12 [u]Isa. 17:5; Hos. 6:11; Joel 3:13; Rev. 14:15
51:34 [v]ch. 50:17
51:36 [w]ch. 50:34 [x]ch. 50:38
51:37 [y]Isa. 13:22; ch. 50:39; Rev. 18:2 [z]ch. 25:9
51:39 [a]ver. 57
51:41 [b]ch. 25:26 [c]Isa. 13:19; ch. 49:25; Dan. 4:30
51:42 [d]Isa. 8:7
51:43 [e]ch. 50:39; ver. 29
51:44 [f]Isa. 46:1; ch. 50:2 [g]ver. 58
51:45 [h]ver. 6; ch. 50:8; Rev. 18:4
51:46 [i]2 Kings 19:7
51:47 [j]ch. 50:2; ver. 52
51:48 [k]Isa. 44:23; Rev. 18:20 [l]ch. 50:3
51:50 [m]ch. 44:28
51:51 [n]Ps. 44:15
51:52 [o]ver. 47
51:53 [p]ch. 49:16; Am. 9:2; Obad. 4
51:54 [q]ch. 50:22
51:56 [r]Ps. 94:1; ch. 50:29; ver. 24
51:57 [s]ver. 39 [t]ch. 46:18
51:58 [u]ver. 44 [v]Hab. 2:13
51:62 [w]ch. 50:3; ver. 29

an end of reading this book, [x]*that* thou
shalt bind a stone to it, and cast it into the
midst of Euphrates:
64 And thou shalt say, Thus shall Babylon sink, and shall not rise from the evil
that I will bring upon her: [y]and they shall
be weary. Thus far *are* the words of Jeremiah.

52 Zedekiah *was* [z]one and twenty
years old when he began to reign,
and he reigned eleven years in Jerusalem.
And his mother's name *was* Hamutal the
daughter of Jeremiah of Libnah.
2 And he did *that which was* evil in the
eyes of the LORD, according to all that Jehoiakim had done.
3 For through the anger of the LORD it
came to pass in Jerusalem and Judah, till he
had cast them out from his presence, that
Zedekiah rebelled against the king of Babylon.
4 ¶ And it came to pass in the [a]ninth year
of his reign, in the tenth month, in the tenth
day of the month, *that* Nebuchadrezzar
king of Babylon came, he and all his army,
against Jerusalem, and pitched against it,
and built forts against it round about.
5 So the city was besieged unto the eleventh year of king Zedekiah.
6 And in the fourth month, in the ninth
day of the month, the famine was sore in the
city, so that there was no bread for the people of the land.
7 Then the city was broken up, and all the
men of war fled, and went forth out of the
city by night by the way of the gate between
the two walls, which *was* by the king's garden; (now the Chaldeans *were* by the city
round about:) and they went by the way of
the plain.
8 ¶ But the army of the Chaldeans pursued after the king, and overtook Zedekiah
in the plains of Jericho; and all his army
was scattered from him.
9 [b]Then they took the king, and carried
him up unto the king of Babylon to Riblah
in the land of Hamath; where he gave judgment upon him.
10 [c]And the king of Babylon slew the
sons of Zedekiah before his eyes: he slew
also all the princes of Judah in Riblah.
11 Then he put out the eyes of Zedekiah;
and the king of Babylon bound him in
chains, and carried him to Babylon, and put
him in prison till the day of his death.
12 ¶ [d]Now in the fifth month, in the tenth
day of the month, [e]which *was* the nineteenth year of Nebuchadrezzar king of Babylon, [f]came Nebuzar-adan, captain of the
guard, *which* served the king of Babylon,
into Jerusalem,
13 And burned the house of the LORD,
and the king's house; and all the houses of
Jerusalem, and all the houses of the great
men, burned he with fire:
14 And all the army of the Chaldeans,
that *were* with the captain of the guard,
brake down all the walls of Jerusalem
round about.
15 [g]Then Nebuzar-adan the captain of
the guard carried away captive *certain* of
the poor of the people, and the residue of
the people that remained in the city, and
those that fell away, that fell to the king of
Babylon, and the rest of the multitude.
16 But Nebuzar-adan the captain of the
guard left *certain* of the poor of the land for
vinedressers and for husbandmen.
17 [h]Also the [i]pillars of brass that *were* in
the house of the LORD, and the bases, and
the brasen sea that *was* in the house of the
LORD, the Chaldeans brake, and carried all
the brass of them to Babylon.
18 [j]The caldrons also, and the shovels,
and the snuffers, and the bowls, and the
spoons, and all the vessels of brass wherewith they ministered, took they away.
19 And the basons, and the firepans, and
the bowls, and the caldrons, and the candlesticks, and the spoons, and the cups; *that*
which *was* of gold *in* gold, and *that* which
was of silver *in* silver, took the captain of
the guard away.
20 The two pillars, one sea, and twelve
brasen bulls that *were* under the bases,
which king Solomon had made in the house
of the LORD: [k]the brass of all these vessels
was without weight.
21 And *concerning* the [l]pillars, the
height of one pillar *was* eighteen cubits; and
a fillet of twelve cubits did compass it; and
the thickness thereof *was* four fingers: *it*
was hollow.
22 And a chapiter of brass *was* upon it;
and the height of one chapiter *was* five cubits, with network and pomegranates upon
the chapiters round about, all *of* brass. The
second pillar also and the pomegranates
were like unto these.
23 And there were ninety and six pomegranates on a side; *and* [m]all the pomegranates upon the network *were* an hundred
round about.
24 ¶ And [n]the captain of the guard took
Seraiah the chief priest, [o]and Zephaniah
the second priest, and the three keepers of
the door:
25 He took also out of the city an eunuch,
which had the charge of the men of war,
and seven men of them that were near the
king's person, which were found in the city;
and the principal scribe of the host, who
mustered the people of the land; and threescore men of the people of the land, that
were found in the midst of the city.
26 So Nebuzar-adan the captain of the
guard took them, and brought them to the
king of Babylon to Riblah.
27 And the king of Babylon smote them,
and put them to death in Riblah in the land
of Hamath. Thus Judah was carried away
captive out of his own land.
28 [p]This *is* the people whom Nebuchadrezzar carried away captive: in the

51:63 [x]Rev. 18:21
51:64 [y]ver. 58
52:1 [z]2 Kings 24:18
52:4 [a]2 Kings 25:1-27; ch. 39:1; Zech. 8:19
52:9 [b]ch. 32:4
52:10 [c]Ezek. 12:13
52:12 [d]Zech. 7:5 [e]ver. 29 [f]ch. 39:9
52:15 [g]ch. 39:8
52:17 [h]ch. 27:19 [i]1 Kings 7:15
52:18 [j]Ex. 27:3; 2 Kings 25:14
52:20 [k]1 Kings 7:47
52:21 [l]1 Kings 7:15; 2 Kings 25:17; 2 Chron. 3:15
52:23 [m]1 Kings 7:20
52:24 [n]2 Kings 25:18 [o]ch. 21:1
52:28 [p]2 Kings 24:2

[q]seventh year [r]three thousand Jews and
three and twenty:
29 [s]In the eighteenth year of Nebuchadrezzar he carried away captive from
Jerusalem eight hundred thirty and two
persons:
30 In the three and twentieth year of
Nebuchadrezzar, Nebuzar-adan the captain of the guard carried away captive of the
Jews seven hundred forty and five persons:
all the persons *were* four thousand and six
hundred.
31 ¶ [t]And it came to pass in the seven
and thirtieth year of the captivity of Jehoiachin king of Judah, in the twelfth month, in
the five and twentieth *day* of the month,
that Evil-merodach king of Babylon in the
first year of his reign [u]lifted up the head of
Jehoiachin king of Judah, and brought him
forth out of prison,
32 And spake kindly unto him, and set his
throne above the throne of the kings that
were with him in Babylon,
33 And changed his prison garments:
[v]and he did continually eat bread before
him all the days of his life.
34 And *for* his diet, there was a continual
diet given him of the king of Babylon, every
day a portion until the day of his death, all
the days of his life.

52:28 [q]2 Kings 24:12 [r]2 Kings 24:14
52:29 [s]ver. 12; ch. 39:9
52:31 [t]2 Kings 25:27 [u]Gen. 40:13
52:33 [v]2 Sam. 9:13

LAMENTATIONS

Jeremiah is the author of this book, written about 586 B.C. Lamentations consists of five poems describing the misery and desolation in Jerusalem following its fall, God's anger with his people and the consequences for the people.

I. Distress in Jerusalem, 1:1–1:22
II. The destruction of Jerusalem, 2:1–2:22
III. The lament of the prophet, 3:1–3:66
IV. The siege of the city, 4:1–4:22
V. The appeal for forgiveness, 5:1–5:22

---

1 How doth the city sit solitary, *that was*
full of people! [a]*how* is she become as a
widow! she *that was* great among the nations, *and* [b]princess among the provinces,
how is she become tributary!
2 She [c]weepeth sore in the [d]night, and
her tears *are* on her cheeks: [e]among all her
lovers [f]she hath none to comfort *her:* all
her friends have dealt treacherously with
her, they are become her enemies.
3 [g]Judah is gone into captivity because of
affliction, and because of great servitude:
[h]she dwelleth among the heathen, she findeth no rest: all her persecutors overtook her
between the straits.
4 The ways of Zion do mourn, because
none come to the solemn feasts: all her
gates are desolate: her priests sigh, her virgins are afflicted, and she *is* in bitterness.
5 Her adversaries [i]are the chief, her enemies prosper; for the LORD hath afflicted
her [j]for the multitude of her transgressions: her [k]children are gone into captivity
before the enemy.
6 And from the daughter of Zion all her
beauty is departed: her princes are become
like harts *that* find no pasture, and they are
gone without strength before the pursuer.
7 Jerusalem remembered in the days of
her affliction and of her miseries all her
pleasant things that she had in the days of
old, when her people fell into the hand of
the enemy, and none did help her: the adversaries saw her, *and* did mock at her sabbaths.
8 [l]Jerusalem hath grievously sinned;
therefore she is removed: all that honoured
her despise her, because [m]they have seen
her nakedness: yea, she sigheth, and turneth backward.
9 Her filthiness *is* in her skirts; she [n]re-
membereth not her last end; therefore she
came down wonderfully: [o]she had no comforter. O LORD, behold my affliction: for the
enemy hath magnified *himself.*
10 The adversary hath spread out his
hand upon [p]all her pleasant things: for she
hath seen *that* [q]the heathen entered into
her sanctuary, whom thou didst command
that [r]they should not enter into thy congregation.
11 All her people sigh, [s]they seek bread;
they have given their pleasant things for
meat to relieve the soul: see, O LORD, and
consider; for I am become vile.
12 ¶ *Is it* nothing to you, all ye that pass
by? behold, and see [t]if there be any sorrow
like unto my sorrow, which is done unto me,
wherewith the LORD hath afflicted *me* in the
day of his fierce anger.
13 From above hath he sent fire into my
bones, and it prevaileth against them: he

1:1 [a]Isa. 47:7 [b]Ezra 4:20
1:2 [c]Jer. 13:17 [d]Job 7:3; Ps. 6:6 [e]Jer. 4:30; ver. 19 [f]ver. 9
1:3 [g]Jer. 52:27 [h]Deut. 28:64; ch. 2:9
1:5 [i]Deut. 28:43 [j]Jer. 30:14; Dan. 9:7 [k]Jer. 52:28
1:8 [l]1 Kings 8:46 [m]Jer. 13:22; Ezek. 16:37; Hos. 2:10
1:9 [n]Deut. 32:29; Isa. 47:7 [o]ver. 2
1:10 [p]ver. 7 [q]Jer. 51:51 [r]Deut. 23:3; Neh. 13:1
1:11 [s]Jer. 38:9; ch. 2:12
1:12 [t]Dan. 9:12

hath [u]spread a net for my feet, he hath
turned me back: he hath made me desolate
and faint all the day.
14 [v]The yoke of my transgressions is
bound by his hand: they are wreathed, *and*
come up upon my neck: he hath made my
strength to fall, the Lord hath delivered me
into *their* hands, *from whom* I am not able
to rise up.
15 The Lord hath trodden under foot all
my mighty *men* in the midst of me: he hath
called an assembly against me to crush my
young men: [w]the Lord hath trodden the virgin, the daughter of Judah, *as* in a winepress.
16 For these *things* I weep; [x]mine eye,
mine eye runneth down with water, because
[y]the comforter that should relieve my soul
is far from me: my children are desolate,
because the enemy prevailed.
17 [z]Zion spreadeth forth her hands, *and*
[a]*there is* none to comfort her: the LORD
hath commanded concerning Jacob, *that*
his adversaries *should be* round about him:
Jerusalem is as a menstruous woman
among them.
18 ¶ The LORD is [b]righteous; for I have
[c]rebelled against his commandment: hear,
I pray you, all people, and behold my sorrow: my virgins and my young men are
gone into captivity.
19 I called for my lovers, *but* [d]they deceived me: my priests and mine elders gave
up the ghost in the city, [e]while they sought
their meat to relieve their souls.
20 Behold, O LORD; for I *am* in distress:
my [f]bowels are troubled; mine heart is
turned within me; for I have grievously rebelled: [g]abroad the sword bereaveth, at
home *there is* as death.
21 They have heard that I sigh: [h]*there is*
none to comfort me: all mine enemies have
heard of my trouble; they are glad that thou
hast done *it:* thou wilt bring [i]the day *that*
thou hast called, and they shall be like
unto me.
22 [j]Let all their wickedness come before
thee; and do unto them, as thou hast done
unto me for all my transgressions: for my
sighs *are* many, and [k]my heart *is* faint.

2 How hath the Lord covered the daughter of Zion with a cloud in his anger,
[l]*and* cast down from heaven unto the earth
[m]the beauty of Israel, and remembered not
[n]his footstool in the day of his anger!
2 The Lord hath swallowed up all the
habitations of Jacob, [o]and hath not pitied:
he hath thrown down in his wrath the
strong holds of the daughter of Judah; he
hath brought *them* down to the ground: [p]he
hath polluted the kingdom and the princes
thereof.
3 He hath cut off in *his* fierce anger all the
horn of Israel: [q]he hath drawn back his
right hand from before the enemy, [r]and he
burned against Jacob like a flaming fire,
which devoureth round about.
4 [s]He hath bent his bow like an enemy:

1:13 [u]Ezek. 12:13
1:14 [v]Deut. 28:48
1:15 [w]Isa. 63:3; Rev. 14:19
1:16 [x]Jer. 13:17; ch. 2:18 [y]ver. 2
1:17 [z]Jer. 4:31 [a]ver. 2
1:18 [b]Neh. 9:33; Dan. 9:7 [c]1 Sam. 12:14
1:19 [d]ver. 2; Jer. 30:14 [e]ver. 11
1:20 [f]Job 30:27; Isa. 16:11; Jer. 4:19; ch. 2:11; Hos. 11:8 [g]Deut. 32:25; Ezek. 7:15
1:21 [h]ver. 2 [i]Isa. 13; Jer. 46
1:22 [j]Ps. 109:15 [k]ch. 5:17
2:1 [l]Matt. 11:23 [m]2 Sam. 1:19 [n]1 Chron. 28:2; Ps. 99:5
2:2 [o]ver. 17; ch. 3:43 [p]Ps. 89:39
2:3 [q]Ps. 74:11 [r]Ps. 89:46
2:4 [s]Isa. 63:10; ver. 5 [t]Ezek. 24:25
2:5 [u]ver. 4; Jer. 30:14 [v]2 Kings 25:9; Jer. 52:13
2:6 [w]Ps. 80:12; Isa. 5:5 [x]Isa. 1:8 [y]ch. 1:4; Zeph. 3:18
2:7 [z]Ps. 74:4
2:8 [a]2 Kings 21:13; Isa. 34:11
2:9 [b]Jer. 51:30 [c]Deut. 28:36; 2 Kings 24:15; ch. 1:3 [d]2 Chron. 15:3 [e]Ps. 74:9; Ezek. 7:26
2:10 [f]Job 2:13; Isa. 3:26; ch. 3:28 [g]Job 2:12 [h]Isa. 15:3; Ezek. 7:18
2:11 [i]Ps. 6:7; ch. 3:48 [j]ch. 1:20 [k]Job 16:13; Ps. 22:14 [l]ver. 19; ch. 4:4
2:13 [m]ch. 1:12; Dan. 9:12
2:14 [n]Jer. 2:8; Ezek. 13:2 [o]Isa. 58:1
2:15 [p]1 Kings 9:8; Jer. 18:16; Nah. 3:19 [q]Ezek. 25:6 [r]2 Kings 19:21; Ps. 44:14 [s]Ps. 48:2
2:16 [t]Job 16:9; Ps. 22:13; ch. 3:46

he stood with his right hand as an adversary, and slew [t]all *that were* pleasant to
the eye in the tabernacle of the daughter of
Zion: he poured out his fury like fire.
5 [u]The Lord was as an enemy: he hath
swallowed up Israel, [v]he hath swallowed
up all her palaces: he hath destroyed his
strong holds, and hath increased in the
daughter of Judah mourning and lamentation.
6 And he hath violently [w]taken away his
tabernacle, [x]as *if it were of* a garden: he
hath destroyed his places of the assembly:
[y]the LORD hath caused the solemn feasts
and sabbaths to be forgotten in Zion, and
hath despised in the indignation of his anger the king and the priest.
7 The Lord hath cast off his altar, he hath
abhorred his sanctuary, he hath given up
into the hand of the enemy the walls of her
palaces; [z]they have made a noise in the
house of the LORD, as in the day of a solemn
feast.
8 The LORD hath purposed to destroy the
wall of the daughter of Zion: [a]he hath
stretched out a line, he hath not withdrawn
his hand from destroying: therefore he
made the rampart and the wall to lament;
they languished together.
9 Her gates are sunk into the ground; he
hath destroyed and [b]broken her bars: [c]her
king and her princes *are* among the Gentiles: [d]the law *is* no *more;* her [e]prophets
also find no vision from the LORD.
10 The elders of the daughter of Zion [f]sit
upon the ground, *and* keep silence: they
have [g]cast up dust upon their heads; they
have [h]girded themselves with sackcloth:
the virgins of Jerusalem hang down their
heads to the ground.
11 [i]Mine eyes do fail with tears, [j]my
bowels are troubled, [k]my liver is poured
upon the earth, for the destruction of the
daughter of my people; because [l]the children and the sucklings swoon in the streets
of the city.
12 They say to their mothers, Where *is*
corn and wine? when they swooned as the
wounded in the streets of the city, when
their soul was poured out into their mothers' bosom.
13 What thing shall I take to witness for
thee? [m]what thing shall I liken to thee,
O daughter of Jerusalem? what shall I equal
to thee, that I may comfort thee, O virgin
daughter of Zion? for thy breach *is* great
like the sea: who can heal thee?
14 Thy [n]prophets have seen vain and
foolish things for thee: and they have [o]not
discovered thine iniquity, to turn away thy
captivity; but have seen for thee false burdens and causes of banishment.
15 [p]All that pass by [q]clap *their* hands
at thee; they hiss [r]and wag their head at
the daughter of Jerusalem, *saying, Is* this
the city that *men* call [s]The perfection of
beauty, The joy of the whole earth?
16 [t]All thine enemies have opened their

mouth against thee: they hiss and gnash the teeth: they say, [u]We have swallowed *her* up: certainly this *is* the day that we looked for; we have found, [v]we have seen *it*.

17 The LORD hath done *that* which he had [w]devised; he hath fulfilled his word that he had commanded in the days of old: [x]he hath thrown down, and hath not pitied: and he hath caused *thine* enemy to [y]rejoice over thee, he hath set up the horn of thine adversaries.

18 Their heart cried unto the Lord, O [z]wall of the daughter of Zion, [a]let tears run down like a river day and night: give thyself no rest; let not the apple of thine eye cease.

19 Arise, [b]cry out in the night: in the beginning of the watches [c]pour out thine heart like water before the face of the Lord: lift up thy hands toward him for the life of thy young children, [d]that faint for hunger [e]in the top of every street.

20 ¶ Behold, O LORD, and consider to whom thou hast done this. [f]Shall the women eat their fruit, *and* children of a span long? [g]shall the priest and the prophet be slain in the sanctuary of the Lord?

21 [h]The young and the old lie on the ground in the streets: my virgins and my young men are fallen by the sword; thou hast slain *them* in the day of thine anger; [i]thou hast killed, *and* not pitied.

22 Thou hast called as in a solemn day [j]my terrors round about, so that in the day of the LORD's anger none escaped nor remained: [k]those that I have swaddled and brought up hath mine enemy consumed.

3 I *am* the man *that* hath seen affliction by the rod of his wrath.

2 He hath led me, and brought *me into* darkness, but not *into* light.

3 Surely against me is he turned; he turneth his hand *against me* all the day.

4 [l]My flesh and my skin hath he made old; he hath [m]broken my bones.

5 He hath builded against me, and compassed *me* with gall and travail.

6 [n]He hath set me in dark places, as *they that be* dead of old.

7 [o]He hath hedged me about, that I cannot get out: he hath made my chain heavy.

8 Also [p]when I cry and shout, he shutteth out my prayer.

9 He hath inclosed my ways with hewn stone, he hath made my paths crooked.

10 [q]He *was* unto me *as* a bear lying in wait, *and as* a lion in secret places.

11 He hath turned aside my ways, and [r]pulled me in pieces: he hath made me desolate.

12 He hath bent his bow, and [s]set me as a mark for the arrow.

13 He hath caused [t]the arrows of his quiver to enter into my reins.

14 I was a [u]derision to all my people; *and* [v]their song all the day.

15 [w]He hath filled me with bitterness, he hath made me drunken with wormwood.

16 He hath also broken my teeth [x]with gravel stones, he hath covered me with ashes.

17 And thou hast removed my soul far off from peace: I forgat prosperity.

18 [y]And I said, My strength and my hope is perished from the LORD:

19 Remembering mine affliction and my misery, [z]the wormwood and the gall.

20 My soul hath *them* still in remembrance, and is humbled in me.

21 This I recall to my mind, therefore have I hope.

22 ¶ [a]*It is of* the LORD's mercies that we are not consumed, because his compassions fail not.

23 *They are* new [b]every morning: great *is* thy faithfulness.

24 The LORD *is* my [c]portion, saith my soul; therefore will I hope in him.

25 The LORD *is* good unto them that [d]wait for him, to the soul *that* seeketh him.

26 *It is* good that *a man* should both hope [e]and quietly wait for the salvation of the LORD.

27 [f]*It is* good for a man that he bear the yoke in his youth.

28 [g]He sitteth alone and keepeth silence, because he hath borne *it* upon him.

29 [h]He putteth his mouth in the dust; if so be there may be hope.

30 [i]He giveth *his* cheek to him that smiteth him: he is filled full with reproach.

31 [j]For the Lord will not cast off for ever:

32 But though he cause grief, yet will he have compassion according to the multitude of his mercies.

33 For [k]he doth not afflict willingly nor grieve the children of men.

34 To crush under his feet all the prisoners of the earth,

35 To turn aside the right of a man before the face of the most High,

36 To subvert a man in his cause, [l]the Lord approveth not.

37 ¶ Who *is* he [m]*that* saith, and it cometh to pass, *when* the Lord commandeth *it* not?

38 Out of the mouth of the most High proceedeth not [n]evil and good?

39 [o]Wherefore doth a living man complain, [p]a man for the punishment of his sins?

40 Let us search and try our ways, and turn again to the LORD.

41 [q]Let us lift up our heart with *our* hands unto God in the heavens.

42 [r]We have transgressed and have rebelled: thou hast not pardoned.

43 Thou hast covered with anger, and persecuted us: [s]thou hast slain, thou hast not pitied.

44 Thou hast covered thyself with a cloud, [t]that *our* prayer should not pass through.

45 Thou hast made us *as* the [u]offscouring and refuse in the midst of the people.

46 [v]All our enemies have opened their mouths against us.

2:16 [u]Ps. 56:2 [v]Ps. 35:21
2:17 [w]Lev. 26:16; Deut. 28:15 [x]ver. 2 [y]Ps. 38:16
2:18 [z]ver. 8 [a]Jer. 14:17; ch. 1:16
2:19 [b]Ps. 119:147 [c]Ps. 62:8 [d]ver. 11 [e]Isa. 51:20; ch. 4:1; Nah. 3:10
2:20 [f]Lev. 26:29; Deut. 28:53; Jer. 19:9; ch. 4:10; Ezek. 5:10 [g]ch. 4:13
2:21 [h]2 Chron. 36:17 [i]ch. 3:43
2:22 [j]Ps. 31:13; Jer. 6:25 [k]Hos. 9:12
3:4 [l]Job 16:8 [m]Ps. 51:8; Isa. 38:13; Jer. 50:17
3:6 [n]Ps. 88:5
3:7 [o]Job 3:23; Hos. 2:6
3:8 [p]Job 30:20; Ps. 22:2
3:10 [q]Job 10:16; Isa. 38:13; Hos. 5:14
3:11 [r]Hos. 6:1
3:12 [s]Job 7:20; Ps. 38:2
3:13 [t]Job 6:4
3:14 [u]Jer. 20:7 [v]Job 30:9; Ps. 69:12; ver. 63
3:15 [w]Jer. 9:15
3:16 [x]Prov. 20:17
3:18 [y]Ps. 31:22
3:19 [z]Jer. 9:15
3:22 [a]Mal. 3:6
3:23 [b]Isa. 33:2
3:24 [c]Ps. 16:5; Jer. 10:16
3:25 [d]Ps. 130:6; Isa. 30:18; Mic. 7:7
3:26 [e]Ps. 37:7
3:27 [f]Ps. 90:12
3:28 [g]Jer. 15:17; ch. 2:10
3:29 [h]Job 42:6
3:30 [i]Isa. 50:6; Matt. 5:39
3:31 [j]Ps. 94:14
3:33 [k]Ezek. 33:11; Heb. 12:10
3:36 [l]Hab. 1:13
3:37 [m]Ps. 33:9
3:38 [n]Job 2:10; Isa. 45:7; Am. 3:6
3:39 [o]Prov. 19:3 [p]Mic. 7:9
3:41 [q]Ps. 86:4
3:42 [r]Dan. 9:5
3:43 [s]ch. 2:2
3:44 [t]ver. 8
3:45 [u]1 Cor. 4:13
3:46 [v]ch. 2:16

47 [w]Fear and a snare is come upon us, [x]desolation and destruction.

48 [y]Mine eye runneth down with rivers of water for the destruction of the daughter of my people.

49 [z]Mine eye trickleth down, and ceaseth not, without any intermission,

50 Till the LORD [a]look down, and behold from heaven.

51 Mine eye affecteth mine heart because of all the daughters of my city.

52 Mine enemies chased me sore, like a bird, [b]without cause.

53 They have cut off my life [c]in the dungeon, and [d]cast a stone upon me.

54 [e]Waters flowed over mine head; *then* [f]I said, I am cut off.

55 ¶ [g]I called upon thy name, O LORD, out of the low dungeon.

56 [h]Thou hast heard my voice: hide not thine ear at my breathing, at my cry.

57 Thou [i]drewest near in the day *that* I called upon thee: thou saidst, Fear not.

58 O Lord, thou hast [j]pleaded the causes of my soul; [k]thou hast redeemed my life.

59 O LORD, thou hast seen my wrong: [l]judge thou my cause.

60 Thou hast seen all their vengeance *and* all their [m]imaginations against me.

61 Thou hast heard their reproach, O LORD, *and* all their imaginations against me;

62 The lips of those that rose up against me, and their device against me all the day.

63 Behold their [n]sitting down, and their rising up; [o]I *am* their musick.

64 ¶ [p]Render unto them a recompence, O LORD, according to the work of their hands.

65 Give them sorrow of heart, thy curse unto them.

66 Persecute and destroy them in anger [q]from under the [r]heavens of the LORD.

4 How is the gold become dim! *how* is the most fine gold changed! the stones of the sanctuary are poured out [s]in the top of every street.

2 The precious sons of Zion, comparable to fine gold, how are they esteemed [t]as earthen pitchers, the work of the hands of the potter!

3 Even the sea monsters draw out the breast, they give suck to their young ones: the daughter of my people *is become* cruel, [u]like the ostriches in the wilderness.

4 [v]The tongue of the sucking child cleaveth to the roof of his mouth for thirst: [w]the young children ask bread, *and* no man breaketh *it* unto them.

5 They that did feed delicately are desolate in the streets: they that were brought up in scarlet [x]embrace dunghills.

6 For the punishment of the iniquity of the daughter of my people is greater than the punishment of the sin of Sodom, that was [y]overthrown as in a moment, and no hands stayed on her.

7 Her Nazarites were purer than snow, they were whiter than milk, they were more ruddy in body than rubies, their polishing *was* of sapphire:

8 Their visage is [z]blacker than a coal; they are not known in the streets: [a]their skin cleaveth to their bones; it is withered, it is become like a stick.

9 *They that be* slain with the sword are better than *they that be* slain with hunger: for these pine away, stricken through for *want of* the fruits of the field.

10 [b]The hands of the [c]pitiful women have sodden their own children: they were their [d]meat in the destruction of the daughter of my people.

11 The LORD hath accomplished his fury; [e]he hath poured out his fierce anger, and [f]hath kindled a fire in Zion, and it hath devoured the foundations thereof.

12 The kings of the earth, and all the inhabitants of the world, would not have believed that the adversary and the enemy should have entered into the gates of Jerusalem.

13 ¶ [g]For the sins of her prophets, *and* the iniquities of her priests, [h]that have shed the blood of the just in the midst of her,

14 They have wandered *as* blind *men* in the streets, [i]they have polluted themselves with blood, [j]so that men could not touch their garments.

15 They cried unto them, Depart ye; *it is* [k]unclean; depart, depart, touch not: when they fled away and wandered, they said among the heathen, They shall no more sojourn *there*.

16 The anger of the LORD hath divided them; he will no more regard them: [l]they respected not the persons of the priests, they favoured not the elders.

17 As for us, [m]our eyes as yet failed for our vain help: in our watching we have watched for a nation *that* could not save *us*.

18 [n]They hunt our steps, that we cannot go in our streets: our end is near, our days are fulfilled; for [o]our end is come.

19 Our persecutors are [p]swifter than the eagles of the heaven: they pursued us upon the mountains, they laid wait for us in the wilderness.

20 The [q]breath of our nostrils, the anointed of the LORD, [r]was taken in their pits, of whom we said, Under his shadow we shall live among the heathen.

21 ¶ [s]Rejoice and be glad, O daughter of Edom, that dwellest in the land of Uz; [t]the cup also shall pass through unto thee: thou shalt be drunken, and shalt make thyself naked.

22 ¶ [u]The punishment of thine iniquity is accomplished, O daughter of Zion; he will no more carry thee away into captivity: [v]he will visit thine iniquity, O daughter of Edom; he will discover thy sins.

5 [w]Remember, O LORD, what is come upon us: consider, and behold [x]our reproach.

3:47 [w]Isa. 24:17; Jer. 48:43 [x]Isa. 51:19
3:48 [y]Jer. 4:19; ch. 2:11
3:49 [z]Ps. 77:2; ch. 1:16
3:50 [a]Isa. 63:15
3:52 [b]Ps. 35:7
3:53 [c]Jer. 37:16 [d]Dan. 6:17
3:54 [e]Ps. 69:2 [f]Ps. 31:22; Isa. 38:10; ver. 18
3:55 [g]Ps. 130:1; Jonah 2:2
3:56 [h]Ps. 3:4
3:57 [i]Jam. 4:8
3:58 [j]Ps. 35:1; Jer. 51:36 [k]Ps. 71:23
3:59 [l]Ps. 9:4
3:60 [m]Jer. 11:19
3:63 [n]Ps. 139:2 [o]ver. 14
3:64 [p]Ps. 28:4; Jer. 11:22; 2 Tim. 4:14
3:66 [q]Deut. 25:19; Jer. 10:11 [r]Ps. 8:3
4:1 [s]ch. 2:19
4:2 [t]Isa. 30:14; Jer. 19:11; 2 Cor. 4:7
4:3 [u]Job 39:14
4:4 [v]Ps. 22:15 [w]ch. 2:11
4:5 [x]Job 24:8
4:6 [y]Gen. 19:25
4:8 [z]ch. 5:10; Joel 2:6; Nah. 2:10 [a]Ps. 102:5
4:10 [b]ch. 2:20 [c]Isa. 49:15 [d]Deut. 28:57; 2 Kings 6:29
4:11 [e]Jer. 7:20 [f]Deut. 32:22; Jer. 21:14
4:13 [g]Jer. 5:31; Ezek. 22:26; Zeph. 3:4 [h]Matt. 23:31
4:14 [i]Jer. 2:34 [j]Num. 19:16
4:15 [k]Lev. 13:45
4:16 [l]ch. 5:12
4:17 [m]2 Kings 24:7; Isa. 20:5; Jer. 37:7; Ezek. 29:16
4:18 [n]2 Kings 25:4 [o]Ezek. 7:2; Am. 8:2
4:19 [p]Deut. 28:49; Jer. 4:13
4:20 [q]Gen. 2:7; ch. 2:9 [r]Jer. 52:9; Ezek. 12:13
4:21 [s]Eccl. 11:9 [t]Jer. 25:15; Obad. 10
4:22 [u]Isa. 40:2 [v]Ps. 137:7
5:1 [w]Ps. 89:50 [x]ch. 2:15; Ps. 79:4

2 [y]Our inheritance is turned to strangers, our houses to aliens.

3 We are orphans and fatherless, our mothers *are* as widows.

4 We have drunken our water for money; our wood is sold unto us.

5 [z]Our necks *are* under persecution: we labour, *and* have no rest.

6 [a]We have given the hand [b]*to* the Egyptians, *and to* the Assyrians, to be satisfied with bread.

7 [c]Our fathers have sinned, *and* [d]*are* not; and we have borne their iniquities.

8 [e]Servants have ruled over us: *there is* none that doth deliver *us* out of their hand.

9 We gat our bread with *the peril of* our lives because of the sword of the wilderness.

10 Our [f]skin was black like an oven because of the terrible famine.

11 [g]They ravished the women in Zion, *and* the maids in the cities of Judah.

12 Princes are hanged up by their hand: [h]the faces of elders were not honoured.

13 They took the young men [i]to grind, and the children fell under the wood.

14 The elders have ceased from the gate, the young men from their musick.

15 The joy of our heart is ceased; our dance is turned into mourning.

16 [j]The crown is fallen *from* our head: woe unto us, that we have sinned!

17 For this [k]our heart is faint; [l]for these *things* our eyes are dim.

18 Because of the mountain of Zion, which is desolate, the foxes walk upon it.

19 Thou, O LORD, [m]remainest for ever; [n]thy throne from generation to generation.

20 [o]Wherefore dost thou forget us for ever, *and* forsake us so long time?

21 [p]Turn thou us unto thee, O LORD, and we shall be turned; renew our days as of old.

22 But thou hast utterly rejected us; thou art very wroth against us.

5:2 [y]Ps. 79:1
5:5 [z]Deut. 28:48; Jer. 28:14
5:6 [a]Gen. 24:2; Jer. 50:15 [b]Hos. 12:1
5:7 [c]Jer. 31:29; Ezek. 18:2 [d]Gen. 42:13; Zech. 1:5
5:8 [e]Neh. 5:15
5:10 [f]Job 30:30; Ps. 119:83; ch. 4:8
5:11 [g]Isa. 13:16; Zech. 14:2
5:12 [h]Isa. 47:6; ch. 4:16
5:13 [i]Judg. 16:21
5:16 [j]Job 19:9; Ps. 89:39
5:17 [k]ch. 1:22 [l]Ps. 6:7; ch. 2:11
5:19 [m]Ps. 9:7; Hab. 1:12 [n]Ps. 45:6
5:20 [o]Ps. 13:1
5:21 [p]Ps. 80:3; Jer. 31:18

EZEKIEL

Ezekiel is the author of this book, written about 571 B.C. or earlier. In the first thirty-two chapters of Ezekiel, the prophecies focus on the imminent destruction of Judah and Jerusalem. Chapters 33 through 48 describe a two part future restoration of Israel. Much of the writing consists of visions, parables, and signs.

I. Ezekiel's commission, 1:1–3:27
II. Prophecies concerning the fall of Judah and Jerusalem, 4:1–11:25
III. Judgment and its causes, 12:1–24:27
IV. Prophecies concerning other nations, 25:1–32:32
V. Israel's future restoration, 33:1–39:29
VI. Vision of the restoration of the Temple and worship, 40:1–48:35

1 Now it came to pass in the thirtieth year, in the fourth *month,* in the fifth *day* of the month, as I *was* among the captives [a]by the river of Chebar, *that* [b]the heavens were opened, and I saw [c]visions of God.

2 In the fifth *day* of the month, which *was* the fifth year of [d]king Jehoiachin's captivity,

3 The word of the LORD came expressly unto Ezekiel the priest, the son of Buzi, in the land of the Chaldeans by the river Chebar; and [e]the hand of the LORD was there upon him.

4 ¶ And I looked, and, behold, [f]a whirlwind came [g]out of the north, a great cloud, and a fire infolding itself, and a brightness *was* about it, and out of the midst thereof as the colour of amber, out of the midst of the fire.

5 [h]Also out of the midst thereof *came* the likeness of four living creatures. And [i]this *was* their appearance; they had [j]the likeness of a man.

6 And every one had four faces, and every one had four wings.

7 And their feet *were* straight feet; and the sole of their feet *was* like the sole of a calf's foot: and they sparkled [k]like the colour of burnished brass.

8 [l]And *they had* the hands of a man under their wings on their four sides; and they four had their faces and their wings.

9 [m]Their wings *were* joined one to another; [n]they turned not when they went; they went every one straight forward.

10 As for [o]the likeness of their faces, they four [p]had the face of a man, [q]and the face of a lion, on the right side: [r]and they four had the face of an ox on the left side; [s]they four also had the face of an eagle.

11 Thus *were* their faces: and their wings *were* stretched upward; two *wings* of every

1:1 [a]ver. 3; ch. 3:15 [b]Matt. 3:16; Acts 7:56; Rev. 19:11 [c]ch. 8:3
1:2 [d]2 Kings 24:12
1:3 [e]1 Kings 18:46; 2 Kings 3:15; ch. 3:14
1:4 [f]Jer. 23:19 [g]Jer. 1:14
1:5 [h]Rev. 4:6 [i]ch. 10:8 [j]ver. 10; ch. 10:14
1:7 [k]Dan. 10:6; Rev. 1:15
1:8 [l]ch. 10:18
1:9 [m]ver. 11 [n]ver. 12; ch. 10:11
1:10 [o]Rev. 4:7 [p]Num. 2:10 [q]Num. 2:3 [r]Num. 2:18 [s]Num. 2:25

one *were* joined one to another, and [t]two
covered their bodies.
12 And [u]they went every one straight forward: [v]whither the spirit was to go, they
went; *and* [w]they turned not when they went.
13 As for the likeness of the living creatures, their appearance *was* like burning
coals of fire, [x]*and* like the appearance of
lamps: it went up and down among the living creatures; and the fire was bright, and
out of the fire went forth lightning.
14 And the living creatures [y]ran and returned [z]as the appearance of a flash of
lightning.
15 ¶ Now as I beheld the living creatures,
behold [a]one wheel upon the earth by the
living creatures, with his four faces.
16 [b]The appearance of the wheels and
their work *was* [c]like unto the colour of a
beryl: and they four had one likeness: and
their appearance and their work *was* as it
were a wheel in the middle of a wheel.
17 When they went, they went upon their
four sides: [d]*and* they turned not when they
went.
18 As for their rings, they were so high
that they were dreadful; and their rings
were [e]full of eyes round about them four.
19 And [f]when the living creatures went,
the wheels went by them: and when the living creatures were lifted up from the earth,
the wheels were lifted up.
20 [g]Whithersoever the spirit was to go,
they went, thither *was their* spirit to go; and
the wheels were lifted up over against them:
[h]for the spirit of the living creature *was* in
the wheels.
21 [i]When those went, *these* went; and
when those stood, *these* stood; and when
those were lifted up from the earth, the
wheels were lifted up over against them: for
the spirit of the living creature *was* in the
wheels.
22 [j]And the likeness of the firmament
upon the heads of the living creature *was* as
the colour of the terrible crystal, stretched
forth over their heads above.
23 And under the firmament *were* their
wings straight, the one toward the other:
every one had two, which covered on this
side, and every one had two, which covered
on that side, their bodies.
24 [k]And when they went, I heard the
noise of their wings, [l]like the noise of great
waters, as [m]the voice of the Almighty, the
voice of speech, as the noise of an host:
when they stood, they let down their wings.
25 And there was a voice from the firmament that *was* over their heads, when they
stood, *and* had let down their wings.
26 ¶ [n]And above the firmament that *was*
over their heads *was* the likeness of a
throne, [o]as the appearance of a sapphire
stone: and upon the likeness of the throne
was the likeness as the appearance of a man
above upon it.
27 [p]And I saw as the colour of amber, as
the appearance of fire round about within it,
from the appearance of his loins even upward, and from the appearance of his loins
even downward, I saw as it were the appearance of fire, and it had brightness
round about.
28 [q]As the appearance of the bow that is
in the cloud in the day of rain, so *was* the
appearance of the brightness round about.
[r]This *was* the appearance of the likeness of
the glory of the LORD. And when I saw *it*, [s]I
fell upon my face, and I heard a voice of one
that spake.

2 And he said unto me, Son of man,
[t]stand upon thy feet, and I will speak
unto thee.
2 And [u]the spirit entered into me when
he spake unto me, and set me upon my feet,
that I heard him that spake unto me.
3 And he said unto me, Son of man, I send
thee to the children of Israel, to a rebellious
nation that hath rebelled against me: [v]they
and their fathers have transgressed against
me, *even* unto this very day.
4 [w]For *they are* impudent children and
stiffhearted. I do send thee unto them; and
thou shalt say unto them, Thus saith the
Lord GOD.
5 [x]And they, whether they will hear, or
whether they will forbear, (for they *are* a
rebellious house,) yet [y]shall know that
there hath been a prophet among them.
6 ¶ And thou, son of man, [z]be not afraid
of them, neither be afraid of their words,
though [a]briers and thorns *be* with thee, and
thou dost dwell among scorpions: [b]be not
afraid of their words, nor be dismayed at
their looks, [c]though they *be* a rebellious
house.
7 [d]And thou shalt speak my words unto
them, [e]whether they will hear, or whether
they will forbear: for they *are* most rebellious.
8 But thou, son of man, hear what I say
unto thee; Be not thou rebellious like that
rebellious house: open thy mouth, and [f]eat
that I give thee.
9 ¶ And when I looked, behold, [g]an hand
was sent unto me; and, lo, [h]a roll of a book
was therein;
10 And he spread it before me; and it *was*
written within and without: and *there was*
written therein lamentations, and mourning, and woe.

3 Moreover he said unto me, Son of man,
eat that thou findest; [i]eat this roll, and
go speak unto the house of Israel.
2 So I opened my mouth, and he caused
me to eat that roll.
3 And he said unto me, Son of man, cause
thy belly to eat, and fill thy bowels with this
roll that I give thee. Then did I [j]eat *it;* and
it was in my mouth [k]as honey for sweetness.
4 ¶ And he said unto me, Son of man, go,
get thee unto the house of Israel, and speak
with my words unto them.
5 For thou *art* not sent to a people of a

1:11 [t]Isa. 6:2
1:12 [u]ver. 9; ch. 10:22 [v]ver. 20 [w]ver. 9
1:13 [x]Rev. 4:5
1:14 [y]Zech. 4:10 [z]Matt. 24:27
1:15 [a]ch. 10:9
1:16 [b]ch. 10:9 [c]Dan. 10:6
1:17 [d]ver. 12
1:18 [e]ch. 10:12; Zech. 4:10
1:19 [f]ch. 10:16
1:20 [g]ver. 12 [h]ch. 10:17
1:21 [i]ver. 19; ch. 10:17
1:22 [j]ch. 10:1
1:24 [k]ch. 10:5 [l]ch. 43:2; Dan. 10:6; Rev. 1:15 [m]Job 37:4; Ps. 29:3
1:26 [n]ch. 10:1 [o]Ex. 24:10
1:27 [p]ch. 8:2
1:28 [q]Rev. 4:3 [r]ch. 3:23 [s]ch. 3:23; Dan. 8:17; Acts 9:4; Rev. 1:17
2:1 [t]Dan. 10:11
2:2 [u]ch. 3:24
2:3 [v]Jer. 3:25; ch. 20:18
2:4 [w]ch. 3:7
2:5 [x]ch. 3:11 [y]ch. 33:33
2:6 [z]Jer. 1:8; Luke 12:4 [a]Isa. 9:18; Jer. 6:28; Mic. 7:4 [b]ch. 3:9; 1 Pet. 3:14 [c]ch. 3:9
2:7 [d]Jer. 1:7 [e]ver. 5
2:8 [f]Rev. 10:9
2:9 [g]ch. 8:3; Jer. 1:9 [h]ch. 3:1
3:1 [i]ch. 2:8
3:3 [j]Jer. 15:16; Rev. 10:9 [k]Ps. 19:10

strange speech and of an hard language, *but* to the house of Israel;

6 Not to many people of a strange speech and of an hard language, whose words thou canst not understand. Surely, [l]had I sent thee to them, they would have hearkened unto thee.

7 But the house of Israel will not hearken unto thee; [m]for they will not hearken unto me: [n]for all the house of Israel *are* impudent and hardhearted.

8 Behold, I have made thy face strong against their faces, and thy forehead strong against their foreheads.

9 [o]As an adamant harder than flint have I made thy forehead: [p]fear them not, neither be dismayed at their looks, though they *be* a rebellious house.

10 Moreover he said unto me, Son of man, all my words that I shall speak unto thee receive in thine heart, and hear with thine ears.

11 And go, get thee to them of the captivity, unto the children of thy people, and speak unto them, and tell them, [q]Thus saith the Lord GOD; whether they will hear, or whether they will forbear.

12 Then the [r]spirit took me up, and I heard behind me a voice of a great rushing, *saying,* Blessed *be* the glory of the LORD from his place.

13 *I heard* also the noise of the wings of the living creatures that touched one another, and the noise of the wheels over against them, and a noise of a great rushing.

14 So [s]the spirit lifted me up, and took me away, and I went in bitterness, in the heat of my spirit; but [t]the hand of the LORD was strong upon me.

15 ¶ Then I came to them of the captivity at Tel-abib, that dwelt by the river of Chebar, and [u]I sat where they sat, and remained there astonished among them seven days.

16 And it came to pass at the end of seven days, that the word of the LORD came unto me, saying,

17 [v]Son of man, I have made thee [w]a watchman unto the house of Israel: therefore hear the word at my mouth, and give them warning from me.

18 When I say unto the wicked, Thou shalt surely die; and thou givest him not warning, nor speakest to warn the wicked from his wicked way, to save his life; the same wicked *man* [x]shall die in his iniquity; but his blood will I require at thine hand.

19 Yet if thou warn the wicked, and he turn not from his wickedness, nor from his wicked way, he shall die in his iniquity; [y]but thou hast delivered thy soul.

20 Again, When a [z]righteous *man* doth turn from his righteousness, and commit iniquity, and I lay a stumblingblock before him, he shall die: because thou hast not given him warning, he shall die in his sin, and his righteousness which he hath done shall not be remembered; but his blood will I require at thine hand.

21 Nevertheless if thou warn the righteous *man,* that the righteous sin not, and he doth not sin, he shall surely live, because he is warned; also thou hast delivered thy soul.

22 ¶ [a]And the hand of the LORD was there upon me; and he said unto me, Arise, go forth [b]into the plain, and I will there talk with thee.

23 Then I arose, and went forth into the plain: and, behold, [c]the glory of the LORD stood there, as the glory which I [d]saw by the river of Chebar: [e]and I fell on my face.

24 Then [f]the spirit entered into me, and set me upon my feet, and spake with me, and said unto me, Go, shut thyself within thine house.

25 But thou, O son of man, behold, [g]they shall put bands upon thee, and shall bind thee with them, and thou shalt not go out among them:

26 And [h]I will make thy tongue cleave to the roof of thy mouth, that thou shalt be dumb, and shalt not be to them a reprover: [i]for they *are* a rebellious house.

27 [j]But when I speak with thee, I will open thy mouth, and thou shalt say unto them, [k]Thus saith the Lord GOD; He that heareth, let him hear; and he that forbeareth, let him forbear: [l]for they *are* a rebellious house.

4 Thou also, son of man, take thee a tile, and lay it before thee, and pourtray upon it the city, *even* Jerusalem:

2 And lay siege against it, and build a fort against it, and cast a mount against it; set the camp also against it, and set *battering* rams against it round about.

3 Moreover take thou unto thee an iron pan, and set it *for* a wall of iron between thee and the city: and set thy face against it, and it shall be besieged, and thou shalt lay siege against it. [m]This *shall be* a sign to the house of Israel.

4 Lie thou also upon thy left side, and lay the iniquity of the house of Israel upon it: *according* to the number of the days that thou shalt lie upon it thou shalt bear their iniquity.

5 For I have laid upon thee the years of their iniquity, according to the number of the days, three hundred and ninety days: [n]so shalt thou bear the iniquity of the house of Israel.

6 And when thou hast accomplished them, lie again on thy right side, and thou shalt bear the iniquity of the house of Judah forty days: I have appointed thee each day for a year.

7 Therefore thou shalt set thy face toward the siege of Jerusalem, and thine arm *shall be* uncovered, and thou shalt prophesy against it.

8 [o]And, behold, I will lay bands upon thee, and thou shalt not turn thee from one side to another, till thou hast ended the days of thy siege.

3:6 *l*Matt. 11:21
3:7 *m*John 15:20 *n*ch. 2:4
3:9 *o*Isa. 50:7; Jer. 1:18; Mic. 3:8 *p*Jer. 1:8; ch. 2:6
3:11 *q*ch. 2:5; ver. 27
3:12 *r*1 Kings 18:12; 2 Kings 2:16; ver. 14; ch. 8:3; Acts 8:39
3:14 *s*ver. 12; ch. 8:3 *t*2 Kings 3:15; ch. 1:3
3:15 *u*Job 2:13; Ps. 137:1
3:17 *v*ch. 33:7 *w*Isa. 52:8; Jer. 6:17
3:18 *x*ch. 33:6; John 8:21
3:19 *y*Isa. 49:4; Acts 20:26
3:20 *z*ch. 18:24
3:22 *a*ver. 14; ch. 1:3 *b*ch. 8:4
3:23 *c*ch. 1:28 *d*ch. 1:1 *e*ch. 1:28
3:24 *f*ch. 2:2
3:25 *g*ch. 4:8
3:26 *h*ch. 24:27; Luke 1:20 *i*ch. 2:5
3:27 *j*ch. 24:27 *k*ver. 11 *l*ver. 9; ch. 12:2
4:3 *m*ch. 12:6
4:5 *n*Num. 14:34
4:8 *o*ch. 3:25

9 ¶ Take thou also unto thee wheat, and
barley, and beans, and lentiles, and millet,
and fitches, and put them in one vessel, and
make thee bread thereof, *according* to the
number of the days that thou shalt lie upon
thy side, three hundred and ninety days
shalt thou eat thereof.
10 And thy meat which thou shalt eat
shall be by weight, twenty shekels a day:
from time to time shalt thou eat it.
11 Thou shalt drink also water by measure, the sixth part of an hin: from time to
time shalt thou drink.
12 And thou shalt eat it *as* barley cakes,
and thou shalt bake it with dung that cometh out of man, in their sight.
13 And the LORD said, Even thus [p]shall
the children of Israel eat their defiled bread
among the Gentiles, whither I will drive
them.
14 Then said I, [q]Ah Lord GOD! behold,
my soul hath not been polluted: for from my
youth up even till now have I not eaten of
[r]that which dieth of itself, or is torn in
pieces; neither came there [s]abominable
flesh into my mouth.
15 Then he said unto me, Lo, I have given
thee cow's dung for man's dung, and thou
shalt prepare thy bread therewith.
16 Moreover he said unto me, Son of man,
behold, I will break the [t]staff of bread in
Jerusalem: and they shall [u]eat bread by
weight, and with care; and they shall
[v]drink water by measure, and with astonishment:
17 That they may want bread and water,
and be astonied one with another, and
[w]consume away for their iniquity.

5 And thou, son of man, take thee a sharp
knife, take thee a barber's razor, [x]and
cause *it* to pass upon thine head and upon
thy beard: then take thee balances to weigh,
and divide the *hair*.
2 [y]Thou shalt burn with fire a third part
in the midst of [z]the city, when [a]the days of
the siege are fulfilled: and thou shalt take a
third part, *and* smite about it with a knife:
and a third part thou shalt scatter in the
wind; and I will draw out a sword after
them.
3 [b]Thou shalt also take thereof a few in
number, and bind them in thy skirts.
4 Then take of them again, and [c]cast
them into the midst of the fire, and burn
them in the fire; *for* thereof shall a fire come
forth into all the house of Israel.
5 ¶ Thus saith the Lord GOD; This *is* Jerusalem: I have set it in the midst of the nations and countries *that are* round about
her.
6 And she hath changed my judgments
into wickedness more than the nations, and
my statutes more than the countries that *are*
round about her: for they have refused my
judgments and my statutes, they have not
walked in them.
7 Therefore thus saith the Lord GOD; Because ye multiplied more than the nations
that *are* round about you, *and* have not
walked in my statutes, neither have kept my
judgments, [d]neither have done according
to the judgments of the nations that *are*
round about you;
8 Therefore thus saith the Lord GOD; Behold, I, even I, *am* against thee, and will
execute judgments in the midst of thee in
the sight of the nations.
9 [e]And I will do in thee that which I have
not done, and whereunto I will not do any
more the like, because of all thine abominations.
10 Therefore the fathers [f]shall eat the
sons in the midst of thee, and the sons shall
eat their fathers; and I will execute judgments in thee, and the whole remnant of
thee will I [g]scatter into all the winds.
11 Wherefore, *as* I live, saith the Lord
GOD; Surely, because thou hast [h]defiled my
sanctuary with all thy [i]detestable things,
and with all thine abominations, therefore
will I also diminish *thee;* [j]neither shall
mine eye spare, neither will I have any pity.
12 ¶ [k]A third part of thee shall die with
the pestilence, and with famine shall they
be consumed in the midst of thee: and a
third part shall fall by the sword round
about thee; and [l]I will scatter a third part
into all the winds, and [m]I will draw out a
sword after them.
13 Thus shall mine anger [n]be accomplished, and I will [o]cause my fury to rest
upon them, [p]and I will be comforted: [q]and
they shall know that I the LORD have spoken *it* in my zeal, when I have accomplished
my fury in them.
14 Moreover [r]I will make thee waste, and
a reproach among the nations that *are*
round about thee, in the sight of all that
pass by.
15 So it shall be a [s]reproach and a taunt,
an instruction and an astonishment unto
the nations that *are* round about thee, when
I shall execute judgments in thee in anger
and in fury and in [t]furious rebukes. I the
LORD have spoken *it*.
16 When I shall [u]send upon them the evil
arrows of famine, which shall be for *their*
destruction, *and* which I will send to destroy
you: and I will increase the famine upon
you, and will break your [v]staff of bread:
17 So will I send upon you famine and
[w]evil beasts, and they shall bereave thee;
and [x]pestilence and blood shall pass
through thee; and I will bring the sword
upon thee. I the LORD have spoken *it*.

6 And the word of the LORD came unto
me, saying,
2 Son of man, [y]set thy face toward the
[z]mountains of Israel, and prophesy against
them,
3 And say, Ye mountains of Israel, hear
the word of the Lord GOD; Thus saith the
Lord GOD to the mountains, and to the hills,
to the rivers, and to the valleys; Behold, I,
even I, will bring a sword upon you, and [a]I
will destroy your high places.

4:13 [p]Hos. 9:3
4:14 [q]Acts 10:14 [r]Ex. 22:31; Lev. 11:40 [s]Deut. 14:3; Isa. 65:4
4:16 [t]Lev. 26:26; Ps. 105:16; Isa. 3:1; ch. 5:16 [u]ver. 10; ch. 12:19 [v]ver. 11
4:17 [w]Lev. 26:39; ch. 24:23
5:1 [x]Lev. 21:5; Isa. 7:20; ch. 44:20
5:2 [y]ver. 12 [z]ch. 4:1 [a]ch. 4:8
5:3 [b]Jer. 40:6
5:4 [c]Jer. 41:1
5:7 [d]Jer. 2:10; ch. 16:47
5:9 [e]Lam. 4:6; Dan. 9:12; Am. 3:2
5:10 [f]Lev. 26:29; Deut. 28:53; 2 Kings 6:29; Jer. 19:9; Lam. 2:20 [g]ver. 12; Lev. 26:33; Deut. 28:64; ch. 12:14; Zech. 2:6
5:11 [h]2 Chron. 36:14; ch. 7:20 [i]ch. 11:21 [j]ch. 7:4
5:12 [k]ver. 2; Jer. 15:2; ch. 6:12 [l]Jer. 9:16; ver. 2; ch. 6:8 [m]Lev. 26:33; ver. 2; ch. 12:14
5:13 [n]Lam. 4:11; ch. 6:12 [o]ch. 21:17 [p]Deut. 32:36; Isa. 1:24 [q]ch. 36:6
5:14 [r]Lev. 26:31; Neh. 2:17
5:15 [s]Deut. 28:37; 1 Kings 9:7; Ps. 79:4; Jer. 24:9; Lam. 2:15 [t]ch. 25:17
5:16 [u]Deut. 32:23 [v]Lev. 26:26; ch. 4:16
5:17 [w]Lev. 26:22; Deut. 32:24; ch. 14:21 [x]ch. 38:22
6:2 [y]ch. 20:46 [z]ch. 36:1
6:3 [a]Lev. 26:30

4 And your altars shall be desolate, and your images shall be broken: and [b]I will cast down your slain *men* before your idols.

5 And I will lay the dead carcases of the children of Israel before their idols; and I will scatter your bones round about your altars.

6 In all your dwellingplaces the cities shall be laid waste, and the high places shall be desolate; that your altars may be laid waste and made desolate, and your idols may be broken and cease, and your images may be cut down, and your works may be abolished.

7 And the slain shall fall in the midst of you, and [c]ye shall know that I *am* the LORD.

8 ¶ [d]Yet will I leave a remnant, that ye may have *some* that shall escape the sword among the nations, when ye shall be scattered through the countries.

9 And they that escape of you shall remember me among the nations whither they shall be carried captives, because [e]I am broken with their whorish heart, which hath departed from me, and [f]with their eyes, which go a whoring after their idols: and [g]they shall lothe themselves for the evils which they have committed in all their abominations.

10 And they shall know that I *am* the LORD, *and that* I have not said in vain that I would do this evil unto them.

11 ¶ Thus saith the Lord GOD; Smite [h]with thine hand, and stamp with thy foot, and say, Alas for all the evil abominations of the house of Israel! [i]for they shall fall by the sword, by the famine, and by the pestilence.

12 He that is far off shall die of the pestilence; and he that is near shall fall by the sword; and he that remaineth and is besieged shall die by the famine: [j]thus will I accomplish my fury upon them.

13 Then [k]shall ye know that I *am* the LORD, when their slain *men* shall be among their idols round about their altars, [l]upon every high hill, [m]in all the tops of the mountains, and [n]under every green tree, and under every thick oak, the place where they did offer sweet savour to all their idols.

14 So will I [o]stretch out my hand upon them, and make the land desolate, yea, more desolate than the wilderness toward [p]Diblath, in all their habitations: and they shall know that I *am* the LORD.

7 Moreover the word of the LORD came unto me, saying,

2 Also, thou son of man, thus saith the Lord GOD unto the land of Israel; [q]An end, the end is come upon the four corners of the land.

3 Now *is* the end *come* upon thee, and I will send mine anger upon thee, and [r]will judge thee according to thy ways, and will recompense upon thee all thine abominations.

4 And [s]mine eye shall not spare thee, neither will I have pity: but I will recompense thy ways upon thee, and thine abominations shall be in the midst of thee: [t]and ye shall know that I *am* the LORD.

5 Thus saith the Lord GOD; An evil, an only evil, behold, is come.

6 An end is come, the end is come: it watcheth for thee; behold, it is come.

7 [u]The morning is come unto thee, O thou that dwellest in the land: [v]the time is come, the day of trouble *is* near, and not the sounding again of the mountains.

8 Now will I shortly [w]pour out my fury upon thee, and accomplish mine anger upon thee: [x]and I will judge thee according to thy ways, and will recompense thee for all thine abominations.

9 And [y]mine eye shall not spare, neither will I have pity: I will recompense thee according to thy ways and thine abominations *that* are in the midst of thee; [z]and ye shall know that I *am* the LORD that smiteth.

10 Behold the day, behold, it is come: [a]the morning is gone forth; the rod hath blossomed, pride hath budded.

11 [b]Violence is risen up into a rod of wickedness: none of them *shall remain,* nor of their multitude, nor of any of theirs: [c]neither *shall there be* wailing for them.

12 [d]The time is come, the day draweth near: let not the buyer rejoice, nor the seller mourn: for wrath *is* upon all the multitude thereof.

13 For the seller shall not return to that which is sold, although they were yet alive: for the vision *is* touching the whole multitude thereof, *which* shall not return; neither shall any strengthen himself in the iniquity of his life.

14 They have blown the trumpet, even to make all ready; but none goeth to the battle: for my wrath *is* upon all the multitude thereof.

15 [e]The sword *is* without, and the pestilence and the famine within: he that *is* in the field shall die with the sword; and he that *is* in the city, famine and pestilence shall devour him.

16 ¶ But [f]they that escape of them shall escape, and shall be on the mountains like doves of the valleys, all of them mourning, every one for his iniquity.

17 All [g]hands shall be feeble, and all knees shall be weak *as* water.

18 They shall also [h]gird *themselves* with sackcloth, and [i]horror shall cover them; and shame *shall be* upon all faces, and baldness upon all their heads.

19 They shall cast their silver in the streets, and their gold shall be removed: their [j]silver and their gold shall not be able to deliver them in the day of the wrath of the LORD: they shall not satisfy their souls, neither fill their bowels: because it is [k]the stumblingblock of their iniquity.

20 ¶ As for the beauty of his ornament, he set it in majesty: [l]but they made the images of their abominations *and* of their detest-

6:4 [b]Lev. 26:30
6:7 [c]ver. 13; ch. 7:4
6:8 [d]Jer. 44:28; ch. 5:2
6:9 [e]Ps. 78:40; Isa. 7:13 [f]Num. 15:39; ch. 20:7 [g]Lev. 26:39; Job 42:6; ch. 20:43
6:11 [h]ch. 21:14 [i]ch. 5:12
6:12 [j]ch. 5:13
6:13 [k]ver. 7 [l]Jer. 2:20 [m]Hos. 4:13 [n]Isa. 57:5
6:14 [o]Isa. 5:25 [p]Num. 33:46; Jer. 48:22
7:2 [q]ver. 3; Am. 8:2; Matt. 24:6
7:3 [r]ver. 8
7:4 [s]ver. 9; ch. 5:11 [t]ver. 27; ch. 6:7
7:7 [u]ver. 10 [v]ver. 12; Zeph. 1:14
7:8 [w]ch. 20:8 [x]ver. 3
7:9 [y]ver. 4 [z]ver. 4
7:10 [a]ver. 7
7:11 [b]Jer. 6:7 [c]Jer. 16:5; ch. 24:16
7:12 [d]ver. 7
7:15 [e]Deut. 32:25; Lam. 1:20; ch. 5:12
7:16 [f]ch. 6:8
7:17 [g]Isa. 13:7; Jer. 6:24; ch. 21:7
7:18 [h]Isa. 3:24; Jer. 48:37; Am. 8:10 [i]Ps. 55:5
7:19 [j]Prov. 11:4; Zeph. 1:18 [k]ch. 14:3
7:20 [l]Jer. 7:30

able things therein: therefore have I set it far from them.

21 And I will give it into the hands of the strangers for a prey, and to the wicked of the earth for a spoil; and they shall pollute it.

22 My face will I turn also from them, and they shall pollute my secret *place:* for the robbers shall enter into it, and defile it.

23 ¶ Make a chain: for [m]the land is full of bloody crimes, and the city is full of violence.

24 Wherefore I will bring the worst of the heathen, and they shall possess their houses: I will also make the pomp of the strong to cease; and their holy places shall be defiled.

25 Destruction cometh; and they shall seek peace, and *there shall be* none.

26 [n]Mischief shall come upon mischief, and rumour shall be upon rumour; [o]then shall they seek a vision of the prophet; but the law shall perish from the priest, and counsel from the ancients.

27 The king shall mourn, and the prince shall be clothed with desolation, and the hands of the people of the land shall be troubled: I will do unto them after their way, and according to their deserts will I judge them; [p]and they shall know that I *am* the LORD.

8 And it came to pass in the sixth year, in the sixth *month,* in the fifth *day* of the month, *as* I sat in mine house, and [q]the elders of Judah sat before me, that [r]the hand of the Lord GOD fell there upon me.

2 [s]Then I beheld, and lo a likeness as the appearance of fire: from the appearance of his loins even downward, fire; and from his loins even upward, as the appearance of brightness, [t]as the colour of amber.

3 And he [u]put forth the form of an hand, and took me by a lock of mine head; and [v]the spirit lifted me up between the earth and the heaven, and [w]brought me in the visions of God to Jerusalem, to the door of the inner gate that looketh toward the north; [x]where *was* the seat of the image of jealousy, which [y]provoketh to jealousy.

4 And, behold, the glory of the God of Israel *was* there, according to the vision that I [z]saw in the plain.

5 ¶ Then said he unto me, Son of man, lift up thine eyes now the way toward the north. So I lifted up mine eyes the way toward the north, and behold northward at the gate of the altar this image of jealousy in the entry.

6 He said furthermore unto me, Son of man, seest thou what they do? *even* the great abominations that the house of Israel committeth here, that I should go far off from my sanctuary? but turn thee yet again, *and* thou shalt see greater abominations.

7 ¶ And he brought me to the door of the court; and when I looked, behold a hole in the wall.

8 Then said he unto me, Son of man, dig now in the wall: and when I had digged in the wall, behold a door.

9 And he said unto me, Go in, and behold the wicked abominations that they do here.

10 So I went in and saw; and behold every form of creeping things, and abominable beasts, and all the idols of the house of Israel, pourtrayed upon the wall round about.

11 And there stood before them seventy men of the ancients of the house of Israel, and in the midst of them stood Jaazaniah the son of Shaphan, with every man his censer in his hand; and a thick cloud of incense went up.

12 Then said he unto me, Son of man, hast thou seen what the ancients of the house of Israel do in the dark, every man in the chambers of his imagery? for they say, [a]The LORD seeth us not; the LORD hath forsaken the earth.

13 ¶ He said also unto me, Turn thee yet again, *and* thou shalt see greater abominations that they do.

14 Then he brought me to the door of the gate of the LORD's house which *was* toward the north; and, behold, there sat women weeping for Tammuz.

15 ¶ Then said he unto me, Hast thou seen *this,* O son of man? turn thee yet again, *and* thou shalt see greater abominations than these.

16 And he brought me into the inner court of the LORD's house, and, behold, at the door of the temple of the LORD, [b]between the porch and the altar, [c]*were* about five and twenty men, [d]with their backs toward the temple of the LORD, and their faces toward the east; and they worshipped [e]the sun toward the east.

17 ¶ Then he said unto me, Hast thou seen *this,* O son of man? Is it a light thing to the house of Judah that they commit the abominations which they commit here? for they have [f]filled the land with violence, and have returned to provoke me to anger: and, lo, they put the branch to their nose.

18 [g]Therefore will I also deal in fury: mine [h]eye shall not spare, neither will I have pity: and though they [i]cry in mine ears with a loud voice, *yet* will I not hear them.

9 He cried also in mine ears with a loud voice, saying, Cause them that have charge over the city to draw near, even every man *with* his destroying weapon in his hand.

2 And, behold, six men came from the way of the higher gate, which lieth toward the north, and every man a slaughter weapon in his hand; [j]and one man among them *was* clothed with linen, with a writer's inkhorn by his side: and they went in, and stood beside the brasen altar.

3 And [k]the glory of the God of Israel was gone up from the cherub, whereupon he was, to the threshold of the house. And he called to the man clothed with linen, which *had* the writer's inkhorn by his side;

7:23 [m]2 Kings 21:16; ch. 9:9
7:26 [n]Deut. 32:23; Jer. 4:20 [o]Ps. 74:9; Lam. 2:9; ch. 20:1
7:27 [p]ver. 4
8:1 [q]ch. 14:1 [r]ch. 1:3
8:2 [s]ch. 1:26 [t]ch. 1:4
8:3 [u]Dan. 5:5 [v]ch. 3:14 [w]ch. 11:1 [x]Jer. 7:30; ch. 5:11 [y]Deut. 32:16
8:4 [z]ch. 1:28
8:12 [a]ch. 9:9
8:16 [b]Joel 2:17 [c]ch. 11:1 [d]Jer. 2:27 [e]Deut. 4:19; 2 Kings 23:5; Job 31:26; Jer. 44:17
8:17 [f]ch. 9:9
8:18 [g]ch. 5:13 [h]ch. 5:11 [i]Prov. 1:28; Isa. 1:15; Jer. 11:11; Mic. 3:4; Zech. 7:13
9:2 [j]Lev. 16:4; ch. 10:2; Rev. 15:6
9:3 [k]ch. 3:23

4 And the LORD said unto him, Go through the midst of the city, through the midst of Jerusalem, and set [l]a mark upon the foreheads of the men [m]that sigh and that cry for all the abominations that be done in the midst thereof.

5 ¶ And to the others he said in mine hearing, Go ye after him through the city, and smite: [n]let not your eye spare, neither have ye pity:

6 [o]Slay utterly old *and* young, both maids, and little children, and women: but [p]come not near any man upon whom *is* the mark; and [q]begin at my sanctuary. [r]Then they began at the ancient men which *were* before the house.

7 And he said unto them, Defile the house, and fill the courts with the slain: go ye forth. And they went forth, and slew in the city.

8 ¶ And it came to pass, while they were slaying them, and I was left, that I [s]fell upon my face, and cried, and said, [t]Ah Lord GOD! wilt thou destroy all the residue of Israel in thy pouring out of thy fury upon Jerusalem?

9 Then said he unto me, The iniquity of the house of Israel and Judah *is* exceeding great, and [u]the land is full of blood, and the city full of perverseness: for they say, [v]The LORD hath forsaken the earth, and [w]the LORD seeth not.

10 And as for me also, mine [x]eye shall not spare, neither will I have pity, *but* [y]I will recompense their way upon their head.

11 And, behold, the man clothed with linen, which *had* the inkhorn by his side, reported the matter, saying, I have done as thou hast commanded me.

10 Then I looked, and, behold, in the [z]firmament that was above the head of the cherubims there appeared over them as it were a sapphire stone, as the appearance of the likeness of a throne.

2 [a]And he spake unto the man clothed with linen, and said, Go in between the wheels, *even* under the cherub, and fill thine hand with [b]coals of fire from between the cherubims, and [c]scatter *them* over the city. And he went in in my sight.

3 Now the cherubims stood on the right side of the house, when the man went in; and the cloud filled the inner court.

4 [d]Then the glory of the LORD went up from the cherub, *and stood* over the threshold of the house; and [e]the house was filled with the cloud, and the court was full of the brightness of the LORD's glory.

5 And the [f]sound of the cherubims' wings was heard *even* to the outer court, as [g]the voice of the Almighty God when he speaketh.

6 And it came to pass, *that* when he had commanded the man clothed with linen, saying, Take fire from between the wheels, from between the cherubims; then he went in, and stood beside the wheels.

7 And *one* cherub stretched forth his hand from between the cherubims unto the fire that *was* between the cherubims, and took *thereof*, and put *it* into the hands of *him that was* clothed with linen: who took *it*, and went out.

8 ¶ [h]And there appeared in the cherubims the form of a man's hand under their wings.

9 [i]And when I looked, behold the four wheels by the cherubims, one wheel by one cherub, and another wheel by another cherub: and the appearance of the wheels *was* as the colour of a [j]beryl stone.

10 And *as for* their appearances, they four had one likeness, as if a wheel had been in the midst of a wheel.

11 [k]When they went, they went upon their four sides; they turned not as they went, but to the place whither the head looked they followed it; they turned not as they went.

12 And their whole body, and their backs, and their hands, and their wings, and [l]the wheels, *were* full of eyes round about, *even* the wheels that they four had.

13 As for the wheels, it was cried unto them in my hearing, O wheel.

14 [m]And every one had four faces: the first face *was* the face of a cherub, and the second face *was* the face of a man, and the third the face of a lion, and the fourth the face of an eagle.

15 And the cherubims were lifted up. This *is* [n]the living creature that I saw by the river of Chebar.

16 [o]And when the cherubims went, the wheels went by them: and when the cherubims lifted up their wings to mount up from the earth, the same wheels also turned not from beside them.

17 [p]When they stood, *these* stood; and when they were lifted up, *these* lifted up themselves *also:* for the spirit of the living creature *was* in them.

18 Then [q]the glory of the LORD [r]departed from off the threshold of the house, and stood over the cherubims.

19 And [s]the cherubims lifted up their wings, and mounted up from the earth in my sight: when they went out, the wheels also *were* beside them, and *every one* stood at the door of the east gate of the LORD's house; and the glory of the God of Israel *was* over them above.

20 [t]This *is* the living creature that I saw under the God of Israel [u]by the river of Chebar; and I knew that they *were* the cherubims.

21 [v]Every one had four faces apiece, and every one four wings; [w]and the likeness of the hands of a man *was* under their wings.

22 And [x]the likeness of their faces *was* the same faces which I saw by the river of Chebar, their appearances and themselves: [y]they went every one straight forward.

11 Moreover [z]the spirit lifted me up, and brought me unto [a]the east gate of the LORD's house, which looketh east-

9:4 [l]Ex. 12:7; Rev. 7:3 [m]Ps. 119:53; Jer. 13:17; 2 Cor. 12:21; 2 Pet. 2:8
9:5 [n]ver. 10; ch. 5:11
9:6 [o]2 Chron. 36:17 [p]Rev. 9:4 [q]Jer. 25:29; 1 Pet. 4:17 [r]ch. 8:11
9:8 [s]Num. 14:5; Josh. 7:6 [t]ch. 11:13
9:9 [u]2 Kings 21:16; ch. 8:17 [v]ch. 8:12 [w]Ps. 10:11; Isa. 29:15
9:10 [x]ch. 5:11 [y]ch. 11:21
10:1 [z]ch. 1:22
10:2 [a]ch. 9:2 [b]ch. 1:13 [c]Rev. 8:5
10:4 [d]ver. 18; ch. 1:28 [e]1 Kings 8:10; ch. 43:5
10:5 [f]ch. 1:24 [g]Ps. 29:3
10:8 [h]ch. 1:8; ver. 21
10:9 [i]ch. 1:15 [j]ch. 1:16
10:11 [k]ch. 1:17
10:12 [l]ch. 1:18
10:14 [m]ch. 1:6
10:15 [n]ch. 1:5
10:16 [o]ch. 1:19
10:17 [p]ch. 1:12
10:18 [q]ver. 4 [r]Hos. 9:12
10:19 [s]ch. 11:22
10:20 [t]ch. 1:22; ver. 15 [u]ch. 1:1
10:21 [v]ch. 1:6; ver. 14 [w]ch. 1:8; ver. 8
10:22 [x]ch. 1:10 [y]ch. 1:12
11:1 [z]ch. 3:12; ver. 24 [a]ch. 10:19

ward: and behold [b]at the door of the gate
five and twenty men; among whom I saw
Jaazaniah the son of Azur, and Pelatiah the
son of Benaiah, princes of the people.
2 Then said he unto me, Son of man, these
are the men that devise mischief, and give
wicked counsel in this city:
3 Which say, *It is* not [c]near; let us build
houses: [d]this *city is* the caldron, and we *be*
the flesh.
4 ¶ Therefore prophesy against them,
prophesy, O son of man.
5 And [e]the Spirit of the LORD fell upon
me, and said unto me, Speak; Thus saith the
LORD; Thus have ye said, O house of Israel:
for I know the things that come into your
mind, *every one of* them.
6 [f]Ye have multiplied your slain in this
city, and ye have filled the streets thereof
with the slain.
7 Therefore thus saith the Lord GOD;
[g]Your slain whom ye have laid in the midst
of it, they *are* the flesh, and this *city is* the
caldron: [h]but I will bring you forth out of
the midst of it.
8 Ye have feared the sword; and I will
bring a sword upon you, saith the Lord
GOD.
9 And I will bring you out of the midst
thereof, and deliver you into the hands of
strangers, and [i]will execute judgments
among you.
10 [j]Ye shall fall by the sword; I will judge
you in [k]the border of Israel; [l]and ye shall
know that I *am* the LORD.
11 [m]This *city* shall not be your caldron,
neither shall ye be the flesh in the midst
thereof; *but* I will judge you in the border of
Israel:
12 And [n]ye shall know that I *am* the
LORD: for ye have not walked in my statutes, neither executed my judgments, but
[o]have done after the manners of the heathen that *are* round about you.
13 ¶ And it came to pass, when I prophesied, that [p]Pelatiah the son of Benaiah died.
Then [q]fell I down upon my face, and cried
with a loud voice, and said, Ah Lord GOD!
wilt thou make a full end of the remnant of
Israel?
14 Again the word of the LORD came unto
me, saying,
15 Son of man, thy brethren, *even* thy
brethren, the men of thy kindred, and all the
house of Israel wholly, *are* they unto whom
the inhabitants of Jerusalem have said, Get
you far from the LORD: unto us is this land
given in possession.
16 Therefore say, Thus saith the Lord
GOD; Although I have cast them far off
among the heathen, and although I have
scattered them among the countries, [r]yet
will I be to them as a little sanctuary in the
countries where they shall come.
17 Therefore say, Thus saith the Lord
GOD; [s]I will even gather you from the people, and assemble you out of the countries

11:1 [b]ch. 8:16
11:3 [c]ch. 12:22; 2 Pet. 3:4 [d]Jer. 1:13; ch. 24:3
11:5 [e]ch. 2:2
11:6 [f]ch. 7:23
11:7 [g]ch. 24:3; Mic. 3:3 [h]ver. 9
11:9 [i]ch. 5:8
11:10 [j]2 Kings 25:19; Jer. 39:6 [k]1 Kings 8:65; 2 Kings 14:25 [l]Ps. 9:16; ch. 6:7
11:11 [m]ver. 3
11:12 [n]ver. 10 [o]Lev. 18:3; Deut. 12:30; ch. 8:10
11:13 [p]ver. 1; Acts 5:5 [q]ch. 9:8
11:16 [r]Ps. 90:1; Isa. 8:14
11:17 [s]Jer. 24:5; ch. 28:25
11:18 [t]ch. 37:23
11:19 [u]Jer. 32:39; ch. 36:26; Zeph. 3:9 [v]Ps. 51:10; Jer. 31:33; ch. 18:31 [w]Zech. 7:12
11:20 [x]Ps. 105:45 [y]Jer. 24:7; ch. 14:11
11:21 [z]ch. 9:10
11:22 [a]ch. 1:19
11:23 [b]ch. 8:4 [c]Zech. 14:4 [d]ch. 43:2
11:24 [e]ch. 8:3
12:2 [f]ch. 2:3 [g]Isa. 6:9; Jer. 5:21; Matt. 13:13 [h]ch. 2:5
12:6 [i]Isa. 8:18; ch. 4:3; ver. 11
12:9 [j]ch. 2:5 [k]ch. 17:12

where ye have been scattered, and I will
give you the land of Israel.
18 And they shall come thither, and [t]they
shall take away all the detestable things
thereof and all the abominations thereof
from thence.
19 And [u]I will give them one heart, and I
will put [v]a new spirit within you; and I will
take [w]the stony heart out of their flesh, and
will give them an heart of flesh:
20 [x]That they may walk in my statutes,
and keep mine ordinances, and do them:
[y]and they shall be my people, and I will be
their God.
21 But *as for them* whose heart walketh
after the heart of their detestable things and
their abominations, [z]I will recompense
their way upon their own heads, saith the
Lord GOD.
22 ¶ Then did the cherubims [a]lift up their
wings, and the wheels beside them; and the
glory of the God of Israel *was* over them
above.
23 And [b]the glory of the LORD went up
from the midst of the city, and stood [c]upon
the mountain [d]which *is* on the east side of
the city.
24 ¶ Afterwards [e]the spirit took me up,
and brought me in a vision by the Spirit of
God into Chaldea, to them of the captivity.
So the vision that I had seen went up
from me.
25 Then I spake unto them of the captivity
all the things that the LORD had shewed me.

12 The word of the LORD also came unto
me, saying,
2 Son of man, thou dwellest in the midst
of [f]a rebellious house, which [g]have eyes to
see, and see not; they have ears to hear, and
hear not: [h]for they *are* a rebellious house.
3 Therefore, thou son of man, prepare
thee stuff for removing, and remove by day
in their sight; and thou shalt remove from
thy place to another place in their sight: it
may be they will consider, though they *be* a
rebellious house.
4 Then shalt thou bring forth thy stuff by
day in their sight, as stuff for removing: and
thou shalt go forth at even in their sight, as
they that go forth into captivity.
5 Dig thou through the wall in their sight,
and carry out thereby.
6 In their sight shalt thou bear *it* upon *thy*
shoulders, *and* carry *it* forth in the twilight:
thou shalt cover thy face, that thou see not
the ground: [i]for I have set thee *for* a sign
unto the house of Israel.
7 And I did so as I was commanded: I
brought forth my stuff by day, as stuff for
captivity, and in the even I digged through
the wall with mine hand; I brought *it* forth
in the twilight, *and* I bare *it* upon *my* shoulder in their sight.
8 ¶ And in the morning came the word of
the LORD unto me, saying,
9 Son of man, hath not the house of Israel,
[j]the rebellious house, said unto thee,
[k]What doest thou?

10 Say thou unto them, Thus saith the
Lord GOD; This [l]burden *concerneth* the
prince in Jerusalem, and all the house of
Israel that *are* among them.
11 Say, [m]I *am* your sign: like as I have
done, so shall it be done unto them: [n]they
shall remove *and* go into captivity.
12 And [o]the prince that *is* among them
shall bear upon *his* shoulder in the twilight,
and shall go forth: they shall dig through
the wall to carry out thereby: he shall cover
his face, that he see not the ground with *his*
eyes.
13 My [p]net also will I spread upon him,
and he shall be taken in my snare: and [q]I
will bring him to Babylon *to* the land of the
Chaldeans; yet shall he not see it, though he
shall die there.
14 And [r]I will scatter toward every wind
all that *are* about him to help him, and all
his bands; and [s]I will draw out the sword
after them.
15 [t]And they shall know that I *am* the
LORD, when I shall scatter them among the
nations, and disperse them in the countries.
16 [u]But I will leave a few men of them
from the sword, from the famine, and from
the pestilence; that they may declare all
their abominations among the heathen
whither they come; and they shall know
that I *am* the LORD.
17 ¶ Moreover the word of the LORD came
to me, saying,
18 Son of man, [v]eat thy bread with quaking, and drink thy water with trembling and
with carefulness;
19 And say unto the people of the land,
Thus saith the Lord GOD of the inhabitants
of Jerusalem, *and* of the land of Israel; They
shall eat their bread with carefulness, and
drink their water with astonishment, that
her land may [w]be desolate from all that is
therein, [x]because of the violence of all them
that dwell therein.
20 And the cities that are inhabited shall
be laid waste, and the land shall be desolate;
and ye shall know that I *am* the LORD.
21 ¶ And the word of the LORD came unto
me, saying,
22 Son of man, what *is* that proverb *that*
ye have in the land of Israel, saying, [y]The
days are prolonged, and every vision faileth?
23 Tell them therefore, Thus saith the
Lord GOD; I will make this proverb to cease,
and they shall no more use it as a proverb in
Israel; but say unto them, [z]The days are at
hand, and the effect of every vision.
24 For [a]there shall be no more any [b]vain
vision nor flattering divination within the
house of Israel.
25 For I *am* the LORD: I will speak, and
[c]the word that I shall speak shall come to
pass; it shall be no more prolonged: for in
your days, O rebellious house, will I say the
word, and will perform it, saith the Lord
GOD.

12:10 [l]Mal. 1:1
12:11 [m]ver. 6 [n]2 Kings 25:4
12:12 [o]Jer. 39:4
12:13 [p]Job 19:6; Lam. 1:13; Jer. 52:9; ch. 17:20 [q]2 Kings 25:7; Jer. 52:11; ch. 17:16
12:14 [r]2 Kings 25:4; ch. 5:10 [s]ch. 5:2
12:15 [t]Ps. 9:16; ch. 6:7; ver. 16
12:16 [u]ch. 6:8
12:18 [v]ch. 4:16
12:19 [w]Zech. 7:14 [x]Ps. 107:34
12:22 [y]ver. 27; ch. 11:3; Am. 6:3; 2 Pet. 3:4
12:23 [z]Joel 2:1; Zeph. 1:14
12:24 [a]ch. 13:23 [b]Lam. 2:14
12:25 [c]Isa. 55:11; ver. 28; Dan. 9:12; Luke 21:33
12:27 [d]ver. 22 [e]2 Pet. 3:4
12:28 [f]ver. 23
13:2 [g]ver. 17 [h]Jer. 14:14
13:4 [i]SSol. 2:15
13:5 [j]Ps. 106:23; ch. 22:30
13:6 [k]ver. 23; ch. 12:24
13:9 [l]Ezra 2:59; Neh. 7:5; Ps. 69:28 [m]ch. 20:38 [n]ch. 11:10
13:10 [o]Jer. 6:14 [p]ch. 22:28
13:11 [q]ch. 38:22

26 ¶ Again the word of the LORD came to
me, saying,
27 [d]Son of man, behold, *they of* the house
of Israel say, The vision that he seeth *is* [e]for
many days *to come*, and he prophesieth of
the times *that are* far off.
28 [f]Therefore say unto them, Thus saith
the Lord GOD; There shall none of my
words be prolonged any more, but the word
which I have spoken shall be done, saith the
Lord GOD.

13 And the word of the LORD came unto
me, saying,
2 Son of man, prophesy against the
prophets of Israel that prophesy, and say
thou unto [g]them that prophesy out of their
own [h]hearts, Hear ye the word of the LORD;
3 Thus saith the Lord GOD; Woe unto the
foolish prophets, that follow their own
spirit, and have seen nothing!
4 O Israel, thy prophets are [i]like the
foxes in the deserts.
5 Ye [j]have not gone up into the gaps, neither made up the hedge for the house of
Israel to stand in the battle in the day of the
LORD.
6 [k]They have seen vanity and lying divination, saying, The LORD saith: and the
LORD hath not sent them: and they have
made *others* to hope that they would confirm the word.
7 Have ye not seen a vain vision, and have
ye not spoken a lying divination, whereas
ye say, The LORD saith *it;* albeit I have not
spoken?
8 Therefore thus saith the Lord GOD; Because ye have spoken vanity, and seen lies,
therefore, behold, I *am* against you, saith
the Lord GOD.
9 And mine hand shall be upon the prophets that see vanity, and that divine lies: they
shall not be in the assembly of my people,
[l]neither shall they be written in the writing
of the house of Israel, [m]neither shall they
enter into the land of Israel; [n]and ye shall
know that I *am* the Lord GOD.
10 ¶ Because, even because they have seduced my people, saying, [o]Peace; and *there
was* no peace; and one built up a wall, and,
lo, others [p]daubed it with untempered
morter:
11 Say unto them which daub *it* with untempered *morter,* that it shall fall: [q]there
shall be an overflowing shower; and ye,
O great hailstones, shall fall; and a stormy
wind shall rend *it.*
12 Lo, when the wall is fallen, shall it not
be said unto you, Where *is* the daubing
wherewith ye have daubed *it?*
13 Therefore thus saith the Lord GOD; I
will even rend *it* with a stormy wind in my
fury; and there shall be an overflowing
shower in mine anger, and great hailstones
in *my* fury to consume *it.*
14 So will I break down the wall that ye
have daubed with untempered *morter,* and
bring it down to the ground, so that the
foundation thereof shall be discovered, and

it shall fall, and ye shall be consumed in the midst thereof: [r]and ye shall know that I *am* the LORD.

15 Thus will I accomplish my wrath upon the wall, and upon them that have daubed it with untempered *morter,* and will say unto you, The wall *is* no *more,* neither they that daubed it;

16 *To wit,* the prophets of Israel which prophesy concerning Jerusalem, and which [s]see visions of peace for her, and *there is* no peace, saith the Lord GOD.

17 ¶ Likewise, thou son of man, [t]set thy face against the daughters of thy people, [u]which prophesy out of their own heart; and prophesy thou against them,

18 And say, Thus saith the Lord GOD; Woe to the *women* that sew pillows to all armholes, and make kerchiefs upon the head of every stature to hunt souls! Will ye [v]hunt the souls of my people, and will ye save the souls alive *that come* unto you?

19 And will ye pollute me among my people [w]for handfuls of barley and for pieces of bread, to slay the souls that should not die, and to save the souls alive that should not live, by your lying to my people that hear *your* lies?

20 Wherefore thus saith the Lord GOD; Behold, I *am* against your pillows, wherewith ye there hunt the souls to make *them* fly, and I will tear them from your arms, and will let the souls go, *even* the souls that ye hunt to make *them* fly.

21 Your kerchiefs also will I tear, and deliver my people out of your hand, and they shall be no more in your hand to be hunted; [x]and ye shall know that I *am* the LORD.

22 Because with lies ye have made the heart of the righteous sad, whom I have not made sad; and [y]strengthened the hands of the wicked, that he should not return from his wicked way, by promising him life:

23 Therefore [z]ye shall see no more vanity, nor divine divinations: for I will deliver my people out of your hand: [a]and ye shall know that I *am* the LORD.

14 Then [b]came certain of the elders of Israel unto me, and sat before me.

2 And the word of the LORD came unto me, saying,

3 Son of man, these men have set up their idols in their heart, and put [c]the stumblingblock of their iniquity before their face: [d]should I be enquired of at all by them?

4 Therefore speak unto them, and say unto them, Thus saith the Lord GOD; Every man of the house of Israel that setteth up his idols in his heart, and putteth the stumblingblock of his iniquity before his face, and cometh to the prophet; I the LORD will answer him that cometh according to the multitude of his idols;

5 That I may take the house of Israel in their own heart, because they are all estranged from me through their idols.

6 ¶ Therefore say unto the house of Israel, Thus saith the Lord GOD; Repent, and turn *yourselves* from your idols; and turn away your faces from all your abominations.

7 For every one of the house of Israel, or of the stranger that sojourneth in Israel, which separateth himself from me, and setteth up his idols in his heart, and putteth the stumblingblock of his iniquity before his face, and cometh to a prophet to enquire of him concerning me; I the LORD will answer him by myself:

8 And [e]I will set my face against that man, and will make him a [f]sign and a proverb, and I will cut him off from the midst of my people; [g]and ye shall know that I *am* the LORD.

9 And if the prophet be deceived when he hath spoken a thing, I the LORD [h]have deceived that prophet, and I will stretch out my hand upon him, and will destroy him from the midst of my people Israel.

10 And they shall bear the punishment of their iniquity: the punishment of the prophet shall be even as the punishment of him that seeketh *unto him;*

11 That the house of Israel may [i]go no more astray from me, neither be polluted any more with all their transgressions; [j]but that they may be my people, and I may be their God, saith the Lord GOD.

12 ¶ The word of the LORD came again to me, saying,

13 Son of man, when the land sinneth against me by trespassing grievously, then will I stretch out mine hand upon it, and will break the [k]staff of the bread thereof, and will send famine upon it, and will cut off man and beast from it:

14 [l]Though these three men, Noah, Daniel, and Job, were in it, they should deliver *but* their own souls [m]by their righteousness, saith the Lord GOD.

15 ¶ If I cause [n]noisome beasts to pass through the land, and they spoil it, so that it be desolate, that no man may pass through because of the beasts:

16 [o]*Though* these three men *were* in it, *as* I live, saith the Lord GOD, they shall deliver neither sons nor daughters; they only shall be delivered, but the land shall be desolate.

17 ¶ Or *if* [p]I bring a sword upon that land, and say, Sword, go through the land; so that I [q]cut off man and beast from it:

18 [r]Though these three men *were* in it, *as* I live, saith the Lord GOD, they shall deliver neither sons nor daughters, but they only shall be delivered themselves.

19 ¶ Or *if* I send [s]a pestilence into that land, and [t]pour out my fury upon it in blood, to cut off from it man and beast:

20 [u]Though Noah, Daniel, and Job *were* in it, *as* I live, saith the Lord GOD, they shall deliver neither son nor daughter; they shall *but* deliver their own souls by their righteousness.

21 For thus saith the Lord GOD; How much more when [v]I send my four sore judgments upon Jerusalem, the sword, and the famine, and the noisome beast, and the

13:14 r ver. 9; ch. 14:8
13:16 s Jer. 6:14
13:17 t ch. 20:46 u ver. 2
13:18 v 2 Pet. 2:14
13:19 w Prov. 28:21; Mic. 3:5
13:21 x ver. 9
13:22 y Jer. 23:14
13:23 z ver. 6; ch. 12:24; Mic. 3:6 a ver. 9; ch. 14:8
14:1 b ch. 8:1
14:3 c ch. 7:19; ver. 4 d 2 Kings 3:13
14:8 e Lev. 17:10; Jer. 44:11; ch. 15:7 f Num. 26:10; Deut. 28:37; ch. 5:15 g ch. 6:7
14:9 h 1 Kings 22:23; Job 12:16; Jer. 4:10; 2 Thess. 2:11
14:11 i 2 Pet. 2:15 j ch. 11:20
14:13 k Lev. 26:26; Isa. 3:1; ch. 4:16
14:14 l Jer. 7:16; ver. 16 m Prov. 11:4
14:15 n Lev. 26:22; ch. 5:17
14:16 o ver. 14
14:17 p Lev. 26:25; ch. 5:12 q ch. 25:13; Zeph. 1:3
14:18 r ver. 14
14:19 s 2 Sam. 24:15; ch. 38:22 t ch. 7:8
14:20 u ver. 14
14:21 v ch. 5:17

pestilence, to cut off from it man and beast?

22 ¶ [w]Yet, behold, therein shall be left a remnant that shall be brought forth, *both* sons and daughters: behold, they shall come forth unto you, and [x]ye shall see their way and their doings: and ye shall be comforted concerning the evil that I have brought upon Jerusalem, *even* concerning all that I have brought upon it.

23 And they shall comfort you, when ye see their ways and their doings: and ye shall know that I have not done [y]without cause all that I have done in it, saith the Lord GOD.

15 And the word of the LORD came unto me, saying,

2 Son of man, What is the vine tree more than any tree, *or than* a branch which is among the trees of the forest?

3 Shall wood be taken thereof to do any work? or will *men* take a pin of it to hang any vessel thereon?

4 Behold, [z]it is cast into the fire for fuel; the fire devoureth both the ends of it, and the midst of it is burned. Is it meet for *any* work?

5 Behold, when it was whole, it was meet for no work: how much less shall it be meet yet for *any* work, when the fire hath devoured it, and it is burned?

6 ¶ Therefore thus saith the Lord GOD; As the vine tree among the trees of the forest, which I have given to the fire for fuel, so will I give the inhabitants of Jerusalem.

7 And [a]I will set my face against them; [b]they shall go out from *one* fire, and *another* fire shall devour them; [c]and ye shall know that I *am* the LORD, when I set my face against them.

8 And I will make the land desolate, because they have committed a trespass, saith the Lord GOD.

16 Again the word of the LORD came unto me, saying,

2 Son of man, [d]cause Jerusalem to know her abominations,

3 And say, Thus saith the Lord GOD unto Jerusalem; Thy birth [e]and thy nativity *is* of the land of Canaan; [f]thy father *was* an Amorite, and thy mother an Hittite.

4 And *as for* thy nativity, [g]in the day thou wast born thy navel was not cut, neither wast thou washed in water to supple *thee;* thou wast not salted at all, nor swaddled at all.

5 None eye pitied thee, to do any of these unto thee, to have compassion upon thee; but thou wast cast out in the open field, to the lothing of thy person, in the day that thou wast born.

6 ¶ And when I passed by thee, and saw thee polluted in thine own blood, I said unto thee *when thou wast* in thy blood, Live; yea, I said unto thee *when thou wast* in thy blood, Live.

7 [h]I have caused thee to multiply as the bud of the field, and thou hast increased and waxen great, and thou art come to excellent ornaments: *thy* breasts are fashioned, and thine hair is grown, whereas thou *wast* naked and bare.

8 Now when I passed by thee, and looked upon thee, behold, thy time *was* the time of love; [i]and I spread my skirt over thee, and covered thy nakedness: yea, I sware unto thee, and entered into a covenant with thee, saith the Lord GOD, and [j]thou becamest mine.

9 Then washed I thee with water; yea, I throughly washed away thy blood from thee, and I anointed thee with oil.

10 I clothed thee also with broidered work, and shod thee with badgers' skin, and I girded thee about with fine linen, and I covered thee with silk.

11 I decked thee also with ornaments, and I [k]put bracelets upon thy hands, [l]and a chain on thy neck.

12 And I put a jewel on thy forehead, and earrings in thine ears, and a beautiful crown upon thine head.

13 Thus wast thou decked with gold and silver; and thy raiment *was of* fine linen, and silk, and broidered work; [m]thou didst eat fine flour, and honey, and oil: and thou wast exceeding [n]beautiful, and thou didst prosper into a kingdom.

14 And [o]thy renown went forth among the heathen for thy beauty: for it *was* perfect through my comeliness, which I had put upon thee, saith the Lord GOD.

15 ¶ [p]But thou didst trust in thine own beauty, [q]and playedst the harlot because of thy renown, and pouredst out thy fornications on every one that passed by; his it was.

16 [r]And of thy garments thou didst take, and deckedst thy high places with divers colours, and playedst the harlot thereupon: *the like things* shall not come, neither shall it be *so.*

17 Thou hast also taken thy fair jewels of my gold and of my silver, which I had given thee, and madest to thyself images of men, and didst commit whoredom with them,

18 And tookest thy broidered garments, and coveredst them: and thou hast set mine oil and mine incense before them.

19 [s]My meat also which I gave thee, fine flour, and oil, and honey, *wherewith* I fed thee, thou hast even set it before them for a sweet savour: and *thus* it was, saith the Lord GOD.

20 [t]Moreover thou hast taken thy sons and thy daughters, whom thou hast borne unto me, and these hast thou sacrificed unto them to be devoured. *Is this* of thy whoredoms a small matter,

21 That thou hast slain my children, and delivered them to cause them to pass through *the fire* for them?

22 And in all thine abominations and thy whoredoms thou hast not remembered the days of thy [u]youth, [v]when thou wast naked and bare, *and* wast polluted in thy blood.

23 And it came to pass after all thy wickedness, (woe, woe unto thee! saith the Lord GOD;)

14:22 w ch. 6:8 x ch. 20:43
14:23 y Jer. 22:8
15:4 z John 15:6
15:7 a Lev. 17:10; ch. 14:8 b Isa. 24:18 c ch. 6:7
16:2 d ch. 20:4
16:3 e ch. 21:30 f ver. 45
16:4 g Hos. 2:3
16:7 h Ex. 1:7
16:8 i Ruth 3:9 j Ex. 19:5; Jer. 2:2
16:11 k Gen. 24:22 l Prov. 1:9
16:13 m Deut. 32:13 n Ps. 48:2
16:14 o Lam. 2:15
16:15 p Deut. 32:15; Jer. 7:4; Mic. 3:11 q Isa. 1:21; Jer. 2:20; ch. 23:3; Hos. 1:2
16:16 r 2 Kings 23:7; ch. 7:20; Hos. 2:8
16:19 s Hos. 2:8
16:20 t 2 Kings 16:3; Ps. 106:37; Isa. 57:5; Jer. 7:31; ch. 20:26
16:22 u Jer. 2:2; ver. 43; Hos. 11:1 v ver. 4

24 *That* [w]thou hast also built unto thee an eminent place, and [x]hast made thee an high place in every street.

25 Thou hast built thy high place [y]at every head of the way, and hast made thy beauty to be abhorred, and hast opened thy feet to every one that passed by, and multiplied thy whoredoms.

26 Thou hast also committed fornication with [z]the Egyptians thy neighbours, great of flesh; and hast increased thy whoredoms, to provoke me to anger.

27 Behold, therefore I have stretched out my hand over thee, and have diminished thine ordinary *food,* and delivered thee unto the will of them that hate thee, [a]the daughters of the Philistines, which are ashamed of thy lewd way.

28 [b]Thou hast played the whore also with the Assyrians, because thou wast unsatiable; yea, thou hast played the harlot with them, and yet couldest not be satisfied.

29 Thou hast moreover multiplied thy fornication in the land of Canaan [c]unto Chaldea; and yet thou wast not satisfied herewith.

30 How weak is thine heart, saith the Lord GOD, seeing thou doest all these *things,* the work of an imperious whorish woman;

31 In that [d]thou buildest thine eminent place in the head of every way, and makest thine high place in every street; and hast not been as an harlot, in that thou scornest hire;

32 *But as* a wife that committeth adultery, *which* taketh strangers instead of her husband!

33 They give gifts to all whores: but [e]thou givest thy gifts to all thy lovers, and hirest them, that they may come unto thee on every side for thy whoredom.

34 And the contrary is in thee from *other* women in thy whoredoms, whereas none followeth thee to commit whoredoms: and in that thou givest a reward, and no reward is given unto thee, therefore thou art contrary.

35 ¶ Wherefore, O harlot, hear the word of the LORD:

36 Thus saith the Lord GOD; Because thy filthiness was poured out, and thy nakedness discovered through thy whoredoms with thy lovers, and with all the idols of thy abominations, and by [f]the blood of thy children, which thou didst give unto them;

37 Behold, therefore [g]I will gather all thy lovers, with whom thou hast taken pleasure, and all *them* that thou hast loved, with all *them* that thou hast hated; I will even gather them round about against thee, and will discover thy nakedness unto them, that they may see all thy nakedness.

38 And I will judge thee, as [h]women that break wedlock and [i]shed blood are judged; and I will give thee blood in fury and jealousy.

39 And I will also give thee into their hand, and they shall throw down [j]thine eminent place, and shall break down thy high places: [k]they shall strip thee also of thy clothes, and shall take thy fair jewels, and leave thee naked and bare.

40 [l]They shall also bring up a company against thee, [m]and they shall stone thee with stones, and thrust thee through with their swords.

41 And they shall [n]burn thine houses with fire, and [o]execute judgments upon thee in the sight of many women: and I will cause thee to [p]cease from playing the harlot, and thou also shalt give no hire any more.

42 So [q]will I make my fury toward thee to rest, and my jealousy shall depart from thee, and I will be quiet, and will be no more angry.

43 Because [r]thou hast not remembered the days of thy youth, but hast fretted me in all these *things;* behold, therefore [s]I also will recompense thy way upon *thine* head, saith the Lord GOD: and thou shalt not commit this lewdness above all thine abominations.

44 ¶ Behold, every one that useth proverbs shall use *this* proverb against thee, saying, As *is* the mother, *so is* her daughter.

45 Thou *art* thy mother's daughter, that lotheth her husband and her children; and thou *art* the sister of thy sisters, which lothed their husbands and their children: [t]your mother *was* an Hittite, and your father an Amorite.

46 And thine elder sister *is* Samaria, she and her daughters that dwell at thy left hand: and [u]thy younger sister, that dwelleth at thy right hand, *is* Sodom and her daughters.

47 Yet hast thou not walked after their ways, nor done after their abominations: but, as *if that were* a very little *thing,* [v]thou wast corrupted more than they in all thy ways.

48 *As* I live, saith the Lord GOD, [w]Sodom thy sister hath not done, she nor her daughters, as thou hast done, thou and thy daughters.

49 Behold, this was the iniquity of thy sister Sodom, pride, [x]fulness of bread, and abundance of idleness was in her and in her daughters, neither did she strengthen the hand of the poor and needy.

50 And they were haughty, and [y]committed abomination before me: therefore [z]I took them away as I saw *good.*

51 Neither hath Samaria committed half of thy sins; but thou hast multiplied thine abominations more than they, and [a]hast justified thy sisters in all thine abominations which thou hast done.

52 Thou also, which hast judged thy sisters, bear thine own shame for thy sins that thou hast committed more abominable than they: they are more righteous than thou: yea, be thou confounded also, and bear thy shame, in that thou hast justified thy sisters.

53 [b]When I shall bring again their captiv-

16:24 [w]ver. 31 [x]Isa. 57:5; Jer. 2:20
16:25 [y]Prov. 9:14
16:26 [z]ch. 8:10
16:27 [a]2 Chron. 28:18; ver. 57
16:28 [b]2 Kings 16:7; 2 Chron. 28:23; Jer. 2:18; ch. 23:12
16:29 [c]ch. 23:14
16:31 [d]ver. 24
16:33 [e]Isa. 30:3; Hos. 8:9
16:36 [f]ver. 20; Jer. 2:34
16:37 [g]Jer. 13:22; Lam. 1:8; ch. 23:9; Hos. 2:10; Nah. 3:5
16:38 [h]Lev. 20:10; Deut. 22:22; ch. 23:45 [i]Gen. 9:6; Ex. 21:12; ver. 20
16:39 [j]ver. 24 [k]ch. 23:26; Hos. 2:3
16:40 [l]ch. 23:10 [m]John 8:5
16:41 [n]Deut. 13:16; 2 Kings 25:9; Jer. 39:8 [o]ch. 5:8 [p]ch. 23:27
16:42 [q]ch. 5:13
16:43 [r]ver. 22; Ps. 78:42 [s]ch. 9:10
16:45 [t]ver. 3
16:46 [u]Deut. 32:32; Isa. 1:10
16:47 [v]2 Kings 21:9; ch. 5:6; ver. 48
16:48 [w]Matt. 10:15
16:49 [x]Gen. 13:10
16:50 [y]Gen. 13:13 [z]Gen. 19:24
16:51 [a]Jer. 3:11; Matt. 12:41
16:53 [b]Isa. 1:9

ity, [c]the captivity of Sodom and her daughters, and the captivity of Samaria and her daughters, then *will I bring again* the captivity of thy captives in the midst of them:

54 That thou mayest bear thine own shame, and mayest be confounded in all that thou hast done, in that thou art [d]a comfort unto them.

55 When thy sisters, Sodom and her daughters, shall return to their former estate, and Samaria and her daughters shall return to their former estate, then thou and thy daughters shall return to your former estate.

56 For thy sister Sodom was not mentioned by thy mouth in the day of thy pride,

57 Before thy wickedness was discovered, as at the time of *thy* [e]reproach of the daughters of Syria, and all *that are* round about her, [f]the daughters of the Philistines, which despise thee round about.

58 [g]Thou hast borne thy lewdness and thine abominations, saith the LORD.

59 For thus saith the Lord GOD; I will even deal with thee as thou hast done, which hast [h]despised [i]the oath in breaking the covenant.

60 ¶ Nevertheless I will [j]remember my covenant with thee in the days of thy youth, and I will establish unto thee [k]an everlasting covenant.

61 Then [l]thou shalt remember thy ways, and be ashamed, when thou shalt receive thy sisters, thine elder and thy younger: and I will give them unto thee for [m]daughters, [n]but not by thy covenant.

62 [o]And I will establish my covenant with thee; and thou shalt know that I *am* the LORD:

63 That thou mayest [p]remember, and be confounded, [q]and never open thy mouth any more because of thy shame, when I am pacified toward thee for all that thou hast done, saith the Lord GOD.

17

And the word of the LORD came unto me, saying,

2 Son of man, put forth a riddle, and speak a parable unto the house of Israel;

3 And say, Thus saith the Lord GOD; [r]A great eagle with great wings, longwinged, full of feathers, which had divers colours, came unto Lebanon, and [s]took the highest branch of the cedar:

4 He cropped off the top of his young twigs, and carried it into a land of traffick; he set it in a city of merchants.

5 He took also of the seed of the land, and planted it in [t]a fruitful field; he placed *it* by great waters, *and* set it [u]*as* a willow tree.

6 And it grew, and became a spreading vine [v]of low stature, whose branches turned toward him, and the roots thereof were under him: so it became a vine, and brought forth branches, and shot forth sprigs.

7 There was also another great eagle with great wings and many feathers: and, behold, [w]this vine did bend her roots toward him, and shot forth her branches toward him, that he might water it by the furrows of her plantation.

8 It was planted in a good soil by great waters, that it might bring forth branches, and that it might bear fruit, that it might be a goodly vine.

9 Say thou, Thus saith the Lord GOD; Shall it prosper? [x]shall he not pull up the roots thereof, and cut off the fruit thereof, that it wither? it shall wither in all the leaves of her spring, even without great power or many people to pluck it up by the roots thereof.

10 Yea, behold, *being* planted, shall it prosper? [y]shall it not utterly wither, when the east wind toucheth it? it shall wither in the furrows where it grew.

11 ¶ Moreover the word of the LORD came unto me, saying,

12 Say now to [z]the rebellious house, Know ye not what these *things mean?* tell *them,* Behold, [a]the king of Babylon is come to Jerusalem, and hath taken the king thereof, and the princes thereof, and led them with him to Babylon;

13 [b]And hath taken of the king's seed, and made a covenant with him, [c]and hath taken an oath of him: he hath also taken the mighty of the land:

14 That the kingdom might be [d]base, that it might not lift itself up, *but* that by keeping of his covenant it might stand.

15 But [e]he rebelled against him in sending his ambassadors into Egypt, [f]that they might give him horses and much people. [g]Shall he prosper? shall he escape that doeth such *things?* or shall he break the covenant, and be delivered?

16 *As* I live, saith the Lord GOD, surely [h]in the place *where* the king *dwelleth* that made him king, whose oath he despised, and whose covenant he brake, *even* with him in the midst of Babylon he shall die.

17 [i]Neither shall Pharaoh with *his* mighty army and great company make for him in the war, [j]by casting up mounts, and building forts, to cut off many persons:

18 Seeing he despised the oath by breaking the covenant, when, lo, he had [k]given his hand, and hath done all these *things,* he shall not escape.

19 Therefore thus saith the Lord GOD; *As* I live, surely mine oath that he hath despised, and my covenant that he hath broken, even it will I recompense upon his own head.

20 And I will [l]spread my net upon him, and he shall be taken in my snare, and I will bring him to Babylon, and [m]will plead with him there for his trespass that he hath trespassed against me.

21 And [n]all his fugitives with all his bands shall fall by the sword, and they that remain shall be scattered toward all winds: and ye shall know that I the LORD have spoken *it.*

22 ¶ Thus saith the Lord GOD; I will also

16:53 [c]Jer. 20:16
16:54 [d]ch. 14:22
16:57 [e]2 Kings 16:5; 2 Chron. 28:18; Isa. 7:1 [f]ver. 27
16:58 [g]ch. 23:49
16:59 [h]ch. 17:13 [i]Deut. 29:12
16:60 [j]Ps. 106:45 [k]Jer. 32:40
16:61 [l]ch. 20:43 [m]Isa. 54:1; Gal. 4:26 [n]Jer. 31:31
16:62 [o]Hos. 2:19
16:63 [p]ver. 61 [q]Rom. 3:19
17:3 [r]ver. 12 [s]2 Kings 24:12
17:5 [t]Deut. 8:7 [u]Isa. 44:4
17:6 [v]ver. 14
17:7 [w]ver. 15
17:9 [x]2 Kings 25:7
17:10 [y]ch. 19:12; Hos. 13:15
17:12 [z]ch. 2:5 [a]ver. 3; 2 Kings 24:11-16
17:13 [b]2 Kings 24:17 [c]2 Chron. 36:13
17:14 [d]ver. 6; ch. 29:14
17:15 [e]2 Kings 24:20; 2 Chron. 36:13 [f]Deut. 17:16; Isa. 31:1 [g]ver. 9
17:16 [h]Jer. 32:5; ch. 12:13
17:17 [i]Jer. 37:7 [j]Jer. 52:4; ch. 4:2
17:18 [k]1 Chron. 29:24; Lam. 5:6
17:20 [l]ch. 12:13 [m]ch. 20:36
17:21 [n]ch. 12:14

FOCUS ON EZEKIEL

Spunky and full of righteous indignation at foolishness are two descriptions that fit the prophet Ezekiel. For 22 years he shouted a warning on the streets of Babylon that Jerusalem and the temple were doomed to be destroyed because of the Israelites' "abominations and . . . whoredoms" (16:22). "Turn or burn" was his call. The people who had experienced the judgment of God did not seem to get the message! He lived out of the "holiness codes" of Leviticus. He was determined to live a righteous life. God used him in dramatic ways to show the world what "thus says the Lord." For 390 days, he was called to lie on his left side. This time period stood for "the years of their [Israel's] iniquity, according to the number of the days, three hundred and ninety days: so shalt thou bear the iniquity of the house of Israel. And when thou hast accomplished them, lie again on thy right side, and thou shalt bear the iniquity of the house of Judah forty days: I have appointed thee each day for a year" (4:5–6). During this period, he was to be tied up so that he could not move. Then he was told what food to eat, and he was to "bake it with dung that cometh out of man, in their sight. . . . And the Lord said, Even thus shall the children of Israel eat their defiled bread among the Gentiles, whither I will drive them" (vv. 12–13). God later allowed Ezekiel to use cow dung, rather than human dung (v. 15).

Ezekiel had one of the harshest messages to proclaim. As a contemporary of Jeremiah, who prophesied in Jerusalem, Ezekiel was to preach repentance to exiles who already felt deserted by God. One of his more punitive warnings was called out to false prophets who tried to make the people believe that they had heard from the Lord. "Woe to the foolish prophets, that follow their own spirit, and have seen nothing! O Israel, thy prophets are like the foxes in the deserts" (13:3–4). We find women specifically mentioned in this matter. "Woe to the women that sew pillows to all armholes, and make kerchiefs upon the head of every stature to hunt souls! Will ye hunt the souls of my people, and will ye save the souls alive that come unto you?" (v. 18). This is a serious charge against the fortunetellers and "palm readers" who were the forerunners to those we know today!

When Ezekiel's wife died, God told him: "Son of man, behold, I take away from thee the desire of thine eyes with a stroke: yet neither shalt thou mourn nor weep, neither shall they tears run down. Forbear to cry make no mourning for the dead, bind the tire of thine head upon thee, and put on thy shoes upon thy feet, and cover not thy lips, and eat not the bread of men" (24:16–17). This was another sign of God's warning that the temple in Jerusalem was about to be destroyed and that tears would not save it!

Ezekiel was an "equal opportunity" preacher who warned Israel and other world powers of impending judgment. Yet he also proclaimed hope for the restoration of Israel and gave us a wonderful image of resurrection in his prophetic message concerning the valley of dry bones (see chpt. 37).

He made the Israelites look beyond the physical temple in Jerusalem to a new city, whose name is "The LORD is there" (48:35). He did his assigned job and remained always, the "watchman" (3:17) and spokesman for God.

HISTORICAL BACKGROUND TO EZEKIEL

Ezekiel prophesied during a time when the north African-Asian international scene was in chaos. The northern kingdom of Israel had gone into captivity in 722 B.C., taken there by the Assyrians, the dominant power at the time. Egypt, fearing the rise of the Babylonians, tried to come to the defense of the Assyrians. King Josiah of Judah tried to intercept and stop the Egyptians from assisting Assyria and was killed at Megiddo by the Egyptians. The Babylonians defeated Egypt in 605 B.C., chasing them all the way to the border of Egypt. On the way back to Babylon, Nebuchadnezzar stopped in Judah, captured Jerusalem, and took many of the ruling people to Babylon. He then placed Jehoiakim on the throne in Judah.

Nebuchadnezzar made a second trip to Judah in 597 B.C. This time he carried other Judeans away, including Ezekiel the prophet. The Babylonian general left Zedekiah on the throne in Judah as a puppet king. Ezekiel counseled Zedekiah to submit to Babylonia, but Zedekiah refused. As a result, Nebuchadnezzar made a third trip to Jerusalem in 586 B.C. This time, he burned the place down, destroying the temple, and leaving only a hand full of poor people to take care of the land.

THE BLACK PRESENCE IN EZEKIEL

Amorites: Mentioned in chapter 16. The Amorites were a tall and strong black people (Amos 2:9–10), descended from Ham through Canaan. See Genesis 10:15–16.

Assyria, Assyrians: Mentioned in chapters 16, 23, 31. In the Table of Nations (Gen. 10) Assyria (Asshur) is identified as a descendant of Shem. The people of this Mesopotamian area were Semitic, Hamitic, and Cushite—all of whom were black. (See the Introduction to Genesis.)

Babylon, Babylonians: Mentioned in chapters 12, 17, 19, 21, 23, 24, 26, 29, 30, 32. The histories of Babylon and Assyria are intertwined together because Assyria is located on the Tigris River and Babylon on the nearby Euphrates River. Nimrod, son of Cush, whose name means "black," built both cities. Indications are that as early as 3000 to 2500 B.C. a group of people known as Sumerians settled the area. According to Henry Rawlinson, the father of Assyriology, these Sumerians migrated there from Africa.

Canaanites: Mentioned in 16:3, 29. Canaan was a son of Ham.

Chaldeans: Mentioned in chapters 1, 12, 23. One of the names given to the people who had Babylon as their capital. They lived in Ur, the area south of Babylon (Shinar) where Abraham lived prior to his departure to Haran and later to Canaan. Their language was very similar to Galla (Oromo), the scientific and religious Cushite language of Africa. They were likely a part of the migration that

took place from Africa into the Mesopotamian area between 5000 and 2500 B.C.

Egypt: Mentioned in chapters 18–20. According to Genesis 10:6, Egyptians were the descendants of Ham. Prior to the arrival of Alexander the Great in 332 B.C., the people of that area called themselves *Kemet,* which means "black." Herodotus, a noted Greek historian who visited Egypt in the centuries prior to the birth of Christ, described the Egyptians as "black with wooly hair." Both Greeks and Romans occupied Egypt at different periods of their history from 322 B.C.

Ethiopia: Mentioned in chapters 30 and 38. *Ethiopia* is the Greek word for "Cush" and describes the descendants of one of the sons of Ham. Ethiopians settled in Egypt and the Mesopotamian area, although some European scholars have sought to limit them to the area just south of Egypt. In chapter 30 their judgment along with that of their powerful neighbor, Egypt, is described. Such destruction would occur when Nebuchadnezzar of Babylon invaded their country.

Hittites: Mentioned in chapter 16. Hittites were the descendants of Canaan. At one time certain scholars minimized their presence and significance. Today they are known to have been very numerous and powerful.

Kedar: Mentioned in 27:21. They are the descendants of Abraham and Hagar (Gen. 25:13).

Pathros: Mentioned in chapters 29 and 30. Pathros was located in southern Egypt where Cushites lived.

Philistia: Mentioned in chapters 16 and 25. Philistines were the descendants of Ham through Egypt (In Hebrew, *Mizraim*); see Genesis 10:13–14.

Phut (Put): Mentioned in 27:10. Phut or Put was the third son of Ham (Gen. 10:6) whose name means "black."

Sheba: Mentioned in chapters 27 and 38. Sheba is mentioned as a son of Cush (Gen. 10:7) as well as a son of Abraham and Keturah (Gen. 25:3).

Tyre: Mentioned in chapters 26–29. The city was located in Phoenicia near Sidon. Sidon was a descendant of Canaan, a son of Ham. Ezekiel speaks of the city's commerce with Spain, India, Greece, Palestine, Arabia, Persia, and other areas. The city also boasted ancient riches such as gold, silver, iron, lead, tin, copper, wheat, cereal, wool, linen, ebony, dye, and so on.

Life Lessons

EZEKIEL 1–3

With the opening of Ezekiel's message, we are immediately caught up in his visions. "This was the appearance of the likeness of the glory of the LORD. And when I saw it, I fell upon my face, and I heard a voice of one that spake. . . . Son of man, stand upon thy feet and I will speak unto thee" (1:28–2:1). Ezekiel then details his call and God's instructions: "Be not afraid of them, neither be afraid of their words . . . thou dost dwell among scorpions . . . thou shalt speak my words unto them, whether they will hear, or whether they will forbear . . . But thou, son of man, hear what I say unto thee; Be not thou rebellious . . . eat that I give thee" (2:6–8). Ezekiel eats the scroll, which fills him and tastes "as honey for sweetness" (3:3).

You Who Are Sweeter than Honey in the Honeycomb, fill my mouth with Your words.

EZEKIEL 4–24

Chapters 4–24 provide us with the symbolic messages. Ezekiel is called to "show" the unrepentant, exiled people their sin and God's just judgment because of the rebellion of their hearts. First, Ezekiel lies on his left side to symbolize the captivity of Israel; then he lies on his right side to symbolize God's judgment against Judah (4:4–9). "Wherefore, as I live, saith the Lord GOD; Surely, because thou hast defiled my sanctuary with all thy detestable things, and with all thine abominations, therefore will I also diminish thee; neither shall mine eye spare, neither will I have any pity. A third part of thee shall die with the pestilence, and with famine shall they be consumed in the midst of thee: and a their part shall fall by the sword round about thee; and I will scatter a third part into all the winds, and I will draw out a sword after them" (5:11–12). This is the punishment Israel and Judah have "earned" due to disobedience and failure to live up to their covenant with God.

In a vision Ezekiel sees the destruction of the temple at Jerusalem because of idol worship. There is judgment on Israel's lying, unjust leaders. False prophets are singled out for punishment and those who practice idol worship are condemned. Jerusalem is pictured as a useless vine (chap. 15) and an unfaithful woman (chap. 16). The overall curse of the entire nation is broken! "Behold, all souls are mine . . . the soul that sinneth, it shall die" (18:4).

The "professional" mourners are called again to "take thou up a lamentation for the princes of Israel, And say, What is thy mother? A lioness: she lay down among the lions. . . his voice should no more be heard upon the mountains of Israel" (19:1–2). In chapter 23, the analogy of Aholah and Aholibah is used to represent the whoredom of Samaria and Jerusalem who are both handed over to the Assyrians. "Thus will I cause lewdness to cease out of the land, that all women may be taught not to do

after your lewdness. And they shall recompense your lewdness upon you, an dye shall bear the sins of your idols: and ye shall know that I am the Lord GOD" (vv. 48–49).

Strong Deliverer, save us from ourselves!

EZEKIEL 25–37

Ezekiel pronounces judgment against a series of foreign nations in the laments of chapters 25–32. In chapter 33, we hear God speak again to Ezekiel. "So thou, O son of man, I have set thee a watchman unto the house of Israel; therefore thou shalt hear the word at my mouth, and warn them from me" (v. 7).

Chapter 34 is a prophecy against the shepherds of Israel who are concerned only about their own welfare. "Behold, I am against the shepherds; and I will require my flock at their hand, and cause them to cease from feeding the flock; neither shall the shepherds feed themselves any more; for I will deliver my flock from their mouth, that they may not be meat for them" (v. 10). Chapter 37 is one of the most well-known passages, describing the valley of the dry bones that are restored to life with the Spirit of the Living God.

Breath of Life, breathe on me, fill me with Your Holy Spirit that I might live fully.

EZEKIEL 39–48

The message of Ezekiel closes with a series of visions. "In the five and twentieth year of our captivity, in the beginning of the year . . . behold a wall on the outside of the house round about" (40:1, 5). It is the hope of restoration. It is the promise of God. "Now will I bring again the captivity of Jacob, and have mercy upon the whole house of Israel, and will be jealous for my holy name. . . . Then shall they know that I am the LORD their God, which caused them to be led into captivity among the heathen: but I have gathered them unto their own land, and have left none of them any more there. Neither will I hide my face any more from them: for I have poured out my spirit upon the house of Israel, saith the Lord GOD" (39:25–29).

FOCUS ON DANIEL

Belteshazzar, Hananiah, Mishael, and Azariah are not names that easily slip off our lips in most Christian circles! We know them more commonly as "Daniel and the Three Hebrew Boys." Their "slave" names were Daniel, Shadrach, Meshach, and Abednego. It seems to be a recurring practice that enslavers will take you into exile, change your name, then strip you of the customs and religious practices that make up your heritage.

These four Israelite men teach us the value of holding on to our "roots"! They show us that loyalty to our heritage, in the midst of our enslavers, can allow God to show up and show out on our behalf. As we read the six short stories about them and their exploits in a foreign land,

we can more clearly understand Daniel's angelic message in chapter 11:32: "The people that do know their God shall be strong, and do exploits." We get to watch these excellent specimens of "Israel's finest" hold to their dietary customs, their prayer lives, and their God while they advance politically and prosper in the midst of exile.

We see their wisdom in action. We see their convictions at work. And we watch God work miracles on their behalf. These stories are our classic Sunday school stories: "The Three Hebrew Boys in the Fiery Furnace"; "Daniel in the Lions' Den." We were taught them. Our children are learning them. And, women of God can extract valuable pearls from the experiences of the Israelites in exile.

HISTORICAL BACKGROUND TO DANIEL

The northern kingdom of Israel went into Assyrian captivity in 722 B.C., a judgment against them by the God whose covenant they had broken. The southern kingdom of Judah was warned that if they continued in idolatry and immorality they, too, would be sent away into captivity. They did not listen, despite the warnings from various prophets. Finally, when the Neo-Babylonian empire rose to power, the conquerors made several incursions into Judah: in 605, 597, and 586 B.C. Each time they inflicted more damage on the city. Daniel apparently was taken during the first incursion when Nebuchadnezzar was on his return trip from chasing the Egyptian army back home.

Following the Babylonian rule, the Persians came to power in 539 B.C. The latter diverted the water course of the Euphrates River leading into the city. While Belshazzar (second in command to Nabonidus) was having a "swinging" party, God sent a bodiless hand to write his nation's doom on the wall (chap. 5). The Persians under Darius the Mede (see 11:1) captured Babylon that same night (5:30–31), and the Persian dynasty lasted until they, in turn, were defeated by Alexander the Great in 330 B.C.

Daniel's prophecies revealed that Medo-Persia would follow Babylon; that the Greeks under Alexander would follow the Persians; that the Romans would follow the Greeks (chap. 7). During the rule of Rome "one like the Son of man" would set up His own rule which would last forever (7:13–14). This is a messianic reference. It is fitting that Jesus often used this title to describe himself (see, for example, Mark 2:28).

THE BLACK PRESENCE IN DANIEL

Babylon: Mentioned in chapters 1–5, 7. Nimrod, son of Cush, who also built Assyria (Gen. 10), founded Babylon. Much of Babylonian history is intertwined with Assyrian history because the two capitals were so close together since the capital of Assyria was located on the Tigris River and Babylon on the Euphrates River. During Daniel's time, the Neo-Babylonian Empire had established itself under Nabopolassar and Nebuchadnezzar. Babylon was noted for its building expertise, especially the Hanging Gardens—one of the Seven Wonders of the ancient World.

Chaldeans: Mentioned in chaps. 1–5, 7. One of the names given to the people who had Babylon as their capital. They lived in Ur, the area south of Babylon (Shinar) where Abraham lived prior to his departure

to Haran and later to Canaan. Their language was very similar to Galla (Oromo), the scientific and religious Cushite language of Africa. They were likely a part of the migration which took place from Africa into the Mesopotamian area between 5000 and 2500 B.C. Noted for their wisdom and knowledge, they appeared in strategic situations during the times of Daniel. It is also possible that the Chaldeans were the "wise men from the east" who visited the Christ child (Matt. 2).

Life Lessons

DANIEL 1–3

The first three chapters are teaching texts about loyalty. "And the king spake unto Ashpenaz the master of his eunuchs, that he should bring certain of the children of Israel, and of the king's seed, and of the princes; children in whom was no blemish, but well favoured, and skilful in all wisdom and cunning in knowledge, and understanding science, and such as had ability in them to stand in the king's palace, and whom they might teach the learning and the tongue of the Chaldeans. . . . But Daniel purposed in his heart that he would not defile himself with the portion of the king's meat, nor with the wine he drank: therefore he requested of the prince of the eunuchs that he might not defile himself" (1:3–4, 8).

The enemy wants to find "the cream of the crop" and make that person assimilate, take off her own identity and become "one of the crowd." God has commanded that we be different, that we be role models set apart to show God's glory wherever we happen to be—even in slavery or exile!

When Nebuchadnezzar made a golden image and demanded that everyone bow down and worship it, Shadrach, Meshach, and Abednego respond, "O Nebuchadnezzar, we are not careful to answer thee in this matter. If it be so, our God whom we serve is able to deliver us from the burning fiery furnace, and he will deliver us out of thine hand, O king. But if not, be it known unto thee, O king, that we will not serve thy gods, nor worship the golden image which thou hast set up" (3:16–18).

O God, help me pass the test of loyalty by remaining steadfast in my faith expression in this foreign land.

DANIEL 2–5

Three of the chapters display God's wisdom at work through them. In chapter two, Daniel interprets the king's dream about the crumbling of a metal statue: "Then the king made Daniel a great man, and gave him many great gifts. . . . Then Daniel requested of the king and he set Shadrach, Meshach, and Abednego, over the affairs of the province of Babylon: but Daniel sat in the gate of the king" (2:48–49). King Nebuchadnezzar dreamed of a big tree which was cut down and stripped bare. Daniel interpreted the dream, and challenged political power: "O, King, let my counsel be acceptable unto thee, and break off thy sins by righteousness, and thine iniquities by shewing mercy to the poor; if it may be a lengthening of thy tranquillity" (4:27). And the dream was fulfilled

In chapter five, King Belshazzar gave a great drinking party, using the goblets from God's holy temple. "In that same hour came forth fingers of a man's hand, and wrote over against the plaister of the wall. . . . And this is the writing that was written, *MENE, MENE, TEKEL,UPHARSIN*" (5:5, 25). Daniel gave the interpretation: "MENE; God hath numbered thy kingdom, and finished it. TEKEL; Thou art weighed in the balances, and art found wanting. PERES; Thy kingdom is divided, and given to the Medes and the Persians. Then commanded Belshazzar, and they clothed Daniel with scarlet, and put a chain of gold about his neck, and made a proclamation concerning him, that he should be the third ruler in the kingdom" (vv. 26–29). It pays to heed God's wisdom and to speak it when necessary, even to those who consider themselves to be "power"! We know who has the ultimate power!

Power of the Powerless, empower me to do what You command, wherever, whenever, and to whomever!

DANIEL 6–12

The most fascinating part of the visions that Daniel receive is the apocalypse, or end-time revelation, he sees. Daniel is approached by an angelic being who details how God is already at work, intervening in history to destroy evil. Enemies plot against Daniel to stop his practice of praying three times daily to his God. The conspiracy works and Daniel is forced into a den of lions as a consequence. God intervenes and delivers (chap. 6). Then Daniel has a series of visions.

"When I, even I Daniel, had seen the vision, and sought for the meaning, then, behold, there stood before me as the appearance of a man. And I heard a man's voice . . . which called, and said, Gabriel, make this man to understand the vision. . . . He said unto me, Understand, O son of man: for at the time of the end shall be the vision. . . . And I Daniel fainted, and was sick certain days; afterward I rose up, and did the king's business; and I was astonished at the vision, but none understood" (7:1, 15; 8:17, 27). Daniel continued to receive revelations and to interpret them. He is promised at the end of the book, "Go thou thy way till the end be: for thou shalt rest, and stand in thy lot at the end of the days" (12:13). That is a great reward for loyalty and wisdom. Perhaps it's worth telling Jesus that it's all right to change your name!

Revealer of Hidden Things, thank You for trusting us with Your wisdom.

FOCUS ON HOSEA

The people of the Living God are likened to a prostitute in the Book of Hosea! Hosea is a real love story about a man who deliberately selects a "street woman" as his bride. However, this is not simply a story about another unfaithful woman. This is a personification of unfaithful Israel—God's sign to the world!

The narrative begins with God's instructions to Hosea: "Go, take unto thee a wife of whoredoms and children of whoredoms: for the land hath committed great whoredom, departing from the LORD. So he went and took Gomer the daughter of Diblaim; which conceived, and bare him a son" (1:2–3).

Although this painful portrait of deceit and the betrayal of sacred marriage vows is a true story, it is also an allegory about God's covenant vows with the "unfaithful" wife, Israel. Israel has a constant habit of seeking other lovers in idols, false gods, and allegiances to other nations. Preaching to the northern kingdom of Israel, God strives to illustrate through Hosea and Gomer's relationship a faithful love for a sinful, backsliding nation.

At the close of Jeroboam's reign in the eighth century, we discover a period marked by political and religious turmoil. Upper-class Jews are prospering from their oppression of the poor, which is a clear perversion of God's will. Therefore, Hosea employs diverse images to evidence God's unfailing mercy, despite the illicit dealings of the unjust.

Hosea is a living testimony of God's open arms of restoration, forgiveness, and salvation to a spouse who wanders off, brings home three "illegitimate" children, and ends up having to be rescued—saved not only from herself but also from life's garbage dump of immorality.

The family situation is a clear-cut portrait of the promiscuous behavior of the entire nation. We must be clear that the harlotry of Hosea's wife is not an indictment of the female gender! The lessons of this story are aimed at the entire people of God—males included.

HISTORICAL BACKGROUND TO HOSEA

After the death of David around 970 B.C., his son Solomon ruled for 40 years. Following Solomon's death, Rehoboam provoked the ten northern tribes to rebel and choose Jeroboam as their king. This northern kingdom deteriorated into idolatry and lawlessness. Assyria, under the leadership of Tiglath-pileser, became dominant about 733 B.C. and began a series of raids into the northern kingdom and the Transjordan area. In 722 B.C., Tiglath-pileser conquered Samaria, the capital of the northern kingdom, and deported some 27,000 people to Assyria. Deporting captives was a common strategy of discouraging revolts by conquered people.

THE BLACK PRESENCE IN HOSEA

Assyria: Mentioned in chapters 5, 10, and 14. In the Table of Nations (Gen. 10) Assyria (Asshur) is identified as a descendant of Shem. The people of this Mesopotamian area were Semitic, Hamitic, and Cushite—all of whom were black (see Introduction to Genesis). According to Genesis 10, Nimrod, a son of Cush, built Asshur. Assyria retained a long, sometimes interrupted, empire.

Baal worship: Mentioned in 2:8. Baal worship preceded the entry of Israelites into the land of Canaan. The worship can be traced back to the Semites to at least 1700 B.C. Baal was worshiped on elevated plateaus as the male source of life and all good things. The female counterpart was Ashtaroth, who was worshiped along with Baal. In both religious experiences, people became very vulgar and in some cases sacrificed their children to the gods.

Egypt: Mentioned in chapters 2, 3, 12, and 13. According to Genesis 10:6, Egyptians were the descendants of Ham. The history of Egypt can be traced back at least 10,000 years B.C. Prior to the arrival of Alexander the Great in 332 B.C., the people of that area called themselves *Kemet,* which means "black." Herodotus, a noted Greek historian who visited Egypt in the centuries prior to the birth of Christ, described the Egyptians as "black with wooly hair."

Memphis: Mentioned in 9:6. Memphis was located on the west bank of the Nile River about 400 miles south of the Mediterranean coast. Hosea foretold a return to Memphis by the Israelites.

Tyre: Mentioned in 9:6. Tyre, located on the Phoenician coast, is frequently identified with Sidon who was a descendant of Ham through Canaan (Gen. 10:15). According to Herodotus, the city was founded in 2750 B.C. The people of Tyre were creative and industrious. They maintained extensive commerce, trading in cedar, gold, silver, iron, copper, dyes, and other commodities. (See Ezekiel 27–28 for more on Tyre's power and wealth.)

Life Lessons

HOSEA 1–3

Chapters 1–3 illustrate Hosea's call to marry Gomer, an unfaithful wife. She bears a son. God instructs Hosea to name the child, Jezreel, indicating the coming punishment for Israel in the valley of Jezreel (1:1–4). Gomer's second child is a daughter. God instructs Hosea to name her Lo-ruhamah, meaning, "I will no more have mercy on the house of Israel" (v. 6). After weaning this infant, Gomer conceives a third time and has another son. The child is named Lo-ammi, meaning "Ye are not my people, and I will not be your God" (v. 8). Gomer leaves home after this. "She shall follow after her lovers, but she shall not overtake them; and she shall seek them, but shall not find them" (2:7).

There is immediate sympathy for Hosea—a husband who has been done wrong! He symbolizes a brokenhearted God who has entered into covenant with Israel only to be rejected time after time. Yet there must be consideration of the pain of Gomer, constantly caught in adultery and loved despite her sin. Every mother can understand the guilt that lived inside her. To leave your children in order to "seek other lovers" suggests a deep-seated, unexplainable pain which commentators have yet to truly uncover. Also there must be some consideration for the three children named to bear the guilt and shame of their mother's sin. The grand reality is that sin hurts all of us!

The covenant with Israel is dissolved because of unfaithful behavior on Israel's part. In chapter three, after Gomer's departure and shameful exposure to the world, God says to Hosea, "Go yet, love a woman beloved of her friend, yet an adulteress, according to the love of the LORD toward the children of Israel . . . So I bought her" (3:11–12). How wonderful it is for us to

know that God still loves and is willing to redeem the person who sins.

Redeemer of Wanderers, how many times I've cheated on You! Forgive me. Cleanse me of my unfaithful ways. I want to be faithful to our covenant. I desire to be true to You.

FOCUS ON JOEL

"Get ready! Get ready! Get ready! The day of the Lord is coming!" No, it's not the voice of Bishop T. D. Jakes pumping up a waiting crowd in some packed-out stadium. This is the voice of the early postexilic prophet, Joel. Joel is talking to a complacent and prosperous Judah who took for granted God's command for justice and mercy as they lived in self-centeredness, self-righteousness, and idolatry. "Get ready," Joel pleads. "Also now, saith the LORD, turn ye even to me with all your heart, and with fasting, and with weeping, and with mourning: And rend your heart, and not your garments, and turn unto the LORD, your God" (2:12–13). Of course, the people refused to heed Joel's urgent message—again!

As to living in Jerusalem, Joel discloses very little. But because of the many references to the blowing of the *shofar*—solemn assembly at the temple, invoking of the fast, and frequent mention of priests and sacrifices—some regard the oracles as a collection of temple liturgies, and Joel as a Jerusalem priest. The urgency of Joel's voice is that God is coming with a vengeance! The day of the Lord would establish God's universal sovereign rule. When that day arrived, judgment and curses for the nations who had forsaken God would be in order. On the other hand, the faithful would be vindicated and receive abundant blessings.

If there was ever a period in which Joel's call to "Get ready" needs to be heard, it is today! The reign of God is soon at hand.

HISTORICAL BACKGROUND TO JOEL

The uncertainty of the date makes identification of the historical background difficult. The reference to Israel's enemies of Tyre, Sidon, Philistia, Edom, and Egypt suggests an early date. References to the invading army from the north suggests the impending Babylonian invasion into Judah around 606 B.C.

THE BLACK PRESENCE IN JOEL

Eden: Mentioned in 2:3. Though some biblical scholars believe the Garden of Eden was located in the Mesopotamian area because two rivers mentioned in Genesis 2 are located there (Tigris and Euphrates), recent discoveries have led other scholars to conclude that the geography referred to more easily fits into the area of East Africa. The earliest remains of humankind were found in Tanzania. It is believed that humankind began here and migrated up the Nile River to other parts of the world. Furthermore, according to some historians, Africa, in ancient times, was called Eden.

Egypt: Mentioned in chapter 3. According to Genesis 10:6, Egyptians were the descendants of Ham whose name means "black" or "burnt face." The history of Egypt can be traced back at least 10,000 years B.C. Prior to the arrival of Alexander the Great in 332 B.C., the people of that area called themselves *Kemet,* which means "black." Herodotus, a noted Greek historian who visited Egypt in the centuries prior to the birth of Christ, described the Egyptians as "black with wooly hair."

Sidon and Tyre: Mentioned in chapter 3. The two cities, Sidon and Tyre, were located on the Phoenician coast. According to Herodotus, Tyre was founded in 2750 B.C. The people of that northern Mediterranean Sea coast were very creative and industrious. They maintained extensive commerce, trading in cedar, gold, silver, iron, copper, dyes, and other commodities. (See Ezekiel 27–28 for more on Tyre's power and wealth.)

Philistia (seacoast): Mentioned in chapter 3. Philistines were the descendants of Ham through Egypt (*Mizraim* in Hebrew). See Genesis 10:13–14.

Sabeans: Mentioned in chapter 3. Sabeans, descendants of Sheba, are mentioned as descendants of Cush (Gen. 10:7), as well as of Abraham and Keturah (Gen. 25:3). They occupied land in northeast Africa sometimes called Arabia.

Life Lessons

JOEL 1

Chapter one opens with a plea to "ye old men, and give ear, all ye inhabitants of the land. Hath this been in your days, or even in the days of your fathers?" (1:2). The approaching enemy is compared to invading locusts. Joel wants to "wake up" his sleeping religious community and make them respond to the severe consequences of their behavior in forgetting their covenant with Yahweh.

> To represent the grief of the people at the devastation of their country, Joel invokes the image of a young woman mourning her husband in widow's weeds of sackcloth (v. 8). Joel's rallying cry is to "return wholeheartedly" to Yahweh (2:12). For Joel, repentance is no guarantee of deliverance. (*WBC,* 203–204)

"Sanctify ye a fast, call a solemn assembly, gather the elders and all the inhabitants of the land into the house of the LORD your God . . . Alas for the day! for the day of the LORD is at hand, and as a destruction from the Almighty shall it come" (2:14–15).

Zion's Deliverer, hear our pleas. Search our repentant hearts. Listen to our cries for mercy.

JOEL 2

The Lord answers and takes pity on Zion (2:18). Material blessings of grain, new wine, and oil are promised (v. 19). Then three additional blessings are listed—blessings to be dispensed before the day of the Lord. There is the outpouring of the Holy Spirit upon all flesh (vv. 28–29). Cosmic signs are announced (vv. 30–31). Salvation is promised for Zion (v. 32). "Whereas in the past, the gift of prophecy was the prerogative of a few, in the future it will be an inclusive gift. Distinctions of age (old men and young men) gender (sons and daughters) social class (male and female servants) will be swept away in this common spiritual endowment." And everyone who calls on the name of the Lord shall be saved (*WBC*, 204; Joel 2:32).

Sweet Salvation, thank You for specifically including women in the Day of the Lord's outpouring!

FOCUS ON AMOS

"Pay me now or pay me later!" was the warning Amos called out to the wealthy and powerful people of Samaria, the capital of Israel. Amos, a confrontational layperson, was both fiery and fearless as he challenged his nation to return to God's command of justice and right living. His message was centered on the fact that while they were complacent at present, they were in for a disastrous future.

Of course, his warnings were in stark contrast to the phony religious leaders in town. Why should anyone listen to a man who had no formal theological training and was not a member of the temple clique?

Amos, a sheepherder and tender of fig trees, was called by God. Like another humble shepherd of old, he took on the mantle of becoming the spokesperson for Yahweh. From the rural area in Tekoa, the southern kingdom, Amos was sent to confront the idol-worshiping, oppressive system that took hold in a politically prospering Jerusalem. Bold as a lion, Amos proclaimed how "the LORD will roar from Zion, and utter his voice from Jerusalem" (1:2). Amos then made this indictment: "Hear this word that the LORD has spoken against you, O children of Israel, against the whole family which I brought up from the land of Egypt" (3:1). Amos was a staunch advocate for the poor, oppressed, and marginalized. He took specific aim at wealthy women who "oppress the poor, which crush the needy" (4:1). For if there was any one class of people who knew what being oppressed, suppressed, and depressed felt like, it was—and is—women!

Amos did not stop with announcing judgment against Israel. He also spoke against every nation because of its sin in the sight of God. Dr. Martin Luther King, Jr. popularized several lines from this prophet in his challenge to the political powers of America in the 1960s. These powerful words continue to echo loudly and clearly today. "Let judgment run down as waters, and righteousness as a mighty stream" (5:24). A pious-sound-

ing, "feel good," religious veneer would not provide sufficient cover for the sin of oppression, said Amos. God told Amos to tell "the sinful" to pay up now or know that they would indeed pay later!

The words of Amos are rich, alive, and well in our world, for he proclaimed that "The days come, saith the Lord God, that I will send a famine in the land, not a famine of bread, nor a thirst for water, but of hearing the words of the Lord" (8:11). African-American women really do want to hear a fresh word from God!

HISTORICAL BACKGROUND TO AMOS

Amos prophesied during the extended reign of Jeroboam II (about 786–746 B.C.). Syria, Israel's northern neighbor, no longer posed a military threat, thanks to the Assyrians. As a result Israel expanded and consolidated its own borders to the south, north, and east, and developed its own internal business. Assyria was not a great threat to them because of their own security problems. As a result, Israel became complacent and deteriorated into shameless idolatry and wickedness. Baal worship flourished with its drunkenness, sensuality, and child sacrifice. Injustice and luxurious living were the order of the day. Amos was sent to preach against this heedless and heartless lifestyle.

THE BLACK PRESENCE IN AMOS

Amorites: Mentioned in 2:9–10. Amorites were the descendants of Ham through Canaan. They are described as a tall people, strong as oak trees.

Egypt: Mentioned in 3:9; 4:10; 9:5. According to Genesis 10:6, Egyptians were the descendants of Ham whose name means "black" or "burnt face." The history of Egypt can be traced back at least 10,000 years B.C. Prior to the arrival of Alexander the Great in 332 B.C., the people of that area called themselves *Kemet,* which means "black." Herodotus, a noted Greek historian who visited Egypt in the centuries prior to the birth of Christ, described the Egyptians as "black with wooly hair."

Ethiopia (Cush): Mentioned in 9:7. *Ethiopia* is the Greek word for Cush and describes the descendants of one of the sons of Ham. Cush means "black" and describes people who lived in Egypt and the Mesopotamian area, some European scholars have sought to limit Ethiopians to the area just south of Egypt.

Gath (6:2), Gaza (1:6), Ashdod (1:8), Ashkelon (1:8), and Ekron (1:8): All of these cities were located in Philistia along the eastern Mediterranean Sea. Philistines were the descendants of Ham through Egypt (in Hebrew, *Mizraim*; Gen. 10:14).

Tyre: Mentioned in 1:9–10. The twin cities of Sidon and Tyre were located on the Phoenician coast. Tyre is frequently identified with Sidon, who was a descendant of Ham through Canaan (Gen. 10:15). According to Herodotus, Tyre was founded in 2750 B.C. The people of that northern Mediterranean Sea coast were creative and industrious. They maintained extensive commerce, trading in cedar,

gold, silver, iron, copper, dyes, and other commodities. (See Ezekiel 27–28 for more on Tyre's power and wealth.)

Sabeans (Sheba): Mentioned in chapter 3. Sabeans, descendants of Sheba, are mentioned as descendants of Cush (Gen. 10:7) as well as of Abraham and Keturah (Gen. 25:3). They occupied land in northeast Africa, which is sometimes called Arabia.

Life Lessons

AMOS 1–2

Chapters one and two are volatile warnings for repeated sins. There is judgment against Israel as God recounts their deliverance from Egypt, the prophets who led them, and the gift of the Promised Land. God's anger is clear. "Is it not even thus, O ye children of Israel? saith the LORD. But ye gave the Nazarites wine to drink; and commanded the prophets, saying, Prophesy not. Behold I am pressed under you, as a cart is pressed that is full of sheaves. Therefore the flight shall perish from the swift, and the strong shall not strengthen his force, neither shall the mighty deliver himself" (2:10–16). The Judge has called the court to order. There is no defense. Justice will be metered out and the punishment will be severe. The reasons for God's anger are pointed out with specificity: "They sold the righteous for silver, and the poor for a pair of shoes; That pant after the dust of the earth on the head of the poor, and turn aside the way of the meek: and a man and his father will go in unto the same maid, to profane my holy name . . . and they drink the wine of the condemned in the house of their god" (vv. 6–8). The people of Israel, from priest to commoner, have become unjust, uncaring, and unholy idol worshipers!

God of Grace and Mercy, help us!

AMOS 7

Chapter seven records Amos's visions of locusts, fire, and a plumbline. The first not to measure up to the straight, strict standards of the plumbline is Amaziah, the priest of Bethel. Amaziah sends words to King Jeroboam: "Amos hath conspired against thee in the midst of the house of Israel: the land is not able to bear it" (7:10–11). Amos prophesies against Amaziah and his entire house for standing against the word of God. "Thy wife shall be an harlot in the city, and thy sons and thy daughters shall fall by the sword, and thy land shall be divided by" (7:17).

This is a socioeconomic curse that strips Amaziah of family and land, two items that were part of God's favor in the past. To signify that his wife would become a prostitute was the ultimate shame of a priest, who was forbidden by the Leviticus holy codes to marry one. In this particular case, the wife and sons are "victims" of their father's sin. It is clear that the innocent suffer with the guilty when judgment is brought upon the land.

Holy One, help me to keep my focus on You and bring only honor to those of my house.

AMOS 8

Chapter eight repeats the warnings of coming destruction, "They shall run to and fro . . . the fair virgins and young men faint for thirst . . . and, The manner of Beer-sheba liveth; even they shall fall, and never rise up again" (8:12–14). Chapter nine begins with the same tone of devastation, but there is a hint of God's grace: "I will destroy it off the face of the earth; saving that I will not utterly destroy the house of Jacob, saith the LORD" (9:8). Finally, Amos pronounces his benediction: God will "plant them upon their land, and they shall no more be pulled up out of their land which I have given them" (v. 15).

Consoler of the Condemned, we exalt Your extension of amazing grace!

FOCUS ON OBADIAH

Short, simple, and to the point! The Book of Obadiah is the shortest book in the canon, only twenty-one verses. It is a concentrated and powerful indictment against sibling rivalry! If there is ever a need for women to heed the call to solidarity, community, and mutual support, this message brings it home loud and clear. "As thou hast done, it shall be done unto thee: thy reward shall return upon thine own head" (1:5). Short, simple, and to the point!

HISTORICAL BACKGROUND TO OBADIAH

Animosity between Edom and Israel is traceable to the birth of Jacob and Esau (which means Edom or "red") when the two struggled in the womb of Rebekah (Gen. 25:21–26). The brothers later were in conflict when they sought the birthright and blessing from their father, Isaac (Gen. 27). Following these incidents Jacob fled to Haran to avoid Esau's wrath, returning years later when Esau's wrath had cooled. Esau moved to the mountainous region of southern Canaan where he remained isolated and protected by the impregnable mountains.

Archaeological evidence points to the founding of Edom's kingdom around the thirteenth century B.C. Other evidence shows the Edomites' entry into the Nile Delta area around 1400 B.C. When Israel attempted to pass through Edomite territory on their way from Egypt to the Promised Land, Edom refused them passage (Num. 20:14-21). Edom remained antagonistic to any Israelite interests, opposed them at every opportunity, and encouraged the Babylonians to destroy them.

THE BLACK PRESENCE IN OBADIAH

Canaanites: Mentioned in verse 20. Canaanites were the descendants of Ham through his son Canaan (Gen. 10:6). Ham means "black" or "swarthy."

Philistines: Mentioned in verse 19. Philistines were the descen-

dants of Ham through Egypt (Gen. 10:13–14). *Mizraim* is the Hebrew name for Egypt.

Zeraphath: Mentioned in verse 20. Zeraphath was located in the Phoenician area of Sidon. Sidon was a descendant of Ham through Canaan (Gen. 10:6, 15).

Life Lessons

OBADIAH 1

The pride of the Edomites resulted in God's judgment (v. 3). They thought that because their country was situated among the rocks, they were safe from all attacks by outside armies. Through Obadiah, God warns them that their high and lofty position would not prevent His judgment upon them (v. 4). We must be ever careful of pride. The surest antidote for pride is to always give the proper honor to the Lord. When God is in His proper place, our attitude will be one of humility. We see ourselves as God sees us.

Dear God, please help me to remember that pride always precedes a fall. Help me to give You Your rightful place in my life so that I will not fall victim to the sin of pride.

OBADIAH 1

The Edomites rejoiced when Israel was judged, when the invaders carried off people and wealth (vv. 11–14). God shows His displeasure at such an arrogant attitude. We must be careful never to gloat over the misfortunes of others. Except for the grace of God, we could be in the same condition or worse.

Dear God, please help me never to look down on the misfortunes of others. Help me remember that instead of gloating over the misfortunes of others, I should instead seek to help them and be ever grateful for the mercy You have bestowed on me.

OBADIAH 1

Family feuds and sibling rivalry are not taken lightly by God. Competition and division are open invitations to danger and destruction. Arrogance and self-sufficiency smack against "family interdependence," which is modeled for the Christian church. We are an interlocked, dependent unit and God will not suffer us to be indifferent, harmful, or destructive toward each other. For women who have a tendency toward "petty jealousy" of each other, the warning is clear in verse 4: "thence will I bring thee down."

Architect of the Family, help me to be supportive, helpful, and loving to every sibling.

Focus on JONAH

We know him as the runaway prophet who ends up in the belly of a whale! The truth is that the historical narrative of Jonah is deeper than one man and a big fish! The Mississippi Mass Choir has made famous the song, "Your Grace and Mercy." But it's been sung by many more recipients of God's unmerited favor than by members of this choir! Jonah's taking the word of grace and mercy to the Assyrians, who were deserving of "death, hell, and destruction," surely should have inspired the Ninevites to sing words that sounded close to these.

Only Israel had a covenant with Yahweh. Only Israel was required to "live holy." Only Israel had the obligations to confess, repent, and walk in holiness before the Lord. The Israelites were God's chosen. They were God's favored. They were God's delivered. So, why would God send Jonah to preach repentance to heathens? Surely God could not be ready or willing to grant grace and mercy to those heathens who had treated the Israelites worse than any other military foe! There had to be a mistake. There had to have been confusion. There must have been a mix-up in the messed-up message. A comparison could be made to the situation of asking a woman who has been embarrassed, as well as physically, sexually, and emotionally violated, to find the perpetrator and tell him about God's love! No way!

So Jonah runs away! Jonah goes in the opposite direction. Jonah will have no part in this mission. This is the only record of a man called by God who goes completely in the opposite direction, trying to outdistance himself and move away from the eyes of the Almighty! But, if you were the woman in the scenario above, what would you do?

HISTORICAL BACKGROUND TO JONAH

Jonah is sent to Nineveh, that awesome nation located on the Tigris River in Mesopotamia. While the Assyrians prior to Jonah's time had dominated the northeastern area and would subsequently do it again, at the time of Jonah, the nation was in a state of decline. The nation had experienced two devastating famines and a total eclipse of the sun, perhaps preparing them for the repentance they displayed at the preaching of Jonah. The mercy of God toward the nation and their king, Ashur-dan III, spared them from destruction for another 200 years.

THE BLACK PRESENCE IN JONAH

Nineveh: Mentioned in chapters 1, 3, and 4. Nineveh was the capital of Assyria. In the Table of Nations (Gen. 10:22), Assyria (Asshur) is identified as a descendant of Shem. The people of this Mesopotamian area were Semitic and Hamitic—both of whom were black (see Introduction to Genesis). According to Genesis 10:8–11, Nimrod, a son of Cush, built Asshur. Assyria retained a long, though sometimes interrupted, empire. During the time of Jonah, the

nation was in a state of decline. It did recover, and in 722 B.C. defeated the northern kingdom of Israel, carrying off some 27,000 Israelites. Later in its history (612 B.C.), Nineveh was defeated during a fierce battle when Babylon (also built by Nimrod) and Persia joined forces to defeat it.

Mariners: Mentioned in 1:5. Jonah boarded the ship in Joppa, located along the Mediterranean Sea. Most likely the ship Jonah boarded was a ship staffed by men of Phoenicia who were noted for their seafaring expertise. Phoenicians were descendants of Ham through Canaan. Their principal cities were Tyre and Sidon. Ezekiel speaks of the city's commerce with Spain, India, Greece, Palestine, Arabia, Persia, and other nations. They had a wealth of gold, silver, iron, lead, tin, copper, wheat, cereal, wool, linen, ebony, dyes, and other commodities.

Life Lessons

JONAH 1

Chapter one details Jonah's running away from his assigned mission. He gets others in trouble for his disobedience. The only thing left to do with the disobedient prophet comes from Jonah himself: "Take me up, and cast me forth into the sea. . . . I know that for my sake this great tempest is upon you" (1:11). The consequence was that "the LORD had prepared a great fish to swallow up Jonah. And Jonah was in the belly of the fish three days and three nights" (v. 17).

Miracle Working Wonder, is this a sign of Your gracious, loving compassion for us in Jesus Christ?

JONAH 2

Chapter two finds Jonah praying in distress. God answers his prayer. "And the Lord spake unto the fish, and it vomited out Jonah upon the dry land" (2:10).

Answering God, in my distress I lift my voice of supplication to You.

JONAH 3

Chapter three finds Jonah going to Nineveh, accomplishing his mission. "So Jonah arose, and went unto Nineveh, according to the word of the LORD" (3:3). He made a three-day journey in one day. As a result: "So the people of Nineveh believed God, and proclaimed a fast, and put on sackcloth, from the greatest of them even to the least of them" (v. 5). "And God saw their works, that they turned from their evil way; and God repented of the evil, that he had said that he would do unto them; and he did it not" (v. 10).

Compassionate Heart, thank You for Your grace and mercy!

JONAH 4

"But it displeased Jonah exceedingly" (4:1). Jonah wants God to annihilate the Ninevites. It's the same attitude that an abused and violated

woman would have about her abuser! Please take notice that Jonah makes no attempt to sound "nice" or "pious" or "holy." He is just plain mad! God allows Jonah his honest, human, and understandable anger. But, grace and mercy have already been dispatched!

Gracious and Merciful Creator, thank You for caring for even the worst of us. And, thank You for understanding the authentic feelings of my heart. Work in me in order to work through me to declare the unsearchable riches of Your love, even to those who have hurt me the most.

FOCUS ON MICAH

In America, we are so limited in vocabulary that accurately conveys what we are attempting to say. It's not uncommon to hear one of us declare that "I love shopping at Sax Fifth Avenue." Or we will declare, "I love your new hair style." And, we all have our own personal "love" affair with some food or home furnishing. The point is that the word *love* is overused. And, so is the word *hate.* Some of us "hate" vegetables. Others of us "hate" our jobs. And, too many of us "hate" some type of music that is not our preferred selection. Once again, a word is overused.

So, when we hear that God "loves" us, the meaning may seem somewhat vague. And, when we hear that God "hates" sin and the practices are detailed, once again our comprehension is clouded. For we have a limited concept of both *love* and *hate.* What we basically try to clarify is our likes and dislikes of people and things using the words that are available to us.

When God spoke of love, Jesus was the tangible result! Love for God was about self-giving, self-limiting, and selflessness. God so loved the world until God gave Jesus to a world condemned to death, hell, and destruction (see John 3:16). Love moved God to intervene on our unworthy behalf! Conversely, when God spoke of *hate* the word meant something totally unacceptable in the eyes or presence of a holy God. The two words—*love* and *hate*—are not about "like" and "dislike" with God.

The prophet Micah comes to give us real images of what God loves and what God hates. When Israel moved into Canaan, a common practice was for cities to imagine their capital cities as female gods married to the male patron god. It is not difficult to understand how prophets would use the female imagery for their discussions about and arguments against Jerusalem, Samaria, and even the church. It's not easy for women readers to see women as the personification of evil in this prophetic book! However, the church is also referred to as "the Bride of Christ." Micah describes God's love, justice, and mercy, as we first see God's wrath in action.

HISTORICAL BACKGROUND TO MICAH

Tiglath-pileser came to power in Assyria in 745 B.C. and immediately set about to restore the lost glory of Assyria. He came to Damascus,

Israel's northern neighbor, and demanded tribute from them. King Menahem of Israel extracted money from the wealthy to pay Tiglath-pileser tribute to keep from being deported to Assyria.

In 722 B.C., Tiglath-pileser died. His successor, Sargon II, returned to the area because King Ahaz of Israel rebelled against Assyria, thinking that Egypt would help defend them. Egypt never showed up to help. The Assyrian king carried away 27,290 people to Assyria and brought into Samaria people he had conquered in other areas. The policy of replacing conquered people with other conquered people was intended to keep down rebellion.

Sargon's successor, Sennacherib, marched into Judah about 701 B.C. and exacted tribute from many of the towns. He was unable to defeat Jerusalem because an angel of the Lord slew 185,000 of his soldiers in one night (2 Kings 19:35), causing him to return to Assyria. According to the historian Herodotus, a horde of field mice swarmed over the Assyrian camp and ate up their weapons. Micah prophesied during this period of time, focusing his message primarily toward the northern kingdom, warning them of the coming devastation by the Assyrians.

THE BLACK PRESENCE IN MICAH

Assyria/Nimrod: Mentioned in 5:6. According to Genesis 10, Nimrod, a son of Cush, built Ashur (Assyria). Assyria retained a long, sometimes interrupted, empire. Nineveh, the capital of Assyria, was defeated during the fierce battle of 612 B.C., when Babylon (also built by Nimrod) and Persia joined forces to defeat it.

Egypt: Mentioned in 6:4 and 7:15. According to Genesis 10:6, Egyptians were the descendants of Ham, whose name means "black" or "burnt face." The history of Egypt can be traced back at least 10,000 years B.C. Prior to the arrival of Alexander the Great in 332 B.C., the people of that area called themselves *Kemet*, which means "black." Herodotus, a noted Greek historian who visited Egypt in the centuries prior to the birth of Christ, described the Egyptians as "black with wooly hair."

Gath: Mentioned in 1:10. Gath was one of the principal cities of Philistia. Philistines were descended from Ham through Egypt (Gen. 10:6–14). *Mizraim* is the Hebrew word for Egypt (Gen. 10:13).

Life Lessons

MICAH 1–2

Chapters one and two describe the judgment that God will bring upon Jerusalem because of its incurable practice of sin. "Therefore I will make Samaria as an heap of the field . . . and all the graven images thereof shall be beaten to pieces, and all the hires thereof shall be burned with the fire, and all the idols thereof will I lay desolate: for she gathered it of the hire of an harlot, and they shall return to the hire of an harlot"

(1:6–7). The major charges of God against the people include the ways they pervert worship and their injustice toward the poor. Micah outlines the charges of God against city after city, with bitter complaints and warnings of that which is to come as judgment. "Woe" is pronounced upon the false prophets who say, "They shall not prophesy to them, that they shall not take shame" (2:6). Even those whose responsibility is to care for the house of God have fallen into sin. They go so far as to make others feel comfortable with their sin! "The women of my people have ye cast out from their pleasant houses; from their children have ye taken away my glory for ever" (v. 9).

Uncovering God, strip away my longing for only my personal comfort. Make me uncomfortable with the things You hate! I want Your blessing to rest, rule, and abide upon me and my house.

MICAH 3–4

Chapters three and four find Micah tearing away at the despicable deeds of the leaders and prophets. "Is it not for you to know judgment? Who hate the good, and love the evil; who pluck off their skin from off them, and their flesh from off their bones; Who also eat the flesh of my people, and flay their skin from off them; and they break their bones, and chop them in pieces, as for the pot, and as flesh within the caldron" (3:1–3). God hates ugly! When you decide to "do the wrong thing" which jeopardizes the small and insignificant in society, there is no out for you with God. God's anger is boiling and the declaration is made that "the seers be ashamed, and the diviners confounded; yea, they shall all cover their lips; for there is no answer of God" (v. 7). As with other prophets, the word of grace is extended: "In the last days . . . many nations shall come, and say, 'Come, and let us go up to the mountain of the LORD, and to the house of the God of Jacob' " (4:1–2). Micah's message is not all doom and gloom! There is always a way of repentance and forgiveness. God hates sin, yet loves sinners!

Loving Creator, thank You for being God and for providing the second, third, fourth, and fifth chance if needed for me to obey You!

MICAH 5–7

Chapter five outlines the coming of the Messiah who will come from Bethlehem and be a shepherd, "in the strength of the LORD, in the majesty of the name of the LORD his God, . . . this man shall be the peace" (5:4–5). Both the right living and the evildoers are given their destiny in this chapter. In chapter six, God sets a solid case against backsliding Israel: "He hath shewed thee, O man, what is good; and what doth the LORD require of thee, but to do justly, and to love mercy, and to walk humbly with thy God" (6:8). No excuse will be allowed, for the covenant and the Ten Commandments outline the way Israel is to behave and serve as a role model for the rest of the world. Her misery is detailed in chapter seven: "Woe is me! . . . I will bear the indignation of the Lord, because I have sinned against him" (7:1, 9). Yet all is not lost. Micah waits in confidence that Israel will rise. "In the day that thy walls are to be built, in that day shall the decree be far removed" (v. 11). He concludes his message with a reminder to a loving and merciful God, "Thou wilt perform the truth to

Jacob and the mercy to Abraham, which thou hast sworn unto our fathers from the days of old" (v. 20). God loved us enough to come in the person of Jesus! That's what *love* means!

O Loving God, I confidently wait on You to act.

Women in EZEKIEL

EZEKIEL'S WIFE: ON THE STAGE OF GOD

The details of this priest's wife are very limited. We only learn of her by reading, "So I spake unto the people in the morning: and at even my wife died; and I did in the morning as I was commanded" (Ezek. 24:18). Ezekiel was forewarned of his wife's death, but he was compelled by God not to mourn or do the normal ceremonial things. The death of his wife was a sign unto the people of the death and doom to come to Israel.

Ezekiel's wife is unnamed in the Book of Ezekiel, but we may assume that she was a godly woman. She was spoken of as the "desire of [his] eyes" (v. 16). It is obvious that in the eyes of Ezekiel she was beloved. Ezekiel was one of the most dramatic prophets in the Scriptures. His ministry was one of acting out God's Word to the people. It appears that the wife of Ezekiel was accustomed to having her life portrayed as if on stage. Ezekiel entertained the elders of the people, therefore, we might assume that his wife was a great hostess. Because of the dramatic demonstrations Ezekiel performed before the people to demonstrate God's will, his wife must surely have had a keen sense of God herself. From one moment to the next, Ezekiel was caught up in demonstrations. Much of the book is prophetic, poetic, and symbolic; therefore, we might assume that Ezekiel's wife had experienced firsthand the actions and poetry of love.

When she died suddenly, Ezekiel was told that his grief was to be silent. This was because God wanted to demonstrate to Israel that what they have loved would be destroyed and they would not mourn it. Ezekiel and his wife were instruments in the hands of God to demonstrate the heartbreak of disobedience.

We often do not know what role we are playing on this stage of life. God has a purpose for all that is done in our lives. Yet because we are often not the *main* character, we feel obscure. The story of Ezekiel's wife speaks to those of us who maintain our place of love but never see its impact during this lifetime. She died to promote God's truth that all of us must love the Lord, and obey the Lord no matter what the circumstances.

Read Ezekiel 24.

Read the insight essay on Grief.

—D. JaPhia

Insights

PURPOSEFUL GIVING

The inequity of wealth distribution in the United States is often reflected within our faith communities. The recent phenomenon that some have labeled a "prosperity ministry" suggests that if one is not wealthy (with *wealth* defined as the acquisition of material goods), then one's faith requires strengthening.

While Scriptures do state that God will bless the godly in all sorts of ways, we discover that emphasis is often placed on areas that lead to relationship building and compassion for one another, rather than self-serving goals and idolatry. God, through the prophet Amos, issues a strong warning to women who oppress the poor (Amos 4:1–3).

When we focus on personal prosperity as a sign of God's providence, we forget that Jesus requires us to care for those who are incapable of caring for themselves (see Luke 14:13). Fulfilling this requirement is often difficult but not impossible. Honoring the commitment sometimes requires that we rethink our understanding and application of tithing and stewardship, which might direct us away from "blind" giving.

If the Holy Spirit is working in a woman's life, His presence will be evident by her generous heart. When a woman realizes she has been blessed with God's grace and mercy, she will give her time, energies, and financial resources.

Ultimately, we are accountable for contributing to kingdom building. Do our contributions make a difference in the communities in which we worship? Are we involved with ministries that meet the needs of the community that they serve? It's time to rethink our giving in order to make a difference in someone else's life.

How blessed we are when we realize that everything we have belongs to God and has been loaned to us to share with others. When we arrive at this point, we are able to discern and to apply the liberating principle: be in bondage to no one—individually and collectively. For Christ has set us free. Let us therefore handle money in our private and corporate lives in a manner that reflects the liberty that is found in our relationship with Jesus Christ. Giving to others without a judging attitude will bring a woman abundant joy!

Read Amos 4:1–3; see also Luke 14:13; 18:12.
Read the portrait on The Widow's Mite.

—*A. Sims*

take of the highest [o]branch of the high cedar, and will set *it;* I will crop off from the top of his young twigs [p]a tender one, and will [q]plant *it* upon an high mountain and eminent:

23 [r]In the mountain of the height of Israel will I plant it: and it shall bring forth boughs, and bear fruit, and be a goodly cedar: and [s]under it shall dwell all fowl of every wing; in the shadow of the branches thereof shall they dwell.

24 And all the trees of the field shall know that I the LORD [t]have brought down the high tree, have exalted the low tree, have dried up the green tree, and have made the dry tree to flourish: [u]I the LORD have spoken and have done *it.*

18 The word of the LORD came unto me again, saying,

2 What mean ye, that ye use this proverb concerning the land of Israel, saying, The [v]fathers have eaten sour grapes, and the children's teeth are set on edge?

3 *As* I live, saith the Lord GOD, ye shall not have *occasion* any more to use this proverb in Israel.

4 Behold, all souls are mine; as the soul of the father, so also the soul of the son is mine: [w]the soul that sinneth, it shall die.

5 ¶ But if a man be just, and do that which is lawful and right,

6 [x]*And* hath not eaten upon the mountains, neither hath lifted up his eyes to the idols of the house of Israel, neither hath [y]defiled his neighbour's wife, neither hath come near to [z]a menstruous woman,

7 And hath not [a]oppressed any, *but* hath restored to the debtor his [b]pledge, hath spoiled none by violence, hath [c]given his bread to the hungry, and hath covered the naked with a garment;

8 He *that* hath not given forth upon [d]usury, neither hath taken any increase, *that* hath withdrawn his hand from iniquity, [e]hath executed true judgment between man and man,

9 Hath walked in my statutes, and hath kept my judgments, to deal truly; he *is* just, he shall surely [f]live, saith the Lord GOD.

10 ¶ If he beget a son *that is* a robber, [g]a shedder of blood, and *that* doeth the like to *any* one of these *things,*

11 And that doeth not any of those *duties,* but even hath eaten upon the mountains, and defiled his neighbour's wife,

12 Hath oppressed the poor and needy, hath spoiled by violence, hath not restored the pledge, and hath lifted up his eyes to the idols, hath [h]committed abomination,

13 Hath given forth upon usury, and hath taken increase: shall he then live? he shall not live: he hath done all these abominations; he shall surely die; [i]his blood shall be upon him.

14 ¶ Now, lo, *if* he beget a son, that seeth all his father's sins which he hath done, and considereth, and doeth not such like,

15 [j]*That* hath not eaten upon the mountains, neither hath lifted up his eyes to the idols of the house of Israel, hath not defiled his neighbour's wife,

16 Neither hath oppressed any, hath not withholden the pledge, neither hath spoiled by violence, *but* hath given his bread to the hungry, and hath covered the naked with a garment,

17 *That* hath taken off his hand from the poor, *that* hath not received usury nor increase, hath executed my judgments, hath walked in my statutes; he shall not die for the iniquity of his father, he shall surely live.

18 *As for* his father, because he cruelly oppressed, spoiled his brother by violence, and did *that* which *is* not good among his people, lo, even [k]he shall die in his iniquity.

19 ¶ Yet say ye, Why? [l]doth not the son bear the iniquity of the father? When the son hath done that which is lawful and right, *and* hath kept all my statutes, and hath done them, he shall surely live.

20 [m]The soul that sinneth, it shall die. [n]The son shall not bear the iniquity of the father, neither shall the father bear the iniquity of the son: [o]the righteousness of the righteous shall be upon him, [p]and the wickedness of the wicked shall be upon him.

21 But [q]if the wicked will turn from all his sins that he hath committed, and keep all my statutes, and do that which is lawful and right, he shall surely live, he shall not die.

22 [r]All his transgressions that he hath committed, they shall not be mentioned unto him: in his righteousness that he hath done he shall live.

23 [s]Have I any pleasure at all that the wicked should die? saith the Lord GOD: *and* not that he should return from his ways, and live?

24 ¶ But [t]when the righteous turneth away from his righteousness, and committeth iniquity, *and* doeth according to all the abominations that the wicked *man* doeth, shall he live? [u]All his righteousness that he hath done shall not be mentioned: in his trespass that he hath trespassed, and in his sin that he hath sinned, in them shall he die.

25 ¶ Yet ye say, [v]The way of the Lord is not equal. Hear now, O house of Israel; Is not my way equal? are not your ways unequal?

26 [w]When a righteous *man* turneth away from his righteousness, and committeth iniquity, and dieth in them; for his iniquity that he hath done shall he die.

27 Again, [x]when the wicked *man* turneth away from his wickedness that he hath committed, and doeth that which is lawful and right, he shall save his soul alive.

28 Because he [y]considereth, and turneth away from all his transgressions that he hath committed, he shall surely live, he shall not die.

29 [z]Yet saith the house of Israel, The way of the Lord is not equal. O house of Israel,

17:22 [o]Isa. 11:1; Jer. 23:5; Zech. 3:8 [p]Isa. 53:2 [q]Ps. 2:6
17:23 [r]Isa. 2:2; ch. 20:40; Mic. 4:1 [s]ch. 31:6; Dan. 4:12
17:24 [t]Luke 1:52 [u]ch. 22:14
18:2 [v]Jer. 31:29; Lam. 5:7
18:4 [w]ver. 20; Rom. 6:23
18:6 [x]ch. 22:9 [y]Lev. 18:20 [z]Lev. 18:19
18:7 [a]Ex. 22:21; Lev. 19:15 [b]Ex. 22:26; Deut. 24:12 [c]Deut. 15:7; Isa. 58:7; Matt. 25:35
18:8 [d]Ex. 22:25; Lev. 25:36; Deut. 23:19; Neh. 5:7; Ps. 15:5 [e]Deut. 1:16; Zech. 8:16
18:9 [f]ch. 20:11; Am. 5:4
18:10 [g]Gen. 9:6; Ex. 21:12; Num. 35:31
18:12 [h]ch. 8:6
18:13 [i]Lev. 20:9; ch. 3:18; Acts 18:6
18:15 [j]ver. 6
18:18 [k]ch. 3:18
18:19 [l]Ex. 20:5; Deut. 5:9; 2 Kings 23:26
18:20 [m]ver. 4 [n]Deut. 24:16; 2 Kings 14:6; 2 Chron. 25:4; Jer. 31:29 [o]Isa. 3:10 [p]Rom. 2:9
18:21 [q]ver. 27; ch. 33:12
18:22 [r]ch. 33:16
18:23 [s]ver. 32; ch. 33:11; 1 Tim. 2:4; 2 Pet. 3:9
18:24 [t]ch. 3:20 [u]2 Pet. 2:20
18:25 [v]ver. 29; ch. 33:17
18:26 [w]ver. 24
18:27 [x]ver. 21
18:28 [y]ver. 14
18:29 [z]ver. 25

are not my ways equal? are not your ways
unequal?
30 [a]Therefore I will judge you, O house
of Israel, every one according to his ways,
saith the Lord GOD. [b]Repent, and turn *yourselves* from all your transgressions; so iniquity shall not be your ruin.
31 ¶ [c]Cast away from you all your transgressions, whereby ye have transgressed;
and make you a [d]new heart and a new
spirit: for why will ye die, O house of Israel?
32 For [e]I have no pleasure in the death of
him that dieth, saith the Lord GOD: wherefore turn *yourselves*, and live ye.
19 Moreover [f]take thou up a lamentation for the princes of Israel,
2 And say, What *is* thy mother? A lioness:
she lay down among lions, she nourished
her whelps among young lions.
3 And she brought up one of her whelps:
[g]it became a young lion, and it learned to
catch the prey; it devoured men.
4 The nations also heard of him; he was
taken in their pit, and they brought him
with chains unto the land of [h]Egypt.
5 Now when she saw that she had waited,
and her hope was lost, then she took [i]an-
other of her whelps, *and* made him a young
lion.
6 [j]And he went up and down among the
lions, [k]he became a young lion, and learned
to catch the prey, *and* devoured men.
7 And he knew their desolate palaces,
and he laid waste their cities; and the land
was desolate, and the fulness thereof, by the
noise of his roaring.
8 [l]Then the nations set against him on
every side from the provinces, and spread
their net over him: [m]he was taken in their
pit.
9 [n]And they put him in ward in chains,
and brought him to the king of Babylon:
they brought him into holds, that his voice
should no more be heard upon [o]the mountains of Israel.
10 ¶ Thy mother *is* [p]like a vine in thy
blood, planted by the waters: she was
[q]fruitful and full of branches by reason of
many waters.
11 And she had strong rods for the scep-
tres of them that bare rule, and her [r]stature
was exalted among the thick branches, and
she appeared in her height with the multitude of her branches.
12 But she was plucked up in fury, she
was cast down to the ground, and the [s]east
wind dried up her fruit: her strong rods
were broken and withered; the fire consumed them.
13 And now she *is* planted in the wilderness, in a dry and thirsty ground.
14 [t]And fire is gone out of a rod of her
branches, *which* hath devoured her fruit, so
that she hath no strong rod *to be* a sceptre
to rule. [u]This *is* a lamentation, and shall be
for a lamentation.
20 And it came to pass in the seventh
year, in the fifth *month*, the tenth *day*

18:30 [a]ch. 7:3 [b]Matt. 3:2; Rev. 2:5
18:31 [c]Eph. 4:22 [d]Jer. 32:39; ch. 11:19
18:32 [e]Lam. 3:33; ver. 23; ch. 33:11; 2 Pet. 3:9
19:1 [f]ch. 26:17
19:3 [g]ver. 6; 2 Kings 23:31
19:4 [h]2 Kings 23:33; 2 Chron. 36:4; Jer. 22:11
19:5 [i]2 Kings 23:34
19:6 [j]Jer. 22:13-17 [k]ver. 3
19:8 [l]2 Kings 24:2 [m]ver. 4
19:9 [n]2 Chron. 36:6; Jer. 22:18 [o]Ezek. 6:2
19:10 [p]ch. 17:6 [q]Deut. 8:7
19:11 [r]ch. 31:3; Dan. 4:11
19:12 [s]ch. 17:10; Hos. 13:15
19:14 [t]Judg. 9:15; 2 Kings 24:20; ch. 17:18 [u]Lam. 4:20
20:1 [v]ch. 8:1
20:3 [w]ver. 31; ch. 14:3
20:4 [x]ch. 22:2 [y]ch. 16:2
20:5 [z]Ex. 6:7; Deut. 7:6 [a]Ex. 3:8; Deut. 4:34 [b]Ex. 20:2
20:6 [c]Ex. 3:8; Deut. 8:7; Jer. 32:22 [d]Ps. 48:2; ver. 15; Dan. 8:9; Zech. 7:14
20:7 [e]ch. 18:31 [f]2 Chron. 15:8 [g]Lev. 17:7; Deut. 29:16; Josh. 24:14
20:8 [h]ch. 7:8; ver. 13
20:9 [i]Ex. 32:12; Num. 14:13; Deut. 9:28; ver. 14; ch. 36:21
20:10 [j]Ex. 13:18
20:11 [k]Deut. 4:8; Neh. 9:13; Ps. 147:19 [l]Lev. 18:5; ver. 13:21; Rom. 10:5; Gal. 3:12
20:12 [m]Ex. 20:8; Deut. 5:12; Neh. 9:14
20:13 [n]Num. 14:22; Ps. 78:40 [o]ver. 16; Prov. 1:25 [p]Ex. 16:27 [q]Num. 14:29; Ps. 106:23
20:14 [r]ver. 9
20:15 [s]Num. 14:28; Ps. 95:11 [t]ver. 6
20:16 [u]ver. 13

of the month, *that* [v]certain of the elders of
Israel came to enquire of the LORD, and sat
before me.
2 Then came the word of the LORD unto
me, saying,
3 Son of man, speak unto the elders of
Israel, and say unto them, Thus saith the
Lord GOD; Are ye come to enquire of me?
As I live, saith the Lord GOD, [w]I will not be
enquired of by you.
4 Wilt thou [x]judge them, son of man, wilt
thou judge *them*? [y]cause them to know the
abominations of their fathers:
5 ¶ And say unto them, Thus saith the
Lord GOD; In the day when [z]I chose Israel,
and lifted up mine hand unto the seed of the
house of Jacob, and made myself [a]known
unto them in the land of Egypt, when I lifted
up mine hand unto them, saying, [b]I *am* the
LORD your God;
6 In the day *that* I lifted up mine hand
unto them, [c]to bring them forth of the land
of Egypt into a land that I had espied for
them, flowing with milk and honey, [d]which
is the glory of all lands:
7 Then said I unto them, [e]Cast ye away
every man [f]the abominations of his eyes,
and defile not yourselves with [g]the idols of
Egypt: I *am* the LORD your God.
8 But they rebelled against me, and would
not hearken unto me: they did not every
man cast away the abominations of their
eyes, neither did they forsake the idols of
Egypt: then I said, I will [h]pour out my fury
upon them, to accomplish my anger against
them in the midst of the land of Egypt.
9 [i]But I wrought for my name's sake,
that it should not be polluted before the heathen, among whom they *were*, in whose
sight I made myself known unto them, in
bringing them forth out of the land of Egypt.
10 ¶ Wherefore I [j]caused them to go
forth out of the land of Egypt, and brought
them into the wilderness.
11 [k]And I gave them my statutes, and
shewed them my judgments, [l]which *if* a
man do, he shall even live in them.
12 Moreover also I gave them my [m]sab-
baths, to be a sign between me and them,
that they might know that I *am* the LORD
that sanctify them.
13 But the house of Israel [n]rebelled
against me in the wilderness: they walked
not in my statutes, and they [o]despised my
judgments, which *if* a man do, he shall even
live in them; and my sabbaths they greatly
[p]polluted: then I said, I would pour out my
fury upon them in the [q]wilderness, to consume them.
14 [r]But I wrought for my name's sake,
that it should not be polluted before the heathen, in whose sight I brought them out.
15 Yet also [s]I lifted up my hand unto
them in the wilderness, that I would not
bring them into the land which I had given
them, flowing with milk and honey, [t]which
is the glory of all lands;
16 [u]Because they despised my judg-

ments, and walked not in my statutes, but
polluted my sabbaths: for [v]their heart went
after their idols.
17 [w]Nevertheless mine eye spared them
from destroying them, neither did I make an
end of them in the wilderness.
18 But I said unto their children in the
wilderness, Walk ye not in the statutes of
your fathers, neither observe their judgments, nor defile yourselves with their
idols:
19 I *am* the LORD your God; [x]walk in my
statutes, and keep my judgments, and do
them;
20 [y]And hallow my sabbaths; and they
shall be a sign between me and you, that ye
may know that I *am* the LORD your God.
21 Notwithstanding [z]the children rebelled against me: they walked not in my
statutes, neither kept my judgments to do
them, [a]which *if* a man do, he shall even live
in them; they polluted my sabbaths: then I
said, [b]I would pour out my fury upon them,
to accomplish my anger against them in the
wilderness.
22 [c]Nevertheless I withdrew mine hand,
and [d]wrought for my name's sake, that it
should not be polluted in the sight of the
heathen, in whose sight I brought them
forth.
23 I lifted up mine hand unto them also in
the wilderness, that [e]I would scatter them
among the heathen, and disperse them
through the countries;
24 [f]Because they had not executed my
judgments, but had despised my statutes,
and had polluted my sabbaths, and [g]their
eyes were after their fathers' idols.
25 Wherefore [h]I gave them also statutes
that were not good, and judgments whereby they should not live;
26 And I polluted them in their own gifts,
in that they caused to pass [i]through *the fire*
all that openeth the womb, that I might
make them desolate, to the end that they
[j]might know that I *am* the LORD.
27 ¶ Therefore, son of man, speak unto
the house of Israel, and say unto them, Thus
saith the Lord GOD; Yet in this your fathers
have [k]blasphemed me, in that they have
committed a trespass against me.
28 *For* when I had brought them into the
land, *for* the which I lifted up mine hand to
give it to them, then [l]they saw every high
hill, and all the thick trees, and they offered
there their sacrifices, and there they presented the provocation of their offering:
there also they made their [m]sweet savour,
and poured out there their drink offerings.
29 Then I said unto them, What *is* the
high place whereunto ye go? And the name
thereof is called Bamah unto this day.
30 Wherefore say unto the house of Israel, Thus saith the Lord GOD; Are ye polluted after the manner of your fathers? and
commit ye whoredom after their abominations?
31 For when ye offer [n]your gifts, when ye
make your sons to pass through the fire, ye
pollute yourselves with all your idols, even
unto this day: and [o]shall I be enquired of by
you, O house of Israel? *As* I live, saith the
Lord GOD, I will not be enquired of by you.
32 And that [p]which cometh into your
mind shall not be at all, that ye say, We will
be as the heathen, as the families of the
countries, to serve wood and stone.
33 ¶ *As* I live, saith the Lord GOD, surely
with a mighty hand, and [q]with a stretched
out arm, and with fury poured out, will I
rule over you:
34 And I will bring you out from the people, and will gather you out of the countries
wherein ye are scattered, with a mighty
hand, and with a stretched out arm, and
with fury poured out.
35 And I will bring you into the wilderness of the people, and there [r]will I plead
with you face to face.
36 [s]Like as I pleaded with your fathers in
the wilderness of the land of Egypt, so will
I plead with you, saith the Lord GOD.
37 And I will cause you to [t]pass under
the rod, and I will bring you into the bond of
the covenant:
38 And [u]I will purge out from among you
the rebels, and them that transgress against
me: I will bring them forth out of the country where they sojourn, and [v]they shall not
enter into the land of Israel: [w]and ye shall
know that I *am* the LORD.
39 As for you, O house of Israel, thus
saith the Lord GOD; [x]Go ye, serve ye every
one his idols, and hereafter *also*, if ye will
not hearken unto me: [y]but pollute ye my
holy name no more with your gifts, and
with your idols.
40 For [z]in mine holy mountain, in the
mountain of the height of Israel, saith the
Lord GOD, there shall all the house of Israel,
all of them in the land, serve me: there [a]will
I accept them, and there will I require your
offerings, and the firstfruits of your oblations, with all your holy things.
41 I will accept you with your [b]sweet savour, when I bring you out from the people,
and gather you out of the countries wherein
ye have been scattered; and I will be sanctified in you before the heathen.
42 [c]And ye shall know that I *am* the
LORD, [d]when I shall bring you into the land
of Israel, into the country *for* the which I
lifted up mine hand to give it to your fathers.
43 And [e]there shall ye remember your
ways, and all your doings, wherein ye have
been defiled; and [f]ye shall lothe yourselves
in your own sight for all your evils that ye
have committed.
44 [g]And ye shall know that I *am* the
LORD, when I have wrought with you [h]for
my name's sake, not according to your
wicked ways, nor according to your corrupt
doings, O ye house of Israel, saith the Lord
GOD.

20:16 [v]Num. 15:39; Ps. 78:37; Am. 5:25; Acts 7:42
20:17 [w]Ps. 78:38
20:19 [x]Deut. 5:32
20:20 [y]ver. 12; Jer. 17:22
20:21 [z]Num. 25:1; Deut. 9:23 [a]ver. 11 [b]ver. 8
20:22 [c]Ps. 78:38; ver. 17 [d]ver. 9
20:23 [e]Lev. 26:33; Deut. 28:64; Ps. 106:27; Jer. 15:4
20:24 [f]ver. 13 [g]ch. 6:9
20:25 [h]Ps. 81:12; ver. 39; Rom. 1:24; 2 Thess. 2:11
20:26 [i]2 Kings 17:17; 2 Chron. 28:3; Jer. 32:35; ch. 16:20 [j]ch. 6:7
20:27 [k]Rom. 2:24
20:28 [l]Isa. 57:5; ch. 6:13 [m]ch. 16:19
20:31 [n]ver. 26 [o]ver. 3
20:32 [p]ch. 11:5
20:33 [q]Jer. 21:5
20:35 [r]Jer. 2:9; ch. 17:20
20:36 [s]Num. 14:21
20:37 [t]Lev. 27:32; Jer. 33:13
20:38 [u]ch. 34:17; Matt. 25:32 [v]Jer. 44:14 [w]ch. 6:7
20:39 [x]Judg. 10:14; Ps. 81:12; Am. 4:4 [y]Isa. 1:13; ch. 23:38
20:40 [z]Isa. 2:2; ch. 17:23; Mic. 4:1 [a]Isa. 56:7; Zech. 8:20; Mal. 3:4; Rom. 12:1
20:41 [b]Eph. 5:2; Phil. 4:18
20:42 [c]ver. 38; ch. 36:23 [d]ch. 11:17
20:43 [e]ch. 16:61 [f]Lev. 26:39; ch. 6:9; Hos. 5:15
20:44 [g]ver. 38; ch. 24:24 [h]ch. 36:22

45 ¶ Moreover the word of the LORD came unto me, saying,

46 [i]Son of man, set thy face toward the south, and drop *thy word* toward the south, and prophesy against the forest of the south field;

47 And say to the forest of the south, Hear the word of the LORD; Thus saith the Lord GOD; Behold, [j]I will kindle a fire in thee, and it shall devour [k]every green tree in thee, and every dry tree: the flaming flame shall not be quenched, and all faces [l]from the south to the north shall be burned therein.

48 And all flesh shall see that I the LORD have kindled it: it shall not be quenched.

49 Then said I, Ah Lord GOD! they say of me, Doth he not speak parables?

21 And the word of the LORD came unto me, saying,

2 [m]Son of man, set thy face toward Jerusalem, and [n]drop *thy word* toward the holy places, and prophesy against the land of Israel,

3 And say to the land of Israel, Thus saith the LORD; Behold, I *am* against thee, and will draw forth my sword out of his sheath, and will cut off from thee [o]the righteous and the wicked.

4 Seeing then that I will cut off from thee the righteous and the wicked, therefore shall my sword go forth out of his sheath against all flesh [p]from the south to the north:

5 That all flesh may know that I the LORD have drawn forth my sword out of his sheath: it [q]shall not return any more.

6 [r]Sigh therefore, thou son of man, with the breaking of *thy* loins; and with bitterness sigh before their eyes.

7 And it shall be, when they say unto thee, Wherefore sighest thou? that thou shalt answer, For the tidings; because it cometh: and every heart shall melt, and [s]all hands shall be feeble, and every spirit shall faint, and all knees shall be weak *as* water: behold, it cometh, and shall be brought to pass, saith the Lord GOD.

8 ¶ Again the word of the LORD came unto me, saying,

9 Son of man, prophesy, and say, Thus saith the LORD; Say, [t]A sword, a sword is sharpened, and also furbished:

10 It is sharpened to make a sore slaughter; it is furbished that it may glitter: should we then make mirth? it contemneth the rod of my son, *as* every tree.

11 And he hath given it to be furbished, that it may be handled: this sword is sharpened, and it is furbished, to give it into the hand of [u]the slayer.

12 Cry and howl, son of man: for it shall be upon my people, it *shall be* upon all the princes of Israel: terrors by reason of the sword shall be upon my people: [v]smite therefore upon *thy* thigh.

13 Because *it is* [w]a trial, and what if the *sword* contemn even the rod? [x]it shall be no *more,* saith the Lord GOD.

14 Thou therefore, son of man, prophesy, and [y]smite *thine* hands together, and let the sword be doubled the third time, the sword of the slain: it *is* the sword of the great *men that are* slain, which entereth into their [z]privy chambers.

15 I have set the point of the sword against all their gates, that *their* heart may faint, and *their* ruins be multiplied: ah! [a]*it is* made bright, *it is* wrapped up for the slaughter.

16 [b]Go thee one way or other, *either* on the right hand, *or* on the left, whithersoever thy face *is* set.

17 I will also [c]smite mine hands together, and [d]I will cause my fury to rest: I the LORD have said *it.*

18 ¶ The word of the LORD came unto me again, saying,

19 Also, thou son of man, appoint thee two ways, that the sword of the king of Babylon may come: both twain shall come forth out of one land: and choose thou a place, choose *it* at the head of the way to the city.

20 Appoint a way, that the sword may come to [e]Rabbath of the Ammonites, and to Judah in Jerusalem the defenced.

21 For the king of Babylon stood at the parting of the way, at the head of the two ways, to use divination: he made *his* arrows bright, he consulted with images, he looked in the liver.

22 At his right hand was the divination for Jerusalem, to appoint captains, to open the mouth in the slaughter, to [f]lift up the voice with shouting, [g]to appoint *battering* rams against the gates, to cast a mount, *and* to build a fort.

23 And it shall be unto them as a false divination in their sight, to them that [h]have sworn oaths: but he will call to remembrance the iniquity, that they may be taken.

24 Therefore thus saith the Lord GOD; Because ye have made your iniquity to be remembered, in that your transgressions are discovered, so that in all your doings your sins do appear; because, *I say,* that ye are come to remembrance, ye shall be taken with the hand.

25 ¶ And thou, [i]profane wicked prince of Israel, [j]whose day is come, when iniquity *shall have* an end,

26 Thus saith the Lord GOD; Remove the diadem, and take off the crown: this *shall* not *be* the same: [k]exalt *him that is* low, and abase *him that is* high.

27 I will overturn, overturn, overturn, it: [l]and it shall be no *more,* until he come whose right it is; and I will give it *him.*

28 ¶ And thou, son of man, prophesy and say, Thus saith the Lord GOD [m]concerning the Ammonites, and concerning their reproach; even say thou, [n]The sword, the sword *is* drawn: for the slaughter *it is* furbished, to consume because of the glittering:

20:46 [i]ch. 6:2
20:47 [j]Jer. 21:14 [k]Luke 23:31 [l]ch. 21:4
21:2 [m]ch. 20:46 [n]Deut. 32:2; Am. 7:16; Mic. 2:6
21:3 [o]Job 9:22
21:4 [p]ch. 20:47
21:5 [q]Isa. 45:23
21:6 [r]Isa. 22:4
21:7 [s]ch. 7:17
21:9 [t]Deut. 32:41; ver. 15
21:11 [u]ver. 19
21:12 [v]Jer. 31:19
21:13 [w]Job 9:23; 2 Cor. 8:2 [x]ver. 27
21:14 [y]Num. 24:10; ver. 17; ch. 6:11 [z]1 Kings 20:30
21:15 [a]ver. 10
21:16 [b]ch. 14:17
21:17 [c]ver. 14; ch. 22:13 [d]ch. 5:13
21:20 [e]Jer. 49:2; ch. 25:5; Am. 1:14
21:22 [f]Jer. 51:14 [g]ch. 4:2
21:23 [h]ch. 17:13
21:25 [i]2 Chron. 36:13; Jer. 52:2; ch. 17:19 [j]ver. 29; ch. 35:5
21:26 [k]ch. 17:24; Luke 1:52
21:27 [l]Gen. 49:10; ver. 13; Luke 1:32; John 1:49
21:28 [m]Jer. 49:1; ch. 25:2; Zeph. 2:8 [n]ver. 9

29 Whiles they [o]see vanity unto thee, whiles they divine a lie unto thee, to bring thee upon the necks of *them that are* slain, of the wicked, [p]whose day is come, when their iniquity *shall have* an end.

30 [q]Shall I cause *it* to return into his sheath? [r]I will judge thee in the place where thou wast created, [s]in the land of thy nativity.

31 And I will [t]pour out mine indignation upon thee, I will [u]blow against thee in the fire of my wrath, and deliver thee into the hand of brutish men, *and* skilful to destroy.

32 Thou shalt be for fuel to the fire; thy blood shall be in the midst of the land; [v]thou shalt be no *more* remembered: for I the LORD have spoken *it*.

22 Moreover the word of the LORD came unto me, saying,

2 Now, thou son of man, [w]wilt thou judge, wilt thou judge [x]the bloody city? yea, thou shalt shew her all her abominations.

3 Then say thou, Thus saith the Lord GOD, The city sheddeth blood in the midst of it, that her time may come, and maketh idols against herself to defile herself.

4 Thou art become guilty in thy blood that thou hast [y]shed; and hast defiled thyself in thine idols which thou hast made; and thou hast caused thy days to draw near, and art come *even* unto thy years: [z]therefore have I made thee a reproach unto the heathen, and a mocking to all countries.

5 *Those that be* near, and *those that be* far from thee, shall mock thee, *which art* infamous *and* much vexed.

6 Behold, [a]the princes of Israel, every one were in thee to their power to shed blood.

7 In thee have they [b]set light by father and mother: in the midst of thee have they [c]dealt by oppression with the stranger: in thee have they vexed the fatherless and the widow.

8 Thou hast [d]despised mine holy things, and hast [e]profaned my sabbaths.

9 In thee are [f]men that carry tales to shed blood: [g]and in thee they eat upon the mountains: in the midst of thee they commit lewdness.

10 In thee have they [h]discovered their fathers' nakedness: in thee have they humbled her that was [i]set apart for pollution.

11 And one hath committed abomination [j]with his neighbour's wife; and another [k]hath lewdly defiled his daughter in law; and another in thee hath humbled his [l]sister, his father's daughter.

12 In thee [m]have they taken gifts to shed blood; [n]thou hast taken usury and increase, and thou hast greedily gained of thy neighbours by extortion, and [o]hast forgotten me, saith the Lord GOD.

13 ¶ Behold, therefore I have [p]smitten mine hand at thy dishonest gain which thou hast made, and at thy blood which hath been in the midst of thee.

14 [q]Can thine heart endure, or can thine hands be strong, in the days that I shall deal with thee? [r]I the LORD have spoken *it*, and will do *it*.

15 And [s]I will scatter thee among the heathen, and disperse thee in the countries, and [t]will consume thy filthiness out of thee.

16 And thou shalt take thine inheritance in thyself in the sight of the heathen, and [u]thou shalt know that I *am* the LORD.

17 And the word of the LORD came unto me, saying,

18 Son of man, [v]the house of Israel is to me become dross: all they *are* brass, and tin, and iron, and lead, in the midst of the furnace; they are *even* the dross of silver.

19 Therefore thus saith the Lord GOD; Because ye are all become dross, behold, therefore I will gather you into the midst of Jerusalem.

20 *As* they gather silver, and brass, and iron, and lead, and tin, into the midst of the furnace, to blow the fire upon it, to melt *it;* so will I gather *you* in mine anger and in my fury, and I will leave *you there*, and melt you.

21 Yea, I will gather you, and [w]blow upon you in the fire of my wrath, and ye shall be melted in the midst therof.

22 As silver is melted in the midst of the furnace, so shall ye be melted in the midst thereof; and ye shall know that I the LORD have [x]poured out my fury upon you.

23 ¶ And the word of the LORD came unto me, saying,

24 Son of man, say unto her, Thou *art* the land that is not cleansed, nor rained upon in the day of indignation.

25 [y]*There is* a conspiracy of her prophets in the midst thereof, like a roaring lion ravening the prey; they [z]have devoured souls; [a]they have taken the treasure and precious things; they have made her many widows in the midst thereof.

26 [b]Her priests have violated my law, and have [c]profaned mine holy things: they have put no [d]difference between the holy and profane, neither have they shewed *difference* between the unclean and the clean, and have hid their eyes from my sabbaths, and I am profaned among them.

27 Her [e]princes in the midst thereof *are* like wolves ravening the prey, to shed blood, *and* to destroy souls, to get dishonest gain.

28 And [f]her prophets have daubed them with untempered *morter*, [g]seeing vanity, and divining lies unto them, saying, Thus saith the Lord GOD, when the LORD hath not spoken.

29 [h]The people of the land have used oppression, and exercised robbery, and have vexed the poor and needy: yea, they have [i]oppressed the stranger wrongfully.

30 [j]And I sought for a man among them, that should [k]make up the hedge, and [l]stand in the gap before me for the land,

21:29 [o]ch. 12:24 [p]ver. 25; Job 18:20; Ps. 37:13
21:30 [q]Jer. 47:6 [r]Gen. 15:14; ch. 16:38 [s]ch. 16:3
21:31 [t]ch. 7:8 [u]ch. 22:20
21:32 [v]ch. 25:10
22:2 [w]ch. 20:4 [x]ch. 24:6; Nah. 3:1
22:4 [y]2 Kings 21:16 [z]Deut. 28:37; 1 Kings 9:7; ch. 5:14; Dan. 9:16
22:6 [a]Isa. 1:23; Mic. 3:1; Zeph. 3:3
22:7 [b]Deut. 27:16 [c]Ex. 22:21
22:8 [d]ver. 26 [e]Lev. 19:30; ch. 23:38
22:9 [f]Ex. 23:1; Lev. 19:16 [g]ch. 18:6
22:10 [h]Lev. 18:7; 1 Cor. 5:1 [i]Lev. 18:19; ch. 18:6
22:11 [j]Lev. 18:20; Deut. 22:22; Jer. 5:8; ch. 18:11 [k]Lev. 18:15 [l]Lev. 18:9
22:12 [m]Ex. 23:8; Deut. 16:19 [n]Ex. 22:25; Lev. 25:36; Deut. 23:19; ch. 18:13 [o]Deut. 32:18; Jer. 3:21; ch. 23:35
22:13 [p]ch. 21:17
22:14 [q]ch. 21:7 [r]ch. 17:24
22:15 [s]Deut. 4:27; ch. 12:14 [t]ch. 23:27
22:16 [u]Ps. 9:16; ch. 6:7
22:18 [v]Ps. 119:119; Isa. 1:22; Jer. 6:28
22:21 [w]ch. 22:20
22:22 [x]ch. 20:8; ver. 31
22:25 [y]Hos. 6:9 [z]Matt. 23:14 [a]Mic. 3:11; Zeph. 3:3
22:26 [b]Mal. 2:8 [c]Lev. 22:2; 1 Sam. 2:29 [d]Lev. 10:10; Jer. 15:19; ch. 44:23
22:27 [e]Isa. 1:23; ch. 22:6; Mic. 3:2; Zeph. 3:3
22:28 [f]ch. 13:10 [g]ch. 13:6
22:29 [h]Jer. 5:26; ch. 18:12 [i]Ex. 22:21; Lev. 19:33; ch. 22:7
22:30 [j]Jer. 5:1 [k]ch. 13:5 [l]Ps. 106:23

that I should not destroy it: but I found none.

31 Therefore have I [m]poured out mine indignation upon them; I have consumed them with the fire of my wrath: [n]their own way have I recompensed upon their heads, saith the Lord GOD.

23 The word of the LORD came again unto me, saying,

2 Son of man, there were [o]two women, the daughters of one mother:

3 And [p]they committed whoredoms in Egypt; they committed whoredoms in [q]their youth: there were their breasts pressed, and there they bruised the teats of their virginity.

4 And the names of them *were* Aholah the elder, and Aholibah her sister: and [r]they were mine, and they bare sons and daughters. Thus *were* their names; Samaria *is* Aholah, and Jerusalem Aholibah.

5 And Aholah played the harlot when she was mine; and she doted on her lovers, on [s]the Assyrians *her* neighbours,

6 *Which were* clothed with blue, captains and rulers, all of them desirable young men, horsemen riding upon horses.

7 Thus she committed her whoredoms with them, with all them *that were* the chosen men of Assyria, and with all on whom she doted: with all their idols she defiled herself.

8 Neither left she her whoredoms *brought* [t]from Egypt: for in her youth they lay with her, and they bruised the breasts of her virginity, and poured their whoredom upon her.

9 Wherefore I have delivered her into the hand of her lovers, into the hand of the [u]Assyrians, upon whom she doted.

10 These [v]discovered her nakedness: they took her sons and her daughters, and slew her with the sword: and she became famous among women; for they had executed judgment upon her.

11 And [w]when her sister Aholibah saw *this*, [x]she was more corrupt in her inordinate love than she, and in her whoredoms more than her sister in *her* whoredoms.

12 She doted upon the [y]Assyrians *her* neighbours, [z]captains and rulers clothed most gorgeously, horsemen riding upon horses, all of them desirable young men.

13 Then I saw that she was defiled, *that* they *took* both one way,

14 And *that* she increased her whoredoms: for when she saw men pourtrayed upon the wall, the images of the Chaldeans pourtrayed with vermilion,

15 Girded with girdles upon their loins, exceeding in dyed attire upon their heads, all of them princes to look to, after the manner of the Babylonians of Chaldea, the land of their nativity:

16 [a]And as soon as she saw them with her eyes, she doted upon them, and sent messengers unto them into Chaldea.

17 And the Babylonians came to her into the bed of love, and they defiled her with their whoredom, and she was polluted with them, and [b]her mind was alienated from them.

18 So she discovered her whoredoms, and discovered her nakedness: then [c]my mind was alienated from her, like as my mind was alienated from her sister.

19 Yet she multiplied her whoredoms, in calling to remembrance the days of her youth, [d]wherein she had played the harlot in the land of Egypt.

20 For she doted upon their paramours, [e]whose flesh *is as* the flesh of asses, and whose issue *is like* the issue of horses.

21 Thus thou calledst to remembrance the lewdness of thy youth, in bruising thy teats by the Egyptians for the paps of thy youth.

22 ¶ Therefore, O Aholibah, thus saith the Lord GOD; [f]Behold, I will raise up thy lovers against thee, from whom thy mind is alienated, and I will bring them against thee on every side;

23 The Babylonians, and all the Chaldeans, [g]Pekod, and Shoa, and Koa, *and* all the Assyrians with them: [h]all of them desirable young men, captains and rulers, great lords and renowned, all of them riding upon horses.

24 And they shall come against thee with chariots, wagons, and wheels, and with an assembly of people, *which* shall set against thee buckler and shield and helmet round about: and I will set judgment before them, and they shall judge thee according to their judgments.

25 And I will set my jealousy against thee, and they shall deal furiously with thee: they shall take away thy nose and thine ears; and thy remnant shall fall by the sword: they shall take thy sons and thy daughters; and thy residue shall be devoured by the fire.

26 [i]They shall also strip thee out of thy clothes, and take away thy fair jewels.

27 Thus [j]will I make thy lewdness to cease from thee, and [k]thy whoredom *brought* from the land of Egypt: so that thou shalt not lift up thine eyes unto them, nor remember Egypt any more.

28 For thus saith the Lord GOD; Behold, I will deliver thee into the hand *of them* [l]whom thou hatest, into the hand *of them* [m]from whom thy mind is alienated:

29 And they shall deal with thee hatefully, and shall take away all thy labour, and [n]shall leave thee naked and bare: and the nakedness of thy whoredoms shall be discovered, both thy lewdness and thy whoredoms.

30 I will do these *things* unto thee, because thou hast [o]gone a whoring after the heathen, *and* because thou art polluted with their idols.

31 Thou hast walked in the way of thy sister; therefore will I give her [p]cup into thine hand.

32 Thus saith the Lord GOD; Thou shalt drink of thy sister's cup deep and large:

22:31 [m]ver. 22 [n]ch. 9:10
23:2 [o]Jer. 3:7; ch. 16:46
23:3 [p]Lev. 17:7; Josh. 24:14; ch. 20:8 [q]ch. 16:22
23:4 [r]ch. 16:8
23:5 [s]2 Kings 15:19; Hos. 8:9
23:8 [t]ver. 3
23:9 [u]2 Kings 17:3
23:10 [v]ch. 16:37
23:11 [w]Jer. 3:8 [x]Jer. 3:11; ch. 16:47
23:12 [y]2 Kings 16:7; 2 Chron. 28:16-23; ch. 16:28 [z]ver. 6
23:16 [a]2 Kings 24:1; ch. 16:29
23:17 [b]ver. 22
23:18 [c]Jer. 6:8
23:19 [d]ver. 3
23:20 [e]ch. 16:26
23:22 [f]ch. 16:37; ver. 28
23:23 [g]Jer. 50:21 [h]ver. 12
23:26 [i]ch. 16:39
23:27 [j]ch. 16:41 [k]ver. 3
23:28 [l]ch. 16:37 [m]ver. 17
23:29 [n]ch. 16:39; ver. 26
23:30 [o]ch. 6:9
23:31 [p]Jer. 25:15

[q]thou shalt be laughed to scorn and had in derision; it containeth much.

33 Thou shalt be filled with drunkenness and sorrow, with the cup of astonishment and desolation, with the cup of thy sister Samaria.

34 Thou shalt [r]even drink it and suck *it* out, and thou shalt break the sherds thereof, and pluck off thine own breasts: for I have spoken *it*, saith the Lord GOD.

35 Therefore thus saith the Lord GOD; Because thou [s]hast forgotten me, and [t]cast me behind thy back, therefore bear thou also thy lewdness and thy whoredoms.

36 ¶ The LORD said moreover unto me; Son of man, wilt thou [u]judge Aholah and Aholibah? yea, [v]declare unto them their abominations;

37 That they have committed adultery, and [w]blood *is* in their hands, and with their idols have they committed adultery, and have also caused their sons, [x]whom they bare unto me, to pass for them through *the fire*, to devour *them*.

38 Moreover this they have done unto me: they have defiled my sanctuary in the same day, and [y]have profaned my sabbaths.

39 For when they had slain their children to their idols, then they came the same day into my sanctuary to profane it; and, lo, [z]thus have they done in the midst of mine house.

40 And furthermore, that ye have sent for men to come from far, [a]unto whom a messenger *was* sent; and, lo, they came: for whom thou didst [b]wash thyself, [c]paintedst thy eyes, and deckedst thyself with ornaments,

41 And satest upon a stately [d]bed, and a table prepared before it, [e]whereupon thou hast set mine incense and mine oil.

42 And a voice of a multitude being at ease *was* with her: and with the men of the common sort *were* brought Sabeans from the wilderness, which put bracelets upon their hands, and beautiful crowns upon their heads.

43 Then said I unto *her that was* old in adulteries, Will they now commit whoredoms with her, and she *with them?*

44 Yet they went in unto her, as they go in unto a woman that playeth the harlot: so went they in unto Aholah and unto Aholibah, the lewd women.

45 ¶ And the righteous men, they shall [f]judge them after the manner of adulteresses, and after the manner of women that shed blood; because they *are* adulteresses, and [g]blood *is* in their hands.

46 For thus saith the Lord GOD; [h]I will bring up a company upon them, and will give them to be removed and spoiled.

47 [i]And the company shall stone them with stones, and dispatch them with their swords; [j]they shall slay their sons and their daughters, and burn up their houses with fire.

48 Thus [k]will I cause lewdness to cease out of the land, [l]that all women may be taught not to do after your lewdness.

49 And they shall recompense your lewdness upon you, and ye shall [m]bear the sins of your idols: [n]and ye shall know that I *am* the Lord GOD.

24 Again in the ninth year, in the tenth month, in the tenth *day* of the month, the word of the LORD came unto me, saying,

2 Son of man, write thee the name of the day, *even* of this same day: the king of Babylon set himself against Jerusalem [o]this same day.

3 [p]And utter a parable unto the rebellious house, and say unto them, Thus saith the Lord GOD; [q]Set on a pot, set *it* on, and also pour water into it:

4 Gather the pieces thereof into it, *even* every good piece, the thigh, and the shoulder; fill *it* with the choice bones.

5 Take the choice of the flock, and burn also the bones under it, *and* make it boil well, and let them seethe the bones of it therein.

6 ¶ Wherefore thus saith the Lord GOD; Woe to [r]the bloody city, to the pot whose scum *is* therein, and whose scum is not gone out of it! bring it out piece by piece; let no [s]lot fall upon it.

7 For her blood is in the midst of her; she set it upon the top of a rock; [t]she poured it not upon the ground, to cover it with dust;

8 That it might cause fury to come up to take vengeance; [u]I have set her blood upon the top of a rock, that it should not be covered.

9 Therefore thus saith the Lord GOD; [v]Woe to the bloody city! I will even make the pile for fire great.

10 Heap on wood, kindle the fire, consume the flesh, and spice it well, and let the bones be burned.

11 Then set it empty upon the coals thereof, that the brass of it may be hot, and may burn, and *that* [w]the filthiness of it may be molten in it, *that* the scum of it may be consumed.

12 She hath wearied *herself* with lies, and her great scum went not forth out of her: her scum *shall be* in the fire.

13 In thy filthiness *is* lewdness: because I have purged thee, and thou wast not purged, thou shalt not be purged from thy filthiness any more, [x]till I have caused my fury to rest upon thee.

14 [y]I the LORD have spoken *it:* it shall come to pass, and I will do *it;* I will not go back, [z]neither will I spare, neither will I repent; according to thy ways, and according to thy doings, shall they judge thee, saith the Lord GOD.

15 ¶ Also the word of the LORD came unto me, saying,

16 Son of man, behold, I take away from thee the desire of thine eyes with a stroke: yet neither shalt thou mourn nor weep, neither shall thy tears run down.

17 Forbear to cry, [a]make no mourning

23:32 [q]ch. 22:4
23:34 [r]Ps. 75:8; Isa. 51:17
23:35 [s]Jer. 2:32; ch. 22:12 [t]1 Kings 14:9; Neh. 9:26
23:36 [u]ch. 20:4 [v]Isa. 58:1
23:37 [w]ch. 16:38; ver. 45 [x]ch. 16:20
23:38 [y]ch. 22:8
23:39 [z]2 Kings 21:4
23:40 [a]Isa. 57:9 [b]Ruth 3:3 [c]2 Kings 9:30; Jer. 4:30
23:41 [d]Esth. 1:6; Isa. 57:7; Am. 2:8 [e]Prov. 7:17; ch. 16:18; Hos. 2:8
23:45 [f]ch. 16:38 [g]ver. 37
23:46 [h]ch. 16:40
23:47 [i]ch. 16:41 [j]2 Chron. 36:17; ch. 24:21
23:48 [k]ch. 22:15; ver. 27 [l]Deut. 13:11; 2 Pet. 2:6
23:49 [m]ver. 35 [n]ch. 20:38
24:2 [o]2 Kings 25:1; Jer. 39:1
24:3 [p]ch. 17:12 [q]Jer. 1:13; ch. 11:3
24:6 [r]ch. 22; ver. 9 [s]2 Sam. 8:2; Joel 3:3; Obad. 11; Nah. 3:10
24:7 [t]Lev. 17:13; Deut. 12:16
24:8 [u]Matt. 7:2
24:9 [v]ver. 6; Nah. 3:1; Hab. 2:12
24:11 [w]ch. 22:15
24:13 [x]ch. 5:13
24:14 [y]1 Sam. 15:29 [z]ch. 5:11
24:17 [a]Jer. 16:5

for the dead, [b]bind the tire of thine head
upon thee, and [c]put on thy shoes upon thy
feet, and [d]cover not *thy* lips, and eat not the
bread of men.
18 So I spake unto the people in the morning: and at even my wife died; and I did in
the morning as I was commanded.
19 ¶ And the people said unto me, [e]Wilt
thou not tell us what these *things are* to us,
that thou doest *so?*
20 Then I answered them, The word of
the LORD came unto me, saying,
21 Speak unto the house of Israel, Thus
saith the Lord GOD; Behold, [f]I will profane
my sanctuary, the excellency of your
strength, [g]the desire of your eyes, and that
which your soul pitieth; [h]and your sons and
your daughters whom ye have left shall fall
by the sword.
22 And ye shall do as I have done: [i]ye
shall not cover *your* lips, nor eat the bread
of men.
23 And your tires *shall be* upon your
heads, and your shoes upon your feet: [j]ye
shall not mourn nor weep; but [k]ye shall
pine away for your iniquities, and mourn
one toward another.
24 Thus [l]Ezekiel is unto you a sign: according to all that he hath done shall ye do:
[m]and when this cometh, [n]ye shall know
that I *am* the Lord GOD.
25 Also, thou son of man, *shall it* not *be*
in the day when I take from them [o]their
strength, the joy of their glory, the desire
of their eyes, and that whereupon they set
their minds, their sons and their daughters,
26 *That* [p]he that escapeth in that day
shall come unto thee, to cause *thee* to hear
it with *thine* ears?
27 [q]In that day shall thy mouth be
opened to him which is escaped, and thou
shalt speak, and be no more dumb: and
[r]thou shalt be a sign unto them; and they
shall know that I *am* the LORD.

25 The word of the LORD came again
unto me, saying,
2 Son of man, [s]set thy face [t]against the
Ammonites, and prophesy against them;
3 And say unto the Ammonites, Hear the
word of the Lord GOD; Thus saith the Lord
GOD; [u]Because thou saidst, Aha, against
my sanctuary, when it was profaned; and
against the land of Israel, when it was desolate; and against the house of Judah, when
they went into captivity;
4 Behold, therefore I will deliver thee to
the men of the east for a possession, and
they shall set their palaces in thee, and
make their dwellings in thee: they shall eat
thy fruit, and they shall drink thy milk.
5 And I will make [v]Rabbah [w]a stable for
camels, and the Ammonites a couching-
place for flocks: [x]and ye shall know that I
am the LORD.
6 For thus saith the Lord GOD; Because
thou [y]hast clapped *thine* hands, and
stamped with the feet, and [z]rejoiced in
heart with all thy despite against the land of
Israel;
7 Behold, therefore I will [a]stretch out
mine hand upon thee, and will deliver thee
for a spoil to the heathen; and I will cut thee
off from the people, and I will cause thee to
perish out of the countries: I will destroy
thee; and thou shalt know that I *am* the
LORD.
8 ¶ Thus saith the Lord GOD; Because that
[b]Moab and [c]Seir do say, Behold, the house
of Judah *is* like unto all the heathen;
9 Therefore, behold, I will open the side of
Moab from the cities, from his cities *which
are* on his frontiers, the glory of the country, Beth-jeshimoth, Baal-meon, and Kiriathaim,
10 [d]Unto the men of the east with the
Ammonites, and will give them in possession, that the Ammonites [e]may not be remembered among the nations.
11 And I will execute judgments upon
Moab; and they shall know that I *am* the
LORD.
12 ¶ Thus saith the Lord GOD; [f]Because
that Edom hath dealt against the house of
Judah by taking vengeance, and hath
greatly offended, and revenged himself
upon them;
13 Therefore thus saith the Lord GOD; I
will also stretch out mine hand upon Edom,
and will cut off man and beast from it; and
I will make it desolate from Teman; and
they of Dedan shall fall by the sword.
14 And [g]I will lay my vengeance upon
Edom by the hand of my people Israel: and
they shall do in Edom according to mine
anger and according to my fury; and they
shall know my vengeance, saith the Lord
GOD.
15 ¶ Thus saith the Lord GOD; [h]Because
[i]the Philistines have dealt by revenge, and
have taken vengeance with a despiteful
heart, to destroy *it* for the old hatred;
16 Therefore thus saith the Lord GOD; Behold, [j]I will stretch out mine hand upon the
Philistines, and I will cut off the [k]Chere-
thims, [l]and destroy the remnant of the sea
coast.
17 And I will [m]execute great vengeance
upon them with furious rebukes; [n]and they
shall know that I *am* the LORD, when I shall
lay my vengeance upon them.

26 And it came to pass in the eleventh
year, in the first *day* of the month,
that the word of the LORD came unto me,
saying,
2 Son of man, [o]because that Tyrus hath
said against Jerusalem, [p]Aha, she is broken
that was the gates of the people: she is
turned unto me: I shall be replenished, *now*
she is laid waste:
3 Therefore thus saith the Lord GOD; Behold, I *am* against thee, O Tyrus, and will
cause many nations to come up against
thee, as the sea causeth his waves to
come up.
4 And they shall destroy the walls of

24:17 [b]Lev. 10:6 [c]2 Sam. 15:30 [d]Mic. 3:7
24:19 [e]ch. 12:9
24:21 [f]Jer. 7:14; ch. 7:20 [g]Ps. 27:4 [h]ch. 23:47
24:22 [i]Jer. 16:6; ver. 17
24:23 [j]Job 27:15; Ps. 78:64 [k]Lev. 26:39; ch. 33:10
24:24 [l]Isa. 20:3; ch. 4:3 [m]Jer. 17:15; John 13:19 [n]ch. 6:7
24:25 [o]ver. 21
24:26 [p]ch. 33:21
24:27 [q]ch. 3:26 [r]ver. 24
25:2 [s]ch. 6:2 [t]Jer. 49:1; ch. 21:28; Am. 1:13; Zeph. 2:9
25:3 [u]Prov. 17:5; ch. 26:2
25:5 [v]ch. 21:20 [w]Isa. 17:2; Zeph. 2:14 [x]ch. 24:24
25:6 [y]Job 27:23; Lam. 2:15; Zeph. 2:15 [z]ch. 36:5; Zeph. 2:8
25:7 [a]ch. 35:3
25:8 [b]Isa. 15; Jer. 48:1; Am. 2:1 [c]ch. 35:2
25:10 [d]ver. 4 [e]ch. 21:32
25:12 [f]2 Chron. 28:17; Ps. 137:7; Jer. 49:7; ch. 35:2; Am. 1:11; Obad. 10
25:14 [g]Isa. 11:14; Jer. 49:2
25:15 [h]Jer. 25:20; Joel 3:4; Am. 1:6 [i]2 Chron. 28:18
25:16 [j]Zeph. 2:4 [k]1 Sam. 30:14 [l]Jer. 47:4
25:17 [m]ch. 5:15 [n]Ps. 9:16
26:2 [o]Isa. 23; Jer. 25:22; Am. 1:9; Zech. 9:2 [p]ch. 25:3

Tyrus, and break down her towers: I will
also scrape her dust from her, and [q]make
her like the top of a rock.
5 It shall be *a place for* the spreading of
nets [r]in the midst of the sea: for I have spoken *it,* saith the Lord GOD: and it shall become a spoil to the nations.
6 And her daughters which *are* in the
field shall be slain by the sword; [s]and they
shall know that I *am* the LORD.
7 ¶ For thus saith the Lord GOD; Behold,
I will bring upon Tyrus Nebuchadrezzar
king of Babylon, [t]a king of kings, from the
north, with horses, and with chariots, and
with horsemen, and companies, and much
people.
8 He shall slay with the sword thy daughters in the field: and he shall [u]make a fort
against thee, and cast a mount against thee,
and lift up the buckler against thee.
9 And he shall set engines of war against
thy walls, and with his axes he shall break
down thy towers.
10 By reason of the abundance of his
horses their dust shall cover thee: thy walls
shall shake at the noise of the horsemen,
and of the wheels, and of the chariots, when
he shall enter into thy gates, as men enter
into a city wherein is made a breach.
11 With the hoofs of his horses shall he
tread down all thy streets: he shall slay thy
people by the sword, and thy strong garrisons shall go down to the ground.
12 And they shall make a spoil of thy
riches, and make a prey of thy merchandise: and they shall break down thy walls,
and destroy thy pleasant houses: and they
shall lay thy stones and thy timber and thy
dust in the midst of the water.
13 [v]And I will cause the noise of [w]thy
songs to cease; and the sound of thy harps
shall be no more heard.
14 And [x]I will make thee like the top of a
rock: thou shalt be *a place* to spread nets
upon; thou shalt be built no more: for I the
LORD have spoken *it,* saith the Lord GOD.
15 ¶ Thus saith the Lord GOD to Tyrus;
Shall not the isles [y]shake at the sound of
thy fall, when the wounded cry, when the
slaughter is made in the midst of thee?
16 Then all the [z]princes of the sea shall
[a]come down from their thrones, and lay
away their robes, and put off their broidered garments: they shall clothe themselves with trembling; [b]they shall sit upon
the ground, and [c]shall tremble at *every* moment, and [d]be astonished at thee.
17 And they shall take up a [e]lamentation
for thee, and say to thee, How art thou destroyed, *that wast* inhabited of seafaring
men, the renowned city, which wast
[f]strong in the sea, she and her inhabitants,
which cause their terror *to be* on all that
haunt it!
18 Now shall [g]the isles tremble in the day
of thy fall; yea, the isles that *are* in the sea
shall be troubled at thy departure.
19 For thus saith the Lord GOD; When I

26:4 [q]ver. 14
26:5 [r]ch. 27:32
26:6 [s]ch. 25:5
26:7 [t]Ezra 7:12; Dan. 2:37
26:8 [u]ch. 21:22
26:13 [v]Isa. 14:11; Jer. 7:34 [w]Isa. 23:16; ch. 28:13; Rev. 18:22
26:14 [x]ver. 4
26:15 [y]Jer. 49:21; ver. 18; ch. 27:28
26:16 [z]Isa. 23:8 [a]Jonah 3:6 [b]Job 2:13 [c]ch. 32:10 [d]ch. 27:35
26:17 [e]ch. 27:32; Rev. 18:9 [f]Isa. 23:4
26:18 [g]ver. 15
26:20 [h]ch. 32:18 [i]ch. 32:23
26:21 [j]ch. 27:36 [k]Ps. 37:36
27:2 [l]ch. 19:1
27:3 [m]ch. 28:2 [n]Isa. 23:3 [o]ch. 28:12
27:5 [p]Deut. 3:9
27:6 [q]Jer. 2:10
27:9 [r]1 Kings 5:18; Ps. 83:7
27:10 [s]Jer. 46:9; ch. 30:5
27:11 [t]ver. 3
27:12 [u]Gen. 10:4; 2 Chron. 20:36
27:13 [v]Gen. 10:2 [w]Rev. 18:13
27:14 [x]Gen. 10:3; ch. 38:6
27:15 [y]Gen. 10:7

shall make thee a desolate city, like the cities that are not inhabited; when I shall bring
up the deep upon thee, and great waters
shall cover thee;
20 When I shall bring thee down [h]with
them that descend into the pit, with the people of old time, and shall set thee in the low
parts of the earth, in places desolate of old,
with them that go down to the pit, that thou
be not inhabited; and I shall set glory [i]in
the land of the living;
21 [j]I will make thee a terror, and thou
shalt be no *more:* [k]though thou be sought
for, yet shalt thou never be found again,
saith the Lord GOD.
27 The word of the LORD came again
unto me, saying,
2 Now, thou son of man, [l]take up a lamentation for Tyrus;
3 And say unto Tyrus, [m]O thou that art
situate at the entry of the sea, *which art* [n]a
merchant of the people for many isles, Thus
saith the Lord GOD; O Tyrus, thou hast said,
[o]I *am* of perfect beauty.
4 Thy borders *are* in the midst of the seas,
thy builders have perfected thy beauty.
5 They have made all thy *ship* boards of
fir trees of [p]Senir: they have taken cedars
from Lebanon to make masts for thee.
6 *Of* the oaks of Bashan have they made
thine oars; the company of the Ashurites
have made thy benches *of* ivory, *brought*
out of [q]the isles of Chittim.
7 Fine linen with broidered work from
Egypt was that which thou spreadest forth
to be thy sail; blue and purple from the isles
of Elishah was that which covered thee.
8 The inhabitants of Zidon and Arvad
were thy mariners: thy wise *men,* O Tyrus,
that were in thee, were thy pilots.
9 The ancients of [r]Gebal and the wise
men thereof were in thee thy calkers: all the
ships of the sea with their mariners were in
thee to occupy thy merchandise.
10 They of Persia and of Lud and of
[s]Phut were in thine army, thy men of war:
they hanged the shield and helmet in thee;
they set forth thy comeliness.
11 The men of Arvad with thine army
were upon thy walls round about, and the
Gammadims were in thy towers: they
hanged their shields upon thy walls round
about; they have made [t]thy beauty perfect.
12 [u]Tarshish *was* thy merchant by reason of the multitude of all *kind* of riches;
with silver, iron, tin, and lead, they traded in
thy fairs.
13 [v]Javan, Tubal, and Meshech, they
were thy merchants: they traded [w]the persons of men and vessels of brass in thy market.
14 They of the house of [x]Togarmah
traded in thy fairs with horses and horsemen and mules.
15 The men of [y]Dedan *were* thy merchants; many isles *were* the merchandise of
thine hand: they brought thee *for* a present
horns of ivory and ebony.

16 Syria *was* thy merchant by reason of the multitude of the wares of thy making: they occupied in thy fairs with emeralds, purple, and broidered work, and fine linen, and coral, and agate.

17 Judah, and the land of Israel, they *were* thy merchants: they traded in thy market [z]wheat of [a]Minnith, and Pannag, and honey, and oil, and [b]balm.

18 Damascus *was* thy merchant in the multitude of the wares of thy making, for the multitude of all riches; in the wine of Helbon, and white wool.

19 Dan also and Javan going to and fro occupied in thy fairs: bright iron, cassia, and calamus, were in thy market.

20 [c]Dedan *was* thy merchant in precious clothes for chariots.

21 Arabia, and all the princes of [d]Kedar, they occupied with thee in lambs, and rams, and goats: in these *were they* thy merchants.

22 The merchants of [e]Sheba and Raamah, they *were* thy merchants: they occupied in thy fairs with chief of all spices, and with all precious stones, and gold.

23 [f]Haran, and Canneh, and Eden, the merchants of [g]Sheba, Asshur, *and* Chilmad, *were* thy merchants.

24 These *were* thy merchants in all sorts *of things,* in blue clothes, and broidered work, and in chests of rich apparel, bound with cords, and made of cedar, among thy merchandise.

25 [h]The ships of Tarshish did sing of thee in thy market: and thou wast replenished, and made very glorious in [i]the midst of the seas.

26 ¶ Thy rowers have brought thee into great waters: [j]the east wind hath broken thee in the midst of the seas.

27 Thy [k]riches, and thy fairs, thy merchandise, thy mariners, and thy pilots, thy calkers, and the occupiers of thy merchandise, and all thy men of war, that *are* in thee, and in all thy company which *is* in the midst of thee, shall fall into the midst of the seas in the day of thy ruin.

28 The suburbs [l]shall shake at the sound of the cry of thy pilots.

29 And [m]all that handle the oar, the mariners, *and* all the pilots of the sea, shall come down from their ships, they shall stand upon the land;

30 And shall cause their voice to be heard against thee, and shall cry bitterly, and shall [n]cast up dust upon their heads, they [o]shall wallow themselves in the ashes:

31 And they shall [p]make themselves utterly bald for thee, and gird them with sackcloth, and they shall weep for thee with bitterness of heart *and* bitter wailing.

32 And in their wailing they shall [q]take up a lamentation for thee, and lament over thee, *saying,* [r]What *city is* like Tyrus, like the destroyed in the midst of the sea?

33 [s]When thy wares went forth out of the seas, thou filledst many people; thou didst enrich the kings of the earth with the multitude of thy riches and of thy merchandise.

34 In the time *when* [t]thou shalt be broken by the seas in the depths of the waters [u]thy merchandise and all thy company in the midst of thee shall fall.

35 [v]All the inhabitants of the isles shall be astonished at thee, and their kings shall be sore afraid, they shall be troubled in *their* countenance.

36 The merchants among the people [w]shall hiss at thee; [x]thou shalt be a terror, and never *shalt be* any more.

28 The word of the LORD came again unto me, saying,

2 Son of man, say unto the prince of Tyrus, Thus saith the Lord GOD; Because thine heart *is* lifted up, and [y]thou hast said, I *am* a God, I sit *in* the seat of God, [z]in the midst of the seas; [a]yet thou *art* a man, and not God, though thou set thine heart as the heart of God:

3 Behold, [b]thou *art* wiser than Daniel; there is no secret that they can hide from thee:

4 With thy wisdom and with thine understanding thou hast gotten thee riches, and hast gotten gold and silver into thy treasures:

5 [c]By thy great wisdom *and* by thy traffick hast thou increased thy riches, and thine heart is lifted up because of thy riches:

6 Therefore thus saith the Lord GOD; Because thou hast set thine heart as the heart of God;

7 Behold, therefore I will bring strangers upon thee, [d]the terrible of the nations: and they shall draw their swords against the beauty of thy wisdom, and they shall defile thy brightness.

8 They shall bring thee down to the pit, and thou shalt die the deaths of *them that are* slain in the midst of the seas.

9 Wilt thou yet [e]say before him that slayeth thee, I *am* God? but thou *shalt be* a man, and no God, in the hand of him that slayeth thee.

10 Thou shalt die the deaths of [f]the uncircumcised by the hand of strangers: for I have spoken *it,* saith the Lord GOD.

11 ¶ Moreover the word of the LORD came unto me, saying,

12 Son of man, [g]take up a lamentation upon the king of Tyrus, and say unto him, Thus saith the Lord GOD; [h]Thou sealest up the sum, full of wisdom, and perfect in beauty.

13 Thou hast been in [i]Eden the garden of God; every precious stone *was* thy covering, the sardius, topaz, and the diamond, the beryl, the onyx, and the jasper, the sapphire, the emerald, and the carbuncle, and gold: the workmanship of [j]thy tabrets and of thy pipes was prepared in thee in the day that thou wast created.

14 Thou *art* the anointed [k]cherub that covereth; and I have set thee *so:* thou wast upon [l]the holy mountain of God; thou hast

27:17 [z]1 Kings 5:9; Ezra 3:7; Acts 12:20 [a]Judg. 11:33 [b]Jer. 8:22
27:20 [c]Gen. 25:3
27:21 [d]Gen. 25:13; Isa. 60:7
27:22 [e]Gen. 10:7; 1 Kings 10:1; Ps. 72:10; Isa. 60:6
27:23 [f]Gen. 11:31; 2 Kings 19:12 [g]Gen. 25:3
27:25 [h]Ps. 48:7 [i]ver. 4
27:26 [j]Ps. 48:7
27:27 [k]Prov. 11:4; ver. 34; Rev. 18:9
27:28 [l]ch. 26:15
27:29 [m]Rev. 18:17
27:30 [n]Job 2:12; Rev. 18:19 [o]Esth. 4:1; Jer. 6:26
27:31 [p]Jer. 16:6; Mic. 1:16
27:32 [q]ch. 26:17; ver. 2 [r]Rev. 18:18
27:33 [s]Rev. 18:19
27:34 [t]ch. 26:19 [u]ver. 27
27:35 [v]ch. 26:15
27:36 [w]Jer. 18:16 [x]ch. 26:21
28:2 [y]ver. 9 [z]ch. 27:3 [a]Isa. 31:3
28:3 [b]Zech. 9:2
28:5 [c]Ps. 62:10; Zech. 9:3
28:7 [d]ch. 30:11
28:9 [e]ver. 2
28:10 [f]ch. 31:18
28:12 [g]ch. 27:2 [h]ch. 27:3; ver. 3
28:13 [i]ch. 31:8 [j]ch. 26:13
28:14 [k]Ex. 25:20; ver. 16 [l]ch. 20:40

walked up and down in the midst of the
stones of fire.
15 Thou *wast* perfect in thy ways from
the day that thou wast created, till iniquity
was found in thee.
16 By the multitude of thy merchandise
they have filled the midst of thee with violence, and thou hast sinned: therefore I will
cast thee as profane out of the mountain of
God: and I will destroy thee, [m]O covering
cherub, from the midst of the stones of fire.
17 [n]Thine heart was lifted up because of
thy beauty, thou hast corrupted thy wisdom
by reason of thy brightness: I will cast thee
to the ground, I will lay thee before kings,
that they may behold thee.
18 Thou hast defiled thy sanctuaries by
the multitude of thine iniquities, by the iniquity of thy traffick; therefore will I bring
forth a fire from the midst of thee, it shall
devour thee, and I will bring thee to ashes
upon the earth in the sight of all them that
behold thee.
19 All they that know thee among the
people shall be astonished at thee: [o]thou
shalt be a terror, and never *shalt* thou *be*
any more.
20 ¶ Again the word of the LORD came
unto me, saying,
21 Son of man, [p]set thy face [q]against Zidon, and prophesy against it,
22 And say, Thus saith the Lord GOD;
[r]Behold, I *am* against thee, O Zidon; and I
will be glorified in the midst of thee: and
[s]they shall know that I *am* the LORD, when
I shall have executed judgments in her, and
shall be [t]sanctified in her.
23 [u]For I will send into her pestilence,
and blood into her streets; and the wounded
shall be judged in the midst of her by the
sword upon her on every side; and they
shall know that I *am* the LORD.
24 ¶ And there shall be no more [v]a prick-
ing brier unto the house of Israel, nor *any*
grieving thorn of all *that are* round about
them, that despised them; and they shall
know that I *am* the Lord GOD.
25 Thus saith the Lord GOD; When I shall
have [w]gathered the house of Israel from the
people among whom they are scattered,
and shall be [x]sanctified in them in the sight
of the heathen, then shall they dwell in their
land that I have given to my servant Jacob.
26 And they shall [y]dwell safely therein,
and shall [z]build houses, and [a]plant vineyards; yea, they shall dwell with confidence, when I have executed judgments
upon all those that despise them round
about them; and they shall know that I *am*
the LORD their God.

29 In the tenth year, in the tenth *month*,
in the twelfth *day* of the month, the
word of the LORD came unto me, saying,
2 Son of man, [b]set thy face against Pharaoh king of Egypt, and prophesy against
him, and [c]against all Egypt:
3 Speak, and say, Thus saith the Lord
GOD; [d]Behold, I *am* against thee, Pharaoh
king of Egypt, the great [e]dragon that lieth
in the midst of his rivers, [f]which hath said,
My river *is* mine own, and I have made *it* for
myself.
4 But [g]I will put hooks in thy jaws, and I
will cause the fish of thy rivers to stick unto
thy scales, and I will bring thee up out of the
midst of thy rivers, and all the fish of thy
rivers shall stick unto thy scales.
5 And I will leave thee *thrown* into the
wilderness, thee and all the fish of thy rivers: thou shalt fall upon the open fields;
[h]thou shalt not be brought together, nor
gathered: [i]I have given thee for meat to the
beasts of the field and to the fowls of the
heaven.
6 And all the inhabitants of Egypt shall
know that I *am* the LORD, because they have
been a [j]staff of reed to the house of Israel.
7 [k]When they took hold of thee by thy
hand, thou didst break, and rend all their
shoulder: and when they leaned upon thee,
thou brakest, and madest all their loins to
be at a stand.
8 ¶ Therefore thus saith the Lord GOD;
Behold, I will bring [l]a sword upon thee,
and cut off man and beast out of thee.
9 And the land of Egypt shall be desolate
and waste; and they shall know that I *am*
the LORD: because he hath said, The river *is*
mine, and I have made *it*.
10 Behold, therefore I *am* against thee,
and against thy rivers, [m]and I will make the
land of Egypt utterly waste *and* desolate,
[n]from the tower of Syene even unto the
border of Ethiopia.
11 [o]No foot of man shall pass through it,
nor foot of beast shall pass through it, neither shall it be inhabited forty years.
12 [p]And I will make the land of Egypt
desolate in the midst of the countries *that*
are desolate, and her cities among the cities
that are laid waste shall be desolate forty
years: and I will scatter the Egyptians
among the nations, and will disperse them
through the countries.
13 ¶ Yet thus saith the Lord GOD; At the
[q]end of forty years will I gather the Egyptians from the people whither they were
scattered:
14 And I will bring again the captivity of
Egypt, and will cause them to return *into*
the land of Pathros, into the land of their
habitation; and they shall be there a [r]base
kingdom.
15 It shall be the basest of the kingdoms;
neither shall it exalt itself any more above
the nations: for I will diminish them, that
they shall no more rule over the nations.
16 And it shall be no more [s]the confidence of the house of Israel, which bringeth
their iniquity to remembrance, when they
shall look after them: but they shall know
that I *am* the Lord GOD.
17 ¶ And it came to pass in the seven and
twentieth year, in the first *month*, in the
first *day* of the month, the word of the LORD
came unto me, saying,

28:16 [m]ver. 14
28:17 [n]ver. 2
28:19 [o]ch. 26:21
28:21 [p]ch. 6:2 [q]Isa. 23:4; Jer. 25:22; ch. 32:30
28:22 [r]Ex. 14:4; ch. 39:13 [s]Ps. 9:16 [t]ch. 20:41; ver. 25
28:23 [u]ch. 38:22
28:24 [v]Num. 33:55; Josh. 23:13
28:25 [w]Isa. 11:12; ch. 11:17 [x]ver. 22
28:26 [y]Jer. 23:6; ch. 36:28 [z]Isa. 65:21; Am. 9:14 [a]Jer. 31:5
29:2 [b]ch. 28:21 [c]Isa. 19:1; Jer. 25:19
29:3 [d]Jer. 44:30; ch. 28:22; ver. 10 [e]Ps. 74:13; Isa. 27:1; ch. 32:2 [f]ch. 28:2
29:4 [g]Isa. 37:29; ch. 38:4
29:5 [h]Jer. 8:2 [i]Jer. 7:33
29:6 [j]2 Kings 18:21; Isa. 36:6
29:7 [k]Jer. 37:5; ch. 17:17
29:8 [l]ch. 14:17
29:10 [m]ch. 30:12 [n]ch. 30:6
29:11 [o]ch. 32:13
29:12 [p]ch. 30:7
29:13 [q]Isa. 19:23; Jer. 46:26
29:14 [r]ch. 17:6
29:16 [s]Isa. 30:2

18 Son of man, [t]Nebuchadrezzar king of
Babylon caused his army to serve a great
service against Tyrus: every head *was* made
bald, and every shoulder *was* peeled: yet
had he no wages, nor his army, for Tyrus,
for the service that he had served against it:
19 Therefore thus saith the Lord GOD; Behold, I will give the land of Egypt unto
Nebuchadrezzar king of Babylon; and he
shall take her multitude, and take her spoil,
and take her prey; and it shall be the wages
for his army.
20 I have given him the land of Egypt *for*
his labour wherewith he [u]served against it,
because they wrought for me, saith the Lord
GOD.
21 ¶ In that day [v]will I cause the horn of
the house of Israel to bud forth, and I will
give thee [w]the opening of the mouth in the
midst of them; and they shall know that I
am the LORD.

30 The word of the LORD came again
unto me, saying,
2 Son of man, prophesy and say, Thus
saith the Lord GOD; [x]Howl ye, Woe worth
the day!
3 For [y]the day *is* near, even the day of the
LORD *is* near, a cloudy day; it shall be the
time of the heathen.
4 And the sword shall come upon Egypt,
and great pain shall be in Ethiopia, when
the slain shall fall in Egypt, and they [z]shall
take away her multitude, and [a]her foundations shall be broken down.
5 Ethiopia, and Libya, and Lydia, and
[b]all the mingled people, and Chub, and the
men of the land that is in league, shall fall
with them by the sword.
6 Thus saith the LORD; They also that uphold Egypt shall fall; and the pride of her
power shall come down: [c]from the tower of
Syene shall they fall in it by the sword, saith
the Lord GOD.
7 [d]And they shall be desolate in the midst
of the countries *that are* desolate, and her
cities shall be in the midst of the cities *that
are* wasted.
8 And they shall know that I *am* the LORD,
when I have set a fire in Egypt, and *when* all
her helpers shall be destroyed.
9 In that day [e]shall messengers go forth
from me in ships to make the careless Ethiopians afraid, and great pain shall come
upon them, as in the day of Egypt: for, lo, it
cometh.
10 Thus saith the Lord GOD; [f]I will also
make the multitude of Egypt to cease by the
hand of Nebuchadrezzar king of Babylon.
11 He and his people with him, [g]the terrible of the nations, shall be brought to destroy the land: and they shall draw their
swords against Egypt, and fill the land with
the slain.
12 And [h]I will make the rivers dry, and
[i]sell the land into the hand of the wicked:
and I will make the land waste, and all that
is therein, by the hand of strangers: I the
LORD have spoken *it*.

29:18 [t]Jer. 27:6; ch. 26:7
29:20 [u]Jer. 25:9
29:21 [v]Ps. 132:17 [w]ch. 24:27
30:2 [x]Isa. 13:6
30:3 [y]ch. 7:7; Joel 2:1; Zeph. 1:7
30:4 [z]ch. 29:19 [a]Jer. 50:15
30:5 [b]Jer. 25:20
30:6 [c]ch. 29:10
30:7 [d]ch. 29:12
30:9 [e]Isa. 18:1
30:10 [f]ch. 29:19
30:11 [g]ch. 28:7
30:12 [h]Isa. 19:5 [i]Isa. 19:4
30:13 [j]Isa. 19:1; Jer. 43:12; Zech. 13:2 [k]Zech. 10:11 [l]Isa. 19:16
30:14 [m]ch. 29:14 [n]Ps. 78:12 [o]Nah. 3:8
30:15 [p]Jer. 46:25
30:16 [q]ver. 8
30:18 [r]Jer. 2:16
30:21 [s]Jer. 48:25 [t]Jer. 46:11
30:22 [u]Ps. 37:17
30:23 [v]ver. 26; ch. 29:12
30:25 [w]Ps. 9:16
30:26 [x]ver. 23; ch. 29:12
31:2 [y]ver. 18
31:3 [z]Dan. 4:10

13 Thus saith the Lord GOD; I will also
[j]destroy the idols, and I will cause *their*
images to cease out of Noph; [k]and there
shall be no more a prince of the land of
Egypt: [l]and I will put a fear in the land of
Egypt.
14 And I will make [m]Pathros desolate,
and will set fire in [n]Zoan, [o]and will execute
judgments in No.
15 And I will pour my fury upon Sin, the
strength of Egypt; and [p]I will cut off the
multitude of No.
16 And I will [q]set fire in Egypt: Sin shall
have great pain, and No shall be rent asunder, and Noph *shall have* distresses daily.
17 The young men of Aven and of Pi-
beseth shall fall by the sword: and these *cities* shall go into captivity.
18 [r]At Tehaphnehes also the day shall
be darkened, when I shall break there the
yokes of Egypt: and the pomp of her
strength shall cease in her: as for her, a
cloud shall cover her, and her daughters
shall go into captivity.
19 Thus will I execute judgments in
Egypt: and they shall know that I *am* the
LORD.
20 ¶ And it came to pass in the eleventh
year, in the first *month,* in the seventh *day*
of the month, *that* the word of the LORD
came unto me, saying,
21 Son of man, I have [s]broken the arm of
Pharaoh king of Egypt; and, lo, [t]it shall not
be bound up to be healed, to put a roller to
bind it, to make it strong to hold the sword.
22 Therefore thus saith the Lord GOD; Behold, I *am* against Pharaoh king of Egypt,
and will [u]break his arms, the strong, and
that which was broken; and I will cause the
sword to fall out of his hand.
23 [v]And I will scatter the Egyptians
among the nations, and will disperse them
through the countries.
24 And I will strengthen the arms of the
king of Babylon, and put my sword in his
hand: but I will break Pharaoh's arms, and
he shall groan before him with the groanings of a deadly wounded *man.*
25 But I will strengthen the arms of the
king of Babylon, and the arms of Pharaoh
shall fall down; and [w]they shall know that
I *am* the LORD, when I shall put my sword
into the hand of the king of Babylon, and he
shall stretch it out upon the land of Egypt.
26 [x]And I will scatter the Egyptians
among the nations, and disperse them
among the countries; and they shall know
that I *am* the LORD.

31 And it came to pass in the eleventh
year, in the third *month,* in the first
day of the month, *that* the word of the LORD
came unto me, saying,
2 Son of man, speak unto Pharaoh king of
Egypt, and to his multitude; [y]Whom art
thou like in thy greatness?
3 ¶ [z]Behold, the Assyrian *was* a cedar
in Lebanon with fair branches, and with a

shadowing shroud, and of an high stature;
and his top was among the thick boughs.
4 [a]The waters made him great, the deep
set him up on high with her rivers running
round about his plants, and sent out her little rivers unto all the trees of the field.
5 Therefore [b]his height was exalted
above all the trees of the field, and his
boughs were multiplied, and his branches
became long because of the multitude of
waters, when he shot forth.
6 All the [c]fowls of heaven made their
nests in his boughs, and under his branches
did all the beasts of the field bring forth
their young, and under his shadow dwelt all
great nations.
7 Thus was he fair in his greatness, in the
length of his branches: for his root was by
great waters.
8 The cedars in the [d]garden of God could
not hide him: the fir trees were not like his
boughs, and the chestnut trees were not like
his branches; nor any tree in the garden of
God was like unto him in his beauty.
9 I have made him fair by the multitude of
his branches: so that all the trees of Eden,
that *were* in the garden of God, envied him.
10 ¶ Therefore thus saith the Lord GOD;
Because thou hast lifted up thyself in
height, and he hath shot up his top among
the thick boughs, and [e]his heart is lifted up
in his height;
11 I have therefore delivered him into the
hand of the mighty one of the heathen; he
shall surely deal with him: I have driven
him out for his wickedness.
12 And strangers, [f]the terrible of the nations, have cut him off, and have left him:
[g]upon the mountains and in all the valleys
his branches are fallen, and his boughs are
broken by all the rivers of the land; and all
the people of the earth are gone down from
his shadow, and have left him.
13 [h]Upon his ruin shall all the fowls of
the heaven remain, and all the beasts of the
field shall be upon his branches:
14 To the end that none of all the trees by
the waters exalt themselves for their height,
neither shoot up their top among the thick
boughs, neither their trees stand up in their
height, all that drink water: for [i]they are all
delivered unto death, [j]to the nether parts of
the earth, in the midst of the children of
men, with them that go down to the pit.
15 Thus saith the Lord GOD; In the day
when he went down to the grave I caused a
mourning: I covered the deep for him, and I
restrained the floods thereof, and the great
waters were stayed: and I caused Lebanon
to mourn for him, and all the trees of the
field fainted for him.
16 I made the nations to [k]shake at the
sound of his fall, when I [l]cast him down to
hell with them that descend into the pit: and
[m]all the trees of Eden, the choice and best of
Lebanon, all that drink water, [n]shall be
comforted in the nether parts of the earth.
17 They also went down into hell with

31:4 [a]Jer. 51:36
31:5 [b]Dan. 4:11
31:6 [c]ch. 17:23; Dan. 4:12
31:8 [d]Gen. 2:8; ch. 28:13
31:10 [e]Dan. 5:20
31:12 [f]ch. 28:7 [g]ch. 32:5
31:13 [h]Isa. 18:6; ch. 32:4
31:14 [i]Ps. 82:7 [j]ch. 32:18
31:16 [k]ch. 26:15 [l]Isa. 14:15 [m]Isa. 14:8 [n]ch. 32:31
31:17 [o]Lam. 4:20
31:18 [p]ver. 2; ch. 32:19 [q]ch. 28:10
32:2 [r]ch. 27:2; ver. 16 [s]ch. 19:3 [t]ch. 29:3 [u]ch. 34:18
32:3 [v]ch. 12:13; Hos. 7:12
32:4 [w]ch. 29:5 [x]ch. 31:13
32:5 [y]ch. 31:12
32:7 [z]Isa. 13:10; Joel 2:31; Am. 8:9; Rev. 6:12; Matt. 24:29
32:10 [a]ch. 27:35 [b]ch. 26:16
32:11 [c]Jer. 46:26; ch. 30:4
32:12 [d]ch. 28:7 [e]ch. 29:19
32:13 [f]ch. 29:11

him unto *them that be* slain with the sword;
and *they that were* his arm, *that* [o]dwelt
under his shadow in the midst of the heathen.
18 ¶ [p]To whom art thou thus like in glory
and in greatness among the trees of Eden?
yet shalt thou be brought down with the
trees of Eden unto the nether parts of the
earth: [q]thou shalt lie in the midst of the uncircumcised with *them that be* slain by the
sword. This *is* Pharaoh and all his multitude, saith the Lord GOD.

32 And it came to pass in the twelfth
year, in the twelfth month, in the first
day of the month, *that* the word of the LORD
came unto me, saying,
2 Son of man, [r]take up a lamentation for
Pharaoh king of Egypt, and say unto him,
[s]Thou art like a young lion of the nations,
[t]and thou *art* as a whale in the seas: and
thou camest forth with thy rivers, and trou-
bledst the waters with thy feet, and [u]fou-
ledst their rivers.
3 Thus saith the Lord GOD; I will therefore [v]spread out my net over thee with a
company of many people; and they shall
bring thee up in my net.
4 Then [w]will I leave thee upon the land, I
will cast thee forth upon the open field, and
[x]will cause all the fowls of the heaven to
remain upon thee, and I will fill the beasts of
the whole earth with thee.
5 And I will lay thy flesh [y]upon the
mountains, and fill the valleys with thy
height.
6 I will also water with thy blood the land
wherein thou swimmest, *even* to the mountains; and the rivers shall be full of thee.
7 And when I shall put thee out, [z]I will
cover the heaven, and make the stars
thereof dark; I will cover the sun with a
cloud, and the moon shall not give her light.
8 All the bright lights of heaven will I
make dark over thee, and set darkness upon
thy land, saith the Lord GOD.
9 I will also vex the hearts of many people, when I shall bring thy destruction
among the nations, into the countries which
thou hast not known.
10 Yea, I will make many people
[a]amazed at thee, and their kings shall be
horribly afraid for thee, when I shall bran-
dish my sword before them; and [b]they shall
tremble at *every* moment, every man for his
own life, in the day of thy fall.
11 ¶ [c]For thus saith the Lord GOD; The
sword of the king of Babylon shall come
upon thee.
12 By the swords of the mighty will I
cause thy multitude to fall, [d]the terrible of
the nations, all of them: and [e]they shall
spoil the pomp of Egypt, and all the multitude thereof shall be destroyed.
13 I will destroy also all the beasts thereof
from beside the great waters; [f]neither shall
the foot of man trouble them any more, nor
the hoofs of beasts trouble them.
14 Then will I make their waters deep,

nd cause their rivers to run like oil, saith he Lord GOD.

15 When I shall make the land of Egypt desolate, and the country shall be destitute of that whereof it was full, when I shall smite all them that dwell therein, [g]then shall they know that I *am* the LORD.

16 This *is* the [h]lamentation wherewith they shall lament her: the daughters of the nations shall lament her: they shall lament for her, *even* for Egypt, and for all her multitude, saith the Lord GOD.

17 ¶ It came to pass also in the twelfth year, in the fifteenth *day* of the month, *that* the word of the LORD came unto me, saying,

18 Son of man, wail for the multitude of Egypt, and [i]cast them down, *even* her, and the daughters of the famous nations, unto the nether parts of the earth, with them that go down into the pit.

19 [j]Whom dost thou pass in beauty? [k]go down, and be thou laid with the uncircumcised.

20 They shall fall in the midst of *them that are* slain by the sword: she is delivered to the sword: draw her and all her multitudes.

21 [l]The strong among the mighty shall speak to him out of the midst of hell with them that help him: they are [m]gone down, they lie uncircumcised, slain by the sword.

22 [n]Asshur *is* there and all her company: his graves *are* about him: all of them slain, fallen by the sword:

23 [o]Whose graves are set in the sides of the pit, and her company is round about her grave: all of them slain, fallen by the sword, which [p]caused terror in the land of the living.

24 There *is* [q]Elam and all her multitude round about her grave, all of them slain, fallen by the sword, which are [r]gone down uncircumcised into the nether parts of the earth, [s]which caused their terror in the land of the living; yet have they borne their shame with them that go down to the pit.

25 They have set her a bed in the midst of the slain with all her multitude: her graves *are* round about him: all of them uncircumcised, slain by the sword: though their terror was caused in the land of the living, yet have they borne their shame with them that go down to the pit: he is put in the midst of *them that be* slain.

26 There *is* [t]Meshech, Tubal, and all her multitude: her graves *are* round about him: all of them [u]uncircumcised, slain by the sword, though they caused their terror in the land of the living.

27 [v]And they shall not lie with the mighty *that are* fallen of the uncircumcised, which are gone down to hell with their weapons of war: and they have laid their swords under their heads, but their iniquities shall be upon their bones, though *they were* the terror of the mighty in the land of the living.

28 Yea, thou shalt be broken in the midst of the uncircumcised, and shalt lie with *them that are* slain with the sword.

29 There *is* [w]Edom, her kings, and all her princes, which with their might are laid by *them that were* slain by the sword: they shall lie with the uncircumcised, and with them that go down to the pit.

30 [x]There *be* the princes of the north, all of them, and all the [y]Zidonians, which are gone down with the slain; with their terror they are ashamed of their might; and they lie uncircumcised with *them that be* slain by the sword, and bear their shame with them that go down to the pit.

31 Pharaoh shall see them, and shall be [z]comforted over all his multitude, *even* Pharaoh and all his army slain by the sword, saith the Lord GOD.

32 For I have caused my terror in the land of the living: and he shall be laid in the midst of the uncircumcised with *them that are* slain with the sword, *even* Pharaoh and all his multitude, saith the Lord GOD.

33 Again the word of the LORD came unto me, saying,

2 Son of man, speak to [a]the children of thy people, and say unto them, [b]When I bring the sword upon a land, if the people of the land take a man of their coasts, and set him for their [c]watchman:

3 If when he seeth the sword come upon the land, he blow the trumpet, and warn the people;

4 Then whosoever heareth the sound of the trumpet, and taketh not warning; if the sword come, and take him away, [d]his blood shall be upon his own head.

5 He heard the sound of the trumpet, and took not warning; his blood shall be upon him. But he that taketh warning shall deliver his soul.

6 But if the watchman see the sword come, and blow not the trumpet, and the people be not warned; if the sword come, and take *any* person from among them, [e]he is taken away in his iniquity; but his blood will I require at the watchman's hand.

7 ¶ [f]So thou, O son of man, I have set thee a watchman unto the house of Israel; therefore thou shalt hear the word at my mouth, and warn them from me.

8 When I say unto the wicked, O wicked *man*, thou shalt surely die; if thou dost not speak to warn the wicked from his way, that wicked *man* shall die in his iniquity; but his blood will I require at thine hand.

9 Nevertheless, if thou warn the wicked of his way to turn from it; if he do not turn from his way, he shall die in his iniquity; but thou hast delivered thy soul.

10 Therefore, O thou son of man, speak unto the house of Israel; Thus ye speak, saying, If our transgressions and our sins *be* upon us, and we [g]pine away in them, [h]how should we then live?

11 Say unto them, *As* I live, saith the Lord GOD, [i]I have no pleasure in the death of the wicked; but that the wicked turn from his

32:15 [g]Ex. 7:5; Ps. 9:16; ch. 6:7
32:16 [h]ver. 2; 2 Sam. 1:17; 2 Chron. 35:25; ch. 26:17
32:18 [i]ch. 26:20
32:19 [j]ch. 31:2 [k]ver. 21; ch. 28:10
32:21 [l]Isa. 1:31; ver. 27 [m]ver. 19
32:22 [n]ver. 24
32:23 [o]Isa. 14:15 [p]ch. 26:17; ver. 24
32:24 [q]Jer. 49:34 [r]ver. 21 [s]ver. 23
32:26 [t]Gen. 10:2; ch. 27:13 [u]ver. 19
32:27 [v]ver. 21; Isa. 14:18
32:29 [w]ch. 25:12
32:30 [x]ch. 38:6 [y]ch. 28:21
32:31 [z]ch. 31:16
33:2 [a]ch. 3:11 [b]ch. 14:17 [c]2 Sam. 18:24; 2 Kings 9:17; ver. 7; Hos. 9:8
33:4 [d]ch. 18:13
33:6 [e]ver. 8
33:7 [f]ch. 3:17
33:10 [g]ch. 24:23 [h]Isa. 49:14; ch. 37:11
33:11 [i]2 Sam. 14:14; ch. 18:23; 2 Pet. 3:9

way and live: turn ye, turn ye from your evil ways; for [j]why will ye die, O house of Israel?

12 Therefore, thou son of man, say unto the children of thy people, The [k]righteousness of the righteous shall not deliver him in the day of his transgression: as for the wickedness of the wicked, [l]he shall not fall thereby in the day that he turneth from his wickedness; neither shall the righteous be able to live for his *righteousness* in the day that he sinneth.

13 When I shall say to the righteous, *that* he shall surely live; [m]if he trust to his own righteousness, and commit iniquity, all his righteousnesses shall not be remembered; but for his iniquity that he hath committed, he shall die for it.

14 Again, [n]when I say unto the wicked, Thou shalt surely die; if he turn from his sin, and do that which is lawful and right;

15 *If* the wicked [o]restore the pledge, [p]give again that he had robbed, walk in [q]the statutes of life, without committing iniquity; he shall surely live, he shall not die.

16 [r]None of his sins that he hath committed shall be mentioned unto him: he hath done that which is lawful and right; he shall surely live.

17 ¶ [s]Yet the children of thy people say, The way of the Lord is not equal: but as for them, their way is not equal.

18 [t]When the righteous turneth from his righteousness, and committeth iniquity, he shall even die thereby.

19 But if the wicked turn from his wickedness, and do that which is lawful and right, he shall live thereby.

20 ¶ Yet ye say, [u]The way of the Lord is not equal. O ye house of Israel, I will judge you every one after his ways.

21 ¶ And it came to pass in the twelfth year [v]of our captivity, in the tenth *month,* in the fifth *day* of the month, [w]*that* one that had escaped out of Jerusalem came unto me, saying, [x]The city is smitten.

22 Now [y]the hand of the LORD was upon me in the evening, afore he that was escaped came; and had opened my mouth, until he came to me in the morning; [z]and my mouth was opened, and I was no more dumb.

23 Then the word of the LORD came unto me, saying,

24 Son of man, [a]they that inhabit those [b]wastes of the land of Israel speak, saying, [c]Abraham was one, and he inherited the land: [d]but we *are* many; the land is given us for inheritance.

25 Wherefore say unto them, Thus saith the Lord GOD; [e]Ye eat with the blood, and [f]lift up your eyes toward your idols, and [g]shed blood: and shall ye possess the land?

26 Ye stand upon your sword, ye work abomination, and ye [h]defile every one his neighbour's wife: and shall ye possess the land?

27 Say thou thus unto them, Thus saith the Lord GOD; *As* I live, surely [i]they that *are* in the wastes shall fall by the sword, and him that *is* in the open field [j]will I give to the beasts to be devoured, and they that *be* in the forts and [k]in the caves shall die of the pestilence.

28 [l]For I will lay the land most desolate, and the [m]pomp of her strength shall cease; and [n]the mountains of Israel shall be desolate, that none shall pass through.

29 Then shall they know that I *am* the LORD, when I have laid the land most desolate because of all their abominations which they have committed.

30 ¶ Also, thou son of man, the children of thy people still are talking against thee by the walls and in the doors of the houses, and [o]speak one to another, every one to his brother, saying, Come, I pray you, and hear what is the word that cometh forth from the LORD.

31 And [p]they come unto thee as the people cometh, and they [q]sit before thee *as* my people, and they hear thy words, but they will not do them: [r]for with their mouth they shew much love, *but* [s]their heart goeth after their covetousness.

32 And, lo, thou *art* unto them as a very lovely song of one that hath a pleasant voice, and can play well on an instrument: for they hear thy words, but they do them not.

33 [t]And when this cometh to pass, (lo, it will come,) then [u]shall they know that a prophet hath been among them.

34 And the word of the LORD came unto me, saying,

2 Son of man, prophesy against the [v]shepherds of Israel, prophesy, and say unto them, Thus saith the Lord GOD unto the shepherds; [w]Woe *be* to the shepherds of Israel that do feed themselves! should not the shepherds feed the flocks?

3 [x]Ye eat the fat, and ye clothe you with the wool, [y]ye kill them that are fed: *but* ye feed not the flock.

4 [z]The diseased have ye not strengthened, neither have ye healed that which was sick, neither have ye bound up *that which was* broken, neither have ye brought again that which was driven away, neither have ye [a]sought that which was lost; but with [b]force and with cruelty have ye ruled them.

5 [c]And they were [d]scattered, because *there is* no shepherd: [e]and they became meat to all the beasts of the field, when they were scattered.

6 My sheep wandered through all the mountains, and upon every high hill: yea, my flock was scattered upon all the face of the earth, and none did search or seek *after them.*

7 ¶ Therefore, ye shepherds, hear the word of the LORD;

8 *As* I live, saith the Lord GOD, surely because my flock became a prey, and my flock [f]became meat to every beast of the field, because *there was* no shepherd, neither did

33:11 [j]ch. 18:31
33:12 [k]ch. 3:20 [l]2 Chron. 7:14
33:13 [m]ch. 3:20
33:14 [n]ch. 3:18
33:15 [o]ch. 18:7 [p]Ex. 22:1; Lev. 6:2; Num. 5:6; Luke 19:8 [q]Lev. 18:5; ch. 20:11
33:16 [r]ch. 18:22
33:17 [s]ver. 20; ch. 18:25
33:18 [t]ch. 18:26
33:20 [u]ver. 17; ch. 18:25
33:21 [v]ch. 1:2 [w]ch. 24:26 [x]2 Kings 25:4
33:22 [y]ch. 1:3 [z]ch. 24:27
33:24 [a]ch. 34:2 [b]ver. 27; ch. 36:4 [c]Isa. 51:2; Acts 7:5 [d]Mic. 3:11; Matt. 3:9; John 8:39
33:25 [e]Gen. 9:4; Lev. 3:17; Deut. 12:16 [f]ch. 18:6 [g]ch. 22:6
33:26 [h]ch. 18:6
33:27 [i]ver. 24 [j]ch. 39:4 [k]Judg. 6:2; 1 Sam. 13:6
33:28 [l]Jer. 44:2; ch. 36:34 [m]ch. 7:24 [n]ch. 6:2
33:30 [o]Isa. 29:13
33:31 [p]ch. 14:1 [q]ch. 8:1 [r]Ps. 78:36; Isa. 29:13 [s]Matt. 13:22
33:33 [t]1 Sam. 3:20 [u]ch. 2:5
34:2 [v]ch. 33:24 [w]Jer. 23:1; Zech. 11:17
34:3 [x]Isa. 56:11; Zech. 11:16 [y]ch. 33:25; Mic. 3:1; Zech. 11:5
34:4 [z]ver. 16; Zech. 11:16 [a]Luke 15:4 [b]1 Pet. 5:3
34:5 [c]ch. 33:21 [d]1 Kings 22:17; Matt. 9:36 [e]Isa. 56:9; Jer. 12:9; ver. 8
34:8 [f]ver. 5

my shepherds search for my flock, [g]but the shepherds fed themselves, and fed not my flock;

9 Therefore, O ye shepherds, hear the word of the LORD;

10 Thus saith the Lord GOD; Behold, I *am* against the shepherds; and [h]I will require my flock at their hand, and cause them to cease from feeding the flock; neither shall the shepherds [i]feed themselves any more; for I will deliver my flock from their mouth, that they may not be meat for them.

11 ¶ For thus saith the Lord GOD; Behold, I, *even* I, will both search my sheep, and seek them out.

12 As a shepherd seeketh out his flock in the day that he is among his sheep *that are* scattered; so will I seek out my sheep, and will deliver them out of all places where they have been scattered in [j]the cloudy and dark day.

13 And [k]I will bring them out from the people, and gather them from the countries, and will bring them to their own land, and feed them upon the mountains of Israel by the rivers, and in all the inhabited places of the country.

14 [l]I will feed them in a good pasture, and upon the high mountains of Israel shall their fold be: [m]there shall they lie in a good fold, and *in* a fat pasture shall they feed upon the mountains of Israel.

15 I will feed my flock, and I will cause them to lie down, saith the Lord GOD.

16 [n]I will seek that which was lost, and bring again that which was driven away, and will bind up *that which was* broken, and will strengthen that which was sick: but I will destroy [o]the fat and the strong; I will feed them [p]with judgment.

17 And *as for* you, O my flock, thus saith the Lord GOD; [q]Behold, I judge between cattle and cattle, between the rams and the he goats.

18 *Seemeth it* a small thing unto you to have eaten up the good pasture, but ye must tread down with your feet the residue of your pastures? and to have drunk of the deep waters, but ye must foul the residue with your feet?

19 And *as for* my flock, they eat that which ye have trodden with your feet; and they drink that which ye have fouled with your feet.

20 ¶ Therefore thus saith the Lord GOD unto them; [r]Behold, I, *even* I, will judge between the fat cattle and between the lean cattle.

21 Because ye have thrust with side and with shoulder, and pushed all the diseased with your horns, till ye have scattered them abroad;

22 Therefore will I save my flock, and they shall no more be a prey; and [s]I will judge between cattle and cattle.

23 And I will set up one [t]shepherd over them, and he shall feed them, [u]*even* my servant David; he shall feed them, and he shall be their shepherd.

24 And [v]I the LORD will be their God, and my servant David [w]a prince among them; I the LORD have spoken *it*.

25 And [x]I will make with them a covenant of peace, and [y]will cause the evil beasts to cease out of the land: and they [z]shall dwell safely in the wilderness, and sleep in the woods.

26 And I will make them and the places round about [a]my hill [b]a blessing; and I will [c]cause the shower to come down in his season; there shall be [d]showers of blessing.

27 And [e]the tree of the field shall yield her fruit, and the earth shall yield her increase, and they shall be safe in their land, and shall know that I *am* the LORD, when I have [f]broken the bands of their yoke, and delivered them out of the hand of those that [g]served themselves of them.

28 And they shall no more [h]be a prey to the heathen, neither shall the beast of the land devour them; but [i]they shall dwell safely, and none shall make *them* afraid.

29 And I will raise up for them a [j]plant of renown, and they shall be no more consumed with hunger in the land, [k]neither bear the shame of the heathen any more.

30 Thus shall they know that [l]I the LORD their God *am* with them, and that they, *even* the house of Israel, *are* my people, saith the Lord GOD.

31 And ye my [m]flock, the flock of my pasture, *are* men, *and* I *am* your God, saith the Lord GOD.

35

Moreover the word of the LORD came unto me, saying,

2 Son of man, [n]set thy face against [o]mount Seir, and [p]prophesy against it,

3 And say unto it, Thus saith the Lord GOD; Behold, O mount Seir, I *am* against thee, and [q]I will stretch out mine hand against thee, and I will make thee most desolate.

4 [r]I will lay thy cities waste, and thou shalt be desolate, and thou shalt know that I *am* the LORD.

5 [s]Because thou hast had a perpetual hatred, and hast shed *the blood of* the children of Israel by the force of the sword in the time of their calamity, [t]in the time *that their* iniquity *had* an end:

6 Therefore, *as* I live, saith the Lord GOD, I will prepare thee unto blood, and blood shall pursue thee: [u]sith thou hast not hated blood, even blood shall pursue thee.

7 Thus will I make mount Seir most desolate, and cut off from it [v]him that passeth out and him that returneth.

8 [w]And I will fill his mountains with his slain *men:* in thy hills, and in thy valleys, and in all thy rivers, shall they fall that are slain with the sword.

9 [x]I will make thee perpetual desolations, and thy cities shall not return: [y]and ye shall know that I *am* the LORD.

10 Because thou hast said, These two na-

34:8 [g]ver. 2
34:10 [h]ch. 3:18; Heb. 13:17 [i]ver. 2
34:12 [j]ch. 30:3; Joel 2:2
34:13 [k]Isa. 65:9; Jer. 23:3; ch. 28:25
34:14 [l]Ps. 23:2 [m]Jer. 33:12
34:16 [n]ver. 4; Isa. 40:11; Mic. 4:6; Matt. 18:11; Mark 2:17; Luke 5:32 [o]Isa. 10:16; Am. 4:1 [p]Jer. 10:24
34:17 [q]ch. 20:37; ver. 20; Zech. 10:3; Matt. 25:32
34:20 [r]ver. 17
34:22 [s]ver. 17
34:23 [t]Isa. 40:11; Jer. 23:4; John 10:11; Heb. 13:20; 1 Pet. 2:25 [u]Jer. 30:9; ch. 37:24; Hos. 3:5
34:24 [v]ver. 30; Ex. 29:45; ch. 37:27 [w]ch. 37:22; Luke 1:32
34:25 [x]ch. 37:26 [y]Lev. 26:6; Isa. 11:6-9; Hos. 2:18 [z]ver. 28; Jer. 23:6
34:26 [a]Isa. 56:7; ch. 20:40 [b]Gen. 12:2; Isa. 19:24; Zech. 8:13 [c]Lev. 26:4 [d]Ps. 68:9; Mal. 3:10
34:27 [e]Lev. 26:4; Ps. 85:12; Isa. 4:2 [f]Lev. 26:13; Jer. 2:20 [g]Jer. 25:14
34:28 [h]ver. 8; ch. 36:4 [i]ver. 25; Jer. 30:10
34:29 [j]Isa. 11:1; Jer. 23:5 [k]ch. 36:3
34:30 [l]ver. 24; ch. 37:27
34:31 [m]Ps. 100:3; John 10:11
35:2 [n]ch. 6:2 [o]Deut. 2:5 [p]Jer. 49:7; ch. 25:12; Am. 1:11; Obad. 10
35:3 [q]ch. 6:14
35:4 [r]ver. 9
35:5 [s]ch. 25:12; Obad. 10 [t]Ps. 137:7; ch. 21:25; Dan. 9:24; Obad. 11
35:6 [u]Ps. 109:17
35:7 [v]Judg. 5:6; ch. 29:11
35:8 [w]ch. 31:12
35:9 [x]Jer. 49:17; ver. 4; ch. 25:13; Mal. 1:3 [y]ch. 6:7

tions and these two countries shall be mine,
and we will [z]possess it; whereas [a]the LORD
was there:
11 Therefore, *as* I live, saith the Lord
GOD, I will even do [b]according to thine anger, and according to thine envy which thou
hast used out of thy hatred against them;
and I will make myself known among them,
when I have judged thee.
12 [c]And thou shalt know that I *am* the
LORD, *and that* I have heard all thy blasphemies which thou hast spoken against the
mountains of Israel, saying, They are laid
desolate, they are given us to consume.
13 Thus [d]with your mouth ye have
boasted against me, and have multiplied
your words against me: I have heard *them*.
14 Thus saith the Lord GOD; [e]When the
whole earth rejoiceth, I will make thee desolate.
15 [f]As thou didst rejoice at the inheritance of the house of Israel, because it was
desolate, so will I do unto thee: [g]thou shalt
be desolate, O mount Seir, and all Idumea,
even all of it: and they shall know that I *am*
the LORD.

36 Also, thou son of man, prophesy
unto the [h]mountains of Israel, and
say, Ye mountains of Israel, hear the word
of the LORD:
2 Thus saith the Lord GOD; Because [i]the
enemy hath said against you, Aha, [j]even
the ancient high places [k]are ours in possession:
3 Therefore prophesy and say, Thus saith
the Lord GOD; Because they have made *you*
desolate, and swallowed you up on every
side, that ye might be a possession unto the
residue of the heathen, [l]and ye are taken
up in the lips of talkers, and *are* an infamy
of the people:
4 Therefore, ye mountains of Israel, hear
the word of the Lord GOD; Thus saith the
Lord GOD to the mountains, and to the hills,
to the rivers, and to the valleys, to the desolate wastes, and to the cities that are forsaken, which [m]became a prey and [n]deri-
sion to the residue of the heathen that *are*
round about;
5 Therefore thus saith the Lord GOD;
[o]Surely in the fire of my jealousy have I
spoken against the residue of the heathen,
and against all Idumea, [p]which have appointed my land into their possession with
the joy of all *their* heart, with despiteful
minds, to cast it out for a prey.
6 Prophesy therefore concerning the land
of Israel, and say unto the mountains, and
to the hills, to the rivers, and to the valleys,
Thus saith the Lord GOD; Behold, I have
spoken in my jealousy and in my fury, because ye have [q]borne the shame of the heathen:
7 Therefore thus saith the Lord GOD; I
have [r]lifted up mine hand, Surely the heathen that are about you, they shall bear
their shame.
8 ¶ But ye, O mountains of Israel, ye shall
shoot forth your branches, and yield your
fruit to my people of Israel; for they are at
hand to come.
9 For, behold, I *am* for you, and I will turn
unto you, and ye shall be tilled and sown:
10 And I will multiply men upon you, all
the house of Israel, *even* all of it: and the
cities shall be inhabited, and [s]the wastes
shall be builded:
11 And [t]I will multiply upon you man
and beast; and they shall increase and bring
fruit: and I will settle you after your old estates, and will do better *unto you* than at
your beginnings; [u]and ye shall know that I
am the LORD.
12 Yea, I will cause men to walk upon
you, *even* my people Israel; [v]and they shall
possess thee, and thou shalt be their inheritance, and thou shalt no more henceforth
[w]bereave them *of men*.
13 Thus saith the Lord GOD; Because they
say unto you, [x]Thou *land* devourest up
men, and hast bereaved thy nations;
14 Therefore thou shalt devour men no
more, neither bereave thy nations any
more, saith the Lord GOD.
15 [y]Neither will I cause *men* to hear in
thee the shame of the heathen any more,
neither shalt thou bear the reproach of the
people any more, neither shalt thou cause
thy nations to fall any more, saith the Lord
GOD.
16 ¶ Moreover the word of the LORD came
unto me, saying,
17 Son of man, when the house of Israel
dwelt in their own land, [z]they defiled it by
their own way and by their doings: their
way was before me as the [a]uncleanness of
a removed woman.
18 Wherefore I poured my fury upon
them [b]for the blood that they had shed
upon the land, and for their idols *wherewith*
they had polluted it:
19 And I [c]scattered them among the heathen, and they were dispersed through the
countries: [d]according to their way and according to their doings I judged them.
20 And when they entered unto the heathen, whither they went, they [e]profaned
my holy name, when they said to them,
These *are* the people of the LORD, and are
gone forth out of his land.
21 ¶ But I had pity [f]for mine holy name,
which the house of Israel had profaned
among the heathen, whither they went.
22 Therefore say unto the house of Israel,
Thus saith the Lord GOD; I do not *this* for
your sakes, O house of Israel, [g]but for mine
holy name's sake, which ye have profaned
among the heathen, whither ye went.
23 And I will sanctify my great name,
which was profaned among the heathen,
which ye have profaned in the midst of
them; and the heathen shall know that I *am*
the LORD, saith the Lord GOD, when I shall
be [h]sanctified in you before their eyes.
24 For [i]I will take you from among the

35:10 [z]Ps. 83:4; ch. 36:5; Obad. 13 [a]Ps. 48:1; ch. 48:35
35:11 [b]Matt. 7:2; Jam. 2:13
35:12 cch. 6:7; Ps. 9:16
35:13 [d]1 Sam. 2:3; Rev. 13:6
35:14 [e]Isa. 65:13
35:15 [f]Obad. 12 [g]ver. 3
36:1 [h]ch. 6:2
36:2 [i]ch. 25:3 [j]Deut. 32:13 [k]ch. 35:10
36:3 [l]Deut. 28:37; 1 Kings 9:7; Lam. 2:15; Dan. 9:16
36:4 [m]ch. 34:28 [n]Ps. 79:4
36:5 [o]Deut. 4:24; ch. 38:19 [p]ch. 35:10
36:6 [q]Ps. 123:3; ch. 34:29; ver. 15
36:7 [r]ch. 20:5
36:10 [s]ver. 33; Isa. 58:12; Am. 9:14
36:11 [t]Jer. 31:27 [u]ch. 35:9
36:12 [v]Obad. 17 [w]Jer. 15:7
36:13 [x]Num. 13:32
36:15 [y]ch. 34:29
36:17 [z]Lev. 18:25; Jer. 2:7 [a]Lev. 15:19
36:18 [b]ch. 16:36
36:19 [c]ch. 22:15 [d]ch. 7:3
36:20 [e]Isa. 52:5; Rom. 2:24
36:21 [f]ch. 20:9
36:22 [g]Ps. 106:8
36:23 [h]ch. 20:41
36:24 [i]ch. 34:13

heathen, and gather you out of all countries,
and will bring you into your own land.
25 ¶ [j]Then will I sprinkle clean water
upon you, and ye shall be clean: [k]from all
your filthiness, and from all your idols, will
I cleanse you.
26 A [l]new heart also will I give you, and
a new spirit will I put within you: and I will
take away the stony heart out of your flesh,
and I will give you an heart of flesh.
27 And I will put my [m]spirit within you,
and cause you to walk in my statutes, and
ye shall keep my judgments, and do *them.*
28 [n]And ye shall dwell in the land that I
gave to your fathers; [o]and ye shall be my
people, and I will be your God.
29 I will also [p]save you from all your un-
cleannesses: and [q]I will call for the corn,
and will increase it, and [r]lay no famine
upon you.
30 [s]And I will multiply the fruit of the
tree, and the increase of the field, that ye
shall receive no more reproach of famine
among the heathen.
31 Then [t]shall ye remember your own
evil ways, and your doings that *were* not
good, and [u]shall lothe yourselves in your
own sight for your iniquities and for your
abominations.
32 [v]Not for your sakes do I *this,* saith
the Lord GOD, be it known unto you: be
ashamed and confounded for your own
ways, O house of Israel.
33 Thus saith the Lord GOD; In the day
that I shall have cleansed you from all your
iniquities I will also cause *you* to dwell in
the cities, [w]and the wastes shall be builded.
34 And the desolate land shall be tilled,
whereas it lay desolate in the sight of all
that passed by.
35 And they shall say, This land that was
desolate is become like the garden of
[x]Eden; and the waste and desolate and ruined cities *are become* fenced, *and* are inhabited.
36 Then the heathen that are left round
about you shall know that I the LORD build
the ruined *places, and* plant that that was
desolate: [y]I the LORD have spoken *it,* and I
will do *it.*
37 Thus saith the Lord GOD; [z]I will yet *for*
this be enquired of by the house of Israel, to
do *it* for them; I will [a]increase them with
men like a flock.
38 As the holy flock, as the flock of Jerusalem in her solemn feasts; so shall the
waste cities be filled with flocks of men: and
they shall know that I *am* the LORD.

37 The [b]hand of the LORD was upon me,
and carried me out [c]in the spirit of
the LORD, and set me down in the midst of
the valley which *was* full of bones,
2 And caused me to pass by them round
about: and, behold, *there were* very many in
the open valley; and, lo, *they were* very dry.
3 And he said unto me, Son of man, can
these bones live? And I answered, O Lord
GOD, [d]thou knowest.
4 Again he said unto me, Prophesy upon
these bones, and say unto them, O ye dry
bones, hear the word of the LORD.
5 Thus saith the Lord GOD unto these
bones; Behold, I will [e]cause breath to enter
into you, and ye shall live:
6 And I will lay sinews upon you, and will
bring up flesh upon you, and cover you with
skin, and put breath in you, and ye shall
live; [f]and ye shall know that I *am* the LORD.
7 So I prophesied as I was commanded:
and as I prophesied, there was a noise, and
behold a shaking, and the bones came together, bone to his bone.
8 And when I beheld, lo, the sinews and
the flesh came up upon them, and the skin
covered them above: but *there was* no
breath in them.
9 Then said he unto me, Prophesy unto
the wind, prophesy, son of man, and say to
the wind, Thus saith the Lord GOD; [g]Come
from the four winds, O breath, and breathe
upon these slain, that they may live.
10 So I prophesied as he commanded me,
[h]and the breath came into them, and they
lived, and stood up upon their feet, an exceeding great army.
11 ¶ Then he said unto me, Son of man,
these bones are the whole house of Israel:
behold, they say, [i]Our bones are dried, and
our hope is lost: we are cut off for our parts.
12 Therefore prophesy and say unto
them, Thus saith the Lord GOD; Behold, [j]O
my people, I will open your graves, and
cause you to come up out of your graves,
and [k]bring you into the land of Israel.
13 And ye shall know that I *am* the LORD,
when I have opened your graves, O my people, and brought you up out of your graves,
14 And [l]shall put my spirit in you, and ye
shall live, and I shall place you in your own
land: then shall ye know that I the LORD
have spoken *it,* and performed *it,* saith the
LORD.
15 ¶ The word of the LORD came again
unto me, saying,
16 Moreover, thou son of man, [m]take thee
one stick, and write upon it, For Judah, and
for [n]the children of Israel his companions:
then take another stick, and write upon it,
For Joseph, the stick of Ephraim and *for* all
the house of Israel his companions:
17 And [o]join them one to another into
one stick; and they shall become one in
thine hand.
18 ¶ And when the children of thy people
shall speak unto thee, saying, [p]Wilt thou
not shew us what thou *meanest* by these?
19 [q]Say unto them, Thus saith the Lord
GOD; Behold, I will take the [r]stick of Joseph, which *is* in the hand of Ephraim, and
the tribes of Israel his fellows, and will put
them with him, *even* with the stick of Judah,
and make them one stick, and they shall be
one in mine hand.
20 ¶ And the sticks whereon thou writest
shall be in thine hand [s]before their eyes.
21 And say unto them, Thus saith the

36:25 [j]Isa. 52:15; Heb. 10:22 [k]Jer. 33:8
36:26 [l]Jer. 32:39; ch. 11:19
36:27 [m]ch. 11:19
36:28 [n]ch. 28:25 [o]Jer. 30:22; ch. 11:20
36:29 [p]Matt. 1:21; Rom. 11:26 [q]Ps. 105:16 [r]ch. 34:29
36:30 [s]ch. 34:27
36:31 [t]ch. 16:61 [u]Lev. 26:39; ch. 6:9
36:32 [v]Deut. 9:5; ver. 22
36:33 [w]ver. 10
36:35 [x]Isa. 51:3; ch. 28:13; Joel 2:3
36:36 [y]ch. 17:24
36:37 [z]ch. 14:3 [a]ver. 10
37:1 [b]ch. 1:3 [c]ch. 3:14; Luke 4:1
37:3 [d]Deut. 32:39; 1 Sam. 2:6; John 5:21; Rom. 4:17; 2 Cor. 1:9
37:5 [e]Ps. 104:30; ver. 9
37:6 [f]ch. 6:7; Joel 2:27
37:9 [g]Ps. 104:30; ver. 5
37:10 [h]Rev. 11:11
37:11 [i]Ps. 141:7; Isa. 49:14
37:12 [j]Isa. 26:19; Hos. 13:14 [k]ch. 36:24; ver. 25
37:14 [l]ch. 36:27
37:16 [m]Num. 17:2 [n]2 Chron. 11:12
37:17 [o]ver. 22
37:18 [p]ch. 12:9
37:19 [q]Zech. 10:6 [r]ver. 16
37:20 [s]ch. 12:3

Lord GOD; Behold, [t]I will take the children of Israel from among the heathen, whither they be gone, and will gather them on every side, and bring them into their own land:

22 And [u]I will make them one nation in the land upon the mountains of Israel; and [v]one king shall be king to them all: and they shall be no more two nations, neither shall they be divided into two kingdoms any more at all.

23 [w]Neither shall they defile themselves any more with their idols, nor with their detestable things, nor with any of their transgressions: but [x]I will save them out of all their dwellingplaces, wherein they have sinned, and will cleanse them: so shall they be my people, and I will be their God.

24 And [y]David my servant *shall be* king over them; and [z]they all shall have one shepherd: [a]they shall also walk in my judgments, and observe my statutes, and do them.

25 [b]And they shall dwell in the land that I have given unto Jacob my servant, wherein your fathers have dwelt; and they shall dwell therein, *even* they, and their children, and their children's children [c]for ever: and [d]my servant David *shall be* their prince for ever.

26 Moreover I will make a [e]covenant of peace with them; it shall be an everlasting covenant with them: and I will place them, and [f]multiply them, and will set my [g]sanctuary in the midst of them for evermore.

27 [h]My tabernacle also shall be with them: yea, I will be [i]their God, and they shall be my people.

28 [j]And the heathen shall know that I the LORD do [k]sanctify Israel, when my sanctuary shall be in the midst of them for evermore.

38

And the word of the LORD came unto me, saying,

2 [l]Son of man, [m]set thy face against [n]Gog, the land of Magog, the chief prince of [o]Meshech and Tubal, and prophesy against him,

3 And say, Thus saith the Lord GOD; Behold, I *am* against thee, O Gog, the chief prince of Meshech and Tubal:

4 And [p]I will turn thee back, and put hooks into thy jaws, and I will bring thee forth, and all thine army, horses and horsemen, [q]all of them clothed with all sorts *of armour, even* a great company *with* bucklers and shields, all of them handling swords:

5 Persia, Ethiopia, and Libya with them; all of them with shield and helmet:

6 [r]Gomer, and all his bands; the house of [s]Togarmah of the north quarters, and all his bands: *and* many people with thee.

7 [t]Be thou prepared, and prepare for thyself, thou, and all thy company that are assembled unto thee, and be thou a guard unto them.

8 ¶ [u]After many days [v]thou shalt be visited: in the latter years thou shalt come into the land *that is* brought back from the sword, [w]*and is* gathered out of many people, against [x]the mountains of Israel, which have been always waste: but it is brought forth out of the nations, and they shall [y]dwell safely all of them.

9 Thou shalt ascend and come [z]like a storm, thou shalt be [a]like a cloud to cover the land, thou, and all thy bands, and many people with thee.

10 Thus saith the Lord GOD; It shall also come to pass, *that* at the same time shall things come into thy mind, and thou shalt think an evil thought:

11 And thou shalt say, I will go up to the land of unwalled villages; I will [b]go to them that are at rest, [c]that dwell safely, all of them dwelling without walls, and having neither bars nor gates,

12 To take a spoil, and to take a prey; to turn thine hand upon [d]the desolate places *that are now* inhabited, [e]and upon the people *that are* gathered out of the nations, which have gotten cattle and goods, that dwell in the midst of the land.

13 [f]Sheba, and [g]Dedan, and the merchants [h]of Tarshish, with all [i]the young lions thereof, shall say unto thee, Art thou come to take a spoil? hast thou gathered thy company to take a prey? to carry away silver and gold, to take away cattle and goods, to take a great spoil?

14 ¶ Therefore, son of man, prophesy and say unto Gog, Thus saith the Lord GOD; [j]In that day when my people of Israel [k]dwelleth safely, shalt thou not know *it?*

15 [l]And thou shalt come from thy place out of the north parts, thou, and [m]many people with thee, all of them riding upon horses, a great company, and a mighty army:

16 [n]And thou shalt come up against my people of Israel, as a cloud to cover the land; [o]it shall be in the latter days, and I will bring thee against my land, [p]that the heathen may know me, when I shall be sanctified in thee, O Gog, before their eyes.

17 Thus saith the Lord GOD; *Art* thou he of whom I have spoken in old time by my servants the prophets of Israel, which prophesied in those days *many* years that I would bring thee against them?

18 And it shall come to pass at the same time when Gog shall come against the land of Israel, saith the Lord GOD, *that* my fury shall come up in my face.

19 For [q]in my jealousy [r]*and* in the fire of my wrath have I spoken, [s]Surely in that day there shall be a great shaking in the land of Israel;

20 So that [t]the fishes of the sea, and the fowls of the heaven, and the beasts of the field, and all creeping things that creep upon the earth, and all the men that *are* upon the face of the earth, shall shake at my presence, [u]and the mountains shall be thrown down, and the steep places shall fall, and every wall shall fall to the ground.

37:21 [t]ch. 36:24
37:22 [u]Isa. 11:13; Jer. 3:18; Hos. 1:11 [v]ch. 34:23; John 10:16
37:23 [w]ch. 36:25 [x]ch. 36:28
37:24 [y]Isa. 40:11; Jer. 23:5; ch. 34:23; Hos. 3:5; Luke 1:32 [z]ver. 22; John 10:16 [a]ch. 36:27
37:25 [b]ch. 36:28 [c]Isa. 60:21; Joel 3:20; Am. 9:15 [d]ver. 24; John 12:34
37:26 [e]Ps. 89:3; Isa. 55:3; Jer. 32:40; ch. 34:25 [f]ch. 36:10 [g]2 Cor. 6:16
37:27 [h]Lev. 26:11; ch. 43:7; John 1:14 [i]ch. 11:20
37:28 [j]ch. 36:23 [k]ch. 20:12
38:2 [l]ch. 39:1 [m]ch. 35:2 [n]Rev. 20:8 [o]ch. 32:26
38:4 [p]2 Kings 19:28; ch. 29:4 [q]ch. 23:12
38:6 [r]Gen. 10:2 [s]ch. 27:14
38:7 [t]Isa. 8:9; Jer. 46:3
38:8 [u]Gen. 49:1; Deut. 4:30; ver. 16 [v]Isa. 29:6 [w]ver. 12; ch. 34:13 [x]ch. 36:1 [y]Jer. 23:6; ch. 28:26; ver. 11
38:9 [z]Isa. 28:2 [a]Jer. 4:13; ver. 16
38:11 [b]Jer. 49:31 [c]ver. 8
38:12 [d]ch. 36:34 [e]ver. 8
38:13 [f]ch. 27:22 [g]ch. 27:15 [h]ch. 27:12 [i]ch. 19:3
38:14 [j]Isa. 4:1 [k]ver. 8
38:15 [l]ch. 39:2 [m]ver. 6
38:16 [n]ver. 9 [o]ver. 8 [p]Ex. 14:4; ch. 36:23
38:19 [q]ch. 36:5 [r]Ps. 89:46 [s]Hag. 2:6; Rev. 16:18
38:20 [t]Hos. 4:3 [u]Jer. 4:24; Nah. 1:5

21 And I will [v]call for [w]a sword against
him throughout all my mountains, saith the
Lord GOD: [x]every man's sword shall be
against his brother.
22 And I will [y]plead against him with
[z]pestilence and with blood; and [a]I will rain
upon him, and upon his bands, and upon the
many people that *are* with him, an overflowing rain, and [b]great hailstones, fire,
and brimstone.
23 Thus will I magnify myself, and [c]sanc-
tify myself; [d]and I will be known in the eyes
of many nations, and they shall know that I
am the LORD.
39 Therefore, [e]thou son of man, prophesy against Gog, and say, Thus saith
the Lord GOD; Behold, I *am* against thee,
O Gog, the chief prince of Meshech and Tubal:
2 And I will turn thee back, and leave but
the sixth part of thee, [f]and will cause thee
to come up from the north parts, and will
bring thee upon the mountains of Israel:
3 And I will smite thy bow out of thy left
hand, and will cause thine arrows to fall out
of thy right hand.
4 [g]Thou shalt fall upon the mountains of
Israel, thou, and all thy bands, and the people that *is* with thee: [h]I will give thee unto
the ravenous birds of every sort, and *to* the
beasts of the field to be devoured.
5 Thou shalt fall upon the open field: for
I have spoken *it*, saith the Lord GOD.
6 [i]And I will send a fire on Magog, and
among them that dwell carelessly in [j]the
isles: and they shall know that I *am* the
LORD.
7 [k]So will I make my holy name known
in the midst of my people Israel; and I will
not *let them* [l]pollute my holy name any
more: [m]and the heathen shall know that I
am the LORD, the Holy One in Israel.
8 ¶ [n]Behold, it is come, and it is done,
saith the Lord GOD; this *is* the day [o]whereof
I have spoken.
9 And they that dwell in the cities of Israel
shall go forth, and shall set on fire and burn
the weapons, both the shields and the bucklers, the bows and the arrows, and the hand-
staves, and the spears, and they shall burn
them with fire seven years:
10 So that they shall take no wood out of
the field, neither cut down *any* out of the
forests; for they shall burn the weapons
with fire: [p]and they shall spoil those that
spoiled them, and rob those that robbed
them, saith the Lord GOD.
11 ¶ And it shall come to pass in that day,
that I will give unto Gog a place there of
graves in Israel, the valley of the passengers
on the east of the sea: and it shall stop the
noses of the passengers: and there shall
they bury Gog and all his multitude: and
they shall call *it* The valley of Hamon-gog.
12 And seven months shall the house of
Israel be burying of them, [q]that they may
cleanse the land.
13 Yea, all the people of the land shall
bury *them;* and it shall be to them a renown
the day that [r]I shall be glorified, saith the
Lord GOD.
14 And they shall sever out men of continual employment, passing through the
land to bury with the passengers those that
remain upon the face of the earth, [s]to
cleanse it: after the end of seven months
shall they search.
15 And the passengers *that* pass through
the land, when *any* seeth a man's bone, then
shall he set up a sign by it, till the buriers
have buried it in the valley of Hamon-gog.
16 And also the name of the city *shall be*
Hamonah. Thus shall they [t]cleanse the
land.
17 ¶ And, thou son of man, thus saith the
Lord GOD; [u]Speak unto every feathered
fowl, and to every beast of the field, [v]As-
semble yourselves, and come; gather yourselves on every side to my sacrifice that I
do sacrifice for you, *even* a great sacrifice
[w]upon the mountains of Israel, that ye may
eat flesh, and drink blood.
18 [x]Ye shall eat the flesh of the mighty,
and drink the blood of the princes of the
earth, of rams, of lambs, and of goats, of
bullocks, all of them [y]fatlings of Bashan.
19 And ye shall eat fat till ye be full, and
drink blood till ye be drunken, of my sacrifice which I have sacrificed for you.
20 [z]Thus ye shall be filled at my table
with horses and chariots, [a]with mighty
men, and with all men of war, saith the Lord
GOD.
21 [b]And I will set my glory among the
heathen, and all the heathen shall see my
judgment that I have executed, and [c]my
hand that I have laid upon them.
22 [d]So the house of Israel shall know that
I *am* the LORD their God from that day and
forward.
23 ¶ [e]And the heathen shall know that
the house of Israel went into captivity for
their iniquity: because they trespassed
against me, therefore [f]hid I my face from
them, and [g]gave them into the hand of their
enemies: so fell they all by the sword.
24 [h]According to their uncleanness and
according to their transgressions have I
done unto them, and hid my face from them.
25 Therefore thus saith the Lord GOD;
[i]Now will I bring again the captivity of
Jacob, and have mercy upon the [j]whole
house of Israel, and will be jealous for my
holy name;
26 [k]After that they have borne their
shame, and all their trespasses whereby
they have trespassed against me, when they
[l]dwelt safely in their land, and none made
them afraid.
27 [m]When I have brought them again
from the people, and gathered them out of
their enemies' lands, and [n]am sanctified in
them in the sight of many nations;
28 [o]Then shall they know that I *am* the
LORD their God, which caused them to be
led into captivity among the heathen: but I

38:21 *v*Ps. 105:16 *w*ch. 14:17 *x*Judg. 7:22; 1 Sam. 14:20; 2 Chron. 20:23
38:22 *y*Isa. 66:16; Jer. 25:31 *z*ch. 5:17 *a*Ps. 11:6; Isa. 29:6 *b*ch. 13:11; Rev. 16:21
38:23 *c*ch. 36:23 *d*Ps. 9:16; ch. 37:28; ver. 16
39:1 *e*ch. 38:2
39:2 *f*ch. 38:15
39:4 *g*ch. 38:21; ver. 17 *h*ch. 33:27
39:6 *i*ch. 38:22; Am. 1:4 *j*Ps. 72:10
39:7 *k*ver. 22 *l*Lev. 18:21; ch. 20:39 *m*ch. 38:16
39:8 *n*Rev. 16:17 *o*ch. 38:17
39:10 *p*Isa. 14:2
39:12 *q*Deut. 21:23; ver. 14
39:13 *r*ch. 28:22
39:14 *s*ver. 12
39:16 *t*ver. 12
39:17 *u*Rev. 19:17 *v*Isa. 18:6; Jer. 12:9; Zeph. 1:7 *w*ver. 4
39:18 *x*Rev. 19:18 *y*Deut. 32:14; Ps. 22:12
39:20 *z*Ps. 76:6; ch. 38:4 *a*Rev. 19:18
39:21 *b*ch. 38:16 *c*Ex. 7:4
39:22 *d*ver. 7
39:23 *e*ch. 36:18 *f*Deut. 31:17; Isa. 59:2 *g*Lev. 26:25
39:24 *h*ch. 36:19
39:25 *i*Jer. 30:3; ch. 34:13 *j*ch. 20:40; Hos. 1:11
39:26 *k*Dan. 9:16 *l*Lev. 26:5
39:27 *m*ch. 28:25 *n*ch. 36:23
39:28 *o*ch. 34:30; ver. 22

have gathered them unto their own land,
and have left none of them any more there.
29 [p]Neither will I hide my face any more
from them: for I have [q]poured out my spirit
upon the house of Israel, saith the Lord
GOD.
40 In the five and twentieth year of our
captivity, in the beginning of the
year, in the tenth *day* of the month, in the
fourteenth year after that [r]the city was
smitten, in the selfsame day [s]the hand of
the LORD was upon me, and brought me
thither.
2 [t]In the visions of God brought he me
into the land of Israel, [u]and set me upon a
very high mountain, by which *was* as the
frame of a city on the south.
3 And he brought me thither, and, behold,
there was a man, whose appearance *was*
[v]like the appearance of brass, [w]with a line
of flax in his hand, [x]and a measuring reed;
and he stood in the gate.
4 And the man said unto me, [y]Son of
man, behold with thine eyes, and hear with
thine ears, and set thine heart upon all that
I shall shew thee; for to the intent that I
might shew *them* unto thee *art* thou
brought hither: [z]declare all that thou seest
to the house of Israel.
5 And behold [a]a wall on the outside of
the house round about, and in the man's
hand a measuring reed of six cubits *long* by
the cubit and an hand breadth: so he measured the breadth of the building, one reed;
and the height, one reed.
6 ¶ Then came he unto the gate which
looketh toward the east, and went up the
stairs thereof, and measured the threshold
of the gate, *which was* one reed broad; and
the other threshold *of the gate, which was*
one reed broad.
7 And *every* little chamber *was* one reed
long, and one reed broad; and between the
little chambers *were* five cubits; and the
threshold of the gate by the porch of
the gate within *was* one reed.
8 He measured also the porch of the gate
within, one reed.
9 Then measured he the porch of the gate,
eight cubits; and the posts thereof, two cubits; and the porch of the gate *was* inward.
10 And the little chambers of the gate
eastward *were* three on this side, and three
on that side; they three *were* of one measure: and the posts had one measure on this
side and on that side.
11 And he measured the breadth of the
entry of the gate, ten cubits; *and* the length
of the gate, thirteen cubits.
12 The space also before the little chambers *was* one cubit *on this side*, and the
space *was* one cubit on that side: and the
little chambers *were* six cubits on this side,
and six cubits on that side.
13 He measured then the gate from the
roof of *one* little chamber to the roof of another: the breadth *was* five and twenty cubits, door against door.

39:29 [p]Isa. 54:8 [q]Joel 2:28; Zech. 12:10; Acts 2:17
40:1 [r]ch. 33:21 [s]ch. 1:3
40:2 [t]ch. 8:3 [u]Rev. 21:10
40:3 [v]ch. 1:7; Dan. 10:6 [w]ch. 47:3 [x]Rev. 11:1
40:4 [y]ch. 44:5 [z]ch. 43:10
40:5 [a]ch. 42:20
40:16 [b]1 Kings 6:4
40:17 [c]Rev. 11:2 [d]1 Kings 6:5 [e]ch. 45:5
40:30 [f]ver. 21

14 He made also posts of threescore cubits, even unto the post of the court round
about the gate.
15 And from the face of the gate of the
entrance unto the face of the porch of the
inner gate *were* fifty cubits.
16 And *there were* [b]narrow windows to
the little chambers, and to their posts within
the gate round about, and likewise to the
arches: and windows *were* round about inward: and upon *each* post *were* palm trees.
17 Then brought he me into [c]the outward
court, and, lo, *there were* [d]chambers, and a
pavement made for the court round about:
[e]thirty chambers *were* upon the pavement.
18 And the pavement by the side of the
gates over against the length of the gates
was the lower pavement.
19 Then he measured the breadth from
the forefront of the lower gate unto the forefront of the inner court without, an hundred
cubits eastward and northward.
20 ¶ And the gate of the outward court
that looked toward the north, he measured
the length thereof, and the breadth thereof.
21 And the little chambers thereof *were*
three on this side and three on that side; and
the posts thereof and the arches thereof
were after the measure of the first gate: the
length thereof *was* fifty cubits, and the
breadth five and twenty cubits.
22 And their windows, and their arches,
and their palm trees, *were* after the measure
of the gate that looketh toward the east; and
they went up unto it by seven steps; and the
arches thereof *were* before them.
23 And the gate of the inner court *was*
over against the gate toward the north, and
toward the east; and he measured from gate
to gate an hundred cubits.
24 ¶ After that he brought me toward the
south, and behold a gate toward the south:
and he measured the posts thereof and the
arches thereof according to these measures.
25 And *there were* windows in it and in
the arches thereof round about, like those
windows: the length *was* fifty cubits, and
the breadth five and twenty cubits.
26 And *there were* seven steps to go up to
it, and the arches thereof *were* before them:
and it had palm trees, one on this side, and
another on that side, upon the posts thereof.
27 And *there was* a gate in the inner court
toward the south: and he measured from
gate to gate toward the south an hundred
cubits.
28 And he brought me to the inner court
by the south gate: and he measured the
south gate according to these measures;
29 And the little chambers thereof, and
the posts thereof, and the arches thereof,
according to these measures: and *there*
were windows in it and in the arches thereof
round about: *it was* fifty cubits long, and
five and twenty cubits broad.
30 And the arches round about *were*
[f]five and twenty cubits long, and five cubits
broad.

31 And the arches thereof *were* toward the utter court; and palm trees *were* upon the posts thereof: and the going up to it *had* eight steps.

32 ¶ And he brought me into the inner court toward the east: and he measured the gate according to these measures.

33 And the little chambers thereof, and the posts thereof, and the arches thereof, *were* according to these measures: and *there were* windows therein and in the arches thereof round about: *it was* fifty cubits long, and five and twenty cubits broad.

34 And the arches thereof *were* toward the outward court; and palm trees *were* upon the posts thereof, on this side, and on that side: and the going up to it *had* eight steps.

35 ¶ And he brought me to the north gate, and measured *it* according to these measures;

36 The little chambers thereof, the posts thereof, and the arches thereof, and the windows to it round about: the length *was* fifty cubits, and the breadth five and twenty cubits.

37 And the posts thereof *were* toward the utter court; and palm trees *were* upon the posts thereof, on this side, and on that side: and the going up to it *had* eight steps.

38 And the chambers and the entries thereof *were* by the posts of the gates, where they washed the burnt offering.

39 ¶ And in the porch of the gate *were* two tables on this side, and two tables on that side, to slay thereon the burnt offering and [g]the sin offering and [h]the trespass offering.

40 And at the side without, as one goeth up to the entry of the north gate, *were* two tables; and on the other side, which *was* at the porch of the gate, *were* two tables.

41 Four tables *were* on this side, and four tables on that side, by the side of the gate; eight tables, whereupon they slew *their sacrifices*.

42 And the four tables *were* of hewn stone for the burnt offering, of a cubit and an half long, and a cubit and an half broad, and one cubit high: whereupon also they laid the instruments wherewith they slew the burnt offering and the sacrifice.

43 And within *were* hooks, an hand broad, fastened round about: and upon the tables *was* the flesh of the offering.

44 ¶ And without the inner gate *were* the chambers of [i]the singers in the inner court, which *was* at the side of the north gate; and their prospect *was* toward the south: one at the side of the east gate *having* the prospect toward the north.

45 And he said unto me, This chamber, whose prospect *is* toward the south, *is* for the priests, [j]the keepers of the charge of the house.

46 And the chamber whose prospect *is* toward the north *is* for the priests, [k]the keepers of the charge of the altar: these *are* the sons of [l]Zadok among the sons of Levi, which come near to the LORD to minister unto him.

47 So he measured the court, an hundred cubits long, and an hundred cubits broad, foursquare; and the altar *that was* before the house.

48 ¶ And he brought me to the porch of the house, and measured *each* post of the porch, five cubits on this side, and five cubits on that side: and the breadth of the gate *was* three cubits on this side, and three cubits on that side.

49 [m]The length of the porch *was* twenty cubits, and the breadth eleven cubits; and *he brought me* by the steps whereby they went up to it: and *there were* [n]pillars by the posts, one on this side, and another on that side.

41

Afterward he brought me to the temple, and measured the posts, six cubits broad on the one side, and six cubits broad on the other side, *which was* the breadth of the tabernacle.

2 And the breadth of the door *was* ten cubits; and the sides of the door *were* five cubits on the one side, and five cubits on the other side: and he measured the length thereof, forty cubits: and the breadth, twenty cubits.

3 Then went he inward, and measured the post of the door, two cubits; and the door, six cubits; and the breadth of the door, seven cubits.

4 So [o]he measured the length thereof, twenty cubits; and the breadth, twenty cubits, before the temple: and he said unto me, This *is* the most holy *place*.

5 After he measured the wall of the house, six cubits; and the breadth of *every* side chamber, four cubits, round about the house on every side.

6 [p]And the side chambers *were* three, one over another, and thirty in order; and they entered into the wall which *was* of the house for the side chambers round about, that they might have hold, but they had not hold in the wall of the house.

7 And [q]*there was* an enlarging, and a winding about still upward to the side chambers: for the winding about of the house went still upward round about the house: therefore the breadth of the house *was still* upward, and so increased *from* the lowest *chamber* to the highest by the midst.

8 I saw also the height of the house round about: the foundations of the side chambers *were* [r]a full reed of six great cubits.

9 The thickness of the wall, which *was* for the side chamber without, *was* five cubits: and *that* which *was* left *was* the place of the side chambers that *were* within.

10 And between the chambers *was* the wideness of twenty cubits round about the house on every side.

11 And the doors of the side chambers *were* toward *the place that was* left, one door toward the north, and another door

40:39 [g]Lev. 4:2 [h]Lev. 5:6
40:44 [i]1 Chron. 6:31
40:45 [j]Lev. 8:35; Num. 3:27; 1 Chron. 9:23; 2 Chron. 13:11; Ps. 134:1
40:46 [k]Num. 18:5; ch. 44:15 [l]1 Kings 2:35; ch. 43:19
40:49 [m]1 Kings 6:3 [n]1 Kings 7:21
41:4 [o]1 Kings 6:20; 2 Chron. 3:8
41:6 [p]1 Kings 6:5
41:7 [q]1 Kings 6:8
41:8 [r]ch. 40:5

toward the south: and the breadth of the place that was left *was* five cubits round about.

12 Now the building that *was* before the separate place at the end toward the west *was* seventy cubits broad; and the wall of the building *was* five cubits thick round about, and the length thereof ninety cubits.

13 So he measured the house, an hundred cubits long; and the separate place, and the building, with the walls thereof, an hundred cubits long;

14 Also the breadth of the face of the house, and of the separate place toward the east, an hundred cubits.

15 And he measured the length of the building over against the separate place which *was* behind it, and the galleries thereof on the one side and on the other side, an hundred cubits, with the inner temple, and the porches of the court;

16 The door posts, and [s]the narrow windows, and the galleries round about on their three stories, over against the door, cieled with wood round about, and from the ground up to the windows, and the windows *were* covered;

17 To that above the door, even unto the inner house, and without, and by all the wall round about within and without, by measure.

18 And *it was* made [t]with cherubims and palm trees, so that a palm tree *was* between a cherub and a cherub; and *every* cherub had two faces;

19 [u]So that the face of a man *was* toward the palm tree on the one side, and the face of a young lion toward the palm tree on the other side: *it was* made through all the house round about.

20 From the ground unto above the door *were* cherubims and palm trees made, and *on* the wall of the temple.

21 The posts of the temple *were* squared, *and* the face of the sanctuary; the appearance *of the one* as the appearance *of the other*.

22 [v]The altar of wood *was* three cubits high, and the length thereof two cubits; and the corners thereof, and the length thereof, and the walls thereof, *were* of wood: and he said unto me, This *is* [w]the table that *is* [x]before the LORD.

23 [y]And the temple and the sanctuary had two doors.

24 And the doors had two leaves *apiece*, two turning leaves; two *leaves* for the one door, and two leaves for the other *door*.

25 And *there were* made on them, on the doors of the temple, cherubims and palm trees, like as *were* made upon the walls; and *there were* thick planks upon the face of the porch without.

26 And *there were* [z]narrow windows and palm trees on the one side and on the other side, on the sides of the porch, and *upon* the side chambers of the house, and thick planks.

41:16 [s]ch. 40:16; ver. 26
41:18 [t]1 Kings 6:29
41:19 [u]ch. 1:10
41:22 [v]Ex. 30:1 [w]ch. 44:16; Mal. 1:7 [x]Ex. 30:8
41:23 [y]1 Kings 6:31-35
41:26 [z]ch. 40:16; ver. 16
42:1 [a]ch. 41:12
42:3 [b]ch. 41:16
42:11 [c]ver. 4
42:13 [d]Lev. 6:16 [e]Lev. 2:3; Num. 18:9
42:14 [f]ch. 44:19

42 Then he brought me forth into the utter court, the way toward the north: and he brought me into [a]the chamber that *was* over against the separate place, and which *was* before the building toward the north.

2 Before the length of an hundred cubits *was* the north door, and the breadth *was* fifty cubits.

3 Over against the twenty *cubits* which *were* for the inner court, and over against the pavement which *was* for the utter court, *was* [b]gallery against gallery in three *stories*.

4 And before the chambers *was* a walk of ten cubits breadth inward, a way of one cubit; and their doors toward the north.

5 Now the upper chambers *were* shorter: for the galleries were higher than these, than the lower, and than the middlemost of the building.

6 For they *were* in three *stories*, but had not pillars as the pillars of the courts: therefore *the building* was straitened more than the lowest and the middlemost from the ground.

7 And the wall that *was* without over against the chambers, toward the utter court on the forepart of the chambers, the length thereof *was* fifty cubits.

8 For the length of the chambers that *were* in the utter court *was* fifty cubits: and, lo, before the temple *were* an hundred cubits.

9 And from under these chambers *was* the entry on the east side, as one goeth into them from the utter court.

10 The chambers *were* in the thickness of the wall of the court toward the east, over against the separate place, and over against the building.

11 And [c]the way before them *was* like the appearance of the chambers which *were* toward the north, as long as they, *and* as broad as they: and all their goings out *were* both according to their fashions, and according to their doors.

12 And according to the doors of the chambers that *were* toward the south *was* a door in the head of the way, *even* the way directly before the wall toward the east, as one entereth into them.

13 ¶ Then said he unto me, The north chambers *and* the south chambers, which *are* before the separate place, they *be* holy chambers, where the priests that approach unto the LORD [d]shall eat the most holy things: there shall they lay the most holy things, and [e]the meat offering, and the sin offering, and the trespass offering; for the place *is* holy.

14 [f]When the priests enter therein, then shall they not go out of the holy *place* into the utter court, but there they shall lay their garments wherein they minister; for they *are* holy; and shall put on other garments, and shall approach to *those things* which *are* for the people.

15 Now when he had made an end of
measuring the inner house, he brought me
forth toward the gate whose prospect *is* toward the east, and measured it round about.
16 He measured the east side with the
measuring reed, five hundred reeds, with
the measuring reed round about.
17 He measured the north side, five hundred reeds, with the measuring reed round
about.
18 He measured the south side, five hundred reeds, with the measuring reed.
19 ¶ He turned about to the west side, *and*
measured five hundred reeds with the measuring reed.
20 He measured it by the four sides: [g]it
had a wall round about, [h]five hundred
reeds long, and five hundred broad, to make
a separation between the sanctuary and the
profane place.

43 Afterward he brought me to the gate,
even the gate [i]that looketh toward
the east.
2 [j]And, behold, the glory of the God of
Israel came from the way of the east: and
[k]his voice *was* like a noise of many waters:
[l]and the earth shined with his glory.
3 And *it was* [m]according to the appearance of the vision which I saw, *even* according to the vision that I saw [n]when I came
[o]to destroy the city: and the visions *were*
like the vision that I saw [p]by the river Chebar; and I fell upon my face.
4 [q]And the glory of the LORD came into
the house by the way of the gate whose
prospect *is* toward the east.
5 [r]So the spirit took me up, and brought
me into the inner court; and, behold, [s]the
glory of the LORD filled the house.
6 And I heard *him* speaking unto me out
of the house; and [t]the man stood by me.
7 ¶ And he said unto me, Son of man,
[u]the place of my throne, and [v]the place of
the soles of my feet, [w]where I will dwell in
the midst of the children of Israel for ever,
and my holy name, shall the house of Israel
[x]no more defile, *neither* they, nor their
kings, by their whoredom, nor by [y]the carcases of their kings in their high places.
8 [z]In their setting of their threshold by
my thresholds, and their post by my posts,
and the wall between me and them, they
have even defiled my holy name by their
abominations that they have committed:
wherefore I have consumed them in mine
anger.
9 Now let them put away their whoredom, and [a]the carcases of their kings, far
from me, [b]and I will dwell in the midst of
them for ever.
10 ¶ Thou son of man, [c]shew the house
to the house of Israel, that they may be
ashamed of their iniquities: and let them
measure the pattern.
11 And if they be ashamed of all that they
have done, shew them the form of the
house, and the fashion thereof, and the goings out thereof, and the comings in thereof,
and all the forms thereof, and all the ordinances thereof, and all the forms thereof,
and all the laws thereof: and write *it* in their
sight, that they may keep the whole form
thereof, and all the ordinances thereof, and
do them.
12 This *is* the law of the house; Upon [d]the
top of the mountain the whole limit thereof
round about *shall be* most holy. Behold, this
is the law of the house.
13 ¶ And these *are* the measures of the
altar after the cubits: [e]The cubit *is* a cubit
and an hand breadth; even the bottom *shall
be* a cubit, and the breadth a cubit, and the
border thereof by the edge thereof round
about *shall be* a span: and this *shall be* the
higher place of the altar.
14 And from the bottom *upon* the ground
even to the lower settle *shall be* two cubits,
and the breadth one cubit; and from the
lesser settle *even* to the greater settle *shall
be* four cubits, and the breadth *one* cubit.
15 So the altar *shall be* four cubits; and
from the altar and upward *shall be* four
horns.
16 And the altar *shall be* twelve *cubits*
long, twelve broad, square in the four
squares thereof.
17 And the settle *shall be* fourteen *cubits*
long and fourteen broad in the four squares
thereof; and the border about it *shall be* half
a cubit; and the bottom thereof *shall be* a
cubit about; and [f]his stairs shall look toward the east.
18 ¶ And he said unto me, Son of man,
thus saith the Lord GOD; These *are* the ordinances of the altar in the day when they
shall make it, to offer burnt offerings
thereon, and to [g]sprinkle blood thereon.
19 And thou shalt give to [h]the priests the
Levites that be of the seed of Zadok, which
approach unto me, to minister unto me,
saith the Lord GOD, [i]a young bullock for a
sin offering.
20 And thou shalt take of the blood
thereof, and put *it* on the four horns of it,
and on the four corners of the settle, and
upon the border round about: thus shalt
thou cleanse and purge it.
21 Thou shalt take the bullock also of the
sin offering, and he [j]shall burn it in the
appointed place of the house, [k]without the
sanctuary.
22 And on the second day thou shalt offer
a kid of the goats without blemish for a sin
offering; and they shall cleanse the altar, as
they did cleanse *it* with the bullock.
23 When thou hast made an end of
cleansing *it*, thou shalt offer a young bullock without blemish, and a ram out of the
flock without blemish.
24 And thou shalt offer them before the
LORD, [l]and the priests shall cast salt upon
them, and they shall offer them up *for* a
burnt offering unto the LORD.
25 [m]Seven days shalt thou prepare every
day a goat *for* a sin offering: they shall also

42:20 [g]ch. 40:5 [h]ch. 45:2
43:1 [i]ch. 10:19
43:2 [j]ch. 11:23 [k]ch. 1:24; Rev. 1:15 [l]ch. 10:4; Rev. 18:1
43:3 [m]ch. 1:4 [n]ch. 9:1 [o]Jer. 1:10 [p]ch. 1:3
43:4 [q]ch. 10:19
43:5 [r]ch. 3:12 [s]1 Kings 8:10; ch. 44:4
43:6 [t]ch. 40:3
43:7 [u]Ps. 99:1 [v]1 Chron. 28:2; Ps. 99:5 [w]Ex. 29:45; Ps. 68:16; Joel 3:17; John 1:14; 2 Cor. 6:16 [x]ch. 39:7 [y]Lev. 26:30; Jer. 16:18
43:8 [z]2 Kings 16:14; ch. 8:3
43:9 [a]ver. 7 [b]ver. 7
43:10 [c]ch. 40:4
43:12 [d]ch. 40:2
43:13 [e]ch. 40:5
43:17 [f]Ex. 20:26
43:18 [g]Lev. 1:5
43:19 [h]ch. 44:15 [i]Ex. 29:10; Lev. 8:14; ch. 45:18
43:21 [j]Ex. 29:14 [k]Heb. 13:11
43:24 [l]Lev. 2:13
43:25 [m]Ex. 29:35; Lev. 8:33

prepare a young bullock, and a ram out of
the flock, without blemish.
26 Seven days shall they purge the altar
and purify it; and they shall consecrate
themselves.
27 [n]And when these days are expired, it
shall be, *that* upon the eighth day, and *so*
forward, the priests shall make your burnt
offerings upon the altar, and your peace offerings; and I will [o]accept you, saith the
Lord GOD.

44

Then he brought me back the way of
the gate of the outward sanctuary
[p]which looketh toward the east; and it *was*
shut.
2 Then said the LORD unto me; This gate
shall be shut, it shall not be opened, and no
man shall enter in by it; [q]because the LORD,
the God of Israel, hath entered in by it,
therefore it shall be shut.
3 *It is* for the prince; the prince, he shall
sit in it to [r]eat bread before the LORD; [s]he
shall enter by the way of the porch of *that*
gate, and shall go out by the way of the
same.
4 ¶ Then brought he me the way of the
north gate before the house: and I looked,
and, [t]behold, the glory of the LORD filled
the house of the LORD: [u]and I fell upon my
face.
5 And the LORD said unto me, [v]Son of
man, mark well, and behold with thine eyes,
and hear with thine ears all that I say unto
thee concerning all the ordinances of the
house of the LORD, and all the laws thereof;
and mark well the entering in of the house,
with every going forth of the sanctuary.
6 And thou shalt say to the [w]rebellious,
even to the house of Israel, Thus saith the
Lord GOD; O ye house of Israel, [x]let it suffice you of all your abominations,
7 [y]In that ye have brought *into my sanc-*
tuary [z]strangers, [a]uncircumcised in heart,
and uncircumcised in flesh, to be in my
sanctuary, to pollute it, *even* my house,
when ye offer [b]my bread, [c]the fat and the
blood, and they have broken my covenant
because of all your abominations.
8 And ye have not [d]kept the charge of
mine holy things: but ye have set keepers of
my charge in my sanctuary for yourselves.
9 ¶ Thus saith the Lord GOD; [e]No
stranger, uncircumcised in heart, nor uncircumcised in flesh, shall enter into my sanctuary, of any stranger that *is* among the
children of Israel.
10 [f]And the Levites that are gone away
far from me, when Israel went astray, which
went astray away from me after their idols;
they shall even bear their iniquity.
11 Yet they shall be ministers in my sanctuary, [g]*having* charge at the gates of the
house, and ministering to the house: [h]they
shall slay the burnt offering and the sacrifice for the people, and [i]they shall stand
before them to minister unto them.
12 Because they ministered unto them before their idols, and [j]caused the house of
Israel to fall into iniquity; therefore have I
[k]lifted up mine hand against them, saith the
Lord GOD, and they shall bear their iniquity.
13 [l]And they shall not come near unto
me, to do the office of a priest unto me, nor
to come near to any of my holy things, in the
most holy *place:* but they shall [m]bear their
shame, and their abominations which they
have committed.
14 But I will make them [n]keepers of the
charge of the house, for all the service
thereof, and for all that shall be done
therein.
15 ¶ [o]But the priests the Levites, [p]the
sons of Zadok, that kept the charge of my
sanctuary [q]when the children of Israel
went astray from me, they shall come near
to me to minister unto me, and they [r]shall
stand before me to offer unto me [s]the fat
and the blood, saith the Lord GOD:
16 They shall enter into my sanctuary,
and they shall come near to [t]my table, to
minister unto me, and they shall keep my
charge.
17 ¶ And it shall come to pass, *that* when
they enter in at the gates of the inner court,
[u]they shall be clothed with linen garments;
and no wool shall come upon them, whiles
they minister in the gates of the inner court,
and within.
18 [v]They shall have linen bonnets upon
their heads, and shall have linen breeches
upon their loins; they shall not gird *them-*
selves with any thing that causeth sweat.
19 And when they go forth into the utter
court, *even* into the utter court to the people,
[w]they shall put off their garments wherein
they ministered, and lay them in the holy
chambers, and they shall put on other garments; and they shall [x]not sanctify the people with their garments.
20 [y]Neither shall they shave their heads,
nor suffer their locks to grow long; they
shall only poll their heads.
21 [z]Neither shall any priest drink wine,
when they enter into the inner court.
22 Neither shall they take for their wives
a [a]widow, nor her that is put away: but they
shall take maidens of the seed of the house
of Israel, or a widow that had a priest before.
23 And [b]they shall teach my people *the*
difference between the holy and profane,
and cause them to discern between the unclean and the clean.
24 And [c]in controversy they shall stand
in judgment; *and* they shall judge it according to my judgments: and they shall keep
my laws and my statutes in all mine assemblies; [d]and they shall hallow my sabbaths.
25 And they shall come at no [e]dead person to defile themselves: but for father, or
for mother, or for son, or for daughter, for
brother, or for sister that hath had no husband, they may defile themselves.
26 And [f]after he is cleansed, they shall
reckon unto him seven days.
27 And in the day that he goeth into the

43:27 [n]Lev. 9:1 [o]Job 42:8; ch. 20:40; Rom. 12:1; 1 Pet. 2:5
44:1 [p]ch. 43:1
44:2 [q]ch. 43:4
44:3 [r]Gen. 31:54; 1 Cor. 10:18 [s]ch. 46:2
44:4 [t]ch. 3:23 [u]ch. 1:28
44:5 [v]ch. 40:4
44:6 [w]ch. 2:5 [x]ch. 45:9; 1 Pet. 4:3
44:7 [y]ch. 43:8; ver. 9; Acts 21:28 [z]Lev. 22:25 [a]Lev. 26:41; Deut. 10:16; Acts 7:51 [b]Lev. 21:6 [c]Lev. 3:16
44:8 [d]Lev. 22:2
44:9 [e]ver. 7
44:10 [f]2 Kings 23:8; 2 Chron. 29:4; ch. 48:11
44:11 [g]1 Chron. 26:1 [h]2 Chron. 29:34 [i]Num. 16:9
44:12 [j]Isa. 9:16; Mal. 2:8 [k]Ps. 106:26
44:13 [l]2 Kings 23:9; Num. 18:3 [m]ch. 32:30
44:14 [n]Num. 18:4; 1 Chron. 23:28
44:15 [o]ch. 40:46 [p]1 Sam. 2:35 [q]ver. 10 [r]Deut. 10:8 [s]ver. 7
44:16 [t]ch. 41:22
44:17 [u]Ex. 28:39
44:18 [v]Ex. 28:40
44:19 [w]ch. 42:14 [x]Ex. 29:37; Lev. 6:27; ch. 46:20; Matt. 23:17
44:20 [y]Lev. 21:5
44:21 [z]Lev. 10:9
44:22 [a]Lev. 21:7
44:23 [b]Lev. 10:10; ch. 22:26; Mal. 2:7
44:24 [c]Deut. 17:8; 2 Chron. 19:8 [d]ch. 22:26
44:25 [e]Lev. 21:1
44:26 [f]Num. 6:10

sanctuary, [g]unto the inner court, to minister in the sanctuary, [h]he shall offer his sin offering, saith the Lord GOD.

28 And it shall be unto them for an inheritance: I [i]*am* their inheritance: and ye shall give them no possession in Israel: I *am* their possession.

29 [j]They shall eat the meat offering, and the sin offering, and the trespass offering; and [k]every dedicated thing in Israel shall be theirs.

30 And the [l]first of all the firstfruits of all *things,* and every oblation of all, of every *sort* of your oblations, shall be the priest's: [m]ye shall also give unto the priest the first of your dough, [n]that he may cause the blessing to rest in thine house.

31 The priests shall not eat of any thing that is [o]dead of itself, or torn, whether it be fowl or beast.

45 Moreover, when ye shall [p]divide by lot the land for inheritance, ye shall [q]offer an oblation unto the LORD, an holy portion of the land: the length *shall be* the length of five and twenty thousand *reeds,* and the breadth *shall be* ten thousand. This *shall be* holy in all the borders thereof round about.

2 Of this there shall be for the sanctuary [r]five hundred *in length,* with five hundred *in breadth,* square round about; and fifty cubits round about for the suburbs thereof.

3 And of this measure shalt thou measure the length of five and twenty thousand, and the breadth of ten thousand: [s]and in it shall be the sanctuary *and* the most holy *place.*

4 [t]The holy *portion* of the land shall be for the priests the ministers of the sanctuary, which shall come near to minister unto the LORD: and it shall be a place for their houses, and an holy place for the sanctuary.

5 [u]And the five and twenty thousand of length, and the ten thousand of breadth, shall also the Levites, the ministers of the house, have for themselves, for a possession for [v]twenty chambers.

6 ¶ [w]And ye shall appoint the possession of the city five thousand broad, and five and twenty thousand long, over against the oblation of the holy *portion:* it shall be for the whole house of Israel.

7 ¶ [x]And *a portion shall be* for the prince on the one side and on the other side of the oblation of the holy *portion,* and of the possession of the city, before the oblation of the holy *portion,* and before the possession of the city, from the west side westward, and from the east side eastward: and the length *shall be* over against one of the portions, from the west border unto the east border.

8 In the land shall be his possession in Israel: and [y]my princes shall no more oppress my people; and *the rest of* the land shall they give to the house of Israel according to their tribes.

9 ¶ Thus saith the Lord GOD; [z]Let it suffice you, O princes of Israel: [a]remove violence and spoil, and execute judgment and justice, take away your exactions from my people, saith the Lord GOD.

10 Ye shall have just [b]balances, and a just ephah, and a just bath.

11 The ephah and the bath shall be of one measure, that the bath may contain the tenth part of an homer, and the ephah the tenth part of an homer: the measure thereof shall be after the homer.

12 And the [c]shekel *shall be* twenty gerahs: twenty shekels, five and twenty shekels, fifteen shekels, shall be your maneh.

13 This *is* the oblation that ye shall offer; the sixth part of an ephah of an homer of wheat, and ye shall give the sixth part of an ephah of an homer of barley:

14 Concerning the ordinance of oil, the bath of oil, *ye shall offer* the tenth part of a bath out of the cor, *which is* an homer of ten baths; for ten baths *are* an homer:

15 And one lamb out of the flock, out of two hundred, out of the fat pastures of Israel; for a meat offering, and for a burnt offering, and for peace offerings, [d]to make reconciliation for them, saith the Lord GOD.

16 All the people of the land shall give this oblation for the prince in Israel.

17 And it shall be the prince's part to *give* burnt offerings, and meat offerings, and drink offerings, in the feasts, and in the new moons, and in the sabbaths, in all solemnities of the house of Israel: he shall prepare the sin offering, and the meat offering, and the burnt offering, and the peace offerings, to make reconciliation for the house of Israel.

18 Thus saith the Lord GOD; In the first *month,* in the first *day* of the month, thou shalt take a young bullock without blemish, and [e]cleanse the sanctuary:

19 [f]And the priest shall take of the blood of the sin offering, and put *it* upon the posts of the house, and upon the four corners of the settle of the altar, and upon the posts of the gate of the inner court.

20 And so thou shalt do the seventh *day* of the month [g]for every one that erreth, and for *him that is* simple: so shall ye reconcile the house.

21 [h]In the first *month,* in the fourteenth day of the month, ye shall have the passover, a feast of seven days; unleavened bread shall be eaten.

22 And upon that day shall the prince prepare for himself and for all the people of the land [i]a bullock *for* a sin offering.

23 And [j]seven days of the feast he shall prepare a burnt offering to the LORD, seven bullocks and seven rams without blemish daily the seven days; [k]and a kid of the goats daily *for* a sin offering.

24 [l]And he shall prepare a meat offering of an ephah for a bullock, and an ephah for a ram, and an hin of oil for an ephah.

25 In the seventh *month,* in the fifteenth day of the month, shall he do the like in the [m]feast of the seven days, according to the sin offering, according to the burnt offering,

44:27 [g]ver. 17 [h]Lev. 4:3
44:28 [i]Num. 18:20; Deut. 10:9; Josh. 13:14
44:29 [j]Lev. 6:18 [k]Lev. 27:21; Num. 18:14
44:30 [l]Ex. 13:2; Num. 3:13 [m]Num. 15:20; Neh. 10:37 [n]Prov. 3:9; Mal. 3:10
44:31 [o]Ex. 22:31; Lev. 22:8
45:1 [p]ch. 47:22 [q]ch. 48:8
45:2 [r]ch. 42:20
45:3 [s]ch. 48:10
45:4 [t]ver. 1; ch. 48:10
45:5 [u]ch. 48:13 [v]ch. 40:17
45:6 [w]ch. 48:15
45:7 [x]ch. 48:21
45:8 [y]Jer. 22:17; ch. 22:27; ch. 46:18
45:9 [z]ch. 44:6 [a]Jer. 22:3
45:10 [b]Lev. 19:35; Prov. 11:1
45:12 [c]Ex. 30:13; Lev. 27:25; Num. 3:47
45:15 [d]Lev. 1:4
45:18 [e]Lev. 16:16
45:19 [f]ch. 43:20
45:20 [g]Lev. 4:27
45:21 [h]Ex. 12:18; Lev. 23:5; Num. 9:2; Deut. 16:1
45:22 [i]Lev. 4:14
45:23 [j]Lev. 23:8 [k]Num. 28:15
45:24 [l]ch. 46:5
45:25 [m]Lev. 23:33; Num. 29:12; Deut. 16:13

and according to the meat offering, and according to the oil.

46 Thus saith the Lord GOD; The gate of
the inner court that looketh toward
the east shall be shut the six working days;
but on the sabbath it shall be opened, and in
the day of the new moon it shall be opened.
2 [n]And the prince shall enter by the way
of the porch of *that* gate without, and shall
stand by the post of the gate, and the priests
shall prepare his burnt offering and his
peace offerings, and he shall worship at the
threshold of the gate: then he shall go forth;
but the gate shall not be shut until the evening.
3 Likewise the people of the land shall
worship at the door of this gate before the
LORD in the sabbaths and in the new moons.
4 And the burnt offering that [o]the prince
shall offer unto the LORD in the sabbath day
shall be six lambs without blemish, and a
ram without blemish.
5 [p]And the meat offering *shall be* an
ephah for a ram, and the meat offering for
the lambs as he shall be able to give, and an
hin of oil to an ephah.
6 And in the day of the new moon *it shall
be* a young bullock without blemish, and six
lambs, and a ram: they shall be without
blemish.
7 And he shall prepare a meat offering, an
ephah for a bullock, and an ephah for a ram,
and for the lambs according as his hand
shall attain unto, and an hin of oil to an
ephah.
8 [q]And when the prince shall enter, he
shall go in by the way of the porch of *that*
gate, and he shall go forth by the way
thereof.
9 ¶ But when the people of the land [r]shall
come before the LORD in the solemn feasts,
he that entereth in by the way of the north
gate to worship shall go out by the way of
the south gate; and he that entereth by the
way of the south gate shall go forth by the
way of the north gate: he shall not return by
the way of the gate whereby he came in, but
shall go forth over against it.
10 And the prince in the midst of them,
when they go in, shall go in; and when they
go forth, shall go forth.
11 And in the feasts and in the solemnities [s]the meat offering shall be an ephah to
a bullock, and an ephah to a ram, and to the
lambs as he is able to give, and an hin of oil
to an ephah.
12 Now when the prince shall prepare a
voluntary burnt offering or peace offerings
voluntarily unto the LORD, [t]*one* shall then
open him the gate that looketh toward the
east, and he shall prepare his burnt offering
and his peace offerings, as he did on the
sabbath day: then he shall go forth; and after his going forth *one* shall shut the gate.
13 [u]Thou shalt daily prepare a burnt offering unto the LORD *of* a lamb of the first
year without blemish: thou shalt prepare it
every morning.
14 And thou shalt prepare a meat offering
for it every morning, the sixth part of an
ephah, and the third part of an hin of oil, to
temper with the fine flour; a meat offering
continually by a perpetual ordinance unto
the LORD.
15 Thus shall they prepare the lamb, and
the meat offering, and the oil, every morning *for* a continual burnt offering.
16 ¶ Thus saith the Lord GOD; If the
prince give a gift unto any of his sons, the
inheritance thereof shall be his sons'; it
shall be their possession by inheritance.
17 But if he give a gift of his inheritance to
one of his servants, then it shall be his to
[v]the year of liberty; after it shall return to
the prince: but his inheritance shall be his
sons' for them.
18 Moreover [w]the prince shall not take of
the people's inheritance by oppression, to
thrust them out of their possession; *but* he
shall give his sons inheritance out of his
own possession: that my people be not scattered every man from his possession.
19 ¶ After he brought me through the entry, which *was* at the side of the gate, into
the holy chambers of the priests, which
looked toward the north: and, behold, there
was a place on the two sides westward.
20 Then said he unto me, This *is* the place
where the priests shall [x]boil the trespass
offering and the sin offering, where they
shall [y]bake the meat offering; that they
bear *them* not out into the utter court, [z]to
sanctify the people.
21 Then he brought me forth into the utter
court, and caused me to pass by the four
corners of the court; and, behold, in every
corner of the court *there was* a court.
22 In the four corners of the court *there
were* courts joined of forty *cubits* long and
thirty broad: these four corners *were* of one
measure.
23 And *there was* a row *of building* round
about in them, round about them four, and
it was made with boiling places under the
rows round about.
24 Then said he unto me, These *are* the
places of them that boil, where the ministers of the house shall [a]boil the sacrifice of
the people.

47 Afterward he brought me again unto
the door of the house; and, behold,
[b]waters issued out from under the threshold of the house eastward: for the forefront
of the house *stood toward* the east, and the
waters came down from under from the
right side of the house, at the south *side* of
the altar.
2 Then brought he me out of the way of
the gate northward, and led me about the
way without unto the utter gate by the way
that looketh eastward; and, behold, there
ran out waters on the right side.
3 And when [c]the man that had the line in
his hand went forth eastward, he measured
a thousand cubits, and he brought me

46:2 [n]ch. 44:3; ver. 8
46:4 [o]ch. 45:17
46:5 [p]ch. 45:29; ver. 7
46:8 [q]ver. 2
46:9 [r]Ex. 23:14-17; Deut. 16:16
46:11 [s]ver. 5
46:12 [t]ch. 44:3; ver. 2
46:13 [u]Ex. 29:38; Num. 28:3
46:17 [v]Lev. 25:10
46:18 [w]ch. 45:8
46:20 [x]2 Chron. 35:13 [y]Lev. 2:4 [z]ch. 44:19
46:24 [a]ver. 20
47:1 [b]Joel 3:18; Zech. 13:1; Rev. 22:1
47:3 [c]ch. 40:3

through the waters; the waters *were* to the
ankles.
4 Again he measured a thousand, and
brought me through the waters; the waters
were to the knees. Again he measured a
thousand, and brought me through; the waters *were* to the loins.
5 Afterward he measured a thousand;
and it was a river that I could not pass over:
for the waters were risen, waters to swim in,
a river that could not be passed over.
6 ¶ And he said unto me, Son of man, hast
thou seen *this?* Then he brought me, and
caused me to return to the brink of the river.
7 Now when I had returned, behold, at the
bank of the river *were* very many [d]trees on
the one side and on the other.
8 Then said he unto me, These waters issue out toward the east country, and go
down into the desert, and go into the sea:
which being brought forth into the sea, the
waters shall be healed.
9 And it shall come to pass, *that* every
thing that liveth, which moveth, whithersoever the rivers shall come, shall live: and
there shall be a very great multitude of fish,
because these waters shall come thither: for
they shall be healed; and every thing shall
live whither the river cometh.
10 And it shall come to pass, *that* the fishers shall stand upon it from En-gedi even
unto En-eglaim; they shall be a *place* to
spread forth nets; their fish shall be according to their kinds, as the fish [e]of the great
sea, exceeding many.
11 But the miry places thereof and the
marishes thereof shall not be healed; they
shall be given to salt.
12 And [f]by the river upon the bank
thereof, on this side and on that side, shall
grow all trees for meat, [g]whose leaf shall
not fade, neither shall the fruit thereof be
consumed: it shall bring forth new fruit according to his months, because their waters
they issued out of the sanctuary: and the
fruit thereof shall be for meat, and the leaf
thereof for [h]medicine.
13 ¶ Thus saith the Lord GOD; This *shall
be* the border, whereby ye shall inherit the
land according to the twelve tribes of Israel:
[i]Joseph *shall have two* portions.
14 And ye shall inherit it, one as well as
another: *concerning* the which I [j]lifted up
mine hand to give it unto your fathers: and
this land shall [k]fall unto you for inheritance.
15 And this *shall be* the border of the land
toward the north side, from the great sea,
[l]the way of Hethlon, as men go to [m]Zedad;
16 [n]Hamath, [o]Berothah, Sibraim, which
is between the border of Damascus and the
border of Hamath; Hazar-hatticon, which *is*
by the coast of Hauran.
17 And the border from the sea shall be
[p]Hazar-enan, the border of Damascus, and
the north northward, and the border of Hamath. And *this is* the north side.
18 And the east side ye shall measure

47:7 [d]ver. 12; Rev. 22:2
47:10 [e]Num. 34:6; Josh. 23:4; ch. 48:28
47:12 [f]ver. 7 [g]Job 8:16; Ps. 1:3; Jer. 17:8 [h]Rev. 22:2
47:13 [i]Gen. 48:5; 1 Chron. 5:1; ch. 48:4
47:14 [j]Gen. 12:7; ch. 20:5 [k]ch. 48:29
47:15 [l]ch. 48:1 [m]Num. 34:8
47:16 [n]Num. 34:8 [o]2 Sam. 8:8
47:17 [p]Num. 34:9; ch. 48:1
47:19 [q]Num. 20:13; Deut. 32:51; Ps. 81:7; ch. 48:28
47:22 [r]Eph. 3:6; Rev. 7:9 [s]Rom. 10:12; Gal. 3:28; Col. 3:11
48:1 [t]ch. 47:15
48:8 [u]ch. 45:1-6
48:11 [v]ch. 44:15

from Hauran, and from Damascus, and
from Gilead, and from the land of Israel *by*
Jordan, from the border unto the east sea.
And *this is* the east side.
19 And the south side southward, from
Tamar *even* to [q]the waters of strife *in* Kadesh, the river to the great sea. And *this is*
the south side southward.
20 The west side also *shall be* the great
sea from the border, till a man come over
against Hamath. This *is* the west side.
21 So shall ye divide this land unto you
according to the tribes of Israel.
22 ¶ And it shall come to pass, *that* ye
shall divide it by lot for an inheritance unto
you, [r]and to the strangers that sojourn
among you, which shall beget children
among you: [s]and they shall be unto you as
born in the country among the children of
Israel; they shall have inheritance with you
among the tribes of Israel.
23 And it shall come to pass, *that* in what
tribe the stranger sojourneth, there shall ye
give *him* his inheritance, saith the Lord
GOD.

48 Now these *are* the names of the
tribes. [t]From the north end to the
coast of the way of Hethlon, as one goeth to
Hamath, Hazar-enan, the border of Damascus northward, to the coast of Hamath; for
these are his sides east *and* west; a *portion
for* Dan.
2 And by the border of Dan, from the east
side unto the west side, a *portion for* Asher.
3 And by the border of Asher, from the
east side even unto the west side, a *portion
for* Naphtali.
4 And by the border of Naphtali, from the
east side unto the west side, a *portion for*
Manasseh.
5 And by the border of Manasseh, from
the east side unto the west side, a *portion
for* Ephraim.
6 And by the border of Ephraim, from the
east side even unto the west side, a *portion
for* Reuben.
7 And by the border of Reuben, from the
east side unto the west side, a *portion for*
Judah.
8 ¶ And by the border of Judah, from the
east side unto the west side, shall be [u]the
offering which ye shall offer of five and
twenty thousand *reeds in* breadth, and *in*
length as one of the *other* parts, from the
east side unto the west side: and the sanctuary shall be in the midst of it.
9 The oblation that ye shall offer unto the
LORD *shall be* of five and twenty thousand
in length, and of ten thousand in breadth.
10 And for them, *even* for the priests,
shall be *this* holy oblation; toward the north
five and twenty thousand *in length,* and toward the west ten thousand in breadth, and
toward the east ten thousand in breadth,
and toward the south five and twenty thousand in length: and the sanctuary of the
LORD shall be in the midst thereof.
11 [v]*It shall be* for the priests that are

sanctified of the sons of Zadok; which have kept my charge, which went not astray when the children of Israel went astray, [w]as the Levites went astray.

12 And *this* oblation of the land that is offered shall be unto them a thing most holy by the border of the Levites.

13 And over against the border of the priests the Levites *shall have* five and twenty thousand in length, and ten thousand in breadth: all the length *shall be* five and twenty thousand, and the breadth ten thousand.

14 [x]And they shall not sell of it, neither exchange, nor alienate the firstfruits of the land: for *it is* holy unto the LORD.

15 ¶ [y]And the five thousand, that are left in the breadth over against the five and twenty thousand, shall be [z]a profane *place* for the city, for dwelling, and for suburbs: and the city shall be in the midst thereof.

16 And these *shall be* the measures thereof; the north side four thousand and five hundred, and the south side four thousand and five hundred, and on the east side four thousand and five hundred, and the west side four thousand and five hundred.

17 And the suburbs of the city shall be toward the north two hundred and fifty, and toward the south two hundred and fifty, and toward the east two hundred and fifty, and toward the west two hundred and fifty.

18 And the residue in length over against the oblation of the holy *portion shall be* ten thousand eastward, and ten thousand westward: and it shall be over against the oblation of the holy *portion;* and the increase thereof shall be for food unto them that serve the city.

19 [a]And they that serve the city shall serve it out of all the tribes of Israel.

20 All the oblation *shall be* five and twenty thousand by five and twenty thousand: ye shall offer the holy oblation foursquare, with the possession of the city.

21 ¶ [b]And the residue *shall be* for the prince, on the one side and on the other of the holy oblation, and of the possession of the city, over against the five and twenty thousand of the oblation toward the east border, and westward over against the five and twenty thousand toward the west border, over against the portions for the prince: and it shall be the holy oblation; [c]and the sanctuary of the house *shall be* in the midst thereof.

22 Moreover from the possession of the Levites, and from the possession of the city, *being* in the midst *of that* which is the prince's, between the border of Judah and the border of Benjamin, shall be for the prince.

23 As for the rest of the tribes, from the east side unto the west side, Benjamin *shall have* a *portion.*

24 And by the border of Benjamin, from the east side unto the west side, Simeon *shall have* a *portion.*

25 And by the border of Simeon, from the east side unto the west side, Issachar a *portion.*

26 And by the border of Issachar, from the east side unto the west side, Zebulun a *portion.*

27 And by the border of Zebulun, from the east side unto the west side, Gad a *portion.*

28 And by the border of Gad, at the south side southward, the border shall be even from Tamar *unto* [d]the waters of strife *in* Kadesh, *and* to the river toward the great sea.

29 [e]This *is* the land which ye shall divide by lot unto the tribes of Israel for inheritance, and these *are* their portions, saith the Lord GOD.

30 ¶ And these *are* the goings out of the city on the north side, four thousand and five hundred measures.

31 [f]And the gates of the city *shall be* after the names of the tribes of Israel: three gates northward; one gate of Reuben, one gate of Judah, one gate of Levi.

32 And at the east side four thousand and five hundred: and three gates; and one gate of Joseph, one gate of Benjamin, one gate of Dan.

33 And at the south side four thousand and five hundred measures: and three gates; one gate of Simeon, one gate of Issachar, one gate of Zebulun.

34 At the west side four thousand and five hundred, *with* their three gates; one gate of Gad, one gate of Asher, one gate of Naphtali.

35 *It was* round about eighteen thousand *measures:* [g]and the name of the city from *that* day *shall be,* [h]The LORD *is* there.

48:11 [w]ch. 44:10
48:14 [x]Ex. 22:29; Lev. 27:10
48:15 [y]ch. 45:6 [z]ch. 42:20
48:19 [a]ch. 45:6
48:21 [b]ch. 45:7 [c]ver. 8
48:28 [d]ch. 47:19
48:29 [e]ch. 47:14
48:31 [f]Rev. 21:12
48:35 [g]Jer. 33:16 [h]Jer. 3:17; Joel 3:21; Zech. 2:10; Rev. 21:3

DANIEL

Daniel identifies himself several times as the author of this book. It was written about 537 B.C. The book of Daniel appears to be made up of two separate parts. The first six chapters tell about Daniel, and the second six chapters contain the prophecies related through Daniel.

Several well known stories found in Daniel include the three young men delivered from the fiery furnace (Chapter 3), the handwriting on the wall (Chapter 5), Daniel in the lion's den (Chapter 6), and the prophecy of Daniel's seventy weeks (Chapter 9).

I. Daniel's early life, 1:1–6:28
II. Daniel's prophecies, 7:1–12:13

---

1 In the third year of the reign of Jehoiakim king of Judah [a]came Nebuchadnezzar king of Babylon unto Jerusalem, and besieged it.

2 And the Lord gave Jehoiakim king of Judah into his hand, with [b]part of the vessels of the house of God: which he carried [c]into the land of Shinar to the house of his god; [d]and he brought the vessels into the treasure house of his god.

3 ¶ And the king spake unto Ashpenaz the master of his eunuchs, that he should bring *certain* of the children of Israel, and of the king's seed, and of the princes;

4 Children [e]in whom *was* no blemish, but well favoured, and skilful in all wisdom, and cunning in knowledge, and understanding science, and such as *had* ability in them to stand in the king's palace, and [f]whom they might teach the learning and the tongue of the Chaldeans.

5 And the king appointed them a daily provision of the king's meat, and of the wine which he drank: so nourishing them three years, that at the end thereof they might [g]stand before the king.

6 Now among these were of the children of Judah, Daniel, Hananiah, Mishael, and Azariah:

7 [h]Unto whom the prince of the eunuchs gave names: [i]for he gave unto Daniel *the name* of Belteshazzar; and to Hananiah, of Shadrach; and to Mishael, of Meshach; and to Azariah, of Abed-nego.

8 ¶ But Daniel purposed in his heart that he would not defile himself [j]with the portion of the king's meat, nor with the wine which he drank: therefore he requested of the prince of the eunuchs that he might not defile himself.

9 Now [k]God had brought Daniel into favour and tender love with the prince of the eunuchs.

10 And the prince of the eunuchs said unto Daniel, I fear my lord the king, who hath appointed your meat and your drink: for why should he see your faces worse liking than the children which *are* of your sort? then shall ye make *me* endanger my head to the king.

1:1 [a]2 Kings 24:1; 2 Chron. 36:6
1:2 [b]Jer. 27:19 [c]Gen. 10:10; Isa. 11:11; Zech. 5:11 [d]2 Chron. 36:7
1:4 [e]Lev. 24:19 [f]Acts 7:22
1:5 [g]ver. 19; Gen. 41:46; 1 Kings 10:8
1:7 [h]Gen. 41:45; 2 Kings 24:17 [i]ch. 4:8
1:8 [j]Deut. 32:38; Ezek. 4:13; Hos. 9:3
1:9 [k]Gen. 39:21; Ps. 106:46; Prov. 16:7
1:17 [l]1 Kings 3:12; Jam. 1:5 [m]Acts 7:22 [n]Num. 12:6; 2 Chron. 26:5; ch. 5:11
1:19 [o]Gen. 41:46; ver. 5
1:20 [p]1 Kings 10:1
1:21 [q]Ps. 110:1; ch. 6:28
2:1 [r]Gen. 41:8; ch. 4:5 [s]Esth. 6:1; ch. 6:18
2:2 [t]Gen. 41:8; Ex. 7:11; ch. 5:7

11 Then said Daniel to Melzar, whom the prince of the eunuchs had set over Daniel, Hananiah, Mishael, and Azariah,

12 Prove thy servants, I beseech thee, ten days; and let them give us pulse to eat, and water to drink.

13 Then let our countenances be looked upon before thee, and the countenance of the children that eat of the portion of the king's meat: and as thou seest, deal with thy servants.

14 So he consented to them in this matter, and proved them ten days.

15 And at the end of ten days their countenances appeared fairer and fatter in flesh than all the children which did eat the portion of the king's meat.

16 Thus Melzar took away the portion of their meat, and the wine that they should drink; and gave them pulse.

17 ¶ As for these four children, [l]God gave them [m]knowledge and skill in all learning and wisdom: and Daniel had [n]understanding in all visions and dreams.

18 Now at the end of the days that the king had said he should bring them in, then the prince of the eunuchs brought them in before Nebuchadnezzar.

19 And the king communed with them; and among them all was found none like Daniel, Hananiah, Mishael, and Azariah: therefore [o]stood they before the king.

20 [p]And in all matters of wisdom *and* understanding, that the king enquired of them, he found them ten times better than all the magicians *and* astrologers that *were* in all his realm.

21 [q]And Daniel continued *even* unto the first year of king Cyrus.

2 And in the second year of the reign of Nebuchadnezzar, Nebuchadnezzar dreamed dreams, [r]wherewith his spirit was troubled, and [s]his sleep brake from him.

2 [t]Then the king commanded to call the magicians, and the astrologers, and the sorcerers, and the Chaldeans, for to shew the king his dreams. So they came and stood before the king.

3 And the king said unto them, I have

dreamed a dream, and my spirit was troubled to know the dream.

4 Then spake the Chaldeans to the king in Syriack, [u]O king, live for ever: tell thy servants the dream, and we will shew the interpretation.

5 The king answered and said to the Chaldeans, The thing is gone from me: if ye will not make known unto me the dream, with the interpretation thereof, ye shall be [v]cut in pieces, and your houses shall be made a dunghill.

6 [w]But if ye shew the dream, and the interpretation thereof, ye shall receive of me gifts and rewards and great honour: therefore shew me the dream, and the interpretation thereof.

7 They answered again and said, Let the king tell his servants the dream, and we will shew the interpretation of it.

8 The king answered and said, I know of certainty that ye would gain the time, because ye see the thing is gone from me.

9 But if ye will not make known unto me the dream, [x]*there is but* one decree for you: for ye have prepared lying and corrupt words to speak before me, till the time be changed: therefore tell me the dream, and I shall know that ye can shew me the interpretation thereof.

10 ¶ The Chaldeans answered before the king, and said, There is not a man upon the earth that can shew the king's matter: therefore *there is* no king, lord, nor ruler, *that* asked such things at any magician, or astrologer, or Chaldean.

11 And *it is* a rare thing that the king requireth, and there is none other that can shew it before the king, [y]except the gods, whose dwelling is not with flesh.

12 For this cause the king was angry and very furious, and commanded to destroy all the wise *men* of Babylon.

13 And the decree went forth that the wise *men* should be slain; and they sought Daniel and his fellows to be slain.

14 ¶ Then Daniel answered with counsel and wisdom to Arioch the captain of the king's guard, which was gone forth to slay the wise *men* of Babylon:

15 He answered and said to Arioch the king's captain, Why *is* the decree *so* hasty from the king? Then Arioch made the thing known to Daniel.

16 Then Daniel went in, and desired of the king that he would give him time, and that he would shew the king the interpretation.

17 Then Daniel went to his house, and made the thing known to Hananiah, Mishael, and Azariah, his companions:

18 [z]That they would desire mercies of the God of heaven concerning this secret; that Daniel and his fellows should not perish with the rest of the wise *men* of Babylon.

19 ¶ Then was the secret revealed unto Daniel [a]in a night vision. Then Daniel blessed the God of heaven.

20 Daniel answered and said, [b]Blessed be the name of God for ever and ever: [c]for wisdom and might are his:

21 And he changeth [d]the times and the seasons: [e]he removeth kings, and setteth up kings: [f]he giveth wisdom unto the wise, and knowledge to them that know understanding:

22 [g]He revealeth the deep and secret things: [h]he knoweth what *is* in the darkness, and [i]the light dwelleth with him.

23 I thank thee, and praise thee, O thou God of my fathers, who hast given me wisdom and might, and hast made known unto me now what we [j]desired of thee: for thou hast *now* made known unto us the king's matter.

24 ¶ Therefore Daniel went in unto Arioch, whom the king had ordained to destroy the wise *men* of Babylon: he went and said thus unto him; Destroy not the wise *men* of Babylon: bring me in before the king, and I will shew unto the king the interpretation.

25 Then Arioch brought in Daniel before the king in haste, and said thus unto him, I have found a man of the captives of Judah, that will make known unto the king the interpretation.

26 The king answered and said to Daniel, whose name *was* Belteshazzar, Art thou able to make known unto me the dream which I have seen, and the interpretation thereof?

27 Daniel answered in the presence of the king, and said, The secret which the king hath demanded cannot the wise *men,* the astrologers, the magicians, the soothsayers, shew unto the king;

28 [k]But there is a God in heaven that revealeth secrets, and maketh known to the king Nebuchadnezzar [l]what shall be in the latter days. Thy dream, and the visions of thy head upon thy bed, are these;

29 As for thee, O king, thy thoughts came *into thy mind* upon thy bed, what should come to pass hereafter: [m]and he that revealeth secrets maketh known to thee what shall come to pass.

30 [n]But as for me, this secret is not revealed to me for *any* wisdom that I have more than any living, but for *their* sakes that shall make known the interpretation to the king, [o]and that thou mightest know the thoughts of thy heart.

31 ¶ Thou, O king, sawest, and behold a great image. This great image, whose brightness *was* excellent, stood before thee; and the form thereof *was* terrible.

32 [p]This image's head *was* of fine gold, his breast and his arms of silver, his belly and his thighs of brass,

33 His legs of iron, his feet part of iron and part of clay.

34 Thou sawest till that a stone was cut out [q]without hands, which smote the image upon his feet *that were* of iron and clay, and brake them to pieces.

35 Then was the iron, the clay, the brass,

2:4 [u]1 Kings 1:31; ch. 3:9
2:5 [v]Ezra 6:11; 2 Kings 10:27; ch. 3:29
2:6 [w]ch. 5:16
2:9 [x]Esth. 4:11
2:11 [y]ver. 28; ch. 5:11
2:18 [z]Matt. 18:12
2:19 [a]Num. 12:6; Job 33:15
2:20 [b]Ps. 113:2 [c]Jer. 32:19
2:21 [d]Esth. 1:13; 1 Chron. 29:30; ch. 7:25 [e]Job 12:18; Ps. 75:6; Jer. 27:5; ch. 4:17 [f]Jam. 1:5
2:22 [g]Job 12:22; Ps. 25:14; ver. 28 [h]Ps. 139:11; Heb. 4:13 [i]ch. 5:11; Jam. 1:17
2:23 [j]ver. 18
2:28 [k]Gen. 40:8; ver. 18; Am. 4:13 [l]Gen. 49:1
2:29 [m]ver. 22
2:30 [n]Gen. 41:16; Acts 3:12 [o]ver. 47
2:32 [p]ver. 38
2:34 [q]ch. 8:25; Zech. 4:6; 2 Cor. 5:1; Heb. 9:24

the silver, and the gold, broken to pieces
together, and became [r]like the chaff of the
summer threshingfloors; and the wind carried them away, that [s]no place was found
for them: and the stone that smote the image [t]became a great mountain, [u]and filled
the whole earth.
36 ¶ This *is* the dream; and we will tell the
interpretation thereof before the king.
37 [v]Thou, O king, *art* a king of kings:
[w]for the God of heaven hath given thee a
kingdom, power, and strength, and glory.
38 [x]And wheresoever the children of
men dwell, the beasts of the field and the
fowls of the heaven hath he given into thine
hand, and hath made thee ruler over them
all. [y]Thou *art* this head of gold.
39 And after thee shall arise [z]another
kingdom [a]inferior to thee, and another
third kingdom of brass, which shall bear
rule over all the earth.
40 And [b]the fourth kingdom shall be
strong as iron: forasmuch as iron breaketh
in pieces and subdueth all *things*: and as
iron that breaketh all these, shall it break in
pieces and bruise.
41 And whereas thou sawest [c]the feet
and toes, part of potters' clay, and part of
iron, the kingdom shall be divided; but
there shall be in it of the strength of the iron,
forasmuch as thou sawest the iron mixed
with miry clay.
42 And *as* the toes of the feet *were* part of
iron, and part of clay, *so* the kingdom shall
be partly strong, and partly broken.
43 And whereas thou sawest iron mixed
with miry clay, they shall mingle themselves with the seed of men: but they shall
not cleave one to another, even as iron is
not mixed with clay.
44 And in the days of these kings [d]shall
the God of heaven set up a kingdom,
[e]which shall never be destroyed: and the
kingdom shall not be left to other people,
[f]*but* it shall break in pieces and consume
all these kingdoms, and it shall stand for
ever.
45 [g]Forasmuch as thou sawest that the
stone was cut out of the mountain without
hands, and that it brake in pieces the iron,
the brass, the clay, the silver, and the gold;
the great God hath made known to the king
what shall come to pass hereafter: and the
dream *is* certain, and the interpretation
thereof sure.
46 ¶ [h]Then the king Nebuchadnezzar fell
upon his face, and worshipped Daniel, and
commanded that they should offer an oblation [i]and sweet odours unto him.
47 The king answered unto Daniel, and
said, Of a truth *it is*, that your God *is* a God
of gods, and a Lord of kings, [j]and a revealer of secrets, seeing thou couldest reveal this secret.
48 Then the king made Daniel a great
man, [k]and gave him many great gifts, and
made him ruler over the whole province of

2:35 [r]Ps. 1:4; Hos. 13:3 [s]Ps. 37:10 [t]Isa. 2:2 [u]Ps. 80:9
2:37 [v]Ezra 7:12; Isa. 47:5; Jer. 27:6; Ezek. 26:7; Hos. 8:10 [w]Ezra 1:2
2:38 [x]ch. 4:21; Jer. 27:6 [y]ver. 32
2:39 [z]ch. 5:28 [a]ver. 32
2:40 [b]ch. 7:7
2:41 [c]ver. 33
2:44 [d]ver. 28 [e]ch. 4:3; Mic. 4:7; Luke 1:32 [f]Ps. 2:9; Isa. 60:12; 1 Cor. 15:24
2:45 [g]ver. 35; Isa. 28:16
2:46 [h]Acts 10:25 [i]Ezra 6:10
2:47 [j]ver. 28
2:48 [k]ver. 6 [l]ch. 4:9
2:49 [m]ch. 3:12 [n]Esth. 2:19
3:4 [o]ch. 4:1
3:6 [p]Jer. 29:22; Rev. 13:15
3:8 [q]ch. 6:12
3:9 [r]ch. 2:4
3:12 [s]ch. 2:49

Babylon, and [l]chief of the governors over
all the wise *men* of Babylon.
49 Then Daniel requested of the king,
[m]and he set Shadrach, Meshach, and Abed-
nego, over the affairs of the province of
Babylon: but Daniel [n]*sat* in the gate of the
king.
3 Nebuchadnezzar the king made an image of gold, whose height *was* threescore cubits, *and* the breadth thereof six
cubits: he set it up in the plain of Dura, in
the province of Babylon.
2 Then Nebuchadnezzar the king sent to
gather together the princes, the governors,
and the captains, the judges, the treasurers,
the counsellors, the sheriffs, and all the rulers of the provinces, to come to the dedication of the image which Nebuchadnezzar
the king had set up.
3 Then the princes, the governors, and
captains, the judges, the treasurers, the
counsellors, the sheriffs, and all the rulers
of the provinces, were gathered together
unto the dedication of the image that Nebuchadnezzar the king had set up; and they
stood before the image that Nebuchadnezzar had set up.
4 Then an herald cried aloud, To you it is
commanded, [o]O people, nations, and languages,
5 *That* at what time ye hear the sound of
the cornet, flute, harp, sackbut, psaltery,
dulcimer, and all kinds of musick, ye fall
down and worship the golden image that
Nebuchadnezzar the king hath set up:
6 And whoso falleth not down and worshippeth shall the same hour [p]be cast into
the midst of a burning fiery furnace.
7 Therefore at that time, when all the people heard the sound of the cornet, flute,
harp, sackbut, psaltery, and all kinds of musick, all the people, the nations, and the
languages, fell down *and* worshipped the
golden image that Nebuchadnezzar the
king had set up.
8 ¶ Wherefore at that time certain Chaldeans [q]came near, and accused the Jews.
9 They spake and said to the king Nebuchadnezzar, [r]O king, live for ever.
10 Thou, O king, hast made a decree, that
every man that shall hear the sound of the
cornet, flute, harp, sackbut, psaltery, and
dulcimer, and all kinds of musick, shall fall
down and worship the golden image:
11 And whoso falleth not down and worshippeth, *that* he should be cast into the
midst of a burning fiery furnace.
12 [s]There are certain Jews whom thou
hast set over the affairs of the province of
Babylon, Shadrach, Meshach, and Abed-
nego; these men, O king, have not regarded
thee: they serve not thy gods, nor worship
the golden image which thou hast set up.
13 ¶ Then Nebuchadnezzar in *his* rage
and fury commanded to bring Shadrach,
Meshach, and Abed-nego. Then they
brought these men before the king.
14 Nebuchadnezzar spake and said unto

them, *Is it* true, O Shadrach, Meshach, and Abed-nego, do not ye serve my gods, nor worship the golden image which I have set up?

15 Now if ye be ready that at what time ye hear the sound of the cornet, flute, harp, sackbut, psaltery, and dulcimer, and all kinds of musick, ye fall down and worship the image which I have made; [t]*well:* but if ye worship not, ye shall be cast the same hour into the midst of a burning fiery furnace; [u]and who *is* that God that shall deliver you out of my hands?

16 Shadrach, Meshach, and Abed-nego, answered and said to the king, O Nebuchadnezzar, [v]we *are* not careful to answer thee in this matter.

17 If it be *so,* our God whom we serve is able to deliver us from the burning fiery furnace, and he will deliver *us* out of thine hand, O king.

18 But if not, be it known unto thee, O king, that we will not serve thy gods, nor worship the golden image which thou hast set up.

19 ¶ Then was Nebuchadnezzar full of fury, and the form of his visage was changed against Shadrach, Meshach, and Abed-nego: *therefore* he spake, and commanded that they should heat the furnace one seven times more than it was wont to be heated.

20 And he commanded the most mighty men that *were* in his army to bind Shadrach, Meshach, and Abed-nego, *and* to cast *them* into the burning fiery furnace.

21 Then these men were bound in their coats, their hosen, and their hats, and their *other* garments, and were cast into the midst of the burning fiery furnace.

22 Therefore because the king's commandment was urgent, and the furnace exceeding hot, the flame of the fire slew those men that took up Shadrach, Meshach, and Abed-nego.

23 And these three men, Shadrach, Meshach, and Abed-nego, fell down bound into the midst of the burning fiery furnace.

24 Then Nebuchadnezzar the king was astonied, and rose up in haste, *and* spake, and said unto his counsellors, Did not we cast three men bound into the midst of the fire? They answered and said unto the king, True, O king.

25 He answered and said, Lo, I see four men loose, [w]walking in the midst of the fire, and they have no hurt; and the form of the fourth is like [x]the Son of God.

26 Then Nebuchadnezzar came near to the mouth of the burning fiery furnace, *and* spake, and said, Shadrach, Meshach, and Abed-nego, ye servants of the most high God, come forth, and come *hither.* Then Shadrach, Meshach, and Abed-nego, came forth of the midst of the fire.

27 And the princes, governors, and captains, and the king's counsellors, being gathered together, saw these men, [y]upon whose bodies the fire had no power, nor was an hair of their head singed, neither were their coats changed, nor the smell of fire had passed on them.

28 *Then* Nebuchadnezzar spake, and said, Blessed *be* the God of Shadrach, Meshach, and Abed-nego, who hath sent his angel, and delivered his servants that [z]trusted in him, and have changed the king's word, and yielded their bodies, that they might not serve nor worship any god, except their own God.

29 [a]Therefore I make a decree, That every people, nation, and language, which speak any thing amiss against the God of Shadrach, Meshach, and Abed-nego, shall be [b]cut in pieces, and their houses shall be made a dunghill: [c]because there is no other God that can deliver after this sort.

30 Then the king promoted Shadrach, Meshach, and Abed-nego, in the province of Babylon.

4 Nebuchadnezzar the king, [d]unto all people, nations, and languages, that dwell in all the earth; Peace be multiplied unto you.

2 I thought it good to shew the signs and wonders [e]that the high God hath wrought toward me.

3 [f]How great *are* his signs! and how mighty *are* his wonders! his kingdom *is* [g]an everlasting kingdom, and his dominion *is* from generation to generation.

4 ¶ I Nebuchadnezzar was at rest in mine house, and flourishing in my palace:

5 I saw a dream which made me afraid, [h]and the thoughts upon my bed and the visions of my head [i]troubled me.

6 Therefore made I a decree to bring in all the wise *men* of Babylon before me, that they might make known unto me the interpretation of the dream.

7 [j]Then came in the magicians, the astrologers, the Chaldeans, and the soothsayers: and I told the dream before them; but they did not make known unto me the interpretation thereof.

8 ¶ But at the last Daniel came in before me, [k]whose name *was* Belteshazzar, according to the name of my god, [l]and in whom *is* the spirit of the holy gods: and before him I told the dream, *saying,*

9 O Belteshazzar, [m]master of the magicians, because I know that the spirit of the holy gods *is* in thee, and no secret troubleth thee, tell me the visions of my dream that I have seen, and the interpretation thereof.

10 Thus *were* the visions of mine head in my bed; I saw, and behold [n]a tree in the midst of the earth, and the height thereof *was* great.

11 The tree grew, and was strong, and the height thereof reached unto heaven, and the sight thereof to the end of all the earth:

12 The leaves thereof *were* fair, and the fruit thereof much, and in it *was* meat for all: [o]the beasts of the field had shadow under it, and the fowls of the heaven dwelt in

3:15 [t]Ex. 32:32; Luke 13:9 [u]Ex. 5:2; 2 Kings 18:35
3:16 [v]Matt. 10:19
3:25 [w]Isa. 43:2 [x]Job 1:6; Ps. 34:7; ver. 28
3:27 [y]Heb. 11:34
3:28 [z]Ps. 34:7; Jer. 17:7; ch. 6:22
3:29 [a]ch. 6:26 [b]ch. 2:5 [c]ch. 6:27
4:1 [d]ch. 3:4
4:2 [e]ch. 3:26
4:3 [f]ch. 6:27 [g]ver. 34; ch. 2:44
4:5 [h]ch. 2:28 [i]ch. 2:1
4:7 [j]ch. 2:2
4:8 [k]ch. 1:7 [l]Isa. 63:11; ver. 18; ch. 2:11
4:9 [m]ch. 2:48
4:10 [n]Ezek. 31:3; ver. 20
4:12 [o]Lam. 4:20; Ezek. 17:23

the boughs thereof, and all flesh was fed of it.

13 I saw in the visions of my head upon my bed, and, behold, [p]a watcher and [q]an holy one came down from heaven;

14 He cried aloud, and said thus, [r]Hew down the tree, and cut off his branches, shake off his leaves, and scatter his fruit: [s]let the beasts get away from under it, and the fowls from his branches:

15 Nevertheless leave the stump of his roots in the earth, even with a band of iron and brass, in the tender grass of the field; and let it be wet with the dew of heaven, and *let* his portion *be* with the beasts in the grass of the earth:

16 Let his heart be changed from man's, and let a beast's heart be given unto him; and let seven [t]times pass over him.

17 This matter *is* by the decree of the watchers, and the demand by the word of the holy ones: to the intent [u]that the living may know [v]that the most High ruleth in the kingdom of men, and giveth it to whomsoever he will, and setteth up over it the basest of men.

18 This dream I king Nebuchadnezzar have seen. Now thou, O Belteshazzar, declare the interpretation thereof, [w]forasmuch as all the wise *men* of my kingdom are not able to make known unto me the interpretation: but thou *art* able; [x]for the spirit of the holy gods *is* in thee.

19 ¶ Then Daniel, [y]whose name *was* Belteshazzar, was astonied for one hour, and his thoughts troubled him. The king spake, and said, Belteshazzar, let not the dream, or the interpretation thereof, trouble thee. Belteshazzar answered and said, My lord, [z]the dream *be* to them that hate thee, and the interpretation thereof to thine enemies.

20 [a]The tree that thou sawest, which grew, and was strong, whose height reached unto the heaven, and the sight thereof to all the earth;

21 Whose leaves *were* fair, and the fruit thereof much, and in it *was* meat for all; under which the beasts of the field dwelt, and upon whose branches the fowls of the heaven had their habitation:

22 [b]It *is* thou, O king, that art grown and become strong: for thy greatness is grown, and reacheth unto heaven, [c]and thy dominion to the end of the earth.

23 [d]And whereas the king saw a watcher and an holy one coming down from heaven, and saying, Hew the tree down, and destroy it; yet leave the stump of the roots thereof in the earth, even with a band of iron and brass, in the tender grass of the field; and let it be wet with the dew of heaven, [e]and *let* his portion *be* with the beasts of the field, till seven times pass over him;

24 This *is* the interpretation, O king, and this *is* the decree of the most High, which is come upon my lord the king:

25 That they shall [f]drive thee from men, and thy dwelling shall be with the beasts of the field, and they shall make thee [g]to eat grass as oxen, and they shall wet thee with the dew of heaven, and seven times shall pass over thee, [h]till thou know that the most High ruleth in the kingdom of men, and [i]giveth it to whomsoever he will.

26 And whereas they commanded to leave the stump of the tree roots; thy kingdom shall be sure unto thee, after that thou shalt have known that the [j]heavens do rule.

27 Wherefore, O king, let my counsel be acceptable unto thee, and [k]break off thy sins by righteousness, and thine iniquities by shewing mercy to the poor; [l]if it may be [m]a lengthening of thy tranquillity.

28 ¶ All this came upon the king Nebuchadnezzar.

29 At the end of twelve months he walked in the palace of the kingdom of Babylon.

30 The king [n]spake, and said, Is not this great Babylon, that I have built for the house of the kingdom by the might of my power, and for the honour of my majesty?

31 [o]While the word *was* in the king's mouth, there fell [p]a voice from heaven, *saying,* O king Nebuchadnezzar, to thee it is spoken; The kingdom is departed from thee.

32 And [q]they shall drive thee from men, and thy dwelling *shall be* with the beasts of the field: they shall make thee to eat grass as oxen, and seven times shall pass over thee, until thou know that the most High ruleth in the kingdom of men, and giveth it to whomsoever he will.

33 The same hour was the thing fulfilled upon Nebuchadnezzar: and he was driven from men, and did eat grass as oxen, and his body was wet with the dew of heaven, till his hairs were grown like eagles' *feathers,* and his nails like birds' *claws.*

34 And [r]at the end of the days I Nebuchadnezzar lifted up mine eyes unto heaven, and mine understanding returned unto me, and I blessed the most High, and I praised and honoured him [s]that liveth for ever, whose dominion *is* [t]an everlasting dominion, and his kingdom *is* from generation to generation:

35 And [u]all the inhabitants of the earth *are* reputed as nothing: and [v]he doeth according to his will in the army of heaven, and *among* the inhabitants of the earth: and [w]none can stay his hand, or say unto him, [x]What doest thou?

36 At the same time my reason returned unto me; [y]and for the glory of my kingdom, mine honour and brightness returned unto me; and my counsellors and my lords sought unto me; and I was established in my kingdom, and excellent majesty was [z]added unto me.

37 Now I Nebuchadnezzar praise and extol and honour the King of heaven, [a]all whose works *are* truth, and his ways judgment: [b]and those that walk in pride he is able to abase.

4:13 [p]Ps. 103:20; ver. 17 [q]Deut. 33:2; ch. 8:13; Zech. 14:5; Jude 14
4:14 [r]Matt. 3:10 [s]Ezek. 31:12
4:16 [t]ch. 11:13
4:17 [u]Ps. 9:16 [v]ch. 2:21; ver. 25
4:18 [w]Gen. 41:8; ch. 5:8 [x]ver. 8
4:19 [y]ver. 8 [z]2 Sam. 18:32; Jer. 29:7
4:20 [a]ver. 10
4:22 [b]ch. 2:38 [c]Jer. 27:6
4:23 [d]ver. 13 [e]ch. 5:21
4:25 [f]ver. 32; ch. 5:21 [g]Ps. 106:20 [h]ver. 17; Ps. 83:18 [i]Jer. 27:5
4:26 [j]Matt. 21:25; Luke 15:18
4:27 [k]1 Pet. 4:8 [l]Ps. 41:1 [m]1 Kings 21:29
4:30 [n]Prov. 16:18; ch. 5:20
4:31 [o]ch. 5:5; Luke 12:20 [p]ver. 24
4:32 [q]ver. 25
4:34 [r]ver. 26 [s]ch. 12:7; Rev. 4:10 [t]Ps. 10:16; ch. 2:44; Mic. 4:7; Luke 1:33
4:35 [u]Isa. 40:15 [v]Ps. 115:3 [w]Job 34:29 [x]Job 9:12; Isa. 45:9; Rom. 9:20
4:36 [y]ver. 26 [z]Job 42:12; Prov. 22:4; Matt. 6:33
4:37 [a]Ps. 33:4; Rev. 15:3 [b]Ex. 18:11; ch. 5:20

5 Belshazzar the king [c]made a great feast to a thousand of his lords, and drank wine before the thousand.

2 Belshazzar, while he tasted the wine, commanded to bring the golden and silver vessels [d]which his father Nebuchadnezzar had taken out of the temple which *was* in Jerusalem; that the king, and his princes, his wives, and his concubines, might drink therein.

3 Then they brought the golden vessels that were taken out of the temple of the house of God which *was* at Jerusalem; and the king, and his princes, his wives, and his concubines, drank in them.

4 They drank wine, [e]and praised the gods of gold, and of silver, of brass, of iron, of wood, and of stone.

5 ¶ [f]In the same hour came forth fingers of a man's hand, and wrote over against the candlestick upon the plaister of the wall of the king's palace: and the king saw the part of the hand that wrote.

6 Then the king's countenance was changed, and his thoughts troubled him, so that the joints of his loins were loosed, and his [g]knees smote one against another.

7 [h]The king cried aloud to bring in [i]the astrologers, the Chaldeans, and the soothsayers. *And* the king spake, and said to the wise *men* of Babylon, Whosoever shall read this writing, and shew me the interpretation thereof, shall be clothed with scarlet, and *have* a chain of gold about his neck, [j]and shall be the third ruler in the kingdom.

8 Then came in all the king's wise *men:* [k]but they could not read the writing, nor make known to the king the interpretation thereof.

9 Then was king Belshazzar greatly [l]troubled, and his countenance was changed in him, and his lords were astonied.

10 ¶ *Now* the queen, by reason of the words of the king and his lords, came into the banquet house: *and* the queen spake and said, [m]O king, live for ever: let not thy thoughts trouble thee, nor let thy countenance be changed:

11 [n]There is a man in thy kingdom, in whom *is* the spirit of the holy gods; and in the days of thy father light and understanding and wisdom, like the wisdom of the gods, was found in him; whom the king Nebuchadnezzar thy father, the king, *I say,* thy father, made [o]master of the magicians, astrologers, Chaldeans, *and* soothsayers;

12 [p]Forasmuch as an excellent spirit, and knowledge, and understanding, interpreting of dreams, and shewing of hard sentences, and dissolving of doubts, were found in the same Daniel, [q]whom the king named Belteshazzar: now let Daniel be called, and he will shew the interpretation.

13 Then was Daniel brought in before the king. *And* the king spake and said unto Daniel, *Art* thou that Daniel, which *art* of the children of the captivity of Judah, whom the king my father brought out of Jewry?

14 I have even heard of thee, that [r]the spirit of the gods *is* in thee, and *that* light and understanding and excellent wisdom is found in thee.

15 And now [s]the wise *men,* the astrologers, have been brought in before me, that they should read this writing, and make known unto me the interpretation thereof: but they could not shew the interpretation of the thing:

16 And I have heard of thee, that thou canst make interpretations, and dissolve doubts: [t]now if thou canst read the writing, and make known to me the interpretation thereof, thou shalt be clothed with scarlet, and *have* a chain of gold about thy neck, and shalt be the third ruler in the kingdom.

17 ¶ Then Daniel answered and said before the king, Let thy gifts be to thyself, and give thy rewards to another; yet I will read the writing unto the king, and make known to him the interpretation.

18 O thou king, [u]the most high God gave Nebuchadnezzar thy father a kingdom, and majesty, and glory, and honour:

19 And for the majesty that he gave him, [v]all people, nations, and languages, trembled and feared before him: whom he would he slew; and whom he would he kept alive; and whom he would he set up; and whom he would he put down.

20 [w]But when his heart was lifted up, and his mind hardened in pride, he was deposed from his kingly throne, and they took his glory from him:

21 And he was [x]driven from the sons of men; and his heart was made like the beasts, and his dwelling *was* with the wild asses: they fed him with grass like oxen, and his body was wet with the dew of heaven; [y]till he knew that the most high God ruled in the kingdom of men, and *that* he appointeth over it whomsoever he will.

22 And thou his son, O Belshazzar, [z]hast not humbled thine heart, though thou knewest all this;

23 [a]But hast lifted up thyself against the Lord of heaven; and they have brought the vessels of his house before thee, and thou, and thy lords, thy wives, and thy concubines, have drunk wine in them; and thou hast praised the gods of silver, and gold, of brass, iron, wood, and stone, [b]which see not, nor hear, nor know: and the God in whose hand thy breath *is,* [c]and whose *are* all thy ways, hast thou not glorified:

24 Then was the part of the hand sent from him; and this writing was written.

25 ¶ And this *is* the writing that was written, MENE, MENE, TEKEL, UPHARSIN.

26 This *is* the interpretation of the thing: MENE; God hath numbered thy kingdom, and finished it.

27 TEKEL; [d]Thou art weighed in the balances, and art found wanting.

5:1 [c]Esth. 1:3
5:2 [d]ch. 1:2; Jer. 52:19
5:4 [e]Rev. 9:20
5:5 [f]ch. 4:31
5:6 [g]Nah. 2:10
5:7 [h]ch. 2:2 [i]Isa. 47:13 [j]ch. 6:2
5:8 [k]ch. 2:27
5:9 [l]ch. 2:1
5:10 [m]ch. 2:4
5:11 [n]ch. 2:48 [o]ch. 4:9
5:12 [p]ch. 6:3 [q]ch. 1:7
5:14 [r]ver. 11
5:15 [s]ver. 7
5:16 [t]ver. 7
5:18 [u]ch. 2:37
5:19 [v]Jer. 27:7; ch. 3:4
5:20 [w]ch. 4:30
5:21 [x]ch. 4:32 [y]ch. 4:17
5:22 [z]2 Chron. 33:23
5:23 [a]ver. 3 [b]Ps. 115:5 [c]Jer. 10:23
5:27 [d]Job 31:6; Ps. 62:9; Jer. 6:30

28 PERES; Thy kingdom is divided, and
given to the [e]Medes and [f]Persians.
29 Then commanded Belshazzar, and
they clothed Daniel with scarlet, and *put* a
chain of gold about his neck, and made a
proclamation concerning him, [g]that he
should be the third ruler in the kingdom.
30 ¶ [h]In that night was Belshazzar the
king of the Chaldeans slain.
31 [i]And Darius the Median took the
kingdom, *being* about threescore and two
years old.

6 It pleased Darius to set [j]over the kingdom an hundred and twenty princes,
which should be over the whole kingdom;
2 And over these three presidents; of
whom Daniel *was* first: that the princes
might give accounts unto them, and the
king should have no damage.
3 Then this Daniel was preferred above
the presidents and princes, [k]because an excellent spirit *was* in him; and the king
thought to set him over the whole realm.
4 ¶ [l]Then the presidents and princes
sought to find occasion against Daniel concerning the kingdom; but they could find
none occasion nor fault; forasmuch as he
was faithful, neither was there any error or
fault found in him.
5 Then said these men, We shall not find
any occasion against this Daniel, except we
find *it* against him concerning the law of his
God.
6 Then these presidents and princes assembled together to the king, and said thus
unto him, [m]King Darius, live for ever.
7 All the presidents of the kingdom, the
governors, and the princes, the counsellors,
and the captains, have consulted together to
establish a royal statute, and to make a firm
decree, that whosoever shall ask a petition
of any God or man for thirty days, save of
thee, O king, he shall be cast into the den of
lions.
8 Now, O king, establish the decree, and
sign the writing, that it be not changed, according to the [n]law of the Medes and Persians, which altereth not.
9 Wherefore king Darius signed the writing and the decree.
10 ¶ Now when Daniel knew that the
writing was signed, he went into his house;
and his windows being open in his chamber
[o]toward Jerusalem, he kneeled upon his
knees [p]three times a day, and prayed, and
gave thanks before his God, as he did aforetime.
11 Then these men assembled, and found
Daniel praying and making supplication
before his God.
12 [q]Then they came near, and spake before the king concerning the king's decree;
Hast thou not signed a decree, that every
man that shall ask *a petition* of any God
or man within thirty days, save of thee,
O king, shall be cast into the den of lions?
The king answered and said, The thing *is*
true, [r]according to the law of the Medes
and Persians, which altereth not.
13 Then answered they and said before
the king, That Daniel, [s]which *is* of the children of the captivity of Judah, [t]regardeth
not thee, O king, nor the decree that thou
hast signed, but maketh his petition three
times a day.
14 Then the king, when he heard *these*
words, [u]was sore displeased with himself,
and set *his* heart on Daniel to deliver him:
and he laboured till the going down of the
sun to deliver him.
15 Then these men assembled unto the
king, and said unto the king, Know, O king,
that [v]the law of the Medes and Persians *is*,
That no decree nor statute which the king
establisheth may be changed.
16 Then the king commanded, and they
brought Daniel, and cast *him* into the den of
lions. *Now* the king spake and said unto
Daniel, Thy God whom thou servest continually, he will deliver thee.
17 [w]And a stone was brought, and laid
upon the mouth of the den; [x]and the king
sealed it with his own signet, and with the
signet of his lords; that the purpose might
not be changed concerning Daniel.
18 ¶ Then the king went to his palace, and
passed the night fasting: neither were instruments of musick brought before him:
[y]and his sleep went from him.
19 Then the king arose very early in the
morning, and went in haste unto the den of
lions.
20 And when he came to the den, he cried
with a lamentable voice unto Daniel: *and*
the king spake and said to Daniel, O Daniel,
servant of the living God, [z]is thy God,
whom thou servest continually, able to deliver thee from the lions?
21 Then said Daniel unto the king, [a]O
king, live for ever.
22 [b]My God hath sent his angel, and hath
[c]shut the lions' mouths, that they have not
hurt me: forasmuch as before him innocency was found in me; and also before
thee, O king, have I done no hurt.
23 Then was the king exceedingly glad
for him, and commanded that they should
take Daniel up out of the den. So Daniel was
taken up out of the den, and no manner of
hurt was found upon him, [d]because he believed in his God.
24 ¶ And the king commanded, [e]and they
brought those men which had accused Daniel, and they cast *them* into the den of lions,
them, [f]their children, and their wives; and
the lions had the mastery of them, and
brake all their bones in pieces or ever they
came at the bottom of the den.
25 ¶ [g]Then king Darius wrote unto all
people, nations, and languages, that dwell
in all the earth; Peace be multiplied unto
you.
26 [h]I make a decree, That in every dominion of my kingdom men [i]tremble and
fear before the God of Daniel: [j]for he *is* the

5:28 [e]Isa. 21:2; ver. 31; ch. 9:1 [f]ch. 6:28
5:29 [g]ver. 7
5:30 [h]Jer. 51:31
5:31 [i]ch. 9:1
6:1 [j]Esth. 1:1
6:3 [k]ch. 5:12
6:4 [l]Eccl. 4:4
6:6 [m]Neh. 2:3; ver. 21; ch. 2:4
6:8 [n]Esth. 1:19; ver. 12
6:10 [o]1 Kings 8:44; Ps. 5:7; Jonah 2:4 [p]Ps. 55:17; Acts 2:1
6:12 [q]ch. 3:8 [r]ver. 8
6:13 [s]ch. 1:6 [t]ch. 3:12
6:14 [u]Mark 6:26
6:15 [v]ver. 8
6:17 [w]Lam. 3:53 [x]Matt. 27:66
6:18 [y]ch. 2:1
6:20 [z]ch. 3:15
6:21 [a]ch. 2:4
6:22 [b]ch. 3:28 [c]Heb. 11:33
6:23 [d]Heb. 11:33
6:24 [e]Deut. 19:19 [f]Deut. 24:16; 2 Kings 14:16; Esth. 9:10
6:25 [g]ch. 4:1
6:26 [h]ch. 3:29 [i]Ps. 99:1 [j]ch. 4:34

living God, and steadfast for ever, and his
kingdom *that* which shall not be [k]de-
stroyed, and his dominion *shall be even*
unto the end.
27 He delivereth and rescueth, [l]and he
worketh signs and wonders in heaven and
in earth, who hath delivered Daniel from
the power of the lions.
28 So this Daniel prospered in the reign
of Darius, [m]and in the reign of [n]Cyrus the
Persian.

7 In the first year of Belshazzar king of
Babylon [o]Daniel had a dream and [p]vi-
sions of his head upon his bed: then he
wrote the dream, *and* told the sum of the
matters.
2 Daniel spake and said, I saw in my vision by night, and, behold, the four winds of
the heaven strove upon the great sea.
3 And four great beasts [q]came up from
the sea, diverse one from another.
4 The first *was* [r]like a lion, and had eagle's wings: I beheld till the wings thereof
were plucked, and it was lifted up from the
earth, and made stand upon the feet as a
man, and a man's heart was given to it.
5 [s]And behold another beast, a second,
like to a bear, and it raised up itself on one
side, and *it had* three ribs in the mouth of it
between the teeth of it: and they said thus
unto it, Arise, devour much flesh.
6 After this I beheld, and lo another, like
a leopard, which had upon the back of it
four wings of a fowl; the beast had also
[t]four heads; and dominion was given to it.
7 After this I saw in the night visions, and
behold [u]a fourth beast, dreadful and terrible, and strong exceedingly; and it had
great iron teeth: it devoured and brake in
pieces, and stamped the residue with the
feet of it: and it *was* diverse from all the
beasts that *were* before it; [v]and it had ten
horns.
8 I considered the horns, and, behold,
[w]there came up among them another little
horn, before whom there were three of the
first horns plucked up by the roots: and, behold, in this horn *were* eyes like the eyes
[x]of man, [y]and a mouth speaking great
things.
9 ¶ [z]I beheld till the thrones were cast
down, and [a]the Ancient of days did sit,
[b]whose garment *was* white as snow, and
the hair of his head like the pure wool: his
throne *was like* the fiery flame, [c]*and* his
wheels *as* burning fire.
10 [d]A fiery stream issued and came forth
from before him: [e]thousand thousands
ministered unto him, and ten thousand
times ten thousand stood before him: [f]the
judgment was set, and the books were
opened.
11 I beheld then because of the voice of
the great words which the horn spake: [g]I
beheld *even* till the beast was slain, and his
body destroyed, and given to the burning
flame.
12 As concerning the rest of the beasts,
they had their dominion taken away: yet
their lives were prolonged for a season and
time.
13 I saw in the night visions, and, behold,
[h]*one* like the Son of man came with the
clouds of heaven, and came to [i]the Ancient
of days, and they brought him near before
him.
14 [j]And there was given him dominion,
and glory, and a kingdom, that all [k]people,
nations, and languages, should serve him:
his dominion *is* [l]an everlasting dominion,
which shall not pass away, and his kingdom
that which shall not be destroyed.
15 ¶ I Daniel [m]was grieved in my spirit in
the midst of *my* body, and the visions of my
head troubled me.
16 I came near unto one of them that
stood by, and asked him the truth of all this.
So he told me, and made me know the interpretation of the things.
17 [n]These great beasts, which are four,
are four kings, *which* shall arise out of the
earth.
18 But [o]the saints of the most High shall
take the kingdom, and possess the kingdom
for ever, even for ever and ever.
19 Then I would know the truth of [p]the
fourth beast, which was diverse from all the
others, exceeding dreadful, whose teeth
were of iron, and his nails *of* brass; *which*
devoured, brake in pieces, and stamped the
residue with his feet;
20 And of the ten horns that *were* in his
head, and *of* the other which came up, and
before whom three fell; even *of* that horn
that had eyes, and a mouth that spake very
great things, whose look *was* more stout
than his fellows.
21 I beheld, [q]and the same horn made
war with the saints, and prevailed against
them;
22 [r]Until the Ancient of days came, [s]and
judgment was given to the saints of the
most High; and the time came that the
saints possessed the kingdom.
23 Thus he said, The fourth beast shall be
[t]the fourth kingdom upon earth, which
shall be diverse from all kingdoms, and
shall devour the whole earth, and shall
tread it down, and break it in pieces.
24 [u]And the ten horns out of this kingdom *are* ten kings *that* shall arise: and another shall rise after them; and he shall be
diverse from the first, and he shall subdue
three kings.
25 [v]And he shall speak *great* words
against the most High, and shall [w]wear out
the saints of the most High, and [x]think to
change times and laws: and [y]they shall be
given into his hand [z]until a time and times
and the dividing of time.
26 [a]But the judgment shall sit, and they
shall take away his dominion, to consume
and to destroy *it* unto the end.
27 And the [b]kingdom and dominion, and
the greatness of the kingdom under the
whole heaven, shall be given to the people

6:26 [k]ch. 2:44; Luke 1:33
6:27 [l]ch. 4:3
6:28 [m]ch. 1:21 [n]Ezra 1:1
7:1 [o]Num. 12:6; Am. 3:7 [p]ch. 2:28
7:3 [q]Rev. 13:1
7:4 [r]Deut. 28:49; 2 Sam. 1:23; Jer. 4:7; Ezek. 17:3; Hab. 1:8
7:5 [s]ch. 2:39
7:6 [t]ch. 8:8
7:7 [u]ch. 2:40; ver. 19:23 [v]ch. 2:41; Rev. 13:1
7:8 [w]ver. 20; ch. 8:9 [x]Rev. 9:7 [y]Ps. 12:3; ver. 25; Rev. 13:5
7:9 [z]Rev. 20:4 [a]Ps. 90:2; ver. 13:22 [b]Ps. 104:2; Rev. 1:14 [c]Ezek. 1:15
7:10 [d]Ps. 50:3; Isa. 30:33 [e]1 Kings 22:19; Ps. 68:17; Heb. 12:22; Rev. 5:11 [f]Rev. 20:4
7:11 [g]Rev. 19:20
7:13 [h]Ezek. 1:26; Matt. 24:30; Rev. 1:7 [i]ver. 9
7:14 [j]Ps. 2:6; Matt. 11:27; John 3:35; 1 Cor. 15:27; Eph. 1:22 [k]ch. 3:4 [l]Ps. 145:13; ch. 2:44; ver. 27; Mic. 4:7; Luke 1:33; John 12:34; Heb. 12:28
7:15 [m]ver. 28
7:17 [n]ver. 3
7:18 [o]Isa. 60:12; ver. 22; 2 Tim. 2:11; Rev. 2:26
7:19 [p]ver. 7
7:21 [q]ch. 8:12; Rev. 11:7
7:22 [r]ver. 9 [s]ver. 18; 1 Cor. 6:2; Rev. 1:6
7:23 [t]ch. 2:40
7:24 [u]ver. 7; Rev. 17:12
7:25 [v]Isa. 37:23; ch. 8:24; Rev. 13:5 [w]Rev. 17:6 [x]ch. 2:21 [y]Rev. 13:7 [z]ch. 12:7; Rev. 12:14
7:26 [a]ver. 10
7:27 [b]ver. 14

of the saints of the most High, [c]whose kingdom *is* an everlasting kingdom, [d]and all dominions shall serve and obey him.

28 Hitherto *is* the end of the matter. As for me Daniel, [e]my cogitations much troubled me, and my countenance changed in me: but I [f]kept the matter in my heart.

8 In the third year of the reign of king Belshazzar a vision appeared unto me, *even unto* me Daniel, after that which appeared unto me [g]at the first.

2 And I saw in a vision; and it came to pass, when I saw, that I *was* at [h]Shushan *in* the palace, which *is* in the province of Elam; and I saw in a vision, and I was by the river of Ulai.

3 Then I lifted up mine eyes, and saw, and, behold, there stood before the river a ram which had *two* horns: and the *two* horns *were* high; but one *was* higher than the other, and the higher came up last.

4 I saw the ram pushing westward, and northward, and southward; so that no beasts might stand before him, neither *was there any* that could deliver out of his hand; [i]but he did according to his will, and became great.

5 And as I was considering, behold, an he goat came from the west on the face of the whole earth, and touched not the ground: and the goat *had* [j]a notable horn between his eyes.

6 And he came to the ram that had *two* horns, which I had seen standing before the river, and ran unto him in the fury of his power.

7 And I saw him come close unto the ram, and he was moved with choler against him, and smote the ram, and brake his two horns: and there was no power in the ram to stand before him, but he cast him down to the ground, and stamped upon him: and there was none that could deliver the ram out of his hand.

8 Therefore the he goat waxed very great: and when he was strong, the great horn was broken; and for it came up [k]four notable ones toward the four winds of heaven.

9 [l]And out of one of them came forth a little horn, which waxed exceeding great, [m]toward the south, and toward the east, and toward the [n]pleasant *land.*

10 [o]And it waxed great, *even* to [p]the host of heaven; and [q]it cast down *some* of the host and of the stars to the ground, and stamped upon them.

11 Yea, [r]he magnified *himself* even to [s]the prince of the host, [t]and by him [u]the daily *sacrifice* was taken away, and the place of his sanctuary was cast down.

12 And [v]an host was given *him* against the daily *sacrifice* by reason of transgression, and it cast down [w]the truth to the ground; and it [x]practised, and prospered.

13 ¶ Then I heard [y]one saint speaking, and another saint said unto that certain *saint* which spake, How long *shall be* the vision *concerning* the daily *sacrifice,* and

7:27 [c]ch. 2:44; Luke 1:33; John 12:34; Rev. 11:15 [d]Isa. 60:12
7:28 [e]ver. 15; ch. 8:27 [f]Luke 2:19
8:1 [g]ch. 7:1
8:2 [h]Esth. 1:2
8:4 [i]ch. 5:19
8:5 [j]ver. 21
8:8 [k]ch. 7:6; ver. 22
8:9 [l]ch. 7:8 [m]ch. 11:25 [n]Ps. 48:2; Ezek. 20:6; ch. 11:16
8:10 [o]ch. 11:28 [p]Isa. 14:13 [q]Rev. 12:4
8:11 [r]Jer. 48:26; ch. 11:36; ver. 25 [s]Josh. 5:14 [t]ch. 11:31 [u]Ex. 29:38; Num. 28:3; Ezek. 46:13
8:12 [v]ch. 11:31 [w]Ps. 119:43; Isa. 59:14 [x]ver. 4; ch. 11:28
8:13 [y]ch. 4:13; 1 Pet. 1:12
8:15 [z]ch. 12:8; 1 Pet. 1:10 [a]Ezek. 1:26
8:16 [b]ch. 12:6 [c]ch. 9:21; Luke 1:19
8:17 [d]Ezek. 1:28; Rev. 1:17
8:18 [e]ch. 10:9; Luke 9:32 [f]Ezek. 2:2
8:19 [g]ch. 9:27; Hab. 2:3
8:20 [h]ver. 3
8:21 [i]ver. 5 [j]ch. 11:3
8:22 [k]ver. 8; ch. 11:4
8:23 [l]Deut. 28:50 [m]ver. 6
8:24 [n]Rev. 17:13 [o]ver. 12; ch. 11:36 [p]ver. 10; ch. 7:25
8:25 [q]ch. 11:21 [r]ver. 11; ch. 11:36 [s]ver. 11; ch. 11:36 [t]Job 34:20; Lam. 4:6; ch. 2:34
8:26 [u]ch. 10:1 [v]Ezek. 12:27; ch. 10:14; Rev. 22:10
8:27 [w]ch. 7:28 [x]ch. 6:2 [y]ver. 16
9:1 [z]ch. 1:21
9:2 [a]2 Chron. 36:21; Jer. 25:11

the transgression of desolation, to give both the sanctuary and the host to be trodden under foot?

14 And he said unto me, Unto two thousand and three hundred days; then shall the sanctuary be cleansed.

15 ¶ And it came to pass, when I, *even* I Daniel, had seen the vision, and [z]sought for the meaning, then, behold, there stood before me [a]as the appearance of a man.

16 And I heard a man's voice [b]between *the banks of* Ulai, which called, and said, [c]Gabriel, make this *man* to understand the vision.

17 So he came near where I stood: and when he came, I was afraid, and [d]fell upon my face: but he said unto me, Understand, O son of man: for at the time of the end *shall be* the vision.

18 [e]Now as he was speaking with me, I was in a deep sleep on my face toward the ground: [f]but he touched me, and set me upright.

19 And he said, Behold, I will make thee know what shall be in the last end of the indignation: [g]for at the time appointed the end *shall be.*

20 [h]The ram which thou sawest having *two* horns *are* the kings of Media and Persia.

21 [i]And the rough goat *is* the king of Grecia: and the great horn that *is* between his eyes [j]*is* the first king.

22 [k]Now that being broken, whereas four stood up for it, four kingdoms shall stand up out of the nation, but not in his power.

23 And in the latter time of their kingdom, when the transgressors are come to the full, a king [l]of fierce countenance, and understanding dark sentences, [m]shall stand up.

24 And his power shall be mighty, [n]but not by his own power: and he shall destroy wonderfully, [o]and shall prosper, and practise, [p]and shall destroy the mighty and the holy people.

25 And [q]through his policy also he shall cause craft to prosper in his hand; [r]and he shall magnify *himself* in his heart, and by peace shall destroy many: [s]he shall also stand up against the Prince of princes; but he shall be [t]broken without hand.

26 [u]And the vision of the evening and the morning which was told *is* true: [v]wherefore shut thou up the vision; for it *shall be* for many days.

27 [w]And I Daniel fainted, and was sick *certain* days; afterward I rose up, [x]and did the king's business; and I was astonished at the vision, [y]but none understood *it.*

9 In the first year [z]of Darius the son of Ahasuerus, of the seed of the Medes, which was made king over the realm of the Chaldeans;

2 In the first year of his reign I Daniel understood by books the number of the years, whereof the word of the LORD came to [a]Jeremiah the prophet, that he would ac-

complish seventy years in the desolations of Jerusalem.

3 ¶ [b]And I set my face unto the Lord God, to seek by prayer and supplications, with fasting, and sackcloth, and ashes:

4 And I prayed unto the LORD my God, and made my confession, and said, O [c]Lord, the great and dreadful God, keeping the covenant and mercy to them that love him, and to them that keep his commandments;

5 [d]We have sinned, and have committed iniquity, and have done wickedly, and have rebelled, even by departing from thy precepts and from thy judgments:

6 [e]Neither have we hearkened unto thy servants the prophets, which spake in thy name to our kings, our princes, and our fathers, and to all the people of the land.

7 O Lord, [f]righteousness *belongeth* unto thee, but unto us confusion of faces, as at this day; to the men of Judah, and to the inhabitants of Jerusalem, and unto all Israel, *that are* near, and *that are* far off, through all the countries whither thou hast driven them, because of their trespass that they have trespassed against thee.

8 O Lord, to us *belongeth* [g]confusion of face, to our kings, to our princes, and to our fathers, because we have sinned against thee.

9 [h]To the Lord our God *belong* mercies and forgivenesses, though we have rebelled against him;

10 [i]Neither have we obeyed the voice of the LORD our God, to walk in his laws, which he set before us by his servants the prophets.

11 Yea, [j]all Israel have transgressed thy law, even by departing, that they might not obey thy voice; therefore the curse is poured upon us, and the oath that *is* written in the [k]law of Moses the servant of God, because we have sinned against him.

12 And he hath [l]confirmed his words, which he spake against us, and against our judges that judged us, by bringing upon us a great evil: [m]for under the whole heaven hath not been done as hath been done upon Jerusalem.

13 [n]As *it is* written in the law of Moses, all this evil is come upon us: [o]yet made we not our prayer before the LORD our God, that we might turn from our iniquities, and understand thy truth.

14 Therefore hath the LORD [p]watched upon the evil, and brought it upon us: for [q]the LORD our God *is* righteous in all his works which he doeth: [r]for we obeyed not his voice.

15 And now, O Lord our God, [s]that hast brought thy people forth out of the land of Egypt with a mighty hand, and hast gotten thee [t]renown, as at this day; [u]we have sinned, we have done wickedly.

16 ¶ O Lord, [v]according to all thy righteousness, I beseech thee, let thine anger and thy fury be turned away from thy city Jerusalem, [w]thy holy mountain: because for our sins, [x]and for the iniquities of our fathers, [y]Jerusalem and thy people [z]*are become* a reproach to all *that are* about us.

17 Now therefore, O our God, hear the prayer of thy servant, and his supplications, [a]and cause thy face to shine upon thy sanctuary [b]that is desolate, [c]for the Lord's sake.

18 [d]O my God, incline thine ear, and hear; open thine eyes, [e]and behold our desolations, and the city [f]which is called by thy name: for we do not present our supplications before thee for our righteousnesses, but for thy great mercies.

19 O Lord, hear; O Lord, forgive; O Lord, hearken and do; defer not, [g]for thine own sake, O my God: for thy city and thy people are called by thy name.

20 ¶ [h]And whiles I *was* speaking, and praying, and confessing my sin and the sin of my people Israel, and presenting my supplication before the LORD my God for the holy mountain of my God;

21 Yea, whiles I *was* speaking in prayer, even the man [i]Gabriel, whom I had seen in the vision at the beginning, being caused to fly swiftly, [j]touched me [k]about the time of the evening oblation.

22 And he informed *me*, and talked with me, and said, O Daniel, I am now come forth to give thee skill and understanding.

23 At the beginning of thy supplications the commandment came forth, and [l]I am come to shew *thee;* [m]for thou *art* greatly beloved: therefore [n]understand the matter, and consider the vision.

24 Seventy weeks are determined upon thy people and upon thy holy city, to finish the transgression, and to make an end of sins, [o]and to make reconciliation for iniquity, [p]and to bring in everlasting righteousness, and to seal up the vision and prophecy, [q]and to anoint the most Holy.

25 [r]Know therefore and understand, *that* [s]from the going forth of the commandment to restore and to build Jerusalem unto [t]the Messiah [u]the Prince, *shall be* seven weeks, and threescore and two weeks: the street shall be built again, and the wall, [v]even in troublous times.

26 And after threescore and two weeks [w]shall Messiah be cut off, [x]but not for himself: and [y]the people of the prince that shall come [z]shall destroy the city [a]and the sanctuary; [b]and the end thereof *shall be* [c]with a flood, and unto the end of the war desolations are determined.

27 And he shall confirm [d]the covenant with [e]many for one week: and in the midst of the week he shall cause the sacrifice and the oblation to cease, and for the overspreading of [f]abominations he shall make *it* desolate, [g]even until the consummation,

9:3 [b]Neh. 1:4; ch. 6:10; Jer. 29:12; Jam. 4:8
9:4 [c]Ex. 20:6; Deut. 7:9; Neh. 1:5
9:5 [d]1 Kings 8:47; Neh. 1:6; Ps. 106:6; Isa. 64:5; Jer. 14:7; ver. 15
9:6 [e]2 Chron. 36:15; ver. 10
9:7 [f]Neh. 9:33
9:8 [g]ver. 7
9:9 [h]Neh. 9:17; Ps. 130:4
9:10 [i]ver. 6
9:11 [j]Isa. 1:4; Jer. 8:5 [k]Lev. 26:14; Deut. 27:15; Lam. 2:17
9:12 [l]Zech. 1:6 [m]Lam. 1:12; Ezek. 5:9; Am. 3:2
9:13 [n]Lev. 26:14; Deut. 28:15; Lam. 2:17 [o]Isa. 9:13; Jer. 2:30; Hos. 7:7
9:14 [p]Jer. 31:28 [q]Neh. 9:33; ver. 7 [r]ver. 10
9:15 [s]Ex. 6:1; 1 Kings 8:51; Neh. 1:10; Jer. 32:21 [t]Ex. 14:18; Neh. 9:10; Jer. 32:20 [u]ver. 5
9:16 [v]1 Sam. 12:7; Ps. 31:1; Mic. 6:4 [w]ver. 20; Zech. 8:3 [x]Ex. 20:5 [y]Lam. 2:15 [z]Ps. 44:13
9:17 [a]Num. 6:25; Ps. 67:1 [b]Lam. 5:18 [c]ver. 19; John 16:24
9:18 [d]Isa. 37:17 [e]Ex. 3:7; Ps. 80:14 [f]Jer. 25:29
9:19 [g]Ps. 79:9
9:20 [h]Ps. 32:5; Isa. 65:24
9:21 [i]ch. 8:16 [j]ch. 8:18 [k]1 Kings 18:36
9:23 [l]ch. 10:12 [m]ch. 10:11 [n]Matt. 24:15
9:24 [o]Isa. 53:10 [p]Isa. 53:11; Jer. 23:5; Heb. 9:12; Rev. 14:6 [q]Ps. 45:7; Luke 1:35; John 1:41; Heb. 9:11
9:25 [r]ver. 23; Matt. 24:15 [s]Ezra 4:24; Neh. 2:1 [t]John 1:41 [u]Isa. 55:4 [v]Neh. 4:8
9:26 [w]Isa. 53:8; Mark 9:12; Luke 24:26 [x]1 Pet. 2:21 [y]Matt. 22:7 [z]Luke 19:44 [a]Matt. 24:2 [b]Matt. 24:6 [c]Isa. 8:7; ch. 11:10; Nah. 1:8
9:27 [d]Isa. 42:6; Jer. 31:31; Ezek. 16:60 [e]Isa. 53:11; Matt. 26:28; Rom. 5:15; Heb. 9:28 [f]Matt. 24:15; Mark 13:14; Luke 21:20 [g]Isa. 10:22; ch. 11:36; Luke 21:24; Rom. 11:26

and that determined shall be poured upon
the desolate.

10 In the third year of Cyrus king of Persia a thing was revealed unto Daniel,
[h]whose name was called Belteshazzar;
[i]and the thing *was* true, [j]but the time appointed *was* long: and [k]he understood the
thing, and had understanding of the vision.
2 In those days I Daniel was mourning
three full weeks.
3 I ate no pleasant bread, neither came
flesh nor wine in my mouth, [l]neither did I
anoint myself at all, till three whole weeks
were fulfilled.
4 And in the four and twentieth day of the
first month, as I was by the side of the great
river, which *is* [m]Hiddekel;
5 Then [n]I lifted up mine eyes, and looked,
and behold [o]a certain man clothed in linen,
whose loins *were* [p]girded with [q]fine gold of
Uphaz:
6 His body also *was* [r]like the beryl, and
his face [s]as the appearance of lightning,
[t]and his eyes as lamps of fire, and his arms
[u]and his feet like in colour to polished
brass, [v]and the voice of his words like the
voice of a multitude.
7 And I Daniel [w]alone saw the vision: for
the men that were with me saw not the vision; but a great quaking fell upon them, so
that they fled to hide themselves.
8 Therefore I was left alone, and saw this
great vision, [x]and there remained no
strength in me: for my [y]comeliness was
turned in me into corruption, and I retained
no strength.
9 Yet heard I the voice of his words: [z]and
when I heard the voice of his words, then
was I in a deep sleep on my face, and my
face toward the ground.
10 ¶ [a]And, behold, an hand touched me,
which set me upon my knees and *upon* the
palms of my hands.
11 And he said unto me, O Daniel, [b]a
man greatly beloved, understand the words
that I speak unto thee, and stand upright:
for unto thee am I now sent. And when he
had spoken this word unto me, I stood trembling.
12 Then said he unto me, [c]Fear not, Daniel: for from the first day that thou didst set
thine heart to understand, and to chasten
thyself before thy God, [d]thy words were
heard, and I am come for thy words.
13 [e]But the prince of the kingdom of Persia withstood me one and twenty days: but,
lo, [f]Michael, one of the chief princes, came
to help me; and I remained there with the
kings of Persia.
14 Now I am come to make thee understand what shall befall thy people [g]in the
latter days: [h]for yet the vision *is* for *many*
days.
15 And when he had spoken such words
unto me, [i]I set my face toward the ground,
and I became dumb.
16 And, behold, [j]*one* like the similitude
of the sons of men [k]touched my lips: then I
opened my mouth, and spake, and said unto
him that stood before me, O my lord, by the
vision [l]my sorrows are turned upon me,
and I have retained no strength.
17 For how can the servant of this my
lord talk with this my lord? for as for me,
straightway there remained no strength in
me, neither is there breath left in me.
18 Then there came again and touched
me *one* like the appearance of a man, and
he strengthened me,
19 And said, [m]O man greatly beloved,
[n]fear not: peace *be* unto thee; be strong,
yea, be strong. And when he had spoken
unto me, I was strengthened, and said, Let
my lord speak; for thou hast strengthened me.
20 Then said he, Knowest thou wherefore
I come unto thee? and now will I return to
fight [o]with the prince of Persia: and when
I am gone forth, lo, the prince of Grecia
shall come.
21 But I will shew thee that which is noted
in the scripture of truth: and *there is* none
that holdeth with me in these things, [p]but
Michael your prince.

11 Also I [q]in the first year of [r]Darius
the Mede, *even* I, stood to confirm
and to strengthen him.
2 And now will I shew thee the truth. Behold, there shall stand up yet three kings in
Persia; and the fourth shall be far richer
than *they* all: and by his strength through
his riches he shall stir up all against the
realm of Grecia.
3 And [s]a mighty king shall stand up, that
shall rule with great dominion, and [t]do according to his will.
4 And when he shall stand up, [u]his kingdom shall be broken, and shall be divided
toward the four winds of heaven; and not to
his posterity, [v]nor according to his dominion which he ruled: for his kingdom shall be
plucked up, even for others beside those.
5 ¶ And the king of the south shall be
strong, and *one* of his princes; and he shall
be strong above him, and have dominion;
his dominion *shall be* a great dominion.
6 And in the end of years they shall join
themselves together; for the king's daughter of the south shall come to the king of the
north to make an agreement: but she shall
not retain the power of the arm; neither
shall he stand, nor his arm: but she shall be
given up, and they that brought her, and he
that begat her, and he that strengthened her
in *these* times.
7 But out of a branch of her roots shall
one stand up in his estate, which shall come
with an army, and shall enter into the fortress of the king of the north, and shall deal
against them, and shall prevail:
8 And shall also carry captives into Egypt
their gods, with their princes, *and* with their
precious vessels of silver and of gold; and
he shall continue *more* years than the king
of the north.
9 So the king of the south shall come into

10:1 [h]ch. 1:7 [i]ch. 8:26; Rev. 19:9 [j]ver. 14 [k]ch. 1:17
10:3 [l]Matt. 6:17
10:4 [m]Gen. 2:14
10:5 [n]Josh. 5:13 [o]ch. 12:6 [p]Rev. 1:13 [q]Jer. 10:9
10:6 [r]Ezek. 1:16 [s]Ezek. 1:14 [t]Rev. 1:14 [u]Ezek. 1:7; Rev. 1:15 [v]Ezek. 1:24; Rev. 1:15
10:7 [w]2 Kings 6:17; Acts 9:7
10:8 [x]ch. 8:27 [y]ch. 7:28
10:9 [z]ch. 8:18
10:10 [a]Jer. 1:9; ch. 9:21; Rev. 1:17
10:11 [b]ch. 9:23
10:12 [c]Rev. 1:17 [d]ch. 9:3; Acts 10:4
10:13 [e]ver. 20 [f]ver. 21; ch. 12:1; Jude 9; Rev. 12:7
10:14 [g]Gen. 49:1; ch. 2:28 [h]ch. 8:26; ver. 1; Hab. 2:3
10:15 [i]ver. 9; ch. 8:18
10:16 [j]ch. 8:15 [k]ver. 10; Jer. 1:9 [l]ver. 8
10:19 [m]ver. 11 [n]Judg. 6:23
10:20 [o]ver. 13
10:21 [p]ver. 13; Jude 9; Rev. 12:7
11:1 [q]ch. 9:1 [r]ch. 5:31
11:3 [s]ch. 7:6 [t]ch. 8:4; ver. 16
11:4 [u]ch. 8:8 [v]ch. 8:22

his kingdom, and shall return into his own land.

10 But his sons shall be stirred up, and shall assemble a multitude of great forces: and *one* shall certainly come, [w]and overflow, and pass through: then shall he return, and be stirred up, [x]*even* to his fortress.

11 And the king of the south shall be moved with choler, and shall come forth and fight with him, *even* with the king of the north: and he shall set forth a great multitude; but the multitude shall be given into his hand.

12 *And* when he hath taken away the multitude, his heart shall be lifted up; and he shall cast down *many* ten thousands: but he shall not be strengthened *by it*.

13 For the king of the north shall return, and shall set forth a multitude greater than the former, and shall certainly come after certain years with a great army and with much riches.

14 And in those times there shall many stand up against the king of the south: also the robbers of thy people shall exalt themselves to establish the vision; but they shall fall.

15 So the king of the north shall come, and cast up a mount, and take the most fenced cities: and the arms of the south shall not withstand, neither his chosen people, neither *shall there be any* strength to withstand.

16 But he that cometh against him [y]shall do according to his own will, and [z]none shall stand before him: and he shall stand in the glorious land, which by his hand shall be consumed.

17 He shall also [a]set his face to enter with the strength of his whole kingdom, and upright ones with him; thus shall he do: and he shall give him the daughter of women, corrupting her: but she shall not stand *on his side*, [b]neither be for him.

18 After this shall he turn his face unto the isles, and shall take many: but a prince for his own behalf shall cause the reproach offered by him to cease; without his own reproach he shall cause *it* to turn upon him.

19 Then he shall turn his face toward the fort of his own land: but he shall stumble and fall, [c]and not be found.

20 Then shall stand up in his estate a raiser of taxes *in* the glory of the kingdom: but within few days he shall be destroyed, neither in anger, nor in battle.

21 And in his estate [d]shall stand up a vile person, to whom they shall not give the honour of the kingdom: but he shall come in peaceably, and obtain the kingdom by flatteries.

22 [e]And with the arms of a flood shall they be overflown from before him, and shall be broken; [f]yea, also the prince of the covenant.

23 And after the league *made* with him [g]he shall work deceitfully: for he shall come up, and shall become strong with a small people.

24 He shall enter peaceably even upon the fattest places of the province; and he shall do *that* which his fathers have not done, nor his fathers' fathers; he shall scatter among them the prey, and spoil, and riches: *yea,* and he shall forecast his devices against the strong holds, even for a time.

25 And he shall stir up his power and his courage against the king of the south with a great army; and the king of the south shall be stirred up to battle with a very great and mighty army; but he shall not stand: for they shall forecast devices against him.

26 Yea, they that feed of the portion of his meat shall destroy him, and his army shall [h]overflow: and many shall fall down slain.

27 And both these kings' hearts *shall be* to do mischief, and they shall speak lies at one table; but it shall not prosper: for [i]yet the end *shall be* at the time appointed.

28 Then shall he return into his land with great riches; and [j]his heart *shall be* against the holy covenant; and he shall do *exploits*, and return to his own land.

29 At the time appointed he shall return, and come toward the south; [k]but it shall not be as the former, [l]or as the latter.

30 ¶ [m]For the ships of Chittim shall come against him: therefore he shall be grieved, and return, and have indignation [n]against the holy covenant: so shall he do; he shall even return, and have intelligence with them that forsake the holy covenant.

31 And arms shall stand on his part, [o]and they shall pollute the sanctuary of strength, and shall take away the daily *sacrifice*, and they shall place the abomination that maketh desolate.

32 And such as do wickedly against the covenant shall he corrupt by flatteries: but the people that do know their God shall be strong, and do *exploits*.

33 [p]And they that understand among the people shall instruct many: [q]yet they shall fall by the sword, and by flame, by captivity, and by spoil, *many* days.

34 Now when they shall fall, they shall be holpen with a little help: but many shall cleave to them with flatteries.

35 And *some* of them of understanding shall fall, [r]to try them, and to purge, and to make *them* white, [s]*even* to the time of the end: [t]because *it is* yet for a time appointed.

36 And the king [u]shall do according to his will; and he shall [v]exalt himself, and magnify himself above every god, and shall speak marvellous things [w]against the God of gods, and shall prosper [x]till the indignation be accomplished: for that that is determined shall be done.

37 Neither shall he regard the God of his fathers, [y]nor the desire of women, [z]nor regard any god: for he shall magnify himself above all.

38 But in his estate shall he honour the God of forces: and a god whom his fathers

11:10 [w]Isa. 8:8; ch. 9:26 [x]ver. 7
11:16 [y]ch. 8:4; ver. 3 [z]Josh. 1:5
11:17 [a]2 Chron. 20:3 [b]ch. 9:26
11:19 [c]Job 20:8; Ps. 37:36; Ezek. 26:21
11:21 [d]ch. 7:8
11:22 [e]ver. 10 [f]ch. 8:10
11:23 [g]ch. 8:25
11:26 [h]ver. 10
11:27 [i]ver. 29; ch. 8:19
11:28 [j]ver. 22
11:29 [k]ver. 23 [l]ver. 25
11:30 [m]Num. 24:24; Jer. 2:10 [n]ver. 28
11:31 [o]ch. 8:11
11:33 [p]Mal. 2:7 [q]Heb. 11:35
11:35 [r]ch. 12:10; 1 Pet. 1:7 [s]ch. 8:17; ver. 40 [t]ver. 29
11:36 [u]ver. 16 [v]ch. 7:8; 2 Thess. 2:4; Rev. 13:5 [w]ch. 8:11 [x]ch. 9:27
11:37 [y]1 Tim. 4:3 [z]Isa. 14:13; 2 Thess. 2:4

knew not shall he honour with gold, and silver, and with precious stones, and pleasant things.

39 Thus shall he do in the most strong holds with a strange god, whom he shall acknowledge *and* increase with glory: and he shall cause them to rule over many, and shall divide the land for gain.

40 [a]And at the time of the end shall the king of the south push at him: and the king of the north shall come against him [b]like a whirlwind, with chariots, [c]and with horsemen, and with many ships; and he shall enter into the countries, [d]and shall overflow and pass over.

41 He shall enter also into the glorious land, and many *countries* shall be overthrown: but these shall escape out of his hand, [e]*even* Edom, and Moab, and the chief of the children of Ammon.

42 He shall stretch forth his hand also upon the countries: and the land of Egypt shall not escape.

43 But he shall have power over the treasures of gold and of silver, and over all the precious things of Egypt: and the Libyans and the Ethiopians *shall be* [f]at his steps.

44 But tidings out of the east and out of the north shall trouble him: therefore he shall go forth with great fury to destroy, and utterly to make away many.

45 And he shall plant the tabernacles of his palace between the seas in [g]the glorious holy mountain; [h]yet he shall come to his end, and none shall help him.

12 And at that time shall [i]Michael stand up, the great prince which standeth for the children of thy people: [j]and there shall be a time of trouble, such as never was since there was a nation *even* to that same time: and at that time thy people [k]shall be delivered, every one that shall be found [l]written in the book.

2 And many of them that sleep in the dust of the earth shall awake, [m]some to everlasting life, and some to shame [n]*and* everlasting contempt.

11:40 [a]ver. 35 [b]Isa. 21:1; Zech. 9:14 [c]Ezek. 38:4; Rev. 9:16 [d]ver. 10
11:41 [e]Isa. 11:14
11:43 [f]Ex. 11:8; Judg. 4:10
11:45 [g]Ps. 48:2; ver. 16; 2 Thess. 2:4 [h]2 Thess. 2:8; Rev. 19:20
12:1 [i]ch. 10:13 [j]Isa. 26:20; Jer. 30:7; Matt. 24:21; Rev. 16:18 [k]Rom. 11:26 [l]Ex. 32:32; Ps. 56:8; Ezek. 13:9; Luke 19:10; Phil. 4:3; Rev. 3:5
12:2 [m]Matt. 25:46; John 5:28; Acts 24:15 [n]Isa. 66:24; Rom. 9:21
12:3 [o]ch. 11:33 [p]Prov. 4:18; Matt. 13:43 [q]Jam. 5:20 [r]1 Cor. 15:41
12:4 [s]ch. 8:26; ver. 9 [t]Rev. 10:4 [u]ch. 10:1; ver. 9
12:5 [v]ch. 10:4
12:6 [w]ch. 10:5 [x]ch. 8:13
12:7 [y]Deut. 32:40; Rev. 10:5 [z]ch. 4:34 [a]ch. 7:25; Rev. 12:14 [b]Luke 21:24; Rev. 10:7 [c]ch. 8:24
12:9 [d]ver. 4
12:10 [e]ch. 11:35; Zech. 13:9 [f]Hos. 14:9; Rev. 9:20 [g]ch. 11:33; John 7:17
12:11 [h]ch. 8:11
12:13 [i]ver. 9 [j]Isa. 57:2; Rev. 14:13 [k]Ps. 1:5

3 And [o]they that be wise shall [p]shine as the brightness of the firmament; [q]and they that turn many to righteousness [r]as the stars for ever and ever.

4 [s]But thou, O Daniel, [t]shut up the words, and seal the book, *even* to [u]the time of the end: many shall run to and fro, and knowledge shall be increased.

5 ¶ Then I Daniel looked, and, behold, there stood other two, the one on this side of the bank of the river, and the other on that side of the bank [v]of the river.

6 And *one* said to [w]the man clothed in linen, which *was* upon the waters of the river, [x]How long *shall it be* to the end of these wonders?

7 And I heard the man clothed in linen, which *was* upon the waters of the river, when he [y]held up his right hand and his left hand unto heaven, and sware by him [z]that liveth for ever [a]that *it shall be* for a time, times, and an half; [b]and when he shall have accomplished to scatter the power of [c]the holy people, all these *things* shall be finished.

8 And I heard, but I understood not: then said I, O my Lord, what *shall be* the end of these *things?*

9 And he said, Go thy way, Daniel: for the words *are* closed up and sealed [d]till the time of the end.

10 [e]Many shall be purified, and made white, and tried; [f]but the wicked shall do wickedly: and none of the wicked shall understand; but [g]the wise shall understand.

11 And from the time [h]*that* the daily *sacrifice* shall be taken away, and the abomination that maketh desolate set up, *there shall be* a thousand two hundred and ninety days.

12 Blessed *is* he that waiteth, and cometh to the thousand three hundred and five and thirty days.

13 But [i]go thou thy way till the end *be:* [j]for thou shalt rest, [k]and stand in thy lot at the end of the days.

HOSEA

Hosea is the author of this book, written sometime between 722 B.C. to 710 B.C. The first three chapters of Hosea tell the story of Hosea's marriage that was nearly destroyed by an unfaithful wife. In the end it was saved because of Hosea's faithfulness to his wife. Many believe this story illustrates Israel's unfaithfulness to God that eventually ends in reconciliation because of God's faithfulness.

I. Hosea's marriage and Israel compared, 1:1–3:5
II. Israel's unfaithfulness, 4:1–10:15
III. God's steadfast love for his people, 11:1–14:9

---

1 The word of the LORD that came unto
Hosea, the son of Beeri, in the days of
Uzziah, Jotham, Ahaz, *and* Hezekiah, kings
of Judah, and in the days of Jeroboam the
son of Joash, king of Israel.
2 The beginning of the word of the LORD
by Hosea. And the LORD said to Hosea,
[a]Go, take unto thee a wife of whoredoms
and children of whoredoms: for [b]the land
hath committed great whoredom, *departing*
from the LORD.
3 So he went and took Gomer the daughter of Diblaim; which conceived, and bare
him a son.
4 And the LORD said unto him, Call his
name Jezreel; for yet a little *while,* [c]and I
will avenge the blood of Jezreel upon the
house of Jehu, [d]and will cause to cease the
kingdom of the house of Israel.
5 [e]And it shall come to pass at that day,
that I will break the bow of Israel, in the
valley of Jezreel.
6 ¶ And she conceived again, and bare a
daughter. And *God* said unto him, Call her
name Lo-ruhamah: [f]for I will no more have
mercy upon the house of Israel; but I will
utterly take them away.
7 [g]But I will have mercy upon the house
of Judah, and will save them by the LORD
their God, and [h]will not save them by bow,
nor by sword, nor by battle, by horses, nor
by horsemen.
8 ¶ Now when she had weaned Lo-
ruhamah, she conceived, and bare a son.
9 Then said *God,* Call his name Lo-ammi:
for ye *are* not my people, and I will not be
your *God.*
10 Yet [i]the number of the children of Israel shall be as the sand of the sea, which
cannot be measured nor numbered; [j]and it
shall come to pass, *that* in the place where
it was said unto them, [k]Ye *are* not my people, *there* it shall be said unto them, *Ye are*
[l]the sons of the living God.
11 [m]Then shall the children of Judah and
the children of Israel be gathered together,
and appoint themselves one head, and they
shall come up out of the land: for great *shall*
be the day of Jezreel.
2 Say ye unto your brethren, Ammi; and
to your sisters, Ruhamah.

2 Plead with your mother, plead: for [n]she
is not my wife, neither *am* I her husband: let
her therefore put away her [o]whoredoms
out of her sight, and her adulteries from between her breasts;
3 Lest [p]I strip her naked, and set her as in
the day that she was [q]born, and make her
[r]as a wilderness, and set her like a dry
land, and slay her with [s]thirst.
4 And I will not have mercy upon her children; for they *be* the [t]children of whoredoms.
5 [u]For their mother hath played the harlot: she that conceived them hath done
shamefully: for she said, I will go after my
lovers, [v]that give *me* my bread and my water, my wool and my flax, mine oil and my
drink.
6 ¶ Therefore, behold, [w]I will hedge up
thy way with thorns, and make a wall, that
she shall not find her paths.
7 And she shall follow after her lovers,
but she shall not overtake them; and she
shall seek them, but shall not find *them:*
then shall she say, [x]I will go and return to
my [y]first husband; for then *was it* better
with me than now.
8 For she did not [z]know that [a]I gave her
corn, and wine, and oil, and multiplied her
silver and gold, *which* they prepared for
Baal.
9 Therefore will I return, and [b]take away
my corn in the time thereof, and my wine
in the season thereof, and will recover my
wool and my flax *given* to cover her nakedness.
10 And now [c]will I discover her lewdness
in the sight of her lovers, and none shall
deliver her out of mine hand.
11 [d]I will also cause all her mirth to
cease, her [e]feast days, her new moons, and
her sabbaths, and all her solemn feasts.
12 And I will destroy her vines and her fig
trees, [f]whereof she hath said, These *are* my
rewards that my lovers have given me: and
[g]I will make them a forest, and the beasts of
the field shall eat them.
13 And I will visit upon her the days of
Baalim, wherein she burned incense to
them, and she [h]decked herself with her ear-

1:2 [a]ch. 3:1 [b]Deut. 31:16; Ps. 73:27; Jer. 2:13; Ezek. 23:3
1:4 [c]2 Kings 10:11 [d]2 Kings 15:10
1:5 [e]2 Kings 15:29
1:6 [f]2 Kings 17:6
1:7 [g]2 Kings 19:35 [h]Zech. 4:6
1:10 [i]Gen. 32:12; Rom. 9:27 [j]Rom. 9:25; 1 Pet. 2:10 [k]ch. 2:23 [l]Jonah 1:12; 1 John 3:1
1:11 [m]Isa. 11:12; Jer. 3:18; Ezek. 34:23
2:2 [n]Isa. 50:1 [o]Ezek. 16:25
2:3 [p]Jer. 13:22; Ezek. 16:37 [q]Ezek. 16:4 [r]Ezek. 19:13 [s]Am. 8:11
2:4 [t]John 8:41
2:5 [u]Isa. 1:21; Jer. 3:1; Ezek. 16:15 [v]ver. 8; Jer. 44:17
2:6 [w]Job 3:23; Lam. 3:7
2:7 [x]ch. 5:15; Luke 15:18 [y]Ezek. 16:8
2:8 [z]Isa. 1:3 [a]Ezek. 16:17
2:9 [b]ver. 3
2:10 [c]Ezek. 16:37
2:11 [d]Am. 8:10 [e]1 Kings 12:32; Am. 8:5
2:12 [f]ver. 5 [g]Ps. 80:12; Isa. 5:5
2:13 [h]Ezek. 23:40

rings and her jewels, and she went after her lovers, and forgat me, saith the LORD.

14 ¶ Therefore, behold, I will allure her, and [i]bring her into the wilderness, and speak comfortably unto her.

15 And I will give her her vineyards from thence, and [j]the valley of Achor for a door of hope: and she shall sing there, as in [k]the days of her youth, and [l]as in the day when she came up out of the land of Egypt.

16 And it shall be at that day, saith the LORD, *that* thou shalt call me Ishi; and shalt call me no more Baali.

17 For [m]I will take away the names of Baalim out of her mouth, and they shall no more be remembered by their name.

18 And in that day will I make a [n]covenant for them with the beasts of the field and with the fowls of heaven, and *with* the creeping things of the ground: and [o]I will break the bow and the sword and the battle out of the earth, and will make them to [p]lie down safely.

19 And I will betroth thee unto me for ever; yea, I will betroth thee unto me in righteousness, and in judgment, and in lovingkindness, and in mercies.

20 I will even betroth thee unto me in faithfulness: and [q]thou shalt know the LORD.

21 And it shall come to pass in that day, [r]I will hear, saith the LORD, I will hear the heavens, and they shall hear the earth;

22 And the earth shall hear the corn, and the wine, and the oil; [s]and they shall hear Jezreel.

23 And [t]I will sow her unto me in the earth; [u]and I will have mercy upon her that had not obtained mercy; and I [v]will say to *them which were* not my people, Thou *art* my people; and they shall say, *Thou art* my God.

3 Then said the LORD unto me, [w]Go yet, love a woman beloved of *her* [x]friend, yet an adulteress, according to the love of the LORD toward the children of Israel, who look to other gods, and love flagons of wine.

2 So I bought her to me for fifteen *pieces* of silver, and *for* an homer of barley, and an half homer of barley:

3 And I said unto her, Thou shalt [y]abide for me many days; thou shalt not play the harlot, and thou shalt not be for *another* man: so *will* I also *be* for thee.

4 For the children of Israel shall abide many days [z]without a king, and without a prince, and without a sacrifice, and without an image, and without an [a]ephod, and *without* [b]teraphim:

5 Afterward shall the children of Israel return, and [c]seek the LORD their God, and [d]David their king; and shall fear the LORD and his goodness in the [e]latter days.

4 Hear the word of the LORD, ye children of Israel: for the LORD hath a [f]controversy with the inhabitants of the land, because *there is* no truth, nor mercy, nor [g]knowledge of God in the land.

2:14 *i*Ezek. 20:35
2:15 *j*Josh. 7:26; Isa. 65:10 *k*Jer. 2:2; Ezek. 16:8 *l*Ex. 15:1
2:17 *m*Ex. 23:13; Josh. 23:7; Ps. 16:4; Zech. 13:2
2:18 *n*Job 5:23; Isa. 11:6-9; Ezek. 34:25 *o*Ps. 46:9; Isa. 2:4; Ezek. 39:9; Zech. 9:10 *p*Lev. 26:5; Jer. 23:6
2:20 *q*Jer. 31:33; John 17:3
2:21 *r*Zech. 8:12
2:22 *s*ch. 1:4
2:23 *t*Jer. 31:27; Zech. 10:9 *u*ch. 1:6 *v*ch. 1:10; Zech. 13:9; Rom. 9:26; 1 Pet. 2:10
3:1 *w*ch. 1:2 *x*Jer. 3:30
3:3 *y*Deut. 21:13
3:4 *z*ch. 10:3 *a*Ex. 28:6 *b*Judg. 17:5
3:5 *c*Jer. 50:4; ch. 5:6 *d*Jer. 30:9; Ezek. 34:23 *e*Isa. 2:2; Jer. 30:24; Ezek. 38:8; Dan. 2:28; Mic. 4:1
4:1 *f*Isa. 1:18; Jer. 25:31; ch. 12:2; Mic. 6:2 *g*Jer. 4:22
4:3 *h*Jer. 4:28; Am. 5:16 *i*Zeph. 1:3
4:4 *j*Deut. 17:12
4:5 *k*Jer. 6:4
4:6 *l*Isa. 5:13
4:7 *m*ch. 13:6 *n*1 Sam. 2:30; Mal. 2:9; Phil. 3:19
4:9 *o*Isa. 24:2; Jer. 5:31
4:10 *p*Lev. 26:26; Mic. 6:14; Hag. 1:6
4:11 *q*Eccl. 7:7; Isa. 28:7
4:12 *r*Jer. 2:27; Hab. 2:19 *s*Isa. 44:20; ch. 5:4
4:13 *t*Isa. 1:29; Ezek. 6:13 *u*Am. 7:17; Rom. 1:28
4:14 *v*ver. 1
4:15 *w*ch. 9:15; Am. 4:4 *x*1 Kings 12:29; ch. 10:5 *y*Am. 8:14; Zeph. 1:5
4:16 *z*Jer. 3:6; Zech. 7:11
4:17 *a*Matt. 15:14
4:18 *b*Mic. 3:11
4:19 *c*Jer. 4:11 *d*Isa. 1:29; Jer. 2:26

2 By swearing, and lying, and killing, and stealing, and committing adultery, they break out, and blood toucheth blood.

3 Therefore [h]shall the land mourn, and [i]every one that dwelleth therein shall languish, with the beasts of the field, and with the fowls of heaven; yea, the fishes of the sea also shall be taken away.

4 Yet let no man strive, nor reprove another: for thy people *are* as they [j]that strive with the priest.

5 Therefore shalt thou fall [k]in the day, and the prophet also shall fall with thee in the night, and I will destroy thy mother.

6 ¶ [l]My people are destroyed for lack of knowledge: because thou hast rejected knowledge, I will also reject thee, that thou shalt be no priest to me: seeing thou hast forgotten the law of thy God, I will also forget thy children.

7 [m]As they were increased, so they sinned against me: [n]*therefore* will I change their glory into shame.

8 They eat up the sin of my people, and they set their heart on their iniquity.

9 And there shall be, [o]like people, like priest: and I will punish them for their ways, and reward them their doings.

10 For [p]they shall eat, and not have enough: they shall commit whoredom, and shall not increase: because they have left off to take heed to the LORD.

11 Whoredom and wine and new wine [q]take away the heart.

12 ¶ My people ask counsel at their [r]stocks, and their staff declareth unto them: for [s]the spirit of whoredoms hath caused *them* to err, and they have gone a whoring from under their God.

13 [t]They sacrifice upon the tops of the mountains, and burn incense upon the hills, under oaks and poplars and elms, because the shadow thereof *is* good: [u]therefore your daughters shall commit whoredom, and your spouses shall commit adultery.

14 I will not punish your daughters when they commit whoredom, nor your spouses when they commit adultery: for themselves are separated with whores, and they sacrifice with harlots: therefore the people *that* [v]doth not understand shall fall.

15 ¶ Though thou, Israel, play the harlot, *yet* let not Judah offend; [w]and come not ye unto Gilgal, neither go ye up to [x]Beth-aven, [y]nor swear, The LORD liveth.

16 For Israel [z]slideth back as a backsliding heifer: now the LORD will feed them as a lamb in a large place.

17 Ephraim *is* joined to idols: [a]let him alone.

18 Their drink is sour: they have committed whoredom continually: [b]her rulers *with* shame do love, Give ye.

19 [c]The wind hath bound her up in her wings, and [d]they shall be ashamed because of their sacrifices.

5 Hear ye this, O priests; and hearken, ye house of Israel; and give ye ear,

O house of the king; for judgment *is* toward
you, because [e]ye have been a snare on Mizpah, and a net spread upon Tabor.
2 And the revolters are [f]profound to
make slaughter, though I *have been* a
rebuker of them all.
3 [g]I know Ephraim, and Israel is not hid
from me: for now, O Ephraim, [h]thou com-
mittest whoredom, *and* Israel is defiled.
4 They will not frame their doings to turn
unto their God: for [i]the spirit of whoredoms *is* in the midst of them, and they have
not known the LORD.
5 And [j]the pride of Israel doth testify to
his face: therefore shall Israel and Ephraim
fall in their iniquity: Judah also shall fall
with them.
6 [k]They shall go with their flocks and
with their herds to seek the LORD; but they
shall not find *him;* he hath withdrawn himself from them.
7 They have [l]dealt treacherously against
the LORD: for they have begotten strange
children: now shall [m]a month devour them
with their portions.
8 [n]Blow ye the cornet in Gibeah, *and* the
trumpet in Ramah: [o]cry aloud *at* [p]Beth-
aven, [q]after thee, O Benjamin.
9 Ephraim shall be desolate in the day of
rebuke: among the tribes of Israel have I
made known that which shall surely be.
10 The princes of Judah were like them
that [r]remove the bound: *therefore* I will
pour out my wrath upon them like water.
11 Ephraim *is* [s]oppressed *and* broken in
judgment, because he willingly walked after [t]the commandment.
12 Therefore *will* I *be* unto Ephraim as a
moth, and to the house of Judah [u]as rottenness.
13 When Ephraim saw his sickness, and
Judah *saw* his [v]wound, then went Ephraim
[w]to the Assyrian, [x]and sent to king Jareb:
yet could he not heal you, nor cure you of
your wound.
14 For [y]I *will be* unto Ephraim as a lion,
and as a young lion to the house of Judah:
[z]I, *even* I, will tear and go away; I will take
away, and none shall rescue *him.*
15 ¶ I will go *and* return to my place, till
[a]they acknowledge their offence, and seek
my face: [b]in their affliction they will seek
me early.

6 Come, and let us return unto the LORD:
for [c]he hath torn, and [d]he will heal us;
he hath smitten, and he will bind us up.
2 [e]After two days will he revive us: in the
third day he will raise us up, and we shall
live in his sight.
3 [f]Then shall we know, *if* we follow on to
know the LORD: his going forth is prepared
[g]as the morning; and [h]he shall come unto
us [i]as the rain, as the latter *and* former rain
unto the earth.
4 ¶ [j]O Ephraim, what shall I do unto
thee? O Judah, what shall I do unto thee?
for your goodness *is* [k]as a morning cloud,
and as the early dew it goeth away.

5:1 [e]ch. 6:9
5:2 [f]Isa. 29:15
5:3 [g]Am. 3:2
[h]Ezek. 23:5;
ch. 4:17
5:4 [i]ch. 4:12
5:5 [j]ch. 7:10
5:6 [k]Prov. 1:28;
Isa. 1:15;
Jer. 11:11;
Ezek. 8:18;
Mic. 3:4; John 7:34
5:7 [l]Isa. 48:8;
Jer. 3:20; ch. 6:7;
Mal. 2:11
[m]Zech. 11:8
5:8 [n]ch. 8:1;
Joel 2:1
[o]Isa. 10:30
[p]Josh. 7:2;
ch. 4:15
[q]Judg. 5:14
5:10 [r]Deut. 19:14
5:11 [s]Deut. 28:33
[t]1 Kings 12:28;
Mic. 6:16
5:12 [u]Prov. 12:4
5:13 [v]Jer. 30:12
[w]2 Kings 15:19;
ch. 7:11 [x]ch. 10:6
5:14 [y]Lam. 3:10;
ch. 13:7
[z]Ps. 50:22
5:15 [a]Lev. 26:40;
Jer. 29:12;
Ezek. 6:9
[b]Ps. 72:34
6:1 [c]Deut. 32:39;
1 Sam. 2:6;
Job 5:18; ch. 5:14
[d]Jer. 30:17
6:2 [e]1 Cor. 15:4
6:3 [f]Isa. 54:13
[g]2 Sam. 23:4
[h]Ps. 72:6
[i]Job 29:23
6:4 [j]ch. 8:11
[k]ch. 13:3
6:5 [l]Jer. 1:10
[m]Jer. 23:29;
Heb. 4:12
6:6
[n]1 Sam. 15:22;
Eccl. 5:1; Mic. 6:8;
Matt. 9:13
[o]Ps. 50:8;
Prov. 21:3;
Isa. 1:11
[p]Jer. 22:16;
John 17:3
6:7 [q]ch. 8:1
[r]ch. 5:7
6:8 [s]ch. 12:11
6:9 [t]Jer. 11:9;
Ezek. 22:25; ch. 5:1
6:10 [u]Jer. 5:30
[v]ch. 4:12
6:11 [w]Jer. 51:33;
Joel 3:13;
Rev. 14:15
[x]Ps. 126:1
7:1 [y]ch. 5:1
7:2 [z]Jer. 17:1
[a]Ps. 9:16;
Prov. 5:22
[b]Ps. 90:8
7:3 [c]Rom. 1:32
7:4 [d]Jer. 9:2
7:7 [e]ch. 8:4
[f]2 Kings 15:10
[g]Isa. 64:7
7:8 [h]Ps. 106:35
7:9 [i]ch. 8:7
7:10 [j]ch. 5:5
[k]Isa. 9:13
7:11 [l]ch. 11:11
[m]2 Kings 15:19;
ch. 5:13
7:12 [n]Ezek. 12:13
[o]Lev. 26:14;
Deut. 28:15;
2 Kings 17:13

5 Therefore have I hewed *them* [l]by the
prophets; I have slain them by [m]the words
of my mouth: and thy judgments *are as* the
light *that* goeth forth.
6 For I desired [n]mercy, and [o]not sacrifice; and the [p]knowledge of God more than
burnt offerings.
7 But they like men [q]have transgressed
the covenant: [r]there have they dealt treacherously against me.
8 [s]Gilead *is* a city of them that work iniquity, *and is* polluted with blood.
9 And as troops of robbers wait for a man,
so [t]the company of priests murder in the
way by consent: for they commit lewdness.
10 I have seen [u]an horrible thing in the
house of Israel: there *is* [v]the whoredom of
Ephraim, Israel is defiled.
11 Also, O Judah, [w]he hath set an harvest
for thee, [x]when I returned the captivity of
my people.

7 When I would have healed Israel, then
the iniquity of Ephraim was discovered,
and the wickedness of Samaria: for [y]they
commit falsehood; and the thief cometh in,
and the troop of robbers spoileth without.
2 And they consider not in their hearts
that I [z]remember all their wickedness: now
[a]their own doings have beset them about;
they are [b]before my face.
3 They make the king glad with their
wickedness, and the princes [c]with their
lies.
4 [d]They *are* all adulterers, as an oven
heated by the baker, *who* ceaseth from raising after he hath kneaded the dough, until it
be leavened.
5 In the day of our king the princes have
made *him* sick with bottles of wine; he
stretched out his hand with scorners.
6 For they have made ready their heart
like an oven, whiles they lie in wait: their
baker sleepeth all the night; in the morning
it burneth as a flaming fire.
7 They are all hot as an oven, and have
devoured their judges; [e]all their kings [f]are
fallen: [g]*there is* none among them that calleth unto me.
8 Ephraim, he [h]hath mixed himself
among the people; Ephraim is a cake not
turned.
9 [i]Strangers have devoured his strength,
and he knoweth *it* not: yea, gray hairs are
here and there upon him, yet he knoweth
not.
10 And the [j]pride of Israel testifieth to
his face: and [k]they do not return to the
LORD their God, nor seek him for all this.
11 ¶ [l]Ephraim also is like a silly dove
without heart: [m]they call to Egypt, they go
to Assyria.
12 When they shall go, [n]I will spread my
net upon them; I will bring them down as
the fowls of the heaven; I will chastise them,
[o]as their congregation hath heard.
13 Woe unto them! for they have fled
from me: destruction unto them! because
they have transgressed against me: though

[p]I have redeemed them, yet they have spoken lies against me.

14 [q]And they have not cried unto me with their heart, when they howled upon their beds: they assemble themselves for corn and wine, *and* they rebel against me.

15 Though I have bound *and* strengthened their arms, yet do they imagine mischief against me.

16 [r]They return, *but* not to the most High: [s]they are like a deceitful bow: their princes shall fall by the sword for the [t]rage of their tongue: this *shall be* their derision [u]in the land of Egypt.

8 *Set* [v]the trumpet to thy mouth. *He shall come* [w]as an eagle against the house of the LORD, because [x]they have transgressed my covenant, and trespassed against my law.

2 [y]Israel shall cry unto me, My God, [z]we know thee.

3 Israel hath cast off *the thing that is* good: the enemy shall pursue him.

4 [a]They have set up kings, but not by me: they have made princes, and I knew *it* not: [b]of their silver and their gold have they made them idols, that they may be cut off.

5 ¶ Thy calf, O Samaria, hath cast *thee* off; mine anger is kindled against them: [c]how long *will it be* ere they attain to innocency?

6 For from Israel *was* it also: the workman made it; therefore it *is* not God: but the calf of Samaria shall be broken in pieces.

7 For [d]they have sown the wind, and they shall reap the whirlwind: it hath no stalk: the bud shall yield no meal: if so be it yield, [e]the strangers shall swallow it up.

8 [f]Israel is swallowed up: now shall they be among the Gentiles [g]as a vessel wherein *is* no pleasure.

9 For [h]they are gone up to Assyria, [i]a wild ass alone by himself: Ephraim [j]hath hired lovers.

10 Yea, though they have hired among the nations, now [k]will I gather them, and they shall sorrow a little for the burden of [l]the king of princes.

11 Because Ephraim hath made [m]many altars to sin, altars shall be unto him to sin.

12 I have written to him [n]the great things of my law, *but* they were counted as a strange thing.

13 [o]They sacrifice flesh *for* the sacrifices of mine offerings, and eat *it;* [p]*but* the LORD accepteth them not; [q]now will he remember their iniquity, and visit their sins: [r]they shall return to Egypt.

14 [s]For Israel hath forgotten [t]his Maker, and [u]buildeth temples; and Judah hath multiplied fenced cities: but [v]I will send a fire upon his cities, and it shall devour the palaces thereof.

9 Rejoice not, O Israel, for joy, as *other* people: for thou [w]hast gone a whoring from thy God, thou hast loved a [x]reward upon every cornfloor.

2 [y]The floor and the winepress shall not feed them, and the new wine shall fail in her.

3 They shall not dwell in [z]the LORD's land; [a]but Ephraim shall return to Egypt, and [b]they shall eat unclean *things* [c]in Assyria.

4 [d]They shall not offer wine *offerings* to the LORD, [e]neither shall they be pleasing unto him: [f]their sacrifices *shall be* unto them as the bread of mourners; all that eat thereof shall be polluted: for their bread [g]for their soul shall not come into the house of the LORD.

5 What will ye do in [h]the solemn day, and in the day of the feast of the LORD?

6 For, lo, they are gone because of destruction: [i]Egypt shall gather them up, Memphis shall bury them: the pleasant *places* for their silver, [j]nettles shall possess them: thorns *shall be* in their tabernacles.

7 The days of visitation are come, the days of recompence are come; Israel shall know *it:* the prophet *is* a fool, [k]the spiritual man *is* mad, for the multitude of thine iniquity, and the great hatred.

8 The [l]watchman of Ephraim *was* with my God: *but* the prophet *is* a snare of a fowler in all his ways, *and* hatred in the house of his God.

9 [m]They have deeply corrupted *themselves,* as in the days of [n]Gibeah: [o]*therefore* he will remember their iniquity, he will visit their sins.

10 I found Israel like grapes in the wilderness; I saw your fathers as [p]the firstripe in the fig tree [q]at her first time: *but* they went to [r]Baal-peor, and [s]separated themselves [t]unto *that* shame; [u]and *their* abominations were according as they loved.

11 *As for* Ephraim, their glory shall fly away like a bird, from the birth, and from the womb, and from the conception.

12 [v]Though they bring up their children, yet [w]will I bereave them, *that there shall* not *be* a man *left:* yea, [x]woe also to them when I [y]depart from them!

13 Ephraim, [z]as I saw Tyrus, *is* planted in a pleasant place: [a]but Ephraim shall bring forth his children to the murderer.

14 Give them, O LORD: what wilt thou give? give them [b]a miscarrying womb and dry breasts.

15 All their wickedness [c]*is* in Gilgal: for there I hated them: [d]for the wickedness of their doings I will drive them out of mine house, I will love them no more: [e]all their princes *are* revolters.

16 Ephraim is smitten, their root is dried up, they shall bear no fruit: yea, [f]though they bring forth, yet will I slay *even* the beloved *fruit* of their womb.

17 My God will cast them away, because they did not hearken unto him: and they shall be [g]wanderers among the nations.

10 Israel *is* [h]an empty vine, he bringeth forth fruit unto himself: according to the multitude of his fruit [i]he hath increased

7:13 [p]Mic. 6:4
7:14 [q]Job 35:9; Ps. 78:36; Jer. 3:10; Zech. 7:5
7:16 [r]ch. 11:7 [s]Ps. 78:57 [t]Ps. 73:9 [u]ch. 9:3
8:1 [v]ch. 5:8 [w]Deut. 28:49; Jer. 4:13; Hab. 1:8 [x]ch. 6:7
8:2 [y]Ps. 78:34; ch. 5:15 [z]Tit. 1:16
8:4 [a]2 Kings 15:13 [b]ch. 2:8
8:5 [c]Jer. 13:27
8:7 [d]Prov. 22:8; ch. 10:12 [e]ch. 7:9
8:8 [f]2 Kings 17:6 [g]Jer. 22:28
8:9 [h]2 Kings 15:19 [i]Jer. 2:24 [j]Isa. 30:6; Ezek. 16:33
8:10 [k]Ezek. 16:37 [l]Isa. 10:8; Ezek. 26:7; Dan. 2:37
8:11 [m]ch. 12:11
8:12 [n]Deut. 4:6; Ps. 119:18
8:13 [o]Jer. 7:21; Zech. 7:6 [p]Jer. 14:10; ch. 5:6; Am. 5:22 [q]ch. 9:9; Am. 8:7 [r]Deut. 28:68; ch. 9:3
8:14 [s]Deut. 32:18 [t]Isa. 29:23; Eph. 2:10 [u]1 Kings 12:31 [v]Jer. 17:27; Am. 2:5
9:1 [w]ch. 4:12 [x]Jer. 44:17; ch. 2:12
9:2 [y]ch. 2:9
9:3 [z]Lev. 25:23; Jer. 2:7 [a]ch. 8:13 [b]Ezek. 4:13; Dan. 1:8 [c]2 Kings 17:6; ch. 11:11
9:4 [d]ch. 3:4 [e]Jer. 6:20; ch. 8:13 [f]Deut. 26:14 [g]Lev. 17:11
9:5 [h]ch. 2:11
9:6 [i]ch. 7:16; ver. 3 [j]Isa. 5:6; ch. 10:8
9:7 [k]Ezek. 13:3; Mic. 2:11; Zeph. 3:4
9:8 [l]Jer. 6:17; Ezek. 3:17
9:9 [m]Isa. 31:6; ch. 10:9 [n]Judg. 19:22 [o]ch. 8:13
9:10 [p]Isa. 28:4; Mic. 7:1 [q]ch. 2:15 [r]Num. 25:3; Ps. 106:28 [s]ch. 4:14 [t]Judg. 6:32; Jer. 11:13 [u]Ps. 81:12; Ezek. 20:8; Am. 4:5
9:12 [v]Job 27:14 [w]Deut. 28:41 [x]Deut. 31:17; 2 Kings 7:18; ch. 5:6 [y]1 Sam. 28:15
9:13 [z]Ezek. 26 [a]ver. 16; ch. 13:16
9:14 [b]Luke 23:29
9:15 [c]ch. 4:15 [d]ch. 1:6 [e]Isa. 1:23
9:16 [f]ver. 13
9:17 [g]Deut. 28:64
10:1 [h]Nah. 2:2 [i]ch. 8:11

the altars; according to the goodness of his land [j]they have made goodly images.

2 Their heart is [k]divided; now shall they be found faulty: he shall break down their altars, he shall spoil their images.

3 [l]For now they shall say, We have no king, because we feared not the LORD; what then should a king do to us?

4 They have spoken words, swearing falsely in making a covenant: thus judgment springeth up [m]as hemlock in the furrows of the field.

5 The inhabitants of Samaria shall fear because of [n]the calves of [o]Beth-aven: for the people thereof shall mourn over it, and the priests thereof *that* rejoiced on it, [p]for the glory thereof, because it is departed from it.

6 It shall be also carried unto Assyria *for* a present to [q]king Jareb: Ephraim shall receive shame, and Israel shall be ashamed [r]of his own counsel.

7 [s]*As for* Samaria, her king is cut off as the foam upon the water.

8 [t]The high places also of Aven, [u]the sin of Israel, shall be destroyed: [v]the thorn and the thistle shall come up on their altars; [w]and they shall say to the mountains, Cover us; and to the hills, Fall on us.

9 [x]O Israel, thou hast sinned from the days of Gibeah: there they stood: [y]the battle in Gibeah against the children of iniquity did not overtake them.

10 [z]*It is* in my desire that I should chastise them; and [a]the people shall be gathered against them, when they shall bind themselves in their two furrows.

11 And Ephraim *is as* [b]an heifer *that is* taught, *and* loveth to tread out *the corn;* but I passed over upon her fair neck: I will make Ephraim to ride; Judah shall plow, *and* Jacob shall break his clods.

12 [c]Sow to yourselves in righteousness, reap in mercy; [d]break up your fallow ground: for *it is* time to seek the LORD, till he come and rain righteousness upon you.

13 [e]Ye have plowed wickedness, ye have reaped iniquity; ye have eaten the fruit of lies: because thou didst trust in thy way, in the multitude of thy mighty men.

14 [f]Therefore shall a tumult arise among thy people, and all thy fortresses shall be spoiled, as Shalman spoiled [g]Beth-arbel in the day of battle: [h]the mother was dashed in pieces upon *her* children.

15 So shall Beth-el do unto you because of your great wickedness: in a morning [i]shall the king of Israel utterly be cut off.

11 When [j]Israel *was* a child, then I loved him, and [k]called my [l]son out of Egypt.

2 *As* they called them, so they went from them: [m]they sacrificed unto Baalim, and burned incense to graven images.

3 [n]I taught Ephraim also to go, taking them by their arms; but they knew not that [o]I healed them.

4 I drew them with cords of a man, with bands of love: and [p]I was to them as they that take off the yoke on their jaws, and [q]I laid meat unto them.

5 ¶ [r]He shall not return into the land of Egypt, but the Assyrian shall be his king, [s]because they refused to return.

6 And the sword shall abide on his cities, and shall consume his branches, and devour *them,* [t]because of their own counsels.

7 And my people are bent to [u]backsliding from me: [v]though they called them to the most High, none at all would exalt *him.*

8 [w]How shall I give thee up, Ephraim? *how* shall I deliver thee, Israel? how shall I make thee as [x]Admah? *how* shall I set thee as Zeboim? [y]mine heart is turned within me, my repentings are kindled together.

9 I will not execute the fierceness of mine anger, I will not return to destroy Ephraim: [z]for I *am* God, and not man; the Holy One in the midst of thee: and I will not enter into the city.

10 They shall walk after the LORD: [a]he shall roar like a lion: when he shall roar, then the children shall tremble [b]from the west.

11 They shall tremble as a bird out of Egypt, [c]and as a dove out of the land of Assyria: [d]and I will place them in their houses, saith the LORD.

12 [e]Ephraim compasseth me about with lies, and the house of Israel with deceit: but Judah yet ruleth with God, and is faithful with the saints.

12 Ephraim [f]feedeth on wind, and followeth after the east wind: he daily increaseth lies and desolation; [g]and they do make a covenant with the Assyrians, and [h]oil is carried into Egypt.

2 [i]The LORD hath also a controversy with Judah, and will punish Jacob according to his ways; according to his doings will he recompense him.

3 ¶ He took his brother [j]by the heel in the womb, and by his strength he [k]had power with God:

4 Yea, he had power over the angel, and prevailed: he wept, and made supplication unto him: he found him *in* [l]Beth-el, and there he spake with us;

5 Even the LORD God of hosts; the LORD *is* his [m]memorial.

6 [n]Therefore turn thou to thy God: keep mercy and judgment and [o]wait on thy God continually.

7 ¶ *He is* a merchant, [p]the balances of deceit *are* in his hand: he loveth to oppress.

8 And Ephraim said, [q]Yet I am become rich, I have found me out substance: *in* all my labours they shall find none iniquity in me that *were* sin.

9 And [r]I *that am* the LORD thy God from the land of Egypt [s]will yet make thee to dwell in tabernacles, as in the days of the solemn feast.

10 [t]I have also spoken by the prophets,

10:1 [j]ch. 8:4
10:2 [k]1 Kings 18:21; Matt. 6:24
10:3 [l]ch. 3:4; Mic. 4:9; ver. 7
10:4 [m]Deut. 29:18; Am. 5:7; Acts 8:23; Heb. 12:15
10:5 [n]1 Kings 12:28; ch. 8:5 [o]ch. 4:15 [p]1 Sam. 4:21; ch. 9:11
10:6 [q]ch. 5:13 [r]ch. 11:6
10:7 [s]ver. 3
10:8 [t]ch. 4:15 [u]Deut. 9:21; 1 Kings 12:30 [v]ch. 9:6 [w]Isa. 2:19; Luke 23:30; Rev. 6:16
10:9 [x]ch. 9:9 [y]Judg. 20
10:10 [z]Deut. 28:63 [a]Jer. 16:16; Ezek. 23:46; ch. 8:10
10:11 [b]Jer. 50:11; Mic. 4:13
10:12 [c]Prov. 18:21 [d]Jer. 4:3
10:13 [e]Job 4:8; Prov. 22:8; ch. 8:7; Gal. 6:7
10:14 [f]ch. 13:16 [g]2 Kings 18:34 [h]ch. 13:16
10:15 [i]ver. 7
11:1 [j]ch. 2:15 [k]Matt. 2:15 [l]Ex. 4:22
11:2 [m]2 Kings 17:16; ch. 2:13
11:3 [n]Deut. 1:31; Isa. 46:3 [o]Ex. 15:26
11:4 [p]Lev. 26:13 [q]Ps. 78:25; ch. 2:8
11:5 [r]ch. 8:13 [s]2 Kings 17:13
11:6 [t]ch. 10:6
11:7 [u]Jer. 3:6; ch. 4:16 [v]ch. 7:16
11:8 [w]Jer. 9:7; ch. 6:4 [x]Gen. 14:8; Deut. 29:23; Am. 4:11 [y]Deut. 32:36; Isa. 63:15; Jer. 31:20
11:9 [z]Num. 23:19; Isa. 55:8; Mal. 3:6
11:10 [a]Isa. 31:4; Joel 3:16; Am. 1:2 [b]Zech. 8:7
11:11 [c]Isa. 60:8; ch. 7:11 [d]Ezek. 28:25
11:12 [e]ch. 12:1
12:1 [f]ch. 8:7 [g]2 Kings 17:4; ch. 5:13; ch. 7:11 [h]Isa. 30:6
12:2 [i]ch. 4:1; Mic. 6:2
12:3 [j]Gen. 25:26 [k]Gen. 32:24
12:4 [l]Gen. 28:12
12:5 [m]Ex. 3:15
12:6 [n]ch. 14:1; Mic. 6:8 [o]Ps. 37:7
12:7 [p]Prov. 11:1; Am. 8:5
12:8 [q]Zech. 11:5; Rev. 3:17
12:9 [r]ch. 13:4 [s]Lev. 23:42; Neh. 8:17; Zech. 14:16
12:10 [t]2 Kings 17:13

and I have multiplied visions, and used
similitudes, by the ministry of the prophets.
11 [u]*Is there* iniquity *in* Gilead? surely
they are vanity: they sacrifice bullocks in
[v]Gilgal; yea, [w]their altars *are* as heaps in
the furrows of the fields.
12 And Jacob [x]fled into the country of
Syria, and Israel [y]served for a wife, and for
a wife he kept *sheep*.
13 [z]And by a prophet the LORD brought
Israel out of Egypt, and by a prophet was he
preserved.
14 [a]Ephraim provoked *him* to anger most
bitterly: therefore shall he leave his blood
upon him, [b]and his [c]reproach shall his
Lord return unto him.

13

When Ephraim spake trembling, he
exalted himself in Israel; but [d]when
he offended in Baal, he died.
2 And now they sin more and more, and
[e]have made them molten images of their
silver, *and* idols according to their own understanding, all of it the work of the craftsmen: they say of them, Let the men that
sacrifice [f]kiss the calves.
3 Therefore they shall be [g]as the morning
cloud and as the early dew that passeth
away, [h]as the chaff *that* is driven with the
whirlwind out of the floor, and as the smoke
out of the chimney.
4 Yet [i]I *am* the LORD thy God from the
land of Egypt, and thou shalt know no god
but me: for [j]*there is* no saviour beside me.
5 ¶ [k]I did know thee in the wilderness,
[l]in the land of great drought.
6 [m]According to their pasture, so were
they filled; they were filled, and their heart
was exalted; therefore [n]have they forgotten me.
7 Therefore [o]I will be unto them as a lion:
as [p]a leopard by the way will I observe
them:
8 I will meet them [q]as a bear *that is* bereaved *of her whelps,* and will rend the caul
of their heart, and there will I devour them
like a lion: the wild beast shall tear them.
9 ¶ O Israel, [r]thou hast destroyed thyself; [s]but in me *is* thine help.
10 I will be thy king: [t]where *is any other*
that may save thee in all thy cities? and thy
judges of whom [u]thou saidst, Give me a
king and princes?
11 [v]I gave thee a king in mine anger, and
took *him* away in my wrath.
12 [w]The iniquity of Ephraim *is* bound up;
his sin *is* hid.
13 [x]The sorrows of a travailing woman
shall come upon him: he *is* [y]an unwise son;
for he should not [z]stay long in *the place of*
the breaking forth of children.
14 [a]I will ransom them from the power of
the grave; I will redeem them from death:
[b]O death, I will be thy plagues; O grave, I
will be thy destruction: [c]repentance shall
be hid from mine eyes.
15 ¶ Though [d]he be fruitful among *his*
brethren, [e]an east wind shall come, the
wind of the LORD shall come up from the
wilderness, and his spring shall become
dry, and his fountain shall be dried up: he
shall spoil the treasure of all pleasant vessels.
16 Samaria shall become desolate; [f]for
she hath rebelled against her God: [g]they
shall fall by the sword: their infants shall be
dashed in pieces, and their women with
child shall be ripped up.

14

O Israel, [h]return unto the LORD thy
God; [i]for thou hast fallen by thine
iniquity.
2 Take with you words, and turn to the
LORD: say unto him, Take away all iniquity,
and receive *us* graciously: so will we render
the [j]calves of our lips.
3 [k]Asshur shall not save us; [l]we will not
ride upon horses: [m]neither will we say any
more to the work of our hands, *Ye are* our
gods: [n]for in thee the fatherless findeth
mercy.
4 ¶ I will heal [o]their backsliding, I will
love them [p]freely: for mine anger is turned
away from him.
5 I will be as [q]the dew unto Israel: he
shall grow as the lily, and cast forth his
roots as Lebanon.
6 His branches shall spread, and [r]his
beauty shall be as the olive tree, and [s]his
smell as Lebanon.
7 [t]They that dwell under his shadow
shall return; they shall revive *as* the corn,
and grow as the vine: the scent thereof *shall*
be as the wine of Lebanon.
8 Ephraim *shall say,* [u]What have I to do
any more with idols? [v]I have heard *him,*
and observed him: I *am* like a green fir tree.
[w]From me is thy fruit found.
9 [x]Who *is* wise, and he shall understand
these *things?* prudent, and he shall know
them? for [y]the ways of the LORD *are* right,
and the just shall walk in them: but the
transgressors shall fall therein.

12:11 [u]ch. 5:1 [v]ch. 4:15; Am. 4:4 [w]ch. 8:11 **12:12** [x]Gen. 28:5; Deut. 26:5 [y]Gen. 29:20 **12:13** [z]Ex. 12:50; Ps. 77:20; Isa. 63:11; Mic. 6:4 **12:14** [a]2 Kings 17:11-18 [b]Dan. 11:18 [c]Deut. 28:37 **13:1** [d]2 Kings 17:16; ch. 11:2 **13:2** [e]ch. 2:8 [f]1 Kings 19:18 **13:3** [g]ch. 6:4 [h]Dan. 2:35 **13:4** [i]Isa. 43:11; ch. 12:9 [j]Isa. 43:11 **13:5** [k]Deut. 2:7 [l]Deut. 8:15 **13:6** [m]Deut. 8:12 [n]ch. 8:14 **13:7** [o]Lam. 3:10; ch. 5:14 [p]Jer. 5:6 **13:8** [q]2 Sam. 17:8; Prov. 17:12 **13:9** [r]Prov. 6:32; ch. 14:1; Mal. 1:9 [s]ver. 4 **13:10** [t]Deut. 32:38; ch. 10:3; ver. 4 [u]1 Sam. 8:5 **13:11** [v]1 Sam. 8:7; ch. 10:3 **13:12** [w]Deut. 32:34; Job 14:17 **13:13** [x]Isa. 13:8; Jer. 30:6 [y]Prov. 22:3 [z]2 Kings 19:3 **13:14** [a]Isa. 25:8; Ezek. 37:12 [b]1 Cor. 15:54 [c]Jer. 15:6; Rom. 11:29 **13:15** [d]Gen. 41:52 [e]Jer. 4:11; Ezek. 17:10; ch. 4:19 **13:16** [f]2 Kings 18:12 [g]2 Kings 8:12; Isa. 13:16; ch. 10:14; Am. 1:13; Nah. 3:10 **14:1** [h]ch. 12:6; Joel 2:13 [i]ch. 13:9 **14:2** [j]Heb. 13:15 **14:3** [k]Jer. 31:18; ch. 5:13 [l]Deut. 17:16; Ps. 33:17; Isa. 30:2 [m]ch. 2:17; ver. 8 [n]Ps. 10:14 **14:4** [o]Jer. 5:6; ch. 11:7 [p]Eph. 1:6 **14:5** [q]Job 29:19; Prov. 19:12 **14:6** [r]Ps. 52:8 [s]Gen. 27:27; SSol. 4:11 **14:7** [t]Ps. 91:1 **14:8** [u]ver. 3 [v]Jer. 31:18 [w]Jam. 1:17 **14:9** [x]Ps. 107:43; Jer. 9:12; Dan. 12:10; John 8:47 [y]Prov. 10:29; Luke 2:34; 2 Cor. 2:16; 1 Pet. 2:7

JOEL

Joel is the author of this book. The time when it was written is uncertain, but the ninth century B.C. seems most likely. The book opens with a description of the locust plague which is then compared to a great army. Following a call to repentance, the prophet tells of the future when God's spirit will be poured out on the earth—possibly at Pentecost. Finally the scene shifts again to a future time when God will judge wicked nations and establish his kingdom following the "Day of the Lord."

I. The plague of locusts, 1:1–2:17
II. God's promise for the future, 2:18–3:21

---

1 The word of the LORD that came to Joel
the son of Pethuel.
2 Hear this, ye old men, and give ear, all
ye inhabitants of the land. [a]Hath this been
in your days, or even in the days of your
fathers?
3 [b]Tell ye your children of it, and *let* your
children *tell* their children, and their children another generation.
4 [c]That which the palmerworm hath left
hath the locust eaten; and that which the
locust hath left hath the cankerworm eaten;
and that which the cankerworm hath left
hath the caterpiller eaten.
5 Awake, ye drunkards, and weep; and
howl, all ye drinkers of wine, because of the
new wine; [d]for it is cut off from your mouth.
6 For [e]a nation is come up upon my land,
strong, and without number, [f]whose teeth
are the teeth of a lion, and he hath the cheek
teeth of a great lion.
7 He hath [g]laid my vine waste, and
barked my fig tree: he hath made it clean
bare, and cast *it* away; the branches thereof
are made white.
8 ¶ [h]Lament like a virgin girded with
sackcloth for [i]the husband of her youth.
9 [j]The meat offering and the drink offering is cut off from the house of the LORD; the
priests, the LORD's ministers, mourn.
10 The field is wasted, [k]the land mourneth; for the corn is wasted: [l]the new wine is
dried up, the oil languisheth.
11 [m]Be ye ashamed, O ye husbandmen;
howl, O ye vinedressers, for the wheat and
for the barley; because the harvest of the
field is perished.
12 [n]The vine is dried up, and the fig tree
languisheth; the pomegranate tree, the
palm tree also, and the apple tree, *even* all
the trees of the field, are withered: because
[o]joy is withered away from the sons of
men.
13 [p]Gird yourselves, and lament, ye
priests: howl, ye ministers of the altar:
come, lie all night in sackcloth, ye ministers
of my God: for [q]the meat offering and the
drink offering is withholden from the house
of your God.
14 ¶ [r]Sanctify ye a fast, call [s]a solemn
assembly, gather the elders *and* [t]all the inhabitants of the land *into* the house of the
LORD your God, and cry unto the LORD,
15 [u]Alas for the day! for [v]the day of the
LORD *is* at hand, and as a destruction from
the Almighty shall it come.
16 Is not the meat cut off before our eyes,
yea, [w]joy and gladness from the house of
our God?
17 The seed is rotten under their clods,
the garners are laid desolate, the barns are
broken down; for the corn is withered.
18 How do [x]the beasts groan! the herds
of cattle are perplexed, because they have
no pasture; yea, the flocks of sheep are
made desolate.
19 O LORD, to thee [y]will I cry: for [z]the
fire hath devoured the pastures of the wilderness, and the flame hath burned all the
trees of the field.
20 The beasts of the field [a]cry also unto
thee: for [b]the rivers of waters are dried up,
and the fire hath devoured the pastures of
the wilderness.
2 Blow [c]ye the trumpet in Zion, and
[d]sound an alarm in my holy mountain:
let all the inhabitants of the land tremble:
for [e]the day of the LORD cometh, for *it is*
nigh at hand;
2 [f]A day of darkness and of gloominess,
a day of clouds and of thick darkness, as the
morning spread upon the mountains: [g]a
great people and a strong; [h]there hath not
been ever the like, neither shall be any more
after it, *even* to the years of many generations.
3 [i]A fire devoureth before them; and behind them a flame burneth: the land *is* as
[j]the garden of Eden before them, [k]and behind them a desolate wilderness; yea, and
nothing shall escape them.
4 [l]The appearance of them *is* as the appearance of horses; and as horsemen, so
shall they run.
5 [m]Like the noise of chariots on the tops
of mountains shall they leap, like the noise
of a flame of fire that devoureth the stubble,
[n]as a strong people set in battle array.
6 Before their face the people shall be
much pained: [o]all faces shall gather blackness.
7 They shall run like mighty men; they

1:2 [a]ch. 2:2
1:3 [b]Ps. 78:4
1:4 [c]Deut. 28:38; ch. 2:25
1:5 [d]Isa. 32:10
1:6 [e]Prov. 30:25; ch. 2:2 [f]Rev. 9:8
1:7 [g]Isa. 5:6
1:8 [h]Isa. 22:12 [i]Prov. 2:17; Jer. 3:4
1:9 [j]ver. 13; ch. 2:14
1:10 [k]Jer. 12:11 [l]Isa. 24:7; ver. 12
1:11 [m]Jer. 14:3
1:12 [n]ver. 10 [o]Ps. 4:7; Isa. 9:3; Jer. 48:33
1:13 [p]ver. 8; Jer. 4:8 [q]ver. 9
1:14 [r]2 Chron. 20:3; ch. 2:15 [s]Lev. 23:36 [t]2 Chron. 20:13
1:15 [u]Jer. 30:7 [v]Isa. 13:6; ch. 2:1
1:16 [w]Deut. 12:6
1:18 [x]Hos. 4:3
1:19 [y]Ps. 50:15 [z]Jer. 9:10; ch. 2:3
1:20 [a]Job 38:41; Ps. 104:21 [b]1 Kings 17:7
2:1 [c]Jer. 4:5; ver. 15 [d]Num. 10:5 [e]ch. 1:15; Obad. 15; Zeph. 1:14
2:2 [f]Am. 5:18 [g]ver. 5; ch. 1:6 [h]Ex. 10:14
2:3 [i]ch. 1:19 [j]Gen. 2:8; Isa. 51:3 [k]Zech. 7:14
2:4 [l]Rev. 9:7
2:5 [m]Rev. 9:9 [n]ver. 2
2:6 [o]Jer. 8:21; Lam. 4:8; Nah. 2:10

shall climb the wall like men of war; and they shall march every one on his ways, and they shall not break their ranks:

8 Neither shall one thrust another; they shall walk every one in his path: and *when* they fall upon the sword, they shall not be wounded.

9 They shall run to and fro in the city; they shall run upon the wall, they shall climb up upon the houses; they shall [p]enter in at the windows [q]like a thief.

10 [r]The earth shall quake before them; the heavens shall tremble: [s]the sun and the moon shall be dark, and the stars shall withdraw their shining:

11 [t]And the LORD shall utter his voice before [u]his army: for his camp *is* very great: [v]for *he is* strong that executeth his word: for the [w]day of the LORD *is* great and very terrible; and [x]who can abide it?

12 ¶ Therefore also now, saith the LORD, [y]turn ye *even* to me with all your heart, and with fasting, and with weeping, and with mourning:

13 And [z]rend your heart, and not [a]your garments, and turn unto the LORD your God: for he *is* [b]gracious and merciful, slow to anger, and of great kindness, and repenteth him of the evil.

14 [c]Who knoweth *if* he will return and repent, and leave [d]a blessing behind him; *even* [e]a meat offering and a drink offering unto the LORD your God?

15 ¶ [f]Blow the trumpet in Zion, [g]sanctify a fast, call a solemn assembly:

16 Gather the people, [h]sanctify the congregation, [i]assemble the elders, [j]gather the children, and those that suck the breasts: [k]let the bridegroom go forth of his chamber, and the bride out of her closet.

17 Let the priests, the ministers of the LORD, weep [l]between the porch and the altar, and let them say, [m]Spare thy people, O LORD, and give not thine heritage to reproach, that the heathen should rule over them: [n]wherefore should they say among the people, Where *is* their God?

18 ¶ Then will the LORD [o]be jealous for his land, [p]and pity his people.

19 Yea, the LORD will answer and say unto his people, Behold, I will send you [q]corn, and wine, and oil, and ye shall be satisfied therewith: and I will no more make you a reproach among the heathen:

20 But [r]I will remove far off from you [s]the northern *army*, and will drive him into a land barren and desolate, with his face [t]toward the east sea, and his hinder part [u]toward the utmost sea, and his stink shall come up, and his ill savour shall come up, because he hath done great things.

21 ¶ Fear not, O land; be glad and rejoice: for the LORD will do great things.

22 Be not afraid, [v]ye beasts of the field: for [w]the pastures of the wilderness do spring, for the tree beareth her fruit, the fig tree and the vine do yield their strength.

23 Be glad then, ye children of Zion, and [x]rejoice in the LORD your God: for he hath given you the former rain moderately, and he [y]will cause to come down for you [z]the rain, the former rain, and the latter rain in the first *month*.

24 And the floors shall be full of wheat, and the fats shall overflow with wine and oil.

25 And I will restore to you the years [a]that the locust hath eaten, the cankerworm, and the caterpiller, and the palmerworm, [b]my great army which I sent among you.

26 And ye shall [c]eat in plenty, and be satisfied, and praise the name of the LORD your God, that hath dealt wondrously with you: and my people shall never be ashamed.

27 [d]And ye shall know that I *am* [e]in the midst of Israel, and *that* [f]I *am* the LORD your God, and none else: and my people shall never be ashamed.

28 ¶ [g]And it shall come to pass afterward, *that* I [h]will pour out my spirit upon all flesh; [i]and your sons and [j]your daughters shall prophesy, your old men shall dream dreams, your young men shall see visions:

29 And also upon [k]the servants and upon the handmaids in those days will I pour out my spirit.

30 And [l]I will shew wonders in the heavens and in the earth, blood, and fire, and pillars of smoke.

31 [m]The sun shall be turned into darkness, and the moon into blood, [n]before the great and the terrible day of the LORD come.

32 And it shall come to pass, *that* [o]whosoever shall call on the name of the LORD shall be delivered: for [p]in mount Zion and in Jerusalem shall be deliverance, as the LORD hath said, and in [q]the remnant whom the LORD shall call.

3 For, behold, [r]in those days, and in that time, when I shall bring again the captivity of Judah and Jerusalem,

2 [s]I will also gather all nations, and will bring them down into [t]the valley of Jehoshaphat, and [u]will plead with them there for my people and *for* my heritage Israel, whom they have scattered among the nations, and parted my land.

3 And they have [v]cast lots for my people; and have given a boy for an harlot, and sold a girl for wine, that they might drink.

4 Yea, and what have ye to do with me, [w]O Tyre, and Zidon, and all the coasts of Palestine? [x]will ye render me a recompence? and if ye recompense me, swiftly *and* speedily will I return your recompence upon your own head;

5 Because ye have taken my silver and my gold, and have carried into your temples my goodly pleasant things:

6 The children also of Judah and the chil-

2:9 [p]Jer. 9:21 [q]John 10:1 **2:10** [r]Ps. 18:7 [s]Isa. 13:10; Ezek. 32:7; ver. 31; ch. 3:15; Matt. 24:29 **2:11** [t]Jer. 25:30; ch. 3:16; Am. 1:2 [u]ver. 25 [v]Jer. 50:34; Rev. 18:8 [w]Jer. 30:7; Am. 5:18; Zeph. 1:15 [x]Num. 24:23; Mal. 3:2 **2:12** [y]Jer. 4:1; Hos. 12:6 **2:13** [z]Ps. 34:18 [a]Gen. 37:34; 2 Sam. 1:11; Job 1:20 [b]Ex. 34:6; Ps. 86:5; Jonah 4:2 **2:14** [c]Josh. 14:12; 2 Sam. 12:22; 2 Kings 19:4; Am. 5:15; Jonah 3:9; Zeph. 2:3 [d]Isa. 65:8; Hag. 2:19 [e]ch. 1:9 **2:15** [f]Num. 10:3; ver. 1 [g]ch. 1:14 **2:16** [h]Ex. 19:10 [i]ch. 1:14 [j]2 Chron. 20:13 [k]1 Cor. 7:5 **2:17** [l]Ezek. 8:16; Matt. 23:35 [m]Ex. 32:11; Deut. 9:26-29 [n]Ps. 42:10; Mic. 7:10 **2:18** [o]Zech. 1:14 [p]Deut. 32:36; Isa. 60:10 **2:19** [q]ch. 1:10; Mal. 3:10 **2:20** [r]Ex. 10:19 [s]Jer. 1:14 [t]Ezek. 47:18; Zech. 14:8 [u]Deut. 11:24 **2:22** [v]ch. 1:18 [w]ch. 1:19; Zech. 8:12 **2:23** [x]Isa. 41:16; Hab. 3:18; Zech. 10:7 [y]Lev. 26:4; Deut. 11:14 [z]Jam. 5:7 **2:25** [a]ch. 1:4 [b]ver. 11 **2:26** [c]Lev. 26:5; Ps. 22:26; Mic. 6:14 **2:27** [d]ch. 3:17 [e]Lev. 26:11; Ezek. 37:26 [f]Isa. 45:5; Ezek. 39:22 **2:28** [g]Isa. 44:3; Ezek. 39:29; Acts 2:17 [h]Zech. 12:10; John 7:39 [i]Isa. 54:13 [j]Acts 21:9 **2:29** [k]1 Cor. 12:13; Gal. 3:28; Col. 3:11 **2:30** [l]Matt. 24:29; Mark 13:24; Luke 21:11 **2:31** [m]ver. 10; Isa. 13:9; ch. 3:1; Matt. 24:29; Mark 13:24; Luke 21:25; Rev. 6:12 [n]Mal. 4:5 **2:32** [o]Rom. 10:13 [p]Isa. 46:13; Obad. 17; Rom. 11:26 [q]Isa. 11:11; Jer. 31:7; Mic. 4:7; Rom. 9:27

3:1 [r]Jer. 30:3; Ezek. 38:14 **3:2** [s]Zech. 14:2 [t]2 Chron. 20:26; ver. 12 [u]Isa. 66:16; Ezek. 38:22 **3:3** [v]Obad. 11; Nah. 3:10 **3:4** [w]Am. 1:6 [x]Ezek. 25:15

dren of Jerusalem have ye sold unto the
Grecians, that ye might remove them far
from their border.
7 Behold, [y]I will raise them out of the
place whither ye have sold them, and will
return your recompence upon your own
head:
8 And I will sell your sons and your
daughters into the hand of the children of
Judah, and they shall sell them to the [z]Sa-
beans, to a people [a]far off: for the LORD
hath spoken *it*.
9 ¶ [b]Proclaim ye this among the Gentiles;
Prepare war, wake up the mighty men, let
all the men of war draw near; let them
come up:
10 [c]Beat your plowshares into swords,
and your pruninghooks into spears: [d]let the
weak say, I *am* strong.
11 [e]Assemble yourselves, and come, all
ye heathen, and gather yourselves together
round about: thither cause [f]thy mighty
ones to come down, O LORD.
12 Let the heathen be wakened, [g]and
come up to the valley of Jehoshaphat: for
there will I sit to [h]judge all the heathen
round about.
13 [i]Put ye in the sickle, for [j]the harvest
is ripe: come, get you down; for the [k]press
is full, the fats overflow; for their wickedness *is* great.
14 Multitudes, multitudes in [l]the valley
of decision: for [m]the day of the LORD *is* near
in the valley of decision.
15 The [n]sun and the moon shall be darkened, and the stars shall withdraw their
shining.
16 The LORD also shall [o]roar out of Zion,
and utter his voice from Jerusalem; and
[p]the heavens and the earth shall shake:
[q]but the LORD *will be* the hope of his people, and the strength of the children of Israel.
17 So [r]shall ye know that I *am* the LORD
your God dwelling in Zion, [s]my holy mountain: then shall Jerusalem be holy, and there
shall [t]no strangers pass through her any
more.
18 ¶ And it shall come to pass in that day,
that the mountains shall [u]drop down new
wine, and the hills shall flow with milk,
[v]and all the rivers of Judah shall flow with
waters, and [w]a fountain shall come forth of
the house of the LORD, and shall water [x]the
valley of Shittim.
19 [y]Egypt shall be a desolation, and
[z]Edom shall be a desolate wilderness, for
the violence *against* the children of Judah,
because they have shed innocent blood in
their land.
20 But Judah shall dwell [a]for ever, and
Jerusalem from generation to generation.
21 For I will [b]cleanse their blood *that* I
have not cleansed: [c]for the LORD dwelleth
in Zion.

3:7 [y]Isa. 43:5; Jer. 23:8
3:8 [z]Ezek. 23:42 [a]Jer. 6:20
3:9 [b]Isa. 8:9; Jer. 46:3; Ezek. 38:7
3:10 [c]Isa. 2:4; Mic. 4:3 [d]Zech. 12:8
3:11 [e]ver. 2 [f]Ps. 103:20; Isa. 13:3
3:12 [g]ver. 2 [h]Ps. 96:13; Isa. 2:4; Mic. 4:3
3:13 [i]Matt. 13:39; Rev. 14:15 [j]Jer. 51:33; Hos. 6:11 [k]Isa. 63:3; Lam. 1:15; Rev. 14:19
3:14 [l]ver. 2 [m]ch. 2:1
3:15 [n]ch. 2:10
3:16 [o]Jer. 25:30; ch. 2:11; Am. 1:2 [p]Hag. 2:6 [q]Isa. 51:5
3:17 [r]ch. 2:27 [s]Dan. 11:45; Obad. 16; Zech. 8:3 [t]Isa. 35:8; Nah. 1:15; Zech. 14:21; Rev. 21:27
3:18 [u]Am. 9:13 [v]Isa. 30:25 [w]Ps. 46:4; Ezek. 47:1; Zech. 14:8; Rev. 22:1 [x]Num. 25:1
3:19 [y]Isa. 19:1 [z]Jer. 49:17; Ezek. 25:12; Am. 1:11; Obad. 10
3:20 [a]Am. 9:15
3:21 [b]Isa. 4:4 [c]Ezek. 48:35; ver. 17; Rev. 21:3

AMOS

Amos is the author of this book written about 760 to 755 B.C. Amos contains prophecies concerning several nations, prophecies concerning Israel, and prophetic visions that extend into the future. The majority of the book (2:6–6:14) tells the story of a depraved Israel, successful but lacking moral character and seeking to use outward piety to cover up their deeds.

I. Prophecies against other nations, 1:1–2:3
II. Prophecies against Israel, 2:3–6:14
III. Prophetic visions, 7:1–9:15

---

1 The words of Amos, [a]who was among the herdmen of [b]Tekoa, which he saw concerning Israel [c]in the days of Uzziah king of Judah, and in the days of [d]Jeroboam the son of Joash king of Israel, two years before the [e]earthquake.

2 And he said, The LORD will [f]roar from Zion, and utter his voice from Jerusalem; and the habitations of the shepherds shall mourn, and the top of [g]Carmel shall wither.

3 Thus saith the LORD; For three transgressions of [h]Damascus, and for four, I will not turn away *the punishment* thereof; [i]because they have threshed Gilead with threshing instruments of iron:

4 [j]But I will send a fire into the house of Hazael, which shall devour the palaces of Ben-hadad.

5 I will break also the [k]bar of Damascus, and cut off the inhabitant from the plain of Aven, and him that holdeth the sceptre from the house of Eden: and [l]the people of Syria shall go into captivity [m]unto Kir, saith the LORD.

6 ¶ Thus saith the LORD; For three transgressions of [n]Gaza, and for four, I will not turn away *the punishment* thereof; because they carried away captive the whole captivity, to deliver *them* up to Edom:

7 But I will send a fire on the wall of Gaza, which shall devour the palaces thereof:

8 And I will cut off the inhabitant from Ashdod, and him that holdeth the sceptre from Ashkelon, and I will turn mine hand against Ekron: and the remnant of the Philistines shall perish, saith the Lord GOD.

9 ¶ Thus saith the LORD; For three transgressions of [o]Tyrus, and for four, I will not turn away *the punishment* thereof; [p]because they delivered up the whole captivity to Edom, and remembered not the brotherly covenant:

10 [q]But I will send a fire on the wall of Tyrus, which shall devour the palaces thereof.

11 ¶ Thus saith the LORD; For three transgressions of [r]Edom, and for four, I will not turn away *the punishment* thereof; because he did pursue [s]his brother [t]with the sword, and did cast off all pity, [u]and his anger did tear perpetually, and he kept his wrath for ever:

12 But [v]I will send a fire upon Teman, which shall devour the palaces of Bozrah.

13 ¶ Thus saith the LORD; For three transgressions of [w]the children of Ammon, and for four, I will not turn away *the punishment* thereof; because they have [x]ripped up the women with child of Gilead, [y]that they might enlarge their border:

14 But I will kindle a fire in the wall of [z]Rabbah, and it shall devour the palaces thereof, [a]with shouting in the day of battle, with a tempest in the day of the whirlwind:

15 And [b]their king shall go into captivity, he and his princes together, saith the LORD.

2 Thus saith the LORD; For three transgressions of [c]Moab, and for four, I will not turn away *the punishment* thereof; because he [d]burned the bones of the king of Edom into lime:

2 But I will send a fire upon Moab, and it shall devour the palaces of [e]Kirioth: and Moab shall die with tumult, [f]with shouting, *and* with the sound of the trumpet:

3 And I will cut off [g]the judge from the midst thereof, and will slay all the princes thereof with him, saith the LORD.

4 ¶ Thus saith the LORD; For three transgressions of Judah, and for four, I will not turn away *the punishment* thereof; [h]because they have despised the law of the LORD, and have not kept his commandments, and [i]their lies caused them to err, [j]after the which their fathers have walked:

5 [k]But I will send a fire upon Judah, and it shall devour the palaces of Jerusalem.

6 ¶ Thus saith the LORD; For three transgressions of Israel, and for four, I will not turn away *the punishment* thereof; because [l]they sold the righteous for silver, and the poor for a pair of shoes;

7 That pant after the dust of the earth on the head of the poor, and [m]turn aside the way of the meek: [n]and a man and his father will go in unto the *same* maid, [o]to profane my holy name:

8 And they lay *themselves* down upon clothes [p]laid to pledge [q]by every altar, and

1:1 [a]ch. 7:14 [b]2 Sam. 14; 2 Chron. 20:20 [c]Hos. 1:1 [d]ch. 7:10 [e]Zech. 14:5
1:2 [f]Jer. 25:30; Joel 3:16 [g]1 Sam. 25; Isa. 33:9
1:3 [h]Isa. 8:4; Jer. 49:23; Zech. 9:1 [i]2 Kings 10:33
1:4 [j]Jer. 17:27; ver. 7; ch. 2:2
1:5 [k]Jer. 51:30; Lam. 2:9 [l]2 Kings 16 [m]ch. 9:7
1:6 [n]2 Chron. 28:18; Isa. 14:29; Jer. 47:4; Ezek. 25:15; Zeph. 2:4
1:9 [o]Isa. 23:1; Jer. 47:4; Ezek. 26; Joel 3:4 [p]ver. 6
1:10 [q]ver. 4
1:11 [r]Isa. 21:11; Jer. 49:8; Ezek. 25:12; Joel 3:19; Obad. 1; Mal. 1:4 [s]Gen. 27:41; Deut. 23:7; Mal. 1:2 [t]2 Chron. 28:17 [u]Ezek. 35:5
1:12 [v]Obad. 9
1:13 [w]Jer. 49:1; Ezek. 25:2; Zeph. 2:9 [x]Hos. 13:16 [y]Jer. 49:1
1:14 [z]Deut. 3:11; 2 Sam. 12:26 [a]ch. 2:2
1:15 [b]Jer. 49:3
2:1 [c]Isa. 15; Jer. 48; Ezek. 25:8; Zeph. 2:8 [d]2 Kings 3:27
2:2 [e]Jer. 48:41 [f]ch. 1:14
2:3 [g]Num. 24:17; Jer. 48:7
2:4 [h]Lev. 26:14; Neh. 1:7; Dan. 9:11 [i]Isa. 28:15; Jer. 16:19; Rom. 1:25 [j]Ezek. 20:13
2:5 [k]Jer. 17:27; Hos. 8:14
2:6 [l]Isa. 29:21; ch. 8:6
2:7 [m]Isa. 10:2; ch. 5:12 [n]Ezek. 22:11 [o]Lev. 20:3; Ezek. 36:20; Rom. 2:24
2:8 [p]Ex. 22:26 [q]Ezek. 23:41; 1 Cor. 8:10

they drink the wine of the condemned *in* the
house of their god.
9 ¶ Yet destroyed I the [r]Amorite before
them, [s]whose height *was* like the height of
the cedars, and he *was* strong as the oaks;
yet I [t]destroyed his fruit from above, and
his roots from beneath.
10 Also [u]I brought you up from the land
of Egypt, and [v]led you forty years through
the wilderness, to possess the land of the
Amorite.
11 And I raised up of your sons for prophets, and of your young men for [w]Nazarites.
Is it not even thus, O ye children of Israel?
saith the LORD.
12 But ye gave the Nazarites wine to
drink; and commanded the prophets, [x]say-
ing, Prophesy not.
13 [y]Behold, I am pressed under you, as a
cart is pressed *that is* full of sheaves.
14 [z]Therefore the flight shall perish from
the swift, and the strong shall not
strengthen his force, [a]neither shall the
mighty deliver himself:
15 Neither shall he stand that handleth
the bow; and *he that is* swift of foot shall not
deliver *himself:* [b]neither shall he that rideth
the horse deliver himself.
16 And *he that is* courageous among the
mighty shall flee away naked in that day,
saith the LORD.
3 Hear this word that the LORD hath spoken against you, O children of Israel,
against the whole family which I brought up
from the land of Egypt, saying,
2 [c]You only have I known of all the families of the earth: [d]therefore I will punish
you for all your iniquities.
3 Can two walk together, except they be
agreed?
4 Will a lion roar in the forest, when he
hath no prey? will a young lion cry out of his
den, if he have taken nothing?
5 Can a bird fall in a snare upon the earth,
where no gin *is* for him? shall *one* take up a
snare from the earth, and have taken nothing at all?
6 Shall a trumpet be blown in the city, and
the people not be afraid? [e]shall there be evil
in a city, and the LORD hath not done *it?*
7 Surely the Lord GOD will do nothing,
but [f]he revealeth his secret unto his servants the prophets.
8 [g]The lion hath roared, who will not
fear? the Lord GOD hath spoken, [h]who can
but prophesy?
9 ¶ Publish in the palaces at Ashdod, and
in the palaces in the land of Egypt, and say,
Assemble yourselves upon the mountains
of Samaria, and behold the great tumults in
the midst thereof, and the oppressed in the
midst thereof.
10 For they [i]know not to do right, saith
the LORD, who store up violence and robbery in their palaces.
11 Therefore thus saith the Lord GOD;
[j]An adversary *there shall be* even round
about the land; and he shall bring down thy
strength from thee, and thy palaces shall be
spoiled.
12 Thus saith the LORD; As the shepherd
taketh out of the mouth of the lion two legs,
or a piece of an ear; so shall the children of
Israel be taken out that dwell in Samaria in
the corner of a bed, and in Damascus *in* a
couch.
13 Hear ye, and testify in the house of Jacob, saith the Lord GOD, the God of hosts,
14 That in the day that I shall visit the
transgressions of Israel upon him I will also
visit the altars of Beth-el: and the horns of
the altar shall be cut off, and fall to the
ground.
15 And I will smite [k]the winter house
with [l]the summer house; and [m]the houses
of ivory shall perish, and the great houses
shall have an end, saith the LORD.
4 Hear this word, ye [n]kine of Bashan,
that *are* in the mountain of Samaria,
which oppress the poor, which crush the
needy, which say to their masters, Bring,
and let us drink.
2 [o]The Lord GOD hath sworn by his holiness, that, lo, the days shall come upon you,
that he will take you away [p]with hooks, and
your posterity with fishhooks.
3 And [q]ye shall go out at the breaches,
every *cow at that which is* before her; and
ye shall cast *them* into the palace, saith the
LORD.
4 ¶ [r]Come to Beth-el, and transgress; at
[s]Gilgal multiply transgression; and [t]bring
your sacrifices every morning, [u]*and* your
tithes after three years:
5 [v]And offer a sacrifice of thanksgiving
with leaven, and proclaim *and* publish [w]the
free offerings: [x]for this liketh you, O ye
children of Israel, saith the Lord GOD.
6 ¶ And I also have given you cleanness
of teeth in all your cities, and want of bread
in all your places: [y]yet have ye not returned
unto me, saith the LORD.
7 And also I have withholden the rain
from you, when *there were* yet three
months to the harvest: and I caused it to rain
upon one city, and caused it not to rain upon
another city: one piece was rained upon,
and the piece whereupon it rained not withered.
8 So two *or* three cities wandered unto
one city, to drink water; but they were not
satisfied: [z]yet have ye not returned unto
me, saith the LORD.
9 [a]I have smitten you with blasting and
mildew: when your gardens and your vineyards and your fig trees and your olive trees
increased, [b]the palmerworm devoured
them: yet have ye not returned unto me,
saith the LORD.
10 I have sent among you the pestilence
[c]after the manner of Egypt: your young
men have I slain with the sword, and have
taken away your horses; and I have made
the stink of your camps to come up unto
your nostrils: [d]yet have ye not returned
unto me, saith the LORD.

2:9 *r*Num. 21:24; Deut. 2:31; Josh. 24:8 *s*Num. 13:28 *t*Isa. 5:24; Mal. 4:1
2:10 *u*Ex. 12:51; Mic. 6:4 *v*Deut. 2:7
2:11 *w*Num. 6:2; Judg. 13:5
2:12 *x*Isa. 30:10; Jer. 11:21; ch. 7:12; Mic. 2:6
2:13 *y*Isa. 1:14
2:14 *z*ch. 9:1; Jer. 9:23 *a*Ps. 33:16
2:15 *b*Ps. 33:17
3:2 *c*Deut. 7:6; Ps. 147:19 *d*Dan. 9:12; Matt. 11:22; Luke 12:47; Rom. 2:9; 1 Pet. 4:17
3:6 *e*Isa. 45:7
3:7 *f*Gen. 6:13; Ps. 25:14; John 15:15
3:8 *g*ch. 1:2 *h*Acts 4:20; 1 Cor. 9:16
3:10 *i*Jer. 4:22
3:11 *j*2 Kings 17:3
3:15 *k*Jer. 36:22 *l*Judg. 3:20 *m*1 Kings 22:39
4:1 *n*Ps. 22:12; Ezek. 39:18
4:2 *o*Ps. 89:35 *p*Jer. 16:16; Hab. 1:15
4:3 *q*Ezek. 12:5
4:4 *r*Ezek. 20:39 *s*Hos. 4:15; ch. 5:5 *t*Num. 28:3 *u*Deut. 14:28
4:5 *v*Lev. 7:13 *w*Lev. 22:18; Deut. 12:6 *x*Ps. 81:12
4:6 *y*Isa. 26:11; Jer. 5:3; Hag. 2:17; ver. 8
4:8 *z*ver. 6
4:9 *a*Deut. 28:22; Hag. 2:17 *b*Joel 1:4
4:10 *c*Ex. 9:3; Deut. 28:27; Ps. 78:50 *d*ver. 6

11 I have overthrown *some* of you, as God
overthrew [e]Sodom and Gomorrah, [f]and ye
were as a firebrand plucked out of the burning: [g]yet have ye not returned unto me,
saith the LORD.
12 Therefore thus will I do unto thee,
O Israel: *and* because I will do this unto
thee, [h]prepare to meet thy God, O Israel.
13 For, lo, he that formeth the mountains,
and createth the wind, [i]and declareth unto
man what *is* his thought, [j]that maketh the
morning darkness, [k]and treadeth upon the
high places of the earth, [l]The LORD, The
God of hosts, *is* his name.
5 Hear ye this word which I [m]take up
against you, *even* a lamentation, O
house of Israel.
2 The virgin of Israel is fallen; she shall
no more rise: she is forsaken upon her land;
there is none to raise her up.
3 For thus saith the Lord GOD; The city
that went out *by* a thousand shall leave an
hundred, and that which went forth *by* an
hundred shall leave ten, to the house of Israel.
4 ¶ For thus saith the LORD unto the house
of Israel, [n]Seek ye me, [o]and ye shall live:
5 But seek not [p]Beth-el, nor enter into
Gilgal, and pass not to [q]Beer-sheba: for
Gilgal shall surely go into captivity, and
[r]Beth-el shall come to nought.
6 [s]Seek the LORD, and ye shall live; lest
he break out like fire in the house of Joseph,
and devour *it,* and *there be* none to quench
it in Beth-el.
7 Ye who [t]turn judgment to wormwood,
and leave off righteousness in the earth,
8 *Seek him* that maketh the [u]seven stars
and Orion, and turneth the shadow of death
into the morning, [v]and maketh the day
dark with night: that [w]calleth for the waters
of the sea, and poureth them out upon the
face of the earth: [x]The LORD *is* his name:
9 That strengtheneth the spoiled against
the strong, so that the spoiled shall come
against the fortress.
10 [y]They hate him that rebuketh in the
gate, and they [z]abhor him that speaketh
uprightly.
11 Forasmuch therefore as your treading
is upon the poor, and ye take from him burdens of wheat: [a]ye have built houses of
hewn stone, but ye shall not dwell in them;
ye have planted pleasant vineyards, but ye
shall not drink wine of them.
12 For I know your manifold transgressions and your mighty sins: [b]they afflict the
just, they take a bribe, and they [c]turn aside
the poor in the gate *from their right.*
13 Therefore [d]the prudent shall keep silence in that time; for it *is* an evil time.
14 Seek good, and not evil, that ye may
live: and so the LORD, the God of hosts, shall
be with you, [e]as ye have spoken.
15 [f]Hate the evil, and love the good, and
establish judgment in the gate: [g]it may be
that the LORD God of hosts will be gracious
unto the remnant of Joseph.

16 Therefore the LORD, the God of hosts,
the Lord, saith thus; Wailing *shall be* in all
streets; and they shall say in all the highways, Alas! alas! and they shall call the husbandman to mourning, and [h]such as are
skilful of lamentation to wailing.
17 And in all vineyards *shall be* wailing:
for [i]I will pass through thee, saith the
LORD.
18 [j]Woe unto you that desire the day of
the LORD! to what end *is* it for you? [k]the day
of the LORD *is* darkness, and not light.
19 [l]As if a man did flee from a lion, and
a bear met him; or went into the house, and
leaned his hand on the wall, and a serpent
bit him.
20 *Shall* not the day of the LORD *be* darkness, and not light? even very dark, and no
brightness in it?
21 ¶ [m]I hate, I despise your feast days,
and [n]I will not smell in your solemn assemblies.
22 [o]Though ye offer me burnt offerings
and your meat offerings, I will not accept
them: neither will I regard the peace offerings of your fat beasts.
23 Take thou away from me the noise of
thy songs; for I will not hear the melody of
thy viols.
24 [p]But let judgment run down as waters,
and righteousness as a mighty stream.
25 [q]Have ye offered unto me sacrifices
and offerings in the wilderness forty years,
O house of Israel?
26 But ye have borne the tabernacle [r]of
your Moloch and Chiun your images, the
star of your god, which ye made to yourselves.
27 Therefore will I cause you to go into
captivity [s]beyond Damascus, saith the
LORD, [t]whose name *is* The God of hosts.
6 Woe [u]to them *that are* at ease in Zion,
and trust in the mountain of Samaria,
which are named [v]chief of the nations, to
whom the house of Israel came!
2 [w]Pass ye unto [x]Calneh, and see; and
from thence go ye to [y]Hamath the great:
then go down to [z]Gath of the Philistines:
[a]*be they* better than these kingdoms? or
their border greater than your border?
3 Ye that [b]put far away the [c]evil day,
[d]and cause [e]the seat of violence to come
near;
4 That lie upon beds of ivory, and stretch
themselves upon their couches, and eat the
lambs out of the flock, and the calves out of
the midst of the stall;
5 [f]That chant to the sound of the viol,
and invent to themselves instruments of
musick, [g]like David;
6 That drink wine in bowls, and anoint
themselves with the chief ointments: [h]but
they are not grieved for the affliction of Joseph.
7 ¶ Therefore now shall they go captive
with the first that go captive, and the banquet of them that stretched themselves shall
be removed.

4:11 [e]Gen. 19:24; Isa. 13:19; Jer. 49:18 [f]Zech. 3:2; Jude 23 [g]ver. 6
4:12 [h]Ezek. 13:5; Luke 14:31
4:13 [i]Ps. 139:2; Dan. 2:28 [j]ch. 5:8 [k]Deut. 32:13; Mic. 1:3 [l]Isa. 47:4; Jer. 10:16; ch. 5:8
5:1 [m]Jer. 7:29; Ezek. 19:1
5:4 [n]2 Chron. 15:2; Jer. 29:13; ver. 6 [o]Isa. 55:3
5:5 [p]ch. 4:4 [q]ch. 8:14 [r]Hos. 4:15
5:6 [s]ver. 4
5:7 [t]ch. 6:12
5:8 [u]Job 9:9 [v]Ps. 104:20 [w]Job 38:34; ch. 9:6 [x]ch. 4:13
5:10 [y]Isa. 29:21 [z]1 Kings 22:8
5:11 [a]Deut. 28:30; Mic. 6:15; Zeph. 1:13; Hag. 1:6
5:12 [b]ch. 2:26 [c]Isa. 29:21; ch. 2:7
5:13 [d]ch. 6:10
5:14 [e]Mic. 3:11
5:15 [f]Ps. 34:14; Rom. 12:9 [g]Ex. 32:30; 2 Kings 19:4; Joel 2:14
5:16 [h]Jer. 9:17
5:17 [i]Ex. 12:12; Nah. 1:12
5:18 [j]Isa. 5:19; Jer. 17:15; Ezek. 12:22; 2 Pet. 3:4 [k]Jer. 30:7; Joel 2:2; Zeph. 1:15
5:19 [l]Jer. 48:44
5:21 [m]Prov. 21:27; Isa. 1:11-16; Jer. 6:20; Hos. 8:13 [n]Lev. 26:31
5:22 [o]Isa. 66:3; Mic. 6:6
5:24 [p]Hos. 6:6; Mic. 6:8
5:25 [q]Deut. 32:17; Josh. 24:14; Isa. 43:23; Ezek. 20:8; Acts 7:42
5:26 [r]1 Kings 11:33
5:27 [s]2 Kings 17:6 [t]ch. 4:13
6:1 [u]Luke 6:24 [v]Ex. 19:5
6:2 [w]Jer. 2:10 [x]Isa. 10:9 [y]2 Kings 18:34 [z]2 Chron. 26:6 [a]Nah. 3:8
6:3 [b]Ezek. 12:27 [c]ch. 5:18 [d]ch. 5:12; ver. 12 [e]Ps. 94:20
6:5 [f]Isa. 5:12 [g]1 Chron. 23:5
6:6 [h]Gen. 37:25

8 [i]The Lord GOD hath sworn by himself, saith the LORD the God of hosts, I abhor [j]the excellency of Jacob, and hate his palaces: therefore will I deliver up the city with all that is therein.

9 And it shall come to pass, if there remain ten men in one house, that they shall die.

10 And a man's uncle shall take him up, and he that burneth him, to bring out the bones out of the house, and shall say unto him that *is* by the sides of the house, *Is there* yet *any* with thee? and he shall say, No. Then shall he say, [k]Hold thy tongue: [l]for we may not make mention of the name of the LORD.

11 For, behold, [m]the LORD commandeth, [n]and he will smite the great house with breaches, and the little house with clefts.

12 ¶ Shall horses run upon the rock? will *one* plow *there* with oxen? for [o]ye have turned judgment into gall, and the fruit of righteousness into hemlock:

13 Ye which rejoice in a thing of nought, which say, Have we not taken to us horns by our own strength?

14 But, behold, [p]I will raise up against you a nation, O house of Israel, saith the LORD the God of hosts; and they shall afflict you from the [q]entering in of Hemath unto the river of the wilderness.

7

Thus hath the Lord GOD shewed unto me; and, behold, he formed grasshoppers in the beginning of the shooting up of the latter growth; and, lo, *it was* the latter growth after the king's mowings.

2 And it came to pass, *that* when they had made an end of eating the grass of the land, then I said, O Lord GOD, forgive, I beseech thee: [r]by whom shall Jacob arise? for he *is* small.

3 [s]The LORD repented for this: It shall not be, saith the LORD.

4 ¶ Thus hath the Lord GOD shewed unto me: and, behold, the Lord GOD called to contend by fire, and it devoured the great deep, and did eat up a part.

5 Then said I, O Lord GOD, cease, I beseech thee: [t]by whom shall Jacob arise? for he *is* small.

6 The LORD repented for this: This also shall not be, saith the Lord GOD.

7 ¶ Thus he shewed me: and, behold, the Lord stood upon a wall *made* by a plumbline, with a plumbline in his hand.

8 And the LORD said unto me, Amos, what seest thou? And I said, A plumbline. Then said the Lord, Behold, [u]I will set a plumbline in the midst of my people Israel: [v]I will not again pass by them any more:

9 [w]And the high places of Isaac shall be desolate, and the sanctuaries of Israel shall be laid waste; and [x]I will rise against the house of Jeroboam with the sword.

10 ¶ Then Amaziah [y]the priest of Beth-el sent to [z]Jeroboam king of Israel, saying, Amos hath conspired against thee in the midst of the house of Israel: the land is not able to bear all his words.

11 For thus Amos saith, Jeroboam shall die by the sword, and Israel shall surely be led away captive out of their own land.

12 Also Amaziah said unto Amos, O thou seer, go, flee thee away into the land of Judah, and there eat bread, and prophesy there:

13 But [a]prophesy not again any more at Beth-el: [b]for it *is* the king's chapel, and it *is* the king's court.

14 ¶ Then answered Amos, and said to Amaziah, I *was* no prophet, neither *was* I [c]a prophet's son; [d]but I *was* an herdman, and a gatherer of sycomore fruit:

15 And the LORD took me as I followed the flock, and the LORD said unto me, Go, prophesy unto my people Israel.

16 ¶ Now therefore hear thou the word of the LORD: Thou sayest, Prophesy not against Israel, and [e]drop not *thy word* against the house of Isaac.

17 [f]Therefore thus saith the LORD; [g]Thy wife shall be an harlot in the city, and thy sons and thy daughters shall fall by the sword, and thy land shall be divided by line; and thou shalt die in a polluted land: and Israel shall surely go into captivity forth of his land.

8

Thus hath the Lord GOD shewed unto me: and behold a basket of summer fruit.

2 And he said, Amos, what seest thou? And I said, A basket of summer fruit. Then said the LORD unto me, [h]The end is come upon my people of Israel; [i]I will not again pass by them any more.

3 And [j]the songs of the temple shall be howlings in that day, saith the Lord GOD: *there shall be* many dead bodies in every place; [k]they shall cast *them* forth with silence.

4 ¶ Hear this, O ye that [l]swallow up the needy, even to make the poor of the land to fail,

5 Saying, When will the new moon be gone, that we may sell corn? and [m]the sabbath, that we may set forth wheat, [n]making the ephah small, and the shekel great, and falsifying the balances by deceit?

6 That we may buy the poor for [o]silver, and the needy for a pair of shoes; *yea,* and sell the refuse of the wheat?

7 The LORD hath sworn by [p]the excellency of Jacob, Surely [q]I will never forget any of their works.

8 [r]Shall not the land tremble for this, and every one mourn that dwelleth therein? and it shall rise up wholly as a flood; and it shall be cast out and drowned, [s]as *by* the flood of Egypt.

9 And it shall come to pass in that day, saith the Lord GOD, [t]that I will cause the sun to go down at noon, and I will darken the earth in the clear day:

10 And I will turn your feasts into mourning, and all your songs into lamentation;

6:8 [i]Jer. 51:14; Heb. 6:13 [j]Ps. 47:4; Ezek. 24:21; ch. 8:7
6:10 [k]ch. 5:13 [l]ch. 8:3
6:11 [m]Isa. 55:11 [n]ch. 3:15
6:12 [o]Hos. 10:4; ch. 5:7
6:14 [p]Jer. 5:15 [q]Num. 34:8; 1 Kings 8:65
7:2 [r]Isa. 51:19; ver. 5
7:3 [s]Deut. 32:36; ver. 6; Jonah 3:10; Jam. 5:16
7:5 [t]ver. 2
7:8 [u]2 Kings 21:13; Isa. 28:17; Lam. 2:8 [v]ch. 8:2; Mic. 7:18
7:9 [w]Gen. 26:23; ch. 5:5 [x]2 Kings 15:10
7:10 [y]1 Kings 12:32 [z]2 Kings 14:23
7:13 [a]ch. 2:12 [b]1 Kings 12:32
7:14 [c]1 Kings 20:35; 2 Kings 2:5 [d]ch. 1:1; Zech. 13:5
7:16 [e]Ezek. 21:2; Mic. 2:6
7:17 [f]Jer. 28:12 [g]Isa. 13:16; Lam. 5:11; Hos. 4:13; Zech. 14:2
8:2 [h]Ezek. 7:2 [i]ch. 7:8
8:3 [j]ch. 5:23 [k]ch. 6:9
8:4 [l]Ps. 14:4; Prov. 30:14
8:5 [m]Neh. 13:15 [n]Mic. 6:10
8:6 [o]ch. 2:6
8:7 [p]ch. 6:8 [q]Hos. 8:13
8:8 [r]Hos. 4:3 [s]ch. 9:5
8:9 [t]Job 5:14; Isa. 13:10; Jer. 15:9; Mic. 3:6

[u]and I will bring up sackcloth upon all loins, and baldness upon every head; [v]and I will make it as the mourning of an only *son,* and the end thereof as a bitter day.

11 ¶ Behold, the days come, saith the Lord GOD, that I will send a famine in the land, not a famine of bread, nor a thirst for water, but [w]of hearing the words of the LORD:

12 And they shall wander from sea to sea, and from the north even to the east, they shall run to and fro to seek the word of the LORD, and shall not find *it.*

13 In that day shall the fair virgins and young men faint for thirst.

14 They that [x]swear by [y]the sin of Samaria, and say, Thy god, O Dan, liveth; and, The manner [z]of Beer-sheba liveth; even they shall fall, and never rise up again.

9

I saw the Lord standing upon the altar: and he said, Smite the lintel of the door, that the posts may shake: and [a]cut them in the head, all of them; and I will slay the last of them with the sword: [b]he that fleeth of them shall not flee away, and he that escapeth of them shall not be delivered.

2 [c]Though they dig into hell, thence shall mine hand take them; [d]though they climb up to heaven, thence will I bring them down:

3 And though they hide themselves in the top of Carmel, I will search and take them out thence; and though they be hid from my sight in the bottom of the sea, thence will I command the serpent, and he shall bite them:

4 And though they go into captivity before their enemies, [e]thence will I command the sword, and it shall slay them: and [f]I will set mine eyes upon them for evil, and not for good.

5 And the Lord GOD of hosts *is* he that toucheth the land, and it shall [g]melt, [h]and all that dwell therein shall mourn: and it shall rise up wholly like a flood; and shall be drowned, as *by* the flood of Egypt.

6 *It is* he that buildeth his [i]stories in the heaven, and hath founded his troop in the earth; he that [j]calleth for the waters of the sea, and poureth them out upon the face of the earth: [k]The LORD *is* his name.

7 *Are* ye not as children of the Ethiopians unto me, O children of Israel? saith the LORD. Have not I brought up Israel out of the land of Egypt? and the [l]Philistines from [m]Caphtor, and the Syrians from [n]Kir?

8 Behold, [o]the eyes of the Lord GOD *are* upon the sinful kingdom, and I [p]will destroy it from off the face of the earth; saving that I will not utterly destroy the house of Jacob, saith the LORD.

9 For, lo, I will command, and I will sift the house of Israel among all nations, like as *corn* is sifted in a sieve, yet shall not the least grain fall upon the earth.

10 All the sinners of my people shall die by the sword, [q]which say, The evil shall not overtake nor prevent us.

11 ¶ [r]In that day will I raise up the tabernacle of David that is fallen, and close up the breaches thereof; and I will raise up his ruins, and I will build it as in the days of old:

12 [s]That they may possess the remnant of [t]Edom, and of all the heathen, which are called by my name, saith the LORD that doeth this.

13 Behold, [u]the days come, saith the LORD, that the plowman shall overtake the reaper, and the treader of grapes him that soweth seed; [v]and the mountains shall drop sweet wine, and all the hills shall melt.

14 [w]And I will bring again the captivity of my people of Israel, and [x]they shall build the waste cities, and inhabit *them;* and they shall plant vineyards, and drink the wine thereof; they shall also make gardens, and eat the fruit of them.

15 And I will plant them upon their land, and [y]they shall no more be pulled up out of their land which I have given them, saith the LORD thy God.

8:10 [u]Isa. 15:2; Jer. 48:37; Ezek. 7:18 [v]Jer. 6:26; Zech. 12:10
8:11 [w]1 Sam. 3:1; Ps. 74:9; Ezek. 7:26
8:14 [x]Hos. 4:15 [y]Deut. 9:21 [z]ch. 5:5
9:1 [a]Ps. 68:21; Hab. 3:13 [b]ch. 2:14
9:2 [c]Ps. 139:8 [d]Job 20:6; Jer. 51:53; Obad. 4
9:4 [e]Lev. 26:33; Deut. 28:65; Ezek. 5:12 [f]Lev. 17:10; Jer. 44:11
9:5 [g]Mic. 1:4 [h]ch. 8:8
9:6 [i]Ps. 104:3 [j]ch. 5:8 [k]ch. 4:13
9:7 [l]Jer. 47:4 [m]Deut. 2:23; Jer. 47:4 [n]ch. 1:5
9:8 [o]ver. 4 [p]Jer. 30:11; Obad. 16
9:10 [q]ch. 6:3
9:11 [r]Acts 15:16
9:12 [s]Obad. 19 [t]Num. 24:18
9:13 [u]Lev. 26:5 [v]Joel 3:18
9:14 [w]Jer. 30:3 [x]Isa. 61:4; Ezek. 36:33-36
9:15 [y]Isa. 60:21; Jer. 32:41; Ezek. 34:28; Joel 3:20

OBADIAH

Obadiah identifies himself as the writer of the book in the first verse. It was probably written at two different times prior to 840 B.C. and 586 B.C. The nation of Edom watched as Jerusalem was invaded and destroyed by the Babylonians. It even helped the invaders. The Edomites were descendants of Esau and thus were related to the Israelites which made their actions particularly distressing. Obadiah announces judgment on Edom through this book.

I. Edom prophesied to be destroyed, 1–9
II. Edom's sins exposed, 10–14
III. The time and nature of Edom's judgment, 15–21

---

1 The vision of Obadiah. Thus saith the
Lord GOD [a]concerning Edom; [b]We have
heard a rumour from the LORD, and an ambassador is sent among the heathen, Arise
ye, and let us rise up against her in battle.
2 Behold, I have made thee small among
the heathen: thou art greatly despised.
3 ¶ The pride of thine heart hath deceived
thee, thou that dwellest in the clefts [c]of the
rock, whose habitation *is* high; [d]that saith
in his heart, Who shall bring me down to the
ground?
4 [e]Though thou exalt *thyself* as the eagle,
and though thou [f]set thy nest among the
stars, thence will I bring thee down, saith
the LORD.
5 If [g]thieves came to thee, if robbers by
night, (how art thou cut off!) would they not
have stolen till they had enough? if the
grapegatherers came to thee, [h]would they
not leave *some* grapes?
6 How are *the things* of Esau searched
out! *how* are his hidden things sought up!
7 All the men of thy confederacy have
brought thee *even* to the border: [i]the men
that were at peace with thee have deceived
thee, *and* prevailed against thee; *that they
eat* thy bread have laid a wound under thee:
[j]*there is* none understanding in him.
8 [k]Shall I not in that day, saith the LORD,
even destroy the wise *men* out of Edom, and
understanding out of the mount of Esau?
9 And thy [l]mighty *men*, O [m]Teman, shall
be dismayed, to the end that every one of
the mount of Esau may be cut off by slaughter.
10 ¶ For *thy* [n]violence against thy
brother Jacob shame shall cover thee, and
[o]thou shalt be cut off for ever.
11 In the day that thou stoodest on the
other side, in the day that the strangers carried away captive his forces, and foreigners
entered into his gates, and [p]cast lots upon
Jerusalem, even thou *wast* as one of them.
12 But thou shouldest not have [q]looked
on [r]the day of thy brother in the day that he
became a stranger; neither shouldest thou
have [s]rejoiced over the children of Judah in
the day of their destruction; neither shouldest thou have spoken proudly in the day of
distress.
13 Thou shouldest not have entered into
the gate of my people in the day of their
calamity; yea, thou shouldest not have
looked on their affliction in the day of their
calamity, nor have laid *hands* on their substance in the day of their calamity;
14 Neither shouldest thou have stood in
the crossway, to cut off those of his that did
escape; neither shouldest thou have delivered up those of his that did remain in the
day of distress.
15 [t]For the day of the LORD *is* near upon
all the heathen: [u]as thou hast done, it shall
be done unto thee: thy reward shall return
upon thine own head.
16 [v]For as ye have drunk upon my holy
mountain, *so* shall all the heathen drink
continually, yea, they shall drink, and they
shall swallow down, and they shall be as
though they had not been.
17 ¶ [w]But upon mount Zion [x]shall be deliverance, and there shall be holiness; and
the house of Jacob shall possess their possessions.
18 And the house of Jacob [y]shall be a
fire, and the house of Joseph a flame, and
the house of Esau for stubble, and they shall
kindle in them, and devour them; and there
shall not be *any* remaining of the house of
Esau; for the LORD hath spoken *it*.
19 And *they of* the south [z]shall possess
the mount of Esau; [a]and *they of* the plain
the Philistines: and they shall possess the
fields of Ephraim, and the fields of Samaria:
and Benjamin *shall possess* Gilead.
20 And the captivity of this host of the
children of Israel *shall possess* that of the
Canaanites, *even* [b]unto Zarephath; and the
captivity of Jerusalem, which *is* in Sepha-
rad, [c]shall possess the cities of the south.
21 And [d]saviours shall come up on
mount Zion to judge the mount of Esau; and
the [e]kingdom shall be the LORD's.

1:1 [a]Isa. 21:11; Ezek. 25:12; Joel 3:19; Mal. 1:3 [b]Jer. 49:14
1:3 [c]2 Kings 14:7 [d]Isa. 14:13; Rev. 18:7
1:4 [e]Job 20:6; Jer. 49:16; Am. 9:2 [f]Hab. 2:9
1:5 [g]Jer. 49:9 [h]Deut. 24:21; Isa. 17:6
1:7 [i]Jer. 38:22 [j]Isa. 19:11
1:8 [k]Job 5:12; Isa. 29:14; Jer. 49:7
1:9 [l]Ps. 76:5; Am. 2:16 [m]Jer. 49:7
1:10 [n]Gen. 27:11; Ps. 137:7; Ezek. 25:12; Am. 1:11 [o]Ezek. 35:9; Mal. 1:4
1:11 [p]Joel 3:3; Nah. 3:10
1:12 [q]Ps. 22:17; Mic. 4:11 [r]Ps. 37:13 [s]Job 31:29; Mic. 7:8; Prov. 17:5
1:15 [t]Ezek. 30:3; Joel 3:14 [u]Ezek. 35:15; Hab. 2:8
1:16 [v]Jer. 25:28; Joel 3:17; 1 Pet. 4:17
1:17 [w]Joel 2:32 [x]Am. 9:8
1:18 [y]Isa. 10:17; Zech. 12:6
1:19 [z]Am. 9:12 [a]Zeph. 2:7
1:20 [b]1 Kings 17:9 [c]Jer. 32:44
1:21 [d]1 Tim. 4:16; Jam. 5:20 [e]Ps. 22:28; Dan. 2:44; Zech. 14:9; Luke 1:33; Rev. 11:15

JONAH

The author of this book is unknown but it was written probably during the eighth century B.C. Jonah is picked by God to go to the city of Nineveh and preach the message of repentance lest the city be destroyed. Jonah refuses and tries to flee from God. Jonah finally travels to Nineveh where the people listen and Nineveh is spared. Despite the success of the mission, Jonah continues to complain and is chastened by God.

I. Jonah's calling and his flight from God, 1:1–1:17
II. Jonah inside the fish, 2:1–2:11
III. Jonah travels to Ninevah and preaches, 3:1–3:10
IV. Jonah dislikes the outcome, 4:1–4:3
V. God chastises Jonah, 4:4–4:11

1 Now the word of the LORD came unto
[a]Jonah the son of Amittai, saying,
2 Arise, go to Nineveh, that [b]great city,
and cry against it; for [c]their wickedness is
come up before me.
3 But Jonah [d]rose up to flee unto Tarshish from the presence of the LORD, and
went down to [e]Joppa; and he found a ship
going to Tarshish: so he paid the fare
thereof, and went down into it, to go with
them unto Tarshish [f]from the presence of
the LORD.
4 ¶ But [g]the LORD sent out a great wind
into the sea, and there was a mighty tempest in the sea, so that the ship was like to
be broken.
5 Then the mariners were afraid, and
cried every man unto his god, and [h]cast
forth the wares that *were* in the ship into the
sea, to lighten *it* of them. But Jonah was
gone down [i]into the sides of the ship; and
he lay, and was fast asleep.
6 So the shipmaster came to him, and said
unto him, What meanest thou, O sleeper?
arise, [j]call upon thy God, [k]if so be that God
will think upon us, that we perish not.
7 And they said every one to his fellow,
Come, and let us [l]cast lots, that we may
know for whose cause this evil *is* upon us.
So they cast lots, and the lot fell upon Jonah.
8 Then said they unto him, [m]Tell us, we
pray thee, for whose cause this evil *is* upon
us; What *is* thine occupation? and whence
comest thou? what *is* thy country? and of
what people *art* thou?
9 And he said unto them, I *am* an Hebrew;
and I fear the LORD, the God of heaven,
[n]which hath made the sea and the dry *land.*
10 Then were the men exceedingly afraid,
and said unto him, Why hast thou done
this? For the men knew that he fled from the
presence of the LORD, because he had told
them.
11 ¶ Then said they unto him, What shall
we do unto thee, that the sea may be calm
unto us? for the sea wrought, and was tempestuous.
12 And he said unto them, [o]Take me up,
and cast me forth into the sea; so shall the
sea be calm unto you: for I know that for my
sake this great tempest *is* upon you.
13 Nevertheless the men rowed hard to
bring *it* to the land; [p]but they could not:
for the sea wrought, and was tempestuous
against them.
14 Wherefore they cried unto the LORD,
and said, We beseech thee, O LORD, we beseech thee, let us not perish for this man's
life, and [q]lay not upon us innocent blood:
for thou, O LORD, [r]hast done as it pleased
thee.
15 So they took up Jonah, and cast him
forth into the sea: [s]and the sea ceased from
her raging.
16 Then the men [t]feared the LORD exceedingly, and offered a sacrifice unto the
LORD, and made vows.
17 ¶ Now the LORD had prepared a great
fish to swallow up Jonah. And [u]Jonah was
in the belly of the fish three days and three
nights.
2 Then Jonah prayed unto the LORD his
God out of the fish's belly,
2 And said, I [v]cried by reason of mine
affliction unto the LORD, [w]and he heard me;
out of the belly of hell cried I, *and* thou
heardest my voice.
3 [x]For thou hadst cast me into the deep,
in the midst of the seas; and the floods compassed me about: [y]all thy billows and thy
waves passed over me.
4 [z]Then I said, I am cast out of thy sight;
yet I will look again [a]toward thy holy temple.
5 The [b]waters compassed me about, *even*
to the soul: the depth closed me round
about, the weeds were wrapped about my
head.
6 I went down to the bottoms of the mountains; the earth with her bars *was* about me
for ever: yet hast thou brought up my life
[c]from corruption, O LORD my God.
7 When my soul fainted within me I remembered the LORD: [d]and my prayer came
in unto thee, into thine holy temple.
8 They that observe [e]lying vanities forsake their own mercy.

1:1 [a]2 Kings 14:25
1:2 [b]Gen. 10:11; ch. 3:2 [c]Gen. 18:20; Ezra 9:6; Jam. 5:4; Rev. 18:5
1:3 [d]ch. 4:2 [e]Josh. 19:46; 2 Chron. 2:16; Acts 9:36 [f]Gen. 4:16; Job 1:12
1:4 [g]Ps. 107:25
1:5 [h]Acts 27:18 [i]1 Sam. 24:3
1:6 [j]Ps. 107:28 [k]Joel 2:14
1:7 [l]Josh. 7:14; 1 Sam. 10:20; Prov. 16:33; Acts 1:26
1:8 [m]Josh. 7:19; 1 Sam. 14:43
1:9 [n]Ps. 146:6; Acts 17:24
1:12 [o]John 11:50
1:13 [p]Prov. 21:30
1:14 [q]Deut. 21:8 [r]Ps. 115:3
1:15 [s]Ps. 89:9; Luke 8:24
1:16 [t]Mark 4:41; Acts 5:11
1:17 [u]Matt. 12:40; Luke 11:30
2:2 [v]Ps. 120:1; Lam. 3:55 [w]Ps. 65:2
2:3 [x]Ps. 88:6 [y]Ps. 42:7
2:4 [z]Ps. 31:22 [a]1 Kings 8:38
2:5 [b]Ps. 69:1; Lam. 3:54
2:6 [c]Ps. 16:10
2:7 [d]Ps. 18:6
2:8 [e]2 Kings 17:15; Ps. 31:6; Jer. 10:8

9 But I will [f]sacrifice unto thee with the
voice of thanksgiving; I will pay *that* that I
have vowed. [g]Salvation *is* of the LORD.
10 ¶ And the LORD spake unto the fish,
and it vomited out Jonah upon the dry *land*.

3 And the word of the LORD came unto
Jonah the second time, saying,
2 Arise, go unto Nineveh, that great city,
and preach unto it the preaching that I bid
thee.
3 So Jonah arose, and went unto Nineveh, according to the word of the LORD.
Now Nineveh was an exceeding great city
of three days' journey.
4 And Jonah began to enter into the city
a day's journey, and [h]he cried, and said,
Yet forty days, and Nineveh shall be overthrown.
5 ¶ So the people of Nineveh [i]believed
God, and proclaimed a fast, and put on
sackcloth, from the greatest of them even to
the least of them.
6 For word came unto the king of Nineveh, and he arose from his throne, and he
laid his robe from him, and covered *him*
with sackcloth, [j]and sat in ashes.
7 [k]And he caused *it* to be proclaimed and
published through Nineveh by the decree of
the king and his nobles, saying, Let neither
man nor beast, herd nor flock, taste any
thing: let them not feed, nor drink water:
8 But let man and beast be covered with
sackcloth, and cry mightily unto God: yea,
[l]let them turn every one from his evil way,
and from [m]the violence that *is* in their
hands.
9 [n]Who can tell *if* God will turn and repent, and turn away from his fierce anger,
that we perish not?
10 ¶ [o]And God saw their works, that they
turned from their evil way; and God repented of the evil, that he had said that he
would do unto them; and he did *it* not.

4 But it displeased Jonah exceedingly,
and he was very angry.
2 And he prayed unto the LORD, and said,
I pray thee, O LORD, *was* not this my saying,
when I was yet in my country? Therefore I
[p]fled before unto Tarshish: for I knew that
thou *art* a [q]gracious God, and merciful,
slow to anger, and of great kindness, and
repentest thee of the evil.
3 [r]Therefore now, O LORD, take, I beseech thee, my life from me; for [s]*it is* better
for me to die than to live.
4 ¶ Then said the LORD, Doest thou well
to be angry?
5 So Jonah went out of the city, and sat on
the east side of the city, and there made him
a booth, and sat under it in the shadow, till
he might see what would become of the city.
6 And the LORD God prepared a gourd,
and made *it* to come up over Jonah, that it
might be a shadow over his head, to deliver
him from his grief. So Jonah was exceeding
glad of the gourd.
7 But God prepared a worm when the
morning rose the next day, and it smote the
gourd that it withered.
8 And it came to pass, when the sun did
arise, that God prepared a vehement east
wind; and the sun beat upon the head of
Jonah, that he fainted, and wished in himself to die, and said, [t]*It is* better for me to
die than to live.
9 And God said to Jonah, Doest thou well
to be angry for the gourd? And he said, I do
well to be angry, *even* unto death.
10 Then said the LORD, Thou hast had
pity on the gourd, for the which thou hast
not laboured, neither madest it grow; which
came up in a night, and perished in a night:
11 And should not I spare Nineveh, [u]that
great city, wherein are more than sixscore
thousand persons [v]that cannot discern between their right hand and their left hand;
and *also* much [w]cattle?

2:9 [f]Ps. 50:14; Hos. 14:2; Heb. 13:15 [g]Ps. 3:8
3:4 [h]Deut. 18:22
3:5 [i]Matt. 12:41; Luke 11:32
3:6 [j]Job 2:8
3:7 [k]2 Chron. 20:3; Joel 2:15
3:8 [l]Isa. 58:6 [m]Isa. 59:6
3:9 [n]2 Sam. 12:22; Joel 2:14
3:10 [o]Jer. 18:8; Am. 7:3
4:2 [p]ch. 1:3 [q]Ex. 34:6; Ps. 86:5; Joel 2:13
4:3 [r]1 Kings 19:4 [s]ver. 8
4:8 [t]ver. 3
4:11 [u]ch. 1:2 [v]Deut. 1:39 [w]Ps. 36:6

MICAH

Micah is specifically identified as the author in the first verse of the book. A date of 700 B.C. seems the most likely date of writing. Micah opens his book with a message of judgment and destruction for Samaria and Judah. He focuses on the judgment of rulers, false teachers and the city of Jerusalem. He then gives a message of hope for the coming kingdom including the promise of the Messiah's first and second coming. Micah 5:2 identifies Bethlehem as the birthplace of the Messiah.

I. Judgment on Samaria and Jerusalem, 1:1–2:13
II. Pronouncements concerning the judgment, 3:1–3:12
III. Promises of deliverance, 4:1–5:1
IV. The coming Messiah, 5:2–5:15
V. God's ultimate plan of victory, 6:1–7:20

---

1 The word of the LORD that came to [a]Mi-
cah the Morasthite in the days of Jotham, Ahaz, *and* Hezekiah, kings of Judah,
[b]which he saw concerning Samaria and Jerusalem.
2 Hear, all ye people; [c]hearken, O earth,
and all that therein is: and let the Lord GOD
[d]be witness against you, the Lord from [e]his
holy temple.
3 For, behold, [f]the LORD cometh forth
out of his [g]place, and will come down, and
tread upon the [h]high places of the earth.
4 And [i]the mountains shall be molten
under him, and the valleys shall be cleft, as
wax before the fire, *and* as the waters *that*
are poured down a steep place.
5 For the transgression of Jacob *is* all this,
and for the sins of the house of Israel. What
is the transgression of Jacob? *is it* not Samaria? and what *are* the high places of Judah? *are they* not Jerusalem?
6 Therefore I will make Samaria [j]as an
heap of the field, *and* as plantings of a vineyard: and I will pour down the stones
thereof into the valley, and I will [k]discover
the foundations thereof.
7 And all the graven images thereof shall
be beaten to pieces, and all the [l]hires
thereof shall be burned with the fire, and all
the idols thereof will I lay desolate: for she
gathered *it* of the hire of an harlot, and they
shall return to the hire of an harlot.
8 Therefore [m]I will wail and howl, [n]I will
go stripped and naked: [o]I will make a wailing like the dragons, and mourning as the
owls.
9 For her wound *is* incurable; for [p]it is
come unto Judah; he is come unto the gate
of my people, *even* to Jerusalem.
10 ¶ [q]Declare ye *it* not at Gath, weep ye
not at all: in the house of Aphrah [r]roll thyself in the dust.
11 Pass ye away, thou inhabitant of Sa-
phir, having thy [s]shame naked: the inhabitant of Zaanan came not forth in the
mourning of Beth-ezel; he shall receive of
you his standing.
12 For the inhabitant of Maroth waited
carefully for good: but [t]evil came down
from the LORD unto the gate of Jerusalem.
13 O thou inhabitant of [u]Lachish, bind
the chariot to the swift beast: she *is* the beginning of the sin to the daughter of Zion:
for the transgressions of Israel were found
in thee.
14 Therefore shalt thou [v]give presents
to Moresheth-gath: the houses of [w]Achzib
shall be a lie to the kings of Israel.
15 Yet will I bring an heir unto thee,
O inhabitant of [x]Mareshah: he shall come
unto [y]Adullam the glory of Israel.
16 Make thee [z]bald, and poll thee for thy
[a]delicate children; enlarge thy baldness as
the eagle; for they are gone into captivity
from thee.
2 Woe to them [b]that devise iniquity, and
[c]work evil upon their beds! when the
morning is light, they practise it, because
[d]it is in the power of their hand.
2 And they covet [e]fields, and take *them*
by violence; and houses, and take *them*
away: so they oppress a man and his house,
even a man and his heritage.
3 Therefore thus saith the LORD; Behold,
against [f]this family do I devise an evil,
from which ye shall not remove your necks;
neither shall ye go haughtily: [g]for this time
is evil.
4 ¶ In that day shall *one* [h]take up a parable against you, and [i]lament with a doleful
lamentation, *and* say, We be utterly spoiled:
[j]he hath changed the portion of my people:
how hath he removed *it* from me! turning
away he hath divided our fields.
5 Therefore thou shalt have none that
shall [k]cast a cord by lot in the congregation
of the LORD.
6 [l]Prophesy ye not, *say they to them*
that prophesy: they shall not prophesy to
them, *that* they shall not take shame.
7 ¶ O *thou that art* named the house of
Jacob, is the spirit of the LORD straitened?
are these his doings? do not my words do
good to him that walketh uprightly?
8 Even of late my people is risen up as an
enemy: ye pull off the robe with the garment

1:1 [a]Jer. 26:18 [b]Am. 1:1
1:2 [c]Deut. 32:1; Isa. 1:2 [d]Ps. 50:7; Mal. 3:5 [e]Ps. 11:4; Jonah 2:7; Hab. 2:20
1:3 [f]Isa. 26:21 [g]Ps. 115 [h]Deut. 32:13; Am. 4:13
1:4 [i]Judg. 5:5; Ps. 97:5; Isa. 64:1; Am. 9:5; Hab. 3:6
1:6 [j]2 Kings 19:25; ch. 3:12 [k]Ezek. 13:14
1:7 [l]Hos. 2:5
1:8 [m]Isa. 21:3; Jer. 4:19 [n]Isa. 20:2 [o]Job 30:29; Ps. 102:6
1:9 [p]2 Kings 18:13; Isa. 8:7
1:10 [q]2 Sam. 1:20 [r]Jer. 6:26
1:11 [s]Isa. 20:4; Jer. 13:22; Nah. 3:5
1:12 [t]Am. 3:6
1:13 [u]2 Kings 18:14
1:14 [v]2 Sam. 8:2; 2 Kings 18:14 [w]Josh. 15:44
1:15 [x]Josh. 15:44 [y]2 Chron. 11:7
1:16 [z]Job 1:20; Isa. 15:2; Jer. 7:29 [a]Lam. 4:5
2:1 [b]Hos. 7:6 [c]Ps. 36:4 [d]Gen. 31:29
2:2 [e]Isa. 5:8
2:3 [f]Jer. 8:3 [g]Am. 5:13; Eph. 5:16
2:4 [h]Hab. 2:6 [i]2 Sam. 1:17 [j]ch. 1:15
2:5 [k]Deut. 32:8
2:6 [l]Isa. 30:10; Am. 2:12

from them that pass by securely as men averse from war.

9 The women of my people have ye cast out from their pleasant houses; from their children have ye taken away my glory for ever.

10 Arise ye, and depart; for this *is* not *your* [m]rest: because it is [n]polluted, it shall destroy *you*, even with a sore destruction.

11 If a man [o]walking in the spirit and falsehood do lie, *saying*, I will prophesy unto thee of wine and of strong drink; he shall even be the prophet of this people.

12 ¶ [p]I will surely assemble, O Jacob, all of thee; I will surely gather the remnant of Israel; I will put them together [q]as the sheep of Bozrah, as the flock in the midst of their fold: [r]they shall make great noise by reason of *the multitude of* men.

13 The breaker is come up before them: they have broken up, and have passed through the gate, and are gone out by it: and [s]their king shall pass before them, [t]and the LORD on the head of them.

3 And I said, Hear, I pray you, O heads of Jacob, and ye princes of the house of Israel; [u]*Is it* not for you to know judgment?

2 Who hate the good, and love the evil; who pluck off their skin from off them, and their flesh from off their bones;

3 Who also [v]eat the flesh of my people, and flay their skin from off them; and they break their bones, and chop them in pieces, as for the pot, and [w]as flesh within the caldron.

4 Then [x]shall they cry unto the LORD, but he will not hear them: he will even hide his face from them at that time, as they have behaved themselves ill in their doings.

5 ¶ Thus saith the LORD [y]concerning the prophets that make my people err, that [z]bite with their teeth, and cry, Peace; and [a]he that putteth not into their mouths, they even prepare war against him.

6 [b]Therefore night *shall be* unto you, that ye shall not have a vision; and it shall be dark unto you, that ye shall not divine; [c]and the sun shall go down over the prophets, and the day shall be dark over them.

7 Then shall the seers be ashamed, and the diviners confounded: yea, they shall all cover their lips; [d]for *there is* no answer of God.

8 ¶ But truly I am full of power by the spirit of the LORD, and of judgment, and of might, [e]to declare unto Jacob his transgression, and to Israel his sin.

9 Hear this, I pray you, ye heads of the house of Jacob, and princes of the house of Israel, that abhor judgment, and pervert all equity.

10 [f]They build up Zion with [g]blood, and Jerusalem with iniquity.

11 [h]The heads thereof judge for reward, and [i]the priests thereof teach for hire, and the prophets thereof divine for money: [j]yet will they lean upon the LORD, and say, *Is* not the LORD among us? none evil can come upon us.

12 Therefore shall Zion for your sake be [k]plowed *as* a field, [l]and Jerusalem shall become heaps, and [m]the mountain of the house as the high places of the forest.

4 But [n]in the last days it shall come to pass, *that* the mountain of the house of the LORD shall be established in the top of the mountains, and it shall be exalted above the hills; and people shall flow unto it.

2 And many nations shall come, and say, Come, and let us go up to the mountain of the LORD, and to the house of the God of Jacob; and he will teach us of his ways, and we will walk in his paths: for the law shall go forth of Zion, and the word of the LORD from Jerusalem.

3 ¶ And he shall judge among many people, and rebuke strong nations afar off; and they shall beat their swords into [o]plowshares, and their spears into pruninghooks: nation shall not lift up a sword against nation, [p]neither shall they learn war any more.

4 [q]But they shall sit every man under his vine and under his fig tree; and none shall make *them* afraid: for the mouth of the LORD of hosts hath spoken *it*.

5 For [r]all people will walk every one in the name of his god, and [s]we will walk in the name of the LORD our God for ever and ever.

6 In that day, saith the LORD, [t]will I assemble her that halteth, [u]and I will gather her that is driven out, and her that I have afflicted;

7 And I will make her that halted [v]a remnant, and her that was cast far off a strong nation: and the LORD [w]shall reign over them in mount Zion from henceforth, even for ever.

8 ¶ And thou, O tower of the flock, the strong hold of the daughter of Zion, unto thee shall it come, even the first dominion; the kingdom shall come to the daughter of Jerusalem.

9 ¶ Now why dost thou cry out aloud? [x]*is there* no king in thee? is thy counsellor perished? for [y]pangs have taken thee as a woman in travail.

10 Be in pain, and labour to bring forth, O daughter of Zion, like a woman in travail: for now shalt thou go forth out of the city, and thou shalt dwell in the field, and thou shalt go *even* to Babylon; there shalt thou be delivered; there the LORD shall redeem thee from the hand of thine enemies.

11 ¶ [z]Now also many nations are gathered against thee, that say, Let her be defiled, and let our eye [a]look upon Zion.

12 But they know not [b]the thoughts of the LORD, neither understand they his counsel: for he shall gather them [c]as the sheaves into the floor.

13 [d]Arise and thresh, O daughter of Zion: for I will make thine horn iron, and I will make thy hoofs brass: and thou shalt

2:10 [m]Deut. 12:9 [n]Lev. 18:25; Jer. 3:2
2:11 [o]Ezek. 13:3
2:12 [p]ch. 4:6 [q]Jer. 31:10 [r]Ezek. 36:37
2:13 [s]Hos. 3:5 [t]Isa. 52:12
3:1 [u]Jer. 5:4
3:3 [v]Ps. 14:4 [w]Ezek. 11:3
3:4 [x]Ps. 18:41; Prov. 1:28; Isa. 1:15; Ezek. 8:18; Zech. 7:13
3:5 [y]Isa. 56:10; Ezek. 13:10 [z]ch. 2:11; Matt. 7:15 [a]Ezek. 13:18
3:6 [b]Isa. 8:20; Ezek. 13:23; Zech. 13:4 [c]Am. 8:9
3:7 [d]Ps. 74:9; Am. 8:11
3:8 [e]Isa. 58:1
3:10 [f]Jer. 22:13 [g]Ezek. 22:27; Hab. 2:12; Zeph. 3:3
3:11 [h]Isa. 1:23; Ezek. 22:12; Hos. 4:18; ch. 7:3 [i]Jer. 6:13 [j]Isa. 48:2; Jer. 7:4; Rom. 2:17
3:12 [k]Jer. 26:18; ch. 1:6 [l]Ps. 79:1 [m]ch. 4:2
4:1 [n]Isa. 2:2; Ezek. 17:22
4:3 [o]Isa. 2:5; Joel 3:10 [p]Ps. 72:7
4:4 [q]1 Kings 4:25; Zech. 3:10
4:5 [r]Jer. 2:11 [s]Zech. 10:12
4:6 [t]Ezek. 34:16; Zeph. 3:19 [u]Ps. 147:2; Ezek. 34:13
4:7 [v]ch. 2:12 [w]Isa. 9:6; Dan. 7:14; Luke 1:33; Rev. 11:15
4:9 [x]Jer. 8:19 [y]Isa. 13:8; Jer. 30:6
4:11 [z]Lam. 2:16 [a]Obad. 12; ch. 7:10
4:12 [b]Isa. 55:8; Rom. 11:33 [c]Isa. 21:10
4:13 [d]Isa. 41:15; Jer. 51:33

[e]beat in pieces many people: [f]and I will
consecrate their gain unto the LORD, and
their substance unto [g]the Lord of the whole
earth.
5 Now gather thyself in troops, O
daughter of troops: he hath laid siege
against us: they shall [h]smite the judge of
Israel with a rod upon the cheek.
2 But thou, [i]Beth-lehem Ephratah,
though thou be little [j]among the [k]thou-
sands of Judah, *yet* out of thee shall he
come forth unto me *that is* to be [l]ruler in
Israel; [m]whose goings forth *have been* from
of old, from everlasting.
3 Therefore will he give them up, until
the time *that* [n]she which travaileth hath
brought forth: then [o]the remnant of his
brethren shall return unto the children of
Israel.
4 ¶ And he shall stand and [p]feed in the
strength of the LORD, in the majesty of the
name of the LORD his God; and they shall
abide: for now [q]shall he be great unto the
ends of the earth.
5 And this *man* [r]shall be the peace, when
the Assyrian shall come into our land: and
when he shall tread in our palaces, then
shall we raise against him seven shepherds,
and eight principal men.
6 And they shall waste the land of Assyria
with the sword, and the land of [s]Nimrod in
the entrances thereof: thus shall he [t]deliver
us from the Assyrian, when he cometh into
our land, and when he treadeth within our
borders.
7 And [u]the remnant of Jacob shall be in
the midst of many people [v]as a dew from
the LORD, as the showers upon the grass,
that tarrieth not for man, nor waiteth for the
sons of men.
8 ¶ And the remnant of Jacob shall be
among the Gentiles in the midst of many
people as a lion among the beasts of the
forest, as a young lion among the flocks of
sheep: who, if he go through, both treadeth
down, and teareth in pieces, and none can
deliver.
9 Thine hand shall be lifted up upon thine
adversaries, and all thine enemies shall be
cut off.
10 [w]And it shall come to pass in that day,
saith the LORD, that I will cut off thy horses
out of the midst of thee, and I will destroy
thy chariots:
11 And I will cut off the cities of thy land,
and throw down all thy strong holds:
12 And I will cut off witchcrafts out of
thine hand; and thou shalt have no *more*
[x]soothsayers:
13 [y]Thy graven images also will I cut off,
and thy standing images out of the midst of
thee; and thou shalt [z]no more worship the
work of thine hands.
14 And I will pluck up thy groves out of
the midst of thee: so will I destroy thy cities.
15 And I will [a]execute vengeance in anger and fury upon the heathen, such as they
have not heard.

6 Hear ye now what the LORD saith;
Arise, contend thou before the mountains, and let the hills hear thy voice.
2 [b]Hear ye, O mountains, [c]the LORD's
controversy, and ye strong foundations of
the earth: for [d]the LORD hath a controversy
with his people, and he will plead with Israel.
3 O my people, [e]what have I done unto
thee? and wherein have I wearied thee? testify against me.
4 [f]For I brought thee up out of the land of
Egypt, and redeemed thee out of the house
of servants; and I sent before thee Moses,
Aaron, and Miriam.
5 O my people, remember now what [g]Ba-
lak king of Moab consulted, and what Balaam the son of Beor answered him from
[h]Shittim unto Gilgal; that ye may know
[i]the righteousness of the LORD.
6 ¶ Wherewith shall I come before the
LORD, *and* bow myself before the high God?
shall I come before him with burnt offerings, with calves of a year old?
7 [j]Will the LORD be pleased with thousands of rams, *or* with ten thousands of
[k]rivers of oil? [l]shall I give my firstborn *for*
my transgression, the fruit of my body *for*
the sin of my soul?
8 He hath [m]shewed thee, O man, what *is*
good; and what doth the LORD require of
thee, but [n]to do justly, and to love mercy,
and to walk humbly with thy God?
9 The LORD's voice crieth unto the city,
and *the man of* wisdom shall see thy name:
hear ye the rod, and who hath appointed it.
10 ¶ Are there yet the treasures of wickedness in the house of the wicked, and the
scant measure [o]*that is* abominable?
11 Shall I count *them* pure with [p]the
wicked balances, and with the bag of deceitful weights?
12 For the rich men thereof are full of violence, and the inhabitants thereof have spoken lies, and [q]their tongue *is* deceitful in
their mouth.
13 Therefore also will I [r]make *thee* sick
in smiting thee, in making *thee* desolate because of thy sins.
14 [s]Thou shalt eat, but not be satisfied;
and thy casting down *shall be* in the midst
of thee; and thou shalt take hold, but shalt
not deliver; and *that* which thou deliverest
will I give up to the sword.
15 Thou shalt [t]sow, but thou shalt not
reap; thou shalt tread the olives, but thou
shalt not anoint thee with oil; and sweet
wine, but shalt not drink wine.
16 ¶ For the statutes of [u]Omri are [v]kept,
and all the works of the house of [w]Ahab,
and ye walk in their counsels; that I should
make thee [x]a desolation, and the inhabitants thereof an hissing: therefore ye shall
bear the [y]reproach of my people.
7 Woe is me! for I am as when they have
gathered the summer fruits, as [z]the
grapegleanings of the vintage: *there is* no

4:13 [e]Dan. 2:44 [f]Isa. 18:7 [g]Zech. 4:14
5:1 [h]Lam. 3:30; Matt. 5:39
5:2 [i]Matt. 2:6; John 7:42 [j]1 Sam. 23:23 [k]Ex. 18:25 [l]Gen. 49:10; Isa. 9:6 [m]Ps. 90:2; Prov. 8:22; John 1:1
5:3 [n]ch. 4:10 [o]ch. 4:7
5:4 [p]Isa. 40:11; Ezek. 34:23; ch. 7:14 [q]Ps. 72:8; Isa. 52:13; Zech. 9:10; Luke 1:32
5:5 [r]Ps. 72:7; Isa. 9:6; Zech. 9:10; Luke 2:14; Eph. 2:14
5:6 [s]Gen. 10:8 [t]Luke 1:71
5:7 [u]ver. 3 [v]Deut. 32:2; Ps. 72:6
5:10 [w]Zech. 9:10
5:12 [x]Isa. 2:6
5:13 [y]Zech. 13:2 [z]Isa. 2:8
5:15 [a]Ps. 149:7; ver. 8; 2 Thess. 1:8
6:2 [b]Deut. 32:1; Ps. 50:1; Isa. 1:2 [c]Hos. 12:2 [d]Isa. 1:18; Hos. 4:1
6:3 [e]Jer. 2:5
6:4 [f]Ex. 12:51; Deut. 4:20; Am. 2:10
6:5 [g]Num. 22:5; Deut. 23:4; Josh. 24:9; Rev. 2:14 [h]Num. 25:1; Josh. 4:19 [i]Judg. 5:11
6:7 [j]Ps. 50:9; Isa. 1:11 [k]Job 29:6 [l]2 Kings 16:3; Jer. 7:31; Ezek. 23:37
6:8 [m]Deut. 10:12; 1 Sam. 15:22; Hos. 6:6 [n]Gen. 18:19; Isa. 1:17
6:10 [o]Deut. 25:13-16; Prov. 11:1
6:11 [p]Hos. 12:7
6:12 [q]Jer. 9:3
6:13 [r]Lev. 26:16; Ps. 107:17
6:14 [s]Lev. 26:26; Hos. 4:10
6:15 [t]Deut. 28:38; Am. 5:11; Zeph. 1:13; Hag. 1:6
6:16 [u]1 Kings 16:25 [v]Hos. 5:11 [w]1 Kings 16:30; 2 Kings 21:3 [x]1 Kings 9:8; Jer. 19:8 [y]Isa. 25:8; Jer. 51:51; Lam. 5:1
7:1 [z]Isa. 17:6

cluster to eat: [a]my soul desired the firstripe fruit.

2 The [b]good *man* is perished out of the earth: and *there is* none upright among men: they all lie in wait for blood; [c]they hunt every man his brother with a net.

3 ¶ That they may do evil with both hands earnestly, [d]the prince asketh, [e]and the judge *asketh* for a reward; and the great *man*, he uttereth his mischievous desire: so they wrap it up.

4 The best of them [f]*is* as a brier: the most upright *is sharper* than a thorn hedge: the day of thy watchmen *and* thy visitation cometh; now shall be their perplexity.

5 ¶ [g]Trust ye not in a friend, put ye not confidence in a guide: keep the doors of thy mouth from her that lieth in thy bosom.

6 For [h]the son dishonoureth the father, the daughter riseth up against her mother, the daughter in law against her mother in law; a man's enemies *are* the men of his own house.

7 Therefore [i]I will look unto the LORD; I will wait for the God of my salvation: my God will hear me.

8 ¶ [j]Rejoice not against me, O mine enemy: [k]when I fall, I shall arise; when I sit in darkness, [l]the LORD *shall be* a light unto me.

9 [m]I will bear the indignation of the LORD, because I have sinned against him, until he plead my cause, and execute judgment for me: [n]he will bring me forth to the light, *and* I shall behold his righteousness.

10 Then *she that is* mine enemy shall see *it*, and [o]shame shall cover her which said unto me, [p]Where is the LORD thy God? [q]mine eyes shall behold her: now shall she be trodden down [r]as the mire of the streets.

11 *In* the day that thy [s]walls are to be built, *in* that day shall the decree be far removed.

12 *In* that day *also* [t]he shall come even to thee from Assyria, and *from* the fortified cities, and from the fortress even to the river, and from sea to sea, and *from* mountain to mountain.

13 Notwithstanding the land shall be desolate because of them that dwell therein, [u]for the fruit of their doings.

14 ¶ Feed thy people with thy rod, the flock of thine heritage, which dwell solitarily *in* [v]the wood, in the midst of Carmel: let them feed *in* Bashan and Gilead, as in the days of old.

15 [w]According to the days of thy coming out of the land of Egypt will I shew unto him marvellous *things*.

16 ¶ The nations [x]shall see and be confounded at all their might: [y]they shall lay *their* hand upon *their* mouth, their ears shall be deaf.

17 They shall lick the [z]dust like a serpent, [a]they shall move out of their holes like worms of the earth: [b]they shall be afraid of the LORD our God, and shall fear because of thee.

18 [c]Who *is* a God like unto thee, that [d]pardoneth iniquity, and passeth by the transgression of [e]the remnant of his heritage? [f]he retaineth not his anger for ever, because he delighteth *in* mercy.

19 He will turn again, he will have compassion upon us; he will subdue our iniquities; and thou wilt cast all their sins into the depths of the sea.

20 [g]Thou wilt perform the truth to Jacob, *and* the mercy to Abraham, [h]which thou hast sworn unto our fathers from the days of old.

7:1 [a]Isa. 28:4; Hos. 9:10
7:2 [b]Ps. 12:1; Isa. 57:1 [c]Hab. 1:15
7:3 [d]Hos. 4:18 [e]Isa. 1:23; ch. 3:11
7:4 [f]2 Sam. 23:6; Isa. 55:13; Ezek. 2:6
7:5 [g]Jer. 9:4
7:6 [h]Ezek. 22:7; Matt. 10:21; Luke 12:53; 2 Tim. 3:2
7:7 [i]Isa. 8:17
7:8 [j]Prov. 24:17; Lam. 4:21 [k]Ps. 37:24; Prov. 24:16 [l]Ps. 27:1
7:9 [m]Lam. 3:39 [n]Ps. 37:6
7:10 [o]Ps. 35:26 [p]Ps. 42:3; Joel 2:17 [q]ch. 4:11 [r]2 Sam. 22:43; Zech. 10:5
7:11 [s]Am. 9:11
7:12 [t]Isa. 11:16; Hos. 11:11
7:13 [u]Jer. 21:14; ch. 3:12
7:14 [v]Isa. 37:24
7:15 [w]Ps. 68:22
7:16 [x]Isa. 26:11 [y]Job 21:5
7:17 [z]Ps. 72:9; Isa. 49:23 [a]Ps. 18:45 [b]Jer. 33:9
7:18 [c]Ex. 15:11 [d]Ex. 34:6; Jer. 50:20 [e]ch. 4:7 [f]Ps. 103:9; Isa. 57:10; Jer. 3:5
7:20 [g]Luke 1:72 [h]Ps. 105:9

NAHUM

Nahum is the writer of this book. It was written after 663 B.C. and before 612 B.C. The first chapter of Nahum describes God and his righteous anger. The rest of the book details the proclamation of judgment on Nineveh, a description of the judgment, and the reasons for the judgment.

I. A description of God, 1:1–1:14
II. The judgment of God against Nineveh, 1:15–3:19

1 The burden [a]of Nineveh. The book of
the vision of Nahum the Elkoshite.
2 God *is* [b]jealous, and [c]the LORD revengeth; the LORD revengeth, and *is* furious; the
LORD will take vengeance on his adversaries, and he reserveth *wrath* for his enemies.
3 The LORD *is* [d]slow to anger, and [e]great
in power, and will not at all acquit *the*
wicked: [f]the LORD *hath* his way in the
whirlwind and in the storm, and the clouds
are the dust of his feet.
4 [g]He rebuketh the sea, and maketh it
dry, and drieth up all the rivers: [h]Bashan
languisheth, and Carmel, and the flower of
Lebanon languisheth.
5 [i]The mountains quake at him, and [j]the
hills melt, and [k]the earth is burned at his
presence, yea, the world, and all that dwell
therein.
6 Who can stand before his indignation?
and [l]who can abide in the fierceness of his
anger? [m]his fury is poured out like fire, and
the rocks are thrown down by him.
7 [n]The LORD *is* good, a strong hold in the
day of trouble; and [o]he knoweth them that
trust in him.
8 [p]But with an overrunning flood he will
make an utter end of the place thereof, and
darkness shall pursue his enemies.
9 [q]What do ye imagine against the LORD?
[r]he will make an utter end: affliction shall
not rise up the second time.
10 For while *they be* folden together [s]*as*
thorns, [t]and while they are drunken *as*
drunkards, [u]they shall be devoured as stubble fully dry.
11 There is *one* come out of thee, [v]that
imagineth evil against the LORD, a wicked
counsellor.
12 Thus saith the LORD; Though *they be*
quiet, and likewise many, yet thus [w]shall
they be cut down, when he shall [x]pass
through. Though I have afflicted thee, I will
afflict thee no more.
13 For now will I [y]break his yoke from
off thee, and will burst thy bonds in sunder.
14 And the LORD hath given a commandment concerning thee, *that* no more of thy
name be sown: out of the house of thy gods
will I cut off the graven image and the molten image: [z]I will make thy grave; for thou
art vile.
15 Behold [a]upon the mountains the feet
of him that bringeth good tidings, that publisheth peace! O Judah, keep thy solemn
feasts, perform thy vows: for [b]the wicked
shall no more pass through thee; [c]he is utterly cut off.

2 He [d]that dasheth in pieces is come up
before thy face: [e]keep the munition,
watch the way, make *thy* loins strong, fortify *thy* power mightily.
2 [f]For the LORD hath turned away the excellency of Jacob, as the excellency of Israel: for [g]the emptiers have emptied them
out, and marred their vine branches.
3 The shield of his mighty men is made
[h]red, the valiant men *are* in scarlet: the
chariots *shall be* with flaming torches in the
day of his preparation, and the fir trees
shall be terribly shaken.
4 The chariots shall rage in the streets,
they shall justle one against another in the
broad ways: they shall seem like torches,
they shall run like the lightnings.
5 He shall recount his worthies: they shall
stumble in their walk; they shall make haste
to the wall thereof, and the defence shall be
prepared.
6 The gates of the rivers shall be opened,
and the palace shall be dissolved.
7 And Huzzab shall be led away captive,
she shall be brought up, and her maids shall
lead *her* as with the voice of [i]doves, taber-
ing upon their breasts.
8 But Nineveh *is* of old like a pool of water: yet they shall flee away. Stand, stand,
shall they cry; but none shall look back.
9 Take ye the spoil of silver, take the spoil
of gold: for *there is* none end of the store
and glory out of all the pleasant furniture.
10 She is empty, and void, and waste: and
the [j]heart melteth, and [k]the knees smite
together, [l]and much pain *is* in all loins, and
[m]the faces of them all gather blackness.
11 Where *is* the dwelling of [n]the lions,
and the feedingplace of the young lions,
where the lion, *even* the old lion, walked,
and the lion's whelp, and none made *them*
afraid?
12 The lion did tear in pieces enough for
his whelps, and strangled for his lionesses,
and filled his holes with prey, and his dens
with ravin.
13 [o]Behold, I *am* against thee, saith the
LORD of hosts, and I will burn her chariots
in the smoke, and the sword shall devour
thy young lions: and I will cut off thy prey

1:1 [a]Zeph. 2:13
1:2 [b]Ex. 20:5; Deut. 4:24; Josh. 24:19 [c]Deut. 32:35; Ps. 94:1; Isa. 59:18
1:3 [d]Ex. 34:6; Neh. 9:17; Ps. 103:8; Jonah 4:2 [e]Job 9:4 [f]Ps. 18:7; Hab. 3:5
1:4 [g]Ps. 106:9; Isa. 50:2; Matt. 8:26 [h]Isa. 33:9
1:5 [i]Ps. 68:8 [j]Judg. 5:5; Ps. 97:5; Mic. 1:4 [k]2 Pet. 3:10
1:6 [l]Mal. 3:2 [m]Rev. 16:1
1:7 [n]1 Chron. 16:34; Ps. 100:5; Jer. 33:11; Lam. 3:25 [o]Ps. 1:6; 2 Tim. 2:19
1:8 [p]Dan. 9:26
1:9 [q]Ps. 2:1 [r]1 Sam. 3:12
1:10 [s]2 Sam. 23:6 [t]ch. 3:11 [u]Mal. 4:1
1:11 [v]2 Kings 19:22
1:12 [w]2 Kings 19:35 [x]Isa. 8:8; Dan. 11:10
1:13 [y]Jer. 2:20
1:14 [z]2 Kings 19:37
1:15 [a]Isa. 52:7; Rom. 10:15 [b]ver. 11 [c]ver. 14
2:1 [d]Jer. 50:23 [e]Jer. 51:11; ch. 3:14
2:2 [f]Isa. 10:12; Jer. 25:29 [g]Ps. 80:12; Hos. 10:1
2:3 [h]Isa. 63:2
2:7 [i]Isa. 38:14
2:10 [j]Isa. 13:7 [k]Dan. 5:6 [l]Jer. 30:9 [m]Joel 2:6
2:11 [n]Job 4:10; Ezek. 19:2-7
2:13 [o]Ezek. 29:3; ch. 3:5

FOCUS ON NAHUM

We live in an age in which the "invincible" wall in Berlin has come down; students in China rebelled in Tiananmen Square against a strong patriarchal government; and the president of the United States was brought to a humiliating public trial! Those who have felt self-sufficient and arrogant in their power status, military might, political domination, and "money" have found themselves humbled and changed by circumstances heretofore inconceivable. It sounds as if we are living in the age of Nahum who prophesied against the cruel nation of Assyria and its capital, Nineveh. Those who oppress God's people will be brought down! Disobedience, rebellion, injustice, cruelty, treachery, exploitation, and arrogance last just so long. God's vengeance will come.

As mothers, we know how often we must repeat warnings, restate "house rules," and reinforce what we have said over and over and over again. Our families know how to push the rules, to break out of established boundaries, and to overstep assigned curfews. But our job is to raise responsible, respectful children into adulthood. It requires, even demands, that we practice the art of disciplinary behaviors. There is only one mother to a family! There is only one God in this sin-sick world. When a nation decides to break the rules, forget God's limits, and overstep established boundaries, God will discipline that nation. Make no mistake about it!

HISTORICAL BACKGROUND TO NAHUM

Tiglath-pileser came to power in Assyria in 745 B.C. and immediately set about to restore the lost glory of Assyria. He came to Damascus, Israel's northern neighbor, and demanded tribute from them. King Menahem of Israel extracted money from the wealthy to pay him tribute to keep from being deported to Assyria.

In 722 B.C., Tiglath-pileser died. His successor, Sargon II, returned to the area because King Ahaz of Israel rebelled against Assyria, thinking that Egypt would help defend them. Egypt never showed up to help. The Assyrian king carried away 27,290 people to Assyria and brought into Samaria people he had conquered in other areas. The policy of replacing conquered people with other conquered people was intended to keep down rebellion. Assyrians treated their captives very cruelly. In some cases they staked their captives to the ground and skinned them alive.

Sargon's successor, Sennacherib, marched into Judah about 701 B.C. and exacted tribute from many of the towns. He deported some 200,000 people at the time. He was unable to defeat Jerusalem because an angel of the Lord slew 185,000 of his soldiers in one night (2 Kings 19:35), causing him to return to Assyria. According to Herodotus, a horde of field mice swarmed over the Assyrian camp and ate their weapons.

Sennacherib was succeeded by Esarhaddon who ruled from 681–669 B.C. Ashurbanipal succeeded Esarhaddon and ruled until 633 B.C. During his rule the Assyrian empire reached its zenith. In 625 B.C. the Assyrians were driven out of Babylon by the Chaldean ruler Nabopolassar. Nineveh, the capital of Assyria, fell to a coalition of Medes and Babylonians in 612 B.C. With the fall of Nineveh, the Assyrian Empire ceased to exist. Nahum prophesied its destruction.

THE BLACK PRESENCE IN NAHUM

Assyria/Nineveh: Mentioned in 2:8; 3:7, 18. In the Table of Nations (Gen. 10), Assyria (Asshur) is identified as a descendant of Shem. The people of this Mesopotamian area were Semitic, Hamitic, and Cushite—all of whom were black (see Introduction to Genesis).

Egypt: According to Genesis 10:6, Egyptians were the descendants of Ham, whose name means "black" or "burnt face." The history of Egypt can be traced back at least 10,000 years B.C. Prior to the arrival of Alexander the Great in 332 B.C., the people of that area called themselves *Kemet,* which means "black." Herodotus, a noted Greek historian who visited Egypt in the centuries prior to the birth of Christ, described the Egyptians as "black with wooly hair."

Ethiopia (Cush): Mentioned in 3:9. *Ethiopia* is the Greek word for Cush, and describes the descendants of one of the sons of Ham. Cush means "black" and describes people who settled in Egypt and the Mesopotamian area. Some European scholars have sought to limit Ethiopians to the area just south of Egypt.

No (Thebes): Mentioned in 3:8. The city was located on both sides of the Nile River in Africa and was the capital of Egypt at one time. Its complete name was No-amon in honor of the Egyptian god Amon who was worshiped in a temple built for his honor

Lubim (Libyans): Mentioned in 3:9. These people are apparently the same as Phut (also mentioned in 3:9). Phut, or Put, was the third son of Ham (Gen. 10:6). They occupied the area just west of Egypt on the Mediterranean Sea. Libyans were frequently associated with the Egyptians and Cushites. They were apparently good fighting men, because they served as mercenary soldiers in various battles

Life Lessons

NAHUM 1

Chapter one is clear and direct: "God is jealous, and the LORD revengeth; the LORD revengeth, and is furious; the LORD will take vengeance on his adversaries, and he reserveth wrath for his enemies. The LORD is slow to anger, and great in power, and will not at all acquit the wicked" (1:2–3). Judgment and punishment will come to those who mistreat God's people. This punishment may not come as soon as we

would like it to, but God has promised that vengeance will occur. Our hands will be clean!

Avenging God, thank You for relieving me of the responsibility to think of ways to "pay back" my enemies. Those who attack me also attack You. I leave them in Your hands.

NAHUM 2–3

Judgment is declared against the greatest, most fearsome enemy Israel had ever encountered. This chapter predicts the time when the Babylonians will come and destroy Nineveh. What they have done to both the northern and southern kingdoms of Israel is lightweight compared to what God has in mind for them. "Nineveh is of old like a pool of water: yet they shall flee away. Stand, stand, shall they cry; but none shall look back. . . . She is empty, and void, and waste: and the heart melteth, and the knees smite together, and much pain is in all loins, and the faces of them all gather blackness. . . . and the voice of they messengers shall no more be heard" (2:8, 10, 13).

Great rejoicing is heard and felt in Israel: "There is no healing of thy bruise; and thy wound is grievous: all that hear the bruit of thee shall clap the hands over thee: for upon whom hath not thy wickedness passed continually?" (3:19). This is bad news for the enemy and good news for those God loves!

Wealth of the Nations, I run to You for refuge in frightening times, for You are a secure place of safety. Thank You for protection as well as comfort.

FOCUS ON HABAKKUK

Two sermon topics come to mind as we contemplate this book of human questions and divine answers. Reverend Cynthia Williams Bryant, teacher and theologian extraordinare, began the early 1970s conferences of African-American "church women" while pastoring historic Bethel AME Church in Baltimore, Maryland with her spouse, Bishop John Bryant. Cynthia is a woman who dares to question God. She also is a woman who dares to wait for God's response.

As she stood facing a sea of expectant black female faces at a conference in Texas, she used this small book to challenge the sisterhood. She preached, "If you're seeing it, why ain't you saying it?" For Habakkuk was told by God, "Write the vision, and make it plain upon tables, that he may run that readeth it" (2:2). Her premise was that as Habakkuk stood on his watch, comfortable in waiting for God to respond to his questions, his close relationship gave him the confidence to believe that an answer was surely forthcoming. Habakkuk, looking and preaching about the violence within Judah, challenges God to come and do something about the backsliding and perverted nation. Bryant's challenge to the sisterhood was basically the same!

We live in a nation much like Judah. Right is called wrong. Wrong is called right. Popular opinion, as opposed to the written Word of God, dictates our response to most situations! The church is silent on too many issues. Reverend Bryant, like Habakkuk, had asked God "Why?" The revelation came that too many women are "called" to teach and to preach, but they are not "talking" about the sin in Zion! "If you're seeing it, why ain't you saying it?" The vision is to be "published" in order to save lives.

Bishop Cornelius Henderson of the United Methodist Church was asked to preach for a prestigious gathering in the hallowed chapel at Garrett-Evangelical Theological Seminary in Evanston, Illinois. That august body was assembled to hear some erudite, dry lecture on some dead theologians' "thoughts." As the bishop had wrestled with the book of Habakkuk, he proclaimed, "There is much to say, and somebody ought to be saying something!" God declared to Habakkuk, "The vision is yet for an appointed time, but at the end it shall speak, and not lie" (2:3). The Babylonians had committed serious violence upon the people of Judah, but Habakkuk was chosen to tell the people that "the just shall live by faith" (v. 4).

God is working even when we can't see evidence of His movement or don't understand what He is doing. Living by faith is difficult. Faith requires a personal, consistent, and well-developed relationship with God. Faith to wait in times of pain is cultivated by "going through." Faith to endure when things seem hopeless requires believing that God knows, cares, and will take care of the situation at the appointed time. Habukkuk is not given to talking about himself. He is predisposed to be a man of few words; what he sees, he reports. There is much to report, and he says so! If you are seeing wrong, are you openly speaking against it? There is much wrong; yet there is too much silence! "If you're seeing it, why ain't you saying it?" For there is much to be said, and you ought to be saying something on behalf of God and right!

HISTORICAL BACKGROUND TO HABAKKUK

The Neo-Babylonian Empire had just emerged following Assyria's defeat at the hands of the Babylonians and Medes in 612 B.C. God was about to permit the Babylonians to control Judah and the surrounding nations. In 605 B.C., Nebuchadnezzar made his first incursion into the eastern Mediterranean area as he chased the Egyptians back to their border. On his way back from defeating the Egyptians, Nebuchadnezzar stopped at Judah and rounded up several thousand people whom he then carried back to Babylon. Habakkuk foresaw the Babylonian invasion and questioned the Lord as to why He would use such a brutal nation to punish Judah, His own people.

THE BLACK PRESENCE IN HABAKKUK

Chaldeans: Mentioned in 1:6. One of the names given to people who had Babylon as their capital. They lived in Ur, the area south of Babylon (Shinar) where Abraham lived prior to his departure to Haran and Canaan. Their language was very similar to Galla (Oromo), the scientific and religious Cushite language of Africa. They were likely a part of the migration which took place from Africa into the Mesopotamian area between 5000 and 2500 B.C.

Noted for their wisdom and knowledge, they appeared in strategic situations during the times of Daniel. It also is possible that the Chaldeans were the "wise men from the east" who came to visit the Christ child (Matt. 2).

Life Lessons

HABAKKUK 1–2

Chapters one and two contain dialogue with the prophet framing some harsh and difficult questions for God. He wants to understand how the Creator of heaven and earth could tolerate the wickedness going on in Judah. Habakkuk is concerned about the violence that the people of Judah are doing to themselves by departing from the covenant relationship, as well as the violence that is sure to come in judgment. The sin within Judah is painful. "Why dost thou shew me iniquity, and cause me to behold grievance? for spoiling and violence are before me: and there are that rise up strife and contention. Therefore the law is slacked, and judgment doth never go forth: for the wicked doth compass about the righteous; therefore wrong judgment" (1:3–4). Standing at the top of the city wall, Habakkuk has the advantage of being able to "look down" and get a true view of what is going on both within and around the city where God is to reign. Sick and tired of being sick and tired, Habakkuk decides to have a little talk with his "companion." So he asks a series of questions. And, his "friend" speaks an answer. "I will work a work in your days, which ye will not believe, though it be told you. For lo, I raise up the Chaldeans" (vv. 5–6). Violence begets violence!

Wall of Protection, take away the spirit of violence. Help me to speak out against violence.

HABAKKUK 1–2

Chapter one draws to a close with Habakkuk's second complaint. "Art thou not from everlasting, O LORD my God, mine Holy One? we shall not die, O LORD, thou hast ordained them for judgment; and O mighty God, thou hast established them for correction. Thou art of purer eyes than to behold evil, and canst not look on iniquity" (1:12–13). That's a good question for women to grapple with as the ravages of racism, sexism, and classism try to hem us in on every side! We all want an answer regarding God's timeframe of "getting" those who have done us wrong! This is when God instructs Habakkuk to "write the vision, and make it plain" (2:2). Payday is coming. Payback also is coming! The righteous must live out their days in faith. Evil will not triumph! "The LORD is in his holy temple: let all the earth keep silence before him" (v. 20).

Rock of Ages, cleft for me, let me hide myself in Thee!

HABAKKUK 3

The book closes with Habakkuk's prayer of praise for God's faithfulness. The prophet has been told that Judah would pay the penalties for her sin and it would not be a pretty sight! But his questions are given

answers. Like the psalms of David, the word *Selah,* which indicates a time of reflection and affirmation of the truth, appears. "O LORD, I have heard thy speech, and was afraid: O LORD, revive thy work in the midst of the years, in the midst of the years make known; in wrath remember mercy" (3:2). We each have days and seasons when it seems that "evil" and the wicked have the upper hand. It can be difficult to "see" why God permits things and people to get so bad and to act so ugly! Habakkuk is seeing what's on the way. In full confidence of the God he serves and questions, Habakkuk includes these reassuring words for our "waiting" hearts.

> *Coming Savior, "Although the fig tree shall not blossom, neither shall fruit be in the vines; the labour of the olive shall fail, and the fields shall yield no meat; the flock shall be cut off from the fold, and there shall be no herd in the stalls: Yet I will rejoice in the LORD, I will joy in the God of my salvation. The LORD God is my strength . . . and he will make me to walk upon mine high places" (vv. 17–19).*

FOCUS ON ZEPHANIAH

There is nothing worse than depression! When the gray, cloudy skies won't clear up; when the sun can't break through the steady downpour of rain; and when nothing is attractive or uplifting, depression has taken hold. When you don't want to get up, go out, or be involved in any social activities—beware! Depression is settling in for the long haul. Today, Zephaniah would be declared "clinically depressed." His words of judgment come from years of watching decline and backsliding. His opening statements are filled with desolation. God has declared "I will utterly consume all things from off the land. . . . Hold thy peace at the presence of the Lord GOD: for the day of the LORD is at hand" (1:2, 7). Once again we hear the terror of the prophet's heart as God speaks words of judgment.

Nothing can be more heart shattering than watching a beloved child die. It is somehow unexplainable to return a "piece" of your very self to the earth from which it came. This is just not how it's supposed to be! Women birth the children. Women nurse and nurture the children. Women care for and tend to the children. Women teach and discipline the children. And somewhere along the way toward adulthood, somebody else begins to influence them, to instruct them, and to "carry them off" into strange customs, habits, and practices. Mothers, particularly in urban areas, are burying their children at earlier ages due to increasing poverty and hopelessness, the influence of gangs and drugs, and the rising violence of child against child. It's depressing to watch one's own child take the path of destruction. Zephaniah knew this "mother's-type" of depression. His words came from the tender heart of a grieving God who had birthed Israel and tended to her every need.

A mother went to court with her son on six different occasions. The social workers had termed him "incorrigible" or worthless, without hope

for salvation. On each visit before the judge, the mother had spoken a word in her child's defense. On the sixth occasion, the judge stopped the proceedings and said to the mother, "Madam, you keep coming here, saying that your child is "a good boy." By now you ought to know that he is a hoodlum. How long can you keep up this same defense?" The mother answered, "Until he's not my boy, your honor." She had undying hope.

In the midst of dire predictions of total destruction, the hope of restoration is raised.

"Seek ye the LORD, all ye meek of the earth, which have wrought his judgment; seek righteousness, seek meekness; it may be ye shall be hid in the day of the LORD's anger" (2:3). God is the hope of Zion!

HISTORICAL BACKGROUND TO ZEPHANIAH

Zephaniah prophesied during the time when the Assyrian Empire was crumbling at the hands of the Babylonians and Medes. After the northern kingdom of Israel went into captivity in 722 B.C., God continued to warn the southern kingdom that they too would go into captivity if they did not heed His warnings to turn from their idolatry and wickedness. About this time, Hilkiah the priest found a copy of the Law in the temple and brought it to Josiah. The king immediately called for repentance and revival (2 Kings 22–23). Even though the nation went through a revival under King Josiah, it soon became clear that the people really were intent on following their own ways. Zephaniah was one of the prophets God sent to give clear warning that judgment was imminent.

THE BLACK PRESENCE IN ZEPHANIAH

Assyria: Mentioned in 2:13. In the Table of Nations (Gen. 10), Assyria (Asshur) is identified as a descendant of Shem. The people of this Mesopotamian area were Semitic, Hamitic, and Cushite—all of whom were black. According to Genesis 10, Nimrod, a son of Cush, built Ashur. Assyria retained a long, sometimes interrupted, empire. In 722 B.C., Assyria defeated the northern kingdom of Israel, carrying off some 27,000 Israelites. Nineveh, the capital of Assyria, was defeated during the fierce battle of 612 B.C. when Babylon (also built by Nimrod) and Persia joined forces to defeat it.

Ethiopia (Cush): Mentioned in 2:12; 3:10. *Ethiopia* is the Greek word for Cush and describes the descendants of one of the sons of Ham. Cush means "black" and describes people who settled in Egypt and the Mesopotamian area. Some European scholars have erroneously sought to limit Ethiopians to the area just south of Egypt.

Philistia (Gaza, Askelon, Ashdod): Mentioned in 2:4–7. Philistines were the descendants of Ham through Egypt (Gen. 10:13–14). *Mizraim* is the Hebrew name for Egypt.

Life Lessons

ZEPHANIAH 1

Chapter one rings out a severe warning of coming destruction aimed at Judah and those who lived in sight of the temple where the name of the Holy One of Israel was to be worshiped. Yet the people worship idols. "I will cut off the remnant of Baal from this place, and the name of the Chemarims with the priests; And them that worship the host of heaven upon the housetops; and them that worship and swear . . . by Malcham . . . and those that have not sought the LORD, not enquired for him" (1:4–6). Idol worship is the first sin that God mentions in the Ten Commandments. Checking our horoscopes, calling "the psychic hotline," and going to visit those who can "read" your future are ways of participating in idolatry! The "starry host" is alive! When we put anything before God—a spouse or significant other, children, a job, the acquisition of wealth—we engage in the practice of idol worship! Beware!

Creator of the sun, moon, and stars, help me know and practice true worship of You who holds my life and future within Your capable hands.

ZEPHANIAH 2–3

Chapter two commands the calling together of a sacred assembly. "Gather yourselves together, yea, gather together, O nation not desired; Before the decree bring forth . . . before the day of the LORD's anger come upon you. Seek ye the LORD" (2:1–3). A series of pronouncements against the "enemies" of the Lord is metered out. Chapter three begins to outline the future of Jerusalem when the destruction has occurred and restoration is provided. God promises: "In that day shalt thou not be ashamed for all thy doings . . . I will also leave in the midst of thee an afflicted and poor people, and they shall trust in the name of the LORD. The remnant of Israel shall not do iniquity, not speak lies, neither shall a deceitful tongue be found in their mouth . . . Sing, O daughter of Zion" (3:8–14).

Keeper of the Remnant, work meekness and humility within me. I want to be ready when You come! My heart sings and rejoices in Your saving grace.

Focus on HAGGAI

Home! It's a place. Home! It's a feeling. Home! It's an attitude. Home! It's about family. Home! It's about a sense of security. Home! It's love and acceptance. The Israelites had been able to return home. Home! It's about the temple and a place to worship God. It's time to rebuild home! God had assigned

the refugees the task of completing the work on the temple. The Israelites who have been in exile return. Those who have been living under "foreign occupation" began to reclaim their property. The work of rebuilding their community in the Promised Land had been a sweet dream to each group.

Fifteen years after their return and resettling, the Lord God asked through the prophet Haggai, "Is it time for you, O ye, to dwell in your cieled houses, and this house lie waste? Now therefore thus saith the LORD of hosts; Consider your ways" (1:4–5). God's "house" is not finished and God is angry!

Babylon had completely destroyed the temple, which was the place that housed the name of Israel's God. Although they recognized that God could not be confined to one building, the temple was the place of worship and sacrifice, as well as their place of being restored to right relationship with God on the annual Day of Atonement (see Leviticus 16). However, their priorities had been focused on themselves—their homes and their needs. Even after being allowed to return to Jerusalem by Darius in order to rebuild their sacred place of worship, the temple of God had not been completed. It stood as a partial monument to a complete God!

Haggai calls them to action: "Thus saith the LORD of hosts . . . Go up to the mountain, and bring wood, and build the house; and I will take pleasure in it, and I will be glorified, saith the LORD" (1:7–8). As the primary "keepers" of our homes, we know internally what it means to have our "house in order." One of the biggest pleasures in life is the ability to have a home built to your personal specifications. Most of us never have this dream realized. Yet that doesn't stop us from daydreaming! Our homes represent us. Our homes stand as a testimony to our economic "worth." A partially built structure is demoralizing. It only serves to remind us of dreams unfulfilled, of hope deferred. The comparison between our home and God's temple is certainly not exact. But that illustration can help us understand a little why God wanted the temple to be completely restored.

This book is a call to challenge the way we set our priorities. The "temple" today that God is calling us to rebuild is our spiritual state. We don't need to build homes. We need to build our souls on God and His truths. It's about making sure that the inner space within us, where God dwells, is "complete." This is also a call for us to give and sacrifice to ensure that our local place of worship—that place where God's name is worshiped—is kept in a condition that reflects God's "corporate" worth, to those who worship and those who pass by it. God's call to finish and complete His "house" is a call to us!

HISTORICAL BACKGROUND TO HAGGAI

The captivity of Judah began in 605 B.C. when Nebuchadnezzar deported thousands of people to Babylon but left the city and temple standing. He made another incursion in 597 B.C. and placed Zedekiah on the throne as a puppet king. Zedekiah rebelled against Nebuchadnezzar. In 586 B.C., the Babylonian king returned to destroy the city and burn the temple. The nation remained in captivity for 70 years until Darius the Great, the Persian king, permitted 50,000 people to return to the land. When they returned, they used a makeshift altar for worship, then laid the

foundation for a temple. After laying the foundation, however, they neglected to complete the building. God sent Haggai with four messages to encourage the people to complete the temple.

THE BLACK PRESENCE IN HAGGAI

Darius: Mentioned in 1:1. This Persian ruler who permitted the Jews to rebuild the temple was perhaps Semitic. Semites were typically black people from the region of Mesopotamia.

Life Lessons

HAGGAI 1

Chapter one begins with the people's excuse for not completing the work assigned them by God. "The time is not come, the time that the LORD's house should be built" (1:2). Their own priorities took precedent over God, who had delivered them once again. Happy to be "home," but caught in great community tension, the people decided that God's house could wait! Coming "home" was not a picnic. Those who had been displaced by foreign occupation and those who had been taken into captivity were at odds over who owned what land, house, or well. Property issues consumed much of their time and caused much community infighting. These social tensions were set against too little rain, poor crop cultivation, and a rate of inflation that rendered them unable to return to "business as usual." Things were tough and not getting any better. They were "doing the best they could" to get their personal houses in order and trying to survive. God's house was put off as a project "on the back burner." God says through Haggai, "Consider your ways. Ye have sown much, and bring in little; ye ear, but ye have not enough; ye drink, but ye are not filled with drink; ye clothe you, but there is none warm; and he that earneth wages earneth wages to put it into a bag with holes. . . . Ye looked for much, and, lo it came to little; and when ye brought it home, I did blow upon it. Why? saith the LORD of hosts. Because of mine house that is waste, and ye run every man unto his won house, Therefore the heaven over you is stayed from dew, and the earth is stayed from her fruit" (vv. 5–6, 9–11). The indictment against Israel is serious.

There is no mistake. They set their priorities wrongly. God works against them as fast as they work for themselves. They cannot win! Their labors are futile!

Harvest Giver, I work diligently to earn my daily bread. Yet I hear You say that when I remember to honor You first, You will provide all that I need. Help me to always establish You as the very first of my priorities! I don't want to work against my own blessings that You desire to send my way!

HAGGAI 2

Chapter two contains the key verse for our prosperity and continued blessing. As the people begin work on God's house with renewed vigor and commitment, God speaks a word of encouragement. "Yet now be strong . . .be

strong . . . be strong, all ye people of the land, saith the LORD, and work: for I am with you . . . According to the word that I covenanted with you . . . so my spirit remaineth among you: Fear ye not" (vv. 4–5). The word of God to "Be strong" came to the leader, Zerubbabel, who had been appointed by the foreign King Darius to do the work of rebuilding. The word of God, "Be strong" came to the high priest, Joshua. The word of God, "Be strong" came also to all the people of the land. The reason behind their being able to do the work assigned and take care of their homes and families was due to the covenant God had made with them years ago. They were to simply "work"—do their part, follow instructions, and rely upon the provisions of an able God. Dannibelle Hall sang it best: "*Little becomes much when you place it in the Master's hand.*" As the people return to work on God's house their blessing is promised again: "From this day will I bless you" (2:19). "[I] will make thee as a signet ring, for I have chosen thee" (v. 23).

Faithful Sovereign, all that I have belongs to You. I covenant to make You my first priority as I "work" on my physical temple and work in my local congregation to uplift Your glorious name.

Focus on ZECHARIAH

"I have a dream!" These words swiftly carry our minds to one man who dared to "see" more than was actual in his life span. "I have a dream!" These words have caused the death of men and women across the ages who dared articulate to "the powers that be" what had been revealed to them by God. "I have a dream!" What a wonderful expression of hope and aspirations which require careful thought and much work to bring to fruition. "I have a dream!" Dreams speak about what has been and what is to come. Dreams can provide inspiration, answer perplexing questions, and offer alternatives that have escaped us during our waking hours. "I have a dream!" The words signify a lofty ambition that mandates that the dreamer have a purpose in order to achieve the longing of his or her yearning heart. God has a habit of giving revelation through dreams. Zechariah was a dreamer in the immediate days after Israel's return from Babylonian captivity.

Born in captivity in Babylonia, yet a prophet and priest among the exiles, Zechariah had both dreams and visions given to him by God. Using apocalyptic imagery and symbolic language, some have called many of Zechariah's dreams "nightmares" because of the way they describe the end of time. There is not much personal information given prior to his voice being uplifted in telling the nation that "the Messiah is coming!" (See Zechariah 6:12; 9:9.) Zechariah adds a series of encouraging words to the exiles who are beginning the work of rebuilding the temple. The people are discouraged that the work they are engaged in will not match the former temple. Although they are working again at God's command, they cannot shake the memories of their yesterdays and the temple's glory. They know how things had been for them when Yahweh was "in the house!" They feel

that a smaller, less grand temple would inhibit the great God from doing miracles again on their behalf. Zechariah comes with words of enlightenment that point them beyond the physical Temple into the grand future God has for the whole world.

Zechariah tells us about a glorious "family reunion" where God declares, "There shall yet old men and old women dwell in the streets of Jerusalem, and every man with his staff in his hand for very age. And the streets of the city shall be full of boys and girls playing in the streets thereof. . . . It also be marvellous in mine eyes? saith the LORD of hosts" (8:4–6). You really do want to be there!

HISTORICAL BACKGROUND TO ZECHARIAH

The captivity of Judah began in 605 B.C. when Nebuchadnezzar deported thousands of people to Babylon but left the city and temple standing. He made another incursion in 597 B.C. and placed Zedekiah on the throne as a puppet king. Zedekiah rebelled against Nebuchadnezzar and in 586 B.C., the Babylonian king returned to destroy the city and burn the temple. The nation remained in captivity for 70 years until the Persian king, Darius the Great, permitted 50,000 people to return to the land. When they returned in 520 B.C., they worshiped on a makeshift altar, laying the foundation for a temple. After laying the foundation, however, they neglected to complete the building. God sent Zechariah to encourage the people to complete the temple. Additionally, the prophet prophesied some of God's future dealings with Israel and the world.

THE BLACK PRESENCE IN ZECHARIAH

Assyria: Mentioned in 10:10. In the Table of Nations (Gen. 10), Assyria (Asshur) is identified as a descendant of Shem. The people of this Mesopotamian area were Semitic, Hamitic, and Cushite—all of whom were black. According to Genesis 10, Nimrod, a son of Cush, built Ashur. Assyria retained a long, sometimes interrupted, empire. In 722 B.C., Assyria defeated the northern kingdom of Israel, carrying off some 27,000 Israelites. Nineveh, the capital of Assyria, was defeated during the fierce battle of 612 B.C., when Babylon (also built by Nimrod) and Persia joined forces to defeat it. In 605 B.C., Babylon defeated Egypt giving Babylon undisputed domination of the Fertile Crescent, the territory extending from Egypt to the Persian Gulf.

Babylon, Babylonians: Mentioned in 2:7. The histories of Babylon and Assyria are intertwined, with Assyria being located on the Tigris River and Babylon on the Euphrates River. Both cities were built by Nimrod. Indications are that as early as 3000 to 2500 B.C., a group of black people known as Sumerians settled the area. According to Henry Rawlinson, the father of Assyriology, these Sumerians migrated there from Africa. By 747 B.C., Babylon was independent. In 699 B.C., Babylon became subject to Assyria and remained so until 625 B.C. when Nabopolassar asserted his independence from Assyria. His son, Nebuchadnezzar, became king in 605 B.C., and immediately began his conquest of the surrounding nations.

Canaanites: Mentioned in 14:21. Canaan was a son of Ham.

Egypt: Mentioned in 10:10. According to Genesis 10:6, Egyptians were the descendants of Ham. The history of Egypt can be traced back at least 10,000 years B.C. Prior to the arrival of Alexander the Great in 332 B.C., the people of that area called themselves *Kemet*, which means "black." Herodotus, a noted Greek historian who visited Egypt in the centuries prior to the birth of Christ, described the Egyptians as "black with wooly hair."

Shinar: Mentioned in 5:11. The area south of Babylon (Shinar) where Abraham lived prior to his departure to Haran and Canaan. The language of the people who lived there was very similar to Galla (Oromo), the scientific and religious Cushite language of Africa. They were likely a part of the migration which took place from Africa into the Mesopotamian area between 5000 and 2500 B.C. Noted for their wisdom and knowledge, they appeared in strategic situations during the time of Daniel. It was also possible that the Chaldeans were the "wise men from the east" who visited the Christ child (Matt. 2).

Philistia (Ashkelon, Gaza, Ekron, Ashdod): Mentioned in 9:5–6. The Philistines were the descendants of Ham through Egypt (*Mizraim* in Hebrew). (See Genesis 10:13–14.)

Phoenicia (Tyre, Sidon): Mentioned in 9:2–3. Tyre and Sidon were twin cities located in Phoenicia on the eastern coast of the Mediterranean Sea. Sidon was a descendant of Canaan, a son of Ham. Ezekiel speaks of the city's commerce with Spain, India, Greece, Palestine, Arabia, Persia, and other nations, as well as its wealth, consisting of gold, silver, iron, lead, tin, copper, wheat, cereal, wool, linen, ebony, dyes, and other commodities.

Life Lessons

ZECHARIAH 1–8

Chapter one is a repeat of Haggai's prophecy of God's anger over the ways of Israel that resulted in her exile. We are introduced again to a thread of hope in the midst of their return. "I am returned to Jerusalem with mercies: my house shall be built in it, saith the LORD of hosts, and a line shall be stretched forth upon Jerusalem. . . . My cities through prosperity shall yet be spread abroad; and the LORD shall yet comfort Zion, and shall yet choose Jerusalem" (1:16–17). Then we get a view of Zechariah's visions: messengers reporting to God all who have oppressed Judah; four horns representing the world powers who will be scattered; a man with a measuring line who declares that Jerusalem will be too small for all the people who will come to fill her walls; clean clothes for the priest which speak of garments of sin exchanged for garments of righteousness; a lampstand which has unlimited supply of oil, foretelling the indwelling of the Holy Spirit in living souls; a flying scroll, which represents God's Word

which will judge the world; a woman who represents the idol worshipers shipped back to Babylonia in a basket (which shows that sin is removed from Israel); and four horses and chariots which will execute God's world judgment. Chapter eight provides God's promise to bless Jerusalem and another call to the people not to stop the work. "Let your hands be strong . . . that the temple might be built. . . . fear not, but let your hands be strong" (8:9, 13).

Temple Builder, work on this building, called me, so that it is worthy of carrying Your great name.

ZECHARIAH 9–14

Chapter nine foretells the coming of the Messiah after work on the temple is complete: "Rejoice greatly, O daughter of Zion; shout, O daughter of Jerusalem: behold, thy King cometh unto thee: he is just, and having salvation; lowly, and riding upon an ass . . . he shall speak peace unto the heathen; and his dominion shall be from sea even to sea, and from the river even to the ends of the earth" (9:9–10). The temple in Jerusalem is only a "dream" to signify the rule of Jesus Christ over the whole of God's people. "And men shall dwell in it, and there shall be no more utter destruction; but Jerusalem shall be safely inhabited" (14:11).

Focus On MALACHI

"I'm sick and tired! And I'm sick and tired of being sick and tired!" Many women have said these words after repeated warnings to others who refuse to pay attention to them. You may be one of those women. It may be a spouse or significant other who has closed ears and does not pay attention. Perhaps the children of your womb or those of the classroom, who can't seem to "get it," have triggered this outburst. Perhaps a supervisor who has failed to comprehend your dissatisfactions that have been both stated and written has set you off. You may feel discouraged after playing "repeat" without any change in behavior. But after saying the same thing a hundred times, perhaps the light bulb comes on in the person's head. Then perhaps like God, you just go stone silent!

Malachi, which means, "my messenger," is the concluding prophet to postexilic Judah. God is "sick and tired" of priests who don't get it and won't do the job they have been appointed to perform. God is "sick and tired" of the people's indifference to meaningful worship and deeds of justice. God is "sick and tired" of their continual intermarriage with foreign women who worship idols. And God is "sick and tired of being sick and tired" of those who have been blessed and yet refuse to return the tithe to uphold the work of the temple. God is about to go stone silent on these hardheaded, backsliding children.

What woman can't identify with God's being "sick and tired of being sick and tired," of not being heard, of not being treated with respect, and of not being appreciated? What woman can't "feel" God's pain at being

rejected for other gods after giving all to the relationship? What woman can't sense God's hurt at children who just won't learn to act right?

Malachi is only another echo of the past. But what woman wouldn't try "just one last time"?

HISTORICAL BACKGROUND TO MALACHI

The people are now back in their land after their 70-year exile. Darius the Great had issued the decree in 530 B.C., permitting them to return. They are now under the rulership of the Persians. Life is not easy. The temple has been rebuilt and perhaps most, if not all, of the wall surrounding it. Crops were not very productive, and religious apathy has set in. Their prolonged captivity had perhaps created doubt about the validity of God's covenant promises. Morals become lax and worship empty. Malachi is sent to address these issues and to encourage faithfulness to the Lord.

THE BLACK PRESENCE IN MALACHI

There are no specific references to the black presence in the Book of Malachi. We know, however, that the entire drama of redemption takes place in an African-Asiatic environment.

Life Lessons

MALACHI 1–3

Chapter one is a harsh denouncement of the priests who offer blemished sacrifices unto God. "Who is there even among you that would shut the doors for nought? neither do ye kindle fire on mine altar for nought, I have no pleasure in you, saith the LORD of hosts, neither will I accept an offering at your" (1:10). Chapter two continues with additional curses: "I will even send a curse upon you, and I will curse your blessings: yea, I have cursed them already, because ye do not lay it to heart" (2:2). Judah's unfaithfulness is set in the context of a marriage covenant being broken. "Judah hath dealt treacherously, and an abomination is committed in Israel and in Jerusalem; for Judah hath profaned the holiness of the LORD which he loved, and hath married the daughter of a strange god. . . . For the LORD, the God of Israel, saith that he hateth putting away" (vv. 11, 16). Useless tears and empty words "have wearied the LORD" (v. 17). So God sends "my messenger and he shall prepare the way before me" (3:1).

"But who may abide the day of his coming? . . . he is like a refiner's fire, and like fullers' soap . . . And I will come near to you to judgment; and I will be a swift witness against the sorcerers, and against false swearers, and against those that oppress the hireling in his wages, the widow, and the fatherless, and that turn aside the stranger from his right, and fear not me, saith the LORD of hosts" (3:2–5).

Lord Almighty, purify me, cleanse me, and give me open ears to hear what You say to me, Your child.

MALACHI 3

The book draws to a close. The last words from God for this covenant people ends with a detailed explanation of tithing, a practice that is deliberately misunderstood today. As God gets ready to shut up the heavens, the "last word" is not about "pledges." It is not about tipping. It is not even about "stewardship Sundays." This "word" is about the way God's people were involved in robbing the One who was their source. How do we rob God? "In tithes and offerings. Ye are cursed with a curse: for ye have robbed me, even this whole nation. Bring ye all the tithes . . . prove me now herewith . . . if I will not open you the windows of heaven, and pour you out a blessing, that there shall not be room enough to receive it" (3:8–12). The tithe is ten percent of whatever we receive as income or gain. The tithe belongs to God! The tithe comes off the top! The tithe is from gross income and not net, after taxes, Social Security, and so on have been removed! For all of what you have received, whether from a well-paying position or from the rolls of public aid, the tithe is a way that all of us can be equal in our giving unto the Lord!

Generous God, You have given me all! Prepare my heart to return unto You the tithe of my resources, my time, and my gifts. It's the least I can do!

MALACHI 4

Because God is compassionate and loving, the promise of grace and mercy is found within this last book: "But unto you that fear my name shall the Sun of righteousness arise with healing in his wings; and ye shall go forth, and grow up as calves of the stall" (4:2).

from the earth, and the voice of [p]thy messengers shall no more be heard.

3 Woe to the [q]bloody city! it *is* all full of
lies *and* robbery; the prey departeth not;
2 The noise of a whip, and [r]the noise of
the rattling of the wheels, and of the prans-
ing horses, and of the jumping chariots.
3 The horseman lifteth up both the bright
sword and the glittering spear: and *there is*
a multitude of slain, and a great number
of carcases; and *there is* none end of *their*
corpses; they stumble upon their corpses:
4 Because of the multitude of the whoredoms of the wellfavoured harlot, [s]the mistress of witchcrafts, that selleth nations
through her whoredoms, and families
through her witchcrafts.
5 [t]Behold, I *am* against thee, saith the
LORD of hosts; and [u]I will discover thy
skirts upon thy face, [v]and I will shew the
nations thy nakedness, and the kingdoms
thy shame.
6 And I will cast abominable filth upon
thee, and [w]make thee vile, and will set thee
as [x]a gazingstock.
7 And it shall come to pass, *that* all they
that look upon thee [y]shall flee from thee,
and say, Nineveh is laid waste: [z]who will
bemoan her? whence shall I seek comforters for thee?
8 [a]Art thou better than populous [b]No,
that was situate among the rivers, *that had*
the waters round about it, whose rampart
was the sea, *and* her wall *was* from the sea?
9 Ethiopia and Egypt *were* her strength,
and *it was* infinite; Put and Lubim were thy
helpers.
10 Yet *was* she carried away, she went
into captivity: [c]her young children also
were dashed in pieces [d]at the top of all the
streets: and they [e]cast lots for her honourable men, and all her great men were bound
in chains.
11 Thou also shalt be [f]drunken: thou
shalt be hid, thou also shalt seek strength
because of the enemy.
12 All thy strong holds *shall be like* [g]fig
trees with the firstripe figs: if they be
shaken, they shall even fall into the mouth
of the eater.
13 Behold, [h]thy people in the midst of
thee *are* women: the gates of thy land shall
be set wide open unto thine enemies: the
fire shall devour thy [i]bars.
14 Draw thee waters for the siege, [j]for-
tify thy strong holds: go into clay, and tread
the morter, make strong the brickkiln.
15 There shall the fire devour thee; the
sword shall cut thee off, it shall eat thee up
like [k]the cankerworm: make thyself many
as the cankerworm, make thyself many as
the locusts.
16 Thou hast multiplied thy merchants
above the stars of heaven: the cankerworm
spoileth, and fleeth away.
17 [l]Thy crowned *are* as the locusts, and
thy captains as the great grasshoppers,
which camp in the hedges in the cold day,
but when the sun ariseth they flee away,
and their place is not known where they
are.
18 [m]Thy shepherds slumber, O [n]king of
Assyria: thy nobles shall dwell *in the dust*:
thy people is [o]scattered upon the mountains, and no man gathereth *them*.
19 *There is* no healing of thy bruise; [p]thy
wound is grievous: [q]all that hear the bruit
of thee shall clap the hands over thee: for
upon whom hath not thy wickedness
passed continually?

2:13 [p]2 Kings 18:17
3:1 [q]Ezek. 22:2; Hab. 2:12
3:2 [r]Jer. 47:3
3:4 [s]Isa. 47:9; Rev. 18:2
3:5 [t]ch. 2:13 [u]Isa. 47:2; Jer. 13:22; Ezek. 16:37; Mic. 1:11 [v]Hab. 2:16
3:6 [w]Mal. 2:9 [x]Heb. 10:33
3:7 [y]Rev. 18:10 [z]Jer. 15:5
3:8 [a]Am. 6:2 [b]Jer. 46:25; Ezek. 30:14-16
3:10 [c]Ps. 137:9; Isa. 13:16; Hos. 13:16 [d]Lam. 2:19 [e]Joel 3:3; Obad. 11
3:11 [f]Jer. 25:17; ch. 1:10
3:12 [g]Rev. 6:13
3:13 [h]Jer. 50:37 [i]Ps. 147:13; Jer. 51:30
3:14 [j]ch. 2:1
3:15 [k]Joel 1:4
3:17 [l]Rev. 9:7
3:18 [m]Ex. 15:16; Ps. 76:6 [n]Jer. 50:18; Ezek. 31:3 [o]1 Kings 22:17
3:19 [p]Mic. 1:9 [q]Isa. 14:8; Lam. 2:15; Zeph. 2:15

HABAKKUK

Habakkuk is the author of this book. It was written around 607 B.C. Habakkuk asks God two questions: "Why does God permit wickedness to continue in Judah?" and "Why does God use wicked people to punish those perceived as more righteous than the invaders?" God responds by assuring Habakkuk that what he (God) has chosen to do is right and that the faith of the people will be rewarded. Habakkuk 3:17–19 is a profound statement of faith in God's dealing with his people.

I. Habakkuk's first question and God's answer, 1:1–1:11
II. Habakkuk's second question and God's answer, 1:12–2:20
III. Habakkuk's response of praise, 3:1–3:19

---

1 The burden which Habakkuk the prophet did see.

2 O LORD, how long shall I cry, [a]and thou wilt not hear! *even* cry out unto thee *of* violence, and thou wilt not save!

3 Why dost thou shew me iniquity, and cause *me* to behold grievance? for spoiling and violence *are* before me: and there are *that* raise up strife and contention.

4 Therefore the law is slacked, and judgment doth never go forth: for the [b]wicked doth compass about the righteous; therefore wrong judgment proceedeth.

5 ¶ [c]Behold ye among the heathen, and regard, and wonder marvellously: for *I* will work a work in your days, *which* ye will not believe, though it be told *you*.

6 For, lo, [d]I raise up the Chaldeans, *that* bitter and hasty nation, which shall march through the breadth of the land, to possess the dwellingplaces *that are* not theirs.

7 They *are* terrible and dreadful: their judgment and their dignity shall proceed of themselves.

8 Their horses also are swifter than the leopards, and are more fierce than the [e]evening wolves: and their horsemen shall spread themselves, and their horsemen shall come from far; [f]they shall fly as the eagle *that* hasteth to eat.

9 They shall come all for violence: their faces shall sup up *as* the east wind, and they shall gather the captivity as the sand.

10 And they shall scoff at the kings, and the princes shall be a scorn unto them: they shall deride every strong hold; for they shall heap dust, and take it.

11 Then shall *his* mind change, and he shall pass over, and offend, [g]*imputing* this his power unto his god.

12 ¶ [h]*Art* thou not from everlasting, O LORD my God, mine Holy One? we shall not die. O LORD, [i]thou hast ordained them for judgment; and, O mighty God, thou hast established them for correction.

13 [j]*Thou art* of purer eyes than to behold evil, and canst not look on iniquity: [k]wherefore lookest thou upon them that deal treacherously, *and* holdest thy tongue when the wicked devoureth *the man that is* more righteous than he?

14 And makest men as the fishes of the sea, as the creeping things, *that have* no ruler over them?

15 They [l]take up all of them with the angle, they catch them in their net, and gather them in their drag: therefore they rejoice and are glad.

16 Therefore [m]they sacrifice unto their net, and burn incense unto their drag; because by them their portion *is* fat, and their meat plenteous.

17 Shall they therefore empty their net, and not spare continually to slay the nations?

2 I will [n]stand upon my watch, and set me upon the tower, [o]and will watch to see what he will say unto me, and what I shall answer when I am reproved.

2 And the LORD answered me, and said, [p]Write the vision, and make *it* plain upon tables, that he may run that readeth it.

3 For [q]the vision *is* yet for an appointed time, but at the end it shall speak, and not lie: though it tarry, wait for it; because it will [r]surely come, it will not tarry.

4 Behold, his soul *which* is lifted up is not upright in him: but the [s]just shall live by his faith.

5 ¶ Yea also, because he transgresseth by wine, *he is* a proud man, neither keepeth at home, who enlargeth his desire [t]as hell, and *is* as death, and cannot be satisfied, but gathereth unto him all nations, and heapeth unto him all people:

6 Shall not all these [u]take up a parable against him, and a taunting proverb against him, and say, Woe to him that increaseth *that which is* not his! how long? and to him that ladeth himself with thick clay!

7 Shall they not rise up suddenly that shall bite thee, and awake that shall vex thee, and thou shalt be for booties unto them?

8 [v]Because thou hast spoiled many nations, all the remnant of the people shall spoil thee; [w]because of men's blood, and *for* the violence of the land, of the city, and of all that dwell therein.

1:2 [a]Lam. 3:8
1:4 [b]Job 21:7; Ps. 94:3; Jer. 12:1
1:5 [c]Isa. 29:14; Acts 13:41
1:6 [d]Deut. 28:49; Jer. 5:15
1:8 [e]Jer. 5:6; Zeph. 3:3 [f]Jer. 4:13
1:11 [g]Dan. 5:4
1:12 [h]Ps. 90:2; Lam. 5:19 [i]2 Kings 19:25; Ps. 17:13; Isa. 10:5; Ezek. 30:25
1:13 [j]Ps. 5:5 [k]Jer. 12:1
1:15 [l]Jer. 16:16; Am. 4:2
1:16 [m]Deut. 8:17; Isa. 10:13
2:1 [n]Isa. 21:8 [o]Ps. 85:8
2:2 [p]Isa. 8:1
2:3 [q]Dan. 10:14 [r]Heb. 10:37
2:4 [s]John 3:36; Rom. 1:17; Gal. 3:11; Heb. 10:38
2:5 [t]Prov. 27:20
2:6 [u]Mic. 2:4
2:8 [v]Isa. 33:1 [w]ver. 17

9 ¶ Woe to him that [x]coveteth an evil covetousness to his house, that he may [y]set his nest on high, that he may be delivered from the power of evil!

10 Thou hast consulted shame to thy house by cutting off many people, and hast sinned *against* thy soul.

11 For the stone shall cry out of the wall, and the beam out of the timber shall answer it.

12 ¶ Woe to him that buildeth a town with [z]blood, and stablisheth a city by iniquity!

13 Behold, *is it* not of the LORD of hosts [a]that the people shall labour in the very fire, and the people shall weary themselves for very vanity?

14 For the earth shall be filled with the [b]knowledge of the glory of the LORD, as the waters cover the sea.

15 ¶ Woe unto him that giveth his neighbour drink, that puttest thy [c]bottle to *him,* and makest *him* drunken also, that thou mayest [d]look on their nakedness!

16 Thou art filled with shame for glory: [e]drink thou also, and let thy foreskin be uncovered: the cup of the LORD's right hand shall be turned unto thee, and shameful spewing *shall be* on thy glory.

17 For the violence of Lebanon shall cover thee, and the spoil of beasts, *which* made them afraid, [f]because of men's blood, and for the violence of the land, of the city, and of all that dwell therein.

18 ¶ [g]What profiteth the graven image that the maker thereof hath graven it; the molten image, and a [h]teacher of lies, that the maker of his work trusteth therein, to make [i]dumb idols?

19 Woe unto him that saith to the wood, Awake; to the dumb stone, Arise, it shall teach! Behold, it *is* laid over with gold and silver, [j]and *there is* no breath at all in the midst of it.

20 But [k]the LORD *is* in his holy temple: [l]let all the earth keep silence before him.

3 A prayer of Habakkuk the prophet [m]upon Shigionoth.

2 O LORD, I have heard thy speech, *and* was afraid: O LORD, [n]revive thy work in the midst of the years, in the midst of the years make known; in wrath remember mercy.

3 God came from Teman, [o]and the Holy One from mount Paran. Selah. His glory covered the heavens, and the earth was full of his praise.

4 And *his* brightness was as the light; he had horns *coming* out of his hand: and there *was* the hiding of his power.

5 [p]Before him went the pestilence, and [q]burning coals went forth at his feet.

2:9 [x]Jer. 22:13 [y]Jer. 49:16; Obad. 4
2:12 [z]Jer. 22:13; Ezek. 24:9; Mic. 3:10; Nah. 3:1
2:13 [a]Jer. 51:58
2:14 [b]Isa. 11:9
2:15 [c]Hos. 7:5 [d]Gen. 9:22
2:16 [e]Jer. 25:26
2:17 [f]ver. 8
2:18 [g]Isa. 44:9 [h]Jer. 10:8; Zech. 10:2 [i]Ps. 115:5; 1 Cor. 12:2
2:19 [j]Ps. 135:17
2:20 [k]Ps. 11:4 [l]Zeph. 1:7; Zech. 2:13
3:1 [m]Ps. 7, title
3:2 [n]Ps. 85:6
3:3 [o]Deut. 33:2; Judg. 5:4; Ps. 68:7
3:5 [p]Nah. 1:3 [q]Ps. 18:8
3:6 [r]Nah. 1:5 [s]Gen. 49:26
3:8 [t]Deut. 33:26; Ps. 68:4; ver. 15
3:9 [u]Ps. 78:15
3:10 [v]Ex. 19:16; Judg. 5:4; Ps. 68:8 [w]Ex. 14:22; Josh. 3:16
3:11 [x]Josh. 10:12 [y]Josh. 10:11; Ps. 18:14
3:12 [z]Jer. 51:33; Am. 1:3; Mic. 4:13
3:13 [a]Josh. 10:24; Ps. 68:21
3:15 [b]ver. 8; Ps. 77:19
3:16 [c]Ps. 119:120; Jer. 23:9
3:18 [d]Job 13:15 [e]Isa. 41:16
3:19 [f]Ps. 27:1 [g]2 Sam. 22; Ps. 18:33 [h]Deut. 32:13

6 He stood, and measured the earth: he beheld, and drove asunder the nations; [r]and the [s]everlasting mountains were scattered, the perpetual hills did bow: his ways *are* everlasting.

7 I saw the tents of Cushan in affliction: *and* the curtains of the land of Midian did tremble.

8 Was the LORD displeased against the rivers? *was* thine anger against the rivers? *was* thy wrath against the sea, [t]that thou didst ride upon thine horses *and* thy chariots of salvation?

9 Thy bow was made quite naked, *according* to the oaths of the tribes, *even thy* word. Selah. [u]Thou didst cleave the earth with rivers.

10 [v]The mountains saw thee, *and* they trembled: the overflowing of the water passed by: the deep uttered his voice, *and* [w]lifted up his hands on high.

11 [x]The sun *and* moon stood still in their habitation: at the light of thine [y]arrows they went, *and* at the shining of thy glittering spear.

12 Thou didst march through the land in indignation, [z]thou didst thresh the heathen in anger.

13 Thou wentest forth for the salvation of thy people, *even* for salvation with thine anointed; [a]thou woundedst the head out of the house of the wicked, by discovering the foundation unto the neck. Selah.

14 Thou didst strike through with his staves the head of his villages: they came out as a whirlwind to scatter me: their rejoicing *was* as to devour the poor secretly.

15 [b]Thou didst walk through the sea with thine horses, *through* the heap of great waters.

16 When I heard, [c]my belly trembled; my lips quivered at the voice: rottenness entered into my bones, and I trembled in myself, that I might rest in the day of trouble: when he cometh up unto the people, he will invade them with his troops.

17 ¶ Although the fig tree shall not blossom, neither *shall* fruit *be* in the vines; the labour of the olive shall fail, and the fields shall yield no meat; the flock shall be cut off from the fold, and *there shall be* no herd in the stalls:

18 [d]Yet I will [e]rejoice in the LORD, I will joy in the God of my salvation.

19 The LORD God *is* [f]my strength, and he will make my feet like [g]hinds' *feet,* and he will make me to [h]walk upon mine high places. To the chief singer on my stringed instruments.

ZEPHANIAH

Zephaniah identifies himself as the author of this book, written about 625 B.C. Zephaniah contains prophecies concerning Judah's coming judgment, first under Babylon and ultimately under God's judgment and prophecies concerning the Gentile nations including Philistia, Moab, Ethiopia, and Assyria. Chapter three begins with a judgment against Jerusalem, followed by a judgment against Gentile nations, but the chapter closes with prophetic blessings on both Jews and Gentiles.

- I. Judah condemned, 1:1–1:18
- II. Judgment against certain Gentile nations, 2:1–2:15
- III. Judgment on Jerusalem, 3:1–3:7
- IV. Ultimate judgment on Gentiles and Jews, 3:8–3:20

---

1 The word of the LORD which came unto
Zephaniah the son of Cushi, the son of
Gedaliah, the son of Amariah, the son of
Hizkiah, in the days of Josiah the son
of Amon, king of Judah.
2 I will utterly consume all *things* from off
the land, saith the LORD.
3 [a]I will consume man and beast; I will
consume the fowls of the heaven, and the
fishes of the sea, and [b]the stumblingblocks
with the wicked; and I will cut off man from
off the land, saith the LORD.
4 I will also stretch out mine hand upon
Judah, and upon all the inhabitants of Jerusalem; and [c]I will cut off the remnant of
Baal from this place, *and* the name of [d]the
Chemarims with the priests;
5 And them [e]that worship the host of
heaven upon the housetops; [f]and them that
worship *and* [g]that swear by the LORD, and
that swear [h]by Malcham;
6 And [i]them that are turned back from
the LORD; and *those* that [j]have not sought
the LORD, nor enquired for him.
7 [k]Hold thy peace at the presence of the
Lord GOD: [l]for the day of the LORD *is* at
hand: for [m]the LORD hath prepared a sacrifice, he hath bid his guests.
8 And it shall come to pass in the day of
the LORD's sacrifice, that I will punish [n]the
princes, and the king's children, and all
such as are clothed with strange apparel.
9 In the same day also will I punish all
those that leap on the threshold, which fill
their masters' houses with violence and deceit.
10 And it shall come to pass in that day,
saith the LORD, *that there shall be* the noise
of a cry from [o]the fish gate, and an howling
from the second, and a great crashing from
the hills.
11 [p]Howl, ye inhabitants of Maktesh, for
all the merchant people are cut down; all
they that bear silver are cut off.
12 And it shall come to pass at that time,
that I will search Jerusalem with candles,
and punish the men that are [q]settled on
their lees: [r]that say in their heart, The LORD
will not do good, neither will he do evil.
13 Therefore their goods shall become a
booty, and their houses a desolation: they
shall also build houses, but [s]not inhabit
them; and they shall plant vineyards, but
[t]not drink the wine thereof.
14 [u]The great day of the LORD *is* near, *it*
is near, and hasteth greatly, *even* the voice
of the day of the LORD: the mighty man shall
cry there bitterly.
15 [v]That day *is* a day of wrath, a day of
trouble and distress, a day of wasteness and
desolation, a day of darkness and gloominess, a day of clouds and thick darkness,
16 A day of [w]the trumpet and alarm
against the fenced cities, and against the
high towers.
17 And I will bring distress upon men,
that they shall [x]walk like blind men, because they have sinned against the LORD:
and [y]their blood shall be poured out as
dust, and their flesh [z]as the dung.
18 [a]Neither their silver nor their gold
shall be able to deliver them in the day of
the LORD's wrath; but the whole land shall
be [b]devoured by the fire of his jealousy: for
[c]he shall make even a speedy riddance of
all them that dwell in the land.

2 Gather [d]yourselves together, yea,
gather together, O nation not desired;
2 Before the decree bring forth, *before* the
day pass [e]as the chaff, before [f]the fierce
anger of the LORD come upon you, before
the day of the LORD's anger come upon you.
3 [g]Seek ye the LORD, [h]all ye meek of the
earth, which have wrought his judgment;
seek righteousness, seek meekness: [i]it may
be ye shall be hid in the day of the LORD's
anger.
4 ¶ For [j]Gaza shall be forsaken, and Ashkelon a desolation: they shall drive out Ashdod [k]at the noon day, and Ekron shall be
rooted up.
5 Woe unto the inhabitants of [l]the
sea coast, the nation of the Cherethites!
the word of the LORD *is* against you;
O [m]Canaan, the land of the Philistines, I
will even destroy thee, that there shall be no
inhabitant.
6 And the sea coast shall be dwellings

1:3 [a]Hos. 4:3 [b]Ezek. 7:19; Matt. 13:41
1:4 [c]2 Kings 23:4 [d]Hos. 10:5
1:5 [e]2 Kings 23:12; Jer. 19:13 [f]1 Kings 18:21; 2 Kings 17:33 [g]Isa. 48:1; Hos. 4:15 [h]Josh. 23:7; 1 Kings 11:33
1:6 [i]Isa. 1:4; Jer. 2:13 [j]Hos. 7:7
1:7 [k]Hab. 2:20; Zech. 2:13 [l]Isa. 13:6 [m]Isa. 34:6; Jer. 46:10; Ezek. 39:17; Rev. 19:17
1:8 [n]Jer. 39:6
1:10 [o]2 Chron. 33:14
1:11 [p]Jam. 5:1
1:12 [q]Jer. 48:11; Am. 6:1 [r]Ps. 94:7
1:13 [s]Deut. 28:30; Am. 5:11 [t]Mic. 6:15
1:14 [u]Joel 2:1
1:15 [v]Isa. 22:5; Jer. 30:7; Joel 2:2; Am. 5:18; ver. 18
1:16 [w]Jer. 4:19
1:17 [x]Deut. 28:29; Isa. 59:10 [y]Ps. 79:3 [z]Ps. 83:10; Jer. 9:22
1:18 [a]Prov. 11:4; Ezek. 7:19 [b]ch. 3:8 [c]ver. 2
2:1 [d]Joel 2:16
2:2 [e]Job 21:18; Ps. 1:4; Isa. 17:13; Hos. 13:3 [f]2 Kings 23:26
2:3 [g]Ps. 105:4; Am. 5:6 [h]Ps. 76:9 [i]Joel 2:14; Am. 5:15; Jonah 3:9
2:4 [j]Jer. 47:4; Ezek. 25:15; Am. 1:6; Zech. 9:5 [k]Jer. 6:4
2:5 [l]Ezek. 25:16 [m]Josh. 13:3

and cottages for shepherds, [n]and folds for flocks.

7 And the coast shall be for [o]the remnant of the house of Judah; they shall feed thereupon: in the houses of Ashkelon shall they lie down in the evening: for the LORD their God shall [p]visit them, and [q]turn away their captivity.

8 ¶ [r]I have heard the reproach of Moab, and [s]the revilings of the children of Ammon, whereby they have reproached my people, and [t]magnified *themselves* against their border.

9 Therefore *as* I live, saith the LORD of hosts, the God of Israel, Surely [u]Moab shall be as Sodom, and [v]the children of Ammon as Gomorrah, [w]*even* the breeding of nettles, and saltpits, and a perpetual desolation: [x]the residue of my people shall spoil them, and the remnant of my people shall possess them.

10 This shall they have [y]for their pride, because they have reproached and magnified *themselves* against the people of the LORD of hosts.

11 The LORD *will be* terrible unto them: for he will famish all the gods of the earth; [z]and *men* shall worship him, every one from his place, *even* all [a]the isles of the heathen.

12 ¶ [b]Ye Ethiopians also, ye *shall be* slain by [c]my sword.

13 And he will stretch out his hand against the north, and [d]destroy Assyria; and will make Nineveh a desolation, *and* dry like a wilderness.

14 And [e]flocks shall lie down in the midst of her, all [f]the beasts of the nations: both the [g]cormorant and the bittern shall lodge in the upper lintels of it; *their* voice shall sing in the windows; desolation *shall be* in the thresholds; for he shall uncover the [h]cedar work.

15 This *is* the rejoicing city [i]that dwelt carelessly, [j]that said in her heart, I *am*, and *there is* none beside me: how is she become a desolation, a place for beasts to lie down in! every one that passeth by her [k]shall hiss, *and* [l]wag his hand.

3 Woe to her that is filthy and polluted, to the oppressing city!

2 She [m]obeyed not the voice; she [n]received not correction; she trusted not in the LORD; she drew not near to her God.

3 [o]Her princes within her *are* roaring lions; her judges *are* [p]evening wolves; they gnaw not the bones till the morrow.

4 Her [q]prophets *are* light *and* treacherous persons: her priests have polluted the sanctuary, they have done [r]violence to the law.

5 [s]The just LORD [t]*is* in the midst thereof; he will not do iniquity: every morning doth he bring his judgment to light, he faileth not; but [u]the unjust knoweth no shame.

6 I have cut off the nations: their towers are desolate; I made their streets waste, that none passeth by: their cities are destroyed, so that there is no man, that there is none inhabitant.

7 [v]I said, Surely thou wilt fear me, thou wilt receive instruction; so their dwelling should not be cut off, howsoever I punished them: but they rose early, *and* [w]corrupted all their doings.

8 ¶ Therefore [x]wait ye upon me, saith the LORD, until the day that I rise up to the prey: for my determination *is* to [y]gather the nations, that I may assemble the kingdoms, to pour upon them mine indignation, *even* all my fierce anger: for all the earth [z]shall be devoured with the fire of my jealousy.

9 For then will I turn to the people [a]a pure language, that they may all call upon the name of the LORD, to serve him with one consent.

10 [b]From beyond the rivers of Ethiopia my suppliants, *even* the daughter of my dispersed, shall bring mine offering.

11 In that day shalt thou not be ashamed for all thy doings, wherein thou hast transgressed against me: for then I will take away out of the midst of thee them that [c]rejoice in thy pride, and thou shalt no more be haughty because of my holy mountain.

12 I will also leave in the midst of thee [d]an afflicted and poor people, and they shall trust in the name of the LORD.

13 [e]The remnant of Israel [f]shall not do iniquity, [g]nor speak lies; neither shall a deceitful tongue be found in their mouth: for [h]they shall feed and lie down, and none shall make *them* afraid.

14 ¶ [i]Sing, O daughter of Zion; shout, O Israel; be glad and rejoice with all the heart, O daughter of Jerusalem.

15 The LORD hath taken away thy judgments, he hath cast out thine enemy: [j]the king of Israel, *even* the LORD, [k]*is* in the midst of thee: thou shalt not see evil any more.

16 In that day [l]it shall be said to Jerusalem, Fear thou not: *and to* Zion, [m]Let not thine hands be slack.

17 The LORD thy God [n]in the midst of thee *is* mighty; he will save, [o]he will rejoice over thee with joy; he will rest in his love, he will joy over thee with singing.

18 I will gather *them that* [p]*are* sorrowful for the solemn assembly, *who* are of thee, *to whom* the reproach of it *was* a burden.

19 Behold, at that time I will undo all that afflict thee: and I will save her that [q]halteth, and gather her that was driven out; and I will get them praise and fame in every land where they have been put to shame.

20 At that time [r]will I bring you *again*, even in the time that I gather you: for I will make you a name and a praise among all people of the earth, when I turn back your captivity before your eyes, saith the LORD.

2:6 [n]Isa. 17:2; ver. 14
2:7 [o]Isa. 11:11; Mic. 4:7; Hag. 1:12; ver. 9 [p]Ex. 4:31; Luke 1:68 [q]Ps. 126:1; Jer. 29:14; ch. 3:20
2:8 [r]Jer. 48:27; Ezek. 25:8 [s]Ezek. 25:3 [t]Jer. 49:1
2:9 [u]Isa. 15; Jer. 48; Ezek. 25:9; Am. 2:1 [v]Am. 1:13 [w]Gen. 19:25; Deut. 29:23; Isa. 13:19; Jer. 49:18 [x]ver. 7
2:10 [y]Isa. 16:6; Jer. 48:29
2:11 [z]Mal. 1:11; John 4:21 [a]Gen. 10:5
2:12 [b]Isa. 18:1; Jer. 46:9; Ezek. 30:9 [c]Ps. 17:13
2:13 [d]Isa. 10:12; Ezek. 31:3; Nah. 1:1
2:14 [e]ver. 6 [f]Isa. 13:21 [g]Isa. 34:11 [h]Jer. 22:14
2:15 [i]Isa. 47:8 [j]Rev. 18:7 [k]Job 27:23; Lam. 2:15; Ezek. 27:36 [l]Nah. 3:19
3:2 [m]Jer. 22:21 [n]Jer. 5:3
3:3 [o]Ezek. 22:27; Mic. 3:9 [p]Hab. 1:8
3:4 [q]Jer. 23:11; Lam. 2:14; Hos. 9:7 [r]Ezek. 22:26
3:5 [s]Deut. 32:4 [t]Mic. 3:11; ver. 15 [u]Jer. 3:3
3:7 [v]Jer. 8:6 [w]Gen. 6:12
3:8 [x]Ps. 27:14; Prov. 20:22 [y]Joel 3:2 [z]ch. 1:18
3:9 [a]Isa. 19:18
3:10 [b]Ps. 68:31; Isa. 18:1; Mal. 1:11; Acts 8:27
3:11 [c]Jer. 7:4; Mic. 3:11; Matt. 3:9
3:12 [d]Isa. 14:32; Zech. 11:11; Matt. 5:3; 1 Cor. 1:27; Jam. 2:5
3:13 [e]Mic. 4:7; ch. 2:7 [f]Isa. 60:21 [g]Isa. 63:8; Rev. 14:5 [h]Ezek. 34:28; Mic. 4:4
3:14 [i]Isa. 12:6; Zech. 2:10
3:15 [j]John 1:49 [k]ver. 5; Ezek. 48:35; Rev. 7:15
3:16 [l]Isa. 35:3 [m]Heb. 12:12
3:17 [n]ver. 15 [o]Deut. 30:9; Isa. 62:5; Jer. 32:41
3:18 [p]Lam. 2:6
3:19 [q]Ezek. 34:16; Mic. 4:6 **3:20** [r]Isa. 11:12; Ezek. 28:25; Am. 9:14

HAGGAI

Haggai identifies himself as the author of this book. It was written in 520 B.C. Haggai contains four appeals from the Lord, spoken to the people through the prophet to continue rebuilding the Temple, which had been started many years earlier and was never finished. Haggai has to appeal to the people and their leaders, which had both lost interest in the Temple.

I. A call to rebuild the Temple, 1:1–1:15
II. A call to courage, 2:1–2:9
III. A call to change lives, 2:10–2:19
IV. A call to faith in the future, 2:20–2:23

---

1 In [a]the second year of Darius the king, in the sixth month, in the first day of the month, came the word of the LORD by Haggai the prophet unto [b]Zerubbabel the son of Shealtiel, governor of Judah, and to [c]Joshua the son of [d]Josedech, the high priest, saying,

2 Thus speaketh the LORD of hosts, saying, This people say, The time is not come, the time that the LORD's house should be built.

3 Then came the word of the LORD [e]by Haggai the prophet, saying,

4 [f]*Is it* time for you, O ye, to dwell in your cieled houses, and this house *lie* waste?

5 Now therefore thus saith the LORD of hosts; [g]Consider your ways.

6 Ye have [h]sown much, and bring in little; ye eat, but ye have not enough; ye drink, but ye are not filled with drink; ye clothe you, but there is none warm; and [i]he that earneth wages earneth wages *to put it* into a bag with holes.

7 ¶ Thus saith the LORD of hosts; Consider your ways.

8 Go up to the mountain, and bring wood, and build the house; and I will take pleasure in it, and I will be glorified, saith the LORD.

9 [j]Ye looked for much, and, lo *it came* to little; and when ye brought *it* home, [k]I did blow upon it. Why? saith the LORD of hosts. Because of mine house that *is* waste, and ye run every man unto his own house.

10 Therefore [l]the heaven over you is stayed from dew, and the earth is stayed *from* her fruit.

11 And I [m]called for a drought upon the land, and upon the mountains, and upon the corn, and upon the new wine, and upon the oil, and upon *that* which the ground bringeth forth, and upon men, and upon cattle, and [n]upon all the labour of the hands.

12 ¶ [o]Then Zerubbabel the son of Shealtiel, and Joshua the son of Josedech, the high priest, with all the remnant of the people, obeyed the voice of the LORD their God, and the words of Haggai the prophet, as the LORD their God had sent him, and the people did fear before the LORD.

13 Then spake Haggai the LORD's messenger in the LORD's message unto the people, saying, [p]I *am* with you, saith the LORD.

14 And [q]the LORD stirred up the spirit of Zerubbabel the son of Shealtiel, [r]governor of Judah, and the spirit of Joshua the son of Josedech, the high priest, and the spirit of all the remnant of the people; [s]and they came and did work in the house of the LORD of hosts, their God,

15 In the four and twentieth day of the sixth month, in the second year of Darius the king.

2 In the seventh *month,* in the one and twentieth *day* of the month, came the word of the LORD by the prophet Haggai, saying,

2 Speak now to Zerubbabel the son of Shealtiel, governor of Judah, and to Joshua the son of Josedech, the high priest, and to the residue of the people, saying,

3 [t]Who *is* left among you that saw this house in her first glory? and how do ye see it now? [u]*is it* not in your eyes in comparison of it as nothing?

4 Yet now [v]be strong, O Zerubbabel, saith the LORD; and be strong, O Joshua, son of Josedech, the high priest; and be strong, all ye people of the land, saith the LORD, and work: for I *am* with you, saith the LORD of hosts:

5 [w]*According to* the word that I covenanted with you when ye came out of Egypt, so [x]my spirit remaineth among you: fear ye not.

6 For thus saith the LORD of hosts; [y]Yet once, it *is* a little while, and [z]I will shake the heavens, and the earth, and the sea, and the dry *land;*

7 And I will shake all nations, [a]and the desire of all nations shall come: and I will fill this house with glory, saith the LORD of hosts.

8 The silver *is* mine, and the gold *is* mine, saith the LORD of hosts.

9 [b]The glory of this latter house shall be greater than of the former, saith the LORD of hosts: and in this place will I give [c]peace, saith the LORD of hosts.

10 ¶ In the four and twentieth *day* of the

1:1 [a]Ezra 4:24; Zech. 1:1 [b]1 Chron. 3:17; Ezra 3:2; Matt. 1:12; Luke 3:27 [c]Ezra 3:2 [d]1 Chron. 6:15
1:3 [e]Ezra 5:1
1:4 [f]2 Sam. 7:2; Ps. 132:3
1:5 [g]Lam. 3:40; ver. 7
1:6 [h]Deut. 28:38; Hos. 4:10; Mic. 6:14; ch. 2:16 [i]Zech. 8:10
1:9 [j]ch. 2:16 [k]ch. 2:17
1:10 [l]Lev. 26:19; Deut. 28:23; 1 Kings 8:35
1:11 [m]1 Kings 17:1; 2 Kings 8:1 [n]ch. 2:17
1:12 [o]Ezra 5:2
1:13 [p]Matt. 28:20; Rom. 8:31
1:14 [q]2 Chron. 36:22; Ezra 1:1 [r]ch. 2:21 [s]Ezra 5:2
2:3 [t]Ezra 3:12 [u]Zech. 4:10
2:4 [v]Zech. 8:9
2:5 [w]Ex. 29:45 [x]Neh. 9:20; Isa. 63:11
2:6 [y]ver. 21; Heb. 12:26 [z]Joel 3:13
2:7 [a]Gen. 49:10; Mal. 3:1
2:9 [b]John 1:14 [c]Ps. 85:8; Luke 2:14; Eph. 2:14

ninth *month,* in the second year of Darius, came the word of the LORD by Haggai the prophet, saying,

11 Thus saith the LORD of hosts; [d]Ask now the priests *concerning* the law, saying,

12 If one bear holy flesh in the skirt of his garment, and with his skirt do touch bread, or pottage, or wine, or oil, or any meat, shall it be holy? And the priests answered and said, No.

13 Then said Haggai, If *one that is* [e]unclean by a dead body touch any of these, shall it be unclean? And the priests answered and said, It shall be unclean.

14 Then answered Haggai, and said, [f]So *is* this people, and so *is* this nation before me, saith the LORD; and so *is* every work of their hands; and that which they offer there *is* unclean.

15 And now, I pray you, [g]consider from this day and upward, from before a stone was laid upon a stone in the temple of the LORD:

16 Since those *days* were, [h]when *one* came to an heap of twenty *measures,* there were *but* ten: when *one* came to the pressfat for to draw out fifty *vessels* out of the press, there were *but* twenty.

17 [i]I smote you with blasting and with mildew and with hail [j]in all the labours of your hands; [k]yet ye *turned* not to me, saith the LORD.

18 Consider now from this day and upward, from the four and twentieth day of the ninth *month, even* from [l]the day that the foundation of the LORD's temple was laid, consider *it.*

19 [m]Is the seed yet in the barn? yea, as yet the vine, and the fig tree, and the pomegranate, and the olive tree, hath not brought forth: from this day will I bless *you.*

20 ¶ And again the word of the LORD came unto Haggai in the four and twentieth *day* of the month, saying,

21 Speak to Zerubbabel, [n]governor of Judah, saying, [o]I will shake the heavens and the earth;

22 And [p]I will overthrow the throne of kingdoms, and I will destroy the strength of the kingdoms of the heathen; and [q]I will overthrow the chariots, and those that ride in them; and the horses and their riders shall come down, every one by the sword of his brother.

23 In that day, saith the LORD of hosts, will I take thee, O Zerubbabel, my servant, the son of Shealtiel, saith the LORD, [r]and will make thee as a signet: for [s]I have chosen thee, saith the LORD of hosts.

2:11 [d]Lev. 10:10; Deut. 33:10; Mal. 2:7
2:13 [e]Num. 19:11
2:14 [f]Tit. 1:15
2:15 [g]ch. 1:5
2:16 [h]ch. 1:6; Zech. 8:10
2:17 [i]Deut. 28:22; 1 Kings 8:37; ch. 1:9; Am. 4:9 [j]ch. 1:11 [k]Jer. 5:3; Am. 4:6
2:18 [l]Zech. 8:9
2:19 [m]Zech. 8:12
2:21 [n]ch. 1:14 [o]ver. 6; Heb. 12:26
2:22 [p]Dan. 2:44; Matt. 24:7 [q]Mic. 5:10; Zech. 4:6
2:23 [r]SSol. 8:6; Jer. 22:24 [s]Isa. 42:1

ZECHARIAH

Zechariah is the author of the book. It was probably written in 520 B.C. The first eight chapters of Zechariah contain a series of prophetic visions. The remainder of the book contains additional prophecies, some of which have been fulfilled, but many are considered apocalyptic and are unfulfilled. Included in these chapters are apparent references to the Messiah's first coming (Chapters 9-11), and his second coming (Chapters 12-14).

I. A call for repentance, 1:1–1:6
II. Zechariah's visions, 1:7–6:8
III. Crowning of Joshua, 6:9–6:15
IV. The problems of fasting, 7:1–8:23
V. Prophecies for Israel in Zechariah's day, 9:1–11:17
VI. Prophecies not yet fulfilled, 12:1–14:21

1 In the eighth month, [a]in the second year of Darius, came the word of the LORD [b]unto Zechariah, the son of Berechiah, the son of Iddo the prophet, saying,

2 The LORD hath been sore displeased with your fathers.

3 Therefore say thou unto them, Thus saith the LORD of hosts; Turn [c]ye unto me, saith the LORD of hosts, and I will turn unto you, saith the LORD of hosts.

4 Be ye not as your fathers, [d]unto whom the former prophets have cried, saying, Thus saith the LORD of hosts; [e]Turn ye now from your evil ways, and *from* your evil doings: but they did not hear, nor hearken unto me, saith the LORD.

5 Your fathers, where *are* they? and the prophets, do they live for ever?

6 But [f]my words and my statutes, which I commanded my servants the prophets, did they not take hold of your fathers? and they returned and said, [g]Like as the LORD of hosts thought to do unto us, according to our ways, and according to our doings, so hath he dealt with us.

7 ¶ Upon the four and twentieth day of

1:1 [a]Ezra 4:24; Hag. 1:1 [b]Ezra 5:1; Matt. 23:35
1:3 [c]Jer. 25:5; Mic. 7:19; Mal. 3:7; Luke 15:20; Jam. 4:8
1:4 [d]2 Chron. 36:15 [e]Isa. 31:6; Jer. 3:12; Ezek. 18:30; Hos. 14:1
1:6 [f]Isa. 55:1 [g]Lam. 1:18

the eleventh month, which *is* the month
Sebat, in the second year of Darius, came
the word of the LORD unto Zechariah, the
son of Berechiah, the son of Iddo the
prophet, saying,
8 I saw by night, and behold [h]a man riding upon a red horse, and he stood among
the myrtle trees that *were* in the bottom;
and behind him *were there* [i]red horses,
speckled, and white.
9 Then said I, O my lord, what *are* these?
And the angel that talked with me said unto
me, I will shew thee what these *be*.
10 And the man that stood among the
myrtle trees answered and said, [j]These *are*
they whom the LORD hath sent to walk to
and fro through the earth.
11 [k]And they answered the angel of the
LORD that stood among the myrtle trees,
and said, We have walked to and fro
through the earth, and, behold, all the earth
sitteth still, and is at rest.
12 ¶ Then the angel of the LORD answered
and said, [l]O LORD of hosts, how long wilt
thou not have mercy on Jerusalem and on
the cities of Judah, against which thou hast
had indignation [m]these threescore and ten
years?
13 And the LORD answered the angel that
talked with me *with* [n]good words *and* comfortable words.
14 So the angel that communed with me
said unto me, Cry thou, saying, Thus saith
the LORD of hosts; I am [o]jealous for Jerusalem and for Zion with a great jealousy.
15 And I am very sore displeased with the
heathen *that are* at ease: for [p]I was but a
little displeased, and they helped forward
the affliction.
16 Therefore thus saith the LORD; [q]I am
returned to Jerusalem with mercies: my
house shall be built in it, saith the LORD of
hosts, and [r]a line shall be stretched forth
upon Jerusalem.
17 Cry yet, saying, Thus saith the LORD of
hosts; My cities through prosperity shall yet
be spread abroad; [s]and the LORD shall yet
comfort Zion, and [t]shall yet choose Jerusalem.
18 ¶ Then lifted I up mine eyes, and saw,
and behold four horns.
19 And I said unto the angel that talked
with me, What *be* these? And he answered
me, [u]These *are* the horns which have scattered Judah, Israel, and Jerusalem.
20 And the LORD shewed me four carpenters.
21 Then said I, What come these to do?
And he spake, saying, These *are* the horns
which have scattered Judah, so that no man
did lift up his head: but these are come to
fray them, to cast out the horns of the Gentiles, which [v]lifted up *their* horn over the
land of Judah to scatter it.

2 I lifted up mine eyes again, and looked,
and behold [w]a man with a measuring
line in his hand.
2 Then said I, Whither goest thou? And he
said unto me, [x]To measure Jerusalem, to
see what *is* the breadth thereof, and what *is*
the length thereof.
3 And, behold, the angel that talked with
me went forth, and another angel went out
to meet him,
4 And said unto him, Run, speak to this
young man, saying, [y]Jerusalem shall be inhabited *as* towns without walls for the multitude of men and cattle therein:
5 For I, saith the LORD, will be unto her [z]a
wall of fire round about, [a]and will be the
glory in the midst of her.
6 ¶ Ho, ho, *come forth*, and flee [b]from the
land of the north, saith the LORD: for I have
[c]spread you abroad as the four winds of the
heaven, saith the LORD.
7 [d]Deliver thyself, O Zion, that dwellest
with the daughter of Babylon.
8 For thus saith the LORD of hosts; After
the glory hath he sent me unto the nations
which spoiled you: for he that [e]toucheth
you toucheth the apple of his eye.
9 For, behold, I will [f]shake mine hand
upon them, and they shall be a spoil to their
servants: and [g]ye shall know that the LORD
of hosts hath sent me.
10 ¶ [h]Sing and rejoice, O daughter of
Zion: for, lo, I come, and I [i]will dwell in the
midst of thee, saith the LORD.
11 [j]And many nations shall be joined to
the LORD [k]in that day, and shall be [l]my
people: and I will dwell in the midst of thee,
and [m]thou shalt know that the LORD of
hosts hath sent me unto thee.
12 And the LORD shall [n]inherit Judah his
portion in the holy land, and [o]shall choose
Jerusalem again.
13 [p]Be silent, O all flesh, before the
LORD: for he is raised up [q]out of his holy
habitation.

3 And he shewed me [r]Joshua the high
priest standing before the angel of the
LORD, and [s]Satan standing at his right
hand to resist him.
2 And the LORD said unto Satan, [t]The
LORD rebuke thee, O Satan; even the LORD
that [u]hath chosen Jerusalem rebuke thee:
[v]*is* not this a brand plucked out of the fire?
3 Now Joshua was clothed with [w]filthy
garments, and stood before the angel.
4 And he answered and spake unto those
that stood before him, saying, Take away
the filthy garments from him. And unto him
he said, Behold, I have caused thine iniquity
to pass from thee, [x]and I will clothe thee
with change of raiment.
5 And I said, Let them set a fair [y]mitre
upon his head. So they set a fair mitre upon
his head, and clothed him with garments.
And the angel of the LORD stood by.
6 And the angel of the LORD protested
unto Joshua, saying,
7 Thus saith the LORD of hosts; If thou
wilt walk in my ways, and if thou wilt [z]keep
my charge, then thou shalt also [a]judge my
house, and shalt also keep my courts, and I

1:8 [h]Josh. 5:13; Rev. 6:4 [i]ch. 6:2-7
1:10 [j]Heb. 1:14
1:11 [k]Ps. 103:20
1:12 [l]Ps. 102:13; Rev. 6:10 [m]Jer. 25:11; Dan. 9:2; ch. 7:5
1:13 [n]Jer. 29:10
1:14 [o]Joel 2:18; ch. 8:2
1:15 [p]Isa. 47:6
1:16 [q]Isa. 12:1; ch. 2:10 [r]ch. 2:1
1:17 [s]Isa. 51:3 [t]Isa. 14:1; ch. 2:12
1:19 [u]Ezra 4:1
1:21 [v]Ps. 75:4
2:1 [w]Ezek. 40:3
2:2 [x]Rev. 11:1
2:4 [y]Jer. 31:27; Ezek. 36:10
2:5 [z]Isa. 26:1; ch. 9:8 [a]Isa. 60:19; Rev. 21:23
2:6 [b]Isa. 48:20; Jer. 1:14 [c]Deut. 28:64; Ezek. 17:21
2:7 [d]Rev. 18:4
2:8 [e]Deut. 32:10; Ps. 17:8; 2 Thess. 1:6
2:9 [f]Isa. 11:15 [g]ch. 4:9
2:10 [h]Isa. 12:6; Zeph. 3:14 [i]Lev. 26:12; Ezek. 37:27; ch. 8:3; John 1:14; 2 Cor. 6:16
2:11 [j]Isa. 2:2; ch. 8:22 [k]ch. 3:10 [l]Ex. 12:49 [m]Ezek. 33:33; ver. 9
2:12 [n]Deut. 32:9 [o]ch. 1:17
2:13 [p]Hab. 2:20; Zeph. 1:7 [q]Ps. 68:5; Isa. 57:15
3:1 [r]Hag. 1:1 [s]Ps. 109:6; Rev. 12:10
3:2 [t]Jude 9 [u]ch. 1:17; Rom. 8:33 [v]Am. 4:11; Rom. 11:5; Jude 23
3:3 [w]Isa. 64:6
3:4 [x]Isa. 61:10; Rev. 19:8; Luke 15:22
3:5 [y]Ex. 29:6; ch. 6:11
3:7 [z]Lev. 8:35; 1 Kings 2:3; Ezek. 44:16 [a]Deut. 17:9; Mal. 2:7

will give thee places to walk among these
that [b]stand by.
8 Hear now, O Joshua the high priest,
thou, and thy fellows that sit before thee:
for they are [c]men wondered at: for, behold,
I will bring forth [d]my servant the
[e]BRANCH.
9 For behold the stone that I have laid
before Joshua; [f]upon one stone *shall be*
[g]seven eyes: behold, I will engrave the
graving thereof, saith the LORD of hosts,
and [h]I will remove the iniquity of that land
in one day.
10 [i]In that day, saith the LORD of hosts,
shall ye call every man his neighbour [j]un-
der the vine and under the fig tree.

4 And [k]the angel that talked with me
came again, and waked me, [l]as a man
that is wakened out of his sleep,
2 And said unto me, What seest thou?
And I said, I have looked, and behold [m]a
candlestick all *of* gold, with a bowl upon the
top of it, [n]and his seven lamps thereon, and
seven pipes to the seven lamps, which *are*
upon the top thereof:
3 [o]And two olive trees by it, one upon the
right *side* of the bowl, and the other upon
the left *side* thereof.
4 So I answered and spake to the angel
that talked with me, saying, What *are* these,
my lord?
5 Then the angel that talked with me answered and said unto me, Knowest thou not
what these be? And I said, No, my lord.
6 Then he answered and spake unto me,
saying, This *is* the word of the LORD unto
Zerubbabel, saying, [p]Not by might, nor by
power, but by my spirit, saith the LORD of
hosts.
7 Who *art* thou, [q]O great mountain? before Zerubbabel *thou shalt become* a plain:
and he shall bring forth [r]the headstone
thereof [s]*with* shoutings, *crying,* Grace,
grace unto it.
8 Moreover the word of the LORD came
unto me, saying,
9 The hands of Zerubbabel [t]have laid the
foundation of this house; his hands [u]shall
also finish it; and [v]thou shalt know that the
[w]LORD of hosts hath sent me unto you.
10 For who hath despised the day of
[x]small things? for they shall rejoice, and
shall see the plummet in the hand of Zerubbabel *with* those seven; [y]they *are* the eyes
of the LORD, which run to and fro through
the whole earth.
11 ¶ Then answered I, and said unto him,
What *are* these [z]two olive trees upon the
right *side* of the candlestick and upon the
left *side* thereof?
12 And I answered again, and said unto
him, What *be these* two olive branches
which through the two golden pipes empty
the golden *oil* out of themselves?
13 And he answered me and said, Knowest thou not what these *be?* And I said, No,
my lord.
14 Then said he, [a]These *are* the two
anointed ones, [b]that stand by [c]the Lord of
the whole earth.

5 Then I turned, and lifted up mine eyes,
and looked, and behold a flying [d]roll.
2 And he said unto me, What seest thou?
And I answered, I see a flying roll; the
length thereof *is* twenty cubits, and the
breadth thereof ten cubits.
3 Then said he unto me, This *is* the [e]curse
that goeth forth over the face of the whole
earth: for every one that stealeth shall be
cut off *as* on this side according to it; and
every one that sweareth shall be cut off *as*
on that side according to it.
4 I will bring it forth, saith the LORD of
hosts, and it shall enter into the house of
the thief, and into the house of [f]him that
sweareth falsely by my name: and it shall
remain in the midst of his house, and [g]shall
consume it with the timber thereof and the
stones thereof.
5 ¶ Then the angel that talked with me
went forth, and said unto me, Lift up now
thine eyes, and see what *is* this that goeth
forth.
6 And I said, What *is* it? And he said, This
is an ephah that goeth forth. He said moreover, This *is* their resemblance through all
the earth.
7 And, behold, there was lifted up a talent
of lead: and this *is* a woman that sitteth in
the midst of the ephah.
8 And he said, This *is* wickedness. And he
cast it into the midst of the ephah; and he
cast the weight of lead upon the mouth
thereof.
9 Then lifted I up mine eyes, and looked,
and, behold, there came out two women,
and the wind *was* in their wings; for they
had wings like the wings of a stork: and
they lifted up the ephah between the earth
and the heaven.
10 Then said I to the angel that talked
with me, Whither do these bear the ephah?
11 And he said unto me, To [h]build it an
house in [i]the land of Shinar: and it shall be
established, and set there upon her own
base.

6 And I turned, and lifted up mine eyes,
and looked, and, behold, there came
four chariots out from between two mountains; and the mountains *were* mountains of
brass.
2 In the first chariot *were* [j]red horses;
and in the second chariot [k]black horses;
3 And in the third chariot [l]white horses;
and in the fourth chariot grisled and bay
horses.
4 Then I answered [m]and said unto the angel that talked with me, What *are* these, my
lord?
5 And the angel answered and said unto
me, [n]These *are* the four spirits of the heavens, which go forth from [o]standing before
the Lord of all the earth.
6 The black horses which *are* therein go
forth into [p]the north country; and the white

3:7 [b]ch. 4:14
3:8 [c]Ps. 71:7; Isa. 8:18 [d]Isa. 42:1; Ezek. 34:23 [e]Isa. 4:2; Jer. 23:5; ch. 6:12; Luke 1:78
3:9 [f]Ps. 118:22; Isa. 28:16 [g]ch. 4:10; Rev. 5:6 [h]Jer. 31:34; Mic. 7:18; ch. 13:1
3:10 [i]ch. 2:11 [j]1 Kings 4:25; Isa. 36:16; Mic. 4:4
4:1 [k]ch. 2:3 [l]Dan. 8:18
4:2 [m]Ex. 25:31; Rev. 1:12 [n]Ex. 25:37; Rev. 4:5
4:3 [o]ver. 11; Rev. 11:4
4:6 [p]Hos. 1:7
4:7 [q]Jer. 51:25; Matt. 21:21 [r]Ps. 118:22 [s]Ezra 3:11
4:9 [t]Ezra 3:10 [u]Ezra 6:15 [v]ch. 2:9 [w]Isa. 48:16; ch. 2:8
4:10 [x]Hag. 2:3 [y]2 Chron. 16:9; Prov. 15:3; ch. 3:9
4:11 [z]ver. 3
4:14 [a]Rev. 11:4 [b]ch. 3:7; Luke 1:19 [c]Josh. 3:11; ch. 6:5
5:1 [d]Ezek. 2:9
5:3 [e]Mal. 4:6
5:4 [f]Lev. 19:12; ch. 8:17; Mal. 3:5 [g]Lev. 14:45
5:11 [h]Jer. 29:5 [i]Gen. 10:10
6:2 [j]ch. 1:8; Rev. 6:4 [k]Rev. 6:5
6:3 [l]Rev. 6:2
6:4 [m]ch. 5:10
6:5 [n]Ps. 104:4; Heb. 1:7 [o]1 Kings 22:19; Dan. 7:10; ch. 4:14; Luke 1:19
6:6 [p]Jer. 1:14

go forth after them; and the grisled go forth
toward the south country.
7 And the bay went forth, and sought to
go that they might [q]walk to and fro through
the earth: and he said, Get you hence, walk
to and fro through the earth. So they walked
to and fro through the earth.
8 Then cried he upon me, and spake unto
me, saying, Behold, these that go toward
the north country have quieted my [r]spirit
in the north country.
9 ¶ And the word of the LORD came unto
me, saying,
10 Take of *them of* the captivity, *even* of
Heldai, of Tobijah, and of Jedaiah, which
are come from Babylon, and come thou the
same day, and go into the house of Josiah
the son of Zephaniah;
11 Then take silver and gold, and make
[s]crowns, and set *them* upon the head of
Joshua the son of Josedech, the high priest;
12 And speak unto him, saying, Thus
speaketh the LORD of hosts, saying, Behold
[t]the man whose name *is* The [u]BRANCH;
and he shall grow up out of his place, [v]and
he shall build the temple of the LORD:
13 Even he shall build the temple of the
LORD; and he [w]shall bear the glory, and
shall sit and rule upon his throne; and [x]he
shall be a priest upon his throne: and the
counsel of peace shall be between them
both.
14 And the crowns shall be to Helem, and
to Tobijah, and to Jedaiah, and to Hen the
son of Zephaniah, [y]for a memorial in the
temple of the LORD.
15 And [z]they *that are* far off shall come
and build in the temple of the LORD, and
[a]ye shall know that the LORD of hosts hath
sent me unto you. And *this* shall come to
pass, if ye will diligently obey the voice of
the LORD your God.

7

7 And it came to pass in the fourth year of
king Darius, *that* the word of the LORD
came unto Zechariah in the fourth *day* of
the ninth month, *even* in Chisleu;
2 When they had sent unto the house of
God Sherezer and Regem-melech, and their
men, to pray before the LORD,
3 *And* to [b]speak unto the priests which
were in the house of the LORD of hosts, and
to the prophets, saying, Should I weep in
[c]the fifth month, separating myself, as I
have done these so many years?
4 ¶ Then came the word of the LORD of
hosts unto me, saying,
5 Speak unto all the people of the land,
and to the priests, saying, When ye [d]fasted
and mourned in the fifth [e]and seventh
month, [f]even those seventy years, did ye at
all fast [g]unto me, *even* to me?
6 And when ye did eat, and when ye did
drink, did not ye eat *for yourselves*, and
drink *for yourselves*?
7 *Should ye* not *hear* the words which the
LORD hath cried by the former prophets,
when Jerusalem was inhabited and in prosperity, and the cities thereof round about
her, when *men* inhabited [h]the south and the
plain?
8 ¶ And the word of the LORD came unto
Zechariah, saying,
9 Thus speaketh the LORD of hosts, saying, [i]Execute true judgment, and shew
mercy and compassions every man to his
brother:
10 And [j]oppress not the widow, nor the
fatherless, the stranger, nor the poor; [k]and
let none of you imagine evil against his
brother in your heart.
11 But they refused to hearken, and
[l]pulled away the shoulder, and [m]stopped
their ears, that they should not hear.
12 Yea, they made their [n]hearts *as* an
adamant stone, [o]lest they should hear the
law, and the words which the LORD of hosts
hath sent in his spirit by the former prophets: [p]therefore came a great wrath from the
LORD of hosts.
13 Therefore it is come to pass, *that* as he
cried, and they would not hear; so [q]they
cried, and I would not hear, saith the LORD
of hosts:
14 But [r]I scattered them with a whirlwind among all the nations [s]whom they
knew not. Thus [t]the land was desolate after them, that no man passed through nor
returned: for they laid [u]the pleasant land
desolate.

8

8 Again the word of the LORD of hosts
came *to me*, saying,
2 Thus saith the LORD of hosts; [v]I was
jealous for Zion with great jealousy, and I
was jealous for her with great fury.
3 Thus saith the LORD; [w]I am returned
unto Zion, and [x]will dwell in the midst of
Jerusalem: and Jerusalem [y]shall be called a
city of truth; and [z]the mountain of the LORD
of hosts [a]the holy mountain.
4 Thus saith the LORD of hosts; [b]There
shall yet old men and old women dwell in
the streets of Jerusalem, and every man
with his staff in his hand for very age.
5 And the streets of the city shall be full of
boys and girls playing in the streets thereof.
6 Thus saith the LORD of hosts; If it be
marvellous in the eyes of the remnant of
this people in these days, [c]should it also be
marvellous in mine eyes? saith the LORD of
hosts.
7 Thus saith the LORD of hosts; Behold, [d]I
will save my people from the east country,
and from the west country;
8 And I will bring them, and they shall
dwell in the midst of Jerusalem: [e]and they
shall be my people, and I will be their God,
[f]in truth and in righteousness.
9 ¶ Thus saith the LORD of hosts; [g]Let
your hands be strong, ye that hear in these
days these words by the mouth of [h]the
prophets, which *were* in [i]the day *that* the
foundation of the house of the LORD of hosts
was laid, that the temple might be built.
10 For before these days there was no
[j]hire for man, nor any hire for beast; [k]nei-
ther *was there any* peace to him that went

6:7 [q]Gen. 13:17; ch. 1:10
6:8 [r]Judg. 8:3; Eccl. 10:4
6:11 [s]Ex. 28:36; Lev. 8:9; ch. 3:5
6:12 [t]Luke 1:78; John 1:45 [u]ch. 3:8 [v]ch. 4:9; Matt. 16:18; Eph. 2:20; Heb. 3:3
6:13 [w]Isa. 22:24 [x]Ps. 110:4; Heb. 3:1
6:14 [y]Ex. 12:14; Mark 14:9
6:15 [z]Isa. 57:19; Eph. 2:13 [a]ch. 2:9
7:3 [b]Deut. 17:9; Mal. 2:7 [c]Jer. 52:12; ch. 8:19
7:5 [d]Isa. 58:5 [e]Jer. 41:1; ch. 8:19 [f]ch. 1:12 [g]Rom. 14:6
7:7 [h]Jer. 17:26
7:9 [i]Isa. 58:6; Jer. 7:23; Mic. 6:8; ch. 8:16; Matt. 23:23
7:10 [j]Ex. 22:21; Deut. 24:17; Isa. 1:17; Jer. 5:28 [k]Ps. 36:4; Mic. 2:1; ch. 8:17
7:11 [l]Neh. 9:29; Jer. 7:24; Hos. 4:16 [m]Acts 7:57
7:12 [n]Ezek. 11:19 [o]Neh. 9:29 [p]2 Chron. 36:16; Dan. 9:11
7:13 [q]Prov. 1:24-28; Isa. 1:15; Jer. 11:11; Mic. 3:4
7:14 [r]Deut. 4:27; Ezek. 36:19; ch. 2:6 [s]Deut. 28:33 [t]Lev. 26:22 [u]Dan. 8:9
8:2 [v]Nah. 1:2; ch. 1:14
8:3 [w]ch. 1:16 [x]ch. 2:10 [y]Isa. 1:21 [z]Isa. 2:2 [a]Jer. 31:23
8:4 [b]1 Sam. 2:31; Isa. 65:20; Lam. 2:20
8:6 [c]Gen. 18:14; Luke 1:37; Rom. 4:21
8:7 [d]Isa. 11:11; Ezek. 37:21; Am. 9:14
8:8 [e]Jer. 30:22; ch. 13:9 [f]Jer. 4:2
8:9 [g]Hag. 2:4; ver. 18 [h]Ezra 5:1 [i]Hag. 2:18
8:10 [j]Hag. 1:6 [k]2 Chron. 15:5

out or came in because of the affliction: for I set all men every one against his neighbour.

11 But now I *will* not *be* unto the residue of this people as in the former days, saith the LORD of hosts.

12 [l]For the seed *shall be* prosperous; the vine shall give her fruit, and [m]the ground shall give her increase, and [n]the heavens shall give their dew; and I will cause the remnant of this people to possess all these *things*.

13 And it shall come to pass, *that* as ye were [o]a curse among the heathen, O house of Judah, and house of Israel; so will I save you, and [p]ye shall be a blessing: fear not, *but* [q]let your hands be strong.

14 For thus saith the LORD of hosts; [r]As I thought to punish you, when your fathers provoked me to wrath, saith the LORD of hosts, [s]and I repented not:

15 So again have I thought in these days to do well unto Jerusalem and to the house of Judah: fear ye not.

16 ¶ These *are* the things that ye shall do; [t]Speak ye every man the truth to his neighbour; execute the judgment of truth and peace in your gates:

17 [u]And let none of you imagine evil in your hearts against his neighbour; and [v]love no false oath: for all these *are things* that I hate, saith the LORD.

18 ¶ And the word of the LORD of hosts came unto me, saying,

19 Thus saith the LORD of hosts; [w]The fast of the fourth *month*, [x]and the fast of the fifth, [y]and the fast of the seventh, [z]and the fast of the tenth, shall be to the house of Judah [a]joy and gladness, and cheerful feasts; [b]therefore love the truth and peace.

20 Thus saith the LORD of hosts; *It shall* yet *come to pass*, that there shall come people, and the inhabitants of many cities:

21 And the inhabitants of one *city* shall go to another, saying, [c]Let us go speedily to pray before the LORD, and to seek the LORD of hosts: I will go also.

22 Yea, [d]many people and strong nations shall come to seek the LORD of hosts in Jerusalem, and to pray before the LORD.

23 Thus saith the LORD of hosts; In those days *it shall come to pass*, that ten men shall [e]take hold out of all languages of the nations, even shall take hold of the skirt of him that is a Jew, saying, We will go with you: for we have heard [f]*that* God *is* with you.

9

The [g]burden of the word of the LORD in the land of Hadrach, and [h]Damascus *shall be* the rest thereof: when [i]the eyes of man, as of all the tribes of Israel, *shall be* toward the LORD.

2 And [j]Hamath also shall border thereby; [k]Tyrus, and [l]Zidon, though it be very [m]wise.

3 And Tyrus did build herself a strong hold, and [n]heaped up silver as the dust, and fine gold as the mire of the streets.

4 Behold, [o]the Lord will cast her out, and he will smite [p]her power in the sea; and she shall be devoured with fire.

5 [q]Ashkelon shall see *it*, and fear; Gaza also *shall see it*, and be very sorrowful, and Ekron; for her expectation shall be ashamed; and the king shall perish from Gaza, and Ashkelon shall not be inhabited.

6 And a bastard shall dwell [r]in Ashdod, and I will cut off the pride of the Philistines.

7 And I will take away his blood out of his mouth, and his abominations from between his teeth: but he that remaineth, even he, *shall be* for our God, and he shall be as a governor in Judah, and Ekron as a Jebusite.

8 And [s]I will encamp about mine house because of the army, because of him that passeth by, and because of him that returneth: and [t]no oppressor shall pass through them any more: for now [u]have I seen with mine eyes.

9 ¶ [v]Rejoice greatly, O daughter of Zion; shout, O daughter of Jerusalem: behold, [w]thy King cometh unto thee: he *is* just, and having salvation; lowly, and riding upon an ass, and upon a colt the foal of an ass.

10 And I [x]will cut off the chariot from Ephraim, and the horse from Jerusalem, and the battle bow shall be cut off: and he shall speak [y]peace unto the heathen: and his dominion *shall be* [z]from sea *even* to sea, and from the river *even* to the ends of the earth.

11 As for thee also, by the blood of thy covenant I have sent forth thy [a]prisoners out of the pit wherein *is* no water.

12 ¶ Turn you to the strong hold, [b]ye prisoners of hope: even to day do I declare *that* [c]I will render double unto thee;

13 When I have bent Judah for me, filled the bow with Ephraim, and raised up thy sons, O Zion, against thy sons, O Greece, and made thee as the sword of a mighty man.

14 And the LORD shall be seen over them, and [d]his arrow shall go forth as the lightning: and the Lord GOD shall blow the trumpet, and shall go [e]with whirlwinds of the south.

15 The LORD of hosts shall defend them; and they shall devour, and subdue with sling stones; and they shall drink, *and* make a noise as through wine; and they shall be filled like bowls, *and* as [f]the corners of the altar.

16 And the LORD their God shall save them in that day as the flock of his people: for [g]*they shall be as* the stones of a crown, [h]lifted up as an ensign upon his land.

17 For [i]how great *is* his goodness, and how great *is* his beauty! [j]corn shall make the young men cheerful, and new wine the maids.

10

Ask ye [k]of the LORD [l]rain [m]in the time of the latter rain, *so* the LORD shall make bright clouds, and give them showers of rain, to every one grass in the field.

8:12 [l]Hos. 2:21; Joel 2:22; Hag. 2:19 [m]Ps. 67:6 [n]Hag. 1:10
8:13 [o]Jer. 42:18 [p]Gen. 12:2; Ruth 4:11; Isa. 19:24; Zeph. 3:20; Hag. 2:19 [q]ver. 9
8:14 [r]Jer. 31:28 [s]2 Chron. 36:16; ch. 1:6
8:16 [t]ch. 7:9; ver. 19; Eph. 4:25
8:17 [u]Prov. 3:29; ch. 7:10 [v]ch. 5:3
8:19 [w]Jer. 52:6 [x]Jer. 52:12; ch. 7:3 [y]2 Kings 25:25; Jer. 41:1 [z]Jer. 52:4 [a]Esth. 8:17; Isa. 35:10 [b]ver. 16
8:21 [c]Isa. 2:3; Mic. 4:1
8:22 [d]Isa. 60:3
8:23 [e]Isa. 3:6 [f]1 Cor. 14:25
9:1 [g]Jer. 23:33 [h]Am. 1:3 [i]2 Chron. 20:12; Ps. 145:15
9:2 [j]Jer. 49:23 [k]Isa. 23; Ezek. 26; Am. 1:9 [l]1 Kings 17:9; Ezek. 28:21; Obad. 20 [m]Ezek. 28:3
9:3 [n]Job 27:16; Ezek. 28:4
9:4 [o]Isa. 23:1 [p]Ezek. 26:17
9:5 [q]Jer. 47:1; Zeph. 2:4
9:6 [r]Am. 1:8
9:8 [s]Ps. 34:7; ch. 2:5 [t]Isa. 60:18; Ezek. 28:24 [u]Ex. 3:7
9:9 [v]Isa. 62:11; ch. 2:10; Matt. 21:5; John 12:15 [w]Jer. 23:5; John 1:49; Luke 19:38
9:10 [x]Hos. 1:7; Mic. 5:10; Hag. 2:22 [y]Eph. 2:14 [z]Ps. 72:8
9:11 [a]Isa. 42:7
9:12 [b]Isa. 49:9 [c]Isa. 61:7
9:14 [d]Ps. 18:14 [e]Isa. 21:1
9:15 [f]Lev. 4:18; Deut. 12:27
9:16 [g]Isa. 62:3; Mal. 3:17 [h]Isa. 11:12
9:17 [i]Ps. 31:19 [j]Joel 3:18; Am. 9:14
10:1 [k]Jer. 14:22 [l]Deut. 11:14 [m]Job 29:23; Joel 2:23

2 For the [n]idols have spoken vanity, and the diviners have seen a lie, and have told false dreams; they [o]comfort in vain: therefore they went their way as a flock, they were troubled, [p]because *there was* no shepherd.

3 Mine anger was kindled against the shepherds, [q]and I punished the goats: for the LORD of hosts [r]hath visited his flock the house of Judah, and [s]hath made them as his goodly horse in the battle.

4 Out of him came forth [t]the corner, out of him [u]the nail, out of him the battle bow, out of him every oppressor together.

5 ¶ And they shall be as mighty *men*, which [v]tread down *their enemies* in the mire of the streets in the battle: and they shall fight, because the LORD *is* with them, and the riders on horses shall be confounded.

6 And I will strengthen the house of Judah, and I will save the house of Joseph, and [w]I will bring them again to place them; for I [x]have mercy upon them: and they shall be as though I had not cast them off: for I *am* the LORD their God, and [y]will hear them.

7 And *they* of Ephraim shall be like a mighty *man*, and their [z]heart shall rejoice as through wine: yea, their children shall see *it*, and be glad; their heart shall rejoice in the LORD.

8 I will [a]hiss for them, and gather them; for I have redeemed them: [b]and they shall increase as they have increased.

9 And [c]I will sow them among the people: and they shall [d]remember me in far countries; and they shall live with their children, and turn again.

10 [e]I will bring them again also out of the land of Egypt, and gather them out of Assyria; and I will bring them into the land of Gilead and Lebanon; and [f]*place* shall not be found for them.

11 [g]And he shall pass through the sea with affliction, and shall smite the waves in the sea, and all the deeps of the river shall dry up: and [h]the pride of Assyria shall be brought down, and [i]the sceptre of Egypt shall depart away.

12 And I will strengthen them in the LORD; and [j]they shall walk up and down in his name, saith the LORD.

11 Open [k]thy doors, O Lebanon, that the fire may devour thy cedars.

2 Howl, fir tree; for the cedar is fallen; because the mighty are spoiled: howl, O ye oaks of Bashan; [l]for the forest of the vintage is come down.

3 ¶ *There is* a voice of the howling of the shepherds; for their glory is spoiled: a voice of the roaring of young lions; for the pride of Jordan is spoiled.

4 Thus saith the LORD my God; [m]Feed the flock of the slaughter;

5 Whose possessors slay them, and [n]hold themselves not guilty: and they that sell them [o]say, Blessed *be* the LORD; for I am rich: and their own shepherds pity them not.

6 For I will no more pity the inhabitants of the land, saith the LORD: but, lo, I will deliver the men every one into his neighbour's hand, and into the hand of his king: and they shall smite the land, and out of their hand I will not deliver *them*.

7 And I will [p]feed the flock of slaughter, *even* you, [q]O poor of the flock. And I took unto me two staves; the one I called Beauty, and the other I called Bands; and I fed the flock.

8 Three shepherds also I cut off [r]in one month; and my soul lothed them, and their soul also abhorred me.

9 Then said I, I will not feed you: [s]that that dieth, let it die; and that that is to be cut off, let it be cut off; and let the rest eat every one the flesh of another.

10 ¶ And I took my staff, *even* Beauty, and cut it asunder, that I might break my covenant which I had made with all the people.

11 And it was broken in that day: and so [t]the poor of the flock that waited upon me knew that it *was* the word of the LORD.

12 And I said unto them, If ye think good, give *me* my price; and if not, forbear. So they [u]weighed for my price thirty *pieces* of silver.

13 And the LORD said unto me, Cast it unto the [v]potter: a goodly price that I was prised at of them. And I took the thirty *pieces* of silver, and cast them to the potter in the house of the LORD.

14 Then I cut asunder mine other staff, *even* Bands, that I might break the brotherhood between Judah and Israel.

15 ¶ And the LORD said unto me, [w]Take unto thee yet the instruments of a foolish shepherd.

16 For, lo, I will raise up a shepherd in the land, *which* shall not visit those that be cut off, neither shall seek the young one, nor heal that that is broken, nor feed that that standeth still: but he shall eat the flesh of the fat, and tear their claws in pieces.

17 [x]Woe to the idol shepherd that leaveth the flock! the sword *shall be* upon his arm, and upon his right eye: his arm shall be clean dried up, and his right eye shall be utterly darkened.

12 The burden of the word of the LORD for Israel, saith the LORD, [y]which stretcheth forth the heavens, and layeth the foundation of the earth, and [z]formeth the spirit of man within him.

2 Behold, I will make Jerusalem [a]a cup of trembling unto all the people round about, when they shall be in the siege both against Judah *and* against Jerusalem.

3 ¶ [b]And in that day will I make Jerusalem [c]a burdensome stone for all people: all that burden themselves with it shall be cut in pieces, though all the people of the earth be gathered together against it.

4 In that day, saith the LORD, [d]I will smite

10:2 [n]Jer. 10:8; Hab. 2:18 [o]Job 13:4 [p]Ezek. 34:5
10:3 [q]Ezek. 34:17 [r]Luke 1:68 [s]SSol. 1:9
10:4 [t]Num. 24:17; 1 Sam. 14:38; Isa. 19:13 [u]Isa. 22:23
10:5 [v]Ps. 18:42
10:6 [w]Jer. 3:18; Ezek. 37:21 [x]Hos. 1:7 [y]ch. 13:9
10:7 [z]Ps. 104:15; ch. 9:15
10:8 [a]Isa. 5:26 [b]Isa. 49:19; Ezek. 36:37
10:9 [c]Hos. 2:23 [d]Deut. 30:1
10:10 [e]Isa. 11:11; Hos. 11:11 [f]Isa. 49:20
10:11 [g]Isa. 11:15 [h]Isa. 14:25 [i]Ezek. 30:13
10:12 [j]Mic. 4:5
11:1 [k]ch. 10:10
11:2 [l]Isa. 32:19
11:4 [m]ver. 7
11:5 [n]Jer. 2:3 [o]Deut. 29:19; Hos. 12:8
11:7 [p]ver. 4 [q]Zeph. 3:12; Matt. 11:5
11:8 [r]Hos. 5:7
11:9 [s]Jer. 15:2
11:11 [t]Zeph. 3:12; ver. 7
11:12 [u]Ex. 21:32; Matt. 26:15
11:13 [v]Matt. 27:9
11:15 [w]Ezek. 34:2
11:17 [x]Jer. 23:1; Ezek. 34:2; John 10:12
12:1 [y]Isa. 42:5 [z]Num. 16:22; Eccl. 12:7; Isa. 57:16; Heb. 12:9
12:2 [a]Isa. 51:17
12:3 [b]ver. 4 [c]Matt. 21:44
12:4 [d]Ps. 76:6; Ezek. 38:4

every horse with astonishment, and his
rider with madness: and I will open mine
eyes upon the house of Judah, and will
smite every horse of the people with blindness.
5 And the governors of Judah shall say in
their heart, The inhabitants of Jerusalem
shall be my strength in the LORD of hosts
their God.
6 ¶ In that day will I make the governors
of Judah [e]like an hearth of fire among the
wood, and like a torch of fire in a sheaf; and
they shall devour all the people round
about, on the right hand and on the left: and
Jerusalem shall be inhabited again in her
own place, *even* in Jerusalem.
7 The LORD also shall save the tents of
Judah first, that the glory of the house of
David and the glory of the inhabitants of
Jerusalem do not magnify *themselves*
against Judah.
8 In that day shall the LORD defend the
inhabitants of Jerusalem; and [f]he that is
feeble among them at that day shall be as
David; and the house of David *shall be* as
God, as the angel of the LORD before them.
9 ¶ And it shall come to pass in that day,
that I will seek to [g]destroy all the nations
that come against Jerusalem.
10 [h]And I will pour upon the house of
David, and upon the inhabitants of Jerusalem, the spirit of grace and of supplications:
and they shall [i]look upon me whom they
have pierced, and they shall mourn for him,
[j]as one mourneth for *his* only *son*, and
shall be in bitterness for him, as one that is
in bitterness for *his* firstborn.
11 In that day shall there be a great
[k]mourning in Jerusalem, [l]as the mourning
of Hadadrimmon in the valley of Megiddon.
12 [m]And the land shall mourn, every family apart; the family of the house of David
apart, and their wives apart; the family of
the house of [n]Nathan apart, and their wives
apart;
13 The family of the house of Levi apart,
and their wives apart; the family of Shimei
apart, and their wives apart;
14 All the families that remain, every
family apart, and their wives apart.

13 In [o]that day there shall be [p]a fountain opened to the house of David
and to the inhabitants of Jerusalem for sin
and for uncleanness.
2 ¶ And it shall come to pass in that day,
saith the LORD of hosts, *that* I will [q]cut off
the names of the idols out of the land, and
they shall no more be remembered and also
I will cause [r]the prophets and the unclean
spirit to pass out of the land.
3 And it shall come to pass, *that* when
any shall yet prophesy, then his father and
his mother that begat him shall say unto
him, Thou shalt not live; for thou speakest
lies in the name of the LORD: and his father
and his mother that begat him [s]shall thrust
him through when he prophesieth.
4 And it shall come to pass in that day,

12:6 [e]Obad. 18
12:8 [f]Joel 3:10
12:9 [g]Hag. 2:22; ver. 3
12:10 [h]Jer. 31:9; Ezek. 39:29; Joel 2:28 [i]John 19:34; Rev. 1:7 [j]Jer. 6:26; Am. 8:10
12:11 [k]Acts 2:37 [l]2 Kings 23:29; 2 Chron. 35:24
12:12 [m]Matt. 24:30; Rev. 1:7 [n]2 Sam. 5:14; Luke 3:31
13:1 [o]ch. 12:3 [p]Heb. 9:14; 1 Pet. 1:19; Rev. 1:5
13:2 [q]Ex. 23:13; Josh. 23:7; Ps. 16:4; Ezek. 30:13; Hos. 2:17; Mic. 5:12 [r]2 Pet. 2:1
13:3 [s]Deut. 13:6
13:4 [t]Mic. 3:6 [u]2 Kings 1:8; Isa. 20:2; Matt. 3:4
13:5 [v]Am. 7:14
13:7 [w]Isa. 40:11; Ezek. 34:23 [x]John 10:30; Phil. 2:6 [y]Matt. 26:31; Mark 14:27 [z]Matt. 18:10; Luke 12:32
13:8 [a]Rom. 11:5
13:9 [b]Isa. 48:10 [c]1 Pet. 1:6 [d]Ps. 50:15; ch. 10:6 [e]Ps. 144:15; Jer. 30:22; Ezek. 11:20; Hos. 2:23; ch. 8:8
14:1 [f]Isa. 13:9; Joel 2:31; Acts 2:20
14:2 [g]Joel 3:2 [h]Isa. 13:16
14:4 [i]Ezek. 11:23 [j]Joel 3:12
14:5 [k]Am. 1:1 [l]Matt. 16:27; Jude 14 [m]Joel 3:11
14:7 [n]Rev. 22:5 [o]Matt. 24:36 [p]Isa. 30:26; Rev. 21:23
14:8 [q]Ezek. 47:1; Joel 3:18; Rev. 22:1
14:9 [r]Dan. 2:44; Rev. 11:15 [s]Eph. 4:5

that [t]the prophets shall be ashamed every
one of his vision, when he hath prophesied;
neither shall they wear [u]a rough garment to
deceive:
5 [v]But he shall say, I *am* no prophet, I *am*
an husbandman; for man taught me to keep
cattle from my youth.
6 And *one* shall say unto him, What *are*
these wounds in thine hands? Then he shall
answer, *Those* with which I was wounded *in*
the house of my friends.
7 ¶ Awake, O sword, against [w]my shepherd, and against the man [x]*that is* my fellow, saith the LORD of hosts: [y]smite the
shepherd, and the sheep shall be scattered:
and I will turn mine hand upon [z]the little
ones.
8 And it shall come to pass, *that* in all the
land, saith the LORD, two parts therein shall
be cut off *and* die; [a]but the third shall be left
therein.
9 And I will bring the third part [b]through
the fire, and will [c]refine them as silver is
refined, and will try them as gold is tried:
[d]they shall call on my name, and I will hear
them: [e]I will say, It *is* my people: and they
shall say, The LORD *is* my God.

14 Behold, [f]the day of the LORD cometh, and thy spoil shall be divided in
the midst of thee.
2 For [g]I will gather all nations against
Jerusalem to battle; and the city shall be
taken, and the [h]houses rifled, and the
women ravished; and half of the city shall
go forth into captivity, and the residue of
the people shall not be cut off from the city.
3 Then shall the LORD go forth, and fight
against those nations, as when he fought in
the day of battle.
4 ¶ And his feet shall stand in that day
[i]upon the mount of Olives, which *is* before
Jerusalem on the east, and the mount of Olives shall cleave in the midst thereof toward
the east and toward the west, [j]*and there
shall be* a very great valley; and half of the
mountain shall remove toward the north,
and half of it toward the south.
5 And ye shall flee *to* the valley of the
mountains; for the valley of the mountains
shall reach unto Azal: yea, ye shall flee, like
as ye fled from before the [k]earthquake in
the days of Uzziah king of Judah: [l]and the
LORD my God shall come, *and* [m]all the
saints with thee.
6 And it shall come to pass in that day,
that the light shall not be clear, *nor* dark:
7 But it shall be [n]one day [o]which shall be
known to the LORD, not day, nor night: but
it shall come to pass, *that* at [p]evening time
it shall be light.
8 And it shall be in that day, *that* living
[q]waters shall go out from Jerusalem; half of
them toward the former sea, and half of
them toward the hinder sea: in summer and
in winter shall it be.
9 And the LORD shall be [r]king over all
the earth: in that day shall there be [s]one
LORD, and his name one.

10 All the land shall be turned [t]as a plain from Geba to Rimmon south of Jerusalem: and it shall be lifted up, and [u]inhabited in her place, from Benjamin's gate unto the place of the first gate, unto the corner gate, [v]and *from* the tower of Hananeel unto the king's winepresses.

11 And *men* shall dwell in it, and there shall be [w]no more utter destruction; [x]but Jerusalem shall be safely inhabited.

12 ¶ And this shall be the plague wherewith the LORD will smite all the people that have fought against Jerusalem; Their flesh shall consume away while they stand upon their feet, and their eyes shall consume away in their holes, and their tongue shall consume away in their mouth.

13 And it shall come to pass in that day, *that* [y]a great tumult from the LORD shall be among them; and they shall lay hold every one on the hand of his neighbour, and [z]his hand shall rise up against the hand of his neighbour.

14 And Judah also shall fight at Jerusalem; [a]and the wealth of all the heathen round about shall be gathered together, gold, and silver, and apparel, in great abundance.

15 And [b]so shall be the plague of the horse, of the mule, of the camel, and of the ass, and of all the beasts that shall be in these tents, as this plague.

16 ¶ And it shall come to pass, *that* every one that is left of all the nations which came against Jerusalem shall even [c]go up from year to year to worship the King, the LORD of hosts, and to keep [d]the feast of tabernacles.

17 [e]And it shall be, *that* whoso will not come up of *all* the families of the earth unto Jerusalem to worship the King, the LORD of hosts, even upon them shall be no rain.

18 And if the family of Egypt go not up, and come not, [f]that *have* no *rain;* there shall be the plague, wherewith the LORD will smite the heathen that come not up to keep the feast of tabernacles.

19 This shall be the punishment of Egypt, and the punishment of all nations that come not up to keep the feast of tabernacles.

20 ¶ In that day shall there be upon the bells of the horses, [g]HOLINESS UNTO THE LORD; and the pots in the LORD's house shall be like the bowls before the altar.

21 Yea, every pot in Jerusalem and in Judah shall be holiness unto the LORD of hosts: and all they that sacrifice shall come and take of them, and seethe therein: and in that day there shall be no more the [h]Canaanite in [i]the house of the LORD of hosts.

14:10 [t]Isa. 40:4 [u]ch. 12:6 [v]Neh. 3:1; Jer. 31:38
14:11 [w]Jer. 31:40 [x]Jer. 23:6
14:13 [y]1 Sam. 14:15 [z]Judg. 7:22; 2 Chron. 20:23; Ezek. 38:21
14:14 [a]Ezek. 39:10
14:15 [b]ver. 12
14:16 [c]Isa. 60:6 [d]Lev. 23:34; Neh. 8:14; Hos. 12:9; John 7:2
14:17 [e]Isa. 60:12
14:18 [f]Deut. 11:10
14:20 [g]Isa. 23:18
14:21 [h]Isa. 35:8; Joel 3:17; Rev. 21:27 [i]Eph. 2:19

MALACHI

Malachi identifies himself as the author of the book. It was written sometime between 450 B.C. and 400 B.C. Disillusionment had settled over the Jews causing a general apathy toward God and his commands. Malachi tells the people of God's commitment to them and calls for their repentance, in light of God's compassion for them. Included in Malachi's book is a prophetic reference to the work of John the Baptist (Chapter 3). The best known verse in the book is Malachi 3:6.

I. God's love for Israel retold, 1:1–1:5
II. The problem with Israel, 1:6–2:17
III. Prophecy concerning the coming messenger, 3:1–3:6
IV. Other problems with Israel, 3:7–3:15
V. God's judgment, 3:16–4:6

1 The burden of the word of the LORD to
Israel by Malachi.
2 [a]I have loved you, saith the LORD. Yet
ye say, Wherein hast thou loved us? *Was*
not Esau Jacob's brother? saith the LORD:
yet [b]I loved Jacob,
3 And I hated Esau, and [c]laid his mountains and his heritage waste for the dragons
of the wilderness.
4 Whereas Edom saith, We are impoverished, but we will return and build the desolate places; thus saith the LORD of hosts,
They shall build, but I will throw down; and
they shall call them, The border of wickedness, and, The people against whom the
LORD hath indignation for ever.
5 And your eyes shall see, and ye shall
say, [d]The LORD will be magnified from the
border of Israel.
6 ¶ A son [e]honoureth *his* father, and a
servant his master: [f]if then I *be* a father,
where *is* mine honour? and if I *be* a master,
where *is* my fear? saith the LORD of hosts
unto you, O priests, that despise my name.
[g]And ye say, Wherein have we despised
thy name?
7 Ye offer [h]polluted bread upon mine altar; and ye say, Wherein have we polluted
thee? In that ye say, [i]The table of the LORD
is contemptible.
8 And [j]if ye offer the blind for sacrifice,
is it not evil? and if ye offer the lame and
sick, *is it* not evil? offer it now unto thy governor; will he be pleased with thee, or [k]ac-
cept thy person? saith the LORD of hosts.
9 And now, I pray you, beseech God that
he will be gracious unto us: [l]this hath been
by your means: will he regard your persons? saith the LORD of hosts.
10 Who *is there* even among you that
would shut the doors *for nought?* [m]neither
do ye kindle *fire* on mine altar for nought. I
have no pleasure in you, saith the LORD of
hosts, [n]neither will I accept an offering at
your hand.
11 For [o]from the rising of the sun even
unto the going down of the same my name
shall be great [p]among the Gentiles; [q]and in
every place [r]incense *shall be* offered unto
my name, and a pure offering: [s]for my
name *shall be* great among the heathen,
saith the LORD of hosts.
12 ¶ But ye have profaned it, in that ye
say, [t]The table of the LORD *is* polluted; and
the fruit thereof, *even* his meat, *is* contemptible.
13 Ye said also, Behold, what a weariness
is it! and ye have snuffed at it, saith the
LORD of hosts; and ye brought *that which
was* torn, and the lame, and the sick; thus ye
brought an offering: [u]should I accept this of
your hand? saith the LORD.
14 But cursed *be* [v]the deceiver, which
hath in his flock a male, and voweth, and
sacrificeth unto the Lord a corrupt thing: for
[w]I *am* a great King, saith the LORD of hosts,
and my name *is* dreadful among the heathen.

2 And now, O ye priests, this commandment *is* for you.
2 [x]If ye will not hear, and if ye will not lay
it to heart, to give glory unto my name, saith
the LORD of hosts, I will even send a curse
upon you, and I will curse your blessings:
yea, I have cursed them already, because ye
do not lay *it* to heart.
3 Behold, I will corrupt your seed, and
spread dung upon your faces, *even* the dung
of your solemn feasts; and *one* shall [y]take
you away with it.
4 And ye shall know that I have sent this
commandment unto you, that my covenant
might be with Levi, saith the LORD of hosts.
5 [z]My covenant was with him of life and
peace; and I gave them to him [a]*for* the fear
wherewith he feared me, and was afraid before my name.
6 [b]The law of truth was in his mouth, and
iniquity was not found in his lips: he walked
with me in peace and equity, and did [c]turn
many away from iniquity.
7 [d]For the priest's lips should keep
knowledge, and they should seek the law at
his mouth: [e]for he *is* the messenger of the
LORD of hosts.
8 But ye are departed out of the way; ye

1:2 [a]Deut. 7:8 [b]Rom. 9:13
1:3 [c]Jer. 49:18; Ezek. 35:3; Obad. 10
1:5 [d]Ps. 35:27
1:6 [e]Ex. 20:12 [f]Luke 6:46 [g]ch. 2:14
1:7 [h]Deut. 15:21 [i]Ezek. 41:22; ver. 12
1:8 [j]Lev. 22:22; Deut. 15:21; ver. 14 [k]Job 42:8
1:9 [l]Hos. 13:9
1:10 [m]1 Cor. 9:13 [n]Isa. 1:11; Jer. 6:20; Am. 5:21
1:11 [o]Ps. 113:3; Isa. 59:19 [p]Isa. 60:3 [q]John 4:21; 1 Tim. 2:8 [r]Rev. 8:3 [s]Isa. 66:19
1:12 [t]ver. 7
1:13 [u]Lev. 22:20
1:14 [v]ver. 8 [w]Ps. 47:2; 1 Tim. 6:15
2:2 [x]Lev. 26:14; Deut. 28:15
2:3 [y]1 Kings 14:10
2:5 [z]Num. 25:12; Ezek. 34:25 [a]Deut. 33:8
2:6 [b]Deut. 33:10 [c]Jer. 23:22; Jam. 5:20
2:7 [d]Deut. 17:9; Lev. 10:11; Ezra 7:10; Jer. 18:18; Hag. 2:11 [e]Gal. 4:14

[f]have caused many to stumble at the law;
[g]ye have corrupted the covenant of Levi,
saith the LORD of hosts.
9 Therefore [h]have I also made you contemptible and base before all the people, according as ye have not kept my ways, but
have been partial in the law.
10 [i]Have we not all one father? [j]hath
not one God created us? why do we deal
treacherously every man against his
brother, by profaning the covenant of our
fathers?
11 ¶ Judah hath dealt treacherously, and
an abomination is committed in Israel and
in Jerusalem; for Judah hath profaned the
holiness of the LORD which he loved, [k]and
hath married the daughter of a strange god.
12 The LORD will cut off the man that doeth this, the master and the scholar, out of
the tabernacles of Jacob, [l]and him that offereth an offering unto the LORD of hosts.
13 And this have ye done again, covering
the altar of the LORD with tears, with weeping, and with crying out, insomuch that he
regardeth not the offering any more, or receiveth *it* with good will at your hand.
14 ¶ Yet ye say, Wherefore? Because the
LORD hath been witness between thee and
[m]the wife of thy youth, against whom thou
hast dealt treacherously: [n]yet *is* she thy
companion, and the wife of thy covenant.
15 And [o]did not he make one? Yet had he
the residue of the spirit. And wherefore
one? That he might seek [p]a godly seed.
Therefore take heed to your spirit, and let
none deal treacherously against the wife of
his youth.
16 For [q]the LORD, the God of Israel, saith
that he hateth putting away: for *one* covereth violence with his garment, saith the
LORD of hosts: therefore take heed to your
spirit, that ye deal not treacherously.
17 ¶ [r]Ye have wearied the LORD with
your words. Yet ye say, Wherein have we
wearied *him?* When ye say, Every one that
doeth evil *is* good in the sight of the LORD,
and he delighteth in them; or, Where *is* the
God of judgment?

3 Behold, [s]I will send my messenger, and
he shall [t]prepare the way before me:
and the Lord, whom ye seek, shall suddenly
come to his temple, [u]even the messenger of
the covenant, whom ye delight in: behold,
[v]he shall come, saith the LORD of hosts.
2 But who may abide [w]the day of his coming? and [x]who shall stand when he appeareth? for [y]he *is* like a refiner's fire, and like
fullers' soap:
3 And [z]he shall sit *as a* refiner and purifier of silver: and he shall purify the sons of
Levi, and purge them as gold and silver,
that they may [a]offer unto the LORD an offering in righteousness.
4 Then [b]shall the offering of Judah and
Jerusalem be pleasant unto the LORD, as in
the days of old, and as in former years.
5 And I will come near to you to judgment; and I will be a swift witness against
the sorcerers, and against the adulterers,
[c]and against false swearers, and against
those that oppress the hireling in *his* wages,
the widow, and the fatherless, and that turn
aside the stranger *from his right,* and fear
not me, saith the LORD of hosts.
6 For I *am* the LORD, [d]I change not;
[e]therefore ye sons of Jacob are not consumed.
7 ¶ Even from the days of [f]your fathers
ye are gone away from mine ordinances,
and have not kept *them.* [g]Return unto me,
and I will return unto you, saith the LORD of
hosts. [h]But ye said, Wherein shall we return?
8 ¶ Will a man rob God? Yet ye have
robbed me. But ye say, Wherein have we
robbed thee? [i]In tithes and offerings.
9 Ye *are* cursed with a curse: for ye have
robbed me, *even* this whole nation.
10 [j]Bring ye all the tithes into [k]the storehouse, that there may be meat in mine
house, and prove me now herewith, saith
the LORD of hosts, if I will not open you the
[l]windows of heaven, and [m]pour you out
a blessing, that *there shall* not *be room*
enough *to receive it.*
11 And I will rebuke [n]the devourer for
your sakes, and he shall not destroy the
fruits of your ground; neither shall your
vine cast her fruit before the time in the
field, saith the LORD of hosts.
12 And all nations shall call you blessed:
for ye shall be [o]a delightsome land, saith
the LORD of hosts.
13 ¶ [p]Your words have been stout
against me, saith the LORD. Yet ye say,
What have we spoken *so much* against
thee?
14 [q]Ye have said, It *is* vain to serve God:
and what profit *is it* that we have kept his
ordinance, and that we have walked mournfully before the LORD of hosts?
15 And now [r]we call the proud happy;
yea, they that work wickedness are set up;
yea, *they that* [s]tempt God are even delivered.
16 ¶ Then they [t]that feared the LORD
[u]spake often one to another: and the LORD
hearkened, and heard *it,* and [v]a book of
remembrance was written before him for
them that feared the LORD, and that thought
upon his name.
17 And [w]they shall be mine, saith the
LORD of hosts, in that day when I make up
my [x]jewels; and [y]I will spare them, as a
man spareth his own son that serveth him.
18 [z]Then shall ye return, and discern between the righteous and the wicked, between him that serveth God and him that
serveth him not.

4 For, behold, [a]the day cometh, that shall
burn as an oven; and all [b]the proud,
yea, and all that do wickedly, shall be
[c]stubble: and the day that cometh shall
burn them up, saith the LORD of hosts, that
it shall [d]leave them neither root nor
branch.

2:8 f1 Sam. 2:17; Jer. 18:15 gNeh. 13:29
2:9 h1 Sam. 2:30
2:10 i1 Cor. 8:6; Eph. 4:6 jJob 31:15
2:11 kEzra 9:1; Neh. 13:23
2:12 lNeh. 13:28
2:14 mProv. 5:18 nProv. 2:17
2:15 oMatt. 19:4 pEzra 9:2; 1 Cor. 7:14
2:16 qDeut. 24:1; Matt. 5:32
2:17 rIsa. 43:24; Am. 2:13; ch. 3:13
3:1 sMatt. 11:10; Mark 1:2; Luke 1:76 tIsa. 40:3 uIsa. 63:9 vHag. 2:7
3:2 wch. 4:1 xRev. 6:17 yIsa. 4:4; Matt. 3:10
3:3 zIsa. 1:25; Zech. 13:9 a1 Pet. 2:5
3:4 bch. 1:11
3:5 cZech. 5:4; Jam. 5:4
3:6 dNum. 23:19; Rom. 11:29; Jam. 1:17 eLam. 3:22
3:7 fActs 7:51 gZech. 1:3 hch. 1:6
3:8 iNeh. 13:10
3:10 jProv. 3:9 k1 Chron. 26:20; 2 Chron. 31:11; Neh. 10:38 lGen. 7:11; 2 Kings 7:2 m2 Chron. 31:10
3:11 nAm. 4:9
3:12 oDan. 8:9
3:13 pch. 2:17
3:14 qJob 21:14; Ps. 73:13; Zeph. 1:12
3:15 rPs. 73:12; ch. 2:17 sPs. 95:9
3:16 tPs. 66:16; ch. 4:2 uHeb. 3:13 vPs. 56:8; Isa. 65:6; Rev. 20:12
3:17 wEx. 19:5; Deut. 7:6; Ps. 135:4; Tit. 2:14; 1 Pet. 2:9 xIsa. 62:3 yPs. 103:13
3:18 zPs. 58:11
4:1 aJoel 2:31; ch. 3:2; 2 Pet. 3:7 bch. 3:18 cObad. 18 dAm. 2:9

2 ¶ But unto you that [e]fear my name shall
the [f]Sun of righteousness arise with healing in his wings; and ye shall go forth, and
grow up as calves of the stall.
3 [g]And ye shall tread down the wicked;
for they shall be ashes under the soles of
your feet in the day that I shall do *this,* saith
the LORD of hosts.
4 ¶ Remember ye the [h]law of Moses my
servant, which I commanded unto him [i]in
Horeb for all Israel, *with* [j]the statutes and
judgments.
5 ¶ Behold, I will send you [k]Elijah the
prophet [l]before the coming of the great
and dreadful day of the LORD:
6 And he shall turn the heart of the fathers to the children, and the heart of the
children to their fathers, lest I come and
[m]smite the earth with [n]a curse.

4:2 [e]ch. 3:16 [f]Luke 1:78; Eph. 5:14; 2 Pet. 1:19; Rev. 2:28 **4:3** [g]2 Sam. 22:43; Mic. 7:10; Zech. 10:5 **4:4** [h]Ex. 20:3 [i]Deut. 4:10 [j]Ps. 147:19 **4:5** [k]Matt. 11:14; Mark 9:11; Luke 1:17 [l]Joel 2:31 **4:6** [m]Zech. 14:12 [n]Zech. 5:3

NEW TESTAMENT

MATTHEW

Matthew, one of Jesus' disciples, is the author of this book. It was written during the 60s A.D. Matthew opens with a genealogy of Christ through his legal, though not natural father, Joseph. Following a brief description of Jesus' birth and childhood, Matthew tells of Jesus' baptism and the beginning of his ministry. Chapters 5 through 28 describe the three years of Jesus' public ministry from his Sermon on the Mount (Chapters 5–7), to his ascension to heaven (Chapter 28). The description of Jesus' birth (1:18–2:12), and the Sermon on the Mount (4:1–7:29) are the best known scriptures in Matthew.

I. The coming of the Messiah, 1:1–2:23
II. Jesus' public ministry, 3:1–15:39
III. Jesus' closing ministries, 16:1–23:39
IV. The prophecies of the destruction of Jerusalem and the end, 24:1–25:46
V. Jesus' arrest, crucifixion, and resurrection, 26:1–28:20

1 The book of the [a]generation of Jesus
Christ, [b]the son of David, [c]the son of
Abraham.
2 [d]Abraham begat Isaac; and [e]Isaac begat Jacob; and [f]Jacob begat Judas and his
brethren;
3 And [g]Judas begat Phares and Zara of
Thamar; and [h]Phares begat Esrom; and Esrom begat Aram;
4 And Aram begat Aminadab; and
Aminadab begat Naasson; and Naasson begat Salmon;
5 And Salmon begat Booz of Rachab; and
Booz begat Obed of Ruth; and Obed begat
Jesse;
6 And [i]Jesse begat David the king; and
[j]David the king begat Solomon of her *that
had been the wife* of Urias;
7 And [k]Solomon begat Roboam; and Roboam begat Abia; and Abia begat Asa;
8 And Asa begat Josaphat; and Josaphat
begat Joram; and Joram begat Ozias;
9 And Ozias begat Joatham; and Joatham
begat Achaz; and Achaz begat Ezekias;
10 And [l]Ezekias begat Manasses; and
Manasses begat Amon; and Amon begat
Josias;
11 And [m]Josias begat Jechonias and his
brethren, about the time they were [n]carried
away to Babylon:
12 And after they were brought to Babylon, [o]Jechonias begat Salathiel; and Salathiel begat [p]Zorobabel;
13 And Zorobabel begat Abiud; and
Abiud begat Eliakim; and Eliakim begat
Azor;
14 And Azor begat Sadoc; and Sadoc begat Achim; and Achim begat Eliud;
15 And Eliud begat Eleazar; and Eleazar
begat Matthan; and Matthan begat Jacob;
16 And Jacob begat Joseph the husband
of Mary, of whom was born Jesus, who is
called Christ.
17 So all the generations from Abraham
to David *are* fourteen generations; and from
David until the carrying away into Babylon

1:1 [a]Luke 3:23 [b]Ps. 132:11; Isa. 11:1; Jer. 23:5; ch. 22:42; John 7:42; Acts 2:30; Rom. 1:3 [c]Gen. 12:3; Gal. 3:16
1:2 [d]Gen. 21:2 [e]Gen. 25:26 [f]Gen. 29:35
1:3 [g]Gen. 38:27 [h]Ruth 4:18; 1 Chron. 2:5
1:6 [i]1 Sam. 16:1 [j]2 Sam. 12:24
1:7 [k]1 Chron. 3:10
1:10 [l]2 Kings 20:21; 1 Chron. 3:13
1:11 [m]1 Chron. 3:15 [n]2 Kings 24:14; 2 Chron. 36:10; Jer. 27:20; Dan. 1:2
1:12 [o]1 Chron. 3:17 [p]Ezra 3:2; Neh. 12:1; Hag. 1:1
1:18 [q]Luke 1:27 [r]Luke 1:35
1:19 [s]Deut. 24:1
1:20 [t]Luke 1:35
1:21 [u]Luke 1:31 [v]Acts 4:12
1:23 [w]Isa. 7:14
1:25 [x]Ex. 13:2; Luke 2:7
2:1 [y]Luke 2:4 [z]Gen. 10:30; 1 Kings 4:30
2:2 [a]Luke 2:11 [b]Num. 24:17; Isa. 60:3
2:4 [c]2 Chron. 36:14 [d]2 Chron. 34:13

are fourteen generations; and from the carrying away into Babylon unto Christ *are*
fourteen generations.
18 ¶ Now the [q]birth of Jesus Christ was
on this wise: When as his mother Mary was
espoused to Joseph, before they came together, she was found with child [r]of the
Holy Ghost.
19 Then Joseph her husband, being a just
man, and not willing [s]to make her a pub-
lick example, was minded to put her away
privily.
20 But while he thought on these things,
behold, the angel of the Lord appeared unto
him in a dream, saying, Joseph, thou son of
David, fear not to take unto thee Mary thy
wife: [t]for that which is conceived in her is
of the Holy Ghost.
21 [u]And she shall bring forth a son, and
thou shalt call his name JESUS: for [v]he
shall save his people from their sins.
22 Now all this was done, that it might be
fulfilled which was spoken of the Lord by
the prophet, saying,
23 [w]Behold, a virgin shall be with child,
and shall bring forth a son, and they shall
call his name Emmanuel, which being interpreted is, God with us.
24 Then Joseph being raised from sleep
did as the angel of the Lord had bidden him,
and took unto him his wife:
25 And knew her not till she had brought
forth [x]her firstborn son: and he called his
name JESUS.

2 Now when [y]Jesus was born in Bethlehem of Judaea in the days of Herod the
king, behold, there came wise men [z]from
the east to Jerusalem,
2 Saying, [a]Where is he that is born King
of the Jews? for we have seen [b]his star in
the east, and are come to worship him.
3 When Herod the king had heard *these
things,* he was troubled, and all Jerusalem
with him.
4 And when he had gathered all [c]the
chief priests and [d]scribes of the people to-

gether, [e]he demanded of them where Christ should be born.

5 And they said unto him, In Bethlehem of Judaea: for thus it is written by the prophet,

6 [f]And thou Bethlehem, *in* the land of Juda, art not the least among the princes of Juda: for out of thee shall come a Governor, [g]that shall rule my people Israel.

7 Then Herod, when he had privily called the wise men, enquired of them diligently what time the star appeared.

8 And he sent them to Bethlehem, and said, Go and search diligently for the young child; and when ye have found *him*, bring me word again, that I may come and worship him also.

9 When they had heard the king, they departed; and, lo, the star, which they saw in the east, went before them, till it came and stood over where the young child was.

10 When they saw the star, they rejoiced with exceeding great joy.

11 ¶ And when they were come into the house, they saw the young child with Mary his mother, and fell down, and worshipped him: and when they had opened their treasures, [h]they presented unto him gifts; gold, and frankincense, and myrrh.

12 And being warned of God [i]in a dream that they should not return to Herod, they departed into their own country another way.

13 And when they were departed, behold, the angel of the Lord appeareth to Joseph in a dream, saying, Arise, and take the young child and his mother, and flee into Egypt, and be thou there until I bring thee word: for Herod will seek the young child to destroy him.

14 When he arose, he took the young child and his mother by night, and departed into Egypt:

15 And was there until the death of Herod: that it might be fulfilled which was spoken of the Lord by the prophet, saying, [j]Out of Egypt have I called my son.

16 ¶ Then Herod, when he saw that he was mocked of the wise men, was exceeding wroth, and sent forth, and slew all the children that were in Bethlehem, and in all the coasts thereof, from two years old and under, according to the time which he had diligently enquired of the wise men.

17 Then was fulfilled that which was spoken by [k]Jeremy the prophet, saying,

18 In Rama was there a voice heard, lamentation, and weeping, and great mourning, Rachel weeping *for* her children, and would not be comforted, because they are not.

19 ¶ But when Herod was dead, behold, an angel of the Lord appeareth in a dream to Joseph in Egypt,

20 Saying, Arise, and take the young child and his mother, and go into the land of Israel: for they are dead which sought the young child's life.

21 And he arose, and took the young child and his mother, and came into the land of Israel.

22 But when he heard that Archelaus did reign in Judaea in the room of his father Herod, he was afraid to go thither: notwithstanding, being warned of God in a dream, he turned aside [l]into the parts of Galilee:

23 And he came and dwelt in a city called [m]Nazareth: that it might be fulfilled [n]which was spoken by the prophets, He shall be called a Nazarene.

3 In those days came [o]John the Baptist, preaching [p]in the wilderness of Judaea,

2 And saying, Repent ye: for [q]the kingdom of heaven is at hand.

3 For this is he that was spoken of by the prophet Esaias, saying, [r]The voice of one crying in the wilderness, [s]Prepare ye the way of the Lord, make his paths straight.

4 And [t]the same John [u]had his raiment of camel's hair, and a leathern girdle about his loins; and his meat was [v]locusts and [w]wild honey.

5 [x]Then went out to him Jerusalem, and all Judaea, and all the region round about Jordan,

6 [y]And were baptized of him in Jordan, confessing their sins.

7 ¶ But when he saw many of the Pharisees and Sadducees come to his baptism, he said unto them, [z]O generation of vipers, who hath warned you to flee from [a]the wrath to come?

8 Bring forth therefore fruits meet for repentance:

9 And think not to say within yourselves, [b]We have Abraham to *our* father: for I say unto you, that God is able of these stones to raise up children unto Abraham.

10 And now also the axe is laid unto the root of the trees: [c]therefore every tree which bringeth not forth good fruit is hewn down, and cast into the fire.

11 [d]I indeed baptize you with water unto repentance: but he that cometh after me is mightier than I, whose shoes I am not worthy to bear: [e]he shall baptize you with the Holy Ghost, and *with* fire:

12 [f]Whose fan *is* in his hand, and he will throughly purge his floor, and gather his wheat into the garner; but he will [g]burn up the chaff with unquenchable fire.

13 ¶ [h]Then cometh Jesus [i]from Galilee to Jordan unto John, to be baptized of him.

14 But John forbad him, saying, I have need to be baptized of thee, and comest thou to me?

15 And Jesus answering said unto him, Suffer *it to be so* now: for thus it becometh us to fulfil all righteousness. Then he suffered him.

16 [j]And Jesus, when he was baptized, went up straightway out of the water: and, lo, the heavens were opened unto him, and he saw [k]the Spirit of God descending like a dove, and lighting upon him:

17 [l]And lo a voice from heaven, saying,

2:4 [e]Mal. 2:7
2:6 [f]Mic. 5:2; John 7:42 [g]Rev. 2:27
2:11 [h]Ps. 72:10; Isa. 60:6
2:12 [i]ch. 1:20
2:15 [j]Hos. 11:1
2:17 [k]Jer. 31:15
2:22 [l]ch. 3:13; Luke 2:39
2:23 [m]John 1:45 [n]Judg. 13:5; 1 Sam. 1:11
3:1 [o]Mark 1:4; Luke 3:2; John 1:28 [p]Josh. 14:10
3:2 [q]Dan. 2:44; ch. 4:17
3:3 [r]Isa. 40:3; Mark 1:3; Luke 3:4; John 1:23 [s]Luke 1:76
3:4 [t]Mark 1:6 [u]2 Kings 1:8; Zech. 13:4 [v]Lev. 11:22 [w]1 Sam. 14:25
3:5 [x]Mark 1:5; Luke 3:7
3:6 [y]Acts 19:4
3:7 [z]ch. 12:34; Luke 3:7 [a]Rom. 5:9; 1 Thess. 1:10
3:9 [b]John 8:33; Acts 13:26; Rom. 4:1
3:10 [c]ch. 7:19; Luke 13:7; John 15:6
3:11 [d]Mark 1:8; Luke 3:16; John 1:15; Acts 1:5 [e]Isa. 4:4; Mal. 3:2; Acts 2:3; 1 Cor. 12:13
3:12 [f]Mal. 3:3 [g]Mal. 4:1; ch. 13:30
3:13 [h]Mark 1:9; Luke 3:21 [i]ch. 2:22
3:16 [j]Mark 1:10 [k]Isa. 11:2; Luke 3:22; John 1:32
3:17 [l]John 12:28

[m]This is my beloved Son, in whom I am well pleased.

4 Then was [n]Jesus led up of [o]the Spirit into the wilderness to be tempted of the devil.

2 And when he had fasted forty days and forty nights, he was afterward an hungred.

3 And when the tempter came to him, he said, If thou be the Son of God, command that these stones be made bread.

4 But he answered and said, It is written, [p]Man shall not live by bread alone, but by every word that proceedeth out of the mouth of God.

5 Then the devil taketh him up [q]into the holy city, and setteth him on a pinnacle of the temple,

6 And saith unto him, If thou be the Son of God, cast thyself down: for it is written, [r]He shall give his angels charge concerning thee: and in *their* hands they shall bear thee up, lest at any time thou dash thy foot against a stone.

7 Jesus said unto him, It is written again, [s]Thou shalt not tempt the Lord thy God.

8 Again, the devil taketh him up into an exceeding high mountain, and sheweth him all the kingdoms of the world, and the glory of them;

9 And saith unto him, All these things will I give thee, if thou wilt fall down and worship me.

10 Then saith Jesus unto him, Get thee hence, Satan: for it is written, [t]Thou shalt worship the Lord thy God, and him only shalt thou serve.

11 Then the devil leaveth him, and, behold, [u]angels came and ministered unto him.

12 ¶ [v]Now when Jesus had heard that John was cast into prison, he departed into Galilee;

13 And leaving Nazareth, he came and dwelt in Capernaum, which is upon the sea coast, in the borders of Zabulon and Nephthalim:

14 That it might be fulfilled which was spoken by Esaias the prophet, saying,

15 [w]The land of Zabulon, and the land of Nephthalim, *by* the way of the sea, beyond Jordan, Galilee of the Gentiles;

16 [x]The people which sat in darkness saw great light; and to them which sat in the region and shadow of death light is sprung up.

17 ¶ [y]From that time Jesus began to preach, and to say, [z]Repent: for the kingdom of heaven is at hand.

18 ¶ [a]And Jesus, walking by the sea of Galilee, saw two brethren, Simon [b]called Peter, and Andrew his brother, casting a net into the sea: for they were fishers.

19 And he saith unto them, Follow me, and [c]I will make you fishers of men.

20 [d]And they straightway left *their* nets, and followed him.

21 [e]And going on from thence, he saw other two brethren, James *the son* of Zebedee, and John his brother, in a ship with Zebedee their father, mending their nets; and he called them.

22 And they immediately left the ship and their father, and followed him.

23 ¶ And Jesus went about all Galilee, [f]teaching in their synagogues, and preaching [g]the gospel of the kingdom, [h]and healing all manner of sickness and all manner of disease among the people.

24 And his fame went throughout all Syria: and they brought unto him all sick people that were taken with divers diseases and torments, and those which were possessed with devils, and those which were lunatick, and those that had the palsy; and he healed them.

25 [i]And there followed him great multitudes of people from Galilee, and *from* Decapolis, and *from* Jerusalem, and *from* Judea, and *from* beyond Jordan.

5 And seeing the multitudes, [j]he went up into a mountain: and when he was set, his disciples came unto him:

2 And he opened his mouth, and taught them, saying,

3 [k]Blessed *are* the poor in spirit: for theirs is the kingdom of heaven.

4 [l]Blessed *are* they that mourn: for they shall be comforted.

5 [m]Blessed *are* the meek: for [n]they shall inherit the earth.

6 Blessed *are* they which do hunger and thirst after righteousness: [o]for they shall be filled.

7 Blessed *are* the merciful: [p]for they shall obtain mercy.

8 [q]Blessed *are* the pure in heart: for [r]they shall see God.

9 Blessed *are* the peacemakers: for they shall be called the children of God.

10 [s]Blessed *are* they which are persecuted for righteousness' sake: for theirs is the kingdom of heaven.

11 [t]Blessed are ye, when *men* shall revile you, and persecute *you,* and shall say all manner of [u]evil against you falsely, for my sake.

12 [v]Rejoice, and be exceeding glad for great *is* your reward in heaven: for [w]so persecuted they the prophets which were before you.

13 ¶ Ye are the salt of the earth: [x]but if the salt have lost his savour, wherewith shall it be salted? it is thenceforth good for nothing, but to be cast out, and to be trodden under foot of men.

14 [y]Ye are the light of the world. A city that is set on an hill cannot be hid.

15 Neither do men [z]light a candle, and put it under a bushel, but on a candlestick; and it giveth light unto all that are in the house.

16 Let your light so shine before men, [a]that they may see your good works, and [b]glorify your Father which is in heaven.

17 ¶ [c]Think not that I am come to destroy

3:17 *m*Ps. 2:7; Isa. 42:1; ch. 12:18; Mark 1:11; Luke 9:35; Eph. 1:6; Col. 1:13; 2 Pet. 1:17
4:1 *n*Mark 1:12; Luke 4:1 *o*1 Kings 18:12; Ezek. 3:14; Acts 8:39
4:4 *p*Deut. 8:3
4:5 *q*Neh. 11:1; Isa. 48:2; ch. 27:53; Rev. 11:2
4:6 *r*Ps. 91:11
4:7 *s*Deut. 6:16
4:10 *t*Deut. 6:13; Josh. 24:14; 1 Sam. 7:3
4:11 *u*Heb. 1:14
4:12 *v*Mark 1:14; Luke 3:30; John 4:43
4:15 *w*Isa. 9:1
4:16 *x*Isa. 42:7; Luke 2:32
4:17 *y*Mark 1:14 *z*ch. 3:2
4:18 *a*Mark 1:16; Luke 5:2 *b*John 1:42
4:19 *c*Luke 5:10
4:20 *d*Mark 10:28; Luke 18:28
4:21 *e*Mark 1:19; Luke 5:10
4:23 *f*ch. 9:35; Mark 1:21; Luke 4:15 *g*ch. 24:14; Mark 1:14 *h*Mark 1:34
4:25 *i*Mark 3:7
5:1 *j*Mark 3:13
5:3 *k*Ps. 51:17; Prov. 16:19; Isa. 57:15; Luke 6:20
5:4 *l*Isa. 61:2; Luke 6:21; John 16:20; 2 Cor. 1:7; Rev. 21:4
5:5 *m*Ps. 37:11 *n*Rom. 4:13
5:6 *o*Isa. 55:1
5:7 *p*Ps. 41:1; ch. 6:14; Mark 11:25; 2 Tim. 1:16; Heb. 6:10; Jam. 2:13
5:8 *q*Ps. 15:2; Heb. 12:14 *r*1 Cor. 13:12; 1 John 3:2
5:10 *s*2 Cor. 4:17; 2 Tim. 2:12; 1 Pet. 3:14
5:11 *t*Luke 6:22 *u*1 Pet. 4:14
5:12 *v*Luke 6:23; Acts 5:41; Rom. 5:3; Jam. 1:2; 1 Pet. 4:13 *w*Neh. 9:26; 2 Chron. 36:16; ch. 23:34; Acts 7:52; 1 Thess. 2:15
5:13 *x*Mark 9:50; Luke 14:34
5:14 *y*Prov. 4:18; Phil. 2:15
5:15 *z*Mark 4:21; Luke 8:16
5:16 *a*1 Pet. 2:12 *b*John 15:8; 1 Cor. 14:25
5:17 *c*Rom. 3:31; Gal. 3:24

the law, or the prophets: I am not come to destroy, but to fulfil.

18 For verily I say unto you, [d]Till heaven and earth pass, one jot or one tittle shall in no wise pass from the law, till all be fulfilled.

19 [e]Whosoever therefore shall break one of these least commandments, and shall teach men so, he shall be called the least in the kingdom of heaven: but whosoever shall do and teach *them,* the same shall be called great in the kingdom of heaven.

20 For I say unto you, That except your righteousness shall exceed [f]*the righteousness* of the scribes and Pharisees, ye shall in no case enter into the kingdom of heaven.

21 ¶ Ye have heard that it was said by them of old time, [g]Thou shalt not kill; and whosoever shall kill shall be in danger of the judgment:

22 But I say unto you, That [h]whosoever is angry with his brother without a cause shall be in danger of the judgment: and whosoever shall say to his brother, [i]Raca, shall be in danger of the council: but whosoever shall say, Thou fool, shall be in danger of hell fire.

23 Therefore [j]if thou bring thy gift to the altar, and there rememberest that thy brother hath ought against thee;

24 [k]Leave there thy gift before the altar, and go thy way; first be reconciled to thy brother, and then come and offer thy gift.

25 [l]Agree with thine adversary quickly, [m]whiles thou art in the way with him; lest at any time the adversary deliver thee to the judge, and the judge deliver thee to the officer, and thou be cast into prison.

26 Verily I say unto thee, Thou shalt by no means come out thence, till thou hast paid the uttermost farthing.

27 ¶ Ye have heard that it was said by them of old time, [n]Thou shalt not commit adultery:

28 But I say unto you, That whosoever [o]looketh on a woman to lust after her hath committed adultery with her already in his heart.

29 [p]And if thy right eye offend thee, [q]pluck it out, and cast *it* from thee: for it is profitable for thee that one of thy members should perish, and not *that* thy whole body should be cast into hell.

30 And if thy right hand offend thee, cut it off, and cast *it* from thee: for it is profitable for thee that one of thy members should perish, and not *that* thy whole body should be cast into hell.

31 It hath been said, [r]Whosoever shall put away his wife, let him give her a writing of divorcement:

32 But I say unto you, That [s]whosoever shall put away his wife, saving for the cause of fornication, causeth her to commit adultery: and whosoever shall marry her that is divorced committeth adultery.

33 ¶ Again, ye have heard that [t]it hath been said by them of old time, [u]Thou shalt not forswear thyself, but [v]shalt perform unto the Lord thine oaths:

34 But I say unto you, [w]Swear not at all; neither by heaven; for it is [x]God's throne:

35 Nor by the earth; for it is his footstool: neither by Jerusalem; for it is [y]the city of the great King.

36 Neither shalt thou swear by thy head, because thou canst not make one hair white or black.

37 [z]But let your communication be, Yea, yea; Nay, nay: for whatsoever is more than these cometh of evil.

38 ¶ Ye have heard that it hath been said, [a]An eye for an eye, and a tooth for a tooth:

39 But I say unto you, [b]That ye resist not evil: [c]but whosoever shall smite thee on thy right cheek, turn to him the other also.

40 And if any man will sue thee at the law, and take away thy coat, let him have *thy* cloke also.

41 And whosoever [d]shall compel thee to go a mile, go with him twain.

42 Give to him that asketh thee, and [e]from him that would borrow of thee turn not thou away.

43 ¶ Ye have heard that it hath been said, [f]Thou shalt love thy neighbour, [g]and hate thine enemy.

44 But I say unto you, [h]Love your enemies, bless them that curse you, do good to them that hate you, and pray [i]for them which despitefully use you, and persecute you;

45 That ye may be the children of your Father which is in heaven: for [j]he maketh his sun to rise on the evil and on the good, and sendeth rain on the just and on the unjust.

46 [k]For if ye love them which love you, what reward have ye? do not even the publicans the same?

47 And if ye salute your brethren only, what do ye more *than others?* do not even the publicans so?

48 [l]Be ye therefore perfect, even [m]as your Father which is in heaven is perfect.

6 Take heed that ye do not your alms before men, to be seen of them: otherwise ye have no reward of your Father which is in heaven.

2 Therefore [n]when thou doest *thine* alms, do not sound a trumpet before thee, as the hypocrites do in the synagogues and in the streets, that they may have glory of men. Verily I say unto you, They have their reward.

3 But when thou doest alms, let not thy left hand know what thy right hand doeth:

4 That thine alms may be in secret: and thy Father which seeth in secret himself [o]shall reward thee openly.

5 ¶ And when thou prayest, thou shalt not be as the hypocrites *are:* for they love to pray standing in the synagogues and in the corners of the streets, that they may be seen of men. Verily I say unto you, They have their reward.

5:18 [d]Luke 16:17
5:19 [e]Jam. 2:10
5:20 [f]Rom. 9:31
5:21 [g]Ex. 20:13; Deut. 5:17
5:22 [h]1 John 3:15 [i]Jam. 2:20
5:23 [j]ch. 8:4
5:24 [k]Job 42:8; ch. 18:19; 1 Tim. 2:8; 1 Pet. 3:7
5:25 [l]Prov. 25:8; Luke 12:58 [m]Ps. 32:6; Isa. 55:6
5:27 [n]Ex. 20:14; Deut. 5:18
5:28 [o]Gen. 34:2; 2 Sam. 11:2; Job 31:1; Prov. 6:25
5:29 [p]ch. 18:8; Mark 9:43-47 [q]ch. 19:12; Rom. 8:13; 1 Cor. 9:27; Col. 3:5
5:31 [r]Deut. 24:1; Jer. 3:1; ch. 19:3; Mark 10:2
5:32 [s]ch. 19:9; Luke 16:18; Rom. 7:3; 1 Cor. 7:10
5:33 [t]ch. 23:16 [u]Ex. 20:7; Lev. 19:12; Num. 30:2; Deut. 5:11 [v]Deut. 23:23
5:34 [w]ch. 23:16; Jam. 5:12 [x]Isa. 66:1
5:35 [y]Ps. 48:2
5:37 [z]Col. 4:6; Jam. 5:12
5:38 [a]Ex. 21:24; Lev. 24:20; Deut. 19:21
5:39 [b]Prov. 20:22; Luke 6:29; Rom. 12:17; 1 Cor. 6:7; 1 Thess. 5:15; 1 Pet. 3:9 [c]Isa. 50:6; Lam. 3:30
5:41 [d]ch. 27:32; Mark 15:21
5:42 [e]Deut. 15:8; Luke 6:30
5:43 [f]Lev. 19:18 [g]Deut. 23:6; Ps. 41:10
5:44 [h]Luke 6:27; Rom. 12:14 [i]Luke 23:34; Acts 7:60; 1 Cor. 4:12; 1 Pet. 2:23
5:45 [j]Job 25:3
5:46 [k]Luke 6:32
5:48 [l]Gen. 17:1; Lev. 11:44; Luke 6:36; Col. 1:28; Jam. 1:4; 1 Pet. 1:15 [m]Eph. 5:1
6:2 [n]Rom. 12:8
6:4 [o]Luke 14:14

6 But thou, when thou prayest, [p]enter into thy closet, and when thou hast shut thy door, pray to thy Father which is in secret; and thy Father which seeth in secret shall reward thee openly.

7 But when ye pray, [q]use not vain repetitions, as the heathen *do:* [r]for they think that they shall be heard for their much speaking.

8 Be not ye therefore like unto them: for your Father knoweth what things ye have need of, before ye ask him.

9 After this manner therefore pray ye: [s]Our Father which art in heaven, Hallowed be thy name.

10 Thy kingdom come. [t]Thy will be done in earth, [u]as *it is* in heaven.

11 Give us this day our [v]daily bread.

12 And [w]forgive us our debts, as we forgive our debtors.

13 [x]And lead us not into temptation, but [y]deliver us from evil: [z]For thine is the kingdom, and the power, and the glory, for ever. Amen.

14 [a]For if ye forgive men their trespasses, your heavenly Father will also forgive you:

15 But [b]if ye forgive not men their trespasses, neither will your Father forgive your trespasses.

16 ¶ Moreover [c]when ye fast, be not, as the hypocrites, of a sad countenance: for they disfigure their faces, that they may appear unto men to fast. Verily I say unto you, They have their reward.

17 But thou, when thou fastest, [d]anoint thine head, and wash thy face;

18 That thou appear not unto men to fast, but unto thy Father which is in secret: and thy Father, which seeth in secret, shall reward thee openly.

19 ¶ [e]Lay not up for yourselves treasures upon earth, where moth and rust doth corrupt, and where thieves break through and steal:

20 [f]But lay up for yourselves treasures in heaven, where neither moth nor rust doth corrupt, and where thieves do not break through nor steal:

21 For where your treasure is, there will your heart be also.

22 [g]The light of the body is the eye: if therefore thine eye be single, thy whole body shall be full of light.

23 But if thine eye be evil, thy whole body shall be full of darkness. If therefore the light that is in thee be darkness, how great *is* that darkness!

24 ¶ [h]No man can serve two masters: for either he will hate the one, and love the other; or else he will hold to the one, and despise the other. [i]Ye cannot serve God and mammon.

25 Therefore I say unto you, [j]Take no thought for your life, what ye shall eat, or what ye shall drink; nor yet for your body, what ye shall put on. Is not the life more than meat, and the body than raiment?

26 [k]Behold the fowls of the air: for they sow not, neither do they reap, nor gather into barns; yet your heavenly Father feedeth them. Are ye not much better than they?

27 Which of you by taking thought can add one cubit unto his stature?

28 And why take ye thought for raiment? Consider the lilies of the field, how they grow; they toil not, neither do they spin:

29 And yet I say unto you, That even Solomon in all his glory was not arrayed like one of these.

30 Wherefore, if God so clothe the grass of the field, which to day is, and to morrow is cast into the oven, *shall he* not much more *clothe* you, O ye of little faith?

31 Therefore take no thought, saying, What shall we eat? or, What shall we drink? or, Wherewithal shall we be clothed?

32 (For after all these things do the Gentiles seek:) for your heavenly Father knoweth that ye have need of all these things.

33 But [l]seek ye first the kingdom of God, and his righteousness; and all these things shall be added unto you.

34 Take therefore no thought for the morrow: for the morrow shall take thought for the things of itself. Sufficient unto the day *is* the evil thereof.

7 Judge [m]not, that ye be not judged.

2 For with what judgment ye judge, ye shall be judged: [n]and with what measure ye mete, it shall be measured to you again.

3 [o]And why beholdest thou the mote that is in thy brother's eye, but considerest not the beam that is in thine own eye?

4 Or how wilt thou say to thy brother, Let me pull out the mote out of thine eye; and, behold, a beam *is* in thine own eye?

5 Thou hypocrite, first cast out the beam out of thine own eye; and then shalt thou see clearly to cast out the mote out of thy brother's eye.

6 ¶ [p]Give not that which is holy unto the dogs, neither cast ye your pearls before swine, lest they trample them under their feet, and turn again and rend you.

7 ¶ [q]Ask, and it shall be given you; seek, and ye shall find; knock, and it shall be opened unto you:

8 For [r]every one that asketh receiveth; and he that seeketh findeth; and to him that knocketh it shall be opened.

9 [s]Or what man is there of you, whom if his son ask bread, will he give him a stone?

10 Or if he ask a fish, will he give him a serpent?

11 If ye then, [t]being evil, know how to give good gifts unto your children, how much more shall your Father which is in heaven give good things to them that ask him?

12 Therefore all things [u]whatsoever ye would that men should do to you, do ye even so to them: for [v]this is the law and the prophets.

13 ¶ [w]Enter ye in at the strait gate: for wide *is* the gate, and broad *is* the way, that

6:6 [p]2 Kings 4:33
6:7 [q]Eccl. 5:2 [r]1 Kings 18:26
6:9 [s]Luke 11:2
6:10 [t]ch. 26:39; Acts 21:14 [u]Ps. 103:20
6:11 [v]Job 23:12; Prov. 30:8
6:12 [w]ch. 18:21
6:13 [x]ch. 26:41; Luke 22:40; 1 Cor. 10:13; 2 Pet. 2:9; Rev. 3:10 [y]John 17:15 [z]1 Chron. 29:11
6:14 [a]Mark 11:25; Eph. 4:32; Col. 3:13
6:15 [b]ch. 18:35; Jam. 2:13
6:16 [c]Isa. 58:5
6:17 [d]Ruth 3:3; Dan. 10:3
6:19 [e]Prov. 23:4; 1 Tim. 6:17; Heb. 13:5; Jam. 5:1
6:20 [f]ch. 19:21; Luke 12:33; 1 Tim. 6:19; 1 Pet. 1:4
6:22 [g]Luke 11:34
6:24 [h]Luke 16:13 [i]Gal. 1:10; 1 Tim. 6:17; Jam. 4:4; 1 John 2:15
6:25 [j]Ps. 55:22; Luke 12:22; Phil. 4:6; 1 Pet. 5:7
6:26 [k]Job 38:41; Ps. 147:9; Luke 12:24
6:33 [l]1 Kings 3:13; Ps. 37:25; Mark 10:30; Luke 12:31; 1 Tim. 4:8
7:1 [m]Luke 6:37; Rom. 2:1; 1 Cor. 4:3; Jam. 4:11
7:2 [n]Mark 4:24; Luke 6:38
7:3 [o]Luke 6:41
7:6 [p]Prov. 9:7; Acts 13:45
7:7 [q]ch. 21:22; Mark 11:24; Luke 11:9; John 14:13; Jam. 1:5; 1 John 3:22
7:8 [r]Prov. 8:17; Jer. 29:12
7:9 [s]Luke 11:11
7:11 [t]Gen. 6:5
7:12 [u]Luke 6:31 [v]Lev. 19:18; ch. 22:40; Rom. 13:8; Gal. 5:14; 1 Tim. 1:5
7:13 [w]Luke 13:24

leadeth to destruction, and many there be which go in thereat:

14 Because strait *is* the gate, and narrow *is* the way, which leadeth unto life, and few there be that find it.

15 ¶ [x]Beware of false prophets, [y]which come to you in sheep's clothing, but inwardly they are [z]ravening wolves.

16 [a]Ye shall know them by their fruits. [b]Do men gather grapes of thorns, or figs of thistles?

17 Even so [c]every good tree bringeth forth good fruit; but a corrupt tree bringeth forth evil fruit.

18 A good tree cannot bring forth evil fruit, neither *can* a corrupt tree bring forth good fruit.

19 [d]Every tree that bringeth not forth good fruit is hewn down, and cast into the fire.

20 Wherefore by their fruits ye shall know them.

21 ¶ Not every one that saith unto me, [e]Lord, Lord, shall enter into the kingdom of heaven; but he that doeth the will of my Father which is in heaven.

22 Many will say to me in that day, Lord, Lord, have we [f]not prophesied in thy name? and in thy name have cast out devils? and in thy name done many wonderful works?

23 And [g]then will I profess unto them, I never knew you: [h]depart from me, ye that work iniquity.

24 ¶ Therefore [i]whosoever heareth these sayings of mine, and doeth them, I will liken him unto a wise man, which built his house upon a rock:

25 And the rain descended, and the floods came, and the winds blew, and beat upon that house; and it fell not: for it was founded upon a rock.

26 And every one that heareth these sayings of mine, and doeth them not, shall be likened unto a foolish man, which built his house upon the sand:

27 And the rain descended, and the floods came, and the winds blew, and beat upon that house; and it fell: and great was the fall of it.

28 And it came to pass, when Jesus had ended these sayings, [j]the people were astonished at his doctrine:

29 [k]For he taught them as *one* having authority, and not as the scribes.

8 When he was come down from the mountain, great multitudes followed him.

2 [l]And, behold, there came a leper and worshipped him, saying, Lord, if thou wilt, thou canst make me clean.

3 And Jesus put forth *his* hand, and touched him, saying, I will; be thou clean. And immediately his leprosy was cleansed.

4 And Jesus saith unto him, [m]See thou tell no man; but go thy way, shew thyself to the priest, and offer the gift that [n]Moses commanded, for a testimony unto them.

5 ¶ [o]And when Jesus was entered into Capernaum, there came unto him a centurion, beseeching him,

6 And saying, Lord, my servant lieth at home sick of the palsy, grievously tormented.

7 And Jesus saith unto him, I will come and heal him.

8 The centurion answered and said, Lord, [p]I am not worthy that thou shouldest come under my roof: but [q]speak the word only, and my servant shall be healed.

9 For I am a man under authority, having soldiers under me: and I say to this *man*, Go, and he goeth; and to another, Come, and he cometh; and to my servant, Do this, and he doeth *it*.

10 When Jesus heard *it*, he marvelled, and said to them that followed, Verily I say unto you, I have not found so great faith, no, not in Israel.

11 And I say unto you, That [r]many shall come from the east and west, and shall sit down with Abraham, and Isaac, and Jacob, in the kingdom of heaven.

12 But [s]the children of the kingdom [t]shall be cast out into outer darkness: there shall be weeping and gnashing of teeth.

13 And Jesus said unto the centurion, Go thy way; and as thou hast believed, *so* be it done unto thee. And his servant was healed in the selfsame hour.

14 ¶ [u]And when Jesus was come into Peter's house, he saw [v]his wife's mother laid, and sick of a fever.

15 And he touched her hand, and the fever left her: and she arose, and ministered unto them.

16 ¶ [w]When the even was come, they brought unto him many that were possessed with devils: and he cast out the spirits with *his* word, and healed all that were sick:

17 That it might be fulfilled which was spoken by Esaias the prophet, saying, [x]Himself took our infirmities, and bare *our* sicknesses.

18 ¶ Now when Jesus saw great multitudes about him, he gave commandment to depart unto the other side.

19 [y]And a certain scribe came, and said unto him, Master, I will follow thee whithersoever thou goest.

20 And Jesus saith unto him, The foxes have holes, and the birds of the air *have* nests; but the Son of man hath not where to lay *his* head.

21 [z]And another of his disciples said unto him, Lord, [a]suffer me first to go and bury my father.

22 But Jesus said unto him, Follow me; and let the dead bury their dead.

23 ¶ And when he was entered into a ship, his disciples followed him.

24 [b]And, behold, there arose a great tempest in the sea, insomuch that the ship was covered with the waves: but he was asleep.

25 And his disciples came to *him*, and

7:15 [x]Deut. 13:3; Jer. 23:16; ch. 24:4; Mark 13:22; Rom. 16:17; Eph. 5:6; Col. 2:8; 2 Pet. 2:1; 1 John 4:1 [y]Mic. 3:5; 2 Tim. 3:5 [z]Acts 20:29
7:16 [a]ver. 20; ch. 12:33 [b]Luke 6:43
7:17 [c]Jer. 11:19; ch. 12:33
7:19 [d]ch. 3:10; Luke 3:9; John 15:2
7:21 [e]Hos. 8:2; ch. 25:11; Luke 6:46; Acts 19:13; Rom. 2:13; Jam. 1:22
7:22 [f]Num. 24:4; John 11:51; 1 Cor. 13:2
7:23 [g]ch. 25:12; Luke 13:25; 2 Tim. 2:19 [h]Ps. 5:5; ch. 25:41
7:24 [i]Luke 6:47
7:28 [j]ch. 13:54; Mark 1:22; Luke 4:32
7:29 [k]John 7:46
8:2 [l]Mark 1:40; Luke 5:12
8:4 [m]ch. 9:30; Mark 5:43 [n]Lev. 14:3; Luke 5:14
8:5 [o]Luke 7:1
8:8 [p]Luke 15:19 [q]Ps. 107:20
8:11 [r]Gen. 12:3; Isa. 2:2; Mal. 1:11; Luke 13:29; Acts 10:45; Rom. 15:9; Eph. 3:6
8:12 [s]ch. 21:43 [t]ch. 13:42; Luke 13:28; 2 Pet. 2:17; Jude 13
8:14 [u]Mark 1:29; Luke 4:38 [v]1 Cor. 9:5
8:16 [w]Mark 1:32; Luke 4:40
8:17 [x]Isa. 53:4; 1 Pet. 2:24
8:19 [y]Luke 9:57
8:21 [z]Luke 9:59 [a]1 Kings 19:20
8:24 [b]Mark 4:37; Luke 8:23

awoke him, saying, Lord, save us: we perish.
26 And he saith unto them, Why are ye
fearful, O ye of little faith? Then [c]he arose,
and rebuked the winds and the sea; and
there was a great calm.
27 But the men marvelled, saying, What
manner of man is this, that even the winds
and the sea obey him!
28 ¶ [d]And when he was come to the other
side into the country of the Gergesenes,
there met him two possessed with devils,
coming out of the tombs, exceeding fierce,
so that no man might pass by that way.
29 And, behold, they cried out, saying,
What have we to do with thee, Jesus, thou
Son of God? art thou come hither to torment
us before the time?
30 And there was a good way off from
them an herd of many swine feeding.
31 So the devils besought him, saying, If
thou cast us out, suffer us to go away into
the herd of swine.
32 And he said unto them, Go. And when
they were come out, they went into the herd
of swine: and, behold, the whole herd of
swine ran violently down a steep place into
the sea, and perished in the waters.
33 And they that kept them fled, and went
their ways into the city, and told every
thing, and what was befallen to the possessed of the devils.
34 And, behold, the whole city came out
to meet Jesus: and when they saw him,
[e]they besought *him* that he would depart
out of their coasts.

9 And he entered into a ship, and passed
over, [f]and came into his own city.
2 [g]And, behold, they brought to him a
man sick of the palsy, lying on a bed: [h]and
Jesus seeing their faith said unto the sick of
the palsy; Son, be of good cheer; thy sins be
forgiven thee.
3 And, behold, certain of the scribes said
within themselves, This *man* blasphemeth.
4 And Jesus [i]knowing their thoughts
said, Wherefore think ye evil in your
hearts?
5 For whether is easier, to say, *Thy* sins be
forgiven thee; or to say, Arise, and walk?
6 But that ye may know that the Son of
man hath power on earth to forgive sins,
(then saith he to the sick of the palsy,) Arise,
take up thy bed, and go unto thine house.
7 And he arose, and departed to his
house.
8 But when the multitudes saw *it*, they
marvelled, and glorified God, which had
given such power unto men.
9 ¶ [j]And as Jesus passed forth from
thence, he saw a man, named Matthew, sitting at the receipt of custom: and he saith
unto him, Follow me. And he arose, and followed him.
10 ¶ [k]And it came to pass, as Jesus sat at
meat in the house, behold, many publicans
and sinners came and sat down with him
and his disciples.

8:26 *c*Ps. 65:7
8:28 *d*Mark 5:1; Luke 8:26
8:34 *e*Deut. 5:25; 1 Kings 17:18; Luke 5:8; Acts 16:39
9:1 *f*ch. 4:13
9:2 *g*Mark 2:3; Luke 5:18 *h*ch. 8:10
9:4 *i*Ps. 139:2; ch. 12:25; Mark 12:15; Luke 5:22
9:9 *j*Mark 2:14; Luke 5:27
9:10 *k*Mark 2:15; Luke 5:29
9:11 *l*ch. 11:19; Luke 5:30 *m*Gal. 2:15
9:13 *n*Hos. 6:6; Mic. 6:6; ch. 12:7 *o*1 Tim. 1:15
9:14 *p*Mark 2:18; Luke 5:33
9:15 *q*John 3:29 *r*Acts 13:2; 1 Cor. 7:5
9:18 *s*Mark 5:22; Luke 8:41
9:20 *t*Mark 5:25; Luke 8:43
9:22 *u*Luke 7:50
9:23 *v*Mark 5:38; Luke 8:51 *w*2 Chron. 35:25
9:24 *x*Acts 20:10
9:27 *y*ch. 15:22; Mark 10:47; Luke 18:38

11 And when the Pharisees saw *it*, they
said unto his disciples, Why eateth your
Master with [l]publicans and [m]sinners?
12 But when Jesus heard *that*, he said
unto them, They that be whole need not a
physician, but they that are sick.
13 But go ye and learn what *that* meaneth, [n]I will have mercy, and not sacrifice:
for I am not come to call the righteous, [o]but
sinners to repentance.
14 ¶ Then came to him the disciples of
John, saying, [p]Why do we and the Pharisees fast oft, but thy disciples fast not?
15 And Jesus said unto them, Can [q]the
children of the bridechamber mourn, as
long as the bridegroom is with them? but
the days will come, when the bridegroom
shall be taken from them, and [r]then shall
they fast.
16 No man putteth a piece of new cloth
unto an old garment, for that which is put in
to fill it up taketh from the garment, and the
rent is made worse.
17 Neither do men put new wine into old
bottles: else the bottles break, and the wine
runneth out, and the bottles perish: but they
put new wine into new bottles, and both are
preserved.
18 ¶ [s]While he spake these things unto
them, behold, there came a certain ruler,
and worshipped him, saying, My daughter
is even now dead: but come and lay thy
hand upon her, and she shall live.
19 And Jesus arose, and followed him,
and *so did* his disciples.
20 ¶ [t]And, behold, a woman, which was
diseased with an issue of blood twelve
years, came behind *him*, and touched the
hem of his garment:
21 For she said within herself, If I may but
touch his garment, I shall be whole.
22 But Jesus turned him about, and when
he saw her, he said, Daughter, be of good
comfort; [u]thy faith hath made thee whole.
And the woman was made whole from that
hour.
23 [v]And when Jesus came into the ruler's
house, and saw [w]the minstrels and the people making a noise,
24 He said unto them, [x]Give place: for the
maid is not dead, but sleepeth. And they
laughed him to scorn.
25 But when the people were put forth, he
went in, and took her by the hand, and the
maid arose.
26 And the fame hereof went abroad into
all that land.
27 ¶ And when Jesus departed thence,
two blind men followed him, crying, and
saying, [y]*Thou* Son of David, have mercy
on us.
28 And when he was come into the house,
the blind men came to him: and Jesus saith
unto them, Believe ye that I am able to do
this? They said unto him, Yea, Lord.
29 Then touched he their eyes, saying,
According to your faith be it unto you.
30 And their eyes were opened; and Jesus

straitly charged them, saying, [z]See *that* no man know *it*.

31 [a]But they, when they were departed, spread abroad his fame in all that country.

32 ¶ [b]As they went out, behold, they brought to him a dumb man possessed with a devil.

33 And when the devil was cast out, the dumb spake: and the multitudes marvelled, saying, It was never so seen in Israel.

34 But the Pharisees said, [c]He casteth out devils through the prince of the devils.

35 [d]And Jesus went about all the cities and villages, [e]teaching in their synagogues, and preaching the gospel of the kingdom, and healing every sickness and every disease among the people.

36 ¶ [f]But when he saw the multitudes, he was moved with compassion on them, because they fainted, and were scattered abroad, [g]as sheep having no shepherd.

37 Then saith he unto his disciples, [h]The harvest truly *is* plenteous, but the labourers *are* few;

38 [i]Pray ye therefore the Lord of the harvest, that he will send forth labourers into his harvest.

10 And [j]when he had called unto *him* his twelve disciples, he gave them power *against* unclean spirits, to cast them out, and to heal all manner of sickness and all manner of disease.

2 Now the names of the twelve apostles are these; The first, Simon, [k]who is called Peter, and Andrew his brother; James *the son* of Zebedee, and John his brother;

3 Philip, and Bartholomew; Thomas, and Matthew the publican; James *the son* of Alphaeus, and Lebbaeus, whose surname was Thaddaeus;

4 [l]Simon the Canaanite, and Judas [m]Iscariot, who also betrayed him.

5 These twelve Jesus sent forth, and commanded them, saying, [n]Go not into the way of the Gentiles, and into *any* city of [o]the Samaritans enter ye not:

6 [p]But go rather to the [q]lost sheep of the house of Israel.

7 [r]And as ye go, preach, saying, [s]The kingdom of heaven is at hand.

8 Heal the sick, cleanse the lepers, raise the dead, cast out devils: [t]freely ye have received, freely give.

9 [u]Provide neither gold, nor silver, nor [v]brass in your purses,

10 Nor scrip for *your* journey, neither two coats, neither shoes, nor yet staves: [w]for the workman is worthy of his meat.

11 [x]And into whatsoever city or town ye shall enter, enquire who in it is worthy; and there abide till ye go thence.

12 And when ye come into an house, salute it.

13 [y]And if the house be worthy, let your peace come upon it: [z]but if it be not worthy, let your peace return to you.

14 [a]And whosoever shall not receive you, nor hear your words, when ye depart out of that house or city, [b]shake off the dust of your feet.

15 Verily I say unto you, [c]It shall be more tolerable for the land of Sodom and Gomorrha in the day of judgment, than for that city.

16 ¶ [d]Behold, I send you forth as sheep in the midst of wolves: [e]be ye therefore wise as serpents, and [f]harmless as doves.

17 But beware of men: for [g]they will deliver you up to the councils, and [h]they will scourge you in their synagogues;

18 And [i]ye shall be brought before governors and kings for my sake, for a testimony against them and the Gentiles.

19 [j]But when they deliver you up, take no thought how or what ye shall speak: for [k]it shall be given you in that same hour what ye shall speak.

20 [l]For it is not ye that speak, but the Spirit of your Father which speaketh in you.

21 [m]And the brother shall deliver up the brother to death, and the father the child: and the children shall rise up against *their* parents, and cause them to be put to death.

22 And [n]ye shall be hated of all *men* for my name's sake: [o]but he that endureth to the end shall be saved.

23 But [p]when they persecute you in this city, flee ye into another: for verily I say unto you, Ye shall not have gone over the cities of Israel, [q]till the Son of man be come.

24 [r]The disciple is not above *his* master, nor the servant above his lord.

25 It is enough for the disciple that he be as his master, and the servant as his lord. If [s]they have called the master of the house Beelzebub, how much more *shall they call* them of his household?

26 Fear them not therefore: [t]for there is nothing covered, that shall not be revealed; and hid, that shall not be known.

27 What I tell you in darkness, *that* speak ye in light: and what ye hear in the ear, *that* preach ye upon the housetops.

28 [u]And fear not them which kill the body, but are not able to kill the soul: but rather fear him which is able to destroy both soul and body in hell.

29 Are not two sparrows sold for a farthing? and one of them shall not fall on the ground without your Father.

30 [v]But the very hairs of your head are all numbered.

31 Fear ye not therefore, ye are of more value than many sparrows.

32 [w]Whosoever therefore shall confess me before men, [x]him will I confess also before my Father which is in heaven.

33 [y]But whosoever shall deny me before men, him will I also deny before my Father which is in heaven.

34 [z]Think not that I am come to send peace on earth: I came not to send peace, but a sword.

9:30 [z]ch. 8:4; Luke 5:14
9:31 [a]Mark 7:36
9:32 [b]ch. 12:22; Luke 11:14
9:34 [c]ch. 12:24; Mark 3:22; Luke 11:15
9:35 [d]Mark 6:6; Luke 13:22 [e]ch. 4:23
9:36 [f]Mark 6:34 [g]Num. 27:17; 1 Kings 22:17; Ezek. 34:5; Zech. 10:2
9:37 [h]Luke 10:2; John 4:35
9:38 [i]2 Thess. 3:1
10:1 [j]Mark 3:13; Luke 6:13
10:2 [k]John 1:42
10:4 [l]Luke 6:15; Acts 1:13 [m]John 13:26
10:5 [n]ch. 4:15 [o]2 Kings 17:24; John 4:9
10:6 [p]ch. 15:24; Acts 13:46 [q]Isa. 53:6; Jer. 50:6; Ezek. 34:5; 1 Pet. 2:25
10:7 [r]Luke 9:2 [s]ch. 3:2; Luke 10:9
10:8 [t]Acts 8:18
10:9 [u]1 Sam. 9:7; Mark 6:8; Luke 9:3 [v]Mark 6:8
10:10 [w]Luke 10:7; 1 Cor. 9:7; 1 Tim. 5:18
10:11 [x]Luke 10:8
10:13 [y]Luke 10:5 [z]Ps. 35:13
10:14 [a]Mark 6:11; Luke 9:5 [b]Neh. 5:13; Acts 13:51
10:15 [c]ch. 11:22
10:16 [d]Luke 10:3 [e]Rom. 16:19; Eph. 5:15 [f]1 Cor. 14:20; Phil. 2:15
10:17 [g]ch. 24:9; Mark 13:9; Luke 12:11 [h]Acts 5:40
10:18 [i]Acts 12:1; 2 Tim. 4:16
10:19 [j]Mark 13:11; Luke 12:11 [k]Ex. 4:12; Jer. 1:7
10:20 [l]2 Sam. 23:2; Acts 4:8; 2 Tim. 4:17
10:21 [m]Mic. 7:6; ver. 35; Luke 21:16
10:22 [n]Luke 21:17 [o]Dan. 12:12; ch. 24:13; Mark 13:13
10:23 [p]ch. 2:13; Acts 8:1 [q]ch. 16:28
10:24 [r]Luke 6:40; John 13:16
10:25 [s]ch. 12:24; Mark 3:22; Luke 11:15; John 8:48
10:26 [t]Mark 4:22; Luke 8:17
10:28 [u]Isa. 8:12; Luke 12:4; 1 Pet. 3:14
10:30 [v]1 Sam. 14:45; 2 Sam. 14:11; Luke 21:18; Acts 27:34
10:32 [w]Luke 12:8; Rom. 10:9 [x]Rev. 3:5
10:33 [y]Mark 8:38; Luke 9:26; 2 Tim. 2:12
10:34 [z]Luke 12:49

35 For I am come to set a man at variance [a]against his father, and the daughter against her mother, and the daughter in law against her mother in law.

36 [b]And a man's foes *shall be* they of his own household.

37 [c]He that loveth father or mother more than me is not worthy of me: and he that loveth son or daughter more than me is not worthy of me.

38 [d]And he that taketh not his cross, and followeth after me, is not worthy of me.

39 [e]He that findeth his life shall lose it: and he that loseth his life for my sake shall find it.

40 ¶ [f]He that receiveth you receiveth me, and he that receiveth me receiveth him that sent me.

41 [g]He that receiveth a prophet in the name of a prophet shall receive a prophet's reward; and he that receiveth a righteous man in the name of a righteous man shall receive a righteous man's reward.

42 [h]And whosoever shall give to drink unto one of these little ones a cup of cold *water* only in the name of a disciple, verily I say unto you, he shall in no wise lose his reward.

11 And it came to pass, when Jesus had made an end of commanding his twelve disciples, he departed thence to teach and to preach in their cities.

2 [i]Now when John had heard [j]in the prison the works of Christ, he sent two of his disciples,

3 And said unto him, Art thou [k]he that should come, or do we look for another?

4 Jesus answered and said unto them, Go and shew John again those things which ye do hear and see:

5 [l]The blind receive their sight, and the lame walk, the lepers are cleansed, and the deaf hear, the dead are raised up, and [m]the poor have the gospel preached to them.

6 And blessed is *he,* whosoever shall not [n]be offended in me.

7 ¶ [o]And as they departed, Jesus began to say unto the multitudes concerning John, What went ye out into the wilderness to see? [p]A reed shaken with the wind?

8 But what went ye out for to see? A man clothed in soft raiment? behold, they that wear soft *clothing* are in kings' houses.

9 But what went ye out for to see? A prophet? yea, I say unto you, [q]and more than a prophet.

10 For this is *he,* of whom it is written, [r]Behold, I send my messenger before thy face, which shall prepare thy way before thee.

11 Verily I say unto you, Among them that are born of women there hath not risen a greater than John the Baptist: notwithstanding he that is least in the kingdom of heaven is greater than he.

12 [s]And from the days of John the Baptist until now the kingdom of heaven suffereth violence, and the violent take it by force.

10:35 [a]Mic. 7:6
10:36 [b]Ps. 41:9; Mic. 7:6; John 13:18
10:37 [c]Luke 14:26
10:38 [d]ch. 16:24; Mark 8:34; Luke 9:23
10:39 [e]ch. 16:25; Luke 17:33; John 12:25
10:40 [f]ch. 18:5; Luke 9:48; John 12:44; Gal. 4:14
10:41 [g]1 Kings 17:10; 2 Kings 4:8
10:42 [h]ch. 8:5; Mark 9:41; Heb. 6:10
11:2 [i]Luke 7:18 [j]ch. 14:3
11:3 [k]Gen. 49:10; Num. 24:17; Dan. 9:24; John 6:14
11:5 [l]Isa. 29:18; John 2:23 [m]Ps. 22:26; Isa. 61:1; Luke 4:18; Jam. 2:5
11:6 [n]Isa. 8:14; ch. 13:57; Rom. 9:32; 1 Cor. 1:23; Gal. 5:11; 1 Pet. 2:8
11:7 [o]Luke 7:24 [p]Eph. 4:14
11:9 [q]ch. 14:5; Luke 1:76
11:10 [r]Mal. 3:1; Mark 1:2; Luke 1:76
11:12 [s]Luke 16:16
11:13 [t]Mal. 4:6
11:14 [u]Mal. 4:5; ch. 17:12; Luke 1:17
11:15 [v]ch. 13:9; Luke 8:8; Rev. 2:7
11:16 [w]Luke 7:31
11:19 [x]ch. 9:10 [y]Luke 7:35
11:20 [z]Luke 10:13
11:21 [a]Jonah 3:7
11:22 [b]ch. 10:15; ver. 24
11:23 [c]Isa. 14:13; Lam. 2:1
11:24 [d]ch. 10:15
11:25 [e]Luke 10:21 [f]Ps. 8:2; 1 Cor. 1:19; 2 Cor. 3:14 [g]ch. 16:17
11:27 [h]ch. 28:18; Luke 10:22; John 3:35; 1 Cor. 15:27 [i]John 1:18
11:29 [j]John 13:15; Phil. 2:5; 1 Pet. 2:21; 1 John 2:6 [k]Zech. 9:9; Phil. 2:7 [l]Jer. 6:16
11:30 [m]1 John 5:3
12:1 [n]Deut. 23:25; Mark 2:23; Luke 6:1
12:3 [o]1 Sam. 21:6

13 [t]For all the prophets and the law prophesied until John.

14 And if ye will receive *it,* this is [u]Elias, which was for to come.

15 [v]He that hath ears to hear, let him hear.

16 ¶ [w]But whereunto shall I liken this generation? It is like unto children sitting in the markets, and calling unto their fellows,

17 And saying, We have piped unto you, and ye have not danced; we have mourned unto you, and ye have not lamented.

18 For John came neither eating nor drinking, and they say, He hath a devil.

19 The Son of man came eating and drinking, and they say, Behold a man gluttonous, and a winebibber, [x]a friend of publicans and sinners. [y]But wisdom is justified of her children.

20 ¶ [z]Then began he to upbraid the cities wherein most of his mighty works were done, because they repented not:

21 Woe unto thee, Chorazin! woe unto thee, Bethsaida! for if the mighty works, which were done in you, had been done in Tyre and Sidon, they would have repented long ago [a]in sackcloth and ashes.

22 But I say unto you, [b]It shall be more tolerable for Tyre and Sidon at the day of judgment, than for you.

23 And thou, Capernaum, [c]which art exalted unto heaven, shalt be brought down to hell: for if the mighty works, which have been done in thee, had been done in Sodom, it would have remained until this day.

24 But I say unto you, [d]That it shall be more tolerable for the land of Sodom in the day of judgment, than for thee.

25 ¶ [e]At that time Jesus answered and said, I thank thee, O Father, Lord of heaven and earth, because [f]thou hast hid these things from the wise and prudent, [g]and hast revealed them unto babes.

26 Even so, Father: for so it seemed good in thy sight.

27 [h]All things are delivered unto me of my Father: and no man knoweth the Son, but the Father; [i]neither knoweth any man the Father, save the Son, and *he* to whomsoever the Son will reveal *him.*

28 ¶ Come unto me, all *ye* that labour and are heavy laden, and I will give you rest.

29 Take my yoke upon you, [j]and learn of me; for I am meek and [k]lowly in heart: [l]and ye shall find rest unto your souls.

30 [m]For my yoke *is* easy, and my burden is light.

12 At that time [n]Jesus went on the sabbath day through the corn; and his disciples were an hungred, and began to pluck the ears of corn, and to eat.

2 But when the Pharisees saw *it,* they said unto him, Behold, thy disciples do that which is not lawful to do upon the sabbath day.

3 But he said unto them, Have ye not read [o]what David did, when he was an hungred, and they that were with him;

4 How he entered into the house of God,
and did eat [p]the shewbread, which was not
lawful for him to eat, neither for them which
were with him, [q]but only for the priests?
5 Or have ye not read in the [r]law, how
that on the sabbath days the priests in the
temple profane the sabbath, and are blameless?
6 But I say unto you, That in this place is
[s]*one* greater than the temple.
7 But if ye had known what *this* meaneth,
[t]I will have mercy, and not sacrifice, ye
would not have condemned the guiltless.
8 For the Son of man is Lord even of the
sabbath day.
9 [u]And when he was departed thence, he
went into their synagogue:
10 ¶ And, behold, there was a man which
had *his* hand withered. And they asked him,
saying, [v]Is it lawful to heal on the sabbath
days? that they might accuse him.
11 And he said unto them, What man
shall there be among you, that shall have
one sheep, and [w]if it fall into a pit on the
sabbath day, will he not lay hold on it, and
lift *it* out?
12 How much then is a man better than a
sheep? Wherefore it is lawful to do well on
the sabbath days.
13 Then saith he to the man, Stretch forth
thine hand. And he stretched *it* forth; and it
was restored whole, like as the other.
14 ¶ Then [x]the Pharisees went out, and
held a council against him, how they might
destroy him.
15 But when Jesus knew *it*, [y]he withdrew
himself from thence: [z]and great multitudes
followed him, and he healed them all;
16 And [a]charged them that they should
not make him known:
17 That it might be fulfilled which was
spoken by Esaias the prophet, saying,
18 [b]Behold my servant, whom I have
chosen; my beloved, [c]in whom my soul is
well pleased: I will put my spirit upon him,
and he shall shew judgment to the Gentiles.
19 He shall not strive, nor cry; neither
shall any man hear his voice in the streets.
20 A bruised reed shall he not break, and
smoking flax shall he not quench, till he
send forth judgment unto victory.
21 And in his name shall the Gentiles
trust.
22 ¶ [d]Then was brought unto him one
possessed with a devil, blind, and dumb:
and he healed him, insomuch that the blind
and dumb both spake and saw.
23 And all the people were amazed, and
said, Is not this the son of David?
24 [e]But when the Pharisees heard *it*, they
said, This *fellow* doth not cast out devils, but
by Beelzebub the prince of the devils.
25 And Jesus [f]knew their thoughts, and
said unto them, Every kingdom divided
against itself is brought to desolation; and
every city or house divided against itself
shall not stand:
26 And if Satan cast out Satan, he is divided against himself; how shall then his
kingdom stand?
27 And if I by Beelzebub cast out devils,
by whom do your children cast *them* out?
therefore they shall be your judges.
28 But if I cast out devils by the Spirit of
God, then [g]the kingdom of God is come
unto you.
29 [h]Or else how can one enter into a
strong man's house, and spoil his goods, except he first bind the strong man? and then
he will spoil his house.
30 He that is not with me is against me;
and he that gathereth not with me scattereth abroad.
31 ¶ Wherefore I say unto you, [i]All manner of sin and blasphemy shall be forgiven
unto men: [j]but the blasphemy *against* the
Holy Ghost shall not be forgiven unto men.
32 And whosoever [k]speaketh a word
against the Son of man, [l]it shall be forgiven
him: but whosoever speaketh against the
Holy Ghost, it shall not be forgiven him,
neither in this world, neither in the *world* to
come.
33 Either make the tree good, and [m]his
fruit good; or else make the tree corrupt,
and his fruit corrupt: for the tree is known
by *his* fruit.
34 O [n]generation of vipers, how can ye,
being evil, speak good things? [o]for out of
the abundance of the heart the mouth
speaketh.
35 A good man out of the good treasure of
the heart bringeth forth good things: and an
evil man out of the evil treasure bringeth
forth evil things.
36 But I say unto you, That every idle
word that men shall speak, they shall give
account thereof in the day of judgment.
37 For by thy words thou shalt be justified, and by thy words thou shalt be condemned.
38 ¶ [p]Then certain of the scribes and of
the Pharisees answered, saying, Master, we
would see a sign from thee.
39 But he answered and said unto them,
An evil and [q]adulterous generation seeketh
after a sign; and there shall no sign be given
to it, but the sign of the prophet Jonas:
40 [r]For as Jonas was three days and
three nights in the whale's belly; so shall the
Son of man be three days and three nights
in the heart of the earth.
41 [s]The men of Nineveh shall rise in
judgment with this generation, and [t]shall
condemn it: [u]because they repented at the
preaching of Jonas; and, behold, a greater
than Jonas *is* here.
42 [v]The queen of the south shall rise up
in the judgment with this generation, and
shall condemn it: for she came from the uttermost parts of the earth to hear the wisdom of Solomon; and, behold, a greater
than Solomon *is* here.
43 [w]When the unclean spirit is gone out
of a man, [x]he walketh through dry places,
seeking rest, and findeth none.

12:4 [p]Ex. 25:30; Lev. 24:5 [q]Ex. 29:32; Lev. 8:31
12:5 [r]Num. 28:9; John 7:22
12:6 [s]2 Chron. 6:18; Mal. 3:1
12:7 [t]Hos. 6:6; Mic. 6:6; ch. 9:13
12:9 [u]Mark 3:1; Luke 6:6
12:10 [v]Luke 13:14; John 9:16
12:11 [w]Ex. 23:4; Deut. 22:4
12:14 [x]ch. 27:1; Mark 3:6; Luke 6:11; John 5:18
12:15 [y]ch. 10:23; Mark 3:7 [z]ch. 19:2
12:16 [a]ch. 9:30
12:18 [b]Isa. 42:1 [c]ch. 3:17
12:22 [d]ch. 9:32; Mark 3:11; Luke 11:14
12:24 [e]ch. 9:34; Mark 3:22; Luke 11:15
12:25 [f]ch. 9:4; John 2:25; Rev. 2:23
12:28 [g]Dan. 2:44; Luke 1:33
12:29 [h]Isa. 49:24; Luke 11:21
12:31 [i]Mark 3:28; Luke 12:10; Heb. 6:4; 1 John 5:16 [j]Acts 7:51
12:32 [k]ch. 11:19; John 7:12 [l]1 Tim. 1:13
12:33 [m]ch. 7:17; Luke 6:43
12:34 [n]ch. 3:7 [o]Luke 6:45
12:38 [p]ch. 16:1; Mark 8:11; Luke 11:16; John 2:18; 1 Cor. 1:22
12:39 [q]Isa. 57:3; ch. 16:4; Mark 8:38; John 4:48
12:40 [r]Jonah 1:17
12:41 [s]Luke 11:32 [t]Jer. 3:11; Ezek. 16:51; Rom. 2:27 [u]Jonah 3:5
12:42 [v]1 Kings 10:1; 2 Chron. 9:1; Luke 11:31
12:43 [w]Luke 11:24 [x]Job 1:7; 1 Pet. 5:8

44 Then he saith, I will return into my house from whence I came out; and when he is come, he findeth *it* empty, swept, and garnished.

45 Then goeth he, and taketh with himself seven other spirits more wicked than himself, and they enter in and dwell there: [y]and the last *state* of that man is worse than the first. Even so shall it be also unto this wicked generation.

46 ¶ While he yet talked to the people, [z]behold, *his* mother and [a]his brethren stood without, desiring to speak with him.

47 Then one said unto him, Behold, thy mother and thy brethren stand without, desiring to speak with thee.

48 But he answered and said unto him that told him, Who is my mother? and who are my brethren?

49 And he stretched forth his hand toward his disciples, and said, Behold my mother and my brethren!

50 For [b]whosoever shall do the will of my Father which is in heaven, the same is my brother, and sister, and mother.

13 The same day went Jesus out of the house, [c]and sat by the sea side.

2 [d]And great multitudes were gathered together unto him, so that [e]he went into a ship, and sat; and the whole multitude stood on the shore.

3 And he spake many things unto them in parables, saying, [f]Behold, a sower went forth to sow;

4 And when he sowed, some *seeds* fell by the way side, and the fowls came and devoured them up:

5 Some fell upon stony places, where they had not much earth: and forthwith they sprung up, because they had no deepness of earth:

6 And when the sun was up, they were scorched; and because they had no root, they withered away.

7 And some fell among thorns; and the thorns sprung up, and choked them:

8 But other fell into good ground, and brought forth fruit, some [g]an hundredfold, some sixtyfold, some thirtyfold.

9 [h]Who hath ears to hear, let him hear.

10 And the disciples came, and said unto him, Why speakest thou unto them in parables?

11 He answered and said unto them, Because [i]it is given unto you to know the mysteries of the kingdom of heaven, but to them it is not given.

12 [j]For whosoever hath, to him shall be given, and he shall have more abundance: but whosoever hath not, from him shall be taken away even that he hath.

13 Therefore speak I to them in parables: because they seeing see not; and hearing they hear not, neither do they understand.

14 And in them is fulfilled the prophecy of Esaias, which saith, [k]By hearing ye shall hear, and shall not understand; and seeing ye shall see, and shall not perceive:

12:45 [y]Heb. 6:4; 2 Pet. 2:20
12:46 [z]Mark 3:31; Luke 8:19 [a]ch. 13:55; Mark 6:3; John 2:12; Acts 1:14; 1 Cor. 9:5; Gal. 1:19
12:50 [b]John 15:14; Gal. 5:6; Col. 3:11; Heb. 2:11
13:1 [c]Mark 4:1
13:2 [d]Luke 8:4 [e]Luke 5:3
13:3 [f]Luke 8:5
13:8 [g]Gen. 26:12
13:9 [h]ch. 11:15; Mark 4:9
13:11 [i]ch. 11:25; Mark 4:11; 1 Cor. 2:10; 1 John 2:27
13:12 [j]ch. 25:29; Mark 4:25; Luke 8:18
13:14 [k]Isa. 6:9; Ezek. 12:2; Mark 4:12; Luke 8:10; John 12:40; Acts 28:26; Rom. 11:8; 2 Cor. 3:14
13:15 [l]Heb. 5:11
13:16 [m]ch. 16:17; Luke 10:23; John 20:29
13:17 [n]Heb. 11:13; 1 Pet. 1:10
13:18 [o]Mark 4:14; Luke 8:11
13:19 [p]ch. 4:23
13:20 [q]Isa. 58:2; Ezek. 33:31; John 5:35
13:21 [r]ch. 11:6; 2 Tim. 1:15
13:22 [s]ch. 19:23; Mark 10:23; Luke 18:24; 1 Tim. 6:9; 2 Tim. 4:10 [t]Jer. 4:3
13:30 [u]ch. 3:12
13:31 [v]Isa. 2:2; Mic. 4:1; Mark 4:30; Luke 13:18

15 For this people's heart is waxed gross, and *their* ears [l]are dull of hearing, and their eyes they have closed; lest at any time they should see with *their* eyes, and hear with *their* ears, and should understand with *their* heart, and should be converted, and I should heal them.

16 But [m]blessed *are* your eyes, for they see: and your ears, for they hear.

17 For verily I say unto you, [n]That many prophets and righteous *men* have desired to see *those things* which ye see, and have not seen *them;* and to hear *those things* which ye hear, and have not heard *them.*

18 ¶ [o]Hear ye therefore the parable of the sower.

19 When any one heareth the word [p]of the kingdom, and understandeth *it* not, then cometh the wicked *one,* and catcheth away that which was sown in his heart. This is he which received seed by the way side.

20 But he that received the seed into stony places, the same is he that heareth the word, and anon [q]with joy receiveth it;

21 Yet hath he not root in himself, but dureth for a while: for when tribulation or persecution ariseth because of the word, by and by [r]he is offended.

22 [s]He also that received seed [t]among the thorns is he that heareth the word; and the care of this world, and the deceitfulness of riches, choke the word, and he becometh unfruitful.

23 But he that received seed into the good ground is he that heareth the word, and understandeth *it;* which also beareth fruit, and bringeth forth, some an hundredfold, some sixty, some thirty.

24 ¶ Another parable put he forth unto them, saying, The kingdom of heaven is likened unto a man which sowed good seed in his field:

25 But while men slept, his enemy came and sowed tares among the wheat, and went his way.

26 But when the blade was sprung up, and brought forth fruit, then appeared the tares also.

27 So the servants of the householder came and said unto him, Sir, didst not thou sow good seed in thy field? from whence then hath it tares?

28 He said unto them, An enemy hath done this. The servants said unto him, Wilt thou then that we go and gather them up?

29 But he said, Nay; lest while ye gather up the tares, ye root up also the wheat with them.

30 Let both grow together until the harvest: and in the time of harvest I will say to the reapers, Gather ye together first the tares, and bind them in bundles to burn them: but [u]gather the wheat into my barn.

31 ¶ Another parable put he forth unto them, saying, [v]The kingdom of heaven is like to a grain of mustard seed, which a man took, and sowed in his field:

32 Which indeed is the least of all seeds:

but when it is grown, it is the greatest among herbs, and becometh a tree, so that the birds of the air come and lodge in the branches thereof.

33 ¶ [w]Another parable spake he unto them; The kingdom of heaven is like unto leaven, which a woman took, and hid in three measures of meal, till the whole was leavened.

34 [x]All these things spake Jesus unto the multitude in parables; and without a parable spake he not unto them:

35 That it might be fulfilled which was spoken by the prophet, saying, [y]I will open my mouth in parables; [z]I will utter things which have been kept secret from the foundation of the world.

36 Then Jesus sent the multitude away, and went into the house: and his disciples came unto him, saying, Declare unto us the parable of the tares of the field.

37 He answered and said unto them, He that soweth the good seed is the Son of man;

38 [a]The field is the world; the good seed are the children of the kingdom; but the tares are [b]the children of the wicked *one;*

39 The enemy that sowed them is the devil; [c]the harvest is the end of the world; and the reapers are the angels.

40 As therefore the tares are gathered and burned in the fire; so shall it be in the end of this world.

41 The Son of man shall send forth his angels, [d]and they shall gather out of his kingdom all things that offend, and them which do iniquity;

42 [e]And shall cast them into a furnace of fire: [f]there shall be wailing and gnashing of teeth.

43 [g]Then shall the righteous shine forth as the sun in the kingdom of their Father. [h]Who hath ears to hear, let him hear.

44 ¶ Again, the kingdom of heaven is like unto treasure hid in a field; the which when a man hath found, he hideth, and for joy thereof goeth and [i]selleth all that he hath, and [j]buyeth that field.

45 ¶ Again, the kingdom of heaven is like unto a merchant man, seeking goodly pearls:

46 Who, when he had found [k]one pearl of great price, went and sold all that he had, and bought it.

47 ¶ Again, the kingdom of heaven is like unto a net, that was cast into the sea, and [l]gathered of every kind:

48 Which, when it was full, they drew to shore, and sat down, and gathered the good into vessels, but cast the bad away.

49 So shall it be at the end of the world: the angels shall come forth, and [m]sever the wicked from among the just,

50 [n]And shall cast them into the furnace of fire: there shall be wailing and gnashing of teeth.

51 Jesus saith unto them, Have ye understood all these things? They say unto him, Yea, Lord.

52 Then said he unto them, Therefore every scribe *which is* instructed unto the kingdom of heaven is like unto a man *that is* an householder, which bringeth forth out of his treasure [o]*things* new and old.

53 ¶ And it came to pass, *that* when Jesus had finished these parables, he departed thence.

54 [p]And when he was come into his own country, he taught them in their synagogue, insomuch that they were astonished, and said, Whence hath this *man* this wisdom, and *these* mighty works?

55 [q]Is not this the carpenter's son? is not his mother called Mary? and [r]his brethren, [s]James, and Joses, and Simon, and Judas?

56 And his sisters, are they not all with us? Whence then hath this *man* all these things?

57 And they [t]were offended in him. But Jesus said unto them, [u]A prophet is not without honour, save in his own country, and in his own house.

58 And [v]he did not many mighty works there because of their unbelief.

14 At that time [w]Herod the tetrarch heard of the fame of Jesus,

2 And said unto his servants, This is John the Baptist; he is risen from the dead; and therefore mighty works do shew forth themselves in him.

3 ¶ [x]For Herod had laid hold on John, and bound him, and put *him* in prison for Herodias' sake, his brother Philip's wife.

4 For John said unto him, [y]It is not lawful for thee to have her.

5 And when he would have put him to death, he feared the multitude, [z]because they counted him as a prophet.

6 But when Herod's birthday was kept, the daughter of Herodias danced before them, and pleased Herod.

7 Whereupon he promised with an oath to give her whatsoever she would ask.

8 And she, being before instructed of her mother, said, Give me here John Baptist's head in a charger.

9 And the king was sorry: nevertheless for the oath's sake, and them which sat with him at meat, he commanded *it* to be given *her.*

10 And he sent, and beheaded John in the prison.

11 And his head was brought in a charger, and given to the damsel: and she brought *it* to her mother.

12 And his disciples came, and took up the body, and buried it, and went and told Jesus.

13 ¶ [a]When Jesus heard *of it,* he departed thence by ship into a desert place apart: and when the people had heard *thereof,* they followed him on foot out of the cities.

14 And Jesus went forth, and saw a great multitude, and [b]was moved with compassion toward them, and he healed their sick.

15 ¶ [c]And when it was evening, his disciples came to him, saying, This is a desert

13:33 [w]Luke 13:20
13:34 [x]Mark 4:33
13:35 [y]Ps. 78:2 [z]Rom. 16:25; 1 Cor. 2:7; Eph. 3:9; Col. 1:26
13:38 [a]ch. 24:14; Mark 16:15; Luke 24:47; Rom. 10:18; Col. 1:6 [b]Gen. 3:13; John 8:44; Acts 13:10; 1 John 3:8
13:39 [c]Joel 3:13; Rev. 14:15
13:41 [d]ch. 18:7; 2 Pet. 2:1
13:42 [e]ch. 3:12; Rev. 19:20 [f]ch. 8:12; ver. 50
13:43 [g]Dan. 12:3; 1 Cor. 15:42 [h]ver. 9
13:44 [i]Phil. 3:7 [j]Isa. 55:1; Rev. 3:18
13:46 [k]Prov. 2:4
13:47 [l]ch. 22:10
13:49 [m]ch. 25:32
13:50 [n]ver. 42
13:52 [o]SSol. 7:13
13:54 [p]ch. 2:23; Mark 6:1; Luke 4:16
13:55 [q]Isa. 49:7; Mark 6:3; Luke 3:23; John 6:42 [r]ch. 12:46 [s]Mark 15:40
13:57 [t]ch. 11:6; Mark 6:3 [u]Luke 4:24; John 4:44
13:58 [v]Mark 6:5
14:1 [w]Mark 6:14; Luke 9:7
14:3 [x]Mark 6:17; Luke 3:19
14:4 [y]Lev. 18:16
14:5 [z]ch. 21:26; Luke 20:6
14:13 [a]ch. 10:23; Mark 6:32; Luke 9:19; John 6:1
14:14 [b]ch. 9:36; Mark 6:34
14:15 [c]Mark 6:35; Luke 9:12; John 6:5

Focus on MATTHEW

The purpose of the Gospel of Matthew is to show that Jesus is the fulfillment of Old Testament prophecies, a descendent of Abraham, and heir to the throne of David. As the husband of Mary, the mother of Jesus, Joseph is Jesus' legal father.

Matthew introduces Jesus as a legitimate heir to the throne of David. He is worshiped by the Magi, who come looking for the king in Jerusalem. Matthew shows how Jesus sets forth His statement of kingdom righteousness (The Sermon on the Mount), then establishes His credentials by the miracles He performs (Matt. 8–11). However, His popularity provokes opposition from the Jewish leaders (Matt. 12–16:12). Knowing that He will be rejected by the Jewish leaders, Jesus prepares His disciples for His crucifixion and death at Jerusalem. Jesus formally presents Himself to the nation with the triumphal entry into Jerusalem (Matt. 21). The people adore Him, but the chief priests and scribes are displeased, so they plot against Him and, with the cooperation of Rome, crucify Him. His resurrection on the third day vindicates His claims, and He commissions His disciples to proclaim the Gospel to the entire world (28:16–20).

THE BLACK PRESENCE IN MATTHEW

Among the African people mentioned in the Gospel of Matthew are Rahab, Uriah, the people of Babylon, the people of Egypt, the people of Sheba, a Canaanite woman, Simon of Cyrene, and the people of Cyrene. Rahab (Rachab) was the prostitute of Canaan (Matt. 1:5), who hid the Israelite spies in numbers. Recall that Canaanites were the descendants of Ham whose name means "black" or "burnt face." Uriah (Urias) (Matt. 1:6), was a Hittite. Hittites were the descendants of Heth, a son of Canaan who, in turn, was a descendant of Ham (Gen. 10:6, 15). Babylon (Matt. 1:12, 17) was settled by Nimrod the son of Cush. Cush means "black." Egypt (Matt. 2:13) was the Greek name for Ham's son Mizraim. (Gen. 10:6)

The Canaanite woman (Matt. 15:21–28) lived in the area of the Phoenician twin cities, Tyre and Sidon. She lived near the Mediterranean Sea. She was a Canaanite—a descendant of Ham. Phoenicians gave civilization our alphabet and numbering system. They were noted for their commerce and inventiveness. The queen of Sheba was the queen of the south (see Matt. 12:42). Sheba was located to the far south of Palestine, and the people of Sheba were descendants of Cush, whose name means "black."

Simon of Cyrene (Matt. 27:32) came from Cyrene, a city located on the northern coast of Africa. The population of the city was approximately 25 percent Jewish, the remainder being native Africans.

These are some of the outstanding Africans who appear in the Gospel of Matthew.

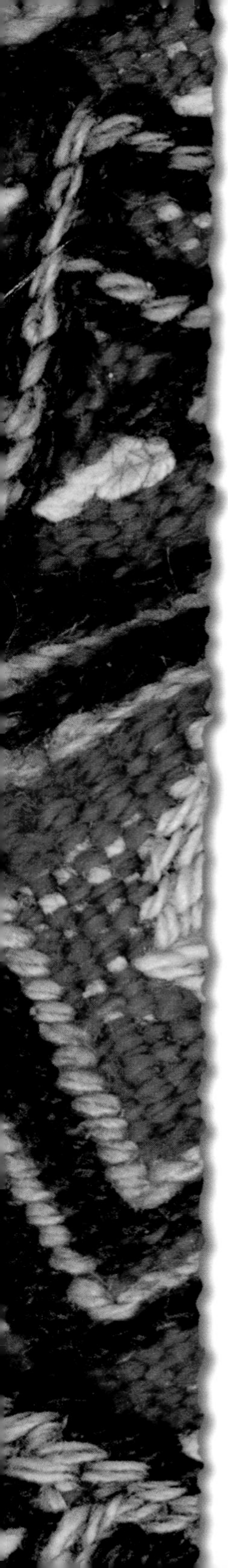

Life Lessons

MATTHEW 1

Matthew includes four women besides Mary in his genealogy of Jesus: Tamar, Rahab, Ruth, and Uriah's wife Bathsheba. This shows the inclusive attitude of Matthew toward women. Tamar and Rahab were Canaanites, Ruth was a Moabite, Bathsheba's husband Uriah was a Hittite. All of this reflects the grace of God in implementing His plan of redemption. It leads us to the conclusion that just as God has demonstrated His grace in the past, so He continues to do so in the present age. He is a God of grace and is available to each one who calls on Him in sincerity and truth.

Dear God, I praise You for Your unchanging grace. Help me to claim Your grace for my daily needs. Amen.

MATTHEW 4

In the account of Jesus' temptation by Satan (Matt. 4:1–11), we notice how the tempter appealed to the fundamental drives of human nature, hunger, self-protection, and desire for power—the same areas where Satan tempts us. Notice also that Jesus resisted the temptation through His appeal to God's Word, "It is written . . ." Our knowledge of and confidence in the written Word of God will be critical when we are faced with Satan's temptations.

Dear God, when I am tempted by Satan, help me to rely on Your word to resist. May Your Holy Spirit give me strength to say "No" to his attacks. Amen.

MATTHEW 6

The prayer our Lord taught His disciples (Matt. 6:9–13) is a pattern for our prayers. The priority should be as follows: acknowledging and affirming God as the sovereign one whose name should be elevated and hallowed, praying that His will should prevail on earth as it is in heaven; praying for our daily needs, for forgiveness, and for deliverance from Satan, the evil one. Keeping the priority as Jesus outlined in this prayer will keep us focused properly.

Dear God, Thank You for providing this model for our prayers. Help me always to give You and Your will top priority when I pray. Amen.

MATTHEW 9

As Jesus went about teaching, preaching, and healing people, He was deeply moved by their condition. He saw them as harassed and helpless like sheep without a shepherd. We as His followers should be moved as He was.

Dear God, please help me to see people as Jesus saw them. Give me the desire and ability to help someone along life's highway so You will be pleased. Amen.

MATTHEW 14

Jesus was concerned about the masses of people who had remained with Him all day to hear the Word of God and were now hungry (Matt. 14:15–21). He took the five loaves and two fish—all that was available—and gave thanks. Rather than complain that He had *only* five loaves and two fish, He thanked God for what He did have. This reminds us that when we take whatever we have and place it (money, abilities, and time) in the hands of Jesus, He can take our little and multiply it to satisfy the needs of others.

Dear God, I give you what I have. I pray that you would multiply it.

MATTHEW 27

We are told that many women were at the cross, having come from Galilee to use their resources to care for Jesus. Their devotion to our Lord is remarkable. When many of the disciples fled, these women were still there watching from a distance, agonizing over the suffering of their Master, whom they knew was innocent. Through the years, women have repeated acts such as these as they have agonized over the suffering of the innocent, using their resources to relieve the hurting.

Dear God, may I, like these women, continue the tradition of serving those who are hurting, knowing that You do not overlook the least cup of water given in Your name Amen.

FOCUS ON MARK

Mark appears to present his material as though he is relying on Peter for much of the sequence, if not the content. The Gospel follows the outline of Peter's sermons, especially Acts 10, and, indeed, one church father, Eusebius (A.D. 140) writes that Mark was the interpreter of Peter. The Gospel displays intense action as the writer gives a brief introduction of Jesus and shows how He immediately went to work as God's Servant. Mark's introduction is followed by an extended account of Jesus' ministry in Galilee. Then comes His ministry in Perea, east of the Jordan River. The last week of Jesus' life prior to the crucifixion occupies five chapters. The Gospel ends with the Resurrection. Frequently the writer uses the term "straightway" which means "immediately." In so doing, he demonstrates that Jesus is the faithful Servant who does God's bidding unwaveringly and without hesitation.

THE BLACK PRESENCE IN MARK

The affirmation of the black presence in biblical history is critical so all people will know the truth of history, and that people of color, in particular, can reclaim their past in order to function more effectively today.

The location of Palestine in the northeast quarter of Africa, on the border of Asia, may be assumed to be a sign of black presence. According to anthropologists, the area was originally populated by a

people who migrated from Africa around 2,500 to 5,000 B.C. There has been a continuous presence of people of Hamitic and Semitic roots since that time, though by the time of the New Testament some Greeks and Romans were added to the population. The name Ham means "black" or "burnt face." Ham's sons, Cush, Phut, Mizraim, and Canaan were no doubt black. Again we must point out that the issue of color in biblical days was a nonissue. People simply accepted others without regard for skin color. Only in recent years (since the 17th century), have attempts been made to deny with pen, ink, and artwork, the presence of blacks in biblical history.

In addition to the general black presence in the Gospel of Mark, there are two particularly noticeable Africans—the Syrophoenician woman and Simon of Cyrene. The Syrophoenician woman (Mark 7:24–30) lived in the area of the twin cities of Tyre and Sidon. These two cities were on the eastern Mediterranean coast. Tyre and Sidon were closely associated with each other in Scripture because of their proximity. Sidon was a descendant of Canaan (Gen. 10:15). Canaan, in turn, was a son of Ham whose name means "black." While, due to sexual intermixing throughout the later generations, the shades of brown may have varied, all of these descendants possessed the genes of their ancestors.

Another African, Simon of Cyrene (Matt. 15:21) lived in Cyrene, which was an African country on its northern coast, west of Egypt. The city was home to a large population of Jewish immigrants. However, it was also home to an even larger population of other "native" Africans. Since Jews at the time were both Semitic and Hamitic through intermarriage and integration, Simon of Cyrene was doubtless black or swarthy. According to some ancient traditions this same Simon is to be identified with Simeon the Niger mentioned in Acts 13:1.

Life Lessons

MARK 1

Mark tells us that Jesus went out to pray while it was still dark (Mark 1:35). Jesus maintained a practice of communing with God. He knew the value of worship and communication with His heavenly Father. Doubtlessly from this fellowship with God He derived strength and direction for accomplishing His mission here on earth.

Dear God, teach me to spend time with You in prayer and meditation, knowing that from such times I will gain emotional, spiritual, and physical strength to accomplish Your purpose for my life. Amen.

MARK 2

Jesus' healing of the paralytic (2:1–12) teaches us that Jesus can both heal and forgive sins. 1 John 1:9 tells us, "If we confess our sins, he is faithful and just to forgive us our sins and to cleanse us from all unrighteousness."

Dear Jesus, when I fail You, please give me the grace to confess my sins so I can experience the joy of Your forgiveness. Amen.

MARK 2

Jesus challenged the Pharisees to place the needy people above their traditions. He did so by refusing to condemn His disciples for plucking grain on the Sabbath and also by healing a man with a shriveled hand on the Sabbath (Mark 2:23–3:5). We should not allow our traditions to prevent us from helping those who are in need.

Dear God, please give me wisdom to never allow traditions to stand in the way of my helping others who are in need. Amen.

MARK 4

Jesus calmed the raging sea, then asked the disciples, "Why are ye so fearful? How is it that ye have no faith?" (Mark 4:40). Is that not the same question Jesus would ask us when we are faced with great turmoil in life? The antidote for fear is trust in a loving God. Certainly the cares of life often test our faith and cause us to fear. In those moments we can call on God and anticipate peace and calmness in our inner selves. Learning to trust is a growing process, but a rewarding one.

Dear Storm-calming God, when the cares of this life overwhelm me, please remind me to come to You for solace and peace. Amen.

MARK 5

Jesus healed the demon-possessed man (Mark 5:1–20). Mark portrays this man as desperate, helpless, and hopeless—until Jesus came! "Sitting, clothed, and in his right mind" (v. 15) describes how completely Jesus had changed his condition. No person is beyond the reach of God's power.

Dear God, help me to know that no situation is beyond Your power to overcome. Help me to trust You in my most difficult situations, and when in Your wisdom You delay an answer, give me the grace to wait on You. Amen.

MARK 5

Jesus raised a dead girl (Mark 5:21–24, 35–42). Jairus, the synagogue ruler, came with a request for Jesus to heal his daughter. When she died, the messengers concluded it was useless for Jesus to come to the man's house. The mourners made fun of Jesus' statement that the damsel was asleep. Jesus proceeded because He knew what none of them knew—His power over death. Not only does this incident give us encouragement for trusting Jesus' power in this life, it lets us know that He can raise us at the appropriate time.

Dear God, I praise You for Your unlimited power. Please remind me of Your power when I'm tempted to believe my situation is hopeless.

MARK 5

A woman who had a very intimate feminine problem discovered that just by touching the hem of Jesus' garment, she was made whole. On the one hand her faith was very small, on the other it was very strong. Jesus said the faith of a mustard seed is all we need. The critical difference is not the amount of the faith but the Person in whom we trust.

Dear Great Physician, show me how to bring my most intimate concerns to You, knowing that it is not how much faith I have as it is that I have faith in You. Help me to know that You alone are the great Healer, and when You choose not to heal, You can give grace to help me endure what You permit to come into my experience Amen.

MARK 5

We learn in Mark's Gospel, that Jesus is a healer! Jesus also healed a sick woman (5:25–34). This woman had been bleeding for 12 years, unable to get relief from the many physicians who attended her. Her faith in the power of Jesus' garment without His conscious attention is remarkable and resulted in total healing.

Dear Lord, help me to remember You can heal me both physically and emotionally.

MARK 9

Jesus used a little child to teach His disciples the need for humility in serving Him (Mark 9:33–39). We often get caught up in the desire for power and recognition for what we do for Christ. On one occasion, Jesus taught that people who do things for recognition are at that very time receiving all the reward they will ever get (Matt. 6:2, 5). Only what we do for Christ will earn His "well done."

Dear God, teach me to serve You without expecting recognition from people. Amen.

MARK 10

We also learn, in the Gospel of Mark that God knows what our true motives are. This is shown when the rich young ruler wanted to know what he needed to do to make sure of eternal life (Mark 10:17–31). Hearing him say he had kept all the commandments, Jesus sought to help this young man see that he really hadn't. He did not really love God with all his heart because he was not willing to sell his possessions and follow Jesus. His trust was really in his material possessions.

Dear God, please teach me to trust in You, not my possessions, knowing that if my trust is in You, I will not be devastated when material losses come.

MARK 14

"Jesus said, Let her alone" (Mark 14:6). He was rebuking those who criticized the woman (Mary) who had anointed His head with expensive perfume (John 12:1–8). Jesus said Mary anointed Him to prepare His body for burial. Did Mary have insight into the destiny of Jesus that others apparently did not have? Jesus understood her motive when others did not.

Dear God, Thank You for understanding my motives when others

do not Give me grace to bear with those who may not understand my deepest emotions Amen.

MARK 16

Three women arrive at Jesus' tomb early in the morning to anoint His body properly. There had not been time to do so when He was buried. So, these women lovingly arose early on the first day of the week to show their care for Jesus. On their way to do what they regarded as proper, they were rewarded with being the first to learn that the tomb was empty. Often God reserves unexpected, special blessings for those who faithfully do the things they know are right.

Dear God, May I faithfully do what You want me to do, knowing that You sometimes reserve blessings for those who faithfully serve You. Amen.

Women in MATTHEW AND MARK

WISE AND FOOLISH VIRGINS: OBEDIENTLY PREPARING FOR CHRIST

Many who read this parable wonder how it can fit with the notion of Jesus Christ as the compassionate, merciful Savior. After all, was it not Jesus Himself who, when asked about how often we should forgive those who wronged us, admonished Peter, seventy times seven? Did not Paul plead with us to be kind, tenderhearted, and forgiving of each other? Is not one of the most tender and moving passages in the New Testament the one where Paul requests Philemon to take Onesimus back and not punish him? Think of the Good Samaritan, who took care of an enemy, or the rich servant who was punished because he showed no mercy when he himself had received mercy. The Bible is so full of people who were merciful that it seems that the five foolish virgins got a raw deal.

The five foolish virgins, like the five wise virgins, were given explicit instructions regarding what they needed to do: "Get the oil. Trim the wicks. Wash the jars. See that you are ready." For whatever reason, they chose not to do so. The five wise virgins, on the other hand, were obedient. They did as they were told and were prepared when the time came.

This tells me several things. First, perhaps I should not question instructions, suggestions, and directions I am given because they seem mundane, trivial, boring, or "beneath" someone with my creativity, uniqueness, and specialness. I just shouldn't have to follow the rules!

Second, obedience is better than sacrifice. Didn't it make you mad and get on your nerves when the old people told you that? Don't you hate to admit that, once again, "mother wit" and common sense win out? Don't you wish you could "work it" just a little?

This parable tells us to be ready, because we don't know when God will call us. Just because He didn't come today doesn't mean He's not

coming tonight or tomorrow. Therefore, we must be obedient, consistent, and committed to the glory and honor of God. We cannot be found unprepared like the five foolish virgins.

Read Matthew 24:42–51; 25:1–13; 1 Thessalonians 5:1–3.
Read the insight essay on Commitment.

—A. Bouie

MARY, THE MOTHER OF JAMES: SACRIFICING FOR CHRIST

Scripture does not tell us much about Mary. In fact, she is also referred to as "the other Mary." We do know that her son, James (known as "James the Just" and "James the Little") was Jesus' apostle.

Mary was one of the women who followed Jesus, a woman of affluence who ministered to the physical needs of Jesus and His disciples during His ministry.

Mary, having followed Jesus throughout His ministry, was a witness to His death on the cross, and was among the first to bring spices to the tomb of her Lord. Even after death, she continued to serve Him.

Having sacrificed her wealth and her son for the service of Jesus, Mary did not have any regrets. Instead, she continued to give to others out of faith and trusting love, and with unrestrained joy.

Mary was among those in the upper room awaiting the arrival of the promised Holy Spirit on the day of Pentecost, when 3,000 members were added to the church.

At a time when women were not given much consideration or prominence, Mary counted the cost of serving Jesus and felt that whatever she had to forsake was worth the sacrifice. God honored Mary in a special way: She was among the women who were the first to receive the news that Jesus had risen from the dead.

Mary is an example of a liberated woman, yet she knew that Jesus Christ alone was her liberator. Therefore, she had no need to make demands of anyone for her equality. She knew all too well that God is impartial; He is merciful and full of grace, and exalts whom He will.

Mary is an excellent example of one who receives the rewards that faith brings. Through her we know that every deed that we do for God counts.

Read Matthew 27; Mark 15:40, 47; 16:1; Luke 24:10.
Read the insight essays on Influence and Motherhood.

—J. Josey

MARY MAGDALENE: SETTING HER REPUTATION STRAIGHT

Mary Magdalene's name is mentioned fifteen times in the Gospels, and on nine occasions while in the company of other women. Because she is usually mentioned before other women, this position suggests that she more than likely played a leadership role among Jesus' followers.

All four Gospels note that she was among the witnesses of the risen Christ. And depending on which Gospel you are reading, either Jesus or the angel commissioned her to go tell the disciples that He had risen from the dead (Matt. 28:5–7; Mark 16:5–7; John 20:14–17).

This commissioning to "go tell" is an affirmation for contemporary women in that Jesus was, and is, intentionally gender-inclusive, establishing the woman's place in the proclamation of the Gospel through Mary. However, if Mary was indeed a prostitute, to have omitted this important fact is contrary to how biblical writers typically reported the stories in the Scriptures. A case in point is Rahab, an Old Testament character (Josh. 2; 6:22–25), who is listed in the New Testament among the faithful servants, yet never shakes the stigma of the title of prostitute (Heb. 11:31).

More importantly, however, than the fact that Mary Magdalene is presumed to have been a prostitute, is the condition from which Jesus liberates her: She was possessed with seven demons (Mark 16:9; Luke 8:2). Old Testament scholar Renita Weems, in *Just a Sister Away,*[1] trys to name those seven demons—names that collectively describe mental, emotional, and spiritual conditions that women of all ages have struggled with. They are depression, fear, low self-esteem, doubt, procrastination, bitterness, and self-pity. We could add to this list, jealousy, guilt, envy, discord, idolatry, and an unforgiving spirit.

But the Great Physician touched Mary Magdalene and made her whole. She became a leader among women, a proclaimer of the Gospel to the apostles, an evangelist to the marginalized, and a servant in God's kingdom.

For all women, Mary Magdalene is a model of a wounded person, who was healed and made whole by the love of Christ, and called and commissioned by Him to serve in His kingdom.

Read Matthew 27:56, 61; 28:1; Mark 15:40, 47; 16:9; Luke 8:2; 24:10.
Read the insight essay on Commitment.

—K. Johnson

Notes

[1] Renita Weems, *Just a Sister Away* (San Diego: LuraMedia, 1988), 90.

DAUGHTER OF JAIRUS: ONLY BELIEVE

Each of the synoptic Gospels (Matthew, Mark, and Luke) records the miracle of Jairus' daughter and these words: "Do not be afraid, only believe."

A Christian mother, father, grandmother, grandfather, and/or guardian(s) will spend their child's lifetime—from infancy to adulthood—embracing this phrase: *"only believe."*

Adults concerned for their beloved children's lives often find themselves going in prayer to Jesus, the miraculous Master Healer. These adults know that drugs, peer pressure, alcohol, gangs, suicide, depression, low self-esteem, violence, etc., have seemingly killed off the innocent or sickened the sons and daughters given to them by God.

These believers know there are surely so many needs the Lord must attend to. Yet these believers know, without a shadow of a doubt, that if anyone can raise their precious children from these deadly ills of society, Jesus certainly can.

We learn in Mark 5:21–24, 35–43, that Jairus' pleading for his daughter to Jesus made a difference. Jairus loved his daughter and lifted her name up to Jesus. This caring and loving father continued to believe

and have patience when Jesus stopped on His way to Jairus' house. Someone had touched Him. A desperately ill woman with an issue of blood for 12 years had touched the hem of His garment and her faith made her well. With the touch she was healed of her affliction (Mark 5:25–34).

During the rejoicing, Jairus' servants arrived. They informed him that his daughter was dead. As soon as Jesus heard these words, He gave Jairus the encouragement he needed: "Be not afraid, only believe" (Mark 5:36).

When Jesus arrived at Jairus' house, people were weeping because the girl was dead. Jesus instructed them to stop weeping, for she was only sleeping (Mark 5:39). After He removed the doubters and unbelievers from the room, He took the little girl's hand and said, "*Talitha cumi,*" which means "Damsel, I say unto thee, arise" (Mark 5:41). Immediately, she did. She rose from the grips of death.

In other words, she got up. She got up after Jesus took her hand and instructed her to arise. She got up because her parent believed. Yes, Jairus' daughter got up because even when others said, "Don't trouble Jesus," this child's parent went through the trouble of going to Him anyhow.

I am certain every adult child who has experienced drugs, alcohol, suicidal thoughts, and other deadly temptations can thank God for their parents' desperate pleas, prayers, and petitions to a heavenly Healer and Redeemer who called them to rise above the things that wanted to destroy them.

Now, they too can thank God for Jesus. So parents, pray and plead, plead and pray, and believe.

Read Mark 5:21–43; see also Matthew 9:18–26; Luke 8:41–56.

Read the insight essays on Attributes of God, Children, Faith, Love, and Prayer.

—D. Moore-James

A HEMORRHAGING WOMAN: KNOWN BY JESUS

Jesus had just come back across the Sea of Galilee. The crowds thronged around Him and followed Him, pressing in on Him and His disciples from all sides, trying to get close to Him, to touch Him, just to be near Him. The woman was there, too, trying to get through. She was ill and weak. She had been suffering with menustrual bleeding, non-stop for twelve years. She was poor. She had spent all her resources on medicines and doctors, but instead of getting better, she only got worse. She was an untouchable. In her society, the law said that women who bled like her were unclean. Anyone who touched her had to bathe and to wash their clothes, and remain in a state of "uncleanness" until evening. Her bed, her clothes, and anything she sat on were all unclean. She had been an untouchable twelve years, and you would think that she would have lost heart.

But she heard about the man who could heal with just a touch, and she believed. She knew if she could get through the crowd to touch the hem of His garment, she would be made well. It was her belief in Jesus that gave her hope that she could become well again. It was her belief in Jesus that made her brave enough to push though the crowds, even though she was unclean. When she did get through to Jesus, she knew immediately that she had been made well. She was afraid that she might be scolded for violating the law of uncleanness, so she said nothing.

Jesus knew who she was and what happened. He knew also that she needed to overcome her fear and to testify about what happened to her. He wanted others to know the kind of faith she had. And He wanted her to know that her faith had not only healed her body, but that it had also saved her soul.

Read Mark 5:25–34; see also Leviticus 15:25–33; Luke 8:43–48.
Read the insight essay on Fear.

—A. Davis

HERODIAS AND SALOME: DECEIT AND SEDUCTION

Herodias was a woman out of control. She was politically astute, ambitious, cunning, greedy, and would stop at nothing to get what she wanted. Initially married to Philip, a ruler over the Trachontis and Idumea territories, she eventually married his brother Herod, who was the ruler over Galilee and more powerful than Phillip. John the Baptist spoke against this marriage (Mark 6:18; see also Leviticus 18:16; 20:21), and it infuriated her. Herodias became angry to the point of wanting to kill John.

Herod was in awe of John and realized that the people revered him, so he was afraid of killing John. Herod had a birthday celebration where Salome, the daughter of Herodias, danced sensuously for him and his guests. He became so intoxicated with her dancing that he agreed to give her anything she asked for, up to one-half of his kingdom (Mark 6:22–23). Herodias saw this as an opportunity to get what she wanted—a chance to have John the Baptist killed. Salome's request caused Herod great sorrow, but he honored his word (Mark 6:26). As she requested, John's head was delivered on a platter.

The mother-daughter relationship among African-Americans can be godly and productive, or ungodly and destructive. For the daughter, her relationship with her mother is the foundation upon which she learns how to relate to others. She should be taught to appreciate her beauty (Ps. 45:9–13), to be honest (1 Peter 2:12), and to practice godliness in her life. For the African-American mother life may, at times, bring unpleasant and disappointing occurrences. But, it is important for a mother to heed the voice of God, which may come through the Scriptures or other people led by God. She can receive correction and direction for every area of life. It opens the door for repentance and forgiveness.

Words are powerful! Words can bring life or death (Prov. 18:21). A mother should speak words of godly instruction to her daughter's life (Titus 2:3–5). Words of manipulation, deceit, and seduction only bring devastation and death (Prov. 5:3–4).

Read Mark 6:14–29; see also Matthew 14; Luke 3:19–20.
Read the insight essays on Influence and Motherhood.

—G. London

THE SYROPHOENICIAN WOMAN: PERSISTENCE PAYS OFF

When the worst of our troubles attack us, as wise women, we know whom to go to get help. Our sister, the Syrophoenician woman, knew where to go and who to see. She knew what Jesus could do. Can you see

her? A small woman, nothing notable, just hot and tired, lines of worry deeply etched in her face. She's walked miles. She gets to Jesus, and the disciples have the nerve to try and send her away because she is bothering them! The poor disciples did not recognize that the Syrophoenician woman was on a mission. It did not matter that Jesus was trying to rest. It didn't matter that the disciples did not want her there. She wasn't going anywhere. She refused to leave—she couldn't. Just see her as she looked at them with that look and told them, "Brothers, I don't have time for this, okay?" When we are worried and scared for our children, we don't tolerate obstacles put in our way.

The disciples sound like whiny babies and her child was gravely ill—with a spirit of anger, rage, and disobedience.

When the Syrophenician woman faces Jesus (as recorded in Mark 7:24–30, see also Matthew 15:21–28), He responds to her request negatively. He compares her to a dog. These words probably hit her hard, but they didn't stop her. Jesus' words don't seem to be from the compassionate Jesus we love to worship. Most likely, Jesus was provoking her to see how she would respond. Most likely, He was testing her faith, so the disciples could clearly see that non-Jews could have faith too.

But Jesus' seemingly harsh words did not deter the Syrophoenician woman from her goal. She was respectful to Him. Jesus threw out a crumb, and she said she would gladly take the crumb. The Syrophoenician woman had heart! She was like a strong black woman. She was not going to let cruel words, negativity, or haughty attitudes deny her daughter new life. We cannot allow mere words to keep us from believing in Jesus and placing our trust in Him. She could be witty—whatever it took—she could do it, for she wanted real life for both her daughter and herself.

She was persistent. She was determined. She pressed her case. She stayed in Jesus' face. She was saying, "Look at me. You are my last hope, and You know it. Can you really turn me away? Can you really let my child continue to suffer?" Sisters, have you been there?

The Syrophenician woman persisted. Jesus relented. Jesus was impressed with her great faith. It was a faith that was so great that she could withstand disparaging remarks. She did not yield. She placed her trust soundly in Christ. Like her, we cannot give up, turn around, or turn away—no matter what. Like her, we must have a strong faith in Christ. We must persist and move the obstacles out of our way!

Read Matthew 15:21–28; Mark 7:24–30.

Read the insight essays on Motherhood, Perseverance, and Prayer.

—M. Bellinger

THE WIDOW'S MITE: SELFLESS GIVING

Jesus stood in the temple watching the multitude of people bring their monetary gifts to one of the seven treasury boxes. Many of the people were wealthy and gave large sums of money. Others gave according to tradition, calculated to the penny by the laws of tithing. One by one they dropped their offerings into the treasury boxes. Quietly, Jesus watched them give funds they did not need for survival.

Jesus also noticed a poor widow approach one of the treasury boxes. One could imagine her as an older woman, slightly bent from age. Her head

may have been covered with an old cloth and she probably wore a torn, dull-colored dress. Her fragile, withered hand would have been pressed against her breast, clutching her gift as she walked slowly toward the treasury box. Yet, it was not her appearance that drew Jesus' attention. It was her willingness to be obedient to God to the point of giving everything she had.

This poor widow dropped two copper coins, or a mite, into the box. This was not much money then, and today would equal a fraction of a penny in U.S. currency. But, those coins were all she had.

In Jesus' eyes, this woman's gift was greater than all the other gifts combined because it was all she had. The spirit in which her gift was given made it priceless, for this poor woman had given from her heart. She had given her last in gratitude to God. Jesus was touched by her giving spirit and remarked to His disciples how great her sacrifice was in comparison to the others.

Like the multitude, many of us may give in abundance for self-glorification. Jesus desires that we give of ourselves—time, talent, and money. Jesus calls us to reach beyond the comfortable and give sacrificially to God. Jesus calls us to be willing to give even our last mite, in gratitude to God.

Read Mark 12:41–44; Luke 21:1–4.

Read the insight essays on Commitment and Influence.

—T. Wade

THE LITTLE MAID: THE TRUTH, THE WHOLE TRUTH, AND NOTHING BUT THE TRUTH

We say we are strong, brave, proud of our accomplishments, independent, opinionated, intelligent, and loyal to our friends. This is the picture we'd like to paint of ourselves. This is the portrait we'd like to show God.

Throughout most of his time with Jesus, the apostle Peter showed himself strong, brave, loyal, and faithful. He appeared to be a warrior when he cut off the ear of the guard in the Garden of Gethsemane, right before Jesus was arrested (John 10:10–11). And he had vowed never to deny Jesus, even under the most strenuous circumstances. But who was he really? What did God know the truth about Peter to really be? Little did Peter know that an unnamed maid would reveal a side of him that not even he knew existed.

While warming himself by a fire in the courtyard of the high priest after the arrest of Jesus, Peter was approached by a maid girl whose name is unknown. "And thou also wast with Jesus of Nazareth," she said. It was then that Peter first denied any association with Jesus.

A second time, she declared, "This is one of them." Peter again denied his relationship to Jesus because he had just witnessed Jesus' interrogation and beating, and feared for his own life. The maid and those with her commented a third time, "Surely, thou are one of them" And again—this time raging, ranting, and swearing—Peter rebuked them.

While Peter had three opportunities to speak the truth, he allowed a spirit of fear and self-preservation to control him. But by lying to the little maid, he was really lying to himself. However, he couldn't lie to God. God used both Peter and the little maid to illustrate to us that even those who profess to love Jesus—even those who follow Him and promise to give up their lives for Him—can fall into the trap of fear and hopelessness if they

do not abide with Him. He also spotlighted the frailties of man, even when he has the best intentions.

Consider how often we lie to others and to ourselves in the midst of unpleasant situations. How often do we deny God, compromising our trust, loyalty, and strength of character in an effort to alleviate the pain or discomfort of a given situation? God's grace told Peter that he was forgiven, and the same grace allows us to be forgiven, too. Let's just remember that when we learn to tell the truth, the whole truth, and nothing but the truth—no matter the circumstances—that God is better able to use us for His glorification.

Read Mark 14:66–72; see also Matthew 26:69–75; Luke 22:56–57; John 18:17.

—M. Cotton Bohanon

Insights

FRUIT OF THE SPIRIT—GOODNESS

In my church, the children often sing, "This little light of mine, I'm gonna let is shine, let it shine, let it shine, let it shine!" This song comes from Scripture, "Let your light so shine before men, that they may see your good works, and glorify your Father which is in heaven" (Matt. 5:16). The fruit of goodness expresses itself in good works. It is manifested when we do good to our neighbors, when we shelter the homeless, when we help the helpless. Service to others is counted as evidence of the goodness of God at work in the life of women (2 Thess. 1:11–12). It expresses itself when we go out of our way for another, not expecting anything in return. First Timothy 6:17–19 admonishes Christians to be rich in good works, ready to distribute, willing to communicate. It is by these actions that we lay up for ourselves a good treasure in heaven.

Each Christian woman has a responsibility to exhibit goodness in her life. However, this goodness can only be cultivated when we abide in Jesus Christ. The Bible tells us that when we dwell in the Lord's house, goodness and mercy shall follow us all the days of our lives. When was the last time you reached out and helped another sister or brother? We live in a world where we are taught to look out for number one, to take care of our own, and to let others fend for themselves. But God calls us to another standard. We are told to maintain good works, to show a pattern of good works, and to be zealous of good works. Many persons will only see the goodness of God as they witness that goodness in us. As a Fruit of the Spirit, goodness is a natural result of love, joy, peace, longsuffering, and kindness at work in a woman's life (Gal. 5:22–23).

Read Matthew 5:13–16.

Read the insight essays on Attributes of God, Fruit of the Spirit, and Sacrificial Living.

—*C. Belt*

FRUIT OF THE SPIRIT—PEACE

Peace is often illusive. We look for it at work, but instead we are often confronted with every imaginable scenario, from co-workers who are friendly, frustrated, irate, or frightened. We yearn for peace at home, but must answer the questions of our children and attend to the needs of a husband.

The Old and New Testaments describe peace as the result of a right relationship with God and with others. The peace we long for comes from God alone and is dependent upon His presence in our lives.

The peace that we yearn for can be experienced by walking in the Spirit despite having turmoil in our lives. The peace of God protects our hearts and minds from anxiety (Phil. 4:7).

The peace that Jesus promises is not simply the absence of conflict. It is the confident assurance, the quietness of spirit, and the steadiness of being that comes from knowing who God is, and who we are in God. Peace

is one of the fruits of the Spirit (Gal. 5:22) as well as part of the "whole armour of God" (Eph. 6:11-17).

The Bible not only talks about this peace which passes all understanding, but offers practical advice on how to truly know peace in our everyday lives. We can bring peace into play by:

Knowing God. Ephesians 2:14 says, "For [Christ] is our peace."

Loving God's Law. Psalm 119:165 says, "Great peace have they which love thy law: and nothing shall offend them."

Practicing Peace. Colossians 3:15 says, "And let the peace of God rule in your hearts."

Making Peace. James 3:18 says, "And the fruit of righteousness is sown in peace of them that make peace." And Matthew 5:9 says "Blessed are the peacemakers: for they shall be called the children of God."

In our culture of violence, it is essential for women of color to cultivate the fruit of peace—peace that dispels violence, opens prison doors, counteracts weapons of war, and brings reconciliation.

Read Matthew 5:9; Philippians 4:7; Colossians 3:15.

Read the insight essays on Confidence, Distress, and Fruit of the Spirit.

—B. Whipple

FORGIVENESS: THE DOORWAY TO HEALING AND RECONCILIATION

One of life's greatest challenges is to forgive someone who has hurt us. Offenses range from the unspeakable to the unbearable. The pain can be deadly. Yet when someone asks you for forgiveness, you have an obligation to grant it. Forgiveness of others is a prerequisite for God to forgive you (Matt. 6:14; James 2:13).

Love is the primary ingredient for forgiveness. It is giving the gift that God brought to us in Christ! We forgive by faith, not by feelings. Luke 11:4 reminds us that we are to forgive others as God has forgiven us. By faith, God creates the capacity in us to forgive those who have trespassed against us. We must forgive others if we don't want to disobey God and break our fellowship with Him (Matt. 6:14–15; Mark 11:25–26; Luke 17:3–4).

The gift of forgiveness is here. It came at Calvary! It was given to us before we asked. Paul writes in Romans 5:10–11 "When we were enemies [of God], we were reconciled to God . . . through our Lord Jesus Christ." Just as God, in Christ, forgave us before we knew to ask, we may need to forgive others before we are asked. In many cases the person or people may never ask for our forgiveness. They may never deserve our forgiveness. However, if we wish to be healed from the hurt, we will give the gift that makes reconciliation and healing possible.

To forgive is not easy, but it is possible! You must be willing to forget past hurts (Phil. 3:13), pray for the offender (1 Sam. 12:23), and give God your hurt (1 Peter 2:21–23), as well as serve as a channel for God's grace. Most importantly, we are learning that forgiveness is the doorway to reconciliation. If we desire to live reconciled lives—at peace with God and creation—we will share this gift as often as necessary. Giving it away sets us free to be healed and made whole! A forgiving spirit will bring blessings to you and others (Prov. 11:17, 15:23).

Read Matthew 6:14–15; Mark 11:25–26.

Read the insight essay on Friendship. Read the portraits on Bathsheba and The Forgiven Adulteress.

—C. Belt

PRAYER: A GOD-GIVEN PROVISION

As powerful, promising, productive, passionate women we must not settle in the valley and shadow of worrying. Matthew reminds us not to worry about what we shall eat, or what we shall drink, or how we shall be clothed, meet our financial setback, or manage our health issues (Matt. 6:25). We are more valuable than sparrows, more precious than purple lilies of the field (Matt. 6:26–28), and wiser than industrious ants.

Worrying can paralyze. We can counteract this by being concerned and creating an action plan—pray. Anxiety can damage our health, disrupt our productivity, alter our perception, and ultimately reduce our ability to trust totally in God. God does not ignore those who depend on Him (Ps. 40:4–5). Prayer is a prelude to promises that develop into provisions (Ps. 18:1–2, 6). God does not promise to provide all we want; He promises to provide all we need (Phil. 4:19).

Prayer for provision is expressed through personal petition or intercession. Personal petitions are the requests women, or other believers, make on their own behalf for their own needs. Intercessions are petitions women, or other believers, make on behalf of others for the needs of others.

Begin to pray for provision by starting with a plan. First, stop worrying and start praying (Ps. 37:1–6). Second, with prayers, supplication, thanksgiving, let your request be made known to God (Phil. 4:6). Next, reflect and examine your circumstances and find contentment. Things might not be as bad as you thought (Phil. 4:9–13). Observe how other Christian women found favor through prayers (2 Kin. 4:1–7; Matt. 9:20–22). Then give yourself permission to ask and seek a solution. If a child or a friend comes to you and asks for bread would you give them a stone? No! God also gives what is good unto those that ask (Matt. 7:7–11). Finally, renew your faith, release your fears (Heb. 12:1–3), and believe (Matt. 9:23; 21:21–22; Mark 9:23; John 20:25).

God desires to provide for the well-being of our soul spiritually, our body physically and materially, and our mind mentally. At times it may appear we are afflicted in every way but not crushed; perplexed but not despairing; persecuted by not forsaken; struck down but not destroyed (2 Cor. 4:7–10; 13–14).

Study and apply the prayer plan and remember God will take care of you through every day, every experience, every change, and every challenge—even impossibility. He is our all-sufficient Provider!

Read Matthew 6:25–28; 9:23; 21:21–22; see also John 20:25.
Read the insight essay on Prayer.

—N. Peete

ADULTERY

"This is now bone of my bones, and flesh of my flesh: she shall be called woman. . . Therefore shall a man leave his father and his mother, and shall cleave unto his wife: and they shall be one flesh." (Gen. 2:23–24)

God provided a woman as a helpmate for Adam. God ordained marriage and blessed it, "Be fruitful and multiply, and replenish the earth, and subdue it" (Gen. 1:28a). To preserve the fidelity of marriage, God gave Israel the seventh commandment: "Thou shalt not commit adultery" (Ex. 20:14). "Marriage is honourable in all, and the bed undefiled: but whoremongers and adulterers God will judge" (Heb. 13:4).

God's intent for husbands and wives is for them to be faithful to each other. Adultery is sexual intercourse between a married man and a female not his wife, or sexual intercourse between a married woman and a man who is not her husband. If a man was found with another man's wife, both the man who slept with her and the woman were to die by stoning (Deut. 22:22; John 8:3–5). A husband and wife are no longer two, but one. "What therefore God has joined together, let not man put asunder" (Matt. 19:6b).

Adultery occurred in the early church. "It is reported commonly that there is fornication among you . . . and such fornication as is not so much as named among the gentiles, that one should have his father's wife. And ye are puffed up, and have not rather mourned, that he that done this deed might be taken away from among you" (1 Cor. 5:1–2). Church leadership is to correct, rebuke, and instruct the adulterer.

A lifestyle of adultery keeps one from inheriting the kingdom of God. "Do not be deceived: neither fornicators, nor idolater, nor adulterers, nor effeminate, nor abusers of themselves with mankind, nor thieves, nor covetous, nor drunkards, nor revilers, nor extortioners, shall inherit the kingdom of God. And such were some of you, but ye are washed, but ye are sanctified, but ye are justified in the name of the Lord Jesus, and by the Spirit of our God" (1 Cor. 6:9–11). A woman who commits adultery can receive God's forgiveness. God forgives those who repent. A woman was caught in the act of adultery and Jesus said, "Go and sin no more" (John 8:11b). Believers are to practice faithfulness to God and in their personal relationships. God uses the faithfulness between a woman and her husband to demonstrate His faithfulness to His children. Adultery destroys the relationship God wants to have with His children whom He loves!

Read Matthew 19:4–6; see also Deuteronomy 22:22.

Read the portraits on the Adulteress of Proverbs, Bathsheba, and the Forgiven Adulteress. See also the insight essays on Commitment, Submission, and Temptation.

—J. Webster

THE PARADOX OF LIFE AND SUFFERING

Suffering covers a wide spectrum of human experiences. My suffering may not be yours, but we share a common bond since a woman's life is inextricably tied to suffering. Suffering is an experience of desolation and aloneness. You might feel separated from God, from people, and from the act of living. Suffering is an experience of desperation—a longing for life as we once knew it, yet understanding that life will never be the same. Suffering is life threatening. It threatens our souls, our minds, and our hearts. The disappointment and disillusionment of life poisons our thinking, our feelings, and threatens our ability to live an abundant life.

Hannah and Elisabeth suffered with the emptiness of barrenness. American slaves experienced suffering. The Meserete Kristos Church in

Ethiopia experienced suffering. Victims of domestic violence experience suffering. Jesus experienced suffering. Although a person may suffer, the sovereignty of God prevails. God is able to bring meaning into the worst situations of suffering.

Suffering causes one to withdraw. We become disheartened as we search for understanding. We question and cry out in great despair only to discover a self we may have not known before—an angry self, a hateful self, a vengeful self, but a true self. We discover a weak self, a humble self, a needful self, a dependent self, and a longing self. In our suffering, we discover a self who understands that without God, there is no life.

In the Garden of Gethsemane, Jesus understood that unless He died, we would not have life (Matt. 26:36–46). Until His hands and feet were nailed to the cross, until He hung, bled, and died, we would not have life. His death brought life. He is the Resurrection and the Life. Because He lives, I can face tomorrow in my suffering. Because He lives, we may be "troubled on every side, yet not distressed" (1 Cor. 4:8). Because He lives, we may be "perplexed, but not in despair; persecuted, but not forsaken; cast down, but not destroyed." Because He lives, we are "always bearing about in the body the dying of the Lord Jesus, that the life also of Jesus might be made manifest in our body. For we which live are always delivered unto death for Jesus' sake, that the life also of Jesus might be made manifest in our mortal flesh. So then death worketh in us, but life in you" (2 Cor. 4:10–12).

The thread that maintains a sense of balance between life and suffering is our faith. Faith becomes the hinge to the door of life, or the vein that carries life to the soul. Our suffering comes as a test of our profession of faith in God through Christ Jesus. It comes as a unique opportunity to glorify God. Our suffering is our testament that "neither death, nor life, nor angels, nor principalities, nor powers, nor things present, nor things to come, nor height, nor depth, nor any other creature, shall be able to separate us from the love of God, which is in Christ Jesus our Lord" (Rom. 8:38–39).

Yes, the paradox of life and suffering is one that humanity cannot answer. Also, the Bible does not provide any easy answers for suffering, but "we know that all things work together for good to them that love God, to them who are the called according to his purpose" (Rom. 8:28).

Read Matthew 26:36–46; see also 2 Corinthians 4:7–12.

Read the insight essays on Faith, Forgiveness, Sacrificial Living, and Suffering. Read the portraits on Leah, Miriam, Rachel, and Tamar.

—L. Wooden

SUICIDE: WHEN GOD'S PROMISES DON'T SEEM LIKE ENOUGH

My first brush with suicide occurred when I saw a beautiful, eerie piece of cut glass in my friend's room when I was in college. I noticed she was uncomfortable when I asked where she had bought it. Eventually I realized that she had used this glass to cut her wrists. While hugging her, I angrily asked how dare she try to take her life, didn't she know how much she meant to me?

There was a time when suicide was rare in our community. And yet, the rate of suicide has skyrocketed more than 100 percent in the past 20 years in the black community, particularly among youth between the ages

of 15–24. How can the people who endured the Middle Passage and more than 200 years of slavery succumb to suicide?

A lot has changed in our community in the past 20 years. With the progress made from the Civil Rights Movement, we saw a simultaneous rise in unemployment, underemployment, domestic violence, divorce, single parents, incarcerations, and families living below the poverty line. With integration, we've lost a lot of our family and community support systems: Grandma and auntie don't live around the corner anymore, and Miss Mabel no longer feels comfortable correcting our children. This lack of family and community support leads to greater despair and anguish among men and women in the black community.

Where is God in the midst of this despair, and what does God have to say about suicide? There are only six accounts of known suicides in the Bible: Saul (1 Sam. 31:1–4; 2 Sam. 1:1–6), Ahithophel (2 Sam. 17:23), Zimri (1 Kin. 16:18–19), Samson (Judg. 16:28–31), Abimelech (Judg. 9:52–54), and Judas (Matt. 27:3–5; Acts 1:18). Surprisingly, suicide is not directly condemned anywhere in the Bible. Our modern understanding of theologically based condemnation of suicide comes from Augustine.

We gain a better understanding of how God views suicide by looking at the testimony of biblical figures who felt depressed and suicidal but chose not to commit suicide. We can learn from Elijah's journey in the wilderness (1 Kin. 19), that God will send an angel to feed us and watch over us when we are in the wilderness. That angel may be a friend, spouse, coworker, stranger, or even a counselor.

When Elijah was so low that he refused to help the angel, God brought him to Mt. Horeb so he could experience the awesome power of God's love (the "sound of sheer silence").

Job's torment is finally ended when he realizes that while God does not promise a rose garden, God does promise to never forsake him. What saves Job is that, even in the midst of his anguish, he continually seeks God for answers. Job often feels tired and angry with God (Job 9:35), but he never gives up (Job 10:1–2). He constantly seeks to maintain his relationship with God (Job 2; 42:2). It is when we are at our lowest that God hears our cries (Jer. 31:15; Matt. 2:18). As Christian women, we must learn to invite God into our states of depression and stop viewing depression and even suicidal thoughts as a sign of lapsed faith. Even the great prophets (e.g., Moses, Elijah, Jonah, Jeremiah) experienced depression and had suicidal thoughts. The sin is not feeling suicidal, but in not seeking God to help you through the crisis. God is ever faithful to His promise to never forsake us. If God is willing to sacrifice His only begotten Son to save us, surely He will come to our aid in the midst of our despair. We have only to call on Him.

Read Matthew 27:3–5; see also 1 Samuel 31:1–13; 2 Samuel 1:1–16; Acts 1:18.

Read the insight essays on Aging and Suffering.

—S. Molock

ABANDONMENT

Sometimes the biggest battle we must fight is within our own soul. The soul is the repository where life's issues are stored—issues that were born out of our life experiences. These issues either bring us joy or pain. They can cause us to grow or decay. They can illicit transformation or stagnancy. One of the life issues that plague all women, particularly women of color, is abandonment. *Abandonment* is defined as "being forsaken or deserted." For many of us it was the father we never really knew, or perhaps the mother whom we feel never really cared for us. For others, it might have been the dissolution of a marriage we thought would last forever. For some, it was the betrayal of a friend, or the unexpected death of a loved one. Regardless of its genesis, each experience can leave us doubting our self-worth or questioning our judgment. It can cause us to become distrustful and guarded in our interactions with others, whether romantic, platonic, or familial. Unresolved life issues like abandonment leave holes in our souls that need to be filled. In desperation, we try to fill those holes with things that are only temporal, like alcohol, drugs, food, sex, money, and other worldly pleasures. In the end we find ourselves feeling deserted, dissatisfied, and alone.

But there is hope! God specializes in healing the holes in our souls and helping us handle life issues. Who better to heal our souls than the One who created us and gave us life? We can take comfort in knowing that God understands and God cares. The Bible teaches that we do not have a high priest that cannot be touched by the feeling of our infirmity (Heb. 4:14–16). During God's time on earth in the Person of Jesus Christ, He too struggled with issues of abandonment. Members of His own community and family rejected Him (John 7:1–5). Jesus' own followers deserted Him in His darkest hour (Mark 14:66–72). He was betrayed unto death by one of His own disciples (vv. 10–11). In addition, during the time He needed His Father the most, He felt alone, and cried out in anguish, "My God, My God why hast thou forsaken me?" (Matt. 27:46). Have you ever felt abandoned by God? You are not alone.

Situations will occur in life that will cause us to feel God has forsaken us. But like Jesus Christ arose from the dead in victory, we too can arise from the grip of despair and experience victory over our feelings of abandonment. First, we must relieve ourselves of guilt and responsibility. Whether it was the husband who walked out or the father who never showed up—accept that it is not your fault. You are fearfully and wonderfully made (Ps. 139:14), created in the image of God and worthy of love and attention. Second, we must find comfort in the love of God. The Bible reminds us that when our mothers and fathers forsake us that God will take care of us (Ps. 27:10). God loves us so much that He sent His only begotten Son to die that we might enter into an everlasting love relationship with Him (John 3:16). Finally, we must embrace and believe that God will never leave us or forsake us (Heb. 13:5). God has promised to be with us even unto the end of the world (Matt. 28:20).

Read Matthew 27:46; Hebrews 4:14–16; 13:5.

Read the portrait on Hagar. Read the insight essay on Grief.

—J. Thompson

EVANGELISM: GONE FISHIN'

"Now as he walked by the sea of Galilee, he saw Simon and Andrew his brother casting a net into the sea; for they were fishers" (Mark 1:16) "And Jesus said unto them, Come ye after me, and I will make you to become fishers of men" (Mark 1:17).

As I was engaging in conversation with my intern, we began to explore the idea of taking our mentoring group on a fishing trip. The girls had talked about asking some of the elders and senior citizens if they would teach them to fish. Some of them spoke of being squeemish when it came to baiting the hook. Some of them talked about the excitement they felt just thinking about it. All of them were totally jazzed at the idea of going to a body of water, maybe boarding a boat, and actually catching a fish. We compared the idea of the trip with that of evangelizing and discipling youngsters in our community. I said to her, there's got to be a way for us to tie this fishing trip in with spreading the Gospel.

It was at that time we began to explore our options: Yes, we could ask those trailblazers to share with us tricks of the trade, but we would also ask them to share with us biblical stories as well as their own testimonies. We would talk about the fact that Jesus chose some of His disciples from this very profession. We would talk about the net that initially came up empty, but once given to the master broke with the abundance of the catch.

Today, the harvest is plentiful. It is the laborers that are few. Could it be because we have not utilized the resources we have in our own backyard? When was the last time you went fishing for Christ? When was the last time you took a young person along with you? When was the last time you baited your rod? Or has your rod, your reel, your pole simply gathered cobwebs in your shed? Is it because your net is broken? Is it because you're out of practice? Is it because you're out of bait? Well, Jesus said, "If you will simply lift me up before men, I'll do the drawing!" (paraphrased). Let me take this time out to remind you that if you give one a fish, you supply her with a meal, but if you teach her to fish, you equip her for life—both practically and spiritually.

Are you waiting to have some time off—vacation time, spare time? Or are you willing to fish for Christ on a regular basis—in the pond nearest you, in your neighborhood creek? If Christ came to your house on any given day, would He find you vegging out in front of the tube, or would He find you out by the lake?

Remember there's peace by the river. So go on, take your gear, pick up a couple of others (preferably youth) or maybe another veteran. Head for the creek, the river, or wherever, then cast your nets and see if you don't find that net breaking because of the increase. May Christ find you at His return, out on the shores, having hung a sign on your door that says: "GONE FISHIN'."

Read Mark 1:16–17; see also Psalm 126:6; Luke 10:2; John 4:39; Romans 10:9–10.

Read the insight essays on Influence, Salvation, and Women's Ministries.

—L. Melton-Dolberry

CHILDREN: A BLESSED HERITAGE FROM GOD

"Children should be seen and not heard." This is an old saying that implies that children are insignificant—they may be cute to look at, but they don't have anything meaningful to say. This saying is contrary to the way God sees children. Children are important, a "heritage of the LORD" (Ps. 127:3).

Children are important to God. They are a blessing from God. Jesus taught that to receive children is to receive Him (Mark 9:37). To give to children is to give to Him (Matt. 10:42), and to be like a child is the key to conversion (Mark 10:15). In the Bible, children were significant, and teachings about God were important to their daily lives (Deut. 6:1). Mothers would bring their children to Jesus for a blessing. He welcomed the children (Mark 9:36–37; 10:13–15). Parents are instructed not to harm their children in any way (Matt. 18:5–10), especially in ways that would result in their becoming angry adults (Eph. 6:4).

Throughout the African-American culture, children have been valued. To assure their children's rightful place in society and in the kingdom of God, parents must introduce them to Jesus. Children must be prepared to fulfill God's call (1 Chron. 22:7–10), encouraged to follow wisdom (Prov. 4:3–4), taught to make their own choices (Prov. 22:6), and instructed to obey their parents in the Lord (Eph. 6:1, 4). In African-American families, destructive criticism, stereotyping, unrealistic expectations, and dysfunctional environments can destroy the relationship between parents and children.

To build meaningful relationships with children, parents should provide a living environment that is filled with encouragement and spoken love. Our children will then "build" strong, godly sons and daughters into the generations. African-American children are a blessed heritage from God.

Read Mark 9:37–42; 10:13–16, 42; see also Psalm 127:3–5; Matthew 10:42; 18:3.

Read the insight essays on Children, Motherhood, and Parenting.

—G. London

PRAYER: A GOD-GIVEN PROMISE

> "Therefore I say unto you, What things soever ye desire, when ye pray, believe that ye receive them, and ye shall have them." (Mark 11:24)

These words from the Gospel according to Mark leave us breathless. God promises to hear and answer our prayers when we pray in faith. In John 16:23–24, Jesus says, "Verily, verily, I say unto you, Whatsoever ye shall ask the Father in my name, he will give it you. Hitherto have ye asked nothing in my name: ask, and ye shall receive, that your joy may be full." Here again is an awesome, God-given promise for prayer. God will respond to requests made in Jesus' name. These promises are given as gifts from God. If we were to take them out of the context of the rest of the New Testament, they would appear to be a "carte blanche" for our every desire. Prayer is one way in which women and other believers claim the promises of God.

God's promises are not "stand-alone" texts. They are part of our God-given new relationship in Jesus Christ. In John 15:7, Jesus says, "If ye

abide in me, and my words abide in you, ye shall ask what ye will, and it shall be done unto you." We must understand that the God-given promise of prayer is not for our selfish whims, the destruction of others, or the arbitrary manipulation of our own lives. God will not break His Word to answer our prayers. God's answers may not always appear in the form or at the time we expect. The challenge to our faith is to trust God is faithful, and will work all things for our good no matter what happens.

In Matthew chapter six, Jesus teaches His disciples about prayer—what we have come to call The Lord's Prayer. At the end of the chapter, Jesus emphasizes that we should pray and not worry, because God is more than able to care for our material and physical needs. God's will is to supply our needs through Jesus Christ, in this life as well as the next. In verse 33, Jesus s ays, "But seek ye first the kingdom of God and His righteousness, and all these things shall be added unto you."

God's prayer promises are part of God's play to redeem all creation through the life, death, and resurrection of Jesus Christ. We are expected to pray based upon a knowledge of and belief in God's Word as revealed to us in Christ. We are to come to God in faith, believing that God is faithful to hear and answer our prayers as God's story continues to be revealed in us.

Read Mark 11:24; see also Jeremiah 33:3; John 14:13–14; Acts 2:33; 2 Peter 1:2–4; Jude 20.

Read the insight essays on Faith, God's Promises, and Prayer.

—W. Bullock

place, and the time is now past; send the multitude away, that they may go into the villages, and buy themselves victuals.

16 But Jesus said unto them, They need not depart; give ye them to eat.

17 And they say unto him, We have here but five loaves, and two fishes.

18 He said, Bring them hither to me.

19 And he commanded the multitude to sit down on the grass, and took the fives loaves, and the two fishes, and looking up to heaven, [d]he blessed, and brake, and gave the loaves to *his* disciples, and the disciples to the multitude.

20 And they did all eat, and were filled: and they took up of the fragments that remained twelve baskets full.

21 And they that had eaten were about five thousand men, beside women and children.

22 ¶ And straightway Jesus constrained his disciples to get into a ship, and to go before him unto the other side, while he sent the multitudes away.

23 [e]And when he had sent the multitudes away, he went up into a mountain apart to pray: [f]and when the evening was come, he was there alone.

24 But the ship was now in the midst of the sea, tossed with waves: for the wind was contrary.

25 And in the fourth watch of the night Jesus went unto them, walking on the sea.

26 And when the disciples saw him [g]walking on the sea, they were troubled, saying, It is a spirit; and they cried out for fear.

27 But straightway Jesus spake unto them, saying, Be of good cheer; it is I; be not afraid.

28 And Peter answered him and said, Lord, if it be thou, bid me come unto thee on the water.

29 And he said, Come. And when Peter was come down out of the ship, he walked on the water, to go to Jesus.

30 But when he saw the wind boisterous, he was afraid; and beginning to sink, he cried, saying, Lord, save me.

31 And immediately Jesus stretched forth *his* hand, and caught him, and said unto him, O thou of little faith, wherefore didst thou doubt?

32 And when they were come into the ship, the wind ceased.

33 Then they that were in the ship came and worshipped him, saying, Of a truth [h]thou art the Son of God.

34 ¶ [i]And when they were gone over, they came into the land of Gennesaret.

35 And when the men of that place had knowledge of him, they sent out into all that country round about, and brought unto him all that were diseased;

36 And besought him that they might only touch the hem of his garment: and [j]as many as touched were made perfectly whole.

15 Then [k]came to Jesus scribes and Pharisees, which were of Jerusalem, saying,

2 [l]Why do thy disciples transgress [m]the tradition of the elders? for they wash not their hands when they eat bread.

3 But he answered and said unto them, Why do ye also transgress the commandment of God by your tradition?

4 For God commanded, saying, [n]Honour thy father and mother: and, [o]He that curseth father or mother, let him die the death.

5 But ye say, Whosoever shall say to *his* father or *his* mother, [p]*It is* a gift, by whatsoever thou mightest be profited by me;

6 And honour not his father or his mother, *he shall be free*. Thus have ye made the commandment of God of none effect by your tradition.

7 [q]*Ye* hypocrites, well did Esaias prophesy of you, saying,

8 [r]This people draweth nigh unto me with their mouth, and honoreth me with *their* lips; but their heart is far from me.

9 But in vain they do worship me, [s]teaching *for* doctrines the commandments of men.

10 ¶ [t]And he called the multitude, and said unto them, Hear, and understand:

11 [u]Not that which goeth into the mouth defileth a man; but that which cometh out of the mouth, this defileth a man.

12 Then came his disciples, and said unto him, Knowest thou that the Pharisees were offended, after they heard this saying?

13 But he answered and said, [v]Every plant, which my heavenly Father hath not planted, shall be rooted up.

14 Let them alone: [w]they be blind leaders of the blind. And if the blind lead the blind, both shall fall into the ditch.

15 [x]Then answered Peter and said unto him, Declare unto us this parable.

16 And Jesus said, [y]Are ye also yet without understanding?

17 Do not ye yet understand, that [z]whatsoever entereth in at the mouth goeth into the belly, and is cast out into the draught?

18 But [a]those things which proceed out of the mouth come forth from the heart; and they defile the man.

19 [b]For out of the heart proceed evil thoughts, murders, adulteries, fornications, thefts, false witness, blasphemies:

20 These are *the things* which defile a man: but to eat with unwashen hands defileth not a man.

21 ¶ [c]Then Jesus went thence, and departed into the coasts of Tyre and Sidon.

22 And, behold, a woman of Canaan came out of the same coasts, and cried unto him, saying, Have mercy on me, O Lord, *thou* Son of David; my daughter is grievously vexed with a devil.

23 But he answered her not a word. And his disciples came and besought him, saying, Send her away; for she crieth after us.

24 But he answered and said, [d]I am not

14:19 [d]ch. 15:36
14:23 [e]Mark 6:46 [f]John 6:16
14:26 [g]Job 9:8
14:33 [h]Ps. 2:7; Mark 1:1; ch. 16:16; Luke 4:41; John 1:49; Acts 8:37; Rom. 1:4
14:34 [i]Mark 6:53
14:36 [j]ch. 9:20; Mark 3:10; Luke 6:19; Acts 19:12
15:1 [k]Mark 7:1
15:2 [l]Mark 7:5 [m]Col. 2:8
15:4 [n]Ex. 20:12; Lev. 19:3; Deut. 5:16; Prov. 23:22; Eph. 6:2 [o]Ex. 21:17; Lev. 20:9; Deut. 27:16; Prov. 20:20
15:5 [p]Mark 7:11
15:7 [q]Mark 7:6
15:8 [r]Isa. 29:13; Ezek. 33:31
15:9 [s]Isa. 29:13; Col. 2:18-22; Tit. 1:14
15:10 [t]Mark 7:14
15:11 [u]Acts 10:15; Rom. 14:14; 1 Tim. 4:4; Tit. 1:15
15:13 [v]John 15:2; 1 Cor. 3:12
15:14 [w]Isa. 9:16; Mal. 2:8; ch. 23:16; Luke 6:39
15:15 [x]Mark 7:17
15:16 [y]ch. 16:9; Mark 7:18
15:17 [z]1 Cor. 6:13
15:18 [a]Jam. 3:6
15:19 [b]Gen. 6:5; Prov. 6:14; Jer. 17:9; Mark 7:21
15:21 [c]Mark 7:24
15:24 [d]ch. 10:5; Acts 8:25; Rom. 15:8

sent but unto the lost sheep of the house of Israel.

25 Then came she and worshipped him, saying, Lord, help me.

26 But he answered and said, It is not meet to take the children's bread, and to cast *it* to [e]dogs.

27 And she said, Truth, Lord: yet the dogs eat of the crumbs which fall from their masters' table.

28 Then Jesus answered and said unto her, O woman, great *is* thy faith: be it unto thee even as thou wilt. And her daughter was made whole from that very hour.

29 [f]And Jesus departed from thence, and came nigh [g]unto the sea of Galilee; and went up into a mountain, and sat down there.

30 [h]And great multitudes came unto him, having with them *those that were* lame, blind, dumb, maimed, and many others, and cast them down at Jesus' feet; and he healed them:

31 Insomuch that the multitude wondered, when they saw the dumb to speak, the maimed to be whole, the lame to walk, and the blind to see: and they glorified the God of Israel.

32 ¶ [i]Then Jesus called his disciples *unto him,* and said, I have compassion on the multitude, because they continue with me now three days, and have nothing to eat: and I will not send them away fasting, lest they faint in the way.

33 [j]And his disciples say unto him, Whence should we have so much bread in the wilderness, as to fill so great a multitude?

34 And Jesus saith unto them, How many loaves have ye? And they said, Seven, and a few little fishes.

35 And he commanded the multitude to sit down on the ground.

36 And [k]he took the seven loaves and the fishes, and [l]gave thanks, and brake *them,* and gave to his disciples, and the disciples to the multitude.

37 And they did all eat, and were filled: and they took up of the broken *meat* that was left seven baskets full.

38 And they that did eat were four thousand men, beside women and children.

39 [m]And he sent away the multitude, and took ship, and came into the coasts of Magdala.

16 The [n]Pharisees also with the Sadducees came, and tempting desired him that he would shew them a sign from heaven.

2 He answered and said unto them, When it is evening, ye say, *It will be* fair weather: for the sky is red.

3 And in the morning, *It will be* foul weather to day: for the sky is red and lowring. O *ye* hypocrites, ye can discern the face of the sky; but can ye not *discern* the signs of the times?

4 [o]A wicked and adulterous generation seeketh after a sign; and there shall no sign be given unto it, but the sign of the prophet Jonas. And he left them, and departed.

5 And [p]when his disciples were come to the other side, they had forgotten to take bread.

6 ¶ Then Jesus said unto them, [q]Take heed and beware of the leaven of the Pharisees and of the Sadducees.

7 And they reasoned among themselves, saying, *It is* because we have taken no bread.

8 *Which* when Jesus perceived, he said unto them, O ye of little faith, why reason ye among yourselves, because ye have brought no bread?

9 [r]Do ye yet not understand, neither remember the five loaves of the five thousand, and how many baskets ye took up?

10 [s]Neither the seven loaves of the four thousand, and how many baskets ye took up?

11 How is it that ye do not understand that I spake *it* not to you concerning bread, that ye should beware of the leaven of the Pharisees and of the Sadducees?

12 Then understood they how that he bade *them* not beware of the leaven of bread, but of the doctrine of the Pharisees and of the Sadducees.

13 ¶ When Jesus came into the coasts of Caesarea Philippi, he asked his disciples, saying, [t]Whom do men say that I the Son of man am?

14 And they said, [u]Some *say that thou art* John the Baptist: some, Elias; and others, Jeremias, or one of the prophets.

15 He saith unto them, But whom say ye that I am?

16 And Simon Peter answered and said, [v]Thou art the Christ, the Son of the living God.

17 And Jesus answered and said unto him, Blessed art thou, Simon Bar-jona: [w]for flesh and blood hath not revealed *it* unto thee, but [x]my Father which is in heaven.

18 And I say also unto thee, That [y]thou art Peter, and [z]upon this rock I will build my church; and [a]the gates of hell shall not prevail against it.

19 [b]And I will give unto thee the keys of the kingdom of heaven: and whatsoever thou shalt bind on earth shall be bound in heaven; and whatsoever thou shalt loose on earth shall be loosed in heaven.

20 [c]Then charged he his disciples that they should tell no man that he was Jesus the Christ.

21 ¶ From that time forth began Jesus [d]to shew unto his disciples, how that he must go unto Jerusalem, and suffer many things of the elders and chief priests and scribes, and be killed, and be raised again the third day.

22 Then Peter took him, and began to rebuke him, saying, Be it far from thee, Lord: this shall not be unto thee.

23 But he turned, and said unto Peter, Get

15:26 [e]ch. 7:6; Phil. 8:2
15:29 [f]Mark 7:31 [g]ch. 4:18
15:30 [h]Isa. 35:5; ch. 11:5; Luke 7:22
15:32 [i]Mark 8:1
15:33 [j]2 Kings 4:43
15:36 [k]ch. 14:19 [l]1 Sam. 9:13; Luke 22:19
15:39 [m]Mark 8:10
16:1 [n]ch. 12:38; Mark 8:11; Luke 11:16; 1 Cor. 1:22
16:4 [o]ch. 12:39
16:5 [p]Mark 8:14
16:6 [q]Luke 12:1
16:9 [r]ch. 14:17; John 6:9
16:10 [s]ch. 15:34
16:13 [t]Mark 8:27; Luke 9:18
16:14 [u]ch. 14:2; Luke 9:7
16:16 [v]ch. 14:33; Mark 8:29; Luke 9:20; John 6:69; Acts 8:37; 1 John 4:15; Heb. 1:2
16:17 [w]Eph. 2:8 [x]1 Cor. 2:10; Gal. 1:16
16:18 [y]John 1:42 [z]Eph. 2:20; Rev. 21:14 [a]Job 38:17; Ps. 9:13; Isa. 38:10
16:19 [b]ch. 18:18; John 20:23
16:20 [c]ch. 17:9; Mark 8:30; Luke 9:21
16:21 [d]ch. 20:17; Mark 8:31; Luke 9:22

thee behind me, [e]Satan: [f]thou art an offense unto me: for thou savourest not the
things that be of God, but those that be of
men.
24 ¶ [g]Then said Jesus unto his disciples,
If any *man* will come after me, let him deny
himself, and take up his cross, and follow me.
25 For [h]whosoever will save his life shall
lose it: and whosoever will lose his life for
my sake shall find it.
26 For what is a man profited, if he shall
gain the whole world, and lose his own
soul? or [i]what shall a man give in exchange for his soul?
27 For [j]the Son of man shall come in the
glory of his Father [k]with his angels; [l]and
then he shall reward every man according
to his works.
28 Verily I say unto you, [m]There be some
standing here, which shall not taste of
death, till they see the Son of man coming in
his kingdom.
17 And [n]after six days Jesus taketh Peter, James, and John his brother, and
bringeth them up into an high mountain
apart,
2 And was transfigured before them: and
his face did shine as the sun, and his raiment was white as the light.
3 And, behold, there appeared unto them
Moses and Elias talking with him.
4 Then answered Peter, and said unto
Jesus, Lord, it is good for us to be here: if
thou wilt, let us make here three tabernacles; one for thee, and one for Moses, and
one for Elias.
5 [o]While he yet spake, behold, a bright
cloud overshadowed them: and behold a
voice out of the cloud, which said, [p]This
is my beloved Son, [q]in whom I am well
pleased; [r]hear ye him.
6 [s]And when the disciples heard *it*, they
fell on their face, and were sore afraid.
7 And Jesus came and [t]touched them,
and said, Arise, and be not afraid.
8 And when they had lifted up their eyes,
they saw no man, save Jesus only.
9 And as they came down from the mountain, [u]Jesus charged them, saying, Tell the
vision to no man, until the Son of man be
risen again from the dead.
10 And his disciples asked him, saying,
[v]Why then say the scribes that Elias must
first come?
11 And Jesus answered and said unto
them, Elias truly shall first come, and [w]re-
store all things.
12 [x]But I say unto you, That Elias is come
already, and they knew him not, but [y]have
done unto him whatsoever they listed. Likewise [z]shall also the Son of man suffer of
them.
13 [a]Then the disciples understood that he
spake unto them of John the Baptist.
14 ¶ [b]And when they were come to the
multitude, there came to him a *certain* man,
kneeling down to him, and saying,

16:23 [e]2 Sam. 19:22 [f]Rom. 8:7
16:24 [g]ch. 10:38; Mark 8:34; Luke 9:23; Acts 14:22; 1 Thess. 3:3; 2 Tim. 3:12
16:25 [h]Luke 17:33; John 12:25
16:26 [i]Ps. 49:7
16:27 [j]ch. 26:64; Mark 8:38; Luke 9:26 [k]Dan. 7:10; Zech. 14:5; ch. 25:31; Jude 14 [l]Job 34:11; Ps. 62:12; Prov. 24:12; Jer. 17:10; Rom. 2:6; 1 Cor. 3:8; 2 Cor. 5:10; 1 Pet. 1:17; Rev. 2:23
16:28 [m]Mark 9:1; Luke 9:27
17:1 [n]Mark 9:2; Luke 9:28
17:5 [o]2 Pet. 1:17 [p]ch. 3:17; Mark 1:11; Luke 3:22 [q]Isa. 42:1 [r]Deut. 18:15; Acts 3:22
17:6 [s]2 Pet. 1:18
17:7 [t]Dan. 8:18
17:9 [u]ch. 16:20; Mark 8:30
17:10 [v]Mal. 4:5; ch. 11:14; Mark 9:11
17:11 [w]Mal. 4:6; Luke 1:16; Acts 3:21
17:12 [x]ch. 11:14; Mark 9:12 [y]ch. 14:3 [z]ch. 16:21
17:13 [a]ch. 11:14
17:14 [b]Mark 9:14; Luke 9:37
17:20 [c]ch. 21:21; Mark 11:23; Luke 17:6; 1 Cor. 12:9
17:22 [d]ch. 16:21; Mark 8:31; Luke 9:22
17:24 [e]Mark 9:33
18:1 [f]Mark 9:33; Luke 9:46
18:3 [g]Ps. 131:2; ch. 19:14; Mark 10:14; Luke 18:16; 1 Cor. 14:20; 1 Pet. 2:2
18:4 [h]ch. 20:27
18:5 [i]ch. 10:42; Luke 9:48
18:6 [j]Mark 9:42; Luke 17:1
18:7 [k]Luke 17:1; 1 Cor. 11:19

15 Lord, have mercy on my son: for he is
lunatick, and sore vexed: for ofttimes he
falleth into the fire, and oft into the water.
16 And I brought him to thy disciples, and
they could not cure him.
17 Then Jesus answered and said, O
faithless and perverse generation, how long
shall I be with you? how long shall I suffer
you? bring him hither to me.
18 And Jesus rebuked the devil; and he
departed out of him: and the child was
cured from that very hour.
19 Then came the disciples to Jesus apart,
and said, Why could not we cast him out?
20 And Jesus said unto them, Because of
your unbelief: for verily I say unto you, [c]If
ye have faith as a grain of mustard seed, ye
shall say unto this mountain, Remove hence
to yonder place; and it shall remove; and
nothing shall be impossible unto you.
21 Howbeit this kind goeth not out but by
prayer and fasting.
22 ¶ [d]And while they abode in Galilee,
Jesus said unto them, The Son of man shall
be betrayed into the hands of men:
23 And they shall kill him, and the third
day he shall be raised again. And they were
exceeding sorry.
24 ¶ And [e]when they were come to Capernaum, they that received tribute *money*
came to Peter, and said, Doth not your master pay tribute?
25 He saith, Yes. And when he was come
into the house, Jesus prevented him, saying,
What thinkest thou, Simon? of whom do the
kings of the earth take custom or tribute? of
their own children, or of strangers?
26 Peter saith unto him, Of strangers.
Jesus saith unto him, Then are the children
free.
27 Notwithstanding, lest we should offend them, go thou to the sea, and cast an
hook, and take up the fish that first cometh
up; and when thou hast opened his mouth,
thou shalt find a piece of money: that take,
and give unto them for me and thee.
18 At [f]the same time came the disciples
unto Jesus, saying, Who is the greatest in the kingdom of heaven?
2 And Jesus called a little child unto him,
and set him in the midst of them,
3 And said, Verily I say unto you, [g]Ex-
cept ye be converted, and become as little
children, ye shall not enter into the kingdom of heaven.
4 [h]Whosoever therefore shall humble
himself as this little child, the same is greatest in the kingdom of heaven.
5 And whoso [i]shall receive one such little child in my name receiveth me.
6 [j]But whoso shall offend one of these
little ones which believe in me, it were better for him that a millstone were hanged
about his neck, and *that* he were drowned
in the depth of the sea.
7 ¶ Woe unto the world because of offences! for [k]it must needs be that offences

come; but [l]woe to that man by whom the offence cometh!

8 [m]Wherefore if thy hand or thy foot offend thee, cut them off, and cast *them* from thee: it is better for thee to enter into life halt or maimed, rather than having two hands or two feet to be cast into everlasting fire.

9 And if thine eye offend thee, pluck it out, and cast *it* from thee: it is better for thee to enter into life with one eye, rather than having two eyes to be cast into hell fire.

10 Take heed that ye despise not one of these little ones; for I say unto you, That in heaven [n]their angels do always [o]behold the face of my Father which is in heaven.

11 [p]For the Son of man is come to save that which was lost.

12 [q]How think ye? if a man have an hundred sheep, and one of them be gone astray, doth he not leave the ninety and nine, and goeth into the mountains, and seeketh that which is gone astray?

13 And if so be that he find it, verily I say unto you, he rejoiceth more of that *sheep,* than of the ninety and nine which went not astray.

14 Even so it is not the will of your Father which is in heaven, that one of these little ones should perish.

15 ¶ Moreover [r]if thy brother shall trespass against thee, go and tell him his fault between thee and him alone: if he shall hear thee, [s]thou hast gained thy brother.

16 But if he will not hear *thee, then* take with thee one or two more, that in [t]the mouth of two or three witnesses every word may be established.

17 And if he shall neglect to hear them, tell *it* unto the church: but if he neglect to hear the church, let him be unto thee as an [u]heathen man and a publican.

18 Verily I say unto you, [v]Whatsoever ye shall bind on earth shall be bound in heaven: and whatsoever ye shall loose on earth shall be loosed in heaven.

19 [w]Again I say unto you, That if two of you shall agree on earth as touching any thing that they shall ask, [x]it shall be done for them of my Father which is in heaven.

20 For where two or three are gathered together in my name, there am I in the midst of them.

21 ¶ Then came Peter to him, and said, Lord, how oft shall my brother sin against me, and I forgive him? [y]till seven times?

22 Jesus saith unto him, I say not unto thee, Until seven times: [z]but, Until seventy times seven.

23 ¶ Therefore is the kingdom of heaven likened unto a certain king, which would take account of his servants.

24 And when he had begun to reckon, one was brought unto him, which owed him ten thousand talents.

25 But forasmuch as he had not to pay, his lord commanded him [a]to be sold, and his wife, and children, and all that he had, and payment to be made.

26 The servant therefore fell down, and worshipped him, saying, Lord, have patience with me, and I will pay thee all.

27 Then the lord of that servant was moved with compassion, and loosed him, and forgave him the debt.

28 But the same servant went out, and found one of his fellowservants, which owed him an hundred pence: and he laid hands on him, and took *him* by the throat, saying, Pay me that thou owest.

29 And his fellowservant fell down at his feet, and besought him, saying, Have patience with me, and I will pay thee all.

30 And he would not: but went and cast him into prison, till he should pay the debt.

31 So when his fellowservants saw what was done, they were very sorry, and came and told unto their lord all that was done.

32 Then his lord, after that he had called him, said unto him, O thou wicked servant, I forgave thee all that debt, because thou desiredst me:

33 Shouldest not thou also have had compassion on thy fellowservant, even as I had pity on thee?

34 And his lord was wroth, and delivered him to the tormentors, till he should pay all that was due unto him.

35 [b]So likewise shall my heavenly Father do also unto you, if ye from your hearts forgive not every one his brother their trespasses.

19 And it came to pass, [c]*that* when Jesus had finished these sayings, he departed from Galilee, and came into the coasts of Judaea beyond Jordan;

2 [d]And great multitudes followed him; and he healed them there.

3 ¶ The Pharisees also came unto him, tempting him, and saying unto him, Is it lawful for a man to put away his wife for every cause?

4 And he answered and said unto them, Have ye not read, [e]that he which made *them* at the beginning made them male and female,

5 And said, [f]For this cause shall a man leave father and mother, and shall cleave to his wife: and [g]they twain shall be one flesh?

6 Wherefore they are no more twain, but one flesh. What therefore God hath joined together, let not man put asunder.

7 They say unto him, [h]Why did Moses then command to give a writing of divorcement, and to put her away?

8 He saith unto them, Moses because of the hardness of your hearts suffered you to put away your wives: but from the beginning it was not so.

9 [i]And I say unto you, Whosoever shall put away his wife, except *it be* for fornication, and shall marry another, committeth adultery: and whoso marrieth her which is put away doth commit adultery.

10 ¶ His disciples say unto him, [j]If the case of the man be so with *his* wife, it is not good to marry.

18:7 [l]ch. 26:24
18:8 [m]ch. 5:29; Mark 9:43
18:10 [n]Ps. 34:7; Zech. 13:7; Heb. 1:14 [o]Esth. 1:14; Luke 1:19
18:11 [p]Luke 9:56; John 3:17
18:12 [q]Luke 15:4
18:15 [r]Lev. 19:17; Luke 17:3 [s]Jam. 5:20; 1 Pet. 3:1
18:16 [t]Deut. 17:6; John 8:17; 2 Cor. 13:1; Heb. 10:28
18:17 [u]Rom. 16:17; 1 Cor. 5:9; 2 Thess. 3:6; 2 John 10
18:18 [v]ch. 16:19; John 20:23; 1 Cor. 5:4
18:19 [w]ch. 5:24 [x]1 John 3:22
18:21 [y]Luke 17:4
18:22 [z]ch. 6:14; Mark 11:25; Col. 3:13
18:25 [a]2 Kings 4:1; Neh. 5:8
18:35 [b]Prov. 21:13; ch. 6:12; Mark 11:26; Jam. 2:13
19:1 [c]Mark 10:1; John 10:40
19:2 [d]ch. 12:15
19:4 [e]Gen. 1:27; Mal. 2:15
19:5 [f]Gen. 2:24; Mark 10:5-9; Eph. 5:31 [g]1 Cor. 6:16
19:7 [h]Deut. 24:1; ch. 5:31
19:9 [i]ch. 5:32; Mark 10:11; Luke 16:18; 1 Cor. 7:10
19:10 [j]Prov. 21:19

11 But he said unto them, [k]All *men* cannot receive this saying, save *they* to whom it is given.

12 For there are some eunuchs, which were so born from *their* mother's womb: and there are some eunuchs, which were made eunuchs of men: and [l]there be eunuchs, which have made themselves eunuchs for the kingdom of heaven's sake. He that is able to receive *it*, let him receive *it*.

13 ¶ [m]Then were there brought unto him little children, that he should put *his* hands on them, and pray: and the disciples rebuked them.

14 But Jesus said, Suffer little children, and forbid them not, to come unto me: for [n]of such is the kingdom of heaven.

15 And he laid *his* hands on them, and departed thence.

16 ¶ [o]And, behold, one came and said unto him, [p]Good Master, what good thing shall I do, that I may have eternal life?

17 And he said unto him, Why callest thou me good? *there is* none good but one, *that is*, God: but if thou wilt enter into life, keep the commandments.

18 He saith unto him, Which? Jesus said, [q]Thou shalt do no murder, Thou shalt not commit adultery, Thou shalt not steal, Thou shalt not bear false witness,

19 [r]Honour thy father and *thy* mother: and, [s]Thou shalt love thy neighbour as thyself.

20 The young man saith unto him, All these things have I kept from my youth up: what lack I yet?

21 Jesus said unto him, If thou wilt be perfect, [t]go *and* sell that thou hast, and give to the poor, and thou shalt have treasure in heaven: and come *and* follow me.

22 But when the young man heard that saying, he went away sorrowful: for he had great possessions.

23 ¶ Then said Jesus unto his disciples, Verily I say unto you, That [u]a rich man shall hardly enter into the kingdom of heaven.

24 And again I say unto you, It is easier for a camel to go through the eye of a needle, than for a rich man to enter into the kingdom of God.

25 When his disciples heard *it*, they were exceedingly amazed, saying, Who then can be saved?

26 But Jesus beheld *them*, and said unto them, With men this is impossible; but [v]with God all things are possible.

27 ¶ [w]Then answered Peter and said unto him, Behold, [x]we have forsaken all, and followed thee; what shall we have therefore?

28 And Jesus said unto them, Verily I say unto you, That ye which have followed me, in the regeneration when the Son of man shall sit in the throne of his glory, [y]ye also shall sit upon twelve thrones, judging the twelve tribes of Israel.

29 [z]And every one that hath forsaken houses, or brethren, or sisters, or father, or mother, or wife, or children, or lands, for my name's sake, shall receive an hundredfold, and shall inherit everlasting life.

30 [a]But many *that are* first shall be last; and the last *shall be* first.

20 For the kingdom of heaven is like unto a man *that is* an householder, which went out early in the morning to hire labourers into his vineyard.

2 And when he had agreed with the labourers for a penny a day, he sent them into his vineyard.

3 And he went out about the third hour, and saw others standing idle in the marketplace,

4 And said unto them; Go ye also into the vineyard, and whatsoever is right I will give you. And they went their way.

5 Again he went out about the sixth and ninth hour, and did likewise.

6 And about the eleventh hour he went out, and found others standing idle, and saith unto them, Why stand ye here all the day idle?

7 They say unto him, Because no man hath hired us. He saith unto them, Go ye also into the vineyard; and whatsoever is right, *that* shall ye receive.

8 So when even was come, the lord of the vineyard saith unto his steward, Call the labourers, and give them *their* hire, beginning from the last unto the first.

9 And when they came that *were hired* about the eleventh hour, they received every man a penny.

10 But when the first came, they supposed that they should have received more; and they likewise received every man a penny.

11 And when they had received *it*, they murmured against the goodman of the house,

12 Saying, These last have wrought *but* one hour, and thou hast made them equal unto us, which have borne the burden and heat of the day.

13 But he answered one of them, and said, Friend, I do thee no wrong: didst not thou agree with me for a penny?

14 Take *that* thine *is*, and go thy way: I will give unto this last, even as unto thee.

15 [b]Is it not lawful for me to do what I will with mine own? [c]Is thine eye evil, because I am good?

16 [d]So the last shall be first, and the first last: [e]for many be called, but few chosen.

17 ¶ [f]And Jesus going up to Jerusalem took the twelve disciples apart in the way, and said unto them,

18 [g]Behold, we go up to Jerusalem; and the Son of man shall be betrayed unto the chief priests and unto the scribes, and they shall condemn him to death,

19 [h]And shall deliver him to the Gentiles to mock, and to scourge, and to crucify *him*: and the third day he shall rise again.

20 ¶ [i]Then came to him the mother of [j]Zebedee's children with her sons, wor-

19:11 [k]1 Cor. 7:2
19:12 [l]1 Cor. 7:32
19:13 [m]Mark 10:13; Luke 18:15
19:14 [n]ch. 18:3
19:16 [o]Mark 10:17; Luke 18:18 [p]Luke 10:25
19:18 [q]Ex. 20:13; Deut. 5:17
19:19 [r]ch. 15:4 [s]Lev. 19:18; ch. 22:39; Rom. 13:9; Gal. 5:14; Jam. 2:8
19:21 [t]ch. 6:20; Luke 12:33; Acts 2:45; 1 Tim. 6:18
19:23 [u]ch. 13:22; Mark 10:24; 1 Cor. 1:26; 1 Tim. 6:9
19:26 [v]Gen. 18:14; Job 42:2; Jer. 32:17; Zech. 8:6; Luke 1:37
19:27 [w]Mark 10:28; Luke 18:28 [x]Deut. 33:9; ch. 4:20; Luke 5:11
19:28 [y]ch. 20:21; Luke 22:28; 1 Cor. 6:2; Rev. 2:26
19:29 [z]Mark 10:29; Luke 18:29
19:30 [a]ch. 20:16; Mark 10:31; Luke 13:30
20:15 [b]Rom. 9:21 [c]Deut. 15:9; Prov. 23:6; ch. 6:23
20:16 [d]ch. 19:30 [e]ch. 22:14
20:17 [f]Mark 10:32; Luke 18:31; John 12:12
20:18 [g]ch. 16:21
20:19 [h]ch. 27:2; Mark 15:1; Luke 23:1; John 18:28; Acts 3:13
20:20 [i]Mark 10:35 [j]ch. 4:21

shipping *him*, and desiring a certain thing of him.

21 And he said unto her, What wilt thou? She saith unto him, Grant that these my two sons [k]may sit, the one on thy right hand, and the other on the left, in thy kingdom.

22 But Jesus answered and said, Ye know not what ye ask. Are ye able to drink of [l]the cup that I shall drink of, and to be baptized with [m]the baptism that I am baptized with? They say unto him, We are able.

23 And he saith unto them, [n]Ye shall drink indeed of my cup, and be baptized with the baptism that I am baptized with: but to sit on my right hand, and on my left, is not mine to [o]give, but *it shall be given to them* for whom it is prepared of my Father.

24 [p]And when the ten heard *it*, they were moved with indignation against the two brethren.

25 But Jesus called them *unto him*, and said, Ye know that the princes of the Gentiles exercise dominion over them, and they that are great exercise authority upon them.

26 But [q]it shall not be so among you: but [r]whosoever will be great among you, let him be your minister;

27 [s]And whosoever will be chief among you, let him be your servant:

28 [t]Even as the [u]Son of man came not to be ministered unto, [v]but to minister, and [w]to give his life a ransom [x]for many.

29 [y]And as they departed from Jericho, a great multitude followed him.

30 ¶ And, behold, [z]two blind men sitting by the way side, when they heard that Jesus passed by, cried out, saying, Have mercy on us, O Lord, *thou* son of David.

31 And the multitude rebuked them, because they should hold their peace: but they cried the more, saying, Have mercy on us, O Lord, *thou* son of David.

32 And Jesus stood still, and called them, and said, What will ye that I shall do unto you?

33 They say unto him, Lord, that our eyes may be opened.

34 So Jesus had compassion *on them*, and touched their eyes: and immediately their eyes received sight, and they followed him.

21 And [a]when they drew nigh unto Jerusalem, and were come to Bethphage, unto [b]the mount of Olives, then sent Jesus two disciples,

2 Saying unto them, Go into the village over against you, and straightway ye shall find an ass tied, and a colt with her: loose *them*, and bring *them* unto me.

3 And if any *man* say ought unto you, ye shall say, The Lord hath need of them; and straightway he will send them.

4 All this was done, that it might be fulfilled which was spoken by the prophet, saying,

5 [c]Tell ye the daughter of Sion, Behold, thy King cometh unto thee, meek, and sitting upon an ass, and a colt the foal of an ass.

6 [d]And the disciples went, and did as Jesus commanded them,

7 And brought the ass, and the colt, and [e]put on them their clothes, and they set *him* thereon.

8 And a very great multitude spread their garments in the way; [f]others cut down branches from the trees, and strawed *them* in the way.

9 And the multitudes that went before, and that followed, cried, saying, [g]Hosanna to the son of David: [h]Blessed *is* he that cometh in the name of the Lord; Hosanna in the highest.

10 [i]And when he was come into Jerusalem, all the city was moved, saying, Who is this?

11 And the multitude said, This is Jesus [j]the prophet of Nazareth of Galilee.

12 ¶ [k]And Jesus went into the temple of God, and cast out all them that sold and bought in the temple, and overthrew the tables of the [l]moneychangers, and the seats of them that sold doves,

13 And said unto them, It is written, [m]My house shall be called the house of prayer; [n]but ye have made it a den of thieves.

14 And the blind and the lame came to him in the temple; and he healed them.

15 And when the chief priests and scribes saw the wonderful things that he did, and the children crying in the temple, and saying, Hosanna to the son of David; they were sore displeased,

16 And said unto him, Hearest thou what these say? And Jesus saith unto them, Yea; have ye never read, [o]Out of the mouth of babes and sucklings thou hast perfected praise?

17 ¶ And he left them, and went out of the city into [p]Bethany; and he lodged there.

18 [q]Now in the morning as he returned into the city, he hungered.

19 [r]And when he saw a fig tree in the way, he came to it, and found nothing thereon, but leaves only, and said unto it, Let no fruit grow on thee henceforward for ever. And presently the fig tree withered away.

20 [s]And when the disciples saw *it*, they marvelled, saying, How soon is the fig tree withered away!

21 Jesus answered and said unto them, Verily I say unto you, [t]If ye have faith, and [u]doubt not, ye shall not only do this *which is done* to the fig tree, [v]but also if ye shall say unto this mountain, Be thou removed, and be thou cast into the sea; it shall be done.

22 And [w]all things, whatsoever ye shall ask in prayer, believing, ye shall receive.

23 ¶ [x]And when he was come into the temple, the chief priests and the elders of the people came unto him as he was teaching, and [y]said, By what authority doest thou these things? and who gave thee this authority?

24 And Jesus answered and said unto

20:21 [k]ch. 19:28
20:22 [l]ch. 26:39; Mark 14:36; Luke 22:42; John 18:11 [m]Luke 12:50
20:23 [n]Acts 12:2; Rom. 8:17; 2 Cor. 1:7; Rev. 1:9 [o]ch. 25:34
20:24 [p]Mark 10:41; Luke 22:24
20:26 [q]1 Pet. 5:3 [r]ch. 23:11; Mark 9:35
20:27 [s]ch. 18:4
20:28 [t]John 13:4 [u]Phil. 2:7 [v]Luke 22:27; John 13:14 [w]Isa. 53:10; Dan. 9:24; John 11:51; 1 Tim. 2:6; Tit. 2:14; 1 Pet. 1:19 [x]ch. 26:28; Rom. 5:15; Heb. 9:28
20:29 [y]Mark 10:46; Luke 18:35
20:30 [z]ch. 9:27
21:1 [a]Mark 11:1; Luke 19:29 [b]Zech. 14:4
21:5 [c]Isa. 62:11; Zech. 9:9; John 12:15
21:6 [d]Mark 11:4
21:7 [e]2 Kings 9:13
21:8 [f]Lev. 23:40; John 12:13
21:9 [g]Ps. 118:25 [h]Ps. 118:26; ch. 23:39
21:10 [i]Mark 11:15; Luke 19:45; John 2:13
21:11 [j]ch. 2:23; Luke 7:16; John 6:14
21:12 [k]Mark 11:11; Luke 19:45; John 2:15 [l]Deut. 14:25
21:13 [m]Isa. 56:7 [n]Jer. 7:11; Mark 11:17; Luke 19:46
21:16 [o]Ps. 8:2
21:17 [p]Mark 11:11; John 11:18
21:18 [q]Mark 11:12
21:19 [r]Mark 11:13
21:20 [s]Mark 11:20
21:21 [t]ch. 17:20; Luke 17:6 [u]Jam. 1:6 [v]1 Cor. 13:2
21:22 [w]ch. 7:7; Mark 11:24; Luke 11:9; Jam. 5:16; 1 John 3:22
21:23 [x]Mark 11:27; Luke 20:1 [y]Ex. 2:14; Acts 4:7

them, I also will ask you one thing, which if ye tell me, I in like wise will tell you by what authority I do these things.

25 The baptism of John, whence was it? from heaven, or of men? And they reasoned with themselves, saying, If we shall say, From heaven; he will say unto us, Why did ye not then believe him?

26 But if we shall say, Of men; we fear the people; [z]for all hold John as a prophet.

27 And they answered Jesus, and said, We cannot tell. And he said unto them, Neither tell I you by what authority I do these things.

28 ¶ But what think ye? A *certain* man had two sons; and he came to the first, and said, Son, go work to day in my vineyard.

29 He answered and said, I will not: but afterward he repented, and went.

30 And he came to the second, and said likewise. And he answered and said, I *go,* sir: and went not.

31 Whether of them twain did the will of *his* father? They say unto him, The first. Jesus saith unto them, [a]Verily I say unto you, That the publicans and the harlots go into the kingdom of God before you.

32 For [b]John came unto you in the way of righteousness, and ye believed him not: [c]but the publicans and the harlots believed him: and ye, when ye had seen *it,* repented not afterward, that ye might believe him.

33 ¶ Hear another parable: There was a certain householder, [d]which planted a vineyard, and hedged it round about, and digged a winepress in it, and built a tower, and let it out to husbandmen, and [e]went into a far country:

34 And when the time of the fruit drew near, he sent his servants to the husbandmen, [f]that they might receive the fruits of it.

35 [g]And the husbandmen took his servants, and beat one, and killed another, and stoned another.

36 Again, he sent other servants more than the first: and they did unto them likewise.

37 But last of all he sent unto them his son, saying, They will reverence my son.

38 But when the husbandmen saw the son, they said among themselves, [h]This is the heir; [i]come, let us kill him, and let us seize on his inheritance.

39 [j]And they caught him, and cast *him* out of the vineyard, and slew *him.*

40 When the lord therefore of the vineyard cometh, what will he do unto those husbandmen?

41 [k]They say unto him, [l]He will miserably destroy those wicked men, [m]and will let out *his* vineyard unto other husbandmen, which shall render him the fruits in their seasons.

42 Jesus saith unto them, [n]Did ye never read in the scriptures, The stone which the builders rejected, the same is become the head of the corner: this is the Lord's doing, and it is marvellous in our eyes?

43 Therefore say I unto you, [o]The kingdom of God shall be taken from you, and given to a nation bringing forth the fruits thereof.

44 And whosoever [p]shall fall on this stone shall be broken: but on whomsoever it shall fall, [q]it will grind him to powder.

45 And when the chief priests and Pharisees had heard his parables, they perceived that he spake of them.

46 But when they sought to lay hands on him, they feared the multitude, because [r]they took him for a prophet.

22 And Jesus answered [s]and spake unto them again by parables, and said,

2 The kingdom of heaven is like unto a certain king, which made a marriage for his son,

3 And sent forth his servants to call them that were bidden to the wedding: and they would not come.

4 Again, he sent forth other servants, saying, Tell them which are bidden, Behold, I have prepared my dinner: [t]my oxen and *my* fatlings *are* killed, and all things *are* ready: come unto the marriage.

5 But they made light of *it,* and went their ways, one to his farm, another to his merchandise:

6 And the remnant took his servants, and entreated *them* spitefully, and slew *them.*

7 But when the king heard *thereof,* he was wroth: and he sent forth [u]his armies, and destroyed those murderers, and burned up their city.

8 Then saith he to his servants, The wedding is ready, but they which were bidden were not [v]worthy.

9 Go ye therefore into the highways, and as many as ye shall find, bid to the marriage.

10 So those servants went out into the highways, and [w]gathered together all as many as they found, both bad and good: and the wedding was furnished with guests.

11 ¶ And when the king came in to see the guests, he saw there a man [x]which had not on a wedding garment:

12 And he saith unto him, Friend, how camest thou in hither not having a wedding garment? And he was speechless.

13 Then said the king to the servants, Bind him hand and foot, and take him away, and cast *him* [y]into outer darkness; there shall be weeping and gnashing of teeth.

14 [z]For many are called, but few *are* chosen.

15 ¶ [a]Then went the Pharisees, and took counsel how they might entangle him in *his* talk.

16 And they sent out unto him their disciples with the Herodians, saying, Master, we know that thou art true, and teachest the way of God in truth, neither carest thou for

21:26 *z* ch. 14:5; Mark 6:20; Luke 20:6
21:31 *a* Luke 7:29
21:32 *b* ch. 3:1 *c* Luke 3:12
21:33 *d* Ps. 80:9; SSol. 8:11; Isa. 5:1; Jer. 2:21; Mark 12:1; Luke 20:9 *e* ch. 25:14
21:34 *f* SSol. 8:11
21:35 *g* 2 Chron. 24:21; Neh. 9:26; ch. 5:12; Acts 7:52; 1 Thess. 2:15; Heb. 11:36
21:38 *h* Ps. 2:8; Heb. 1:2 *i* Ps. 2:2; ch. 26:3; John 11:53; Acts 4:27
21:39 *j* ch. 26:50; Mark 14:46; Luke 22:54; John 18:12; Acts 2:23
21:41 *k* Luke 20:16 *l* Luke 21:24; Heb. 2:3 *m* Acts 13:46; Rom. 9
21:42 *n* Ps. 118:22; Isa. 28:16; Mark 12:10; Luke 20:17; Acts 4:11; Eph. 2:20; 1 Pet. 2:6
21:43 *o* ch. 8:12
21:44 *p* Isa. 8:14; Zech. 12:3; Luke 20:18; Rom. 9:33; 1 Pet. 2:8 *q* Isa. 60:12; Dan. 2:44
21:46 *r* ver. 11; Luke 7:16; John 7:40
22:1 *s* Luke 14:16; Rev. 19:7
22:4 *t* Prov. 9:2
22:7 *u* Dan. 9:26; Luke 19:27
22:8 *v* ch. 10:11; Acts 13:46
22:10 *w* ch. 13:38
22:11 *x* 2 Cor. 5:3; Eph. 4:24; Col. 3:10; Rev. 3:4
22:13 *y* ch. 8:12
22:14 *z* ch. 20:16
22:15 *a* Mark 12:13; Luke 20:20

any *man:* for thou regardest not the person
of men.
17 Tell us therefore, What thinkest thou?
Is it lawful to give tribute unto Caesar, or
not?
18 But Jesus perceived their wickedness,
and said, Why tempt ye me, *ye* hypocrites?
19 Shew me the tribute money. And they
brought unto him a penny.
20 And he saith unto them, Whose *is* this
image and superscription?
21 They say unto him, Caesar's. Then
saith he unto them, [b]Render therefore unto
Caesar the things which are Caesar's; and
unto God the things that are God's.
22 When they had heard *these words,*
they marvelled, and left him, and went their
way.
23 ¶ [c]The same day came to him the Sadducees, [d]which say that there is no resurrection, and asked him,
24 Saying, Master, [e]Moses said, If a man
die, having no children, his brother shall
marry his wife, and raise up seed unto his
brother.
25 Now there were with us seven brethren: and the first, when he had married a
wife, deceased, and, having no issue, left his
wife unto his brother:
26 Likewise the second also, and the
third, unto the seventh.
27 And last of all the woman died also.
28 Therefore in the resurrection whose
wife shall she be of the seven? for they all
had her.
29 Jesus answered and said unto them,
Ye do err, [f]not knowing the scriptures, nor
the power of God.
30 For in the resurrection they neither
marry, nor are given in marriage, but [g]are
as the angels of God in heaven.
31 But as touching the resurrection of the
dead, have ye not read that which was spoken unto you by God, saying,
32 [h]I am the God of Abraham, and the
God of Isaac, and the God of Jacob? God is
not the God of the dead, but of the living.
33 And when the multitude heard *this,*
[i]they were astonished at his doctrine.
34 ¶ [j]But when the Pharisees had heard
that he had put the Sadducees to silence,
they were gathered together.
35 Then one of them, *which was* [k]a lawyer, asked *him a question,* tempting him,
and saying,
36 Master, which *is* the great commandment in the law?
37 Jesus said unto him, [l]Thou shalt love
the Lord thy God with all thy heart, and
with all thy soul, and with all thy mind.
38 This is the first and great commandment.
39 And the second *is* like unto it, [m]Thou
shalt love thy neighbour as thyself.
40 [n]On these two commandments hang
all the law and the prophets.
41 ¶ [o]While the Pharisees were gathered
together, Jesus asked them,

22:21 [b]ch. 17:25; Rom. 13:7
22:23 [c]Mark 12:18; Luke 20:27 [d]Acts 23:8
22:24 [e]Deut. 25:5
22:29 [f]John 20:9
22:30 [g]1 John 3:2
22:32 [h]Ex. 3:6; Mark 12:26; Luke 20:37; Acts 7:32; Heb. 11:16
22:33 [i]ch. 7:28
22:34 [j]Mark 12:28
22:35 [k]Luke 10:25
22:37 [l]Deut. 6:5; Luke 10:27
22:39 [m]Lev. 19:18; ch. 19:19; Mark 12:31; Luke 10:27; Rom. 13:9; Gal. 5:14; Jam. 2:8
22:40 [n]ch. 7:12; 1 Tim. 1:5
22:41 [o]Mark 12:35; Luke 20:41
22:44 [p]Ps. 110:1; Acts 2:34; 1 Cor. 15:25; Heb. 1:13
22:46 [q]Luke 14:6 [r]Mark 12:34; Luke 20:40
23:2 [s]Neh. 8:4; Mal. 2:7; Mark 12:38; Luke 20:45
23:3 [t]Rom. 2:19
23:4 [u]Luke 11:46; Acts 15:10; Gal. 6:13
23:5 [v]ch. 6:1 [w]Num. 15:38; Deut. 6:8; Prov. 3:3
23:6 [x]Mark 12:38; Luke 11:43; 3 John 9
23:8 [y]Jam. 3:1; 2 Cor. 1:24; 1 Pet. 5:3
23:9 [z]Mal. 1:6
23:11 [a]ch. 20:26
23:12 [b]Job 22:29; Prov. 15:33; Luke 14:11; Jam. 4:6; 1 Pet. 5:5
23:13 [c]Luke 11:52
23:14 [d]Mark 12:40; Luke 20:47; 2 Tim. 3:6; Tit. 1:11
23:16 [e]ch. 15:14; ver. 24 [f]ch. 5:33
23:17 [g]Ex. 30:29

42 Saying, What think ye of Christ?
whose son is he? They say unto him, *The
son* of David.
43 He saith unto them, How then doth David in spirit call him Lord, saying,
44 [p]The LORD said unto my Lord, Sit thou
on my right hand, till I make thine enemies
thy footstool?
45 If David then call him Lord, how is he
his son?
46 [q]And no man was able to answer him
a word, [r]neither durst any *man* from that
day forth ask him any more *questions.*
23 Then spake Jesus to the multitude,
and to his disciples,
2 Saying, [s]The scribes and the Pharisees
sit in Moses' seat:
3 All therefore whatsoever they bid you
observe, *that* observe and do; but do not ye
after their works: for [t]they say, and do not.
4 [u]For they bind heavy burdens and
grievous to be borne, and lay *them* on men's
shoulders; but they *themselves* will not
move them with one of their fingers.
5 But [v]all their works they do for to be
seen of men: [w]they make broad their phy-
lacteries, and enlarge the borders of their
garments,
6 [x]And love the uppermost rooms at
feasts, and the chief seats in the synagogues,
7 And greetings in the markets, and to be
called of men, Rabbi, Rabbi.
8 [y]But be not ye called Rabbi: for one is
your Master, *even* Christ; and all ye are
brethren.
9 And call no *man* your father upon the
earth: [z]for one is your Father, which is in
heaven.
10 Neither be ye called masters: for one is
your Master, *even* Christ.
11 But [a]he that is greatest among you
shall be your servant.
12 [b]And whosoever shall exalt himself
shall be abased; and he that shall humble
himself shall be exalted.
13 ¶ But [c]woe unto you, scribes and
Pharisees, hypocrites! for ye shut up the
kingdom of heaven against men: for ye neither go in *yourselves,* neither suffer ye them
that are entering to go in.
14 Woe unto you, scribes and Pharisees,
hypocrites! [d]for ye devour widows' houses,
and for a pretence make long prayer: therefore ye shall receive the greater damnation.
15 Woe unto you, scribes and Pharisees,
hypocrites! for ye compass sea and land to
make one proselyte, and when he is made,
ye make him twofold more the child of hell
than yourselves.
16 Woe unto you, [e]*ye* blind guides, which
say, [f]Whosoever shall swear by the temple,
it is nothing; but whosoever shall swear by
the gold of the temple, he is a debtor!
17 *Ye* fools and blind: for whether is
greater, the gold, [g]or the temple that sanctifieth the gold?
18 And, Whosoever shall swear by the al-

r, it is nothing; but whosoever sweareth by the gift that is upon it, he is guilty.

19 *Ye* fools and blind: for whether *is* greater, the gift, or [h]the altar that sanctifieth the gift?

20 Whoso therefore shall swear by the altar, sweareth by it, and by all things thereon.

21 And whoso shall swear by the temple, sweareth by it, and by [i]him that dwelleth therein.

22 And he that shall swear by heaven, sweareth by [j]the throne of God, and by him that sitteth thereon.

23 Woe unto you, scribes and Pharisees, hypocrites! [k]for ye pay tithe of mint and anise and cummin, and [l]have omitted the weightier *matters* of the law, judgment, mercy, and faith: these ought ye to have done, and not to leave the other undone.

24 *Ye* blind guides, which strain at a gnat, and swallow a camel.

25 Woe unto you, scribes and Pharisees, hypocrites! [m]for ye make clean the outside of the cup and of the platter, but within they are full of extortion and excess.

26 *Thou* blind Pharisee, cleanse first that *which is* within the cup and platter, that the outside of them may be clean also.

27 Woe unto you, scribes and Pharisees, hypocrites! [n]for ye are like unto whited sepulchres, which indeed appear beautiful outward, but are within full of dead *men's* bones, and of all uncleanness.

28 Even so ye also outwardly appear righteous unto men, but within ye are full of hypocrisy and iniquity.

29 [o]Woe unto you, scribes and Pharisees, hypocrites! because ye build the tombs of the prophets, and garnish the sepulchres of the righteous,

30 And say, If we had been in the days of our fathers, we would not have been partakers with them in the blood of the prophets.

31 Wherefore ye be witnesses unto yourselves, that [p]ye are the children of them which killed the prophets.

32 [q]Fill ye up then the measure of your fathers.

33 *Ye* serpents, *ye* [r]generation of vipers, how can ye escape the damnation of hell?

34 ¶ [s]Wherefore, behold, I send unto you prophets, and wise men, and scribes: and [t]*some* of them ye shall kill and crucify; and [u]*some* of them shall ye scourge in your synagogues, and persecute *them* from city to city:

35 [v]That upon you may come all the righteous blood shed upon the earth, [w]from the blood of righteous Abel unto [x]the blood of Zacharias son of Barachias, whom ye slew between the temple and the altar.

36 Verily I say unto you, All these things shall come upon this generation.

37 [y]O Jerusalem, Jerusalem, *thou* that killest the prophets, [z]and stonest them which are sent unto thee, how often would [a]I have gathered thy children together, even as a hen gathereth her chickens [b]under *her* wings, and ye would not!

38 Behold, your house is left unto you desolate.

39 For I say unto you, Ye shall not see me henceforth, till ye shall say, [c]Blessed *is* he that cometh in the name of the Lord.

24

And [d]Jesus went out, and departed from the temple: and his disciples came to *him* for to shew him the buildings of the temple.

2 And Jesus said unto them, See ye not all these things? verily I say unto you, [e]There shall not be left here one stone upon another, that shall not be thrown down.

3 ¶ And as he sat upon the mount of Olives, [f]the disciples came unto him privately, saying, [g]Tell us, when shall these things be? and what *shall be* the sign of thy coming, and of the end of the world?

4 And Jesus answered and said unto them, [h]Take heed that no man deceive you.

5 For [i]many shall come in my name, saying, I am Christ; [j]and shall deceive many.

6 And ye shall hear of wars and rumours of wars: see that ye be not troubled: for all *these things* must come to pass, but the end is not yet.

7 For [k]nation shall rise against nation, and kingdom against kingdom: and there shall be famines, and pestilences, and earthquakes, in divers places.

8 All these *are* the beginning of sorrows.

9 [l]Then shall they deliver you up to be afflicted, and shall kill you: and ye shall be hated of all nations for my name's sake.

10 And then shall many [m]be offended, and shall betray one another, and shall hate one another.

11 And [n]many false prophets shall rise, and [o]shall deceive many.

12 And because iniquity shall abound, the love of many shall wax cold.

13 [p]But he that shall endure unto the end, the same shall be saved.

14 And this [q]gospel of the kingdom [r]shall be preached in all the world for a witness unto all nations; and then shall the end come.

15 [s]When ye therefore shall see the abomination of desolation, spoken of by [t]Daniel the prophet, stand in the holy place, ([u]whoso readeth, let him understand:)

16 Then let them which be in Judaea flee into the mountains:

17 Let him which is on the housetop not come down to take any thing out of his house:

18 Neither let him which is in the field return back to take his clothes.

19 And [v]woe unto them that are with child, and to them that give suck in those days!

20 But pray ye that your flight be not in the winter, neither on the sabbath day:

21 For [w]then shall be great tribulation,

23:19 [h]Ex. 29:37
23:21 [i]1 Kings 8:13; 2 Chron. 6:2; Ps. 26:8
23:22 [j]ch. 5:34; Ps. 11:4; Acts 7:49
23:23 [k]Luke 11:42 [l]1 Sam. 15:22; Hos. 6:6; Mic. 6:8; ch. 9:13
23:25 [m]Mark 7:4; Luke 11:39
23:27 [n]Luke 11:44; Acts 23:3
23:29 [o]Luke 11:47
23:31 [p]Acts 7:51; 1 Thess. 2:15
23:32 [q]Gen. 15:16; 1 Thess. 2:16
23:33 [r]ch. 3:7
23:34 [s]ch. 21:34; Luke 11:49 [t]Acts 5:40 [u]ch. 10:17; 2 Cor. 11:24
23:35 [v]Rev. 18:24 [w]Gen. 4:8; 1 John 3:12 [x]2 Chron. 24:20
23:37 [y]Luke 13:34 [z]2 Chron. 24:21 [a]Deut. 32:11 [b]Ps. 17:8
23:39 [c]Ps. 118:26; ch. 21:9
24:1 [d]Mark 13:1; Luke 21:5
24:2 [e]1 Kings 9:7; Jer. 26:18; Mic. 3:12; Luke 19:44
24:3 [f]Mark 13:3 [g]1 Thess. 5:1
24:4 [h]Eph. 5:6; Col. 2:8; 2 Thess. 2:3; 1 John 4:1
24:5 [i]Jer. 14:14; ver. 24; John 5:43 [j]ver. 11
24:7 [k]2 Chron. 15:6; Isa. 19:2; Hag. 2:22; Zech. 14:13
24:9 [l]ch. 10:17; Mark 13:9; Luke 21:12; John 15:20; Acts 4:2; 1 Pet. 4:16; Rev. 2:10
24:10 [m]ch. 11:6; 2 Tim. 1:15
24:11 [n]ch. 7:15; Acts 20:29; 2 Pet. 2:1 [o]1 Tim. 4:1; ver. 5
24:13 [p]ch. 10:22; Mark 13:13; Heb. 3:6; Rev. 2:10
24:14 [q]ch. 4:23 [r]Rom. 10:18; Col. 1:6
24:15 [s]Mark 13:14; Luke 21:20 [t]Dan. 9:27 [u]Dan. 9:23
24:19 [v]Luke 23:29
24:21 [w]Dan. 9:26; Joel 2:2

such as was not since the beginning of the world to this time, no, nor ever shall be.

22 And except those days should be shortened, there should no flesh be saved: [x]but for the elect's sake those days shall be shortened.

23 [y]Then if any man shall say unto you, Lo, here *is* Christ, or there; believe *it* not.

24 For [z]there shall arise false Christs, and false prophets, and shall shew great signs and wonders; insomuch that, [a]if *it were* possible, they shall deceive the very elect.

25 Behold, I have told you before.

26 Wherefore if they shall say unto you, Behold, he is in the desert; go not forth: behold, *he is* in the secret chambers; believe *it* not.

27 [b]For as the lightning cometh out of the east, and shineth even unto the west; so shall also the coming of the Son of man be.

28 [c]For wheresoever the carcase is, there will the eagles be gathered together.

29 ¶ [d]Immediately after the tribulation of those days [e]shall the sun be darkened, and the moon shall not give her light, and the stars shall fall from heaven, and the powers of the heavens shall be shaken:

30 [f]And then shall appear the sign of the Son of man in heaven: [g]and then shall all the tribes of the earth mourn, [h]and they shall see the Son of man coming in the clouds of heaven with power and great glory.

31 [i]And he shall send his angels with a great sound of a trumpet, and they shall gather together his elect from the four winds, from one end of heaven to the other.

32 Now learn [j]a parable of the fig tree; When his branch is yet tender, and putteth forth leaves, ye know that summer *is* nigh:

33 So likewise ye, when ye shall see all these things, know [k]that it is near, *even* at the doors.

34 Verily I say unto you, [l]This generation shall not pass, till all these things be fulfilled.

35 [m]Heaven and earth shall pass away, but my words shall not pass away.

36 ¶ [n]But of that day and hour knoweth no *man*, no, not the angels of heaven, [o]but my Father only.

37 But as the days of Noe *were*, so shall also the coming of the Son of man be.

38 [p]For as in the days that were before the flood they were eating and drinking, marrying and giving in marriage, until the day that Noe entered into the ark,

39 And knew not until the flood came, and took them all away; so shall also the coming of the Son of man be.

40 [q]Then shall two be in the field; the one shall be taken, and the other left.

41 Two *women shall be* grinding at the mill; the one shall be taken, and the other left.

42 ¶ [r]Watch therefore: for ye know not what hour your Lord doth come.

43 [s]But know this, that if the goodman of the house had known in what watch the thief would come, he would have watched, and would not have suffered his house to be broken up.

44 [t]Therefore be ye also ready: for in such an hour as ye think not the Son of man cometh.

45 [u]Who then is a faithful and wise servant, whom his lord hath made ruler over his household, to give them meat in due season?

46 [v]Blessed *is* that servant, whom his lord when he cometh shall find so doing.

47 Verily I say unto you, That [w]he shall make him ruler over all his goods.

48 But and if that evil servant shall say in his heart, My lord delayeth his coming;

49 And shall begin to smite *his* fellowservants, and to eat and drink with the drunken;

50 The lord of that servant shall come in a day when he looketh not for *him*, and in an hour that he is not aware of,

51 And shall cut him asunder, and appoint *him* his portion with the hypocrites: [x]there shall be weeping and gnashing of teeth.

25

Then shall the kingdom of heaven be likened unto ten virgins, which took their lamps, and went forth to meet [y]the bridegroom.

2 [z]And five of them were wise, and five *were* foolish.

3 They that *were* foolish took their lamps, and took no oil with them:

4 But the wise took oil in their vessels with their lamps.

5 While the bridegroom tarried, [a]they all slumbered and slept.

6 And at midnight [b]there was a cry made, Behold, the bridegroom cometh; go ye out to meet him.

7 Then all those virgins arose, and [c]trimmed their lamps.

8 And the foolish said unto the wise, Give us of your oil; for our lamps are gone out.

9 But the wise answered, saying, *Not so;* lest there be not enough for us and you: but go ye rather to them that sell, and buy for yourselves.

10 And while they went to buy, the bridegroom came; and they that were ready went in with him to the marriage: and [d]the door was shut.

11 Afterward came also the other virgins, saying, [e]Lord, Lord, open to us.

12 But he answered and said, Verily I say unto you, [f]I know you not.

13 [g]Watch therefore, for ye know neither the day nor the hour wherein the Son of man cometh.

14 ¶ [h]For *the kingdom of heaven is* [i]as a man travelling into a far country, *who* called his own servants, and delivered unto them his goods.

15 And unto one he gave five talents, to

24:22 [x]Isa. 65:8; Zech. 14:2
24:23 [y]Mark 13:21; Luke 17:23
24:24 [z]Deut. 13:1; ver. 5; 2 Thess. 2:9; Rev. 13:13 [a]John 6:37; Rom. 8:28; 2 Tim. 2:19
24:27 [b]Luke 17:24
24:28 [c]Job 29:30; Luke 17:37
24:29 [d]Dan. 7:11 [e]Isa. 13:10; Ezek. 32:7; Joel 2:10; Am. 5:20; Mark 13:24; Luke 21:25; Acts 2:20; Rev. 6:12
24:30 [f]Dan. 7:13 [g]Zech. 12:12 [h]ch. 16:27; Mark 13:26; Rev. 1:7
24:31 [i]ch. 13:41; 1 Cor. 15:52; 1 Thess. 4:16
24:32 [j]Luke 21:29
24:33 [k]Jam. 5:9
24:34 [l]ch. 16:28; Mark 13:30; Luke 21:32
24:35 [m]Ps. 102:26; Isa. 51:6; Jer. 31:35; ch. 5:18; Mark 13:31; Luke 21:33; Heb. 1:11
24:36 [n]Mark 13:32; Acts 1:7; 1 Thess. 5:2; 2 Pet. 3:10 [o]Zech. 14:7
24:38 [p]Gen. 6:3; Luke 17:26; 1 Pet. 3:20
24:40 [q]Luke 17:34
24:42 [r]ch. 13; Mark 13:33; Luke 21:36
24:43 [s]Luke 12:39; 1 Thess. 5:2; 2 Pet. 3:10; Rev. 3:3
24:44 [t]ch. 25:13; 1 Thess. 5:6
24:45 [u]Luke 12:42; Acts 20:28; 1 Cor. 4:2; Heb. 3:5
24:46 [v]Rev. 16:15
24:47 [w]ch. 25:21; Luke 22:29
24:51 [x]ch. 8:12
25:1 [y]Eph. 5:29; Rev. 19:7
25:2 [z]ch. 13:47
25:5 [a]1 Thess. 5:6
25:6 [b]ch. 24:31; 1 Thess. 4:16
25:7 [c]Luke 12:35
25:10 [d]Luke 13:25
25:11 [e]ch. 7:21
25:12 [f]Ps. 5:5; Hab. 1:13; John 9:31
25:13 [g]ch. 24:42; Mark 13:33; Luke 21:36; 1 Cor. 16:13; 1 Thess. 5:6; 1 Pet. 5:8; Rev. 16:15
25:14 [h]Luke 19:12 [i]ch. 21:33

another two, and to another one; [j]to every man according to his several ability; and straightway took his journey.

16 Then he that had received the five talents went and traded with the same, and made *them* other five talents.

17 And likewise he that *had received* two, he also gained other two.

18 But he that had received one went and digged in the earth, and hid his lord's money.

19 After a long time the lord of those servants cometh, and reckoneth with them.

20 And so he that had received five talents came and brought other five talents, saying, Lord, thou deliveredst unto me five talents: behold, I have gained beside them five talents more.

21 His lord said unto him, Well done, *thou* good and faithful servant: thou hast been faithful over a few things, [k]I will make thee ruler over many things: enter thou into [l]the joy of thy lord.

22 He also that had received two talents came and said, Lord, thou deliveredst unto me two talents: behold, I have gained two other talents beside them.

23 His lord said unto him, [m]Well done, good and faithful servant; thou hast been faithful over a few things, I will make thee ruler over many things: enter thou into the joy of thy lord.

24 Then he which had received the one talent came and said, Lord, I knew thee that thou art an hard man, reaping where thou hast not sown, and gathering where thou hast not strawed:

25 And I was afraid, and went and hid thy talent in the earth: lo, *there* thou hast *that is* thine.

26 His lord answered and said unto him, *Thou* wicked and slothful servant, thou knewest that I reap where I sowed not, and gather where I have not strawed:

27 Thou oughtest therefore to have put my money to the exchangers, and *then* at my coming I should have received mine own with usury.

28 Take therefore the talent from him, and give *it* unto him which hath ten talents.

29 [n]For unto every one that hath shall be given, and he shall have abundance: but from him that hath not shall be taken away even that which he hath.

30 And cast ye the unprofitable servant [o]into outer darkness: there shall be weeping and gnashing of teeth.

31 ¶ [p]When the Son of man shall come in his glory, and all the holy angels with him, then shall he sit upon the throne of his glory:

32 And [q]before him shall be gathered all nations: and [r]he shall separate them one from another, as a shepherd divideth *his* sheep from the goats:

33 And he shall set the sheep on his right hand, but the goats on the left.

34 Then shall the King say unto them on his right hand, Come, ye blessed of my Father, [s]inherit the kingdom [t]prepared for you from the foundation of the world:

35 [u]For I was an hungred, and ye gave me meat: I was thirsty, and ye gave me drink: [v]I was a stranger, and ye took me in:

36 [w]Naked, and ye clothed me: I was sick, and ye visited me: [x]I was in prison, and ye came unto me.

37 Then shall the righteous answer him, saying, Lord, when saw we thee an hungred, and fed *thee?* or thirsty, and gave *thee* drink?

38 When saw we thee a stranger, and took *thee* in? or naked, and clothed *thee?*

39 Or when saw we thee sick, or in prison, and came unto thee?

40 And the King shall answer and say unto them, Verily I say unto you, [y]Inasmuch as ye have done *it* unto one of the least of these my brethren, ye have done *it* unto me.

41 Then shall he say also unto them on the left hand, [z]Depart from me, ye cursed, [a]into everlasting fire, prepared for [b]the devil and his angels:

42 For I was an hungred, and ye gave me no meat: I was thirsty, and ye gave me no drink:

43 I was a stranger, and ye took me not in: naked, and ye clothed me not: sick, and in prison, and ye visited me not.

44 Then shall they also answer him, saying, Lord, when saw we thee an hungred, or athirst, or a stranger, or naked, or sick, or in prison, and did not minister unto thee?

45 Then shall he answer them, saying, Verily I say unto you, [c]Inasmuch as ye did *it* not to one of the least of these, ye did *it* not to me.

46 And [d]these shall go away into everlasting punishment: but the righteous into life eternal.

26 And it came to pass, when Jesus had finished all these sayings, he said unto his disciples,

2 [e]Ye know that after two days is *the feast of* the passover, and the Son of man is betrayed to be crucified.

3 [f]Then assembled together the chief priests, and the scribes, and the elders of the people, unto the palace of the high priest, who was called Caiaphas,

4 And consulted that they might take Jesus by subtilty, and kill *him.*

5 But they said, Not on the feast *day,* lest there be an uproar among the people.

6 ¶ [g]Now when Jesus was in [h]Bethany, in the house of Simon the leper,

7 There came unto him a woman having an alabaster box of very precious ointment, and poured it on his head, as he sat *at meat.*

8 [i]But when his disciples saw *it,* they had indignation, saying, To what purpose *is* this waste?

9 For this ointment might have been sold for much, and given to the poor.

10 When Jesus understood *it,* he said

25:15 [j]Rom. 12:6; 1 Cor. 12:7; Eph. 4:11
25:21 [k]ch. 24:47; ver. 34; Luke 12:44 [l]Heb. 12:2; 2 Tim. 2:12; 1 Pet. 1:8
25:23 [m]ver. 21
25:29 [n]ch. 13:12; Mark 4:25; Luke 8:18; John 15:2
25:30 [o]ch. 8:12
25:31 [p]Zech. 14:5; ch. 16:27; Mark 8:38; Acts 1:11; 1 Thess. 4:16; 2 Thess. 1:7; Jude 14; Rev. 1:7
25:32 [q]Rom. 14:10; 2 Cor. 5:10; Rev. 20:12 [r]Ezek. 20:38; ch. 13:49
25:34 [s]Rom. 8:17; 1 Pet. 1:4; Rev. 21:7 [t]ch. 20:23; Mark 10:40; 1 Cor. 2:9; Heb. 11:16
25:35 [u]Isa. 58:7; Ezek. 18:7; Jam. 1:27 [v]Heb. 13:2; 3 John 5
25:36 [w]Jam. 2:15 [x]2 Tim. 1:16
25:40 [y]Prov. 14:31; ch. 10:42; Mark 9:41; Heb. 6:10
25:41 [z]Ps. 6:8; ch. 7:23; Luke 13:27 [a]ch. 13:40 [b]2 Pet. 2:4; Jude 6
25:45 [c]Prov. 14:31; Zech. 2:8; Acts 9:5
25:46 [d]Dan. 12:2; John 5:29; Rom. 2:7
26:2 [e]Mark 14:1; Luke 22:1; John 12:1
26:3 [f]Ps. 2:2; John 11:47; Acts 4:25
26:6 [g]Mark 14:3; John 11:1 [h]ch. 21:17
26:8 [i]John 12:4

unto them, Why trouble ye the woman? for
she hath wrought a good work upon me.

11 [j]For ye have the poor always with
you; but [k]me ye have not always.

12 For in that she hath poured this ointment on my body, she did *it* for my burial.

13 Verily I say unto you, Wheresoever
this gospel shall be preached in the whole
world, *there* shall also this, that this woman
hath done, be told for a memorial of her.

14 ¶ [l]Then one of the twelve, called [m]Ju-
das Iscariot, went unto the chief priests,

15 And said *unto them,* [n]What will ye
give me, and I will deliver him unto you?
And they convenanted with him for thirty
pieces of silver.

16 And from that time he sought opportunity to betray him.

17 ¶ [o]Now the first *day* of the *feast of*
unleavened bread the disciples came to
Jesus, saying unto him, Where wilt thou
that we prepare for thee to eat the passover?

18 And he said, Go into the city to such a
man, and say unto him, The Master saith,
My time is at hand; I will keep the passover
at thy house with my disciples.

19 And the disciples did as Jesus had appointed them; and they made ready the
passover.

20 [p]Now when the even was come, he sat
down with the twelve.

21 And as they did eat, he said, Verily I
say unto you, that one of you shall betray
me.

22 And they were exceeding sorrowful,
and began every one of them to say unto
him, Lord, is it I?

23 And he answered and said, [q]He that
dippeth *his* hand with me in the dish, the
same shall betray me.

24 The Son of man goeth [r]as it is written
of him: but [s]woe unto that man by whom
the Son of man is betrayed! it had been
good for that man if he had not been born.

25 Then Judas, which betrayed him, answered and said, Master, is it I? He said unto
him, Thou hast said.

26 ¶ [t]And as they were eating, [u]Jesus
took bread, and blessed *it,* and brake *it,* and
gave *it* to the disciples, and said, Take, eat;
[v]this is my body.

27 And he took the cup, and gave thanks,
and gave *it* to them, saying, [w]Drink ye all
of it;

28 For [x]this is my blood [y]of the new testament, which is shed [z]for many for the
remission of sins.

29 But [a]I say unto you, I will not drink
henceforth of this fruit of the vine, [b]until
that day when I drink it new with you in my
Father's kingdom.

30 [c]And when they had sung an hymn,
they went out into the mount of Olives.

31 Then saith Jesus unto them, [d]All ye
shall [e]be offended because of me this night:
for it is written, [f]I will smite the shepherd,
and the sheep of the flock shall be scattered
abroad.

26:11 [j]Deut. 15:11; John 12:8 [k]ch. 18:20; John 13:33
26:14 [l]Mark 14:10; Luke 22:3; John 13:2 [m]ch. 10:4
26:15 [n]Zech. 11:12; ch. 27:3
26:17 [o]Ex. 12:6; Mark 14:12; Luke 22:7
26:20 [p]Mark 14:17-21; Luke 22:14; John 13:21
26:23 [q]Ps. 41:9; Luke 22:21; John 13:18
26:24 [r]Ps. 22; Isa. 53; Dan. 9:26; Mark 9:12; Luke 24:25; Acts 17:2; 1 Cor. 15:3 [s]John 17:12
26:26 [t]Mark 14:22; Luke 22:19 [u]1 Cor. 11:23 [v]1 Cor. 10:16
26:27 [w]Mark 14:23
26:28 [x]Ex. 24:8; Lev. 17:11 [y]Jer. 31:31 [z]ch. 20:28; Rom. 5:15; Heb. 9:22
26:29 [a]Mark 14:25; Luke 22:18 [b]Acts 10:41
26:30 [c]Mark 14:26
26:31 [d]Mark 14:27; John 16:32 [e]ch. 11:6 [f]Zech. 13:7
26:32 [g]ch. 28:7; Mark 14:28
26:34 [h]Mark 14:30; Luke 22:34; John 13:38
26:36 [i]Mark 14:32-35; Luke 22:39; John 18:1
26:37 [j]ch. 4:21
26:38 [k]John 12:27
26:39 [l]Mark 14:36; Luke 22:42; Heb. 5:7 [m]John 12:27 [n]ch. 20:22 [o]John 5:30; Phil. 2:8
26:41 [p]Mark 13:33; Luke 22:40; Eph. 6:18
26:47 [q]Mark 14:43; Luke 22:47; John 18:3; Acts 1:16
26:49 [r]2 Sam. 20:9
26:50 [s]Ps. 41:9
26:51 [t]John 18:10
26:52 [u]Gen. 9:6; Rev. 13:10

32 But after I am risen again, [g]I will go
before you into Galilee.

33 Peter answered and said unto him,
Though all *men* shall be offended because
of thee, *yet* will I never be offended.

34 Jesus said unto him, [h]Verily I say unto
thee, That this night, before the cock crow,
thou shalt deny me thrice.

35 Peter said unto him, Though I should
die with thee, yet will I not deny thee. Likewise also said all the disciples.

36 ¶ [i]Then cometh Jesus with them unto
a place called Gethsemane, and saith unto
the disciples, Sit ye here, while I go and
pray yonder.

37 And he took with him Peter and [j]the
two sons of Zebedee, and began to be sorrowful and very heavy.

38 Then saith he unto them, [k]My soul is
exceeding sorrowful, even unto death: tarry
ye here, and watch with me.

39 And he went a little further, and fell on
his face, and [l]prayed, saying, [m]O my Father, if it be possible, [n]let this cup pass from
me: nevertheless [o]not as I will, but as thou
wilt.

40 And he cometh unto the disciples, and
findeth them asleep, and saith unto Peter,
What, could ye not watch with me one
hour?

41 [p]Watch and pray, that ye enter not
into temptation: the spirit indeed *is* willing,
but the flesh *is* weak.

42 He went away again the second time,
and prayed, saying, O my Father, if this cup
may not pass away from me, except I drink
it, thy will be done.

43 And he came and found them asleep
again: for their eyes were heavy.

44 And he left them, and went away
again, and prayed the third time, saying the
same words.

45 Then cometh he to his disciples, and
saith unto them, Sleep on now, and take
your rest: behold, the hour is at hand, and
the Son of man is betrayed into the hands of
sinners.

46 Rise, let us be going: behold, he is at
hand that doth betray me.

47 ¶ And [q]while he yet spake, lo, Judas,
one of the twelve, came, and with him a
great multitude with swords and staves,
from the chief priests and elders of the people.

48 Now he that betrayed him gave them a
sign, saying, Whomsoever I shall kiss, that
same is he: hold him fast.

49 And forthwith he came to Jesus, and
said, Hail, master; [r]and kissed him.

50 And Jesus said unto him, [s]Friend,
wherefore art thou come? Then came they,
and laid hands on Jesus, and took him.

51 And, behold, [t]one of them which were
with Jesus stretched out *his* hand, and drew
his sword, and struck a servant of the high
priest's, and smote off his ear.

52 Then said Jesus unto him, Put up again
thy sword into his place: [u]for all they that

take the sword shall perish with the sword.
53 Thinkest thou that I cannot now pray
to my Father, and he shall presently give me
[v]more than twelve legions of angels?
54 But how then shall the scriptures be
fulfilled, [w]that thus it must be?
55 In that same hour said Jesus to the
multitudes, Are ye come out as against a
thief with swords and staves for to take me?
I sat daily with you teaching in the temple,
and ye laid no hold on me.
56 But all this was done, that the [x]scrip-
tures of the prophets might be fulfilled.
Then [y]all the disciples forsook him, and
fled.
57 ¶ [z]And they that had laid hold on
Jesus led *him* away to Caiaphas the high
priest, where the scribes and the elders
were assembled.
58 But Peter followed him afar off unto
the high priest's palace, and went in, and sat
with the servants, to see the end.
59 Now the chief priests, and elders, and
all the council, sought false witness against
Jesus, to put him to death;
60 But found none: yea, though [a]many
false witnesses came, *yet* found they none.
At the last came [b]two false witnesses,
61 And said, This *fellow* said, [c]I am able
to destroy the temple of God, and to build it
in three days.
62 [d]And the high priest arose, and said
unto him, Answerest thou nothing? what *is*
it which these witness against thee?
63 But [e]Jesus held his peace. And the
high priest answered and said unto him, [f]I
adjure thee by the living God, that thou tell
us whether thou be the Christ, the Son of
God.
64 Jesus saith unto him, Thou hast said:
nevertheless I say unto you, [g]Hereafter
shall ye see the Son of man [h]sitting on the
right hand of power, and coming in the
clouds of heaven.
65 [i]Then the high priest rent his clothes,
saying, He hath spoken blasphemy; what
further need have we of witnesses? behold,
now ye have heard his blasphemy.
66 What think ye? They answered and
said, [j]He is guilty of death.
67 [k]Then did they spit in his face, and
buffeted him; and [l]others smote *him* with
the palms of their hands,
68 Saying, [m]Prophesy unto us, thou
Christ, Who is he that smote thee?
69 ¶ [n]Now Peter sat without in the palace: and a damsel came unto him, saying,
Thou also wast with Jesus of Galilee.
70 But he denied before *them* all, saying,
I know not what thou sayest.
71 And when he was gone out into the
porch, another *maid* saw him, and said unto
them that were there, This *fellow* was also
with Jesus of Nazareth.
72 And again he denied with an oath, I do
not know the man.
73 And after a while came unto *him* they
that stood by, and said to Peter, Surely thou
also art *one* of them; for thy [o]speech bewrayeth thee.
74 Then [p]began he to curse and to swear,
saying, I know not the man. And immediately the cock crew.
75 And Peter remembered the word of
Jesus, which said unto him, [q]Before the
cock crow, thou shalt deny me thrice. And
he went out, and wept bitterly.

27 When the morning was come, [r]all
the chief priests and elders of the
people took counsel against Jesus to put
him to death:
2 And when they had bound him, they led
him away, and [s]delivered him to Pontius
Pilate the governor.
3 ¶ [t]Then Judas, which had betrayed
him, when he saw that he was condemned,
repented himself, and brought again the
thirty pieces of silver to the chief priests and
elders,
4 Saying, I have sinned in that I have betrayed the innocent blood. And they said,
What *is that* to us? see thou *to that*.
5 And he cast down the pieces of silver in
the temple, [u]and departed, and went and
hanged himself.
6 And the chief priests took the silver
pieces, and said, It is not lawful for to put
them into the treasury, because it is the
price of blood.
7 And they took counsel, and bought with
them the potter's field, to bury strangers in.
8 Wherefore that field was called, [v]The
field of blood, unto this day.
9 Then was fulfilled that which was spoken by Jeremy the prophet, saying, [w]And
they took the thirty pieces of silver, the
price of him that was valued, whom they of
the children of Israel did value;
10 And gave them for the potter's field, as
the Lord appointed me.
11 And Jesus stood before the governor:
[x]and the governor asked him, saying, Art
thou the King of the Jews? And Jesus said
unto him, [y]Thou sayest.
12 And when he was accused of the chief
priests and elders, [z]he answered nothing.
13 Then said Pilate unto him, [a]Hearest
thou not how many things they witness
against thee?
14 And he answered him to never a word;
insomuch that the governor marvelled
greatly.
15 [b]Now at *that* feast the governor was
wont to release unto the people a prisoner,
whom they would.
16 And they had then a notable prisoner,
called Barabbas.
17 Therefore when they were gathered
together, Pilate said unto them, Whom will
ye that I release unto you? Barabbas, or
Jesus which is called Christ?
18 For he knew that for envy they had
delivered him.
19 ¶ When he was set down on the judgment seat, his wife sent unto him, saying,
Have thou nothing to do with that just man:

26:53 [v]2 Kings 6:17; Dan. 7:10
26:54 [w]Isa. 53:7; ver. 24; Luke 24:25
26:56 [x]Lam. 4:20; ver. 54 [y]John 18:15
26:57 [z]Mark 14:53; Luke 22:54; John 18:12
26:60 [a]Ps. 27:12; Mark 14:55; Acts 6:13 [b]Deut. 19:15
26:61 [c]ch. 27:40; John 2:19
26:62 [d]Mark 14:60
26:63 [e]Isa. 53:7; ch. 27:12 [f]Lev. 5:1; 1 Sam. 14:24
26:64 [g]Dan. 7:13; ch. 16:27; Luke 21:27; John 1:51; Rom. 14:10; 1 Thess. 4:16; Rev. 1:7 [h]Ps. 110:1; Acts 7:55
26:65 [i]2 Kings 18:37
26:66 [j]Lev. 24:16; John 19:7
26:67 [k]Isa. 50:6; ch. 27:30 [l]Luke 22:63; John 19:3
26:68 [m]Mark 14:65; Luke 22:64
26:69 [n]Mark 14:66; Luke 22:55; John 18:16
26:73 [o]Luke 22:59
26:74 [p]Mark 14:71
26:75 [q]ver. 34; Mark 14:30; Luke 22:61; John 13:38
27:1 [r]Ps. 2:2; Mark 15:1; Luke 22:66; John 18:28
27:2 [s]ch. 20:19; Acts 3:13
27:3 [t]ch. 26:14
27:5 [u]2 Sam. 17:23; Acts 1:18
27:8 [v]Acts 1:19
27:9 [w]Zech. 11:12
27:11 [x]Mark 15:2; Luke 23:3; John 18:33 [y]John 18:37; 1 Tim. 6:13
27:12 [z]ch. 26:63; John 19:9
27:13 [a]ch. 26:62; John 19:10
27:15 [b]Mark 15:6; Luke 23:17; John 18:39

for I have suffered many things this day in a dream because of him.

20 [c]But the chief priests and elders persuaded the multitude that they should ask Barabbas, and destroy Jesus.

21 The governor answered and said unto them, Whether of the twain will ye that I release unto you? They said, Barabbas.

22 Pilate saith unto them, What shall I do then with Jesus which is called Christ? *They* all say unto him, Let him be crucified.

23 And the governor said, Why, what evil hath he done? But they cried out the more, saying, Let him be crucified.

24 ¶ When Pilate saw that he could prevail nothing, but *that* rather a tumult was made, he [d]took water, and washed *his* hands before the multitude, saying, I am innocent of the blood of this just person: see ye *to it*.

25 Then answered all the people, and said, [e]His blood *be* on us, and on our children.

26 ¶ Then released he Barabbas unto them: and when [f]he had scourged Jesus, he delivered *him* to be crucified.

27 [g]Then the soldiers of the governor took Jesus into the common hall, and gathered unto him the whole band *of soldiers*.

28 And they stripped him, and [h]put on him a scarlet robe.

29 ¶ [i]And when they had platted a crown of thorns, they put *it* upon his head, and a reed in his right hand: and they bowed the knee before him, and mocked him, saying, Hail, King of the Jews!

30 And [j]they spit upon him, and took the reed, and smote him on the head.

31 And after that they had mocked him, they took the robe off from him, and put his own raiment on him, [k]and led him away to crucify *him*.

32 [l]And as they came out, [m]they found a man of Cyrene, Simon by name: him they compelled to bear his cross.

33 [n]And when they were come unto a place called Golgotha, that is to say, a place of a skull,

34 ¶ [o]They gave him vinegar to drink mingled with gall: and when he had tasted *thereof*, he would not drink.

35 [p]And they crucified him, and parted his garments, casting lots: that it might be fulfilled which was spoken by the prophet, [q]They parted my garments among them, and upon my vesture did they cast lots.

36 [r]And sitting down they watched him there;

37 And [s]set up over his head his accusation written, THIS IS JESUS THE KING OF THE JEWS.

38 [t]Then were there two thieves crucified with him, one on the right hand, and another on the left.

39 ¶ And [u]they that passed by reviled him, wagging their heads,

40 And saying, [v]Thou that destroyest the temple, and buildest *it* in three days, save thyself. [w]If thou be the Son of God, come down from the cross.

41 Likewise also the chief priests mocking *him*, with the scribes and elders, said,

42 He saved others; himself he cannot save. If he be the King of Israel, let him now come down from the cross, and we will believe him.

43 [x]He trusted in God; let him deliver him now, if he will have him: for he said, I am the Son of God.

44 [y]The thieves also, which were crucified with him, cast the same in his teeth.

45 [z]Now from the sixth hour there was darkness over all the land unto the ninth hour.

46 And about the ninth hour [a]Jesus cried with a loud voice, saying, Eli, Eli, lama sabachthani? that is to say, [b]My God, my God, why hast thou forsaken me?

47 Some of them that stood there, when they heard *that*, said, This *man* calleth for Elias.

48 And straightway one of them ran, and took a spunge, [c]and filled *it* with vinegar, and put *it* on a reed, and gave him to drink.

49 The rest said, Let be, let us see whether Elias will come to save him.

50 ¶ [d]Jesus, when he had cried again with a loud voice, yielded up the ghost.

51 And, behold, [e]the veil of the temple was rent in twain from the top to the bottom; and the earth did quake, and the rocks rent;

52 And the graves were opened; and many bodies of the saints which slept arose,

53 And came out of the graves after his resurrection, and went into the holy city, and appeared unto many.

54 [f]Now when the centurion, and they that were with him, watching Jesus, saw the earthquake, and those things that were done, they feared greatly, saying, Truly this was the Son of God.

55 And many women were there beholding afar off, [g]which followed Jesus from Galilee, ministering unto him:

56 [h]Among which was Mary Magdalene, and Mary the mother of James and Joses, and the mother of Zebedee's children.

57 [i]When the even was come, there came a rich man of Arimathea, named Joseph, who also himself was Jesus' disciple:

58 He went to Pilate, and begged the body of Jesus. Then Pilate commanded the body to be delivered.

59 And when Joseph had taken the body, he wrapped it in a clean linen cloth,

60 And [j]laid it in his own new tomb, which he had hewn out in the rock: and he rolled a great stone to the door of the sepulchre, and departed.

61 And there was Mary Magdalene, and the other Mary, sitting over against the sepulchre.

62 ¶ Now the next day, that followed the day of the preparation, the chief priests and Pharisees came together unto Pilate,

27:20 [c]Mark 15:11; Luke 23:18; John 18:40; Acts 3:14
27:24 [d]Deut. 21:6
27:25 [e]Deut. 19:10; Josh. 2:19; 1 Kings 2:32; 2 Sam. 1:16; Acts 5:28
27:26 [f]Isa. 53:5; Mark 15:15; Luke 23:16; John 19:1
27:27 [g]Mark 15:15; John 19:2
27:28 [h]Luke 23:11
27:29 [i]Ps. 69:19; Isa. 53:3
27:30 [j]Isa. 50:6; ch. 26:67
27:31 [k]Isa. 53:7
27:32 [l]Num. 15:35; 1 Kings 21:13; Acts 7:58; Heb. 13:12 [m]Mark 15:21; Luke 23:26
27:33 [n]Mark 15:22; Luke 23:33; John 19:17
27:34 [o]Ps. 69:21; ver. 48
27:35 [p]Mark 15:24; Luke 23:34; John 19:24 [q]Ps. 22:18
27:36 [r]ver. 54
27:37 [s]Mark 15:26; Luke 23:38; John 19:19
27:38 [t]Isa. 53:12; Mark 15:27; Luke 23:32; John 19:18
27:39 [u]Ps. 22:7; Mark 15:29; Luke 23:35
27:40 [v]ch. 26:61; John 2:19 [w]ch. 26:63
27:43 [x]Ps. 22:8
27:44 [y]Mark 15:32; Luke 23:39
27:45 [z]Am. 8:9; Mark 15:33; Luke 23:44
27:46 [a]Heb. 5:7 [b]Ps. 22:1
27:48 [c]Ps. 69:21; Mark 15:36; Luke 23:36; John 19:29
27:50 [d]Mark 15:37; Luke 23:46
27:51 [e]Ex. 26:31; 2 Chron. 3:14; Mark 15:38; Luke 23:45
27:54 [f]ver. 36; Mark 15:39; Luke 23:47
27:55 [g]Luke 8:2
27:56 [h]Mark 15:40
27:57 [i]Mark 15:42; Luke 23:50; John 19:38
27:60 [j]Isa. 53:9

63 Saying, Sir, we remember that that deceiver said, while he was yet alive, [k]After three days I will rise again.

64 Command therefore that the sepulchre be made sure until the third day, lest his disciples come by night, and steal him away, and say unto the people, He is risen from the dead: so the last error shall be worse than the first.

65 Pilate said unto them, Ye have a watch: go your way, make *it* as sure as ye can.

66 So they went, and made the sepulchre sure, [l]sealing the stone, and setting a watch.

28 In the [m]end of the sabbath, as it began to dawn toward the first *day* of the week, came Mary Magdalene [n]and the other Mary to see the sepulchre.

2 And, behold, there was a great earthquake: for [o]the angel of the Lord descended from heaven, and came and rolled back the stone from the door, and sat upon it.

3 [p]His countenance was like lightning, and his raiment white as snow:

4 And for fear of him the keepers did shake, and became as dead *men*.

5 And the angel answered and said unto the women, Fear not ye: for I know that ye seek Jesus, which was crucified.

6 He is not here: for he is risen, [q]as he said. Come, see the place where the Lord lay.

7 And go quickly, and tell his disciples that he is risen from the dead; and, behold, [r]he goeth before you into Galilee; there shall ye see him: lo, I have told you.

8 And they departed quickly from the sepulchre with fear and great joy; and did run to bring his disciples word.

9 ¶ And as they went to tell his disciples, behold, [s]Jesus met them, saying, All hail. And they came and held him by the feet, and worshipped him.

10 Then said Jesus unto them, Be not afraid: go tell [t]my brethren that they go into Galilee, and there shall they see me.

11 ¶ Now when they were going, behold, some of the watch came into the city, and shewed unto the chief priests all the things that were done.

12 And when they were assembled with the elders, and had taken counsel, they gave large money unto the soldiers,

13 Saying, Say ye, His disciples came by night, and stole him *away* while we slept.

14 And if this come to the governor's ears, we will persuade him, and secure you.

15 So they took the money, and did as they were taught: and this saying is commonly reported among the Jews until this day.

16 ¶ Then the eleven disciples went away into Galilee, into a mountain [u]where Jesus had appointed them.

17 And when they saw him, they worshipped him: but some doubted.

18 And Jesus came and spake unto them, saying, [v]All power is given unto me in heaven and in earth.

19 ¶ [w]Go ye therefore, and [x]teach all nations, baptizing them in the name of the Father, and of the Son, and of the Holy Ghost:

20 [y]Teaching them to observe all things whatsoever I have commanded you: and, lo, I am with you alway, *even* unto the end of the world. Amen.

27:63 [k]ch. 16:21; Mark 8:31; Luke 9:22; John 2:19
27:66 [l]Dan. 6:17
28:1 [m]Mark 16:1; Luke 24:1; John 20:1 [n]ch. 27:56
28:2 [o]Mark 16:5; Luke 24:4; John 20:12
28:3 [p]Dan. 10:6
28:6 [q]ch. 12:40
28:7 [r]ch. 26:32; Mark 16:7
28:9 [s]Mark 16:9; John 20:14
28:10 [t]John 20:17; Rom. 8:29; Heb. 2:11
28:16 [u]ch. 26:32; ver. 7
28:18 [v]Dan. 7:13; ch. 11:27; Luke 1:32; John 3:35; Acts 2:36; Rom. 14:9; 1 Cor. 15:27; Eph. 1:10; Phil. 2:9; Heb. 1:2; 1 Pet. 3:22; Rev. 17:14
28:19 [w]Mark 16:15 [x]Isa. 52:10; Luke 24:47; Acts 2:38; Rom. 10:18; Col. 1:23
28:20 [y]Acts 2:42

MARK

Mark is the writer of this book, written sometime during the mid-50s to 60s A.D. Mark begins his book at the time of Jesus' baptism and moves quickly through Jesus' public ministry, his death, and his victory in the resurrection.

I. Jesus begins his public ministry, 1:1–1:20
II. Jesus' public ministry, 1:21–10:52
III. Jesus' last week, 11:1–15:47
IV. Jesus' resurrection and ascension, 16:1–16:20

1 The beginning of the gospel of Jesus Christ, [a]the Son of God;
2 As it is written in the prophets, [b]Behold, I send my messenger before thy face, which shall prepare thy way before thee.
3 [c]The voice of one crying in the wilderness, Prepare ye the way of the Lord, make his paths straight.
4 [d]John did baptize in the wilderness, and preach the baptism of repentance for the remission of sins.
5 [e]And there went out unto him all the land of Judaea, and they of Jerusalem, and were all baptized of him in the river of Jordan, confessing their sins.
6 And John was [f]clothed with camel's hair, and with a girdle of a skin about his loins; and he did eat [g]locusts and wild honey;
7 And preached, saying, [h]There cometh one mightier than I after me, the latchet of whose shoes I am not worthy to stoop down and unloose.
8 [i]I indeed have baptized you with water: but he shall baptize you [j]with the Holy Ghost.
9 [k]And it came to pass in those days, that Jesus came from Nazareth of Galilee, and was baptized of John in Jordan.
10 [l]And straightway coming up out of the water, he saw the heavens opened, and the Spirit like a dove descending upon him:
11 And there came a voice from heaven, *saying,* [m]Thou art my beloved Son, in whom I am well pleased.
12 [n]And immediately the Spirit driveth him into the wilderness.
13 And he was there in the wilderness forty days, tempted of Satan; and was with the wild beasts; [o]and the angels ministered unto him.
14 [p]Now after that John was put in prison, Jesus came into Galilee, [q]preaching the gospel of the kingdom of God,
15 And saying, [r]The time is fulfilled, and [s]the kingdom of God is at hand: repent ye, and believe the gospel.
16 [t]Now as he walked by the sea of Galilee, he saw Simon and Andrew his brother casting a net into the sea: for they were fishers.
17 And Jesus said unto them, Come ye after me, and I will make you to become fishers of men.
18 And straightway [u]they forsook their nets, and followed him.
19 [v]And when he had gone a little further thence, he saw James the *son* of Zebedee, and John his brother, who also were in the ship mending their nets.
20 And straightway he called them: and they left their father Zebedee in the ship with the hired servants, and went after him.
21 [w]And they went into Capernaum; and straightway on the sabbath day he entered into the synagogue, and taught.
22 [x]And they were astonished at his doctrine: for he taught them as one that had authority, and not as the scribes.
23 [y]And there was in their synagogue a man with an unclean spirit; and he cried out,
24 Saying, Let *us* alone; [z]what have we to do with thee, thou Jesus of Nazareth? art thou come to destroy us? I know thee who thou art, the Holy One of God.
25 And Jesus [a]rebuked him, saying, Hold thy peace, and come out of him.
26 And when the unclean spirit [b]had torn him, and cried with a loud voice, he came out of him.
27 And they were all amazed, insomuch that they questioned among themselves, saying, What thing is this? what new doctrine *is* this? for with authority commandeth he even the unclean spirits, and they do obey him.
28 And immediately his fame spread abroad throughout all the region round about Galilee.
29 [c]And forthwith, when they were come out of the synagogue, they entered into the house of Simon and Andrew, with James and John.
30 But Simon's wife's mother lay sick of a fever, and anon they tell him of her.
31 And he came and took her by the hand, and lifted her up; and immediately the fever left her, and she ministered unto them.
32 [d]And at even, when the sun did set, they brought unto him all that were diseased, and them that were possessed with devils.

1:1 [a]Matt. 14:33; Luke 1:35; John 1:34
1:2 [b]Mal. 3:1; Matt. 11:10; Luke 7:27
1:3 [c]Isa. 40:3; Matt. 3:3; Luke 3:4; John 1:15
1:4 [d]Matt. 3:1; Luke 3:3; John 3:23
1:5 [e]Matt. 3:5
1:6 [f]Matt. 3:4 [g]Lev. 11:22
1:7 [h]Matt. 3:11; John 1:27; Acts 13:25
1:8 [i]Acts 1:5 [j]Isa. 44:3; Joel 2:28; Acts 2:4; 1 Cor. 12:13
1:9 [k]Matt. 3:13; Luke 3:21
1:10 [l]Matt. 3:16; John 1:32
1:11 [m]Ps. 2:7; Matt. 3:17; ch. 9:7
1:12 [n]Matt. 4:1; Luke 4:1
1:13 [o]Matt. 4:11
1:14 [p]Matt. 4:12 [q]Matt. 4:23
1:15 [r]Dan. 9:25; Gal. 4:4; Eph. 1:10 [s]Matt. 3:2
1:16 [t]Matt. 4:18; Luke 5:4
1:18 [u]Matt. 19:27; Luke 5:11
1:19 [v]Matt. 4:21
1:21 [w]Matt. 4:13; Luke 4:31
1:22 [x]Matt. 7:28
1:23 [y]Luke 4:33
1:24 [z]Matt. 8:29
1:25 [a]ver. 34
1:26 [b]ch. 9:20
1:29 [c]Matt. 8:14; Luke 4:38
1:32 [d]Matt. 8:16; Luke 4:40

33 And all the city was gathered together at the door.

34 And he healed many that were sick of divers diseases, and cast out many devils; and [e]suffered not the devils to speak, because they knew him.

35 And [f]in the morning, rising up a great while before day, he went out, and departed into a solitary place, and there prayed.

36 And Simon and they that were with him followed after him.

37 And when they had found him, they said unto him, All *men* seek for thee.

38 And he said unto them, [g]Let us go into the next towns, that I may preach there also: for [h]therefore came I forth.

39 [i]And he preached in their synagogues throughout all Galilee, and cast out devils.

40 [j]And there came a leper to him, beseeching him, and kneeling down to him, and saying unto him, If thou wilt, thou canst make me clean.

41 And Jesus, moved with compassion, put forth *his* hand, and touched him, and saith unto him, I will; be thou clean.

42 And as soon as he had spoken, immediately the leprosy departed from him, and he was cleansed.

43 And he straitly charged him, and forthwith sent him away;

44 And saith unto him, See thou say nothing to any man: but go thy way, shew thyself to the priest, and offer for thy cleansing those things [k]which Moses commanded, for a testimony unto them.

45 [l]But he went out, and began to publish *it* much, and to blaze abroad the matter, insomuch that Jesus could no more openly enter into the city, but was without in desert places: [m]and they came to him from every quarter.

2 And again [n]he entered into Capernaum after *some* days; and it was noised that he was in the house.

2 And straightway many were gathered together, insomuch that there was no room to receive *them,* no, not so much as about the door: and he preached the word unto them.

3 And they come unto him, bringing one sick of the palsy, which was borne of four.

4 And when they could not come nigh unto him for the press, they uncovered the roof where he was: and when they had broken *it* up, they let down the bed wherein the sick of the palsy lay.

5 When Jesus saw their faith, he said unto the sick of the palsy, Son, thy sins be forgiven thee.

6 But there were certain of the scribes sitting there, and reasoning in their hearts,

7 Why doth this *man* thus speak blasphemies? [o]who can forgive sins but God only?

8 And immediately [p]when Jesus perceived in his spirit that they so reasoned within themselves, he said unto them, Why reason ye these things in your hearts?

9 [q]Whether is it easier to say to the sick of the palsy, *Thy* sins be forgiven thee; or to say, Arise, and take up thy bed, and walk?

10 But that ye may know that the Son of man hath power on earth to forgive sins, (he saith to the sick of the palsy,)

11 I say unto thee, Arise, and take up thy bed, and go thy way into thine house.

12 And immediately he arose, took up the bed, and went forth before them all; insomuch that they were all amazed, and glorified God, saying, We never saw it on this fashion.

13 [r]And he went forth again by the sea side; and all the multitude resorted unto him, and he taught them.

14 [s]And as he passed by, he saw Levi the *son* of Alpheus sitting at the receipt of custom, and said unto him, Follow me. And he arose and followed him.

15 [t]And it came to pass, that, as Jesus sat at meat in his house, many publicans and sinners sat also together with Jesus and his disciples: for there were many, and they followed him.

16 And when the scribes and Pharisees saw him eat with publicans and sinners, they said unto his disciples, How is it that he eateth and drinketh with publicans and sinners?

17 When Jesus heard *it,* he saith unto them, [u]They that are whole have no need of the physician, but they that are sick: I came not to call the righteous, but sinners to repentance.

18 [v]And the disciples of John and of the Pharisees used to fast: and they come and say unto him, Why do the disciples of John and of the Pharisees fast, but thy disciples fast not?

19 And Jesus said unto them, Can the children of the bridechamber fast, while the bridegroom is with them? as long as they have the bridegroom with them, they cannot fast.

20 But the days will come, when the bridegroom shall be taken away from them, and then shall they fast in those days.

21 No man also seweth a piece of new cloth on an old garment: else the new piece that filled it up taketh away from the old, and the rent is made worse.

22 And no man putteth new wine into old bottles: else the new wine doth burst the bottles, and the wine is spilled, and the bottles will be marred: but new wine must be put into new bottles.

23 [w]And it came to pass, that he went through the corn fields on the sabbath day; and his disciples began, as they went, [x]to pluck the ears of corn.

24 And the Pharisees said unto him, Behold, why do they on the sabbath day that which is not lawful?

25 And he said unto them, Have ye never read [y]what David did, when he had need, and was an hungred, he, and they that were with him?

26 How he went into the house of God in

1:34 [e]ch. 3:12; Luke 4:41; Acts 16:17
1:35 [f]Luke 4:42
1:38 [g]Luke 4:43 [h]Isa. 61:1; John 16:28
1:39 [i]Matt. 4:23; Luke 4:44
1:40 [j]Matt. 8:2; Luke 5:12
1:44 [k]Lev. 14:3; Luke 5:14
1:45 [l]Luke 5:15 [m]ch. 2:13
2:1 [n]Matt. 9:1; Luke 5:18
2:7 [o]Job 14:4; Isa. 43:25
2:8 [p]Matt. 9:4
2:9 [q]Matt. 9:5
2:13 [r]Matt. 9:9
2:14 [s]Matt. 9:9; Luke 5:27
2:15 [t]Matt. 9:10
2:17 [u]Matt. 9:12; Luke 5:31; 1 Tim. 1:15
2:18 [v]Matt. 9:14; Luke 5:33
2:23 [w]Matt. 12:1; Luke 6:1 [x]Deut. 23:25
2:25 [y]1 Sam. 21:6

the days of Abiathar the high priest, and did eat the shewbread, [z]which is not lawful to eat but for the priests, and gave also to them which were with him?

27 And he said unto them, The sabbath was made for man, and not man for the sabbath:

28 Therefore [a]the Son of man is Lord also of the sabbath.

3 And [b]he entered again into the synagogue; and there was a man there which had a withered hand.

2 And they watched him, whether he would heal him on the sabbath days; that they might accuse him.

3 And he saith unto the man which had the withered hand, Stand forth.

4 And he saith unto them, Is it lawful to do good on the sabbath day, or to do evil? to save life, or to kill? But they held their peace.

5 And when he had looked round about on them with anger, being grieved for the hardness of their hearts, he saith unto the man, Stretch forth thine hand. And he stretched *it* out: and his hand was restored whole as the other.

6 [c]And the Pharisees went forth, and straightway took counsel with [d]the Herodians against him, how they might destroy him.

7 But Jesus withdrew himself with his disciples to the sea: and a great multitude from Galilee followed him, [e]and from Judaea,

8 And from Jerusalem, and from Idumaea, and *from* beyond Jordan; and they about Tyre and Sidon, a great multitude, when they had heard what great things he did, came unto him.

9 And he spake to his disciples, that a small ship should wait on him because of the multitude, lest they should throng him.

10 For he had healed many; insomuch that they pressed upon him for to touch him, as many as had plagues.

11 [f]And unclean spirits, when they saw him, fell down before him, and cried, saying, [g]Thou art the Son of God.

12 And [h]he straitly charged them that they should not make him known.

13 [i]And he goeth up into a mountain, and calleth *unto him* whom he would: and they came unto him.

14 And he ordained twelve, that they should be with him, and that he might send them forth to preach,

15 And to have power to heal sicknesses, and to cast out devils:

16 And Simon [j]he surnamed Peter;

17 And James the *son* of Zebedee, and John the brother of James; and he surnamed them Boanerges, which is, The sons of thunder:

18 And Andrew, and Philip, and Bartholomew, and Matthew, and Thomas, and James the *son* of Alpheus, and Thaddaeus, and Simon the Canaanite,

19 And Judas Iscariot, which also betrayed him: and they went into an house.

20 And the multitude cometh together again, [k]so that they could not so much as eat bread.

21 And when his friends heard *of it*, they went out to lay hold on him: [l]for they said, He is beside himself.

22 ¶ And the scribes which came down from Jerusalem said, [m]He hath Beelzebub, and by the prince of the devils casteth he out devils.

23 [n]And he called them *unto him*, and said unto them in parables, How can Satan cast out Satan?

24 And if a kingdom be divided against itself, that kingdom cannot stand.

25 And if a house be divided against itself, that house cannot stand.

26 And if Satan rise up against himself, and be divided, he cannot stand, but hath an end.

27 [o]No man can enter into a strong man's house, and spoil his goods, except he will first bind the strong man; and then he will spoil his house.

28 [p]Verily I say unto you, All sins shall be forgiven unto the sons of men, and blasphemies wherewith soever they shall blaspheme:

29 But he that shall blaspheme against the Holy Ghost hath never forgiveness, but is in danger of eternal damnation:

30 Because they said, He hath an unclean spirit.

31 ¶ [q]There came then his brethren and his mother, and, standing without, sent unto him, calling him.

32 And the multitude sat about him, and they said unto him, Behold, thy mother and thy brethren without seek for thee.

33 And he answered them, saying, Who is my mother, or my brethren?

34 And he looked round about on them which sat about him, and said, Behold my mother and my brethren!

35 For whosoever shall do the will of God, the same is my brother, and my sister, and mother.

4 And [r]he began again to teach by the sea side: and there was gathered unto him a great multitude, so that he entered into a ship, and sat in the sea; and the whole multitude was by the sea on the land.

2 And he taught them many things by parables, [s]and said unto them in his doctrine,

3 Hearken; Behold, there went out a sower to sow:

4 And it came to pass, as he sowed, some fell by the way side, and the fowls of the air came and devoured it up.

5 And some fell on stony ground, where it had not much earth; and immediately it sprang up, because it had no depth of earth:

6 But when the sun was up, it was scorched; and because it had no root, it withered away.

2:26 [z]Ex. 29:32; Lev. 24:9
2:28 [a]Matt. 12:8
3:1 [b]Matt. 12:9; Luke 6:6
3:6 [c]Matt. 12:14 [d]Matt. 22:16
3:7 [e]Luke 6:17
3:11 [f]ch. 1:23; Luke 4:41 [g]Matt. 14:33; ch. 1:1
3:12 [h]ch. 1:25; Matt. 12:16
3:13 [i]Matt. 10:1; Luke 6:12
3:16 [j]John 1:42
3:20 [k]ch. 6:31
3:21 [l]John 7:5
3:22 [m]Matt. 9:34; Luke 11:15; John 7:20
3:23 [n]Matt. 12:25
3:27 [o]Isa. 49:24; Matt. 12:29
3:28 [p]Matt. 12:31; Luke 12:10; 1 John 5:16
3:31 [q]Matt. 12:46; Luke 8:19
4:1 [r]Matt. 13:1; Luke 8:4
4:2 [s]ch. 12:38

7 And some fell among thorns, and the thorns grew up, and choked it, and it yielded no fruit.

8 And other fell on good ground, [t]and did yield fruit that sprang up and increased; and brought forth, some thirty, and some sixty, and some an hundred.

9 And he said unto them, He that hath ears to hear, let him hear.

10 [u]And when he was alone, they that were about him with the twelve asked of him the parable.

11 And he said unto them, Unto you it is given to know the mystery of the kingdom of God: but unto [v]them that are without, all *these* things are done in parables:

12 [w]That seeing they may see, and not perceive; and hearing they may hear, and not understand; lest at any time they should be converted, and *their* sins should be forgiven them.

13 And he said unto them, Know ye not this parable? and how then will ye know all parables?

14 ¶ [x]The sower soweth the word.

15 And these are they by the way side, where the word is sown; but when they have heard, Satan cometh immediately, and taketh away the word that was sown in their hearts.

16 And these are they likewise which are sown on stony ground; who, when they have heard the word, immediately receive it with gladness;

17 And have no root in themselves, and so endure but for a time: afterward, when affliction or persecution ariseth for the word's sake, immediately they are offended.

18 And these are they which are sown among thorns; such as hear the word,

19 And the cares of this world, [y]and the deceitfulness of riches, and the lusts of other things entering in, choke the word, and it becometh unfruitful.

20 And these are they which are sown on good ground; such as hear the word, and receive *it*, and bring forth fruit, some thirtyfold, some sixty, and some an hundred.

21 ¶ [z]And he said unto them, Is a candle brought to be put under a bushel, or under a bed? and not to be set on a candlestick?

22 [a]For there is nothing hid, which shall not be manifested; neither was any thing kept secret, but that it should come abroad.

23 [b]If any man have ears to hear, let him hear.

24 And he said unto them, Take heed what ye hear: [c]with what measure ye mete, it shall be measured to you: and unto you that hear shall more be given.

25 [d]For he that hath, to him shall be given: and he that hath not, from him shall be taken even that which he hath.

26 ¶ And he said, [e]So is the kingdom of God, as if a man should cast seed into the ground;

27 And should sleep, and rise night and day, and the seed should spring and grow up, he knoweth not how.

28 For the earth bringeth forth fruit of herself; first the blade, then the ear, after that the full corn in the ear.

29 But when the fruit is brought forth, immediately [f]he putteth in the sickle, because the harvest is come.

30 ¶ And he said, [g]Whereunto shall we liken the kingdom of God? or with what comparison shall we compare it?

31 *It is* like a grain of mustard seed, which, when it is sown in the earth, is less than all the seeds that be in the earth:

32 But when it is sown, it groweth up, and becometh greater than all herbs, and shooteth out great branches; so that the fowls of the air may lodge under the shadow of it.

33 [h]And with many such parables spake he the word unto them, as they were able to hear *it*.

34 But without a parable spake he not unto them: and when they were alone, he expounded all things to his disciples.

35 [i]And the same day, when the even was come, he saith unto them, Let us pass over unto the other side.

36 And when they had sent away the multitude, they took him even as he was in the ship. And there were also with him other little ships.

37 And there arose a great storm of wind, and the waves beat into the ship, so that it was now full.

38 And he was in the hinder part of the ship, asleep on a pillow: and they awake him, and say unto him, Master, carest thou not that we perish?

39 And he arose, and rebuked the wind, and said unto the sea, Peace, be still. And the wind ceased, and there was a great calm.

40 And he said unto them, Why are ye so fearful? how is it that ye have no faith?

41 And they feared exceedingly, and said one to another, What manner of man is this, that even the wind and the sea obey him?

5 And [j]they came over unto the other side of the sea, into the country of the Gadarenes.

2 And when he was come out of the ship, immediately there met him out of the tombs a man with an unclean spirit,

3 Who had *his* dwelling among the tombs; and no man could bind him, no, not with chains:

4 Because that he had been often bound with fetters and chains, and the chains had been plucked asunder by him, and the fetters broken in pieces: neither could any *man* tame him.

5 And always, night and day, he was in the mountains, and in the tombs, crying, and cutting himself with stones.

6 But when he saw Jesus afar off, he ran and worshipped him,

7 And cried with a loud voice, and said, What have I to do with thee, Jesus, *thou* Son

4:8 [t]John 15:5; Col. 1:6
4:10 [u]Matt. 13:10; Luke 8:9
4:11 [v]1 Cor. 5:12; Col. 4:5; 1 Thess. 4:12; 1 Tim. 3:7
4:12 [w]Isa. 6:9; Matt. 13:14; Luke 8:10; John 12:40; Acts 28:26; Rom. 11:8
4:14 [x]Matt. 13:19
4:19 [y]1 Tim. 6:9
4:21 [z]Matt. 5:15; Luke 8:16
4:22 [a]Matt. 10:26; Luke 12:2
4:23 [b]Matt. 11:15; ver. 9
4:24 [c]Matt. 7:2; Luke 6:38
4:25 [d]Matt. 13:12; Luke 8:18
4:26 [e]Matt. 13:24
4:29 [f]Rev. 14:15
4:30 [g]Matt. 13:31; Luke 13:18; Acts 2:41
4:33 [h]Matt. 13:34; John 16:12
4:35 [i]Matt. 8:18; Luke 8:22
5:1 [j]Matt. 8:28; Luke 8:26

of the most high God? I adjure thee by God,
that thou torment me not.
8 For he said unto him, Come out of the
man, *thou* unclean spirit.
9 And he asked him, What *is* thy name?
And he answered, saying, My name *is* Legion: for we are many.
10 And he besought him much that he
would not send them away out of the country.
11 Now there was there nigh unto the
mountains a great herd of swine feeding.
12 And all the devils besought him, saying, Send us into the swine, that we may
enter into them.
13 And forthwith Jesus gave them leave.
And the unclean spirits went out, and entered into the swine: and the herd ran violently down a steep place into the sea, (they
were about two thousand;) and were
choked in the sea.
14 And they that fed the swine fled, and
told *it* in the city, and in the country. And
they went out to see what it was that was
done.
15 And they come to Jesus, and see him
that was possessed with the devil, and had
the legion, sitting, and clothed, and in his
right mind: and they were afraid.
16 And they that saw *it* told them how it
befell to him that was possessed with the
devil, and *also* concerning the swine.
17 And [k]they began to pray him to depart
out of their coasts.
18 And when he was come into the ship,
[l]he that had been possessed with the devil
prayed him that he might be with him.
19 Howbeit Jesus suffered him not, but
saith unto him, Go home to thy friends, and
tell them how great things the Lord hath
done for thee, and hath had compassion on
thee.
20 And he departed, and began to publish
in Decapolis how great things Jesus had
done for him: and all *men* did marvel.
21 [m]And when Jesus was passed over
again by ship unto the other side, much people gathered unto him: and he was nigh
unto the sea.
22 [n]And, behold, there cometh one of the
rulers of the synagogue, Jairus by name;
and when he saw him, he fell at his feet,
23 And besought him greatly, saying, My
little daughter lieth at the point of death: *I
pray thee,* come and lay thy hands on her,
that she may be healed; and she shall live.
24 And *Jesus* went with him; and much
people followed him, and thronged him.
25 And a certain woman, [o]which had an
issue of blood twelve years,
26 And had suffered many things of many
physicians, and had spent all that she had,
and was nothing bettered, but rather grew
worse,
27 When she had heard of Jesus, came in
...press behind, and touched his garment.
...r she said, If I may touch but his
... I shall be whole.

5:17 [k]Matt. 8:34; Acts 16:39
5:18 [l]Luke 8:38
5:21 [m]Matt. 9:1; Luke 8:40
5:22 [n]Matt. 9:18; Luke 8:41
5:25 [o]Lev. 15:25; Matt. 9:20
5:30 [p]Luke 6:19
5:34 [q]Matt. 9:22; ch. 10:52; Acts 14:9
5:35 [r]Luke 8:49
5:39 [s]John 11:11
5:40 [t]Acts 9:40
5:43 [u]Matt. 8:4; ch. 3:12; Luke 5:14
6:1 [v]Matt. 13:54; Luke 4:16
6:2 [w]John 6:42
6:3 [x]Matt. 12:46; Gal. 1:19 [y]Matt. 11:6

29 And straightway the fountain of her
blood was dried up; and she felt in *her* body
that she was healed of that plague.
30 And Jesus, immediately knowing in
himself that [p]virtue had gone out of him,
turned him about in the press, and said,
Who touched my clothes?
31 And his disciples said unto him, Thou
seest the multitude thronging thee, and sayest thou, Who touched me?
32 And he looked round about to see her
that had done this thing.
33 But the woman fearing and trembling,
knowing what was done in her, came and
fell down before him, and told him all the
truth.
34 And he said unto her, Daughter, [q]thy
faith hath made thee whole; go in peace,
and be whole of thy plague.
35 [r]While he yet spake, there came from
the ruler of the synagogue's *house certain*
which said, Thy daughter is dead: why trou-
blest thou the Master any further?
36 As soon as Jesus heard the word that
was spoken, he saith unto the ruler of the
synagogue, Be not afraid, only believe.
37 And he suffered no man to follow him,
save Peter, and James, and John the brother
of James.
38 And he cometh to the house of the
ruler of the synagogue, and seeth the tumult, and them that wept and wailed
greatly.
39 And when he was come in, he saith
unto them, Why make ye this ado, and
weep? the damsel is not dead, but [s]sleep-
eth.
40 And they laughed him to scorn. [t]But
when he had put them all out, he taketh the
father and the mother of the damsel, and
them that were with him, and entereth in
where the damsel was lying.
41 And he took the damsel by the hand,
and said unto her, Talitha cumi; which is,
being interpreted, Damsel, I say unto thee,
arise.
42 And straightway the damsel arose,
and walked; for she was *of the age* of twelve
years. And they were astonished with a
great astonishment.
43 And [u]he charged them straitly that no
man should know it; and commanded that
something should be given her to eat.

6 And [v]he went out from thence, and
came into his own country; and his disciples follow him.
2 And when the sabbath day was come,
he began to teach in the synagogue: and
many hearing *him* were astonished, saying,
[w]From whence hath this *man* these things?
and what wisdom *is* this which is given unto
him, that even such mighty works are
wrought by his hands?
3 Is not this the carpenter, the son of
Mary, [x]the brother of James, and Joses,
and of Juda, and Simon? and are not his
sisters here with us? And they [y]were offended at him.

4 But Jesus said unto them, [z]A prophet is not without honour, but in his own country, and among his own kin, and in his own house.

5 [a]And he could there do no mighty work, save that he laid his hands upon a few sick folk, and healed *them.*

6 And [b]he marvelled because of their unbelief. [c]And he went round about the villages, teaching.

7 ¶ [d]And he called *unto him* the twelve, and began to send them forth by two and two; and gave them power over unclean spirits;

8 And commanded them that they should take nothing for *their* journey, save a staff only; no scrip, no bread, no money in *their* purse:

9 But [e]*be* shod with sandals; and not put on two coats.

10 [f]And he said unto them, In what place soever ye enter into an house, there abide till ye depart from that place.

11 [g]And whosoever shall not receive you, nor hear you, when ye depart thence, [h]shake off the dust under your feet for a testimony against them. Verily I say unto you, It shall be more tolerable for Sodom and Gomorrha in the day of judgment, than for that city.

12 And they went out, and preached that men should repent.

13 And they cast out many devils, [i]and anointed with oil many that were sick, and healed *them.*

14 [j]And king Herod heard *of him;* (for his name was spread abroad:) and he said, That John the Baptist was risen from the dead, and therefore mighty works do shew forth themselves in him.

15 [k]Others said, That it is Elias. And others said, That it is a prophet, or as one of the prophets.

16 [l]But when Herod heard *thereof,* he said, It is John, whom I beheaded: he is risen from the dead.

17 For Herod himself had sent forth and laid hold upon John, and bound him in prison for Herodias' sake, his brother Philip's wife: for he had married her.

18 For John had said unto Herod, [m]It is not lawful for thee to have thy brother's wife.

19 Therefore Herodias had a quarrel against him, and would have killed him; but she could not:

20 For Herod [n]feared John, knowing that he was a just man and an holy, and observed him; and when he heard him, he did many things, and heard him gladly.

21 [o]And when a convenient day was come, that Herod [p]on his birthday made a supper to his lords, high captains, and chief *estates* of Galilee;

22 And when the daughter of the said Herodias came in, and danced, and pleased Herod and them that sat with him, the king

6:4 [z]Matt. 13:57; John 4:44
6:5 [a]Gen. 19:22; Matt. 13:58; ch. 9:23
6:6 [b]Isa. 59:16 [c]Matt. 9:35; Luke 13:22
6:7 [d]Matt. 10:1; ch. 3:13; Luke 9:1
6:9 [e]Acts 12:8
6:10 [f]Matt. 10:11; Luke 9:4
6:11 [g]Matt. 10:14; Luke 10:10 [h]Acts 13:51
6:13 [i]Jam. 5:14
6:14 [j]Matt. 14:1; Luke 9:7
6:15 [k]Matt. 16:14; ch. 8:28
6:16 [l]Matt. 14:2; Luke 3:19
6:18 [m]Lev. 18:16
6:20 [n]Matt. 14:5
6:21 [o]Matt. 14:6 [p]Gen. 40:20
6:23 [q]Esth. 5:3
6:26 [r]Matt. 14:9
6:30 [s]Luke 9:10
6:31 [t]Matt. 14:13 [u]ch. 3:20
6:32 [v]Matt. 14:13
6:34 [w]Matt. 9:36 [x]Luke 9:11
6:35 [y]Matt. 14:15; Luke 9:12
6:37 [z]Num. 11:13; 2 Kings 4:43
6:38 [a]Matt. 14:17; ch. 8:5; John 6:9
6:41 [b]1 Sam. 9:13; Matt. 26:26

said unto the damsel, Ask of me whatsoever thou wilt, and I will give *it* thee.

23 And he sware unto her, [q]Whatsoever thou shalt ask of me, I will give *it* thee, unto the half of my kingdom.

24 And she went forth, and said unto her mother, What shall I ask? And she said, The head of John the Baptist.

25 And she came in straightway with haste unto the king, and asked, saying, I will that thou give me by and by in a charger the head of John the Baptist.

26 [r]And the king was exceeding sorry; *yet* for his oath's sake, and for their sakes which sat with him, he would not reject her.

27 And immediately the king sent an executioner, and commanded his head to be brought: and he went and beheaded him in the prison,

28 And brought his head in a charger, and gave it to the damsel: and the damsel gave it to her mother.

29 And when his disciples heard *of it,* they came and took up his corpse, and laid it in a tomb.

30 [s]And the apostles gathered themselves together unto Jesus, and told him all things, both what they had done, and what they had taught.

31 [t]And he said unto them, Come ye yourselves apart into a desert place, and rest a while: for [u]there were many coming and going, and they had no leisure so much as to eat.

32 [v]And they departed into a desert place by ship privately.

33 And the people saw them departing, and many knew him, and ran afoot thither out of all cities, and outwent them, and came together unto him.

34 [w]And Jesus, when he came out, saw much people, and was moved with compassion toward them, because they were as sheep not having a shepherd: and [x]he began to teach them many things.

35 [y]And when the day was now far spent, his disciples came unto him, and said, This is a desert place, and now the time *is* far passed:

36 Send them away, that they may go into the country round about, and into the villages, and buy themselves bread: for they have nothing to eat.

37 He answered and said unto them, Give ye them to eat. And they say unto him, [z]Shall we go and buy two hundred pennyworth of bread, and give them to eat?

38 He saith unto them, How many loaves have ye? go and see. And when they knew, they say, [a]Five, and two fishes.

39 And he commanded them to make all sit down by companies upon the green grass.

40 And they sat down in ranks, by hundreds, and by fifties.

41 And when he had taken the five loaves and the two fishes, he looked up to heaven, [b]and blessed, and brake the loaves, and

gave *them* to his disciples to set before
them; and the two fishes divided he among
them all.
42 And they did all eat, and were filled.
43 And they took up twelve baskets full of
the fragments, and of the fishes.
44 And they that did eat of the loaves
were about five thousand men.
45 [c]And straightway he constrained his
disciples to get into the ship, and to go to the
other side before unto Bethsaida, while he
sent away the people.
46 And when he had sent them away, he
departed into a mountain to pray.
47 [d]And when even was come, the ship
was in the midst of the sea, and he alone on
the land.
48 And he saw them toiling in rowing; for
the wind was contrary unto them: and about
the fourth watch of the night he cometh
unto them, walking upon the sea, and
[e]would have passed by them.
49 But when they saw him walking upon
the sea, they supposed it had been a spirit,
and cried out:
50 For they all saw him, and were troubled. And immediately he talked with them,
and saith unto them, Be of good cheer: it is
I; be not afraid.
51 And he went up unto them into the
ship; and the wind ceased: and they were
sore amazed in themselves beyond measure, and wondered.
52 For [f]they considered not *the miracle*
of the loaves: for their [g]heart was hardened.
53 [h]And when they had passed over, they
came into the land of Gennesaret, and drew
to the shore.
54 And when they were come out of the
ship, straightway they knew him,
55 And ran through that whole region
round about, and began to carry about in
beds those that were sick, where they heard
he was.
56 And whithersoever he entered, into
villages, or cities, or country, they laid the
sick in the streets, and besought him that
[i]they might touch if it were but the border
of his garment: and as many as touched him
were made whole.

7 Then [j]came together unto him the
Pharisees, and certain of the scribes,
which came from Jerusalem.
2 And when they saw some of his disciples eat bread with defiled, that is to say,
with unwashen, hands, they found fault.
3 For the Pharisees, and all the Jews, except they wash *their* hands oft, eat not,
holding the tradition of the elders.
4 And *when they come* from the market,
except they wash, they eat not. And many
other things there be, which they have received to hold, *as* the washing of cups, and
pots, brasen vessels, and of tables.
5 [k]Then the Pharisees and scribes asked
him, Why walk not thy disciples according
to the tradition of the elders, but eat bread
with unwashen hands?
6 He answered and said unto them, Well
hath Esaias prophesied of you hypocrites,
as it is written, [l]This people honoureth me
with *their* lips, but their heart is far
from me.
7 Howbeit in vain do they worship me,
teaching *for* doctrines the commandments
of men.
8 For laying aside the commandment of
God, ye hold the tradition of men, *as* the
washing of pots and cups: and many other
such like things ye do.
9 And he said unto them, Full well ye reject the commandment of God, that ye may
keep your own tradition.
10 For Moses said, [m]Honour thy father
and thy mother; and, [n]Whoso curseth father or mother, let him die the death:
11 But ye say, If a man shall say to his
father or mother, *It is* [o]Corban, that is to
say, a gift, by whatsoever thou mightest be
profited by me; *he shall be free.*
12 And ye suffer him no more to do ought
for his father or his mother;
13 Making the word of God of none effect
through your tradition, which ye have delivered: and many such like things do ye.
14 ¶ [p]And when he had called all the people *unto him,* he said unto them, Hearken
unto me every one *of you,* and understand:
15 There is nothing from without a man,
that entering into him can defile him: but
the things which come out of him, those are
they that defile the man.
16 [q]If any man have ears to hear, let him
hear.
17 [r]And when he was entered into the
house from the people, his disciples asked
him concerning the parable.
18 And he saith unto them, Are ye so
without understanding also? Do ye not perceive, that whatsoever thing from without
entereth into the man, *it* cannot defile him;
19 Because it entereth not into his heart,
but into the belly, and goeth out into the
draught, purging all meats?
20 And he said, That which cometh out of
the man, that defileth the man.
21 [s]For from within, out of the heart of
men, proceed evil thoughts, adulteries, fornications, murders,
22 Thefts, covetousness, wickedness, deceit, lasciviousness, an evil eye, blasphemy,
pride, foolishness:
23 All these evil things come from within,
and defile the man.
24 ¶ [t]And from thence he arose, and
went into the borders of Tyre and Sidon,
and entered into an house, and would have
no man know *it:* but he could not be hid.
25 For a *certain* woman, whose young
daughter had an unclean spirit, heard of
him, and came and fell at his feet:
26 The woman was a Greek, a Syrophenician by nation; and she besought him that

6:45 [c]Matt. 14:22; John 6:17
6:47 [d]Matt. 14:23; John 6:16
6:48 [e]Luke 24:28
6:52 [f]ch. 8:17 [g]ch. 3:5
6:53 [h]Matt. 14:34
6:56 [i]Matt. 9:20; ch. 5:27; Acts 19:12
7:1 [j]Matt. 15:1
7:5 [k]Matt. 15:2
7:6 [l]Isa. 29:13; Matt. 15:8
7:10 [m]Ex. 20:12; Deut. 5:16; Matt. 15:4 [n]Ex. 21:17; Lev. 20:9; Prov. 20:20
7:11 [o]Matt. 15:5
7:14 [p]Matt. 15:10
7:16 [q]Matt. 11:15
7:17 [r]Matt. 15:15
7:21 [s]Gen. 6:5; Matt. 15:19
7:24 [t]Matt. 15:21

he would cast forth the devil out of her daughter.

27 But Jesus said unto her, Let the children first be filled: for it is not meet to take the children's bread, and to cast *it* unto the dogs.

28 And she answered and said unto him, Yes, Lord: yet the dogs under the table eat of the children's crumbs.

29 And he said unto her, For this saying go thy way; the devil is gone out of thy daughter.

30 And when she was come to her house, she found the devil gone out, and her daughter laid upon the bed.

31 ¶ [u]And again, departing from the coasts of Tyre and Sidon, he came unto the sea of Galilee, through the midst of the coasts of Decapolis.

32 And [v]they bring unto him one that was deaf, and had an impediment in his speech; and they beseech him to put his hand upon him.

33 And he took him aside from the multitude, and put his fingers into his ears, and [w]he spit, and touched his tongue;

34 And looking [x]up to heaven, [y]he sighed, and saith unto him, Ephphatha, that is, Be opened.

35 [z]And straightway his ears were opened, and the string of his tongue was loosed, and he spake plain.

36 And [a]he charged them that they should tell no man: but the more he charged them, so much the more a great deal they published *it;*

37 And were beyond measure astonished, saying, He hath done all things well: he maketh both the deaf to hear, and the dumb to speak.

8 In those days [b]the multitude being very great, and having nothing to eat, Jesus called his disciples *unto him,* and saith unto them,

2 I have compassion on the multitude, because they have now been with me three days, and have nothing to eat:

3 And if I send them away fasting to their own houses, they will faint by the way: for divers of them came from far.

4 And his disciples answered him, From whence can a man satisfy these *men* with bread here in the wilderness?

5 [c]And he asked them, How many loaves have ye? And they said, Seven.

6 And he commanded the people to sit down on the ground: and he took the seven loaves, and gave thanks, and brake, and gave to his disciples to set before *them;* and they did set *them* before the people.

7 And they had a few small fishes: and [d]he blessed, and commanded to set them also before *them.*

8 So they did eat, and were filled: and they took up of the broken *meat* that was left seven baskets.

9 And they that had eaten were about four thousand: and he sent them away.

10 ¶ And [e]straightway he entered into a ship with his disciples, and came into the parts of Dalmanutha.

11 [f]And the Pharisees came forth, and began to question with him, seeking of him a sign from heaven, tempting him.

12 And he sighed deeply in his spirit, and saith, Why doth this generation seek after a sign? verily I say unto you, There shall no sign be given unto this generation.

13 And he left them, and entering into the ship again departed to the other side.

14 ¶ [g]Now *the disciples* had forgotten to take bread, neither had they in the ship with them more than one loaf.

15 [h]And he charged them, saying, Take heed, beware of the leaven of the Pharisees, and *of* the leaven of Herod.

16 And they reasoned among themselves, saying, *It is* [i]because we have no bread.

17 And when Jesus knew *it,* he saith unto them, Why reason ye, because ye have no bread? [j]perceive ye not yet, neither understand? have ye your heart yet hardened?

18 Having eyes, see ye not? and having ears, hear ye not? and do ye not remember?

19 [k]When I brake the five loaves among five thousand, how many baskets full of fragments took ye up? They say unto him, Twelve.

20 And [l]when the seven among four thousand, how many baskets full of fragments took ye up? And they said, Seven.

21 And he said unto them, How is it that [m]ye do not understand?

22 ¶ And he cometh to Bethsaida; and they bring a blind man unto him, and besought him to touch him.

23 And he took the blind man by the hand, and led him out of the town; and when [n]he had spit on his eyes, and put his hands upon him, he asked him if he saw ought.

24 And he looked up, and said, I see men as trees, walking.

25 After that he put *his* hands again upon his eyes, and made him look up: and he was restored, and saw every man clearly.

26 And he sent him away to his house, saying, Neither go into the town, [o]nor tell *it* to any in the town.

27 ¶ [p]And Jesus went out, and his disciples, into the towns of Caesarea Philippi: and by the way he asked his disciples, saying unto them, Whom do men say that I am?

28 And they answered, [q]John the Baptist: but some *say,* Elias; and others, One of the prophets.

29 And he saith unto them, But whom say ye that I am? And Peter answereth and saith unto him, [r]Thou art the Christ.

30 [s]And he charged them that they should tell no man of him.

31 And [t]he began to teach them, that the Son of man must suffer many things, and be rejected of the elders, and *of* the chief priests, and scribes, and be killed, and after three days rise again.

7:31 *u*Matt. 15:29
7:32 *v*Matt. 9:32; Luke 11:14
7:33 *w*ch. 8:23; John 9:6
7:34 *x*ch. 6:41; John 11:41 *y*John 11:33
7:35 *z*Isa. 35:5; Matt. 11:5
7:36 *a*ch. 5:43
8:1 *b*Matt. 15:32
8:5 *c*Matt. 15:34; ch. 6:38
8:7 *d*Matt. 14:19; ch. 6:41
8:10 *e*Matt. 15:39
8:11 *f*Matt. 12:38; John 6:30
8:14 *g*Matt. 16:5
8:15 *h*Matt. 16:6; Luke 12:1
8:16 *i*Matt. 16:7
8:17 *j*ch. 6:52
8:19 *k*Matt. 14:20; ch. 6:43; Luke 9:17; John 6:13
8:20 *l*Matt. 15:37; ver. 8
8:21 *m*ch. 6:52; ver. 17
8:23 *n*ch. 7:33
8:26 *o*Matt. 8:4; ch. 5:43
8:27 *p*Matt. 16:13; Luke 9:18
8:28 *q*Matt. 14:2
8:29 *r*Matt. 16:6; John 6:69
8:30 *s*Matt. 16:20
8:31 *t*Matt. 16:21; Luke 9:22

32 And he spake that saying openly. And Peter took him, and began to rebuke him.

33 But when he had turned about and looked on his disciples, he rebuked Peter, saying, Get thee behind me, Satan: for thou savourest not the things that be of God, but the things that be of men.

34 ¶ And when he had called the people *unto him* with his disciples also, he said unto them, [u]Whosoever will come after me, let him deny himself, and take up his cross, and follow me.

35 For [v]whosoever will save his life shall lose it; but whosoever shall lose his life for my sake and the gospel's, the same shall save it.

36 For what shall it profit a man, if he shall gain the whole world, and lose his own soul?

37 Or what shall a man give in exchange for his soul?

38 [w]Whosoever therefore [x]shall be ashamed of me and of my words in this adulterous and sinful generation; of him also shall the Son of man be ashamed, when he cometh in the glory of his Father with the holy angels.

9 And he said unto them, [y]Verily I say unto you, That there be some of them that stand here, which shall not taste of death, till they have seen [z]the kingdom of God come with power.

2 ¶ [a]And after six days Jesus taketh *with him* Peter, and James, and John, and leadeth them up into an high mountain apart by themselves: and he was transfigured before them.

3 And his raiment became shining, exceeding [b]white as snow; so as no fuller on earth can white them.

4 And there appeared unto them Elias with Moses: and they were talking with Jesus.

5 And Peter answered and said to Jesus, Master, it is good for us to be here: and let us make three tabernacles; one for thee, and one for Moses, and one for Elias.

6 For he wist not what to say; for they were sore afraid.

7 And there was a cloud that overshadowed them: and a voice came out of the cloud, saying, This is my beloved Son: hear him.

8 And suddenly, when they had looked round about, they saw no man any more, save Jesus only with themselves.

9 [c]And as they came down from the mountain, he charged them that they should tell no man what things they had seen, till the Son of man were risen from the dead.

10 And they kept that saying with themselves, questioning one with another what the rising from the dead should mean.

11 ¶ And they asked him, saying, Why say the scribes [d]that Elias must first come?

12 And he answered and told them, Elias verily cometh first, and restoreth all things; and [e]how it is written of the Son of man, that he must suffer many things, and [f]be set at nought.

13 But I say unto you, That [g]Elias is indeed come, and they have done unto him whatsoever they listed, as it is written of him.

14 ¶ [h]And when he came to *his* disciples, he saw a great multitude about them, and the scribes questioning with them.

15 And straightway all the people, when they beheld him, were greatly amazed, and running to *him* saluted him.

16 And he asked the scribes, What question ye with them?

17 And [i]one of the multitude answered and said, Master, I have brought unto thee my son, which hath a dumb spirit;

18 And wheresoever he taketh him, he teareth him: and he foameth, and gnasheth with his teeth, and pineth away: and I spake to thy disciples that they should cast him out; and they could not.

19 He answereth him, and saith, O faithless generation, how long shall I be with you? how long shall I suffer you? bring him unto me.

20 And they brought him unto him: and [j]when he saw him, straightway the spirit tare him; and he fell on the ground, and wallowed foaming.

21 And he asked his father, How long is it ago since this came unto him? And he said, Of a child.

22 And ofttimes it hath cast him into the fire, and into the waters, to destroy him: but if thou canst do any thing, have compassion on us, and help us.

23 Jesus said unto him, [k]If thou canst believe, all things *are* possible to him that believeth.

24 And straightway the father of the child cried out, and said with tears, Lord, I believe; help thou mine unbelief.

25 When Jesus saw that the people came running together, he rebuked the foul spirit, saying unto him, *Thou* dumb and deaf spirit, I charge thee, come out of him, and enter no more into him.

26 And *the spirit* cried, and rent him sore, and came out of him: and he was as one dead; insomuch that many said, He is dead.

27 But Jesus took him by the hand, and lifted him up; and he arose.

28 [l]And when he was come into the house, his disciples asked him privately, Why could not we cast him out?

29 And he said unto them, This kind can come forth by nothing, but by prayer and fasting.

30 ¶ And they departed thence, and passed through Galilee; and he would not that any man should know *it*.

31 [m]For he taught his disciples, and said unto them, The Son of man is delivered into the hands of men, and they shall kill him; and after that he is killed, he shall rise the third day.

8:34 [u]Matt. 10:38; Luke 9:23
8:35 [v]John 12:25
8:38 [w]Matt. 10:33; Luke 9:26 [x]Rom. 1:16; 2 Tim. 1:8
9:1 [y]Matt. 16:28; Luke 9:27 [z]Matt. 24:30; Luke 22:18
9:2 [a]Matt. 17:1; Luke 9:28
9:3 [b]Dan. 7:9; Matt. 28:3
9:9 [c]Matt. 17:9
9:11 [d]Mal. 4:5; Matt. 17:10
9:12 [e]Ps. 22:6; Isa. 53:2; Dan. 9:26 [f]Luke 23:11; Phil. 2:7
9:13 [g]Matt. 11:14; Luke 1:17
9:14 [h]Matt. 17:14; Luke 9:37
9:17 [i]Matt. 17:14; Luke 9:38
9:20 [j]ch. 1:26; Luke 9:42
9:23 [k]Matt. 17:20; ch. 11:23; Luke 17:6; John 11:40
9:28 [l]Matt. 17:19
9:31 [m]Matt. 17:22; Luke 9:44

32 But they understood not that saying, and were afraid to ask him.

33 ¶ [n]And he came to Capernaum: and being in the house he asked them, What was it that ye disputed among yourselves by the way?

34 But they held their peace: for by the way they had disputed among themselves, who *should be* the greatest.

35 And he sat down, and called the twelve, and saith unto them, [o]If any man desire to be first, *the same* shall be last of all, and servant of all.

36 And [p]he took a child, and set him in the midst of them: and when he had taken him in his arms, he said unto them,

37 Whosoever shall receive one of such children in my name, receiveth me: and [q]whosoever shall receive me, receiveth not me, but him that sent me.

38 ¶ [r]And John answered him, saying, Master, we saw one casting out devils in thy name, and he followeth not us: and we forbad him, because he followeth not us.

39 But Jesus said, Forbid him not: [s]for there is no man which shall do a miracle in my name, that can lightly speak evil of me.

40 For [t]he that is not against us is on our part.

41 [u]For whosoever shall give you a cup of water to drink in my name, because ye belong to Christ, verily I say unto you, he shall not lose his reward.

42 [v]And whosoever shall offend one of *these* little ones that believe in me, it is better for him that a millstone were hanged about his neck, and he were cast into the sea.

43 [w]And if thy hand offend thee, cut it off: it is better for thee to enter into life maimed, than having two hands to go into hell, into the fire that never shall be quenched:

44 [x]Where their worm dieth not, and the fire is not quenched.

45 And if thy foot offend thee, cut if off: it is better for thee to enter halt into life, than having two feet to be cast into hell, into the fire that never shall be quenched:

46 Where their worm dieth not, and the fire is not quenched.

47 And if thine eye offend thee, pluck it out: it is better for thee to enter into the kingdom of God with one eye, than having two eyes to be cast into hell fire:

48 Where their worm dieth not, and the fire is not quenched.

49 For every one shall be salted with fire, [y]and every sacrifice shall be salted with salt.

50 [z]Salt *is* good: but if the salt have lost his saltness, wherewith will ye season it? [a]Have salt in yourselves, and [b]have peace one with another.

10 And [c]he arose from thence, and cometh into the coasts of Judaea by the farther side of Jordan: and the people resort unto him again; and, as he was wont, he taught them again.

9:33 [n]Matt. 18:1; Luke 9:46
9:35 [o]Matt. 20:26; ch. 10:43
9:36 [p]Matt. 18:2; ch. 10:16
9:37 [q]Matt. 10:40; Luke 9:48
9:38 [r]Num. 11:28; Luke 9:49
9:39 [s]1 Cor. 12:3
9:40 [t]Matt. 12:30
9:41 [u]Matt. 10:42
9:42 [v]Matt. 18:6; Luke 17:1
9:43 [w]Deut. 13:6; Matt. 5:29
9:44 [x]Isa. 66:24
9:49 [y]Lev. 2:13; Ezek. 43:24
9:50 [z]Matt. 5:13; Luke 14:34 [a]Eph. 4:29; Col. 4:6 [b]Rom. 12:18; 2 Cor. 13:11; Heb. 12:14
10:1 [c]Matt. 19:1; John 10:40
10:2 [d]Matt. 19:3
10:4 [e]Deut. 24:1; Matt. 5:31
10:6 [f]Gen. 1:27
10:7 [g]Gen. 2:24; 1 Cor. 6:16; Eph. 5:31
10:11 [h]Matt. 5:32; Luke 16:18; Rom. 7:3; 1 Cor. 7:10
10:13 [i]Matt. 19:13; Luke 18:15
10:14 [j]1 Cor. 14:20; 1 Pet. 2:2
10:15 [k]Matt. 18:3
10:17 [l]Matt. 19:16; Luke 18:18
10:19 [m]Ex. 20; Rom. 13:9
10:21 [n]Matt. 6:19; Luke 12:33
10:23 [o]Matt. 19:23; Luke 18:24

2 ¶ [d]And the Pharisees came to him, and asked him, Is it lawful for a man to put away *his* wife? tempting him.

3 And he answered and said unto them, What did Moses command you?

4 And they said, [e]Moses suffered to write a bill of divorcement, and to put *her* away.

5 And Jesus answered and said unto them, For the hardness of your heart he wrote you this precept.

6 But from the beginning of the creation [f]God made them male and female.

7 [g]For this cause shall a man leave his father and mother, and cleave to his wife;

8 And they twain shall be one flesh: so then they are no more twain, but one flesh.

9 What therefore God hath joined together, let not man put asunder.

10 And in the house his disciples asked him again of the same *matter.*

11 And he saith unto them, [h]Whosoever shall put away his wife, and marry another, committeth adultery against her.

12 And if a woman shall put away her husband, and be married to another, she committeth adultery.

13 ¶ [i]And they brought young children to him, that he should touch them: and *his* disciples rebuked those that brought *them.*

14 But when Jesus saw *it,* he was much displeased, and said unto them, Suffer the little children to come unto me, and forbid them not: for [j]of such is the kingdom of God.

15 Verily I say unto you, [k]Whosoever shall not receive the kingdom of God as a little child, he shall not enter therein.

16 And he took them up in his arms, put *his* hands upon them, and blessed them.

17 ¶ [l]And when he was gone forth into the way, there came one running, and kneeled to him, and asked him, Good Master, what shall I do that I may inherit eternal life?

18 And Jesus said unto him, Why callest thou me good? *there is* none good but one, *that is,* God.

19 Thou knowest the commandments, [m]Do not commit adultery, Do not kill, Do not steal, Do not bear false witness, Defraud not, Honour thy father and mother.

20 And he answered and said unto him, Master, all these have I observed from my youth.

21 Then Jesus beholding him loved him, and said unto him, One thing thou lackest: go thy way, sell whatsoever thou hast, and give to the poor, and thou shalt have [n]treasure in heaven: and come, take up the cross, and follow me.

22 And he was sad at that saying, and went away grieved: for he had great possessions.

23 ¶ [o]And Jesus looked round about, and saith unto his disciples, How hardly shall they that have riches enter into the kingdom of God!

24 And the disciples were astonished at

his words. But Jesus answereth again, and saith unto them, Children, how hard is it for them [p]that trust in riches to enter into the kingdom of God!

25 It is easier for a camel to go through the eye of a needle, than for a rich man to enter into the kingdom of God.

26 And they were astonished out of measure, saying among themselves, Who then can be saved?

27 And Jesus looking upon them saith, With men *it is* impossible, but not with God: for [q]with God all things are possible.

28 ¶ [r]Then Peter began to say unto him, Lo, we have left all, and have followed thee.

29 And Jesus answered and said, Verily I say unto you, There is no man that hath left house, or brethren, or sisters, or father, or mother, or wife, or children, or lands, for my sake, and the gospel's,

30 [s]But he shall receive an hundredfold now in this time, houses, and brethren, and sisters, and mothers, and children, and lands, with persecutions; and in the world to come eternal life.

31 [t]But many *that are* first shall be last; and the last first.

32 ¶ [u]And they were in the way going up to Jerusalem; and Jesus went before them: and they were amazed; and as they followed, they were afraid. [v]And he took again the twelve, and began to tell them what things should happen unto him,

33 *Saying,* Behold, we go up to Jerusalem; and the Son of man shall be delivered unto the chief priests, and unto the scribes; and they shall condemn him to death, and shall deliver him to the Gentiles:

34 And they shall mock him, and shall scourge him, and shall spit upon him, and shall kill him: and the third day he shall rise again.

35 ¶ [w]And James and John, the sons of Zebedee, come unto him, saying, Master, we would that thou shouldest do for us whatsoever we shall desire.

36 And he said unto them, What would ye that I should do for you?

37 They said unto him, Grant unto us that we may sit, one on thy right hand, and the other on thy left hand, in thy glory.

38 But Jesus said unto them, Ye know not what ye ask: can ye drink of the cup that I drink of? and be baptized with the baptism that I am baptized with?

39 And they said unto him, We can. And Jesus said unto them, Ye shall indeed drink of the cup that I drink of; and with the baptism that I am baptized withal shall ye be baptized:

40 But to sit on my right hand and on my left hand is not mine to give; but *it shall be given to them* for whom it is prepared.

41 [x]And when the ten heard *it,* they began to be much displeased with James and John.

42 But Jesus called them *to him,* and saith unto them, [y]Ye know that they which are

10:24 [p]Job 31:24; Ps. 52:7; 1 Tim. 6:17
10:27 [q]Jer. 32:17; Matt. 19:26; Luke 1:37
10:28 [r]Matt. 19:27; Luke 18:28
10:30 [s]2 Chron. 25:9; Luke 18:30
10:31 [t]Matt. 19:30; Luke 13:30
10:32 [u]Matt. 20:17; Luke 18:31; [v]ch. 8:31; Luke 9:22
10:35 [w]Matt. 20:20
10:41 [x]Matt. 20:24
10:42 [y]Luke 22:25
10:43 [z]Matt. 20:26; ch. 9:35; Luke 9:48
10:45 [a]John 13:14; Phil. 2:7; [b]Matt. 20:28; 1 Tim. 2:6; Tit. 2:14
10:46 [c]Matt. 20:29; Luke 18:35
10:52 [d]Matt. 9:22; ch. 5:34
11:1 [e]Matt. 21:1; Luke 19:29; John 12:14
11:8 [f]Matt. 21:8
11:9 [g]Ps. 118:26

accounted to rule over the Gentiles exercise lordship over them; and their great ones exercise authority upon them.

43 [z]But so shall it not be among you: but whosoever will be great among you, shall be your minister:

44 And whosoever of you will be the chiefest, shall be servant of all.

45 For even [a]the Son of man came not to be ministered unto, but to minister, and [b]to give his life a ransom for many.

46 ¶ [c]And they came to Jericho: and as he went out of Jericho with his disciples and a great number of people, blind Bartimaeus, the son of Timaeus, sat by the highway side begging.

47 And when he heard that it was Jesus of Nazareth, he began to cry out, and say, Jesus, *thou* son of David, have mercy on me.

48 And many charged him that he should hold his peace: but he cried the more a great deal, *Thou* son of David, have mercy on me.

49 And Jesus stood still, and commanded him to be called. And they call the blind man, saying unto him, Be of good comfort, rise; he calleth thee.

50 And he, casting away his garment, rose, and came to Jesus.

51 And Jesus answered and said unto him, What wilt thou that I should do unto thee? The blind man said unto him, Lord, that I might receive my sight.

52 And Jesus said unto him, Go thy way; [d]thy faith hath made thee whole. And immediately he received his sight, and followed Jesus in the way.

11 And [e]when they came nigh to Jerusalem, unto Bethphage and Bethany, at the mount of Olives, he sendeth forth two of his disciples,

2 And saith unto them, Go your way into the village over against you: and as soon as ye be entered into it, ye shall find a colt tied, whereon never man sat; loose him, and bring *him.*

3 And if any man say unto you, Why do ye this? say ye that the Lord hath need of him; and straightway he will send him hither.

4 And they went their way, and found the colt tied by the door without in a place where two ways met; and they loose him.

5 And certain of them that stood there said unto them, What do ye, loosing the colt?

6 And they said unto them even as Jesus had commanded: and they let them go.

7 And they brought the colt to Jesus, and cast their garments on him; and he sat upon him.

8 [f]And many spread their garments in the way: and others cut down branches off the trees, and strawed *them* in the way.

9 And they that went before, and they that followed, cried, saying, [g]Hosanna; Blessed *is* he that cometh in the name of the Lord:

10 Blessed *be* the kingdom of our father David, that cometh in the name of the Lord: [h]Hosanna in the highest.

11 [i]And Jesus entered into Jerusalem, and into the temple: and when he had looked round about upon all things, and now the eventide was come, he went out unto Bethany with the twelve.

12 ¶ [j]And on the morrow, when they were come from Bethany, he was hungry:

13 [k]And seeing a fig tree afar off having leaves, he came, if haply he might find any thing thereon: and when he came to it, he found nothing but leaves; for the time of figs was not *yet*.

14 And Jesus answered and said unto it, No man eat fruit of thee hereafter for ever. And his disciples heard *it*.

15 ¶ [l]And they come to Jerusalem: and Jesus went into the temple, and began to cast out them that sold and bought in the temple, and overthrew the tables of the moneychangers, and the seats of them that sold doves;

16 And would not suffer that any man should carry *any* vessel through the temple.

17 And he taught, saying unto them, Is it not written, [m]My house shall be called of all nations the house of prayer? but [n]ye have made it a den of thieves.

18 And [o]the scribes and chief priests heard *it*, and sought how they might destroy him: for they feared him, because [p]all the people was astonished at his doctrine.

19 And when even was come, he went out of the city.

20 ¶ [q]And in the morning, as they passed by, they saw the fig tree dried up from the roots.

21 And Peter calling to remembrance saith unto him, Master, behold, the fig tree which thou cursedst is withered away.

22 And Jesus answering saith unto them, Have faith in God.

23 For [r]verily I say unto you, That whosoever shall say unto this mountain, Be thou removed, and be thou cast into the sea; and shall not doubt in his heart, but shall believe that those things which he saith shall come to pass; he shall have whatsoever he saith.

24 Therefore I say unto you, [s]What things soever ye desire, when ye pray, believe that ye receive *them*, and ye shall have *them*.

25 And when ye stand praying, [t]forgive, if ye have ought against any: that your Father also which is in heaven may forgive you your trespasses.

26 But [u]if ye do not forgive, neither will your Father which is in heaven forgive your trespasses.

27 ¶ And they come again to Jerusalem: [v]and as he was walking in the temple, there come to him the chief priests, and the scribes, and the elders,

28 And say unto him, By what authority doest thou these things? and who gave thee this authority to do these things?

29 And Jesus answered and said unto them, I will also ask of you one question, and answer me; and I will tell you by what authority I do these things.

30 The baptism of John, was *it* from heaven, or of men? answer me.

31 And they reasoned with themselves, saying, If we shall say, From heaven; he will say, Why then did ye not believe him?

32 But if we shall say, Of men; they feared the people: for [w]all *men* counted John, that he was a prophet indeed.

33 And they answered and said unto Jesus, We cannot tell. And Jesus answering saith unto them, Neither do I tell you by what authority I do these things.

12 And [x]he began to speak unto them by parables. A *certain* man planted a vineyard, and set an hedge about *it*, and digged *a place for* the winefat, and built a tower, and let it out to husbandmen, and went into a far country.

2 And at the season he sent to the husbandmen a servant, that he might receive from the husbandmen of the fruit of the vineyard.

3 And they caught *him*, and beat him, and sent *him* away empty.

4 And again he sent unto them another servant; and at him they cast stones, and wounded *him* in the head, and sent *him* away shamefully handled.

5 And again he sent another; and him they killed, and many others; beating some, and killing some.

6 Having yet therefore one son, his wellbeloved, he sent him also last unto them, saying, They will reverence my son.

7 But those husbandmen said among themselves, This is the heir; come, let us kill him, and the inheritance shall be ours.

8 And they took him, and killed *him*, and cast *him* out of the vineyard.

9 What shall therefore the lord of the vineyard do? he will come and destroy the husbandmen, and will give the vineyard unto others.

10 And have ye not read this scripture; [y]The stone which the builders rejected is become the head of the corner:

11 This was the Lord's doing, and it is marvellous in our eyes?

12 [z]And they sought to lay hold on him, but feared the people: for they knew that he had spoken the parable against them: and they left him, and went their way.

13 ¶ [a]And they send unto him certain of the Pharisees and of the Herodians, to catch him in *his* words.

14 And when they were come, they say unto him, Master, we know that thou art true, and carest for no man: for thou regardest not the person of men, but teachest the way of God in truth: Is it lawful to give tribute to Caesar, or not?

15 Shall we give, or shall we not give? But he, knowing their hypocrisy, said unto

11:10 [h]Ps. 148:1
11:11 [i]Matt. 21:12
11:12 [j]Matt. 21:18
11:13 [k]Matt. 21:19
11:15 [l]Matt. 21:12; Luke 19:45; John 2:14
11:17 [m]Isa. 56:7 [n]Jer. 7:11
11:18 [o]Matt. 21:45; Luke 19:47 [p]Matt. 7:28; ch. 1:22; Luke 4:32
11:20 [q]Matt. 21:19
11:23 [r]Matt. 17:20; Luke 17:6
11:24 [s]Matt. 7:7; Luke 11:9; John 14:13; Jam. 1:5
11:25 [t]Matt. 6:14; Col. 3:13
11:26 [u]Matt. 18:35
11:27 [v]Matt. 21:23; Luke 20:1
11:32 [w]Matt. 3:5; ch. 6:20
12:1 [x]Matt. 21:33; Luke 22:9
12:10 [y]Ps. 118:22
12:12 [z]Matt. 21:45; ch. 11:18; John 7:25
12:13 [a]Matt. 22:15; Luke 20:20

them, Why tempt ye me? bring me a penny, that I may see *it*.

16 And they brought *it*. And he saith unto them, Whose *is* this image and superscription? And they said unto him, Caesar's.

17 And Jesus answering said unto them, Render to Caesar the things that are Caesar's, and to God the things that are God's. And they marvelled at him.

18 ¶ [b]Then come unto him the Sadducees, [c]which say there is no resurrection; and they asked him, saying,

19 Master, [d]Moses wrote unto us, If a man's brother die, and leave *his* wife *behind him*, and leave no children, that his brother should take his wife, and raise up seed unto his brother.

20 Now there were seven brethren: and the first took a wife, and dying left no seed.

21 And the second took her, and died, neither left he any seed: and the third likewise.

22 And the seven had her, and left no seed: last of all the woman died also.

23 In the resurrection therefore, when they shall rise, whose wife shall she be of them? for the seven had her to wife.

24 And Jesus answering said unto them, Do ye not therefore err, because ye know not the scriptures, neither the power of God?

25 For when they shall rise from the dead, they neither marry, nor are given in marriage; but [e]are as the angels which are in heaven.

26 And as touching the dead, that they rise: have ye not read in the book of Moses, how in the bush God spake unto him, saying, [f]I *am* the God of Abraham, and the God of Isaac, and the God of Jacob?

27 He is not the God of the dead, but the God of the living: ye therefore do greatly err.

28 ¶ [g]And one of the scribes came, and having heard them reasoning together, and perceiving that he had answered them well, asked him, Which is the first commandment of all?

29 And Jesus answered him, The first of all the commandments *is*, [h]Hear, O Israel; The Lord our God is one Lord:

30 And thou shalt love the Lord thy God with all thy heart, and with all thy soul, and with all thy mind, and with all thy strength: this *is* the first commandment.

31 And the second *is* like, *namely* this, [i]Thou shalt love thy neighbour as thyself. There is none other commandment greater than these.

32 And the scribe said unto him, Well, Master, thou hast said the truth: for there is one God; [j]and there is none other but he:

33 And to love him with all the heart, and with all the understanding, and with all the soul, and with all the strength, and to love *his* neighbour as himself, [k]is more than all whole burnt offerings and sacrifices.

34 And when Jesus saw that he answered discreetly, he said unto him, Thou art not far from the kingdom of God. [l]And no man after that durst ask him *any question*.

35 ¶ [m]And Jesus answered and said, while he taught in the temple, How say the scribes that Christ is the son of David?

36 For David himself said [n]by the Holy Ghost, [o]The LORD said to my Lord, Sit thou on my right hand, till I make thine enemies thy footstool.

37 David therefore himself calleth him Lord; and whence is he *then* his son? And the common people heard him gladly.

38 ¶ And [p]he said unto them in his doctrine, [q]Beware of the scribes, which love to go in long clothing, and [r]*love* salutations in the marketplaces,

39 And the chief seats in the synagogues, and the uppermost rooms at feasts:

40 [s]Which devour widows' houses, and for a pretence make long prayers: these shall receive greater damnation.

41 ¶ [t]And Jesus sat over against the treasury, and beheld how the people cast money [u]into the treasury: and many that were rich cast in much.

42 And there came a certain poor widow, and she threw in two mites, which make a farthing.

43 And he called *unto him* his disciples, and saith unto them, Verily I say unto you, That [v]this poor widow hath cast more in, than all they which have cast into the treasury:

44 For all *they* did cast in of their abundance; but she of her want did cast in all that she had, [w]*even* all her living.

13 And [x]as he went out of the temple, one of his disciples saith unto him, Master, see what manner of stones and what buildings *are here!*

2 And Jesus answering said unto him, Seest thou these great buildings? [y]there shall not be left one stone upon another, that shall not be thrown down.

3 And as he sat upon the mount of Olives over against the temple, Peter and James and John and Andrew asked him privately,

4 [z]Tell us, when shall these things be? and what *shall be* the sign when all these things shall be fulfilled?

5 And Jesus answering them began to say, [a]Take heed lest any *man* deceive you:

6 For many shall come in my name, saying, I am *Christ;* and shall deceive many.

7 And when ye shall hear of wars and rumours of wars, be ye not troubled: for *such things* must needs be; but the end *shall* not *be* yet.

8 For nation shall rise against nation, and kingdom against kingdom: and there shall be earthquakes in divers places, and there shall be famines and troubles: [b]these *are* the beginnings of sorrows.

9 ¶ But [c]take heed to yourselves: for they shall deliver you up to councils; and in the synagogues ye shall be beaten: and ye shall be brought before rulers and kings for my sake, for a testimony against them.

12:18 [b]Matt. 22:23; Luke 20:27 [c]Acts 23:8
12:19 [d]Deut. 25:5
12:25 [e]1 Cor. 15:42
12:26 [f]Ex. 3:6
12:28 [g]Matt. 22:35
12:29 [h]Deut. 6:4; Luke 10:27
12:31 [i]Lev. 19:18; Matt. 22:39; Rom. 13:9; Gal. 5:14; Jam. 2:8
12:32 [j]Deut. 4:39; Isa. 45:6
12:33 [k]1 Sam. 15:22; Hos. 6:6; Mic. 6:6
12:34 [l]Matt. 22:46
12:35 [m]Matt. 22:41; Luke 20:41
12:36 [n]2 Sam. 23:2 [o]Ps. 110:1
12:38 [p]ch. 4:2 [q]Matt. 23:1; Luke 20:46 [r]Luke 11:43
12:40 [s]Matt. 23:14
12:41 [t]Luke 21:1 [u]2 Kings 12:9
12:43 [v]2 Cor. 8:12
12:44 [w]Deut. 24:6; 1 John 3:17
13:1 [x]Matt. 24:1; Luke 21:5
13:2 [y]Luke 19:44
13:4 [z]Matt. 24:3; Luke 21:7
13:5 [a]Jer. 29:8; Eph. 5:6; 1 Thess. 2:3
13:8 [b]Matt. 24:8
13:9 [c]Matt. 10:17; Rev. 2:10

10 And [d]the gospel must first be published among all nations.

11 [e]But when they shall lead *you,* and deliver you up, take no thought beforehand what ye shall speak, neither do ye premeditate: but whatsoever shall be given you in that hour, that speak ye: for it is not ye that speak, [f]but the Holy Ghost.

12 Now [g]the brother shall betray the brother to death, and the father the son; and children shall rise up against *their* parents, and shall cause them to be put to death.

13 [h]And ye shall be hated of all *men* for my name's sake: but [i]he that shall endure unto the end, the same shall be saved.

14 ¶ [j]But when ye shall see the abomination of desolation, [k]spoken of by Daniel the prophet, standing where it ought not, (let him that readeth understand,) then [l]let them that be in Judaea flee to the mountains:

15 And let him that is on the housetop not go down into the house, neither enter *therein,* to take any thing out of his house:

16 And let him that is in the field not turn back again for to take up his garment.

17 [m]But woe to them that are with child, and to them that give suck in those days!

18 And pray ye that your flight be not in the winter.

19 [n]For *in* those days shall be affliction, such as was not from the beginning of the creation which God created unto this time, neither shall be.

20 And except that the Lord had shortened those days, no flesh should be saved: but for the elect's sake, whom he hath chosen, he hath shortened the days.

21 [o]And then if any man shall say to you, Lo, here *is* Christ; or, lo, *he is* there; believe *him* not:

22 For false Christs and false prophets shall rise, and shall shew signs and wonders, to seduce, if *it were* possible, even the elect.

23 But [p]take ye heed: behold, I have foretold you all things.

24 ¶ [q]But in those days, after that tribulation, the sun shall be darkened, and the moon shall not give her light,

25 And the stars of heaven shall fall, and the powers that are in heaven shall be shaken.

26 [r]And then shall they see the Son of man coming in the clouds with great power and glory.

27 And then shall he send his angels, and shall gather together his elect from the four winds, from the uttermost part of the earth to the uttermost part of heaven.

28 [s]Now learn a parable of the fig tree; When her branch is yet tender, and putteth forth leaves, ye know that summer is near:

29 So ye in like manner, when ye shall see these things come to pass, know that it is nigh, *even* at the doors.

30 Verily I say unto you, that this generation shall not pass, till all these things be done.

31 Heaven and earth shall pass away: but [t]my words shall not pass away.

32 ¶ But of that day and *that* hour knoweth no man, no, not the angels which are in heaven, neither the Son, but the Father.

33 [u]Take ye heed, watch and pray: for ye know not when the time is.

34 [v]*For the Son of man is* as a man taking a far journey, who left his house, and gave authority to his servants, and to every man his work, and commanded the porter to watch.

35 [w]Watch ye therefore: for ye know not when the master of the house cometh, at even, or at midnight, or at the cockcrowing, or in the morning:

36 Lest coming suddenly he find you sleeping.

37 And what I say unto you I say unto all, Watch.

14 After [x]two days was *the feast of* the passover, and of unleavened bread: and the chief priests and the scribes sought how they might take him by craft, and put *him* to death.

2 But they said, Not on the feast *day,* lest there be an uproar of the people.

3 ¶ [y]And being in Bethany in the house of Simon the leper, as he sat at meat, there came a woman having an alabaster box of ointment of spikenard very precious; and she brake the box, and poured *it* on his head.

4 And there were some that had indignation within themselves, and said, Why was this waste of the ointment made?

5 For it might have been sold for more than three hundred pence, and have been given to the poor. And they murmured against her.

6 And Jesus said, Let her alone; why trouble ye her? she hath wrought a good work on me.

7 For [z]ye have the poor with you always, and whensoever ye will ye may do them good: but me ye have not always.

8 She hath done what she could: she is come aforehand to anoint my body to the burying.

9 Verily I say unto you, Wheresoever this gospel shall be preached throughout the whole world, *this* also that she hath done shall be spoken of for a memorial of her.

10 ¶ [a]And Judas Iscariot, one of the twelve, went unto the chief priests, to betray him unto them.

11 And when they heard *it,* they were glad, and promised to give him money. And he sought how he might conveniently betray him.

12 ¶ [b]And the first day of unleavened bread, when they killed the passover, his disciples said unto him, Where wilt thou that we go and prepare that thou mayest eat the passover?

13 And he sendeth forth two of his disci-

13:10 [d]Matt. 24:14
13:11 [e]Matt. 10:19; Luke 12:11 [f]Acts 2:4
13:12 [g]Mic. 7:6; Matt. 10:21; Luke 21:16
13:13 [h]Matt. 24:9; Luke 21:17 [i]Dan. 12:12; Matt. 10:22; Rev. 2:10
13:14 [j]Matt. 24:15 [k]Dan. 9:27 [l]Luke 21:21
13:17 [m]Luke 21:23
13:19 [n]Dan. 9:26; Joel 2:2; Matt. 24:21
13:21 [o]Matt. 24:23; Luke 17:23
13:23 [p]2 Pet. 3:17
13:24 [q]Dan. 7:10; Zeph. 1:15; Matt. 24:29; Luke 21:25
13:26 [r]Dan. 7:13; Matt. 16:27; ch. 14:62; Acts 1:11; 1 Thess. 4:16; 2 Thess. 1:7; Rev. 1:7
13:28 [s]Matt. 24:32; Luke 21:29
13:31 [t]Isa. 40:8
13:33 [u]Matt. 24:42; Luke 12:40; Rom. 13:11; 1 Thess. 5:6
13:34 [v]Matt. 24:45
13:35 [w]Matt. 24:42
14:1 [x]Matt. 26:2; Luke 22:1; John 11:55
14:3 [y]Matt. 26:6; John 12:1; Luke 7:37
14:7 [z]Deut. 15:11
14:10 [a]Matt. 26:14; Luke 22:3
14:12 [b]Matt. 26:17; Luke 22:7

ples, and saith unto them, Go ye into the city, and there shall meet you a man bearing a pitcher of water: follow him.

14 And wheresoever he shall go in, say ye to the goodman of the house, The Master saith, Where is the guestchamber, where I shall eat the passover with my disciples?

15 And he will shew you a large upper room furnished *and* prepared: there make ready for us.

16 And his disciples went forth, and came into the city, and found as he had said unto them: and they made ready the passover.

17 [c]And in the evening he cometh with the twelve.

18 And as they sat and did eat, Jesus said, Verily I say unto you, One of you which eateth with me shall betray me.

19 And they began to be sorrowful, and to say unto him one by one, *Is* it I? and another *said, Is* it I?

20 And he answered and said unto them, *It is* one of the twelve, that dippeth with me in the dish.

21 [d]The Son of man indeed goeth, as it is written of him: but woe to that man by whom the Son of man is betrayed! good were it for that man if he had never been born.

22 ¶ [e]And as they did eat, Jesus took bread, and blessed, and brake *it,* and gave to them, and said, Take, eat: this is my body.

23 And he took the cup, and when he had given thanks, he gave *it* to them: and they all drank of it.

24 And he said unto them, This is my blood of the new testament, which is shed for many.

25 Verily I say unto you, I will drink no more of the fruit of the vine, until that day that I drink it new in the kingdom of God.

26 ¶ [f]And when they had sung an hymn, they went out into the mount of Olives.

27 [g]And Jesus saith unto them, All ye shall be offended because of me this night: for it is written, [h]I will smite the shepherd, and the sheep shall be scattered.

28 But [i]after that I am risen, I will go before you into Galilee.

29 [j]But Peter said unto him, Although all shall be offended, yet *will* not I.

30 And Jesus saith unto him, Verily I say unto thee, That this day, *even* in this night, before the cock crow twice, thou shalt deny me thrice.

31 But he spake the more vehemently, If I should die with thee, I will not deny thee in any wise. Likewise also said they all.

32 [k]And they came to a place which was named Gethsemane: and he saith to his disciples, Sit ye here, while I shall pray.

33 And he taketh with him Peter and James and John, and began to be sore amazed, and to be very heavy;

34 And saith unto them, [l]My soul is exceeding sorrowful unto death: tarry ye here, and watch.

35 And he went forward a little, and fell on the ground, and prayed that, if it were possible, the hour might pass from him.

36 And he said, [m]Abba, Father, [n]all things *are* possible unto thee; take away this cup from me: [o]nevertheless not what I will, but what thou wilt.

37 And he cometh, and findeth them sleeping, and saith unto Peter, Simon, sleepest thou? couldest not thou watch one hour?

38 Watch ye and pray, lest ye enter into temptation. [p]The spirit truly *is* ready, but the flesh *is* weak.

39 And again he went away, and prayed, and spake the same words.

40 And when he returned, he found them asleep again, (for their eyes were heavy,) neither wist they what to answer him.

41 And he cometh the third time, and saith unto them, Sleep on now, and take *your* rest: it is enough, [q]the hour is come; behold, the Son of man is betrayed into the hands of sinners.

42 [r]Rise up, let us go; lo, he that betrayeth me is at hand.

43 ¶ [s]And immediately, while he yet spake, cometh Judas, one of the twelve, and with him a great multitude with swords and staves, from the chief priests and the scribes and the elders.

44 And he that betrayed him had given them a token, saying, Whomsoever I shall kiss, that same is he; take him, and lead *him* away safely.

45 And as soon as he was come, he goeth straightway to him, and saith, Master, master; and kissed him.

46 ¶ And they laid their hands on him, and took him.

47 And one of them that stood by drew a sword, and smote a servant of the high priest, and cut off his ear.

48 [t]And Jesus answered and said unto them, Are ye come out, as against a thief, with swords and *with* staves to take me?

49 I was daily with you in the temple teaching, and ye took me not: but [u]the scriptures must be fulfilled.

50 [v]And they all forsook him, and fled.

51 And there followed him a certain young man, having a linen cloth cast about *his* naked *body;* and the young men laid hold on him:

52 And he left the linen cloth, and fled from them naked.

53 ¶ [w]And they led Jesus away to the high priest: and with him were assembled all the chief priests and the elders and the scribes.

54 And Peter followed him afar off, even into the palace of the high priest: and he sat with the servants, and warmed himself at the fire.

55 [x]And the chief priests and all the council sought for witness against Jesus to put him to death; and found none.

56 For many bare false witness against him, but their witness agreed not together.

14:17 [c]Matt. 26:20
14:21 [d]Matt. 26:24; Luke 22:22
14:22 [e]Matt. 26:26; Luke 22:19; 1 Cor. 11:23
14:26 [f]Matt. 26:30
14:27 [g]Matt. 26:31 [h]Zech. 13:7
14:28 [i]ch. 16:7
14:29 [j]Matt. 26:33; Luke 22:33; John 13:37
14:32 [k]Matt. 26:36; Luke 22:39; John 18:1
14:34 [l]John 12:27
14:36 [m]Rom. 8:15; Gal. 4:6 [n]Heb. 5:7 [o]John 5:30
14:38 [p]Rom. 7:23; Gal. 5:17
14:41 [q]John 13:1
14:42 [r]Matt. 26:46; John 18:1
14:43 [s]Matt. 26:47; Luke 22:47; John 18:3
14:48 [t]Matt. 26:55; Luke 22:52
14:49 [u]Ps. 22:6; Isa. 53:7; Luke 22:37
14:50 [v]Ps. 88:8; ver. 27
14:53 [w]Matt. 26:57; Luke 22:54; John 18:13
14:55 [x]Matt. 26:59

57 And there arose certain, and bare false witness against him, saying,

58 We heard him say, [y]I will destroy this temple that is made with hands, and within three days I will build another made without hands.

59 But neither so did their witness agree together.

60 [z]And the high priest stood up in the midst, and asked Jesus, saying, Answerest thou nothing? what *is it which* these witness against thee?

61 But [a]he held his peace, and answered nothing. [b]Again the high priest asked him, and said unto him, Art thou the Christ, the Son of the Blessed?

62 And Jesus said, I am: [c]and ye shall see the Son of man sitting on the right hand of power, and coming in the clouds of heaven.

63 Then the high priest rent his clothes, and saith, What need we any further witnesses?

64 Ye have heard the blasphemy: what think ye? And they all condemned him to be guilty of death.

65 And some began to spit on him, and to cover his face, and to buffet him, and to say unto him, Prophesy: and the servants did strike him with the palms of their hands.

66 ¶ [d]And as Peter was beneath in the palace, there cometh one of the maids of the high priest:

67 And when she saw Peter warming himself, she looked upon him, and said, And thou also wast with Jesus of Nazareth.

68 But he denied, saying, I know not, neither understand I what thou sayest. And he went out into the porch; and the cock crew.

69 [e]And a maid saw him again, and began to say to them that stood by, This is *one* of them.

70 And he denied it again. [f]And a little after, they that stood by said again to Peter, Surely thou art *one* of them: [g]for thou art a Galilaean, and thy speech agreeth *thereto*.

71 But he began to curse and to swear, *saying*, I know not this man of whom ye speak.

72 [h]And the second time the cock crew. And Peter called to mind the word that Jesus said unto him, Before the cock crow twice, thou shalt deny me thrice. And when he thought thereon, he wept.

15

And [i]straightway in the morning the chief priests held a consultation with the elders and scribes and the whole council, and bound Jesus, and carried *him* away, and delivered *him* to Pilate.

2 [j]And Pilate asked him, Art thou the King of the Jews? And he answering said unto him, Thou sayest *it*.

3 And the chief priests accused him of many things: but he answered nothing.

4 [k]And Pilate asked him again, saying, Answerest thou nothing? behold how many things they witness against thee.

5 [l]But Jesus yet answered nothing; so that Pilate marvelled.

6 Now [m]at *that* feast he released unto them one prisoner, whomsoever they desired.

7 And there was *one* named Barabbas, *which lay* bound with them that had made insurrection with him, who had committed murder in the insurrection.

8 And the multitude crying aloud began to desire *him to do* as he had ever done unto them.

9 But Pilate answered them, saying, Will ye that I release unto you the King of the Jews?

10 For he knew that the chief priests had delivered him for envy.

11 But [n]the chief priests moved the people, that he should rather release Barabbas unto them.

12 And Pilate answered and said again unto them, What will ye then that I shall do *unto him* whom ye call the King of the Jews?

13 And they cried out again, Crucify him.

14 Then Pilate said unto them, Why, what evil hath he done? And they cried out the more exceedingly, Crucify him.

15 ¶ [o]And *so* Pilate, willing to content the people, released Barabbas unto them, and delivered Jesus, when he had scourged *him*, to be crucified.

16 [p]And the soldiers led him away into the hall, called Praetorium; and they call together the whole band.

17 And they clothed him with purple, and platted a crown of thorns, and put it about his *head*,

18 And began to salute him, Hail, King of the Jews!

19 And they smote him on the head with a reed, and did spit upon him, and bowing *their* knees worshipped him.

20 And when they had mocked him, they took off the purple from him, and put his own clothes on him, and led him out to crucify him.

21 [q]And they compel one Simon a Cyrenian, who passed by, coming out of the country, the father of Alexander and Rufus, to bear his cross

22 [r]And they bring him unto the place Golgotha, which is, being interpreted, The place of a skull.

23 [s]And they gave him to drink wine mingled with myrrh: but he received *it* not.

24 And when they had crucified him, [t]they parted his garments, casting lots upon them, what every man should take.

25 And [u]it was the third hour, and they crucified him.

26 And [v]the superscription of his accusation was written over, THE KING OF THE JEWS.

27 And [w]with him they crucify two thieves; the one on his right hand, and the other on his left.

28 And the scripture was fulfilled, which saith, [x]And he was numbered with the transgressors.

14:58 [y]ch. 15:29; John 2:19
14:60 [z]Matt. 26:62
14:61 [a]Isa. 53:7 [b]Matt. 26:63
14:62 [c]Matt. 24:30; Luke 22:69
14:66 [d]Matt. 26:58; Luke 22:55; John 18:16
14:69 [e]Matt. 26:71; Luke 22:58; John 18:25
14:70 [f]Matt. 26:73; Luke 22:59; John 18:26 [g]Acts 2:7
14:72 [h]Matt. 26:75
15:1 [i]Ps. 2:2; Matt. 27:1; Luke 22:66; John 18:28; Acts 3:13
15:2 [j]Matt. 27:11
15:4 [k]Matt. 27:13
15:5 [l]Isa. 53:7; John 19:9
15:6 [m]Matt. 27:15; Luke 23:17; John 18:39
15:11 [n]Matt. 27:20; Acts 3:14
15:15 [o]Matt. 27:26; John 19:1
15:16 [p]Matt. 27:27
15:21 [q]Matt. 27:32; Luke 23:26
15:22 [r]Matt. 27:33; Luke 23:33; John 19:17
15:23 [s]Matt. 27:34
15:24 [t]Ps. 22:18; Luke 23:34; John 19:23
15:25 [u]Matt. 27:45; Luke 23:44; John 19:14
15:26 [v]Matt. 27:37; John 19:19
15:27 [w]Matt. 27:38
15:28 [x]Isa. 53:12; Luke 22:37

29 And [y]they that passed by railed on him, wagging their heads, and saying, Ah, [z]thou that destroyest the temple, and buildest *it* in three days,

30 Save thyself, and come down from the cross.

31 Likewise also the chief priests mocking said among themselves with the scribes, He saved others; himself he cannot save.

32 Let Christ the King of Israel descend now from the cross, that we may see and believe. And [a]they that were crucified with him reviled him.

33 And [b]when the sixth hour was come, there was darkness over the whole land until the ninth hour.

34 And at the ninth hour Jesus cried with a loud voice, saying, [c]Eloi, Eloi, lama sabachthani? which is, being interpreted, My God, my God, why hast thou forsaken me?

35 And some of them that stood by, when they heard *it*, said, Behold, he calleth Elias.

36 And [d]one ran and filled a spunge full of vinegar, and put *it* on a reed, and [e]gave him to drink, saying, Let alone; let us see whether Elias will come to take him down.

37 [f]And Jesus cried with a loud voice, and gave up the ghost.

38 And [g]the veil of the temple was rent in twain from the top to the bottom.

39 ¶ And [h]when the centurion, which stood over against him, saw that he so cried out, and gave up the ghost, he said, Truly this man was the Son of God.

40 [i]There were also women looking on [j]afar off: among whom was Mary Magdalene, and Mary the mother of James the less and of Joses, and Salome;

41 (Who also, when he was in Galilee, [k]followed him, and ministered unto him;) and many other women which came up with him unto Jerusalem.

42 ¶ [l]And now when the even was come, because it was the preparation, that is, the day before the sabbath,

43 Joseph of Arimathea, an honourable counsellor, which also [m]waited for the kingdom of God, came, and went in boldly unto Pilate, and craved the body of Jesus.

44 And Pilate marvelled if he were already dead: and calling *unto him* the centurion, he asked him whether he had been any while dead.

45 And when he knew *it* of the centurion, he gave the body to Joseph.

46 [n]And he bought fine linen, and took him down, and wrapped him in the linen, and laid him in a sepulchre which was hewn out of a rock, and rolled a stone unto the door of the sepulchre.

47 And Mary Magdalene and Mary *the mother* of Joses beheld where he was laid.

16 And [o]when the sabbath was past, Mary Magdalene, and Mary the *mother* of James, and Salome, [p]had bought sweet spices, that they might come and anoint him.

2 [q]And very early in the morning the first *day* of the week, they came unto the sepulchre at the rising of the sun.

3 And they said among themselves, Who shall roll us away the stone from the door of the sepulchre?

4 And when they looked, they saw that the stone was rolled away: for it was very great.

5 [r]And entering into the sepulchre, they saw a young man sitting on the right side, clothed in a long white garment; and they were affrighted.

6 [s]And he saith unto them, Be not affrighted: Ye seek Jesus of Nazareth, which was crucified: he is risen; he is not here: behold the place where they laid him.

7 But go your way, tell his disciples and Peter that he goeth before you into Galilee: there shall ye see him, [t]as he said unto you.

8 And they went out quickly, and fled from the sepulchre; for they trembled and were amazed: [u]neither said they any thing to any *man;* for they were afraid.

9 ¶ Now when *Jesus* was risen early the first *day* of the week, [v]he appeared first to Mary Magdalene, [w]out of whom he had cast seven devils.

10 [x]*And* she went and told them that had been with him, as they mourned and wept.

11 [y]And they, when they had heard that he was alive, and had been seen of her, believed not.

12 ¶ After that he appeared in another form [z]unto two of them, as they walked, and went into the country.

13 And they went and told *it* unto the residue: neither believed they them.

14 ¶ [a]Afterward he appeared unto the eleven as they sat at meat, and upbraided them with their unbelief and hardness of heart, because they believed not them which had seen him after he was risen.

15 [b]And he said unto them, Go ye into all the world, [c]and preach the gospel to every creature.

16 [d]He that believeth and is baptized shall be saved; [e]but he that believeth not shall be damned.

17 And these signs shall follow them that believe; [f]In my name shall they cast out devils; [g]they shall speak with new tongues;

18 [h]They shall take up serpents; and if they drink any deadly thing, it shall not hurt them; [i]they shall lay hands on the sick, and they shall recover.

19 ¶ So then [j]after the Lord had spoken unto them, he was [k]received up into heaven, and [l]sat on the right hand of God.

20 And they went forth, and preached every where, the Lord working with *them*, [m]and confirming the word with signs following. Amen.

15:29 yPs. 22:7 zch. 14:58; John 2:19
15:32 aMatt. 27:44; Luke 23:39
15:33 bMatt. 27:45; Luke 23:44
15:34 cPs. 21:1; Matt. 27:46
15:36 dMatt. 27:48; John 19:29 ePs. 69:21
15:37 fMatt. 27:50; Luke 23:45; John 19:30
15:38 gMatt. 27:51; Luke 23:45
15:39 hMatt. 27:54; Luke 23:46
15:40 iMatt. 27:55; Luke 23:49 jPs. 38:11
15:41 kLuke 8:2
15:42 lMatt. 27:57; Luke 23:50; John 19:38
15:43 mLuke 2:25
15:46 nMatt. 27:59; Luke 23:53; John 19:40
16:1 oMatt. 28:1; Luke 24:1; John 20:1 pLuke 23:56
16:2 qLuke 24:1; John 20:1
16:5 rLuke 24:3; John 20:11
16:6 sMatt. 28:5
16:7 tMatt. 26:32; ch. 14:28
16:8 uMatt. 28:8; Luke 24:9
16:9 vJohn 20:14 wLuke 8:2
16:10 xLuke 24:10; John 20:18
16:11 yLuke 24:11
16:12 zLuke 24:13
16:14 aLuke 24:36; John 20:19; 1 Cor. 15:5
16:15 bMatt. 28:19; John 15:16 cCol. 1:23
16:16 dJohn 3:18; Acts 2:38; Rom. 10:9; 1 Pet. 3:21 eJohn 12:48
16:17 fLuke 10:17; Acts 5:16 gActs 2:4; 1 Cor. 12:10
16:18 hLuke 10:19; Acts 28:5 iActs 5:15; Jam. 5:14
16:19 jActs 1:2 kLuke 24:51 lPs. 110:1; Acts 7:55
16:20 mActs 5:12; 1 Cor. 2:4; Heb. 2:4

Focus on LUKE

The contents of the Gospel as recorded by Luke is designed to assure Theophilus that the message of Christ had a solid foundation. Theophilus may have been a benevolent benefactor who was paying the expense of Luke's research. Luke traces the events of Christ from His forerunner's birth (John the Baptist) through the birth of Christ Himself to a virgin. More is recorded about Jesus' life than in any of the other Gospels. Luke shows how Christ was prepared for His mission through His wilderness experience and His temptation by Satan. Christ's work in northern Palestine is recorded in chapters 4:14–9:50. His southern Palestine work is detailed in 9:51–21:38. His death and resurrection is vividly narrated in chapters 22–24.

THE BLACK PRESENCE IN LUKE

Among the most prominent Africans in the Gospel of Luke are Adam, the Samaritans, the queen of Sheba, Simon of Cyrene, and the people of Tyre and Sidon. The Samaritans, people of Samaria, (Luke 9:52; 10:33; 17:11, 16) were of mixed blood. They were a combination of Hebrew and other ethnic groups—groups that were brought into the land by Sennacherib when he deported Israelites from the northern kingdom (722 B.C.). Since most of the surrounding nations were either black Cushites or Shemites, it is probable that this ethnic mixture included "black" blood. In addition to their mixed marriages, this group rejected all Hebrew scriptures except the Pentateuch. Consequently, orthodox Jews rejected them. However, Jesus showed a special interest in them. Moreover, the Great Commission specified that Samaritans were to be targeted in the proclamation of the Gospel.

Queen of Sheba: Mentioned in 11:31 ("the queen of the south"). Sheba was located on both sides of the Red Sea: the west side being Africa proper, the east being Arabia. They traded precious stones, incense, and slaves. Genesis 10:7 indicates that Sheba (Seba) was a son of Cush whose name means "black."

Life Lessons

LUKE 1

In the birth of John the Baptist (1:5–25), we learn many life lessons. The appearance of an angel to announce the birth of John, the Messiah's forerunner, was the fulfillment of prophecy made by the prophet Malachi (4:5). Luke shows the continuity of God's activity from the Old Testament

into the New. We learn that God keeps His word. God kept His word in relationship to Abraham, Isaac, and Jacob, and this was repeated many times during the history of Israel.

Dear God, I praise You for Your faithfulness in always keeping Your word. May I never doubt Your promises to be faithful to me. Amen.

LUKE 1

From the point where Jesus' birth is announced, we learn that God will use ordinary people to fulfill His promises (1:26–38). Jesus' birth is foretold. Mary's response to the angel's announcement was greeted with a resounding, "I am available to You, Lord" (paraphrased). God used her readiness to obey as the means of bringing salvation to the world. God still looks for people like Mary who are eager to be vessels for accomplishing His will.

Dear God, please grant me the willingness to be available to You for whatever Your will is for my life. Help me to believe that "where You guide You will provide." Amen.

LUKE 1

We also learn important lessons from Mary's visit to Elisabeth and Mary's song (Luke 1:39–55). Certainly the angel's announcement to Mary that she would give birth to Jesus was sufficient to assure her of the significance of her child's birth. But now Elisabeth gave her further confirmation. This elderly relative called Mary's child her "Lord" (Luke 1:43). Furthermore, Elisabeth seemed aware that Mary had a heavenly visitor appear even before Mary had told her. Sometimes God gives us more than one confirmation of His will.

Dear God, thank You for those times when You give me added confirmation that I am doing Your will. Amen.

Women in LUKE

ANNA: A MODEL OF SPIRITUAL DEVOTION

Anna was a prophet. She was a woman through whom God spoke. When she spoke, those in the temple listened. She was a messianic watcher and a leader. She represents God calling women to be prophetic leaders. She is so respected that her attestation of Jesus is highly regarded, alongside that of an angel and a righteous man.

Anna was the model of spiritual devotion who kept vigil in the temple—fasted, prayed, and offered thanksgivings. According to Luke 19:45–48, Jesus says that the temple shall be the house of prayer. Jesus teaches daily and follows the example of Anna. Jesus is called prophet (Luke 24:19), as was Anna (Luke 2:36–38).

Finally, Anna is the forerunner to the apostles, who are commissioned to witness to the entire world beginning with Jerusalem. According to Luke 24:52, the apostles returned to Jerusalem and were continually in the temple blessing God, just as Anna had done earlier.

Anna represents hopeful expectation. She is a model who shows women today how to live their lives in a righteous and godly way.

Read Luke 2:36–38; see also Isaiah 9:6–7.

Read the insight essay on Prayer.

—P. Williamson

PETER'S MOTHER-IN-LAW: FREE FROM PAIN!

Peter's mother-in-law's healing by Jesus is recorded in the synoptic Gospels: Matthew, Mark, and Luke. Each recording gives a different perspective depicting certain characteristics of Jesus: Matthew, God's sovereignty; Mark, God's servanthood; Luke, God's compassionate humanity. Peter's mother-in-law was confined and afflicted with a great fever. It must have been very painful because he sought Jesus on her behalf (Luke 4:38). She was important to her family and to Jesus. He took her by the hand, and she was healed and immediately rose to minister to them. As a form of gratitude, she served the needs of the Lord and those with Him. Her gratitude not only said thank you, but it humbled her for service.

Jesus understood the value of a mother to a family. He also valued women even though society considered them inferior.

Each recorded account speaks to the unique way a woman's life can encounter Jesus to receive healing. For the African-American woman, the synoptic Gospels assure her of three things:

1. Jesus can *touch her* and bring healing to any area of life on a continual basis (Matt. 8:3, 14–17). His touch allows her to feel and experience something other than pain.

2. Jesus can *lift her up*—bringing healing to the many painful areas of her life. She can raise her standards emotionally (Matt. 11:28–29), spiritually (2 Pet. 1:3), and physically (Rom. 12:1–2).

3. Jesus can *speak to her* life and bring complete healing (Luke 4:38–39; 13:10–13). His words can change her.

Jesus is the only One who can free the African-American woman from the pains of life that may have confined her to a certain position or mindset (Prov. 23:7). Once Jesus touches her life, it brings healing and raises her to a position of servanthood. She can service the needs of others in deeds and words. She is to be hospitable towards other Christians and to minister her gift to another as a good steward of the manifold grace of God (1 Pet. 4:9–10). Her gratitude can be seen as she strengthens and encourages other believers by servicing them. Jesus can free her from any physical, emotional, or spiritual pains. When the Son sets her free, she is free indeed!

Read Luke 4:38–39; see also Matthew 8:1–15; Mark 1:29–31.

Read the insight essays on Attributes of God, Faith, Love, and Prayer. See the insight chart on Jesus' Miracles Among Women.

—G. London

THE WIDOW OF NAIN: A MOTHER'S RESTORATION

When Luke wrote his Gospel, he was addressing a primitive community of Christians, and he wrote for the purpose of ensuring that they would "know the certainty of those things, wherein [they had] been instructed" (Luke 1:4). His writing, then, is confirmation of their prior instruction. As he outlines the life, ministry, death, and resurrection of Jesus Christ, Luke presents the historical facts about Jesus, but also adds his own unique perspective on those events. In this story, Luke wants to present to his readers a Jesus who is the essence of love and divine power. He is a servant who brings deliverance to the poor, the brokenhearted, the ostracized, and even those who are victimized. Jesus is represented to Luke's audience as one who sees the needs of the desolate, comforts in moments of grief, is victorious over death, and reunites those who are separated.

In order not to be reduced to pauperism, and in order to have a voice within the community, this nameless widow needed her son. Without him, she would be ostracized and relegated to life on the fringes of society. While I abhor the social practices that relegated this woman to an insignificant and difficult existence after her son's death, I also see a similarity between this woman's predicament and that of Black America. To help his mother survive, this young man simply could not die—even though his death was natural. He couldn't retreat from this difficult life on earth to the silent grave. No, her survival was dependent on his survival—her existence was so tied to his—that Jesus was compelled to respond to her need. Recognizing that when her son's life was over, so was hers, Jesus restores both of their lives.

For African-American women, there is a need to understand that our existence is tied to the life of every woman in our community—so much so, that not one of us can afford the luxury of the detachment and independence that often characterizes the mindless acceptance of a lifeless existence. Just as Luke's character didn't determine her lifelessness, in many cases the death that exists in the lives of women of color is one that is inflicted upon us by male-dominated society. Racism, classism, and corruption are the forces that are draining the life out of our being. What is worse is that, instead of engaging in the struggle for authentic living, there are so many in our community who, of their own will, opt for death. Too many choose apathy, self-hatred, mediocrity, and insensitivity, instead of human involvement, pride, excellence, and awareness. And because so many have made that choice and have dropped out, run away, and given up, our survival is in question. Just as the mother needed her son, so does the black community need its collective offspring—its youth, its men, and its women—to be alive and whole. Therein lies the "social security" needed for survival.

As the voice of Jesus speaks life and liberation to those who are among the living dead declaring, "Get up, I tell you," our deliverance lies in our willingness to respond to the divine call and sit up. The call to life is in vain when there is no response from the called. The command goes forth, and Jesus stands ready to give a whole and revived child back to its mother.

Read Luke 7:11–17; see also 1 Kings 17:23.

Read the insight essays on Children and Widows.

—*M. Flake*

THE PERSISTENT WIDOW: IN DUE SEASON YOU WILL REAP

We are to pray without ceasing. No matter what we are going through or what we need, we must be determined to obtain what we need to make it in this world. Persistence is a virtue. With one thing on our minds, and being very, very persistent, we must do what our widow sister did—wait until our change comes.

When you are in dire need of something, you do not care how far you have to go to get it, how much it's going to cost, or what you have to sacrifice in order to get it. A deeply felt need will have you crawling, taking risks, and using any means necessary to get it met. In spite of who this widow was, what she was, where she was, she had a need and knew where to go to get it met. So, if there's anything you need from Jesus, go to Him, look to Him. He can be found.

This woman was able to persist because she was doing so based on faith. If no one else knows, certainly the African-American woman knows what it's like to be persistent. If you want something or need something bad enough, then live a little longer. Our widow sister lets us know that if you pray long and hard enough, He will give us wings as an eagle and feet that won't become weary. In due season you will reap.

Read Luke 18:1–8.

Read the insight essays on Perseverance, Prayer, and Widows.

—J. Wharton

Insights

GOD'S PROMISES ARE ALWAYS— "YEA" AND "AMEN"

God always promises with "Yea" and "Amen" (2 Cor. 1:20). "Yea" assures that His promise will truly come into being, while "Amen" comforts us with the knowledge of God's assurance that the promise is complete in Him. In other words, God's promises are a reality from the moment that they are made. For our part, we must believe God's promises to be "yea" and "amen."

For example, God promised both Mary and Elisabeth that they would become parents. Elisabeth was skeptical because she thought she and her husband, Zacharias, were past the age of childbearing (Luke 1:18). Mary questioned God's promise because she could not fathom how a virgin could give birth. In each case, their skepticism was grounded in fact, but God required submission to His promise from them—not reliance on human logic. Thus, when Zacharias questioned God's word, he was struck dumb because he did not believe (Luke 1:20). Elisabeth's acceptance and subsequent conception of John exemplified faith.

Similarly, Mary submitted herself to God in faith and conceived the Christ Child. Her submission is expressed like this, "Behold the handmaid of the Lord; be it unto me according to thy word" (Luke 1:38).

These women became spiritual vessels for bringing John and Jesus

into the world. In this way, their submission to God's promise resulted in fulfillment for themselves and for humanity. Women today must still heed the call of the Lord and submit their bodies as vessels to bring forth God's word, life, and presence. As long as God's promises are "Yea" and "Amen," truth and completion, reality and fulfillment, women must look to Him in faith, humble themselves, pray, seek God's will for their lives, and cease from doing evil.

Read Luke 1; see also John 13:3–5; 14:13.

—M. V. Stephens

SPIRITUALLY NAMING OUR CHILDREN

Spiritually, what's in a name? Our ancestors believed that a child's name would have a direct influence on the character of that child. It behooves each of us then, as chosen children of a gracious God, to research names. We must know their original meaning. In naming our children, we must have insight into our spiritual and earthly heritage. Then, if necessary, we can use original names or create names that we have defined and given our own special meanings.

The Old Testament provides more than 50 examples where children are given names with special meanings. Sometimes the names would relate to the child's birth or conception (see Gen. 17:19; 25:26; 1 Sam. 4:21). The New Testament provides examples of parents being told exactly what to name their children. Luke 1:57–66 describes the naming of John the Baptist by Elisabeth and Zacharias, and Luke 2:21 tells of the most notable naming—the naming of Jesus.

When people's lives changed, or when their character changed, their names were sometimes changed to reflect their new identity. Such was the case when Jesus changed Simon's name to Peter (John 1:42), and Saul's name to Paul (Acts 13:9).

In essence, the time is right for sisters to reclaim our spiritual heritage of poise, polish, and panache, and define who and what we are, and who our children are as children of a living God.

Read Luke 1:57–66.

Read the insight essay on Children.

—L. Hall

WOOLY HAIR

There are no more than 50 to 60 references to hair in the entire Bible, as opposed to thousands of references to God, and hundreds to love and giving and other hallmark terms of the Christian faith. Hair is mentioned as a detail in biblical stories—an incidental detail. Occasionally it assumes central importance, as in the Old Testament story of Samson and Delilah (Judg. 16) and the New Testament stories of the women who wiped Jesus' feet with their hair: the unnamed woman (Luke 7:38, 44) and Mary of Bethany (John 11:2; 12:3).

Artists' depictions of women in biblical times show them with long and flowing hair. According to Paul's writing in 1 Corinthians 11:14–15, whether the hair is flowing or not, long hair is considered a shame for a man, but the glory of a woman. Nowhere in English translations of the New Testament is there a reference to the texture of hair, except in

Revelation 1:14, where the glorified Savior of John's vision has hair that is "white like wool," but this reference is more to color than to texture. A similar, but more direct, comparison to texture is made in the Old Testament (Dan. 7:9), where the risen and ruling Savior's hair is described as being like "pure wool."

The woman of Luke 7:38, 44 who washes Jesus' feet with her tears and dries them with her hair, does so with her *thrixin.* And the similar story in John 11:2; 12:3 with Mary of Bethany who anoints Jesus' feet with oil, then wipes them with her hair, also uses the word *thrixin* for hair. When one thinks about it, silky hair, because of its lack of absorbency, would hardly be the choice for drying anything wet or oil-based. Had these women had silky hair, they would, in all practical probability, have dried Jesus' feet with the ends of their long dresses. It is reasonable to believe that wooly hair was common for the men and women of Palestine during biblical times.

African-American women have faced a challenge in the United States in the acceptance of the predominantly wooly texture of our hair. Because we were systematically made to feel inferior about both our dark skin hues and our wooly hair, we have learned to dislike it and to straighten it. While women should enjoy the freedom in hairstyling, far too many rule out styles in their natural texture because of a deeply ingrained self-hatred of that texture. This is a rejection of the wisdom of God, whose creation is flawless (Gen. 1:31), and who, with great intention, created skin colors from the darkest black to the palest white, and hair textures from the thickest wool to the thinnest silk. As African-American women, we should delight in displaying the glories of our wooly-textured hair. It looks beautiful in braids and locks and twists, and equally lovely in creative geometric, stationary shapes that strikingly frame our faces and excellently maintain their form, without the aid of holding sprays and hair teasing. Different (from majority culture) does not mean deficient. We should look with grateful pride to the woman of Luke 7 and Mary of Bethany, our sisters in Christ, who had supreme honor of wiping dry our Lord's feet with their bounteous, wooly hair.

Read Luke 7.

Read the portrait on Mary of Bethany.

—J. Ross

DEPRESSION: HOW CAN I MAKE IT ONE MORE DAY?

The word "depressed" means pressed down. Often the pressures of this world press us down, engulf us, and cause us to fall into hopelessness and despair. The images that bombard us tell us that what is right, good, and worthwhile are diametrically opposed to the life many African-American women live.

We—as most women—desire to be loved, cared for, and cherished. However, African-American women many times find themselves alone and struggling to earn a living to support themselves and their children.

When we feel depressed, there is something we can do to avert hopelessness. We can pray and hold the Word of God deep in our souls and spirits. We can let God, through His Word and Holy Spirit, minister to us.

We can recall the psalmist's words in Psalm 34:17–18 and hold on to our hope in God and Christ Jesus. (See also Psalm 31:24; Romans 4:18–22; Hebrews 6:18–19.)

We can remember 2 Corinthians 1:20–22, where we are told the promises of God are "Yea" in Christ, and "Amen" is spoken by us to the glory of God. We must, by the Holy Spirit, call to remembrance the promises of God. (See Matthew 6:25–34; 11:28–30; Luke 12:22–31.)

So let us begin to rest in Jesus and God, and let the Holy Spirit comfort us. Meditate on Nehemiah 8:10; Psalm 62:1–2; Matthew 11:28–30; John 14:16–18; 16:12–15; and Philippians 4:5–8. Remember Psalm 68:5–6 where we are told the Lord is a father to the fatherless and sets the lonely in families.

In all things praise and worship the Lord. Put on the full armor of God and think of those things that demonstrate the love of Christ. Remember Psalm 100 and Ephesians 6:10–18. We must be about doing the will of our Father, which is to glorify God through services to Him and our fellow human beings, and then our joy will be restored.

Read Luke 12:22–31.

Read the insight essays on Prayer and Suffering.

—*A. Manuel*

VANITY

The Bible mentions many women of great beauty: Sarah, Rebekah, Rachel, Abigail, Bathsheba, and Esther. Esther 2:9 tells of Queen Esther's daily beauty regimen. As Christian women, our appearance should be a compliment to our inner spirit and never a hindrance to the kingdom of God. We should be concerned more about our inner beauty than our outer beauty. Beauty is more than an appealing face. It is a Christlike spirit that personifies God's love.

In our vanity, we should remember the stooped woman in Luke 13:10–17, who carried her visible affliction for 18 years. She wasn't always bent and crooked. She had once stood straight and tall. She was elegant and balanced. Her body did not fight against her, and her eyes could look straight up to the heavens. Now we have been humbled in our bodies and must find other things to think on. We have been falsely led to believe that who we are is what we look like in the midst of our youth. But Jesus tells us that the presentation of our lives is what honors the gifts that have been given to us.

Vanity is a product of our will. As women, we must choose whether the center of our affections will be self or God. In our vanity, we misunderstand the gifts that God has given to us. We make them into idols and worship them. They, in turn, serve to separate us from ourselves, each other, and from God. We are gifted—not by the mere appearance of our face and bodies—but by the love of God who created us, the forgiveness of Christ Jesus who liberates us, and the presence of the Holy Spirit who sustains us.

Read Luke 13:10–17.

See also the insight essays on Aging and Graciousness.

—*D. Taylor*

LUKE

Luke is the author of this book, written in the 60s A.D. Luke opens with the brief history of John the Baptist followed by the best known description of the birth of Jesus. Luke provides a genealogy of Christ through Jesus' mother, Mary. Beginning in chapter 4 is the detailed description of Jesus' public ministry culminating in the day-by-day report of the events of the last week of Jesus' ministry. The book closes with Christ's ministry following his resurrection.

I. The birth of John the Baptist, 1:1–1:80
II. The birth of Jesus and his childhood, 2:1–2:52
III. Jesus' baptism and his genealogy, 3:1–3:38
IV. Jesus' public ministry, 4:1–19:27
V. Jesus' final week, 19:28–23:56
VI. Jesus' resurrection and ascension, 24:1–24:53

1 Forasmuch as many have taken in hand
to set forth in order a declaration of
those things which are most surely believed
among us,
2 [a]Even as they delivered them unto us,
which [b]from the beginning were eyewitnesses, and ministers of the word;
3 [c]It seemed good to me also, having had
perfect understanding of all things from the
very first, to write unto thee [d]in order,
[e]most excellent Theophilus,
4 [f]That thou mightest know the certainty
of those things, wherein thou hast been instructed.
5 ¶ There was [g]in the days of Herod, the
king of Judaea, a certain priest named
Zacharias, [h]of the course of Abia: and his
wife *was* of the daughters of Aaron, and her
name *was* Elisabeth.
6 And they were both [i]righteous before
God, walking in all the commandments and
ordinances of the Lord blameless.
7 And they had no child, because that
Elisabeth was barren, and they both were
now well stricken in years.
8 And it came to pass, that while he executed the priest's office before God [j]in the
order of his course,
9 According to the custom of the priest's
office, his lot was [k]to burn incense when he
went into the temple of the Lord.
10 [l]And the whole multitude of the people were praying without at the time of incense.
11 And there appeared unto him an angel
of the Lord standing on the right side of
[m]the altar of incense.
12 And when Zacharias saw *him*, [n]he
was troubled, and fear fell upon him.
13 But the angel said unto him, Fear not,
Zacharias: for thy prayer is heard; and thy
wife Elisabeth shall bear thee a son, and
[o]thou shalt call his name John.
14 And thou shalt have joy and gladness;
and [p]many shall rejoice at his birth.
15 For he shall be great in the sight of the
Lord, and [q]shall drink neither wine nor
strong drink; and he shall be filled with
the Holy Ghost, [r]even from his mother's
womb.
16 [s]And many of the children of Israel
shall he turn to the Lord their God.
17 [t]And he shall go before him in the
spirit and power of Elias, to turn the hearts
of the fathers to the children, and the disobedient to the wisdom of the just; to make
ready a people prepared for the Lord.
18 And Zacharias said unto the angel,
[u]Whereby shall I know this? for I am an old
man, and my wife well stricken in years.
19 And the angel answering said unto
him, I am [v]Gabriel, that stand in the presence of God; and am sent to speak unto
thee, and to shew thee these glad tidings.
20 And, behold, [w]thou shalt be dumb, and
not able to speak, until the day that these
things shall be performed, because thou believest not my words, which shall be fulfilled in their season.
21 And the people waited for Zacharias,
and marvelled that he tarried so long in the
temple.
22 And when he came out, he could not
speak unto them: and they perceived that he
had seen a vision in the temple: for he beckoned unto them, and remained speechless.
23 And it came to pass, that, as soon as
[x]the days of his ministration were accomplished, he departed to his own house.
24 And after those days his wife Elisabeth
conceived, and hid herself five months, saying,
25 Thus hath the Lord dealt with me in
the days wherein he looked on *me*, to [y]take
away my reproach among men.
26 And in the sixth month the angel Gabriel was sent from God unto a city of Galilee, named Nazareth,
27 To a virgin [z]espoused to a man whose
name was Joseph, of the house of David;
and the virgin's name *was* Mary.
28 And the angel came in unto her, and

1:2 [a]Heb. 2:3; 1 Pet. 5:1; 2 Pet. 1:16; 1 John 1:1 [b]Mark 1:1; John 15:27
1:3 [c]Acts 15:19; 1 Cor. 7:40 [d]Acts 11:4 [e]Acts 1:1
1:4 [f]John 20:31
1:5 [g]Matt. 2:1 [h]1 Chron. 24:10; Neh. 12:4
1:6 [i]Gen. 7:1; 1 Kings 9:4; 2 Kings 20:3; Job 1:1; Acts 23:1; Phil. 3:6
1:8 [j]1 Chron. 24:19; 2 Chron. 8:14
1:9 [k]Ex. 30:7; 1 Sam. 2:28; 1 Chron. 23:13; 2 Chron. 29:11
1:10 [l]Lev. 16:17; Rev. 8:3
1:11 [m]Ex. 30:1
1:12 [n]Judg. 6:22; Dan. 10:8; ver. 29; ch. 2:9; Acts 10:4; Rev. 1:17
1:13 [o]ver. 60
1:14 [p]ver. 58
1:15 [q]Num. 6:3; Judg. 13:4; ch. 7:33 [r]Jer. 1:5; Gal. 1:15
1:16 [s]Mal. 4:5
1:17 [t]Mal. 4:5; Matt. 11:14; Mark 9:12
1:18 [u]Gen. 17:17
1:19 [v]Dan. 8:16; Matt. 18:10; Heb. 1:14
1:20 [w]Ezek. 3:26
1:23 [x]2 Kings 11:5; 1 Chron. 9:25
1:25 [y]Gen. 30:23; Isa. 4:1
1:27 [z]Matt. 1:18; ch. 2:4

said, [a]Hail, *thou that art* highly favoured, [b]the Lord *is* with thee: blessed *art* thou among women.

29 And when she saw *him*, [c]she was troubled at his saying, and cast in her mind what manner of salutation this should be.

30 And the angel said unto her, Fear not, Mary: for thou hast found favour with God.

31 [d]And, behold, thou shalt conceive in thy womb, and bring forth a son, and [e]shalt call his name JESUS.

32 He shall be great, [f]and shall be called the Son of the Highest: and [g]the Lord God shall give unto him the throne of his father David:

33 [h]And he shall reign over the house of Jacob for ever; and of his kingdom there shall be no end.

34 Then said Mary unto the angel, How shall this be, seeing I know not a man?

35 And the angel answered and said unto her, [i]The Holy Ghost shall come upon thee, and the power of the Highest shall overshadow thee: therefore also that holy thing which shall be born of thee shall be called [j]the Son of God.

36 And, behold, thy cousin Elisabeth, she hath also conceived a son in her old age: and this is the sixth month with her, who was called barren.

37 For [k]with God nothing shall be impossible.

38 And Mary said, Behold the handmaid of the Lord; be it unto me according to thy word. And the angel departed from her.

39 And Mary arose in those days, and went into the hill country with haste, [l]into a city of Juda;

40 And entered into the house of Zacharias, and saluted Elisabeth.

41 And it came to pass, that, when Elisabeth heard the salutation of Mary, the babe leaped in her womb; and Elisabeth was filled with the Holy Ghost:

42 And she spake out with a loud voice, and said, [m]Blessed *art* thou among women, and blessed *is* the fruit of thy womb.

43 And whence *is* this to me, that the mother of my Lord should come to me?

44 For, lo, as soon as the voice of thy salutation sounded in mine ears, the babe leaped in my womb for joy.

45 And blessed *is* she that believed: for there shall be a performance of those things which were told her from the Lord.

46 And Mary said, [n]My soul doth magnify the Lord,

47 And my spirit hath rejoiced in God my Saviour.

48 For [o]he hath regarded the low estate of his handmaiden: for, behold, from henceforth [p]all generations shall call me blessed.

49 For he that is mighty [q]hath done to me great things; and [r]holy *is* his name.

50 And [s]his mercy *is* on them that fear him from generation to generation.

51 [t]He hath shewed strength with his arm; [u]he hath scattered the proud in the imagination of their hearts.

52 [v]He hath put down the mighty from *their* seats, and exalted them of low degree.

53 [w]He hath filled the hungry with good things; and the rich he hath sent empty away.

54 He hath holpen his servant Israel, [x]in remembrance of *his* mercy;

55 [y]As he spake to our fathers, to Abraham, and to his seed for ever.

56 And Mary abode with her about three months, and returned to her own house.

57 Now Elisabeth's full time came that she should be delivered; and she brought forth a son.

58 And her neighbours and her cousins heard how the Lord had shewed great mercy upon her; and [z]they rejoiced with her.

59 And it came to pass, that [a]on the eighth day they came to circumcise the child; and they called him Zacharias, after the name of his father.

60 And his mother answered and said, [b]Not *so;* but he shall be called John.

61 And they said unto her, There is none of thy kindred that is called by this name.

62 And they made signs to his father, how he would have him called.

63 And he asked for a writing table, and wrote, saying, [c]His name is John. And they marvelled all.

64 [d]And his mouth was opened immediately, and his tongue *loosed,* and he spake, and praised God.

65 And fear came on all that dwelt round about them: and all these sayings were noised abroad throughout all [e]the hill country of Judaea.

66 And all they that heard *them* [f]laid *them* up in their hearts, saying, What manner of child shall this be! And [g]the hand of the Lord was with him.

67 And his father Zacharias [h]was filled with the Holy Ghost, and prophesied, saying,

68 [i]Blessed *be* the Lord God of Israel; for [j]he hath visited and redeemed his people,

69 [k]And hath raised up an horn of salvation for us in the house of his servant David;

70 [l]As he spake by the mouth of his holy prophets, which have been since the world began:

71 That we should be saved from our enemies, and from the hand of all that hate us;

72 [m]To perform the mercy *promised* to our fathers, and to remember his holy covenant;

73 [n]The oath which he sware to our father Abraham,

74 That he would grant unto us, that we being delivered out of the hand of our enemies might [o]serve him without fear,

75 [p]In holiness and righteousness before him, all the days of our life.

76 And thou, child, shalt be called the

1:28 *a*Dan. 9:23 *b*Judg. 6:12
1:29 *c*ver. 12
1:31 *d*Isa. 7:14; Matt. 1:21 *e*ch. 2:21
1:32 *f*Mark 5:7 *g*2 Sam. 7:11; Isa. 9:6; Jer. 23:5; Ps. 132:11; Rev. 3:7
1:33 *h*Dan. 2:44; Obad. 21; Mic. 4:7; John 12:34; Heb. 1:8
1:35 *i*Matt. 1:20 *j*Matt. 14:33; Mark 1:1; John 1:34; Acts 8:37; Rom. 1:4
1:37 *k*Gen. 18:14; Jer. 32:17; Zech. 8:6; Matt. 19:26; Mark 10:27; ch. 18:27; Rom. 4:21
1:39 *l*Josh. 21:9
1:42 *m*ver. 28; Judg. 5:24
1:46 *n*1 Sam. 2:1; Ps. 34:2; Hab. 3:18
1:48 *o*1 Sam. 1:11; Ps. 138:6 *p*Mal. 3:12; ch. 11:27
1:49 *q*Ps. 71:19 *r*Ps. 111:9
1:50 *s*Gen. 17:7; Ex. 20:6; Ps. 103:17
1:51 *t*Ps. 98:1; Isa. 40:10 *u*Ps. 33:10; 1 Pet. 5:5
1:52 *v*1 Sam. 2:6; Job 5:11; Ps. 113:6
1:53 *w*1 Sam. 2:5; Ps. 34:10
1:54 *x*Ps. 98:3; Jer. 31:3
1:55 *y*Gen. 17:19; Ps. 132:11; Rom. 11:28; Gal. 3:16
1:58 *z*ver. 14
1:59 *a*Gen. 17:12; Lev. 12:3
1:60 *b*ver. 13
1:63 *c*ver. 13
1:64 *d*ver. 20
1:65 *e*ver. 39
1:66 *f*ch. 2:19 *g*Gen. 39:2; Ps. 80:17; Acts 11:21
1:67 *h*Joel 2:28
1:68 *i*1 Kings 1:48; Ps. 41:13 *j*Ex. 3:16; Ps. 111:9; ch. 7:16
1:69 *k*Ps. 132:17
1:70 *l*Jer. 23:5; Dan. 9:24; Acts 3:21; Rom. 1:2
1:72 *m*Lev. 26:42; Ps. 98:3; Ezek. 16:60; ver. 54
1:73 *n*Gen. 12:3; Heb. 6:13
1:74 *o*Rom. 6:18; Heb. 9:14
1:75 *p*Jer. 32:39; Eph. 4:24; 2 Thess. 2:13; 2 Tim. 1:9; Tit. 2:12; 1 Pet. 1:15; 2 Pet. 1:4

prophet of the Highest: for [q]thou shalt go
before the face of the Lord to prepare his
ways;
77 To give knowledge of salvation unto
his people [r]by the remission of their sins,
78 Through the tender mercy of our God;
whereby the dayspring from on high hath
visited us,
79 [s]To give light to them that sit in darkness and *in* the shadow of death, to guide
our feet into the way of peace.
80 And [t]the child grew, and waxed
strong in spirit, and [u]was in the deserts till
the day of his shewing unto Israel.
2 And it came to pass in those days, that
there went out a decree from Caesar
Augustus, that all the world should be
taxed.
2 ([v]*And* this taxing was first made when
Cyrenius was governor of Syria.)
3 And all went to be taxed, every one into
his own city.
4 And Joseph also went up from Galilee,
out of the city of Nazareth, into Judaea,
unto [w]the city of David, which is called
Bethlehem; ([x]because he was of the house
and lineage of David:)
5 To be taxed with Mary [y]his espoused
wife, being great with child.
6 And so it was, that, while they were
there, the days were accomplished that she
should be delivered.
7 And [z]she brought forth her firstborn
son, and wrapped him in swaddling clothes,
and laid him in a manger; because there
was no room for them in the inn.
8 And there were in the same country
shepherds abiding in the field, keeping
watch over their flock by night.
9 And, lo, the angel of the Lord came
upon them, and the glory of the Lord shone
round about them: [a]and they were sore
afraid.
10 And the angel said unto them, Fear
not: for, behold, I bring you good tidings of
great joy, [b]which shall be to all people.
11 [c]For unto you is born this day in the
city of David [d]a Saviour, [e]which is Christ
the Lord.
12 And this *shall be* a sign unto you; Ye
shall find the babe wrapped in swaddling
clothes, lying in a manger.
13 [f]And suddenly there was with the angel a multitude of the heavenly host praising God, and saying,
14 [g]Glory to God in the highest, and on
earth [h]peace, [i]good will toward men.
15 And it came to pass, as the angels were
gone away from them into heaven, the
shepherds said one to another, Let us now
go even unto Bethlehem, and see this thing
which is come to pass, which the Lord hath
made known unto us.
16 And they came with haste, and found
Mary, and Joseph, and the babe lying in a
manger.
17 And when they had seen *it*, they made
known abroad the saying which was told
them concerning this child.
18 And all they that heard *it* wondered at
those things which were told them by the
shepherds.
19 [j]But Mary kept all these things, and
pondered *them* in her heart.
20 And the shepherds returned, glorifying and praising God for all the things that
they had heard and seen, as it was told unto
them.
21 [k]And when eight days were accomplished for the circumcising of the child, his
name was called [l]JESUS, which was so
named of the angel before he was conceived
in the womb.
22 And when [m]the days of her purification according to the law of Moses were accomplished, they brought him to Jerusalem,
to present *him* to the Lord;
23 (As it is written in the law of the Lord,
[n]Every male that openeth the womb shall
be called holy to the Lord;)
24 And to offer a sacrifice according to
[o]that which is said in the law of the Lord, A
pair of turtledoves, or two young pigeons.
25 And, behold, there was a man in Jerusalem, whose name *was* Simeon; and the
same man *was* just and devout, [p]waiting
for the consolation of Israel: and the Holy
Ghost was upon him.
26 And it was revealed unto him by the
Holy Ghost, that he should not [q]see death,
before he had seen the Lord's Christ.
27 And he came [r]by the Spirit into the
temple: and when the parents brought in
the child Jesus, to do for him after the custom of the law,
28 Then took he him up in his arms, and
blessed God, and said,
29 Lord, [s]now lettest thou thy servant depart in peace, according to thy word:
30 For mine eyes [t]have seen thy salvation,
31 Which thou hast prepared before the
face of all people;
32 [u]A light to lighten the Gentiles, and
the glory of thy people Israel.
33 And Joseph and his mother marvelled
at those things which were spoken of him.
34 And Simeon blessed them, and said
unto Mary his mother, Behold, this *child* is
set for the [v]fall and rising again of many in
Israel; and for [w]a sign which shall be spoken against;
35 (Yea, [x]a sword shall pierce through
thy own soul also,) that the thoughts of
many hearts may be revealed.
36 And there was one Anna, a prophetess, the daughter of Phanuel, of the tribe of
Aser: she was of a great age, and had lived
with an husband seven years from her virginity;
37 And she *was* a widow of about fourscore and four years, which departed not
from the temple, but served *God* with fastings and prayers [y]night and day.
38 And she coming in that instant gave

1:76 [q]Isa. 40:3; Mal. 3:1; Matt. 11:10; ver. 17
1:77 [r]Mark 1:4; ch. 3:3
1:79 [s]Isa. 9:2; Matt. 4:16; Acts 26:18
1:80 [t]ch. 2:40 [u]Matt. 3:1
2:2 [v]Acts 5:37
2:4 [w]1 Sam. 16:1; John 7:42 [x]Matt. 1:16; ch. 1:27
2:5 [y]Matt. 1:16; ch. 1:27
2:7 [z]Matt. 1:25
2:9 [a]ch. 1:12
2:10 [b]Gen. 12:3; Matt. 28:19; Mark 1:15; ver. 31; ch. 24:47; Col. 1:23
2:11 [c]Isa. 9:6 [d]Matt. 1:21 [e]Matt. 1:16; ch. 1:43; Acts 2:36; Phil. 2:11
2:13 [f]Gen. 28:12; Ps. 103:20; Dan. 7:10; Heb. 1:14; Rev. 5:11
2:14 [g]ch. 19:38; Eph. 1:6; Rev. 5:13 [h]Isa. 57:19; ch. 1:79; Rom. 5:1; Eph. 2:17; Col. 1:20 [i]John 3:16; Eph. 2:4; 2 Thess. 2:16; 1 John 4:9
2:19 [j]Gen. 37:11; ch. 1:66; ver. 51
2:21 [k]Gen. 17:12; Lev. 12:3; ch. 1:59 [l]Matt. 1:21; ch. 1:31
2:22 [m]Lev. 12:2
2:23 [n]Ex. 13:2; Num. 3:13
2:24 [o]Lev. 12:2
2:25 [p]Isa. 40:1; Mark 15:43; ver. 38
2:26 [q]Ps. 89:48; Heb. 11:5
2:27 [r]Matt. 4:1
2:29 [s]Gen. 46:30; Phil. 1:23
2:30 [t]Isa. 52:10; ch. 3:6
2:32 [u]Isa. 9:2; Matt. 4:16; Acts 13:47
2:34 [v]Isa. 8:14; Hos. 14:9; Matt. 21:44; Rom. 9:32; 1 Cor. 1:23; 2 Cor. 2:16; 1 Pet. 2:7 [w]Acts 28:22
2:35 [x]Ps. 42:10; John 19:25
2:37 [y]Acts 26:7; 1 Tim. 5:5

thanks likewise unto the Lord, and spake of
him to all them that [z]looked for redemption
in Jerusalem.
39 And when they had performed all
things according to the law of the Lord, they
returned into Galilee, to their own city Nazareth.
40 [a]And the child grew, and waxed
strong in spirit, filled with wisdom: and the
grace of God was upon him.
41 Now his parents went to Jerusalem
[b]every year at the feast of the passover.
42 And when he was twelve years old,
they went up to Jerusalem after the custom
of the feast.
43 And when they had fulfilled the days,
as they returned, the child Jesus tarried behind in Jerusalem; and Joseph and his
mother knew not *of it*.
44 But they, supposing him to have been
in the company, went a day's journey; and
they sought him among *their* kinsfolk and
acquaintance.
45 And when they found him not, they
turned back again to Jerusalem, seeking
him.
46 And it came to pass, that after three
days they found him in the temple, sitting in
the midst of the doctors, both hearing them,
and asking them questions.
47 And [c]all that heard him were astonished at his understanding and answers.
48 And when they saw him, they were
amazed: and his mother said unto him, Son,
why hast thou thus dealt with us? behold,
thy father and I have sought thee sorrowing.
49 And he said unto them, How is it that
ye sought me? wist ye not that I must be
about [d]my Father's business?
50 And [e]they understood not the saying
which he spake unto them.
51 And he went down with them, and
came to Nazareth, and was subject unto
them: but his mother [f]kept all these sayings in her heart.
52 And Jesus [g]increased in wisdom and
stature, and in favour with God and man.

3 Now in the fifteenth year of the reign of
Tiberius Caesar, Pontius Pilate being
governor of Judaea, and Herod being tetrarch of Galilee, and his brother Philip tetrarch of Ituraea and of the region of
Trachonitis, and Lysanias the tetrarch of
Abilene,
2 [h]Annas and Caiaphas being the high
priests, the word of God came unto John the
son of Zacharias in the wilderness.
3 [i]And he came into all the country about
Jordan, preaching the baptism of repentance [j]for the remission of sins;
4 As it is written in the book of the words
of Esaias the prophet, saying, [k]The voice of
one crying in the wilderness, Prepare ye the
way of the Lord, make his paths straight.
5 Every valley shall be filled, and every
mountain and hill shall be brought low; and
the crooked shall be made straight, and the
rough ways *shall be* made smooth;
6 And [l]all flesh shall see the salvation of
God.
7 Then said he to the multitude that came
forth to be baptized of him, [m]O generation
of vipers, who hath warned you to flee from
the wrath to come?
8 Bring forth therefore fruits worthy of
repentance, and begin not to say within
yourselves, We have Abraham to *our* father: for I say unto you, That God is able of
these stones to raise up children unto Abraham.
9 And now also the axe is laid unto the
root of the trees: [n]every tree therefore
which bringeth not forth good fruit is hewn
down, and cast into the fire.
10 And the people asked him, saying,
[o]What shall we do then?
11 He answereth and saith unto them,
[p]He that hath two coats, let him impart to
him that hath none; and he that hath meat,
let him do likewise.
12 Then [q]came also publicans to be baptized, and said unto him, Master, what shall
we do?
13 And he said unto them, [r]Exact no
more than that which is appointed you.
14 And the soldiers likewise demanded of
him, saying, And what shall we do? And he
said unto them, Do violence to no man,
[s]neither accuse *any* falsely; and be content
with your wages.
15 And as the people were in expectation,
and all men mused in their hearts of John,
whether he were the Christ, or not;
16 John answered, saying unto *them* all,
[t]I indeed baptize you with water; but one
mightier than I cometh, the latchet of whose
shoes I am not worthy to unloose: he shall
baptize you with the Holy Ghost and with
fire:
17 Whose fan *is* in his hand, and he will
throughly purge his floor, and [u]will gather
the wheat into his garner; but the chaff he
will burn with fire unquenchable.
18 And many other things in his exhortation preached he unto the people.
19 [v]But Herod the tetrarch, being reproved by him for Herodias his brother
Philip's wife, and for all the evils which
Herod had done,
20 Added yet this above all, that he shut
up John in prison.
21 Now when all the people were baptized, [w]it came to pass, that Jesus also being
baptized, and praying, the heaven was
opened,
22 And the Holy Ghost descended in a
bodily shape like a dove upon him, and a
voice came from heaven, which said, Thou
art my beloved Son; in thee I am well
pleased.
23 And Jesus himself began to be [x]about
thirty years of age, being (as was supposed)
[y]the son of Joseph, which was *the son* of
Heli,

2:38 [z]Mark 15:43; ver. 25; ch. 24:21
2:40 [a]ver. 52; ch. 1:80
2:41 [b]Ex. 23:15; Deut. 16:1
2:47 [c]Matt. 7:28; Mark 1:22; ch. 4:22; John 7:15
2:49 [d]John 2:16
2:50 [e]ch. 9:45
2:51 [f]ver. 19; Dan. 7:28
2:52 [g]1 Sam. 2:26; ver. 40
3:2 [h]John 11:49; Acts 4:6
3:3 [i]Matt. 3:1; Mark 1:4 [j]ch. 1:77
3:4 [k]Isa. 40:3; Matt. 3:3; Mark 1:3; John 1:23
3:6 [l]Ps. 98:2; Isa. 52:10; ch. 2:10
3:7 [m]Matt. 3:7
3:9 [n]Matt. 7:19
3:10 [o]Acts 2:37
3:11 [p]ch. 11:41; 2 Cor. 8:14; Jam. 2:15; 1 John 3:17
3:12 [q]Matt. 21:32; ch. 7:29
3:13 [r]ch. 19:8
3:14 [s]Ex. 23:1; Lev. 19:11
3:16 [t]Matt. 3:11
3:17 [u]Mic. 4:12; Matt. 13:30
3:19 [v]Matt. 14:3; Mark 6:17
3:21 [w]Matt. 3:13; John 1:32
3:23 [x]Num. 4:3 [y]Matt. 13:55; John 6:42

24 Which was *the son* of Matthat, which was *the son* of Levi, which was *the son* of Melchi, which was *the son* of Janna, which was *the son* of Joseph,

25 Which was *the son* of Mattathias, which was *the son* of Amos, which was *the son* of Naum, which was *the son* of Esli, which was *the son* of Nagge,

26 Which was *the son* of Maath, which was *the son* of Mattathias, which was *the son* of Semei, which was *the son* of Joseph, which was *the son* of Juda,

27 Which was *the son* of Joanna, which was *the son* of Rhesa, which was *the son* of Zorobabel, which was *the son* of Salathiel, which was *the son* of Neri,

28 Which was *the son* of Melchi, which was *the son* of Addi, which was *the son* of Cosam, which was *the son* of Elmodam, which was *the son* of Er,

29 Which was *the son* of Jose, which was *the son* of Eliezer, which was *the son* of Jorim, which was *the son* of Matthat, which was *the son* of Levi,

30 Which was *the son* of Simeon, which was *the son* of Juda, which was *the son* of Joseph, which was *the son* of Jonan, which was *the son* of Eliakim,

31 Which was *the son* of Melea, which was *the son* of Menan, which was *the son* of Mattatha, which was *the son* of [z]Nathan, [a]which was *the son* of David,

32 [b]Which was *the son* of Jesse, which was *the son* of Obed, which was *the son* of Booz, which was *the son* of Salmon, which was *the son* of Naasson,

33 Which was *the son* of Aminadab, which was *the son* of Aram, which was *the son* of Esrom, which was *the son* of Phares, which was *the son* of Juda,

34 Which was *the son* of Jacob, which was *the son* of Isaac, which was *the son* of Abraham, [c]which was *the son* of Thara, which was *the son* of Nachor,

35 Which was *the son* of Saruch, which was *the son* of Ragau, which was *the son* of Phalec, which was *the son* of Heber, which was *the son* of Sala,

36 [d]Which was *the son* of Cainan, which was *the son* of Arphaxad, [e]which was *the son* of Sem, which was *the son* of Noe, which was *the son* of Lamech,

37 Which was *the son* of Mathusala, which was *the son* of Enoch, which was *the son* of Jared, which was *the son* of Maleleel, which was *the son* of Cainan,

38 Which was *the son* of Enos, which was *the son* of Seth, which was *the son* of Adam, [f]which was *the son* of God.

4 And [g]Jesus being full of the Holy Ghost returned from Jordan, and [h]was led by the Spirit into the wilderness,

2 Being forty days tempted of the devil. And [i]in those days he did eat nothing: and when they were ended, he afterward hungered.

3 And the devil said unto him, If thou be the Son of God, command this stone that it be made bread.

4 And Jesus answered him, saying, [j]It is written, That man shall not live by bread alone, but by every word of God.

5 And the devil, taking him up into an high mountain, shewed unto him all the kingdoms of the world in a moment of time.

6 And the devil said unto him, All this power will I give thee, and the glory of them: for [k]that is delivered unto me; and to whomsoever I will I give it.

7 If thou therefore wilt worship me, all shall be thine.

8 And Jesus answered and said unto him, Get thee behind me, Satan: for [l]it is written, Thou shalt worship the Lord thy God, and him only shalt thou serve.

9 [m]And he brought him to Jerusalem, and set him on a pinnacle of the temple, and said unto him, If thou be the Son of God, cast thyself down from hence:

10 For [n]it is written, He shall give his angels charge over thee, to keep thee:

11 And in *their* hands they shall bear thee up, lest at any time thou dash thy foot against a stone.

12 And Jesus answering said unto him, [o]It is said, Thou shalt not tempt the Lord thy God.

13 And when the devil had ended all the temptation, he departed from him [p]for a season.

14 ¶ [q]And Jesus returned [r]in the power of the Spirit into [s]Galilee: and there went out a fame of him through all the region round about.

15 And he taught in their synagogues, being glorified of all.

16 ¶ And he came to [t]Nazareth, where he had been brought up: and, as his custom was, [u]he went into the synagogue on the sabbath day, and stood up for to read.

17 And there was delivered unto him the book of the prophet Esaias. And when he had opened the book, he found the place where it was written,

18 [v]The Spirit of the Lord *is* upon me, because he hath anointed me to preach the gospel to the poor; he hath sent me to heal the brokenhearted, to preach deliverance to the captives, and recovering of sight to the blind, to set at liberty them that are bruised,

19 To preach the acceptable year of the Lord.

20 And he closed the book, and he gave *it* again to the minister, and sat down. And the eyes of all them that were in the synagogue were fastened on him.

21 And he began to say unto them, This day is this scripture fulfilled in your ears.

22 And all bare him witness, and [w]wondered at the gracious words which proceeded out of his mouth. And they said, [x]Is not this Joseph's son?

23 And he said unto them, Ye will surely say unto me this proverb, Physician, heal thyself: whatsoever we have heard done in

3:31 [z]Zech. 12:12 [a]2 Sam. 5:14; 1 Chron. 3:5
3:32 [b]Ruth 4:18; 1 Chron. 2:10
3:34 [c]Gen. 11:24
3:36 [d]Gen. 11:12 [e]Gen. 5:6
3:38 [f]Gen. 5:1
4:1 [g]Matt. 4:1; Mark 1:12 [h]ver. 14; ch. 2:27
4:2 [i]Ex. 34:28; 1 Kings 19:8
4:4 [j]Deut. 8:3
4:6 [k]John 12:31; Rev. 13:2
4:8 [l]Deut. 6:13
4:9 [m]Matt. 4:5
4:10 [n]Ps. 91:11
4:12 [o]Deut. 6:16
4:13 [p]John 14:30; Heb. 4:15
4:14 [q]Matt. 4:12; John 4:43 [r]ver. 1 [s]Acts 10:37
4:16 [t]Matt. 2:23; Mark 6:1 [u]Acts 13:14
4:18 [v]Isa. 61:1
4:22 [w]Ps. 45:2; Matt. 13:54; Mark 6:2; ch. 2:47 [x]John 6:42

[y]Capernaum, do also here in [z]thy country.

24 And he said, Verily I say unto you, No [a]prophet is accepted in his own country.

25 But I tell you of a truth, [b]many widows were in Israel in the days of Elias, when the heaven was shut up three years and six months, when great famine was throughout all the land;

26 But unto none of them was Elias sent, save unto Sarepta, *a city* of Sidon, unto a woman *that was* a widow.

27 [c]And many lepers were in Israel in the time of Eliseus the prophet; and none of them was cleansed, saving Naaman the Syrian.

28 And all they in the synagogue, when they heard these things, were filled with wrath,

29 And rose up, and thrust him out of the city, and led him unto the brow of the hill whereon their city was built, that they might cast him down headlong.

30 But he [d]passing through the midst of them went his way,

31 And [e]came down to Capernaum, a city of Galilee, and taught them on the sabbath days.

32 And they were astonished at his doctrine: [f]for his word was with power.

33 ¶ [g]And in the synagogue there was a man, which had a spirit of an unclean devil, and cried out with a loud voice,

34 Saying, Let *us* alone; what have we to do with thee, *thou* Jesus of Nazareth? art thou come to destroy us? [h]I know thee who thou art; [i]the Holy One of God.

35 And Jesus rebuked him, saying, Hold thy peace, and come out of him. And when the devil had thrown him in the midst, he came out of him, and hurt him not.

36 And they were all amazed, and spake among themselves, saying, What a word *is* this! for with authority and power he commandeth the unclean spirits, and they come out.

37 And the fame of him went out into every place of the country round about.

38 ¶ [j]And he arose out of the synagogue, and entered into Simon's house. And Simon's wife's mother was taken with a great fever; and they besought him for her.

39 And he stood over her, and rebuked the fever; and it left her: and immediately she arose and ministered unto them.

40 ¶ [k]Now when the sun was setting, all they that had any sick with divers diseases brought them unto him; and he laid his hands on every one of them, and healed them.

41 [l]And devils also came out of many, crying out, and saying, Thou art Christ the Son of God. And [m]he rebuking *them* suffered them not to speak: for they knew that he was Christ.

42 And [n]when it was day, he departed and went into a desert place: and the people sought him, and came unto him, and stayed him, that he should not depart from them.

43 And he said unto them, I must preach the kingdom of God to other cities also: for therefore am I sent.

44 [o]And he preached in the synagogues of Galilee.

5 And [p]it came to pass, that, as the people pressed upon him to hear the word of God, he stood by the lake of Gennesaret,

2 And saw two ships standing by the lake: but the fishermen were gone out of them, and were washing *their* nets.

3 And he entered into one of the ships, which was Simon's, and prayed him that he would thrust out a little from the land. And he sat down, and taught the people out of the ship.

4 Now when he had left speaking, he said unto Simon, [q]Launch out into the deep, and let down your nets for a draught.

5 And Simon answering said unto him, Master, we have toiled all the night, and have taken nothing: nevertheless at thy word I will let down the net.

6 And when they had this done, they inclosed a great multitude of fishes: and their net brake.

7 And they beckoned unto *their* partners, which were in the other ship, that they should come and help them. And they came, and filled both the ships, so that they began to sink.

8 When Simon Peter saw *it*, he fell down at Jesus' knees, saying, [r]Depart from me; for I am a sinful man, O Lord.

9 For he was astonished, and all that were with him, at the draught of the fishes which they had taken:

10 And so *was* also James, and John, the sons of Zebedee, which were partners with Simon. And Jesus said unto Simon, Fear not; [s]from henceforth thou shalt catch men.

11 And when they had brought their ships to land, [t]they forsook all, and followed him.

12 ¶ [u]And it came to pass, when he was in a certain city, behold a man full of leprosy: who seeing Jesus fell on *his* face, and besought him, saying, Lord, if thou wilt, thou canst make me clean.

13 And he put forth *his* hand, and touched him, saying, I will: be thou clean. And immediately the leprosy departed from him.

14 [v]And he charged him to tell no man: but go, and shew thyself to the priest, and offer for thy cleansing, [w]according as Moses commanded, for a testimony unto them.

15 But so much the more went there a fame abroad of him: [x]and great multitudes came together to hear, and to be healed by him of their infirmities.

16 ¶ [y]And he withdrew himself into the wilderness, and prayed.

17 And it came to pass on a certain day, as he was teaching, that there were Pharisees and doctors of the law sitting by, which were come out of every town of Galilee, and Judaea, and Jerusalem: and the power of the Lord was *present* to heal them.

4:23 [y]Matt. 4:13 [z]Matt. 13:54; Mark 6:1
4:24 [a]Matt. 13:57; Mark 6:4; John 4:44
4:25 [b]1 Kings 17:9; Jam. 5:17
4:27 [c]2 Kings 5:14
4:30 [d]John 8:59
4:31 [e]Matt. 4:13; Mark 1:21
4:32 [f]Matt. 6:28; Tit. 2:15
4:33 [g]Mark 1:23
4:34 [h]ver. 41 [i]Ps. 16:10; Dan. 9:24; ch. 1:35
4:38 [j]Matt. 8:14; Mark 1:29
4:40 [k]Matt. 8:16; Mark 1:32
4:41 [l]Mark 1:34 [m]Mark 1:25; ver. 34
4:42 [n]Mark 1:35
4:44 [o]Mark 1:39
5:1 [p]Matt. 4:18; Mark 1:16
5:4 [q]John 21:6
5:8 [r]2 Sam. 6:9; 1 Kings 17:18
5:10 [s]Matt. 4:19; Mark 1:17
5:11 [t]Matt. 4:20; Mark 1:18; ch. 18:28
5:12 [u]Matt. 8:2; Mark 1:40
5:14 [v]Matt. 8:4 [w]Lev. 14:4
5:15 [x]Matt. 4:25; Mark 3:7; John 6:2
5:16 [y]Matt. 14:23; Mark 6:46

18 ¶ [z]And, behold, men brought in a bed
a man which was taken with a palsy: and
they sought *means* to bring him in, and to
lay *him* before him.
19 And when they could not find by what
way they might bring him in because of the
multitude, they went upon the housetop,
and let him down through the tiling with *his*
couch into the midst before Jesus.
20 And when he saw their faith, he said
unto him, Man, thy sins are forgiven thee.
21 [a]And the scribes and the Pharisees began to reason, saying, Who is this which
speaketh blasphemies? [b]Who can forgive
sins, but God alone?
22 But when Jesus perceived their
thoughts, he answering said unto them,
What reason ye in your hearts?
23 Whether is easier, to say, Thy sins be
forgiven thee; or to say, Rise up and walk?
24 But that ye may know that the Son of
man hath power upon earth to forgive sins,
(he said unto the sick of the palsy,) I say
unto thee, Arise, and take up thy couch, and
go into thine house.
25 And immediately he rose up before
them, and took up that whereon he lay, and
departed to his own house, glorifying God.
26 And they were all amazed, and they
glorified God, and were filled with fear, saying, We have seen strange things to day.
27 ¶ [c]And after these things he went
forth, and saw a publican, named Levi, sitting at the receipt of custom: and he said
unto him, Follow me.
28 And he left all, rose up, and followed
him.
29 [d]And Levi made him a great feast in
his own house: and [e]there was a great company of publicans and of others that sat
down with them.
30 But their scribes and Pharisees murmured against his disciples, saying, Why do
ye eat and drink with publicans and sinners?
31 And Jesus answering said unto them,
They that are whole need not a physician;
but they that are sick.
32 [f]I came not to call the righteous, but
sinners to repentance.
33 ¶ And they said unto him, [g]Why do
the disciples of John fast often, and make
prayers, and likewise *the disciples* of the
Pharisees; but thine eat and drink?
34 And he said unto them, Can ye make
the children of the bridechamber fast, while
the bridegroom is with them?
35 But the days will come, when the
bridegroom shall be taken away from them,
and then shall they fast in those days.
36 ¶ [h]And he spake also a parable unto
them; No man putteth a piece of a new garment upon an old; if otherwise, then both
the new maketh a rent, and the piece that
was *taken* out of the new agreeth not with
the old.
37 And no man putteth new wine into old
bottles; else the new wine will burst the bottles, and be spilled, and the bottles shall perish.
38 But new wine must be put into new
bottles; and both are preserved.
39 No man also having drunk old *wine*
straightway desireth new: for he saith, The
old is better.

6 And [i]it came to pass on the second sabbath after the first, that he went through
the corn fields; and his disciples plucked the
ears of corn, and did eat, rubbing *them* in
their hands.
2 And certain of the Pharisees said unto
them, Why do ye that [j]which is not lawful
to do on the sabbath days?
3 And Jesus answering them said, Have
ye not read so much as this, [k]what David
did, when himself was an hungred, and they
which were with him;
4 How he went into the house of God, and
did take and eat the shewbread, and gave
also to them that were with him; [l]which it
is not lawful to eat but for the priests alone?
5 And he said unto them, That the Son of
man is Lord also of the sabbath.
6 [m]And it came to pass also on another
sabbath, that he entered into the synagogue
and taught: and there was a man whose
right hand was withered.
7 And the scribes and Pharisees watched
him, whether he would heal on the sabbath
day; that they might find an accusation
against him.
8 But he knew their thoughts, and said to
the man which had the withered hand, Rise
up, and stand forth in the midst. And he
arose and stood forth.
9 Then said Jesus unto them, I will ask
you one thing; Is it lawful on the sabbath
days to do good, or to do evil? to save life,
or to destroy *it*?
10 And looking round about upon them
all, he said unto the man, Stretch forth thy
hand. And he did so: and his hand was restored whole as the other.
11 And they were filled with madness;
and communed one with another what they
might do to Jesus.
12 [n]And it came to pass in those days,
that he went out into a mountain to pray,
and continued all night in prayer to God.
13 ¶ And when it was day, he called *unto*
him his disciples: [o]and of them he chose
twelve, whom also he named apostles;
14 Simon, ([p]whom he also named Peter,)
and Andrew his brother, James and John,
Philip and Bartholomew,
15 Matthew and Thomas, James the *son*
of Alpheus, and Simon called Zelotes,
16 And Judas [q]*the brother* of James, and
Judas Iscariot, which also was the traitor.
17 ¶ And he came down with them, and
stood in the plain, and the company of his
disciples, [r]and a great multitude of people
out of all Judaea and Jerusalem, and from
the sea coast of Tyre and Sidon, which
came to hear him, and to be healed of their
diseases;

5:18 [z]Matt. 9:2; Mark 2:3
5:21 [a]Matt. 9:3; Mark 2:6 [b]Ps. 32:5; Isa. 43:25
5:27 [c]Matt. 9:9; Mark 2:13
5:29 [d]Matt. 9:10; Mark 2:15 [e]ch. 15:1
5:32 [f]Matt. 9:13; 1 Tim. 1:15
5:33 [g]Matt. 9:14; Mark 2:18
5:36 [h]Matt. 9:16; Mark 2:21
6:1 [i]Matt. 12:1; Mark 2:23
6:2 [j]Ex. 20:10
6:3 [k]1 Sam. 21:6
6:4 [l]Lev. 24:9
6:6 [m]Matt. 12:9; Mark 3:1; ch. 13:14; John 9:16
6:12 [n]Matt. 14:23
6:13 [o]Matt. 10:1
6:14 [p]John 1:42
6:16 [q]Jude 1
6:17 [r]Matt. 4:25; Mark 3:7

18 And they that were vexed with unclean spirits: and they were healed.

19 And the whole multitude [s]sought to touch him: for [t]there went virtue out of him, and healed *them* all.

20 ¶ And he lifted up his eyes on his disciples, and said, [u]Blessed *be ye* poor: for yours is the kingdom of God.

21 [v]Blessed *are ye* that hunger now: for ye shall be filled. [w]Blessed *are ye* that weep now: for ye shall laugh.

22 [x]Blessed are ye, when men shall hate you, and when they [y]shall separate you *from their company*, and shall reproach *you*, and cast out your name as evil, for the Son of man's sake.

23 [z]Rejoice ye in that day, and leap for joy: for, behold, your reward *is* great in heaven: for [a]in the like manner did their fathers unto the prophets.

24 [b]But woe unto you [c]that are rich! for [d]ye have received your consolation.

25 [e]Woe unto you that are full! for ye shall hunger. [f]Woe unto you that laugh now! for ye shall mourn and weep.

26 [g]Woe unto you, when all men shall speak well of you! for so did their fathers to the false prophets.

27 ¶ [h]But I say unto you which hear, Love your enemies, do good to them which hate you,

28 Bless them that curse you, and [i]pray for them which despitefully use you.

29 [j]And unto him that smiteth thee on the *one* cheek offer also the other; [k]and him that taketh away thy cloke forbid not *to take thy* coat also.

30 [l]Give to every man that asketh of thee; and of him that taketh away thy goods ask *them* not again.

31 [m]And as ye would that men should do to you, do ye also to them likewise.

32 [n]For if ye love them which love you, what thank have ye? for sinners also love those that love them.

33 And if ye do good to them which do good to you, what thank have ye? for sinners also do even the same.

34 [o]And if ye lend *to them* of whom ye hope to receive, what thank have ye? for sinners also lend to sinners, to receive as much again.

35 But [p]love ye your enemies, and do good, and [q]lend, hoping for nothing again; and your reward shall be great, and [r]ye shall be the children of the Highest: for he is kind unto the unthankful and *to* the evil.

36 [s]Be ye therefore merciful, as your Father also is merciful.

37 [t]Judge not, and ye shall not be judged: condemn not, and ye shall not be condemned: forgive, and ye shall be forgiven:

38 [u]Give, and it shall be given unto you; good measure, pressed down, and shaken together, and running over, shall men give into your [v]bosom. For [w]with the same measure that ye mete withal it shall be measured to you again.

39 And he spake a parable unto them, [x]Can the blind lead the blind? shall they not both fall into the ditch?

40 [y]The disciple is not above his master: but every one that is perfect shall be as his master.

41 [z]And why beholdest thou the mote that is in thy brother's eye, but perceivest not the beam that is in thine own eye?

42 Either how canst thou say to thy brother, Brother, let me pull out the mote that is in thine eye, when thou thyself beholdest not the beam that is in thine own eye? Thou hypocrite, [a]cast out first the beam out of thine own eye, and then shalt thou see clearly to pull out the mote that is in thy brother's eye.

43 [b]For a good tree bringeth not forth corrupt fruit; neither doth a corrupt tree bring forth good fruit.

44 For [c]every tree is known by his own fruit. For of thorns men do not gather figs, nor of a bramble bush gather they grapes.

45 [d]A good man out of the good treasure of his heart bringeth forth that which is good; and an evil man out of the evil treasure of his heart bringeth forth that which is evil: for [e]of the abundance of the heart his mouth speaketh.

46 ¶ [f]And why call ye me, Lord, Lord, and do not the things which I say?

47 [g]Whosoever cometh to me, and heareth my sayings, and doeth them, I will shew you to whom he is like:

48 He is like a man which built an house, and digged deep, and laid the foundation on a rock: and when the flood arose, the stream beat vehemently upon that house, and could not shake it: for it was founded upon a rock.

49 But he that heareth, and doeth not, is like a man that without a foundation built an house upon the earth; against which the stream did beat vehemently, and immediately it fell; and the ruin of that house was great.

7 Now when he had ended all his sayings in the audience of the people, [h]he entered into Capernaum.

2 And a certain centurion's servant, who was dear unto him, was sick, and ready to die.

3 And when he heard of Jesus, he sent unto him the elders of the Jews, beseeching him that he would come and heal his servant.

4 And when they came to Jesus, they besought him instantly, saying, That he was worthy for whom he should do this:

5 For he loveth our nation, and he hath built us a synagogue.

6 Then Jesus went with them. And when he was now not far from the house, the centurion sent friends to him, saying unto him, Lord, trouble not thyself: for I am not worthy that thou shouldest enter under my roof:

7 Wherefore neither thought I myself worthy to come unto thee: but say in a word, and my servant shall be healed.

6:19 [s]Matt. 14:36 [t]Mark 5:30; ch. 8:46
6:20 [u]Matt. 5:3; Jam. 2:5
6:21 [v]Isa. 55:1; Matt. 5:6 [w]Isa. 61:3; Matt. 5:4
6:22 [x]Matt. 5:11; 1 Pet. 2:19 [y]John 16:2
6:23 [z]Matt. 5:12; Acts 5:41; Col. 1:24; Jam. 1:2 [a]Acts 7:51
6:24 [b]Am. 6:1; Jam. 5:1 [c]ch. 12:21 [d]Matt. 6:2; ch. 16:25
6:25 [e]Isa. 65:13 [f]Prov. 14:13
6:26 [g]John 15:19; 1 John 4:5
6:27 [h]Ex. 23:4; Prov. 25:2; Matt. 5:44; ver. 35; Rom. 12:20
6:28 [i]ch. 23:34; Acts 7:60
6:29 [j]Matt. 5:39 [k]1 Cor. 6:7
6:30 [l]Deut. 15:7; Prov. 21:26; Matt. 5:42
6:31 [m]Matt. 7:12
6:32 [n]Matt. 5:46
6:34 [o]Matt. 5:42
6:35 [p]ver. 27 [q]Ps. 37:26; ver. 30 [r]Matt. 5:45
6:36 [s]Matt. 5:48
6:37 [t]Matt. 7:1
6:38 [u]Prov. 19:17 [v]Ps. 79:12 [w]Matt. 7:2; Mark 4:24; Jam. 2:13
6:39 [x]Matt. 15:14
6:40 [y]Matt. 10:24; John 13:16
6:41 [z]Matt. 7:3
6:42 [a]Prov. 18:17
6:43 [b]Matt. 7:16
6:44 [c]Matt. 12:33
6:45 [d]Matt. 12:35 [e]Matt. 12:34
6:46 [f]Mal. 1:6; Matt. 7:21; ch. 13:25
6:47 [g]Matt. 7:24
7:1 [h]Matt. 8:5

8 For I also am a man set under authority, having under me soldiers, and I say unto one, Go, and he goeth; and to another, Come, and he cometh; and to my servant, Do this, and he doeth *it*.

9 When Jesus heard these things, he marvelled at him, and turned him about, and said unto the people that followed him, I say unto you, I have not found so great faith, no, not in Israel.

10 And they that were sent, returning to the house, found the servant whole that had been sick.

11 ¶ And it came to pass the day after, that he went into a city called Nain; and many of his disciples went with him, and much people.

12 Now when he came nigh to the gate of the city, behold, there was a dead man carried out, the only son of his mother, and she was a widow: and much people of the city was with her.

13 And when the Lord saw her, he had compassion on her, and said unto her, Weep not.

14 And he came and touched the bier: and they that bare *him* stood still. And he said, Young man, I say unto thee, [i]Arise.

15 And he that was dead sat up, and began to speak. And he delivered him to his mother.

16 [j]And there came a fear on all: and they glorified God, saying, [k]That a great prophet is risen up among us; and, [l]That God hath visited his people.

17 And this rumour of him went forth throughout all Judaea, and throughout all the region round about.

18 [m]And the disciples of John shewed him of all these things.

19 ¶ And John calling *unto him* two of his disciples sent *them* to Jesus, saying, Art thou he that should come? or look we for another?

20 When the men were come unto him, they said, John Baptist hath sent us unto thee, saying, Art thou he that should come? or look we for another?

21 And in that same hour he cured many of *their* infirmities and plagues, and of evil spirits; and unto many *that were* blind he gave sight.

22 [n]Then Jesus answering said unto them, Go your way, and tell John what things ye have seen and heard; [o]how that the blind see, the lame walk, the lepers are cleansed, the deaf hear, the dead are raised, [p]to the poor the gospel is preached.

23 And blessed is *he*, whosoever shall not be offended in me.

24 ¶ [q]And when the messengers of John were departed, he began to speak unto the people concerning John, What went ye out into the wilderness for to see? A reed shaken with the wind?

25 But what went ye out for to see? A man clothed in soft raiment? Behold, they which are gorgeously apparelled, and live delicately, are in kings' courts.

26 But what went ye out for to see? A prophet? Yea, I say unto you, and much more than a prophet.

27 This is *he*, of whom it is written, [r]Behold, I send my messenger before thy face, which shall prepare thy way before thee.

28 For I say unto you, Among those that are born of women there is not a greater prophet than John the Baptist: but he that is least in the kingdom of God is greater than he.

29 And all the people that heard *him*, and the publicans, justified God, [s]being baptized with the baptism of John.

30 But the Pharisees and lawyers rejected [t]the counsel of God against themselves, being not baptized of him.

31 ¶ And the Lord said, [u]Whereunto then shall I liken the men of this generation? and to what are they like?

32 They are like unto children sitting in the marketplace, and calling one to another, and saying, We have piped unto you, and ye have not danced; we have mourned to you, and ye have not wept.

33 For [v]John the Baptist came neither eating bread nor drinking wine; and ye say, He hath a devil.

34 The Son of man is come eating and drinking; and ye say, Behold a gluttonous man, and a winebibber, a friend of publicans and sinners!

35 [w]But wisdom is justified of all her children.

36 ¶ [x]And one of the Pharisees desired him that he would eat with him. And he went into the Pharisee's house, and sat down to meat.

37 And, behold, a woman in the city, which was a sinner, when she knew that *Jesus* sat at meat in the Pharisee's house, brought an alabaster box of ointment,

38 And stood at his feet behind *him* weeping, and began to wash his feet with tears, and did wipe *them* with the hairs of her head, and kissed his feet, and anointed *them* with the ointment.

39 Now when the Pharisee which had bidden him saw *it*, he spake within himself, saying, [y]This man, if he were a prophet, would have known who and what manner of woman *this is* that toucheth him: for she is a sinner.

40 And Jesus answering said unto him, Simon, I have somewhat to say unto thee. And he saith, Master, say on.

41 There was a certain creditor which had two debtors: the one owed five hundred pence, and the other fifty.

42 And when they had nothing to pay, he frankly forgave them both. Tell me therefore, which of them will love him most?

43 Simon answered and said, I suppose that *he*, to whom he forgave most. And he said unto him, Thou hast rightly judged.

44 And he turned to the woman, and said

7:14 [i]ch. 8; John 11:43; Acts 9:40; Rom. 4:17
7:16 [j]ch. 1:65 [k]ch. 24:19; John 4:19 [l]ch. 1:68
7:18 [m]Matt. 11:2
7:22 [n]Matt. 11:5 [o]Isa. 35:5 [p]ch. 4:18
7:24 [q]Matt. 11:7
7:27 [r]Mal. 3:1
7:29 [s]Matt. 3:5; ch. 3:12
7:30 [t]Acts 20:27
7:31 [u]Matt. 11:16
7:33 [v]Matt. 3:4; Mark 1:6; ch. 1:15
7:35 [w]Matt. 11:19
7:36 [x]Matt. 26:6; Mark 14:3; John 11:2
7:39 [y]ch. 15:2

unto Simon, Seest thou this woman? I entered into thine house, thou gavest me no water for my feet: but she hath washed my feet with tears, and wiped *them* with the hairs of her head.

45 Thou gavest me no kiss: but this woman since the time I came in hath not ceased to kiss my feet.

46 [z]My head with oil thou didst not anoint: but this woman hath anointed my feet with ointment.

47 [a]Wherefore I say unto thee, Her sins, which are many, are forgiven; for she loved much: but to whom little is forgiven, *the same* loveth little.

48 And he said unto her, [b]Thy sins are forgiven.

49 And they that sat at meat with him began to say within themselves, [c]Who is this that forgiveth sins also?

50 And he said to the woman, [d]Thy faith hath saved thee; go in peace.

8 And it came to pass afterward, that he went throughout every city and village, preaching and shewing the glad tidings of the kingdom of God: and the twelve *were* with him,

2 And [e]certain women, which had been healed of evil spirits and infirmities, Mary called Magdalene, [f]out of whom went seven devils,

3 And Joanna the wife of Chuza Herod's steward, and Susanna, and many others, which ministered unto him of their substance.

4 ¶ [g]And when much people were gathered together, and were come to him out of every city, he spake by a parable:

5 A sower went out to sow his seed: and as he sowed, some fell by the way side; and it was trodden down, and the fowls of the air devoured it.

6 And some fell upon a rock; and as soon as it was sprung up, it withered away, because it lacked moisture.

7 And some fell among thorns; and the thorns sprang up with it, and choked it.

8 And other fell on good ground, and sprang up, and bare fruit an hundredfold. And when he had said these things, he cried, He that hath ears to hear, let him hear.

9 [h]And his disciples asked him, saying, What might this parable be?

10 And he said, Unto you it is given to know the mysteries of the kingdom of God: but to others in parables; [i]that seeing they might not see, and hearing they might not understand.

11 [j]Now the parable is this: The seed is the word of God.

12 Those by the way side are they that hear; then cometh the devil, and taketh away the word out of their hearts, lest they should believe and be saved.

13 They on the rock *are they,* which, when they hear, receive the word with joy; and these have no root, which for a while

7:46 [z]Ps. 23:5
7:47 [a]1 Tim. 1:14
7:48 [b]Matt. 9:2; Mark 2:5
7:49 [c]Matt. 9:3; Mark 2:7
7:50 [d]Matt. 9:22; Mark 5:34; ch. 8:48
8:2 [e]Matt. 27:55 [f]Mark 16:9
8:4 [g]Matt. 13:2; Mark 4:1
8:9 [h]Matt. 13:10; Mark 4:10
8:10 [i]Isa. 6:9; Mark 4:12
8:11 [j]Matt. 13:18; Mark 4:14
8:16 [k]Matt. 5:15; Mark 4:21; ch. 11:33
8:17 [l]Matt. 10:26; ch. 12:2
8:18 [m]Matt. 13:12; ch. 19:26
8:19 [n]Matt. 12:46; Mark 3:31
8:22 [o]Matt. 8:23; Mark 4:35
8:26 [p]Matt. 8:28; Mark 5:1

believe, and in time of temptation fall away.

14 And that which fell among thorns are they, which, when they have heard, go forth, and are choked with cares and riches and pleasures of *this* life, and bring no fruit to perfection.

15 But that on the good ground are they, which in an honest and good heart, having heard the word, keep *it,* and bring forth fruit with patience.

16 ¶ [k]No man, when he hath lighted a candle, covereth it with a vessel, or putteth *it* under a bed; but setteth *it* on a candlestick, that they which enter in may see the light.

17 [l]For nothing is secret, that shall not be made manifest; neither *any thing* hid, that shall not be known and come abroad.

18 Take heed therefore how ye hear: [m]for whosoever hath, to him shall be given; and whosoever hath not, from him shall be taken even that which he seemeth to have.

19 ¶ [n]Then came to him *his* mother and his brethren, and could not come at him for the press.

20 And it was told him *by certain* which said, Thy mother and thy brethren stand without, desiring to see thee.

21 And he answered and said unto them, My mother and my brethren are these which hear the word of God, and do it.

22 ¶ [o]Now it came to pass on a certain day, that he went into a ship with his disciples: and he said unto them, Let us go over unto the other side of the lake. And they launched forth.

23 But as they sailed he fell asleep: and there came down a storm of wind on the lake; and they were filled *with water,* and were in jeopardy.

24 And they came to him, and awoke him, saying, Master, master, we perish. Then he arose, and rebuked the wind and the raging of the water: and they ceased, and there was a calm.

25 And he said unto them, Where is your faith? And they being afraid wondered, saying one to another, What manner of man is this! for he commandeth even the winds and water, and they obey him.

26 ¶ [p]And they arrived at the country of the Gadarenes, which is over against Galilee.

27 And when he went forth to land, there met him out of the city a certain man, which had devils long time, and ware no clothes, neither abode in *any* house, but in the tombs.

28 When he saw Jesus, he cried out, and fell down before him, and with a loud voice said, What have I to do with thee, Jesus, *thou* Son of God most high? I beseech thee, torment me not.

29 (For he had commanded the unclean spirit to come out of the man. For oftentimes it had caught him: and he was kept bound with chains and in fetters; and he brake the

bands, and was driven of the devil into the wilderness.)

30 And Jesus asked him, saying, What is thy name? And he said, Legion: because many devils were entered into him.

31 And they besought him that he would not command them to go out [q]into the deep.

32 And there was there an herd of many swine feeding on the mountain: and they besought him that he would suffer them to enter into them. And he suffered them.

33 Then went the devils out of the man, and entered into the swine: and the herd ran violently down a steep place into the lake, and were choked.

34 When they that fed *them* saw what was done, they fled, and went and told *it* in the city and in the country.

35 Then they went out to see what was done; and came to Jesus, and found the man, out of whom the devils were departed, sitting at the feet of Jesus, clothed, and in his right mind: and they were afraid.

36 They also which saw *it* told them by what means he that was possessed of the devils was healed.

37 ¶ [r]Then the whole multitude of the country of the Gadarenes round about [s]besought him to depart from them; for they were taken with great fear: and he went up into the ship, and returned back again.

38 Now [t]the man out of whom the devils were departed besought him that he might be with him: but Jesus sent him away, saying,

39 Return to thine own house, and shew how great things God hath done unto thee. And he went his way, and published throughout the whole city how great things Jesus had done unto him.

40 And it came to pass, that, when Jesus was returned, the people *gladly* received him: for they were all waiting for him.

41 ¶ [u]And, behold, there came a man named Jairus, and he was a ruler of the synagogue: and he fell down at Jesus' feet, and besought him that he would come into his house:

42 For he had one only daughter, about twelve years of age, and she lay a dying. But as he went the people thronged him.

43 ¶ [v]And a woman having an issue of blood twelve years, which had spent all her living upon physicians, neither could be healed of any,

44 Came behind *him,* and touched the border of his garment: and immediately her issue of blood stanched.

45 And Jesus said, Who touched me? When all denied, Peter and they that were with him said, Master, the multitude throng thee and press *thee,* and sayest thou, Who touched me?

46 And Jesus said, Somebody hath touched me: for I perceive that [w]virtue is gone out of me.

47 And when the woman saw that she was not hid, she came trembling, and falling down before him, she declared unto him before all the people for what cause she had touched him, and how she was healed immediately.

48 And he said unto her, Daughter, be of good comfort: thy faith hath made thee whole; go in peace.

49 ¶ [x]While he yet spake, there cometh one from the ruler of the synagogue's *house,* saying to him, Thy daughter is dead; trouble not the Master.

50 But when Jesus heard *it,* he answered him, saying, Fear not: believe only, and she shall be made whole.

51 And when he came into the house, he suffered no man to go in, save Peter, and James, and John, and the father and the mother of the maiden.

52 And all wept, and bewailed her: but he said, Weep not; she is not dead, [y]but sleepeth.

53 And they laughed him to scorn, knowing that she was dead.

54 And he put them all out, and took her by the hand, and called, saying, Maid, [z]arise.

55 And her spirit came again, and she arose straightway: and he commanded to give her meat.

56 And her parents were astonished: but [a]he charged them that they should tell no man what was done.

9 Then [b]he called his twelve disciples together, and gave them power and authority over all devils, and to cure diseases.

2 And [c]he sent them to preach the kingdom of God, and to heal the sick.

3 [d]And he said unto them, Take nothing for *your* journey, neither staves, nor scrip, neither bread, neither money; neither have two coats apiece.

4 [e]And whatsoever house ye enter into, there abide, and thence depart.

5 [f]And whosoever will not receive you, when ye go out of that city, [g]shake off the very dust from your feet for a testimony against them.

6 [h]And they departed, and went through the towns, preaching the gospel, and healing every where.

7 ¶ [i]Now Herod the tetrarch heard of all that was done by him: and he was perplexed, because that it was said of some, that John was risen from the dead;

8 And of some, that Elias had appeared; and of others, that one of the old prophets was risen again.

9 And Herod said, John have I beheaded: but who is this, of whom I hear such things? [j]And he desired to see him.

10 ¶ [k]And the apostles, when they were returned, told him all that they had done. [l]And he took them, and went aside privately into a desert place belonging to the city called Bethsaida.

11 And the people, when they knew *it,* followed him: and he received them, and spake unto them of the kingdom of God,

8:31 [q]Rev. 20:3
8:37 [r]Matt. 8:34 [s]Acts 16:39
8:38 [t]Mark 5:18
8:41 [u]Matt. 9:18; Mark 5:22
8:43 [v]Matt. 9:20
8:46 [w]Mark 5:30; ch. 6:19
8:49 [x]Mark 5:35
8:52 [y]John 11:11
8:54 [z]ch. 7:14; John 11:43
8:56 [a]Matt. 8:4; Mark 5:43
9:1 [b]Matt. 10:1; Mark 3:13
9:2 [c]Matt. 10:7; Mark 6:12; ch. 10:1
9:3 [d]Matt. 10:9; Mark 6:8; ch. 10:4
9:4 [e]Matt. 10:11; Mark 6:10
9:5 [f]Matt. 10:14 [g]Acts 13:51
9:6 [h]Mark 6:12
9:7 [i]Matt. 14:1; Mark 6:14
9:9 [j]ch. 23:8
9:10 [k]Mark 6:30 [l]Matt. 14:13

and healed them that had need of healing.

12 [m]And when the day began to wear away, then came the twelve, and said unto him, Send the multitude away, that they may go into the towns and country round about, and lodge, and get victuals: for we are here in a desert place.

13 But he said unto them, Give ye them to eat. And they said, We have no more but five loaves and two fishes; except we should go and buy meat for all this people.

14 For they were about five thousand men. And he said to his disciples, Make them sit down by fifties in a company.

15 And they did so, and made them all sit down.

16 Then he took the five loaves and the two fishes, and looking up to heaven, he blessed them, and brake, and gave to the disciples to set before the multitude.

17 And they did eat, and were all filled: and there was taken up of fragments that remained to them twelve baskets.

18 ¶ [n]And it came to pass, as he was alone praying, his disciples were with him: and he asked them, saying, Whom say the people that I am?

19 They answering said, [o]John the Baptist; but some *say*, Elias; and others *say*, that one of the old prophets is risen again.

20 He said unto them, But whom say ye that I am? [p]Peter answering said, The Christ of God.

21 [q]And he straitly charged them, and commanded *them* to tell no man that thing;

22 Saying, [r]The Son of man must suffer many things, and be rejected of the elders and chief priests and scribes, and be slain, and be raised the third day.

23 ¶ [s]And he said to *them* all, If any *man* will come after me, let him deny himself, and take up his cross daily, and follow me.

24 For whosoever will save his life shall lose it: but whosoever will lose his life for my sake, the same shall save it.

25 [t]For what is a man advantaged, if he gain the whole world, and lose himself, or be cast away?

26 [u]For whosoever shall be ashamed of me and of my words, of him shall the Son of man be ashamed, when he shall come in his own glory, and *in his* Father's, and of the holy angels.

27 [v]But I tell you of a truth, there be some standing here, which shall not taste of death, till they see the kingdom of God.

28 ¶ [w]And it came to pass about an eight days after these sayings, he took Peter and John and James, and went up into a mountain to pray.

29 And as he prayed, the fashion of his countenance was altered, and his raiment *was* white *and* glistering.

30 And, behold, there talked with him two men, which were Moses and Elias:

31 Who appeared in glory, and spake of his decease which he should accomplish at Jerusalem.

32 But Peter and they that were with him [x]were heavy with sleep: and when they were awake, they saw his glory, and the two men that stood with him.

33 And it came to pass, as they departed from him, Peter said unto Jesus, Master, it is good for us to be here: and let us make three tabernacles; one for thee, and one for Moses, and one for Elias: not knowing what he said.

34 While he thus spake, there came a cloud, and overshadowed them: and they feared as they entered into the cloud.

35 And there came a voice out of the cloud, saying, [y]This is my beloved Son: [z]hear him.

36 And when the voice was past, Jesus was found alone. [a]And they kept *it* close, and told no man in those days any of those things which they had seen.

37 ¶ [b]And it came to pass, that on the next day, when they were come down from the hill, much people met him.

38 And, behold, a man of the company cried out, saying, Master, I beseech thee, look upon my son: for he is mine only child.

39 And, lo, a spirit taketh him, and he suddenly crieth out; and it teareth him that he foameth again, and bruising him hardly departeth from him.

40 And I besought thy disciples to cast him out; and they could not.

41 And Jesus answering said, O faithless and perverse generation, how long shall I be with you, and suffer you? Bring thy son hither.

42 And as he was yet a coming, the devil threw him down, and tare *him*. And Jesus rebuked the unclean spirit, and healed the child, and delivered him again to his father.

43 ¶ And they were all amazed at the mighty power of God. But while they wondered every one at all things which Jesus did, he said unto his disciples,

44 [c]Let these sayings sink down into your ears: for the Son of man shall be delivered into the hands of men.

45 [d]But they understood not this saying, and it was hid from them, that they perceived it not: and they feared to ask him of that saying.

46 ¶ [e]Then there arose a reasoning among them, which of them should be greatest.

47 And Jesus, perceiving the thought of their heart, took a child, and set him by him,

48 And said unto them, [f]Whosoever shall receive this child in my name receiveth me: and whosoever shall receive me receiveth him that sent me: [g]for he that is least among you all, the same shall be great.

49 ¶ [h]And John answered and said, Master, we saw one casting out devils in thy name; and we forbad him, because he followeth not with us.

50 And Jesus said unto him, Forbid *him* not: for [i]he that is not against us is for us.

51 ¶ And it came to pass, when the time

9:12 [m]Matt. 14:15; Mark 6:35; John 6:1
9:18 [n]Matt. 16:13; Mark 8:27
9:19 [o]Matt. 14:2; ver. 7
9:20 [p]Matt. 16:16; John 6:69
9:21 [q]Matt. 16:20
9:22 [r]Matt. 16:21
9:23 [s]Matt. 10:38; Mark 8:34; ch. 14:27
9:25 [t]Matt. 16:26; Mark 8:36
9:26 [u]Matt. 10:33; Mark 8:38; 2 Tim. 2:12
9:27 [v]Matt. 16:28; Mark 9:1
9:28 [w]Matt. 17:1; Mark 9:2
9:32 [x]Dan. 8:18
9:35 [y]Matt. 3:17 [z]Acts 3:22
9:36 [a]Matt. 17:9
9:37 [b]Matt. 17:14; Mark 9:14
9:44 [c]Matt. 17:22
9:45 [d]Mark 9:32; ch. 2:50
9:46 [e]Matt. 18:1; Mark 9:34
9:48 [f]Matt. 10:40; Mark 9:37; John 12:44 [g]Matt. 23:11
9:49 [h]Num. 11:28; Mark 9:38
9:50 [i]Matt. 12:30; ch. 11:23

was come that [j]he should be received up,
he stedfastly set his face to go to Jerusalem,
52 And sent messengers before his face:
and they went, and entered into a village of
the Samaritans, to make ready for him.
53 And [k]they did not receive him, because his face was as though he would go to
Jerusalem.
54 And when his disciples James and
John saw *this*, they said, Lord, wilt thou
that we command fire to come down from
heaven, and consume them, even as [l]Elias
did?
55 But he turned, and rebuked them, and
said, Ye know not what manner of spirit ye
are of.
56 For [m]the Son of man is not come to
destroy men's lives, but to save *them*. And
they went to another village.
57 ¶ [n]And it came to pass, that, as they
went in the way, a certain *man* said unto
him, Lord, I will follow thee whithersoever
thou goest.
58 And Jesus said unto him, Foxes have
holes, and birds of the air *have* nests; but
the Son of man hath not where to lay *his*
head.
59 [o]And he said unto another, Follow me.
But he said, Lord, suffer me first to go and
bury my father.
60 Jesus said unto him, Let the dead bury
their dead: but go thou and preach the kingdom of God.
61 And another also said, Lord, [p]I will
follow thee; but let me first go bid them farewell, which are at home at my house.
62 And Jesus said unto him, No man, having put his hand to the plough, and looking
back, is fit for the kingdom of God.

10 After these things the Lord appointed other seventy also, and
[q]sent them two and two before his face into
every city and place, whither he himself
would come.
2 Therefore said he unto them, [r]The harvest truly *is* great, but the labourers *are* few:
[s]pray ye therefore the Lord of the harvest,
that he would send forth labourers into his
harvest.
3 Go your ways: [t]behold, I send you forth
as lambs among wolves.
4 [u]Carry neither purse, nor scrip, nor
shoes: and [v]salute no man by the way.
5 [w]And into whatsoever house ye enter,
first say, Peace *be* to this house.
6 And if the son of peace be there, your
peace shall rest upon it: if not, it shall turn
to you again.
7 [x]And in the same house remain, [y]eat-
ing and drinking such things as they give:
for [z]the labourer is worthy of his hire. Go
not from house to house.
8 And into whatsoever city ye enter, and
they receive you, eat such things as are set
before you:
9 [a]And heal the sick that are therein, and
say unto them, [b]The kingdom of God is
come nigh unto you.

9:51 [j]Mark 16:19; Acts 1:2
9:53 [k]John 4:4
9:54 [l]2 Kings 1:10
9:56 [m]John 3:17
9:57 [n]Matt. 8:19
9:59 [o]Matt. 8:21
9:61 [p]1 Kings 19:20
10:1 [q]Matt. 10:1; Mark 6:7
10:2 [r]Matt. 9:37; John 4:35 [s]2 Thess. 3:1
10:3 [t]Matt. 10:16
10:4 [u]Matt. 10:9; Mark 6:8; ch. 9:3 [v]2 Kings 4:29
10:5 [w]Matt. 10:12
10:7 [x]Matt. 10:11 [y]1 Cor. 10:27 [z]Matt. 10:10; 1 Cor. 9:4; 1 Tim. 5:18
10:9 [a]ch. 9:2 [b]Matt. 3:2; ver. 11
10:11 [c]Matt. 10:14; ch. 9:5; Acts 13:51
10:12 [d]Matt. 10:15; Mark 6:11
10:13 [e]Matt. 11:21 [f]Ezek. 3:6
10:15 [g]Matt. 11:23 [h]Gen. 11:4; Deut. 1:28; Isa. 14:13; Jer. 51:53 [i]Ezek. 26:20
10:16 [j]Matt. 10:40; Mark 9:37; John 13:20 [k]1 Thess. 4:8 [l]John 5:23
10:17 [m]ver. 1
10:18 [n]John 12:31; Rev. 9:1
10:19 [o]Mark 16:18; Acts 28:5
10:20 [p]Ex. 32:32; Ps. 69:28; Isa. 4:3; Dan. 12:1; Phil. 4:3; Heb. 12:23; Rev. 13:8
10:21 [q]Matt. 11:25
10:22 [r]Matt. 28:18; John 3:35 [s]John 1:18
10:23 [t]Matt. 13:16
10:24 [u]1 Pet. 1:10
10:25 [v]Matt. 19:16
10:27 [w]Deut. 6:5 [x]Lev. 19:18

10 But into whatsoever city ye enter, and
they receive you not, go your ways out into
the streets of the same, and say,
11 [c]Even the very dust of your city,
which cleaveth on us, we do wipe off
against you: notwithstanding be ye sure of
this, that the kingdom of God is come nigh
unto you.
12 But I say unto you, that [d]it shall be
more tolerable in that day for Sodom, than
for that city.
13 [e]Woe unto thee, Chorazin! woe unto
thee, Bethsaida! [f]for if the mighty works
had been done in Tyre and Sidon, which
have been done in you, they had a great
while ago repented, sitting in sackcloth and
ashes.
14 But it shall be more tolerable for Tyre
and Sidon at the judgment, than for you.
15 [g]And thou, Capernaum, which art
[h]exalted to heaven, [i]shalt be thrust down
to hell.
16 [j]He that heareth you heareth me; and
[k]he that despiseth you despiseth me; [l]and
he that despiseth me despiseth him that sent
me.
17 ¶ And [m]the seventy returned again
with joy, saying, Lord, even the devils are
subject unto us through thy name.
18 And he said unto them, [n]I beheld Satan as lightning fall from heaven.
19 Behold, [o]I give unto you power to
tread on serpents and scorpions, and over
all the power of the enemy: and nothing
shall by any means hurt you.
20 Notwithstanding in this rejoice not,
that the spirits are subject unto you; but
rather rejoice, because [p]your names are
written in heaven.
21 ¶ [q]In that hour Jesus rejoiced in spirit,
and said, I thank thee, O Father, Lord of
heaven and earth, that thou hast hid these
things from the wise and prudent, and hast
revealed them unto babes: even so, Father;
for so it seemed good in thy sight.
22 [r]All things are delivered to me of my
Father: and [s]no man knoweth who the Son
is, but the Father; and who the Father is, but
the Son, and *he* to whom the Son will reveal
him.
23 ¶ And he turned him unto *his* disciples,
and said privately, [t]Blessed *are* the eyes
which see the things that ye see:
24 For I tell you, [u]that many prophets
and kings have desired to see those things
which ye see, and have not seen *them;* and
to hear those things which ye hear, and
have not heard *them*.
25 ¶ And, behold, a certain lawyer stood
up, and tempted him, saying, [v]Master, what
shall I do to inherit eternal life?
26 He said unto him, What is written in
the law? how readest thou?
27 And he answering said, [w]Thou shalt
love the Lord thy God with all thy heart, and
with all thy soul, and with all thy strength,
and with all thy mind; and [x]thy neighbour
as thyself.

28 And he said unto him, Thou hast answered right: this do, and [y]thou shalt live.

29 But he, willing to [z]justify himself, said unto Jesus, And who is my neighbour?

30 And Jesus answering said, A certain *man* went down from Jerusalem to Jericho, and fell among thieves, which stripped him of his raiment, and wounded *him,* and departed, leaving *him* half dead.

31 And by chance there came down a certain priest that way: and when he saw him, [a]he passed by on the other side.

32 And likewise a Levite, when he was at the place, came and looked *on him,* and passed by on the other side.

33 But a certain [b]Samaritan, as he journeyed, came where he was: and when he saw him, he had compassion *on him,*

34 And went to *him,* and bound up his wounds, pouring in oil and wine, and set him on his own beast, and brought him to an inn, and took care of him.

35 And on the morrow when he departed, he took out two pence, and gave *them* to the host, and said unto him, Take care of him; and whatsoever thou spendest more, when I come again, I will repay thee.

36 Which now of these three, thinkest thou, was neighbour unto him that fell among the thieves?

37 And he said, He that shewed mercy on him. Then said Jesus unto him, Go, and do thou likewise.

38 ¶ Now it came to pass, as they went, that he entered into a certain village: and a certain woman named [c]Martha received him into her house.

39 And she had a sister called Mary, [d]which also [e]sat at Jesus' feet, and heard his word.

40 But Martha was cumbered about much serving, and came to him, and said, Lord, dost thou not care that my sister hath left me to serve alone? bid her therefore that she help me.

41 And Jesus answered and said unto her, Martha, Martha, thou art careful and troubled about many things:

42 But [f]one thing is needful: and Mary hath chosen that good part, which shall not be taken away from her.

11 And it came to pass, that, as he was praying in a certain place, when he ceased, one of his disciples said unto him, Lord, teach us to pray, as John also taught his disciples.

2 And he said unto them, When ye pray, say, [g]Our Father which art in heaven, Hallowed be thy name. Thy kingdom come. Thy will be done, as in heaven, so in earth.

3 Give us day by day our daily bread.

4 And forgive us our sins; for we also forgive every one that is indebted to us. And lead us not into temptation; but deliver us from evil.

5 And he said unto them, Which of you shall have a friend, and shall go unto him at midnight, and say unto him, Friend, lend me three loaves;

6 For a friend of mine in his journey is come to me, and I have nothing to set before him?

7 And he from within shall answer and say, Trouble me not: the door is now shut, and my children are with me in bed; I cannot rise and give thee.

8 I say unto you, [h]Though he will not rise and give him, because he is his friend, yet because of his importunity he will rise and give him as many as he needeth.

9 [i]And I say unto you, Ask, and it shall be given you; seek, and ye shall find; knock, and it shall be opened unto you.

10 For every one that asketh receiveth; and he that seeketh findeth; and to him that knocketh it shall be opened.

11 [j]If a son shall ask bread of any of you that is a father, will he give him a stone? or if *he ask* a fish, will he for a fish give him a serpent?

12 Or if he shall ask an egg, will he offer him a scorpion?

13 If ye then, being evil, know how to give good gifts unto your children: how much more shall *your* heavenly Father give the Holy Spirit to them that ask him?

14 ¶ [k]And he was casting out a devil, and it was dumb. And it came to pass, when the devil was gone out, the dumb spake; and the people wondered.

15 But some of them said, [l]He casteth out devils through Beelzebub the chief of the devils.

16 And others, tempting *him,* [m]sought of him a sign from heaven.

17 [n]But [o]he, knowing their thoughts, said unto them, Every kingdom divided against itself is brought to desolation; and a house *divided* against a house falleth.

18 If Satan also be divided against himself, how shall his kingdom stand? because ye say that I cast out devils through Beelzebub.

19 And if I by Beelzebub cast out devils, by whom do your sons cast *them* out? therefore shall they be your judges.

20 But if I [p]with the finger of God cast out devils, no doubt the kingdom of God is come upon you.

21 [q]When a strong man armed keepeth his palace, his goods are in peace:

22 But [r]when a stronger than he shall come upon him, and overcome him, he taketh from him all his armour wherein he trusted, and divideth his spoils.

23 [s]He that is not with me is against me: and he that gathereth not with me scattereth.

24 [t]When the unclean spirit is gone out of a man, he walketh through dry places, seeking rest; and finding none, he saith, I will return unto my house whence I came out.

25 And when he cometh, he findeth *it* swept and garnished.

10:28 [y]Lev. 18:5; Neh. 9:29; Ezek. 20:11; Rom. 10:5
10:29 [z]ch. 16:15
10:31 [a]Ps. 38:11
10:33 [b]John 4:9
10:38 [c]John 11:1
10:39 [d]1 Cor. 7:32 [e]Luke 8:35; Acts 22:3
10:42 [f]Ps. 27:4
11:2 [g]Matt. 6:9
11:8 [h]ch. 18:1
11:9 [i]Matt. 7:7; Mark 11:24; John 15:7; Jam. 1:6; 1 John 3:22
11:11 [j]Matt. 7:9
11:14 [k]Matt. 9:32
11:15 [l]Matt. 9:34
11:16 [m]Matt. 12:38
11:17 [n]Matt. 12:25; Mark 3:24 [o]John 2:25
11:20 [p]Ex. 8:19
11:21 [q]Matt. 12:29; Mark 3:27
11:22 [r]Isa. 53:12; Col. 2:15
11:23 [s]Matt. 12:30
11:24 [t]Matt. 12:43

26 Then goeth he, and taketh *to him* seven other spirits more wicked than himself; and they enter in, and dwell there: and [u]the last *state* of that man is worse than the first.

27 ¶ And it came to pass, as he spake these things, a certain woman of the company lifted up her voice, and said unto him, [v]Blessed *is* the womb that bare thee, and the paps which thou hast sucked.

28 But he said, Yea [w]rather, blessed *are* they that hear the word of God, and keep it.

29 ¶ [x]And when the people were gathered thick together, he began to say, This is an evil generation: they seek a sign; and there shall no sign be given it, but the sign of Jonas the prophet.

30 For as [y]Jonas was a sign unto the Ninevites, so shall also the Son of man be to this generation.

31 [z]The queen of the south shall rise up in the judgment with the men of this generation, and condemn them: for she came from the utmost parts of the earth to hear the wisdom of Solomon; and, behold, a greater than Solomon *is* here.

32 The men of Nineve shall rise up in the judgment with this generation, and shall condemn it: for [a]they repented at the preaching of Jonas; and, behold, a greater than Jonas *is* here.

33 [b]No man, when he hath lighted a candle, putteth *it* in a secret place, neither under a bushel, but on a candlestick, that they which come in may see the light.

34 [c]The light of the body is the eye: therefore when thine eye is single, thy whole body also is full of light; but when *thine eye* is evil, thy body also *is* full of darkness.

35 Take heed therefore that the light which is in thee be not darkness.

36 If thy whole body therefore *be* full of light, having no part dark, the whole shall be full of light, as when the bright shining of a candle doth give thee light.

37 ¶ And as he spake, a certain Pharisee besought him to dine with him: and he went in, and sat down to meat.

38 And [d]when the Pharisee saw *it*, he marvelled that he had not first washed before dinner.

39 [e]And the Lord said unto him, Now do ye Pharisees make clean the outside of the cup and the platter; but [f]your inward part is full of ravening and wickedness.

40 *Ye* fools, did not he that made that which is without make that which is within also?

41 [g]But rather give alms of such things as ye have; and, behold, all things are clean unto you.

42 [h]But woe unto you, Pharisees! for ye tithe mint and rue and all manner of herbs, and pass over judgment and the love of God: these ought ye to have done, and not to leave the other undone.

43 [i]Woe unto you, Pharisees! for ye love the uppermost seats in the synagogues, and greetings in the markets.

44 [j]Woe unto you, scribes and Pharisees, hypocrites! [k]for ye are as graves which appear not, and the men that walk over *them* are not aware *of them.*

45 ¶ Then answered one of the lawyers, and said unto him, Master, thus saying thou reproachest us also.

46 And he said, Woe unto you also, *ye* lawyers! [l]for ye lade men with burdens grievous to be borne, and ye yourselves touch not the burdens with one of your fingers.

47 [m]Woe unto you! for ye build the sepulchres of the prophets, and your fathers killed them.

48 Truly ye bear witness that ye allow the deeds of your fathers: for they indeed killed them, and ye build their sepulchres.

49 Therefore also said the wisdom of God, [n]I will send them prophets and apostles, and *some* of them they shall slay and persecute:

50 That the blood of all the prophets which was shed from the foundation of the world, may be required of this generation;

51 [o]From the blood of Abel unto [p]the blood of Zacharias, which perished between the altar and the temple: verily I say unto you, It shall be required of this generation.

52 [q]Woe unto you, lawyers! for ye have taken away the key of knowledge: ye entered not in yourselves, and them that were entering in ye hindered.

53 And as he said these things unto them, the scribes and the Pharisees began to urge *him* vehemently, and to provoke him to speak of many things:

54 Laying wait for him, and [r]seeking to catch something out of his mouth, that they might accuse him.

12 In [s]the mean time, when there were gathered together an innumerable multitude of people, insomuch that they trode one upon another, he began to say unto his disciples first of all, [t]Beware ye of the leaven of the Pharisees, which is hypocrisy.

2 [u]For there is nothing covered, that shall not be revealed; neither hid, that shall not be known.

3 Therefore whatsoever ye have spoken in darkness shall be heard in the light; and that which ye have spoken in the ear in closets shall be proclaimed upon the housetops.

4 [v]And I say unto you [w]my friends, Be not afraid of them that kill the body, and after that have no more that they can do.

5 But I will forewarn you whom ye shall fear: Fear him, which after he hath killed hath power to cast into hell; yea, I say unto you, Fear him.

6 Are not five sparrows sold for two farthings, and not one of them is forgotten before God?

11:26 [u]John 5:14; Heb. 6:4; 2 Pet. 2:20
11:27 [v]ch. 1:28
11:28 [w]Matt. 7:21; ch. 8:21; Jam. 1:25
11:29 [x]Matt. 12:38
11:30 [y]Jonah 1:17
11:31 [z]1 Kings 10:1
11:32 [a]Jonah 3:5
11:33 [b]Matt. 5:15; Mark 4:21; ch. 8:16
11:34 [c]Matt. 6:22
11:38 [d]Mark 7:3
11:39 [e]Matt. 23:25 [f]Tit. 1:15
11:41 [g]Isa. 58:7; Dan. 4:27; ch. 12:33
11:42 [h]Matt. 23:23
11:43 [i]Matt. 23:6; Mark 12:38
11:44 [j]Matt. 23:27 [k]Ps. 5:9
11:46 [l]Matt. 23:4
11:47 [m]Matt. 23:29
11:49 [n]Matt. 23:34
11:51 [o]Gen. 4:8 [p]2 Chron. 24:20
11:52 [q]Matt. 23:13
11:54 [r]Mark 12:13
12:1 [s]Matt. 16:6; Mark 8:15 [t]Matt. 16:12
12:2 [u]Matt. 10:26; Mark 4:22; ch. 8:17
12:4 [v]Matt. 10:28; Isa. 51:7; Jer. 1:8 [w]John 15:14

7 But even the very hairs of your head are all numbered. Fear not therefore: ye are of more value than many sparrows.

8 [x]Also I say unto you, Whosoever shall confess me before men, him shall the Son of man also confess before the angels of God:

9 But he that denieth me before men shall be denied before the angels of God.

10 And [y]whosoever shall speak a word against the Son of man, it shall be forgiven him: but unto him that blasphemeth against the Holy Ghost it shall not be forgiven.

11 [z]And when they bring you unto the synagogues, and *unto* magistrates, and powers, take ye no thought how or what thing ye shall answer, or what ye shall say:

12 For the Holy Ghost shall teach you in the same hour what ye ought to say.

13 ¶ And one of the company said unto him, Master, speak to my brother, that he divide the inheritance with me.

14 And he said unto him, [a]Man, who made me a judge or a divider over you?

15 And he said unto them, [b]Take heed, and beware of covetousness: for a man's life consisteth not in the abundance of the things which he possesseth.

16 And he spake a parable unto them, saying, The ground of a certain rich man brought forth plentifully:

17 And he thought within himself, saying, What shall I do, because I have no room where to bestow my fruits?

18 And he said, This will I do: I will pull down my barns, and build greater; and there will I bestow all my fruits and my goods.

19 And I will say to my soul, [c]Soul, thou hast much goods laid up for many years; take thine ease, eat, drink, *and* be merry.

20 But God said unto him, *Thou* fool, this night [d]thy soul shall be required of thee: [e]then whose shall those things be, which thou hast provided?

21 So *is* he that layeth up treasure for himself, [f]and is not rich toward God.

22 ¶ And he said unto his disciples, Therefore I say unto you, [g]Take no thought for your life, what ye shall eat; neither for the body, what ye shall put on.

23 The life is more than meat, and the body *is more* than raiment.

24 Consider the ravens: for they neither sow nor reap; which neither have storehouse nor barn; and [h]God feedeth them: how much more are ye better than the fowls?

25 And which of you with taking thought can add to his stature one cubit?

26 If ye then be not able to do that thing which is least, why take ye thought for the rest?

27 Consider the lilies how they grow: they toil not, they spin not; and yet I say unto you, that Solomon in all his glory was not arrayed like one of these.

28 If then God so clothe the grass, which is to day in the field, and to morrow is cast into the oven; how much more *will he clothe* you, O ye of little faith?

29 And seek not ye what ye shall eat, or what ye shall drink, neither be ye of doubtful mind.

30 For all these things do the nations of the world seek after: and your Father knoweth that ye have need of these things.

31 ¶ [i]But rather seek ye the kingdom of God; and all these things shall be added unto you.

32 Fear not, little flock; for [j]it is your Father's good pleasure to give you the kingdom.

33 [k]Sell that ye have, and give alms; [l]provide yourselves bags which wax not old, a treasure in the heavens that faileth not, where no thief approacheth, neither moth corrupteth.

34 For where your treasure is, there will your heart be also.

35 [m]Let your loins be girded about, and [n]*your* lights burning;

36 And ye yourselves like unto men that wait for their lord, when he will return from the wedding; that when he cometh and knocketh, they may open unto him immediately.

37 [o]Blessed *are* those servants, whom the lord when he cometh shall find watching: verily I say unto you, that he shall gird himself, and make them to sit down to meat, and will come forth and serve them.

38 And if he shall come in the second watch, or come in the third watch, and find *them* so, blessed are those servants.

39 [p]And this know, that if the goodman of the house had known what hour the thief would come, he would have watched, and not have suffered his house to be broken through.

40 [q]Be ye therefore ready also: for the Son of man cometh at an hour when ye think not.

41 ¶ Then Peter said unto him, Lord, speakest thou this parable unto us, or even to all?

42 And the Lord said, [r]Who then is that faithful and wise steward, whom *his* lord shall make ruler over his household, to give *them their* portion of meat in due season?

43 Blessed *is* that servant, whom his lord when he cometh shall find so doing.

44 [s]Of a truth I say unto you, that he will make him ruler over all that he hath.

45 [t]But and if that servant say in his heart, My lord delayeth his coming; and shall begin to beat the menservants and maidens, and to eat and drink and to be drunken;

46 The lord of that servant will come in a day when he looketh not for *him,* and at an hour when he is not aware, and will cut him in sunder, and will appoint him his portion with the unbelievers.

47 And [u]that servant, which knew his lord's will, and prepared not *himself,* nei-

12:8 [x]Matt. 10:32; Mark 8:38; 2 Tim. 2:12; 1 John 2:23
12:10 [y]Matt. 12:31; Mark 3:28; 1 John 5:16
12:11 [z]Matt. 10:19; Mark 13:11; ch. 21:14
12:14 [a]John 18:36
12:15 [b]1 Tim. 6:7
12:19 [c]Eccl. 11:9; 1 Cor. 15:32; Jam. 5:5
12:20 [d]Job 20:22; Ps. 52:7; Jam. 4:14 [e]Ps. 39:6; Jer. 17:11
12:21 [f]Matt. 6:20; ver. 33; 1 Tim. 6:18; Jam. 2:5
12:22 [g]Matt. 6:25
12:24 [h]Job 38:41; Ps. 147:9
12:31 [i]Matt. 6:33
12:32 [j]Matt. 11:25
12:33 [k]Matt. 19:21; Acts 2:45 [l]Matt. 6:20; ch. 16:9; 1 Tim. 6:19
12:35 [m]Eph. 6:14; 1 Pet. 1:13 [n]Matt. 25:1
12:37 [o]Matt. 24:46
12:39 [p]Matt. 24:43; 1 Thess. 5:2; 2 Pet. 3:10; Rev. 3:3
12:40 [q]Matt. 24:44; Mark 13:33; ch. 21:34; 1 Thess. 5:6; 2 Pet. 3:12
12:42 [r]Matt. 24:45; 1 Cor. 4:2
12:44 [s]Matt. 24:47
12:45 [t]Matt. 24:48
12:47 [u]Num. 15:30; Deut. 25:2; John 9:41; Acts 17:30; Jam. 4:17

ther did according to his will, shall be beaten with many *stripes.*

48 [v]But he that knew not, and did commit things worthy of stripes, shall be beaten with few *stripes.* For unto whomsoever much is given, of him shall be much required; and to whom men have committed much, of him they will ask the more.

49 ¶ [w]I am come to send fire on the earth; and what will I, if it be already kindled?

50 But [x]I have a baptism to be baptized with; and how am I straitened till it be accomplished!

51 [y]Suppose ye that I am come to give peace on earth? I tell you, Nay; [z]but rather division:

52 [a]For from henceforth there shall be five in one house divided, three against two, and two against three.

53 The father shall be divided against the son, and the son against the father; the mother against the daughter, and the daughter against the mother; the mother in law against her daughter in law, and the daughter in law against her mother in law.

54 ¶ And he said also to the people, [b]When ye see a cloud rise out of the west, straightway ye say, There cometh a shower; and so it is.

55 And when *ye see* the south wind blow, ye say, There will be heat; and it cometh to pass.

56 *Ye* hypocrites, ye can discern the face of the sky and of the earth; but how is it that ye do not discern this time?

57 Yea, and why even of yourselves judge ye not what is right?

58 ¶ [c]When thou goest with thine adversary to the magistrate, [d]*as thou art* in the way, give diligence that thou mayest be delivered from him; lest he hale thee to the judge, and the judge deliver thee to the officer, and the officer cast thee into prison.

59 I tell thee, thou shalt not depart thence, till thou hast paid the very last mite.

13 There were present at that season some that told him of the Galileans, whose blood Pilate had mingled with their sacrifices.

2 And Jesus answering said unto them, Suppose ye that these Galileans were sinners above all the Galileans, because they suffered such things?

3 I tell you, Nay: but, except ye repent, ye shall all likewise perish.

4 Or those eighteen, upon whom the tower in Siloam fell, and slew them, think ye that they were sinners above all men that dwelt in Jerusalem?

5 I tell you, Nay: but, except ye repent, ye shall all likewise perish.

6 ¶ He spake also this parable; [e]A certain *man* had a fig tree planted in his vineyard; and he came and sought fruit thereon, and found none.

7 Then said he unto the dresser of his vineyard, Behold, these three years I come seeking fruit on this fig tree, and find none: cut it down; why cumbereth it the ground?

8 And he answering said unto him, Lord, let it alone this year also, till I shall dig about it, and dung *it:*

9 And if it bear fruit, *well:* and if not, *then* after that thou shalt cut it down.

10 And he was teaching in one of the synagogues on the sabbath.

11 ¶ And, behold, there was a woman which had a spirit of infirmity eighteen years, and was bowed together, and could in no wise lift up *herself.*

12 And when Jesus saw her, he called *her to him,* and said unto her, Woman, thou art loosed from thine infirmity.

13 [f]And he laid *his* hands on her: and immediately she was made straight, and glorified God.

14 And the ruler of the synagogue answered with indignation, because that Jesus had healed on the sabbath day, and said unto the people, [g]There are six days in which men ought to work: in them therefore come and be healed, and [h]not on the sabbath day.

15 The Lord then answered him, and said, *Thou* hypocrite, [i]doth not each one of you on the sabbath loose his ox or *his* ass from the stall, and lead *him* away to watering?

16 And ought not this woman, [j]being a daughter of Abraham, whom Satan hath bound, lo, these eighteen years, be loosed from this bond on the sabbath day?

17 And when he had said these things, all his adversaries were ashamed: and all the people rejoiced for all the glorious things that were done by him.

18 ¶ [k]Then said he, Unto what is the kingdom of God like? and whereunto shall I resemble it?

19 It is like a grain of mustard seed, which a man took, and cast into his garden; and it grew, and waxed a great tree; and the fowls of the air lodged in the branches of it.

20 And again he said, Whereunto shall I liken the kingdom of God?

21 It is like leaven, which a woman took and hid in three measures of meal, till the whole was leavened.

22 [l]And he went through the cities and villages, teaching, and journeying toward Jerusalem.

23 Then said one unto him, Lord, are there few that be saved? And he said unto them,

24 ¶ [m]Strive to enter in at the strait gate: for [n]many, I say unto you, will seek to enter in, and shall not be able.

25 [o]When once the master of the house is risen up, and [p]hath shut to the door, and ye begin to stand without, and to knock at the door, saying, [q]Lord, Lord, open unto us; and he shall answer and say unto you, [r]I know you not whence ye are:

26 Then shall ye begin to say, We have eaten and drunk in thy presence, and thou hast taught in our streets.

27 [s]But he shall say, I tell you, I know

12:48 [v]Lev. 5:17; 1 Tim. 1:13
12:49 [w]ver. 51
12:50 [x]Matt. 20:22; Mark 10:38
12:51 [y]Matt. 10:34; ver. 49 [z]Mic. 7:6; John 7:43
12:52 [a]Matt. 10:35
12:54 [b]Matt. 16:2
12:58 [c]Prov. 25:8; Matt. 5:25 [d]Ps. 32:6; Isa. 55:6
13:6 [e]Isa. 5:2; Matt. 21:19
13:13 [f]Mark 16:18; Acts 9:17
13:14 [g]Ex. 20:9 [h]Matt. 12:10; Mark 3:2; ch. 6:7
13:15 [i]ch. 14:5
13:16 [j]ch. 19:9
13:18 [k]Matt. 13:31; Mark 4:30
13:22 [l]Matt. 9:35; Mark 6:6
13:24 [m]Matt. 7:13 [n]John 7:34; Rom. 9:31
13:25 [o]Ps. 32:6; Isa. 55:6 [p]Matt. 25:10 [q]ch. 6:46 [r]Matt. 7:23
13:27 [s]Matt. 7:23; ver. 25

you not whence ye are; [t]depart from me, all *ye* workers of iniquity.

28 [u]There shall be weeping and gnashing of teeth, [v]when ye shall see Abraham, and Isaac, and Jacob, and all the prophets, in the kingdom of God, and you *yourselves* thrust out.

29 And they shall come from the east, and *from* the west, and from the north, and *from* the south, and shall sit down in the kingdom of God.

30 [w]And, behold, there are last which shall be first, and there are first which shall be last.

31 ¶ The same day there came certain of the Pharisees, saying unto him, Get thee out, and depart hence: for Herod will kill thee.

32 And he said unto them, Go ye, and tell that fox, Behold, I cast out devils, and I do cures to day and to morrow, and the third *day* [x]I shall be perfected.

33 Nevertheless I must walk to day, and to morrow, and the *day* following: for it cannot be that a prophet perish out of Jerusalem.

34 [y]O Jerusalem, Jerusalem, which killest the prophets, and stonest them that are sent unto thee; how often would I have gathered thy children together, as a hen *doth gather* her brood under *her* wings, and ye would not!

35 Behold, [z]your house is left unto you desolate: and verily I say unto you, Ye shall not see me, until *the time* come when ye shall say, [a]Blessed *is* he that cometh in the name of the Lord.

14 And it came to pass, as he went into the house of one of the chief Pharisees to eat bread on the sabbath day, that they watched him.

2 And, behold, there was a certain man before him which had the dropsy.

3 And Jesus answering spake unto the lawyers and Pharisees, saying, [b]Is it lawful to heal on the sabbath day?

4 And they held their peace. And he took *him,* and healed him, and let him go;

5 And answered them, saying, [c]Which of you shall have an ass or an ox fallen into a pit, and will not straightway pull him out on the sabbath day?

6 And they could not answer him again to these things.

7 ¶ And he put forth a parable to those which were bidden, when he marked how they chose out the chief rooms; saying unto them,

8 When thou art bidden of any *man* to a wedding, sit not down in the highest room; lest a more honourable man than thou be bidden of him;

9 And he that bade thee and him come and say to thee, Give this man place; and thou begin with shame to take the lowest room.

10 [d]But when thou art bidden, go and sit down in the lowest room; that when he that bade thee cometh, he may say unto thee, Friend, go up higher: then shalt thou have worship in the presence of them that sit at meat with thee.

11 [e]For whosoever exalteth himself shall be abased; and he that humbleth himself shall be exalted.

12 ¶ Then said he also to him that bade him, When thou makest a dinner or a supper, call not thy friends, nor thy brethren, neither thy kinsmen, nor *thy* rich neighbours; lest they also bid thee again, and a recompence be made thee.

13 But when thou makest a feast, call [f]the poor, the maimed, the lame, the blind:

14 And thou shalt be blessed; for they cannot recompense thee: for thou shalt be recompensed at the resurrection of the just.

15 ¶ And when one of them that sat at meat with him heard these things, he said unto him, [g]Blessed *is* he that shall eat bread in the kingdom of God.

16 [h]Then said he unto him, A certain man made a great supper, and bade many:

17 And [i]sent his servant at supper time to say to them that were bidden, Come; for all things are now ready.

18 And they all with one *consent* began to make excuse. The first said unto him, I have bought a piece of ground, and I must needs go and see it: I pray thee have me excused.

19 And another said, I have bought five yoke of oxen, and I go to prove them: I pray thee have me excused.

20 And another said, I have married a wife, and therefore I cannot come.

21 So that servant came, and shewed his lord these things. Then the master of the house being angry said to his servant, Go out quickly into the streets and lanes of the city, and bring in hither the poor, and the maimed, and the halt, and the blind.

22 And the servant said, Lord, it is done as thou hast commanded, and yet there is room.

23 And the lord said unto the servant, Go out into the highways and hedges, and compel *them* to come in, that my house may be filled.

24 For I say unto you, [j]That none of those men which were bidden shall taste of my supper.

25 ¶ And there went great multitudes with him: and he turned, and said unto them,

26 [k]If any *man* come to me, [l]and hate not his father, and mother, and wife, and children, and brethren, and sisters, [m]yea, and his own life also, he cannot be my disciple.

27 And [n]whosoever doth not bear his cross, and come after me, cannot be my disciple.

28 For [o]which of you, intending to build a tower, sitteth not down first, and counteth the cost, whether he have *sufficient* to finish *it?*

29 Lest haply, after he hath laid the foun-

13:27 [t]Ps. 6:8; Matt. 25:41
13:28 [u]Matt. 8:12 [v]Matt. 8:11
13:30 [w]Matt. 19:30; Mark 10:31
13:32 [x]Heb. 2:10
13:34 [y]Matt. 23:37
13:35 [z]Lev. 26:31; Ps. 69:25; Isa. 1:7; Dan. 9:27; Mic. 3:12 [a]Ps. 118:26; Matt. 21:9; Mark 11:10; ch. 19:38; John 12:13
14:3 [b]Matt. 12:10
14:5 [c]Ex. 23:5; Deut. 22:4; ch. 13:15
14:10 [d]Prov. 25:6
14:11 [e]Job 22:29; Ps. 18:27; Prov. 29:23; Matt. 23:12; ch. 18:14; Jam. 4:6; 1 Pet. 5:5
14:13 [f]Neh. 8:10
14:15 [g]Rev. 19:9
14:16 [h]Matt. 22:2
14:17 [i]Prov. 9:2
14:24 [j]Matt. 21:43; Acts 13:46
14:26 [k]Deut. 13:6; Matt. 10:37 [l]Rom. 9:13 [m]Rev. 12:11
14:27 [n]Matt. 16:24; Mark 8:34; ch. 9:23; 2 Tim. 3:12
14:28 [o]Prov. 24:27

dation, and is not able to finish *it,* all that behold *it* begin to mock him,

30 Saying, This man began to build, and was not able to finish.

31 Or what king, going to make war against another king, sitteth not down first, and consulteth whether he be able with ten thousand to meet him that cometh against him with twenty thousand?

32 Or else, while the other is yet a great way off, he sendeth an ambassage, and desireth conditions of peace.

33 So likewise, whosoever he be of you that forsaketh not all that he hath, he cannot be my disciple.

34 ¶ [p]Salt *is* good: but if the salt have lost his savour, wherewith shall it be seasoned?

35 It is neither fit for the land, nor yet for the dunghill; *but* men cast it out. He that hath ears to hear, let him hear.

15 Then [q]drew near unto him all the publicans and sinners for to hear him.

2 And the Pharisees and scribes murmured, saying, This man receiveth sinners, [r]and eateth with them.

3 ¶ And he spake this parable unto them, saying,

4 [s]What man of you, having an hundred sheep, if he lose one of them, doth not leave the ninety and nine in the wilderness, and go after that which is lost, until he find it?

5 And when he hath found *it,* he layeth *it* on his shoulders, rejoicing.

6 And when he cometh home, he calleth together *his* friends and neighbours, saying unto them, Rejoice with me; for I have found my sheep [t]which was lost.

7 I say unto you, that likewise joy shall be in heaven over one sinner that repenteth, [u]more than over ninety and nine just persons, which need no repentance.

8 ¶ Either what woman having ten pieces of silver, if she lose one piece, doth not light a candle, and sweep the house, and seek diligently till she find *it?*

9 And when she hath found *it,* she calleth *her* friends and *her* neighbours together, saying, Rejoice with me; for I have found the piece which I had lost.

10 Likewise, I say unto you, there is joy in the presence of the angels of God over one sinner that repenteth.

11 ¶ And he said, A certain man had two sons:

12 And the younger of them said to *his* father, Father, give me the portion of goods that falleth *to me.* And he divided unto them [v]*his* living.

13 And not many days after the younger son gathered all together, and took his journey into a far country, and there wasted his substance with riotous living.

14 And when he had spent all, there arose a mighty famine in that land; and he began to be in want.

15 And he went and joined himself to a citizen of that country; and he sent him into his fields to feed swine.

16 And he would fain have filled his belly with the husks that the swine did eat: and no man gave unto him.

17 And when he came to himself, he said, How many hired servants of my father's have bread enough and to spare, and I perish with hunger!

18 I will arise and go to my father, and will say unto him, Father, I have sinned against heaven, and before thee,

19 And am no more worthy to be called thy son: make me as one of thy hired servants.

20 And he arose, and came to his father. But [w]when he was yet a great way off, his father saw him, and had compassion, and ran, and fell on his neck, and kissed him.

21 And the son said unto him, Father, I have sinned against heaven, [x]and in thy sight, and am no more worthy to be called thy son.

22 But the father said to his servants, Bring forth the best robe, and put *it* on him; and put a ring on his hand, and shoes on *his* feet:

23 And bring hither the fatted calf, and kill *it;* and let us eat, and be merry:

24 [y]For this my son was dead, and is alive again; he was lost, and is found. And they began to be merry.

25 Now his elder son was in the field: and as he came and drew nigh to the house, he heard musick and dancing.

26 And he called one of the servants, and asked what these things meant.

27 And he said unto him, Thy brother is come; and thy father hath killed the fatted calf, because he hath received him safe and sound.

28 And he was angry, and would not go in: therefore came his father out, and intreated him.

29 And he answering said to *his* father, Lo, these many years do I serve thee, neither transgressed I at any time thy commandment: and yet thou never gavest me a kid, that I might make merry with my friends:

30 But as soon as this thy son was come, which hath devoured thy living with harlots, thou hast killed for him the fatted calf.

31 And he said unto him, Son, thou art ever with me, and all that I have is thine.

32 It was meet that we should make merry, and be glad: [z]for this thy brother was dead, and is alive again; and was lost, and is found.

16 And he said also unto his disciples, There was a certain rich man, which had a steward; and the same was accused unto him that he had wasted his goods.

2 And he called him, and said unto him, How is it that I hear this of thee? give an account of thy stewardship; for thou mayest be no longer steward.

3 Then the steward said within himself,

14:34 [p]Matt. 5:13; Mark 9:50
15:1 [q]Matt. 9:10
15:2 [r]Acts 11:3; Gal. 2:12
15:4 [s]Matt. 18:12
15:6 [t]1 Pet. 2:10
15:7 [u]ch. 5:32
15:12 [v]Mark 12:44
15:20 [w]Acts 2:39; Eph. 2:13
15:21 [x]Ps. 51:4
15:24 [y]ver. 32; Eph. 2:1; Rev. 3:1
15:32 [z]ver. 24

What shall I do? for my lord taketh away from me the stewardship: I cannot dig; to beg I am ashamed.

4 I am resolved what to do, that, when I am put out of the stewardship, they may receive me into their houses.

5 So he called every one of his lord's debtors *unto him,* and said unto the first, How much owest thou unto my lord?

6 And he said, An hundred measures of oil. And he said unto him, Take thy bill, and sit down quickly, and write fifty.

7 Then said he to another, And how much owest thou? And he said, An hundred measures of wheat. And he said unto him, Take thy bill, and write fourscore.

8 And the lord commended the unjust steward, because he had done wisely: for the children of this world are in their generation wiser than [a]the children of light.

9 And I say unto you, [b]Make to yourselves friends of the mammon of unrighteousness; that, when ye fail, they may receive you into everlasting habitations.

10 [c]He that is faithful in that which is least is faithful also in much: and he that is unjust in the least is unjust also in much.

11 If therefore ye have not been faithful in the unrighteous mammon, who will commit to your trust the true *riches*?

12 And if ye have not been faithful in that which is another man's, who shall give you that which is your own?

13 ¶ [d]No servant can serve two masters: for either he will hate the one, and love the other; or else he will hold to the one, and despise the other. Ye cannot serve God and mammon.

14 And the Pharisees also, [e]who were covetous, heard all these things: and they derided him.

15 And he said unto them, Ye are they which [f]justify yourselves before men; but [g]God knoweth your hearts: for [h]that which is highly esteemed among men is abomination in the sight of God.

16 [i]The law and the prophets *were* until John: since that time the kingdom of God is preached, and every man presseth into it.

17 [j]And it is easier for heaven and earth to pass, than one tittle of the law to fail.

18 [k]Whosoever putteth away his wife, and marrieth another, committeth adultery: and whosoever marrieth her that is put away from *her* husband committeth adultery.

19 ¶ There was a certain rich man, which was clothed in purple and fine linen, and fared sumptuously every day:

20 And there was a certain beggar named Lazarus, which was laid at his gate, full of sores,

21 And desiring to be fed with the crumbs which fell from the rich man's table: moreover the dogs came and licked his sores.

22 And it came to pass, that the beggar died, and was carried by the angels into Abraham's bosom: the rich man also died, and was buried;

23 And in hell he lift up his eyes, being in torments, and seeth Abraham afar off, and Lazarus in his bosom.

24 And he cried and said, Father Abraham, have mercy on me, and send Lazarus, that he may dip the tip of his finger in water, and [l]cool my tongue; for I [m]am tormented in this flame.

25 But Abraham said, Son, [n]remember that thou in thy lifetime receivedst thy good things, and likewise Lazarus evil things: but now he is comforted, and thou art tormented.

26 And beside all this, between us and you there is a great gulf fixed: so that they which would pass from hence to you cannot; neither can they pass to us, that *would come* from thence.

27 Then he said, I pray thee therefore, father, that thou wouldest send him to my father's house:

28 For I have five brethren; that he may testify unto them, lest they also come into this place of torment.

29 Abraham saith unto him, [o]They have Moses and the prophets; let them hear them.

30 And he said, Nay, father Abraham: but if one went unto them from the dead, they will repent.

31 And he said unto him, If they hear not Moses and the prophets, [p]neither will they be persuaded, though one rose from the dead.

17 Then said he unto the disciples, [q]It is impossible but that offences will come: but woe *unto him,* through whom they come!

2 It were better for him that a millstone were hanged about his neck, and he cast into the sea, than that he should offend one of these little ones.

3 ¶ Take heed to yourselves: [r]If thy brother trespass against thee, [s]rebuke him; and if he repent, forgive him.

4 And if he trespass against thee seven times in a day, and seven times in a day turn again to thee, saying, I repent; thou shalt forgive him.

5 And the apostles said unto the Lord, Increase our faith.

6 [t]And the Lord said, If ye had faith as a grain of mustard seed, ye might say unto this sycamine tree, Be thou plucked up by the root, and be thou planted in the sea; and it should obey you.

7 But which of you, having a servant plowing or feeding cattle, will say unto him by and by, when he is come from the field, Go and sit down to meat?

8 And will not rather say unto him, Make ready wherewith I may sup, and gird thyself, [u]and serve me, till I have eaten and drunken; and afterward thou shalt eat and drink?

9 Doth he thank that servant because he

16:8 [a]John 12:36; Eph. 5:8; 1 Thess. 5:5
16:9 [b]Dan. 4:27; Matt. 6:19; ch. 11:41; 1 Tim. 6:17
16:10 [c]Matt. 25:21; ch. 19:27
16:13 [d]Matt. 6:24
16:14 [e]Matt. 23:14
16:15 [f]ch. 10:29 [g]Ps. 7:9 [h]1 Sam. 16:7
16:16 [i]Matt. 4:17; Luke 7:29
16:17 [j]Ps. 102:27; Isa. 40:8; Matt. 5:18; 1 Pet. 1:25
16:18 [k]Matt. 5:32; Mark 10:11; 1 Cor. 7:10
16:24 [l]Zech. 14:12 [m]Isa. 66:24; Mark 9:44
16:25 [n]Job 21:13; ch. 6:24
16:29 [o]Isa. 8:20; John 5:39; Acts 15:21
16:31 [p]John 12:10
17:1 [q]Matt. 18:6; Mark 9:42; 1 Cor. 11:19
17:3 [r]Matt. 18:15 [s]Lev. 19:17; Prov. 17:10; Jam. 5:19
17:6 [t]Matt. 17:20; Mark 9:23
17:8 [u]ch. 12:37

did the things that were commanded him? I trow not.

10 So likewise ye, when ye shall have done all those things which are commanded you, say, We are [v]unprofitable servants: we have done that which was our duty to do.

11 ¶ And it came to pass, [w]as he went to Jerusalem, that he passed through the midst of Samaria and Galilee.

12 And as he entered into a certain village, there met him ten men that were lepers, [x]which stood afar off:

13 And they lifted up *their* voices, and said, Jesus, Master, have mercy on us.

14 And when he saw *them,* he said unto them, [y]Go shew yourselves unto the priests. And it came to pass, that, as they went, they were cleansed.

15 And one of them, when he saw that he was healed, turned back, and with a loud voice glorified God,

16 And fell down on *his* face at his feet, giving him thanks: and he was a Samaritan.

17 And Jesus answering said, Were there not ten cleansed? but where *are* the nine?

18 There are not found that returned to give glory to God, save this stranger.

19 [z]And he said unto him, Arise, go thy way: thy faith hath made thee whole.

20 ¶ And when he was demanded of the Pharisees, when the kingdom of God should come, he answered them and said, The kingdom of God cometh not with observation:

21 [a]Neither shall they say, Lo here! or, lo there! for, behold, [b]the kingdom of God is within you.

22 And he said unto the disciples, [c]The days will come, when ye shall desire to see one of the days of the Son of man, and ye shall not see *it.*

23 [d]And they shall say to you, See here; or, see there: go not after *them,* nor follow *them.*

24 [e]For as the lightning, that lighteneth out of the one *part* under heaven, shineth unto the other *part* under heaven; so shall also the Son of man be in his day.

25 [f]But first must he suffer many things, and be rejected of this generation.

26 [g]And as it was in the days of Noe, so shall it be also in the days of the Son of man.

27 They did eat, they drank, they married wives, they were given in marriage, until the day that Noe entered into the ark, and the flood came, and destroyed them all.

28 [h]Likewise also as it was in the days of Lot; they did eat, they drank, they bought, they sold, they planted, they builded;

29 But [i]the same day that Lot went out of Sodom it rained fire and brimstone from heaven, and destroyed *them* all.

30 Even thus shall it be in the day when the Son of man [j]is revealed.

31 In that day, he [k]which shall be upon the housetop, and his stuff in the house, let him not come down to take it away: and he

17:10 [v]Job 22:3; Ps. 16:2; Matt. 25:30; Rom. 3:12; 1 Cor. 9:16; Philem. 11
17:11 [w]Luke 9:51; John 4:4
17:12 [x]Lev. 13:46
17:14 [y]Lev. 13:2; Matt. 8:4; ch. 5:14
17:19 [z]Matt. 9:22; Mark 5:34; ch. 7:50
17:21 [a]ver. 23 [b]Rom. 14:17
17:22 [c]Matt. 9:15; John 17:12
17:23 [d]Matt. 24:23; Mark 13:21; ch. 21:8
17:24 [e]Matt. 24:27
17:25 [f]Mark 8:31; ch. 9:22
17:26 [g]Gen. 7; Matt. 24:37
17:28 [h]Gen. 19
17:29 [i]Gen. 19:16
17:30 [j]2 Thess. 1:7
17:31 [k]Matt. 24:17; Mark 13:15
17:32 [l]Gen. 19:26
17:33 [m]Matt. 10:39; Mark 8:35; ch. 9:24; John 12:25
17:34 [n]Matt. 24:40; 1 Thess. 4:17
17:37 [o]Job 39:30; Matt. 24:28
18:1 [p]ch. 11:5; Rom. 12:12; Eph. 6:18; Col. 4:2; 1 Thess. 5:17
18:5 [q]ch. 11:8
18:7 [r]Rev. 6:10
18:8 [s]Heb. 10:37; 2 Pet. 3:8
18:9 [t]ch. 10:29
18:11 [u]Ps. 135:2 [v]Isa. 1:15; Rev. 3:17
18:14 [w]Job 22:29; Matt. 23:12; ch. 14:11; Jam. 4:6; 1 Pet. 5:5
18:15 [x]Matt. 19:13; Mark 10:13

that is in the field, let him likewise not return back.

32 [l]Remember Lot's wife.

33 [m]Whosoever shall seek to save his life shall lose it; and whosoever shall lose his life shall preserve it.

34 [n]I tell you, in that night there shall be two *men* in one bed; the one shall be taken, and the other shall be left.

35 Two *women* shall be grinding together; the one shall be taken, and the other left.

36 Two *men* shall be in the field; the one shall be taken, and the other left.

37 And they answered and said unto him, [o]Where, Lord? And he said unto them, Wheresoever the body *is,* thither will the eagles be gathered together.

18 And he spake a parable unto them *to this end,* that men ought [p]always to pray, and not to faint;

2 Saying, There was in a city a judge, which feared not God, neither regarded man:

3 And there was a widow in that city; and she came unto him, saying, Avenge me of mine adversary.

4 And he would not for a while: but afterward he said within himself, Though I fear not God, nor regard man;

5 [q]Yet because this widow troubleth me, I will avenge her, lest by her continual coming she weary me.

6 And the Lord said, Hear what the unjust judge saith.

7 And [r]shall not God avenge his own elect, which cry day and night unto him, though he bear long with them?

8 I tell you [s]that he will avenge them speedily. Nevertheless when the Son of man cometh, shall he find faith on the earth?

9 And he spake this parable unto certain [t]which trusted in themselves that they were righteous, and despised others:

10 Two men went up into the temple to pray; the one a Pharisee, and the other a publican.

11 The Pharisee [u]stood and prayed thus with himself, [v]God, I thank thee, that I am not as other men *are,* extortioners, unjust, adulterers, or even as this publican.

12 I fast twice in the week, I give tithes of all that I possess.

13 And the publican, standing afar off, would not lift up so much as *his* eyes unto heaven, but smote upon his breast, saying, God be merciful to me a sinner.

14 I tell you, this man went down to his house justified *rather* than the other: [w]for every one that exalteth himself shall be abased; and he that humbleth himself shall be exalted.

15 [x]And they brought unto him also infants, that he would touch them: but when *his* disciples saw *it,* they rebuked them.

16 But Jesus called them *unto him,* and said, Suffer little children to come unto me,

and forbid them not: for [y]of such is the kingdom of God.

17 [z]Verily I say unto you, Whosoever shall not receive the kingdom of God as a little child shall in no wise enter therein.

18 [a]And a certain ruler asked him, saying, Good Master, what shall I do to inherit eternal life?

19 And Jesus said unto him, Why callest thou me good? none *is* good, save one, *that is,* God.

20 Thou knowest the commandments, [b]Do not commit adultery, Do not kill, Do not steal, Do not bear false witness, [c]Honour thy father and thy mother.

21 And he said, All these have I kept from my youth up.

22 Now when Jesus heard these things, he said unto him, Yet lackest thou one thing: [d]sell all that thou hast, and distribute unto the poor, and thou shalt have treasure in heaven: and come, follow me.

23 And when he heard this, he was very sorrowful: for he was very rich.

24 And when Jesus saw that he was very sorrowful, he said, [e]How hardly shall they that have riches enter into the kingdom of God!

25 For it is easier for a camel to go through a needle's eye, than for a rich man to enter into the kingdom of God.

26 And they that heard *it* said, Who then can be saved?

27 And he said, [f]The things which are impossible with men are possible with God.

28 [g]Then Peter said, Lo, we have left all, and followed thee.

29 And he said unto them, Verily I say unto you, [h]There is no man that hath left house, or parents, or brethren, or wife, or children, for the kingdom of God's sake,

30 [i]Who shall not receive manifold more in this present time, and in the world to come life everlasting.

31 ¶ [j]Then he took *unto him* the twelve, and said unto them, Behold, we go up to Jerusalem, and all things [k]that are written by the prophets concerning the Son of man shall be accomplished.

32 For [l]he shall be delivered unto the Gentiles, and shall be mocked, and spitefully entreated, and spitted on:

33 And they shall scourge *him,* and put him to death: and the third day he shall rise again.

34 [m]And they understood none of these things: and this saying was hid from them, neither knew they the things which were spoken.

35 ¶ [n]And it came to pass, that as he was come nigh unto Jericho, a certain blind man sat by the way side begging:

36 And hearing the multitude pass by, he asked what it meant.

37 And they told him, that Jesus of Nazareth passeth by.

38 And he cried, saying, Jesus, *thou* son of David, have mercy on me.

39 And they which went before rebuked him, that he should hold his peace: but he cried so much the more, *Thou* son of David, have mercy on me.

40 And Jesus stood, and commanded him to be brought unto him: and when he was come near, he asked him,

41 Saying, What wilt thou that I shall do unto thee? And he said, Lord, that I may receive my sight.

42 And Jesus said unto him, Receive thy sight: [o]thy faith hath saved thee.

43 And immediately he received his sight, and followed him, [p]glorifying God: and all the people, when they saw *it,* gave praise unto God.

19 And *Jesus* entered and passed through Jericho.

2 And, behold, *there was* a man named Zaccheus, which was the chief among the publicans, and he was rich.

3 And he sought to see Jesus who he was; and could not for the press, because he was little of stature.

4 And he ran before, and climbed up into a sycomore tree to see him: for he was to pass that *way.*

5 And when Jesus came to the place, he looked up, and saw him, and said unto him, Zaccheus, make haste, and come down; for to day I must abide at thy house.

6 And he made haste, and came down, and received him joyfully.

7 And when they saw *it,* they all murmured, saying, [q]That he was gone to be guest with a man that is a sinner.

8 And Zaccheus stood, and said unto the Lord; Behold, Lord, the half of my goods I give to the poor; and if I have taken any thing from any man by [r]false accusation, [s]I restore *him* fourfold.

9 And Jesus said unto him, This day is salvation come to this house, forsomuch as [t]he also is [u]a son of Abraham.

10 [v]For the Son of man is come to seek and to save that which was lost.

11 And as they heard these things, he added and spake a parable, because he was nigh to Jerusalem, and because [w]they thought that the kingdom of God should immediately appear.

12 [x]He said therefore, A certain nobleman went into a far country to receive for himself a kingdom, and to return.

13 And he called his ten servants, and delivered them ten pounds, and said unto them, Occupy till I come.

14 [y]But his citizens hated him, and sent a message after him, saying, We will not have this *man* to reign over us.

15 And it came to pass, that when he was returned, having received the kingdom, then he commanded these servants to be called unto him, to whom he had given the money, that he might know how much every man had gained by trading.

16 Then came the first, saying, Lord, thy pound hath gained ten pounds.

18:16 [y]1 Cor. 14:20; 1 Pet. 2:2
18:17 [z]Mark 10:15
18:18 [a]Matt. 19:16; Mark 10:17
18:20 [b]Ex. 20:12; Deut. 5:16-20; Rom. 13:9 [c]Eph. 6:2; Col. 3:20
18:22 [d]Matt. 6:19; 1 Tim. 6:19
18:24 [e]Prov. 11:28; Matt. 19:23; Mark 10:23
18:27 [f]Jer. 32:17; Zech. 8:6; Matt. 19:26; ch. 1:37
18:28 [g]Matt. 19:27
18:29 [h]Deut. 33:9
18:30 [i]Job 42:10
18:31 [j]Matt. 16:21; Mark 10:32 [k]Ps. 22; Isa. 53
18:32 [l]Matt. 27:2; ch. 23:1; John 18:28; Acts 3:13
18:34 [m]Mark 9:32; ch. 2:50; John 10:6
18:35 [n]Matt. 20:29; Mark 10:46
18:42 [o]ch. 17:19
18:43 [p]ch. 5:26; Acts 4:21
19:7 [q]Matt. 9:11; ch. 5:30
19:8 [r]ch. 3:14 [s]Ex. 22:1; 1 Sam. 12:3; 2 Sam. 12:6
19:9 [t]Rom. 4:11; Gal. 3:7 [u]ch. 13:16
19:10 [v]Matt. 10:6
19:11 [w]Acts 1:6
19:12 [x]Matt. 25:14; Mark 13:34
19:14 [y]John 1:11

17 And he said unto him, Well, thou good servant: because thou hast been [z]faithful in a very little, have thou authority over ten cities.

18 And the second came, saying, Lord, thy pound hath gained five pounds.

19 And he said likewise to him, Be thou also over five cities.

20 And another came, saying, Lord, behold, *here is* thy pound, which I have kept laid up in a napkin:

21 [a]For I feared thee, because thou art an austere man: thou takest up that thou layedst not down, and reapest that thou didst not sow.

22 And he saith unto him, [b]Out of thine own mouth will I judge thee, *thou* wicked servant. [c]Thou knewest that I was an austere man, taking up that I laid not down, and reaping that I did not sow:

23 Wherefore then gavest not thou my money into the bank, that at my coming I might have required mine own with usury?

24 And he said unto them that stood by, Take from him the pound, and give *it* to him that hath ten pounds.

25 (And they said unto him, Lord, he hath ten pounds.)

26 For I say unto you, [d]That unto every one which hath shall be given; and from him that hath not, even that he hath shall be taken away from him.

27 But those mine enemies, which would not that I should reign over them, bring hither, and slay *them* before me.

28 ¶ And when he had thus spoken, [e]he went before, ascending up to Jerusalem.

29 [f]And it came to pass, when he was come nigh to Bethphage and Bethany, at the mount called *the mount* of Olives, he sent two of his disciples,

30 Saying, Go ye into the village over against *you;* in the which at your entering ye shall find a colt tied, whereon yet never man sat: loose him, and bring *him hither.*

31 And if any man ask you, Why do ye loose *him?* thus shall ye say unto him, Because the Lord hath need of him.

32 And they that were sent went their way, and found even as he had said unto them.

33 And as they were loosing the colt, the owners thereof said unto them, Why loose ye the colt?

34 And they said, The Lord hath need of him.

35 And they brought him to Jesus: [g]and they cast their garments upon the colt, and they set Jesus thereon.

36 [h]And as he went, they spread their clothes in the way.

37 And when he was come nigh, even now at the descent of the mount of Olives, the whole multitude of the disciples began to rejoice and praise God with a loud voice for all the mighty works that they had seen;

38 Saying, [i]Blessed *be* the King that cometh in the name of the Lord: [j]peace in heaven, and glory in the highest.

39 And some of the Pharisees from among the multitude said unto him, Master, rebuke thy disciples.

40 And he answered and said unto them, I tell you that, if these should hold their peace, [k]the stones would immediately cry out.

41 ¶ And when he was come near, he beheld the city, and [l]wept over it,

42 Saying, If thou hadst known, even thou, at least in this thy day, the things *which belong* unto thy peace! but now they are hid from thine eyes.

43 For the days shall come upon thee, that thine enemies shall [m]cast a trench about thee, and compass thee round, and keep thee in on every side,

44 And [n]shall lay thee even with the ground, and thy children within thee; and [o]they shall not leave in thee one stone upon another; [p]because thou knewest not the time of thy visitation.

45 [q]And he went into the temple, and began to cast out them that sold therein, and them that bought;

46 Saying unto them, [r]It is written, My house is the house of prayer: but [s]ye have made it a den of thieves.

47 And he taught daily in the temple. But [t]the chief priests and the scribes and the chief of the people sought to destroy him,

48 And could not find what they might do: for all the people were very attentive to hear him.

20

And [u]it came to pass, *that* on one of those days, as he taught the people in the temple, and preached the gospel, the chief priests and the scribes came upon *him* with the elders,

2 And spake unto him, saying, Tell us, [v]by what authority doest thou these things? or who is he that gave thee this authority?

3 And he answered and said unto them, I will also ask you one thing; and answer me:

4 The baptism of John, was it from heaven, or of men?

5 And they reasoned with themselves, saying, If we shall say, From heaven; he will say, Why then believed ye him not?

6 But and if we say, Of men; all the people will stone us: [w]for they be persuaded that John was a prophet.

7 And they answered, that they could not tell whence *it was.*

8 And Jesus said unto them, Neither tell I you by what authority I do these things.

9 Then began he to speak to the people this parable; [x]A certain man planted a vineyard, and let it forth to husbandmen, and went into a far country for a long time.

10 And at the season he sent a servant to the husbandmen, that they should give him of the fruit of the vineyard: but the husbandmen beat him, and sent *him* away empty.

11 And again he sent another servant:

19:17 [z]Matt. 25:21; ch. 16:10
19:21 [a]Matt. 25:24
19:22 [b]2 Sam. 1:16; Job 15:6; Matt. 12:37 [c]Matt. 25:26
19:26 [d]Matt. 13:12; Mark 4:25; ch. 8:18
19:28 [e]Mark 10:32
19:29 [f]Matt. 21:1; Mark 11:1
19:35 [g]2 Kings 9:13; Matt. 21:7; Mark 11:7; John 12:14
19:36 [h]Matt. 21:8
19:38 [i]Ps. 118:26; ch. 13:35 [j]ch. 2:14; Eph. 2:14
19:40 [k]Hab. 2:11
19:41 [l]John 11:35
19:43 [m]Isa. 29:3; Jer. 6:3; ch. 21:20
19:44 [n]1 Kings 9:7; Mic. 3:12 [o]Matt. 24:2; Mark 13:2; ch. 21:6 [p]Dan. 9:24; ch. 1:68; 1 Pet. 2:12
19:45 [q]Matt. 21:12; Mark 11:11; John 2:14
19:46 [r]Isa. 56:7 [s]Jer. 7:11
19:47 [t]Mark 11:18; John 7:19
20:1 [u]Matt. 21:23
20:2 [v]Acts 4:7
20:6 [w]Matt. 14:5; ch. 7:29
20:9 [x]Matt. 21:33; Mark 12:1

and they beat him also, and entreated *him*
shamefully, and sent *him* away empty.
12 And again he sent a third: and they
wounded him also, and cast *him* out.
13 Then said the lord of the vineyard,
What shall I do? I will send my beloved son:
it may be they will reverence *him* when they
see him.
14 But when the husbandmen saw him,
they reasoned among themselves, saying,
This is the heir: come, let us kill him, that
the inheritance may be ours.
15 So they cast him out of the vineyard,
and killed *him*. What therefore shall the
lord of the vineyard do unto them?
16 He shall come and destroy these husbandmen, and shall give the vineyard to
others. And when they heard *it*, they said,
God forbid.
17 And he beheld them, and said, What is
this then that is written, [y]The stone which
the builders rejected, the same is become
the head of the corner?
18 Whosoever shall fall upon that stone
shall be broken; but [z]on whomsoever it
shall fall, it will grind him to powder.
19 ¶ And the chief priests and the scribes
the same hour sought to lay hands on him;
and they feared the people: for they perceived that he had spoken this parable
against them.
20 [a]And they watched *him*, and sent
forth spies, which should feign themselves
just men, that they might take hold of his
words, that so they might deliver him unto
the power and authority of the governor.
21 And they asked him, saying, [b]Master,
we know that thou sayest and teachest
rightly, neither acceptest thou the person *of*
any, but teachest the way of God truly:
22 Is it lawful for us to give tribute unto
Caesar, or no?
23 But he perceived their craftiness, and
said unto them, Why tempt ye me?
24 Shew me a penny. Whose image and
superscription hath it? They answered and
said, Caesar's.
25 And he said unto them, Render therefore unto Caesar the things which be Caesar's, and unto God the things which be
God's.
26 And they could not take hold of his
words before the people: and they marvelled at his answer, and held their peace.
27 ¶ [c]Then came to *him* certain of the
Sadducees, [d]which deny that there is any
resurrection; and they asked him,
28 Saying, Master, [e]Moses wrote unto us,
If any man's brother die, having a wife, and
he die without children, that his brother
should take his wife, and raise up seed unto
his brother.
29 There were therefore seven brethren:
and the first took a wife, and died without
children.
30 And the second took her to wife, and
he died childless.
31 And the third took her; and in like

20:17 [y]Ps. 118:22; Matt. 21:42
20:18 [z]Dan. 2:34; Matt. 21:44
20:20 [a]Matt. 22:15
20:21 [b]Matt. 22:16; Mark 12:14
20:27 [c]Matt. 22:23; Mark 12:18 [d]Acts 23:6
20:28 [e]Deut. 25:5
20:36 [f]1 Cor. 15:42; 1 John 3:2 [g]Rom. 8:23
20:37 [h]Ex. 3:6
20:38 [i]Rom. 6:10
20:41 [j]Matt. 22:42; Mark 12:35
20:42 [k]Ps. 110:1; Acts 2:34
20:45 [l]Matt. 23:1; Mark 12:38
20:46 [m]Matt. 23:5 [n]ch. 11:43
20:47 [o]Matt. 23:14
21:1 [p]Mark 12:41
21:3 [q]2 Cor. 8:12
21:5 [r]Matt. 24:1; Mark 13:1
21:6 [s]ch. 19:44
21:8 [t]Matt. 24:4; Mark 13:5; Eph. 5:6; 2 Thess. 2:3

manner the seven also: and they left no children, and died.
32 Last of all the woman died also.
33 Therefore in the resurrection whose
wife of them is she? for seven had her to
wife.
34 And Jesus answering said unto them,
The children of this world marry, and are
given in marriage:
35 But they which shall be accounted
worthy to obtain that world, and the resurrection from the dead, neither marry, nor
are given in marriage:
36 Neither can they die any more: for
[f]they are equal unto the angels; and are the
children of God, [g]being the children of the
resurrection.
37 Now that the dead are raised, [h]even
Moses shewed at the bush, when he calleth
the Lord the God of Abraham, and the God
of Isaac, and the God of Jacob.
38 For he is not a God of the dead, but of
the living: for [i]all live unto him.
39 ¶ Then certain of the scribes answering said, Master, thou hast well said.
40 And after that they durst not ask him
any *question at all*.
41 And he said unto them, [j]How say they
that Christ is David's son?
42 And David himself saith in the book of
Psalms, [k]The LORD said unto my Lord, Sit
thou on my right hand,
43 Till I make thine enemies thy footstool.
44 David therefore calleth him Lord, how
is he then his son?
45 ¶ [l]Then in the audience of all the people he said unto his disciples,
46 [m]Beware of the scribes, which desire
to walk in long robes, and [n]love greetings
in the markets, and the highest seats in the
synagogues, and the chief rooms at feasts;
47 [o]Which devour widows' houses, and
for a shew make long prayers: the same
shall receive greater damnation.

21

And he looked up, [p]and saw the rich
men casting their gifts into the treasury.
2 And he saw also a certain poor widow
casting in thither two mites.
3 And he said, Of a truth I say unto you,
[q]that this poor widow hath cast in more
than they all:
4 For all these have of their abundance
cast in unto the offerings of God: but she of
her penury hath cast in all the living that
she had.
5 ¶ [r]And as some spake of the temple,
how it was adorned with goodly stones and
gifts, he said,
6 *As for* these things which ye behold, the
days will come, in the which [s]there shall
not be left one stone upon another, that
shall not be thrown down.
7 And they asked him, saying, Master,
but when shall these things be? and what
sign *will there be* when these things shall
come to pass?
8 And he said, [t]Take heed that ye be not

deceived: for many shall come in my name, saying, I am *Christ;* and the time draweth near: go ye not therefore after them.

9 But when ye shall hear of wars and commotions, be not terrified: for these things must first come to pass; but the end *is* not by and by.

10 [u]Then said he unto them, Nation shall rise against nation, and kingdom against kingdom:

11 And great earthquakes shall be in divers places, and famines, and pestilences; and fearful sights and great signs shall there be from heaven.

12 [v]But before all these, they shall lay their hands on you, and persecute *you,* delivering *you* up to the synagogues, and [w]into prisons, [x]being brought before kings and rulers [y]for my name's sake.

13 And [z]it shall turn to you for a testimony.

14 [a]Settle *it* therefore in your hearts, not to meditate before what ye shall answer:

15 For I will give you a mouth and wisdom, [b]which all your adversaries shall not be able to gainsay nor resist.

16 [c]And ye shall be betrayed both by parents, and brethren, and kinsfolks, and friends; and [d]*some* of you shall they cause to be put to death.

17 And [e]ye shall be hated of all *men* for my name's sake.

18 [f]But there shall not an hair of your head perish.

19 In your patience possess ye your souls.

20 [g]And when ye shall see Jerusalem compassed with armies, then know that the desolation thereof is nigh.

21 Then let them which are in Judaea flee to the mountains; and let them which are in the midst of it depart out; and let not them that are in the countries enter thereinto.

22 For these be the days of vengeance, that [h]all things which are written may be fulfilled.

23 [i]But woe unto them that are with child, and to them that give suck, in those days! for there shall be great distress in the land, and wrath upon this people.

24 And they shall fall by the edge of the sword, and shall be led away captive into all nations: and Jerusalem shall be trodden down of the Gentiles, [j]until the times of the Gentiles be fulfilled.

25 ¶ [k]And there shall be signs in the sun, and in the moon, and in the stars; and upon the earth distress of nations, with perplexity; the sea and the waves roaring;

26 Men's hearts failing them for fear, and for looking after those things which are coming on the earth: [l]for the powers of heaven shall be shaken.

27 And then shall they see the Son of man [m]coming in a cloud with power and great glory.

28 And when these things begin to come to pass, then look up, and lift up your heads; for [n]your redemption draweth nigh.

29 [o]And he spake to them a parable; Behold the fig tree, and all the trees;

30 When they now shoot forth, ye see and know of your own selves that summer is now nigh at hand.

31 So likewise ye, when ye see these things come to pass, know ye that the kingdom of God is nigh at hand.

32 Verily I say unto you, This generation shall not pass away, till all be fulfilled.

33 [p]Heaven and earth shall pass away: but my words shall not pass away.

34 ¶ And [q]take heed to yourselves, lest at any time your hearts be overcharged with surfeiting, and drunkenness, and cares of this life, and *so* that day come upon you unawares.

35 For [r]as a snare shall it come on all them that dwell on the face of the whole earth.

36 [s]Watch ye therefore, and [t]pray always, that ye may be accounted worthy to escape all these things that shall come to pass, and [u]to stand before the Son of man.

37 [v]And in the day time he was teaching in the temple; and [w]at night he went out, and abode in the mount that is called *the mount* of Olives.

38 And all the people came early in the morning to him in the temple, for to hear him.

22 Now [x]the feast of unleavened bread drew nigh, which is called the Passover.

2 And [y]the chief priests and scribes sought how they might kill him; for they feared the people.

3 ¶ [z]Then entered Satan into Judas surnamed Iscariot, being of the number of the twelve.

4 And he went his way, and communed with the chief priests and captains, how he might betray him unto them.

5 And they were glad, and [a]covenanted to give him money.

6 And he promised, and sought opportunity to betray him unto them in the absence of the multitude.

7 ¶ [b]Then came the day of unleavened bread, when the passover must be killed.

8 And he sent Peter and John, saying, Go and prepare us the passover, that we may eat.

9 And they said unto him, Where wilt thou that we prepare?

10 And he said unto them, Behold, when ye are entered into the city, there shall a man meet you, bearing a pitcher of water; follow him into the house where he entereth in.

11 And ye shall say unto the goodman of the house, The Master saith unto thee, Where is the guestchamber, where I shall eat the passover with my disciples?

12 And he shall shew you a large upper room furnished: there make ready.

13 And they went, and found as he had

21:10 [u]Matt. 24:7
21:12 [v]Mark 13:9; Rev. 2:10 [w]Acts 4:3 [x]Acts 25:23 [y]1 Pet. 2:13
21:13 [z]Phil. 1:28; 2 Thess. 1:5
21:14 [a]Matt. 10:19; Mark 13:11; ch. 12:11
21:15 [b]Acts 6:10
21:16 [c]Mic. 7:6; Mark 13:12 [d]Acts 7:59
21:17 [e]Matt. 10:22
21:18 [f]Matt. 10:30
21:20 [g]Matt. 24:15; Mark 13:14
21:22 [h]Dan. 9:26; Zech. 11:1
21:23 [i]Matt. 24:19
21:24 [j]Dan. 9:27; Rom. 11:25
21:25 [k]Matt. 24:29; Mark 13:24; 2 Pet. 3:10
21:26 [l]Matt. 24:29
21:27 [m]Matt. 24:30; Rev. 1:7
21:28 [n]Rom. 8:19
21:29 [o]Matt. 24:32; Mark 13:28
21:33 [p]Matt. 24:35
21:34 [q]Rom. 13:13; 1 Thess. 5:6; 1 Pet. 4:7
21:35 [r]1 Thess. 5:2; 2 Pet. 3:10; Rev. 3:3
21:36 [s]Matt. 24:42; Mark 13:33 [t]ch. 18:1 [u]Ps. 1:5; Eph. 6:13
21:37 [v]John 8:1 [w]ch. 22:39
22:1 [x]Matt. 26:2; Mark 14:1
22:2 [y]Ps. 2:2; John 11:47; Acts 4:27
22:3 [z]Matt. 26:14; Mark 14:10; John 13:2
22:5 [a]Zech. 11:12
22:7 [b]Matt. 26:17; Mark 14:12

said unto them: and they made ready the passover.

14 [c]And when the hour was come, he sat down, and the twelve apostles with him.

15 And he said unto them, With desire I have desired to eat this passover with you before I suffer:

16 For I say unto you, I will not any more eat thereof, [d]until it be fulfilled in the kingdom of God.

17 And he took the cup, and gave thanks, and said, Take this, and divide *it* among yourselves:

18 For [e]I say unto you, I will not drink of the fruit of the vine, until the kingdom of God shall come.

19 ¶ [f]And he took bread, and gave thanks, and brake *it*, and gave unto them, saying, This is my body which is given for you: [g]this do in remembrance of me.

20 Likewise also the cup after supper, saying, [h]This cup *is* the new testament in my blood, which is shed for you.

21 ¶ [i]But, behold, the hand of him that betrayeth me *is* with me on the table.

22 [j]And truly the Son of man goeth, [k]as it was determined: but woe unto that man by whom he is betrayed!

23 [l]And they began to enquire among themselves, which of them it was that should do this thing.

24 ¶ [m]And there was also a strife among them, which of them should be accounted the greatest.

25 [n]And he said unto them, The kings of the Gentiles exercise lordship over them; and they that exercise authority upon them are called benefactors.

26 [o]But ye *shall* not *be* so: [p]but he that is greatest among you, let him be as the younger; and he that is chief, as he that doth serve.

27 [q]For whether *is* greater, he that sitteth at meat, or he that serveth? *is* not he that sitteth at meat? but [r]I am among you as he that serveth.

28 Ye are they which have continued with me in [s]my temptations.

29 And [t]I appoint unto you a kingdom, as my Father hath appointed unto me;

30 That [u]ye may eat and drink at my table in my kingdom, [v]and sit on thrones judging the twelve tribes of Israel.

31 ¶ And the Lord said, Simon, Simon, behold, [w]Satan hath desired *to have* you, that he may [x]sift *you* as wheat:

32 But [y]I have prayed for thee, that thy faith fail not: [z]and when thou art converted, strengthen thy brethren.

33 And he said unto him, Lord, I am ready to go with thee, both into prison, and to death.

34 [a]And he said, I tell thee, Peter, the cock shall not crow this day, before that thou shalt thrice deny that thou knowest me.

35 [b]And he said unto them, When I sent you without purse, and scrip, and shoes, lacked ye any thing? And they said, Nothing.

36 Then said he unto them, But now, he that hath a purse, let him take *it*, and likewise *his* scrip: and he that hath no sword, let him sell his garment, and buy one.

37 For I say unto you, that this that is written must yet be accomplished in me, [c]And he was reckoned among the transgressors: for the things concerning me have an end.

38 And they said, Lord, behold, here *are* two swords. And he said unto them, It is enough.

39 ¶ [d]And he came out, and [e]went, as he was wont, to the mount of Olives; and his disciples also followed him.

40 [f]And when he was at the place, he said unto them, Pray that ye enter not into temptation.

41 [g]And he was withdrawn from them about a stone's cast, and kneeled down, and prayed,

42 Saying, Father, if thou be willing, remove this cup from me: nevertheless [h]not my will, but thine, be done.

43 And there appeared [i]an angel unto him from heaven, strengthening him.

44 [j]And being in an agony he prayed more earnestly: and his sweat was as it were great drops of blood falling down to the ground.

45 And when he rose up from prayer, and was come to his disciples, he found them sleeping for sorrow,

46 And said unto them, Why sleep ye? rise and [k]pray, lest ye enter into temptation.

47 ¶ And while he yet spake, [l]behold a multitude, and he that was called Judas, one of the twelve, went before them, and drew near unto Jesus to kiss him.

48 But Jesus said unto him, Judas, betrayest thou the Son of man with a kiss?

49 When they which were about him saw what would follow, they said unto him, Lord, shall we smite with the sword?

50 ¶ And [m]one of them smote the servant of the high priest, and cut off his right ear.

51 And Jesus answered and said, Suffer ye thus far. And he touched his ear, and healed him.

52 [n]Then Jesus said unto the chief priests, and captains of the temple, and the elders, which were come to him, Be ye come out, as against a thief, with swords and staves?

53 When I was daily with you in the temple, ye stretched forth no hands against me: [o]but this is your hour, and the power of darkness.

54 ¶ [p]Then took they him, and led *him*, and brought him into the high priest's house. [q]And Peter followed afar off.

55 [r]And when they had kindled a fire in

22:14 [c]Matt. 26:20; Mark 14:17
22:16 [d]ch. 14:15; Acts 10:41; Rev. 19:9
22:18 [e]Matt. 26:29; Mark 14:25
22:19 [f]Matt. 26:26; Mark 14:22 [g]1 Cor. 11:24
22:20 [h]1 Cor. 10:16
22:21 [i]Ps. 41:9; Matt. 26:21; Mark 14:18; John 13:21
22:22 [j]Matt. 26:24 [k]Acts 2:23
22:23 [l]Matt. 26:22; John 13:22
22:24 [m]Mark 9:34; Luke 9:46
22:25 [n]Matt. 20:25; Mark 10:42
22:26 [o]Matt. 20:26; 1 Pet. 5:3 [p]ch. 9:48
22:27 [q]ch. 12:37 [r]Matt. 20:28; John 13:13; Phil. 2:7
22:28 [s]Heb. 4:15
22:29 [t]Matt. 24:47; ch. 12:32; 2 Cor. 1:7; 2 Tim. 2:12
22:30 [u]Matt. 8:11; ch. 14:15; Rev. 19:9 [v]Ps. 49:14; Matt. 19:28; 1 Cor. 6:2; Rev. 3:21
22:31 [w]1 Pet. 5:8 [x]Am. 9:9
22:32 [y]John 17:9 [z]Ps. 51:13; John 21:15
22:34 [a]Matt. 26:34; Mark 14:30; John 13:38
22:35 [b]Matt. 10:9; ch. 9:3
22:37 [c]Isa. 53:12; Mark 15:28
22:39 [d]Matt. 26:36; Mark 14:32; John 18:1 [e]ch. 21:37
22:40 [f]Matt. 6:13; Mark 14:38; ver. 46
22:41 [g]Matt. 26:39; Mark 14:35
22:42 [h]John 5:30
22:43 [i]Matt. 4:11
22:44 [j]John 12:27; Heb. 5:7
22:46 [k]ver. 40
22:47 [l]Matt. 26:47; Mark 14:43; John 18:3
22:50 [m]Matt. 26:51; Mark 14:47; John 18:10
22:52 [n]Matt. 26:55; Mark 14:48
22:53 [o]John 12:27 **22:54** [p]Matt. 26:57 [q]Matt. 26:58; John 18:15
22:55 [r]Matt. 26:69; Mark 14:66; John 18:17

the midst of the hall, and were set down together, Peter sat down among them.

56 But a certain maid beheld him as he sat by the fire, and earnestly looked upon him, and said, This man was also with him.

57 And he denied him, saying, Woman, I know him not.

58 [s]And after a little while another saw him, and said, Thou art also of them. And Peter said, Man, I am not.

59 [t]And about the space of one hour after another confidently affirmed, saying, Of a truth this *fellow* also was with him: for he is a Galilean.

60 And Peter said, Man, I know not what thou sayest. And immediately, while he yet spake, the cock crew.

61 And the Lord turned, and looked upon Peter. [u]And Peter remembered the word of the Lord, how he had said unto him, [v]Before the cock crow, thou shalt deny me thrice.

62 And Peter went out, and wept bitterly.

63 ¶ [w]And the men that held Jesus mocked him, and smote *him*.

64 And when they had blindfolded him, they struck him on the face, and asked him, saying, Prophesy, who is it that smote thee?

65 And many other things blasphemously spake they against him.

66 ¶ [x]And as soon as it was day, [y]the elders of the people and the chief priests and the scribes came together, and led him into their council, saying,

67 [z]Art thou the Christ? tell us. And he said unto them, If I tell you, ye will not believe:

68 And if I also ask *you*, ye will not answer me, nor let *me* go.

69 [a]Hereafter shall the Son of man sit on the right hand of the power of God.

70 Then said they all, Art thou then the Son of God? And he said unto them, [b]Ye say that I am.

71 [c]And they said, What need we any further witness? for we ourselves have heard of his own mouth.

23 And [d]the whole multitude of them arose, and led him unto Pilate.

2 And they began to accuse him, saying, We found this *fellow* [e]perverting the nation, and [f]forbidding to give tribute to Caesar, saying [g]that he himself is Christ a King.

3 [h]And Pilate asked him, saying, Art thou the King of the Jews? And he answered him and said, Thou sayest *it*.

4 Then said Pilate to the chief priests and *to* the people, [i]I find no fault in this man.

5 And they were the more fierce, saying, He stirreth up the people, teaching throughout all Jewry, beginning from Galilee to this place.

6 When Pilate heard of Galilee, he asked whether the man were a Galilean.

7 And as soon as he knew that he belonged unto [j]Herod's jurisdiction, he sent him to Herod, who himself also was at Jerusalem at that time.

8 ¶ And when Herod saw Jesus, he was exceeding glad: for [k]he was desirous to see him of a long *season*, because [l]he had heard many things of him; and he hoped to have seen some miracle done by him.

9 Then he questioned with him in many words; but he answered him nothing.

10 And the chief priests and scribes stood and vehemently accused him.

11 [m]And Herod with his men of war set him at nought, and mocked *him*, and arrayed him in a gorgeous robe, and sent him again to Pilate.

12 ¶ And the same day [n]Pilate and Herod were made friends together: for before they were at enmity between themselves.

13 ¶ [o]And Pilate, when he had called together the chief priests and the rulers and the people,

14 Said unto them, [p]Ye have brought this man unto me, as one that perverteth the people: and, behold, [q]I, having examined *him* before you, have found no fault in this man touching those things whereof ye accuse him:

15 No, nor yet Herod: for I sent you to him; and, lo, nothing worthy of death is done unto him.

16 [r]I will therefore chastise him, and release *him*.

17 [s](For of necessity he must release one unto them at the feast.)

18 And [t]they cried out all at once, saying, Away with this *man*, and release unto us Barabbas:

19 (Who for a certain sedition made in the city, and for murder, was cast into prison.)

20 Pilate therefore, willing to release Jesus, spake again to them.

21 But they cried, saying, Crucify *him*, crucify him.

22 And he said unto them the third time, Why, what evil hath he done? I have found no cause of death in him: I will therefore chastise him, and let *him* go.

23 And they were instant with loud voices, requiring that he might be crucified. And the voices of them and of the chief priests prevailed.

24 And [u]Pilate gave sentence that it should be as they required.

25 And he released unto them him that for sedition and murder was cast into prison, whom they had desired; but he delivered Jesus to their will.

26 [v]And as they led him away, they laid hold upon one Simon, a Cyrenian, coming out of the country, and on him they laid the cross, that he might bear *it* after Jesus.

27 ¶ And there followed him a great company of people, and of women, which also bewailed and lamented him.

28 But Jesus turning unto them said, Daughters of Jerusalem, weep not for me, but weep for yourselves, and for your children.

22:58 [s]Matt. 26:71; Mark 14:69; John 18:25
22:59 [t]Matt. 26:73; Mark 14:70; John 18:26
22:61 [u]Matt. 26:75; Mark 14:72 [v]Matt. 26:34; John 13:38
22:63 [w]Matt. 26:67; Mark 14:65
22:66 [x]Matt. 27:1 [y]Acts 4:26
22:67 [z]Matt. 26:63; Mark 14:61
22:69 [a]Matt. 26:64; Mark 14:62; Heb. 1:3
22:70 [b]Matt. 26:64; Mark 14:62
22:71 [c]Matt. 26:65; Mark 14:62
23:1 [d]Matt. 27:2; Mark 15:1; John 18:28
23:2 [e]Acts 17:7 [f]Matt. 17:27; Mark 12:17 [g]John 19:12
23:3 [h]Matt. 27:11; 1 Tim. 6:13
23:4 [i]1 Pet. 2:22
23:7 [j]ch. 3:1
23:8 [k]ch. 9:9 [l]Matt. 14:1; Mark 6:14
23:11 [m]Isa. 53:3
23:12 [n]Acts 4:27
23:13 [o]Matt. 27:23; Mark 15:14; John 18:38
23:14 [p]ver. 1 [q]ver. 4
23:16 [r]Matt. 27:26; John 19:1
23:17 [s]Matt. 27:15; Mark 15:6; John 18:39
23:18 [t]Acts 3:14
23:24 [u]Matt. 27:26; Mark 15:15; John 19:16
23:26 [v]Matt. 27:32; Mark 15:21; John 19:17

29 [w]For, behold, the days are coming, in the which they shall say, Blessed *are* the barren, and the wombs that never bare, and the paps which never gave suck.

30 [x]Then shall they begin to say to the mountains, Fall on us; and to the hills, Cover us.

31 [y]For if they do these things in a green tree, what shall be done in the dry?

32 [z]And there were also two other, malefactors, led with him to be put to death.

33 And [a]when they were come to the place, which is called Calvary, there they crucified him, and the malefactors, one on the right hand, and the other on the left.

34 ¶ Then said Jesus, Father, [b]forgive them; for [c]they know not what they do. And [d]they parted his raiment, and cast lots.

35 And [e]the people stood beholding. And the [f]rulers also with them derided *him,* saying, He saved others; let him save himself, if he be Christ, the chosen of God.

36 And the soldiers also mocked him, coming to him, and offering him vinegar,

37 And saying, If thou be the king of the Jews, save thyself.

38 [g]And a superscription also was written over him in letters of Greek, and Latin, and Hebrew, THIS IS THE KING OF THE JEWS.

39 ¶ [h]And one of the malefactors which were hanged railed on him, saying, If thou be Christ, save thyself and us.

40 But the other answering rebuked him, saying, Dost not thou fear God, seeing thou art in the same condemnation?

41 And we indeed justly; for we receive the due reward of our deeds: but this man hath done nothing amiss.

42 And he said unto Jesus, Lord, remember me when thou comest into thy kingdom.

43 And Jesus said unto him, Verily I say unto thee, To day shalt thou be with me in paradise.

44 [i]And it was about the sixth hour, and there was a darkness over all the earth until the ninth hour.

45 And the sun was darkened, and [j]the veil of the temple was rent in the midst.

46 ¶ And when Jesus had cried with a loud voice, he said, [k]Father, into thy hands I commend my spirit: [l]and having said thus, he gave up the ghost.

47 [m]Now when the centurion saw what was done, he glorified God, saying, Certainly this was a righteous man.

48 And all the people that came together to that sight, beholding the things which were done, smote their breasts, and returned.

49 [n]And all his acquaintance, and the women that followed him from Galilee, stood afar off, beholding these things.

50 ¶ [o]And, behold, *there was* a man named Joseph, a counsellor; *and he was* a good man, and a just:

51 (The same had not consented to the counsel and deed of them;) *he was* of Arimathea, a city of the Jews: [p]who also himself waited for the kingdom of God.

52 This *man* went unto Pilate, and begged the body of Jesus.

53 [q]And he took it down, and wrapped it in linen, and laid it in a sepulchre that was hewn in stone, wherein never man before was laid.

54 And that day was [r]the preparation, and the sabbath drew on.

55 And the women also, [s]which came with him from Galilee, followed after, and [t]beheld the sepulchre, and how his body was laid.

56 And they returned, and [u]prepared spices and ointments; and rested the sabbath day [v]according to the commandment.

24 Now [w]upon the first *day* of the week, very early in the morning, they came unto the sepulchre, [x]bringing the spices which they had prepared, and certain *others* with them.

2 [y]And they found the stone rolled away from the sepulchre.

3 [z]And they entered in, and found not the body of the Lord Jesus.

4 And it came to pass, as they were much perplexed thereabout, [a]behold, two men stood by them in shining garments:

5 And as they were afraid, and bowed down *their* faces to the earth, they said unto them, Why seek ye the living among the dead?

6 He is not here, but is risen: [b]remember how he spake unto you when he was yet in Galilee,

7 Saying, The Son of man must be delivered into the hands of sinful men, and be crucified, and the third day rise again.

8 And [c]they remembered his words,

9 [d]And returned from the sepulchre, and told all these things unto the eleven, and to all the rest.

10 It was Mary Magdalene, and [e]Joanna, and Mary *the mother* of James, and other *women that were* with them, which told these things unto the apostles.

11 [f]And their words seemed to them as idle tales, and they believed them not.

12 [g]Then arose Peter, and ran unto the sepulchre; and stooping down, he beheld the linen clothes laid by themselves, and departed, wondering in himself at that which was come to pass.

13 ¶ [h]And, behold, two of them went that same day to a village called Emmaus, which was from Jerusalem *about* threescore furlongs.

14 And they talked together of all these things which had happened.

15 And it came to pass, that, while they communed *together* and reasoned, [i]Jesus himself drew near, and went with them.

16 But [j]their eyes were holden that they should not know him.

17 And he said unto them, What manner

23:29 [w]Matt. 24:19; ch. 21:23
23:30 [x]Isa. 2:19; Hos. 10:8; Rev. 6:16
23:31 [y]Prov. 11:31; Jer. 25:29; Ezek. 20:47; 1 Pet. 4:17
23:32 [z]Isa. 53:12; Matt. 27:38
23:33 [a]Matt. 27:33; Mark 15:22; John 19:17
23:34 [b]Matt. 5:44; Acts 7:60; 1 Cor. 4:12 [c]Acts 3:17 [d]Matt. 27:35; Mark 15:24; John 19:23
23:35 [e]Ps. 22:17; Zech. 12:10 [f]Matt. 27:39; Mark 15:29
23:38 [g]Matt. 27:37; Mark 15:26; John 19:19
23:39 [h]Matt. 27:44; Mark 15:32
23:44 [i]Matt. 27:45; Mark 15:33
23:45 [j]Matt. 27:51; Mark 15:38
23:46 [k]Ps. 31:5; 1 Pet. 2:23 [l]Matt. 27:50; Mark 15:37; John 19:30
23:47 [m]Matt. 27:54; Mark 15:39
23:49 [n]Ps. 38:11; Matt. 27:55; Mark 15:40; John 19:25
23:50 [o]Matt. 27:57; Mark 15:42; John 19:38
23:51 [p]Mark 15:43; ch. 2:25
23:53 [q]Matt. 27:59; Mark 15:46
23:54 [r]Matt. 27:62
23:55 [s]ch. 8:2 [t]Mark 15:47
23:56 [u]Mark 16:1 [v]Ex. 20:10
24:1 [w]Matt. 28:1; Mark 16:1; John 20:2 [x]ch. 23:56
24:2 [y]Matt. 28:2; Mark 16:4
24:3 [z]ver. 23; Mark 16:5
24:4 [a]John 20:12; Acts 1:10
24:6 [b]Matt. 16:21; Mark 8:31; ch. 9:22
24:8 [c]John 2:22
24:9 [d]Matt. 28:8; Mark 16:10
24:10 [e]ch. 8:3
24:11 [f]Mark 16:11; ver. 25
24:12 [g]John 20:3
24:13 [h]Mark 16:12

24:15 [i]Matt. 18:20; ver. 36 **24:16** [j]John 20:14

of communications *are* these that ye have one to another, as ye walk, and are sad?

18 And the one of them, [k]whose name was Cleopas, answering said unto him, Art thou only a stranger in Jerusalem, and hast not known the things which are come to pass there in these days?

19 And he said unto them, What things? And they said unto him, Concerning Jesus of Nazareth, [l]which was a prophet [m]mighty in deed and word before God and all the people:

20 [n]And how the chief priests and our rulers delivered him to be condemned to death, and have crucified him.

21 But we trusted [o]that it had been he which should have redeemed Israel: and beside all this, to day is the third day since these things were done.

22 Yea, and [p]certain women also of our company made us astonished, which were early at the sepulchre;

23 And when they found not his body, they came, saying, that they had also seen a vision of angels, which said that he was alive.

24 And [q]certain of them which were with us went to the sepulchre, and found *it* even so as the women had said: but him they saw not.

25 Then he said unto them, O fools, and slow of heart to believe all that the prophets have spoken:

26 [r]Ought not Christ to have suffered these things, and to enter into his glory?

27 [s]And beginning at [t]Moses and [u]all the prophets, he expounded unto them in all the scriptures the things concerning himself.

28 And they drew nigh unto the village, whither they went: and [v]he made as though he would have gone further.

29 But [w]they constrained him, saying, Abide with us: for it is toward evening, and the day is far spent. And he went in to tarry with them.

30 And it came to pass, as he sat at meat with them, [x]he took bread, and blessed *it*, and brake, and gave to them.

31 And their eyes were opened, and they knew him; and he vanished out of their sight.

32 And they said one to another, Did not our heart burn within us, while he talked with us by the way, and while he opened to us the scriptures?

33 And they rose up the same hour, and returned to Jerusalem, and found the eleven gathered together, and them that were with them,

34 Saying, The Lord is risen indeed, and [y]hath appeared to Simon.

35 And they told what things *were done* in the way, and how he was known of them in breaking of bread.

36 ¶ [z]And as they thus spake, Jesus himself stood in the midst of them, and saith unto them, Peace *be* unto you.

37 But they were terrified and affrighted, and supposed that they had seen [a]a spirit.

38 And he said unto them, Why are ye troubled? and why do thoughts arise in your hearts?

39 Behold my hands and my feet, that it is I myself: [b]handle me, and see; for a spirit hath not flesh and bones, as ye see me have.

40 And when he had thus spoken, he shewed them *his* hands and *his* feet.

41 And while they yet believed not [c]for joy, and wondered, he said unto them, [d]Have ye here any meat?

42 And they gave him a piece of a broiled fish, and of an honeycomb.

43 [e]And he took *it*, and did eat before them.

44 And he said unto them, [f]These *are* the words which I spake unto you, while I was yet with you, that all things must be fulfilled, which were written in the law of Moses, and *in* the prophets, and *in* the psalms, concerning me.

45 Then [g]opened he their understanding, that they might understand the scriptures,

46 And said unto them, [h]Thus it is written, and thus it behoved Christ to suffer, and to rise from the dead the third day:

47 And that repentance and [i]remission of sins should be preached in his name [j]among all nations, beginning at Jerusalem.

48 And [k]ye are witnesses of these things.

49 ¶ [l]And, behold, I send the promise of my Father upon you: but tarry ye in the city of Jerusalem, until ye be endued with power from on high.

50 ¶ And he led them out as [m]far as to Bethany, and he lifted up his hands, and blessed them.

51 [n]And it came to pass, while he blessed them, he was parted from them, and carried up into heaven.

52 [o]And they worshipped him, and returned to Jerusalem with great joy:

53 And were continually [p]in the temple, praising and blessing God. Amen.

24:18 [k]John 19:25
24:19 [l]Matt. 21:11; ch. 7:16; John 3:2; Acts 2:22 [m]Acts 7:22
24:20 [n]ch. 23:1; Acts 13:27
24:21 [o]ch. 1:68; Acts 1:6
24:22 [p]Matt. 28:8; Mark 16:10; ver. 9; John 20:18
24:24 [q]ver. 12
24:26 [r]ver. 46; Acts 17:3; 1 Pet. 1:11
24:27 [s]ver. 45 [t]Gen. 3:15; Num. 21:9; Deut. 18:15 [u]Ps. 16:9; Isa. 7:14; Jer. 23:5; Ezek. 34:23; Dan. 9:24; Mic. 7:20; Mal. 3:1; John 1:45
24:28 [v]Gen. 32:26; Mark 6:48
24:29 [w]Gen. 19:3; Acts 16:15
24:30 [x]Matt. 14:19
24:34 [y]1 Cor. 15:5
24:36 [z]Mark 16:14; John 20:19; 1 Cor. 15:5
24:37 [a]Mark 6:49
24:39 [b]John 20:20
24:41 [c]Gen. 45:26 [d]John 21:5
24:43 [e]Acts 10:41
24:44 [f]Matt. 16:21; Mark 8:31; ch. 9:22; ver. 6
24:45 [g]Acts 16:14
24:46 [h]ver. 26; Ps. 22; Isa. 50:6; Acts 17:3
24:47 [i]Dan. 9:24; Acts 13:38; 1 John 2:12 [j]Gen. 12:3; Ps. 22:27; Isa. 49:6; Jer. 31:34; Hos. 2:23; Mic. 4:2; Mal. 1:11
24:48 [k]John 15:27; Acts 1:8
24:49 [l]Isa. 44:3; Joel 2:28; John 14:16; Acts 1:4
24:50 [m]Acts 1:12
24:51 [n]2 Kings 2:11; Mark 16:19; John 20:17; Acts 1:9; Eph. 4:8
24:52 [o]Matt. 28:9
24:53 [p]Acts 2:46

JOHN

The writer of John is identified as "the disciple Jesus loved," the apostle John. It was probably written sometime between A.D. 85 and A.D. 90. John centers on the teachings of Christ and their applicability to all men. Additionally, John focuses on the humanity of Christ while never losing sight of Christ's divine nature. In the latter chapters, John provides information concerning the arrest, trial, and crucifixion of Jesus that the other gospels do not contain.

John contains the shortest verse in the Bible, John 11:35, and the most often quoted verse, John 3:16.

I. The relationship of God and Christ, 1:1–1:18
II. John the Baptist and Jesus, 1:19–1:51
III. Jesus' public ministry, 2:1–12:11
IV. Jesus' last week of public ministry, 12:12-19:42
V. The resurrection, 20:1–21:25

---

1 In the beginning [a]was the Word, and
the Word was [b]with God, [c]and the
Word was God.
2 [d]The same was in the beginning with
God.
3 [e]All things were made by him; and
without him was not any thing made that
was made.
4 [f]In him was life; and [g]the life was the
light of men.
5 And [h]the light shineth in darkness; and
the darkness comprehended it not.
6 ¶ [i]There was a man sent from God,
whose name *was* John.
7 [j]The same came for a witness, to bear
witness of the Light, that all *men* through
him might believe.
8 He was not that Light, but *was sent* to
bear witness of that Light.
9 [k]*That* was the true Light, which lighteth every man that cometh into the world.
10 He was in the world, and [l]the world
was made by him, and the world knew him
not.
11 [m]He came unto his own, and his own
received him not.
12 But [n]as many as received him, to them
gave he power to become the sons of God,
even to them that believe on his name:
13 [o]Which were born, not of blood, nor of
the will of the flesh, nor of the will of man,
but of God.
14 [p]And the Word [q]was made [r]flesh,
and dwelt among us, (and [s]we beheld his
glory, the glory as of the only begotten of
the Father,) [t]full of grace and truth.
15 ¶ [u]John bare witness of him, and
cried, saying, This was he of whom I spake,
[v]He that cometh after me is preferred before me: [w]for he was before me.
16 And of his [x]fulness have all we received, and grace for grace.
17 For [y]the law was given by Moses, *but*
[z]grace and [a]truth came by Jesus Christ.
18 [b]No man hath seen God at any time;
[c]the only begotten Son, which is in the bosom of the Father, he hath declared *him*.
19 ¶ And this is [d]the record of John,
when the Jews sent priests and Levites from
Jerusalem to ask him, Who art thou?
20 And [e]he confessed, and denied not;
but confessed, I am not the Christ.
21 And they asked him, What then? Art
thou [f]Elias? And he saith, I am not. Art
thou [g]that prophet? And he answered, No.
22 Then said they unto him, Who art
thou? that we may give an answer to them
that sent us. What sayest thou of thyself?
23 [h]He said, I *am* the voice of one crying
in the wilderness, Make straight the way of
the Lord, as [i]said the prophet Esaias.
24 And they which were sent were of the
Pharisees.
25 And they asked him, and said unto
him, Why baptizest thou then, if thou be not
that Christ, nor Elias, neither that prophet?
26 John answered them, saying, [j]I baptize with water: [k]but there standeth one
among you, whom ye know not;
27 [l]He it is, who coming after me is preferred before me, whose shoe's latchet I am
not worthy to unloose.
28 These things were done [m]in Bethabara
beyond Jordan, where John was baptizing.
29 ¶ The next day John seeth Jesus coming unto him, and saith, Behold [n]the Lamb
of God, [o]which taketh away the sin of the
world.
30 [p]This is he of whom I said, After me
cometh a man which is preferred before me:
for he was before me.
31 And I knew him not: but that he should

1:1 *a*Prov. 8:22; Col. 1:17; 1 John 1:1; Rev. 1:2 *b*Prov. 8:30; ch. 17:5; 1 John 1:2 *c*Phil. 2:6; 1 John 5:7 **1:2** *d*Gen. 1:1 **1:3** *e*Ps. 33:6; Col. 1:16; ver. 10; Eph. 3:9; Heb. 1:2; Rev. 4:11 **1:4** *f*ch. 5:26; 1 John 5:11 *g*ch. 8:12 **1:5** *h*ch. 3:19 **1:6** *i*Mal. 3:1; Matt. 3:1; Luke 3:2; ver. 33 **1:7** *j*Acts 19:4 **1:9** *k*ver. 4; Isa. 49:6; 1 John 2:8 **1:10** *l*ver. 3; Heb. 1:2 **1:11** *m*Luke 19:14; Acts 3:26 **1:12** *n*Isa. 56:5; Rom. 8:15; Gal. 3:26; 2 Pet. 1:4; 1 John 3:1 **1:13** *o*ch. 3:5; Jam. 1:18; 1 Pet. 1:23 **1:14** *p*Matt. 1:16; Luke 1:31; 1 Tim. 3:16 *q*Rom. 1:3; Gal. 4:4 *r*Heb. 2:11 *s*Isa. 40:5; Matt. 17:2; ch. 2:11; 2 Pet. 1:17 *t*Col. 1:19 **1:15** *u*ver. 32; ch. 3:32 *v*Matt. 3:11; Mark 1:7; Luke 3:16; ver. 27; ch. 3:31 *w*ch. 8:58; Col. 1:17 **1:16** *x*ch. 3:34; Eph. 1:6; Col. 1:19 **1:17** *y*Ex. 20:1; Deut. 4:44 *z*Rom. 3:24 *a*ch. 8:32 **1:18** *b*Ex. 33:20; Deut. 4:12; Matt. 11:27; Luke 10:22; ch. 6:46; 1 Tim. 1:17; 1 John 4:12 *c*ver. 14; ch. 3:16; 1 John 4:9 **1:19** *d*ch. 5:33 **1:20** *e*Luke 3:15; ch. 3:28; Acts 13:25 **1:21** *f*Mal. 4:5; Matt. 17:10 *g*Deut. 18:15 **1:23** *h*Matt. 3:3; Mark 1:3; Luke 3:4; ch. 3:28 *i*Isa. 40:3 **1:26** *j*Matt. 3:11 *k*Mal. 3:1 **1:27** *l*ver. 15; Acts 19:4 **1:28** *m*Judg. 7:24; ch. 10:40 **1:29** *n*Ex. 12:3; Isa. 53:7; ver. 36; Acts 8:32; 1 Pet. 1:19; Rev. 5:6 *o*Isa. 53:11; 1 Cor. 15:3; Gal. 1:4; Heb. 1:3; 1 Pet. 2:24; 1 John 2:2; Rev. 1:5 **1:30** *p*ver. 15

be made manifest to Israel, [q]therefore am I come baptizing with water.

32 [r]And John bare record, saying, I saw the Spirit descending from heaven like a dove, and it abode upon him.

33 And I knew him not: but he that sent me to baptize with water, the same said unto me, Upon whom thou shalt see the Spirit descending, and remaining on him, [s]the same is he which baptizeth with the Holy Ghost.

34 And I saw, and bare record that this is the Son of God.

35 ¶ Again the next day after John stood, and two of his disciples;

36 And looking upon Jesus as he walked, he saith, [t]Behold the Lamb of God!

37 And the two disciples heard him speak, and they followed Jesus.

38 Then Jesus turned, and saw them following, and saith unto them, What seek ye? They said unto him, Rabbi, (which is to say, being interpreted, Master,) where dwellest thou?

39 He saith unto them, Come and see. They came and saw where he dwelt, and abode with him that day: for it was about the tenth hour.

40 One of the two which heard John *speak*, and followed him, was [u]Andrew, Simon Peter's brother.

41 He first findeth his own brother Simon, and saith unto him, We have found the Messias, which is, being interpreted, the Christ.

42 And he brought him to Jesus. And when Jesus beheld him, he said, Thou art Simon the son of Jona: [v]thou shalt be called Cephas, which is by interpretation, A stone.

43 ¶ The day following Jesus would go forth into Galilee, and findeth Philip, and saith unto him, Follow me.

44 Now [w]Philip was of Bethsaida, the city of Andrew and Peter.

45 Philip findeth [x]Nathanael, and saith unto him, We have found him, of whom [y]Moses in the law, and the [z]prophets, did write, Jesus [a]of Nazareth, the son of Joseph.

46 And Nathanael said unto him, [b]Can there any good thing come out of Nazareth? Philip saith unto him, Come and see.

47 Jesus saw Nathanael coming to him, and saith of him, Behold [c]an Israelite indeed, in whom is no guile!

48 Nathanael saith unto him, Whence knowest thou me? Jesus answered and said unto him, Before that Philip called thee, when thou wast under the fig tree, I saw thee.

49 Nathanael answered and saith unto him, Rabbi, [d]thou art the Son of God; thou art [e]the King of Israel.

50 Jesus answered and said unto him, Because I said unto thee, I saw thee under the fig tree, believest thou? thou shalt see greater things than these.

51 And he saith unto him, Verily, verily, I say unto you, [f]Hereafter ye shall see heaven open, and the angels of God ascending and descending upon the Son of man.

2 And the third day there was a marriage in [g]Cana of Galilee; and the mother of Jesus was there:

2 And both Jesus was called, and his disciples, to the marriage.

3 And when they wanted wine, the mother of Jesus saith unto him, They have no wine.

4 Jesus saith unto her, [h]Woman, [i]what have I to do with thee? [j]mine hour is not yet come.

5 His mother saith unto the servants, Whatsoever he saith unto you, do *it*.

6 And there were set there six waterpots of stone, [k]after the manner of the purifying of the Jews, containing two or three firkins apiece.

7 Jesus saith unto them, Fill the waterpots with water. And they filled them up to the brim.

8 And he saith unto them, Draw out now, and bear unto the governor of the feast. And they bare *it*.

9 When the ruler of the feast had tasted [l]the water that was made wine, and knew not whence it was: (but the servants which drew the water knew;) the governor of the feast called the bridegroom,

10 And saith unto him, Every man at the beginning doth set forth good wine; and when men have well drunk, then that which is worse: *but* thou hast kept the good wine until now.

11 This beginning of miracles did Jesus in Cana of Galilee, [m]and manifested forth his glory; and his disciples believed on him.

12 ¶ After this he went down to Capernaum, he, and his mother, and [n]his brethren, and his disciples: and they continued there not many days.

13 ¶ [o]And the Jews' passover was at hand, and Jesus went up to Jerusalem,

14 [p]And found in the temple those that sold oxen and sheep and doves, and the changers of money sitting:

15 And when he had made a scourge of small cords, he drove them all out of the temple, and the sheep, and the oxen; and poured out the changers' money, and overthrew the tables;

16 And said unto them that sold doves, Take these things hence; make not [q]my Father's house an house of merchandise.

17 And his disciples remembered that it was written, [r]The zeal of thine house hath eaten me up.

18 ¶ Then answered the Jews and said unto him, [s]What sign shewest thou unto us, seeing that thou doest these things?

19 Jesus answered and said unto them, [t]Destroy this temple, and in three days I will raise it up.

20 Then said the Jews, Forty and six years was this temple in building, and wilt thou rear it up in three days?

1:31 [q]Mal. 3:1; Matt. 3:6; Luke 1:17
1:32 [r]Matt. 3:16; Mark 1:10; Luke 3:22; ch. 5:32
1:33 [s]Matt. 3:11; Acts 1:5
1:36 [t]ver. 29
1:40 [u]Matt. 4:18
1:42 [v]Matt. 16:18
1:44 [w]ch. 12:21
1:45 [x]ch. 21:2 [y]Gen. 3:15; Deut. 18:18; Luke 24:27 [z]Isa. 4:2; Mic. 5:2; Zech. 6:12; Luke 24:27 [a]Matt. 2:23; Luke 2:4
1:46 [b]ch. 7:41
1:47 [c]Ps. 32:2; ch. 8:39; Rom. 2:28
1:49 [d]Matt. 14:33 [e]Matt. 21:5; ch. 18:37
1:51 [f]Gen. 28:12; Matt. 4:11; Luke 2:9; Acts 1:10
2:1 [g]Josh. 19:28
2:4 [h]ch. 19:26 [i]2 Sam. 16:10 [j]ch. 7:6
2:6 [k]Mark 7:3
2:9 [l]ch. 4:46
2:11 [m]ch. 1:14
2:12 [n]Matt. 12:46
2:13 [o]Ex. 12:14; Deut. 16:1; ver. 23; ch. 5:1
2:14 [p]Matt. 21:12; Mark 11:15; Luke 19:45
2:16 [q]Luke 2:49
2:17 [r]Ps. 69:9
2:18 [s]Matt. 12:38; ch. 6:30
2:19 [t]Matt. 26:61; Mark 14:58

21 But he spake [u]of the temple of his body.

22 When therefore he was risen from the dead, [v]his disciples remembered that he had said this unto them; and they believed the scripture, and the word which Jesus had said.

23 ¶ Now when he was in Jerusalem at the passover, in the feast *day*, many believed in his name, when they saw the miracles which he did.

24 But Jesus did not commit himself unto them, because he knew all *men*,

25 And needed not that any should testify of man: for [w]he knew what was in man.

3 There was a man of the Pharisees, named Nicodemus, a ruler of the Jews:

2 [x]The same came to Jesus by night, and said unto him, Rabbi, we know that thou art a teacher come from God: for [y]no man can do these miracles that thou doest, except [z]God be with him.

3 Jesus answered and said unto him, Verily, verily, I say unto thee, [a]Except a man be born again, he cannot see the kingdom of God.

4 Nicodemus saith unto him, How can a man be born when he is old? can he enter the second time into his mother's womb, and be born?

5 Jesus answered, Verily, verily, I say unto thee, [b]Except a man be born of water and *of* the Spirit, he cannot enter into the kingdom of God.

6 That which is born of the flesh is flesh; and that which is born of the Spirit is spirit.

7 Marvel not that I said unto thee, Ye must be born again.

8 [c]The wind bloweth where it listeth, and thou hearest the sound thereof, but canst not tell whence it cometh, and whither it goeth: so is every one that is born of the Spirit.

9 Nicodemus answered and said unto him, [d]How can these things be?

10 Jesus answered and said unto him, Art thou a master of Israel, and knowest not these things?

11 [e]Verily, verily, I say unto thee, We speak that we do know, and testify that we have seen; and [f]ye receive not our witness.

12 If I have told you earthly things, and ye believe not, how shall ye believe, if I tell you *of* heavenly things?

13 And [g]no man hath ascended up to heaven, but he that came down from heaven, *even* the Son of man which is in heaven.

14 ¶ [h]And as Moses lifted up the serpent in the wilderness, even so [i]must the Son of man be lifted up:

15 That whosoever believeth in him should not perish, but [j]have eternal life.

16 ¶ [k]For God so loved the world, that he gave his only begotten Son, that whosoever believeth in him should not perish, but have everlasting life.

17 [l]For God sent not his Son into the world to condemn the world; but that the world through him might be saved.

18 ¶ [m]He that believeth on him is not condemned: but he that believeth not is condemned already, because he hath not believed in the name of the only begotten Son of God.

19 And this is the condemnation, [n]that light is come into the world, and men loved darkness rather than light, because their deeds were evil.

20 For [o]every one that doeth evil hateth the light, neither cometh to the light, lest his deeds should be reproved.

21 But he that doeth truth cometh to the light, that his deeds may be made manifest, that they are wrought in God.

22 ¶ After these things came Jesus and his disciples into the land of Judea; and there he tarried with them, [p]and baptized.

23 ¶ And John also was baptizing in Aenon near to [q]Salim, because there was much water there: [r]and they came, and were baptized.

24 For [s]John was not yet cast into prison.

25 ¶ Then there arose a question between *some* of John's disciples and the Jews about purifying.

26 And they came unto John, and said unto him, Rabbi, he that was with thee beyond Jordan, [t]to whom thou bearest witness, behold, the same baptizeth, and all *men* come to him.

27 John answered and said, [u]A man can receive nothing, except it be given him from heaven.

28 Ye yourselves bear me witness, that I said, [v]I am not the Christ, but [w]that I am sent before him.

29 [x]He that hath the bride is the bridegroom: but [y]the friend of the bridegroom, which standeth and heareth him, rejoiceth greatly because of the bridegroom's voice: this my joy therefore is fulfilled.

30 He must increase, but I *must* decrease.

31 [z]He that cometh from above [a]is above all: [b]he that is of the earth is earthly, and speaketh of the earth: [c]he that cometh from heaven is above all.

32 And [d]what he hath seen and heard, that he testifieth; and no man receiveth his testimony.

33 He that hath received his testimony [e]hath set to his seal that God is true.

34 [f]For he whom God hath sent speaketh the words of God: for God giveth not the Spirit [g]by measure *unto him*.

35 [h]The Father loveth the Son, and hath given all things into his hand.

36 [i]He that believeth on the Son hath everlasting life: and he that believeth not the Son shall not see life; but the wrath of God abideth on him.

4 When therefore the Lord knew how the Pharisees had heard that Jesus made and [j]baptized more disciples than John,

2 (Though Jesus himself baptized not, but his disciples,)

2:21 [u]1 Cor. 3:16; 2 Cor. 6:16; Col. 2:9; Heb. 8:2
2:22 [v]Luke 24:8
2:25 [w]1 Sam. 16:7; 1 Chron. 28:9; Matt. 9:4; Mark 2:8; ch. 6:64; Acts 1:24; Rev. 2:23
3:2 [x]ch. 7:50 [y]ch. 9:16; Acts 2:22 [z]Acts 10:38
3:3 [a]ch. 1:13; Gal. 6:15; Tit. 3:5; Jam. 1:18; 1 Pet. 1:23; 1 John 3:9
3:5 [b]Mark 16:16; Acts 2:38
3:8 [c]Eccl. 11:5; 1 Cor. 2:11
3:9 [d]ch. 6:52
3:11 [e]Matt. 11:27; ch. 1:18 [f]ver. 32
3:13 [g]Prov. 30:4; ch. 6:33; Acts 2:34; 1 Cor. 15:47; Eph. 4:9
3:14 [h]Num. 21:9 [i]ch. 8:28
3:15 [j]ver. 36; ch. 6:47
3:16 [k]Rom. 5:8; 1 John 4:9
3:17 [l]Luke 9:56; ch. 5:45; 1 John 4:14
3:18 [m]ch. 5:24
3:19 [n]ch. 1:4
3:20 [o]Job 24:13; Eph. 5:13
3:22 [p]ch. 4:2
3:23 [q]1 Sam. 9:4 [r]Matt. 3:5
3:24 [s]Matt. 14:3
3:26 [t]ch. 1:7
3:27 [u]1 Cor. 4:7; Heb. 5:4; Jam. 1:17
3:28 [v]ch. 1:20 [w]Mal. 3:1; Mark 1:2; Luke 1:17
3:29 [x]Matt. 22:2; 2 Cor. 11:2; Eph. 5:25; Rev. 21:9 [y]SSol. 5:1
3:31 [z]ver. 13; ch. 8:23 [a]Matt. 28:18; ch. 1:15; Rom. 9:5 [b]1 Cor. 15:47 [c]ch. 6:33; 1 Cor. 15:47; Eph. 1:21; Phil. 2:9
3:32 [d]ver. 11; ch. 8:26
3:33 [e]Rom. 3:4; 1 John 5:10
3:34 [f]ch. 7:16 [g]ch. 1:16
3:35 [h]Matt. 11:27; Luke 10:22; ch. 5:20; Heb. 2:8
3:36 [i]Hab. 2:4; ch. 1:12; ver. 15; Rom. 1:17; 1 John 5:10
4:1 [j]ch. 3:22

Focus on JOHN

The Gospel of John begins with a prologue (1:1–18) in which John introduces Jesus as the "Word" who became flesh. He maintains that the Word existed in eternity and, in time, became human so that those who believe in Him might have life eternal. Through the skillful use of eight selected miracles and discourses of our Lord, the author shows how the impact of Christ's ministry grew. Then it drew opposition from the Jewish scholars until they finally engineered Christ's crucifixion. Thus rejected, in chapters 13 through 17, Jesus spends considerable time with His disciples preparing them for His death, ultimate victory, and ascension. A number of divine titles are ascribed to Christ by others. Jesus affirmed His own deity with the use of titles like: Lamb of God, the Vine, the Shepherd, the Door, the Water of Life, Bread from heaven, Son of God, the Way, the Truth, the Life, and the Resurrection.

THE BLACK PRESENCE IN JOHN

The location of Palestine, in the northeast quarter of Africa on the border of Asia, assumes a black presence. According to anthropologists the area was originally populated by a people who migrated from Africa around 2,500 to 5,000 B.C. There has been a continuous presence in the area since that time, though by the time of the New Testament, Greeks and Romans were added to the population. The early people of that area were Hamites and Semites. The word Ham means "black" or "burnt face." His sons were Cush, Phut, Mizraim, and Canaan. They were also black. Again we must point out that the issue of color in biblical days was a nonissue. People simply accepted others without regard to skin color. Only in recent years (since the 17th century) have attempts been made to deny the presence of blacks in biblical history.

The apostle John, of course, though born in Palestine, eventually settled in Ephesus. While we do not have access to specific references to the population of Ephesus, we can infer the presence of people of color. We know that the entire Mediterranean world derived much of its knowledge from Africa, and specifically from Alexandria, which was built by Alexander the Great. The library at Alexandria held 700,000 books and scrolls, and people from all over the Greek world, including Ephesus, came to Africa to study and obtain their education.

Life Lessons

JOHN 1

John's purpose in writing was to show that Jesus Christ is from God, speaks for God, and is the only way of access to God. The prologue to his Gospel makes the identity of Christ quite clear. Christ was in the beginning with God, and was, in fact, God. He came to the earth to show us the way back to God. Every person in the world must come to grips with who Jesus is and decide whether to trust Him for life, or reject Him.

Dear God, please open my eyes to the truth of Your Son's identity. Help me to trust Him as my own personal Savior and life according to Your will and way. Amen.

JOHN 4

Jesus challenged His disciples to lift their eyes to see the enormity of human need and accept the challenge of being workers who will help bring in the harvest.

Dear God, please open my eyes to see someone in need today. Give me the love and ability to help someone who needs Your love in a special way.

JOHN 6

Five thousand men plus women and children were hungry, and Jesus fed them.

Holy Provider, thank You for attending to all my physical needs.

Women in JOHN

THE FORGIVEN ADULTERESS: CAUGHT, BUT NOT CONDEMNED

She was caught. She was dragged before the men of the community. She was accused. She waited to be stoned—to be destroyed by anything they decided to throw at her. But had she loved him? Had he told her it would be all right, that he would fix everything, that he loved her? But when the witnesses burst in on them, he apparently didn't protest, didn't defend her, and conveniently escaped prosecution.

He left her to face her accusers alone. There was nothing she could say that they were willing to hear. The community let him escape—she would be stoned to her death.

The guys may have laughed behind their hands when they saw him, but he had his life. On the other hand, all her friends and acquaintances

pulled away. After all, she might be after their man. Can't you hear them—her sisters—their words pouring acid into the wound of her shame? There was no one to stand by her side in her defense. Oh, the pain of being the one caught—exposed for the world to see.

You may have tried drugs and were out there for awhile. Finally, enough was enough, but now your family doesn't trust you and has trouble believing in you.

Your destructive relationships almost cost you your life—black eyes and swollen lips, hospital visits, and the inability to hold a job. You are always hiding, afraid, and ashamed.

You have felt everyone knew your business and thought you were unworthy. Our sister must have felt belittled, judged by the self-righteous, and found guilty. But out of the crowd, at the point of our deepest fear, steps Jesus!

God is willing to forgive when you repent and turn to Him, writing in the dust of our broken lives and challenging the finger-pointers to check out the four fingers pointing back at them!

We might be caught, but Jesus does not condemn us! He forgives us! Jesus paid the price for the adulteress and for all of us.

Jesus challenges each of us to make new choices, and His grace provides hope for all our lives.

Read John 7:53–8:11; see also Exodus 20:14; Leviticus 20:10; Deuteronomy 17:5–6.

Read the insight essays on Adultery and Forgiveness.

—M. Bellinger

MARY OF BETHANY: THE UNFORGOTTEN WOMAN

Overwhelmed by the cares of the world, the African-American woman is frequently caring for children, elderly parents, or even the extended family. She obtains the necessities, but wishes for the finer things of life and also searches for stability and success. Mary of Bethany is one example to be followed concerning what is most important for a believer to care about. Her Hebrew name means "bitterness resulting from trouble, sorrow, disobedience, and rebellion." Like so many women, she probably had her share of all of these. Nevertheless, this Mary did not allow the circumstances of life to hold her back. She is portrayed as a disciple and a worshiper. Twice Jesus commended her actions by profoundly saying that she knew what to choose and that she would not be forgotten.

Mary's identity was always in the shadow of her siblings, Martha and Lazarus—but especially in her sister's. One can view these sisters as two sides of our inner selves. At one moment, we may see some of Mary's attributes in our lives, and at another time her sister's. It is not a matter of good or bad, but rather good and better concerning the decisions. There are choices and priorities, and hopefully we will make the better one in a particular situation.

In the case of Luke 10:38–42, Mary makes the better choice. Seated at the feet of Jesus, she is a true disciple. For the first century Jew, this position symbolized a level of higher education, which was not the norm for women. It was revolutionary for Jesus to even consider a woman capable

of intellectual learning. There would always be tables to set and meals to prepare, but how many opportunities would there be to spend time with the Lord in the flesh in your home? Hopefully, Mary's sister did not regret her choice, since Jesus said that Mary's choice would not be taken from her.

Another aspect of Mary's character is that of a worshiper. In John 11:2, 12:1–3 (see also Matt. 26:6–13), Mary is the woman who uses the costly perfume to anoint Jesus. Her action would not be forgotten. It was Mary's sister who declared the great theological truth of Jesus as Messiah and the resurrection. Although, after being taught by Jesus, Mary seemed to understand that He had to endure the cross before the resurrection. She was symbolizing His preparation for burial. Could she have had a deeper understanding than her male counterparts? In both situations as disciple and worshiper, Mary had the insight or intuition that Jesus would not always be with them. She seized the day and enjoyed being in His presence.

Read John 11:28–36, 45; 12:3–8; see also Mark 14:1–9; Luke 10:38–42.

Read the insight essays on Commitment and Faith.

—A. Aubry

MARY AND MARTHA: DETERMINED SISTERS

"Jesus said unto her, I am the resurrection, and the life: he that believeth in me, though he were dead, yet shall he live" (John 11:25).

It is difficult to believe that death could happen to a sister, brother, or someone significant to us that we love. Death, we think, always happens to someone else and at some other time. But all too often we realize that death happens to us and our loved ones at the most unexpected times. We then began to realize that the loss of a loved one touches every one of us.

One of the most remarkable and memorable stories in the Bible about siblings dealing with death is found in the Gospel of John (John 11:1–44). It is the story of Mary of Bethany, her sister Martha, and their brother Lazarus.

At first glance, this biblical story of two women provides a glimpse of the beautiful sisters that they are. But we soon learn that they are suffering sisters (John 11:1–2). They've experienced sickness, shame, and persecution, yet there is something special about how God has protected them by giving them a strong, protective friend in Jesus.

The powerful lesson in this story is that Mary and Martha weathered many trials yet triumphed because they were willing to cast their burdens upon Jesus, which is why they sent for Him when Lazarus was dying: "Lord behold, he whom you love is sick" (John 11:3).

When Lazarus dies, Jesus comforts them. But He also demonstrates His power to them by raising Lazarus from the dead. It was a miracle that these two sisters had to experience in order to realize the true glory and compassion of Christ.

Read John 11:28–36, 45; 12:1–8; see also Matthew 26:6–13; Mark 14:1–9; Luke 10:38–42.

—D. Moore-James

MARY, THE MOTHER OF JESUS: TRUE MOTHERHOOD

She is described as a virgin (Luke 1:27), highly favored (Luke 1:28), and blessed (Luke 1:42). Her total trust earned God's pleasure (Luke 1:26–28). In the Magnificat (Luke 1:46–55), even in the face of social ridicule, Mary rejoices at being chosen by God. Her song reveals an understanding of the theology of reversals in the messianic age—how the lowly are lifted high, the mighty are brought low, the hungry are filled, and the rich are sent away empty.

Jesus was closer to His mother than He was to any other person, even His father Joseph. Each one of the Gospels shows Mary in a different light. Jesus, in the genealogy in Matthew, is listed as Mary's son—and Joseph is given a secondary status, merely mentioned as her husband. Within Jewish culture, being mentioned as a son of a woman would have been considered demeaning. However, in this instance, it heightens the importance of Mary and honors her. In Mark, the family of Jesus is rarely mentioned. Joseph is not mentioned at all. Mark 3:20–27, 31–35 and 6:1–6 present the remainder of the family unfavorably. According to Jesus, the new definition of His family is whoever does the will of God. John (19:25–27) positions the mother of Jesus (who is unnamed in this Gospel) at the cross where she now has achieved true motherhood. Jesus confers a title upon her that transcends their familial connection—Jesus makes her John's mother.

Finally, according to Acts 1:14, Mary is included as one of the devoted disciples in the upper room. She receives the Holy Spirit, which came upon her when Jesus was conceived (compare Luke 1:35; Acts 2:1–4).

Mothers today should follow Mary's example and provide their own children, and those they nurture spiritually, with the messages of God's love and faithfulness.

Read John 2:1–5; 19:25–27; see also Matthew 1:16–25; Mark 3:31; Luke 1–2; Acts 1:14.

See also the insight essays on Motherhood and Widows.

—P. Williamson

Insights

DOMESTIC VIOLENCE

"For God so loved the world that he gave his only begotten Son, that whosoever believeth in Him should not perish but have everlasting life" (John 3:16). "And thou shalt love the Lord thy God with all thy heart, . . . this is the first commandment. . . . Thou shalt love thy neighbour as thyself. There is none other commandment greater than these" (Mark 12:30–31). "[Charity (love)] doth not behave itself unseemly" (1 Cor. 13:5). "If ye love me, keep my commandments" (John 14:15).

The great God of the universe loves us. He wants us to love Him, each other, and ourselves. God never intended for us to be victimized. The texts above illustrate how important the principle of love is to Him.

Too often African-American women overlook or forget the part of the commandment that requires that we love ourselves. The culture does not embrace us, and we are sent messages not to love ourselves. Furthermore, we sometimes do not fully understand what love does and does not require, particularly in intimate relationships. We cannot love another in the way God desires if we do not love, respect, and protect ourselves first.

Violence is incompatible with love. Domestic violence (physical, psychological, economic, sexual) is sin. Violent relationships break the greatest commandment. Furthermore, we know that the Holy Spirit neither produces nor condones abuse, for love and gentleness are fruits of the Spirit (see Gal. 5:22). In the New Testament, husbands are admonished to love their wives unconditionally and sacrificially (Eph. 5:25).

You are valuable to God. His sacrifice for you demonstrates that. No matter what you have been told, what you have experienced, what mistakes you may have made, God loves you and wants you to be loved. He also wants you to take care of your life. No one has His authority to demean and brutalize you. No earthly promise can supersede His commands. If you are in a relationship that threatens your mental or physical health (your soul and your temple), seek guidance and strength from the Spirit as to how to bring your life in accordance with God's will, that all His children "should prosper and be in health" (3 John 2). Consult with trained professionals to assist you in adopting a lifestyle that will bring you in compliance with God's command to love yourself.

Read John 3:16; 14:15.

Read essays on Marriage, Overcoming Abuse, and Suffering.

—L. Ammons

WOMEN'S MINISTRIES—EVANGELIST

My first encounter with a woman evangelist was probably the day I was born. My mother, though not a minister, taught me the Scriptures and drilled into me the love of God expressed through God's Son, Jesus Christ. Her testimony kept me from straying too far from the truth and was instrumental in my own call to ministry. Jesus affirmed women in the ministry and the ministry of women evangelists. This was evident in His interaction with the Samaritan woman at the well (John 4:1–39). The Samaritan woman was instrumental in evangelizing her entire town. She did not use fancy words or profound theological statements; she simply said, "Come, see a man which told me all things that I ever did: is not this the Christ?" (John 4:29).

There are many examples of women evangelists in the New Testament. In Matthew 5:13–16, Jesus stated that His followers were "salt" and "light" for the world. We can assume this includes women as well. Matthew 28:1–8 informs us that the angel at the empty tomb directed the women to go tell the disciples that Jesus was alive. They became witnesses to His resurrection.

African-American women have evangelized their communities and their children for a long time. As our world continues to devalue human beings, we must still be willing to go forward and declare that "Jesus saves" to the utmost. Jesus saves from domestic violence, racism, sexism,

poverty, low self-esteem, brokenheartedness, loneliness, and drug addiction. Jesus saves!

Read John 4:1–30; 20:15–18; see also Acts 1:8; 5:11–15; 17:12.
Read the insight essays on Evangelism and Women's Ministries.

—C. Belt

PEACE

So often in life we've heard others (or even ourselves) say, "I'm looking for some peace," or "If only I can find peace," or "I wish peace would come." These very words imply that peace is somewhere far off. They imply that peace is something to be given from some abstract place or by some unknown person. So we act out these words and define what peace means from some external source.

In one sense, we hear politicians speak of world peace in a context of it's being the absence of conflict. Yet, wars occur in the name of gaining peace. People lose their lives believing in the cause of peace. They go to battle with codes of honor to fight for the cause of peace.

Then there is the concern for peace that leads many of us to believe that it comes in the following ways:

When we are free of financial cares;
When we have good jobs or are doing well in our entrepreneurial endeavors;
When we have great comfortable places to call home;
When we have significant others (husbands/wives);
When we belong to prestigious civic groups;
When we are in charge of our lives, and the list goes on and on.

Finally, there is the notion that we can escape to a place of peace by smoking, drinking, using drugs, having sex, or wielding power.

The truth of the matter is, many of us teach ourselves that peace is attainable through some, or all, of these ways. We allow these things to make us high. Our lives are replete with a searching and meandering that keeps us completely unsatisfied and afraid of losing our worldly acquisitions. Fear, panic, and/or desperation lead us into conflict with others and ourselves. When the rush of the high is gone, we are desperate for its return. We repeat the cycle, become depressed, and tell ourselves to be comfortable and content with the habits we have formed. We say to ourselves, "This is Life!"

Many of the things we do on a daily basis have merit and they are indeed worthwhile. But they must be placed in their proper context, however, or peace will continue to evade us. We must come to learn that peace does not come through worldly things or pleasures if it is to last. We must go to its Source.

Jesus said, "Peace I leave with you, my peace I give unto you: not as the world giveth, give I unto you. Let not your heart be troubled, neither let it be afraid" (John 14:27). Learning God's Word and applying it to our hearts and lives will engage this Fruit of the Spirit for us. It will teach us how to place all worldly necessities and pleasures in their proper places. It will teach us that in this world we will have trials, tribulations, and disappointments, as well as pleasures, successes, and happiness. However, we can have peace in any of these of conditions because the peace given

to us in our Lord and Savior Jesus Christ is the basis of our contentment in whatever condition we find ourselves. It is the peace that takes us beyond our human understanding. The secret of overcoming the anxiety we face (the absence of peace) is to constantly rejoice in the Lord and to pray to Him, giving thanks for His provision, His grace, and His mercy, now and in the future. When we come to know that God is taking care of our affairs, we can allow the peace of God to fill our lives. God's peace is not dependent on outward circumstances. Supernatural peace comes from the confidence of knowing that God is in control. Paul describes it best, "And the peace of God, which passeth all understanding, shall keep your hearts and minds through Jesus Christ" (Phil. 4:7).

Read John 14:27.

Read the insight essays on Confidence, Distress, Fruit of the Spirit, and Peace.

—C. Richards

SACRIFICIAL LIVING—MY LIFE IS NOT MY OWN

"Wait on the LORD: be of good courage, and he shall strengthen thine heart: wait, I say, on the LORD" (Ps. 27:14). Sometimes I believe I can almost hear the souls of African-American women crying out, "How long O Lord must we wait!" We have waited for hundreds of years for inclusion in the benefits of our nation. We have sacrificed our wants, desires, and needs for the good of the whole, and still we are in many ways disenfranchised.

However, the Word instructs us that the "system" we must seek inclusion in—and the benefits of—is the kingdom of God. No earthly system, government, or culture can compare to that of God.

Even though we, by earthly standards, have sacrificed a great deal, it cannot compare to the sacrifice of Christ Jesus (Matt. 26:52–54; Mark 14:36). Just as Jesus laid down His life for us, we must lay down our lives for others (1 John 3:16–17), giving it completely and wholeheartedly.

African-American women have a unique opportunity to illustrate to the remainder of the body of Christ and the world: the godly principle of denying oneself and living for Christ and others (John 15:12–17). This is the legacy of our foreparents—a legacy not of gold, silver, and worldly riches, but one of sacrifice, service, and love for Christ and the body of Christ (John 12:25–26; Rom. 12:10; 1 Cor. 13:1–3). We must again remove ourselves from the standards of success set by the world and look to the Word of God for our validation (John 6:27; Rom. 12:1–2).

Read John 15:12–17.

Read the insight essays on Commitment, and Suffering.

—A. Manuel

3 He left Judaea, and departed again into Galilee.

4 And he must needs go through Samaria.

5 Then cometh he to a city of Samaria, which is called Sychar, near to the parcel of ground [k]that Jacob gave to his son Joseph.

6 Now Jacob's well was there. Jesus therefore, being wearied with *his* journey, sat thus on the well: *and* it was about the sixth hour.

7 There cometh a woman of Samaria to draw water: Jesus saith unto her, Give me to drink.

8 (For his disciples were gone away unto the city to buy meat.)

9 Then saith the woman of Samaria unto him, How is it that thou, being a Jew, askest drink of me, which am a woman of Samaria? for [l]the Jews have no dealings with the Samaritans.

10 Jesus answered and said unto her, If thou knewest the gift of God, and who it is that saith to thee, Give me to drink; thou wouldest have asked of him, and he would have given thee [m]living water.

11 The woman saith unto him, Sir, thou hast nothing to draw with, and the well is deep: from whence then hast thou that living water?

12 Art thou greater than our father Jacob, which gave us the well, and drank thereof himself, and his children, and his cattle?

13 Jesus answered and said unto her, Whosoever drinketh of this water shall thirst again:

14 But [n]whosoever drinketh of the water that I shall give him shall never thirst; but the water that I shall give him [o]shall be in him a well of water springing up into everlasting life.

15 [p]The woman saith unto him, Sir, give me this water, that I thirst not, neither come hither to draw.

16 Jesus saith unto her, Go, call thy husband, and come hither.

17 The woman answered and said, I have no husband. Jesus said unto her, Thou hast well said, I have no husband:

18 For thou hast had five husbands; and he whom thou now hast is not thy husband: in that saidst thou truly.

19 The woman saith unto him, Sir, [q]I perceive that thou art a prophet.

20 Our fathers worshipped in [r]this mountain; and ye say, that in [s]Jerusalem is the place where men ought to worship.

21 Jesus saith unto her, Woman, believe me, the hour cometh, [t]when ye shall neither in this mountain, nor yet at Jerusalem, worship the Father.

22 Ye worship [u]ye know not what: we know what we worship: for [v]salvation is of the Jews.

23 But the hour cometh, and now is, when the true worshippers shall worship the Father in [w]spirit [x]and in truth: for the Father seeketh such to worship him.

24 [y]God *is* a Spirit: and they that worship him must worship *him* in spirit and in truth.

25 The woman saith unto him, I know that Messias cometh, which is called Christ: when he is come, [z]he will tell us all things.

26 Jesus saith unto her, [a]I that speak unto thee am *he*.

27 ¶ And upon this came his disciples, and marvelled that he talked with the woman: yet no man said, What seekest thou? or, Why talkest thou with her?

28 The woman then left her waterpot, and went her way into the city, and saith to the men,

29 Come, see a man, [b]which told me all things that ever I did: is not this the Christ?

30 Then they went out of the city, and came unto him.

31 ¶ In the mean while his disciples prayed him, saying, Master, eat.

32 But he said unto them, I have meat to eat that ye know not of.

33 Therefore said the disciples one to another, Hath any man brought him *ought* to eat?

34 Jesus saith unto them, [c]My meat is to do the will of him that sent me, and to finish his work.

35 Say not ye, There are yet four months, and *then* cometh harvest? behold, I say unto you, Lift up your eyes, and look on the fields; [d]for they are white already to harvest.

36 [e]And he that reapeth receiveth wages, and gathereth fruit unto life eternal: that both he that soweth and he that reapeth may rejoice together.

37 And herein is that saying true, One soweth, and another reapeth.

38 I sent you to reap that whereon ye bestowed no labour: other men laboured, and ye are entered into their labours.

39 ¶ And many of the Samaritans of that city believed on him [f]for the saying of the woman, which testified, He told me all that ever I did.

40 So when the Samaritans were come unto him, they besought him that he would tarry with them: and he abode there two days.

41 And many more believed because of his own word;

42 And said unto the woman, Now we believe, not because of thy saying: for [g]we have heard *him* ourselves, and know that this is indeed the Christ, the Saviour of the world.

43 ¶ Now after two days he departed thence, and went into Galilee.

44 For [h]Jesus himself testified, that a prophet hath no honour in his own country.

45 Then when he was come into Galilee, the Galileans received him, [i]having seen all the things that he did at Jerusalem at the feast: [j]for they also went unto the feast.

46 So Jesus came again into Cana of Galilee, [k]where he made the water wine. And there was a certain nobleman, whose son was sick at Capernaum.

4:5 [k]Gen. 33:19; Josh. 24:32
4:9 [l]2 Kings 17:24; Luke 9:52; Acts 10:28
4:10 [m]Isa. 12:3; Jer. 2:13; Zech. 13:1
4:14 [n]ch. 6:35 [o]ch. 7:38
4:15 [p]ch. 6:34; Rom. 6:23; 1 John 5:20
4:19 [q]Luke 7:16; ch. 6:14
4:20 [r]Judg. 9:7 [s]Deut. 12:5; 1 Kings 9:3; 2 Chron. 7:12
4:21 [t]Mal. 11; 1 Tim. 2:8
4:22 [u]2 Kings 17:29 [v]Isa. 2:3; Luke 24:47; Rom. 9:4
4:23 [w]Phil. 3:3 [x]ch. 1:17
4:24 [y]2 Cor. 3:17
4:25 [z]ver. 29
4:26 [a]ch. 9:37; Matt. 26:63; Mark 14:61
4:29 [b]ver. 25
4:34 [c]Job 23:12; ch. 6:38
4:35 [d]Matt. 9:37; Luke 10:2
4:36 [e]Dan. 12:3
4:39 [f]ver. 29
4:42 [g]ch. 17:8; 1 John 4:14
4:44 [h]Matt. 13:57; Mark 6:4; Luke 4:24
4:45 [i]ch. 2:23 [j]Deut. 16:16
4:46 [k]ch. 2:1

47 When he heard that Jesus was come out of Judaea into Galilee, he went unto him, and besought him that he would come down, and heal his son: for he was at the point of death.

48 Then said Jesus unto him, [l]Except ye see signs and wonders, ye will not believe.

49 The nobleman saith unto him, Sir, come down ere my child die.

50 Jesus saith unto him, Go thy way; thy son liveth. And the man believed the word that Jesus had spoken unto him, and he went his way.

51 And as he was now going down, his servants met him, and told *him*, saying, Thy son liveth.

52 Then enquired he of them the hour when he began to amend. And they said unto him, Yesterday at the seventh hour the fever left him.

53 So the father knew that *it was* at the same hour, in the which Jesus said unto him, Thy son liveth: and himself believed, and his whole house.

54 This *is* again the second miracle *that* Jesus did, when he was come out of Judaea into Galilee.

5 After [m]this there was a feast of the Jews; and Jesus went up to Jerusalem.

2 Now there is at Jerusalem [n]by the sheep *market* a pool, which is called in the Hebrew tongue Bethesda, having five porches.

3 In these lay a great multitude of impotent folk, of blind, halt, withered, waiting for the moving of the water.

4 For an angel went down at a certain season into the pool, and troubled the water: whosoever then first after the troubling of the water stepped in was made whole of whatsoever disease he had.

5 And a certain man was there, which had an infirmity thirty and eight years.

6 When Jesus saw him lie, and knew that he had been now a long time *in that case*, he saith unto him, Wilt thou be made whole?

7 The impotent man answered him, Sir, I have no man, when the water is troubled, to put me into the pool: but while I am coming, another steppeth down before me.

8 Jesus saith unto him, [o]Rise, take up thy bed, and walk.

9 And immediately the man was made whole, and took up his bed, and walked: and [p]on the same day was the sabbath.

10 ¶ The Jews therefore said unto him that was cured, It is the sabbath day: [q]it is not lawful for thee to carry *thy* bed.

11 He answered them, He that made me whole, the same said unto me, Take up thy bed, and walk.

12 Then asked they him, What man is that which said unto thee, Take up thy bed, and walk?

13 And he that was healed wist not who it was: for Jesus had conveyed himself away, a multitude being in *that* place.

14 Afterward Jesus findeth him in the temple, and said unto him, Behold, thou art made whole: [r]sin no more, lest a worse thing come unto thee.

15 The man departed, and told the Jews that it was Jesus, which had made him whole.

16 And therefore did the Jews persecute Jesus, and sought to slay him, because he had done these things on the sabbath day.

17 ¶ But Jesus answered them, [s]My Father worketh hitherto, and I work.

18 Therefore the Jews [t]sought the more to kill him, because he not only had broken the sabbath, but said also that God was his Father, [u]making himself equal with God.

19 Then answered Jesus and said unto them, Verily, verily, I say unto you, [v]The Son can do nothing of himself, but what he seeth the Father do: for what things soever he doeth, these also doeth the Son likewise.

20 For [w]the Father loveth the Son, and sheweth him all things that himself doeth: and he will shew him greater works than these, that ye may marvel.

21 For as the Father raiseth up the dead, and quickeneth *them;* [x]even so the Son quickeneth whom he will.

22 For the Father judgeth no man, but [y]hath committed all judgment unto the Son:

23 That all *men* should honour the Son, even as they honour the Father. [z]He that honoureth not the Son honoureth not the Father which hath sent him.

24 Verily, verily, I say unto you, [a]He that heareth my word, and believeth on him that sent me, hath everlasting life, and shall not come into condemnation; [b]but is passed from death unto life.

25 Verily, verily, I say unto you, The hour is coming, and now is, when [c]the dead shall hear the voice of the Son of God: and they that hear shall live.

26 For as the Father hath life in himself; so hath he given to the Son to have life in himself;

27 And [d]hath given him authority to execute judgment also, [e]because he is the Son of man.

28 Marvel not at this: for the hour is coming, in the which all that are in the graves shall hear his voice,

29 [f]And shall come forth; [g]they that have done good, unto the resurrection of life; and they that have done evil, unto the resurrection of damnation.

30 [h]I can of mine own self do nothing: as I hear, I judge: and my judgment is just; because [i]I seek not mine own will, but the will of the Father which hath sent me.

31 [j]If I bear witness of myself, my witness is not true.

32 ¶ [k]There is another that beareth witness of me; and I know that the witness which he witnesseth of me is true.

33 Ye sent unto John, [l]and he bare witness unto the truth.

34 But I receive not testimony from man:

4:48 [l]1 Cor. 1:22
5:1 [m]Lev. 23:2; Deut. 16:1; ch. 2:13
5:2 [n]Neh. 3:1
5:8 [o]Matt. 9:6; Mark 2:11; Luke 5:24
5:9 [p]ch. 9:14
5:10 [q]Ex. 20:10; Neh. 13:19; Jer. 17:21; Matt. 12:2; Mark 2:24; Luke 6:2
5:14 [r]Matt. 12:45; ch. 8:11
5:17 [s]ch. 9:4
5:18 [t]ch. 7:19 [u]ch. 10:30; Phil. 2:6
5:19 [v]ver. 30; ch. 8:28
5:20 [w]Matt. 3:17; ch. 3:35; 2 Pet. 1:17
5:21 [x]Luke 7:14; ch. 11:25
5:22 [y]Matt. 11:27; ver. 27; ch. 3:35; Acts 17:31; 1 Pet. 4:5
5:23 [z]1 John 2:23
5:24 [a]ch. 3:16 [b]1 John 3:14
5:25 [c]ver. 28; Eph. 2:1; Col. 2:13
5:27 [d]ver. 22; Acts 10:42 [e]Dan. 7:13
5:29 [f]Isa. 26:19; 1 Thess. 4:16; 1 Cor. 15:52 [g]Dan. 12:2; Matt. 25:32
5:30 [h]ver. 19 [i]Matt. 26:39; ch. 4:34
5:31 [j]ch. 8:14; Rev. 3:14
5:32 [k]Matt. 3:17; ch. 8:18; 1 John 5:6
5:33 [l]ch. 1:15

but these things I say, that ye might be saved.

35 He was a burning and [m]a shining light: and [n]ye were willing for a season to rejoice in his light.

36 ¶ But [o]I have greater witness than *that* of John: for [p]the works which the Father hath given me to finish, the same works that I do, bear witness of me, that the Father hath sent me.

37 And the Father himself, which hath sent me, [q]hath borne witness of me. Ye have neither heard his voice at any time, [r]nor seen his shape.

38 And ye have not his word abiding in you: for whom he hath sent, him ye believe not.

39 ¶ [s]Search the scriptures; for in them ye think ye have eternal life: and [t]they are they which testify of me.

40 [u]And ye will not come to me, that ye might have life.

41 [v]I receive not honour from men.

42 But I know you, that ye have not the love of God in you.

43 I am come in my Father's name, and ye receive me not: if another shall come in his own name, him ye will receive.

44 [w]How can ye believe, which receive honour one of another, and seek not [x]the honour that *cometh* from God only?

45 Do not think that I will accuse you to the Father: [y]there is *one* that accuseth you, *even* Moses, in whom ye trust.

46 For had ye believed Moses, ye would have believed me: [z]for he wrote of me.

47 But if ye believe not his writings, how shall ye believe my words?

6 After [a]these things Jesus went over the sea of Galilee, which is *the sea* of Tiberias.

2 And a great multitude followed him, because they saw his miracles which he did on them that were diseased.

3 And Jesus went up into a mountain, and there he sat with his disciples.

4 [b]And the passover, a feast of the Jews, was nigh.

5 ¶ [c]When Jesus then lifted up *his* eyes, and saw a great company come unto him, he saith unto Philip, Whence shall we buy bread, that these may eat?

6 And this he said to prove him: for he himself knew what he would do.

7 Philip answered him, [d]Two hundred pennyworth of bread is not sufficient for them, that every one of them may take a little.

8 One of his disciples, Andrew, Simon Peter's brother, saith unto him,

9 There is a lad here, which hath five barley loaves, and two small fishes: [e]but what are they among so many?

10 And Jesus said, Make the men sit down. Now there was much grass in the place. So the men sat down, in number about five thousand.

11 And Jesus took the loaves; and when he had given thanks, he distributed to the disciples, and the disciples to them that were set down; and likewise of the fishes as much as they would.

12 When they were filled, he said unto his disciples, Gather up the fragments that remain, that nothing be lost.

13 Therefore they gathered *them* together, and filled twelve baskets with the fragments of the five barley loaves, which remained over and above unto them that had eaten.

14 Then those men, when they had seen the miracle that Jesus did, said, This is of a truth [f]that prophet that should come into the world.

15 ¶ When Jesus therefore perceived that they would come and take him by force, to make him a king, he departed again into a mountain himself alone.

16 [g]And when even was *now* come, his disciples went down unto the sea,

17 And entered into a ship, and went over the sea toward Capernaum. And it was now dark, and Jesus was not come to them.

18 And the sea arose by reason of a great wind that blew.

19 So when they had rowed about five and twenty or thirty furlongs, they see Jesus walking on the sea, and drawing nigh unto the ship: and they were afraid.

20 But he saith unto them, It is I; be not afraid.

21 Then they willingly received him into the ship: and immediately the ship was at the land whither they went.

22 ¶ The day following, when the people which stood on the other side of the sea saw that there was none other boat there, save that one whereinto his disciples were entered, and that Jesus went not with his disciples into the boat, but *that* his disciples were gone away alone;

23 (Howbeit there came other boats from Tiberias nigh unto the place where they did eat bread, after that the Lord had given thanks:)

24 When the people therefore saw that Jesus was not there, neither his disciples, they also took shipping, and came to Capernaum, seeking for Jesus.

25 And when they had found him on the other side of the sea, they said unto him, Rabbi, when camest thou hither?

26 Jesus answered them and said, Verily, verily, I say unto you, Ye seek me, not because ye saw the miracles, but because ye did eat of the loaves, and were filled.

27 Labour not for the meat which perisheth, but [h]for that meat which endureth unto everlasting life, which the Son of man shall give unto you: [i]for him hath God the Father sealed.

28 Then said they unto him, What shall we do, that we might work the works of God?

29 Jesus answered and said unto them,

5:35 [m]2 Pet. 1:19 [n]Matt. 13:20; Mark 6:20
5:36 [o]1 John 5:9 [p]ch. 3:2
5:37 [q]Matt. 3:17; ch. 6:27 [r]Deut. 4:12; ch. 1:18; 1 Tim. 1:17; 1 John 4:12
5:39 [s]Isa. 8:20; Luke 16:29; ver. 46; Acts 17:11 [t]Deut. 18:15; Luke 24:27; ch. 1:45
5:40 [u]ch. 1:11
5:41 [v]ver. 34; 1 Thess. 2:6
5:44 [w]ch. 12:43 [x]Rom. 2:29
5:45 [y]Rom. 2:12
5:46 [z]Gen. 3:15; Deut. 18:15; ch. 1:45; Acts 26:22
6:1 [a]Matt. 14:15; Mark 6:35; Luke 9:10
6:4 [b]Lev. 23:5; Deut. 16:1; ch. 2:13
6:5 [c]Matt. 14:14; Mark 6:35; Luke 9:12
6:7 [d]Num. 11:21
6:9 [e]2 Kings 4:43
6:14 [f]Gen. 49:10; Deut. 18:15; Matt. 11:3; ch. 1:21
6:16 [g]Matt. 14:23; Mark 6:47
6:27 [h]ver. 54; ch. 4:14 [i]Matt. 3:17; Mark 1:11; Luke 3:22; ch. 1:33; Acts 2:22; 2 Pet. 1:17

[j]This is the work of God, that ye believe on him whom he hath sent.

30 They said therefore unto him, [k]What sign shewest thou then, that we may see, and believe thee? what dost thou work?

31 [l]Our fathers did eat manna in the desert; as it is written, [m]He gave them bread from heaven to eat.

32 Then Jesus said unto them, Verily, verily, I say unto you, Moses gave you not that bread from heaven; but my Father giveth you the true bread from heaven.

33 For the bread of God is he which cometh down from heaven, and giveth life unto the world.

34 [n]Then said they unto him, Lord, evermore give us this bread.

35 And Jesus said unto them, [o]I am the bread of life: [p]he that cometh to me shall never hunger; and he that believeth on me shall never thirst.

36 [q]But I said unto you, That ye also have seen me, and believe not.

37 [r]All that the Father giveth me shall come to me; and [s]him that cometh to me I will in no wise cast out.

38 For I came down from heaven, [t]not to do mine own will, [u]but the will of him that sent me.

39 And this is the Father's will which hath sent me, [v]that of all which he hath given me I should lose nothing, but should raise it up again at the last day.

40 And this is the will of him that sent me, [w]that every one which seeth the Son, and believeth on him, may have everlasting life: and I will raise him up at the last day.

41 The Jews then murmured at him, because he said, I am the bread which came down from heaven.

42 And they said, [x]Is not this Jesus, the son of Joseph, whose father and mother we know? how is it then that he saith, I came down from heaven?

43 Jesus therefore answered and said unto them, Murmur not among yourselves.

44 [y]No man can come to me, except the Father which hath sent me draw him: and I will raise him up at the last day.

45 [z]It is written in the prophets, And they shall be all taught of God. [a]Every man therefore that hath heard, and hath learned of the Father, cometh unto me.

46 [b]Not that any man hath seen the Father, [c]save he which is of God, he hath seen the Father.

47 Verily, verily, I say unto you, [d]He that believeth on me hath everlasting life.

48 [e]I am that bread of life.

49 [f]Your fathers did eat manna in the wilderness, and are dead.

50 [g]This is the bread which cometh down from heaven, that a man may eat thereof, and not die.

51 I am the living bread [h]which came down from heaven: if any man eat of this bread, he shall live for ever: and [i]the bread that I will give is my flesh, which I will give for the life of the world.

52 The Jews therefore [j]strove among themselves, saying, [k]How can this man give us *his* flesh to eat?

53 Then Jesus said unto them, Verily, verily, I say unto you, Except [l]ye eat the flesh of the Son of man, and drink his blood, ye have no life in you.

54 [m]Whoso eateth my flesh, and drinketh my blood, hath eternal life; and I will raise him up at the last day.

55 For my flesh is meat indeed, and my blood is drink indeed.

56 He that eateth my flesh, and drinketh my blood, [n]dwelleth in me, and I in him.

57 As the living Father hath sent me, and I live by the Father: so he that eateth me, even he shall live by me.

58 [o]This is that bread which came down from heaven: not as your fathers did eat manna, and are dead: he that eateth of this bread shall live for ever.

59 These things said he in the synagogue, as he taught in Capernaum.

60 [p]Many therefore of his disciples, when they had heard *this,* said, This is an hard saying; who can hear it?

61 When Jesus knew in himself that his disciples murmured at it, he said unto them, Doth this offend you?

62 [q]*What* and if ye shall see the Son of man ascend up where he was before?

63 [r]It is the spirit that quickeneth; the flesh profiteth nothing: the words that I speak unto you, *they* are spirit, and *they* are life.

64 But [s]there are some of you that believe not. For [t]Jesus knew from the beginning who they were that believed not, and who should betray him.

65 And he said, Therefore [u]said I unto you, that no man can come unto me, except it were given unto him of my Father.

66 ¶ [v]From that *time* many of his disciples went back, and walked no more with him.

67 Then said Jesus unto the twelve, Will ye also go away?

68 Then Simon Peter answered him, Lord, to whom shall we go? thou hast [w]the words of eternal life.

69 [x]And we believe and are sure that thou art that Christ, the Son of the living God.

70 Jesus answered them, [y]Have not I chosen you twelve, [z]and one of you is a devil?

71 He spake of Judas Iscariot *the son* of Simon: for he it was that should betray him, being one of the twelve.

7 After these things Jesus walked in Galilee: for he would not walk in Jewry, [a]because the Jews sought to kill him.

2 [b]Now the Jews' feast of tabernacles was at hand.

3 [c]His brethren therefore said unto him, Depart hence, and go into Judaea, that thy

6:29 [j]1 John 3:23
6:30 [k]Matt. 12:38; Mark 8:11; 1 Cor. 1:22
6:31 [l]Ex. 16:15; Num. 11:7; Neh. 9:15; 1 Cor. 10:3 [m]Ps. 78:24
6:34 [n]ch. 4:15
6:35 [o]ver. 48 [p]ch. 4:14
6:36 [q]ver. 26
6:37 [r]ver. 45 [s]Matt. 24:24; ch. 10:28; 2 Tim. 2:19; 1 John 2:19
6:38 [t]Matt. 26:39; ch. 5:30 [u]ch. 4:34
6:39 [v]ch. 10:28
6:40 [w]ver. 27; ch. 3:15
6:42 [x]Matt. 13:55; Mark 6:3; Luke 4:22
6:44 [y]SSol. 1:4; ver. 65
6:45 [z]Isa. 54:13; Jer. 31:34; Mic. 4:2; Heb. 8:10 [a]ver. 37
6:46 [b]ch. 1:18 [c]Matt. 11:27; Luke 10:22; ch. 1:18
6:47 [d]ch. 3:16; ver. 40
6:48 [e]ver. 33
6:49 [f]ver. 31
6:50 [g]ver. 51
6:51 [h]ch. 3:13 [i]Heb. 10:5
6:52 [j]ch. 7:43 [k]ch. 3:9
6:53 [l]Matt. 26:26
6:54 [m]ver. 27; ch. 4:14
6:56 [n]1 John 3:24
6:58 [o]ver. 49
6:60 [p]ver. 66; Matt. 11:6
6:62 [q]ch. 3:13; Mark 16:19; Acts 1:9; Eph. 4:8
6:63 [r]2 Cor. 3:6
6:64 [s]ver. 36 [t]ch. 2:24
6:65 [u]ver. 44
6:66 [v]ver. 60
6:68 [w]Acts 5:20
6:69 [x]Matt. 16:16; Mark 8:29; Luke 9:20; ch. 1:49
6:70 [y]Luke 6:13 [z]ch. 13:27
7:1 [a]ch. 5:16
7:2 [b]Lev. 23:34
7:3 [c]Matt. 12:46; Mark 3:31; Acts 1:14

disciples also may see the works that thou
doest.
4 For *there is* no man *that* doeth any
thing in secret, and he himself seeketh to be
known openly. If thou do these things, shew
thyself to the world.
5 For [d]neither did his brethren believe in
him.
6 Then Jesus said unto them, [e]My time is
not yet come: but your time is alway ready.
7 [f]The world cannot hate you; but me it
hateth, [g]because I testify of it, that the
works thereof are evil.
8 Go ye up unto this feast: I go not up yet
unto this feast; [h]for my time is not yet full
come.
9 When he had said these words unto
them, he abode *still* in Galilee.
10 ¶ But when his brethren were gone up,
then went he also up unto the feast, not
openly, but as it were in secret.
11 Then [i]the Jews sought him at the
feast, and said, Where is he?
12 And [j]there was much murmuring
among the people concerning him: for
[k]some said, He is a good man: others said,
Nay; but he deceiveth the people.
13 Howbeit no man spake openly of him
[l]for fear of the Jews.
14 ¶ Now about the midst of the feast
Jesus went up into the temple, and taught.
15 [m]And the Jews marvelled, saying,
How knoweth this man letters, having
never learned?
16 Jesus answered them, and said, [n]My
doctrine is not mine, but his that sent me.
17 [o]If any man will do his will, he shall
know of the doctrine, whether it be of God,
or *whether* I speak of myself.
18 [p]He that speaketh of himself seeketh
his own glory: but he that seeketh his glory
that sent him, the same is true, and no unrighteousness is in him.
19 [q]Did not Moses give you the law, and
yet none of you keepeth the law? [r]Why go
ye about to kill me?
20 The people answered and said, [s]Thou
hast a devil: who goeth about to kill thee?
21 Jesus answered and said unto them, I
have done one work, and ye all marvel.
22 [t]Moses therefore gave unto you circumcision; (not because it is of Moses, [u]but
of the fathers;) and ye on the sabbath day
circumcise a man.
23 If a man on the sabbath day receive
circumcision, that the law of Moses should
not be broken; are ye angry at me, because
[v]I have made a man every whit whole on
the sabbath day?
24 [w]Judge not according to the appearance, but judge righteous judgment.
25 Then said some of them of Jerusalem,
Is not this he, whom they seek to kill?
26 But, lo, he speaketh boldly, and they
say nothing unto him. [x]Do the rulers know
indeed that this is the very Christ?
27 [y]Howbeit we know this man whence

7:5 *d*Mark 3:21
7:6 *e*ch. 2:4; ver. 8
7:7 *f*ch. 15:19 *g*ch. 3:19
7:8 *h*ch. 8:30; ver. 6
7:11 *i*ch. 11:56
7:12 *j*ch. 9:16 *k*Matt. 21:46; Luke 7:16; ch. 6:14; ver. 40
7:13 *l*ch. 9:22
7:15 *m*Matt. 13:54; Mark 6:2; Luke 4:22; Acts 2:7
7:16 *n*ch. 3:11
7:17 *o*ch. 8:43
7:18 *p*ch. 5:41
7:19 *q*Ex. 24:3; Deut. 33:4; John 1:17; Acts 7:38 *r*Matt. 12:14; Mark 3:6; ch. 5:16
7:20 *s*ch. 8:48
7:22 *t*Lev. 12:3 *u*Gen. 17:10
7:23 *v*ch. 5:8
7:24 *w*Deut. 1:16; Prov. 24:23; ch. 8:15; Jam. 2:1
7:26 *x*ver. 48
7:27 *y*Matt. 13:55; Mark 6:3; Luke 4:22
7:28 *z*ch. 8:14 *a*ch. 5:43 *b*ch. 5:32; Rom. 3:4 *c*ch. 1:18
7:29 *d*Matt. 11:27; ch. 10:15
7:30 *e*Mark 11:18; Luke 19:47; ver. 19; ch. 8:37 *f*ver. 44; ch. 8:20
7:31 *g*Matt. 12:23; ch. 3:2
7:33 *h*ch. 13:33
7:34 *i*Hos. 5:6; ch. 8:21
7:35 *j*Isa. 11:12; Jam. 1:1; 1 Pet. 1:1
7:37 *k*Lev. 23:36 *l*Isa. 55:1; ch. 6:35; Rev. 22:17
7:38 *m*Deut. 18:15 *n*Prov. 18:4; Isa. 12:3; ch. 4:14
7:39 *o*Isa. 44:3; Joel 2:28; ch. 16:7; Acts 2:17 *p*ch. 12:16
7:40 *q*Deut. 18:15; ch. 1:21
7:41 *r*ch. 4:42 *s*ver. 52; ch. 1:46
7:42 *t*Ps. 132:11; Jer. 23:5; Mic. 5:2; Matt. 2:5; Luke 2:4 *u*1 Sam. 16:1
7:43 *v*ver. 12; ch. 9:16
7:44 *w*ver. 30
7:46 *x*Matt. 7:29
7:48 *y*ch. 12:42; Acts 6:7; 1 Cor. 1:20

he is: but when Christ cometh, no man
knoweth whence he is.
28 Then cried Jesus in the temple as he
taught, saying, [z]Ye both know me, and ye
know whence I am: and [a]I am not come of
myself, but he that sent me [b]is true, [c]whom
ye know not.
29 But [d]I know him: for I am from him,
and he hath sent me.
30 Then [e]they sought to take him: but
[f]no man laid hands on him, because his
hour was not yet come.
31 And [g]many of the people believed on
him, and said, When Christ cometh, will he
do more miracles than these which this *man*
hath done?
32 ¶ The Pharisees heard that the people
murmured such things concerning him; and
the Pharisees and the chief priests sent officers to take him.
33 Then said Jesus unto them, [h]Yet a little while am I with you, and *then* I go unto
him that sent me.
34 Ye [i]shall seek me, and shall not find
me: and where I am, *thither* ye cannot
come.
35 Then said the Jews among themselves,
Whither will he go, that we shall not find
him? will he go unto [j]the dispersed among
the Gentiles, and teach the Gentiles?
36 What *manner of* saying is this that he
said, Ye shall seek me, and shall not find
me: and where I am, *thither* ye cannot
come?
37 [k]In the last day, that great *day* of the
feast, Jesus stood and cried, saying, [l]If any
man thirst, let him come unto me, and
drink.
38 [m]He that believeth on me, as the scripture hath said, [n]out of his belly shall flow
rivers of living water.
39 ([o]But this spake he of the Spirit, which
they that believe on him should receive: for
the Holy Ghost was not yet *given;* because
that Jesus was not yet [p]glorified.)
40 ¶ Many of the people therefore, when
they heard this saying, said, Of a truth this
is [q]the Prophet.
41 Others said, [r]This is the Christ. But
some said, Shall Christ come [s]out of Galilee?
42 [t]Hath not the scripture said, That
Christ cometh of the seed of David, and out
of the town of Bethlehem, [u]where David
was?
43 So [v]there was a division among the
people because of him.
44 And [w]some of them would have taken
him; but no man laid hands on him.
45 ¶ Then came the officers to the chief
priests and Pharisees; and they said unto
them, Why have ye not brought him?
46 The officers answered, [x]Never man
spake like this man.
47 Then answered them the Pharisees,
Are ye also deceived?
48 [y]Have any of the rulers or of the Pharisees believed on him?

49 But this people who knoweth not the law are cursed.

50 Nicodemus saith unto them, ([z]he that came to Jesus by night, being one of them,)

51 [a]Doth our law judge *any* man, before it hear him, and know what he doeth?

52 They answered and said unto him, Art thou also of Galilee? Search, and look: for [b]out of Galilee ariseth no prophet.

53 And every man went unto his own house.

8 Jesus went unto the mount of Olives.

2 And early in the morning he came again into the temple, and all the people came unto him; and he sat down, and taught them.

3 And the scribes and Pharisees brought unto him a woman taken in adultery; and when they had set her in the midst,

4 They say unto him, Master, this woman was taken in adultery, in the very act.

5 [c]Now Moses in the law commanded us, that such should be stoned: but what sayest thou?

6 This they said, tempting him, that they might have to accuse him. But Jesus stooped down, and with *his* finger wrote on the ground, *as though he heard them not*.

7 So when they continued asking him, he lifted up himself, and said unto them, [d]He that is without sin among you, let him first cast a stone at her.

8 And again he stooped down, and wrote on the ground.

9 And they which heard *it*, [e]being convicted by *their own* conscience, went out one by one, beginning at the eldest, *even* unto the last: and Jesus was left alone, and the woman standing in the midst.

10 When Jesus had lifted up himself, and saw none but the woman, he said unto her, Woman, where are those thine accusers? hath no man condemned thee?

11 She said, No man, Lord. And Jesus said unto her, [f]Neither do I condemn thee: go, and [g]sin no more.

12 ¶ Then spake Jesus again unto them, saying, [h]I am the light of the world: he that followeth me shall not walk in darkness, but shall have the light of life.

13 The Pharisees therefore said unto him, [i]Thou bearest record of thyself; thy record is not true.

14 Jesus answered and said unto them, Though I bear record of myself, *yet* my record is true: for I know whence I came, and whither I go; but [j]ye cannot tell whence I come, and whither I go.

15 [k]Ye judge after the flesh; [l]I judge no man.

16 And yet if I judge, my judgment is true: for [m]I am not alone, but I and the Father that sent me.

17 [n]It is also written in your law, that the testimony of two men is true.

18 I am one that bear witness of myself, and [o]the Father that sent me beareth witness of me.

19 Then said they unto him, Where is thy Father? Jesus answered, [p]Ye neither know me, nor my Father: [q]if ye had known me, ye should have known my Father also.

20 These words spake Jesus in [r]the treasury, as he taught in the temple: and [s]no man laid hands on him; for [t]his hour was not yet come.

21 Then said Jesus again unto them, I go my way, and [u]ye shall seek me, and [v]shall die in your sins: whither I go, ye cannot come.

22 Then said the Jews, Will he kill himself? because he saith, Whither I go, ye cannot come.

23 And he said unto them, [w]Ye are from beneath; I am from above: [x]ye are of this world; I am not of this world.

24 [y]I said therefore unto you, that ye shall die in your sins: [z]for if ye believe not that I am *he*, ye shall die in your sins.

25 Then said they unto him, Who art thou? And Jesus saith unto them, Even *the same* that I said unto you from the beginning.

26 I have many things to say and to judge of you: but [a]he that sent me is true; and [b]I speak to the world those things which I have heard of him.

27 They understood not that he spake to them of the Father.

28 Then said Jesus unto them, When ye have [c]lifted up the Son of man, [d]then shall ye know that I am *he*, and [e]*that* I do nothing of myself; but [f]as my Father hath taught me, I speak these things.

29 And [g]he that sent me is with me: [h]the Father hath not left me alone; [i]for I do always those things that please him.

30 As he spake these words, [j]many believed on him.

31 Then said Jesus to those Jews which believed on him, If ye continue in my word, *then* are ye my disciples indeed;

32 And ye shall know the truth, and [k]the truth shall make you free.

33 ¶ They answered him, [l]We be Abraham's seed, and were never in bondage to any man: how sayest thou, Ye shall be made free?

34 Jesus answered them, Verily, verily, I say unto you, [m]Whosoever committeth sin is the servant of sin.

35 And [n]the servant abideth not in the house for ever: *but* the Son abideth ever.

36 [o]If the Son therefore shall make you free, ye shall be free indeed.

37 I know that ye are Abraham's seed; but [p]ye seek to kill me, because my word hath no place in you.

38 [q]I speak that which I have seen with my Father: and ye do that which ye have seen with your father.

39 They answered and said unto him, [r]Abraham is our father. Jesus saith unto them, [s]If ye were Abraham's children, ye would do the works of Abraham.

40 [t]But now ye seek to kill me, a man

7:50 [z]ch. 3:2
7:51 [a]Deut. 1:17
7:52 [b]Isa. 9:1; Matt. 4:15; ch. 1:46; ver. 41
8:5 [c]Lev. 20:10; Deut. 22:22
8:7 [d]Deut. 17:7; Rom. 2:1
8:9 [e]Rom. 2:22
8:11 [f]Luke 9:56; ch. 3:17 [g]ch. 5:14
8:12 [h]ch. 1:4
8:13 [i]ch. 5:31
8:14 [j]ch. 7:28
8:15 [k]ch. 7:24 [l]ch. 3:17
8:16 [m]ver. 29; ch. 16:32
8:17 [n]Deut. 17:6; Matt. 18:16; 2 Cor. 13:1; Heb. 10:28
8:18 [o]ch. 5:37
8:19 [p]ver. 55; ch. 16:3 [q]ch. 14:7
8:20 [r]Mark 12:41 [s]ch. 7:30 [t]ch. 7:8
8:21 [u]ch. 7:34 [v]ver. 24
8:23 [w]ch. 3:31 [x]ch. 15:19; 1 John 4:5
8:24 [y]ver. 21 [z]Mark 16:16
8:26 [a]ch. 7:28 [b]ch. 3:32
8:28 [c]ch. 3:14 [d]Rom. 1:4 [e]ch. 5:19 [f]ch. 3:11
8:29 [g]ch. 14:10 [h]ver. 16 [i]ch. 4:34
8:30 [j]ch. 7:31
8:32 [k]Rom. 6:14; Jam. 1:25
8:33 [l]Lev. 25:42; Matt. 3:9; ver. 39
8:34 [m]Rom. 6:16; 2 Pet. 2:19
8:35 [n]Gal. 4:30
8:36 [o]Rom. 8:2; Gal. 5:1
8:37 [p]ch. 7:19; ver. 40
8:38 [q]ch. 3:32
8:39 [r]Matt. 3:9; ver. 33 [s]Rom. 2:28; Gal. 3:7
8:40 [t]ver. 37

that hath told you the truth, [u]which I have
heard of God: this did not Abraham.
41 Ye do the deeds of your father. Then
said they to him, We be not born of fornication; [v]we have one Father, *even* God.
42 Jesus said unto them, [w]If God were
your Father, ye would love me: [x]for I proceeded forth and came from God; [y]neither
came I of myself, but he sent me.
43 [z]Why do ye not understand my
speech? *even* because ye cannot hear my
word.
44 [a]Ye are of *your* father the devil, and
the lusts of your father ye will do. He was a
murderer from the beginning, and [b]abode
not in the truth, because there is no truth in
him. When he speaketh a lie, he speaketh of
his own: for he is a liar, and the father of it.
45 And because I tell *you* the truth, ye believe me not.
46 Which of you convinceth me of sin?
And if I say the truth, why do ye not believe me?
47 [c]He that is of God heareth God's
words: ye therefore hear *them* not, because
ye are not of God.
48 Then answered the Jews, and said
unto him, Say we not well that thou art a
Samaritan, and [d]hast a devil?
49 Jesus answered, I have not a devil;
but I honour my Father, and ye do dishonour me.
50 And I [e]seek not mine own glory: there
is one that seeketh and judgeth.
51 Verily, verily, I say unto you, [f]If a man
keep my saying, he shall never see death.
52 Then said the Jews unto him, Now we
know that thou hast a devil. [g]Abraham is
dead, and the prophets; and thou sayest, If
a man keep my saying, he shall never taste
of death.
53 Art thou greater than our father Abraham, which is dead? and the prophets are
dead: whom makest thou thyself?
54 Jesus answered, [h]If I honour myself,
my honour is nothing: [i]it is my Father that
honoureth me; of whom ye say, that he is
your God:
55 Yet [j]ye have not known him; but I
know him: and if I should say, I know him
not, I shall be a liar like unto you: but I know
him, and keep his saying.
56 Your father Abraham [k]rejoiced to see
my day: [l]and he saw *it*, and was glad.
57 Then said the Jews unto him, Thou art
not yet fifty years old, and hast thou seen
Abraham?
58 Jesus said unto them, Verily, verily, I
say unto you, Before Abraham was, [m]I am.
59 Then [n]took they up stones to cast at
him: but Jesus hid himself, and went out of
the temple, [o]going through the midst of
them, and so passed by.

9 And as *Jesus* passed by, he saw a man
which was blind from *his* birth.
2 And his disciples asked him, saying,
Master, [p]who did sin, this man, or his parents, that he was born blind?

8:40 [u]ver. 26
8:41 [v]Isa. 63:16; Mal. 1:6
8:42 [w]1 John 5:1 [x]ch. 16:27 [y]ch. 5:43
8:43 [z]ch. 7:17
8:44 [a]Matt. 13:38; 1 John 3:8 [b]Jude 6
8:47 [c]ch. 10:26; 1 John 4:6
8:48 [d]ch. 7:20; ver. 52
8:50 [e]ch. 5:41
8:51 [f]ch. 5:24
8:52 [g]Zech. 1:5; Heb. 11:13
8:54 [h]ch. 5:31 [i]ch. 5:41; Acts 3:13
8:55 [j]ch. 7:28
8:56 [k]Luke 10:24 [l]Heb. 11:13
8:58 [m]Ex. 3:14; Isa. 43:13; ch. 17:5; Col. 1:17; Rev. 1:8
8:59 [n]ch. 10:31 [o]Luke 4:30
9:2 [p]ver. 34
9:3 [q]ch. 11:4
9:4 [r]ch. 4:34
9:5 [s]ch. 1:5
9:6 [t]Mark 7:33
9:7 [u]Neh. 3:15 [v]2 Kings 5:14
9:11 [w]ver. 6
9:16 [x]ver. 33; ch. 3:2 [y]ch. 7:12
9:17 [z]ch. 4:19
9:22 [a]ch. 7:13; Acts 5:13 [b]ver. 34; ch. 16:2

3 Jesus answered, Neither hath this man
sinned, nor his parents: [q]but that the works
of God should be made manifest in him.
4 [r]I must work the works of him that sent
me, while it is day: the night cometh, when
no man can work.
5 As long as I am in the world, [s]I am the
light of the world.
6 When he had thus spoken, [t]he spat on
the ground, and made clay of the spittle,
and he anointed the eyes of the blind man
with the clay,
7 And said unto him, Go, wash [u]in the
pool of Siloam, (which is by interpretation,
Sent.) [v]He went his way therefore, and
washed, and came seeing.
8 ¶ The neighbours therefore, and they
which before had seen him that he was
blind, said, Is not this he that sat and
begged?
9 Some said, This is he: others *said*, He is
like him: *but* he said, I am *he*.
10 Therefore said they unto him, How
were thine eyes opened?
11 He answered and said, [w]A man that is
called Jesus made clay, and anointed mine
eyes, and said unto me, Go to the pool of
Siloam, and wash: and I went and washed,
and I received sight.
12 Then said they unto him, Where is he?
He said, I know not.
13 ¶ They brought to the Pharisees him
that aforetime was blind.
14 And it was the sabbath day when Jesus
made the clay, and opened his eyes.
15 Then again the Pharisees also asked
him how he had received his sight. He said
unto them, He put clay upon mine eyes, and
I washed, and do see.
16 Therefore said some of the Pharisees,
This man is not of God, because he keepeth
not the sabbath day. Others said, [x]How can
a man that is a sinner do such miracles?
And [y]there was a division among them.
17 They say unto the blind man again,
What sayest thou of him, that he hath
opened thine eyes? He said, [z]He is a
prophet.
18 But the Jews did not believe concerning him, that he had been blind, and received his sight, until they called the
parents of him that had received his sight.
19 And they asked them, saying, Is this
your son, who ye say was born blind? how
then doth he now see?
20 His parents answered them and said,
We know that this is our son, and that he
was born blind:
21 But by what means he now seeth, we
know not; or who hath opened his eyes, we
know not: he is of age; ask him: he shall
speak for himself.
22 These *words* spake his parents, because [a]they feared the Jews: for the Jews
had agreed already, that if any man did confess that he was Christ, he [b]should be put
out of the synagogue.

23 Therefore said his parents, He is of age; ask him.

24 Then again called they the man that was blind, and said unto him, [c]Give God the praise: [d]we know that this man is a sinner.

25 He answered and said, Whether he be a sinner *or no*, I know not: one thing I know, that, whereas I was blind, now I see.

26 Then said they to him again, What did he to thee? how opened he thine eyes?

27 He answered them, I have told you already, and ye did not hear: wherefore would ye hear *it* again? will ye also be his disciples?

28 Then they reviled him, and said, Thou art his disciple; but we are Moses' disciples.

29 We know that God spake unto Moses: *as for* this *fellow*, [e]we know not from whence he is.

30 The man answered and said unto them, [f]Why herein is a marvellous thing, that ye know not from whence he is, and *yet* he hath opened mine eyes.

31 Now we know that [g]God heareth not sinners: but if any man be a worshipper of God, and doeth his will, him he heareth.

32 Since the world began was it not heard that any man opened the eyes of one that was born blind.

33 [h]If this man were not of God, he could do nothing.

34 They answered and said unto him, [i]Thou wast altogether born in sins, and dost thou teach us? And they cast him out.

35 Jesus heard that they had cast him out; and when he had found him, he said unto him, Dost thou believe on [j]the Son of God?

36 He answered and said, Who is he, Lord, that I might believe on him?

37 And Jesus said unto him, Thou hast both seen him, and [k]it is he that talketh with thee.

38 And he said, Lord, I believe. And he worshipped him.

39 ¶ And Jesus said, [l]For judgment I am come into this world, [m]that they which see not might see; and that they which see might be made blind.

40 And *some* of the Pharisees which were with him heard these words, [n]and said unto him, Are we blind also?

41 Jesus said unto them, [o]If ye were blind, ye should have no sin: but now ye say, We see; therefore your sin remaineth.

10 Verily, verily, I say unto you, He that entereth not by the door into the sheepfold, but climbeth up some other way, the same is a thief and a robber.

2 But he that entereth in by the door is the shepherd of the sheep.

3 To him the porter openeth; and the sheep hear his voice: and he calleth his own sheep by name, and leadeth them out.

4 And when he putteth forth his own sheep, he goeth before them, and the sheep follow him: for they know his voice.

5 And a stranger will they not follow, but will flee from him: for they know not the voice of strangers.

6 This parable spake Jesus unto them: but they understood not what things they were which he spake unto them.

7 Then said Jesus unto them again, Verily, verily, I say unto you, I am the door of the sheep.

8 All that ever came before me are thieves and robbers: but the sheep did not hear them.

9 [p]I am the door: by me if any man enter in, he shall be saved, and shall go in and out, and find pasture.

10 The thief cometh not, but for to steal, and to kill, and to destroy: I am come that they might have life, and that they might have *it* more abundantly.

11 [q]I am the good shepherd: the good shepherd giveth his life for the sheep.

12 But he that is an hireling, and not the shepherd, whose own the sheep are not, seeth the wolf coming, and [r]leaveth the sheep, and fleeth: and the wolf catcheth them, and scattereth the sheep.

13 The hireling fleeth, because he is an hireling, and careth not for the sheep.

14 I am the good shepherd, and [s]know my *sheep*, and am known of mine.

15 [t]As the Father knoweth me, even so know I the Father: [u]and I lay down my life for the sheep.

16 And [v]other sheep I have, which are not of this fold: them also I must bring, and they shall hear my voice; [w]and there shall be one fold, *and* one shepherd.

17 Therefore doth my Father love me, [x]because I lay down my life, that I might take it again.

18 No man taketh it from me, but I lay it down of myself. I have power to lay it down, and I [y]have power to take it again. [z]This commandment have I received of my Father.

19 ¶ [a]There was a division therefore again among the Jews for these sayings.

20 And many of them said, [b]He hath a devil, and is mad; why hear ye him?

21 Others said, These are not the words of him that hath a devil. [c]Can a devil [d]open the eyes of the blind?

22 ¶ And it was at Jerusalem the feast of the dedication, and it was winter.

23 And Jesus walked in the temple [e]in Solomon's porch.

24 Then came the Jews round about him, and said unto him, How long dost thou make us to doubt? If thou be the Christ, tell us plainly.

25 Jesus answered them, I told you, and ye believed not: [f]the works that I do in my Father's name, they bear witness of me.

26 But [g]ye believe not, because ye are not of my sheep, as I said unto you.

27 [h]My sheep hear my voice, and I know them, and they follow me:

28 And I give unto them eternal life; and

9:24 [c]Josh. 7:19; 1 Sam. 6:5 [d]ver. 16
9:29 [e]ch. 8:14
9:30 [f]ch. 3:10
9:31 [g]Job 27:9; Ps. 18:41; Prov. 1:28; Isa. 1:15; Jer. 11:11; Ezek. 8:18; Mic. 3:4; Zech. 7:13
9:33 [h]ver. 16
9:34 [i]ver. 2
9:35 [j]Matt. 14:33; Mark 1:1; ch. 10:36; 1 John 5:13
9:37 [k]ch. 4:26
9:39 [l]ch. 3:17 [m]Matt. 13:13
9:40 [n]Rom. 2:19
9:41 [o]ch. 15:22
10:9 [p]ch. 14:6; Eph. 2:18
10:11 [q]Isa. 40:11; Ezek. 34:12; Heb. 13:20; 1 Pet. 2:25
10:12 [r]Zech. 11:16
10:14 [s]2 Tim. 2:19
10:15 [t]Matt. 11:27 [u]ch. 15:13
10:16 [v]Isa. 56:8 [w]Ezek. 37:22; Eph. 2:14; 1 Pet. 2:25
10:17 [x]Isa. 53:7; Heb. 2:9
10:18 [y]ch. 2:19 [z]ch. 6:38; Acts 2:24
10:19 [a]ch. 7:43
10:20 [b]ch. 7:20
10:21 [c]Ex. 4:11; Ps. 94:9 [d]ch. 9:6
10:23 [e]Acts 3:11
10:25 [f]ver. 38; ch. 3:2
10:26 [g]ch. 8:47; 1 John 4:6
10:27 [h]ver. 4

[i]they shall never perish, neither shall any *man* pluck them out of my hand.

29 [j]My Father, [k]which gave *them* me, is greater than all; and no *man* is able to pluck *them* out of my Father's hand.

30 [l]I and *my* Father are one.

31 Then [m]the Jews took up stones again to stone him.

32 Jesus answered them, Many good works have I shewed you from my Father; for which of those works do ye stone me?

33 The Jews answered him, saying, For a good work we stone thee not; but for blasphemy; and because that thou, being a man, [n]makest thyself God.

34 Jesus answered them, [o]Is it not written in your law, I said, Ye are gods?

35 If he called them gods, [p]unto whom the word of God came, and the scripture cannot be broken;

36 Say ye of him, [q]whom the Father hath sanctified, and [r]sent into the world, Thou blasphemest; [s]because I said, I am [t]the Son of God?

37 [u]If I do not the works of my Father, believe me not.

38 But if I do, though ye believe not me, [v]believe the works: that ye may know, and believe, [w]that the Father *is* in me, and I in him.

39 [x]Therefore they sought again to take him: but he escaped out of their hand,

40 And went away again beyond Jordan into the place [y]where John at first baptized; and there he abode.

41 And many resorted unto him, and said, John did no miracle: [z]but all things that John spake of this man were true.

42 [a]And many believed on him there.

11 Now a certain *man* was sick, *named* Lazarus, of Bethany, the town of [b]Mary and her sister Martha.

2 ([c]It was *that* Mary which anointed the Lord with ointment, and wiped his feet with her hair, whose brother Lazarus was sick.)

3 Therefore his sisters sent unto him, saying, Lord, behold, he whom thou lovest is sick.

4 When Jesus heard *that*, he said, This sickness is not unto death, [d]but for the glory of God, that the Son of God might be glorified thereby.

5 Now Jesus loved Martha, and her sister, and Lazarus.

6 When he had heard therefore that he was sick, [e]he abode two days still in the same place where he was.

7 Then after that saith he to *his* disciples, Let us go into Judaea again.

8 *His* disciples say unto him, Master, [f]the Jews of late sought to stone thee; and goest thou thither again?

9 Jesus answered, Are there not twelve hours in the day? [g]If any man walk in the day, he stumbleth not, because he seeth the light of this world.

10 But [h]if a man walk in the night, he stumbleth, because there is no light in him.

11 These things said he: and after that he saith unto them, Our friend Lazarus [i]sleepeth; but I go, that I may awake him out of sleep.

12 Then said his disciples, Lord, if he sleep, he shall do well.

13 Howbeit Jesus spake of his death: but they thought that he had spoken of taking of rest in sleep.

14 Then said Jesus unto them plainly, Lazarus is dead.

15 And I am glad for your sakes that I was not there, to the intent ye may believe; nevertheless let us go unto him.

16 Then said Thomas, which is called Didymus, unto his fellowdisciples, Let us also go, that we may die with him.

17 Then when Jesus came, he found that he had *lain* in the grave four days already.

18 Now Bethany was nigh unto Jerusalem, about fifteen furlongs off:

19 And many of the Jews came to Martha and Mary, to comfort them concerning their brother.

20 Then Martha, as soon as she heard that Jesus was coming, went and met him: but Mary sat *still* in the house.

21 Then said Martha unto Jesus, Lord, if thou hadst been here, my brother had not died.

22 But I know, that even now, [j]whatsoever thou wilt ask of God, God will give *it* thee.

23 Jesus saith unto her, Thy brother shall rise again.

24 Martha saith unto him, [k]I know that he shall rise again in the resurrection at the last day.

25 Jesus said unto her, I am [l]the resurrection, and the [m]life: [n]he that believeth in me, though he were dead, yet shall he live:

26 And whosoever liveth and believeth in me shall never die. Believest thou this?

27 She saith unto him, Yea, Lord: [o]I believe that thou art the Christ, the Son of God, which should come into the world.

28 And when she had so said, she went her way, and called Mary her sister secretly, saying, The Master is come, and calleth for thee.

29 As soon as she heard *that*, she arose quickly, and came unto him.

30 Now Jesus was not yet come into the town, but was in that place where Martha met him.

31 [p]The Jews then which were with her in the house, and comforted her, when they saw Mary, that she rose up hastily and went out, followed her, saying, She goeth unto the grave to weep there.

32 Then when Mary was come where Jesus was, and saw him, she fell down at his feet, saying unto him, [q]Lord, if thou hadst been here, my brother had not died.

33 When Jesus therefore saw her weeping, and the Jews also weeping which came with her, he groaned in the spirit, and was troubled,

10:28 [i]ch. 6:37
10:29 [j]ch. 14:28 [k]ch. 17:2
10:30 [l]ch. 17:11
10:31 [m]ch. 8:59
10:33 [n]ch. 5:18
10:34 [o]Ps. 82:6
10:35 [p]Rom. 13:1
10:36 [q]ch. 6:27 [r]ch. 3:17 [s]ch. 5:17; ver. 30 [t]Luke 1:35; ch. 9:35
10:37 [u]ch. 15:24
10:38 [v]ch. 5:36 [w]ch. 14:10
10:39 [x]ch. 7:30
10:40 [y]ch. 1:28
10:41 [z]ch. 3:30
10:42 [a]ch. 8:30
11:1 [b]Luke 10:38
11:2 [c]Matt. 26:7; Mark 14:3; ch. 12:3
11:4 [d]ch. 9:3; ver. 40
11:6 [e]ch. 10:40
11:8 [f]ch. 10:31
11:9 [g]ch. 9:4
11:10 [h]ch. 12:35
11:11 [i]Deut. 31:16; Dan. 12:2; Matt. 9:24; Acts 7:60; 1 Cor. 15:18
11:22 [j]ch. 9:31
11:24 [k]Luke 14:14; ch. 5:29
11:25 [l]ch. 5:21 [m]ch. 1:4; Col. 3:4; 1 John 1:1 [n]ch. 3:36; 1 John 5:10
11:27 [o]Matt. 16:16; ch. 4:42
11:31 [p]ver. 19
11:32 [q]ver. 21

34 And said, Where have ye laid him? They said unto him, Lord, come and see.

35 [r]Jesus wept.

36 Then said the Jews, Behold how he loved him!

37 And some of them said, Could not this man, [s]which opened the eyes of the blind, have caused that even this man should not have died?

38 Jesus therefore again groaning in himself cometh to the grave. It was a cave, and a stone lay upon it.

39 Jesus said, Take ye away the stone. Martha, the sister of him that was dead, saith unto him, Lord, by this time he stinketh: for he hath been *dead* four days.

40 Jesus saith unto her, Said I not unto thee, that, if thou wouldest believe, thou shouldest [t]see the glory of God?

41 Then they took away the stone *from the place* where the dead was laid. And Jesus lifted up *his* eyes, and said, Father, I thank thee that thou hast heard me.

42 And I knew that thou hearest me always: but [u]because of the people which stand by I said *it*, that they may believe that thou hast sent me.

43 And when he thus had spoken, he cried with a loud voice, Lazarus, come forth.

44 And he that was dead came forth, bound hand and foot with graveclothes: and [v]his face was bound about with a napkin. Jesus saith unto them, Loose him, and let him go.

45 Then many of the Jews which came to Mary, [w]and had seen the things which Jesus did, believed on him.

46 But some of them went their ways to the Pharisees, and told them what things Jesus had done.

47 ¶ [x]Then gathered the chief priests and the Pharisees a council, and said, [y]What do we? for this man doeth many miracles.

48 If we let him thus alone, all *men* will believe on him: and the Romans shall come and take away both our place and nation.

49 And one of them, *named* [z]Caiaphas, being the high priest that same year, said unto them, Ye know nothing at all,

50 [a]Nor consider that it is expedient for us, that one man should die for the people, and that the whole nation perish not.

51 And this spake he not of himself: but being high priest that year, he prophesied that Jesus should die for that nation;

52 And [b]not for that nation only, [c]but that also he should gather together in one the children of God that were scattered abroad.

53 Then from that day forth they took counsel together for to put him to death.

54 Jesus [d]therefore walked no more openly among the Jews; but went thence unto a country near to the wilderness, into a city called [e]Ephraim, and there continued with his disciples.

55 ¶ [f]And the Jews' passover was nigh at hand: and many went out of the country up to Jerusalem before the passover, to purify themselves.

56 [g]Then sought they for Jesus, and spake among themselves, as they stood in the temple, What think ye, that he will not come to the feast?

57 Now both the chief priests and the Pharisees had given a commandment, that, if any man knew where he were, he should shew *it*, that they might take him.

12

Then Jesus six days before the passover came to Bethany, [h]where Lazarus was which had been dead, whom he raised from the dead.

2 [i]There they made him a supper; and Martha served: but Lazarus was one of them that sat at the table with him.

3 Then took [j]Mary a pound of ointment of spikenard, very costly, and anointed the feet of Jesus, and wiped his feet with her hair: and the house was filled with the odour of the ointment.

4 Then saith one of his disciples, Judas Iscariot, Simon's *son*, which should betray him,

5 Why was not this ointment sold for three hundred pence, and given to the poor?

6 This he said, not that he cared for the poor; but because he was a thief, and [k]had the bag, and bare what was put therein.

7 Then said Jesus, Let her alone: against the day of my burying hath she kept this.

8 For [l]the poor always ye have with you; but me ye have not always.

9 Much people of the Jews therefore knew that he was there: and they came not for Jesus' sake only, but that they might see Lazarus also, [m]whom he had raised from the dead.

10 ¶ [n]But the chief priest consulted that they might put Lazarus also to death;

11 [o]Because that by reason of him many of the Jews went away, and believed on Jesus.

12 ¶ [p]On the next day much people that were come to the feast, when they heard that Jesus was coming to Jerusalem,

13 Took branches of palm trees, and went forth to meet him, and cried, [q]Hosanna: Blessed *is* the King of Israel that cometh in the name of the Lord.

14 [r]And Jesus, when he had found a young ass, sat thereon; as it is written,

15 [s]Fear not, daughter of Sion: behold, thy King cometh, sitting on an ass's colt.

16 These things [t]understood not his disciples at the first: [u]but when Jesus was glorified, [v]then remembered they that these things were written of him, and *that* they had done these things unto him.

17 The people therefore that was with him when he called Lazarus out of his grave, and raised him from the dead, bare record.

18 [w]For this cause the people also met him, for that they heard that he had done this miracle.

11:35 [r]Luke 19:41
11:37 [s]ch. 9:6
11:40 [t]ver. 4
11:42 [u]ch. 12:30
11:44 [v]ch. 20:7
11:45 [w]ch. 2:23
11:47 [x]Ps. 2:2; Matt. 26:3; Mark 14:1; Luke 22:2 [y]ch. 12:19; Acts 4:16
11:49 [z]Luke 3:2; ch. 18:14; Acts 4:6
11:50 [a]ch. 18:14
11:52 [b]Isa. 49:6; 1 John 2:2 [c]ch. 10:16; Eph. 2:14
11:54 [d]ch. 4:1 [e]2 Chron. 13:19
11:55 [f]ch. 2:13
11:56 [g]ch. 11:7
12:1 [h]ch. 11:1
12:2 [i]Matt. 26:6; Mark 14:3
12:3 [j]Luke 10:38; ch. 11:2
12:6 [k]ch. 13:29
12:8 [l]Matt. 26:11; Mark 14:7
12:9 [m]ch. 11:43
12:10 [n]Luke 16:31
12:11 [o]ch. 11:45; ver. 18
12:12 [p]Matt. 21:8; Mark 11:8; Luke 19:35
12:13 [q]Ps. 118:25
12:14 [r]Matt. 21:7
12:15 [s]Zech. 9:9
12:16 [t]Luke 18:34 [u]ch. 7:39 [v]ch. 14:26
12:18 [w]ver. 11

19 The Pharisees therefore said among themselves, [x]Perceive ye how ye prevail nothing? behold, the world is gone after him.

20 ¶ And there [y]were certain Greeks among them [z]that came up to worship at the feast:

21 The same came therefore to Philip, [a]which was of Bethsaida of Galilee, and desired him, saying, Sir, we would see Jesus.

22 Philip cometh and telleth Andrew: and again Andrew and Philip tell Jesus.

23 ¶ And Jesus answered them, saying, [b]The hour is come, that the Son of man should be glorified.

24 Verily, verily, I say unto you, [c]Except a corn of wheat fall into the ground and die, it abideth alone: but if it die, it bringeth forth much fruit.

25 [d]He that loveth his life shall lose it; and he that hateth his life in this world shall keep it unto life eternal.

26 If any man serve me, let him follow me; and [e]where I am, there shall also my servant be: if any man serve me, him will *my* Father honour.

27 [f]Now is my soul troubled; and what shall I say? Father, save me from this hour: [g]but for this cause came I unto this hour.

28 Father, glorify thy name. [h]Then came there a voice from heaven, *saying,* I have both glorified *it,* and will glorify *it* again.

29 The people therefore, that stood by, and heard *it,* said that it thundered: others said, An angel spake to him.

30 Jesus answered and said, [i]This voice came not because of me, but for your sakes.

31 Now is the judgment of this world: now shall [j]the prince of this world be cast out.

32 And I, [k]if I be lifted up from the earth, will draw [l]all *men* unto me.

33 [m]This he said, signifying what death he should die.

34 The people answered him, [n]We have heard out of the law that Christ abideth for ever: and how sayest thou, The Son of man must be lifted up? who is this Son of man?

35 Then Jesus said unto them, Yet a little while [o]is the light with you. [p]Walk while ye have the light, lest darkness come upon you: for [q]he that walketh in darkness knoweth not whither he goeth.

36 While ye have light, believe in the light, that ye may be [r]the children of light. These things spake Jesus, and departed, and [s]did hide himself from them.

37 ¶ But though he had done so many miracles before them, yet they believed not on him:

38 That the saying of Esaias the prophet might be fulfilled, which he spake, [t]Lord, who hath believed our report? and to whom hath the arm of the Lord been revealed?

39 Therefore they could not believe, because that Esaias said again,

40 [u]He hath blinded their eyes, and hardened their heart; that they should not see with *their* eyes, nor understand with *their* heart, and be converted, and I should heal them.

41 [v]These things said Esaias, when he saw his glory, and spake of him.

42 ¶ Nevertheless among the chief rulers also many believed on him; but [w]because of the Pharisees they did not confess *him,* lest they should be put out of the synagogue:

43 [x]For they loved the praise of men more than the praise of God.

44 ¶ Jesus cried and said, [y]He that believeth on me, believeth not on me, but on him that sent me.

45 And he [z]that seeth me seeth him that sent me.

46 [a]I am come a light into the world, that whosoever believeth on me should not abide in darkness.

47 And if any man hear my words, and believe not, [b]I judge him not: for [c]I came not to judge the world, but to save the world.

48 [d]He that rejecteth me, and receiveth not my words, hath one that judgeth him: [e]the word that I have spoken, the same shall judge him in the last day.

49 For [f]I have not spoken of myself; but the Father which sent me, he gave me a commandment, [g]what I should say, and what I should speak.

50 And I know that his commandment is life everlasting: whatsoever I speak therefore, even as the Father said unto me, so I speak.

13 Now [h]before the feast of the passover, when Jesus knew that [i]his hour was come that he should depart out of this world unto the Father, having loved his own which were in the world, he loved them unto the end.

2 And supper being ended, [j]the devil having now put into the heart of Judas Iscariot, Simon's *son,* to betray him;

3 Jesus knowing [k]that the Father had given all things into his hands, and [l]that he was come from God, and went to God;

4 [m]He riseth from supper, and laid aside his garments; and took a towel, and girded himself.

5 After that he poureth water into a bason, and began to wash the disciples' feet, and to wipe *them* with the towel wherewith he was girded.

6 Then cometh he to Simon Peter: and Peter saith unto him, Lord, [n]dost thou wash my feet?

7 Jesus answered and said unto him, What I do thou knowest not now; [o]but thou shalt know hereafter.

8 Peter saith unto him, Thou shalt never wash my feet. Jesus answered him, [p]If I wash thee not, thou hast no part with me.

9 Simon Peter saith unto him, Lord, not my feet only, but also *my* hands and *my* head.

10 Jesus saith to him, He that is washed needeth not save to wash *his* feet, but is

12:19 [x]ch. 11:47
12:20 [y]Acts 17:4 [z]1 Kings 8:41; Acts 8:27
12:21 [a]ch. 1:44
12:23 [b]ch. 13:32
12:24 [c]1 Cor. 15:36
12:25 [d]Matt. 10:39; Mark 8:35; Luke 9:24
12:26 [e]ch. 14:3; 1 Thess. 4:17
12:27 [f]Matt. 26:38; Luke 12:50; ch. 13:21 [g]Luke 22:53; ch. 18:37
12:28 [h]Matt. 3:17
12:30 [i]ch. 11:42
12:31 [j]Matt. 12:29; Luke 10:18; ch. 14:30; Acts 26:18; 2 Cor. 4:4; Eph. 2:2
12:32 [k]ch. 3:14 [l]Rom. 5:18; Heb. 2:9
12:33 [m]ch. 18:32
12:34 [n]Ps. 89:36; Isa. 9:7; Ezek. 37:25; Dan. 2:44; Mic. 4:7
12:35 [o]ch. 1:9; ver. 46 [p]Jer. 13:16; Eph. 5:8 [q]ch. 11:10; 1 John 2:11
12:36 [r]Luke 16:8; Eph. 5:8; 1 Thess. 5:5; 1 John 2:9 [s]ch. 8:59
12:38 [t]Isa. 53:1; Rom. 10:16
12:40 [u]Isa. 6:9; Matt. 13:14
12:41 [v]Isa. 6:1
12:42 [w]ch. 7:13
12:43 [x]ch. 5:44
12:44 [y]Mark 9:37; 1 Pet. 1:21
12:45 [z]ch. 14:9
12:46 [a]ver. 35; ch. 3:19
12:47 [b]ch. 5:45 [c]ch. 3:17
12:48 [d]Luke 10:16 [e]Deut. 18:19; Mark 16:16
12:49 [f]ch. 8:38 [g]Deut. 18:18
13:1 [h]Matt. 26:2 [i]ch. 12:23
13:2 [j]Luke 22:3; ver. 27
13:3 [k]Matt. 11:27; ch. 3:35; Acts 2:36; 1 Cor. 15:27; Heb. 2:8 [l]ch. 8:42
13:4 [m]Luke 22:27; Phil. 2:7
13:6 [n]Matt. 3:14
13:7 [o]ver. 12
13:8 [p]ch. 3:5; 1 Cor. 6:11; Eph. 5:26; Tit. 3:5; Heb. 10:22

clean every whit: and [q]ye are clean, but not all.

11 For [r]he knew who should betray him; therefore said he, Ye are not all clean.

12 So after he had washed their feet, and had taken his garments, and was set down again, he said unto them, Know ye what I have done to you?

13 [s]Ye call me Master and Lord: and ye say well; for *so* I am.

14 [t]If I then, *your* Lord and Master, have washed your feet; [u]ye also ought to wash one another's feet.

15 For [v]I have given you an example, that ye should do as I have done to you.

16 [w]Verily, verily, I say unto you, The servant is not greater than his lord; neither he that is sent greater than he that sent him.

17 [x]If ye know these things, happy are ye if ye do them.

18 ¶ I speak not of you all: I know whom I have chosen: but that the scripture may be fulfilled, [y]He that eateth bread with me hath lifted up his heel against me.

19 [z]Now I tell you before it come, that, when it is come to pass, ye may believe that I am *he*.

20 [a]Verily, verily, I say unto you, He that receiveth whomsoever I send receiveth me; and he that receiveth me receiveth him that sent me.

21 [b]When Jesus had thus said, [c]he was troubled in spirit, and testified, and said, Verily, verily, I say unto you, that [d]one of you shall betray me.

22 Then the disciples looked one on another, doubting of whom he spake.

23 Now [e]there was leaning on Jesus' bosom one of his disciples, whom Jesus loved.

24 Simon Peter therefore beckoned to him, that he should ask who it should be of whom he spake.

25 He then lying on Jesus' breast saith unto him, Lord, who is it?

26 Jesus answered, He it is, to whom I shall give a sop, when I have dipped *it*. And when he had dipped the sop, he gave *it* to Judas Iscariot, *the son* of Simon.

27 [f]And after the sop Satan entered into him. Then said Jesus unto him, That thou doest, do quickly.

28 Now no man at the table knew for what intent he spake this unto him.

29 For some *of them* thought, because [g]Judas had the bag, that Jesus had said unto him, Buy *those things* that we have need of against the feast; or, that he should give something to the poor.

30 He then having received the sop went immediately out: and it was night.

31 ¶ Therefore, when he was gone out, Jesus said, [h]Now is the Son of man glorified, and [i]God is glorified in him.

32 [j]If God be glorified in him, God shall also glorify him in himself, and [k]shall straightway glorify him.

33 Little children, yet a little while I am with you. Ye shall seek me: [l]and as I said unto the Jews, Whither I go, ye cannot come; so now I say to you.

34 [m]A new commandment I give unto you, That ye love one another; as I have loved you, that ye also love one another.

35 [n]By this shall all *men* know that ye are my disciples, if ye have love one to another.

36 ¶ Simon Peter said unto him, Lord, whither goest thou? Jesus answered him, Whither I go, thou canst not follow me now; but [o]thou shalt follow me afterwards.

37 Peter said unto him, Lord, why cannot I follow thee now? I will [p]lay down my life for thy sake.

38 Jesus answered him, Wilt thou lay down thy life for my sake? Verily, verily, I say unto thee, The cock shall not crow, till thou hast denied me thrice.

14 Let [q]not your heart be troubled: ye believe in God, believe also in me.

2 In my Father's house are many mansions: if *it were* not *so*, I would have told you. [r]I go to prepare a place for you.

3 And if I go and prepare a place for you, [s]I will come again, and receive you unto myself; that [t]where I am, *there* ye may be also.

4 And whither I go ye know, and the way ye know.

5 Thomas saith unto him, Lord, we know not whither thou goest; and how can we know the way?

6 Jesus saith unto him, I am [u]the way, [v]the truth, and [w]the life: [x]no man cometh unto the Father, but by me.

7 [y]If ye had known me, ye should have known my Father also: and from henceforth ye know him, and have seen him.

8 Philip saith unto him, Lord, shew us the Father, and it sufficeth us.

9 Jesus saith unto him, Have I been so long time with you, and yet hast thou not known me, Philip? [z]he that hath seen me hath seen the Father; and how sayest thou *then*, Shew us the Father?

10 Believest thou not that [a]I am in the Father, and the Father in me? the words that I speak unto you [b]I speak not of myself: but the Father that dwelleth in me, he doeth the works.

11 Believe me that I *am* in the Father, and the Father in me: [c]or else believe me for the very works' sake.

12 [d]Verily, verily, I say unto you, He that believeth on me, the works that I do shall he do also; and greater *works* than these shall he do; because I go unto my Father.

13 [e]And whatsoever ye shall ask in my name, that will I do, that the Father may be glorified in the Son.

14 If ye shall ask any thing in my name, I will do *it*.

15 ¶ [f]If ye love me, keep my commandments.

16 And I will pray the Father, and [g]he shall give you another Comforter, that he may abide with you for ever;

17 *Even* [h]the Spirit of truth; [i]whom the

13:10 q ch. 15:3
13:11 r ch. 6:64
13:13 s Matt. 23:8; Luke 6:46; 1 Cor. 8:6; Phil. 2:11
13:14 t Luke 22:27 u Rom. 12:10; Gal. 6:1; 1 Pet. 5:5
13:15 v Matt. 11:29; Phil. 2:5; 1 Pet. 2:21; 1 John 2:6
13:16 w Matt. 10:24; Luke 6:40; ch. 15:20
13:17 x Jam. 1:25
13:18 y Ps. 41:9; Matt. 26:23; ver. 21
13:19 z ch. 14:29
13:20 a Matt. 10:40; Luke 10:16
13:21 b Matt. 26:21; Mark 14:18; Luke 22:21 c ch. 12:27 d Acts 1:17; 1 John 2:19
13:23 e ch. 19:26
13:27 f Luke 22:3; ch. 6:70
13:29 g ch. 12:6
13:31 h ch. 12:23 i ch. 14:13; 1 Pet. 4:11
13:32 j ch. 17:1 k ch. 12:23
13:33 l ch. 7:34
13:34 m Lev. 19:18; ch. 15:12; Eph. 5:2; 1 Thess. 4:9; Jam. 2:8; 1 Pet. 1:22; 1 John 2:7
13:35 n 1 John 2:5
13:36 o ch. 21:18; 2 Pet. 1:14
13:37 p Matt. 26:33; Mark 14:29; Luke 22:33
14:1 q ver. 27; ch. 16:3
14:2 r ch. 13:33
14:3 s ver. 18; Acts 1:11 t ch. 12:26; 1 Thess. 4:17
14:6 u Heb. 9:8 v ch. 1:17 w ch. 1:4 x ch. 10:9
14:7 y ch. 8:19
14:9 z ch. 12:45; Col. 1:15; Heb. 1:3
14:10 a ver. 20; ch. 10:38 b ch. 5:19
14:11 c ch. 5:36
14:12 d Matt. 21:21; Mark 16:17; Luke 10:17
14:13 e Matt. 7:7; Mark 11:24; Luke 11:9; ch. 15:7; Jam. 1:5; 1 John 3:22
14:15 f ver. 21; ch. 15:10; 1 John 5:3
14:16 g ch. 15:26; Rom. 8:15
14:17 h ch. 15:26; 1 John 4:6 i 1 Cor. 2:14

world cannot receive, because it seeth him not, neither knoweth him: but ye know him; for he dwelleth with you, [j]and shall be in you.

18 [k]I will not leave you comfortless: [l]I will come to you.

19 Yet a little while, and the world seeth me no more; but [m]ye see me: [n]because I live, ye shall live also.

20 At that day ye shall know that [o]I *am* in my Father, and ye in me, and I in you.

21 [p]He that hath my commandments, and keepeth them, he it is that loveth me: and he that loveth me shall be loved of my Father, and I will love him, and will manifest myself to him.

22 [q]Judas saith unto him, not Iscariot, Lord, how is it that thou wilt manifest thyself unto us, and not unto the world?

23 Jesus answered and said unto him, [r]If a man love me, he will keep my words: and my Father will love him, [s]and we will come unto him, and make our abode with him.

24 He that loveth me not keepeth not my sayings: and [t]the word which ye hear is not mine, but the Father's which sent me.

25 These things have I spoken unto you, being *yet* present with you.

26 But [u]the Comforter, *which is* the Holy Ghost, whom the Father will send in my name, [v]he shall teach you all things, and bring all things to your remembrance, whatsoever I have said unto you.

27 [w]Peace I leave with you, my peace I give unto you: not as the world giveth, give I unto you. [x]Let not your heart be troubled, neither let it be afraid.

28 Ye have heard how [y]I said unto you, I go away, and come *again* unto you. If ye loved me, ye would rejoice, because I said, [z]I go unto the Father: for [a]my Father is greater than I.

29 And [b]now I have told you before it come to pass, that, when it is come to pass, ye might believe.

30 Hereafter I will not talk much with you: [c]for the prince of this world cometh, and hath nothing in me.

31 But that the world may know that I love the Father; and [d]as the Father gave me commandment, even so I do. Arise, let us go hence.

15

I am the true vine, and my Father is the husbandman.

2 [e]Every branch in me that beareth not fruit he taketh away: and every *branch* that beareth fruit, he purgeth it, that it may bring forth more fruit.

3 [f]Now ye are clean through the word which I have spoken unto you.

4 [g]Abide in me, and I in you. As the branch cannot bear fruit of itself, except it abide in the vine; no more can ye, except ye abide in me.

5 I am the vine, ye *are* the branches: He that abideth in me, and I in him, the same bringeth forth much [h]fruit: for without me ye can do nothing.

14:17 [j]1 John 2:27
14:18 [k]Matt. 28:20 [l]ver. 3
14:19 [m]ch. 16:16 [n]1 Cor. 15:20
14:20 [o]ver. 10; ch. 10:38
14:21 [p]ver. 15; 1 John 2:5
14:22 [q]Luke 6:16
14:23 [r]ver. 15 [s]1 John 2:24; Rev. 3:20
14:24 [t]ver. 10; ch. 5:19
14:26 [u]ver. 16; Luke 24:49; ch. 15:26 [v]ch. 2:22; 1 John 2:20
14:27 [w]Phil. 4:7; Col. 3:15 [x]ver. 1
14:28 [y]ver. 3 [z]ver. 12; ch. 16:16 [a]ch. 5:18; Phil. 2:6
14:29 [b]ch. 13:19
14:30 [c]ch. 12:31
14:31 [d]ch. 10:18; Phil. 2:8; Heb. 5:8
15:2 [e]Matt. 15:13
15:3 [f]ch. 13:10; Eph. 5:26; 1 Pet. 1:22
15:4 [g]Col. 1:23; 1 John 2:6
15:5 [h]Hos. 14:8; Phil. 1:11
15:6 [i]Matt. 3:10
15:7 [j]ver. 16; ch. 14:13
15:8 [k]Matt. 5:16; Phil. 1:11 [l]ch. 8:31
15:10 [m]ch. 14:15
15:11 [n]ch. 16:24; 1 John 1:4
15:12 [o]ch. 13:34; 1 Thess. 4:9; 1 Pet. 4:8; 1 John 3:11
15:13 [p]ch. 10:11; Rom. 5:7; Eph. 5:2; 1 John 3:16
15:14 [q]Matt. 12:50; ch. 14:15
15:15 [r]Gen. 18:17; ch. 17:26; Acts 20:27
15:16 [s]ch. 6:70; 1 John 4:10 [t]Matt. 28:19; Mark 16:15; Col. 1:6 [u]ver. 7; ch. 14:13
15:17 [v]ver. 12
15:18 [w]1 John 3:1
15:19 [x]1 John 4:5 [y]ch. 17:14
15:20 [z]Matt. 10:24; Luke 6:40; ch. 13:16 [a]Ezek. 3:7
15:21 [b]Matt. 10:22; ch. 16:3
15:22 [c]ch. 9:41 [d]Rom. 1:20; Jam. 4:17
15:23 [e]1 John 2:23
15:24 [f]ch. 3:2
15:25 [g]Ps. 35:19
15:26 [h]Luke 24:49; ch. 14:17; Acts 2:33 [i]1 John 5:6

6 If a man abide not in me, [i]he is cast forth as a branch, and is withered; and men gather them, and cast *them* into the fire, and they are burned.

7 If ye abide in me, and my words abide in you, [j]ye shall ask what ye will, and it shall be done unto you.

8 [k]Herein is my Father glorified, that ye bear much fruit; [l]so shall ye be my disciples.

9 As the Father hath loved me, so have I loved you: continue ye in my love.

10 [m]If ye keep my commandments, ye shall abide in my love; even as I have kept my Father's commandments, and abide in his love.

11 These things have I spoken unto you, that my joy might remain in you, and [n]*that* your joy might be full.

12 [o]This is my commandment, That ye love one another, as I have loved you.

13 [p]Greater love hath no man than this, that a man lay down his life for his friends.

14 [q]Ye are my friends, if ye do whatsoever I command you.

15 Henceforth I call you not servants; for the servant knoweth not what his lord doeth: but I have called you friends; [r]for all things that I have heard of my Father I have made known unto you.

16 [s]Ye have not chosen me, but I have chosen you, and [t]ordained you, that ye should go and bring forth fruit, and *that* your fruit should remain: that [u]whatsoever ye shall ask of the Father in my name, he may give it you.

17 [v]These things I command you, that ye love one another.

18 [w]If the world hate you, ye know that it hated me before *it hated* you.

19 [x]If ye were of the world, the world would love his own: but [y]because ye are not of the world, but I have chosen you out of the world, therefore the world hateth you.

20 Remember the word that I said unto you, [z]The servant is not greater than his lord. If they have persecuted me, they will also persecute you; [a]if they have kept my saying, they will keep yours also.

21 But [b]all these things will they do unto you for my name's sake, because they know not him that sent me.

22 [c]If I had not come and spoken unto them, they had not had sin: [d]but now they have no cloke for their sin.

23 [e]He that hateth me hateth my Father also.

24 If I had not done among them [f]the works which none other man did, they had not had sin: but now have they both seen and hated both me and my Father.

25 But *this cometh to pass*, that the word might be fulfilled that is written in their law, [g]They hated me without a cause.

26 [h]But when the Comforter is come, whom I will send unto you from the Father, *even* the Spirit of truth, which proceedeth from the Father, [i]he shall testify of me:

27 And [j]ye also shall bear witness, because [k]ye have been with me from the beginning.

16 These things have I spoken unto you, that ye [l]should not be offended.

2 [m]They shall put you out of the synagogues: yea, the time cometh, [n]that whosoever killeth you will think that he doeth God service.

3 And [o]these things will they do unto you, because they have not known the Father, nor me.

4 But [p]these things have I told you, that when the time shall come, ye may remember that I told you of them. And [q]these things I said not unto you at the beginning, because I was with you.

5 But now [r]I go my way to him that sent me; and none of you asketh me, Whither goest thou?

6 But because I have said these things unto you, [s]sorrow hath filled your heart.

7 Nevertheless I tell you the truth; It is expedient for you that I go away: for if I go not away, [t]the Comforter will not come unto you; but [u]if I depart, I will send him unto you.

8 And when he is come, he will reprove the world of sin, and of righteousness, and of judgment:

9 [v]Of sin, because they believe not on me;

10 [w]Of righteousness, [x]because I go to my Father, and ye see me no more;

11 [y]Of judgment, because [z]the prince of this world is judged.

12 I have yet many things to say unto you, [a]but ye cannot bear them now.

13 Howbeit when he, [b]the Spirit of truth, is come, [c]he will guide you into all truth: for he shall not speak of himself; but whatsoever he shall hear, *that* shall he speak: and he will shew you things to come.

14 He shall glorify me: for he shall receive of mine, and shall shew *it* unto you.

15 [d]All things that the Father hath are mine: therefore said I, that he shall take of mine, and shall shew *it* unto you.

16 [e]A little while, and ye shall not see me: and again, a little while, and ye shall see me, [f]because I go to the Father.

17 Then said *some* of his disciples among themselves, What is this that he saith unto us, A little while, and ye shall not see me: and again, a little while, and ye shall see me: and, Because I go to the Father?

18 They said therefore, What is this that he saith, A little while? we cannot tell what he saith.

19 Now Jesus knew that they were desirous to ask him, and said unto them, Do ye enquire among yourselves of that I said, A little while, and ye shall not see me: and again, a little while, and ye shall see me?

20 Verily, verily, I say unto you, That ye shall weep and lament, but the world shall rejoice: and ye shall be sorrowful, but your sorrow shall be turned into joy.

15:27 [j]Luke 24:48; Acts 1:8; 1 Pet. 5:1; 2 Pet. 1:16 [k]Luke 1:2; 1 John 1:1
16:1 [l]Matt. 11:6
16:2 [m]ch. 9:22 [n]Acts 8:1
16:3 [o]ch. 15:21; Rom. 10:2; 1 Cor. 2:8; 1 Tim. 1:13
16:4 [p]ch. 13:19 [q]Matt. 9:15
16:5 [r]ver. 10; ch. 7:33
16:6 [s]ver. 22; ch. 14:1
16:7 [t]ch. 7:39 [u]Acts 2:33; Eph. 4:8
16:9 [v]Acts 2:22-37
16:10 [w]Acts 2:32 [x]ch. 3:14
16:11 [y]Acts 26:18 [z]Luke 10:18; ch. 12:31; Eph. 2:2; Col. 2:15; Heb. 2:14
16:12 [a]Mark 4:33; 1 Cor. 3:2; Heb. 5:12
16:13 [b]ch. 14:17 [c]ch. 14:26; 1 John 2:20
16:15 [d]Matt. 11:27; ch. 3:35
16:16 [e]ver. 10; ch. 7:33 [f]ver. 28; ch. 13:3
16:21 [g]Isa. 26:17
16:22 [h]ver. 6 [i]Luke 24:41; ch. 14:1; Acts 2:46; 1 Pet. 1:8
16:23 [j]Matt. 7:7; ch. 14:13
16:24 [k]ch. 15:11
16:26 [l]ver. 23
16:27 [m]ch. 14:21 [n]ver. 30; ch. 3:13
16:28 [o]ch. 13:3
16:30 [p]ch. 21:17 [q]ver. 27; ch. 17:8
16:32 [r]Matt. 26:31; Mark 14:27 [s]ch. 20:10 [t]ch. 8:29
16:33 [u]Isa. 9:6; ch. 14:27; Rom. 5:1; Eph. 2:14; Col. 1:20 [v]ch. 15:19; 2 Tim. 3:12 [w]ch. 14:1 [x]Rom. 8:37; 1 John 4:4
17:1 [y]ch. 12:23
17:2 [z]Dan. 7:14; Matt. 11:27; ch. 3:35; 1 Cor. 15:25; Phil. 2:10; Heb. 2:8 [a]ver. 6; ch. 6:37
17:3 [b]Isa. 53:11; Jer. 9:24 [c]1 Cor. 8:4; 1 Thess. 1:9 [d]ch. 3:34
17:4 [e]ch. 13:31 [f]ch. 4:34 [g]ch. 14:31
17:5 [h]ch. 1:1; Phil. 2:6; Col. 1:15; Heb. 1:3
17:6 [i]ver. 26; Ps. 22:22 [j]ver. 2; ch. 6:37

21 [g]A woman when she is in travail hath sorrow, because her hour is come: but as soon as she is delivered of the child, she remembereth no more the anguish, for joy that a man is born into the world.

22 [h]And ye now therefore have sorrow: but I will see you again, and [i]your heart shall rejoice, and your joy no man taketh from you.

23 And in that day ye shall ask me nothing. [j]Verily, verily, I say unto you, Whatsoever ye shall ask the Father in my name, he will give *it* you.

24 Hitherto have ye asked nothing in my name: ask, and ye shall receive, [k]that your joy may be full.

25 These things have I spoken unto you in proverbs: but the time cometh, when I shall no more speak unto you in proverbs, but I shall shew you plainly of the Father.

26 [l]At that day ye shall ask in my name: and I say not unto you, that I will pray the Father for you:

27 [m]For the Father himself loveth you, because ye have loved me, and [n]have believed that I came out from God.

28 [o]I came forth from the Father, and am come into the world: again, I leave the world, and go to the Father.

29 His disciples said unto him, Lo, now speakest thou plainly, and speakest no proverb.

30 Now are we sure that [p]thou knowest all things, and needest not that any man should ask thee: by this [q]we believe that thou camest forth from God.

31 Jesus answered them, Do ye now believe?

32 [r]Behold, the hour cometh, yea, is now come, that ye shall be scattered, [s]every man to his own, and shall leave me alone: and [t]yet I am not alone, because the Father is with me.

33 These things I have spoken unto you, that [u]in me ye might have peace. [v]In the world ye shall have tribulation: [w]but be of good cheer; [x]I have overcome the world.

17 These words spake Jesus, and lifted up his eyes to heaven, and said, Father, [y]the hour is come; glorify thy Son, that thy Son also may glorify thee:

2 [z]As thou hast given him power over all flesh, that he should give eternal life to as many [a]as thou hast given him.

3 And [b]this is life eternal, that they might know thee [c]the only true God, and Jesus Christ, [d]whom thou hast sent.

4 [e]I have glorified thee on the earth: [f]I have finished the work [g]which thou gavest me to do.

5 And now, O Father, glorify thou me with thine own self with the glory [h]which I had with thee before the world was.

6 [i]I have manifested thy name unto the men [j]which thou gavest me out of the world: thine they were, and thou gavest them me; and they have kept thy word.

7 Now they have known that all things

whatsoever thou hast given me are of thee.

8 For I have given unto them the words [k]which thou gavest me; and they have received *them,* [l]and have known surely that I came out from thee, and they have believed that thou didst send me.

9 I pray for them: [m]I pray not for the world, but for them which thou hast given me; for they are thine.

10 And all mine are thine, and [n]thine are mine; and I am glorified in them.

11 [o]And now I am no more in the world, but these are in the world, and I come to thee. Holy Father, [p]keep through thine own name those whom thou hast given me, [q]that they may be one, [r]as we *are.*

12 While I was with them in the world, [s]I kept them in thy name: those that thou gavest me I have kept, and [t]none of them is lost, [u]but the son of perdition; [v]that the scripture might be fulfilled.

13 And now come I to thee; and these things I speak in the world, that they might have my joy fulfilled in themselves.

14 [w]I have given them thy word; [x]and the world hath hated them, because they are not of the world, [y]even as I am not of the world.

15 I pray not that thou shouldest take them out of the world, but [z]that thou shouldest keep them from the evil.

16 [a]They are not of the world, even as I am not of the world.

17 [b]Sanctify them through thy truth: [c]thy word is truth.

18 [d]As thou hast sent me into the world, even so have I also sent them into the world.

19 And [e]for their sakes I sanctify myself, that they also might be sanctified through the truth.

20 Neither pray I for these alone, but for them also which shall believe on me through their word;

21 [f]That they all may be one; [g]as thou, Father, *art* in me, and I in thee, that they also may be one in us: that the world may believe that thou hast sent me.

22 And the glory which thou gavest me I have given them; [h]that they may be one, even as we are one:

23 I in them, and thou in me, [i]that they may be made perfect in one; and that the world may know that thou hast sent me, and hast loved them, as thou hast loved me.

24 [j]Father, I will that they also, whom thou hast given me, be with me where I am; that they may behold my glory, which thou hast given me: [k]for thou lovedst me before the foundation of the world.

25 O righteous Father, [l]the world hath not known thee: but [m]I have known thee, and [n]these have known that thou hast sent me.

26 [o]And I have declared unto them thy name, and will declare *it:* that the love [p]wherewith thou hast loved me may be in them, and I in them.

17:8 *k*ch. 8:28 *l*ver. 25; ch. 16:27
17:9 *m*1 John 5:19
17:10 *n*ch. 16:15
17:11 *o*ch. 13:1 *p*1 Pet. 1:5; Jude 1 *q*ver. 21 *r*ch. 10:30
17:12 *s*ch. 6:39; Heb. 2:13 *t*ch. 18:9; 1 John 2:19 *u*ch. 6:70 *v*Ps. 109:8; Acts 1:20
17:14 *w*ver. 8 *x*ch. 15:18; 1 John 3:13 *y*ch. 8:23; ver. 16
17:15 *z*Matt. 6:13; Gal. 1:4; 2 Thess. 3:3; 1 John 5:18
17:16 *a*ver. 14
17:17 *b*ch. 15:3; Acts 15:9; Eph. 5:26; 1 Pet. 1:22 *c*2 Sam. 7:28; Ps. 119:142; ch. 8:40
17:18 *d*ch. 20:21
17:19 *e*1 Cor. 1:2; 1 Thess. 4:7; Heb. 10:10
17:21 *f*ver. 11; ch. 10:16; Rom. 12:5; Gal. 3:28 *g*ch. 10:38
17:22 *h*ch. 14:20; 1 John 1:3
17:23 *i*Col. 3:14
17:24 *j*ch. 12:26; 1 Thess. 4:17 *k*ver. 5
17:25 *l*ch. 15:21 *m*ch. 7:29 *n*ver. 8; ch. 16:27
17:26 *o*ver. 6; ch. 15:15 *p*ch. 15:9
18:1 *q*Matt. 26:36; Mark 14:32; Luke 22:39 *r*2 Sam. 15:23
18:2 *s*Luke 21:37
18:3 *t*Matt. 26:47; Mark 14:43; Luke 22:47; Acts 1:16
18:9 *u*ch. 17:12
18:10 *v*Matt. 26:51; Mark 14:47; Luke 22:49
18:11 *w*Matt. 20:22
18:13 *x*Matt. 26:57 *y*Luke 3:2
18:14 *z*ch. 11:50
18:15 *a*Matt. 26:58; Mark 14:54; Luke 22:54
18:16 *b*Matt. 26:69; Mark 14:66; Luke 22:54
18:20 *c*Matt. 26:55; Luke 4:15; ch. 7:14

18 When Jesus had spoken these words, [q]he went forth with his disciples over [r]the brook Cedron, where was a garden, into the which he entered, and his disciples.

2 And Judas also, which betrayed him, knew the place: [s]for Jesus ofttimes resorted thither with his disciples.

3 [t]Judas then, having received a band of *men* and officers from the chief priests and Pharisees, cometh thither with lanterns and torches and weapons.

4 Jesus therefore, knowing all things that should come upon him, went forth, and said unto them, Whom seek ye?

5 They answered him, Jesus of Nazareth. Jesus saith unto them, I am *he.* And Judas also, which betrayed him, stood with them.

6 As soon then as he had said unto them, I am *he,* they went backward, and fell to the ground.

7 Then asked he them again, Whom seek ye? And they said, Jesus of Nazareth.

8 Jesus answered, I have told you that I am *he:* if therefore ye seek me, let these go their way:

9 That the saying might be fulfilled, which he spake, [u]Of them which thou gavest me have I lost none.

10 [v]Then Simon Peter having a sword drew it, and smote the high priest's servant, and cut off his right ear. The servant's name was Malchus.

11 Then said Jesus unto Peter, Put up thy sword into the sheath: [w]the cup which my Father hath given me, shall I not drink it?

12 Then the band and the captain and officers of the Jews took Jesus, and bound him,

13 And [x]led him away to [y]Annas first; for he was father in law to Caiaphas, which was the high priest that same year.

14 [z]Now Caiaphas was he, which gave counsel to the Jews, that it was expedient that one man should die for the people.

15 ¶ [a]And Simon Peter followed Jesus, and *so did* another disciple: that disciple was known unto the high priest, and went in with Jesus into the palace of the high priest.

16 [b]But Peter stood at the door without. Then went out that other disciple, which was known unto the high priest, and spake unto her that kept the door, and brought in Peter.

17 Then saith the damsel that kept the door unto Peter, Art not thou also *one* of this man's disciples? He saith, I am not.

18 And the servants and officers stood there, who had made a fire of coals; for it was cold: and they warmed themselves: and Peter stood with them, and warmed himself.

19 ¶ The high priest then asked Jesus of his disciples, and of his doctrine.

20 Jesus answered him, [c]I spake openly to the world; I ever taught in the synagogue, and in the temple, whither the Jews always resort; and in secret have I said nothing.

21 Why askest thou me? ask them which heard me, what I have said unto them: behold, they know what I said.

22 And when he had thus spoken, one of the officers which stood by [d]struck Jesus with the palm of his hand, saying, Answerest thou the high priest so?

23 Jesus answered him, If I have spoken evil, bear witness of the evil: but if well, why smitest thou me?

24 [e]Now Annas had sent him bound unto Caiaphas the high priest.

25 And Simon Peter stood and warmed himself. [f]They said therefore unto him, Art not thou also *one* of his disciples? He denied *it*, and said, I am not.

26 One of the servants of the high priest, being *his* kinsman whose ear Peter cut off, saith, Did not I see thee in the garden with him?

27 Peter then denied again: and [g]immediately the cock crew.

28 ¶ [h]Then led they Jesus from Caiaphas unto the hall of judgment: and it was early; [i]and they themselves went not into the judgment hall, lest they should be defiled; but that they might eat the passover.

29 Pilate then went out unto them, and said, What accusation bring ye against this man?

30 They answered and said unto him, If he were not a malefactor, we would not have delivered him up unto thee.

31 Then said Pilate unto them, Take ye him, and judge him according to your law. The Jews therefore said unto him, It is not lawful for us to put any man to death:

32 [j]That the saying of Jesus might be fulfilled, which he spake, signifying what death he should die.

33 [k]Then Pilate entered into the judgment hall again, and called Jesus, and said unto him, Art thou the King of the Jews?

34 Jesus answered him, Sayest thou this thing of thyself, or did others tell it thee of me?

35 Pilate answered, Am I a Jew? Thine own nation and the chief priests have delivered thee unto me: what hast thou done?

36 [l]Jesus answered, [m]My kingdom is not of this world: if my kingdom were of this world, then would my servants fight, that I should not be delivered to the Jews: but now is my kingdom not from hence.

37 Pilate therefore said unto him, Art thou a king then? Jesus answered, Thou sayest that I am a king. To this end was I born, and for this cause came I into the world, that I should bear witness unto the truth. Every one that [n]is of the truth heareth my voice.

38 Pilate saith unto him, What is truth? And when he had said this, he went out again unto the Jews, and saith unto them, [o]I find in him no fault *at all*.

39 [p]But ye have a custom, that I should release unto you one at the passover: will ye therefore that I release unto you the King of the Jews?

40 [q]Then cried they all again, saying, Not this man, but Barabbas. [r]Now Barabbas was a robber.

19 Then [s]Pilate therefore took Jesus, and scourged *him*.

2 And the soldiers platted a crown of thorns, and put *it* on his head, and they put on him a purple robe,

3 And said, Hail, King of the Jews! and they smote him with their hands.

4 Pilate therefore went forth again, and saith unto them, Behold, I bring him forth to you, [t]that ye may know that I find no fault in him.

5 Then came Jesus forth, wearing the crown of thorns, and the purple robe. And *Pilate* saith unto them, Behold the man!

6 [u]When the chief priests therefore and officers saw him, they cried out, saying, Crucify *him*, crucify *him*. Pilate saith unto them, Take ye him, and crucify *him*: for I find no fault in him.

7 The Jews answered him, [v]We have a law, and by our law he ought to die, because [w]he made himself the Son of God.

8 ¶ When Pilate therefore heard that saying, he was the more afraid;

9 And went again into the judgment hall, and saith unto Jesus, Whence art thou? [x]But Jesus gave him no answer.

10 Then saith Pilate unto him, Speakest thou not unto me? knowest thou not that I have power to crucify thee, and have power to release thee?

11 Jesus answered, [y]Thou couldest have no power *at all* against me, except it were given thee from above: therefore he that delivered me unto thee hath the greater sin.

12 And from thenceforth Pilate sought to release him: but the Jews cried out, saying, [z]If thou let this man go, thou art not Caesar's friend: [a]whosoever maketh himself a king speaketh against Caesar.

13 ¶ When Pilate therefore heard that saying, he brought Jesus forth, and sat down in the judgment seat in a place that is called the Pavement, but in the Hebrew, Gabbatha.

14 And [b]it was the preparation of the passover, and about the sixth hour: and he saith unto the Jews, Behold your King!

15 But they cried out, Away with *him*, away with *him*, crucify him. Pilate saith unto them, Shall I crucify your King? The chief priests answered, [c]We have no king but Caesar.

16 [d]Then delivered he him therefore unto them to be crucified. And they took Jesus, and led *him* away.

17 [e]And he bearing his cross [f]went forth into a place called *the place* of a skull, which is called in the Hebrew Golgotha:

18 Where they crucified him, and two other with him, on either side one, and Jesus in the midst.

19 ¶ [g]And Pilate wrote a title, and put *it*

18:22 [d]Jer. 20:2; Acts 23:2
18:24 [e]Matt. 26:57
18:25 [f]Matt. 26:69; Mark 14:69; Luke 22:58
18:27 [g]Matt. 26:74; Mark 14:72; Luke 22:60; ch. 13:38
18:28 [h]Matt. 27:2; Mark 15:1; Luke 23:1; Acts 3:13 [i]Acts 10:28
18:32 [j]Matt. 20:19; ch. 12:32
18:33 [k]Matt. 27:11
18:36 [l]1 Tim. 6:13 [m]Dan. 2:44; Luke 12:14; ch. 6:15
18:37 [n]ch. 8:47; 1 John 3:19
18:38 [o]Matt. 27:24; Luke 23:4; ch. 19:4
18:39 [p]Matt. 27:15; Mark 15:6; Luke 23:17
18:40 [q]Acts 3:14 [r]Luke 23:19
19:1 [s]Matt. 20:19; Mark 15:15; Luke 18:33
19:4 [t]ch. 18:38; ver. 6
19:6 [u]Acts 3:13
19:7 [v]Lev. 24:16 [w]Matt. 26:65; ch. 5:18
19:9 [x]Isa. 53:7; Matt. 27:12
19:11 [y]Luke 22:53; ch. 7:30
19:12 [z]Luke 23:2 [a]Acts 17:7
19:14 [b]Matt. 27:62
19:15 [c]Gen. 49:10
19:16 [d]Matt. 27:26; Mark 15:15; Luke 23:24
19:17 [e]Matt. 27:31; Mark 15:21; Luke 23:26 [f]Num. 15:36; Heb. 13:12
19:19 [g]Matt. 27:37; Mark 15:26; Luke 23:38

on the cross. And the writing was, JESUS OF NAZARETH THE KING OF THE JEWS.

20 This title then read many of the Jews: for the place where Jesus was crucified was nigh to the city: and it was written in Hebrew, *and* Greek, *and* Latin.

21 Then said the chief priests of the Jews to Pilate, Write not, The King of the Jews; but that he said, I am King of the Jews.

22 Pilate answered, What I have written I have written.

23 ¶ [h]Then the soldiers, when they had crucified Jesus, took his garments, and made four parts, to every soldier a part; and also *his* coat: now the coat was without seam, woven from the top throughout.

24 They said therefore among themselves, Let us not rend it, but cast lots for it, whose it shall be: that the scripture might be fulfilled, which saith, [i]They parted my raiment among them, and for my vesture they did cast lots. These things therefore the soldiers did.

25 ¶ [j]Now there stood by the cross of Jesus his mother, and his mother's sister, Mary the *wife* of [k]Cleophas, and Mary Magdalene.

26 When Jesus therefore saw his mother, and [l]the disciple standing by, whom he loved, he saith unto his mother, [m]Woman, behold thy son!

27 Then saith he to the disciple, Behold thy mother! And from that hour that disciple took her [n]unto his own *home*.

28 ¶ After this, Jesus knowing that all things were now accomplished, [o]that the scripture might be fulfilled, saith, I thirst.

29 Now there was set a vessel full of vinegar: and [p]they filled a spunge with vinegar, and put *it* upon hyssop, and put *it* to his mouth.

30 When Jesus therefore had received the vinegar, he said, [q]It is finished: and he bowed his head, and gave up the ghost.

31 The Jews therefore, [r]because it was the preparation, [s]that the bodies should not remain upon the cross on the sabbath day, (for that sabbath day was an high day,) besought Pilate that their legs might be broken, and *that* they might be taken away.

32 Then came the soldiers, and brake the legs of the first, and of the other which was crucified with him.

33 But when they came to Jesus, and saw that he was dead already, they brake not his legs:

34 But one of the soldiers with a spear pierced his side, and forthwith [t]came there out blood and water.

35 And he that saw *it* bare record, and his record is true: and he knoweth that he saith true, that ye might believe.

36 For these things were done, [u]that the scripture should be fulfilled, A bone of him shall not be broken.

37 And again another scripture saith, [v]They shall look on him whom they pierced.

38 ¶ [w]And after this Joseph of Arimathaea, being a disciple of Jesus, but secretly [x]for fear of the Jews, besought Pilate that he might take away the body of Jesus: and Pilate gave *him* leave. He came therefore, and took the body of Jesus.

39 And there came also [y]Nicodemus, which at the first came to Jesus by night, and brought a mixture of myrrh and aloes, about an hundred pound *weight*.

40 Then took they the body of Jesus, and [z]wound it in linen clothes with the spices, as the manner of the Jews is to bury.

41 Now in the place where he was crucified there was a garden; and in the garden a new sepulchre, wherein was never man yet laid.

42 [a]There laid they Jesus therefore [b]because of the Jews' preparation *day;* for the sepulchre was nigh at hand.

20 The [c]first *day* of the week cometh Mary Magdalene early, when it was yet dark, unto the sepulchre, and seeth the stone taken away from the sepulchre.

2 Then she runneth, and cometh to Simon Peter, and to the [d]other disciple, whom Jesus loved, and saith unto them, They have taken away the Lord out of the sepulchre, and we know not where they have laid him.

3 [e]Peter therefore went forth, and that other disciple, and came to the sepulchre.

4 So they ran both together: and the other disciple did outrun Peter, and came first to the sepulchre.

5 And he stooping down, *and looking in,* saw [f]the linen clothes lying; yet went he not in.

6 Then cometh Simon Peter following him, and went into the sepulchre, and seeth the linen clothes lie,

7 And [g]the napkin, that was about his head, not lying with the linen clothes, but wrapped together in a place by itself.

8 Then went in also that other disciple, which came first to the sepulchre, and he saw, and believed.

9 For as yet they knew not the [h]scripture, that he must rise again from the dead.

10 Then the disciples went away again unto their own home.

11 ¶ [i]But Mary stood without at the sepulchre weeping: and as she wept, she stooped down, *and looked* into the sepulchre,

12 And seeth two angels in white sitting, the one at the head, and the other at the feet, where the body of Jesus had lain.

13 And they say unto her, Woman, why weepest thou? She saith unto them, Because they have taken away my Lord, and I know not where they have laid him.

14 [j]And when she had thus said, she turned herself back, and saw Jesus standing, and [k]knew not that it was Jesus.

15 Jesus saith unto her, Woman, why weepest thou? whom seekest thou? She, supposing him to be the gardener, saith unto him, Sir, if thou have borne him hence,

19:23 [h]Matt. 27:35; Mark 15:24; Luke 23:34
19:24 [i]Ps. 22:18
19:25 [j]Matt. 27:55; Mark 15:40; Luke 23:49 [k]Luke 24:18
19:26 [l]ch. 13:23 [m]ch. 2:4
19:27 [n]ch. 1:11
19:28 [o]Ps. 69:21
19:29 [p]Matt. 27:48
19:30 [q]ch. 17:4
19:31 [r]ver. 42; Mark 15:42 [s]Deut. 21:23
19:34 [t]1 John 5:6
19:36 [u]Ex. 12:46; Num. 9:12; Ps. 34:20
19:37 [v]Ps. 22:16; Zech. 12:10; Rev. 1:7
19:38 [w]Matt. 27:57; Mark 15:42; Luke 23:50 [x]ch. 9:22
19:39 [y]ch. 3:1
19:40 [z]Acts 5:6
19:42 [a]Isa. 53:9 [b]ver. 31
20:1 [c]Matt. 28:1; Mark 16:1; Luke 24:1
20:2 [d]ch. 13:23
20:3 [e]Luke 24:12
20:5 [f]ch. 19:40
20:7 [g]ch. 11:44
20:9 [h]Ps. 16:10; Acts 2:25-31
20:11 [i]Mark 16:5
20:14 [j]Matt. 28:9; Mark 16:9 [k]Luke 24:16; ch. 21:4

tell me where thou hast laid him, and I will take him away.

16 Jesus saith unto her, Mary. She turned herself, and saith unto him, Rabboni; which is to say, Master.

17 Jesus saith unto her, Touch me not; for I am not yet ascended to my Father: but go to [l]my brethren, and say unto them, [m]I ascend unto my Father, and your Father; and *to* [n]my God, and your God.

18 [o]Mary Magdalene came and told the disciples that she had seen the Lord, and *that* he had spoken these things unto her.

19 ¶ [p]Then the same day at evening, being the first *day* of the week, when the doors were shut where the disciples were assembled for fear of the Jews, came Jesus and stood in the midst, and saith unto them, Peace *be* unto you.

20 And when he had so said, he shewed unto them *his* hands and his side. [q]Then were the disciples glad, when they saw the Lord.

21 Then said Jesus to them again, Peace *be* unto you: [r]as *my* Father hath sent me, even so send I you.

22 And when he had said this, he breathed on *them,* and saith unto them, Receive ye the Holy Ghost:

23 [s]Whose soever sins ye remit, they are remitted unto them; *and* whose soever *sins* ye retain, they are retained.

24 ¶ But Thomas, one of the twelve, [t]called Didymus, was not with them when Jesus came.

25 The other disciples therefore said unto him, We have seen the Lord. But he said unto them, Except I shall see in his hands the print of the nails, and put my finger into the print of the nails, and thrust my hand into his side, I will not believe.

26 ¶ And after eight days again his disciples were within, and Thomas with them: *then* came Jesus, the doors being shut, and stood in the midst, and said, Peace *be* unto you.

27 Then saith he to Thomas, Reach hither thy finger, and behold my hands; and [u]reach hither thy hand, and thrust *it* into my side: and be not faithless, but believing.

28 And Thomas answered and said unto him, My Lord and my God.

29 Jesus saith unto him, Thomas, because thou hast seen me, thou hast believed: [v]blessed *are* they that have not seen, and *yet* have believed.

30 ¶ [w]And many other signs truly did Jesus in the presence of his disciples, which are not written in this book:

31 [x]But these are written, that ye might believe that Jesus is the Christ, the Son of God; [y]and that believing ye might have life through his name.

21

After these things Jesus shewed himself again to the disciples at the sea of Tiberias; and on this wise shewed he *himself.*

2 There were together Simon Peter, and Thomas called Didymus, and [z]Nathanael of Cana in Galilee, and [a]the *sons* of Zebedee, and two other of his disciples.

3 Simon Peter saith unto them, I go afishing. They say unto him, We also go with thee. They went forth, and entered into a ship immediately; and that night they caught nothing.

4 But when the morning was now come, Jesus stood on the shore: but the disciples [b]knew not that it was Jesus.

5 Then [c]Jesus saith unto them, Children, have ye any meat? They answered him, No.

6 And he said unto them, [d]Cast the net on the right side of the ship, and ye shall find. They cast therefore, and now they were not able to draw it for the multitude of fishes.

7 Therefore [e]that disciple whom Jesus loved saith unto Peter, It is the Lord. Now when Simon Peter heard that it was the Lord, he girt *his* fisher's coat *unto him,* (for he was naked,) and did cast himself into the sea.

8 And the other disciples came in a little ship; (for they were not far from land, but as it were two hundred cubits,) dragging the net with fishes.

9 As soon then as they were come to land, they saw a fire of coals there, and fish laid thereon, and bread.

10 Jesus saith unto them, Bring of the fish which ye have now caught.

11 Simon Peter went up, and drew the net to land full of great fishes, an hundred and fifty and three: and for all there were so many, yet was not the net broken.

12 Jesus saith unto them, [f]Come *and* dine. And none of the disciples durst ask him, Who art thou? knowing that it was the Lord.

13 Jesus then cometh, and taketh bread, and giveth them, and fish likewise.

14 This is now [g]the third time that Jesus shewed himself to his disciples, after that he was risen from the dead.

15 ¶ So when they had dined, Jesus saith to Simon Peter, Simon, *son* of Jonas, lovest thou me more than these? He saith unto him, Yea, Lord; thou knowest that I love thee. He saith unto him, Feed my lambs.

16 He saith to him again the second time, Simon, *son* of Jonas, lovest thou me? He saith unto him, Yea, Lord; thou knowest that I love thee. [h]He saith unto him, Feed my sheep.

17 He saith unto him the third time, Simon, *son* of Jonas, lovest thou me? Peter was grieved because he said unto him the third time, Lovest thou me? And he said unto him, Lord, [i]thou knowest all things; thou knowest that I love thee. Jesus saith unto him, Feed my sheep.

18 [j]Verily, verily, I say unto thee, When thou wast young, thou girdedst thyself, and walkedst whither thou wouldest: but when thou shalt be old, thou shalt stretch forth thy hands, and another shall gird thee, and carry *thee* whither thou wouldest not.

20:17 [l]Ps. 22:22; Matt. 28:10; Rom. 8:29; Heb. 2:11 [m]ch. 16:28 [n]Eph. 1:17
20:18 [o]Matt. 28:10; Luke 24:10
20:19 [p]Mark 16:14; Luke 24:36; 1 Cor. 15:5
20:20 [q]ch. 16:22
20:21 [r]Matt. 28:18; ch. 17:18; Heb. 3:1; 2 Tim. 2:2
20:23 [s]Matt. 16:19
20:24 [t]ch. 11:16
20:27 [u]1 John 1:1
20:29 [v]2 Cor. 5:7; 1 Pet. 1:8
20:30 [w]ch. 21:25
20:31 [x]Luke 1:4 [y]ch. 3:15; 1 Pet. 1:9
21:2 [z]ch. 1:45 [a]Matt. 4:21
21:4 [b]ch. 20:14
21:5 [c]Luke 24:41
21:6 [d]Luke 5:4
21:7 [e]ch. 13:23
21:12 [f]Acts 10:41
21:14 [g]ch. 20:19
21:16 [h]Acts 20:28; Heb. 13:20; 1 Pet. 2:25
21:17 [i]ch. 2:24
21:18 [j]ch. 13:36; Acts 12:3

19 This spake he, signifying [k]by what death he should glorify God. And when he had spoken this, he saith unto him, Follow me.

20 Then Peter, turning about, seeth the disciple [l]whom Jesus loved following; which also leaned on his breast at supper and said, Lord, which is he that betrayeth thee?

21 Peter seeing him saith to Jesus, Lord, and what *shall* this man *do?*

22 Jesus saith unto him, If I will that he tarry [m]till I come, what *is that* to thee? follow thou me.

23 Then went this saying abroad among the brethren, that that disciple should not die: yet Jesus said not unto him, He shall not die; but, If I will that he tarry till I come, what *is that* to thee?

24 This is the disciple which testifieth of these things, and wrote these things: and [n]we know that his testimony is true.

25 [o]And there are also many other things which Jesus did, the which, if they should be written every one, [p]I suppose that even the world itself could not contain the books that should be written. Amen.

21:19 [k]2 Pet. 1:14
21:20 [l]ch. 13:23
21:22 [m]Matt. 16:27; 1 Cor. 4:5; Rev. 2:25
21:24 [n]ch. 19:35; 3 John 12
21:25 [o]ch. 20:30 [p]Am. 7:10

ACTS

Luke has long been recognized as the author of Acts. The date of A.D. 61 is widely accepted as the date of writing. The book begins with Christ's final instructions before his ascension and the giving of the Holy Spirit. The book then divides into two distinct parts. The first twelve chapters tell of the travels and teachings of Peter, Stephen, and James. The remainder of the book details Paul's conversion and subsequent ministry.

I. Pentecost and the giving of the Holy Spirit, 1:1–2:47
II. The ministry of Peter, Stephen, Barnabas and others, 3:1–8:40
III. The conversion of Paul, 9:1–9:31
IV. Peter and the Gentiles, 10:1–11:30
V. Persecution under Herod, 12:1–12:25
VI. Paul's ministry, 13:1–28:31

1 The former treatise have I made, O [a]Theophilus, of all that Jesus began both to do and teach,

2 [b]Until the day in which he was taken up, after that he through the Holy Ghost [c]had given commandments unto the apostles whom he had chosen:

3 [d]To whom also he shewed himself alive after his passion by many infallible proofs, being seen of them forty days, and speaking of the things pertaining to the kingdom of God:

4 [e]And, being assembled together with *them,* commanded them that they should not depart from Jerusalem, but wait for the promise of the Father, which, [f]*saith he,* ye have heard of me.

5 [g]For John truly baptized with water; [h]but ye shall be baptized with the Holy Ghost not many days hence.

6 When they therefore were come together, they asked of him, saying, [i]Lord, wilt thou at this time [j]restore again the kingdom to Israel?

7 And he said unto them, [k]It is not for you to know the times or the seasons, which the Father hath put in his own power.

8 [l]But ye shall receive power, [m]after that the Holy Ghost is come upon you: and [n]ye shall be witnesses unto me both in Jerusalem, and in all Judaea, and in Samaria, and unto the uttermost part of the earth.

9 [o]And when he had spoken these things, while they beheld, [p]he was taken up; and a cloud received him out of their sight.

10 And while they looked stedfastly toward heaven as he went up, behold, two men stood by them [q]in white apparel;

11 Which also said, [r]Ye men of Galilee, why stand ye gazing up into heaven? this same Jesus, which is taken up from you into heaven, [s]shall so come in like manner as ye have seen him go into heaven.

12 [t]Then returned they unto Jerusalem from the mount called Olivet, which is from Jerusalem a sabbath day's journey.

13 And when they were come in, they went up [u]into an upper room, where abode both [v]Peter, and James, and John, and Andrew, Philip, and Thomas, Bartholomew, and Matthew, James *the son* of Alphaeus, and [w]Simon Zelotes, and [x]Judas *the brother* of James.

14 [y]These all continued with one accord in prayer and supplication, with [z]the

1:1 [a]Luke 1:3
1:2 [b]Mark 16:19; Luke 9:51; ver. 9; 1 Tim. 3:16 [c]Matt. 28:19; Mark 16:15; John 20:21; ch. 10:41
1:3 [d]Mark 16:14; Luke 24:36; John 20:19; 1 Cor. 15:5
1:4 [e]Luke 24:43 [f]Luke 24:49; John 14:16; ch. 2:33
1:5 [g]Matt. 3:11; ch. 11:16 [h]Joel 3:18; ch. 2:4
1:6 [i]Matt. 24:3 [j]Isa. 1:26; Dan. 7:27; Am. 9:11
1:7 [k]Matt. 24:36; Mark 13:32; 1 Thess. 5:1
1:8 [l]ch. 2:1 [m]Luke 24:49 [n]Luke 24:48; John 15:27; ver. 22; ch. 2:32
1:9 [o]Luke 24:51; John 6:62 [p]ver. 2
1:10 [q]Matt. 28:3; Mark 16:5; Luke 24:4; John 20:12; ch. 10:3
1:11 [r]ch. 2:7 [s]Dan. 7:13; Matt. 24:30; Mark 13:26; Luke 21:27; John 14:3; 1 Thess. 1:10; 2 Thess. 1:10; Rev. 1:7
1:12 [t]Luke 24:52 **1:13** [u]ch. 9:37 [v]Matt. 10:2 [w]Luke 6:15 [x]Jude 1
1:14 [y]ch. 2:1 [z]Luke 23:49

women, and Mary the mother of Jesus, and
with [a]his brethren.
15 ¶ And in those days Peter stood up in
the midst of the disciples, and said, (the
number [b]of names together were about an
hundred and twenty,)
16 Men *and* brethren, this scripture must
needs have been fulfilled, [c]which the Holy
Ghost by the mouth of David spake before
concerning Judas, [d]which was guide to
them that took Jesus.
17 For [e]he was numbered with us, and
had obtained part of [f]this ministry.
18 [g]Now this man purchased a field with
[h]the reward of iniquity; and falling headlong, he burst asunder in the midst, and all
his bowels gushed out.
19 And it was known unto all the dwellers
at Jerusalem; insomuch as that field is
called in their proper tongue, Aceldama,
that is to say, The field of blood.
20 For it is written in the book of Psalms,
[i]Let his habitation be desolate, and let no
man dwell therein: and [j]his bishoprick let
another take.
21 Wherefore of these men which have
companied with us all the time that the Lord
Jesus went in and out among us,
22 [k]Beginning from the baptism of John,
unto that same day that [l]he was taken up
from us, must one be ordained [m]to be a witness with us of his resurrection.
23 And they appointed two, Joseph called
[n]Barsabas, who was surnamed Justus, and
Matthias.
24 And they prayed, and said, Thou,
Lord, [o]which knowest the hearts of all *men*,
shew whether of these two thou hast chosen,
25 [p]That he may take part of this ministry and apostleship, from which Judas by
transgression fell, that he might go to his
own place.
26 And they gave forth their lots; and the
lot fell upon Matthias; and he was numbered with the eleven apostles.

2 And when [q]the day of Pentecost was
fully come, [r]they were all with one accord in one place.
2 And suddenly there came a sound from
heaven as of a rushing mighty wind, and [s]it
filled all the house where they were sitting.
3 And there appeared unto them cloven
tongues like as of fire, and it sat upon each
of them.
4 And [t]they were all filled with the Holy
Ghost, and began [u]to speak with other
tongues, as the Spirit gave them utterance.
5 And there were dwelling at Jerusalem
Jews, devout men, out of every nation under
heaven.
6 Now when this was noised abroad, the
multitude came together, and were confounded, because that every man heard
them speak in his own language.
7 And they were all amazed and marvelled, saying one to another, Behold, are
not all these which speak [v]Galileans?
8 And how hear we every man in our own
tongue, wherein we were born?
9 Parthians, and Medes, and Elamites,
and the dwellers in Mesopotamia, and in
Judea, and Cappadocia, in Pontus, and
Asia,
10 Phrygia, and Pamphylia, in Egypt, and
in the parts of Libya about Cyrene, and
strangers of Rome, Jews and proselytes,
11 Cretes and Arabians, we do hear them
speak in our tongues the wonderful works
of God.
12 And they were all amazed, and were in
doubt, saying one to another, What meaneth this?
13 Others mocking said, These men are
full of new wine.
14 ¶ But Peter, standing up with the
eleven, lifted up his voice, and said unto
them, Ye men of Judaea, and all *ye* that
dwell at Jerusalem, be this known unto you,
and hearken to my words:
15 For these are not drunken, as ye suppose, [w]seeing it is *but* the third hour of the
day.
16 But this is that which was spoken by
the prophet Joel;
17 [x]And it shall come to pass in the last
days, saith God, [y]I will pour out of my
Spirit upon all flesh: and your sons and
[z]your daughters shall prophesy, and your
young men shall see visions, and your old
men shall dream dreams:
18 And on my servants and on my handmaidens I will pour out in those days of my
Spirit; [a]and they shall prophesy:
19 [b]And I will shew wonders in heaven
above, and signs in the earth beneath;
blood, and fire, and vapour of smoke:
20 [c]The sun shall be turned into darkness, and the moon into blood, before that
great and notable day of the Lord come:
21 And it shall come to pass, *that* [d]who-
soever shall call on the name of the Lord
shall be saved.
22 Ye men of Israel, hear these words;
Jesus of Nazareth, a man approved of God
among you [e]by miracles and wonders and
signs, which God did by him in the midst of
you, as ye yourselves also know:
23 Him, [f]being delivered by the determi-
nate counsel and foreknowledge of God,
[g]ye have taken, and by wicked hands have
crucified and slain:
24 [h]Whom God hath raised up, having
loosed the pains of death: because it was not
possible that he should be holden of it.
25 For David speaketh concerning him,
[i]I foresaw the Lord always before my face,
for he is on my right hand, that I should not
be moved:
26 Therefore did my heart rejoice, and my
tongue was glad; moreover also my flesh
shall rest in hope:
27 Because thou wilt not leave my soul in
hell, neither wilt thou suffer thine Holy One
to see corruption.
28 Thou hast made known to me the ways

1:14 [a]Matt. 13:55
1:15 [b]Rev. 3:4
1:16 [c]Ps. 41:9; John 13:18 [d]Luke 22:47; John 18:3
1:17 [e]Matt. 10:4; Luke 6:16 [f]ver. 25; ch. 12:25
1:18 [g]Matt. 27:5 [h]Matt. 26:15; 2 Pet. 2:15
1:20 [i]Ps. 69:25 [j]Ps. 109:8
1:22 [k]Mark 1:1 [l]ver. 9 [m]John 15:27; ver. 8; ch. 4:33
1:23 [n]ch. 15:22
1:24 [o]1 Sam. 16:7; 1 Chron. 28:9; Jer. 11:20; ch. 15:8; Rev. 2:23
1:25 [p]ver. 17
2:1 [q]Lev. 23:15; Deut. 16:9; ch. 20:16 [r]ch. 1:14
2:2 [s]ch. 4:31
2:4 [t]ch. 1:5 [u]Mark 16:17; ch. 10:46; 1 Cor. 12:10
2:7 [v]ch. 1:11
2:15 [w]1 Thess. 5:7
2:17 [x]Isa. 44:3; Ezek. 11:19; Joel 2:28; Zech. 12:10; John 7:38 [y]ch. 10:45 [z]ch. 21:9
2:18 [a]ch. 21:4; 1 Cor. 12:10
2:19 [b]Joel 2:30
2:20 [c]Matt. 24:29; Mark 13:24; Luke 21:25
2:21 [d]Rom. 10:13
2:22 [e]John 3:2; ch. 10:38; Heb. 2:4
2:23 [f]Matt. 26:24; Luke 22:22; ch. 3:18 [g]ch. 5:30
2:24 [h]ver. 32; ch. 3:15; Rom. 4:24; 1 Cor. 6:14; 2 Cor. 4:14; Gal. 1:1; Eph. 1:20; Col. 2:12; 1 Thess. 1:10; Heb. 13:20; 1 Pet. 1:21
2:25 [i]Ps. 16:8

of life; thou shalt make me full of joy with
thy countenance.
29 Men *and* brethren, let me freely speak
unto you [j]of the patriarch David, that he is
both dead and buried, and his sepulchre is
with us unto this day.
30 Therefore being a prophet, [k]and
knowing that God had sworn with an oath
to him, that of the fruit of his loins, according to the flesh, he would raise up Christ to
sit on his throne;
31 He seeing this before spake of the resurrection of Christ, [l]that his soul was not
left in hell, neither his flesh did see corruption.
32 [m]This Jesus hath God raised up,
[n]whereof we all are witnesses.
33 Therefore [o]being by the right hand of
God exalted, and [p]having received of the
Father the promise of the Holy Ghost, he
[q]hath shed forth this, which ye now see and
hear.
34 For David is not ascended into the
heavens: but he saith himself, [r]The LORD
said unto my Lord, Sit thou on my right
hand,
35 Until I make thy foes thy footstool.
36 Therefore let all the house of Israel
know assuredly, that God [s]hath made that
same Jesus, whom ye have crucified, both
Lord and Christ.
37 ¶ Now when they heard *this,* [t]they
were pricked in their heart, and said unto
Peter and to the rest of the apostles, Men
and brethren, what shall we do?
38 Then Peter said unto them, [u]Repent,
and be baptized every one of you in the
name of Jesus Christ for the remission of
sins, and ye shall receive the gift of the Holy
Ghost.
39 For the promise is unto you, and [v]to
your children, and [w]to all that are afar off,
even as many as the Lord our God shall call.
40 And with many other words did he testify and exhort, saying, Save yourselves
from this untoward generation.
41 ¶ Then they that gladly received his
word were baptized: and the same day there
were added *unto them* about three thousand souls.
42 [x]And they continued stedfastly in the
apostles' doctrine and fellowship, and in
breaking of bread, and in prayers.
43 And fear came upon every soul: and
[y]many wonders and signs were done by the
apostles.
44 And all that believed were together,
and [z]had all things common;
45 And sold their possessions and goods,
and [a]parted them to all *men,* as every man
had need.
46 [b]And they, continuing daily with one
accord [c]in the temple, and [d]breaking bread
from house to house, did eat their meat with
gladness and singleness of heart,
47 Praising God, and [e]having favour
with all the people. And [f]the Lord added to
the church daily such as should be saved.

3 Now Peter and John went up together
[g]into the temple at the hour of prayer,
[h]*being* the ninth *hour.*
2 And [i]a certain man lame from his
mother's womb was carried, whom they
laid daily at the gate of the temple which is
called Beautiful, [j]to ask alms of them that
entered into the temple;
3 Who seeing Peter and John about to go
into the temple asked an alms.
4 And Peter, fastening his eyes upon him
with John, said, Look on us.
5 And he gave heed unto them, expecting
to receive something of them.
6 Then Peter said, Silver and gold have I
none; but such as I have give I thee: [k]In the
name of Jesus Christ of Nazareth rise up
and walk.
7 And he took him by the right hand, and
lifted *him* up: and immediately his feet and
ankle bones received strength.
8 And he [l]leaping up stood, and walked,
and entered with them into the temple,
walking, and leaping, and praising God.
9 [m]And all the people saw him walking
and praising God:
10 And they knew that it was he which
[n]sat for alms at the Beautiful gate of the
temple: and they were filled with wonder
and amazement at that which had happened unto him.
11 And as the lame man which was
healed held Peter and John, all the people
ran together unto them in the porch [o]that is
called Solomon's, greatly wondering.
12 ¶ And when Peter saw *it,* he answered
unto the people, Ye men of Israel, why marvel ye at this? or why look ye so earnestly
on us, as though by our own power or holiness we had made this man to walk?
13 [p]The God of Abraham, and of Isaac,
and of Jacob, the God of our fathers, [q]hath
glorified his Son Jesus; whom ye [r]delivered
up, and [s]denied him in the presence of Pilate, when he was determined to let *him* go.
14 But ye denied [t]the Holy One [u]and the
Just, and desired a murderer to be granted
unto you;
15 And killed the Prince of life, [v]whom
God hath raised from the dead; [w]whereof
we are witnesses.
16 [x]And his name through faith in his
name hath made this man strong, whom ye
see and know: yea, the faith which is by him
hath given him this perfect soundness in the
presence of you all.
17 And now, brethren, I wot that
[y]through ignorance ye did *it,* as *did* also
your rulers.
18 But [z]those things, which God before
had shewed [a]by the mouth of all his prophets, that Christ should suffer, he hath so fulfilled.
19 ¶ [b]Repent ye therefore, and be converted, that your sins may be blotted out,
when the times of refreshing shall come
from the presence of the Lord;

2:29 [j]1 Kings 2:10; ch. 13:36
2:30 [k]2 Sam. 7:12; Ps. 132:11; Luke 1:32; Rom. 1:3; 2 Tim. 2:8
2:31 [l]Ps. 16:10; ch. 13:35
2:32 [m]ver. 24 [n]ch. 1:8
2:33 [o]ch. 5:31; Phil. 2:9; Heb. 10:12 [p]John 14:26; ch. 1:4 [q]ch. 10:45; Eph. 4:8
2:34 [r]Ps. 110:1; Matt. 22:44; 1 Cor. 15:25; Eph. 1:20; Heb. 1:13
2:36 [s]ch. 5:31
2:37 [t]Zech. 12:10; Luke 3:10; ch. 9:6
2:38 [u]Luke 24:47; ch. 3:19
2:39 [v]Joel 2:28; ch. 3:25 [w]ch. 10:45; Eph. 2:13
2:42 [x]ver. 46; ch. 1:14; Rom. 12:12; Eph. 6:18; Col. 4:2; Heb. 10:25
2:43 [y]Mark 16:17; ch. 4:33
2:44 [z]ch. 4:32
2:45 [a]Isa. 58:7
2:46 [b]ch. 1:14 [c]Luke 24:53; ch. 5:42 [d]ch. 20:7
2:47 [e]Luke 2:52; ch. 4:33; Rom. 14:18 [f]ch. 5:14
3:1 [g]ch. 2:46 [h]Ps. 55:17
3:2 [i]ch. 14:8 [j]John 9:8
3:6 [k]ch. 4:10
3:8 [l]Isa. 35:6
3:9 [m]ch. 4:16
3:10 [n]John 9:8
3:11 [o]John 10:23; ch. 5:12
3:13 [p]ch. 5:30 [q]John 7:39 [r]Matt. 27:2 [s]Matt. 27:20; Mark 15:11; Luke 23:18; John 18:40; ch. 13:28
3:14 [t]Ps. 16:10; Mark 1:24; Luke 1:35; ch. 2:27 [u]ch. 7:52
3:15 [v]ch. 2:24 [w]ch. 2:32
3:16 [x]Matt. 9:22; ch. 4:10
3:17 [y]Luke 23:34; John 16:3; ch. 13:27; 1 Cor. 2:8; 1 Tim. 1:13
3:18 [z]Luke 24:44; ch. 26:22 [a]Ps. 22; Isa. 50:6; Dan. 9:26; 1 Pet. 1:10
3:19 [b]ch. 2:38

20 And he shall send Jesus Christ, which before was preached unto you:

21 [c]Whom the heaven must receive until the times of [d]restitution of all things, [e]which God hath spoken by the mouth of all his holy prophets since the world began.

22 For Moses truly said unto the fathers, [f]A prophet shall the Lord your God raise up unto you of your brethren, like unto me; him shall ye hear in all things whatsoever he shall say unto you.

23 And it shall come to pass, *that* every soul, which will not hear that prophet, shall be destroyed from among the people.

24 Yea, and all the prophets from Samuel and those that follow after, as many as have spoken, have likewise foretold of these days.

25 [g]Ye are the children of the prophets, and of the covenant which God made with our fathers, saying unto Abraham, [h]And in thy seed shall all the kindreds of the earth be blessed.

26 [i]Unto you first God, having raised up his Son Jesus, [j]sent him to bless you, [k]in turning away every one of you from his iniquities.

4

And as they spake unto the people, the priests, and the captain of the temple, and the Sadducees, came upon them,

2 [l]Being grieved that they taught the people, and preached through Jesus the resurrection from the dead.

3 And they laid hands on them, and put *them* in hold unto the next day: for it was now eventide.

4 Howbeit many of them which heard the word believed; and the number of the men was about five thousand.

5 ¶ And it came to pass on the morrow, that their rulers, and elders, and scribes,

6 And [m]Annas the high priest, and Caiaphas, and John, and Alexander, and as many as were of the kindred of the high priest, were gathered together at Jerusalem.

7 And when they had set them in the midst, they asked, [n]By what power, or by what name, have ye done this?

8 [o]Then Peter, filled with the Holy Ghost, said unto them, Ye rulers of the people, and elders of Israel,

9 If we this day be examined of the good deed done to the impotent man, by what means he is made whole;

10 Be it known unto you all, and to all the people of Israel, [p]that by the name of Jesus Christ of Nazareth, whom ye crucified, [q]whom God raised from the dead, *even* by him doth this man stand here before you whole.

11 [r]This is the stone which was set at nought of you builders, which is become the head of the corner.

12 [s]Neither is there salvation in any other: for there is none other name under heaven given among men, whereby we must be saved.

13 ¶ Now when they saw the boldness of Peter and John, [t]and perceived that they were unlearned and ignorant men, they marvelled; and they took knowledge of them, that they had been with Jesus.

14 And beholding the man which was healed [u]standing with them, they could say nothing against it.

15 But when they had commanded them to go aside out of the council, they conferred among themselves,

16 Saying, [v]What shall we do to these men? for that indeed a notable miracle hath been done by them *is* [w]manifest to all them that dwell in Jerusalem; and we cannot deny *it*.

17 But that it spread no further among the people, let us straitly threaten them, that they speak henceforth to no man in this name.

18 [x]And they called them, and commanded them not to speak at all nor teach in the name of Jesus.

19 But Peter and John answered and said unto them, [y]Whether it be right in the sight of God to hearken unto you more than unto God, judge ye.

20 [z]For we cannot but speak the things which [a]we have seen and heard.

21 So when they had further threatened them, they let them go, finding nothing how they might punish them, [b]because of the people: for all *men* glorified God for [c]that which was done.

22 For the man was above forty years old, on whom this miracle of healing was shewed.

23 ¶ And being let go, [d]they went to their own company, and reported all that the chief priests and elders had said unto them.

24 And when they heard that, they lifted up their voice to God with one accord, and said, Lord, [e]thou *art* God, which hast made heaven, and earth, and the sea, and all that in them is:

25 Who by the mouth of thy servant David hast said, [f]Why did the heathen rage, and the people imagine vain things?

26 The kings of the earth stood up, and the rulers were gathered together against the Lord, and against his Christ.

27 For [g]of a truth against [h]thy holy child Jesus, [i]whom thou hast anointed, both Herod, and Pontius Pilate, with the Gentiles, and the people of Israel, were gathered together,

28 [j]For to do whatsoever thy hand and thy counsel determined before to be done.

29 And now, Lord, behold their threatenings: and grant unto thy servants, [k]that with all boldness they may speak thy word,

30 By stretching forth thine hand to heal; [l]and that signs and wonders may be done [m]by the name of [n]thy holy child Jesus.

31 ¶ And when they had prayed, [o]the place was shaken where they were assembled together; and they were all filled with the Holy Ghost, [p]and they spake the word of God with boldness.

3:21 [c]ch. 1:11 [d]Matt. 17:11 [e]Luke 1:70
3:22 [f]Deut. 18:15; ch. 7:37
3:25 [g]ch. 2:39; Rom. 9:4; Gal. 3:26 [h]Gen. 12:3; Gal. 3:8
3:26 [i]Matt. 10:5; Luke 24:47; ch. 13:32 [j]ver. 22 [k]Matt. 1:21
4:2 [l]Matt. 22:23; Acts 23:8
4:6 [m]Luke 3:2; John 11:49
4:7 [n]Ex. 2:14; Matt. 21:23; ch. 7:27
4:8 [o]Luke 12:11
4:10 [p]ch. 3:6 [q]ch. 2:24
4:11 [r]Ps. 118:22; Isa. 28:16; Matt. 21:42
4:12 [s]Matt. 1:21; ch. 10:43; 1 Tim. 2:5
4:13 [t]Matt. 11:25; 1 Cor. 1:27
4:14 [u]ch. 3:11
4:16 [v]John 11:47 [w]ch. 3:9
4:18 [x]ch. 5:40
4:19 [y]ch. 5:29
4:20 [z]ch. 1:8 [a]ch. 22:15; 1 John 1:1
4:21 [b]Matt. 21:26; Luke 20:6; ch. 5:26 [c]ch. 3:7
4:23 [d]ch. 12:12
4:24 [e]2 Kings 19:15
4:25 [f]Ps. 2:1
4:27 [g]Matt. 26:3; Luke 22:2 [h]Luke 1:35 [i]Luke 4:18; John 10:36
4:28 [j]ch. 2:23
4:29 [k]ver. 13; ch. 9:27; Eph. 6:19
4:30 [l]ch. 2:43 [m]ch. 3:6 [n]ver. 27
4:31 [o]ch. 2:2 [p]ver. 29

32 And the multitude of them that believed [q]were of one heart and of one soul: [r]neither said any *of them* that ought of the things which he possessed was his own; but they had all things common.

33 And with [s]great power gave the apostles [t]witness of the resurrection of the Lord Jesus: and [u]great grace was upon them all.

34 Neither was there any among them that lacked: [v]for as many as were possessors of lands or houses sold them, and brought the prices of the things that were sold,

35 [w]And laid *them* down at the apostles' feet: [x]and distribution was made unto every man according as he had need.

36 And Joses, who by the apostles was surnamed Barnabas, (which is, being interpreted, The son of consolation,) a Levite, *and* of the country of Cyprus,

37 [y]Having land, sold *it,* and brought the money, and laid *it* at the apostles' feet.

5

But a certain man named Ananias, with Sapphira his wife, sold a possession,

2 And kept back *part* of the price, his wife also being privy *to it,* [z]and brought a certain part, and laid *it* at the apostles' feet.

3 [a]But Peter said, Ananias, why hath [b]Satan filled thine heart to lie to the Holy Ghost, and to keep back *part* of the price of the land?

4 Whiles it remained, was it not thine own? and after it was sold, was it not in thine own power? why hast thou conceived this thing in thine heart? thou hast not lied unto men, but unto God.

5 And Ananias hearing these words [c]fell down, and gave up the ghost: and great fear came on all them that heard these things.

6 And the young men arose, [d]wound him up, and carried *him* out, and buried *him.*

7 And it was about the space of three hours after, when his wife, not knowing what was done, came in.

8 And Peter answered unto her, Tell me whether ye sold the land for so much? And she said, Yea, for so much.

9 Then Peter said unto her, How is it that ye have agreed together [e]to tempt the Spirit of the Lord? behold, the feet of them which have buried thy husband *are* at the door, and shall carry thee out.

10 [f]Then fell she down straightway at his feet, and yielded up the ghost: and the young men came in, and found her dead, and, carrying *her* forth, buried *her* by her husband.

11 [g]And great fear came upon all the church, and upon as many as heard these things.

12 ¶ And [h]by the hands of the apostles were many signs and wonders wrought among the people; ([i]and they were all with one accord in Solomon's porch.

13 And [j]of the rest durst no man join himself to them: [k]but the people magnified them.

14 And believers were the more added to the Lord, multitudes both of men and women.)

15 Insomuch that they brought forth the sick into the streets, and laid *them* on beds and couches, [l]that at the least the shadow of Peter passing by might overshadow some of them.

16 There came also a multitude *out* of the cities round about unto Jerusalem, bringing [m]sick folks, and them which were vexed with unclean spirits: and they were healed every one.

17 ¶ [n]Then the high priest rose up, and all they that were with him, (which is the sect of the Sadducees,) and were filled with indignation,

18 [o]And laid their hands on the apostles, and put them in the common prison.

19 But [p]the angel of the Lord by night opened the prison doors, and brought them forth, and said,

20 Go, stand and speak in the temple to the people [q]all the words of this life.

21 And when they heard *that,* they entered into the temple early in the morning, and taught. [r]But the high priest came, and they that were with him, and called the council together, and all the senate of the children of Israel, and sent to the prison to have them brought.

22 But when the officers came, and found them not in the prison, they returned, and told,

23 Saying, The prison truly found we shut with all safety, and the keepers standing without before the doors: but when we had opened, we found no man within.

24 Now when the high priest and [s]the captain of the temple and the chief priests heard these things, they doubted of them whereunto this would grow.

25 Then came one and told them, saying, Behold, the men whom ye put in prison are standing in the temple, and teaching the people.

26 Then went the captain with the officers, and brought them without violence: [t]for they feared the people, lest they should have been stoned.

27 And when they had brought them, they set *them* before the council: and the high priest asked them,

28 Saying, [u]Did not we straitly command you that ye should not teach in this name? and, behold, ye have filled Jerusalem with your doctrine, [v]and intend to bring this man's [w]blood upon us.

29 ¶ Then Peter and the *other* apostles answered and said, [x]We ought to obey God rather than men.

30 [y]The God of our fathers raised up Jesus, whom ye slew and [z]hanged on a tree.

31 [a]Him hath God exalted with his right hand *to be* [b]a Prince and [c]a Saviour, [d]for to give repentance to Israel, and forgiveness of sins.

32 And [e]we are his witnesses of these

4:32 [q]ch. 5:12; Rom. 15:5; 2 Cor. 13:11; Phil. 1:27; 1 Pet. 3:8 [r]ch. 2:44
4:33 [s]ch. 1:8 [t]ch. 1:22 [u]ch. 2:47
4:34 [v]ch. 2:45
4:35 [w]ver. 37; ch. 5:2 [x]ch. 2:45
4:37 [y]ver. 34; ch. 5:1
5:2 [z]ch. 4:37
5:3 [a]Num. 30:2; Deut. 23:21; Eccl. 5:4 [b]Luke 22:3
5:5 [c]ver. 10
5:6 [d]John 19:40
5:9 [e]ver. 3; Matt. 4:7
5:10 [f]ver. 5
5:11 [g]ver. 5; ch. 2:43
5:12 [h]ch. 2:43; Rom. 15:19; 2 Cor. 12:12; Heb. 2:4 [i]ch. 3:11
5:13 [j]John 9:22 [k]ch. 2:47
5:15 [l]Matt. 9:21; ch. 19:12
5:16 [m]Mark 16:17; John 14:12
5:17 [n]ch. 4:1
5:18 [o]Luke 21:12
5:19 [p]ch. 12:7
5:20 [q]John 6:68; 1 John 5:11
5:21 [r]ch. 4
5:24 [s]Luke 22:4; ch. 4:1
5:26 [t]Matt. 21:26
5:28 [u]ch. 4:18 [v]ch. 2:23 [w]Matt. 23:35
5:29 [x]ch. 4:19
5:30 [y]ch. 3:13 [z]ch. 10:39; Gal. 3:13; 1 Pet. 2:24
5:31 [a]ch. 2:33; Phil. 2:9; Heb. 2:10 [b]ch. 3:15 [c]Matt. 1:21 [d]Luke 24:47; ch. 3:26; Eph. 1:7; Col. 1:14
5:32 [e]John 15:26

things; and *so is* also the Holy Ghost, [f]whom God hath given to them that obey him.

33 ¶ [g]When they heard *that,* they were cut *to the heart,* and took counsel to slay them.

34 Then stood there up one in the council, a Pharisee, named [h]Gamaliel, a doctor of the law, had in reputation among all the people, and commanded to put the apostles forth a little space;

35 And said unto them, Ye men of Israel, take heed to yourselves what ye intend to do as touching these men.

36 For before these days rose up Theudas, boasting himself to be somebody; to whom a number of men, about four hundred, joined themselves: who was slain; and all, as many as obeyed him, were scattered, and brought to nought.

37 After this man rose up Judas of Galilee in the days of the taxing, and drew away much people after him: he also perished; and all, *even* as many as obeyed him, were dispersed.

38 And now I say unto you, Refrain from these men, and let them alone: [i]for if this counsel or this work be of men, it will come to nought:

39 [j]But if it be of God, ye cannot overthrow it; lest haply ye be found even [k]to fight against God.

40 And to him they agreed: and when they had [l]called the apostles, [m]and beaten *them,* they commanded that they should not speak in the name of Jesus, and let them go.

41 ¶ And they departed from the presence of the council, [n]rejoicing that they were counted worthy to suffer shame for his name.

42 And daily [o]in the temple, and in every house, [p]they ceased not to teach and preach Jesus Christ.

6 And in those days, [q]when the number of the disciples was multiplied, there arose a murmuring of the [r]Grecians against the Hebrews, because their widows were neglected [s]in the daily ministration.

2 Then the twelve called the multitude of the disciples *unto them,* and said, [t]It is not reason that we should leave the word of God, and serve tables.

3 Wherefore, brethren, [u]look ye out among you seven men of honest report, full of the Holy Ghost and wisdom, whom we may appoint over this business.

4 But we [v]will give ourselves continually to prayer, and to the ministry of the word.

5 ¶ And the saying pleased the whole multitude: and they chose Stephen, [w]a man full of faith and of the Holy Ghost, and [x]Philip, and Prochorus, and Nicanor, and Timon, and Parmenas, and [y]Nicolas a proselyte of Antioch:

6 Whom they set before the apostles: and [z]when they had prayed, [a]they laid *their* hands on them.

7 And [b]the word of God increased; and the number of the disciples multiplied in Jerusalem greatly; and a great company [c]of the priests were obedient to the faith.

8 And Stephen, full of faith and power, did great wonders and miracles among the people.

9 ¶ Then there arose certain of the synagogue, which is called *the synagogue* of the Libertines, and Cyrenians, and Alexandrians, and of them of Cilicia and of Asia, disputing with Stephen.

10 And [d]they were not able to resist the wisdom and the spirit by which he spake.

11 [e]Then they suborned men, which said, We have heard him speak blasphemous words against Moses, and *against* God.

12 And they stirred up the people, and the elders, and the scribes, and came upon *him,* and caught him, and brought *him* to the council,

13 And set up false witnesses, which said, This man ceaseth not to speak blasphemous words against this holy place, and the law:

14 [f]For we have heard him say, that this Jesus of Nazareth shall [g]destroy this place, and shall change the customs which Moses delivered us.

15 And all that sat in the council, looking stedfastly on him, saw his face as it had been the face of an angel.

7 Then said the high priest, Are these things so?

2 And he said, [h]Men, brethren, and fathers, hearken; The God of glory appeared unto our father Abraham, when he was in Mesopotamia, before he dwelt in Charran,

3 And said unto him, [i]Get thee out of thy country, and from thy kindred, and come into the land which I shall shew thee.

4 Then [j]came he out of the land of the Chaldeans, and dwelt in Charran: and from thence, when his father was dead, he removed him into this land, wherein ye now dwell.

5 And he gave him none inheritance in it, no, not *so much as* to set his foot on: [k]yet he promised that he would give it to him for a possession, and to his seed after him, when *as yet* he had no child.

6 And God spake on this wise, [l]That his seed should sojourn in a strange land; and that they should bring them into bondage, and entreat *them* evil [m]four hundred years.

7 And the nation to whom they shall be in bondage will I judge, said God: and after that shall they come forth, and [n]serve me in this place.

8 [o]And he gave him the covenant of circumcision: [p]and so *Abraham* begat Isaac, and circumcised him the eighth day; [q]and Isaac *begat* Jacob; and [r]Jacob *begat* the twelve patriarchs.

9 [s]And the patriarchs, moved with envy, sold Joseph into Egypt: [t]but God was with him,

10 And delivered him out of all his afflictions, [u]and gave him favour and wisdom in

5:32 f ch. 2:4
5:33 g ch. 2:37
5:34 h ch. 22:3
5:38 i Prov. 21:30; Isa. 8:10; Matt. 15:13
5:39 j Luke 21:15; 1 Cor. 1:25 k ch. 7:51
5:40 l ch. 4:18 m Matt. 10:17; Mark 13:9
5:41 n Matt. 5:12; Rom. 5:3; 2 Cor. 12:10; Phil. 1:29; Heb. 10:34; Jam. 1:2; 1 Pet. 4:13
5:42 o ch. 2:46 p ch. 4:20
6:1 q ch. 2:41 r ch. 9:29 s ch. 4:35
6:2 t Ex. 18:17
6:3 u Deut. 1:13; ch. 1:21; 1 Tim. 3:7
6:4 v ch. 2:42
6:5 w ch. 11:24 x ch. 8:5 y Rev. 2:6
6:6 z ch. 1:24 a ch. 8:17; 1 Tim. 4:14; 2 Tim. 1:6
6:7 b ch. 12:24; Col. 1:6 c John 12:42
6:10 d Ex. 4:12; Isa. 54:17; Luke 21:15; ch. 5:39
6:11 e 1 Kings 21:10; Matt. 26:59
6:14 f ch. 25:8 g Dan. 9:26
7:2 h ch. 22:1
7:3 i Gen. 12:1
7:4 j Gen. 11:31
7:5 k Gen. 12:7
7:6 l Gen. 15:13 m Ex. 12:40; Gal. 3:17
7:7 n Ex. 3:12
7:8 o Gen. 17:9 p Gen. 21:2 q Gen. 25:26 r Gen. 29:31
7:9 s Gen. 37:4; Ps. 105:17 t Gen. 39:2
7:10 u Gen. 41:37

the sight of Pharaoh king of Egypt; and he made him governor over Egypt and all his house.

11 [v]Now there came a dearth over all the land of Egypt and Chanaan, and great affliction: and our fathers found no sustenance.

12 [w]But when Jacob heard that there was corn in Egypt, he sent out our fathers first.

13 [x]And at the second *time* Joseph was made known to his brethren; and Joseph's kindred was made known unto Pharaoh.

14 [y]Then sent Joseph, and called his father Jacob to *him,* and [z]all his kindred, threescore and fifteen souls.

15 [a]So Jacob went down into Egypt, [b]and died, he, and our fathers,

16 And [c]were carried over into Sychem, and laid in [d]the sepulchre that Abraham bought for a sum of money of the sons of Emmor *the father* of Sychem.

17 But when [e]the time of the promise drew nigh, which God had sworn to Abraham, [f]the people grew and multiplied in Egypt,

18 Till another king arose, which knew not Joseph.

19 The same dealt subtilly with our kindred, and evil entreated our fathers, [g]so that they cast out their young children, to the end they might not live.

20 [h]In which time Moses was born, and [i]was exceeding fair, and nourished up in his father's house three months:

21 And [j]when he was cast out, Pharaoh's daughter took him up, and nourished him for her own son.

22 And Moses was learned in all the wisdom of the Egyptians, and was [k]mighty in words and in deeds.

23 [l]And when he was full forty years old, it came into his heart to visit his brethren the children of Israel.

24 And seeing one *of them* suffer wrong, he defended *him,* and avenged him that was oppressed, and smote the Egyptian:

25 For he supposed his brethren would have understood how that God by his hand would deliver them: but they understood not.

26 [m]And the next day he shewed himself unto them as they strove, and would have set them at one again, saying, Sirs, ye are brethren; why do ye wrong one to another?

27 But he that did his neighbour wrong thrust him away, saying, [n]Who made thee a ruler and a judge over us?

28 Wilt thou kill me, as thou diddest the Egyptian yesterday?

29 [o]Then fled Moses at this saying, and was a stranger in the land of Madian, where he begat two sons.

30 [p]And when forty years were expired, there appeared to him in the wilderness of mount Sina an angel of the Lord in a flame of fire in a bush.

31 When Moses saw *it,* he wondered at the sight: and as he drew near to behold *it,* the voice of the Lord came unto him,

32 *Saying,* [q]I *am* the God of thy fathers, the God of Abraham, and the God of Isaac, and the God of Jacob. Then Moses trembled, and durst not behold.

33 [r]Then said the Lord to him, Put off thy shoes from thy feet: for the place where thou standest is holy ground.

34 [s]I have seen, I have seen the affliction of my people which is in Egypt, and I have heard their groaning, and am come down to deliver them. And now come, I will send thee into Egypt.

35 This Moses whom they refused, saying, Who made thee a ruler and a judge? the same did God send *to be* a ruler and a deliverer [t]by the hand of the angel which appeared to him in the bush.

36 [u]He brought them out, after that he had [v]shewed wonders and signs in the land of Egypt, [w]and in the Red sea, [x]and in the wilderness forty years.

37 ¶ This is that Moses, which said unto the children of Israel, [y]A prophet shall the Lord your God raise up unto you of your brethren, like unto me; [z]him shall ye hear.

38 [a]This is he, that was in the church in the wilderness with [b]the angel which spake to him in the mount Sina, and *with* our fathers: [c]who received the lively [d]oracles to give unto us:

39 To whom our fathers would not obey, but thrust *him* from them, and in their hearts turned back again into Egypt,

40 [e]Saying unto Aaron, Make us gods to go before us: for *as for* this Moses, which brought us out of the land of Egypt, we wot not what is become of him.

41 [f]And they made a calf in those days, and offered sacrifice unto the idol, and rejoiced in the works of their own hands.

42 Then [g]God turned, and gave them up to worship [h]the host of heaven; as it is written in the book of the prophets, [i]O ye house of Israel, have ye offered to me slain beasts and sacrifices *by the space of* forty years in the wilderness?

43 Yea, ye took up the tabernacle of Moloch, and the star of your god Remphan, figures which ye made to worship them: and I will carry you away beyond Babylon.

44 Our fathers had the tabernacle of witness in the wilderness, as he had appointed, speaking unto Moses, [j]that he should make it according to the fashion that he had seen.

45 [k]Which also our fathers that came after brought in with Jesus into the possession of the Gentiles, [l]whom God drave out before the face of our fathers, unto the days of David;

46 [m]Who found favour before God, and [n]desired to find a tabernacle for the God of Jacob.

47 [o]But Solomon built him an house.

48 Howbeit [p]the most High dwelleth not in temples made with hands; as saith the prophet

7:11 [v]Gen. 41:54
7:12 [w]Gen. 42:1
7:13 [x]Gen. 45:4
7:14 [y]Gen. 45:9 [z]Gen. 46:27; Deut. 10:22
7:15 [a]Gen. 46:5 [b]Gen. 49:33; Ex. 1:6
7:16 [c]Ex. 13:19; Josh. 24:32 [d]Gen. 23:16
7:17 [e]Gen. 15:13; ver. 6 [f]Ex. 1:7; Ps. 105:24
7:19 [g]Ex. 1:22
7:20 [h]Ex. 2:2 [i]Heb. 11:23
7:21 [j]Ex. 2:3-10
7:22 [k]Luke 24:19
7:23 [l]Ex. 2:11
7:26 [m]Ex. 2:13
7:27 [n]Luke 12:14; ch. 4:7
7:29 [o]Ex. 2:15
7:30 [p]Ex. 3:2
7:32 [q]Matt. 22:32; Heb. 11:16
7:33 [r]Ex. 3:5; Josh. 5:15
7:34 [s]Ex. 3:7
7:35 [t]Ex. 14:19; Num. 20:16
7:36 [u]Ex. 12:41 [v]Ex. 7; Ps. 105:27 [w]Ex. 14:21 [x]Ex. 16:1
7:37 [y]Deut. 18:15; ch. 3:22 [z]Matt. 15:5
7:38 [a]Ex. 19:3 [b]Isa. 63:9; Gal. 3:19; Heb. 2:2 [c]Ex. 21:1; Deut. 5:27; John 1:17 [d]Rom. 3:2
7:40 [e]Ex. 32:1
7:41 [f]Deut. 9:16; Ps. 106:19
7:42 [g]Ps. 81:12; Ezek. 20:25; Rom. 1:24; 2 Thess. 2:11 [h]Deut. 4:19; 2 Kings 17:16; Jer. 19:13 [i]Am. 5:25
7:44 [j]Ex. 25:40; Heb. 8:5
7:45 [k]Josh. 3:14 [l]Neh. 9:24; Ps. 44:2; ch. 13:19
7:46 [m]1 Sam. 16:1; 2 Sam. 7:1; Ps. 89:19; ch. 13:22 [n]1 Kings 8:17; 1 Chron. 22:7; Ps. 132:4
7:47 [o]1 Kings 6:1; 1 Chron. 17:12; 2 Chron. 3:1
7:48 [p]1 Kings 8:27; 2 Chron. 2:6; ch. 17:24

49 [q]Heaven *is* my throne, and earth *is* my
footstool: what house will ye build me?
saith the Lord: or what *is* the place of my
rest?
50 Hath not my hand made all these
things?
51 ¶ Ye [r]stiffnecked and [s]uncircumcised
in heart and ears, ye do always resist the
Holy Ghost: as your fathers *did,* so *do* ye.
52 [t]Which of the prophets have not your
fathers persecuted? and they have slain
them which shewed before of the coming of
[u]the Just One; of whom ye have been now
the betrayers and murderers:
53 [v]Who have received the law by the
disposition of angels, and have not kept *it.*
54 ¶ [w]When they heard these things, they
were cut to the heart, and they gnashed on
him with *their* teeth.
55 But he, [x]being full of the Holy Ghost,
looked up stedfastly into heaven, and saw
the glory of God, and Jesus standing on the
right hand of God,
56 And said, Behold, [y]I see the heavens
opened, and the [z]Son of man standing on
the right hand of God.
57 Then they cried out with a loud voice,
and stopped their ears, and ran upon him
with one accord,
58 And [a]cast *him* out of the city, [b]and
stoned *him:* and [c]the witnesses laid down
their clothes at a young man's feet, whose
name was Saul.
59 And they stoned Stephen, [d]calling
upon *God,* and saying, Lord Jesus, [e]receive
my spirit.
60 And he [f]kneeled down, and cried with
a loud voice, [g]Lord, lay not this sin to their
charge. And when he had said this, he fell
asleep.

8 And [h]Saul was consenting unto his
death. And at that time there was a
great persecution against the church which
was at Jerusalem; and [i]they were all scattered abroad throughout the regions of Judaea and Samaria, except the apostles.
2 And devout men carried Stephen *to his*
burial, and [j]made great lamentation over
him.
3 As for Saul, [k]he made havock of the
church, entering into every house, and haling men and women committed *them* to
prison.
4 Therefore [l]they that were scattered
abroad went every where preaching the
word.
5 Then [m]Philip went down to the city of
Samaria, and preached Christ unto them.
6 And the people with one accord gave
heed unto those things which Philip spake,
hearing and seeing the miracles which he
did.
7 For [n]unclean spirits, crying with loud
voice, came out of many that were possessed *with them:* and many taken with pal-
sies, and that were lame, were healed.
8 And there was great joy in that city.
9 But there was a certain man, called Simon, which beforetime in the same city
[o]used sorcery, and bewitched the people of
Samaria, [p]giving out that himself was some
great one:
10 To whom they all gave heed, from the
least to the greatest, saying, This man is the
great power of God.
11 And to him they had regard, because
that of long time he had bewitched them
with sorceries.
12 But when they believed Philip preaching the things [q]concerning the kingdom of
God, and the name of Jesus Christ, they
were baptized, both men and women.
13 Then Simon himself believed also: and
when he was baptized, he continued with
Philip, and wondered, beholding the miracles and signs which were done.
14 Now when the apostles which were at
Jerusalem heard that Samaria had received
the word of God, they sent unto them Peter
and John:
15 Who, when they were come down,
prayed for them, [r]that they might receive
the Holy Ghost:
16 (For [s]as yet he was fallen upon none
of them: only [t]they were baptized in [u]the
name of the Lord Jesus.)
17 Then [v]laid they *their* hands on them,
and they received the Holy Ghost.
18 And when Simon saw that through
laying on of the apostles' hands the Holy
Ghost was given, he offered them money,
19 Saying, Give me also this power, that
on whomsoever I lay hands, he may receive
the Holy Ghost.
20 But Peter said unto him, Thy money
perish with thee, because [w]thou hast
thought that [x]the gift of God may be purchased with money.
21 Thou hast neither part nor lot in this
matter: for thy heart is not right in the sight
of God.
22 Repent therefore of this thy wickedness, and pray God, [y]if perhaps the thought
of thine heart may be forgiven thee.
23 For I perceive that thou art in [z]the gall
of bitterness, and *in* the bond of iniquity.
24 Then answered Simon, and said,
[a]Pray ye to the Lord for me, that none of
these things which ye have spoken come
upon me.
25 And they, when they had testified and
preached the word of the Lord, returned
to Jerusalem, and preached the gospel in
many villages of the Samaritans.
26 And the angel of the Lord spake unto
Philip, saying, Arise, and go toward the
south unto the way that goeth down from
Jerusalem unto Gaza, which is desert.
27 And he arose and went: and, behold,
[b]a man of Ethiopia, an eunuch of great authority under Candace queen of the Ethiopians, who had the charge of all her treasure,
and [c]had come to Jerusalem for to worship,
28 Was returning, and sitting in his chariot read Esaias the prophet.

7:49 [q]Isa. 66:1; Matt. 5:34
7:51 [r]Ex. 32:9; Isa. 48:4 [s]Lev. 26:41; Deut. 10:16; Jer. 4:4; Ezek. 44:9
7:52 [t]2 Chron. 36:16; Matt. 21:35; 1 Thess. 2:15 [u]ch. 3:14
7:53 [v]Ex. 20:1; Gal. 3:19; Heb. 2:2
7:54 [w]ch. 5:33
7:55 [x]ch. 6:5
7:56 [y]Ezek. 1:1; Matt. 3:16; ch. 10:11 [z]Dan. 7:13
7:58 [a]1 Kings 21:13; Luke 4:29; Heb. 13:12 [b]Lev. 24:16 [c]Deut. 13:9; ch. 8:1
7:59 [d]ch. 9:14 [e]Ps. 31:5; Luke 23:45
7:60 [f]ch. 9:40 [g]Matt. 5:44; Luke 6:28
8:1 [h]ch. 7:58 [i]ch. 11:19
8:2 [j]Gen. 23:2; 2 Sam. 3:31
8:3 [k]ch. 7:58; 1 Cor. 15:9; Gal. 1:13; Phil. 3:6; 1 Tim. 1:13
8:4 [l]Matt. 10:23; ch. 11:19
8:5 [m]ch. 6:5
8:7 [n]Mark 16:17
8:9 [o]ch. 13:6 [p]ch. 5:36
8:12 [q]ch. 1:3
8:15 [r]ch. 2:38
8:16 [s]ch. 19:2 [t]Matt. 28:19; ch. 2:38 [u]ch. 10:48
8:17 [v]ch. 6:6; Heb. 6:2
8:20 [w]2 Kings 5:16; Matt. 10:8 [x]ch. 2:38
8:22 [y]Dan. 4:27; 2 Tim. 2:25
8:23 [z]Heb. 12:15
8:24 [a]Gen. 20:7; Ex. 8:8; Num. 21:7; 1 Kings 13:6; Job 42:8; Jam. 5:16
8:27 [b]Zeph. 3:10 [c]John 12:20

29 Then the Spirit said unto Philip, Go near, and join thyself to this chariot.

30 And Philip ran thither to *him,* and heard him read the prophet Esaias, and said, Understandest thou what thou readest?

31 And he said, How can I, except some man should guide me? And he desired Philip that he would come up and sit with him.

32 The place of the scripture which he read was this, [d]He was led as a sheep to the slaughter; and like a lamb dumb before his shearer, so opened he not his mouth:

33 In his humiliation his judgment was taken away: and who shall declare his generation? for his life is taken from the earth.

34 And the eunuch answered Philip, and said, I pray thee, of whom speaketh the prophet this? of himself, or of some other man?

35 Then Philip opened his mouth, [e]and began at the same scripture, and preached unto him Jesus.

36 And as they went on *their* way, they came unto a certain water: and the eunuch said, See, *here is* water; [f]what doth hinder me to be baptized?

37 And Philip said, [g]If thou believest with all thine heart, thou mayest. And he answered and said, [h]I believe that Jesus Christ is the Son of God.

38 And he commanded the chariot to stand still: and they went down both into the water, both Philip and the eunuch; and he baptized him.

39 And when they were come up out of the water, [i]the Spirit of the Lord caught away Philip, that the eunuch saw him no more: and he went on his way rejoicing.

40 But Philip was found at Azotus: and passing through he preached in all the cities, till he came to Caesarea.

9 And [j]Saul, yet breathing out threatenings and slaughter against the disciples of the Lord, went unto the high priest,

2 And desired of him letters to Damascus to the synagogues, that if he found any of this way, whether they were men or women, he might bring them bound unto Jerusalem.

3 And [k]as he journeyed, he came near Damascus: and suddenly there shined round about him a light from heaven:

4 And he fell to the earth, and heard a voice saying unto him, Saul, Saul, [l]why persecutest thou me?

5 And he said, Who art thou, Lord? And the Lord said, I am Jesus whom thou persecutest: [m]*it is* hard for thee to kick against the pricks.

6 And he trembling and astonished said, Lord, [n]what wilt thou have me to do? And the Lord *said* unto him, Arise, and go into the city, and it shall be told thee what thou must do.

7 And [o]the men which journeyed with him stood speechless, hearing a voice, but seeing no man.

8 And Saul arose from the earth; and when his eyes were opened, he saw no man: but they led him by the hand, and brought *him* into Damascus.

9 And he was three days without sight, and neither did eat nor drink.

10 ¶ And there was a certain disciple at Damascus, [p]named Ananias; and to him said the Lord in a vision, Ananias. And he said, Behold, I *am here,* Lord.

11 And the Lord *said* unto him, Arise, and go into the street which is called Straight, and enquire in the house of Judas for *one* called Saul, [q]of Tarsus: for, behold, he prayeth,

12 And hath seen in a vision a man named Ananias coming in, and putting *his* hand on him, that he might receive his sight.

13 Then Ananias answered, Lord, I have heard by many of this man, [r]how much evil he hath done to thy saints at Jerusalem:

14 And here he hath authority from the chief priests to bind all [s]that call on thy name.

15 But the Lord said unto him, Go thy way: for [t]he is a chosen vessel unto me, to bear my name before [u]the Gentiles, and [v]kings, and the children of Israel:

16 For [w]I will shew him how great things he must suffer for my name's sake.

17 [x]And Ananias went his way, and entered into the house; and [y]putting his hands on him said, Brother Saul, the Lord, *even* Jesus, that appeared unto thee in the way as thou camest, hath sent me, that thou mightest receive thy sight, and [z]be filled with the Holy Ghost.

18 And immediately there fell from his eyes as it had been scales: and he received sight forthwith, and arose, and was baptized.

19 And when he had received meat, he was strengthened. [a]Then was Saul certain days with the disciples which were at Damascus.

20 And straightway he preached Christ in the synagogues, [b]that he is the Son of God.

21 But all that heard *him* were amazed, and said; [c]Is not this he that destroyed them which called on this name in Jerusalem, and came hither for that intent, that he might bring them bound unto the chief priests?

22 But Saul increased the more in strength, [d]and confounded the Jews which dwelt at Damascus, proving that this is very Christ.

23 ¶ And after that many days were fulfilled, [e]the Jews took counsel to kill him:

24 [f]But their laying await was known of Saul. And they watched the gates day and night to kill him.

25 Then the disciples took him by night, and [g]let *him* down by the wall in a basket.

26 [h]And when Saul was come to Jerusalem, he assayed to join himself to the disci-

8:32 [d]Isa. 53:7
8:35 [e]Luke 24:27; ch. 18:28
8:36 [f]ch. 10:47
8:37 [g]Matt. 28:19; Mark 16:16 [h]Matt. 16:16; John 6:69; ch. 9:20; 1 John 4:15
8:39 [i]1 Kings 18:12; 2 Kings 2:16; Ezek. 3:12
9:1 [j]ch. 8:3; Gal. 1:13; 1 Tim. 1:13
9:3 [k]ch. 22:6; 1 Cor. 15:8
9:4 [l]Matt. 25:40
9:5 [m]ch. 5:39
9:6 [n]Luke 3:10; ch. 2:37
9:7 [o]Dan. 10:7; ch. 22:9
9:10 [p]ch. 22:12
9:11 [q]ch. 21:39
9:13 [r]ver. 1
9:14 [s]ver. 21; ch. 7:59; 1 Cor. 1:2; 2 Tim. 2:22
9:15 [t]ch. 13:2; Rom. 1:1; 1 Cor. 15:10; Gal. 1:15; Eph. 3:7; 1 Tim. 2:7; 2 Tim. 1:11 [u]Rom. 1:5; Gal. 2:7 [v]ch. 25:22
9:16 [w]ch. 20:23; 2 Cor. 11:23
9:17 [x]ch. 22:12 [y]ch. 8:17 [z]ch. 2:4
9:19 [a]ch. 26:20
9:20 [b]ch. 8:37
9:21 [c]ch. 8:3; ver. 1; Gal. 1:13
9:22 [d]ch. 18:28
9:23 [e]ch. 23:12; 2 Cor. 11:26
9:24 [f]2 Cor. 11:32
9:25 [g]Josh. 2:15; 1 Sam. 19:12
9:26 [h]ch. 22:17; Gal. 1:17

ples: but they were all afraid of him, and believed not that he was a disciple.

27 [i]But Barnabas took him, and brought *him* to the apostles, and declared unto them how he had seen the Lord in the way, and that he had spoken to him, [j]and how he had preached boldly at Damascus in the name of Jesus.

28 And [k]he was with them coming in and going out at Jerusalem.

29 And he spake boldly in the name of the Lord Jesus, and disputed against the [l]Grecians: [m]but they went about to slay him.

30 *Which* when the brethren knew, they brought him down to Caesarea, and sent him forth to Tarsus.

31 [n]Then had the churches rest throughout all Judaea and Galilee and Samaria, and were edified; and walking in the fear of the Lord, and in the comfort of the Holy Ghost, were multiplied.

32 ¶ And it came to pass, as Peter passed [o]throughout all *quarters*, he came down also to the saints which dwelt at Lydda.

33 And there he found a certain man named Aeneas, which had kept his bed eight years, and was sick of the palsy.

34 And Peter said unto him, Aeneas, [p]Jesus Christ maketh thee whole: arise, and make thy bed. And he arose immediately.

35 And all that dwelt at Lydda and [q]Saron saw him, and [r]turned to the Lord.

36 ¶ Now there was at Joppa a certain disciple named Tabitha, which by interpretation is called Dorcas: this woman was full [s]of good works and almsdeeds which she did.

37 And it came to pass in those days, that she was sick, and died: whom when they had washed, they laid *her* in [t]an upper chamber.

38 And forasmuch as Lydda was nigh to Joppa, and the disciples had heard that Peter was there, they sent unto him two men, desiring *him* that he would not delay to come to them.

39 Then Peter arose and went with them. When he was come, they brought him into the upper chamber: and all the widows stood by him weeping, and shewing the coats and garments which Dorcas made, while she was with them.

40 But Peter [u]put them all forth, and [v]kneeled down, and prayed; and turning *him* to the body [w]said, Tabitha, arise. And she opened her eyes: and when she saw Peter, she sat up.

41 And he gave her *his* hand, and lifted her up, and when he had called the saints and widows, presented her alive.

42 And it was known throughout all Joppa; [x]and many believed in the Lord.

43 And it came to pass, that he tarried many days in Joppa with one [y]Simon a tanner.

10

There was a certain man in Caesarea called Cornelius, a centurion of the band called the Italian *band,*

2 [z]*A* devout *man,* and one that [a]feared God with all his house, which gave much alms to the people, and prayed to God alway.

3 [b]He saw in a vision evidently about the ninth hour of the day an angel of God coming in to him, and saying unto him, Cornelius.

4 And when he looked on him, he was afraid, and said, What is it, Lord? And he said unto him, Thy prayers and thine alms are come up for a memorial before God.

5 And now send men to Joppa, and call for *one* Simon, whose surname is Peter:

6 He lodgeth with one [c]Simon a tanner, whose house is by the sea side: [d]he shall tell thee what thou oughtest to do.

7 And when the angel which spake unto Cornelius was departed, he called two of his household servants, and a devout soldier of them that waited on him continually;

8 And when he had declared all *these* things unto them, he sent them to Joppa.

9 ¶ On the morrow, as they went on their journey, and drew nigh unto the city, [e]Peter went up upon the housetop to pray about the sixth hour:

10 And he became very hungry, and would have eaten: but while they made ready, he fell into a trance,

11 And [f]saw heaven opened, and a certain vessel descending unto him, as it had been a great sheet knit at the four corners, and let down to the earth:

12 Wherein were all manner of fourfooted beasts of the earth, and wild beasts, and creeping things, and fowls of the air.

13 And there came a voice to him, Rise, Peter; kill, and eat.

14 But Peter said, Not so, Lord; [g]for I have never eaten any thing that is common or unclean.

15 And the voice *spake* unto him again the second time, [h]What God hath cleansed, *that* call not thou common.

16 This was done thrice: and the vessel was received up again into heaven.

17 Now while Peter doubted in himself what this vision which he had seen should mean, behold, the men which were sent from Cornelius had made enquiry for Simon's house, and stood before the gate,

18 And called, and asked whether Simon, which was surnamed Peter, were lodged there.

19 ¶ While Peter thought on the vision, [i]the Spirit said unto him, Behold, three men seek thee.

20 [j]Arise therefore, and get thee down, and go with them, doubting nothing: for I have sent them.

21 Then Peter went down to the men which were sent unto him from Cornelius; and said, Behold, I am he whom ye seek: what *is* the cause wherefore ye are come?

9:27 [i]ch. 4:36 [j]ver. 20:22
9:28 [k]Gal. 1:18
9:29 [l]ch. 6:1 [m]ver. 23; 2 Cor. 11:26
9:31 [n]ch. 8:1
9:32 [o]ch. 8:14
9:34 [p]ch. 3:6
9:35 [q]1 Chron. 5:16 [r]ch. 11:21
9:36 [s]1 Tim. 2:10; Tit. 3:8
9:37 [t]ch. 1:13
9:40 [u]Matt. 9:25 [v]ch. 7:60 [w]Mark 5:41; John 11:43
9:42 [x]John 11:45
9:43 [y]ch. 10:6
10:2 [z]ver. 22; ch. 8:2 [a]ver. 35
10:3 [b]ver. 30; ch. 11:13
10:6 [c]ch. 9:43 [d]ch. 11:14
10:9 [e]ch. 11:5
10:11 [f]ch. 7:56; Rev. 19:11
10:14 [g]Lev. 11:4; Deut. 14:3; Ezek. 4:14
10:15 [h]Matt. 15:11; ver. 28; Rom. 14:14; 1 Cor. 10:25; 1 Tim. 4:4; Tit. 1:15
10:19 [i]ch. 11:12
10:20 [j]ch. 15:7

22 And they said, [k]Cornelius the centurion, a just man, and one that feareth God,
and [l]of good report among all the nation of
the Jews, was warned from God by an holy
angel to send for thee into his house, and to
hear words of thee.
23 Then called he them in, and lodged
them. And on the morrow Peter went away
with them, [m]and certain brethren from
Joppa accompanied him.
24 And the morrow after they entered
into Caesarea. And Cornelius waited for
them, and had called together his kinsmen
and near friends.
25 And as Peter was coming in, Cornelius
met him, and fell down at his feet, and worshipped *him.*
26 But Peter took him up, saying, [n]Stand
up; I myself also am a man.
27 And as he talked with him, he went in,
and found many that were come together.
28 And he said unto them, Ye know how
[o]that it is an unlawful thing for a man that
is a Jew to keep company, or come unto one
of another nation; but [p]God hath shewed
me that I should not call any man common
or unclean.
29 Therefore came I *unto you* without
gainsaying, as soon as I was sent for: I ask
therefore for what intent ye have sent
for me?
30 And Cornelius said, Four days ago I
was fasting until this hour; and at the ninth
hour I prayed in my house, and behold, [q]a
man stood before me [r]in bright clothing,
31 And said, Cornelius, [s]thy prayer is
heard, [t]and thine alms are had in remembrance in the sight of God.
32 Send therefore to Joppa, and call
hither Simon, whose surname is Peter; he is
lodged in the house of *one* Simon a tanner
by the sea side: who, when he cometh, shall
speak unto thee.
33 Immediately therefore I sent to thee;
and thou hast well done that thou art come.
Now therefore are we all here present before God, to hear all things that are commanded thee of God.
34 ¶ Then Peter opened *his* mouth, and
said, [u]Of a truth I perceive that God is no
respecter of persons:
35 But [v]in every nation he that feareth
him, and worketh righteousness, is accepted with him.
36 The word which *God* sent unto the
children of Israel, [w]preaching peace by
Jesus Christ: ([x]he is Lord of all:)
37 That word, *I say,* ye know, which was
published throughout all Judaea, and [y]be-
gan from Galilee, after the baptism which
John preached;
38 How [z]God anointed Jesus of Nazareth
with the Holy Ghost and with power: who
went about doing good, and healing all that
were oppressed of the devil; [a]for God was
with him.
39 And [b]we are witnesses of all things
which he did both in the land of the Jews,

10:22 [k]ver. 1 [l]ch. 22:12
10:23 [m]ver. 45; ch. 11:12
10:26 [n]ch. 14:14; Rev. 19:10
10:28 [o]John 4:9; ch. 11:3; Gal. 2:12 [p]ch. 15:8; Eph. 3:6
10:30 [q]ch. 1:10 [r]Matt. 28:3; Mark 16:5; Luke 24:4
10:31 [s]ver. 4; Dan. 10:12 [t]Heb. 6:10
10:34 [u]Deut. 10:17; 2 Chron. 19:7; Job 34:19; Rom. 2:11; Gal. 2:6; Eph. 6:9; Col. 3:25; 1 Pet. 1:17
10:35 [v]ch. 15:9; Rom. 2:13; 1 Cor. 12:13; Gal. 3:28; Eph. 2:13
10:36 [w]Isa. 57:19; Eph. 2:14; Col. 1:20 [x]Matt. 28:18; Rom. 10:12; 1 Cor. 15:27; Eph. 1:20; 1 Pet. 3:22; Rev. 17:14
10:37 [y]Luke 4:14
10:38 [z]Luke 4:18; ch. 2:22; Heb. 1:9 [a]John 3:2
10:39 [b]ch. 2:32 [c]ch. 5:30
10:40 [d]ch. 2:24
10:41 [e]John 14:17; ch. 13:31 [f]Luke 24:30; John 21:13
10:42 [g]Matt. 28:19; ch. 1:8 [h]John 5:22; ch. 17:31 [i]Rom. 14:9; 2 Cor. 5:10; 2 Tim. 4:1; 1 Pet. 4:5
10:43 [j]Isa. 53:11; Jer. 31:34; Dan. 9:24; Mic. 7:18; Zech. 13:1; Mal. 4:2; ch. 26:22 [k]ch. 15:9; Rom. 10:11; Gal. 3:22
10:44 [l]ch. 4:31
10:45 [m]ver. 23 [n]ch. 11:18; Gal. 3:14
10:47 [o]ch. 11:17; Rom. 10:12
10:48 [p]1 Cor. 1:17 [q]ch. 2:38
11:2 [r]ch. 10:45; Gal. 2:12
11:3 [s]ch. 10:28 [t]Gal. 2:12
11:4 [u]Luke 1:3
11:5 [v]ch. 10:9
11:12 [w]John 16:13; ch. 10:19 [x]ch. 10:23

and in Jerusalem; [c]whom they slew and
hanged on a tree:
40 Him [d]God raised up the third day, and
shewed him openly;
41 [e]Not to all the people, but unto witnesses chosen before of God, *even* to us,
[f]who did eat and drink with him after he
rose from the dead.
42 And [g]he commanded us to preach
unto the people, and to testify [h]that it is he
which was ordained of God *to be* the Judge
[i]of quick and dead.
43 [j]To him give all the prophets witness,
that through his name [k]whosoever believeth in him shall receive remission of sins.
44 ¶ While Peter yet spake these words,
[l]the Holy Ghost fell on all them which
heard the word.
45 [m]And they of the circumcision which
believed were astonished, as many as came
with Peter, [n]because that on the Gentiles
also was poured out the gift of the Holy
Ghost.
46 For they heard them speak with
tongues, and magnify God. Then answered
Peter,
47 Can any man forbid water, that these
should not be baptized, which have received the Holy Ghost [o]as well as we?
48 [p]And he commanded them to be baptized [q]in the name of the Lord. Then prayed
they him to tarry certain days.
11 And the apostles and brethren that
were in Judaea heard that the Gentiles had also received the word of God.
2 And when Peter was come up to Jerusalem, [r]they that were of the circumcision
contended with him,
3 Saying, [s]Thou wentest in to men uncircumcised, [t]and didst eat with them.
4 But Peter rehearsed *the matter* from
the beginning, and expounded *it* [u]by order
unto them, saying,
5 [v]I was in the city of Joppa praying: and
in a trance I saw a vision, A certain vessel
descend, as it had been a great sheet, let
down from heaven by four corners; and it
came even to me:
6 Upon the which when I had fastened
mine eyes, I considered, and saw fourfooted
beasts of the earth, and wild beasts, and
creeping things, and fowls of the air.
7 And I heard a voice saying unto me,
Arise, Peter; slay and eat.
8 But I said, Not so, Lord: for nothing
common or unclean hath at any time entered into my mouth.
9 But the voice answered me again from
heaven, What God hath cleansed, *that* call
not thou common.
10 And this was done three times: and all
were drawn up again into heaven.
11 And, behold, immediately there were
three men already come unto the house
where I was, sent from Caesarea unto me.
12 And [w]the Spirit bade me go with them,
nothing doubting. Moreover [x]these six

brethren accompanied me, and we entered into the man's house:

13 [y]And he shewed us how he had seen an angel in his house, which stood and said unto him, Send men to Joppa, and call for Simon, whose surname is Peter;

14 Who shall tell thee words, whereby thou and all thy house shall be saved.

15 And as I began to speak, the Holy Ghost fell on them, [z]as on us at the beginning.

16 Then remembered I the word of the Lord, how that he said, [a]John indeed baptized with water; but [b]ye shall be baptized with the Holy Ghost.

17 [c]Forasmuch then as God gave them the like gift as *he did* unto us, who believed on the Lord Jesus Christ; [d]what was I, that I could withstand God?

18 When they heard these things, they held their peace, and glorified God, saying, [e]Then hath God also to the Gentiles granted repentance unto life.

19 ¶ [f]Now they which were scattered abroad upon the persecution that arose about Stephen travelled as far as Phenice, and Cyprus, and Antioch, preaching the word to none but unto the Jews only.

20 And some of them were men of Cyprus and Cyrene, which, when they were come to Antioch, spake unto [g]the Grecians, preaching the Lord Jesus.

21 And [h]the hand of the Lord was with them: and a great number believed, and [i]turned unto the Lord.

22 ¶ Then tidings of these things came unto the ears of the church which was in Jerusalem: and they sent forth [j]Barnabas, that he should go as far as Antioch.

23 Who, when he came, and had seen the grace of God, was glad, and [k]exhorted them all, that with purpose of heart they would cleave unto the Lord.

24 For he was a good man, and [l]full of the Holy Ghost and of faith: [m]and much people was added unto the Lord.

25 Then departed Barnabas to [n]Tarsus, for to seek Saul:

26 And when he had found him, he brought him unto Antioch. And it came to pass, that a whole year they assembled themselves with the church, and taught much people. And the disciples were called Christians first in Antioch.

27 ¶ And in these days came [o]prophets from Jerusalem unto Antioch.

28 And there stood up one of them named [p]Agabus, and signified by the Spirit that there should be great dearth throughout all the world: which came to pass in the days of Claudius Caesar.

29 Then the disciples, every man according to his ability, determined to send [q]relief unto the brethren which dwelt in Judaea:

30 [r]Which also they did, and sent it to the elders by the hands of Barnabas and Saul.

12 Now about that time Herod the king stretched forth *his* hands to vex certain of the church.

2 And he killed James [s]the brother of John with the sword.

3 And because he saw it pleased the Jews, he proceeded further to take Peter also. (Then were [t]the days of unleavened bread.)

4 And [u]when he had apprehended him, he put *him* in prison, and delivered *him* to four quaternions of soldiers to keep him; intending after Easter to bring him forth to the people.

5 Peter therefore was kept in prison: but prayer was made without ceasing of the church unto God for him.

6 And when Herod would have brought him forth, the same night Peter was sleeping between two soldiers, bound with two chains: and the keepers before the door kept the prison.

7 And, behold, [v]the angel of the Lord came upon *him*, and a light shined in the prison: and he smote Peter on the side, and raised him up, saying, Arise up quickly. And his chains fell off from *his* hands.

8 And the angel said unto him, Gird thyself, and bind on thy sandals. And so he did. And he saith unto him, Cast thy garment about thee, and follow me.

9 And he went out, and followed him; and [w]wist not that it was true which was done by the angel; but thought [x]he saw a vision.

10 When they were past the first and the second ward, they came unto the iron gate that leadeth unto the city; [y]which opened to them of his own accord: and they went out, and passed on through one street; and forthwith the angel departed from him.

11 And when Peter was come to himself, he said, Now I know of a surety, that [z]the Lord hath sent his angel, and [a]hath delivered me out of the hand of Herod, and *from* all the expectation of the people of the Jews.

12 And when he had considered *the thing*, [b]he came to the house of Mary the mother of [c]John, whose surname was Mark; where many were gathered together [d]praying.

13 And as Peter knocked at the door of the gate, a damsel came to hearken, named Rhoda.

14 And when she knew Peter's voice, she opened not the gate for gladness, but ran in, and told how Peter stood before the gate.

15 And they said unto her, Thou art mad. But she constantly affirmed that it was even so. Then said they, [e]It is his angel.

16 But Peter continued knocking: and when they had opened *the door*, and saw him, they were astonished.

17 But he, [f]beckoning unto them with the hand to hold their peace, declared unto them how the Lord had brought him out of the prison. And he said, Go shew these things unto James, and to the brethren. And he departed, and went into another place.

18 Now as soon as it was day, there was

11:13 [y]ch. 10:30
11:15 [z]ch. 2:4
11:16 [a]Matt. 3:11; John 1:26; ch. 1:5 [b]Isa. 44:3; Joel 2:28
11:17 [c]ch. 15:8 [d]ch. 10:47
11:18 [e]Rom. 10:12
11:19 [f]ch. 8:1
11:20 [g]ch. 6:1
11:21 [h]Luke 1:66; ch. 2:47 [i]ch. 9:35
11:22 [j]ch. 9:27
11:23 [k]ch. 13:43
11:24 [l]ch. 6:5 [m]ver. 21; ch. 5:14
11:25 [n]ch. 9:30
11:27 [o]ch. 2:17; 1 Cor. 12:28; Eph. 4:11
11:28 [p]ch. 21:10
11:29 [q]Rom. 15:26; 1 Cor. 16:1; 2 Cor. 9:1
11:30 [r]ch. 12:25
12:2 [s]Matt. 4:21
12:3 [t]Ex. 12:14
12:4 [u]John 21:18
12:7 [v]ch. 5:19
12:9 [w]Ps. 126:1 [x]ch. 10:3
12:10 [y]ch. 16:26
12:11 [z]Ps. 34:7; Dan. 3:28; Heb. 1:14 [a]Job 5:19; Ps. 33:18; 2 Cor. 1:10; 2 Pet. 2:9
12:12 [b]ch. 4:23 [c]ch. 15:37 [d]ver. 5
12:15 [e]Gen. 48:16; Matt. 18:10
12:17 [f]ch. 13:16

no small stir among the soldiers, what was
become of Peter.
19 And when Herod had sought for him,
and found him not, he examined the keepers, and commanded that *they* should be
put to death. And he went down from Judaea to Caesarea, and *there* abode.
20 ¶ And Herod was highly displeased
with them of Tyre and Sidon: but they came
with one accord to him, and, having made
Blastus the king's chamberlain their friend,
desired peace; because [g]their country was
nourished by the king's *country*.
21 And upon a set day Herod, arrayed
in royal apparel, sat upon his throne, and
made an oration unto them.
22 And the people gave a shout, *saying, It
is* the voice of a god, and not of a man.
23 And immediately the angel of the Lord
[h]smote him, because [i]he gave not God the
glory: and he was eaten of worms, and gave
up the ghost.
24 ¶ But [j]the word of God grew and multiplied.
25 And Barnabas and Saul returned from
Jerusalem, when they had fulfilled *their*
ministry, and [k]took with them [l]John,
whose surname was Mark.

13 Now there were [m]in the church that
was at Antioch certain prophets and
teachers; as [n]Barnabas, and Simeon that
was called Niger, and [o]Lucius of Cyrene,
and Manaen, which had been brought up
with Herod the tetrarch, and Saul.
2 As they ministered to the Lord, and
fasted, the Holy Ghost said, [p]Separate me
Barnabas and Saul for the work [q]where-
unto I have called them.
3 And [r]when they had fasted and prayed,
and laid *their* hands on them, they sent
them away.
4 ¶ So they, being sent forth by the Holy
Ghost, departed unto Seleucia; and from
thence they sailed to [s]Cyprus.
5 And when they were at Salamis, [t]they
preached the word of God in the synagogues of the Jews: and they had also
[u]John to *their* minister.
6 And when they had gone through the
isle unto Paphos, they found [v]a certain sorcerer, a false prophet, a Jew, whose name
was Bar-jesus:
7 Which was with the deputy of the country, Sergius Paulus, a prudent man; who
called for Barnabas and Saul, and desired to
hear the word of God.
8 But [w]Elymas the sorcerer (for so is his
name by interpretation) withstood them,
seeking to turn away the deputy from the
faith.
9 Then Saul, (who also *is called* Paul,)
[x]filled with the Holy Ghost, set his eyes on
him,
10 And said, O full of all subtilty and all
mischief, [y]*thou* child of the devil, *thou* enemy of all righteousness, wilt thou not cease
to pervert the right ways of the Lord?
11 And now, behold, [z]the hand of the
Lord *is* upon thee, and thou shalt be blind,
not seeing the sun for a season. And immediately there fell on him a mist and a darkness; and he went about seeking some to
lead him by the hand.
12 Then the deputy, when he saw what
was done, believed, being astonished at the
doctrine of the Lord.
13 Now when Paul and his company
loosed from Paphos, they came to Perga in
Pamphylia: and [a]John departing from them
returned to Jerusalem.
14 ¶ But when they departed from Perga,
they came to Antioch in Pisidia, and [b]went
into the synagogue on the sabbath day, and
sat down.
15 And [c]after the reading of the law and
the prophets the rulers of the synagogue
sent unto them, saying, *Ye* men *and* brethren, if ye have [d]any word of exhortation for
the people, say on.
16 Then Paul stood up, and [e]beckoning
with *his* hand said, Men of Israel, and [f]ye
that fear God, give audience.
17 The God of this people of Israel [g]chose
our fathers, and exalted the people [h]when
they dwelt as strangers in the land of Egypt,
[i]and with an high arm brought he them out
of it.
18 And [j]about the time of forty years suffered he their manners in the wilderness.
19 And when [k]he had destroyed seven
nations in the land of Chanaan, [l]he divided
their land to them by lot.
20 And after that [m]he gave *unto them*
judges about the space of four hundred and
fifty years, [n]until Samuel the prophet.
21 [o]And afterward they desired a king:
and God gave unto them Saul the son of Cis,
a man of the tribe of Benjamin, by the space
of forty years.
22 And [p]when he had removed him, [q]he
raised up unto them David to be their king;
to whom also he gave testimony, and said,
[r]I have found David the *son* of Jesse, [s]a
man after mine own heart, which shall fulfill all my will.
23 [t]Of this man's seed hath God according [u]to *his* promise raised unto Israel [v]a
Saviour, Jesus:
24 [w]When John had first preached before
his coming the baptism of repentance to all
the people of Israel.
25 And as John fulfilled his course, he
said, [x]Whom think ye that I am? I am not
he. But, behold, there cometh one after me,
whose shoes of *his* feet I am not worthy to
loose.
26 Men *and* brethren, children of the
stock of Abraham, and whosoever among
you feareth God, [y]to you is the word of this
salvation sent.
27 For they that dwell at Jerusalem, and
their rulers, [z]because they knew him not,
nor yet the voices of the prophets [a]which
are read every sabbath day, [b]they have fulfilled *them* in condemning *him*.
28 [c]And though they found no cause of

12:20 [g]1 Kings 5:9; Ezek. 27:17
12:23 [h]1 Sam. 25:38; 2 Sam. 24:17 [i]Ps. 115:1
12:24 [j]Isa. 55:11; ch. 6:7; Col. 1:6
12:25 [k]ch. 13:5 [l]ver. 12
13:1 [m]ch. 11:27 [n]ch. 11:22-26 [o]Rom. 16:21
13:2 [p]Num. 8:14; ch. 9:15; Rom. 1:1; Gal. 1:15 [q]Matt. 9:38; ch. 14:26; Rom. 10:15; Eph. 3:7; 1 Tim. 2:7; 2 Tim. 1:11; Heb. 5:4
13:3 [r]ch. 6:6
13:4 [s]ch. 4:36
13:5 [t]ver. 46 [u]ch. 12:25
13:6 [v]ch. 8:9
13:8 [w]Ex. 7:11; 2 Tim. 3:8
13:9 [x]ch. 4:8
13:10 [y]Matt. 13:38; John 8:44; 1 John 3:8
13:11 [z]Ex. 9:3; 1 Sam. 5:6
13:13 [a]ch. 15:38
13:14 [b]ch. 16:13
13:15 [c]Luke 4:16; ver. 27 [d]Heb. 13:22
13:16 [e]ch. 12:17 [f]ver. 26; ch. 10:35
13:17 [g]Deut. 7:6 [h]Ex. 1:1; Ps. 105:23; ch. 7:17 [i]Ex. 6:6
13:18 [j]Ex. 16:35; Num. 14:33; Ps. 95:9; ch. 7:36
13:19 [k]Deut. 7:1 [l]Josh. 14:1; Ps. 78:55
13:20 [m]Judg. 2:16 [n]1 Sam. 3
13:21 [o]1 Sam. 8:5
13:22 [p]1 Sam. 15:23; Hos. 13:11 [q]1 Sam. 16:13; 2 Sam. 2:4 [r]Ps. 89:20 [s]1 Sam. 13:14; ch. 7:46
13:23 [t]Isa. 11:1; Luke 1:32; ch. 2:30; Rom. 1:3 [u]2 Sam. 7:12; Ps. 132:11 [v]Matt. 1:21; Rom. 11:26
13:24 [w]Matt. 3:1; Luke 3:3
13:25 [x]Matt. 3:11; Mark 1:7; Luke 3:16; John 1:20
13:26 [y]Matt. 10:6; Luke 24:47; ver. 46; ch. 3:26
13:27 [z]Luke 23:34; ch. 3:17; 1 Cor. 2:8 [a]ver. 14; ch. 15:21 [b]Luke 24:20; ch. 26:22
13:28 [c]Matt. 27:22; Mark 15:13; Luke 23:21; John 19:6

death *in him*, [d]yet desired they Pilate that he should be slain.

29 [e]And when they had fulfilled all that was written of him, [f]they took *him* down from the tree, and laid *him* in a sepulchre.

30 [g]But God raised him from the dead:

31 And [h]he was seen many days of them which came up with him [i]from Galilee to Jerusalem, [j]who are his witnesses unto the people.

32 And we declare unto you glad tidings, how that [k]the promise which was made unto the fathers,

33 God hath fulfilled the same unto us their children, in that he hath raised up Jesus again; as it is also written in the second psalm, [l]Thou art my Son, this day have I begotten thee.

34 And as concerning that he raised him up from the dead, *now* no more to return to corruption, he said on this wise, [m]I will give you the sure mercies of David.

35 Wherefore he saith also in another *psalm*, [n]Thou shalt not suffer thine Holy One to see corruption.

36 For David, after he had served his own generation by the will of God, [o]fell on sleep, and was laid unto his fathers, and saw corruption:

37 But he, whom God raised again, saw no corruption.

38 ¶ Be it known unto you therefore, men *and* brethren, that [p]through this man is preached unto you the forgiveness of sins:

39 And [q]by him all that believe are justified from all things, from which ye could not be justified by the law of Moses.

40 Beware therefore, lest that come upon you, which is spoken of in [r]the prophets;

41 Behold, ye despisers, and wonder, and perish: for I work a work in your days, a work which ye shall in no wise believe, though a man declare it unto you.

42 And when the Jews were gone out of the synagogue, the Gentiles besought that these words might be preached to them the next sabbath.

43 Now when the congregation was broken up, many of the Jews and religious proselytes followed Paul and Barnabas: who, speaking to them, [s]persuaded them to continue in [t]the grace of God.

44 ¶ And the next sabbath day came almost the whole city together to hear the word of God.

45 But when the Jews saw the multitudes, they were filled with envy, and [u]spake against those things which were spoken by Paul, contradicting and blaspheming.

46 Then Paul and Barnabas waxed bold, and said, [v]It was necessary that the word of God should first have been spoken to you: but [w]seeing ye put it from you, and judge yourselves unworthy of everlasting life, lo, [x]we turn to the Gentiles.

47 For so hath the Lord commanded us, *saying*, [y]I have set thee to be a light of the Gentiles, that thou shouldest be for salvation unto the ends of the earth.

48 And when the Gentiles heard this, they were glad, and glorified the word of the Lord: and [z]as many as were ordained to eternal life believed.

49 And the word of the Lord was published throughout all the region.

50 But the Jews stirred up the devout and honourable women, and the chief men of the city, and [a]raised persecution against Paul and Barnabas, and expelled them out of their coasts.

51 [b]But they shook off the dust of their feet against them, and came unto Iconium.

52 And the disciples [c]were filled with joy, and with the Holy Ghost.

14 And it came to pass in Iconium, that they went both together into the synagogue of the Jews, and so spake, that a great multitude both of the Jews and also of the Greeks believed.

2 But the unbelieving Jews stirred up the Gentiles, and made their minds evil affected against the brethren.

3 Long time therefore abode they speaking boldly in the Lord, [d]which gave testimony unto the word of his grace, and granted signs and wonders to be done by their hands.

4 But the multitude of the city was divided: and part held with the Jews, and part with the [e]apostles.

5 And when there was an assault made both of the Gentiles, and also of the Jews with their rulers, [f]to use *them* despitefully, and to stone them,

6 They were ware of *it*, and [g]fled unto Lystra and Derbe, cities of Lycaonia, and unto the region that lieth round about:

7 And there they preached the gospel.

8 ¶ [h]And there sat a certain man at Lystra, impotent in his feet, being a cripple from his mother's womb, who never had walked:

9 The same heard Paul speak: who stedfastly beholding him, and [i]perceiving that he had faith to be healed,

10 Said with a loud voice, [j]Stand upright on thy feet. And he leaped and walked.

11 And when the people saw what Paul had done, they lifted up their voices, saying in the speech of Lycaonia, [k]The gods are come down to us in the likeness of men.

12 And they called Barnabas, Jupiter; and Paul, Mercurius, because he was the chief speaker.

13 Then the priest of Jupiter, which was before their city, brought oxen and garlands unto the gates, [l]and would have done sacrifice with the people.

14 *Which* when the apostles, Barnabas and Paul, heard *of*, [m]they rent their clothes, and ran in among the people, crying out,

15 And saying, Sirs, [n]why do ye these things? [o]We also are men of like passions with you, and preach unto you that ye should turn from [p]these vanities [q]unto the

13:28 *d*ch. 3:13
13:29 *e*Luke 18:31; John 19:28 *f*Matt. 27:59; Mark 15:46; Luke 23:53; John 19:38
13:30 *g*Matt. 28:6; ch. 2:24
13:31 *h*Matt. 28:16; ch. 1:3; 1 Cor. 15:5 *i*ch. 1:11 *j*ch. 1:8
13:32 *k*Gen. 3:15; ch. 26:6; Rom. 4:13; Gal. 3:16
13:33 *l*Ps. 2:7; Heb. 1:5
13:34 *m*Isa. 55:3
13:35 *n*Ps. 16:10; ch. 2:31
13:36 *o*1 Kings 2:10; ch. 2:29
13:38 *p*Jer. 31:34; Dan. 9:24; Luke 24:47; 1 John 2:12
13:39 *q*Isa. 53:11; Rom. 3:28; Heb. 7:19
13:40 *r*Isa. 29:14; Hab. 1:5
13:43 *s*ch. 11:23 *t*Tit. 2:11; Heb. 12:15; 1 Pet. 5:12
13:45 *u*ch. 18:6; 1 Pet. 4:4; Jude 10
13:46 *v*Matt. 10:6; ch. 3:26; ver. 26; Rom. 1:16 *w*Ex. 32:10; Deut. 32:21; Isa. 55:5; Matt. 21:43; Rom. 10:19 *x*ch. 18:6
13:47 *y*Isa. 42:6; Luke 2:32
13:48 *z*ch. 2:47
13:50 *a*2 Tim. 3
13:51 *b*Matt. 10:14; Mark 6:11; Luke 9:5; ch. 18:6
13:52 *c*Matt. 5:12; John 16:22; ch. 2:46
14:3 *d*Mark 16:20; Heb. 2:4
14:4 *e*ch. 13:3
14:5 *f*2 Tim. 3:11
14:6 *g*Matt. 10:23
14:8 *h*ch. 3:2
14:9 *i*Matt. 8:10
14:10 *j*Isa. 35:6
14:11 *k*ch. 8:10
14:13 *l*Dan. 2:46
14:14 *m*Matt. 26:65
14:15 *n*ch. 10:26 *o*Jam. 5:17; Rev. 19:10 *p*1 Sam. 12:21; 1 Kings 16:13; Jer. 14:22; Am. 2:4; 1 Cor. 8:4 *q*1 Thess. 1:9

FOCUS ON ACTS

Acts is the continuing chronicle of Jesus' story as lived out by those whose lives He touched. This book is a sequel of Luke's careful research and documentation regarding the emerging church of Jesus and the resurrected and ascended Christ. The same scared people, who had been hiding in a locked upper room, go out into the streets witnessing a new reality—the presence of the Holy Spirit in their lives.

The Holy Spirit is a gift sent by Jesus Christ on the day of Pentecost. The powerful presence, anointing touch, and unifying ability, which was bestowed upon each person in that place, spilled over and then out into the streets and to the known world. The Holy Spirit made such a difference that others came running to inquire, "What is this?" Those who were formerly afraid and hidden were challenged to answer, to explain, and to testify about the resulting change in their lives. For Jesus had already decreed, "But, ye shall receive power, after that Holy Ghost is come upon you: and ye shall be witnesses unto me both in Jerusalem, and in all Judaea, and in Samaria, and unto the uttermost part of the earth." (Acts 1:8)

The twelve had multiplied to about 120 people (Acts 1:15). They all joined together constantly in prayer, along with the women and Mary the mother of Jesus and with his brothers (Acts 1:12–15). How delightful it is to women to have it stated that the women were there. We have known that women played a significant part in the ministry of Jesus. We know that they stood at the foot of the cross, came to "roll the stone away," and sought His body. It is recorded that it was to the women that Jesus first appeared and who were told to go and tell "my brothers" that the Resurrection has occurred! Therefore, it is only proper that Luke, the historian, recorded it. He recorded that, on the day of Pentecost, when the Holy Spirit rushed in like wind, kissed the apostles with fire, and gave them power to come out of hiding, that the women were mentioned as "present"!

The presence of empowered women is not new or surprising. Contemporary history brings us role models such as Harriet Tubman, Sojourner Truth, Mary McCloud Bethune, and Rosa Parks. These women were filled with God's power and presence, and were emboldened with God's wise words. They were emboldened to go and proclaim that a new day, a new creation, and a new reality had come! It required a "fresh touch" for Harriet to escape and return to carry others with her to freedom. It required a "bold kiss" for Sojourner to tell Jesus it would be all right to change her name. It required a "rushing mighty wind" for Mary to look at a garbage dump and envision a place of higher education for African-American students. It took "tongues of fire" for Rosa Parks to declare, "I shall not be moved!" This all happened because the promise was given: "I will pour out my Spirit on all flesh, your sons and your daughters shall prophesy, . . . and whosoever shall call on the name of the LORD shall be delivered" (Joel 2:28–32).

The Book of Acts, then, is a continuation of Luke's writings, which began with the Gospel ascribed to Luke. Using the Lord's statement that the disciples were to be witnesses in Jerusalem, Judaea, Samaria, and unto the ends of the earth (Acts 1:8), Luke shows how the early church endeavored to make that happen. The Day of Pentecost was the occasion of the arrival of the Holy Spirit. On that day Peter preached, three thousand people responded to the Gospel and were baptized. Thus the church was born and the witness to the Gospel in Jerusalem was ignited. Philip took the Gospel to Samaria and introduced it to the Ethiopian eunuch who carried it back to his country. Peter witnessed to the Roman centurion, but persecution and the conversion of Saul were primary events that triggered the spread of the Gospel throughout the Mediterranean world. Luke described the founding of the church at Antioch and of Paul's missionary journeys into Asia and Europe.

African historians have observed that the Holy Spirit led Paul to take the Gospel west into Asia Minor instead of south into Africa because the Gospel had already found such a ready acceptance with the African nations. As evidence, they point to the many African martyrs who died for the cause of Christ, as well as to the prevalence of such prominent early African church fathers as Tertullian, Augustine, and Origen.

THE BLACK PRESENCE IN ACTS

Antiochian church: Mentioned in Acts 13:1 and elsewhere. The church at Antioch had broken out of a Jewish-only attitude to embrace Gentiles. Among its leadership were Simeon, called Niger, and Lucius of Cyrene, a city on the northern coast of Africa. Barnabas was from Cyprus; Manean was a foster brother of Herod the Tetrarch. Saul was from Cilicia.

Apollos: Mentioned in Acts 8:24. Apollos was from the city of Alexandria, a city built by Alexander the Great on the northern coast of Africa. Two of the five districts of Alexandria were heavily populated by Jews. Many others were native Africans.

Azotus: Mentioned in Acts 8:40. Azotus was one of the Philistine cities. Philistines were descendants of Egyptians who, in turn, were descendants from Ham.

Elamites: Mentioned in Acts 2:9. Elamites were a Semitic group of people living in the Mesopotamian area. Most ancient Semitic people were black.

Egypt/Egyptians: Mentioned in Acts 2:10; 7:9–39. Egyptian is the Greek term for the people the Hebrews called Mizraim. They were the descendants of Ham whose name means "black."

Ethiopian eunuch: Mentioned in Acts 8:26–38. Ethiopian is the Greek word for Cush which means "black." Eunuch originally referred to a castrated male, but later designated an officer in the service of a king or magistrate. Since a eunuch could not be a full member of the Jewish community, some think this worshiping eunuch was a Gentile. If so, he is the first Gentile to become a believer and not the Roman centurion (Acts 10).

Libya: **Mentioned in Acts 2:10. Libya is the Greek name for Put who was a son of Ham. Libya was a country on the northern coast of Africa, west of Egypt, where both Jews and Africans lived. One of its chief cities was Cyrene.**

Mesopotamia: **Mentioned in Acts 2:9 and 7:2. According to Henry Rawlinson, Mesopotamia was settled by migrants from Africa around 2500 to 3000 B.C. Both Semites and Cushites occupied the area, but according to many scholars, they were both black. This is based on language, artifacts, and other archaeological evidence.**

Samaritans: **Mentioned in Acts 8. Samaritans were a mixed race of people created when Sennecherib deported Israelites from Samaria in 722 B.C. and brought in other people from the surrounding area. Since most surrounding nations were Cushite, it can be inferred that those brought into Samaria were black and that they intermarried with Israelites to produce the mixed population.**

Life Lessons

ACTS 1–2

In Acts, Luke continues his detailed report to Theophilus by testifying about the acts of the Holy Spirit, who had been sent, as promised by Jesus on the day of His ascension. We find an historical narrative of the life, growth, and struggle in the early days of the church of Christ, which began on the day of Pentecost in Jerusalem and then spread abroad. The Gospel was spread because the Holy Spirit started working in the life of those believers who had waited in the upper room until they were empowered by a supernatural force. They were empowered to "run and tell" the wonderful story of Jesus Christ. Matthias was chosen to replace Judas, and "they all continued with one accord in prayer and supplication, with the women, and Mary the mother of Jesus" (Acts 1:14).

Peter became the chief spokesperson to a waiting crowd that sought an explanation of what had happened to the group of 120. As he drew his message to a close, he charged, "Therefore let all the house of Israel know assuredly, that God hath made that same Jesus, whom ye have crucified, both Lord and Christ. Now when they heard this, they were pricked in their heart, and said unto Peter and to the rest of the apostles, Men and brethren, what shall we do? Then Peter said unto them, "Repent, and be baptized every one of you in the name of Jesus Christ for the remission of sins . . . and the same day there were added unto them about three thousand souls . . . And the Lord added to the church daily such as should be saved" (2:36–38, 41, 47).

Life and Resurrection, thank You for Your saving grace that covers me.

ACTS 4–5

As the group of believers came together, there was a communal spirit where "neither said any of them that ought of the things which he possessed was his own, but they had all things" (Acts 4:32). However, the spirit of greed was present. Ananias and his wife Sapphira were the first two persons who tried to make a profit from withholding possessions, and lied about it. Both, on separate occasions, lied to the Holy Spirit (5:3 and 5:10). Both dropped dead and "great fear came upon all the church, and upon as many as heard about these things" (Acts 5:11).

Spirit of Truth, rid me of the spirit of deceitfulness.

ACTS 6–9

As the numbers of believers increased, there was strife between cultures. "And in those days . . . there arose a murmuring of the Grecians against the Hebrews because their widows were neglected in the daily ministration [distribution of food]" (Acts 6:1). The role of "deacon" was arranged by the twelve apostles to care for the needs of the women. The church grew and persecution broke out against the church in Jerusalem, and "they were all scattered abroad throughout the regions of Judaea and Samaria, except the apostles" (Acts 8:1). Saul began an all-out campaign to destroy the church, "entering into every house, and haling men and women committed them to prison" (Acts 8:3). There was no respect of person there! Our sisters suffered for the spread of the "Realm of God." Eventually, Saul was apprehended by God (Acts 9:1–17). It is recorded, "Saul increased the more in strength, and confounded the Jews which dwelt at Damascus, proving that this is very Christ. . . . Then had the churches rest throughout all Judaea and Galilee and Samaria, and were edified, and walking in the fear of the Lord, and in the comfort of the Holy Ghost, were multiplied" (Acts 9:22, 31).

God of Increase, how I magnify Your name for coming to use one like me!

ACTS 9

Peter traveled the area, preaching and healing. "Now there was at Joppa a certain disciple named Tabitha, which by interpretation is called Dorcas: this woman was full of good works and almsdeeds which she did" (Acts 9:36). Tabitha was the first and only woman specifically called a "disciple" in Scripture! Her "good works" for the widows in Joppa out of her own resources was well-known. She had not been commissioned, like the "deacons" in Jerusalem, but how often do women receive the same role value and public acclaim for the ministry they perform? It seemed to make little difference that her ministry was called "good works." What mattered was that "Peter . . . kneeled down, and prayed, and turning him to the body said, Tabitha, arise. And she opened her eyes: and when she saw Peter, she sat up. And he gave her his hand, and lifted her up, and when he had called the saints and widows, presented her alive. And it was known throughout all Joppa; and many believed in the Lord" (Acts 9:40–42).

Power of Good Works, sustain me in what You have called me to do in Your name.

ACTS 12

Peter was arrested by Herod and kept in prison, bound with chains, and placed between two guards. "Peter therefore was kept in prison: but prayer was made without ceasing of the church unto God for him (Acts 12:5). When God sent an angel to answer their prayers and Peter showed up at the house of Mary the mother of John Mark, a servant named Rhoda answered the door, but didn't open it upon hearing Peter's voice. She ran back to inform the prayer group that Peter was at the door and they responded, "Thou art mad" (Acts 12:15).

As she kept insisting that it was Peter, but failed to let him into the house, they decided, "It is his angel" (Acts 12:15). Finally, the door was opened and Rhoda's announcement was seen to be true. It seems that regardless of the news that women bring, it must first be discounted. Usually, the authority of a woman's word is challenged and put to the test.

Voice of the Unheard, help me to keep making Your unbelievable announcements!

ACTS 16

On a second missionary journey, God sent Paul and his companions to Philippi where a church was planted. "On the Sabbath we went out of the city by a river side, where prayer was wont to be made; and we sat down, and spake unto the women which resorted thither. And a certain woman named Lydia, a seller of purple [cloth], from the city of Thyatira, which worshipped God heard us" (Acts 16:13–15). These women constituted the initial church! They were already praying, in worship, and were ready to receive the news of Jesus Christ. It is interesting to note that they were at the river, at the water, at the source of refreshment where women have always gathered to share news. The men, "expected" to find a captive audience there! In 16:40 we read that Lydia's house becomes a "house church" and "[Paul and Silas] went out of prison, and entered into the house of Lydia: and when they had seen the brethren, they comforted them."

Fountain of Life, fall afresh upon me!

ACTS 18

In Corinth, Paul met a clergy couple, Aquila and his wife Priscilla, who were well-known missionaries in both Corinth and Ephesus. They were a pair, on fire for God. They were partners who allowed Paul to live with them. They traveled with him on a sea journey to Ephesus, where they remained to build up the body of believers. As Paul wrote to the churches in Rome and in Corinth, he always sent greetings and honored this indispensable team. They were instrumental in teaching Apollos, an educator, about the role of the Holy Spirit in the church (Acts 18:24–27). Their home became the "house church" in Ephesus (1 Cor. 16:19).

Testimony of Truth, speak through my life to the power of the Holy Spirit.

FOCUS ON ROMANS

How many frogs have you kissed—trying to find "the prince"? It's a story with which we are all familiar as we go through life on a search for "the one"! We seek the one who will love us unconditionally, the one who will make our lives complete, the one who will satisfy our inner urges. We seek the one who will be a delightful companion, a trusted soul-mate, a loyal and faithful friend. The Lord only knows how many frogs we have kissed! We kiss and kiss, but "the prince" still does not appear! That is because life is not that easy and love is much more complicated than a kiss that makes everything all right.

Paul addressed the church at Rome as a group of people who needed to be made aware that frogs were plentiful! These new converts knew a variety of gods. They lived in a cosmopolitan area where theology, religion, and cultic practices were all around them. Yet, they had been introduced to the Prince of Peace—Jesus the Christ. Out of all their seeking and exploring wrong paths, they had finally come upon the Way. So, Paul wrote to encourage them in the Lord. He said, "All have sinned, and come short of the glory of God" (Rom. 3:23). He included Jews in his "all." He included every ethnic group and racial tribe in his "all." Surely he included us in his "all." There are no exceptions.

It's part and parcel of the human experience to seek out and to kiss frogs! There's no shame to bear. There's no finger to point. There's no guilt to hide behind. Just "fess up." However, the Prince has come. This is Paul's good news! It's time to stop choosing the wrong in order to find the right. The search is over. Meaning has come. Purpose has shown up. Direction has been provided. Love wants to claim us, to enfold us, and to give us guidance for our lives. "For we know that all things work together for good to them that who love God" (Rom. 8:28). Therefore, part of our "need" to kiss all the frogs in the past is to now have a better appreciation for the Prince of Peace! Part of our being lost is the ability to now rejoice over being found. Part of our seeking love in all the wrong places is to be able to "know" it and to identify it when it comes!

Paul wrote a life-changing letter to let us know that it's a common practice to kiss frogs! And, he wrote it to let us know that the time is over for chasing, finding, and kissing those frogs! "Let love be without dissimulation. Abhor that which is evil; cleave to that which is good; Be kindly affectioned one to another with brotherly love, in honour preferring one another . . . Be not overcome of evil, but overcome evil with good" (Rom. 12:9, 21). Stop kissing and keeping those frogs!

In Romans, then, the apostle sets forth the most logical and clearest presentation of the Gospel we have in the New Testament. After an introduction explaining his personal circumstances, he sets forth the conviction that all people—Gentiles and Jews—are sinful and fall short of God's

glory. To him, evidence of Gentile sinfulness is the pagan practices. Jewish sinfulness is seen in that Jews profess a relationship with God, but fail to live up to their profession.

Having declared all people sinful, Paul explains that God has proclaimed the Way of justification. It is a plan based on the atoning sacrifice of Jesus. It is to be received by faith without the necessity or usefulness of works. This new plan has been provided by the Ancient of Days. Some objected to faith as a means of justification because such a position might encourage sinfulness. However, Paul urged righteous behavior that would spring from faith in God. He also explained the ministry of the Holy Spirit to empower believers for Christlike behavior and service.

Having set forth the doctrine of justification by faith for all who believe, the apostle addresses the issue of Israel's place in God's plan since they were no longer at center stage in God's activity. The book climaxes with a plea to believers that in view of God's superb plan of salvation, we ought to present our bodies to Him as living sacrifices and live lives worthy of such a divine provision.

THE BLACK PRESENCE IN ROMANS

While there are no specific references to the Black presence within the Book of Romans, it must be borne in mind that the Gospel preached by Paul had its origin in Palestine and North Africa, where there was a significant Black presence. Not until the Greeks and Romans began to migrate into the biblical lands during the second and first centuries before the birth of Christ do we find any significant presence of other racial groups. However, once again, it must be stressed that in biblical times racial identification did not have the significance it carries today. It only becomes crucial today because during the last two centuries efforts have been made to eliminate or distort the reality of the biblical Black presence. This has been to the detriment of people of color. Additionally, some have concluded that since Paul was mistaken for an Egyptian (see Acts 21:38) that he himself must have been black.

Life Lessons

ROMANS 1

This is both the longest and the first of Paul's epistles to be written. In it, we find a two-part message of what Christians are to believe and how they are to behave out of their new belief system. He begins with an opening statement of why he put pen to paper in this particular instance. "Paul, a servant of Jesus Christ, called to be an apostle, separated unto the gospel of God, . . . (which he had promised afore by his prophets in the holy scriptures,) Concerning his Son Jesus Christ our Lord, which was made of the seed of David according to the flesh, And declared to be the Son of God with power, according to the Spirit of holiness, by the resurrection from the dead" (Rom. 1:1–4). Paul had never been to Rome.

Neither had any of the other disciples. Yet the Word had spread into Rome by those who had been in Jerusalem on the Day of Pentecost. This is the first systematic approach to a Christian's understanding of faith in Christ. It is logical. It is orderly. Its approach is set forth in sequence, listing both blessings and consequences of "right belief." Paul testified to this with boldness. "I am not ashamed of the gospel of Christ: for it is the power of God unto salvation to every one that believeth: to the Jew first, and also to the Greek. For therein is the righteousness of God revealed from faith to faith: as it is written, The just shall live by faith" (Rom. 1:16–17).

Living Testimony, let my life be a witness to the world I touch and affect.

ROMANS 1

Paul is adamant in his teaching that "the wrath of God is revealed from heaven against all ungodliness and unrighteousness of men, who hold the truth in unrighteousness, Because that which may be know of God is manifest in them, for God hath shewed it unto them" (Rom. 1:18–19). The consequences for choosing the wrong god, worshiping the wrong gods, and not turning to the True and Living God has resulted the fact that "wherefore God also gave [humans] up to uncleanness through the lusts of their own hearts, to dishonour their own bodies between themselves: Who changed the truth of God into a lie . . . For this cause God gave them up unto vile affections: for even their women did change the use into that which is against nature . . . God gave them over to a reprobate mind, to do those things . . ." (Rom. 1:24–29). It's a serious indictment! It's a clear statement of how degrading sexual passions came into being. Although Paul is not setting out to specifically deal with particular degrading sexual passions, he provides the underlying reason for perverted sexual relationships: "[they] became vain in their imaginations, and their foolish heart was darkened. Professing themselves to be wise, they became fools, And change the glory of the uncorruptible God into an image made like to corruptible man" (Rom. 1:21–23).

World Wisdom, help me to see You clearly, love You dearly and obey Your will for my life.

ROMANS 2–3

There is no room for any of us to condemn another. "Thou are inexcusable, O man, whosoever thou are that judgest: for wherein thou judgest another, thou condemnest thyself; for thou that judgest doest the same things" (Rom. 2:1). Although perverted sexual relationships are clearly, for Paul, a result of rebellion against God, Paul does not allow for any of us to "bash and trash" another who continues to live out of their current "wisdom." "For all have sinned, and come short of the glory of God, Being justified freely by his grace through the redemption that is in Christ Jesus: Whom God hath set forth to be a propitiation through faith in his blood" (Rom. 3:23–25).

Atoning Sacrifice, thank You for the blood that bought my pardon.

ROMANS 2–4

"The [promise of God] is of faith, that it might be by grace; to the end the promise might be sure to all the seed; not to that only which is of the

law, but that also which is of the faith of Abraham" (Rom. 4:16). There was no Jewish nation when God made a covenant promise with Abram! However, in faith, Abram believed God and a Jewish nation was created through him! Now we, believers, are Jews! "He is not a Jew which is one outwardly; neither is that circumcision, which is outward in the flesh: But he is a Jew, which is one inwardly, and circumcision is that of the heart, in the spirit, and not in the letter" (Rom. 2:28). The Law demanded that all male Jews be circumcised. It showed their distinct difference from other nations. Yet, Jewish women by definition could not perform this rite. Today, however, circumcision of the heart allows us full admittance into the family of God and to the benefits that come with being God's royal heirs!

Great Physician, thank You for the work that You've done within my heart. I know that I've been changed!

ROMANS 16

As Paul drew his letter to a close, he extended personal greetings to folks who had assisted him in various means and those whom he held dear to his heart. It is of great interest that he listed first, Phebe, "a servant of the church" and "a succourer of many." He named a total of nine women: Priscilla, Mary, Junia, Tryphena, Tryphosa, Persis, the mother of Rufus, Julia, and the sister of Nereus. He gave some specifics to a few; Priscilla (and Aquila) fellow workers; Mary, who was a diligent worker; and Tryphena and Tryphosa, hard workers in the Lord. All of these women were intermingled among the names of "brothers" that he greeted as "colaborers" in the ministry of spreading the Word of Jesus Christ. Paul remembered the women, and he did it with fondness and gratitude!

Dear Lord Jesus, use me to spread Your Good News.

Women in ACTS AND ROMANS

SAPPHIRA, THE WIFE OF ANANIAS: A LOST OPPORTUNITY FOR TRUTH

During the time that the early Church was selling property and voluntarily laying the monies at the apostle Peter's feet (Acts 4:34–37), selfishness, greed, and deceit entered into the hearts of Sapphira and her husband Ananias, who decided to keep part of the money for themselves (Acts 5:2). This couple sold some of their property and agreed to cheat and lie about it. In doing so, they ultimately lied to God (Acts 5:4).

Sapphira's husband approached Peter first, and, without a chance to explain, his heart was exposed to the apostle by the Holy Spirit. As a result of his evil intent, he died immediately (Acts 5:5). After three hours, Sapphira came before Peter, not knowing about her husband's death (Acts 5:7). Peter's approach with her was different. He questioned her about the sale of the land, giving her an opportunity to speak truthfully (Acts 5:8). But Sapphira chose to keep lying (Acts 5:8). Like her husband, her lie resulted in her immediate death (Acts 5:9–10). Sapphira placed more confidence in her husband's evil plan than in God. What could have been a blessing to the church turned into a disaster (Acts 5:11).

The death of Sapphira and her husband shocked the church. God showed them all that He will not tolerate dishonesty in relationships.

The African-American wife is certainly instructed by God to love and submit to her husband as unto the Lord (Eph. 5:22). A woman's relationship with God and her husband should be based on integrity and commitment. She is to respect him and agree to godly decisions. She is not told to submit to ungodly or wicked schemes, especially ones that would cause her to lie to God. It is important for her to keep the marriage covenant—something ordained by God. More importantly, her covenant with God should be kept at all times, never putting herself willingly in a position to break that covenant. By chance, if she finds herself faced with an ungodly decision made by her spouse, she should speak the truth in love so they can grow together spiritually (Eph. 4:15).

Read Acts 4:32–35; 5:1–11.

Read the insight essays on, Commitment, and Submission.

—G. London

CANDACE: THE QUEEN OF ETHIOPIA

Candace was a title given to the queen of Ethiopia. Without knowing Queen Candace's full name, it is difficult to place her exactly in history, but she was probably one of the successors of the queen of Sheba. As a ruler in Ethiopia, she led one of the oldest African nations.

The finance chairman of Queen Candace's treasury came to Jerusalem to worship. As he returned to go home, he sat in his chariot, attempting to read the Word of God. Philip, a disciple led by the Spirit of God, came and explained the scriptures to him.

The fact that he was allowed to go to Jerusalem to worship speaks volumes about Candace's leadership. As a leader, she was an individual who worked for the good of the kingdom on earth and God's kingdom yet to come.

The eunuch's understanding of the Scriptures was paramount to his ability to manage the financial affairs of the queen. With greater understanding, he could put his Lord, his life, and his job in the proper perspective.

The queen benefited from the spirituality of her finance chairman. Believing in God enabled him to deal fairly with others, and thus enhance the integrity of her kingdom. Believing in God, the eunuch could be longsuffering and kind to those he met.

It is quite possible that his strong faith and beliefs were qualities the queen recognized and applauded. She looked beyond his managerial capabilities to his heart, and she found a man compassionate and loving. She sought and found an individual whom she could trust because he worked to please God first and then others.

Queen Candace was confident in who she was, so she did not feel threatened by the eunuch's service to someone else. And today, 40 percent of Ethiopians belong to the Ethiopian Orthodox Church, a Christian faith. That faith spread, and African-Americans today are strong soldiers in the Lord's army.

Read Acts 8:27–39.

Read essay on Evangelism.

—J. Chambers

TABITHA (DORCAS)—DOING HER PART

Tabitha, also known as Dorcas, wasn't merely a busy person, she was an industry. Her presence left a feeling of well-being in its wake. She gave to the poor. She helped others. She was known around Joppa as a disciple of Jesus. Her generosity apparently extended to anyone in need, particularly widows. Her death caused everyone to realize just how valuable her contributions had been, and the Christians in Joppa needed help in order to deal with this loss (see Acts 9:36–39). Since the apostle Peter was in the area, they asked him to help them.

When Peter arrived, the people introduced the dead woman by showing him the many handmade items she had given them. The widows were especially sad. They cried as Peter was told the wonderful things Tabitha had done. Peter then asked to be alone with the body. We are told that he prayed. We don't know what he prayed, but we know that God answered by bringing Tabitha back to life.

When the believers had gathered at Peter's request, he brought Tabitha to them. The people witnessed a joyful, life-giving miracle, and when the news spread, "many believed in the Lord" (Acts 9:42). Tabitha's

life of service and sacrifice brought people knowledge of Jesus, but God's power, revealed when Peter raised Tabitha to life, brought them to faith.

Read Acts 9:36–43

RHODA: AN OBEDIENT CHILD

Little Rhoda, the servant of Mary the mother of John Mark, was attending a prayer meeting one evening and had the duty of keeping the door secure. Christ's followers were under persecution and although they were praying, they certainly didn't want those who might harm them to know it!

Rhoda was doing her duty. She could be complaining about being a servant. She could be preoccupied with her own thoughts and not attending to her task. She could even wander off to her own devices—for after all, although there was a group assembled, their eyes were closed!

But Rhoda was doing her duty. She was listening for sounds beyond the door and warning those gathered of impending danger. The group's prayer is for Peter's safety, for he has again been taken to prison for his courageous preaching.

During the prayer session, Rhoda hears a knock at the door. She recognizes Peter's voice and immediately goes to ask for permission to open the door. Those praying would not believe her. They told her that the knocking was done by Peter's angel. But, Rhoda never doubted that it was Peter's voice that she heard. She knew that God heard their prayers.

We can follow this example of simple, childlike faith.

Read Acts 12:12–19.

Read the insight essay on Prayer.

—E. Watson

LYDIA: A MODEL FOR WOMEN IN MINISTRY

Lydia was a fascinating woman. A successful businesswoman, she traded in dye and dyed goods. Purple was her specialty—a color of fabric that few could afford. She probably had a love for texture and design in fabric.

On the Sabbath, Lydia was with a group of women by the shores of the river. Lydia obviously impressed Paul and the others with her strong leadership. They accepted her invitation to stay at her home.

Lydia receives brief recognition in the Book of Acts, yet she symbolizes the importance of strong and capable women in the church's earliest history. She was among the first Gentile converts in Europe, one of the first known Christian businesswomen, and one of the first believers to open her home for Christian service.

Women were converts to Christ from the start. From the beginning of church history, women publicly declared themselves followers of Jesus. Even while the disciples were in hiding, it was to women that the risen Christ was first revealed. Women were the ones who searched out the men to bring them the Good News.

Read Acts 16:13–15, 40.

—R.. Walker

FORTUNE-TELLING SLAVE: A SURPRISING TESTIMONY TO GOD'S WORK

Fortune-telling was a common practice in the Greek and Roman cultures. Divination was the attempt to foretell the unknown and the future. Many beliefs of superstition were used to do so. It is a system of fraud (Ezra 13:6–7), abomination (Deut. 18:11–12), condemnation (Jer. 27:9), and was punishable by death (Lev. 20:6, 27). Those who practiced it were astrologers (Isa. 47:13), charmers (Deut. 18:11), false prophets (Jer. 14:14), and sorcerers (Acts 13:6, 8).

A young slave girl possessed with a spirit of divination approached Paul and Silas one day when they went to preach at Philippi (Acts 16:16). The demonic spirit gave her the power to tell the future. The spirit spoke the truth mockingly. Her masters profited from her unfortunate condition by using her for their own gain.

She followed Paul and Silas for several days, yelling that these men were servants of the most high God, showing the way of salvation (v. 17). Being grieved in his spirit, Paul took spiritual authority over the unclean spirit and commanded it to leave the young girl (v. 18). In the name of Jesus, the girl was freed. Her owners were angry when they realized that their chances to make more money had ceased (v. 19). As a result, Paul and Silas were taken before the magistrates (v. 20), beaten and imprisoned (vv. 22–23), and were watched carefully by the prison guard (v. 23). Through prayer and singing the miraculous occurred. An earthquake shook the prison doors open and the prisoners' chains became unfastened. Grateful that the prisoners did not escape and that he was stopped from committing suicide by Paul, the guard along with his entire family was saved and baptized.

This is the only time Acts mentions the fortune-telling slave girl. Her testimony, however, will stand forever, proving that God can bring glory out of the most unfair, abusive and harsh situations.

In today's society, divination is subtly camouflaged as entertainment. The commercials and infomercials are creative enough to raise a woman's curiosity. The most important areas of life are targeted: love, sex, and work. The African-American woman must be careful not to fall prey to demonic spirits (Lev. 19:31; Deut. 18:11; Is. 8:19). She must trust in the true God for the plans for her life (Jer. 29:11–13), because His voice is truth (John 16:13).

Read Acts 16:16–28.

—G. London

LOIS AND EUNICE: FAITH THROUGH THE GENERATIONS

Lois and Eunice were women who lived out their faith as an example for their friends and family, including young Timothy. As his grandmother and mother, these Christian women influenced Timothy and shaped the character of a great preacher. The apostle Paul commended them in his letter to their child, "I'm reminded of how sincere your faith is. That faith first lived in your grandmother Lois and your mother Eunice. I'm convinced that it also lives in you" (2 Timothy 1:5). Lois and Eunice raised Timothy.

As his caregivers, they taught him, disciplined him, loved him, and cared for him. Through their example, Timothy saw faith at work. Through their choices and actions, he learned what it meant to believe in God.

From infancy, little Timothy knew the Scriptures because he knew Lois and Eunice. They not only spoke about the Scriptures, they also lived out the love of God as Timothy grew from a boy to a man. From the fire-place where they prepared meals to his bedside where they talked and prayed, their faith shone brightly enough to touch his life and bring him firmly into the family of God.

Lois and Eunice nurtured generations beyond the walls where they lived and worked. They passed on their knowledge and faith by being trustworthy caregivers and teachers. Through their influence upon Timothy, they helped change the world because they were faithful with what God gave them.

Read Acts 16:1; 2 Timothy 1:5.

PRISCILLA: A WITNESS TO CHRIST

Priscilla was a bold and courageous woman whose tentmaking business was flourishing in Rome at the time that she met the apostle Paul in Corinth.

Priscilla wore a familiar crown: She was not afraid to speak and stand up for what she believed in. Without ever elevating herself above others, she faithfully took her instructions from the Lord, and the Gospel was taken further because of her. Luke, in his writings, could not ignore or neglect the importance of this Christian leader's work in Corinth, Ephesus, and in the church in Rome (Acts 18:2, 18, 26).

Priscilla's home was a meeting place for new Christians. She was loyal and devoted. According to A. E. Gaebelein in his book, *Acts of the Apostles,* it must have brought joy to the soul of Paul to be in a place where conversations about the Lord flowed daily.

Just like a woman, Priscilla, with her husband Aquila, labored for the Gospel. She was a valuable preacher whom Paul felt comfortable leaving in charge. When he returned to Ephesus, Paul found that his interim pastor had born much fruit and the church had made great progress.

Even Apollos humbled himself and sat at Priscilla and Aquila's feet to receive the full Gospel. Apollos may not have been able to convince the Jews that Jesus was the Savior if it had not been for Priscilla. This wise woman could have found fault in him, but instead, she helped him. Just like a woman, she filled this half-empty man until he overflowed with the true Gospel, making him a blessing to Corinth.

Just like a woman—full of love, wisdom and courage—Priscilla remained a witness and a student of the Gospel. She worked side by side with her husband, spreading the Word while also managing her business, church, and home. She also heavily influenced the lives of three men: Paul, Aquila, and Apollos. Priscilla radiated courage and strength.

Read Acts 18; see also Romans 16:3–4; 1 Corinthians 16:15, 19; 2 Timothy 4:19.

Read the insight essay on Women's Ministries.

—W. Johnson

PHILLIP'S DAUGHTERS: THOSE PREACHING WOMEN

In the world of the Bible, women were often only mentioned in passing, if at all. Yet their gifts and contributions to the life of the community and the work of the ministry often shine through like a candle in a dark room. Such is the case with the daughters of Phillip. Acts 21:8–9 makes a cursory reference to these women. As a matter of fact, one could read this chapter and completely overlook the significance of these women's ministry. Phillip had four daughters (no mention is made of his wife). They were young women of high moral character who had chosen to be single and celibate. These women were a part of Paul's company. (There were apparently men and women who traveled with Paul on his preaching tours as he moved from city to city.) They were not merely present to provide Paul with financial or spiritual support. Instead, they were preaching women—women who spoke inspired utterances from God in a culture that denied the personhood and presence of women.

Historical, as well as contemporary, African-American women have faced a similar situation. Too often our contributions have been paled in the light of the achievements of African-American men. Yet the powerful public preaching of women such as Jarena Lee, Florence Spearing Randolph, and Vashti McKenzie continue to break through. As a community of believers, we must work together as women and men of God who have as their primary focus the spreading of the Gospel. Supportive of the gifts that we each bring to the task, we model inclusion, thereby advancing God's kingdom. Whether you are called by God to preach the Gospel from the pulpit or to serve faithfully in the pew, women continue to play a significant role in the church, in society, and in the advancement of God's kingdom. We cannot allow culture, tradition, denomination, or gender to hinder us from that which God has called and anointed us to do. Black women preach on.

Read Acts 21:8–9, 17; see also Joel 2:28; Matthew 19:12; 1 Corinthians 7:25–34.

Read the insight essay on Women's Ministries.

—A. E. Crawford

PHEBE: A FAITHFUL MESSENGER

An artist with paintbrush in hand smiles, visualizing a masterpiece. God is like that. While we gather the broken pieces of our lives, desiring to be mended, God sees the finished product. He works from the end to the beginning, gently and lovingly taking the shattered bits of our fragmented lives and putting them together again. His hand forms masterpieces worthy of praise and admiration.

Phebe, like other women in the early church and even women today, volunteered countless hours for the advancement of God's kingdom through her various church ministries (Rom. 16:1–2). She remained focused on the goal of spreading the Good News, and accomplished this task against insurmountable odds.

Driven by her deep sense of desire, purpose, faith, and commitment, Phebe traveled many miles in order to deliver the apostle Paul's letter to

the Christians at Rome. This letter was important, for its contents would be the bridge to understanding God's plan for future Christians. Phebe's steadfast motivation touched the hearts of countless people who would not have been receptive to her otherwise.

Phebe teaches us that with unwavering faith in God, we are sustained.

Read Romans 16:1–2.

Read the insight essays on Commitment, Faith, and Women's Ministries.

—K. Davis

Insights

WOMEN'S MINISTRIES—PREACHER

Since the women of the Gospels returned from the tomb, women have been proclaimers of the Good News of Jesus Christ (see John 20:1–18). The Scriptures provide numerous examples—in both the Old and New Testaments—of women who were prophets. Women preached and prophesied. Examples of biblical women, like Deborah, Miriam, Huldah, Esther, Mary Magdalene, Lydia, and many more, provide the biblical witness that God does indeed use women to stand and declare what the Lord says! The apostle Paul encouraged women to exercise their gift of prophecy. He also taught them how to do so in the public assembly of the church (1 Cor. 11:5). However, as we were growing up, young girls were never exposed to women in ministry.

Acts 2:17 says, "In the last days . . . I will pour out of my Spirit upon all flesh: and your sons and your daughters shall prophesy." God is still using women to bring the Word in due season. As women continue to answer God's call, communities are transformed, churches are revived, and women are empowered. Women like Sojourner Truth, Jarena Lee, Amanda Berry Smith, and Julia Foote were God's preaching women long before it was acceptable for women to preach. These women are trailblazers and role models as we stand on the brink of the 21st century. God is still calling and using women to proclaim God's Word. God has called us for such a time as this!

Read Acts 2:17; see also John 20.

Read the insight essays on Women's Ministries. Read the portraits on Anna, Deborah, Huldah, and Miriam.

—*C. Woods*

WOMEN'S MINISTRIES—TEACHER

Teaching is identified as one of the spiritual gifts in each of Paul's lists (Rom. 12:7; 1 Cor. 12:28–29; Eph. 4:11). All Christians are to teach others (Col. 3:16). The purpose of the gift is "for the work of the ministry, for the edifying of the body of Christ . . . unto the measure of the stature of the fulness of Christ . . . henceforth be no more children . . . may grow up into him in all things" (Eph. 4:12–15). The teacher is a nurturer and developer, one who is called to train persons from infancy to maturity. The office of teacher has long been a socially acceptable place for women, particularly in the church. It is considered the natural outgrowth of what a woman is "supposed to do." Thus, in the church, it has been acceptable for women to be Sunday school teachers (particularly for women and children) or workshop leaders, but being preachers was considered taboo for women for a long while.

In the Book of Acts, a Jew named Apollos, a man very learned in the Scriptures and one who spoke boldly from his limited knowledge of "the Way," was taught by a woman named Priscilla (Prisca) and her husband Aquila (see Acts 18). Some Bible scholars have determined that Priscilla

was probably the main teacher because her name is listed first in a number of translations of the Bible. (It is a custom for the most notable name to be listed first).

Certainly, the apostle Paul encouraged older women to teach younger women (Titus 2:3–5). In 2 Timothy 1:3–5, he applauded Timothy's grandmother, Lois, and his mother, Eunice, for teaching him in the faith. For many Christians, their first memory of church and of the love of God was expressed through the loving sister who taught them in Sunday school. Some of my most challenging and rewarding experiences as an ordained minister have come from sisters who taught me in seminary, in workshops and seminars, and through their witness. Thank God for the teaching ministry of these gifted women.

Read Acts 18; Romans 12:7; Titus 2:3–5.

—C. Woods

NURTURING SPIRITUAL GIFTS IN OUR CHILDREN

As a single mother of five teenagers, I often ask the Lord to raise these children for His glory. Children are a gift from God, but sometimes we get a gift—and in frustration we try to return it!

But God is faithful; He will never give us more than we can bear. God says that every child has spiritual gifts, which He ordained since the foundations of the world. If we nurture those gifts through prayer, faith in Jesus Christ, and godly associations, our children will become the men and women of God that He purposed them to be.

God provides role models for nurturing spiritual gifts, both in the life of Christ and the lives of ordinary people. There is a powerful principle at work here—impartation. Paul speaks of this principle in Romans 1:11, "I long to see you, that I may impart unto you some spiritual gift."

In Matthew 19:13–15, Jesus laid hands on the children and prayed. In 2 Timothy 1:5, Paul speaks to young Timothy about "unfeigned" faith in Christ, modeled by his grandmother, Lois, and mother Eunice. As a result of this "unfeigned" faith, Timothy was a mighty warrior for the Lord. Paul stirred up the gift of God, which was in Timothy "by the laying on of hands." Paul, a godly associate, laid hands on Timothy, imparting the apostolic Spirit he would need to lead the early church at Ephesus.

God instructs us through these examples to "lay hands" on our children—not the hands of violence that the enemy tries to "stress" us into, but hands guided by God's love to impart some spiritual gift. As we ask God to raise our children to glorify Him, mediate on the examples of Jesus, Lois, Eunice, and Paul. Teach children undying faith in the Father, provide them with godly associations, and lay hands on them and pray.

Read Romans 1:11; 8:29, see also Genesis 1:26–27; 1 Timothy 4:12; Hebrews 11:35–38.

Read the insight essays on Children, Influence, and Motherhood.

—J. Scott

RECOVERY WITH DIGNITY—ADDICTION

It is both inspirational and comforting when African-American women can call to mind the experiences of their sisters in meeting the crushing

challenges of life. From the slave traders' auction blocks to the concrete corridors of inner cities—African-American women have forged the tradition of the strong Black woman that helps them to lay claim to human dignity.

Yet, there are times when this tradition can work to the disservice of the African-American woman. One of these times is when she falls victim to the destructive disorders of addiction—addiction to alcohol and other drugs, to compulsive overeating, shopping, abusive relationships, and other things damaging her health and disrupting her life.

When this happens, she finds herself scalded by shame and remorse, and filled with the constantly growing fear of losing the dignity that makes her a strong Black woman. She does not understand why she continues to do what she is doing. Yet, she cannot seem to admit her powerlessness, because, she, after all, is a strong Black woman. She has survived because she refuses to accept that she is powerless. To admit powerlessness is to lose her dignity and her life.

Then one day, she stumbles upon Romans 7:15–25. It is then that she begins to understand what every truly strong Black woman knows: an admission of personal powerlessness is a willingness to rely on the One who has all power. From this moment on, she begins to be open to God for direction in obtaining the medical, emotional, and spiritual help needed for a recovery with dignity for a strong Black woman.

Read Romans 7:15–25.

—L. J. Hood

SALVATION

Salvation is best described as "God's deliverance." Salvation is the noun form of the word *saved.* But what are we, as Christians, saved from, and what does salvation mean to us personally? For many of us, being saved and having salvation simply means that we are born again; we were baptized and we are now able to sit at the table with fellow believers and partake of Holy Communion and say "I'm saved." But is that all that salvation means? Is that all our salvation encompasses? Is that all that Jesus could do? Salvation is all-encompassing. It is our healing, our preservation, our protection, our welfare, our deliverance, our health, our help. God, in His infinite wisdom and power and mercy, knew that we needed to be saved from sickness, disease, calamity, bondage, and the ultimate—eternal death. Christ came and saved us from everything that is ungodly, everything that is not like Him. This is our salvation. Jesus, Hebrew for Joshua or *yeshua,* means "salvation." He is our salvation.

How can we obtain such great salvation? By a part of our bodies that so easily besets and ensnares us. It is also the part of our bodies that can help us to leave the power of darkness and bring us into the marvelous light: by our mouths. The mouth is a powerful weapon. Life and death exist in it. Salvation does as well. But we must confess. We must say it with our mouths. It's a simple truth, but when we were saved, we had to say it—confess that Jesus, the Son of God, died and was raised from the dead three days later. We did not get saved just by thinking that we were saved; we confessed our salvation. But do not stop at salvation. We are urged to confess, acknowledge Christ before men—so that He can confess us before His Father which is in heaven (see Romans 10:9–12). Being a

silent Christian, just like silently being saved, is impossible. We must confess—if not now, very soon. For saved or unsaved, every knee will bow and every tongue shall confess that Jesus is Lord.

Read Romans 10:9–12.

Read the insight essays on Evangelism, Prayer, and Women's Ministries

—*C. Byrd*

ATTRIBUTES OF GOD—OMNISCIENCE

"O the depth of the riches both of the wisdom and knowledge of God! how unsearchable are his judgments, and his ways past finding out." (Rom. 11:33)

God has perfect knowledge of all that transpires in human experiences. God does not have to reason, or find things out, or learn gradually. God's knowledge of past, present, and future is simultaneous. He learns from no one. He is never surprised and He never forgets (Isa. 46:9–10). Every now and then, God chooses to share that knowledge with us.

God knows His children completely. God prepares them from the beginning for ministry, for marriage, and for employment. Through God's own knowledge, God works into our life all of the characteristics we would need to grow and thrive as Black women, in a world that is hostile toward us. God equipped us with strength, with courage, with independence, and with vigilance. Even though your upbringing may have been filled with the ups and downs of life, you should be thankful that God in His wisdom knew exactly what you would need and when the need would become apparent. God knows woman fully (Ps. 33:15): her past (Rev. 2:2–3), where she goes, what she does, what she thinks and says (Ps. 33:13–15). God even knows what motivates every woman (1 Sam. 16:7).

Your strength is made perfect in weakness; your courage comes from knowing that you are loved and accepted by God; your independence is forged through your dependence on God; and your vigilance comes from understanding your call to be a watch woman of God. I thank God that He always knows just what we need.

Read Romans 11:33.

—*B. Whipple*

COMMITMENT

Romans 12:1–2 describes the kind of commitment God desires and deserves from us. Our lives should be totally committed to God—a commitment that completely focuses on God's will in our lives. This means that our first and last priorities must be to please God. The implication of such commitment is that we no longer belong to the world or ourselves; our free will has to be consumed by God's will. Every aspect of our lives should be in God's control—this is a "living" sacrifice. It is important to understand how such a commitment unfolds in our lives. The first question is, "Are we where God wants us? Assuming the answer is yes, the second question is, "Are we following God's instructions in the situations he has placed us in (i.e., marriage, community, church, employment)?

Paul suggests that this kind of commitment is only reasonable. This is not reasonable simply because of God's priceless gift of grace and mercy

through Jesus Christ, but also because of the social and spiritual benefit we gain. Turning our lives over to God brings about a renewing of our minds and a separation from the world and its destruction. A renewed mind improves our reactions to life situations, shifts our perspective of right and wrong, and enhances our expectation to live a peaceful life. Separation from the world gives us complete freedom to be what God wants us to be without being concerned about the world's opinion; we dare to be different. This kind of separation keeps us from being anxious if we are alone in our thinking because we know God will never let us be lonely. This kind of commitment transforms every aspect of our life. For example, our response in marriage would be based on our commitment and trust in God first and foremost. The commitment in the marriage would be driven by the commitment to God "for better or worse." Our duties in the church will be defined by God and not by position. There would be no compromising of the Gospel or fear in presenting God's truth. As we function in the community, God would define our social standards and—without question—we would be set apart from others. It would be obvious to all we encounter that our perspective on and response to life is different in a very reassuring way.

As a living sacrifice our lives belong to God, and the reward becomes ours. Those who are truly committed have the full joy of knowing that they do not have to journey this life alone. Fully committed Christians benefit in a daily walk with a God who is fully committed in His endless love demonstrated in His plan of salvation.

Commitment builds faith and develops strong character. It is a spiritual discipline, (Prov. 16:3). It is a lifetime venture requiring time, work, and determination (Matt. 16:24). Commitment requires some action, and it cannot be separated from responsibility. Commitment extends beyond our relationship to the heavenly Father to other aspects of our life.

Read Romans 12:1–2; see also Matthew 5:33, 37; Mark 8:34; Luke 9:62; 14:27.

Read portraits on Mary Magdalene, Naomi, Phoebe, Ruth, and the Widow's Mite.

—B. Whitaker

POSITIVE THINKING

Life can be tough! It can be hard to handle at times. As African-American women, there are so many issues for us to deal with. There are health issues, relationship challenges, family issues, and career challenges—to name a few—that sap our strength, our sense of well-being, and keep us from achieving our highest potential as women.

Given all that we have to go through, sometimes we say to ourselves, like the psalmist David said in Psalm 55:6, after pouring out his pain to God, "Oh, that I had wings like a dove! for then would I fly away, and be at rest." With the wings of a dove, we could simply escape. But I want to suggest that it is much more beneficial for us not to run from our pain, but rather to go through it and rise above it.

Attitude determines altitude! The writer of Proverbs says in verse 23:7, "As he [man or woman] thinketh in his heart, so is he [or she]." Psychologists believe that what people think affects their emotions, their

ability to relate to others, and the ability to cope in difficult circumstances. What is it that is weighing you down, keeping you from living up to your fullest potential, and hindering you from enjoying the abundant life in Christ (John 10:10)? What is your attitude toward it? Is it an impossible situation? Can you rise above it? What you think about it will determine your ability to cope with it.

If you think you can, you will. But if you think you can't, you won't. Christian women should be positive thinkers (Phil. 4:11–13). We should keep our minds on things that are true, noble, just, pure, lovely, and of good report (Phil. 4:8). Negative thinking will always keep you from overcoming the obstacles in your life, achieving your highest potential, and being free. The key to rising above your circumstances is to be renewed in your mind: "And be not conformed to this world: but be ye transformed by the renewing of your mind, that ye may prove what is that good, and acceptable, and perfect, will of God" (Rom. 12:2). Change your way of thinking from the negative to the positive (Phil. 4:8), and finally live each day by faith in God with whom nothing is impossible. Nothing will be impossible to the person who believes (Matt. 17:20; Mark 10:27).

Read Romans 12:1–2; Philippians 4:11–13.

Read the insight essays on Fruit of the Spirit.

—*C. Belt*

RELATIONSHIP BUILDERS

The Bible is a book all about relationships—relating to God and relating to other people. Consider how the following Biblical qualities might serve as better building blocks to friendships with others:

- DEVOTION: Be kindly affectionate to one another with brotherly love (Rom. 12:10)
- HONOR: Honor others above yourself (Rom. 12:10)
- GENEROSITY: Share with Christian friends who have needs (Rom. 12:13)
- A COMMITMENT TO UNITY AND PEACE: Be of the same mind. Live in harmony with one another (Rom. 12:16; 1 Thess. 5:14; 1 Pet. 3:8)
- HUMILITY: Don't be arrogant, proud, or conceited (Rom. 12:16; 1 Pet. 5:5)
- A NON-CRITICAL ATTITUDE: Don't judge one another (Rom. 14:13)
- ACCEPTANCE: Accept one another (Rom. 15:7)
- HELPFULNESS: Carry each other's burdens (Gal. 6:2)
- GOODNESS: Do good to others (Gal. 6:10)
- HONESTY: Speak truthfully to others (Eph. 4:25)
- ENCOURAGEMENT: Attempt to build up and encourage others (Eph. 4:29; 5:19; 1 Thess. 5:11)
- KINDNESS: Be kind and compassionate to one another (Eph. 4:32; 1 Thess. 5:15)
- FORGIVENESS: Forgive each other (Eph. 4:32)
- UNSELFISHNESS: Consider others better than yourself (Phil. 2:3); Submit to one another (Eph. 5:21)
- THOUGHTFULNESS: Look out for the interests of others (Phil. 2:4)
- PATIENCE: Bear with each other (Col. 3:13)
- LOVE: Love one another deeply, from the heart (1 Pet. 1:22)
- RESPECT: Show proper respect to everyone (1 Pet. 2:17)
- HOSPITALITY: Offer hospitality to one another without grumbling (1 Pet 4:9)
- SERVANTHOOD: Serve one another in love (Gal 5:13; 1 Pet 4:10)

HOW THE HOLY SPIRIT HELPS US

The disciples did not understand how it could be "good" for Jesus to leave them and to send the "Comforter" or Holy Spirit to take His place (John 16:6–7). Here's why the sending of the Spirit is such a blessing:

- He *regenerates* us (makes us alive spiritually)
  John 3:3–8; Titus 3:5
- He *indwells* us (takes up residence inside us)
  John 14:17; Rom. 8:9,11; 1 Cor. 6:19
- He *baptizes* us (joins us to the body of Christ)
  1 Cor. 12:13; Luke 3:16
- He *seals* us (marks us as His/makes us secure)
  2 Cor. 1:22; Eph. 1:13; 4:30; Rom. 8:16
- He *fills* us (empowers us for life & ministry)
  Eph. 5:18; Acts 4:8, 31; 6:3; 9:17; 11:24
- He *teaches* us (keeps us from error)
  John 14:26; 16:13; 1 John 2:20,27
- He *guides* us (shows us how to live)
  Gal. 5:16, 25; Acts 13:2; Rom. 8:14
- He *convicts* us (points out our sins)
  John 16:7–8
- He *prays* for us (strengthens us in weakness)
  Rom. 8:26–27
- He *assures* us (reminds us we belong to God)
  Rom. 8:16; Gal. 4:6
- He *reproduces* Christ in us (makes us holy)
  Gal. 5:22–23
- He *gifts* us (equips us to serve others)
  Rom. 12:3–8; 1 Cor. 12:4–31

living God, [r]which made heaven, and
earth, and the sea, and all things that are
therein:
16 [s]Who in times past suffered all nations to walk in their own ways.
17 [t]Nevertheless he left not himself without witness, in that he did good, and [u]gave
us rain from heaven, and fruitful seasons,
filling our hearts with food and gladness.
18 And with these sayings scarce restrained they the people, that they had not
done sacrifice unto them.
19 ¶ [v]And there came thither *certain*
Jews from Antioch and Iconium, who persuaded the people, [w]and, having stoned
Paul, drew *him* out of the city, supposing he
had been dead.
20 Howbeit, as the disciples stood round
about him, he rose up, and came into the
city: and the next day he departed with Barnabas to Derbe.
21 And when they had preached the gospel to that city, [x]and had taught many, they
returned again to Lystra, and *to* Iconium,
and Antioch,
22 Confirming the souls of the disciples,
and [y]exhorting them to continue in the
faith, and that [z]we must through much tribulation enter into the kingdom of God.
23 And when they had [a]ordained them
elders in every church, and had prayed with
fasting, they commended them to the Lord,
on whom they believed.
24 And after they had passed throughout
Pisidia, they came to Pamphylia.
25 And when they had preached the word
in Perga, they went down into Attalia:
26 And thence sailed to Antioch, [b]from
whence they had been [c]recommended to
the grace of God for the work which they
fulfilled.
27 And when they were come, and had
gathered the church together, [d]they rehearsed all that God had done with them,
and how he had [e]opened the door of faith
unto the Gentiles.
28 And there they abode long time with
the disciples.

15 And [f]certain men which came down
from Judaea taught the brethren,
and said, [g]Except ye be circumcised [h]after
the manner of Moses, ye cannot be saved.
2 When therefore Paul and Barnabas had
no small dissension and disputation with
them, they determined that [i]Paul and Barnabas, and certain other of them, should go
up to Jerusalem unto the apostles and elders about this question.
3 And [j]being brought on their way by the
church, they passed through Phenice and
Samaria, [k]declaring the conversion of the
Gentiles: and they caused great joy unto all
the brethren.
4 And when they were come to Jerusalem, they were received of the church, and
of the apostles and elders, and [l]they declared all things that God had done with
them.
5 But there rose up certain of the sect of
the Pharisees which believed, saying,
[m]That it was needful to circumcise them,
and to command *them* to keep the law of
Moses.
6 ¶ And the apostles and elders came together for to consider of this matter.
7 And when there had been much disputing, Peter rose up, and said unto them,
[n]Men *and* brethren, ye know how that a
good while ago God made choice among us,
that the Gentiles by my mouth should hear
the word of the gospel, and believe.
8 And God, [o]which knoweth the hearts,
bare them witness, [p]giving them the Holy
Ghost, even as *he did* unto us;
9 [q]And put no difference between us and
them, [r]purifying their hearts by faith.
10 Now therefore why tempt ye God, [s]to
put a yoke upon the neck of the disciples,
which neither our fathers nor we were able
to bear?
11 But [t]we believe that through the grace
of the Lord Jesus Christ we shall be saved,
even as they.
12 ¶ Then all the multitude kept silence,
and gave audience to Barnabas and Paul,
declaring what miracles and wonders God
had [u]wrought among the Gentiles by them.
13 ¶ And after they had held their peace,
[v]James answered, saying, Men *and* brethren, hearken unto me:
14 [w]Simeon hath declared how God at
the first did visit the Gentiles, to take out of
them a people for his name.
15 And to this agree the words of the
prophets; as it is written,
16 [x]After this I will return, and will build
again the tabernacle of David, which is
fallen down; and I will build again the ruins
thereof, and I will set it up:
17 That the residue of men might seek
after the Lord, and all the Gentiles, upon
whom my name is called, saith the Lord,
who doeth all these things.
18 Known unto God are all his works
from the beginning of the world.
19 Wherefore [y]my sentence is, that we
trouble not them, which from among the
Gentiles [z]are turned to God:
20 But that we write unto them, that they
abstain [a]from pollutions of idols, and
[b]*from* fornication, and *from* things strangled, [c]and *from* blood.
21 For Moses of old time hath in every
city them that preach him, [d]being read in
the synagogues every sabbath day.
22 Then pleased it the apostles and elders, with the whole church, to send chosen
men of their own company to Antioch with
Paul and Barnabas; *namely,* Judas surnamed [e]Barsabas, and Silas, chief men
among the brethren:
23 And they wrote *letters* by them after
this manner; The apostles and elders and
brethren *send* greeting unto the brethren
which are of the Gentiles in Antioch and
Syria and Cilicia:

14:15 [r]Gen. 1:1; Ps. 33:6; Rev. 14:7
14:16 [s]Ps. 81:12; ch. 17:30; 1 Pet. 4:3
14:17 [t]ch. 17:27; Rom. 1:20 [u]Lev. 26:4; Deut. 11:14; Job 5:10; Ps. 65:10; Jer. 14:22; Matt. 5:45
14:19 [v]ch. 13:45 [w]2 Cor. 11:25; 2 Tim. 3:11
14:21 [x]Matt. 28:19
14:22 [y]ch. 11:23 [z]Matt. 10:38; Luke 22:28; Rom. 8:17; 2 Tim. 2:11
14:23 [a]Tit. 1:5
14:26 [b]ch. 13:1 [c]ch. 15:40
14:27 [d]ch. 15:4 [e]1 Cor. 16:9; 2 Cor. 2:12; Col. 4:3; Rev. 3:8
15:1 [f]Gal. 2:12 [g]John 7:22; ver. 5; Gal. 5:2; Phil. 3:2; Col. 2:8 [h]Gen. 17:10; Lev. 12:3
15:2 [i]Gal. 2:1
15:3 [j]Rom. 15:24; 1 Cor. 16:6 [k]ch. 14:27
15:4 [l]ver. 12; ch. 14:27
15:5 [m]ver. 1
15:7 [n]ch. 10:20
15:8 [o]1 Chron. 28:9; ch. 1:24 [p]ch. 10:44
15:9 [q]Rom. 10:11 [r]ch. 10:15; 1 Cor. 1:2; 1 Pet. 1:23
15:10 [s]Matt. 23:4; Gal. 5:1
15:11 [t]Rom. 3:24; Eph. 2:8; Tit. 2:11
15:12 [u]ch. 14:27
15:13 [v]ch. 12:17
15:14 [w]ver. 7
15:16 [x]Am. 9:11
15:19 [y]ver. 28 [z]1 Thess. 1:9
15:20 [a]Gen. 35:2; Ex. 20:3; Ezek. 20:30; 1 Cor. 8:1; Rev. 2:14 [b]1 Cor. 6:9; Gal. 5:19; Eph. 5:3; Col. 3:5; 1 Thess. 4:3; 1 Pet. 4:3 [c]Gen. 9:4; Lev. 3:17; Deut. 12:16
15:21 [d]ch. 13:15
15:22 [e]ch. 1:23

24 Forasmuch as we have heard, that [f]certain which went out from us have troubled you with words, subverting your souls, saying, *Ye must* be circumcised, and keep the law: to whom we gave no *such* commandment:

25 It seemed good unto us, being assembled with one accord, to send chosen men unto you with our beloved Barnabas and Paul,

26 [g]Men that have hazarded their lives for the name of our Lord Jesus Christ.

27 We have sent therefore Judas and Silas, who shall also tell *you* the same things by mouth.

28 For it seemed good to the Holy Ghost, and to us, to lay upon you no greater burden than these necessary things;

29 [h]That ye abstain from meats offered to idols, and [i]from blood, and from things strangled, and from fornication: from which if ye keep yourselves, ye shall do well. Fare ye well.

30 So when they were dismissed, they came to Antioch: and when they had gathered the multitude together, they delivered the epistle:

31 *Which* when they had read, they rejoiced for the consolation.

32 And Judas and Silas, being prophets also themselves, [j]exhorted the brethren with many words, and confirmed *them.*

33 And after they had tarried *there* a space, they were let [k]go in peace from the brethren unto the apostles.

34 Notwithstanding it pleased Silas to abide there still.

35 [l]Paul also and Barnabas continued in Antioch, teaching and preaching the word of the Lord, with many others also.

36 ¶ And some days after Paul said unto Barnabas, Let us go again and visit our brethren [m]in every city where we have preached the word of the Lord, *and see* how they do.

37 And Barnabas determined to take with them [n]John, whose surname was Mark.

38 But Paul thought not good to take him with them, [o]who departed from them from Pamphylia, and went not with them to the work.

39 And the contention was so sharp between them, that they departed asunder one from the other: and so Barnabas took Mark, and sailed unto Cyprus;

40 And Paul chose Silas, and departed, [p]being recommended by the brethren unto the grace of God.

41 And he went through Syria and Cilicia, [q]confirming the churches.

16 Then came he to [r]Derbe and Lystra: and, behold, a certain disciple was there, [s]named Timotheus, [t]the son of a certain woman, which was a Jewess, and believed; but his father *was* a Greek:

2 Which [u]was well reported of by the brethren that were at Lystra and Iconium.

3 Him would Paul have to go forth with him; and [v]took and circumcised him because of the Jews which were in those quarters: for they knew all that his father was a Greek.

4 And as they went through the cities, they delivered them the decrees for to keep, [w]that were ordained of the apostles and elders which were at Jerusalem.

5 And [x]so were the churches established in the faith, and increased in number daily.

6 Now when they had gone throughout Phrygia and the region of Galatia, and were forbidden of the Holy Ghost to preach the word in Asia,

7 After they were come to Mysia, they assayed to go into Bithynia: but the Spirit suffered them not.

8 And they passing by Mysia [y]came down to Troas.

9 And a vision appeared to Paul in the night; There stood a [z]man of Macedonia, and prayed him, saying, Come over into Macedonia, and help us.

10 And after he had seen the vision, immediately we endeavoured to go [a]into Macedonia, assuredly gathering that the Lord had called us for to preach the gospel unto them.

11 Therefore loosing from Troas, we came with a straight course to Samothracia, and the next *day* to Neapolis;

12 And from thence to [b]Philippi, which is the chief city of that part of Macedonia, *and* a colony: and we were in that city abiding certain days.

13 And on the sabbath we went out of the city by a river side, where prayer was wont to be made; and we sat down, and spake unto the women which resorted *thither.*

14 ¶ And a certain woman named Lydia, a seller of purple, of the city of Thyatira, which worshipped God, heard *us:* whose [c]heart the Lord opened, that she attended unto the things which were spoken of Paul.

15 And when she was baptized, and her household, she besought *us,* saying, If ye have judged me to be faithful to the Lord, come into my house, and abide *there.* And [d]she constrained us.

16 ¶ And it came to pass, as we went to prayer, a certain damsel [e]possessed with a spirit of divination met us, which brought her masters [f]much gain by soothsaying:

17 The same followed Paul and us, and cried, saying, These men are the servants of the most high God, which shew unto us the way of salvation.

18 And this did she many days. But Paul, [g]being grieved, turned and said to the spirit, I command thee in the name of Jesus Christ to come out of her. [h]And he came out the same hour.

19 ¶ And [i]when her masters saw that the hope of their gains was gone, [j]they caught Paul and Silas, and [k]drew *them* into the marketplace unto the rulers,

20 And brought them to the magistrates,

15:24 [f]ver. 1; Gal. 2:4; Tit. 1:10
15:26 [g]ch. 13:50; 1 Cor. 15:30; 2 Cor. 11:23
15:29 [h]ver. 20; ch. 21:25; Rev. 2:14 [i]Lev. 17:14
15:32 [j]ch. 14:22
15:33 [k]1 Cor. 16:11; Heb. 11:31
15:35 [l]ch. 13:1
15:36 [m]ch. 13:4
15:37 [n]ch. 12:12; Col. 4:10; 2 Tim. 4:11; Philem. 24
15:38 [o]ch. 13:13
15:40 [p]ch. 14:26
15:41 [q]ch. 16:5
16:1 [r]ch. 14:6 [s]ch. 19:22; Rom. 16:21; 1 Cor. 4:17; Phil. 2:19; 1 Thess. 3:2; 1 Tim. 1:2; 2 Tim. 1:2 [t]2 Tim. 1:5
16:2 [u]ch. 6:3
16:3 [v]1 Cor. 9:20; Gal. 2:3
16:4 [w]ch. 15:28
16:5 [x]ch. 15:41
16:8 [y]2 Cor. 2:12; 2 Tim. 4:13
16:9 [z]ch. 10:30
16:10 [a]2 Cor. 2:13
16:12 [b]Phil. 1:1
16:14 [c]Luke 24:45
16:15 [d]Gen. 19:3; Judg. 19:21; Luke 24:29; Heb. 13:2
16:16 [e]1 Sam. 28:7 [f]ch. 19:24
16:18 [g]Mark 1:25 [h]Mark 16:17
16:19 [i]ch. 19:25 [j]2 Cor. 6:5 [k]Matt. 10:18

saying, These men, being Jews, [l]do exceedingly trouble our city,
21 And teach customs, which are not lawful for us to receive, neither to observe, being Romans.
22 And the multitude rose up together against them: and the magistrates rent off their clothes, [m]and commanded to beat *them*.
23 And when they had laid many stripes upon them, they cast *them* into prison, charging the jailor to keep them safely:
24 Who, having received such a charge, thrust them into the inner prison, and made their feet fast in the stocks.
25 ¶ And at midnight Paul and Silas prayed, and sang praises unto God: and the prisoners heard them.
26 [n]And suddenly there was a great earthquake, so that the foundations of the prison were shaken: and immediately [o]all the doors were opened, and every one's bands were loosed.
27 And the keeper of the prison awaking out of his sleep, and seeing the prison doors open, he drew out his sword, and would have killed himself, supposing that the prisoners had been fled.
28 But Paul cried with a loud voice, saying, Do thyself no harm: for we are all here.
29 Then he called for a light, and sprang in, and came trembling, and fell down before Paul and Silas,
30 And brought them out, and said, [p]Sirs, what must I do to be saved?
31 And they said, [q]Believe on the Lord Jesus Christ, and thou shalt be saved, and thy house.
32 And they spake unto him the word of the Lord, and to all that were in his house.
33 And he took them the same hour of the night, and washed *their* stripes; and was baptized, he and all his, straightway.
34 And when he had brought them into his house, [r]he set meat before them, and rejoiced, believing in God with all his house.
35 And when it was day, the magistrates sent the serjeants, saying, Let those men go.
36 And the keeper of the prison told this saying to Paul, The magistrates have sent to let you go: now therefore depart, and go in peace.
37 But Paul said unto them, They have beaten us openly uncondemned, [s]being Romans, and have cast *us* into prison; and now do they thrust us out privily? nay verily; but let them come themselves and fetch us out.
38 And the serjeants told these words unto the magistrates: and they feared, when they heard that they were Romans.
39 And they came and besought them, and brought *them* out, and [t]desired *them* to depart out of the city.
40 And they went out of the prison, [u]and entered into *the house of* Lydia: and when they had seen the brethren, they comforted them, and departed.

16:20 [l]1 Kings 18:17; ch. 17:6
16:22 [m]2 Cor. 6:5; 1 Thess. 2:2
16:26 [n]ch. 4:31 [o]ch. 5:19
16:30 [p]Luke 3:10; ch. 2:37
16:31 [q]John 3:16; 1 John 5:10
16:34 [r]Luke 5:29
16:37 [s]ch. 22:25
16:39 [t]Matt. 8:34
16:40 [u]ver. 14
17:2 [v]Luke 4:16; ch. 9:20
17:3 [w]Luke 24:26; ch. 18:28; Gal. 3:1
17:4 [x]ch. 28:24 [y]ch. 15:22
17:5 [z]Rom. 16:21
17:6 [a]ch. 16:20
17:7 [b]Luke 23:2; John 19:12; 1 Pet. 2:15
17:10 [c]ch. 9:25; ver. 14
17:11 [d]Isa. 34:16; Luke 16:29; John 5:39
17:14 [e]Matt. 10:23
17:15 [f]ch. 18:5
17:16 [g]2 Pet. 2:8

17 Now when they had passed through Amphipolis and Apollonia, they came to Thessalonica, where was a synagogue of the Jews:
2 And Paul, as his manner was, [v]went in unto them, and three sabbath days reasoned with them out of the scriptures,
3 Opening and alleging, [w]that Christ must needs have suffered, and risen again from the dead; and that this Jesus, whom I preach unto you, is Christ.
4 [x]And some of them believed, and consorted with Paul and [y]Silas; and of the devout Greeks a great multitude, and of the chief women not a few.
5 ¶ But the Jews which believed not, moved with envy, took unto them certain lewd fellows of the baser sort, and gathered a company, and set all the city on an uproar, and assaulted the house of [z]Jason, and sought to bring them out to the people.
6 And when they found them not, they drew Jason and certain brethren unto the rulers of the city, crying, [a]These that have turned the world upside down are come hither also;
7 Whom Jason hath received: and these all do contrary to the decrees of Caesar, [b]saying that there is another king, *one* Jesus.
8 And they troubled the people and the rulers of the city, when they heard these things.
9 And when they had taken security of Jason, and of the other, they let them go.
10 ¶ And [c]the brethren immediately sent away Paul and Silas by night unto Berea: who coming *thither* went into the synagogue of the Jews.
11 These were more noble than those in Thessalonica, in that they received the word with all readiness of mind, and [d]searched the scriptures daily, whether those things were so.
12 Therefore many of them believed; also of honourable women which were Greeks, and of men, not a few.
13 But when the Jews of Thessalonica had knowledge that the word of God was preached of Paul at Berea, they came thither also, and stirred up the people.
14 [e]And then immediately the brethren sent away Paul to go as it were to the sea: but Silas and Timotheus abode there still.
15 And they that conducted Paul brought him unto Athens: and [f]receiving a commandment unto Silas and Timotheus for to come to him with all speed, they departed.
16 ¶ Now while Paul waited for them at Athens, [g]his spirit was stirred in him, when he saw the city wholly given to idolatry.
17 Therefore disputed he in the synagogue with the Jews, and with the devout persons, and in the market daily with them that met with him.
18 Then certain philosophers of the Epicureans, and of the Stoicks, encountered him. And some said, What will this babbler

say? other some, He seemeth to be a setter forth of strange gods: because he preached unto them Jesus, and the resurrection.

19 And they took him, and brought him unto Areopagus, saying, May we know what this new doctrine, whereof thou speakest, *is?*

20 For thou bringest certain strange things to our ears: we would know therefore what these things mean.

21 (For all the Athenians and strangers which were there spent their time in nothing else, but either to tell, or to hear some new thing.)

22 ¶ Then Paul stood in the midst of Mars' hill, and said, *Ye* men of Athens, I perceive that in all things ye are too superstitious.

23 For as I passed by, and beheld your devotions, I found an altar with this inscription, TO THE UNKNOWN GOD. Whom therefore ye ignorantly worship, him declare I unto you.

24 [h]God that made the world and all things therein, seeing that he is [i]Lord of heaven and earth, [j]dwelleth not in temples made with hands;

25 Neither is worshipped with men's hands, [k]as though he needed any thing, seeing [l]he giveth to all life, and breath, and all things;

26 And hath made of one blood all nations of men for to dwell on all the face of the earth, and hath determined the times before appointed, and [m]the bounds of their habitation;

27 [n]That they should seek the Lord, if haply they might feel after him, and find him, [o]though he be not far from every one of us:

28 For [p]in him we live, and move, and have our being; [q]as certain also of your own poets have said, For we are also his offspring.

29 Forasmuch then as we are the offspring of God, [r]we ought not to think that the Godhead is like unto gold, or silver, or stone, graven by art and man's device.

30 And [s]the times of this ignorance God winked at; but [t]now commandeth all men every where to repent:

31 Because he hath appointed a day, in the which [u]he will judge the world in righteousness by *that* man whom he hath ordained; *whereof* he hath given assurance unto all *men,* in that [v]he hath raised him from the dead.

32 ¶ And when they heard of the resurrection of the dead, some mocked: and others said, We will hear thee again of this *matter.*

33 So Paul departed from among them.

34 Howbeit certain men clave unto him, and believed: among the which *was* Dionysius the Areopagite, and a woman named Damaris, and others with them.

18 After these things Paul departed from Athens, and came to Corinth;

2 And found a certain Jew named [w]Aquila, born in Pontus, lately come from Italy, with his wife Priscilla; (because that Claudius had commanded all Jews to depart from Rome:) and came unto them.

3 And because he was of the same craft, he abode with them, [x]and wrought: for by their occupation they were tentmakers.

4 [y]And he reasoned in the synagogue every sabbath, and persuaded the Jews and the Greeks.

5 And [z]when Silas and Timotheus were come from Macedonia, Paul was [a]pressed in the spirit, and testified to the Jews *that* Jesus *was* Christ.

6 And [b]when they opposed themselves, and blasphemed, [c]he shook *his* raiment, and said unto them, [d]Your blood *be* upon your own heads; [e]I *am* clean: [f]from henceforth I will go unto the Gentiles.

7 ¶ And he departed thence, and entered into a certain *man's* house, named Justus, *one* that worshipped God, whose house joined hard to the synagogue.

8 [g]And Crispus, the chief ruler of the synagogue, believed on the Lord with all his house; and many of the Corinthians hearing believed, and were baptized.

9 Then [h]spake the Lord to Paul in the night by a vision, Be not afraid, but speak, and hold not thy peace:

10 [i]For I am with thee, and no man shall set on thee to hurt thee: for I have much people in this city.

11 And he continued *there* a year and six months, teaching the word of God among them.

12 ¶ And when Gallio was the deputy of Achaia, the Jews made insurrection with one accord against Paul, and brought him to the judgment seat,

13 Saying, This *fellow* persuadeth men to worship God contrary to the law.

14 And when Paul was now about to open *his* mouth, Gallio said unto the Jews, [j]If it were a matter of wrong or wicked lewdness, O *ye* Jews, reason would that I should bear with you:

15 But if it be a question of words and names, and *of* your law, look ye *to it;* for I will be no judge of such *matters.*

16 And he drave them from the judgment seat.

17 Then all the Greeks took [k]Sosthenes, the chief ruler of the synagogue, and beat *him* before the judgment seat. And Gallio cared for none of those things.

18 ¶ And Paul *after this* tarried *there* yet a good while, and then took his leave of the brethren, and sailed thence into Syria, and with him Priscilla and Aquila; having [l]shorn *his* head in [m]Cenchrea: for he had a vow.

19 And he came to Ephesus, and left them there: but he himself entered into the synagogue, and reasoned with the Jews.

20 When they desired *him* to tarry longer time with them, he consented not;

21 But bade them farewell, saying, [n]I

17:24 [h]ch. 14:15 [i]Matt. 11:25 [j]ch. 7:48
17:25 [k]Ps. 50:8 [l]Gen. 2:7; Num. 16:22; Job 12:10; Isa. 42:5; Zech. 12:1
17:26 [m]Deut. 32:8
17:27 [n]Rom. 1:20 [o]ch. 14:17
17:28 [p]Col. 1:17; Heb. 1:3 [q]Tit. 1:12
17:29 [r]Isa. 40:18
17:30 [s]ch. 14:16; Rom. 3:25 [t]Luke 24:47; Tit. 2:11; 1 Pet. 1:14
17:31 [u]ch. 10:42; Rom. 2:16 [v]ch. 2:24
18:2 [w]Rom. 16:3; 1 Cor. 16:19; 2 Tim. 4:19
18:3 [x]ch. 20:34; 1 Cor. 4:12; 1 Thess. 2:9; 2 Thess. 3:8
18:4 [y]ch. 17:2
18:5 [z]ch. 17:14 [a]Job 32:18; ch. 17:3; ver. 28
18:6 [b]ch. 13:45; 1 Pet. 4:4 [c]Neh. 5:13; Matt. 10:14; ch. 13:51 [d]Lev. 20:9; 2 Sam. 1:16; Ezek. 18:13 [e]Ezek. 3:18; ch. 20:26 [f]ch. 13:46
18:8 [g]1 Cor. 1:14
18:9 [h]ch. 23:11
18:10 [i]Jer. 1:18; Matt. 28:20
18:14 [j]ch. 23:29
18:17 [k]1 Cor. 1:1
18:18 [l]Num. 6:18; ch. 21:24 [m]Rom. 16:1
18:21 [n]ch. 19:21

must by all means keep this feast that cometh in Jerusalem: but I will return again unto you, [o]if God will. And he sailed from Ephesus.

22 And when he had landed at Caesarea, and gone up, and saluted the church, he went down to Antioch.

23 And after he had spent some time *there,* he departed, and went over *all* the country of [p]Galatia and Phrygia in order, [q]strengthening all the disciples.

24 ¶ [r]And a certain Jew named Apollos, born at Alexandria, an eloquent man, *and* mighty in the scriptures, came to Ephesus.

25 This man was instructed in the way of the Lord; and being [s]fervent in the spirit, he spake and taught diligently the things of the Lord, [t]knowing only the baptism of John.

26 And he began to speak boldly in the synagogue: whom when Aquila and Priscilla had heard, they took him unto *them,* and expounded unto him the way of God more perfectly.

27 And when he was disposed to pass into Achaia, the brethren wrote, exhorting the disciples to receive him: who, when he was come, [u]helped them much which had believed through grace:

28 For he mightily convinced the Jews, *and that* publickly, [v]shewing by the scriptures that Jesus was Christ.

19 And it came to pass, that, while [w]Apollos was at Corinth, Paul having passed through the upper coasts came to Ephesus: and finding certain disciples,

2 He said unto them, Have ye received the Holy Ghost since ye believed? And they said unto him, [x]We have not so much as heard whether there be any Holy Ghost.

3 And he said unto them, Unto what then were ye baptized? And they said, [y]Unto John's baptism.

4 Then said Paul, [z]John verily baptized with the baptism of repentance, saying unto the people, that they should believe on him which should come after him, that is, on Christ Jesus.

5 When they heard *this,* they were baptized [a]in the name of the Lord Jesus.

6 And when Paul had [b]laid *his* hands upon them, the Holy Ghost came on them; and [c]they spake with tongues, and prophesied.

7 And all the men were about twelve.

8 [d]And he went into the synagogue, and spake boldly for the space of three months, disputing and persuading the things [e]concerning the kingdom of God.

9 But [f]when divers were hardened, and believed not, but spake evil [g]of that way before the multitude, he departed from them, and separated the disciples, disputing daily in the school of one Tyrannus.

10 And [h]this continued by the space of two years; so that all they which dwelt in Asia heard the word of the Lord Jesus, both Jews and Greeks.

11 And [i]God wrought special miracles by the hands of Paul:

12 [j]So that from his body were brought unto the sick handkerchiefs or aprons, and the diseases departed from them, and the evil spirits went out of them.

13 ¶ [k]Then certain of the vagabond Jews, exorcists, [l]took upon them to call over them which had evil spirits the name of the Lord Jesus, saying, We adjure you by Jesus whom Paul preacheth.

14 And there were seven sons of *one* Sceva, a Jew, *and* chief of the priests, which did so.

15 And the evil spirit answered and said, Jesus I know, and Paul I know; but who are ye?

16 And the man in whom the evil spirit was leaped on them, and overcame them, and prevailed against them, so that they fled out of that house naked and wounded.

17 And this was known to all the Jews and Greeks also dwelling at Ephesus; and [m]fear fell on them all, and the name of the Lord Jesus was magnified.

18 And many that believed came, and [n]confessed, and shewed their deeds.

19 Many of them also which used curious arts brought their books together, and burned them before all *men:* and they counted the price of them, and found *it* fifty thousand *pieces* of silver.

20 [o]So mightily grew the word of God and prevailed.

21 ¶ [p]After these things were ended, Paul [q]purposed in the spirit, when he had passed through Macedonia and Achaia, to go to Jerusalem, saying, After I have been there, [r]I must also see Rome.

22 So he sent into Macedonia two of [s]them that ministered unto him, Timotheus and [t]Erastus; but he himself stayed in Asia for a season.

23 And [u]the same time there arose no small stir about [v]that way.

24 For a certain *man* named Demetrius, a silversmith, which made silver shrines for Diana, brought [w]no small gain unto the craftsmen;

25 Whom he called together with the workmen of like occupation, and said, Sirs, ye know that by this craft we have our wealth.

26 Moreover ye see and hear, that not alone at Ephesus, but almost throughout all Asia, this Paul hath persuaded and turned away much people, saying that [x]they be no gods, which are made with hands:

27 So that not only this our craft is in danger to be set at nought; but also that the temple of the great goddess Diana should be despised, and her magnificence should be destroyed, whom all Asia and the world worshippeth.

28 And when they heard *these sayings,* they were full of wrath, and cried out, saying, Great *is* Diana of the Ephesians.

29 And the whole city was filled with con-

18:21 [o]1 Cor. 4:19; Heb. 6:3; Jam. 4:15
18:23 [p]Gal. 1:2 [q]ch. 14:22
18:24 [r]1 Cor. 1:12; Tit. 3:13
18:25 [s]Rom. 12:11 [t]ch. 19:3
18:27 [u]1 Cor. 3:6
18:28 [v]ch. 9:22
19:1 [w]1 Cor. 1:12
19:2 [x]1 Sam. 3:7; ch. 8:16
19:3 [y]ch. 18:25
19:4 [z]Matt. 3:11; John 1:15; ch. 1:5
19:5 [a]ch. 8:16
19:6 [b]ch. 6:6 [c]ch. 2:4
19:8 [d]ch. 17:2 [e]ch. 1:3
19:9 [f]2 Tim. 1:15; 2 Pet. 2:2; Jude 10 [g]ch. 9:2; ver. 23
19:10 [h]ch. 20:31
19:11 [i]Mark 16:20; ch. 14:3
19:12 [j]2 Kings 4:29; ch. 5:15
19:13 [k]Matt. 12:27 [l]Mark 9:38; Luke 9:49
19:17 [m]Luke 1:65; ch. 2:43
19:18 [n]Matt. 3:6
19:20 [o]ch. 6:7
19:21 [p]Rom. 15:25; Gal. 2:1 [q]ch. 20:22 [r]ch. 18:21; Rom. 15:24-28
19:22 [s]ch. 13:5 [t]Rom. 16:23; 2 Tim. 4:20
19:23 [u]2 Cor. 1:8 [v]ch. 9:2
19:24 [w]ch. 16:16
19:26 [x]Ps. 115:4; Isa. 44:10-20; Jer. 10:3

fusion: and having caught [y]Gaius and [z]Aristarchus, men of Macedonia, Paul's companions in travel, they rushed with one accord into the theatre.

30 And when Paul would have entered in unto the people, the disciples suffered him not.

31 And certain of the chief of Asia, which were his friends, sent unto him, desiring *him* that he would not adventure himself into the theatre.

32 Some therefore cried one thing, and some another: for the assembly was confused; and the more part knew not wherefore they were come together.

33 And they drew Alexander out of the multitude, the Jews putting him forward. And [a]Alexander [b]beckoned with the hand, and would have made his defence unto the people.

34 But when they knew that he was a Jew, all with one voice about the space of two hours cried out, Great *is* Diana of the Ephesians.

35 And when the townclerk had appeased the people, he said, *Ye* men of Ephesus, what man is there that knoweth not how that the city of the Ephesians is a worshipper of the great goddess Diana, and of the *image* which fell down from Jupiter?

36 Seeing then that these things cannot be spoken against, ye ought to be quiet, and to do nothing rashly.

37 For ye have brought hither these men, which are neither robbers of churches, nor yet blasphemers of your goddess.

38 Wherefore if Demetrius, and the craftsmen which are with him, have a matter against any man, the law is open, and there are deputies: let them implead one another.

39 But if ye enquire any thing concerning other matters, it shall be determined in a lawful assembly.

40 For we are in danger to be called in question for this day's uproar, there being no cause whereby we may give an account of this concourse.

41 And when he had thus spoken, he dismissed the assembly.

20 And after the uproar was ceased, Paul called unto *him* the disciples, and embraced *them,* and [c]departed for to go into Macedonia.

2 And when he had gone over those parts, and had given them much exhortation, he came into Greece,

3 And *there* abode three months. And [d]when the Jews laid wait for him, as he was about to sail into Syria, he purposed to return through Macedonia.

4 And there accompanied him into Asia Sopater of Berea; and of the Thessalonians, [e]Aristarchus and Secundus; and [f]Gaius of Derbe, and [g]Timotheus; and of Asia, [h]Tychicus and [i]Trophimus.

5 These going before tarried for us at Troas.

6 And we sailed away from Philippi after [j]the days of unleavened bread, and came unto them [k]to Troas in five days; where we abode seven days.

7 And upon [l]the first *day* of the week, when the disciples came together [m]to break bread, Paul preached unto them, ready to depart on the morrow; and continued his speech until midnight.

8 And there were many lights [n]in the upper chamber, where they were gathered together.

9 And there sat in a window a certain young man named Eutychus, being fallen into a deep sleep: and as Paul was long preaching, he sunk down with sleep, and fell down from the third loft, and was taken up dead.

10 And Paul went down, and [o]fell on him, and embracing *him* said, [p]Trouble not yourselves; for his life is in him.

11 When he therefore was come up again, and had broken bread, and eaten, and talked a long while, even till break of day, so he departed.

12 And they brought the young man alive, and were not a little comforted.

13 ¶ And we went before to ship, and sailed unto Assos, there intending to take in Paul: for so had he appointed, minding himself to go afoot.

14 And when he met with us at Assos, we took him in, and came to Mitylene.

15 And we sailed thence, and came the next *day* over against Chios; and the next *day* we arrived at Samos, and tarried at Trogyllium; and the next *day* we came to Miletus.

16 For Paul had determined to sail by Ephesus, because he would not spend the time in Asia: [q]for he hasted, if it were possible for him, [r]to be at Jerusalem [s]the day of Pentecost.

17 ¶ And from Miletus he sent to Ephesus, and called the elders of the church.

18 And when they were come to him, he said unto them, Ye know, [t]from the first day that I came into Asia, after what manner I have been with you at all seasons,

19 Serving the Lord with all humility of mind, and with many tears, and temptations, which befell me [u]by the lying in wait of the Jews:

20 *And* how [v]I kept back nothing that was profitable *unto you,* but have shewed you, and have taught you publickly, and from house to house,

21 [w]Testifying both to the Jews, and also to the Greeks, [x]repentance toward God, and faith toward our Lord Jesus Christ.

22 And now, behold, [y]I go bound in the spirit unto Jerusalem, not knowing the things that shall befall me there:

23 Save that [z]the Holy Ghost witnesseth in every city, saying that bonds and afflictions abide me.

24 But [a]none of these things move me, neither count I my life dear unto myself, [b]so

19:29 [y]Rom. 16:23; 1 Cor. 1:14 [z]ch. 20:4; Col. 4:10; Phil. 24
19:33 [a]1 Tim. 1:20; 2 Tim. 4:14 [b]ch. 12:17
20:1 [c]1 Cor. 16:5; 1 Tim. 1:3
20:3 [d]ch. 9:23; 2 Cor. 11:26
20:4 [e]ch. 19:29; Col. 4:10 [f]ch. 19:29 [g]ch. 16:1 [h]Eph. 6:21; Col. 4:7; 2 Tim. 4:12; Tit. 3:12 [i]ch. 21:29; 2 Tim. 4:20
20:6 [j]Ex. 12:14 [k]ch. 16:8; 2 Cor. 2:12; 2 Tim. 4:13
20:7 [l]1 Cor. 16:2; Rev. 1:10 [m]ch. 2:42; 1 Cor. 10:16
20:8 [n]ch. 1:13
20:10 [o]1 Kings 17:21; 2 Kings 4:34 [p]Matt. 9:24
20:16 [q]ch. 18:21 [r]ch. 24:17 [s]ch. 2:1; 1 Cor. 16:8
20:18 [t]ch. 18:19
20:19 [u]ver. 3
20:20 [v]ver. 27
20:21 [w]ch. 18:5 [x]Mark 1:15; Luke 24:47; ch. 2:38
20:22 [y]ch. 19:21
20:23 [z]ch. 21:4; 1 Thess. 3:3
20:24 [a]ch. 21:13; Rom. 8:35; 2 Cor. 4:16 [b]2 Tim. 4:7

that I might finish my course with joy, [c]and
the ministry, [d]which I have received of the
Lord Jesus, to testify the gospel of the grace
of God.
25 And now, behold, [e]I know that ye all,
among whom I have gone preaching the
kingdom of God, shall see my face no more.
26 Wherefore I take you to record this
day, that I *am* [f]pure from the blood of all
men.
27 For [g]I have not shunned to declare
unto you all [h]the counsel of God.
28 ¶ [i]Take heed therefore unto yourselves, and to all the flock, over the which
the Holy Ghost [j]hath made you overseers,
to feed the church of God, [k]which he hath
purchased [l]with his own blood.
29 For I know this, that after my departing [m]shall grievous wolves enter in among
you, not sparing the flock.
30 Also [n]of your own selves shall men
arise, speaking perverse things, to draw
away disciples after them.
31 Therefore watch, and remember, that
[o]by the space of three years I ceased not to
warn every one night and day with tears.
32 And now, brethren, I commend you to
God, and [p]to the word of his grace, which
is able [q]to build you up, and to give you [r]an
inheritance among all them which are sanctified.
33 [s]I have coveted no man's silver, or
gold, or apparel.
34 Yea, ye yourselves know, [t]that these
hands have ministered unto my necessities,
and to them that were with me.
35 I have shewed you all things, [u]how
that so labouring ye ought to support the
weak, and to remember the words of the
Lord Jesus, how he said, It is more blessed
to give than to receive.
36 ¶ And when he had thus spoken, he
[v]kneeled down, and prayed with them all.
37 And they all wept sore, and [w]fell on
Paul's neck, and kissed him,
38 Sorrowing most of all for the words
[x]which he spake, that they should see his
face no more. And they accompanied him
unto the ship.

21 And it came to pass, that after we
were gotten from them, and had
launched, we came with a straight course
unto Coos, and the *day* following unto
Rhodes, and from thence unto Patara:
2 And finding a ship sailing over unto
Phenicia, we went aboard, and set forth.
3 Now when we had discovered Cyprus,
we left it on the left hand, and sailed into
Syria, and landed at Tyre: for there the ship
was to unlade her burden.
4 And finding disciples, we tarried there
seven days: [y]who said to Paul through the
Spirit, that he should not go up to Jerusalem.
5 And when we had accomplished those
days, we departed and went our way; and
they all brought us on our way, with wives
and children, till *we were* out of the city:
and [z]we kneeled down on the shore, and
prayed.
6 And when we had taken our leave one
of another, we took ship; and they returned
[a]home again.
7 And when we had finished *our* course
from Tyre, we came to Ptolemais, and saluted the brethren, and abode with them
one day.
8 And the next *day* we that were of Paul's
company departed, and came unto Caesarea: and we entered into the house of Philip
[b]the evangelist, [c]which was *one* of the
seven; and abode with him.
9 And the same man had four daughters,
virgins, [d]which did prophesy.
10 And as we tarried *there* many days,
there came down from Judaea a certain
prophet, named [e]Agabus.
11 And when he was come unto us, he
took Paul's girdle, and bound his own
hands and feet, and said, Thus saith the
Holy Ghost, [f]So shall the Jews at Jerusalem bind the man that owneth this girdle,
and shall deliver *him* into the hands of the
Gentiles.
12 And when we heard these things, both
we, and they of that place, besought him not
to go up to Jerusalem.
13 Then Paul answered, [g]What mean ye
to weep and to break mine heart? for I am
ready not to be bound only, but also to die
at Jerusalem for the name of the Lord Jesus.
14 And when he would not be persuaded,
we ceased, saying, [h]The will of the Lord be
done.
15 And after those days we took up our
carriages, and went up to Jerusalem.
16 There went with us also *certain* of the
disciples of Caesarea, and brought with
them one Mnason of Cyprus, an old disciple, with whom we should lodge.
17 [i]And when we were come to Jerusalem, the brethren received us gladly.
18 And the *day* following Paul went in
with us unto [j]James; and all the elders
were present.
19 And when he had saluted them, [k]he
declared particularly what things God had
wrought among the Gentiles [l]by his ministry.
20 And when they heard *it*, they glorified
the Lord, and said unto him, Thou seest,
brother, how many thousands of Jews there
are which believe; and they are all [m]zealous
of the law:
21 And they are informed of thee, that
thou teachest all the Jews which are among
the Gentiles to forsake Moses, saying that
they ought not to circumcise *their* children,
neither to walk after the customs.
22 What is it therefore? the multitude
must needs come together: for they will
hear that thou art come.
23 Do therefore this that we say to thee:
We have four men which have a vow on
them;
24 Them take, and purify thyself with

20:24 [c]ch. 1:17; 2 Cor. 4:1 [d]Gal. 1:1; Tit. 1:3
20:25 [e]ver. 38; Rom. 15:23
20:26 [f]ch. 18:6; 2 Cor. 7:2
20:27 [g]ver. 20 [h]Luke 7:30; John 15:15; Eph. 1:11
20:28 [i]1 Tim. 4:16; 1 Pet. 5:2 [j]1 Cor. 12:28 [k]Eph. 1:7; Col. 1:14; Heb. 9:12; 1 Pet. 1:19; Rev. 5:9 [l]Heb. 9:14
20:29 [m]Matt. 7:15; 2 Pet. 2:1
20:30 [n]1 Tim. 1:20; 1 John 2:19
20:31 [o]ch. 19:10
20:32 [p]Heb. 13:9 [q]ch. 9:31 [r]ch. 26:18; Eph. 1:18; Col. 1:12; Heb. 9:15; 1 Pet. 1:4
20:33 [s]1 Sam. 12:3; 1 Cor. 9:12; 2 Cor. 7:2
20:34 [t]ch. 18:3; 1 Cor. 4:12; 1 Thess. 2:9; 2 Thess. 3:8
20:35 [u]Rom. 15:1; 1 Cor. 9:12; 2 Cor. 11:9; Eph. 4:28; 1 Thess. 4:11; 2 Thess. 3:8
20:36 [v]ch. 7:60
20:37 [w]Gen. 45:14
20:38 [x]ver. 25
21:4 [y]ver. 12; ch. 20:23
21:5 [z]ch. 20:36
21:6 [a]John 1:11
21:8 [b]Eph. 4:11; 2 Tim. 4:5 [c]ch. 6:5
21:9 [d]Joel 2:28; ch. 2:17
21:10 [e]ch. 11:28
21:11 [f]ver. 33; ch. 20:23
21:13 [g]ch. 20:24
21:14 [h]Matt. 6:10; Luke 11:2
21:17 [i]ch. 15:4
21:18 [j]ch. 15:13; Gal. 1:19
21:19 [k]ch. 15:4; Rom. 15:18 [l]ch. 1:17; ch. 20:24
21:20 [m]ch. 22:3; Rom. 10:2; Gal. 1:14

them, and be at charges with them, that they may [n]shave *their* heads: and all may know that those things, whereof they were informed concerning thee, are nothing; but *that* thou thyself also walkest orderly, and keepest the law.

25 As touching the Gentiles which believe, [o]we have written *and* concluded that they observe no such thing, save only that they keep themselves from *things* offered to idols, and from blood, and from strangled, and from fornication.

26 Then Paul took the men, and the next day purifying himself with them [p]entered into the temple, [q]to signify the accomplishment of the days of purification, until that an offering should be offered for every one of them.

27 And when the seven days were almost ended, [r]the Jews which were of Asia, when they saw him in the temple, stirred up all the people, and [s]laid hands on him,

28 Crying out, Men of Israel, help: This is the man, [t]that teacheth all *men* every where against the people, and the law, and this place: and further brought Greeks also into the temple, and hath polluted this holy place.

29 (For they had seen before with him in the city [u]Trophimus an Ephesian, whom they supposed that Paul had brought into the temple.)

30 And [v]all the city was moved, and the people ran together: and they took Paul, and drew him out of the temple: and forthwith the doors were shut.

31 And as they went about to kill him, tidings came unto the chief captain of the band, that all Jerusalem was in an uproar.

32 [w]Who immediately took soldiers and centurions, and ran down unto them: and when they saw the chief captain and the soldiers, they left beating of Paul.

33 Then the chief captain came near, and took him, and [x]commanded *him* to be bound with two chains; and demanded who he was, and what he had done.

34 And some cried one thing, some another, among the multitude: and when he could not know the certainty for the tumult, he commanded him to be carried into the castle.

35 And when he came upon the stairs, so it was, that he was borne of the soldiers for the violence of the people.

36 For the multitude of the people followed after, crying, [y]Away with him.

37 And as Paul was to be led into the castle, he said unto the chief captain, May I speak unto thee? Who said, Canst thou speak Greek?

38 [z]Art not thou that Egyptian, which before these days madest an uproar, and leddest out into the wilderness four thousand men that were murderers?

39 But Paul said, [a]I am a man *which am* a Jew of Tarsus, *a city* in Cilicia, a citizen of no mean city: and, I beseech thee, suffer me to speak unto the people.

40 And when he had given him licence, Paul stood on the stairs, and [b]beckoned with the hand unto the people. And when there was made a great silence, he spake unto *them* in the Hebrew tongue, saying,

22 Men, [c]brethren, and fathers, hear ye my defence *which I make* now unto you.

2 (And when they heard that he spake in the Hebrew tongue to them, they kept the more silence: and he saith,)

3 [d]I am verily a man *which am* a Jew, born in Tarsus, *a city* in Cilicia, yet brought up in this city [e]at the feet of [f]Gamaliel, *and* taught [g]according to the perfect manner of the law of the fathers, and [h]was zealous toward God, [i]as ye all are this day.

4 [j]And I persecuted this way unto the death, binding and delivering into prisons both men and women.

5 As also the high priest doth bear me witness, and [k]all the estate of the elders: [l]from whom also I received letters unto the brethren, and went to Damascus, to bring them which were there bound unto Jerusalem, for to be punished.

6 And [m]it came to pass, that, as I made my journey, and was come nigh unto Damascus about noon, suddenly there shone from heaven a great light round about me.

7 And I fell unto the ground, and heard a voice saying unto me, Saul, Saul, why persecutest thou me?

8 And I answered, Who art thou, Lord? And he said unto me, I am Jesus of Nazareth, whom thou persecutest.

9 And [n]they that were with me saw indeed the light, and were afraid; but they heard not the voice of him that spake to me.

10 And I said, What shall I do, Lord? And the Lord said unto me, Arise, and go into Damascus; and there it shall be told thee of all things which are appointed for thee to do.

11 And when I could not see for the glory of that light, being led by the hand of them that were with me, I came into Damascus.

12 And [o]one Ananias, a devout man according to the law, [p]having a good report of all the [q]Jews which dwelt *there*,

13 Came unto me, and stood, and said unto me, Brother Saul, receive thy sight. And the same hour I looked up upon him.

14 And he said, [r]The God of our fathers [s]hath chosen thee, that thou shouldest know his will, and [t]see [u]that Just One, and [v]shouldest hear the voice of his mouth.

15 [w]For thou shalt be his witness unto all men of [x]what thou hast seen and heard.

16 And now why tarriest thou? arise, and be baptized, [y]and wash away thy sins, [z]calling on the name of the Lord.

17 And [a]it came to pass, that, when I was come again to Jerusalem, even while I prayed in the temple, I was in a trance;

18 And [b]saw him saying unto me, [c]Make

21:24 [n]Num. 6:2; ch. 18:18
21:25 [o]ch. 15:20
21:26 [p]ch. 24:18 [q]Num. 6:13
21:27 [r]ch. 24:18 [s]ch. 26:21
21:28 [t]ch. 24:5
21:29 [u]ch. 20:4
21:30 [v]ch. 26:21
21:32 [w]ch. 23:27
21:33 [x]ver. 11; ch. 20:23
21:36 [y]Luke 23:18; John 19:15; ch. 22:22
21:38 [z]ch. 5:36
21:39 [a]ch. 9:11
21:40 [b]ch. 12:17
22:1 [c]ch. 7:2
22:3 [d]ch. 21:39; 2 Cor. 11:22; Phil. 3:5 [e]Deut. 33:3; 2 Kings 4:38; Luke 10:39 [f]ch. 5:34 [g]ch. 26:5 [h]ch. 21:20; Gal. 1:14 [i]Rom. 10:2
22:4 [j]ch. 8:3; Phil. 3:6; 1 Tim. 1:13
22:5 [k]Luke 22:66; ch. 4:5 [l]ch. 9:2
22:6 [m]ch. 9:3
22:9 [n]ch. 9:7; Dan. 10:7
22:12 [o]ch. 9:17 [p]ch. 10:22 [q]1 Tim. 3:7
22:14 [r]ch. 3:13 [s]ch. 9:15 [t]1 Cor. 9:1 [u]ch. 3:14 [v]1 Cor. 11:23; Gal. 1:12
22:15 [w]ch. 23:11 [x]ch. 4:20
22:16 [y]ch. 2:38; Heb. 10:22 [z]ch. 9:14; Rom. 10:13
22:17 [a]ch. 9:26; 2 Cor. 12:2
22:18 [b]ver. 14 [c]Matt. 10:14

haste, and get thee quickly out of Jerusalem: for they will not receive thy testimony
concerning me.
19 And I said, Lord, [d]they know that I
imprisoned and [e]beat in every synagogue
them that believed on thee:
20 [f]And when the blood of thy martyr
Stephen was shed, I also was standing by,
and [g]consenting unto his death, and kept
the raiment of them that slew him.
21 And he said unto me, Depart: [h]for I
will send thee far hence unto the Gentiles.
22 And they gave him audience unto this
word, and *then* lifted up their voices, and
said, [i]Away with such a *fellow* from the
earth: for it is not fit that [j]he should live.
23 And as they cried out, and cast off
their clothes, and threw dust into the air,
24 The chief captain commanded him to
be brought into the castle, and bade that he
should be examined by scourging; that he
might know wherefore they cried so against
him.
25 And as they bound him with thongs,
Paul said unto the centurion that stood by,
[k]Is it lawful for you to scourge a man that
is a Roman, and uncondemned?
26 When the centurion heard *that*, he
went and told the chief captain, saying,
Take heed what thou doest: for this man is
a Roman.
27 Then the chief captain came, and said
unto him, Tell me, art thou a Roman? He
said, Yea.
28 And the chief captain answered, With
a great sum obtained I this freedom. And
Paul said, But I was *free* born.
29 Then straightway they departed from
him which should have examined him: and
the chief captain also was afraid, after he
knew that he was a Roman, and because he
had bound him.
30 On the morrow, because he would
have known the certainty wherefore he was
accused of the Jews, he loosed him from *his*
bands, and commanded the chief priests
and all their council to appear, and brought
Paul down, and set him before them.
23 And Paul, earnestly beholding the
council, said, Men *and* brethren, [l]I
have lived in all good conscience before
God until this day.
2 And the high priest Ananias commanded them that stood by him [m]to smite
him on the mouth.
3 Then said Paul unto him, God shall
smite thee, *thou* whited wall: for sittest thou
to judge me after the law, and [n]command-
est me to be smitten contrary to the law?
4 And they that stood by said, Revilest
thou God's high priest?
5 Then said Paul, [o]I wist not, brethren,
that he was the high priest: for it is written,
[p]Thou shalt not speak evil of the ruler of
thy people.
6 But when Paul perceived that the one
part were Sadducees, and the other Pharisees, he cried out in the council, Men *and*
brethren, [q]I am a Pharisee, the son of a
Pharisee: [r]of the hope and resurrection of
the dead I am called in question.
7 And when he had so said, there arose a
dissension between the Pharisees and the
Sadducees: and the multitude was divided.
8 [s]For the Sadducees say that there is no
resurrection, neither angel, nor spirit: but
the Pharisees confess both.
9 And there arose a great cry: and the
scribes *that were* of the Pharisees' part
arose, and strove, saying, [t]We find no evil
in this man: but [u]if a spirit or an angel hath
spoken to him, [v]let us not fight against God.
10 And when there arose a great dissension, the chief captain, fearing lest Paul
should have been pulled in pieces of them,
commanded the soldiers to go down, and to
take him by force from among them, and to
bring *him* into the castle.
11 And [w]the night following the Lord
stood by him, and said, Be of good cheer,
Paul: for as thou hast testified of me in Jerusalem, so must thou bear witness also at
Rome.
12 And when it was day, [x]certain of the
Jews banded together, and bound themselves under a curse, saying that they would
neither eat nor drink till they had killed
Paul.
13 And they were more than forty which
had made this conspiracy.
14 And they came to the chief priests and
elders, and said, We have bound ourselves
under a great curse, that we will eat nothing
until we have slain Paul.
15 Now therefore ye with the council signify to the chief captain that he bring him
down unto you to morrow, as though ye
would enquire something more perfectly
concerning him: and we, or ever he come
near, are ready to kill him.
16 And when Paul's sister's son heard of
their lying in wait, he went and entered into
the castle, and told Paul.
17 Then Paul called one of the centurions
unto *him*, and said, Bring this young man
unto the chief captain: for he hath a certain
thing to tell him.
18 So he took him, and brought *him* to the
chief captain, and said, Paul the prisoner
called me unto *him*, and prayed me to bring
this young man unto thee, who hath something to say unto thee.
19 Then the chief captain took him by the
hand, and went *with him* aside privately,
and asked *him*, What is that thou hast to
tell me?
20 And he said, [y]The Jews have agreed to
desire thee that thou wouldest bring down
Paul to morrow into the council, as though
they would enquire somewhat of him more
perfectly.
21 But do not thou yield unto them: for
there lie in wait for him of them more than
forty men, which have bound themselves
with an oath, that they will neither eat nor
drink till they have killed him: and now are

22:19 [d]ver. 4; ch. 8:3 [e]Matt. 10:17
22:20 [f]ch. 7:58 [g]Luke 11:48; ch. 8:1; Rom. 1:32
22:21 [h]ch. 9:15; Rom. 1:5; Gal. 1:15; Eph. 3:7; 1 Tim. 2:7; 2 Tim. 1:11
22:22 [i]ch. 21:36 [j]ch. 25:24
22:25 [k]ch. 16:37
23:1 [l]ch. 24:16; 1 Cor. 4:4; 2 Cor. 1:12; 2 Tim. 1:3; Heb. 13:18
23:2 [m]1 Kings 22:24; Jer. 20:2; John 18:22
23:3 [n]Lev. 19:35; Deut. 25:1; John 7:51
23:5 [o]ch. 24:17 [p]Ex. 22:28; Eccl. 10:20; 2 Pet. 2:10; Jude 8
23:6 [q]ch. 26:5; Phil. 3:5 [r]ch. 24:15
23:8 [s]Matt. 22:23; Mark 12:18; Luke 20:27
23:9 [t]ch. 25:25 [u]ch. 22:7 [v]ch. 5:39
23:11 [w]ch. 18:9
23:12 [x]ver. 21; ch. 25:3
23:20 [y]ver. 12

they ready, looking for a promise from thee.

22 So the chief captain *then* let the young man depart, and charged *him, See thou* tell no man that thou hast shewed these things to me.

23 And he called unto *him* two centurions, saying, Make ready two hundred soldiers to go to Caesarea, and horsemen threescore and ten, and spearmen two hundred, at the third hour of the night;

24 And provide *them* beasts, that they may set Paul on, and bring *him* safe unto Felix the governor.

25 And he wrote a letter after this manner:

26 Claudius Lysias unto the most excellent governor Felix *sendeth* greeting.

27 [z]This man was taken of the Jews, and should have been killed of them: then came I with an army, and rescued him, having understood that he was a Roman.

28 [a]And when I would have known the cause wherefore they accused him, I brought him forth into their council:

29 Whom I perceived to be accused [b]of questions of their law, [c]but to have nothing laid to his charge worthy of death or of bonds.

30 And [d]when it was told me how that the Jews laid wait for the man, I sent straightway to thee, and [e]gave commandment to his accusers also to say before thee what *they had* against him. Farewell.

31 Then the soldiers, as it was commanded them, took Paul, and brought *him* by night to Antipatris.

32 On the morrow they left the horsemen to go with him, and returned to the castle:

33 Who, when they came to Caesarea, and delivered the epistle to the governor, presented Paul also before him.

34 And when the governor had read *the letter*, he asked of what province he was. And when he understood that *he was* of [f]Cilicia;

35 [g]I will hear thee, said he, when thine accusers are also come. And he commanded him to be kept in [h]Herod's judgment hall.

24

24 And after [i]five days [j]Ananias the high priest descended with the elders, and *with* a certain orator *named* Tertullus, who informed the governor against Paul.

2 And when he was called forth, Tertullus began to accuse *him*, saying, Seeing that by thee we enjoy great quietness, and that very worthy deeds are done unto this nation by thy providence,

3 We accept *it* always, and in all places, most noble Felix, with all thankfulness.

4 Notwithstanding, that I be not further tedious unto thee, I pray thee that thou wouldest hear us of thy clemency a few words.

5 [k]For we have found this man *a* pestilent *fellow*, and a mover of sedition among all the Jews throughout the world, and a ringleader of the sect of the Nazarenes:

6 [l]Who also hath gone about to profane the temple: whom we took, and would [m]have judged according to our law.

7 [n]But the chief captain Lysias came *upon us*, and with great violence took *him* away out of our hands,

8 [o]Commanding his accusers to come unto thee: by examining of whom thyself mayest take knowledge of all these things, whereof we accuse him.

9 And the Jews also assented, saying that these things were so.

10 Then Paul, after that the governor had beckoned unto him to speak, answered, Forasmuch as I know that thou hast been of many years a judge unto this nation, I do the more cheerfully answer for myself:

11 Because that thou mayest understand, that there are yet but twelve days since I went up to Jerusalem [p]for to worship.

12 [q]And they neither found me in the temple disputing with any man, neither raising up the people, neither in the synagogues, nor in the city:

13 Neither can they prove the things whereof they now accuse me.

14 But this I confess unto thee, that after [r]the way which they call heresy, so worship I the [s]God of my fathers, believing all things which are written in [t]the law and in the prophets:

15 And [u]have hope toward God, which they themselves also allow, [v]that there shall be a resurrection of the dead, both of the just and unjust.

16 And [w]herein do I exercise myself, to have always a conscience void of offense toward God, and *toward* men.

17 Now after many years [x]I came to bring alms to my nation, and offerings.

18 [y]Whereupon certain Jews from Asia found me purified in the temple, neither with multitude, nor with tumult.

19 [z]Who ought to have been here before thee, and object, if they had ought against me.

20 Or else let these same *here* say, if they have found any evil doing in me, while I stood before the council,

21 Except it be for this one voice, that I cried standing among them, [a]Touching the resurrection of the dead I am called in question by you this day.

22 And when Felix heard these things, having more perfect knowledge of *that* way, he deferred them, and said, When [b]Lysias the chief captain shall come down, I will know the uttermost of your matter.

23 And he commanded a centurion to keep Paul, and to let *him* have liberty, and [c]that he should forbid none of his acquaintance to minister or come unto him.

24 And after certain days, when Felix came with his wife Drusilla, which was a Jewess, he sent for Paul, and heard him concerning the faith in Christ.

23:27 *z*ch. 21:33
23:28 *a*ch. 22:30
23:29 *b*ch. 18:15 *c*ch. 26:31
23:30 *d*ver. 20 *e*ch. 24:8
23:34 *f*ch. 21:39
23:35 *g*ch. 24:1 *h*Matt. 27:27
24:1 *i*ch. 21:27 *j*ch. 23:2
24:5 *k*Luke 23:2; ch. 6:13; 1 Pet. 2:12
24:6 *l*ch. 21:28 *m*John 18:31
24:7 *n*ch. 21:33
24:8 *o*ch. 23:30
24:11 *p*ver. 17; ch. 21:26
24:12 *q*ch. 25:8
24:14 *r*Am. 8:14; ch. 9:2 *s*2 Tim. 1:3 *t*ch. 26:22
24:15 *u*ch. 28:23 *v*Dan. 12:2; John 5:28
24:16 *w*ch. 23:1
24:17 *x*ch. 11:29; Rom. 15:25; 2 Cor. 8:4; Gal. 2:10
24:18 *y*ch. 21:26
24:19 *z*ch. 23:30
24:21 *a*ch. 23:6
24:22 *b*ver. 7
24:23 *c*ch. 27:3

25 And as he reasoned of righteousness, temperance, and judgment to come, Felix trembled, and answered, Go thy way for this time; when I have a convenient season, I will call for thee.

26 He hoped also that [d]money should have been given him of Paul, that he might loose him: wherefore he sent for him the oftener, and communed with him.

27 But after two years Porcius Festus came into Felix' room: and Felix, [e]willing to shew the Jews a pleasure, left Paul bound.

25 Now when Festus was come into the province, after three days he ascended from Caesarea to Jerusalem.

2 [f]Then the high priest and the chief of the Jews informed him against Paul, and besought him,

3 And desired favour against him, that he would send for him to Jerusalem, [g]laying wait in the way to kill him.

4 But Festus answered, that Paul should be kept at Caesarea, and that he himself would depart shortly *thither.*

5 Let them therefore, said he, which among you are able, go down with *me,* and accuse this man, [h]if there be any wickedness in him.

6 And when he had tarried among them more than ten days, he went down unto Caesarea; and the next day sitting on the judgment seat commanded Paul to be brought.

7 And when he was come, the Jews which came down from Jerusalem stood round about, [i]and laid many and grievous complaints against Paul, which they could not prove.

8 While he answered for himself, [j]Neither against the law of the Jews, neither against the temple, nor yet against Caesar, have I offended any thing at all.

9 But Festus, [k]willing to do the Jews a pleasure, answered Paul, and said, [l]Wilt thou go up to Jerusalem, and there be judged of these things before me?

10 Then said Paul, I stand at Caesar's judgment seat, where I ought to be judged: to the Jews have I done no wrong, as thou very well knowest.

11 [m]For if I be an offender, or have committed any thing worthy of death, I refuse not to die: but if there be none of these things whereof these accuse me, no man may deliver me unto them. [n]I appeal unto Caesar.

12 Then Festus, when he had conferred with the council, answered, Hast thou appealed unto Caesar? unto Caesar shalt thou go.

13 And after certain days king Agrippa and Bernice came unto Caesarea to salute Festus.

14 And when they had been there many days, Festus declared Paul's cause unto the king, saying, [o]There is a certain man left in bonds by Felix:

15 [p]About whom, when I was at Jerusalem, the chief priests and the elders of the Jews informed *me,* desiring *to have* judgment against him.

16 [q]To whom I answered, It is not the manner of the Romans to deliver any man to die, before that he which is accused have the accusers face to face, and have licence to answer for himself concerning the crime laid against him.

17 Therefore, when they were come hither, [r]without any delay on the morrow I sat on the judgment seat, and commanded the man to be brought forth.

18 Against whom when the accusers stood up, they brought none accusation of such things as I supposed:

19 [s]But had certain questions against him of their own superstition, and of one Jesus, which was dead, whom Paul affirmed to be alive.

20 And because I doubted of such manner of questions, I asked *him* whether he would go to Jerusalem, and there be judged of these matters.

21 But when Paul had appealed to be reserved unto the hearing of Augustus, I commanded him to be kept till I might send him to Caesar.

22 Then [t]Agrippa said unto Festus, I would also hear the man myself. To morrow, said he, thou shalt hear him.

23 And on the morrow, when Agrippa was come, and Bernice, with great pomp, and was entered into the place of hearing, with the chief captains, and principal men of the city, at Festus' commandment Paul was brought forth.

24 And Festus said, King Agrippa, and all men which are here present with us, ye see this man, about whom [u]all the multitude of the Jews have dealt with me, both at Jerusalem, and *also* here, crying that he ought [v]not to live any longer.

25 But when I found that [w]he had committed nothing worthy of death, [x]and that he himself hath appealed to Augustus, I have determined to send him.

26 Of whom I have no certain thing to write unto my lord. Wherefore I have brought him forth before you, and specially before thee, O king Agrippa, that, after examination had, I might have somewhat to write.

27 For it seemeth to me unreasonable to send a prisoner, and not withal to signify the crimes *laid* against him.

26 Then Agrippa said unto Paul, Thou art permitted to speak for thyself. Then Paul stretched forth the hand, and answered for himself:

2 I think myself happy, king Agrippa, because I shall answer for myself this day before thee touching all the things whereof I am accused of the Jews:

3 Especially *because I know* thee to be expert in all customs and questions which are among the Jews: wherefore I beseech thee to hear me patiently.

24:26 [d]Ex. 23:8
24:27 [e]Ex. 23:2; ch. 12:3
25:2 [f]ch. 24:1; ver. 15
25:3 [g]ch. 23:12
25:5 [h]ch. 18:14; ver. 18
25:7 [i]Mark 15:3; Luke 23:2; ch. 24:5
25:8 [j]ch. 6:13
25:9 [k]ch. 24:27 [l]ver. 20
25:11 [m]ver. 25; ch. 18:14 [n]ch. 26:32
25:14 [o]ch. 24:27
25:15 [p]ver. 2
25:16 [q]ver. 4
25:17 [r]ver. 6
25:19 [s]ch. 18:15
25:22 [t]ch. 9:15
25:24 [u]ver. 2 [v]ch. 22:22
25:25 [w]ch. 23:9 [x]ver. 11

4 My manner of life from my youth, which was at the first among mine own nation at Jerusalem, know all the Jews;

5 Which knew me from the beginning, if they would testify, that after [y]the most straitest sect of our religion I lived a Pharisee.

6 [z]And now I stand and am judged for the hope of [a]the promise made of God unto our fathers:

7 Unto which *promise* [b]our twelve tribes, instantly serving *God* [c]day and night, [d]hope to come. For which hope's sake, king Agrippa, I am accused of the Jews.

8 Why should it be thought a thing incredible with you, that God should raise the dead?

9 [e]I verily thought with myself, that I ought to do many things contrary to the name of Jesus of Nazareth.

10 [f]Which thing I also did in Jerusalem: and many of the saints did I shut up in prison, having received authority [g]from the chief priests; and when they were put to death, I gave my voice against *them*.

11 [h]And I punished them oft in every synagogue, and compelled *them* to blaspheme; and being exceedingly mad against them, I persecuted *them* even unto strange cities.

12 [i]Whereupon as I went to Damascus with authority and commission from the chief priests,

13 At midday, O king, I saw in the way a light from heaven, above the brightness of the sun, shining round about me and them which journeyed with me.

14 And when we were all fallen to the earth, I heard a voice speaking unto me, and saying in the Hebrew tongue, Saul, Saul, why persecutest thou me? *it is* hard for thee to kick against the pricks.

15 And I said, Who art thou, Lord? And he said, I am Jesus whom thou persecutest.

16 But rise, and stand upon thy feet: for I have appeared unto thee for this purpose, [j]to make thee a minister and a witness both of these things which thou hast seen, and of those things in the which I will appear unto thee;

17 Delivering thee from the people, and *from* the Gentiles, [k]unto whom now I send thee,

18 [l]To open their eyes, *and* [m]to turn *them* from darkness to light, and *from* the power of Satan unto God, [n]that they may receive forgiveness of sins, and [o]inheritance among them which are [p]sanctified by faith that is in me.

19 Whereupon, O king Agrippa, I was not disobedient unto the heavenly vision:

20 But [q]shewed first unto them of Damascus, and at Jerusalem, and throughout all the coasts of Judaea, and *then* to the Gentiles, that they should repent and turn to God, and do [r]works meet for repentance.

21 For these causes [s]the Jews caught me in the temple, and went about to kill *me*.

22 Having therefore obtained help of God, I continue unto this day, witnessing both to small and great, saying none other things than those [t]which the prophets and [u]Moses did say should come:

23 [v]That Christ should suffer, *and* [w]that he should be the first that should rise from the dead, and [x]should shew light unto the people, and to the Gentiles.

24 And as he thus spake for himself, Festus said with a loud voice, Paul, [y]thou art beside thyself; much learning doth make thee mad.

25 But he said, I am not mad, most noble Festus; but speak forth the words of truth and soberness.

26 For the king knoweth of these things, before whom also I speak freely: for I am persuaded that none of these things are hidden from him; for this thing was not done in a corner.

27 King Agrippa, believest thou the prophets? I know that thou believest.

28 Then Agrippa said unto Paul, Almost thou persuadest me to be a Christian.

29 And Paul said, [z]I would to God, that not only thou, but also all that hear me this day, were both almost, and altogether such as I am, except these bonds.

30 And when he had thus spoken, the king rose up, and the governor, and Bernice, and they that sat with them:

31 And when they were gone aside, they talked between themselves, saying, [a]This man doeth nothing worthy of death or of bonds.

32 Then said Agrippa unto Festus, This man might have been set at liberty, [b]if he had not appealed unto Caesar.

27 And when [c]it was determined that we should sail into Italy, they delivered Paul and certain other prisoners unto *one* named Julius, a centurion of Augustus' band.

2 And entering into a ship of Adramyttium, we launched, meaning to sail by the coasts of Asia; *one* [d]Aristarchus, a Macedonian of Thessalonica, being with us.

3 And the next *day* we touched at Sidon. And Julius [e]courteously entreated Paul, and gave *him* liberty to go unto his friends to refresh himself.

4 And when we had launched from thence, we sailed under Cyprus, because the winds were contrary.

5 And when we had sailed over the sea of Cilicia and Pamphylia, we came to Myra, *a city* of Lycia.

6 And there the centurion found a ship of Alexandria sailing into Italy; and he put us therein.

7 And when we had sailed slowly many days, and scarce were come over against Cnidus, the wind not suffering us, we sailed under Crete, over against Salmone;

8 And, hardly passing it, came unto a place which is called The fair havens; nigh whereunto was the city *of* Lasea.

9 Now when much time was spent, and

26:5 [y]ch. 22:3; Phil. 3:5
26:6 [z]ch. 23:6 [a]Gen. 3:15; Deut. 18:15; 2 Sam. 7:12; Ps. 132:11; Isa. 4:2; Jer. 23:5; Ezek. 34:23; Dan. 9:24; Mic. 7:20; ch. 13:32; Rom. 15:8; Tit. 2:13
26:7 [b]Jam. 1:1 [c]Luke 2:37; 1 Tim. 5:5; 1 Thess. 3:10 [d]Phil. 3:11
26:9 [e]John 16:2; 1 Tim. 1:13
26:10 [f]ch. 8:3; Gal. 1:13 [g]ch. 9:14
26:11 [h]ch. 22:19
26:12 [i]ch. 9:3
26:16 [j]ch. 22:15
26:17 [k]ch. 22:21
26:18 [l]Isa. 35:5; Luke 1:79; John 8:12; 2 Cor. 4:4; Eph. 1:18; 1 Thess. 5:5 [m]2 Cor. 6:14; Eph. 4:18; Col. 1:13; 1 Pet. 2:9 [n]Luke 1:77 [o]Eph. 1:11; Col. 1:12 [p]ch. 20:32
26:20 [q]ch. 9:20 [r]Matt. 3:8
26:21 [s]ch. 21:30
26:22 [t]Luke 24:27; ch. 24:14; Rom. 3:21 [u]John 5:46
26:23 [v]Luke 24:26 [w]1 Cor. 15:20; Col. 1:18; Rev. 1:5 [x]Luke 2:32
26:24 [y]2 Kings 9:11; John 10:20; 1 Cor. 1:23
26:29 [z]1 Cor. 7:7
26:31 [a]ch. 23:9
26:32 [b]ch. 25:11
27:1 [c]ch. 25:12
27:2 [d]ch. 19:29
27:3 [e]ch. 24:23

when sailing was now dangerous, [f]because the fast was now already past, Paul admonished *them,*

10 And said unto them, Sirs, I perceive that this voyage will be with hurt and much damage, not only of the lading and ship, but also of our lives.

11 Nevertheless the centurion believed the master and the owner of the ship, more than those things which were spoken by Paul.

12 And because the haven was not commodious to winter in, the more part advised to depart thence also, if by any means they might attain to Phenice, *and there* to winter; *which is* an haven of Crete, and lieth toward the south west and north west.

13 And when the south wind blew softly, supposing that they had obtained *their* purpose, loosing *thence,* they sailed close by Crete.

14 But not long after there arose against it a tempestuous wind, called Euroclydon.

15 And when the ship was caught, and could not bear up into the wind, we let *her* drive.

16 And running under a certain island which is called Clauda, we had much work to come by the boat:

17 Which when they had taken up, they used helps, undergirding the ship; and, fearing lest they should fall into the quicksands, strake sail, and so were driven.

18 And we being exceedingly tossed with a tempest, the next *day* they lightened the ship;

19 And the third *day* [g]we cast out with our own hands the tackling of the ship.

20 And when neither sun nor stars in many days appeared, and no small tempest lay on *us,* all hope that we should be saved was then taken away.

21 But after long abstinence, Paul stood forth in the midst of them, and said, Sirs, ye should have hearkened unto me, and not have loosed from Crete, and to have gained this harm and loss.

22 And now I exhort you to be of good cheer: for there shall be no loss of *any man's* life among you, but of the ship.

23 [h]For there stood by me this night the angel of God, whose I am, and [i]whom I serve,

24 Saying, Fear not, Paul; thou must be brought before Caesar: and, lo, God hath given thee all them that sail with thee.

25 Wherefore, sirs, be of good cheer: [j]for I believe God, that it shall be even as it was told me.

26 Howbeit [k]we must be cast upon a certain island.

27 But when the fourteenth night was come, as we were driven up and down in Adria, about midnight the shipmen deemed that they drew near to some country;

28 And sounded, and found *it* twenty fathoms: and when they had gone a little further, they sounded again, and found *it* fifteen fathoms.

29 Then fearing lest we should have fallen upon rocks, they cast four anchors out of the stern, and wished for the day.

30 And as the shipmen were about to flee out of the ship, when they had let down the boat into the sea, under colour as though they would have cast anchors out of the foreship,

31 Paul said to the centurion and to the soldiers, Except these abide in the ship, ye cannot be saved.

32 Then the soldiers cut off the ropes of the boat, and let her fall off.

33 And while the day was coming on, Paul besought *them* all to take meat, saying, This day is the fourteenth day that ye have tarried and continued fasting, having taken nothing.

34 Wherefore I pray you to take *some* meat: for this is for your health: for [l]there shall not an hair fall from the head of any of you.

35 And when he had thus spoken, he took bread, and [m]gave thanks to God in presence of them all: and when he had broken *it,* he began to eat.

36 Then were they all of good cheer, and they also took *some* meat.

37 And we were in all in the ship two hundred threescore and sixteen [n]souls.

38 And when they had eaten enough, they lightened the ship, and cast out the wheat into the sea.

39 And when it was day, they knew not the land: but they discovered a certain creek with a shore, into the which they were minded, if it were possible, to thrust in the ship.

40 And when they had taken up the anchors, they committed *themselves* unto the sea, and loosed the rudder bands, and hoised up the mainsail to the wind, and made toward shore.

41 And falling into a place where two seas met, [o]they ran the ship aground; and the forepart stuck fast, and remained unmoveable, but the hinder part was broken with the violence of the waves.

42 And the soldiers' counsel was to kill the prisoners, lest any of them should swim out, and escape.

43 But the centurion, willing to save Paul, kept them from *their* purpose; and commanded that they which could swim should cast *themselves* first *into the sea,* and get to land:

44 And the rest, some on boards, and some on *broken pieces* of the ship. And so it came to pass, [p]that they escaped all safe to land.

28

And when they were escaped, then they knew that [q]the island was called Melita.

2 And the [r]barbarous people shewed us no little kindness: for they kindled a fire,

27:9 [f]Lev. 23:27
27:19 [g]Jonah 1:5
27:23 [h]ch. 23:11 [i]Dan. 6:16; Rom. 1:9; 2 Tim. 1:3
27:25 [j]Luke 1:45; Rom. 4:20; 2 Tim. 1:12
27:26 [k]ch. 28:1
27:34 [l]1 Kings 1:52; Matt. 10:30; Luke 12:7
27:35 [m]1 Sam. 9:13; Matt. 15:36; Mark 8:6; John 6:11; 1 Tim. 4:3
27:37 [n]ch. 2:41; Rom. 13:1; 1 Pet. 3:20
27:41 [o]2 Cor. 11:25
27:44 [p]ver. 22
28:1 [q]ch. 27:26
28:2 [r]Rom. 1:14; 1 Cor. 14:11; Col. 3:11

and received us every one, because of the
present rain, and because of the cold.
3 And when Paul had gathered a bundle
of sticks, and laid *them* on the fire, there
came a viper out of the heat, and fastened
on his hand.
4 And when the barbarians saw the *venomous* beast hang on his hand, they said
among themselves, No doubt this man is a
murderer, whom, though he hath escaped
the sea, yet vengeance suffereth not to live.
5 And he shook off the beast into the fire,
and [s]felt no harm.
6 Howbeit they looked when he should
have swollen, or fallen down dead suddenly: but after they had looked a great
while, and saw no harm come to him, they
changed their minds, and [t]said that he was
a god.
7 In the same quarters were possessions
of the chief man of the island, whose name
was Publius; who received us, and lodged
us three days courteously.
8 And it came to pass, that the father of
Publius lay sick of a fever and of a bloody
flux: to whom Paul entered in, and [u]prayed,
and [v]laid his hands on him, and healed him.
9 So when this was done, others also,
which had diseases in the island, came, and
were healed:
10 Who also honoured us with many
[w]honours; and when we departed, they
laded *us* with such things as were necessary.
11 And after three months we departed in
a ship of Alexandria, which had wintered in
the isle, whose sign was Castor and Pollux.
12 And landing at Syracuse, we tarried
there three days.
13 And from thence we fetched a compass, and came to Rhegium: and after one
day the south wind blew, and we came the
next day to Puteoli:
14 Where we found brethren, and were
desired to tarry with them seven days: and
so we went toward Rome.
15 And from thence, when the brethren
heard of us, they came to meet us as far as
Appii forum, and The three taverns: whom
when Paul saw, he thanked God, and took
courage.
16 And when we came to Rome, the centurion delivered the prisoners to the captain
of the guard: but [x]Paul was suffered to
dwell by himself with a soldier that kept
him.
17 And it came to pass, that after three
days Paul called the chief of the Jews together: and when they were come together,
he said unto them, Men *and* brethren,

28:5 [s]Mark 16:18; Luke 10:19
28:6 [t]ch. 14:11
28:8 [u]Jam. 5:14 [v]Mark 6:5; Luke 4:40; ch. 19:11; 1 Cor. 12:9
28:10 [w]Matt. 15:6; 1 Tim. 5:17
28:16 [x]ch. 24:25
28:17 [y]ch. 24:12 [z]ch. 21:33
28:18 [a]ch. 22:24
28:19 [b]ch. 25:11
28:20 [c]ch. 26:6 [d]ch. 26:29; Eph. 3:1; 2 Tim. 1:16; Philem. 10
28:22 [e]Luke 2:34; ch. 24:5; 1 Pet. 2:12
28:23 [f]Luke 24:27; ch. 17:3 [g]ch. 26:6
28:24 [h]ch. 14:4
28:26 [i]Isa. 6:9; Jer. 5:21; Ezek. 12:2; Matt. 13:14; Mark 4:12; Luke 8:10; John 12:40; Rom. 11:8
28:28 [j]Matt. 21:41; ch. 13:46; Rom. 11:11
28:31 [k]ch. 4:31; Eph. 6:19

[y]though I have committed nothing against
the people, or customs of our fathers, yet
[z]was I delivered prisoner from Jerusalem
into the hands of the Romans.
18 Who, [a]when they had examined me,
would have let *me* go, because there was no
cause of death in me.
19 But when the Jews spake against *it*, [b]I
was constrained to appeal unto Caesar; not
that I had ought to accuse my nation of.
20 For this cause therefore have I called
for you, to see *you*, and to speak with *you*:
because that [c]for the hope of Israel I am
bound with [d]this chain.
21 And they said unto him, We neither
received letters out of Judaea concerning
thee, neither any of the brethren that came
shewed or spake any harm of thee.
22 But we desire to hear of thee what thou
thinkest: for as concerning this sect, we
know that every where [e]it is spoken
against.
23 And when they had appointed him a
day, there came many to him into *his* lodging; [f]to whom he expounded and testified
the kingdom of God, persuading them concerning Jesus, [g]both out of the law of Moses, and *out of* the prophets, from morning
till evening.
24 And [h]some believed the things which
were spoken, and some believed not.
25 And when they agreed not among
themselves, they departed, after that Paul
had spoken one word, Well spake the Holy
Ghost by Esaias the prophet unto our fathers,
26 Saying, [i]Go unto this people, and say,
Hearing ye shall hear, and shall not understand; and seeing ye shall see, and not perceive:
27 For the heart of this people is waxed
gross, and their ears are dull of hearing, and
their eyes have they closed; lest they should
see with *their* eyes, and hear with *their* ears,
and understand with *their* heart, and should
be converted, and I should heal them.
28 Be it known therefore unto you, that
the salvation of God is sent [j]unto the Gentiles, and *that* they will hear it.
29 And when he had said these words, the
Jews departed, and had great reasoning
among themselves.
30 And Paul dwelt two whole years in his
own hired house, and received all that came
in unto him,
31 [k]Preaching the kingdom of God, and
teaching those things which concern the
Lord Jesus Christ, with all confidence, no
man forbidding him.

ROMANS

Paul identifies himself as the writer of Romans. It was written in A.D. 57 or A.D. 58. Paul begins his letter to the Romans with a greeting to the church at Rome, followed by a litany of sins that befall mankind. From that basis, Paul begins a detailed argument and description of God's intervention in the person of Jesus Christ. Included in this discussion is its applicability to Jews an Gentiles alike, where righteousness comes from, how it is obtained, the lifelong experience that is sanctification, and the struggles everyone faces in life. He then focuses on the problem of Israel's rejection of the Messiah and its meaning. Finally, Paul closes with additional discussion of righteousness and the sanctified life.

I. Greetings to the church at Rome, 1:1–1:17
II. The universality of sin, 1:18–3:20
III. Righteousness and justification, 3:21–5:21
IV. The principle of sanctification, 6:1–8:39
V. The problem of Israel, 9:1–11:36
VI. The practical teachings on sanctification, 12:1–15:13
VII. Paul's closing remarks and personal messages, 15:14–16:27

---

1 Paul, a servant of Jesus Christ, [a]called
to be an apostle, [b]separated unto the
gospel of God,
2 ([c]Which he had promised afore [d]by his
prophets in the holy scriptures,)
3 Concerning his Son Jesus Christ our
Lord, [e]which was [f]made of the seed of David according to the flesh;
4 And [g]declared *to be* the Son of God
with power, according [h]to the spirit of holiness, by the resurrection from the dead:
5 By whom [i]we have received grace and
apostleship, for [j]obedience to the faith
among all nations, [k]for his name:
6 Among whom are ye also the called of
Jesus Christ:
7 To all that be in Rome, beloved of God,
[l]called *to be* saints: [m]Grace to you and
peace from God our Father, and the Lord
Jesus Christ.
8 First, [n]I thank my God through Jesus
Christ for you all, that [o]your faith is spoken
of throughout the whole world.
9 For [p]God is my witness, [q]whom I serve
with my spirit in the gospel of his Son, that
[r]without ceasing I make mention of you always in my prayers;
10 [s]Making request, if by any means now
at length I might have a prosperous journey
[t]by the will of God to come unto you.
11 For I long to see you, that I may impart
unto you some spiritual gift, to the end ye
may be established;
12 That is, that I may be comforted together with you by [u]the mutual faith both
of you and me.
13 Now I would not have you ignorant,
brethren, that oftentimes I purposed to
come unto you, (but [v]was let hitherto,) that
I might have some [w]fruit among you also,
even as among other Gentiles.
14 [x]I am debtor both to the Greeks, and
to the Barbarians; both to the wise, and to
the unwise.
15 So, as much as in me is, I am ready to
preach the gospel to you that are at Rome
also.
16 For [y]I am not ashamed of the gospel of
Christ: for [z]it is the power of God unto sal
vation to every one that believeth; [a]to the
Jew first, and also to the Greek.
17 For therein is the righteousness of God
revealed from faith to faith: as it is written,
[b]The just shall live by faith.
18 [c]For the wrath of God is revealed from
heaven against all ungodliness and unrighteousness of men, who hold the truth in unrighteousness;
19 Because [d]that which may be known
of God is manifest in them; for [e]God hath
shewed *it* unto them.
20 For [f]the invisible things of him from
the creation of the world are clearly seen,
being understood by the things that are
made, *even* his eternal power and Godhead;
so that they are without excuse:
21 Because that, when they knew God,
they glorified *him* not as God, neither were
thankful; but [g]became vain in their imaginations, and their foolish heart was darkened.
22 [h]Professing themselves to be wise,
they became fools,
23 And changed the glory of the uncorruptible [i]God into an image made like to
corruptible man, and to birds, and fourfooted beasts, and creeping things.
24 [j]Wherefore God also gave them up to
uncleanness through the lusts of their own
hearts, [k]to dishonour their own bodies [l]be-
tween themselves:
25 Who changed [m]the truth of God [n]into

1:1 [a]Acts 22:21; Gal. 1:1; 1 Tim. 1:11 [b]Acts 9:15 **1:2** [c]Acts 26:6 [d]Gal. 3:8 **1:3** [e]Matt. 1:6; Acts 2:30; 2 Tim. 2:8 [f]John 1:14 **1:4** [g]Acts 13:33 [h]Heb. 9:14 **1:5** [i]1 Cor. 15:10; Eph. 3:8 [j]Acts 6:7 [k]Acts 9:15 **1:7** [l]1 Cor. 1:2 [m]1 Cor. 1:3; Gal. 1:3 **1:8** [n]1 Cor. 1:4; Col. 1:3; 1 Thess. 1:2 [o]1 Thess. 1:8 **1:9** [p]2 Cor. 1:23; 1 Thess. 2:5 [q]Acts 27:23 [r]1 Thess. 3:10 **1:10** [s]1 Thess. 3:10 [t]Jam. 4:15 **1:12** [u]Tit. 1:4 **1:13** [v]Acts 16:7 [w]Phil. 4:17 **1:14** [x]1 Cor. 9:16 **1:16** [y]Ps. 40:9; 2 Tim. 1:8 [z]1 Cor. 1:18 [a]Luke 2:30 **1:17** [b]Hab. 2:4; Gal. 3:11; Phil. 3:9 **1:18** [c]Acts 17:30; Col. 3:6 **1:19** [d]Acts 14:17 [e]John 1:9 **1:20** [f]Ps. 19:1 **1:21** [g]2 Kings 17:15; Eph. 4:17 **1:22** [h]Jer. 10:14 **1:23** [i]Deut. 4:16; Isa. 40:18; Jer. 2:11; Acts 17:29 **1:24** [j]Ps. 81:12; Eph. 4:18; 2 Thess. 2:11 [k]1 Cor. 6:18; 1 Pet. 4:3 [l]Lev. 18:22

1:25 [m]1 Thess. 1:9 [n]Isa. 44:20; Am. 2:4

a lie, and worshipped and served the creature more than the Creator, who is blessed
for ever. Amen.
26 For this cause God gave them up unto
[o]vile affections: for even their women did
change the natural use into that which is
against nature:
27 And likewise also the men, leaving the
natural use of the woman, burned in their
lust one toward another; men with men
working that which is unseemly, and receiving in themselves that recompence of
their error which was meet.
28 And even as they did not like to retain
God in *their* knowledge, God gave them
over to a reprobate mind, to do those things
[p]which are not convenient;
29 Being filled with all unrighteousness,
fornication, wickedness, covetousness,
maliciousness; full of envy, murder, debate,
deceit, malignity; whisperers,
30 Backbiters, haters of God, despiteful,
proud, boasters, inventors of evil things,
disobedient to parents,
31 Without understanding, covenant-
breakers, without natural affection, impla-
cable, unmerciful:
32 Who knowing the judgment of God,
that they which commit such things are
worthy of death, not only do the same, but
[q]have pleasure in them that do them.

2 Therefore thou art inexcusable, O man,
whosoever thou art that judgest: [r]for
wherein thou judgest another, thou condemnest thyself; for thou that judgest doest
the same things.
2 But we are sure that the judgment of
God is according to truth against them
which commit such things.
3 And thinkest thou this, O man, that
judgest them which do such things, and doest the same, that thou shalt escape the
judgment of God?
4 Or despisest thou [s]the riches of his
goodness and forbearance and [t]longsuffer-
ing; [u]not knowing that the goodness of God
leadeth thee to repentance?
5 But after thy hardness and impenitent
heart [v]treasurest up unto thyself wrath
against the day of wrath and revelation of
the righteous judgment of God;
6 [w]Who will render to every man according to his deeds:
7 To them who by patient continuance in
well doing seek for glory and honour and
immortality, eternal life:
8 But unto them that are contentious, and
[x]do not obey the truth, but obey unrighteousness, indignation and wrath,
9 Tribulation and anguish, upon every
soul of man that doeth evil, of the Jew
[y]first, and also of the Gentile;
10 [z]But glory, honour, and peace, to every man that worketh good, to the Jew first,
and also to the Gentile:
11 For [a]there is no respect of persons
with God.
12 For as many as have sinned without
law shall also perish without law: and as
many as have sinned in the law shall be
judged by the law;
13 (For [b]not the hearers of the law *are*
just before God, but the doers of the law
shall be justified.
14 For when the Gentiles, which have not
the law, do by nature the things contained
in the law, these, having not the law, are a
law unto themselves:
15 Which shew the work of the law written in their hearts, their conscience also
bearing witness, and *their* thoughts the
mean while accusing or else excusing one
another;)
16 [c]In the day when God shall judge the
secrets of men [d]by Jesus Christ [e]according
to my gospel.
17 Behold, [f]thou art called a Jew, and
[g]restest in the law, [h]and makest thy boast
of God,
18 And [i]knowest *his* will, and [j]approv-
est the things that are more excellent, being
instructed out of the law;
19 And [k]art confident that thou thyself
art a guide of the blind, a light of them
which are in darkness,
20 An instructor of the foolish, a teacher
of babes, [l]which hast the form of knowledge and of the truth in the law.
21 [m]Thou therefore which teachest another, teachest thou not thyself? thou that
preachest a man should not steal, dost thou
steal?
22 Thou that sayest a man should not
commit adultery, dost thou commit adultery? thou that abhorrest idols, [n]dost thou
commit sacrilege?
23 Thou that makest thy boast of the law,
through breaking the law dishonourest
thou God?
24 For the name of God is blasphemed
among the Gentiles through you, as it is
[o]written.
25 [p]For circumcision verily profiteth, if
thou keep the law: but if thou be a breaker
of the law, thy circumcision is made uncircumcision.
26 Therefore [q]if the uncircumcision keep
the righteousness of the law, shall not his
uncircumcision be counted for circumcision?
27 And shall not uncircumcision which is
by nature, if it fulfil the law, [r]judge thee,
who by the letter and circumcision dost
transgress the law?
28 For [s]he is not a Jew, which is one outwardly; neither *is that* circumcision, which
is outward in the flesh:
29 But he *is* a Jew, [t]which is one inwardly; and [u]circumcision *is that* of the
heart, [v]in the spirit, *and* not in the letter;
[w]whose praise *is* not of men, but of God.

3 What advantage then hath the Jew? or
what profit *is there* of circumcision?
2 Much every way: chiefly, because that
[x]unto them were committed the oracles of
God.

1:26 [o]Lev. 18:22; Jude 10
1:28 [p]Eph. 5:4
1:32 [q]Hos. 7:3
2:1 [r]2 Sam. 12:5; John 8:9
2:4 [s]Eph. 1:7 [t]Ex. 34:6 [u]Isa. 30:18
2:5 [v]Deut. 32:34
2:6 [w]Job 34:11; Prov. 24:12; Jer. 17:10; 1 Cor. 3:8; 2 Cor. 5:10
2:8 [x]Job 24:13
2:9 [y]Am. 3:2; 1 Pet. 4:17
2:10 [z]1 Pet. 1:7
2:11 [a]Deut. 10:17; Job 34:19; Acts 10:34; Eph. 6:9; Col. 3:25
2:13 [b]Matt. 7:21; 1 John 3:7
2:16 [c]Eccl. 12:14; John 12:48; 1 Cor. 4:5 [d]John 5:22; 2 Tim. 4:1; 1 Pet. 4:5 [e]1 Tim. 1:11
2:17 [f]Matt. 3:9; 2 Cor. 11:22 [g]Mic. 3:11 [h]Isa. 45:25
2:18 [i]Deut. 4:8 [j]Phil. 1:10
2:19 [k]Matt. 15:14
2:20 [l]2 Tim. 1:13
2:21 [m]Ps. 50:16
2:22 [n]Mal. 3:8
2:24 [o]2 Sam. 12:14; Ezek. 36:20
2:25 [p]Gal. 5:3
2:26 [q]Acts 10:34
2:27 [r]Matt. 12:41
2:28 [s]Matt. 3:9; Gal. 6:15; Rev. 2:9
2:29 [t]1 Pet. 3:4 [u]Col. 2:11 [v]2 Cor. 3:6 [w]1 Cor. 4:5; 1 Thess. 2:4
3:2 [x]Deut. 4:7

3 For what if [y]some did not believe?
[z]shall their unbelief make the faith of God
without effect?
4 [a]God forbid: yea, let [b]God be true, but
[c]every man a liar; as it is written, [d]That
thou mightest be justified in thy sayings,
and mightest overcome when thou art
judged.
5 But if our unrighteousness commend
the righteousness of God, what shall we
say? *Is* God unrighteous who taketh vengeance? ([e]I speak as a man)
6 God forbid: for then [f]how shall God
judge the world?
7 For if the truth of God hath more
abounded through my lie unto his glory;
why yet am I also judged as a sinner?
8 And not *rather,* (as we be slanderously
reported, and as some affirm that we say,)
Let us do evil that good may come? whose
damnation is just.
9 What then? are we better *than they?*
No, in no wise: for we have before proved
both Jews and Gentiles, that [g]they are all
under sin;
10 As it is written, [h]There is none righteous, no, not one:
11 There is none that understandeth,
there is none that seeketh after God.
12 They are all gone out of the way, they
are together become unprofitable; there is
none that doeth good, no, not one.
13 [i]Their throat *is* an open sepulchre;
with their tongues they have used deceit;
[j]the poison of asps *is* under their lips:
14 [k]Whose mouth *is* full of cursing and
bitterness:
15 [l]Their feet *are* swift to shed blood:
16 Destruction and misery *are* in their
ways:
17 And the way of peace have they not
known:
18 [m]There is no fear of God before their
eyes.
19 Now we know that what things soever
[n]the law saith, it saith to them who are
under the law: that [o]every mouth may be
stopped, and all the world may become
guilty before God.
20 Therefore [p]by the deeds of the law
there shall no flesh be justified in his sight:
for by the law *is* the knowledge of sin.
21 But [q]now the righteousness of God
without the law is manifested, [r]being witnessed by the law [s]and the prophets;
22 Even the righteousness of God *which*
is by faith of Jesus Christ unto all and upon
all them that believe: for [t]there is no difference:
23 For [u]all have sinned, and come short
of the glory of God;
24 Being justified freely [v]by his grace
[w]through the redemption that is in Christ
Jesus:
25 Whom God hath set forth [x]*to be* a
propitiation through faith [y]in his blood, to
declare his righteousness [z]for the remission of [a]sins that are past, through the forbearance of God;
26 To declare, *I say,* at this time his righteousness: that he might be just, and the
justifier of him which believeth in Jesus.
27 [b]Where *is* boasting then? It is ex-
cluded. By what law? of works? Nay: but by
the law of faith.
28 Therefore we conclude [c]that a man is
justified by faith without the deeds of the
law.
29 *Is he* the God of the Jews only? *is he*
not also of the Gentiles? Yes, of the Gentiles
also:
30 Seeing [d]*it is* one God, which shall justify the circumcision by faith, and uncircumcision through faith.
31 Do we then make void the law through
faith? God forbid: yea, we establish the law.
4 What shall we say then that [e]Abraham
our father, as pertaining to the flesh,
hath found?
2 For if Abraham were justified by works,
he hath *whereof* to glory; but not before
God.
3 For what saith the scripture? [f]Abra-
ham believed God, and it was counted unto
him for righteousness.
4 Now to him that worketh is the reward
not reckoned of grace, but of debt.
5 But to him that worketh not, but believeth on him that justifieth [g]the ungodly, his
faith is counted for righteousness.
6 Even as David also describeth the
blessedness of the man, unto whom God imputeth righteousness without works,
7 *Saying,* [h]Blessed *are* they whose iniquities are forgiven, and whose sins are covered.
8 Blessed *is* the man to whom the Lord
will not impute sin.
9 *Cometh* this blessedness then upon the
circumcision *only,* or upon the uncircumcision also? for we say that faith was reckoned to Abraham for righteousness.
10 How was it then reckoned? when he
was in circumcision, or in uncircumcision?
Not in circumcision, but in uncircumcision.
11 And [i]he received the sign of circumcision, a seal of the righteousness of the faith
which *he had yet* being uncircumcised: that
[j]he might be the father of all them that believe, though they be not circumcised; that
righteousness might be imputed unto them
also:
12 And the father of circumcision to them
who are not of the circumcision only, but
who also walk in the steps of that faith of
our father Abraham, which *he had* being
yet uncircumcised.
13 For the promise, that he should be the
[k]heir of the world, *was* not to Abraham, or
to his seed, through the law, but through the
righteousness of faith.
14 For [l]if they which are of the law *be*
heirs, faith is made void, and the promise
made of none effect:
15 Because [m]the law worketh wrath: for

3:3 [y]Heb. 4:2 [z]Num. 23:19
3:4 [a]Job 40:8 [b]John 3:33 [c]Ps. 62:9 [d]Ps. 51:4
3:5 [e]Gal. 3:15
3:6 [f]Gen. 18:25
3:9 [g]Gal. 3:22
3:10 [h]Ps. 14:1
3:13 [i]Ps. 5:9 [j]Ps. 140:3
3:14 [k]Ps. 10:7
3:15 [l]Prov. 1:16
3:18 [m]Ps. 36:1
3:19 [n]John 10:34 [o]Job 5:16; Ezek. 16:63
3:20 [p]Ps. 143:2; Gal. 2:16; Eph. 2:8
3:21 [q]Acts 15:11; Heb. 11:4 [r]John 5:46 [s]1 Pet. 1:10
3:22 [t]Gal. 3:28
3:23 [u]Gal. 3:22
3:24 [v]Eph. 2:8 [w]Matt. 20:28; Col. 1:14; 1 Tim. 2:6; 1 Pet. 1:18
3:25 [x]Lev. 16:15 [y]Col. 1:20 [z]Acts 13:38 [a]Acts 17:30
3:27 [b]1 Cor. 1:29
3:28 [c]Acts 13:38
3:30 [d]Gal. 3:8
4:1 [e]Isa. 51:2; John 8:33; 2 Cor. 11:22
4:3 [f]Gen. 15:6; Jam. 2:23
4:5 [g]Josh. 24:2
4:7 [h]Ps. 32:1
4:11 [i]Gen. 17:10 [j]Luke 19:9
4:13 [k]Gen. 17:4
4:14 [l]Gal. 3:18
4:15 [m]1 Cor. 15:56; Gal. 3:10; 1 John 3:4

where no law is, *there is* no transgression.

16 Therefore *it is* of faith, that *it might be* by grace; [n]to the end the promise might be sure to all the seed; not to that only which is of the law, but to that also which is of the faith of Abraham; [o]who is the father of us all,

17 (As it is written, [p]I have made thee a father of many nations,) before him whom he believed, *even* God, [q]who quickeneth the dead, and calleth those [r]things which be not as though they were.

18 Who against hope believed in hope, that he might become the father of many nations, according to that which was spoken, [s]So shall thy seed be.

19 And being not weak in faith, [t]he considered not his own body now dead, when he was about an hundred years old, neither yet the deadness of Sarah's womb:

20 He staggered not at the promise of God through unbelief; but was strong in faith, giving glory to God;

21 And being fully persuaded that, what he had promised, [u]he was able also to perform.

22 And therefore it was imputed to him for righteousness.

23 Now [v]it was not written for his sake alone, that it was imputed to him;

24 But for us also, to whom it shall be imputed, if we believe [w]on him that raised up Jesus our Lord from the dead;

25 [x]Who was delivered for our offences, and [y]was raised again for our justification.

5

Therefore [z]being justified by faith, we have [a]peace with God through our Lord Jesus Christ:

2 [b]By whom also we have access by faith into this grace [c]wherein we stand, and [d]rejoice in hope of the glory of God.

3 And not only *so*, but [e]we glory in tribulations also: [f]knowing that tribulation worketh patience;

4 [g]And patience, experience; and experience, hope:

5 [h]And hope maketh not ashamed; [i]because the love of God is shed abroad in our hearts by the Holy Ghost which is given unto us.

6 For when we were yet without strength, in due time Christ died for the ungodly.

7 For scarcely for a righteous man will one die: yet peradventure for a good man some would even dare to die.

8 But [j]God commendeth his love toward us, in that, while we were yet sinners, Christ died for us.

9 Much more then, being now justified [k]by his blood, we shall be saved [l]from wrath through him.

10 For if, when we were enemies, [m]we were reconciled to God by the death of his Son, much more, being reconciled, we shall be saved [n]by his life.

11 And not only *so*, but we also [o]joy in God through our Lord Jesus Christ, by whom we have now received the atonement.

12 Wherefore, as [p]by one man sin entered into the world, and [q]death by sin; and so death passed upon all men, for that all have sinned:

13 (For until the law sin was in the world: but [r]sin is not imputed when there is no law.

14 Nevertheless death reigned from Adam to Moses, even over them that had not sinned after the similitude of Adam's transgression, [s]who is the figure of him that was to come.

15 But not as the offence, so also *is* the free gift. For if through the offence of one many be dead, much more the grace of God, and the gift by grace, *which is* by one man, Jesus Christ, hath abounded [t]unto many.

16 And not as *it was* by one that sinned, *so is* the gift: for the judgment *was* by one to condemnation, but the free gift *is* of many offences unto justification.

17 For if by one man's offence death reigned by one; much more they which receive abundance of grace and of the gift of righteousness shall reign in life by one, Jesus Christ.)

18 Therefore as by the offence of one *judgment came* upon all men to condemnation; even so by the righteousness of one *the free gift came* [u]upon all men unto justification of life.

19 For as by one man's disobedience many were made sinners, so by the obedience of one shall many be made righteous.

20 Moreover [v]the law entered, that the offence might abound. But where sin abounded, grace did much [w]more abound:

21 That as sin hath reigned unto death, even so might grace reign through righteousness unto eternal life by Jesus Christ our Lord.

6

What shall we say then? Shall we continue in sin, that grace may abound?

2 God forbid. How shall we, that are [x]dead to sin, live any longer therein?

3 Know ye not, that [y]so many of us as were baptized into Jesus Christ [z]were baptized into his death?

4 Therefore we are [a]buried with him by baptism into death: that [b]like as Christ was raised up from the dead by [c]the glory of the Father, [d]even so we also should walk in newness of life.

5 [e]For if we have been planted together in the likeness of his death, we shall be also *in the likeness* of *his* resurrection:

6 Knowing this, that [f]our old man is crucified with *him*, that [g]the body of sin might be destroyed, that henceforth we should not serve sin.

7 For [h]he that is dead is freed from sin.

8 Now [i]if we be dead with Christ, we believe that we shall also live with him:

9 Knowing that [j]Christ being raised from the dead dieth no more; death hath no more dominion over him.

4:16 [n]Gal. 3:22 [o]Isa. 51:2
4:17 [p]Gen. 17:5 [q]Eph. 2:1 [r]1 Cor. 1:28
4:18 [s]Gen. 15:5
4:19 [t]Gen. 17:17
4:21 [u]Ps. 115:3; Heb. 11:19
4:23 [v]1 Cor. 10:6
4:24 [w]Acts 2:24
4:25 [x]Isa. 53:5; Gal. 1:4; 1 Pet. 2:24 [y]1 Cor. 15:17
5:1 [z]Isa. 32:17 [a]Eph. 2:14
5:2 [b]John 10:9; Heb. 10:19 [c]1 Cor. 15:1 [d]Heb. 3:6
5:3 [e]Matt. 5:11; 2 Cor. 12:10; Phil. 2:17; 1 Pet. 3:14 [f]Jam. 1:3
5:4 [g]Jam. 1:12
5:5 [h]Phil. 1:20 [i]2 Cor. 1:22; Eph. 1:13
5:8 [j]John 15:13; 1 John 3:16
5:9 [k]Eph. 2:13; 1 John 1:7 [l]1 Thess. 1:10
5:10 [m]2 Cor. 5:18; Col. 1:20 [n]John 5:26
5:11 [o]Gal. 4:9
5:12 [p]Gen. 3:6 [q]Gen. 2:17
5:13 [r]1 John 3:4
5:14 [s]1 Cor. 15:21
5:15 [t]Isa. 53:11
5:18 [u]John 12:32
5:20 [v]John 15:22 [w]Luke 7:47
6:2 [x]Gal. 2:19
6:3 [y]Col. 3:3 [z]1 Cor. 15:29
6:4 [a]Col. 2:12 [b]1 Cor. 6:14 [c]John 2:11 [d]Gal. 6:15; Col. 3:10
6:5 [e]Phil. 3:10
6:6 [f]Gal. 2:20; Col. 3:5 [g]Col. 2:11
6:7 [h]1 Pet. 4:1
6:8 [i]2 Tim. 2:11
6:9 [j]Rev. 1:18

10 For in that he died, [k]he died unto sin once: but in that he liveth, [l]he liveth unto God.

11 Likewise reckon ye also yourselves to be dead indeed unto sin, but [m]alive unto God through Jesus Christ our Lord.

12 [n]Let not sin therefore reign in your mortal body, that ye should obey it in the lusts thereof.

13 Neither yield ye your [o]members *as* instruments of unrighteousness unto sin: but [p]yield yourselves unto God, as those that are alive from the dead, and your members *as* instruments of righteousness unto God.

14 For [q]sin shall not have dominion over you: for ye are not under the law, but under grace.

15 What then? shall we sin, [r]because we are not under the law, but under grace? God forbid.

16 Know ye not, that [s]to whom ye yield yourselves servants to obey, his servants ye are to whom ye obey; whether of sin unto death, or of obedience unto righteousness?

17 But God be thanked, that ye were the servants of sin, but ye have obeyed from the heart [t]that form of doctrine which was delivered you.

18 Being then [u]made free from sin, ye became the servants of righteousness.

19 I speak after the manner of men because of the infirmity of your flesh: for as ye have yielded your members servants to uncleanness and to iniquity unto iniquity; even so now yield your members servants to righteousness unto holiness.

20 For when ye were [v]the servants of sin, ye were free from righteousness.

21 What fruit had ye then in those things whereof ye are now ashamed? for the end of those things *is* death.

22 But now [w]being made free from sin, and become servants to God, ye have your fruit unto holiness, and the end everlasting life.

23 For [x]the wages of sin *is* death; but [y]the gift of God *is* eternal life through Jesus Christ our Lord.

7 Know ye not, brethren, (for I speak to them that know the law,) how that the law hath dominion over a man as long as he liveth?

2 For [z]the woman which hath an husband is bound by the law to *her* husband so long as he liveth; but if the husband be dead, she is loosed from the law of *her* husband.

3 So then [a]if, while *her* husband liveth, she be married to another man, she shall be called an adulteress: but if her husband be dead, she is free from that law; so that she is no adulteress, though she be married to another man.

4 Wherefore, my brethren, ye also are become [b]dead to the law by the body of Christ; that ye should be married to another, *even* to him who is raised from the dead, that we should [c]bring forth fruit unto God.

5 For when we were in the flesh, the motions of sins, which were by the law, did work in our members [d]to bring forth fruit unto death.

6 But now we are delivered from the law, that being dead wherein we were held; that we should serve [e]in newness of spirit, and not *in* the oldness of the letter.

7 What shall we say then? *Is* the law sin? God forbid. Nay, I had not known sin, but by the law: for I had not known lust, except the law had said, [f]Thou shalt not covet.

8 But sin, taking occasion by the commandment, wrought in me all manner of concupiscence. For [g]without the law sin *was* dead.

9 For I was alive without the law once: but when the commandment came, sin revived, and I died.

10 And the commandment, [h]which *was ordained* to life, I found *to be* unto death.

11 For sin, taking occasion by the commandment, deceived me, and by it slew *me.*

12 Wherefore [i]the law *is* holy, and the commandment holy, and just, and good.

13 Was then that which is good made death unto me? God forbid. But sin, that it might appear sin, working death in me by that which is good; that sin by the commandment might become exceeding sinful.

14 For we know that the law is spiritual: but I am carnal, [j]sold under sin.

15 For that which I do I allow not: for [k]what I would, that do I not; but what I hate, that do I.

16 If then I do that which I would not, I consent unto the law that *it is* good.

17 Now then it is no more I that do it, but sin that dwelleth in me.

18 For I know that [l]in me (that is, in my flesh,) dwelleth no good thing: for to will is present with me; but *how* to perform that which is good I find not.

19 For the good that I would I do not: but the evil which I would not, that I do.

20 Now if I do that I would not, it is no more I that do it, but sin that dwelleth in me.

21 I find then a law, that, when I would do good, evil is present with me.

22 For I [m]delight in the law of God after [n]the inward man:

23 But [o]I see another law in my members, warring against the law of my mind, and bringing me into captivity to the law of sin which is in my members.

24 O wretched man that I am! who shall deliver me from the body of this death?

25 [p]I thank God through Jesus Christ our Lord. So then with the mind I myself serve the law of God; but with the flesh the law of sin.

8 *There is* therefore now no condemnation to them which are in Christ Jesus, who [q]walk not after the flesh, but after the Spirit.

2 For [r]the law of [s]the Spirit of life in Christ Jesus hath made me free from the law of sin and death.

6:10 [k]Heb. 9:27 [l]Luke 20:38
6:11 [m]Gal. 2:19
6:12 [n]Ps. 19:13
6:13 [o]Col. 3:5 [p]1 Pet. 2:24
6:14 [q]Gal. 5:18
6:15 [r]1 Cor. 9:21
6:16 [s]Matt. 6:24; 2 Pet. 2:19
6:17 [t]2 Tim. 1:13
6:18 [u]John 8:32; Gal. 5:1; 1 Pet. 2:16
6:20 [v]John 8:34
6:22 [w]John 8:32
6:23 [x]Gen. 2:17 [y]1 Pet. 1:4
7:2 [z]1 Cor. 7:39
7:3 [a]Matt. 5:32
7:4 [b]Gal. 2:19; Col. 2:14 [c]Gal. 5:22
7:5 [d]Gal. 5:19
7:6 [e]2 Cor. 3:6
7:7 [f]Ex. 20:17; Acts 20:33
7:8 [g]1 Cor. 15:56
7:10 [h]Lev. 18:5; 2 Cor. 3:7
7:12 [i]Ps. 19:8
7:14 [j]1 Kings 21:20
7:15 [k]Gal. 5:17
7:18 [l]Gen. 6:5
7:22 [m]Ps. 1:2 [n]2 Cor. 4:16; Col. 3:9
7:23 [o]Gal. 5:17
7:25 [p]1 Cor. 15:57
8:1 [q]Gal. 5:16
8:2 [r]John 8:36 [s]1 Cor. 15:45

3 For [t]what the law could not do, in that it was weak through the flesh, [u]God sending his own Son in the likeness of sinful flesh, and for sin, condemned sin in the flesh:

4 That the righteousness of the law might be fulfilled in us, who walk not after the flesh, but after the Spirit.

5 For [v]they that are after the flesh do mind the things of the flesh; but they that are after the Spirit, [w]the things of the Spirit.

6 For [x]to be carnally minded *is* death: but to be spiritually minded *is* life and peace.

7 Because [y]the carnal mind *is* enmity against God: for it is not subject to the law of God, [z]neither indeed can be.

8 So then they that are in the flesh cannot please God.

9 But ye are not in the flesh, but in the Spirit, if so be that [a]the Spirit of God dwell in you. Now if any man have not [b]the Spirit of Christ, he is none of his.

10 And if Christ *be* in you, the body *is* dead because of sin; but the Spirit *is* life because of righteousness.

11 But if the Spirit of [c]him that raised up Jesus from the dead dwell in you, [d]he that raised up Christ from the dead shall also quicken your mortal bodies by his Spirit that dwelleth in you.

12 Therefore, brethren, we are debtors, not to the flesh, to live after the flesh.

13 For [e]if ye live after the flesh, ye shall die: but if ye through the Spirit do [f]mortify the deeds of the body, ye shall live.

14 For [g]as many as are led by the Spirit of God, they are the sons of God.

15 For [h]ye have not received the spirit of bondage again [i]to fear; but ye have received the [j]Spirit of adoption, whereby we cry, [k]Abba, Father.

16 [l]The Spirit itself beareth witness with our spirit, that we are the children of God:

17 And if children, then heirs; [m]heirs of God, and joint-heirs with Christ; [n]if so be that we suffer with *him*, that we may be also glorified together.

18 For I reckon that [o]the sufferings of this present time *are* not worthy *to be compared* with the glory which shall be revealed in us.

19 For [p]the earnest expectation of the creature waiteth for the [q]manifestation of the sons of God.

20 For [r]the creature was made subject to vanity, not willingly, but by reason of him who hath subjected *the same* in hope,

21 Because the creature itself also shall be delivered from the bondage of corruption into the glorious liberty of the children of God.

22 For we know that the whole creation [s]groaneth and travaileth in pain together until now.

23 And not only *they*, but ourselves also, which have [t]the firstfruits of the Spirit, [u]even we ourselves groan within ourselves, [v]waiting for the adoption, *to wit*, the [w]redemption of our body.

24 For we are saved by hope: but [x]hope that is seen is not hope: for what a man seeth, why doth he yet hope for?

25 But if we hope for that we see not, *then* do we with patience wait for *it*.

26 Likewise the Spirit also helpeth our infirmities: for [y]we know not what we should pray for as we ought: but [z]the Spirit itself maketh intercession for us with groanings which cannot be uttered.

27 And [a]he that searcheth the hearts knoweth what *is* the mind of the Spirit, because he maketh intercession for the saints [b]according to *the will of* God.

28 And we know that all things work together for good to them that love God, to them [c]who are the called according to *his* purpose.

29 For whom [d]he did foreknow, [e]he also did predestinate [f]*to be* conformed to the image of his Son, [g]that he might be the firstborn among many brethren.

30 Moreover whom he did predestinate, them he also [h]called: and whom he called, them he also [i]justified: and whom he justified, them he also [j]glorified.

31 What shall we then say to these things? [k]If God *be* for us, who *can be* against us?

32 He that spared not his own Son, but delivered him up for us all, how shall he not with him also freely give us all things?

33 Who shall lay any thing to the charge of God's elect? [l]*It is* God that justifieth.

34 [m]Who *is* he that condemneth? *It is* Christ that died, yea rather, that is risen again, [n]who is even at the right hand of God, [o]who also maketh intercession for us.

35 Who shall separate us from the love of Christ? *shall* tribulation, or distress, or persecution, or famine, or nakedness, or peril, or sword?

36 As it is written, [p]For thy sake we are killed all the day long; we are accounted as sheep for the slaughter.

37 [q]Nay, in all these things we are more than conquerors through him that loved us.

38 For I am persuaded, that neither death, nor life, nor angels, nor [r]principalities, nor powers, nor things present, nor things to come,

39 Nor height, nor depth, nor any other creature, shall be able to separate us from the love of God, which is in Christ Jesus our Lord.

9 I [s]say the truth in Christ, I lie not, my conscience also bearing me witness in the Holy Ghost,

2 That I have great heaviness and continual sorrow in my heart.

3 For [t]I could wish that myself were accursed from Christ for my brethren, my kinsmen according to the flesh:

4 [u]Who are Israelites; [v]to whom *pertaineth* the adoption, and [w]the glory, and [x]the

8:3 [t]Acts 13:39 [u]Gal. 3:13
8:5 [v]John 3:6 [w]Gal. 5:22
8:6 [x]Gal. 6:8
8:7 [y]Jam. 4:4 [z]1 Cor. 2:14
8:9 [a]1 Cor. 3:16 [b]John 3:34; Phil. 1:19; 1 Pet. 1:11
8:11 [c]Acts 2:24 [d]1 Cor. 6:14; Eph. 2:5
8:13 [e]Gal. 6:8 [f]Eph. 4:22
8:14 [g]Gal. 5:18
8:15 [h]1 Cor. 2:12 [i]2 Tim. 1:7 [j]Isa. 56:5 [k]Mark 14:36
8:16 [l]2 Cor. 1:22
8:17 [m]Acts 26:18 [n]Acts 14:22; 2 Tim. 2:11
8:18 [o]2 Cor. 4:17
8:19 [p]2 Pet. 3:13 [q]1 John 3:2
8:20 [r]Gen. 3:19
8:22 [s]Jer. 12:11
8:23 [t]2 Cor. 5:5 [u]2 Cor. 5:2 [v]Luke 20:36 [w]Luke 21:28
8:24 [x]2 Cor. 5:7
8:26 [y]Matt. 20:22 [z]Zech. 12:10
8:27 [a]1 Chron. 28:9; Prov. 17:3; Jer. 11:20; 1 Thess. 2:4; Rev. 2:23 [b]1 John 5:14
8:28 [c]2 Tim. 1:9
8:29 [d]Ex. 33:12; Jer. 1:5; Matt. 7:23; 1 Pet. 1:2 [e]Eph. 1:5 [f]John 17:22; Phil. 3:21; 1 John 3:2 [g]Col. 1:15; Rev. 1:5
8:30 [h]Eph. 4:4; 1 Pet. 2:9 [i]1 Cor. 6:11 [j]John 17:22
8:31 [k]Num. 14:9
8:33 [l]Isa. 50:8
8:34 [m]Job 34:29 [n]Mark 16:19; Heb. 1:3; 1 Pet. 3:22 [o]Heb. 7:25
8:36 [p]Ps. 44:22; 2 Cor. 4:11
8:37 [q]1 Cor. 15:57; 1 John 4:4; Rev. 12:11
8:38 [r]Eph. 1:21; 1 Pet. 3:22
9:1 [s]2 Cor. 1:23; Phil. 1:8; 1 Tim. 2:7
9:3 [t]Ex. 32:32
9:4 [u]Deut. 7:6 [v]Ex. 4:22; Jer. 31:9 [w]1 Sam. 4:21; Ps. 63:2 [x]Acts 3:25

covenants, and [y]the giving of the law, and
[z]the service *of God,* and [a]the promises;
5 [b]Whose *are* the fathers, and [c]of whom
as concerning the flesh Christ *came,* [d]who
is over all, God blessed for ever. Amen.
6 [e]Not as though the word of God hath
taken none effect. For [f]they *are* not all Israel, which are of Israel:
7 [g]Neither, because they are the seed of
Abraham, *are they* all children: but, In
[h]Isaac shall thy seed be called.
8 That is, They which are the children of
the flesh, these *are* not the children of God:
but [i]the children of the promise are
counted for the seed.
9 For this *is* the word of promise, [j]At this
time will I come, and Sarah shall have a son.
10 And not only *this;* but when [k]Rebecca
also had conceived by one, *even* by our father Isaac;
11 (For *the children* being not yet born,
neither having done any good or evil, that
the purpose of God according to election
might stand, not of works, but of him that
calleth;)
12 It was said unto her, [l]The elder shall
serve the younger.
13 As it is written, [m]Jacob have I loved,
but Esau have I hated.
14 What shall we say then? [n]*Is there* unrighteousness with God? God forbid.
15 For he saith to Moses, [o]I will have
mercy on whom I will have mercy, and I will
have compassion on whom I will have compassion.
16 So then *it is* not of him that willeth, nor
of him that runneth, but of God that sheweth mercy.
17 For [p]the scripture saith unto Pharaoh,
[q]Even for this same purpose have I raised
thee up, that I might shew my power in
thee, and that my name might be declared
throughout all the earth.
18 Therefore hath he mercy on whom he
will *have mercy,* and whom he will he hardeneth.
19 Thou wilt say then unto me, Why doth
he yet find fault? For [r]who hath resisted his
will?
20 Nay but, O man, who art thou that re-
pliest against God? [s]Shall the thing formed
say to him that formed *it,* Why hast thou
made me thus?
21 Hath not the [t]potter power over the
clay, of the same lump to make [u]one vessel
unto honour, and another unto dishonour?
22 *What* if God, willing to shew *his* wrath,
and to make his power known, endured
with much longsuffering [v]the vessels of
wrath [w]fitted to destruction:
23 And that he might make known [x]the
riches of his glory on the vessels of mercy,
which he had afore prepared unto glory,
24 Even us, whom he hath called, not of
the Jews only, but also of the Gentiles?
25 As he saith also in Osee, [y]I will call
them my people, which were not my people;
and her beloved, which was not beloved.

9:4 [y]Ps. 147:19 [z]Heb. 9:1 [a]Acts 13:32
9:5 [b]Deut. 10:15 [c]Luke 3:23 [d]Jer. 23:6; Acts 20:28; Heb. 1:8
9:6 [e]Num. 23:19 [f]John 8:39
9:7 [g]Gal. 4:23 [h]Gen. 21:12
9:8 [i]Gal. 4:28
9:9 [j]Gen. 18:10
9:10 [k]Gen. 25:21
9:12 [l]Gen. 25:23
9:13 [m]Deut. 21:15; Mal. 1:2; Matt. 10:37; John 12:25
9:14 [n]Deut. 32:4; Job 8:3; Ps. 92:15
9:15 [o]Ex. 33:19
9:17 [p]Gal. 3:8 [q]Ex. 9:16
9:19 [r]2 Chron. 20:6; Dan. 4:35
9:20 [s]Isa. 29:16
9:21 [t]Prov. 16:4 [u]2 Tim. 2:20
9:22 [v]1 Thess. 5:9 [w]1 Pet. 2:8
9:23 [x]Eph. 1:7
9:25 [y]Hos. 2:23
9:26 [z]Hos. 1:10
9:27 [a]Isa. 10:22
9:28 [b]Isa. 28:22
9:29 [c]Isa. 1:9 [d]Isa. 13:19
9:31 [e]Gal. 5:4
9:32 [f]Luke 2:34
9:33 [g]Ps. 118:22; Matt. 21:42; 1 Pet. 2:6
10:2 [h]Acts 21:20
10:3 [i]Phil. 3:9
10:4 [j]Matt. 5:17
10:5 [k]Lev. 18:5; Ezek. 20:11; Gal. 3:12
10:6 [l]Deut. 30:12
10:8 [m]Deut. 30:14
10:9 [n]Matt. 10:32; Acts 8:37
10:11 [o]Isa. 28:16
10:12 [p]Acts 15:9 [q]Acts 10:36 [r]Eph. 1:7

26 [z]And it shall come to pass, *that* in the
place where it was said unto them, Ye *are*
not my people; there shall they be called the
children of the living God.
27 Esaias also crieth concerning Israel,
[a]Though the number of the children of Israel be as the sand of the sea, a remnant
shall be saved:
28 For he will finish the work, and cut *it*
short in righteousness: [b]because a short
work will the Lord make upon the earth.
29 And as Esaias said before, [c]Except the
Lord of Sabaoth had left us a seed, [d]we had
been as Sodoma, and been made like unto
Gomorrha.
30 What shall we say then? That the Gentiles, which followed not after righteousness, have attained to righteousness, even
the righteousness which is of faith.
31 But Israel, which followed after the
law of righteousness, [e]hath not attained to
the law of righteousness.
32 Wherefore? Because *they sought it* not
by faith, but as it were by the works of the
law. For [f]they stumbled at that stumblingstone;
33 As it is written, [g]Behold, I lay in Sion
a stumblingstone and rock of offence: and
whosoever believeth on him shall not be
ashamed.

10 Brethren, my heart's desire and
prayer to God for Israel is, that they
might be saved.
2 For I bear them record [h]that they have
a zeal of God, but not according to knowledge.
3 For they being ignorant of God's righteousness, and going about to establish
their own [i]righteousness, have not submitted themselves unto the righteousness of
God.
4 For [j]Christ *is* the end of the law for
righteousness to every one that believeth.
5 For Moses describeth the righteousness
which is of the law, [k]That the man which
doeth those things shall live by them.
6 But the righteousness which is of faith
speaketh on this wise, [l]Say not in thine
heart, Who shall ascend into heaven? (that
is, to bring Christ down *from above:*)
7 Or, Who shall descend into the deep?
(that is, to bring up Christ again from the
dead.)
8 But what saith it? [m]The word is nigh
thee, *even* in thy mouth, and in thy heart:
that is, the word of faith, which we preach;
9 That [n]if thou shalt confess with thy
mouth the Lord Jesus, and shalt believe in
thine heart that God hath raised him from
the dead, thou shalt be saved.
10 For with the heart man believeth unto
righteousness; and with the mouth confession is made unto salvation.
11 For the scripture saith, [o]Whosoever
believeth on him shall not be ashamed.
12 For [p]there is no difference between
the Jew and the Greek: for [q]the same Lord
over all [r]is rich unto all that call upon him.

13 [s]For whosoever shall call [t]upon the name of the Lord shall be saved.

14 How then shall they call on him in whom they have not believed? and how shall they believe in him of whom they have not heard? and how shall they hear [u]without a preacher?

15 And how shall they preach, except they be sent? as it is written, [v]How beautiful are the feet of them that preach the gospel of peace, and bring glad tidings of good things!

16 But [w]they have not all obeyed the gospel. For Esaias saith, [x]Lord, who hath believed our report?

17 So then faith *cometh* by hearing, and hearing by the word of God.

18 But I say, Have they not heard? Yes verily, [y]their sound went into all the earth, [z]and their words unto the ends of the world.

19 But I say, Did not Israel know? First Moses saith, [a]I will provoke you to jealousy by *them that are* no people, *and* by a [b]foolish nation I will anger you.

20 But Esaias is very bold, and saith, [c]I was found of them that sought me not; I was made manifest unto them that asked not after me.

21 But to Israel he saith, [d]All day long I have stretched forth my hands unto a disobedient and gainsaying people.

11 I say then, [e]Hath God cast away his people? God forbid. For [f]I also am an Israelite, of the seed of Abraham, *of* the tribe of Benjamin.

2 God hath not cast away his people which he foreknew. Wot ye not what the scripture saith of Elias? how he maketh intercession to God against Israel, saying,

3 [g]Lord, they have killed thy prophets, and digged down thine altars; and I am left alone, and they seek my life.

4 But what saith the answer of God unto him? [h]I have reserved to myself seven thousand men, who have not bowed the knee to *the image of* Baal.

5 Even so then at this present time also there is a remnant according to the election of grace.

6 And [i]if by grace, then *is it* no more of works: otherwise grace is no more grace. But if *it be* of works, then is it no more grace: otherwise work is no more work.

7 What then? Israel hath not obtained that which he seeketh for; but the election hath obtained it, and the rest were blinded

8 (According as it is written, [j]God hath given them the spirit of slumber, [k]eyes that they should not see, and ears that they should not hear;) unto this day.

9 And David saith, [l]Let their table be made a snare, and a trap, and a stumblingblock, and a recompence unto them:

10 [m]Let their eyes be darkened, that they may not see, and bow down their back alway.

11 I say then, Have they stumbled that they should fall? God forbid: but *rather* [n]through their fall salvation *is come* unto the Gentiles, for to provoke them to jealousy.

12 Now if the fall of them *be* the riches of the world, and the diminishing of them the riches of the Gentiles; how much more their fulness?

13 For I speak to you Gentiles, inasmuch as [o]I am the apostle of the Gentiles, I magnify mine office:

14 If by any means I may provoke to emulation *them which are* my flesh, and [p]might save some of them.

15 For if the casting away of them *be* the reconciling of the world, what *shall* the receiving *of them be,* but life from the dead?

16 For if [q]the firstfruit *be* holy, the lump *is* also *holy:* and if the root *be* holy, so *are* the branches.

17 And if [r]some of the branches be broken off, [s]and thou, being a wild olive tree, wert graffed in among them, and with them partakest of the root and fatness of the olive tree;

18 [t]Boast not against the branches. But if thou boast, thou bearest not the root, but the root thee.

19 Thou wilt say then, The branches were broken off, that I might be graffed in.

20 Well; because of unbelief they were broken off, and thou standest by faith. Be not highminded, but [u]fear:

21 For if God spared not the natural branches, *take heed* lest he also spare not thee.

22 Behold therefore the goodness and severity of God: on them which fell, severity; but toward thee, goodness, [v]if thou continue in *his* goodness: otherwise [w]thou also shalt be cut off.

23 And they also, [x]if they abide not still in unbelief, shall be graffed in: for God is able to graff them in again.

24 For if thou wert cut out of the olive tree which is wild by nature, and wert graffed contrary to nature into a good olive tree: how much more shall these, which be the natural *branches,* be graffed into their own olive tree?

25 For I would not, brethren, that ye should be ignorant of this mystery, lest ye should be wise in your own conceits, that [y]blindness in part is happened to Israel, [z]until the fulness of the Gentiles be come in.

26 And so all Israel shall be saved: as it is written, [a]There shall come out of Sion the Deliverer, and shall turn away ungodliness from Jacob:

27 [b]For this *is* my covenant unto them, when I shall take away their sins.

28 As concerning the gospel, *they are* enemies for your sakes: but as touching the election, *they are* [c]beloved for the fathers' sakes.

29 For the gifts and calling of God *are* [d]without repentance.

10:13 [s]Joel 2:32 [t]Acts 9:14
10:14 [u]Tit. 1:3
10:15 [v]Isa. 52:7
10:16 [w]Heb. 4:2 [x]Isa. 53:1
10:18 [y]Ps. 19:4; Mark 16:15; Col. 1:6 [z]1 Kings 18:10
10:19 [a]Deut. 32:21 [b]Tit. 3:3
10:20 [c]Isa. 65:1
10:21 [d]Isa. 65:2
11:1 [e]1 Sam. 12:22 [f]2 Cor. 11:22
11:3 [g]1 Kings 19:10
11:4 [h]1 Kings 19:18
11:6 [i]Deut. 9:4
11:8 [j]Isa. 29:10 [k]Deut. 29:4; Jer. 5:21; Ezek. 12:2; John 12:40; Acts 28:26
11:9 [l]Ps. 69:22
11:10 [m]Ps. 69:23
11:11 [n]Acts 13:46
11:13 [o]Acts 9:15; Eph. 3:8; 1 Tim. 2:7
11:14 [p]1 Cor. 7:16; Jam. 5:20
11:16 [q]Lev. 23:10
11:17 [r]Jer. 11:16 [s]Acts 2:39
11:18 [t]1 Cor. 10:12
11:20 [u]Prov. 28:14; Phil. 2:12
11:22 [v]1 Cor. 15:2 [w]John 15:2
11:23 [x]2 Cor. 3:16
11:25 [y]2 Cor. 3:14 [z]Luke 21:24
11:26 [a]Ps. 14:7
11:27 [b]Isa. 27:9; Heb. 8:8
11:28 [c]Deut. 7:8
11:29 [d]Num. 23:19

30 For as ye [e]in times past have not believed God, yet have now obtained mercy through their unbelief:

31 Even so have these also now not believed, that through your mercy they also may obtain mercy.

32 For [f]God hath concluded them all in unbelief, that he might have mercy upon all.

33 O the depth of the riches both of the wisdom and knowledge of God! [g]how unsearchable *are* his judgments, and [h]his ways past finding out!

34 [i]For who hath known the mind of the Lord? or [j]who hath been his counsellor?

35 Or [k]who hath first given to him, and it shall be recompensed unto him again?

36 For [l]of him, and through him, and to him, *are* all things: [m]to whom *be* glory for ever. Amen.

12 I [n]beseech you therefore, brethren, by the mercies of God, [o]that ye [p]present your bodies [q]a living sacrifice, holy, acceptable unto God, *which is* your reasonable service.

2 And [r]be not conformed to this world: but [s]be ye transformed by the renewing of your mind, that ye may [t]prove what *is* that good, and acceptable, and perfect, will of God.

3 For I say, [u]through the grace given unto me, to every man that is among you, [v]not to think *of himself* more highly than he ought to think; but to think soberly, according as God hath dealt [w]to every man the measure of faith.

4 For [x]as we have many members in one body, and all members have not the same office:

5 So [y]we, *being* many, are one body in Christ, and every one members one of another.

6 [z]Having then gifts differing according to the grace that is given to us, whether [a]prophecy, *let us prophesy* according to the proportion of faith;

7 Or ministry, *let us wait* on *our* ministering; or [b]he that teacheth, on teaching;

8 Or [c]he that exhorteth, on exhortation: [d]he that giveth, *let him do it* with simplicity; [e]he that ruleth, with diligence; he that sheweth mercy, [f]with cheerfulness.

9 [g]*Let* love be without dissimulation. [h]Abhor that which is evil; cleave to that which is good.

10 [i]*Be* kindly affectioned one to another with brotherly love; [j]in honour preferring one another;

11 Not slothful in business; fervent in spirit; serving the Lord;

12 [k]Rejoicing in hope; [l]patient in tribulation; [m]continuing instant in prayer;

13 [n]Distributing to the necessity of saints; [o]given to hospitality.

14 [p]Bless them which persecute you: bless, and curse not.

15 [q]Rejoice with them that do rejoice, and weep with them that weep.

16 [r]*Be* of the same mind one toward another. [s]Mind not high things, but condescend to men of low estate. [t]Be not wise in your own conceits.

17 [u]Recompense to no man evil for evil. [v]Provide things honest in the sight of all men.

18 If it be possible, as much as lieth in you, [w]live peaceably with all men.

19 Dearly beloved, [x]avenge not yourselves, but *rather* give place unto wrath: for it is written, [y]Vengeance *is* mine; I will repay, saith the Lord.

20 [z]Therefore if thine enemy hunger, feed him; if he thirst, give him drink: for in so doing thou shalt heap coals of fire on his head.

21 Be not overcome of evil, but overcome evil with good.

13 Let every soul [a]be subject unto the higher powers. For [b]there is no power but of God: the powers that be are ordained of God.

2 Whosoever therefore resisteth [c]the power, resisteth the ordinance of God: and they that resist shall receive to themselves damnation.

3 For rulers are not a terror to good works, but to the evil. Wilt thou then not be afraid of the power? [d]do that which is good, and thou shalt have praise of the same:

4 For he is the minister of God to thee for good. But if thou do that which is evil, be afraid; for he beareth not the sword in vain: for he is the minister of God, a revenger to *execute* wrath upon him that doeth evil.

5 Wherefore [e]*ye* must needs be subject, not only for wrath, [f]but also for conscience sake.

6 For for this cause pay ye tribute also: for they are God's ministers, attending continually upon this very thing.

7 [g]Render therefore to all their dues: tribute to whom tribute *is due;* custom to whom custom; fear to whom fear; honour to whom honour.

8 Owe no man any thing, but to love one another: for [h]he that loveth another hath fulfilled the law.

9 For this, [i]Thou shalt not commit adultery, Thou shalt not kill, Thou shalt not steal, Thou shalt not bear false witness, Thou shalt not covet; and if *there be* any other commandment, it is briefly comprehended in this saying, namely, [j]Thou shalt love thy neighbour as thyself.

10 Love worketh no ill to his neighbour: therefore [k]love *is* the fulfilling of the law.

11 And that, knowing the time, that now *it is* high time [l]to awake out of sleep: for now *is* our salvation nearer than when we believed.

12 The night is far spent, the day is at hand: [m]let us therefore cast off the works of darkness, and [n]let us put on the armour of light.

11:30 [e]Eph. 2:2
11:32 [f]Gal. 3:22
11:33 [g]Ps. 36:6 [h]Job 11:7
11:34 [i]Job 15:8; Jer. 23:18; 1 Cor. 2:16 [j]Job 36:22
11:35 [k]Job 35:7
11:36 [l]1 Cor. 8:6 [m]Gal. 1:5; 2 Tim. 4:18; Heb. 13:21; 2 Pet. 3:18; Jude 25
12:1 [n]2 Cor. 10:1 [o]1 Pet. 2:5 [p]Ps. 50:13 [q]Heb. 10:20
12:2 [r]1 Pet. 1:14 [s]Eph. 1:18 [t]Eph. 5:10
12:3 [u]1 Cor. 3:10; Eph. 3:2 [v]Prov. 25:27 [w]1 Cor. 12:7
12:4 [x]1 Cor. 12:12
12:5 [y]1 Cor. 10:17
12:6 [z]1 Cor. 12:4 [a]Acts 11:27
12:7 [b]Acts 13:1; Gal. 6:6; 1 Tim. 5:17
12:8 [c]Acts 15:32 [d]Matt. 6:1 [e]Acts 20:28; Heb. 13:7; 1 Pet. 5:2 [f]2 Cor. 9:7
12:9 [g]1 Tim. 1:5 [h]Ps. 34:14
12:10 [i]Heb. 13:1; 2 Pet. 1:7 [j]Phil. 2:3
12:12 [k]Luke 10:20; 1 Thess. 5:16; Heb. 3:6 [l]Luke 21:19; Heb. 10:36; Jam. 1:4 [m]Luke 18:1; Col. 4:2; Eph. 6:18
12:13 [n]1 Cor. 16:1; Heb. 6:10; 1 John 3:17 [o]1 Tim. 3:2; Heb. 13:2; 1 Pet. 4:9
12:14 [p]Matt. 5:44; Acts 7:60; 1 Cor. 4:12
12:15 [q]1 Cor. 12:26
12:16 [r]1 Cor. 1:10; 1 Pet. 3:8 [s]Ps. 131:1 [t]Prov. 3:7
12:17 [u]Prov. 20:22; 1 Thess. 5:15; 1 Pet. 3:9 [v]2 Cor. 8:21
12:18 [w]Mark 9:50
12:19 [x]Lev. 19:18 [y]Deut. 32:35
12:20 [z]Ex. 23:4; Matt. 5:44
13:1 [a]Tit. 3:1 [b]Prov. 8:15; John 19:11
13:2 [c]Tit. 3:1
13:3 [d]1 Pet. 2:14
13:5 [e]Eccl. 8:2 [f]1 Pet. 2:19
13:7 [g]Matt. 22:21; Luke 20:35
13:8 [h]Gal. 5:14; 1 Tim. 1:5; Jam. 2:8
13:9 [i]Ex. 20:13; Matt. 19:18 [j]Lev. 19:18; Mark 12:31; Gal. 5:14
13:10 [k]Matt. 22:40
13:11 [l]1 Cor. 15:34; 1 Thess. 5:5
13:12 [m]Eph. 5:11 [n]Eph. 6:13

13 [o]Let us walk honestly, as in the day; [p]not in rioting and drunkenness, [q]not in chambering and wantonness, [r]not in strife and envying.

14 But [s]put ye on the Lord Jesus Christ, and [t]make not provision for the flesh, to *fulfil* the lusts *thereof*.

14

Him that [u]is weak in the faith receive ye, *but* not to doubtful disputations.

2 For one believeth that he [v]may eat all things: another, who is weak, eateth herbs.

3 Let not him that eateth despise him that eateth not; and [w]let not him which eateth not judge him that eateth: for God hath received him.

4 [x]Who art thou that judgest another man's servant? to his own master he standeth or falleth. Yea, he shall be holden up: for God is able to make him stand.

5 [y]One man esteemeth one day above another: another esteemeth every day *alike*. Let every man be fully persuaded in his own mind.

6 He that [z]regardeth the day, regardeth *it* unto the Lord; and he that regardeth not the day, to the Lord he doth not regard *it*. He that eateth, eateth to the Lord, for [a]he giveth God thanks; and he that eateth not, to the Lord he eateth not, and giveth God thanks.

7 For [b]none of us liveth to himself, and no man dieth to himself.

8 For whether we live, we live unto the Lord; and whether we die, we die unto the Lord: whether we live therefore, or die, we are the Lord's.

9 For [c]to this end Christ both died, and rose, and revived, that he might be [d]Lord both of the dead and living.

10 But why dost thou judge thy brother? or why dost thou set at nought thy brother? for [e]we shall all stand before the judgment seat of Christ.

11 For it is written, [f]*As* I live, saith the Lord, every knee shall bow to me, and every tongue shall confess to God.

12 So then [g]every one of us shall give account of himself to God.

13 Let us not therefore judge one another any more: but judge this rather, that [h]no man put a stumblingblock or an occasion to fall in *his* brother's way.

14 I know, and am persuaded by the Lord Jesus, [i]that *there is* nothing unclean of itself: but [j]to him that esteemeth any thing to be unclean, to him *it is* unclean.

15 But if thy brother be grieved with *thy* meat, now walkest thou not charitably. [k]Destroy not him with thy meat, for whom Christ died.

16 Let not then your good be evil spoken of:

17 [l]For the kingdom of God is not meat and drink; but righteousness, and peace, and joy in the Holy Ghost.

18 For he that in these things serveth Christ [m]*is* acceptable to God, and approved of men.

19 [n]Let us therefore follow after the things which make for peace, and things wherewith [o]one may edify another.

20 For meat destroy not the work of God. [p]All things indeed *are* pure; [q]but *it is* evil for that man who eateth with offence.

21 *It is* good neither to eat [r]flesh, nor to drink wine, nor *any thing* whereby thy brother stumbleth, or is offended, or is made weak.

22 Hast thou faith? have *it* to thyself before God. [s]Happy *is* he that condemneth not himself in that thing which he alloweth.

23 And he that doubteth is damned if he eat, because *he eateth* not of faith: for [t]whatsoever *is* not of faith is sin.

15

We [u]then that are strong ought to bear the infirmities of the weak, and not to please ourselves.

2 [v]Let every one of us please *his* neighbour for *his* good to edification.

3 [w]For even Christ pleased not himself; but, as it is written, [x]The reproaches of them that reproached thee fell on me.

4 For [y]whatsoever things were written aforetime were written for our learning, that we through patience and comfort of the scriptures might have hope.

5 [z]Now the God of patience and consolation grant you to be likeminded one toward another according to Christ Jesus:

6 That ye may [a]with one mind *and* one mouth glorify God, even the Father of our Lord Jesus Christ.

7 Wherefore receive ye one another, as Christ also received us to the glory of God.

8 Now I say that [b]Jesus Christ was a minister of the circumcision for the truth of God, [c]to confirm the promises *made* unto the fathers:

9 And [d]that the Gentiles might glorify God for *his* mercy; as it is written, [e]For this cause I will confess to thee among the Gentiles, and sing unto thy name.

10 And again he saith, [f]Rejoice, ye Gentiles, with his people.

11 And again, [g]Praise the Lord, all ye Gentiles; and laud him, all ye people.

12 And again, Esaias saith, [h]There shall be a root of Jesse, and he that shall rise to reign over the Gentiles; in him shall the Gentiles trust.

13 Now the God of hope fill you with all joy and peace in believing, that ye may abound in hope, through the power of the Holy Ghost.

14 And [i]I myself also am persuaded of you, my brethren, that ye also are full of goodness, [j]filled with all knowledge, able also to admonish one another.

15 Nevertheless, brethren, I have written the more boldly unto you in some sort, as putting you in mind, [k]because of the grace that is given to me of God,

16 That [l]I should be the minister of Jesus Christ to the Gentiles, ministering the gos-

13:13 [o]Phil. 4:8; 1 Pet. 2:12 [p]Prov. 23:20; 1 Pet. 4:3 [q]1 Cor. 6:9 [r]Jam. 3:14
13:14 [s]Gal. 3:27; Col. 3:10 [t]Gal. 5:16
14:1 [u]1 Cor. 8:9
14:2 [v]1 Cor. 10:25; Tit. 1:15
14:3 [w]Col. 2:16
14:4 [x]Jam. 4:12
14:5 [y]Gal. 4:10
14:6 [z]Gal. 4:10 [a]1 Cor. 10:31
14:7 [b]1 Cor. 6:19; 1 Thess. 5:10; 1 Pet. 4:2
14:9 [c]2 Cor. 5:15 [d]Acts 10:36
14:10 [e]Matt. 25:31; 2 Cor. 5:10; Jude 14
14:11 [f]Isa. 45:23
14:12 [g]Matt. 12:36; 1 Pet. 4:5
14:13 [h]1 Cor. 8:9
14:14 [i]Acts 10:15; 1 Tim. 4:4; Tit. 1:15 [j]1 Cor. 8:7
14:15 [k]1 Cor. 8:11
14:17 [l]1 Cor. 8:8
14:18 [m]2 Cor. 8:21
14:19 [n]Ps. 34:14 [o]1 Cor. 14:12
14:20 [p]Matt. 15:11; Tit. 1:15 [q]1 Cor. 8:9
14:21 [r]1 Cor. 8:13
14:22 [s]1 John 3:21
14:23 [t]Tit. 1:15
15:1 [u]Gal. 6:1
15:2 [v]1 Cor. 9:19
15:3 [w]Matt. 26:39 [x]Ps. 69:9
15:4 [y]1 Cor. 9:9
15:5 [z]1 Cor. 1:10
15:6 [a]Acts 4:24
15:8 [b]Matt. 15:24; Acts 3:25 [c]2 Cor. 1:20
15:9 [d]John 10:16 [e]Ps. 18:49
15:10 [f]Deut. 32:43
15:11 [g]Ps. 117:1
15:12 [h]Isa. 11:1
15:14 [i]2 Pet. 1:12 [j]1 Cor. 8:1
15:15 [k]Gal. 1:15
15:16 [l]Gal. 2:7; 2 Tim. 1:11; Phil. 2:17

pel of God, that the [m]offering up of the Gentiles might be acceptable, being sanctified
by the Holy Ghost.
17 I have therefore whereof I may glory
through Jesus Christ [n]in those things
which pertain to God.
18 For I will not dare to speak of any of
those things [o]which Christ hath not
wrought by me, to make the Gentiles obedient, by word and deed,
19 [p]Through mighty signs and wonders,
by the power of the Spirit of God; so that
from Jerusalem, and round about unto Illyr-
icum, I have fully preached the gospel of
Christ.
20 Yea, so have I strived to preach the
gospel, not where Christ was named, [q]lest
I should build upon another man's foundation:
21 But as it is written, [r]To whom he was
not spoken of, they shall see: and they that
have not heard shall understand.
22 For which cause also [s]I have been
much hindered from coming to you.
23 But now having no more place in these
parts, and [t]having a great desire these
many years to come unto you;
24 Whensoever I take my journey into
Spain, I will come to you: for I trust to see
you in my journey, [u]and to be brought on
my way thitherward by you, if first I be
somewhat filled with your *company*.
25 But now [v]I go unto Jerusalem to minister unto the saints.
26 For [w]it hath pleased them of Macedonia and Achaia to make a certain contribution for the poor saints which are at
Jerusalem.
27 It hath pleased them verily; and their
debtors they are. For if the Gentiles have
been made partakers of their spiritual
things, [x]their duty is also to minister unto
them in carnal things.
28 When therefore I have performed this,
and have sealed to them [y]this fruit, I will
come by you into Spain.
29 And I am sure that, when I come unto
you, I shall come in the fulness of the blessing of the gospel of Christ.
30 Now I beseech you, brethren, for the
Lord Jesus Christ's sake, and [z]for the love
of the Spirit, [a]that ye strive together with
me in *your* prayers to God for me;
31 [b]That I may be delivered from them
that do not believe in Judaea; and that [c]my
service which *I have* for Jerusalem may be
accepted of the saints;
32 That I may come unto you with joy [d]by
the will of God, and may with you [e]be refreshed.
33 Now [f]the God of peace *be* with you
all. Amen.

16 I commend unto you Phebe our sister, which is a servant of the church
which is at [g]Cenchrea:
2 [h]That ye receive her in the Lord, as
becometh saints, and that ye assist her in
whatsoever business she hath need of you:
for she hath been a succourer of many, and
of myself also.
3 Greet [i]Priscilla and Aquila my helpers
in Christ Jesus:
4 Who have for my life laid down their
own necks: unto whom not only I give
thanks, but also all the churches of the Gentiles.
5 Likewise *greet* [j]the church that is in
their house. Salute my wellbeloved Epaene-
tus, who is [k]the firstfruits of Achaia unto
Christ.
6 Greet Mary, who bestowed much labour on us.
7 Salute Andronicus and Junia, my kinsmen, and my fellowprisoners, who are of
note among the apostles, who also [l]were in
Christ before me.
8 Greet Amplias my beloved in the Lord.
9 Salute Urbane, our helper in Christ, and
Stachys my beloved.
10 Salute Apelles approved in Christ. Salute them which are of Aristobulus' *household*.
11 Salute Herodion my kinsman. Greet
them that be of the *household* of Narcissus,
which are in the Lord.
12 Salute Tryphena and Tryphosa, who
labour in the Lord. Salute the beloved Persis, which laboured much in the Lord.
13 Salute Rufus [m]chosen in the Lord, and
his mother and mine.
14 Salute Asyncritus, Phlegon, Hermas,
Patrobas, Hermes, and the brethren which
are with them.
15 Salute Philologus, and Julia, Nereus,
and his sister, and Olympas, and all the
saints which are with them.
16 [n]Salute one another with an holy kiss.
The churches of Christ salute you.
17 Now I beseech you, brethren, mark
them [o]which cause divisions and offences
contrary to the doctrine which ye have
learned; and [p]avoid them.
18 For they that are such serve not our
Lord Jesus Christ, but [q]their own belly; and
[r]by good words and fair speeches deceive
the hearts of the simple.
19 For your obedience is come abroad
unto all *men*. I am glad therefore on your
behalf: but yet I would have you [s]wise unto
that which is good, and simple concerning
evil.
20 And the God of peace [t]shall bruise Satan under your feet shortly. [u]The grace of
our Lord Jesus Christ *be* with you. Amen.
21 [v]Timotheus my workfellow, and [w]Lu-
cius, and [x]Jason, and [y]Sosipater, my kinsmen, salute you.
22 I Tertius, who wrote *this* epistle, salute
you in the Lord.
23 [z]Gaius mine host, and of the whole
church, saluteth you. [a]Erastus the chamberlain of the city saluteth you, and Quartus
a brother.
24 [b]The grace of our Lord Jesus Christ *be*
with you all. Amen.
25 Now [c]to him that is of power to stab-

15:16 [m]Isa. 66:20
15:17 [n]Heb. 5:1
15:18 [o]Acts 21:19
15:19 [p]Acts 19:11
15:20 [q]2 Cor. 10:13
15:21 [r]Isa. 52:15
15:22 [s]1 Thess. 2:17
15:23 [t]Acts 19:21
15:24 [u]Acts 15:3
15:25 [v]Acts 19:21
15:26 [w]1 Cor. 16:1
15:27 [x]1 Cor. 9:11
15:28 [y]Phil. 4:17
15:30 [z]Phil. 2:1 [a]2 Cor. 1:11
15:31 [b]2 Thess. 3:2 [c]2 Cor. 8:4
15:32 [d]Acts 18:21; Jam. 4:15 [e]1 Cor. 16:18; 2 Tim. 1:16; Philem. 7
15:33 [f]1 Cor. 14:33; Phil. 4:9; 1 Thess. 5:23; Heb. 13:20
16:1 [g]Acts 18:18
16:2 [h]Phil. 2:29
16:3 [i]Acts 18:2
16:5 [j]1 Cor. 16:19; Philem. 2 [k]1 Cor. 16:15
16:7 [l]Gal. 1:22
16:13 [m]2 John 1
16:16 [n]1 Cor. 16:20; 1 Thess. 5:26; 1 Pet. 5:14
16:17 [o]Acts 15:1 [p]1 Cor. 5:9; 2 Tim. 3:5; Tit. 3:10
16:18 [q]Phil. 3:19 [r]Col. 2:4; Tit. 1:10; 2 Pet. 2:3
16:19 [s]Matt. 10:16
16:20 [t]Gen. 3:15 [u]1 Cor. 16:23; Phil. 4:23; 1 Thess. 5:28; Rev. 22:21
16:21 [v]Acts 16:1; Phil. 2:19; 1 Thess. 3:2; Heb. 13:23 [w]Acts 13:1 [x]Acts 17:5 [y]Acts 20:4
16:23 [z]1 Cor. 1:14 [a]Acts 19:22
16:24 [b]1 Thess. 5:28
16:25 [c]Eph. 3:20; 2 Thess. 2:17; Jude 24

lish you according to my gospel, and the preaching of Jesus Christ, [d]according to the revelation of the mystery, [e]which was kept secret since the world began,

26 But [f]now is made manifest, and by the scriptures of the prophets, according to the commandment of the everlasting God, made known to all nations for [g]the obedience of faith:

27 To [h]God only wise, *be* glory through Jesus Christ for ever. Amen.

16:25 [d]Eph. 1:9 [e]1 Cor. 2:7; Col. 1:26
16:26 [f]Eph. 1:9; Tit. 1:2; 1 Pet. 1:20 [g]Acts 6:7
16:27 [h]1 Tim. 1:17

1 CORINTHIANS

Paul acknowledges himself as the author of 1 and 2 Corinthians. First Corinthians was probably written in A.D. 55 or A.D. 56 and is Paul's letter to the church at Corinth, which had experienced a great deal of turmoil within the church, as well as trying to determine the proper application of the new doctrines of Christianity to everyday life. Paul addresses the issues involving the church, then moves on to the moral questions. He closes with a discussion of the resurrection as it applies to Christ and the Christian. The thirteenth chapter, often referred to as the love chapter, is probably the best loved chapter of this book.

I. Greetings to the church from Paul, 1:1–1:9
II. The problems of the church, 1:10–6:20
III. Marriage relationships, 7:1–7:40
IV. Pagan rituals and corrupted religious practices, 8:1–10:22
V. Other instructions for the church, 11:1–14:40
VI. The resurrection, 15:1–15:58
VII. Paul's parting instructions and greetings, 16:1–16:24

1 Paul, [a]called *to be* an apostle of Jesus Christ [b]through the will of God, and [c]Sosthenes *our* brother,

2 Unto the church of God which is at Corinth, [d]to them that [e]are sanctified in Christ Jesus, [f]called *to be* saints, with all that in every place [g]call upon the name of Jesus Christ our Lord, [h]both theirs and ours:

3 [i]Grace *be* unto you, and peace, from God our Father, and *from* the Lord Jesus Christ.

4 [j]I thank my God always on your behalf, for the grace of God which is given you by Jesus Christ;

5 That in every thing ye are enriched by him, [k]in all utterance, and *in* all knowledge;

6 Even as [l]the testimony of Christ was confirmed in you:

7 So that ye come behind in no gift; [m]waiting for the coming of our Lord Jesus Christ:

8 [n]Who shall also confirm you unto the end, [o]*that ye may be* blameless in the day of our Lord Jesus Christ.

9 [p]God *is* faithful, by whom ye were called unto [q]the fellowship of his Son Jesus Christ our Lord.

10 Now I beseech you, brethren, by the name of our Lord Jesus Christ, [r]that ye all speak the same thing, and *that* there be no divisions among you; but *that* ye be perfectly joined together in the same mind and in the same judgment.

11 For it hath been declared unto me of you, my brethren, by them *which are of the house* of Chloe, that there are contentions among you.

12 Now this I say, that every one of you saith, I am of Paul; and I of [s]Apollos; and I of [t]Cephas; and I of Christ.

13 [u]Is Christ divided? was Paul crucified for you? or were ye baptized in the name of Paul?

14 I thank God that I baptized none of you, but [v]Crispus and [w]Gaius;

15 Lest any should say that I had baptized in mine own name.

16 And I baptized also the household of Stephanas: besides, I know not whether I baptized any other.

17 For Christ sent me not to baptize, but to preach the gospel: [x]not with wisdom of words, lest the cross of Christ should be made of none effect.

18 For the preaching of the cross is to [y]them that perish [z]foolishness; but unto us which are saved it is the [a]power of God.

19 For it is written, [b]I will destroy the wisdom of the wise, and will bring to nothing the understanding of the prudent.

20 [c]Where *is* the wise? where *is* the scribe? where *is* the disputer of this world?

1:1 [a]Rom. 1:1 [b]2 Cor. 1:1; Col. 1:1 [c]Acts 18:17
1:2 [d]Jude 1 [e]John 17:19 [f]Rom. 1:7 [g]Acts 9:14 [h]Rom. 3:22
1:3 [i]Rom. 1:7; Eph. 1:2; 1 Pet. 1:2
1:4 [j]Rom. 1:8
1:5 [k]2 Cor. 8:7
1:6 [l]2 Tim. 1:8
1:7 [m]Phil. 3:20; 2 Pet. 3:12
1:8 [n]1 Thess. 3:13 [o]Col. 1:22
1:9 [p]Isa. 49:7; 2 Thess. 3:3; Heb. 10:23 [q]John 15:4
1:10 [r]Rom. 12:16; Phil. 2:2; 1 Pet. 3:8
1:12 [s]Acts 18:24 [t]John 1:42
1:13 [u]2 Cor. 11:4
1:14 [v]Acts 18:8 [w]Rom. 16:23
1:17 [x]2 Pet. 1:16
1:18 [y]2 Cor. 2:15 [z]Acts 17:18 [a]Rom. 1:16
1:19 [b]Job 5:12; Jer. 8:9
1:20 [c]Isa. 33:18

[d]hath not God made foolish the wisdom of this world?

21 [e]For after that in the wisdom of God the world by wisdom knew not God, it pleased God by the foolishness of preaching to save them that believe.

22 For the [f]Jews require a sign, and the Greeks seek after wisdom:

23 But we preach Christ crucified, [g]unto the Jews a stumblingblock, and unto the Greeks foolishness;

24 But unto them which are called, both Jews and Greeks, Christ [h]the power of God, and [i]the wisdom of God.

25 Because the foolishness of God is wiser than men; and the weakness of God is stronger than men.

26 For ye see your calling, brethren, how that [j]not many wise men after the flesh, not many mighty, not many noble, *are called:*

27 But [k]God hath chosen the foolish things of the world to confound the wise; and God hath chosen the weak things of the world to confound the things which are mighty;

28 And base things of the world, and things which are despised, hath God chosen, *yea,* and [l]things which are not, to bring to nought things that are:

29 [m]That no flesh should glory in his presence.

30 But of him are ye in Christ Jesus, who of God is made unto us wisdom, and [n]righteousness, and [o]sanctification, and [p]redemption:

31 That, according as it is written, [q]He that glorieth, let him glory in the Lord.

2 And I, brethren, when I came to you, [r]came not with excellency of speech or of wisdom, declaring unto you the testimony of God.

2 For I determined not to know any thing among you, [s]save Jesus Christ, and him crucified.

3 And [t]I was with you [u]in weakness, and in fear, and in much trembling.

4 And my speech and my preaching [v]*was* not with enticing words of man's wisdom, [w]but in demonstration of the Spirit and of power:

5 That your faith should not stand in the wisdom of men, but [x]in the power of God.

6 Howbeit we speak wisdom among them [y]that are perfect: yet not [z]the wisdom of this world, nor of the princes of this world, that come to nought:

7 But we speak the wisdom of God in a mystery, *even* the hidden *wisdom,* [a]which God ordained before the world unto our glory:

8 [b]Which none of the princes of this world knew: for [c]had they known *it,* they would not have crucified the Lord of glory.

9 But as it is written, [d]Eye hath not seen, nor ear heard, neither have entered into the heart of man, the things which God hath prepared for them that love him.

10 But [e]God hath revealed *them* unto us by his Spirit: for the Spirit searcheth all things, yea, the deep things of God.

11 For what man knoweth the things of a man, [f]save the spirit of man which is in him? [g]even so the things of God knoweth no man, but the Spirit of God.

12 Now we have received, not the spirit of the world, but [h]the spirit which is of God; that we might know the things that are freely given to us of God.

13 [i]Which things also we speak, not in the words which man's wisdom teacheth, but which the Holy Ghost teacheth; comparing spiritual things with spiritual.

14 [j]But the natural man receiveth not the things of the Spirit of God: for they are foolishness unto him: [k]neither can he know *them,* because they are spiritually discerned.

15 [l]But he that is spiritual judgeth all things, yet he himself is judged of no man.

16 [m]For who hath known the mind of the Lord, that he may instruct him? [n]But we have the mind of Christ.

3 And I, brethren, could not speak unto you as unto spiritual, but as unto carnal, *even* as unto [o]babes in Christ.

2 I have fed you with [p]milk, and not with meat: [q]for hitherto ye were not able *to bear it,* neither yet now are ye able.

3 For ye are yet carnal: for [r]whereas *there is* among you envying, and strife, and divisions, are ye not carnal, and walk as men?

4 For while one saith, I am of Paul; and another, I *am* of Apollos; are ye not carnal?

5 Who then is Paul, and who *is* Apollos, but [s]ministers by whom ye believed, [t]even as the Lord gave to every man?

6 [u]I have planted, [v]Apollos watered; [w]but God gave the increase.

7 So then [x]neither is he that planteth any thing, neither he that watereth; but God that giveth the increase.

8 Now he that planteth and he that watereth are one: [y]and every man shall receive his own reward according to his own labour.

9 For [z]we are labourers together with God: ye are God's husbandry, *ye are* [a]God's building.

10 [b]According to the grace of God which is given unto me, as a wise masterbuilder, I have laid [c]the foundation, and another buildeth thereon. But [d]let every man take heed how he buildeth thereupon.

11 For other foundation can no man lay than [e]that is laid, [f]which is Jesus Christ.

12 Now if any man build upon this foundation gold, silver, precious stones, wood, hay, stubble;

13 Every man's work shall be made manifest: for the day [g]shall declare it, because [h]it shall be revealed by fire; and the fire shall try every man's work of what sort it is.

14 If any man's work abide which he hath built thereupon, he shall receive a reward.

15 If any man's work shall be burned, he

1:20 [d]Job 12:17; Rom. 1:22
1:21 [e]Matt. 11:25; Rom. 1:20
1:22 [f]Matt. 12:38; Luke 11:16; John 4:48
1:23 [g]Isa. 8:14; Luke 2:34; John 6:60; Gal. 5:11; 1 Pet. 2:8
1:24 [h]Rom. 1:4 [i]Col. 2:3
1:26 [j]John 7:48
1:27 [k]Ps. 8: Jam. 2:5
1:28 [l]Rom. 4:17
1:29 [m]Rom. 3:27
1:30 [n]Jer. 23:5; 2 Cor. 5:21; Phil. 3:9 [o]John 17:19 [p]Eph. 1:7
1:31 [q]Jer. 9:23
2:1 [r]2 Cor. 10:10
2:2 [s]Gal. 6:14
2:3 [t]Acts 18:1 [u]2 Cor. 4:7
2:4 [v]2 Pet. 1:16 [w]Rom. 15:19
2:5 [x]2 Cor. 4:7
2:6 [y]Eph. 4:13; Heb. 5:14 [z]2 Cor. 1:12
2:7 [a]Rom. 16:25; Col. 1:26; 2 Tim. 1:9
2:8 [b]Matt. 11:25; Acts 13:27; 2 Cor. 3:14 [c]Luke 23:34; Acts 3:17
2:9 [d]Isa. 64:4
2:10 [e]Matt. 13:11; 1 John 2:27
2:11 [f]Prov. 20:27 [g]Rom. 11:33
2:12 [h]Rom. 8:15
2:13 [i]2 Pet. 1:16
2:14 [j]Matt. 16:23 [k]Rom. 8:5
2:15 [l]Prov. 28:5; 1 John 4:1
2:16 [m]Job 15:8; Jer. 23:18; Rom. 11:34 [n]John 15:15
3:1 [o]Heb. 5:13
3:2 [p]Heb. 5:12 [q]John 16:12
3:3 [r]Gal. 5:20
3:5 [s]2 Cor. 3:3 [t]Rom. 12:3
3:6 [u]Acts 18:4 [v]Acts 18:24 [w]2 Cor. 3:5
3:7 [x]2 Cor. 12:11
3:8 [y]Ps. 62:12; Gal. 6:4; Rev. 2:23
3:9 [z]Acts 15:4 [a]Eph. 2:20; Heb. 3:3; 1 Pet. 2:5
3:10 [b]Rom. 1:5 [c]Rom. 15:20 [d]1 Pet. 4:11
3:11 [e]Isa. 28:16; 2 Cor. 11:4; Gal. 1:7 [f]Eph. 2:20
3:13 [g]1 Pet. 1:7 [h]Luke 2:35

COR GAL EPH

shall suffer loss: but he himself shall be saved; [i]yet so as by fire.

16 [j]Know ye not that ye are the temple of God, and *that* the Spirit of God dwelleth in you?

17 If any man defile the temple of God, him shall God destroy; for the temple of God is holy, which *temple* ye are.

18 [k]Let no man deceive himself. If any man among you seemeth to be wise in this world, let him become a fool, that he may be wise.

19 For the wisdom of this world is foolishness with God. For it is written, [l]He taketh the wise in their own craftiness.

20 And again, [m]The Lord knoweth the thoughts of the wise, that they are vain.

21 Therefore let no man glory in men. For [n]all things are yours;

22 Whether Paul, or Apollos, or Cephas, or the world, or life, or death, or things present, or things to come; all are yours;

23 And [o]ye are Christ's; and Christ *is* God's.

4 Let a man so account of us, as of [p]the ministers of Christ, [q]and stewards of the mysteries of God.

2 Moreover it is required in stewards, that a man be found faithful.

3 But with me it is a very small thing that I should be judged of you, or of man's judgment: yea, I judge not mine own self.

4 For I know nothing by myself; [r]yet am I not hereby justified: but he that judgeth me is the Lord.

5 [s]Therefore judge nothing before the time, until the Lord come, who both will bring to light the hidden things of darkness, and will make manifest the counsels of the hearts: and [t]then shall every man have praise of God.

6 And these things, brethren, I have in a figure transferred to myself and *to* Apollos for your sakes; [u]that ye might learn in us not to think *of men* above that which is written, that no one of you be puffed up for one against another.

7 For who maketh thee to differ *from another?* and [v]what hast thou that thou didst not receive? now if thou didst receive *it,* why dost thou glory, as if thou hadst not received *it?*

8 Now ye are full, [w]now ye are rich, ye have reigned as kings without us: and I would to God ye did reign, that we also might reign with you.

9 For I think that God hath set forth us the apostles last, [x]as it were appointed to death: for [y]we are made a spectacle unto the world, and to angels, and to men.

10 We *are* [z]fools for Christ's sake, but *ye are* wise in Christ; [a]we *are* weak, but ye *are* strong; ye *are* honourable, but we *are* despised.

11 [b]Even unto this present hour we both hunger, and thirst, and [c]are naked, and [d]are buffeted, and have no certain dwellingplace;

12 [e]And labour, working with our own hands: [f]being reviled, we bless; being persecuted, we suffer it:

13 Being defamed, we intreat: [g]we are made as the filth of the world, *and are* the offscouring of all things unto this day.

14 I write not these things to shame you, but [h]as my beloved sons I warn *you.*

15 For though ye have ten thousand instructors in Christ, yet *have ye* not many fathers: for [i]in Christ Jesus I have begotten you through the gospel.

16 Wherefore I beseech you, [j]be ye followers of me.

17 For this cause have I sent unto you [k]Timotheus, [l]who is my beloved son, and faithful in the Lord, who shall bring you into remembrance of my ways which be in Christ, as I teach every where in every church.

18 Now some are puffed up, as though I would not come to you.

19 [m]But I will come to you shortly, [n]if the Lord will, and will know, not the speech of them which are puffed up, but the power.

20 For [o]the kingdom of God *is* not in word, but in power.

21 What will ye? [p]shall I come unto you with a rod, or in love, and *in* the spirit of meekness?

5 It is reported commonly *that there is* fornication among you, and such fornication as is not so much as [q]named among the Gentiles, [r]that one should have his [s]father's wife.

2 And ye are puffed up, and have not rather [t]mourned, that he that hath done this deed might be taken away from among you.

3 [u]For I verily, as absent in body, but present in spirit, have judged already, as though I were present, *concerning* him that hath so done this deed,

4 In the name of our Lord Jesus Christ, when ye are gathered together, and my spirit, [v]with the power of our Lord Jesus Christ,

5 [w]To deliver such an one unto [x]Satan for the destruction of the flesh, that the spirit may be saved in the day of the Lord Jesus.

6 [y]Your glorying *is* not good. Know ye not that [z]a little leaven leaveneth the whole lump?

7 Purge out therefore the old leaven, that ye may be a new lump, as ye are unleavened. For even [a]Christ our [b]passover is sacrificed for us:

8 Therefore [c]let us keep the feast, [d]not with old leaven, neither [e]with the leaven of malice and wickedness; but with the unleavened *bread* of sincerity and truth.

9 I wrote unto you in an epistle [f]not to company with fornicators:

10 Yet not altogether with the fornicators of this world, or with the covetous, or with the extortioners, or with idolaters; for then must ye needs go [g]out of the world.

3:15 [i]Jude 23
3:16 [j]2 Cor. 6:16; Heb. 3:6; 1 Pet. 2:5
3:18 [k]Prov. 5:7
3:19 [l]Job 5:13
3:20 [m]Ps. 94:11
3:21 [n]2 Cor. 4:5
3:23 [o]Rom. 14:8; Gal. 3:29
4:1 [p]Matt. 24:45; Col. 1:25 [q]Luke 12:42; 1 Pet. 4:10
4:4 [r]Job 9:2; Prov. 21:2; Rom. 3:20
4:5 [s]Matt. 7:1; Rev. 20:12 [t]Rom. 2:29
4:6 [u]Rom. 12:3
4:7 [v]John 3:27; 1 Pet. 4:10
4:8 [w]Rev. 3:17
4:9 [x]Ps. 44:22; 2 Cor. 4:11 [y]Heb. 10:33
4:10 [z]2 Kings 9:11 [a]2 Cor. 13:9
4:11 [b]2 Cor. 4:8 [c]Job 22:6 [d]Acts 23:2
4:12 [e]Acts 18:3; 2 Thess. 3:8; 1 Tim. 4:10 [f]Matt. 5:44; Acts 7:60; Rom. 12:14
4:13 [g]Lam. 3:45
4:14 [h]1 Thess. 2:11
4:15 [i]Acts 18:11; Gal. 4:19; Philem. 10
4:16 [j]Phil. 3:17; 2 Thess. 3:9
4:17 [k]Acts 19:22; 1 Thess. 3:2 [l]1 Tim. 1:2
4:19 [m]Acts 19:21 [n]Acts 18:21; Heb. 6:3; Jam. 4:15
4:20 [o]1 Thess. 1:5
4:21 [p]2 Cor. 10:2
5:1 [q]Eph. 5:3 [r]Lev. 18:8 [s]2 Cor. 7:12
5:2 [t]2 Cor. 7:7
5:3 [u]Col. 2:5
5:4 [v]Matt. 16:19; 2 Cor. 2:10
5:5 [w]Job 2:6; 1 Tim. 1:20 [x]Acts 26:18
5:6 [y]Jam. 4:16 [z]Gal. 5:9
5:7 [a]Isa. 53:7; 1 Pet. 1:19; Rev. 5:6 [b]John 19:14
5:8 [c]Ex. 12:15 [d]Deut. 16:3 [e]Matt. 16:6; Luke 12:1
5:9 [f]2 Cor. 6:14; 2 Thess. 3:14
5:10 [g]John 17:15

11 But now I have written unto you not to keep company, [h]if any man that is called a brother be a fornicator, or covetous, or an idolater, or a railer, or a drunkard, or an extortioner; with such an one [i]no not to eat.

12 For what have I to do to judge [j]them also that are without? do not ye judge them that are within?

13 But them that are without God judgeth. Therefore [k]put away from among yourselves that wicked person.

6 Dare any of you, having a matter against another, go to law before the unjust, and not before the saints?

2 Do ye not know that [l]the saints shall judge the world? and if the world shall be judged by you, are ye unworthy to judge the smallest matters?

3 Know ye not that we shall [m]judge angels? how much more things that pertain to this life?

4 If then ye have judgments of things pertaining to this life, set them to judge who are least esteemed in the church.

5 I speak to your shame. Is it so, that there is not a wise man among you? no, not one that shall be able to judge between his brethren?

6 But brother goeth to law with brother, and that before the unbelievers.

7 Now therefore there is utterly a fault among you, because ye go to law one with another. [n]Why do ye not rather take wrong? why do ye not rather *suffer yourselves to* be defrauded?

8 Nay, ye do wrong, and defraud, [o]and that *your* brethren.

9 Know ye not that the unrighteous shall not inherit the kingdom of God? Be not deceived: [p]neither fornicators, nor idolaters, nor adulterers, nor effeminate, nor abusers of themselves with mankind,

10 Nor thieves, nor covetous, nor drunkards, nor revilers, nor extortioners, shall inherit the kingdom of God.

11 And such were [q]some of you: [r]but ye are washed, but ye are sanctified, but ye are justified in the name of the Lord Jesus, and by the Spirit of our God.

12 All things are lawful unto me, but all things are not expedient: all things are lawful for me, but I will not be brought under the power of any.

13 [s]Meats for the belly, and the belly for meats: but God shall destroy both it and them. Now the body *is* not for fornication, but [t]for the Lord; [u]and the Lord for the body.

14 And [v]God hath both raised up the Lord, and will also raise up us [w]by his own power.

15 Know ye not that [x]your bodies are the members of Christ? shall I then take the members of Christ, and make *them* the members of an harlot? God forbid.

16 What? know ye not that he which is joined to an harlot is one body? for [y]two, saith he, shall be one flesh.

5:11 [h]Matt. 18:17; 2 Thess. 3:6; 2 John 10 [i]Gal. 2:12
5:12 [j]Mark 4:11; 1 Thess. 4:12; 1 Tim. 3:7
5:13 [k]Deut. 13:5
6:2 [l]Ps. 49:14; Matt. 19:28; Luke 22:30
6:3 [m]2 Pet. 2:4
6:7 [n]Prov. 20:22; Luke 6:29; Rom. 12:17
6:8 [o]1 Thess. 4:6
6:9 [p]Gal. 5:21; 1 Tim. 1:9; Heb. 12:14
6:11 [q]Eph. 2:2; Tit. 3:3 [r]Heb. 10:22
6:13 [s]Matt. 15:17; Col. 2:22 [t]1 Thess. 4:3 [u]Eph. 5:23
6:14 [v]Rom. 6:5 [w]Eph. 1:19
6:15 [x]Rom. 12:5
6:16 [y]Gen. 2:24; Eph. 5:31
6:17 [z]John 17:21
6:18 [a]Rom. 6:12 [b]Rom. 1:24
6:19 [c]2 Cor. 6:16 [d]Rom. 14:7
6:20 [e]Acts 20:28; Heb. 9:12; 1 Pet. 1:18; Rev. 5:9
7:3 [f]Ex. 21:10
7:5 [g]Ex. 19:15; Joel 2:16; Zech. 7:3 [h]1 Thess. 3:5
7:6 [i]2 Cor. 8:8
7:7 [j]Acts 26:29 [k]Matt. 19:12
7:9 [l]1 Tim. 5:14
7:10 [m]Mal. 2:14; Mark 10:11; Luke 16:18
7:14 [n]Mal. 2:15
7:15 [o]Rom. 12:18
7:16 [p]1 Pet. 3:1

17 [z]But he that is joined unto the Lord is one spirit.

18 [a]Flee fornication. Every sin that a man doeth is without the body; but he that committeth fornication sinneth [b]against his own body.

19 What? [c]know ye not that your body is the temple of the Holy Ghost *which is* in you, which ye have of God, [d]and ye are not your own?

20 For [e]ye are bought with a price: therefore glorify God in your body, and in your spirit, which are God's.

7 Now concerning the things whereof ye wrote unto me: *It is* good for a man not to touch a woman.

2 Nevertheless, *to avoid* fornication, let every man have his own wife, and let every woman have her own husband.

3 [f]Let the husband render unto the wife due benevolence: and likewise also the wife unto the husband.

4 The wife hath not power of her own body, but the husband: and likewise also the husband hath not power of his own body, but the wife.

5 [g]Defraud ye not one the other, except *it be* with consent for a time, that ye may give yourselves to fasting and prayer; and come together again, that [h]Satan tempt you not for your incontinency.

6 But I speak this by permission, [i]*and* not of commandment.

7 For [j]I would that all men were even as I myself. But [k]every man hath his proper gift of God, one after this manner, and another after that.

8 I say therefore to the unmarried and widows, It is good for them if they abide even as I.

9 But [l]if they cannot contain, let them marry: for it is better to marry than to burn.

10 And unto the married I command, *yet* not I, but the Lord, [m]Let not the wife depart from *her* husband:

11 But and if she depart, let her remain unmarried, or be reconciled to *her* husband: and let not the husband put away *his* wife.

12 But to the rest speak I, not the Lord: If any brother hath a wife that believeth not, and she be pleased to dwell with him, let him not put her away.

13 And the woman which hath an husband that believeth not, and if he be pleased to dwell with her, let her not leave him.

14 For the unbelieving husband is sanctified by the wife, and the unbelieving wife is sanctified by the husband: else [n]were your children unclean; but now are they holy.

15 But if the unbelieving depart, let him depart. A brother or a sister is not under bondage in such *cases:* but God hath called us [o]to peace.

16 For what knowest thou, O wife, whether thou shalt [p]save *thy* husband? or how knowest thou, O man, whether thou shalt save *thy* wife?

17 But as God hath distributed to every

man, as the Lord hath called every one, so let him walk. And [q]so ordain I in all churches.

18 Is any man called being circumcised? let him not become uncircumcised. Is any called in uncircumcision? [r]let him not be circumcised.

19 [s]Circumcision is nothing, and uncircumcision is nothing, but [t]the keeping of the commandments of God.

20 Let every man abide in the same calling wherein he was called.

21 Art thou called *being* a servant? care not for it: but if thou mayest be made free, use *it* rather.

22 For he that is called in the Lord, *being* a servant, is [u]the Lord's freeman: likewise also he that is called, *being* free, is [v]Christ's servant.

23 [w]Ye are bought with a price; be not ye the servants of men.

24 Brethren, let every man, wherein he is called, therein abide with God.

25 Now concerning virgins [x]I have no commandment of the Lord: yet I give my judgment, as one [y]that hath obtained mercy of the Lord [z]to be faithful.

26 I suppose therefore that this is good for the present distress, *I say,* that *it is* good for a man so to be.

27 Art thou bound unto a wife? seek not to be loosed. Art thou loosed from a wife? seek not a wife.

28 But and if thou marry, thou hast not sinned; and if a virgin marry, she hath not sinned. Nevertheless such shall have trouble in the flesh: but I spare you.

29 But [a]this I say, brethren, the time *is* short: it remaineth, that both they that have wives be as though they had none;

30 And they that weep, as though they wept not; and they that rejoice, as though they rejoiced not; and they that buy, as though they possessed not;

31 And they that use this world, as not abusing *it:* for [b]the fashion of this world passeth away.

32 But I would have you without carefulness. [c]He that is unmarried careth for the things that belong to the Lord, how he may please the Lord:

33 But he that is married careth for the things that are of the world, how he may please *his* wife.

34 There is difference *also* between a wife and a virgin. The unmarried woman [d]careth for the things of the Lord, that she may be holy both in body and in spirit: but she that is married careth for the things of the world, how she may please *her* husband.

35 And this I speak for your own profit; not that I may cast a snare upon you, but for that which is comely, and that ye may attend upon the Lord without distraction.

36 But if any man think that he behaveth himself uncomely toward his virgin, if she pass the flower of *her* age, and need so require, let him do what he will, he sinneth not: let them marry.

37 Nevertheless he that standeth stedfast in his heart, having no necessity, but hath power over his own will, and hath so decreed in his heart that he will keep his virgin, doeth well.

38 [e]So then he that giveth *her* in marriage doeth well; but he that giveth *her* not in marriage doeth better.

39 [f]The wife is bound by the law as long as her husband liveth; but if her husband be dead, she is at liberty to be married to whom she will; [g]only in the Lord.

40 But she is happier if she so abide, after my judgment: and [h]I think also that I have the Spirit of God.

8 Now [i]as touching things offered unto idols, we know that we all have [j]knowledge. [k]Knowledge puffeth up, but charity edifieth.

2 And [l]if any man think that he knoweth any thing, he knoweth nothing yet as he ought to know.

3 But if any man love God, [m]the same is known of him.

4 As concerning therefore the eating of those things that are offered in sacrifice unto idols, we know that [n]an idol *is* nothing in the world, [o]and that *there is* none other God but one.

5 For though there be that are [p]called gods, whether in heaven or in earth, (as there be gods many, and lords many,)

6 But [q]to us *there is but* one God, the Father, [r]of whom *are* all things, and we in him; and [s]one Lord Jesus Christ, [t]by whom *are* all things, and we by him.

7 Howbeit *there is* not in every man that knowledge: for some with conscience of the idol unto this hour eat *it* as a thing offered unto an idol; and their conscience being weak is [u]defiled.

8 But [v]meat commendeth us not to God: for neither, if we eat, are we the better; neither, if we eat not, are we the worse.

9 But [w]take heed lest by any means this liberty of yours become [x]a stumblingblock to them that are weak.

10 For if any man see thee which hast knowledge sit at meat in the idol's temple, shall not the conscience of him which is weak be emboldened to eat those things which are offered to idols;

11 And [y]through thy knowledge shall the weak brother perish, for whom Christ died?

12 But [z]when ye sin so against the brethren, and wound their weak conscience, ye sin against Christ.

13 Wherefore, [a]if meat make my brother to offend, I will eat no flesh while the world standeth, lest I make my brother to offend.

9 Am [b]I not an apostle? am I not free? [c]have I not seen Jesus Christ our Lord? are not ye my work in the Lord?

2 If I be not an apostle unto others, yet doubtless I am to you: for [d]the seal of mine apostleship are ye in the Lord.

7:17 [q]2 Cor. 11:28
7:18 [r]Acts 15:1
7:19 [s]Gal. 5:6 [t]John 15:14
7:22 [u]John 8:36; Philem. 16 [v]Gal. 5:13; 1 Pet. 2:16
7:23 [w]Lev. 25:42
7:25 [x]2 Cor. 8:8 [y]1 Tim. 1:16 [z]1 Tim. 1:12
7:29 [a]Rom. 13:11; 2 Pet. 3:8
7:31 [b]Ps. 39:6; 1 Pet. 1:24; 1 John 2:17
7:32 [c]1 Tim. 5:5
7:34 [d]Luke 10:40
7:38 [e]Heb. 13:4
7:39 [f]Rom. 7:2 [g]2 Cor. 6:14
7:40 [h]1 Thess. 4:8
8:1 [i]Acts 15:20 [j]Rom. 14:14 [k]Rom. 14:3
8:2 [l]Gal. 6:3
8:3 [m]Ex. 33:12; Matt. 7:23; Gal. 4:9
8:4 [n]Isa. 41:24 [o]Deut. 4:39; Mark 12:29; Eph. 4:6
8:5 [p]John 10:34
8:6 [q]Mal. 2:10 [r]Acts 17:28 [s]John 13:13; Eph. 4:5; Phil. 2:11 [t]John 1:3; Heb. 1:2
8:7 [u]Rom. 14:14
8:8 [v]Rom. 14:17
8:9 [w]Gal. 5:13 [x]Rom. 14:13
8:11 [y]Rom. 14:15
8:12 [z]Matt. 25:40
8:13 [a]Rom. 14:21
9:1 [b]Acts 9:15; Gal. 2:7; 1 Tim. 2:7 [c]Acts 9:3
9:2 [d]2 Cor. 3:2

3 Mine answer to them that do examine me is this,

4 [e]Have we not power to eat and to drink?

5 Have we not power to lead about a sister, a wife, as well as other apostles, and *as* [f]the brethren of the Lord, and [g]Cephas?

6 Or I only and Barnabas, [h]have not we power to forbear working?

7 Who [i]goeth a warfare any time at his own charges? who [j]planteth a vineyard, and eateth not of the fruit thereof? or who [k]feedeth a flock, and eateth not of the milk of the flock?

8 Say I these things as a man? or saith not the law the same also?

9 For it is written in the law of Moses, [l]Thou shalt not muzzle the mouth of the ox that treadeth out the corn. Doth God take care for oxen?

10 Or saith he *it* altogether for our sakes? For our sakes, no doubt, *this* is written: that [m]he that ploweth should plow in hope; and that he that thresheth in hope should be partaker of his hope.

11 [n]If we have sown unto you spiritual things, *is it* a great thing if we shall reap your carnal things?

12 If others be partakers of *this* power over you, *are* not we rather? [o]Nevertheless we have not used this power; but suffer all things, [p]lest we should hinder the gospel of Christ.

13 [q]Do ye not know that they which minister about holy things live *of the things* of the temple? and they which wait at the altar are partakers with the altar?

14 Even so [r]hath the Lord ordained [s]that they which preach the gospel should live of the gospel.

15 But [t]I have used none of these things: neither have I written these things, that it should be so done unto me: for [u]*it were* better for me to die, than that any man should make my glorying void.

16 For though I preach the gospel, I have nothing to glory of: for [v]necessity is laid upon me; yea, woe is unto me, if I preach not the gospel!

17 For if I do this thing willingly, I have a reward: but if against my will, [w]a dispensation *of the gospel* is committed unto me.

18 What is my reward then? *Verily* that, [x]when I preach the gospel, I may make the gospel of Christ without charge, that I abuse not my power in the gospel.

19 For though I be free from all *men*, yet have [y]I made myself servant unto all, [z]that I might gain the more.

20 And [a]unto the Jews I became as a Jew, that I might gain the Jews; to them that are under the law, as under the law, that I might gain them that are under the law;

21 [b]To [c]them that are without law, as without law, (being not without law to God, but under the law to Christ,) that I might gain them that are without law.

22 [d]To the weak became I as weak, that I might gain the weak: I am made all things to all *men*, [e]that I might by all means save some.

23 And this I do for the gospel's sake, that I might be partaker thereof with *you*.

24 Know ye not that they which run in a race run all, but one receiveth the prize? [f]So run, that ye may obtain.

25 And every man that [g]striveth for the mastery is temperate in all things. Now they *do it* to obtain a corruptible crown; but we [h]an incorruptible.

26 I therefore so run, [i]not as uncertainly; so fight I, not as one that beateth the air:

27 [j]But I keep under my body, and [k]bring *it* into subjection: lest that by any means, when I have preached to others, I myself should be [l]a castaway.

10 Moreover, brethren, I would not that ye should be ignorant, how that all our fathers were under [m]the cloud, and all passed through [n]the sea;

2 And were all baptized unto Moses in the cloud and in the sea;

3 And did all eat the same [o]spiritual meat;

4 And did all drink the same [p]spiritual drink: for they drank of that spiritual Rock that followed them: and that Rock was Christ.

5 But with many of them God was not well pleased: for they [q]were overthrown in the wilderness.

6 Now these things were our examples, to the intent we should not lust after evil things, as [r]they also lusted.

7 Neither be ye idolaters, as *were* some of them; as it is written, [s]The people sat down to eat and drink, and rose up to play.

8 [t]Neither let us commit fornication, as some of them committed, and [u]fell in one day three and twenty thousand.

9 Neither let us tempt Christ, as [v]some of them also tempted, and [w]were destroyed of serpents.

10 Neither murmur ye, as [x]some of them also murmured, and [y]were destroyed of [z]the destroyer.

11 Now all these things happened unto them for ensamples: and [a]they are written for our admonition, [b]upon whom the ends of the world are come.

12 Wherefore [c]let him that thinketh he standeth take heed lest he fall.

13 There hath no temptation taken you but such as is common to man: but God *is* faithful, [d]who will not suffer you to be tempted above that ye are able; but will with the temptation also [e]make a way to escape, that ye may be able to bear *it*.

14 Wherefore, my dearly beloved, [f]flee from idolatry.

15 I speak as to wise men; judge ye what I say.

16 [g]The cup of blessing which we bless, is it not the communion of the blood of Christ? [h]The bread which we break, is it not the communion of the body of Christ?

9:4 [e]1 Thess. 2:6
9:5 [f]Matt. 13:55; Luke 6:15; Gal. 1:19 [g]Matt. 8:14
9:6 [h]2 Thess. 3:8
9:7 [i]2 Cor. 10:4; 2 Tim. 2:3 [j]Deut. 20:6 [k]John 21:15
9:9 [l]Deut. 25:4
9:10 [m]2 Tim. 2:6
9:11 [n]Rom. 15:27
9:12 [o]Acts 20:33; 1 Thess. 2:6 [p]2 Cor. 11:12
9:13 [q]Lev. 6:16; Deut. 10:9
9:14 [r]Matt. 10:10 [s]Gal. 6:6
9:15 [t]Acts 18:3; 2 Thess. 3:8 [u]2 Cor. 11:10
9:16 [v]Rom. 1:14
9:17 [w]Gal. 2:7; Col. 1:25
9:18 [x]2 Cor. 4:5
9:19 [y]Gal. 5:13 [z]Matt. 18:15
9:20 [a]Acts 16:3
9:21 [b]Gal. 3:2 [c]Rom. 2:12
9:22 [d]Rom. 15:1 [e]Rom. 11:14
9:24 [f]Gal. 2:2; 2 Tim. 4:7; Heb. 12:1
9:25 [g]Eph. 6:12; 2 Tim. 2:5 [h]2 Tim. 4:8; 1 Pet. 1:4; Rev. 2:10
9:26 [i]2 Tim. 2:5
9:27 [j]Rom. 8:13 [k]Rom. 6:18 [l]Jer. 6:30
10:1 [m]Ex. 13:21; Deut. 1:33; Neh. 9:12 [n]Ex. 14:22; Josh. 4:23; Ps. 78:13
10:3 [o]Ex. 16:15; Ps. 78:24
10:4 [p]Ex. 17:6; Ps. 78:15
10:5 [q]Num. 14:29; Heb. 3:17; Jude 5
10:6 [r]Num. 11:4
10:7 [s]Ex. 32:6
10:8 [t]Rev. 2:14 [u]Num. 25:1
10:9 [v]Ex. 17:2; Deut. 6:16; Ps. 78:18 [w]Num. 21:6
10:10 [x]Ex. 16:2 [y]Num. 14:37 [z]Ex. 12:23; 1 Chron. 21:15
10:11 [a]Rom. 15:4 [b]Phil. 4:5; 1 John 2:18
10:12 [c]Rom. 11:20
10:13 [d]Ps. 125:3 [e]Jer. 29:11
10:14 [f]2 Cor. 6:17
10:16 [g]Matt. 26:26 [h]Acts 2:42

17 For [i]we *being* many are one bread, *and* one body: for we are all partakers of that one bread.

18 Behold [j]Israel [k]after the flesh: [l]are not they which eat of the sacrifices partakers of the altar?

19 What say I then? that the idol is any thing, or that which is offered in sacrifice to idols is any thing?

20 But *I say,* that the things which the Gentiles [m]sacrifice, they sacrifice to devils, and not to God: and I would not that ye should have fellowship with devils.

21 [n]Ye cannot drink the cup of the Lord, and [o]the cup of devils: ye cannot be partakers of the Lord's table, and of the table of devils.

22 Do we [p]provoke the Lord to jealousy? [q]are we stronger than he?

23 All things are lawful for me, but all things are not expedient: all things are lawful for me, but all things edify not.

24 [r]Let no man seek his own, but every man another's *wealth.*

25 [s]Whatsoever is sold in the shambles, *that* eat, asking no question for conscience sake:

26 For [t]the earth *is* the Lord's, and the fulness thereof.

27 If any of them that believe not bid you *to a feast,* and ye be disposed to go; [u]whatsoever is set before you, eat, asking no question for conscience sake.

28 But if any man say unto you, This is offered in sacrifice unto idols, eat not for his sake that shewed it, and for conscience sake: for [v]the earth *is* the Lord's, and the fulness thereof:

29 Conscience, I say, not thine own, but of the other: for [w]why is my liberty judged of another *man's* conscience?

30 For if I by grace be a partaker, why am I evil spoken of for that [x]for which I give thanks?

31 [y]Whether therefore ye eat, or drink, or whatsoever ye do, do all to the glory of God.

32 [z]Give none offence, neither to the Jews, nor to the Gentiles, nor to [a]the church of God:

33 Even as [b]I please all *men* in all *things,* not seeking mine own profit, but the *profit* of many, that they may be saved.

11 Be [c]ye followers of me, even as I also *am* of Christ.

2 Now I praise you, brethren, that ye remember me in all things, and keep the ordinances, as I delivered *them* to you.

3 But I would have you know, that [d]the head of every man is Christ; and [e]the head of the woman *is* the man; and [f]the head of Christ *is* God.

4 Every man praying or prophesying, having *his* head covered, dishonoureth his head.

5 But [g]every woman that prayeth or prophesieth with *her* head uncovered dishonoureth her head: for that is even all one as if she were [h]shaven.

6 For if the woman be not covered, let her also be shorn: but if it be [i]a shame for a woman to be shorn or shaven, let her be covered.

7 For a man indeed ought not to cover *his* head, forasmuch as [j]he is the image and glory of God: but the woman is the glory of the man.

8 For [k]the man is not of the woman; but the woman of the man.

9 [l]Neither was the man created for the woman; but the woman for the man.

10 For this cause ought the woman [m]to have power on *her* head [n]because of the angels.

11 Nevertheless [o]neither is the man without the woman, neither the woman without the man, in the Lord.

12 For as the woman *is* of the man, even so *is* the man also by the woman; [p]but all things of God.

13 Judge in yourselves: is it comely that a woman pray unto God uncovered?

14 Doth not even nature itself teach you, that, if a man have long hair, it is a shame unto him?

15 But if a woman have long hair, it is a glory to her: for *her* hair is given her for a covering.

16 But [q]if any man seem to be contentious, we have no such custom, neither the churches of God.

17 Now in this that I declare *unto you* I praise *you* not, that ye come together not for the better, but for the worse.

18 For first of all, when ye come together in the church, I hear that there be divisions among you; and I partly believe it.

19 For [r]there must be also heresies among you, [s]that they which are approved may be made manifest among you.

20 When ye come together therefore into one place, *this* is not to eat the Lord's supper.

21 For in eating every one taketh before *other* his own supper: and one is hungry, and [t]another is drunken.

22 What? have ye not houses to eat and to drink in? or despise ye the church of God, and [u]shame them that have not? What shall I say to you? shall I praise you in this? I praise *you* not.

23 For [v]I have received of the Lord that which also I delivered unto you, [w]That the Lord Jesus the *same* night in which he was betrayed took bread:

24 And when he had given thanks, he brake *it,* and said, Take, eat: this is my body, which is broken for you: this do in remembrance of me.

25 After the same manner also *he took* the cup, when he had supped, saying, This cup is the new testament in my blood: this do ye, as oft as ye drink *it,* in remembrance of me.

26 For as often as ye eat this bread, and drink this cup, ye do shew the Lord's death [x]till he come.

10:17 [i]Rom. 12:5
10:18 [j]Rom. 4:12 [k]Rom. 4:1 [l]Lev. 3:3
10:20 [m]Lev. 17:7; Ps. 106:37; Rev. 9:20
10:21 [n]2 Cor. 6:15 [o]Deut. 32:38
10:22 [p]Deut. 32:21 [q]Ezek. 22:14
10:24 [r]Rom. 15:1
10:25 [s]1 Tim. 4:4
10:26 [t]Ex. 19:5; Ps. 24:1
10:27 [u]Luke 10:7
10:28 [v]Deut. 10:14
10:29 [w]Rom. 14:16
10:30 [x]Rom. 14:6
10:31 [y]Col. 3:17
10:32 [z]Rom. 14:13 [a]Acts 20:28
10:33 [b]Rom. 15:2
11:1 [c]Eph. 5:1; 1 Thess. 1:6; 2 Thess. 3:9
11:3 [d]Eph. 5:23 [e]Gen. 3:16; 1 Pet. 3:1 [f]John 14:28
11:5 [g]Acts 21:9 [h]Deut. 21:12
11:6 [i]Num. 5:18
11:7 [j]Gen. 1:26
11:8 [k]Gen. 2:21
11:9 [l]Gen. 2:18
11:10 [m]Gen. 24:65 [n]Eccl. 5:6
11:11 [o]Gal. 3:28
11:12 [p]Rom. 11:36
11:16 [q]1 Tim. 6:4
11:19 [r]Matt. 18:7; Acts 20:30; 1 Tim. 4:1 [s]Deut. 13:3; 1 John 2:19
11:21 [t]2 Pet. 2:13
11:22 [u]Jam. 2:6
11:23 [v]Gal. 1:1 [w]Matt. 26:26; Luke 22:19
11:26 [x]John 14:3; 1 Thess. 4:16; 2 Thess. 1:10; Rev. 1:7

FOCUS ON FIRST CORINTHIANS

Most of us probably had a wise grandmother who would talk about how people are so easily deceived by appearances. "Gal, folks come into our communities with suits, white shirts, and briefcases and carry out more of our money than bandits wearing a mask and carrying a gun! A snake is still a snake." We continue to be deceived by snakes! Sure, they can look good, dress well, talk persuasively, and even behave correctly—for a while! However, a snake is still a snake regardless of how it's dressed. A snake will always return to its slithering ways. Paul wrote this first letter to the church at Corinth because the people of the Way had become enamored with some snakes.

False teachings, heresy, and even out-and-out lies were being spread throughout the church that Paul had founded and pastored. Paul's reputation had been smeared, his teaching has been challenged, and his authority questioned. Therefore he wrote to expose the snakes.

Deceit is subtle. Evil is not always obvious. Lies can be veiled or twisted with pieces of the truth. "We are easily conned," Granny would say. We have "itching ears" that are tuned to hear a new and easier method for our love relationship with God! Snakes come and tell us what we want to hear. Do you want to count the times you've been deceived by a good-looking snake?

Stripping away falsehoods to reach the heart of the truth was a difficult challenge for Paul. How does one chastise and encourage one's child at the same time? How does one spank and hug one's child in the same motion? Paul made a gallant attempt. Eventually he fell back to redirecting the church's attention to the manifest love of God in Jesus Christ. For Paul, repentance, conversion, transformation, and salvation are all about love! Read chapter thirteen. Read it until you fall in love with Jesus Christ all over again! Snakes and snakeskins will seem less attractive!

THE BLACK PRESENCE IN FIRST AND SECOND CORINTHIANS

While there are few references to the Black presence within the Epistles to the Corinthians, we must bear in mind that the Gospel preached by Paul had its origin in North Africa and Palestine, where there was a significant black presence. Not until the Greeks and Romans began to migrate into the biblical lands during the centuries prior to the birth of Christ do we find any significant presence of other racial groups. Bear in mind once again that in biblical times racial identification did not have the significance it carries today. This significance is more critical today because of efforts made within the last two centuries to eliminate or distort the reality of the biblical Black presence to the detriment of people of color.

Apollos: Mentioned in chapters 1, 3, 4 and 16. Apollos was born in Alexandria (Acts 18:24) which is located on the northern coast of Africa. As an African Jew he was versed in Jewish Scriptures, but also in the African culture. He was knowledgeable about the Scriptures, and was made even more knowledgeable by the tutoring he received form Priscilla (Prisca) and Aquila (Acts 18:24). Additionally, some have concluded that since Paul was mistaken for an Egyptian (Acts 21:38), he must have been black.

Life Lessons

1 CORINTHIANS 1

The key verse in this letter is found at the beginning of it. "I beseech you, brethren, by the name of our Lord Jesus Christ, that ye speak the same thing, and that there be no divisions among you; but that ye be perfectly joined together in the same mind and in the same judgment" (1:10). Paul proclaims that unity in the church is essential for believers. He does not call for uniformity, for he goes on to declare, "All things are lawful for me, but all things are not expedient: all things are lawful for me, but all things edify not" (10:23). Unity is mandatory for this church in shambles! Ego, pride, immorality, eating meat offered to idols, and internal divisions are just a few of the matters that Paul tries to address in this circulating letter. He attempts once more to teach the believers in Corinth what he had taught them while with them: "For the preaching of the cross is to them that perish foolishness; but unto us which are saved it is the power of God" (1:18). They had argued over who was "the leader" in the church, but Paul refuses to be dragged into that messy situation. "Christ sent me not to baptize, but to preach the gospel: not with wisdom of words, lest the cross of Christ should be made of none effect" (v. 17).

Ultimate Power, may Your resurrection power be displayed in my life.

1 CORINTHIANS 3–5

Paul calls us again to unity by reminding the church, "I have planted, Apollos watered; but God gave the increase" (3:6). We are called to work together for the good of the body. It really makes no difference who gets the credit as long as God gets the glory! "For we are laborers together with God" (v. 9). Paul asks the church: "Know ye not that ye are the temple of God, and that the Spirit of God dwelleth in you?" (v. 16). We are God's dwelling—a sacred holding space for the Holy One to inhabit! How we treat our bodies makes a difference. What we put into our bodies makes a difference. How we act in our bodies makes a difference. The people at Corinth had begun to believe that they were "above" living lives that demonstrated that they were the people of God.

Because of wrong teaching from those who considered themselves wise, they had begun to live lives of great immorality. The result is reported to Paul. "It is reported that there is fornication among you, and such forni-

cation as is not so much as named among the Gentiles, that one should have his father's wife" (5:1). Flagrant sin is rampant and pastor Paul calls it to a quick halt! "Put away from among yourselves that wicked person" (v. 13).

Temple Dwelling God, keep me from immorality. Keep my mind pure.

1 CORINTHIANS 7

In chapter seven as Paul begins to address issues that the Corinthians had brought to his attention, he calls on both men and women in the community to be faithful to marital vows. He is forthright in his call to the sexual rights of each one in the marriage relationship. "Let the husband render unto the wife due benevolence: and likewise also the wife unto the husband" (7:3). In a lengthy discourse on marriage, sex, and divorce, we have a Paul that we hear little of from today's pulpit! In these passages, Paul is an equal-opportunity advocate! Far too many of the Corinthians had gone so far as to abstain from marital sex as a form of rigorous asceticism, which was a "sign" that they had been "delivered" from bodily functions. Paul's pastoral wisdom contradicts this behavior.

Spirit of Love, keep me holy, in whatever state I find myself.

1 CORINTHIANS 11–14

Understanding all that Paul wrote about the appropriate behavior of women in the church requires an understanding of the times and the circumstances of the first century. Suffice it to say, that his most often misquoted passage against the role of women in ministry comes from 1 Corinthians 14:32–35, which includes his injunction "Let your women keep silence in the churches . . . they are commanded to be under obedience, as also saith the law" (v. 34). However, it is seldom quoted that prior to this Paul had already said, "Nevertheless neither is the man without the woman, neither the woman without the man, in the Lord. For as the woman is of the man, even so is the man also by the woman; but all things of God" (11:11–12). Paul's whole argument in this letter is based on "the rib" story of Genesis 2.

What happens when you follow the creation story of chapter one of Genesis, where both male and female are created in the image of God? What happens when you recall that Jesus came to women after His resurrection and gave them His message? If women had kept silent at that time, waiting for permission to "speak," would the Good News have been spread to the ends of the earth as Jesus commanded?

Commissioning Christ, thank You for giving us voice and a command to use it in service for your Realm!

FOCUS ON
SECOND CORINTHIANS

Do you know anything about being lonely? Is there some faint remembrance of a time in your life when you actually felt all alone? Do you have

a memory of a time that you felt that there was not another living soul who cared about you, had your interest at heart, and was concerned for your well-being? Did you ever stop and think, "Maybe I'm adopted. Perhaps that's why no one cares!" Has it ever seemed as if even the stars refused to shine for you and the skies turned gray whenever you came out to play? Can you even remotely identify with that character in *Peanuts* who walks around with a dismal cloud hanging over his shoulders? By now are you saying, "Been there; done that"? Don't worry. We each have experiences like this in our days "before Christ!"

Paul addressed the issue of self-examination as he wrote again to the "puffed-up" church at Corinth. It seems as if they had forgotten that they had been orphans like the rest of us! There was discord among the membership as they struggled to prove their worth through their achievements and possessions. Paul reminded them that all we have, all we are, and all that we can ever hope to become is only made possible through our adoption into God's family. Jesus Christ made this adoption possible. Without Christ, not one of us would have a sense of belonging. Without Christ, we would once again be alienated from God.

As the church wrestled with their "giftedness," they continued to have disharmony among themselves over Paul's leadership and ministry. Majoring in minor issues, the plight of sin and sinfulness played havoc among them. Paul urges them to remember their adoption into a royal family. He motivated them to recall their salvation through Christ. He encouraged them to relax and let go of yesterday's "stuff" which would not take them into a better tomorrow. "Therefore if any man be in Christ, he is a new creature: old things are passed away; behold, all things are become new" (5:17). When those old feelings of loneliness try to creep back into your thought-life, this is an excellent verse to recall! We have a new family; we are never left alone! This is a guaranteed promise because Jesus Christ cared enough to die in our place and rose to offer us life eternal. No! Never alone!

Life Lessons

2 CORINTHIANS 2–5

Paul's advice from the previous letter had not been followed. The problems he had addressed remained. Division in the church continued and now Paul's authority is being questioned further. The letter he had written had been received as a severe rebuke, feelings had been hurt, and anger had flared. Yet Paul remains confident that sinful practices have to cease. "For out of much affliction and anguish of heart I wrote unto you with many tears; not that ye should be grieved, but that ye might know the love which I have more abundantly unto you" (2:4). He asks for forgiveness and forgives the one who had been punished because of his sexual misconduct. He goes to great lengths to discuss the issue of forgiveness "lest Satan should get an advantage of us: for we are not ignorant of his devices" (v. 11). Division is always a problem, even in math! It cannot be left to simply go

away. We must work toward reconciliation. Paul leads the way.

We have been given "the ministry of reconciliation" through Christ (5:18). This is a charge we must strive diligently to keep.

Minister of Reconciliation, work this ministry way down on the inside of me. It is so difficult to let go and let God!

2 CORINTHIANS 6–12

With painful, difficult and often rambling arguments, the apostle Paul struggles to reestablish himself as "an ambassador" and the "official agent" for Jesus Christ who came and brought them the Word of Truth. "Our mouth is open unto you, our heart is enlarged. Ye are not straitened in us, but ye are straitened in your own bowels" (6:11–12). He exhorts them not to heed the counsel of those who challenge his authority and uses chapter 10 to defend himself. "Not to boast in another man's line of things made ready to our hand" (10:16). He charges those causing the divisions with being "false apostles, deceitful workers, transforming themselves into the apostles of Christ" (11:13), and says, "And no marvel; for Satan himself is transformed into an angel of light" (v. 14). He reminds them about Eve, who was "beguiled . . . through [Satan's] subtilty" as the reason for their minds' being led astray from "the simplicity that is in Christ" (v. 3). Yet, Paul goes on to lift up the power of the cross of Christ, which makes redemption possible for all of us. "Most gladly therefore will I rather glory in my infirmities, that the power of Christ may rest upon me. Therefore I take pleasure in infirmities, in reproaches, in necessities, in persecutions, in distresses for Christ's sake: for when I am weak, then am I strong" (12:9–10). We thrive because of the cross. Paul also admonishes us to "be of good comfort, be of one mind, live in peace; and the God of love and peace shall with you" (13:11). Isn't that good news?

May "the grace of the Lord Jesus Christ, and the love of God, and the communion of the Holy Ghost" be with us all! (13:14)

FOCUS ON GALATIANS

The story is told that on the day when President Lincoln was to sign the Emancipation Proclamation, his hands were swollen from handshaking with guests. He looked at the document that would make a solemn statement to the entire United States about slavery being "evil." He made the witnesses wait. For he didn't want his handwriting to appear shaky and unstable as he set our ancestors free from slavery! He wanted history to view him as confident in this move, which had caused a split between the states.

Jesus wasn't shaken and unstable as he went to Calvary to atone for our sin and break the hold of sin that had us in bondage! He went forth to battle sin, death, and hell on our behalf and He won!

History also has recorded the facts of many bold black women who have never been shaky about their freedom in spite of racist systems and laws that said differently. Harriet Tubman, Sojourner Truth, Mary Church

Terrill, Rosa Parks, Shirley Chisholm, and Barbara Jordan are a few of the legendary women who have internalized and acted out of the Magna Carta given by Paul in the Epistle to the Galatians.

All of them lived lives which rang with the majestic words of the Negro spiritual, "Before I'll be a slave, I'll be buried in my grave and go home to my Lord, and be free!" For deep down inside of them, freedom was straining to be unleashed. Paul knew this constraint to go against the grain, against public opinion, and against the popular religious trend. As he sat thinking of the conflict between law and Gospel, he wrote: "I stand fast therefore in the liberty wherewith Christ hath made us free, and be not entangled again with the yoke of bondage" (5:1). He wrote it with a confident, steady hand!

It is reported that Harriet Tubman ran away to Canada to be freed of the yokes of slavery. However, when she arrived, she was neither happy nor satisfied. She wanted others like herself to experience freedom at its fullness. This inner prompting for liberty is what made her keep returning to the South to bring out other African slaves. The same is true for Sojourner Truth, whose slave name was given as Isabella Bumphry. However the push for freedom that stoked her inner fire had God speak the name Sojourner to her as she was sent on a mission to preach about this freedom on behalf of slaves. Her famous "Ain't I a Woman" speech was given at an all Anglo-American women's convention where they were seeking equal rights for white women, but the hundreds of thousands of Negro slaves had been forgotten! Sojourner asked God to give her a second name like "the white folks." That name was given as a charge to always proclaim Truth!

Freedom, liberty, and equal rights are not simply matters of laws on books, rules on paper, and regulations that do not touch hearts and spirits. With our conversion experience, a personal relationship with Jesus Christ, and baptism in the Holy Spirit, we are compelled to seek not only our personal security as equals in the world, but we are forced by love to stand firm and unshaken as we work on behalf of people everywhere. We work for access to all that is ours from a generous God. Women who are "free" within themselves don't have to wait for any human being to put a pen to paper in order for them to act! Women who are "free" don't need permission to work on behalf of God whenever, however, and wherever the Holy Spirit moves! Although Lincoln signed the proclamation on a shaky-handed day, his confidence or lack thereof was not what made the ultimate difference!

Paul began the Galatians Epistle by reasserting his authority as an apostle. He does this by recounting his experiences of God having revealed Himself to Paul along the Damascus Road and of Paul's subsequent acceptance by the other apostles and Jerusalem leaders (chaps. 1–2). Paul restated his primary teaching that people are made right with God on the basis of faith in the atoning work of Christ. He repudiated the notion that the Mosaic Law and circumcision are necessary to be put right with God (chaps. 3–5). After explaining the doctrine of justification by faith the apostle wrote about the application of the teaching (chaps. 5–6). This doctrine was misunderstood, Paul explained, if people used it as an excuse to sin. The apostle pointed out that if believers lived according to the Spirit

they would not fulfil the sinful desires of the flesh. He encouraged the believers to bear one another's burdens and not be weary in doing well.

THE BLACK PRESENCE IN GALATIANS

The black presence in the Epistle to the Galatians appears in the mention of Arabia (1:17; 4:25). Paul mentions Arabia as the place where he spent time after visiting Jerusalem and before returning to Damascus. He also refers to Arabia as the location of Mt. Sinai. This large tract of land is located south of Palestine between Africa and the Indian Ocean. The people of Arabia were the descendants of Abraham through Sarah's handmaid Hagar. Hagar was African-Egyptian. Abraham, a Semite from the land of Mesopotamia, also was a person of color. These descendants of Abraham occupied Arabia.

Additionally, some have concluded that since Paul was mistaken for an Egyptian (Acts 21:38), he must have been black.

Life Lessons

GALATIANS 1–3

Paul understood being misunderstood and attacked. His teachings were undermined by those known as Judaizers. These Judaizers taught the Galatians that in order for them to be "true" Christians, they had to follow all the constraints of the Law of Moses. Chapters one and two reaffirm Paul's authority as "an apostle, (not of men, neither by man, but by Jesus Christ, and God the Father, who raised him from the dead)" (1:1) and detail his systematic theology of freedom in Christ. In chapter three, he asks the essential question, "O foolish Galatians, who hath bewitched you, that ye should not obey the truth . . .?" (v. 1).

The "new" teachers persuaded the Christians that circumcision and other rites were necessary to achieve salvation. However, Paul reminds them, "He therefore that ministereth to you the Spirit, and worketh miracles among you, doeth he it by the works of the law, or by the hearing of faith?" (3:5). He also asserts, "But after that faith is come, we are no longer under a schoolmaster" (v. 25). In other words, we are no longer under the supervision of the Law. Paul then writes: "Ye are all the children of God by faith in Christ Jesus. For as many of you as have been baptized into Christ have put on Christ. There is neither Jew nor Greek, there is neither bond nor free, there is neither male nor female: for ye are all one in Christ Jesus" (vv. 26–28).

Adopting and Accepting God, I give You thanks for making me an heir to the promise made to Abraham and Sarah. Through Jesus Christ I am included!

GALATIANS 4

As he tries to reach the hearts and spirits of this confused congregation, Paul uses the metaphor of his being "the mother" of this people. "My little children, of whom I travail in birth again until Christ be formed in

you, I desire to be present with you now, and to change my voice; for I stand in doubt of you" (4:19–20).

Loving God, help me in my times of confusion to feel Your mother-like concern for me.

Focus on EPHESIANS

The story is told of three little piglets who grew up in the same family. Each one received love, education, wisdom, and encouragement from their home. The time came when each piglet had to move out on its own. The first piglet was a party animal and threw up a shoddy construction in order to run and find a party. The middle piglet was greedy. There is no nice way to put it! After having a good and filling breakfast, she set out to build herself a nice home. She drew up good plans and even laid a solid foundation. However, a grumbling stomach took priority. She finished her home with sticks, held together by mud. Off to fix a feast she went. Now, the last piglet was conscientious and hardworking. Parties didn't attract her and eating was not high on her list. She was determined to have a solidly built home.

Night came—time for the piglets to go to bed in their new homes. Of course, watching and waiting on the sidelines was their fierce enemy, the wolf. As soon as the sun went down and the moon began to shine, off to the first house went the hungry wolf. With great huffing and puffing, the house of the first little piglet was completely demolished. She ran out the back door to her sister's house to escape. After a midnight snack the two sisters went to bed. The hungry wolf came and found it difficult to enter through the well-constructed basement. However, when the wolf got to the flimsy sticks, the huffing and puffing brought the second house down. Off to their sister's home they ran. The relentless wolf came the third time. However, the huffing and puffing did not do any good. The house was well fortified. The wolf had to slink away, hungry still.

In the fairy tale version, the wolf and the pigs never have another confrontation. The story is marked "The End," but we know that hungry wolves don't give up that easily. Even when they confront a solidly built construction, they simply slink away to refocus on a different strategy! So, we can be certain that the wolf is not completely gone, even at the conclusion of our fairy tales.

Jesus knows about the wolves, and warns "little piglets" to be on guard for those who will come in sheep's clothing, but are really ferocious wolves! Paul knew about the wolves firsthand. Paul wrote the letter to the Ephesian believers from a Roman prison cell where the huffing and puffing of death breathed down his neck! In it he encourages Christians to "put on the whole armour of God" (6:11). He then gives some added protection against the cagey wolf—the Enemy of all believers. "Praying always with all prayer and supplication in the Spirit, and watching thereunto with all perseverance and supplication for all saints; and for me" (6:18–19).

Prevailing prayer is an often overlooked weapon for us.

Today the piglets and the wolves are yet engaged in battles. The question is which little piglet are you?

THE BLACK PRESENCE IN EPHESIANS

While there are no specific references to the black presence within the Epistle to the Ephesians, it must be borne in mind that the Gospel preached by Paul had its origin in North Africa and Palestine where there was a significant black presence. Not until the Greeks and Romans began to migrate into the biblical lands during the centuries prior to the birth of Christ do we find any significant presence of other racial groups. Bear in mind once again that in biblical times racial identification did not have the significance it carries today. This significance is more critical today because of efforts made within the last two centuries to eliminate or distort the reality of the biblical black presence to the detriment of people of color.

Life Lessons

EPHESIANS 1–5

Chapter one begins this letter of encouragement as Paul greets the saints and offers thanksgiving and prayer for their faithful response to the good news of Jesus Christ. He reminds them that "we all had our conversation in times past in the lusts of our flesh, fulfilling the desires of the flesh and of the mind; and were by nature the children of wrath, even as others. But God, who is rich in mercy, for his great love wherewith he loved us, even when we were dead in sins, hath quickened us together with Christ, (by grace ye are saved;)" (2:3–5). Paul then details the unity of Jews and Gentiles in the body of Christ: "For he is our peace, who hath made both one, and hath broken down the middle wall of partition between us; having abolished in his flesh the enmity, even the law of commandments contained in ordinances; for to make in himself of twain one new man, so making peace" (vv. 14–15). His prayer is that the Ephesians will "walk worthy of the vocation wherewith ye are called" (4:1). He appeals to them as a "prisoner of the Lord" (v. 1) and calls for them to live lives of righteousness to "grieve not the holy Spirit of God" (v. 30). Paul then admonishes, "Be ye therefore followers of God, as dear children" (5:1). They are to "[submit] yourselves one to another in the fear of God" (v. 21). That's good advice!

Lord of All, to Thee we raise our humble voice of grateful praise for Your amazing love.

FOCUS ON PHILIPPIANS

Anita Baker sings, "You bring me joy!" She offers accolades to the one who brings the sunshine into her day. She lifts her voice in testimony of the way her state of mind changes in the presence of the "joy bringer." When he is absent, there is a profound loss in her life.

We are well aware of the fact that someone who brings joy today can also be the creator of nightmares tomorrow—nightmares which last longer than the hint of sunlight we thought we saw upon his arrival into our lives!

Joy is a deep and abiding sense of peace and fulfillment that few of us can find or sustain in a human being. It is rare that we ourselves are the bringers of constant joy. Joy comes from intimacy with another, which outlasts the tests of time and the storms of life. However, most of us get joy confused with happiness, which is based on happenstance and is fickle and fleeting!

Happiness depends on circumstances. Therefore, it is an illusive attainment, at best. Happiness doesn't come to stay. For happiness doesn't produce the strength of character which calls forth joy and inner peace. Happiness will run away when your situation changes and you are no longer "on top of the world." The Ferris wheel of life must turn and go around. None of us can remain "on top" forever!

Paul sat in jail, facing a trial that he knew could end in a death sentence. He'd had a rough life since his conversion. He knew the journey of walking with sorrow. Through his trials, temptations, and troubles, Paul had learned about abiding joy. Philippians is a letter of joy written from a Roman jail. The joy does not come from circumstances. The joy comes from Paul's intimate relationship with Jesus Christ. He is the only One who brings us consistent and everlasting joy!

Most of us talk about intimacy, but we don't really experience it. For "in-to-me-see" calls for a pulling off of every mask. It requires a shedding of all our pretensions. It demands that we drop our defenses and be known at our core. It allows another to see the good, the bad, and the ugly! "In-to-me-see" says, "I want you to take a good, hard, long look at the authentic me in the raw. Tell me if you love me now." It's a scary position to take. For rejection is a possibility! It takes vulnerability and risk-taking to call someone to know you at your worst and trust that person will love you when the looking is over! The truth of the matter is that most of us don't really know ourselves that well!

Paul was comfortable with his "whole" self! He knew that God knew him at his worst when he wreaked havoc on people of the Way (see Acts 7:58; 9:1–2). Yet God had used him to build the realm of Christ among the Gentiles. He was humbled, now he shares his joy. "Rejoice in the Lord alway: and again I say, Rejoice" (Phil. 4:4). The joy comes in knowing that

your worst won't turn God away from you! That's reason enough to rejoice and take the occasion to encourage the saints toward faithfulness, humility, and joy in serving the Lord.

The Epistle to the Philippians begins with expressions of thanksgiving for the Philippians and the hopeful thought that despite his imprisonment Paul is glad that the Gospel is advancing (1:12). He encourages the Philippians to remain true to God—no matter what happened—even if it means suffering for the sake of the Good News of Jesus Christ (1:27–30). The second chapter urges them to humility using the profound humiliation experienced by Christ when He put aside the outward display of glory to take upon Himself human flesh in order to atone for the sins of humankind (2:5–11). Pointing to Timothy and Epaphroditus as his faithful fellow servants (vv. 19, 25), the apostle urges the saints at Philippi to welcome and honor them. Paul encourages the believers to aim high as he has done, to press toward the upward prize which God offers to those who are faithful (3:14). He pleads with them to rejoice in the Lord always (4:4), and to think good thoughts about Christ (v. 8). He closes with expressions of thanks for the generous gift they had sent him, reminding them that God would supply all their needs because they had been so generous to him (v. 19).

THE BLACK PRESENCE IN PHILIPPIANS

There are no specific references to the black presence within the Epistle to the Philippians. However, we must bear in mind that the Gospel preached by Paul had its origin in North Africa and Palestine where there was a significant black presence. Not until the Greeks and Romans began to migrate into the biblical lands during the centuries prior to the birth of Christ do we find any significant presence of other racial groups. Bear in mind once again that in biblical times racial identification did not have the significance it carries today. This significance is more critical today because of efforts made within the last two centuries to eliminate or distort the reality of the biblical black presence to the detriment of people of color.

Additionally, some have concluded that since Paul was mistaken for an Egyptian (Acts 21:38), he must have been black.

Life Lessons

PHILIPPIANS 1

Chapter one introduces us to "Paul and Timotheus, the servants of Jesus Christ" (1:1). Paul gives God thanks for the people in Philippi who have entered into partnership with them on behalf of the Good News (v. 3–4, 7). Paul mentions his confidence that the Lord would continue to work in the hearts of the Philippian believers (v. 6). The Philippians worked in different ways to assure that the ministry was advanced. They had not only witnessed in Philippi but also helped to support the traveling

team of Paul and Timothy. Paul wants them to understand that his imprisonment has not hindered the work of God. Instead: "many of the brethren in the Lord, waxing confident by my bonds, are much more bold to speak the word without fear" (v. 14). Here Paul helps us to understand that our circumstances can always promote the Good News. Our attitude, which shapes how we handle situations which life brings our way, can give glory and honor to God.

Joy Giver, let me always rejoice in Your ability to bring me through difficult situations. Keep me focused on You.

PHILIPPIANS 4

We are provided with a vivid portrait of women at work in the church at Philippi. In chapter four, Paul pleads with Euodias and Syntyche "be of the same mind in the Lord" (v. 2).

"My brethren dearly beloved and longed for . . . I intreat thee also, true yokefellow, help those women which laboured with me in the gospel, with Clement also, and with other my fellowlabourers, whose names are in the book of life" (4:1, 3). This admonition from Paul gives us a different view of his appreciation, respect, and acceptance of women involved in the ministry of the local church. There is no doubt we have the names of "sisters" because he specifically requests, "help those women." What is essential for us to note is that the women, whose influence has helped the growth of the church, have a broken relationship that has been brought to the attention of Paul.

These are not unnamed women, but we know that Euodias and Syntyche have had a significant falling out which has not been reconciled. As Paul writes about joy in Christ, he begs for reconciliation between the sisters. It is imperative, if we desire abiding joy in our life that we not get caught up in the "E & S" syndrome of petty infighting, which detracts from our witness.

Great One, let us always remember our unity in the body. Keep us mindful that You have more than enough love to go around for every sibling!

PHILIPPIANS 4

Paul concludes his letter by giving thanks to the congregation for the great contribution they have sent through Epaphroditus. Telling them "whatsoever things are true, whatsoever things are honest, whatsoever things are just, whatsoever things are pure, whatsoever things are lovely, whatsoever things are of good report; if there be any virtue, and if there be any praise, think on these things" (4:8). He thanks them and shares with them that he "[has] learned, in whatever state [he is], therewith to be content" (v. 11), all because "I can do all things through Christ which strengtheneth me" (v. 13). He concludes by greeting them in the name of Christ Jesus and sending them hellos; "all the saints salute you, chiefly they that are of Caesar's household" (v. 22). This reminds them that even in jail, he is winning souls for Christ! There is no spot that Christ is not!

Lord, may we always be aware of the privilege of being able to say to another, "the grace of the Lord Jesus Christ be with you all. Amen" (v. 23).

Focus on Colossians

To be a member of your favorite sorority requires application, a get-acquainted tea for being looked over and "classified." It is a time of going on-line and, hopefully, preparing for the great day of "crossing over." However, before that happens, there is the paying of local and national dues, purchasing the right colors, getting the right recommendations, having the correct background, remembering the right dates and people, and being willing to keep up the right type of social activities. After all of that, you still might not be allowed into the sorority of your choice!

Perhaps you're not into the whole "black Greek scene." You simply want to work hard and keep up with the Joneses. You might be concerned about the right degree, the right position, the right salary, the right mentor, and the right assignment. You need the right support staff, the right visibility, and the right outcomes. This outlook requires that you have the right clothes, the right car, the right address, and the right social standing to be noticed. However, even if all that happens, you may or may not be accepted by the Joneses!

Maybe this is not your story. Maybe you find yourself struggling to just make it from day to day. In this country you need certain things to even be assisted with your needs. You need a Social Security number, a birth certificate, a telephone, and an address. Even with all of the necessary documentation, getting the help you need is not guaranteed. If you do receive help, there are the continuing certification processes to follow. It's the way of every culture to have you follow the rules, "jump the hoops," and fit in our mold. So it's no wonder that many of us are just like the folks at Colosse who thought that salvation required certain rituals in order to stay connected to Jesus Christ.

What in the world can be received without falling in line with the status quo? The Latin phrase *status quo* means "to find oneself in the middle of a mess"! Jesus comes to get us out of the mess, to stop the need for rules, regulations, and rituals to prove a right relationship. There is no "thing" that we do to qualify for God's grace. It is a free gift to us through the shed blood of Jesus Christ (see Eph. 2:8–9). It's hard to believe. It sounds too good to be true. There are many who teach that the "things" can save us and bring us closer to Christ. They make the rituals seem primary and ultimate. It's this teaching that Paul addresses in the letter to the Colossians.

Syncretism is the practice of mixing ideas from other religions and philosophies. Syncretic false teachers had come into the church with a "mixed bag" of rituals from strains of Judaism, Greek philosophies, and even paganism. The type of heresy these false teachers taught in Colosse became known as *Gnosticism* centuries later. It emphasized Greek knowledge as paramount and denied the work of Jesus Christ on Calvary. In

other words, one's "rightness" had nothing to do with being in the right club, living in the right section of town, or even knowing the right set of people, but everything to do with knowledge.

In this epistle Paul asks God to fill us with the knowledge of that perfect will through spiritual wisdom and understanding so that we might live a life worthy of Jesus Christ. Through a right relationship and belief in the power of the Cross, we can please the Lord in every way by bearing fruit in our good works, growing in our relationship with God, being strengthened with all power so that we might have great endurance and patience to joyfully give thanks to God who has qualified us to share in the inheritance of the saints (1:9–12). All of this can be accomplished without an application form or references! Just go for it!

After a brief greeting at the beginning of the letter, the apostle expresses thanksgiving to God and to the Colossian saints for their love and faith (vv. 4–6). He prays for their increased knowledge and wisdom to fulfill God's will (v. 9). He then launches into a remarkable description concerning the supremacy of Christ over all ideologies, beings, or philosophies (vv. 15–19). He then challenges them to reject as heresy any teaching which is inconsistent with what he presents (chap. 2). The apostle follows this plea with the admonition to rid their lives of any conduct which is unbecoming of a follower of Jesus Christ (chap. 3). This admonition is addressed to all believers.

THE BLACK PRESENCE IN COLOSSIANS

There are no specific references to the black presence within the Epistle to the Colossians. However, we must bear in mind that the Gospel preached by Paul had its origin in North Africa and Palestine where there was a significant black presence. Not until the Greeks and Romans began to migrate into the biblical lands during the centuries prior to the birth of Christ do we find any significant presence of other racial groups. Bear in mind once again that in biblical times racial identification did not have the significance it carries today. This significance is more critical today because of efforts made within the last two centuries to eliminate or distort the reality of the biblical black presence to the detriment of people of color.

Additionally, some have concluded that since Paul was mistaken for an Egyptian (Acts 21:38), he must have been black.

Life Lessons

COLOSSIANS 1–2

Colossians, Philippians, Ephesians, and Philemon are called the Prison Letters, written while Paul was jailed in Rome. The greeting to this letter is an identification and authority of the apostle (1:1–2). This is followed by a prayer of thanksgiving for their love, faith, and hope—the cornerstones of

Christianity (vv. 3–8). Knowledge is not listed until he prays for them to be filled with the knowledge of God's perfect will through belief in Jesus Christ (vv. 9–10). For Paul, it was a time to reinforce the fact that "what" one knew was not as important as "who" one knew. The One to know was Jesus Christ.

Knowledge had become a central focus of controversy in the church. Paul lifts up the supremacy of Christ, who "is the image of the invisible God, the firstborn over all creation. For by him were all things created, that are in heaven, and that are in earth . . . He is before all things, and by him all things consist. And he is the head of the body, the church" (vv. 15–18). Paul is well aware of the "enticing words" (2:4) being taught which declared that secret knowledge was being withheld from most believers. The Gnostics also taught that the body was evil and that Jesus had only appeared to be human but was not. Paul encourages the saints to "beware lest any man spoil you through philosophy and vain deceit, after the tradition of men, after the rudiments of the world, and not after Christ" (v. 8).

Christ of All, keep me firmly rooted in my belief that You alone are sufficient for my salvation. Let the world and its traditions not invade and cloud my mind.

COLOSSIANS 3

Paul exhorts the saints: "If ye then be risen with Christ, seek those things which are above, where Christ sitteth on the right hand of God. Set your affection on things above, not on things on the earth" (3:1–2). He goes on to describe rules for right living for believers to follow. He instructs us to take off the old sinful garments and to put on the new clothing, which comes from a relationship with Jesus Christ (vv. 12–14). He gives us a basic Christian Education program to work through. He talks about the need for forgiveness to be at work in us so that reconciliation and unity might be evident for all to see. "Above all these things put on charity, which is the bond of perfectness. And let the peace of God rule in your hearts" (vv. 14–15). Forgiveness is the key! When we remember that God loved us enough to forgive us for our sinful nature and practices, it ought to make it easier to forgive others for their sins against us. Forgiveness requires diligence and practice.

Forgiving God, help me to always remember Your willingness to forgive me!

COLOSSIANS 4

Paul concludes his letter with firm instructions: "Continue in prayer, and watch in the same with thanksgiving; withal praying also for us" (4:2–3). He uplifts the brothers and sisters ministering in Laodicea, especially noting "Nymphas, and the church which is in his house" (v. 15). Finally, he sends a firm warning to Archippus and to each of us! "Say to Archippus, Take heed to the ministry which thou hast received in the Lord, that thou fulfil it" (v. 17). Too many of us know what God has called us to do, but allow other people and situations to retard our progress with a given assignment. It is clear that Archippus had started doing something that had the potential to be significant within the life of the church. However, he had stopped working. We are each given specific roles to play

within the body. This is the function of spiritual gifts (see 1 Cor. 12). When we don't do our job, others suffer! See to it that you complete the work you have received in the Lord!

Assigning Savior, You finished Your job on a rugged tree on Calvary. Despite the suffering and agony, You did not stop. Help me to get up and get busy. Help me to finish my task with joy!

FOCUS ON FIRST THESSALONIANS

Women of color know the exhausting pain of waiting! We have a history of surviving continuing onslaughts of terror, tyranny, subjection, abandonment, and rejection. We know that we live wholly dependent upon the strength and wisdom of God to conquer the challenges that life presents. Waiting and hoping are twin aunts in each of our families. They are part of our family tree. We know them as well as we know Sorrow, our mother. We know how to begin again, for Suffering is our grandmother, while Striving is among our sisters. We are women who know their experiences for our name is Wait!

We have lived our lives under whips, fire hoses, and before howling and growling dogs. Too often we have lived under the fist and under the feet of the men in our lives. We have lived our lives within the walls, within the narrow constrictions known as bondage—bondage that is too often self-inflicted by our fantasies. We have waited in the lush forest of Ethiopia, in the tropical wilds of Kenya, and in the palaces of Egypt. We have waited through the forced exodus from Africa and during the voyages of many slave ships. We have landed and waited on the shores of the land of the free and the home of the slaves in chains. We have waited.

We have waited in the seasoning pens, on the auction blocks, in the big houses, and in the shanties. We have waited as we washed, cooked, cleaned, chopped, plowed, and hoed. We have waited, embraced by loneliness; wracked by pain and despair; kissed by poverty and misery; caressed by anxiety, fear, and disease. We know how to wait.

We have pleaded and we have hurt. We have loved and longed for dreams to come true. We have had our bodies stolen. We have been traded, bartered, sold, abused, raped, bred, exploited, married off, and been taken advantage of simply because of our color and our gender. We have given birth and we have suffered loss as we raised our babies and "maimed" others.

We have sheltered the orphan, welcomed the stranger, and embraced the lonely and unlovely. We have known the essence of despair. We have stood, crying as we waited in the throes of death. We have known throats parched as we thirsted for justice. Our feet have grown bloody, cutting paths and making ways where there have been no ways, no means, and no money. Yes, without a doubt, we know how to wait and to hope.

Our only hope has been in Jesus Christ and his victory over sin, death, and hell. However, our waiting has not been in vain. There is a better life.

If not here, then in eternity. This is the story of the people called Christians in Thessalonica who were tortured and slain for their faith. Paul's encouragement to them is ours. "We believe that Jesus died and rose again, even so them also which sleep in Jesus will God bring with him" (4:14).

Sisters, keep the faith!

Paul thanks God for the faith of the Thessalonians in the face of much persecution (1:3; 2:14). He recounts his experience at Philippi where he was beaten and thrown into prison (2:2). Yet he faithfully preached the same Gospel to them that he had preached at Philippi (v. 13). They had responded positively to his message and he was glad. The letter becomes personal as he expresses his longing for them and the action he took in sending Timothy to see how they were doing (3:2). Timothy's report encouraged him (vv. 6–8). He admonishes the believers to maintain sexual purity (4:1–8) and to work with their hands (vv. 11–12) in order to avoid disgracing the people of God.

After discovering their confusion about believers who had died, the apostle clarifies his teaching by asserting that dead believers would, in fact, rise first when the Lord Jesus returns in glory to receive believers (vv. 13–18). Dead believers would join live ones and together they will meet the Lord in the air (v. 17). Paul then explains to the believers that no one knows when this will happen, so they should encourage and build up each other (5:1–11).

THE BLACK PRESENCE IN FIRST THESSALONIANS

There are no specific references to the black presence within Paul's first letter to the believers in Thessalonica. However, we must bear in mind that the Gospel preached by Paul had its origin in North Africa and Palestine where there was a significant black presence. Not until the Greeks and Romans began to migrate into the biblical lands during the centuries prior to the birth of Christ do we find any significant presence of other racial groups. Bear in mind once again that in biblical times racial identification did not have the significance it carries today. This significance is more critical today because of efforts made within the last two centuries to eliminate or distort the reality of the biblical black presence to the detriment of people of color.

Life Lessons

1 THESSALONIANS 2

Paul writes to people who had suffered persecution for their faith. As he recalls his time with the believers at Thessalonica, after offering thanksgiving for their steadfast faith, he reminds them, "We might have been burdensome, as the apostles of Christ. But we were gentle among you, even as a nurse cherisheth her children: So being affectionately desirous of you, we were willing to have imparted unto you, not the gospel

of God only, but also our own souls, because ye were dear unto us" (2:6–8). Here Paul does not resort to "manly power" to lord over the church. He affirms the womanly qualities of gentleness and the ability to share, like a loving mother. Relationships among the people of Christ must always be characterized by a gentle spirit that exhibits love.

Gentle Redeemer, work the quality of gentleness throughout my relationships, especially the very difficult ones!

1 THESSALONIANS 4

Paul tells the believers that "This is the will of God, even your sanctification, that ye should abstain from fornication: That every one of you should know how to possess his vessel in sanctification and honour; Not in the lust of concupiscence, even as the Gentiles which know not God. . . . For God hath not called us unto uncleanness, but unto holiness" (4:3–5, 7). Keeping our bodies under subjection is not always easy. Yet it is required. It is possible with the help of the Holy Spirit. A holy life honors God. Unfortunately, sexual sin was an expected and accepted way of life in the Greco-Roman world.

God calls us to live at a higher standard. To be sanctified means to be set apart for Christ through the Holy Spirit working in us to bring us into conformity with the will of God—not in conformity with the low standards of the world.

Sanctifying Spirit, move me to do God's perfect will.

1 THESSALONIANS 5

When the going gets rough there must be a place and a community where comfort and solace may be found. Paul knew firsthand the severity of the suffering being experienced by the church. Therefore he encouraged them to "comfort yourselves together, and edify one another, even as also ye do" (5:11). The gift of encouragement is a necessary one for the church of God today. If it's missing in your local assembly, perhaps it can start with you!

Lord, this is my prayer for all I know: May "the very God of peace sanctify you wholly; and I pray God your whole spirit and soul and body be preserved blameless unto the coming of our Lord Jesus Christ. Faithful is he that calleth you, who also will do it" (vv. 23–24).

FOCUS ON

SECOND THESSALONIANS

Miscommunication is at the root of many estranged relationships. Often we feel that someone has said or inferred something that has caused us great pain. It happens often between females and males in conversations. It occurs in parent-child conversations.

It is a present dynamic in on-the-job situations. When we finally sit down and talk about what we thought was said, we find that what we heard was not what was stated or intended!

Too often, instead of authentically communicating with each other, we become two "talking heads," speaking *at* each other, not *with* each other! As one individual is speaking, the other person is nodding, acting as if she is listening, while what's really going on is that the silent person is formulating the "head" conversation which will be spoken when the other stops talking. When the second person begins talking, the no-listening act is repeated! We miss much of what is being said to us as we come in and out of our own thoughts, which are impacted by the perceptions and baggage we bring to the moment. Active listening requires deliberate concentration and diligence. Active listening demands putting our agendas aside and being serious about being fully present in the conversation. Active listening calls for us to pause, ask for clarification, and even repeat a statement to ensure that what we heard was what was intended. That is hard work!

As women we approach situations with many things on our plates and in our minds. We live multifaceted lives, which require that we play many roles. It is not easy to "empty our minds and be "here" right now! We are either rehearsing what has happened already or planning what needs to happen next. We miss much in conversations! We accuse our significant males of not listening, when in all honesty, none of us can fully listen without making a concentrated effort.

The people at Thessalonica had listened to Paul's first letter of encouragement and consolation. Some had misunderstood his teaching about the Second Coming of Jesus Christ.

Many thought Paul was saying Jesus was on His way back "now." They stopped working. They gave up planning for tomorrow and began to sit and wait for Christ's return. Of course they were tired of the struggle and the persecution. Surely, the next life would be better. "Let it come now!" Tensions rose as these nonworkers were not able to contribute to the welfare of the church. Paul wrote Second Thessalonians in hopes of clearing up what he meant to say the first time! He wanted to clarify teachings presented in his first letter.

After greeting the believers (1:1–2), Paul offers thanks to God for them, and assures them that those who persecuted them would be punished on the day the Lord Jesus arrived (vv. 4–10). He prays that God will fulfill His purposes in and for them (vv. 11–12). The apostle then explains that the day of the Lord will be preceded by the appearance of "that man of sin . . . the son of perdition" (2:3) who will exalt himself above everything that is worshiped. He will proclaim himself to be God (2:1–6). Paul indicates they already knew what held this lawless one back (v. 6). Bible scholars have longed through the ages that Paul would have repeated here what he had previously told the Thessalonians as to the identity of this power, which restrained him. Consequently various possibilities have been offered, including the church, the Roman government, the preaching of Paul himself, the Holy Spirit, and so on. Whichever it is, the ultimate source of the restraint has to be the power of God.

Paul encourages them to stand fast and to pray for him that the word of the Lord might spread rapidly (2:15; 3:1–5). He also addresses the issue of those who refused to work, apparently expecting the imminent return of Christ. Paul urges them to settle down and work, counseling them that if a person did not work he should not eat (3:6–10). His final

greeting includes the assurance that any letter from him will bear his signature to authenticate its authorship (v. 17).

THE BLACK PRESENCE IN SECOND THESSALONIANS

There are no specific references to the black presence within Paul's second letter to the believers in Thessalonica. However, we must bear in mind that the Gospel preached by Paul had its origin in North Africa and Palestine where there was a significant black presence. Not until the Greeks and Romans began to migrate into the biblical lands during the centuries prior to the birth of Christ do we find any significant presence of other racial groups. Bear in mind once again that in biblical times racial identification did not have the significance it carries today. This significance is more critical today because of efforts made within the last two centuries to eliminate or distort the reality of the biblical black presence to the detriment of people of color.

Additionally, some have concluded that since Paul was mistaken for an Egyptian (Acts 21:38), he must have been black.

Life Lessons

2 THESSALONIANS 2–3

Much of what we heard and read in Paul's first letter is repeated as he attempts to clarify his teachings. "Remember ye not, that, when I was yet with you, I told you these things?" (2:5) "Therefore, brethren, stand fast, and hold the traditions which ye have been taught, whether by word, or our epistle. Now our Lord Jesus Christ himself, and God, even our Father, which hath loved us, and hath given us everlasting consolation and good hope through grace, comfort your hearts, and stablish you in every good word and work" (vv. 15–17). Paul realizes that some of the congregation has grown weary of the unceasing persecution of the church. The words of encouragement are repeated in order to strengthen believers for the difficult days ahead. Apathy is to be expected when difficulties continue. It is a defense mechanism, which allows us to let down our guards and be further deceived by the enemy of our souls! "But the Lord is faithful, who shall stablish you, and keep you from evil" (3:3) Our faithfulness is the expected response.

Faithful One, hard times cause me to seek ways of escape. Help me to remain faithful to You.

2 THESSALONIANS 3

Those who anticipated the immediate return of Christ used this as an excuse to cease working. They became a burden to the rest of the community. Paul calls the church to remember that "when we were with you, this we commanded you, that if any would not work, neither should he eat" (3:10). The church should not support the lazy. This speaks to women who allow adult sons to return home without making every attempt to find

gainful employment. It surely addresses those sisters who allow adult men—significant others—to live in their homes without working. If we do this, we're supporting and encouraging that man's sinful habits.

The grace of our Lord Jesus Christ be with [us] all! (v. 18)

Women in PHILIPPIANS

EUODIAS AND SYNTYCHE: WOMEN IN CONFLICT

The apostle Paul held Euodias in high esteem. He told the saints in the church at Philippi to "help those women [Euodias and Syntyche] which laboured with me in the gospel" (Phil. 4:3). The only other person who received such admiration was Timothy.

However, in Philippians 4:2, we find Paul addressing the church about the conduct of these two women. Euodias and Syntyche feuded about a matter that disrupted the life of the church. Therefore, he wrote asking the saints to assist in bringing about a reconciliation between these two women.

Euodias and Syntyche were truly an asset to Paul's ministry. They contributed greatly to the local church, which is why Paul was adamant about bringing wholeness and healing to this situation. If left unchecked, this conflict would cause harm to the church.

When there is division in the household of faith, the work of the church is hindered. Whatever the issue was between Euodias and Syntyche, Paul put it to rest, and he wanted the other saints to assist in making that happen.

As women of color and of faith, we must focus on important matters and not dwell on the minor issues. The time we waste arguing about insignificant matters could be better used doing something that would advance the work of the Lord.

Instead of feuding, Paul encourages the saints to rejoice. How can we attract others to the church if we are at odds with each other? They see enough of that outside the church! While we may not always agree with one another, we can strive to compromise. Things do not always have to go our way. We must remember that everyone is someone important to Christ. When we do, we will respect each other just as He respects us.

When we rejoice in the Lord, we will find ways to encourage someone else. We will consider the other person's well-being just as we would our own. Strife is a tool of our adversary. So, we must continue to lift up the cross and proclaim Christ's love, until all the world adores His sacred name.

Read Philippians 4.

Read the insight essay on Prayer.

—D. Stroman

Insights

CELIBACY

Celibacy is the act of dedicating one's life to God's service and maintaining sexual purity while single. For some women, celibacy becomes a life-long vow so that they might give themselves completely to the Lord and His church (1 Cor. 7:32–34). It is a vow to be totally "holy both in body and in spirit" (v. 34). As our Lord clearly states, this calling is not for everyone. However, celibacy can lead to deeper faith and a closer relationship with God.

Instead of looking for security in tangible things that are only temporary, God wants us to know, love, and lean on Him, not just as Father and Savior but as soul mate, first love, best friend, and comforter (see Isa. 54:1–6; John 14:26). He may use marriage to picture for us the eternal relationship between ourselves and our Savior, or He may call us to a single-minded, wholehearted focus on Him through celibacy (1 Cor. 7:32–34). God points us through both callings to a final eternal union with Him, which He is preparing for us all.

Whether married or single, we are called to be imitators of God (Eph. 5:1–10), and to keep our bodies as the temple of God's Spirit (1 Cor. 6:13–14, 18–20). Through Christ's redeeming blood and intercession (Heb. 4: 14–16), we receive the grace we need to resist temptation and lead a life that is pleasing to God.

Read 1 Corinthians 6:13–14, 18–20; 7:32–34.

Read the insight essays on Commitment and Singleness.

—C. Richards

SINGLENESS: A CALL TO HOLINESS

Man appears before us in the Scriptures as a fallen being, someone who by nature is unholy and sinful. Though created in the image of God, mankind lost one of the most important features of the image—holiness. Holiness is an outcome of God's benevolent work in salvation (see Eph. 4:22–24). Holiness is possible for women—married or single (Luke 1:75; 2 Cor. 7:1; 1 Thess. 3:13).

The New Testament teaches that Christians are sanctified positionally when we are saved by the virtue of being presented "in Christ Jesus" (1 Cor. 1:2, 30). On a daily basis, we are being sanctified by experiences as we consider our position (Rom. 6:11). In the end, we will be sanctified by experiences in the sense of being fully conformed in the glory of God (Rom. 8:30).

The Christian single is "a chosen person" and one of God's elect people. Just as Israel was a chosen race, under the Old Covenant, Christian singles now have better and more excellent privileges under the New Covenant (1 Pet. 2:9). As members of a holy nation, all Christian singles can apply the use of the word *saint.* Our born-again nature implies that

we are the ones who have high ethical characters (1 Cor. 1:2, 24). The Holy Spirit takes residence in the heart of every Christian single woman and begins the positive work of sanctification (Rom. 5:5). According to the Scriptures, holiness cannot exist in the absence of the moral qualities that God demands from those whom He calls His people (Eph. 4:24).

No longer do we have to focus our attention on past failures or hurts. We can look forward with singleness of purpose. Singleness of purpose does not mean being a stranger of the covenant of promise. The promise of God's Word to women is that we will experience the fullness of His presence in our lives as we seek to know the Lord, love the Lord, and follow His Word. We may be single, but we are never alone. In fact, our state is the opposite (Gal. 3:29). Attentively and purposefully, holiness drives one to the mercy of God (Luke 1:50, 58; 2 Cor. 7:1). For it is God's call to holiness that the believer can always find purpose. It provides the ultimate refuge in seeking security and the best benefits of being single-minded and dedicated to the call as Paul was (Rom. 1:4–6; 6:19, 22; 1 Cor. 7:1–9).

Read 1 Corinthians 7:1–9; see also 1 Peter 2:9.

Read the insight essays on Attributes of God, Prayer, Sacrificial Living, and Singleness.

—*A.* ***Hobbs***

SINGLENESS: UNIQUE OPPORTUNITY FOR SERVICE

Singleness is not a stigma but the best opportunity to display the ultimate in a vertical relationship with God (1 Cor. 7:34). Singleness is simply submission—a unique opportunity for service.

The surrender of your natural self to a spiritual position with God is more important than anything else. According to Galatians 5:24, you have "crucified the flesh" and submitted to God.

Submitting to God's will can affect us monumentally. It is the ultimate in giving one's life, sacrificially, to God. With that commitment, the believer becomes intertwined with God and knows Him intimately. Concomitantly, she becomes secure and "mature in Christ." Perhaps the best example of this is Mother Teresa. She was a vessel of honor (2 Tim. 2:21). During this century, no one has touched the hearts of the world more than Mother Teresa. Her singleness provided her the opportunity to serve others. She exemplified 1 Corinthians 15:58, "Be ye steadfast, unmovable, always abounding in the work of the Lord, forasmuch as ye know that your labor is not in vain in the Lord."

Mother Teresa had the best husband, partner, and brother: the Lord Jesus Christ. The most honored woman in the world lived according to Isaiah 3:10. She was a righteous woman who was enjoying the "fruit of their doings." For her faithfulness, God promoted her and caused mankind to honor her (Rom. 13:6–7). She was single in purpose and "given" to the opportunity to serve (1 Cor. 7:34).

Mother Teresa's heart emanated the heart of God. His purpose and desires became hers—loving people like Christ loved the church. After all has been said and done, she became a friend of God because of her singleness and willingness to serve (James 2:23). What an example!

Read 1 Corinthians 7:32–34; see also Ephesians 4:11–16; Philippians 3:15–21; Colossians 1:3–10.

Read the insight essays on Celibacy, Sacrificial Living, and Singleness.

—*A. Hobbs*

FRUIT OF THE SPIRIT: LOVE

Tina Turner, in her song "What's Love Got To Do with It," raised a question about the validity of the emotion called love. According to Tina, love was something that one could do without; unfortunately, some Christians feel the same way.

According to Tina, love is based in the emotions. However, the Bible speaks of another kind of love—one that is not an emotion at all. It is an act of the will, whereby we line our wills with God's will, and we do right by one another, regardless of how we feel.

Biblical love is not envious, proud, self-centered, rude, or provoking. It is:

patient—slow to anger;
kind—gentle to all;
unselfish;
truthful;
hopeful and encouraging; and
enduring—without end (1 Cor. 13:4–8).

The Bible speaks of three kinds of love: (1) *eros,* which is sensual love; (2) *phileo,* which relates to friendship, parental, or family love; and (3) *agape,* which is Christlike, selfless, self-sacrificing. It is God's love. *Agape* love relates to the will, not the emotions. God calls us to have *agape* love for one another. In 1 Corinthians 13:13, Paul calls unselfish, loyal, and benevolent concern for the well-being of others the greatest gift of all.

This love confirms our Christianity. John 13:35 says, "By this shall all men know that ye are my disciples, if ye have love one to another." First John 4:20 notes, "He that loveth not his brother whom he hath seen, how can he love God whom he hath not seen?"

As we look at the challenges facing the black community, we must understand that love is the only power that will save us. God's love can look at the worse situation and see hope. God's love can stand in the midst of hate and poverty and speak a word of deliverance. God's love can transform communities and transform minds. "The fruit of the Spirit is love . . . against such there is no law" (Gal. 5:22–23).

Read 1 Corinthians 13.

Read the insight essays on Attributes of God, Fruit of the Spirit, Love, and Romance.

—*C. Belt*

INTIMACY: RELATIONSHIPS WITH OTHER CHRISTIANS

The genuine, open communication of one heart to another is, perhaps, the most fitting definition of intimacy. The word *intimacy* does not appear in Scripture; yet it is evident from many passages that God is interested in the kind of genuine relationship that intimacy denotes. He desires it in His deal-

ings with His people, as well as in the personal dealings of individuals with family, friends, and other Christians. True intimacy always involves a spiritual dimension. Unfortunately, it is a characteristic that sometimes eludes even our most treasured relationships, and because of this we are worse off.

Intimacy is that essential element of our lives that sustains us. Newborn babies crave intimate contact as much as they desire milk. Without it they cannot thrive. Every human heart yearns for the opportunity to "know even as also I am known" (1 Cor. 13:12), because this is how we were created. When human or spiritual intimacy is missing, we are not complete. We attempt to fill that void with things or activities that are less than satisfying.

While we cannot be intimate with a host of people, there is a level of intimacy or communion that Christians can enjoy with each other based on our common heritage and faith. This kind of intimate love is not superficial—it comes from the heart (1 Pet. 1:22). Jesus desired that all members of the church share in this kind of closeness that would allow the world to see a different way of being in relationship. His prayer was that we would be one, knitted together in love, as He and the Father are one (John 10:30).

Read 1 Corinthians 13.

—E. Alexander

GRIEF: MOURNING THE LOSS OF A STILLBORN CHILD

Grief is certainly something most of us will experience at some time in life. Grief is universal and the method by which one handles pain. Grief is a normal response to the loss of a significant person—especially an unborn child. You will face the emptiness and the difficult task of readjusting. This period will include viewing the reality of the loss, admitting the pain, and adjusting to a home environment in which the child never came home from the hospital. The most difficult part will be answering the question, "Where is the new baby?" or "What did you have—a boy or a girl?"

The grief over the death of a stillborn child is more difficult because the loss is unexpected, untimely, and sudden. Daily you will battle the feelings of unfinished business, guilt, failure, and shame. For parents, the death of a child is one of life's most devastating losses. Only someone who has had this experience can fully understand the feelings associated with the loss of a child.

This experience should bring the parents closer to one another in an effort to cope. It doesn't always, however. Some couples who were unable to cope with their loss soon watched their marriages flounder as the unrealistic "blame game" began. That's why couples facing the loss of a child need to rely heavily on their relationships to God.

Your relationship with Christ will give you support, meaning, and hope for the future. Through a daily personal encounter with Christ, you will find His comfort and peace in times of mourning. When a grieving person refuses to consider the claims of Christ (healing, strength, and comfort), there is no hope. You will experience prolonged periods of shock, numbness, denial,

intense crying, restlessness, loneliness, and insomnia. However, daily prayer, singing, verbal statements of God's promises, positive thoughts of overcoming, and reading the Scriptures will help soften the pain. Accepting God's strength and support can ease the grieving process. The quiet support of others can help sustain you through these difficult times.

As you begin to recognize the stages of grief, you will learn how to walk and grow through this experience. For parents, that is no easy task. Grief comes without warning. Grief can only be conquered when it is faced honestly, with divine help and the support of other people. Thank God for the widely available sources of help from family members, friends, ministers, and physicians. After many days of hopelessness, you will learn to live with the memory of your loss. This experience will help you mature and make you better equipped to reach out to others. You can go through this experience with God, who provides all the comfort you'll need.

Read 1 Corinthians 15; see also Psalm 23:3–4; 55:17; 61:1–2; 63; 119:28; Isaiah 53:3–4; 2 Corinthians 4:14; 5:8; 1 Thessalonians 4:14, 18.

Read the insight essays on Children, Grief, Motherhood, Parenting, and Suffering.

—C. Love

BON VOYAGE: THE COURAGE TO SAY GOOD-BYE

It must have been around February when we found out that what was supposed to be a bruise, and then a cyst, was really a tumor. We could not believe it! Just two months earlier my nephew had come back to San Diego to hang out with his friends and cousins for Christmas. Sure, he was on crutches, but everybody knew that Larry was dramatic. He was in pain but he played it off so well. Nothing stopped him. He was a determined young black man.

The tumor was malignant. They'd given him three months, and two had already passed. Larry wasn't running anymore. He used to play practical jokes on the nurses. They couldn't find him regularly. But no more. He was trying to breathe and trying to eat. My nephew was trying to live. He'd given his life to the Lord and long since repented for his follies and sins. "I'm going to live, Aunt Sandra! I'm going to beat this thing. God's gonna heal me. Nothing's too hard for God—*nothing!* Not even *this!*"

But that wasn't God's plan for Larry. By early May, he was no longer eating or talking. Breathing was his biggest challenge. He was on a morphine drip, and he no longer responded to the questions. We had shared many secrets in the last two months. I'd been with him almost daily. I loved him, but now it was time to let him go. He was suffering, struggling to stay here for us. Like many families, we wanted him to hang on. But the Holy Spirit spoke to my heart and asked, "Why?" Why should he stay on this side? By then everyone else was gone home. So I kissed him and gave him permission to go. "We'll be fine, sweetie," I said. "Don't stay for us. Jesus has something better for you on the other side. We'll see you there. I'll miss you so much." Then I climbed in his bed and began to sing a song to him just as I'd done when the kids were young. I turned my face to the

window so that he wouldn't see my cry. When I turned back, he was easing out. I caught him just in time to say, "Babe, babe . . . I love you." He squeezed my hand, took four good breaths. *Four.* Then he stepped over.

God gives us the courage to trust Him even in the face of death—courage to believe that He is too wise to make a mistake and too good to do wrong. May God continually remind us that this world is not our home. We're only to pitch a tent, not build a homestead (see 2 Cor. 5:1). And when it's our time, we too will hear a song and cross over.

Read 2 Corinthians 5:1–9.

Read the insight essays on Depression, Fear, and Grief.

—L. Melton-Dolberry

ROMANCE: THE MISUNDERSTOOD GIFT

Romance is God's gift to mankind. Yet romance is made up of many elements. God sanctioned romance in His Word by giving us three books on the mysteries of romance: Ruth, Esther, and Song of Solomon. In these books, we see man wooing woman. But we also see God wooing us—sinful people—to repent—turn from our wicked ways—and accept Christ Jesus by faith to be our Lord and Savior.

In the earlier days, most Jewish marriages were arranged by the parents and were called "love matches." These matches were usually done when the children were of a very young age. They would have many years to get to know each other before the marriage ceremony, plenty of time to decide if the marriage should take place.

God knew we would need that "certain something" in our relationships for it to go from a courting relationship to a loving marriage relationship. That certain something is romance. As God's love has many virtues, so has romance its many elements; yet all is worthwhile and rewarding.

One of romance's elements is confession. Just as we confess Jesus Christ as our Lord, and witness to the world of His sacrifice (Rom. 10:8–10), we also confess our feelings for "that man" to him and others. We are proud to be known as "his woman," and want the world to know.

Wonder, trust, anticipation, hope, respect, faithfulness, compassion, gentleness, admiration, and abstinence are but a few of the elements of romance. All of these are very much present in our marriages, and each should be examined prayerfully during the courtship phase. Romance is the seed; these elements are the fruit of that seed. Only through Christ Jesus can our romances produce marriages of a lasting nature.

Romance can be hypocritical also. Ask yourself these questions and allow the Holy Spirit to show you the answers:

Is he opportunistic?

Is his focus on this opportunity to compromise you and your faith?

Is he seeking to fulfill his own selfish lusts?

Is he a man who gives "lip service" for his own gain?

Are all of his answers truthful? Can you trust him?

Accept good answers with praise.

God sees both sides of our faces and loves us in spite of our duality. But, we should not "romantically sin" in order to keep or get a man. With

each new relationship, we are to set priorities, knowing that God always knows what is best for us.

Someone said, "Everyone needs the acts of love for life and growth. Sincere admiration must be felt and shared on a regular basis. Differences between men and women must be acknowledged. Romance moves beyond the needs of the lover to minister to the beloved."

Read Galatians 5:22–25; Ephesians 5:2

Read the insight essays on Dating and Love.

—J. Josey

IMAGE OF GOD AND THE BEAUTY OF THE HEART

One of the most important lessons a child can learn is that God made humankind in His image (Gen. 1:26–27; 9:6). Therefore, each of us is uniquely beautiful. This does not pertain to the physical image, but rather the spiritual and moral images of our being. We are healers, prophets, teachers, and lovers. Our self-image, which is based on God's love for us, can be learned early in life. It can be the life force that gives us strength in the depths of life's valleys and humility during the joy of the mountain-top experiences.

In today's world, women of color awake each morning confronting the demons associated with society's images and definitions of beauty. Beauty gets quietly empowered within institutions and relationships to suggest who is in and who is out, who is worthy and who is not, who is good and who is bad. In disobedience to God's Word, which says that beauty and intelligence are of the heart and the good action which flows from the heart, we often allow our self-image to get entangled with the materialistic commercial representation of notions of beauty. And though Euro-Americans amount to less than ten percent of the world's population, beauty gets defined by Euro-American standards of skin color, hair texture, hair length, size of nose and lips.

For women of color, reclaiming the power of self-image is one of the first steps to discovering a loving relationship with God. Self-image is intricately connected to standards of beauty; and for African women the world over, images and definitions of beauty are used to separate us from the love of God and ourselves.

Each day we must awaken to rediscover our true selves, reclaim our positive self-image, and teach our children that real beauty is of the heart and of one's actions (see Eph. 4:23–24; Col. 3:10). Let no one destroy your image of God or your self-image.

Read Colossians 3:10; see also Genesis 1:26; 9:6; Ephesians 4:24.

—I. Carruthers

FRUIT OF THE SPIRIT: GENTLENESS

Gentleness begins with genuine humility. Its technical meaning is "great power held in control." Being gentle is about knowing one's power, and knowing when and how to use it. Gentleness is not weakness; it is strength that is directed toward God and expressed in action with service to others. Jesus is our example of gentleness. He is the one "who, being in

the form of God, thought it not robbery to be equal with God: but made himself of no reputation, and took upon him the form of a servant, and was made in the likeness of men: and being found in fashion as a man, he humbled himself, and became obedient unto death, even the death of the cross" (Phil 2:6–8).

Gentleness shows great strength of character, because people who are gentle are often laughed at. Jesus courageously cut through longstanding social practices by refusing to ignore little children even though His disciples wanted Him to. He included those who the church of His day had rejected: women, tax collectors, and sinners (cf., Matthew 11:19). To walk in gentleness means to use one's power to lift up, to encourage, and to uphold! A gentle woman is one who is humble and has a submissive attitude.

African-American women wield great power, in spite of our often low status in this world. The Bible tells us that "greater is he that is in you, than he that is in the world" (1 John 4:4). Through Jesus Christ, we have been given the power to bind and loose on earth, and to have what we do on earth be approved by heaven. What would it look like, if African-American women began to walk in the gentleness of Jesus Christ, binding the power of the enemy in our communities, over our children and in our homes, and loosing them to their full potential in Jesus Christ?

Read Philippians 2:6–8; see Psalm 18:35; Matthew 11:29; Ephesians 4:1–3; 1 Timothy 6:11.

Read the insight essays on Fruit of the Spirit and Submission.

—C. Belt

SINGLENESS: A STAGE IN LIFE

Being single has become a "thorn in the flesh" of many women. Each day their prayers are filled with questions like "How long, Lord?" or "When, Lord?" and "Is this the one, Lord?" or "Why me, Lord?" Many women become frustrated and restless during this period in their lives and as a result find themselves in relationships that are unproductive and unhealthy emotionally, spiritually, and sometimes physically. But the Bible clearly teaches us that we are to be anxious for nothing because God knows what we have need of (Matt. 6:32; Phil. 4:6). What, then, does one do in the meantime?

The key to successful single life is contentment. The apostle Paul teaches us that no matter what state we find ourselves in, we must learn to be content (Phil. 4:12). Contentment means being satisfied with the way things are until God changes them. This is often a difficult task for the single woman. We are often plagued with feelings of inadequacy, loneliness, and doubt. But the Bible teaches us three essential truths that will help us find contentment.

First, the single woman can find rest in knowing that God created her for companionship. God said in Genesis 2:18: "It is not good that the man should be alone; I will make him an help meet for him." Adam experienced singleness in the Garden of Eden, but God decided when his period of singleness should end.

Second, the single woman can find contentment in realizing that God

has a specific purpose for this stage in her life. Ecclesiastes 3:1 teaches us that to everything there is a season: a time for every purpose under heaven. The responsibility of the single woman is to discover what God's purpose for her life is during this stage. This is the time during which we can diligently seek God's will for our lives through Bible study, prayer and Christian fellowship and service (Matt. 6:33).

Lastly, the single woman must realize that this stage of singleness is a period of preparation. The Bible says in Genesis 2:18 that God had to make or "fashion" a mate for Adam. In what ways is God fashioning you? This is the period in which we can fully avail ourselves of God's transforming power.

We can use this time to prepare ourselves spiritually. How is your walk with God? Are you faithful in your study of God's Word and your communication with God? This is the time to draw near to God, believing that He will draw near to you.

We can use this time to prepare ourselves financially. Have you set financial goals? How is your credit? Are you preparing for your retirement?

We can prepare ourselves physically. Are you satisfied with your appearance? How is your health? Our period of singleness is the time when God can prepare us for the next stage in life.

For most African-American women, singleness is a permanent state. For some, it is a temporary state. Regardless of whether you are single by choice, widowed, or divorced, the key to a successful, fulfilling single life is learning to be satisfied with where you are now until God moves you to where He would have you to be. "Delight thyself also in the LORD; and he shall give thee the desires of thine heart. Commit thy way unto the LORD; trust also in him; and he shall bring it to pass. . . . Rest in the LORD, and wait patiently for him" (Ps. 37:4–5, 7a).

Read Psalm 37; Philippians 4:12.

Read the insight essays on Celibacy, Dating, Romance, and Singleness.

—J. Thompson

PRAYER

Pray without ceasing, we are told in 1 Thessalonians 5:17. Prayer is the opportunity God provides us to become intimately acquainted with Him. In our conversations with God, through prayer, we develop a personal relationship with God. Prayer is the greatest power on earth. It is communication between the soul of man and the heart of God. This personal contact with God's living presence is an exclusive privilege granted to all. Prayer causes us to have hope in hopeless situations, and empowers us to invade and eradicate all impossibilities.

Prayer is our expression of dependence on God. It is also our affirmation of God's promises to us. The sincerity and potency of our prayer is often indicated by our acknowledgment of a willingness to change. We openly become venerable as we bow before the mysterious, tremendous awesome presence of the indwelling Spirit of God and listen as God speaks quietly or sometimes violently to the center of our souls.

Draw close to God through prayer. The transition may leave you confused or overawed. True prayer will cause us in our smallness to tremble before the greatness of an omnipotent, omniscient God. Yet there is always that assurance that God is not only willing, but also able, and always knows best.

Often we utter ardent requests and become discouraged when God's timing does not coincide with our own, and His ways do not surrender to our meager understanding. At these moments, we should "let go" and "let God." It is always better to wait than to force things. God's yoke is easy and God's burden is light (see Matt. 11:28–30). When God directs a situation, we don't have to force circumstances. They flow. Prayer is not intended to be a means of manipulating God, but as a way of seeking God's strength, direction, and will.

There is no limitation in God. All limitations are human misconceptions. Pray! May your life be filled with unspeakable joy fortified by the peace "which passeth all understanding" (Phil. 4:7) as you relinquish what you are for what God would have you be. "Not what I will, but what thou wilt" (see Mark 14:36).

Read 1 Thessalonians 5:17.

Read the insight essay on Evangelism. Read the portraits of Anna and Rhoda.

—C. Archibald

27 [y]Wherefore whosoever shall eat this bread, and drink *this* cup of the Lord, unworthily, shall be guilty of the body and blood of the Lord.

28 But [z]let a man examine himself, and so let him eat of *that* bread, and drink of *that* cup.

29 For he that eateth and drinketh unworthily, eateth and drinketh damnation to himself, not discerning the Lord's body.

30 For this cause many *are* weak and sickly among you, and many sleep.

31 For [a]if we would judge ourselves, we should not be judged.

32 But when we are judged, [b]we are chastened of the Lord, that we should not be condemned with the world.

33 Wherefore, my brethren, when ye come together to eat, tarry one for another.

34 And if any man hunger, let him eat at home; that ye come not together unto condemnation. And the rest [c]will I set in order when I come.

12 Now concerning spiritual *gifts*, brethren, I would not have you ignorant.

2 Ye know [d]that ye were Gentiles, carried away unto these [e]dumb idols, even as ye were led.

3 Wherefore I give you to understand, [f]that no man speaking by the Spirit of God calleth Jesus accursed: and [g]*that* no man can say that Jesus is the Lord, but by the Holy Ghost.

4 Now [h]there are diversities of gifts, but [i]the same Spirit.

5 [j]And there are differences of administrations, but the same Lord.

6 And there are diversities of operations, but it is the same God [k]which worketh all in all.

7 [l]But the manifestation of the Spirit is given to every man to profit withal.

8 For to one is given by the Spirit the word of wisdom; to another [m]the word of knowledge by the same Spirit;

9 [n]To another faith by the same Spirit; to another [o]the gifts of healing by the same Spirit;

10 [p]To another the working of miracles; to another [q]prophecy; [r]to another discerning of spirits; to another [s]*divers* kinds of tongues; to another the interpretation of tongues:

11 But all these worketh that one and the selfsame Spirit, [t]dividing to every man severally [u]as he will.

12 For [v]as the body is one, and hath many members, and all the members of that one body, being many, are one body: [w]so also *is* Christ.

13 For [x]by one Spirit are we all baptized into one body, [y]whether *we be* Jews or Gentiles, whether *we be* bond or free; and [z]have been all made to drink into one Spirit.

14 For the body is not one member, but many.

11:27 [y]Num. 9:10
11:28 [z]2 Cor. 13:5
11:31 [a]Ps. 32:5
11:32 [b]Ps. 94:12
11:34 [c]Tit. 1:5
12:2 [d]Eph. 2:11; Tit. 3:3; 1 Pet. 4:3 [e]Ps. 115:5
12:3 [f]Mark 9:39 [g]Matt. 16:17; 2 Cor. 3:5
12:4 [h]Rom. 12:4; 1 Pet. 4:10 [i]Eph. 4:4
12:5 [j]Rom. 12:6
12:6 [k]Eph. 1:23
12:7 [l]Rom. 12:6; 1 Pet. 4:10
12:8 [m]2 Cor. 8:7
12:9 [n]Matt. 17:19 [o]Mark 16:18
12:10 [p]Mark 16:17 [q]Rom. 12:6 [r]1 John 4:1 [s]Acts 2:4
12:11 [t]Rom. 12:6; Eph. 4:7 [u]John 3:8
12:12 [v]Rom. 12:4 [w]Gal. 3:16
12:13 [x]Rom. 6:5 [y]Gal. 3:28; Col. 3:11 [z]John 6:63
12:18 [a]Rom. 12:3
12:27 [b]Rom. 12:5; Col. 1:24 [c]Eph. 5:30
12:28 [d]Eph. 4:11 [e]Eph. 2:20 [f]Acts 13:1 [g]Num. 11:17 [h]Rom. 12:8; Heb. 13:17
13:2 [i]Matt. 7:22 [j]Matt. 17:20; Luke 17:6
13:3 [k]Matt. 6:1
13:4 [l]Prov. 10:12
13:5 [m]Phil. 2:4

15 If the foot shall say, Because I am not the hand, I am not of the body; is it therefore not of the body?

16 And if the ear shall say, Because I am not the eye, I am not of the body; is it therefore not of the body?

17 If the whole body *were* an eye, where *were* the hearing? If the whole *were* hearing, where *were* the smelling?

18 But now hath God set the members every one of them in the body, [a]as it hath pleased him.

19 And if they were all one member, where *were* the body?

20 But now *are they* many members, yet but one body.

21 And the eye cannot say unto the hand, I have no need of thee: nor again the head to the feet, I have no need of you.

22 Nay, much more those members of the body, which seem to be more feeble, are necessary:

23 And those *members* of the body, which we think to be less honourable, upon these we bestow more abundant honour; and our uncomely *parts* have more abundant comeliness.

24 For our comely *parts* have no need: but God hath tempered the body together, having given more abundant honour to that *part* which lacked:

25 That there should be no schism in the body, but *that* the members should have the same care one for another.

26 And whether one member suffer, all the members suffer with it; or one member be honoured, all the members rejoice with it.

27 Now [b]ye are the body of Christ, and [c]members in particular.

28 And [d]God hath set some in the church, first [e]apostles, secondarily [f]prophets, thirdly teachers, after that miracles, then gifts of healings, [g]helps, [h]governments, diversities of tongues.

29 *Are* all apostles? *are* all prophets? *are* all teachers? *are* all workers of miracles?

30 Have all the gifts of healing? do all speak with tongues? do all interpret?

31 But covet earnestly the best gifts: and yet shew I unto you a more excellent way.

13 Though I speak with the tongues of men and of angels, and have not charity, I am become *as* sounding brass, or a tinkling cymbal.

2 And though I have *the gift of* [i]prophecy, and understand all mysteries, and all knowledge; and though I have all faith, [j]so that I could remove mountains, and have not charity, I am nothing.

3 And [k]though I bestow all my goods to feed *the poor*, and though I give my body to be burned, and have not charity, it profiteth me nothing.

4 [l]Charity suffereth long, *and* is kind; charity envieth not; charity vaunteth not itself, is not puffed up,

5 Doth not behave itself unseemly, [m]seek-

eth not her own, is not easily provoked, thinketh no evil;

6 [n]Rejoiceth not in iniquity, but [o]rejoiceth in the truth;

7 [p]Beareth all things, believeth all things, hopeth all things, endureth all things.

8 Charity never faileth: but whether *there be* prophecies, they shall fail; whether *there be* tongues, they shall cease; whether *there be* knowledge, it shall vanish away.

9 For we know in part, and we prophesy in part.

10 But when that which is perfect is come, then that which is in part shall be done away.

11 When I was a child, I spake as a child, I understood as a child, I thought as a child: but when I became a man, I put away childish things.

12 For [q]now we see through a glass, darkly; but then [r]face to face: now I know in part; but then shall I know even as also I am known.

13 And now abideth faith, hope, charity, these three; but the greatest of these *is* charity.

14 Follow after charity, and desire spiritual *gifts,* [s]but rather that ye may prophesy.

2 For he that [t]speaketh in an *unknown* tongue speaketh not unto men, but unto God: for no man understandeth *him;* howbeit in the spirit he speaketh mysteries.

3 But he that prophesieth speaketh unto men *to* edification, and exhortation, and comfort.

4 He that speaketh in an *unknown* tongue edifieth himself; but he that prophesieth edifieth the church.

5 I would that ye all spake with tongues, but rather that ye prophesied: for greater *is* he that prophesieth than he that speaketh with tongues, except he interpret, that the church may receive edifying.

6 Now, brethren, if I come unto you speaking with tongues, what shall I profit you, except I shall speak to you either by revelation, or by knowledge, or by prophesying, or by doctrine?

7 And even things without life giving sound, whether pipe or harp, except they give a distinction in the sounds, how shall it be known what is piped or harped?

8 For if the trumpet give an uncertain sound, who shall prepare himself to the battle?

9 So likewise ye, except ye utter by the tongue words easy to be understood, how shall it be known what is spoken? for ye shall speak into the air.

10 There are, it may be, so many kinds of voices in the world, and none of them *is* without signification.

11 Therefore if I know not the meaning of the voice, I shall be unto him that speaketh a barbarian, and he that speaketh *shall be* a barbarian unto me.

12 Even so ye, forasmuch as ye are zealous of spiritual *gifts,* seek that ye may excel to the edifying of the church.

13 Wherefore let him that speaketh in an *unknown* tongue pray that he may interpret.

14 For if I pray in an *unknown* tongue, my spirit prayeth, but my understanding is unfruitful.

15 What is it then? I will pray with the spirit, and I will pray with the understanding also: [u]I will sing with the spirit, and I will sing [v]with the understanding also.

16 Else when thou shalt bless with the spirit, how shall he that occupieth the room of the unlearned say Amen at thy giving of thanks, seeing he understandeth not what thou sayest?

17 For thou verily givest thanks well, but the other is not edified.

18 I thank my God, I speak with tongues more than ye all:

19 Yet in the church I had rather speak five words with my understanding, that *by my voice* I might teach others also, than ten thousand words in an *unknown* tongue.

20 Brethren, [w]be not children in understanding: howbeit in malice [x]be ye children, but in understanding be men.

21 [y]In the law it is [z]written, With *men of* other tongues and other lips will I speak unto this people; and yet for all that will they not hear me, saith the Lord.

22 Wherefore tongues are for a sign, not to them that believe, but to them that believe not: but prophesying *serveth* not for them that believe not, but for them which believe.

23 If therefore the whole church be come together into one place, and all speak with tongues, and there come in *those that are* unlearned, or unbelievers, [a]will they not say that ye are mad?

24 But if all prophesy, and there come in one that believeth not, or *one* unlearned, he is convinced of all, he is judged of all:

25 And thus are the secrets of his heart made manifest; and so falling down on *his* face he will worship God, and report [b]that God is in you of a truth.

26 How is it then, brethren? when ye come together, every one of you hath a psalm, hath a doctrine, hath a tongue, hath a revelation, hath an interpretation. [c]Let all things be done unto edifying.

27 If any man speak in an *unknown* tongue, *let it be* by two, or at the most *by* three, and *that* by course; and let one interpret.

28 But if there be no interpreter, let him keep silence in the church; and let him speak to himself, and to God.

29 Let the prophets speak two or three, and let the other judge.

30 If *any thing* be revealed to another that sitteth by, [d]let the first hold his peace.

31 For ye may all prophesy one by one, that all may learn, and all may be comforted.

13:6 [n]Ps. 10:3 [o]2 John 4
13:7 [p]Rom. 15:1; 2 Tim. 2:24
13:12 [q]2 Cor. 3:18 [r]Matt. 18:10
14:1 [s]Num. 11:25
14:2 [t]Acts 2:4
14:15 [u]Eph. 5:19 [v]Ps. 47:7
14:20 [w]Ps. 131:2; Rom. 16:19; Eph. 4:14 [x]Matt. 18:3
14:21 [y]John 10:34 [z]Isa. 28:11
14:23 [a]Acts 2:13
14:25 [b]Isa. 45:14
14:26 [c]2 Cor. 12:19
14:30 [d]1 Thess. 5:19

32 And [e]the spirits of the prophets are
subject to the prophets.
33 For God is not *the author* of confusion,
but of peace, as in all churches of the saints.
34 [f]Let your women keep silence in the
churches: for it is not permitted unto them
to speak; but [g]*they are commanded* to be
under obedience, as also saith the [h]law.
35 And if they will learn any thing, let
them ask their husbands at home: for it is a
shame for women to speak in the church.
36 What? came the word of God out from
you? or came it unto you only?
37 [i]If any man think himself to be a
prophet, or spiritual, let him acknowledge
that the things that I write unto you are the
commandments of the Lord.
38 But if any man be ignorant, let him be
ignorant.
39 Wherefore, brethren, [j]covet to prophesy,
and forbid not to speak with tongues.
40 Let all things be done decently and in
order.

15 Moreover, brethren, I declare unto
you the gospel [k]which I preached
unto you, which also ye have received, and
[l]wherein ye stand;
2 [m]By which also ye are saved, if ye keep
in memory what I preached unto you, unless
[n]ye have believed in vain.
3 For I delivered unto you first of all that
[o]which I also received, how that Christ died
for our sins [p]according to the scriptures;
4 And that he was buried, and that he rose
again the third day [q]according to the scriptures:
5 [r]And that he was seen of Cephas, then
[s]of the twelve:
6 After that, he was seen of above five
hundred brethren at once; of whom the
greater part remain unto this present, but
some are fallen asleep.
7 After that, he was seen of James; then
[t]of all the apostles.
8 [u]And last of all he was seen of me also,
as of one born out of due time.
9 For I am [v]the least of the apostles, that
am not meet to be called an apostle, because
[w]I persecuted the church of God.
10 But [x]by the grace of God I am what
I am: and his grace which *was bestowed*
upon me was not in vain; but [y]I laboured
more abundantly than they all: [z]yet not I,
but the grace of God which was with me.
11 Therefore whether *it were* I or they, so
we preach, and so ye believed.
12 Now if Christ be preached that he rose
from the dead, how say some among you
that there is no resurrection of the dead?
13 But if there be no resurrection of the
dead, [a]then is Christ not risen:
14 And if Christ be not risen, then *is* our
preaching vain, and your faith *is* also vain.
15 Yea, and we are found false witnesses
of God; because [b]we have testified of God
that he raised up Christ: whom he raised not
up, if so be that the dead rise not.

14:32 [e]1 John 4:1
14:34 [f]1 Tim. 2:11 [g]Eph. 5:22; Tit. 2:5; 1 Pet. 3:1 [h]Gen. 3:16
14:37 [i]2 Cor. 10:7
14:39 [j]1 Thess. 5:20
15:1 [k]Gal. 1:11 [l]Rom. 5:2
15:2 [m]Rom. 1:16 [n]Gal. 3:4
15:3 [o]Gal. 1:12 [p]Ps. 22:15; Dan. 9:26; Zech. 13:7; Acts 3:18; 1 Pet. 1:11
15:4 [q]Ps. 2:7; Hos. 6:2; Luke 24:26; 1 Pet. 1:11
15:5 [r]Luke 24:34 [s]Matt. 28:17; Luke 24:36; John 20:19
15:7 [t]Luke 24:50
15:8 [u]Acts 9:4
15:9 [v]Eph. 3:8 [w]Acts 8:3; Phil. 3:6; 1 Tim. 1:13
15:10 [x]Eph. 2:7 [y]2 Cor. 11:23 [z]Matt. 10:20; 2 Cor. 3:5; Gal. 2:8; Phil. 2:13
15:13 [a]1 Thess. 4:14
15:15 [b]Acts 2:24
15:17 [c]Rom. 4:25
15:19 [d]2 Tim. 3:12
15:20 [e]1 Pet. 1:3 [f]Acts 26:23; Rev. 1:5
15:21 [g]Rom. 5:12 [h]John 11:25
15:23 [i]1 Thess. 4:15
15:24 [j]Dan. 7:14
15:25 [k]Ps. 110:1; Eph. 1:22; Heb. 1:13
15:26 [l]2 Tim. 1:10
15:27 [m]Ps. 8:6; Heb. 2:8; 1 Pet. 3:22
15:28 [n]Phil. 3:21
15:30 [o]2 Cor. 11:26
15:31 [p]1 Thess. 2:19 [q]Rom. 8:36
15:32 [r]2 Cor. 1:8 [s]Isa. 22:13; Luke 12:19
15:34 [t]Rom. 13:11 [u]1 Thess. 4:5
15:35 [v]Ezek. 37:3
15:36 [w]John 12:24

16 For if the dead rise not, then is not
Christ raised:
17 And if Christ be not raised, your faith
is vain; [c]ye are yet in your sins.
18 Then they also which are fallen asleep
in Christ are perished.
19 [d]If in this life only we have hope in
Christ, we are of all men most miserable.
20 But now [e]is Christ risen from the
dead, *and* become [f]the firstfruits of them
that slept.
21 For [g]since by man *came* death, [h]by
man *came* also the resurrection of the dead.
22 For as in Adam all die, even so in
Christ shall all be made alive.
23 But [i]every man in his own order:
Christ the firstfruits; afterward they that are
Christ's at his coming.
24 Then *cometh* the end, when he shall
have delivered up [j]the kingdom to God,
even the Father; when he shall have put
down all rule and all authority and power.
25 For he must reign, [k]till he hath put all
enemies under his feet.
26 [l]The last enemy *that* shall be destroyed
is death.
27 For he [m]hath put all things under his
feet. But when he saith all things are put
under *him, it is* manifest that he is excepted,
which did put all things under him.
28 [n]And when all things shall be subdued
unto him, then shall the Son also himself be
subject unto him that put all things under
him, that God may be all in all.
29 Else what shall they do which are baptized
for the dead, if the dead rise not at all?
why are they then baptized for the dead?
30 And [o]why stand we in jeopardy every
hour?
31 I protest by [p]your rejoicing which I
have in Christ Jesus our Lord, [q]I die daily.
32 If after the manner of men [r]I have
fought with beasts at Ephesus, what advantageth
it me, if the dead rise not? [s]let us eat
and drink; for to morrow we die.
33 Be not deceived: evil communications
corrupt good manners.
34 [t]Awake to righteousness, and sin not;
[u]for some have not the knowledge of God:
I speak *this* to your shame.
35 But some *man* will say, [v]How are the
dead raised up? and with what body do they
come?
36 *Thou* fool, [w]that which thou sowest is
not quickened, except it die:
37 And that which thou sowest, thou sowest
not that body that shall be, but bare
grain, it may chance of wheat, or of some
other *grain:*
38 But God giveth it a body as it hath
pleased him, and to every seed his own
body.
39 All flesh *is* not the same flesh: but
there is one *kind of* flesh of men, another
flesh of beasts, another of fishes, *and* another
of birds.
40 *There are* also celestial bodies, and
bodies terrestrial: but the glory of the celes-

tial *is* one, and the *glory* of the terrestrial *is* another.

41 *There is* one glory of the sun, and another glory of the moon, and another glory of the stars: for *one* star differeth from *another* star in glory.

42 [x]So also *is* the resurrection of the dead. It is sown in corruption; it is raised in incorruption:

43 [y]It is sown in dishonour; it is raised in glory: it is sown in weakness; it is raised in power:

44 It is sown a natural body; it is raised a spiritual body. There is a natural body, and there is a spiritual body.

45 And so it is written, The first man Adam [z]was made a living soul; [a]the last Adam *was made* [b]a quickening spirit.

46 Howbeit that *was* not first which is spiritual, but that which is natural; and afterward that which is spiritual.

47 [c]The first man *is* of the earth, [d]earthy: the second man *is* the Lord [e]from heaven.

48 As *is* the earthy, such *are* they also that are earthy: [f]and as *is* the heavenly, such *are* they also that are heavenly.

49 And [g]as we have borne the image of the earthy, [h]we shall also bear the image of the heavenly.

50 Now this I say, brethren, that [i]flesh and blood cannot inherit the kingdom of God; neither doth corruption inherit incorruption.

51 Behold, I shew you a mystery; [j]We shall not all sleep, [k]but we shall all be changed,

52 In a moment, in the twinkling of an eye, at the last trump: [l]for the trumpet shall sound, and the dead shall be raised incorruptible, and we shall be changed.

53 For this corruptible must put on incorruption, and [m]this mortal *must* put on immortality.

54 So when this corruptible shall have put on incorruption, and this mortal shall have put on immortality, then shall be brought to pass the saying that is written, [n]Death is swallowed up in victory.

55 [o]O death, where *is* thy sting? O grave, where *is* thy victory?

56 The sting of death *is* sin; and [p]the strength of sin *is* the law.

57 [q]But thanks *be* to God, which giveth us [r]the victory through our Lord Jesus Christ.

58 [s]Therefore, my beloved brethren, be ye stedfast, unmoveable, always abounding in the work of the Lord, forasmuch as ye know that your labour is not in vain in the Lord.

16

Now concerning [t]the collection for the saints, as I have given order to the churches of Galatia, even so do ye.

2 [u]Upon the first *day* of the week let every one of you lay by him in store, as *God* hath prospered him, that there be no gatherings when I come.

3 And when I come, [v]whomsoever ye shall approve by *your* letters, them will I send to bring your liberality unto Jerusalem.

4 [w]And if it be meet that I go also, they shall go with me.

5 Now I will come unto you, [x]when I shall pass through Macedonia: for I do pass through Macedonia.

6 And it may be that I will abide, yea, and winter with you, that ye may [y]bring me on my journey whithersoever I go.

7 For I will not see you now by the way; but I trust to tarry a while with you, [z]if the Lord permit.

8 But I will tarry at Ephesus until Pentecost.

9 For [a]a great door and effectual is opened unto me, and [b]*there are* many adversaries.

10 Now [c]if Timotheus come, see that he may be with you without fear: for [d]he worketh the work of the Lord, as I also *do*.

11 [e]Let no man therefore despise him: but conduct him forth [f]in peace, that he may come unto me: for I look for him with the brethren.

12 As touching *our* brother Apollos, I greatly desired him to come unto you with the brethren: but his will was not at all to come at this time; but he will come when he shall have convenient time.

13 [g]Watch ye, [h]stand fast in the faith, quit you like men, [i]be strong.

14 [j]Let all your things be done with charity.

15 I beseech you, brethren, (ye know the house of Stephanas, that it is [k]the firstfruits of Achaia, and *that* they have addicted themselves to [l]the ministry of the saints,)

16 [m]That ye submit yourselves unto such, and to every one that helpeth with *us*, and [n]laboureth.

17 I am glad of the coming of Stephanas and Fortunatus and Achaicus: [o]for that which was lacking on your part they have supplied.

18 [p]For they have refreshed my spirit and yours: therefore [q]acknowledge ye them that are such.

19 The churches of Asia salute you. Aquila and Priscilla salute you much in the Lord, [r]with the church that is in their house.

20 All the brethren greet you. [s]Greet ye one another with an holy kiss.

21 [t]The salutation of *me* Paul with mine own hand.

22 If any man [u]love not the Lord Jesus Christ, [v]let him be Anathema. [w]Maranatha.

23 [x]The grace of our Lord Jesus Christ *be* with you.

24 My love *be* with you all in Christ Jesus. Amen.

15:42 [x]Dan. 12:3
15:43 [y]Phil. 3:21
15:45 [z]Gen. 2:7 [a]Rom. 5:14 [b]John 5:21; Col. 3:4
15:47 [c]John 3:31 [d]Gen. 2:7 [e]John 3:13
15:48 [f]Phil. 3:20
15:49 [g]Gen. 5:3 [h]Rom. 8:29; Phil. 3:21; 1 John 3:2
15:50 [i]Matt. 16:17
15:51 [j]1 Thess. 4:15 [k]Phil. 3:21
15:52 [l]Zech. 9:14; John 5:25; 1 Thess. 4:16
15:53 [m]2 Cor. 5:4
15:54 [n]Isa. 25:8; Rev. 20:14
15:55 [o]Hos. 13:14
15:56 [p]Rom. 4:15
15:57 [q]Rom. 7:25 [r]1 John 5:4
15:58 [s]2 Pet. 3:14
16:1 [t]Acts 11:29; 2 Cor. 8:4; Gal. 2:10
16:2 [u]Acts 20:7
16:3 [v]2 Cor. 8:19
16:4 [w]2 Cor. 8:4
16:5 [x]Acts 19:21
16:6 [y]Acts 15:3; 2 Cor. 1:16
16:7 [z]Acts 18:21
16:9 [a]Acts 14:27; Col. 4:3; Rev. 3:8 [b]Acts 19:9
16:10 [c]Acts 19:22 [d]Rom. 16:21; 1 Thess. 3:2
16:11 [e]1 Tim. 4:12 [f]Acts 15:33
16:13 [g]Matt. 24:42; 1 Pet. 5:8 [h]Phil. 1:27; 2 Thess. 2:15 [i]Eph. 6:10
16:14 [j]1 Pet. 4:8
16:15 [k]Rom. 16:5 [l]2 Cor. 8:4
16:16 [m]Heb. 13:17 [n]Heb. 6:10
16:17 [o]2 Cor. 11:9; Philem. 13
16:18 [p]Col. 4:8 [q]1 Thess. 5:12
16:19 [r]Rom. 16:5
16:20 [s]Rom. 16:16
16:21 [t]Col. 4:18
16:22 [u]Eph. 6:24 [v]Gal. 1:8 [w]Jude 14
16:23 [x]Rom. 16:20

2 CORINTHIANS

Paul acknowledges himself as the author of 1 and 2 Corinthians. Second Corinthians was probably written in A.D. 56 or A.D. 57. Paul first deals with some particular problems in the church and their resolution. Then he pleads for the Corinthian church to remember its promise to provide assistance to the Christians in Judea. Finally Paul offers a defense of his apostleship and authority. Second Corinthians 5:20–21, 6:14, and 12:9 are all very familiar verses in the book.

I. Greetings from Paul to the church, 1:1–1:11
II. A problem dealt with in the church, 1:12–2:13
III. The ministry of an apostle, 2:14–7:16
IV. Concepts of giving, 8:1–9:15
V. Paul's defense of his apostleship, 10:1–12:18
VI. Paul's closing remarks and greetings, 12:19–13:14

1 Paul, ^aan apostle of Jesus Christ by the will of God, and Timothy *our* brother, unto the church of God which is at Corinth, ^bwith all the saints which are in all Achaia:

2 ^cGrace *be* to you and peace from God our Father, and *from* the Lord Jesus Christ.

3 ^dBlessed *be* God, even the Father of our Lord Jesus Christ, the Father of mercies, and the God of all comfort;

4 Who comforteth us in all our tribulation, that we may be able to comfort them which are in any trouble, by the comfort wherewith we ourselves are comforted of God.

5 For as ^ethe sufferings of Christ abound in us, so our consolation also aboundeth by Christ.

6 And whether we be afflicted, *it is* for your consolation and salvation, which is effectual in the enduring of the same sufferings which we also suffer: or whether we be comforted, *it is* for your consolation and salvation.

7 And our hope of you *is* stedfast, knowing, that ^fas ye are partakers of the sufferings, so *shall ye be* also of the consolation.

8 For we would not, brethren, have you ignorant of ^gour trouble which came to us in Asia, that we were pressed out of measure, above strength, insomuch that we despaired even of life:

9 But we had the sentence of death in ourselves, that we should ^hnot trust in ourselves, but in God which raiseth the dead:

10 ⁱWho delivered us from so great a death, and doth deliver: in whom we trust that he will yet deliver *us*;

11 Ye also ^jhelping together by prayer for us, that for the gift *bestowed* upon us by the means of many persons thanks may be given by many on our behalf.

12 For our rejoicing is this, the testimony of our conscience, that in simplicity and godly sincerity, ^knot with fleshly wisdom, but by the grace of God, we have had our conversation in the world, and more abundantly to you-ward

13 For we write none other things unto you, than what ye read or acknowledge; and I trust ye shall acknowledge even to the end;

14 As also ye have acknowledged us in part, that we are your rejoicing, even as ^lye also *are* ours in the day of the Lord Jesus.

15 And in this confidence ^mI was minded to come unto you before, that ye might have ⁿa second benefit;

16 And to pass by you into Macedonia, and ^oto come again out of Macedonia unto you, and of you to be brought on my way toward Judaea.

17 When I therefore was thus minded, did I use lightness? or the things that I purpose, do I purpose according to the flesh, that with me there should be yea yea, and nay nay?

18 But *as* God *is* true, our word toward you was not yea and nay.

19 For ^pthe Son of God, Jesus Christ, who was preached among you by us, *even* by me and Silvanus and Timotheus, was not yea and nay, ^qbut in him was yea.

20 ^rFor all the promises of God in him *are* yea, and in him Amen, unto the glory of God by us.

21 Now he which stablisheth us with you in Christ, and ^shath anointed us, *is* God;

22 Who ^thath also sealed us, and ^ugiven the earnest of the Spirit in our hearts.

23 Moreover ^vI call God for a record upon my soul, ^wthat to spare you I came not as yet unto Corinth.

24 Not for ^xthat we have dominion over your faith, but are helpers of your joy: for ^yby faith ye stand.

2 But I determined this with myself, that I would not come again to you in heaviness.

2 For if I make you sorry, who is he then that maketh me glad, but the same which is made sorry by me?

1:1 ^a1 Cor. 1:1; Col. 1:1; 1 Tim. 1:1 ^bPhil. 1:1

1:2 ^cRom. 1:7; Gal. 1:3; Phil. 1:2; 1 Thess. 1:1; 2 Thess. 1:2

1:3 ^dEph. 1:3

1:5 ^eActs 9:4

1:7 ^fRom. 8:17

1:8 ^gActs 19:23

1:9 ^hJer. 17:5

1:10 ⁱ2 Pet. 2:9

1:11 ^jRom. 15:30; Philem. 22

1:12 ^k1 Cor. 2:4

1:14 ^lPhil. 2:16

1:15 ^m1 Cor. 4:19 ⁿRom. 1:11

1:16 ^o1 Cor. 16:5

1:19 ^pMark 1:1; Acts 9:20 ^qHeb. 13:8

1:20 ^rRom. 15:8

1:21 ^s1 John 2:20

1:22 ^tEph. 1:13; Rev. 2:17 ^uEph. 1:14

1:23 ^vRom. 1:9; Phil. 1:8 ^w1 Cor. 4:21

1:24 ^x1 Cor. 3:5 ^yRom. 11:20

3 And I wrote this same unto you, lest, when I came, I should have sorrow from them of whom I ought to rejoice; [z]having confidence in you all, that my joy is *the joy* of you all.

4 For out of much affliction and anguish of heart I wrote unto you with many tears; not that ye should be grieved, but that ye might know the love which I have more abundantly unto you.

5 But [a]if any have caused grief, he hath not [b]grieved me, but in part: that I may not overcharge you all.

6 Sufficient to such a man *is* this punishment, which *was inflicted* [c]of many.

7 [d]So that contrariwise ye *ought* rather to forgive *him,* and comfort *him,* lest perhaps such a one should be swallowed up with overmuch sorrow.

8 Wherefore I beseech you that ye would confirm *your* love toward him.

9 For to this end also did I write, that I might know the proof of you, whether ye be obedient in all things.

10 To whom ye forgive any thing, I *forgive* also: for if I forgave any thing, to whom I forgave *it,* for your sakes *forgave I it* in the person of Christ;

11 Lest Satan should get an advantage of us: for we are not ignorant of his devices.

12 Furthermore, [e]when I came to Troas to *preach* Christ's gospel, and [f]a door was opened unto me of the Lord,

13 I had no rest in my spirit, because I found not Titus my brother: but taking my leave of them, I went from thence into Macedonia.

14 Now thanks *be* unto God, which always causeth us to triumph in Christ, and maketh manifest [g]the savour of his knowledge by us in every place.

15 For we are unto God a sweet savour of Christ, [h]in them that are saved, and in them that perish:

16 [i]To the one *we are* the savour of death unto death; and to the other the savour of life unto life. And [j]who *is* sufficient for these things?

17 For we are not as many, which [k]corrupt the word of God: but as of sincerity, but as of God, in the sight of God speak we in Christ.

3 Do we begin again to commend ourselves? or need we, as some *others,* [l]epistles of commendation to you, or *letters* of commendation from you?

2 [m]Ye are our epistle written in our hearts, known and read of all men:

3 *Forasmuch as ye are* manifestly declared to be the epistle of Christ [n]ministered by us, written not with ink, but with the Spirit of the living God; not [o]in tables of stone, but [p]in fleshy tables of the heart.

4 And such trust have we through Christ to God-ward:

5 [q]Not that we are sufficient of ourselves to think any thing as of ourselves; but [r]our sufficiency *is* of God;

6 Who also hath made us able [s]ministers of [t]the new testament; not [u]of the letter, but of the spirit: for [v]the letter killeth, [w]but the spirit giveth life.

7 But if [x]the ministration of death, [y]written *and* engraven in stones, was glorious, [z]so that the children of Israel could not stedfastly behold the face of Moses for the glory of his countenance; which *glory* was to be done away:

8 How shall not [a]the ministration of the spirit be rather glorious?

9 For if the ministration of condemnation *be* glory, much more doth the ministration [b]of righteousness exceed in glory.

10 For even that which was made glorious had no glory in this respect, by reason of the glory that excelleth.

11 For if that which is done away *was* glorious, much more that which remaineth *is* glorious.

12 Seeing then that we have such hope, [c]we use great plainness of speech:

13 And not as Moses, [d]*which* put a vail over his face, that the children of Israel could not stedfastly look to [e]the end of that which is abolished:

14 But [f]their minds were blinded: for until this day remaineth the same vail untaken away in the reading of the old testament; which *vail* is done away in Christ.

15 But even unto this day, when Moses is read, the vail is upon their heart.

16 Nevertheless [g]when it shall turn to the Lord, [h]the vail shall be taken away.

17 Now [i]the Lord is that Spirit: and where the Spirit of the Lord *is,* there *is* liberty.

18 But we all, with open face beholding [j]as in a glass [k]the glory of the Lord, [l]are changed into the same image from glory to glory, *even* as by the Spirit of the Lord.

4 Therefore seeing we have this ministry, [m]as we have received mercy, we faint not;

2 But have renounced the hidden things of dishonesty, not walking in craftiness, [n]nor handling the word of God deceitfully; but by manifestation of the truth commending ourselves to every man's conscience in the sight of God.

3 But if our gospel be hid, [o]it is hid to them that are lost:

4 In whom [p]the god of this world [q]hath blinded the minds of them which believe not, lest the light of the glorious gospel of Christ, [r]who is the image of God, should shine unto them.

5 [s]For we preach not ourselves, but Christ Jesus the Lord; and [t]ourselves your servants for Jesus' sake.

6 For God, [u]who commanded the light to shine out of darkness, hath [v]shined in our hearts, to *give* [w]the light of the knowledge of the glory of God in the face of Jesus Christ.

7 But we have this treasure in earthen

2:3 [z]Gal. 5:10
2:5 [a]1 Cor. 5:1 [b]Gal. 4:12
2:6 [c]1 Cor. 5:4
2:7 [d]Gal. 6:1
2:12 [e]Acts 16:8 [f]1 Cor. 16:9
2:14 [g]SSol. 1:3
2:15 [h]1 Cor. 1:18
2:16 [i]Luke 2:34; 1 Pet. 2:7 [j]1 Cor. 15:10
2:17 [k]2 Pet. 2:3
3:1 [l]Acts 18:27
3:2 [m]1 Cor. 9:2
3:3 [n]1 Cor. 3:5 [o]Ex. 24:12 [p]Ps. 40:8; Ezek. 11:19; Heb. 8:10
3:5 [q]John 15:5 [r]1 Cor. 15:10
3:6 [s]1 Cor. 3:5; Col. 1:25; 1 Tim. 1:11 [t]Jer. 31:31; Heb. 8:6 [u]Rom. 2:27 [v]Rom. 3:20 [w]John 6:63
3:7 [x]Rom. 7:10 [y]Ex. 34:1 [z]Ex. 34:29
3:8 [a]Gal. 3:5
3:9 [b]Rom. 1:17
3:12 [c]Eph. 6:19
3:13 [d]Ex. 34:33 [e]Rom. 10:4
3:14 [f]Isa. 6:10; John 12:40; Acts 28:26
3:16 [g]Ex. 34:34 [h]Isa. 25:7
3:17 [i]1 Cor. 15:45
3:18 [j]1 Cor. 13:12 [k]1 Tim. 1:11 [l]Rom. 8:29; Col. 3:10
4:1 [m]1 Cor. 7:25
4:2 [n]1 Thess. 2:3
4:3 [o]1 Cor. 1:18
4:4 [p]John 12:31 [q]Isa. 6:10 [r]John 1:18; Col. 1:15; Heb. 1:3
4:5 [s]1 Cor. 1:13 [t]1 Cor. 9:19
4:6 [u]Gen. 1:3 [v]2 Pet. 1:19 [w]1 Pet. 2:9

vessels, [x]that the excellency of the power
may be of God, and not of us.
8 *We are* troubled on every side, yet not
distressed; *we are* perplexed, but not in despair;
9 Persecuted, but not forsaken; [y]cast
down, but not destroyed;
10 [z]Always bearing about in the body the
dying of the Lord Jesus, [a]that the life also
of Jesus might be made manifest in our
body.
11 For we which live [b]are alway delivered unto death for Jesus' sake, that the life
also of Jesus might be made manifest in our
mortal flesh.
12 So then death worketh in us, but life in
you.
13 We having [c]the same spirit of faith,
according as it is written, [d]I believed, and
therefore have I spoken; we also believe,
and therefore speak;
14 Knowing that [e]he which raised up the
Lord Jesus shall raise up us also by Jesus,
and shall present *us* with you.
15 For [f]all things *are* for your sakes, that
the abundant grace might through the
thanksgiving of many redound to the glory
of God.
16 For which cause we faint not; but
though our outward man perish, yet [g]the
inward *man* is renewed day by day.
17 For [h]our light affliction, which is but
for a moment, worketh for us a far more
exceeding *and* eternal weight of glory;
18 [i]While we look not at the things
which are seen, but at the things which are
not seen: for the things which are seen *are*
temporal; but the things which are not seen
are eternal.
5 For we know that if [j]our earthly house
of *this* tabernacle were dissolved, we
have a building of God, an house not made
with hands, eternal in the heavens.
2 For in this [k]we groan, earnestly desiring to be clothed upon with our house which
is from heaven:
3 If so be that [l]being clothed we shall not
be found naked.
4 For we that are in *this* tabernacle do
groan, being burdened: not for that we
would be unclothed, but [m]clothed upon,
that mortality might be swallowed up of
life.
5 Now [n]he that hath wrought us for the
selfsame thing *is* God, who also [o]hath given
unto us the earnest of the Spirit.
6 Therefore *we are* always confident,
knowing that, whilst we are at home in the
body, we are absent from the Lord:
7 (For [p]we walk by faith, not by sight:)
8 We are confident, *I say,* and [q]willing
rather to be absent from the body, and to be
present with the Lord.
9 Wherefore we labour, that, whether
present or absent, we may be accepted of
him.
10 [r]For we must all appear before the
judgment seat of Christ; [s]that every one

4:7 [x]1 Cor. 2:5
4:9 [y]Ps. 37:24
4:10 [z]1 Cor. 15:31; Phil. 3:10 [a]Rom. 8:17; 1 Pet. 4:13
4:11 [b]Ps. 44:22; 1 Cor. 15:31
4:13 [c]Rom. 1:12 [d]Ps. 116:10
4:14 [e]Rom. 8:11
4:15 [f]1 Cor. 3:21; 2 Tim. 2:10
4:16 [g]Rom. 7:22; Col. 3:10; 1 Pet. 3:4
4:17 [h]Matt. 5:12; 1 Pet. 1:6
4:18 [i]Rom. 8:24
5:1 [j]Job 4:19
5:2 [k]Rom. 8:23
5:3 [l]Rev. 3:18
5:4 [m]1 Cor. 15:53
5:5 [n]Isa. 29:23 [o]Rom. 8:23
5:7 [p]Rom. 8:24; Heb. 11:1
5:8 [q]Phil. 1:23
5:10 [r]Matt. 25:31 [s]Rom. 2:6; Eph. 6:8; Col. 3:24
5:11 [t]Job 31:23; Jude 23
5:14 [u]Rom. 5:15
5:15 [v]Rom. 6:11; Gal. 2:20; 1 Thess. 5:10
5:16 [w]Matt. 12:50; Gal. 5:6; Phil. 3:7 [x]John 6:63
5:17 [y]Rom. 8:9 [z]Gal. 5:6 [a]Isa. 43:18; Rev. 21:5
5:18 [b]Rom. 5:10; Col. 1:20; 1 John 2:2
5:19 [c]Rom. 3:24
5:20 [d]Job 33:23; Eph. 6:20
5:21 [e]Isa. 53:6; 1 Pet. 2:22; 1 John 3:5 [f]Rom. 1:17
6:1 [g]1 Cor. 3:9 [h]Heb. 12:15
6:2 [i]Isa. 49:8
6:3 [j]Rom. 14:13
6:4 [k]1 Cor. 4:1
6:7 [l]1 Cor. 2:4 [m]Eph. 6:11
6:9 [n]1 Cor. 4:9

may receive the things *done* in *his* body,
according to that he hath done, whether *it
be* good or bad.
11 Knowing therefore [t]the terror of the
Lord, we persuade men; but we are made
manifest unto God; and I trust also are
made manifest in your consciences.
12 For we commend not ourselves again
unto you, but give you occasion to glory on
our behalf, that ye may have somewhat to
answer them which glory in appearance,
and not in heart.
13 For whether we be beside ourselves, *it
is* to God: or whether we be sober, *it is* for
your cause.
14 For the love of Christ constraineth us;
because we thus judge, that [u]if one died for
all, then were all dead:
15 And *that* he died for all, [v]that they
which live should not henceforth live unto
themselves, but unto him which died for
them, and rose again.
16 [w]Wherefore henceforth know we no
man after the flesh: yea, though we have
known Christ after the flesh, [x]yet now
henceforth know we *him* no more.
17 Therefore if any man [y]*be* in Christ, *he
is* [z]a new creature: [a]old things are passed
away; behold, all things are become new.
18 And all things *are* of God, [b]who hath
reconciled us to himself by Jesus Christ,
and hath given to us the ministry of reconciliation;
19 To wit, that [c]God was in Christ, reconciling the world unto himself, not imputing
their trespasses unto them; and hath committed unto us the word of reconciliation.
20 Now then we are [d]ambassadors for
Christ, as though God did beseech *you* by
us: we pray *you* in Christ's stead, be ye reconciled to God.
21 For [e]he hath made him *to be* sin for us,
who knew no sin; that we might be made
[f]the righteousness of God in him.
6 We then, *as* [g]workers together *with
him,* beseech *you* also [h]that ye receive
not the grace of God in vain.
2 (For he saith, [i]I have heard thee in a
time accepted, and in the day of salvation
have I succoured thee: behold, now *is* the
accepted time; behold, now *is* the day of salvation.)
3 [j]Giving no offence in any thing, that
the ministry be not blamed:
4 But in all *things* approving ourselves
[k]as the ministers of God, in much patience,
in afflictions, in necessities, in distresses,
5 In stripes, in imprisonments, in tumults,
in labours, in watchings, in fastings;
6 By pureness, by knowledge, by longsuffering, by kindness, by the Holy Ghost, by
love unfeigned,
7 By the word of truth, by [l]the power of
God, by [m]the armour of righteousness on
the right hand and on the left,
8 By honour and dishonour, by evil report
and good report: as deceivers, and *yet* true;
9 As unknown, and *yet* well known; [n]as

dying, and, behold, we live; [o]as chastened, and not killed;

10 As sorrowful, yet alway rejoicing; as poor, yet making many rich; as having nothing, and *yet* possessing all things.

11 O *ye* Corinthians, our mouth is open unto you, our heart is enlarged.

12 Ye are not straitened in us, but ye are straitened in your own bowels.

13 Now for a recompence in the same, ([p]I speak as unto *my* children,) be ye also enlarged.

14 [q]Be ye not unequally yoked together with unbelievers: for [r]what fellowship hath righteousness with unrighteousness? and what communion hath light with darkness?

15 And what concord hath Christ with Belial? or what part hath he that believeth with an infidel?

16 And what agreement hath the temple of God with idols? for [s]ye are the temple of the living God; as God hath said, [t]I will dwell in them, and walk in *them;* and I will be their God, and they shall be my people.

17 [u]Wherefore come out from among them, and be ye separate, saith the Lord, and touch not the unclean *thing;* and I will receive you,

18 [v]And will be a Father unto you, and ye shall be my sons and daughters, saith the Lord Almighty.

7

Having [w]therefore these promises, dearly beloved, let us cleanse ourselves from all filthiness of the flesh and spirit, perfecting holiness in the fear of God.

2 Receive us; we have wronged no man, we have corrupted no man, [x]we have defrauded no man.

3 I speak not *this* to condemn *you:* for I have said before, that ye are in our hearts to die and live with *you.*

4 Great *is* my boldness of speech toward you, [y]great *is* my glorying of you: [z]I am filled with comfort, I am exceeding joyful in all our tribulation.

5 For, when we were come into Macedonia, our flesh had no rest, but we were troubled on every side; [a]without *were* fightings, within *were* fears.

6 Nevertheless God, that comforteth those that are cast down, comforted us by the coming of Titus;

7 And not by his coming only, but by the consolation wherewith he was comforted in you, when he told us your earnest desire, your mourning, your fervent mind toward me; so that I rejoiced the more.

8 For though I made you sorry with a letter, I do not repent, though I did repent: for I perceive that the same epistle hath made you sorry, though *it were* but for a season.

9 Now I rejoice, not that ye were made sorry, but that ye sorrowed to repentance: for ye were made sorry after a godly manner, that ye might receive damage by us in nothing.

10 For [b]godly sorrow worketh repentance to salvation not to be repented of: [c]but the sorrow of the world worketh death.

11 For behold this selfsame thing, that ye sorrowed after a godly sort, what carefulness it wrought in you, yea, *what* clearing of yourselves, yea, *what* indignation, yea, *what* fear, yea, *what* vehement desire, yea, *what* zeal, yea, *what* revenge! In all *things* ye have approved yourselves to be clear in this matter.

12 Wherefore, though I wrote unto you, *I did it* not for his cause that had done the wrong, nor for his cause that suffered wrong, but that our care for you in the sight of God might appear unto you.

13 Therefore we were comforted in your comfort: yea, and exceedingly the more joyed we for the joy of Titus, because his spirit [d]was refreshed by you all.

14 For if I have boasted any thing to him of you, I am not ashamed; but as we spake all things to you in truth, even so our boasting, which *I made* before Titus, is found a truth.

15 And his inward affection is more abundant toward you, whilst he remembereth [e]the obedience of you all, how with fear and trembling ye received him.

16 I rejoice therefore that [f]I have confidence in you in all *things.*

8

Moreover, brethren, we do you to wit of the grace of God bestowed on the churches of Macedonia;

2 How that in a great trial of affliction the abundance of their joy and [g]their deep poverty abounded unto the riches of their liberality.

3 For to *their* power, I bear record, yea, and beyond *their* power *they were* willing of themselves;

4 Praying us with much intreaty that we would receive the gift, and *take upon us* [h]the fellowship of the ministering to the saints.

5 And *this they did,* not as we hoped, but first gave their own selves to the Lord, and unto us by the will of God.

6 Insomuch that we desired Titus, that as he had begun, so he would also finish in you the same grace also.

7 Therefore, as [i]ye abound in every *thing, in* faith, and utterance, and knowledge, and *in* all diligence, and *in* your love to us, *see* that ye abound in this grace also.

8 [j]I speak not by commandment, but by occasion of the forwardness of others, and to prove the sincerity of your love.

9 For ye know the grace of our Lord Jesus Christ, [k]that, though he was rich, yet for your sakes he became poor, that ye through his poverty might be rich.

10 And herein [l]I give *my* advice: for [m]this is expedient for you, who have begun before, not only to do, but also to be forward a year ago.

11 Now therefore perform the doing *of it;* that as *there was* a readiness to will, so

6:9 [o]Ps. 118:18
6:13 [p]1 Cor. 4:14
6:14 [q]Deut. 7:2 [r]1 Sam. 5:2; 1 Cor. 10:21; Eph. 5:7
6:16 [s]1 Cor. 3:16; Heb. 3:6 [t]Ex. 29:45; Jer. 31:33; Ezek. 11:20
6:17 [u]Isa. 52:11
6:18 [v]Jer. 31:1
7:1 [w]1 John 3:3
7:2 [x]Acts 20:33
7:4 [y]1 Cor. 1:4 [z]Phil. 2:17
7:5 [a]Deut. 32:25
7:10 [b]2 Sam. 12:13 [c]Prov. 17:22
7:13 [d]Rom. 15:32
7:15 [e]Phil. 2:12
7:16 [f]2 Thess. 3:4
8:2 [g]Mark 12:44
8:4 [h]Acts 11:29; 1 Cor. 16:1
8:7 [i]1 Cor. 1:5
8:8 [j]1 Cor. 7:6
8:9 [k]Matt. 8:20; Phil. 2:6
8:10 [l]1 Cor. 7:25 [m]Prov. 19:17; 1 Tim. 6:18; Heb. 13:16

there may be a performance also out of that
which ye have.
12 For [n]if there be first a willing mind, *it
is* accepted according to that a man hath,
and not according to that he hath not.
13 For *I mean* not that other men be
eased, and ye burdened:
14 But by an equality, *that* now at this
time your abundance *may be a supply* for
their want, that their abundance also may
be *a supply* for your want: that there may be
equality:
15 As it is written, [o]He that *had gathered*
much had nothing over; and he that *had
gathered* little had no lack.
16 But thanks *be* to God, which put the
same earnest care into the heart of Titus for
you.
17 For indeed he accepted the exhortation; but being more forward, of his own
accord he went unto you.
18 And we have sent with him the
brother, whose praise *is* in the gospel
throughout all the churches;
19 And not *that* only, but who was also
[p]chosen of the churches to travel with us
with this grace, which is administered by us
to the glory of the same Lord, and *declaration of* your ready mind:
20 Avoiding this, that no man should
blame us in this abundance which is administered by us:
21 [q]Providing for honest things, not only
in the sight of the Lord, but also in the sight
of men.
22 And we have sent with them our
brother, whom we have oftentimes proved
diligent in many things, but now much more
diligent, upon the great confidence which *I
have* in you.
23 Whether *any do enquire* of Titus, *he is*
my partner and fellowhelper concerning
you: or our brethren *be enquired of, they are*
[r]the messengers of the churches, *and* the
glory of Christ.
24 Wherefore shew ye to them, and before the churches, the proof of your love,
and of our boasting on your behalf.

9 For as touching [s]the ministering to the
saints, it is superfluous for me to write
to you:
2 For I know the forwardness of your
mind, for which I boast of you to them of
Macedonia, that Achaia was ready a year
ago; and your zeal hath provoked very
many.
3 Yet have I sent the brethren, lest our
boasting of you should be in vain in this
behalf; that, as I said, ye may be ready:
4 Lest haply if they of Macedonia come
with me, and find you unprepared, we (that
we say not, ye) should be ashamed in this
same confident boasting.
5 Therefore I thought it necessary to exhort the brethren, that they would go before
unto you, and make up beforehand your
bounty, whereof ye had notice before, that
the same might be ready, as *a matter of*
bounty, and not as *of* covetousness.
6 [t]But this *I say,* He which soweth sparingly shall reap also sparingly; and he
which soweth bountifully shall reap also
bountifully.
7 Every man according as he purposeth
in his heart, *so let him give;* [u]not grudg-
ingly, or of necessity: for [v]God loveth a
cheerful giver.
8 [w]And God *is* able to make all grace
abound toward you; that ye, always having
all sufficiency in all *things,* may abound to
every good work:
9 (As it is written, [x]He hath dispersed
abroad; he hath given to the poor: his righteousness remaineth for ever.
10 Now he that [y]ministereth seed to the
sower both minister bread for *your* food,
and multiply your seed sown, and increase
the fruits of your [z]righteousness;)
11 Being enriched in every thing to all
bountifulness, which causeth through us
thanksgiving to God.
12 For the administration of this service
not only supplieth the want of the saints,
but is abundant also by many thanksgivings
unto God;
13 Whiles by the experiment of this
ministration they [a]glorify God for your professed subjection unto the gospel of Christ,
and for *your* liberal [b]distribution unto
them, and unto all *men;*
14 And by their prayer for you, which
long after you for the exceeding grace of
God in you.
15 Thanks *be* unto God [c]for his unspeakable gift.

10 Now [d]I Paul myself beseech you by
the meekness and gentleness of
Christ, who in presence *am* base among
you, but being absent am bold toward you:
2 But I beseech *you,* [e]that I may not be
bold when I am present with that confidence, wherewith I think to be bold against
some, which think of us as if we walked
according to the flesh.
3 For though we walk in the flesh, we do
not war after the flesh:
4 ([f]For the weapons [g]of our warfare *are*
not carnal, but [h]mighty through God [i]to
the pulling down of strong holds;)
5 [j]Casting down imaginations, and every
high thing that exalteth itself against the
knowledge of God, and bringing into captivity every thought to the obedience of
Christ;
6 And having in a readiness to revenge all
disobedience, when your obedience is fulfilled.
7 [k]Do ye look on things after the outward
appearance? [l]If any man trust to himself
that he is Christ's, let him of himself think
this again, that, as he *is* Christ's, even so *are*
[m]we Christ's.
8 For though I should boast somewhat
more of our authority, which the Lord hath

8:12 [n]Mark 12:43
8:15 [o]Ex. 16:18
8:19 [p]1 Cor. 16:3
8:21 [q]Rom. 12:17; 1 Pet. 2:12
8:23 [r]Phil. 2:25
9:1 [s]Acts 11:29; 1 Cor. 16:1; Gal. 2:10
9:6 [t]Prov. 11:24
9:7 [u]Deut. 15:7 [v]Ex. 25:2; Rom. 12:8
9:8 [w]Prov. 11:24
9:9 [x]Ps. 112:9
9:10 [y]Isa. 55:19 [z]Hos. 10:12
9:13 [a]Matt. 5:16 [b]Heb. 13:16
9:15 [c]Jam. 1:17
10:1 [d]Rom. 12:1
10:2 [e]1 Cor. 4:21
10:4 [f]Eph. 6:13 [g]1 Tim. 1:18 [h]Acts 7:22 [i]Jer. 1:10
10:5 [j]1 Cor. 1:19
10:7 [k]John 7:24 [l]1 Cor. 14:37 [m]1 Cor. 3:23

given us for edification, and not for your destruction, I should not be ashamed:

9 That I may not seem as if I would terrify you by letters.

10 For *his* letters, say they, *are* weighty and powerful; but [n]*his* bodily presence *is* weak, and *his* [o]speech contemptible.

11 Let such an one think this, that, such as we are in word by letters when we are absent, such *will we be* also in deed when we are present.

12 For we dare not make ourselves of the number, or compare ourselves with some that commend themselves: but they measuring themselves by themselves, and comparing themselves among themselves, are not wise.

13 But we will not boast of things without *our* measure, but according to the measure of the rule which God hath distributed to us, a measure to reach even unto you.

14 For we stretch not ourselves beyond *our measure,* as though we reached not unto you: [p]for we are come as far as to you also in *preaching* the gospel of Christ:

15 Not boasting of things without *our* measure, *that is,* [q]of other men's labours; but having hope, when your faith is increased, that we shall be enlarged by you according to our rule abundantly,

16 To preach the gospel in the *regions* beyond you, *and* not to boast in another man's line of things made ready to our hand.

17 [r]But he that glorieth, let him glory in the Lord.

18 For [s]not he that commendeth himself is approved, but [t]whom the Lord commendeth.

11 Would to God ye could bear with me a little in *my* folly: and indeed bear with me.

2 For I am [u]jealous over you with godly jealousy: for [v]I have espoused you to one husband, [w]that I may present *you* [x]*as* a chaste virgin to Christ.

3 But I fear, lest by any means, as [y]the serpent beguiled Eve through his subtilty, so your minds [z]should be corrupted from the simplicity that is in Christ.

4 For if he that cometh preacheth another Jesus, whom we have not preached, or *if* ye receive another spirit, which ye have not received, or [a]another gospel, which ye have not accepted, ye might well bear with *him.*

5 For I suppose [b]I was not a whit behind the very chiefest apostles.

6 But though [c]*I be* rude in speech, yet not [d]in knowledge; but we have been throughly made manifest among you in all things.

7 Have I committed an offence [e]in abasing myself that ye might be exalted, because I have preached to you the gospel of God freely?

8 I robbed other churches, taking wages *of them,* to do you service.

9 And when I was present with you, and wanted, [f]I was chargeable to no man: for that which was lacking to me [g]the brethren which came from Macedonia supplied: and in all *things* I have kept myself from being burdensome unto you, and *so* will I keep *myself.*

10 [h]As the truth of Christ is in me, [i]no man shall stop me of this boasting in the regions of Achaia.

11 Wherefore? because I love you not? God knoweth.

12 But what I do, that I will do, [j]that I may cut off occasion from them which desire occasion; that wherein they glory, they may be found even as we.

13 For such [k]*are* false apostles, [l]deceitful workers, transforming themselves into the apostles of Christ.

14 And no marvel; for Satan himself is transformed into [m]an angel of light.

15 Therefore *it is* no great thing if his ministers also be transformed as the ministers of righteousness; [n]whose end shall be according to their works.

16 I say again, Let no man think me a fool; if otherwise, yet as a fool receive me, that I may boast myself a little.

17 That which I speak, [o]I speak *it* not after the Lord, but as it were foolishly, in this confidence of boasting.

18 [p]Seeing that many glory after the flesh, I will glory also.

19 For ye suffer fools gladly, [q]seeing ye *yourselves* are wise.

20 For ye suffer, [r]if a man bring you into bondage, if a man devour *you,* if a man take *of you,* if a man exalt himself, if a man smite you on the face.

21 I speak as concerning reproach, as though we had been weak. Howbeit [s]whereinsoever any is bold, (I speak foolishly,) I am bold also.

22 Are they Hebrews? [t]so *am* I. Are they Israelites? so *am* I. Are they the seed of Abraham? so *am* I.

23 Are they ministers of Christ? (I speak as a fool) I *am* more; [u]in labours more abundant, [v]in stripes above measure, in prisons more frequent, [w]in deaths oft.

24 Of the Jews five times received I [x]forty *stripes* save one.

25 Thrice was I [y]beaten with rods, [z]once was I stoned, thrice I [a]suffered shipwreck, a night and a day I have been in the deep;

26 *In* journeyings often, *in* perils of waters, *in* perils of robbers, [b]*in* perils by *mine own* countrymen, [c]*in* perils by the heathen, *in* perils in the city, *in* perils in the wilderness, *in* perils in the sea, *in* perils among false brethren;

27 In weariness and painfulness, [d]in watchings often, [e]in hunger and thirst, in fastings often, in cold and nakedness.

28 Beside those things that are without, that which cometh upon me daily, [f]the care of all the churches.

29 [g]Who is weak, and I am not weak? who is offended, and I burn not?

10:10 n1 Cor. 2:3 o1 Cor. 1:17
10:14 p1 Cor. 3:5
10:15 qRom. 15:20
10:17 rIsa. 65:16; 1 Cor. 1:31
10:18 sProv. 27:2 tRom. 2:29
11:2 uGal. 4:17 vHos. 2:19 wCol. 1:28 xLev. 21:13
11:3 yGen. 3:4 zEph. 6:24; 1 Tim. 1:3; Heb. 13:9
11:4 aGal. 1:7
11:5 b1 Cor. 15:10
11:6 c1 Cor. 1:17 dEph. 3:4
11:7 eActs 18:3
11:9 fActs 20:33; 2 Thess. 3:8 gPhil. 4:10
11:10 hRom. 9:1 i1 Cor. 9:15
11:12 j1 Cor. 9:12
11:13 kActs 15:24; Gal. 1:7; Phil. 1:15; 1 John 4:1; Rev. 2:2 lPhil. 3:2
11:14 mGal. 1:8
11:15 nPhil. 3:19
11:17 o1 Cor. 7:6
11:18 pPhil. 3:3
11:19 q1 Cor. 4:10
11:20 rGal. 2:4
11:21 sPhil. 3:4
11:22 tActs 22:3; Phil. 3:5
11:23 u1 Cor. 15:10 vActs 9:16 w1 Cor. 15:30
11:24 xDeut. 25:3
11:25 yActs 16:22 zActs 14:19 aActs 27:41
11:26 bActs 9:23 cActs 14:5
11:27 dActs 20:31 e1 Cor. 4:11
11:28 fActs 20:18
11:29 g1 Cor. 8:13

30 If I must needs glory, I will glory of the things which concern mine infirmities.

31 [h]The God and Father of our Lord Jesus Christ, [i]which is blessed for evermore, knoweth that I lie not.

32 [j]In Damascus the governor under Aretas the king kept the city of the Damascenes with a garrison, desirous to apprehend me:

33 And through a window in a basket was I let down by the wall, and escaped his hands.

12 It is not expedient for me doubtless to glory. I will come to visions and revelations of the Lord.

2 I knew a man [k]in Christ above fourteen years ago, (whether in the body, I cannot tell; or whether out of the body, I cannot tell: God knoweth;) such an one [l]caught up to the third heaven.

3 And I knew such a man, (whether in the body, or out of the body, I cannot tell: God knoweth;)

4 How that he was caught up into [m]paradise, and heard unspeakable words, which it is not lawful for a man to utter.

5 Of such an one will I glory: yet of myself I will not glory, but in mine infirmities.

6 For though I would desire to glory, I shall not be a fool; for I will say the truth: but *now* I forbear, lest any man should think of me above that which he seeth me *to be,* or *that* he heareth of me.

7 And lest I should be exalted above measure through the abundance of the revelations, there was given to me a [n]thorn in the flesh, [o]the messenger of Satan to buffet me, lest I should be exalted above measure.

8 [p]For this thing I besought the Lord thrice, that it might depart from me.

9 And he said unto me, My grace is sufficient for thee: for my strength is made perfect in weakness. Most gladly therefore will I rather glory in my infirmities, [q]that the power of Christ may rest upon me.

10 Therefore [r]I take pleasure in infirmities, in reproaches, in necessities, in persecutions, in distresses for Christ's sake: for when I am weak, then am I strong.

11 I am become a fool in glorying; ye have compelled me: for I ought to have been commended of you: for [s]in nothing am I behind the very chiefest apostles, though [t]I be nothing.

12 [u]Truly the signs of an apostle were wrought among you in all patience, in signs, and wonders, and mighty deeds.

13 [v]For what is it wherein ye were inferior to other churches, except *it be* that [w]I myself was not burdensome to you? forgive me this wrong.

14 Behold, the third time I am ready to come to you; and I will not be burdensome to you: for [x]I seek not yours, but you: [y]for the children ought not to lay up for the parents, but the parents for the children.

15 And [z]I will very gladly spend and be spent [a]for you; though the more abundantly I love you, the less I be loved.

16 But be it so, I did not burden you: nevertheless, being crafty, I caught you with guile.

17 Did I make a gain of you by any of them whom I sent unto you?

18 I desired Titus, and with *him* I sent a brother. Did Titus make a gain of you? walked we not in the same spirit? *walked we* not in the same steps?

19 Again, think ye that we excuse ourselves unto you? [b]we speak before God in Christ: [c]but *we do* all things, dearly beloved, for your edifying.

20 For I fear, lest, when I come, I shall not find you such as I would, and *that* [d]I shall be found unto you such as ye would not: lest *there be* debates, envyings, wraths, strifes, backbitings, whisperings, swellings, tumults:

21 *And* lest, when I come again, my God will humble me among you, and *that* I shall bewail many which have sinned already, and have not repented of the uncleanness and [e]fornication and lasciviousness which they have committed.

13 This *is* the third *time* I am coming to you. [f]In the mouth of two or three witnesses shall every word be established.

2 I told you before, and foretell you, as if I were present, the second time; and being absent now I write to them which heretofore have sinned, and to all other, that, if I come again, I will not spare:

3 Since ye seek a proof of Christ [g]speaking in me, which to you-ward is not weak, but is mighty [h]in you.

4 [i]For though he was crucified through weakness, yet [j]he liveth by the power of God. For we also are weak in him, but we shall live with him by the power of God toward you.

5 [k]Examine yourselves, whether ye be in the faith; prove your own selves. Know ye not your own selves, [l]how that Jesus Christ is in you, except ye be [m]reprobates?

6 But I trust that ye shall know that we are not reprobates.

7 Now I pray to God that ye do no evil; not that we should appear approved, but that ye should do that which is honest, though we be as reprobates.

8 For we can do nothing against the truth, but for the truth.

9 For we are glad, [n]when we are weak, and ye are strong: and this also we wish, [o]*even* your perfection.

10 [p]Therefore I write these things being absent, lest being present [q]I should use sharpness, according to the power which the Lord hath given me to edification, and not to destruction.

11 Finally, brethren, farewell. Be perfect,

11:31 [h]Rom. 1:9; 1 Thess. 2:5 [i]Rom. 9:5
11:32 [j]Acts 9:24
12:2 [k]Rom. 16:7 [l]Acts 22:17
12:4 [m]Luke 23:43
12:7 [n]Ezek. 28:24 [o]Job 2:7
12:8 [p]Deut. 3:23-27
12:9 [q]1 Pet. 4:14
12:10 [r]Rom. 5:3
12:11 [s]Gal. 2:6 [t]1 Cor. 3:7
12:12 [u]Rom. 15:18
12:13 [v]1 Cor. 1:7 [w]1 Cor. 9:12
12:14 [x]Acts 20:33 [y]1 Cor. 4:14
12:15 [z]1 Thess. 2:8 [a]John 10:11; 2 Tim. 2:10
12:19 [b]Rom. 9:1 [c]1 Cor. 10:33
12:20 [d]1 Cor. 4:21
12:21 [e]1 Cor. 5:1
13:1 [f]Num. 35:30; Matt. 18:16; John 8:17
13:3 [g]Matt. 10:20 [h]1 Cor. 9:2
13:4 [i]Phil. 2:7 [j]Rom. 6:4
13:5 [k]1 Cor. 11:28 [l]Rom. 8:10 [m]1 Cor. 9:27
13:9 [n]1 Cor. 4:10 [o]1 Thess. 3:10
13:10 [p]1 Cor. 4:21 [q]Tit. 1:13

be of good comfort, [r]be of one mind, live in peace; and the God of love and peace shall be with you.

12 [s]Greet one another with an holy kiss.

13 All the saints salute you.

14 [t]The grace of the Lord Jesus Christ, and the love of God, and the communion of the Holy Ghost, *be* with you all. Amen.

13:11 [r]Rom. 12:16
13:12 [s]Rom. 16:16
13:14 [t]Rom. 16:24

GALATIANS

Paul is the author of Galatians. It was probably written in A.D. 49. Paul begins this book with a reaffirmation of his apostolic authority, then quickly proceeds to explain the doctrine of justification by faith. He carefully defines and argues the doctrine from several viewpoints: from experience, from law, from Abraham, from personal testimony, and from allegory. In the final two chapters, Paul offers practical advice concerning the application of justification by faith in day to day life. Galatians 5:7 and 6:14 are two of the best known verses in Galatians.

I. Greetings to the church, 1:1–1:5
II. The problem in the church defined, 1:6–1:10
III. Paul's authority to speak on the issue, 1:11–2:21
IV. Justification by faith defended, 3:1–4:31
V. Justification by faith applied in daily life, 5:1–6:10
VI. Closing remarks, 6:11–6:18

1 Paul, an apostle, (not of men, neither by man, but [a]by Jesus Christ, and God the Father, [b]who raised him from the dead;)

2 And all the brethren [c]which are with me, [d]unto the churches of Galatia:

3 [e]Grace *be* to you and peace from God the Father, and *from* our Lord Jesus Christ,

4 [f]Who gave himself for our sins, that he might deliver us [g]from this present evil world, according to the will of God and our Father:

5 To whom *be* glory for ever and ever. Amen.

6 I marvel that ye are so soon removed from him that called you into the grace of Christ unto another gospel:

7 [h]Which is not another; but there be some [i]that trouble you, and would pervert the gospel of Christ.

8 But though [j]we, or an angel from heaven, preach any other gospel unto you than that which we have preached unto you, let him be accursed.

9 As we said before, so say I now again, If any *man* preach any other gospel unto you [k]than that ye have received, let him be accursed.

10 For [l]do I now [m]persuade men, or God? or [n]do I seek to please men? for if I yet pleased men, I should not be the servant of Christ.

11 [o]But I certify you, brethren, that the gospel which was preached of me is not after man.

12 For [p]I neither received it of man, neither was I taught *it*, but [q]by the revelation of Jesus Christ.

13 For ye have heard of my conversation in time past in the Jews' religion, how that [r]beyond measure I persecuted the church of God, and [s]wasted it:

14 And profited in the Jews' religion above many my equals in mine own nation, [t]being more exceedingly zealous [u]of the traditions of my fathers.

15 But when it pleased God, [v]who separated me from my mother's womb, and called *me* by his grace,

16 [w]To reveal his Son in me, that [x]I might preach him among the heathen; immediately I conferred not with [y]flesh and blood:

17 Neither went I up to Jerusalem to them which were apostles before me; but I went into Arabia, and returned again unto Damascus.

18 Then after three years [z]I went up to Jerusalem to see Peter, and abode with him fifteen days.

19 But [a]other of the apostles saw I none, save [b]James the Lord's brother.

20 Now the things which I write unto you, [c]behold, before God, I lie not.

21 [d]Afterwards I came into the regions of Syria and Cilicia;

22 And was unknown by face [e]unto the churches of Judaea which [f]were in Christ:

23 But they had heard only, That he which persecuted us in times past now preacheth the faith which once he destroyed.

24 And they glorified God in me.

2 Then fourteen years after [g]I went up again to Jerusalem with Barnabas, and took Titus with *me* also.

1:1 [a]Acts 9:6; [b]Acts 2:24
1:2 [c]Phil. 2:22; [d]1 Cor. 16:1
1:3 [e]Rom. 1:7; 2 Cor. 1:2; Eph. 1:2; Col. 1:2; 1 Thess. 1:1; 2 John 3
1:4 [f]Matt. 20:28; Tit. 2:14; [g]Isa. 65:17; Heb. 2:5; 1 John 5:19
1:7 [h]2 Cor. 11:4; [i]Acts 15:1
1:8 [j]1 Cor. 16:22
1:9 [k]Deut. 4:2; Rev. 22:18
1:10 [l]1 Thess. 2:4; [m]1 Sam. 24:7; 1 John 3:9; [n]1 Thess. 2:4
1:11 [o]1 Cor. 15:1
1:12 [p]1 Cor. 15:1; [q]Eph. 3:3
1:13 [r]Acts 9:1; [s]Acts 8:3
1:14 [t]Acts 22:3; [u]Jer. 9:14; Mark 7:5
1:15 [v]Isa. 49:1; Acts 9:15; Rom. 1:1
1:16 [w]2 Cor. 4:6; [x]Acts 9:15; Eph. 3:8; [y]Matt. 16:17; Eph. 6:12
1:18 [z]Acts 9:26
1:19 [a]1 Cor. 9:5; [b]Matt. 13:55
1:20 [c]Rom. 9:1
1:21 [d]Acts 9:30
1:22 [e]1 Thess. 2:14; [f]Rom. 16:7
2:1 [g]Acts 15:2

2 And I went up by revelation, [h]and communicated unto them that gospel which I preach among the Gentiles, but privately to them which were of reputation, lest by any means [i]I should run, or had run, in vain.

3 But neither Titus, who was with me, being a Greek, was compelled to be circumcised:

4 And that because of [j]false brethren unawares brought in, who came in privily to spy out our liberty which we have in Christ Jesus, [k]that they might bring us into bondage:

5 To whom we gave place by subjection, no, not for an hour; that the truth of the gospel might continue with you.

6 But of these who seemed to be somewhat, (whatsoever they were, it maketh no matter to me: [l]God accepteth no man's person:) for they who seemed *to be somewhat* [m]in conference added nothing to me:

7 But contrariwise, [n]when they saw that the gospel of the uncircumcision [o]was committed unto me, as *the gospel* of the circumcision *was* unto Peter;

8 (For he that wrought effectually in Peter to the apostleship of the circumcision, [p]the same was mighty in me toward the Gentiles:)

9 And when James, Cephas, and John, who seemed to be [q]pillars, perceived [r]the grace that was given unto me, they gave to me and Barnabas the right hands of fellowship; that we *should go* unto the heathen, and they unto the circumcision.

10 Only *they would* that we should remember the poor; [s]the same which I also was forward to do.

11 [t]But when Peter was come to Antioch, I withstood him to the face, because he was to be blamed.

12 For before that certain came from James, [u]he did eat with the Gentiles: but when they were come, he withdrew and separated himself, fearing them which were of the circumcision.

13 And the other Jews dissembled likewise with him; insomuch that Barnabas also was carried away with their dissimulation.

14 But when I saw that they walked not uprightly according to the truth of the gospel, I said unto Peter [v]before *them* all, [w]If thou, being a Jew, livest after the manner of Gentiles, and not as do the Jews, why compellest thou the Gentiles to live as do the Jews?

15 [x]We *who are* Jews by nature, and not [y]sinners of the Gentiles,

16 [z]Knowing that a man is not justified by the works of the law, but [a]by the faith of Jesus Christ, even we have believed in Jesus Christ, that we might be justified by the faith of Christ, and not by the works of the law: for [b]by the works of the law shall no flesh be justified.

17 But if, while we seek to be justified by Christ, we ourselves also are found [c]sinners, *is* therefore Christ the minister of sin? God forbid.

18 For if I build again the things which I destroyed, I make myself a transgressor.

19 For I [d]through the law [e]am dead to the law, that I might [f]live unto God.

20 I am [g]crucified with Christ: nevertheless I live; yet not I, but Christ liveth in me: and the life which I now live in the flesh [h]I live by the faith of the Son of God, [i]who loved me, and gave himself for me.

21 I do not frustrate the grace of God: for [j]if righteousness *come* by the law, then Christ is dead in vain.

3 O foolish Galatians, who hath bewitched you, that ye should not obey the truth, before whose eyes Jesus Christ hath been evidently set forth, crucified among you?

2 This only would I learn of you, Received ye [k]the Spirit by the works of the law, [l]or by the hearing of faith?

3 Are ye so foolish? having begun in the Spirit, are ye now made perfect by the [m]flesh?

4 [n]Have ye suffered so many things in vain? if *it be* yet in vain.

5 He therefore [o]that ministereth to you the Spirit, and worketh miracles among you, *doeth he it* by the works of the law, or by the hearing of faith?

6 Even as [p]Abraham believed God, and it was accounted to him for righteousness.

7 Know ye therefore that [q]they which are of faith, the same are the children of Abraham.

8 And [r]the scripture, foreseeing that God would justify the heathen through faith, preached before the gospel unto Abraham, *saying,* [s]In thee shall all nations be blessed.

9 So then they which be of faith are blessed with faithful Abraham.

10 For as many as are of the works of the law are under the curse: for it is written, [t]Cursed *is* every one that continueth not in all things which are written in the book of the law to do them.

11 But that no man is justified by the law in the sight of God, *it is* evident: for, [u]The just shall live by faith.

12 And [v]the law is not of faith: but, [w]The man that doeth them shall live in them.

13 [x]Christ hath redeemed us from the curse of the law, being made a curse for us: for it is written, [y]Cursed *is* every one that hangeth on a tree:

14 [z]That the blessing of Abraham might come on the Gentiles through Jesus Christ; that we might receive [a]the promise of the Spirit through faith.

15 Brethren, I speak after the manner of men; [b]Though *it be* but a man's covenant, yet *if it be* confirmed, no man disannulleth, or addeth thereto.

16 Now [c]to Abraham and his seed were the promises made. He saith not, And to seeds, as of many; but as of one, And to thy seed, which is [d]Christ.

2:2 [h]Acts 15:12 [i]Phil. 2:16
2:4 [j]Acts 15:1 [k]2 Cor. 11:20
2:6 [l]Acts 10:34 [m]2 Cor. 12:11
2:7 [n]Acts 13:46; 1 Tim. 2:7; 2 Tim. 1:11 [o]1 Thess. 2:4
2:8 [p]Acts 9:15; Col. 1:29
2:9 [q]Matt. 16:18; Rev. 21:14 [r]Rom. 1:5; Eph. 3:8
2:10 [s]Acts 11:30; 1 Cor. 16:1; 2 Cor. 8
2:11 [t]Acts 15:35
2:12 [u]Acts 10:28
2:14 [v]1 Tim. 5:20 [w]Acts 10:28
2:15 [x]Acts 15:10 [y]Matt. 9:11
2:16 [z]Acts 13:38 [a]Rom. 1:17 [b]Ps. 143:2
2:17 [c]1 John 3:8
2:19 [d]Rom. 8:2 [e]Rom. 6:14 [f]Rom. 6:11; 1 Thess. 5:10; Heb. 9:14
2:20 [g]Rom. 6:6 [h]2 Cor. 5:15; 1 Pet. 4:2 [i]Eph. 5:2
2:21 [j]Rom. 11:6
3:2 [k]Acts 2:38; Heb. 6:4 [l]Rom. 10:16
3:3 [m]Heb. 7:16
3:4 [n]Heb. 10:35
3:5 [o]2 Cor. 3:8
3:6 [p]Gen. 15:6; Jam. 2:23
3:7 [q]John 8:39
3:8 [r]Rom. 9:17 [s]Gen. 12:3
3:10 [t]Deut. 27:26
3:11 [u]Hab. 2:4; Heb. 10:38
3:12 [v]Rom. 4:4 [w]Lev. 18:5; Ezek. 20:11; Rom. 10:5
3:13 [x]Rom. 8:3 [y]Deut. 21:23
3:14 [z]Rom. 4:9 [a]Isa. 32:15; Ezek. 11:19; Joel 2:28; John 7:39; Acts 2:33
3:15 [b]Heb. 9:17
3:16 [c]Gen. 12:3 [d]1 Cor. 12:12

17 And this I say, *that* the covenant, that was confirmed before of God in Christ, the law, [e]which was four hundred and thirty years after, cannot disannul, [f]that it should make the promise of none effect.

18 For if [g]the inheritance *be* of the law, [h]*it is* no more of promise: but God gave *it* to Abraham by promise.

19 Wherefore then *serveth* the law? [i]It was added because of transgressions, till the seed should come to whom the promise was made; *and it was* [j]ordained by angels in the hand [k]of a mediator.

20 Now a mediator is not *a mediator* of one, [l]but God is one.

21 *Is* the law then against the promises of God? God forbid: for if there had been a law given which could have given life, verily righteousness should have been by the law.

22 But the scripture hath concluded [m]all under sin, [n]that the promise by faith of Jesus Christ might be given to them that believe.

23 But before faith came, we were kept under the law, shut up unto the faith which should afterwards be revealed.

24 Wherefore [o]the law was our schoolmaster *to bring us* unto Christ, [p]that we might be justified by faith.

25 But after that faith is come, we are no longer under a schoolmaster.

26 For ye [q]are all the children of God by faith in Christ Jesus.

27 For [r]as many of you as have been baptized into Christ [s]have put on Christ.

28 [t]There is neither Jew nor Greek, there is neither bond nor free, there is neither male nor female: for ye are all [u]one in Christ Jesus.

29 And [v]if ye *be* Christ's, then are ye Abraham's seed, and [w]heirs according to the promise.

4 Now I say, *That* the heir, as long as he is a child, differeth nothing from a servant, though he be lord of all;

2 But is under tutors and governors until the time appointed of the father.

3 Even so we, when we were children, [x]were in bondage under the elements of the world:

4 But [y]when the fulness of the time was come, God sent forth his Son, [z]made [a]of a woman, [b]made under the law,

5 [c]To redeem them that were under the law, [d]that we might receive the adoption of sons.

6 And because ye are sons, God hath sent forth [e]the Spirit of his Son into your hearts, crying, Abba, Father.

7 Wherefore thou art no more a servant, but a son; [f]and if a son, then an heir of God through Christ.

8 Howbeit then, [g]when ye knew not God, [h]ye did service unto them which by nature are no gods.

9 But now, [i]after that ye have known God, or rather are known of God, [j]how turn ye again to [k]the weak and beggarly elements, whereunto ye desire again to be in bondage?

10 [l]Ye observe days, and months, and times, and years.

11 I am afraid of you, [m]lest I have bestowed upon you labour in vain.

12 Brethren, I beseech you, be as I *am;* for I *am* as ye *are:* [n]ye have not injured me at all.

13 Ye know how [o]through infirmity of the flesh I preached the gospel unto you at the first.

14 And my temptation which was in my flesh ye despised not, nor rejected; but received me [p]as an angel of God, [q]*even* as Christ Jesus.

15 Where is then the blessedness ye spake of? for I bear you record, that, if *it had been* possible, ye would have plucked out your own eyes, and have given them to me.

16 Am I therefore become your enemy, because I tell you the truth?

17 They [r]zealously affect you, *but* not well; yea, they would exclude you, that ye might affect them.

18 But *it is* good to be zealously affected always in *a* good *thing,* and not only when I am present with you.

19 [s]My little children, of whom I travail in birth again until Christ be formed in you,

20 I desire to be present with you now, and to change my voice; for I stand in doubt of you.

21 Tell me, ye that desire to be under the law, do ye not hear the law?

22 For it is written, that Abraham had two sons, [t]the one by a bondmaid, [u]the other by a freewoman.

23 But he *who was* of the bondwoman [v]was born after the flesh; [w]but he of the freewoman *was* by promise.

24 Which things are an allegory: for these are the two covenants; the one from the mount [x]Sinai, which gendereth to bondage, which is Agar.

25 For this Agar is mount Sinai in Arabia, and answereth to Jerusalem which now is, and is in bondage with her children.

26 But [y]Jerusalem which is above is free, which is the mother of us all.

27 For it is written, [z]Rejoice, *thou* barren that bearest not; break forth and cry, thou that travailest not: for the desolate hath many more children than she which hath an husband.

28 Now we, brethren, as Isaac was, are [a]the children of promise.

29 But as then [b]he that was born after the flesh persecuted him *that was born* after the Spirit, even so *it is* now.

30 Nevertheless what saith the scripture? [c]Cast out the bondwoman and her son: for [d]the son of the bondwoman shall not be heir with the son of the freewoman.

31 So then, brethren, we are not children of the bondwoman, [e]but of the free.

3:17 [e]Ex. 12:40 [f]Rom. 4:13
3:18 [g]Rom. 8:17 [h]Rom. 4:14
3:19 [i]John 15:22; 1 Tim. 1:9 [j]Acts 7:53 [k]Ex. 20:19; John 1:17; Acts 7:38
3:20 [l]Rom. 3:29
3:22 [m]Rom. 3:9 [n]Rom. 4:11
3:24 [o]Matt. 5:17; Col. 2:17; Heb. 9:9 [p]Acts 13:39
3:26 [q]John 1:12; 1 John 3:1
3:27 [r]Rom. 6:3 [s]Rom. 13:14
3:28 [t]Rom. 10:12; Col. 3:11 [u]John 10:16
3:29 [v]Gen. 21:10; Heb. 11:18 [w]Rom. 8:17
4:3 [x]Col. 2:8
4:4 [y]Gen. 49:10; Mark 1:15; Eph. 1:10 [z]John 1:14; Phil. 2:7; Heb. 2:14 [a]Gen. 3:15; Mic. 5:3; Matt. 1:23 [b]Matt. 5:17
4:5 [c]Matt. 20:28; Heb. 9:12; Eph. 1:7 [d]John 1:12
4:6 [e]Rom. 5:5
4:7 [f]Rom. 8:16
4:8 [g]Eph. 2:12 [h]Rom. 1:25; Eph. 2:11; 1 Thess. 1:9
4:9 [i]1 Cor. 8:3 [j]Col. 2:20 [k]Rom. 8:3
4:10 [l]Rom. 14:5
4:11 [m]1 Thess. 3:5
4:12 [n]2 Cor. 2:5
4:13 [o]1 Cor. 2:3
4:14 [p]2 Sam. 19:27; Mal. 2:7 [q]Matt. 10:40; John 13:20; 1 Thess. 2:13
4:17 [r]Rom. 10:2
4:19 [s]1 Cor. 4:15; Jam. 1:18
4:22 [t]Gen. 16:15 [u]Gen. 21:2
4:23 [v]Rom. 9:7 [w]Gen. 18:10
4:24 [x]Deut. 33:2
4:26 [y]Isa. 2:2; Rev. 3:12
4:27 [z]Isa. 54:1
4:28 [a]Acts 3:25
4:29 [b]Gen. 21:9
4:30 [c]Gen. 21:10 [d]John 8:35
4:31 [e]John 8:36

5 Stand fast therefore in [f]the liberty wherewith Christ hath made us free, and be not entangled again [g]with the yoke of bondage.

2 Behold, I Paul say unto you, that [h]if ye be circumcised, Christ shall profit you nothing.

3 For I testify again to every man that is circumcised, that he is a debtor to do the whole law.

4 [i]Christ is become of no effect unto you, whosoever of you are justified by the law; [j]ye are fallen from grace.

5 For we through the Spirit [k]wait for the hope of righteousness by faith.

6 For [l]in Jesus Christ neither circumcision availeth any thing, nor uncircumcision; but [m]faith which worketh by love.

7 Ye [n]did run well; who did hinder you that ye should not obey the truth?

8 This persuasion *cometh* not of him that calleth you.

9 [o]A little leaven leaveneth the whole lump.

10 [p]I have confidence in you through the Lord, that ye will be none otherwise minded: but he that troubleth you [q]shall bear his judgment, whosoever he be.

11 And I, brethren, if I yet preach circumcision, [r]why do I yet suffer persecution? then is [s]the offence of the cross ceased.

12 [t]I would they were even cut off [u]which trouble you.

13 For, brethren, ye have been called unto liberty; only [v]*use* not liberty for an occasion to the flesh, but [w]by love serve one another.

14 For [x]all the law is fulfilled in one word, *even* in this; [y]Thou shalt love thy neighbour as thyself.

15 But if ye bite and devour one another, take heed that ye be not consumed one of another.

16 *This* I say then, [z]Walk in the Spirit, and ye shall not fulfil the lust of the flesh.

17 For [a]the flesh lusteth against the Spirit, and the Spirit against the flesh: and these are contrary the one to the other: [b]so that ye cannot do the things that ye would.

18 But [c]if ye be led of the Spirit, ye are not under the law.

19 Now [d]the works of the flesh are manifest, which are *these;* Adultery, fornication, uncleanness, lasciviousness,

20 Idolatry, witchcraft, hatred, variance, emulations, wrath, strife, seditions, heresies,

21 Envyings, murders, drunkenness, revellings, and such like: of the which I tell you before, as I have also told *you* in time past, that [e]they which do such things shall not inherit the kingdom of God.

22 But [f]the fruit of the Spirit is love, joy, peace, longsuffering, [g]gentleness, [h]goodness, [i]faith,

23 Meekness, temperance: [j]against such there is no law.

24 And they that are Christ's [k]have crucified the flesh with the affections and lusts.

25 [l]If we live in the Spirit, let us also walk in the Spirit.

26 [m]Let us not be desirous of vain glory, provoking one another, envying one another.

6 Brethren, [n]if a man be overtaken in a fault, ye [o]which are spiritual, restore such an one [p]in the spirit of meekness; considering thyself, [q]lest thou also be tempted.

2 [r]Bear ye one another's burdens, and so fulfil [s]the law of Christ.

3 For [t]if a man think himself to be something, when [u]he is nothing, he deceiveth himself.

4 But [v]let every man prove his own work, and then shall he have rejoicing in himself alone, and [w]not in another.

5 [x]For every man shall bear his own burden.

6 [y]Let him that is taught in the word communicate unto him that teacheth in all good things.

7 [z]Be not deceived; [a]God is not mocked: for [b]whatsoever a man soweth, that shall he also reap.

8 [c]For he that soweth to his flesh shall of the flesh reap corruption; but he that soweth to the Spirit shall of the Spirit reap life everlasting.

9 And [d]let us not be weary in well doing: for in due season we shall reap, [e]if we faint not.

10 [f]As we have therefore opportunity, [g]let us do good unto all *men*, especially unto them who are of [h]the household of faith.

11 Ye see how large a letter I have written unto you with mine own hand.

12 As many as desire to make a fair shew in the flesh, they constrain you to be circumcised; [i]only lest they should suffer persecution for the cross of Christ.

13 For neither they themselves who are circumcised keep the law; but desire to have you circumcised, that they may glory in your flesh.

14 [j]But God forbid that I should glory, save in the cross of our Lord Jesus Christ, by whom the world is [k]crucified unto me, and I unto the world.

15 For [l]in Christ Jesus neither circumcision availeth any thing, nor uncircumcision, but [m]a new creature.

16 [n]And as many as walk [o]according to this rule, peace *be* on them, and mercy, and upon [p]the Israel of God.

17 From henceforth let no man trouble me: for [q]I bear in my body the marks of the Lord Jesus.

18 Brethren, [r]the grace of our Lord Jesus Christ *be* with your spirit. Amen.

5:1 fJohn 8:32; 1 Pet. 2:16 gActs 15:10
5:2 hActs 15:1
5:4 iRom. 9:31 jHeb. 12:15
5:5 kRom. 8:24
5:6 l1 Cor. 7:19 m1 Thess. 1:3
5:7 n1 Cor. 9:24
5:9 o1 Cor. 5:6
5:10 p2 Cor. 2:3 q2 Cor. 10:6
5:11 r1 Cor. 15:30 s1 Cor. 1:23
5:12 tJosh. 7:25 uActs 15:1
5:13 v1 Cor. 8:9; 2 Pet. 2:19; Jude 4 w1 Cor. 9:19
5:14 xMatt. 7:12 yLev. 19:18; Rom. 13:8
5:16 zRom. 6:12
5:17 aRom. 7:23 bRom. 7:15
5:18 cRom. 6:14
5:19 d1 Cor. 3:3; Col. 3:5; Jam. 3:14
5:21 e1 Cor. 6:9; Col. 3:6; Rev. 22:15
5:22 fJohn 15:2 gCol. 3:12 hRom. 15:14 i1 Cor. 13:7
5:23 j1 Tim. 1:9
5:24 kRom. 6:6
5:25 lRom. 8:4
5:26 mPhil. 2:3
6:1 nRom. 14:1; Jam. 5:19 o1 Cor. 2:15 p1 Cor. 4:21; 2 Tim. 2:25 q1 Cor. 7:5
6:2 rRom. 15:1 sJohn 13:14; 1 John 4:21
6:3 tRom. 12:3 u2 Cor. 3:5
6:4 v1 Cor. 11:28 wLuke 18:11
6:5 xRom. 2:6
6:6 yRom. 15:27
6:7 z1 Cor. 6:9 aJob 13:9 bLuke 16:25; 2 Cor. 9:6
6:8 cJob 4:8; Hos. 8:7; Rom. 8:13
6:9 d2 Thess. 3:13 eMatt. 24:13; Rev. 2:10
6:10 fJohn 9:4 g1 Thess. 5:15; Tit. 3:8 hEph. 2:19
6:12 iPhil. 3:18
6:14 jPhil. 3:3 kRom. 6:6
6:15 l1 Cor. 7:19 m2 Cor. 5:17
6:16 nPs. 125:5 oPhil. 3:16 pRom. 2:29
6:17 q2 Cor. 1:5
6:18 r2 Tim. 4:22

EPHESIANS

Paul is the author of Ephesians, which was probably written about A.D. 60. Paul begins this letter with blessings to those who have accepted Christ as their Savior. Paul then discusses salvation by grace and the uniting of those in Christ into a single body of believers. The last three chapters of Ephesians are devoted to the practical application of this new life in Christ.

Beginning in verse 10 of chapter 6, Paul details how the believer should prepare for battle with Satan by putting on the "armor of God." These verses are the most widely recognized verses in Ephesians.

I. Greetings to the church at Ephesus, 1:1–1:2
II. The blessings of being in Christ, 1:3–1:23
III. Salvation through grace, 2:1–2:10
IV. United and equal in Christ, 2:11-3:21
V. Practical considerations for the believer, 4:1–6:9
VI. The armor of God, 6:10-6:20
VII. Closing remarks, 6:21–6:24

---

1 Paul, an apostle of Jesus Christ [a]by the
will of God, [b]to the saints which are
at Ephesus, [c]and to the faithful in Christ
Jesus:
2 [d]Grace *be* to you, and peace, from God
our Father, and *from* the Lord Jesus Christ.
3 [e]Blessed *be* the God and Father of our
Lord Jesus Christ, who hath blessed us with
all spiritual blessings in heavenly *places* in
Christ:
4 According as [f]he hath chosen us in him
[g]before the foundation of the world, that
we should [h]be holy and without blame before him in love:
5 [i]Having predestinated us unto [j]the
adoption of children by Jesus Christ to himself, [k]according to the good pleasure of his
will,
6 To the praise of the glory of his grace,
[l]wherein he hath made us accepted in [m]the
beloved.
7 [n]In whom we have redemption through
his blood, the forgiveness of sins, according
to [o]the riches of his grace;
8 Wherein he hath abounded toward us in
all wisdom and prudence;
9 [p]Having made known unto us the mystery of his will, according to his good pleasure [q]which he hath purposed in himself:
10 That in the dispensation of [r]the fulness of times [s]he might gather together in
one [t]all things in Christ, both which are in
heaven, and which are on earth; *even*
in him:
11 [u]In whom also we have obtained an
inheritance, being predestinated according
to [v]the purpose of him who worketh all
things after the counsel of his own will:
12 [w]That we should be to the praise of his
glory, [x]who first trusted in Christ.
13 In whom ye also *trusted*, after that ye
heard [y]the word of truth, the gospel of your
salvation: in whom also after that ye believed, [z]ye were sealed with that holy Spirit
of promise,
14 [a]Which is the earnest of our inheritance [b]until the redemption of [c]the purchased possession, [d]unto the praise of his
glory.
15 Wherefore I also, [e]after I heard of
your faith in the Lord Jesus, and love unto
all the saints,
16 [f]Cease not to give thanks for you,
making mention of you in my prayers;
17 That [g]the God of our Lord Jesus
Christ, the Father of glory, [h]may give unto
you the spirit of wisdom and revelation in
the knowledge of him:
18 [i]The eyes of your understanding being enlightened; that ye may know what is
the hope of his calling, and what the riches
of the glory of his inheritance in the saints,
19 And what *is* the exceeding greatness of
his power to us-ward who believe, [j]accord-
ing to the working of his mighty power,
20 Which he wrought in Christ, when [k]he
raised him from the dead, and [l]set *him* at
his own right hand in the heavenly *places*,
21 [m]Far above all [n]principality, and
power, and might, and dominion, and every
name that is named, not only in this world,
but also in that which is to come:
22 And [o]hath put all *things* under his
feet, and gave him [p]*to be* the head over all
things to the church,
23 [q]Which is his body, [r]the fulness of
him [s]that filleth all in all.

2 And [t]you *hath he quickened*, who were
dead in trespasses and sins;
2 [u]Wherein in time past ye walked according to the course of this world, according to the prince of the power of the air, the

1:1 [a]2 Cor. 1:1 [b]Rom. 1:7 [c]1 Cor. 4:17 **1:2** [d]Gal. 1:3 **1:3** [e]2 Cor. 1:3 **1:4** [f]Rom. 8:28; 2 Tim. 1:9; Jam. 2:5 [g]1 Pet. 1:2 [h]Luke 1:75; 1 Thess. 4:7; Tit. 2:12 **1:5** [i]Rom. 8:29 [j]John 1:12; 2 Cor. 6:18; Gal. 4:5 [k]Matt. 1:26; 1 Cor. 1:21 **1:6** [l]Rom. 3:24 [m]Matt. 3:17 **1:7** [n]Acts 20:28; Col. 1:14; Heb. 9:12; Rev. 5:9 [o]Rom. 2:4 **1:9** [p]Rom. 16:25 [q]2 Tim. 1:9 **1:10** [r]Gal. 4:4; 1 Pet. 1:20 [s]1 Cor. 3:22 [t]Phil. 2:9 **1:11** [u]Acts 20:32; Col. 1:12; Tit. 3:7; 1 Pet. 1:4 [v]Isa. 46:10 **1:12** [w]2 Thess. 2:13 [x]Jam. 1:18 **1:13** [y]John 1:17 [z]2 Cor. 1:22 **1:14** [a]2 Cor. 1:22 [b]Luke 21:28 [c]Acts 20:28 [d]1 Pet. 2:9 **1:15** [e]Col. 1:4 **1:16** [f]Rom. 1:9; Col. 1:3; 1 Thess. 1:2 **1:17** [g]John 20:17 [h]Col. 1:9 **1:18** [i]Acts 26:18 **1:19** [j]Col. 1:29 **1:20** [k]Acts 2:24 [l]Ps. 110:1; Col. 3:1; Heb. 1:3 **1:21** [m]Phil. 2:9; Heb. 1:4 [n]Rom. 8:38 **1:22** [o]Ps. 8:6; 1 Cor. 15:27; Heb. 2:8 [p]Col. 1:18

1:23 [q]Rom. 12:5; Col. 1:18 [r]Col. 2:10 [s]1 Cor. 12:6 **2:1** [t]John 5:24
2:2 [u]1 Cor. 6:11; 1 John 5:19

spirit that now worketh in [v]the children of disobedience:

3 [w]Among whom also we all had our conversation in times past in [x]the lusts of our flesh, fulfilling the desires of the flesh and of the mind; and [y]were by nature the children of wrath, even as others.

4 But God, [z]who is rich in mercy, for his great love wherewith he loved us,

5 [a]Even when we were dead in sins, hath [b]quickened us together with Christ, (by grace ye are saved;)

6 And hath raised *us* up together, and made *us* sit together in heavenly *places* in Christ Jesus:

7 That in the ages to come he might shew the exceeding riches of his grace in [c]*his* kindness toward us through Christ Jesus.

8 [d]For by grace are ye saved [e]through faith; and that not of yourselves: [f]*it is* the gift of God:

9 [g]Not of works, lest any man should boast.

10 For we are his [h]workmanship, created in Christ Jesus unto good works, which God hath before ordained that we should walk in them.

11 Wherefore [i]remember, that ye *being* in time past Gentiles in the flesh, who are called Uncircumcision by that which is called [j]the Circumcision in the flesh made by hands;

12 [k]That at that time ye were without Christ, [l]being aliens from the commonwealth of Israel, and strangers from [m]the covenants of promise, [n]having no hope, [o]and without God in the world:

13 [p]But now in Christ Jesus ye who sometimes were [q]far off are made nigh by the blood of Christ.

14 For [r]he is our peace, [s]who hath made both one, and hath broken down the middle wall of partition *between us;*

15 [t]Having abolished [u]in his flesh the enmity, *even* the law of commandments *contained* in ordinances; for to make in himself of twain one [v]new man, *so* making peace;

16 And that he might [w]reconcile both unto God in one body by the cross, [x]having slain the enmity thereby:

17 And came [y]and preached peace to you which were afar off, and to [z]them that were nigh.

18 For [a]through him we both have access [b]by one Spirit unto the Father.

19 Now therefore ye are no more strangers and foreigners, but [c]fellowcitizens with the saints, and of [d]the household of God;

20 And are [e]built [f]upon the foundation of the [g]apostles and prophets, Jesus Christ himself being [h]the chief corner *stone;*

21 In whom all the building fitly framed together groweth unto [i]an holy temple in the Lord:

22 [j]In whom ye also are builded together for an habitation of God through the Spirit.

3 For this cause I Paul, [k]the prisoner of Jesus Christ [l]for you Gentiles,

2 If ye have heard of [m]the dispensation of the grace of God [n]which is given me to you-ward:

3 [o]How that [p]by revelation [q]he made known unto me the mystery; (as I wrote afore in few words,

4 Whereby, when ye read, ye may understand my knowledge [r]in the mystery of Christ)

5 [s]Which in other ages was not made known unto the sons of men, as it is now revealed unto his holy apostles and prophets by the Spirit;

6 That the Gentiles [t]should be fellowheirs, and of the same body, and [u]partakers of his promise in Christ by the gospel:

7 [v]Whereof I was made a minister, [w]according to the gift of the grace of God given unto me by [x]the effectual working of his power.

8 Unto me, [y]who am less than the least of all saints, is this grace given, that [z]I should preach among the Gentiles [a]the unsearchable riches of Christ;

9 And to make all *men* see what *is* the fellowship of the mystery, [b]which from the beginning of the world hath been hid in God, [c]who created all things by Jesus Christ:

10 [d]To the intent that now [e]unto the principalities and powers in heavenly *places* [f]might be known by the church the manifold wisdom of God,

11 According to the eternal purpose which he purposed in Christ Jesus our Lord:

12 In whom we have boldness and access [g]with confidence by the faith of him.

13 [h]Wherefore I desire that ye faint not at my tribulations for you, [i]which is your glory.

14 For this cause I bow my knees unto the Father of our Lord Jesus Christ,

15 Of whom [j]the whole family in heaven and earth is named,

16 That he would grant you, [k]according to the riches of his glory, [l]to be strengthened with might by his Spirit in [m]the inner man;

17 [n]That Christ may dwell in your hearts by faith; that ye, [o]being rooted and grounded in love,

18 May be able to comprehend with all saints [p]what *is* the breadth, and length, and depth, and height;

19 And to know the love of Christ, which passeth knowledge, that ye might be filled [q]with all the fulness of God.

20 Now [r]unto him that is able to do exceeding abundantly [s]above all that we ask or think, [t]according to the power that worketh in us,

21 [u]Unto him *be* glory in the church by

2:2 [v]Col. 3:6
2:3 [w]Tit. 3:3 [x]Gal. 5:16 [y]Ps. 51:5
2:4 [z]Rom. 10:12
2:5 [a]Rom. 5:6 [b]Rom 6:4
2:7 [c]Tit. 3:4
2:8 [d]Rom. 3:24 [e]Rom. 4:16 [f]Matt. 16:17; Rom. 10:14; Phil. 1:29
2:9 [g]Rom. 3:20; 2 Tim. 1:9; Tit. 3:5
2:10 [h]Deut. 32:6; Isa. 19:25; John 3:3; 2 Cor. 5:5; Tit. 2:14
2:11 [i]1 Cor. 12:2 [j]Rom. 2:28
2:12 [k]Col. 1:21 [l]Ezek. 13:9 [m]Rom. 9:4 [n]1 Thess. 4:13 [o]Gal. 4:8
2:13 [p]Gal. 3:28 [q]Acts 2:39
2:14 [r]Mic. 5:5; Acts 10:36; Rom. 5:1 [s]John 10:16
2:15 [t]Col. 2:14 [u]Col. 1:22 [v]2 Cor. 5:17
2:16 [w]Col. 1:20 [x]Rom. 6:6
2:17 [y]Isa. 57:19; Acts 2:39; Rom. 5:1 [z]Ps. 148:14
2:18 [a]John 10:9; Heb. 4:16; 1 Pet. 3:18 [b]1 Cor. 12:13
2:19 [c]Phil. 3:20 [d]Gal. 6:10
2:20 [e]1 Cor. 3:9 [f]Matt. 16:18; Rev. 21:14 [g]1 Cor. 12:28 [h]Ps. 118:22; Matt. 21:42
2:21 [i]1 Cor. 3:17
2:22 [j]1 Pet. 2:5
3:1 [k]Acts 21:33; Col. 4:3; 2 Tim. 1:8 [l]Gal. 5:11; 2 Tim. 2:10
3:2 [m]Rom. 1:5; Col. 1:25 [n]Acts 9:15; Gal. 1:16
3:3 [o]Acts 22:17 [p]Gal. 1:12 [q]Rom. 16:25
3:4 [r]1 Cor. 4:1
3:5 [s]Acts 10:28
3:6 [t]Gal. 3:28 [u]Gal. 3:14
3:7 [v]Rom. 15:16 [w]Rom. 1:5 [x]Rom. 15:18
3:8 [y]1 Cor. 15:9 [z]Gal. 1:16; 2 Tim. 1:11 [a]Col. 1:27
3:9 [b]Rom. 16:25; Col. 1:26 [c]Ps. 33:6; Col. 1:16; Heb. 1:2
3:10 [d]1 Pet. 1:12 [e]Rom. 8:38; 1 Pet. 3:22 [f]1 Cor. 2:7
3:12 [g]Heb. 4:16
3:13 [h]Acts 14:22; 1 Thess. 3:3 [i]2 Cor. 1:6
3:15 [j]Phil. 2:9
3:16 [k]Rom. 9:23; Col. 1:27 [l]Col. 1:11 [m]Rom. 7:22
3:17 [n]John 14:23 [o]Col. 1:23
3:18 [p]Rom. 10:3 **3:19** [q]John 1:16 **3:20** [r]Rom. 16:25 [s]1 Cor. 2:9 [t]Col. 1:29 **3:21** [u]Rom. 11:36

Christ Jesus throughout all ages, world
without end. Amen.

4

I therefore, [v]the prisoner of the Lord,
beseech you that ye [w]walk worthy of
the vocation wherewith ye are called,
2 [x]With all lowliness and meekness, with
longsuffering, forbearing one another in
love;
3 Endeavouring to keep the unity of the
Spirit [y]in the bond of peace.
4 [z]*There is* one body, and [a]one Spirit,
even as ye are called in one hope of your
calling;
5 [b]One Lord, [c]one faith, [d]one baptism,
6 [e]One God and Father of all, who *is*
above all, and [f]through all, and in you all.
7 But [g]unto every one of us is given grace
according to the measure of the gift of
Christ.
8 Wherefore he saith, [h]When he ascended up on high, [i]he led captivity captive, and gave gifts unto men.
9 ([j]Now that he ascended, what is it but
that he also descended first into the lower
parts of the earth?
10 He that descended is the same also
[k]that ascended up far above all heavens,
[l]that he might fill all things.)
11 [m]And he gave some, apostles; and
some, prophets; and some, [n]evangelists;
and some, [o]pastors and [p]teachers;
12 [q]For the perfecting of the saints, for
the work of the ministry, [r]for the edifying
of [s]the body of Christ:
13 Till we all come in the unity of the
faith, [t]and of the knowledge of the Son of
God, unto [u]a perfect man, unto the measure
of the stature of the fulness of Christ:
14 That we *henceforth* be no more [v]chil-
dren, [w]tossed to and fro, and carried about
with every [x]wind of doctrine, by the sleight
of men, *and* cunning craftiness, [y]whereby
they lie in wait to deceive;
15 But [z]speaking the truth in love, may
grow up into him in all things, [a]which is the
head, *even* Christ:
16 [b]From whom the whole body fitly
joined together and compacted by that
which every joint supplieth, according to
the effectual working in the measure of every part, maketh increase of the body unto
the edifying of itself in love.
17 This I say therefore, and testify in the
Lord, that [c]ye henceforth walk not as other
Gentiles walk, [d]in the vanity of their mind,
18 [e]Having the understanding darkened,
[f]being alienated from the life of God
through the ignorance that is in them, because of the [g]blindness of their heart:
19 [h]Who being past feeling [i]have given
themselves over unto lasciviousness, to
work all uncleanness with greediness.
20 But ye have not so learned Christ;
21 If so be that ye have heard him, and
have been taught by him, as the truth is in
Jesus:
22 That ye [j]put off concerning [k]the former conversation [l]the old man, which is
corrupt according to the deceitful lusts;
23 And [m]be renewed in the spirit of your
mind;
24 And that ye [n]put on the new man,
which after God is created in righteousness
and true holiness.
25 Wherefore putting away lying, [o]speak
every man truth with his neighbour: for
[p]we are members one of another.
26 [q]Be ye angry, and sin not: let not the
sun go down upon your wrath:
27 [r]Neither give place to the devil.
28 Let him that stole steal no more: but
rather [s]let him labour, working with *his*
hands the thing which is good, that he may
have to give [t]to him that needeth.
29 [u]Let no corrupt communication proceed out of your mouth, but [v]that which is
good to the use of edifying, [w]that it may
minister grace unto the hearers.
30 And [x]grieve not the holy Spirit of God,
whereby ye are sealed unto the day of [y]re-
demption.
31 [z]Let all bitterness, and wrath, and anger, and clamour, and [a]evil speaking, be
put away from you, [b]with all malice:
32 And [c]be ye kind one to another, tenderhearted, [d]forgiving one another, even as
God for Christ's sake hath forgiven you.

5

Be [e]ye therefore followers of God, as
dear children;
2 And [f]walk in love, [g]as Christ also hath
loved us, and hath given himself for us an
offering and a sacrifice to God [h]for a sweet-
smelling savour.
3 But [i]fornication, and all uncleanness,
or covetousness, [j]let it not be once named
among you, as becometh saints;
4 [k]Neither filthiness, nor foolish talking,
nor jesting, [l]which are not convenient: but
rather giving of thanks.
5 For this ye know, that [m]no whore-
monger, nor unclean person, nor covetous
man, [n]who is an idolater, [o]hath any inheritance in the kingdom of Christ and of God.
6 [p]Let no man deceive you with vain
words: for because of these things [q]cometh
the wrath of God upon the children of disobedience.
7 Be not ye therefore partakers with
them.
8 [r]For ye were sometimes darkness, but
now [s]*are ye* light in the Lord: walk as [t]chil-
dren of light:
9 (For [u]the fruit of the Spirit *is* in all goodness and righteousness and truth;)
10 [v]Proving what is acceptable unto the
Lord.
11 And [w]have no fellowship with [x]the
unfruitful works of darkness, but rather
[y]reprove *them*.
12 [z]For it is a shame even to speak of
those things which are done of them in secret.

4:1 [v]Philem. 1 [w]Phil. 1:27; 1 Thess. 2:12 **4:2** [x]Acts 20:19; Col. 3:12 **4:3** [y]Col. 3:14 **4:4** [z]Rom. 12:5 [a]1 Cor. 12:4 **4:5** [b]1 Cor. 1:13 [c]Jude 3 [d]Gal. 3:27 **4:6** [e]Mal. 2:10 [f]Rom. 11:36 **4:7** [g]Rom. 12:3 **4:8** [h]Ps. 68:18 [i]Judg. 5:12 **4:9** [j]John 3:13 **4:10** [k]Acts 1:9; Heb. 4:14 [l]Acts 2:33 **4:11** [m]1 Cor. 12:28 [n]Acts 21:8 [o]Acts 20:28 [p]Rom. 12:7 **4:12** [q]1 Cor. 12:7 [r]1 Cor. 14:26 [s]Col. 1:24 **4:13** [t]Col. 2:2 [u]1 Cor. 14:20 **4:14** [v]Isa. 28:9 [w]Heb. 13:9 [x]Matt. 11:7 [y]Rom. 16:18 **4:15** [z]Zech. 8:16; 1 John 3:18 [a]Col. 1:18 **4:16** [b]Col. 2:19 **4:17** [c]Col. 3:7 [d]Rom. 1:21 **4:18** [e]Acts 26:18 [f]Gal. 4:8 [g]Rom. 1:21 **4:19** [h]1 Tim. 4:2 [i]Rom. 1:24 **4:22** [j]Col. 2:11; 1 Pet. 2:1 [k]Col. 3:7 [l]Rom. 6:6 **4:23** [m]Rom. 12:2 **4:24** [n]Rom. 6:4; Gal. 6:15; Col. 3:10 **4:25** [o]Zech. 8:16 [p]Rom. 12:5 **4:26** [q]Ps. 4:4 **4:27** [r]2 Cor. 2:10; 1 Pet. 5:9 **4:28** [s]Acts 20:35; 2 Thess. 3:8 [t]Luke 3:11 **4:29** [u]Matt. 12:36 [v]Col. 4:6 [w]Col. 3:16 **4:30** [x]Isa. 7:13; 1 Thess. 5:19 [y]Luke 21:28 **4:31** [z]Col. 3:8 [a]Tit. 3:2; 1 Pet. 2:1 [b]Tit. 3:3 **4:32** [c]2 Cor. 2:10 [d]Matt. 6:14 **5:1** [e]Matt. 5:45 **5:2** [f]John 13:34; 1 John 3:11 [g]Gal. 1:4; 1 John 3:16 [h]Gen. 8:21; 2 Cor. 2:15 **5:3** [i]Rom. 6:13; 2 Cor. 12:21; Col. 3:5 [j]1 Cor. 5:1 **5:4** [k]Matt. 12:35 [l]Rom. 1:28 **5:5** [m]1 Cor. 6:9 [n]Col. 3:5 [o]Gal. 5:21 **5:6** [p]Jer. 29:8; Col. 2:4; 2 Thess. 2:3 [q]Rom. 1:18 **5:8** [r]Isa. 9:2; Acts 26:18; Rom. 1:21; 1 Pet. 2:9 [s]John 8:12; 1 Thess. 5:5; 1 John 2:9 [t]Luke 16:8 **5:9** [u]Gal. 5:22 **5:10** [v]Rom. 12:2; 1 Thess. 5:21; 1 Tim. 2:3 **5:11** [w]1 Cor. 5:9; 2 Thess. 3:6 [x]Rom. 6:21 [y]Lev. 19:17 **5:12** [z]Rom. 1:24

13 But [a]all things that are reproved are made manifest by the light: for whatsoever doth make manifest is light.

14 Wherefore he saith, [b]Awake thou that sleepest, and [c]arise from the dead, and Christ shall give thee light.

15 [d]See then that ye walk circumspectly, not as fools, but as wise,

16 [e]Redeeming the time, [f]because the days are evil.

17 [g]Wherefore be ye not unwise, but [h]understanding [i]what the will of the Lord *is*.

18 And [j]be not drunk with wine, wherein is excess; but be filled with the Spirit;

19 Speaking to yourselves [k]in psalms and hymns and spiritual songs, singing and making melody in your heart to the Lord;

20 [l]Giving thanks always for all things unto God and the Father [m]in the name of our Lord Jesus Christ;

21 [n]Submitting yourselves one to another in the fear of God.

22 [o]Wives, submit yourselves unto your own husbands, as unto the Lord.

23 For [p]the husband is the head of the wife, even as [q]Christ is the head of the church: and he is the saviour of the body.

24 Therefore as the church is subject unto Christ, so *let* the wives *be* to their own husbands [r]in every thing.

25 [s]Husbands, love your wives, even as Christ also loved the church, and [t]gave himself for it;

26 That he might sanctify and cleanse it [u]with the washing of water [v]by the word,

27 [w]That he might present it to himself a glorious church, [x]not having spot, or wrinkle, or any such thing; but that it should be holy and without blemish.

28 So ought men to love their wives as their own bodies. He that loveth his wife loveth himself.

29 For no man ever yet hated his own flesh; but nourisheth and cherisheth it, even as the Lord the church:

30 For [y]we are members of his body, of his flesh, and of his bones.

31 [z]For this cause shall a man leave his father and mother, and shall be joined unto his wife, and they [a]two shall be one flesh.

32 This is a great mystery: but I speak concerning Christ and the church.

33 Nevertheless [b]let every one of you in particular so love his wife even as himself; and the wife *see* that she [c]reverence *her* husband.

6 Children, [d]obey your parents in the Lord: for this is right.

2 [e]Honour thy father and mother; (which is the first commandment with promise;)

3 That it may be well with thee, and thou mayest live long on the earth.

4 And, [f]ye fathers, provoke not your children to wrath: but [g]bring them up in the nurture and admonition of the Lord.

5 [h]Servants, be obedient to them that are *your* masters according to the flesh, [i]with fear and trembling, [j]in singleness of your heart, as unto Christ;

6 [k]Not with eyeservice, as menpleasers; but as the servants of Christ, doing the will of God from the heart;

7 With good will doing service, as to the Lord, and not to men:

8 [l]Knowing that whatsoever good thing any man doeth, the same shall he receive of the Lord, [m]whether *he be* bond or free.

9 And, ye [n]masters, do the same things unto them, [o]forbearing threatening: knowing that [p]your Master also is in heaven; [q]neither is there respect of persons with him.

10 Finally, my brethren, be strong in the Lord, and [r]in the power of his might.

11 [s]Put on the whole armour of God, that ye may be able to stand against the wiles of the devil.

12 For we wrestle not against [t]flesh and blood, but against [u]principalities, against powers, against [v]the rulers of the darkness of this world, against spiritual wickedness in high *places*.

13 [w]Wherefore take unto you the whole armour of God, that ye may be able to withstand in the evil day, and having done all, to stand.

14 Stand therefore, [x]having your loins girt about with truth, and [y]having on the breastplate of righteousness;

15 [z]And your feet shod with the preparation of the gospel of peace;

16 Above all, taking [a]the shield of faith, wherewith ye shall be able to quench all the fiery darts of the wicked.

17 And [b]take the helmet of salvation, and [c]the sword of the Spirit, which is the word of God:

18 [d]Praying always with all prayer and supplication in the Spirit, and [e]watching thereunto with all perseverance and [f]supplication for all saints;

19 [g]And for me, that utterance may be given unto me, that I may open my mouth [h]boldly, to make known the mystery of the gospel,

20 For which [i]I am an ambassador [j]in bonds: that therein [k]I may speak boldly, as I ought to speak.

21 But [l]that ye also may know my affairs, *and* how I do, [m]Tychicus, a beloved brother and faithful minister in the Lord, shall make known to you all things:

22 [n]Whom I have sent unto you for the same purpose, that ye might know our affairs, and *that* he might comfort your hearts.

23 [o]Peace *be* to the brethren, and love with faith, from God the Father and the Lord Jesus Christ.

24 Grace *be* with all them that love our Lord Jesus Christ [p]in sincerity. Amen.

5:13 *a*John 3:20
5:14 *b*Isa. 60:1; 1 Cor. 15:34; 1 Thess. 5:6 *c*John 5:25; Col. 3:1
5:15 *d*Col. 4:5
5:16 *e*Col. 4:5 *f*Eccl. 11:2
5:17 *g*Col. 4:5 *h*Rom. 12:2 *i*1 Thess. 4:3
5:18 *j*Prov. 20:1; Luke 21:34
5:19 *k*Acts 16:25; Col. 3:16; Jam. 5:13
5:20 *l*Ps. 34:1; Col. 3:17; 1 Thess. 5:18 *m*Heb. 13:15
5:21 *n*Phil. 2:3
5:22 *o*Gen. 3:16; Col. 3:18; Tit. 2:5
5:23 *p*1 Cor. 11:3 *q*Col. 1:18
5:24 *r*Col. 3:20
5:25 *s*Col. 3:19 *t*Acts 20:28
5:26 *u*John 3:5; Heb. 10:22; 1 John 5:6 *v*John 15:3
5:27 *w*2 Cor. 11:2 *x*SSol. 4:7
5:30 *y*Gen. 2:23; 1 Cor. 6:15
5:31 *z*Gen. 2:24; Mark 10:7 *a*1 Cor. 6:16
5:33 *b*Col. 3:19 *c*1 Pet. 3:6
6:1 *d*Prov. 23:22
6:2 *e*Ex. 20:12; Jer. 35:18; Ezek. 22:7; Matt. 15:4; Mark 7:10
6:4 *f*Col. 3:21 *g*Gen. 18:19; Ps. 78:4; Prov. 19:18
6:5 *h*Col. 3:22; Tit. 2:9; 1 Pet. 2:18 *i*2 Cor. 7:15 *j*1 Chron. 29:17
6:6 *k*Col. 3:22
6:8 *l*Rom. 2:6; Col. 3:24 *m*Gal. 3:28
6:9 *n*Col. 4:1 *o*Lev. 25:43 *p*John 13:13 *q*Rom. 2:11
6:10 *r*Col. 1:11
6:11 *s*Rom. 13:12; 1 Thess. 5:8
6:12 *t*Matt. 16:17 *u*Rom. 8:38 *v*Luke 22:53; Col. 1:13
6:13 *w*2 Cor. 10:4
6:14 *x*Isa. 11:5; 1 Pet. 1:13 *y*Isa. 59:17; 1 Thess. 5:8
6:15 *z*Isa. 52:7
6:16 *a*1 John 5:4
6:17 *b*Isa. 59:17 *c*Heb. 4:12
6:18 *d*Luke 18:1; Col. 4:2; 1 Thess. 5:17 *e*Matt. 26:41 *f*Phil. 1:4
6:19 *g*Acts 4:29; 2 Thess. 3:1 *h*2 Cor. 3:12
6:20 *i*2 Cor. 5:20 *j*Acts 26:29; 2 Tim. 1:16; Philem. 10 *k*Acts 28:31; 1 Thess. 2:2
6:21 *l*Col. 4:7 *m*Acts 20:4; Tit. 3:12
6:22 *n*Col. 4:8
6:23 *o*1 Pet. 5:14
6:24 *p*Tit. 2:7

PHILIPPIANS

Paul acknowledges himself as the author of Philippians, which was probably written about A.D. 61. Philippians begins with a greeting and prayer for the church at Philippi followed by a brief description of Paul's current circumstances. Chapter two presents an exhortation for humility using Christ as the example. Philippians 2:5–11 provides a clear picture of Christ as the humble servant. Chapters three and four contain various warnings against Judaizers, other examples of Paul's own life in Christ, and exhortations concerning peace and prayer.

I. Greetings and intercessory prayer to Philippi, 1:1–1:11
II. Paul's circumstances at that time, 1:12–1:30
III. The humility of Christ, 2:1–2:11
IV. Practicing humility, 2:12–2:30
V. Warning against Judaizers, 3:1–3:3
VI. Paul reflects on his own life, 3:4–4:1
VII. Exhortations to the church at Philippi, 4:2–4:23

1 Paul and Timotheus, the servants of
Jesus Christ, To all the saints [a]in Christ
Jesus which are at Philippi, with the bish-
ops and deacons:
2 [b]Grace *be* unto you, and peace, from
God our Father, and *from* the Lord Jesus
Christ.
3 [c]I thank my God upon every remembrance of you,
4 Always in every prayer of mine for you
all making request with joy,
5 [d]For your fellowship in the gospel from
the first day until now;
6 Being confident of this very thing, that
he which hath begun [e]a good work in you
will perform *it* until the day of Jesus Christ:
7 Even as it is meet for me to think this of
you all, because I have you [f]in my heart;
inasmuch as both in [g]my bonds, and in the
defense and confirmation of the gospel, ye
all are partakers of my grace.
8 For [h]God is my record, how greatly I
long after you all in the bowels of Jesus
Christ.
9 And this I pray, [i]that your love may
abound yet more and more in knowledge
and *in* all judgment;
10 That [j]ye may approve things that are
excellent; [k]that ye may be sincere and without offence [l]till the day of Christ;
11 Being filled with the fruits of righteousness, [m]which are by Jesus Christ,
[n]unto the glory and praise of God.
12 But I would ye should understand,
brethren, that the things *which happened*
unto me have fallen out rather unto the furtherance of the gospel;
13 So that my bonds in Christ are manifest in all the palace, and in all other *places;*
14 And many of the brethren in the Lord,
waxing confident by my bonds, are much
more bold to speak the word without fear.
15 Some indeed preach Christ even of
envy and strife; and some also of good will:
16 The one preach Christ of contention,
not sincerely, supposing to add affliction to
my bonds:
17 But the other of love, knowing that I
am set for the defence of the gospel.
18 What then? notwithstanding, every
way, whether in pretence, or in truth, Christ
is preached; and I therein do rejoice, yea,
and will rejoice.
19 For I know that this shall turn to my
salvation [o]through your prayer, and the
supply of [p]the Spirit of Jesus Christ,
20 According to my [q]earnest expectation
and *my* hope, that [r]in nothing I shall be
ashamed, but *that* [s]with all boldness, as
always, *so* now also Christ shall be magnified in my body, whether *it be* by life, or by
death.
21 For to me to live *is* Christ, and to die *is*
gain.
22 But if I live in the flesh, this *is* the fruit
of my labour: yet what I shall choose I wot
not.
23 For [t]I am in a strait betwixt two, having a desire to [u]depart, and to be with
Christ; which is far better:
24 Nevertheless to abide in the flesh *is*
more needful for you.
25 And having this confidence, I know
that I shall abide and continue with you all
for your furtherance and joy of faith;
26 That [v]your rejoicing may be more
abundant in Jesus Christ for me by my coming to you again.
27 Only [w]let your conversation be as it
becometh the gospel of Christ: that whether
I come and see you, or else be absent, I may
hear of your affairs, that ye stand fast in one
spirit, [x]with one mind [y]striving together
for the faith of the gospel;
28 And in nothing terrified by your adversaries: [z]which is to them an evident token
of perdition, [a]but to you of salvation, and
that of God.

1:1 [a]1 Cor. 1:2
1:2 [b]Rom. 1:7; 1 Pet. 1:2
1:3 [c]Rom. 1:8; Eph. 1:15; Col. 1:3; 2 Thess. 1:3
1:5 [d]Rom. 12:13
1:6 [e]John 6:29
1:7 [f]2 Cor. 3:2 [g]Eph. 3:1; 2 Tim. 1:8
1:8 [h]Rom. 1:9; 1 Thess. 2:5
1:9 [i]1 Thess. 3:12
1:10 [j]Rom. 2:18 [k]Acts 24:16 [l]1 Cor. 1:8
1:11 [m]John 15:4; Col. 1:6 [n]John 15:8
1:19 [o]2 Cor. 1:11 [p]Rom. 8:9
1:20 [q]Rom. 8:19 [r]Rom. 5:5 [s]Eph. 6:19
1:23 [t]2 Cor. 5:8 [u]2 Tim. 4:6
1:26 [v]2 Cor. 1:14
1:27 [w]Eph. 4:1; 1 Thess. 2:12 [x]1 Cor. 1:10 [y]Jude 3
1:28 [z]2 Thess. 1:5 [a]Rom. 8:17

29 For unto you [b]it is given in the behalf of Christ, [c]not only to believe on him, but also to suffer for his sake;

30 [d]Having the same conflict [e]which ye saw in me, and now hear *to be* in me.

2 If *there be* therefore any consolation in Christ, if any comfort of love, [f]if any fellowship of the Spirit, if any [g]bowels and mercies,

2 [h]Fulfil ye my joy, [i]that ye be likeminded, having the same love, *being* of one accord, of one mind.

3 [j]*Let* nothing *be done* through strife or vainglory; but [k]in lowliness of mind let each esteem other better than themselves.

4 [l]Look not every man on his own things, but every man also on the things of others.

5 [m]Let this mind be in you, which was also in Christ Jesus:

6 Who, [n]being in the form of God, [o]thought it not robbery to be equal with God:

7 [p]But made himself of no reputation, and took upon him the form [q]of a servant, and [r]was made in the likeness of men:

8 And being found in fashion as a man, he humbled himself, and [s]became obedient unto death, even the death of the cross.

9 Wherefore God also [t]hath highly exalted him, and [u]given him a name which is above every name:

10 [v]That at the name of Jesus every knee should bow, of *things* in heaven, and *things* in earth, and *things* under the earth;

11 And [w]*that* every tongue should confess that Jesus Christ *is* Lord, to the glory of God the Father.

12 Wherefore, my beloved, as ye have always obeyed, not as in my presence only, but now much more in my absence, work out your own salvation with [x]fear and trembling.

13 For [y]it is God which worketh in you both to will and to do of *his* good pleasure.

14 Do all things [z]without murmurings and [a]disputings:

15 That ye may be blameless and harmless, [b]the sons of God, without rebuke, [c]in the midst of [d]a crooked and perverse nation, among whom [e]ye shine as lights in the world;

16 Holding forth the word of life; that [f]I may rejoice in the day of Christ, that [g]I have not run in vain, neither laboured in vain.

17 Yea, and if [h]I be offered upon the sacrifice [i]and service of your faith, [j]I joy, and rejoice with you all.

18 For the same cause also do ye joy, and rejoice with me.

19 But I trust in the Lord Jesus to send [k]Timotheus shortly unto you, that I also may be of good comfort, when I know your state.

20 For I have no man [l]likeminded, who will naturally care for your state.

21 For all [m]seek their own, not the things which are Jesus Christ's.

22 But ye know the proof of him, [n]that, as a son with the father, he hath served with me in the gospel.

23 Him therefore I hope to send presently, so soon as I shall see how it will go with me.

24 But [o]I trust in the Lord that I also myself shall come shortly.

25 Yet I supposed it necessary to send to you Epaphroditus, my brother, and companion in labour, and [p]fellowsoldier, [q]but your messenger, and [r]he that ministered to my wants.

26 For he longed after you all, and was full of heaviness, because that ye had heard that he had been sick.

27 For indeed he was sick nigh unto death: but God had mercy on him; and not on him only, but on me also, lest I should have sorrow upon sorrow.

28 I sent him therefore the more carefully, that, when ye see him again, ye may rejoice, and that I may be the less sorrowful.

29 Receive him therefore in the Lord with all gladness; and [s]hold such in reputation:

30 Because for the work of Christ he was nigh unto death, not regarding his life, [t]to supply your lack of service toward me.

3 Finally, my brethren, [u]rejoice in the Lord. To write the same things to you, to me indeed *is* not grievous, but for you *it is* safe.

2 [v]Beware of dogs, beware of [w]evil workers, [x]beware of the concision.

3 For we are [y]the circumcision, [z]which worship God in the spirit, and [a]rejoice in Christ Jesus, and have no confidence in the flesh.

4 Though [b]I might also have confidence in the flesh. If any other man thinketh that he hath whereof he might trust in the flesh, I more:

5 [c]Circumcised the eighth day, [d]of the stock of Israel, [e]*of* the tribe of Benjamin, [f]an Hebrew of the Hebrews; as touching the law, [g]a Pharisee;

6 [h]Concerning zeal, [i]persecuting the church; [j]touching the righteousness which is in the law, [k]blameless.

7 But [l]what things were gain to me, those I counted loss for Christ.

8 Yea doubtless, and I count all things *but* loss [m]for the excellency of the knowledge of Christ Jesus my Lord: for whom I have suffered the loss of all things, and do count them *but* dung, that I may win Christ,

9 And be found in him, not having [n]mine own righteousness, which is of the law, but [o]that which is through the faith of Christ, the righteousness which is of God by faith:

10 That I may know him, and the power of his resurrection, and [p]the fellowship of his sufferings, being made conformable unto his death;

1:29 [b]Acts 5:41 [c]Eph. 2:8
1:30 [d]Col. 2:1 [e]Acts 16:19
2:1 [f]2 Cor. 13:14 [g]Col. 3:12
2:2 [h]John 3:29 [i]Rom. 12:16; 2 Cor. 13:11; 1 Pet. 3:8
2:3 [j]Gal. 5:26 [k]Rom. 12:10; 1 Pet. 5:5
2:4 [l]1 Cor. 10:24
2:5 [m]Matt. 11:29; 1 Pet. 2:21; 1 John 2:6
2:6 [n]John 1:1; Col. 1:15; Heb. 1:3 [o]John 5:18
2:7 [p]Ps. 22:6; Dan. 9:26; Mark 9:12 [q]Isa. 42:1; Zech. 3:8; Matt. 20:28 [r]John 1:14; Gal. 4:4; Heb. 2:14
2:8 [s]Matt. 26:39; Heb. 5:8
2:9 [t]John 17:1; Heb. 2:9 [u]Eph. 1:20
2:10 [v]Isa. 45:23; Rom. 14:11; Rev. 5:13
2:11 [w]John 13:13; Rom. 14:9; 1 Cor. 8:6
2:12 [x]Eph. 6:5
2:13 [y]2 Cor. 3:5
2:14 [z]1 Cor. 10:10 [a]Rom. 14:1
2:15 [b]Matt. 5:45 [c]1 Pet. 2:12 [d]Deut. 32:5 [e]Matt. 5:14
2:16 [f]2 Cor. 1:14 [g]Gal. 2:2
2:17 [h]2 Tim. 4:6 [i]Rom. 15:16 [j]2 Cor. 7:4
2:19 [k]Rom. 16:21
2:20 [l]Ps. 55:13
2:21 [m]1 Cor. 10:24
2:22 [n]1 Cor. 4:17; 2 Tim. 1:2
2:24 [o]Philem. 22
2:25 [p]Philem. 2 [q]2 Cor. 8:23 [r]2 Cor. 11:9
2:29 [s]1 Cor. 16:18; 1 Tim. 5:17
2:30 [t]1 Cor. 16:17
3:1 [u]2 Cor. 13:11
3:2 [v]Isa. 56:10 [w]2 Cor. 11:13 [x]Rom. 2:28
3:3 [y]Deut. 10:16; Rom. 2:29; Col. 2:11 [z]John 4:23 [a]Gal. 6:14
3:4 [b]2 Cor. 11:18
3:5 [c]Gen. 17:12 [d]2 Cor. 11:22 [e]Rom. 11:1 [f]2 Cor. 11:22 [g]Acts 23:6
3:6 [h]Acts 22:3 [i]Acts 8:3 [j]Rom. 10:5 [k]Luke 1:6
3:7 [l]Matt. 13:44
3:8 [m]Isa. 53:11; John 17:3; 1 Cor. 2:2
3:9 [n]Rom. 10:3 [o]Rom. 1:17
3:10 [p]Rom. 6:3; 2 Tim. 2:11; 1 Pet. 4:13

11 If by any means I might [q]attain unto
the resurrection of the dead.
12 Not as though I had already [r]attained,
either were already [s]perfect: but I follow
after, if that I may apprehend that for which
also I am apprehended of Christ Jesus.
13 Brethren, I count not myself to have
apprehended: but *this* one thing *I do*, [t]for-
getting those things which are behind, and
[u]reaching forth unto those things which are
before,
14 [v]I press toward the mark for the prize
of [w]the high calling of God in Christ Jesus.
15 Let us therefore, as many as be [x]per-
fect, [y]be thus minded: and if in any thing ye
be otherwise minded, God shall reveal even
this unto you.
16 Nevertheless, whereto we have already attained, [z]let us walk [a]by the same
rule, let us mind the same thing.
17 Brethren, [b]be followers together of
me, and mark them which walk so as [c]ye
have us for an ensample.
18 (For many walk, of whom I have told
you often, and now tell you even weeping,
that they are [d]the enemies of the cross of
Christ:
19 [e]Whose end *is* destruction, [f]whose
God *is their* belly, and [g]*whose* glory *is* in
their shame, [h]who mind earthly things.)
20 For [i]our conversation is in heaven;
[j]from whence also we [k]look for the Saviour, the Lord Jesus Christ:
21 [l]Who shall change our vile body, that
it may be fashioned like unto his glorious
body, [m]according to the working whereby
he is able [n]even to subdue all things unto
himself.

4 Therefore, my brethren dearly beloved
and longed for, [o]my joy and crown, so
stand fast in the Lord, *my* dearly beloved.
2 I beseech Euodias, and beseech Syntyche, that they be of the same mind in the
Lord.
3 And I intreat thee also, true yokefellow,
help those women which [p]laboured with
me in the gospel, with Clement also, and
with other my fellowlabourers, whose
names *are* in [q]the book of life.
4 [r]Rejoice in the Lord alway: *and* again I
say, Rejoice.
5 Let your moderation be known unto all
men. [s]The Lord *is* at hand.
6 [t]Be careful for nothing; but in every
thing by prayer and supplication with
thanksgiving let your requests be made
known unto God.

3:11 [q]Acts 26:7
3:12 [r]1 Tim. 6:12 [s]Heb. 12:23
3:13 [t]Ps. 45:10; 2 Cor. 5:16 [u]1 Cor. 9:24
3:14 [v]2 Tim. 4:7 [w]Heb. 3:1
3:15 [x]1 Cor. 2:6 [y]Gal. 5:10
3:16 [z]Rom. 12:16 [a]Gal. 6:16
3:17 [b]1 Cor. 4:16 [c]1 Pet. 5:3
3:18 [d]Gal. 1:7
3:19 [e]2 Cor. 11:15 [f]Rom. 16:18; Tit. 1:11 [g]Hos. 4:7; Gal. 6:13 [h]Rom. 8:5
3:20 [i]Eph. 2:6 [j]Acts 1:11 [k]1 Cor. 1:7; Tit. 2:13
3:21 [l]1 Cor. 15:43; 1 John 3:2 [m]Eph. 1:19 [n]1 Cor. 15:26
4:1 [o]2 Cor. 1:14
4:3 [p]Rom. 16:3 [q]Ex. 32:32; Dan. 12:1; Luke 10:20
4:4 [r]Rom. 12:12; 1 Pet. 4:13
4:5 [s]2 Thess. 2:2; Jam. 5:8; 1 Pet. 4:7
4:6 [t]Ps. 55:22; Matt. 6:25; Luke 12:22
4:7 [u]John 14:27; Col. 3:15
4:8 [v]1 Thess. 5:22
4:9 [w]Rom. 15:33; 2 Cor. 13:11; 1 Thess. 5:23
4:10 [x]2 Cor. 11:9
4:11 [y]1 Tim. 6:6
4:12 [z]1 Cor. 4:11
4:13 [a]John 15:5
4:15 [b]2 Cor. 11:8
4:17 [c]Rom. 15:28
4:18 [d]Heb. 13:16 [e]2 Cor. 9:12
4:19 [f]Ps. 23:1 [g]Eph. 1:7
4:20 [h]Rom. 16:27
4:21 [i]Gal. 1:2
4:23 [j]Rom. 16:24

7 And [u]the peace of God, which passeth
all understanding, shall keep your hearts
and minds through Christ Jesus.
8 Finally, brethren, whatsoever things
are true, whatsoever things *are* honest,
whatsoever things *are* just, whatsoever
things *are* pure, whatsoever things *are*
lovely, [v]whatsoever things *are* of good report; if *there be* any virtue, and if *there be*
any praise, think on these things.
9 Those things, which ye have both
learned, and received, and heard, and seen
in me, do: and [w]the God of peace shall be
with you.
10 But I rejoiced in the Lord greatly, that
now at the last [x]your care of me hath flourished again; wherein ye were also careful,
but ye lacked opportunity.
11 Not that I speak in respect of want: for
I have learned, in whatsoever state I am,
[y]*therewith* to be content.
12 [z]I know both how to be abased, and I
know how to abound: every where and in
all things I am instructed both to be full and
to be hungry, both to abound and to suffer
need.
13 I can do all things [a]through Christ
which strengtheneth me.
14 Notwithstanding ye have well done,
that ye did communicate with my affliction.
15 Now ye Philippians know also, that
in the beginning of the gospel, when I departed from Macedonia, [b]no church communicated with me as concerning giving
and receiving, but ye only.
16 For even in Thessalonica ye sent once
and again unto my necessity.
17 Not because I desire a gift: but I desire
[c]fruit that may abound to your account.
18 But I have all, and abound: I am full,
having received of Epaphroditus the things
which were sent from you, [d]an odour of a
sweet smell, [e]a sacrifice acceptable, well-
pleasing to God.
19 But my God [f]shall supply all your
need [g]according to his riches in glory by
Christ Jesus.
20 [h]Now unto God and our Father *be*
glory for ever and ever. Amen.
21 Salute every saint in Christ Jesus. The
brethren [i]which are with me greet you.
22 All the saints salute you, chiefly they
that are of Caesar's household.
23 [j]The grace of our Lord Jesus Christ *be*
with you all. Amen.

COLOSSIANS

Paul is the author of Colossians, which was probably written about A.D. 61. A form of heresy had crept into the Colosse church that involved forms of mysticism, elevation of ceremony, secret or hidden knowledge, and the worship of angels. Although the heresy is not addressed specifically, Paul preaches the sufficiency of Christ in all things, and a list of rules for a Christ-centered life. Colossians 1:15–18 is a particularly powerful statement of who Christ is.

I. Greetings and prayer for the Colosse church, 1:1–1:14
II. The supremacy of Christ, 1:15–1:29
III. Christ better than philosophy, 2:1–2:10
IV. Christ better than legalism, 2:11–2:17
V. Christ better than mysticism, 2:18–2:23
VI. The Christian life, 3:1–4:6
VII. Closing remarks and greetings, 4:7–4:18

---

1 Paul, [a]an apostle of Jesus Christ by the
will of God, and Timotheus *our* brother,
2 To the saints [b]and faithful brethren in
Christ which are at Colosse: [c]Grace *be* unto
you, and peace, from God our Father and
the Lord Jesus Christ.
3 [d]We give thanks to God and the Father
of our Lord Jesus Christ, praying always for
you,
4 [e]Since we heard of your faith in Christ
Jesus, and of [f]the love *which ye have* to all
the saints,
5 For the hope [g]which is laid up for you
in heaven, whereof ye heard before in the
word of the truth of the gospel;
6 Which is come unto you, [h]as *it is* in all
the world; and [i]bringeth forth fruit, as *it*
doth also in you, since the day ye heard *of*
it, and knew [j]the grace of God in truth:
7 As ye also learned of [k]Epaphras our
dear fellowservant, who is for you [l]a faithful minister of Christ;
8 Who also declared unto us your [m]love
in the Spirit.
9 [n]For this cause we also, since the day
we heard *it*, do not cease to pray for you,
and to desire [o]that ye might be filled with
[p]the knowledge of his will [q]in all wisdom
and spiritual understanding;
10 [r]That ye might walk worthy of the
Lord [s]unto all pleasing, [t]being fruitful in
every good work, and increasing in the
knowledge of God;
11 [u]Strengthened with all might, according to his glorious power, [v]unto all patience
and longsuffering [w]with joyfulness;
12 [x]Giving thanks unto the Father, which
hath made us meet to be partakers of [y]the
inheritance of the saints in light:
13 Who hath delivered us from [z]the
power of darkness, [a]and hath translated *us*
into the kingdom of his dear Son:
14 [b]In whom we have redemption
through his blood, *even* the forgiveness of
sins:
15 Who is [c]the image of the invisible
God, [d]the firstborn of every creature:
16 For [e]by him were all things created,
that are in heaven, and that are in earth,
visible and invisible, whether *they be*
thrones, or [f]dominions, or principalities, or
powers: all things were created [g]by him,
and for him:
17 [h]And he is before all things, and by
him all things consist.
18 And [i]he is the head of the body, the
church: who is the beginning, [j]the firstborn
from the dead; that in all *things* he might
have the preeminence.
19 For it pleased *the Father* that [k]in him
should all fulness dwell;
20 And, [l]having made peace through the
blood of his cross, [m]by him to reconcile [n]all
things unto himself; by him, *I say*, whether
they be things in earth, or things in heaven.
21 And you, [o]that were sometime alienated and enemies in *your* mind [p]by wicked
works, yet now hath he reconciled
22 [q]In the body of his flesh through
death, [r]to present you holy and unblameable and unreproveable in his sight:
23 If ye continue in the faith [s]grounded
and settled, and *be* [t]not moved away from
the hope of the gospel, which ye have heard,
[u]*and* which was preached to every creature
which is under heaven; [v]whereof I Paul am
made a minister;
24 [w]Who now rejoice in my sufferings
[x]for you, and fill up [y]that which is behind
of the afflictions of Christ in my flesh for
[z]his body's sake, which is the church:
25 Whereof I am made a minister, according to [a]the dispensation of God which is
given to me for you, to fulfil the word of
God;
26 *Even* [b]the mystery which hath been
hid from ages and from generations, [c]but
now is made manifest to his saints:

1:1 [a]Eph. 1:1
1:2 [b]1 Cor. 4:17 [c]Gal. 1:3
1:3 [d]1 Cor. 1:4; Philem. 1:3
1:4 [e]Eph. 1:15 [f]Heb. 6:10
1:5 [g]2 Tim. 4:8
1:6 [h]Matt. 24:14; Rom. 10:18 [i]Mark 4:8; Phil. 1:11 [j]2 Cor. 6:1; Tit. 2:11; 1 Pet. 5:12
1:7 [k]Philem. 23 [l]2 Cor. 11:23
1:8 [m]Rom. 15:30
1:9 [n]Eph. 1:15 [o]1 Cor. 1:5 [p]Rom. 12:2 [q]Eph. 1:8
1:10 [r]Eph. 4:1; 1 Thess. 2:12 [s]1 Thess. 4:1 [t]John 15:16; Phil. 1:11; Tit. 3:1
1:11 [u]Eph. 3:16 [v]Eph. 4:2 [w]Acts 5:41
1:12 [x]Eph. 5:20 [y]Acts 26:18
1:13 [z]Eph. 6:12; 1 Pet. 2:9 [a]1 Thess. 2:12
1:14 [b]Eph. 1:7
1:15 [c]2 Cor. 4:4 [d]Rev. 3:14
1:16 [e]John 1:3; Eph. 3:9; Heb. 1:2 [f]Rom. 8:38; 1 Pet. 3:22 [g]Rom. 11:36
1:17 [h]John 1:1
1:18 [i]Eph. 1:10 [j]Acts 26:23; Rev. 1:5
1:19 [k]John 1:16
1:20 [l]Eph. 2:14 [m]2 Cor. 5:18 [n]Eph. 1:10
1:21 [o]Eph. 2:1 [p]Tit. 1:15
1:22 [q]Eph. 2:15 [r]Luke 1:75; 1 Thess. 4:7; Tit. 2:14
1:23 [s]Eph. 3:17 [t]John 15:6 [u]Rom. 10:18 [v]Acts 1:17; Eph. 3:7; 1 Tim. 2:7
1:24 [w]Rom. 5:3 [x]Eph. 3:1 [y]2 Cor. 1:5; 2 Tim. 1:8 [z]Eph. 1:23
1:25 [a]1 Cor. 9:17; Eph. 3:2
1:26 [b]Rom. 16:25; Eph. 3:9 [c]Matt. 13:11

27 [d]To whom God would make known what *is* [e]the riches of the glory of this mystery among the Gentiles; which is Christ in you, [f]the hope of glory:

28 Whom we preach, [g]warning every man, and teaching every man in all wisdom; [h]that we may present every man perfect in Christ Jesus:

29 [i]Whereunto I also labour, striving [j]according to his working, which worketh in me mightily.

2 For I would that ye knew what great [k]conflict I have for you, and *for* them at Laodicea, and *for* as many as have not seen my face in the flesh;

2 [l]That their hearts might be comforted, being knit together in love, and unto all riches of the full assurance of understanding, [m]to the acknowledgement of the mystery of God, and of the Father, and of Christ;

3 [n]In whom are hid all the treasures of wisdom and knowledge.

4 And this I say, [o]lest any man should beguile you with enticing words.

5 For [p]though I be absent in the flesh, yet am I with you in the spirit, joying and beholding [q]your order, and the [r]stedfastness of your faith in Christ.

6 [s]As ye have therefore received Christ Jesus the Lord, *so* walk ye in him:

7 [t]Rooted and built up in him, and stablished in the faith, as ye have been taught, abounding therein with thanksgiving.

8 [u]Beware lest any man spoil you through philosophy and vain deceit, after [v]the tradition of men, after the [w]rudiments of the world, and not after Christ.

9 For [x]in him dwelleth all the fulness of the Godhead bodily.

10 [y]And ye are complete in him, [z]which is the head of all principality and power:

11 In whom also ye are [a]circumcised with the circumcision made without hands, in [b]putting off the body of the sins of the flesh by the circumcision of Christ:

12 [c]Buried with him in baptism, wherein also ye are risen with *him* through [d]the faith of the operation of God, [e]who hath raised him from the dead.

13 [f]And you, being dead in your sins and the uncircumcision of your flesh, hath he quickened together with him, having forgiven you all trespasses;

14 [g]Blotting out the handwriting of ordinances that was against us, which was contrary to us, and took it out of the way, nailing it to his cross;

15 *And* [h]having spoiled [i]principalities and powers, he made a shew of them openly, triumphing over them in it.

16 Let no man therefore [j]judge you [k]in meat, or in drink, or in respect [l]of an holyday, or of the new moon, or of the sabbath *days*:

17 [m]Which are a shadow of things to come; but the body *is* of Christ.

18 Let no man beguile you of your reward in a voluntary humility and worshipping of angels, intruding into those things [n]which he hath not seen, vainly puffed up by his fleshly mind,

19 And not holding [o]the Head, from which all the body by joints and bands having nourishment ministered, and knit together, increaseth with the increase of God.

20 Wherefore if ye be [p]dead with Christ from the rudiments of the world, [q]why, as though living in the world, are ye subject to ordinances,

21 ([r]Touch not; taste not; handle not;

22 Which all are to perish with the using;) [s]after the commandments and doctrines of men?

23 [t]Which things have indeed a shew of wisdom in will worship, and humility, and neglecting of the body; not in any honour to the satisfying of the flesh.

3 If ye then [u]be risen with Christ, seek those things which are above, where [v]Christ sitteth on the right hand of God.

2 Set your affection on things above, not on things on the earth.

3 [w]For ye are dead, [x]and your life is hid with Christ in God.

4 [y]When Christ, *who is* [z]our life, shall appear, then shall ye also appear with him [a]in glory.

5 [b]Mortify therefore [c]your members which are upon the earth; [d]fornication, uncleanness, inordinate affection, [e]evil concupiscence, and covetousness, [f]which is idolatry:

6 [g]For which things' sake the wrath of God cometh on [h]the children of disobedience:

7 [i]In the which ye also walked some time, when ye lived in them.

8 [j]But now ye also put off all these; anger, wrath, malice, blasphemy, [k]filthy communication out of your mouth.

9 [l]Lie not one to another, [m]seeing that ye have put off the old man with his deeds;

10 And have put on the new *man*, which [n]is renewed in knowledge [o]after the image of him that [p]created him:

11 Where there is neither [q]Greek nor Jew, circumcision nor uncircumcision, Barbarian, Scythian, bond *nor* free: [r]but Christ *is* all, and in all.

12 [s]Put on therefore, [t]as the elect of God, holy and beloved, [u]bowels of mercies, kindness, humbleness of mind, meekness, longsuffering;

13 [v]Forbearing one another, and forgiving one another, if any man have a quarrel against any: even as Christ forgave you, so also *do* ye.

14 [w]And above all these things [x]*put on* charity, which is the [y]bond of perfectness.

15 And let [z]the peace of God rule in your hearts, [a]to the which also ye are called [b]in one body; and be ye thankful.

16 Let the word of Christ dwell in you richly in all wisdom; teaching and admon-

1:27 d2 Cor. 2:14
eRom. 9:23
f1 Tim. 1:1
1:28 gActs 20:20
h2 Cor. 11:2
1:29 i1 Cor. 15:10
jEph. 1:19
2:1 kPhil. 1:30
2:2 l2 Cor. 1:6
mPhil. 3:8
2:3 n1 Cor. 1:24
2:4 oRom. 16:18;
Eph. 4:14
2:5 p1 Cor. 5:3
q1 Cor. 14:40
r1 Pet. 5:9
2:6 s1 Thess. 4:1
2:7 tEph. 2:21
2:8 uJer. 29:8;
Eph. 5:6; Heb. 13:9
vMatt. 15:2
wGal. 4:3
2:9 xJohn 1:14
2:10 yJohn 1:16
zEph. 1:20
2:11
aDeut. 10:16;
Rom. 2:29; Phil. 3:3
bRom. 6:6
2:12 cRom. 6:4
dEph. 1:19
eActs 2:24
2:13 fEph. 2:1
2:14 gEph. 2:15
2:15 hGen. 3:15;
Isa. 53:12;
Matt. 12:29;
John 12:31;
Eph. 4:8 iEph. 6:12
2:16 jRom. 14:3
kRom. 14:2
lRom. 14:5
2:17 mHeb. 8:5
2:18 nEzek. 13:3
2:19 oEph. 4:15
2:20 pRom. 6:3;
Eph. 2:15 qGal. 4:3
2:21 r1 Tim. 4:3
2:22 sIsa. 29:13;
Tit. 1:14
2:23 t1 Tim. 4:8
3:1 uRom. 6:5
vRom. 8:34
3:3 wRom. 6:2
x2 Cor. 5:7
3:4 y1 John 3:2
zJohn 11:25
a1 Cor. 15:43
3:5 bRom. 8:13
cRom. 6:13
dEph. 5:3
e1 Thess. 4:5
fEph. 5:5
3:6 gRom. 1:18;
Rev. 22:15
hEph. 2:2
3:7 iRom. 6:19;
Eph. 2:2; Tit. 3:3
3:8 jEph. 4:22;
Heb. 12:1;
Jam. 1:21
kEph. 4:29
3:9 lLev. 19:11
mEph. 4:22
3:10 nRom. 12:2
oEph. 4:23
pEph. 2:10
3:11 qRom. 10:12;
Gal. 3:28; Eph. 6:8
rEph. 1:23
3:12 sEph. 4:24
t1 Thess. 1:4;
2 Pet. 1:10
uGal. 5:22;
Eph. 4:2
3:13 vMark 11:25
3:14 w1 Pet. 4:8
xJohn 13:34;
1 Cor. 13; Eph. 5:2;
1 Tim. 1:5;
1 John 3:23
yEph. 4:3
3:15 zRom. 14:17
a1 Cor. 7:15
bEph. 2:16

ishing one another [c]in psalms and hymns and spiritual songs, singing with grace in your hearts to the Lord.

17 And [d]whatsoever ye do in word or deed, *do* all in the name of the Lord Jesus, [e]giving thanks to God and the Father by him.

18 [f]Wives, submit yourselves unto your own husbands, [g]as it is fit in the Lord.

19 [h]Husbands, love *your* wives, and be not [i]bitter against them.

20 [j]Children, obey *your* parents [k]in all things: for this is well pleasing unto the Lord.

21 [l]Fathers, provoke not your children *to anger*, lest they be discouraged.

22 [m]Servants, obey in all things *your* masters [n]according to the flesh; not with eyeservice, as menpleasers; but in singleness of heart, fearing God:

23 [o]And whatsoever ye do, do *it* heartily, as to the Lord, and not unto men;

24 [p]Knowing that of the Lord ye shall receive the reward of the inheritance: [q]for ye serve the Lord Christ.

25 But he that doeth wrong shall receive for the wrong which he hath done: and [r]there is no respect of persons.

4 Masters, [s]give unto *your* servants that which is just and equal; knowing that ye also have a Master in heaven.

2 [t]Continue in prayer, and watch in the same with thanksgiving;

3 [u]Withal praying also for us, that God would [v]open unto us a door of utterance, to speak [w]the mystery of Christ, [x]for which I am also in bonds:

4 That I may make it manifest, as I ought to speak.

5 [y]Walk in wisdom toward them that are without, [z]redeeming the time.

6 Let your speech *be* alway [a]with grace, [b]seasoned with salt, [c]that ye may know how ye ought to answer every man.

3:16 [c]1 Cor. 14:26
3:17 [d]1 Cor. 10:31 [e]Rom. 1:8; 1 Thess. 5:18; Heb. 13:15
3:18 [f]Eph. 5:22; 1 Pet. 3:1 [g]Eph. 5:3
3:19 [h]Eph. 5:25 [i]Eph. 4:31
3:20 [j]Eph. 6:1 [k]Eph. 5:24
3:21 [l]Eph. 6:4
3:22 [m]Eph. 6:5; Tit. 2:9; 1 Pet. 2:18 [n]Philem. 16
3:23 [o]Eph. 6:6
3:24 [p]Eph. 6:8 [q]1 Cor. 7:22
3:25 [r]Deut. 10:17; Eph. 6:9; 1 Pet. 1:17
4:1 [s]Eph. 6:9
4:2 [t]Luke 18:1; Eph. 6:18; 1 Thess. 5:17
4:3 [u]Eph. 6:19 [v]1 Cor. 16:9 [w]Matt. 13:11; Eph. 6:19 [x]Eph. 6:20
4:5 [y]Eph. 5:15 [z]Eph. 5:16
4:6 [a]Eccl. 10:12 [b]Mark 9:50 [c]1 Pet. 3:15
4:7 [d]Eph. 6:21
4:8 [e]Eph. 6:22
4:9 [f]Philem. 10
4:10 [g]Acts 19:29 [h]Acts 15:37
4:12 [i]Philem. 23 [j]Rom. 15:30 [k]Matt. 5:48; Phil. 3:15; Heb. 5:14
4:14 [l]2 Tim. 4:11 [m]2 Tim. 4:10
4:15 [n]Rom. 16:5
4:16 [o]1 Thess. 5:27
4:17 [p]Philem. 2 [q]1 Tim. 4:6
4:18 [r]1 Cor. 16:21 [s]Heb. 13:3 [t]Heb. 13:25

7 [d]All my state shall Tychicus declare unto you, *who is* a beloved brother, and a faithful minister and fellowservant in the Lord:

8 [e]Whom I have sent unto you for the same purpose, that he might know your estate, and comfort your hearts;

9 With [f]Onesimus, a faithful and beloved brother, who is *one* of you. They shall make known unto you all things which *are done* here.

10 [g]Aristarchus my fellowprisoner saluteth you, and [h]Marcus, sister's son to Barnabas, (touching whom ye received commandments: if he come unto you, receive him;)

11 And Jesus, which is called Justus, who are of the circumcision. These only *are my* fellowworkers unto the kingdom of God, which have been a comfort unto me.

12 [i]Epaphras, who is *one* of you, a servant of Christ, saluteth you, always [j]labouring fervently for you in prayers, that ye may stand [k]perfect and complete in all the will of God.

13 For I bear him record, that he hath a great zeal for you, and them *that are* in Laodicea, and them in Hierapolis.

14 [l]Luke, the beloved physician, and [m]Demas, greet you.

15 Salute the brethren which are in Laodicea, and Nymphas, and [n]the church which is in his house.

16 And when [o]this epistle is read among you, cause that it be read also in the church of the Laodiceans; and that ye likewise read the *epistle* from Laodicea.

17 And say to [p]Archippus, Take heed to [q]the ministry which thou hast received in the Lord, that thou fulfil it.

18 [r]The salutation by the hand of me Paul. [s]Remember my bonds. [t]Grace *be* with you. Amen.

1 THESSALONIANS

Paul acknowledges himself as the author of 1 Thessalonians, which was probably written about A.D. 51. Paul begins his letter to the church at Thessalonica by commending them for their steadfastness. He then reaffirms his own ministry toward the church and his concerns for their sufferings and testings. Chapters four and five contain practical instructions concerning daily living and proceed to a discussion of events to take place in the end times. First Thessalonians 4:13–5:11 contains some of the most vivid descriptions of Christ's return.

I. Greetings and commendations for the church at Thessalonica, 1:1–1:10
II. Paul reaffirms the validity of his ministry, 2:1–2:12
III. Paul's concern for the church, 2:13–3:13
IV. Daily living as a Christian, 4:1–4:12
V. Christ's return, 4:13–5:11
VI. Further instructions for daily living as a Christian, 5:12–5:22
VII. Closing prayer and greetings, 5:23–5:28

---

1 Paul, and [a]Silvanus, and Timotheus, unto the church of the Thessalonians *which is* in God the Father and *in* the Lord Jesus Christ: [b]Grace *be* unto you, and peace, from God our Father, and the Lord Jesus Christ.

2 [c]We give thanks to God always for you all, making mention of you in our prayers;

3 Remembering without ceasing [d]your work of faith, [e]and labour of love, and patience of hope in our Lord Jesus Christ, in the sight of God and our Father;

4 Knowing, brethren beloved, [f]your election of God.

5 For [g]our gospel came not unto you in word only, but also in power, and [h]in the Holy Ghost, [i]and in much assurance; as [j]ye know what manner of men we were among you for your sake.

6 And [k]ye became followers of us, and of the Lord, having received the word in much affliction, [l]with joy of the Holy Ghost:

7 So that ye were ensamples to all that believe in Macedonia and Achaia.

8 For from you [m]sounded out the word of the Lord not only in Macedonia and Achaia, but also [n]in every place your faith to God-ward is spread abroad; so that we need not to speak any thing.

9 For they themselves shew of us what manner of entering in we had unto you, [o]and how ye turned to God from idols to serve the living and true God;

10 And [p]to wait for his Son [q]from heaven, [r]whom he raised from the dead, *even* Jesus, which delivered us [s]from the wrath to come.

2 For yourselves, brethren, know our entrance in unto you, that it was not in vain:

2 But even after that we had suffered before, and were shamefully entreated, as ye know, at [t]Philippi, we were bold in our God [u]to speak unto you the gospel of God [v]with much contention.

3 [w]For our exhortation *was* not of deceit, nor of uncleanness, nor in guile:

4 But as [x]we were allowed of God [y]to be put in trust with the gospel, even so we speak; [z]not as pleasing men, but God, [a]which trieth our hearts.

5 For [b]neither at any time used we flattering words, as ye know, nor a cloke of covetousness; [c]God *is* witness:

6 [d]Nor of men sought we glory, neither of you, nor *yet* of others, when [e]we might have been [f]burdensome, [g]as the apostles of Christ.

7 But [h]we were gentle among you, even as a nurse cherisheth her children:

8 So being affectionately desirous of you, we were willing [i]to have imparted unto you, not the gospel of God only, but also [j]our own souls, because ye were dear unto us.

9 For ye remember, brethren, our labour and travail: for [k]labouring night and day, [l]because we would not be chargeable unto any of you, we preached unto you the gospel of God.

10 Ye *are* witnesses, and God *also*, [m]how holily and justly and unblameably we behaved ourselves among you that believe:

11 As ye know how we exhorted and comforted and charged every one of you, as a father *doth* his children,

12 [n]That ye would walk worthy of God, [o]who hath called you unto his kingdom and glory.

13 For this cause also thank we God without ceasing, because, when ye received the word of God which ye heard of us, ye received *it* [p]not *as* the word of men, but as it is in truth, the word of God, which effectually worketh also in you that believe.

14 For ye, brethren, became followers [q]of the churches of God which in Judaea are in

1:1 *a*2 Cor. 1:19; 1 Pet. 5:12 *b*Eph. 1:2
1:2 *c*Rom. 1:8; Philem. 4
1:3 *d*John 6:29; 2 Thess. 1:3; Jam. 2:17 *e*Rom. 16:6
1:4 *f*Col. 3:12
1:5 *g*Mark 16:20 *h*2 Cor. 6:6 *i*Col. 2:2 *j*2 Thess. 3:7
1:6 *k*1 Cor. 4:16; 2 Thess. 3:9 *l*Acts 5:41
1:8 *m*Rom. 10:18 *n*Rom. 1:8
1:9 *o*1 Cor. 12:2
1:10 *p*Rom. 2:7; Tit. 2:13; 2 Pet. 3:12 *q*Acts 1:11 *r*Acts 2:24 *s*Matt. 3:7
2:2 *t*Acts 16:22 *u*Acts 17:2 *v*Phil. 1:30
2:3 *w*2 Cor. 7:2
2:4 *x*1 Cor. 7:25 *y*1 Cor. 9:17; Tit. 1:3 *z*Gal. 1:10 *a*Prov. 17:3
2:5 *b*Acts 20:33 *c*Rom. 1:9
2:6 *d*John 5:41 *e*1 Cor. 9:4; 2 Thess. 3:9; Philem. 8 *f*2 Cor. 11:9 *g*1 Cor. 9:1
2:7 *h*1 Cor. 2:3; 2 Tim. 2:24
2:8 *i*Rom. 1:11 *j*2 Cor. 12:15
2:9 *k*Acts 20:34; 2 Cor. 11:9; 2 Thess. 3:8 *l*2 Cor. 12:13
2:10 *m*2 Cor. 7:2
2:12 *n*Eph. 4:1; Col. 1:10 *o*1 Cor. 1:9; 2 Tim. 1:9
2:13 *p*Matt. 10:40; 2 Pet. 3:2
2:14 *q*Gal. 1:22

Christ Jesus: for [r]ye also have suffered like things of your own countrymen, [s]even as they *have* of the Jews:

15 [t]Who both killed the Lord Jesus, and [u]their own prophets, and have persecuted us; and they please not God, [v]and are contrary to all men:

16 [w]Forbidding us to speak to the Gentiles that they might be saved, [x]to fill up their sins alway: [y]for the wrath is come upon them to the uttermost.

17 But we, brethren, being taken from you for a short time [z]in presence, not in heart, endeavoured the more abundantly to see your face with great desire.

18 Wherefore we would have come unto you, even I Paul, once and again; but [a]Satan hindered us.

19 For [b]what *is* our hope, or joy, or [c]crown of rejoicing? *Are* not even ye in the presence of our Lord Jesus Christ [d]at his coming?

20 For ye are our glory and joy.

3 Wherefore when we could no longer forbear, [e]we thought it good to be left at Athens alone;

2 And sent [f]Timotheus, our brother, and minister of God, and our fellowlabourer in the gospel of Christ, to establish you, and to comfort you concerning your faith:

3 [g]That no man should be moved by these afflictions: for yourselves know that [h]we are appointed thereunto.

4 [i]For verily, when we were with you, we told you before that we should suffer tribulation; even as it came to pass, and ye know.

5 For this cause, when I could no longer forbear, I sent to know your faith, [j]lest by some means the tempter have tempted you, and [k]our labour be in vain.

6 [l]But now when Timotheus came from you unto us, and brought us good tidings of your faith and charity, and that ye have good remembrance of us always, desiring greatly to see us, [m]as we also *to see* you:

7 Therefore, brethren, [n]we were comforted over you in all our affliction and distress by your faith:

8 For now we live, if ye [o]stand fast in the Lord.

9 For what thanks can we render to God again for you, for all the joy wherewith we joy for your sakes before our God;

10 [p]Night and day [q]praying exceedingly that we might see your face, [r]and might perfect that which is lacking in your faith?

11 Now God himself and our Father, and our Lord Jesus Christ, [s]direct our way unto you.

12 And the Lord make you to increase and abound in love [t]one toward another, and toward all *men*, even as we *do* toward you:

13 To the end he may [u]stablish your hearts unblameable in holiness before God, even our Father, at the coming of our Lord Jesus Christ [v]with all his saints.

2:14 [r]Acts 17:5 [s]Heb. 10:33
2:15 [t]Acts 2:23 [u]Matt. 5:12; Acts 7:52 [v]Esth. 3:8
2:16 [w]Luke 11:52 [x]Gen. 15:16 [y]Matt. 24:6
2:17 [z]1 Cor. 5:3
2:18 [a]Rom. 1:13
2:19 [b]2 Cor. 1:14 [c]Prov. 16:31 [d]1 Cor. 15:23
3:1 [e]Acts 17:15
3:2 [f]Rom. 16:21; 2 Cor. 1:19
3:3 [g]Eph. 3:13 [h]Acts 9:16; 2 Tim. 3:12; 1 Pet. 2:21
3:4 [i]Acts 20:24
3:5 [j]1 Cor. 7:5 [k]Gal. 2:2
3:6 [l]Acts 18:1 [m]Phil. 1:8
3:7 [n]2 Cor. 1:4
3:8 [o]Phil. 4:1
3:10 [p]Acts 26:7 [q]Rom. 1:10 [r]2 Cor. 13:9
3:11 [s]Mark 1:3
3:12 [t]2 Pet. 1:7
3:13 [u]1 Cor. 1:8; 2 Thess. 2:17; 1 John 3:20 [v]Zech. 14:5
4:1 [w]Phil. 1:27 [x]Col. 1:10
4:3 [y]Rom. 12:2 [z]Eph. 5:27 [a]1 Cor. 6:15; Col. 3:5
4:4 [b]Rom. 6:19
4:5 [c]Col. 3:5 [d]Eph. 4:17 [e]1 Cor. 15:34; Eph. 2:12; 2 Thess. 1:8
4:6 [f]Lev. 19:11 [g]2 Thess. 1:8
4:7 [h]Lev. 11:44; Heb. 12:14; 1 Pet. 1:14
4:8 [i]Luke 10:16 [j]1 Cor. 2:10
4:9 [k]Jer. 31:34; Heb. 8:11; 1 John 2:20 [l]Matt. 22:39; Eph. 5:2; 1 Pet. 4:8
4:11 [m]2 Thess. 3:11 [n]Acts 20:35; 2 Thess. 3:7
4:12 [o]Rom. 13:13; Col. 4:5; 1 Pet. 2:12
4:13 [p]Lev. 19:28; 2 Sam. 12:20 [q]Eph. 2:12
4:14 [r]1 Cor. 15:13 [s]1 Cor. 15:18
4:15 [t]1 Kings 13:17 [u]1 Cor. 15:51
4:16 [v]Matt. 24:30; 2 Thess. 1:7 [w]1 Cor. 15:52 [x]1 Cor. 15:23
4:17 [y]1 Cor. 15:51 [z]Acts 1:9 [a]John 12:26
5:1 [b]Matt. 24:3
5:2 [c]Matt. 24:43; 2 Pet. 3:10; Rev. 3:3
5:3 [d]Isa. 13:6-9; 2 Thess. 1:9

4 Furthermore then we beseech you, brethren, and exhort *you* by the Lord Jesus, [w]that as ye have received of us how ye ought to walk [x]and to please God, *so* ye would abound more and more.

2 For ye know what commandments we gave you by the Lord Jesus.

3 For this is [y]the will of God, *even* [z]your sanctification, [a]that ye should abstain from fornication:

4 [b]That every one of you should know how to possess his vessel in sanctification and honour;

5 [c]Not in the lust of concupiscence, [d]even as the Gentiles [e]which know not God:

6 [f]That no *man* go beyond and defraud his brother in *any* matter: because that the Lord [g]*is* the avenger of all such, as we also have forewarned you and testified.

7 For God hath not called us unto uncleanness, [h]but unto holiness.

8 [i]He therefore that despiseth, despiseth not man, but God, [j]who hath also given unto us his holy Spirit.

9 But as touching brotherly love ye need not that I write unto you: for [k]ye yourselves are taught of God [l]to love one another.

10 And indeed ye do it toward all the brethren which are in all Macedonia: but we beseech you, brethren, that ye increase more and more;

11 And that ye study to be quiet, and [m]to do your own business, and [n]to work with your own hands, as we commanded you;

12 [o]That ye may walk honestly toward them that are without, and *that* ye may have lack of nothing.

13 But I would not have you to be ignorant, brethren, concerning them which are asleep, that ye sorrow not, [p]even as others [q]which have no hope.

14 For [r]if we believe that Jesus died and rose again, even so [s]them also which sleep in Jesus will God bring with him.

15 For this we say unto you [t]by the word of the Lord, [u]that we which are alive *and* remain unto the coming of the Lord shall not prevent them which are asleep.

16 For [v]the Lord himself shall descend from heaven with a shout, with the voice of the archangel, and with [w]the trump of God: [x]and the dead in Christ shall rise first:

17 [y]Then we which are alive *and* remain shall be caught up together with them [z]in the clouds, to meet the Lord in the air: and so [a]shall we ever be with the Lord.

18 Wherefore comfort one another with these words.

5 But of [b]the times and the seasons, brethren, ye have no need that I write unto you.

2 For yourselves know perfectly that [c]the day of the Lord so cometh as a thief in the night.

3 For when they shall say, Peace and safety; then [d]sudden destruction cometh

upon them, [e]as travail upon a woman with
child; and they shall not escape.
4 [f]But ye, brethren, are not in darkness,
that that day should overtake you as a thief.
5 Ye are all [g]the children of light, and the
children of the day: we are not of the night,
nor of darkness.
6 [h]Therefore let us not sleep, as *do* others; but [i]let us watch and be sober.
7 For [j]they that sleep sleep in the night;
and they that be drunken [k]are drunken in
the night.
8 But let us, who are of the day, be sober,
[l]putting on the breastplate of faith and
love; and for an helmet, the hope of salvation.
9 For [m]God hath not appointed us to
wrath, [n]but to obtain salvation by our Lord
Jesus Christ,
10 [o]Who died for us, that, whether we
wake or sleep, we should live together with
him.
11 Wherefore comfort yourselves together, and edify one another, even as also
ye do.
12 And we beseech you, brethren, [p]to
know them which labour among you, and
are over you in the Lord, and admonish you;
13 And to esteem them very highly in love
for their work's sake. [q]*And* be at peace
among yourselves.
14 Now we exhort you, brethren, [r]warn
them that are unruly, [s]comfort the feeble-
minded, [t]support the weak, [u]be patient toward all *men.*
15 [v]See that none render evil for evil unto
any *man;* but ever [w]follow that which is
good, both among yourselves, and to all
men.
16 [x]Rejoice evermore.
17 [y]Pray without ceasing.
18 [z]In every thing give thanks: for this is
the will of God in Christ Jesus concerning
you.
19 [a]Quench not the Spirit.
20 [b]Despise not prophesyings.
21 [c]Prove all things; [d]hold fast that
which is good.
22 Abstain from all appearance of evil.
23 And [e]the very God of peace sanctify
you wholly; and *I pray God* your whole
spirit and soul and body [f]be preserved
blameless unto the coming of our Lord
Jesus Christ.
24 [g]Faithful *is* he that calleth you, who
also will do *it.*
25 Brethren, [h]pray for us.
26 [i]Greet all the brethren with an holy
kiss.
27 I charge you by the Lord that this
[j]epistle be read unto all the holy brethren.
28 [k]The grace of our Lord Jesus Christ *be*
with you. Amen.

5:3 [e]Jer. 13:21
5:4 [f]Rom. 13:12
5:5 [g]Eph. 5:8
5:6 [h]Matt. 25:5 [i]Matt. 24:42; 1 Pet. 5:8
5:7 [j]Luke 21:34; 1 Cor. 15:34; Eph. 5:14 [k]Acts 2:15
5:8 [l]Isa. 59:17
5:9 [m]Rom. 9:22; Jude 4 [n]2 Thess. 2:13
5:10 [o]Rom. 14:8
5:12 [p]1 Cor. 16:18; 1 Tim. 5:17; Heb. 13:7
5:13 [q]Mark 9:50
5:14 [r]2 Thess. 3:11 [s]Heb. 12:12 [t]Rom. 14:1 [u]Gal. 5:22; Col. 3:12; 2 Tim. 4:2
5:15 [v]Lev. 19:18; Matt. 5:39; Rom. 12:17; 1 Pet. 3:9 [w]Gal. 6:10
5:16 [x]2 Cor. 6:10
5:17 [y]Luke 18:1; Eph. 6:18; Col. 4:2
5:18 [z]Eph. 5:20
5:19 [a]1 Cor. 14:30; 1 Tim. 4:14; 2 Tim. 1:6
5:20 [b]1 Cor. 14:1
5:21 [c]1 Cor. 2:11 [d]Phil. 4:8
5:23 [e]Phil. 4:9 [f]1 Cor. 1:8
5:24 [g]1 Cor. 1:9
5:25 [h]Col. 4:3
5:26 [i]Rom. 16:16 **5:27** [j]Col. 4:16 **5:28** [k]Rom. 16:20

2 THESSALONIANS

Paul acknowledges himself as the author of 2 Thessalonians, which was probably written about A.D. 51. Chapter 1 contains Paul's greeting and encouragement. Chapter 2 describes the final days, its events and people and information concerning Satan and the Antichrist. Chapter 3 encourages the church at Thessalonica to continue to pray and stand fast in the face of adversity.

- I. Greetings and words of encouragement, 1:1–1:12
- II. Prophecies concerning the final days, 2:1–2:17
- III. Exhortations and closing greetings, 3:1–3:18

---

1 Paul, [a]and Silvanus, and Timotheus, unto the the church of the Thessalonians [b]in God our Father and the Lord Jesus Christ:

2 [c]Grace unto you, and peace, from God our Father and the Lord Jesus Christ.

3 [d]We are bound to thank God always for you, brethren, as it is meet, because that your faith groweth exceedingly, and the charity of every one of you all toward each other aboundeth;

4 So that [e]we ourselves glory in you in the churches of God [f]for your patience and faith [g]in all your persecutions and tribulations that ye endure:

5 *Which is* [h]a manifest token of the righteous judgment of God, that ye may be counted worthy of the kingdom of God, [i]for which ye also suffer:

6 [j]Seeing *it is* a righteous thing with God to recompense tribulation to them that trouble you;

7 And to you who are troubled [k]rest with us, when [l]the Lord Jesus shall be revealed from heaven with his mighty angels,

8 [m]In flaming fire taking vengeance on them [n]that know not God, and [o]that obey not the gospel of our Lord Jesus Christ:

9 [p]Who shall be punished with everlasting destruction from the presence of the Lord, and [q]from the glory of his power;

10 [r]When he shall come to be glorified in his saints, [s]and to be admired in all them that believe (because our testimony among you was believed) in that day.

11 Wherefore also we pray always for you, that our God would count you worthy of *this* calling, and fulfil all the good pleasure of *his* goodness, and [t]the work of faith with power:

12 [u]That the name of our Lord Jesus Christ may be glorified in you, and ye in him, according to the grace of our God and the Lord Jesus Christ.

2 Now we beseech you, brethren, [v]by the coming of our Lord Jesus Christ, [w]and *by* our gathering together unto him,

2 [x]That ye be not soon shaken in mind, or be troubled, neither by spirit, nor by word, nor by letter as from us, as that the day of Christ is at hand.

3 [y]Let no man deceive you by any means: for *that day shall not come,* [z]except there come a falling away first, and [a]that man of sin be revealed, [b]the son of perdition;

4 Who opposeth and [c]exalteth himself [d]above all that is called God, or that is worshipped; so that he as God sitteth in the temple of God, shewing himself that he is God.

5 Remember ye not, that, when I was yet with you, I told you these things?

6 And now ye know what withholdeth that he might be revealed in his time.

7 For [e]the mystery of iniquity doth already work: only he who now letteth *will let,* until he be taken out of the way.

8 And then shall that Wicked be revealed, [f]whom the Lord shall consume [g]with the spirit of his mouth, and shall destroy [h]with the brightness of his coming:

9 *Even him,* whose coming is [i]after the working of Satan with all power and [j]signs and lying wonders,

10 And with all deceivableness of unrighteousness in [k]them that perish; because they received not the love of the truth, that they might be saved.

11 And [l]for this cause God shall send them strong delusion, [m]that they should believe a lie:

12 That they all might be damned who believed not the truth, but [n]had pleasure in unrighteousness.

13 But we are bound to give thanks alway to God for you, brethren beloved of the Lord, because God [o]hath [p]from the beginning chosen you to salvation [q]through sanctification of the Spirit and belief of the truth:

14 Whereunto he called you by our gospel, to [r]the obtaining of the glory of our Lord Jesus Christ.

15 Therefore, brethren, [s]stand fast, and hold [t]the traditions which ye have been taught, whether by word, or our epistle.

16 Now our Lord Jesus Christ himself, and God, even our Father, [u]which hath loved us, and hath given *us* everlasting consolation and [v]good hope through grace,

17 Comfort your hearts, [w]and stablish you in every good word and work.

1:1 [a]2 Cor. 1:19 [b]1 Thess. 1:1
1:2 [c]1 Cor. 1:3
1:3 [d]1 Thess. 1:2
1:4 [e]2 Cor. 7:14 [f]1 Thess. 1:3 [g]1 Thess. 2:14
1:5 [h]Phil. 1:28 [i]1 Thess. 2:14
1:6 [j]Rev. 6:10
1:7 [k]Rev. 14:13 [l]1 Thess. 4:16
1:8 [m]Heb. 10:27; Rev. 21:8 [n]Ps. 79:6 [o]Rom. 2:8
1:9 [p]Phil. 3:19 [q]Deut. 33:2
1:10 [r]Ps. 89:7 [s]Ps. 68:35
1:11 [t]1 Thess. 1:3
1:12 [u]1 Pet. 1:7
2:1 [v]1 Thess. 4:16 [w]Matt. 24:31; 1 Thess. 4:17
2:2 [x]Matt. 24:4; 1 John 4:1
2:3 [y]Matt. 24:4 [z]1 Tim. 4:1 [a]Dan. 7:25; Rev. 13:11 [b]John 17:12
2:4 [c]Isa. 14:13; Dan. 7:25; Rev. 13:6 [d]1 Cor. 8:5
2:7 [e]1 John 2:18
2:8 [f]Dan. 7:10 [g]Job 4:9; Hos. 6:5; Rev. 2:16 [h]Heb. 10:27
2:9 [i]John 8:41; Rev. 18:23 [j]Deut. 13:1; Rev. 13:13
2:10 [k]2 Cor. 2:15
2:11 [l]1 Kings 22:22; Rom. 1:24 [m]Matt. 24:5
2:12 [n]Rom. 1:32
2:13 [o]1 Thess. 1:4 [p]Eph. 1:4 [q]Luke 1:75
2:14 [r]John 17:22; 1 Pet. 5:10
2:15 [s]1 Cor. 16:13 [t]1 Cor. 11:2
2:16 [u]1 John 4:10 [v]1 Pet. 1:3
2:17 [w]1 Cor. 1:8; 1 Pet. 5:10

3 Finally, brethren, [x]pray for us, that the word of the Lord may have *free* course, and be glorified, even as *it is* with you:

2 And [y]that we may be delivered from unreasonable and wicked men: [z]for all *men* have not faith.

3 But [a]the Lord is faithful, who shall stablish you, and [b]keep *you* from evil.

4 And [c]we have confidence in the Lord touching you, that ye both do and will do the things which we command you.

5 And [d]the Lord direct your hearts into the love of God, and into the patient waiting for Christ.

6 Now we command you, brethren, in the name of our Lord Jesus Christ, [e]that ye withdraw yourselves [f]from every brother that walketh [g]disorderly, and not after the tradition which he received of us.

7 For yourselves know [h]how ye ought to follow us: for [i]we behaved not ourselves disorderly among you;

8 Neither did we eat any man's bread for nought; but [j]wrought with labour and travail night and day, that we might not be chargeable to any of you:

9 [k]Not because we have not power, but to make ourselves an ensample unto you to follow us.

10 For even when we were with you, this we commanded you, [l]that if any would not work, neither should he eat.

11 For we hear that there are some which walk among you disorderly, [m]working not at all, but are busybodies.

12 [n]Now them that are such we command and exhort by our Lord Jesus Christ, [o]that with quietness they work, and eat their own bread.

13 But ye, brethren, [p]be not weary in well doing.

14 And if any man obey not our word by this epistle, note that man, and [q]have no company with him, that he may be ashamed.

15 [r]Yet count *him* not as an enemy, [s]but admonish *him* as a brother.

16 Now [t]the Lord of peace himself give you peace always by all means. The Lord *be* with you all.

17 [u]The salutation of Paul with mine own hand, which is the token in every epistle: so I write.

18 [v]The grace of our Lord Jesus Christ *be* with you all. Amen.

3:1 [x]Eph. 6:19; 1 Thess. 5:25
3:2 [y]Rom. 15:31 [z]Acts 28:24
3:3 [a]1 Cor. 1:9 [b]John 17:15
3:4 [c]2 Cor. 7:16
3:5 [d]1 Chron. 29:18
3:6 [e]Rom. 16:17; 2 John 10 [f]1 Cor. 5:11 [g]1 Thess. 4:11
3:7 [h]1 Cor. 4:16 [i]1 Thess. 2:10
3:8 [j]Acts 18:3; 1 Thess. 2:9
3:9 [k]1 Cor. 9:6
3:10 [l]Gen. 3:19
3:11 [m]1 Thess. 4:11; 1 Pet. 4:15
3:12 [n]1 Thess. 4:11 [o]Eph. 4:28
3:13 [p]Gal. 6:9
3:14 [q]Matt. 18:17
3:15 [r]Lev. 19:17 [s]Tit. 3:10
3:16 [t]Rom. 15:33; 2 Cor. 13:11; 1 Thess. 5:23
3:17 [u]1 Cor. 16:21
3:18 [v]Rom. 16:24

1 TIMOTHY

Paul is the author of 1 Timothy, which was probably written about A.D. 63. First Timothy contains information on the proper operation of a church, including the organization and requirements for church leadership. Practical advice such as dealing with various age groups in the church, proper public worship, the handling of money, and refuting false doctrines and teachers, make up the bulk of 1 Timothy.

I. Greetings to Timothy, 1:1–1:2
II. Contrast of sound and false doctrine, 1:3–1:11
III. Paul's personal testimony to Timothy, 1:12–1:20
IV. Pastoral instructions, 2:1–6:21

1 Paul, an apostle of Jesus Christ [a]by the commandment [b]of God our Saviour, and Lord Jesus Christ, [c]*which is* our hope;

2 Unto [d]Timothy, [e]*my* own son in the faith: [f]Grace, mercy, *and* peace, from God our Father and Jesus Christ our Lord.

3 As I besought thee to abide still at Ephesus, [g]when I went into Macedonia, that thou mightest charge some [h]that they teach no other doctrine,

4 [i]Neither give heed to fables and endless genealogies, which minister questions, rather than godly edifying which is in faith: *so do.*

5 Now [j]the end of the commandment is charity [k]out of a pure heart, and *of* a good conscience, and *of* faith unfeigned:

6 From which some having swerved have turned aside unto vain jangling;

7 Desiring to be teachers of the law; understanding neither what they say, nor whereof they affirm.

8 But we know that [l]the law *is* good, if a man use it lawfully;

9 [m]Knowing this, that the law is not made for a righteous man, but for the lawless and disobedient, for the ungodly and for sinners, for unholy and profane, for murderers of fathers and murderers of mothers, for manslayers,

10 For whoremongers, for them that defile themselves with mankind, for menstealers, for liars, for perjured persons, and if

1:1 [a]Acts 9:15 [b]Tit. 1:3 [c]Col. 1:27
1:2 [d]Acts. 16:1; Phil. 2:19; 1 Thess. 3:2 [e]Tit. 1:4 [f]Gal. 1:3; 1 Pet. 1:2
1:3 [g]Acts. 20:1 [h]Gal. 1:6
1:4 [i]2 Tim. 2:14
1:5 [j]Rom. 13:8 [k]2 Tim. 2:22
1:8 [l]Rom. 7:12
1:9 [m]Gal. 3:19

there be any other thing that is contrary [n]to sound doctrine;

11 According to the glorious gospel of the blessed God, [o]which was committed to my trust.

12 And I thank Christ Jesus our Lord, [p]who hath enabled me, [q]for that he counted me faithful, [r]putting me into the ministry;

13 [s]Who was before a blasphemer, and a persecutor, and injurious: but I obtained mercy, because [t]I did *it* ignorantly in unbelief.

14 [u]And the grace of our Lord was exceeding abundant [v]with faith [w]and love which is in Christ Jesus.

15 [x]This *is* a faithful saying, and worthy of all acceptation, that [y]Christ Jesus came into the world to save sinners; of whom I am chief.

16 Howbeit for this cause [z]I obtained mercy, that in me first Jesus Christ might shew forth all longsuffering, [a]for a pattern to them which should hereafter believe on him to life everlasting.

17 Now unto [b]the King eternal, [c]immortal, [d]invisible, [e]the only wise God, [f]*be* honour and glory for ever and ever. Amen.

18 This charge [g]I commit unto thee, son Timothy, according to the prophecies which went before on thee, that thou by them mightest [h]war a good warfare;

19 Holding faith, and a good conscience; which some having put away concerning faith have made shipwreck:

20 Of whom is [i]Hymenaeus and [j]Alexander; whom I have [k]delivered unto Satan, that they may learn not to [l]blaspheme.

2 I exhort therefore, that, first of all, supplications, prayers, intercessions, *and* giving of thanks, be made for all men;

2 [m]For kings, and [n]*for* all that are in authority; that we may lead a quiet and peaceable life in all godliness and honesty.

3 For this *is* [o]good and acceptable in the sight [p]of God our Saviour;

4 [q]Who will have all men to be saved, [r]and to come unto the knowledge of the truth.

5 [s]For *there is* one God, and [t]one mediator between God and men, the man Christ Jesus;

6 [u]Who gave himself a ransom for all, [v]to be testified [w]in due time.

7 [x]Whereunto I am ordained a preacher, and an apostle, ([y]I speak the truth in Christ, *and* lie not;) [z]a teacher of the Gentiles in faith and verity.

8 I will therefore that men pray [a]every where, [b]lifting up holy hands, without wrath and doubting.

9 In like manner also, that [c]women adorn themselves in modest apparel, with shamefacedness and sobriety; not with braided hair, or gold, or pearls, or costly array;

10 [d]But (which becometh women professing godliness) with good works.

1:10 [n]2 Tim. 4:3
1:11 [o]1 Cor. 9:17; Col. 1:25; 1 Thess. 2:4; Tit. 1:3
1:12 [p]2 Cor. 12:9 [q]1 Cor. 7:25 [r]2 Cor. 3:5
1:13 [s]Acts 8:3; Phil. 3:6 [t]Luke 23:34; Acts 3:17
1:14 [u]Rom. 5:20 [v]2 Tim. 1:13 [w]Luke 7:47
1:15 [x]2 Tim. 2:11 [y]Matt. 9:13; Luke 5:32; Rom. 5:8
1:16 [z]2 Cor. 4:1 [a]Acts 13:39
1:17 [b]Ps. 10:16 [c]Rom. 1:23 [d]John 1:18; 1 John 4:12 [e]Rom. 16:27 [f]1 Chron. 29:11
1:18 [g]2 Tim. 2:2 [h]2 Tim. 2:3
1:20 [i]2 Tim. 2:17 [j]2 Tim. 2:14 [k]1 Cor. 5:5 [l]Acts 13:45
2:2 [m]Ezra 6:10 [n]Rom. 13:1
2:3 [o]Rom. 12:2 [p]2 Tim. 1:9
2:4 [q]Ezek. 18:23; Tit. 2:11; 2 Pet. 3:9 [r]John 17:3
2:5 [s]Rom. 3:29 [t]Heb. 8:6
2:6 [u]Matt. 20:28; Eph. 1:7; Tit. 2:14 [v]1 Cor. 1:6; 2 Tim. 1:8 [w]Rom. 5:6; Eph. 1:9; Tit. 1:3
2:7 [x]Eph. 3:7 [y]Rom. 9:1 [z]Rom. 11:13
2:8 [a]Mal 1:11 [b]Ps. 134:2
2:9 [c]1 Pet. 3:3
2:10 [d]1 Pet. 3:4
2:12 [e]1 Cor. 14:34 [f]Eph. 5:24
2:13 [g]Gen. 1:27
2:14 [h]Gen. 3:6
3:1 [i]Acts 20:28 [j]Eph. 4:12
3:2 [k]Tit. 1:6 [l]2 Tim. 2:24
3:3 [m]Tit. 1:7 [n]2 Tim. 2:24 [o]1 Pet. 5:2 [p]2 Tim. 2:24
3:4 [q]Tit. 1:6
3:6 [r]Isa. 14:12
3:7 [s]Acts 22:12; 1 Thess. 4:12 [t]2 Tim. 2:26
3:8 [u]Acts 6:3 [v]Lev. 10:9
3:11 [w]Tit. 2:3
3:13 [x]Matt. 25:21
3:15 [y]Eph. 2:21
3:16 [z]John 1:14 [a]Matt. 3:16; Rom. 1:4; 1 Pet. 3:18 [b]Matt. 28:2; Luke 2:13; John 20:12; 1 Pet. 1:12 [c]Acts 10:34; Eph. 3:5; Rom. 10:18 [d]Col. 1:6 [e]Luke 24:51; 1 Pet. 3:22
4:1 [f]John 16:13; 2 Pet. 3:3; Jude 4 [g]1 Pet. 1:20

11 Let the woman learn in silence with all subjection.

12 But [e]I suffer not a woman to teach, [f]nor to usurp authority over the man, but to be in silence.

13 For [g]Adam was first formed, then Eve.

14 And [h]Adam was not deceived, but the woman being deceived was in the transgression.

15 Notwithstanding she shall be saved in childbearing, if they continue in faith and charity and holiness with sobriety.

3 This *is* a true saying, If a man desire the office of a [i]bishop, he desireth a good [j]work.

2 [k]A bishop then must be blameless, the husband of one wife, vigilant, sober, of good behaviour, given to hospitality, [l]apt to teach;

3 [m]Not given to wine, [n]no striker, [o]not greedy of filthy lucre; but [p]patient, not a brawler, not covetous;

4 One that ruleth well his own house, [q]having his children in subjection with all gravity;

5 (For if a man know not how to rule his own house, how shall he take care of the church of God?)

6 Not a novice, lest being lifted up with pride [r]he fall into the condemnation of the devil.

7 Moreover he must have a good report [s]of them which are without; lest he fall into reproach [t]and the snare of the devil.

8 Likewise *must* [u]the deacons *be* grave, not doubletongued, [v]not given to much wine, not greedy of filthy lucre;

9 Holding the mystery of the faith in a pure conscience.

10 And let these also first be proved; then let them use the office of a deacon, being *found* blameless.

11 [w]Even so *must their* wives *be* grave, not slanderers, sober, faithful in all things.

12 Let the deacons be the husbands of one wife, ruling their children and their own houses well.

13 For [x]they that have used the office of a deacon well purchase to themselves a good degree, and great boldness in the faith which is in Christ Jesus.

14 These things write I unto thee, hoping to come unto thee shortly:

15 But if I tarry long, that thou mayest know how thou oughtest to behave thyself [y]in the house of God, which is the church of the living God, the pillar and ground of the truth.

16 And without controversy great is the mystery of godliness: [z]God was manifest in the flesh, [a]justified in the Spirit, [b]seen of angels, [c]preached unto the Gentiles, [d]believed on in the world, [e]received up into glory.

4 Now the Spirit [f]speaketh expressly, that [g]in the latter times some shall de-

part from the faith, giving heed [h]to seduc-
ing spirits, [i]and doctrines of devils;
2 [j]Speaking lies in hypocrisy; [k]having
their conscience seared with a hot iron;
3 [l]Forbidding to marry, [m]*and command-*
ing to abstain from meats, which God hath
created [n]to be received [o]with thanksgiving
of them which believe and know the truth.
4 For [p]every creature of God *is* good, and
nothing to be refused, if it be received with
thanksgiving:
5 For it is sanctified by the word of God
and prayer.
6 If thou put the brethren in remembrance of these things, thou shalt be a good
minister of Jesus Christ, [q]nourished up in
the words of faith and of good doctrine,
whereunto thou hast attained.
7 But [r]refuse profane and old wives' fables, and [s]exercise thyself *rather* unto godliness.
8 For [t]bodily exercise profiteth little: but
godliness is profitable unto all things, [u]hav-
ing promise of the life that now is, and of
that which is to come.
9 This *is* a faithful saying and worthy of
all acceptation.
10 For therefore [v]we both labour and suffer reproach, because we trust in the living
God, [w]who is the Saviour of all men, specially of those that believe.
11 These things command and teach.
12 [x]Let no man despise thy youth; but
[y]be thou an example of the believers, in
word, in conversation, in charity, in spirit,
in faith, in purity.
13 Till I come, give attendance to reading,
to exhortation, to doctrine.
14 [z]Neglect not the gift that is in thee,
which was given thee by prophecy, [a]with
the laying on of the hands of the presbytery.
15 Meditate upon these things; give thyself wholly to them; that thy profiting may
appear to all.
16 [b]Take heed unto thyself, and unto the
doctrine; continue in them: for in doing this
thou shalt both [c]save thyself, and [d]them
that hear thee.

5

Rebuke [e]not an elder, but intreat *him* as
a father; *and* the younger men as brethren;
2 The elder women as mothers; the younger as sisters, with all purity.
3 Honour widows that are widows indeed.
4 But if any widow have children or nephews, let them learn first to shew piety at
home, and [f]to requite their parents: for that
is good and acceptable before God.
5 [g]Now she that is a widow indeed, and
desolate, trusteth in God, and [h]continueth
in supplications and prayers [i]night and
day.
6 [j]But she that liveth in pleasure is dead
while she liveth.
7 And these things give in charge, that
they may be blameless.
8 But if any provide not for his own, [k]and
specially for those of his own house, [l]he
hath denied the faith, [m]and is worse than an
infidel.
9 Let not a widow be taken into the number under threescore years old, [n]having
been the wife of one man,
10 Well reported of for good works; if she
have brought up children, if she have
[o]lodged strangers, if she have [p]washed the
saints' feet, if she have relieved the afflicted, if she have diligently followed every
good work.
11 But the younger widows refuse: for
when they have begun to wax wanton
against Christ, they will marry;
12 Having damnation, because they have
cast off their first faith.
13 [q]And withal they learn *to be* idle,
wandering about from house to house; and
not only idle, but tattlers also and busybodies, speaking things which they ought not.
14 [r]I will therefore that the younger
women marry, bear children, guide the
house, [s]give none occasion to the adversary to speak reproachfully.
15 For some are already turned aside after Satan.
16 If any man or woman that believeth
have widows, let them relieve them, and let
not the church be charged; that it may relieve them that are widows indeed.
17 [t]Let the elders that rule well [u]be
counted worthy of double honour, especially they who labour in the word and doctrine.
18 For the scripture saith, [v]Thou shalt
not muzzle the ox that treadeth out the corn.
And, [w]The labourer *is* worthy of his reward.
19 Against an elder receive not an accusation, but [x]before two or three witnesses.
20 [y]Them that sin rebuke before all,
[z]that others also may fear.
21 [a]I charge *thee* before God, and the
Lord Jesus Christ, and the elect angels, that
thou observe these things without preferring one before another, doing nothing by
partiality.
22 [b]Lay hands suddenly on no man,
[c]neither be partaker of other men's sins:
keep thyself pure.
23 Drink no longer water, but use a little
wine [d]for thy stomach's sake and thine often infirmities.
24 [e]Some men's sins are open beforehand, going before to judgment; and some
men they follow after.
25 Likewise also the good works *of some*
are manifest beforehand; and they that are
otherwise cannot be hid.

6

Let as many [f]servants as are under the
yoke count their own masters worthy of
all honour, [g]that the name of God and *his*
doctrine be not blasphemed.
2 And they that have believing masters,
let them not despise *them*, [h]because they
are brethren; but rather do *them* service,
because they are faithful and beloved, par-

4:1 [h]2 Tim. 3:13; Rev. 16:14 [i]Dan. 11:35
4:2 [j]Matt. 7:15; 2 Pet. 2:3 [k]Eph. 4:19
4:3 [l]1 Cor. 7:28; Heb. 13:4 [m]Rom. 14:3 [n]Gen. 1:29 [o]Rom. 14:6
4:4 [p]Rom. 14:14; Tit. 1:15
4:6 [q]2 Tim. 3:14
4:7 [r]2 Tim. 2:16 [s]Heb. 5:14
4:8 [t]1 Cor. 8:8 [u]Ps. 37:4; Mark 10:30; Rom. 8:28
4:10 [v]1 Cor. 4:11 [w]Ps. 36:6
4:12 [x]1 Cor. 16:11 [y]Tit. 2:7
4:14 [z]2 Tim. 1:6 [a]Acts 6:6
4:16 [b]Acts 20:28 [c]Ezek. 33:9 [d]Rom. 11:14; Jam. 5:20
5:1 [e]Lev. 19:32
5:4 [f]Gen. 45:10; Eph. 6:1
5:5 [g]1 Cor. 7:32 [h]Luke 2:37 [i]Acts 26:7
5:6 [j]Jam. 5:5
5:8 [k]Isa. 58:7 [l]2 Tim. 3:5 [m]Matt. 18:17
5:9 [n]Luke 2:36
5:10 [o]Acts 16:15; 1 Pet. 4:9 [p]Gen. 18:4; John 13:5
5:13 [q]2 Thess. 3:11
5:14 [r]1 Cor. 7:9 [s]Tit. 2:8
5:17 [t]Rom. 12:8; Gal. 6:6; Phil. 2:29; Heb. 13:7 [u]Acts 28:10
5:18 [v]Deut. 25:4 [w]Lev. 19:13; Matt. 10:10; Luke 10:7
5:19 [x]Deut 19:15
5:20 [y]Gal. 2:11 [z]Deut. 13:11
5:21 [a]2 Tim. 2:14
5:22 [b]Acts 6:6 [c]2 John 11
5:23 [d]Ps. 104:15
5:24 [e]Gal. 5:19
6:1 [f]Eph. 6:5; Tit. 2:9; 1 Pet. 2:18 [g]Isa. 52:5; Tit. 2:5
6:2 [h]Col. 4:1

FOCUS ON FIRST TIMOTHY

The same womb that cramps with monthly menses is the origin of all our "in the beginnings!" The breast that offers milk sustains life. The hand that rocks the cradle rules the world, "they" say. And, we are fully aware that the mother's touch that eases our pain will also correct our behavior! It seems that the labor that brings forth birth seldom ceases, for being a mother means a lifetime commitment. *Mother* is another word for love.

Our mothers were the ones who traveled that forced exodus from Africa, cradling dying or starving babies to their breasts. They emerged from the dank holes of slave ships, on the shores of the "land of the free and the home of the slave" with chains on their necks and ankles, but holding the babies who survived on their ample hips. These children may not have been the children they had birthed, but they claimed them all the same. *Mother* is a word to be remembered.

As Paul writes to Pastor Timothy, his protégé, he uplifts Timothy's mother, Eunice, and grandmother, Lois, the godly women who shaped his life and modeled Christian behavior (2 Tim. 1:5). They had invested their lives in Timothy. Paul recognized their gifts.

May God continue to bless happy, healthy mothers; matriarchal heads of families; single, struggling, adoptive mothers and stepmothers; old, established, community mothers; moving-on-up mothers; educated, cultured, pearl-wearing, sophisticated mothers; finger-snapping, gospel-loving, shucking-and-jiving mothers; pace-setting, ghetto-living, trying-hard-to-survive mothers; friend-mothers; sister-mothers; rapping, tiptoe tapping, too young mothers; and the "sho'-nuff" church mother! They are all God's amazing gifts of ebony, sable, swarthy brown, chocolate, nutmeg, brown sugar, and coal-black. God has made mothers multicolored, multiethnic, curly-, straight-, long-, short-, weaved-, faded-, and shaved-haired. Mothers come in all colors, shapes, and sizes. Yet in the end, they are God's gifts to us—their children.

Paul's first letter to Timothy was written to give the young leader instructions on how to shepherd the church at Ephesus. Paul talks about the church's organization as well as its requirements for leadership. Paul deals with public worship, the proper use of money, and how to deal with false teachers and false doctrine.

THE BLACK PRESENCE IN FIRST TIMOTHY

There are no specific references to the black presence within Paul's first letter to Timothy. However, we must bear in mind that the Gospel preached by Paul had its origin in North Africa and Palestine where there was a significant black presence. Not until the Greeks and Romans began to migrate into the biblical lands during the centuries prior to the birth of Christ do we find any significant presence of other racial groups. Bear in mind once again that in bibli-

cal times racial identification did not have the significance it carries today. This significance is more critical today because of efforts made within the last two centuries to eliminate or distort the reality of the biblical black presence to the detriment of people of color.

Additionally, some have concluded that since Paul was mistaken for an Egyptian (Acts 21:38), he must have been black.

Life Lessons

1 TIMOTHY 1

As Paul writes to a younger man who pastors the church Paul had founded in Ephesus, he reflects upon the grace of God: "And I thank Christ Jesus our Lord, who hath enabled me, for that he counted me faithful, putting me into the ministry; Who was before a blasphemer, and a persecutor, and injurious: but I obtained mercy, because I did it ignorantly in unbelief. And the grace of our Lord was exceeding abundant with faith and love which is in Christ Jesus. This is a faithful saying, and worthy of all acceptation, that Christ Jesus came into the world to save sinners; of whom I am chief. Howbeit for this cause I obtained mercy, that in me first Jesus Christ might shew forth all longsuffering, for a pattern to them which should hereafter believe on him to life everlasting" (1:12–16). Paul chooses not to begin his teaching from an exalted position of seniority, but by recalling where grace found him as he persecuted the people of God! (See Acts 7:58; 9:1–2.)

Amazing Grace, thank You for loving, choosing and using a sinner like me!

1 TIMOTHY 2

Chapter two provides instructions on the order of worship. "I exhort therefore, that, first of all, supplications, prayers, intercessions, and giving of thanks, be made for all men; For kings, and for all that are in authority; that we may lead a quiet and peaceable life in all godliness" (2:1–2). In a time period when severe persecutions are taking place, praying for "peace and quiet" is wise.

Paul also provides instructions about the dress of women. The following verses about women in the church are included: "Let the woman learn in silence with all subjection. But I suffer not a woman to teach, nor to usurp authority over the man, but to be in silence" (vv. 11–12). This passage must be interpreted in light of Paul's statement that there is "neither male nor female" in the Body of Christ. (See Galatians 3:28.)

Supreme Guide, help me worship You in spirit and in truth!

1 TIMOTHY 5

In chapter five, Paul's advice encompasses widows, elder, and servants. Paul admonishes Timothy to "honour widows that are widows indeed. But if any widow have children or nephews, let them learn first to

shew piety at home, and to requite their parents: for that is good and acceptable before God" (5:2–3). In other words, Paul suggests that families help support the widows. As we would say today, "Charity begins at home!" Real piety or devotion for God can be seen in one's actions. After all, "faith without works is dead" (James 2:26). This is not to say that one has to earn salvation by works. Rather, one shows her obedience to God by her actions.

Provider of the widowed, let me not overlook those in need, whether they are in my family or in my community.

FOCUS ON SECOND TIMOTHY

After his opening greeting, the apostle immediately encourages Timothy to remain faithful to his calling and not be ashamed of Paul who is now a prisoner. He urges faithfulness because the mission to proclaim the Gospel is too important and too urgent. He uses the analogies of a soldier, an athlete, and a farmer to encourage faithfulness (2:1–7). As in 1 Timothy Paul warns this young brother to flee youthful desires, and pursue righteousness and godliness, to anticipate that in the latter days people would not endure sound doctrine but will deteriorate into gross ungodliness as they focused on self (3:1–9). He ends the letter with a charge to preach the Word at all times because the aged apostle is about to depart this life to be with the Lord (4:1–5). Paul expresses confidence that he has fought the good fight, having finished his course and having guarded the faith (v. 7). As a result he expects to receive the crown of life which the righteous Judge (unlike Nero and the other unjust judges) would give him on the day of accountability (v. 8).

THE BLACK PRESENCE IN SECOND TIMOTHY

There are no specific references to the black presence within Paul's second letter to Timothy. However, we must bear in mind that the Gospel preached by Paul had its origin in North Africa and Palestine where there was a significant black presence. Not until the Greeks and Romans began to migrate into the biblical lands during the centuries prior to the birth of Christ do we find any significant presence of other racial groups. Bear in mind once again that in biblical times racial identification did not have the significance it carries today. This significance is more critical today because of efforts made within the last two centuries to eliminate or distort the reality of the biblical black presence to the detriment of people of color.

Additionally, some have concluded that since Paul was mistaken for an Egyptian (Acts 21:38), he must have been black.

Life Lessons

2 TIMOTHY 1

Facing death for his life as a follower of Jesus, the apostle Paul writes, "passing the torch" to "Timothy, my dearly beloved son" (1:2). Persecution under Nero is in full swing; Paul is imprisoned and awaiting execution. He writes to Timothy to encourage him to keep the faith and carry out the ministry at his hand without apology. Reminding Timothy of "the unfeigned faith that is in thee, which dwelt first in thy grandmother Lois, and thy mother," Paul urges this younger man to "stir up the gift of God, which is in thee by the putting on of my hands. For God hath not given us the spirit of fear; but of power, and of love, and of a sound" (vv. 5–7).

Spirit of Power, Love and Sound Mind, live strong in me!

2 TIMOTHY 2

Giving a young man the wisdom of both his years and live experience, Paul attempts to provide Timothy with a manual for church administration. Paul knew Timothy would need grace in abundance. So, he writes, "Be strong in the grace that is in Christ Jesus" (2:1). This is a reminder to Timothy to trust completely in the undeserved favor and merit of the One who was "of the seed of David was raised from the dead" (v. 8). As an elder in the church Paul charges Timothy to "put them in remembrance . . . Study to shew thyself approved unto God, a workman that needeth not to be ashamed, rightly dividing the word of truth" (vv. 14–15). Vital leaders are those who remain faithful and diligent to the reading, studying, internalizing, and living of the Word of God.

Living Word, speak to my heart. Give me the words that will bring new life.

2 TIMOTHY 3

There will be difficult days ahead, Paul assures Timothy. "For men shall be lovers of their own selves, covetous, boasters, proud, blasphemers, disobedient to parents, unthankful, unholy, . . . lovers of pleasures more than lovers of God; having a form of godliness, but denying the power thereof: from such turn away" (3:2–5). This passage warns Timothy about the false teachers who come with untruth and cause women to abandon the faith (v. 6). Since women were not allowed formal education, their study was limited to what was taught in the house churches. Many false teachers led women astray. To be called "silly" (v. 6) might sound insulting; nevertheless, it's true today! We need to be grounded in God's truth in Jesus Christ in order that we might not be fooled by good-looking, nice-sounding liars who claim to speak for God!

Spirit of Truth, teach me wisdom so that I might discern truth from error.

2 TIMOTHY 4

Paul closes his letter with a final greeting. "Salute Prisca and Aquila" (4:19). Prisca "is mentioned first, which perhaps indicates her greater importance among Christians, since normally in antiquity the person with greater status—the man, for example, or the person with a higher social class—would be named first" (*WBC*, 359–60). At the end of his life, Paul remembers those who have worked faithfully with him, prayerfully supported him, and sustained him with lodging and financial assistance. He had given his life for the sake of the Gospel and he recognized that many others had interwoven their lives with his. Community was important to the apostle Paul. It was another piece of the legacy he left for his son in Christ, Timothy.

Weaving God, let the threads of my life be knit with others who are working to cover the world with a tapestry of love in the blessed name of Your Son, Jesus Christ.

FOCUS ON TITUS

Storms are inevitable! Storms are a reality of life. They don't necessarily warn us of their approach. The sun can be shining, flowers blooming, and trees gently swaying in the wind. Suddenly, out of nowhere, a storm hits! Storms come because of a change in weather patterns, as a result of a collision of two different types of air (warm and cool). Of course, you know that some storms can cause great destruction. Hurricanes, tropical storms, and tornadoes frighten the most seasoned folks who live in their annual paths. A storm's ending brings a change in living patterns for those affected. Communities share resources. Volunteers come to serve. Life is changed. But life goes on after a storm.

That's why storms are metaphors for the troubles of life. All of us are either just emerging from a "storm." Or we're in the middle of a storm—or one is brewing "off shore."

Our focus in life ought not to not be how to avoid storms but how to behave in the midst of them. Many of us have been in the situation of praying for a change in our "weather conditions." Storms not only come in our personal lives, they also hit our local congregations. We want to pretend that all of us are Christians, but the reality is that there is much conflict present in our local congregations. When your home life is affected by a storm, all of the other areas of your life will reap the impact. When your personal life is fraught with difficulty, you will find storm clouds hovering at your job. As hard as we attempt to compartmentalize our lives and keep them separate, a storm has the ability to sweep over all that is present, rearranging and changing us.

Thank God for Jesus Christ who is present with us in every storm. Praise God for the haven we have in Jesus who longs to be our place of refuge in the time of storms. Glory to the Sender of Storms who knows

both us and the type of storm we need to bring out the potential for abundant living which is within us. Storms don't come to destroy us. They come to build character. They come to show us just what we're made of and help us see how we react to the pressure. They come and allow us to experience the grace of God which is a strong tower upon which we can depend, regardless to the size, sound, and fury of the storm!

Titus, a Greek convert of Paul's faced a storm in his job as overseer of the churches on the island of Crete. Dealing with false teachers is a recurring theme of the Pastoral Letters. Paul begins his letter with a ringing affirmation of his own role of being a proclaimer of a message that has no equal—the hope of eternal life which God, who cannot lie, promised before He created the world (1:1–3). The affirmation is intended to remind Titus that his role of overseeing the work in Crete is of utmost importance. A part of Titus's responsibility was to identify and install reliable leadership (vv. 5–10). Experience had certainly taught the apostle that good leadership was essential to maintaining the ministry. This was especially crucial in Crete where the cultural norm was characterized by lying, gluttony, and monetary greed. Paul identifies specific emphases for the elderly men, elderly women, young men, and slaves (2:1–10). He expects Christian believers to set the example for the entire citizenry (2:8; 3:2, 8) In every case he appeals to the grace of God as the motivation for holy living (2:11–14; 3:3–8).

THE BLACK PRESENCE IN TITUS

Crete is the island from which Philistines came to settle in the land of Canaan. According to Genesis 10:13–14, the Philistines are the descendants of Ham through Mizraim (Egypt). Both Ham and Egypt mean "black." We must bear in mind that the Gospel preached by Paul had its origin in North Africa and Palestine where there was a significant black presence. Not until the Greeks and Romans began to migrate into the biblical lands during the centuries prior to the birth of Christ do we find any significant presence of other racial groups. Bear in mind also that in biblical times racial identification did not have the significance it carries today. This significance is more critical today because of efforts made within the last two centuries to eliminate or distort the reality of the biblical black presence to the detriment of people of color.

Additionally, some have concluded that since Paul was mistaken for an Egyptian (Acts 21:38), he must have been black.

Life Lessons

TITUS 1–2

Leadership in the church is Paul's agenda. Titus is a Gentile, a Greek who was of great assistance to Paul between his first and second imprisonments in Rome. After a typical "Pauline" greeting, acknowledging Titus

as "mine own son after the common faith" (v. 4), we are not left in doubt about the purpose of this letter. "For this cause I left thee in Crete, that thou shouldest set in order the things that are wanting, and ordain elders in every city, as I had appointed thee" (v. 5). Because "one of themselves, even a prophet of their own, said, The Cretans are always liars, evil beasts, slow bellies. This witness is true. Wherefore rebuke them sharply, that they may be sound in the faith" (v. 12). This "storm" of wrong doctrine had to be dealt with. The Judaizers taught the new Gentile converts that they had to be followers of Jewish Law before they could be Christians. Paul wants these converts to receive the truth. "But speak thou the things which become sound" (2:1).

Source of Truth, lead me in the way everlasting. Let my leadership be a model worthy of emulation, I pray.

TITUS 2

Duties for various members in the church are outlined. The older men and women are listed. Young men are instructed. Younger women are called to "love their husbands, to love their children, to be discreet, chaste, keepers at home, good, obedient to their own husbands, that the word of God be not blasphemed" (2:4–5). Titus is challenged to teach the young men in order "that he that is of the contrary part may be ashamed, having no evil thing to say of you" (v. 8). Titus also is to "exhort servants to be obedient unto their own masters, and to please them well in all things . . . that they may adorn the doctrine of God our Savior in all" (vv. 9–10).

Liberating Savior, thank You for the power to live a life that is pleasing to You.

FOCUS ON PHILEMON

Before I'll be a slave, I'll be buried in my grave, go home to my Lord and be free!

Liberty is not a legal concept. Freedom is planted within our very "isness." Being made in the image of God prompts us to grow and achieve. Human beings were created in order that they might become reflections of God. When another human being decides to prevent our being all that God would have us be, something within us begins to churn.

Harriet Tubman was the daughter of African slaves. Although born into the institution of slavery, Harriet inwardly knew that being a slave was not her manifest destiny. She longed to be free. She couldn't read or write. She did not have access to a school, books, or debates that would sharpen her cogent argument for her right to life, liberty, and the pursuit of happiness. She just knew that slavery would not be her life-long status. So she ran away.

Outrunning slave traders and their dogs, Harriet made it all the way to Canada. She tasted freedom. She looked around and could sniff freedom in the air. Overhead the birds sang, the sun shone, and the stars twinkled

brightly in their freedom. Harriet should have been satisfied. After all, she was free. But her freedom reminded her of the others who were yet enslaved. She wanted to experience freedom from life's restraint called slavery.

Chased like a fugitive from justice, with "wanted" posters displayed along public routes, Harriet made many return trips south to conduct the Underground Railroad toward freedom. She was called the "Black Moses" for her efforts. This Mother of Freedom made freedom a reality for herself and over three hundred others. It made her no difference that laws, customs, and traditions demanded her acceptance of the practice of slavery! Something within Harriet Tubman broke open and propelled her to be a self-emancipated woman. May her spirit of free expression continue to rise in us!

In Philemon, Paul recognized that urge in people to free themselves and he used tact and persuasive power to convince Philemon to treat the runaway slave Onesimus kindly. He refers to Philemon as his dear friend and fellow worker (v. 1). He expresses appreciation for Philemon's faith and love for people (v. 5). Such strong affirmation, while genuine, is meant to prepare Philemon's heart for the bold request Paul would make.

The apostle pleads, on the basis of love, that Philemon would receive back his runaway slave—without punishing him. While Paul does not state outright that Philemon should set Onesimus free, many Bible students see in his language a suggestion to do so. Paul certainly implores for the abolition of the slave *status*—"thou shouldst receive him for ever; not now as a servant, but above a servant, a brother beloved" (vv. 15–16). Paul declares how helpful Onesimus had been in his ministry (vv. 11–14).

We do not know why Paul does not attack slavery as a system in this short letter. However, the principle of regarding slaves as brothers was like an injection of a serum into slave society. It was a serum that centuries later resulted in the abolition of slavery.

THE BLACK PRESENCE IN PHILEMON

There are no specific references to the black presence within the letter to Philemon. However, we must bear in mind that the Gospel preached by Paul had its origin in North Africa and Palestine where there was a significant black presence. Not until the Greeks and Romans began to migrate into the biblical lands during the centuries prior to the birth of Christ do we find any significant presence of other racial groups. Bear in mind once again that in biblical times racial identification did not have the significance it carries today. This significance is more critical today because of efforts made within the last two centuries to eliminate or distort the reality of the biblical black presence to the detriment of people of color.

Additionally, some have concluded that since Paul was mistaken for an Egyptian (Acts 21:38), he must have been black.

Life Lessons

PHILEMON 1

Paul begins this short letter by greeting a friend and co-laborer, Apphia, whom scholars believe was a female patron of the house church. She is called "beloved" (v. 2). This is not a meaningless designation from Paul. This title indicates that Apphia has been greatly involved and even highly influential in the spread of the Gospel in Colossse. Apphia also may have been Philemon's wife.

> Paul's strategy is to use persons (Beloved Apphia and our fellow soldier, Archippus, v. 2) who are Philemon's equals as well as the larger community as an audience who will judge whether or not Philemon has taken the apostle's advice. (WBC, 362)

Paul is wise enough and skilled enough to pull out all the stops when it comes to having Onesimus treated as a member of the Body of Christ. The matter was serious enough for Brother Paul to ask Sister Apphia for help!

Connecting Bond of Love, thank You for allowing the sisterhood to be of assistance in the spread of Your Good News for the entire family.

PHILEMON 1

Paul called Philemon "brother" (v. 20) after calling him a beloved friend and fellow laborer (v. 2). He addresses Onesimus, a slave, as his "son" (v. 10) and "beloved brother" (v. 20). He does not speak against slavery, which is an accepted practice of the culture, but instead admonishes Philemon to "receive him for ever; not now as a servant, but above a servant, a brother beloved (vv. 15–16). The connection Paul uses is that of family. It is not simply a family of origin, one in which we have no choice, but it is the family of blood ties! For the shed blood of Jesus connected us at the cross. Paul renames the relationships and redefines the boundaries. "If thou count me therefore a partner, receive him as myself" (v. 17). Onesimus is uplifted by Paul as his equal. Philemon is called upon to do the same.

God of All, to Thee we raise this our voice of grateful praise for being part of Your beloved family.

FOCUS ON HEBREWS

"Gooder than good" is one of those expressions we hear around the tables during family gatherings. When Mama puts her famous fried chicken, potato salad, ham-simmered string beans, cornbread muffins, and sweet potato pie in front of you, the taste is in your eyes. "It's not just good—it's gooder than good!"

"Gooder than good" is one of those expressions we hear as the "sistas" brag about the bargains they found at the discount mall. When the famous labels have gone from half price to the end-of-the-season clearance racks and you can find your size, in a color that sets off your skin tones and you have the necessary accessories already in your closet at home, the joy is in your credit card savings. It's not just good—it's gooder than good!

"Gooder than good!" is one of those expressions we hear at work as a "sista" tries hard not to brag about the new promotion, outstanding evaluation, merit bonus and new corner office being prepared just after the completion of a hard-earned move up the corporate ladder. Oh, the victory of those still outstanding student loans and staying up all night to stay two steps ahead of the competition! It's not just good—it's gooder than good!

God created an entire world, placed a man and a woman in place as co-managers. It was good. When they messed up and deserved to be scrapped and a new model designed, God announced His grace. Through the woman's "seed," deliverance would come (see Gen. 3:15). So God didn't destroy Adam and Eve. When their children who followed them in acts of sin and rebellion—priests, prophets, and kings came to warn them and lead them back to a right relationship with God. That was good. But, it wasn't enough. The preaching, teaching, rituals, and symbols didn't do the job of reaching and transforming their hearts. They were God's chosen people; yet their sinful hearts often separated them from God. That was not good!

So God decided to move into their community. In Jesus, the Infinite was disguised in finite flesh. The power that had created the universe reversed itself and became dependent and powerless in order to show us the way back to God. There was no longer competition between the old covenant, old rituals, and old habits. The "new" came in Jesus Christ and gave us instant access to a relationship with God through confession, repentance, and acceptance of our redemption. At-one-ment (atonement) is ours! Thank God for salvation through the redeeming work of Jesus. It's gooder than good!

HISTORICAL BACKGROUND TO HEBREWS

The believers to whom this letter is directed were apparently primarily Jewish, though some scholars have questioned this. They lived either in a large Jewish community such as existed in Alexandria, Egypt, or in Palestine

itself. Based on the way in which the letter is developed, they had apparently accepted Christ. Due to either persecution or the influence of Judaizers, they were tempted to leave their faith and return to Judaism (Heb. 6:1–6).

The letter begins by showing that the revelation brought by Jesus is superior to all other revelations (1:1–4). The writer goes on to show that Christ is superior to Moses who introduced the Old Testament priesthood (3:1–4:13). He is superior to the Aaronic priesthood (4:14–7:28), and any other human way of approaching the Almighty God (see chapters 8–10). The writer points out that access to God is based on faith (11:1, 6), and demonstrates by citing the faith of many Old Testament patriarchs. The letter concludes by encouraging faithfulness to God and to those who have the responsibility of being shepherds.

THE BLACK PRESENCE IN HEBREWS

There are few references to specific black people in the Epistle to the Hebrews. If the recipients of the letter were Jews living in Alexandria, Egypt, they lived in a largely black community. They likely were Jews of African descent. It is known that the entire geographic area was populated by people who were descendants of Ham and Shem, both of whom were of African descent.

Life Lessons

HEBREWS 1–2

In chapter one, the writer of Hebrews explains that the New Covenant was come, thanks to the coming of Christ. In chapter two, the author urges that the people of the Way avoid returning to their old beliefs and habits of depending upon rituals as a way to establish a relationship with God. He reminds them that Jesus is superior to the angels (1:4; 2:5–18). Jesus is "gooder than good." The best of the "old" covenant could not compare to Jesus. "But we see Jesus, who was made a little lower than the angels for the suffering of death, crowned with glory and honour; that he by the grace of God should taste death for every man" (2:9).

Taster of Death, thank You for taking the victory from the jaws of death for me!

HEBREWS 4

"Let us therefore come boldly unto the throne of grace, that we may obtain mercy, and find grace to help in time of need" (4:16). This is one of those verses we need to commit to memory for the hard times. There is no spot where God is not, and there is nothing too hard for Him! This verse assures us that that we can't wear out God's grace or mercy. Every time we approach God's throne, His grace and mercy is also there to cover our sins. And, when we come seeking intervention, we don't have to come begging. We are to come with bold confidence that our God is more than able to assist us.

Jehovah-jireh, my Provider, You have more than enough to meet my every need!

HEBREWS 5

"We have many things to say, and hard to be uttered, seeing ye are dull of hearing" (5:11). Sometimes a rebuke is necessary to get one's point across. Instead of being able to write more about Jesus' role as High Priest, the author is forced to cease because the readers are "dull of hearing." In other words, they were slow to learn or slow to make progress in their Christian walk. May this never be said of us!

Patient Instructor, help me not to be satisfied with where I am in my walk with You. Instead, may I have joy in growing more and more like You.

HEBREWS 10

The superiority of Christ and the superiority of faith in Christ are repeated over and over again as an encouragement against returning to the old familiar rituals and patterns of worship. "Sacrifice and offering thou wouldest not . . . in burnt offerings and sacrifices for sin thou hast had no pleasure" (10:5–6). "Cast not away therefore your confidence, which hath great recompence of reward" (v. 35). The saints are encouraged to hold on to their faith despite the persecution that continues. "But we are not of them who draw back unto perdition; but of them that believe to the saving of the soul" (v. 39).

Promise Keeper, I holding onto my faith in every promise You have made.

HEBREWS 11

The chapter is known as the "Hebrews Hall of Faith." The words "by faith" in many of the verses in this chapter call to mind an image of an active faith. This famous chapter is both a litany and roll call for the patriarchs and matriarchs of our Christian faith. It includes flesh-and-blood men and women who were risk takers for God. None of them had faith in what they could literally see. They made it to these pages of ancient history due to their faith in the precious promises of God. "These all died in the faith, not having received the promises, but having see them afar off, and were persuaded of them, and embraced them, and confessed that they were strangers and pilgrims on the earth" (11:13). We find the names of precious few women. Among those mentioned are Sara (v. 11); Jochebed, the mother of Moses (v. 23; she is not named here, however); the nameless Pharaoh's daughter who named Moses (v. 24); and Rahab, the harlot (v. 31). A fascinating sentence is found in verse 35: "Women received their dead raised to life again." This includes many sisters in Old Testament Scriptures as well as those who encountered both Jesus and the apostles (see, for example, Luke 7:11–17). Their names are not called, but their faith is noted for us today! They did it because "God having provided some better thing for us, that they without us should not be made perfect" (v. 40).

Faithful One, help me to be a woman who actually lives by my words of faith.

HEBREWS 13

"Let brotherly love continue. Be not forgetful to entertain strangers: for thereby some have entertained angels unawares" (13:1–2). Love includes the stranger, regards the nameless, and is hospitable to everyone

without regard for status. Hospitality is a spiritual gift! Hospitality is a mark of the average woman of color. This ability to include others within the open circle of our love is a good example of the way God has drawn the circle wider to pull us inside.

Grace Greater Than All Our Sin, thank You for including us!

Focus On James

One of those womanish and sassy sayings from the mouth of the foremothers goes like this: "I said it, I meant it, and I'll step back in it." This means, "Yes, you *really* heard what you *thought* you heard that I said! And I mean it!" Such a reply goes on to answer a hearer's question as to whether or not the speaker was serious about what she said. This reply is another way of saying, "If you want me to prove my belief in what I said, here I am! Recall what I've done before. Try me! Now, watch what I do from this moment on." For this is the essence of saying what you mean, meaning what you say, as well as proving it by following through with consistent actions.

We know another familiar saying: "Talk is cheap." This means that many of us have the power of articulation that is not seen in our subsequent behaviors. We claim much and do little is another way of looking at the phenomenon of just using language. Many of us know the language of the church. But, in the final analysis, most of us are not dependable to "put up" after we speak up. James, the brother of Jesus, and the writer of the work that bears his name, comes to challenge us.

The question James puts before Christians is "How does your talk match your walk?" The word on the street says that we don't live like we talk! We are basically people of our world. We have become spin-doctors, word-crafters and empty phrase-spouters. Granny used to say, "The proof is in the pudding, gal!" James says, "Shew me thy faith without thy works, and I will shew thee my faith by my works" (2:18). We are confronted with the need to make our word our bond. If we dare to call ourselves Christians—people who imitate Jesus Christ—our walk had better match our talk.

For the word on the street is that too many so-called Christians are simply representing one—trying to fool others while being deceived themselves! James says that believing is more than joining a congregation and being baptized a dry devil and coming up a wet one! This business of being a Christian means that we are women like our foremothers. We say it. We mean it. We prove it with our very lives, twenty-four/seven! Word up!

James is a very practical and succinct writer. He begins by encouraging faithfulness in the midst of temptation and persecution, assuring readers that God is able to help them through any and all troubles (chap. 1). Other practical issues include partiality, boastfulness, worldliness, and wealth (chaps. 2–5). He concludes the instruction for dealing with a variety of situations including sickness, interpersonal relationships, and the effectiveness of prayer (5:13–20).

THE BLACK PRESENCE IN JAMES

There are no specific references to the black presence in the Epistle of James. It must be remembered, however, that the Gospel undergirding James's writing is rooted in the African-Asian corridor where the black and Asian presence predominated. By the time of Christ and the founding of the Christian church, a Caucasian presence became integrated into the culture as Greeks and Romans conquered and migrated into the area. Their presence, however, did not overshadow the predominant black and Semitic culture, which preceded their arrival by thousands of years. It is the opinion of some that James directed his epistle primarily to Jews who were scattered east of Palestine in the Mesopotamian area.

Life Lessons

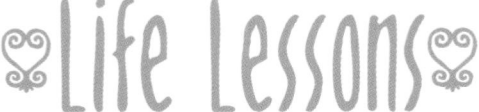

JAMES 1

James is the "wisdom" epistle of the New Testament. It is filled with practical advice for living as a Christian ought. For James, a "living faith" is essential to make a difference in the world. Since he is fully aware of the persecutions against the people of the Way (Christians), he does not begin this letter with false hope and chitchat. Also, he does not offer the slightest possibility that the living for Christ will ever get any easier! He assumes that trials, persecution, and death are part of the lifestyle of Jesus' people. "Count it all joy when ye fall into divers temptations; knowing this, that the trying of your faith worketh patience. But let patience have her perfect work, that ye may be perfect and entire, wanting nothing. If any of you lack wisdom, let him ask of God, that giveth to all men liberally, and upbraideth not" (1:2–5). It's not a matter of "if" we will face severe challenges, but "when" we do. James exhorts us to go to God for help to make it through each trial. Wisdom will be our guide through the storms of life that are sure to come and will continue to come.

Wisdom of the Ages, fill me with directions and instructions to steer me through the storms of my life.

JAMES 2

Chapter two says that genuine faith forbids favoritism. This chapter is not couched in theological language. James says simply, "My brethren, have not the faith of our Lord Jesus Christ, the Lord of glory, with respect of persons" (2:1).

> James addressed Christians who were experiencing community conflict that had reached crisis proportions. The root cause of this crisis seems to have been the community's adoption of questionable social values derived from the world rather than from God's law. (Cain Hope Felder, *Troubling Biblical Waters* [Maryknoll, NY: Orbis Press, 1997], 118–120)

Lifter of Our Heads, thank You for not showing favoritism but counting me as Your own.

JAMES 2

"Shew me thy faith without thy works, and I will shew thee my faith by my works . . . Abraham believed God, and it was imputed unto him for righteousness: and he was called the Friend of God. . . . Likewise also was not Rahab the harlot justified by works, when she had received the messengers, and had sent them out another way?" (2:18, 23–25). James calls for us to "put up or shut up"! Empty words, reciting creeds of faith, carelessly mouthing Scriptures, and speaking Christian vernacular do not a Christian make! Rahab, the prostitute who shielded the spies as the Israelites entered the Promised Land (Josh. 2) is used as an example of how a "living faith" works (v. 25).

Savior of Sinners, help my walk to match my talk in every circumstance.

JAMES 4

Submission is a Christian virtue. Our true submission is unto God. "God resisteth the proud, but giveth grace unto the humble. Submit yourselves therefore to God. Resist the devil, and he will flee from you. Draw nigh to God, and he will draw nigh to you. Cleanse your hands, ye sinners; and purify your hearts, ye double minded. . . . Humble yourselves in the sight of the Lord, and he shall lift you up" (4:6–10). Submission—yielding and committing our whole selves, mind, body, and soul—brings us near to the heart of God. Many of us, especially women of color, have great difficulty with the phrase "humble yourselves" in verse 10. What we need to remember is that the word *humble* in the Greek language of the New Testament does not mean "doormat"! To be humble is to recognize that our worth comes from God alone. It means that we know that we are solely dependent on God. We live, move, and have our being in God. Knowing this helps us understand that we are not independent nor are we left alone. We are wholly dependent upon the grace of a loving, long-suffering and beneficent God. It's all right to be humble under the mighty hand of the Almighty!

Merciful and Beneficent One, I bow in humble submission with awe and reverence.

JAMES 5

"Is any among you afflicted? let him pray. Is any merry? let him sing psalms. Is any sick among you? let him call for the elders of the church; and let them pray over him, anointing him with oil in the name of the Lord: And the prayer of faith shall save the sick, and the Lord shall raise him up; and if he hath committed sins, they shall be forgiven him. Confess your faults one to another, and pray one for another, that ye may be healed. The effectual fervent prayer of a righteous man availeth much" (5:13–16). Prayer is our most powerful resource. Too many times we do all that we can do first and resort to prayer as a "last resort"! James gives us a formula for which results are guaranteed. A key portion of being "raised up" (v. 15) is confession, which means to agree with God's Word about where you are at the moment. "Confess your faults one to another" (v. 16). This is not a call to empty out all the various sinful things you have done to everyone. But it is a call to find those who are

trusted and proven intercessors who can receive your confession without judgment, but in grace pray with you for a place of restoration. All of us reach a place of brokenness in the realm of our spiritual lives. During these times, the presence of God might seem absent. This is a time to call for the saints and to share your brokenness. For the promise is that "the Lord shall raise him up." It is your privilege. It is God's will for us to be whole. Follow the formula and benefit from God's divine intervention in your situations.

Healing God, pour Your oil of anointing upon my head. Let it run down like the needed rain. Let it overflow the dry places in my life. Anointing, fall on me!

FOCUS ON FIRST PETER

The young woman did not understand. All of her life she had honored her teachers. Her Sunday school teacher had been a family friend who made a special effort to engage her young class around the truths of Scripture. Her youth leader had been a role model whom she adored and imitated, which is the highest form of praise. Her high school English teacher had paid special attention to her, taught her much more than the school board paid her for. This "special" woman had laid the foundation for her early social formation by introducing her to the *Ebony* Fashion Show and teaching her how to eat at "the" little town restaurant, The Copper Kettle. Teachers had always held a place of high esteem in her heart. Why was she so angry with this instructor, a college professor who taught a class called "Introduction to Biblical Literacy"?

Everything she had held as sacred was being ridiculed. The professor said that the Bible had errors, contradicting statements, and was a collection of stories. She didn't understand. The professor had stood one day and challenged God. "If there is a God, why doesn't this God just come and strike me dead?" When death didn't come, the instructor laughed. She didn't understand why her faith was being belittled. She didn't understand why an agnostic taught this particular course. She surely didn't understand why God didn't just send a bolt of lightning and stop this foolish discourse which was so insulting to both her and God! It was too late to withdraw. She would endure. She had many questions. She did not understand.

Was she ever shocked to pick up a Sunday paper and see the photo of the professor on the front page. The headline read: "University professor felled by gnat while moving lawn"! The story detailed that while doing a routine chore, a tiny gnat, a teeny-weeny insect, had flown up from the grass, flew up the teacher's nose and somehow cut off his air passage. God had not sent anything dramatic like a thunderbolt or a flash of lightning!

Persecution for our faith has not stopped. In little and big ways we are attacked for our belief in the Invisible Majesty which we call God. Sometimes persecution is subtle and other times, it's outright malicious and even embarrassing. The world has not changed since Peter wrote to

the people of Jesus Christ to offer encouragement to those who continue to suffer for their faith. The Epistle of First Peter is a survival manual in order that we may endure in praise unto God. Second Peter is a warning against false teachers and false teaching. They continue to mix lies and truth in their attempts to deceive us into believing error. Peter's counsel holds true today: "Blessed be the God and Father of our Lord Jesus Christ, which according to his abundant mercy hath begotten us again unto a lively hope by the resurrection of Jesus Christ from the dead" (1:3). All false prophets need to be warned to watch out for those gnats!

The apostle begins his letter with a strong affirmation of the unshakable inheritance believers in Jesus Christ possess—no persecution can rob believers of this eternal inheritance. It is "incorruptible"(cannot perish), "undefiled" (cannot spoil), "fadeth not away," is "reserved in heaven," and "kept by the power of God" (1:4–5). Therefore believers ought to be holy because the God who called them is holy (v. 15). They should crave spiritual milk so they will grow (2:2). They are to submit to authorities (vv. 13–25). Peter counsels wives to submit to their husbands and husbands to be considerate of their wives, treating them with respect (3:1–7). Believers are advised on how to live as part of a minority in the midst of an evil environment (3:8–4:19). Elders are admonished to feed the flocks under their care (5:1–3). Young men are to submit to the elders (5:5).

THE BLACK PRESENCE IN FIRST PETER

There are no specific references to the black presence in the Epistle of 1 Peter. It must be remembered, however, that the Gospel had its origin in the African-Asian corridor where the black and Asian presence predominated. By the time of Christ and the founding of the Christian church, a Caucasian presence became integrated into the culture as Greeks and Romans conquered and migrated into the area. Their presence, however, did not overshadow the predominant black and Semitic culture, which preceded their arrival by thousands of years. The affirmation of the Black presence in biblical times is made necessary because of the attempts during the last two hundred years to distort or minimize that presence to the detriment of people of color.

Life Lessons

1 PETER 1

This letter is addressed to "the strangers scattered throughout Pontus, Galatia, Cappadocia, Asia, and Bithynia, elect according to the foreknowledge of God the Father" (1:1–2). Our ancestors used to sing a spiritual that goes, "I'm just a stranger here, heaven is my home." They were assured of the fact that suffering came for only a season and that they had "an inheritance incorruptible, and undefiled, and that fadeth not away, reserved in heaven for you, who are kept by the power of God through faith unto salvation ready to be revealed in the last time" (1:4–5).

Through the tribulations and persecution of slavery, our ancestors realized that God prepared them for something better in the homeland of their soul. That's why they could sing with gusto and conviction, "One glad morning, when this life is over, I will fly away and be at rest!" "Wherefore gird up the loins of your mind, be sober, and hope to the end for the grace that is to be brought unto you at the revelation of Jesus Christ; As obedient children, not fashioning yourselves according to the former lusts in your ignorance. . . . Be holy in all manner of" (vv. 13–15). It's easy to retaliate and do "tit for tat" living when you know the oppressor! Yet Peter calls for a higher standard. For you have been "born again!" (v. 23).

Strong Deliverer, You are worthy to be praised for preparing us for new life in Your Kingdom.

1 PETER 2

"Ye are a chosen generation, a royal priesthood, an holy nation, a peculiar people; that ye should shew forth the praises of him who hath called you out of darkness into his marvelous light: which in time past were not a people, but are now the people of God" (2:9–10). What a high privilege to be adopted into a royal family. Adoption comes not as a result of our doing. Our noteworthy accomplishments, class backgrounds, our gender or our ethnic group will never bring us to this status before God! God chose us. Christ redeemed us. And the Holy Spirit is at work in us, with us and on our behalf to win others as "they may by your good works, which they shall behold, glorify God" (v. 12).

King of Glory, be glorified in my life.

1 PETER 3

God does not need, want or desire "CIA Christians." CIA Christians are undercover Christians. God does not want cowards as witnesses to His glory. God allows our trials to come and uses them to evidence our trust in Him. That's why in the midst of a trial or after we have gained victory, Peter reminds us to "be ready always to give an answer to every man that asketh you a reason of the hope that is in you with meekness and fear" (3:15). Storms are coming. The world is watching how we go through our storms. Let them see through our lifestyle that our hope is anchored in the One who turned a cross into a symbol of victorious triumph!

Seer of All Things, may I be willing "to give an answer to every man that asketh" concerning the hope that is in me (v. 15).

1 PETER 4

"The end of all things is at hand: be ye therefore sober, and watch unto prayer. And above al things have fervent charity among yourselves: for charity shall cover the multitude of sins" (4:7–8). This love is not an erotic, self-absorbed feeling. This love is not even a "family" type, a certain attitude of "I've got to love them, but I sure don't like them." This love is God's accepting, selfless love that goes beyond "I've done all I'm willing to do" to "what more can I do?" We are impoverished in the English language and use the word *love* very loosely. We "love" clothes, hairdos, and nail colors! Peter calls us to use the love of God when dealing with each other. This will end the petty infighting that crops up so easily between sisters. God is love. And God has enough love for each of us in the family. Let love hide the

faults of the individual you are most angry with today. Ask God to allow love to hide your faults as you "work" somebody else's nerve!

Lover of My Soul, let me to Your bosom fly as I seek the love which hides others' faults!

FOCUS ON SECOND PETER

The apostle Peter, after his brief greeting, urges believers to add various virtues to their faith, all of which will empower a believer to be effective in his Christian walk. He assures them that the faith they exercised in Jesus Christ is rooted in fact. They were "eyewitnesses of his majesty" (1:16). "This voice which came from heaven we heard"(v. 18). And we have a more sure word—"For the prophecy came not in old time by the will of man: but holy men of God spake as they were moved by the Holy Ghost (v. 21).

He warns of greedy false teachers who will secretly introduce "damnable heresies"(2:1) to exploit the unsuspecting (2:3). Readers of this epistle are reminded that God will judge them as He did the angels that sinned, people in Noah's day, and people in the days of Sodom and Gomorrah (Jude 1:6). Peter anticipates the coming of scoffers who disdain the promise of Christ's return (3:3). He follows this up with words of encouragement concerning God's faithfulness in keeping His promises (v. 9). He patiently waits for all who are willing to repent.

THE BLACK PRESENCE IN SECOND PETER

There are no specific references to the black presence in the Epistle of 2 Peter. It must be remembered, however, that the Gospel had its origin in the African-Asian corridor where the black and Asian presence predominated. By the time of Christ and the founding of the Christian church, a Caucasian presence became integrated into the culture as Greeks and Romans conquered and migrated into the area. Their presence, however, did not overshadow the predominant black and Semitic culture, which preceded their arrival by thousands of years. The affirmation of the Black presence in biblical times is made necessary because of the attempts during the last two hundred years to distort or minimize that presence to the detriment of people of color.

Life Lessons

2 PETER 1

This letter is a warning against false teachers who try to undermine the teachings of Jesus Christ. "His divine power hath given unto us all things that pertain unto life and godliness, through the knowledge of him that hath called us to glory and virtue: Whereby are given unto us exceeding great and precious promises . . . For we have not followed cunningly devised fables, when we made known unto you the power and coming of our Lord Jesus Christ, but were eyewitnesses of his majesty" (1:3–4, 16). We are not telling lies, spinning yarns, or engaging in fairy tales, says Peter. Lying teachers instructed that self-control in sexual matters was not necessary since the body and its deeds were not important. Peter admonishes, "Add to your faith virtue; and to virtue knowledge; and to knowledge temperance; and to temperance patience. . . for if these things be in you, and abound, they make you that ye shall neither be barren not unfruitful in the knowledge of our Lord Jesus Christ" (vv. 5–6, 8). A living, dynamic faith is one controlled by the work of the Holy Spirit in us, bringing glory to God in all we do. It is essential that we "give diligence to make your calling and election sure: for if ye do these things, ye shall never fall: for so an entrance shall be ministered unto you abundantly into the everlasting kingdom of our Lord and Savior Jesus Christ" (v. 10). Sisters, self-control is not an option!

Spirit of Truth, lead me in ways that are life giving and glory producing!

2 PETER 1–3

Peter spends the first chapter of this epistle giving us a "math lesson"—qualities to add to our faith (1:5–7). These qualities will keep a believer discerning—a necessary commodity when false teachers are about! Peter's argument that "if God spared not the angels that sinned, but cast them down to hell, and delivered them into chains of darkness, to be reserved unto judgment" (2:4) demonstrates that God is going to punish those who deceive Christians and lead them into sin and error. "Through covetousness shall they with feigned words make merchandise of you" (v. 3). We need to evaluate our teachers and what they are teaching. All teachings should measure up to the Word of God. It makes no difference how good these teachings sounds. We are called to be careful about what teachings we allow to guide our conduct, especially our sexual conduct. If it sounds too good to be true, most likely it's not! "Therefore, beloved, seeing ye know these things before, beware . . . grow in the grace, and in the knowledge of our Lord and Savior Jesus Christ" (3:17–18).

Wise Counselor, guide me to know Your truth.

FOCUS ON
FIRST, SECOND, AND THIRD JOHN

Memory is a gift from God. Modern computers are built to simulate the intelligence "system" that God has provided in the human brain. We store information in the recesses called *memory*. That information is often "retrieved" by us to remember what we have learned in days gone past. We learned how to talk, to do math, to read, and to pass science tests by adding to what we already knew! Without memory we would always be a process of starting over.

Sometimes memories comes in the form of flashbacks. Something in our present will trigger a memory from days past. All memories are not pleasant. Some things we would prefer to forget suddenly appear upon the screen of our minds. As diligently as we strive to "delete" some difficult events, they will never be forgotten. When we can remember what happened "once upon a time," we are better prepared to prevent a reoccurrence in our lives.

Memory is a gift from God.

When a dear one dies, our memories allow us to survive our grief. For those who have touched our lives with meaning, purpose, and direction become part of our stored memory. Our "memory banks" keep them alive and fresh, daily with us in thought. Along our life's journey we encounter many diverse personalities. Some people may not leave a strong impression upon our lives. They breeze in and breeze out. Others come and don't have to stay long, but they influence us for the rest of our lives. Our lives have been impacted due to the strong impressions of others. Sunday school teachers, public school teachers, neighbors, family, friends, pastors, high school and college counselors are among those who most affect our impressionable young lives. We are the way we are today; we act the way we act today, we dress the way we dress today, and enjoy many of things we do today due to what we experienced in the life and behavior of another in days gone by.

Memory is a gift from God.

The writings of John come to the church as a gift of memory. The apostle John had only spent three and one-half years with Jesus Christ. However, those years changed his life. He writes out of his appreciation for the memory of a good friend, the Teacher who had led him to God. John had walked, talked, and eaten with Jesus. He had stood with the women and watched his friend die upon a cruel cross. And he had been in the Upper Room when the resurrected Lord came and spoke "Peace" to the disciples and later gave them the Great Commission before His ascension. Many years later, this senior statesman of the church writes out of his gift of memory. He remembers Jesus as light (1 John 1:5–7; 2:10–11). He remembers Jesus as love (chaps. 3–4). He remembers Jesus as a healer.

He remembers Jesus as life. He writes to remind these new "little children" (2:28): "These things have I written unto you that believe on the name of the Son of God; that ye may know that ye have eternal life" (5:13). We are the recipients of John's memory. For memory is a gift from God!

John begins his first letter with a strong statement concerning the certainty of the Word of life (1:1–4). He affirms the reality of sin (which the Gnostics denied) and declares God's provision: forgiveness based on the atoning sacrifice of Jesus Christ (1:5–2:2). He pleads that his readers will not live according to the world because it with its pleasures is passing away. Only those who do the will of God will live forever (2:15). John intimates that a split has taken place within the church as he speaks of those who "went out from us" (v. 19). He describes as the antichrist any person who rejects the identity of the person of Christ—that is, anyone who denies that Jesus Christ is God in the flesh. Reminding them of the great love God has shown toward us (3:1–3), John challenges the readers to demonstrate their sincerity of their faith by loving each other (3:11–5:5). He assures them that in applying the standards of righteousness pointed out in his letter, they will have the assurance of possessing eternal life (5:12–21).

Second John also contains the exhortation to love and to watch out for the deceptive teaching concerning the person of Jesus Christ. The "apostle of love" explains that unless followers of Christ practice love toward God and toward others, their faith is hollow. John is so passionate concerning adherence to the identity of Jesus that he discourages fellowship with anyone whose teaching is not consistent with "that which we had from the beginning"(v. 5).

Third John is addressed to Gaius, a beloved Christian brother of the writer. John expresses appreciation for the way that Gaius showed hospitality to those who served the Lord (vv. 5–8). John then reproves Diotrephes for the arrogant way that he treated people in the church. He not only refused to welcome servants of the Lord who had come from John, but put out of the church those who welcomed anyone sent from John (vv. 9–10). Finally, John commends Demetrius for his good behavior (vv. 11–12).

THE BLACK PRESENCE IN FIRST, SECOND, AND THIRD JOHN

There are no specific references to the black presence in John's Epistles. It must be remembered, however, that the Gospel had its origin in the African-Asian corridor where the black and Asian presence predominated. By the time of Christ and the founding of the Christian church, a Caucasian presence became integrated into the culture as Greeks and Romans conquered and migrated into the area. Their presence, however, did not overshadow the predominant black and Semitic culture, which preceded their arrival by thousands of years. The affirmation of the black presence in biblical times is made necessary because of the attempts during the last two hundred years to distort or minimize that presence to the detriment of people of color.

Life Lessons

1 JOHN 1

John writes to remind us that Jesus is the Light. He talks of his own personal witness to the Living Christ. "We have seen with our eyes, which we have looked upon, and out hands have handled, of the Word of life . . . We have seen it, and bear witness, and shew unto you that eternal life" (1:1–2). Declining commitment to the practices taught by Jesus prompts John's letter. John writes to correct error in judgment and behaviors among those calling themselves Christians yet living by lower standards. His letter includes words of loving encouragement for true believers. He begins with two strong references to his lasting impressions of Jesus, that of "Light" and "Living Word." John testifies to what he has seen and experienced. This is what we are called to do!

Light of the World, shine in me and through me that others will know that my experience with You is authentic and enduring.

1 JOHN 2

"Love not the world, neither the things that are in the world. . . . For all that is in the world, the lust of the flesh, and the lust of the eyes, and the pride of life, is not of the Father, but is of the world" (2:15–16). John writes to assist us in severing our strong and fatal attachment to the "strings" of the world. He deals with inward cravings—the pull toward things that are not satisfying or eternal. He refers us back to the Garden of Eden where Adam and Eve craved equality with God, looked at the forbidden tree, and yielded to temptation and sin. The tricks of the enemy of our soul has not changed! The things or objects may be different, but John warns us to be on the alert.

Eternal Life, keep me focused on You!

1 JOHN 3

"For this is the message that ye heard from the beginning, that we should love one another" (3:11). The message of Jesus is constant (see John 13:34). It is a message of loving embrace and inclusion. Love is not a warm, fuzzy feeling that comes when others behave in ways we find acceptable. Love is not an ego-satisfying impulse that seeks to dominate another. The love of Jesus is a sharing, empowering, accepting activity which as constant and consistent, born of His self-giving nature. Jesus is love in action. His actions were and are those of generosity, healing, and inclusion. We are called to a consistency in our thoughts and behaviors.

Love Incarnate, live through me.

1 JOHN 4

"Beloved, believe not every spirit, but try the spirits whether they are of God: because many false prophets are gone out into the world" (4:1). We are urged by John to "try" the spirits. We are urged not to be naïve

enough to accept everything we hear in church as gospel! Heresies and false teachings were plentiful then and continue today. Many dare to stand and declare that they have "a word form the Lord." Yet, we know that all belief systems are not God's truth. So, John encourages us to "try" the spirits. We can test them by seeing whether they meet the criteria of "whatsoever things are true, whatsoever things are honest, whatsoever things are just, whatsoever things are pure, whatsoever things are lovely, whatsoever things are of good report; if there be any virtue, and if there be any praise, think on these things" (Phil. 4:8).

Excellence, I am not ashamed of the Gospel. I want to be a living testimony!

2 JOHN 1

Doolittle is a character from the play *Pygmalion* (later, the movie *My Fair Lady*), who happens to embody the spirit of Second John's message. Professor Henry Higgins, a major word craftsman who came into her life, spun tales with his expansive vocabulary. In trying to work his magic of articulation upon this lady, she gets tired of his many empty words. Finally, in a huff she tells him, "Words, words! I'm sick of words. If you love me, prove it!" The apostle John had experienced true love in Jesus Christ. He knew love's virtues and manner of behaving. Jesus was the embodiment of love in truth and self-giving. So, as John remembers his Teacher and Friend, he writes to encourage the church to be like Jesus; to imitate His life and to follow His leadership in truthful love. "And this is love, that we walk after his commandments. This is the commandment, That as ye have heard from the beginning, ye should walk in it" (v. 6).

Lover of the Loveless, work in me that Your divine image is reflected in my deeds and not simply in my words.

3 JOHN 1

Moving from issues of doctrine to the ethical matter of hospitality, John recalls the many individuals who had opened themselves, their homes, and their means to Jesus and the roving band of disciples for over three and one-half years. Without hospitality, their work would have been greatly impeded. So, hospitality was of primary concern as the mission ministry of the church. Gaius, a "wellbeloved" friend (v. 1), had been faithful in caring for the needs of visiting teachers sent by John (vv. 5–6). John's greeting is both a commendation and prayer for the one who lived out the mode of sharing love. "I wish above all things that thou mayest prosper and be in health, even as thy soul prospereth" (v. 2). Our spiritual and physical well-being are connected, for we are mind, body, and spirit. There is no separation of how we treat others and how that impacts us in various ways. "Diotrephes, who loveth to have the preeminence among them, receiveth us not. . . . neither doth he himself receive the brethren . . .Follow not that which is evil, but that which is good" (vv. 9–11).

A warm and gracious sign of welcome is a benchmark of the church of Jesus. Is it any wonder that in the average African-American church, the usher board is comprised of smiling sisters?

Hospitable Host of Heaven, thank You for flinging open the door to eternity and inviting me to come and be a welcome guest.

Focus on JUDE

News that false teachers infiltrated the church prompted Jude to switch from writing about "the common salvation" (v. 3) to addressing this encroaching heresy. Some believe the heresy was at least related to the doctrine of Gnosticism. Gnosticism taught that getting to know God required more than simple faith in the Lord Jesus. A person had to have a series of "knowledge" experiences that gradually brought him or her ever closer to God. Its adherents concluded that the human body was unimportant to God. This doctrine resulted in two practices: neglect of the body through the denial of food to gain this "higher" experience with God, and lustful activities—gluttony, fornication, and so on. Though this heresy reached its peak later in the Christian era, it had its beginning during the time of Paul and John. Jude writes to refute this distortion of the Christian message. He warns that just as God judged those who sought to justify immoral behavior in the past, God would do it again (v. 5). He cites the examples of the angels who rebelled, the Israelites who followed Moses from Egypt but rebelled against his leadership, and Sodom and Gomorrah (vv. 6–7). After encouraging them to keep themselves in the love of God, Jude ends the letter by assuring the readers that God was able to keep from falling those whose hearts were steadfast (vv. 24–25)—a benediction that many churches use today.

THE BLACK PRESENCE IN JUDE

Adam: Mentioned in verse 14. See the Introduction to the Book of Genesis.

Egypt: Mentioned in verse 5. Egypt (*Mizraim* in Hebrew) is a Greek term meaning "black." Prior to the conquering of that land by Alexander the Great in 332 B.C., the people along the Nile River called themselves *Kemet*, which means "black."

Life Lessons

JUDE 1

Jude, a servant of Jesus Christ and brother of James, a leader in the early church, writes to those who have been "sanctified," "preserved," and "called" by the life, words, and ministry of the Living Lord. He writes to encourage their faithful living of the doctrines and practices of the people of the Way. "It was needful for me to write unto you, and exhort you that ye should earnestly contend for the faith which was once delivered unto the saints" (v. 3). He prompts the church to return to the basics of salvation: trust in Jesus Christ.

Christ, My Solid Rock, help me to be firmly planted in the truth of Your Word.

JUDE 1

Apostasy means turning away form the truth of Christ and following "ways" that suit our individual fancy! False teachers had secretly "crept in unawares . . . ungodly men, turning the grace of our God into lasciviousness, and denying the only Lord God, and our Lord Jesus Christ" (v. 4). The primary issue among the theologians of this period centered among the human-divine nature of Jesus. From this debate many concluded that what they believed far superseded how they lived and behaved. Ungodly living was practiced and encouraged. It was cheap grace at its best. Jude, however, warns: "These filthy dreamers defile the flesh, despise dominion, and speak evil of dignities. . . . Woe unto them!" (vv. 8, 11). These messages found listeners and practitioners! Jude calls the faithful to stand firm on truth. He also calls for the wayward to return to God's way of right living. "But ye, beloved, building up yourselves on your most holy faith, praying in the Holy Ghost. . . . Of some have compassion, making a difference: And others save with fear, pulling them out of the fire; hating even the garment spotted by the flesh" (vv. 20–23) Stand! Persevere! Hold on to your faith!

Lord, my prayer for all is this: "Unto him that is able to keep you from falling, and to present you faultless before the presence of his glory with exceeding joy, to the only wise God our Savior, be glory and majesty, dominion and power, both now and ever. Amen" (vv. 24–25).

Women in SECOND TIMOTHY AND SECOND JOHN

CLAUDIA: A SINCERE SUPPORTER

One story that was told to me when I was child has meant more to me as an adult than when I first heard it as a child. That story focused on a woman who had three daughters. Each daughter was considered a valuable member of society: a prominent physician, a leading criminal attorney, and a renowned vocalist. Life provided its challenges to each daughter. There were times when they doubted themselves; their abilities to handle situations and their understanding of what their system taught were challenged. Yet there was a praying mother, grandmother, aunt, niece, or daughter who offered encouragement or never stopped praying. Everyone needs a cheering squad and a support base. As an adult, we can say that we can appreciate the value of stored prayers and those who keep the faith in our stead. Claudia was such an ambassador to young Timothy and Paul. (See 2 Timothy 4:21.)

Claudia was the type of person who supported her leader despite what others thought. She is one of the most respected and influential women of Gentile background. She was an encourager, nurturer, and

strong supporter. What Claudia had going for her was the fact that she did not put her total trust in the messenger, but in the message. Faith was the key to her maintaining a positive base. Understanding who you are in Christ—understanding the purchase price—really puts into perspective who you are and to whom you belong. Claudia could have been our great-grandmother, grandmother, or mother who prevailed through many tribulations, and whose travails continue. Despite it all, our "Claudias" continue to look toward the hills for their help (see Ps. 121).

Read 2 Timothy 4:21; see also John 17:20–23.

Read the insight essay on Influence.

—B. Kitt

THE ELECT LADY

Let love be without dissimulation. . . . Distributing to the necessity of the saints; given to hospitality (Rom. 12:9, 13).

There is some debate whether the "elect lady" of 2 John is literal or figurative. Taken literally, the epistle is written to a particular lady and her children. Taken figuratively, it could refer to the local church and its membership. Whether the church or one special lady, the "elect lady" is to be emulated by all. This priceless narrative of the elect lady exemplifies for us what it means to live, love, walk, and serve in the spirit of truth. She is a lady of saintly character and distinguished privilege.

The elect lady is commended for her virtuous and religious education of her children; also, she is exhorted to abide in the doctrine of Christ to preserve the truth, and carefully to avoid the delusions of false teachers. The apostle John commends her and the other believers for remaining faithful to the truth of the Gospel and urges them to obey the command to love one another. "That, as ye have heard from the beginning, ye should walk in it. For many deceivers are entered into the world, who confess not that Jesus Christ is come in the flesh" (2 John: 6–7). There were many false teachers who were dangerous and twisted the truth. The lady was admonished not to show hospitality to these perpetrators; instead, she was to practice the great commandment of Christian love and charity. The Scriptures admonish us to "be ye therefore wise as serpents, and harmless as doves" (Matt. 10:16).

Others loved this lady too, not for her rank but for her holiness. She was not only a choice one, but also a chosen one—a woman of refinement and good manners. Good manners are a very important virtue. Being honest and treating people with integrity are also essential. There are enough hypocrites. We are to be leaders of a strong support system to build our church and communities from the inside out. We are the church, so it is imperative that we are included as role models.

Read 2 John 1.

Read the insight essay on Evangelism.

—P. George

Insights

PARENTING

Since there is no handbook that automatically comes when children are born into the world, many people rely on family and friends for guidance. It helps if you have had good role models and can follow in your parents' footsteps—with appropriate changes to fit your own identity.

Parenting is frightening, but it is one of the most rewarding experiences that God has created for humankind. There is no perfect way of parenting. Some people have a natural instinct for parenting and others grow into it through the experience.

Parenting is an awesome responsibility. When God formed us in the image of Himself, He raised us—as a parent raises a child. God provided everything for the first family, Adam and Eve. God provided water, fruit, vegetables, shelter from the sun (trees), and light. They had full use of the Garden of Eden. God looked over them—monitoring what they did. Once when He approached the Garden of Eden to communicate with Adam and Eve, He saw that they had disobeyed His instructions (see Gen. 3). God had given them free will. But He had warned them to not eat of the tree of good and evil (see Gen. 2:16–17). God had guided them in the right direction. They had everything they needed to shelter them from the storms of life, but as many children do, they did not listen. They let the serpent influence their thinking and deceive them into ignoring God's prohibition concerning eating the fruit. They rebelled against God, but He never stopped loving them.

God is our example of a loving parent. Parenting is praising, advising, reminding, encouraging, nurturing, teaching/training (Ps. 78:1–8; Prov. 22:6; 2 Tim. 1:3–5); influencing, nourishing, giving, and disciplining children (Prov. 13:24; Heb. 12:5–8). It is teaching them to live a Christian life by word and example. Parenting requires patience and compassion. You have to mirror the attributes of God (persistence, patience, mercy) and demonstrate a good Christian marriage (1 Tim. 3:4, 12). It helps if you are reliable and trustworthy, like God. Your children depend on you to be there for them.

Sometimes it's just plain hard being a parent. But during those hard times we must walk in faith. Sometimes you go without certain things so that your children will have what they need for school and other necessities. But God always provides the necessities of life.

Parenting is a full-time, life-long position. Although some may think parenting stops when children become of age, it really does not. Parenting is what you make of it. It can be fun or it can be frightening. Married or single, parenting is hard work!

Read 2 Timothy 1:3-5; see also Deuteronomy 6:4-9; Proverbs 19:18; 22:6, 15; Titus 2:1–6.

Read the insight essays on Children, and Motherhood.

—S. Demby

FRUIT OF THE SPIRIT—SELF-CONTROL

When a woman chooses to control her thoughts, feelings, and actions rather than allowing them to master her, she is exercising self-control (see Titus 2:4–5). Self-control is a personal discipline that allows us to say no to things that are ungodly and say yes to God's will for our lives. If we want to be successful, we must exercise self-control. This fruit of the Spirit is what makes us stay in and do our homework when we'd rather be outside playing; it is what gives us the strength to say no to drugs and sex when everyone around us is saying yes.

Self-control allows us to be obedient to our parents and to God when the world is telling us to do our own thing. Self-control gives us the courage to walk away from a fight and helps us stand when everyone is calling us punks and sissies. Self-control keeps our mouths shut and our attitudes in check; and it allows us to take a stand for Jesus, even if we must stand alone. Self-control is necessary if we are to stay focused and be successful in life. God gives us this character trait as we listen to the Holy Spirit and allow Him to guide our lives.

As a young African-American woman, I know that in order to stay in control I must study God's Word and allow it to sink into my heart. I know that self-control is necessary for my personal development, my spiritual growth, and my Christian service. Sometimes that is hard, especially when many of my friends try to put me down. I believe that my generation is called for a special purpose in God. When we live our lives with self-control, we acknowledge that God a plan for our lives; thus, we tell the world that we have chosen to honor God's purpose. Without self-control, we have little opportunity to experience God's blessings.

Read Titus 2:4–5; see also Psalm 19:14; Galatians 5:22–23; 1 Timothy 4:7–8; 2 Peter 1:5–8.

Read the insight essays on Fruit of the Spirit, Perseverance, and Spiritual Discipline.

—K. Belt

FAITH

"Faith is the substance of things hoped for, the evidence of things not seen" (Heb. 11:1). Faith is a present act that is oriented toward a future hope. Faith is intangible, but manifests itself in tangible results. We are told that "without faith it is impossible to please him" (Heb. 11:6). God is the object of all faith and only "the fool hath said in his heart, There is no God" (Ps. 14:1).

God has given each person a measure of faith (Rom. 12:3). It can remain stagnant or it can grow. Do nothing with faith, and even that which you have will be taken away. However, if used, like muscle, it will grow and become strong. In a world fraught with anxiety brought on by challenges, expectations, conflicts, problems, fears, strengths, hopes, and dreams, faith is essential for survival. We must posture ourselves to strengthen our faith through constantly saturating our consciousness with the Word of God until it penetrates and fills the hollow places of our souls.

With God all things are possible (Matt. 19:26). The Bible lists many heroes and heroines who did unimaginable things because they stepped out in faith. This group (Heb, 11:4–39) has been labeled as "so great a

cloud of witnesses" (Heb. 12:1). A brief review of their faith indicates: (1) we must believe that God exists, and (2) God rewards those who diligently seek Him (Heb. 11:6) and follow His guidance.

We must add to this cloud of witnesses God's ebony children—Harriet Tubman, Sojourner Truth, Mary Bethune, Ida B. Wells, Rosa Parks, Fannie Lou Hamer, and millions of unsung heroines who operate daily in faith. God honors those who honor Him.

Read Hebrews 11.

Read the portraits on Hannah, Phoebe, and Rahab.

—C. Archibald

PERSEVERANCE—HELP! I'M RUNNING TO SAVE MY LIFE!

Perseverance is not a choice—it is a must for those who choose to survive. In addition, if we are going to achieve our goals in life or become successful in any way, we must choose to persevere. We must stay focused on our goals by keeping them in view while we run the race to save our lives. Bear in mind we are going to experience many failures, run into many obstacles, and encounter many barriers on the road to our destination. But we must continue to persevere. God has already given us the power to be overcomers.

Faith, prayer, self-control, and obedience are critical elements that help us persevere. We must be fully aware that if we complete the race with faith and commitment we will be rewarded with God's blessings, both now and in eternity (Matt. 24:13; Heb. 11:6; Rev. 21:7).

There was once a geologist who was an experienced Mt. Everest climber. On one occasion he got caught in a storm with his team. Eight people on his team died because of the subzero temperatures and lack of oxygen. He knew that he, too, would die if he did not throw off the excess weight that caused him to slow his pace. Consequently, he dropped his backpack that contained all the essentials for life, including food, water, and liquid oxygen. The geologist did however, retain one essential item—a radio. His hands were frostbitten to the point that he couldn't feel them anymore and his legs were numb; yet he continued to place one foot in front of the other. The geologist knew that he walked to save his life. He was able to stay on course using the radio. His friends were on the other end of the radio encouraging him to continue walking. When he stopped, his friends would keep him talking and alert. They knew if he got comfortable and fell asleep he was not going to win the race to save his life. After many hours of walking, the geologist made it back to camp. He lost both hands to frostbite, but he saved his life. The difference between the geologist that made it back to camp and those who died was perseverance and determination.

Many of us, like the geologist, are in a storm that could cause us to lose our life, a marriage, children, or jobs if we don't persevere. There may be a storm in our marriage, or our spouse may be ready to walk out the door, but perseverance will make the difference between those marriages that end in divorce and those that survive. Sure, we are going to be tossed about because of financial difficulty, neglect, and fatigue. All our desires are not going to be reached. But remember: we are in a race to

save our lives. We must drop everything that burdens us and makes us feel like giving up. We must lay aside pride, selfishness, disappointment, broken promises, and disillusionment, and give those burdens to God.

Yes, we must endure pain, suffering, hurt, and embarrassment in our quest to win the race. What is perseverance but staying our course despite failure and disappointment? To persevere is to try, try, and try again regardless of circumstances or conditions. We may get tired and frustrated along the way, but we must continue to place one foot in front of the other. Anyone who has experienced success has also experienced failure, setback, disillusionment, and pain prior to winning the race.

Whether we are in the race toward a good marriage, financial stability, a college degree, certification, or other challenges, we must persevere. Life's victories are not won by those with the best plans but by those who, through faith, persevere in the race. If you stay focused on Jesus you can hold up under any load.

In life, if you have a purpose in which you can believe, there's no end to the amount of things you can accomplish. — Marian Anderson

Read Hebrews 11:1; 12:1; see also Matthew 6:33; Luke 14:28–30.
Read the insight essays on Commitment, Faith, and Prayer.

—C. Grace-Scott

TEMPTATION

Life is full of temptation! Everyone will struggle with some kind of temptation throughout the course of her life. Temptation is an enticement to sin. However, the example of Jesus Christ and the Word of God teach us how we can overcome temptation. The Bible teaches us that God does not tempt us, but states rather that temptation arises from two sources: our own passions (James 1:13–15), and Satan, often called the "tempter" (Luke 4:2). God allows us to be tempted to teach us obedience, trust, and loyalty to Him. Although being a Christian does not exempt us from experiencing temptation, God does promise not to tempt us beyond what we can bear. Instead He provides a way of escape (1 Cor. 10:13). Jesus shows us that using the Word of God is an effective means of overcoming temptation (Matt. 4:1–11). The Bible says, "Thy word is a lamp unto my feet, and a light unto my path" (Ps. 119:105). When we submit ourselves to God, through obedience to His Word, we find strength to resist the devil. When we resist, he will flee (James 4:7).

Read James 1:13–15.
Read the insight essay on Abuse. Read the portrait on Delilah.

—J. Thompson

LOVE

"Let us not love in word, neither in tongue; but in deed and in truth." (1 John 3:18)

Across the TV screen comes an ad, and a little girl, accustomed to turning off her feelings, watches. As the harried businessman on TV receives one harassment after another, she is amused at all of the people fussing at him—his secretary, his boss, and other coworkers.

The little girl has a twisted sense of what is funny. She has been left

alone to amuse herself too much and has learned to laugh at the pain of others. She finds the same humor in real hurt as she finds in the violence in cartoons, which is, unfortunately, intended to be funny. She also has been fussed at and shamed so much when in her father's company, that she has not experienced many healthy joys.

So when the man on TV receives a phone call from his wife, the little girl expects he will receive yet another browbeating. She is surprised when the wife's message is a simple "I love you." She sees his face light up as his wife demonstrated in words her love for him. Love should be demonstrated (1 John 3:14, 18; 4:7, 20). He stops frowning and takes a deep breath. There is a far away look in his eyes as if he is no longer bothered by the maltreatment he has just received. As 1 John 3:11 suggests, love is not an option. The man even looks like he's feeling positive about the people around him.

The little girl is amazed. A strange feeling comes over her. She likes it. She feels—for a brief moment—warm and special inside. Perhaps she feels God's impression of love in her heart (1 John 3:17), and she wonders what it would be like to be loved—to hear those words said to her.

As a bright 12-year-old, she reads and writes adequately, and has lots of time to think. She wonders how she could make that feeling come again. She turns off the TV, then looks around for a pencil and some paper. She finds some in her school bag, all balled up and written on one side. *This will do,* she thinks.

At first she just writes the words *I love you, I love you,* over and over. Then she whispers them. It feels nice to say those three little words. Unbeknownst to her, she is beginning to feel God's love for her (see 1 John 4:19). Because of this, a thought comes to her mind. Perhaps she will get someone to love her—one day. But what must she do?

We know the Bible says, "Thy word have I hid in my heart" (Ps. 119:11). The little girl is impressed that she can receive love if she dares to give love. She writes a note to her dad. It says, *Dear Dad, I love you. Your girl, Jamelle.*

When we express our love to others, we allow God's love to shine through us (1 John 3:14; 4:7, 20). All through the Bible we are shown God's love and told to show His love to others: our friends and family—even those who may not like us or whom we dislike. The Bible not only tells us to love, it tells us *how* to love (1 John 3:18; 4:7–8). This day, why not sing out loud, or just in your mind, the little song: " 'Tis Love That Makes Us Happy." The words are:

> God is love; we're His little children.
> God is love; we would be like Him.
> 'Tis love that makes us happy,
> 'Tis love that smoothes the way;
> It helps us mind, it makes us kind
> To others every day.
>
> —F. E. Belden, 1892

Read 1 John 3:16–18.

Read the insight essays on Attributes of God, Fruit of the Spirit, Marriage, and Romance.

—E. Watson

takers of the benefit. These things teach and
exhort.
3 If any man teach otherwise, and consent [i]not to wholesome words, *even* the
words of our Lord Jesus Christ, [j]and to the
doctrine which is according to godliness;
4 He is proud, [k]knowing nothing, but dot-
ing about [l]questions and strifes of words,
whereof cometh envy, strife, railings, evil
surmisings,
5 [m]Perverse disputings of [n]men of corrupt minds, and destitute of the truth, [o]sup-
posing that gain is godliness: [p]from such
withdraw thyself.
6 But [q]godliness with contentment is
great gain.
7 For [r]we brought nothing into *this*
world, *and it is* certain we can carry nothing
out.
8 And [s]having food and raiment let us be
therewith content.
9 But [t]they that will be rich fall into
temptation and a snare, and *into* many foolish and hurtful lusts, which drown men in
destruction and perdition.
10 [u]For the love of money is the root of all
evil: which while some coveted after, they
have erred from the faith, and pierced themselves through with many sorrows.
11 [v]But thou, [w]O man of God, flee these
things; and follow after righteousness, godliness, faith, love, patience, meekness.
12 [x]Fight the good fight of faith, [y]lay
hold on eternal life, whereunto thou art also
called, [z]and hast professed a good profession before many witnesses.
13 I give thee charge in the sight of God,
[a]who quickeneth all things, and *before*
Christ Jesus, [b]who before Pontius Pilate
witnessed a good confession;
14 That thou keep *this* commandment
without spot, unrebukeable, [c]until the appearing of our Lord Jesus Christ:
15 Which in his times he shall shew, *who
is* the blessed and only Potentate, [d]the King
of kings, and Lord of lords;
16 Who only hath immortality, dwelling
in the light which no man can approach
unto; [e]whom no man hath seen, nor can
see: [f]to whom *be* honour and power everlasting. Amen.
17 Charge them that are rich in this
world, that they be not highminded, [g]nor
trust in [h]uncertain riches, but in [i]the living
God, [j]who giveth us richly all things to enjoy;
18 That they do good, that [k]they be rich
in good works, [l]ready to distribute, [m]will-
ing to communicate;
19 [n]Laying up in store for themselves a
good foundation against the time to come,
that they may lay hold on eternal life.
20 O Timothy, [o]keep that which is committed to thy trust, [p]avoiding profane *and*
vain babblings, and oppositions of science
falsely so called:
21 Which some professing [q]have erred
concerning the faith. Grace *be* with thee.
Amen.

6:3 *i*2 Tim. 1:13 *j*Tit. 1:1
6:4 *k*1 Cor. 8:2 *l*2 Tim. 2:23
6:5 *m*1 Cor. 11:16 *n*2 Tim. 3:8 *o*Tit. 1:11 *p*Rom. 16:17
6:6 *q*Ps. 37:16; Heb. 13:5
6:7 *r*Job 1:21; Prov. 27:24; Eccl. 5:15
6:8 *s*Gen. 28:20
6:9 *t*Prov. 15:27; Jam. 5:1
6:10 *u*Ex. 23:8
6:11 *v*2 Tim. 2:22 *w*Deut. 33:1
6:12 *x*1 Cor. 9:25 *y*Phil. 3:12 *z*Heb. 13:23
6:13 *a*Deut. 32:39; John 5:21 *b*Matt. 27:11; Rev. 1:5
6:14 *c*Phil. 1:6
6:15 *d*Rev. 17:14
6:16 *e*Ex. 33:20 *f*Eph. 3:21; Jude 25; Rev. 1:6
6:17 *g*Job 31:24; Mark 10:24; Luke 12:21 *h*Prov. 23:5 *i*1 Thess. 1:9 *j*Acts 14:17
6:18 *k*Luke 12:21; Jam. 2:5 *l*Rom. 12:13 *m*Gal. 6:6
6:19 *n*Matt. 6:20
6:20 *o*2 Tim. 1:14; Rev. 3:3 *p*2 Tim. 2:14
6:21 *q*2 Tim. 2:18

2 TIMOTHY

Paul is the author of 2 Timothy, which was probably written about A.D. 66. Paul's customary greeting is followed by his encouragement to Timothy to have courage and remain faithful to sound doctrine. In the second chapter, Paul describes the attributes of a man of God. Included in this description is the best known verse in 2 Timothy (2:15). The third chapter describes the apostasy that would mark the Last Days and the means of overcoming that apostasy. Second Timothy closes with additional instructions on preaching the gospel and a brief statement concerning the afterlife.

I. Greetings to Timothy, 1:1–1:17
II. Exhortations to Timothy, 1:8–1:18
III. The attributes of a man of God, 2:1–2:26
IV. The Last Days, 3:1–3:17
V. Further exhortations to Timothy, 4:1–4:8
VI. Closing greetings, 4:9–4:22

---

1 Paul, [a]an apostle of Jesus Christ by the
will of God, according to [b]the promise
of life which is in Christ Jesus,
2 [c]To Timothy, *my* dearly beloved son:
Grace, mercy, *and* peace, from God the Father and Christ Jesus our Lord.
3 [d]I thank God, [e]whom I serve from *my*
forefathers with pure conscience, that
[f]without ceasing I have remembrance of
thee in my prayers night and day;
4 Greatly desiring to see thee, being
mindful of thy tears, that I may be filled
with joy;
5 When I call to remembrance [g]the unfeigned faith that is in thee, which dwelt
first in thy grandmother Lois, and [h]thy
mother Eunice; and I am persuaded that in
thee also.
6 Wherefore I put thee in remembrance
[i]that thou stir up the gift of God, which is
in thee by the putting on of my hands.
7 For [j]God hath not given us the spirit of
fear; [k]but of power, and of love, and of a
sound mind.
8 [l]Be not thou therefore ashamed of [m]the
testimony of our Lord, nor of me [n]his prisoner: [o]but be thou partaker of the afflictions of the gospel according to the power of
God;
9 [p]Who hath saved us, and [q]called *us*
with an holy calling, [r]not according to our
works, but [s]according to his own purpose
and grace, which was given us in Christ
Jesus [t]before the world began,
10 But [u]is now made manifest by the appearing of our Saviour Jesus Christ, [v]who
hath abolished death, and hath brought life
and immortality to light through the gospel:
11 [w]Whereunto I am appointed a
preacher, and an apostle, and a teacher of
the Gentiles.
12 [x]For the which cause I also suffer
these things: nevertheless I am not
ashamed: [y]for I know whom I have believed, and am persuaded that he is able to
[z]keep that which I have committed unto
him against that day.
13 [a]Hold fast [b]the form of [c]sound
words, which thou hast heard of me, [d]in
faith and love which is in Christ Jesus.
14 [e]That good thing which was committed unto thee keep by the Holy Ghost
[f]which dwelleth in us.
15 This thou knowest, that [g]all they
which are in Asia be turned away from me;
of whom are Phygellus and Hermogenes.
16 The Lord [h]give mercy unto the house
of Onesiphorus; [i]for he oft refreshed me,
and was not ashamed of [j]my chain:
17 But, when he was in Rome, he sought
me out very diligently, and found *me.*
18 The Lord grant unto him [k]that he may
find mercy of the Lord [l]in that day: and in
how many things he [m]ministered unto me at
Ephesus, thou knowest very well.

2 Thou therefore, [n]my son, [o]be strong in
the grace that is in Christ Jesus.
2 And the things that thou hast heard of
me among many witnesses, [p]the same commit thou to faithful men, who shall be [q]able
to teach others also.
3 Thou therefore endure hardness, [r]as a
good soldier of Jesus Christ.
4 [s]No man that warreth entangleth himself with the affairs of *this* life; that he may
please him who hath chosen him to be a
soldier.
5 And [t]if a man also strive for masteries,
yet is he not crowned, except he strive lawfully.
6 [u]The husbandman that laboureth must
be first partaker of the fruits.
7 Consider what I say; and the Lord give
thee understanding in all things.
8 Remember that Jesus Christ [v]of the
seed of David [w]was raised from the dead
[x]according to my gospel:
9 [y]Wherein I suffer trouble, as an evildoer, [z]*even* unto bonds; [a]but the word of
God is not bound.

1:1 *a*2 Cor. 1:1 *b*Eph. 3:6; Heb. 9:15
1:2 *c*1 Tim. 1:2
1:3 *d*Rom. 1:8 *e*Acts 22:3; Gal. 1:14 *f*1 Thess. 1:2
1:5 *g*1 Tim. 1:5 *h*Acts 16:1
1:6 *i*1 Thess. 5:19
1:7 *j*Rom. 8:15 *k*Luke 24:49
1:8 *l*Rom. 1:16 *m*1 Tim. 2:6 *n*Eph. 3:1 *o*Col. 1:24
1:9 *p*1 Tim. 1:1 *q*1 Thess. 4:7 *r*Rom. 3:20 *s*Rom. 8:28 *t*Rom. 16:25; Tit. 1:2; 1 Pet. 1:20
1:10 *u*Rom. 16:26; Col. 1:26; Tit. 1:3 *v*1 Cor. 15:54
1:11 *w*Acts 9:15; 1 Tim. 2:7
1:12 *x*Eph. 3:1 *y*1 Pet. 4:19 *z*1 Tim. 6:20
1:13 *a*Tit. 1:9; Rev. 2:25 *b*Rom. 2:20 *c*1 Tim. 1:10 *d*1 Tim. 1:14
1:14 *e*1 Tim. 6:20 *f*Rom. 8:11
1:15 *g*Acts 19:10
1:16 *h*Matt. 5:7 *i*Philem. 7 *j*Acts 28:20
1:18 *k*Matt. 25:34-40 *l*2 Thess. 1:10 *m*Heb. 6:10
2:1 *n*1 Tim. 1:2 *o*Eph. 6:10
2:2 *p*1 Tim. 1:18 *q*1 Tim. 3:2
2:3 *r*1 Tim. 1:18
2:4 *s*1 Cor. 9:25
2:5 *t*1 Cor. 9:25
2:6 *u*1 Cor. 9:10
2:8 *v*Rom. 1:3 *w*1 Cor. 15:1 *x*Rom. 2:16
2:9 *y*Acts 9:16 *z*Eph. 3:1; Col. 4:3 *a*Acts 28:31; Phil. 1:13

10 Therefore [b]I endure all things for the elect's sakes, [c]that they may also obtain the salvation which is in Christ Jesus with eternal glory.

11 [d]*It is* a faithful saying: For [e]if we be dead with *him*, we shall also live with *him:*

12 [f]If we suffer, we shall also reign with *him:* [g]if we deny *him*, he also will deny us:

13 [h]If we believe not, *yet* he abideth faithful: [i]he cannot deny himself.

14 Of these things put *them* in remembrance, [j]charging *them* before the Lord [k]that they strive not about words to no profit, *but* to the subverting of the hearers.

15 Study to shew thyself approved unto God, a workman that needeth not to be ashamed, rightly dividing the word of truth.

16 But [l]shun profane *and* vain babblings: for they will increase unto more ungodliness.

17 And their word will eat as doth a canker: of whom is [m]Hymenaeus and Philetus;

18 Who [n]concerning the truth have erred, [o]saying that the resurrection is past already; and overthrow the faith of some.

19 Nevertheless [p]the foundation of God standeth sure, having this seal, The Lord [q]knoweth them that are his. And, Let every one that nameth the name of Christ depart from iniquity.

20 [r]But in a great house there are not only vessels of gold and of silver, but also of wood and of earth; [s]and some to honour, and some to dishonour.

21 [t]If a man therefore purge himself from these, he shall be a vessel unto honour, sanctified, and meet for the master's use, *and* [u]prepared unto every good work.

22 Flee also youthful lusts: but [v]follow righteousness, faith, charity, peace, with them that [w]call on the Lord [x]out of a pure heart.

23 But [y]foolish and unlearned questions avoid, knowing that they do gender strifes.

24 And [z]the servant of the Lord must not strive; but be gentle unto all *men*, [a]apt to teach, patient,

25 [b]In meekness instructing those that oppose themselves; [c]if God peradventure will give them repentance [d]to the acknowledging of the truth;

26 And *that* they may recover themselves [e]out of the snare of the devil, who are taken captive by him at his will.

3 This know also, that [f]in the last days perilous times shall come.

2 For men shall be [g]lovers of their own selves, [h]covetous, [i]boasters, [j]proud, [k]blasphemers, [l]disobedient to parents, unthankful, unholy,

3 [m]Without natural affection, [n]trucebreakers, false accusers, [o]incontinent, fierce, despisers of those that are good,

4 [p]Traitors, heady, highminded, [q]lovers of pleasures more than lovers of God;

5 Having a form of godliness, but [r]denying the power thereof: [s]from such turn away.

6 For [t]of this sort are they which creep into houses, and lead captive silly women laden with sins, led away with divers lusts,

7 Ever learning, and never able [u]to come to the knowledge of the truth.

8 [v]Now as Jannes and Jambres withstood Moses, so do these also resist the truth: [w]men of corrupt minds, [x]reprobate concerning the faith.

9 But they shall proceed no further: for their folly shall be manifest unto all *men*, [y]as theirs also was.

10 [z]But thou hast fully known my doctrine, manner of life, purpose, faith, longsuffering, charity, patience,

11 Persecutions, afflictions, which came unto me [a]at Antioch, [b]at Iconium, [c]at Lystra; what persecutions I endured: but [d]out of *them* all the Lord delivered me.

12 Yea, and [e]all that will live godly in Christ Jesus shall suffer persecution.

13 [f]But evil men and seducers shall wax worse and worse, deceiving, and being deceived.

14 But continue thou in the things which thou hast learned and hast been assured of, knowing of whom thou hast learned *them;*

15 And that from a child thou hast known [g]the holy scriptures, which are able to make thee wise unto salvation through faith which is in Christ Jesus.

16 [h]All scripture *is* given by inspiration of God, [i]and *is* profitable for doctrine, for reproof, for correction, for instruction in righteousness:

17 [j]That the man of God may be perfect, throughly furnished unto all good works.

4 I [k]charge *thee* therefore before God, and the Lord Jesus Christ, [l]who shall judge the quick and the dead at his appearing and his kingdom;

2 Preach the word; be instant in season, out of season; reprove, [m]rebuke, [n]exhort with all longsuffering and doctrine.

3 For the time will come when they will not endure [o]sound doctrine; but after their own lusts shall they heap to themselves teachers, having itching ears;

4 And they shall turn away *their* ears from the truth, and [p]shall be turned unto fables.

5 But watch thou in all things, endure afflictions, do the work of [q]an evangelist, make full proof of thy ministry.

6 For [r]I am now ready to be offered, and the time of [s]my departure is at hand.

7 [t]I have fought a good fight, I have finished *my* course, I have kept the faith:

8 Henceforth there is laid up for me [u]a crown of righteousness, which the Lord, the righteous judge, shall give me at that day: and not to me only, but unto all them also that love his appearing.

9 Do thy diligence to come shortly unto me:

10 For [v]Demas hath forsaken me, [w]having loved this present world, and is de-

2:10 [b]Eph. 3:13 [c]2 Cor. 1:6
2:11 [d]1 Tim. 1:15 [e]Rom. 6:5
2:12 [f]Rom. 8:17 [g]Matt. 10:33; Luke 12:9
2:13 [h]Rom. 3:3 [i]Num. 23:19
2:14 [j]1 Tim. 5:21 [k]1 Tim. 1:4
2:16 [l]1 Tim. 4:7
2:17 [m]1 Tim. 1:20
2:18 [n]1 Tim. 6:21 [o]1 Cor. 15:12
2:19 [p]Matt. 24:24; 1 John 2:19 [q]Num. 16:5; John 10:14
2:20 [r]1 Tim. 3:15 [s]Rom. 9:21
2:21 [t]Isa. 52:11 [u]Tit. 3:1
2:22 [v]1 Tim. 6:11 [w]Acts 9:14 [x]1 Tim. 1:5
2:23 [y]1 Tim. 1:4
2:24 [z]Tit. 3:2 [a]1 Tim. 3:2
2:25 [b]Gal. 6:1; 1 Pet. 3:15 [c]Acts 8:22 [d]1 Tim. 2:4
2:26 [e]1 Tim. 3:7
3:1 [f]1 Tim. 4:1; 1 John 2:18; Jude 18
3:2 [g]Phil. 2:21 [h]2 Pet. 2:3 [i]Jude 16 [j]1 Tim. 6:4 [k]1 Tim. 1:20; Jude 10 [l]Rom. 1:30
3:3 [m]Rom. 1:31 [n]Rom. 1:31 [o]2 Pet. 3:3
3:4 [p]2 Pet. 2:10 [q]Phil. 3:19; Jude 4
3:5 [r]1 Tim. 5:8 [s]2 Thess. 3:6
3:6 [t]Matt. 23:14
3:7 [u]1 Tim. 2:4
3:8 [v]Ex. 7:11 [w]1 Tim. 6:5 [x]Rom. 1:28; Tit. 1:16
3:9 [y]Ex. 7:12
3:10 [z]Phil. 2:22
3:11 [a]Acts 13:45 [b]Acts 14:2 [c]Acts 14:19 [d]Ps. 34:19
3:12 [e]Ps. 34:19; Matt. 16:24; Josh. 17:14; 1 Thess. 3:3
3:13 [f]2 Thess. 2:11
3:15 [g]John 5:39
3:16 [h]2 Pet. 1:20 [i]Rom. 15:4
3:17 [j]1 Tim. 6:11
4:1 [k]1 Tim. 5:21 [l]Acts 10:42
4:2 [m]1 Tim. 5:20 [n]1 Tim. 4:13
4:3 [o]1 Tim. 1:10
4:4 [p]1 Tim. 1:4
4:5 [q]Acts 21:8
4:6 [r]Phil. 2:17 [s]Phil. 1:23
4:7 [t]1 Cor. 9:24; 1 Tim. 6:12; Heb. 12:1
4:8 [u]1 Cor. 9:25; 1 Pet. 5:4; Rev. 2:10
4:10 [v]Col. 4:15 [w]1 John 2:15

parted unto Thessalonica; Crescens to Galatia, Titus unto Dalmatia.

11 Only [x]Luke is with me. Take [y]Mark, and bring him with thee: for he is profitable to me for the ministry.

12 And [z]Tychicus have I sent to Ephesus.

13 The cloke that I left at Troas with Carpus, when thou comest, bring *with thee,* and the books, *but* especially the parchments.

14 [a]Alexander the coppersmith did me much evil: [b]the Lord reward him according to his works:

15 Of whom be thou ware also; for he hath greatly withstood our words.

16 At my first answer no man stood with me, but all *men* forsook me: [c]*I pray God* that it may not be laid to their charge.

17 [d]Notwithstanding the Lord stood with me, and strengthened me; [e]that by me the preaching might be fully known, and *that* all the Gentiles might hear: and I was delivered [f]out of the mouth of the lion.

18 [g]And the Lord shall deliver me from every evil work, and will preserve *me* unto his heavenly kingdom: [h]to whom *be* glory for ever and ever. Amen.

19 Salute [i]Prisca and Aquila, and the [j]household of Onesiphorus.

20 [k]Erastus abode at Corinth: but [l]Trophimus have I left at Miletum sick.

21 Do thy diligence to come before winter. Eubulus greeteth thee, and Pudens, and Linus, and Claudia, and all the brethren.

22 [m]The Lord Jesus Christ *be* with thy spirit. Grace *be* with you. Amen.

4:11 [x]Col. 4:14 [y]Acts 12:25
4:12 [z]Acts 20:4; Col. 4:7; Tit. 3:12
4:14 [a]Acts 19:33 [b]2 Sam. 3:39; Rev. 18:6
4:16 [c]Acts 7:60
4:17 [d]Matt. 10:19 [e]Acts 9:15 [f]Ps. 22:21
4:18 [g]Ps. 121:7 [h]Rom. 11:36; Heb. 13:21
4:19 [i]Acts 18:2 [j]2 Tim. 1:16
4:20 [k]Acts 19:22 [l]Acts 20:4
4:22 [m]Gal. 6:18

TITUS

Paul acknowledges himself as the author of Titus, which was probably written about A.D. 65. The book of Titus opens with Paul's greetings to Titus followed by directions for appointing church leaders, dealing with false teachers, and a description of the duties of a minister. In the last part of chapter two, Paul reaffirms the proper response to the grace of God. Titus concludes with information concerning godly conduct and several personal messages from Paul to various people.

I. Greetings to Titus, 1:1–1:4
II. Church requirements, 1:5–2:10
III. God's grace, 2:11-2:15
IV. Godly conduct, 3:1–3:11
V. Closing greetings and personal messages, 3:12–3:15

---

1 Paul, a servant of God, and an apostle of Jesus Christ, according to the faith of God's elect, and [a]the acknowledging of the truth [b]which is after godliness;

2 [c]In hope of eternal life, which God, [d]that cannot lie, promised [e]before the world began;

3 [f]But hath in due times manifested his word through preaching, [g]which is committed unto me [h]according to the commandment of God our Saviour;

4 To [i]Titus, [j]*mine* own son after [k]the common faith: [l]Grace, mercy, *and* peace, from God the Father and the Lord Jesus Christ our Saviour.

5 For this cause left I thee in Crete, that thou shouldest [m]set in order the things that are wanting, and [n]ordain elders in every city, as I had appointed thee:

6 [o]If any be blameless, [p]the husband of one wife, [q]having faithful children not accused of riot or unruly.

7 For a bishop must be blameless, as [r]the steward of God; not selfwilled, not soon angry, [s]not given to wine, no striker, [t]not given to filthy lucre;

8 [u]But a lover of hospitality, a lover of good men, sober, just, holy, temperate;

9 [v]Holding fast [w]the faithful word as he hath been taught, that he may be able [x]by sound doctrine both to exhort and to convince the gainsayers.

10 For [y]there are many unruly and vain talkers and [z]deceivers, [a]specially they of the circumcision:

11 Whose mouths must be stopped, [b]who subvert whole houses, teaching things which they ought not, [c]for filthy lucre's sake.

12 [d]One of themselves, *even* a prophet of their own, said, The Cretians *are* alway liars, evil beasts, slow bellies.

13 This witness is true. [e]Wherefore rebuke them sharply, that they may be sound in the faith;

14 [f]Not giving heed to Jewish fables, and

1:1 [a]2 Tim. 2:25 [b]1 Tim. 3:16
1:2 [c]2 Tim. 1:1 [d]Num. 23:19 [e]Rom. 16:25; 1 Pet. 1:20
1:3 [f]2 Tim. 1:10 [g]1 Thess. 2:4 [h]1 Tim. 1:1
1:4 [i]2 Cor. 2:13 [j]1 Tim. 1:2 [k]Rom. 1:12; 2 Pet. 1:1 [l]Eph. 1:2; 1 Tim. 1:2; 2 Tim. 1:2
1:5 [m]1 Cor. 11:34 [n]Acts 14:23
1:6 [o]1 Tim. 3:2 [p]1 Tim. 3:12 [q]1 Tim. 3:4
1:7 [r]Matt. 24:45 [s]Lev. 10:9; Eph. 5:18 [t]1 Tim. 3:3
1:8 [u]1 Tim. 3:2
1:9 [v]2 Thess. 2:15 [w]1 Tim. 1:15 [x]1 Tim. 1:10
1:10 [y]1 Tim. 1:6 [z]Rom. 16:18 [a]Acts 15:1
1:11 [b]Matt. 23:14 [c]1 Tim. 6:5
1:12 [d]Acts 17:28
1:13 [e]2 Cor. 13:10
1:14 [f]1 Tim. 1:4

[g]commandments of men, that turn from the truth.

15 [h]Unto the pure all things *are* pure: but [i]unto them that are defiled and unbelieving *is* nothing pure; but even their mind and conscience is defiled.

16 They profess that they know God; but [j]in works they deny *him*, being abominable, and disobedient, [k]and unto every good work reprobate.

2 But speak thou the things which become [l]sound doctrine:

2 That the aged men be sober, grave, temperate, sound in faith, in charity, in patience.

3 [m]The aged women likewise, that *they be* in behaviour as becometh holiness, not false accusers, not given to much wine, teachers of good things;

4 That they may teach the young women to be sober, [n]to love their husbands, to love their children,

5 *To be* discreet, chaste, keepers at home, good, [o]obedient to their own husbands, [p]that the word of God be not blasphemed.

6 Young men likewise exhort to be sober minded.

7 [q]In all things shewing thyself a pattern of good works: in doctrine *shewing* uncorruptness, gravity, [r]sincerity,

8 [s]Sound speech, that cannot be condemned; [t]that he that is of the contrary part [u]may be ashamed, having no evil thing to say of you.

9 *Exhort* [v]servants to be obedient unto their own masters, *and* to please *them* well [w]in all *things;* not answering again;

10 Not purloining, but shewing all good fidelity; [x]that they may adorn the doctrine of God our Saviour in all things.

11 For [y]the grace of God that bringeth salvation [z]hath appeared to all men,

12 Teaching us [a]that, denying ungodliness [b]and worldly lusts, we should live soberly, righteously, and godly, in this present world;

13 [c]Looking for that blessed [d]hope, and the glorious [e]appearing of the great God and our Saviour Jesus Christ;

14 [f]Who gave himself for us, that he might redeem us from all iniquity, [g]and purify unto himself [h]a peculiar people, [i]zealous of good works.

15 These things speak, and [j]exhort, and rebuke with all authority. [k]Let no man despise thee.

3 Put them in mind [l]to be subject to principalities and powers, to obey magistrates, [m]to be ready to every good work,

2 [n]To speak evil of no man, [o]to be no brawlers, *but* [p]gentle, shewing all [q]meekness unto all men.

3 For [r]we ourselves also were sometimes foolish, disobedient, deceived, serving divers lusts and pleasures, living in malice and envy, hateful, *and* hating one another.

4 But after that the kindness and love of [s]God our Saviour toward man appeared,

5 [t]Not by works of righteousness which we have done, but according to his mercy he saved us, by [u]the washing of regeneration, and renewing of the Holy Ghost;

6 [v]Which he shed on us abundantly through Jesus Christ our Saviour;

7 [w]That being justified by his grace, [x]we should be made heirs according to the hope of eternal life.

8 [y]*This is* a faithful saying, and these things I will that thou affirm constantly, that they which have believed in God might be careful to maintain good works. These things are good and profitable unto men.

9 But [z]avoid foolish questions, and genealogies, and contentions, and strivings about the law; [a]for they are unprofitable and vain.

10 A man that is an heretick [b]after the first and second admonition [c]reject;

11 Knowing that he that is such is subverted, and sinneth, [d]being condemned of himself.

12 When I shall send Artemas unto thee, or [e]Tychicus, be diligent to come unto me to Nicopolis: for I have determined there to winter.

13 Bring Zenas the lawyer and [f]Apollos on their journey diligently, that nothing be wanting unto them.

14 And let ours also learn to maintain good works for necessary uses, that they be [g]not unfruitful.

15 All that are with me salute thee. Greet them that love us in the faith. Grace *be* with you all. Amen.

1:14 [g]Isa. 29:13; Col. 2:22
1:15 [h]Luke 11:39; 1 Cor. 6:12; 1 Tim. 4:3 [i]Rom. 14:23
1:16 [j]2 Tim. 3:5 [k]Rom. 1:28
2:1 [l]1 Tim. 1:10
2:3 [m]1 Tim. 2:9
2:4 [n]1 Tim. 5:14
2:5 [o]1 Cor. 14:34; Col. 3:18; 1 Tim. 2:11 [p]Rom. 2:24
2:7 [q]1 Tim. 4:12 [r]Eph. 6:24
2:8 [s]1 Tim. 6:3 [t]Neh. 5:9; 1 Pet. 2:12 [u]2 Thess. 3:14
2:9 [v]Eph. 6:5; 1 Tim. 6:1; 1 Pet. 2:18 [w]Eph. 5:24
2:10 [x]Matt. 5:16
2:11 [y]Rom. 5:15 [z]Luke 3:6; 1 Tim. 2:4
2:12 [a]Luke 1:75; Eph. 1:4; Col. 1:22 [b]1 Pet. 4:2
2:13 [c]1 Cor. 1:7; 2 Pet. 3:12 [d]Acts 24:15 [e]Col. 3:4; Heb. 9:28; 1 Pet. 1:7
2:14 [f]Gal. 1:4; 1 Tim. 2:6 [g]Heb. 9:14 [h]Ex. 15:16; 1 Pet. 2:9 [i]Eph. 2:10
2:15 [j]2 Tim. 4:2 [k]1 Tim. 4:12
3:1 [l]Rom. 13:1 [m]Col. 1:10; Heb. 13:21
3:2 [n]Eph. 4:31 [o]2 Tim. 2:24 [p]Phil. 4:5 [q]Eph. 4:2
3:3 [r]1 Cor. 6:11; Col. 1:21; 1 Pet. 4:3
3:4 [s]1 Tim. 2:3
3:5 [t]Rom. 3:20; Eph. 2:4; 2 Tim. 1:9 [u]John 3:3; 1 Pet. 3:21
3:6 [v]Ezek. 36:25; John 1:16; Acts 2:33
3:7 [w]Rom. 3:24 [x]Rom. 8:23
3:8 [y]1 Tim. 1:15
3:9 [z]1 Tim. 1:4 [a]2 Tim. 2:14
3:10 [b]2 Cor. 13:2 [c]Matt. 18:17; 2 Thess. 3:6; 2 Tim. 3:5
3:11 [d]Acts 13:46
3:12 [e]Acts 20:4
3:13 [f]Acts 18:24 **3:14** [g]Rom. 15:28; Col. 1:10; 2 Pet. 1:8

PHILEMON

Paul is the author of Philemon, which was probably written about A.D. 61. This is Paul's letter to Philemon concerning Onesimus, a former slave of Philemon's. The letter begins with a greeting to Philemon followed by a plea on behalf of Onesimus. Although there is no positive statement of the outcome of this plea, it is reasonable to assume that Philemon did as Paul asked in the context of forgiveness as demonstrated by Christ's death on the cross.

I. Greeting to Philemon, 1–3
II. Prayer for Philemon, 4–7
III. Paul's plea on behalf of Onesimus, 8–21
IV. Paul' plan to visit Philemon and his benediction, 22–25

---

1 Paul, [a]a prisoner of Jesus Christ, and Timothy *our* brother, unto Philemon our dearly beloved, [b]and fellowlabourer,

2 And to *our* beloved Apphia, and [c]Archippus [d]our fellowsoldier, and to [e]the church in thy house:

3 [f]Grace to you, and peace, from God our Father and the Lord Jesus Christ.

4 [g]I thank my God, making mention of thee always in my prayers,

5 [h]Hearing of thy love and faith, which thou hast toward the Lord Jesus, and toward all saints;

6 That the communication of thy faith may become effectual [i]by the acknowledging of every good thing which is in you in Christ Jesus.

7 For we have great joy and consolation in thy love, because the bowels of the saints [j]are refreshed by thee, brother.

8 Wherefore, [k]though I might be much bold in Christ to enjoin thee that which is convenient,

9 Yet for love's sake I rather beseech *thee*, being such an one as Paul the aged, and now also a prisoner of Jesus Christ.

10 I beseech thee for my son [l]Onesimus, [m]whom I have begotten in my bonds:

11 Which in time past was to thee unprofitable, but now profitable to thee and to me:

12 Whom I have sent again: thou therefore receive him, that is, mine own bowels:

13 Whom I would have retained with me, [n]that in thy stead he might have ministered unto me in the bonds of the gospel:

14 But without thy mind would I do nothing; [o]that thy benefit should not be as it were of necessity, but willingly.

15 [p]For perhaps he therefore departed for a season, that thou shouldest receive him for ever;

16 Not now as a servant, but above a servant, [q]a brother beloved, specially to me, but how much more unto thee, [r]both in the flesh, and in the Lord?

17 If thou count me therefore [s]a partner, receive him as myself.

18 If he hath wronged thee, or oweth *thee* ought, put that on mine account;

19 I Paul have written *it* with mine own hand, I will repay *it:* albeit I do not say to thee how thou owest unto me even thine own self besides.

20 Yea, brother, let me have joy of thee in the Lord: refresh my bowels in the Lord.

21 [t]Having confidence in thy obedience I wrote unto thee, knowing that thou wilt also do more than I say.

22 But withal prepare me also a lodging: for [u]I trust that [v]through your prayers I shall be given unto you.

23 There salute thee [w]Epaphras, my fellowprisoner in Christ Jesus;

24 [x]Marcus, [y]Aristarchus, [z]Demas, [a]Lucas, my fellowlabourers.

25 [b]The grace of our Lord Jesus Christ *be* with your spirit. Amen.

1:1 [a]Eph. 3:1 [b]Phil. 2:25
1:2 [c]Col. 4:17 [d]Phil. 2:25 [e]Rom. 16:5
1:3 [f]Eph. 1:2
1:4 [g]Eph. 1:16; 2 Thess. 4:3
1:5 [h]Eph. 1:15
1:6 [i]Phil. 1:9
1:7 [j]2 Cor. 7:13
1:8 [k]1 Thess. 2:6
1:10 [l]Col. 4:9 [m]1 Cor. 4:15
1:13 [n]1 Cor. 16:17
1:14 [o]2 Cor. 9:7
1:15 [p]Gen. 45:5
1:16 [q]Matt. 23:8 [r]Col. 3:22
1:17 [s]2 Cor. 8:23
1:21 [t]2 Cor. 7:16
1:22 [u]Phil. 1:25 [v]2 Cor. 1:11
1:23 [w]Col. 1:7
1:24 [x]Acts 12:12 [y]Acts 19:29 [z]Col. 4:14 [a]2 Tim. 4:11
1:25 [b]2 Tim. 4:22

HEBREWS

Traditionally, Paul has been credited with writing the book sometime before A.D. 70. Hebrews contains a lengthy discussion of the Old Testament sacrificial system and the reason for its existence. There is a continual comparison of this Old Testament system with the superior sacrifice made by Christ on the cross as the sacrificial Lamb, offered on the altar of atonement. Beginning in chapter 11, the writer focuses on faith as the mechanism by which all people, past, present, and future, come to trust in God and his son Jesus Christ. The most famous chapter in Hebrews is chapter 11, often simply referred to as the "faith chapter."

I. Christ is superior to all others, 1:1–10:39
II. Faith that is strong, 11:1–12:29
III. Proper conduct, 13:1–13:19
IV. Closing and farewell, 13:20–13:25

---

1 God, who at sundry times and [a]in divers manners spake in time past unto the fathers by the prophets,

2 Hath [b]in these last days [c]spoken unto us by *his* Son, [d]whom he hath appointed heir of all things, [e]by whom also he made the worlds;

3 [f]Who being the brightness of *his* glory, and the express image of his person, and [g]upholding all things by the word of his power, when he had by himself purged our sins, [h]sat down on the right hand of the Majesty on high;

4 Being made so much better than the angels, as [i]he hath by inheritance obtained a more excellent name than they.

5 For unto which of the angels said he at any time, [j]Thou art my Son, this day have I begotten thee? And again, [k]I will be to him a Father, and he shall be to me a Son?

6 And again, when he bringeth in [l]the firstbegotten into the world, he saith, [m]And let all the angels of God worship him.

7 And of the angels he saith, [n]Who maketh his angels spirits, and his ministers a flame of fire.

8 But unto the Son *he saith,* [o]Thy throne, O God, *is* for ever and ever: a sceptre of righteousness *is* the sceptre of thy kingdom.

9 Thou hast loved righteousness, and hated iniquity; therefore God, *even* thy God, [p]hath anointed thee with the oil of gladness above thy fellows.

10 And, [q]Thou, Lord, in the beginning hast laid the foundation of the earth; and the heavens are the works of thine hands:

11 [r]They shall perish; but thou remainest; and they all shall wax old as doth a garment;

12 And as a vesture shalt thou fold them up, and they shall be changed: but thou art the same, and thy years shall not fail.

13 But to which of the angels said he at any time, [s]Sit on my right hand, until I make thine enemies thy footstool?

14 [t]Are they not all ministering spirits, sent forth to minister for them who shall be [u]heirs of salvation?

2 Therefore we ought to give the more earnest heed to the things which we have heard, lest at any time we should let *them* slip.

2 For if the word [v]spoken by angels was stedfast, and [w]every transgression and disobedience received a just recompence of reward;

3 How shall we escape, if we neglect so great salvation; [x]which at the first began to be spoken by the Lord, and was [y]confirmed unto us by them that heard *him;*

4 [z]God also bearing *them* witness, [a]both with signs and wonders, and with divers miracles, and [b]gifts of the Holy Ghost, [c]according to his own will?

5 For unto the angels hath he not put in subjection [d]the world to come, whereof we speak.

6 But one in a certain place testified, saying, [e]What is man, that thou art mindful of him? or the son of man, that thou visitest him?

7 Thou madest him a little lower than the angels; thou crownedst him with glory and honour, and didst set him over the works of thy hands:

8 [f]Thou hast put all things in subjection under his feet. For in that he put all in subjection under him, he left nothing *that is* not put under him. But now [g]we see not yet all things put under him.

9 But we see Jesus, [h]who was made a little lower than the angels for the suffering of death, [i]crowned with glory and honour; that he by the grace of God should taste death [j]for every man.

10 [k]For it became him, [l]for whom *are* all things, and by whom *are* all things, in bringing many sons unto glory, to make [m]the captain of their salvation [n]perfect through sufferings.

11 For both he that sanctifieth and they

1:1 [a]Num. 12:6 **1:2** [b]Deut. 4:30; Eph. 1:10 [c]John 1:17 [d]Ps. 2:8; John 3:35; Rom. 8:17 [e]John 1:3; Col. 1:16 **1:3** [f]John 1:14; Col. 1:15 [g]John 1:4; Rev. 4:11 [h]Ps. 110:1; 1 Pet. 3:22 **1:4** [i]Eph. 1:21 **1:5** [j]Ps. 2:7 [k]2 Sam. 7:14; Ps. 89:26 **1:6** [l]Rom. 8:29; Rev. 1:5 [m]Deut. 32:43; 1 Pet. 3:22 **1:7** [n]Ps. 104:4 **1:8** [o]Ps. 45:6 **1:9** [p]Isa. 61:1 **1:10** [q]Ps. 102:25 **1:11** [r]Isa. 34:4; 2 Pet. 3:7; Rev. 21:1 **1:13** [s]Ps. 110:1; Mark 12:36; Luke 20:42 **1:14** [t]Gen. 19:16; Dan. 3:28; Matt. 18:10; Acts 12:7 [u]Rom. 8:17; Jam. 2:5; 1 Pet. 3:7 **2:2** [v]Deut. 33:2; Acts 7:53; Gal. 3:19 [w]Num. 15:30 **2:3** [x]Matt. 4:17 [y]Luke 1:2 **2:4** [z]Mark 16:20; Rom. 15:18; 1 Cor. 2:4 [a]Acts 2:22 [b]1 Cor. 12:4 [c]Eph. 1:5 **2:5** [d]2 Pet. 3:13 **2:6** [e]Job 7:17 **2:8** [f]Matt. 28:18; Eph. 1:22 [g]1 Cor. 15:25 **2:9** [h]Phil. 2:7 [i]Acts 2:33 [j]John 3:16; 2 Cor. 5:15; 1 Tim. 2:6; Rev. 5:9 **2:10** [k]Luke 24:46 [l]Rom. 11:36 [m]Acts 3:15 [n]Luke 13:32

who are sanctified [o]*are* all of one: for which cause [p]he is not ashamed to call them brethren,

12 Saying, [q]I will declare thy name unto my brethren, in the midst of the church will I sing praise unto thee.

13 And again, [r]I will put my trust in him. And again, [s]Behold I and the children [t]which God hath given me.

14 Forasmuch then as the children are partakers of flesh and blood, he [u]also himself likewise took part of the same; [v]that through death he might destroy him that had the power of death, that is, the devil;

15 And deliver them who [w]through fear of death were all their lifetime subject to bondage.

16 For verily he took not on *him the nature of* angels; but he took on *him* the seed of Abraham.

17 Wherefore in all things it behoved him [x]to be made like unto *his* brethren, that he might be a merciful and faithful high priest in things *pertaining* to God, to make reconciliation for the sins of the people.

18 For in that he himself hath suffered being tempted, he is able to succour them that are tempted.

3 Wherefore, holy brethren, partakers of [y]the heavenly calling, consider [z]the Apostle and High Priest of our profession, Christ Jesus;

2 Who was faithful to him that appointed him, as also [a]Moses *was faithful* in all his house.

3 For this *man* was counted worthy of more glory than Moses, inasmuch as [b]he who hath builded the house hath more honour than the house.

4 For every house is builded by some *man;* but [c]he that built all things *is* God.

5 And Moses verily *was* faithful in all his house, as [d]a servant, [e]for a testimony of those things which were to be spoken after;

6 But Christ as a son over his own house; [f]whose house are we, [g]if we hold fast the confidence and the rejoicing of the hope firm unto the end.

7 Wherefore (as [h]the Holy Ghost saith, [i]To day if ye will hear his voice,

8 Harden not your hearts, as in the provocation, in the day of temptation in the wilderness:

9 When your fathers tempted me, proved me, and saw my works forty years.

10 Wherefore I was grieved with that generation, and said, They do alway err in *their* heart; and they have not known my ways.

11 So I sware in my wrath, They shall not enter into my rest.)

12 Take heed, brethren, lest there be in any of you an evil heart of unbelief, in departing from the living God.

13 But exhort one another daily, while it is called To day; lest any of you be hardened through the deceitfulness of sin.

14 For we are made partakers of Christ, if we hold the beginning of our confidence stedfast unto the end;

15 While it is said, To day if ye will hear his voice, harden not your hearts, as in the provocation.

16 [j]For some, when they had heard, did provoke: howbeit not all that came out of Egypt by Moses.

17 But with whom was he grieved forty years? *was it* not with them that had sinned, [k]whose carcases fell in the wilderness?

18 And [l]to whom sware he that they should not enter into his rest, but to them that believed not?

19 So we see that they could not enter in because of unbelief.

4 Let us therefore fear, lest, a promise being left *us* of entering into his rest, any of you should seem to come short of it.

2 For unto us was the gospel preached, as well as unto them: but the word preached did not profit them, not being mixed with faith in them that heard *it*.

3 For we which have believed do enter into rest, as he said, [m]As I have sworn in my wrath, if they shall enter into my rest: although the works were finished from the foundation of the world.

4 For he spake in a certain place of the seventh *day* on this wise, [n]And God did rest the seventh day from all his works.

5 And in this *place* again, If they shall enter into my rest.

6 Seeing therefore it remaineth that some must enter therein, and they to whom it was first preached entered not in because of unbelief:

7 Again, he limiteth a certain day, saying in David, To day, after so long a time; as it is said, [o]To day if ye will hear his voice, harden not your hearts.

8 For if Jesus had given them rest, then would he not afterward have spoken of another day.

9 There remaineth therefore a rest to the people of God.

10 For he that is entered into his rest, he also hath ceased from his own works, as God *did* from his.

11 Let us labour therefore to enter into that rest, lest any man fall after the same example of unbelief.

12 For the word of God *is* [p]quick, and powerful, and [q]sharper than any [r]twoedged sword, piercing even to the dividing asunder of soul and spirit, and of the joints and marrow, and *is* [s]a discerner of the thoughts and intents of the heart.

13 [t]Neither is there any creature that is not manifest in his sight: but all things *are* naked [u]and opened unto the eyes of him with whom we have to do.

14 Seeing then that we have a great high priest, that is passed into the heavens, Jesus the Son of God, let us hold fast *our* profession.

15 For [v]we have not an high priest which cannot be touched with the feeling of our

2:11 [o]Acts 17:26 [p]Matt. 28:10; Rom. 8:29
2:12 [q]Ps. 22:22
2:13 [r]Ps. 18:2 [s]Isa. 8:18 [t]John 20:29
2:14 [u]John 1:14; Phil. 2:7 [v]1 Cor. 15:54; 2 Tim. 1:10
2:15 [w]Luke 1:74; 2 Tim. 1:7
2:17 [x]Phil. 2:7
3:1 [y]Rom. 1:7; Eph. 4:1; Phil. 3:14; 2 Tim. 1:9; 2 Pet. 1:10 [z]Rom. 15:8
3:2 [a]Num. 12:7
3:3 [b]Zech. 6:12
3:4 [c]Eph. 2:10
3:5 [d]Ex. 14:31; Deut. 3:24; Josh. 1:2 [e]Deut. 18:15
3:6 [f]1 Cor. 3:16; Eph. 2:21; 1 Tim. 3:15 [g]Matt. 10:22; Col. 1:23
3:7 [h]2 Sam. 23:2 [i]Ps. 95:7
3:16 [j]Num. 14:2
3:17 [k]Num. 14:22; 1 Cor. 10:5; Jude 5
3:18 [l]Num. 14:30
4:3 [m]Ps. 95:11
4:4 [n]Gen. 2:2
4:7 [o]Ps. 95:7
4:12 [p]Isa. 49:2; 2 Cor. 10:4; 1 Pet. 1:23 [q]Prov. 5:4 [r]Eph. 6:17 [s]1 Cor. 14:24
4:13 [t]Ps. 33:13 [u]Job 26:6
4:15 [v]Isa. 53:3

infirmities; but [w]was in all points tempted like as *we are,* [x]*yet* without sin.

16 [y]Let us therefore come boldly unto the throne of grace, that we may obtain mercy, and find grace to help in time of need.

5 For every high priest taken from among men is ordained for men in things *pertaining* to God, that he may offer both gifts and sacrifices for sins:

2 Who can have compassion on the ignorant, and on them that are out of the way; for that he himself also is compassed with infirmity.

3 And [z]by reason hereof he ought, as for the people, so also for himself, to offer for sins.

4 [a]And no man taketh this honour unto himself, but he that is called of God, as [b]*was* Aaron.

5 [c]So also Christ glorified not himself to be made an high priest; but he that said unto him, [d]Thou art my Son, to day have I begotten thee.

6 As he saith also in another *place,* [e]Thou *art* a priest for ever after the order of Melchisedec.

7 Who in the days of his flesh, when he had [f]offered up prayers and supplications [g]with strong crying and tears unto him [h]that was able to save him from death, and was heard [i]in that he feared;

8 Though he were a Son, yet learned he [j]obedience by the things which he suffered;

9 And being made perfect, he became the author of eternal salvation unto all them that obey him;

10 Called of God an high priest after the order of Melchisedec.

11 Of whom [k]we have many things to say, and hard to be uttered, seeing ye are [l]dull of hearing.

12 For when for the time ye ought to be teachers, ye have need that one teach you again which *be* the first principles of the oracles of God; and are become such as have need of [m]milk, and not of strong meat.

13 For every one that useth milk *is* unskilful in the word of righteousness: for he is [n]a babe.

14 But strong meat belongeth to them that are of full age, *even* those who by reason of use have their senses exercised [o]to discern both good and evil.

6 Therefore [p]leaving the principles of the doctrine of Christ, let us go on unto perfection; not laying again the foundation of repentance from dead works, and of faith toward God,

2 [q]Of the doctrine of baptisms, [r]and of laying on of hands, [s]and of resurrection of the dead, [t]and of eternal judgment.

3 And this will we do, [u]if God permit.

4 For [v]*it is* impossible for those who were once enlightened, and have tasted of [w]the heavenly gift, and [x]were made partakers of the Holy Ghost,

5 And have tasted the good word of God, and the powers of the world to come,

6 If they shall fall away, to renew them again unto repentance; seeing they crucify to themselves the Son of God afresh, and put *him* to an open shame.

7 For the earth which drinketh in the rain that cometh oft upon it, and bringeth forth herbs meet for them by whom it is dressed, [y]receiveth blessing from God:

8 [z]But that which beareth thorns and briers *is* rejected, and *is* nigh unto cursing; whose end *is* to be burned.

9 But, beloved, we are persuaded better things of you, and things that accompany salvation, though we thus speak.

10 [a]For [b]God *is* not unrighteous to forget [c]your work and labour of love, which ye have shewed toward his name, in that ye have [d]ministered to the saints, and do minister.

11 And we desire that every one of you do shew the same diligence [e]to the full assurance of hope unto the end:

12 That ye be not slothful, but followers of them who through faith and patience inherit the promises.

13 For when God made promise to Abraham, because he could swear by no greater, [f]he sware by himself,

14 Saying, Surely blessing I will bless thee, and multiplying I will multiply thee.

15 And so, after he had patiently endured, he obtained the promise.

16 For men verily swear by the greater: and [g]an oath for confirmation *is* to them an end of all strife.

17 Wherein God, willing more abundantly to shew unto the heirs of promise [h]the immutability of his counsel, confirmed *it* by an oath:

18 That by two immutable things, in which *it was* impossible for God to lie, we might have a strong consolation, who have fled for refuge to lay hold upon the hope set before us:

19 Which *hope* we have as an anchor of the soul, both sure and stedfast, [i]and which entereth into that within the veil;

20 Whither the forerunner is for us entered, *even* Jesus, made an high priest for ever after the order of Melchisedec.

7 For this [j]Melchisedec, king of Salem, priest of the most high God, who met Abraham returning from the slaughter of the kings, and blessed him;

2 To whom also Abraham gave a tenth part of all; first being by interpretation King of righteousness, and after that also King of Salem, which is, King of peace;

3 Without father, without mother, without descent, having neither beginning of days, nor end of life; but made like unto the Son of God; abideth a priest continually.

4 Now consider how great this man *was,* [k]unto whom even the patriarch Abraham gave the tenth of the spoils.

5 And verily [l]they that are of the sons of

4:15 [w]Luke 22:28 [x]2 Cor. 5:21; 1 John 3:5
4:16 [y]Eph. 2:18
5:3 [z]Lev. 4:3
5:4 [a]2 Chron. 26:18 [b]Ex. 28:1; 1 Chron. 23:13
5:5 [c]John 8:54 [d]Ps. 2:7
5:6 [e]Ps. 110:4
5:7 [f]Matt. 26:39; John 17:1 [g]Ps. 22:1; Mark 15:34 [h]Matt. 26:53 [i]Matt. 26:37; Luke 22:43; John 12:27
5:8 [j]Phil. 2:8
5:11 [k]John 16:12 [l]Matt. 13:15
5:12 [m]1 Cor. 3:1
5:13 [n]1 Cor. 13:11; 1 Pet. 2:2
5:14 [o]Isa. 7:15
6:1 [p]Phil. 3:12
6:2 [q]Acts 19:4 [r]Acts 8:14 [s]Acts 17:31 [t]Acts 24:25
6:3 [u]Acts 18:21
6:4 [v]Matt. 12:31; 1 John 5:16 [w]John 4:10 [x]Gal. 3:2
6:7 [y]Ps. 65:10
6:8 [z]Isa. 5:6
6:10 [a]Prov. 14:31; John 13:20 [b]Rom. 3:4 [c]1 Thess. 1:3 [d]Rom. 15:25; 2 Tim. 1:18
6:11 [e]Col. 2:2
6:13 [f]Gen. 22:16; Luke 1:73
6:16 [g]Ex. 22:11
6:17 [h]Rom. 11:29
6:19 [i]Lev. 16:15
7:1 [j]Gen. 14:18
7:4 [k]Gen. 14:20
7:5 [l]Num. 18:21

Levi, who receive the office of the priesthood, have a commandment to take tithes of the people according to the law, that is, of their brethren, though they come out of the loins of Abraham:

6 But he whose descent is not counted from them received tithes of Abraham, [m]and blessed [n]him that had the promises.

7 And without all contradiction the less is blessed of the better.

8 And here men that die receive tithes; but there he *receiveth them,* of whom it is witnessed that he liveth.

9 And as I may so say, Levi also, who receiveth tithes, paid tithes in Abraham.

10 For he was yet in the loins of his father, when Melchisedec met him.

11 [o]If therefore perfection were by the Levitical priesthood, (for under it the people received the law,) what further need *was there* that another priest should rise after the order of Melchisedec, and not be called after the order of Aaron?

12 For the priesthood being changed, there is made of necessity a change also of the law.

13 For he of whom these things are spoken pertaineth to another tribe, of which no man gave attendance at the altar.

14 For *it is* evident that [p]our Lord sprang out of Juda; of which tribe Moses spake nothing concerning priesthood.

15 And it is yet far more evident: for that after the similitude of Melchisedec there ariseth another priest,

16 Who is made, not after the law of a carnal commandment, but after the power of an endless life.

17 For he testifieth, [q]Thou *art* a priest for ever after the order of Melchisedec.

18 For there is verily a disannulling of the commandment going before for [r]the weakness and unprofitableness thereof.

19 For [s]the law made nothing perfect, but the bringing in of a better hope *did;* by the which we [t]draw nigh unto God.

20 And inasmuch as not without an oath *he was made priest:*

21 (For those priests were made without an oath; but this with an oath by him that said unto him, [u]The Lord sware and will not repent, Thou *art* a priest for ever after the order of Melchisedec:)

22 By so much was Jesus made a surety of a better testament.

23 And they truly were many priests, because they were not suffered to continue by reason of death:

24 But this *man,* because he continueth ever, hath an unchangeable priesthood.

25 Wherefore he is able also to save them to the uttermost that come unto God by him, seeing he ever liveth [v]to make intercession for them.

26 For such an high priest became us, *who is* holy, harmless, undefiled, separate from sinners, [w]and made higher than the heavens;

27 Who needeth not daily, as those high priests, to offer up sacrifice, [x]first for his own sins, [y]and then for the people's: for [z]this he did once, when he offered up himself.

28 For the law maketh men high priests which have infirmity; but the word of the oath, which was since the law, *maketh* the Son, who is consecrated for evermore.

8 Now of the things which we have spoken *this is* the sum: We have such an high priest, [a]who is set on the right hand of the throne of the Majesty in the heavens;

2 A minister of the sanctuary, and of the true tabernacle, which the Lord pitched, and not man.

3 For every high priest is ordained to offer gifts and sacrifices: wherefore [b]*it is* of necessity that this man have somewhat also to offer.

4 For if he were on earth, he should not be a priest, seeing that there are priests that offer gifts according to the law:

5 Who serve unto the example and [c]shadow of heavenly things, as Moses was admonished of God when he was about to make the tabernacle: [d]for, See, saith he, *that* thou make all things according to the pattern shewed to thee in the mount.

6 But now [e]hath he obtained a more excellent ministry, by how much also he is the mediator of a better covenant, which was established upon better promises.

7 For if that first *covenant* had been faultless, then should no place have been sought for the second.

8 For finding fault with them, he saith, [f]Behold, the days come, saith the Lord, when I will make a new covenant with the house of Israel and with the house of Judah:

9 Not according to the covenant that I made with their fathers in the day when I took them by the hand to lead them out of the land of Egypt; because they continued not in my covenant, and I regarded them not, saith the Lord.

10 For this *is* the covenant that I will make with the house of Israel after those days, saith the Lord; I will put my laws into their mind, and write them in their hearts: and [g]I will be to them a God, and they shall be to me a people:

11 And [h]they shall not teach every man his neighbour, and every man his brother, saying, Know the Lord: for all shall know me, from the least to the greatest.

12 For I will be merciful to their unrighteousness, [i]and their sins and their iniquities will I remember no more.

13 [j]In that he saith, A new *covenant,* he hath made the first old. Now that which decayeth and waxeth old *is* ready to vanish away.

9 Then verily the first *covenant* had also ordinances of divine service, and [k]a worldly sanctuary.

2 [l]For there was a tabernacle made; the first, [m]wherein *was* [n]the candlestick, and

7:6 [m]Gen. 14:19 [n]Rom. 4:13
7:11 [o]Gal. 2:21
7:14 [p]Isa. 11:1; Luke 3:33; Rom. 1:3
7:17 [q]Ps. 110:4
7:18 [r]Rom. 8:3
7:19 [s]Acts 13:39; Gal. 2:16 [t]Rom. 5:2
7:21 [u]Ps. 110:4
7:25 [v]Rom. 8:34; 1 John 2:1
7:26 [w]Eph. 1:20
7:27 [x]Lev. 9:7 [y]Lev. 16:15 [z]Rom. 6:10
8:1 [a]Eph. 1:20
8:3 [b]Eph. 5:2
8:5 [c]Col. 2:17 [d]Ex. 25:40; Acts 7:44
8:6 [e]2 Cor. 3:6
8:8 [f]Jer. 31:31
8:10 [g]Zech. 8:8
8:11 [h]Isa. 54:13; 1 John 2:27
8:12 [i]Rom. 11:27
8:13 [j]2 Cor. 5:17
9:1 [k]Ex. 25:8
9:2 [l]Ex. 26:1 [m]Ex. 26:35 [n]Ex. 25:31

[o]the table, and the shewbread; which is called the sanctuary.

3 [p]And after the second veil, the tabernacle which is called the Holiest of all;

4 Which had the golden censer, and [q]the ark of the covenant overlaid round about with gold, wherein *was* [r]the golden pot that had manna, and [s]Aaron's rod that budded, and [t]the tables of the covenant;

5 And [u]over it the cherubims of glory shadowing the mercyseat; of which we cannot now speak particularly.

6 Now when these things were thus ordained, [v]the priests went always into the first tabernacle, accomplishing the service *of God.*

7 But into the second *went* the high priest alone [w]once every year, not without blood, which he offered for himself, and *for* the errors of the people:

8 The Holy Ghost this signifying, that [x]the way into the holiest of all was not yet made manifest, while as the first tabernacle was yet standing:

9 Which *was* a figure for the time then present, in which were offered both gifts and sacrifices, [y]that could not make him that did the service perfect, as pertaining to the conscience;

10 *Which stood* only in [z]meats and drinks, and [a]divers washings, [b]and carnal ordinances, imposed *on them* until the time of reformation.

11 But Christ being come an high priest of good things to come, by a greater and more perfect tabernacle, not made with hands, that is to say, not of this building;

12 Neither by the blood of goats and calves, but [c]by his own blood he entered in [d]once into the holy place, [e]having obtained eternal redemption *for us.*

13 For if [f]the blood of bulls and of goats, and [g]the ashes of an heifer sprinkling the unclean, sanctifieth to the purifying of the flesh:

14 How much more [h]shall the blood of Christ, [i]who through the eternal Spirit [j]offered himself without spot to God, purge your conscience from dead works [k]to serve the living God?

15 [l]And for this cause he is the mediator of the new testament, [m]that by means of death, for the redemption of the transgressions *that were* under the first testament, they which are called might receive the promise of eternal inheritance.

16 For where a testament *is,* there must also of necessity be the death of the testator.

17 For [n]a testament *is* of force after men are dead: otherwise it is of no strength at all while the testator liveth.

18 [o]Whereupon neither the first *testament* was dedicated without blood.

19 For when Moses had spoken every precept to all the people according to the law, [p]he took the blood of calves and of goats, [q]with water, and scarlet wool, and hyssop, and sprinkled both the book, and all the people,

20 Saying, [r]This *is* the blood of the testament which God hath enjoined unto you.

21 Moreover [s]he sprinkled with blood both the tabernacle, and all the vessels of the ministry.

22 And almost all things are by the law purged with blood; and [t]without shedding of blood is no remission.

23 *It was* therefore necessary that the patterns of things in the heavens should be purified with these; but the heavenly things themselves with better sacrifices than these.

24 For Christ is not entered into the holy places made with hands, *which are* the figures of the true; but into heaven itself, now [u]to appear in the presence of God for us:

25 Nor yet that he should offer himself often, as the high priest entereth into the holy place every year with blood of others;

26 For then must he often have suffered since the foundation of the world: but now [v]once [w]in the end of the world hath he appeared to put away sin by the sacrifice of himself.

27 [x]And as it is appointed unto men once to die, [y]but after this the judgment:

28 So [z]Christ was once [a]offered to bear the sins [b]of many; and unto them that [c]look for him shall he appear the second time without sin unto salvation.

10 For the law having [d]a shadow of good things to come, *and* not the very image of the things, can never with those sacrifices which they offered year by year continually make the comers thereunto perfect.

2 For then would they not have ceased to be offered? because that the worshippers once purged should have had no more conscience of sins.

3 [e]But in those *sacrifices there is* a remembrance again *made* of sins every year.

4 For [f]*it is* not possible that the blood of bulls and of goats should take away sins.

5 Wherefore when he cometh into the world, he saith, [g]Sacrifice and offering thou wouldest not, but a body hast thou prepared me:

6 In burnt offerings and *sacrifices* for sin thou hast had no pleasure.

7 Then said I, Lo, I come (in the volume of the book it is written of me,) to do thy will, O God.

8 Above when he said, Sacrifice and offering and burnt offerings and *offering* for sin thou wouldest not, neither hadst pleasure *therein;* which are offered by the law;

9 Then said he, Lo, I come to do thy will, O God. He taketh away the first, that he may establish the second.

10 [h]By the which will we are sanctified through the offering of the body of Jesus Christ once *for all.*

11 And every priest standeth [i]daily ministering and offering oftentimes the same

9:2 [o]Ex. 25:23
9:3 [p]Ex. 26:31
9:4 [q]Ex. 25:10 [r]Ex. 16:33 [s]Num. 17:10 [t]Ex. 25:16; 1 Kings 8:9; 2 Chron. 5:10
9:5 [u]Ex. 25:18; 1 Kings 8:6
9:6 [v]Num. 28:3
9:7 [w]Ex. 30:10
9:8 [x]John 14:6
9:9 [y]Gal. 3:21
9:10 [z]Lev. 11:2 [a]Num. 19:7 [b]Eph. 2:15
9:12 [c]Acts 20:28; Col. 1:14; 1 Pet. 1:19 [d]Zech. 3:9 [e]Dan. 9:24
9:13 [f]Lev. 16:14 [g]Num. 19:2
9:14 [h]1 Pet. 1:19; Rev. 1:5 [i]Rom. 1:4 [j]Eph. 2:5 [k]Luke 1:74; 1 Pet. 4:2
9:15 [l]1 Tim. 2:5 [m]Rom. 3:25
9:17 [n]Gal. 3:15
9:18 [o]Ex. 24:6
9:19 [p]Ex. 24:5 [q]Lev. 14:4
9:20 [r]Ex. 24:8
9:21 [s]Ex. 29:12
9:22 [t]Lev. 17:11
9:24 [u]Rom. 8:34
9:26 [v]1 Pet. 3:18 [w]1 Cor. 10:11; Eph. 1:10
9:27 [x]Gen. 3:19 [y]2 Cor. 5:10
9:28 [z]Rom. 6:10 [a]1 Pet. 2:24 [b]Matt. 26:28 [c]Tit. 2:13
10:1 [d]Col. 2:17
10:3 [e]Lev. 16:21
10:4 [f]Mic. 6:6
10:5 [g]Ps. 40:6; Jer. 6:20; Am. 5:21
10:10 [h]John 17:19
10:11 [i]Num. 28:3

sacrifices, which can never take away sins:

12 [j]But this man, after he had offered one sacrifice for sins for ever, sat down on the right hand of God;

13 From henceforth expecting [k]till his enemies be made his footstool.

14 For by one offering he hath perfected for ever them that are sanctified.

15 *Whereof* the Holy Ghost also is a witness to us: for after that he had said before,

16 [l]This *is* the covenant that I will make with them after those days, saith the Lord, I will put my laws into their hearts, and in their minds will I write them;

17 And their sins and iniquities will I remember no more.

18 Now where remission of these *is, there is* no more offering for sin.

19 Having therefore, brethren, [m]boldness to enter into the holiest by the blood of Jesus,

20 By [n]a new and living way, which he hath consecrated for us, through the veil, that is to say, his flesh;

21 And *having* an high priest over [o]the house of God;

22 Let us draw near with a true heart [p]in full assurance of faith, having our hearts sprinkled from an evil conscience, and [q]our bodies washed with pure water.

23 Let us hold fast the profession of *our* faith without wavering; (for [r]he *is* faithful that promised;)

24 And let us consider one another to provoke unto love and to good works:

25 [s]Not forsaking the assembling of ourselves together, as the manner of some *is;* but exhorting *one another:* and [t]so much the more, as ye see [u]the day approaching.

26 For [v]if we sin wilfully [w]after that we have received the knowledge of the truth, there remaineth no more sacrifice for sins,

27 But a certain fearful looking for of judgment and [x]fiery indignation, which shall devour the adversaries.

28 He that despised Moses' law died without mercy [y]under two or three witnesses:

29 Of how much sorer punishment, suppose ye, shall he be thought worthy, who hath trodden under foot the Son of God, and [z]hath counted the blood of the covenant, wherewith he was sanctified, an unholy thing, [a]and hath done despite unto the Spirit of grace?

30 For we know him that hath said, [b]Vengeance *belongeth* unto me, I will recompense, saith the Lord. And again, [c]The Lord shall judge his people.

31 [d]*It is* a fearful thing to fall into the hands of the living God.

32 But [e]call to remembrance the former days, in which, after ye were illuminated, ye endured [f]a great fight of afflictions;

33 Partly, whilst ye were made [g]a gazingstock both by reproaches and afflictions; and partly, whilst [h]ye became companions of them that were so used.

34 For ye had compassion of me [i]in my bonds, and [j]took joyfully the spoiling of your goods, knowing in yourselves that [k]ye have in heaven a better and an enduring substance.

35 Cast not away therefore your confidence, [l]which hath great recompence of reward.

36 [m]For ye have need of patience, that, after ye have done the will of God, [n]ye might receive the promise.

37 For [o]yet a little while, and [p]he that shall come will come, and will not tarry.

38 Now [q]the just shall live by faith: but if *any man* draw back, my soul shall have no pleasure in him.

39 But we are not of them [r]who draw back unto perdition; but of them that [s]believe to the saving of the soul.

11 Now faith is the substance of things hoped for, the evidence [t]of things not seen.

2 For by it the elders obtained a good report.

3 Through faith we understand that [u]the worlds were framed by the word of God, so that things which are seen were not made of things which do appear.

4 By faith [v]Abel offered unto God a more excellent sacrifice than Cain, by which he obtained witness that he was righteous, God testifying of his gifts: and by it he being dead [w]yet speaketh.

5 By faith [x]Enoch was translated that he should not see death; and was not found, because God had translated him: for before his translation he had this testimony, that he pleased God.

6 But without faith *it is* impossible to please *him:* for he that cometh to God must believe that he is, and *that* he is a rewarder of them that diligently seek him.

7 By faith [y]Noah, being warned of God of things not seen as yet, moved with fear, [z]prepared an ark to the saving of his house; by the which he condemned the world, and became heir of [a]the righteousness which is by faith.

8 By faith [b]Abraham, when he was called to go out into a place which he should after receive for an inheritance, obeyed; and he went out, not knowing whither he went.

9 By faith he sojourned in the land of promise, as *in* a strange country, [c]dwelling in tabernacles with Isaac and Jacob, the heirs with him of the same promise:

10 For he looked for a city which hath foundations, [d]whose builder and maker *is* God.

11 Through faith also [e]Sara herself received strength to conceive seed, and [f]was delivered of a child when she was past age, because she judged him [g]faithful who had promised.

12 Therefore sprang there even of one, and [h]him as good as dead, [i]*so many* as the stars of the sky in multitude, and as the sand which is by the sea shore innumerable.

13 These all died in faith, not having re-

10:12 jCol. 3:1
10:13 kPs. 110:1; 1 Cor. 15:25
10:16 lJer. 31:33
10:19 mRom. 5:2
10:20 nJohn 10:9
10:21 o1 Tim. 3:15
10:22 pEph. 3:12; 1 John 3:21 qEzek. 36:25
10:23 r1 Cor. 1:9; 2 Thess. 3:3
10:25 sActs 2:42 tRom. 13:11 uPhil. 4:5
10:26 vNum. 15:30 w2 Pet. 2:20
10:27 xEzek. 36:5; 2 Thess. 1:8
10:28 yDeut. 17:2; John 8:17; 2 Cor. 13:1
10:29 z1 Cor. 11:29 aMatt. 12:31
10:30 bDeut. 32:35 cDeut. 32:36
10:31 dLuke 12:5
10:32 eGal. 3:4 fPhil. 1:29
10:33 g1 Cor. 4:9 hPhil. 1:7
10:34 iPhil. 1:7 jMatt. 5:12; Jam. 1:2 kMatt. 6:20; 1 Tim. 6:19
10:35 lMatt. 5:12
10:36 mLuke 21:19 nCol. 3:24
10:37 oLuke 18:8 pHab. 2:3
10:38 qRom. 1:17
10:39 r2 Pet. 2:20 sActs 16:30; 2 Thess. 2:14
11:1 tRom. 8:24
11:3 uGen. 1:1; John 1:3; 2 Pet. 3:5
11:4 vGen. 4:4 wGen. 4:10
11:5 xGen. 5:22
11:7 yGen. 6:13 z1 Pet. 3:20 aRom. 3:22
11:8 bGen. 12:1
11:9 cGen. 12:8
11:10 dRev. 21:2
11:11 eGen. 17:19 fLuke 1:36 gRom. 4:21
11:12 hRom. 4:19 iGen. 22:17

ceived the promises, but [j]having seen them afar off, and were persuaded of *them,* and embraced *them,* and [k]confessed that they were strangers and pilgrims on the earth.

14 For they that say such things declare plainly that they seek a country.

15 And truly, if they had been mindful of that *country* from whence they came out, they might have had opportunity to have returned.

16 But now they desire a better *country,* that is, an heavenly: wherefore God is not ashamed [l]to be called their God: for [m]he hath prepared for them a city.

17 By faith [n]Abraham, when he was tried, offered up Isaac: and he that had received the promises [o]offered up his only begotten *son,*

18 Of whom it was said, [p]That in Isaac shall thy seed be called:

19 Accounting that God [q]*was* able to raise *him* up, even from the dead; from whence also he received him in a figure.

20 By faith [r]Isaac blessed Jacob and Esau concerning things to come.

21 By faith Jacob, when he was a dying, [s]blessed both the sons of Joseph; and [t]worshipped, *leaning* upon the top of his staff.

22 By faith [u]Joseph, when he died, made mention of the departing of the children of Israel; and gave commandment concerning his bones.

23 By faith [v]Moses, when he was born, was hid three months of his parents, because they saw *he was* a proper child; and they were not afraid of the king's [w]commandment.

24 By faith [x]Moses, when he was come to years, refused to be called the son of Pharaoh's daughter;

25 [y]Choosing rather to suffer affliction with the people of God, than to enjoy the pleasures of sin for a season;

26 Esteeming the reproach of Christ greater riches than the treasures in Egypt: for he had respect unto the recompence of the reward.

27 By faith [z]he forsook Egypt, not fearing the wrath of the king: for he endured, as seeing him who is invisible.

28 Through faith [a]he kept the passover, and the sprinkling of blood, lest he that destroyed the firstborn should touch them.

29 By faith [b]they passed through the Red sea as by dry *land:* which the Egyptians assaying to do were drowned.

30 By faith [c]the walls of Jericho fell down, after they were compassed about seven days.

31 By faith [d]the harlot Rahab perished not with them that believed not, when [e]she had received the spies with peace.

32 And what shall I more say? for the time would fail me to tell of [f]Gedeon, and *of* [g]Barak, and *of* [h]Samson, and *of* [i]Jephthae; *of* [j]David also, and [k]Samuel, and *of* the prophets:

33 Who through faith subdued kingdoms, wrought righteousness, [l]obtained promises, [m]stopped the mouths of lions,

34 [n]Quenched the violence of fire, [o]escaped the edge of the sword, [p]out of weakness were made strong, waxed valiant in fight, [q]turned to flight the armies of the aliens.

35 [r]Women received their dead raised to life again: and others were [s]tortured, not accepting deliverance; that they might obtain a better resurrection:

36 And others had trial of *cruel* mockings and scourgings, yea, moreover [t]of bonds and imprisonment:

37 [u]They were stoned, they were sawn asunder, were tempted, were slain with the sword: [v]they wandered about [w]in sheepskins and goatskins; being destitute, afflicted, tormented;

38 (Of whom the world was not worthy:) they wandered in deserts, and *in* mountains, and [x]*in* dens and caves of the earth.

39 And these all, having obtained a good report through faith, received not the promise:

40 God having provided some better thing for us, that they without us should not be [y]made perfect.

12 Wherefore seeing we also are compassed about with so great a cloud of witnesses, [z]let us lay aside every weight, and the sin which doth so easily beset *us,* and [a]let us run [b]with patience the race that is set before us,

2 Looking unto Jesus the author and finisher of *our* faith; [c]who for the joy that was set before him endured the cross, despising the shame, and [d]is set down at the right hand of the throne of God.

3 [e]For consider him that endured such contradiction of sinners against himself, [f]lest ye be wearied and faint in your minds.

4 [g]Ye have not yet resisted unto blood, striving against sin.

5 And ye have forgotten the exhortation which speaketh unto you as unto children, [h]My son, despise not thou the chastening of the Lord, nor faint when thou art rebuked of him:

6 For [i]whom the Lord loveth he chasteneth, and scourgeth every son whom he receiveth.

7 [j]If ye endure chastening, God dealeth with you as with sons; for what son is he whom the father chasteneth not?

8 But if ye be without chastisement, [k]whereof all are partakers, then are ye bastards, and not sons.

9 Furthermore we have had fathers of our flesh which corrected *us,* and we gave *them* reverence: shall we not much rather be in subjection unto [l]the Father of spirits, and live?

10 For they verily for a few days chastened *us* after their own pleasure; but he for *our* profit, [m]that *we* might be partakers of his holiness.

11:13 [j]John 8:56 [k]Gen. 23:4; Ps. 39:12; 1 Pet. 1:17
11:16 [l]Ex. 3:6; Acts 7:32 [m]Phil. 3:20
11:17 [n]Gen. 22:1 [o]Jam. 2:21
11:18 [p]Gen. 21:12
11:19 [q]Rom. 4:17
11:20 [r]Gen. 27:27
11:21 [s]Gen. 48:5 [t]Gen. 47:31
11:22 [u]Gen. 50:24
11:23 [v]Ex. 2:2 [w]Ex. 1:16
11:24 [x]Ex. 2:10
11:25 [y]Ps. 84:10
11:27 [z]Ex. 10:28
11:28 [a]Ex. 12:21
11:29 [b]Ex. 14:22
11:30 [c]Josh. 6:20
11:31 [d]Josh. 6:23 [e]Josh. 1:1
11:32 [f]Judg. 6:11 [g]Judg. 4:6 [h]Judg. 13:24 [i]Judg. 11:1 [j]1 Sam. 16:1 [k]1 Sam. 1:20
11:33 [l]2 Sam. 7:11 [m]Judg. 14:5; Dan. 6:22
11:34 [n]Dan. 3:25 [o]1 Sam. 20:1; 2 Kings 6:16 [p]2 Kings 20:7; Ps. 6:8 [q]Judg. 15:8; 2 Sam. 8:1
11:35 [r]1 Kings 17:22 [s]Acts 22:25
11:36 [t]Gen. 39:20
11:37 [u]1 Kings 21:13; Acts 7:58 [v]2 Kings 1:8 [w]Zech. 13:4
11:38 [x]1 Kings 18:4
11:40 [y]Rev. 6:11
12:1 [z]Col. 3:8 [a]1 Cor. 9:24 [b]Rom. 12:12
12:2 [c]Luke 24:26; 1 Pet. 1:11 [d]Ps. 110:1
12:3 [e]Matt. 10:24 [f]Gal. 6:9
12:4 [g]1 Cor. 10:13
12:5 [h]Job 5:17
12:6 [i]Ps. 94:12; Jam. 1:12; Rev. 3:19
12:7 [j]Deut. 8:5; Prov. 13:24
12:8 [k]Ps. 73:1
12:9 [l]Num. 16:22; Eccl. 12:7; Isa. 42:5
12:10 [m]Lev. 11:44

11 Now no chastening for the present seemeth to be joyous, but grievous: nevertheless afterward it yieldeth [n]the peaceable fruit of righteousness unto them which are exercised thereby.

12 Wherefore [o]lift up the hands which hang down, and the feeble knees;

13 [p]And make straight paths for your feet, lest that which is lame be turned out of the way; [q]but let it rather be healed.

14 [r]Follow peace with all *men,* and holiness, [s]without which no man shall see the Lord:

15 [t]Looking diligently [u]lest any man fail of the grace of God; [v]lest any root of bitterness springing up trouble *you,* and thereby many be defiled;

16 [w]Lest there *be* any fornicator, or profane person, as Esau, [x]who for one morsel of meat sold his birthright.

17 For ye know how that afterward, [y]when he would have inherited the blessing, he was rejected: for he found no place of repentance, though he sought it carefully with tears.

18 For ye are not come unto the [z]mount that might be touched, and that burned with fire, nor unto blackness, and darkness, and tempest,

19 And the sound of a trumpet, and the voice of words; which *voice* they that heard [a]intreated that the word should not be spoken to them any more:

20 (For they could not endure that which was commanded, [b]And if so much as a beast touch the mountain, it shall be stoned, or thrust through with a dart:

21 [c]And so terrible was the sight, *that* Moses said, I exceedingly fear and quake:)

22 But ye are come [d]unto mount Sion, [e]and unto the city of the living God, the heavenly Jerusalem, [f]and to an innumerable company of angels,

23 To the general assembly and church of [g]the firstborn, [h]which are written in heaven, and to God [i]the Judge of all, and to the spirits of just men [j]made perfect,

24 And to Jesus the mediator of the new covenant, and to [k]the blood of sprinkling, that speaketh better things [l]than *that of* Abel.

25 See that ye refuse not him that speaketh. For if they escaped not who refused him that spake on earth, much more *shall not* we *escape,* if we turn away from him that *speaketh* from heaven:

26 [m]Whose voice then shook the earth: but now he hath promised, saying, [n]Yet once more I shake not the earth only, but also heaven.

27 And this *word,* Yet once more, signifieth [o]the removing of those things that are shaken, as of things that are made, that those things which cannot be shaken may remain.

28 Wherefore we receiving a kingdom which cannot be moved, let us have grace, whereby we may serve God acceptably with reverence and godly fear:

29 For [p]our God *is* a consuming fire.

13 Let [q]brotherly love continue.

2 [r]Be not forgetful to entertain strangers: for thereby [s]some have entertained angels unawares.

3 [t]Remember them that are in bonds, as bound with them; *and* them which suffer adversity, as being yourselves also in the body.

4 Marriage *is* honourable in all, and the bed undefiled: [u]but whoremongers and adulterers God will judge.

5 *Let your* conversation *be* without covetousness; *and* [v]*be* content with such things as ye have: for he hath said, [w]I will never leave thee, nor forsake thee.

6 So that we may boldly say, [x]The Lord *is* my helper, and I will not fear what man shall do unto me.

7 Remember them which have the rule over you, who have spoken unto you the word of God: whose faith follow, considering the end of *their* conversation.

8 Jesus Christ [y]the same yesterday, and to day, and for ever.

9 [z]Be not carried about with divers and strange doctrines. For *it is* a good thing that the heart be established with grace; [a]not with meats, which have not profited them that have been occupied therein.

10 [b]We have an altar, whereof they have no right to eat which serve the tabernacle.

11 For [c]the bodies of those beasts, whose blood is brought into the sanctuary by the high priest for sin, are burned without the camp.

12 Wherefore Jesus also, that he might sanctify the people with his own blood, [d]suffered without the gate.

13 Let us go forth therefore unto him without the camp, bearing [e]his reproach.

14 [f]For here have we no continuing city, but we seek one to come.

15 [g]By him therefore let us offer [h]the sacrifice of praise to God continually, that is, [i]the fruit of *our* lips giving thanks to his name.

16 [j]But to do good and to communicate forget not: for [k]with such sacrifices God is well pleased.

17 [l]Obey them that have the rule over you, and submit yourselves: for [m]they watch for your souls, as they that must give account, that they may do it with joy, and not with grief: for that *is* unprofitable for you.

18 [n]Pray for us: for we trust we have [o]a good conscience, in all things willing to live honestly.

19 But I beseech *you* [p]the rather to do this, that I may be restored to you the sooner.

12:11 [n]Jam. 3:18
12:12 [o]Job 4:3
12:13 [p]Prov. 4:26 [q]Gal. 6:1
12:14 [r]Ps. 34:14; 2 Tim. 2:22 [s]Matt. 5:8; Eph. 5:5
12:15 [t]2 Cor. 6:1 [u]Gal. 5:4 [v]Deut. 29:18
12:16 [w]Eph. 5:3; 1 Thess. 4:3 [x]Gen. 25:33
12:17 [y]Gen. 27:34
12:18 [z]Ex. 19:12; Rom. 6:14; 2 Tim. 1:7
12:19 [a]Ex. 20:19
12:20 [b]Ex. 19:13
12:21 [c]Ex. 19:16
12:22 [d]Gal. 4:26 [e]Phil. 3:20 [f]Deut. 33:2; Jude 14
12:23 [g]Ex. 4:22; Rev. 14:4 [h]Luke 10:20; Rev. 13:8 [i]Gen. 18:25 [j]Phil. 3:12
12:24 [k]Ex. 24:8 [l]Gen. 4:10
12:26 [m]Ex. 19:18 [n]Hag. 2:6
12:27 [o]Ps. 102:26; 2 Pet. 3:10; Rev. 21:1
12:29 [p]Ex. 24:17; Ps. 50:3; Isa. 66:15
13:1 [q]Rom. 12:10; 1 Pet. 1:22; 2 Pet. 1:7
13:2 [r]Matt. 25:35; 1 Tim. 3:2; 1 Pet. 4:9 [s]Gen. 18:3
13:3 [t]Matt. 25:36; 1 Cor. 12:26; Col. 4:18
13:4 [u]1 Cor. 6:9; Eph. 5:5; Col. 3:5
13:5 [v]Matt. 6:25; 1 Tim. 6:6 [w]Gen. 28:15; Josh. 1:5; 1 Chron. 28:20
13:6 [x]Ps. 27:1
13:8 [y]John 8:58
13:9 [z]Eph. 4:14; 1 John 4:1 [a]Rom. 14:17; 1 Tim. 4:3
13:10 [b]1 Cor. 9:13
13:11 [c]Ex. 29:14; Num. 19:3
13:12 [d]John 19:17
13:13 [e]1 Pet. 4:14
13:14 [f]Mic. 2:10
13:15 [g]Eph. 5:20 [h]Lev. 7:12 [i]Hos. 14:2
13:16 [j]Rom. 12:13 [k]2 Cor. 9:12
13:17 [l]Phil. 2:29; 1 Tim. 5:17 [m]Ezek. 3:17
13:18 [n]Rom. 15:30; Col. 4:3; 1 Thess. 5:25 [o]Acts 23:1
13:19 [p]Philem. 22

20 Now [q]the God of peace, [r]that brought again from the dead our Lord Jesus, [s]that great shepherd of the sheep, [t]through the blood of the everlasting covenant,

21 [u]Make you perfect in every good work to do his will, [v]working in you that which is wellpleasing in his sight, through Jesus Christ; [w]to whom *be* glory for ever and ever. Amen.

22 And I beseech you, brethren, suffer the word of exhortation: for [x]I have written a letter unto you in few words.

23 Know ye that [y]*our* brother Timothy [z]is set at liberty; with whom, if he come shortly, I will see you.

24 Salute all them that have the rule over you, and all the saints. They of Italy salute you.

25 [a]Grace *be* with you all. Amen.

13:20 qRom. 15:33 rActs 2:24 sIsa. 40:11 tZech. 9:11 **13:21** u2 Thess. 2:17 vPhil. 2:13 wGal. 1:5; Rev. 1:6 **13:22** x1 Pet. 5:12 **13:23** y1 Thess. 3:2 z1 Tim. 6:12 **13:25** aTit. 3:15

JAMES

James, the brother of Jesus, is considered to be the author of this book written between A.D. 40 and A.D. 60. James begins with a discussion of the nature of trials and temptations and why they happen. The remainder of James deals with practical concerns of the Christian life such as partiality, boastfulness, and worldliness. The book concludes with exhortations to be patient in difficult times and to pray continually for each other.

I. The nature of trials and tribulations, 1:1–1:27
II. Avoiding favoritism, 2:1–2:13
III. Faith and works, 2:14–2:26
IV. Christian speaking, 3:1–3:12
V. On obtaining wisdom, 3:13–3:18
VI. Submission to the will of God, 4:1–4:17
VII. Danger of riches, 5:1–5:6
VIII. Suffering and faith, 5:7–5:19

1 [a]James, [b]a servant of God and of the Lord Jesus Christ, [c]to the twelve tribes [d]which are scattered abroad, greeting.

2 My brethren, [e]count it all joy [f]when ye fall into divers temptations;

3 [g]Knowing *this*, that the trying of your faith worketh patience.

4 But let patience have *her* perfect work, that ye may be perfect and entire, wanting nothing.

5 [h]If any of you lack wisdom, [i]let him ask of God, that giveth to all *men* liberally, and upbraideth not; and [j]it shall be given him.

6 [k]But let him ask in faith, nothing wavering. For he that wavereth is like a wave of the sea driven with the wind and tossed.

7 For let not that man think that he shall receive any thing of the Lord.

8 A double minded man *is* unstable in all his ways.

9 Let the brother of low degree rejoice in that he is exalted:

10 But the rich, in that he is made low: because [l]as the flower of the grass he shall pass away.

11 For the sun is no sooner risen with a burning heat, but it withereth the grass, and the flower thereof falleth, and the grace of the fashion of it perisheth: so also shall the rich man fade away in his ways.

12 [m]Blessed *is* the man that endureth temptation: for when he is tried, he shall receive [n]the crown of life, [o]which the Lord hath promised to them that love him.

13 Let no man say when he is tempted, I am tempted of God: for God cannot be tempted with evil, neither tempteth he any man:

14 But every man is tempted, when he is drawn away of his own lust, and enticed.

15 Then [p]when lust hath conceived, it bringeth forth sin: and sin, when it is finished, [q]bringeth forth death.

16 Do not err, my beloved brethren.

17 [r]Every good gift and every perfect gift is from above, and cometh down from the Father of lights, [s]with whom is no variableness, neither shadow of turning.

18 [t]Of his own will begat he us with the word of truth, [u]that we should be a kind of [v]firstfruits of his creatures.

19 Wherefore, my beloved brethren, [w]let every man be swift to hear, [x]slow to speak, [y]slow to wrath:

20 For the wrath of man worketh not the righteousness of God.

21 Wherefore [z]lay apart all filthiness and superfluity of naughtiness, and receive with meekness the engrafted word, [a]which is able to save your souls.

1:1 aActs 12:17; Jude 1 bTit. 1:1 cActs 26:7 dDeut. 32:26; Acts 2:5; 1 Pet. 1:1 **1:2** eMatt. 5:12; Heb. 10:34; 1 Pet. 4:13 f1 Pet. 1:6 **1:3** gRom. 5:3 **1:5** h1 Kings 3:9 iMatt. 7:7; Luke 11:9; John 14:13 jJer. 29:12 **1:6** kMark 11:24 **1:10** lJob 14:2; Isa. 40:6; 1 Cor. 7:31; 1 John 2:17 **1:12** mJob 5:17; Heb. 12:5; Rev. 3:19 n1 Cor. 9:25; 1 Pet. 5:4; Rev. 2:10 oMatt. 10:22 **1:15** pJob 15:35 qRom. 6:21 **1:17** rJohn 3:27 sNum. 23:19; Mal. 3:6; Rom. 11:29 **1:18** tJohn 1:13; 1 Pet. 1:23 uEph. 1:12 vJer. 2:3 **1:19** wEccl. 5:1 xProv. 10:19 yProv. 14:17 **1:21** zCol. 3:8 aActs 13:26; 1 Cor. 15:2; Eph. 1:13; Heb. 2:3; 1 Pet. 1:9

22 But [b]be ye doers of the word, and not hearers only, deceiving your own selves.

23 For [c]if any be a hearer of the word, and not a doer, he is like unto a man beholding his natural face in a glass:

24 For he beholdeth himself, and goeth his way, and straightway forgetteth what manner of man he was.

25 But [d]whoso looketh into the perfect law of liberty, and continueth *therein*, he being not a forgetful hearer, but a doer of the work, [e]this man shall be blessed in his deed.

26 If any man among you seem to be religious, and [f]bridleth not his tongue, but deceiveth his own heart, this man's religion *is* vain.

27 Pure religion and undefiled before God and the Father is this, [g]To visit the fatherless and widows in their affliction, [h]*and* to keep himself unspotted from the world.

2 My brethren, have not the faith of our Lord Jesus Christ, [i]*the Lord* of glory, with [j]respect of persons.

2 For if there come unto your assembly a man with a gold ring, in goodly apparel, and there come in also a poor man in vile raiment;

3 And ye have respect to him that weareth the gay clothing, and say unto him, Sit thou here in a good place; and say to the poor, Stand thou there, or sit here under my footstool:

4 Are ye not then partial in yourselves, and are become judges of evil thoughts?

5 Hearken, my beloved brethren, [k]Hath not God chosen the poor of this world [l]rich in faith, and heirs of the kingdom [m]which he hath promised to them that love him?

6 But [n]ye have despised the poor. Do not rich men oppress you, [o]and draw you before the judgment seats?

7 Do not they blaspheme that worthy name by the which ye are called?

8 If ye fulfil the royal law according to the scripture, [p]Thou shalt love thy neighbour as thyself, ye do well:

9 But if ye have respect to persons, ye commit sin, and are convinced of the law as transgressors.

10 For whosoever shall keep the whole law, and yet offend in one *point*, [q]he is guilty of all.

11 For he that said, [r]Do not commit adultery, said also, Do not kill. Now if thou commit no adultery, yet if thou kill, thou art become a transgressor of the law.

12 So speak ye, and so do, as they that shall be judged by the law of liberty.

13 For [s]he shall have judgment without mercy, that hath shewed no mercy; and [t]mercy rejoiceth against judgment.

14 [u]What *doth it* profit, my brethren, though a man say he hath faith, and have not works? can faith save him?

15 [v]If a brother or sister be naked, and destitute of daily food,

16 And [w]one of you say unto them, Depart in peace, be *ye* warmed and filled; notwithstanding ye give them not those things which are needful to the body; what *doth it* profit?

17 Even so faith, if it hath not works, is dead, being alone.

18 Yea, a man may say, Thou hast faith, and I have works: shew me thy faith without thy works, and I will shew thee my faith by my works.

19 Thou believest that there is one God; thou doest well: [x]the devils also believe, and tremble.

20 But wilt thou know, O vain man, that faith without works is dead?

21 Was not Abraham our father justified by works, [y]when he had offered Isaac his son upon the altar?

22 Seest thou [z]how faith wrought with his works, and by works was faith made perfect?

23 And the scripture was fulfilled which saith, [a]Abraham believed God, and it was imputed unto him for righteousness: and he was called [b]the Friend of God.

24 Ye see then how that by works a man is justified, and not by faith only.

25 Likewise also [c]was not Rahab the harlot justified by works, when she had received the messengers, and had sent *them* out another way?

26 For as the body without the spirit is dead, so faith without works is dead also.

3 My brethren, [d]be not many masters, [e]knowing that we shall receive the greater condemnation.

2 For [f]in many things we offend all. [g]If any man offend not in word, [h]the same *is* a perfect man, *and* able also to bridle the whole body.

3 Behold, [i]we put bits in the horses' mouths, that they may obey us; and we turn about their whole body.

4 Behold also the ships, which though *they be* so great, and *are* driven of fierce winds, yet are they turned about with a very small helm, whithersoever the governor listeth.

5 Even so [j]the tongue is a little member, and [k]boasteth great things. Behold, how great a matter a little fire kindleth!

6 And [l]the tongue *is* a fire, a world of iniquity: so is the tongue among our members, that [m]it defileth the whole body, and setteth on fire the course of nature; and it is set on fire of hell.

7 For every kind of beasts, and of birds, and of serpents, and of things in the sea, is tamed, and hath been tamed of mankind:

8 But the tongue can no man tame; *it is* an unruly evil, [n]full of deadly poison.

9 Therewith bless we God, even the Father; and therewith curse we men, [o]which are made after the similitude of God.

10 Out of the same mouth proceedeth blessing and cursing. My brethren, these things ought not so to be.

1:22 [b]Matt. 7:21; Rom. 2:13; 1 John 3:7
1:23 [c]Luke 6:47
1:25 [d]2 Cor. 3:18 [e]John 13:17
1:26 [f]Ps. 34:13
1:27 [g]Isa. 1:16 [h]Rom. 12:2
2:1 [i]1 Cor. 2:8 [j]Lev. 19:15; Prov. 24:23; Matt. 22:16
2:5 [k]John 7:48 [l]Luke 12:21; Rev. 2:9 [m]Ex. 20:6; Prov. 8:17; Matt. 5:3; 1 Cor. 2:9; 2 Tim. 4:8
2:6 [n]1 Cor. 11:22 [o]Acts 13:50
2:8 [p]Lev. 19:18; Rom. 13:8; Gal. 5:14
2:10 [q]Deut. 27:26; Gal. 3:10
2:11 [r]Ex. 20:13
2:13 [s]Job 22:6; Matt. 6:15 [t]1 John 4:17
2:14 [u]Matt. 7:26
2:15 [v]Job 31:19
2:16 [w]1 John 3:18
2:19 [x]Matt. 8:29; Luke 4:34; Acts 16:17
2:21 [y]Gen. 22:9
2:22 [z]Heb. 11:17
2:23 [a]Gen. 15:6; Gal. 3:6 [b]2 Chron. 20:7
2:25 [c]Josh. 2:1
3:1 [d]Matt. 23:8; 1 Pet. 5:3 [e]Luke 6:37
3:2 [f]1 Kings 8:46; Prov. 20:9; Eccl. 7:20 [g]Ps. 34:13 [h]Matt. 12:37
3:3 [i]Ps. 32:9
3:5 [j]Prov. 12:18 [k]Ps. 12:3
3:6 [l]Prov. 16:27 [m]Matt. 15:11
3:8 [n]Ps. 140:3
3:9 [o]Gen. 1:26

11 Doth a fountain send forth at the same
place sweet *water* and bitter?
12 Can the fig tree, my brethren, bear olive berries? either a vine, figs? so *can* no
fountain both yield salt water and fresh.
13 [p]Who *is* a wise man and endued with
knowledge among you? let him shew out of
a good conversation his works with meekness of wisdom.
14 But if ye have [q]bitter envying and
strife in your hearts, [r]glory not, and lie not
against the truth.
15 [s]This wisdom descendeth not from
above, but *is* earthly, sensual, devilish.
16 For [t]where envying and strife *is*, there
is confusion and every evil work.
17 But [u]the wisdom that is from above is
first pure, then peaceable, gentle, *and* easy
to be intreated, full of mercy and good
fruits, without partiality, [v]and without hypocrisy.
18 [w]And the fruit of righteousness is
sown in peace of them that make peace.
4 From whence *come* wars and fightings
among you? *come they* not hence, *even*
of your lusts [x]that war in your members?
2 Ye lust, and have not: ye kill, and desire
to have, and cannot obtain: ye fight and
war, yet ye have not, because ye ask not.
3 [y]Ye ask, and receive not, [z]because ye
ask amiss, that ye may consume *it* upon
your lusts.
4 [a]Ye adulterers and adulteresses, know
ye not that [b]the friendship of the world is
enmity with God? [c]whosoever therefore
will be a friend of the world is the enemy of
God.
5 Do ye think that the scripture saith in
vain, [d]The spirit that dwelleth in us lusteth
to envy?
6 But he giveth more grace. Wherefore he
saith, [e]God resisteth the proud, but giveth
grace unto the humble.
7 Submit yourselves therefore to God.
[f]Resist the devil, and he will flee from you.
8 [g]Draw nigh to God, and he will draw
nigh to you. [h]Cleanse *your* hands, *ye* sinners; and [i]purify *your* hearts, *ye* double
minded.
9 [j]Be afflicted, and mourn, and weep: let
your laughter be turned to mourning, and
your joy to heaviness.
10 [k]Humble yourselves in the sight of the
Lord, and he shall lift you up.
11 [l]Speak not evil one of another, brethren. He that speaketh evil of *his* brother,
[m]and judgeth his brother, speaketh evil of
the law, and judgeth the law: but if thou
judge the law, thou art not a doer of the law,
but a judge.
12 There is one lawgiver, [n]who is able to
save and to destroy: [o]who art thou that
judgest another?
13 [p]Go to now, ye that say, To day or to
morrow we will go into such a city, and continue there a year, and buy and sell, and get
gain:
14 Whereas ye know not what *shall be* on
the morrow. For what *is* your life? [q]It is
even a vapour, that appeareth for a little
time, and then vanisheth away.
15 For that ye *ought* to say, [r]If the Lord
will, we shall live, and do this, or that.
16 But now ye rejoice in your boastings:
[s]all such rejoicing is evil.
17 Therefore [t]to him that knoweth to do
good, and doeth *it* not, to him it is sin.
5 Go [u]to now, *ye* rich men, weep and
howl for your miseries that shall come
upon *you*.
2 Your riches are corrupted, and [v]your
garments are motheaten.
3 Your gold and silver is cankered; and
the rust of them shall be a witness against
you, and shall eat your flesh as it were fire.
[w]Ye have heaped treasure together for the
last days.
4 Behold, [x]the hire of the labourers who
have reaped down your fields, which is of
you kept back by fraud, crieth: and [y]the
cries of them which have reaped are entered into the ears of the Lord of sabaoth.
5 [z]Ye have lived in pleasure on the earth,
and been wanton; ye have nourished your
hearts, as in a day of slaughter.
6 Ye have condemned *and* killed the just;
and he doth not resist you.
7 Be patient therefore, brethren, unto the
coming of the Lord. Behold, the husbandman waiteth for the precious fruit of the
earth, and hath long patience for it, until he
receive [a]the early and latter rain.
8 Be ye also patient; stablish your hearts:
[b]for the coming of the Lord draweth nigh.
9 Grudge not one against another, brethren, lest ye be condemned: behold, the
judge [c]standeth before the door.
10 [d]Take, my brethren, the prophets,
who have spoken in the name of the Lord,
for an example of suffering affliction, and of
patience.
11 Behold, [e]we count them happy which
endure. Ye have heard of [f]the patience of
Job, and have seen [g]the end of the Lord;
that [h]the Lord is very pitiful, and of tender
mercy.
12 But above all things, my brethren,
[i]swear not, neither by heaven, neither by
the earth, neither by any other oath: but let
your yea be yea; and *your* nay, nay; lest ye
fall into condemnation.
13 Is any among you afflicted? let him
pray. Is any merry? [j]let him sing psalms.
14 Is any sick among you? let him call for
the elders of the church; and let them pray
over him, [k]anointing him with oil in the
name of the Lord:
15 And the prayer of faith shall save the
sick, and the Lord shall raise him up; [l]and
if he hath committed sins, they shall be forgiven him.
16 Confess *your* faults one to another,
and pray one for another, that ye may be
healed. [m]The effectual fervent prayer of a
righteous man availeth much.
17 Elias was a man [n]subject to like pas-

3:13 *p*Gal. 6:4
3:14 *q*Rom. 13:13 *r*Rom. 2:17
3:15 *s*Phil. 3:19
3:16 *t*1 Cor. 3:3
3:17 *u*1 Cor. 2:6 *v*Rom. 12:9; 1 John 3:18
3:18 *w*Prov. 11:18; Matt. 5:9; Phil. 1:11
4:1 *x*Rom. 7:23; 1 Pet. 2:11
4:3 *y*Job 27:9; Prov. 1:28; Isa. 1:15; Mic. 3:4; Zech. 7:13 *z*Ps. 66:18
4:4 *a*Ps. 73:27 *b*1 John 2:15 *c*John 15:19
4:5 *d*Gen. 6:5; Prov. 21:10
4:6 *e*Job 22:29; Prov. 3:34; Matt. 23:12; 1 Pet. 5:5
4:7 *f*Eph. 4:27
4:8 *g*2 Chron. 15:2 *h*Isa. 1:16 *i*1 Pet. 1:22
4:9 *j*Matt. 5:4
4:10 *k*Job 22:29; Luke 14:11; 1 Pet. 5:6
4:11 *l*Eph. 4:31 *m*Matt. 7:1; Rom. 2:1; 1 Cor. 4:5
4:12 *n*Matt. 10:28 *o*Rom. 14:4
4:13 *p*Prov. 27:1
4:14 *q*Job 7:7; 1 Pet. 1:24; 1 John 2:17
4:15 *r*Acts 18:21; Heb. 6:3
4:16 *s*1 Cor. 5:6
4:17 *t*Luke 12:47; Rom. 1:20
5:1 *u*Prov. 11:28; 1 Tim. 6:9
5:2 *v*Job 13:28
5:3 *w*Rom. 2:5
5:4 *x*Lev. 19:13; Jer. 22:13; Mal. 3:5 *y*Deut. 24:15
5:5 *z*Job 21:13; Luke 16:19; 1 Tim. 5:6
5:7 *a*Deut. 11:14; Hos. 6:3; Joel 2:23
5:8 *b*Phil. 4:5; 1 Pet. 4:7
5:9 *c*Matt. 24:33
5:10 *d*Matt. 5:12
5:11 *e*Ps. 94:12 *f*Job 1:21 *g*Job 42:10 *h*Num. 14:18
5:12 *i*Matt. 5:34
5:13 *j*Eph. 5:19
5:14 *k*Mark 6:13
5:15 *l*Isa. 33:24
5:16 *m*Gen. 20:17; Deut. 9:18; Josh. 10:12; 1 Kings 13:6; 2 Kings 4:33; Prov. 15:29; John 9:31
5:17 *n*Acts 14:15

sions as we are, and [o]he prayed earnestly that it might not rain: [p]and it rained not on the earth by the space of three years and six months.

18 And [q]he prayed again, and the heaven gave rain, and the earth brought forth her fruit.

19 Brethren, [r]if any of you do err from the truth, and one convert him;

20 Let him know, that he which converteth the sinner from the error of his way [s]shall save a soul from death, and [t]shall hide a multitude of sins.

5:17 [o]1 Kings 17:1 [p]Luke 4:25
5:18 [q]1 Kings 18:42
5:19 [r]Matt. 18:15
5:20 [s]Rom. 11:14; 1 Tim. 4:16; [t]Prov. 10:12

1 PETER

Peter identifies himself as the author of this book which was probably written A.D. 63 or 64. Peter begins his letter by reaffirming the wonder of salvation. He encourages his readers to remain holy, love one another, continue to seek God's word, and to remember who they are in Christ. He gives instructions on proper Christian conduct in relation to unbelievers, governments, employers, and family. Peter acknowledges that suffering will occur but that there are reasons for it and the believer must be prepared to deal with it. He closes the letter with a statement concerning Christian leadership and service.

I. Greetings, 1:1–1:2
II. The grace of God and salvation, 1:3–1:12
III. The holy life, 1:13–2:10
IV. Christians and relationships, 2:11-3:7
V. Christians and suffering, 3:8–4:19
VI. Christian leaders, 5:1–5:5
VII. Christian service, 5:6–5:11
VIII. Closing greetings, 5:12–5:14

---

1 Peter, an apostle of Jesus Christ, to the strangers [a]scattered throughout Pontus, Galatia, Cappadocia, Asia, and Bithynia,

2 [b]Elect [c]according to the foreknowledge of God the Father, [d]through sanctification of the Spirit, unto obedience and [e]sprinkling of the blood of Jesus Christ: [f]Grace unto you, and peace, be multiplied.

3 [g]Blessed *be* the God and Father of our Lord Jesus Christ, which [h]according to his abundant mercy [i]hath begotten us again unto a lively hope [j]by the resurrection of Jesus Christ from the dead,

4 To an inheritance incorruptible, and undefiled, and that fadeth not away, [k]reserved in heaven for you,

5 [l]Who are kept by the power of God through faith unto salvation ready to be revealed in the last time.

6 [m]Wherein ye greatly rejoice, though now [n]for a season, if need be, [o]ye are in heaviness through manifold temptations:

7 That [p]the trial of your faith, being much more precious than of gold that perisheth, though [q]it be tried with fire, [r]might be found unto praise and honour and glory at the appearing of Jesus Christ:

8 [s]Whom having not seen, ye love; [t]in whom, though now ye see *him* not, yet believing, ye rejoice with joy unspeakable and full of glory:

9 Receiving [u]the end of your faith, *even* the salvation of *your* souls.

10 [v]Of which salvation the prophets have enquired and searched diligently, who prophesied of the grace *that should come* unto you:

11 Searching what, or what manner of time [w]the Spirit of Christ which was in them did signify, when it testified beforehand [x]the sufferings of Christ, and the glory that should follow.

12 [y]Unto whom it was revealed, that [z]not unto themselves, but unto us they did minister the things, which are now reported unto you by them that have preached the gospel unto you with [a]the Holy Ghost sent down from heaven; [b]which things the angels desire to look into.

13 Wherefore [c]gird up the loins of your mind, [d]be sober, and hope to the end for the grace that is to be brought unto you [e]at the revelation of Jesus Christ;

14 As obedient children, [f]not fashioning yourselves according to the former lusts [g]in your ignorance:

15 [h]But as he which hath called you is

1:1 [a]John 7:35; Jam. 1:1
1:2 [b]Eph. 1:4 [c]Rom. 8:29 [d]2 Thess. 2:13 [e]Heb. 10:22 [f]Rom. 1:7; Jude 2
1:3 [g]2 Cor. 1:3 [h]Tit. 3:5 [i]John 3:3 [j]1 Cor. 15:20
1:4 [k]Col. 1:5
1:5 [l]John 10:28
1:6 [m]Matt. 5:12; 2 Cor. 6:10 [n]2 Cor. 4:17 [o]Jam. 1:2
1:7 [p]Jam. 1:3 [q]Job 23:10; Prov. 17:3; Isa. 48:10; 1 Cor. 3:13 [r]Rom. 2:7; 2 Thess. 1:7-12
1:8 [s]1 John 4:20 [t]John 20:29; Heb. 11:1
1:9 [u]Rom. 6:22
1:10 [v]Gen. 49:10; Hag. 2:7; Zech. 6:12; Luke 10:24; 2 Pet. 1:19
1:11 [w]2 Pet. 1:21 [x]Ps. 22:6; Dan. 9:26; Luke 24:25; Acts 26:22
1:12 [y]Dan. 9:24 [z]Heb. 11:13 [a]Acts 2:4 [b]Ex. 25:20; Eph. 3:10
1:13 [c]Luke 12:35 [d]Luke 21:34; 1 Thess. 5:6 [e]Luke 17:30; 2 Thess. 1:7
1:14 [f]Rom. 12:2 [g]Acts 17:30
1:15 [h]Luke 1:74; 1 Thess. 4:3; Heb. 12:14

holy, so be ye holy in all manner of conversation;
16 Because it is written, [i]Be ye holy; for
I am holy.
17 And if ye call on the Father, [j]who
without respect of persons judgeth according to every man's work, [k]pass the time of
your [l]sojourning *here* in fear:
18 Forasmuch as ye know [m]that ye were
not redeemed with corruptible things, *as* silver and gold, from your vain conversation
[n]*received* by tradition from your fathers;
19 But [o]with the precious blood of Christ,
[p]as of a lamb without blemish and without
spot:
20 [q]Who verily was foreordained before
the foundation of the world, but was manifest [r]in these last times for you,
21 Who by him do believe in God, [s]that
raised him up from the dead, and [t]gave him
glory; that your faith and hope might be in
God.
22 Seeing ye [u]have purified your souls in
obeying the truth through the Spirit unto
unfeigned [v]love of the brethren, *see that ye*
love one another with a pure heart fervently:
23 [w]Being born again, not of corruptible
seed, but of incorruptible, [x]by the word of
God, which liveth and abideth for ever.
24 For [y]all flesh *is* as grass, and all the
glory of man as the flower of grass. The
grass withereth, and the flower thereof falleth away:
25 [z]But [a]the word of the Lord endureth
for ever. And this is the word which by the
gospel is preached unto you.

2 Wherefore [b]laying aside all malice, and
all guile, and hypocrisies, and envies,
and all evil speakings,
2 [c]As newborn babes, desire the sincere
[d]milk of the word, that ye may grow
thereby:
3 If so be ye have [e]tasted that the Lord *is*
gracious.
4 To whom coming, *as unto* a living
stone, [f]disallowed indeed of men, but chosen of God, *and* precious,
5 [g]Ye also, as lively stones, are built up
[h]a spiritual house, [i]an holy priesthood, to
offer up [j]spiritual sacrifices, [k]acceptable
to God by Jesus Christ.
6 Wherefore also it is contained in the
scripture, [l]Behold, I lay in Sion a chief corner stone, elect, precious: and he that believeth on him shall not be confounded.
7 Unto you therefore which believe *he is*
precious: but unto them which be disobedient, [m]the stone which the builders disallowed, the same is made the head of the
corner,
8 [n]And a stone of stumbling, and a rock
of offence, [o]*even to them* which stumble at
the word, being disobedient: [p]whereunto
also they were appointed.
9 But ye *are* [q]a chosen generation, [r]a
royal priesthood, [s]an holy nation, [t]a peculiar people; that ye should shew forth the
praises of him who hath called you out of
[u]darkness into his marvellous light:
10 [v]Which in time past *were* not a people,
but *are* now the people of God: which had
not obtained mercy, but now have obtained
mercy.
11 Dearly beloved, I beseech *you* [w]as
strangers and pilgrims, [x]abstain from
fleshly lusts, [y]which war against the soul;
12 [z]Having your conversation honest
among the Gentiles: that, whereas they
speak against you as evildoers, [a]they may
by *your* good works, which they shall behold, glorify God [b]in the day of visitation.
13 [c]Submit yourselves to every ordinance of man for the Lord's sake: whether
it be to the king, as supreme;
14 Or unto governors, as unto them that
are sent by him [d]for the punishment of evildoers, and [e]for the praise of them that do
well.
15 For so is the will of God, that [f]with
well doing ye may put to silence the ignorance of foolish men:
16 [g]As free, and not using *your* liberty for
a cloke of maliciousness, but as [h]the servants of God.
17 [i]Honour all *men.* [j]Love the brotherhood. [k]Fear God. Honour the king.
18 [l]Servants, *be* subject to *your* masters
with all fear; not only to the good and gentle, but also to the froward.
19 For this *is* [m]thankworthy, if a man for
conscience toward God endure grief, suffering wrongfully.
20 For what glory *is it,* if, when ye be buffeted for your faults, ye shall take it patiently? but if, when ye do well, and suffer
for it, ye take it patiently, this *is* acceptable
with God.
21 For [n]even hereunto were ye called: because Christ also suffered for us, [o]leaving
us an example, that ye should follow his
steps:
22 [p]Who did no sin, neither was guile
found in his mouth:
23 [q]Who, when he was reviled, reviled
not again; when he suffered, he threatened
not; but [r]committed *himself* to him that
judgeth righteously:
24 [s]Who his own self bare our sins in his
own body on the tree, [t]that we, being dead
to sins, should live unto righteousness: [u]by
whose stripes ye were healed.
25 For [v]ye were as sheep going astray;
but are now returned [w]unto the Shepherd
and Bishop of your souls.

3 Likewise, [x]ye wives, *be* in subjection to
your own husbands; that, if any obey
not the word, [y]they also may without the
word [z]be won by the conversation of the
wives;

1:16 [i]Lev. 11:44
1:17 [j]Deut. 10:17; Rom. 2:11
[k]2 Cor. 7:1; Heb. 12:28
[l]2 Cor. 5:6
1:18 [m]1 Cor. 6:20
[n]Ezek. 20:18
1:19 [o]Acts 20:28; Heb. 9:12; Rev. 5:9
[p]Ex. 12:5; John 1:29; 1 Cor. 5:7
1:20 [q]Rom. 3:25; Col. 1:26; 2 Tim. 1:9; Rev. 13:8
[r]Gal. 4:4; Heb. 1:2
1:21 [s]Acts 2:24
[t]Matt. 28:18; Eph. 1:20; Phil. 2:9
1:22 [u]Acts 15:9
[v]Rom. 12:9; 1 Tim. 1:5; Heb. 13:1; 1 John 3:18
1:23 [w]John 1:13
[x]Jam. 1:18
1:24 [y]Ps. 103:15; Jam. 1:10
1:25 [z]Ps. 102:12; Luke 16:17
[a]John 1:1
2:1 [b]Eph. 4:22; Heb. 12:1; Jam. 1:21
2:2 [c]Matt. 18:3; Rom. 6:4; 1 Cor. 14:20
[d]1 Cor. 3:2
2:3 [e]Ps. 34:8
2:4 [f]Ps. 118:22; Acts 4:11
2:5 [g]Eph. 2:21
[h]Heb. 3:6
[i]Isa. 61:6
[j]Hos. 14:2; Rom. 12:1; Heb. 13:15
[k]Phil. 4:18
2:6 [l]Isa. 28:16
2:7 [m]Ps. 118:22; Acts 4:11
2:8 [n]Isa. 8:14; Rom. 9:33
[o]1 Cor. 1:23
[p]Ex. 9:16; 1 Thess. 5:9; Jude 4
2:9 [q]Deut. 10:15
[r]Ex. 19:5
[s]John 17:19; 2 Tim. 1:9
[t]Deut. 4:20; Eph. 1:14; Tit. 2:14
[u]Acts 26:18; Col. 1:13; 1 Thess. 5:4
2:10 [v]Hos. 1:9
2:11 [w]1 Chron. 29:15; Heb. 11:13
[x]Rom. 13:14
[y]Jam. 4:1
2:12 [z]Rom. 12:17; Phil. 2:15; Tit. 2:8
[a]Matt. 5:16
[b]Luke 19:44
2:13 [c]Matt. 22:21; Tit. 3:1
2:14 [d]Rom. 13:4
[e]Rom. 13:3
2:15 [f]Tit. 2:8
2:16 [g]Gal. 5:1
[h]1 Cor. 7:22
2:17 [i]Rom. 12:10
[j]Heb. 13:1
[k]Prov. 24:21; Rom. 13:7
2:18 [l]Eph. 6:5; 1 Tim. 6:1; Tit. 2:9
2:19 [m]Matt. 5:10
2:21 [n]Matt. 16:24; 1 Thess. 3:3; 2 Tim. 3:12 [o]John 13:15; 1 John 2:6 **2:22** [p]Isa. 53:9; John 8:46; 2 Cor. 5:21 **2:23** [q]Isa. 53:7; John 8:48; Heb. 12:3 [r]Luke 23:46 **2:24** [s]Isa. 53:4; Heb. 9:28 [t]Rom. 6:2 [u]Isa. 53:5 **2:25** [v]Isa. 53:6 [w]Ezek. 34:23; Heb. 13:20 **3:1** [x]1 Cor. 14:34; Col. 3:18; Tit. 2:5 [y]1 Cor. 7:16 [z]Matt. 18:15

2 While they behold your chaste conversation *coupled* with fear.

3 [a]Whose adorning let it not be that outward *adorning* of plaiting the hair, and of wearing of gold, or of putting on of apparel;

4 But *let it be* [b]the hidden man of the heart, in that which is not corruptible, *even the ornament* of a meek and quiet spirit, which is in the sight of God of great price.

5 For after this manner in the old time the holy women also, who trusted in God, adorned themselves, being in subjection unto their own husbands:

6 Even as Sara obeyed Abraham, [c]calling him lord: whose daughters ye are, as long as ye do well, and are not afraid with any amazement.

7 [d]Likewise, ye husbands, dwell with *them* according to knowledge, giving honour unto the wife, [e]as unto the weaker vessel, and as being heirs together of the grace of life; [f]that your prayers be not hindered.

8 Finally, [g]*be ye* all of one mind, having compassion one of another, [h]love as brethren, [i]*be* pitiful, *be* courteous:

9 [j]Not rendering evil for evil, or railing for railing: but contrariwise blessing; knowing that ye are thereunto called, [k]that ye should inherit a blessing.

10 For [l]he that will love life, and see good days, [m]let him refrain his tongue from evil, and his lips that they speak no guile:

11 Let him [n]eschew evil, and do good; [o]let him seek peace, and ensue it.

12 For the eyes of the Lord *are* over the righteous, [p]and his ears *are open* unto their prayers: but the face of the Lord *is* against them that do evil.

13 [q]And who *is* he that will harm you, if ye be followers of that which is good?

14 [r]But and if ye suffer for righteousness' sake, happy *are ye:* and [s]be not afraid of their terror, neither be troubled;

15 But sanctify the Lord God in your hearts: and [t]*be* ready always to *give* an answer to every man that asketh you a reason of the hope that is in you with meekness and fear:

16 [u]Having a good conscience; [v]that, whereas they speak evil of you, as of evildoers, they may be ashamed that falsely accuse your good conversation in Christ.

17 For *it is* better, if the will of God be so, that ye suffer for well doing, than for evil doing.

18 For Christ also hath [w]once suffered for sins, the just for the unjust, that he might bring us to God, [x]being put to death [y]in the flesh, but [z]quickened by the Spirit:

19 By which also he went and preached unto the spirits [a]in prison;

20 Which sometime were disobedient, [b]when once the longsuffering of God waited in the days of Noah, while [c]the ark was a preparing, [d]wherein few, that is, eight souls were saved by water.

21 [e]The like figure whereunto *even* baptism doth also now save us (not the putting away of [f]the filth of the flesh, [g]but the answer of a good conscience toward God,) by the resurrection of Jesus Christ:

22 Who is gone into heaven, and [h]is on the right hand of God; [i]angels and authorities and powers being made subject unto him.

4 Forasmuch then as Christ hath suffered for us in the flesh, arm yourselves likewise with the same mind: for [j]he that hath suffered in the flesh hath ceased from sin;

2 [k]That he no longer [l]should live the rest of *his* time in the flesh to the lusts of men, [m]but to the will of God.

3 [n]For the time past of *our* life may suffice us [o]to have wrought the will of the Gentiles, when we walked in lasciviousness, lusts, excess of wine, revellings, banquetings, and abominable idolatries:

4 Wherein they think it strange that ye run not with *them* to the same excess of riot, [p]speaking evil of *you:*

5 Who shall give account to him that is ready [q]to judge the quick and the dead.

6 For for this cause was the gospel preached also to them that are dead, that they might be judged according to men in the flesh, but live according to God in the spirit.

7 But [r]the end of all things is at hand: [s]be ye therefore sober, and watch unto prayer.

8 [t]And above all things have fervent charity among yourselves: for [u]charity shall cover the multitude of sins.

9 [v]Use hospitality one to another [w]without grudging.

10 [x]As every man hath received the gift, *even so* minister the same one to another, [y]as good stewards of [z]the manifold grace of God.

11 [a]If any man speak, *let him speak* as the oracles of God; [b]if any man minister, *let him do it* as of the ability which God giveth: that [c]God in all things may be glorified through Jesus Christ, [d]to whom be praise and dominion for ever and ever. Amen.

12 Beloved, think it not strange concerning [e]the fiery trial which is to try you, as though some strange thing happened unto you:

13 [f]But rejoice, inasmuch as [g]ye are partakers of Christ's sufferings; that, when his glory shall be revealed, ye may be glad also with exceeding joy.

14 [h]If ye be reproached for the name of Christ, happy *are ye;* for the spirit of glory and of God resteth upon you: on their part he is evil spoken of, but on your part he is glorified.

15 But let none of you suffer as a murderer, or *as* a thief, or *as* an evildoer, [i]or *as* a busybody in other men's matters.

16 Yet if *any man suffer* as a Christian, let him not be ashamed; [j]but let him glorify God on this behalf.

17 For the time *is come* [k]that judgment must begin at the house of God: and [l]if *it*

3:3 [a]1 Tim. 2:9
3:4 [b]Ps. 45:13; 2 Cor. 4:16
3:6 [c]Gen. 18:12
3:7 [d]1 Cor. 7:3; Col. 3:19 [e]1 Cor. 12:23 [f]Job 42:8
3:8 [g]Rom. 12:16 [h]Rom. 12:10 [i]Col. 3:12
3:9 [j]Prov. 17:13; Rom. 12:14; 1 Cor. 4:12 [k]Matt. 25:34
3:10 [l]Ps. 34:12 [m]Jam. 1:26
3:11 [n]Ps. 37:27; 3 John 11 [o]Rom. 12:18
3:12 [p]John 9:31
3:13 [q]Prov. 16:7
3:14 [r]Matt. 5:10 [s]Isa. 8:12; John 14:1
3:15 [t]Ps. 119:46; Col. 4:6; 2 Tim. 2:25
3:16 [u]Heb. 13:18 [v]Tit. 2:8
3:18 [w]Rom. 5:6 [x]2 Cor. 13:4 [y]Col. 1:21 [z]Rom. 1:4
3:19 [a]Isa. 42:7
3:20 [b]Gen. 6:3 [c]Heb. 11:7 [d]Gen. 7:7
3:21 [e]Eph. 5:26 [f]Tit. 3:5 [g]Rom. 10:10
3:22 [h]Ps. 110:1; Eph. 1:20; Col. 3:1 [i]Rom. 8:38; Eph. 1:21
4:1 [j]Rom. 6:2; Col. 3:3
4:2 [k]Rom. 14:7 [l]Gal. 2:20 [m]John 1:13; 2 Cor. 5:15; Jam. 1:18
4:3 [n]Ezek. 44:6 [o]Eph. 2:2; Tit. 3:3
4:4 [p]Acts 13:45
4:5 [q]Acts 10:42; 1 Cor. 15:51; 2 Tim. 4:1
4:7 [r]Matt. 24:13; Phil. 4:5; Heb. 10:25; 2 Pet. 3:9; 1 John 2:18 [s]Matt. 26:41; Col. 4:2
4:8 [t]Heb. 13:1 [u]Prov. 10:12; Jam. 5:20
4:9 [v]Rom. 12:13 [w]2 Cor. 9:7; Philem. 14
4:10 [x]Rom. 12:6 [y]Matt. 24:45; 1 Cor. 4:1; Tit. 1:7 [z]1 Cor. 12:4
4:11 [a]Jer. 23:22 [b]Rom. 12:6 [c]Eph. 5:20 [d]1 Tim. 6:16
4:12 [e]1 Cor. 3:13
4:13 [f]Acts 5:41 [g]Rom. 8:17; Phil. 3:10; Col. 1:24; Rev. 1:9
4:14 [h]Matt. 5:11; Jam. 1:12
4:15 [i]1 Thess. 4:11
4:16 [j]Acts 5:41
4:17 [k]Isa. 10:12; Ezek. 9:6; Mal. 3:5 [l]Luke 23:31

first *begin* at us, [m]what shall the end *be* of
them that obey not the gospel of God?
18 [n]And if the righteous scarcely be
saved, where shall the ungodly and the sinner appear?
19 Wherefore let them that suffer according to the will of God [o]commit the keeping
of their souls *to him* in well doing, as unto
a faithful Creator.

5 The elders which are among you I exhort, who am also [p]an elder, and [q]a
witness of the sufferings of Christ, and also
[r]a partaker of the glory that shall be revealed:
2 [s]Feed the flock of God which is among
you, taking the oversight *thereof,* [t]not by
constraint, but willingly; [u]not for filthy
lucre, but of a ready mind;
3 Neither as [v]being lords over [w]*God's*
heritage, but [x]being ensamples to the flock.
4 And when [y]the chief Shepherd shall
appear, ye shall receive [z]a crown of glory
that fadeth not away.
5 Likewise, ye younger, submit yourselves unto the elder. Yea, [a]all *of you* be
subject one to another, and be clothed with
humility: for [b]God resisteth the proud, and
[c]giveth grace to the humble.
6 [d]Humble yourselves therefore under
the mighty hand of God, that he may exalt
you in due time:
7 [e]Casting all your care upon him; for he
careth for you.
8 [f]Be sober, be vigilant; because [g]your
adversary the devil, as a roaring lion, walketh about, seeking whom he may devour:
9 [h]Whom resist stedfast in the faith,
[i]knowing that the same afflictions are accomplished in your brethren that are in the
world.
10 But the God of all grace, [j]who hath
called us unto his eternal glory by Christ
Jesus, after that ye have suffered [k]a while,
[l]make you perfect, [m]stablish, strengthen,
settle *you.*
11 [n]To him *be* glory and dominion for
ever and ever. Amen.
12 [o]By Silvanus, a faithful brother unto
you, as I suppose, I have [p]written briefly,
exhorting, and testifying [q]that this is the
true grace of God wherein ye stand.
13 The *church that is* at Babylon, elected
together with *you,* saluteth you; and *so doth*
[r]Marcus my son.
14 [s]Greet ye one another with a kiss of
charity. [t]Peace *be* with you all that are in
Christ Jesus. Amen.

4:17 [m]Luke 10:12 **4:18** [n]Prov. 11:31 **4:19** [o]Ps. 31:5; 2 Tim. 1:12 **5:1** [p]Philem. 9 [q]Luke 24:48 [r]Rom. 8:17 **5:2** [s]John 21:15 [t]1 Cor. 9:17 [u]1 Tim. 3:3 **5:3** [v]Ezek. 34:4; 1 Cor. 3:9; 2 Cor. 1:24 [w]Ps. 33:12 [x]Phil. 3:17; 1 Tim. 4:12; Tit. 2:7 **5:4** [y]Heb. 13:20 [z]1 Cor. 9:25; Jam. 1:12 **5:5** [a]Rom. 12:10; Phil. 2:3 [b]Jam. 4:6 [c]Isa. 57:15 **5:6** [d]Jam. 4:10 **5:7** [e]Ps. 37:5; Luke 12:11; Phil. 4:6 **5:8** [f]Luke 21:34 [g]Job 1:7; Rev. 12:12 **5:9** [h]Eph. 6:11 [i]Acts 14:22; 2 Tim. 3:12 **5:10** [j]1 Cor. 1:9 [k]2 Cor. 4:17 [l]Heb. 13:21 [m]2 Thess. 2:17 **5:11** [n]Rev. 1:6 **5:12** [o]2 Cor. 1:19 [p]Heb. 13:22 [q]Acts 20:24; 2 Pet. 1:12 **5:13** [r]Acts 12:12

5:14 [s]Rom. 16:16; 2 Cor. 13:12; 1 Thess. 5:26 [t]Eph. 6:23

2 PETER

Peter is the author of this book which was probably written in A.D. 66. Each chapter in 2 Peter focuses on a different topic. In chapter 1, Peter encourages the reader to continue to grow spiritually. Chapter 2 deals with false doctrine and false teachers. Chapter 3 is a prophetic chapter relating to the return of Christ, and the judgments that will follow Christ's return. One of the most often quoted scriptures concerning the delay in Christ's return can be found in 2 Peter 3:8–9.

I. Spiritual growth and faithfulness, 1:1–1:21
II. False teachers and false doctrines, 2:1–2:22
III. Christ's return, 3:1–3:18

1 Simon Peter, a servant and an apostle of
Jesus Christ, to them that have obtained
[a]like precious faith with us through the
righteousness of God and our Saviour Jesus
Christ:
2 [b]Grace and peace be multiplied unto
you through the knowledge of God, and of
Jesus our Lord,
3 According as his divine power hath
given unto us all things that *pertain* unto
life and godliness, [c]through the knowledge
of him [d]that hath called us to glory and
virtue:
4 [e]Whereby are given unto us exceeding
great and precious promises: that by these
ye might be [f]partakers of the divine nature,
having escaped the corruption that is in the
world through lust.
5 And beside this, giving all diligence,
add to your faith virtue; and to virtue
[g]knowledge;
6 And to knowledge temperance; and to
temperance patience; and to patience godliness;
7 And to godliness brotherly kindness;
and [h]to brotherly kindness charity.
8 For if these things be in you, and
abound, they make *you that ye shall* neither
be barren [i]nor unfruitful in the knowledge
of our Lord Jesus Christ.
9 But he that lacketh these things [j]is
blind, and cannot see afar off, and hath for-

1:1 [a]Rom. 1:12; Eph. 4:5; Tit. 1:4 **1:2** [b]Dan. 4:1; Jude 2 **1:3** [c]John 17:3 [d]1 Thess. 2:12; 2 Tim. 1:9; 1 Pet. 2:9 **1:4** [e]2 Cor. 7:1 [f]2 Cor. 3:18; Heb. 12:10; 1 John 3:2 **1:5** [g]1 Pet. 3:7 **1:7** [h]Gal. 6:10; 1 John 4:21 **1:8** [i]John 15:2 **1:9** [j]1 John 2:9

gotten that he was [k]purged from his old sins.

10 Wherefore the rather, brethren, give diligence [l]to make your calling and election sure: for if ye do these things, ye shall never fall:

11 For so an entrance shall be ministered unto you abundantly into the everlasting kingdom of our Lord and Saviour Jesus Christ.

12 Wherefore [m]I will not be negligent to put you always in remembrance of these things, [n]though ye know *them,* and be established in the present truth.

13 Yea, I think it meet, as [o]long as I am in this tabernacle, to stir you up by putting *you* in remembrance;

14 [p]Knowing that shortly I must put off *this* my tabernacle, even as [q]our Lord Jesus Christ hath shewed me.

15 Moreover I will endeavour that ye may be able after my decease to have these things always in remembrance.

16 For we have not followed [r]cunningly devised fables, when we made known unto you the power and coming of our Lord Jesus Christ, but [s]were eyewitnesses of his majesty.

17 For he received from God the Father honour and glory, when there came such a voice to him from the excellent glory, [t]This is my beloved Son, in whom I am well pleased.

18 And this voice which came from heaven we heard, when we were with him in [u]the holy mount.

19 We have also a more sure word of prophecy; whereunto ye do well that ye take heed, as unto [v]a light that shineth in a dark place, until the day dawn, and [w]the day star arise in your hearts:

20 Knowing this first, that [x]no prophecy of the scripture is of any private interpretation.

21 For [y]the prophecy came not in old time by the will of man: [z]but holy men of God spake *as they were* moved by the Holy Ghost.

2 But [a]there were false prophets also among the people, even as [b]there shall be false teachers among you, who privily shall bring in damnable heresies, even [c]denying the Lord [d]that bought them, [e]and bring upon themselves swift destruction.

2 And many shall follow their pernicious ways; by reason of whom the way of truth shall be evil spoken of.

3 And [f]through covetousness shall they with feigned words [g]make merchandise of you: [h]whose judgment now of a long time lingereth not, and their damnation slumbereth not.

4 For if God spared not [i]the angels [j]that sinned, but [k]cast *them* down to hell, and delivered *them* into chains of darkness, to be reserved unto judgment;

5 And spared not the old world, but saved [l]Noah the eighth *person,* [m]a preacher of righteousness, bringing in the flood upon the world of the ungodly;

6 And [n]turning the cities of Sodom and Gomorrha into ashes condemned *them* with an overthrow, [o]making *them* an ensample unto those that after should live ungodly;

7 And [p]delivered just Lot, vexed with the filthy conversation of the wicked:

8 (For that righteous man dwelling among them, [q]in seeing and hearing, vexed *his* righteous soul from day to day with *their* unlawful deeds;)

9 [r]The Lord knoweth how to deliver the godly out of temptations, and to reserve the unjust unto the day of judgment to be punished:

10 But chiefly [s]them that walk after the flesh in the lust of uncleanness, and despise government. [t]Presumptuous *are they,* selfwilled, they are not afraid to speak evil of dignities.

11 Whereas [u]angels, which are greater in power and might, bring not railing accusation against them before the Lord.

12 But these, [v]as natural brute beasts, made to be taken and destroyed, speak evil of the things that they understand not; and shall utterly perish in their own corruption;

13 [w]And shall receive the reward of unrighteousness, *as* they that count it pleasure [x]to riot in the day time. [y]Spots *they are* and blemishes, sporting themselves with their own deceivings while [z]they feast with you;

14 Having eyes full of adultery, and that cannot cease from sin; beguiling unstable souls: [a]an heart they have exercised with covetous practices; cursed children:

15 Which have forsaken the right way, and are gone astray, following the way of [b]Balaam *the son* of Bosor, who loved the wages of unrighteousness;

16 But was rebuked for his iniquity: the dumb ass speaking with man's voice forbad the madness of the prophet.

17 [c]These are wells without water, clouds that are carried with a tempest; to whom the mist of darkness is reserved for ever.

18 For when [d]they speak great swelling *words* of vanity, they allure through the lusts of the flesh, *through much* wantonness, those that [e]were clean escaped from them who live in error.

19 While they promise them [f]liberty, they themselves are [g]the servants of corruption: for of whom a man is overcome, of the same is he brought in bondage.

20 For [h]if after they have escaped the pollutions of the world through the knowledge of the Lord and Saviour Jesus Christ, they are again entangled therein, and overcome, the latter end is worse with them than the beginning.

21 For [i]it had been better for them not to have known the way of righteousness, than, after they have known *it,* to turn from the holy commandment delivered unto them.

1:9 [k]Eph. 5:26; 1 John 1:7
1:10 [l]1 John 3:19
1:12 [m]Rom. 15:14; 1 John 2:21; Jude 5 [n]1 Pet. 5:12
1:13 [o]2 Cor. 5:1
1:14 [p]Deut. 4:21 [q]John 21:18
1:16 [r]1 Cor. 1:17 [s]Matt. 17:1; John 1:14; 1 John 1:1
1:17 [t]Matt. 3:17; Luke 3:22
1:18 [u]Ex. 3:5; Matt. 17:6
1:19 [v]Ps. 119:105 [w]2 Cor. 4:4
1:20 [x]Rom. 12:6
1:21 [y]2 Tim. 3:16 [z]2 Sam. 23:2; Acts 1:16
2:1 [a]Deut. 13:1 [b]Matt. 24:11; 1 Cor. 11:19; 1 Tim. 4:1; 1 John 4:1; Jude 18 [c]Jude 4 [d]1 Cor. 6:20; Eph. 1:7; Heb. 10:29; Rev. 5:9 [e]Phil. 3:19
2:3 [f]Rom. 16:18; 1 Tim. 6:5; Tit. 1:11 [g]2 Cor. 2:17 [h]Deut. 32:35
2:4 [i]Job 4:18 [j]John 8:44 [k]Luke 8:31
2:5 [l]Gen. 7:1; 1 Pet. 3:20 [m]1 Pet. 3:19
2:6 [n]Gen. 19:24; Jude 7 [o]Num. 26:10
2:7 [p]Gen. 19:16
2:8 [q]Ps. 119:139
2:9 [r]Ps. 34:17
2:10 [s]Jude 4 [t]Jude 8
2:11 [u]Jude 9
2:12 [v]Jer. 12:3
2:13 [w]Phil. 3:19 [x]Rom. 13:13 [y]Jude 12 [z]1 Cor. 11:20
2:14 [a]Jude 11
2:15 [b]Num. 22:5
2:17 [c]Jude 12
2:18 [d]Jude 16 [e]Acts 2:40
2:19 [f]Gal. 5:13 [g]John 8:34
2:20 [h]Matt. 12:45; Heb. 6:4
2:21 [i]Luke 12:47

22 But it is happened unto them according to the true proverb, [j]The dog *is* turned to his own vomit again; and the sow that was washed to her wallowing in the mire.

3 This second epistle, beloved, I now write unto you; in *both* which I stir up your pure minds by way of remembrance:

2 That ye may be mindful of the words which were spoken before by the holy prophets, [k]and of the commandment of us the apostles of the Lord and Saviour:

3 [l]Knowing this first, that there shall come in the last days scoffers, walking after their own lusts,

4 And saying, [m]Where is the promise of his coming? for since the fathers fell asleep, all things continue as *they were* from the beginning of the creation.

5 For this they willingly are ignorant of, that [n]by the word of God the heavens were of old, and the earth [o]standing out of the water and in the water:

6 [p]Whereby the world that then was, being overflowed with water, perished:

7 But the heavens and the earth, which are now, by the same word are kept in store, reserved unto [q]fire against the day of judgment and perdition of ungodly men.

8 But, beloved, be not ignorant of this one thing, that one day *is* with the Lord as a thousand years, and [r]a thousand years as one day.

9 [s]The Lord is not slack concerning his promise, as some men count slackness; but [t]is longsuffering to us-ward, [u]not willing that any should perish, but [v]that all should come to repentance.

10 But [w]the day of the Lord will come as a thief in the night; in the which [x]the heavens shall pass away with a great noise, and the elements shall melt with fervent heat, the earth also and the works that are therein shall be burned up.

11 *Seeing* then *that* all these things shall be dissolved, what manner *of persons* ought ye to be [y]in *all* holy conversation and godliness,

12 [z]Looking for and hasting unto the coming of the day of God, wherein the heavens being on fire shall [a]be dissolved, and the elements shall [b]melt with fervent heat?

13 Nevertheless we, according to his promise, look for [c]new heavens and a new earth, wherein dwelleth righteousness.

14 Wherefore, beloved, seeing that ye look for such things, be diligent [d]that ye may be found of him in peace, without spot, and blameless.

15 And account *that* [e]the longsuffering of our Lord *is* salvation; even as our beloved brother Paul also according to the wisdom given unto him hath written unto you;

16 As also in all *his* epistles, [f]speaking in them of these things; in which are some things hard to be understood, which they that are unlearned and unstable wrest, as *they do* also the other scriptures, unto their own destruction.

17 Ye therefore, beloved, [g]seeing ye know *these things* before, [h]beware lest ye also, being led away with the error of the wicked, fall from your own stedfastness.

18 [i]But grow in grace, and *in* the knowledge of our Lord and Saviour Jesus Christ. [j]To him *be* glory both now and for ever. Amen.

2:22 [j]Prov. 26:11
3:2 [k]Jude 17
3:3 [l]1 Tim. 4:1; Jude 18
3:4 [m]Isa. 5:19; Ezek. 12:22; Matt. 24:48
3:5 [n]Gen. 1:6; Heb. 11:3 [o]Ps. 24:2
3:6 [p]Gen. 7:11
3:7 [q]Matt. 25:41
3:8 [r]Ps. 90:4
3:9 [s]Hab. 2:3 [t]Isa. 30:18 [u]Ezek. 18:23 [v]Rom. 2:4
3:10 [w]Matt. 24:43; 1 Thess. 5:2; Rev. 3:3 [x]Ps. 102:26; Matt. 24:35; Mark 13:31; Heb. 1:11; Rev. 20:11
3:11 [y]1 Pet. 1:15
3:12 [z]1 Cor. 1:7 [a]Ps. 50:3 [b]Mic. 1:4
3:13 [c]Isa. 65:17
3:14 [d]1 Cor. 1:8; 1 Thess. 3:13
3:15 [e]Rom. 2:4
3:16 [f]Rom. 8:19; 1 Thess. 4:15
3:17 [g]Mark 13:23 [h]Eph. 4:14
3:18 [i]Eph. 4:15 [j]2 Tim. 4:18

1 JOHN

First John was written by John, an apostle of Jesus, between A.D. 85 and A.D. 90. Beginning with the very basic premise of sin, John moves quickly to the truth of salvation through Jesus Christ. Confession, obedience, and love for fellow believers are touted as the necessary ingredients in a Christian's life. Chapter 4 opens with a method of determining false teaching, and continues with a description of love, the power of love, and the results of love. John closes with the assurance of eternal life, instructions concerning prayer, and the believer's relationship to sin.

I. Christ, sin, and the believer, 1:1–2:2
II. The believer's life in Christ, 2:3–2:29
III. The expressions of love, 3:1–3:24
IV. Discerning false teachers and doctrines, 4:1–4:6
V. Further expressions of love, 4:7–5:3
VI. Overcoming the world, 5:4–5:5
VII. The certainty of Christ, 5:6–5:12
VIII. Eternal life, 5:13
IX. Closing remarks, 5:14–5:21

1 That [a]which was from the beginning,
which we have heard, which we have
seen with our eyes, [b]which we have looked
upon, and [c]our hands have handled, of the
Word of life;
2 (For [d]the life [e]was manifested, and we
have seen *it*, [f]and bear witness, and shew
unto you that eternal life, [g]which was with
the Father, and was manifested unto us;)
3 [h]That which we have seen and heard
declare we unto you, that ye also may have
fellowship with us: and truly [i]our fellowship *is* with the Father, and with his Son
Jesus Christ.
4 And these things write we unto you,
[j]that your joy may be full.
5 This then is the message which we have
heard of him, and declare unto you, that
[k]God is light, and in him is no darkness at
all.
6 [l]If we say that we have fellowship with
him, and walk in darkness, we lie, and do
not the truth:
7 But if we walk in the light, as he is in the
light, we have fellowship one with another,
and [m]the blood of Jesus Christ his Son
cleanseth us from all sin.
8 [n]If we say that we have no sin, we deceive ourselves, and the truth is not in us.
9 [o]If we confess our sins, he is faithful
and just to forgive us *our* sins, and to
[p]cleanse us from all unrighteousness.
10 If we say that we have not sinned, we
make him a liar, and his word is not in us.
2 My little children, these things write I
unto you, that ye sin not. And if any
man sin, [q]we have an advocate with the
Father, Jesus Christ the righteous:
2 And [r]he is the propitiation for our sins:
and not for ours only, but [s]also for *the sins
of* the whole world.
3 And hereby we do know that we know
him, if we keep his commandments.
4 He that saith, I know him, and keepeth
not his commandments, is a liar, and the
truth is not in him.
5 But [t]whoso keepeth his word, in him
verily is the love of God perfected: hereby
know we that we are in him.
6 [u]He that saith he abideth in him [v]ought
himself also so to walk, even as he walked.
7 Brethren, [w]I write no new commandment unto you, but an old commandment
[x]which ye had from the beginning. The old
commandment is the word which ye have
heard from the beginning.
8 Again, [y]a new commandment I write
unto you, which thing is true in him and in
you: [z]because the darkness is past, and
[a]the true light now shineth.
9 [b]He that saith he is in the light, and
hateth his brother, is in darkness even until
now.
10 He that loveth his brother abideth in
the light, and [c]there is none occasion of
stumbling in him.
11 But he that hateth his brother is in
darkness, and [d]walketh in darkness, and
knoweth not whither he goeth, because that
darkness hath blinded his eyes.
12 I write unto you, little children, because [e]your sins are forgiven you for his
name's sake.
13 I write unto you, fathers, because ye
have known him *that is* from the beginning.
I write unto you, young men, because ye
have overcome the wicked one. I write unto
you, little children, because ye have known
the Father.
14 I have written unto you, fathers, because ye have known him *that is* from the
beginning. I have written unto you, young
men, because [f]ye are strong, and the word

1:1 [a]John 1:1 [b]John 1:14 [c]Luke 24:39
1:2 [d]John 1:4 [e]Rom. 16:26 [f]John 21:24 [g]John 1:1
1:3 [h]Acts 4:20 [i]John 17:21
1:4 [j]John 15:11
1:5 [k]John 1:9
1:6 [l]2 Cor. 6:14
1:7 [m]1 Cor. 6:11; Heb. 9:14; 1 Pet. 1:19
1:8 [n]1 Kings 8:46; Job 9:2; Prov. 20:9; Jam. 3:2
1:9 [o]Ps. 32:5 [p]Ps. 51:2
2:1 [q]Rom. 8:34; Heb. 7:25
2:2 [r]Rom. 3:25 [s]John 1:29
2:5 [t]John 14:21
2:6 [u]John 15:4 [v]Matt. 11:29; 1 Pet. 2:21
2:7 [w]2 John 5 [x]2 John 5
2:8 [y]John 13:34 [z]Rom. 13:21; 1 Thess. 5:5 [a]John 1:9
2:9 [b]1 Cor. 13:2
2:10 [c]2 Pet. 1:10
2:11 [d]John 12:35
2:12 [e]Luke 24:47
2:14 [f]Eph. 6:10

of God abideth in you, and ye have overcome the wicked one.

15 [g]Love not the world, neither the things *that are* in the world. [h]If any man love the world, the love of the Father is not in him.

16 For all that *is* in the world, the lust of the flesh, [i]and the lust of the eyes, and the pride of life, is not of the Father, but is of the world.

17 And [j]the world passeth away, and the lust thereof: but he that doeth the will of God abideth for ever.

18 [k]Little children, [l]it is the last time: and as ye have heard that [m]antichrist shall come, [n]even now are there many antichrists; whereby we know [o]that it is the last time.

19 [p]They went out from us, but they were not of us; for [q]if they had been of us, they would *no doubt* have continued with us: but *they went out,* [r]that they might be made manifest that they were not all of us.

20 But [s]ye have an unction [t]from the Holy One, and [u]ye know all things.

21 I have not written unto you because ye know not the truth, but because ye know it, and that no lie is of the truth.

22 [v]Who is a liar but he that denieth that Jesus is the Christ? He is antichrist, that denieth the Father and the Son.

23 [w]Whosoever denieth the Son, the same hath not the Father: *[but]* [x]*he that acknowledgeth the Son hath the Father also.*

24 Let that therefore abide in you, [y]which ye have heard from the beginning. If that which ye have heard from the beginning shall remain in you, [z]ye also shall continue in the Son, and in the Father.

25 [a]And this is the promise that he hath promised us, *even* eternal life.

26 These *things* have I written unto you [b]concerning them that seduce you.

27 But the anointing which ye have received of him abideth in you, and [c]ye need not that any man teach you: but as the same anointing [d]teacheth you of all things, and is truth, and is no lie, and even as it hath taught you, ye shall abide in him.

28 And now, little children, abide in him; that, when he shall appear, we may have confidence, and not be ashamed before him at his coming.

29 [e]If ye know that he is righteous, ye know that every one that doeth righteousness is born of him.

3 Behold, what manner of love the Father hath bestowed upon us, that [f]we should be called the sons of God: therefore the world knoweth us not, [g]because it knew him not.

2 Beloved, [h]now are we the sons of God, and [i]it doth not yet appear what we shall be: but we know that, when he shall appear, [j]we shall be like him; for [k]we shall see him as he is.

3 And every man that hath this hope in him purifieth himself, even as he is pure.

4 Whosoever committeth sin transgresseth also the law: for [l]sin is the transgression of the law.

5 And ye know that he was manifested [m]to take away our sins; and [n]in him is no sin.

6 Whosoever abideth in him sinneth not: [o]whosoever sinneth hath not seen him, neither known him.

7 Little children, let no man deceive you: [p]he that doeth righteousness is righteous, even as he is righteous.

8 [q]He that committeth sin is of the devil; for the devil sinneth from the beginning. For this purpose the Son of God was manifested, [r]that he might destroy the works of the devil.

9 Whosoever is born of God doth not commit sin; for [s]his seed remaineth in him: and he cannot sin, because he is born of God.

10 In this the children of God are manifest, and the children of the devil: whosoever doeth not righteousness is not of God, neither he that loveth not his brother.

11 For this is the message that ye heard from the beginning, [t]that we should love one another.

12 Not as [u]Cain, *who* was of that wicked one, and slew his brother. And wherefore slew he him? Because his own works were evil, and his brother's righteous.

13 Marvel not, my brethren, if [v]the world hate you.

14 We know that we have passed from death unto life, because we love the brethren. He that loveth not *his* brother abideth in death.

15 [w]Whosoever hateth his brother is a murderer: and ye know that [x]no murderer hath eternal life abiding in him.

16 [y]Hereby perceive we the love *of God,* because he laid down his life for us: and we ought to lay down *our* lives for the brethren.

17 [z]But whoso hath this world's good, and seeth his brother have need, and shutteth up his bowels *of compassion* from him, how dwelleth the love of God in him?

18 My little children, [a]let us not love in word, neither in tongue; but in deed and in truth.

19 And hereby we know [b]that we are of the truth, and shall assure our hearts before him.

20 [c]For if our heart condemn us, God is greater than our heart, and knoweth all things.

21 [d]Beloved, if our heart condemn us not, [e]*then* have we confidence toward God.

22 And [f]whatsoever we ask, we receive of him, because we keep his commandments, [g]and do those things that are pleasing in his sight.

23 [h]And this is his commandment, That we should believe on the name of his Son

2:15 [g]Rom. 12:2 [h]Matt. 6:24; Jam. 4:4
2:16 [i]Eccl. 5:11
2:17 [j]1 Cor. 7:31; 1 Pet. 1:24
2:18 [k]John 21:5 [l]Heb. 1:2 [m]2 Thess. 2:3 [n]Matt. 24:5 [o]1 Tim. 4:1
2:19 [p]Deut. 13:13; Acts 20:30 [q]Matt. 24:24; 2 Tim. 2:19 [r]1 Cor. 11:19
2:20 [s]2 Cor. 1:21 [t]Mark 1:24 [u]John 10:4
2:22 [v]2 John 7
2:23 [w]John 15:23 [x]John 14:7
2:24 [y]2 John 6 [z]John 14:23
2:25 [a]John 17:3
2:26 [b]2 John 7
2:27 [c]Jer. 31:33 [d]John 14:26
2:29 [e]Acts 22:14
3:1 [f]John 1:12 [g]John 15:18
3:2 [h]Isa. 56:5; Gal. 3:26 [i]Rom. 8:18 [j]Rom. 8:29; Phil. 3:21; Col. 3:4 [k]Job 19:26; Matt. 5:8; 1 Cor. 13:12
3:4 [l]Rom. 4:15
3:5 [m]Isa. 53:5; Heb. 1:3; 1 Pet. 2:24 [n]2 Cor. 5:21; 1 Pet. 2:22
3:6 [o]3 John 11
3:7 [p]Ezek. 18:5-9
3:8 [q]Matt. 13:38 [r]Gen. 3:15; John 16:11; Heb. 2:14
3:9 [s]1 Pet. 1:23
3:11 [t]John 13:34
3:12 [u]Gen. 4:4; Jude 11
3:13 [v]John 15:18
3:15 [w]Matt. 5:21 [x]Gal. 5:21
3:16 [y]John 3:16; Eph. 5:2
3:17 [z]Deut. 15:7
3:18 [a]Ezek. 33:31; Eph. 4:15; Jam. 2:15
3:19 [b]John 18:37
3:20 [c]1 Cor. 4:4
3:21 [d]Job 22:26 [e]Heb. 10:22
3:22 [f]Ps. 34:15; Jer. 29:12; Matt. 7:8; John 14:13; Jam. 5:16 [g]John 8:29
3:23 [h]John 6:29

Jesus Christ, [i]and love one another, as he
gave us commandment.
24 And [j]he that keepeth his commandments [k]dwelleth in him, and he in him. And
[l]hereby we know that he abideth in us, by
the Spirit which he hath given us.

4 Beloved, [m]believe not every spirit, but
[n]try the spirits whether they are of God:
because [o]many false prophets are gone out
into the world.
2 Hereby know ye the Spirit of God: [p]Ev-
ery spirit that confesseth that Jesus Christ is
come in the flesh is of God:
3 And [q]every spirit that confesseth not
that Jesus Christ is come in the flesh is not
of God: and this is that *spirit* of antichrist,
whereof ye have heard that it should come;
and [r]even now already is it in the world.
4 Ye are of God, little children, and have
overcome them: because greater is he that
is in you, than [s]he that is in the world.
5 [t]They are of the world: therefore speak
they of the world, and [u]the world heareth
them.
6 We are of God: [v]he that knoweth God
heareth us; he that is not of God heareth not
us. Hereby know we [w]the spirit of truth, and
the spirit of error.
7 Beloved, let us love one another: for
love is of God; and every one that loveth is
born of God, and knoweth God.
8 He that loveth not knoweth not God; for
God is love.
9 [x]In this was manifested the love of God
toward us, because that God sent his only
begotten Son into the world, that we might
live through him.
10 Herein is love, [y]not that we loved God,
but that he loved us, and sent his Son *to be*
the propitiation for our sins.
11 Beloved, [z]if God so loved us, we ought
also to love one another.
12 [a]No man hath seen God at any time. If
we love one another, God dwelleth in us,
and his love is perfected in us.
13 [b]Hereby know we that we dwell in
him, and he in us, because he hath given us
of his Spirit.
14 And [c]we have seen and do testify that
[d]the Father sent the Son *to be* the Saviour
of the world.
15 [e]Whosoever shall confess that Jesus
is the Son of God, God dwelleth in him, and
he in God.
16 And we have known and believed the
love that God hath to us. God is love; and he
that dwelleth in love dwelleth in God, and
God in him.
17 Herein is our love made perfect, that
[f]we may have boldness in the day of judgment: because as he is, so are we in this
world.
18 There is no fear in love; but perfect
love casteth out fear: because fear hath torment. He that feareth is not made perfect in
love.
19 We love him, because he first loved us.
20 If a man say, I love God, and hateth his
brother, he is a liar: for he that loveth not his
brother whom he hath seen, how can he
love God whom he hath not seen?
21 And [g]this commandment have we
from him, That he who loveth God love his
brother also.

5 Whosoever [h]believeth that Jesus is the
Christ is [i]born of God: [j]and every one
that loveth him that begat loveth him also
that is begotten of him.
2 By this we know that we love the children of God, when we love God, and keep
his commandments.
3 [k]For this is the love of God, that we
keep his commandments: and [l]his commandments are not grievous.
4 For [m]whatsoever is born of God overcometh the world: and this is the victory
that overcometh the world, *even* our faith.
5 Who is he that overcometh the world,
but [n]he that believeth that Jesus is the Son
of God?
6 This is he that came [o]by water and
blood, *even* Jesus Christ; not by water only,
but by water and blood. [p]And it is the Spirit
that beareth witness, because the Spirit is
truth.
7 For there are three that bear record in
heaven, the Father, [q]the Word, and the
Holy Ghost: [r]and these three are one.
8 And there are three that bear witness
in earth, the Spirit, and the water, and the
blood: and these three agree in one.
9 If we receive [s]the witness of men, the
witness of God is greater: [t]for this is the
witness of God which he hath testified of his
Son.
10 He that believeth on the Son of God
[u]hath the witness in himself: he that believeth not God [v]hath made him a liar; because
he believeth not the record that God gave of
his Son.
11 And this is the record, that God hath
given to us eternal life, and [w]this life is in
his Son.
12 [x]He that hath the Son hath life; *and* he
that hath not the Son of God hath not life.
13 [y]These things have I written unto you
that believe on the name of the Son of God;
that ye may know that ye have eternal life,
and that ye may believe on the name of the
Son of God.
14 And this is the confidence that we have
in him, that, if we ask any thing according
to his will, he heareth us:
15 And if we know that he hear us, whatsoever we ask, we know that we have the
petitions that we desired of him.
16 If any man see his brother sin a sin
which is not unto death, he shall ask, and
[z]he shall give him life for them that sin not
unto death. [a]There is a sin unto death: [b]I do
not say that he shall pray for it.
17 All unrighteousness is sin: and there is
a sin not unto death.
18 We know that [c]whosoever is born of
God sinneth not; but he that is begotten of

3:23 [i]Matt. 22:39; Eph. 5:2; 1 Thess. 4:9
3:24 [j]John 14:23 [k]John 17:21 [l]Rom. 8:9
4:1 [m]Jer. 29:8 [n]1 Cor. 14:29; Rev. 2:2 [o]Matt. 24:5; 1 Tim. 4:1; 2 Pet. 2:1
4:2 [p]1 Cor. 12:3
4:3 [q]2 John 7 [r]2 Thess. 2:7
4:4 [s]John 12:31; Eph. 2:2
4:5 [t]John 3:31 [u]John 15:19
4:6 [v]John 8:47; 2 Cor. 10:7 [w]Isa. 8:20
4:9 [x]John 3:16
4:10 [y]John 15:16; Tit. 3:4
4:11 [z]Matt. 18:33
4:12 [a]John 1:18
4:13 [b]John 14:20
4:14 [c]John 1:14 [d]John 3:17
4:15 [e]Rom. 10:9
4:17 [f]Jam. 2:13
4:21 [g]Matt. 22:37
5:1 [h]John 1:12 [i]John 1:13 [j]John 15:23
5:3 [k]John 14:15 [l]Mic. 6:8
5:4 [m]John 16:33
5:5 [n]1 Cor. 15:57
5:6 [o]John 19:34 [p]John 14:17
5:7 [q]John 1:1 [r]John 10:30
5:9 [s]John 8:17 [t]Matt. 3:16
5:10 [u]Rom. 8:16 [v]John 3:33
5:11 [w]John 1:4
5:12 [x]John 3:36
5:13 [y]John 20:31
5:16 [z]Job 42:8 [a]Matt. 12:31; Luke 12:10; Heb. 6:4 [b]Jer. 7:16
5:18 [c]1 Pet. 1:23

God [d]keepeth himself, and that wicked one toucheth him not.

19 *And* we know that we are of God, and [e]the whole world lieth in wickedness.

20 And we know that the Son of God is come, and [f]hath given us an understanding, [g]that we may know him that is true, and we are in him that is true, *even* in his Son Jesus Christ. [h]This is the true God, and eternal life.

21 Little children, [i]keep yourselves from idols. Amen.

5:18 [d]Jam. 1:27
5:19 [e]Gal. 1:4
5:20 [f]Luke 24:45 [g]John 17:3 [h]Isa. 9:6; Rom. 9:5; Tit. 2:13; Heb. 1:8
5:21 [i]1 Cor. 10:14

2 JOHN

Second John was written by John, an apostle of Jesus, between A.D. 85 and A.D. 90. 2 John begins with an admonition to love one another and obey the commandments of Christ. This is followed by a warning against false teachers and doctrines.

I. Greetings, 1–3
II. Observing the commandments of Christ, 4–6
III. Watch for false teachers and doctrines, 7–11
IV. Closing greeting, 12–13

1 The elder unto the elect lady and her children, [a]whom I love in the truth; and not I only, but also all they that have known [b]the truth;

2 For the truth's sake, which dwelleth in us, and shall be with us for ever.

3 [c]Grace be with you, mercy, *and* peace, from God the Father, and from the Lord Jesus Christ, the Son of the Father, in truth and love.

4 I rejoiced greatly that I found of thy children [d]walking in truth, as we have received a commandment from the Father.

5 And now I beseech thee, lady, [e]not as though I wrote a new commandment unto thee, but that which we had from the beginning, [f]that we love one another.

6 And [g]this is love, that we walk after his commandments. This is the commandment, That, [h]as ye have heard from the beginning, ye should walk in it.

7 For [i]many deceivers are entered into the world, [j]who confess not that Jesus Christ is come in the flesh. [k]This is a deceiver and an antichrist.

8 [l]Look to yourselves, [m]that we lose not those things which we have wrought, but that we receive a full reward.

9 [n]Whosoever transgresseth, and abideth not in the doctrine of Christ, hath not God. He that abideth in the doctrine of Christ, he hath both the Father and the Son.

10 If there come any unto you, and bring not this doctrine, receive him not into *your* house, [o]neither bid him God speed:

11 For he that biddeth him God speed is partaker of his evil deeds.

12 [p]Having many things to write unto you, I would not *write* with paper and ink: but I trust to come unto you, and speak face to face, [q]that our joy may be full.

13 [r]The children of thy elect sister greet thee. Amen.

1:1 [a]1 John 3:18 [b]John 8:32; Col. 1:5; 2 Thess. 2:13; Heb. 10:26
1:3 [c]1 Tim. 1:2
1:4 [d]3 John 3
1:5 [e]1 John 2:7 [f]John 13:34; 1 Pet. 4:8; 1 John 3:23
1:6 [g]John 14:15 [h]1 John 2:24
1:7 [i]1 John 4:1 [j]1 John 4:2 [k]1 John 2:22
1:8 [l]Mark 13:9 [m]Gal. 3:4
1:9 [n]1 John 2:23
1:10 [o]Rom. 16:17; Gal. 1:8; 2 Tim. 3:5
1:12 [p]3 John 13 [q]John 17:13
1:13 [r]1 Pet. 5:13

3 JOHN

Third John was written by John, an apostle of Jesus, between A.D. 85 and A.D. 90. This letter commends Gaius for his treatment of the teachers John has sent to the churches and condemns Diotrephes, who has asserted his authority in the church by rejecting these same teachers.

I. Greeting to Gaius, 1
II. Commendations to Gaius, 2–8
III. Reproof of Diotrephes, 9–11
IV. Introduction of Demetrius, 12
V. Closing greetings, 13–14

---

1 The elder unto the wellbeloved Gaius, [a]whom I love in the truth.

2 Beloved, I wish above all things that thou mayest prosper and be in health, even as thy soul prospereth.

3 For I rejoiced greatly, when the brethren came and testified of the truth that is in thee, even as [b]thou walkest in the truth.

4 I have no greater joy than to hear that [c]my children walk in truth.

5 Beloved, thou doest faithfully whatsoever thou doest to the brethren, and to strangers;

6 Which have born witness of thy charity before the church: whom if thou bring forward on their journey after a godly sort, thou shalt do well:

7 Because that for his name's sake they went forth, [d]taking nothing of the Gentiles.

8 We therefore ought to receive such, that we might be fellowhelpers to the truth.

9 I wrote unto the church: but Diotrephes, who loveth to have the preeminence among them, receiveth us not.

10 Wherefore, if I come, I will remember his deeds which he doeth, prating against us with malicious words: and not content therewith, neither doth he himself receive the brethren, and forbiddeth them that would, and casteth *them* out of the church.

11 Beloved, [e]follow not that which is evil, but that which is good. [f]He that doeth good is of God: but he that doeth evil hath not seen God.

12 Demetrius [g]hath good report of all *men*, and of the truth itself: yea, and we *also* bear record; [h]and ye know that our record is true.

13 [i]I had many things to write, but I will not with ink and pen write unto thee:

14 But I trust I shall shortly see thee, and we shall speak face to face. Peace *be* to thee. *Our* friends salute thee. Greet the friends by name.

1:1 *a*2 John 1
1:3 *b*2 John 4
1:4 *c*1 Cor. 4:15
1:7 *d*1 Cor. 9:12
1:11 *e*Ps. 37:27; 1 Pet. 3:11 *f*1 John 2:29
1:12 *g*1 Tim. 3:7 *h*John 21:24
1:13 *i*2 John 12

JUDE

Jude the brother of James wrote this book in the latter half of the first century. Following a greeting, Jude describes the sin and eventual end of godless people or those teaching false doctrines. He closes with the exhortation to persevere and seek the truth of God.

I. Greetings, 1–2
II. Purpose of the letter, 3–4
III. False teachers and doctrines, 5–16
IV. Exhortations for perseverance, 17–23
V. Closing greetings, 24–25

---

1 Jude, the servant of Jesus Christ, and [a]brother of James, to them that are sanctified by God the Father, and [b]preserved in Jesus Christ, *and* [c]called:

2 Mercy unto you, and [d]peace, and love, be multiplied.

3 Beloved, when I gave all diligence to write unto you [e]of the common salvation, it was needful for me to write unto you, and exhort *you* that [f]ye should earnestly contend for the faith which was once delivered unto the saints.

4 [g]For there are certain men crept in unawares, [h]who were before of old ordained to this condemnation, ungodly men, [i]turning [j]the grace of our God into lasciviousness, and [k]denying the only Lord God, and our Lord Jesus Christ.

5 I will therefore put you in remembrance, though ye once knew this, how that [l]the Lord, having saved the people out of the land of Egypt, afterward [m]destroyed them that believed not.

6 And [n]the angels which kept not their first estate, but left their own habitation, [o]he hath reserved in everlasting chains under darkness [p]unto the judgment of the great day.

7 Even as [q]Sodom and Gomorrha, and the cities about them in like manner, giving themselves over to fornication, and going after strange flesh, are set forth for an example, suffering the vengeance of eternal fire.

8 [r]Likewise also these *filthy* dreamers defile the flesh, despise dominion, and [s]speak evil of dignities.

9 Yet [t]Michael the archangel, when contending with the devil he disputed about the body of Moses, [u]durst not bring against him a railing accusation, but said, [v]The Lord rebuke thee.

10 [w]But these speak evil of those things which they know not: but what they know naturally, as brute beasts, in those things they corrupt themselves.

11 Woe unto them! for they have gone in the way [x]of Cain, and [y]ran greedily after the error of Balaam for reward, and perished [z]in the gainsaying of Core.

12 [a]These are spots in your [b]feasts of charity, when they feast with you, feeding themselves without fear: [c]clouds *they are* without water, [d]carried about of winds; trees whose fruit withereth, without fruit, twice dead, [e]plucked up by the roots;

13 [f]Raging waves of the sea, [g]foaming out their own shame; wandering stars, [h]to whom is reserved the blackness of darkness for ever.

14 And Enoch also, [i]the seventh from Adam, prophesied of these, saying, Behold, [j]the Lord cometh with ten thousands of his saints,

15 To execute judgment upon all, and to convince all that are ungodly among them of all their ungodly deeds which they have ungodly committed, and of all their [k]hard *speeches* which ungodly sinners have spoken against him.

16 These are murmurers, complainers, walking after their own lusts; and [l]their mouth speaketh great swelling *words*, [m]having men's persons in admiration because of advantage.

17 [n]But, beloved, remember ye the words which were spoken before of the apostles of our Lord Jesus Christ;

18 How that they told you [o]there should be mockers in the last time, who should walk after their own ungodly lusts.

19 These be they [p]who separate themselves, [q]sensual, having not the Spirit.

20 But ye, beloved, [r]building up yourselves on your most holy faith, [s]praying in the Holy Ghost,

21 Keep yourselves in the love of God, [t]looking for the mercy of our Lord Jesus Christ unto eternal life.

22 And of some have compassion, making a difference:

23 And others [u]save with fear, [v]pulling *them* out of the fire; hating even [w]the garment spotted by the flesh.

24 [x]Now unto him that is able to keep you from falling, and [y]to present *you* faultless before the presence of his glory with exceeding joy,

25 [z]To the only wise God our Saviour, *be* glory and majesty, dominion and power, both now and ever. Amen.

1:1 [a]Luke 6:16 [b]John 17:11 [c]Rom. 1:7
1:2 [d]1 Pet. 1:2
1:3 [e]Tit. 1:4 [f]Phil. 1:27; 2 Tim. 1:13
1:4 [g]Gal. 2:4 [h]Rom. 9:21 [i]2 Pet. 2:10 [j]Tit. 2:11 [k]Tit. 1:16; 1 John 2:22
1:5 [l]1 Cor. 10:9 [m]Num. 14:29; Heb. 3:17
1:6 [n]John 8:44 [o]2 Pet. 2:4 [p]Rev. 20:10
1:7 [q]Gen. 19:24; 2 Pet. 2:6
1:8 [r]2 Pet. 2:10 [s]Ex. 22:28
1:9 [t]Dan. 10:13 [u]2 Pet. 2:11 [v]Zech. 3:2
1:10 [w]2 Pet. 2:12
1:11 [x]Gen. 4:5 [y]Num. 22:7 [z]Num. 16:1
1:12 [a]2 Pet. 2:13 [b]1 Cor. 11:21 [c]Prov. 25:14 [d]Eph. 4:14 [e]Matt. 15:13
1:13 [f]Isa. 57:20 [g]Phil. 3:19 [h]2 Pet. 2:17
1:14 [i]Gen. 5:18 [j]Deut. 33:2; Zech. 14:5; Matt. 25:31; Rev. 1:7
1:15 [k]1 Sam. 2:3; Mal. 3:13
1:16 [l]2 Pet. 2:18 [m]Prov. 28:21
1:17 [n]2 Pet. 3:2
1:18 [o]1 Tim. 4:1; 2 Pet. 2:1
1:19 [p]Prov. 18:1; Hos. 4:14; Heb. 10:25 [q]1 Cor. 2:14
1:20 [r]Col. 2:7 [s]Rom. 8:26
1:21 [t]Tit. 2:13
1:23 [u]Rom. 11:14 [v]Am. 4:11; Zech. 3:2 [w]Zech. 3:4
1:24 [x]Rom. 16:25 [y]Col. 1:22
1:25 [z]Rom. 16:27

REVELATION

The Revelation was written by John while he was in exile on Patmos—probably between A.D. 90 and A.D. 100. The first part of Revelation describes how the book came to be written, and gives information concerning the seven churches in Asia Minor and describes heaven (chapters 21 and 22).

The remainder of Revelation describes the period between Christ's ascension and his second coming as a time of judgment on the earth, culminating in the battle of Armageddon and the second coming of Christ. The last chapters of Revelation describe the future of the Millennium, the battle of Gog and Magog, the Great White Throne Judgment, the Lake of Fire, and the new heaven and the new earth.

I. The Revelation of Christ, 1:1–1:20
II. The messages to the seven churches, 2:1–3:22
III. John's view into heaven, 4:1–5:14
IV. The Tribulation, 6:1–19:21
V. The Millennium, 20:1–20:6
VI. Satan's last stand, 20:7–20:10
VII. Great White Throne Judgment, 20:11–20:15
VIII. The new heaven and the new earth, 21:1–22:21

1 The Revelation of Jesus Christ, [a]which God gave unto him, to shew unto his servants things which [b]must shortly come to pass; and [c]he sent and signified *it* by his angel unto his servant John:

2 [d]Who bare record of the word of God, and of the testimony of Jesus Christ, and of all things [e]that he saw.

3 [f]Blessed *is* he that readeth, and they that hear the words of this prophecy, and keep those things which are written therein: for [g]the time *is* at hand.

4 John to the seven churches which are in Asia: Grace *be* unto you, and peace, from him [h]which is, and [i]which was, and which is to come; [j]and from the seven Spirits which are before his throne;

5 And from Jesus Christ, [k]*who is* the faithful witness, *and* the [l]first begotten of the dead, and [m]the prince of the kings of the earth. Unto him [n]that loved us, [o]and washed us from our sins in his own blood,

6 And hath [p]made us kings and priests unto God and his Father; [q]to him *be* glory and dominion for ever and ever. Amen.

7 [r]Behold, he cometh with clouds; and every eye shall see him, and [s]they *also* which pierced him: and all kindreds of the earth shall wail because of him. Even so, Amen.

8 [t]I am Alpha and Omega, the beginning and the ending, saith the Lord, [u]which is, and which was, and which is to come, the Almighty.

9 I John, who also am your brother, and [v]companion in tribulation, and [w]in the kingdom and patience of Jesus Christ, was in the isle that is called Patmos, [x]for the word of God, and for the testimony of Jesus Christ.

10 [y]I was in the Spirit on [z]the Lord's day, and heard behind me [a]a great voice, as of a trumpet,

11 Saying, [b]I am Alpha and Omega, [c]the first and the last: and, What thou seest, write in a book, and send *it* unto the seven churches which are in Asia; unto Ephesus, and unto Smyrna, and unto Pergamos, and unto Thyatira, and unto Sardis, and unto Philadelphia, and unto Laodicea.

12 And I turned to see the voice that spake with me. And being turned, [d]I saw seven golden candlesticks;

13 [e]And in the midst of the seven candlesticks [f]*one* like unto the Son of man, [g]clothed with a garment down to the foot, and [h]girt about the paps with a golden girdle.

14 His head and [i]*his* hairs *were* white like wool, as white as snow; and [j]his eyes *were* as a flame of fire;

15 [k]And his feet like unto fine brass, as if they burned in a furnace; and [l]his voice as the sound of many waters.

16 [m]And he had in his right hand seven stars: and [n]out of his mouth went a sharp twoedged sword: [o]and his countenance *was* as the sun shineth in his strength.

17 And [p]when I saw him, I fell at his feet as dead. And [q]he laid his right hand upon me, saying unto me, Fear not; [r]I am the first and the last:

18 [s]*I am* he that liveth, and was dead; and, behold, [t]I am alive for evermore, Amen; and [u]have the keys of hell and of death.

1:1 [a]John 3:32 [b]ch. 4:1; ver. 3 [c]ch. 22:16 **1:2** [d]1 Cor. 1:6; ch. 6:9; ver. 9 [e]1 John 1:1 **1:3** [f]Luke 11:28; ch. 22:7 [g]Rom. 13:11; Jam. 5:8; 1 Pet. 4:7; ch. 22:10 **1:4** [h]Ex. 3:14; ver. 8 [i]John 1:1 [j]Zech. 3:9; ch. 3:1 **1:5** [k]John 8:14; 1 Tim. 6:13; ch. 3:14 [l]1 Cor. 15:20; Col. 1:18 [m]Eph. 1:20; ch. 17:14 [n]John 13:34; Gal. 2:20 [o]Heb. 9:14; 1 John 1:7 **1:6** [p]1 Pet. 2:5; ch. 5:10 [q]1 Tim. 6:16; Heb. 13:21; 1 Pet. 4:11 **1:7** [r]Dan. 7:13; Matt. 24:30; Acts 1:11 [s]Zech. 12:10; John 19:37 **1:8** [t]Isa. 41:4; ver. 17; ch. 2:8; ver. 11 [u]ver. 4; ch. 4:8 **1:9** [v]Phil. 1:7; 2 Tim. 1:8 [w]Rom. 8:17; 2 Tim. 2:12 [x]ch. 6:9; ver. 2 **1:10** [y]Acts 10:10; 2 Cor. 12:2; ch. 4:2 [z]John 20:26; Acts 20:7; 1 Cor. 16:2 [a]ch. 4:1 **1:11** [b]ver. 8 [c]ver. 17 **1:12** [d]ver. 20; Ex. 25:37; Zech. 4:2 **1:13** [e]ch. 2:1 [f]Ezek. 1:26; Dan. 7:13; ch. 14:14 [g]Dan. 10:5 [h]ch. 15:6 **1:14** [i]Dan. 7:9 [j]Dan. 10:6; ch. 2:18 **1:15** [k]Ezek. 1:7; Dan. 10:6; ch. 2:18 [l]Ezek. 43:2; Dan. 10:6; ch. 14:2 **1:16** [m]ver. 20; ch. 2:1 [n]Isa. 49:2; Eph. 6:17; Heb. 4:12; ch. 2:12 [o]Acts 26:13; ch. 10:1 **1:17** [p]Ezek. 1:28 [q]Dan. 8:18 [r]Isa. 41:4; ch. 2:8; ver. 11 **1:18** [s]Rom. 6:9 [t]ch. 4:9 [u]Ps. 68:20; ch. 20:1

19 Write [v]the things which thou hast seen, [w]and the things which are, [x]and the things which shall be hereafter;

20 The mystery [y]of the seven stars which thou sawest in my right hand, [z]and the seven golden candlesticks. The seven stars are [a]the angels of the seven churches: and [b]the seven candlesticks which thou sawest are the seven churches.

2 Unto the angel of the church of Ephesus write; These things saith [c]he that holdeth the seven stars in his right hand, [d]who walketh in the midst of the seven golden candlesticks;

2 [e]I know thy works, and thy labour, and thy patience, and how thou canst not bear them which are evil: and [f]thou hast tried them [g]which say they are apostles, and are not, and hast found them liars:

3 And hast borne, and hast patience, and for my name's sake hast laboured, and hast [h]not fainted.

4 Nevertheless I have *somewhat* against thee, because thou hast left thy first love.

5 Remember therefore from whence thou art fallen, and repent, and do the first works; [i]or else I will come unto thee quickly, and will remove thy candlestick out of his place, except thou repent.

6 But this thou hast, that thou hatest the deeds of [j]the Nicolaitans, which I also hate.

7 [k]He that hath an ear, let him hear what the Spirit saith unto the churches; To him that overcometh will I give [l]to eat of [m]the tree of life, which is in the midst of the paradise of God.

8 And unto the angel of the church in Smyrna write; These things saith [n]the first and the last, which was dead, and is alive;

9 [o]I know thy works, and tribulation, and poverty, (but thou art [p]rich) and *I know* the blasphemy of [q]them which say they are Jews, and are not, [r]but *are* the synagogue of Satan.

10 [s]Fear none of those things which thou shalt suffer: behold, the devil shall cast *some* of you into prison, that ye may be tried; and ye shall have tribulation ten days: [t]be thou faithful unto death, and I will give thee [u]a crown of life.

11 [v]He that hath an ear, let him hear what the Spirit saith unto the churches; He that overcometh shall not be hurt of [w]the second death.

12 And to the angel of the church in Pergamos write; These things saith [x]he which hath the sharp sword with two edges;

13 [y]I know thy works, and where thou dwellest, *even* [z]where Satan's seat *is:* and thou holdest fast my name, and hast not denied my faith, even in those days wherein Antipas *was* my faithful martyr, who was slain among you, where Satan dwelleth.

14 But I have a few things against thee, because thou hast there them that hold the doctrine of [a]Balaam, who taught Balac to cast a stumblingblock before the children of Israel, [b]to eat things sacrificed unto idols, [c]and to commit fornication.

15 So hast thou also them that hold the doctrine [d]of the Nicolaitans, which thing I hate.

16 Repent; or else I will come unto thee quickly, and [e]will fight against them with the sword of my mouth.

17 [f]He that hath an ear, let him hear what the Spirit saith unto the churches; To him that overcometh will I give to eat of the hidden manna, and will give him a white stone, and in the stone [g]a new name written, which no man knoweth saving he that receiveth *it*.

18 And unto the angel of the church in Thyatira write; These things saith the Son of God, [h]who hath his eyes like unto a flame of fire, and his feet *are* like fine brass;

19 [i]I know thy works, and charity, and service, and faith, and thy patience, and thy works; and the last *to be* more than the first.

20 Notwithstanding I have a few things against thee, because thou sufferest that woman [j]Jezebel, which calleth herself a prophetess, to teach and to seduce my servants [k]to commit fornication, and to eat things sacrificed unto idols.

21 And I gave her space [l]to repent of her fornication; and she repented not.

22 Behold, I will cast her into a bed, and them that commit adultery with her into great tribulation, except they repent of their deeds.

23 And I will kill her children with death; and all the churches shall know that [m]I am he which searcheth the reins and hearts: and [n]I will give unto every one of you according to your works.

24 But unto you I say, and unto the rest in Thyatira, as many as have not this doctrine, and which have not known the depths of Satan, as they speak; [o]I will put upon you none other burden.

25 But [p]that which ye have *already* hold fast till I come.

26 And he that overcometh, and keepeth [q]my works unto the end, [r]to him will I give power over the nations:

27 [s]And he shall rule them with a rod of iron; as the vessels of a potter shall they be broken to shivers: even as I received of my Father.

28 And I will give him [t]the morning star.

29 [u]He that hath an ear, let him hear what the Spirit saith unto the churches.

3 And unto the angel of the church in Sardis write; These things saith he [v]that hath the seven Spirits of God, and the seven stars; [w]I know thy works, that thou hast a name that thou livest, [x]and art dead.

2 Be watchful, and strengthen the things which remain, that are ready to die: for I have not found thy works perfect before God.

3 [y]Remember therefore how thou hast received and heard, and hold fast, and [z]re-

1:19 [v]ver. 12
[w]ch. 2:1 [x]ch. 4:1
1:20 [y]ver. 16
[z]ver. 12
[a]Mal. 2:7; ch. 2:1
[b]Zech. 4:2;
Matt. 5:15;
Phil. 2:15
2:1 [c]ch. 1:16
[d]ch. 1:13
2:2 [e]Ps. 1:6;
ver. 9; ch. 3:1
[f]1 John 4:1
[g]2 Cor. 11:13;
2 Pet. 2:1
2:3 [h]Gal. 6:9;
Heb. 12:3
2:5 [i]Matt. 21:41
2:6 [j]ver. 15
2:7 [k]Matt. 11:15;
ver. 11; ch. 3:6
[l]ch. 22:2
[m]Gen. 2:9
2:8 [n]ch. 1:8
2:9 [o]ver. 2
[p]Luke 12:21;
1 Tim. 6:18;
Jam. 2:5
[q]Rom. 2:17
[r]ch. 3:9
2:10 [s]Matt. 10:22
[t]Matt. 24:13
[u]Jam. 1:12;
ch. 3:11
2:11 [v]ver. 7;
ch. 13:9
[w]ch. 20:14
2:12 [x]ch. 1:16
2:13 [y]ver. 2
[z]ver. 9
2:14 [a]Num. 24:14;
2 Pet. 2:15;
Jude 11
[b]ver. 20;
Acts 15:29;
1 Cor. 8:9
[c]1 Cor. 6:13
2:15 [d]ver. 6
2:16 [e]Isa. 11:4;
2 Thess. 2:8;
ch. 1:16
2:17 [f]ver. 7
[g]ch. 3:12
2:18 [h]ch. 1:14
2:19 [i]ver. 2
2:20
[j]1 Kings 16:31;
2 Kings 9:7
[k]Ex. 34:15;
Acts 15:20;
1 Cor. 10:19;
ver. 14
2:21 [l]Rom. 2:4;
ch. 9:20
2:23
[m]1 Sam. 16:7;
1 Chron. 28:9;
2 Chron. 6:30;
Ps. 7:9; Jer. 11:20;
John 2:24;
Acts 1:24;
Rom. 8:27
[n]Ps. 62:12;
Matt. 16:27;
Rom. 2:6;
2 Cor. 5:10;
Gal. 6:5; ch. 20:12
2:24 [o]Acts 15:28
2:25 [p]ch. 3:11
2:26 [q]John 6:29;
1 John 3:23
[r]Matt. 19:28;
Luke 22:29;
1 Cor. 6:3; ch. 3:21
2:27 [s]Ps. 2:8;
Dan. 7:22; ch. 12:5
2:28 [t]2 Pet. 1:19;
ch. 22:16
2:29 [u]ver. 7
3:1 [v]ch. 1:4
[w]ch. 2:2
[x]Eph. 2:1;
1 Tim. 5:6
3:3 [y]1 Tim. 6:20;
2 Tim. 1:13; ver. 11
[z]ver. 19

pent. [a]If therefore thou shalt not watch, I will come on thee as a thief, and thou shalt not know what hour I will come upon thee.

4 Thou hast [b]a few names even in Sardis which have not [c]defiled their garments; and they shall walk with me [d]in white: for they are worthy.

5 He that overcometh, [e]the same shall be clothed in white raiment; and I will not [f]blot out his name out of the [g]book of life, but [h]I will confess his name before my Father, and before his angels.

6 [i]He that hath an ear, let him hear what the Spirit saith unto the churches.

7 And to the angel of the church in Philadelphia write; These things saith [j]he that is holy, [k]he that is true, he that hath [l]the key of David, [m]he that openeth, and no man shutteth; and [n]shutteth, and no man openeth;

8 [o]I know thy works: behold, I have set before thee [p]an open door, and no man can shut it: for thou hast a little strength, and hast kept my word, and hast not denied my name.

9 Behold, I will make [q]them of the synagogue of Satan, which say they are Jews, and are not, but do lie; behold, [r]I will make them to come and worship before thy feet, and to know that I have loved thee.

10 Because thou hast kept the word of my patience, [s]I also will keep thee from the hour of temptation, which shall come upon [t]all the world, to try them that dwell [u]upon the earth.

11 Behold, [v]I come quickly; [w]hold that fast which thou hast, that no man take [x]thy crown.

12 Him that overcometh will I make [y]a pillar in the temple of my God, and he shall go no more out: and [z]I will write upon him the name of my God, and the name of the city of my God, *which is* [a]new Jerusalem, which cometh down out of heaven from my God: [b]and *I will write upon him* my new name.

13 [c]He that hath an ear, let him hear what the Spirit saith unto the churches.

14 And unto the angel of the church of the Laodiceans write; [d]These things saith the Amen, [e]the faithful and true witness, [f]the beginning of the creation of God;

15 [g]I know thy works, that thou art neither cold nor hot: I would thou wert cold or hot.

16 So then because thou art lukewarm, and neither cold nor hot, I will spue thee out of my mouth.

17 Because thou sayest, [h]I am rich, and increased with goods, and have need of nothing; and knowest not that thou art wretched, and miserable, and poor, and blind, and naked:

18 I counsel thee [i]to buy of me gold tried in the fire, that thou mayest be rich; and [j]white raiment, that thou mayest be clothed, and *that* the shame of thy nakedness do not appear; and anoint thine eyes with eyesalve, that thou mayest see.

19 [k]As many as I love, I rebuke and chasten: be zealous therefore, and repent.

20 Behold, [l]I stand at the door, and knock: [m]if any man hear my voice, and open the door, [n]I will come in to him, and will sup with him, and he with me.

21 To him that overcometh [o]will I grant to sit with me in my throne, even as I also overcame, and am set down with my Father in his throne.

22 [p]He that hath an ear, let him hear what the Spirit saith unto the churches.

4 After this I looked, and, behold, a door *was* opened in heaven: and [q]the first voice which I heard *was* as it were of a trumpet talking with me; which said, [r]Come up hither, [s]and I will shew thee things which must be hereafter.

2 And immediately [t]I was in the spirit: and, behold, [u]a throne was set in heaven, and *one* sat on the throne.

3 And he that sat was to look upon like a jasper and a sardine stone: [v]and *there was* a rainbow round about the throne, in sight like unto an emerald.

4 [w]And round about the throne *were* four and twenty seats: and upon the seats I saw four and twenty elders sitting, [x]clothed in white raiment; [y]and they had on their heads crowns of gold.

5 And out of the throne proceeded [z]lightnings and thunderings and voices: [a]and *there were* seven lamps of fire burning before the throne, which are [b]the seven Spirits of God.

6 And before the throne *there was* [c]a sea of glass like unto crystal: [d]and in the midst of the throne, and round about the throne, *were* four beasts full of eyes before [e]and behind.

7 [f]And the first beast *was* like a lion, and the second beast like a calf, and the third beast had a face as a man, and the fourth beast *was* like a flying eagle.

8 And the four beasts had each of them [g]six wings about *him;* and *they were* full of eyes [h]within: and they rest not day and night, saying, [i]Holy, holy, holy, [j]Lord God Almighty, [k]which was, and is, and is to come.

9 And when those beasts give glory and honour and thanks to him that sat on the throne, [l]who liveth for ever and ever,

10 [m]The four and twenty elders fall down before him that sat on the throne, [n]and worship him that liveth for ever and ever, [o]and cast their crowns before the throne, saying,

11 [p]Thou art worthy, O Lord, to receive glory and honour and power: [q]for thou hast created all things, and for thy pleasure they are and were created.

5 And I saw in the right hand of him that sat on the throne a [r]book written

3:3 [a]Matt. 24:42; Matt. 25:13; Mark 13:33; Luke 12:39; 1 Thess. 5:2; 2 Pet. 3:10; ch. 16:15
3:4 [b]Acts 1:15 [c]Jude 23 [d]ch. 4:4
3:5 [e]ch. 19:8 [f]Ex. 32:32; Ps. 69:28 [g]Phil. 4:3; ch. 13:8 [h]Matt. 10:32; Luke 12:8
3:6 [i]ch. 2:7
3:7 [j]Acts 3:14 [k]1 John 5:20; ver. 14; ch. 1:5 [l]Isa. 22:22; Luke 1:32; ch. 1:18 [m]Matt. 16:19 [n]Job 12:14
3:8 [o]ver. 1 [p]1 Cor. 16:9; 2 Cor. 2:12
3:9 [q]ch. 2:9 [r]Isa. 49:23
3:10 [s]2 Pet. 2:9 [t]Luke 2:1 [u]Isa. 24:17
3:11 [v]Phil. 4:5; ch. 1:3 [w]ver. 3; ch. 2:25 [x]ch. 2:10
3:12 [y]1 Kings 7:21; Gal. 2:9 [z]ch. 2:17 [a]Gal. 4:26; Heb. 12:22; ch. 21:2 [b]ch. 22:4
3:13 [c]ch. 2:7
3:14 [d]Isa. 65:16 [e]ch. 1:5; ver. 7 [f]Col. 1:15
3:15 [g]ver. 1
3:17 [h]Hos. 12:8; 1 Cor. 4:8
3:18 [i]Isa. 55:1; Matt. 13:44 [j]2 Cor. 5:3; ch. 7:13
3:19 [k]Job 5:17; Prov. 3:11; Heb. 12:5; Jam. 1:12
3:20 [l]SSol. 5:2 [m]Luke 12:37 [n]John 14:23
3:21 [o]Matt. 19:28; Luke 22:30; 1 Cor. 6:2; 2 Tim. 2:12; ch. 2:26
3:22 [p]ch. 2:7
4:1 [q]ch. 1:10 [r]ch. 11:12 [s]ch. 1:19
4:2 [t]ch. 1:10 [u]Isa. 6:1; Jer. 17:12; Ezek. 1:26; Dan. 7:9
4:3 [v]Ezek. 1:28
4:4 [w]ch. 11:16 [x]ch. 3:4 [y]ver. 10
4:5 [z]ch. 8:5 [a]Ex. 37:23; 2 Chron. 4:20; Ezek. 1:13; Zech. 4:2 [b]ch. 1:4
4:6 [c]Ex. 38:8; ch. 15:2 [d]Ezek. 1:5 [e]ver. 8
4:7 [f]Num. 2:2; Ezek. 1:10
4:8 [g]Isa. 6:2 [h]ver. 6 [i]Isa. 6:3 [j]ch. 1:8 [k]ch. 1:4
4:9 [l]ch. 1:18
4:10 [m]ch. 5:8 [n]ver. 9 [o]ver. 4
4:11 [p]ch. 5:12 [q]Gen. 1:1; Acts 17:24; Eph. 3:9; Col. 1:16; ch. 10:6
5:1 [r]Ezek. 2:9

FOCUS ON REVELATION

There are different levels of learning and knowing. All education and knowledge is not internalized the same way. There is a superficial level, where we just hear information. There is the factual level, where we expand on what we already know by adding facts to it. We learn to walk, talk, and spell at this level. Then, there is the intentional level, where we focus, study, research, and internalize specific topics and facts "on purpose." Some things we know because someone told us. Other things we were forced to learn in order to function in society. Yet, there are many things we set our minds on and spend considerable time on it because we have decided to learn it.

None of us can say, with complete accuracy, when we first heard about Jesus! There are hints and pieces of "old" memory, but for the most part, the message of Jesus just "was." The information just came our way. But the seniors among us can recall being taught "Now I lay me down to sleep," Psalm 23, and eventually the Lord's Prayer. The facts were stored in our memory banks and remain there until today, regardless of our complete compression of their meaning. We remember bits of Sunday school lessons, youth group teachings, and Vacation Bible School trivia. However, far too few of us can recount our serious, intentional study of the doctrine of our faith!

On the isle of Patmos, John the Revelator, is given the privileged occasion to do an intentional study of different types of church folks who all claim to be "Christian."

The book opens with a declaration of its true author, Him "which is, and which was, and which is to come" (1:8).

John sees Jesus in His glorified state as opposed to His earthly state in which He had "emptied" Himself (Phil. 2:6–8). The Book of Revelation can be outlined based on John's vision of Christ:

1. "The things which thou hast seen"(1:19);
2. "The things which are" (1:19; chaps. 2–3);
3. "The things which shall be hereafter" (1:19; chaps. 4–22).

Following the letters to the seven churches (chaps. 2–3), John suddenly finds himself in heaven. He is given a vision of the majesty of God and His attendants (chaps. 4–5). In the right hand of "Him who at on the throne a book written within and on the backside, sealed with seven seals" (5:1). When the Lamb prevails to break the seals, seven judgments follow (6:1–8:1). These seal judgments are followed by seven trumpet judgments (8:2–14:20), which are followed by seven bowl judgments (15:1–18:24). Chapter 19 records the celebration that follows the defeat of all forces opposed to the Son, the marriage of the Lamb to His bride, and the coming of Christ to rule. Satan is bound for 1,000 years (20:1–3) after which he is released and goes out to deceive the world and lead a revolt against Christ. He is defeated and cast into the lake of fire, along with those who

have rejected Christ (vv. 14–15). Chapters 21–22 describe the new heaven and the new earth. New Jerusalem is pictured as the abode of the righteous (21:24; 22:14). The book ends with an invitation to anyone who will to come and drink from the fountain that gives life (22:17).

THE BLACK PRESENCE IN REVELATION

There is a strong black presence in the seven churches of Asia Minor. The population of Asia Minor consisted of a mixed breed of people extending back in history several thousands of years. It is interesting to note that from approximately 2000 B.C. into the New Testament times, a people at one time known as Hittites were a significant component of this population. Hittites descended from Canaan (Gen. 10:15; 1 Chron. 1:13). Canaan was a son of Cush, whose name means "black." While not all people in Asia Minor were black, the black heritage of many cannot be ignored. Jezebel (2:20), the wife of King Ahab (1 Kings 16:31–33) is used to typify the teacher in Thyatira who encouraged church members to depart from established Christian behavior and engage in evil practices. Jezebel was a Phoenician whose ancestors sprang from Cush through Canaan, and back to Ham.

The Euphrates River, Egypt, and Babylon are all locations of black people mentioned in the Book of Revelation. The Euphrates River (9:14) is one of two rivers located in Mesopotamia. According to the best authorities, this area was settled by people who migrated from Africa around 5000 B.C. Egypt (11:8) is located in the northeast section of Africa. The land was settled by the descendants of Ham, whose name means "black." Egypt is used figuratively in this text. Babylon (14:8) was settled originally by Nimrod, a son of Cush. Babylon was first a city located on the Euphrates River. Around 606 B.C., Nebuchadnezzar established the Babylonian Empire. Scholars differ in identifying the meaning of Babylon in Revelation. Some believe the term symbolizes the entire world system to be destroyed at Christ's return. Others regard it as symbolic of the struggle between good and evil taking place during this age. Still others have attempted to identify the name with a particular modern city.

Life Lessons

REVELATION 1

"The Revelation of Jesus Christ, which God gave unto him, to shew unto his servants things which must shortly come to pass" (1:1) This book is apocalyptic, meaning it reveals the mystery of Jesus Christ. It is a book of spectacular signs and symbols. It is a vision of the "end time" which Jesus allowed John to see and to share. In it the church is urged to hold and maintain high standards of right living. "Blessed is he that readeth, and they that hear the words of this prophecy, and keep those things

which are written therein: for the time is at hand" (v. 3).

Jesus' identity as God is given: "I am the Alpha and Omega, the beginning and the ending, saith the Lord, which is, and which was, and which is to come, the Almighty" (1:8).

Almighty Coming Sovereign, I bow before You and cry with the host of angelic beings "Holy, holy, holy, Lord God Almighty . . . Thou art worthy, O Lord, to receive glory and honour and power" (4:8, 11).

REVELATION 1

"I John, who also am your brother, and companion in tribulation, and in the kingdom and patience of Jesus Christ, was in the isle that is called Patmos, for the word of God, and for the testimony of Jesus Christ" (1:9). The church has always endured severe persecution for it stood against the social, political, economic, and religious norms of the day. Being a Christian has never been easy. Jesus suffered. The apostles suffered. You and I will suffer because of our faith!

The Roman officials had exiled John to an island about 50 miles from Ephesus. He had refused the Roman mandate to cease preaching the Good News of Jesus Christ. The message of truth is not popular today. Many of us have been "banished" and "exiled."

Suffering Savior, in my times of exile, stand by me!

REVELATION 1–2

The seven golden lampstands represent the congregations in Ephesus, Smyrna, Pergamos, Thyatira, Sardis, Philadelphia, and Laodicea. They faced great difficulty. John sees a vision of someone, "like unto the Son of man" (1:13). Jesus is in their midst with wisdom (white hair), judgment (blazing eyes), the priestly garb of forgiveness (robe and golden sash), and power (sharp double-edged sword and the seven stars).

As the apostle John begins his intentional study, led by the risen Jesus, the truth of the heart's intentions of various church members are exposed. For some, this is not a very pretty picture as Jesus explains: "I know thy works, and thy labour, and thy patience . . . and hast borne, and hast patience, and for my name's sake hast laboured, and hast not fainted. Nevertheless I have somewhat against thee, because thou hast left thy first love" (2:2–4).

First Love, forgive me for straying from You. Draw me back to Your fold. I long to be faithful.

REVELATION 2

Jesus' warnings continue: "Repent; or else I will come unto thee quickly, and will fight against them with the sword of my mouth" (2:16). That is a promise He plans to keep. Sexual immorality ran rampant through the congregation at Pergamos. Many false teachers encouraged loose living. As a result many folks followed their teachings! Jesus follows His a severe rebuke with a haunting plea: "He that hath an ear, let him hear what the Spirit saith unto the churches" (v. 17).

Then Jesus adds this rebuke: "Thou sufferest that woman Jezebel, which calleth herself a prophetess, to teach and to seduce my servants to commit fornication, and to eat things sacrificed unto idols. . . . I will kill her children with death; and all the churches shall know that I am he which searcheth the

reins and hearts: and I will give unto every one of you according to your works. But unto you I say, and unto the rest . . . that which ye have already hold fast till I come" (vv. 20, 23–25). Jezebel symbolizes the pagan queen who worshiped Baal and killed God's prophets (1 Kings 18; 19). She represents a consistent threat of evil that runs through the church. She refuses to repent and be subject unto Israel's God. Her offspring live on! Avoid allowing sexual immorality and idolatry to make themselves at home in you!

Holy One, purify me, in word and in deeds. Rule all of me.

REVELATION 3

Jesus continues with a few words to the church in Sardis: "I know thy works, that thou hast a name that thou livest, and art dead. Be watchful, and strengthen the things which remain, that are ready to die: for I have not found thy works perfect before God" (3:1–2). Good looks don't measure up! The call is to return to basic Christian truths and live the talk!

All Knowing One, help me to live devoted to Your holy ways.

REVELATION 3

Jesus moves on to the church in Philadelphia: "Thou hast little strength, and hast kept my word, and hast not denied my name. . . . Behold, I come quickly; hold that fast which thou hast" (3:8, 11). Here is a commendation to faithful living.

Witness of My Life, help me to hold on!

REVELATION 3

One of the most familiar rebukes in the Revelation is the one Jesus addresses to the church in Laodicea: "I know thy works, that thou art neither cold nor hot: I would thou wert cold or hot. So then because thou art lukewarm, and neither cold nor hot, I will spue thee out of my mouth" (3:15–16). Here is the most serious rebuke against mediocrity and indifference! This congregation was rich with material things and complacent about Christ who implored, "Behold, I stand at the door, and knock: if any man hear my voice, and open the door, I will come in to him, and will sup with him, and he with me" (v. 20).

Holy Presence, I invite you into my life, again and again.

REVELATION 4–5

Chapters four and five are filled with glorious visions of the world to come. "After this I looked, and, behold, a door was opened in heaven: and the first voice which I heard was as it were of a trumpet talking with me; which said, Come up hither, and I will shew thee things which must be hereafter" (4:1–2). The Lamb of God, the Lion of the Tribe of Judah, stands strong as the 24 elders and angelic host sing, "Worthy is the Lamb, that was slain to receive power, and riches, and wisdom, and strength, and honour, and glory, and blessing" (5:12).

Worthy Lamb, my heart, too, sings, "Amen!"

REVELATION 7–12

The revelation continues with a view of the saints in heaven—those who come through the tribulation. "After this I beheld, and lo, a great multitude, which no man could number, of all nations, and kindreds, and peo-

ple, and tongues . . . And one of the elders answered, saying unto me, What are these which are arrayed in white robes? and whence came they? . . . And he said to me, These are they which came out of great tribulation, and have washed their robes, and made them white in the blood of the Lamb" (7:9, 13–14). The people of God come from everywhere. They all come through suffering! "They overcame him by the blood of the Lamb, and by the word of their testimony" (12:11). They all have been washed in the redeeming blood of Jesus Christ. And they have shared their testimony with others. There are two great aspects of our Christian faith that will be recognized through eternity. One is the matchless, redemptive blood of Jesus that has washed away our sin. The second is the record of our life in both word and deeds, which is recorded in the Lamb's Book of Life.

Testimony of truth, I realize that my life is a testimony of our relationship. Help me leave a worthy record of my love for You!

REVELATION 12

"And there appeared a great wonder in heaven; a woman clothed with the sun, and the moon under her feet, and upon her head a crown of twelve stars: And she being with child cried, travailing in birth, and pained to be delivered. . . . The woman fled into the wilderness, where she hath a place prepared of God, that they should feed her there a thousand and two hundred and threescore days" (12:1, 26). John observes a great conflict in the heavens as an enormous red dragon with seven heads, seven horns, and seven crowns on his heads (v. 3) seeks to destroy the child of this pregnant woman. The dragon represents Satan, the evil one who is the power and authority of the kingdoms of this world. The woman represents the people who faithfully waited for the Deliverer, the Messiah. The child she carries is the Messiah.

"She brought forth a man child, who was to rule all nations with a rod of iron: and her child was caught up unto God, and to his throne" (v. 5). As Satan waits to devour the Child of the woman, God has prepared a place for her to be hidden for three and one-half years. This number might stand for the time between Jesus' first and second comings. It might also mean a period of time after the rapture of the church. "The woman were given two wings of a great eagle, that she might fly into the wilderness, into her place" (v. 14).

Overcoming God, You provide protection for me from the enemies' plans. You keep me safe from harm. Thank You!

REVELATION 13

It is no secret that we are involved in a war. Satan hates God and God's people. Satan has followers and authority in this world. Satan knows his destiny and realizes that his time is drawing to a close. Satan understands that he is a defeated foe. "And he opened his mouth in blasphemy against God, to blaspheme his name, and his tabernacle, and them that dwell in heaven. And it was given unto him to make war with the saints, and to overcome them: and power was given him over all kindreds, and tongues, and nations. And all that dwell upon the earth shall worship him, whose names are not written in the book of life of the Lamb slain from the

foundation of the world" (13:6–8).

Holder of the Book, I told Jesus it would be all right to put my name in the Lamb's Book of Life. Daily, I'm checking on my name's registration!

REVELATION 17–19

One of the angels of the seven vials shows John another woman. "Come hither; I will shew unto thee the judgment of the great whore that sitteth upon many waters: With whom the kings of the earth have committed fornication, and the inhabitants of the earth have been made drunk with the wine of her fornication. . . . And upon her forehead was a name written, MYSTERY, BABYLON THE GREAT, THE MOTHER OF HARLOTS AND ABOMINATIONS OF THE EARTH. And I saw the woman was drunk with the blood of the saints, the blood of the martyrs of Jesus" (17:1–2, 5–6). This woman represents the evil "systems" of the world which have oppressed and slain the people of God. The Roman Empire is one that fits the description with its seven emperors. John the Revelator announces the fall of every evil system and the Lamb's seizing the final victory. "And the ten horns which thou sawest upon the beast, these shall hate the whore, and shall make her desolate and naked, and shall eat her flesh, and burn her with fire" (v. 16). As vengeance is enacted upon Babylon, and other sound is heard, that of "the voice of a great multitude, and as the voice of many waters, and as the voice of many thunderings, saying, Alleluia: for the Lord God omnipotent reigneth" (19:6).

Reigning Monarch, I want to sing in the heavenly choir. Attune my heart now to shout forth Your worthy praise.

REVELATION 20–21

"And the devil that deceived them was cast into the lake of fire and brimstone, where the beast and the false prophet are, and shall be tormented day and night for ever and ever. . . . And whosoever was not found written in the book of life was cast into the lake of fire" (20:10, 15). This is the place of eternal punishment for all who do not place their faith in Jesus Christ. There are many different signs and symbols throughout this book. It required an in-depth study of both the prophecies found in Daniel and Ezekiel to begin a full overview of the complexity of these interwoven visions. What we need to remember is that every vision and symbol points us to the final victory of Jesus Christ and the peace that victory renders. John's closing image is of heaven—the final destination for all believers. "And I saw a new heaven and a new earth: for the first heaven and the first earth were passed away; and there was no more sea. And I John saw the holy city, new Jerusalem, coming down from God out of heaven, prepared as a bride adorned for her husband" (21:1–2).

Great God of Heaven and Earth, Oh, I want to be there with You, to be part of this happy day! Thank You for "The End" of the story. Thank You for salvation. Thank You for hope!

REVELATION 22

The last words in Revelation point us to the glorious hope of Jesus' return. "I Jesus have sent mine angel to testify unto you these things in the churches. I am the root and the offspring of David, and the bright and

morning star. And the Spirit and the bride say, Come. . . . He which testifieth these things saith, Surely I come quickly. Amen. Even so, come, Lord Jesus. The grace of our Lord Jesus Christ be with you all. Amen" (22:16–17a, 20–21).

Jesus, I echo John's words, "Even so, come, Lord Jesus!" (v. 21).

Women in REVELATION

THE REVELATION 12 WOMAN: A WOMAN OF FOCUS

> And there appeared a great wonder in heaven; a woman clothed with the sun, and the moon under her feet, and upon her head a crown of twelve stars. (Rev. 12:1)

Picture the moment of delivery: a woman, pregnant and seemingly alone, crying in pain as she anticipates the birth of her child. Suddenly, her worst enemy appears. His breath is on her. He waits to devour the baby as soon as it appears. How he hates her! He could have easily killed them both immediately. But no, he wants her to see her child die.

In extreme peril, she delivers the boy. The child is swept up to God. Still weak from the birth, the woman rises to her feet and runs. Unstable hips, wobbly legs—she runs for her life.

She spoke to no one. She never pleaded with the enemy nor called for help. She ran, even without her baby, to the place where God prepared. And the devil followed. Michael and the angels fought him. He was then hurled from heaven. Still, the devil sought to kill the woman. God gave her the wings of an eagle to speed her escape. Still, the devil was obsessed with killing her. The earth swallowed the flood that the devil spat at the woman. That allowed her to escape the devil's clutches. The devil, defeated and still hating the woman, dedicated his life to killing her seed.

Who was she? Though obviously symbolic in meaning, this woman's attributes are instructive. She was strong, courageous—clearly, a soldier. The woman had been given specific instruction. She understood what she had to do. Once given her mission, she executed it without question or complaint. Her circumstances and her feelings were irrelevant. Help came from unexpected places. Success depended on her staying dedicated to her mission and acting on what she knew—no matter what the circumstance, no matter who opposed her. Timing was everything.

The Revelation 12 woman was a woman of focus. Self-sacrifice was just the beginning of the contribution she made. She gave all she had—and heaven and earth moved.

Read Revelation 12:1–3.

Read the insight essays on Commitment and Perseverance.

—V. Hartsfield

within and on the backside, [s]sealed with
seven seals.
2 And I saw a strong angel proclaiming
with a loud voice, Who is worthy to open
the book, and to loose the seals thereof?
3 And no man [t]in heaven, nor in earth,
neither under the earth, was able to open
the book, neither to look thereon.
4 And I wept much, because no man was
found worthy to open and to read the book,
neither to look thereon.
5 And one of the elders saith unto me,
Weep not: behold, [u]the Lion of the tribe of
Juda, [v]the Root of David, hath prevailed
to open the book, and [w]to loose the seven
seals thereof.
6 And I beheld, and, lo, in the midst of the
throne and of the four beasts, and in the
midst of the elders, stood [x]a Lamb as it had
been slain, having seven horns and [y]seven
eyes, which are [z]the seven Spirits of God
sent forth into all the earth.
7 And he came and took the book out of
the right hand [a]of him that sat upon the
throne.
8 And when he had taken the book, [b]the
four beasts and four *and* twenty elders fell
down before the Lamb, having every one
of them [c]harps, and golden vials full of
odours, [d]which are the prayers of saints.
9 And [e]they sung a new song, saying,
[f]Thou art worthy to take the book, and to
open the seals thereof: [g]for thou wast slain,
and [h]hast redeemed us to God by thy blood
[i]out of every kindred, and tongue, and people, and nation;
10 [j]And hast made us unto our God
kings and priests: and we shall reign on the
earth.
11 And I beheld, and I heard the voice of
many angels [k]round about the throne and
the beasts and the elders: and the number of
them was [l]ten thousand times ten thousand, and thousands of thousands;
12 Saying with a loud voice, [m]Worthy is
the Lamb that was slain to receive power,
and riches, and wisdom, and strength, and
honour, and glory, and blessing.
13 And [n]every creature which is in
heaven, and on the earth, and under the
earth, and such as are in the sea, and all that
are in them, heard I saying, [o]Blessing, and
honour, and glory, and power, *be* unto him
[p]that sitteth upon the throne, and unto the
Lamb for ever and ever.
14 [q]And the four beasts said, Amen. And
the four *and* twenty elders fell down and
worshipped him [r]that liveth for ever and
ever.

6 And [s]I saw when the Lamb opened one
of the seals, and I heard, as it were the
noise of thunder, [t]one of the four beasts
saying, Come and see.
2 And I saw, and behold [u]a white horse:
[v]and he that sat on him had a bow; [w]and a
crown was given unto him: and he went
forth conquering, and to conquer.
3 And when he had opened the second

5:1 [s]Isa. 29:11; Dan. 12:4
5:3 [t]ver. 13
5:5 [u]Gen. 49:9; Heb. 7:14 [v]Isa. 11:1; Rom. 15:12; ch. 22:16 [w]ver. 1; ch. 6:1
5:6 [x]Isa. 53:7; John 1:29; 1 Pet. 1:19; ch. 13:8; ver. 9 [y]Zech. 3:9 [z]ch. 4:5
5:7 [a]ch. 4:2
5:8 [b]ch. 4:8 [c]ch. 14:2 [d]Ps. 141:2; ch. 8:3
5:9 [e]Ps. 40:3; ch. 14:3 [f]ch. 4:11 [g]ver. 6 [h]Acts 20:28; Rom. 3:24; 1 Cor. 6:20; Eph. 1:7; Col. 1:14; Heb. 9:12; 1 Pet. 1:18; 2 Pet. 2:1; 1 John 1:7; ch. 14:4 [i]Dan. 4:1; ch. 7:9
5:10 [j]Ex. 19:6; 1 Pet. 2:5; ch. 1:6
5:11 [k]ch. 4:4 [l]Ps. 68:17; Dan. 7:10; Heb. 12:22
5:12 [m]ch. 4:11
5:13 [n]Phil. 2:10; ver. 3 [o]1 Chron. 29:11; Rom. 9:5; 1 Tim. 6:16; 1 Pet. 4:11; ch. 1:6 [p]ch. 6:16
5:14 [q]ch. 19:4 [r]ch. 4:9
6:1 [s]ch. 5:5 [t]ch. 4:7
6:2 [u]Zech. 6:3; ch. 19:11 [v]Ps. 45:4 [w]Zech. 6:11; ch. 14:14
6:3 [x]ch. 4:7
6:4 [y]Zech. 6:2
6:5 [z]ch. 4:7 [a]Zech. 6:2
6:6 [b]ch. 9:4
6:7 [c]ch. 4:7
6:8 [d]Zech. 6:3 [e]Ezek. 14:21 [f]Lev. 26:22
6:9 [g]ch. 8:3 [h]ch. 20:4 [i]ch. 1:9 [j]2 Tim. 1:8; ch. 12:17
6:10 [k]Zech. 1:12 [l]ch. 3:7 [m]ch. 11:18
6:11 [n]ch. 3:4 [o]Heb. 11:40; ch. 14:13
6:12 [p]ch. 16:18 [q]Joel 2:10; Matt. 24:29; Acts 2:20
6:13 [r]ch. 8:10
6:14 [s]Ps. 102:26; Isa. 34:4; Heb. 1:12 [t]Jer. 3:23; ch. 16:20
6:15 [u]Isa. 2:19
6:16 [v]Hos. 10:8; Luke 23:30; ch. 9:6
6:17 [w]Isa. 13:6; Zeph. 1:14; ch. 16:14 [x]Ps. 76:7
7:1 [y]Dan. 7:2

seal, [x]I heard the second beast say, Come
and see.
4 [y]And there went out another horse *that*
was red: and *power* was given to him that
sat thereon to take peace from the earth,
and that they should kill one another: and
there was given unto him a great sword.
5 And when he had opened the third seal,
[z]I heard the third beast say, Come and see.
And I beheld, and lo [a]a black horse; and he
that sat on him had a pair of balances in his
hand.
6 And I heard a voice in the midst of the
four beasts say, A measure of wheat for a
penny, and three measures of barley for a
penny; and [b]*see* thou hurt not the oil and
the wine.
7 And when he had opened the fourth
seal, [c]I heard the voice of the fourth beast
say, Come and see.
8 [d]And I looked, and behold a pale horse:
and his name that sat on him was Death,
and Hell followed with him. And power was
given unto them over the fourth part of the
earth, [e]to kill with sword, and with hunger,
and with death, [f]and with the beasts of the
earth.
9 And when he had opened the fifth seal,
I saw under [g]the altar [h]the souls of them
that were slain [i]for the word of God, and
for [j]the testimony which they held:
10 And they cried with a loud voice, saying, [k]How long, O Lord, [l]holy and true,
[m]dost thou not judge and avenge our blood
on them that dwell on the earth?
11 And [n]white robes were given unto every one of them; and it was said unto them,
[o]that they should rest yet for a little season,
until their fellowservants also and their
brethren, that should be killed as they *were*,
should be fulfilled.
12 And I beheld when he had opened the
sixth seal, [p]and, lo, there was a great earthquake; and [q]the sun became black as sackcloth of hair, and the moon became as
blood;
13 [r]And the stars of heaven fell unto the
earth, even as a fig tree casteth her untimely
figs, when she is shaken of a mighty wind.
14 [s]And the heaven departed as a scroll
when it is rolled together; and [t]every
mountain and island were moved out of
their places.
15 And the kings of the earth, and the
great men, and the rich men, and the chief
captains, and the mighty men, and every
bondman, and every free man, [u]hid themselves in the dens and in the rocks of the
mountains;
16 [v]And said to the mountains and rocks,
Fall on us, and hide us from the face of him
that sitteth on the throne, and from the
wrath of the Lamb:
17 [w]For the great day of his wrath is
come; [x]and who shall be able to stand?

7 And after these things I saw four angels
standing on the four corners of the
earth, [y]holding the four winds of the earth,

[z]that the wind should not blow on the earth, nor on the sea, nor on any tree.

2 And I saw another angel ascending from the east, having the seal of the living God: and he cried with a loud voice to the four angels, to whom it was given to hurt the earth and the sea,

3 Saying, [a]Hurt not the earth, neither the sea, nor the trees, till we have [b]sealed the servants of our God [c]in their foreheads.

4 [d]And I heard the number of them which were sealed: *and there were* sealed [e]an hundred *and* forty *and* four thousand of all the tribes of the children of Israel.

5 Of the tribe of Juda *were* sealed twelve thousand. Of the tribe of Reuben *were* sealed twelve thousand. Of the tribe of Gad *were* sealed twelve thousand.

6 Of the tribe of Aser *were* sealed twelve thousand. Of the tribe of Nepthalim *were* sealed twelve thousand. Of the tribe of Manasses *were* sealed twelve thousand.

7 Of the tribe of Simeon *were* sealed twelve thousand. Of the tribe of Levi *were* sealed twelve thousand. Of the tribe of Issachar *were* sealed twelve thousand.

8 Of the tribe of Zabulon *were* sealed twelve thousand. Of the tribe of Joseph *were* sealed twelve thousand. Of the tribe of Benjamin *were* sealed twelve thousand.

9 After this I beheld, and, lo, [f]a great multitude, which no man could number, [g]of all nations, and kindreds, and people, and tongues, stood before the throne, and before the Lamb, [h]clothed with white robes, and palms in their hands;

10 And cried with a loud voice, saying, [i]Salvation to our God [j]which sitteth upon the throne, and unto the Lamb.

11 [k]And all the angels stood round about the throne, and *about* the elders and the four beasts, and fell before the throne on their faces, and worshipped God,

12 [l]Saying, Amen: Blessing, and glory, and wisdom, and thanksgiving, and honour, and power, and might, *be* unto our God for ever and ever. Amen.

13 And one of the elders answered, saying unto me, What are these which are arrayed in [m]white robes? and whence came they?

14 And I said unto him, Sir, thou knowest. And he said to me, [n]These are they which came out of great tribulation, and have [o]washed their robes, and made them white in the blood of the Lamb.

15 Therefore are they before the throne of God, and serve him day and night in his temple: and he that sitteth on the throne shall [p]dwell among them.

16 [q]They shall hunger no more, neither thirst any more; [r]neither shall the sun light on them, nor any heat.

17 For the Lamb which is in the midst of the throne [s]shall feed them, and shall lead them unto living fountains of waters: [t]and God shall wipe away all tears from their eyes.

7:1 [z]ch. 9:4
7:3 [a]ch. 6:6 [b]Ezek. 9:4; ch. 14:1 [c]ch. 22:4
7:4 [d]ch. 9:16 [e]ch. 14:1
7:9 [f]Rom. 11:25 [g]ch. 5:9 [h]ch. 3:5; ver. 14
7:10 [i]Ps. 3:8; Isa. 43:11; Jer. 3:23; Hos. 13:4; ch. 19:1 [j]ch. 5:13
7:11 [k]ch. 4:6
7:12 [l]ch. 5:13
7:13 [m]ver. 9
7:14 [n]ch. 6:9 [o]Isa. 1:18; Zech. 3:3; Heb. 9:14; 1 John 1:7; ch. 1:5
7:15 [p]Isa. 4:5; ch. 21:3
7:16 [q]Isa. 49:10 [r]Ps. 121:6; ch. 21:4
7:17 [s]Ps. 23:1; John 10:11 [t]Isa. 25:8; ch. 21:4
8:1 [u]ch. 6:1
8:2 [v]Matt. 18:10; Luke 1:19 [w]2 Chron. 29:25-28
8:3 [x]ch. 5:8 [y]Ex. 30:1; ch. 6:9
8:4 [z]Ps. 141:2; Luke 1:10
8:5 [a]ch. 16:18 [b]2 Sam. 22:8; 1 Kings 19:11; Acts 4:31
8:7 [c]Ezek. 38:22 [d]ch. 16:2 [e]Isa. 2:13; ch. 9:4
8:8 [f]Jer. 51:25; Am. 7:4 [g]ch. 16:3 [h]Ezek. 14:19
8:9 [i]ch. 16:3
8:10 [j]Isa. 14:12; ch. 9:1 [k]ch. 16:4
8:11 [l]Ruth 1:20 [m]Ex. 15:23; Jer. 9:15
8:12 [n]Isa. 13:10; Am. 8:9
8:13 [o]ch. 14:6 [p]ch. 9:12
9:1 [q]Luke 10:18; ch. 8:10 [r]Luke 8:31; ch. 17:8; ver. 2
9:2 [s]Joel 2:2

8 And [u]when he had opened the seventh seal, there was silence in heaven about the space of half an hour.

2 [v]And I saw the seven angels which stood before God; [w]and to them were given seven trumpets.

3 And another angel came and stood at the altar, having a golden censer; and there was given unto him much incense, that he should offer *it* with [x]the prayers of all saints upon [y]the golden altar which was before the throne.

4 And [z]the smoke of the incense, *which came* with the prayers of the saints, ascended up before God out of the angel's hand.

5 And the angel took the censer, and filled it with fire of the altar, and cast *it* into the earth: and [a]there were voices, and thunderings, and lightnings, [b]and an earthquake.

6 And the seven angels which had the seven trumpets prepared themselves to sound.

7 The first angel sounded, [c]and there followed hail and fire mingled with blood, and they were cast [d]upon the earth: and the third part [e]of trees was burnt up, and all green grass was burnt up.

8 And the second angel sounded, [f]and as it were a great mountain burning with fire was cast into the sea: [g]and the third part of the sea [h]became blood;

9 [i]And the third part of the creatures which were in the sea, and had life, died; and the third part of the ships were destroyed.

10 And the third angel sounded, [j]and there fell a great star from heaven, burning as it were a lamp, [k]and it fell upon the third part of the rivers, and upon the fountains of waters;

11 [l]And the name of the star is called Wormwood: [m]and the third part of the waters became wormwood; and many men died of the waters, because they were made bitter.

12 [n]And the fourth angel sounded, and the third part of the sun was smitten, and the third part of the moon, and the third part of the stars; so as the third part of them was darkened, and the day shone not for a third part of it, and the night likewise.

13 And I beheld, [o]and heard an angel flying through the midst of heaven, saying with a loud voice, [p]Woe, woe, woe, to the inhabiters of the earth by reason of the other voices of the trumpet of the three angels, which are yet to sound!

9 And the fifth angel sounded, [q]and I saw a star fall from heaven unto the earth: and to him was given the key of [r]the bottomless pit.

2 And he opened the bottomless pit; [s]and there arose a smoke out of the pit, as the smoke of a great furnace; and the sun and the air were darkened by reason of the smoke of the pit.

3 And there came out of the smoke [t]lo-
custs upon the earth: and unto them was
given power, [u]as the scorpions of the earth
have power.
4 And it was commanded them [v]that they
should not hurt [w]the grass of the earth, neither any green thing, neither any tree; but
only those men which have not [x]the seal of
God in their foreheads.
5 And to them it was given that they
should not kill them, [y]but that they should
be tormented five months: and their torment *was* as the torment of a scorpion,
when he striketh a man.
6 And in those days [z]shall men seek
death, and shall not find it; and shall desire
to die, and death shall flee from them.
7 And [a]the shapes of the locusts *were* like
unto horses prepared unto battle; [b]and on
their heads *were* as it were crowns like
gold, [c]and their faces *were* as the faces of
men.
8 And they had hair as the hair of women,
and [d]their teeth were as *the teeth* of lions.
9 And they had breastplates, as it were
breastplates of iron; and the sound of their
wings *was* [e]as the sound of chariots of
many horses running to battle.
10 And they had tails like unto scorpions,
and there were stings in their tails: [f]and
their power *was* to hurt men five months.
11 [g]And they had a king over them,
which is [h]the angel of the bottomless pit,
whose name in the Hebrew tongue *is* Abad-
don, but in the Greek tongue hath *his* name
Apollyon.
12 [i]One woe is past; *and,* behold, there
come two woes more hereafter.
13 And the sixth angel sounded, and I
heard a voice from the four horns of the
golden altar which is before God,
14 Saying to the sixth angel which had
the trumpet, Loose the four angels which
are bound [j]in the great river Euphrates.
15 And the four angels were loosed,
which were prepared for an hour, and a
day, and a month, and a year, for to slay the
third part of men.
16 And [k]the number of the army [l]of the
horsemen *were* two hundred thousand
thousand: [m]and I heard the number of them.
17 And thus I saw the horses in the vision,
and them that sat on them, having breastplates of fire, and of jacinth, and brimstone:
[n]and the heads of the horses *were* as the
heads of lions; and out of their mouths issued fire and smoke and brimstone.
18 By these three was the third part of
men killed, by the fire, and by the smoke,
and by the brimstone, which issued out of
their mouths.
19 For their power is in their mouth, and
in their tails: [o]for their tails *were* like unto
serpents, and had heads, and with them
they do hurt.
20 And the rest of the men which were
not killed by these plagues [p]yet repented
not of the works of their hands, that they
should not worship [q]devils, [r]and idols of
gold, and silver, and brass, and stone, and
of wood: which neither can see, nor hear,
nor walk:
21 Neither repented they of their murders, [s]nor of their sorceries, nor of their
fornication, nor of their thefts.

10 And I saw another mighty angel
come down from heaven, clothed
with a cloud: [t]and a rainbow *was* upon his
head, and [u]his face *was* as it were the sun,
and [v]his feet as pillars of fire:
2 And he had in his hand a little book
open: [w]and he set his right foot upon the
sea, and *his* left *foot* on the earth,
3 And cried with a loud voice, as *when* a
lion roareth: and when he had cried, [x]seven
thunders uttered their voices.
4 And when the seven thunders had uttered their voices, I was about to write: and
I heard a voice from heaven saying unto me,
[y]Seal up those things which the seven thunders uttered, and write them not.
5 And the angel which I saw stand upon
the sea and upon the earth [z]lifted up his
hand to heaven,
6 And sware by him that liveth for ever
and ever, [a]who created heaven, and the
things that therein are, and the earth, and
the things that therein are, and the sea, and
the things which are therein, [b]that there
should be time no longer:
7 But [c]in the days of the voice of the seventh angel, when he shall begin to sound,
the mystery of God should be finished, as he
hath declared to his servants the prophets.
8 And [d]the voice which I heard from
heaven spake unto me again, and said, Go
and take the little book which is open in the
hand of the angel which standeth upon the
sea and upon the earth.
9 And I went unto the angel, and said
unto him, Give me the little book. And he
said unto me, [e]Take *it*, and eat it up; and it
shall make thy belly bitter, but it shall be in
thy mouth sweet as honey.
10 And I took the little book out of the
angel's hand, and ate it up; [f]and it was in
my mouth sweet as honey: and as soon as I
had eaten it, [g]my belly was bitter.
11 And he said unto me, Thou must
prophesy again before many peoples, and
nations, and tongues, and kings.

11 And there was given me [h]a reed like
unto a rod: and the angel stood, saying, [i]Rise, and measure the temple of God,
and the altar, and them that worship
therein.
2 But [j]the court which is without the temple leave out, and measure it not; [k]for it is
given unto the Gentiles: and the holy city
shall they [l]tread under foot [m]forty *and* two
months.
3 And I will give *power* unto my two [n]wit-
nesses, [o]and they shall prophesy [p]a thousand two hundred *and* threescore days,
clothed in sackcloth.
4 These are the [q]two olive trees, and the

9:3 [t]Ex. 10:4; Judg. 7:12 [u]ver. 10
9:4 [v]ch. 6:6 [w]ch. 8:7 [x]Ex. 12:23; Ezek. 9:4; ch. 7:3
9:5 [y]ch. 11:7; ver. 10
9:6 [z]Job 3:21; Isa. 2:19; Jer. 8:3; ch. 6:16
9:7 [a]Joel 2:4 [b]Nah. 3:17 [c]Dan. 7:8
9:8 [d]Joel 1:6
9:9 [e]Joel 2:5
9:10 [f]ver. 5
9:11 [g]Eph. 2:2 [h]ver. 1
9:12 [i]ch. 8:13
9:14 [j]ch. 16:12
9:16 [k]Ps. 68:17; Dan. 7:10 [l]Ezek. 38:4 [m]ch. 7:4
9:17 [n]1 Chron. 12:8; Isa. 5:28
9:19 [o]Isa. 9:15
9:20 [p]Deut. 31:29 [q]Lev. 17:7; Deut. 32:17; Ps. 106:37; 1 Cor. 10:20 [r]Ps. 115:4; Dan. 5:23
9:21 [s]ch. 22:15
10:1 [t]Ezek. 1:28 [u]Matt. 17:2; ch. 1:16 [v]ch. 1:15
10:2 [w]Matt. 28:18
10:3 [x]ch. 8:5
10:4 [y]Dan. 8:26
10:5 [z]Ex. 6:8; Dan. 12:7
10:6 [a]Neh. 9:6; ch. 4:11 [b]Dan. 12:7; ch. 16:17
10:7 [c]ch. 11:15
10:8 [d]ver. 4
10:9 [e]Jer. 15:16; Ezek. 2:8
10:10 [f]Ezek. 3:3 [g]Ezek. 2:10
11:1 [h]Ezek. 40:3; ch. 21:15 [i]Num. 23:18
11:2 [j]Ezek. 40:17 [k]Ps. 79:1; Luke 21:24 [l]Dan. 8:10 [m]ch. 13:5
11:3 [n]ch. 20:4 [o]ch. 19:10 [p]ch. 12:6
11:4 [q]Ps. 52:8; Jer. 11:16; Zech. 4:3

two candlesticks standing before the God of the earth.

5 And if any man will hurt them, [r]fire proceedeth out of their mouth, and devoureth their enemies: [s]and if any man will hurt them, he must in this manner be killed.

6 These [t]have power to shut heaven, that it rain not in the days of their prophecy: and [u]have power over waters to turn them to blood, and to smite the earth with all plagues, as often as they will.

7 And when they [v]shall have finished their testimony, [w]the beast that ascendeth [x]out of the bottomless pit [y]shall make war against them, and shall overcome them, and kill them.

8 And their dead bodies *shall lie* in the street of [z]the great city, which spiritually is called Sodom and Egypt, [a]where also our Lord was crucified.

9 [b]And they of the people and kindreds and tongues and nations shall see their dead bodies three days and an half, [c]and shall not suffer their dead bodies to be put in graves.

10 [d]And they that dwell upon the earth shall rejoice over them, and make merry, [e]and shall send gifts one to another; [f]because these two prophets tormented them that dwelt on the earth.

11 [g]And after three days and an half [h]the Spirit of life from God entered into them, and they stood upon their feet; and great fear fell upon them which saw them.

12 And they heard a great voice from heaven saying unto them, Come up hither. [i]And they ascended up to heaven [j]in a cloud; [k]and their enemies beheld them.

13 And the same hour [l]was there a great earthquake, [m]and the tenth part of the city fell, and in the earthquake were slain of men seven thousand: and the remnant were affrighted, [n]and gave glory to the God of heaven.

14 [o]The second woe is past; *and,* behold, the third woe cometh quickly.

15 And [p]the seventh angel sounded; [q]and there were great voices in heaven, saying, [r]The kingdoms of this world are become *the kingdoms* of our Lord, and of his Christ; [s]and he shall reign for ever and ever.

16 And [t]the four and twenty elders, which sat before God on their seats, fell upon their faces, and worshipped God,

17 Saying, We give thee thanks, O Lord God Almighty, [u]which art, and wast, and art to come; because thou hast taken to thee thy great power, [v]and hast reigned.

18 [w]And the nations were angry, and thy wrath is come, [x]and the time of the dead, that they should be judged, and that thou shouldest give reward unto thy servants the prophets, and to the saints, and them that fear thy name, [y]small and great; [z]and shouldest destroy them which destroy the earth.

19 And [a]the temple of God was opened in heaven, and there was seen in his temple the ark of his testament: and [b]there were lightnings, and voices, and thunderings, and an earthquake, [c]and great hail.

12 And there appeared a great wonder in heaven; a woman clothed with the sun, and the moon under her feet, and upon her head a crown of twelve stars:

2 And she being with child cried, [d]travailing in birth, and pained to be delivered.

3 And there appeared another wonder in heaven; and behold [e]a great red dragon, [f]having seven heads and ten horns, [g]and seven crowns upon his heads.

4 And [h]his tail drew the third part [i]of the stars of heaven, [j]and did cast them to the earth: and the dragon stood [k]before the woman which was ready to be delivered, [l]for to devour her child as soon as it was born.

5 And she brought forth a man child, [m]who was to rule all nations with a rod of iron: and her child was caught up unto God, and *to* his throne.

6 And [n]the woman fled into the wilderness, where she hath a place prepared of God, that they should feed her there [o]a thousand two hundred *and* threescore days.

7 And there was war in heaven: [p]Michael and his angels fought [q]against the dragon; and the dragon fought and his angels,

8 And prevailed not; neither was their place found any more in heaven.

9 And [r]the great dragon was cast out, [s]that old serpent, called the Devil, and Satan, [t]which deceiveth the whole world: [u]he was cast out into the earth, and his angels were cast out with him.

10 And I heard a loud voice saying in heaven, [v]Now is come salvation, and strength, and the kingdom of our God, and the power of his Christ: for the accuser of our brethren is cast down, [w]which accused them before our God day and night.

11 And [x]they overcame him by the blood of the Lamb, and by the word of their testimony; [y]and they loved not their lives unto the death.

12 Therefore [z]rejoice, *ye* heavens, and ye that dwell in them. [a]Woe to the inhabiters of the earth and of the sea! for the devil is come down unto you, having great wrath, [b]because he knoweth that he hath but a short time.

13 And when the dragon saw that he was cast unto the earth, he persecuted [c]the woman which brought forth the man *child.*

14 [d]And to the woman were given two wings of a great eagle, [e]that she might fly [f]into the wilderness, into her place, where she is nourished [g]for a time, and times, and half a time, from the face of the serpent.

15 And the serpent [h]cast out of his mouth water as a flood after the woman, that he might cause her to be carried away of the flood.

16 And the earth helped the woman, and the earth opened her mouth, and swallowed

11:5 [r]2 Kings 1:10; Jer. 1:10; Ezek. 43:3; Hos. 6:5 [s]Num. 16:29
11:6 [t]1 Kings 17:1; Jam. 5:16 [u]Ex. 7:19
11:7 [v]Luke 13:32 [w]ch. 13:1 [x]ch. 9:2 [y]Dan. 7:21; Zech. 14:2
11:8 [z]ch. 14:8 [a]Heb. 13:12; ch. 18:24
11:9 [b]ch. 17:15 [c]Ps. 79:2
11:10 [d]ch. 12:12 [e]Esth. 9:19 [f]ch. 16:10
11:11 [g]ver. 9 [h]Ezek. 37:5
11:12 [i]Isa. 14:13; ch. 12:5 [j]Isa. 60:8; Acts 1:9 [k]2 Kings 2:1
11:13 [l]ch. 6:12 [m]ch. 16:19 [n]Josh. 7:19; ch. 14:7
11:14 [o]ch. 8:13
11:15 [p]ch. 10:7 [q]Isa. 27:13; ch. 16:17 [r]ch. 12:10 [s]Dan. 2:44
11:16 [t]ch. 4:4
11:17 [u]ch. 1:4 [v]ch. 19:6
11:18 [w]ver. 2 [x]Dan. 7:9; ch. 6:10 [y]ch. 19:5 [z]ch. 23:10
11:19 [a]ch. 15:5 [b]ch. 8:5 [c]ch. 16:21
12:2 [d]Isa. 66:7; Gal. 4:19
12:3 [e]ch. 17:3 [f]ch. 17:9 [g]ch. 13:1
12:4 [h]ch. 9:10 [i]ch. 17:18 [j]Dan. 8:10 [k]ver. 2 [l]Ex. 1:16
12:5 [m]Ps. 2:9; ch. 2:27
12:6 [n]ver. 4 [o]ch. 11:3
12:7 [p]Dan. 10:13 [q]ver. 3; ch. 20:2
12:9 [r]Luke 10:18; John 12:31 [s]Gen. 3:1; ch. 20:2 [t]ch. 20:3 [u]ch. 9:1
12:10 [v]ch. 11:15 [w]Job 1:9; Zech. 3:1
12:11 [x]Rom. 8:33 [y]Luke 14:26
12:12 [z]Ps. 96:11; Isa. 49:13; ch. 18:20 [a]ch. 8:13 [b]ch. 10:6
12:13 [c]ver. 5
12:14 [d]Ex. 19:4 [e]ver. 6 [f]ch. 17:3 [g]Dan. 7:25
12:15 [h]Isa. 59:19

up the flood which the dragon cast out of his
mouth.
17 And the dragon was wroth with the
woman, [i]and went to make war with the
remnant of her seed, [j]which keep the commandments of God, and have [k]the testimony of Jesus Christ.

13 And I stood upon the sand of the sea,
and saw [l]a beast rise up out of the
sea, [m]having seven heads and ten horns,
and upon his horns ten crowns, and upon
his heads the name of blasphemy.
2 [n]And the beast which I saw was like
unto a leopard, [o]and his feet were as *the
feet* of a bear, [p]and his mouth as the mouth
of a lion: and [q]the dragon gave him his
power, [r]and his seat, [s]and great authority.
3 And I saw one of his heads [t]as it were
wounded to death; and his deadly wound
was healed: and [u]all the world wondered
after the beast.
4 And they worshipped the dragon which
gave power unto the beast: and they worshipped the beast, saying, [v]Who *is* like unto
the beast? who is able to make war with
him?
5 And there was given unto him [w]a mouth
speaking great things and blasphemies; and
power was given unto him to continue
[x]forty *and* two months.
6 And he opened his mouth in blasphemy
against God, to blaspheme his name, [y]and
his tabernacle, and them that dwell in
heaven.
7 And it was given unto him [z]to make
war with the saints, and to overcome them:
[a]and power was given him over all kindreds, and tongues, and nations.
8 And all that dwell upon the earth shall
worship him, [b]whose names are not written
in the book of life of the Lamb slain [c]from
the foundation of the world.
9 [d]If any man have an ear, let him hear.
10 [e]He that leadeth into captivity shall
go into captivity: [f]he that killeth with the
sword must be killed with the sword. [g]Here
is the patience and the faith of the saints.
11 And I beheld another beast [h]coming
up out of the earth; and he had two horns
like a lamb, and he spake as a dragon.
12 And he exerciseth all the power of the
first beast before him, and causeth the earth
and them which dwell therein to worship
the first beast, [i]whose deadly wound was
healed.
13 And [j]he doeth great wonders, [k]so
that he maketh fire come down from
heaven on the earth in the sight of men,
14 And [l]deceiveth them that dwell on the
earth [m]by *the means of* those miracles
which he had power to do in the sight of the
beast; saying to them that dwell on the
earth, that they should make an image to
the beast, which had the wound by a sword,
[n]and did live.
15 And he had power to give life unto the
image of the beast, that the image of the
beast should both speak, [o]and cause that as
many as would not worship the image of the
beast should be killed.
16 And he causeth all, both small and
great, rich and poor, free and bond, [p]to receive a mark in their right hand, or in their
foreheads:
17 And that no man might buy or sell,
save he that had the mark, or [q]the name of
the beast, [r]or the number of his name.
18 [s]Here is wisdom. Let him that hath
understanding count [t]the number of the
beast: [u]for it is the number of a man; and
his number *is* Six hundred threescore *and*
six.

14 And I looked, and, lo, [v]a Lamb stood
on the mount Sion, and with him [w]an
hundred forty *and* four thousand, [x]having
his Father's name written in their foreheads.
2 And I heard a voice from heaven, [y]as
the voice of many waters, and as the voice
of a great thunder: and I heard the voice of
[z]harpers harping with their harps:
3 And [a]they sung as it were a new song
before the throne, and before the four
beasts, and the elders: and no man could
learn that song [b]but the hundred *and* forty
and four thousand, which were redeemed
from the earth.
4 These are they which were not defiled
with women; for they are virgins. These are
[c]they [d]which follow the Lamb whithersoever he goeth. These [e]were redeemed from
among men, [f]*being* the firstfruits unto God
and to the Lamb.
5 And [g]in their mouth was found no
guile: for [h]they are without fault before the
throne of God.
6 And I saw another angel [i]fly in the
midst of heaven, [j]having the everlasting
gospel to preach unto them that dwell on
the earth, [k]and to every nation, and kindred, and tongue, and people,
7 Saying with a loud voice, [l]Fear God,
and give glory to him; for the hour of his
judgment is come: [m]and worship him that
made heaven, and earth, and the sea, and
the fountains of waters.
8 And there followed another angel, saying, [n]Babylon is fallen, is fallen, [o]that great
city, because she made all nations drink of
the wine of the wrath of her fornication.
9 And the third angel followed them, saying with a loud voice, [p]If any man worship
the beast and his image, and receive *his*
mark in his forehead, or in his hand,
10 The same [q]shall drink of the wine of
the wrath of God, which is [r]poured out
without mixture into [s]the cup of his indignation; and [t]he shall be tormented with
[u]fire and brimstone in the presence of the
holy angels, and in the presence of the
Lamb:
11 And [v]the smoke of their torment ascendeth up for ever and ever: and they have
no rest day nor night, who worship the
beast and his image, and whosoever receiveth the mark of his name.

12:17 [i]Gen. 3:15; ch. 11:7 [j]ch. 14:13 [k]1 Cor. 2:1; 1 John 5:10; ch. 1:2
13:1 [l]Dan. 7:2 [m]ch. 12:3
13:2 [n]Dan. 7:6 [o]Dan. 7:5 [p]Dan. 7:4 [q]ch. 12:9 [r]ch. 16:10 [s]ch. 12:4
13:3 [t]ver. 12 [u]ch. 17:8
13:4 [v]ch. 18:18
13:5 [w]Dan. 7:8 [x]ch. 11:2
13:6 [y]John 1:14; Col. 2:9
13:7 [z]Dan. 7:21; ch. 11:7 [a]ch. 11:18
13:8 [b]Ex. 32:32; Dan. 12:1; Phil. 4:3; ch. 3:5 [c]ch. 17:8
13:9 [d]ch. 2:7
13:10 [e]Isa. 33:1 [f]Gen. 9:6; Matt. 26:52 [g]ch. 14:12
13:11 [h]ch. 11:7
13:12 [i]ver. 3
13:13 [j]Deut. 13:1; Matt. 24:24; 2 Thess. 2:9; ch. 16:14 [k]1 Kings 18:38; 2 Kings 1:10
13:14 [l]ch. 12:9 [m]2 Thess. 2:9 [n]2 Kings 20:7
13:15 [o]ch. 16:2
13:16 [p]ch. 14:9
13:17 [q]ch. 14:11 [r]ch. 15:2
13:18 [s]ch. 17:9 [t]ch. 15:2 [u]ch. 21:17
14:1 [v]ch. 5:5 [w]ch. 7:4 [x]ch. 7:3
14:2 [y]ch. 1:15 [z]ch. 5:8
14:3 [a]ch. 5:9 [b]ver. 1
14:4 [c]2 Cor. 11:2 [d]ch. 3:4 [e]ch. 5:9 [f]Jam. 1:18
14:5 [g]Ps. 32:2; Zeph. 3:13 [h]Eph. 5:27; Jude 24
14:6 [i]ch. 8:13 [j]Eph. 3:9; Tit. 1:2 [k]ch. 13:7
14:7 [l]ch. 11:18 [m]Neh. 9:6; Ps. 33:6; Acts 14:15
14:8 [n]Isa. 21:9; Jer. 51:8; ch. 18:2 [o]Jer. 51:7; ch. 11:8
14:9 [p]ch. 13:14
14:10 [q]Ps. 75:8; Isa. 51:17; Jer. 25:15 [r]ch. 18:6 [s]ch. 16:19 [t]ch. 20:10 [u]ch. 19:20
14:11 [v]Isa. 34:10; ch. 19:3

12 [w]Here is the patience of the saints: [x]here *are* they that keep the commandments of God, and the faith of Jesus.

13 And I heard a voice from heaven saying unto me, Write, [y]Blessed *are* the dead [z]which die in the Lord from henceforth: Yea, saith the Spirit, [a]that they may rest from their labours; and their works do follow them.

14 And I looked, and behold a white cloud, and upon the cloud *one* sat [b]like unto the Son of man, [c]having on his head a golden crown, and in his hand a sharp sickle.

15 And another angel [d]came out of the temple, crying with a loud voice to him that sat on the cloud, [e]Thrust in thy sickle, and reap: for the time is come for thee to reap; for the harvest [f]of the earth is ripe.

16 And he that sat on the cloud thrust in his sickle on the earth; and the earth was reaped.

17 And another angel came out of the temple which is in heaven, he also having a sharp sickle.

18 And another angel came out from the altar, [g]which had power over fire; and cried with a loud cry to him that had the sharp sickle, saying, [h]Thrust in thy sharp sickle, and gather the clusters of the vine of the earth; for her grapes are fully ripe.

19 And the angel thrust in his sickle into the earth, and gathered the vine of the earth, and cast *it* into [i]the great winepress of the wrath of God.

20 And [j]the winepress was trodden [k]without the city, and blood came out of the winepress, [l]even unto the horse bridles, by the space of a thousand *and* six hundred furlongs.

15 And [m]I saw another sign in heaven, great and marvellous, [n]seven angels having the seven last plagues; [o]for in them is filled up the wrath of God.

2 And I saw as it were [p]a sea of glass [q]mingled with fire: and them that had gotten the victory over the beast, [r]and over his image, and over his mark, *and* over the number of his name, stand on the sea of glass, [s]having the harps of God.

3 And they sing [t]the song of Moses the servant of God, and the song of the Lamb, saying, [u]Great and marvellous *are* thy works, Lord God Almighty; [v]just and true *are* thy ways, thou King of saints.

4 [w]Who shall not fear thee, O Lord, and glorify thy name? for *thou* only *art* holy: for [x]all nations shall come and worship before thee; for thy judgments are made manifest.

5 And after that I looked, and, behold, [y]the temple of the tabernacle of the testimony in heaven was opened:

6 [z]And the seven angels came out of the temple, having the seven plagues, [a]clothed in pure and white linen, and having their breasts girded with golden girdles.

7 [b]And one of the four beasts gave unto the seven angels seven golden vials full of the wrath of God, [c]who liveth for ever and ever.

8 And [d]the temple was filled with smoke [e]from the glory of God, and from his power; and no man was able to enter into the temple, till the seven plagues of the seven angels were fulfilled.

16 And I heard a great voice out of the temple saying [f]to the seven angels, Go your ways, and pour out the vials [g]of the wrath of God upon the earth.

2 And the first went, and poured out his vial [h]upon the earth; and [i]there fell a noisome and grievous sore upon the men [j]which had the mark of the beast, and *upon* them [k]which worshipped his image.

3 And the second angel poured out his vial [l]upon the sea; and [m]it became as the blood of a dead *man:* [n]and every living soul died in the sea.

4 And the third angel poured out his vial [o]upon the rivers and fountains of waters; [p]and they became blood.

5 And I heard the angel of the waters say, [q]Thou art righteous, O Lord, [r]which art, and wast, and shalt be, because thou hast judged thus.

6 For [s]they have shed the blood [t]of saints and prophets, [u]and thou hast given them blood to drink; for they are worthy.

7 And I heard another out of the altar say, Even so, [v]Lord God Almighty, [w]true and righteous *are* thy judgments.

8 And the fourth angel poured out his vial [x]upon the sun; [y]and power was given unto him to scorch men with fire.

9 And men were scorched with great heat, and [z]blasphemed the name of God, which hath power over these plagues: [a]and they repented not [b]to give him glory.

10 And the fifth angel poured out his vial [c]upon the seat of the beast; [d]and his kingdom was full of darkness; [e]and they gnawed their tongues for pain,

11 And [f]blasphemed the God of heaven because of their pains and [g]their sores, [h]and repented not of their deeds.

12 And the sixth angel poured out his vial [i]upon the great river Euphrates; [j]and the water thereof was dried up, [k]that the way of the kings of the east might be prepared.

13 And I saw three unclean [l]spirits like frogs *come* out of the mouth of [m]the dragon, and out of the mouth of the beast, and out of the mouth of [n]the false prophet.

14 [o]For they are the spirits of devils, [p]working miracles, *which* go forth unto the kings of the earth [q]and of the whole world, to gather them to [r]the battle of that great day of God Almighty.

15 [s]Behold, I come as a thief. Blessed *is* he that watcheth, and keepeth his garments, [t]lest he walk naked, and they see his shame.

16 [u]And he gathered them together into a

14:12 [w]ch. 13:10 [x]ch. 12:17
14:13 [y]Eccl. 4:1; ch. 20:6 [z]1 Cor. 15:18; 1 Thess. 4:16 [a]2 Thess. 1:7; Heb. 4:9; ch. 6:11
14:14 [b]Ezek. 1:26; Dan. 7:13; ch. 1:13 [c]ch. 6:2
14:15 [d]ch. 6:17 [e]Joel 3:13; Matt. 13:39 [f]Jer. 51:33; ch. 13:12
14:18 [g]ch. 16:8 [h]Joel 3:13
14:19 [i]ch. 19:15
14:20 [j]Isa. 63:3; Lam. 1:15 [k]ch. 11:8; Heb. 13:12 [l]ch. 19:14
15:1 [m]ch. 12:1 [n]ch. 16:1 [o]ch. 14:10
15:2 [p]ch. 4:6 [q]Matt. 3:11 [r]ch. 13:15 [s]ch. 5:8
15:3 [t]Ex. 15:1; Deut. 31:30; ch. 14:3 [u]Deut. 32:4; Ps. 111:2 [v]Ps. 145:17; Hos. 14:9; ch. 16:7
15:4 [w]Ex. 15:14; Jer. 10:7 [x]Isa. 66:22
15:5 [y]Num. 1:50; ch. 11:19
15:6 [z]ver. 1 [a]Ex. 28:6; Ezek. 44:17; ch. 1:13
15:7 [b]ch. 4:6 [c]1 Thess. 1:9; ch. 4:9
15:8 [d]Ex. 40:34; 1 Kings 8:10; 2 Chron. 5:14; Isa. 6:4 [e]2 Thess. 1:9
16:1 [f]ch. 15:1 [g]ch. 14:10
16:2 [h]ch. 8:7 [i]Ex. 9:9 [j]ch. 13:16 [k]ch. 13:14
16:3 [l]ch. 8:8 [m]Ex. 7:17 [n]ch. 8:9
16:4 [o]ch. 8:10 [p]Ex. 7:20
16:5 [q]ch. 15:3 [r]ch. 1:4
16:6 [s]Matt. 23:34; ch. 3:15 [t]ch. 11:18 [u]Isa. 49:26
16:7 [v]ch. 15:3 [w]ch. 13:10
16:8 [x]ch. 8:12 [y]ch. 9:17
16:9 [z]ver. 11 [a]Dan. 5:22; ch. 9:20 [b]ch. 11:13
16:10 [c]ch. 13:2 [d]ch. 9:2 [e]ch. 11:10
16:11 [f]ver. 9 [g]ver. 2 [h]ver. 9
16:12 [i]ch. 9:14 [j]Jer. 50:38 [k]Isa. 41:2
16:13 [l]1 John 4:1 [m]ch. 12:3 [n]ch. 19:20
16:14 [o]1 Tim. 4:1; Jam. 3:15 [p]2 Thess. 2:9; ch. 13:13 [q]Luke 2:1 [r]ch. 17:14
16:15 [s]Matt. 24:43; 1 Thess. 5:2; 2 Pet. 3:10; ch. 3:3 [t]2 Cor. 5:3; ch. 3:4
16:16 [u]ch. 19:19

place called in the Hebrew tongue Armageddon.
17 And the seventh angel poured out his
vial into the air; and there came a great
voice out of the temple of heaven, from the
throne, saying, [v]It is done.
18 And [w]there were voices, and thunders,
and lightnings; [x]and there was a great
earthquake, [y]such as was not since men
were upon the earth, so mighty an earthquake, *and* so great.
19 And [z]the great city was divided into
three parts, and the cities of the nations fell:
and great Babylon [a]came in remembrance
before God, [b]to give unto her the cup of the
wine of the fierceness of his wrath.
20 And [c]every island fled away, and the
mountains were not found.
21 [d]And there fell upon men a great hail
out of heaven, *every stone* about the weight
of a talent: and [e]men blasphemed God because of [f]the plague of the hail; for the
plague thereof was exceeding great.
17 And there came [g]one of the seven
angels which had the seven vials,
and talked with me, saying unto me, Come
hither; [h]I will shew unto thee the judgment
of [i]the great whore [j]that sitteth upon
many waters:
2 [k]With whom the kings of the earth
have committed fornication, and [l]the inhabitants of the earth have been made
drunk with the wine of her fornication.
3 So he carried me away in the spirit
[m]into the wilderness: and I saw a woman
sit [n]upon a scarlet coloured beast, full of
[o]names of blasphemy, [p]having seven
heads and [q]ten horns.
4 And the woman [r]was arrayed in purple
and scarlet colour, [s]and decked with gold
and precious stones and pearls, [t]having a
golden cup in her hand [u]full of abominations and filthiness of her fornication:
5 And upon her forehead *was* a name
written, [v]MYSTERY, BABYLON [w]THE
GREAT, [x]THE MOTHER OF HARLOTS
AND ABOMINATIONS OF THE EARTH.
6 And I saw [y]the woman drunken [z]with
the blood of the saints, and with the blood of
[a]the martyrs of Jesus: and when I saw her,
I wondered with great admiration.
7 And the angel said unto me, Wherefore
didst thou marvel? I will tell thee the mystery of the woman, and of the beast that
carrieth her, which hath the seven heads
and ten horns.
8 The beast that thou sawest was, and is
not; and [b]shall ascend out of the bottomless
pit, and [c]go into perdition: and they that
dwell on the earth [d]shall wonder, [e]whose
names were not written in the book of life
from the foundation of the world, when
they behold the beast that was, and is not,
and yet is.
9 And [f]here *is* the mind which hath wisdom. [g]The seven heads are seven mountains, on which the woman sitteth.
10 And there are seven kings: five are

16:17 [v]ch. 21:6
16:18 [w]ch. 4:5 [x]ch. 11:13 [y]Dan. 12:1
16:19 [z]ch. 14:8 [a]ch. 18:5 [b]Isa. 51:17; Jer. 25:15; ch. 14:10
16:20 [c]ch. 6:14
16:21 [d]ch. 11:19 [e]ver. 9 [f]Ex. 9:23
17:1 [g]ch. 21:9 [h]ch. 16:19 [i]Nah. 3:4; ch. 19:2 [j]Jer. 51:13; ver. 15
17:2 [k]ch. 18:3 [l]Jer. 51:7; ch. 14:8
17:3 [m]ch. 12:6 [n]ch. 12:3 [o]ch. 13:1 [p]ver. 9 [q]ver. 12
17:4 [r]ch. 18:12 [s]Dan. 11:38 [t]Jer. 51:7; ch. 18:6 [u]ch. 14:8
17:5 [v]2 Thess. 2:7 [w]ch. 11:8 [x]ch. 18:9
17:6 [y]ch. 18:24 [z]ch. 13:15 [a]ch. 6:9
17:8 [b]ch. 11:7 [c]ch. 13:10; ver. 11 [d]ch. 13:3 [e]ch. 13:8
17:9 [f]ch. 13:18 [g]ch. 13:1
17:11 [h]ver. 8
17:12 [i]Dan. 7:20; Zech. 1:18; ch. 13:1
17:14 [j]ch. 16:14 [k]Deut. 10:17; 1 Tim. 6:15; ch. 19:16 [l]Jer. 50:44; ch. 14:4
17:15 [m]Isa. 8:7; ver. 1 [n]ch. 13:7
17:16 [o]Jer. 50:41; ch. 16:12 [p]Ezek. 16:37-44; ch. 18:16 [q]ch. 18:8
17:17 [r]2 Thess. 2:11 [s]ch. 10:7
17:18 [t]ch. 16:19 [u]ch. 12:4
18:1 [v]ch. 17:1 [w]Ezek. 43:2
18:2 [x]Isa. 13:19; Jer. 51:8; ch. 14:8 [y]Isa. 13:21; Jer. 50:39 [z]Isa. 14:23; Mark 5:2
18:3 [a]ch. 14:8 [b]ver. 11; Isa. 47:15
18:4 [c]Isa. 48:20; Jer. 50:8; 2 Cor. 6:17
18:5 [d]Gen. 18:20; Jer. 51:9; Jonah 1:2 [e]ch. 16:19
18:6 [f]Ps. 137:8; Jer. 50:15; 2 Tim. 4:14; ch. 13:10 [g]ch. 14:10 [h]ch. 16:19
18:7 [i]Ezek. 28:2 [j]Isa. 47:7; Zeph. 2:15
18:8 [k]Isa. 47:9; ver. 10 [l]ch. 17:16

fallen, and one is, *and* the other is not yet
come; and when he cometh, he must continue a short space.
11 And the beast that was, and is not,
even he is the eighth, and is of the seven,
and [h]goeth into perdition.
12 And [i]the ten horns which thou sawest
are ten kings, which have received no kingdom as yet; but receive power as kings one
hour with the beast.
13 These have one mind, and shall give
their power and strength unto the beast.
14 [j]These shall make war with the Lamb,
and the Lamb shall overcome them: [k]for he
is Lord of lords, and King of kings: [l]and
they that are with him *are* called, and chosen, and faithful.
15 And he saith unto me, [m]The waters
which thou sawest, where the whore sitteth,
[n]are peoples, and multitudes, and nations,
and tongues.
16 And the ten horns which thou sawest
upon the beast, [o]these shall hate the whore,
and shall make her desolate [p]and naked,
and shall eat her flesh, and [q]burn her with
fire.
17 [r]For God hath put in their hearts to
fulfil his will, and to agree, and give their
kingdom unto the beast, [s]until the words of
God shall be fulfilled.
18 And the woman which thou sawest [t]is
that great city, [u]which reigneth over the
kings of the earth.
18 And [v]after these things I saw another angel come down from heaven,
having great power; [w]and the earth was
lightened with his glory.
2 And he cried mightily with a strong
voice, saying, [x]Babylon the great is fallen,
is fallen, and [y]is become the habitation of
devils, and the hold of every foul spirit, and
[z]a cage of every unclean and hateful bird.
3 For all nations [a]have drunk of the wine
of the wrath of her fornication, and the
kings of the earth have committed fornication with her, [b]and the merchants of the
earth are waxed rich through the abundance of her delicacies.
4 And I heard another voice from heaven,
saying, [c]Come out of her, my people, that
ye be not partakers of her sins, and that ye
receive not of her plagues.
5 [d]For her sins have reached unto
heaven, and [e]God hath remembered her iniquities.
6 [f]Reward her even as she rewarded you,
and double unto her double according to
her works: [g]in the cup which she hath filled
[h]fill to her double.
7 [i]How much she hath glorified herself,
and lived deliciously, so much torment and
sorrow give her: for she saith in her heart,
I sit a [j]queen, and am no widow, and shall
see no sorrow.
8 Therefore shall her plagues come [k]in
one day, death, and mourning, and famine;
and [l]she shall be utterly burned with fire:

[m]for strong *is* the Lord God who judgeth
her.
9 And [n]the kings of the earth, who have
committed fornication and lived deliciously
with her, [o]shall bewail her, and lament for
her, [p]when they shall see the smoke of her
burning,
10 Standing afar off for the fear of her
torment, saying, [q]Alas, alas, that great city
Babylon, that mighty city! [r]for in one hour
is thy judgment come.
11 And [s]the merchants of the earth shall
weep and mourn over her; for no man buyeth their merchandise any more:
12 [t]The merchandise of gold, and silver,
and precious stones, and of pearls, and fine
linen, and purple, and silk, and scarlet, and
all thyine wood, and all manner vessels of
ivory, and all manner vessels of most precious wood, and of brass, and iron, and
marble,
13 And cinnamon, and odours, and ointments, and frankincense, and wine, and oil,
and fine flour, and wheat, and beasts, and
sheep, and horses, and chariots, and slaves,
and [u]souls of men.
14 And the fruits that thy soul lusted after
are departed from thee, and all things
which were dainty and goodly are departed
from thee, and thou shalt find them no more
at all.
15 [v]The merchants of these things, which
were made rich by her, shall stand afar off
for the fear of her torment, weeping and
wailing,
16 And saying, Alas, alas, that great city,
[w]that was clothed in fine linen, and purple,
and scarlet, and decked with gold, and precious stones, and pearls!
17 [x]For in one hour so great riches is
come to nought. And [y]every shipmaster,
and all the company in ships, and sailors,
and as many as trade by sea, stood afar off,
18 [z]And cried when they saw the smoke
of her burning, saying, [a]What *city is* like
unto this great city!
19 And [b]they cast dust on their heads,
and cried, weeping and wailing, saying,
Alas, alas, that great city, wherein were
made rich all that had ships in the sea by
reason of her costliness! [c]for in one hour is
she made desolate.
20 [d]Rejoice over her, *thou* heaven, and
ye holy apostles and prophets; for [e]God
hath avenged you on her.
21 And a mighty angel took up a stone
like a great millstone, and cast *it* into the
sea, saying, [f]Thus with violence shall that
great city Babylon be thrown down, and
[g]shall be found no more at all.
22 [h]And the voice of harpers, and musi-
cians, and of pipers, and trumpeters, shall
be heard no more at all in thee; and no
craftsman, of whatsoever craft *he be,* shall
be found any more in thee; and the sound of
a millstone shall be heard no more at all in
thee;
23 [i]And the light of a candle shall shine
no more at all in thee; [j]and the voice of the
bridegroom and of the bride shall be heard
no more at all in thee: for [k]thy merchants
were the great men of the earth; [l]for by thy
sorceries were all nations deceived.
24 And [m]in her was found the blood of
prophets, and of saints, and of all that
[n]were slain upon the earth.

19 And after these things [o]I heard a
great voice of much people in
heaven, saying, Alleluia; [p]Salvation, and
glory, and honour, and power, unto the
Lord our God:
2 For [q]true and righteous *are* his judgments: for he hath judged the great whore,
which did corrupt the earth with her fornication, and [r]hath avenged the blood of his
servants at her hand.
3 And again they said, Alleluia. And [s]her
smoke rose up for ever and ever.
4 And [t]the four and twenty elders and
the four beasts fell down and worshipped
God that sat on the throne, saying, [u]Amen;
Alleluia.
5 And a voice came out of the throne, saying, [v]Praise our God, all ye his servants,
and ye that fear him, [w]both small and great.
6 [x]And I heard as it were the voice of a
great multitude, and as the voice of many
waters, and as the voice of mighty thunderings, saying, Alleluia: for [y]the Lord God
omnipotent reigneth.
7 Let us be glad and rejoice, and give honour to him: for [z]the marriage of the Lamb
is come, and his wife hath made herself
ready.
8 And [a]to her was granted that she
should be arrayed in fine linen, clean and
white: [b]for the fine linen is the righteousness of saints.
9 And he saith unto me, Write, [c]Blessed
are they which are called unto the marriage
supper of the Lamb. And he saith unto me,
[d]These are the true sayings of God.
10 And [e]I fell at his feet to worship him.
And he said unto me, [f]See *thou do it* not: I
am thy fellowservant, and of thy brethren
[g]that have the testimony of Jesus: worship
God: for the testimony of Jesus is the spirit
of prophecy.
11 [h]And I saw heaven opened, and behold [i]a white horse; and he that sat upon
him *was* called [j]Faithful and True, and [k]in
righteousness he doth judge and make war.
12 [l]His eyes *were* as a flame of fire, [m]and
on his head *were* many crowns; [n]and he
had a name written, that no man knew, but
he himself.
13 [o]And he *was* clothed with a vesture
dipped in blood: and his name is called
[p]The Word of God.
14 [q]And the armies *which were* in
heaven followed him upon white horses,
[r]clothed in fine linen, white and clean.
15 And [s]out of his mouth goeth a sharp
sword, that with it he should smite the nations: and [t]he shall rule them with a rod of

18:8 [m]Jer. 50:34; ch. 11:17
18:9 [n]Ezek. 26:16; ch. 17:2; ver. 3 [o]Jer. 50:46 [p]ver. 18; ch. 19:3
18:10 [q]Isa. 21:9; ch. 14:8 [r]ver. 17
18:11 [s]Ezek. 27:27-36; ver. 3
18:12 [t]ch. 17:4
18:13 [u]Ezek. 27:13
18:15 [v]ver. 3
18:16 [w]ch. 17:4
18:17 [x]ver. 10 [y]Isa. 23:14; Ezek. 27:29
18:18 [z]Ezek. 27:30; ver. 9 [a]ch. 13:4
18:19 [b]Josh. 7:6; 1 Sam. 4:12; Job 2:12; Ezek. 27:30 [c]ver. 8
18:20 [d]Isa. 44:23; Jer. 51:48 [e]Luke 11:49; ch. 19:2
18:21 [f]Jer. 51:64 [g]ch. 12:8
18:22 [h]Isa. 24:8; Jer. 7:34; Ezek. 26:13
18:23 [i]Jer. 25:10 [j]Jer. 7:34 [k]Isa. 23:8 [l]2 Kings 9:22; Nah. 3:4; ch. 17:2
18:24 [m]ch. 17:6 [n]Jer. 51:49
19:1 [o]ch. 11:15 [p]ch. 4:11
19:2 [q]ch. 15:3 [r]Deut. 32:43; ch. 6:10
19:3 [s]Isa. 34:10; ch. 14:11
19:4 [t]ch. 4:4 [u]1 Chron. 16:36; Neh. 5:13; ch. 5:14
19:5 [v]Ps. 134:1 [w]ch. 11:18
19:6 [x]Ezek. 1:24; ch. 14:2 [y]ch. 11:15
19:7 [z]Matt. 22:2; 2 Cor. 11:2; Eph. 5:32; ch. 21:2
19:8 [a]Ps. 45:13; Ezek. 16:10; ch. 3:18 [b]Ps. 132:9
19:9 [c]Matt. 22:2; Luke 14:15 [d]ch. 21:5
19:10 [e]ch. 22:8 [f]Acts 10:26; ch. 22:9 [g]1 John 5:10; ch. 12:17
19:11 [h]ch. 15:5 [i]ch. 6:2 [j]ch. 3:14 [k]Isa. 11:4
19:12 [l]ch. 1:14 [m]ch. 6:2 [n]ch. 2:17; ver. 16
19:13 [o]Isa. 63:2 [p]John 1:1; 1 John 5:7
19:14 [q]ch. 14:20 [r]Matt. 28:3; ch. 4:4
19:15 [s]Isa. 11:4; 2 Thess. 2:8; ch. 1:16; ver. 27 [t]Ps. 2; ch. 2:27

iron: and [u]he treadeth the winepress of the
fierceness and wrath of Almighty God.
16 And [v]he hath on *his* vesture and on his
thigh a name written, [w]KING OF KINGS,
AND LORD OF LORDS.
17 And I saw an angel standing in the sun;
and he cried with a loud voice, saying [x]to
all the fowls that fly in the midst of heaven,
[y]Come and gather yourselves together
unto the supper of the great God;
18 [z]That ye may eat the flesh of kings,
and the flesh of captains, and the flesh of
mighty men, and the flesh of horses, and of
them that sit on them, and the flesh of all
men, both free and bond, both small and
great.
19 [a]And I saw the beast, and the kings of
the earth, and their armies, gathered together to make war against him that sat on
the horse, and against his army.
20 [b]And the beast was taken, and with
him the false prophet that wrought miracles
before him, with which he deceived them
that had received the mark of the beast, and
[c]them that worshipped his image. [d]These
both were cast alive into a lake of fire
[e]burning with brimstone.
21 And the remnant [f]were slain with the
sword of him that sat upon the horse, which
sword proceeded out of his mouth: [g]and all
the fowls [h]were filled with their flesh.

20
And I saw an angel come down from
heaven, [i]having the key of the bottomless pit and a great chain in his hand.
2 And he laid hold on [j]the dragon, that
old serpent, which is the Devil, and Satan,
and bound him a thousand years,
3 And cast him into the bottomless pit,
and shut him up, and [k]set a seal upon him,
[l]that he should deceive the nations no
more, till the thousand years should be fulfilled: and after that he must be loosed a
little season.
4 And I saw [m]thrones, and they sat upon
them, and [n]judgment was given unto them:
and *I saw* [o]the souls of them that were beheaded for the witness of Jesus, and for the
word of God, and [p]which had not worshipped the beast, [q]neither his image, neither had received *his* mark upon their
foreheads, or in their hands; and they lived
and [r]reigned with Christ a thousand years.
5 But the rest of the dead lived not again
until the thousand years were finished. This
is the first resurrection.
6 Blessed and holy *is* he that hath part in
the first resurrection: on such [s]the second
death hath no power, but they shall be
[t]priests of God and of Christ, [u]and shall
reign with him a thousand years.
7 And when the thousand years are expired, [v]Satan shall be loosed out of his
prison,
8 And shall go out [w]to deceive the nations
which are in the four quarters of the earth,
[x]Gog and Magog, [y]to gather them together
to battle: the number of whom *is* as the sand
of the sea.
9 [z]And they went up on the breadth of
the earth, and compassed the camp of the
saints about, and the beloved city: and fire
came down from God out of heaven, and
devoured them.
10 [a]And the devil that deceived them was
cast into the lake of fire and brimstone,
[b]where the beast and the false prophet *are*,
and [c]shall be tormented day and night for
ever and ever.
11 And I saw a great white throne, and
him that sat on it, from whose face [d]the
earth and the heaven fled away; [e]and there
was found no place for them.
12 And I saw the dead, [f]small and great,
stand before God; [g]and the books were
opened: and another [h]book was opened,
which is *the book* of life: and the dead were
judged out of those things which were written in the books, [i]according to their works.
13 And the sea gave up the dead which
were in it; and [j]death and hell delivered up
the dead which were in them: [k]and they
were judged every man according to their
works.
14 And [l]death and hell were cast into the
lake of fire. [m]This is the second death.
15 And whosoever was not found written
in the book of life [n]was cast into the lake of
fire.

21
And [o]I saw a new heaven and a new
earth: [p]for the first heaven and the
first earth were passed away; and there was
no more sea.
2 And I John saw [q]the holy city, new Jerusalem, coming down from God out of
heaven, prepared [r]as a bride adorned for
her husband.
3 And I heard a great voice out of heaven
saying, Behold, [s]the tabernacle of God *is*
with men, and he will dwell with them, and
they shall be his people, and God himself
shall be with them, *and be* their God.
4 [t]And God shall wipe away all tears
from their eyes; [u]and there shall be no
more death, [v]neither sorrow, nor crying,
neither shall there be any more pain: for the
former things are passed away.
5 And [w]he that sat upon the throne said,
[x]Behold, I make all things new. And he said
unto me, Write: for [y]these words are true
and faithful.
6 And he said unto me, [z]It is done. [a]I am
Alpha and Omega, the beginning and the
end. [b]I will give unto him that is athirst of
the fountain of the water of life freely.
7 He that overcometh shall inherit all
things; and [c]I will be his God, and he shall
be my son.
8 [d]But the fearful, and unbelieving, and
the abominable, and murderers, and whoremongers, and sorcerers, and idolaters, and
all liars, shall have their part in [e]the lake
which burneth with fire and brimstone:
which is the second death.
9 And there came unto me one of [f]the

19:15 [u]Isa. 63:3; ch. 14:19
19:16 [v]ver. 12 [w]Dan. 2:47; 1 Tim. 6:15; ch. 17:14
19:17 [x]ver. 21 [y]Ezek. 39:17
19:18 [z]Ezek. 39:18
19:19 [a]ch. 16:16
19:20 [b]ch. 16:13 [c]ch. 13:12 [d]Dan. 7:11; ch. 20:10 [e]ch. 14:10
19:21 [f]ver. 15 [g]ver. 17 [h]ch. 17:16
20:1 [i]ch. 1:18
20:2 [j]2 Pet. 2:4; Jude 6; ch. 12:9
20:3 [k]Dan. 6:17 [l]ch. 16:14; ver. 8
20:4 [m]Dan. 7:9; Matt. 19:28; Luke 22:30 [n]1 Cor. 6:2 [o]ch. 6:9 [p]ch. 13:12 [q]ch. 13:15 [r]Rom. 8:17; 2 Tim. 2:12; ch. 5:10
20:6 [s]ch. 2:11 [t]Isa. 61:6; 1 Pet. 2:9; ch. 1:6 [u]ver. 4
20:7 [v]ver. 2
20:8 [w]ver. 3 [x]Ezek. 38:2 [y]ch. 16:14
20:9 [z]Isa. 8:8; Ezek. 38:9
20:10 [a]ver. 8 [b]ch. 19:20 [c]ch. 14:10
20:11 [d]2 Pet. 3:7; ch. 21:1 [e]Dan. 2:35
20:12 [f]ch. 19:5 [g]Dan. 7:10 [h]Ps. 69:28; Dan. 12:1; Phil. 4:3; ch. 3:5 [i]Jer. 17:10; Matt. 16:27; Rom. 2:6; ch. 2:23; ver. 13
20:13 [j]ch. 6:8 [k]ver. 12
20:14 [l]1 Cor. 15:26 [m]ver. 6; ch. 21:8
20:15 [n]ch. 19:20
21:1 [o]Isa. 65:17; 2 Pet. 3:13 [p]ch. 20:11
21:2 [q]Isa. 52:1; Gal. 4:26; Heb. 11:10; ch. 3:12; ver. 10 [r]Isa. 54:5; 2 Cor. 11:2
21:3 [s]Lev. 26:11; Ezek. 43:7; 2 Cor. 6:16; ch. 7:15
21:4 [t]Isa. 25:8; ch. 7:17 [u]1 Cor. 15:26; ch. 20:14 [v]Isa. 35:10
21:5 [w]ch. 4:2 [x]Isa. 43:19; 2 Cor. 5:17 [y]ch. 19:9
21:6 [z]ch. 16:17 [a]ch. 1:8 [b]Isa. 12:3; John 4:10; ch. 22:17
21:7 [c]Zech. 8:8; Heb. 8:10
21:8 [d]1 Cor. 6:9; Gal. 5:19; Eph. 5:5; 1 Tim. 1:9; Heb. 12:14; ch. 22:15 [e]ch. 20:14
21:9 [f]ch. 15:1

seven angels which had the seven vials full of the seven last plagues, and talked with me, saying, Come hither, I will shew thee [g]the bride, the Lamb's wife.

10 And he carried me away [h]in the spirit to a great and high mountain, and shewed me [i]that great city, the holy Jerusalem, descending out of heaven from God,

11 [j]Having the glory of God: and her light *was* like unto a stone most precious, even like a jasper stone, clear as crystal;

12 And had a wall great and high, *and* had [k]twelve gates, and at the gates twelve angels, and names written thereon, which are *the names* of the twelve tribes of the children of Israel:

13 [l]On the east three gates; on the north three gates; on the south three gates; and on the west three gates.

14 And the wall of the city had twelve foundations, and [m]in them the names of the twelve apostles of the Lamb.

15 And he that talked with me [n]had a golden reed to measure the city, and the gates thereof, and the wall thereof.

16 And the city lieth foursquare, and the length is as large as the breadth: and he measured the city with the reed, twelve thousand furlongs. The length and the breadth and the height of it are equal.

17 And he measured the wall thereof, an hundred *and* forty *and* four cubits, *according to* the measure of a man, that is, of the angel.

18 And the building of the wall of it was *of* jasper: and the city *was* pure gold, like unto clear glass.

19 [o]And the foundations of the wall of the city *were* garnished with all manner of precious stones. The first foundation *was* jasper; the second, sapphire; the third, a chalcedony; the fourth, an emerald;

20 The fifth, sardonyx; the sixth, sardius; the seventh, chrysolyte; the eighth, beryl; the ninth, a topaz; the tenth, a chrysoprasus; the eleventh, a jacinth; the twelfth, an amethyst.

21 And the twelve gates *were* twelve pearls; every several gate was of one pearl: [p]and the street of the city *was* pure gold, as it were transparent glass.

22 [q]And I saw no temple therein: for the Lord God Almighty and the Lamb are the temple of it.

23 [r]And the city had no need of the sun, neither of the moon, to shine in it: for the glory of God did lighten it, and the Lamb *is* the light thereof.

24 [s]And the nations of them which are saved shall walk in the light of it: and the kings of the earth do bring their glory and honour into it.

25 [t]And the gates of it shall not be shut at all by day: for [u]there shall be no night there.

26 [v]And they shall bring the glory and honour of the nations into it.

27 And [w]there shall in no wise enter into it any thing that defileth, neither *whatsoever* worketh abomination, or *maketh* a lie: but they which are written in the Lamb's [x]book of life.

22 And he shewed me [y]a pure river of water of life, clear as crystal, proceeding out of the throne of God and of the Lamb.

2 [z]In the midst of the street of it, and on either side of the river, *was there* [a]the tree of life, which bare twelve *manner of* fruits, *and* yielded her fruit every month: and the leaves of the tree *were* [b]for the healing of the nations.

3 And [c]there shall be no more curse: [d]but the throne of God and of the Lamb shall be in it; and his servants shall serve him:

4 And [e]they shall see his face; and [f]his name *shall be* in their foreheads.

5 [g]And there shall be no night there; and they need no candle, neither light of the sun; for [h]the Lord God giveth them light: [i]and they shall reign for ever and ever.

6 And he said unto me, [j]These sayings *are* faithful and true: and the Lord God of the holy prophets [k]sent his angel to shew unto his servants the things which must shortly be done.

7 [l]Behold, I come quickly: [m]blessed *is* he that keepeth the sayings of the prophecy of this book.

8 And I John saw these things, and heard *them.* And when I had heard and seen, [n]I fell down to worship before the feet of the angel which shewed me these things.

9 Then saith he unto me, [o]See *thou do it* not: for I am thy fellowservant, and of thy brethren the prophets, and of them which keep the sayings of this book: worship God.

10 [p]And he saith unto me, Seal not the sayings of the prophecy of this book: [q]for the time is at hand.

11 [r]He that is unjust, let him be unjust still: and he which is filthy, let him be filthy still: and he that is righteous, let him be righteous still: and he that is holy, let him be holy still.

12 [s]And, behold, I come quickly; and [t]my reward *is* with me, [u]to give every man according as his work shall be.

13 [v]I am Alpha and Omega, the beginning and the end, the first and the last.

14 [w]Blessed *are* they that do his commandments, that they may have right [x]to the tree of life, [y]and may enter in through the gates into the city.

15 For [z]without *are* [a]dogs, and sorcerers, and whoremongers, and murderers, and idolaters, and whosoever loveth and maketh a lie.

16 [b]I Jesus have sent mine angel to testify unto you these things in the churches. [c]I am the root and the offspring of David, *and* [d]the bright and morning star.

17 And the Spirit and [e]the bride say, Come. [f]And let him that heareth say, Come. And let him that is athirst come. And

21:9 [g]ch. 19:7; ver. 2
21:10 [h]ch. 1:10 [i]Ezek. 48; ver. 2
21:11 [j]ch. 22:5; ver. 23
21:12 [k]Ezek. 48:31-34
21:13 [l]Ezek. 48:31-34
21:14 [m]Matt. 16:18; Gal. 2:9; Eph. 2:20
21:15 [n]Ezek. 40:3; Zech. 2:1; ch. 11:1
21:19 [o]Isa. 54:11
21:21 [p]ch. 22:2
21:22 [q]John 4:23
21:23 [r]Isa. 24:23; ch. 22:5; ver. 11
21:24 [s]Isa. 60:3
21:25 [t]Isa. 60:11 [u]Isa. 60:20; Zech. 14:7; ch. 22:5
21:26 [v]ver. 24
21:27 [w]Isa. 35:8; Joel 3:17; ch. 22:14 [x]Phil. 4:3; ch. 3:5
22:1 [y]Ezek. 47:1; Zech. 14:8
22:2 [z]Ezek. 47:12; ch. 21:21 [a]Gen. 2:9; ch. 2:7 [b]ch. 21:24
22:3 [c]Zech. 14:11 [d]Ezek. 48:35
22:4 [e]Matt. 5:8; 1 Cor. 13:12; 1 John 3:2 [f]ch. 3:12
22:5 [g]ch. 21:23 [h]Ps. 36:9 [i]Dan. 7:27; Rom. 5:17; 2 Tim. 2:12; ch. 3:21
22:6 [j]ch. 19:9 [k]ch. 1:1
22:7 [l]ch. 3:11; ver. 10 [m]ch. 1:3
22:8 [n]ch. 19:10
22:9 [o]ch. 19:10
22:10 [p]Dan. 8:26; ch. 10:4 [q]ch. 1:3
22:11 [r]Ezek. 3:27; Dan. 12:10; 2 Tim. 3:13
22:12 [s]ver. 7 [t]Isa. 40:10 [u]Rom. 2:6; ch. 20:12
22:13 [v]Isa. 41:4; ch. 1:8
22:14 [w]Dan. 12:12; 1 John 3:24 [x]ver. 2; ch. 2:7 [y]ch. 21:27
22:15 [z]1 Cor. 6:9; Gal. 5:19; Col. 3:6; ch. 9:20 [a]Phil. 3:2
22:16 [b]ch. 1:1 [c]ch. 5:5 [d]Num. 24:17; Zech. 6:12; 2 Pet. 1:19; ch. 2:28
22:17 [e]ch. 21:2 [f]Isa. 55:1; John 7:37; ch. 21:6

whosoever will, let him take the water of
life freely.
18 For I testify unto every man that heareth the words of the prophecy of this book,
[g]If any man shall add unto these things,
God shall add unto him the plagues that are
written in this book:
19 And if any man shall take away from
the words of the book of this prophecy,
[h]God shall take away his part out of the
book of life, and out of [i]the holy city, and
from the things which are written in this
book.
20 He which testifieth these things saith,
[j]Surely I come quickly. [k]Amen. [l]Even so,
come, Lord Jesus.
21 [m]The grace of our Lord Jesus Christ *be*
with you all. Amen.

22:18 [g]Deut. 4:2; Prov. 30:6
22:19 [h]Ex. 32:33; Ps. 69:28; ch. 3:5 [i]ch. 21:2
22:20 [j]ver. 12 [k]John 21:25 [l]2 Tim. 4:8
22:21 [m]Rom. 16:20; 2 Thess. 3:18

CONCORDANCE

A

ABASE, *make low, humble.*
every one proud *a.* Job 40:11
exalt shall be *a.* Matt. 23:12
how to be *a.* Phil. 4:12

ABHOR, *hate extremely.*
Lord will *a.* bloody Ps. 5:6
I hate and *a.* lying 119:163
nations shall *a.* Prov. 24:24
that *a.* judgment Mic. 3:9
a. that which is evil Rom. 12:9

ABIDE, *continue, bear, await.*
a. ye every man Ex. 16:29
Lord who shall *a.* Ps. 15:1
a. in me John 15:4
any man's work *a.* 1 Cor. 3:14
to *a.* in the flesh Phil. 1:24
little children, *a.*
in him 1 John 2:28

ABIDETH, *continue, bear.*
established earth, it *a.* Ps. 119:90
wrath of God *a.* John 3:36
now *a.* faith 1 Cor. 13:13
whosoever *a.* in him 1 John 3:6

ABIDING, *continuing, bearing.*
shepherds *a.* in field Luke 2:8
have not his word *a.* John 5:38

ABLE, *fit, qualified, talented.*
who is *a.* to judge 1 Kings 3:9
who is *a.* to stand Prov. 27:4
are ye *a.* to drink cup Matt. 20:22
tempted above ye
are *a.* 1 Cor. 10:13
a. to do exceeding Eph. 3:20
a. to subdue all Phil. 3:21
is *a.* to keep that 2 Tim. 1:12
a. to keep you from Jude 24

ABOMINABLE, *very hateful.*
touch any *a.* thing Lev. 7:21
have done *a.* works Ps. 14:1
walked in *a.* idolatries 1 Pet. 4:3

ABOMINATION, *detestable thing.*
wickedness is an *a.* Prov. 8:7
false balance is *a.* 11:1
sacrifice of wicked *a.* 15:8
proud in heart is *a.* 16:5
see *a.* of desolation Matt. 24:15
a. in sight of God Luke 16:15
a. of the earth Rev. 17:5

ABOUND, *have plenty.*
iniquity shall *a.* Matt. 24:12
ye may *a.* in hope Rom. 15:13
always *a.* in work 1 Cor. 15:58
a. in love one 1 Thess. 3:12
charity toward
each *a.* 2 Thess. 1:3

ABOVE, *higher, heaven.*
sent from *a.* Ps. 18:16
servant *a.* his lord Matt. 10:24
cometh from *a.* is *a.* all John 3:31
God who is *a.* all Eph. 4:6
seek things which are *a.* Col. 3:1

ABSTAIN, *hold off from.*
a. from fornication 1 Thess. 4:3
a. from appearance of 5:22
a. from fleshly lusts 1 Pet. 2:11

ABUNDANCE, *great quantity.*
trusted in *a.* of Ps. 52:7
loveth *a.* with increase Eccl. 5:10
life consisteth not
in *a.* Luke 12:15
a. of their joy 2 Cor. 8:2
rich through *a.* Rev. 18:3

ABUNDANT, *ample, plentiful.*
God *a.* in goodness Ex. 34:6
grace of Lord *a.* 1 Tim. 1:14
according to his *a.* 1 Pet. 1:3

ABUNDANTLY, *fully.*
God will *a.* pardon Isa. 55:7
have it more *a.* John 10:10
able do exceeding *a.* Eph. 3:20
willing more *a.* to Heb. 6:17

ACCEPT, *receive kindly.*
thy God *a.* thee 2 Sam. 24:23
him will I *a.* Job 42:8
no prophet *a.* in his Luke 4:24
now is the *a.* time 2 Cor. 6:2

ACCEPTABLE, *well-pleasing.*
shall not be *a.* Lev. 22:20
prayer in an *a.* time Ps. 69:13
a. year of the Lord Isa. 61:2
preach the *a.* year Luke 4:19
holy, *a.* unto God Rom. 12:1
sacrifice *a.* to God Phil. 4:18

ACKNOWLEDGE, *own, confess.*
a. my transgressions Ps. 51:3
all thy ways *a.* him Prov. 3:6
a. thine iniquity Jer. 3:13
let him *a.* that the 1 Cor. 14:37
a. ye them that are such 16:18
what ye read or *a.* 2 Cor. 1:13

ADD, *increase.*
peace shall they *a.* Prov. 3:2
can *a.* one cubit Matt. 6:27
shall be *a.* unto you 6:33
no man *a.* thereto Gal. 3:15
a. affliction to my Phil. 1:16
a. to your faith 2 Pet. 1:5
shall *a.* unto these Rev. 22:18

ADOPTION, *acceptance.*
received Spirit of *a.* Rom. 8:15
waiting for the *a.* 8:23
to whom pertaineth the *a.* 9:4
we receive *a.* of sons Gal. 4:5
predestinated unto *a.* Eph. 1:5

ADULTERER, *unchaste person.*
a. surely put to Lev. 20:10
idolaters, nor *a.* 1 Cor. 6:9
a. God will judge Heb. 13:4
ye *a.* know ye not Jam. 4:4

ADULTERY, *unchaste living.*
not commit *a.* Ex. 20:14
they committed *a.* Ezek. 23:37
committed *a.* in heart Matt. 5:28
dost thou commit *a.* Rom. 2:22
commit no *a.* yet kill Jam. 2:11

ADVERSARY, *antagonist.*
how long shall the *a.* Ps. 74:10
who is mine *a.* Isa. 50:8
shall devour the *a.* Heb. 10:27
your *a.* the devil 1 Pet. 5:8

ADVOCATE, *one interceding.*
a. with the Father 1 John 2:1

AFFECTION, *feeling, passion.*
them unto vile *a.* Rom. 1:26
without natural *a.* 1:31
set your *a.* on things Col. 3:2

AFFLICT, *grieve, trouble.*
they *a.* the just Am. 5:12
they shall *a.* you 6:14
will *a.* thee no more Nah. 1:12

AFFLICTED, *grieved, troubled.*
smitten of God and *a.* Isa. 53:4
a. yet opened not mouth 53:7
whether we be *a.* 2 Cor. 1:6
have relieved the *a.* 1 Tim. 5:10
is any among you *a.* Jam. 5:13

AFFLICTION, *adversity, sorrow.*
have seen the *a.* of my Ex. 3:7
looked upon their *a.* 4:31
look upon mine *a.* Ps. 25:18
perished in mine *a.* 119:92
consider mine *a.* 119:153
comforted in our *a.* 1 Thess. 3:7
partaker of *a.* 2 Tim. 1:8
all things, endure *a.* 4:5
choosing to suffer *a.* Heb. 11:25

AFRAID, *fearful, timid.*
none make you *a.* Lev. 26:6
trust and not be *a.* Isa. 12:2
it is I; be not *a.* Matt. 14:27
not *a.* of them that kill Luke 12:4
neither let it be *a.* John 14:27

AGREE, *approve, give consent.*
except they *a.* Am. 3:3
two of you shall *a.* Matt. 18:19
these three *a.* in one 1 John 5:8

AGREEMENT, *mutual consent.*
with hell are at *a.* Isa. 28:15
what *a.* hath temple 2 Cor. 6:16

ALIVE, *to live, be active.*
Noah only *a.* Gen. 7:23
I kill I make *a.* Deut. 32:39
shewed himself *a.* Acts 1:3
Jesus, Paul affirmed *a.* 25:19
a. through Christ Rom. 6:11
in Christ all made *a.* 1 Cor. 15:22
we which are *a.* 1 Thess. 4:15
a. for evermore Rev. 1:18
was dead is *a.* 2:8
a. into lake of fire 19:20

ALMIGHTY, *all-powerful.*
I am the *A.* God Gen. 17:1
I am God *A.* be 35:11
A. scattered kings Ps. 68:14
shadow of the *A.* 91:1
holy Lord God *A.* Rev. 4:8
God *A.* which wast 11:17
even so Lord God *A.* 16:7
wrath of *A.* God 19:15
God *A.* and Lamb 21:22

ALTAR, *place of sacrifice.*
Noah builded an *a.* Gen. 8:20
compass thine *a.* Ps. 26:6
an *a.* to the Lord Isa. 19:19

partakers with *a.* 1 Cor. 9:13
prayers upon golden *a.* Rev. 8:3

ANCHOR, *that which holds fast.*
would have cast *a.* Acts 27:30
hope as an *a.* of the Heb. 6:19

ANGEL, *heavenly messenger.*
Little lower than *a.* Ps. 8:5
a. of Lord encampeth 34:7
man did eat *a.* food 78:25
a. shut lions' mouths Dan. 6:22
a. of Lord in dream Matt. 1:20
legions of *a.* 26:53
a. rolled back stone 28:2
tongues of men and of *a.* 1 Cor. 13:1
little lower than the *a.* Heb. 2:7
entertained *a.* unawares 13:2
God spared not *a.* 2 Pet. 2:4

ANOINT, *pour upon.*
shalt *a.* them and Ex. 28:41
a. the most Holy Dan. 9:24
come to *a.* my body Mark 14:8
spices that might *a.* 16:1
a. thine eyes with Rev. 3:18

ANOINTED, *consecrated.*
Lord saveth his *a.* Ps. 20:6
touch not mine *a.* 105:15

ANTI-CHRIST, *opponent of Christ.*
heard that *a.* shall 1 John 2:18
he is *a.* that denieth 2:22
this is that spirit of *a.* 4:3
a deceiver and an *a.* 2 John 7

APOSTLE, *one sent forth.*
names of twelve *a.* Matt. 10:2
twelve named *a.* Luke 6:13
signs done by *a.* Acts 2:43
Paul called to be *a.* Rom. 1:1
signs of an *a.* 2 Cor. 12:12
foundation of *a.* Eph. 2:20

APPOINT, *assign, allot.*
a. place for people 2 Sam. 7:10
salvation will God *a.* Isa. 26:1
a. him his portion Matt. 24:51

APPOINTED, *allotted.*
a. his bounds Job 14:5
those *a.* to die Ps. 79:11
did as Jesus *a.* Matt. 26:19
not *a.* us to wrath 1 Thess. 5:9
hath *a.* heir of all Heb. 1:2
faithful to him that *a.* 3:2
a. once to die 9:27

ARISE, *to stand up, to ascend.*
a., O Lord; save Ps. 3:7
a. for our help 44:26
a. false Christs Matt. 24:24
I will *a.* and go Luke 15:18
a. from the dead Eph. 5:14

ARMOUR, *protective covering, garment.*
a. of righteousness 2 Cor. 6:7
whole *a.* of God Eph. 6:11

ASCEND, *to go up, climb.*
I will *a.* into heaven Isa. 14:13
no man hath *a.* John 3:13
I *a.* unto my Father 20:17

ASHAMED, *abashed, confused.*
and were not *a.* Gen. 2:25
whosoever *a.* of me Mark 8:38
not *a.* of gospel Rom. 1:16
I am not *a.* 2 Cor. 7:14
am not *a.* for 2 Tim. 1:12
not *a.* at coming 1 John 2:28

ASK, *inquire, seek counsel.*
God said, *a.* what 1 Kings 3:5
before ye *a.* Matt. 6:8
a. and it shall be given 7:7
know not what ye *a.* 20:22
whatsoever ye *a.* in John 14:13
if abide in me, *a.* 15:7
lack wisdom let him *a.* Jam. 1:5
because ye *a.* not 4:2
whatsoever we *a.* 1 John 3:22
if *a.* according to his 5:14

ASSURANCE, *full conviction.*
a. of understanding Col. 2:2
gospel in much *a.* 1 Thess. 1:5
full *a.* of hope unto Heb. 6:11
true heart in full *a.* 10:22

ATONEMENT, *reconciliation.*
make an *a.* for Lev. 16:11
day of *a.* to make an *a.* 23:28
have now received *a.* Rom. 5:11

AUTHORITY, *right to govern.*
as one having *a.* Matt. 7:29
gave power and *a.* Luke 9:1
for all that are in *a.* 1 Tim. 2:2
woman to usurp *a.* 2:12
dragon gave him *a.* Rev. 13:2

AWAKE, *be roused from sleep.*
when I *a.* with thy Ps. 17:15
when I *a.* I am still 139:18
high time to *a.* Rom. 13:11
a. to righteousness 1 Cor. 15:34
a. thou that sleepest Eph. 5:14

B

BACKSLIDING, *turning to sin.*
b. in heart shall be Prov. 14:14
my people are bent to *b.* Hos. 11:7
I will heal their *b.* 14:4

BAPTISM, *Christian ordinance.*
b. of repentance for Luke 3:3
with the *b.* of John Luke 7:29
John baptized with *b.* of Acts 19:4
buried with him by *b.* Rom. 6:4
one Lord, faith, *b.* Eph. 4:5

BAPTIZE, *perform baptism.*
b. you with water Matt. 3:11
b. with Holy Ghost Luke 3:16
I *b.* with water John 1:26

BAPTIZED, *submission to baptism.*
Jesus unto John to be *b.* Matt. 3:13
be *b.* with Holy Ghost Acts 1:5
repent and be *b.* 2:38
b. into Jesus Christ Rom. 6:3
by one Spirit are all *b.* 1 Cor. 12:13

BAPTIZING, *act of baptism.*
all nations *b.* them Matt. 28:19

BEAR, *carry, endure, yield.*
greater than can *b.* Gen. 4:13
shall *b.* thee up in Ps. 91:12
not worthy to *b.* Matt. 3:11
compelled to *b.* cross Matt. 27:32
cannot *b.* them now John 16:12
be able to *b.* it 1 Cor. 10:13
b. ye one another's Gal. 6:2

BEGINNING, *commencement.*
in *b.* God created Gen. 1:1
fear of Lord the *b.* Ps. 111:10
in the *b.* was Word John 1:1
in the *b.* with God 1:2
b. and the ending Rev. 1:8

BEGOTTEN, *generated.*
this day have I *b.* Ps. 2:7
only *b.* of Father John 1:14
offered only *b.* son Heb. 11:17
sent his only *b.* Son 1 John 4:9

BELIEVE, *trust, rely on, accept.*
they will not *b.* Ex. 4:1
b. in the Lord 2 Chron. 20:20
ye may know and *b.* Isa. 43:10
all through him *b.* John 1:7
b. on him whom he sent 6:29
dost thou *b.* on Son 9:35
light *b.* in light 12:36
b. in thine heart that Rom. 10:9
those that *b.* 1 Tim. 4:10
b. to saving of soul Heb. 10:39
devils also *b.* and Jam. 2:19
b. on his Son Jesus 1 John 3:23
b. not every spirit 4:1

BELIEVED, *trusted, accepted.*
b. thy commandments Ps. 119:66
who hath *b.* report Isa. 53:1
know whom I have *b.* 2 Tim. 1:12
we which have *b.* Heb. 4:3
b. the love that God 1 John 4:16
destroyed that *b.* not Jude 5

BELIEVEST, *trust, accept.*
b. not I am in Father John 14:10
b. there is one God Jam. 2:19

BELIEVETH, *trust, accept.*
b. shall be saved Mark 16:16
b. should not perish John 3:15
b. on him hath life 5:24
b. on me never thirst 6:35
b. on me the works I do 14:12
b. all things 1 Cor. 13:7
b. Jesus is Christ 1 John 5:1

BELIEVING, *trusting, accepting.*
b. ye shall Matt. 21:22
and peace in *b.* Rom. 15:13
yet *b.* ye rejoice 1 Pet. 1:8

BETRAYED, *to disclose, deliver.*
Judas who *b.* him Matt. 10:4
son of man shall be *b.* 17:22
shall be *b.* by Luke 21:16
Judas which *b.* him John 18:2
night he was *b.* 1 Cor. 11:23

BETTER, *preferable.*
b. little with fear Prov. 15:16
good name *b.* than Eccl. 7:1
b. for me to die 1 Cor. 9:15
with Christ is far *b.* Phil. 1:23
made so much *b.* Heb. 1:4

BETWEEN, *in middle.*
enmity *b.* thy seed Gen. 3:15
no difference *b.* Jew Rom. 10:12
mediator *b.* God and 1 Tim. 2:5

BEWARE, *take heed, guard.*
b. lest thou forget Lord Deut. 6:12

b. of scribes Mark 12:38
b. of covetousness Luke 12:15
b. lest ye also 2 Pet. 3:17

BIRTH, *coming into world.*
b. of Jesus Christ Matt. 1:18
many rejoice at his *b.* Luke 1:14
blind from his *b.* John 9:1

BLASPHEME, *speak evil of God.*
thou didst *b.* God 1 Kings 21:10
b. Holy Ghost Mark 3:29
b. his name and his Rev. 13:6

BLASPHEMY, *irreverent words.*
b. shall be forgiven Matt. 12:31
put off malice, *b.* Col. 3:8

BLESS, *make happy, praise.*
b. them that *b.* Gen. 12:3
whom Lord shall *b.* Isa. 19:25
b. which persecute Rom. 12:14

BLESSED, *happy, praised.*
b. are the poor in Matt. 5:3
b. they that mourn 5:4
b. are the meek 5:5
b. are they which hunger 5:6
b. ye when men revile 5:11
more *b.* to give Acts 20:35
that *b.* hope Tit. 2:13

BLESSING, *divine favor.*
thou shalt be a *b.* Gen. 12:2
receive the *b.* from Ps. 24:5
fulness of the *b.* Rom. 15:29
cup of *b.* which 1 Cor. 10:16
b. of Abraham come Gal. 3:14
us with spiritual *b.* Eph. 1:3
worthy receive *b.* Rev. 5:12

BLIND, *destitute of sight, dark.*
openeth eyes of *b.* Ps. 146:8
eyes of *b.* shall see Isa. 29:18
walk like *b.* men Zeph. 1:17
two *b.* men followed Matt. 9:27
b. leaders of the *b.* 15:14
woe unto ye *b.* guides Matt. 23:16
a guide of the *b.* Rom. 2:19

BLINDNESS, *lack of sight.*
b. in part is Rom. 11:25
b. of their heart Eph. 4:18

BLOOD, *vital fluid in the body.*
water become *b.* Ex. 4:9
b. strike on posts 12:7
b. maketh atonement Lev. 17:11
flesh and *b.* hath not Matt. 16:17
this is my *b.* shed Mark 14:24
testament in my *b.* Luke 22:20
born not of *b.* John 1:13
purchased with his *b.* Acts 20:28
justified by his *b.* Rom. 5:9
b. cannot inherit 1 Cor. 15:50
redemption through *b.* Eph. 1:7
not without *b.* Heb. 9:7
into holiest by *b.* 10:19
with precious *b.* of 1 Pet. 1:19

BODY, *physical human.*
flesh and *b.* are Prov. 5:11
b. cast into hell Matt. 5:29
eat, this my *b.* 26:26
light of *b.* is eye Luke 11:34
no thought for *b.* 12:22
the temple of his *b.* John 2:21
b. of sin destroyed Rom. 6:6
b. living sacrifice 12:1
absent from the *b.* 2 Cor. 5:8
edifying *b.* Christ Eph. 4:12
change our vile *b.* Phil. 3:21
head of the *b.* Col. 1:18
offering *b.* of Jesus Heb. 10:10
able bridle whole *b.* Jam. 3:2

BOOK, *writing, scriptures.*
blotted out of *b.* Ps. 69:28
not contain *b.* John 21:25
names in *b.* of life Phil. 4:3
blot out of *b.* life Rev. 3:5
not in *b.* of life 13:8
opened *b.* of life 20:12
Lamb's *b.* of life 21:27

BORN, *brought forth.*
b. king of the Jews Matt. 2:2
where Christ should be *b.* 2:4
good if had not been *b.* 26:24
unto you is *b.* this day Luke 2:11
except man *b.* again John 3:3
to this end was I *b.* 18:37
b. again not of 1 Pet. 1:23
b. of God not commit 1 John 3:9
loveth is *b.* of God 4:7
believeth is *b.* of God 5:1

BOUGHT, *purchased.*
all he had and *b.* Matt. 13:46
cast out them that *b.* 21:12
and *b.* potter's field 27:7
b. with a price 1 Cor. 6:20
the Lord that *b.* 2 Pet. 2:1

BOUND, *made fast, restrained.*
b. in affliction Ps. 107:10
whom Satan hath *b.* Luke 13:16
word of God not *b.* 2 Tim. 2:9
in bonds as *b.* with Heb. 13:3
b. him thousand years Rev. 20:2

BREAD, *necessary food.*
sweat shalt eat *b.* Gen. 3:19
unleavened *b.* Ex. 29:2
not live by *b.* only Deut. 8:3
stones be made *b.* Matt. 4:3
this day our daily *b.* 6:11
ask *b.*, give stone 7:9
took *b.* and blessed 26:26
not live by *b.* alone Luke 4:4
gave *b.* from heaven John 6:31
Jesus taketh *b.* and 21:13
b. we break, is 1 Cor. 10:16
night betrayed took *b.* 11:23

BREASTPLATE, *object worn on chest.*
righteousness as a *b.* Isa. 59:17
b. of righteousness Eph. 6:14
b. of faith and 1 Thess. 5:8
as it were *b.* of iron Rev. 9:9

BREATH, *air inhaled; life.*
God breathed *b.* of Gen. 2:7
by the *b.* of God frost Job 37:10
that hath *b.* Ps. 150:6
to all life and *b.* Acts 17:25

BRIMSTONE, *sulphur.*
upon Gomorrah *b.* Gen. 19:24
whole land *b.* Deut. 29:23
upon wicked rain *b.* Ps. 11:6
rained fire and *b.* Luke 17:29
tormented with *b.* Rev. 14:10

BRING, *to carry, fetch, cause.*
earth *b.* forth Gen. 1:11
b. me unto thy holy Ps. 43:3
what a day may *b.* Prov. 27:1
I *b.* good tidings Luke 2:10
heard, *b.* forth fruit 8:15
b. to nought things 1 Cor. 1:28
b. it into subjection 9:27
might *b.* us to God 1 Pet. 3:18
b. glory of nations Rev. 21:26

BROKEN, *parted by violence.*
them of *b.* heart Ps. 34:18
b. cisterns that can Jer. 2:13
scripture cannot be *b.* John 10:35
bone of him not be *b.* 19:36
body *b.* for you 1 Cor. 11:24

BURDEN, *that which is borne.*
yoke of his *b.* Isa. 9:4
my *b.* is light Matt. 11:30
one another's *b.* Gal. 6:2

BURNT OFFERING, *sacrifice.*
Noah offered *b.* Gen. 8:20
Lord delight in *b.* 1 Sam. 15:22
b. not required Ps. 40:6
delightest not in *b.* 51:16
b. not acceptable Jer. 6:20
knowledge more than *b.* Hos. 6:6
to love more than *b.* Mark 12:33
in *b.* no pleasure Heb. 10:6

C

CALL, *to speak in loud voice.*
will *c.* me blessed Gen. 30:13
hear me when I *c.* Ps. 4:1
mercy unto all that *c.* 86:5
c. upon him while Isa. 55:6
have *c.* you friends John 15:15
them which are *c.* 1 Cor. 1:24
c. sons of God 1 John 3:1

CALLING, *divine summons.*
c. of God without Rom. 11:29
hope of his *c.* Eph. 1:18
high *c.* of God in Phil. 3:14
worthy of this *c.* 2 Thess. 1:11
of heavenly *c.* Heb. 3:1

CAST, *throw, impel.*
why *c.* down soul? Ps. 42:5
c. burden upon Lord 55:22
c. my sins behind Isa. 38:17
c. into furnace Dan. 3:6
c. into den of lions 6:7
c. thyself down Matt. 4:6
c. pearls before swine 7:6
power *c.* out devils Mark 3:15
in no wise *c.* out John 6:37
first *c.* stone at her 8:7
hath God *c.* away his Rom. 11:1
c. off works darkness 13:12
c. all your care upon 1 Pet. 5:7
love *c.* out fear 1 John 4:18

CAUSE, *reason, plea, case.*
maintained my *c.* Ps. 9:4
hate me without *c.* 35:19
Lord plead their *c.* Prov. 22:23
angry without *c.* Matt. 5:22
hated me without *c.* John 15:25
no *c.* of death in Acts 13:28
this *c.* many weak 1 Cor. 11:30
c. obtained mercy 1 Tim. 1:16
which *c.* I suffer 2 Tim. 1:12
which *c.* not ashamed Heb. 2:11

CEASE, *leave off.*
day and night not *c.* Gen. 8:22
maketh wars to *c.* Ps. 46:9

c. from own wisdom Prov. 23:4
c. to do evil Isa. 1:16
offence of cross *c.* Gal. 5:11
c. not to give Eph. 1:16
not *c.* to pray Col. 1:9
pray without *c.* 1 Thess. 5:17

CHARITY, *love, kindness.*
but *c.* edifieth 1 Cor. 8:1
above all put on *c.* Col. 3:14
your faith and *c.* 1 Thess. 3:6
kindness; and to *c.* 2 Pet. 1:7
witness of thy *c.* 3 John 6

CHEER, *reassure, assurance.*
let thy heart *c.* thee Eccl. 11:9
be of good *c.*; thy sins Matt. 9:2
be of good *c.*; it is I 14:27
of good *c.*; I have John 16:33
you to be of good *c.* Acts 27:22

CHILD, *one young in years.*
do not sin against *c.* Gen. 42:22
train up a *c.* in the way Prov. 22:6
unto us a *c.* is born Isa. 9:6
little *c.* lead them 11:6
called little *c.* unto Matt. 18:2
when I was a *c.* 1 Cor. 13:11
from a *c.* hast 2 Tim. 3:15

CHILDREN, *plural of child.*
suffer little *c.* forbid Matt. 19:14
we are the *c.* of God Rom. 8:16
upon *c.* of disobedience Eph. 5:6
c. obey your parents Col. 3:20
c. in subjection 1 Tim. 3:4

CHOOSE, *make choice of.*
therefore *c.* life Deut. 30:19
c. you whom ye Josh. 24:15
way that he shall *c.* Ps. 25:12
c. our inheritance for us 47:4
refuse evil, *c.* good Isa. 7:15
c. rather to suffer Heb. 11:25

CHOSEN, *selected.*
ye have *c.* the Lord Josh. 24:22
many called few *c.* Matt. 20:16
whom he hath *c.* Mark 13:20
ye have not *c.* me John 15:16
a *c.* vessel unto me Acts 9:15
God hath *c.* foolish 1 Cor. 1:27
c. to be soldier 2 Tim. 2:4

CHRIST, *Son of God, Messiah.*
where *C.* be born Matt. 2:4
thou art the *C.* the Son Matt. 16:16
many saying I am *C.* 24:5
prophesy, thou *C.* 26:68
knew he was *C.* Luke 4:41
save himself if *C.* 23:35
ought not *C.* to have 24:26
raise up *C.* to Acts 2:30
preached *C.* unto them 8:5
due time *C.* died Rom. 5:6
as *C.* was raised 6:4
C. being raised 6:9
have not Spirit of *C.* 8:9
C. is end of law 10:4
to this end *C.* died 14:9
C. pleased not himself 15:3
preach *C.* crucified 1 Cor. 1:23
ye are *C.* and *C.* 3:23
C. our passover 5:7
is not *C.* raised 15:16
not I but *C.* liveth Gal. 2:20
heir through *C.* Gal. 4:7
not so learned *C.* Eph. 4:20
C. also loved us and 5:2
C. give thee light 5:14
one preach *C.* of Phil. 1:16
for me to live is *C.* 1:21
C. sitteth on Col. 3:1
C. who is our life 3:4
C. glorified not Heb. 5:5
Spirit of *C.* signify 1 Pet. 1:11
denieth Jesus is *C.* 1 John 2:22
believeth Jesus is *C.* 5:1
reigned with *C.* Rev. 20:4

CHURCH, *body of Christians.*
I will build my *c.* Matt. 16:18
I persecuted *c.* of 1 Cor. 15:9
Christ head of *c.* Eph. 5:23
c. of living God 1 Tim. 3:15

CLEAN, *free from filth, pure.*
every *c.* beast Gen. 7:2
he that hath *c.* hands Ps. 24:4
create in me a *c.* heart 51:10
ways of man *c.* in Prov. 16:2
made my heart *c.* 20:9
thou canst make me *c.* Matt. 8:2
fine linen *c.* and Rev. 19:8

CLEANSE, *render clean.*
c. me from secret Ps. 19:12
c. us from all sin 1 John 1:7
c. from unrighteousness 1:9

CLOUD, *vapor, gloom.*
by day pillar of *c.* Ex. 13:21
glory appeared in *c.* 16:10
Lord descended in *c.* 34:5
his strength is in *c.* Ps. 68:34
Son of man coming in *c.* Matt. 24:30
c. received him Acts 1:9
caught up in *c.* 1 Thess. 4:17
he cometh with *c.* Rev. 1:7

COME, *approach, arrive.*
c. thou into ark Gen. 7:1
my name, I will *c.* Ex. 20:24
c. and declare his Ps. 22:31
all nations shall *c.* 86:9
c. forth rod of Jesse Isa. 11:1
thy kingdom *c.* Matt. 6:10
gospel preached, and *c.* 24:14
any man thirst let him *c.* John 7:37
I will *c.* again and 14:3
tarry till I *c.* 21:22
let us *c.* boldly Heb. 4:16
behold I *c.* quickly Rev. 22:7

COMFORT, *console, consolation.*
thy rod and staff *c.* me Ps. 23:4
my *c.* in my affliction 119:50
c. them concerning John 11:19
c. one another 1 Thess. 4:18

COMFORTED, *consoled, cheered.*
for they shall be *c.* Matt. 5:4
all learn and be *c.* 1 Cor. 14:31
we are *c.* of God 2 Cor. 1:4
hearts might be *c.* Col. 2:2

COMFORTER, *one who comforts.*
looked for *c.* but Ps. 69:20
give you another *C.* John 14:16

COMFORTLESS, *without comfort.*
will not leave you *c.* John 14:18

COMMANDMENT, *a charge.*
thy *c.* are faithful Ps. 119:86
thy *c.* are my delights 119:143
the *c.* is a lamp Prov. 6:23
which is great *c.*? Matt. 22:36
blessed that do *c.* Rev. 22:14

COMMUNION, *fellowship.*
c. of the blood 1 Cor. 10:16
what *c.* hath light 2 Cor. 6:14

COMPASSION, *sympathy, pity.*
Lord will have *c.* Deut. 30:3
Jesus moved with *c.* Mark 1:41
have *c.* on whom Rom. 9:15
have *c.* on ignorant Heb. 5:2
having *c.* one of 1 Pet. 3:8

COMPLETE, *filled, perfect.*
ye are *c.* in him Col. 2:10
stand perfect and *c.* 4:12

CONCEIVE, *form, think, devise.*
they *c.* mischief Job 15:35
in sin my mother *c.* me Ps. 51:5
c. in her is of Matt. 1:20

CONDEMN, *declare guilty, fine.*
who shall *c.* me? Isa. 50:9
shall *c.* him to death Matt. 20:18
Judas, when saw was *c.* 27:3
c. not and ye shall Luke 6:37
delivered him to be *c.* 24:20
sent not Son to *c.* John 3:17
c. not himself in that Rom. 14:22
not *c.* with world 1 Cor. 11:32
our heart *c.* us 1 John 3:20

CONDEMNATION, *declared guilty.*
this is the *c.* that John 3:19
not come into *c.* 5:24
judgment by one to *c.* Rom. 5:16
lest ye fall into *c.* Jam. 5:12

CONFESS, *acknowledge, own.*
c. their iniquity Lev. 26:40
c. I am not Christ John 1:20
every tongue shall *c.* Rom. 14:11
every tongue *c.* Phil. 2:11
c. our sins, he is 1 John 1:9
I will *c.* his name Rev. 3:5

CONGREGATION, *assembly.*
sin offering for *c.* Lev. 4:21
exalt him in *c.* Ps. 107:32

CONSCIENCE, *the moral sense.*
convicted by their *c.* John 8:9
be subject for *c.* sake Rom. 13:5
pure heart, good *c.* 1 Tim. 1:5
faith and good *c.* 1:19
c. seared with hot iron 4:2
mind and *c.* defiled Tit. 1:15
purge *c.* from works Heb. 9:14

CONSIDER, *think, regard.*
I *c.* thy heavens Ps. 8:3
c. my trouble 9:13
c. this, ye that forget God 50:22
c. her ways and be Prov. 6:6
c. diligently what is 23:1
c. lilies of the field Matt. 6:28
c. thyself lest Gal. 6:1

CONSUME, *burn up, destroy.*
bush was not *c.* Ex. 3:2
thy God is a *c.* fire Deut. 4:24
let sinners be *c.* Ps. 104:35
that ye be not *c.* Gal. 5:15
c. it upon lusts Jam. 4:3

CONTENT, *satisfied, willing.*
would God been *c.* Josh. 7:7
be *c.* with wages Luke 3:14
be *c.* with such Heb. 13:5
CONTINUE, *persevere, persist.*
if ye *c.* in my word John 8:31
c. ye in my love 15:9
exhorting to *c.* in faith Acts 14:22
shall we *c.* in sin Rom. 6:1
c. instant in prayer 12:12
if ye *c.* in faith Col. 1:23
not suffered to *c.* Heb. 7:23
let brotherly love *c.* 13:1
CONTRITE, *humble, sorrowful.*
such as be of a *c.* Ps. 34:18
broken and a *c.* heart 51:17
heart of *c.* ones Isa. 57:15
poor and a *c.* spirit 66:2
CONVERSATION, *talk, conduct.*
be of upright *c.* Ps. 37:14
we had our *c.* 2 Cor. 1:12
our *c.* in past Eph. 2:3
our *c.* is in heaven Phil. 3:20
your *c.* be without Heb. 13:5
shew a good *c.* Jam. 3:13
be holy in all *c.* 1 Pet. 1:15
CORRUPT, *from good to bad.*
moth and rust *c.* Matt. 6:19
neither moth *c.* Luke 12:33
fear lest your minds *c.* 2 Cor. 11:3
c. according to the Eph. 4:22
men of *c.* minds 1 Tim. 6:5
CORRUPTIBLE, *tainted, decayable.*
a *c.* crown 1 Cor. 9:25
c. put on incorruption 15:53
born not of *c.* seed 1 Pet. 1:23
CORRUPTION, *depravity, death.*
no more return to *c.* Acts 13:34
it is sown in *c.* 1 Cor. 15:42
shall of flesh reap *c.* Gal. 6:8
escaped the *c.* that 2 Pet. 1:4
perish in their own *c.* 2:12
COUNSEL, *advice, consultation.*
give advice and *c.* Judg. 20:7
not in *c.* of ungodly Ps. 1:1
fall by own *c.* 5:10
c. of Lord standeth 33:11
guide me with thy *c.* 73:24
nor *c.* against the Lord Prov. 21:30
COURAGE, *bravery, firmness.*
be strong, of good *c.* Deut. 31:6
wait, be of good *c.* Ps. 27:14
COURSE, *race, way.*
finish *c.* with joy Acts 20:24
c. of this world Eph. 2:2
finished my *c.* 2 Tim. 4:7
COVENANT, *mutual agreement.*
will remember my *c.* Gen. 9:15
ever mindful of his *c.* Ps. 111:5
confirm *c.* one week Dan. 9:27
strangers from the *c.* Eph. 2:12
mediator of better *c.* Heb. 8:6
CREATED, *formed, made.*
God *c.* heaven and Gen. 1:1
day God *c.* man Deut. 4:32
who *c.* these things Isa. 40:26
he that *c.* heavens 42:5
hath not one God *c.* Mal. 2:10
neither man *c.* for 1 Cor. 11:9
by him all things *c.* Col. 1:16
hast *c.* all things Rev. 4:11
CREATION, *making, thing made.*
beginning of *c.* Mark 10:6
continue as from *c.* 2 Pet. 3:4
beginning of the *c.* Rev. 3:14
CREATOR, *maker, God.*
remember now thy C. Eccl. 12:1
Lord, the C. of the Isa. 40:28
more than C. Rom. 1:25
as unto a faithful C. 1 Pet. 4:19
CROSS, *figuratively affliction.*
bearing his *c.* went John 19:17
lest *c.* of Christ be 1 Cor. 1:17
offence of the *c.* Gal. 5:11
should glory, save in *c.* 6:14
even death of the *c.* Phil. 2:8
enemies of *c.* 3:18
blood of his *c.* Col. 1:20
nailing it to his *c.* 2:14
for joy endured the *c.* Heb. 12:2
CROWN, *emblem of royalty.*
a *c.* of glory shall Prov. 4:9
virtuous woman is a *c.* 12:4
woe to the *c.* of pride Isa. 28:1
be a *c.* of glory 62:3
a *c.* of thorns Matt. 27:29
wearing *c.* thorns John 19:5
c. of rejoicing 1 Thess. 2:19
c. of righteousness 2 Tim. 4:8
receive *c.* glory 1 Pet. 5:4
give *c.* of life Rev. 2:10
cast *c.* before throne Rev. 4:10
on his head many *c.* 19:12
CRUCIFIED, *executed on cross.*
betrayed to be *c.* Matt. 26:2
all say, let him be *c.* 27:22
third hour *c.* him Mark 15:25
wicked hands have *c.* Acts 2:23
our old man is *c.* Rom. 6:6
c. through weakness 2 Cor. 13:4
I am *c.* with Christ Gal. 2:20
CRUCIFY, *to nail to the cross.*
led him away to *c.* him Matt. 27:31
cried out, *c.* him Mark 15:13
saying, *c.* him Luke 23:21
they *c.* Son of God Heb. 6:6
CUP, *drinking vessel.*
my *c.* runneth over Ps. 23:5
c. of salvation 116:13
able to drink of *c.* Matt. 20:22
took *c.* and gave thanks 26:27
c. is new testament Luke 22:20
c. which my Father John 18:11
c. of blessing 1 Cor. 10:16
often as ye drink this *c.* 11:26
c. of his wrath Rev. 16:19

D

DAILY, *day by day, regularly.*
sorrow in heart *d.* Ps. 13:2
our *d.* bread Matt. 6:11
take up his cross *d.* Luke 9:23
I die *d.* Col. 5:31
exhort one another *d.* Heb. 3:13
DARK, *not light, obscure.*
they grope in the *d.* Job 12:25
judge through *d.* cloud 22:13
DARKEN, *to make dark.*
who *d.* counsel Job 38:2
stars be not *d.* Eccl. 12:2
sun be *d.* Matt. 24:29
foolish heart *d.* Rom. 1:21
understanding *d.* Eph. 4:18
DARKLY, *dimly, obscurely.*
see through glass *d.* 1 Cor. 13:12
DARKNESS, *gloom, blackness.*
d. upon face of deep Gen. 1:2
cast into outer *d.* Matt. 8:12
and the power of *d.* Luke 22:53
d. over all earth 23:44
loved *d.* rather than John 3:19
turn from *d.* to light Acts 26:18
light out of *d.* 2 Cor. 4:6
with works of *d.* Eph. 5:11
against rulers of *d.* 6:12
from power of *d.* Col. 1:13
we not of *d.* 1 Thess. 5:5
kingdom full of *d.* Rev. 16:10
DAY, *light time, lifetime.*
God called light *d.* Gen. 1:5
six *d.* shalt labour Ex. 20:9
this *d.* have I begotten Ps. 2:7
more unto perfect *d.* Prov. 4:18
knowest not what a *d.* 27:1
Ancient of *d.* sit Dan. 7:9
this *d.* daily bread Matt. 6:11
ye know neither *d.* nor 25:13
raise again at last *d.* John 6:39
work while it is *d.* 9:4
against *d.* of wrath Rom. 2:5
killed all *d.* long 8:36
d. at hand: let us 13:12
d. of salvation 2 Cor. 6:2
d. cometh as thief 1 Thess. 5:2
DEAD, *inanimate, without life.*
thou art a *d.* man Gen. 20:3
d. praise not the Lord Ps. 115:17
thy *d.* men shall live Isa. 26:19
seek living among *d.* Luke 24:5
d. shall hear voice John 5:25
though he were *d.* yet 11:25
am *d.* to law Gal. 2:19
being *d.* in your sins Col. 2:13
if we be *d.* with 2 Tim. 2:11
d. were judged out of Rev. 20:12
DECEIVE, *lead astray, lie to.*
not God *d.* thee 2 Kings 19:10
d. not yourselves Jer. 37:9
take heed no man *d.* Matt. 24:4
let no man *d.* 1 Cor. 3:18
lie in wait to *d.* Eph. 4:14
d. ourselves and 1 John 1:8
d. nations no more Rev. 20:3
DECEIVED, *made to err.*
heart be not *d.* Deut. 11:16
whosoever *d.* thereby Prov. 20:1
heed ye be not *d.* Luke 21:8
d. me and by it Rom. 7:11
Adam was not *d.* 1 Tim. 2:14
DECEIVER, *one who deceives.*
that *d.* said Matt. 27:63
are many *d.* Tit. 1:10
many *d.* entered into 2 John 7
DECEIVETH, *deceiving.*
man that *d.* his Prov. 26:19
he *d.* himself Gal. 6:3

Devil which *d.* Rev. 12:9
d. them on earth 13:14

DECLARE, *explain, make known.*
heavens *d.* the glory of Ps. 19:1
wondrous works *d.* 75:1
d. works of the Lord 118:17
Son hath *d.* him John 1:18
d. to be Son of God Rom. 1:4
d. his righteousness 3:25
day shall *d.* it 1 Cor. 3:13
d. plainly that they Heb. 11:14

DEFILE, *make unclean, impure.*
neither *d.* yourselves Lev. 11:44
d. with own works Ps. 106:39
would not *d.* himself Dan. 1:8
not into, lest be *d.* John 18:28
thereby many be *d.* Heb. 12:15
tongue *d.* whole body Jam. 3:6

DELIVER, *liberate, give up to.*
I am come to *d.* them Ex. 3:8
none can *d.* out of thine Job 10:7
to *d.* their soul from Ps. 33:19
call upon me I will *d.* 50:15
surely he shall *d.* thee 91:3
cannot *d.* his soul Isa. 44:20
our God able to *d.* Dan. 3:17
tempt God are *d.* Mal. 3:15
d. us from evil Matt. 6:13
time she be *d.* Luke 1:57
d. him be crucified John 19:16
d. for our offences Rom. 4:25
we are *d.* from the law 7:6

DENY, *disown, reject.*
whosoever *d.* me Matt. 10:33
let him *d.* himself 16:24
thou shalt *d.* me thrice 26:34
form godliness, *d.* power 2 Tim. 3:5
d. ungodliness and Tit. 2:12
d. Son hath not the 1 John 2:23
d. the only Lord God Jude 4
kept word not *d.* name Rev. 3:8

DESCEND, *come down.*
his glory shall not *d.* Ps. 49:17
spirit of God *d.* Matt. 3:16
Spirit like a dove *d.* Mark 1:10
Lord shall *d.* from 1 Thess. 4:16

DESIRE, *to wish, long for.*
more to be *d.* are Ps. 19:10
one thing I *d.* of Lord 27:4
d. truth in the inward 51:6
I *d.* mercy, and not Hos. 6:6
do whatsoever we *d.* Mark 10:35
what ye *d.* when ye pray 11:24
d. spiritual gifts 1 Cor. 14:1

DESPISE, *reject, hate.*
contrite heart not *d.* Ps. 51:17
will not *d.* their prayer 102:17
fools *d.* wisdom and Prov. 1:7
fool *d.* instruction 15:5
d. not thy mother 23:22
he is *d.* and rejected Isa. 53:3
d. not one these little Matt. 18:10
things *d.* God chosen 1 Cor. 1:28
no man *d.* youth 1 Tim. 4:12
no man *d.* thee Tit. 2:15

DESTROY, *demolish, ruin, kill.*
I will *d.* man Gen. 6:7
d. cities of plain 19:29
pastors that *d.* sheep Jer. 23:1
which is able to *d.* soul Matt. 10:28
how they might *d.* him 12:14
I will *d.* this temple Mark 14:58
last enemy be *d.* is 1 Cor. 15:26
able save and to *d.* Jam. 4:12

DESTRUCTION, *calamity, ruin.*
d. was of God 2 Chron. 22:7
into *d.* let him fall Ps. 35:8
redeemeth life from *d.* 103:4
fool's mouth his *d.* Prov. 18:7
broad way to *d.* Matt. 7:13
for *d.* of flesh 1 Cor. 5:5
sudden *d.* cometh 1 Thess. 5:3

DEVIL, *wicked angel, Satan.*
tempted of the *d.* Matt. 4:1
in thy name cast out *d.* 7:22
prepared for *d.* and his 25:41
d. besought him Mark 5:12
authority over all *d.* Luke 9:1
d. put into Judas to John 13:2
neither place to *d.* Eph. 4:27
against wiles of the *d.* 6:11
out of snare of *d.* 2 Tim. 2:26
resist the *d.* and he Jam. 4:7
your adversary the *d.* 1 Pet. 5:8
old serpent, the *D.* Rev. 12:9
d. cast into fire 20:10

DEVOUR, *consume, waste.*
fire *d.* them Lev. 10:2
fire *d.* before him Ps. 50:3
shall *d.* adversaries Heb. 10:27
whom he may *d.* 1 Pet. 5:8

DIE, *expire, lose life.*
thou shalt surely *d.* Gen. 2:17
neither touch it lest ye *d.* 3:3
curse God and *d.* Job 2:9
they *d.* without wisdom 4:21
for righteous one *d.* Rom. 5:7
no man *d.* to himself 14:7
as in Adam all *d.* 1 Cor. 15:22
I *d.* daily 15:31
to *d.* is gain Phil. 1:21
appointed once to *d.* Heb. 9:27

DISCERN, *discover, distinguish.*
wise man's heart *d.* Eccl. 8:5
d. between right Jonah 4:11
d. the face of sky Matt. 16:3
spiritually *d.* 1 Cor. 2:14

DISCIPLE, *follower, pupil.*
cannot be my *d.* Luke 14:26
d. believed on him John 2:11
then are ye my *d.* indeed 8:31
so shall ye be my *d.* 15:8
d. whom he loved 19:26

DISCOURAGE, *depress.*
wherefore *d.* ye the heart Num. 32:7
not be *d.* till he Isa. 42:4
lest they be *d.* Col. 3:21

DISPENSATION, *bestowment.*
a *d.* of gospel. 1 Cor. 9:17
d. of fulness Eph. 1:10
heard of *d.* of grace 3:2
according *d.* of God Col. 1:25

DISTRESS, *pain, grief.*
in *d.* I called 2 Sam. 22:7
my soul out of *d.* 1 Kings 1:29
good for present *d.* 1 Cor. 7:26
ourselves in *d.* 2 Cor. 6:4
take pleasure in *d.* for 12:10

DIVIDE, *rend, separate.*
waters were *d.* Ex. 14:21
vail *d.* between holy 26:33
he *d.* the sea Ps. 78:13
d. word of truth 2 Tim. 2:15

DOCTRINE, *teaching, belief.*
astonished at his *d.* Matt. 7:28
what new *d.* is this Mark 1:27
every wind of *d.* Eph. 4:14
contrary to *d.* 1 Tim. 1:10
nourished in good *d.* 4:6
profitable for *d.* 2 Tim. 3:16
not endure sound *d.* 4:3
by sound *d.* to exhort Tit. 1:9

DOMINION, *rule, power.*
have *d.* over fish Gen. 1:26
d. over the works of Ps. 8:6
upright have *d.* over 49:14
death hath no more *d.* Rom. 6:9
have *d.* over your 2 Cor. 1:24

DOOR, *opening, entrance.*
it is near, even at *d.* Matt. 24:33
d. were shut where John 20:19
opened the *d.* of faith Acts 14:27
great *d.* effectual 1 Cor. 16:9

DOUBT, *to lack faith.*
wherefore didst *d.* Matt. 14:31
have faith, and *d.* not 21:21
but some *d.* 28:17
not *d.* in his heart Mark 11:23

DRINK, *to swallow a liquid.*
d. of river of thy Ps. 36:8
d. of the cup I *d.* of Matt. 20:22
saying *d.* ye all of it 26:27
thirst, come and *d.* John 7:37
d. same spiritual 1 Cor. 10:4

DUST, *earthy matter, earth.*
God formed man of *d.* Gen. 2:7
d. shalt thou eat all the 3:14
brought me into *d.* Ps. 22:15
remembereth we are *d.* 103:14

E

EAR, *organ of hearing.*
cause thine *e.* hear Ps. 10:17
incline thine *e.* unto me 17:6
have *e.* but hear not 135:17
incline thine *e.* unto Prov. 2:2
he that hath *e.* to hear Matt. 11:15

EARNEST, *zealous, ardent.*
e. expectation of Rom. 8:19
told *e.* desire 2 Cor. 7:7
my *e.* expectation Phil. 1:20

EARNESTLY, *fervently.*
covet *e.* best gifts 1 Cor. 12:31
groan, *e.* desiring 2 Cor. 5:2
e. contend for faith Jude 3

EARTH, *land, world.*
e. without form Gen. 1:2
e. corrupt before 6:11
Lord of all the *e.* Josh. 3:11
e. yield her increase Ps. 67:6
hadst formed the *e.* 90:2
laid foundation of *e.* Ps. 102:25
Lord hath founded *e.* Prov. 3:19
e. full his glory Isa. 6:3

meek inherit the *e.* Matt. 5:5
treasures upon *e.* where 6:19
come to send peace on *e.* 10:34
thou shalt bind on *e.* 16:19
if two of you agree on *e.* 18:19
I have glorified thee on *e.* John 17:4
e. shall be burned 2 Pet. 3:10
we shall reign on *e.* Rev. 5:10

EAT, *partake of food.*
mayest freely *e.* Gen. 2:16
dust shalt thou *e.* all the 3:14
man did *e.* angels' food Ps. 78:25
life, what ye *e.* Matt. 6:25
take, *e.*, this is my body 26:26
let us *e.* and be merry Luke 15:23
e. the flesh of the Son of John 6:53

ELECT, *chosen.*
mine *e.* in whom my Isa. 42:1
Israel mine *e.*, I have 45:4
mine *e.* shall inherit it 65:9
for the *e.* sake Matt. 24:22
avenge his own *e.* Luke 18:7
charge of God's *e.* Rom. 8:33
e. of God, holy and Col. 3:12

END, *last part, close, purpose.*
wicked come to an *e.* Ps. 7:9
make me know mine *e.* 39:4
years shall have no *e.* 102:27
of his government no *e.* Isa. 9:7
world without *e.* 45:17
endureth to the *e.* Matt. 10:22
but the *e.* is not yet 24:6
of his kingdom no *e.* Luke 1:33
loved unto the *e.* John 13:1
to this *e.* was I born 18:37
e. of those things Rom. 6:21
then cometh *e.* 1 Cor. 15:24
world without *e.* Eph. 3:21
e. of your faith 1 Pet. 1:9
e. of things is at hand 4:7
beginning and *e.* Rev. 21:6

ENDURE, *suffer, withstand.*
children able to *e.* Gen. 33:14
Lord shall *e.* for ever Ps. 9:7
his truth *e.* to all 100:5
he that *e.* to end Matt. 10:22
e. all things 1 Cor. 13:7
e. the cross Heb. 12:2
blessed man that *e.* Jam. 1:12

ENEMY, *adversary, foe.*
in the presence mine *e.* Ps. 23:5
count them mine *e.* 139:22
maketh his *e.* at peace Prov. 16:7
man's *e.* of his own Mic. 7:6
love your *e.* Matt. 5:44
all *e.* under feet 1 Cor. 15:25
friend of world *e.* of Jam. 4:4

ENMITY, *hostility, hatred.*
I will put *e.* between Gen. 3:15
before were at *e.* Luke 23:12
carnal mind is *e.* Rom. 8:7

ENTER, *go in, come in.*
e. into his gates Ps. 100:4
e. ye in at the strait Matt. 7:13
many will seek to *e.* Luke 13:24
and *e.* into his glory 24:26
cannot *e.* into John 3:5
e. into their labours 4:38
e. not by the door into 10:1
by one man sin *e.* Rom. 5:12
e. into holiest by 10:19
e. in through Rev. 22:14

EQUAL, *even, uniform, just.*
things that are *e.* Ps. 17:2
their way is not *e.* Ezek. 33:17
e. unto angels Luke 20:36
himself *e.* with God John 5:18
not robbery to be *e.* Phil. 2:6

ERR, *go astray.*
a people that do *e.* Ps. 95:10
e. from commandments 119:21
cause thee to *e.* Isa. 3:12
concerning truth *e.* 2 Tim. 2:18
if any *e.* from truth Jam. 5:19

ESCAPE, *evade, hasten away.*
wicked shall not *e.* Job 11:20
e. with skin of teeth 19:20
speaketh lies not *e.* Prov. 19:5
worthy to *e.* Luke 21:36
e. judgment of God Rom. 2:3
make a way to *e.* 1 Cor. 10:13
destruction not *e.* 1 Thess. 5:3
how *e.* if we neglect Heb. 2:3

ESTABLISH, *fix, settle, confirm.*
will *e.* covenant Gen. 6:18
throne be *e.* for ever 2 Sam. 7:16
let thy ways be *e.* Prov. 4:26
every word be *e.* Matt. 18:16
that ye may be *e.* Rom. 1:11
e. in truth 2 Pet. 1:12

ETERNAL, *perpetual, everlasting.*
e. God thy refuge Deut. 33:27
I may have *e.* life Mal. 9:16
danger *e.* damnation Mark 3:29
I may inherit *e.* life? 10:17
believeth have *e.* John 3:15
fruit unto life *e.* 4:36
in them ye have *e.* life 5:39
keep it unto life *e.* 12:25
e. power and Godhead Rom. 1:20
for glory, *e.* life 2:7
grace reign unto *e.* life 5:21
an house *e.* in heavens 2 Cor. 5:1
lay hold on *e.* life 1 Tim. 6:12
obtained *e.* redemption Heb. 9:12
e. life with Father 1 John 1:2
promise, even *e.* life 2:25

EVER, *at all times, continually.*
Lord endure for *e.* Ps. 9:7
he is *e.* merciful 37:26
our God for *e.* and *e.* 48:14
shalt endure for *e.* 102:12
keepeth truth for *e.* 146:6
riches not for *e.* Prov. 27:24
trust in Lord for *e.* Isa. 26:4
the glory for *e.*! Matt. 6:13
abideth for *e.* John 12:34

EVERLASTING, *perpetual.*
from *e.* to *e.* thou Ps. 90:2
lead me in the way *e.* Ps. 139:24
an *e.* kingdom 145:13
the *e.* God, the Lord Isa. 40:28
saved with *e.* salvation 45:17
I make *e.* covenant 55:3
some to *e.* life, and Dan. 12:2
cast into *e.* fire Matt. 18:8
shall inherit *e.* life 19:29
have *e.* life John 3:16
believeth hath *e.* life 3:36
the end *e.* life Rom. 6:22
believe to life *e.* 1 Tim. 1:16
having the *e.* gospel Rev. 14:6

EVERMORE, *throughout all time.*
pleasures for *e.* Ps. 16:11
do good; dwell for *e.* 37:27
glorify thy name for *e.* 86:12
seek his face *e.* 105:4
I am alive for *e.* Rev. 1:18

EVIL, *misfortune, iniquity.*
heart only *e.* Gen. 6:5
if *e.* to serve Lord Josh. 24:15
receive good not *e.* Job 2:10
depart from *e.* and Ps. 34:14
rewarded me *e.* for good 35:12
rewardeth *e.* for good, *e.* Prov. 17:13
whether it be good or *e.* Jer. 42:6
e., Lord hath not done Am. 3:6
thinketh no *e.* 1 Cor. 13:5
none render *e.* for *e.* 1 Thess. 5:15
root of all *e.* 1 Tim. 6:10
not rendering *e.* 1 Pet. 3:9

EXCEED, *surpass, excel.*
forty stripes, not *e.* Deut. 25:3
e. righteousness of Matt. 5:20

EXCEEDING, *in great degree.*
thy *e.* great reward Gen. 15:1
unto God my *e.* joy Ps. 43:4
rejoiced with *e.* joy Matt. 2:10
grace *e.* abundant 1 Tim. 1:14
e. great and precious 2 Pet. 1:4

EYE, *organ of sight.*
pleasant to the *e.* Gen. 3:6
e. for *e.* Ex. 21:24
lift up thine *e.* Deut. 3:27
e. of Lord every place Prov. 15:3
woe unto wise in own *e.* Isa. 5:21
having *e.* see not Mark 8:18
e. hath not seen 1 Cor. 2:9
if whole body an *e.* 12:17
twinkling of an *e.* 15:52
every *e.* shall see Rev. 1:7

F

FACE, *countenance.*
from thy *f.* I be hid Gen. 4:14
have seen God *f.* to *f.* 32:30
canst not see my *f.* Ex. 33:20
saidst, seek my *f.* Ps. 27:8
set his *f.* to go to Luke 9:51
they struck him on *f.* 22:64
but then *f.* to *f.* 1 Cor. 13:12
hide us from *f.* of Rev. 6:16
from whose *f.* the 20:11
shall see his *f.* 22:4

FAIL, *be wanting, disappoint.*
he will not *f.* thee Deut. 31:6
my heart *f.* me Ps. 40:12
when strength *f.* 71:9
he shall not *f.* nor be Isa. 42:4
prayed thy faith *f.* not Luke 22:32
charity never *f.* 1 Cor. 13:8

FAINT, *become weak, weary.*
their soul *f.* in them Ps. 107:5
soul *f.* for salvation 119:81

Creator *f.* not Isa. 40:28
shall walk and not *f.* 40:31
always pray, not *f.* Luke 18:1
we *f.* not 2 Cor. 4:1
reap if we *f.* not Gal. 6:9
wearied and *f.* in Heb. 12:3

FAITH, *loyalty, belief, reliance.*
in whom is no *f.* Deut. 32:20
O ye of little *f.* Matt. 6:30
thy *f.* made thee whole 9:22
have *f.* and doubt not 21:21
Lord, increase our *f.* Luke 17:5
for obedience to *f.* Rom. 1:5
f. counted for 4:5
being justified by *f.* we Rom. 5:1
word of *f.* we preach 10:8
every man measure of *f.* 12:3
weak in *f.* receive ye 14:1
though I have all *f.* so 1 Cor. 13:2
your *f.* is also vain 15:14
we walk by *f.*, not sight 2 Cor. 5:7
or by the hearing of *f.*? Gal. 3:2
f. worketh by love 5:6
one Lord, one *f.*, one Eph. 4:5
taking shield of *f.* 6:16
and joy of *f.* Phil. 1:25
your *f.* groweth 2 Thess. 1:3
for all men have not *f.* 3:2
I have kept the *f.* 2 Tim. 4:7
full assurance of *f.* Heb. 10:22
f. is substance things 11:1
trying of your *f.* Jam. 1:3
prayer of *f.* save sick 5:15
stedfast in the *f.* 1 Pet. 5:9

FAITHFUL, *firm in adherence.*
he is God, the *f.* Deut. 7:9
Lord preserveth the *f.* Ps. 31:23
all commandments *f.* 119:86
Lord that is *f.* Isa. 49:7
who is *f.* and wise Matt. 24:45
Lord *f.* who shall 2 Thess. 3:3
counted me *f.* 1 Tim. 1:12
he is *f.* and just 1 John 1:9
Christ, the *f.* witness Rev. 1:5
be thou *f.* unto death 2:10
called *F.* and True 19:11
words are true and *f.* 21:5

FAITHFULNESS, *constancy.*
I have declared thy *f.* Ps. 40:10
make known thy *f.* to all 89:1
my *f.* and my mercy shall 89:24
great is thy *f.* Lam. 3:23

FALL, *drop down, sink into sin.*
thousand shall *f.* at thy Ps. 91:7
wicked *f.* own nets 141:10
prating fool shall *f.* Prov. 10:8
wicked *f.* into mischief 24:16
diggeth pit shall *f.* 26:27
how art thou *f.* from Isa. 14:12
f. and not arise Jer. 8:4
f. down and worship Matt. 4:9
in temptation *f.* away Luke 8:13
Satan as lightning *f.* 10:18
f. into hands of God Heb. 10:31

FALSE, *dishonest, untrue, lying.*
my words not *f.* Job 36:4
hate every *f.* way Ps. 119:104
boasteth *f.* gift Prov. 25:14
prophesy *f.* vision Jer. 14:14
prophesy *f.* dreams 23:32
love no *f.* oath Zech. 8:17
beware of *f.* prophets Matt. 7:15
shall arise *f.* Christs 24:24
are *f.* apostles 2 Cor. 11:13
be *f.* teachers 2 Pet. 2:1

FAST, *to abstain from food.*
in day of your *f.* ye Isa. 58:3
when they *f.* I will Jer. 14:12
when ye *f.* be not Matt. 6:16

FATHER, *male parent, God.*
f. of many nations Gen. 17:4
as a *f.* pitieth children Ps. 103:13
God, everlasting *F.* Isa. 9:6
glorify your *F.* Matt. 5:16
our *F.* which art in heaven 6:9
loveth *f.* or mother 10:37
call no man your *f.* 23:9
as your *F.* is merciful Luke 6:36
said Jesus, *F.* forgive 23:34
F., into thy hands I 23:46
only begotten of *F.* John 1:14
the *F.* loveth the Son 3:35
as the *F.* raiseth up the 5:21
we have one *F.* even God 8:41
my *F.* is greater than 10:29
I and my *F.* are one 10:30
no man cometh unto *F.* 14:6
seen me, seen the *F.* 14:9
my *F.* is greater than I 14:28
one God and *F.* of all Eph. 4:6
fellowship is with *F.* 1 John 1:3
advocate with *F.* 2:1

FAULT, *error, defect.*
no *f.* in this man Luke 23:14
man be overtaken in *f.* Gal. 6:1
confess your *f.* Jam. 5:16
without *f.* before Rev. 14:5

FEAR, *dread, terror, awe.*
f. of God is not in this Gen. 20:11
f. not, God is come to Ex. 20:20
in *f.* will I worship Ps. 5:7
f. of Lord is clean 19:9
will *f.* no evil 23:4
whom shall I *f.*? 27:1
host encamp not *f.* 27:3
blessed man that *f.* 112:1
f. of Lord beginning Prov. 1:7
f. of Lord prolongeth 10:27
f. God and keep his Eccl. 12:13
f. him which is able Matt. 10:28
angel said, *f.* not 28:5
f. not, little flock Luke 12:32
hearts failing for *f.* 21:26
with *f.* and trembling Eph. 6:5
not spirit of *f.* 2 Tim. 1:7
reverence and godly *f.* Heb. 12:28

FELLOWSHIP, *association.*
doctrine and *f.* Acts 2:42
not have *f.* with devils 1 Cor. 10:20
what *f.* hath 2 Cor. 6:14
right hands of *f.* Gal. 2:9
no *f.* with Eph. 5:11
your *f.* in the gospel Phil. 1:5
have *f.* with us 1 John 1:3
if we say we have *f.* with 1:6

FIGHT, *to contest, struggle.*
Lord shall *f.* for you Ex. 14:14
that *f.* against me Ps. 35:1
not *f.* against God Acts 23:9
f. the good *f.* of 1 Tim. 6:12
fought a good *f.* 2 Tim. 4:7
ye *f.* and war, yet ye Jam. 4:2

FILLED, *made full, satisfy.*
earth *f.* violence Gen. 6:13
earth shall be *f.* Num. 14:21
mouth *f.* with praise Ps. 71:8
earth *f.* with glory 72:19
I will *f.* their treasures Prov. 8:21
f. with Holy Ghost Luke 1:15
hath Satan *f.* thine heart Acts 5:3
f. with fornication Rom. 1:29
be *f.* with the Spirit Eph. 5:18

FIND, *discover, detect.*
your sin will *f.* you Num. 32:23
seek ye shall *f.* Matt. 7:7
f. no evil in this man Acts 23:9
good I *f.* not Rom. 7:18
may *f.* grace to help Heb. 4:16

FIRE, *burning light.*
f. goeth before him and Ps. 97:3
Holy Ghost and *f.* Matt. 3:11
f. not quenched Mark 9:44
cloven tongues like *f.* Acts 2:3
f. try every work 1 Cor. 3:13
f. from God Rev. 20:9
was cast into lake of *f.* 20:10

FIRST, *original, highest, chief.*
f. be reconciled to Matt. 5:24
seek ye *f.* the kingdom 6:33
f. great commandment 22:38
if any man desire be *f.* Mark 9:35
gospel *f.* be published 13:10
f. must he suffer Luke 17:25
let him *f.* cast a stone John 8:7
f.-fruits of the spirit Rom. 8:23
if the *f.*-fruit be holy 11:16
in Christ rise *f.* 1 Thess. 4:16
a falling away *f.* 2 Thess. 2:3
Adam was *f.* 1 Tim. 2:13
he *f.* loved us 1 John 4:19
f. heaven and *f.* earth Rev. 21:1

FLEE, *run away from, avoid.*
f. fornication 1 Cor. 6:18
f. from idolatry 10:14
man of God *f.* these 1 Tim. 6:11
f. youthful lusts 2 Tim. 2:22
resist devil will *f.* Jam. 4:7
death shall *f.* from Rev. 9:6

FLESH, *human nature, meat.*
they shall be one *f.* Gen. 2:24
f. and blood not Matt. 16:17
should no *f.* be saved 24:22
all *f.* see salvation Luke 3:6
word was made *f.* John 1:14
no *f.* be justified Rom. 3:20
when we were in the *f.* 7:5
all *f.* not the same *f.* 1 Cor. 15:39
thorn in the *f.* 2 Cor. 12:7
walk after the *f.* 2 Pet. 2:10
Christ is come in *f.* 1 John 4:2

FLOOD, *deluge, overflow.*
neither any more *f.* Gen. 9:11
established it upon *f.* Ps. 24:2
f. came, winds blew Matt. 7:25
as in days before *f.* 24:38
knew not until the *f.* came 24:39

FOLLOW, *go after, pursue.*
he saith *f.* me Matt. 4:19
take cross, *f.* me 16:24
any serve, let him *f.* John 12:26

f. after charity 1 Cor. 14:1
f. that which good 1 Thess. 5:15
f. righteousness 1 Tim. 6:11
f. not that evil 3 John 11
which *f.* the Lamb Rev. 14:4

FOOL, *one deficient in intellect.*
f. said in heart Ps. 14:1
f. despise wisdom Prov. 1:7
shall say, Thou *f.* Matt. 5:22
ye *f.* and blind 23:17
they became *f.* Rom. 1:22
let him become *f.* 1 Cor. 3:18
f. for Christ's 4:10
walk not as *f.* but Eph. 5:15

FOOTSTOOL, *rest for feet.*
worship at his *f.* Ps. 99:5
enemies thy *f.* 110:1
earth is my *f.* Isa. 66:1
till enemies his *f.* Heb. 10:13

FORGAVE, *pardoned.*
thou *f.* iniquity of Ps. 32:5
he *f.* their iniquity 78:38
for your sakes *f.* I 2 Cor. 2:10
as Christ *f.* you, so Col. 3:13

FORGIVE, *to absolve, pardon.*
and *f.* all my sins Ps. 25:18
I will *f.* their iniquity Jer. 31:34
but if ye *f.* not men their Matt. 6:15
hath power to *f.* sins 9:6
how oft sin, I *f.*? 18:21
who can *f.* sins but Mark 2:7
when ye stand praying, *f.* 11:25
Father *f.* them; for 23:34
rather to *f.* him 2 Cor. 2:7
to whom ye *f.* any thing 2:10
faithful and just to *f.* 1 John 1:9

FORGIVEN, *granted pardon.*
thy sins *f.* thee Matt. 9:2
God for Christ's sake *f.* Eph. 4:32
f. all trespasses Col. 2:13
because sins are *f.* 1 John 2:12

FORGIVENESS, *pardon.*
preached *f.* of sins Acts 13:38
may receive *f.* of sins 26:18
f. of sins according Eph. 1:7

FORNICATION, *sexual relations outside marriage.*
saving for *f.* Matt. 5:32
not born of *f.* John 8:41
abstain from *f.* Acts 15:20
f. not be once named Eph. 5:3
abstain from *f.* 1 Thess. 4:3

FOUNDATION, *basis, support.*
f. heaven moved 2 Sam. 22:8
if the *f.* be destroyed Ps. 11:3
laid the *f.* of the earth 104:5
is everlasting *f.* Prov. 10:25
without a *f.* built house Luke 6:48
another man's *f.* Rom. 15:20
I have laid the *f.* 1 Cor. 3:10
other *f.* can no man lay 3:11

FOUNTAIN, *origin, spring.*
the *f.* of life Ps. 36:9
law of wise is a *f.* of Prov. 13:14
fear of the Lord is a *f.* 14:27
f. of living waters Jer. 2:13
give *f.* of water Rev. 21:6

FREE, *at liberty.*
of *f.* heart 2 Chron. 29:31
uphold with *f.* Spirit Ps. 51:12
let oppressed go *f.* Isa. 58:6
truth make you *f.* John 8:32
made *f.* from sin Rom. 6:18
made me *f.* from law of 8:2
am I not *f.*? 1 Cor. 9:1
Christ hath made us *f.* Gal. 5:1

FRUIT, *produce, increase.*
tithe of *f.* Lord's Lev. 27:30
yield *f.* of increase Ps. 107:37
f. of righteous a tree Prov. 11:30
neither *f.* in vines Hab. 3:17
know them by *f.* Matt. 7:16
tree is known by his *f.* 12:33
good ground, beareth *f.* 13:23
branch that beareth *f.* John 15:2
bring forth *f.* unto God Rom. 7:4
f. of Spirit is love Gal. 5:22
mercy and good *f.* Jam. 3:17
yielded *f.* every month Rev. 22:2

FULL, *complete, abounding.*
land *f.* of wickedness Lev. 19:29
earth *f.* thy mercy Ps. 119:64
earth *f.* of his glory Isa. 6:3
valley *f.* of bones Ezek. 37:1
f. power by Spirit Mic. 3:8
your joy might be *f.* John 15:11
instructed to be *f.* Phil. 4:12
your joy may be *f.* 1 John 1:4

FURY, *wrath, frenzy.*
f. is not in me; who Isa. 27:4
in anger, and in *f.* Jer. 21:5
jealous with great *f.* Zech. 8:2

G

GATE, *door, opening.*
your heads, O ye *g.* Ps. 24:7
Lord loveth the *g.* of 87:2
his *g.* with thanksgiving 100:4
thy *g.* shall be open Isa. 60:11
enter at strait *g.* Matt. 7:13
g. of hell not prevail 16:18
had twelve *g.* and Rev. 21:12
every *g.* one pearl 21:21

GIFT, *a present, reward.*
he that hateth *g.* Prov. 15:27
a *g.* is as a precious 17:8
every one loveth *g.* Isa. 1:23
it is a *g.* by whatsoever Matt. 15:5
g. of Holy Ghost Acts 2:38
g. of God purchased 8:20
desire spiritual *g.* 1 Cor. 14:1
neglect not the *g.* 1 Tim. 4:14

GIVE, *confer, grant.*
surely *g.* the tenth Gen. 28:22
g. his angels charge Ps. 91:11
g. to him that asketh Matt. 5:42
g. us this day our daily 6:11
freely received, freely *g.* 10:8
to *g.* you kingdom Luke 12:32
g. eternal life John 17:2
g. us all things Rom. 8:32
God *g.* increase 1 Cor. 3:7
g. attendance to 1 Tim. 4:13
g. to all men liberally Jam. 1:5
g. grace unto the humble 4:6

GIVEN, *bestowed, conferred.*
child born, son *g.* Isa. 9:6
ask, shall be *g.* Matt. 7:7
much *g.*, much required Luke 12:48
Father hath *g.* me John 5:36
g. name above every Phil. 2:9

GLAD, *gratified, joyful.*
will be *g.* in heart Ex. 4:14
I will be *g.* and rejoice Ps. 9:2
therefore my heart is *g.* 16:9
be *g.* in the Lord, and 32:11
maketh *g.* heart of 104:15
I was *g.* when they said 122:1
g. tidings of kingdom Luke 8:1
saw it, and was *g.* John 8:56
declare *g.* tidings Acts 13:32
bring *g.* tidings of Rom. 10:15
g. when are weak 2 Cor. 13:9

GLORIFIED, *from glorify.*
Son of man be *g.* John 12:23
Father *g.* in Son 14:13
God hath *g.* Son Acts 3:13
word may be *g.* 2 Thess. 3:1

GLORIFY, *honor, worship.*
praise *g.* me Ps. 50:23
all nations shall *g.* thy Ps. 86:9
Father, *g.* thy name John 12:28
g. God in body and 1 Cor. 6:20

GLORY, *praise, honor, splendor.*
set thy *g.* above heavens Ps. 8:1
King of *g.* shall come in 24:7
wise inherit *g.* Prov. 3:35
crown of your *g.* Jer. 13:18
Son of man come in *g.* Matt. 16:27
to whom *g.* for ever Rom. 11:36
to God only wise be *g.* 16:27
from *g.* to *g.* 2 Cor. 3:18

GOD, *eternal, infinite Spirit.*
blessed most high *G.* Gen. 14:20
Thou *G.* seest me 16:13
by hands of mighty *G.* 49:24
will be your *G.* Lev. 26:12
G. not a man, that Num. 23:19
thy *G.* is among Deut. 7:21
a *G.* in Israel 1 Sam. 17:46
who is *G.* save 2 Sam. 22:32
if the Lord be *G.* 1 Kings 18:21
great is our *G.* 2 Chron. 2:5
O Lord, thou art our *G.* 14:11
G. greater than man Job 33:12
behold, *G.* is mighty 36:5
Thou art my *G.* Ps. 31:14
after thee, O *G.* 42:1
G. King of all earth 47:7
thou art *G.* alone 86:10
the Lord our *G.* is holy 99:9
G. is in heaven Eccl. 5:2
G. is with us Isa. 8:10
the mighty *G.* the 9:6
G. is my salvation 12:2
this is our *G.*, we have 25:9
behold, your *G.* 40:9
I am *G.* there is none 45:22
thy *G.* reigneth 52:7
I will be their *G.* Jer. 31:33
I am *G.* not man Hos. 11:9
who is a *G.* like Mic. 7:18
interpreted, *G.* with Matt. 1:23
that *G.* is true John 3:33
G. is a Spirit; and they John 4:24

my Lord and my *G.* John 20:28
G. forbid: yea let *G.* Rom. 3:4
if *G.* be for us, who can 8:31
G. is faithful 1 Cor. 1:9
there is but one *G.* the 8:6
be to them a *G.* Heb. 8:10
G. is light, and in 1 John 1:5
G. is greater than our 3:20
for G. is love 4:8
in temple of my *G.* Rev. 3:12
G. shall be with them 21:3

GOOD, *kind, excellent, fit.*
not *g.* man be alone Gen. 2:18
God meant it unto *g.* 50:20
none that doeth *g.* Ps. 14:1
see that the Lord is *g.* 34:8
the Lord is *g.* to all 145:9
but a *g.* word maketh Prov. 12:25
merry heart doeth *g.* 17:22
a *g.* name is rather to 22:1
be of *g.* comfort Matt. 9:22
salt is *g.*: but if Mark 9:50
I am the *g.* shepherd John 10:11
abound to *g.* work 2 Cor. 9:8

GOSPEL, *glad tidings.*
lose his life for *g.* Mark 8:35
not ashamed of *g.* Rom. 1:16
if our *g.* be hid 2 Cor. 4:3
receive another *g.* 11:4
fellowship in *g.* Phil. 1:5
g. came not in word 1 Thess. 1:5

GRACE, *favor, mercy, elegance.*
g. poured into lips Ps. 45:2
G. to you, and peace Rom. 1:7
justified freely by his *g.* 3:24
access by faith into *g.* 5:2
by *g.* a partaker 1 Cor. 10:30
my *g.* is sufficient for 2 Cor. 12:9
by *g.* ye are saved Eph. 2:5
unto me is this *g.* given 3:8
be strong in *g.* 2 Tim. 2:1
g. whereby may serve Heb. 12:28

GRAVE, *burial place, tomb.*
hide me in *g.* Job 14:13
in *g.* who shall give Ps. 6:5
wicked silent in the *g.* 31:17
g. cannot praise thee Isa. 38:18
ransom from *g.* Hos. 13:14
g. were opened Matt. 27:52
O *g.* thy victory 1 Cor. 15:55

GREAT, *large, numerous.*
is *g.* reward Ps. 19:11
g. is the Holy One of Isa. 12:6
g. reward in heaven Matt. 5:12
called *g.* in kingdom 5:19
pearl of *g.* price 13:46
this a *g.* mystery Eph. 5:32
a *g.* white throne Rev. 20:11

GREATER, *superior.*
the Lord *g.* than all Ex. 18:11
thou shalt see *g.* John 1:50
God is *g.* than 1 John 3:20
no *g.* joy than to 3 John 4

GREATEST, *foremost, principal.*
who *g.* in kingdom Matt. 18:1
g. be your servant 23:11
the *g.* is charity 1 Cor. 13:13

GUILTY, *wicked, ill-deserving.*
we are verily *g.* Gen. 42:21
hath sinned and is *g.* Lev. 6:4
he is *g.* of death Matt. 26:66
world become *g.* Rom. 3:19
he is *g.* of all Jam. 2:10

H

HAND, *part of the body, immediate.*
at thy right *h.* Ps. 16:11
clean *h.* and pure heart 24:4
establish work of *h.* 90:17
from the *h.* of God Eccl. 2:24
none can stay his *h.* Dan. 4:35
kingdom is at *h.* Matt. 3:2
let not thy left *h.* know 6:3
my time is at *h.* 26:18
at *h.*, that doth betray 26:46
delivered into *h.* of Luke 9:44
out of Father's *h.* John 10:29
not made with *h.* 2 Cor. 5:1
the Lord is at *h.* Phil. 4:5
day of Christ at *h.* 2 Thess. 2:2

HAPPY, *content.*
h. am I, for Gen. 30:13
h. is that people whose Ps. 144:15
h. is he that hath God 146:5
h. are ye if ye do John 13:17

HARVEST, *time of reaping.*
shall reap the *h.* Lev. 23:10
gathereth in *h.* Prov. 6:8
he that sleepeth in *h.* is 10:5
the *h.* is plenteous Matt. 9:37
h. is end of world 13:39
the *h.* truly is great Luke 10:2

HATE, *dislike, detest, abhor.*
not *h.* thy brother Lev. 19:17
that *h.* thee flee Num. 10:35
love the Lord, *h.* evil Ps. 97:10
I *h.* them that *h.* thee 139:21
fools *h.* knowledge Prov. 1:22
spareth rod *h.* his son 13:24
a time to love, time to *h.* Eccl. 3:8
h. the evil, love Am. 5:15
either he will *h.* the one Matt. 6:24
ye shall be *h.* of all 10:22
shall *h.* one another 24:10
doeth evil *h.* light John 3:20
the world cannot *h.* you 7:7
if world *h.* you 15:18

HEAL, *make whole, reconcile.*
O Lord, *h.* me for Ps. 6:2
time to *h.* Eccl. 3:3
his stripes we are *h.* Isa. 53:5
me and I shall be *h.* Jer. 17:14
I will come and *h.* Matt. 8:7
pray ye may be *h.* Jam. 5:16
stripes ye were *h.* 1 Pet. 2:24

HEAR, *perceive sound.*
h. me when I call, O Ps. 4:1
cause thine ear to *h.* 10:17
they *h.* thy words, but Ezek. 33:31
whosoever *h.* these Matt. 7:24
if he will not *h.* thee 18:16
he that *h.* you, *h.* me Luke 10:16
sheep *h.* his voice John 10:3
the world *h.* them 1 John 4:5

HEARING, *perceiving of sound.*
h. they hear not Matt. 13:13
faith cometh by *h.* Rom. 10:17
or by the *h.* of faith Gal. 3:5

HEART, *seat of moral life.*
with all your *h.* Deut. 11:13
love with all *h.* 13:3
he hath said in his *h.* Ps. 10:6
search me, know my *h.* 139:23
proud *h.* is sin Prov. 21:4
as he thinketh in his *h.* 23:7
wise man's *h.* discerneth Eccl. 8:5
h. is deceitful above Jer. 17:9
blessed the pure in *h.* Matt. 5:8
h. man believeth Rom. 10:10
entered into *h.* 1 Cor. 2:9
Christ dwell in *h.* Eph. 3:17
near with true *h.* Heb. 10:22
purify your *h.* ye Jam. 4:8
the hidden man of *h.* 1 Pet. 3:4

HEAVEN, *sky, abode of bliss.*
windows *h.* opened Gen. 7:11
the gate of *h.* 28:17
when I consider thy *h.* Ps. 8:3
h. and earth praise 69:34
as *h.* high above 103:11
new *h.* and new earth Isa. 65:17
if *h.* be measured Jer. 31:37
h. and earth pass Matt. 5:18
not angels in *h.* Mark 13:32
h. and earth to pass Luke 16:17
other name under *h.* Acts 4:12
eternal in *h.* 2 Cor. 5:1
are written in *h.* Heb. 12:23
earth and *h.* fled Rev. 20:11
new *h.* and new earth 21:1

HEIR, *one who inherits.*
h.; *h.* of God, joint Rom. 8:17
h. according to the Gal. 3:29
h. according to hope Tit. 3:7
h. of salvation Heb. 1:14
h. of the righteousness 11:7
h. of the kingdom Jam. 2:5

HELL, *abode of evil spirits.*
unto lowest *h.* Deut. 32:22
wicked turned into *h.* Ps. 9:17
if I make my bed in *h.* 139:8
deliver his soul from *h.* Prov. 23:14
h. enlarged herself Isa. 5:14
cast down to *h.* Ezek. 31:16
soul and body in *h.* Matt. 10:28
gates *h.* not prevail 16:18
cast down to *h.* 2 Pet. 2:4
keys of *h.* and Rev. 1:18
and *h.* cast into lake 20:14

HELP, *to aid, assistance.*
an *h.* meet for him Gen. 2:18
is none to *h.* Ps. 22:11
he is our *h.* and our 33:20
Lord shall *h.* them 37:40
a present *h.* in trouble 46:1
h. mine unbelief Mark 9:24

HIDE, *withhold, secret.*
h. me under the shadow Ps. 17:8
didst *h.* face 30:7
how long *h.* thyself? 89:46
I will *h.* mine eyes Isa. 1:15
h. multitude of sins Jam. 5:20

HIGH, *lofty, elevated, noble.*
hast ascended on *h.* Ps. 68:18
heaven is *h.* above the 103:11
h. praises of God 149:6
h. look, proud heart Prov. 21:4
he shall dwell on *h.* Isa. 33:16
glorious *h.* throne Jer. 17:12
mind not *h.* things Rom. 12:16
down every *h.* thing 2 Cor. 10:5
prize of *h.* calling Phil. 3:14

HOLY, *pure, hallowed, sacred.*
place is *h.* Ex. 3:5
sabbath day to keep *h.* 20:8
be ye *h.*; I am the Lord Lev. 20:7
thou art *h.* O thou that Ps. 22:3
the Lord is *h.* in all 145:17
filled with *H.* Ghost Luke 1:15
H. Ghost descended in 3:22
H. Ghost shall teach 12:12
all filled with *H.* Ghost Acts 2:4
h. acceptable unto God Rom. 12:1
H. Ghost teacheth 1 Cor. 2:13
we should be *h.* and Eph. 1:4
to present you *h.* and Col. 1:22
lifting up *h.* hands 1 Tim. 2:8
H. Ghost sent down 1 Pet. 1:12

HOPE, *confident expectation.*
hypocrite's *h.* perish Job 8:13
set *h.* in God Ps. 78:7
not ashamed of my *h.* 119:116
whose *h.* is in Lord 146:5
for we are saved by *h.* Rom. 8:24
faith, *h.*, charity 1 Cor. 13:13
we have such *h.* 2 Cor. 3:12
we wait for *h.* Gal. 5:5
h. laid up for Col. 1:5
Christ in you, the *h.* 1:27
which have no *h.* 1 Thess. 4:13
helmet *h.* of salvation 5:8
that blessed *h.* Tit. 2:13
the *h.* of eternal life 3:7
h. we have as an anchor Heb. 6:19
that hath this *h.* 1 John 3:3

HOUSE, *dwelling, temple.*
none but *h.* of God Gen. 28:17
habitation of thy *h.* Ps. 26:8
in my Father's *h.* John 14:2
h. not made with 2 Cor. 5:1

HUMBLE, *not proud, meek.*
h. thee and prove Deut. 8:2
cry of the *h.* Ps. 9:12
forget not the *h.* 10:12
better *h.* spirit Prov. 16:19
lofty looks be *h.* Isa. 2:11
contrite *h.* spirit 57:15
whosoever shall *h.* Matt. 18:4
h. himself be exalted Luke 14:11
h. himself and became Phil. 2:8
giveth grace unto *h.* Jam. 4:6
h. yourselves under 1 Pet. 5:6

HUNGER, *to crave food.*
Blessed they which *h.* Matt. 5:6
for ye shall *h.* Luke 6:25
cometh never *h.* John 6:35
if thine enemy *h.* Rom. 12:20
we both *h.* and 1 Cor. 4:11
shall *h.* no more Rev. 7:16

HYPOCRITE, *pretender, cheat.*
h. hope perish Job 8:13
what is hope of *h.*? 27:8
h. heap up wrath Job 36:13
every one is an *h.* Isa. 9:17
fast, be not as *h.* Matt. 6:16
h. can ye not discern 16:3
appoint portion with *h.* 24:51

I

IDOL, *image of false god.*
turn not unto *i.* Lev. 19:4
make you no *i.* 26:1
i. he shall utterly abolish Isa. 2:18
turn from your *i.* Ezek. 14:6
i. will lay desolate Mic. 1:7
cut off the names of *i.* Zech. 13:2
that abhorrest *i.* Rom. 2:22
an *i.* nothing in 1 Cor. 8:4
yourselves from *i.* 1 John 5:21

IMAGE, *figure, form, idol.*
man in our *i.* Gen. 1:26
glory of God into *i.* Rom. 1:23
conformed to *i.* of his Son 8:29
i. and glory of God 1 Cor. 11:7
Christ *i.* of God 2 Cor. 4:4
i. of him created Col. 3:10

IMMORTALITY, *unending life or existence.*
mortal put on *i.* 1 Cor. 15:53
put on *i.*, then shall be 15:54
who only hath *i.* 1 Tim. 6:16
life and *i.* to light 2 Tim. 1:10

IMPOSSIBLE, *not possible.*
nothing be *i.* Matt. 17:20
with men this is *i.* 19:26
i. for those who were Heb. 6:4
it was *i.* for God to lie 6:18
without faith it is *i.* to 11:6

IMPUTE, *ascribe, attribute.*
be *i.* unto him Lev. 7:18
blood shall be *i.* unto Lev. 17:4
Lord *i.* not iniquity Ps. 32:2
God *i.* righteousness Rom. 4:6
Lord will not *i.* sin 4:8

INFIRMITY, *feebleness.*
this is my *i.* Ps. 77:10
himself took our *i.* Matt. 8:17
because of the *i.* of Rom. 6:19
Spirit helpeth our *i.* 8:26
glory, but in *i.* 2 Cor. 12:5

INHERIT, *to be heir, possess.*
shall *i.* it forever Ex. 32:13
his seed shall *i.* the Ps. 25:13
meek *i.* the earth 37:11
the simple *i.* folly Prov. 14:18
i. everlasting life Matt. 19:29
i. kingdom prepared for 25:34
may *i.* eternal life Mark 10:17
i. the blessing Heb. 12:17

INIQUITY, *wickedness.*
visiting the *i.* of the Ex. 20:5
forgiving *i.* and 34:7
upon me let *i.* be 1 Sam. 25:24
all workers of *i.* no Ps. 14:4
O Lord pardon mine *i.* 25:11
Lord imputeth not *i.* 32:2
mine *i.* have I not hid 32:5
blot out all mine *i.* 51:9
who forgiveth thine *i.* 103:3
let not *i.* have dominion 119:133
by truth *i.* purged Prov. 16:6
thine *i.* is taken away Isa. 6:7
laid on him the *i.* of 53:6
ye that work *i.* Matt. 7:23
mystery of *i.* 2 Thess. 2:7
depart from *i.* 2 Tim. 2:19
redeem us from *i.* Tit. 2:14

INSTRUCT, *teach, educate.*
i. me in the night Ps. 16:7
I will *i.* thee and teach 32:8
knowest, being *i.* Rom. 2:18
I am *i.* to be full Phil. 4:12

INSTRUCTION, *teaching.*
despise wisdom and *i.* Prov. 1:7
take fast hold of *i.* let Prov. 4:13
receive my *i.* 8:10
hear *i.* and be wise, and 8:33
whoso loveth *i.* loveth 12:1
refuseth *i.* despiseth 15:32
i. in righteousness 2 Tim. 3:16

INTERCESSION, *pleading.*
made *i.* for Isa. 53:12
Spirit maketh *i.* Rom. 8:26
how he maketh *i.* to God 11:2
prayers, *i.*, giving 1 Tim. 2:1
liveth to make *i.* Heb. 7:25

J

JEALOUS, *vigilant, zealous.*
I am a *j.* God Ex. 20:5
j. for my holy name Ezek. 39:25
j. over you with 2 Cor. 11:2

JEHOVAH, *name of God.*
by my name *J.* was I Ex. 6:3
whose name is *J.* Ps. 83:18
Lord *J.* is my strength Isa. 12:2
in Lord *J.* is everlasting 26:4

JESUS, *the Messiah, Saviour.*
J. called Christ Matt. 1:16
J. was born in Bethlehem 2:1
J. when he was baptized 3:16
J. began to preach, and 4:17
laid hands on *J.*, and 26:50
J. son of David Mark 10:47
J. entered into 11:11
J. said I am; and ye 14:62
when he saw *J.* he Luke 8:28
J. cried with loud voice 23:46
seeth *J.* coming John 1:29
brought him to *J.* 1:42
J. knew hour was come 13:1
disciple whom *J.* Loved 20:2
all *J.* began to do Acts 1:1
at name of *J.* Phil. 2:10
high priest *J.* Heb. 4:14
confess *J.* is Son 1 John 4:15
I *J.* sent angel Rev. 22:16

JOY, *gladness, pleasure.*
fulness of *j.* Ps. 16:11
j. cometh in morning Ps. 30:5
with voice of *j.* 42:4
j. of the whole earth is 48:2
nations sing for *j.* 67:4
sow tears, reap in *j.* 126:5
everlasting j . upon Isa. 35:10
break forth into *j.* 52:9
with j . receiveth it Matt. 13:20
j. over one sinner Luke 15:7
j. is fulfilled John 3:29
count it all *j.* when Jam. 1:2

ye rejoice with *j.* 1 Pet. 1:8
glad with exceeding *j.* 4:13

JUDGMENT, *act of judging.*
thy *j.* as noonday Ps. 37:6
set *j.* in earth Isa. 42:4
j. unto victory Matt. 12:20
escape *j.* of God Rom. 2:3
stand before *j.* seat 14:10
of eternal *j.* Heb. 6:2
but after this the *j.* 9:27

JUST, *honest, true, upright.*
more *j.* than God Job 4:17
path of the *j.* is as Prov. 4:18
teach a *j.* man 9:9
j. live by faith Hab. 2:4
resurrection of the *j.* Luke 14:14
j. live by faith Rom. 1:17
whatsoever are *j.* Phil. 4:8
that which is *j.* and Col. 4:1
a *j.* recompence Heb. 2:2

JUSTIFY, *defend, make just.*
will not *j.* wicked Ex. 23:7
j. himself rather Job 32:2
thy sight no man *j.* Ps. 143:2
no flesh be *j.* Rom. 3:20
j. by faith, have peace 5:1

K

KEEP, *observe, protect.*
k. me as apple of eye Ps. 17:8
k. tongue from evil 34:13
angels to *k.* thee 91:11
she shall *k.* thee Prov. 4:6
time to *k.*, and Eccl. 3:6
earth *k.* silence Hab. 2:20
angels to *k.* thee Luke 4:10
if ye love me, *k.* my John 14:15
k. thyself pure 1 Tim. 5:22
if we *k.* his 1 John 2:3
I also will *k.* thee Rev. 3:10
k. sayings of this book 22:9

KING, *chief ruler, sovereign.*
a *k.* to judge us 1 Sam. 8:5
have I set my *K.* Ps. 2:6
my *K.* and my God 5:2
the Lord is *K.* for ever 10:16
God is my *K.* of old 74:12
an everlasting *K.* Jer. 10:10
blessed be the *K.* Luke 19:38
he himself is Christ a *k.* 23:2
Jews, Behold your *K.* John 19:14
the *K.* eternal 1 Tim. 1:17
thy ways, thou *K.* of Rev. 15:3

KINGDOM, *dominion of the king.*
thine is the *k.* 1 Chron. 29:11
the *k.* is the Lord's Ps. 22:28
his *k.* everlasting Dan. 4:3
k. an everlasting *k.* 7:27
I appoint unto
you a *k.* Luke 22:29
cannot see *k.* of God John 3:3
my *k.* is not of this 18:36
delivered up *k.* 1 Cor. 15:24
his heavenly *k.* 2 Tim. 4:18
rich in faith, heirs *k.* Jam. 2:5
everlasting *k.* of 2 Pet. 1:11

KNOW, *to be aware of.*
I *k.* that my redeemer Job 19:25
k. that I am God Ps. 46:10
this I *k.* for God is for 56:9
let not left hand *k.* Matt. 6:3
given unto you to *k.* 13:11
it is not for you to *k.* Acts 1:7
we *k.* that all things Rom. 8:28
saith, I *k.* him, and 1 John 2:4
we *k.* that, when he shall 3:2

KNOWLEDGE, *what is known.*
fear Lord beginning *k.* Prov. 1:7
by his *k.* the depths 3:20
a man of *k.* increaseth Prov. 24:5
nor *k.* in grave Eccl. 9:10
earth filled with *k.* Hab. 2:14
give *k.* of salvation Luke 1:77
more perfect *k.* Acts 24:22
retain God in *k.* Rom. 1:28
by law is *k.* of sin 3:20
k. puffeth up, but 1 Cor. 8:1
to another word of *k.* 12:8
add to virtue *k.* 2 Pet. 1:5
grow in grace, and *k.* 3:18

L

LABOUR, *work, toil.*
six days shalt thou *l.* Ex. 20:9
eat the *l.* of thine hands Ps. 128:2
in all *l.* there is profit Prov. 14:23
l. not to be rich; cease 23:4
no end of all his *l.* Eccl. 4:8
they shall not *l.* in vain Isa. 65:23
l. of olive fail Hab. 3:17
your *l.* is not vain in 1 Cor. 15:58
the fruit of my *l.* Phil. 1:22
your *l.* of love 1 Thess. 1:3
let us *l.* to enter into Heb. 4:11

LAMB, *young sheep, Christ.*
as a *l.* to the slaughter Isa. 53:7
behold the *L.* of God John 1:29
a *l.* without blemish 1 Pet. 1:19
the *L.* that was slain Rev. 5:12
wrath of the *L.* 6:16
white in blood of *L.* 7:14
overcame by blood of *L.* 12:11
L. book of life 21:27
throne of God and *L.* 22:1

LAW, *a decree, order, statute.*
in his *l.* meditate Ps. 1:2
l. of Lord perfect 19:7
l. of his God in heart 37:31
thy *l.* is within my heart 40:8
and the *l.* is light Prov. 6:23
l. of truth was in his Mal. 2:6
not to destroy *l.* Matt. 5:17
weightier matters of *l.* 23:23
by *l.* is knowledge
of sin Rom. 3:20
until the *l.* sin was in 5:13
ye are not under the *l.* Rom. 6:14
dead to *l.* by Christ 7:4
free from *l.* of sin and 8:2
the *l.* is not of faith Gal. 3:12
debtor to do whole *l.* 5:3
l. shadow of good Heb. 10:1

LEAD, *guide, direct.*
cloud to *l.* them Ex. 13:21
he *l.* me beside still Ps. 23:2
l. me in a plain path 27:1
little child shall *l.* Isa. 11:6
l. us not into Matt. 6:13
the blind *l.* the blind 15:14

LEAST, *smallest, low degree.*
these *l.* commandments Matt. 5:19
l. in kingdom of heaven 11:11
l. of all seeds 13:32
that which is *l.* Luke 16:10

LIBERTY, *freedom.*
l. throughout land Lev. 25:10
I will walk at *l.* Ps. 119:45
proclaim *l.* to Isa. 61:1
lest this *l.* become 1 Cor. 8:9
where spirit, is *l.* 2 Cor. 3:17
stand fast in the *l.* Gal. 5:1
perfect law of *l.* Jam. 1:25
not using *l.* for a 1 Pet. 2:16

LIFE, *animation, salvation.*
tree of *l.* in midst of Gen. 2:9
give *l.* for *l.* Ex. 21:23
l. of flesh blood Lev. 17:11
blood is the *l.* Deut. 12:23
shew path of *l.* Ps. 16:11
fountain of *l.* 36:9
l. unto thy soul and Prov. 3:22
way of *l.* is above to 15:24
wisdom giveth *l.* Eccl. 7:12
for your *l.* Matt. 6:25
save *l.*, or kill? Mark 3:4
in him was *l.* and John 1:4
I am the bread of *l.* 6:35
lay down thy *l.* for my 13:38
in newness of *l.* Rom. 6:4
spiritually minded is *l.* 8:6
neither death, nor *l.* Rom. 8:38
Spirit giveth *l.* 2 Cor. 3:6
l. of Jesus be 4:10
for what is your *l.*? Jam. 4:14
eat tree of *l.* Rev. 2:7
crown of *l.* 2:10
of water of *l.* 22:1

LIGHT, *illumination.*
l. of wicked put out Job 18:5
the Lord is my *l.* and Ps. 27:1
in thy *l.* shall we see *l.* 36:9
and a *l.* unto my 119:105
path just shining *l.* Prov. 4:18
the law is *l.* 6:23
the *l.* is sweet Eccl. 11:7
have seen great *l.* Isa. 9:2
l. to the Gentiles 49:6
shine for thy *l.* is come 60:1
the *l.* of the world Matt. 5:14
let your *l.* so shine that 5:16
l. of the body is the eye 6:22
life was *l.* of men John 1:4
I am *l.* of the world 8:12
from darkness to *l.* Acts 26:18
l. of the knowledge
of glory 2 Cor. 4:6
Satan angel of *l.* 11:14
Christ shall give thee *l.* Eph. 5:14
God is *l.* and in 1 John 1:5
walk in the *l.* as he is in *l.* 1:7
Lamb the *l.* thereof Rev. 21:23
God giveth them *l.* 22:5

LIVE, *to be alive.*
deceitful shall not *l.* Ps. 55:23
hear, soul shall *l.* Isa. 55:3
can these bones *l.*? Ezek. 37:3
seek me and *l.* Am. 5:4
just *l.* by faith Hab. 2:4
man shall not *l.* by Matt. 4:4
because I *l.* ye shall *l.* John 14:19

just *l.* by faith Rom. 1:17
l. peaceably with 12:18
dying, behold, we *l.* 2 Cor. 6:9
if we *l.* in the Spirit let Gal. 5:25
to *l.* is Christ Phil. 1:21
l. unto righteousness 1 Pet. 2:24

LIVING, *having life.*
man became a *l.* soul Gen. 2:7
fountain of *l.* waters Jer. 2:13
given thee *l.* water John 4:10
I am the *l.* bread 6:51
a *l.* sacrifice Rom. 12:1

LORD, *Jehovah, Jesus Christ.*
L. is my strength Ex. 15:2
the *L.* he is God Deut. 4:35
the *L.* our God is one *L.* 6:4
thou art *L.* alone Neh. 9:6
see that the *L.* is good Ps. 34:8
the *L.* he is God 100:3
the Son of man is *L.* Mark 2:28
the *L.* is risen indeed Luke 24:34
both *L.* and Christ Acts 2:36
same *L.* over all Rom. 10:12
one *L.*, one faith Eph. 4:5

LOST, *not to be found.*
salt *l.* savour Matt. 5:13
go to *l.* sheep 10:6
my son was *l.* Luke 15:24
was *l.* and is found 15:32
hid to them are *l.* 2 Cor. 4:3

LOVE, *regard with affection.*
l. thy neighbour Lev. 19:18
shalt *l.* the Lord Deut. 6:5
I will *l.* thee, O Lord Ps. 18:1
l. the Lord hate evil 97:10
l. covereth all sins Prov. 10:12
l. with everlasting *l.* Jer. 31:3
l. your enemies Matt. 5:44
if ye *l.* them which *l.* 5:46
l. one another as I *l.* John 15:12
greater *l.* hath no man 15:13
l. one another; for Rom. 13:8
fruit of Spirit is *l.* Gal. 5:22
l. of Christ which Eph. 3:19
l. of money root 1 Tim. 6:10
not fear, but *l.* 2 Tim. 1:7
l. is of God 1 John 4:7
God is *l.* 4:8

LOWER, *humble.*
little *l.* than the angels Ps. 8:5
into *l.* parts of earth 63:9

M

MADE, *formed, created.*
day Lord hath *m.* Ps. 118:24
Lord *m.* all things Prov. 16:4
all things *m.* by him John 1:3

MAKER, *one who makes.*
more pure than *M.*? Job 4:17
the Lord our *M.* Ps. 95:6
reproacheth his *M.* Prov. 14:31
the Lord is *M.* of them 22:2
builder and *m.* God Heb. 11:10

MAN, *adult male person.*
m. in our image Gen. 1:26
m. born unto trouble Job 5:7
what is *m.* that thou 7:17
m. to destruction Ps. 90:3
no *m.* serve two Matt. 6:24
no *m.* hath seen John 1:18
behold the *m.* John 19:5
m. is not of the woman 1 Cor. 11:8
m. Christ Jesus 1 Tim. 2:5

MANGER, *feeding trough.*
Laid him in a *m.* Luke 2:7

MANIFEST, *make known.*
m. forth his glory John 2:11
have *m.* thy name 17:6
God *m.* in flesh 1 Tim. 3:16
the life was *m.* 1 John 1:2
m. take away our sins 3:5
in this was *m.* the love 4:9

MARRIAGE, *matrimony.*
in *m.* doeth well 1 Cor. 7:38
m. is honourable Heb. 13:4
m. of the Lamb is Rev. 19:7

MASTER, *one in authority.*
one is your *m.* even Matt. 23:8
ye call me *M.* and Lord John 13:13
wise *m.* builder 1 Cor. 3:10

MEDIATOR, *intercessor.*
one *m.* between 1 Tim. 2:5
m. of better covenant Heb. 8:6
m. of the new testament 9:15
Jesus the *m.* of new 12:24

MEEK, *gentle, mild, humble.*
m. shall eat and be Ps. 22:26
m. inherit the earth 37:11
save all the *m.* of earth 76:9
Lord lifteth up the *m.* 147:6
blessed are the *m.* Matt. 5:5

MERCY, *favor, pity, leniency.*
Lord of great *m.* Num. 14:18
his *m.* endureth 1 Chron. 16:34
according to thy *m.* Ps. 25:7
multitude of *m.* blot 51:1
I trust in *m.* of God 52:8
m. and truth are met 85:10
his *m.* is everlasting 100:5
earth is full of thy *m.* 119:64
great *m.* gather Isa. 54:7
I will have *m.* on Rom. 9:15
God that sheweth *m.* 9:16
by *m.* of God 12:1
received *m.* we faint not 2 Cor. 4:1
God rich in *m.* Eph. 2:4
find *m.* of Lord 2 Tim. 1:18
we may obtain *m.* Heb. 4:16

MESSIAH, *the Saviour.*
M., the Prince Dan. 9:25
shall *M.* be cut off, but 9:26

MIND, *imagination, thought.*
he is in one *m.* and Job 23:13
whose *m.* is stayed Isa. 26:3
love with all *m.* Luke 10:27
a reprobate *m.* Rom. 1:28
carnal *m.* is enmity 8:7
m. not high things but 12:16
we have *m.* of Christ 1 Cor. 2:16
be of one *m.* live in 2 Cor. 13:11
and of a sound *m.* 2 Tim. 1:7

MIRACLE, *a supernatural event.*
have seen great *m.* Deut. 29:3
beginning of *m.* did John 2:11
followed saw *m.* 6:2
working of *m.* 1 Cor. 12:10
worketh *m.* among Gal. 3:5
witness with *m.* Heb. 2:4

MOCK, *deride, ridicule, taunt.*
m. when your fear Prov. 1:26
fools make *m.* at sin 14:9
m. and scourge Mark 10:34
God is not *m.* Gal. 6:7

MONEY, *coin, stamped metal.*
m. is a defence Eccl. 7:12
redeemed without *m.* Isa. 52:3
without *m.* and without 55:1
changers of *m.* John 2:14
thy *m.* perish with Acts 8:20
love of *m.* root of 1 Tim. 6:10

MOTHER, *female parent.*
was *m.* of all living Gen. 3:20
m. comforteth Isa. 66:13
m. of my Lord Luke 1:43
m. of Jesus there John 2:1
m. of harlots Rev. 17:5

MOURN, *grieve, be sorrowful.*
a time to *m.* and a Eccl. 3:4
comfort all that *m.* Isa. 61:2
blessed they that *m.* Matt. 5:4

MOUTH, *opening between lips.*
out of *m.* of babes Ps. 8:2
my *m.* speak of wisdom 49:3
my *m.* shew forth thy 51:15
flattering *m.* worketh Prov. 26:28
draw near with *m.* Isa. 29:13
out of own *m.* will I Luke 19:22
with *m.* confession Rom. 10:10
out of same *m.* Jam. 3:10

MYSTERY, *secret, wonder.*
to know the *m.* Mark 4:11
ignorant of this *m.* Rom. 11:25
I shew you a *m.* 1 Cor. 15:51
m. of God Col. 2:2
m. of iniquity 2 Thess. 2:7
m. of faith in 1 Tim. 3:9
M., Babylon the great Rev. 17:5

N

NAME, *title, appellation.*
I will declare thy *n.* Ps. 22:22
they that love his *n.* 69:36
praise thy *n.* for thy Ps. 138:2
good *n.* rather to be Prov. 22:1
whose *n.* is Holy Isa. 57:15
be called by a new *n.* 62:2
Hallowed be thy *n.* Matt. 6:9
hated for my *n.* sake 10:22
come in Father's *n.* John 5:43
n. in the book of life Phil. 4:3
all in *n.* of Lord Col. 3:17
Father's *n.* written in Rev. 14:1

NEIGHBOUR, *fellow creature.*
Love *n.* as thyself Lev. 19:18
teach man his *n.* Jer. 31:34
to love his *n.* as Mark 12:33
and who is my *n.* Luke 10:29
no ill to his *n.* Rom. 13:10

NEW, *recent, modern, fresh.*
sing a *n.* song Ps. 33:3
no *n.* thing under Eccl. 1:9
called by *n.* name Isa. 62:2
n. heaven and *n.* 65:17
what *n.* doctrine is Mark 1:27
n. commandment John 13:34
a *n.* creature 2 Cor. 5:17

n. and living way Heb. 10:20
n. name written Rev. 2:17
n. heaven, *n.* earth 21:1

NOTHING, *no thing, nonentity.*
thou hast lacked *n.* Deut. 2:7
desireth, hath *n.* Prov. 13:4
n. impossible unto Matt. 17:20
without me can do *n.* John 15:5

O

OBEY, *to comply with orders.*
o. my voice and I Jer. 7:23
winds and sea *o.* Matt. 8:27
o. God rather than Acts 5:29
o. your parents in Eph. 6:1
servants, *o.* masters Col. 3:22

OBTAIN, *to acquire, win, earn.*
o. favour of Lord Prov. 8:35
also may *o.* mercy Rom. 11:31
run, that may *o.* 1 Cor. 9:24
may *o.* mercy Heb. 4:16

OFFEND, *sin against, disturb.*
nothing *o.* them Ps. 119:165
right eye *o.* thee Matt. 5:29
o. one of these little 18:6
yet *o.* in one point Jam. 2:10

OVERCOME, *conquer, subdue.*
able to *o.* it Num. 13:30
I have *o.* the world John 16:33
be not *o.* of evil Rom. 12:21
born of God *o.* 1 John 5:4

OVERTAKE, *catch, come upon.*
blessings *o.* thee Deut. 28:2
curses *o.* thee 28:15
sword *o.* you Jer. 42:16
evil shall not *o.* Am. 9:10
that day *o.* you 1 Thess. 5:4

P

PARADISE, *place of bliss.*
be with me in *p.* Luke 23:43
caught up into *p.* 2 Cor. 12:4

PARDON, *forgive, excuse.*
he will abundantly *p.* Isa. 55:7
like thee, that *p.* Mic. 7:18

PASSOVER, *a feast.*
they kept the *p.* at Num. 9:5
prepare to eat *p.* Matt. 26:17
Christ our *p.* is 1 Cor. 5:7
through faith kept *p.* Heb. 11:28

PATIENCE, *constancy.*
Lord, have *p.*, and Matt. 18:26
your *p.* and faith 2 Thess. 1:4
follow love, *p.* 1 Tim. 6:11
faith, charity, *p.* Tit. 2:2
trying worketh *p.* Jam. 1:3
suffering and *p.* 5:10
and to temperance *p.* 2 Pet. 1:6
the *p.* and the faith Rev. 13:10

PEACE, *calm repose.*
Lord give thee *p.* Num. 6:26
seek *p.* and pursue it Ps. 34:14
keep in perfect *p.* Isa. 26:3
thy *p.* as a river 48:18
p., *p.* when is no *p.* Jer. 6:14
p. be multiplied Dan. 4:1
let your *p.* come Matt. 10:13
p. one with another Mark 9:50
p. I leave with you John 14:27
we have *p.* with God Rom. 5:1
preach the gospel of *p.* 10:15
God of *p.* be with you 15:33
he is our *p.* who Eph. 2:14

PEOPLE, *nation, tribe, race.*
take you for a *p.* Ex. 6:7
bless God, ye *p.* Ps. 66:8
my *p.* would not 81:11
a *p.* that do err 95:10
sin reproach to *p.* Prov. 14:34
save his *p.* from sins Matt. 1:21
purify a peculiar *p.* Tit. 2:14

PERFECT, *complete, faultless.*
be *p.* with Lord Deut. 18:13
law of the Lord is *p.* Ps. 19:7
keep in *p.* peace Isa. 26:3
p. will of God Rom. 12:2
present every man *p.* Col. 1:28
stand *p.* and complete 4:12
man of God be *p.* 2 Tim. 3:17
spirits of just made *p.* Heb. 12:23
p. in every good work 13:21
p. love casteth 1 John 4:18

PERSECUTE, *to afflict, harass.*
from them that *p.* Ps. 7:1
wicked doth *p.* the poor 10:2
blessed when men *p.* Matt. 5:11
why *p.* thou me? Acts 9:4
p. this way unto death 22:4
bless which *p.* you Rom. 12:14

PLEASURE, *that which pleases.*
do good in thy good *p.* Ps. 51:18
taketh *p.* in his people 149:4
he that loveth *p.* Prov. 21:17
p. of Lord prosper Isa. 53:10
Father's *p.* to give Luke 12:32
p. in infirmities 2 Cor. 12:10
lovers of *p.* more 2 Tim. 3:4
enjoy *p.* of sin Heb. 11:25

POOR, *destitute, in need.*
p. never cease Deut. 15:11
I am *p.* and needy Ps. 40:17
rich and *p.* together 49:2
blessed *p.* in spirit Matt. 5:3
p. always with you 26:11
blessed be ye *p.* Luke 6:20
goods to feed *p.* 1 Cor. 13:3
for your sakes became *p.* 2 Cor. 8:9

POUR, *cause to flow.*
p. out your heart Ps. 62:8
p. out my spirit Prov. 1:23
p. out prayer when Isa. 26:16
p. out soul unto death 53:12

POWER, *ability, authority.*
thine is the *p.* and 1 Chron. 29:11
being girded with *p.* Ps. 65:6
hath *p.* over spirit Eccl. 8:8
p. on earth to forgive Matt. 9:6
all *p.* is given unto me 28:18
p. to become sons of John 1:12
receive *p.* after Holy Acts 1:8
it is raised in *p.* 1 Cor. 15:43
p. of his resurrection Phil. 3:10
had *p.* of death Heb. 2:14
p. of an endless life 7:16

PRAISE, *homage.*
my *p.* shall be of Ps. 22:25
p. is comely 33:1
his courts with *p.* 100:4
earth full of *p.* Hab. 3:3
give God the *p.* John 9:24
whose *p.* not of men Rom. 2:29
if there be any *p.* Phil. 4:8

PRAY, *to entreat, implore.*
p. for the peace of Ps. 122:6
p. to Father which is in Matt. 6:6
Lord teach us to *p.* Luke 11:1
men ought always to *p.* 18:1
I will *p.* the Father John 14:16
I *p.* for them; I *p.* not 17:9
I will *p.* with spirit 1 Cor. 14:15
p. without ceasing 1 Thess. 5:17
afflicted? Let him *p.* Jam. 5:13
p. one for another 5:16

PRAYER, *supplication, request.*
thou that hearest *p.* Ps. 65:2
p. be made continually 72:15
p. of upright his Prov. 15:8
by *p.* and fasting Matt. 17:21
praying with all *p.* Eph. 6:18
sanctified by *p.* 1 Tim. 4:5

PREACH, *to deliver a sermon.*
p. good tidings unto Isa. 61:1
Jesus began to *p.* Matt. 4:17
p. kingdom of God Luke 9:60
p. Christ unto them Acts 8:5
p. except be sent? Rom. 10:15
p. Christ crucified 1 Cor. 1:23
p. not ourselves 2 Cor. 4:5
p. the word; be 2 Tim. 4:2

PRECIOUS, *very valuable.*
p. things of heaven Deut. 33:13
my soul was *p.* in 1 Sam. 26:21
p. in sight of Lord Ps. 116:15
more *p.* than rubies Prov. 3:15
a man more *p.* Isa. 13:12
p. blood of Christ 1 Pet. 1:19
like *p.* faith 2 Pet. 1:1

PREVAIL, *persuade, force.*
did waters *p.* Gen. 7:20
Lord, let not man *p.* Ps. 9:19
if one *p.* against Eccl. 4:12
gates of hell not *p.* Matt. 16:18

PREVENT, *come before.*
God of mercy *p.* Ps. 59:10
my prayer *p.* thee 88:13
evil shall not *p.* us Am. 9:10

PRIDE, *unreasonable conceit.*
foot of *p.* come Ps. 36:11
taken in their *p.* 59:12
p. do I hate Prov. 8:13
p. before destruction 16:18
man's *p.* shall bring 29:23
woe to crown of *p.* Isa. 28:1
lifted up with *p.* 1 Tim. 3:6
p. of life not of 1 John 2:16

PROCLAIM, *announce.*
p. name of Lord Ex. 33:19
go *p.* these words Jer. 3:12
p. liberty for you to sword 34:17

PROFIT, *gain, benefit to gain.*
riches *p.* not in day Prov. 11:4
in labour there is *p.* 14:23
no *p.* under the sun Eccl. 2:11
what is a man *p.* Matt. 16:26

PROMISE, *assurance, covenant.*
p. of my Father Luke 24:49
wait for *p.* of the Acts 1:4

p. of none effect Rom. 4:14
p. of life now 1 Tim. 4:8
lest *p.* left us Heb. 4:1

PROSPER, *to succeed, increase.*
God will *p.* us Neh. 2:20
he doeth shall *p.* Ps. 1:3
they *p.* that love thee 122:6
pleasure shall *p.* Isa. 53:10

PURCHASE, *to buy, acquire.*
p. a field with Acts 1:18
p. with his own blood 20:28
redemption of *p.* Eph. 1:14

PURE, *simple, true, genuine.*
shew thyself *p.* 2 Sam. 22:27
words *p.* are Prov. 15:26
p. in own eyes 30:12
all things are *p.* Rom. 14:20
whatsoever things *p.* Phil. 4:8
keep thyself *p.* 1 Tim. 5:22
even as he is *p.* 1 John 3:3

Q

QUENCH, *hinder or extinguish.*
none shall *q.* them Isa. 1:31
none can *q.* it Jer. 4:4
q. not the Spirit 1 Thess. 5:19

QUICK, *speedy, living.*
judge *q.* and dead Acts 10:42
judge *q.* and dead 2 Tim. 4:1

QUICKEN, *revive, stimulate.*
shalt *q.* me again Ps. 71:20
also *q.* your mortal Rom. 8:11

QUICKLY, *with haste, speedily.*
surely I come *q.* Rev. 22:20

R

RAISE, *lift up, elevate.*
r. those bowed Ps. 145:14
third day will *r.* us Hos. 6:2
r. the dead Matt. 10:8
three days I will *r.* John 2:19
Father *r.* up dead 5:21
would *r.* Christ Acts 2:30
God should *r.* dead? 26:8
r. up Christ 1 Cor. 15:15
God which *r.* dead 2 Cor. 1:9

REAP, *receive fruit of labor.*
not *r.* corners of Lev. 19:9
sow tears, *r.* in joy Ps. 126:5
iniquity, *r.* vanity Prov. 22:8
shall *r.* whirlwind Hos. 8:7
sow, but not *r.* Mic. 6:15
sparingly, shall *r.* 2 Cor. 9:6

RECEIVE, *take what is given.*
Lord will *r.* my prayer Ps. 6:9
r. blessing from the Lord 24:5
able to *r.* it, let
him *r.* it Matt. 19:12
believing ye shall *r.* 21:22
this man *r.* sinners Luke 15:2
ask and ye shall *r.* John 16:24
weak in faith *r.* ye Rom. 14:1
r. not grace of 2 Cor. 6:1
r. promise of Spirit Gal. 3:14
called might *r.* Heb. 9:15

RECEIVED, *taken.*
freely *r.*, freely Matt. 10:8
own *r.* him not John 1:11
cloud *r.* him out Acts 1:9
by whom *r.* grace Rom. 1:5
not *r.* spirit bondage 8:15
r. dead raised Heb. 11:35
I *r.* of Father Rev. 2:27

REDEEM, *repurchase, save.*
I will *r.* you Ex. 6:6
Lord *r.* soul of Ps. 34:22
r. them under law Gal. 4:5
r. us from iniquity Tit. 2:14

REDEEMER, *God as Saviour.*
know my *R.* liveth Job 19:25
strength and my *R.* Ps. 19:14
thy *R.* the Holy Isa. 41:14
I the Lord am thy *R.* 49:26

REFUGE, *place of safety.*
eternal God, thy *r.* Deut. 33:27
God is our *r.* Ps. 46:1
thou my strong *r.* 71:7
is my *r.* 91:2
have a place of *r.* Prov. 14:26
made lies our *r.* Isa. 28:15

REJOICE, *delight, joy, exult.*
r. in every good Deut. 26:11
r. with trembling Ps. 2:11
Lord reigneth, earth *r.* 97:1
let thy servant *r.* 109:28
who *r.* to do evil Prov. 2:14
r. and do good in Eccl. 3:12
poor shall *r.* Isa. 29:19
my servants shall *r.* 65:13
your heart shall *r.* 66:14
many *r.* at birth Luke 1:14
the world shall *r.* John 16:20
r. in hope glory Rom. 5:2
r. not in iniquity 1 Cor. 13:6
r. in day of Christ Phil. 2:16
r. evermore 1 Thess. 5:16

REMISSION, *pardon.*
blood for *r.* of Matt. 26:28
salvation by *r.* of sins Luke 1:77
baptized for *r.* of sins Acts 2:38
receive *r.* of sins 10:43
r. of sins past Rom. 3:25
without blood no *r.* Heb. 9:22

RENEW, *make new spiritually.*
r. right spirit within Ps. 51:10
shall *r.* strength Isa. 40:31
O Lord, *r.* our days Lam. 5:21
r. them again unto Heb. 6:6

REPENT, *change of mind and life.*
I will *r.* of the evil Jer. 18:8
neither will I *r.* Ezek. 24:14
God *r.* of evil Jonah 3:10
r. ye and believe Mark 1:15
except ye *r.* ye Luke 13:3
r. and be baptized Acts 2:38
all men to *r.* 17:30
r. and turn to God 26:20

REPENTANCE, *contrition.*
sinners to *r.* Matt. 9:13
r. for remission of Mark 1:4
which need no *r.* Luke 15:7
leadeth to *r.* Rom. 2:4
God give them *r.* 2 Tim. 2:25
foundation of *r.* Heb. 6:1

RESIST, *oppose, hinder.*
that ye *r.* not evil Matt. 5:39
not able to *r.* the Acts 6:10
they that *r.* shall Rom. 13:2
also *r.* the truth 2 Tim. 3:8
God *r.* the proud Jam. 4:6
r. the devil, and he 4:7

REST, *repose, resting-place.*
r. on seventh day Gen. 2:2
sabbath of *r.* holy Ex. 31:15
land had *r.* Josh. 14:15
flesh *r.* in hope Ps. 16:9
r. in the Lord and wait 37:7
return unto thy *r.* O 116:7
spirit of Lord shall *r.* Isa. 11:2
whole earth at *r.* 14:7
may cause weary to *r.* 28:12
ye shall find *r.* for Jer. 6:16
I will give you *r.* Matt. 11:28
place of my *r.* Acts 7:49
not enter into *r.* Heb. 3:11
r. yet for a little Rev. 6:11

RESTORE, *replace, refund.*
he *r.* my soul Ps. 23:3
I will *r.* health unto Jer. 30:17
I *r.* him fourfold Luke 19:8
wilt thou *r.* kingdom Acts 1:6
r. such an one in Gal. 6:1

RESURRECTION, *rising again to life.*
say there is no *r.* Matt. 22:23
preached through
Jesus *r.* Acts 4:2
of the hope and *r.* I am 23:6
in likeness of his *r.* Rom. 6:5
if there be no *r.* 1 Cor. 15:13
power of his *r.* Phil. 3:10
obtain better *r.* Heb. 11:35
lively hope, by *r.* 1 Pet. 1:3
this is the first *r.* Rev. 20:5

REVEAL, *disclose, discover.*
things *r.* unto us Deut. 29:29
glory of Lord *r.* Isa. 40:5
be *r.* by fire 1 Cor. 3:13
to *r.* his Son in me Gal. 1:16
God *r.* even this Phil. 3:15
man of sin be *r.* 2 Thess. 2:3

REWARD, *remuneration, pay.*
exceeding great *r.* Gen. 15:1
keeping, great *r.* Ps. 19:11
a *r.* for righteous 58:11
shalt see *r.* of wicked 91:8
great is your *r.* in Matt. 5:12
r. every man according 16:27
receive due *r.* of Luke 23:41
with *r.* of iniquity Acts 1:18
my *r.* is with me Rev. 22:12

RIGHTEOUS, *godly, virtuous.*
r. with wicked Gen. 18:23
shall justify the *r.* Deut. 25:1
Lord knoweth way of *r.* Ps. 1:6
be glad, ye *r.* 32:11
many afflictions of *r.* 34:19
Lord upholdeth the *r.* 37:17
r. be in everlasting 112:6
Lord is *r.* in all ways 145:17
Lord not suffer *r.* to Prov. 10:3
desire of *r.* only good 11:23
r. more excellent than 12:26
there is none *r.* Rom. 3:10
scarcely for *r.* man will 5:7
advocate, Jesus the *r.* 1 John 2:1
r. even as he is *r.* 3:7
true and *r.* are thy Rev. 16:7
r. let him be *r.* still 22:11

RIGHTEOUSNESS, *holiness.*
offer sacrifices of *r.* Ps. 4:5
righteous Lord loveth *r.* 11:7
in paths of *r.* Ps. 23:3
right hand full of *r.* 48:10
heavens declare his *r.* 50:6
his *r.* endureth for ever 111:3
r. delivereth from Prov. 10:2
followeth *r.* findeth life 21:21
I will declare thy *r.* Isa. 57:12
and thirst after *r.* Matt. 5:6
except *r.* exceed *r.* 5:20
God imputeth *r.* Rom. 4:6
of the gift of *r.* 5:17
heart believeth unto *r.* 10:10
awake to *r.* 1 Cor. 15:34
fruit of Spirit is *r.* Eph. 5:9
having breastplate of *r.* 6:14
follow after *r.* 1 Tim. 6:11
a crown of *r.* 2 Tim. 4:8
became heir of *r.* Heb. 11:7
a preacher of *r.* 2 Pet. 2:5

ROCK, *stone, a defense, refuge.*
he is the *R.* Deut. 32:4
set me upon a *r.* Ps. 27:5
r. of salvation 89:26
built house upon *r.* Matt. 7:24
upon this *r.* I build my 16:18
lay in Sion *r.* of Rom. 9:33
that *R.* was Christ 1 Cor. 10:4

RUN, *move with swift pace.*
strong to *r.* race Ps. 19:5
rivers *r.* into sea Eccl. 1:7
r. not be weary Isa. 40:31
many shall *r.* to and Dan. 12:4
r. or had *r.* in vain Gal. 2:2
I have not *r.* in Phil. 2:16
r. with patience Heb. 12:1

S

SABBATH, *day of rest.*
is rest of holy *s.* Ex. 16:23
man that keepeth *s.* Isa. 56:2
call *s.* a delight, the 58:13

SACRIFICE, *offering to God.*
let us do *s.* to Lord Ex. 5:17
offer *s.* and put trust Ps. 4:5
covenant by *s.* 50:5
more acceptable
 than *s.* Prov. 21:3
than *s.* of fools Eccl. 5:1
love more than *s.* Mark 12:33
present living *s.* Rom. 12:1
Christ is *s.* for us 1 Cor. 5:7
upon *s.* of your faith Phil. 2:17
put away sin by *s.* Heb. 9:26
remaineth no more *s.* 10:26
more excellent *s.* 11:4

SALVATION, *redemption.*
waited for thy *s.* O Gen. 49:18
see *s.* of the Lord Ex. 14:13
s. belongeth unto Ps. 3:8
an everlasting *s.* Isa. 45:17
horn of *s.* for us Luke 1:69
power unto *s.* Rom. 1:16
now is day of *s.* 2 Cor. 6:2
gospel of your *s.* Eph. 1:13
work out own *s.* Phil. 2:12
us to obtain *s.* 1 Thess. 5:9
chosen you to *s.* 2 Thess. 2:13
grace bringeth *s.* Tit. 2:11
shall be heirs of *s.* Heb. 1:14
author of eternal *s.* 5:9
through faith unto *s.* 1 Pet. 1:5
S. to our God Rev. 7:10

SANCTIFY, *make holy, purify.*
shall *s.* yourselves Lev. 11:44
s. and cleanse Eph. 5:26
God of peace *s.* 1 Thess. 5:23
s. the people with Heb. 13:12
s. Lord God in your 1 Pet. 3:15

SATAN, *devil, fallen angel.*
S. provoked David 1 Chron. 21:1
S. went forth from Job 1:12
S. stand at his right Ps. 109:6
Get thee hence *S.* Matt. 4:10
if *S.* cast out *S.* he is 12:26
then entered *S.* into Luke 22:3
God shall bruise *S.* Rom. 16:20
lest *S.* should get 2 Cor. 2:11
S. transformed into 11:14
S. hindered us 1 Thess. 2:18

SAVE, *rescue, deliver, protect.*
s. Lord; let the king Ps. 20:9
s. thy people, and bless Ps. 28:9
thy right hand shall *s.* 138:7
your God will *s.* you Isa. 35:4
look unto me and be *s.* 45:22
s. his people from Matt. 1:21
s. life, or kill? Mark 3:4
thy faith hath *s.* Luke 7:50
not to destroy but to *s.* 9:56
whereby we be *s.* Acts 4:12
what must I do to be *s.*? 16:30
we are *s.* by hope Rom. 8:24
to *s.* from death Heb. 5:7
can faith *s.* Jam. 2:14
prayer faith shall *s.* 5:15
scarcely be *s.* 1 Pet. 4:18

SAVIOUR, *God, Jesus Christ.*
Lord gave Israel *s.* 2 Kings 13:5
rejoiced in God my *S.* Luke 1:47
this is Christ the *S.* John 4:42
Christ *s.* of body Eph. 5:23
we look for the *S.* Phil. 3:20
of God our *S.* 1 Tim. 2:3
appearing of our *S.* 2 Tim. 1:10
Son to be the *S.* 1 John 4:14
only wise God our *S.* Jude 25

SCRIPTURE, *written revelation.*
err, not knowing
 the *s.* Matt. 22:29
s. must be fulfilled Mark 14:49
search *s.*; for in John 5:39
s. cannot be broken 10:35
shewing by *s.*
 Jesus was Acts 18:28
what saith the *s.* Rom. 4:3
all *s.* given by
 inspiration 2 Tim. 3:16
law, according to *s.* Jam. 2:8
no *s.* of private 2 Pet. 1:20

SEARCH, *inquire after, seek.*
s. me O God, know Ps. 139:23
s. the scriptures John 5:39
s. scriptures daily Acts 17:11

SECRET, *concealed, private.*
s. of Lord with them Ps. 25:14
his *s.* is with the Prov. 3:32
revealeth his *s.* unto Am. 3:7
thine alms be in *s.* Matt. 6:4
s. of heart made 1 Cor. 14:25

SEEK, *search for, try to find.*
s. not after your Num. 15:39
heart to *s.* God 2 Chron. 19:3
early will I *s.* thee Ps. 63:1
s. me but not find Prov. 1:28
s. me early shall find 8:17
s. ye first kingdom Matt. 6:33
all men *s.* for thee Mark 1:37
whom they *s.* to kill John 7:25
who *s.* for glory Rom. 2:7
all *s.* own things Phil. 2:21
s. things above Col. 3:1
of them that *s.* him Heb. 11:6
s. whom he may 1 Pet. 5:8
shall men *s.* death Rev. 9:6

SERVANT, *helper, slave.*
fool shall be *s.* Prov. 11:29
s. justify many Isa. 53:11
s. as his Lord Matt. 10:25
be *s.* of all Mark 9:35
is the *s.* of sin John 8:34
were *s.* of sin Rom. 6:17
called being a *s.* 1 Cor. 7:21
no more *s.* but a son Gal. 4:7
took form of a *s.* Phil. 2:7

SERVE, *obey, minister, assist.*
fear Lord and *s.* Deut. 6:13
all nations *s.* him Ps. 72:11
s. him with one Zeph. 3:9
no man can *s.* two Matt. 6:24
if any *s.* me, let John 12:26
should not *s.* sin Rom. 6:6
myself *s.* Law of God 7:25
by love *s.* one another Gal. 5:13
ye *s.* Lord Christ Col. 3:24
s. day and night Rev. 7:15

SHEEP, *woolly, timid animal.*
Abel was keeper of *s.* Gen. 4:2
all *s.* and oxen Ps. 8:7
counted as *s.* for 44:22
like *s.* have gone Isa. 53:6
pastors scatter *s.* Jer. 23:1
in *s.* clothing Matt. 7:15
s. hear his voice John 10:3
unto him, feed my *s.* John 21:16
as *s.* going astray 1 Pet. 2:25

SHEPHERD, *keeper of sheep.*
Lord is my *s.* Ps. 23:1
feed flock like *s.* Isa. 40:11
set up *s.* over Jer. 23:4
s. caused to go astray 50:6
one *s.* over them Ezek. 34:23
in same country *s.* Luke 2:8
I am the good *s.* John 10:14

SHOUT, *sudden and loud outcry.*
s. so that earth rang 1 Sam. 4:5
s. when praised Ezra 3:11
s. unto God with Ps. 47:1
s. O Israel be glad Zeph. 3:14

SIGN, *token, symbol, omen.*
Lord give you a *s.* Isa. 7:14
for an everlasting *s.* 55:13
discern the *s.* Matt. 16:3
what *s.* of thy coming 24:3
s. in sun, moon Luke 21:25
other *s.* did Jesus John 20:30
Jews require a *s.* 1 Cor. 1:22
witness with *s.* Heb. 2:4

SIN, *contrary to law of God.*
s. lieth at the door Gen. 4:7
stand in awe, *s.* not Ps. 4:4

remember not *s.* of my Ps. 25:7
my *s.* ever before me 51:3
may add *s.* to *s.* Isa. 30:1
not remember thy *s.* 43:25
they *s.* more and Hos. 13:2
all *s.* be forgiven Matt. 12:31
taketh away *s.* of John 1:29
reprove world of *s.* 16:8
where *s.* abounded Rom. 5:20
we continue in *s.* 6:1
awake and *s.* not 1 Cor. 15:34
made be *s.* for 2 Cor. 5:21
man of *s.* revealed 2 Thess. 2:3

SINNER, *a transgressor, an offender.*
standeth in way of *s.* Ps. 1:1
if *s.* entice thee Prov. 1:10
one *s.* destroyeth Eccl. 9:18
call *s.* to repentance Matt. 9:13
which was a *s.* Luke 7:37
joy in heaven over one *s.* 15:7
we were yet *s.* Christ Rom. 5:8
separate from *s.* Heb. 7:26
cleanse hands, ye *s.* Jam. 4:8

SLEEP, *state of repose.*
in peace and *s.* Ps. 4:8
thy *s.* be sweet Prov. 3:24
yet a little *s.* a little 6:10
to awake out of *s.* Rom. 13:11
s. in Jesus 1 Thess. 4:14

SLUMBER, *sleep.*
keepeth thee not *s.* Ps. 121:3
give not *s.* to thine Prov. 6:4
none shall *s.* nor Isa. 5:27
them spirit of *s.* Rom. 11:8

SON, *male child, Christ.*
kiss the *S.*, lest he be Ps. 2:12
wise *s.* maketh glad Prov. 10:1
unto us a *s.* is given Isa. 9:6
bring forth a *s.* Matt. 1:21
S. of the Blessed Mark 14:61
S. of the Highest Luke 1:32
only begotten *S.* John 1:18
Woman behold thy *s.* 19:26
spared not his own *S.* Rom. 8:32
S. himself be 1 Cor. 15:28
sent forth his *S.* Gal. 4:4
be to me a *S.*? Heb. 1:5
denieth *S.*, the same 1 John 2:23

SOUL, *person, spiritual part.*
became living *s.* Gen. 2:7
my *s.* is weary Job 10:1
not leave *s.* in hell Ps. 16:10
his *s.* dwell at ease 25:13
my *s.* waiteth upon 62:1
s. offering for sin Isa. 53:10
destroy both *s.* and Matt. 10:28
and lose his own *s.*? 16:26
every *s.* be subject Rom. 13:1
to saving of the *s.* Heb. 10:39
save a *s.* from death Jam. 5:20

SPEAK, *talk, utter words.*
that God would *s.* Job 11:5
s. every man truth Zech. 8:16
what ye shall *s.* Matt. 10:19
men *s.* well of you Luke 6:26
and therefore *s.* 2 Cor. 4:13
slow to *s.* Jam. 1:19

SPIRIT, *breath of life; third person of the trinity.*
my *s.* not always Gen. 6:3
I commit my *s.* Ps. 31:5
Lord weigheth *s.* Prov. 16:2
s. indeed is willing Matt. 26:41
S. like a dove Mark 1:10
God is a *S.* John 4:24
even the *S.* of truth 14:17
when *S.* of truth is 16:13
speak as *S.* gave Acts 2:4
after the *S.* Rom. 8:1
s. giveth life 2 Cor. 3:6
walk in the *S.* Gal. 5:16
soweth to *S.* shall of *S.* 6:8
access by one *S.* Eph. 2:18
keep unity of *S.* 4:3
filled with the *S.* 5:18
your love in the *S.* Col. 1:8
quench not the *s.* 1 Thess. 5:19
sanctification of *S.* 2 Thess. 2:13
justified in *S.* 1 Tim. 3:16
without *s.* is dead Jam. 2:26
S. he hath given 1 John 3:24
believe not every *s.* 4:1

STAND, *remain erect, be firm.*
s. still and see Ex. 14:13
s. up for mine help Ps. 35:2
s. not in evil thing Eccl. 8:3
it shall not *s.* Isa. 7:7
who shall *s.* when Mal. 3:2
house divided not *s.* Matt. 12:25
wherein we *s.* Rom. 5:2
s. fast in faith 1 Cor. 16:13
having done all, to *s.* Eph. 6:13
s. fast in the Lord Phil. 4:1
live, if ye *s.* fast 1 Thess. 3:8
I *s.* at door Rev. 3:20

STEDFAST, *firm, resolute.*
thou shalt be *s.* Job 11:15
brethren, be ye *s.* 1 Cor. 15:58
hope of you *s.* 2 Cor. 1:7
word by angels *s.* Heb. 2:2
s. in the faith 1 Pet. 5:9

STONE, *rock, piece of rock.*
this *s.* shall be a Josh. 24:27
s. which builders Ps. 118:22
for foundation a *s.* Isa. 28:16
s. cut out without Dan. 2:34
command this *s.* be Luke 4:3
him first cast a *s.* John 8:7

STRAIGHT, *direct, upright.*
make thy way *s.* Ps. 5:8
make *s.* in desert a Isa. 40:3
make his paths *s.* Matt. 3:3
made *s.* glorified God Luke 13:13
make *s.* paths for Heb. 12:13

STRANGER, *foreigner.*
s. risen up against Ps. 54:3
s. doth not intermeddle Prov. 14:10
I was a *s.* and ye Matt. 25:35
glory, save this *s.* Luke 17:18
to entertain *s.* Heb. 13:2

STRENGTH, *support, security.*
the Lord is my *s.* Ex. 15:2
wisdom and *s.* Job 12:13
Lord is *s.* of my life Ps. 27:1
God is our refuge and *s.* 46:1
way of Lord is *s.* Prov. 10:29
wisdom better than *s.* Eccl. 9:16
without *s.*, in due Rom. 5:6
s. of sin is law 1 Cor. 15:56

SUBJECT, *under authority.*
even devils are *s.* Luke 10:17
not *s.* to law of God Rom. 8:7
every soul *s.* unto higher 13:1
Son himself be *s.* 1 Cor. 15:28

SUBMIT, *yield to, surrender.*
strangers *s.* unto Ps. 18:44
s. yourselves unto Eph. 5:22
s. yourselves Heb. 13:17
s. yourselves to God Jam. 4:7
s. to ordinance 1 Pet. 2:13

SUFFER, *permit, undergo pain.*
s. Holy One to see Ps. 16:10
idle soul *s.* hunger Prov. 19:15
s. not mouth cause sin Eccl. 5:6
s. little children Mark 10:14
beloved Christ to *s.* Luke 24:46
if so be that we *s.* Rom. 8:17
not *s.* you to be 1 Cor. 10:13
to believe but *s.* Phil. 1:29
to *s.* affliction Heb. 11:25
ye do well and *s.* 1 Pet. 2:20

SUN, *source of light.*
S. stand thou still Josh. 10:12
s. to rule by day Ps. 136:8
s. be no more thy Isa. 60:19
Lord giveth *s.* for Jer. 31:35
maketh *s.* rise on Matt. 5:45
let not *s.* go down Eph. 4:26
city no need of *s.* Rev. 21:23

SUPPLICATION, *petition.*
thy *s.* to Almighty Job 8:5
Lord hath heard my *s.* Ps. 6:9
let my *s.* be accepted Jer. 37:20
in prayer and *s.* Acts 1:14
and *s.* for saints Eph. 6:18

SWORD, *offensive weapon.*
flaming *s.* which Gen. 3:24
tongue a sharp *s.* Ps. 57:4
s. shall pierce thy Luke 2:35
than two edged *s.* Heb. 4:12
killeth with *s.* must Rev. 13:10

T

TEACH, *instruct.*
t. them diligently Deut. 6:7
O Lord; *t.* me thy Ps. 25:4
instruct him and *t.* Isa. 28:26
t. all nations Matt. 28:19
Lord *t.* us to pray Luke 11:1
he shall *t.* you all John 14:26
t. every where in 1 Cor. 4:17
t. every man in Col. 1:28
t. things which they Tit. 1:11

TEMPT, *entice, put to test.*
God did *t.* Abraham Gen. 22:1
wherefore *t.* Lord? Ex. 17:2
not *t.* the Lord Deut. 6:16
Thou shalt not *t.* the Matt. 4:7
Why *t.* ye me 22:18
agreed to *t.* Spirit Acts 5:9
Satan *t.* you not 1 Cor. 7:5

TEMPTATION, *entice to evil.*
as in day of *t.* in Ps. 95:8
lead us not into *t.* Matt. 6:13
that enter not into *t.* 26:41
hath no *t.* taken 1 Cor. 10:13
godly out of *t.* 2 Pet. 2:9

TESTAMENT, *covenant, will.*
my blood of new *t.* Matt. 26:28

This cup is new *t.* Luke 22:20
minister of new *t.* 2 Cor. 3:6
surety of better *t.* Heb. 7:22
the ark of his *t.* Rev. 11:19

TESTIFY, *bear witness.*
t. falsely against Deut. 19:18
our sins *t.* against Isa. 59:12
t. unto them lest Luke 16:28
t. in the Lord, that Eph. 4:17
t. beforehand the 1 Pet. 1:11
have seen and do *t.* 1 John 4:14
sent mine angel to *t.* Rev. 22:16

THANKSGIVING, *express gratitude.*
offer it for a *t.* Lev. 7:12
offer unto God *t.* Ps. 50:14
into gates with *t.* 100:4
with *t.* sing praise 147:7
abounding with *t.* Col. 2:7
be received with *t.* 1 Tim. 4:4

THINK, *reflect, meditate.*
t. on me when Gen. 40:14
t. they shall be Matt. 6:7
what *t.* ye of Christ? 22:42
ye *t.* ye have John 5:39
not *t.* of himself Rom. 12:3
t. no evil 1 Cor. 13:5
if man *t.* himself Gal. 6:3
above all ask or *t.* Eph. 3:20
t. it not strange 1 Pet. 4:12

THIRST, *desire for drink.*
in my *t.* they gave Ps. 69:21
hunger and *t.* after Matt. 5:6
if thine enemy *t.* Rom. 12:20
in hunger and *t.* 2 Cor. 11:27

THRONE, *royal seat.*
prepared his *t.* for Ps. 9:7
Lord's *t.* is in heaven 11:4
Lord sitting upon a *t.* Isa. 6:1
heaven is my *t.* 66:1
come boldly unto *t.* Heb. 4:16
great white *t.* Rev. 20:11

TIME, *duration, season.*
t. not hidden from Job 24:1
Lord deliver him in *t.* of Ps. 41:1
t. every purpose Eccl. 3:1
t. to seek the Lord Hos. 10:12
my *t.* is at hand Matt. 26:18
t. of thy visitation Luke 19:44
my *t.* not come John 7:6

TONGUE, *organ of speech.*
under *t.* mischief Ps. 10:7
keep *t.* from evil 34:13
their *t.* a sword 57:4
wholesome *t.* tree life Prov. 15:4
keepeth his *t.* 21:23
his *t.* as devouring Isa. 30:27
speak other *t.* Acts 2:4
divers kinds of *t.* 1 Cor. 12:10
t. of men and angels 13:1
bridleth not his *t.* Jam. 1:26
t. is a little member 3:5

TRANSGRESSION, *crime, sin.*
because of the *t.* Ezra 10:6
innocent great *t.* Ps. 19:13
wounded for our *t.* Isa. 53:5
his *t.* shall not be Ezek. 18:22

TRAVAIL, *labor.*
see *t.* of his soul Isa. 53:11
compassed me with *t.* Lam. 3:5
creation *t.* in pain Rom. 8:22
remember our *t.* 1 Thess. 2:9
wrought with *t.* 2 Thess. 3:8

TRESPASS, *misdeed, offense.*
forgive *t.* of thy Gen. 50:17
forgive men their *t.* Matt. 6:14
imputing their *t.* 2 Cor. 5:19
quickened dead in *t.* Eph. 2:1

TRIBULATION, *affliction.*
shall be great *t.* Matt. 24:21
in word have *t.* John 16:33
through much *t.* Acts 14:22
comforteth us in *t.* 2 Cor. 1:4
we should suffer *t.* 1 Thess. 3:4

TROUBLE, *afflict, affliction.*
let not all *t.* seem Neh. 9:32
refuge in times of *t.* Ps. 9:9
my soul is full of *t.* 88:3
be with him in *t.* 91:15
walk in midst of *t.* 138:7
former *t.* are forgotten Isa. 65:16
comfort in *t.* 2 Cor. 1:4

TRUE, *faithful, loyal, right.*
a *t.* witness Prov. 14:25
Lord is the *t.* God Jer. 10:10
was the *t.* Light John 1:9
Father giveth *t.* bread 6:32
I am the *t.* vine 15:1
created in *t.* holiness Eph. 4:24
whatsoever things *t.* Phil. 4:8
near with *t.* heart Heb. 10:22

TRUTH, *fact, real, right.*
Lord, abundant in *t.* Ex. 34:6
his *t.* shall be thy shield Ps. 91:4
t. of Lord endureth 117:2
buy the *t.* and sell Prov. 23:23
Speak every man *t.* Zech. 8:16
full of grace and *t.* John 1:14
I am the way, the *t.* 14:6
men, who hold *t.* in Rom. 1:18
sincerity and *t.* 1 Cor. 5:8
dividing word of *t.* 2 Tim. 2:15
any err from *t.* Jam. 5:19
t. not in him 1 John 2:4

U

UNBELIEF, *want of faith.*
help thou mine *u.* Mark 9:24
u. make faith without Rom. 3:3
ignorantly in *u.* 1 Tim. 1:13
evil heart of *u.* Heb. 3:12

UNDERSTAND, *comprehend.*
who *u.* his errors? Ps. 19:12
how can man *u.* his Prov. 20:24
readeth let him *u.* Matt. 24:15
there is none that *u.* Rom. 3:11
u. all mysteries 1 Cor. 13:2

UNDERSTANDING, *wisdom.*
Almighty giveth *u.* Job 32:8
his *u.* is infinite Ps. 147:5
lean not unto thine own *u.* Prov. 3:5
love with all *u.* Mark 12:33
passeth all *u.* Phil. 4:7
Lord give thee *u.* 2 Tim. 2:7
that hath *u.* count Rev. 13:18

UNGODLY, *wicked, sinful.*
deliver me to *u.* Job 16:11
not in counsel of *u.* Ps. 1:1
law is for the *u.* 1 Tim. 1:9
where *u.* and 1 Pet. 4:18
u. men turning grace Jude 4

UNRIGHTEOUSNESS, *not upright or just; sinful.*
no *u.* in judgment Lev. 19:15
true, no *u.* is in him John 7:18
hold the truth in *u.* Rom. 1:18
had pleasure in *u.* 2 Thess. 2:12
receive reward of *u.* 2 Pet. 2:13
cleanse from all *u.* 1 John 1:9

V

VAIL, or **VEIL,** *cover for face.*
a *v.* of blue Ex. 26:31
holy place within *v.* Lev. 16:2
that within the *v.* Heb. 6:19
the *v.*, his flesh 10:20

VAIN, *ineffectual, idle.*
name of Lord in *v.* Ex. 20:7
not a *v.* thing for Deut. 32:47
people imagine a *v.* Ps. 2:1
I hate *v.* thoughts Ps. 119:113
beauty is *v.* but a Prov. 31:30
not *v.* repetitions Matt. 6:7
have believed in *v.* 1 Cor. 15:2
grace of God in *v.* 2 Cor. 6:1
man's religion is *v.* Jam. 1:26

VANITY, *worthlessness, pride.*
how long will ye love *v.* Ps. 4:2
thoughts of man are *v.* 94:11
remove from me *v.* Prov. 30:8
v. of *v.* all is *v.* Eccl. 1:2
behold they are *v.* Isa. 41:29

VENGEANCE, *retribution.*
Lord hath taken *v.* Judg. 11:36
execute *v.* upon Ps. 149:7
God will come with *v.* Isa. 35:4
unrighteous taketh *v.* Rom. 3:5
suffering *v.* eternal Jude 7

VICTORY, *triumph.*
Lord wrought *v.* 2 Sam. 23:10
holy arm gotten *v.* Ps. 98:1
swallow death in *v.* Isa. 25:8

VIRGIN, *young woman.*
v. shall conceive Isa. 7:14
v. espoused to a man Luke 1:27

VOICE, *speech, utterance.*
a still, small *v.* 1 Kings 19:12
fool's *v.* is known Eccl. 5:3
v. of him that crieth Isa. 40:3
any hear his *v.* Matt. 12:19
to change my *v.* Gal. 4:20
if any hear my *v.* Rev. 3:20

W

WAGES, *payment for service.*
what shall thy *w.* Gen. 29:15
I will give thee *w.* Ex. 2:9
be content with *w.* Luke 3:14
reapeth receiveth *w.* John 4:36
w. of sin is death Rom. 6:23
w. of unrighteousness 2 Pet. 2:15

WAIT, *stay, remain.*
should I *w.* for Lord 2 Kings 6:33
none that *w.* on thee Ps. 25:3
w. patiently for him 37:7
I will *w.* on thy name 52:9
I *w.* for the Lord 130:5
though it tarry, *w.* Hab. 2:3

w. for kingdom Mark 15:43
w. for the adoption Rom. 8:23
w. for hope of Gal. 5:5
w. for his Son 1 Thess. 1:10

WALK, *advance by steps.*
though I *w.* through Ps. 23:4
I will *w.* in mine 26:11
let us *w.* in light Isa. 2:5
w. and not faint 40:31
not *w.* in darkness John 8:12
W. while ye have light 12:35
w. in steps of faith Rom. 4:12
w. by faith 2 Cor. 5:7
w. worthy of the Eph. 4:1
w. worthy of Lord Col. 1:10
if we *w.* in the light 1 John 1:7
they shall *w.* with me Rev. 3:4
nations saved *w.* in light 21:24

WAR, *armed conflict.*
though *w.* rise Ps. 27:3
made *w.* with saints Dan. 7:21
not *w.* after flesh 2 Cor. 10:3
beast shall make *w.* Rev. 11:7
was *w.* in heaven 12:7

WATCH, *keep guard.*
W., ye know not Matt. 24:42
w. ye stand fast 1 Cor. 16:13
let us *w.* and be 1 Thess. 5:6
w. thou in all 2 Tim. 4:5
w. for your souls Heb. 13:17

WATER, *fluid necessary to life.*
iniquity like *w.* Job 15:16
poured out like *w.* Ps. 22:14
me beside still *w.* 23:2
blood they shed like *w.* 79:3
as the *w.* cover the sea Isa. 11:9
baptize you with *w.* Matt. 3:11
w. was made wine John 2:9
man be born of *w.* John 3:5
souls saved by *w.* 1 Pet. 3:20
he that came by *w.* 1 John 5:6
w. of life freely Rev. 22:17

WAY, *path, manner of life.*
keep me in this *w.* Gen. 28:20
walk in his *w.* Deut. 8:6
Lord knoweth *w.* of Ps. 1:6
lead in *w.* everlasting 139:24
w. of fool right in Prov. 12:15
w. called *w.* of Isa. 35:8
spread garments in *w.* Mark 11:8
all gone out of *w.* Rom. 3:12
make a *w.* to 1 Cor. 10:13
new and living *w.* Heb. 10:20

WEAK, *feeble, not strong.*
O Lord, for I am *w.* Ps. 6:2
strengthen *w.* hands Isa. 35:3
w. say, am strong Joel 3:10
not *w.* in faith Rom. 4:19
w. in faith receive ye 14:1
when *w.* then strong 2 Cor. 12:10

WEARY, *tired, fatigued.*
I am *w.* of my life Gen. 27:46
w. with groaning Ps. 6:6
lest he be *w.* of thee Prov. 25:17
will ye *w.* my God Isa. 7:13
run and not be *w.* 40:31
to him that is *w.* 50:4
w. in well doing Gal. 6:9

WEEP, *to shed tears.*
a time to *w.* Eccl. 3:4
w. not for the dead Jer. 22:10
blessed are ye that *w.* Luke 6:21
w. with them that *w.* Rom. 12:15
w. as though they 1 Cor. 7:30

WHITE, *color of snow.*
garments always *w.* Eccl. 9:8
purified and made *w.* Dan. 12:10
two in *w.* apparel Acts 1:10

WHITER, *more white.*
I be *w.* than snow Ps. 51:7

WHORE, *harlot.*
w. is a deep ditch Prov. 23:27
adulterer and *w.* Isa. 57:3
the great *w.* Rev. 17:1

WICKED, *sinful.*
w. cease from Job 3:17
God is angry with *w.* Ps. 7:11
evil shall slay *w.* 34:21
w. perish at presence 68:2
punish *w.* for Isa. 13:11
fiery darts of *w.* Eph. 6:16
w. be revealed 2 Thess. 2:8

WICKEDNESS, *sinfulness.*
God saw *w.* of man Gen. 6:5
w. proceedeth 1 Sam. 24:13
let *w.* of wicked come Ps. 7:9
thou hatest *w.* 45:7
w. burneth as fire Isa. 9:18
covetousness, *w.* Mark 7:22
inward full of *w.* Luke 11:39
filled with all *w.* Rom. 1:29
of malice and *w.* 1 Cor. 5:8
spiritual *w.* in Eph. 6:12
world lieth in *w.* 1 John 5:19

WIFE, *married woman.*
findeth *w.* findeth Prov. 18:22
prudent *w.* from Lord 19:14
remember Lot's *w.* Luke 17:32
love *w.* as himself Eph. 5:33
honour unto *w.* 1 Pet. 3:7
bride, the Lamb's *w.* Rev. 21:9

WILL, *desire to do.*
shall do *w.* of God Mark 3:35
w. of flesh nor of *w.* John 1:13
My meat is to do *w.* of 4:34
w. of Lord be done Acts 21:14

WIND, *current of air.*
God made *w.* to pass Gen. 8:1
my life is *w.* Job 7:7
like chaff *w.* driveth Ps. 1:4
as chaff before *w.* 35:5
w. shall carry Isa. 41:16
w. was contrary Matt. 14:24
w. bloweth where John 3:8
sound as of *w.* Acts 2:2
w. of doctrine Eph. 4:14
wave driven with *w.* Jam. 1:6
of a mighty *w.* Rev. 6:13

WISDOM, *knowledge, sagacity.*
w. is principal Prov. 4:7
cease from own *w.* 23:4
in much *w.* is Eccl. 1:18
w. is justified Matt. 11:19
not with *w.* of 1 Cor. 1:17
w. of world foolishness 3:19
be filled with *w.* Col. 1:9
if any lack *w.* Jam. 1:5
here is *w.* Rev. 13:18

WISE, *learned, discreet.*
great not always *w.* Job 32:9
making *w.* simple Ps. 19:7
w. man attain *w.* Prov. 1:5
w. in hand of God Eccl. 9:1
five *w.*, five foolish Matt. 25:2
w. in own conceits Rom. 11:25
foolish confound *w.* 1 Cor. 1:27
ye are *w.* in Christ 4:10
w. unto salvation 2 Tim. 3:15

WITNESS, *testimony.*
God is *w.* betwixt Gen. 31:50
my *w.* is in heaven Job 16:19
faithful *w.* in heaven Ps. 89:37
faithful *w.* not lie Prov. 14:5
bear *w.* of Light John 1:7
conscience bearing *w.* Rom. 2:15
w. of God greater 1 John 5:9

WOMAN, *female person.*
shall be called *W.* Gen. 2:23
foolish *w.* is Prov. 9:13
virtuous *w.* crown to 12:4
O *w.*, great is thy Matt. 15:28
w. behold thy son John 19:26
his Son, made of *w.* Gal. 4:4

WORD, *language, scripture.*
let *w.* of my Ps. 19:14
w. spoken in due Prov. 15:23
how to speak *w.* in Isa. 50:4
by every *w.* that Matt. 4:4
That every idle *w.* men Matt. 12:36
my *w.* shall not 24:35
sower soweth *w.* Mark 4:14
w. of eternal life John 6:68
fulfilled in one *w.* Gal. 5:14
holding forth *w.* Phil. 2:16
not in *w.* only 1 Thess. 1:5
w. of faith 1 Tim. 4:6
preach the *w.* 2 Tim. 4:2
be ye doers of *w.* Jam. 1:22
of the *W.* of life 1 John 1:1

WORK, *performance of duty.*
ended his *w.* Gen. 2:2
the *w.* of thy fingers Ps. 8:3
thy wonderful *w.* 40:5
w. of Lord are great 111:2
trusted in thy *w.* Jer. 48:7
w. the *w.* of God? John 6:28
w. I do in my Father's 10:25
without *w.* Rom. 4:6
tribulations *w.* patience 5:3
every man's *w.* 1 Cor. 3:13
not of *w.* lest any Eph. 2:9
w. out your own Phil. 2:12
good word and *w.* 2 Thess. 2:17
do *w.* of 2 Tim. 4:5
destroy *w.* of devil 1 John 3:8
keepeth my *w.* Rev. 2:26

WORLD, *creation, universe.*
the earth and the *w.* Ps. 90:2
God so loved the *w.* John 3:16
w. cannot hate you 7:7
if *w.* hate you 15:18
I pray not for *w.* 17:9
w. is crucified Gal. 6:14
without God in *w.* Eph. 2:12
loved present *w.* 2 Tim. 4:10
love not *w.* 1 John 2:15
w. wondered after Rev. 13:3

WORSHIP, *reverence, honor.*
let us *w.* and bow Ps. 95:6

w. Lord in holy Isa. 27:13
fall down and *w.* Matt. 4:9
w. God in spirit Phil. 3:3

WRATH, *violent anger.*
by thy *w.* are we Ps. 90:7
great *w.* suffer Prov. 19:19
reserveth *w.* for his Nah. 1:2
flee from *w.* Matt. 3:7
go down upon your *w.* Eph. 4:26
appointed us to *w.* 1 Thess. 5:9
w. of man worketh Jam. 1:20

Y

YOUTH, *state of being young.*
evil from *y.* Gen. 8:21
not sins of my *y.* Ps. 25:7
rejoice in thy *y.* Eccl. 11:9
kept from my *y.* Matt. 19:20

Z

ZEAL, *active interest.*
my *z.* for Lord 2 Kings 10:16
where is thy *z.* Isa. 63:15
have *z.* of God Rom. 10:2
hath great *z.* for you Col. 4:13

Concluding Notes

Hebrew Scriptures begin with a picture of mother Eve. The New Testament begins with a portrait of Mary, the virgin mother of Jesus. We conclude the biblical canon with the Bride of Christ, a symbol of the very best of womanhood—regal and holy. What a journey for God's female creation, both the highs and the lows of our corporate experiences! We were created with possibilities and potential—yet, we willingly participated in the Fall. The church is pictured in Revelation as a woman—the bride of Christ—who offers an invitation to all: "Come, to the heavenly banquet" (see Rev. 22:17, 20).

In spite of the Fall, the righteousness of God prevailed and Mary was found worthy to bear the Son of God. Although women have been defamed and vilified throughout history, Jesus, while dying on the cross, included Mary in the community of faith. On the day of crucifixion, women were there. When the command was given to "Go tell," women were there. On the day of Pentecost, when the Holy Spirit was poured out on believers, women were there. And, the record stands that when the invitation is given to come to the Great Feast—Jesus, the Holy Spirit, and the bride of Christ, will jointly say, "Come!"

God's ways are mysterious. The mind of God is greater, more exalted, and more complex than we can even imagine. The Book of Revelation declares that a great woman was hidden away, by God, until it was safe (chap. 12). Perhaps this illustrates our time. It is clear that God has chosen to include women in His great plan. Religion may denounce us, history may dismiss us, our culture may demean us, and our personal psyches may find it difficult to accept it—but God does loves us—the females of creation.

A careful study of the canon of Scriptures reveals the many roles and tasks of women. Hagar received God's promise of a great nation (Gen. 16); a nameless slave girl helped save the life of Naaman (2 Kin. 5), a foreign dignitary; Esther, a parentless child, becomes queen and saves her nation; Deborah becomes a warrior-judge (Judg. 5); and a queen mother teaches her son the worth and value of a virtuous woman (Prov. 31). In Scripture, Women are seen as both foolish and wise, as harlot and as saint, as an insignificant and as the worthy matron who births the wisest man on earth. The result is that throughout the unveiling of God's interactions with humans—women are seen!

Through snippets of conversations, careful "digging," and deliberate analysis, we discover Hannah, whose prayer caused her to rise in victory (1 Sam 1–2); Rizpah, who stands tall and strong in the public's eye for the five months until God sends rain (2 Sam. 21); Abigail, who reminded King David that vengeance belonged to God (1 Sam. 25); Queen Athaliah, who ruled Israel for six years (2 Kin. 11); and the unfortunate concubine whose hacked body caused tribal war in Israel (Judg. 19).

These wise and witty women of the Scriptures provide us with information, insight, and windows of opportunity to view God at work in our contemporary lives. And, they help us to be prepared for the strong and determined sisterhood we meet in Mary and Elizabeth, who are outstanding witnesses in Jesus' birth narratives in the Gospels. We are not shocked when we encounter the female followers of Jesus—the women who financially supported His mission ministry and watched as He suffered, bled, and died. They were also there when He rose from the dead! We anticipate Lydia and her praying sisters, whom Paul encounters down at the riverside at Philippi (Acts 16:13). And, we see clearly Paul's regard for women in ministry, when we read Romans 16, where Paul commends Phebe and other women for working with Him to advance the gospel.

Perhaps many of our "undiscovered" sisters startle us with their bodacious behaviors. This may be due to the silence of the pulpit. And, it could possibly be from our neglecting to "search the scriptures; for in them ye think ye have eternal life"(John 5:39). Regardless of our reasons heretofore, these women now belong to us. Their stories have and will continue to impact our lives.

Thank God for the *Women of Color Study Bible.* Thank God for women of color who study the Bible. Thank God for the Holy Bible which holds the stories of the matriarchs and patriarchs of our faith. Thank God for continuing opportunities to live our lives in their shadows; to learn from their mistakes; to cry over their plights; to delight in their triumphs; and to be inspired by their discoveries of our God who continues to create, use, and include women!

Shalom!

—Sista Linda H. Hollies
Woman to Woman Commentator

God's Plan for Saving People

In a nutshell, people receive salvation when they turn to God with all their heart, soul, mind, and will, asking God to save them. But let's break that process down.

WHY WE NEED GOD'S SALVATION

The Bible teaches that all persons are sinners and are out of fellowship with God because our original parents (Adam and Eve) sinned; and that original sin has passed from one generation to another and from one person to another (see Isaiah 53:6; Romans 3:23; 5:12). Of course, we're also sinners because we sin every time we think or act contrary to God's perfect holy will. The consequence of being sinners is that we are out of favor with God—both now and forever (John 3:36).

WHAT GOD HAS DONE

The good news is that God has done something to bring us back into favor and fellowship with Himself. He sent His only Son, Jesus, to pay the penalty for the sins of the whole world. Jesus, the Christ, said He "came . . . to give his life a ransom for many" (Mark 10:45). "For God so loved the world, that he gave his only begotten Son, that whosoever believeth in him should not perish, but have everlasting life" (John 3:16). God showed His approval of His Son's atoning death by raising Him from the dead (Romans 1:4).

WHAT WE MUST DO

God has made provision for our salvation. Our part is to turn to Him in faith and accept His death upon the cross, as payment for our sins. By turning to God in repentance and faith, the broken relationship between God and us is healed. In turning to Him, we acknowledge our sinfulness and turn away from sin. This is called repentance. Romans 10:9 reads, "That if thou shalt confess with thy mouth the Lord Jesus, and shalt believe in thine heart that God hath raised him from the dead, thou shalt be saved." By accepting Jesus into one's heart, a person is "born again," or born from above (John 3:3), and becomes a member of God's special family—the church.

Jesus said that persons who accept Him should be baptized as a public confession of their decision to accept Him (Matthew 28:19). In the Book of Acts, when people accepted Christ, they joined with other believers in the fellowship of the church, where they devoted themselves to the apostles' teaching, to fellowship with other believers, to the breaking of bread (communion), and to prayer. These disciplines help believers to strengthen their faith and deepen their relationship with God.

Breaking the Silence

Feminist scholar Bell Hooks writes, "Each time a woman begins to speak, a liberating process begins."[1] These words offer tremendous encouragement, given the relentless attempts, historically and currently, to silence the female voice and oppress her will.

Sadly, the silencing of women has even involved the misinterpretation and misuse of God's Word. Traditionally, in the Black church, there has been a code of silence that women not speak publicly or with authority. While the code is not as prevalent as it has been, too many women continue to suffer under this oppression. Today, many Black women, within and outside the church, bear the physical, mental, and spiritual scars, left by men who resented these Black women's unwillingness to remain silent.

The effect of such errors on the psyche and behavior of the Christian church, in general, and the Bible-loving Black church, in particular, has been brutal. The biblical interpretations used by white slave owners to suppress African slaves in order to elevate the white race to a status of power and privilege is one such example. Equally erroneous has been the biblical interpretations used by Black men to oppress Black women in order to elevate their male identity.

One source for this view is found in 1 Corinthians 14:34–35, "Let your women keep silence in the churches: for it is not permitted unto them to speak; but they are commanded to be under obedience, as also saith the law. And if they will learn any thing, let them ask their husbands at home: for it is a shame for women to speak in the church." Many New Testament scholars have examined these two verses for their authenticity.

The excluding and muffling of the voices of women in the church today is counter to the general tone of Paul's letters. In one of Paul's first letters, addressed to the church at Rome and written at the height of his career between A.D. 54 and 58, Paul's vision of inclusivity is captured in his salutation "To all that be in Rome, beloved of God" (Rom. 1:7). Included among Paul's beloved are the women preachers, teachers, and prophets he acknowledges in this letter—women, such as Deaconess Phebe (Rom. 16:1); fellow worker and church house convenor Priscilla (Rom. 16:3); and hard working co-servant Mary (Rom. 16:6). In Paul's letter to the Philippians, the first congregation established by Paul on European soil, the work of fellow females Euodias and Syntyche, is acknowledged (Phil. 4:2–3). Nowhere in his letters does Paul describe these female prophets, whom Paul says labored hard on behalf of the Gospel (Phil. 4:3), as less than equal, less than free, or less than vocal.

Clearly, given the visible and acknowledged track record of these female leaders and Gospel laborers by Paul during the first-generation Pauline churches, there is reason to doubt that Paul would be an advocate for female silence and oppression in the church. To prohibit women from speaking in the church would have limited the number of people Paul could recruit to become Gospel coworkers with him. It would appear that

during certain phases in the life of the early church, certainly at the time of Paul, there existed a visible dependency on the active and vocal participation of women in ministry. The sheer number of women actively participating in the church today confirms that type of dependency still exists today.

A passage that is hard to understand and has been misused by people is 1 Corinthians 14:34–35. The church in Corinth certainly experienced many painful divisions among its members. Admittedly, there was a problem in the church at Corinth that needed to be corrected. It was a problem of the entire church—not some of its members, and surely not limited to its female members. At issue for Paul was that both male and female members, in the name of being spiritual (Gr. *pneumatikos*), were creating disorder in the worship service.[2] In this passage, Paul is expressing his vision of Christian worship, in which the gifts of the Spirit are given to all members of the church—men and women alike—for the unity of the church and community building[3] (1 Corinthians 14:26–33). Given the presence of the Holy Spirit and the divine gifts granted to all members in the church—Paul was saying to the Corinthians that, even in the most Spirit-filled worship, each man and each woman is expected to honor the community's worship standards.

As more and more women find their voices, the code of silence is broken. Many women, including myself, have intuitively understood the evil, undergirding the incorrect use of Scripture to oppress women. Now, we join ranks and use our liberating voices to fight against error. The revolution is here to stay. The silence is broken forever.

—L. Fitchue

Notes

[1]Hooks, Bell, Talking Back: Thinking Feminist, Thinking Black (Boston: South End Press, 1989), 12.

[2]Fee, Gordon D., First Epistle to the Corinthians (Grand Rapids, Mich.: W. B. Eerdmans, 1987), 701.

[3]Hays, Richard B., First Corinthians, Interpretation: A Bible Commentary for Teaching and Preaching (Louisville, KY: John Knox Press, 1997), 249.

Contributors

Reverend Estrelda Alexander is currently Associate Dean for Community Life at Wesley Theological Seminary, and cofounder and President of the Association of Full Gospel Women Clergy. She is also an Adjunct Professor of Theology at Trinity College. She is a graduate of Wesley Theological Seminary (MDiv.), Columbia University (MA), and currently a Ph.D candidate in Political Theology at the Catholic University of America.

Mrs. Maude A. Alexander is a retired early childhood education teacher, storyteller, and workshop leader. She is a graduate of the University of Louisville with a BA and graduate studies in Early Childhood Education, Education of the Black Child, Multicultural Education, and the Infusion of African-American Education into Curriculums.

Professor Linda L. Ammons is Associate Professor of Law at the Cleveland-Marshall College of Law in Cleveland, OH, where she teaches Administrative Law, Legislation, and Women and the Law. Ms. Ammons was the principle person in the Governor's office responsible for the battered women's clemency project in Ohio. When this project was completed, twenty-eight Ohio women received clemencies. She has also served as a legal expert for the California legislature and numerous organizations on the subject of battered women. Before entering the legal profession, Ms. Ammons worked in the communications field where she was an anchorperson and talk show host. She has published numerous articles for national scholarly and popular press publications.

Dr. Pamela June Anderson is a graduate of Johns Hopkins University (BS), Howard University Divinity School (MDiv.), and United Theological Seminary (DMin.) She is the National Secretary for Ministers for Racial and Social Justice, Jeremiah A. Wright, Jr./Molefi K. Asante/Cornell West Scholar, author, and highly acclaimed seminar/workshop leader, preacher, and pastor. Dr. Anderson has contributed to a number of publications including Urban Ministries' *Precepts for Living, The Michigan Chronicle, The Columbus Post,* various Untied Church of Christ's publications, and *The Book of Daily Prayer.* She is the author of *Heavenly Hints/Earthly Events: A Chat with Churchfolk.*

Reverend Chestina M. Archibald, lecturer, educator, editor, and author is Pastor of Braden United Methodist Church and serves as Director of the Wesley Foundation at Fisk University. She is the editor of *Say Amen: The African-American Family's Book of Prayers*, coeditor of *Divine Inspiration*, and author of *Secret of the Psalms*. She was selected by the Staley Foundation as one of its distinguished Christian Scholar Lecturers.

Mrs. Marcia B. Armstead, born and raised in Jamaica, West Indies, is founder and president of the Complete Family Seminars, a consulting service to improve the spiritual, psychosocial, and physical quality of life

for families. She authors, designs, and conducts seminars nationally and internationally. She is scriptwriter and producer of an employee training video, a former columnist for an Orlando business magazine, and a talk-show guest on two television programs. She is a businesswoman, published free-lance writer, and poet.

Dr. Rhoenna P. Armster has thirty-two years of successful teaching experience in private and public schools, and at the college and university level. She has a Ph.D in Leadership and Human Behavior from the United States International University, a MBA from National University, and a MBA in Business Education from the University of Northern Colorado. She has traveled extensively throughout the world.

Reverend Angela D. Aubry currently teaches in the New Orleans Public Schools, the Greater St. Stephen College of Ministry and Theological Seminary, and the Victory Bible School. She is a graduate of Oral Roberts University with a MTh. in Theological/Historical Studies and an MA in Biblical Literature. She is a member of Victory Fellowship where she is a leader in the Singles' and Women's Ministries, Music Ministry, and Evangelism Ministry.

Reverend Karen E. Mosby-Avery, writer, consultant, and the mother of twins, is Pastor of Good News Community Church United Church of Christ in Chicago, IL, which is a multiracial, multicultural, bilingual inner-city congregation. She is a graduate of Garrett-Evangelical Theological Seminary (MDiv.). She serves on various local and national committees and advisory boards for the United Church of Christ, the National Council of Churches of Christ, and the Center for the Church and the Black Experience at Garrett-Evangelical Theological Seminary.

Reverend Mary Anne Allen Bellinger a native of the Republic of Panama, is an advisor, consultant, and a member of numerous local and national programs and boards, who has traveled widely as a preacher for political observation and religious dialogue in Cuba, West Africa, England, Guyana, and other countries. She is an ordained minister in the Baptist church and an ordained Itinerant Elder in the A.M.E. church. She is a graduate of Andover Newton Theological School (MDiv.).

Reverend Cynthia B. Belt is currently serving as Pastor of Mt. Tabor United Methodist Church in Gambrills, MD, and New Beginnings Fellowship United Methodist Church in Severn, MD. Reverend Belt has over fifteen years experience in the computer field. She has traveled nationally and internationally providing computer training and installation for small businesses, corporations, and computer-user groups. Reverend Belt is a graduate of Wesley Theological Seminary (MDiv.), and is currently enrolled in the Doctor of Ministry program, with an emphasis on the African-American Church and Its Ministries.

Ms. Keya Belt is a junior attending Old Mill High School in Millersvile, MD, where she is a member of the Student Council, the Marching Band, the Concert Band, and the Future Business Leaders of America. She is the daughter of Reverend Cynthia B. Belt. Keya serves on the leadership team of

her church, New Beginnings United Methodist Church, where her mother is the pastor. She also serves on the Youth Council for the Annapolis District.

Reverend Bridgette Annette Black is Pastor of Coppin Chapel African Methodist Episcopal Church in Indianapolis, IN. She completed her MDiv. at Garrett-Evangelical Theological Seminary and is currently pursuing a DMin. in Pastoral Care and Counseling at Christian Theological Seminary. In 1998 she portrayed "Ain't Baby" in the critically acclaimed production of "From the Mississippi Delta."

Reverend Winfred Blagmond is a graduate of Wesley Theological Seminary (MDiv.) with a focus on Urban Ministry. She is currently serving as Pastor of Strawbridge United Methodist Church in New Windsor, MD.

Ms. Jetola Anderson-Blair, fluent in Spanish and French is a regional Human Resources Advisor for a major chemical company in Houston, TX. She holds a BA in Psychology from the State University of New York at Plattaburgh and an MBA in Management from Villanova University. Ms. Anderson-Blair is a member of Friendship Community Bible Church, Houston ,where she is a member of the teaching and ushering staff. In 1991 she was listed as one of "The Top 10 to Watch" in the Guide to Black Resources in New York City. Her essay, "Presumed Incompetent," was published in the inspirational book, *Sister to Sister: Devotions for African-American Women*, by Suzan Johnson-Cook.

Reverend Michele Cotton Bohanon serves as an Assistant in the Prayer Ministry at the First Institutional Baptist Church in Phoenix, AZ, and is involved in the social justice and civic organizations for the Paradise Valley School District.

Reverend Toni R. Booker, mother of three is the Youth Minister at Martin Luther King, Jr. Memorial Baptist Church in Renton, WA. Her ministry involves education of young people about God and their accountability to Him. She has a BA in Psychology from Portland State University, Portland, OR.

Reverend Linda E. Boston is Pastor of Grace Lutheran Church, San Jose, CA. She is a graduate of Pacific Lutheran Theological Seminary (MDiv.), and United Theological Seminary (DMin). She has had several articles and sermons published including "A Womanist Reflection on 1 Corinthians" published by the Center for Women and Religion, Graduate Theological Union, Berkeley, CA.

Dr. Ann Bouie currently serves as Visiting Scholar for the U.S. Department of Education National Institute on the Education of At-Risk Students in Washington, DC. She assists policy makers and practitioners in designing and implementing programs and support services in the area of education. She has taught at the university level, has published several articles on education, and is in demand as a trainer and facilitator for school districts, educational policy-making and reform projects, governmental agencies, and youth-serving organizations. She holds a PhD. in Policy Administration and Analysis, an MA in Secondary Education, and an MA in African and African-American History from Stanford University.

Reverend Cookie Frances Lee Bracey is a pastor, chaplain, and professor. She serves as Pastor of the St. Matthew United Methodist Church, Trevose, PA, chaplain of the United States Air Force Civil Air Patrol, the Methodist Hospital and Pennsylvania Hospital in Philadelphia, PA. Reverend Bracey is an Adjunct Professor at Eastern Baptist Seminary, Field Education Department, and a Professor at Philadelphia School of Developing Ministries. She is a graduate of Temple University (BSW) and Wesley Theological Seminary (MDiv.).

Reverend Nina Bryant is a chaplain and a clinical pastoral educator serving in ministry at Alta Bates Medical Center in Oakland, CA. She is a trainer of seminary students, lay leaders, and clergy in grief counseling, and other compassionate care ministries. She is a graduate of San Francisco Theological Seminary (MDiv.).

Reverend Marion Wyvetta Bullock, is the Executive Director of the Division for Congregational Ministries (DCM) of the Evangelical Lutheran Church In America (ELCA). She has served on the church-wide staff for sixteen years. Her duties include directing church-wide ministries in the areas of worship, Christian education, evangelism, youth, social ministry, hunger education, and multicultural and language/culture specific resources. She is a graduate of the Lutheran School of Theology and Hartford Seminary.

Attorney Candace Lorelle Byrd, an active member of the State Bar of Georgia, American Bar Association, the Gate City Bar, and Georgia Trial Lawyers Association, received her law degree from Howard University. She has been active in the State Bar of Georgia's Moot Court Committee and the High School Mock Trial Program, a program in which high school students conduct a trial and compete on the local and state level. She is an active member of the music ministry at World Changers Church International in College Park, GA.

Minister Terri L. Byrd, is a graduate of Southern University A & M College. She is a member of Church Point Ministries, Inc. Minister Byrd is a writer of short stories, poems, songs, and plays.

Reverend LaJuana D. Caldwell, a gifted speaker and soloist, is a minister with the Church of God. She holds a MTh. from the International Seminary, Plymouth, FL. She is currently the Director of Christian Education at Harvest Temple Church of God in Forestville, MD.

Dr. Iva E. Carruthers, former Chairperson and Professor of the Sociology Department at Northeastern Illinois University, has more than 25 years experience in education, educational planning, policy analysis, program design and evaluation, as well as human resource management and training. She is founder and President of Nexus Unlimited, Inc., an information management, training, and consulting firm. She is a noted researcher, historian, and published writer. As co-producer of "Know Your Heritage" television show, Dr. Carruthers has produced fifteen study guides on African-Americans and African History. Dr. Carruthers is a frequent guest speaker for various national and international forums. She is

a graduate of Northwestern University with an MA in Counselor Education and a Ph.D in Sociology.

Reverend Jacquetta Chambers, an active United Methodist, is pastor of McMillian United Methodist Church in Fort Worth, TX. A speaker, teacher, and counselor, she has served on the Black Clergy Women's Steering Committee BMCR, Tarrant County Clergy for Interracial Peace and Justice, and is now a member of the Commission on Inter-Religious Concerns and Christian Unity. She is a graduate of Texas Christian University Brite School of Divinity with a MDiv. in Pastoral Care and Counseling, and has currently completed the course work for her DDiv. degree.

Reverend DeeDee M. Coleman is the Assistant to the Pastor in Liturgical Ministries at the Russell Street Missionary Baptist Church. She earned a MA in Pastoral Ministry from Marygrove College and is currently a doctoral candidate at Ashland Seminary with a dual degree of a MDiv. and a DMin. with special studies in Liturgical Structure and Planning of the World Church.

Reverend Monica Anita Coleman, was ordained an Itinerant Deacon in the A.M.E. Church, currently serves as a Pastoral Assistant at Metropolitan Interdenominational Church in Nashville, TN. She is founder and coordinator of "The Dinah Project," an organized church response to the crisis of sexual violence in the community. She is a graduate of Vanderbilt Divinity School (MDiv.) and certification in the study of religion, gender, and sexuality.

Dr. Suzan D. Johnson Cook after thirteen years at the historic Mariners' Temple in Manhattan, she became the founder and Senior Pastor of the Bronx Christian Fellowship. She is a graduate of New York's Columbia University Teacher's College and Union Theological Seminary (MA and MDiv.) and United Theological Seminary (DMin.). Dr. Cook has combined her academic preparation and communications skills to teach at Harvard and other institutions and can often be seen and heard hosting radio and television shows. She is the only African-American woman and faith community leader appointed by President Clinton to the National Advisory Board on Race. She is the author or editor of several books, including *Sister Strength: Devotions For and From African-American Women.*

Reverend Charmayne Cooke is a native of Boston, MA who has worked in the field of broadcasting for the last twenty-five years. An ordained Baptist minister, Reverend Cooke presently resides in the Washington, DC area.

Reverend Maria-Alma Rainey Copeland is Pastor of Mizpah Lutheran Church in St. Louis, MO. She is a graduate of Pacific Lutheran University (BA) and Luther Northwestern Theological Seminary (MDiv.). She recently completed her academic studies for the DMin. degree at Eden Theological Seminary. Her undergraduate work included interim study in Israel, Japan, and Germany. During her pastorate in Jacksonville, FL, she was Religious Talk Show Hostess for the Morning Talk Show, WJAZ, and morning devotions for WJKS. She was also guest writer for Religious News for

the *Jacksonville Times*. Presently she is the guest columnist for the *Gaston Gazette* in Gastonia North Carolina.

Dr. A. Elaine Crawford is a graduate of Virginia Union University School of Theology (MDiv.) where she was named a Benjamin E. Mays Scholar and was the recipient of the Samuel Horace James Theological Award. She earned her Ph.D in Historical/Theological Studies from Union Theological Seminary. Currently she serves as Program Coordinator for the Womanist Scholars Program, in the Office of Black Women in Church and Society at the ITC, and Adjunct Professor in the Religion and Philosophy Department at Spelman College. Her recent publications include the article "Womanist Christology: Where Have We Come From and Where Are We Going?" in the journal *Review and Expositor*.

Reverend Alice J. Burnette Davis, attorney, is the Minister of Community Outreach, Executive Director of the Family Life Center Foundation, Sunday school teacher, Bible study teacher, and member of the Economic and Community Development Corporation. She is responsible for working with various church and community groups to plan and implement church-related community activities. She earned her MDiv. from Wesley Theological Seminary.

Reverend Katherine J. Davis is an ordained Elder, Central Texas Conference, United Methodist Church, and Associate Pastor of First United Methodist Church, Arlington, TX. Her areas of responsibility included the Singles Ministry, Commission on Religion and Race, Church and Society, AIDS Care Team, and Better Home Ministry to Homeless Families. She is a graduate of the Interdenominational Theological Center at Gammon Theological Seminary (MDiv.).

Reverend Sandra Demby, mother and grandmother is Pastor of the Hereford Charge in Baltimore County, MD. She is a graduate of Morgan University (BS) and Wesley Theological Seminary (MDiv.).

Reverend Alice Dise is a member of Vernon Park Church of God, Chicago, IL where she is a member of the ministerial staff and Superintendent of Sunday School. She is also Director of Editorial, Writer, and editor of vacation Bible school curriculum for Urban Ministries, Inc. Reverend Dise is author of *Black Women In Ministry In the Church of God, Preparation For Teaching: The Inner Life*, and contributing author in *Called To Minister, Empowered To Serve*.

Reverend Troy Janel Harrison-Dixon is Pastor of Calvary Presbyterian Church in Wilson, NC. She earned a MDiv. and a Masters of Theology degree from Eastern Theological Seminary. She is a Bible study teacher, Christian educator, and seminar/workshop leader.

Reverend LaSandra Melton-Dolberry's recent areas of ministry include Associate Minister, New Creation Church where she has enjoyed a multifaceted ministry as Director in the areas of Children, Youth, Young Adult, and Women's Ministries. She is a Certified Crisis Counselor completing the Crisis Intervention Counseling Program at University of California, San Diego. Reverend Dolberry previously was the writer of the

religious column in the *San Diego Voice and Viewpoint* and is presently author of "SisterSpirit," a column in *Aspire Viewpoint Contemporary Gospel* magazine. Most recently she became a contributing author in the second volume of *Sister to Sister,* a woman's devotional.

Reverend Marcia L. Dyson a contributing writer for *Essence* magazine is a native of Chicago, IL who presently lives and writes in New York City. She is a social and cultural critic, writer, public relations, and marketing specialist. She is a graduate of Chicago State University. Her most provocative essay to date is her honest, self-critical, and deeply probing examination of ministerial misconduct, sexual exploitation, and gender oppression in the Black church which was featured in the May, 1998 issue of *Essence* magazine, entitled "When Preachers Prey."

Dr. Violet Lucinda Fisher's ministry began at age 16 when she became a licensed minister in the Holiness Church of God conference. She is currently an ordained Elder and serving as Associate Pastor at St. Daniel's United Methodist Church in Chester, PA. Her ministry has extended throughout the islands of Bermuda, Jamaica, Haiti, and Africa, where she served as a missionary in Kenya, Uganda, and Tanzania.

Dr. Leah Gaskin Fitchue, listed on *Ebony* magazine's Honor Roll of Great Black Women Preachers, has served as Associate Minister to three urban churches: Mt. Zion A.M.E. Church in Trenton, NJ; Jones Tabernacle A.M.E. Church in Philadelphia; and Mother Bethel A.M.E. Church, the first African Methodist Episcopal Church in Philadelphia, where she serves today. Dr. Fitchue is also Associate Professor of Urban Ministry at Eastern Seminary ,where she was the first full-time African-American female faculty member (1992). In 1995 she was appointed Director of the Doctor of Ministry program in the Renewal of the Church for Mission. Dr. Fitchue is the first African-American woman to serve as director of a Doctor of Ministry program in the Association of Doctor of Ministry Educators (ADME). In 1995 she became the first African-American woman in the 70-year history of the seminary to receive tenure. Dr. Fitchue is also a published poet and a licensed marriage and family therapist.

Dr. Margaret Elaine McCollins Flake, listed on the Honor Roll of *Ebony* magazine's list of America's 15 Greatest Black Women Preachers, has distinguished herself as an effective leader in Christian Education, Evangelistic, and Outreach Ministry. She is an Itinerant Elder in the A.M.E. Church and currently serves as Assistant Pastor at Allen A.M.E. Church, Jamaica, NY. She is also the Educational Director of the Allen Christian School, which she co-founded with her husband and Pastor, Dr. Floyd H. Flake. She received a MA in English from Boston University, a MDiv. from Union Theological Seminary, and a DMin. from Union Theological Seminary.

Reverend Andrea Beaden Foster is on the ministerial staff of Ebenezer African Methodist Episcopal Church in Fort Washington, MD. She is a twenty-year member of the Army National Guard and holds the rank of Major. She is also the first African-American female chaplain in the history of the District of Columbia Army National Guard. She is cur-

rently the Drug Deman Reduction Administrator for the DC National Guard and the Deputy State Chaplain. She holds several diplomas from the U.S. Army Chaplain Center and School, a BS in Dental Hygiene from the University of Maryland and MDiv. from the Wesley Theological Seminary.

Dr. Abena Safiyah Fosua and her husband, Dr. Kwasi I. Kena are Directors of the Resource Development and Training Unit for the Methodist Church, with the General Board of Global Ministries serving in Ghana, West Africa, where they provide curriculum and leadership training materials for the Methodist Church. She is a professor, speaker, and author who has written for Upper Room Publications, Cokesbury's Daily Bible Study, and Urban Ministries. Her first book was titled *Mother Wit: 365 Meditations for African-American Women.* She earned a MDiv. from Oral Roberts Seminary and a DMin. from United Theological Seminary in Afrocentric Pastoring and Preaching.

Reverend Beverly Jackson Garvin, teacher, preacher, trainer currently serves as Minister to Youth at Christ United Methodist Church in Detroit, MI, and she is Executive Director of Lifelines Ministries, Inc., International—a womanist ministry for mother-daughter relationships. She is a graduate of Garrett-Evangelical Theological Seminary (MDiv.).

Ms. Portia George, formerly served as marketing sales representative for Judson Press, has been active in Christian education for more than twenty-five years. She is founder of "Kingdom Kids," a program designed to help children of all ages in their journey to know Christ. The sole proprietor of PG Enterprises, the author of three African-American Christian Children's books, and other products, is the director of the American Baptist Mission Speakers Bureau.

Reverend Bridget Goines, teacher, preacher, and workshop leader is founder of Glorious Warriors Young Adult Ministry, which meets the needs of young adults between the ages of 18 and 35. Currently she is an Intern Pastor at Friendship West Baptist Church in Dallas, TX. She holds a BS in Social Work from Morgan State University and is currently pursuing a MDiv. from Perkins School of Theology at Southern Methodist University.

Reverend Yar D. G. Bratcher Gono, born in Liberia, West Africa, she is an instructor at Georgia State University in Atlanta, GA. She serves on the Steering Committee of Black Clergy Women Consultation, and was listed among the Who's Who Among Students in American Universities and Colleges. She earned a MDiv. from Interdenominational Theological Center, a MTh. from Candler School of Theology, Emory University, and is currently a Ph.D candidate with a major in Psychology of Moral Development and African Women's Studies at Emory University. She has pastored United Methodist Churches in Liberia, West Africa, and conducted workshops and vacation Bible school in Monrovia, Nimba, and Liberia.

Dr. Arlene W. Gordon is Associate for Resource Center Development and Educational Ministry Advocates Support in the Congregational Ministries Division of the Presbyterian Church (USA). Previously she served as Associate Pastor of Sojourner Truth Presbyterian Church in

Richmond, CA. She has mentored and worked with youth and young adults and led numerous workshops across denominations. She is a graduate of United Theological Seminary (DMin), and San Francisco Theological Seminary (MDiv.).

Dr. Deborah Denise Graham, a graduate of Central Hower High and Upward Bound, she has since earned degrees from the Duke University (MDiv.), and the University of Akron (Ph.D). She is an ordained Elder in the United Methodist Church and is serving as Pastor of Holy Trinity United Methodist Church in Akron, OH.

Mrs. Easter M. Green is a retired business owner, having owned and operated a beauty salon for thirty years. She is a member of the Allen Temple Baptist Church where she serves as a Deaconess. Mrs. Green raised four children as a single mother and in fifteen years she has been a foster mother to over 158 children in Alameda County.

Dr. Faye S. Gunn is a ministerial daughter of the historic Alfred Street Baptist Church in Alexandria, VA, where she is actively involved in community affairs. As the Assistant Pastor for Program Planning, her responsibilities include directing seasonal, revival, and special programs of the church. In addition she initiated, designed, and implemented significant ministries, including the church's Commission on Evangelism, the 100 student tutorial program, and the Cancer Ministry. Dr. Gunn received her DMin. from the Wesley Theological Seminary in Washington, DC. She has earned a MDiv. from the School of Theology at Virginia Union University, and a MEd. in Secondary Educational Administration from Bowie State College.

Dr. Cynthia L. Hale is the founding pastor of the Ray of Hope Christian Church in Decatur, GA. Beginning with only four persons meeting for Bible study, 3000 plus persons have joined during the last eleven years, making it the fastest growing Disciple church in Georgia. A native of Roanoke, VA, Dr. Hale's natural talent in music led her to study at Hollins College in Virginia. She holds a MDiv. from Duke University and a DMin. from United Theological Seminary. Dr. Hale was inducted into the African-American Biographies Hall of Fame, and was the recipient of the Martin Luther King's Board of Preachers Award. Dr. Hale was also listed on *Ebony* magazine's Honor Roll of Great Black Women Preachers.

Reverend Laverne C. Hall, writer, artist, and poet, is Associate Minister at Mount Zion Baptist Church in Seattle, WA and currently enrolled at the Institute of Theological Studies at Seattle University. She teaches and trains youth and adults and has coordinated workshops in women's prisons. Her published books include *The Mahji Paper Doll Series, Contemporary Collectibles, Hair's What It's All About,* and *The Quiet Brilliance of Onyx.* She is publisher of the thirteen year old *DollArtVenture,* the only magazine worldwide featuring African-American Doll Artists and Collectors.

Reverend Cecelia Swafford Harris is Pastor of the Hazel Crest Community Church and an ordained Elder in the United Methodist Church. Reverend Harris has designed curriculum and taught at the Pembroke

Institute; a week intensive class on Leadership Development and Ministerial Recruitment for High School and Freshmen College Students. She is a graduate of Garrett-Evangelical Theological Seminary (MDiv.).

Reverend Gloria Harris has a BS in Nursing from the University of Detroit, a MTh. in Christian Education from Oral Roberts University in Tulsa, OK, and a MA Journalism Mass Communication in Information and News Gathering from the University of Oklahoma in Norman, OK. She has worked as a staff writer for the *Tulsa Christian Times*, has published articles in the *Christian Journal of Nursing*, worked as a ghost writer for "Victory Christian Center Pastor's Lending Library." She has created, developed, written, and edited for Christian InfoNet, a Christian information service over the Internet—and she is currently a writer and editor of the "Nurses Notes Newsletter" for the Harris Methodist Hospital Oncology Unit. She is a member of Calvary Cathedral Church in Fort Worth, TX.

Mrs. Hattie G. Harris is a retired educator who received her formal training from Benedict College, Columbia, SC and Furman University, Greenville, SC. She is currently pursuing a MA of Christian Education from Erskine Theological Seminary, Due West, SC. She is a member of the Cedar Grove Baptist Church, Simpsonville, SC where she serves as Director of Christian Education.

Ms. Vanessa Hartsfield author, speaker, seminar leader, and massage therapist has a Physics Degree from Spelman College, a Mechanical Engineering degree from the Georgia Institute of Technology, and a Certificate in Massage Therapy from the Atlanta School of Massage. She is also certified in Deep Tissue, Neuromuscular Therapy, Sports Massage, and Cranial Sacral Balancing. She studied Tuina in Beijing China, and has taught at the Atlanta School of Massage.

Reverend Kellie V. Hayes, pastor's wife, Bible study teacher, and mother of three is Co-Pastor of New Liberation A.M.E. Church (with her husband) in Landover, MD. She is a graduate of Hampton University where she studied Fashion Merchandising/Marketing and received her BA degree. She received her MTh. with an emphasis in Systematic Theology from Wesley Theological Seminary. While serving as Assistant Youth Pastor at Ebenezer A.M.E. Church, along with her husband, she was instrumental in the development and implementation of a Manhood/Womanhood Adolescent Rites of Passage Ministry.

Reverend Raye Evelyn Haynes is an active member of Second Baptist Church in Vallejo, CA where her goal is to establish a Christian Counseling Center for women. She is a graduate of California State University, Sacramento with an MS degree in Counseling and Pupil Personnel. She is active in mission work in Senegal West Africa.

Reverend Barbara Ann Heard is currently Associate Pastor at Trinity United Church of Christ where she is active in the community. Reverend Heard is a supporter of "Family Rescue" a shelter for abused women and children. She was previously employed as Instructor of Clinical Pastoral Education at the University of Chicago Medical Center. She is a graduate of Garrett-Evangelical Theological Seminary (MDiv.).

Reverend Vanessa Henderson is currently the Assistant in Prayer Ministry at First Institutional Baptist Church, Phoenix, AZ. She has also served with the Street Ministry and the Nursing Home Ministry. Reverend Henderson is a graduate of Carlow College in Pittsburgh, PA where she received her BS in Psychology.

Dr. Avaneda Dorenza Hobbs, author, musician, and marketing and product developer is a licensed and ordained minister and a lecturer on issues facing the church. She earned a MA in Educational Administration and a MA in Church Administration. She is also the recipient of a Ph.D in Educational Administration and Communications, and Counseling from SOT Institute. She has authored or co-authored numerous books ,including *From the Garden of Eden to America* and *Who Are We? Building A Knowledge Base About Different Racial, Ethnic, and Cultural Groups in America.*

Dr. Linda H. Hollies, wife, mother, and author is an ordained Elder and Director of Outreach Ministry in the United Methodist West Michigan Annual Conference. In addition to her pastoral ministry, she has given extensive devotion to the needs of women. She is founder and Executive Director of Woman to Woman Ministries, Inc., which is an educational resource agency for women of color. Dr. Hollies has authored six books—the most widely circulated being *Inner Healing for Broken Vessels*. In the November 1997, edition of *Ebony* magazine, she was listed on the Honor Roll of Great Black Women Preachers.

Dr. Lottie Jones Hood is the author of numerous books including *Stigma, Its Effect on the Woman Alcoholic* and *The Role of the African-American Church in the Prevention of Drug Abuse*. She is the recipient of numerous outstanding women awards, and the developer of one of 10 Best National Drug Prevention Programs (BA; BES). She is the Pastor of First Congregational Church in Detroit, MI, where she lives with her husband the Honorable Harold Hood, Judge on the Bench of the Michigan Court of Appeals. She has a MA in Management, Supervision and Public Administration; a MA of Social Work; a MDiv.; a Ph.D in Education, Human Services Administration; and a DDiv.

Dr. Janet Hopkins pastors two churches on the West Side of Chicago. She received her Doctorate from McCormick Theological Seminary and is an ordained Elder in the United Methodist Church.

Mrs. Joan E. Jackson was employed as Professor of English Composition and Public Speaking, and African-American Literature at Mesa Community College for twenty-five years. She is the author of two college English composition textbooks and numerous religious writings. These writings include tips for wives, women, mothers, newly weds, and drug addicted individuals. She is also a playwright and poet, and has published a number of plays, poems, dramas, musicals, and essays. Her ministry "Master Teachers for the Master" informs individuals of His Word and His way, particularly in male/female and family relationships.

Reverend Darlene Moore-James is the first female Pastor of Hartzell Mount Zion United Methodist Church in Slidell, LA, a member of the St. Tammany Ministerial Alliance and a Mentoring Pastor for incoming pastors

for the St. Tammany Ministerial Alliance. She is a speaker and workshop leader, and the recipient of the "Women Who Have Made a Difference" Award. She is a graduate of Gammon Theological Seminary at the Interdenominational Theological Center (MDiv.). She is the author of *Sista Pearl* and *I Am the Preacher's Child.*

Reverend Deborah L. Shumake JaPhia, author, playwright, producer, director, and retreat coordinator, is a member of the Greater Christ Baptist Church in Detroit, MI. She is Founder/CEO of *God's Woman, The Magazine For Women Who Love and Serve Jesus Christ,* the radio talk show of *God's Woman* magazine "On The Air," and proprietor of God's Woman Publishing, Inc., Company. She is currently enrolled at the University of Chicago, Graham School of Publishing.

Dr. Diane H. Johnson licensed to preach and is ordained an itinerant Elder by the African Methodist Episcopal Church she currently serves as Associate Minister at Galilee A.M.E. Church. She was formerly on the ministerial staff of Ebenezer A.M.E. Church in Fort Washington, MD, where she served as Minister to the Christian Business Network Ministry, the Deaf Ministry, and the Tennis Ministry. Formerly the General Sales Manager for Howard University's radio station, WHUR-FM, she along with her husband, are the proud owners of Gospel Notes Records and Books in Oxon Hill, MD. She is the founding member and Chairman of the Board of Directors of the Christian African-American Booksellers Association. She has earned the MA in Education, the MBA, and the MDiv. degrees from Howard University, and the DMin. from United Theological Seminary.

Reverend Frankye Anthea Sourie Johnson is an ordained Elder and member of the Oklahoma Annual Conference of the United Methodist Church. She has been the Pastor of the Warren Memorial United Methodist Church in Ardmore, OK for three years where she is leading the church in reaching out to all those, especially African-American women, who have been overlooked by the church and society.

Reverend Katurah Worrill Johnson is currently serving at College Avenue United Methodist Church as its Associate Pastor. Reverend Johnson received her MDiv., concentrating in Biblical Studies from Gammon Theological Seminary at Interdenominational Theological Center, and holds a BA in Journalism from Georgia State University. She is a member of the Mayor's Steering Committee Against Domestic Violence and serves as workshop co-leader of Children Coping with Divorce for the county's divorcing parents.

Reverend Wilma R. Johnson currently serves as Pastor of New Prospect Baptist Church in Detroit, MI. She is the first woman in the city of Detroit to pastor a prominent, traditional Black Baptist church. She previously served as Assistant Pastor at Hartford Memorial Baptist Church where her ministry included Christian counseling and teaching the evening Bible study class. She has taught, conducted workshops, and preached for twenty-three years. She and her husband David have two sons. She is a storyteller of Black Folktales, collects African-American books for children, and writes children's stories. She is a graduate of Marygrove College with a MA in Pastoral Ministry.

Reverend Jolene Josey, Associate Minister at Eastside Baptist Church in Tacoma, WA, has worked for twenty-two years in a nontraditional job for women, commonly called "The Trades," where she has been the only African-American female in the Tacoma area. She is also working with other women who are interested in entering the trades, and women in transition, whose lives have been one of drugs, alcohol, prostitution, and abuse.

Mrs. Marjorie L. Kimbrough holds a MA, summa cum laude in Christian Education from Interdenominational Theological Center. She worked for twenty-eight years in the data processing industry. Her background includes positions as Mathematical Engineer, Systems Representative, and Programming Languages Consultant, and Lecturer. She has written several programming language textbooks, taught on videotape, and conducted seminars and training courses. In addition, she held the positions of Instructor in Christian Education for ITC and Professor of Religion at Clark Atlanta University. Her book, *Accept No Limitations: A Black Woman Encounters Corporate America* won the 1991 Georgia Author of the Year Award in the area of nonfiction.

Dr. Barbara Lewis King is the founder and pastor of Hillside Chapel and Truth Center in Atlanta, GA. She abandoned an academic career and began her nondenominational, ecumenical ministry in her living room. Dr. King earned a BA in Sociology from Texas Southern University. She is also a professionally trained social worker, having earned the MSW degree from Atlanta University. She has been awarded three Honorary DDiv. degrees and has completed the course work for a Ph.D in Educational Administration. Dr. King was listed by *Ebony* magazine as one of America's Greatest Black Women Preachers and one of the 100 most fascinating women of the 20th Century. She has her own television program "Transform Your Life" and has appeared in the "Remembering the Spirit" segment of the Oprah Winfrey Show.

Reverend Bonita A. Kitt is a graduate of the American Baptist Seminary of the West, Berkeley, CA where she earned two master degrees. Reverend Kitt is the Minister of Comfort at the Allen Temple Baptist Church in Oakland, CA. This ministry provides grief support to the congregation and the community through counseling and referrals. Reverend Kitt is also currently a Hospice Chaplain and Volunteer Coordinator with GranCare Home Health and Hospice.

Dr. Janette Chandler Kotey is the Associate Pastor and Minister of Music and the Arts at St. Paul United Methodist Church in Dallas, TX. She holds a DMin., MDiv., and an MA in Education from Oral Roberts University.

Dr. Linda Lee, a pastor's wife is currently the District Superintendent of the Detroit East District Annual Conference. Previously for three years she was the Pastor of the Covenant Avenue Methodist Church in Detroit, MI. Dr. Lee holds a DMin. and an MDiv. from the United Theological Seminary in Dayton, OH. She is the mother of three children.

Reverend Vanessa Stephens Lee, author of two books and a theatrical production titled *Esther: A Womanist Perspective* is part of a clergy

couple, and Pastor of the Federalsburg-Denton Charge, United Methodist Churches in the Peninsula-Delaware Conference. A graduate of Wesley Theological Seminary with a MDiv., she is currently a student in the Doctor of Ministry program in African-American Studies, also at Wesley Seminary.

Reverend Ginger D. London, Bible study teacher, author, and counselor is the founder and host of "Heart To Heart," a Christian radio talk show and host of the "Word of Live" radio music program on WNDC 910/AM in Baton Rouge, LA. She earned two MA degrees from Oral Roberts University Graduate School of Theology and Missions. For several years she worked with battered women's programs as a telephone crisis counselor and an outpatient counselor for abused women and their families. She is the author of *Understanding Your Calling, Discerning Your Boaz,* and *The Making Of A Spiritual Diamond.*

Dr. Carolyn B. Love co-pastors with her husband of twenty-seven years at the Truth For Living Ministries in Jacksonville, FL, where her personal deliverance from drugs, alcohol, and depression are all tremendous witnesses to the awesome power of God. She is President and Founder of Truth Bible College and Seminary, President and Founder of Fresh Word Outreach Ministries, and serves as a local host for the Trinity Broadcasting Network (TBN). She is an elementary school principal, conference/seminar speaker, and mother of two children.

Mrs. Dinah Page Manns, volunteer counselor, high school teacher, and Director of a halfway house, is the Assistant Director of the Educational Opportunity Center at Rogers State University. She earned a MA in Counseling from Oral Roberts University. Currently she is a doctoral candidate in Adult Education at Oklahoma State University.

Mrs. Ann Shenethia Manuel holds a degree in Social Studies and Education from the University of Oklahoma, and a JD from the University of Texas. She is currently an administrator at Carl Albert State College and is pursuing a limited license in the ministry.

Reverend Rosita Mathews, a writer, classically trained pianist with a green belt in karate, is Chief of Chaplain Service at the VA Medical Center in Northampton, MA. She is the first African-American woman and the second woman in the country to serve as a Chief of Chaplain Service. She completed her undergraduate studies at the University of Michigan in Ann Arbor, MI, and earned her MDiv. at Southern Baptist Theological Seminary. She has also completed some postgraduate doctoral work at Princeton Theological Seminary. She is published in several texts including *A Troubling in My Soul: Womanist Perspectives on Evil and Suffering,* and *Embracing the Spirit.*

Ms. Loretta E. McBride, listed in the Who's Who for Teachers, is a graduate of Mills College in Oakland, CA, with a degree in Early Childhood Education and Sociology. She is currently Vice Principal of Fellowship Academy, a Christian school in San Francisco, and a member of Gethsemane Community Church in Berkeley, CA.

Dr. Dolores E. Lee McCabe, Minister of Evangelism at Zion Baptist Church of Ardmore, PA, is also Assistant Professor of Social Justice and Counseling and Assistant to the Provost for Multicultural Affairs at Eastern College in St. Davids, PA. She received a MA of Education in Counseling from Antioch University, a MDiv., and a DMin. in Marriage and Family Counseling from Eastern Baptist Theological Seminary. She also studied at the Jungian Institute in Switzerland, specializing in dream interpretation.

Chaplain Emma Louise McNair is the mother of six children; three girls and three boys, and the grandmother of eight. She is currently serving as Staff Chaplain at the Methodist Medical Center. She is the first Black woman in the Mississippi Conference and the state of Mississippi to receive a certificate as a certified Chaplain (fellow) of the College Chaplains, Inc.

Reverend Bernadine Grant McRipley is a writer for *PC* (USA), *Stewardship of Public Life* (SPL) *Health Care Quarterly,* and editor for *EcoJustice Quarterly* magazine. She is a graduate of Princeton Theological Seminary (MDiv.) and an ordained clergywoman in the Presbyterian Church (USA).

Reverend Andrea L. Middleton is Pastor of John Wesley United Methodist Church in Clarksburg, MD. She is a graduate of Wesley Theological Seminary (MDiv.) and the Citadel (the Military College of South Carolina) (MA of Education). She has worked in the field of Telecommunications, as a tutor of English composition and literature, and as a word processing instructor.

Dr. Ella Pearson Mitchell, former Dean of the Chapel at Spelman College, has preached and taught across America for over five decades, is visiting professor/mentor for Homiletics majors in the Doctor of Ministry program at the Interdenominational Theological Center in Atlanta. Previously she was also visiting professor of homiletics, Adjunct Professor for the In-Service Doctor of Ministry Program at United Theological Seminary. In addition to preaching, she team-teaches and leads workshops and seminars with her husband Henry. She holds an MA in Religious Education from Columbia University Teachers College and Union Theological Seminary; and a DMin from the School of Theology, Claremont, CA. She is the editor of three volumes of *Those Preaching Women,* a contributor to *Black Church Lifestyles,* and a writer of various articles for church-related publications. She was listed by *Ebony* magazine as one of America's Greatest Black Women Preachers.

Dr. Sherry Davis Molock, author and speaker, is Associate Professor of Psychology at George Washington University in Washington, DC. She is the former director of the Clinical Psychology Program at Howard University. She also conducts research in the areas of suicidal behaviors, and on infertility and adoption in the African-American community. She has made numerous presentations and written articles in *The Journal of Negro Education, The Journal of Black Psychology,* and *The Journal of the National Medical Association.* She earned a MA and a Ph.D in Psychology

from the University of Maryland, College Park, and is currently working on her Masters of Divinity degree at Howard University Divinity School.

Evangelist Alberiene Riene Adams-Morris, poet and licensed missionary in the Church of God in Christ in Gary, IN, holds a degree in Culinary Arts and Owning. She is also a teacher in the Gary school system, program counselor for the mentally and physically challenged in various group homes in the area. She is a contributor author in *Sister to Sister Devotions* edited by Dr. Linda Hollies.

Dr. Camille Williams-Neal, a registered nurse is currently serving the Presbyterian Church USA National Ministries Division as the Associate for Evangelism and Racial and Cultural Diversity. Prior to this she served as Interim Associate Pastor of First Presbyterian Church in Wooster, OH. Other ministry experience include mission coworker to Brazil, South America ,along with her husband Reverend Robert Williams-Neal and their two daughters. She combined her nursing and pastoral ministry during a seminary intern year in Zaire, Africa ,where she served as Chaplain at the Kellersberger Hospital at Bibanga, Zaire. She is a graduate of Louisville Presbyterian Seminary (MDiv.), McCormick Theological Seminary (DMin.).

Reverend Naomi E. Peete, author, evangelist, preacher, artist, and singer is currently Associate Minister at Mount Zion Baptist Church in Seattle, WA, and Senior Faculty Member and Professor of Biology at City University Graduate School of Education in Tacoma, WA. She received a MS from Morgan State University in Science Education and a MA in Pastoral Studies from Seattle University.

Reverend Anita Adams Powell, has been a public school teacher, counselor, college administrator, and director of community agencies. Presently she is an Associate Pastor/Minister of Faith Development and previously served as Associate Director of Admissions and Adjunct Professor at the Eastern Baptist Theological Seminary. She holds a MA from Wesleyan University and a MDiv. from Eastern Baptist Theological Seminary.

Ms. Constance A. Richards is a junior high and high school teacher. She is Jamaican by birth and began her university education at the University of the West Indies where she obtained a BS in Physics. She holds a MA in Music from Howard University in Piano Performance and is presently completing another MA in Vocal Performance.

Ms. Shewanda Riley, has been a producer for Armed Forces Radio and Television, radio host and announcer, and writer. Currently works as Executive Assistant/Scheduler for a Texas congresswoman. Previously she was Adjunct Professor in writing at Richland Community College, Assistant Director of Communications for New Creation Christian Fellowship. She is a member of The Potter's House and works with PHASE, the Singles' Ministry.

Reverend Sheila Ford Robinson, Director of religious programming, and a religious announcer is the Creator of an audiotape and book of Christian poems and songs for children. She is an active member of the Bible Way Christian Center in San Jose, CA, where she is Director of the

Singles' Ministry. She is also a frequent speaker for youth and young adult organizations, detention facilities, residential homes, and prisons.

Reverend Jini Kilgore Ross co-pastors with her husband Earl of the New Vision Baptist Church in Katy, TX, and teaches in the English department at Houston Community College. She is also a Christian writer and editor. Reverend Ross is a graduate of Occidental College, the University of California-Berkeley, and the American Baptist Seminary of the West, and has done post-graduate studies at the University of Houston. Reverend Ross' ministries include: Director of a shelter for homeless persons in Los Angeles, CA, Associate Pastor at Wheeler Avenue Baptist Church in Houston, TX, and co-author and editor of a number of books.

Mrs. Cordelia Grace-Scott is an Administrative Auditor who lives with her husband Dallas and two children in Laurel, MD. She is a member of Faith Temple COGIC where she is a Sunday school teacher, and Director of the summer camp program. Mrs. Scott holds an MBA Degree from Clark Atlanta University.

Reverend Jannah Scott has worked as a researcher, writer, and designated public lobbyist. Currently, she serves as Assistant in Evangelism and Community Outreach Ministry at First Institutional Baptist Church and Research and Statistical Analysis Chief for the Arizona Department of Health Services. She received both undergraduate and graduate degrees from the University of California, Berkeley in Health Policy Studies. She also completed doctoral course work in Political Science at Brown University.

Reverend Angela Stewart Sims is an Accounting Manager in Bethesda, MD. She is a graduate of Howard University School of Divinity (MDiv.).

Reverend Claudette Elaine Sims is a full-time motivational speaker, writer, trainer, and communications consultant in Houston, TX. She is a licensed minister and member of the Wheeler Avenue Baptist Church. A former television and radio talk show host, she is a poet, and author of four books; *The Rainbow People, Keep Heaven in View, Don't Weep For Me, and Loving Me.* She has taught theater and drama to inner-city children and is the producer and star of a one-woman show entitled "Voices of My Sisters." She has been featured in *Essence* magazine and made national appearances on Phil Donahue and Sally Jessy Raphael.

Dr. Kathryn R. Smallwood is a widow with three adult children and three granddaughters. She is a graduate of Pittsburgh Theological Seminary (MDiv.), and an ordained minister in the Presbyterian Church, USA. She has designed a mentoring program for Family Resources and East End Cooperative Ministries, and served as Interim Pastor in Richwood, WV of an "all-white" congregation. She now shares her skills independently in multi-cultural sensitivity, relationship building, and church group dynamics.

Dr. Malvina V. Stephens is a native of Port Arthur, TX. She is a full-time staff member of Allen Temple Baptist Church in Oakland, CA. She is the Director of Prison Ministry and Coordinator of Congregational Care. She earned her MDiv. from the American Baptist Seminary of the West

and her DMin. from San Francisco Theological Seminary.

Reverend Dorothea J. Belt Stroman, a pastor's wife, is an ordained Deacon and Elder presently serving as Pastor of Albright Memorial United Methodist Church in Washington, DC. She is a graduate of Howard University Divinity School (MDiv.).

Reverend Deborah Tinsley Taylor, registered nurse, poet, singer, and liturgist, writes and performs original works which celebrate God's love. She has conducted Bible studies based on the "Silent Voices of Women in the Bible, Woman's Word," a monthly discussion of writings by women biblical scholars and theologians. She writes workshop-based curriculums for intergenerational Sunday schools, and is an advocate for women. Several of her poems were published in *Taking Back My Yesterdays* edited by Dr. Linda H. Hollies.

Reverend Meriann Taylor is an author, a psychotherapist, and family therapist, who specializes in pastoral care, counseling, couples and family therapy, HIV/AIDS, and women's health. Reverend Taylor is Director of the Black Church HIV/AIDS National Technical Assistance Center of The Balm in Gilead, Inc., Instructor of Pastoral Care and Counseling at Blanton-Peale Institute and New York Theological Seminary. She is a graduate of Vanderbilt University Divinity School (MDiv.).

Reverend Jacqueline Thompson is a graduate of Howard University School of Divinity where she earned a MDiv. While at Howard she received numerous honors and awards for exhibiting qualities of excellence in scholarship, preaching, and ministry. Currently she serves as the Minister of Youth at Shiloh Baptist Church in Washington, DC.

Ms. Maxine Thompson enjoys writing poetry. She resides in San Pablo, CA with her adult son. She is a graduate of the University of California at Berkeley with a BA in Sociology. She is a member of Berkeley Mt. Zion Baptist Church where her father is the pastor.

Dr. Lisa M. Smith-Vosper has been a legislative assistant, a seventh grade English and drop-out prevention teacher, a community college instructor, and a regional coordinator with a tri-state organization which works to revitalize impoverished areas and to improve the quality of life for the communities of Arkansas, Louisiana, and Mississippi. In her church she assists with the development and organization of a worldwide ministry; is an Associate Youth and Young Adult Ministry Director and Bible Teacher, is founder of the church's Ministry of the Arts, and serves as a consultant, motivational speaker, and presenter.

Reverend Tanya S. Wade is the first African-American female ordained in the Presbytery of Baltimore. She also became the first female Assistant Pastor ordained and installed in the Madison Avenue Presbyterian Church's 149-year history. Currently she is Director of the Baltimore County Delta Community Outreach Center in Randallstown, MD. and the Parish Associate of Cherry Hill Presbyterian Church. She has developed, written, and implemented several enrichment curriculums, Christian education studies, and Christian plays.

Reverend N. S. "Robin" Walker is administrator at Beth Eden Housing Development in Oakland, CA. Reverend Walker is a graduate of the American Baptist Seminary of the West (MDiv.). She is an active member of Allen Temple Baptist Church where she serves as Research Assistant to the senior pastor and the co-pastor.

Reverend Elaine P. Walters is a nationally known speaker, preacher, and teacher. She is Assistant Pastor and Church Administrator for St. Paul A.M.E. Church in Indianapolis, IN, consultant to Indiana University Purdue University School of Social Work, and Executive Director of Indiana One Church, One Child Program, Inc, a program that prepares families for foster care licensing and adoption. A pastor's wife, mother of three, grandmother of seven, and great-grandmother of one, she holds a MA in Urban Ministry. She is the founder of women's ministry groups in Anderson and Indianapolis. Under her leadership both groups conduct annual statewide conference focusing on empowering women, spiritually, politically, socially, and psychologically. She was the first female to deliver the citywide Martin Luther King, Jr. Day address in Anderson.

Reverend Cheryl D. Ward, a native of Oakland, CA was called to preach at the age of twelve. She is founder and Pastor of New Liberation Community Church in Oakland, CA. The church is non-denominational and ethnically diverse. Reverend Ward was featured in *Ebony* magazine in 1997 as one of the Top 25 Most Eligible Bachelorettes, and is the author of *I Have Fallen and I Can Get Up*. She holds a MA in Preaching from the Pacific School of Religion in Berkeley and plans to pursue a Ph.D in Homiletics.

Linda M. Washington is a freelance writer/editor living in Carol Stream, IL. She has worked in publishing for nearly eighteen years in various capacities, after receiving a BA (English/writing) from Northwestern University in Evanston, Illinois. She worked as a curriculum editor full-time (David C. Cook/Ligature Creative Studios) for eight years. She has written fifteen books, including *Hands On Nature* (Rainbow); *Jesus and Friends;* and *The Lord's Prayer* (David C. Cook Church Resources), and co-authored a number of others, including: *Ready for Life* (Tyndale); *God and Me* (Rainbow/Legacy Press). She was among a group of writers who worked on *Voices of Faith*, a Women's Study Bible for World Publishing (1998).

Dr. Elizabeth D. Watson, with a grant from the Whirlpool Foundation, has provided diversity seminars and workshops for the Center for Intercultural Relations. She is Associate Professor of Social Work, and the Director of Admissions in the Department of Social Work at Andrews University, in Berrien Springs, MI. She teaches at both the graduate and undergraduate levels. She is a frequent presenter and speaker on a variety of topics, including women's issues, single parenting, motivation, and change. She earned a MA in Social Work from Howard University and is currently in the dissertation stage of a Ph.D program in Educational Leadership. She has written for several magazines and contributed to a series of women's devotional books.

Reverend Vanessa Weatherspoon, a licensed financial planner, received her undergraduate education in Atlanta, GA with degrees in

Mathematics and Industrial Engineering Technology from Spelman College and Southern Technical Institute. She completed her MA in Christian Education and a MDiv. from Oral Roberts University. While at Oral Roberts she was involved in the development of the Christian Education Department at Higher Dimensions Family Church. In her ministry, VanNet Works, she strives to help equip Christians in becoming effective witnesses for the Lord.

Reverend Joan C. Webster is an anointed worship leader, intercessor, teacher/preacher, counselor, and church administrator. She earned an MDiv. and MA in Christian Education from Oral Roberts University. In 1993 she began Shalom (Peace) Family Fun Camp, a violence prevention summer camp. Shalom has grown and is now a year-round program under the umbrella of Operation 2008 Bridges for Youth, Inc.

Dr. Joan L. Wharton served as the first woman Secretary of the historic A.M.E. Ministerial Alliance of Baltimore and Vicinity. She received a MDiv. from Howard University Divinity School, and a Ph.D from United Theological Seminary. She is an ordained Itinerant Elder in the African Methodist Episcopal Church and serves a Pastor of Mt. Zion A.M.E. Church in Long Green, MD. She is also an educator in the Baltimore City Public Schools. She has written articles for the National Council of Churches and a handbook for churches to use in developing an effective youth ministry.

Reverend Barbara J. Whipple, pastor's wife, mother of three sons, is a graduate of Coppin State College, Family Bible Institute College and Seminary ,and the College of Notre Dame. Currently she serves, along with her husband as Associate Minister at the Mt. Zion Baptist Church where she is also apart of the Prayer Ministry, Missionary Outreach Ministry, and the Evangelism Ministry.

Reverend Bessie Whitaker completed her undergraduate studies at Southern University, her graduate studies in engineering at Tuskegee Institute, and her MTh. from Fuller Theological Seminary. Currently she serves as the Assistant Bible study teacher at Allen Temple Baptist Church in Oakland, CA, where she is a member.

Dr. Leah Elizabeth Mosley White, while serving the Greater Faith Baptist Church, also serves as the Administrator of the New Psalmist Christian School, the largest accredited African-American Christian School in the Baltimore area. She is Director of Education for the State of Maryland for the Full Gospel Baptist Church Fellowship and the Financial Secretary for Collective Banking Group of Baltimore. She is the first African-American woman to be called to pastor a Baptist church in Baltimore. She has preached, lectured, conducted retreats, workshops, leadership training seminars, and revivals throughout the country and in the islands. She has been featured in *Who's Who in Black America*, and has a monthly column in *Unity in the Spirit Magazine*. She earned a MS from Johns Hopkins University, a MTh. from Saint Mary's Seminary and University, and a DMin. from United Theological Seminary.

Dr. Bernadette Glover-Williams, a native of Scotch Plains, NJ, is a discerning and articulate interpreter of church and social issues. She is a graduate of Eastern College, Eastern Baptist Theological Seminary, and Blanton-Peal Institute, and holds a DMin. degree from United Theological Seminary. She serves as Assistant Pastor of the Second Baptist Church, Perth Amboy, NJ.

Reverend Mary Newbern-Williams is Associate for Racial Ethnic Schools and Colleges for the Presbyterian Church (USA). She is a graduate of Princeton Theological Seminary with a MA in Christian Education and a MDiv. She is a writer and has performed in a number of plays and theatrical productions.

Reverend Portia Turner Williamson was awarded the prestigious Angier B. Duke Scholarship for full tuition at Duke University, where she majored in Religion and minored in Music. She culminated her undergraduate work at Oxford University in Oxford, England. She earned the MDiv. from Virginia Union, and has completed course work for the Ph.D in Religion at Duke University. She has been Professor of Biblical Studies at the university and graduate school level, graduate school teaching assistant, Professor of New Testament, and Associate Dean of the Master of Divinity Program at several universities and divinity schools.

Reverend Jane E. Wood is the first African-American to serve as Associate Pastor of St. Paul-Lusby United Methodist Church. She is a graduate of Wesley Seminary Course of Study school and continues to work toward her degree in Sociology with a concentration in Family Studies at the University of Maryland University College. She is also a volunteer in the Rockville Detention Center as well as the Homeless Program for the Women in Rockville.

Reverend Lois A. Wooden is Associate Minister at Metropolitan Baptist Church in Washington, DC., having served as its first Church Administrator, President of the Chorus Choir, Administrative Assistant to the Senior Pastor, and has given spiritual leadership to the Praise Team Ministry. She has taught Bible classes through the Metropolitan CDC as well as the Christian Discipleship Institute. Presently she is Associate Minister, retreat facilitator, revivalist, teacher, counselor, and Chaplain of the Chevy Chase Chapter of the Order of Saint Luke the Physician. She is a graduate of Virginia Union University School of Theology (MDiv.).

Reverend Cynthia E. Woods has been a substitute teacher, teacher/advisor for a summer youth program. She holds a BS degree in Human Development from Virginia Polytechnic Institute and State University and an MDiv. from Wesley Theological Seminary with distinction as a Benjamin E. Mays Fellow. Presently, she is the Protestant Chaplain at Georgetown University and Associate Pastor of the National Memorial Church of God, a growing multicultural congregation in Washington, DC.

918-27

Mrs. Beverly Yates, pastor's wife, mother, and grandmother, is a retired Registered Nurse. She is past President of Chicagoland Christian Women's Conference.

Features Index

This index lists the *Insight Essays* **(Ins.)**, which cover subjects of importance to contemporary African-American women; Women's *Portraits* **(Port.)**, which describe the lives of biblical women and apply biblical principles to the life experiences of African-American women.

Abandonment **(Ins.)** **694-20**
Abigail **(Port.)** **246-6**
see Graciousness **(Ins.)**
Achsah **(Port.)** **150-17**
see Zelophehad's Daughters **(Port.)**; The Virtuous Wife of Proverbs **(Port.)**; Adopted Through Love **(Ins.)**; Infertility **(Ins.)**
Adulteress of Proverbs, The **(Port.)** **470-15**
Adultery **(Ins.)** **694-17**
Aging **(Ins.)** **470-20**
Aloneness, The Gift of **(Ins.)**
Anger **(Ins.)** **54-23**
Anna **(Port.)** **758-2**
Athaliah **(Port.)** **278-13**
Attributes of God—Holiness **(Ins.)** **470-22**
Attributes of God—Immutable **(Ins.)** **406-22**
Attributes of God—Jealousy **(Ins.)** **54-21**
Attributes of God—Omnipresent **(Ins.)54-22**
Attributes of God—Omniscience **(Ins.)** **790-20**
Attributes of God—Righteousness **(Ins.)** **246-12**
Attributes of God—Sovereign **(Ins.)** **406-24**
Bath-sheba **(Port.)** **246-9**
see Adultery **(Ins.)**
Bon Voyage: The Courage to Say Goodbye **(Ins.)**
Brokenheartedness **(Ins.)** **246-15**
Brokenness: A Biblical Perspective **(Ins.)** **406-16**
Bumping into Omnipotence **(Ins.)** **406-22**
Candace **(Port.)** **790-10**
Celibacy **(Ins.)** **822-2**
Children: A Blessed Heritage from God **(Ins.)** **694-22**
Children—A Great Challenge: Teaching Our Children **(Ins.)** **150-26**
Children—Nurturing Spiritual Gifts in Our Children **(Ins.)** **790-18**
Children—Spiritually Naming Our Children **(Ins.)** **758-6**
Children—Raising Children: Finding the Disciplinary Balance **470-19**
Claudia **(Port.)** **854-26**
Commitment **(Ins.)** **790-20**
Commitment to Community **(Ins.)** **246-11**
Confidence **(Ins.)** **406-14**
Coping **(Ins.)** **406-21**
see Stress Management **(Ins.)**; Temptation **(Ins.)**
Courage to Heal **(Ins.)** **150-28**
see Rahab **(Port.)**; Fear **(Ins.)**
Creation of Women **(Ins.)** **22-12**
see Eve **(Port.)**
Dance, Sisters, Dance **(Ins.)** **54-21**
Date Rape **(Ins.)** **246-13**
see Dinah **(Port.)**
Dating **(Ins.)** **406-18**
see Dinah **(Port.)**
Daughter of Jairus **(Port.)** **694-9**
Daughters of Job, The **(Port.)** **406-8**
Deborah **(Port.)** **150-19**
Delilah **(Port.)** **150-22**
Depression **(Ins.)** **758-7**
Dinah **(Port.)** **22-10**
see Date Rape **(Ins.)**
Distress **(Ins.)** **406-23**
Domestic Violence **(Ins.)** **758-5**
see Overcoming Abuse **(Ins.)** **406-12**; Suffering **(Ins.)**; **Sexual Abuse (Ins.)** **246-14**
Elect Lady **(Port.)** **854-27**
see Evangelism: Gone Fishin' **(Ins.)**
Euodia and Syntyche **(Port.)**
see Prayer
Evangelism: Gone Fishin' **(Ins.)** **694-21**
Eve **(Port.)** **22-4**
Ezekiel's wife **(Port.)** **598-23**
Grief **(Ins.)**
Faith **(Ins.)** **854-29**
see Hannah **(Port.)**; Phebe **(Port.)**; Rahab **(Port.)**
Fear **(Ins.)** **406-15**
Forgiven Adulteress, The **(Port.)** **758-2**
Forgiveness: The Doorway to Healing and Reconciliation **(Ins.)** **694-16**
Forgiveness: God's Extended Mercy **(Ins.)** **406-20**
Fortune-telling Slave, The **(Port.)** **790-13**
Friendship **(Ins.)** **150-29; 406-11**
Fruit of the Spirit—Faithfulness of God **(Ins.)** **54-20**
Fruit of the Spirit—Gentleness **(Ins.)822-28**
Fruit of the Spirit—Goodness **(Ins.)** **694-15**
Fruit of the Spirit—Joy **(Ins.)** **406-13**

Key: Insight Essays **(Ins.)** Portraits **(Port.)**

Fruit of the Spirit—Kindness **(Ins.)** **406-14**
Fruit of the Spirit—Love **(Ins.)** **822-24**
Fruit of the Spirit—Patience **(Ins.)** **406-20**
Fruit of the Spirit—Peace **(Ins.)** **694-15**
Fruit of the Spirit—Self-Control **(Ins.)** **854-28**
God's Promises Are Always "Yea" and "Amen" **(Ins.)** **758-5**
Grace and Mercy **(Ins.)** **406-14**
Graciousness **(Ins.)** **150-28**
Grief **(Ins.)**
see Rizpah **(Port.)**; Widow of Nain **(Port.); Survival of a Still-Born Child (Ins.)** **822-25**
Hagar **(Port.)** **22-5**
Hannah **(Port.)246-5**
Hemorrhaging Woman, A **(Port.)** **694-10**
Herodias and Salome **(Port.)** **694-11**
Huldah **(Port.)** **278-11**
Image of God and the Beauty of the Heart **(Ins.)** **822-28**
Infertility **(Ins.)** **22-14**
Suffering **(Ins.)**; Hannah **(Port.)**; Rachel **(Port.)**; Sarah **(Port.)**
Influence **(Ins.)** **150-27**
Intimacy—What Is Intimacy **(Ins.)** **150-29**
Intimacy—Relationships with Other Christians **(Ins.)** **822-24**
Intuition **(Ins.)** **246-12**
Jael **(Port.)** **150-20**
Jehoshabeath **(Port.)** **278-14**
Jezebel (Wicked Queen) **(Port.)** **278-12**
Job's Wife **(Port.)** **406-9**
Jochebed **(Port.)** **54-16**
see Motherhood **(Ins.)**
Leadership—Responsible Decisions **(Ins.)** **278-16**
Leadership—Brick by Brick Together **(Ins.)** **374-8**
see Deborah **(Port.)**
Leah Girl **(Port.)** **22-10**
Levite's Concubine, The **(Port.)**
Little Maid **(Port.)** **694-13**
Lois and Eunice **(Port.)** **790-13**
Loneliness **(Ins.)** **406-19**
see Friendship **(Ins.)**; Singleness **(Ins.)**
Love **(Ins.)** **854-31**
Lot's Daughters **(Port.)**
Lot's Wife **(Port.)** **22-7**
Lydia **(Port.)** **790-12**
Marriage **(Ins.)** **246-11**
Mary and Martha **(Port.)** **758-4**
Mary Magdalene **(Port.)** **694-8**
Mary, Mother of James **(Port.)** **694-8**
Mary, Mother of Jesus **(Port.)** **758-5**
Mary of Bethany **(Port.)** **758-3**
Micah's Mother **(Port.)** **150-23**
Michal and the Wives of Benjamin **(Port.)** **246-7**
Miriam **(Port.)** **54-17**
Motherhood **(Ins.)** **54-19; 278-14**
see Micah's Mother **(Port.)**; Samson's Mother **(Port.)**
Naomi **(Port.)** **150-24**
see Widows **(Ins.)**
Parenting **(Ins.)** **854-27**
see Motherhood **(Ins.)**
Peace **(Ins.)** **758-7**
Perseverance—Help I'm Running to Save My Life! **(Ins.)** **854-29**
Persistent Widow, The **(Port.)** **758-5**
Peter's Mother-in-law **(Port.)** **758-3**
Philip's Daughters **(Port.)** **790-15**
Phebe **(Port.)** **790-15**
Positive Thinking **(Ins.)** **790-21**
Prayer **(Ins.)** **822-30**
Prayer: A God-Given Promise **(Ins.)** **694-23**
Prayer: A God-Given Provision **(Ins.)** **694-17**
Priscilla **(Port.)** **790-14**
Prophet's Widow, The **(Port.)** **278-10**
Purposeful Giving **(Ins.)** **598-24**
see Widow's Mite, The **(Port.)**
Queen of Sheba, The **(Port.)** **278-9**
Rachel **(Port.)** **22-9**
see Infertility **(Ins.)**
Rahab **(Port.)** **150-18**
Rebekah **(Port.)** **22-8**
Rebellion **(Ins.)** **54-23**
Recovery with Dignity **(Ins.)** **790-18**
Revelation 12 Woman, The **(Port.)** **886-7**
Rhoda **(Port.)** **790-12**
Rizpah **(Port.)** **246-8**
Romance—A Biblical Perspective **(Ins.)** **470-21**
Romance—The Misunderstood Gift **(Ins.)** **822-27**
see Dating **(Ins.)**; Love **(Ins.)**
Ruth **(Port.)** **150-25**
see Commitment **(Ins.)**; Graciousness **(Ins.)**
Sacrificial Living—My Life Is Not My Own **(Ins.)** **758-8**
Salvation **(Ins.)** **790-19**
Samson's Bride **(Port.)** **150-22**
Samson's Mother **(Port.)** **150-21**
see Infertility **(Ins.)**
Sapphira, the wife of Ananias **(Port.)** **790-10**
Sarah **(Port.)** **22-6**
Infertility **(Ins.)**; Submission **(Ins.)**
Shulamite Bride **(Port.)** **470-16**
Shunammite Woman, The **(Port.)** **278-11**
Singleness—A Call to Holiness **(Ins.)822-22**
Singleness—A Stage in Life **(Ins.)822-29**
Singleness—A Unique Opportunity for Service **(Ins.)** **822-23**
Single Parenting **(Ins.)** **406-17**
Spiritual Discipline **(Ins.)** **470-23**
Spiritual Mothering **(Ins.)**
Stress Management—Learning to Say "No" **(Ins.)** **470-24**
Submission **(Ins.)** **22-15**

918-30

Suffering—Paradox of Life and Suffering (**Ins.**) **694-18**
Suffering—Physical Pain (**Ins.**) 406-11
see Hemorrhaging Woman (**Port.**); Tamar (**Port.**)
Suicide (**Ins.**) **694-19**
Syntyche (**Port.**)
see Euodia and Syntyche (**Port.**)
Syrophoenician Woman (**Port.**) **694-11**
Tabitha (**Port.**) **790-11**
Tamar (**Port.**) **22-11**
Tamar (**Port.**) **22-11**
Tamar (**Port.**) **22-11**
see Date Rape (**Ins.**)
Temptation (**Ins.**) **854-31**
see Adultery (**Ins.**); Delilah (**Port.**)
Three M's: Ministry, Marriage, and Motherhood (**Ins.**)
Unwed Mothers (**Ins.**) **22-16**
see Hagar (**Port.**); Motherhood (**Ins.**)
Vanity (**Ins.**) **758-8**
Queen Vashti (**Port.**)
Virtuous Woman of Proverbs, A (**Port.**) **470-15**
Widow of Nain, The (**Port.**) **758-4**
Widows—Dependence upon God (**Ins.**) **150-30**
Widow's Mite, The (**Port.**) **694-12**
Wisdom Personified (**Port.**) **470-13**
Wise and Foolish Virgins (**Port.**) **694-7**
Wooly Hair (**Ins.**)
Woman of Thebez (**Port.**) **150-20**
Women's Ministries—Evangelist (**Ins.**) **758-6**
Women's Ministries—Preacher (**Ins.**) **790-14**
Women's Ministries—Teacher (**Ins.**) **790-1**
Zelophehad's Daughters (**Port.**) **54-17**
Zipporah (**Port.**) **54-15**

Key: Insight Essays (**Ins.**) Portraits (**Port.**)

Women in the Bible

Abi (Abijah)—2 Kings 18:2; 2 Chronicles 29:1
Abiah—1 Chronicles 2:24
Abigail (David's half-sister)—2 Samuel 17:25; 1 Chronicles 2:16–17
Abigail (Nabal's wife)—1 Samuel 25:1–42; 2 Samuel 3:3
Abihail (Daughter of Eliab)—2 Chronicles 11:18
Abihail (Mother of Zuriel)—Numbers 3:35
Abihail (Wife of Abishur)—1 Chronicles 2:29
Abishag—1 Kings 1:3–4; 2:13–22
Abital—2 Samuel 3:4; 1 Chronicles 3:3
Achsah—Joshua 15:16–17; Judges 1:12–13
Adah (Daughter of Elon)—Genesis 36:2
Adah (Wife of Lamech)—Genesis 4:19–23
Ahinoam (Saul's wife)—1 Samuel 14:50
Ahinoam (Wife of David)—1 Samuel 25:43; 27:3; 30:5; 2 Samuel 2:2; 3:2; 1 Chronicles 3:1
Ahlal (Daughter of Sheshan)—1 Chronicles 2:31
Ahlal (Mother of Zabad)—1 Chronicles 11:41
Aholibamah—Genesis 36:2–14, 18–25
Anah—Genesis 36:2, 18, 25
Anna—Luke 2:36–38
Apphia—Philemon 1:2
Asenath—Genesis 41:45, 50; 46:20
Atarah—1 Chronicles 2:26
Athaliah—2 Kings 8:26; 11; 2 Chronicles 22:1–2, 10–12; 23:13–21; 24:7
Azubah (Wife of Caleb)—1 Chronicles 2:18–19
Azubah (Mother of Jehoshaphat)—1 Kings 22:42; 2 Chronicles 20:31
Baara—1 Chronicles 8:8
Bashemath (Daughter of Solomon)—1 Kings 4:15
Bashemath (Wife of Esau)—Genesis 26:34; 36:10
Bath-sheba—2 Samuel 11:2–3; 12:24; 1 Kings 1:11–31
Bernice—Acts 25:13, 23; 26:30
Bilhah—Genesis 29:29; 30:3–5, 7; 35:22, 25; 37:2; 46:25, 1 Chronicles 4:29; 7:13
Bithiah—1 Chronicles 4:18
Candace—Acts 8:27
Claudia—2 Timothy 4:21
Cozbi—Numbers 25:15–18
Damaris—Acts 17:34
Deborah (Rebekah's nurse)—Genesis 35:8
Deborah (The prophetess)—Judges 4:4–14; 5:1–18
Delilah—Judges 16:4–21
Dinah—Genesis 34:1–19
Dorcas—Acts 9:36–43
Drusilla—Acts 24:24
Eglah—2 Samuel 3:5; 1 Chronicles 3:3
Elisheba—Exodus 6:23
Ephah—1 Chronicles 2:46
Ephrath—Genesis 35:16; 1 Chronicles 2:19, 50; 4:4
Esther—Esther 2:7–8, 10–11, 15–17, 20, 22; 4:5, 8–10, 13, 17; 5:7, 12;

6:14–7:3, 5–8; 8:1–4, 7; 9:12–13, 25, 29, 31–32
Eunice—2 Timothy 1:5
Euodias—Philippians 4:2
Eve—Genesis 3:20; 4:1; 2 Corinthians 11:3; 1 Timothy 2:13
Gomer—Hosea 1:1–3
Hadassah—Esther 2:7
Hagar—Genesis 16:1, 3–4, 8, 15–16; 21:9, 14, 17; 25:12
Haggith—2 Samuel 3:4–5; 1 Kings 1:5, 11; 2:13; 1 Chronicles 3:2
Hannah—1 Samuel 1:2, 5, 8–9, 13, 15, 19–20, 22; 2:1, 21
Hazelelponi—1 Chronicles 4:3
Helah—1 Chronicles 4:5, 7
Hephzi-bah—2 Kings 21:1; Isaiah 62:4
Herodias—Matthew 14:3–12; Mark 6:14–24; Luke 3:19–20
Hodesh—1 Chronicles 8:8–9
Hodiah—1 Chronicles 4:18–19
Hoglah—Numbers 26:33; 27:1; 36:11; Joshua 17:3
Huldah—2 Kings 22:14–20; 2 Chronicles 34:22–23
Hushim—1 Chronicles 7:12; 8:8, 11;
Jecholiah, Jecoliah—2 Kings 15:2; 2 Chronicles 26:3
Jedidah—2 Kings 22:1–2
Jehoaddan—2 Kings 14:2; 2 Chronicles 25:1
Jehosheba, Jehoshebeath—2 Kings 11:2; 2 Chronicles 22:11
Jehudijah—1 Chronicles 4:18
Jemima—Job 42:14
Jerusha, Jerushah—2 Kings 15:33; 2 Chronicles 27:1
Jezebel (Wife of Ahab)—1 Kings 16:31; 18:4; 18:13; 19:1–2; 21:5; 21:7; 21:11; 21:14–15; 21:23; 21:25; 2 King 9:7; 9:10; 9:22; 9:30; 9:36–37; 18:4–19; 19:1–2; 21:5–25
Jezebel (of Revelation)—Revelation 2:18–29
Joanna—Luke 8:1–3; 24:10
Jochebed—Exodus 6:20; Numbers 26:59
Judah—Jeremiah 3:7, 8,10
Judith—Genesis 26:34
Julia—Romans 16:15
Keren-Happuch—Job 42:14
Keturah—Genesis 25:1–4, 1 Chronicles 1:32–33
Kezia—Job 42:14
Leah—Genesis 29:30; 49:31: Ruth 4:11
Lois—2 Timothy 1:5
Lo-Ruhamah—Hosea 1:6, 8
Lydia—Acts 16:14–15, 40
Maachah—2 Samuel 3:3; 1 Kings 15:1–2, 10, 13; 1 Chronicles 2:48; 3:2; 7:15–16; 8:29; 9:35; 2 Chronicles 11:20–22; 15:16
Mahalah (Sister of Machir)–1 Chronicles 7:18
Mahalath (Daughter of Ishmael)–Genesis 28:9
Mahalath (First wife of King Rehoboam)–2 Chronicles 11:18
Mahlah (Daughter of Zelophehad)—Numbers 26:33; 27:1; 36:11, Joshua 17:3
Mara—Ruth 1:20
Martha—Luke 10:38–41; John 11:1, 5, 19–21, 24, 30, 39; 12:1–2
Mary (Mother of James and Joses)—Matthew 27:56, 61; Mark 15:40, 47; 16:1; Luke 24:10
Mary (Mother of Jesus)—Matthew 1:16, 18, 20; 2:11; 12:46; Luke 1:27, 30, 34, 38–39, 41, 46, 56; Luke 2:5, 16, 19, 34; John 19:25; Acts 1:14
Mary (Mother of John Mark)—Acts 12:12
Mary (of Bethany)—Luke 10:38–39; John 11:1–2, 19–20, 28, 31–32, 45; 12:1–3
Mary (of Rome)—Romans 16:6
Mary Magdalene—Matthew 27:56, 61; 28:1; Mark 15:40, 47; 16:1, 9; Luke 8:2; 24:10; John 19:25; 20:1–18
Matred—Genesis 36:39; 1 Chronicles 1:50
Mehetabel—Genesis 36:39; 1 Chronicles 1:50
Merab—1 Samuel 14:49; 18:17, 19
Meshullemeth—2 King 21:19
Michaiah—2 Chronicles 13:2
Michal—1 Samuel 14:49; 18:20–28; 19:11–17; 25:44; 2 Samuel 3:13–14; 6:16–23; 21:8; 1 Chronicles 15:29
Milcah (Daughter of Haran)—Genesis 11:29; 22:20; 24:15, 24, 47
Milcah (Daughter of Zelophehad)—Numbers 26:33, 27:1; 36:11; Joshua 17:3
Miriam (Sister of Moses and Aaron)—Exodus 15:20–21; Numbers 12:1–15; 20:1; 26:59: Deuteronomy 24:9; Micah 6:4
Miriam (Daughter of Ezra)—1 Chronicles 4:17
Naamah (Sister of Tubal-cain)—Genesis 4:22
Naamah (Wife of Solomon, Mother of Rehoboam)—1 King 14:21, 31; 2 Chronicles 12:13
Naarah—1 Chronicles 4:5–6
Naomi—Ruth 1:2, 8, 11, 19–2:2; 6, 20, 22; 3:1; 4:3, 5, 9, 14, 16–17
Nehushta—2 Kings 24:8
Noadiah—Nehemiah 6:14
Noah—Numbers 26:33; 27:1
Orpah—Ruth 1:4, 14
Peninnah—1 Samuel 1:2
Persis—Romans 16:12
Phanuel—Luke 2:36
Phebe—Romans 16:1–2
Priscilla—Acts 18:2, 18, 26; Romans 16:3; 1 Corinthians 16:19; 2 Timothy 4:19
Puah—Exodus 1:15
Rachel—Genesis 29:6, 9–12, 16–18, 20, 25, 28–31; 30:1–2, 6, 8, 14–15, 22, 25; 31:4, 14, 19, 32, 34; 33:1–2, 7; 35:16–26; 46:19, 22; Ruth 4:11; 1 Samuel 10:2; Jeremiah 31:15; Matthew 2:18
Rahab—Joshua 2:1, 3; 6:17, 23, 25; Hebrew 11:31; James 2:25
Rebekah—Genesis 22:23; 24:15, 29–30, 45, 51, 53, 58–61, 64, 67; 25:20–21, 28

Reumah—Genesis 22:24
Rhoda—Acts 12:13
Rizpah—2 Samuel 3:7; 21:8–10
Ruth—Ruth 1:4, 14, 16, 22; 2:2, 8, 21–22; 3:9; 4:5, 10, 13; Matthew 1:5
Salome (Daughter of Herodias)—Matthew 14:6–11; Mark 6:22–28
Salome (Wife of Zebedee)—Mark 15:40–41; 16:1–2
Sapphira—Acts 5:1–11
Sarah—Genesis 11:29–31; 12:5, 11, 17; 16:1–3, 5–6, 8; 17:15, 17, 19, 21; 18:6, 9–15; 20:2, 14, 16; 18–21:3, 6–7, 9, 12; 23:1–2, 19; 24:36; 25:10; 49:31; Isaiah 51:2; Romans 4:19; 9:9; Hebrews 11:11; 1 Peter 3:6
Serah—Genesis 46:17; 1 Chronicles 7:30
Shelomith (Daughter of Dibri)—Leviticus 24:10–11
Shelomith (Daughter of Maachah)—2 Chronicles 11:20
Shelomith (Daughter of Zerubbabel)—1 Chronicles 3:19
Sherah—1 Chronicles 7:24
Shimeath—2 Kings 12:21; 2 Chronicles 24:26
Shiphrah—Exodus 1:15
Shomer—2 Kings 12:21
Shua—Genesis 38:1–2; 1 Chronicles 7:32
Susanna—Luke 8:2–3
Syntyche—Philippians 4:2
Tahpenes—1 Kings 11:19–20
Tamar (Daughter of Absalom)—2 Samuel 14:27
Tamar (Daughter of David)—2 Samuel 13:1–20; 1 Chronicles 3:9
Tamar (Who married into the family of Judah)—Genesis 38:6–30; Ruth 4:12; 1 Chronicles 2:4
Taphath—1 King 4:11
Tirzah—Numbers 26:33
Tryphena, Tryphosa—Romans 16:12
Vashti—Esther 1:9, 11–12, 15–17, 19; 2:1, 4, 17
Zebudah—2 Kings 23:36
Zeresh—Esther 5:10, 14; 6:13
Zeuah—1 Kings 11:26
Zeruiah—2 Samuel 17:25; 1 Chronicles 2:16
Zibiah—2 Kings 12:1; 2 Chronicles 24:1
Zillah—Genesis 4:19–23
Zilpah—Genesis 29:24; 30:9–10; 35:26; 37:2; 46:18
Zipporah—Exodus 2:21, 22; 4:24, 25; 18:1–6

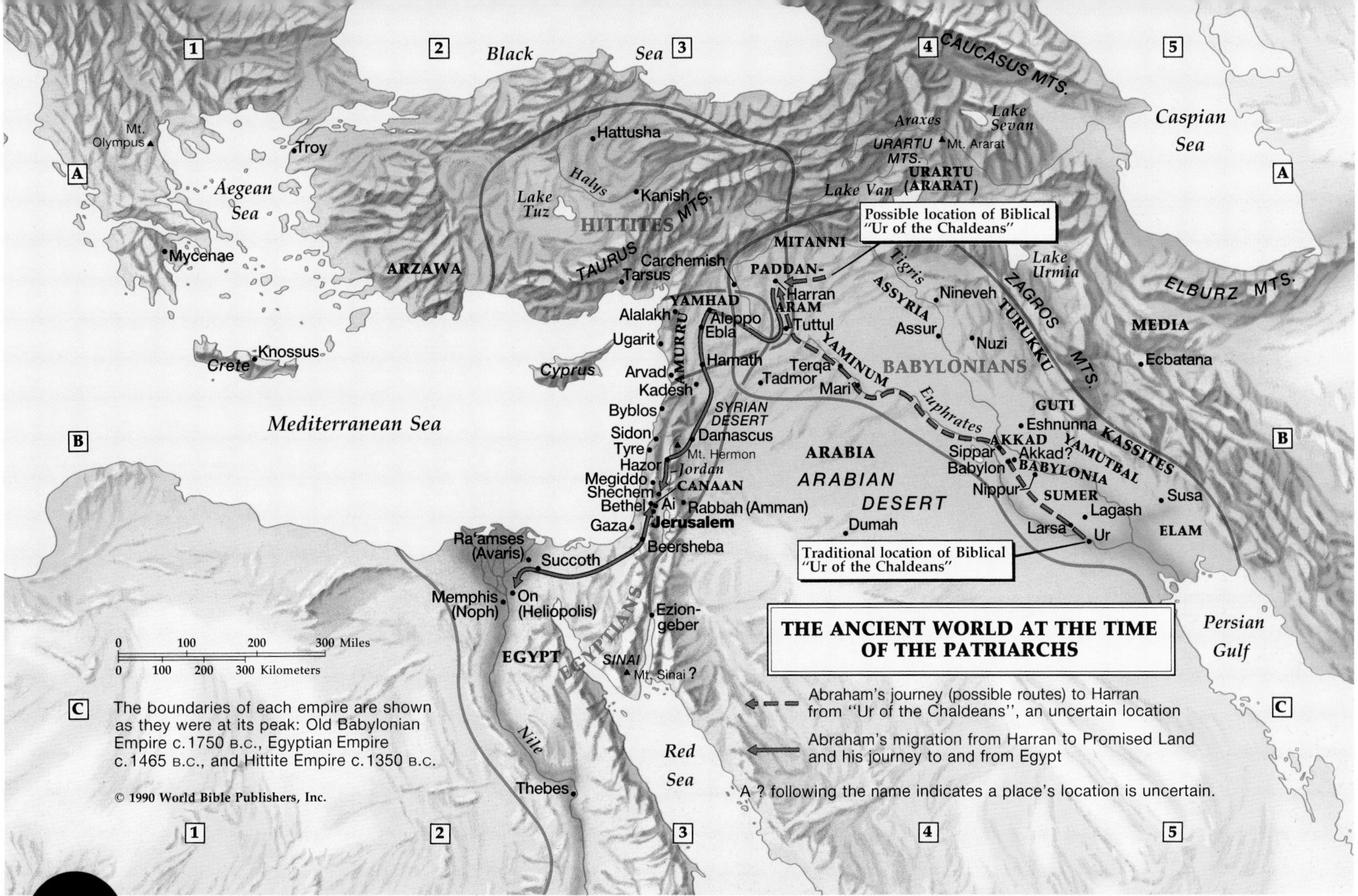

THE ANCIENT WORLD AT THE TIME
OF THE PATRIARCHS

- - - ▶ Abraham's journey (possible routes) to Harran
from "Ur of the Chaldeans", an uncertain location

──▶ Abraham's migration from Harran to Promised Land
and his journey to and from Egypt

A ? following the name indicates a place's location is uncertain.

Possible location of Biblical
"Ur of the Chaldeans"

Traditional location of Biblical
"Ur of the Chaldeans"

The boundaries of each empire are shown
as they were at its peak: Old Babylonian
Empire c. 1750 B.C., Egyptian Empire
c. 1465 B.C., and Hittite Empire c. 1350 B.C.

© 1990 World Bible Publishers, Inc.

| 0 | 100 | 200 | 300 Miles |
| 0 | 100 | 200 | 300 Kilometers |

Caspian
Sea

ELBURZ MTS.

CAUCASUS MTS.

Lake
Sevan

Araxes

URARTU ▲Mt. Ararat
MTS.

URARTU (ARARAT)

Lake Van

MEDIA

•Ecbatana

Lake
Urmia

ZAGROS
MTS.

TURUKKU

GUTI

•Eshnunna

KASSITES

Nineveh• AKKAD YAMUTBAL

ASSYRIA •Nuzi Sippar• Akkad?

•Assur Babylon BABYLONIA

Tigris Nippur• SUMER •Susa

Euphrates •Larsa Lagash• ELAM

BABYLONIANS •Ur

Persian
Gulf

MITANNI

PADDAN-
ARAM •Harran
•Tuttul

YAMINUM

Terqa• Tadmor Mari•

ARABIA

ARABIAN
DESERT

•Dumah

Black
Sea

HITTITES

TAURUS MTS.

•Hattusha •Kanish

Halys

Lake
Tuz

Carchemish•

Tarsus•

YAMHAD

Aleppo• Ebla•

Alalakh•

Ugarit•

Arvad•

AMURRU

SYRIAN
DESERT

Damascus•

Hamath•

Kadesh•

Mt. Hermon▲

Jordan

CANAAN

Rabbah (Amman)•

ARZAWA

Troy•

Aegean
Sea

Mt.
Olympus▲

•Mycenae

•Knossus

Crete

Cyprus

Mediterranean Sea

Byblos•

Sidon•

Tyre•

Megiddo• Hazor•

Shechem•

Bethel• •Ai Jerusalem•

Gaza•

•Beersheba

Succoth•

Ezion-
geber•

SINAI ▲Mt. Sinai ?

EGYPT

EGYPTIANS

Ra'amses
(Avaris)•

•On
(Heliopolis)

Memphis•
(Noph)

Nile

•Thebes

Red
Sea

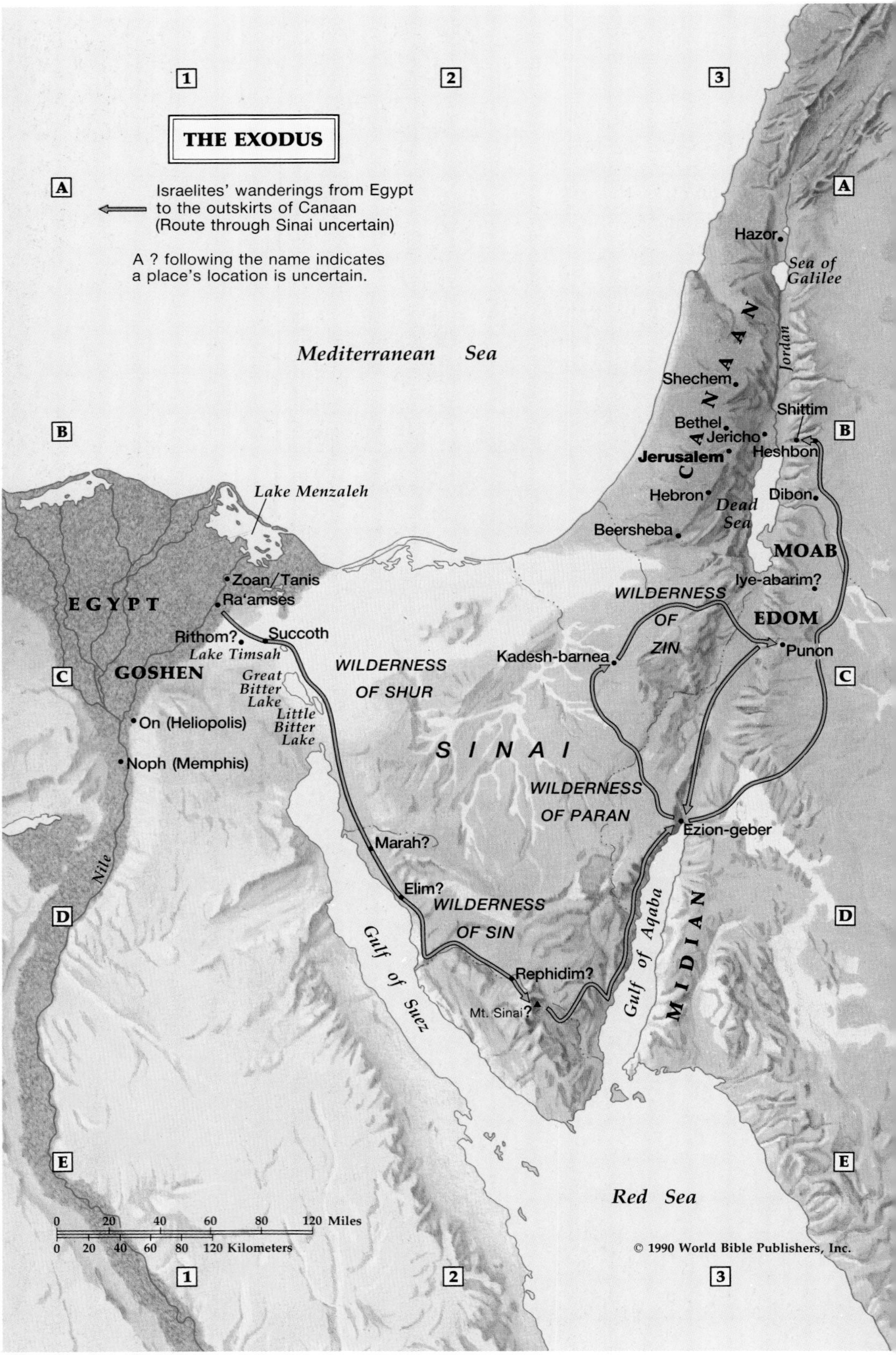
THE EXODUS
Israelites' wanderings from Egypt to the outskirts of Canaan (Route through Sinai uncertain)
A ? following the name indicates a place's location is uncertain.
Mediterranean Sea
Hazor
Sea of Galilee
CANAAN
Jordan
Shechem
Bethel
Jericho
Shittim
Heshbon
Jerusalem
Hebron
Dead Sea
Dibon
Beersheba
MOAB
Iye-abarim?
WILDERNESS OF ZIN
EDOM
Kadesh-barnea
Punon
Lake Menzaleh
Zoan/Tanis
Ra'amses
EGYPT
Rithom?
Succoth
Lake Timsah
GOSHEN
Great Bitter Lake
Little Bitter Lake
WILDERNESS OF SHUR
On (Heliopolis)
Noph (Memphis)
SINAI
WILDERNESS OF PARAN
Ezion-geber
Marah?
Elim?
WILDERNESS OF SIN
Nile
Gulf of Suez
Rephidim?
Mt. Sinai?
Gulf of Aqaba
MIDIAN
Red Sea
0 20 40 60 80 120 Miles
0 20 40 60 80 120 Kilometers
1
2
3
A
B
C
D
E
© 1990 World Bible Publishers, Inc.

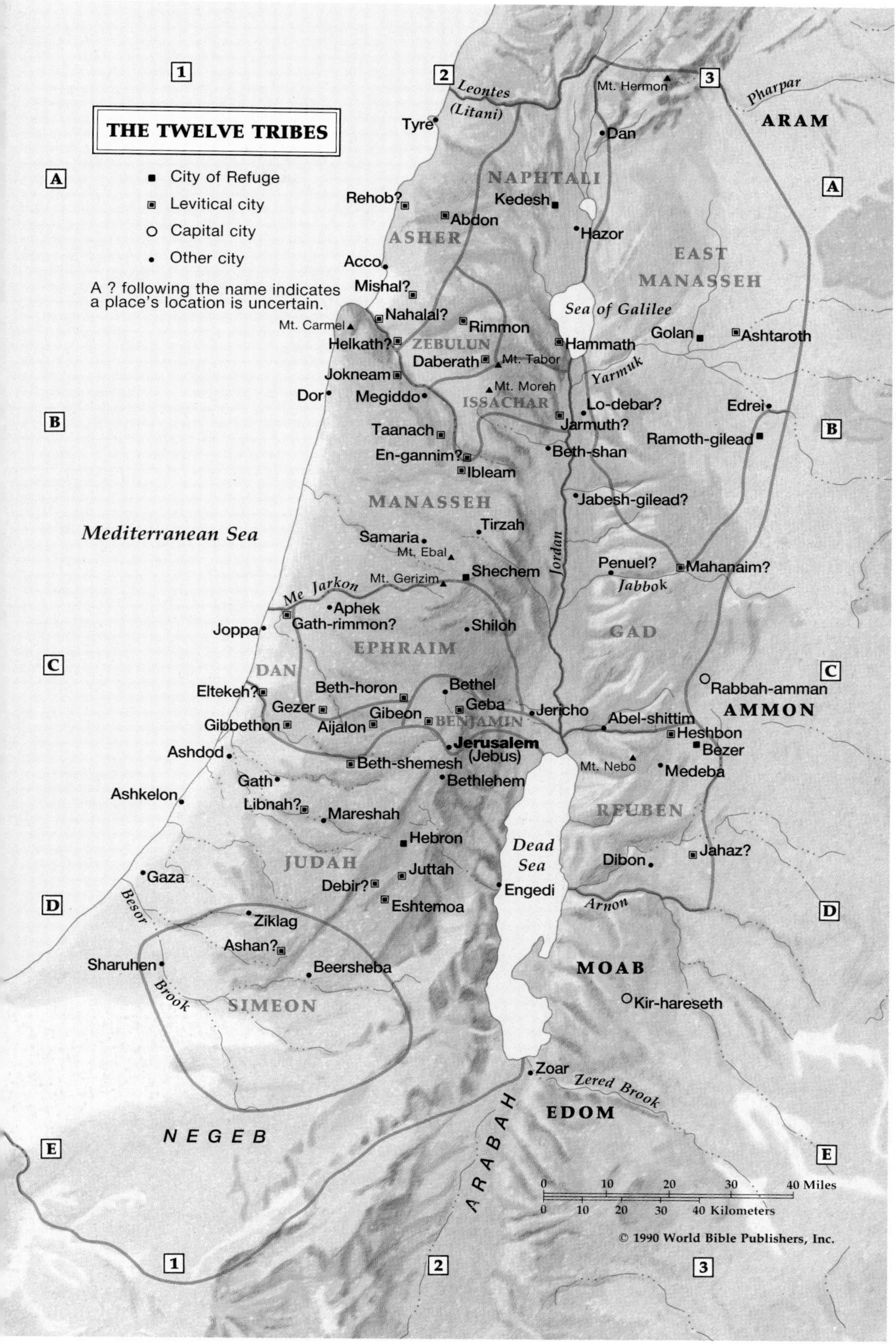
THE TWELVE TRIBES
City of Refuge
Levitical city
Capital city
Other city
A ? following the name indicates a place's location is uncertain.
1
2
3
A
B
C
D
E
Leontes
(Litani)
Tyre
Mt. Hermon
Pharpar
ARAM
Dan
NAPHTALI
Kedesh
Rehob?
Abdon
Hazor
ASHER
EAST
MANASSEH
Acco
Mishal?
Sea of Galilee
Nahalal?
Mt. Carmel
Rimmon
Helkath?
ZEBULUN
Hammath
Golan
Ashtaroth
Daberath
Mt. Tabor
Yarmuk
Jokneam
Mt. Moreh
Dor
Megiddo
ISSACHAR
Lo-debar?
Edrei
Jarmuth?
Taanach
Ramoth-gilead
En-gannim?
Beth-shan
Ibleam
MANASSEH
Jabesh-gilead?
Mediterranean Sea
Tirzah
Samaria
Mt. Ebal
Jordan
Penuel?
Mahanaim?
Shechem
Mt. Gerizim
Jabbok
Me Jarkon
Aphek
Gath-rimmon?
Joppa
Shiloh
GAD
EPHRAIM
DAN
Bethel
Rabbah-amman
Elteketh?
Beth-horon
Geba
Gezer
Gibeon
Jericho
AMMON
BENJAMIN
Abel-shittim
Gibbethon
Aijalon
Heshbon
Jerusalem
(Jebus)
Bezer
Ashdod
Beth-shemesh
Mt. Nebo
Medeba
Gath
Bethlehem
Ashkelon
Libnah?
Mareshah
REUBEN
Hebron
Dead
Sea
Jahaz?
JUDAH
Dibon
Gaza
Juttah
Debir?
Engedi
Besor
Eshtemoa
Arnon
Ziklag
Ashan?
Sharuhen
Beersheba
MOAB
Brook
SIMEON
Kir-hareseth
Zoar
Zered Brook
ARABAH
EDOM
NEGEB
0
10
20
30
40 Miles
0
10
20
30
40 Kilometers
© 1990 World Bible Publishers, Inc.

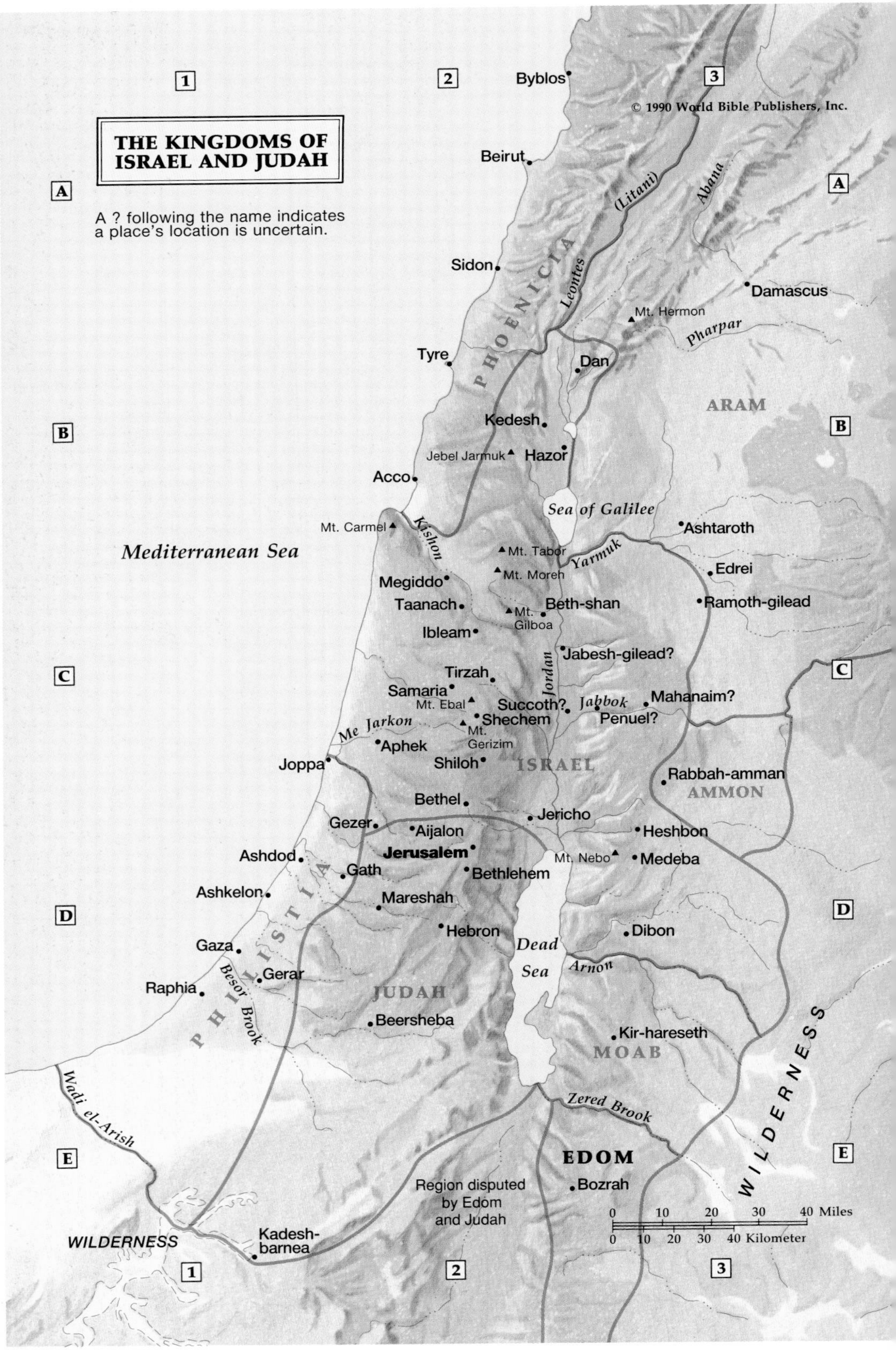
THE KINGDOMS OF ISRAEL AND JUDAH
A ? following the name indicates a place's location is uncertain.
© 1990 World Bible Publishers, Inc.
1
2
3
A
B
C
D
E
Byblos
Beirut
(Litani)
Abana
Sidon
PHOENICIA
Leontes
Damascus
Mt. Hermon
Pharpar
Tyre
Dan
ARAM
Kedesh
Jebel Jarmuk
Hazor
Acco
Sea of Galilee
Mt. Carmel
Kishon
Ashtaroth
Mediterranean Sea
Mt. Tabor
Yarmuk
Edrei
Mt. Moreh
Megiddo
Taanach
Beth-shan
Ramoth-gilead
Mt. Gilboa
Ibleam
Jabesh-gilead?
Jordan
Tirzah
Samaria
Mt. Ebal
Succoth?
Jabbok
Mahanaim?
Penuel?
Shechem
Me Jarkon
Mt. Gerizim
Aphek
Joppa
Shiloh
ISRAEL
Rabbah-amman
AMMON
Bethel
Jericho
Gezer
Aijalon
Heshbon
Ashdod
Jerusalem
Mt. Nebo
Medeba
Gath
Bethlehem
Ashkelon
Mareshah
Hebron
Dibon
Gaza
Dead Sea
Arnon
PHILISTIA
Gerar
Besor Brook
Raphia
JUDAH
Beersheba
Kir-hareseth
MOAB
WILDERNESS
Wadi el-Arish
Zered Brook
EDOM
Bozrah
Region disputed by Edom and Judah
0 10 20 30 40 Miles
0 10 20 30 40 Kilometer
WILDERNESS
Kadesh-barnea

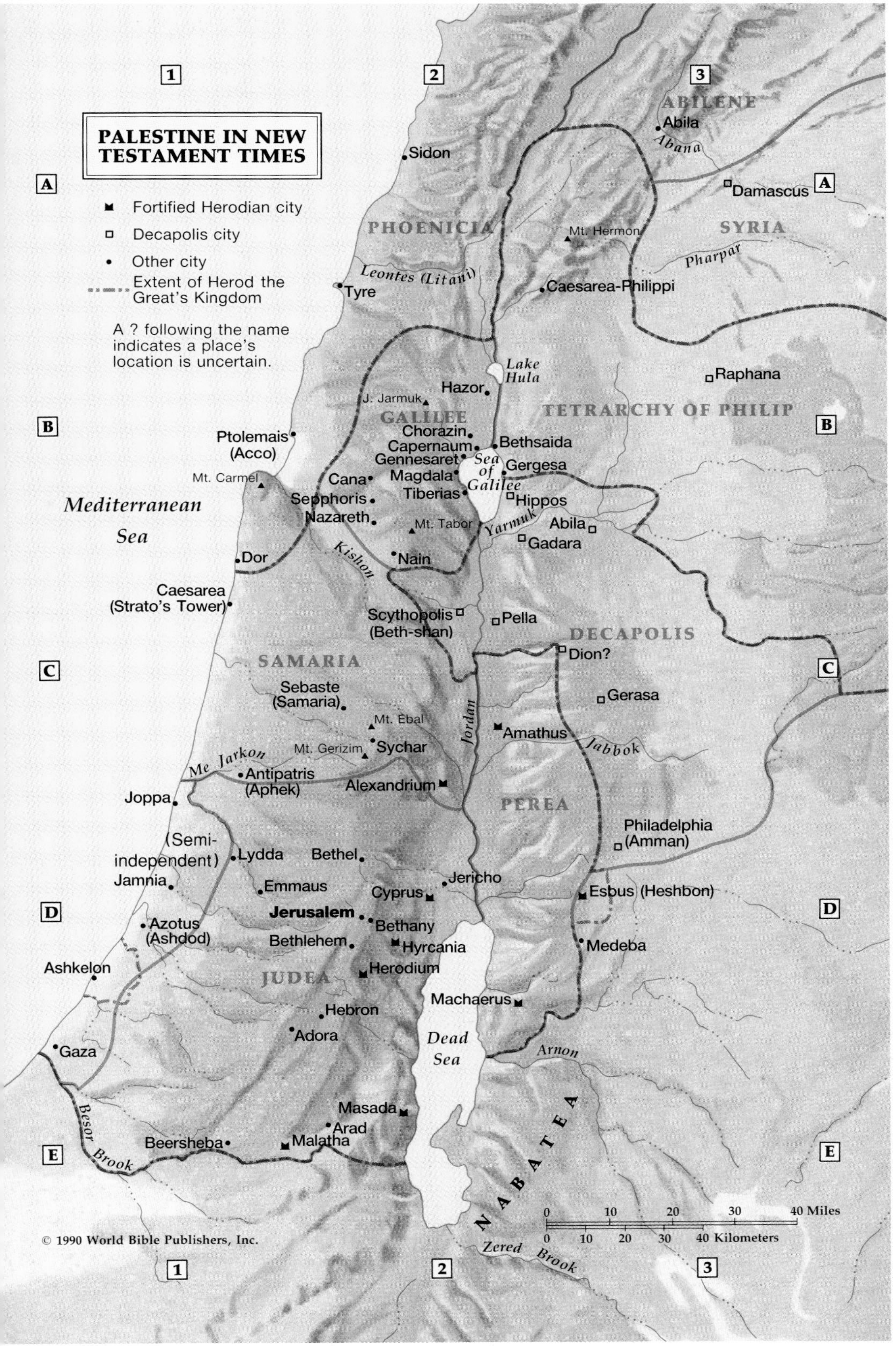

PALESTINE IN NEW TESTAMENT TIMES
Fortified Herodian city
Decapolis city
Other city
Extent of Herod the Great's Kingdom
A ? following the name indicates a place's location is uncertain.
1
2
3
A
B
C
D
E
ABILENE
Abila
Abana
Sidon
Damascus
PHOENICIA
Mt. Hermon
SYRIA
Pharpar
Leontes (Litani)
Tyre
Caesarea-Philippi
Lake Hula
Raphana
Hazor
J. Jarmuk
TETRARCHY OF PHILIP
GALILEE
Chorazin
Ptolemais (Acco)
Capernaum
Bethsaida
Gennesaret
Sea of Galilee
Gergesa
Mt. Carmel
Cana
Magdala
Tiberias
Hippos
Mediterranean Sea
Sepphoris
Nazareth
Mt. Tabor
Yarmuk
Abila
Gadara
Kishon
Dor
Nain
Caesarea (Strato's Tower)
Scythopolis (Beth-shan)
Pella
DECAPOLIS
SAMARIA
Dion?
Sebaste (Samaria)
Gerasa
Mt. Ebal
Jordan
Amathus
Sychar
Mt. Gerizim
Jabbok
Me Jarkon
Antipatris (Aphek)
Alexandrium
Joppa
PEREA
(Semi-independent)
Philadelphia (Amman)
Lydda
Bethel
Jamnia
Emmaus
Jericho
Cyprus
Esbus (Heshbon)
Jerusalem
Bethany
Azotus (Ashdod)
Bethlehem
Hyrcania
Medeba
Ashkelon
Herodium
JUDEA
Machaerus
Hebron
Adora
Dead Sea
Gaza
Arnon
Besor Brook
Masada
Arad
Beersheba
Malatha
NABATEA
0 10 20 30 40 Miles
0 10 20 30 40 Kilometers
Zered Brook

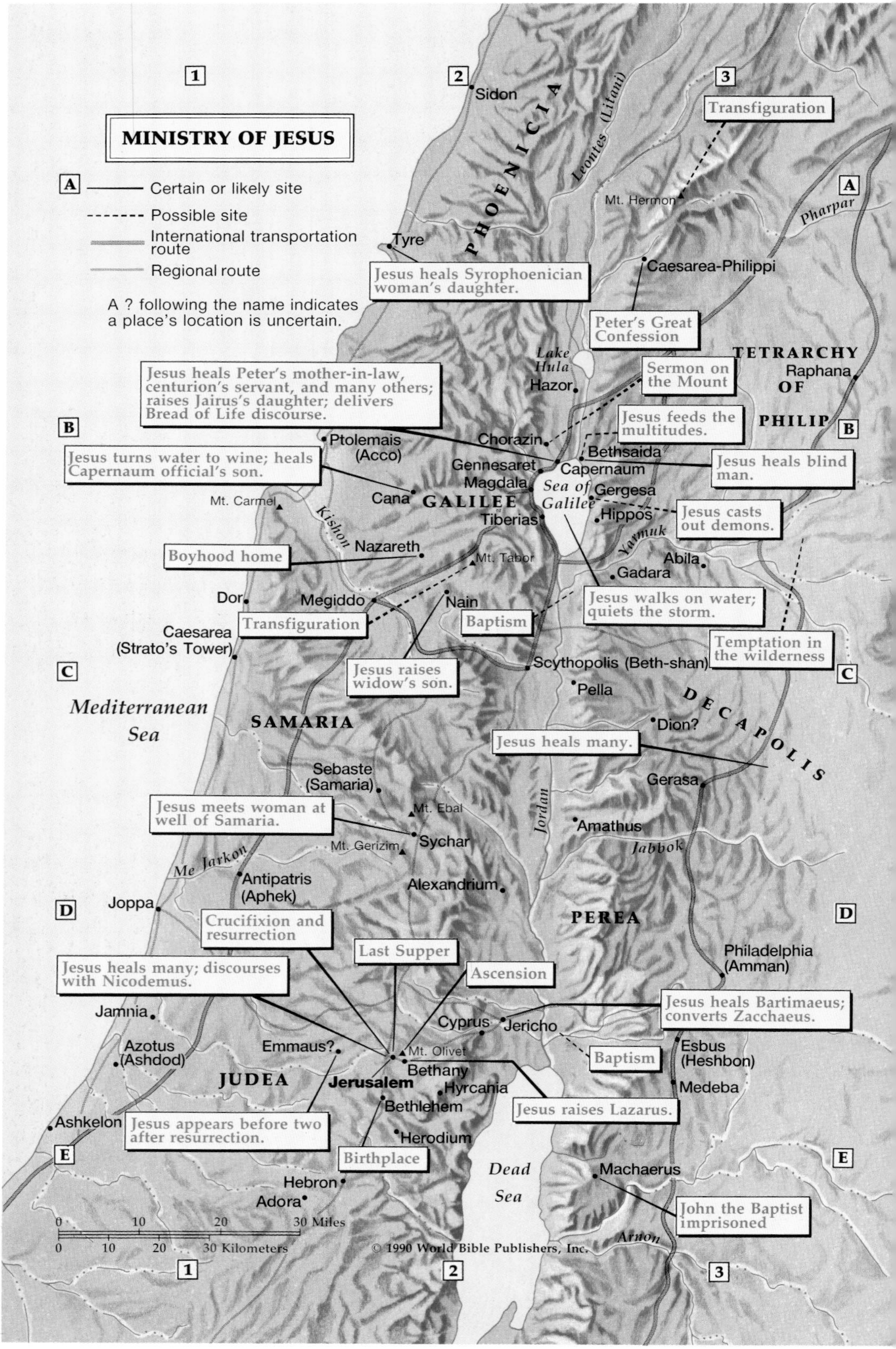

MINISTRY OF JESUS
Certain or likely site
Possible site
International transportation route
Regional route
A ? following the name indicates a place's location is uncertain.
1
2
3
A
B
C
D
E
Sidon
PHOENICIA
Leontes (Litani)
Transfiguration
Mt. Hermon
Pharpar
Tyre
Jesus heals Syrophoenician woman's daughter.
Caesarea-Philippi
Peter's Great Confession
Lake Hula
Hazor
TETRARCHY OF PHILIP
Raphana
Sermon on the Mount
Jesus heals Peter's mother-in-law, centurion's servant, and many others; raises Jairus's daughter; delivers Bread of Life discourse.
Jesus feeds the multitudes.
Chorazin
Ptolemais (Acco)
Bethsaida
Jesus heals blind man.
Jesus turns water to wine; heals Capernaum official's son.
Gennesaret
Capernaum
Magdala
Sea of Galilee
Gergesa
Cana
GALILEE
Mt. Carmel
Kishon
Tiberias
Hippos
Jesus casts out demons.
Yarmuk
Nazareth
Boyhood home
Mt. Tabor
Abila
Gadara
Dor
Megiddo
Nain
Jesus walks on water; quiets the storm.
Transfiguration
Baptism
Caesarea (Strato's Tower)
Temptation in the wilderness
Jesus raises widow's son.
Scythopolis (Beth-shan)
Pella
Mediterranean Sea
SAMARIA
DECAPOLIS
Dion?
Jesus heals many.
Sebaste (Samaria)
Gerasa
Jesus meets woman at well of Samaria.
Mt. Ebal
Jordan
Sychar
Amathus
Mt. Gerizim
Jabbok
Me Jarkon
Antipatris (Aphek)
Alexandrium
Joppa
PEREA
Crucifixion and resurrection
Last Supper
Philadelphia (Amman)
Jesus heals many; discourses with Nicodemus.
Ascension
Jesus heals Bartimaeus; converts Zacchaeus.
Jamnia
Cyprus
Jericho
Azotus (Ashdod)
Emmaus?
Mt. Olivet
Esbus (Heshbon)
Baptism
Bethany
JUDEA
Jerusalem
Hyrcania
Medeba
Bethlehem
Jesus raises Lazarus.
Ashkelon
Jesus appears before two after resurrection.
Herodium
Birthplace
Dead Sea
Machaerus
Hebron
John the Baptist imprisoned
Adora
0 10 20 30 Miles
0 10 20 30 Kilometers
© 1990 World Bible Publishers, Inc.
Arnon

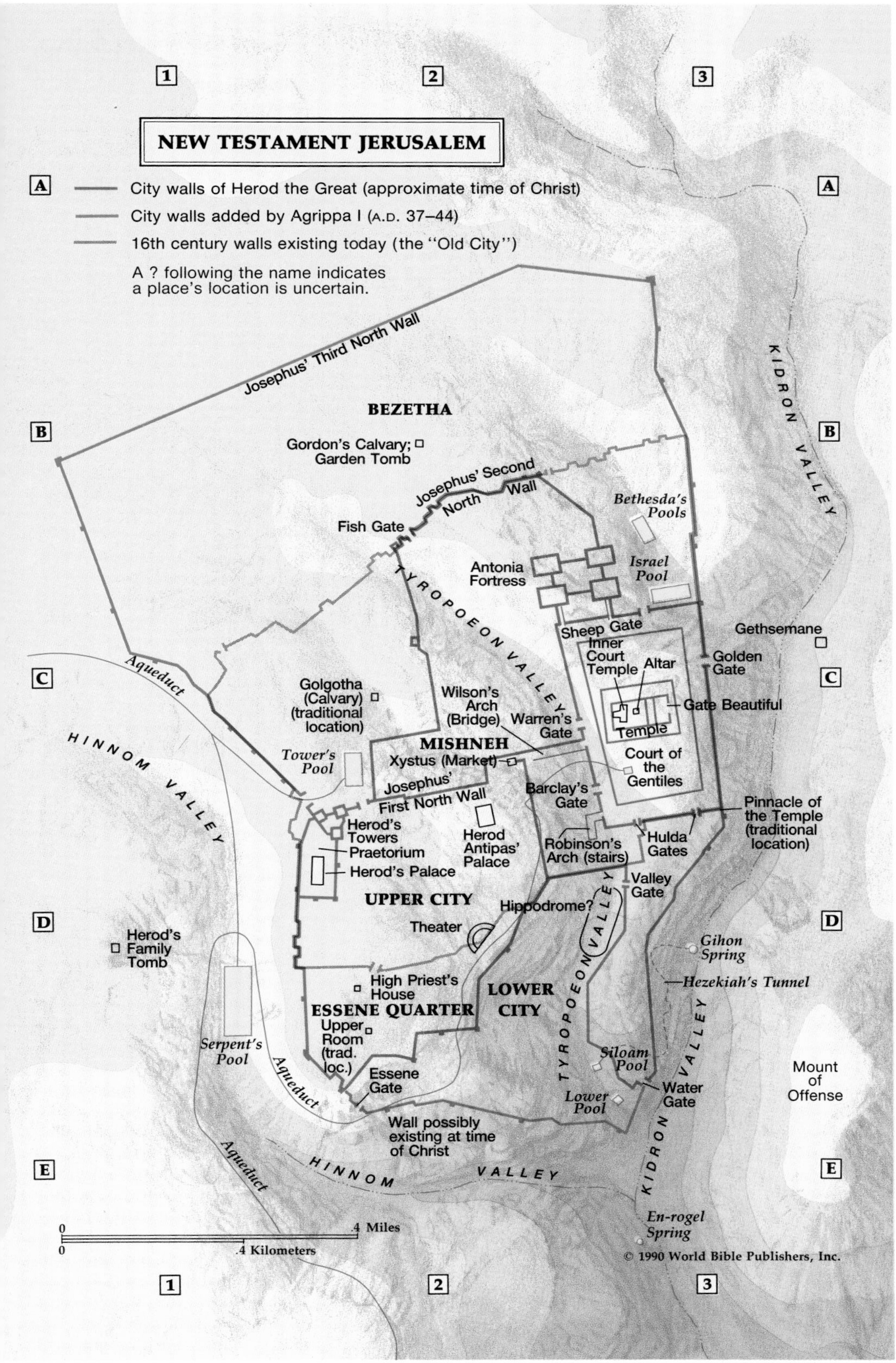

NEW TESTAMENT JERUSALEM
City walls of Herod the Great (approximate time of Christ)
City walls added by Agrippa I (A.D. 37–44)
16th century walls existing today (the "Old City")
A ? following the name indicates a place's location is uncertain.
1
2
3
A
B
C
D
E
Josephus' Third North Wall
BEZETHA
Gordon's Calvary; Garden Tomb
Josephus' Second North Wall
Fish Gate
Bethesda's Pools
Israel Pool
Antonia Fortress
KIDRON VALLEY
TYROPOEON VALLEY
Sheep Gate
Gethsemane
Inner Court
Temple
Altar
Golden Gate
Gate Beautiful
Temple
Golgotha (Calvary) (traditional location)
Wilson's Arch (Bridge)
Warren's Gate
Aqueduct
HINNOM VALLEY
Tower's Pool
MISHNEH
Xystus (Market)
Court of the Gentiles
Josephus' First North Wall
Barclay's Gate
Pinnacle of the Temple (traditional location)
Herod's Towers
Praetorium
Herod's Palace
Herod Antipas' Palace
Robinson's Arch (stairs)
Hulda Gates
Valley Gate
UPPER CITY
Hippodrome?
Theater
Herod's Family Tomb
Gihon Spring
Hezekiah's Tunnel
High Priest's House
ESSENE QUARTER
LOWER CITY
Upper Room (trad. loc.)
Serpent's Pool
Aqueduct
Siloam Pool
Mount of Offense
Essene Gate
Water Gate
Lower Pool
Wall possibly existing at time of Christ
HINNOM VALLEY
KIDRON VALLEY
Aqueduct
En-rogel Spring
0 .4 Miles
0 .4 Kilometers
© 1990 World Bible Publishers, Inc.

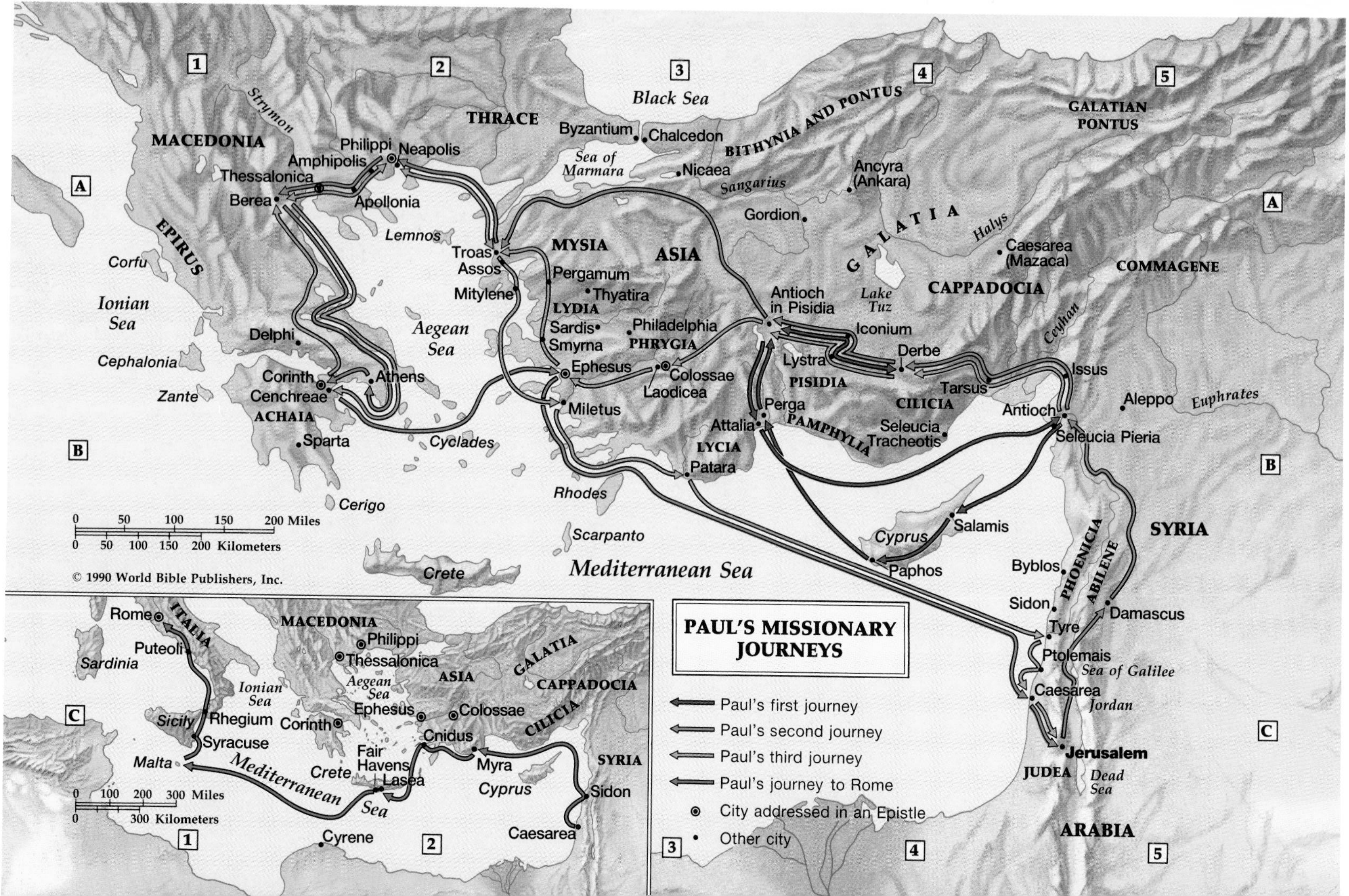
PAUL'S MISSIONARY JOURNEYS
Paul's first journey
Paul's second journey
Paul's third journey
Paul's journey to Rome
City addressed in an Epistle
Other city
Black Sea
THRACE
MACEDONIA
EPIRUS
Strymon
Byzantium
Chalcedon
BITHYNIA AND PONTUS
GALATIAN PONTUS
Sea of Marmara
Nicaea
Sangarius
Ancyra (Ankara)
Gordion
GALATIA
Halys
Caesarea (Mazaca)
COMMAGENE
CAPPADOCIA
Lake Tuz
Philippi
Neapolis
Amphipolis
Thessalonica
Apollonia
Berea
Lemnos
Troas
Assos
Mitylene
MYSIA
ASIA
Pergamum
Thyatira
LYDIA
Sardis
Smyrna
Philadelphia
PHRYGIA
Ephesus
Colossae
Laodicea
Miletus
Antioch in Pisidia
Iconium
Lystra
Derbe
PISIDIA
Tarsus
CILICIA
Issus
Ceyhan
Perga
Attalia
PAMPHYLIA
Seleucia Tracheotis
LYCIA
Patara
Antioch
Seleucia Pieria
Aleppo
Euphrates
Corfu
Ionian Sea
Cephalonia
Zante
Delphi
Corinth
Cenchreae
Athens
ACHAIA
Sparta
Aegean Sea
Cyclades
Rhodes
Cerigo
Scarpanto
Crete
Mediterranean Sea
Cyprus
Salamis
Paphos
SYRIA
Byblos
PHOENICIA
ABILENE
Sidon
Damascus
Tyre
Ptolemais
Sea of Galilee
Caesarea
Jordan
Jerusalem
JUDEA
Dead Sea
ARABIA
0 50 100 150 200 Miles
0 50 100 150 200 Kilometers
© 1990 World Bible Publishers, Inc.
Rome
ITALIA
Puteoli
Sardinia
MACEDONIA
Philippi
Thessalonica
Aegean Sea
ASIA
GALATIA
CAPPADOCIA
Ionian Sea
Ephesus
Colossae
CILICIA
Sicily
Rhegium
Corinth
Cnidus
SYRIA
Syracuse
Malta
Mediterranean Sea
Fair Havens
Lasea
Crete
Myra
Cyprus
Sidon
Caesarea
Cyrene
0 100 200 300 Miles
0 300 Kilometers
1
2
3
4
5
A
B
C